BECKETT

MW01029060

Baseball Card

ALPHABETICAL CHECKLIST

NUMBER 7

Edited by

DR. JAMES BECKETT

RICH KLEIN & GRANT SANDGROUND

with the Price Guide staff of

BECKETT BASEBALL CARD MONTHLY

Beckett Publications • Dallas, Texas

 Prices in this guide reflect current retail rates determined just prior to printing. They do not reflect for-sale prices by the author, publisher, distributors, advertisers, or any card dealers associated with this guide. Every effort has been made to eliminate errors. Readers are invited to write us noting any errors which may be researched and corrected in subsequent printings. The publisher will not be held responsible for losses which may occur in the sale or purchase of cards because of information contained herein.

Manufactured in the United States of America
First Printing
ISBN 1-887432-33-7

Beckett Baseball Card Alphabetical
Table of Contents

About the Author 4
About This Book 4
Introduction 4
How To Collect 5
Obtaining Cards 5
Preserving Your Cards 6
Collecting vs. Investing 6
How To Use the Alphabetical Checklist .. 6
Legend 8
Additional Reading 44
Advertising 45
Acknowledgments 1079

Index to Advertisers

Burbank Sportscards 7
Cardwon 7
Cavalier Cards 7
C & I Collectibles 7
Columbia City Collectibles 7
Dave & Alex's 7
Edward's Baseball Cards Plus........45
Freedman Collectibles 46
Larry Fritsch Cards 7
Stars Company 7
The Striclty Mint 7

Player Listings

A 47
B 82
C 183
D 256
E 303
F 319
G 354
H 421
I 489
J 493
K 528
L 559
M 603
N 708
O 726
P 745
Q 794
R 796
S 860
T 955
U 991
V 993
W 1011
X 1067
Y 1067
Z 1074

About the Author

Jim Beckett, the leading authority on sport card values in the United States, maintains a wide range of activities in the world of sports. He possesses one of the finest collections of sports cards and autographs in the world, has made numerous appearances on radio and television, and has been frequently cited in many national publications. He was awarded the first "Special Achievement Award" for Contributions to the Hobby by the National Sports Collectors Convention in 1980, the "Jock-Jaspersen Award" for Hobby Dedication in 1983, and the "Buck Barker, Spirit of the Hobby" Award in 1991.

Dr. Beckett is the author of *Beckett Baseball Card Price Guide, The Official Price Guide to Baseball Cards, The Sport Americana Price Guide to Baseball Collectibles, The Sport Americana Baseball Memorabilia and Autograph Price Guide, Beckett Football Card Price Guide, The Official Price Guide to Football Cards, Beckett Hockey Card Price Guide, The Official Price Guide to Hockey Cards, Beckett Basketball Card Price Guide, The Official Price Guide to Basketball Cards, and The Sport Americana Baseball Card Alphabetical Checklist.* In addition, he is the founder, publisher, and editor of *Beckett Baseball Card Monthly, Beckett Basketball Card Monthly, Beckett Football Card Monthly, Beckett Hockey Monthly, Beckett Future Stars, Beckett Racing Monthly, and Beckett Tribute* magazines.

Jim Beckett received his Ph.D. in Statistics from Southern Methodist University in 1975. Prior to starting Beckett Publications in 1984, Dr. Beckett served as an Associate Professor of Statistics at Bowling Green State University and as a vice president of a consulting firm in Dallas, Texas. He currently resides in Dallas with his wife, Patti, and their daughters, Christina, Rebecca, and Melissa.

About This Book

Isn't it great? Every year these books get bigger and better with all the new sets coming out. But even more exciting is that every year there are more collectors, more shows, more stores, and more interest in the cards we love so much. Many of the features contained in the other *Beckett Price Guides* have been incorporated into this premier edition since condition grading, terminology, and many other aspects of collecting are common to the card hobby in general. We hope you find the book both interesting and useful in your collecting pursuits.

This alphabetical checklist presents all the cards issued for any particular player (or person) included in the card sets listed in our annual Beckett Baseball Price Guide or Beckett Almanac of Baseball Cards and Collectibles. In some cases, it also includes cards that are checklisted but not yet priced in any of our books. It will prove to be an invaluable tool for seasoned and novice collectors alike. Although this book was carefully compiled and proofread, it is inevitable that errors, misspellings and inconsistencies may occur. Please keep a record of any errors that come to your attention and send them to the author, so that these corrections may be incorporated into future editions of the *Beckett* Football

Welcome to the world of baseball cards.

Introduction

Welcome to the exciting world of baseball card collecting, America's fastest-growing avocation. You have made a good choice in buying this book, since it will open up to you the entire panorama of this field in the simplest, most concise way.

The growth of *Beckett Baseball Card Monthly, Beckett Basketball Card Monthly, Beckett Football Card Monthly, Beckett Hockey Monthly, Beckett Future Stars and Beckett Racing Monthly* is an indication of the unprecedented popularity of sports cards. Founded in 1984 by Dr. James Beckett, the author of this book, *Beckett Baseball Card Monthly* contains the most extensive and accepted monthly Price Guide, collectible glossy superstar covers, colorful feature articles, "Short Prints," Convention Calendar, tips for beginners, "Readers Write" letters to and responses from the editor, information on errors and varieties, autograph collecting tips and profiles of the sport's Hottest stars. Published every month, *BBCM* is the hobby's largest paid circulation periodical. The other five magazines were built on the success of *BBCM*.

So collecting baseball cards — while still pursued as a hobby with youthful exuberance by kids in the neighborhood — has also taken on the trappings of an industry, with thousands of full- and part-time card dealers, as well as vendors of supplies, clubs and conventions. In fact, each year since 1980 thousands of hobbyists have assembled for a National Sports Collectors Convention, at which hundreds of dealers have displayed their wares, seminars have been conducted, autographs penned by sports notables, and millions of cards changed hands. The Beckett Guide is the best annual guide available to the exciting world of football cards. Read it and use it. May your enjoyment and your card collection increase in the coming months and years.

How to Collect

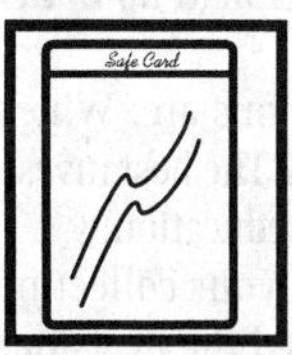
Safe Card

Each collection is personal and reflects the individuality of its owner. There are no set rules on how to collect cards. Since card collecting is a hobby or leisure pastime, what you collect, how much you collect, and how much time and money you spend collecting are entirely up to you. The funds you have available for collecting and your own personal taste should determine how you collect. Information and ideas presented here are intended to help you get the most enjoyment from this hobby.

It is impossible to collect every card ever produced. Therefore, beginners as well as intermediate and advanced collectors usually specialize in some way. One of the reasons this hobby is popular is that individual collectors can define and tailor their collecting methods to match their own tastes. To give you some ideas of the various approaches to collecting, we will list some of the more popular areas of specialization.

Many collectors select complete sets from particular years. For example, they may concentrate on assembling complete sets from all the years since their birth or since they became avid sports fans. They may try to collect a card for every player during that specified period of time.

Many others wish to acquire only certain players. Usually such players are the superstars of the sport, but occasionally collectors will specialize in all the cards of players who attended a particular college or came from a certain town. Some collectors are only interested in the first cards or Rookie Cards of certain players. This is the guide for collectors interested in pursuing the hobby this way.

Obtaining Cards

Several avenues are open to card collectors. Cards still can be purchased in the traditional way: by the pack at the local candy, grocery, drug or major discount stores.

But there are also thousands of card shops across the country that specialize in selling cards individually or by the pack, box, or set. Another alternative is the thousands of card shows held each month around the country, which feature anywhere from eight to 800 tables of sports cards and memorabilia for sale.

For many years, it has been possible to purchase complete sets of baseball cards through mail-order advertisers found in traditional sports media publications, such as *The Sporting News, Baseball Digest, Street & Smith* yearbooks, and others. These sets also are advertised in the card collecting periodicals. Many collectors will begin by subscribing to at least one of the hobby periodicals, all with good up-to-date information. In fact, subscription offers can be found in the advertising section of this book.

Most serious card collectors obtain old (and new) cards from one or more of several main sources: (1) trading or buying from other collectors or dealers; (2) responding to sale or auction ads in the hobby publications; (3) buying at a local hobby store; and/or (4) attending sports collectibles shows or conventions.

We advise that you try all four methods since each has its own distinct advantages: (1) trading is a great way to make new friends; (2) hobby periodicals help you keep up with what's going on in the hobby (including when and where the conventions are happening); (3) stores provide the opportunity to enjoy personalized service and consider a great diversity of material in a relaxed sports-oriented atmosphere; and (4) shows allow you to choose from multiple dealers and thousands of cards under one roof in a competitive situation.

Preserving Your Cards

Cards are fragile. They must be handled properly in order to retain their value. Careless handling can easily result in creased or bent cards. It is, however, not recommended that tweezers or tongs be used to pick up your cards since such utensils might mar or indent card surfaces and thus reduce those cards' conditions and values.

In general, your cards should be handled directly as little as possible. This is sometimes easier to say than to do.

Although there are still many who use custom boxes, storage trays, or even shoe boxes, plastic sheets are the preferred method of many collectors for storing cards.

A collection stored in plastic pages in a three-ring album allows you to view your collection at any time without the need to touch the card itself. Cards can also be kept in single holders (of various types and thickness) designed for the enjoyment of each card individually.

For a large collection, some collectors may use a combination of the above methods. When purchasing plastic sheets for your cards, be sure that you find the pocket size that fits the cards snugly. Don't put your 1994 Extra Bases cards in a sheet designed to fit 1997 Fleer.

Most hobby and collectibles shops and virtually all collectors' conventions will have these plastic pages available in quantity for the various sizes offered, or you can purchase them directly from the advertisers in this book.

Also, remember that pocket size isn't the only factor to consider when looking for plastic sheets. Other factors such as safety, economy, appearance, availability, or personal preference also may indicate which types of sheets a collector may want to buy.

Damp, sunny and/or hot conditions — no, this is not a weather forecast — are three elements to avoid in extremes if you are interested in preserving your collection. Too much (or too little) humidity can cause the gradual deterioration of a card. Direct, bright sun (or fluorescent light) over time will bleach out the color of a card. Extreme heat accelerates the decomposition of the card. On the other hand, many cards have lasted more than 75 years without much scientific intervention. So be cautious, even if the above factors typically present a problem only when present in the extreme. It never hurts to be prudent.

Collecting vs. Investing

Collecting individual players and collecting complete sets are both popular vehicles for investment and speculation.

Most investors and speculators stock up on complete sets or on quantities of players they think have good investment potential.

There is obviously no guarantee in this book, or anywhere else for that matter, that cards will outperform the stock market or other investment alternatives in the future. After all, basketball cards do not pay quarterly dividends and cards cannot be sold at their "current values" as easily as stocks or bonds.

Nevertheless, investors have noticed a favorable long-term trend in the past performance of basketball and other sports collectibles, and certain cards and sets have outperformed just about any other investment in some years.

Many hobbyists maintain that the best investment is and always will be the building of a collection, which traditionally has held up better than outright speculation.

Some of the obvious questions are: Which cards? When to buy? When to sell? The best investment you can make is in your own education.

The more you know about your collection and the hobby, the more informed the decisions you will be able to make. We're not selling investment tips. We're selling information about the current value of baseball cards. It's up to you to use that information to your best advantage.

How to Use the Alphabetical Checklist

This alphabetical checklist has been designed to be user friendly. The set code abbreviations used throughout are easily identified and memorized. The format adopted for card identification is explained below. However, the large number of card sets contained in this volume require that the reader become familiar first with the abbreviations and format used in card identification. PLEASE READ THE FOLLOWING SECTION CAREFULLY BEFORE ATTEMPTING TO USE THE CHECKLIST.

The player cards are listed alphabetically by the player's current last name. Different players with identical first and last names are most often distinguished by middle initials or other additional information. The codes following the player's names are indented and give the set names and numbers of the cards on which the players appeared. When the year of issue extends beyond one calendar year (e.g., 1992-93), an abbreviated form of the earliest date is given for the year of issue (92 for 1992). The set code abbreviations are designed so that each code is distinctive for a particular card set.

Depending on the particular card set, the set code abbreviations consist of from three to four different elements: a) Year of issue (listed in ascending chronological order); b) Producer or sponsor; c) Set code suffixes (commonly used for insert cards); and d) Card number (always preceded by a dash). Here are a few examples of a typical listing:

Aaron, Hank
54Top-128
Year: 1954, Producer: Topps, Card Number: 128

Jr. Griffey, Ken
97PinCerMBlu-53
Year: 1997, Producer: Pinnacle, Set Code Suffix: Certified Mirror Blue, Card Number: 53

Clemente, Roberto
94TopArc1-251
Year: 1994, Producer: Topps, Set Code Suffix: Archives, Card Number: 251

When two different producers issued cards for a player in the same year, the cards are listed alphabetically according to the maker's name (e.g., 1991 Topps precedes 1991 Upper Deck). Note that mainly postal abbreviations have often been used to identify college sets (e.g., VA for Virginia).

The card number typically corresponds to the particular number on the card itself; in some instances, the card number also involves letter prefixes. In playing card sets (e.g., 1991 U.S. Playing Card All-Stars), the letter prefixes "C", "D", "H" and "S" have been added to the card numbers to denote the suits clubs, diamonds, hearts and spades, respectively. Cards in unnumbered sets are usually entered alphabetically according to the player's last name and assigned a number arbitrarily. In sets in which all the cards are numbered, a single unnumbered card is marked either "x(x)" or "NNO" for "no number".

Lastly, the user of this checklist will notice that the cards of players from sports other than baseball (as well as subjects not even from the world of sports) are contained in this checklist. This circumstance arose because of the decision to include multi-sport sets containing baseball cards in this checklist. (With most issues found in our Future Stars magazine, however, a decision was made to include only the baseball-related cards in the alphabetical checklist.) In the price guide, these multi-sport card sets are typically indicated by an asterisk (*), which is placed after the set code suffix in the alphabetical checklist.

Legend

Abbreviations	Set Name
SetAbbrev	SetName
'sA'sPos	A's Postcards
16	W516-1
198TCMSotF	Stars of the Future TCMA
1DiaMatCSB	Diamond Match Co. Silver Border
A's	A's
A'sCHP	A's CHP
A'sFirT20	A's Fireside T208
A'sGraG	A's Granny Goose
A'sGreT	A's Greats TCMA
A'sJacitB	A's Jack in the Box
A'sJayP	A's Jay Publishing
A'sMot	A's Mother's
A'sMotR	A's Mother's ROY's
A'sPos	A's Postcards
A'sRodM	A's Rodeo Meats
A'sRodMC	A's Rodeo Meat Commemorative
A'sSFE	A's S.F. Examiner
A'sSmoC	A's Smokey Colorgrams
A'sTeal	A's Team Issue
A'sUno7P	A's Unocal 76 Pins
AbaYanF	Abany Yankees Fleer/ProCards
AccRegJ	Accel Reggie Jackson
ActPac	Action Packed
ActPac2G	Action Packed 24K Gold
ActPac2GF	Action Packed 24K Gold
ActPacA	Action Packed ASG
ActPacA2	Action Packed ASG 24K
ActPacAC	Action Packed ASG Coke/Amoco
ActPacAP	Action Packed ASG Prototypes
ActPacF	Action Packed
ActPacP	Action Packed Prototypes
ActPacSP	Action Packed Seaver Promos
ActPacT	Action Packed Test
AdeGiaF	Adelaide Giants Futura
AFUMus	AFUD Musial
AGFA	AGFA
AlaGol	Alaska Goldpanners

AlaGolAA'TI	Alaska Goldpanners All-Time AS '60s Team Issue
AlaGolAA'TI	Alaska Goldpanners All-Time AS '70s Team Issue
AlaGolTI	Alaska Goldpanners Team Issue
AlbA'sT	Albany A's TCMA
AlbA'sT	Albany-Colonie A's TCMA
AlbDecGB	Albany Yankees All Decade Best
AlbDukC	Albuquerque Dukes Caruso
AlbDukC	Albuquerque Dukes CMC
AlbDukC	Albuquerque Dukes Cramer
AlbDukF	Albuquerque Dukes Fleer/ProCards
AlbDukF	Alburquerque Dukes Fleer/ProCards
AlbDukLD	Albuquerque Dukes Line Drive
AlbDukP	Albuquerque Dukes Police
AlbDukP	Albuquerque Dukes ProCards
AlbDukS	Albuquerque Dukes SkyBox
AlbDukT	Albuquerque Dukes TCMA
AlbDukT	Albuquerque Dukes Tribune
AlbDukTI	Albuquerque Dukes Caruso
AlbDukTI	Albuquerque Dukes Team Issue
AlbPolC	Albany Polecats Classic
AlbPolC	Albany Polecats Classic/Best
AlbPolF	Albany Polecats Fleer/ProCards
AlbYanB	Albany Yankees Best
AlbYanCB	Albany Yankees Classic/Best Kraft
AlbYanF	Albany Yankees Fleer/ProCards
AlbYanLD	Albany Yankees Line Drive
AlbYanP	Albany Yankees ProCards
AlbYanS	Albany Yankees SkyBox
AlbYanS	Albany Yankees Star
AlbYanT	Albany Yankees TCMA
AlbYanT	Albany-Colonie Yankees TCMA
AlbYanTI	Albany-Colonie Yankees Team Issue
AlDemDCR3	Al Demaree Die Cuts R304
AleDukT	Alexandria Dukes TCMA
AllandGN	Allen and Ginter N28
AllandGN	Allen and Ginter N29
AllandGN	Allen and Ginter N43
AllBasA	All-Star Baseball Album
AllBasT	All-American Baseball Team
AllGamPI	All-Star Game Program Inserts
AllLadBC	All-American Ladies Baseball Club
AllToo1	All-Star Toon-Ups I
AlrGri2TT	Alrak Griffey 24 Taco Time
AlrGriAAS	Alrak Griffey Ace Auto Supply
AlrGrifMVO	Alrak Griffey Mt. Vernon Ohio
AlrGriG	Alrak Griffey Gazette
AlrGriGM	Alrak Griffey Golden Moments
AlrGriGMS	Alrak Griffey Golden Moments Sheet
AlrGriM	Alrak Griffey McDonald's
AlrGriM	Alrak Griffey Metal
AlrGriP	Alrak Griffey Postcard
AlrGriT	Alrak Griffey Two-sided
AlrGriTP	Alrak Griffey Triple Play
AlrTacGJ	Alrak Griffey Jr. Taco Time
aMaa	Star Maas
AmaGolST	Amarillo Gold Sox TCMA
AmeCarE	American Caramel E106
AmeCarE	American Caramel E122
AmeCarE	American Caramel E126
AmeCarE	American Caramel E90-1
AmeCarE	American Caramel E91
AmeLeaPC	American League Publishing Co. PC770
AmeNut&CCP	American Nut and Chocolate Co. Pennant
AmeTraS	American Tract Society
AmeYou	Ameritech Yount
AncBucTI	Anchorage Bucs Team Issue
AncGlaP	Anchorage Glacier Pilots
AncGlaPTI	Anchorage Glacier Pilots Team Issue
AndBraT	Anderson Braves TCMA
AndRanT	Anderson Rangers TCMA
AngAdoF	Angels Adohr Farms
AngAdoFD	Angels Adohr Farms Dairy
AngCHP	Angels CHP
AngDexP	Angels Dexter Press
AngFamF	Angels Family Fun Centers
AngGreT	Angels Greats TCMA
AngGriS	Angels Grich Sheet
AngJacitB	Angels Jack in the Box
AngJayP	Angels Jay Publishing
AngLAT	Angels L.A. Times
AngMot	Angels Mother's
AngPol	Angels Police
AngSmo	Angels Smokey
AngStrH	Angels Straw Hat
AngTeal	Angels Team Issue
AppFoxBS	Appleton Foxes Box Scores
AppFoxC	Appleton Foxes Classic
AppFoxC	Appleton Foxes Classic/Best
AppFoxF	Appleton Foxes Fleer/ProCards
AppFoxF	Appleton Foxes Fritsch
AppFoxP	Appleton Foxes ProCards
AppFoxT	Appleton Foxes TCMA
AppLeaAB	Appalachian League All-Stars Best
AreHol	Arena Holograms *
AreKidGCH	Arena Kid Griffey Comic Holograms
AriBlaDB	Lethbridge Black Diamonds Best
AriFalLS	Arizona Fall League SplitSecond
AriLot	Arizona Lottery
AriWilP	Arizona Wildcats Police
ArkRaz	Arkansas Razorbacks
ArkTraB	Arkansas Travelers Best
ArkTraF	Arkansas Travelers Fleer/ProCards
ArkTraGS	Arkansas Travelers Grand Slam
ArkTraLD	Arkansas Travelers Line Drive
ArkTraP	Arkansas Travelers ProCards
ArkTraS	Arkansas Travelers SkyBox
ArkTraT	Arkansas Travelers TCMA
ArkTraTI	Arkansas Travelers Team Issue
ArmCoi	Armour Coins
ARuFalLS	Arizona Fall League SplitSecond
aSab	Star Saberhagen/Davis
ASAJohM	ASA Johnny Mize
ASASpa	ASA Spahn
AshOil	Ashland Oil
AshTouB	Asheville Tourists Best
AshTouC	Asheville Tourists Classic
AshTouC	Asheville Tourists Classic/Best
AshTouF	Asheville Tourists Fleer/ProCards
AshTouP	Asheville Tourists ProCards
AshTouT	Asheville Tourists TCMA
AshTouTI	Asheville Tourists Team Issue
AshTouUTI	Asheville Tourists Update Team Issue
aSny	Star Snyder
Ast	Astros
AstAstI	Astros Astrosports Inserts
AstBigLBPP	Astros Big League Book Picture Pak
AstBurK	Astros Burger King
AstCok	Astros Coke
AstCol4S	Astros Colt .45s Smokey
AstFouTIP	Astros Four-on-One Team Issue Posters
AstGreT	Astros Greats TCMA
AstHouP	Astros Houston Post
AstLenH	Astros Lennox HSE
AstMilL	Astros Miller Lite
AstMot	Astros Mother's
AstPol	Astros Police
AstPosD	Astros Post Dierker
AstSer1	Astros-Series One
AstShoSO	Astros Shooting Stars-Series One
AstShoSTw	Astros Shooting Stars-Series Two

AstShowSTh	Astros Shooting Stars-Series Three
AstSmo	Astros Smokey
AstTeal	Astros Team Issue
AstTeal1	Astros Team Issue 12
AstTeal2	Astros Team Issue 25
AthJayP	A's Jay Publishing
AthMot	A's Mother's
AtlCon	Atlanta Convention
AtlOil	Atlantic Oil
AtlOilPBCC	Atlantic Oil Play Ball Contest Cards
AubAstB	Auburn Astros Best
AubAstC	Auburn Astros Classic
AubAstC	Auburn Astros Classic/Best
AubAstF	Auburn Astros Fleer/ProCards
AubAstP	Auburn Astros ProCards
AubAstT	Auburn Astros TCMA
AubAstTI	Auburn Astros Team Issue
AubDouB	Auburn Doubledays Best
AugBecN	August Beck N403
AugGreB	Augusta Greenjackets Best
AugGreC	Augusta Greenjackets Classic
AugGreF	Augusta GreenJackets Fleer/ProCards
AugPirC	Augusta Pirates Classic/Best
AugPirF	Augusta Pirates Fleer/ProCards
AugPirP	Augusta Pirates ProCards
AurRec	Auravision Records
AurSpoMK	Aurora Sports Model Kits
AusFut	Australian Futera
AusFut1A	Australian Futera 1993 All-Stars
AusFutGP	Australian Futera Gold Prospect
AusFutL	Australian Futera Legend
AusFutSFP	Australian Futera Strike Force-Fire Power
B18B	B18 Blankets
BabRCCE	Babe Ruth Candy Company E-Unc.
BabRutS	Babe Ruth Story
BakBlaTI	Bakersfield Blaze Team Issue
BakDodC	Bakersfield Dodgers Classic
BakDodCLC	Bakersfield Dodgers Cal League Cards
BakDodP	Bakersfield Dodgers ProCards
BalIntR	Baltimore Orioles Ruth
BalParF	Ball Park Franks
BalParF	Ball Park Franks Will Clark
BasAmeAAB	Baseball America AA All-Stars Best
BasAmeAPB	Baseball America AA Prospects Best
BasBatEU	Baseball Bats E-Unc.
BasBesAotM	Baseball's Best Aces of the Mound
BasBesHM	Baseball's Best Hit Men
BasBesHRK	Baseball's Best Home Run Kings
BasBesRB	Baseball's Best Record Breakers
BasCarN	Baseball Card News
BasCitRC	Baseball City Royals Classic/Best
BasCitRF	Baseball City Royals Fleer/ProCards
BasCitRP	Baseball City Royals ProCards
BasCitRS	Baseball City Royals Star
BasComT	Baseball Comics T203
BasGre	Baseball Greats
BasMagM	Baseball Magazine M118
BasPho	Baseball Photos
BasStaB	Baseball Star Buttons
BasTabP	Baseball Tabs PR1
BasWit	Baseball Wit
BatCliC	Batavia Clippers Classic
BatCliC	Batavia Clippers Classic/Best
BatCliF	Batavia Clippers Fleer/ProCards
BatCliP	Batavia Clippers ProCards
BatCliTI	Batavia Clippers Team Issue
BatR31	Batter-Up R318
BatRouCT	Baton Rouge Cougars TCMA
BatTroT	Batavia Trojans TCMA
BatTroTI	Batavia Trojans Team Issue
Baz	Bazooka
BazA	Bazooka ATG
BazNumT	Bazooka Numbered Test
BazQua5A	Bazooka Quadracard '53 Archives
BazRedH	Bazooka Red Hot
BazTeaU	Bazooka Team USA
BazUnn	Bazooka Unnumbered
BBMJap	BBM Japan
BBMJapAS	BBM Japan All Stars
BBMJapN	BBM Japan Nippon
BBMJapSAG	BBM Japan Sanyo All-Star Game
BeaGolGP	Beaumont Golden Gators ProCards
BeaGolGT	Beaumont Golden Gators TCMA
BelBreB	Beloit Brewers Best
BelBreC	Beloit Brewers Classic
BelBreC	Beloit Brewers Classic/Best
BelBreF	Beloit Brewers Fleer/ProCards
BelBreF	Beloit Brewers Fritsch
BelBreGS	Beloit Brewers Grand Slam
BelBreIS	Beloit Brewers I Star
BelBreIS	Beloit Brewers II Star
BelBreP	Beloit Brewers ProCards
BelBreS	Beloit Brewers Star
BelBreT	Beloit Brewers TCMA
BelBreTI	Beloit Snappers Team Issue
BelGiaTI	Bellingham Giants Team Issue
BelMarC	Bellingham Mariners Classic
BelMarC	Bellingham Mariners Classic/Best
BelMarC	Bellingham Mariners Cramer
BelMarF	Bellingham Mariners Fleer/ProCards
BelMarL	Bellingham Mariners Legoe
BelMarP	Bellingham Mariners ProCards
BelMarTI	Bellingham Mariners Team Issue
BelSnaTI	Beloit Snappers Team Issue
BenBucC	Bend Bucks Classic/Best
BenBucL	Bend Bucks Legoe
BenBucP	Bend Bucks ProCards
BenMusSP	Billings Mustangs Sports Pro
BenPhiC	Bend Phillies Cramer
BenRocC	Bend Rockies Classic/Best
BenRocF	Bend Rockies Fleer/ProCards
BerRos	Berk Ross
BerRos	Berk Ross *
Bes	Best
BesAutS	Best Autograph Series
BesAutS1RP	Best Autograph Series 1st Round Picks
BesAutSA	Best Autograph Series Autographs
BesFra	Best Franchise
BesPlaotYAJ	Best Player of the Year Andruw Jones
BesPlaotYAJA	Best Player of the Year Andruw Jones Autographs
BesWesR	Best Western Ryan
BF2FP	BF2 Felt Pennants
BHCRSpoL	BHCR Sports Legends
BigEatEU	Big Eater E-Unc.
BigLeaC	Big League Chew
BigLeaIS	Big League Inc. Statues
BilMusF	Billings Mustangs Fleer/ProCards
BilMusP	Billings Mustangs ProCards
BilMusSP	Billings Mustangs Sports Pro
BilMusTI	Billings Mustangs Team Issue
BilRedTI	Billings Mustangs Team Issue
BimBreD	Bimbo Bread Discs
BinBeeB	Binghamton Bees Best
BinMetF	Binghamton Mets Fleer/ProCards
BinMetS	Binghamton Mets SkyBox
BinMetTI	Binghamton Mets Team Issue
BirBarB	Birmingham Barons Best
BirBarC	Birmingham Barons Classic
BirBarDGB	Birmingham Barons All Decade Best
BirBarF	Birmingham Barons Fleer/ProCards
BirBarLD	Birmingham Barons Line Drive

BirBarP	Birmingham Barons ProCards
BirBarS	Birmingham Barons SkyBox
BirBarT	Birmingham Barons TCMA
BirBarTI	Birmingham Barons Team Issue
BisCoaLE	Bishop Coast League E100
BisCoaLE	Bishop Coast League E99
BlaBacD	Blank Back Discs
BlaYNPRWL	Blanco Y Negro Puerto Rico Winter League
BlaYNPRWLU	Blanco Y Negro Puerto Rico Winter League Update
Ble23KB	Bleachers 23K Bonds
Ble23KGJ	Bleachers 23K Griffey Jr.
Ble23KJ	Bleachers 23K Justice
Ble23KR	Bleachers 23K Ryan
Ble23KS	Bleachers 23K Sandberg
Ble23KT	Bleachers 23K Thomas
BlePro	Bleachers Promos
BleRya6	Bleachers Ryan 6
BluJay5	Blue Jays 5x7
BluJayAF	Blue Jays Ault Foods
BluJayB	Blue Jays Bookmarks
BluJayBY	Blue Jays Bubble Yum
BluJayCP1	Blue Jays Colla Postcards 15
BluJayD	Blue Jays Dempster's
BluJayD4	Blue Jays Donruss 45
BluJayDM	Blue Jays Donruss McDonald's
BluJayDWS	Blue Jays Donruss World Series
BluJayFS	Blue Jays Fire Safety
BluJayGT	Blue Jays Greats TCMA
BluJayHS	Blue Jays Hostess Stickers
BluJayMH	Blue Jays Maxwell House
BluJayOH	Blue Jays Oh Henry!
BluJayP	Blue Jays Postcards
BluJayPLP	Blue Jays Pepsi/Frito Lay Pennants
BluJayS	Blue Jays Score
BluJayS	Blue Jays Scorebook
BluJayS	Blue Jays Sizzler
BluJayUSPC	Blue Jays U.S. Playing Cards
BluOriB	Bluefield Orioles Best
BluOriC	Bluefield Orioles Classic
BluOriC	Bluefield Orioles Classic/Best
BluOriF	Bluefield Orioles Fleer/ProCards
BluOriP	Bluefield Orioles ProCards
BluOriS	Bluefield Orioles Star
BluTin	Blue Tint R346
BoaandB	Boardwalk and Baseball
BobCamRB	Richmond Braves Bob's Camera
BobParHoF	Bob Parker Hall of Fame
BoiHawB	Boise Hawks Best
BoiHawC	Boise Hawks Classic
BoiHawC	Boise Hawks Classic/Best
BoiHawF	Boise Hawks Fleer/ProCards
BoiHawP	Boise Hawks ProCards
BoiHawTI	Boise Hawks Team Issue
BonBreR	Bond Bread Robinson
BooProC	Book Promotional Cards
Bow	Bowman
Bow	Bowman Foil
Bow195E	Bowman 1952 Extension
Bow98ROY	Bowman 1998 ROY Candidates
BowBanD	Bowery Bank DiMaggio
BowBayB	Bowie Baysox Best
BowBayF	Bowie Baysox Fleer/ProCards
BowBayTI	Bowie Baysox Team Issue
BowBes	Bowman's Best
BowBesA	Bowman's Best Autographs
BowBesAAR	Bowman's Best Autographs Atomic Refractor
BowBesAR	Bowman's Best Atomic Refractors
BowBesAR	Bowman's Best Autographs Refractor
BowBesBC	Bowman's Best Best Cuts
BowBesBCAR	Bowman's Best Best Cuts Atomic Refractor
BowBesBCR	Bowman's Best Best Cuts Refractor
BowBesC	Bowman's Best Cuts
BowBesCAR	Bowman's Best Cuts Atomic Refractors
BowBesCR	Bowman's Best Cuts Refractors
BowBesJR	Bowman's Best Jumbo Refractors
BowBesMI	Bowman's Best Mirror Image
BowBesMIAR	Bowman's Best Mirror Image Atomic Refractor
BowBesMIAR	Bowman's Best Mirror Image Atomic Refractors
BowBesMIARI	Bowman's Best Mirror Image Atomic Refractor Inverted
BowBesMII	Bowman's Best Mirror Image Inverted
BowBesMIR	Bowman's Best Mirror Image Refractor
BowBesMIR	Bowman's Best Mirror Image Refractors
BowBesMIRI	Bowman's Best Mirror Image Refractor Inverted
BowBesP	Bowman's Best Previews
BowBesPAR	Bowman's Best Preview Atomic Refractor
BowBesPAR	Bowman's Best Previews Atomic Refractors
BowBesPR	Bowman's Best Preview Refractor
BowBesPR	Bowman's Best Previews Refractors
BowBesR	Bowman's Best Refractor
BowBesR	Bowman's Best Refractors
BowBW	Bowman B/W
BowC	Bowman Color
BowCerBIA	Bowman Certified Black Ink Autographs
BowCerBIA	Bowman Certified Blue Ink Autographs
BowCerGIA	Bowman Certified Gold Ink Autographs
BowCerGIJA	Bowman Certified Green Ink Jeter Autograph
BowChr	Bowman Chrome
BowChr1RC	Bowman Chrome 1998 ROY Candidates
BowChr1RCR	Bowman Chrome 1998 ROY Candidates Refractors
BowChrI	Bowman Chrome International
BowChrIR	Bowman Chrome International Refractor
BowChrR	Bowman Chrome Refractor
BowChrSHR	Bowman Chrome Scout's Honor Roll
BowChrSHRR	Bowman Chrome Scout's Honor Roll Refractor
BowGolF	Bowman Gold Foil
BowIns	Bowman Inserts
BowInsT	Bowman Inserts Tiffany
BowInsT	Bowman Reprint Inserts Tiffany
BowInt	Bowman International
BowIntB	Bowman International Best
BowIntBAR	Bowman International Best Atomic Refractor
BowIntBR	Bowman International Best Refractors
BowMinLP	Bowman Minor League POY
BowPCL	Bowman PCL
BowPre	Bowman Previews
BowRepI	Bowman Reprint Inserts
BowScoHR	Bowman Scout's Honor Roll
BowTif	Bowman Tiffany
BoyScooAT	Boy Scouts of America Treadway
Bra195T	Braves 1957 TCMA
Bra53 F	Braves 53 Fritsch
BraBilaBP	Braves Bill and Bob Postcards PPC-741
BraBurKL	Braves Burger King Lids
BraCok	Braves Coke
BraDav	Braves Davison's
BraDub	Braves Dubuque
BraDubP	Braves Dubuque Perforated
BraDubS	Braves Dubuque Singles
BraFloA	Braves Florida Agriculture

BraGolS	Braves Golden Stamps
BraGreT	Braves Greats TCMA
BraHos	Braves Hostess
BraIrvD	Braves Irvingdale Dairy
BraJayP	Braves Jay Publishing
BraJohC	Braves Johnston Cookies
BraKryPS	Braves Krystal Postcard Sanders
BraLaktL	Braves Lake to Lake
BraLykP	Braves Lykes Perforated
BraLykS	Braves Lykes Standard
BraMer	Braves Merrell
BraPhoC	Braves Photo Cards
BraPol	Braves Police
BraSmo	Braves Smokey
BraSpiaS	Braves Spic and Span
BraSpiaS3	Braves Spic and Span 3x5
BraSpiaS4	Braves Spic and Span 4x5
BraSpiaS7	Braves Spic and Span 7x10
BraSpiaSD	Braves Spic and Span Die-Cut
BraSpiaSP	Braves Spic and Span Postcards
BraSubS	Braves Dubuque Standard
BraTBSAT	Braves TBS America's Team
BraTCC	Braves TCC
BraUSPC	Braves U.S. Playing Cards
BreA&P	Brewers A and P
BreBro	Brewers Broadcasters
BreBtaTI	Greenville Braves Team Issue
BreCarT	Brewers Carlson Travel
BreCouMB	Brevard County Manatees Best
BreCouMC	Brevard County Manatees Classic
BreCouMF	Brevard County Manatees Fleer/ProCards
BreE10	Breisch-Williams E107
BreGar	Brewers Gardner's
BreGreT	Brewers Greats TCMA
BreMcD	Brewers McDonald's
BreMil	Brewers Milk
BreMilB	Brewers Miller Brewing
BrePol	Brewers Police
BreSen	Brewers Sentry
BreSen5	Brewers Sentry 5x7
BreSenY	Brewers Sentry Yount
BreTeal	Brewers Team Issue
BreUSO	Brewers U.S. Oil
BreYea	Brewers Yearbook
Bri	Briggs
BriBanF	Brisbane Bandits Futura
BriE97	Briggs E97
BriRedST	Bristol Red Sox TCMA
BriTigC	Bristol Tigers Classic
BriTigC	Bristol Tigers Classic/Best
BriTigF	Bristol Tigers Fleer/ProCards
BriTigP	Bristol Tigers ProCards
BriTigS	Bristol Tigers Star
BriWhiSB	Bristol White Sox Best
BriYouC	Brigham Young Cougars
Bro194F	Browns '44 Fritsch
BroPenCB	Browns Pencil Clip Buttons PPC-1
BroW75	Browns W753
BucN28	Buchner N284
BufBisB	Buffalo Bisons Best
BufBisBS	Buffalo Bisons Blue Shield
BufBisC	Buffalo Bisons CMC
BufBisF	Buffalo Bisons Fleer/ProCards
BufBisFJO	Buffalo Bisons F.J. Offerman
BufBisLD	Buffalo Bisons Line Drive
BufBisP	Buffalo Bisons ProCards
BufBisP	Buffalo Bisons Pucko
BufBisS	Buffalo Bisons SkyBox
BufBisT	Buffalo Bisons TCMA
BufBisTI	Buffalo Bisons Team Issue
BulDurM	Bull Durham Movie
BulDurOS	Bull Durham Orion Set
BurAstC	Burlington Astros Classic/Best
BurAstF	Burlington Astros Fleer/ProCards
BurAstP	Burlington Astros ProCards
BurBeeC	Burlington Bees Classic
BurBeeC	Burlington Bees Classic/Best
BurBeeF	Burlington Bees Fleer/ProCards
BurBeeT	Burlington Bees TCMA
BurBeeTI	Burlington Bees Team Issue
BurBraB	Burlington Braves Best
BurBraP	Burlington Braves ProCards
BurBraS	Burlington Braves Star
BurCheD	Burger Chef Discs
BurExpP	Burlington Expos ProCards
BurIndB	Burlington Indians Best
BurIndC	Burlington Indians Classic
BurIndC	Burlington Indians Classic/Best
BurIndF	Burlington Indians Fleer/ProCards
BurIndP	Burlington Indians ProCards
BurIndS	Burlington Indians Star
BurKinA	Burger King All-Pro
BurKinPHR	Burger King Pitch/Hit/Run
BurKinR	Burger King Ripken
BurKinRG	Burger King Ripken Gold
BurRanF	Burlington Rangers Fritsch
BurRanT	Burlington Rangers TCMA
BusBroBPP	Buster Brown Bread Pins PB2
ButCanV	Butterfinger Canadian V94
ButCopKB	Butte Copper Kings Best
ButCopKSP	Butte Copper Kings Sports Pro
ButCopKT	Butte Copper Kings TCMA
ButCopKtI	Butte Copper Kings Team Issue
ButCre	Butter Cream R306
ButPreR	Butterfinger Premiums R310
CadDis	Cadaco Discs
CadEllD	Cadaco Ellis Discs
Cal	Calbee
CalCanC	Calgary Cannons CMC
CalCanC	Calgary Cannons Cramer
CalCanF	Calgary Cannons Fleer/ProCards
CalCanLD	Calgary Cannons Line Drive
CalCanP	Calgary Cannons ProCards
CalCanS	Calgary Cannons SkyBox
CalHOFW	Callahan HOF W576
CalHok	Calbee Hokkaido
CalJap	Calbee Japanese
CalLeaA	California League All-Stars Cal League Cards
CalLeaACL	California League All-Stars Cal League Cards
CalLeaACLC	California League All-Stars Cal League Cards
CalLeLA	California League All-Stars
CamPepP	Cameo Pepsin Pins PE4
CanIndB	Canton-Akron Indians Best
CanIndF	Canton-Akron Indians Fleer/ProCards
CanIndLD	Canton-Akron Indians Line Drive
CanIndP	Canton-Akron Indians ProCards
CanIndS	Canton-Akron Indians SkyBox
CanIndS	Canton-Akron Indians Star
CapCitBC	Capital City Bombers Classic
CapCitBC	Capital City Bombers Classic/Best
CapCitBF	Capital City Bombers Fleer/ProCards
CapCodPB	Cape Cod Prospects Ballpark
CapCodPPaLP	Cape Cod Prospects P and L Promotions
Car	Cardinals
Car	Cardtoons
Car193T	Cardinals 1934 TCMA
Car5	Cardinals 5x7
Car5x7	Cardinals 5x7
CarCoi	Cardinals Coins

CarColBP	Cardinals Colonial Bread Porter
CarColJB	Card Collectors' Justice Boyhood
CarGreT	Cardinals Greats TCMA
CarGuaPG	Card Guard Promo Griffey
CarHawI	Hawaii Islanders Caruso
CarHunW	Cardinals Hunter's Wieners
CarIGAS	Cardinals IGA Stores
CarJayP	Cardinals Jay Publishing
CarKASD	Cardinals KAS Discs
CarLeaA	Carolina League All-Stars
CarLeaA	Carolina League All-Time
CarLeaA1B	Carolina League All-Stars 1 Best
CarLeaA2B	Carolina League All-Stars 2 Best
CarLeaAF	Carolina League All-Stars Fleer/ProCards
CarLeaAGF	Carolina League All-Stars Fleer/ProCards
CarLeaAIB	Carolina League All-Stars Insert Best
CarLeaAP	Carolina League All-Stars ProCards
CarLeaAS	Carolina League All-Stars Star
CarMcD	Cardinals McDonald's/Pacific
CarMudB	Carolina Mudcats Best
CarMudF	Carolina Mudcats Fleer/ProCards
CarMudF	Reading Phillies TCMA
CarMudLD	Carolina Mudcats Line Drive
CarMudP	Carolina Mudcats ProCards
CarMudS	Carolina Mudcats SkyBox
CarMudTI	Carolina Mudcats Team Issue
CarNewE	Carson Newman Eagles
CarPhoG	Phoenix Giants Caruso
CarPol	Cardinals Police
CarSacS	Sacramento Solons Caruso
CarSalLCA	Salt Lake City Angels Caruso
CarSchM	Cardinals Schnucks Milk
CarSmo	Cardinals Smokey
CarSpoI	Spokane Indians Caruso
CarTacT	Tacoma Twins Caruso
CarTeal	Cardinals Team Issue
CarW75	Cardinals W754
CedRapAT	Cedar Rapids Astros TCMA
CedRapCT	Cedar Rapids Cardinals TCMA
CedRapGT	Cedar Rapids Giants TCMA
CedRapKC	Cedar Rapids Kernels Classic
CedRapKC	Cedar Rapids Kernels Classic/Best
CedRapKF	Cedar Rapids Kernels Fleer/ProCards
CedRapKTI	Cedar Rapids Kernels Team Issue
CedRapRB	Cedar Rapids Reds Best
CedRapRC	Cedar Rapids Reds Classic/Best
CedRapRDGB	Cedar Rapids Reds All Decade Best
CedRapRF	Cedar Rapids Reds Fleer/ProCards
CedRapRF	Cedar Rapids Reds Fritsch
CedRapRP	Cedar Rapids Reds ProCards
CedRapRS	Cedar Rapids Reds Star
CedRapRT	Cedar Rapids Reds TCMA
CenFlo	Centennial Flour
CenValRC	Central Valley Rockies Classic
CenValRC	Central Valley Rockies Classic/Best
CenValRF	Central Valley Rockies Fleer/ProCards
CerSup	Cereal Superstars
ChaChaT	Charleston Charlies TCMA
ChaKniB	Charlotte Knights Best
ChaKniF	Charlotte Knights Fleer/ProCards
ChaKniLD	Charlotte Knights Line Drive
ChaKniP	Charlotte Knights ProCards
ChaKniS	Charlotte Knights SkyBox
ChaKniTI	Charlotte Knights Team Issue
ChaLooB	Chattanooga Lookouts Best
ChaLooF	Chattanooga Lookouts Fleer/ProCards
ChaLooGS	Chattanooga Lookouts Grand Slam
ChaLooLD	Chattanooga Lookouts Line Drive
ChaLooLITI	Chattanooga Lookouts Legends II Team Issue
ChaLooLTI	Chattanooga Lookouts Legends Team Issue
ChaLooP	Chattanooga Lookouts ProCards
ChaLooS	Chattanooga Lookouts SkyBox
ChaLooT	Chattanooga Lookouts TCMA
ChaLooTI	Chattanooga Lookouts Team Issue
ChaO'sP	Charlotte O's Police
ChaO'sT	Charlotte O's TCMA
ChaO'sW	Charlotte O's W3TV
ChaO'sW	Charlotte O's WBTV
ChaOriW	Charlotte Orioles WBTV
ChaPatT	Charleston Patriots TCMA
ChaPirT	Charleston Pirates TCMA
ChaRaiB	Charleston Rainbows Best
ChaRaiC	Charleston Rainbows Classic/Best
ChaRaiF	Charleston Rainbows Fleer/ProCards
ChaRaiP	Charleston Rainbows ProCards
ChaRanC	Charlotte Rangers Classic/Best
ChaRanF	Charlotte Rangers Fleer/ProCards
ChaRanP	Charlotte Rangers ProCards
ChaRanS	Charlotte Rangers Star
ChaRivC	Charleston Riverdogs Classic
ChaRivF	Charleston RiverDogs Fleer/ProCards
ChaRivTI	Charleston Riverdogs Team Issue
ChaRivUTIS	Charleston Riverdogs Update Team Issue
ChaRoyT	Charleston Royals TCMA
ChaSupJ	Charboneau Super Joe's
ChaTheY	Challenge The Yankees
ChaWheB	Charleston Wheelers Best
ChaWheC	Charleston Wheelers Classic
ChaWheC	Charleston Wheelers Classic/Best
ChaWheF	Charleston Wheelers Fleer/ProCards
ChaWheP	Charleston Wheelers ProCards
ChaWVWC	Charleston (WV) Wheelers Classic/Best
CheBoy	Chef Boyardee
ChePat	Chemstrand Patches
ChiE	Chicago E90-3
ChiEveAP	Chicago Evening American Pins
ChiGre	Chicago Greats
ChuHomS	Church's Hometown Stars
ChuHomSG	Church's Hometown Stars Gold
ChuShoS	Church's Show Stoppers
CinOraW	Cincinnati Orange/Gray W711-1
Cir	Circa
CirAcc	Circa Access
CirBos	Circa Boss
CirEmeA	Circa Emerald Autographs
CirEmeAR	Circa Emerald Autograph Redemptions
CirFasT	Circa Fast Track
CirIco	Circa Icons
CirK	Circle K
CirLimA	Circa Limited Access
CirRav	Circa Rave
CirRavR	Circa Rave Reviews
CirSupB	Circa Super Boss
CitMetC	Citgo Metal Coins
CitPriC	City Pride Clemente
Cla	Classic
Cla#1DPMF	Classic #1 Draft Pick Mail-In
Cla/Bes	Classic/Best
Cla1	Classic I
Cla2	Classic II
Cla3	Classic III
Cla7/1PC	Classic 7/11 Phone Cards
ClaBenR	Bend Rockies Classic
ClaBlu	Classic Blue
ClaBluBF	Classic/Best Blue Bonus
ClaBonB	Classic Bonus Baby
ClaBreD3	Clark's Bread D-381-2
ClaCP	Classic C-3 Presidential
ClaCreotC	Classic Cream of the Crop
ClaDraP	Classic Draft Picks

ClaDraPFB	Classic Draft Picks Foil Bonus
ClaDraPP	Classic Draft Picks Previews
ClaDraPP	Classic Draft Picks Promos
ClaElmP	Elmira Pioneers Classic
ClaExp#PF	Classic/Best Expansion #1 Picks
ClaFanFPCP	Classic Phone Cards Promos
ClaFisN	Classic/Best Fisher Nuts
ClaFS7	Classic/Best
ClaGam	Classic Game
ClaGolA	Classic/Best Gold Acetates
ClaGolB	Classic/Best Gold Bonus
ClaGolF	Classic/Best Gold
ClaGolLF	Classic/Best Gold LPs
ClaGolN1PLF	Classic/Best Gold #1 Pick LPs
ClaGolP	Classic/Best Gold Promos
ClaGolREF	Classic/Best Gold Rookie Express
ClaHudVR	Hudson Valley Renegades Classic
ClaHunC	Huntington Cubs Classic
ClaLigB	Classic Light Blue
ClaMVPF	Classic/Best MVPs
ClaNolR1	Classic Nolan Ryan 10
ClaPhoC	Classic Phone Cards
ClaPla&MotYF	Classic/Best Player and Manager of the Year
ClaPro	Classic/Best Promo
ClaPro	Classic/Best Promos
ClaRed	Classic Red
ClaRedB	Classic/Best Red Bonus
ClaTraO	Classic Travel Orange
ClaTraP	Classic Travel Purple
ClaTriF	Classic Tri-Cards
ClaUpd	Classic Update
ClaUpdCotC	Classic Update Cream of the Crop
ClaUpdY	Classic Update Yellow
ClaYel	Classic Yellow
ClaYouG	Classic/Best Young Guns
ClePhiC	Clearwater Phillies Classic
ClePhiC	Clearwater Phillies Classic/Best
ClePhiF	Clearwater Phillies Fleer/ProCards
ClePhiP	Clearwater Phillies ProCards
ClePhiS	Clearwater Phillies Star
CliDodT	Clinton Dodgers TCMA
CliGiaB	Clinton Giants Best
CliGiaC	Clinton Giants Classic/Best
CliGiaF	Clinton Giants Fleer/ProCards
CliGiaF	Clinton Giants Fritsch
CliGiaP	Clinton Giants ProCards
CliGiaT	Clinton Giants TCMA
CliGiaUTI	Clinton Giants Update Team Issue
CliLumC	Clinton Lumberkings Classic
CliLumF	Clinton LumberKings Fleer/ProCards
CliLumKTI	Clinton Lumber Kings Team Issue
CliPilT	Clinton Pilots TCMA
CloFotW	Clopay Foto-Fun W626
CloHSS	Clovis HS Smokey
CMC	CMC
CMCBasG	CMC Baseball's Greatest
CMCCan	CMC Canseco
CMCMan	CMC Mantle
CMCMat	CMC Mattingly
CMCRut	CMC Ruth
CocAstT	Cocoa Astros TCMA
CokCapA	Coke Caps All-Stars
CokCapA	Coke Caps Astros
CokCapAAm	Coke Caps All-Stars AL
CokCapAs	Coke Caps Astros
CokCapAt	Coke Caps Athletics
CokCapB	Coke Caps Braves
CokCapBT	Coke Caps Baseball Tips
CokCapC	Coke Caps Cubs
CokCapD	Coke Caps Dodgers
CokCapDA	Coke Caps Dodgers/Angels
CokCapG	Coke Caps Giants
CokCapI	Coke Caps Indians
CokCapNLA	Coke Caps All-Stars NL
CokCapO	Coke Caps Orioles
CokCapPh	Coke Caps Phillies
CokCapPi	Coke Caps Pirates
CokCapR	Coke Caps Reds
CokCapRS	Coke Caps Red Sox
CokCapS	Coke Caps Senators
CokCapT	Coke Caps Tigers
CokCapTi	Coke Caps Tigers
CokCapTw	Coke Caps Twins
CokCapWS	Coke Caps White Sox
CokCapYM	Coke Caps Yankees and Mets
CokCasI	Coke Case Inserts
CokMat	Coke Mattingly
CokTeaS	Coke Team Sets
CokTip	Coke Tips
Col	Collect-A-Books
Col.45B	Colt .45's Booklets
Col.45JP	Colt .45's Jay Publishing
Col45"P	Colt .45's Pepsi-Cola
Col45'HC	Colt .45's Houston Chronicle
Col45'JP	Colt .45's Jay Publishing
ColAllG	Colla All-Star Game
ColAllP	Colla All-Stars Promos
ColAstB	Columbus Astros Best
ColAstP	Columbus Astros ProCards
ColAstT	Columbus Astros TCMA
ColBag	Colla Bagwell
ColBon	Colla Bonds
ColC	Collector's Choice
ColCan	Colla Canseco
ColChiE	Colgan's Chips E254
ColCho	Collector's Choice
ColChoAC	Collector's Choice All-Star Connection
ColChoBS	Collector's Choice Big Shots
ColChoBSGS	Collector's Choice Big Shots Gold Signatures
ColChoCtA	Collector's Choice Crash the All-Star Game
ColChoCtAG	Collector's Choice Crash the All-Star Game Exchange
ColChoCtG	Collector's Choice Crash the Game
ColChoCtGE	Collector's Choice Crash the Game Exchange
ColChoCtGG	Collector's Choice Crash the Game Gold
ColChoCtGGE	Collector's Choice Crash the Game Gold Exchange
ColChoCtGIW	Collector's Choice Crash the Game Instant Win
ColChoGACA	Collector's Choice Griffey A Cut Above
ColChoGriCD	Collector's Choice Griffey Clearly Dominant
ColChoGS	Collector's Choice Gold Signature
ColChoHRA	Collector's Choice Home Run All-Stars
ColChoNF	Collector's Choice New Frontier
ColChoNS	Collector's Choice Nomo Scrapbook
ColChoPP	Collector's Choice Premier Power
ColChoPPG	Collector's Choice Premier Power Gold
ColChoS	Collector's Choice Stick'Ums
ColChoSE	Collector's Choice SE
ColChoSEGS	Collector's Choice SE Gold Signature
ColChoSESS	Collector's Choice SE Silver Signature
ColChoSS	Collector's Choice Silver Signature
ColChoT	Collector's Choice Team vs. Team
ColChoTBS	Collector's Choice The Big Show
ColChoTBSWH	Collector's Choice The Big Show World Headquarters
ColChoTotT	Collector's Choice Toast of the Town

ColChoYMtP	Collector's Choice You Make the Play
ColChoYMtPGS	Collector's Choice You Make the Play Gold Signature
ColCliB	Columbus Clippers Best
ColCliC	Columbus Clippers CMC
ColCliF	Columbus Clippers Fleer/ProCards
ColCliLD	Columbus Clippers Line Drive
ColCliMCTI	Columbus Clippers Milk Caps Team Issue
ColCliP	Columbus Clippers Police
ColCliP	Columbus Clippers ProCards
ColCliS	Columbus Clippers SkyBox
ColCliT	Columbus Clippers TCMA
ColCliTI	Columbus Clippers Team Issue
ColE13	Collins-McCarthy E135
ColEdgDJ	Collector's Edge Dial Justice
ColGoo	Colla Gooden
ColGriJ	Colla Griffey Jr.
ColGwy	Colla Gwynn
ColIndC	Columbus Indians Classic/Best
ColIndP	Columbus Indians ProCards
ColJoeC	Colla Joe Carter
ColJus	Colla Justice
ColMaa	Colla Maas
ColMat	Colla Mattingly
ColMcG	Colla McGwire
ColMeaPP	Colonial Meat Products Piersall
ColMetB	Columbia Mets Best
ColMetC	Columbia Mets Classic/Best
ColMetF	Columbia Mets Fleer/ProCards
ColMetGS	Columbia Mets Grand Slam
ColMetP	Columbia Mets ProCards
ColMetPI	Columbia Mets PLAY II
ColMetPIISPI	Columbia Mets Insert Set PLAY II
ColMetPPI	Columbia Mets Postcards Play II
ColMudB	Columbus Mudcats Best
ColMudP	Columbus Mudcats ProCards
ColMudS	Columbus Mudcats Star
ColPosD	Colla Postcards Dawson
ColPosG	Colla Postcards Grace
ColPosG	Colla Postcards Greenwell
ColPosM	Colla Postcards Mitchell
ColPosMc	Colla Postcards McGwire
ColPosOS	Colla Postcards Ozzie Smith
ColPosP	Colla Postcards Piazza
ColPosRJ	Colla Postcards Ripken Jr.
ColPosS	Colla Postcards Sandberg
ColPosWC	Colla Postcards Will Clark
ColPro	Colla Promos
ColRedB	Colgan's Red Border
ColRedC	Columbus Redstixx Classic
ColRedC	Columbus RedStixx Classic/Best
ColRedF	Columbus Redstixx Fleer/ProCards
ColRobA	Colla Roberto Alomar
ColRya	Colla Ryan
ColSan	Colla Sandberg
ColSilB	Colorado Silver Bullets
ColSilB9	Colorado Silver Bullets
ColSilBC	Colorado Silver Bullets Coors
ColSprSSC	Colorado Springs Sky Sox CMC
ColSprSSF	Colorado Springs Sky Sox Fleer/ProCards
ColSprSSLD	Colorado Springs Sky Sox Line Drive
ColSprSSP	Colorado Springs Sky Sox ProCards
ColSprSSS	Colorado Springs Sky Sox SkyBox
ColSprSSTI	Colorado Springs Sky Sox Team Issue
ColStr	Colla Strawberry
ColtheSBM	Collect the Stars Baseball Magnetables
ColTho	Colla Thomas
ColTinT	Colgans Tin Tops
ColWilC	Colla Will Clark
ComIma	Comic Images
ComImaP	Comic Images Promo
ConAmeA	Conlon American All-Stars
ConHar	Conlon Hardee's/Coke
ConMar	Conlon Marketcom
ConMasB	Conlon Masters BW
ConMasC	Conlon Masters Color
ConNatA	Conlon National All-Stars
ConNegA	Conlon Negro All-Stars
ConSer1	Conlon Series 1
ConSer2	Conlon Series 2
ConSer3	Conlon Series 3
ConSer4	Conlon Series 4
ConSer5	Conlon Series 5
ConT20	Contentnea T209
ConTSN	Conlon TSN
ConTSN1N	Conlon TSN 13th National
ConTSNAP	Conlon TSN All-Star Program
ConTSNB	Conlon TSN Burgundy
ConTSNCI	Conlon TSN Color Inserts
ConTSNCMP	Conlon TSN Club Members Promos
ConTSNGI	Conlon TSN Gold Inserts
ConTSNGJ	Conlon TSN Griffey Jr.
ConTSNP	Conlon TSN Promos
ConTSNP	Conlon TSN Prototypes
CooPapB	Cool Papa Bell
CouT21	Coupon T213
CouTimLBR	Country Time Legends Brooks Robinson
CraDis	Crane Discs
CraJac	Cracker Jack
CraJacE	Cracker Jack E145-1
CraJacE	Cracker Jack E145-2
CraJacP	Cracker Jack Pins PR4
CraSalLCG	Salt Lake City Gulls Cramer
Cub190T	Cubs 1907 TCMA
CubA.CDPP	Cubs A.C. Dietsche Postcards PC765
CubCan	Cubs Canon
CubChi	Cubs Chi-Foursome
CubChiT	Cubs Chicago Tribune
CubDavB	Cubs David Berg
CubDunD	Cubs Dunkin Donuts
CubGat	Cubs Gatorade
CubGFGCP	Cubs G.F. Grignon Co. PC775
CubGreT	Cubs Greats TCMA
CubJayP	Cubs Jay Publishing
CubJewT	Cubs Jewel Tea
CubLea	Cuban League
CubLioP	Cubs Lion Photo
CubMar	Cubs Marathon
CubOldS	Cubs Old Style
CubOldSBW	Cubs Old Style Billy Williams
CubPho	Cubs Photos
CubPos	Cubs Postcards
CubProPS	Cubs Pro's Pizza Supermarket
CubRedL	Cubs Red Lobster
CubRol	Cubs Rolaids
CubSev	Cubs Seven-Up
CubTeal	Cubs Team Issue
CubTealC	Cubs Team Issue Color
CubThoAV	Cubs Thorn Apple Valley
CubUno	Cubs Unocal
CubVanLS	Cubs Vance Law Smokey
CubVinL	Cubs Vine Line
CubWGN	Cubs WGN/Pepsi
CUIMCG	CUI Metal Cards Griffey
CUIMCR	CUI Metal Cards Ripken
D3	D3
D3Zon	D3 Zone
DaiDolF	Daikyo Dolphins Futura
DaiQueKGJ	Dairy Queen Griffey Jr.
DaiQueS	Dairy Queen Statues
DalCon	Dallas Convention
DalNatCC	Dallas National Collectors Convention

DanBraB	Danville Braves Best
DanBraC	Danville Braves Classic
DanBraC	Danville Braves Classic/Best
DanBraF	Danville Braves Fleer/ProCards
DanBraTI	Danville Braves Team Issue
DanDee	Dan Dee
DanSunF	Danville Suns Fritsch
DarChoE	Darby Chocolates E271
DarFar	Darigold Farms
DavLipB	David Lipscomb Bisons
DayBeaAP	Daytona Beach Admirals ProCards
DayBeaAT	Daytona Beach Astros TCMA
DayBeaIP	Daytona Beach Islanders ProCards
DayBeaIT	Daytona Beach Islanders TCMA
DayCubB	Daytona Cubs Best
DayCubC	Daytona Cubs Classic
DayCubC	Daytona Cubs Classic/Best
DayCubF	Daytona Cubs Fleer/ProCards
DayDaiNM	Dayton Daily News M137
DEL	Classic/Best Autographs
DelR33	Delong R333
DelRut	Delphi Ruth
DelShoB	Delmarva Shorebirds Best
DenBal	Denver BallPark
DenHol	Denny's Holograms
DenHolGS	Denny's Holograms Grand Slam
DenHolGSAP	Denny's Holograms Grand Slam Artist's Proofs
DenZepC	Denver Zephrys CMC
DenZepC	Denver Zephrys CMC
DenZepF	Denver Zephyrs Fleer/ProCards
DenZepLD	Denver Zephyrs Line Drive
DenZepP	Denver Zephyrs ProCards
DenZepS	Denver Zephyrs SkyBox
DeSCom	DeSa Commemorative
DexPre	Dexter Press
Dia	Dimanche/Derniere Heure
DiaCla	Diamond Classics
DiaClaS2	Diamond Classics Series 2
DiaGre	Diamond Greats
DiaGumP	Diamond Gum Pins
DiaMar	Diamond Marks
DiaMarA	Diamond Marks Art
DiaMarP	Diamond Marks Prototypes
DiaMatCS2	Diamond Match Co. Series 2
DiaMatCS3T1	Diamond Match Co. Series 3 Type 1
DiaMatCS3T2	Diamond Match Co. Series 3 Type 2
DiaMatCS4	Diamond Match Co. Series 4
DiaStaCD	Diamond Stars Continuation Den's
DiaStaES	Diamond Stars Extension Set
DiaStaR	Diamond Stars R327
Dim2GT	Dimple II Glove Tags
DixLid	Dixie Lids
DixLidP	Dixie Lids Premiums
DixPre	Dixie Premiums
DoctheV	Doc "The Video"
Dod	Dodgers
Dod195T	Dodgers 1955 TCMA
DodBelB	Dodgers Bell Brand
DodBlu	Dodgers Blue
DodCokP	Dodgers Coke Postcards
DodGolS	Dodgers Golden Stamps
DodGreT	Dodgers Greats TCMA
DodHea	Dodgers Heads-Up
DodJayP	Dodgers Jay Publishing
DodMor	Dodgers Morrell
DodMot	Dodgers Mother's
DodPol	Dodgers Police
DodPos	Dodgers Postcards
DodROY	Dodgers ROYs
DodSmo	Dodgers Smokey
DodSmoA	Dodgers Smokey All-Stars
DodSmoG	Dodgers Smokey Greats
DodStaSV	Dodgers Stamps St. Vincent
DodStaTA	Dodgers Stamps Trak Auto
DodTar	Dodgers Target
DodTeaI	Dodgers Team Issue
DodTic	Dodgers Ticketron
DodUniO	Dodgers Union Oil
DodUniOP	Dodgers Union Oil Photos
DodUniOV	Dodgers Union Oil Volpe
DodUno7P	Dodgers Unocal 76 Pins
DodVol	Dodgers Volpe
DogBuiE	Dodgers Builders Emporium
DomDisP	Domino Discs PX7
DomLeaS	Dominican League Stickers
Don	Donruss
DonActA	Donruss Action All-Stars
DonActAS	Donruss Action All-Stars
DonAll	Donruss All-Stars
DonAllB	Donruss All-Star Box
DonAnn8	Donruss Anniversary '84
DonArmaD	Donruss Armed and Dangerous
DonAwaWJ	Donruss Award Winner Jumbos
DonBasB	Donruss Baseball's Best
DonBesA	Donruss Best AL
DonBesN	Donruss Best NL
DonBomS	Donruss Bomb Squad
DonBonC	Donruss Bonus Cards
DonBonM	Donruss Bonus MVP's
DonCha	Donruss Champions
DonCokR	Donruss Coke Ryan
DonCraJ1	Donruss Cracker Jack I
DonCraJ2	Donruss Cracker Jack II
DonDiaK	Donruss Diamond Kings
DonDiaKC	Donruss Diamond Kings Canvas
DonDom	Donruss Dominators
DonEli	Donruss Elite
DonEli	Donruss Elite Inserts
DonEliD	Donruss Elite Dominators
DonEliGS	Donruss Elite Gold Stars
DonEliLaL	Donruss Elite Leather and Lumber
DonEliPtT	Donruss Elite Passing the Torch
DonEliPtTA	Donruss Elite Passing the Torch Autographs
DonEliS	Donruss Elite Supers
DonEliTotC	Donruss Elite Turn of the Century
DonEliTotCDC	Donruss Elite Turn of the Century Die Cuts
DonFraFea	Donruss Franchise Features
DonFreF	Donruss Freeze Frame
DonGraS	Donruss Grand Slammers
DonHig	Donruss Highlights
DonHitL	Donruss Hit List
DonHOFH	Donruss HOF Heroes
DonHOFS	Donruss HOF Sluggers
DonJenHS	Huntsville Stars Jennings
DonLeaS	Donruss Learning Series
DonLim	Donruss Limited
DonLimFotG	Donruss Limited Fabric of the Game
DonLimLE	Donruss Limited Limited Exposure
DonLonBL	Donruss Long Ball Leaders
DonLonL	Donruss Longball Leaders
DonMasotG	Donruss Masters of the Game
DonMat#	Mattingly's #23 Restaurant
DonMcD	Donruss McDonald's
DonMouM	Donruss Mound Marvels
DonMVP	Donruss MVPs
DonOpeD	Donruss Opening Day
DonP	Donruss Pop-Ups
DonPop	Donruss Pop-Ups
DonPowA	Donruss Power Alley

DonPowADC	Donruss Power Alley Die Cuts
DonPre	Donruss Preferred
DonPre	Donruss Previews
DonPreCttC	Donruss Preferred Cut to the Chase
DonPreP	Donruss Press Proofs
DonPrePGold	Donruss Press Proofs Gold
DonPrePM	Donruss Preferred Precious Metals
DonPreS	Donruss Preferred Staremasters
DonPreTB	Donruss Preferred Tin Boxes
DonPreTBG	Donruss Preferred Tin Boxes Gold
DonPreTP	Donruss Preferred Tin Packs
DonPreTPG	Donruss Preferred Tin Packs Gold
DonPreXP	Donruss Preferred X-Ponential Power
DonPro	Donruss Promos
DonPurP	Donruss Pure Power
DonRatR	Donruss Rated Rookies
DonReaBY	Donruss Team Book Yankees
DonRipOWIK	Donruss Ripken The Only Way I Know
DonRocL	Donruss Rocket Launchers
DonRoo	Donruss Rookies
DonRooDK	Donruss Rookie Diamond Kings
DonRooDKC	Donruss Rookie Diamond Kings Canvas
DonRooP	Donruss Rookies Phenoms
DonRouT	Donruss Round Trippers
DonSam	Donruss Samples
DonSho	Donruss Showdown
DonSpeE	Donruss Special Edition
DonSpiotG	Donruss Spirit of the Game
DonSupD	Donruss Super DK's
DonTea	Donruss Team Sets
DonTeaBA	Donruss Team Book Athletics
DonTeaBC	Donruss Team Book Cubs
DonTeaBM	Donruss Team Book Mets
DonTeaBRS	Donruss Team Book Red Sox
DonTeaSMVP	Donruss Team Sets MVP's
DonTeaSPE	Donruss Team Sets Pennant Edition
DonTopotO	Donruss Top of the Order
DonTra	Donruss Traded
DonUpd	Donruss Update
DonWaxBC	Donruss Wax Box Cards
DonWin	Don Wingfield
Dor	Dormand
DorChe	Dorman's Cheese
DouDisP	Doubleheader Discs PX3
DouPlaR	Double Play R330
Dra	Drake's
DubPacT	Dubuque Packers TCMA
DukCabN	Duke Cabinets N142
DukTotDZN	Duke Talk of the Diamond N135
DunBluJB	Dunedin Blue Jays Best
DunBluJC	Dunedin Blue Jays Classic
DunBluJC	Dunedin Blue Jays Classic/Best
DunBluJF	Dunedin Blue Jays Fleer/ProCards
DunBluJFFN	Dunedin Blue Jays Family Fun Night
DunBluJP	Dunedin Blue Jays ProCards
DunBluJS	Dunedin Blue Jays Star
DunBluJT	Dunedin Blue Jays TCMA
DunBluJTI	Dunedin Blue Jays Team Issue
DunBluJUTI	Dunedin Blue Jays Update Team Issue
DunDonPPS	Pawtucket Red Sox Dunkin' Donuts
DurBulBIB	Durham Bulls (Blue) Best
DurBulBrB	Durham Bulls (Brown) Best
DurBulC	Durham Bulls Classic
DurBulC	Durham Bulls Classic/Best
DurBulF	Durham Bulls Fleer/ProCards
DurBulIS	Durham Bulls I Star
DurBulIS	Durham Bulls II Star
DurBulP	Durham Bulls ProCards
DurBulS	Durham Bulls Star
DurBulT	Durham Bulls TCMA
DurBulTI	Durham Bulls Team Issue
DurBulUP	Durham Bulls Update ProCards
DurBulUTI	Durham Bulls Update Team Issue
DurPowP1	Duracell Power Players I
DurPowP2	Duracell Power Players II
DynRos	Dynasty Rose
E&SP	E and S Publishing
E-UOraBSC	E-Unc. Orange Bordered Strip Cards
E101	E101
E102	E102
E120	E120
E121So1	E121 Series of 120
E121So8	E121 Series of 80
E12AmeCDC	American Caramel Die Cuts E125
E94	E94
E98	E98
EagBalL	Eagle Ballpark Legends
EasLeaAP	Eastern League All-Stars ProCards
EasLeaDDP	Eastern League Diamond Diplomacy ProCards
EdgR.WG	Edgerton R. Williams Game
EdmTraC	Edmonton Trappers CMC
EdmTraC	Edmonton Trappers Cramer
EdmTraF	Edmonton Trappers Fleer/ProCards
EdmTraLD	Edmonton Trappers Line Drive
EdmTraP	Edmonton Trappers ProCards
EdmTraRR	Edmonton Trappers Red Rooster
EdmTraS	Edmonton Trappers SkyBox
EdmTraT	Edmonton Trappers TCMA
EdmTraTI	Edmonton Trappers Team Issue
El PasDAGTI	El Paso Diablos All-Time Greats Team Issue
El PasDB	El Paso Diablos Best
El PasDF	El Paso Diablos Fleer/ProCards
El PasDTI	El Paso Diablos Team Issue
EliSenL	Elite Senior League
EliTwiC	Elizabethton Twins Classic
EliTwiC	Elizabethton Twins Classic/Best
EliTwiF	Elizabethton Twins Fleer/ProCards
EliTwiP	Elizabethton Twins ProCards
EliTwiS	Elizabethton Twins Star
ElmPio(C	Elmira Pioneers (Black) Cain
ElmPio(C	Elmira Pioneers (Red) Cain
ElmPio1C	Elmira Pioneers 100th Cain
ElmPioC	Elmira Pioneers Cain
ElmPioC	Elmira Pioneers Classic/Best
ElmPioF	Elmira Pioneers Fleer/ProCards
ElmPioP	Elmira Pioneers ProCards
ElmPioP	Elmira Pioneers Pucko
ElmPioRSP	Elmira Pioneer Red Sox ProCards
ElmPioRST	Elmira Pioneer Red Sox TCMA
ElmPioT	Elmira Pioneers TCMA
ElmPioTI	Elmira Pioneers Team Issue
ElmPioUTI	Elmira Pionners Update Team Issue
ElPasDB	El Paso Diablos Best
ElPasDF	El Paso Diablos Fleer/ProCards
ElPasDGS	El Paso Diablos Grand Slam
ElPasDLD	El Paso Diablos Line Drive
ElPasDP	El Paso Diablos ProCards
ElPasDS	El Paso Diablos SkyBox
ElPasDT	El Paso Diablos TCMA
ElSidPog	El Sid Pogs
Emb	Embossed
EmbGolI	Embossed Golden Idols
Emo	Emotion
EmoLegoB	Emotion-XL Legion of Boom
EmoMas	Emotion Masters
EmoN	Emotion N-Tense
EmoN	Emotion-XL N-Tense
EmoR	Emotion Ripken
EmoRarB	Emotion-XL Rare Breed
EmoRoo	Emotion Rookies

EmoXL	Emotion-XL
EmoXLD	Emotion-XL D-Fense
EquSpoHoF	Equitable Sports Hall of Fame *
EriCarP	Erie Cardinals ProCards
EriCarT	Erie Cardinals TCMA
EriOriS	Erie Orioles Star
EriSaiC	Erie Sailors Classic/Best
EriSaiF	Erie Sailors Fleer/ProCards
EriSaiP	Erie Sailors ProCards
EriSaiS	Erie Sailors Star
EriSeaB	Erie Seawolves Best
EssCoi	Esso Coins
EugEmeB	Eugene Emeralds Best
EugEmeC	Eugene Emeralds Classic
EugEmeC	Eugene Emeralds Classic/Best
EugEmeC	Eugene Emeralds Cramer
EugEmeF	Eugene Emeralds Fleer/ProCards
EugEmeGS	Eugene Emeralds Grand Slam
EugEmeP	Eugene Emeralds Procards
EugEmeTI	Eugene Emeralds Team Issue
EurSta	Eureka Stamps
EvaTriT	Evansville Triplets TCMA
EvaTriT	Evansville Tripletts TCMA
EveAqaTI	Everett Aquasox Team Issue
EveAquB	Everett Aquasox Best
EveGiaB	Everett Giants Best
EveGiaC	Everett Giants Classic
EveGiaC	Everett Giants Classic/Best
EveGiaC	Everett Giants Cramer
EveGiaF	Everett Giants Fleer/ProCards
EveGiaIC	Everett Giants II Cramer
EveGiaP	Everett Giants ProCards
EveGiaPC	Everett Giants Popcorn Cramer
EveGiaS	Everett Giants Star
Exc	Excel
ExcAll	Excel All-Stars
ExcAll	Excel All-Stars
ExcAllF	Excel All-Stars
ExcCli	Excel Climbing
ExcFirYP	Excel First Year Phenoms
ExcFirYPF	Excel First Year Phenoms
ExcFS7	Excel
ExcLeaL	Excel League Leaders
ExcLeaLF	Excel League Leaders
ExcSeaC	Excel Season Crowns
ExcSeaTL	Excel Season Team Leaders
Exh	Exhibits
Exh	Exhibits Four-in-One
ExhCan	Exhibits Canadian
ExhFou	Exhibits Four-in-One
ExhFou	Exhibits Four-in-One W463-4
ExhFou	Exhibits Four-in-One W463-5
ExhFou	Exhibits Four-in-One W463-6
ExhFou	Exhibits Four-in-One W463-7
ExhHoF	Exhibit Hall of Fame
ExhPCL	Exhibits PCL
ExhSal	Exhibits Salutation
ExhStaB	Exhibit Stat Back
ExhTea	Exhibits Team
ExhWriH	Exhibits Wrigley HOF
ExpBoo	Expos Bookmarks
ExpColP7	Expos Postcards
ExpDis	Expos Discs
ExpDonD	Expos Donruss Durivage
ExpDonM	Expos Donruss McDonald's
ExpFudP	Expos Fud's Photography
ExpGreT	Expos Greats TCMA
ExpHygM	Expos Hygrade Meats
ExpLaPR	Expos La Pizza Royale
ExpPin	Expos Pins
ExpPos	Expos Postcards
ExpPosN	Expos Postcards Named
ExpProPa	Expos Provigo Panels
ExpProPo	Expos Provigo Posters
ExpPS	Expos Pro Stars
ExpRed	Expos Redpath
ExpStu	Expos Stuart
ExpWes	Expos Weston
ExpZel	Expos Zellers
ExtBas	Extra Bases
ExtBasGB	Extra Bases Game Breakers
ExtBasMLH	Extra Bases Major League Hopefuls
ExtBasPD	Extra Bases Pitchers Duel
ExtBasRS	Extra Bases Rookie Standouts
ExtBasSYS	Extra Bases Second Year Stars
FanCar	FanFest Carlton
FanCle	FanFest Clemente
FanCraAL	Fan Craze AL WG2
FanCraNL	Fan Craze NL WG3
FanRya	FanFest Ryan
FatPlaT	Fatima Players T222
FatT20	Fatima T200
FayGenB	Fayeteville Generals Best
FayGenC	Fayetteville Generals Classic
FayGenC	Fayetteville Generals Classic/Best
FayGenF	Fayetteville Generals Fleer/ProCards
FayGenP	Fayetteville Generals ProCards
FayGenTI	Fayetteville Generals Team Issue
FBIDis	FBI Discs
FegMurCG	Feg Murray's Cartoon Greats
FifNatC	Fifth National Convention
FifNatCT	Fifth National Convention Tickets
Fin	Finest
FinBro	Finest Bronze
FinEmb	Finest Embossed
FinEmbR	Finest Embossed Refractors
FinFlaT	Finest Flame Throwers
FinJum	Finest Jumbos
FinLan	Finest Landmark
FinPowK	Finest Power Kings
FinPre	Finest Pre-Production
FinPro	Finest Promos
FinProR	Finest Promo Refractors
FinRef	Finest Refractors
FisBakL	Fischer Baking Labels
Fla	Flair
FlaDiaC	Flair Diamond Cuts
FlaHotG	Flair Hot Gloves
FlaHotN	Flair Hot Numbers
FlaInfP	Flair Infield Power
FlaOutP	Flair Outfield Power
FlaPow	Flair Powerline
FlaPro	Flair Promos
FlaRip	Flair Ripken
FlaSho	Flair Showcase
FlaShoARR	Flair Showcase Alex Rodriguez Redemption
FlaShoDC	Flair Showcase Diamond Cuts
FlaShoHG	Flair Showcase Hot Gloves
FlaShoLC	Flair Showcase Legacy Collection
FlaShoLCM	Flair Showcase Legacy Collection Masterpieces
FlaShoWotF	Flair Showcase Wave of the Future
FlaTodS	Flair Today's Spotlight
FlaWavotF	Flair Wave of the Future
Fle	Fleer
FleAll	Fleer All-Stars
FleAllF	Fleer All-Fleer
FleAllR	Fleer All-Rookies
FleAllS	Fleer All-Stars
FleAndJA	Fleer Andruw Jones Autograph
FleASMG	Fleer AS Match Game

FleAtl	Fleer Atlantic
FleAutR	Fleer Autograph Redemption
FleAwaW	Fleer Award Winners
FleBasA	Fleer Baseball All-Stars
FleBasF	Fleer Baseball Firsts
FleBasM	Fleer Baseball MVP's
FleBleB	Fleer Bleacher Blasters
FleBra	Fleer Braves
FleBreD	Fleischmann Bread D381
FleCan	Fleer Canadian
FleChe	Fleer Checklists
FleCitTP	Fleer Citgo The Performer
FleCle	Fleer Clemens
FleCloS	Fleer Cloth Stickers
FleCub	Fleer Cubs
FleDecoE	Fleer Decade of Excellence
FleDecoERT	Fleer Decade of Excellence Rare Traditions
FleDiaT	Fleer Diamond Tribute
FleDod	Fleer Dodgers
FleExcS	Fleer Exciting Stars
FleFamF	Fleer Famous Feats
FleFinE	Fleer Final Edition
FleFinEDT	Fleer Final Edition Diamond Tribute
FleForTR	Fleer For The Record
FleFruotL	Fleer Fruit of the Loom
FleFutHoF	Fleer Future Hall of Famers
FleGamW	Fleer Game Winners
FleGla	Fleer Glavine
FleGlo	Fleer Glossy
FleGolM	Fleer Golden Memories
FleGolM	Fleer Golden Moments
FleGouG	Fleer Goudey Greats
FleGouGF	Fleer Goudey Greats Foil
FleHea	Fleer Headliners
FleHeroB	Fleer Heroes of Baseball
FleHotS	Fleer Hottest Stars
FleInd	Fleer Indians
FleLeaL	Fleer League Leaders
FleLeaS	Fleer League Standouts
FleLimBC	Fleer Limited Box Cards
FleLimE	Fleer Limited Edition
FleLumC	Fleer Lumber Company
FleMajLP	Fleer Major League Prospects
FleMilDM	Fleer Million Dollar Moments
FleMin	Fleer Mini
FleNewH	Fleer New Horizons
FleNig&D	Fleer Night and Day
FleOri	Fleer Orioles
FlePio	Fleer Pioneers
FlePosG	Fleer Postseason Glory
FlePro	Fleer Pro-Visions
FlePro	Fleer Prospects
FleRan	Fleer Rangers
FleRecS	Fleer Record Setters
FleRedS	Fleer Red Sox
FleRoaW	Fleer Road Warriors
FleRoc	Fleer Rockies
FleRooS	Fleer Rookie Sensations
FleSal	Fleer Salmon
FleSlu	Fleer Sluggers/Pitchers
FleSluBC	Fleer Sluggers/Pitchers Box Cards
FleSmo'H	Fleer Smoke 'n Heat
FleSmo'nH	Fleer Smoke 'n Heat
FleSoaS	Fleer Soaring Stars
FleSt.LM	St. Lucie Mets Fleer/ProCards
FleSta	Fleer Stamps
FleStaS	Fleer Star Stickers
FleSti	Fleer Stickers
FleStiC	Fleer Sticker Cards
FleStiWBC	Fleer Stickers Wax Box Cards
FleSun	Fleer Sunoco
FleSup	Fleer Superstars
FleSupBC	Fleer Superstars Box Cards
FleTeaL	Fleer Team Leaders
FleTif	Fleer Tiffany
FleTomL	Fleer Tomorrow's Legends
FleUpd	Fleer Update
FleUpd	Fleer Update Diamond Tribute
FleUpdDT	Fleer Update Diamond Tribute
FleUpdG	Fleer Update Glossy
FleUpdH	Fleer Update Headliners
FleUpdNH	Fleer Update New Horizons
FleUpdRU	Fleer Update Rookie Update
FleUpdSL	Fleer Update Smooth Leather
FleUpdSS	Fleer Update Soaring Stars
FleUpdTC	Fleer Update Tiffany
FleWaxBC	Fleer Wax Box Cards
FleWhiS	Fleer White Sox
FleWil	Fleer Williams
FleWilD	Fleer Wildest Days
FleWorS	Fleer World Series
FleZon	Fleer Zone
Flo	Flopps
FloStaLAF	Florida State League All-Stars Fleer/ProCards
FloStaLAP	Florida State League All-Stars ProCards
FloStaLAS	Florida State League All-Stars Star
FloStaLAS	Florida State League All-Stars Star
ForLauRSC	Fort Lauderdale Red Sox Classic/Best
ForLauRSFP	Fort Lauderdale Red Sox Fleer/ProCards
ForLauYC	Fort Lauderdale Yankees Classic/Best
ForLauYS	Fort Lauderdale Yankees Sussman
ForLauYS	Fort Lauderdale Yanks Sussman
ForLauYTI	Fort Lauderdale Yankees Team Issue
ForMyeMC	Fort Myers Miracle Classic
ForMyeMC	Fort Myers Miracle Classic/Best
ForMyeMF	Fort Myers Miracle Fleer/ProCards
ForMyeMTI	Fort Myers Miracle Team Issue
ForMyeRT	Fort Myers Royals TCMA
ForPosBS1	Forst Postcards Ballpark Series 1
ForPosBS2	Forst Postcards Ballpark Series 2
ForWayWB	Fort Wayne Wizards Best
ForWayWC	Fort Wayne Wizards Classic
ForWayWC	Fort Wayne Wizards Classic/Best
ForWayWF	Fort Wayne Wizards Fleer/ProCards
ForWayWTI	Fort Wayne Wizards Team Issue
FouBal	Foul Ball
FouBasHN	Four Base Hits N-Unc.
FraBabR	Franchise Babe Ruth
FraBroR	Franchise Brooks Robinson
FraGloT	Franklin Glove Tag
FraGloT	Franklin Glove Tags
FraThoC	Frank Thomas Coin
Fre	French's
FreGiaP	Fresno Giants Police
FreKeyB	Frederick Keys Best
FreKeyC	Frederick Keys Classic
FreKeyC	Frederick Keys Classic/Best
FreKeyF	Frederick Keys Fleer/ProCards
FreKeyP	Frederick Keys ProCards
FreKeyS	Frederick Keys Star
FreKeyTI	Frederick Keys Team Issue
FreStaBS	Fresno State Bulldogs Smokey
FreStaLBS	Fresno State Lady Bulldogs Smokey
FreSunCLC	Fresno Suns Cal League Cards
FreSunP	Fresno Suns ProCards
FRIAAG	Fritsch AAGPBL
FriBasCM	Fritsch Baseball Card Museum
FriOneYW	Fritsch One Year Winners
FroJoy	Fro Joy
FroRowAH	Front Row ATG Holograms

FroRowB	Front Row Brock
FroRowBa	Front Row Banks
FroRowBe	Front Row Berra
FroRowBL	Front Row Buck Leonard
FroRowBR	Front Row Brooks Robinson
FroRowC	Front Row Campanella
FroRowCGS	Front Row Campanella Gold Signature
FroRowCH	Front Row Campanella Hologram
FroRowD	Front Row Dandridge
FroRowDP	Front Row Draft Picks
FroRowDPP	Front Row Draft Picks Promos
FroRowDPPC	Front Row Draft Picks Promo Card
FroRowDPPS	Front Row Draft Picks Promo Sheet
FroRowF	Front Row Fingers
FroRowF	Front Row Ford
FroRowFR	Front Row Frankie Rodriguez
FroRowGCH	Front Row Griffey Club House
FroRowGG	Front Row Griffey Gold
FroRowGH	Front Row Griffey Holograms
FroRowGJGC	Front Row Griffey Jr. Gold Collection
FroRowGJOC	Front Row Griffey Jr. Oversized Card
FroRowI	Front Row Irvin
FroRowKGJ	Front Row Ken Griffey Jr.
FroRowN	Front Row Newhouser
FroRowP	Front Row Palmer
FroRowRF	Front Row Rick Ferrell
FroRowSe	Front Row Seaver
FroRowSt	Front Row Stargell
FroRowT	Front Row Thomas
FroRowTG	Front Row Thomas Gold
FroRowTG	Front Row Tyler Green
Ft.LauYC	Ft. Lauderdale Yankees Classic/Best
Ft.LauYF	Fort Lauderdale Yankees Fleer/ProCards
Ft.LauYP	Ft. Lauderdale Yankees ProCards
Ft.LauYS	Ft. Lauderdale Yankees Star
Ft.MyeMCB	Fort Myer Miracle Classic/Best
Ft.MyeMF	Fort Myers Miracle Fleer/ProCards
Ft.MyeRP	Ft. Myers Royals ProCards
Ft.MyeRT	Ft. Myers Royals TCMA
FtMyeMB	Fort Myers Miracle Best
FunBal	Fun Ball
FunFac	Funky Facts
FunFooP	Fun Foods Pins
FUnPac	Fun Pack
FunPacA	Fun Pack All-Stars
FunPacM	Fun Pack Mascots
GadFunC	Gad Fun Cards
GahWilMB	Gahan Wilson Monster Baseball
GalBasGHoF	Galasso Baseball's Great Hall of Fame
GalGloG	Galasso Glossy Greats
GalHaloFRL	Galasso Hall of Famers Ron Lewis
GalRegJ	Galasso Reggie Jackson
GandBCGCE	G and B Chewing Gum Co E223
GasAmeMBD	Gassler's American Maid Bread D381-1
GasRanB	Gastonia Rangers Best
GasRanC	Gastonia Rangers Classic/Best
GasRanF	Gastonia Rangers Fleer/ProCards
GasRanP	Gastonia Rangers ProCards
GasRanS	Gastonia Rangers Star
GasRanT	Gastonia Rangers TCMA
GatCitPP	Gate City Pioneers ProCards
GatCitPSP	Gate City Pioneers Sports Pro
GenCubC	Geneva Cubs Classic/Best
GenCubF	Geneva Cubs Fleer/ProCards
GenCubP	Geneva Cubs ProCards
GenCubS	Geneva Cubs Star
GenMilB	General Mills Booklets
GenMilS	General Mills Stickers
GeoBreP	George Brett Promo
GeoBurP	George Burke PC744
GeoCMil	George C. Miller R300

GeoColC	Georgia College Colonials
GeoSteM	George Steinbrenner Menu
Gia	Giants
Gia195T	Giants 1951 TCMA
GiaActIS	Giants Action Images Stand-Ups
GiaAMC	Giants AMC
GiaArmT	Giants Armour Tabs
GiaATaTTP	Giants AT and T Team Postcards
GiaCheB	Giants Chevrolet Bonds
GiaCheHoFP	Giants Chevron Hall of Famer Pins
GiaEurFS	Giants Eureka Federal Savings
GiaFalBTP	Giants Falstaff Beer Team Photos
GiaFanFFB	Giants Fan Fair Fun Bucks
GiaGolS	Giants Golden Stamps
GiaGreT	Giants Greats TCMA
GiaJayP	Giants Jay Publishing
GiaMot	Giants Mother's
GiaPacGaE	Giants Pacific Gas and Electric
GiaPol	Giants Police
GiaPos	Giants Postcards
GiaSch	Giants Schedule
GiaSFC	Giants S.F. Chronicle
GiaSFCB	Giants S.F. Call-Bulletin
GiaSFE	Giants S.F. Examiner
GiaSmo	Giants Smokey
GiaTarBCI	Giants Target Bottle Caps II
GiaTeal	Giants Team Issue
GiaTic	Giants Ticketron
GiaUllAFS	Giants Ullman's Art Frame Series
GiaUSPC	Giants U.S. Playing Cards
GilRazL	Gillette Razor Label
GleFalRC	Glens Falls Redbirds Classic/Best
GleFalRF	Glens Falls Redbirds Fleer/ProCards
GleFalTP	Glen Falls Tigers ProCards
GleFalTP	Glens Falls Tigers ProCards
GleFalWSBT	Glen Falls White Sox B/W TCMA
GleFalWSCT	Glen Falls White Sox Color TCMA
GleFalWST	Glen Falls White Sox TCMA
GleFalWST	Glens Falls White Sox TCMA
GofPos	Goff Postcards
Gol	Gold-Mine
GolCar	Gold Card
GolEntR	Gold Entertainment Ruth
GolMedFR	Gold Medal Flour R313A
GolPre	Golden Press
GooHumICBLS	Good Humor Ice Cream Big League Sticks
GooN16	Goodwin N162
Gou	Goudey R319
Gou	Goudey R320
Gou	Goudey R324
GouBWR	Goudey B/W R322
GouCanV	Goudey Canadian V353
GouCanV	Goudey Canadian V354
GouCarA	Goudey Card Album
GouFliMR	Goudey Flip Movies R326
GouHeaU	Goudey Heads Up R323
GouKnoHR	Goudey Knot Hole R325
GouPreR	Goudey Premiums R309-1
GouPreR	Goudey Premiums R309-2
GouPreR303A	Goudey Premiums R303A
GouPreR303B	Goudey Premiums R303B
GouPuzR	Goudey Puzzle R321
GouThuMR	Goudey Thum Movies R342
GouWidPPR	Goudey Wide Pen Premiums R314
GreBasS	Grenada Baseball Stamps
GreBatB	Greensboro Bats Best
GreBatC	Greensboro Bats Classic
GreBatF	Greensboro Bats Fleer/ProCards
GreBatTI	Greensboro Bats Team Issue
GreBraB	Greenville Braves Best

GreBraC	Greenville Braves Classic/Best
GreBraF	Greenville Braves Fleer/ProCards
GreBraLD	Greenville Braves Line Drive
GreBraP	Greenville Braves ProCards
GreBraS	Greenville Braves SkyBox
GreBraS	Greenville Braves Star
GreBraT	Greenwood Braves TCMA
GreBraTI	Greenville Braves Team Issue
GreFalDB	Great Falls Dodgers Best
GreFalDSP	Great Falls Dodgers Sports Pro
GreFalDTI	Great Falls Dodgers Sports Pro
GreFalDTI	Great Falls Dodgers Team Issue
GreHeroBP	Greyhound Heroes of Base Paths
GreHorB	Greensboro Hornets Best
GreHorC	Greensboro Hornets Classic/Best
GreHorF	Greensboro Hornets Fleer/ProCards
GreHorP	Greensboro Hornets ProCards
GreHorS	Greensboro Hornets Star
GreHorT	Greensboro Hornets TCMA
GrePlaG	Great Plains Greats
GriNik	Griffey Nike
GSGalAG	GS Gallery All-Time Greats
GulCoaDF	Gulf Coast Dodgers Fleer/ProCards
GulCoaMF	Gulf Coast Mets Fleer/ProCards
GulCoaRSP	Gulf Coast Rangers Sports Pro
GulCoaYF	Gulf Coast Yankees Fleer/ProCards
GuyPotCP	Guy's Potato Chip Pins
H80FouMH	Four Mighty Heroes H801-6
HagSunB	Hagerstown Suns Best
HagSunC	Hagerstown Suns Classic
HagSunC	Hagerstown Suns Classic/Best
HagSunDGB	Hagerstown Suns All Decade Best
HagSunF	Hagerstown Suns Fleer/ProCards
HagSunLD	Hagerstown Suns Line Drive
HagSunP	Hagerstown Suns ProCards
HagSunS	Hagerstown Suns SkyBox
HagSunS	Hagerstown Suns Star
HalHalR	Halsey Hall Recalls
HalofFB	Hall of Fame Busts
HalofFPP	Hall of Fame Picture Pack
HamRedB	Hamilton Redbirds Best
HamRedC	Hamilton Redbirds Classic/Best
HamRedF	Hamilton Redbirds Fleer/ProCards
HamRedP	Hamilton Redbirds ProCards
HamRedS	Hamilton Redbirds Star
HarCitRCB	Hardware City Rock Cats Best
HarCitRCTI	Hardware City Rock Cats Team Issue
HarHarW	Harry Hartman W711-2
HarSenB	Harrisburg Senators Best
HarSenF	Harrisburg Senators Fleer/ProCards
HarSenLD	Harrisburg Senators Line Drive
HarSenP	Harrisburg Senators ProCards
HarSenS	Harrisburg Senators SkyBox
HarSenS	Harrisburg Senators Star
HarSenTI	Harrisburg Senators Team Issue
HarSta	Hartland Statues
HarStaR	Hartland Statue Ryan
HasTriFT	Hassan Triple Folders T202
HawIsIC	Hawaii Islanders Caruso
HawIsIC	Hawaii Islanders Cramer
HawIsIP	Hawaii Islanders ProCards
HawIsIT	Hawaii Islanders TCMA
HawRai	Hawaii Rainbows
HawWomS	Hawaii-Hilo Women's Softball
HayComBP	Hayes Company Bauer PC750
HelBreF	Helena Brewers Fleer/ProCards
HelBreSP	Helena Brewers Sports Pro
HelBreTI	Helena Brewers Team Issue
HenHouW	Henry House Wieners
HicCraB	Hickory Crawdads Best
HicCraC	Hickory Crawdads Classic
HicCraC	Hickory Crawdads Classic/Best
HicCraF	Hickory Crawdads Fleer/ProCards
Hig5	High 5
Hig5S	High 5 Superstars
HigDesMB	High Desert Mavericks Best
HigDesMC	High Desert Mavericks Classic
HigDesMC	High Desert Mavericks Classic/Best
HigDesMF	High Desert Mavericks Fleer/ProCards
HigDesMP	High Desert Mavericks ProCards
HigMinM	Highland Mint Mint-Coins
HigMinMCP	Highland Mint Mint-Cards Pinnacle/UD
HigMinMCT	Highland Mint Mint-Cards Topps
HigMinMM	Highland Mint Mini Mint-Cards
HigMinMSM	Highland Mint Magnum Series Medallions
HigSchPLS	High School Prospects Little Sun
HilStaHWB	Hilo Stars Hawaii Winter Ball
Hir	Hires
HirTes	Hires Test
HitTheBB	Hit The Books Bookmarks
HOFStiB	HOF Sticker Book
HolBreD	Holsum Bread D327
HolMilT	Holyoke Millers TCMA
HomBon	Homogenized Bond *
HomCooC	Homers Cookies Classics
HomRunD	Home Run Derby
HomRunKE	Home Run Kisses E136-1
HonShaHWB	Honolulu Sharks Hawaii Winter Ball
Hos	Hostess
HosSti	Hostess Stickers
HosTwi	Hostess Twinkie
Hot50PS	Hottest 50 Players Stickers
Hot50RS	Hottest 50 Rookies Stickers
HouSho	Houston Show
HowPhoSP	Howard Photo Service PC751
Hoy	Hoyle
HudValRB	Hudson Valley Renegades Best
HudValRF	Hudson Valley Renegades Fleer/ProCards
HudValRTI	Hudson Valley Renegades Team Issue
HumDumC	Humpty Dumpty Canadian
HunCubC	Huntington Cubs Classic/Best
HunCubF	Huntington Cubs Fleer/ProCards
HunCubP	Huntington Cubs ProCards
HunStaB	Huntsville Stars Best
HunStaC	Huntsville Stars Classic/Best
HunStaF	Huntsville Stars Fleer/ProCards
HunStaJ	Huntsville Stars Jennings
HunStaLD	Huntsville Stars Line Drive
HunStaP	Huntsville Stars ProCards
HunStaS	Huntsville Stars SkyBox
HunStaTI	Huntsville Stars Team Issue
HutPop	Hutchinson Popcorn
HygAllG	Hygrade All-Time Greats
HygMea	Hygrade Meats
IBAWorA	IBA World All-Stars
IdaFalAT	Idaho Falls Athletics TCMA
IdaFalATI	Idaho Falls A's Team Issue
IdaFalB	Idaho Falls Braves Team Issue
IdaFalBF	Idaho Falls Braves Fleer/ProCards
IdaFalBP	Idaho Falls Braves ProCards
IdaFalBSP	Idaho Falls Braves Sports Pro
IdaFalBTI	Idaho Falls Braves Team Issue
IdaFalGF	Idaho Falls Gems Fleer/ProCards
IdaFalGSP	Idaho Falls Gems Sports Pro
IllLot	Illinois Lottery
ImpProP	Imprinted Products Pin-Cards
ImpTobC	Imperial Tobacco C46
Ind	Indians
Ind192T	Indians 1920 TCMA
IndBurK	Indians Burger King
IndCarBL	Indians Carling Black Label

IndFanC	Indians Fan Club/McDonald's
IndGat	Indians Gatorade
IndGolS	Indians Golden Stamps
IndGreT	Indians Greats TCMA
IndIndB	Indianapolis Indians Best
IndIndC	Indianapolis Indians CMC
IndIndF	Indianapolis Indians Fleer/ProCards
IndIndLD	Indianapolis Indians Line Drive
IndIndP	Indianapolis Indians ProCards
IndIndS	Indianapolis Indians SkyBox
IndIndTI	Indianapolis Indians Team Issue
IndJayP	Indians Jay Publishing
IndNumN	Indians Num Num
IndOhH	Indians Oh Henry
IndPenCBP	Indians Pencil Clip Buttons PPC-2
IndPol	Indians Polaroid
IndPos	Indians Postcards
IndSoh	Indians Sohio
IndSouPSoCP	Indians Souvenir Postcard Shop of Cleveland PC785
IndTeal	Indians Team Issue
IndVanPP	Indians Van Patrick PC-761
IndVisEI	Indians Vis Ed
IndWhe	Indians Wheaties
IndWUA	Indians WUAB-TV
IntLeaASB	International League All Stars Broder
IntLeaAT	International League All-Stars TCMA
IowCubB	Iowa Cubs Best
IowCubC	Iowa Cubs CMC
IowCubF	Iowa Cubs Fleer/ProCards
IowCubLD	Iowa Cubs Line Drive
IowCubP	Iowa Cubs ProCards
IowCubS	Iowa Cubs SkyBox
IowCubT	Iowa Cubs TCMA
IowCubTI	Iowa Cubs Team Issue
IowOakP	Iowa Oaks Police
IowOakT	Iowa Oaks TCMA
ISCHooHA	ISCA Hoosier Hot-Stove All-Stars
JacExpB	Jacksonville Expos Best
JacExpP	Jacksonville Expos ProCards
JacExpT	Jacksonville Expos TCMA
JacGenB	Jackson Generals Best
JacGenF	Jackson Generals Fleer/ProCards
JacGenLD	Jackson Generals Line Drive
JacGenP	Jackson Generals ProCards
JacGenS	Jackson Generals SkyBox
JacGenTI	Jackson Generals Team Issue
JacMetF	Jackson Mets Feder
JacMetGS	Jackson Mets Grand Slam
JacMetT	Jackson Mets TCMA
JacSunB	Jacksonville Suns Best
JacSunF	Jacksonville Suns Fleer/ProCards
JacSunLD	Jacksonville Suns Line Drive
JacSunP	Jacksonville Suns ProCards
JacSunS	Jacksonville Suns SkyBox
JacSunT	Jacksonville Suns TCMA
JacSunTI	Jacksonville Suns Team Issue
JamExpC	Jamestown Expos Classic/Best
JamExpF	Jamestown Expos Fleer/ProCards
JamExpP	Jamestown Expos ProCards
JamExpP	Jamestown Expos Pucko
JamJamC	Jamestown Jammers Classic
JamJamF	Jamestown Jammers Fleer/ProCards
JapPlaB	Japan Play Ball
JayPubA	Jay Publishing All-Stars
JefCarCC	Jefferies Card Collectors Co.
Jel	Jello
JerJonPC	Jerry Jonas Promotion Cards
JesHSA	Jesuit HS Alumni
JetPos	Jets Postcards
JHDABE	J.H. Dockman All-Star Baseball E-Unc.

JimDea	Jimmy Dean
JimDeaAG	Jimmy Dean All-Time Greats
JimDeaLL	Jimmy Dean Living Legends
JimDeaR	Jimmy Dean Rookies
JimDeaRS	Jimmy Dean Rookie Stars
JJKCopP	J.J.K. Copyart Photographers
JohCitCC	Johnson City Cardinals Classic
JohCitCC	Johnson City Cardinals Classic/Best
JohCitCF	Johnson City Cardinals Fleer/ProCards
JohCitCP	Johnson City Cardinals ProCards
JohCitCS	Johnson City Cardinals Star
JohCitCTI	Johnson City Cardinals Team Issue
JohMiz	Johnny Mize
JosHalC	Joseph Hall Cabinets
JuJuDE	Ju Ju Drums E286
K-M	K-Mart
Kah	Kahn's
KahAtl	Kahn's Atlanta
KahComC	Kahn's Commemorative Coins
KahCoo	Kahn's Cooperstown
KalBatN	Kalamazoo Bats N690-1
KalTeaN	Kalamazoo Teams N690-2
KanCouCC	Kane County Cougars Classic
KanCouCC	Kane County Cougars Classic/Best
KanCouCF	Kane County Cougars Fleer/ProCards
KanCouCLTI	Kane County Cougars Legends Team Issue
KanCouCP	Kane County Cougars ProCards
KanCouCTI	Kane County Cougars Team Issue
KanCouCUTI	Kane County Cougars Update Team Issue
KASDis	KAS Discs
KayB	Kay-Bee
Kel	Kellogg's
Kel2D	Kellogg's 2D
Kel3D	Kellogg's 3D
KelAll	Kellogg's All-Stars
KelATG	Kellogg's ATG
KelCerB	Kellogg's Cereal Boxes
KelCle	Kellogg's Clemente
KelFroFBB	Kellogg's Frosted Flakes Box Back
KelLey	Kellogg's Leyendas
KelPep*	Kellogg's Pep *
KelPepS	Kellogg's Pep Stamps *
KelPin	Kelly's Pins
KelRusSWC	Kelly Russell Studios Will Clark
KelStaU	Kellogg's Stand Ups
KenIndB	Kinston Indians Best
KenTwiB	Kenosha Twins Best
KenTwiC	Kenosha Twins Classic/Best
KenTwiF	Kenosha Twins Fleer/ProCards
KenTwiP	Kenosha Twins ProCards
KenTwiS	Kenosha Twins Star
KeyChal	Key Chain Inserts
KimN18	Kimball's N184
Kin	King-B Discs
KinBluJT	Kinston Blue Jays TCMA
KinBluJTI	Kinston Blue Jays Team Issue
KinDis	King-B Discs
KinEagP	Kinston Eagles ProCards
KinIndC	Kinston Indians Classic
KinIndC	Kinston Indians Classic/Best
KinIndF	Kinston Indians Fleer/ProCards
KinIndP	Kinston Indians ProCards
KinIndS	Kinston Indians Star
KinIndTI	Kinston Indians Team Issue
KinMetB	Kingsport Mets Best
KinMetC	Kingsport Mets Classic
KinMetC	Kingsport Mets Classic/Best
KinMetF	Kingsport Mets Fleer/ProCards
KinMetP	Kingsport Mets ProCards
KinMetS	Kingsport Mets Star

KisCobB	Kissimmee Cobras Best
KisDodD	Kissimmee Dodgers Diamond
KisDodP	Kissimmee Dodgers ProCards
KitCloD	Kitty Clover Discs
KnoBluJB	Knoxville Blue Jays Best
KnoBluJF	Knoxville Blue Jays Fleer/ProCards
KnoBluJLD	Knoxville Blue Jays Line Drive
KnoBluJP	Knoxville Blue Jays ProCards
KnoBluJS	Knoxville Blue Jays SkyBox
KnoBluJS	Knoxville Blue Jays Star
KnoBluJT	Knoxville Blue Jays TCMA
KnoKnoST	Knoxville Knox Sox TCMA
KnoSmoB	Knoxville Smokies Best
KnoSmoF	Knoxville Smokies Fleer/ProCards
KoBreWSI	Koester's Bread World Series Issue D383
KodCelD	Kodak Celebration Denver
KolMotBPP	Kolbs Mothers' Bread Pins PB4
Kra	Kraft
KraFoo	Kraft Foods
L1L	L1 Leathers
LaBouMRD	La Bounty Moscow Red Devils
LafDriT	Lafayette Drillers TCMA
LakElsSB	Lake Elsinore Storm Best
LakElsSC	Lake Elsinore Storm Classic
LakElsSF	Lake Elsinore Storm Fleer/ProCards
LakElsSTI	Lake Elsinore Storm Team Issue
LakTigB	Lakeland Tigers Best
LakTigC	Lakeland Tigers Classic
LakTigC	Lakeland Tigers Classic/Best
LakTigF	Lakeland Tigers Fleer/ProCards
LakTigP	Lakeland Tigers ProCards
LakTigS	Lakeland Tigers Star
LanJetB	Lancaster Jethawks Best
LanLugB	Lansing Lugnuts Best
LaPat	La Patrie
LaPre	La Presse
LasVegSB	Las Vegas Stars Best
LasVegSBHN	Las Vegas Stars Baseball Hobby News
LasVegSC	Las Vegas Stars CMC
LasVegSC	Las Vegas Stars Cramer
LasVegSF	Las Vegas Stars Fleer/ProCards
LasVegSLD	Las Vegas Stars Line Drive
LasVegSP	Las Vegas Stars ProCards
LasVegSS	Las Vegas Stars SkyBox
Lau300	Laughlin 300/400/500
LauAllG	Laughlin All-Star Games
LauBatB	Laughlin Batty Baseball
LauDiaJ	Laughlin Diamond Jubilee
LauEro	Laughlin Erorrs
LauFamF	Laughlin Famous Feats
LauGreF	Laughlin Great Feats
LauIndC	Laughlin Indianapolis Clowns
LauLonABS	Laughlin Long Ago Black Stars
LauOldTBS	Laughlin Old Time Black Stars
LauSpo	Laughlin Sportslang
LauWorS	Laughlin World Series
LavPro	Laval Provinciale
LawSemC	Lawrence Serman Postcards
Lea	Leaf
Lea	Leaf/Donruss
Lea300C	Leaf 300 Club
LeaAllGMC	Leaf All-Star Game MVP Contenders
LeaAllGMCG	Leaf All-Star Game MVP Contenders Gold
LeaBanS	Leaf Banner Season
LeaBlaG	Leaf Black Gold
LeaChe	Leaf Checklists
LeaCleC	Leaf Clean-Up Crew
LeaCor	Leaf Cornerstones
LeaDrefS	Leaf Dress for Success
LeaFas	Leaf Fasttrack
LeaFraM	Leaf Fractal Matrix
LeaFraMDC	Leaf Fractal Matrix Die Cuts
LeaGam	Leaf Gamers
LeaGet	Leaf Get-A-Grip
LeaGolA	Leaf Gold All-Stars
LeaGolP	Leaf Gold Previews
LeaGolR	Leaf Gold Rookies
LeaGolS	Leaf Gold Stars
LeaGreG	Leaf Great Gloves
LeaHatO	Leaf Hats Off
LeaHeaftH	Leaf Heading for the Hall
LeaJacRR	Leaf Jackie Robinson Reprint
LeaJacRSNWG	Leaf Jackie Robinson Scratch 'N Win Game
LeaKnoG	Leaf Knot-Hole Gang
LeaL	Leaf Limited
LeaLeaotN	Leaf Leagues of the Nation
LeaLim	Leaf Limited
LeaLimG	Leaf Limited Gold
LeaLimGA	Leaf Limited Gold All-Stars
LeaLimIBP	Leaf Limited Bat Patrol
LeaLimL	Leaf Limited Lumberjacks
LeaLimLB	Leaf Limited Lumberjacks Black
LeaLimPC	Leaf Limited Pennant Craze
LeaLimR	Leaf Limited Rookies
LeaLimRG	Leaf Limited Rookies Gold
LeaLimRP	Leaf Limited Rookies Phenoms
LeaMVPC	Leaf MVP Contenders
LeaMVPCG	Leaf MVP Contenders Gold
LeaOpeD	Leaf Opening Day
LeaPicP	Leaf Picture Perfect
LeaPowB	Leaf Power Brokers
LeaPre	Leaf Preferred
LeaPre	Leaf Premiums
LeaPre	Leaf Previews
LeaPreP	Leaf Preferred Press Proofs
LeaPrePB	Leaf Press Proofs Bronze
LeaPrePG	Leaf Press Proofs Gold
LeaPrePS	Leaf Press Proofs Silver
LeaPreSG	Leaf Preferred Steel Gold
LeaPreSP	Leaf Preferred Steel Power
LeaPreSta	Leaf Preferred Staremaster
LeaPreSte	Leaf Preferred Steel
LeaPro	Leaf Promos
LeaSig	Leaf Signature
LeaSigA	Leaf Signature Autographs
LeaSigAG	Leaf Signature Autographs Gold
LeaSigAS	Leaf Signature Autographs Silver
LeaSigEA	Leaf Signature Extended Autographs
LeaSigEACM	Leaf Signature Extended Autographs Century Marks
LeaSigPPG	Leaf Signature Press Proofs Gold
LeaSigPPP	Leaf Signature Press Proofs Platinum
LeaSli	Leaf Slideshow
LeaSpeO*	Leaf Special Olympics *
LeaStaS	Leaf Statistical Standouts
LeaTho	Leaf Thomas
LeaThoC	Leaf Thomas Collection
LeaThoGH	Leaf Thomas Greatest Hits
LeaTotB	Leaf Total Bases
LeaWarT	Leaf Warning Track
LegFoi	Legendary Foils
LegFoiHI	Legendary Foils Hawaii IX
LegFoiP	Legendary Foils Promos
LegPosR	Legends Postcard Ryan
LegSpoF	Legends Sports Fingers
LeoDayCC	Leon Day Commemorative Card
LetMouF	Lethbridge Mounties Fleer/ProCards
LetMouSP	Lethbridge Mounties Sports Pro
LimRocDP	Lime Rock Dominican Promos
LimRocDWB	Lime Rock Dominican Winter Baseball
LimRocGH	Lime Rock Griffey Holograms

LinDri	Line Drive
LinDriAA	Line Drive AA
LinDriAAA	Line Drive AAA
LinDriP	Line Drive Previews
LinDriS	Line Drive Sandberg
LinPor	Linnett Portraits
LinSup	Linnett Superstars
LinVen	LineUp Venezuelan Baseball
LinVenB	LineUp Venezuelan Baseball
LitFalMP	Little Falls Mets ProCards
LitFalMP	Little Falls Mets Pucko
LitFalMT	Little Falls Mets TCMA
LitSunMLL	Little Sun Minor League Legends
LitSunW	Little Sun Writers
LodDodT	Lodi Dodgers TCMA
LonBeaPT	Long Beach Press Telegram
LonJacN	Lone Jack N370
LonTigF	London Tigers Fleer/ProCards
LonTigLD	London Tigers Line Drive
LonTigP	London Tigers ProCards
LonTigS	London Tigers SkyBox
LouRedB	Louisville Redbirds Best
LouRedBC	Louisville Red Birds CMC
LouRedBLBC	Louisville Red Birds Louisville Baseball Club
LouRedBP	Louisville Red Birds ProCards
LouRedBTI	Louisville Red Birds Team Issue
LouRedE	Louisville Redbirds Ehrlers
LouRedF	Louisville Redbirds Fleer/ProCards
LouRedLD	Louisville Redbirds Line Drive
LouRedP	Louisville Redbirds ProCards
LouRedR	Louisville Redbirds Riley's
LouRedS	Louisville Redbirds SkyBox
LouRedTI	Louisville Redbirds Team Issue
LouSlu	Louisville Slugger
LowSpiB	Lowell Spinners Best
LSUMcDM	LSU Tigers Ben McDonald McDag
LSUTig	LSU Tigers
LSUTigA	LSU Tigers Anheuser-Busch
LSUTigGM	LSU Tigers Greats McDag
LSUTigM	LSU Tigers McDag
LSUTigMP	LSU Tigers McDag Purple
LSUTigP	LSU Tigers Police
LuxCigPP	Luxello Cigars Pins PT2
LynHilB	Lynchburg Hillcats Best
LynHilTI	Lynchburg Hillcats Team Issue
LynHilUB	Lynchburg Hillcats Update Best
LynMetP	Lynchburg Mets ProCards
LynMetT	Lynchburg Mets TCMA
LynPirT	Lynn Pirates TCMA
LynRanT	Lynchburg Rangers TCMA
LynRedSC	Lynchburg Red Sox Classic
LynRedSC	Lynchburg Red Sox Classic/Best
LynRedSF	Lynchburg Red Sox Fleer/ProCards
LynRedSP	Lynchburg Red Sox ProCards
LynRedSS	Lynchburg Red Sox Star
LynRedSTI	Lynchburg Red Sox Team Issue
LynSaiT	Lynn Sailors TCMA
MacBraB	Macon Braves Best
MacBraC	Macon Braves Classic
MacBraC	Macon Braves Classic/Best
MacBraF	Macon Braves Fleer/ProCards
MacBraP	Macon Braves ProCards
MacBraTI	Macon Braves Team Issue
MacBraUTI	Macon Braves Update Team Issue
MacPirP	Macon Pirates ProCards
MacSta	MacGregor Staff
MadHatC	Madison Hatters Classic
MadHatF	Madison Hatters Fleer/ProCards
MadMusB	Madison Muskies Best
MadMusC	Madison Muskies Classic/Best
MadMusF	Madison Muskies Fleer/ProCards
MadMusF	Madison Muskies Fritsch
MadMusP	Madison Muskies Police
MadMusP	Madison Muskies ProCards
MadMusS	Madison Muskies Star
MadMusT	Madison Muskies TCMA
MaiGuiP	Maine Guides ProCards
MaiGuiT	Maine Guides TCMA
MaiPhiC	Maine Phillies CMC
MaiPhiP	Maine Phillies ProCards
MajLeaCP	Major League Collector Pins
MajLeaM	Major League Movie
Man191BSR	Manning 1919 Black Sox Reprints
MandMSL	M and M's Star Lineup
ManDonC	Mantle Donor Card
MapCriV	Maple Crispette V117
MapLeaBH	Maple Leafs Bee Hive
MapLeaSF	Maple Leafs Shopsy's Frankfurters
MarCouH	Mariners Country Hearth
MarDaiQ	Mariners Dairy Queen
MarExh	Marchant Exhibits
MarExhH	Marchant Exhibits HOF
MarFloA	Marlins Florida Agriculture
MarGreT	Mariners Greats TCMA
MarMot	Mariners Mother's
MarNal	Mariners Nalley's
MarPac	Mariners Pacific
MarPhiB	Martinsville Phillies Best
MarPhiC	Martinsville Phillies Classic
MarPhiC	Martinsville Phillies Classic/Best
MarPhiF	Martinsville Phillies Fleer/ProCards
MarPhiP	Martinsville Phillies ProCards
MarPhiS	Martinsville Phillies Star
MarPhiTI	Martinsville Phillies Team Issue
MarPol	Mariners Police
MarPub	Marlins Publix
MarRedAP	Mariners Red Apple Pin
MarUSPC	Marlins U.S. Playing Cards
MasBreD	Master Bread Discs
MasMan	Mascot Mania
MatMin	Mattel Mini-Records
MauStiHWB	Maui Stingrays Hawaii Winter Ball
MaxPubP	Max Stein/United States Publishing House PC758
May	Mayo N300
McCCob	McCallum Cobb
McDCoi	McDonald's/TCI/Coca-Cola Coin
McGCloT	McGregor Clothes Tags
MCIAmb	MCI Ambassadors
MDAA	MDA All-Stars
MDAMVP	MDA MVP
MeaGolBB	Meadow Gold Blank Back
MeaGolM	Meadow Gold Milk
MeaGolSB	Meadow Gold Stat Back
MecDFT	Mecca Double Folders T201
MedA'sC	Medford A's Cramer
MedAthB	Medford Athletics Best
MedHatBJB	Medicine Hat Blue Jays Best
MedHatBJF	Medicine Hat Blue Jays Fleer/ProCards
MedHatBJP	Medicine Hat Blue Jays ProCards
MedHatBJSP	Medicine Hat Blue Jays Sports Pro
MedHatBJTI	Medicine Hat Blue Jays Team Issue
MegGriJWL	Megacards Griffey Jr. Wish List
MegRut	Megacards Ruth
MegRutP	Megacards Ruth Prototypes
MegRutS	Megacards Ruthian Shots
MelBusF	Melbourne Bushrangers Futura
MelMinE	Mello Mints E105
MemChiB	Memphis Chicks Best
MemChiBC	Memphis Chicks Britling Cafeterias
MemChiF	Memphis Chicks Fleer/ProCards

MemChiLD Memphis Chicks Line Drive
MemChiP Memphis Chicks ProCards
MemChiS Memphis Chicks SkyBox
MemChiS Memphis Chicks Star
MemChiSTOS Memphis Chicks Silver Time Out Sports
MemChiT Memphis Chicks TCMA
MemChiTI Memphis Chicks Team Issue
MemChiTOS Memphis Chicks Time Out Sports
Met196C Mets 1969 Calendar
Met196T Mets 1969 TCMA
Met63 S Mets '63 SSPC
Met69CCPP Mets '69 Capital Cards Postcard Promos
Met69CS Mets '69 Commemorative Sheet
Met69SP Mets '69 Spectrum Promos
Met69T Mets '69 Tribute
Met69Y Mets '69 Year Book
MetAllEB Mets All-Time Ed Broder
MetBak Metz Baking
MetBoyS Mets Boy Scouts
MetCit Mets Citgo
MetCol8 Mets Colla 8x10
MetColP Mets Colla Postcards
MetComR Mets Community Relations
MetDaiPA Mets Dairylea Photo Album
MetFanC Mets Fan Club
MetGal62 Mets Galasso '62
MetGreT Mets Greats TCMA
MetHaloF Mets Hall of Fame
MetIma Metallic Images
MetImpG Metallic Impressions Griffey
MetImpM Metallic Impressions Mantle
MetImpRi Metallic Impressions Ripken
MetImpRy Metallic Impressions Ryan
MetJapEB Mets Japan Ed Broder
MetJayP Mets Jay Publishing
MetKah Mets Kahn's
MetMagM Mets Magic Memory
MetMod Mets Modell
MetMSAP Mets MSA Placemats
MetNewYDN Mets New York Daily News
MetOriEB Mets Original Ed Broder
MetPhoA Mets Photo Album
MetShuST Mets Shultz Chevrolet Spring Training
MetSSP Mets SSPC
MetTCM Mets TCMA
MetTeal Mets Team Issue
MetTra Mets Transogram Statues
MetTriS6S Mets Tribute Sheet '69 Spectrum
MetTro Mets Tropicana
MetUni Metal Universe
MetUniBF Metal Universe Blast Furnace
MetUniEAR Metal Universe Emerald Autograph Redemptions
MetUniHM Metal Universe Heavy Metal
MetUniMF Metal Universe Magnetic Field
MetUniMfG Metal Universe Mining for Gold
MetUniML Metal Universe Mother Lode
MetUniP Metal Universe Platinum
MetUniPP Metal Universe Platinum Portraits
MetUniProS Metal Universe Promo Sheet
MetUniT Metal Universe Titanium
MetWIZ Mets WIZ
MetWorSC Mets World Series Champs
MexCitTT Mexico City Tigers TCMA
MiaHur Miami Hurricanes
MiaHurBB Miami Hurricanes Bumble Bee
MiaMarP Miami Marlins ProCards
MiaMarS Miami Marlins Star
MiaMarT Miami Marlins TCMA
MiaMirC Miami Miracle Classic/Best
MiaMirIS Miami Miracle I Star
MiaMirIS Miami Miracle II Star
MiaMirP Miami Miracles ProCards
MiaOriT Miami Orioles TCMA
MicBatCB Michigan Battle Cats Best
MicBatCTI Michigan Battle Cats Team Issue
MidAngB Midland Angels Best
MidAngF Midland Angels Fleer/ProCards
MidAngGS Midland Angels Grand Slam
MidAngLD Midland Angels Line Drive
MidAngOHP Midland Angels One Hour Photo
MidAngP Midland Angels ProCards
MidAngS Midland Angels SkyBox
MidAngT Midland Angels TCMA
MidAngTI Midland Angels Team Issue
MidCubT Midland Cubs TCMA
MidLeaA Midwest League All-Stars
MidLeaAB Midwest League All-Stars Best
MidLeaAF Midwest League All-Stars Fleer/ProCards
MidLeaAGF Midwest League All-Stars Fleer/ProCards
MidLeaAGS Midwest League All-Stars Grand Slam
MidLeaAP Midwest League All-Stars ProCards
MidLeaASGS Midwest League All-Stars Grand Slam
MidLeaATI Midwest League All-Stars Team Issue
MilBonSS Milk Bone Super Stars
MilBra Milton Bradley
MilDud Milk Duds
MilSau Milwaukee Sausage
Min Minnesota
MinLeaTS1 Minor League Team Sets 1972-Present
MinTwiP Twins Postcards
MisStaB Mississippi State Bulldogs
MJBHolB MJB Holographics Bagwell
MJBHolK MJB Holographics Knoblauch
MJBHolP MJB Holographics Prototypes
MLBBasB MLBPA Baseball Buttons (Pins)
MLBKeyC MLBPA Key Chains
MLBOffS MLB Official Stamps
MLBPin MLB Pins
MLBPin MLBPA Pins
ModA'sB Modesto A's Best
ModA'sC Modesto A's Chong
ModA'sC Modesto A's Chong
ModA'sC Modesto A's Classic
ModA'sC Modesto A's Classic/Best
ModA'sCLC Modesto A's Cal League Cards
ModA'sF Modesto A's Fleer/ProCards
ModA'sP Modesto A's ProCards
ModA'sTI Modesto A's Team Issue
MonNew Montreal News
MonRoyF Montreal Royals FC53
MooGra Moonlight Graham
MooSna MooTown Snackers
MotBag Mother's Bagwell
MotCan Mother's Canseco
MotCoo Mothers Cookies
MotGri Mother's Griffeys
MotGriJ Mother's Griffey Jr.
MotKno Mother's Knoblauch
MotMatW Mother's Matt Williams
MotMcG Mother's McGwire
MotNolR Mother's Nolan Ryan
MotOldT Motorola Old Timers
MotPia Mother's Piazza
MotPia Mother's Piazza/Salmon
MotRya Mother's Ryan
MotRya7N Mother's Ryan 7 No-Hitters
MotRyaF Mother's Ryan Farewell
MotSal Mother's Salmon
MotWilC Mother's Will Clark
MPR302-1 MP and Co. R302-1
MPR302-2 MP and Co. R302-2

Mr.TurS	Mr. Turkey Superstars
MrsShePP	Mrs. Sherlock's Pins PB5-1
MrsShePP	Mrs. Sherlock's Pins PB5-2
MrsShePP	Mrs. Sherlock's Pins PB5-3
MrsShePP	Mrs. Sherlock's Pins PB5-4
MrTurBG	Mr. Turkey Baseball Greats
MSABenSHD	MSA Ben's Super Hitters Discs
MSABenSPD	MSA Ben's Super Pitchers Discs
MSADis	MSA Discs
MSAFanSD	MSA Fantastic Sam's Discs
MSAHolD	MSA Holsum Discs
MSAHosD	MSA Hostess Discs
MSAIceTD	MSA Iced Tea Discs
MSAJayPCD	MSA Jay's Potato Chip Discs
MSAJifPD	MSA Jiffy Pop Discs
MSAMinD	MSA Mini Discs
MSASupS	MSA Super Stars
MTVRocnJ	MTV Rock n' Jock
MusTTC	Musial TTC
MVP	MVP Game
MVP2H	MVP 2 Highlights
MyrBeaBJP	Myrtle Beach Blue Jays ProCards
MyrBeaHC	Myrtle Beach Hurricanes Classic/Best
MyrBeaHF	Myrtle Beach Hurricanes Fleer/ProCards
MyrBeaHP	Myrtle Beach Hurricanes ProCards
N526N7C	N526 No. 7 Cigars
Nab	Nabisco
NabAllA	Nabisco All-Star Autographs
NabTeaF	Nabisco Team Flakes
NadCarE	Nadja Caramel E92
NadE1	Nadja E104
NasAngT	Nashua Angels TCMA
NasHeaF	Nassau Health Ford
NaSouTI	Nashville Sounds Team Issue
NasPirP	Nashua Pirates ProCards
NasPirT	Nashua Pirates TCMA
NasSouB	Nashville Sounds Best
NasSouC	Nashville Sounds CMC
NasSouF	Nashville Sounds Fleer/ProCards
NasSouLD	Nashville Sounds Line Drive
NasSouP	Nashville Sounds ProCards
NasSouS	Nashville Sounds SkyBox
NasSouTI	Nashville Sounds Team Issue
NasXprF	Nashville Xpress Fleer/ProCards
NatCarE	National Caramel E220
NatChiFPR	National Chicle Fine Pen Premiums R313
NatChiMS	National Chicle Maranville Secrets R344
NatGamW	National Game WG5
NatLeaAC	National League All-Stars Commemorative
NatPac	National Packtime
NatPac2	National Packtime 2
NatTeaL	National Tea Labels
NebCor	Nebraska Cornhuskers
NegLeaBMKC	Negro League Baseball Museum Kansas City
NegLeaD	Negro League Duquesne
NegLeaF	Negro League Fritsch
NegLeaFS	Negro League Fritsch Samples
NegLeaK	Negro League Kraft
NegLeaL2	Negro League Legends II
NegLeaLI	Negro League Legends I
NegLeaPD	Negro League Phil Dixon
NegLeaPL	Negro League Paul Lee
NegLeaRL	Negro League Ron Lewis
NegLeaRL2	Negro League Retort Legends II
NegLeaRLI	Negro League Retort Legends I
NegLeaS	Negro League Stars
Nei	Neilson's V61
Nes	Nestle
Nes792	Nestle 792
NesDreT	Nestle Dream Team

NesQuiB	Nestle Quik Bunnies
New	NewSport
NewBriRSB	New Britain Red Sox Best
NewBriRSF	New Britain Red Sox Fleer/ProCards
NewBriRSLD	New Britain Red Sox Line Drive
NewBriRSP	New Britain Red Sox ProCards
NewBriRSS	New Britain Red Sox SkyBox
NewBriRSS	New Britain Red Sox Star
NewCoPT	Newark Co-Pilots TCMA
NewHavRB	New Haven Ravens Best
NewHavRF	New Haven Ravens Fleer/ProCards
NewHavRTI	New Haven Ravens Team Issue
NewHavRUSTI	New Haven Raven Uncut Sheet Team Issue
NewJerCB	New Jersey Cardinals Best
NewJerCC	New Jersey Cardinals Classic
NewJerCF	New Jersey Cardinals Fleer/ProCards
NewJerCTI	New Jersey Cardinals Team Issue
NewN566	Newsboy N566
NewOriP	Newark Orioles ProCards
NewOriT	Newark Orioles TCMA
NewOrlZF	New Orleans Zephyrs Fleer/ProCards
NewPin	New Pinnacle
NewPinAP	New Pinnacle Artist's Proof
NewPinIE	New Pinnacle Interleague Encounter
NewPinKtP	New Pinnacle Keeping the Pace
NewPinMC	New Pinnacle Museum Collection
NewPinPP	New Pinnacle Press Plates
NewPinS	New Pinnacle Spellbound
NewWayCT	Newark Wayne Co-Pilots TCMA
NewYorJA	New York Journal American
NewYorN	New York News M138
NewYorNTDiS	New York News This Day in Sports
NiaFalRC	Niagara Falls Rapids Classic/Best
NiaFalRF	Niagara Falls Rapids Fleer/ProCards
NiaFalRP	Niagara Falls Rapids ProCards
NiaFalRP	Niagara Falls Rapids Pucko
NikMin	Nike Mini-Posters
NinGriJ	Nintendo Griffey Jr.
Nis	Nissen
NoiSatP	NoirTech Satchel Paige
NorBreL	Northland Bread Labels
NorNagUTI	Norwich Navigators Update Team Issue
NorNavB	Norwich Navigators Best
NorNavTI	Norwich Navigators Team Issue
NorTidB	Norfolk Tides Best
NorTidF	Norfolk Tides Fleer/ProCards
NorTidTI	Norfolk Tides Team Issue
NuHi	Nu-Card Hi-Lites
NuSco	Nu-Card Scoops
ObaT21	Obak T212
Oco& SSBG	O'Connell and Son Baseball Greats
OCoandSI	O'Connell and Son Ink
OdgRapTI	Ogden Raptors Team Issue
OgdA'sT	Ogden A's TCMA
OgdRapF	Ogden Raptors Fleer/ProCards
OgdRapSP	Ogden Raptors Sports Pro
OgdRapTI	Ogden Raptors Team Issue
OhiHalofF	Ohio Hall of Fame
OklCit8B	Oklahoma City 89ers Best
OklCit8C	Oklahoma City 89ers CMC
OklCit8F	Oklahoma City 89ers Fleer/ProCards
OklCit8LD	Oklahoma City 89ers Line Drive
OklCit8P	Oklahoma City 89ers ProCards
OklCit8S	Oklahoma City 89ers SkyBox
OklCit8T	Oklahoma City 89ers TCMA
OklCit8TI	Oklahoma City 89ers Team Issue
OklSoo	Oklahoma Sooners
OklStaC	Oklahoma State Cowboys
OklTodML	Oklahoma Today Major Leaguers
OldJudN	Old Judge N167

OldJudN	Old Judge N172
OldLonC	Old London Coins
OldMilT	Old Mill T210
OlmStu	Olmes Studios
OmaRoyB	Omaha Royals Best
OmaRoyC	Omaha Royals CMC
OmaRoyF	Omaha Royals Fleer/ProCards
OmaRoyLD	Omaha Royals Line Drive
OmaRoyP	Omaha Royals Police
OmaRoyP	Omaha Royals ProCards
OmaRoyS	Omaha Royals Shurfine
OmaRoyS	Omaha Royals SkyBox
OmaRoyT	Omaha Royals TCMA
OmaRoyTI	Omaha Royals Team Issue
OmaRoyTT	Omaha Royals Top Trophies
OneYanC	Oneonta Yankees Classic
OneYanC	Oneonta Yankees Classic/Best
OneYanF	Oneonta Yankees Fleer/ProCards
OneYanP	Oneonta Yankees ProCards
OneYanT	Oneonta Yankees TCMA
oPacCLAB	Pacific Coast League All-Stars Broder
OPC	O-Pee-Chee
OPCAllR	O-Pee-Chee All-Star Redemptions
OPCBatUV	O-Pee-Chee Batter Ups V300
OPCBoxB	O-Pee-Chee Box Bottoms
OPCBTC	O-Pee-Chee Blue Team Checklists
OPCDec	O-Pee-Chee Deckle
OPCDiaD	O-Pee-Chee Diamond Dynamos
OPCHotP	O-Pee-Chee Hot Prospects
OPCJumA	O-Pee-Chee Jumbo All-Stars
OPCPapI	O-Pee-Chee Paper Inserts
OPCPos	O-Pee-Chee Posters
OPCPre	O-Pee-Chee Premier
OPCPreSP	O-Pee-Chee Premier Star Performers
OPCPreSPF	O-Pee-Chee Premier Star Performers Foil
OPCPreTDP	O-Pee-Chee Premier Top Draft Picks
OPCTC	O-Pee-Chee Team Checklists
OPCWorC	O-Pee-Chee World Champions
OPCWorSH	O-Pee-Chee World Series Heroes
OrbPinNP	Orbit Pins Numbered PR2
OrbPinUP	Orbit Pins Unnumbered PR3
OrcPhoAP	Orcajo Photo Art PC786
Ori	Orioles
Ori6F	Orioles 1966 Franchise
OriCro	Orioles Crown
OriCroASU	Orioles Crown Action Stand Ups
OriEng	Orioles English's Discs
OriEngCL	Orioles English's Chicken Lids
OriEss	Orioles Esskay
OriFreB	Orioles French Bray
OriGreT	Orioles Greats TCMA
OriHea	Orioles Health
OriJayP	Orioles Jay Publishing
OriJohP	Orioles Johnny Pro
OriofB	Origins of Baseball
OriPol	Orioles Police
OriPos	Orioles Postcards
OriPro	Orioles Program
OriTeal	Orioles Team Issue
OriUSPC	Orioles U.S. Playing Cards
OrlCubB	Orlando Cubs Best
OrlCubF	Orlando Cubs Fleer/ProCards
OrlSunRB	Orlando Sun Rays Best
OrlSunRF	Orlando Sun Rays Fleer/ProCards
OrlSunRLD	Orlando Sun Rays Line Drive
OrlSunRP	Orlando Sun Rays ProCards
OrlSunRS	Orlando Sun Rays SkyBox
OrlSunRS	Orlando Sun Rays Star
OrlTwi8SCT	Orlando Twins 81 SL Champs TCMA
OrlTwiB	Orlando Twins Best
OrlTwiP	Orlando Twins ProCards

OrlTwiT	Orlando Twins TCMA
OrnOvaPP	Ornate Oval Pins PM1
OscAstC	Osceola Astros Classic
OscAstC	Osceola Astros Classic/Best
OscAstF	Osceola Astros Fleer/ProCards
OscAstP	Osceola Astros ProCards
OscAstS	Osceola Astros Star
OscAstTI	Osceola Astros Team Issue
OscMayR	Oscar Mayer Round-Ups
OttLynF	Ottawa Lynx Fleer/ProCards
OurNatGPP	Our National Game Pins PM8
OveCanR	Overland Candy R301
OxfConE	Oxford Confectionery E253
Pac	Pacific
PacAll	Pacific All-Latino
PacBaeS	Pacific Baerga Softball
PacBeiA	Pacific Beisbol Amigos
PacBel	Packard Bell
PacCar	Pacific Card-Supials
PacCarM	Pacific Card-Supials Minis
PacCerCGT	Pinnacle Certified Certified Gold Team
PacCoaBD	Pacific Coast Biscuit D310
PacCoaBD	Pacific Coast Biscuit D311
PacCraC	Pacific Cramer's Choice
PacEigMO	Pacific Eight Men Out
PacEstL	Pacific Estrellas Latinas
PacFirD	Pacific Fireworks Die Cuts
PacGolCD	Pacific Gold Crown Die Cuts
PacGolCDC	Pacific Gold Crown Die Cuts
PacGolP	Pacific Gold Prisms
PacGwyCB	Pacific Gwynn Candy Bar
PacHarR	Pacific Harvey Riebe
PacHom	Pacific Hometowns
PacJugC	Pacific Jugadores Calientes
PacLatD	Pacific Latinos Destacados
PacLatotML	Pacific Latinos of the Major Leagues
PacLeg	Pacific Legends
PacLegI	Pacific Legends I
PacLegI	Pacific Legends II
PacLigB	Pacific Light Blue
PacMil	Pacific Milestones
PacNolR	Pacific/Advil Nolan Ryan
PacOctM	Pacific October Moments
PacPri	Pacific Prisms
PacPriFB	Pacific Prisms Fence Busters
PacPriFT	Pacific Prisms Flame Throwers
PacPriG	Pacific Prisms Gold
PacPriGA	Pacific Prisms Gate Attractions
PacPriGotD	Pacific Prisms Gems of the Diamond
PacPriLB	Pacific Prisms Light Blue
PacPriP	Pacific Prisms Platinum
PacPriRHS	Pacific Prisms Red Hot Stars
PacPriSH	Pacific Prisms Sluggers and Hurlers
PacPriSL	Pacific Prisms Sizzling Lumber
PacPro	Pacific Promos
PacPro	Pacific Prototype
PacRya2S	Pacific Ryan 27th Season
PacRya7N	Pacific Ryan 7th No-Hitter
PacRyaFM	Pacific Ryan Farewell McCormick
PacRyaG	Pacific Ryan Gold
PacRyaI8	Pacific Ryan Inserts 8
PacRyaL	Pacific Ryan Limited
PacRyaM6	Pacific Ryan Magazine 6
PacRyaPI	Pacific Ryan Prism Inserts
PacRyaTEI	Pacific Ryan Texas Express I
PacRyaTEI	Pacific Ryan Texas Express II
PacSea	Pacific Seaver
PacSeaI6	Pacific Seaver Inserts 6
PacSenL	Pacific Senior League
PacSil	Pacific Silver
PacSilP	Pacific Silver Prisms

PacSpa	Pacific Spanish
PacSpaGE	Pacific Spanish Gold Estrellas
PacSpaPI	Pacific Spanish Prism Inserts
PacTriCD	Pacific Triple Crown Die Cuts
PadBohHB	Padres Bohemian Hearth Bread
PadCarJ	Padres Carl's Jr.
PadCHP	Padres CHP
PadCok	Padres Coke
PadDea	Padres Dean's
PadFamF	Padres Family Fun
PadFirPTB	Padres Fire Prevention Tips Booklets
PadGreT	Padres Greats TCMA
PadMag	Padres Magazine
PadMag	Padres Magazine/Rally's
PadMag	Padres Magazine/Unocal
PadMcDD	Padres McDonald Discs
PadMot	Padres Mother's
PadPolD	Padres Police DARE
PadSchC	Padres Schedule Cards
PadSmo	Padres Smokey
PadTeaI	Padres Team Issue
PadVol	Padres Volpe
PalSprAC	Palm Springs Angels Classic/Best
PalSprACLC	Palm Springs Angels Cal League Cards
PalSprAF	Palm Springs Angels Fleer/ProCards
PalSprAP	Palm Springs Angels Police
PalSprAP	Palm Springs Angels ProCards
PalSprP	Palm Springs ProCards
PalStaP	Pallos Stadium Postcards
PanAm TU	Pan Am Team USA Blue INDEP
PanAmTURB	Pan Am Team USA Red BDK
PanCanT1	Panini Canadian Top 15
PanFreS	Panini French Stickers
PanSti	Panini Stickers
PAORelT	PAO Religious Tracts
PapGinD	Papa Gino's Discs
Par	Parkhurst
ParPatF	Parramatta Patriots Futura
ParSpo	Parade Sportive
PatRut	Pathe Ruth
PawRedSC	Pawtucket Red Sox CMC
PawRedSDD	Pawtucket Red Sox Dunkin' Donuts
PawRedSF	Pawtucket Red Sox Fleer/ProCards
PawRedSLD	Pawtucket Red Sox Line Drive
PawRedSP	Pawtucket Red Sox ProCards
PawRedSS	Pawtucket Red Sox SkyBox
PawRedST	Pawtucket Red Sox TCMA
PawRedSTI	Pawtucket Red Sox Dunkin' Donuts
PawRedSTI	Pawtucket Red Sox Team Issue
PawRedTI	Pawtucket Red Sox Team Issue
PC7AlbHoF	Albertype Hall of Fame PC754-2
PC7HFGSS	H.F. Gardner Sports Stars PC768
PC7HHB	H.H. Bregstone PC743
PC7JM	J.D. McCarthy PC753
PCLPin	PCL Pins
PenPilBT	Peninsula Pilots B/W TCMA
PenPilC	Peninsula Pilots Classic/Best
PenPilCT	Peninsula Pilots Color TCMA
PenPilF	Peninsula Pilots Fleer/ProCards
PenPilP	Peninsula Pilots ProCards
PenPilS	Peninsula Pilots Star
PenWhiSP	Peninsula White Sox ProCards
PeoChiB	Peoria Chiefs Best
PeoChiC	Peoria Chiefs Classic
PeoChiC	Peoria Chiefs Classic/Best
PeoChiCTI	Peoria Chiefs Earl Cunningham Team Issue
PeoChiF	Peoria Chiefs Fleer/ProCards
PeoChiP	Peoria Chiefs ProCards
PeoChiPW	Peoria Chiefs Pizza World
PeoChiTI	Peoria Chiefs Team Issue

PeoChiUTI	Peoria Chiefs Update Team Issue
PeoSunF	Peoria Suns Fritsch
PeoT21	People's T216
Pep	Pepsi
PepCan	Pepsi Canseco
PepDieM	Pepsi Diet MSA
PepGloD	Pepsi Glove Discs
PepGri	Pepsi Griffeys
PepMcG	Pepsi McGwire
PepRicH	Pepsi Rickey Henderson
PepRicHD	Pepsi Rickey Henderson Discs
PepSidF	Pepsi Sid Fernandez
PepSup	Pepsi Superstar
PerAll	Perma-Graphic All-Stars
PerCelP	Perez-Steele Celebration Postcards
PerCreC	Perma-Graphic Credit Cards
PerGamC	Perfect Game Canseco
PerGamGJ	Perfect Game Griffey Jr.
PerGreM	Perez-Steele Great Moments
PerHaloFP	Perez-Steele Hall of Fame Postcards
PerHeaF	Perth Heat Futura
PerMasW	Perez-Steele Master Works
PetSta	Petro-Canada Standups
Pew	Pewter
PheGiaCr	Phoenix Giants Cramer
Phi	Phillies
Phi195T	Phillies 1950 TCMA
PhiArcO	Phillies Arco Oil
PhiBul	Philadelphia Bulletin
PhiBurK	Phillies Burger King
PhiCarE	Philadelphia Caramel E95
PhiCarE	Philadelphia Caramel E96
PhiCha	Phillies Champion
PhiCIG	Phillies CIGNA
PhiDaiN	Philadelphia Daily News *
PhiGreT	Phillies Greats TCMA
PhiJayP	Phillies Jay Publishing
PhiJohP	Phillies Johnny Pro
PhiKel	Phillies Keller's
PhiLumPB	Phillies Lummis Peanut Butter
PhiMed	Phillies Medford
PhiMel	Phillies Mellon
PhiPhiB	Phillies Philadelphia Bulletin
PhiPhiI	Phillies Philadelphia Inquirer
PhiPol	Phillies Police
PhiPosGM	Phillies Postcards Great Moments
PhiPosGPaM	Phillies Postcards Great Players and Managers
PhiSSP	Phillies SSPC
PhiTas	Phillies Tastykake
PhiTeaI	Phillies Team Issue
PhiTeaS	Phillies Team Set
PhiTopAS	Phillies Topps Ashburn Sheet
PhiUSPC	Phillies U.S. Playing Cards
PhoFilHoF	Photo File Hall of Fame
PhoFilR	Photo File Ryan
PhoFirB	Phoenix Firebirds Best
PhoFirC	Phoenix Firebirds CMC
PhoFirF	Phoenix Firebirds Fleer/ProCards
PhoFirLD	Phoenix Firebirds Line Drive
PhoFirP	Phoenix Firebirds ProCards
PhoFirS	Phoenix Firebirds SkyBox
PhoFirTI	Phoenix Firebirds Team Issue
PhoGiaBHN	Phoenix Giants Baseball Hobby News
PhoGiaC	Phoenix Giants Caruso
PhoGiaC	Phoenix Giants Cramer
PhoGiaCa	Phoenix Giants Caruso
PhoGiaCC	Phoenix Giants Coca Cola
PhoGiaCC	Phoenix Giants Cramer Coke
PhoGiaCK	Phoenix Giants Circle K
PhoGiaCP	Phoenix Giants Coke Premium

PhoGiaVNB	Phoenix Giants Valley National Bank
PicCle	Pictureform Clemente
PieBolWB	Piedmont Boll Weevils Best
PiePhiF	Piedmont Phillies Fleer/ProCards
PieStaT	Piedmont Stamps T330-2
Pil69G	Pilots 69 Galasso
PilPos	Pilots Post-Intelligencer
Pin	Pinnacle
PinAfi	Pinnacle Aficionado
PinAfiAP	Pinnacle Aficionado Artist's Proofs
PinAfiFPP	Pinnacle Aficionado First Pitch Preview
PinAfiMN	Pinnacle Aficionado Magic Numbers
PinAfiP	Pinnacle Aficionado Promos
PinAfiR	Pinnacle Aficionado Rivals
PinAfiSP	Pinnacle Aficionado Slick Picks
PinArtP	Pinnacle Artist's Proofs
PinArtP	Pinnacle Starburst Artist's Proofs
PinCar	Pinnacle Cardfrontations
PinCer	Pinnacle Certified
PinCerCMGT	Pinnacle Certified Certified Mirror Gold Team
PinCerCT	Pinnacle Certified Certified Team
PinCerLI	Pinnacle Certified Lasting Impressions
PinCerMBla	Pinnacle Certified Mirror Black
PinCerMBlu	Pinnacle Certified Mirror Blue
PinCerMG	Pinnacle Certified Mirror Gold
PinCerMR	Pinnacle Certified Mirror Red
PinCerR	Pinnacle Certified Red
PinChrBC	Pinnacle Christie Brinkley Collection
PinCoo	Pinnacle Cooperstown
PinCooD	Pinnacle Cooperstown Dufex
PinDiM	Pinnacle DiMaggio
PinDiMA	Pinnacle DiMaggio Autographs
PinEssotG	Pinnacle Essence of the Game
PinETA	Pinnacle ETA
PinExpOD	Pinnacle Expansion Opening Day
PinFan	Pinnacle FanFest
PinFirR	Pinnacle First Rate
PinFoil	Pinnacle Foil
PinGatA	Pinnacle Gate Attractions
PinHom	Pinnacle Home/Away
PinHomRC	Pinnacle Home Run Club
PinIns	Pinnacle Inside
PinInsC	Pinnacle Inside Cans
PinInsCE	Pinnacle Inside Club Edition
PinInsDD	Pinnacle Inside Dueling Dugouts
PinInsDE	Pinnacle Inside Diamond Edition
PinInsFS	Pinnacle Inside 40 Something
PinMan	Pinnacle Mantle
PinMin	Pinnacle Mint
PinMinB	Pinnacle Mint Bronze
PinMinCB	Pinnacle Mint Coins Brass
PinMinCG	Pinnacle Mint Coins Gold-Plated
PinMinCGR	Pinnacle Mint Coins Gold Redemption
PinMinCN	Pinnacle Mint Coins Nickel
PinMinCS	Pinnacle Mint Coins Silver
PinMinG	Pinnacle Mint Gold
PinMinS	Pinnacle Mint Silver
PinMusC	Pinnacle Museum Collection
PinNewB	Pinnacle New Blood
PinNewG	Pinnacle New Generation
PinPasttM	Pinnacle Passport to the Majors
PinPer	Pinnacle Performers
PinPin	Pinnacle Pins
PinPinR	Pinnacle Pin Redemption
PinPow	Pinnacle Power
PinPowS	Pinnacle Power Surge
PinPreP	Pinnacle Press Plates
PinProS	Pinnacle Project Stardom
PinRedH	Pinnacle Red Hot
PinRoo	Pinnacle Rookies

PinRooI	Pinnacle Rookie Idols
PinRooTP	Pinnacle Rookie Team Pinnacle
PinRunC	Pinnacle Run Creators
PinSam	Pinnacle Samples
PinSha	Pinnacle Shades
PinSky	Pinnacle Skylines
PinSlu	Pinnacle Slugfest
PinSta	Pinnacle Starburst
PinTea2	Pinnacle Team 2000
PinTea2	Pinnacle Team 2001
PinTeaP	Pinnacle Team Pinnacle
PinTeaS	Pinnacle Team Spirit
PinTeaT	Pinnacle Team Tomorrow
PinTheN	Pinnacle The Naturals
PinTotCPB	Pinnacle Totally Certified Platinum Blue
PinTotCPG	Pinnacle Totally Certified Platinum Gold
PinTotCPR	Pinnacle Totally Certified Platinum Red
PinTotCS	Pinnacle Totally Certified Samples
PinTri	Pinnacle Tribute
PinUps	Pinnacle Upstarts
PinWhiH	Pinnacle White Hot
PinX-P	Pinnacle X-Press
PinX-PF&A	Pinnacle X-Press Far and Away
PinX-PMoS	Pinnacle X-Press Men of Summer
PinX-PMP	Pinnacle X-Press Melting Pot
PinX-PMW	Pinnacle X-Press Metal Works
PinX-PMWG	Pinnacle X-Press Metal Works Gold
PinX-PMWS	Pinnacle X-Press Metal Works Silver
PinX-PSfF	Pinnacle X-Press Swing for the Fences
PinX-PSfFU	Pinnacle X-Press Swing for the Fences Upgrade
Pir	Pirates
Pir196T	Pirates 1960 TCMA
PirActP	Pirates Action Photos
PirAmeCE	Pirates American Caramels E90-2
PirArc	Pirates Arco Oil
PirBloP	Pirates Blockbuster Pins
PirEasH	Pirates East Hills
PirFanT	Pirates FanFest Tokens
PirFil	Pirates Filmet
PirGre	Pirates Greiner
PirGreT	Pirates Greats TCMA
PirHerP	Pirates Hermes Pins
PirHil	Pirates Hills
PirHomC	Pirates Homers Cookies
PirIDL	Pirates IDL
PirJacitB	Pirates Jack in the Box
PirJayP	Pirates Jay Publishing
PirKDK	Pirates KDKA
PirNatI	Pirates Nationwide Insurance
PirPosG	Pirates Post-Gazette
PirPosP	Pirates Post-Gazette Portraits
PirQui	Pirates Quintex
PirRigF	Pirates Riger Ford
PirTag	Pirates Tag-Ons
PirTeaI	Pirates Team Issue
PirTipTD	Pirates Tip-Top D322
PirVerFJ	Pirates Very Fine Juice
PitCubP	Pittsfield Cubs ProCards
PitMetB	Pittsfield Mets Best
PitMetC	Pittsfield Mets Classic
PitMetC	Pittsfield Mets Classic/Best
PitMetF	Pittsfield Mets Fleer/ProCards
PitMetP	Pittsfield Mets ProCards
PitMetP	Pittsfield Mets Pucko
PitMetS	Pittsfield Mets Star
PitMetTI	Pittsfield Mets Team Issue
PitPosH	Pitch Postcards HOF
PlaBal	Play Ball R334
PlaBal	Play Ball R335
PlaBal	Play Ball R336

PlaGriJ	Playball Griffey Jr.
PlaMat	Playball Mattingly
PlaMatG	Playball Mattingly Gold
PlaPri	PlayMakers Prints
PlaStr	Playball Strawberry
PlaWilC	Playball Will Clark
PloCanE	Plow's Candy E300
PM1StaP1	PM10 Stadium Pins 1 3/4'
PMGol	PM Gold
PMGolB	PM Gold Bench
PMGolCP	PM Gold Card Prototype
PMGolRP	PM Gold Ruth Prototype
PocGiaP	Pocatello Giants ProCards
PocGiaTB	Pocatello Giants The Bon
PocPioP	Pocatello Pioneers ProCards
PocPioSP	Pocatello Pioneers Sports Pro
PocPosF	Pocatello Posse Fleer/ProCards
PocPosSP	Pocatello Posse Sports Pro
PolAve	Police Avery
PolGroW	Polo Grounds WG4
PolMcG	Police McGwire
PolMet	Police Mets/Yankees
PomBlaBNLP	Pomegranate Black Ball Negro League Postcards
PomBlaBPB	Pomegranate Black Ball Postcard Book
PomNegLB	Pomegranate Negro League Bookmarks
PorandAR	Portraits and Action R315
PorandAR	Portraits and Action R316
PorBeaC	Portland Beavers CMC
PorBeaC	Portland Beavers Cramer
PorBeaF	Portland Beavers Fleer/ProCards
PorBeaLD	Portland Beavers Line Drive
PorBeaP	Portland Beavers Pins
PorBeaP	Portland Beavers ProCards
PorBeaS	Portland Beavers SkyBox
PorBeaT	Portland Beavers TCMA
PorChaRP	Port Charlotte Rangers ProCards
PorCitRB	Port City Roosters Best
PorCitRTI	Port City Roosters Team Issue
PorRocB	Portland Rockies Best
PorSeaDB	Portland Sea Dogs Best
PorSeaDF	Portland Sea Dogs Fleer/ProCards
PorSeaDTI	Portland Sea Dogs Team Issue
Pos	Post
PosCan	Post Canadian
PosGarT	Post Garvey Tips
PriPatD	Princeton Patriots Diamond
PriPirS	Princeton Pirates Star
PriRedC	Princeton Reds Classic
PriRedC	Princeton Reds Classic/Best
PriRedF	Princeton Reds Fleer/ProCards
PriRedP	Princeton Reds ProCards
PriWilCB	Prince William Cannons Best
PriWilCC	Prince William Cannons Classic
PriWilCC	Prince William Cannons Classic/Best
PriWilCF	Prince William Cannons Fleer/ProCards
PriWilCP	Prince William Cannons ProCards
PriWilCS	Prince William Cannons Star
PriWilCTI	Prince William Cannons Team Issue
PriWilPP	Prince William Pirates ProCards
PriWilPT	Prince William Pirates TCMA
PriWilYP	Prince William Yankees ProCards
PriWilYS	Prince William Yankees Star
Pro	ProMint
Pro22KGB	ProMint 22K Gold Bonds
ProA aaA	ProCards A and AA
ProAAAF	ProCards AAA
ProFS7	ProCards
ProMag	Pro Mags
ProMagA	Pro Mags All-Stars
ProMagDM	Pro Mags Die Cuts

ProMagIM	Pro Mags Inspirational Magnets
ProMagML	Pro Mags Mag Limited
ProMagP	Pro Mags Promo
ProPizC	Pro's Pizza Chicago
ProSta	Pro Stamps
ProStaP	Pro Stars Postcards
PubSti	Pubs.Int'l. Stickers
PulBraB	Pulaski Braves Best
PulBraC	Pulaski Braves Classic/Best
PulBraF	Pulaski Braves Fleer/ProCards
PulBraP	Pulaski Braves ProCards
QuaCitAB	Quad City Angels Best
QuaCitAC	Quad City Angels Classic/Best
QuaCitAGS	Quad City Angels Grand Slam
QuaCitAP	Quad City Angels ProCards
QuaCitAT	Quad City Angels TCMA
QuaCitCT	Quad City Cubs TCMA
QuaCitRB	Quad City River Bandits Best
QuaCitRBC	Quad City River Bandits Classic
QuaCitRBC	Quad City River Bandits Classic/Best
QuaCitRBF	Quad City River Bandits Fleer/ProCards
QuaCitRBTI	Quad City River Bandits Team Issue
QuaGra	Quaker Granola
QuaOatR	Quaker Oats Ruth
R31PasP	R312 Pastel Photos
R31Pre	R311 Premiums
R33So2	R337 Series Of 24
R42SmaS	R423 Small Strip
RaiFooW	Rainbow Foods Winfield
RalPur	Ralston Purina
RamT20	Ramly T204
RanAffF	Rangers Affiliated Food
RanAllP	Rangers All-Stars Pins
RanBurK	Rangers Burger King
RanComS	Rangers Commemorative Sheet
RanCra	Rangers Crayola
RanCucQB	Rancho Cucamonga Quakes Best
RanCucQC	Rancho Cucamonga Quakes Classic
RanCucQC	Rancho Cucamonga Quakes Classic/Best
RanCucQF	Rancho Cucamonga Quakes Fleer/ProCards
RanCucQT	Rancho Cucamonga Quakes Team Issue
RanDrP	Rangers Dr. Pepper
RanGreT	Rangers Greats TCMA
RanJarP	Rangers Jarvis Press
RanKee	Rangers Keebler
RanLit	Rangers Lite
RanMagM	Rangers Magic Marker
RanMot	Rangers Mother's
RanPer	Rangers Performance
RanSmo	Rangers Smokey
RanTeal	Rangers Team Issue
Raw	Rawlings
RawActT	Rawlings Activewear Tags
RawActTS	Rawlings Activewear Tags Seaver
RawGloT	Rawling's Glove Tags
RawGloT	Rawlings Glove Tags
RawMus	Rawlings Musial
RCColC	RC Cola Cans
ReaPhiB	Reading Phillies Best
ReaPhiELC	Reading Phillies Eastern League Champions Team Issue
ReaPhiF	Reading Phillies Fleer/ProCards
ReaPhiLD	Reading Phillies Line Drive
ReaPhiP	Reading Phillies ProCards
ReaPhiS	Reading Phillies SkyBox
ReaPhiS	Reading Phillies Star
ReaPhiT	Reading Phillies TCMA
ReaPhiTI	Reading Phillies Team Issue
ReaRem	Reading Remembers
Red76K	Reds '76 Klosterman

RedBor	Reds Borden's
RedBurB	Reds Burger Beer
RedBurBP	Reds Burger Beer Photos
RedCok	Reds Coke
RedCroT	Red Cross T215
RedEnq	Reds Enquirer
RedFol	Red Foley
RedFolMI	Red Foley's Magazine Inserts
RedFolS	Red Foley Stickers
RedFolSB	Red Foley Sticker Book
RedFreBC	Reds French Bauer Caps
RedGreT	Reds Greats TCMA
RedHeaF	Red Heart
RedIceL	Reds Icee Lids
RedJayP	Reds Jay Publishing
RedKah	Reds Kahn's
RedKro	Reds Kroger
RedMan	Red Man
RedPep	Reds Pepsi
RedPioT	Redwood Pioneers TCMA
RedPos	Reds Posters
RedShiBS	Reds Shillito's Boys Shop
RedSoh	Reds Sohio
RedSox	Red Sox
RedSox1T	Red Sox 1946 TCMA
RedSoxA	Red Sox Arco Oil
RedSoxAO	Red Sox Arco Oil
RedSoxBASP	Red Sox Boston American Series PC742-1
RedSoxBDASP	Red Sox Boston Daily American Souvenir PC742-2
RedSoxBG2S	Red Sox Boston Globe 2nd Series
RedSoxC	Red Sox Coke
RedSoxCPPC	Red Sox Color Photo Post Cards
RedSoxDD	Red Sox Dunkin' Donuts
RedSoxEF	Red Sox Early Favorites
RedSoxFNSMS	Red Sox First National Super Market Stores
RedSoxGT	Red Sox Greats TCMA
RedSoxJP	Red Sox Jay Publishing
RedSoxP	Red Sox Pepsi
RedSoxSAP	Red Sox Sports Action Postcards
RedSoxSM	Red Sox Star Market
RedSoxTI	Red Sox Team Issue
RedSoxUP	Red Sox Union Pins
RedSoxWHP	Red Sox Winter Haven Police
RedSunT	Red Sun T211
RedTexG	Reds Texas Gold
RedWinA	Red Wing Aces/Scarlets
RedWorCP	Reds World's Champions PCs
RedYea	Reds Yearbook
RegGloT	Regent Glove Tags
RemBre	Remar Bread
RemUltK	Rembrandt Ultra-Pro Karros
RemUltP	Rembrandt Ultra-Pro Piazza
RemUltP	Rembrandt Ultra-Pro Promos
RemUltPP	Rembrandt Ultra Pro Piazza
RemUltPP	Rembrandt Ultra-Pro Piazza Promos
RenSilSCLC	Reno Silver Sox Cal League Cards
RevLeg1	Revolutionary Legends 1
RevSup1	Revolutionary Superstars 1
RicBra2ATI	Richmond Braves 25th Anniversary Team Issue
RicBraB	Richmond Braves Best
RicBraBB	Richmond Braves Bleacher Bums
RicBraBC	Richmond Braves Bob's Camera
RicBraC	Richmond Braves CMC
RicBraC	Richmond Braves Crown
RicBraF	Richmond Braves Fleer/ProCards
RicBraLD	Richmond Braves Line Drive
RicBraP	Richmond Braves Pepsi
RicBraP	Richmond Braves ProCards
RicBraRC	Richmond Braves Richmond Camera
RicBraRC	Richmond Braves Richmond Comix
RicBraS	Richmond Braves SkyBox
RicBraT	Richmond Braves TCMA
RicBraTI	Richmond Braves Team Issue
RicBraUB	Richmond Braves Update Best
RinPos1Y1	Rini Postcards 1961 Yankees 1
RinPos1Y2	Rini Postcards 1961 Yankees 2
RinPos1Y3	Rini Postcards 1961 Yankees 3
RinPosBD2	Rini Postcards Brooklyn Dodgers 2
RinPosBD3	Rini Postcards Brooklyn Dodgers 3
RinPosBD4	Rini Postcards Brooklyn Dodgers 4
RinPosC	Rini Postcards Clemente
RinPosD1	Rini Postcards Dodgers 1
RinPosG	Rini Postcards Gehrig
RinPosM	Rini Postcards Mattingly 1
RinPosM	Rini Postcards Munson
RinPosM1	Rini Postcards Mets 1969
RinPosM2	Rini Postcards Mattingly II
RinPosNL1	Rini Postcards Negro League 1
RinPosR1	Rini Postcards Ryan 1
RinPosR2	Rini Postcards Ryan 2
RinPosYMP	Rini Postcards Yankees Monument Park 1
RitCE	Rittenhouse Candy E285
RivPilCLC	Riverside Pilots Cal League Cards
RivRedWB	Riverside Red Wave Best
RivRedWCLC	Riverside Red Wave Cal League Cards
RivRedWP	Riverside Red Wave ProCards
RobGouS	Robert Gould Statues
RobGouW	Robert Gould W605
RocCubTI	Rockford Cubs Team Issue
RocExpC	Rockford Expos Classic/Best
RocExpF	Rockford Expos Fleer/ProCards
RocExpLC	Rockford Expos Litho Center
RocExpP	Rockford Expos ProCards
RocPE3	Rochester PE3
RocPol	Rockies Police
RocRedWB	Rochester Red Wings Best
RocRedWC	Rochester Red Wings CMC
RocRedWF	Rochester Red Wings Fleer/ProCards
RocRedWGC	Rochester Red Wings Governor's Cup
RocRedWGCP	Rochester Red Wings Governor's Cup Pucko
RocRedWLD	Rochester Red Wings Line Drive
RocRedWM	Rochester Red Wings McCurdy's
RocRedWP	Rochester Red Wings ProCards
RocRedWS	Rochester Red Wings SkyBox
RocRedWSP	Rochester Red Wings Schieble Press W745
RocRedWT	Rochester Red Wings TCMA
RocRedWTI	Rochester Red Wings Team Issue
RocRedWW	Rochester Red Wings WTF
RocRoyC	Rockford Royals Classic
RocRoyC	Rockford Royals Classic/Best
RocRoyF	Rockford Royals Fleer/ProCards
RocUSPC	Rockies U.S. Playing Cards
RosComP	Rose Company PC760
RotCP	Rotograph Co. PC782
RotMcG	Rotograph McGinnity
RowExh	Rowe Exhibits
Roy	Royals
RoyDes	Royal Desserts
RoyGreT	Royals Greats TCMA
RoyKitCD	Royals Kitty Clover Discs
RoyMon	Royals Montreal
RoyNatP	Royals National Photo
RoyPol	Royals Police
RoyPre	Royal Premiums
RoySmo	Royals Smokey

RoySol Royals Solon
RoySta2 Royals Star 25th
RoyTasD Royals Tastee Discs
RoyTeal Royals Team Issue
RyaArlYP Ryan Arlington Yellow Pages
RyaSSC Ryan SSCA
S74Sil S74 Silks
S81LarS S81 Large Silks
SacSolC Sacramento Solons Caruso
SafSupLB Safelon Superstar Lunch Bags
SalAngC Salem Angels Cramer
SalAngP Salem Angels ProCards
SalAvaB Salem Avalanche Best
SalAvaTI Salem Avalanche Team Issue
SalBucC Salem Buccaneers Classic
SalBucC Salem Buccaneers Classic/Best
SalBucF Salem Buccaneers Fleer/ProCards
SalBucP Salem Buccaneers ProCards
SalBucS Salem Buccaneers Star
SalDodTI Salem Dodgers Team Issue
SalLakBF Salt Lake Buzz Fleer/ProCards
SalLakCC Salt Lake City Caruso
SalLakCGC Salt Lake City Gulls Caruso
SalLakCGC Salt Lake City Gulls Cramer
SalLakCGT Salt Lake City Gulls TCMA
SalLakCTTI Salt Lake City Trappers Team Issue
SalLakTP Salt Lake Trappers ProCards
SalLakTSP Salt Lake Trappers Sports Pro
SalLakTTI Salt Lake Trappers Team Issue
SalLakTTT Salt Lake Trappers Taco Time
SalMetC Salada Metal Coins
SalPirT Salem Pirates TCMA
SalPlaC Salada Plastic Coins
SalRedBP Salem Red Birds ProCards
SalSpuC Salinas Spurs Classic/Best
SalSpuCLC Salinas Spurs Cal League Cards
SalSpuF Salinas Spurs Fleer/ProCards
SalSpuP Salinas Spurs Police
SalSpuP Salinas Spurs ProCards
SanAntBT San Antonio Brewers TCMA
SanAntBTI San Antonio Brewers Team Issue
SanAntDTI San Antonio Dodgers Team Issue
SanAntMB San Antonio Missions Best
SanAntMF San Antonio Missions Fleer/ProCards
SanAntMGS San Antonio Missions Grand Slam
SanAntMLD San Antonio Missions Line Drive
SanAntMP San Antonio Missions ProCards
SanAntMS San Antonio Missions SkyBox
SanAntMTI San Antonio Missions Team Issue
SanBerC San Bernardino Classic/Best
SanBerSB San Bernadino Spirit Best
SanBerSB San Bernardino Spirit Best
SanBerSB San Bernardino Stampede Best
SanBerSC San Bernardino Spirit Classic
SanBerSC San Bernardino Spirit Classic/Best
SanBerSCLC San Bernadino Spirit Cal League Cards
SanBerSCLC San Bernardino Spirit Cal League Cards
SanBerSF San Bernardino Spirit Fleer/ProCards
SanBerSP San Bernardino Spirit ProCards
SanBerSTI San Bernardino Spirit Team Issue
SanDieSA3 San Diego State Aztecs 3D/Autograph Pro Image
SanDieSAAG San Diego State Aztecs All-Time Greats
SanDieSAG San Diego State All-Time Greats
SanDieSAS San Diego State Aztecs Smokey
SanDieSC San Diego Sports Collectors
SandSW S and S WG8
SanJosBC San Jose Bees Colla
SanJosBP San Jose Bees ProCards
SanJosGB San Jose Giants Best
SanJosGC San Jose Giants Classic
SanJosGC San Jose Giants Classic/Best
SanJosGCLC San Jose Giants Cal League Cards
SanJosGF San Jose Giants Fleer/ProCards
SanJosGP San Jose Giants ProCards
SanJosGS San Jose Giants Star
SanJosMC San Jose Missions Mr. Chef's
SanJosMJitB San Jose Missions Jack in the Box
SanJosMMC San Jose Missions Mr. Chef's
SarRedSB Sarasota Red Sox Best
SarRedSC Sarasota Red Sox Classic
SarRedSF Sarasota Red Sox Fleer/ProCards
SarWhiSC Sarasota White Sox Classic/Best
SarWhiSCB Sarasota White Sox Classic/Best
SarWhiSF Sarasota White Sox Fleer/ProCards
SarWhiSP Sarasota White Sox ProCards
SarWhiSS Sarasota White Sox Star
SavBraT Savannah Braves TCMA
SavCarC Savannah Cardinals Classic
SavCarC Savannah Cardinals Classic/Best
SavCarF Savannah Cardinals Fleer/ProCards
SavCarP Savannah Cardinals ProCards
SavCarT Savannah Cardinals TCMA
SavSanB Savannah Sandgnats Best
SCFOldT SCFS Old Timers
SchDis Schwebels Discs
SchR33 Schutter-Johnson R332
Sco Score
Sco100RS Score 100 Rising Stars
Sco100S Score 100 Superstars
ScoAi Score Airmail
ScoAll Score All-Stars
ScoAllF Score All-Star Fanfest
ScoBigB Score Big Bats
ScoBla Score Blast Masters
ScoBoxC Score Box Cards
ScoBoyoS Score Boys of Summer
ScoBra Score Braves
ScoBraPl Score Braves Platinum
ScoBraPr Score Braves Premier
ScoCokD Score Coke/Hardees Discs
ScoConR Score Contest Redemption
ScoCoo Score Cooperstown
ScoCyc Score Cycle
ScoDiaA Score Diamond Aces
ScoDiM Score DiMaggio
ScoDod Score Dodgers
ScoDodPl Score Dodgers Platinum
ScoDodPr Score Dodgers Premier
ScoDouGC Score Double Gold Champs
ScoDraP Score Draft Picks
ScoDreT Score Dream Team
ScoDugC Score Dugout Collection
ScoDugCAP Score Dugout Collection Artist's Proofs
ScoFacI Score Factory Inserts
ScoFra Score Franchise
ScoFraG Score Franchise Glowing
ScoFutF Score Future Franchise
ScoGlo Score Glossy
ScoGolDT Score Gold Dream Team
ScoGolR Score Gold Rush
ScoGolS Score Gold Stars
ScoHaloG Score Hall of Gold
ScoHaloGYTE Score Hall of Gold You Trade Em
ScoHeaotO Score Heart of the Order
ScoHigZ Score Highlight Zone
ScoHobR Score Hobby Reserve
ScoHot1R Score Hottest 100 Rookies
ScoHot1S Score Hottest 100 Stars
ScoHotR Score Hot Rookies
ScoImpP Score Impact Players
ScoInd Score Indians

ScoIndPl	Score Indians Platinum
ScoIndPr	Score Indians Premier
ScoIndU	Score Indians Update
ScoIndUTC	Score Indians Update Tribe Collection
ScoMan	Score Mantle
ScoMar	Score Mariners
ScoMarPl	Score Mariners Platinum
ScoMarPr	Score Mariners Premier
ScoMcD	Score McDonald's
ScoNumG	Score Numbers Game
ScoOri	Score Orioles
ScoOriPl	Score Orioles Platinum
ScoOriPr	Score Orioles Premier
ScoPitP	Score Pitcher Perfect
ScoPlaTS	Score Platinum Team Sets
ScoPowP	Score Power Pace
ScoPreS	Score Premium Stock
ScoPro	Score Promos
ScoProaG	Score Proctor and Gamble
ScoProP	Score/Pinnacle Promo Panels
ScoRan	Score Rangers
ScoRanPl	Score Rangers Platinum
ScoRanPr	Score Rangers Premier
ScoRedS	Score Red Sox
ScoRedSPl	Score Red Sox Platinum
ScoRedSPr	Score Red Sox Premier
ScoRef	Score Reflextions
ScoResC	Score Reserve Collection
ScoRoc	Score Rockies
ScoRocPl	Score Rockies Platinum
ScoRocPr	Score Rockies Premier
ScoRoo	Score Rookie/Traded
ScoRoo	Score Rookies
ScoRooCP	Score Rookie/Traded Changing Places
ScoRooDT	Score Rookie Dream Team
ScoRooG	Score Rookie/Traded Glossy
ScoRooGR	Score Rookie/Traded Gold Rush
ScoRooS	Score Rookie/Traded Samples
ScoRooSR	Score Rookie/Traded Super Rookies
ScoRul	Score Rules
ScoRulJ	Score Rules Jumbos
ScoRyaLaT	Score Ryan Life and Times
ScoSam	Score Samples
ScoSco	Score Scoremasters
ScoShoS	Score Showcase Series
ScoShoSAP	Score Showcase Series Artist's Proofs
ScoSpoR	Score Sportflics Ryan
ScoStaaD	Score Stand and Deliver
ScoSteS	Score Stellar Season
ScoTitT	Score Titanic Taters
ScoWhiS	Score White Sox
ScoWhiSPl	Score White Sox Platinum
ScoWhiSPr	Score White Sox Premier
ScoYan	Score Yankees
ScoYanPl	Score Yankees Platinum
ScoYanPr	Score Yankees Premier
ScoYouS2	Score Young Superstars II
ScoYouSI	Score Young Superstars I
ScoYouTE	Score You Trade Em
ScrDC	Scraps Die Cuts
ScrRedBB	Scranton/Wilkes-Barre Red Barons Best
ScrRedBC	Scranton Red Barons CMC
ScrRedBF	Scranton/Wilkes-Barre Red Barons Fleer/ProCards
ScrRedBLD	Scranton Red Barons Line Drive
ScrRedBP	Scranton Red Barons ProCards
ScrRedBS	Scranton/Wilkes-Barre Red Barons SkyBox
ScrRedBTI	Scranton/Wilkes-Barre Red Barons Team Issue
SeaPop	Seattle Popcorn
SeaRaiC	Seattle Rainiers Cramer
SeaSLP	Sears-East St. Louis PC783
Sel	Select
SelAce	Select Aces
SelArtP	Select Artist's Proof
SelArtP	Select Artist's Proofs
SelBigS	Select Big Sticks
SelCanM	Select Can't Miss
SelCer	Select Certified
SelCerAP	Select Certified Artist's Proofs
SelCerC	Select Certified Checklists
SelCerCB	Select Certified Certified Blue
SelCerCR	Select Certified Certified Red
SelCerF	Select Certified Future
SelCerGT	Select Certified Gold Team
SelCerIP	Select Certified Interleague Preview
SelCerMB	Select Certified Mirror Blue
SelCerMG	Select Certified Mirror Gold
SelCerMR	Select Certified Mirror Red
SelCerPU	Select Certified Potential Unlimited 1975
SelCerPU9	Select Certified Potential Unlimited 903
SelCerS	Select Certified Samples
SelCerSF	Select Certified Select Few
SelChaR	Select Chase Rookies
SelChaS	Select Chase Stars
SelClaTF	Select Claim To Fame
SelCroC	Select Crown Contenders
SelDufIP	Select Dufex Insert Promos
SelEnF	Select En Fuego
SelRegG	Select Registered Gold
SelRoo	Select Rookie/Traded
SelRooA	Select Rookie Autographs
SelRooAR	Select Rookie/Traded All-Star Rookies
SelRooR	Select Rookie Revolution
SelRooS	Select Rookie Surge
SelSam	Select Samples
SelSki	Select Skills
SelStaL	Select Stat Leaders
SelSurS	Select Sure Shots
SelTeaN	Select Team Nucleus
SelToootT	Select Tools of the Trade
SelToootTMB	Select Tools of the Trade Mirror Blue
SelTriC	Select Triple Crown
SenBarP	Senators Barr-Farnham Postcards
SenGunBP	Senators Gunther Beer PC
SenJayP	Senators Jay Publishing
SenNatPC	Senators National Photo Company
SenNewLP	Senators Newberrys Little Pro
SenOakT	Senators Oakland Tribune
SenPolP	Senators Police Pink
SenPolY	Senators Police Yellow
SenTeaI	Senators Team Issue
SenTeaI8	Senators Team Issue 8x10
SenTeaI81/2	Senators Team Issue 8 1/2x 11
SenTeaIPW	Senators Team Issue Photos W-UNC
SenTeaIW	Senators Team Issue W-UNC
SenUniMC	Senators Universal Match Corp.
SenVasS	Senators Vassar Sweaters
SenWasT	Senators Washington Times
SenWri&D	Senators Wright & Ditson
SepAnoP	Sepia Anon PC796
SerSta	Sertoma Stars
Sev3DCN	Seven-Eleven 3-D Coins National
SevCoi	Seven-Eleven Coins
SevElev	Seven-Eleven
SFHaCN	S.F.Hess and Co. N338-1
SFHesCreN32	S.F. Hess and Co. Creole N321
ShaPiz	Shakey's Pizza
SheGrePG	Sheraton Great Plains Greats
ShiPlaC	Shirriff Plastic Coins
ShrCapF	Shreveport Captains Fleer/ProCards

ShrCapFB	Shreveport Captains First Base
ShrCapLD	Shreveport Captains Line Drive
ShrCapP	Shreveport Captains ProCards
ShrCapS	Shreveport Captains SkyBox
ShrCapS	Shreveport Captains Star
ShrCapT	Shreveport Captains TCMA
SigBatP	Signature Bats Promo
SigOil	Signal Oil
SigRoo	Signature Rookies
SigRooBS	Signature Rookies Bonus Signatures Draft Picks
SigRooCF	Signature Rookies Cliff Floyd
SigRooDDS	Signature Rookies Draft Day Stars
SigRooDDSS	Signature Rookies Draft Day Stars Signatures
SigRooDP	Signature Rookies Draft Picks
SigRooDPS	Signature Rookies Signatures Draft Picks
SigRooFCD	Signature Rookies Flip Cards Draft Picks
SigRooFCS	Signature Rookies Flip Card Signatures Draft Picks
SigRooFD	Signature Rookies Future Dynasty
SigRooFDS	Signature Rookies Future Dynasty Signatures
SigRooHP	Signature Rookies Hottest Prospects
SigRooMR	Signature Rookies Major Rookies
SigRooMRS	Signature Rookies Major Rookies Signatures
SigRooOHKG	Signature Rookies Old Judge Ken Griffey Jr.
SigRooOJ	Signature Rookies Old Judge
SigRooOJA	Signature Rookies Old Judge All-Stars
SigRooOJAS	Signature Rookies Old Judge All-Stars Signatures
SigRooOJHP	Signature Rookies Old Judge Hot Prospects
SigRooOJHPS	Signature Rookies Old Judge Hot Prospects Signatures
SigRooOJMC	Signature Rookies Old Judge Marty Cordova
SigRooOJMR	Signature Rookies Old Judge Major Respect
SigRooOJP	Signature Rookies Old Judge Preview '95
SigRooOJPP	Signature Rookies Old Judge Peak Picks
SigRooOJPS	Signature Rookies Old Judge Preview '95 Signatures
SigRooOJRS	Signature Rookies Old Judge Rising Stars
SigRooOJS	Signature Rookies Old Judge Signatures
SigRooOJSS	Signature Rookies Old Judge Star Squad
SigRooOJSSS	Signature Rookies Old Judge Star Squad Signatures
SigRooOJTP	Signature Rookies Old Judge Top Prospect
SigRooOP	Signature Rookies Organizational Player of the Year
SigRooOPS	Signature Rookies Organizational Player of the Year Signatures
SigRooS	Signature Rookies Signatures
SigRooSig	Signature Rookies Signatures
SigRooTPD	Signature Rookies Top Prospects Draft Picks
SigRooTPS	Signature Rookies Top Prospects Signatures Draft Picks
SilHol	SilverStar Holograms
SimandSMLBL	Simon and Schuster More Little Big Leaguers
SkiBra	Skin Bracer
SkyAA F	SkyBox AA
SkyAAAF	SkyBox AAA
SkyE-X	SkyBox E-X2000
SkyE-XACA	SkyBox E-X2000 A Cut Above
SkyE-XC	Skybox E-X2000 Credentials
SkyE-XEAR	SkyBox E-X2000 Emerald Autograph Redemptions
SkyE-XEC	SkyBox E-X2000 Essential Credentials
SkyE-XHoN	SkyBox E-X2000 Hall or Nothing
SkyE-XSD2	SkyBox E-X2000 Star Date 2000
SmiClo	Smith's Clothing
SmoAmeL	Smokey American League
SmoNatL	Smokey National League
SnaDeaC	Snapple Dean Chance
SocHer	Socko Hershiser
SolHug	Solons Hughes
SolSunP	Solon Sunbeam/Pureta PC759
SomandK	Sommer and Kaufman
SonGre	Sonic/Pepsi Greats
Sou	Southeastern
SouAtlLAF	South Atlantic League All-Stars Fleer/ProCards
SouAtlLAGF	South Atlantic League All-Stars Fleer/ProCards
SouAtlLAGP	South Atlantic League All-Stars ProCards
SouAtlLAGS	South Atlantic League All-Stars Grand Slam
SouAtlLAGS	South Atlantic League All-Stars Grand Slam
SouAtlLAIPI	South Atlantic League All-Stars Inserts Play II
SouAtlLAPI	South Atlantic League All-Stars Play II
SouAtlLAS	South Atlantic League All-Stars Star
SouBenSHC	South Bend Silver Hawks Classic
SouBenSHF	South Bend Silver Hawks Fleer/ProCards
SouBenSHS	South Bend Silver Hawks Best
SouBenWSB	South Bend White Sox Best
SouBenWSC	South Bend White Sox Classic/Best
SouBenWSF	South Bend White Sox Fleer/ProCards
SouBenWSGS	South Bend White Sox Grand Slam
SouBenWSP	South Bend White Sox ProCards
SouCalS	Southern Cal Trojans Smokey
SouLeaAJ	Southern League All-Stars Jennings
SouOreAB	Southern Oregon A's Best
SouOreAC	Southern Oregon A's Classic/Best
SouOreAC	Southern Oregon Athletics Classic
SouOreAF	Southern Oregon A's Fleer/ProCards
SouOreAF	Southern Oregon Athletics Fleer/ProCards
SouOreAP	Southern Oregon A's ProCards
SouOreTI	Southern Oregon Timberjacks Team Issue
SP	SP
SpaGloT	Spalding Glove Tags
SpaPhiB	Spartanburg Phillies Best
SpaPhiC	Spartanburg Phillies Classic/Best
SpaPhiF	Spartanburg Phillies Fleer/ProCards
SpaPhiP	Spartanburg Phillies ProCards
SpaPhiS	Spartanburg Phillies Star
SpaPhiT	Spartanburg Phillies TCMA
SparPhiC	Spartanburg Phillies Classic
SPBasH	SP Baseball Heroes
SPCha	SP Championship
SPChaCP	SP Championship Classic Performances
SPChaCPDC	SP Championship Classic Performances Die Cuts
SPChaDC	SP Championship Die Cuts
SPChaDFC	SP Championship Fall Classic
SPChaFCDC	SP Championship Fall Classic Die Cuts
SPDieC	SP Die Cuts
SpeGolSGJ	Spectrum Gold Signature Griffey Jr.
SpeGolSH	Spectrum Gold Signature Herman
SpeGolSS	Spectrum Gold Signature Seaver
SpeHOF2	Spectrum HOF II
SpeHOFI	Spectrum HOF I

SpeRya1	Spectrum Ryan 10
SpeRya2	Spectrum Ryan 23K
SpeRya5	Spectrum Ryan 5
SpeRyaTS	Spectrum Ryan Tribute Sheet
SPGamF	SP Game Film
SPGriH	SP Griffey Heroes
SPHol	SP Holoviews
SPHolDC	SP Holoviews Die Cuts
SPInsI	SP Inside Info
SPMarM	SP Marquee Matchups
SPMarMDC	SP Marquee Matchup Die Cuts
SPML	SP Minors
SPMLA	SP Minors Autographs
SPMLDtS	SP Minors Destination the Show
SPMLMJC	SP Minors Michael Jordan Time Capsule
Spo	Sportflics
Spo	Sportflix
Spo	Sportscaster
Spo	Sportstix
SpoArtP	Sportflix Artist's Proofs
SpoBre	Spotbilt Brett
SpoComoA	Sport Company of America *
SpoCubG	Sports Cube Game
SpoDeaP	Sportflics Dealer Panels
SpoDecG	Sportflics Decade Greats
SpoDecGS	Sportflics Decade Greats Samples
SpoDesJM	Sports Design J.D. McCarthy
SpoDesPW	Sports Design Products West
SpoDet	Sportflix Detonators
SpoDouT	Sportflix Double Take
SpoExcW	Sports Exchange W603
SpoFanA	Sportflics FanFest All-Stars
SpoGam	Sportflics Gamewinners
SpoHaloF	Sportrait Hall of Fame
SpoHamT	Sportflix Hammer Team
SpoHitP	Sportflix Hit Parade
SpoHobBG	Sports Hobbyist Baseball Greats
SpoIll	Sports Illustrated
SpoIllAC	Sports Illustrated Ad Cards*
SpoIllAM	Sports Illustrated Autographed Mini-Covers
SpoIllCC	Sports Illustrated Cooperstown Collection
SpoIllEE	Sports Illustrated Extra Edition
SpoIllFK1	Sports Illustrated For Kids II
SpoIllFKI	Sports Illustrated For Kids I
SpoIllGS	Sports Illustrated Great Shots
SpoIndB	Spokane Indians Best
SpoIndC	Spokane Indians Caruso
SpoIndC	Spokane Indians Classic
SpoIndC	Spokane Indians Classic/Best
SpoIndC	Spokane Indians Cramer
SpoIndF	Spokane Indians Fleer/ProCards
SpoIndGC	Spokane Indians Greats Cramer
SpoIndP	Spokane Indians ProCards
SpoIndSP	Spokane Indians Sports Pro
SpoIndT	Spokane Indians TCMA
SpoIndTI	Spokane Indians Team Issue
SpoKin	Sport Kings R338 *
SpoLifCW	Sporting Life Cabinets W600
SpoLifM	Sporting Life M116
SpoMagP	Sport Magazine Premiums *
SpoMemAG	Sports Memorabilia All-Time Greats
SpoMov	Sportflics Movers
SpoNewM	Sporting News M101-4
SpoNewM	Sporting News M101-5
SpoNewP	Sporting News PC757
SpoNewSM	Sporting News Supplements M101-2
SpoNewSM	Sporting News Supplements M101-7
SpoNSP	Sporting News Sports Page
SpoPowS	Sportflix Power Surge

SpoPro	Sportflics Prototypes
SpoPro	Sportflix ProMotion
SpoRea	Sports Reading
SpoRoo	Sportflics Rookie/Traded
SpoRoo	Sportflics Rookies
SpoRoo2	Sportflics Rookies II
SpoRooAP	Sportflics Rookie/Traded Artist's Proofs
SpoRooGGG	Sportflics Rookie/Traded Going Going Gone
SpoRooI	Sportflics Rookies I
SpoRooP	Sportflics Rookie Packs
SpoRooRS	Sportflics Rookie/Traded Rookie Starflics
SpoRooS	Sportflics Rookie/Traded Samples
SpoSam	Sportflics Samples
SpoSam	Sportflix Samples
SpoSha	Sportflics Shakers
SpoStaCC	Sports Stars Collector Coins
SpoSupD	Sportflics Superstar Discs
SpoTeaL	Sportflics Team Logo
SpoTeaP	Sportflics Team Preview
SpoTimM	Sporting Times M117
SPPlaP	SP Platinum Power
SPPre	SP Previews
SPPreF	SP Previews FanFest
SprCarB	Springfield Cardinals Best
SprCarC	Springfield Cardinals Classic/Best
SprCarDGB	Springfield Cardinals All Decade Best
SprCarF	Springfield Cardinals Fleer/ProCards
SprCarF	Springfield Cardinals Fritsch
SprCarP	Springfield Cardinals ProCards
SprCarT	Springfield Cardinals TCMA
SprRedWK	Springfield Redbirds Wiener King
SprSulC	Springfield Sultans Classic
SprSulF	Springfield Sultans Fleer/ProCards
SprSulTI	Springfield Sultans Team Issue
SPSil	SP Silver
SPSpeF	SP Special FX
SPSpeFX	SP Special FX
SPSpeFXDC	SP Special FX Die Cuts
SPSpxF	SP SPx Force
SPSPxFA	SP SPx Force Autographs
SPVinAu	SP Vintage Autographs
SPx	SPx
SPxBoufG	SPx Bound for Glory
SPxBoufGSS	SPx Bound for Glory Supreme Signatures
SPxBro	SPx Bronze
SPxCorotG	SPx Cornerstones of the Game
SPxGol	SPx Gold
SPxGraF	SPx Grand Finale
SPxSil	SPx Silver
SPxSte	SPx Steel
Squ	Squirt
SSP	SSPC
SSP18	SSPC 18
SSP188WS	SSPC 1887 World Series
SSP270	SSPC 270
SSP42	SSPC 42
SSPHOF	SSPC HOF
SSPPuzB	SSPC Puzzle Back
SSPSam	SSPC Samples
SSPYanOD	SSPC Yankees Old-Timers Day
St.CatBJC	St. Catharines Blue Jays Classic
St.CatBJC	St. Catharines Blue Jays Classic/Best
St.CatBJF	St. Catharines Blue Jays Fleer/ProCards
St.CatBJP	St. Catharines Blue Jays ProCards
St.LucMC	St. Lucie Mets Classic
St.LucMC	St. Lucie Mets Classic/Best
St.LucMCB	St. Lucie Mets Classic/Best
St.LucMF	St. Lucie Mets Fleer/ProCards
St.LucMP	St. Lucie Mets ProCards
St.LucMS	St. Lucie Mets Star

St.PetCC	St. Petersburg Cardinals Classic
St.PetCC	St. Petersburg Cardinals Classic/Best
St.PetCF	St. Petersburg Cardinals Fleer/ProCards
St.PetCP	St. Petersburg Cardinals ProCards
St.PetCS	St. Pete Cardinals Star
St.PetCS	St. Petersburg Cardinals Star
St.PetCT	St. Petersburg Cardinals TCMA
St.VinHHS	St. Vincent HOF Heroes Stamps
Sta	Star
StaAbb	Star Abbott
StaAloB	Star Alomar Brothers
StaAve	Star Avery
StaAwaW	Star Award Winners
StaBag	Star Bagwell
StaBel	Star Bell
StaBel	Star Belle
StaBelRG	Star Belle Rookie Guild
StaBen	Star Benes
StaBis	Standard Biscuit
StaBlaM	Star Mattingly Blankback
StaBog	Star Boggs
StaBog	Star Boggs Hitman
StaBog/G	Star Boggs/Gwynn
StaBoJ	Star Bo Jackson
StaBre	Star Brett
StaCalL	Star Cal Large
StaCalS	Star Cal Small
StaCan	Star Canseco
StaCar	Star Carlton
StaCarE	Standard Caramel E93
StaCla	Star Clark/Grace
StaCla	Star Will Clark
StaCle	Star Clemens
StaCle	Star Clemens/Gooden
StaCle2	Star Clemens II
StaClu	Stadium Club
StaCluAn	Stadium Club Angels
StaCluAs	Stadium Club Astros
StaCluAt	Stadium Club Athletics
StaCluB	Stadium Club Braves
StaCluB&B	Stadium Club Bash and Burn
StaCluC	Stadium Club Co-Signers
StaCluCa	Stadium Club Cardinals
StaCluCB	Stadium Club Crystal Ball
StaCluCC	Stadium Club Clear Cut
StaCluCM	Stadium Club Charter Member *
StaCluCT	Stadium Club Crunch Time
StaCluCu	Stadium Club Cubs
StaCluD	Stadium Club Dodgers
StaCluD	Stadium Club Dome
StaCluDD	Stadium Club Dugout Dirt
StaCluDP	Stadium Club Draft Picks
StaCluDPFDI	Stadium Club Draft Picks First Day Issue
StaCluECN	Stadium Club East Coast National
StaCluEPB	Stadium Club Extreme Players Bronze
StaCluEPG	Stadium Club Extreme Players Gold
StaCluEPS	Stadium Club Extreme Players Silver
StaCluEWB	Stadium Club Extreme Winners Bronze
StaCluEWG	Stadium Club Extreme Winners Gold
StaCluEWS	Stadium Club Extreme Winners Silver
StaCluF	Stadium Club Finest
StaCluFDI	Stadium Club First Day Issue
StaCluFDP	Stadium Club First Draft Picks
StaCluFR	Stadium Club Firebrand Redemption
StaCluG	Stadium Club Giants
StaCluGR	Stadium Club Golden Rainbow
StaCluI	Stadium Club Inserts
StaCluI	Stadium Club Instavision
StaCluM	Stadium Club Millennium
StaCluM	Stadium Club Murphy
StaCluMa	Stadium Club Mantle
StaCluMari	Stadium Club Mariners
StaCluMarl	Stadium Club Marlins
StaCluMat	Stadium Club Matrix
StaCluMeg	Stadium Club Megaheroes
StaCluMet	Stadium Club Metalists
StaCluMM	Stadium Club Midsummer Matchups
StaCluMMP	Stadium Club Murphy Master Photos
StaCluMO	Stadium Club Members Only
StaCluMO	Stadium Club Members Only *
StaCluMOF	Stadium Club Members Only Finest Bronze
StaCluMOP	Stadium Club Members Only Parallel
StaCluMP	Stadium Club Master Photos
StaCluNC	Stadium Club National Convention
StaCluP	Stadium Club Phillies
StaCluP	Stadium Club Pre-Production
StaCluPC	Stadium Club Phone Cards
StaCluPC	Stadium Club Prime Cuts
StaCluPG	Stadium Club Pure Gold
StaCluPL	Stadium Club Patent Leather
StaCluPP	Stadium Club Power Packed
StaCluPP	Stadium Club Pre-Production
StaCluPS	Stadium Club Power Streak
StaCluPZ	Stadium Club Power Zone
StaCluR	Stadium Club Rangers
StaCluRL	Stadium Club Ring Leaders
StaCluRoc	Stadium Club Rockies
StaCluRoy	Stadium Club Royals
StaCluSS	Stadium Club Super Skills
StaCluST	Stadium Club Super Teams
StaCluSTDW	Stadium Club Super Team Division Winners
StaCluSTMP	Stadium Club Super Team Master Photos
StaCluSTWS	Stadium Club Super Team World Series
StaCluT	Stadium Club Team
StaCluTA	Stadium Club TSC Awards
StaCluTF	Stadium Club Team Finest
StaCluTFDI	Stadium Club Team First Day Issue
StaCluU	Stadium Club Ultra-Pro
StaCluVE	Stadium Club Virtual Extremists
StaCluVR	Stadium Club Virtual Reality
StaCluVRMO	Stadium Club Virtual Reality Members Only
StaCluWS	Stadium Club White Sox
StaCluY	Stadium Club Yankees
StaCon	Star Cone
StaDav	Star Davis/McGwire
StaDaw	Star Dawson
StaEriD	Star Eric Davis
StaFie	Star Fielder
StaFS7	Star
StaGan	Star Gant
StaGar	Star Garvey
StaGarC	Star Gary Carter
StaGonRG	Star Gonzalez Rookie Guild
StaGoo	Star Gooden Orange
StaGooB	Star Gooden Blue
StaGor	Star Gordon
StaGre	Star Greenwell Red
StaGreP	Star Greenwell Purple
StaGri	Star Griffeys
StaGriJ	Star Griffey Jr.
StaGwy	Star Gwynn
StaHen	Star Henderson
StaHer	Star Hernandez
StaHer	Star Hershiser
StaHor	Star Horn
StaJef	Star Jefferies
StaJor	Star Jordan
StaJoyR	Star Joyner Red
StaJus	Star Justice

StaKno	Star Knoblauch
StaLar	Star Larkin
StaLewRG	Star Lewis Rookie Guild
StaLinAl	Starting Lineup All-Stars
StaLinAn	Starting Lineup Angels
StaLinAs	Starting Lineup A's
StaLinAst	Starting Lineup Astros
StaLinBJ	Starting Lineup Blue Jays
StaLinBra	Starting Lineup Braves
StaLinBre	Starting Lineup Brewers
StaLinCa	Starting Lineup Cardinals
StaLinCu	Starting Lineup Cubs
StaLinD	Starting Lineup Dodgers
StaLinE	Starting Lineup Expos
StaLinG	Starting Lineup Giants
StaLinI	Starting Lineup Indians
StaLinMa	Starting Lineup Mariners
StaLinMe	Starting Lineup Mets
StaLinO	Starting Lineup Orioles
StaLinPa	Starting Lineup Padres
StaLinPh	Starting Lineup Phillies
StaLinPi	Starting Lineup Pirates
StaLinRa	Starting Lineup Rangers
StaLinRe	Starting Lineup Reds
StaLinRo	Starting Lineup Royals
StaLinRS	Starting Lineup Red Sox
StaLinTi	Starting Lineup Tigers
StaLinTw	Starting Lineup Twins
StaLinWS	Starting Lineup White Sox
StaLinY	Starting Lineup Yankees
StaLonJS	Starline Long John Silver
StaMat	Star Mattingly
StaMat	Star Sticker Mattingly
StaMat/S	Star Mattingly/Schmidt
StaMatW	Star Matt Williams
StaMcD	Star McDonald
StaMcG	Star McGwire
StaMcGG	Star McGwire Green
StaMcR	Star McReynolds
StaMey	Stahl Meyer
StaMit	Star Mitchell
StaMit	Star Mitchell/Yount
StaMit/C	Star Mitchell/Clark
StaMur	Star Murphy
StaNok	Star Nokes
StaPal	Star Palmer
StaPinB	Starshots Pinback Badges
StaPinP2	PM10 Stadium Pins 2 1/8'
StaPla	Star Plantier
StaPlaCE	Star Player Candy E-Unc.
StaPro	Star Promos
StaPro	Starline Prototypes
StaPuc	Star Puckett
StaRai	Star Raines
StaRic	Star Rice
StaRip	Star Ripken
StaRya	Star Ryan
StaSan	Star Sandberg
StaSan	Star Santiago
StaSanA	Star Sandy Alomar
StaSch	Star Schmidt
StaSco	Star Scott
StaSea	Star Seaver
StaSei	Star Seitzer
StaStiC	Star Stickers Canseco
StaStiGB	Star Stickers George Bell
StaStiJ	Star Stickers Joyner Blue
StaStiS	Star Stickers Snyder
StaStiV	Star Sticker Valenzuela
StaStr	Star Strawberry
StaTar	Star Tartabull
StaThoRG	Star Thomas Rookie Guild
StaTra	Star Trammell
StaVal	Star Valenzuela
StaVanP	Star Van Poppel
StaWal	Star Walton
StaWal/O	Star Walton/Olson
StaWilC	Star Will Clark
StaWin	Star Winfield
StaYou	Star Yount
StCatSB	St. Catharines Stompers Best
StCatSTI	St. Catherines Stompers Team Issue
SteDra	Sterling Dravecky
StLucMTI	St. Lucie Mets Team Issue
StoPop	Stouffer Pop-ups
StoPorB	Stockton Ports Best
StoPorC	Stockton Ports Classic
StoPorC	Stockton Ports Classic/Best
StoPorCLC	Stockton Ports Cal League Cards
StoPorF	Stockton Ports Fleer/ProCards
StoPorP	Stockton Ports ProCards
StoPorS	Stockton Ports Star
StPetCB	St. Petersburg Cardinals Best
Stu	Studio
StuAut	Studio Autographs
StuEdiC	Studio Editor's Choice
StuGolS	Studio Gold Series
StuHarH	Studio Hard Hats
StuHer	Studio Heritage
StuHitP	Studio Hit Parade
StuMas	Studio Masterstrokes
StuMasS	Studio Master Strokes
StuMasS8	Studio Master Strokes 8x10
StuPan	Stuart Panels
StuPlaS	Studio Platinum Series
StuPor8	Studio Portraits 8x10
StuPre	Studio Previews
StuPrePB	Studio Press Proofs Bronze
StuPrePG	Studio Press Proof Gold
StuPrePG	Studio Press Proofs Gold
StuPrePS	Studio Press Proof Silver
StuPrePS	Studio Press Proofs Silver
StuSerS	Studio Series Stars
StuSil	Studio Silhouettes
StuStaGS	Studio Stained Glass Stars
StuSupoC	Studio Superstars on Canvas
StuTho	Studio Thomas
SucSav	Sucker Saver
Sum	Summit
Sum21C	Summit 21 Club
SumAbo&B	Summit Above and Beyond
SumArtP	Summit Artist's Proofs
SumBal	Summit Ballparks
SumBigB	Summit Big Bang
SumBigBM	Summit Big Bang Mirage
SumBraB	Sumter Braves Best
SumBraP	Sumter Braves ProCards
SumFlyC	Sumter Flyers Classic/Best
SumFlyP	Sumter Flyers ProCards
SumFoi	Summit Foil
SumHitI	Summit Hitters Inc.
SumNewA	Summit New Age
SumNthD	Summit Nth Degree
SumPos	Summit Positions
SumSam	Summit Samples
SunBre	Sunbeam Bread
SunPin	Sunoco Pins
SunPopK	Sun-Glo Pop Kaline
SunSee	Sunflower Seeds
SupActM	Superstar Action Marbles
SupBlaB	Superstar Blank Backs
SupMcDP	SuperSlam McDowell Promos

SweBasG	Swell Baseball Greats
SweCapPP	Sweet Caporal Pins P2
SweSpoT	Swell Sport Thrills
SwiFra	Swifts Franks
SydWavF	Sydney Wave Futura
SyrChi1A	Syracuse Chiefs 10th Anniversary
SyrChiC	Syracuse Chiefs CMC
SyrChiF	Syracuse Chiefs Fleer/ProCards
SyrChiK	Syracuse Chiefs Kraft
SyrChiLD	Syracuse Chiefs Line Drive
SyrChiMB	Syracuse Chiefs Merchants Bank
SyrChiP	Syracuse Chiefs ProCards
SyrChiS	Syracuse Chiefs SkyBox
SyrChiT	Syracuse Chiefs TCMA
SyrChiTI	Syracuse Chiefs Team Issue
SyrChiTT	Syracuse Chiefs Tallmadge Tire
T/MSenL	T/M Senior League
T/MUmp	T/M Umpires
T205	T205 Gold Border
T206	T206 White Border
T207	T207 Brown Background
T22SeroC	T227 Series of Champions
TacBan	Tacoma Bank
TacGia	Tacoma Giants
TacRaiB	Tacoma Rainiers Best
TacRaiTI	Tacoma Rainers Team Issue
TacTigC	Tacoma Tigers CMC
TacTigC	Tacoma Tigers Cramer
TacTigF	Tacoma Tigers Fleer/ProCards
TacTigLD	Tacoma Tigers Line Drive
TacTigP	Tacoma Tigers ProCards
TacTigS	Tacoma Tigers SkyBox
TacTigT	Tacoma Tigers TCMA
TacTugT	Tacoma Tugs TCMA
TacTwiC	Tacoma Twins Caruso
TacTwiDQ	Tacoma Twins Dairy Queen
TacTwiK	Tacoma Twins KMMO
TacYanC	Tacoma Yankees Cramer
TamTarP	Tampa Tarpons ProCards
TamTarS	Tampa Tarpons Star
TamTarT	Tampa Tarpons TCMA
TamYanC	Tampa Yankees Classic
TamYanD	Tampa Yankees Diamond
TamYanF	Tampa Yankees Fleer/ProCards
TamYanY	Tampa Yankees Best
TamYanYI	Tampa Yankees Team Issue
TanBraE	Tango Brand Eggs
TarThoBD	Tarzan Thoro Bread D382
TasDis	Tastee-Freez Discs
taStiW	Star Stickers Winfield
TatOrb	Tatoo Orbit R305
TatOrbSDR	Tatoo Orbit Self Develop R308
taVen	Star Ventura
TayBow4	Taylor/Schmierer Bowman 47
TCM	TCMA
TCM50	TCMA 50'S
TCM60I	TCMA 60'S I
TCM60I	TCMA 60's II
TCMAllG	TCMA All-Time Greats
TCMJapPB	TCMA Japanese Pro Baseball
TCMPla1	TCMA Playball 1946
TCMPla1	TCMA Playball 1947
TCMPla1942	TCMA Playball 1942
TCMPla1943	TCMA Playball 1943
TCMPla1944	TCMA Playball 1944
TCMPla1945	TCMA Playball 1945
TCMSupS	TCMA Superstars Simon
TCMTheWY	TCMA The War Years
TealssTT	Tucson Toros Team Issue
TeaOut	Team Out
TedWil	Ted Williams

TedWil5C	Ted Williams 500 Club
TedWilBR	Ted Williams Brooks Robinson
TedWilDGC	Ted Williams Dan Gardiner Collection
TedWilLC	Ted Williams Locklear Collection
TedWilM	Ted Williams Memories
TedWilMS	Ted Williams Mike Schmidt
TedWilP	Ted Williams Promos
TedWilPC	Ted Williams POG Cards
TedWilRC	Ted Williams Roberto Clemente
TedWilRM	Ted Williams Roger Maris
TedWilTfB	Ted Williams Trade for Babe
TenTecGE	Tennessee Tech Golden Eagles
TenVolW	Tennessee Volunteers Wendy's
Tex	Texas Longhorns
TexLeaAB	Texas League All-Stars Best
TexLeaAF	Texas League All-Stars Feder
TexLeaAGS	Texas League All-Stars Grand Slam
TexLon	Texas Longhorns
TexSupRS	Texas Supermarket Ryan Stickers
TexTomE	Texas Tommy E224
ThoMcAD	Thom McAn Discs
ThoMcAF	Thom McAn Feller
TidTidC	Tidewater Tides Candl
TidTidC	Tidewater Tides CMC
TidTidCa	Tidewater Tides Candl
TidTidCM	Tidewater Tides CMC
TidTidF	Tidewater Tides Fleer/ProCards
TidTidLD	Tidewater Tides Line Drive
TidTidP	Tidewater Tides ProCards
TidTidS	Tidewater Tides SkyBox
TidTidT	Tidewater Tides TCMA
TidTidTI	Tidewater Tides Team Issue
Tig	Tigers
TigACDPP	Tigers A.C. Dietsche Postcards PC765
TigAIKS	Tigers Al Kaline Story
TigBurK	Tigers Burger King
TigCaiD	Tigers Cain's Discs
TigCok	Tigers Coke
TigCok	Tigers Coke/Kroger
TigDeaCS	Tigers Dearborn Card Show
TigDetFPB	Tigers Detroit Free Press Bubblegumless
TigDetN	Tigers Detroit News
TigDexP	Tigers Dexter Press
TigDom	Tigers Domino's
TigFarJ	Tigers Farmer Jack
TigFliJ	Tigers Flint Journal
TigFreGWP	Tigers Fred G.Wright Postcards
TigFreP	Tigers Free Press
TigGat	Tigers Gatorade
TigGle	Tigers Glendale
TigGraASP	Tigers Graphic Arts Service PC749
TigGreT	Tigers Greats TCMA
TigHMTP	Tigers H.M. Taylor PC773-2
TigJayP	Tigers Jay Publishing
TigJew	Tigers Jewel
TigLid	Tiger Lids
TigLitC	Tigers Little Caesars
TigMar	Tigers Marathon
TigMilH	Tigers Milk Henneman
TigMorPenWBPP	Tigers Morton's Pennant Winner Bread Pins PB3
TigOldTS	Tigers Old-Timers Troy Show
TigPep	Tigers Pepsi/Kroger
TigPepT	Tigers Pepsi Trammell
TigPol	Tigers Police
TigPosCF	Tiger Post Cards Ford
TigSecNP	Tigers Second National Plymouth
TigSpoD	Tigers Sports Design
TigTaCP	Tigers Topping and Company PC773-1
TigTeal	Tigers Team Issue
TigTealC	Tigers Team Issue Color

TigWavP	Tigers Wave Postcards
TigWen	Tigers Wendy's/Coke
TipTop	Tip Top
TobPosH8	Tobin Postcards H 804-21
TolMudHB	Toledo Mud Hens Best
TolMudHC	Toledo Mud Hens CMC
TolMudHF	Toledo Mud Hens Fleer/ProCards
TolMudHLD	Toledo Mud Hens Line Drive
TolMudHP	Toledo Mud Hens ProCards
TolMudHS	Toledo Mud Hens SkyBox
TolMudHT	Toledo Mud Hens TCMA
TolMudHTI	Toledo Mud Hens Team Issue
TomBarW	Tom Barker WG6
TomPiz	Tombstone Pizza
Top	Topps
Top3-D	Topps 3-D
TopActS	Topps Action Stickers
TopAll	Topps All-Stars
TopAme2C	Topps Ames 20/20 Club
TopAmeA	Topps Ames All-Stars
TopArc1	Topps Archives 1953
TopArc1	Topps Archives 1954
TopArc1G	Topps Archives 1954 Gold
TopArcBD	Topps Archives Brooklyn Dodgers
TopAwaW	Topps Award Winners
TopAweI	Topps Awesome Impact
TopBasT	Topps Baseball Talk
TopBatL	Topps Batting Leaders
TopBig	Topps Big
TopBigC	Topps Big Cards
TopBlaG	Topps Black Gold
TopBluB	Topps Blue Backs
TopBluTC	Topps Blue Team Checklists
TopBoo	Topps Booklets
TopBowK	Topps Bowie Kuhn
TopBroLL	Topps Bronze League Leaders
TopBuc	Topps Bucks
TopCanL	Topps Candy Lids
TopCapC	Topps Cap'n Crunch
TopCas	Topps Cashen
TopCer	Topps Cereal
TopChr	Topps Chrome
TopChrAS	Topps Chrome All Stars
TopChrDD	Topps Chrome Diamond Duos
TopChrDDR	Topps Chrome Diamond Duos Refractors
TopChrMotG	Topps Chrome Masters of the Game
TopChrMotGR	Topps Chrome Masters of the Game Refractors
TopChrR	Topps Chrome Refractors
TopChrSAR	Topps Chrome All Stars Refractors
TopChrSB	Topps Chrome Season's Best
TopChrSBR	Topps Chrome Season's Best Refractors
TopChrWC	Topps Chrome Wrecking Crew
TopChrWCR	Topps Chrome Wrecking Crew Refractors
TopClaC	Topps Classic Confrontations
TopCloS	Topps Cloth Stickers
TopCloT	Topps Cloth Test
TopCoi	Topps Coins
TopCoi	Topps Coins Inserts
TopCom	Topps Comics
TopComotH	Topps Commanders of the Hill
TopConMA	Topps Connie Mack All-Stars
TopCraJ2	Topps Cracker Jack II
TopCraJI	Topps Cracker Jack I
TopCurA	Topps Current All-Stars
TopCyb	Topps Cyberstats
TopCybSiR	Topps Cyber Season in Review
TopDaiQTU	Topps Dairy Queen Team USA
TopDeb89	Topps Debut '89
TopDeb90	Topps Debut '90
TopDeb91	Topps Debut '91
TopDec	Topps Deckle
TopDecE	Topps Deckle Edge
TopDecI	Topps Decal Inserts
TopDesS	Topps Desert Shield
TopDicG	Topps Dice Game
TopDou	Topps Doubleheaders
TopDouA	Topps Doubleheaders All-Stars
TopDouH	Topps Double Header
TopDouM	Topps Doubleheaders Mets/Yankees Test
TopEasCN	Topps East Coast National
TopEmbI	Topps Embossed Inserts
TopFin	Topps Finest
TopFol	Topps Foldouts
TopFou	Topps Four-in-One
TopFulS	Topps Full Shots
TopGal	Topps Gallery
TopGalE	Topps Gallery Expressionists
TopGalGoH	Topps Gallery Gallery of Heroes
TopGaloC	Topps Gallery of Champions
TopGalP	Topps Gallery Promos
TopGalPG	Topps Gallery Photo Gallery
TopGalPMS	Topps Gallery Peter Max Serigraphs
TopGalPMSSS	Topps Gallery Peter Max Signature Series Serigraphs
TopGalPPI	Topps Gallery Player's Private Issue
TopGalPPI	Topps Gallery Players Private Issue
TopGamI	Topps Game Inserts
TopGayP	Topps Gaylord Perry
TopGia	Topps Giants
TopGiaSU	Topps Giant Stand Ups
TopGloA	Topps Glossy All-Stars
TopGloS	Topps Glossy Send-Ins
TopGol	Topps Gold
TopGolPS	Topps Gold Pre-Production Sheet
TopGolS	Topps Golden Spikes
TopGolW	Topps Gold Winners
TopGreM	Topps Greatest Moments
TopHeaU	Topps Heads Up
TopHeaUT	Topps Heads Up Test
TopHilHM	Topps Hills Hit Men
TopHilTM	Topps Hills Team MVP's
TopHobM	Topps Hobby Masters
TopHocF	Topps Hocus Focus
TopInaM	Topps Inaugural Marlins/Rockies
TopIntF	Topps Inter-League Finest
TopIntFR	Topps Inter-League Finest Refractors
TopKid	Topps Kids
TopLas	Topps Laser
TopLasBS	Topps Laser Bright Spots
TopLasPC	Topps Laser Power Cuts
TopLasSS	Topps Laser Stadium Stars
TopLeaL	Topps League Leaders
TopLeaS	Topps Leader Sheet
TopLegot6M	Topps Legends of the '60s Medallions
TopMag	Topps Magazine
TopMagJRC	Topps Magazine Jumbo Rookie Cards
TopMagR	Topps Magic Rub-Offs
TopMan	Topps Mantle
TopManC	Topps Mantle Case
TopManF	Topps Mantle Finest
TopManFR	Topps Mantle Finest Refractors
TopManR	Topps Mantle Redemption
TopMasotG	Topps Masters of the Game
TopMay	Topps Mays
TopMayF	Topps Mays Finest
TopMayFR	Topps Mays Finest Refractors
TopMcD	Topps McDonald's
TopMic	Topps Micro
TopMin	Topps/OPC Minis
TopMinL	Topps Mini Leaders
TopMysF	Topps Mystery Finest

TopMysFR	Topps Mystery Finest Refractors
TopNikH	Topps Nikon House
TopPewB	Topps Pewter Bonuses
TopPho	Topps Photographers
TopPin	Topps Pin-Ups
TopPin	Topps Pins
TopPirS	Topps Pirate Stickers
TopPla	Topps Plaks
TopPor	Topps Porcelain
TopPorP	Topps Porcelain Promo
TopPos	Topps Postcards
TopPos	Topps Poster Inserts
TopPos	Topps Posters
TopPowB	Topps Power Boosters
TopPre	Topps Pre-Production
TopPreS	Topps Pre-Production Sheet
TopPro	Topps Profiles
TopPuz	Topps Puzzles
TopRedB	Topps Red Backs
TopRedSS	Topps Red Sox Stickers
TopRep5	Topps Reprint 52
TopRevLL	Topps Revco League Leaders
TopRitM	Topps Ritz Mattingly
TopRitTM	Topps Rite-Aid Team MVP's
TopRoaW	Topps Road Warriors
TopRoo	Topps Rookies
TopRos	Topps Rose
TopRubD	Topps Rub Downs
TopRubI	Topps Rub-Off Inserts
TopRut	Topps Ruth
TopScr	Topps Scratchoffs
TopScr	Topps Screenplays
TopScrSI	Topps Screenplays Special Inserts
TopSeaB	Topps Season's Best
TopSenL	Topps Senior League
TopSpa	Topps Spanish
TopSpaFI	Topps Spanish Factory Inserts
TopSta	Topps Stamps
TopSta	Topps Stand-Ups
TopSta	Topps Stars
TopSta1AS	Topps Stars 1997 All Stars
TopStaA	Topps Stamp Albums
TopStaAM	Topps Stars Always Mint
TopStaASGM	Topps Stars All Star Game Memories
TopStaFAS	Topps Stars Future All Stars
TopStaHRR	Topps Stars HOF Rookie Reprints
TopStaHRRA	Topps Stars HOF Rookie Reprint Autographs
TopStaI	Topps Stamps Inserts
TopStaRP	Topps Stars Rookie Promos
TopStaU	Topps Stand Ups
TopSti	Topps Stickers
TopSti	Topps/O-Pee-Chee Stickers
TopStiB	Topps Sticker Boxes
TopStiB	Topps/O-Pee-Chee Sticker Backs
TopStiI	Topps Stick-On Inserts
TopStiV	Topps Sticker Variations
TopSup	Topps Super
TopSupHT	Topps Super Home Team
TopSupN	Topps Super National
TopSupS	Topps Superstar Samplers
TopSweS	Topps Sweet Strokes
TopTat	Topps Tattoos
TopTatI	Topps Tattoos Inserts
TopTea	Topps Teams
TopTeaC	Topps Team Checklists
TopTeaCS	Topps Team Checklist Sheet
TopTeaP	Topps Team Posters
TopTeaT	Topps Team Timber
TopTes5	Topps Test 53
TopTesF	Topps Test Foil
TopTesS	Topps Test Stamps
TopTif	Topps Tiffany
TopTifT	Topps Traded Tiffany
TopTra	Topps Traded
TopTraBP	Topps Traded Bronze Premiums
TopTraFI	Topps Traded Finest Inserts
TopTraG	Topps Traded Gold
TopTraI	Topps Transfers Inserts
TopTraPB	Topps Traded Power Boosters
TopTraT	Topps Traded Tiffany
TopTriH	Topps Triple Headers
TopTVA	Topps TV All-Stars
TopTVCa	Topps TV Cardinals
TopTVCu	Topps TV Cubs
TopTVM	Topps TV Mets
TopTVRS	Topps TV Red Sox
TopTVY	Topps TV Yankees
TopUKM	Topps UK Minis
TopUKMT	Topps UK Minis Tiffany
TopVen	Topps Venezuelan
TopWaxBC	Topps Wax Box Cards
TopWreC	Topps Wrecking Crew
TopZes	Topps Zest
Toy	Toys'R'Us
ToyMasP	Toys'R'Us Master Photos
ToyRoo	Toys'R'Us Rookies
TraSta	Transogram Statues
TreThuB	Trenton Thunder Best
TreThuF	Trenton Thunder Fleer/ProCards
TreThuTI	Trenton Thunder Team Issue
TriA AAC	Triple A All-Stars CMC
TriA AAGP	Triple A All-Stars ProCards
TriA AAP	Triple A All-Stars ProCards
TriA AAS	Triple A All-Stars SkyBox
TriAAAC	Triple A All-Stars CMC
TriAAAGF	Triple A All-Stars Fleer/ProCards
TriAAAP	Triple A All-Stars ProCards
TriAAC	Triple A All-Stars CMC
TriAAF	Triple A All-Stars Fleer/ProCards
TriAllGP	Triple A All-Stars ProCards
TriPla	Triple Play
TriPlaA	Triple Play Action
TriPlaBS	Triple Play Bomb Squad
TriPlaG	Triple Play Gallery
TriPlaLL	Triple Play League Leaders
TriPlaM	Triple Play Medalists
TriPlaN	Triple Play Nicknames
TriPlaP	Triple Play Previews
TriPlaP	Triple Play Promos
TriTriC	Tri-Cities Triplets Cramer
TriTriT	Tri-Cities Triplets TCMA
TruVal	True Value
TucTorC	Tucson Toros Caruso
TucTorC	Tucson Toros CMC
TucTorC	Tucson Toros Cramer
TucTorCa	Tucson Toros Caruso
TucTorF	Tucson Toros Fleer/ProCards
TucTorJP	Tucson Toros Jones Photo
TucTorLD	Tucson Toros Line Drive
TucTorP	Tucson Toros ProCards
TucTorS	Tucson Toros SkyBox
TucTorT	Tucson Toros TCMA
TucTorTI	Tucson Toros Team Issue
TulDriDGB	Tulsa Drillers All Decade Best
TulDriF	Tulsa Drillers Fleer/ProCards
TulDriGS	Tulsa Drillers Grand Slam
TulDriLD	Tulsa Drillers Line Drive
TulDriP	Tulsa Drillers ProCards
TulDriS	Tulsa Drillers SkyBox
TulDriT	Tulsa Drillers TCMA
TulDriTI	Tulsa Drillers Team Issue

TulOil	Tulsa Oilers
TulOil7	Tulsa Oilers 7-11
TulOilGP	Tulsa Oilers Goof's Pants
TurRedT	Turkey Red T3
TusTorB	Tucson Toros Best
TusTorCr	Tucson Toros Cramer
TVSpoM	TV Sports Mailbags
TVSpoMF5HRC	TV Sports Mailbag/Photo File 500 Home Run Club
Twi7	Twins 7-Eleven
TwiCloD	Twins Cloverleaf Dairy
TwiFaiG	Twins Fairway Grocery
TwiFri	Twins Frisz
TwiFriP	Twins Frisz Postcards
TwiGreT	Twins Greats TCMA
TwiJayP	Twins Jay Publishing
TwiMasBD	Twins Master Bread Discs
TwiPetM	Twins Peter's Meats
TwiPos	Twins Postcards
TwiSmoC	Twins Smokey Colorgrams
TwiTeal	Twins Team Issue
TwiTealC	Twins Team Issue Color
TwiUniMC	Twins Universal Match Corp.
TwiVol	Twins Volpe
UC3	UC3
UC3ArtP	UC3 Artist's Proofs
UC3CleS	UC3 Clear Shots
UC3CycS	UC3 Cyclone Squad
UC3InM	UC3 In Motion
UllHomRK	Ultra Home Run Kings
Ult	Ultra
UltAllR	Ultra All-Rookies
UltAllRGM	Ultra All-Rookies Gold Medallions
UltAllRJ	Ultra All-Rookies Jumbo
UltAllS	Ultra All-Stars
UltAllSGM	Ultra All-Stars Gold Medallion
UltAutE	Ultra Autographstix Emeralds
UltAwaW	Ultra Award Winners
UltAwaWGM	Ultra Award Winners Gold Medallion
UltBasC	Ultimate Baseball Card
UltBasR	Ultra Baseball Rules
UltCalttH	Ultra Call to the Hall
UltCalttHGM	Ultra Call to the Hall Gold Medallion
UltCarA	Ultra Career Achievement
UltChe	Ultra Checklists
UltCheGM	Ultra Checklists Gold Medallion
UltDiaP	Ultra Diamond Producers
UltDiaPGM	Ultra Diamond Producers Gold Medallion
UltDouT	Ultra Double Trouble
UltEck	Ultra Eckersley
UltFamGam	Ultra Fame Game
UltFieC	Ultra Fielder's Choice
UltFir	Ultra Firemen
UltFreF	Ultra Fresh Foundations
UltFreFGM	Ultra Fresh Foundations Gold Medallions
UltGol	Ultra Gold
UltGolM	Ultra Gold Medallion
UltGolME	Ultra Gold Medallion
UltGolMR	Ultra Gold Medallion Rookies
UltGolP	Ultra Golden Prospects
UltGolP	Ultra Golden Prospects Hobby
UltGolPGM	Ultra Golden Prospects Gold Medallion
UltGolPHGM	Ultra Golden Prospects Hobby Gold Medallion
UltGwy	Ultra Gwynn
UltHitM	Ultra Hitting Machines
UltHitMGM	Ultra Hitting Machines Gold Medallion
UltHomRK	Ultra Home Run Kings
UltHomRKGM	Ultra Home Run Kings Gold Medallion
UltHomRKR	Ultra Home Run Kings Redemption
UltHRK	Ultra Home Run Kings

UltLeaL	Ultra League Leaders
UltLeaLGM	Ultra League Leaders Gold Medallion
UltLeaS	Ultra Leather Shop
UltOn-L	Ultra On-Base Leaders
UltOn-LGM	Ultra On-Base Leaders Gold Medallion
UltOnBL	Ultra On-Base Leaders
UltOnBLGM	Ultra On-Base Leaders Gold Medallion
UltPer	Ultra Performers
UltPhiF	Ultra Phillies Finest
UltPlaME	Ultra Platinum Medallion
UltPowP	Ultra Power Plus
UltPowPGM	Ultra Power Plus Gold Medallion
UltPriL	Ultra Prime Leather
UltPriLGM	Ultra Prime Leather Gold Medallion
UltPro	Ultra Promos
UltRaw	Ultra Rawhide
UltRawGM	Ultra Rawhide Gold Medallion
UltRBIK	Ultra RBI Kings
UltRBIKGM	Ultra RBI Kings Gold Medallion
UltRes	Ultra Respect
UltResGM	Ultra Respect Gold Medallion
UltRisS	Ultra Rising Stars
UltRisSGM	Ultra Rising Stars Gold Medallion
UltRooR	Ultra Rookie Reflections
UltSeaC	Ultra Season Crowns
UltSeaCGM	Ultra Seasons Crowns Gold Medallion
UltSecYS	Ultra Second Year Standouts
UltSecYSGM	Ultra Second Year Standouts Gold Medallion
UltStaR	Ultra Starring Role
UltStrK	Ultra Strikeout Kings
UltStrKGM	Ultra Strikeout Kings Gold Medallion
UltThu	Ultra Thunderclap
UltThuGM	Ultra Thunderclap Gold Medallion
UltTop3	Ultra Top 30
UltTop3GM	Ultra Top 30 Gold Medallion
UltUpd	Ultra Update
UniOil	Union Oil
UniWayS	United Way Sierra
UppDec	Upper Deck
UppDecA	Upper Deck All-Stars
UppDecA	Upper Deck Autographs
UppDecAG	Upper Deck Amazing Greats
UppDecAH	Upper Deck Aaron Heroes
UppDecAH	Upper Deck All-Time Heroes
UppDecAH1	Upper Deck All-Time Heroes 125th
UppDecAH1A	Upper Deck All-Time Heroes 1954 Archives
UppDecAHNIL	Upper Deck All-Time Heroes Next In Line
UppDecAHP	Upper Deck All-Time Heroes Preview
UppDecAJ	Upper Deck All-Star Jumbos
UppDecAJG	Upper Deck All-Star Jumbos Gold
UppDecAWJ	Upper Deck Award Winner Jumbos
UppDecBCP	Upper Deck Blue Chip Prospects
UppDecBH	Upper Deck Bench/Morgan Heroes
UppDecC	Upper Deck Checklists
UppDecCB2	Upper Deck Comic Ball 2
UppDecCB3	Upper Deck Comic Ball 3
UppDecCBP	Upper Deck Comic Ball Promos
UppDecCP	Upper Deck Clutch Performers
UppDecCPH	Upper Deck College POY Holograms
UppDecCRJ	Upper Deck Clark Reggie Jackson
UppDecDC	Upper Deck Diamond Collection
UppDecDD	Upper Deck Diamond Destiny
UppDecDDG	Upper Deck Diamond Destiny Gold
UppDecDDS	Upper Deck Diamond Destiny Silver
UppDecDG	Upper Deck Diamond Gallery
UppDecED	Upper Deck Electric Diamond
UppDecEDG	Upper Deck Electric Diamond Gold
UppDecF	Upper Deck FanFest
UppDecFA	Upper Deck Fifth Anniversary

UppDecFAJ	Upper Deck Fifth Anniversary Jumbo
UppDecFE	Upper Deck Final Edition
UppDecFG	Upper Deck FanFest Gold
UppDecFH	Upper Deck Future Heroes
UppDecFSP	Upper Deck Future Stock Prospects
UppDecG	Upper Deck Gameface
UppDecGJ	Upper Deck Game Jersey
UppDecGJ	Upper Deck Griffey Jumbos
UppDecGold	Upper Deck Gold
UppDecGP	Upper Deck Griffey Promos
UppDecHC	Upper Deck Hot Commodities
UppDecHH	Upper Deck Heroes Highlights
UppDecHoB	Upper Deck Heroes of Baseball
UppDecHoB5	Upper Deck Heroes of Baseball 5x7
UppDecHRH	Upper Deck Home Run Heroes
UppDecIC	Upper Deck Iooss Collection
UppDecICJ	Upper Deck Iooss Collection Jumbo
UppDecJH	Upper Deck Jackson Heroes
UppDecJHJ	Upper Deck Jackson Heroes Jumbo
UppDecKGJHR	Upper Deck Ken Griffey Jr. Highlight Reels
UppDecLDC	Upper Deck Long Distance Connection
UppDecMH	Upper Deck Mantle Heroes
UppDecMH	Upper Deck Mays Heroes
UppDecML	Upper Deck
UppDecML	Upper Deck Minors
UppDecMLFS	Upper Deck Future Stock
UppDecMLMJJ	Upper Deck Michael Jordan Season Highlights Jumbos
UppDecMLMJOoO	Upper Deck Michael Jordan One On One
UppDecMLMJS	Upper Deck Michael Jordan's Scrapbook
UppDecMLMLA	Upper Deck Minor League Autographs
UppDecMLOP	Upper Deck Organizational Profiles
UppDecMLPotY	Upper Deck Minors Player of the Year
UppDecMLPotYF	Upper Deck Minors Player of the Year
UppDecMLS	Upper Deck Mantle's Long Shots
UppDecMLSED	Upper Deck Mantle's Long Shots Electric Diamond
UppDecMLT1PF	Upper Deck Top 10 Prospect
UppDecMLT1PJF	Upper Deck Minors Top 10 Prospect Jumbos
UppDecMLT1PMF	Upper Deck Minors Top 10 Prospect Mail-In
UppDecMLTPHF	Upper Deck Minors Top Prospect Holograms
UppDecMM	Upper Deck Memorable Moments
UppDecMPC	Upper Deck Mantle Phone Cards
UppDecMtSGR	Upper Deck Meet the Stars Griffey Redemption
UppDecNG	Upper Deck Next Generation
UppDecNGED	Upper Deck Next Generation Electric Diamond
UppDecNomH	Upper Deck Nomo Highlights
UppDecNRJ	Upper Deck Nomo ROY Japanese
UppDecOD	Upper Deck On Deck
UppDecP	Upper Deck Predictor
UppDecP	Upper Deck Promos
UppDecPAW	Upper Deck Predictor Award Winners
UppDecPAWE	Upper Deck Predictor Award Winner Exchange
UppDecPC	Upper Deck/GTS Phone Cards
UppDecPD	Upper Deck Power Driven
UppDecPHE	Upper Deck Predictor Hobby Exchange
UppDecPLL	Upper Deck Predictor League Leaders
UppDecPLLE	Upper Deck Predictor League Leaders Exchange
UppDecPP	Upper Deck Power Package
UppDecPPJ	Upper Deck Power Package Jumbo
UppDecPRE	Upper Deck Predictor Retail Exchange
UppDecPreH	Upper Deck Predictor Hobby
UppDecPreR	Upper Deck Predictor Retail
UppDecRCJ	Upper Deck Ripken Collection Jumbos
UppDecRH	Upper Deck Ruth Heroes
UppDecRH	Upper Deck Ryan Heroes
UppDecRipC	Upper Deck Ripken Collection
UppDecRP	Upper Deck Run Producers
UppDecRSF	Upper Deck Rock Solid Foundation
UppDecRunP	Upper Deck Run Producers
UppDecS	Upper Deck Sheet
UppDecS	Upper Deck Sheets
UppDecSDRJ	Upper Deck Sports Drink Jackson
UppDecSE	Upper Deck Special Edition
UppDecSEG	Upper Deck Special Edition Gold
UppDecSH	Upper Deck Season Highlights
UppDecSHoB	Upper Deck Sonic Heroes of Baseball
UppDecSoaD	Upper Deck Steal of a Deal
UppDecSR	Upper Deck Scouting Report
UppDecSS	Upper Deck Silver Sluggers
UppDecTAE	Upper Deck: The American Epic
UppDecTAEGM	Upper Deck: The American Epic GM
UppDecTAELD	Upper Deck: The American Epic Little Debbies
UppDecTAN	Upper Deck Then And Now
UppDecTMH	Upper Deck Team MVP Holograms
UppDecTR	Upper Deck T202 Reprints
UppDecTriCro	Upper Deck Triple Crown
UppDecTTS	Upper Deck Ticket To Stardom
UppDecU	Upper Deck UD3
UppDecUGN	Upper Deck UD3 Generation Next
UppDecUMA	Upper Deck UD3 Marquee Attraction
UppDecUSS	Upper Deck UD3 Superb Signatures
UppDecVJLS	Upper Deck V.J. Lovero Showcase
UppDecWB	Upper Deck Williams Best
UppDecWH	Upper Deck Williams Heroes
UppDecWWB	Upper Deck Williams Wax Boxes
USCar	U.S. Caramel R328
USDepoT	U.S. Department of Transportation
USGamSBL	U.S. Game Systems Baseball Legends
USPlaCA	U.S. Playing Card All-Stars
USPlaCA	U.S. Playing Cards Aces
USPlaCMLA	U.S. Playing Cards Aces
USPlaCR	U.S. Playing Cards Rookies
USPLegSC	USPS Legends Stamp Cards
UtiBluJT	Utica Blue Jays TCMA
UtiBluSC	Utica Blue Sox Classic
UtiBluSC	Utica Blue Sox Classic/Best
UtiBluSF	Utica Blue Sox Fleer/ProCards
UtiBluSP	Utica Blue Sox ProCards
UtiBluSP	Utica Blue Sox Pucko
UtiBluST	Utica Blue Sox TCMA
ValNatBPG	Phoenix Giants Valley National Bank
VanCanB	Vancouver Canadians Best
VanCanC	Vancouver Canadians CMC
VanCanC	Vancouver Canadians Cramer
VanCanF	Vancouver Canadians Fleer/ProCards
VanCanLD	Vancouver Canadians Line Drive
VanCanP	Vancouver Canadians ProCards
VanCanS	Vancouver Canadians SkyBox
VanCanT	Vancouver Canadians TCMA
VenGulP	Ventura Gulls ProCards
VenLeaS	Venezuelan League Stickers
VenLinU	LineUp Venezuelan Baseball
VenSti	Venezuela Stickers
VerBeaDB	Vero Beach Dodgers Best
VerBeaDC	Vero Beach Dodgers Classic
VerBeaDC	Vero Beach Dodgers Classic/Best
VerBeaDF	Vero Beach Dodgers Fleer/ProCards
VerBeaDP	Vero Beach Dodgers ProCards
VerBeaDS	Vero Beach Dodgers Star
VerBeaDT	Vero Beach Dodgers TCMA
VerBeaDTI	Vero Beach Dodgers Team Issue
VerExpB	Vermont Expos Best

VerExpC	Vermont Expos Classic
VerExpF	Vermont Expos Fleer/ProCards
VerMarP	Vermont Mariners ProCards
VerRedP	Vermont Reds ProCards
VicPos	Victory Posters
VicT21	Victory T214
VirGenS	Virginia Generals Star
VisOakC	Visalia Oaks Classic/Best
VisOakCLC	Visalia Oaks Cal League Cards
VisOakF	Visalia Oaks Fleer/ProCards
VisOakF	Visalia Oaks Fritsch
VisOakP	Visalia Oaks ProCards
VisOakT	Visalia Oaks TCMA
VisOakUP	Visalia Oaks Update ProCards
W/RMarG	W/R Mark Grace
W501	W501
W502	W502
W503	W503
W512	W512 *
W513	W513 *
W514	W514
W515	W515
W517	W517
W551	W551
W554	W554
W555	W555
W56PlaC	W560 Playing Cards *
W572	W572
W573	W573
W575	W575
W720HolS	W720 Hollywood Stars
W725AngTI	W725 Angels Team Issue
W72HolS	W720 Hollywood Stars
WalMaiW	Walter Mails WG7
WarBakSP	Ward Baking Sporties Pins PB6
WasVia	Washington Viacom
WatA'sT	Waterbury A's TCMA
WatDiaB	Waterloo Diamonds Best
WatDiaC	Waterloo Diamonds Classic/Best
WatDiaF	Waterloo Diamonds Fleer/ProCards
WatDiaP	Waterloo Diamonds ProCards
WatDiaS	Waterloo Diamonds Star
WatDodT	Waterbury Dodgers TCMA
WatIndC	Watertown Indians Classic
WatIndC	Watertown Indians Classic/Best
WatIndF	Waterloo Indians Fritsch
WatIndF	Watertown Indians Fleer/ProCards
WatIndP	Waterbury Indians ProCards
WatIndP	Waterloo Indians ProCards
WatIndP	Watertown Indians ProCards
WatIndS	Watertown Indians Star
WatIndT	Waterbury Indians TCMA
WatIndT	Waterloo Indians TCMA
WatIndTI	Watertown Indians Team Issue
WatPirP	Watertown Pirates ProCards
WatPirP	Watertown Pirates Pucko
WatRedT	Waterbury Reds TCMA
WatRoyT	Waterloo Royals TCMA
WauMetT	Wausau Mets TCMA
WauTimB	Wausau Timbers Best
WauTimF	Wausau Timbers Fritsch
WauTimGS	Wausau Timbers Grand Slam
WauTimP	Wausau Timbers ProCards
WauTimS	Wausau Timbers Star
WauTimT	Wausau Timbers TCMA
WavRedF	Waverly Reds Futura
WelPirC	Welland Pirates Classic
WelPirC	Welland Pirates Classic/Best
WelPirF	Welland Pirates Fleer/ProCards
WelPirP	Welland Pirates ProCards
WelPirP	Welland Pirates Pucko
WenCle	Wendy's Clemente
WesHavAT	West Haven A's TCMA
WesHavWCT	West Haven White Caps TCMA
WesHavYT	West Haven Yankees TCMA
WesMicWB	West Michigan Whitecaps Best
WesMicWC	West Michigan Whitecaps Classic
WesMicWF	West Michigan Whitecaps Fleer/ProCards
WesMicWTI	West Michigan Whitecaps Team Issue
WesOahCHWB	West Oahu Canefires Hawaii Winter Ball
WesPalBEB	West Palm Beach Expos Best
WesPalBEC	West Palm Beach Expos Classic
WesPalBEC	West Palm Beach Expos Classic/Best
WesPalBEF	West Palm Beach Expos Fleer/ProCards
WesPalBEP	West Palm Beach Expos ProCards
WesPalBES	West Palm Beach Expos Star
WesPalBES	West Palm Beach Expos Sussman
WesVirWC	West Virginia Wheelers Classic/Best
WesVirWF	West Virginia Wheelers Fleer/ProCards
WG1CarG	WG1 Card Game
WhaRya	Whataburger Ryan
Whe	Wheaties *
WheBB1	Wheaties BB1
WheBB10	Wheaties BB10
WheBB11	Wheaties BB11
WheBB12	Wheaties BB12
WheBB13	Wheaties BB13
WheBB14	Wheaties BB14
WheBB15	Wheaties BB15
WheBB3	Wheaties BB3
WheBB4	Wheaties BB4
WheBB5	Wheaties BB5
WheBB6	Wheaties BB6
WheBB7	Wheaties BB7
WheBB8	Wheaties BB8
WheBB9	Wheaties BB9
WheM4	Wheaties M4
WheM5	Wheaties M5
WheSta	Wheaties Stamps
WhiLegtL	Whitehall Legends to Life
WhiPro	Whitehall Prototypes
WhiSox	White Sox
WhiSox1T	White Sox 1919 TCMA
WhiSoxC	White Sox Chi-Foursome
WhiSoxC	White Sox Coke
WhiSoxDS	White Sox Durochrome Stickers
WhiSoxGT	White Sox Greats TCMA
WhiSoxGWH	White Sox George W. Hull
WhiSoxH	White Sox Hawthorn-Mellody
WhiSoxJP	White Sox Jay Publishing
WhiSoxJT	White Sox Jewel Tea
WhiSoxK	White Sox Kodak
WhiSoxL	White Sox Lotshaw's
WhiSoxTAG	White Sox TCMA All-Time Greats
WhiSoxTI	White Sox Team Issue
WhiSoxTI1	White Sox Team Issue
WhiSoxTS	White Sox Ticket Stubs
WhiSoxTV	White Sox True Value
WicAerDS	Wichita Aeros Dog'n Shake
WicAerKSB	Wichita Aeros Kansas State Bank
WicAerODF	Wichita Aeros One Day Film
WicAerRD	Wichita Aeros Rock's Dugout
WicAerT	Wichita Aeros TCMA
WicAerTI	Wichita Aeros Team Issue
WicBonR	Wichita Bonus Rock
WicChaR	Wichita Champions Rock
WicPilRD	Wichita Pilots Rock's Dugout
WicStaR	Wichita Stadium Rock
WicStaSGD	Wichita State Shockers Game Day
WicUpdR	Wichita Update Rock
WicWraB	Wichita Wranglers Best
WicWraF	Wichita Wranglers Fleer/ProCards

WicWraLD	Wichita Wranglers Line Drive
WicWraP	Wichita Wranglers ProCards
WicWraR	Wichita Wranglers Rock
WicWraRD	Wichita Wranglers Rock's Dugout
WicWraS	Wichita Wranglers SkyBox
WicWraTI	Wichita Wranglers Team Issue
WifBalD	Wiffle Ball Discs
Wil	Wilson
WilBilB	Williamsport Bills Best
WilBilLD	Williamsport Bills Line Drive
WilBilP	Williamsport Bills ProCards
WilBilS	Williamsport Bills Star
WilBluRB	Wilmington Blue Rocks Best
WilBluRC	Wilmington Blue Rocks Classic
WilBluRC	Wilmington Blue Rocks Classic/Best
WilBluRF	Wilmington Blue Rocks Fleer/ProCards
WilBluRTI	Wilmington Blue Rocks Team Issue
WilCarE	Williams Caramels E103
WilChoV	Willards Chocolates V100
WilCubC	Williamsport Cubs Classic
WilCubF	Williamsport Cubs Fleer/ProCards
WilGloT	Wilson Glove Tags
WilMay	Willie Mays
WilMulP	Willard Mullin Postcards
WilPatV	William Paterson V89
WilSpoG	Wilson Sporting Goods
WilSpoGH828	Wilson Sporting Goods H828
WilSpoGH828-1	Wilson Sporting Goods H828-1
WilTomT	Williamsport Tomahawks TCMA
WinDis	Windwalker Discs
WinHavRSC	Winter Haven Red Sox Classic/Best
WinHavRSF	Winter Haven Red Sox Fleer/ProCards
WinHavRSP	Winter Haven Red Sox ProCards
WinHavRSS	Winter Haven Red Sox Star
WinSpiC	Winston-Salem Spirits Classic
WinSpiC	Winston-Salem Spirits Classic/Best
WinSpiF	Winston-Salem Spirits Fleer/ProCards
WinSpiP	Winston-Salem Spirits ProCards
WinSpiS	Winston-Salem Spirits Star
WinSpiTI	Winston-Salem Spirits Team Issue
WisRapTF	Wisconsin Rapids Twins Fritsch
WisRapTT	Wisconsin Rapids Twins TCMA
WisTimRB	Wisconsin Timber Rattlers Best
WolNewDTPP	Tigers Wolverine News Postcards PC773-3
WonBreS	Wonder Bread Stars
Woo	Woolworth's
WorUniG	World University Games*
WorWidGTP	World Wide Gum Trimmed Premiums V351B
WorWidGV	World Wide Gum V351A
WorWidGV	World Wide Gum V355
WorWidGV	World Wide Gum V362
WWSmiP	W.W. Smith Postcards
WytCubP	Wytheville Cubs ProCards
WytCubS	Wytheville Cubs Star
YakBeaC	Yakima Bears Classic
YakBeaC	Yakima Bears Classic/Best
YakBeaF	Yakima Bears Fleer/ProCards
YakBeaP	Yakima Bears ProCards
YakBeaTI	Yakima Bears Team Issue
Yan	Yankees
Yan192T	Yankees 1927 TCMA
Yan196T	Yankees 1961 TCMA
Yan61RL	Yankees 61 Ron Lewis
YanArcO	Yankees Arco Oil
YanASFY	Yankee A-S Fifty Years
YanBurK	Yankees Burger King
YanCitAG	Yankee Citgo All-Time Greats
YanCliDP	Yankee Clinic Day Postcards
YanDyn1T	Yankee Dynasty 1936-39 TCMA
YanGreT	Yankees Greats TCMA
YanJayP	Yankees Jay Publishing
YanPicA	Yankees Picture Album
YanReqKP	Yankee Requena K Postcards
YanRoyRD	Yankees Roy Rogers Discs
YanScoNW	Yankees Score Nat West
YanSSP	Yankees SSPC
YanSSPD	Yankees SSPC Diary
YanSta	Yankees Stamps
YanTCM	Yankees TCMA
YanTeal	Yankees Team Issue
YanWIZ6	Yankees WIZ 60s
YanWIZ7	Yankees WIZ 70s
YanWIZ8	Yankees WIZ 80s
YanWIZA	Yankees WIZ All-Stars
YanWIZH	Yankees WIZ HOF
YanYealT	Yankee Yearbook Insert TCMA
YelBasP	Yellow Basepath Pins
Yoo	Yoo-Hoo
YooMatBC	Yoo-Hoo Match Book Cover
YorCarE	York Caramel E210
Yue	Yuenglings
ZCle	Z-Silk Clemente
Zen	Zenith
Zen Z-Z	Zenith Z-Team
Zen8x1	Zenith 8x10
Zen8x1D	Zenith 8x10 Dufex
ZenAllS	Zenith All-Star Salute
ZenArtP	Zenith Artist's Proofs
ZenDiaC	Zenith Diamond Club
ZenDiaCP	Zenith Diamond Club Parallel
ZenMoz	Zenith Mozaics
ZenRooRC	Zenith Rookie Roll Call
ZenV-2	Zenith V-2
ZenZ	Zenith Z-Team
Zip	Ziploc

Additional Reading

Each year Beckett Publications produces comprehensive annual price guides for each of the four major sports: *Beckett Baseball Card Price Guide, Beckett Football Card Price Guide, Beckett Basketball Card Price Guide*, and *Beckett Hockey Card Price Guide.* The aim of these annual guides is to provide information and accurate pricing on a wide array of sports cards, ranging from main issues by the major card manufacturers to various regional, promotional, and food issues. Also other alphabetical checklists, such as *The Beckett Baseball Card Alphabetical, The Beckett Football Card Alphabetical* and *The Beckett Hockey Card Price Guide and Alphabetical*, are published to assist the collector in identifying all the cards of any particular player. The seasoned collector will find these tools valuable sources of information that will enable him to pursue his hobby interests.

In addition, abridged editions of the Beckett Price Guides have been published for each of the four major sports as part of the House of

Collectibles series: *The Official Price Guide to Baseball Cards, The Official Price Guide to Football Cards, The Official Price Guide to Basketball Cards,* and *The Official Price Guide to Hockey Cards.* Published in a convenient mass-market paperback format, these price guides provide information and accurate pricing on all the main issues by the major card manufacturers.

Advertising

Many
Thanks!

Within this Book you will find advertisements for sports memorabilia material, mail order, and retail sports collectibles establishments. All advertisements were accepted in good faith based on the reputation of the advertiser; however, neither the author, the publisher, the distributors, nor the other advertisers in this Book accept any responsibility for any particular advertiser not complying with the terms of his or her ad.

Readers also should be aware that prices in advertisements are subject to change over the annual period before a new edition of this volume is issued each spring. When replying to an advertisement late in the baseball year, the reader should take this into account, and contact the dealer by phone or in writing for up-to-date price information. Should you come into contact with any of the advertisers in this guide as a result of their advertisement herein, please mention this source as your contact.

Acknowledgments

AVAILABLE
HERE

A great deal of diligence, hard work, and dedicated effort went into this year's volume. However, the high standards to which we hold ourselves could not have been met without the expert input and generous amount of time contributed by many people. Our sincere thanks are extended to each and every one of you.

A complete list of these invaluable contributors appears after the alphabetical section.

A's, Chatham
88CapCodPB-23
Aaron, Hank (Henry Louis)
47Exh-1
47PM1StaP1-1
53BraSpiaS3-28
54BraJohC-5
54BraSpiaSP-1
54Top-128
55Bow-179
55BraGolS-25
55BraJohC-44
55BraSpiaSD-1
55Top-47
55TopDouH-105
56BraBilaBP-1
56Top-31
56TopPin-16
56YelBasP-1
57BraSpiaS4-1
57SwiFra-13
57Top-20
58BraJayP-1
58HarSta-3
58Hir-44
58JayPubA-1
58Top-30A
58Top-30B
58Top-351
58Top-418
58Top-488
59ArmCoi-1
59Baz-1
59HomRunD-1
59Top-212
59Top-380
59Top-467
59Top-561
60ArmCoi-1A
60ArmCoi-1B
60Baz-4
60BraDav-1
60BraJayP-1
60BraLaktL-1
60BraSpiaS-1
60KeyChal-1
60MacSta-1
60NuHi-62
60Top-300
60Top-566
60TopTat-1
61NuSco-462
61Pos-107A
61Pos-107B
61Top-43
61Top-415
61Top-484
61Top-577
61TopStaI-37
62Baz-29
62BraJayP-1
62ExhStaB-1
62Jel-149
62PC7HFGSS-1
62Pos-149
62PosCan-149
62SalPlaC-180
62ShiPlaC-180
62Top-320
62Top-394
62TopBuc-1
62TopStaI-143
63BasMagM-1
63Baz-9
63BraJayP-1
63ExhStaB-1
63Jel-152
63Pos-152
63SalMetC-24
63Top-1
63Top-3
63Top-242
63Top-390
63TopStiI-1
64Baz-9
64BraJayP-1
64ChatheY-26
64Top-7
64Top-9
64Top-11
64Top-300
64Top-423
64TopCoi-83
64TopCoi-149
64TopGia-49
64TopSta-84
64TopStaU-1
64TopTatI-21
64TopVen-7
64TopVen-9
64TopVen-11
64TopVen-300
64WheSta-1
65Baz-9
65ChaTheY-24
65Kah-1
65OldLonC-1
65OPC-2
65OPC-170
65Top-2
65Top-170
65TopEmbl-59
65TopTraI-37
66Baz-30
66Kah-1
66Top-215
66Top-500
66TopRubI-1
66TopVen-215
67Baz-30
67CokCapA-19
67CokCapB-3
67CokCapNLA-19
67DexPre-1
67Kah-1A
67Kah-1B
67OPCPapI-15
67Top-242
67Top-244
67Top-250
67TopGiaSU-20
67TopPos-15
67TopTesF-1
67TopVen-284
68AtlOilPBCC-1
68Baz-5
68CokCapB-3
68DexPre-1
68Kah-A1
68Kah-B1
68OPC-3
68OPC-5
68OPC-110
68Top-3
68Top-5
68Top-110
68Top-370
68TopActS-3A
68TopActS-10B
68TopActS-16A
68TopGamI-4
68TopPla-13
68TopPos-14
68TopVen-3
68TopVen-5
68TopVen-110
68TopVen-370
69CitMetC-16
69Kah-A1
69Kah-B1
69MilBra-1
69MLBOffS-109
69MLBPin-31
69NabTeaF-1
69OPC-100
69Top-100
69TopDecI-1
69TopSta-1
69TopSup-34
69TopTeaP-2
69TraSta-53
70DayDaiNM-7
70MilBra-1
70MLBOffS-1
70OPC-65
70OPC-462
70OPC-500
70Top-65
70Top-462
70Top-500
70TopScr-1
70TopSup-24
70TraSta-4A
71AllBasA-1
71BazNumT-23
71BazUnn-32
71MatMin-1
71MatMin-2
71MilDud-33
71MLBOffS-1
71MLBOffS-553
71OPC-400
71Top-400
71TopCoi-137
71TopSup-44
71TopTat-71
71TopTat-72
72Dia-53
72MilBra-1
72OPC-87
72OPC-89
72OPC-299
72OPC-300
72ProStaP-13
72Top-87
72Top-89
72Top-299
72Top-300
72TopCloT-1
72TopPos-9
73LinPor-1
73OPC-1
73OPC-100
73OPC-473
73Top-1
73Top-100
73Top-473
73TopCanL-1
73TopCom-1
73TopPin-1
74BraPhoC-1
74LauAllG-72
74NewYorNTDiS-24
74OPC-1
74OPC-2
74OPC-3
74OPC-4
74OPC-5
74OPC-6
74OPC-7
74OPC-8
74OPC-9
74OPC-332
74Top-1
74Top-2
74Top-3
74Top-4
74Top-5
74Top-6
74Top-332
74TopDecE-57
74TopPuz-1
74TopSta-1
75BlaBacD-1
75Hos-130
75HosTwi-130
75OPC-1
75OPC-195
75OPC-660
75SSPPuzB-1
75SSPSam-1
75Top-1
75Top-195
75Top-660
76BreA&P-1
76CraDis-1
76Hos-94
76LauDiaJ-8
76LauIndC-34
76OPC-1
76OPC-550
76SafSupLB-1
76SafSupLB-2
76SafSupLB-3
76SafSupLB-4
76SafSupLB-5
76SSP-239
76Top-1
76Top-550
77GalGloG-44
77GalGloG-231
77Spo-316
77Spo-1109
78AtlCon-1
78BraTCC-1
78TCM60I-290
79Top-412
79Top-413
80Lau300-16
80PacLeg-7
80PerHaloFP-177
80SSPHOF-177
81BraPol-44
81SanDieSC-2
81TCM60I-356
82BasCarN-6
82CraJac-9
82K-M-43
83DiaClaS2-82
83DonHOFH-34
83KelCerB-9
83MLBPin-19
83Oco& SSBG-1
83TopSti-1
83TopTraBP-7
84DonCha-8
84OCoandSI-36
84OCoandSI-99
84OCoandSI-144
84OCoandSI-160
84WilMay-40
84WilMay-52
85CirK-1
85DonHOFS-7
85Woo-1
86BigLeaC-1
86BraGreT-5
86Don-602
86DonAllB-PUZ
86DonSupD-NNO
86DonWaxBC-PUZ
86Lea-259
86SpoDecG-40
86SpoDesJM-9
86TCM-18
86TCMSupS-2
87Bra195T-1
87HygAllG-1
87K-M-1
87LeaSpeO*-H7
87NesDreT-29
87SpoRea-7
88GreBasS-38
88HouSho-2
88PacLegI-1
89HOFStiB-44
89PerCelP-1
89Top-663
89TopBasT-35
89TopBasT-41
89TopTif-663
90AGFA-6
90BasWit-6
90Col-22
90HOFStiB-81
90PacLeg-1
90PerGreM-9
90SweBasG-2
91Kel3D-2
91KelStaU-1
91SweBasG-102
91TopArc1-317
91TopEasCN-1
91UppDec-HH1
91UppDecAH-19
91UppDecAH-20
91UppDecAH-21
91UppDecAH-22
91UppDecAH-23
91UppDecAH-24
91UppDecAH-25
91UppDecAH-26
91UppDecAH-27
91UppDecAH-AU3
91USGamSBL-4C
91USGamSBL-4D
91USGamSBL-4H
91USGamSBL-4S
92BazQua5A-6
92FroRowAH-1
92MVP-10
92MVP2H-2
92TVSpoMF5HRC-1
92Zip-11
93MetIma-1
93UppDecAH-1
93UppDecAH-149
93UppDecAH-150
94BreMilB-1
94BreSen-1
94TedWil5C-1
94Top-715
94TopArc1-128
94TopArc1-NNO
94TopArc1G-128
94TopArc1G-NNO
94TopGol-715
94TopSpa-715
94UppDecAH-5
94UppDecAH-75
94UppDecAH-121
94UppDecAH-144
94UppDecAH-164
94UppDecAH1-5
94UppDecAH1-75
94UppDecAH1-121
94UppDecAH1-144
94UppDecAH1-164
94UppDecAJ-47
94UppDecAJG-47
94UppDecS-3
94UppDecTAEGM-1
95NegLeaL2-1
95TopLegot6M-2
97SpollIAM-6
97SpollICC-1
97St.VinHHS-1
97TopMan-24
97TopManF-24
97TopManFR-24
Aaron, Tommie Lee
62PC7HFGSS-1
63Top-46
64Top-454
65Top-567
68Top-394
69OPC-128
69Top-128
69TopFou-3
70OPC-278
70Top-278
71MLBOffS-2
71OPC-717
71RicBraTI-1
71Top-717
72MilBra-2
78RicBraT-1
82BraPol-23
90RicBra2ATI-1
Aaron, Wil
75SanAntBT-1
76WilTomT-1
Aase, Don (Donald William)
76OPC-597
76Top-597
77Top-472
78AngFamF-1
78OPC-233
78Top-12
79Top-368
80OPC-126
80Top-239
81Don-411
81Fle-286
81LonBeaPT-15
81Top-601
82Don-267
82Fle-450
82FleSta-212
82OPC-199
82Top-199
83Don-38
83Fle-76
83Top-599
84AngSmo-1
85Don-255
85Fle-293
85FleUpd-1
85OriHea-1
85Top-86
85TopTif-86
85TopTifT-1T
85TopTra-1T
86Don-392
86DonHig-12
86Fle-268
86Top-288
86TopTif-288
87ClaGam-99
87Don-231
87DonAll-47
87Fle-461
87Fle-627
87FleExcS-1
87FleGlo-461
87FleGlo-627
87FleMin-1
87FleStiC-1
87OPC-207

87SevCoi-M4
87Spo-165
87Spo-194
87SpoTeaP-21
87Top-766
87TopMinL-38
87TopSti-228
87TopTif-766
88Fle-553
88FleGlo-553
88OriFreB-41
88Sco-518
88ScoGlo-518
88Top-467
88TopTif-467
89FleUpd-100
89MetColP-20
89MetKah-1
89Sco-524
89TopTra-1T
89TopTraT-1T
89UppDec-450
90DodMot-27
90Fle-196
90FleCan-196
90OPC-301
90Sco-377
90ScoRoo-29T
90Top-301
90TopTif-301
90UppDec-131
91Fle-193
91MetWIZ-1
91OriCro-1
91Sco-289

Abad, Andy
94SarRedSC-2
94SarRedSF-1963
95TreThuTI-24
96SarRedSB-5

Abarbanel, Mickey
68Top-287
68TopVen-287

Abare, Bill
89St.CatBJP-2071
90MyrBeaBJP-2781
91DunBluJC-15
91DunBluJP-212

Abbaticchio, Ed
08RosComP-147
09ColChiE-1
09T206-1
09T206-2
10PirTipTD-14
10SweCapPP-65
11SpoLifM-243
11T205-1
12ColRedB-1
12ColTinT-1

Abbatiello, Pat
87IdaFalBP-26

Abbe, Chris
92YakBeaF-3451
93ExcFS7-51
93SanAntMF-3007
94SanAntMF-2471

Abbey, Bert Wood
90DodTar-1

Abbey, Charlie (Charles S.)
95May-29

Abbott, Bud
93ActPacA-168
93ActPacA2-65G

Abbott, Chuck
96BoiHawB-4

Abbott, Fred (Frederick H.)
09ColChiE-2
09T206-390
12ColRedB-2
12ColTinT-2

Abbott, Glenn (W. Glenn)
74OPC-602
74Top-602
75OPC-591
75Top-591
76OPC-322
76SSP-485
76Top-322
77Hos-147
77OPC-219
77Top-207
78Hos-17
78OPC-92
78Top-31
79OPC-263
79Top-497
80OPC-92
80Top-166
81Don-47
81Fle-615
81MarPol-3
81OPC-174
81Top-699
82Don-302
82Fle-502
82Top-336
82Top-571
84Fle-74
84Nes792-356
84OPC-356
84TigWavP-2
84Top-356
84TopTif-356
86JacMetT-25
86MarGreT-9
87JacMetF-20
88JacMetGS-5
89TidTidC-26
89TidTidP-1947
90HunStaB-25
91LinDriAAA-550
91TacTigLD-550
91TacTigP-2322
92TacTigF-2518
93HunStaF-2098
94HunStaF-1348
95HunStaTI-1
96HunStaTI-1

Abbott, Jeff
94SigRooDP-81
94SigRooDPS-81
95Bes-12
95Bow-243
95BowGolF-243
95PriWilCTI-1
95SPML-36
95Top-599
96Bow-210
96BowBes-125
96BowBesAR-125
96BowBesR-125
96Exc-30
96ExcCli-1
96NasSouB-5
97Bow-128
97Bow98ROY-ROY1
97BowBes-190
97BowBesAR-190
97BowBesR-190
97BowCerBIA-CA1
97BowCerGIA-CA1
97BowChr-140
97BowChr1RC-ROY1
97BowChr1RCR-ROY1
97BowChrI-140
97BowChrIR-140
97BowChrR-140
97BowInt-128
97ColCho-469
97FlaSho-A106
97FlaSho-B106
97FlaSho-C106
97FlaShoLC-106
97FlaShoLC-B106
97FlaShoLC-C106
97FlaShoLCM-A106
97FlaShoLCM-B106
97FlaShoLCM-C106
97FlaShoWotF-6
97Fle-668
97FleTif-668
97Sel-126
97SelArtP-126
97SelRegG-126
97Top-491
97Ult-500
97UltGolME-500
97UltPlaME-500

Abbott, Jim
87PanAmTURB-25
88TopTra-1T
88TopTraT-1T
89Bow-39
89BowTif-39
89ClaTraP-151
89DonBasB-171
89DonRoo-16
89FleUpd-11
89ScoRoo-88T
89Top-573
89TopBig-322
89TopHeaUT-16
89TopTif-573
89TopTra-2T
89TopTraT-2T
89UppDec-755
89UppDecS-1
90AngSmo-1
90Baz-22
90Bow-288
90BowTif-288
90ClaBlu-40
90Col-27
90Don-108
90DonLeaS-44
90Fle-125
90FleCan-125
90FleSoaS-10
90GooHumICBLS-1
90Hot50RS-1
90KinDis-20
90Lea-31
90MLBBasB-95
90OPC-675
90PanSti-34
90Pos-13
90PubSti-362
90Sco-330
90Sco100RS-5
90ScoYouSI-5
90Spo-99
90StaAbb-1
90StaAbb-2
90StaAbb-3
90StaAbb-4
90StaAbb-5
90StaAbb-6
90StaAbb-7
90StaAbb-8
90StaAbb-9
90StaAbb-10
90StaAbb-11
90SupActM-1
90Top-675
90TopBig-329
90TopDeb89-1
90TopDou-1
90TopGloS-50
90TopHeaU-16
90TopMag-19
90TopRoo-1
90TopSti-172
90TopSti-319
90TopTif-675
90ToyRoo-1
90UppDec-645
90VenSti-1
90WonBreS-3
91AngSmo-7
91Bow-200
91Cla3-T1
91ClaGam-5
91Don-78
91Fle-305
91Lea-162
91MajLeaCP-23
91OPC-285
91PanFreS-188
91PanSti-140
91Pos-20
91RedFolS-1
91Sco-105
91Sco100S-69
91SevCoi-SC1
91SimandSMLBL-1
91StaClu-124
91StaPinB-1
91Stu-22
91Top-285
91TopDesS-285
91TopMic-285
91TopSta-1
91TopTif-285
91Ult-43
91UppDec-554
92AngPol-1
92Bow-185
92Bow-572
92Cla1-T1
92Cla2-T1
92ClaGam-109
92Don-130
92DonCraJ1-3
92Fle-50
92FleSmo'nH-S12
92Hig5-11
92HitTheBB-1
92JimDea-1
92Lea-1
92Mr.TurS-1
92OPC-530
92OPCPre-140
92PanSti-12
92Pin-281
92Pin-539
92PinRool-2
92PinTea2-42
92PinTeaP-2
92Sco-620
92Sco100S-19
92ScoImpP-14
92SevCoi-22
92SpoIllFK1-50
92StaClu-210
92Stu-141
92StuPre-21
92SunSee-11
92Top-406
92Top-530
92TopDaiQTU-9
92TopGol-406
92TopGol-530
92TopGolW-406
92TopGolW-530
92TopKid-97
92TopMcD-20
92TopMic-406
92TopMic-530
92TriPla-204
92Ult-321
92UppDec-78
92UppDec-86
92UppDec-325
92UppDec-642
92UppDecS-13
92UppDecTMH-3
93Bow-131
93ClaGam-1
93Don-35
93DurPowP2-16
93Fin-46
93FinRef-46
93Fla-244
93Fle-187
93FleFinE-242
93FunPac-204
93FunPac-205
93HumDumC-13
93Kra-1
93Lea-253
93LeaGolA-R18
93MSABenSPD-18
93OPC-1
93OPCPre-130
93PacSpa-551
93Pin-11
93Sco-646
93Sel-98
93SelRoo-30T
93SP-262
93StaClu-615
93StaCluFDI-615
93StaCluMO-1
93StaCluMOP-615
93StaCluY-2
93Stu-29
93Top-780
93TopComotH-4
93TopGol-780
93TopInaM-780
93TopMic-780
93TopTra-75T
93TriPla-258
93TriPlaG-GS7
93Ult-590
93UppDec-30
93UppDec-31
93UppDec-53
93UppDec-451
93UppDec-554
93UppDecFA-A4
93UppDecFAJ-A4
93UppDecGold-30
93UppDecGold-31
93UppDecGold-53
93UppDecGold-451
93UppDecGold-554
93UppDecOD-D1
94Bow-193
94ColC-450
94ColChoGS-450
94ColChoSS-450
94DenHol-1
94Don-357
94DonSpeE-357
94ExtBas-127
94Fin-149
94FinPre-149P
94FinRef-149
94Fla-318
94Fle-224
94FleGolM-10
94FUnPac-75
94Lea-38
94LeaL-53
94OPC-211
94OscMayR-1
94Pac-420
94PanSti-98
94Pin-110
94PinArtP-110
94PinMusC-110
94PinTri-TR2
94ProMag-86
94RedFolMI-17
94Sco-127
94Sco-626
94ScoGolR-127
94ScoGolR-626
94Sel-78
94SP-195
94SPDieC-195
94Spo-138
94StaClu-516
94StaCluFDI-516
94StaCluGR-516
94StaCluMOP-516
94StaCluT-184
94StaCluTFDI-184
94Stu-211
94SucSav-7
94TomPiz-16
94Top-350
94TopGol-350
94TopSpa-350
94TriPla-271
94Ult-397
94UppDec-310
94UppDecED-310
95AngTeal-1
95ColCho-525
95ColChoGS-525
95ColChoSE-241
95ColChoSEGS-241
95ColChoSESS-241
95ColChoSS-525
95Don-369
95DonPreP-369
95DonTopotO-30
95Emo-24
95Fin-190
95Fin-233
95FinRef-190
95FinRef-233
95Fla-240
95Fle-65
95FleUpd-32
95Lea-374
95Pac-292
95Pin-394
95PinArtP-394
95PinMusC-394
95Sco-452
95ScoGolR-452
95ScoPlaTS-452
95ScoYouTE-452T
95Sel-146
95SelArtP-146
95SP-142
95SPSil-142
95StaClu-7
95StaClu-569
95StaCluFDI-7
95StaCluMOP-7
95StaCluMOP-569
95StaCluSTWS-7
95StaCluSTWS-569
95StaCluVR-3
95Stu-137

95Top-60
95TopCyb-42
95TopTra-75T
95Ult-307
95UltGolM-307
95UppDec-207
95UppDec-438
95UppDec-451T
95UppDecED-207
95UppDecED-438
95UppDecEDG-207
95UppDecEDG-438
95UppDecSE-155
95UppDecSEG-155
95WhiSoxK-1
96AngMot-5
96Cir-16
96CirRav-16
96ColCho-78
96ColChoGS-78
96ColChoSS-78
96Don-177
96DonPreP-177
96EmoXL-21
96Fin-S43
96FinRef-S43
96Fla-31
96Fle-40
96FleTif-40
96Kin-12
96Pac-268
96Pin-76
96Pin-228
96PinAfi-61
96PinAfiAP-61
96PinAfiFPP-61
96PinArtP-128
96PinFoil-228
96PinSta-128
96Sco-130
96ScoDugC-A81
96ScoDugCAP-A81
96Sel-107
96SelArtP-107
96SP-48
96StaClu-241
96StaCluMOP-241
95StaCluVRMC-3
96Sum-13
96SumAbo&B-13
96SumArtP-13
96SumFoi-13
96Top-372
96Ult-323
96UltGolM-323
96UppDec-292
96UppDecVJLS-VJ1
96VanCanB-4
97PacPriGotD-GD1
87PanAmTUBI-38
Abbott, John
85ElmPioT-1
86GreHorP-1
88WinHavRSS-1
Abbott, Kurt
89MedAthB-27
90MadMusB-3
90MadMusP-2274
90MidLeaASGS-1
91HunStaTI-1
91ModA'sC-1
91ModA'sP-3092
92HunStaF-3954
92HunStaS-301
92SkyAA F-126
93TacTigF-3037
93TriAAAGF-50
94Bow-534
94ColC-31
94ColC-389
94ColChoGS-31
94ColChoGS-389
94ColChoSS-31
94ColChoSS-389
94ExtBas-256
94ExtBasRS-1
94Fin-431
94FinJum-431
94FinRef-431
94Fla-160
94FlaWavotF-A1
94FleAllR-M1
94FleMajLP-1
94FleUpd-132
94Lea-346
94LeaLimR-11
94Pin-226
94PinArtP-226
94PinMusC-226
94PinRooTP-5
94Sco-598
94ScoBoyoS-53
94ScoGolR-598
94ScoRoo-RT11
94ScoRooGR-RT11
94ScoRooSR-SU9
94Sel-187
94SelRooS-RS12
94Spo-153
94StaClu-588
94StaCluFDI-588
94StaCluGR-588
94StaCluMOP-588
94StaCluT-86
94StaCluTFDI-86
94Stu-105
94TopGol-773
94TopSpa-773
94Ult-104
94Ult-489
94UltAllR-1
94UltAllRJ-1
94UppDec-313
94UppDecED-313
95ColCho-303
95ColChoGS-303
95ColChoSS-303
95Don-70
95DonPreP-70
95DonTopotO-237
95Fin-2
95FinRef-2
95Fla-349
95Fle-323
95FleRooS-1
95Lea-191
95LeaLim-186
95Pac-164
95Pin-202
95PinArtP-202
95PinMusC-202
95Sco-358
95ScoGolR-358
95ScoPlaTS-358
95Sel-145
95SelArtP-145
95StaClu-327
95StaCluMOP-327
95StaCluSTWS-327
95StaCluVR-169
95Stu-81
95Top-460
95TopCyb-255
95Ult-160
95UltGolM-160
95UppDec-116
95UppDecED-116
95UppDecEDG-116
95UppDecSE-252
95UppDecSEG-252
96ColCho-154
96ColChoGS-154
96ColChoSS-154
96Don-428
96DonPreP-428
96EmoXL-181
96Fla-256
96Fle-380
96FleTif-380
96Lea-164
96LeaPrePB-164
96LeaPrePG-164
96LeaPrePS-164
96LeaSigA-1
96LeaSigAG-1
96LeaSigAS-1
96MetUni-161
96MetUniP-161
96Pac-74
96Pin-314
96PinFoil-314
96Sco-398
96StaClu-200
96StaClu-351
96StaCluEPB-351
96StaCluEPG-351
96StaCluEPS-351
96StaCluMOP-200
96StaCluMOP-351
95StaCluVRMC-169
96Top-118
96Ult-195
96UltGolM-195
96UppDec-334
97Fle-323
97FleTif-323
97Pac-294
97PacLigB-294
97PacSil-294
97Top-454
Abbott, Kyle
89QuaCitAGS-13
90Bow-287
90BowTif-287
90MidAngGS-5
90OPC-444
90Sco-673
90Top-444
90TopTif-444
91Bow-187
91EdmTraLD-151
91EdmTraP-1507
91LinDriAAA-151
91UppDec-51
92Bow-310
92Cla1-T2
92Cla2-T57
92ClaGam-198
92Don-3
92DonRoo-1
92Fle-51
92Lea-495
92OPC-763
92OPCPre-185
92PhiMed-1
92Pin-432
92PinTea2-75
92ProFS7-27
92Sco-849
92ScoRoo-2
92SpoStaCC-1
92StaClu-818
92Top-763
92TopDeb91-1
92TopGol-763
92TopGolW-763
92TopMic-763
92UppDec-8
92UppDec-754
93Bow-652
93Don-676
93Fle-483
93PhiMed-1
93Pin-378
93Sco-403
93ScrRedBF-2537
93ScrRedBTI-1
93Sel-332
93StaClu-201
93StaCluFDI-201
93StaCluMOP-201
93StaCluP-3
93Top-317
93TopGol-317
93TopInaM-317
93TopMic-317
93Ult-82
93UppDec-300
93UppDecGold-300
94Top-773
95Phi-1
95PhiMel-1
Abbott, Paul
86KenTwiP-1
87KenTwiP-24
88VisOakCLC-165
88VisOakP-92
89OrlTwiB-7
89OrlTwiP-1348
89SouLeaAJ-14
90CMC-553
90PorBeaC-1
90PorBeaP-168
90ProAAAF-238
91Bow-329
91Don-639
91LinDriAAA-401
91PorBeaLD-401
91PorBeaP-1558
91Sco-363
91TopDeb90-1
91UppDec-487
92Fle-667
92OPC-781
92Sco-697
92StaClu-567
92Top-781
92TopGol-781
92TopGolW-781
92TopMic-781
93CanIndF-2830
94OmaRoyF-1215
95IowCubTI-1
96LasVegSB-5
Abbott, Terry
78GreBraT-1
89AugPirP-515
90CedRapRB-5
90CedRapRP-2338
90MidLeaASGS-53
92BenMusSP-29
92BilMusF-3374
93BilMusF-3963
93BilMusSP-28
94ChaLooF-1374
95ChaLooTI-26
Abbott, Todd
96WesMicWB-5
Abbs, Steve
94JohCitCC-1
94JohCitCF-3714
ABC's, Indianapolis
93NegLeaRL2-55
93TedWilPC-12
Abe, Keiji
90GatCitPP-3362
90GatCitPSP-23
Abe, Osamu
83SanJosBC-8
Abel, Sid
51BerRos-C16
Abell, Antonio
96JohCitCTI-1
Abell, Scott
92EugEmeC-4
92EugEmeF-3031
Aber, Al (Albert Julius)
53Top-233
54Top-238
55Bow-24
56Top-317
57Top-141
59TigGraASP-1
91TopArc1-233
94TopArc1-238
94TopArc1G-238
Abercrombie, John
91HigDesMC-14
91HigDesMP-2397
92WatDiaC-19
92WatDiaF-2146
93WicWraF-2979
Abernathy, Matt
95IdaFalBTI-18
96CliLumKTI-1
Abernathy, Ted
57Top-293
59Top-169
59TopVen-169
60Top-334
64Top-64
64TopVen-64
65Top-332
66CubTeal-1
66OPC-2
66Top-2
66TopVen-2
67Top-597
68Top-264
68TopVen-264
69CubJewT-1
69CubPho-1
69MilBra-2
69Top-483
69TopSta-21
70RoyTeal-1
70Top-562
71MLBOffS-409
71OPC-187
71Top-187
72MilBra-3
72OPC-519
72Top-519
73OPC-22
73Top-22
84CubUno-9
89ChaLooLITI-1
Abernathy, Tom
36WorWidGV-122
Abernethy, Tom
89GenCubP-1858
Aberson, Cliff (Clifford A.)
49Lea-136A
49Lea-136B
49W725AngTI-1
Abner, Ben
86MacPirP-1
87HarSenP-26
Abner, Shawn
85LynMetT-25
85Top-282
85TopTif-282
86JacMetT-19
86MetTCM-35
87LasVegSP-2
88BlaYNPRWLU-14
88Don-33
88DonBasB-21
88DonRoo-5
88Fle-576
88FleGlo-576
88Lea-33
88PadSmo-1
88Sco-626
88ScoGlo-626
88Spo-223
88StaLinPa-1
89Don-323
89LasVegSC-22
89LasVegSP-21
89Sco-411
90ClaYel-T20
90OPC-122
90Sco-352
90Top-122
90TopTif-122
90UppDec-301
91Don-561
91Fle-522
91Lea-381
91OPC-697
91PadMag-8
91PadSmo-1
91Sco-261
91StaClu-291
91Top-697
91TopDesS-697
91TopMic-697
91TopTif-697
91Ult-300
91UppDec-795
92Don-736
92OPC-338
92Sco-616
92StaClu-197
92Top-338
92TopGol-338
92TopGolW-338
92TopMic-338
92UppDec-502
92VanCanS-626
92WhiSoxK-45
93Don-651
93Fle-579
93OmaRoyF-1689
93Sco-437
93StaClu-403
93StaCluFDI-403
93StaCluMOP-403
93Top-582
93TopGol-582
93TopInaM-582
93TopMic-582
Abone, Joseph
80MemChiT-6
82WicAerTI-1
Abraham, Alan
81WesHavAT-18
Abraham, Brian
77SanJosMC-23
79OgdA'sT-10
80OgdA'sT-9
82WesHavAT-1
Abraham, Glenn
87EveGiaC-10
87PocGiaTB-31
Abraham, Timothy
96MauStiHWB-NNO
96PorSeaDB-3
96PorSeaDB-4

Abrams, Cal (Calvin Ross)
51Bow-152
52Bow-86
52Top-350
53BowC-160
53NorBreL-1
53Top-98
54Bow-91
54OriEss-1
55Bow-55
55OriEss-1
83TopRep5-350
88RinPosD1-10C
90DodTar-2
91OriCro-2
91TopArc1-98
95TopArcBD-34
Abramvicius, Jason
93WelPirF-3346
94AugGreF-2999
94SalBucC-2
94SalBucF-2315
Abrego, Johnny
86Don-32
86IowCubP-1
86StaoftFT-13
Abrell, Thomas
86SumBraP-1
87ChaWheP-26
Abreu, Armand
77SpaPhiT-12
Abreu, Bob
91LinDriAA-26
92AshTouC-19
92ClaFS7-383
93ClaFS7-24
93ClaGolF-105
93LinVenB-194
93LinVenB-277
93OscAstC-2
93OscAstF-638
94ExcFS7-196
94JacGenF-227
94UppDecML-13
94VenLinU-51
95Bes-73
95Bow-4
95BowBes-B3
95BowBesR-B3
95Exc-199
95LinVen-11
95SigRooOJ-1
95SigRooOJP-1
95SigRooOJPS-1
95SigRooOJS-1
95SPML-64
95SPMLA-1
95Sum21C-TC1
95TusTorTI-1
95UppDecML-48
96Bow-199
96BowBes-155
96BowBesAR-155
96BowBesR-155
96BowMinLP-3
96ColCho-450
96ColChoGS-450
96ColChoSS-450
96Exc-169
96Fla-271
96FlaWavotF-1
96FleUpd-U136
96FleUpdNH-1
96FleUpdTC-U136
96Pin-390
96PinAfi-153
96PinAfi-171
96PinAfiAP-153
96PinAfiAP-171
96PinFoil-390
96PinProS-8
96Sel-189
96SelArtP-189
96SelCer-104
96SelCerAP-104
96SelCerCB-104
96SelCerCR-104
96SelCerMB-104
96SelCerMG-104
96SelCerMR-104
96SP-18
96StaClu-256
96StaCluMOP-256
96Sum-166
96SumAbo&B-166
96SumArtP-166
96SumFoi-166
96Top-101
96TusTorB-1
96Ult-483
96UltGolM-483
96UltGolP-1
96UltGolPHGM-1
96UppDec-258
96UppDecPHE-H51
96UppDecPreH-H51
96Zen-105
96ZenArtP-105
97Bow-296
97BowBes-170
97BowBesAR-170
97BowBesBC-BC17
97BowBesBCAR-BC17
97BowBesBCR-BC17
97BowBesMI-MI10
97BowBesMIAR-MI10
97BowBesMIARI-MI10
97BowBesMII-MI10
97BowBesMIR-MI10
97BowBesMIRI-MI10
97BowBesR-170
97BowCerBIA-CA2
97BowCerGIA-CA2
97BowChr-204
97BowChrI-204
97BowChrIR-204
97BowChrR-204
97BowChrSHR-SHR2
97BowChrSHRR-SHR2
97BowInt-296
97BowIntB-BBI16
97BowIntBAR-BBI16
97BowIntBR-BBI16
97BowScoHR-2
97Cir-246
97CirRav-246
97ColCho-120
97Don-353
97DonFraFea-15
97DonLim-15
97DonLim-144
97DonLimFotG-21
97DonLimLE-15
97DonLimLE-144
97DonPre-165
97DonPreCttC-165
97DonPreP-353
97DonPrePGold-353
97Fin-295
97FinEmb-295
97FinEmbR-295
97FinRef-295
97FlaSho-A54
97FlaSho-B54
97FlaSho-C54
97FlaShoLC-54
97FlaShoLC-B54
97FlaShoLC-C54
97FlaShoLCM-A54
97FlaShoLCM-B54
97FlaShoLCM-C54
97FlaShoWotF-10
97Fle-338
97FleNewH-1
97FleRooS-12
97FleTif-338
97Lea-26
97LeaFraM-26
97LeaFraMDC-26
97MetUni-133
97MetUniMfG-1
97NewPin-173
97NewPinAP-173
97NewPinMC-173
97NewPinPP-173
97PacPriGotD-GD148
97Pin-48
97PinArtP-48
97PinCer-117
97PinCerMBlu-117
97PinCerMG-117
97PinCerMR-117
97PinCerR-117
97PinMusC-48
97PinTotCPB-117
97PinTotCPG-117
97PinTotCPR-117
97PinX-P-122
97PinX-PMoS-122
97Sco-486
97ScoHobR-486
97ScoResC-486
97ScoShoS-486
97ScoShoSAP-486
97Sel-138
97SelArtP-138
97SelRegG-138
97SkyE-X-75
97SkyE-XC-75
97SkyE-XEC-75
97SpoIll-1
97SpoIllEE-1
97StaClu-195
97StaClu-300
97StaCluM-M28
97StaCluMOP-195
97StaCluMOP-300
97StaCluMOP-M28
97Stu-161
97StuPrePG-161
97StuPrePS-161
97Top-416
97TopChr-148
97TopChrR-148
97TopGal-148
97TopGalPPI-148
97Ult-203
97UltGolME-203
97UltPlaME-203
97UppDec-363
97UppDecBCP-BC12
95UppDecMLFS-48
97UppDecTTS-TS11
Abreu, Francisco
87DayBeaAP-11
Abreu, Frank (Franklin)
87SavCarP-20
88SprCarB-21
89St.PetCS-1
90ArkTraGS-4
91ArkTraLD-26
92St.PetCC-8
92St.PetCF-2031
Abreu, Guillermo
94EliTwiC-1
94EliTwiF-3737
Abreu, Jose
95BurBeeTI-23
96BelGiaTI-31
Abreu, Juan
93LinVenB-221
95ButCopKtl-2
Abreu, Manny
72CedRapCT-13
80CarMudF-16
Abreu, Winston
95DanBraTI-1
96BesAutS-1
96Exc-121
96MacBraB-1
Abril, Odie (Ernest)
85GreHorT-21
86FloStaLAP-1
86WinHavRSP-1
87WinHavRSP-15
88WinHavRSS-2
89WinHavRSS-1
90LynRedSTI-14
Abshier, Lanny
87SalAngP-27
Abstein, Bill (William H.)
09ColChiE-3A
09ColChiE-3B
09T206-3
10NadE1-1
10PirHerP-1
11MecDFT-7
11SpoLifCW-1
12ColRedB-3A
12ColRedB-3B
12ColTinT-3A
12ColTinT-3B
12ImpTobC-86
Acevedo, Jesus
93EliTwiC-2
93EliTwiF-3418
93LinVenB-170
Acevedo, Juan
93CenValRC-2
94NewHavRF-1540
95Bow-6
95BowBes-B19
95BowBesR-B19
95ColCho-42
95ColChoGS-42
95ColChoSS-42
95Exc-185
95ExcLeaL-1
95Sel-200
95SelArtP-200
95SelCer-130
95SelCerMG-130
95SigRooOP-OP1
95SigRooOPS-OP1
95SP-15
95SPSil-15
95StaClu-599
95StaCluMOP-599
95StaCluSTWS-599
95Sum-149
95SumNthD-149
95Top-316
95UppDec-265
95UppDecED-265
95UppDecEDG-265
95UppDecML-40
95UppDecMLOP-OP9
95Zen-129
96FleUpd-U154
96FleUpdTC-U154
96LeaSigA-2
96LeaSigAG-2
96LeaSigAS-2
96NorTidB-5
96Pin-324
96PinFoil-324
96Sel-148
96SelArtP-148
96SigRooOJTP-T1
96Ult-510
96UltGolM-510
95UppDecMLFS-40
Acevedo, Milton
92LetMouSP-2
Acker, Jim (James Austin)
84BluJayFS-1
84Don-146
84Fle-145
84Nes792-359
84OPC-359
84Top-359
84TopTif-359
85BluJayFS-1
85Fle-96
85OPC-101
85Top-101
85TopTif-101
86BluJayAF-1
86BluJayFS-1
86Don-363
86Fle-50
86OPC-46
86Top-569
86TopTif-569
87BraSmo-10
87Don-659
87Fle-509
87FleGlo-509
87Top-407
87TopTif-407
88Fle-531
88FleGlo-531
88OPC-293
88Sco-576
88ScoGlo-576
88StaLinBra-1
88Top-678
88TopSti-43
88TopTif-678
89BraDub-1
89Top-244
89TopTif-244
89UppDec-52
90BluJayFS-1
90Don-558
90OPC-728
90Top-728
90TopTif-728
91BluJayFS-1
91BluJayS-21
91Don-368
91Fle-167
91OPC-71
91Sco-122
91Top-71
91TopDesS-71
91TopMic-71
91TopTif-71
91UppDec-670
92Fle-322
92MarMot-23
92OPC-178
92Sco-63
92ScoProP-17
92TexLon-1
92Top-178
92TopGol-178
92TopGolW-178
92TopMic-178
Acker, Larry
85TucTorC-55
86TucTorP-1
87BirBarB-8
88MemChiB-7
Acker, Tom (Thomas James)
57Kah-1
57Top-219
58RedEnq-1
58Top-149
59RedEnq-1
59RedShiBS-1
59Top-201
60Top-274
Ackerman, John
84EveGiaC-27
Ackley, Fritz (Florian F.)
64Top-368
64TopVen-368
64WhiSoxTS-1
65Top-477
78TCM60I-27
Ackley, John
80ElmPioRST-12
Acosta, Bert
78NewWayCT-1
Acosta, Carlos
86TamTarP-1
Acosta, Cecilio
73OPC-379
73Top-379
74OPC-22
74Top-22
75OPC-634
75Top-634
Acosta, Clemente
90CMC-711
90PalSprACLC-226
90PalSprAP-2569
91LinDriAA-426
91MidAngLD-426
91MidAngP-426
92MidAngS-451
Acosta, Ed
71OPC-343
71Top-343
72OPC-123
72PadTeal-1
72Top-123
73OPC-244
73Top-244
74HawIsIC-104
Acosta, Eddie
93HelBreF-4100
93HelBreSP-12
96DelShoB-4
Acosta, Jose
87WatPirP-17
88AugPirP-371
89AugPirP-492
Acosta, Oscar
89GasRanP-1025
91LinDriAA-600
91TulDriLD-600
91TulDriP-2789
91TulDriTI-1
92OklCit8F-1930
94DayCubC-28
94DayCubF-2370
Acre, Mark
92RenSilSCLC-36
93MadMusC-2
93MidLeaAGF-11
94A'sMot-22
94Bow-332
94BowBes-B44
94BowBesR-B44
94Cla-168
94ClaGolF-97
94ClaTriF-T58

94ExcFS7-116
94ExtBas-143
94Fla-327
94FlaWavotF-B1
94FleUpd-72
94LeaLimR-22
94ScoRoo-RT163
94ScoRooGR-RT163
94Sel-413
94TacTigF-3165
94TopTra-24T
94Ult-405
94UppDecML-68
95AthMot-26
95ColCho-18
95ColChoGS-18
95ColChoSS-18
95Don-76
95DonPreP-76
95Fla-291
95Fle-238
95Lea-329
95Pac-308
95Sco-501
95ScoGolR-501
95ScoPlaTS-501
95SigRoo-1
95SigRooSig-1
95StaClu-376
95StaCluMOP-376
95StaCluSTWS-376
95Top-224
95TopCyb-126
95Ult-89
95UltGolM-89
95UppDec-279
95UppDecED-279
95UppDecEDG-279
96ColCho-638
96ColChoGS-638
96ColChoSS-638
96Don-181
96DonPreP-181
96Fle-202
96FleTif-202
97Fle-632
97FleTif-632
97PacPriGotD-GD77
Acro, Mascot
91PeoChiTI-29
Acta, Manny (Manuel)
88OscAstS-1
89ColMudB-2
89ColMudP-136
89ColMudS-1
90OscAstS-1
91BurAstC-12
91BurAstP-2806
92AshTouC-29
93AubAstC-28
93AubAstF-3460
94AubAstC-24
94AubAstF-3775
95AubAstTI-28
96AubDouB-24
Acton, Joe
87AllandGN-31
Acton, Wrestler
88GooN16-9
Adachi, Tomo
94BriTigC-1
Adair, Bill
76ExpRed-1
Adair, Jerry (Kenneth Jerry)
59OklTodML-20
60Lea-28
61Top-71
62Top-449
62TopStal-2
63Jel-61
63Pos-61
63Top-488
64Top-22
64TopVen-22
65OPC-231
65Top-231
66Top-533
66TopRubI-2
66WhiSoxTI-1
67CokCapWS-2
67Top-484
67TopVen-264
68CokCapRS-17
68DexPre-2
68Top-346
68TopVen-346
69MilBra-3
69MLBOffS-55
69OPC-159
69RoySol-1
69RoyTeal-1
69Top-159
69TopFou-1
69TopSta-181
69TopTeaP-7
70MLBOffS-217
70OPC-525
70RoyTeal-2
70Top-525
72MilBra-4
73OPC-179
73Top-179A
73Top-179B
81RedSoxBG2S-68
83FraBroR-12
83FraBroR-18
91OriCro-3
Adair, Jimmy (James Aubrey)
67AstTeal2-1
87AstSer1-30
Adair, Rick
81WauTimT-14
82LynSaiT-1
83SalLakCGT-8
84ChaLooT-23
87WatIndP-29
89ColSprSSC-23
89ColSprSSP-247
90CMC-471
90ColSprSSC-19
90ColSprSSP-56
90ProAAAF-237
91ColSprSSLD-100
91ColSprSSP-2201
91LinDriAAA-100
92IndFanC-30
93IndWUA-33
94WicWraF-206
95TolMudHTI-3
Adair, Scott
96IdaFalB-1
Adam, David
92SanBerC-18
92SanBerSF-943
93RivPilCLC-3
94JacSunF-1403
95PorCitRTI-1
Adam, Justin
95SpoIndTI-2
96LanLugB-4
Adamczak, Jim
86JacMetT-1
Adames, Hernan
88TamTarS-1
Adames, Juan
88WytCubP-1997
89PeoChiTI-16
Adams, Ace Townsend
41DouPlaR-137
83TCMPla1943-43
88ConSer3-1
Adams, Art
91BriTigC-29
91BriTigP-3594
92FayGenC-16
93FayGenF-119
Adams, Babe (Charles B.)
09ColChiE-4
09SpoNewSM-28
10E12AmeCDC-1
10NadE1-2
10PirAmeCE-1
10PirHerP-2
10PirTipTD-9
11DiaGumP-1
11PloCanE-1
11SpoLifCW-2
11SpoLifM-244
12ColRedB-4
12ColTinT-4
14B18B-74A
14B18B-74B
14CraJacE-63
15CraJacE-63
15SpoNewM-1
16FleBreD-1
16SpoNewM-1
19W514-54
20NatCarE-1
21E121So1-1
21Exh-1
21Nei-91
22E120-211
22W573-1
22W575-1
23W501-84
23W515-6
23WilChoV-1
26SpoComoA-1
61Fle-90
76ISCHooHA-23
80LauFamF-38
87ConSer2-7
92ConTSN-443
94ConTSN-1245
94ConTSNB-1245
20W516-18
Adams, Bert (John Bertram)
12PhiCarE-1
12T207-1
Adams, Bob
77EvaTriT-1
Adams, Bobby (Robert Henry)
49EurSta-76
49Lea-54
51Bow-288
52Bow-166
52Top-249
53BowC-108
53RedMan-NL2
53Top-152
54Bow-108
54Top-123
55Bow-118
55Top-178
56Top-287
58Top-99
59Top-249
83TopRep5-249
91OriCro-4
91TopArc1-152
94TopArc1-123
94TopArc1G-123
Adams, Brian
90SpaPhiB-12
90SpaPhiP-2493
90SpaPhiS-1
Adams, Bud
87EugEmeP-2665
88BasCitRS-1
Adams, Buster (Elvin Clark)
43PhiTeal-1
46SeaSLP-1
Adams, Carl Ray
79NewCoPT-15
Adams, Craig
77WatIndT-1
81ChaLooT-20
82ChaLooT-22
Adams, Dan
75LafDriT-28
Adams, Daryl
80PenPilBT-2
80PenPilCT-2
Adams, Dave
90QuaCitAGS-12
90SpoIndSP-8
91ChaRaiC-14
91ChaRaiP-99
91QuaCitAC-1
91QuaCitAP-2618
92MidAngF-4018
92MidAngOHP-1
92MidAngS-452
92SkyAA F-191
92WatDiaC-24
92WatDiaF-2147
Adams, Derek
91BluOriC-12
91BluOriP-4132
92KanCouCC-21
92KanCouCF-96
92KanCouCTI-1
Adams, Dick (Richard Leroy)
84EdmTraC-104
Adams, Gary
90GatCitPP-3352
90GatCitPSP-1
91SumFlyC-22
91SumFlyP-2347
Adams, Gerald
84NewOriT-20
85NewOriT-9
Adams, Glenn Charles
74PhoGiaC-85
76OPC-389
76SSP-108
76Top-389
78Top-497
78TwiFriP-1
79Top-193
79TwiFriP-1
80Top-604
81Don-566A
81Don-566B
81Fle-562
81Top-18
82Don-431
82Fle-545
82SyrChiT-19
82SyrChiTI-1
82Top-519
83OPC-374
83Top-574
87WatIndP-10
88CarLeaAS-21
95IowCubTI-2
96IowCubB-3
Adams, Jason
90KinMetS-30
93KinMetC-2
93KinMetF-3807
94PitMetC-2
94PitMetF-3532
95AubAstTI-25
96QuaCitRB-6
Adams, Joe (Joseph Edward)
95OmaRoyTI-1
Adams, Joe (Pres)
96OmaRoyB-6
Adams, John
78BurBeeT-1
80HolMilT-16
83ArkTraT-10
84ArkTraT-12
Adams, Ken
86EugEmeC-46
88BasCitRS-2
89BasCitRS-1
Adams, Lionel
89IdaFalBP-2012
89SumBraP-1098
Adams, Mike
86VisOakP-1
87VisOakP-22
Adams, Mike (Robert Michael)
74OPC-573
74TacTwiC-22
74Top-573
Adams, Moose
91EveGiaC-20
91EveGiaP-3904
Adams, Morgan
90MedHatBJB-16
Adams, Pat
82AppFoxF-27
83AppFoxF-8
85PhoGiaC-186
87PhoFirP-21
88WesPalBES-1
Adams, Ralph
84LitFalMT-6
86LynMetP-1
Adams, Red (Charles Dwight)
47SigOil-21
49BowPCL-24
53MotCoo-53
73OPC-569
73Top-569
74OPC-144
74Top-144
Adams, Ricky Lee
78DayBeaAT-1
80ElPasDT-21
81HolMilT-7
82HolMilT-13
84Don-85
84Nes792-487
84Top-487
84TopTif-487
85PhoGiaC-188
86PhoFirP-1
86Top-153
86TopTif-153
Adams, Rollo
81CliGiaT-26
Adams, Sparky (Earl John)
25Exh-17
26Exh-17
27Exh-9
29ExhFou-13
31Exh-15
33DouDisP-1
33ExhFou-8
33Gou-213
34DiaMatCSB-1
34DiaStaR-24
35GouPuzR-1H
35GouPuzR-3F
35GouPuzR-14F
35GouPuzR-15F
93ConTSN-695
Adams, Steve
86WatPirP-1
87MacPirP-13
88SalBucS-1
89EasLeaDDP-DD27
89HarSenP-295
89HarSenS-1
90EasLeaAP-EL30
90HarSenP-1185
90HarSenS-1
91CarMudLD-101
91CarMudP-1078
91LinDriAA-101
Adams, Terry
76CedRapGT-1
Adams, Terry Wayne
91HunCubC-1
91HunCubP-3324
92ClaFS7-217
92PeoChiC-19
92PeoChiTI-1
92StaCluD-1
93DayCubC-2
93DayCubF-850
94DayCubC-2
94DayCubF-2343
96Bow-207
96ColCho-491
96ColChoGS-491
96ColChoSS-491
96Fin-B212
96FinRef-B212
96FleCub-1
96FleUpd-U108
96FleUpdTC-U108
96LeaSigA-3
96LeaSigAG-3
96LeaSigAS-3
96Pin-389
96PinFoil-389
96Ult-447
96UltGolM-447
96UppDec-488U
97Cir-252
97CirRav-252
97ColCho-54
97Fle-272
97FleTif-272
95OrlCubF-1
97PacPriGotD-GD116
97StaClu-161
97StaCluMOP-161
97Top-191
97Ult-403
97UltGolME-403
97UltPlaME-403
Adams, Tim
89CarNewE-20
Adams, Tommy
91BelMarC-16
91BelMarP-3677
91Cla/Bes-430
91ClaDraP-49
92CalLeaACL-45
92ClaFS7-245
92SanBerC-1
92SanBerSF-969
92StaCluD-2
92UppDecML-247

92UppDecMLPotY-PY13
93Bow-683
93ClaFS7-178
93ClaGolF-141
94UppDecML-222
96SigRooOJ-1
96SigRooOJS-1
Adams, Willie Edward
92TopTra-1T
92TopTraG-1T
93StaCluM-183
94Bow-632
94ModA'sC-2
94ModA'sF-3055
94VerBeaDC-2
94VerBeaDF-85
95Bow-156
95HunStaTI-2
95Top-641
96Bow-133
97Bow-321
97BowCerBIA-CA3
97BowCerGIA-CA3
97BowInt-321
97Cir-314
97CirRav-314
97ColCho-13
97Fin-12
97FinRef-12
97Fle-182
97FleTif-182
97StaClu-375
97StaCluMOP-375
97Top-337
97UppDec-243
Adams, Yank
87AllandGN-42
Adamson, Joel
90PriPatD-1
92ClaFS7-74
92ClePhiC-14
92ClePhiF-2045
93HigDesMC-2
93HigDesMF-31
93Top-613
93TopGol-613
93TopInaM-613
93TopMic-613
94PorSeaDF-669
94PorSeaDTI-7
95ChaKniTI-5
96ChaKniB-6
Adamson, Mike (John Michael)
69OPC-66
69Top-66
71OPC-362
71Top-362
91OriCro-5
Adamson, Tony
91PerHeaF-18
95AusFut-85
95AusFut-104
Adamson, Wade
80OrlTwiT-1
Adcock, Joe (Joseph Wilbur)
47Exh-2A
47Exh-2B
51Bow-323
52Bow-69
52Top-347
53BowC-151
53BraJohC-17
53BraSpiaS3-1
53BraSpiaS7-1
54Bow-96
54BraJohC-9
54BraSpiaSP-2
55Bow-218
55BraGolS-16
55BraJohC-9
55BraSpiaSD-2
56BraBilaBP-2
56Top-320
56YelBasP-2
57BraSpiaS4-2
57Top-117
58BraJayP-2
58Top-325
58Top-351
59Top-315
60BraLaktL-2
60BraSpiaS-2
60NuHi-33
60Top-3
60TopVen-3
61NuSco-433
61Pos-104A
61Pos-104B
61Raw-1
61Top-245
61TopStal-38
62BraJayP-2
62Jel-145
62Pos-145A
62Pos-145B
62PosCan-145
62SalPlaC-125
62ShiPlaC-125
62Top-265
62TopBuc-2
62TopStal-144
63BasMagM-2
63Fle-46
63IndJayP-1
63Jel-148
63Pos-148
63Top-170
67Top-563
72LauGreF-42
78AtlCon-2
78BraTCC-2
78TCM60I-73
78TCM60I-108
82GSGalAG-7
83Bra53F-9
83TopRep5-347
86BraGreT-1
88PacLegI-31
89SweBasG-6
90HOFStiB-50
90LSUTigGM-12
91TopArc1-285
92BazQua5A-1
94TedWil-40
94TedWil-145
Adderly, Ken
87MiaMarP-18
Addis, Bob (Robert Gorden)
52Top-259
53BowC-94
53Top-157
79DiaGre-224
82Bow195E-260
83TopRep5-259
91TopArc1-157
Adduci, Jim (James David)
82ArkTraT-18
83LouRedR-19
84LouRedR-19
85VanCanC-206
86VanCanP-1
87DenZepP-16
87Don-495
88BrePol-14
89Fle-176
89FleGlo-176
89PhiTas-37
89Sco-587
89Top-338
89TopTif-338
90CMC-238
90ProAAAF-306
90ScrRedBC-12
90ScrRedBP-604
94BreMilB-2
Aderholt, Morrie
90DodTar-888
Adge, Jason
95WatIndTI-1
Adkins, Adrian
89PriPirS-1
Adkins, Doc (Merle Theron)
09ColChiE-5
09T206-391
11T205-187
12ColRedB-5
12ColTinT-5
12ImpTobC-18
Adkins, Rob
92MyrBeaHC-4
92St.CatBJC-15
92St.CatBJF-3376
93ClaGolF-176
93MedHatBJF-3729
93MedHatBJSP-11
Adkins, Steve
87Ft.LauYP-22
87PriWilYP-20
88PriWilYS-1
89BasAmeAPB-AA3
89EasLeaAP-11
89Ft.LauYS-1
90AlbDecGB-28
90ClaUpd-T2
90CMC-201
90ColCliC-1
90ColCliP-17
90ColCliP-667
90ProAAAF-317
90TopTVY-35
91ColCliLD-101
91ColCliP-1
91ColCliP-588
91LinDriAAA-101
91Sco-716
91ScoRoo-16
91TopDeb90-2
92IowCubF-4044
92IowCubS-201
93SyrChiF-990
94BowBayF-2404
94RocRedWTI-1
Adkins, Terry
85PriWilPT-6
Adkins, Tim
92HigSchPLS-20
93ClaGolF-171
93St.CatBJC-2
93St.CatBJF-3965
94HagSunC-2
94HagSunF-2721
95DunBluJTI-1
96DunBluJB-1
96DunBluJTI-1
Adler, Felix
40WheM4-13
41WheM5-14
Adler, Jimmy
90BriTigS-1
Adler, Marcus
88FayGenP-1085
89LakTigS-1
Adlesh, Dave (David George)
65AstBigLBPP-1
67Ast-1
67OPC-51
67Top-51
68Top-576
69Top-341
87AstShowSTh-1
87AstShowSTh-27
Adolfo, Carlos
94VerExpC-1
94VerExpF-3919
96DelShoB-5
Adriana, Sharnol
91St.CatBJC-5
91St.CatBJP-3400
92DunBluJF-2004
93KnoSmoF-1255
94SyrChiF-975
94SyrChiTI-1
95KnoSmoF-45
96SyrChiTI-1
Adriance, Dan
86TriTriC-190
87BelBreP-23
88BelBreGS-6
89SalSpuCLC-124
89SalSpuP-1818
Afenir, Tom
95WatIndTI-2
96WatIndTI-1
Afenir, Troy
85OscAstTI-13
86ColAstP-1
87ColAstP-4
88ColAstB-23
89HunStaB-3
90CMC-599
90ProAAAF-142
90TacTigC-22
90TacTigP-95
91Fle-1
91LinDriAAA-526
91Sco-745
91TacTigLD-526
91TacTigP-2308
92Bow-509
92DonRoo-2
92Fle-248
92Lea-525
92NasSouS-276
92RedKah-38
92Sco-407
92StaClu-613
92StaCluECN-613
93IndIndF-1491
Agacinski, Kenny
93ForMyeMC-29
94ForMyeMC-30
Agado, David
89BatCliP-1926
90MarPhiP-3204
Agan, Tim
83TolMudHT-24
84TolMudHT-19
Agar, Jeff
86LakTigP-1
87GleFalTP-12
Agbayani, Benny
93PitMetC-2
93PitMetF-3722
94FloStaLAF-FSL37
94St.LucMC-2
94St.LucMF-1206
95StLucMTI-4
96BinBeeB-1
96HilStaHWB-32
96NorTidB-6
Agee, Tommie Lee
65OPC-166
65Top-166
66OPC-164
66Top-164
66TopVen-164
66WhiSoxTI-2
67Baz-2
67CokCapWS-18
67DexPre-2
67OPCPapI-4
67Top-455
67TopPos-4
67TopVen-224
68AtlOilPBCC-2
68Baz-6
68Baz-15
68Kah-B2
68Top-465
69MetBoyS-3
69MetCit-1
69MetNewYDN-1
69MilBra-4
69MLBOffS-163
69Top-364
69TopSta-61
69TopTeaP-24
70DayDaiNM-84
70Kel-11
70MetTra-23C
70MLBOffS-73
70OPC-50
70OPC-198
70OPC-307
70Top-50
70Top-198
70Top-307
70TopPos-13
70TopSup-42
71BazNumT-16
71BazUnn-1
71Kel-46
71MLBOffS-145
71OPC-310
71Top-310
71TopCoi-91
71TopSup-36
71TopTat-73
72MilBra-5
72OPC-245
72Top-245
73OPC-420
73Top-420
74OPC-630
74Top-630
74TopTra-630T
81TCM60I-315
81TCM60I-322
86MetGreT-6
87AstShoSTw-26
89Met196C-1
89RinPosM1-3
90PacLeg-2
90SweBasG-19
91LinDri-30
91MetWIZ-2
91SweBasG-1
93UppDecAH-2
94Met69CCPP-7
94Met69CS-6
94Met69T-5
94TedWil-57
94UppDecAH-6
94UppDecAH-120
94UppDecAH-207
94UppDecAH1-6
94UppDecAH1-120
94UppDecAH1-207
Agganis, Harry
55Top-152
Agler, Joe (Joseph Abram)
09ColChiE-6
12ColRedB-6
12ColTinT-6
Agnew, Sam (Samuel Lester)
14B18B-29A
14B18B-29B
15SpoNewM-2
16ColE13-1
16SpoNewM-2
Agnoly, Earl
96KanCouCTI-1
Agostinelli, Peter
93BatCliC-2
93BatCliF-3135
93SpaPhiC-2
93SpaPhiF-1046
94ClePhiC-2
94ClePhiF-2516
95ClePhiF-207
Agostinelli, Sal
84SavCarT-22
86St.PetCP-1
87ArkTraP-15
88LouRedBC-21
88LouRedBP-424
88LouRedBTI-5
89ReaPhiB-22
89ReaPhiP-654
89ReaPhiS-1
90CMC-237
90ReaPhiB-13
90ReaPhiP-1222
90ReaPhiS-1
90ScrRedBC-11
91LinDriAAA-476
91ScrRedBLD-476
91ScrRedBP-2540
Agosto, Juan Roberto
81EdmTraRR-5
82EdmTraT-12
84Don-208
84Fle-50
84Nes792-409
84Top-409
84TopTif-409
84WhiSoxTV-1
85Don-526
85Fle-506
85Top-351
85TopTif-351
85WhiSoxC-50
86Don-488
86Fle-197
86Top-657
86TopTif-657
86WhiSoxC-50
87Top-277
87TopTif-277
87TucTorP-1
88AstMot-24
88AstPol-1
88Fle-437
88FleGlo-437
88Sco-558
88ScoGlo-558
88StaLinAst-1
88TopTra-2T
88TopTraT-2T
89AstLenH-17
89AstMot-23
89AstSmo-1
89BlaYNPRWL-70
89Bow-321

89BowTif-321
89Don-354
89Fle-348
89FleGlo-348
89PanSti-81
89Sco-283
89Top-559
89TopTif-559
89UppDec-251
90AstLenH-1
90AstMot-26
90Don-477
90Fle-220
90FleCan-220
90OPC-181
90PubSti-85
90Sco-284
90Top-181
90TopTif-181
90UppDec-450
90VenSti-2
91Bow-402
91CarPol-49
91Don-531
91Fle-497
91Lea-404
91OPC-703
91Sco-591
91StaClu-570
91Top-703
91TopDesS-703
91TopMic-703
91TopTif-703
91TopTra-1T
91TopTraT-1T
91UppDec-569
91UppDec-788
92CarPol-1
92Don-37
92Fle-574
92OPC-421
92Sco-329
92Top-421
92TopGol-421
92TopGolW-421
92TopMic-421
92Ult-562
92UppDec-693
93LasVegSF-935
Agosto, Stevenson
96CedRapKTI-1
Agramonte, Freddy
94GreFalDSP-1
Aguado, Victor
93UtiBluSC-2
93UtiBluSF-3538
Aguayo, Carmelo
82TulDriT-14
Aguayo, Luis
82Don-622
82Fle-238
82Top-449
83Don-546
83PhiTas-1
83PorBeaT-1
83Top-252
84PhiTas-28
85Don-503
85PhiTas-11
85PhiTas-28
85Top-663
85TopTif-663
86Don-503
86Fle-433
86PhiTas-16
86Top-69
86TopTif-69
87Fle-169
87FleGlo-169
87OPC-18
87PhiTas-16
87Top-755
87TopTif-755
88BlaYNPRWL-98
88Don-185
88Fle-297
88FleGlo-297
88PhiTas-1
88Sco-499
88ScoGlo-499
88StaLinPh-1
88Top-356
88TopBig-226
88TopTif-356
89BlaYNPRWL-103
89BlaYNPRWLU-44
89BlaYNPRWLU-57
89Bow-88
89BowTif-88
89Don-551
89Fle-249
89FleGlo-249
89IndTeal-1
89Sco-436
89Top-561
89TopTif-561
89UppDec-156
91LinDriAAA-351
91PawRedSDD-1
91PawRedSLD-351
91PawRedSP-43
92PawRedSS-351
92YanWIZ8-1
93PawRedSDD-1
93PawRedSF-2425
93PawRedSTI-25
94PawRedSDD-1
94PawRedSF-961
95PawRedSDD-1
95PawRedTI-16
97DunDonPPS-1
Aguiar, Douglas
95MarPhiTI-1
96MarPhiB-1
Aguilar, Alonso
96SpoIndB-3
Aguilar, Carlos
95LinVen-129
Aguilar, Jose
85MexCitTT-14
Aguilar, Mark
88StoPorCLC-191
88StoPorP-723
89MadMusS-1
96ColSilB-1
Aguilera, Rick
85TidTidT-11
86BasStaB-1
86Don-441
86Fle-74
86KayB-1
86Lea-216
86MetColP-14
86MetTCM-1
86MetWorSC-6
86Top-599
86TopTif-599
87ClaGam-79
87Don-620
87Fle-1
87FleExcS-2
87FleGlo-1
87Lea-89
87MetColP-22
87OPC-103
87Top-103
87TopTif-103
88Don-446
88DonTeaBM-446
88Fle-127
88FleGlo-127
88Lea-231
88MetColP-13
88MetKah-15
88Sco-521
88ScoGlo-521
88ScoYouS2-21
88Top-434
88TopTif-434
89Don-526
89DonBasB-265
89Fle-27
89FleGlo-27
89MetColP-21
89MetKah-2
89Sco-327
89Top-257
89TopTif-257
89UppDec-563
90Bow-405
90BowTif-405
90Don-391
90DonBesA-79
90Fle-365
90FleCan-365
90Lea-38
90OPC-711
90PubSti-127
90Sco-519
90Top-711
90TopBig-284
90TopTif-711
90UppDec-11
90VenSti-3
91BasBesAotM-1
91Bow-334
91Don-172
91Fle-602
91Lea-471
91MetWIZ-3
91OPC-318
91PanFreS-308
91PanSti-243
91RedFolS-2
91Sco-170
91Sco100S-67
91StaClu-76
91Stu-81
91Top-318
91TopDesS-318
91TopMic-318
91TopTif-318
91Ult-185
91UppDec-542
91USPlaCA-7H
92Bow-89
92Don-95
92Fle-195
92Hig5-81
92Lea-34
92OPC-44
92OPCPre-62
92Pin-211
92Sco-42
92Sco100S-4
92ScoProP-11
92StaClu-726
92StaCluD-3
92StaCluNC-726
92Stu-201
92Top-44
92TopGol-44
92TopGolW-44
92TopKid-114
92TopMic-44
92TriPla-65
92Ult-88
92UppDec-130
93Bow-453
93Don-19
93Fin-22
93FinRef-22
93Fla-233
93Fle-261
93Lea-32
93OPC-25
93PacSpa-168
93Pin-386
93PinTeaP-B11
93Sco-64
93Sel-206
93SelStaL-68
93SP-244
93StaClu-354
93StaCluFDI-354
93StaCluM-122
93StaCluMOP-354
93Top-625
93TopGol-625
93TopInaM-625
93TopMic-625
93Ult-228
93UppDec-303
93UppDecGold-303
94Bow-132
94ColC-473
94ColChoGS-473
94ColChoSS-476
94Don-503
94ExtBas-113
94Fin-280
94FinRef-280
94Fla-311
94Fle-198
94FUnPac-73
94Lea-45
94OPC-92
94Pin-293
94PinArtP-293
94PinMusC-293
94RedFolMI-21
94Sco-129
94ScoGolR-129
94Sel-160
94SP-182
94SPDieC-182
94StaClu-275
94StaCluFDI-275
94StaCluGR-275
94StaCluMOP-275
94Top-280
94TopGol-280
94TopSpa-280
94TriPla-251
94Ult-384
94UppDec-141
94UppDecED-141
95Baz-50
95Bow-391
95ColCho-480
95ColChoGS-480
95ColChoSE-224
95ColChoSEGS-224
95ColChoSESS-224
95ColChoSS-480
95Don-53
95DonPreP-53
95DonTopotO-16
95Emb-62
95EmbGolI-62
95Fin-154
95FinRef-154
95Fla-277
95Fle-196
95FleTeaL-9
95Lea-66
95Pac-244
95PacPri-78
95Pin-325
95PinArtP-325
95PinMusC-325
95RedFol-24
95Sco-122
95ScoGolR-122
95ScoPlaTS-122
95SP-169
95SPCha-128
95SPChaDC-128
95SPSil-169
95StaClu-177
95StaClu-404
95StaCluFDI-177
95StaCluMOP-177
95StaCluMOP-404
95StaCluSTWS-177
95StaCluSTWS-404
95Stu-60
95Top-65
95TopCyb-47
95Ult-71
95UltGolM-71
95UppDec-191
95UppDec-482T
95UppDecED-191
95UppDecEDG-191
95UppDecSE-216
95UppDecSEG-216
96Baz-45
96ColCho-605
96ColChoGS-605
96ColChoSS-605
96Don-14
96DonPreP-14
96EmoXL-79
96Fla-110
96Fle-21
96FleTif-21
96FleUpd-U50
96FleUpdTC-U50
96Lea-133
96LeaPrePB-133
96LeaPrePG-133
96LeaPrePS-133
96Pac-256
96Pin-355
96PinFoil-355
96ProSta-130
96Sco-105
96ScoDugC-A74
96ScoDugCAP-A74
96SP-112
96StaClu-35
96StaClu-264
96StaCluEPB-35
96StaCluEPG-35
96StaCluEPS-35
96StaCluMOP-35
96StaCluMOP-264
96Top-305
96TopGal-65
96TopGalPPI-65
96TopLas-113
96Ult-12
96Ult-371
96UltGolM-12
96UltGolM-371
96UppDec-369
97Cir-202
97CirRav-202
97ColCho-156
97Don-113
97DonPreP-113
97DonPrePGold-113
97Fle-142
97FleTif-142
97Pac-132
97PacLigB-132
97PacSil-132
97Sco-125
97ScoPreS-125
97ScoShoS-125
97ScoShoSAP-125
97StaClu-310
97StaCluMOP-310
97Top-405
97Ult-85
97UltGolME-85
97UltPlaME-85
97UppDec-103
Aguirre, Hank (Henry John)
57Top-96
58Top-337
59TigGraASP-2
59Top-36
59TopVen-36
60Top-546
61Top-324
61TopStal-144
62TigPosCF-1
62Top-407
63Jel-54
63Pos-54
63SalMetC-32
63TigJayP-1
63Top-6
63Top-257
64TigJayP-1
64TigLid-1
64Top-39
64TopCoi-74
64TopSta-38
64TopStaU-2
64TopTatI-23
64TopVen-39
65TigJayP-1
65Top-522
66OPC-113
66Top-113
66TopVen-113
67Top-263
67TopVen-252
68Top-553
69CubJewT-2
69OPC-94
69Top-94
70Top-699
73OPC-81
73Top-81A
73Top-81B
74OPC-354
74Top-354
75TucTorC-21
75TucTorTI-1
78TCM60I-225
81TigDetN-122
90DodTar-3
Aguirre, Jose
94CedRapKC-2
94CedRapKF-1101
95CedRapKTI-12
95LakElsSTI-1
Ahearne, Pat
92LakTigF-2271
93LakTigC-2
93LakTigF-1299
94TreThuF-2111
95BowBes-B30
95BowBesR-B30
95TolMudHTI-5

95TopTra-88T
Ahern, Brian
88CapCodPPaLP-30
89EugEmeB-23
90AppFoxBS-2
90AppFoxP-2086
90CMC-875
92MemChiS-426
92OmaRoyF-2952
92SkyAA F-178
93OmaRoyF-1671
Ahern, Jeff
82DanSunF-3
83RedPioT-1
Ahr, Jeff
87NewOriP-20
88HagSunS-1
Ahrens, Kelly
90BenBucL-6
90CliGiaB-3
90CliGiaP-2551
Aiello, Talbot
81WisRapTT-20
Aikens, Willie Mays
75QuaCitAT-3
77SalLakCGC-22
78SSP270-201
79RoyTeal-1
80OPC-191
80Top-368
81AllGamPI-1
81CokTeaS-73
81Don-220
81Fle-43
81OPC-23
81RoyPol-1
81Top-524
81TopScr-27
81TopSti-84
82Don-412
82Fle-404
82FleSta-206
82OPC-35
82Roy-1
82Top-35
82TopSti-196
82TopStiV-196
83AllGamPI-1
83Don-212
83Fle-104
83FleSta-1
83FleSti-101
83OPC-136
83Roy-1
83RoyPol-1
83Top-136
84BluJayFS-2
84Don-155
84Fle-341
84FleUpd-1
84Nes792-685
84OPC-137
84Top-685
84TopSti-276
84TopTif-685
84TopTra-1T
84TopTraT-1T
85BluJayFS-2
85Fle-97
85OPC-147
85Top-436
85TopTif-436
89PacSenL-147
89T/MSenL-2
89TopSenL-57
90EliSenL-107
78STLakCGC-22
Aikman, Troy
92StaCluMO-37
Ainge, Danny (Daniel Rae)
77Spo-8608
78SyrChiT-1
79SyrChiTI-4
80SyrChiT-20
81Don-569
81Fle-418
81TopTra-727
82Don-638
82Fle-608
82OPC-125
82Top-125
84OCoandSI-223
92SyrChiTT-1
93StaCluMO-29
Ainsmith, Eddie (Edward W.)
10JuJuDE-1
12T207-2
14B18B-38
15SpoNewM-3
16SpoNewM-3
22E120-226
22W572-1
22W573-2
90DodTar-4
Aitcheson, Kevin
83KnoBluJT-15
Aitchison, Raleigh L.
90DodTar-889
Aker, Jack Delane
66Top-287
66TopVen-287
67CokCapAt-7
67DexPre-3
67OPC-110
67Top-110
68Top-224
68TopVen-224
69MLBOffS-91
69PilPos-9
69Top-612
69TopSta-221
69TopTeaP-9
70MLBOffS-241
70OPC-43
70Top-43
71MLBOffS-481
71OPC-593
71Top-593
71YanArcO-1
72Top-769
73OPC-262
73Top-262
74MetDaiPA-6
74OPC-562
74Top-562
77LynMetT-1
78TCM60I-274
81TidTidT-21
82TidTidT-19
83BufBisT-25
83Pil69G-27
84BufBisT-18
85WatIndT-22
86IndOhH-NNO
86IndTeal-1
87IndGat-NNO
88BurBraP-29
91MetWIZ-4
92YanWIZ6-1
92YanWIZ7-1
Akerfelds, Darrel
84MadMusP-25
85HunStaJ-32
86TacTigP-1
87TacTigP-2
88ColSprSSC-1
88ColSprSSP-1537
88Sco-632
88ScoGlo-632
88Top-82
88TopTif-82
89OklCit8C-1
89OklCit8P-1532
89RanSmo-1
90FleUpd-41
90Lea-526
90PhiTas-1
90TopTra-1T
90TopTraT-1T
91Bow-493
91Don-110
91Fle-386
91OPC-524
91PhiMed-1
91Sco-223
91StaClu-581
91Top-524
91TopDesS-524
91TopMic-524
91TopTif-524
91UppDec-619
92OklCit8S-313
93RanKee-45
93SyrChiF-991
95MidAngOHP-1
95MidAngTI-1
Akers, Chad
93BilMusF-3950
93BilMusSP-16
94ChaWheC-3
94ChaWheF-2708
Akers, Howard
86KinEagP-1
Akimoto, Ratoo
87SanJosBP-14
Akin, Aaron
97Bow-432
97BowChr-292
97BowChrI-292
97BowChrIR-292
97BowChrR-292
97BowInt-432
97TopSta-114
97TopStaAM-114
Akins, Carlos
96BluOriB-4
Akins, Daron
86DavLipB-1
Akins, Sid
85BurRanT-12
85Top-390
85TopTif-390
87DurBulP-5
88RicBraC-7
88RicBraP-14
89GreBraP-1151
88RicBraBC-4
Akins, Tom
85IndIndTI-27
89IndIndP-1216
Ako, Gerry
80HolMilT-23
81ElPasDT-9
81VanCanT-22
Ala, Aurelio
52LavPro-106
Alario, Dave
86BakDodP-1
Alayon, Elvis
96LowSpiB-4
Alazaus, Shawn
93OneYanC-2
93OneYanF-3494
Alba, Gibson
85DomLeaS-162
85SyrChiT-1
86SyrChiP-1
87BufBisP-14
88LouRedBC-6
88LouRedBP-442
88LouRedBTI-6
89LouRedBC-1
89LouRedBP-1252
89LouRedBTI-7
90CMC-102
90LouRedBC-2
90LouRedBLBC-5
90LouRedBP-393
90ProAAAF-507
90TopTVCa-37
91RicBraBC-5
91RicBraP-2559
91RicBraTI-7
Albaladejo, Randy
93AshTouC-2
93AshTouF-2278
94AubAstC-1
94AubAstF-3761
94QuaCitRBC-2
94QuaCitRBF-536
Albarado, Marc
94UtiBluSC-1
94UtiBluSF-3824
Albaral, Randy
96MedHatBJTI-1
Alberro, Hector
87BelBreP-20
90JohCitCS-1
Alberro, Jose
91GulCoaRSP-2
92ChaRanF-2217
92GasRanC-6
93TulDriF-2725
94OklCit8F-1487
95FleUpd-80
95RanCra-2
96OklCit8B-4
96Sco-226
93TulDriTI-1
Albert, Gus (August P.)
87OldJudN-1
Albert, James
88AllandGN-41
Albert, Pedestrian
88GooN16-10
Albert, Rashad
96BriWhiSB-8
Albert, Rick (Richard)
75LynRanT-1
83AndBraT-2
85GreBraTI-1
86GreBraTI-1
87RicBraC-26
87RicBraT-26
88SumBraP-416
93DurBulC-27
93DurBulF-504
94DurBulC-29
94DurBulF-346
94DurBulTI-1
96EugEmeB-26
Albert, Tim
92BelBreC-15
92BelBreF-416
Alberts, Butch (Francis Burt)
77SalLakCGC-25
78SyrChiT-2
79SyrChiTI-14
80SyrChiT-10
80SyrChiTI-1
Albertson, John
88IdaFalBP-1839
Alborano, Pete
87EugEmeP-2660
88CarLeaAS-22
88VirGenS-1
89BasCitRS-2
89Sta-62
90MemChiB-3
90MemChiP-1020
90MemChiS-1
90StaFS7-82
91LinDriAA-401
91MemChiLD-401
91MemChiP-665
92ReaPhiF-585
92ReaPhiS-526
Albosta, Ed (Edward John)
47SigOil-1
90DodTar-5
Albrecht, Andy (Andrew)
88CapCodPPaLP-159
91OneYanP-4164
92PriWilCC-7
92PriWilCF-159
93SanJosGC-2
93SanJosGF-22
Albrecht, Jon
95SpoIndTI-3
Albright, Dave
81ChaRoyT-9
Albright, Eric
89NiaFalRP-2
90LakTigS-1
91Cla/Bes-39
91LakTigC-14
92LakTigC-3
Albright, Gilbert
80CliGiaT-25
Albro, Daryl
89MisStaB-1
90MisStaB-1
91MisStaB-1
92MisStaB-1
93MisStaB-1
Albury, Allan
91BriBanF-2
Albury, Vic (Victor)
72Top-778
73TacTwiC-1
74OPC-605
74Top-605
75OPC-368
75Top-368
76OPC-336
76SSP-205
76Top-336
77Top-536
82WatIndF-3
82WatIndT-27
83ChaChaT-20
83WatIndF-27
84MaiGuiT-9
Alcala y porte, Bastidas
Alcala, Jesus
80VenLeaS-13
82OneYanT-12
Alcala, Julio
86FloStaLAP-2
86Ft.MyeRP-1
87MemChiB-5
87MemChiP-24
89MemChiB-6
89MemChiP-1183
89MemChiS-1
Alcala, Santo
76OPC-589
76Top-589
77ExpPos-1
77PepGloD-52
77Top-636
78OPC-36
78Top-321
81PorBeaT-3
Alcantara, Francisco
90NiaFalRP-15
91RenSilSCLC-20
Alcantara, Israel
93BurBeeC-2
93BurBeeF-163
94WesPalBEC-1
94WesPalBEF-45
95HarSenTI-5
95SPML-94
96BesAutSA-1
96FleUpd-U146
96FleUpdTC-U146
96HarSenB-4
96Ult-500
96UltGolM-500
96UltGolP-2
96UltGolPHGM-2
Alcantara, Jose
75ForLauYS-24
76ForLauYS-4
77ForLauYS-4
Alcaraz, Luis (Angel Luis)
69Top-437
70RoyTeal-3
90DodTar-6
Alcazar, Jorge
86PenWhiSP-1
87BirBarB-27
88VanCanC-23
88VanCanP-772
Alcott, Charles
87OldJudN-2
Alder, Jimmy
90BriTigP-3168
91FayGenC-17
91FayGenP-1176
92LakTigC-11
92LakTigF-2284
93LonTigF-2313
Alderman, Kurt
94VerExpC-2
94VerExpF-3911
Aldred, Scott
87FayGenP-11
88LakTigS-1
89LonTigP-1368
90Bow-344
90BowTif-344
90CMC-379
90ProAAAF-371
90TolMudHC-2
90TolMudHP-141
91Bow-147
91Don-422
91LinDriAAA-576
91OPC-658
91Sco-740
91ScoRoo-3
91StaClu-429
91TolMudHLD-576
91TolMudHP-1922
91Top-658
91TopDeb90-3
91TopDesS-658
91TopMic-658
91TopTif-658
91UppDec-7
92Cla1-T3
92Cla2-T75
92ClaGam-147
92Don-486
92Fle-127
92OPC-198

92Pin-354
92ProFS7-66
92Sco-729
92Sco100RS-41
92StaClu-762
92Top-198
92TopGol-198
92TopGolW-198
92TopMic-198
93Don-733
93PacSpa-419
93RocUSPC-4C
93RocUSPC-13H
93StaClu-573
93StaCluFDI-573
93StaCluMOP-573
93StaCluRoc-7
93Top-463
93TopGol-463
93TopInaM-463
93TopMic-463
93Ult-338
96LeaSigEA-1
Aldrete, Mike
86FleUpd-1
86PhoFirP-2
87Don-450
87Fle-264
87FleGlo-264
87GiaMot-24
87Top-71
87TopTif-71
88Don-362
88DonBasB-191
88Fle-76
88FleGlo-76
88GiaMot-5
88OPC-351
88PanSti-426
88RedFolSB-1
88Sco-556
88ScoGlo-556
88ScoYouSI-35
88Spo-80
88StaLinG-1
88Top-602
88TopBig-119
88TopSti-89
88TopTif-602
89Bow-368
89BowTif-368
89Don-140
89DonTra-25
89ExpPos-1
89Fle-323
89FleGlo-323
89FleUpd-95
89OPC-9
89PanSti-219
89Sco-82
89ScoRoo-68T
89Top-158
89TopSti-80
89TopTif-158
89UppDec-239
89UppDec-738
90ExpPos-1
90OPC-589
90Sco-220A
90Sco-220B
90Top-589
90TopTif-589
90UppDec-415
91Fle-224
91OPC-483
91Sco-447
91Top-483
91TopDesS-483
91TopMic-483
91TopTif-483
92ColSprSSF-756
92ColSprSSS-76
92Don-621
92Fle-102
92OPC-256
92PanSti-45
92Sco-351
92StaClu-305
92Top-256
92TopGol-256
92TopGolW-256
92TopMic-256
93TacTigF-3042
94A'sMot-19
94Fle-252
94Sco-277
94ScoGolR-277
95AthMot-8
95Sco-192
95ScoGolR-192
95ScoPlaTS-192
96AngMot-22
96Bow-101
96LeaSigEA-2
86StaoftFT -38
Aldrete, Richard
87EveGiaC-6
88CalLeaACLC-7
88SanJosGCLC-116
88SanJosGP-119
89ShrCapP-1847
90ShrCapP-1448
90ShrCapS-1
91LinDriAAA-376
91PhoFirLD-376
91PhoFirP-78
92ArkTraS-26
Aldrich, Jay
83BelBreF-8
86ElPasDP-1
87DenZepP-4
88BlaYNPRWLU-30
88BrePol-33
88DenZepC-7
88DenZepP-1270
88Don-460
88Fle-155
88FleGlo-155
88Sco-578
88ScoGlo-578
88Top-616
88TopTif-616
89DenZepC-1
89DenZepP-42
90CMC-307
90ProAAAF-452
90RocRedWC-6
90RocRedWP-695
91OriCro-6
94BreMilB-3
Aldrich, Russell
80WatRedT-20
81WatRedT-18
Aldrich, Tom
88BriTigP-1881
89LonTigP-1386
90LonTigP-1272
Aldridge, Steve
93OneYanC-3
93OneYanF-3507
94GreBatF-477
97GreBatC-2
Aldridge, Vic
21Nei-74
22E120-151
22W572-2
22W573-3
28W56PlaC-C12A
94ConTSN-1114
94ConTSNB-1114
Alegre, Paul
90SalSpuCLC-133
90SalSpuP-2729
Alejo, Bob
96A'sMot-28
Alejo, Nigel
94VenLinU-148
95LinVen-131
95MidLeaA-1
96BreCouMB-4
Aleno, Chuck (Charles)
45CenFlo-1
Aleshire, Troy
86AubAstP-1
Alesio, Chris
90HamRedB-22
90HamRedS-1
Alexander, Bob
52LaPat-1
Alexander, Bob (Robert S.)
52Par-63
53ExhCan-34
55OriEss-2
91OriCro-7
Alexander, Chad
95AubAstTI-13
96Bow-330
96QuaCitRB-7
Alexander, Chuck (Charles)
88BurIndP-1785
89WatIndS-1
Alexander, Dale (David Dale)
29ExhFou-23
29PorandAR-2
31Exh-23
32OrbPinNP-27
32OrbPinUP-1
33DouDisP-2
33GeoCMil-1
33Gou-221
33TatOrb-1
33TatOrbSDR-181
61Fle-91
79RedSoxEF-8
81TigDetN-69
81TigSecNP-13
88ConSer4-1
92ConTSN-616
Alexander, Dave
89SalLakTTI-22
90MiaMirIS-1
Alexander, Don
90AubAstB-23
90AubAstP-3418
91AubAstC-25
91AubAstP-4290
93AshTouC-27
93AshTouF-2294
94AubAstC-25
94AubAstF-3776
95AubAstTI-25
95OdgRapTI-1
96QuaCitRB-3
Alexander, Doyle L.
72Top-579
73OPC-109
73OriJohP-13
73Top-109
74OPC-282
74Top-282
75OPC-491
75Top-491
76OPC-638
76SSP-374
76Top-638
77Hos-140
77Top-254
78OPC-52
78RanBurK-4
78RCColC-66
78SSP270-105
78Top-146
79OPC-230
79Top-442
80Top-67
81AllGamPI-163
81Don-448
81Fle-255
81Top-708
81TopTra-728
82Don-96
82Fle-383
82Top-364
82TopTra-1T
83Don-451
83Top-512
84BluJayFS-3
84Don-439
84Fle-146
84Nes792-677
84OPC-112
84Top-677
84TopTif-677
85AllGamPI-73
85BluJayFS-3
85Don-561
85Fle-98
85Lea-134
85OPC-218
85OPCPos-21
85SpoIndGC-1
85Top-218
85TopMin-218
85TopSti-365
85TopTif-218
86BluJayAF-2
86BluJayFS-2
86Don-390
86Fle-51
86FleLimE-1
86Lea-182
86OPC-196
86Spo-133
86Top-196
86TopMinL-34
86TopTif-196
87Don-657
87DonHig-52
87Fle-510
87FleGlo-510
87OPC-249
87Top-686
87TopTif-686
88Don-584
88DonBasB-13
88Fle-51
88FleGlo-51
88FleMin-21
88FleStiC-23
88OPC-316
88Sco-610
88ScoGlo-610
88StaLinTi-1
88TigPep-19
88TigPol-1
88Top-492
88TopBig-34
88TopTif-492
89Bow-94
89BowTif-94
89Don-178
89DonAll-12
89DonBasB-125
89Fle-128
89FleBasA-1
89FleGlo-128
89OPC-77
89RedFolSB-1
89Sco-129
89Spo-211
89TigMar-19
89TigPol-19
89Top-77
89TopBig-182
89TopSti-274
89TopTif-77
89UppDec-298
90DodTar-7
90Don-62
90Fle-599
90FleCan-599
90KayB-1
90OPC-748
90PubSti-467
90Sco-237
90Top-748
90TopTif-748
90UppDec-330
90VenSti-4
91OriCro-8
92YanWIZ7-2
92YanWIZ8-2
93RanKee-46
Alexander, Eric
89BluOriS-1
89Sta-113
91BluOriC-11
91BluOriP-4138
93GleFalRC-2
93GleFalRF-3992
94SavCarC-2
94SavCarF-495
Alexander, Gary
87AriWilP-1
88TexLeaAGS-4
88TulDriTI-12
89TexLeaAGS-31
89TulDriGS-5
89TulDriTI-1
90Bes-291
90EasLeaAP-EL19
90ReaPhiB-14
90ReaPhiP-1224
90ReaPhiS-2
90StaFS7-79
91LinDriAAA-477
91ScrRedBLD-477
91ScrRedBP-2542
92ScrRedBF-2451
92ScrRedBS-476
Alexander, Gary Wayne
75LafDriT-12
76PheGiaCr-25
76PhoGiaCa-11
76PhoGiaCC-1
76PhoGiaVNB-1
77PhoGiaCC-1
77PhoGiaCP-1
77Top-476
78OPC-72
78Top-624
79Hos-57
79OPC-168
79Top-332
80OPC-78
80Top-141
81Don-200
81Fle-398
81Top-416
81TopTra-729
82Fle-475
82Top-11
89PacSenL-141
Alexander, Gerald
90ChaRanS-1
90OklCit8P-422
90ProAAAF-668
91Cla3-T11
91Don-419
91Fle-278
91LinDriAAA-301
91OklCit8LD-301
91OklCit8P-170
91RanMot-27
91Sco-733
91TopDeb90-4
91UppDecFE-72F
92Don-578
92Fle-297
92OklCit8F-1905
92OklCit8S-301
92Sco-163
92Sco100RS-99
92StaClu-185
93RanKee-47
Alexander, Grover C.
09SpoNewSM-74
11L1L-114
11S81LarS-89
13NatGamW-1
13TomBarW-1
14CraJacE-37
14FatPlaT-1
15CraJacE-37
15SpoNewM-4
16BF2FP-83
16ColE13-2
16FleBreD-2
16SpoNewM-4
17HolBreD-1
19W514-65
20NatCarE-2
21E121So1-2
21E121So8-1A
21E121So8-1B
21Exh-2
21Nei-69
21OxfConE-1
22AmeCarE-1
22E120-152
22W572-3
22W573-4
22W575-2
22WilPatV-18
23W501-59
23W503-38
23W515-49
23WilChoV-2
24MrsShePP-1
25Exh-18
26SpoComoA-2
27AmeCarE-13
27Exh-29
27YorCarE-44
28Exh-29
28W502-44
28W512-2
28Yue-44
29ExhFou-15
30SchR33-19
30SchR33-48
31W517-15
36PC7AlbHoF-14
40PlaBal-119
48ExhHoF-1
48SweSpoT-11
49LeaPre-1
50CalHOFW-1

51TopConMA-1
60ExhWriH-1
60Fle-5
61Fle-2
61GolPre-2
63BasMagM-3
63BazA-29
63HalofFB-21
67TopVen-171
68LauWorS-23
69Baz-2
69Baz-3
70FleWorS-23
71FleWorS-13
72FleFamF-13
72LauGreF-41
75SheGrePG-16
76GrePlaG-16
76JerJonPC-7
76MotOldT-10
76RowExh-6
76ShaPiz-14
77BobParHoF-1
77GalGloG-153
77ShaPiz-5
80Lau300-8
80LauFamF-40
80MarExhH-1
80PacLeg-124
80PerHaloFP-14
80SSPHOF-14
81ConTSN-10
83DiaClaS2-94
83DonHOFH-23
83PhiPosGM-7
83PhiPosGPaM-2
84GalHaloFRL-14
84OCoandSI-137
85Woo-2
86ConSer1-3
86PhiGreT-5
87ConSer2-4
87HygAllG-2
88ConSer3-2
88GreBasS-9
89HOFStiB-72
90PerGreM-42
90SweBasG-30
91ConTSN-32
91SweBasG-128
92CarMcD-16
92ConTSN-534
92ConTSN-630
92ConTSNCI-15
92CubOldS-1
93ActPacA-92
93ActPacA2-26G
93ConTSN-932
93CraJac-7
93SpeHOF2-2
94ConTSN-1223
94ConTSNB-1223
94UppDecTAE-38
95ConTSN-1321
20W516-9
Alexander, Jon
88BasCitRS-3
89BasCitRS-3
Alexander, Manny
89BluOriS-2
89Sta-114
90Bes-241
90WauTimB-20
90WauTimP-2135
91CarLeaAP-CAR4
91Cla/Bes-97
91FreKeyC-15
91FreKeyP-2369
92Bow-41
92ClaFS7-119
92HagSunF-2560
92HagSunS-251
92OPC-551
92ProFS7-9
92SkyAA F-104
92Top-551
92TopGol-551
92TopGolW-551
92TopMic-551
93Bow-577
93Don-11
93FleMajLP-A4
93LimRocDWB-49
93LimRocDWB-145
93Pin-244
93PinRooTP-7
93RocRedWF-245
93Sco-234
93Sel-391
93Top-587
93TopGol-587
93TopInaM-587
93TopMic-587
93UppDec-5
93UppDecGold-5
94Bow-215
94Cla-97
94OriPro-1
94OriUSPC-2S
94Pac-24
94Pin-35
94PinArtP-35
94PinMusC-35
94RocRedWF-1002
94RocRedWTI-2
94StaCluT-300
94StaCluTFDI-300
95FleUpd-1
95TopTra-59T
95UltGolMR-M1
96ColCho-53
96ColChoGS-53
96ColChoSS-53
96Don-210
96DonPreP-210
96Fle-1
96FleTif-1
96LeaSigA-4
96LeaSigAG-4
96LeaSigAS-4
96Pac-237
96PacPri-P73
96PacPriG-P73
96Sco-393
96Top-34
96Ult-1
96UltGolM-1
96UppDec-11
97Fle-695
97FleTif-695
97Pac-16
97PacLigB-16
97PacSil-16
Alexander, Matt
92DavLipB-1
93DavLipB-1
Alexander, Matt (Matthew)
73WicAerKSB-1
76OPC-382
76SSP-501
76Top-382
77Top-644
78Top-102
81PorBeaT-4
81Top-68
82Top-528
Alexander, Pat
78CedRapGT-1
81ShrCapT-23
Alexander, Phil
91AdeGiaF-12
Alexander, Rob
88MadMusP-1
89ModA'sC-7
89ModA'sCLC-270
Alexander, Roberto
79CliDodT-4
82VerBeaDT-1
84AlbDukC-166
Alexander, Roger
79RicBraT-12
Alexander, Tim
80AndBraT-6
83DurBulT-27
84DurBulT-10
Alexander, Tommy
85FreGiaP-25
87WicPilRD-3
88JacExpB-9
88JacExpP-982
Alexander, Walt (Walter E.)
16ColE13-3
16FleBreD-3
Alexis, Juan
91MarPhiC-28
91MarPhiP-3442
Aleys, Maximo
89EveGiaS-1
89Sta-187
90CliGiaB-22
90CliGiaP-2548
91Cla/Bes-87
91SanJosGC-13
91SanJosGP-1
Alfano, Donald
49W725AngTI-2
Alfano, Jeff
96OgdRapTI-6
Alfaro, Flavio
85DurBulT-18
85Top-391
85TopTif-391
Alfaro, Hermanos
80VenLeaS-134
Alfaro, Jesus
76VenLeaS-212
80VenLeaS-109
80VenLeaS-239
80WicAerT-14
84ChaO'sT-19
86ElPasDP-3
87ElPasDP-15
87TexLeaAF-30
88MidAngGS-19
89ElPasDGS-20
90El PasDAGTI-4
90ElPasDGS-3
90TexLeaAGS-10
93LinVenB-144
94VenLinU-55
95LinVen-18
Alfaro, Jose
74CedRapAT-14
75DubPacT-22
76VenLeaS-186
80VenLeaS-123
80VenLeaS-233
Alfonseca, Antonio
93JamExpC-2
94KanCouCC-2
94KanCouCF-152
94KanCouCTI-1
95PorSeaDTI-1
96BesAutS-2
96BowBes-107
96BowBesAR-107
96BowBesR-107
96ChaKniB-7
Alfonso, Carlos
75IowOakT-1
76IndIndTI-24
82AubAstT-18
86TucTorP-2
92GiaMot-28
92GiaPacGaE-1
93PhoFirF-1532
94PhoFirF-1535
96GiaMot-28
Alfonso, Ossie
84VisOakT-6
85OrlTwiT-14
Alfonzo, Edgar (Edgardo)
86QuaCitAP-1
87PalSprP-20
88PalSprACLC-96
88QuaCitAGS-19
89PalSprACLC-44
89PalSprAP-464
91MidAngOHP-1
91PalSprAP-2021
92CalLeaACL-43
92PalSprAC-23
92PalSprAF-845
93BowBayF-2193
93ClaGolF-30
93LinVenB-151
94BowBayF-2417
95LinVen-7
95SigRoo-2
95SigRooSig-2
95Zen-128
96MidAngB-5
96MidAngOHP-1
Alfonzo, Edgardo Antonio
92PitMetC-10
92PitMetF-3301
93ClaFS7-92
93ClaGolF-210
93ExcFS7-68
93FloStaLAF-38
93LinVenB-129
93St.LucMC-1
94BinMetF-708
94Bow-156
94BowBes-B13
94BowBesR-B13
94ClaGolF-166
94ExcFS7-232
94MetShuST-3
94UppDecML-241
94VenLinU-16
94VenLinU-52
95Bow-19
95BowBes-R81
95BowBesR-R81
95Emo-157
95EmoRoo-1
95Exc-230
95Fin-246
95FinRef-246
95Fla-380
95FleAllR-M1
95LinVen-76
95SelCer-128
95SelCerMG-128
95SP-22
95SPCha-11
95SPChaDC-11
95SPSil-22
95StaClu-563
95StaCluMOP-563
95StaCluSTWS-563
95Sum-135
95Sum21C-TC3
95SumNthD-135
95TopTra-54T
95UltGolMR-M2
95UppDec-255
95UppDecED-255
95UppDecEDG-255
95UppDecML-49
95UppDecSE-191
95UppDecSEG-191
95ZenRooRC-14
96ColCho-218
96ColChoGS-218
96ColChoSS-218
96Don-195
96DonPreP-195
96Fla-315
96Fle-472
96FleTif-472
96Lea-116
96LeaPre-58
96LeaPreP-58
96LeaPrePB-116
96LeaPrePG-116
96LeaPrePS-116
96MetKah-1
96MetUni-197
96MetUniP-197
96Pac-140
96PacPri-P45
96PacPriG-P45
96PanSti-27
96Pin-239
96PinAfi-149
96PinAfiAP-149
96PinArtP-139
96PinFoil-239
96PinSta-139
96Sco-174
96ScoDugC-A98
96ScoDugCAP-A98
96Sel-85
96SelArtP-85
96SelCer-68
96SelCerAP-68
96SelCerCB-68
96SelCerCR-68
96SelCerMB-68
96SelCerMG-68
96SelCerMR-68
96StaClu-164
96StaCluMOP-164
96Sum-43
96SumAbo&B-43
96SumArtP-43
96SumFoi-43
96Top-99
96Ult-239
96UltGolM-239
96UppDec-142
96Zen-65
96ZenArtP-65
97Cir-58
97CirRav-58
97ColCho-397
97Don-57
97DonLim-72
97DonLimLE-72
97DonPreP-57
97DonPrePGold-57
97Fle-390
93StLucMF-2926
97FleTif-390
97Pac-357
97PacLigB-357
97PacSil-357
97Sco-372
97ScoHobR-372
97ScoResC-372
97ScoShoS-372
97ScoShoSAP-372
97StaClu-89
97StaCluMOP-89
97Top-212
97Ult-410
97UltGolME-410
97UltPlaME-410
95UppDecMLFS-49
Alfonzo, Roberto
94KinMetC-1
94KinMetF-3828
Alford, Mike
89MisStaB-2
90MisStaB-2
Alfredson, Tom
86QuaCitAP-2
87PalSprP-19
88MidAngGS-15
89MidAngGS-4
90BirBarB-5
90BirBarP-1394
Alger, Kevin
92MarPhiC-24
92MarPhiF-3045
93SpaPhiC-3
93SpaPhiF-1047
94ClePhiC-3
94ClePhiF-2517
Alguacil, Jose
94CliLumF-1985
96SanJosGB-2
94CliLumC-2
Ali, Muhammad
92PhiDaiN-9
Alicano, Pedro
91PeoChiC-2
91PeoChiP-1333
91PeoChiTI-4
92WinSpiC-21
92WinSpiF-1198
Alicea, Edwin
88BlaYNPRWL-2
89BlaYNPRWL-170
89GreBraB-6
89GreBraP-1156
89GreBraS-1
90DurBulTI-13
91MiaMirC-26
91MiaMirP-419
92GreBraF-1163
92GreBraS-226
93ColSprSSF-3098
93GreBraF-355
93LinVenB-302
95NorTidTI-5
Alicea, Luis
85AncGlaPTI-1
86EriCarP-1
87ArkTraP-16
88BlaYNPRWLU-37
88CarSmo-24
88DonRoo-52
88FleUpd-116
88FleUpdG-116
88LouRedBC-20
88LouRedBP-436
88LouRedBTI-7
88ScoRoo-98T
88ScoRooG-98T
88TopTra-3T
88TopTraT-3T
89Don-466
89Fle-443
89FleGlo-443
89LouRedBC-14
89LouRedBP-1263

89LouRedBTI-8
89PanSti-175
89RedFolSB-2
89Sco-231
89Top-261
89Top-588
89TopSti-37
89TopTif-261
89TopTif-588
89UppDec-281
90LouRedBLBC-6
91LinDriAAA-226
91LouRedLD-226
91LouRedP-2919
91LouRedTI-17
92Don-560
92Sco-607
92StaClu-103
93CarPol-1
93Don-416
93Fle-507
93PacBeiA-28
93PacBeiA-29
93PacBeiA-30
93PacSpa-293
93Sco-183
93StaClu-178
93StaCluFDI-178
93StaCluMOP-178
93Top-257
93TopGol-257
93TopInaM-257
93TopMic-257
93UppDec-605
93UppDecGold-605
94CarPol-1
94ColC-32
94ColChoGS-32
94ColChoSS-32
94Don-534
94ExtBas-355
94Fin-40
94FinRef-40
94Fle-627
94Lea-203
94Pac-585
94Pin-319
94PinArtP-319
94PinMusC-319
94Sco-522
94ScoGolR-522
94StaClu-146
94StaCluFDI-146
94StaCluGR-146
94StaCluMOP-146
94StaCluT-309
94StaCluTFDI-309
94Top-416
94TopGol-416
94TopSpa-416
94Ult-562
94UppDec-239
94UppDecED-239
95Don-43
95DonPreP-43
95DonTopotO-17
95Fin-243
95FinRef-243
95Fle-493
95Lea-381
95Pac-404
95Sco-173
95ScoGolR-173
95ScoPlaTS-173
95Top-630
95TopCyb-396
95Ult-259
95UltGolM-259
96ColCho-59
96ColChoGS-59
96ColChoSS-59
96Don-221
96DonPreP-221
96Fle-22
96FleTif-22
96FleUpd-U181
96FleUpdTC-U181
96MetUni-11
96MetUniP-11
96Pac-259
96Sco-438
96StaClu-190
96StaClu-365
96StaCluMOP-190
96StaCluMOP-365
96Top-377
96Ult-13
96Ult-539
96UltGolM-13
96UltGolM-539
97Fle-657
97FleTif-657
97Pac-402
97PacLigB-402
97PacSil-402
97Ult-513
97UltGolME-513
97UltPlaME-513

Alicea, Miguel
80PenPilBT-4
80PenPilCT-6
81ReaPhiT-6
85BelBreT-24
87ChaO'sW-16
88BlaYNPRWL-130
88EdmTraC-11
88EdmTraP-582
89BlaYNPRWL-3
89PalSprACLC-55

Alimena, Charles
92CliGiaC-19
93CliGiaC-2
93CliGiaF-2494
94CliLumF-1986
94CliLumC-3

Alkire, Jeff
91MiaHurBB-1
92TopTra-2T
92TopTraG-2T
93ClaFS7-93
93SavCarC-2
93SavCarF-677
93SouAtlLAGF-44
93StaCluM-163
93StaCluM-174
94ClaGolF-157
94ExcFS7-254
94UppDecML-238
96PorSeaDB-6

Allaire, Karl
85OscAstTI-16
86ColAstP-2
87ColAstP-14
88TucTorC-17
88TucTorJP-1
88TucTorP-167
90CMC-499
90EdmTraC-22
90EdmTraP-521
90ProAAAF-97
91LinDriAAA-577
91TolMudHLD-577
91TolMudHP-1937
92TolMudHF-1048
92TolMudHS-576

Allanson, Andy
84BufBisT-7
85WatIndT-24
86DonRoo-43
86FleUpd-2
86IndOhH-6
86IndTeal-2
86TopTra-1T
86TopTraT-1T
87BufBisP-3
87Don-95
87Fle-241
87FleGlo-241
87IndGat-6
87Lea-102
87Top-436
87TopRoo-1
87TopSti-311
87TopTif-436
87ToyRoo-1
88Don-465
88DonBasB-5
88FleUpd-21
88FleUpdG-21
88IndGat-6
88Sco-586
88ScoGlo-586
88StaLinI-1
88Top-728
88TopBig-231
88TopTif-728
89Bow-83
89BowTif-83
89Don-138
89Fle-396
89FleGlo-396
89IndTeal-2
89OPC-283
89PanSti-323
89Sco-46
89Top-283
89TopBig-311
89TopSti-207
89TopTif-283
89UppDec-217
90Fle-483
90FleCan-483
90OPC-514
90PubSti-551
90Sco-452
90Top-514
90TopTif-514
90UppDec-590
90VenSti-5
91Lea-455
91TigCok-10
92BrePol-1
92DenZepF-2642
92Don-42
92Fle-128
92Lea-510
92OPC-167
92Sco-537
92StaClu-238
92Top-167
92TopGol-167
92TopGolW-167
92TopMic-167
93PhoFirF-1517
94BreMilB-4
94SanBerSF-2761
95AngMot-23
95LakElsSTI-2

Allard, Brian M.
77AshTouT-1
79TucTorT-4
80ChaChaT-5
80Top-673
81SpoIndT-10
82Top-283
83SalLakCGT-6
84SalLakCGC-171
85IntLeaAT-43
85MaiGuiT-30
86WatIndP-1
87WilBilP-16
88EasLeaAP-50
88WilBilP-1311
89KenTwiP-1080
89KenTwiS-27
90CalLeaACLC-26
90VisOakCLC-80
90VisOakP-2171
91VisOakC-26
91VisOakP-1758
91VisOakP-1759
92VisOakC-25
92VisOakF-1030
93FayGenC-27
93FayGenF-145
93RanKee-48
94LakTigC-28
94LakTigF-3052
96TolMudHB-4

Allen, Bernie (Bernard Keith)
61TwiCloD-1
62Top-596
63Jel-2
63Pos-2
63Top-427
63TwiJayP-1
63TwiVol-1
64Top-455
65OPC-237
65Top-237
66Top-327
66TopVen-327
66TwiFaiG-1
67CokCapS-2
67DexPre-4
67OPC-118
67SenTeal-1
67Top-118
68Top-548
69MilBra-5
69MLBOffS-100
69OPC-27
69SenTeal8-1
69Top-27
69TopSta-231
69TopTeaP-23
70MLBOffS-277
70Top-577
71MLBOffS-529
71OPC-427
71SenTealW-1
71Top-427
72MilBra-6
72Top-644
73LinPor-126
73OPC-293
73Top-293
77SerSta-1
78TwiFri-26
92YanWIZ7-3

Allen, Bob
88CapCodPPaLP-157

Allen, Bob (Robert Gilman)
87OldJudN-5

Allen, Bob (Robert Gray)
61Top-452
62Top-543
63Top-266
64Top-209
64TopVen-209
66Top-538
67OPC-24
67Top-24
68OPC-176
68Top-176
68TopVen-176

Allen, Bob (Robert)
84AlbDukC-156
86ElPasDP-2
87MidAngP-23

Allen, Brandon
96BatCliTI-18

Allen, Cedric
94PriRedC-2
94PriRedF-3253
95Exc-171
96Exc-144

Allen, Chad
89BurIndS-1
90WatIndS-1
91CarLeaAP-CAR11
91KinIndC-1
91KinIndP-313
92CanIndS-101
92KinIndF-2466
93CanIndF-2831

Allen, Chris
96TreThuB-19

Allen, Clint
91MisStaB-2
92MisStaB-2

Allen, Craig
96GreFalDB-2
96GreFalDTI-1

Allen, Dave
85FreGiaP-5
87UtiBluSP-32
88BatCliP-1684
90AubAstB-16
90AubAstP-3414
91BurAstP-2792

Allen, David
91BurAstC-1
91Cla/Bes-222

Allen, Dell
92MarPhiC-26
92MarPhiF-3062
93MarPhiC-2
93MarPhiF-3480

Allen, Dusty
96CliLumKTI-2

Allen, Edward
83ButCopKT-23
83ChaRoyT-10

Allen, Ethan (Ethan Nathan)
29PorandAR-1
33Gou-46
33GouCanV-46
34DiaMatCSB-2
34BatR31-76
34DiaStaR-92
35DiaMatCS2-1
35DiaMatCS3T1-1
35GouPuzR-6C
36GouWidPPR-A1
79DiaGre-254
92MegRut-150
93ConTSN-779
94ConTSN-1128
94ConTSNB-1128

Allen, Frank Leon
16FleBreD-4
90DodTar-9

Allen, George
43ParSpo-1

Allen, Greg
78WisRapTT-1

Allen, Hank (Harold Andrew)
67Top-569
68Top-426
69MilBra-6
69SenTeal-1
69SenTeal8-2
69Top-623
70OPC-14
70Top-14
71MLBOffS-3
72MilBra-7
94BreMilB-95

Allen, Harold
88AshTouP-1060
89OscAstS-1
90Bes-161
90ColMudB-11
90ColMudP-1337
90ColMudS-1
91LinDriAAA-601
91TucTorLD-601
91TucTorP-2204
92JacGenF-3991
92JacGenS-326

Allen, Jamie (James Bradley)
80LynSaiT-18
81SpoIndT-31
82QuaCitCT-17
82SalLakCGT-2
84SalLakCGC-182
84Don-267
84Fle-604
84Nes792-744
84Top-744
84TopSti-350
84TopTif-744

Allen, Jim
74AlbDukTI-79
75AlbDukC-18
83QuaCitCT-18
89JohCitCS-1

Allen, John Marshall
34Gou-42
34GouCanV-96
93LetMouF-4154
93LetMouSP-1

Allen, Johnny (John Thomas)
32OrbPinNP-103
35GouPuzR-8E
35GouPuzR-9E
35GouPuzR-11E
35GouPuzR-13C
35GouPuzR-15C
36R31PasP-1
37OPCBatUV-122
39WheBB12-2
41BroW75-1
42DodTeal-1
43DodTeal-1
90DodTar-10
92ConTSN-384
93ConTSN-722

Allen, Kim (Kim Bryant)
75QuaCitAT-31
80SpoIndT-19
80VenLeaS-157
81Fle-612
81SpoIndT-27
89PacSenL-99
89TopSenL-53
91PacSenL-99
78STLakCGC-5

Allen, Larry
86PenWhiSP-2
87ChaWheP-11
88SouBenWSGS-2

Allen, Lee
90LitSunW-6

Allen, Lloyd Cecil
71OPC-152
71Top-152
72OPC-102
72Top-102
73OPC-267
73Top-267
74OPC-539
74Top-539
76SSP-140
76TulOilGP-2
79IowOakP-2
93RanKee-49
Allen, Marlon
94PriRedC-3
94PriRedF-3266
97Bow-359
97BowInt-359
Allen, Matt
91JamExpC-7
91JamExpP-3547
92AlbPolC-5
92AlbPolF-2308
92JamExpC-16
92JamExpF-1504
93WesPalBEC-24
93WesPalBEF-1342
94WesPalBEC-2
94WesPalBEF-42
Allen, Mel
48YanTeal-1
92MegRut-146
92MegRut-147
Allen, Mike
80BufBisT-11
80WicAerT-13
Allen, Myron Smith
87OldJudN-4
Allen, Neil
77LynMetT-2A
77LynMetT-2B
78TidTidT-1
80Top-94
81AllGamPI-164
81CokTeaS-85
81Don-276
81Fle-322
81OPC-322
81Top-322
81TopSti-198
81TopSupHT-73
82Don-506
82Fle-520
82FleSta-84
82Kel-20
82MetPhoA-1
82OPC-205
82Top-205
82TopSti-66
83Don-98
83Fle-536
83FleSta-2
83FleSti-236
83Kel-34
83OPC-268
83Top-575
83TopSti-265
83TopTra-1T
84Car-1
84Car5x7-1
84Don-109
84Fle-318
84JacMetF-1
84Nes792-435
84OPC-183
84Top-435
84TopSti-147
84TopTif-435
85CarTeal-1
85Don-205
85Fle-219
85OPC-234
85Top-731
85TopMin-731
85TopSti-144
85TopTif-731
86CarTeal-1
86Don-610
86Fle-98
86FleUpd-3
86Top-663
86TopTif-663
86TopTra-2T
86TopTraT-2T
86WhiSoxC-33
87Don-507
87Fle-484
87FleGlo-484
87OPC-113
87RedFolSB-93
87Top-113
87TopSti-292
87TopTif-113
87WhiSoxC-1
88Don-597
88Top-384
88TopTif-384
89ColSprSSC-6
89Don-196
89Fle-250A
89Fle-250B
89FleGlo-250
89Sco-375
89Top-61
89TopTif-61
89UppDec-567
90CMC-148
90NasSouC-23
90NasSouP-223
90ProAAAF-535
91MetWIZ-5
92YanWIZ8-3
96StCatSB-2
Allen, Newt (Newton)
78LauLonABS-3
86NegLeaF-104
90NegLeaS-30
94TedWil-100
Allen, Nick (Artemus)
20RedWorCP-1
Allen, Paul
89WelPirP-32
Allen, Richie (Richard A.)
47StaPinP2-1
64PhiPhiB-1
64Top-243
64TopVen-243
65OldLonC-2
65Top-460
65TopEmbl-36
65TopTral-38
66Baz-4
66OPC-80
66PhiTeal-1
66Top-80
66TopRubl-3
66TopVen-80
67Baz-4
67CokCapA-1
67CokCapNLA-25
67CokCapPh-1
67DexPre-5
67PhiPol-1
67Top-242
67Top-244
67Top-309
67Top-450
67TopGiaSU-18
67TopVen-311
68Baz-14
68DexPre-3
68Top-225
68TopActS-12A
68TopGamI-23
68TopPla-14
68TopPos-15
68TopVen-225
69CitMetC-17
69MilBra-7
69MLBOffS-172
69MLBPin-33
69NabTeaF-2
69OPC-6
69OPCDec-1
69PhiTeal-1
69Top-6
69Top-350
69TopDec-26
69TopDecl-2
69TopSta-71
69TopSup-53
69TopTeaP-8
69TraSta-57
70CarTeal-1
70DayDaiNM-80
70Kel-33
70MLBOffS-133
70OPC-40
70Top-40
70TopScr-2
71BazNumT-44
71DodTic-1
71Kel-57
71MLBOffS-97
71OPC-650
71Top-650
71TopSup-40
71TopTat-53
72MilBra-8
72OPC-240
72Top-240
72WhiSox-1
72WhiSoxDS-1
72WhiSoxTI1-1
73Kel2D-26
73LinPor-47
73OPC-62
73OPC-63
73OPC-310
73Top-62
73Top-63
73Top-310
73TopCanL-2
73TopCom-2
73TopPin-2
74Kel-33
74OPC-70
74OPC-332
74Top-70
74Top-332
74TopDecE-39
74TopPuz-2
74TopSta-151
75Kel-42
75OPC-210
75OPC-307
75OPC-400
75SSP42-4
75Top-210
75Top-307
75Top-400
76OPC-455
76SSP-473
76Top-455
81TCM60I-415
82K-M-21
83PhiPosGPaM-7
84OCoandSI-203
85WhiSoxC-29
86PhiGreT-10
89WhiSoxK-1
90CedRapRB-8
90DodTar-8
92UppDecS-5
92UppDecS-24
93ActPacA-155
93UppDecS-15
94TedWil-71
Allen, Rick
88AlaGolTI-1
89BilMusP-2045
90CedRapRP-2331
91ChaLooLD-151
91ChaLooP-1964
91LinDriAA-151
92ChaLooS-176
92OrlSunRF-2851
Allen, Robert Earl
82VerBeaDT-15
Allen, Rod (Roderick B.)
78AppFoxT-1
79KnoKnoST-24
81EdmTraRR-21
82SalLakCGT-3
83SalLakCGT-14
85RocRedWT-10
87BufBisP-24
88ColSprSSC-19
88ColSprSSP-1545
88TriAAC-39
89Fle-397
89FleGlo-397
94KanCouCC-29
94KanCouCF-179
94KanCouCTI-2
95KanCouCTI-46
Allen, Rodney
96EugEmeB-24
Allen, Ronnie
91BatCliC-25
91BatCliP-3474
91FroRowDP-13
92ClePhiC-23
92ClePhiF-2046
92StaCluD-4
93ReaPhiF-288
94LynRedSC-2
94LynRedSF-1883
Allen, Scott
88BurIndP-1784
Allen, Shane
81QuaCitCT-7
Allen, Sterling
76BatRouCT-1
Allen, Steve
88ButCopKSP-26
89GasRanP-1022
89GasRanS-1
89Sta-133
90TexLeaAGS-36
90TulDriP-1148
90TulDriTI-1
91LinDriAA-526
91SanAntMLD-526
91SanAntMP-2965
92SanAntMF-3967
92SanAntMS-551
93AlbDukF-1451
93ColSprSSF-3080
94ColSprSSF-724
Allen, Tracy
90WinHavRSS-1
91WinHavRSC-1
91WinHavRSP-481
Allenson, Gary M.
80Top-376
81Don-455
81Top-128
82Don-386
82Fle-287
82OPC-273
82RedSoxC-1
82Top-686
83Don-30
83Fle-177
83Top-472
84Don-335
84Fle-388
84Nes792-56
84OPC-56
84Top-56
84TopTif-56
85Fle-148
85SyrChiT-3
85Top-259
85TopTif-259
87OneYanP-24
88OneYanP-2064
89LynRedSS-23
89PacSenL-41
89T/MSenL-3
90EliSenL-92
90LynRedSTI-27
91LinDriAA-474
91NewBriRSLD-474
91NewBriRSP-367
91PacSenL-111
92RedSoxDD-1
96ChaRivTI-9601
Allensworth, Jermaine
93WelPirF-3371
94CarMudF-1590
94Cla-162
94ExcFirYPF-6
94ExcFS7-250
94Top-616
94TopGol-616
94TopSpa-616
94UppDec-541
94UppDecED-541
95CarMudF-169
95UppDecML-122
97Bow-247
97BowBes-27
97BowBesAR-27
97BowBesR-27
97BowInt-247
97Cir-290
97CirRav-290
97ColCho-6
97Don-155
97DonEli-93
97DonEliGS-93
97DonLim-103
97DonLimLE-103
97DonPreP-155
97DonPrePGold-155
97Fin-67
97FinRef-67
97Fle-423
97FleRooS-1
97FleTif-423
97Lea-23
97LeaFraM-23
97LeaFraMDC-23
97MetUni-236
97Pac-389
97PacLigB-389
97PacPri-132
97PacPriLB-132
97PacPriP-132
97PacSil-389
97PinIns-12
97PinInsCE-12
97PinInsDE-12
97Sco-313
97ScoPreS-313
97ScoShoS-313
97ScoShoSAP-313
97SkyE-X-90
97SkyE-XC-90
97SkyE-XEC-90
97SpoIll-108
97SpoIllEE-108
97StaClu-97
97StaCluM-M14
97StaCluMOP-97
97StaCluMOP-M14
97Stu-65
97StuPrePG-65
97StuPrePS-65
97Top-341
97TopChr-115
97TopChrR-115
97TopGal-153
97TopGalPPI-153
97Ult-258
97UltGolME-258
97UltPlaME-258
97UppDec-226
95UppDecMLFS-122
Alley, Chipper
96AppLeaAB-1
96BluOriB-5
Alley, Gene (Leonard Eugene)
64PirKDK-1
64Top-509
65OPC-121
65Top-121
66PirEasH-14
66Top-336
66TopVen-336
67CokCapPi-2
67DexPre-6
67Kah-2
67PirTeal-1
67Top-283
67TopPirS-1
67TopVen-322
68Kah-A2
68Kah-B3
68OPC-53
68PirKDK-22
68PirTeal-1
68Top-53
68Top-368
68TopGamI-25
68TopVen-53
68TopVen-368
69MilBra-8
69MLBOffS-181
69PirGre-1
69PirJacitB-1
69Top-436
69TopSta-81
69TopTeaP-16
70DayDaiNM-152
70MLBOffS-97
70Top-566
71MLBOffS-193
71OPC-416
71PirActP-1
71PirArc-1
71Top-416
72MilBra-9
72OPC-286
72Top-286
73OPC-635
73Top-635

94UppDecAH-138
94UppDecAH1-138
Alleyne, Isaac
87SalLakTTT-9
88JamExpP-1903
89RocExpLC-1
90ArkTraGS-5
Allie, Gair R.
54Top-179
55Top-59
55TopDouH-71
58JetPos-1
94TopArc1-179
94TopArc1G-179
Allietta, Bob (Robert G.)
76OPC-623
76Top-623
79TacTugT-15
80TacTigT-11
Allinger, Bob
83MiaMarT-21
Allison, Bob (William R.)
55DonWin-10
59HomRunD-2
59Top-116
59TopVen-116
60ArmCoi-2
60KeyChal-2
60NuHi-66
60SenJayP-1
60Top-320
60TopTat-2
61NuSco-466
61Pos-91A
61Pos-91B
61Top-355
61TopStal 176
61TwiJayP-1
61TwiUniMC-1
62AurRec-1
62Baz-1
62Jel-83
62Pos-83
62PosCan-83
62SalPlaC-22
62ShiPlaC-22
62Top-180
62TopStal-73
62TopVen-180
63BasMagM-4
63Jel-7
63Pos-7
63Top-75
63TwiJayP-2
63TwiVol-2
64Top-10
64Top-290
64TopCoi-19
64TopVen-10
64TopVen-290
64TwiJayP-1
64WheSta-2
65OldLonC-21
65OPC-180
65Top-180
65TopEmbl-38
65TopTral-1
66Top-345
66TopVen-345
66TwiFaiG-2
67CokCapTw-2
67DexPre-7
67OPC-194
67Top-194
67Top-334
68DexPre-4
68Top-335
68TopVen-335
69MilBra-9
69MLBOffS-64
69OPC-30
69Top-30
69TopSta-191
69TopTeaP-15
69TwiTealC-1
70DayDaiNM-149
70MLBOffS-229
70Top-635
72MilBra-10
78TCM60I-26
78TwiFri-1
83MLBPin-1
86TwiGreT-5
89ChaLooLITI-2
89PacLegI-165
89SweBasG-27
93UppDecAH-3
Allison, Brad
96AriBlaDB-5
Allison, Bubba
86BenPhiC-151
Allison, Chris
94UtiBluSC-2
94UtiBluSF-3825
95Bes-8
95MicBatCTI-1
95MidLeaA-2
96Exc-10
Allison, Cody
96BurIndB-17
Allison, Dana
89MedAthB-28
90ModA'sCLC-153
90ModA'sP-2203
91Bow-238
91ScoRoo-94T
91TacTigP-2295
91UppDec-771
92HunStaF-3940
92TacTigS-526
92TopDeb91-2
93HunStaF-2074
94TacTigF-3166
Allison, Fritz
94ElmPioF-3480
94ElmPioC-1
Allison, Jamie
88CalLeaACLC-21
88RenSilSCLC-279
89KinIndS-1
90KinIndTI-10
Allison, Jeff
87IdaFalBP-5
88MiaMarS-1
88SalLakCTTI-9
Allison, Jim
83TriTriT-12
85BurRanT-27
85UtiBluST-1
86DayBealP-1
Allison, Tom
90PitMetP-32
91ColMetPI-7
91ColMetPPI-5
92BinMetF-521
92BinMetS-51
93BinMetF-2339
94BinMetF-721
Allred, Beau
88CarLeaAS-23
88KinIndS-1
89BasAmeAPB-AA7
89BlaYNPRWL-56
89CanIndB-4
89CanIndP-1302
89CanIndS-1
89EasLeaAP-6
89Sta-154
90CMC-461
90ColSprSSC-9
90ColSprSSP-48
90Don-691
90FleUpd-88
90IndTeal-1
90OPC-419
90ProAAAF-229
90ScoRoo-70T
90Top-419
90TopDeb89-2
90TopTif-419
91Bow-80
91Fle-358
91IndFanC-1
91Lea-316
91Sco-338
91Sco100RS-56
91ScoRoo-22
91Ult-104
91UppDec-784
92ColSprSSF-762
92ColSprSSS-77
92SkyAAAF-34
93ChaKniF-554
94RicBraF-2857
Almada, Mel (Baldomero M.)
34BatR31-147
35DiaMatCS3T1-2
36GouWidPPR-B1
36NatChiFPR-1
36OveCanR-1
39PlaBal-43
40PlaBal-71
40SolHug-1
90DodTar-11
91ConTSN-234
92ConTSN-550
Almante, Tom
86ArkTraP-1
Almanza, Armando
96PeoChiB-4
Almanzar, Carlos
94MedHatBJF-3672
94MedHatBJSP-12
95KnoSmoF-31
96KnoSmoB-4
Almanzar, Richard
96BesAutS-3
96BesAutSA-2
96Bow-358
96LakTigB-5
97Bow-125
97BowInt-125
Almaraz, Johnny
88BilMusP-1825
89GreHorP-431
Almeida, Rafael D.
12T207-3
Almon, Bill (William F.)
74HawIslC-106
75HawIslC-11
76HawIslC-10
77PadSchC-1A
77PadSchC-1B
77PadSchC-12
77Top-490
78PadFamF-1
78Top-392
79Kel-53
79Top-616
80ExpPos-1
80OPC-225
80Top-436
81Fle-332
81Top-163
81TopTra-730
82Don-637
82Fle-335
82FleSta-185
82OPC-119
82Top-521
82TopSti-167
83Don-356
83Fle-228
83OPC-362
83Top-362
83TopTra-2T
84A'sMot-11
84Don-467
84Fle-436
84Nes792-241
84OPC-241
84Top-241
84TopSti-334
84TopTif-241
85Don-589
85Fle-414
85FleUpd-2
85Pir-1
85Top-273
85Top-607
85TopTif-273
85TopTif-607
85TopTifT-2T
85TopTra-2T
86Don-479
86Fle-602
86OPC-48
86Top-48
86TopSti-131
86TopTif-48
87Don-326
87Fle-601
87FleGlo-601
87OPC-159
87Top-447
87TopTif-447
87TopTra-1T
87TopTraT-1T
88Don-487
88PhiTas-2
88StaLinMe-1
88Top-787
88TopTif-787
91MetWIZ-6
Almond, Greg
93GleFalRC-3
93GleFalRF-4004
94MadHatC-1
94MadHatF-134
96PeoChiB-5
Almonte, Wady
96FreKeyB-2
97FlaShoWotF-4
97Fle-613
97FleTif-613
97Ult-510
97UltGolME-510
97UltPlaME-510
Aloi, Dave
74CedRapAT-7
75DubPacT-24
Aloma, Luis
51Bow-231
52Top-308
54Bow-134
54Top-57
83TopRep5-308
94TopArc1-57
94TopArc1G-57
Alomar, Rafael
61TacBan-1
61UniOil-T30
Alomar, Roberto
87TexLeaAF-8
87WicPilRD-4
88BlaYNPRWL-34
88Don-34
88DonBasB-42
88DonRoo-35
88FleUpd-122
88FleUpdG-122
88LasVegSC-20
88LasVegSP-231
88Lea-34
88PadSmo-2
88ScoRoo-105T
88ScoRooG-105T
88TopTra-4T
88TopTraT-4T
89BimBreD-12
89BlaYNPRWL-104
89Bow-258
89Bow-458
89BowTif-258
89BowTif-458
89ClaTraO-127
89Don-246
89DonBasB-21
89Fle-299
89Fle-630
89FleGlo-299
89FleGlo-630
89FleSup-1
89OPC-206
89PadCok-1
89PadMag-9
89PadMag-14
89PanSti-191
89RedFolSB-3
89Sco-232
89ScoHot1R-72
89ScoYouSI-28
89Spo-20
89Top-206
89Top-231
89TopBig-102
89TopGloS-19
89TopRoo-1
89TopSti-104
89TopTif-206
89TopTif-231
89ToyRoo-1
89TVSpoM-47
89UppDec-471
90Bow-221
90BowTif-221
90ClaBlu-61
90Don-111
90DonBesN-35
90Fle-149
90FleCan-149
90FleLeaL-1
90Lea-75
90OPC-517
90PadCok-1
90PadMag-10
90PanSti-349
90PubSti-43
90PubSti-607
90Sco-12
90Spo-93
90StaAloB-1
90StaAloB-3
90StaAloB-5
90StaAloB-7
90StaAloB-9
90StaAloB-11
90Top-517
90TopBig-9
90TopCoi-37
90TopGloS-27
90TopMag-85
90TopMinL-77
90TopSti-109
90TopStiB-4
90TopTif-517
90TopTVA-35
90UppDec-346
90UppDecS-3
90USPlaCA-4D
90VenSti-6
90VenSti-7
91BluJayFS-2
91BluJayFS-1
91BluJayS-13
91BluJayS-39
91Bow-9
91CadEllD-1
91Cla1-T94
91Cla2-T81
91ClaGam-113
91ColRobA-1
91ColRobA-2
91ColRobA-3
91ColRobA-4
91ColRobA-5
91ColRobA-6
91ColRobA-7
91ColRobA-8
91ColRobA-9
91ColRobA-10
91ColRobA-11
91ColRobA-12
91ColRobA-xx
91Don-12
91Don-682
91DonSupD-12
91Fle-523
91FleUpd-63
91Lea-267
91OPC-315
91OPCPre-1
91PanFreS-92
91PanSti-96
91RedFolS-3
91Sco-25
91Sco-887
91Sco100S-100
91ScoRoo-44T
91StaClu-304
91Stu-131
91SunSee-19
91Top-315
91TopDesS-315
91TopMic-315
91TopTif-315
91TopTra-2T
91TopTraT-2T
91TopTriH-A14
91Ult-358
91UppDec-80
91UppDec-335
91UppDec-763
91UppDecFE-83F
91USPlaCA-12H
92Bow-20
92Cla1-T4
92ClaGam-121
92ColAllG-3
92ColAllP-3
92ColPro-1A
92ColPro-1B
92Don-28
92Don-58
92DonMcD-G1
92Fle-323
92Fle-698
92FleCitTP-24
92Fre-12

92Hig5-116
92Lea-233
92LeaBlaG-233
92MooSna-13
92Mr.TurS-2
92MSABenSHD-3
92New-1
92OPC-225
92OPCPre-130
92PanSti-26
92PanSti-273
92PepDieM-15
92Pin-45
92Pin-306
92Pin-586
92PinTea2-48
92PinTeaP-5
92PosCan-13
92RevSup1-13
92RevSup1-14
92RevSup1-15
92Sco-15
92Sco100S-82
92ScoCokD-1
92ScoImpP-10
92ScoProaG-3
92ScoProP-4
92SevCoi-5
92SpoIllFK1-54
92SpoIllFK1-497
92StaClu-159
92StaCluD-5
92StaPro-1
92Stu-251
92StuPre-13
92Top-225
92TopGol-225
92TopGolW-225
92TopKid-90
92TopMcD-4
92TopMic-225
92TriPla-84
92Ult-143
92UltAllS-2
92UltAwaW-20
92UppDec-81
92UppDec-355
92UppDecF-11
92UppDecFG-11
92UppDecTMH-4
92UppDecWB-T11
93BluJayCP1-1
93BluJayCP1-4
93BluJayD-2
93BluJayD4-2
93BluJayDM-12
93BluJayDM-18A
93BluJayDM-18B
93BluJayDM-28
93BluJayFS-1
93Bow-338
93ClaGam-2
93ColAllG-1
93DiaMar-1
93DiaMarA-1
93DiaMarP-1
93Don-132
93Don-425
93DonDiaK-DK20
93DonEli-26
93DonEliD-20
93DonEliS-8
93DonLonBL-LL8
93DonMasotG-10
93DonMVP-6
93DonPre-22
93DonSpiotG-SG3
93Fin-88
93FinJum-88
93FinPro-88
93FinProR-88
93FinRef-88
93Fla-287
93Fle-330
93Fle-357
93FleAll-AL2
93FleAtl-1
93FleFruotL-1
93FlePro-A1
93FleTeaL-AL9
93FunPac-10
93FunPac-22
93FunPac-54
93FunPac-55
93FunPacA-AS4
93Hos-14
93HumDumC-22
93Kra-2
93Lea-245
93LeaGolA-R13
93LeaGolA-U4
93OPC-4
93OPCPreSP-3
93OPCPreSPF-3
93OPCWorC-1
93PacBeiA-7
93PacSpa-319
93PacSpaPI-7
93PanSti-27
93Pin-30
93PinCoo-29
93PinCooD-29
93Pos-22
93PosCan-5
93Sco-14
93Sco-511
93Sco-542
93ScoFra-14
93ScoGolDT-11
93Sel-8
93SelChaS-14
93SelStaL-39
93SelStaL-51
93SP-1
93StaClu-142
93StaClu-596
93StaCluFDI-142
93StaCluFDI-596
93StaCluM-19
93StaCluM-191
93StaCluMOP-142
93StaCluMOP-596
93Stu-4
93Top-50
93TOPBLAG-23
93TopFulS-5
93TopGol-50
93TopInaM-50
93TopMic-50
93TopMic-P50
93TopPreS-1
93Toy-13
93TriPla-2
93TriPla-200
93TriPlaA-13
93TriPlaP-2
93Ult-639
93UltAwaW-13
93UppDec-42
93UppDec-125
93UppDec-815
93UppDec-840
93UppDecCP-R1
93UppDecDG-4
93UppDecFA-A3
93UppDecFAJ-A3
93UppDecFH-55
93UppDecGold-42
93UppDecGold-125
93UppDecGold-815
93UppDecGold-840
93UppDecIC-WI4
93UppDecICJ-WI4
93UppDecOD-D2
93UppDecSH-HI1
93USPlaCA-2D
93USPlaCA-9H
94BluJayP-1
94BluJayUSPC-1D
94BluJayUSPC-7C
94BluJayUSPC-7S
94Bow-609
94BowBes-R7
94BowBesR-R7
94ChuHomS-11
94ChuHomSG-11
94ColC-33
94ColC-321
94ColC-331
94ColC-631
94ColChoGS-33
94ColChoGS-321
94ColChoGS-331
94ColChoGS-631
94ColChoSS-33
94ColChoSS-321
94ColChoSS-331
94ColChoSS-631
94ColChoT-1
94DenHol-2
94Don-6
94DonSpeE-6
94ExtBas-186
94Fin-205
94FinJum-205
94FinRef-205
94Fla-115
94FlaHotN-1
94Fle-324
94FleAllS-1
94FleSun-1
94FUnPac-12
94FUnPac-178
94FUnPac-201
94FUnPac-211
94FUnPac-217
94KinDis-20
94Lea-225
94LeaGolS-1
94LeaL-75
94LeaLimGA-3
94LeaPro-1
94LeaSli-5
94OPC-96
94OPCAllR-21
94OPCJumA-21
94OPCWorC-6
94Pac-632
94PacAll-17
94PacSilP-5
94PanSti-134
94Pin-287
94PinArtP-287
94PinMusC-287
94PinRunC-RC6
94PinTheN-8
94PinTri-TR16
94Pos-18
94PosCan-3
94PosCanG-3
94ProMag-136
94RedFolMI-1
94Sco-43
94ScoGolR-43
94ScoGolS-42
94Sel-229
94SP-39
94SPDieC-39
94SPHol-1
94SPHolDC-1
94Spo-31
94Spo-177
94SpoFanA-AS2
94SPPre-ER1
94StaClu-10
94StaClu-110
94StaCluFDI-10
94StaCluFDI-110
94StaCluGR-10
94StaCluGR-110
94StaCluMO-33
94StaCluMOP-10
94StaCluMOP-110
94StaCluT-153
94StaCluTF-1
94StaCluTFDI-153
94Stu-24
94Top-385
94Top-675
94TopBlaG-1
94TopGol-385
94TopGol-675
94TopSpa-385
94TopSpa-675
94TopSupS-1
94TriPla-31
94TriPlaM-5
94Ult-434
94UltAllS-3
94UltAwaW-3
94UltHitM-1
94UltOnBL-1
94UppDec-35
94UppDec-455
94UppDecAJ-16
94UppDecAJG-16
94UppDecDC-E1
94UppDecED-35
94UppDecED-455
94UppDecNG-1
94UppDecNGED-1
94USPlaCA-9D
94USPlaCA-12H
95Baz-81
95BazRedH-RH16
95BluJayP-1
95BluJayUSPC-1H
95BluJayUSPC-5C
95Bow-368
95BowBes-R57
95BowBesR-R57
95ClaPhoC-57
95ColCho-140
95ColChoGS-140
95ColChoSE-51
95ColChoSEGS-51
95ColChoSESS-51
95ColChoSS-140
95D3-4
95DenHol-1
95Don-49
95DonAll-AL4
95DonDom-4
95DonPreP-49
95DonTopotO-171
95Emb-91
95EmbGolI-91
95Emo-90
95Fin-137
95FinRef-137
95Fla-94
95FlaHotG-1
95Fle-87
95FleAllF-3
95FleAllS-3
95FleUpdSL-1
95KinDis-1
95Kra-1
95Lea-256
95LeaGreG-2
95LeaLim-4
95LeaLimG-14
95LeaLimIBP-17
95Pac-435
95PacGolCDC-19
95PacLatD-1
95PacPri-138
95PanSti-46
95Pin-222
95PinArtP-222
95PinFan-14
95PinMusC-222
95PinPin-8
95PinPinR-8
95PinRedH-RH23
95PinTeaP-TP4
95PinUps-US2
95PinWhiH-WH23
95Pos-5
95PosCan-2
95RedFol-36
95Sco-2
95Sco-553
95ScoDreT-DG2
95ScoGolR-2
95ScoGolR-553
95ScoHaloG-HG3
95ScoPlaTS-2
95ScoPlaTS-553
95ScoRul-SR8
95ScoRulJ-SR8
95ScoSam-2
95Sel-34
95SelArtP-34
95SelCer-75
95SelCerMG-75
95SelCerS-75
95SelSam-34
95SP-201
95SPCha-100
95SPCha-196
95SPChaCP-CP6
95SPChaCPDC-CP6
95SPChaDC-100
95SPChaDC-196
95Spo-128
95SpoArtP-128
95SpoDouT-3
95SpoSam-128
95SPSil-201
95SPSpeF-23
95StaClu-70
95StaCluFDI-70
95StaCluMOP-70
95StaCluMOP-SS1
95StaCluSS-SS1
95StaCluSTWS-70
95StaCluVR-43
95Stu-17
95StuGolS-17
95StuPlaS-17
95Sum-50
95SumNthD-50
95Top-438
95TopCyb-234
95UC3-78
95UC3ArtP-78
95Ult-116
95UltAwaW-3
95UltAwaWGM-3
95UltGolM-116
95UppDec-40
95UppDecED-40
95UppDecEDG-40
95UppDecPAW-H23
95UppDecPAWE-H23
95UppDecPC-MLB6
95UppDecSE-197
95UppDecSEG-197
95UppDecSoaD-SD6
95Zen-89
96Baz-35
96Bow-45
96BowBes-65
96BowBesAR-65
96BowBesMI-2
96BowBesMIAR-2
96BowBesMIR-2
96BowBesR-65
96Cir-1
96CirBos-1
96CirRav-1
96ColCho-339
96ColCho-463
96ColChoGS-339
96ColChoGS-463
96ColChoSS-339
96ColChoSS-463
96Don-103
96DonDiaK-6
96DonPreP-103
96EmoXL-1
96EmoXLD-1
96Fin-B228
96Fin-G197
96FinRef-B228
96FinRef-G197
96Fla-1
96FlaHotG-1
96Fle-267
96FleOri-1
96FleTif-267
96FleUpd-U1
96FleUpdH-1
96FleUpdSL-1
96FleUpdTC-U1
96Kin-20
96Lea-155
96LeaLim-50
96LeaLimG-50
96LeaPre-61
96LeaPreP-61
96LeaPrePB-155
96LeaPrePG-155
96LeaPrePS-155
96LeaPreSG-12
96LeaPreSte-12
96LeaSig-48
96LeaSigA-5
96LeaSigAG-5
96LeaSigAS-5
96LeaSigPPG-48
96LeaSigPPP-48
96MetUni-1
96MetUniP-1
96MLBPin-1
96Pac-450
96PacBaeS-5
96PacCraC-CC1
96PacEstL-EL1
96PacGolCD-DC1
96PacHom-HP10
96PacPri-P23
96PacPriG-P23
96PacPriRHS-RH1
96PanSti-159
96Pin-242
96PinAfi-97
96PinAfi-160
96PinAfiAP-97

96PinAfiAP-160
96PinAfiFPP-97
96PinArtP-142
96PinFoil-242
96PinSta-142
96Sco-57
96Sco-365
96ScoDugC-A50
96ScoDugC-B90
96ScoDugCAP-A50
96ScoDugCAP-B90
96ScoRef-8
96Sel-122
96SelArtP-122
96SelCer-99
96SelCerAP-99
96SelCerCB-99
96SelCerCR-99
96SelCerMB-99
96SelCerMG-99
96SelCerMR-99
96SP-29
96Spo-73
96SpoArtP-73
96SpoDouT-2
96SPSpeFX-24
96SPSpeFXDC-24
96SPx-6
96SPxBoufG-7
96SPxGol-6
96StaClu-176
96StaCluEPB-176
96StaCluEPG-176
96StaCluEPS-176
96StaCluMOP-176
95StaCluVRMC-43
96Stu-29
96StuPrePB-29
96StuPrePG-29
96StuPrePS-29
96Sum-146
96SumAbo&B-146
96SumArtP-146
96SumFoi-146
96SumPos-2
96TeaOut-1
96TeaOut-C92
96Top-289
96TopChr-115
96TopChrR-115
96TopGal-78
96TopGalPPI-78
96TopLas-33
96TopPro-AL1
96Ult-142
96Ult-301
96Ult-573
96UltGolM-142
96UltGolM-301
96UltGolM-573
96UltPriL-3
96UltPriLGM-3
96UltRaw-1
96UltRawGM-1
96UppDec-275
96UppDec-370
96UppDecA-1
96UppDecDD-DD7
96UppDecDDG-DD7
96UppDecDDS-DD7
96UppDecHC-HC3
96UppDecPRE-R21
96UppDecPreR-R21
96Zen-18
96Zen-141
96ZenArtP-18
96ZenArtP-141
96ZenDiaC-11
96ZenDiaCP-11
96ZenMoz-8
96ZenZ-11
97BluJayS-46
97BluJayS-48
97Bow-35
97BowBes-59
97BowBesAR-59
97BowBesR-59
97BowChr-30
97BowChrI-30
97BowChrIR-30
97BowChrR-30
97BowInt-35
97Cir-163
97CirRav-163
97ColCho-39
97ColCho-219
97ColChoAC-11
97ColChoTBS-6
97ColChoTBSWH-6
97Don-37
97Don-414
97DonArmaD-14
97DonEli-20
97DonEliGS-20
97DonLim-21
97DonLim-62
97DonLim-145
97DonLimFotG-64
97DonLimLE-21
97DonLimLE-62
97DonLimLE-145
97DonPre-106
97DonPreCttC-106
97DonPreP-37
97DonPreP-414
97DonPrePGold-37
97DonPrePGold-414
97DonPreXP-5A
97DonTea-32
97DonTeaSPE-32
97Fin-111
97Fin-205
97FinEmb-111
97FinEmbR-111
97FinRef-111
97FinRef-205
97FlaSho-A58
97FlaSho-B58
97FlaSho-C58
97FlaShoHG-1
97FlaShoLC-58
97FlaShoLC-B58
97FlaShoLC-C58
97FlaShoLCM-A58
97FlaShoLCM-B58
97FlaShoLCM-C58
97Fle-1
97Fle-696
97FleTif-1
97FleTif-696
97Lea-14
97Lea-393
97LeaFraM-14
97LeaFraM-393
97LeaFraMDC-14
97LeaFraMDC-393
97LeaGolS-33
97MetUni-1
97MetUniMF-1
97MetUniML-1
97NewPin-102
97NewPinAP-102
97NewPinMC-102
97NewPinPP-102
97Pac-17
97PacCar-1
97PacCarM-1
97PacCraC-1
97PacFirD-1
97PacGolCD-1
97PacLatotML-2
97PacLigB-17
97PacPri-7
97PacPriGA-GA1
97PacPriGotD-GD9
97PacPriLB-7
97PacPriP-7
97PacPriSL-SL1C
97PacSIl-17
97PinCer-95
97PinCerLI-16
97PinCerMBlu-95
97PinCerMG-95
97PinCerMR-95
97PinCerR-95
97PinIns-75
97PinInsCE-75
97PinInsDD-5
97PinInsDE-75
97PinPasttM-9
97PinTotCPB-95
97PinTotCPG-95
97PinTotCPR-95
97PinX-P-112
97PinX-PMoS-112
97ProMag-43
97ProMagML-43
97Sco-67
97Sco-542
97ScoFra-9
97ScoFraG-9
97ScoHeaotO-11
97ScoHobR-542
97ScoOri-3
97ScoOriPl-3
97ScoOriPr-3
97ScoPreS-67
97ScoResC-542
97ScoShoS-67
97ScoShoS-542
97ScoShoSAP-67
97ScoShoSAP-542
97ScoSteS-11
97Sel-59
97SelArtP-59
97SelRegG-59
97SkyE-X-4
97SkyE-XC-4
97SkyE-XEC-4
97SkyE-XHoN-19
97SP-29
97SpoIll-55
97SpoIllEE-55
97SpoIllGS-6
97SPSpeF-26
97SPSpxF-8
97SPSPxFA-8
97SPx-9
97SPxBro-9
97SPxGraF-9
97SPxSil-9
97SPxSte-9
97StaClu-38
97StaClu-240
97StaCluMat-240
97StaCluMOP-38
97StaCluMOP-240
97StaCluMOP-PL12
97StaCluPL-PL12
97Stu-95
97StuPrePG-95
97StuPrePS-95
97Top-152
97TopChr-58
97TopChrR-58
97TopGal-47
97TopGalPPI-47
97TopSta-31
97TopSta1AS-AS12
97TopStaAM-31
97TopSweS-SS1
97Ult-1
97UltDouT-1
97UltFamGam-15
97UltFieC-1
97UltGolME-1
97UltHitM-14
97UltLeaS-8
97UltPlaME-1
97UltTop3-19
97UltTop3GM-19
97UppDec-19
97UppDec-142
97UppDec-201
97UppDec-249
97UppDec-383
97UppDecAG-AG2
97UppDecU-33
97Zen-5

Alomar, Sandy (Conde Santos) Sr.

65OPC-82
65Top-82
66Top-428
67Top-561
68Top-541
69AngJacitB-1
69Top-283
69TopSta-151
69TopTeaP-11
69WhiSoxTI-1
70DayDaiNM-110
70MLBOffS-169
70OPC-29
70Top-29
71AngJacitB-1
71MLBOffS-337
71OPC-745
71Top-745
71TopCoi-28
72MilBra-11
72OPC-253
72Top-253
73OPC-123
73Top-123
74OPC-347
74Top-347
74TopSta-141
75OPC-266
75Top-266
75YanSSP-19
76OPC-629
76SSP-441
76Top-629
77Top-54
78RanBurK-15
78SSP270-86
78Top-533
79Top-144
86AngGreT-2
88PadSmo-3
89Bow-258
89BowTif-258
89PadMag-9
90PadMag-22
91MetWIZ-7
92Pin-586
92YanWIZ7-4
93RanKee-50

Alomar, Sandy (Santos) Jr.

86BeaGolGP-1
87TexLeaAF-10
87WicPilRD-5
88BlaYNPRWL-33
88LasVegSC-22
88LasVegSP-236
88TriAAAP-20
88TriAAC-31
89BlaYNPRWL-102
89BlaYNPRWL-105
89BlaYNPRWLU-45
89Bow-454
89BowTif-454
89ClaLigB-79
89Don-28
89DonRoo-21
89Fle-300
89Fle-630
89FleGlo-300
89FleGlo-630
89LasVegSC-11
89LasVegSP-7
89PadMag-2
89PadMag-9
89PanSti-192
89Sco-630
89ScoYouS2-1
89Spo-223
89SpoIllFKI-248
89Sta-125
89Top-648
89TopTif-648
89TriA AAC-31
89TriAAP-AAA6
89UppDec-5
90Bow-337
90BowTif-337
90ClaUpd-T3
90ClaYel-T76
90Don-30
90DonBesA-97
90DonLeaS-40
90DonRoo-1
90Fle-150
90FleCan-150
90FleUpd-89
90Hot50RS-2
90IndTeal-2
90Lea-232
90OPC-353
90Sco-577
90ScoMcD-2
90ScoRoo-18T
90StaAloB-1
90StaAloB-2
90StaAloB-4
90StaAloB-6
90StaAloB-8
90StaAloB-10
90StaSanA-1
90StaSanA-2
90StaSanA-3
90StaSanA-4
90StaSanA-5
90StaSanA-6
90StaSanA-7
90StaSanA-8
90StaSanA-9
90StaSanA-10
90StaSanA-11
90Top-353
90TopBig-265
90TopMag-20
90TopTif-353
90TopTra-2T
90TopTraT-2T
90TriAAAC-31
90UppDec-655
90UppDec-756
90USPlaCA-2S
90WinDis-1
91Baz-20
91Bow-57
91Cla1-T39
91Cla2-T68
91ClaGam-194
91Don-13
91Don-51
91Don-489
91Don-693
91DonSupD-13
91Fle-359
91IndFanC-2
91JimDea-8
91KinDis-17
91Lea-189
91Lea-528
91LeaPre-17
91MajLeaCP-18
91MooSna-10
91OPC-165
91OPCPre-2
91PanCanT1-109
91PanFreS-166
91PanFreS-215
91PanSti-172
91PetSta-9
91Pos-6
91PosCan-23
91RedFolS-113
91Sco-400
91Sco-694
91Sco-793
91Sco-851
91Sco-879
91Sco100RS-1
91ScoHotR-6
91StaClu-61
91StaCluCM-1
91StaPinB-2
91Stu-41
91SunSee-21
91Top-165
91TopCraJI-5
91TopDesS-165
91TopGaloC-1
91TopGloA-9
91TopMic-165
91TopRoo-1
91TopSta-2
91TopTif-165
91TopTriH-A5
91ToyRoo-1
91Ult-105
91UppDec-46
91UppDec-144
91UppDecFE-81F
91USPlaCA-11D
91Woo-6
92Bow-140
92Cla2-T50
92ClaGam-46
92ColAllG-13
92ColAllP-13
92Don-29
92Don-203
92DonCraJ1-10
92DonMcD-11
92Fle-103
92Fle-698
92Fre-10
92Hig5-41
92HitTheBB-2
92IndFanC-1
92Lea-9
92Mr.TurS-3
92OPC-420
92OPCPre-164
92PanSti-44
92PanSti-271

92PepDieM-10
92Pin-436
92PinTea2-17
92PosCan-11
92RevSup1-13
92RevSup1-14
92RevSup1-15
92Sco-510
92Sco100S-49
92ScoCokD-2
92ScoImpP-40
92ScoProaG-1
92SevCoi-6
92StaClu-740
92StaCluD-6
92StaCluNC-740
92Stu-161
92Top-420
92TopGol-420
92TopGolW-420
92TopKid-71
92TopMic-420
92TriPla-227
92Ult-45
92UppDec-81
92UppDec-156
92UppDecF-12
92UppDecFG-12
93Bow-93
93DiaMar-2
93Don-39
93Fin-26
93FinRef-26
93Fle-212
93FunPac-106
93HumDumC-5
93IndWUA-1
93KinDis-18
93Kra-3
93Lea-83
93OPC-12
93PacBeiA-5
93PacBeiA-6
93PacBeiA-7
93PacSpa-91
93PacSpaGE-11
93PacSpaPl-8
93PanSti-47
93Pin-211
93Sco-116
93Sel-26
93SelSam-26
93SP-118
93StaClu-400
93StaCluFDI-400
93StaCluM-123
93StaCluMMP-1
93StaCluMOP-400
93Stu-13
93Top-85
93TopGol-85
93TopInaM-85
93TopMic-85
93TriPla-251
93Ult-182
93UppDec-255
93UppDecGold-255
94Bow-139
94ColC-34
94ColChoGS-34
94ColChoSS-34
94Don-65
94ExtBas-55
94Fin-251
94FinRef-251
94Fla-282
94Fle-98
94FUnPac-93
94Lea-223
94OPC-201
94Pac-164
94PanSti-53
94Pin-44
94PinArtP-44
94PinMusC-44
94ProMag-36
94Sco-445
94ScoGolR-445
94Sel-366
94StaClu-144
94StaCluFDI-144
94StaCluGR-144
94StaCluMOP-144
94Stu-90
94Top-273
94TopGol-273
94TopSpa-273
94TriPla-111
94Ult-40
94UppDec-415
94UppDecED-415
95Baz-11
95ColCho-273
95ColChoGS-273
95ColChoSS-273
95Don-3
95DonPreP-3
95DonTopotO-56
95Emb-105
95EmbGolI-105
95Fin-61
95FinRef-61
95Fla-249
95Fle-130
95Lea-121
95Pac-115
95PanSti-26
95Pin-39
95PinArtP-39
95PinMusC-39
95Sco-519
95ScoGolR-519
95ScoPlaTS-519
95StaClu-87
95StaClu-217
95StaCluFDI-87
95StaCluFDI-217
95StaCluMOP-87
95StaCluMOP-217
95StaCluSTWS-87
95StaCluSTWS-217
95StaCluVR-53
95Top-522
95TopCyb-308
95TopPre-PP4
95Ult-35
95UltGolM-35
95UppDec-92
95UppDecED-92
95UppDecEDG-92
96Cir-31
96CirRav-31
96Don-41
96DonPreP-41
96EmoXL-44
96Fla-62
96Fle-80
96FleInd-1
96FleTif-80
96Lea-98
96LeaPrePB-98
96LeaPrePG-98
96LeaPrePS-98
96MetUni-42
96MetUniP-42
96Pac-295
96PinChrBC-13
96SchDis-19
96Sco-103
96StaClu-373
96StaCluEPB-373
96StaCluEPG-373
96StaCluEPS-373
96StaCluMOP-373
95StaCluVRMC-53
96Top-294
96Ult-340
96UltGolM-340
96UppDec-313
96UppDecA-2
97Bow-281
97BowChr-94
97BowChrI-94
97BowChrIR-94
97BowChrR-94
97BowInt-281
97Cir-257
97CirRav-257
97ColCho-93
97Don-314
97DonLim-163
97DonLimLE-163
97DonPreP-314
97DonPrePGold-314
97DonTea-87
97DonTeaSPE-87
97Fin-113
97FinEmb-113
97FinEmbR-113
97FinRef-113
97FlaSho-A115
97FlaSho-B115
97FlaSho-C115
97FlaShoLC-115
97FlaShoLC-B115
97FlaShoLC-C115
97FlaShoLCM-A115
97FlaShoLCM-B115
97FlaShoLCM-C115
97Fle-74
97FleTif-74
97Lea-259
97LeaFraM-259
97LeaFraMDC-259
97NewPin-114
97NewPinAP-114
97NewPinMC-114
97NewPinPP-114
97Pac-66
97PacLigB-66
97PacPri-24
97PacPriLB-24
97PacPriP-24
97PacSil-66
97PinCer-12
97PinCerMBlu-12
97PinCerMG-12
97PinCerMR-12
97PinCerR-12
97PinTotCPB-12
97PinTotCPG-12
97PinTotCPR-12
97PinX-PSfF-4
97PinX-PSfFU-4
97Sco-173
97ScoInd-9
97ScoIndPl-9
97ScoIndPr-9
97ScoIndU-9
97ScoIndUTC-9
97ScoPreS-173
97ScoShoS-173
97ScoShoSAP-173
97SpoIll-34
97SpoIll-56
97SpoIllEE-34
97SpoIllEE-56
97StaClu-101
97StaCluMOP-101
97Top-245
97TopSta-72
97TopSta1AS-AS20
97TopStaAM-72
97TopStaASGM-ASM10
97Ult-45
97UltGolME-45
97UltPlaME-45
97UppDec-343

Alongi, Doug
93GenCubC-2
93GenCubF-3188

Alonso, Julio
77EvaTriT-2

Alonzo, Ray
83MadMusF-6

Alonzo, Steven
94BurBeeC-28
94BurBeeF-1098

Alou, Felipe Rojas
59Top-102
59TopVen-102
60Lea-6
60Top-287
61GiaJayP-1
61Top-565
62AmeTraS-52A
62AmeTraS-52B
62AmeTraS-52C
62AmeTraS-52D
62GiaJayP-1
62Jel-133
62Pos-133
62PosCan-133
62SalPlaC-130
62ShiPlaC-130
62Top-133
62TopStaI-193
62TopVen-133
63GiaJayP-1
63Jel-107
63Pos-107
63Top-270
64Top-65
64TopCoi-11
64TopSta-62
64TopVen-65
65Top-383
66Kah-2
66OPC-96
66Top-96
66TopVen-96
67CokCapB-12
67DexPre-8
67Kah-3
67OPCPapI-30
67Top-240
67Top-530
67TopPos-30
67TopVen-281
68AtlOilPBCC-3
68CokCapB-12
68DexPre-5
68Kah-B4
68OPC-55
68Top-55
68TopVen-55
69MilBra-10
69MLBOffS-110
69MLBPin-32
69OPC-2
69Top-2
69Top-300
69TopDec-17
69TopDecI-3
69TopSta-2
69TopSup-35
69TopTeaP-2
69TraSta-51
70DayDaiNM-65
70MLBOffS-253
70OPC-434
70Top-434
71Kel-7
71MLBOffS-505
71OPC-495
71Top-495
71TopCoi-8
71YanCliDP-9
72MilBra-12
72OPC-263
72Top-263
73LinPor-127
73OPC-650
73SyrChiTI-1
73Top-650
74OPC-485
74Top-485
74TopTra-485T
75SSP42-42
78AtlCon-3
78MemChiBC-1
78TCM60I-74
79ExpPos-1
80ExpPos-2
82Don-650
82WicAerTI-2
83WicAerDS-2
84ExpPos-1
84ExpStu-6
84ExpStu-38
84GiaMot-19
85DomLeaS-145
85IndIndTI-2
86WesPalBEP-1
88FloStaLAS-2
88PacLegI-58
88WesPalBES-2
89WesPalBES-27
90FloStaLAS-23
90WesPalBES-29
91WesPalBEC-1
91WesPalBEP-1244
92ExpDonD-15B
92ExpPos-1
92TopTra-3T
92TopTraG-3T
92YanWIZ7-5
93Bow-701
93ExpDonM-31
93ExpDonM-AU0
93ExpPosN-1
93Top-508
93TopGol-508
93TopInaM-508
93TopMic-508
94BreMilB-96
94TopSpa-L1
96ExpBoo-1
96ExpDis-1

Alou, Jesus M.R.
64Top-47
64TopVen-47
65Top-545
66Top-242
66TopRubI-4
66TopVen-242
67CokCapG-18
67DexPre-9
67Top-332
67TopVen-330
68DexPre-6
68Top-452
69MilBra-11
69MLBOffS-136
69OPC-22
69Top-22
69TopSta-51
70DayDaiNM-141
70MLBOffS-37
70OPC-248
70Top-248
71AstCok-1
71MLBOffS-73
71OPC-337
71Top-337
72MilBra-13
72Top-716
73OPC-93
73Top-93
74OPC-654
74Top-654A
74Top-654B
75MetSSP-6
75OPC-253
75SSP42-42
75Top-253
76OPC-468
76SSP-538
76Top-468
78AstBurK-22
79Top-107
80Top-593
81TCM60I-406
85DomLeaS-143
87AstShoSTw-1
87AstShoSTw-26
91MetWIZ-8

Alou, Jose
87BurExpP-1076
88WesPalBES-3
89WesPalBES-1

Alou, Matty (Mateo Rojas)
60TacBan-1
61Top-327
62Top-413
63SalMetC-25
63Top-128
64Top-204
64TopVen-204
65Top-318
66OPC-94
66PirEasH-18
66Top-94
66TopVen-94
67Baz-47
67CokCapPi-17
67DexPre-10
67Kah-4A
67Kah-4B
67OPC-10
67OPCPapI-29
67PirTeal-2
67Top-10
67Top-240
67TopPirS-2
67TopPirS-28
67TopPos-29
67TopVen-298
68Baz-2
68Kah-B5
68OPC-1
68PirKDK-18
68PirTeal-2
68Top-1
68Top-270
68TopGamI-1
68TopVen-1
68TopVen-270
69Kah-B2
69MilBra-12

69MLBOffS-182
69OPC-2
69PirGre-2
69Top-2
69Top-490
69TopDecI-4
69TopSta-82
69TopSup-56
69TopTeaP-16
69TraSta-58
70DayDaiNM-111
70Kel-28
70MLBOffS-98
70OPC-30
70OPC-460
70Top-30
70Top-460
71CarTeaI-1
71Kel-53
71MLBOffS-265
71OPC-720
71Top-720
71TopCoi-47
72MilBra-14
72OPC-395
72Top-395
73LinPor-128
73NewYorN-19
73OPC-132
73SyrChiTI-2
73Top-132
74OPC-430
74PadDea-1
74PadMcDD-1
74Top-430
75SSP42-42
77PadSchC-2
78TCM60I-75
85DomLeaS-144
86SpoDesJM-15
88PacLegI-37
91SweBasG-2
92YanWIZ7-6
93TedWil-74
93UppDecAH-4
Alou, Moises
86WatPirP-2
87WatPirP-27
88AugPirP-360
89SalBucS-1
89Sta-93
90Bow-178
90BowTif-178
90BufBisTI-1
90CMC-790
90Fle-650
90FleCan-650
90HarSenP-1204
90HarSenS-2
90ProAaA-29
90Sco-592
91Cla1-T60
91Don-38
91OPC-526
91OPCPre-3
91Sco-813
91StaClu-31
91Stu-191
91Top-526A
91Top-526B
91TopDeb90-5
91TopDesS-526
91TopMic-526
91TopTif-526
91UppDec-665
92Cla2-T36
92DonRooP-BC1
92ExpPos-2
92FleUpd-95
92JimDeaRS-9
92Lea-426
92OPC-401
92Pin-572
92PinRoo-16
92Sco100RS-9
92SpoIllFK1-298
92StaClu-519
92TopTra-4T
92TopTraG-4T
92Ult-511
93Bow-452
93Bow-701
93ClaGam-3
93DiaMar-3
93Don-510
93ExpColP7-1
93ExpDonM-1
93ExpPosN-2
93Fin-189
93FinRef-189
93Fla-78
93Fle-70
93FleRooS-RSB1
93HumDumC-39
93Lea-147
93LimRocDWB-112
93LinVenB-303
93LinVenB-321
93OPC-10
93PacBeiA-26
93PacJugC-19
93PacSpa-180
93PacSpaGE-1
93PanSti-232
93Pin-92
93Sco-187
93Sel-272
93SelChaR-2
93SP-100
93StaClu-239
93StaCluFDI-239
93StaCluMOP-239
93Stu-11
93Top-123
93TopGol-123
93TopInaM-123
93TopMic-123
93Toy-96
93ToyMasP-1
93TriPla-244
93Ult-61
93UppDec-297
93UppDecGold-297
93USPlaCR-11S
94Bow-116
94BowBes-R52
94BowBesR-R52
94ColC-35
94ColChoGS-35
94ColChoSS-35
94Don-3
94DonDiaK-DK23
94DonMVP-8
94DonSpeE-3
94ExtBas-299
94Fin-121
94FinPre-121P
94FinRef-121
94Fla-400
94Fle-531
94Lea-252
94LeaL-123
94OPC-266
94Pac-372
94PanSti-206
94Pin-7
94PinArtP-7
94PinMusC-7
94PinSam-7
94PosCan-9
94PosCanG-9
94ProMag-81
94Sco-90
94ScoGolR-90
94Sel-159
94SP-82
94SPDieC-82
94Spo-87
94StaClu-141
94StaCluFDI-141
94StaCluGR-141
94StaCluMOP-141
94Stu-74
94Top-50
94TopGol-50
94TopSpa-50
94TriPla-91
94Ult-222
94UppDec-351
94UppDecED-351
95Baz-70
95Bow-285
95BowBes-R4
95BowBesR-R4
95ColCho-250
95ColChoGS-250
95ColChoSE-104
95ColChoSEGS-104
95ColChoSESS-104
95ColChoSS-250
95D3-13
95DenHol-2
95Don-408
95DonDiaK-DK10
95DonDom-7
95DonPreP-408
95DonTopotO-276
95Emb-24
95EmbGolI-24
95Emo-148
95Fin-128
95FinRef-128
95Fla-160
95Fle-344
95FleAllS-16
95FleTeaL-22
95FleUpdSS-1
95Kra-16
95Lea-288
95Lea300C-4
95LeaLim-158
95Pac-260
95PacLatD-2
95PacPri-84
95PanSti-78
95Pin-321
95PinArtP-321
95PinMusC-321
95PinUps-US23
95PosCan-5
95Sco-19
95Sco-572
95ScoGolR-19
95ScoGolR-572
95ScoHaloG-HG12
95ScoPlaTS-19
95ScoPlaTS-572
95Sel-78
95SelArtP-78
95SelCer-36
95SelCerMG-36
95SP-78
95SPCha-65
95SPChaDC-65
95Spo-115
95SpoArtP-115
95SPSil-78
95StaClu-295
95StaClu-503
95StaCluCC-CC21
95StaCluCT-16
95StaCluMO-1
95StaCluMOP-295
95StaCluMOP-503
95StaCluMOP-CC21
95StaCluSTWS-295
95StaCluSTWS-503
95StaCluVR-153
95Stu-35
95StuGolS-35
95Sum-37
95SumNthD-37
95TomPiz-19
95Top-584
95TopCyb-357
95TopFin-8
95TopLeaL-LL5
95UC3-36
95UC3ArtP-36
95Ult-186
95UltAllS-1
95UltAllSGM-1
95UltAwaW-25
95UltAwaWGM-25
95UltGolM-186
95UltRisS-1
95UltRisSGM-1
95UppDec-79
95UppDecED-79
95UppDecEDG-79
95UppDecPLL-R57
95UppDecPLLE-R57
95UppDecSE-138
95UppDecSEG-138
95USPlaCMLA-6D
95Zen-78
96Baz-52
96Bow-7
96BowBes-64
96BowBesAR-64
96BowBesR-64
96Cir-147
96CirAcc-22
96CirBos-40
96CirRav-147
96ColCho-209
96ColCho-400
96ColChoGS-209
96ColChoGS-400
96ColChoSS-209
96ColChoSS-400
96DenHol-24
96Don-283
96DonPreP-283
96EmoXL-218
96ExpDis-2
96ExpDis-3
96Fin-B157
96Fin-B250
96FinRef-B157
96FinRef-B250
96Fla-301
96Fle-450
96FleTif-450
96Lea-182
96LeaPre-34
96LeaPreP-34
96LeaPrePB-182
96LeaPrePG-182
96LeaPrePS-182
96LeaPreSG-74
96LeaPreSte-74
96LeaSigA-6
96LeaSigAG-6
96LeaSigAS-6
96MetUni-188
96MetUniP-188
96Pac-133
96PacEstL-EL2
96PacPri-P40
96PacPriG-P40
96PanSti-17
96Pin-206
96PinAfi-87
96PinAfiAP-87
96PinAfiFPP-87
96PinArtP-106
96PinFan-26
96PinFoil-206
96PinSta-106
96Sco-75
96ScoDugC-A61
96ScoDugCAP-A61
96Sel-49
96SelArtP-49
96SelCer-65
96SelCerAP-65
96SelCerCB-65
96SelCerCR-65
96SelCerMB-65
96SelCerMG-65
96SelCerMR-65
96SelTeaN-24
96SP-121
96Spo-67
96SpoArtP-67
96StaClu-138
96StaCluEPB-138
96StaCluEPG-138
96StaCluEPS-138
96StaCluMOP-138
96StaCluVRMC-153
96Stu-101
96StuPrePB-101
96StuPrePG-101
96StuPrePS-101
96Sum-73
96SumAbo&B-73
96SumArtP-73
96SumFoi-73
96Top-309
96TopChr-123
96TopChrR-123
96TopGal-6
96TopGalPPI-6
96TopLas-1
96Ult-228
96UltGolM-228
96UppDec-395
96Zen-79
96ZenArtP-79
96ZenMoz-17
97Bow-235
97BowBes-13
97BowBesAR-13
97BowBesR-13
97BowChr-62
97BowChrI-62
97BowChrIR-62
97BowChrR-62
97BowInt-235
97Cir-126
97CirRav-126
97ColCho-341
97Don-66
97Don-279
97DonEli-62
97DonEliGS-62
97DonLim-3
97DonLim-162
97DonLimLE-3
97DonLimLE-162
97DonPre-113
97DonPreCttC-113
97DonPreP-66
97DonPreP-279
97DonPrePGold-66
97DonPrePGold-279
97Fin-297
97FinEmb-297
97FinEmbR-297
97FinRef-297
97FlaSho-A174
97FlaSho-B174
97FlaSho-C174
97FlaShoLC-174
97FlaShoLC-B174
97FlaShoLC-C174
97FlaShoLCM-A174
97FlaShoLCM-B174
97FlaShoLCM-C174
97Fle-374
97Fle-647
97FleTif-374
97FleTif-647
97Lea-219
97LeaFraM-219
97LeaFraMDC-219
97MetUni-152
97NewPin-149
97NewPinAP-149
97NewPinMC-149
97NewPinPP-149
97Pac-341
97PacLigB-341
97PacPri-117
97PacPriGotD-GD164
97PacPriLB-117
97PacPriP-117
97PacSil-341
97Pin-113
97PinArtP-113
97PinCer-71
97PinCerMBlu-71
97PinCerMG-71
97PinCerMR-71
97PinCerR-71
97PinIns-6
97PinInsCE-6
97PinInsDE-6
97PinMusC-113
97PinTotCPB-71
97PinTotCPG-71
97PinTotCPR-71
97PinX-P-58
97PinX-PMoS-58
97PinX-PSfF-35
97PinX-PSfFU-35
97Sco-47
97Sco-358
97ScoHobR-358
97ScoPreS-47
97ScoResC-358
97ScoShoS-47
97ScoShoS-358
97ScoShoSAP-47
97ScoShoSAP-358
97SkyE-X-70
97SkyE-XC-70
97SkyE-XEC-70
97SP-76
97SpoIll-84
97SpoIllEE-84
97StaClu-80
97StaCluMOP-80
97Stu-116
97StuPrePG-116
97StuPrePS-116
97Top-460
97TopChr-161

97TopChrR-161
97TopGal-61
97TopGalPPI-61
97TopSta-14
97TopStaAM-14
97TopStaASGM-ASM7
97Ult-225
97Ult-347
97UltDouT-16
97UltGolME-225
97UltGolME-347
97UltPlaME-225
97UltPlaME-347
97UppDec-534

Alperman, Whitey (Charles A.)
08RosComP-93
09RamT20-1
09T206-4
11SpoLifCW-3
12ColRedB-7
12ColTinT-7
12ImpTobC-7
90DodTar-890

Alpert, George
81BatTroT-25
82WatIndF-27
82WatIndT-20

Alphonzo, Edgar
95RocRedWTI-6

Alstead, Jason
91FreKeyC-21
91FreKeyP-2375
92ClaFS7-106
92FreKeyC-9
92FreKeyF-1816
93FreKeyC-2
93FreKeyF-1038

Alston, Dell (Wendell)
78SSP270-4
78TacYanC-27
78Top-710
78YanSSPD-4
79TacTugT-19
79Top-54
80TacTigT-24
80Top-198
81Don-322
92YanWIZ7-7

Alston, Garvin
92BenRocC-5
92BenRocF-1465
92FroRowDP-54
93Bow-640
93CenValRC-3
93CenValRF-2883
93ClaFS7-163
93Top-661
93TopGol-661
93TopInaM-661
93TopMic-661
94CenValRC-2
94CenValRF-3193
95NewHavRTI-16
96ColSprSSTI-1
97Fle-582
97FleTif-582

Alston, Tom (Thomas E.)
53MotCoo-24
54CarHunW-1
55Bow-257
55CarHunW-1

Alston, Walter E.
52Par-66
53ExhCan-61
55DodGolS-1
56Dod-1
56Top-8
58DodJayP-1
58PacBel-1
58Top-314
59DodTeal-1
59DodVol-1
60DodBelB-18
60DodMor-1
60DodPos-1
60DodTeal-1
60DodUniO-1
60Top-212
61DodBelB-24
61DodJayP-1
61DodUniO-1
61Top-136
62DodBelB-24
62DodJayP-1
62Top-217
63DodJayP-1
63Top-154
64Top-101
64TopVen-101
65DodJayP-1
65DodTeal-1
65OPC-217
65Top-217
66OPC-116
66Top-116
66TopVen-116
67Top-294
68Top-472
69OPC-24
69Top-24
70OPC-242
70Top-242
71DodTic-2
71OPC-567
71Top-567
72Top-749
73OPC-569
73Top-569
74OPC-144
74Top-144
75OPC-361
75Top-361
76OPC-46
76SSP-90
76Top-46
79DiaGre-95
79TCM50-187
80DodGreT-12
80PacLeg-14
80PerHaloFP-181
80SSPHOF-184
81TCM60I-306
82OhiHaloF-15
85UltBasC-14
86SpoDesJM-6
87Dod195T-1
87DodSmoA-1
88DodSmo-1
88WilMulP-16
89DodSmoG-1
90DodTar-12
91RinPosBD4-12
92DodStaTA-6
92DodUno7P-5
95TopArcBD-109
95TopArcBD-141

Altaffer, Todd
91SouBenWSC-12
91SouBenWSP-2848
92WatDiaC-17
92WatDiaF-2132

Altamirano, Porfirio
80VenLeaS-251
81OklCit8T-1
83Fle-153
83PorBeaT-15
83Top-432
84IowCubT-23
84Nes792-101
84Top-101
84TopTif-101

Altenberger, Peter
88CapCodPPaLP-48

Altizer, Dave (David Tildon)
09ColChiE-8A
09ColChiE-8B
12ColRedB-8A
12ColRedB-8B
12ColTinT-8A
12ColTinT-8B

Altizer, Quentin
49W725AngTI-3

Altman, George Lee
59Top-512
60CubJayP-1
60Top-259
61CubJayP-1
61Pos-195A
61Pos-195B
61Top-551
61TopStal-1
62CubJayP-1
62Jel-187
62Pos-187
62PosCan-187
62SalPlaC-128
62ShiPlaC-128
62Top-240
62TopBuc-3
62TopStal-103
63BasMagM-5
63Jel-171
63Pos-171
63SalMetC-31
63Top-357
64Baz-23
64Top-95
64TopSta-69
64TopStaU-3
64TopVen-95
65CubJayP-1
65Top-528
66CubTeal-2
66OPC-146
66Top-146
66TopVen-146
67CokCapC-17
67DexPre-11
67OPC-87
67ProPizC-1
67Top-87
91MetWIZ-9

Altman, Heath
93EveGiaC-1
93EveGiaF-3756
94CliLumF-1970
95BurBeeTI-24
96BreCouMB-5
94CliLumC-4

Altman, John
77VisOakT-1

Altobelli, Joseph S.
63RocRedWSP-1
75IntLeaAT-16
77Gia-1
77Top-211
78Top-256
79GiaPol-6
79Top-356
80ColCliP-16
80ColCliT-8
83OriPos-1
83TopTra-3T
84Don-88
84Fle-643
84Fle-647
84FleSti-125
84Nes792-21
84OriTeal-1
84Top-21
84TopTif-21
85Top-574
85TopGloA-12
85TopTif-574
86YanTCM-39
88CubDavB-NNO
89CubMar-NNO
90CubMar-28
90TopTVCu-2
91CubMar-NNO
91CubVinL-2
93RocRedWF-259

Altrock, Nick (Nicholas)
04FanCraAL-1
07WhiSoxGWH-1
08RosComP-11
09ColChiE-9
11SpoLifCW-4
12ColRedB-9
12ColTinT-9
26SpoComoA-3
27YorCarE-40
31SenTealPW-1
36NatChiFPR-98
36R31PasP-40
46SpoExcW-1-8
60SenUniMC-1
61Fle-3
63GadFunC-45
77GalGloG-178
87ConSer2-8
88ConSer5-1
91ConTSN-226
94ConTSN-1119
94ConTSNB-1119

Alusik, George J.
62Top-261
63Top-51
64Top-431

Alva, John
86SumBraP-2
87DurBulP-25
88GreBraB-6
89GreBraB-7
89GreBraP-1154
89GreBraS-2
90CMC-299
90GreBraS-1
90ProAAAF-408
90RicBraC-23
90RicBraP-263
91LinDriAAA-426
91RicBraBC-19
91RicBraLD-426
91RicBraP-2574
91RicBraTI-13

Alvarado, Arnaldo
75DubPacT-5
76VenLeaS-58
80VenLeaS-66

Alvarado, Basilio
96DelShoB-6
96VerExpB-7

Alvarado, Jose
85MexCitTT-15

Alvarado, Luis
94EliTwiC-2
94EliTwiF-3720
95ForWayWTI-1

Alvarado, Luis Cesar
70OPC-317
70RedSoxCPPC-1
70Top-317
71OPC-489
71Top-489
72Top-774
73OPC-627
73Top-627
74OPC-462
74Top-462
76TulOilGP-14
91MetWIZ-10

Alvarez, Alex
88CapCodPPaLP-7
93LinVenB-14
94VenLinU-65
95LinVen-240

Alvarez, Carlos
95LinVen-160

Alvarez, Carmelo
82VerBeaDT-16

Alvarez, Chris
86FloStaLAP-3
86Ft.LauYP-1
87AlbYanP-15
88ColCliC-24
88ColCliP-13
88ColCliP-323
89ColCliP-739
90LonTigP-1273

Alvarez, Clemente
88UtiBluSP-2
89SouBenWSGS-30
90SarWhiSS-1
91Cla/Bes-142
91SarWhiSC-12
91SarWhiSP-1115
92BirBarF-2585
92BirBarS-76
92ClaFS7-29
92SkyAA F-36
93BirBarF-1195
93Bow-188
93LinVenB-104
94NasSouF-1253
94VenLinU-21
95LinVen-86

Alvarez, David
89ElmPioP-1
90ElmPioP-2

Alvarez, Emenegilda
91MedHatBJP-4112
91MedHatBJSP-21

Alvarez, Gabe
95SPML-101
95SPMLA-2
96BesAutS-4
96Bow-309
96BowBes-140
96BowBesAR-140
96BowBesR-140
96BowMinLP-12
96Exc-233
96ExcFirYP-1
96MemChiB-6
97Bow-397
97BowChr-263
97BowChrI-263
97BowChrIR-263
97BowChrR-263
97BowInt-397
97Top-204

Alvarez, Javier
89EugEmeB-15
90EugEmeGS-1

Alvarez, Joe
75ForLauYS-14
89VerBeaDS-27
90VerBeaDS-30

Alvarez, Jorge
89SalDodTI-5
90VerBeaDS-1
91LinDriAA-527
91SanAntMLD-527
92SanAntMF-3979
92SanAntMS-552
92SkyAA F-241
93LimRocDWB-73
93SanAntMF-3009
94PorSeaDF-683
94PorSeaDTI-8

Alvarez, Jose
76DubPacT-1
77MetDaiPA-1
92SalBucC-12
92SalBucF-54

Alvarez, Jose Lino
79SavBraT-12
81RicBraT-15
82RicBraT-1
83RicBraT-1
84TucTorC-51
86GreBraTI-2
88FleUpd-70
88FleUpdG-70
88RicBraC-8
88RicBraP-12
89BraDub-2
89Don-405
89Fle-585
89FleGlo-585
89PanSti-31
89Top-253
89TopTif-253
89UppDec-734
90Don-389
90Fle-574
90FleCan-574
90OPC-782
90PubSti-106
90Sco-148
90Top-782
90TopTif-782
90UppDec-634
90VenSti-8

Alvarez, Juan
96CedRapKTI-2

Alvarez, Luis
80VenLeaS-186

Alvarez, Mike
81MiaOriT-11
82ForMyeRT-12
83OmaRoyT-1
84OmaRoyT-19
85Ft.MyeRT-27
86Ft.MyeRP-2
87AppFoxP-18
88SavCarP-353
90BasCitRS-29
91LinDriAA-425
91MemChiP-670
92MemChiF-2436
93OmaRoyF-1697
94OmaRoyF-1239
95OmaRoyTI-2
96OmaRoyB-3

Alvarez, Orlando
74AlbDukTI-66
74AlbDukTI-1
75AlbDukC-1
75IntLeaASB-1
75PacCoaLAB-1
76SalLakCGC-11
77SalLakCGC-13
90DodTar-891

Alvarez, Ossie (Oswaldo G.)
59Top-504

60TacBan-2
85MexCitTT-4
Alvarez, Rafael
76VenLeaS-18
95ForWayWTI-21
96ForWayWB-2
96FtMyeMB-26
Alvarez, Robbie
79WatIndT-27
81ChaLooT-3
82MiaMarT-12
Alvarez, Rogelio H.
58RedEnq-2
63Top-158
Alvarez, Shawn
95GreBatTI-1
Alvarez, Tavo
91Cla/Bes-48
91SumFlyC-1
91SumFlyP-2324
92Bow-165
92ClaFS7-439
92ProFS7-267
92UppDecML-262
92WesPalBEC-3
92WesPalBEF-2077
93Bow-16
93ClaFS7-121
93ClaGolF-46
93ExcFS7-55
93ExcLeaLF-12
93FleFinE-88
93OttLynF-2428
93Ult-410
93UppDec-501
93UppDecGold-501
94ColC-654
94ColChoGS-654
94ColChoSS-654
94UppDec-295
94UppDecED-295
94UppDecML-151
94UppDecML-170
96ColCho-612
96ColChoGS-612
96ColChoSS-612
96Don-516
96DonPreP-516
96Pac-122
96SelArtP-193
96Sum-168
96SumAbo&B-168
96SumArtP-168
96SumFoi-168
Alvarez, Wilson
88GasRanP-1017
89ChaRanS-1
89TulDriTI-2
90CMC-628
90ProAAAF-159
90TopDeb89-3
90UppDec-765
90VanCanC-1
90VanCanP-481
91BirBarLD-51
91BirBarP-1446
91Bow-354
91Cla/Bes-285
91LinDriAA-51
91OPC-378
91StaCluMO-1
91Top-378A
91Top-378B
91TopDesS-378
91TopMic-378
91TopTif-378
91UltUpd-13
91UppDecFE-42F
92Bow-69
92Cla1-T5
92ClaGam-114
92Don-495
92Don-630
92Fle-74
92Fle-684
92Lea-78
92OPC-452
92OPCPre-122
92Pin-192
92ProFS7-41
92Sco-428
92Sco-760
92StaClu-761
92StaCluNC-761
92Top-452
92TopGol-452
92TopGolW-452
92TopMic-452
92Ult-32
92UppDec-573
92WhiSoxK-40
93Bow-387
93Don-37
93Fla-180
93Fle-199
93Lea-496
93LinVenB-6
93LinVenB-346
93PacSpa-66
93Pin-441
93RanKee-51
93Sco-609
93StaClu-181
93StaCluFDI-181
93StaCluMOP-181
93StaCluWS-10
93Top-737
93TopGol-737
93TopInaM-737
93TopMic-737
93Ult-170
93UppDec-350
93UppDecGold-350
93WhiSoxK-1
94Bow-54
94BowBes-R26
94BowBesR-R26
94ColC-36
94ColChoGS-36
94ColChoSS-36
94Don-518
94ExtBas-40
94ExtBasPD-5
94Fin-139
94FinRef-139
94Fla-28
94Fle-73
94Lea-71
94LeaL-19
94Pac-118
94Pin-128
94PinArtP-128
94PinMusC-128
94Sco-220
94ScoGolR-220
94Sel-111
94SP-188
94SPDieC-188
94Spo-97
94StaClu-462
94StaCluFDI-462
94StaCluGR-462
94StaCluMO-12
94StaCluMOP-462
94StaCluT-132
94StaCluTFDI-132
94Stu-203
94Top-299
94TopGol-299
94TopSpa-299
94TriPla-261
94Ult-30
94UppDec-204
94UppDecED-204
94USPlaCA-8S
94VenLinU-201
94WhiSoxK-1
95Baz-35
95Bow-412
95ColCho-503
95ColChoGS-503
95ColChoSE-239
95ColChoSEGS-239
95ColChoSESS-239
95ColChoSS-503
95Don-57
95DonPreP-57
95Fin-144
95FinRef-144
95Fla-23
95Fle-109
95FleAllS-23
95Lea-27
95LinVen-40
95Pac-82
95PacLatD-3
95PacPri-27
95PanSti-11
95Pin-123
95PinArtP-123
95PinMusC-123
95RedFol-14
95Sco-90
95ScoGolR-90
95ScoPlaTS-90
95Sel-206
95SelArtP-206
95SP-143
95Spo-138
95SpoArtP-138
95SPSil-143
95StaClu-132
95StaClu-405
95StaCluFDI-132
95StaCluMOP-132
95StaCluMOP-405
95StaCluSTWS-132
95StaCluSTWS-405
95StaCluVR-68
95Stu-56
95Top-186
95TopCyb-106
95Ult-26
95UltGolM-26
95UppDec-197
95UppDecED-197
95UppDecEDG-197
95WhiSoxK-2
96Cir-24
96CirRav-24
96ColCho-89
96ColChoGS-89
96ColChoSS-89
96Don-174
96DonPreP-174
96Fin-B183
96FinRef-B183
96Fla-46
96Fle-61
96FleTif-61
96FleWhiS-1
96Lea-145
96LeaPrePB-145
96LeaPrePG-145
96LeaPrePS-145
96LeaSigA-7
96LeaSigAG-7
96LeaSigAS-7
96Pac-292
96PacPri-P87
96PacPriG-P87
96Sco-66
96StaClu-147
96StaClu-243
96StaCluMOP-147
96StaCluMOP-243
95StaCluVRMC-68
96Top-159
96Ult-35
96UltGolM-35
96UppDec-306
97Cir-156
97CirRav-156
97ColCho-71
97Don-75
97DonLim-98
97DonLimLE-98
97DonPreP-75
97DonPrePGold-75
97DonTea-62
97DonTeaSPE-62
97Fin-74
97FinRef-74
97Fle-54
97FleTif-54
97Lea-68
97LeaFraM-68
97LeaFraMDC-68
97MetUni-52
97NewPin-73
97NewPinAP-73
97NewPinMC-73
97NewPinPP-73
97Pac-49
97PacLatotML-6
97PacLigB-49
97PacPri-18
97PacPriLB-18
97PacPriP-18
97PacPriSH-SH3B
97PacSil-49
97Sco-212
97ScoPreS-212
97ScoShoS-212
97ScoShoSAP-212
97ScoWhiS-9
97ScoWhiSPI-9
97ScoWhiSPr-9
97StaClu-347
97StaCluMOP-347
97Stu-120
97StuPrePG-120
97StuPrePS-120
97Top-176
97TopGal-118
97TopGalPPI-118
97Ult-34
97UltGolME-34
97UltPlaME-34
97UppDec-36
Alvis, Andy
80BatTroT-20
Alvis, Dave
86WatIndP-2
87WatIndP-7
Alvis, Max (Roy Maxwell)
47Exh-3
63Top-228
64IndJayP-1
64Kah-1
64Top-545
64TopCoi-48
64TopGia-46
64TopSta-7
64TopStaU-4
64TopTatI-22
65Kah-2
65OPC-185
65Top-185
65TopEmbl-3
65TopTral-2
66IndTeal-1
66Kah-3
66Top-415
66TopRubl-5
67CokCapA-24
67CokCapAAm-34
67CokCapl-2
67DexPre-12
67Kah-5
67Top-520
67TopGiaSU-16
68AtlOilPBCC-4
68Baz-9
68Kah-A3
68Kah-B6
68Top-340
68TopActS-6A
68TopPla-1
68TopPos-2
68TopVen-340
69Kah-B3
69MilBra-13
69MLBOffS-37
69MLBPin-1
69OPC-145
69Top-145
69TopFou-5
69TopSta-161
69TopTeaP-13
70BreMcD-1
70BreTeal-1
70MLBOffS-193
70OPC-85
70Top-85
71BreTeal-1
72MilBra-15
78TCM60I-83
92TexLon-2
94BreMilB-97
Alvord, Billy (William C.)
87OldJudN-6
Alyea, Brant
88GasRanP-1007
88SouAtlLAGS-16
89St.LucMS-1
90TulDriP-1165
Alyea, Brant (Garrabrant R.)
66OPC-11
66Top-11
66TopVen-11
69OPC-48
69Top-48
69TopTeaP-23
70OPC-303
70Top-303
71MLBOffS-457
71OPC-449
71Top-449
72MilBra-16
72OPC-383
72Top-383
Alzualde, Daniel
95BoiHawTI-1
95LinVen-161
Amado, Jose
94VenLinU-241
95EveAqaTI-1
95LinVen-204
96MidLeaAB-3
96WisTimRB-5
Amador, Bruce
82MadMusF-30
Amador, Manuel
93MarPhiC-3
93MarPhiF-3481
95ClePhiF-220
Amalfitano, Joey (John J.)
55Bow-269
55GiaGolS-25
55Top-144
60Top-356
61Top-87
62Col.45B-1
62Col45'HC-1
62Col45'JP-1
62Jel-144
62Pos-144
62PosCan-144
62SalPlaC-193
62ShiPlaC-193
62Top-456
62TopStal-123
63Fle-36
63Top-199
64Top-451
65Top-402
67CubProPS-1
73OPC-252
73Top-252A
73Top-252B
74OPC-78
74Top-78
76SSP-629
77PadSchC-3
78TCM60I-96
81Don-522
81Top-676
83DodPol-NNO
83PhiTas-2
84DodPol-NNO
85DodCokP-1
86DodCokP-1
87DodMot-27
87DodPol-29
88DodMot-28
89AstCol4S-15
89DodMot-27
89DodPol-1
90DodMot-28
90DodPol-NNO
91DodMot-28
91DodPol-NNO
92DodMot-28
92DodPol-NNO
93DodMot-28
93DodPol-30
94DodMot-28
94DodPol-30
95DodMot-28
95DodPol-30
96DodMot-28
96DodPol-8
Aman, Kevan
77WauMetT-1
Amante, Tom
87St.PetCP-10
90SprCarDGB-4
Amaral, Rich
86PitCubP-1
87PitCubP-22
88PitCubP-1362
89BirBarB-14
89BirBarP-91
90CMC-640
90ProAAAF-171
90VanCanC-13
90VanCanP-493
91CalCanLD-51

91CalCanP-520
91LinDriAAA-51
92Bow-386
92CalCanF-3737
92DonRoo-3
92Pin-581
92SkyAAAF-291
92StaClu-689
92StaCluECN-689
92TopDeb91-3
92Ult-430
93Fla-266
93FleFinE-263
93JimDeaR-1
93Lea-516
93MarMot-27
93OPCPre-114
93PacJugC-1
93PacSpa-617
93Sco-249
93SelRoo-145T
93SP-127
93StaClu-264
93StaCluFDI-264
93StaCluMari-4
93StaCluMOP-264
93Top-431
93TopGol-431
93TopInaM-431
93TopMic-431
93Ult-265
93UppDec-551
93UppDecGold-551
94Bow-389
94ColC-37
94ColChoGS-37
94ColChoSS-37
94Don-66
94ExtBas-158
94Fin-16
94FinJum-16
94FinRef-16
94Fle-278
94Lea-104
94MarMot-11
94OPC-149
94Pac-561
94PanSti-120
94Pin-386
94PinArtP-386
94PinMusC-386
94Sco-210
94ScoGolR-210
94Sel-114
94StaClu-44
94StaCluFDI-44
94StaCluGR-44
94StaCluMOP-44
94Stu-98
94Top-233
94TopGol-233
94TopSpa-233
94TriPla-121
94Ult-116
94UppDec-211
94UppDecED-211
94USPlaCR-8H
94USPlaCR-11D
95ColCho-288
95ColChoGS-288
95ColChoSS-288
95Don-67
95DonPreP-67
95Fle-258
95Lea-177
95MarMot-13
95MarPac-18
95Pac-388
95Sco-539
95ScoGolR-539
95ScoPlaTS-539
95TopTra-142T
96ColCho-724
96ColChoGS-724
96ColChoSS-724
96Don-385
96DonPreP-385
96Fle-225
96FleTif-225
96LeaSigEA-3
96MarMot-6
96Pac-414
96Ult-121
96UltGolM-121
97DonTea-150
97DonTeaSPE-150
97Fle-201
97FleTif-201
97Pac-180
97PacLigB-180
97PacSil-180
97Sco-221
97ScoMar-12
97ScoMarPl-12
97ScoMarPr-12
97ScoPreS-221
97ScoShoS-221
97ScoShoSAP-221

Amaro, Ruben
59Top-178
59TopVen-178
60PhiJayP-1
61Top-103
62Jel-194
62Pos-194
62PosCan-194
62SalPlaC-163
62ShiPlaC-163
62Top-284
62TopStal-163
63Fle-50
63Top-455
64PhiJayP-1
64PhiPhiB-2
64Top-432
65PhiJayP-1
65Top-419
66OPC-186
66Top-186
66TopVen-186
67CokCapYM-V2
67Top-358
68OPC-138
68Top-138
68TopVen-138
69Top-598
69TopTeaP-17
76OklCit8TI-20
78TCM60I-28
83CubThoAV-NNO
83PhiPosGPaM-4
84CubChiT-1
84CubSev-NNO
85CubSev-NNO
86CubGat-NNO
89BriTigS-29
90BriTigP-3175
92YanWIZ6-2
93BriTigC-27
93BriTigF-3666
94TopSpa-L2
95LinVen-71

Amaro, Ruben Jr.
87SalAngP-17
88CalLeaACLC-32
88PalSprACLC-97
88PalSprAP-1434
89QuaCitAB-30
89QuaCitAGS-18
90MidAngGS-4
91Bow-208
91Cla3-T19
91EdmTraLD-152
91EdmTraP-1526
91LinDriAAA-152
91TriA AAGP-AAA12
92Bow-184
92Don-733
92DonRoo-4
92Fle-52
92Lea-339
92OPC-269
92OPCPre-16
92PhiMed-2
92Pin-570
92ProFS7-30
92ScoRoo-98T
92StaClu-870
92Top-269
92TopDeb91-4
92TopGol-269
92TopGolW-269
92TopMic-269
92TopTra-5T
92TopTraG-5T
92Ult-540
92UppDec-752
93Don-488
93Fle-97
93LinVenB-182
93OPC-18
93PacSpa-229
93PhiMed-2
93Sco-341
93ScrRedBTI-2
93StaClu-385
93StaCluFDI-385
93StaCluMOP-385
93Top-43
93TopGol-43
93TopInaM-43
93TopMic-43
93Ult-83
93USPlaCR-9C
94ChaKniF-905
94Fle-581
94Pac-467
94Sco-265
94ScoGolR-265
95LinVen-67
95Pac-116
97PacPriGotD-GD180

Amaya, Ben
86ChaLooP-1

Ambler, Wayne H.
39PlaBal-117
41Gou-7

Ambos, Willie
88SalLakCTTI-13
89SanBerSB-9
89SanBerSCLC-66
91SalLakTP-3202
91SalLakTSP-25
94OgdRapSP-24

Ambos, Willy"Bull"
95OdgRapTI-2

Ambrose, John
94SigRooDP-36
94SigRooDPS-36
95Bow-26

Ambrose, Mark
87ElPasDP-11
88ElPasDB-15
89StoPorB-10
89StoPorCLC-159
89StoPorP-377

Ambrosina, Pete
94JohCitCC-2
94JohCitCF-3707

Ambrosio, Ciro
90St.CatBJP-3467
91MyrBeaHC-15
91MyrBeaHP-2949

Amelung, Ed (Edward)
81VerBeaDT-1
83AlbDukT-19
84AlbDukC-163
85AlbDukC-158
85DomLeaS-23
86AlbDukP-1
87EdmTraP-2071
88SanDieSAAG-1
89SanDieSAG-2
90DodTar-13
86StaoftFT -20

American Giants, Chicago
92NegLeaRLI-87
92NegLeaRLI-88
93NegLeaRL2-49
93NegLeaRL2-73

Amerson, Archie
77OrlTwiT-1
78SanJosMMC-21
79TolMudHT-4

Amerson, Gordon
94SigRooDP-73
94SigRooDPS-73
95IdaFalBTI-28
96CliLumKTI-3

Ames, Doug
86MadMusP-1

Ames, Ken
80AndBraT-10

Ames, Red (Leon Kessling)
06FanCraNL-1
06GiaUllAFS-1
09ColChiE-10A
09ColChiE-10B
09T206-5
09T206-6
09T206-7
10CouT21-69
10CouT21-70
10CouT21-256
10DomDisP-1
10E12AmeCDC-2
10NadE1-3
10RedCroT-1
10RedCroT-89
10RedCroT-168
10StaCarE-1
10SweCapPP-106
10W555-1
11S74Sil-79
11SpoLifCW-5
11SpoLifM-204
11T205-2
11TurRedT-77
12ColRedB-10A
12ColRedB-10B
12ColTinT-10A
12ColTinT-10B
12HasTriFT-48A
12HasTriFT-74A
12PhiCarE-2
15SpoNewM-5
16ColE13-4
16SpoNewM-5
91ConTSN-153
92ConTSN-334

Amezeua, Adan
94AubAstF-3762
96KisCobB-4

Aminoff, Matt
93EugEmeC-2
93EugEmeF-3844
94BelMarC-2
94BelMarF-3223
95SalAvaTI-8

Amman, Matt
94WelPirC-2
94WelPirF-3507

Amoros, Sandy (Edmundo I.)
47PM1StaP1-2
53ExhCan-43
55DodGolS-19
55Top-75
55TopDouH-53
56Dod-2
56Top-42
56TopPin-49
57Top-201
58MonRoyF-1
58Top-93
60Top-531
88RinPosD1-2A
90DodTar-14
95TopArcBD-97
95TopArcBD-143

Amos, Chad
93ForLauRSC-2
93ForLauRSFP-1587
94SarRedSF-1940

Amos, Chris
94OgdRapF-3739
94OgdRapSP-1

Amos, Perry
91HunCubC-2
91HunCubP-3325

Anaya, Mike
89Sta-22
90KinMetB-15
90KinMetS-1
91PitMetC-22
91PitMetP-3414

Anders, Scott
86PeoChiP-1

Andersen, Larry E.
78Top-703
79TacTugT-4
80Top-665
82Don-428
82Top-52
83Don-181
83Fle-470
83PorBeaT-3
83Top-234
84PhiTas-14
85Don-570
85Fle-244
85PhiTas-9
85PhiTas-13
85Top-428
85TopTif-428
86Don-355
86Fle-434
86PhiTas-47
86Top-183
86TopTif-183
87AstMot-21
87AstPol-1
87Don-640
87Fle-49
87FleGlo-49
87Top-503
87TopTif-503
88AstMot-21
88AstPol-2
88Don-332
88Fle-438
88FleGlo-438
88Sco-133A
88Sco-133B
88ScoGlo-133A
88ScoGlo-133B
88StaLinAst-2
88Top-342
88TopTif-342
89AstLenH-18
89AstMot-20
89AstSmo-2
89Bow-325
89BowTif-325
89Don-359
89Fle-349
89FleGlo-349
89Sco-523
89Top-24
89TopTif-24
89UppDec-404
90AstLenH-2
90AstMot-20
90Bow-67
90BowTif-67
90Don-359
90Fle-221
90FleCan-221
90Lea-386
90PubSti-86
90Sco-282
90UppDec-407
90VenSti-9
91Bow-660
91Don-665
91Fle-83
91FleUpd-120
91Lea-407
91OPC-761
91PadMag-17
91PadSmo-2
91Sco-848
91ScoRoo-71T
91StaClu-390
91Stu-241
91Top-761
91TopDesS-761
91TopMic-761
91TopTif-761
91UppDec-41
91UppDec-793
92Don-687
92Fle-597
92OPC-616
92PadCarJ-1
92PadMot-21
92PadPolD-29
92PadSmo-1
92Pin-399
92Sco-263
92StaClu-91
92Top-616
92TopGol-616
92TopGolW-616
92TopMic-616
92UppDec-587
93Fle-518
93FleFinE-108
93Lea-491
93PacSpa-573
93PhiMed-3
93Sco-445
93StaCluP-2
94Don-71
94Fle-582
94Pac-468
94PhiMed-1
94PhiMel-1
94Sco-237

94ScoGolR-237
94StaCluT-223
94StaCluTFDI-223
95Pac-324
95ReaPhiELC-2
95ReaPhiTI-33
96ReaPhiB-27
Andersen, Mark
95BreCouMF-236
Andersen, Morten
93StaCluMO-45
Andersh, Kevin
86MacPirP-2
89AugPirP-512
Anderson, Alf (Alfred W.)
77TCMTheWY-44
Anderson, Allan
83WisRapTF-3
84VisOakT-20
85TolMudHT-1
86DonRoo-3
86TolMudHP-1
87Don-368
87Fle-533
87FleGlo-533
87PorBeaP-4
87Top-336
87TopTif-336
88FleUpd-41
88FleUpdG-41
88PorBeaC-1
88PorBeaP-654
88Top-101
88TopTif-101
89Bow-149
89BowTif-149
89ClaTraP-178
89Don-419
89DonBasB-270
89Fle-102
89FleGlo-102
89FleLeaL-1
89OPC-20
89PanSti-381
89Sco-394
89ScoYouSI-34
89Spo-220
89Top-672
89TopMinL-60
89TopTif-672
89UppDec-85
90Bow-409
90BowTif-409
90Don-64
90DonBesA-52
90Fle-366
90FleCan-366
90Lea-5
90OPC-71
90PanSti-117
90PubSti-320
90PubSti-593
90RedFolSB-1
90Sco-292
90Spo-59
90Top-71
90TopSti-296
90TopTif-71
90UppDec-219
90VenSti-10
90VenSti-11
91Bow-327
91Don-527
91Fle-603
91Lea-259
91OPC-223
91Sco-135
91StaClu-188
91StaCluP-1
91Top-223
91TopDesS-223
91TopMic-223
91TopTif-223
91UppDec-503
92Fle-196
92OPC-417
92Sco-731
92StaClu-204
92StaClu-767
92Top-417
92TopGol-417
92TopGolW-417
92TopMic-417
92UppDec-506
93OklCit8F-1617
94ChaRivF-2690
Anderson, Allen
94ChaRivC-27
Anderson, Andy
88ElPasDB-16
Anderson, Andy Holm
86NegLeaF-41
Anderson, Bernie
86LakTigP-2
87LakTigP-10
88GleFalTP-928
89LonTigP-1364
Anderson, Bill (William)
91PomBlaBPB-2
Anderson, Blake
93MisStaB-2
96PorRocB-4
Anderson, Bob (Robert Carl)
58Top-209
59Top-447
60CubJayP-2
60Top-412
61CubJayP-2
61Top-283
61TopStaI-2
62CubJayP-2
62Top-557
63Top-379
Anderson, Brady
85ElmPioT-2
86FloStaLAP-4
86WinHavRSP-2
87NewBriRSP-7
88DonRoo-14
88DonTeaBBS-NEW
88ScoRoo-70T
88ScoRooG-70T
88TopTra-5T
88TopTraT-5T
89Bow-18
89BowTif-18
89Don-519
89Fle-606
89FleGlo-606
89OPC-161
89OriFreB-9
89Sco-563
89ScoYouSI-26
89Top-757
89TopRoo-2
89TopTif-757
89TopUKM-1
89ToyRoo-2
89TVSpoM-90
89UppDec-408
90Bow-258
90BowTif-258
90Don-638
90Fle-172
90FleCan-172
90MLBBasB-119
90OPC-598
90PubSti-572
90Sco-33
90Top-598
90TopMag-90
90TopTif-598
90UppDec-290
90VenSti-12
91Bow-100
91Don-668
91Fle-466
91OPC-97
91OriCro-9
91Sco-249
91StaClu-410
91Top-97A
91Top-97B
91TopDesS-97
91TopMic-97
91TopTif-97
91UppDec-349
92Fle-1
92Lea-343
92OPC-268
92Pin-452
92Sco-365
92SpoIllFK1-386
92StaClu-303
92Stu-121
92Top-268
92TopGol-268
92TopGolW-268
92TopMic-268
92Ult-301
92UppDec-185
93Bow-409
93ClaGam-4
93DiaMar-4
93Don-89
93DonDiaK-DK23
93DonSpiotG-SG17
93Fin-71
93FinRef-71
93Fla-149
93Fle-163
93FleFruotL-2
93FleTeaL-AL7
93FunPac-131
93Lea-177
93MilBonSS-19
93OPC-16
93PacSpa-14
93PanSti-76
93Pin-70
93Sco-140
93Sel-56
93SelSam-56
93SelStaL-21
93SelStaL-57
93SP-154
93StaClu-507
93StaCluFDI-507
93StaCluM-169
93StaCluMOP-507
93Stu-17
93Top-355
93TOPBLAG-24
93TopGol-355
93TopInaM-355
93TopMic-355
93Toy-52
93TriPla-166
93Ult-138
93UppDec-44
93UppDec-111
93UppDecGold-44
93UppDecGold-111
93USPlaCA-11H
94Bow-233
94ColC-405
94ColChoGS-405
94ColChoSS-405
94Don-592
94ExtBas-1
94Fin-131
94FinRef-131
94Fla-251
94Fle-1
94FUnPac-149
94Lea-66
94OPC-3
94OriPro-2
94OriUSPC-8S
94OriUSPC-13D
94Pac-25
94PanSti-17
94Pin-165
94PinArtP-165
94PinMusC-165
94ProMag-6
94Sco-335
94ScoGolR-335
94Sel-55
94StaClu-53
94StaCluFDI-53
94StaCluGR-53
94StaCluMOP-53
94StaCluT-290
94StaCluTFDI-290
94Top-145
94TopGol-145
94TopSpa-145
94TriPla-151
94Ult-301
94UppDec-63
94UppDecED-63
95Baz-84
95Bow-357
95ColCho-334
95ColChoGS-334
95ColChoSE-154
95ColChoSEGS-154
95ColChoSESS-154
95ColChoSS-334
95Don-201
95DonPreP-201
95DonTopotO-1
95Emb-44
95EmbGolI-44
95Emo-1
95Fin-44
95FinRef-44
95Fla-1
95Fle-1
95Lea-100
95LeaLim-16
95Pac-17
95Pin-188
95PinArtP-188
95PinMusC-188
95Sco-421
95ScoGolR-421
95ScoPlaTS-421
95Sel-227
95SelArtP-227
95SP-118
95SPCha-116
95SPChaDC-116
95Spo-76
95SpoArtP-76
95SPSil-118
95StaClu-268
95StaCluFDI-268
95StaCluMOP-268
95StaCluSTWS-268
95StaCluVR-134
95Stu-187
95Top-613
95TopCyb-381
95TopLeaL-LL18
95Ult-1
95UltGolM-1
95UppDec-132
95UppDecED-132
95UppDecEDG-132
95USPlaCMLA-6H
96Baz-32
96Bow-110
96BowBes-25
96BowBesAR-25
96BowBesR-25
96Cir-2
96CirRav-2
96ColCho-462
96ColChoGS-462
96ColChoSS-462
96Don-538
96DonPreP-538
96EmoXL-2
96Fin-B45
96Fin-S346
96FinRef-B45
96FinRef-S346
96Fla-2
96Fle-2
96FleOri-2
96FleTif-2
96Lea-36
96LeaLim-64
96LeaLimG-64
96LeaPre-78
96LeaPreP-78
96LeaPrePB-36
96LeaPrePG-36
96LeaPrePS-36
96LeaSig-50
96LeaSigPPG-50
96LeaSigPPP-50
96MetUni-2
96MetUniP-2
96MLBPin-2
96Pac-236
96PanSti-134
96Pin-74
96ProMagA-1
96ProSta-78
96Sco-331
96ScoDugC-B56
96ScoDugCAP-B56
96Sel-119
96SelArtP-119
96SelCerIP-25
96SP-36
96StaClu-316
96StaCluEPB-316
96StaCluEPG-316
96StaCluEPS-316
96StaCluMOP-316
95StaCluVRMC-134
96Sum-118
96SumAbo&B-118
96SumArtP-118
96SumFoi-118
96TeaOut-2
96Top-258
96TopChr-102
96TopChrR-102
96TopGal-11
96TopGalPPI-11
96TopLas-97
96Ult-2
96UltGolM-2
96UppDec-278
96UppDecDD-DD9
96UppDecDDG-DD9
96UppDecDDS-DD9
96UppDecVJLS-VJ14
96Zen-92
96ZenArtP-92
97Bow-268
97BowBes-91
97BowBesA-91
97BowBesAAR-91
97BowBesAR-91
97BowBesR-91
97BowChr-86
97BowChrI-86
97BowChrIR-86
97BowChrR-86
97BowInt-268
97Cir-352
97CirRav-352
97ColCho-275
97ColChoAC-6
97ColChoCtG-4A
97ColChoCtG-4B
97ColChoCtG-4C
97ColChoCtGIW-CG4
97ColChoPP-PP2
97ColChoPPG-PP2
97ColChoS-16
97ColChoTotT-T6
97Don-16
97Don-416
97DonEli-36
97DonEliGS-36
97DonLim-129
97DonLim-130
97DonLim-166
97DonLim-184
97DonLimFotG-56
97DonLimLE-129
97DonLimLE-130
97DonLimLE-166
97DonLimLE-184
97DonLonL-4
97DonPre-95
97DonPre-193
97DonPreCttC-95
97DonPreCttC-193
97DonPreP-16
97DonPreP-416
97DonPrePGold-16
97DonPrePGold-416
97DonTea-31
97DonTeaSPE-31
97Fin-154
97Fin-312
97FinEmb-154
97FinEmb-312
97FinEmbR-154
97FinEmbR-312
97FinRef-154
97FinRef-312
97FlaSho-A9
97FlaSho-B9
97FlaSho-C9
97FlaShoLC-9
97FlaShoLC-B9
97FlaShoLC-C9
97FlaShoLCM-A9
97FlaShoLCM-B9
97FlaShoLCM-C9
97Fle-2
97FleLumC-1
97FleTif-2
97Lea-88
97Lea-377
97LeaFraM-88
97LeaFraM-377
97LeaFraMDC-88
97LeaFraMDC-377
97LeaWarT-13

97MetUni-2
97NewPin-78
97NewPin-183
97NewPin-196
97NewPinAP-78
97NewPinAP-183
97NewPinAP-196
97NewPinIE-2
97NewPinMC-78
97NewPinMC-183
97NewPinMC-196
97NewPinPP-78
97NewPinPP-183
97NewPinPP-196
97NewPinPP-I2B
97Pac-18
97PacCar-2
97PacCarM-2
97PacFirD-2
97PacGolCD-2
97PacLigB-18
97PacPri-8
97PacPriGA-GA2
97PacPriLB-8
97PacPriP-8
97PacSil-18
97PacTriCD-1
97Pin-98
97PinArtP-98
97PinCer-27
97PinCerLI-8
97PinCerMBlu-27
97PinCerMG-27
97PinCerMR-27
97PinCerR-27
97PinIns-20
97PinInsCE-20
97PinInsDE-20
97PinInsFS-9
97PinMusC-98
97PinTotCPB-27
97PinTotCPG-27
97PinTotCPR-27
97PinX-P-38
97PinX-PF&A-16
97PinX-PMoS-38
97PinX-PSfF-16
97PinX-PSfFU-16
97ProMag-44
97ProMagML-44
97Sco-96
97ScoHigZ-12
97ScoOri-5
97ScoOriPl-5
97ScoOriPr-5
97ScoPreS-96
97ScoShoS-96
97ScoShoSAP-96
97ScoSteS-14
97ScoTitT-11
97Sel-55
97SelArtP-55
97SelRegG-55
97SkyE-X-5
97SkyE-XC-5
97SkyE-XEC-5
97SP-32
97SpoIll-126
97SpoIllEE-126
97SPSpeF-23
97SPSpxF-2
97SPSPxFA-2
97SPx-11
97SPxBro-11
97SPxGraF-11
97SPxSil-11
97SPxSte-11
97StaClu-253
97StaClu-388
97StaCluFR-F6
97StaCluI-I7
97StaCluI-I20
97StaCluMat-253
97StaCluMOP-253
97StaCluMOP-388
97StaCluMOP-I7
97StaCluMOP-I20
97StaCluMOP-FB6
97StaCluMOP-PG1
97StaCluPG-PG1
97Stu-30
97StuHarH-17
97StuPrePG-30
97StuPrePS-30
97Top-6
97TopChr-3
97TopChrDD-DD7
97TopChrDDR-DD7
97TopChrR-3
97TopChrSB-7
97TopChrSBR-7
97TopGal-57
97TopGalPPI-57
97TopHobM-HM14
97TopSeaB-SB7
97TopSta-44
97TopSta1AS-AS14
97TopStaAM-44
97TopTeaT-TT9
97Ult-2
97UltGolME-2
97UltPlaME-2
97UltTop3-30
97UltTop3GM-30
97UppDec-23
97UppDec-215
97UppDecLDC-LD2
97UppDecP-6
97UppDecRP-RP7
97UppDecU-2
97Zen-39

Anderson, Brian
94AngMot-22
94Bow-39
94Bow-369
94ColC-21
94ColChoGS-21
94ColChoSS-21
94ExtBas-29
94ExtBasRS-2
94Fin-304
94FinRef-304
94Fla-19
94FleMajLP-2
94FleUpd-15
94LeaGolR-17
94LeaL-13
94Pin-432
94PinArtP-432
94PinMusC-432
94Sco-468
94ScoGolR-468
94ScoRoo-RT125
94ScoRooGR-RT125
94ScoRooSR-SU17
94Sel-383
94SP-21
94SPDieC-21
94SpoRoo-94
94SpoRooAP-94
94SpoRooRS-TR10
94StaClu-571
94StaCluFDI-571
94StaCluGR-571
94StaCluMOP-571
94TopTra-10T
94Ult-321
94UppDec-1
94UppDecED-1
95AngCHP-12
95AngMot-22
95Bow-317
95ColCho-104
95ColChoGS-104
95ColChoSE-33
95ColChoSEGS-33
95ColChoSESS-33
95ColChoSS-104
95D3-20
95Don-72
95DonPreP-72
95Emb-11
95EmbGolI-11
95Fin-12
95FinRef-12
95Fle-218
95Lea-118
95Pac-50
95Pin-181
95PinArtP-181
95PinMusC-181
95PinUps-US30
95Sco-361
95ScoGolR-361
95ScoPlaTS-361
95Sel-70
95SelArtP-70
95StaClu-432
95StaCluMOP-432
95StaCluSTWS-432
95StaCluVR-227
95Stu-55
95Sum-103
95SumNthD-103
95Top-542
95TopCyb-323
95Ult-18
95UltGolM-18
95UppDec-18
95UppDecED-18
95UppDecEDG-18
96BufBisB-2
96ColCho-76
96ColChoGS-76
96ColChoSS-76
96Don-194
96DonPreP-194
96Fle-41
96FleTif-41
96ProSta-4
96Sco-204
95StaCluVRMC-227
96Ult-24
96UltGolM-24
96UppDec-29
97MidAngOHP-1

Anderson, Bud (Karl Adam)
79SpoIndT-20
79Top-712
81ChaLooT-25
82ChaChaT-1
82Ind-1
83Fle-408
83IndPos-1
83IndWhe-1
83Top-367
84Don-590
84Fle-533
84MaiGuiT-8
84Nes792-497
84Top-497
84TopTif-497
91PacSenL-4

Anderson, Chad
90MarPhiP-3205
91MarPhiC-27
91MarPhiP-3443
92BatCliC-3
92BatCliF-3254
93SpaPhiC-4
93SpaPhiF-1048

Anderson, Charlie (Charles)
90MisStaB-3
91MisStaB-3
92JohCitCC-7
92JohCitCF-3121
92MisStaB-3
93SavCarC-3
93SavCarF-690
94MadHatC-2
94MadHatF-137
95ArkTraTI-1

Anderson, Chris
91MiaHurBB-2
92BoiHawC-15
92BoiHawF-3634
93PalSprAC-2
93PalSprAF-74
96HudValRB-7

Anderson, Clark
93EveGiaC-2
93EveGiaF-3757

Anderson, Cliff
92YakBeaC-14
92YakBeaF-3455
94VerBeaDC-3
94VerBeaDF-78
95VerBeaDTI-1
96SanBerSB-5

Anderson, Craig (Norman C.)
62Top-593
63Top-59
81TCM60I-295
82MetGal62-15
91MetWIZ-11
92GulCoaRSP-14

Anderson, Dallas
96AriBlaDB-6

Anderson, Dave
76CedRapGT-2
77CedRapGT-3

Anderson, Dave (David C.)
82AlbDukT-14
84DodPol-10
84Don-642
84Nes792-376
84Top-376
84TopTif-376
85DodCokP-2
85Don-275
85Fle-366
85Top-654
85TopTif-654
86BasStaB-2
86DodCokP-2
86DodPol-10
86DodUniOP-1
86Fle-123
86OPC-29
86Top-758
86TopTif-758
87DodMot-17
87DodPol-4
87Fle-436
87FleGlo-436
87Top-73
87TopTif-73
88DodMot-17
88DodPol-10
88Don-475
88Fle-508
88FleGlo-508
88OPC-203
88PanSti-313
88Sco-166
88ScoGlo-166
88StaLinD-1
88Top-456
88TopTif-456
89DodMot-17
89DodPol-7
89DodStaSV-1
89Don-434
89Fle-53
89FleGlo-53
89OPC-117
89Sco-478
89Top-117
89TopTif-117
89UppDec-89
90DodTar-15
90Don-486
90FleUpd-59
90GiaMot-19
90OPC-248
90PubSti-1
90Sco-238
90Top-248
90TopTif-248
90UppDec-510
90VenSti-13
91Fle-252
91GiaMot-19
91GiaPacGaE-18
91OPC-572
91Sco-641
91Stu-251
91Top-572
91TopDesS-572
91TopMic-572
91TopTif-572
91Ult-314
92AlbDukS-1
92Bow-394
92DodSmo-5392
92Don-759
92Fle-625
92Sco-167
92ScoRoo-45T
92UppDec-290
94JamJamC-27
94JamJamF-3984
96LakTigB-1

Anderson, David
92Min-1

Anderson, Doug
91BelMarC-19
91BelMarP-3654

Anderson, Dwain C.
72OPC-268
72Top-268
73OPC-241
73Top-241

Anderson, Ed
77CocAstT-1

Anderson, Eddie
90NebCor-1

Anderson, Edward
76DubPacT-2

Anderson, Eric
82AubAstT-6
94EliTwiC-3
94EliTwiF-3721
95SprSulTI-1
96WilBluRB-15

Anderson, Ferrell J.
52Par-17
90DodTar-16

Anderson, Franklin
96SouBenSHS-4

Anderson, Fred
16FleBreD-5

Anderson, Fred (John Fred)
16ColE13-5

Anderson, Garret
90HigSchPLS-19
91Cla/Bes-258
91QuaCitAC-22
91QuaCitAP-2641
92Bow-298
92CalLeaACL-46
92ClaFS7-209
92MidAngOHP-2
92PalSprAC-12
92PalSprAF-851
92ProFS7-34
92UppDecML-292
92UppDecMLPotY-PY1
93ExcFS7-139
93VanCanF-2608
94Bow-479
94Cla-105
94ExcAllF-7
94ExcFS7-23
94LeaLimR-62
94SigRoo-5
94SigRooS-5
94Top-84
94TopGol-84
94TopSpa-84
94TriAAF-AAA22
94Ult-322
94UppDecML-157
94UppDecML-183
94VanCanF-1873
95AngMot-17
95Bow-250
95BowBes-B46
95BowBesR-B46
95BowGolF-250
95ColCho-23
95ColChoGS-23
95ColChoSE-12
95ColChoSEGS-12
95ColChoSESS-12
95ColChoSS-23
95Don-281
95DonPreP-281
95Fin-30
95FinRef-30
95Fla-233
95FleMajLP-1
95FleUpd-64
95Lea-332
95LeaGolR-2
95LeaLim-167
95Pac-51
95Pin-133
95Pin-289
95PinArtP-133
95PinArtP-289
95PinMusC-133
95PinMusC-289
95PinNewB-NB4
95Sco-310
95ScoGolR-310
95ScoPlaTS-310
95ScoRooDT-RDT8
95Sel-113
95Sel-239
95SelArtP-113
95SelArtP-239
95SelCanM-CM9
95SelCer-135
95SelCerMG-135
95SelCerPU-9

95SelCerPU9-9
95SPCha-6
95Spo-151
95SpoArtP-151
95StaClu-384
95StaCluMOP-384
95StaCluSTWS-384
95Stu-84
95Sum-122
95SumNthD-122
95Ult-265
95UltGolM-265
95UppDec-216
95UppDecED-216
95UppDecEDG-216
95UppDecPAW-H35
95UppDecPAWE-H35
95UppDecSEG-128
95Zen-140
96AngMot-15
96Baz-31
96Bow-94
96BowBes-40
96BowBesAR-40
96BowBesR-40
96Cir-17
96CirRav-17
96ColCho-69
96ColChoGS-69
96ColChoSS-69
96Don-73
96DonPreP-73
96EmoRarB-1
96EmoXL-22
96Fin-S73
96FinRef-S73
96Fla-32
96Fle-42
96FleRooS-1
96FleTif-42
96FleTomL-1
96Lea-114
96LeaLim-40
96LeaLimG-40
96LeaPre-55
96LeaPreP-55
96LeaPrePB-114
96LeaPrePG-114
96LeaPrePS-114
96LeaPreSG-21
96LeaPreSte-21
96LeaSig-125
96LeaSigA-8
96LeaSigAG-8
96LeaSigAS-8
96LeaSigPPG-125
96LeaSigPPP-125
96MetUni-23
96MetUniP-23
96MetUniPP-1
96Pac-274
96PacPri-P83
96PacPriG-P83
96PanSti-207
96PanSti-244
96Pin-5
96Pin-200
96Pin-282
96PinAfi-134
96PinAfiAP-134
96PinAfiSP-31
96PinArtP-5
96PinArtP-182
96PinFoil-282
96PinProS-12
96PinSam-5
96PinSta-5
96PinSta-182
96PinTeaT-7
96Sco-35
96Sco-375
96ScoDiaA-27
96ScoDugC-A34
96ScoDugC-B100
96ScoDugCAP-A34
96ScoDugCAP-B100
96ScoFutF-10
96ScoRef-7
96Sel-38
96SelArtP-38
96SelCer-95
96SelCerAP-95
96SelCerCB-95
96SelCerCR-95
96SelCerMB-95
96SelCerMG-95
96SelCerMR-95
96SelTeaN-23
96SigRooOJMR-M4
96SP-44
96Spo-63
96SpoArtP-63
96SpoPro-20
96StaClu-3
96StaClu-227
96StaCluEPB-3
96StaCluEPG-3
96StaCluEPS-3
96StaCluMO-49
96StaCluMOP-3
96StaCluMOP-227
96Stu-23
96StuPrePB-23
96StuPrePG-23
96StuPrePS-23
96Sum-94
96SumAbo&B-94
96SumArtP-94
96SumBigB-16
96SumBigBM-16
96SumFoi-94
96Top-132
96TopChr-36
96TopChrR-36
96TopGal-95
96TopGalPPI-95
96TopLas-17
96TopMysF-M6
96TopMysFR-M6
96Ult-25
96UltFreF-1
96UltFreFGM-1
96UltGolM-25
96UltRisS-1
96UltRisSGM-1
96UppDec-31
96UppDecBCP-BC19
96UppDecVJLS-VJ16
96Zen-69
96ZenArtP-69
96ZenMoz-7
97Cir-115
97CirRav-115
97ColCho-252
97Don-141
97DonEli-55
97DonEliGS-55
97DonLim-180
97DonLimLE-180
97DonPre-5
97DonPreCttC-5
97DonPreP-141
97DonPrePGold-141
97DonTea-4
97DonTeaSPE-4
97Fin-21
97FinRef-21
97FlaSho-A170
97FlaSho-B170
97FlaSho-C170
97FlaShoLC-170
97FlaShoLC-B170
97FlaShoLC-C170
97FlaShoLCM-A170
97FlaShoLCM-B170
97FlaShoLCM-C170
97Fle-34
97FleTif-34
97Lea-215
97LeaFraM-215
97LeaFraMDC-215
97MetUni-36
97NewPin-31
97NewPinAP-31
97NewPinMC-31
97NewPinPP-31
97Pac-1
97PacLigB-1
97PacSil-1
97Pin-2
97PinArtP-2
97PinIns-88
97PinInsCE-88
97PinInsDE-88
97PinMusC-2
97PinX-P-26
97PinX-PMoS-26
97ProMag-41
97ProMagML-41
97Sco-30
97ScoPreS-30
97ScoShoS-30
97ScoShoSAP-30
97Sel-68
97SelArtP-68
97SelRegG-68
97SP-18
97StaClu-61
97StaCluMOP-61
97Stu-82
97StuPrePG-82
97StuPrePS-82
97Top-24
97TopChr-10
97TopChrR-10
97TopGal-157
97TopGalPPI-157
97Ult-22
97UltGolME-22
97UltPlaME-22
97UppDec-292

Anderson, Glen
86BenPhiC-141

Anderson, Greg
76BurBeeT-1

Anderson, Harry W.
47PM1StaP1-3
57Top-404
58PhiJayP-1
58Top-171
59Top-85
59TopVen-85
60PhiJayP-2
60Top-285
61Top-76

Anderson, Jeff
86PenWhiSP-3

Anderson, Jesse
81AppFoxT-1
82AppFoxF-10
83AlbA'sT-1

Anderson, Jim (James Lea)
79Top-703
80Top-183
80VenLeaS-212
81Don-165
81Fle-598
81MarPol-4
81Top-613
82Don-181
82Don-352A
82Fle-503
82Top-497
83RanAffF-46
84Nes792-353
84RanJarP-14
84Top-353
84TopTif-353
85OklCit8T-6
87CliGiaP-5
88CliGiaP-703
89ShrCapP-1835
93RanKee-52
78STLakCGC-2

Anderson, Jimmy
96CarLeaA1B-4
96CarLeaA2B-4
96LynHilB-1
97Bow-181
97BowBes-139
97BowBesAR-139
97BowBesR-139
97BowInt-181
97Top-492

Anderson, John
84ButCopKT-2
88MarPhiS-1
94AubAstC-2
94AubAstF-3750

Anderson, John C.
62Top-266
81TCM60I-301
91OriCro-10

Anderson, John Joseph
03BreE10-1
03BreE10-2
08RosComP-12
09RamT20-2
09T206-392
90DodTar-17

Anderson, Jon
91QuaCitAP-2629

Anderson, Kelly
79CedRapGT-24

Anderson, Ken
87SpoCubG-3

Anderson, Kent
86PalSprAP-1
88EdmTraC-17
88EdmTraP-574
89EdmTraC-17
89TopTra-3T
89TopTraT-3T
90Don-490
90Hot50RS-3
90OPC-16
90PubSti-363
90Sco-412
90Sco100RS-86
90Top-16
90TopDeb89-4
90TopTif-16
90UppDec-691
90VenSti-14
91Bow-194
91Don-525
91EdmTraLD-153
91EdmTraP-1520
91Fle-306
91LinDriAAA-153
91OPC-667
91Sco-224A
91Sco-224B
91StaClu-241
91Top-667
91TopDesS-667
91TopMic-667
91TopTif-667
92CalCanF-3738
93IowCubF-2138

Anderson, Larry (Lawrence D.)
75OklCit8TI-7
76OPC-593
76SSP-248
76SSP-249
76Top-593
77Top-487
80ChaO'sP-1
80ChaO'sW-1
80PorBeaT-23
94BreMilB-98

Anderson, Marlon
95BatCliTI-1
96BesAutS-5
96Bow-120
96Exc-194
97Bow-302
97BowBes-174
97BowBesAR-174
97BowBesR-174
97BowChr-210
97BowChrI-210
97BowChrIR-210
97BowChrR-210
97BowInt-302

Anderson, Matt (Matthew)
88OklSoo-9
89BluOriS-26
90CMC-872
90WauTimB-6
90WauTimP-2119
90WauTimS-1
91KanCouCC-3
91KanCouCP-2650
91KanCouCTI-1
92ClaFS7-107
92FreKeyC-19
92FreKeyF-1797
92ProFS7-11
92UppDecML-89
94AlbPolC-2
94AlbPolF-2227
94OriPro-3
94FreKeyC-2

Anderson, Mike
85LitFalMT-1
86LitFalMP-1
87ColMetP-20
88PalSprACLC-98
88PalSprAP-1438
89GreHorP-428
89RenSilSCLC-239
90CedRapRP-2318
91ChaLooLD-152
91ChaLooP-1950
91LinDriAA-152
91OriCro-11
91WavRedF-4
92ChaLooF-3810
92ChaLooS-177
93ChaLooF-2352
93ChaRaiC-2
93ChaRaiF-1900
94ChaRanF-2489
94IowCubF-1269
95IowCubTI-3

Anderson, Mike (Michael A.)
72OPC-14
72Top-14
73OPC-147
73Top-147
74OPC-619
74PhiJohP-22
74Top-619
75OPC-118
75Top-118
76OPC-527
76SSP-469
76Top-527
76TopTra-527T
77Car5-1
77CarTeal-1
77Top-72
78Top-714
79Top-102
80BurBeeT-18
80Top-317
81PorBeaT-5
82VanCanT-22
84VanCanC-46
85LouRedR-29
87PalSprP-24
90CedRapRB-20

Anderson, Nub (Steve)
76LauIndC-14
76LauIndC-25

Anderson, Ottis
91StaCluCM-33
91StaCluCM-34

Anderson, Paul
91SprCarC-1
91SprCarP-731
92ArkTraF-1120
93ArkTraF-2803
94LouRedF-2970
95ArkTraTI-2
96HelBreTI-33

Anderson, Rick (Richard A.)
79ColCliT-21
79JacMetT-16
81SpoIndT-28
81TidTidT-26
82TidTidT-12
84TidTidT-19
85IntLeaAT-19
85TidTidT-6
86MetWorSC-17
86TidTidP-1
87Fle-2
87FleGlo-2
87MetColP-23
87OmaRoyP-22
87Top-594
87TopTif-594
88OmaRoyC-1
88OmaRoyP-1512
89Sco-441
90KenTwiB-28
90KenTwiP-2311
90KenTwiS-26
91KenTwiC-20
91KenTwiP-2092
91MetWIZ-12
92KenTwiC-26
92KenTwiF-621
93NasXprF-418
94NasXprF-402

Anderson, Rick (Richard Lee)
76ShrCapT-3
80SpoIndT-20
81Top-282
92YanWIZ7-8

Anderson, Roy
85MadMusP-1
85MadMusT-4

86ModA'sC-1
86ModA'sP-1A
86ModA'sP-1B
87HunStaTI-1
Anderson, Scott
82MadMusF-10
85TulDriTI-33
88OklCit8C-1
89IndIndC-6
89IndIndP-1234
90CMC-57
90IndIndC-7
90IndIndP-280
90ProAAAF-563
91Fle-225
91Sco-734
93EdmTraF-1129
93RanKee-53
94NewOrlZF-1460
95OmaRoyTI-3
Anderson, Sparky (George Lee)
59Top-338
60MapLeaSF-1
60Lea-125
60Top-34
60TopVen-34
61MapLeaBH-1
70OPC-181
70Top-181
71OPC-688
71Top-688
72OPC-358
72Top-358
73OPC-296
73Top-296
74OPC-326
74Top-326
75OPC-531
75Top-531
76OPC-104
76SSP-22
76Top-104
77Top-287
78Pep-1
78SSP270-129
78Top-401
79Top-259
80Top-626
81Don-370
81Fle-460
81TCM60I-300
81TigDetN-18
81Top-666
82Don-29
83Don-533A
83Don-533B
83Tig-1
83Top-666
84Fle-650
84Nes792-259
84TigWavP-1
84Top-259
84TopTif-259
85Fle-628
85FleStaS-125
85SevCoi-D2
85TigWen-1
85Top-307
85TopTif-307
86DonAll-58
86Top-411
86TopGloA-1
86TopTif-411
87Top-218
87TopTif-218
88PacLegI-46
88TigPep-11
88TigPol-2
88Top-14
88TopTif-14
89TigMar-11
89TigPol-NNO
89Top-193
89TopBasT-156
89TopTif-193
90OPC-609
90TigCok-1
90Top-609
90TopTif-609
91OPC-519
91Stu-261
91TigCok-11
91TigPol-1
91Top-519
91TopDesS-519
91TopMic-519
91TopTif-519
92OPC-381
92Top-381
92TopGol-381
92TopGolW-381
92TopMic-381
92UppDecS-30
93TigGat-1
93Top-506
93TopGol-506
93TopInaM-506
93TopMic-506
96Red76K-1
96UppDec-480
Anderson, Spike
90WicStaSGD-2
Anderson, Steve
83BelBreF-12
91OneYanP-4159
92GreHorC-18
92GreHorF-784
93SanBerSC-2
93SanBerSF-776
Anderson, Tim
87BakDodP-22
Anderson, Todd
91PocPioP-3794
91PocPioSP-16
Anderson, Tom
78WatIndT-1
79WatIndT-13
91AubAstC-8
92AshTouC-4
93FloStaLAF-34
93OscAstC-3
93OscAstF-618
94OscAstC-2
94OscAstF-1128
Anderson, Varney S.
87OldJudN-7
Andino, Luis
94MarPhiC-2
94MarPhiF-3306
95MarPhiTI-2
Andrade, Herberto
87GenCubP-8
88PeoChiTI-1
89ChaWheB-13
89ChaWheP-1759
93LinVenB-114
95LinVen-236
Andreopoulos, Alex
95BelBreTI-24
96StoPorB-17
Andres, Ernie (Ernest Henry)
46RedSoxTI-1
Andretta, Holly
89SalLakTTI-10
Andrews, Clayton
96MedHatBJTI-2
Andrews, Daniel
90GreFalDSP-22
91GreFalDSP-19
Andrews, Fred
76OklCit8TI-12
76VenLeaS-17
78TidTidT-2
Andrews, George E.
87BucN28-74A
87BucN28-74B
87OldJudN-8
87OldJudN-9
88GooN16-1
88WG1CarG-46
90KalBatN-1
94OriofB-43
Andrews, Ivy Paul
32OrbPinNP-1
32OrbPinUP-2
33GeoCMil-2
33TatOrb-2
34BatR31-106
34BatR31-115
36ExhFou-15
36NatChiFPR-2
75YanDyn1T-1
92ConTSN-420
Andrews, Jay III
91BasCitRC-23
91BasCitRP-1409
Andrews, Jeff
87PorChaRP-12
88TulDriTI-9
89TulDriGS-3
89TulDriTI-3
90TulDriP-1174
90TulDriTI-2
91LinDriAAA-303
91OklCit8LD-303
91OklCit8P-194
92JacSunS-375
94BilMusF-3672
94BilMusSP-1
94JacSunF-1427
95TacRaiTI-2
96TacRaiB-3
Andrews, John
88SanDieSAAG-2
89SanDieSAG-1
Andrews, Kevin
94HudValRC-28
Andrews, Mike (Michael Jay)
67Top-314
67TopRedSS-7
68CokCapRS-13
68DexPre-7
68Top-502
69MilBra-14
69MLBOffS-10
69OPC-209
69RedSoxAO-1
69RedSoxTI-1
69Top-52
69TopSta-131
69TopTeaP-3
70MLBOffS-157
70OPC-406
70RedSoxCPPC-2
70Top-406
71OPC-191
71Top-191
72MilBra-17
72OPC-361
72Top-361
72WhiSoxC-1
72WhiSoxTI1-2
73OPC-42
73Top-42
81RedSoxBG2S-69
81TCM60I-417
Andrews, Nate (Nathan H.)
79DiaGre-259
93ConTSN-886
Andrews, Rob (Robert P.)
75IntLeaAT-10
76OPC-568
76SSP-54
76Top-568
77Top-209
78Top-461
79GiaPol-21
79Top-34
80Top-279
Andrews, Shane
90ClaDraP-11
90ClaYel-T88
91Bow-452
91OPC-74
91Sco-674
91SumFlyC-10
91SumFlyP-2339
91Top-74
91TopCraJ2-13
91TopDesS-74
91TopMic-74
91TopTif-74
92AlbPolC-1
92AlbPolF-2311
92ClaBluBF-BC3
92ClaFS7-8
92ClaRedB-BC3
92UppDecML-290
93Bow-378
93ClaFS7-122
93ClaGolF-71
93ExcFS7-56
93HarSenF-273
93SouAtlLAIPI-13
93SouAtlLAPI-1
94BowBes-B24
94BowBes-X93
94BowBesR-B24
94BowBesR-X93
94Cla-85
94ClaCreotC-C15
94ClaGolF-90
94ColC-651
94ColChoGS-651
94ColChoSS-651
94ExcFS7-222
94OttLynF-2902
94UppDec-2
94UppDecED-2
94UppDecML-153
94UppDecML-175
95Bow-60
95ColCho-548T
95Fin-271
95FinRef-271
95Fla-372
95FleUpd-103
95FleUpdRU-1
95Pin-410
95PinArtP-410
95PinMusC-410
95Sel-170
95SelArtP-170
95SelCer-108
95SelCerMG-108
95SP-73
95SPSil-73
95StaClu-609
95StaCluMOP-609
95StaCluSTWS-609
95Sum-116
95SumNthD-116
95Top-652
95UppDec-463T
95UppDecML-136
95Zen-120
96ColCho-208
96ColChoGS-208
96ColChoSS-208
96Don-186
96DonPreP-186
96ExpBoo-2
96ExpDis-4
96Fla-302
96Fle-451
96FleTif-451
96Lea-178
96LeaPrePB-178
96LeaPrePG-178
96LeaPrePS-178
96LeaSigA-9
96LeaSigAG-9
96LeaSigAS-9
96Pin-293
96PinFoil-293
96StaClu-443
96StaCluMOP-443
96Ult-501
96UltGolM-501
96UppDec-394
97Cir-91
97CirRav-91
97ColCho-161
97Fle-375
97FleTif-375
97PacPriGotD-GD165
97Sco-422
97ScoHobR-422
97ScoResC-422
97ScoShoS-422
97ScoShoSAP-422
97Top-57
97Ult-366
97UltGolME-366
97UltPlaME-366
97UppDec-108
95UppDecMLFS-136
Andrews, Stan (Stanley J.)
41Gou-24
90DodTar-18
Andrews, Wally (William W.)
87OldJudN-10
Andrezejewski, Joe
89HelBreSP-1
90BelBreB-3
90BelBreS-1
90Bes-52
90MidLeaASGS-2
91EriSaiC-15
91EriSaiP-4059
Andujar, Hector
91WatIndC-16
91WatIndP-3371
Andujar, Joaquin
77Top-67
78AstBurK-7
78Top-158
78TopZes-1
79OPC-246
79Top-471
80Kel-55
80OPC-324
80Top-617
81Don-381
81Fle-63
81FleStiC-48
81OPC-329
81Top-329
81TopTra-731
82Don-607
82Fle-110
82Top-533
83AllGamPI-163
83Car-1
83Don-316
83DonActA-27
83Fle-1
83FleSta-3
83FleSti-7
83OPC-228
83Top-228
83Top-561
83TopSti-179
84AllGamPI-73
84Car-2
84Car5x7-2
84Don-181
84Fle-319
84FunFooP-90
84Nes792-785
84OPC-371
84Top-785
84TopTif-785
85AllGamPI-163
85CarTeal-2
85Don-13
85Don-449
85DonSupD-13
85Fle-220
85FleStaS-85
85Lea-13
85OPC-231
85SevCoi-C6
85Top-655
85TopGloS-12
85TopSti-136
85TopSup-38
85TopTif-655
86A'sMot-4
86AstMot-15
86CarKASD-11
86CarTeal-2
86Don-231
86Fle-26
86FleLimE-2
86FleUpd-4
86OPC-150
86Spo-101
86Spo-133
86Spo-185
86Top-150
86TopMinL-58
86TopSti-44
86TopTif-150
86TopTra-3T
86TopTraT-3T
87A'sSmoC-1
87Don-548
87Fle-385
87FleGlo-385
87FleHotS-1
87FleMin-2
87Lea-162
87OPC-284
87RedFolSB-11
87Top-775
87TopSti-172
87TopTif-775
88AstMot-26
88AstPol-3
88Sco-193
88ScoGlo-193
88Top-47
88TopTif-47
89Sco-472
89TopSenL-93

89UppDec-79
Andujar, Juan
89JohCitCS-2
90Bes-13
90SprCarB-1
91Cla/Bes-80
91SprCarC-2
91SprCarP-746
92St.PetCC-6
92St.PetCF-2032
93CarLeaAGF-25
93KinIndC-2
93KinIndF-2252
93KinIndTI-1
94CarLeaAF-CAR33
94KinIndF-2649
Andujar, Luis
92SouBenWSC-4
92SouBenWSF-168
93SarWhiSC-2
93SarWhiSF-1360
94BirBarC-2
94BirBarF-614
94ExcFS7-33
96BirBarB-23
96Don-425
96DonPreP-425
96Fle-62
96FleTif-62
96NasSouB-6
96Pac-283
Andux, Orlando
52LavPro-107
Angel, Jason
92BenMusSP-4
92BilMusF-3346
92FroRowDP-10
93StaCluM-33
93WinSpiC-2
93WinSpiF-1562
94WinSpiC-2
94WinSpiF-262
Angeli, Doug
93BatCliC-3
93BatCliF-3151
94SpaPhiF-1728
94SparPhiC-2
95ReaPhiELC-1
96ReaPhiB-15
Angelini, Norm (Norman S.)
73OPC-616
73Top-616
75OmaRoyTI-1
Angelo, Mark
83EriCarT-12
84SavCarT-11
Angels, California
64TopTatI-3
65Top-293
66OPC-131
66Top-131
66TopRubI-103
66TopVen-131
67Top-327
68Top-252
68TopVen-252
69FleCloS-4
69TopStaA-4
70OPC-522
70Top-522
71OPC-442
71Top-442
71TopTat-134
72OPC-71
72Top-71
73OPC-243
73OPCBTC-4
73Top-243
73TopBluTC-4
74OPC-114
74OPCTC-4
74Top-114
74TopStaA-4
74TopTeaC-4
78Top-214
83FleSta-228
83FleSti-NNO
87FleWaxBC-C13
87SpoTeaL-11
88PanSti-457
88RedFolSB-129
90PubSti-638
90RedFolSB-120
90VenSti-518
91PanCanT1-132
94ImpProP-3
94Sco-319
94ScoGolR-319
95PanSti-150
96PanSti-211
Angels, Los Angeles
61TopMagR-6
62GuyPotCP-10
62Top-132A
62Top-132B
62TopVen-132
63Top-39
64Top-213
64TopVen-213
Angels, Midland
87MidAngP-30
Angels, Quad City
86QuaCitAP-33
Angerhofer, Chad
96BilMusTI-1
Angero, Jose
87OmaRoyP-2
Anglen, Toby
95DanBraTI-2
Anglero, Jose
88BasCitRS-4
88BlaYNPRWLU-38
89BasCitRS-4
89BlaYNPRWL-137
90BasCitRS-1
91LakTigC-18
91LakTigP-271
Anglin, Russ
83AndBraT-25
Angotti, Donald
90OscAstS-2
91AubAstC-12
91AubAstP-4276
92TucTorF-504
Angulo, Ken
83RedPioT-2
85MidAngT-15
Anicich, Mike
82JacMetT-14
82TidTidT-25
83MidCubT-20
Aniya, Sohachi
79TCMJapPB-88
Ankenman, Pat (Fred N.)
90DodTar-892
Annee, Tim
89MedAthB-23
Annis, Bill (William P.)
87OldJudN-11
Ansley, Willie
89AshTouP-950
89Bow-332
89BowTif-332
89SouAtlLAGS-3
89Top-607
89TopTif-607
90Bes-3
90CMC-810
90ColMudB-1
90ColMudP-1356
90ColMudS-2
90ProAaA-57
90StaFS7-14
91Bow-549
91Cla/Bes-135
91JacGenLD-551
91JacGenP-935
91LinDriAA-551
92JacGenF-4010
93TucTorF-3071
Anson, Cap (Adrian C.)
36PC7AlbHoF-17
50CalHOFW-2
60ExhWriH-2
60Fle-44
61Fle-4
63BazA-39
63HalofFB-22
69Baz-9
75FlePio-1
76GrePlaG-30
76ShaPiz-21
77BobParHoF-2
77ShaPiz-12
80PerHaloFP-17
80SSPHOF-17
84GalHaloFRL-21
87AllandGN-1
87BucN28-18A
87BucN28-18B
87OldJudN-12A
87OldJudN-12B
88GandBCGCE-1
88GooN16-2
88SpoTimM-1
88WG1CarG-10
89EdgR.WG-1
89HOFStiB-5
90BasWit-66
90HOFStiB-9
90PerGreM-96
92CubOldS-2
94OriofB-46
94UppDecTAE-7
95May-1
98CamPepP-1
Anthony, Andy
86VerBeaDP-1
Anthony, Brian
96PorRocB-5
Anthony, Dane
79WatIndT-14
80WatIndT-2
82ChaLooT-8
83WatIndF-21
Anthony, Eric
89BasAmeAPB-AA11
89ColMudB-1
89ColMudP-134
89ColMudS-2
89SouLeaAJ-3
89Sta-1
89TucTorJP-1
90AstLenH-3
90AstMot-3
90Bow-81
90BowTif-81
90ClaBlu-70
90ColMudS-3
90Don-34
90DonBesN-28
90DonRoo-49
90Fle-222
90FleCan-222
90Hot50RS-4
90Lea-82
90LeaPre-7
90OPC-608
90PanSti-379
90Sco-584
90Sco100RS-45
90ScoRooDT-B10
90ScoYouSI-42
90Spo-179
90Top-608
90TopBig-197
90TopDeb89-5
90TopTif-608
90ToyRoo-2
90UppDec-28
91Bow-540
91Cla2-T34
91ClaGam-139
91Don-333
91Fle-498
91Lea-181
91LinDriAAA-602
91MajLeaCP-44
91OPC-331
91Sco-146
91Sco100RS-42
91StaClu-229
91Stu-171
91Top-331
91TopCraJ2-3
91TopDesS-331
91TopMic-331
91TopTif-331
91TucTorLD-602
91TucTorP-2223
91Ult-131
91UppDec-533
92AstMot-7
92Fle-424
92Pin-363
92PinTea2-28
92Sco-315
92Sco100RS-8
92StaClu-575
92TriPla-18
93AstMot-8
93Bow-152
93ClaGam-5
93DenHol-2
93Don-8
93Fin-179
93FinRef-179
93Fla-56
93Fle-45
93Lea-218
93LinVenB-219
93OPC-2
93PacSpa-474
93PanSti-176
93Pin-84
93PinHomRC-34
93Sco-173
93Sel-137
93StaClu-141
93StaCluAs-7
93StaCluFDI-141
93StaCluMOP-141
93Stu-3
93Top-89
93TopGol-89
93TopInaM-89
93TopMic-89
93Toy-49
93ToyMasP-2
93TriPla-109
93Ult-389
93UppDec-183
93UppDecGold-183
93UppDecHRH-HR22
94Bow-445
94ColC-38
94ColC-411
94ColChoGS-38
94ColChoGS-411
94ColChoSS-38
94ColChoSS-411
94Don-480
94ExtBas-159
94Fin-349
94FinRef-349
94Fla-98
94Fle-482
94FleUpd-79
94Lea-229
94LeaL-64
94MarMot-3
94OPC-61
94Pac-256
94PanSti-188
94Pin-75
94PinArtP-75
94PinMusC-75
94ProMag-129
94Sco-400
94ScoGolR-400
94ScoRoo-RT27
94ScoRooGR-RT27
94Sel-286
94SP-102
94SPDieC-102
94SpoRoo-137
94SpoRooAP-137
94StaClu-548
94StaCluFDI-548
94StaCluGR-548
94StaCluMOP-548
94StaCluMOP-ST6
94StaCluST-ST6
94Stu-99
94Top-182
94TopGol-182
94TopSpa-182
94TopTra-27T
94TriPla-122
94Ult-202
94Ult-415
94UppDec-361
94UppDecED-361
95Don-31
95DonPreP-31
95Fle-259
95Pin-306
95PinArtP-306
95PinMusC-306
95RedKah-1
95Sco-506
95ScoGolR-506
95ScoPlaTS-506
95Top-565
95TopCyb-341
95Ult-98
95UltGolM-98
96FleUpd-U116
96FleUpdTC-U116
96Pin-287
96PinFoil-287
96Sco-415
Anthony, Greg Pepper
91ClaDraP-27
91FroRowDP-19
92ChaRaiF-111
92ClaFS7-51
92OPC-336
92StaCluD-7
92Top-336
92TopGol-336
92TopGolW-336
92TopMic-336
93WatDiaC-2
93WatDiaF-1758
Anthony, Lee
49BowPCL-1
50W720HolS-1
Anthony, Mark
90HigSchPLS-9
91SpoIndC-12
91SpoIndP-3959
92Bow-449
92ChaRaiC-3
92ChaRaiF-131
92UppDecML-125
Anthony, Paul
77SalPirT-1
Antigua, Felix
89AugPirP-497
89PriPirS-2
89Sta-173
90AugPirP-2466
90SouAtlLAS-26
Antigua, Jose
93WhiSoxK-30
Antigua, Nilson
96EriSeaB-4
Antolick, Jeff
92OneYanC-26
93GreHorC-2
93GreHorF-876
93SouAtlLAGF-18
94TamYanC-2
94TamYanF-2372
95NorNavTI-40
Antonelli, John L.
47PM1StaP1-4
47PM1StaP1-5
53BraJohC-2
54NewYorJA-20
54RedMan-NL21
55RedMan-NL13
58GiaJayP-1
58GiaSFCB-1
60GiaJayP-1
60RawGloT-1
61Kah-1
61Pos-142A
61Pos-142B
79DiaGre-316
83BelBreF-6
83Bra53F-34
Antonelli, Johnny (John A.)
47Exh-4A
47Exh-4B
49EurSta-3
50Bow-74
50JJKCopP-1
51Bow-243
52Top-140
53BraSpiaS3-2
53Top-106
54Bow-208
54Top-119
55ArmCoi-1
55BigLeaIS-1
55Bow-124
55DaiQueS-1
55GiaGolS-3
56Top-138
57Top-105
58Hir-50
58HirTes-1
58PacBel-2
58Top-152
59ArmCoi-2
59Top-377

60Baz-35
60Top-80
60Top-572
60TopTat-3
60TopVen-80
61Top-115
61TopStal-132
70FleWorS-51
80MarExh-1
83TopRep5-140
84FifNatCT-10
84GiaMot-13
91TopArc1-106
92BazQua5A-22
94TopArc1-119
94TopArc1G-119

Antonello, Bill (William J.)
50W720HolS-2
53Top-272
72TopTes5-3
90DodTar-19
91TopArc1-272
95TopArcBD-57

Antonini, Adrian
92LSUTigM-2
93LSUTigM-9
94BatCliC-1
94BatCliF-3435
94LSUTig-5
94LSUTigMP-7
95BatCliTI-2

Antoon, Jeff
92EugEmeC-5
92EugEmeF-3034
93RocRoyC-2
93RocRoyF-721

Antunez, Martin
82BelBreF-23

Anyzeski, Fred
75AppFoxT-1

Apana, Matt
93BelMarC-2
93BelMarF-3196
94RivPilCLC-1
95Bow-168
95TacRaiTI-4
96PorCitRB-5

Aparicio, Luis E.
47Exh-5A
47Exh-5B
56Top-292
56YelBasP-3
57Top-7
58HarSta-15
58JayPubA-2
58Top-85A
58Top-85B
58Top-483
58WhiSoxJP-1
59Top-310
59Top-408
59Top-560
59WilSpoG-1
60Baz-22
60KeyChal-3
60Lea-1
60Top-240
60Top-389
60Top-559
60WhiSoxJP-1
60WhiSoxTS-1
61Baz-35
61Pos-19A
61Pos-19B
61Top-440
61Top-574
61TopStal-120
61WhiSoxTS-1
62Baz-30
62ExhStaB-2
62Jel-49
62Pos-49
62PosCan-49
62SalPlaC-71
62ShiPlaC-71
62Top-325
62Top-469
62TopStal-22
62TopVen-200
62WhiSoxJP-1
62WhiSoxTS-1
63BasMagM-6
63ExhStaB-2
63Jel-37
63Pos-37
63SalMetC-50
63Top-205
63TopStil-2
64OriJayP-1
64Top-540
64TopCoi-31
64TopCoi-127
64TopGia-39
64WheSta-3
65Top-410
65TopTral-3
66OPC-90
66Top-90
66TopVen-90
67CokCapO-2
67DexPre-13
67OPC-60
67Top-60
67TopVen-189
68CokCapO-2
68Top-310
68TopVen-310
69KelPin-1
69MilBra-15
69MLBOffS-28
69MLBPin-2
69OPC-75
69OPCDec-2
69Top-75
69TopDec-6
69TopDecI-5
69TopSta-152
69TopSup-10
69TopTeaP-11
69TraSta-24
69WhiSoxTI-2
70DayDaiNM-55
70Kel-22
70MLBOffS-181
70OPC-315
70Top-315
70TopScr-3
70TopSup-3
70WhiSoxTI-1
71AllBasA-2
71BazNumT-8
71BazUnn-26
71Kel-19
71MilDud-1
71MLBOffS-313
71MLBOffS-554
71OPC-740
71RedSoxA-1
71RedSoxTI-1
71Top-740
71TopCoi-16
71TopGreM-51
71TopSup-23
71TopTat-44
72EssCoi-1
72MilBra-18
72OPC-313
72OPC-314
72Top-313
72Top-314
72TopCloT-2
73LinPor-14
73OPC-165
73Top-165
74OPC-61
74Top-61
74TopSta-131
76VenLeaS-181
77GalGloG-42
78TCM60I-250
80PerHaloFP-185
80SSPHOF-186
80VenLeaS-136
81Ori6F-3
81TCM60I-358
83DiaClaS2-93
83FraBroR-12
83FraBroR-22
84OCoandSI-67
84SpoDesPW-2
84WhiSoxTV-2
85WhiSoxC-13
86OriGreT-9
86SpoDecG-37
87NesDreT-15
88GreBasS-28
88PacLegI-91
89HOFStiB-18
89PerCelP-2
89WhiSoxK-6
90AGFA-9
90BasWit-23
90PerGreM-43
91OriCro-12
92UppDecS-26
93ActPacA-122
93ActPacA2-56G
93LinVenB-11
93TedWil-25
94TopSpa-L3
94Yoo-1
95MCIAmb-14
97TopStaHRR-1
97TopStaHRRA-1

Apicella, Jamie
94EveGiaC-1
94EveGiaF-3665

Apodaca, Bob (Robert John)
74MetDaiPA-8
74OPC-608
74Top-608A
74Top-608B
75MetSSP-15
75OPC-659
75Top-659
76MetMSAP-3
76OPC-16
76SSP-548
76Top-16
77MetDaiPA-2
77Top-225
78MetDaiPA-27
78Top-592
79OPC-98
79Top-197
80Top-633
82JacMetT-23
86ColMetP-1
87ColMetP-2
89JacMetGS-21
90JacMetGS-4
91LinDriAAA-575
91MetWIZ-13
91TidTidP-2527
92TidTidF-913
93NorTidF-2586
94NorTidF-2937
95NorTidTI-2
96NorTidB-2

Apolinario, Oswaldo
90BurBraB-6
90BurBraP-2354
90BurBraS-1

Aponte, Edwin
80SanJosMJitB-2
81LynSaiT-15
83WatIndF-2
84BufBisT-19

Aponte, Juan
80VenLeaS-71

Aponte, Luis Eduardo
76VenLeaS-46
80VenLeaS-58
80VenLeaS-85
81PawRedST-8
83Don-109
83Fle-178
83Top-577
84Don-371
84Fle-389
84FleUpd-2
84Ind-1
84IndWhe-38
84Nes792-187
84Top-187
84TopTif-187
84TopTra-2T
84TopTraT-2T
85Fle-437
95LinVen-163

Aponte, Newlan
89WytCubS-1

Aponte, Rick (Ricardo)
78DayBeaAT-2
80ColAstT-16
87AubAstP-19
90AshTouC-27
90AshTouP-2765
91AshTouP-585
92BurAstC-27
92BurAstF-564

Appier, Kevin
87EugEmeP-2672
88BasCitRS-5
89FleUpd-35
89OmaRoyC-4
89OmaRoyP-1720
90Bow-367
90BowTif-367
90DonRoo-21
90Fle-100
90FleCan-100
90OPC-167
90Sco-625
90Sco100RS-13
90Top-167
90TopDeb89-6
90TopTif-167
90UppDec-102
91Baz-21
91Bow-309
91Don-740
91Fle-549
91OPC-454
91PanCanT1-72
91PanCanT1-95
91RoyPol-1
91Sco-268
91Sco100RS-73
91StaClu-501
91Top-454A
91Top-454B
91TopDesS-454
91TopMic-454
91TopRoo-2
91TopTif-454
91ToyRoo-2
91Ult-143
91UppDec-566
92Bow-640
92Don-455
92Fle-150
92Lea-31
92OPC-281
92Pin-434
92PinTea2-5
92RoyPol-1
92Sco-542
92StaClu-523
92Top-281
92TopGol-281
92TopGolW-281
92TopMic-281
92TriPla-8
92Ult-66
92UppDec-159
92UppDecTMH-5
93Bow-41
93CadDis-1
93Don-43
93Fin-78
93FinRef-78
93Fla-212
93Fle-235
93FunPac-180
93Lea-101
93OPC-23
93PacSpa-131
93PanSti-101
93Pin-133
93RoyPol-2
93Sco-154
93Sel-102
93SelAce-9
93SelStaL-80
93SP-226
93StaClu-374
93StaCluFDI-374
93StaCluMOP-374
93StaCluRoy-5
93Top-76
93TopComotH-8
93TopGol-76
93TopInaM-76
93TopMic-76
93TriPla-234
93Ult-556
93UppDec-89
93UppDecGold-89
93USPlaCA-10S
94Bow-555
94ColC-351
94ColC-390
94ColChoGS-351
94ColChoGS-390
94ColChoSS-351
94ColChoSS-390
94DenHol-3
94Don-47
94DonSpeE-47
94ExtBas-83
94Fin-174
94FinRef-174
94Fla-54
94Fle-147
94FleLeaL-6
94FUnPac-55
94Lea-70
94OPC-225
94OscMayR-2
94Pac-279
94PanSti-71
94Pin-48
94PinArtP-48
94PinMusC-48
94Sco-359
94ScoGolR-359
94Sel-64
94SP-170
94SPDieC-170
94SPHol-2
94SPHolDC-2
94Spo-84
94StaClu-340
94StaCluFDI-340
94StaCluGR-340
94StaCluMO-14
94StaCluMOP-340
94Top-701
94TopGol-701
94TopSpa-701
94TriPla-231
94Ult-61
94UppDec-133
94UppDecAJ-13
94UppDecAJG-13
94UppDecED-133
94USPlaCA-12S
95Baz-110
95Bow-292
95BowBes-R6
95BowBesR-R6
95ClaPhoC-31
95ColCho-462
95ColChoGS-462
95ColChoSS-462
95Don-542
95DonPreP-542
95DonTopotO-82
95Emb-43
95EmbGolI-43
95Emo-48
95Fin-108
95FinRef-108
95Fla-262
95Fle-152
95Lea-84
95LeaLim-24
95Pac-196
95Pin-70
95PinArtP-70
95PinFan-7
95PinMusC-70
95Sco-520
95ScoGolR-520
95ScoPlaTS-520
95Sel-23
95SelArtP-23
95SelCer-22
95SelCerMG-22
95SP-160
95SPCha-157
95SPCha-160
95SPChaDC-157
95SPChaDC-160
95Spo-62
95SpoArtP-62
95SPSil-160
95StaClu-445
95StaClu-516
95StaCluMOP-445
95StaCluMOP-516
95StaCluSTWS-445
95StaCluSTWS-516
95StaCluVR-236
95Sum-46
95SumNthD-46
95Top-325
95TopCyb-178

95TopLeaL-LL50
95UC3-21
95UC3ArtP-21
95Ult-53
95UltGolM-53
95UppDec-419
95UppDecED-419
95UppDecEDG-419
95Zen-63
96Baz-51
96Bow-68
96BowBes-45
96BowBesAR-45
96BowBesR-45
96Cir-43
96CirRav-43
96ColCho-170
96ColChoGS-170
96ColChoSS-170
96ColChoYMtP-1
96ColChoYMtP-1A
96ColChoYMtPGS-1
96ColChoYMtPGS-1A
96DenHol-22
96Don-439
96DonPreP-439
96EmoXL-64
96Fin-B23
96FinRef-B23
96Fla-86
96Fle-123
96FleSmo'H-1
96FleTif-123
96Lea-108
96LeaPrePB-108
96LeaPrePG-108
96LeaPrePS-108
96LeaSig-135
96LeaSigPPG-135
96LeaSigPPP-135
96MetUni-62
96MetUniP-62
96Pac-329
96PacPri-P104
96PacPriG-P104
96PanSti-185
96Pin-101
96PinAfi-65
96PinAfiAP-65
96PinAfiFPP-65
96PinArtP-38
96PinSta-38
96ProSta-120
96RoyPol-1
96Sco-199
96Sco-284
96ScoDugC-B9
96ScoDugCAP-B9
96Sel-27
96SelArtP-27
96SelTeaN-17
96SP-96
96Spo-75
96SpoArtP-75
96StaClu-362
96StaCluEPB-362
96StaCluEPG-362
96StaCluEPS-362
96StaCluMOP-362
95StaCluVRMC-236
96Stu-111
96StuPrePB-111
96StuPrePG-111
96StuPrePS-111
96Sum-72
96SumAbo&B-72
96SumArtP-72
96SumFoi-72
96TeaOut-3
96Top-364
96TopChr-148
96TopChrR-148
96TopGal-64
96TopGalPPI-64
96TopLas-114
96Ult-67
96UltGolM-67
96UppDec-86
96UppDecPHE-H17
96UppDecPreH-H17
97Bow-26
97BowBes-49
97BowBesAR-49
97BowBesR-49
97BowChr-22
97BowChrI-22
97BowChrIR-22
97BowChrR-22
97BowInt-26
97Cir-158
97CirRav-158
97ColCho-130
97Don-206
97Don-434
97DonEli-106
97DonEliGS-106
97DonLim-147
97DonLim-172
97DonLimLE-147
97DonLimLE-172
97DonPre-66
97DonPreCttC-66
97DonPreP-206
97DonPreP-434
97DonPrePGold-206
97DonPrePGold-434
97Fin-85
97FinRef-85
97FlaSho-A17
97FlaSho-B17
97FlaSho-C17
97FlaShoLC-17
97FlaShoLC-B17
97FlaShoLC-C17
97FlaShoLCM-A17
97FlaShoLCM-B17
97FlaShoLCM-C17
97Fle-109
97Fle-733
97FleTeaL-7
97FleTif-109
97FleTif-733
97Lea-34
97LeaFraM-34
97LeaFraMDC-34
97MetUni-90
97NewPin-59
97NewPinAP-59
97NewPinMC-59
97NewPinPP-59
97Pac-97
97PacLigB-97
97PacSil-97
97PinCar-4
97PinIns-59
97PinInsCE-59
97PinInsDE-59
97PinX-P-55
97PinX-PMoS-55
97ProMag-56
97ProMagML-56
97RoyPol-1
97Sco-42
97ScoPreS-42
97ScoShoS-42
97ScoShoSAP-42
97SkyE-X-23
97SkyE-XC-23
97SkyE-XEC-23
97SP-88
97SpoIll-156
97SpoIllEE-156
97StaClu-22
97StaCluMat-22
97StaCluMOP-22
97Stu-94
97StuPrePG-94
97StuPrePS-94
97Top-30
97TopChr-12
97TopChrR-12
97TopGal-71
97TopGalPPI-71
97TopSta-22
97TopStaAM-22
97Ult-65
97UltGolME-65
97UltPlaME-65
97UppDec-389

Applegate, Russ
84IdaFalATI-1
85MadMusP-2
85MadMusT-5
86ModA'sC-2
86ModA'sP-2

Appleton, Ed (Edward Sam)
16ColE13-6
90DodTar-893

Appleton, Pete (Peter W.)
39PlaBal-137
39WhiSoxTI-1
40PlaBal-128
40WhiSoxL-1
91ConTSN-76

Appling, Luke (Lucas B.)
31Exh-19
34BatR31-124
34DiaStaR-95
34ExhFou-10
34Gou-27
34GouCanV-84
35AlDemDCR3-18
35GouPuzR-1I
35GouPuzR-2F
35GouPuzR-16F
35GouPuzR-17F
36ExhFou-10
36GouWidPPR-B2
36GouWidPPR-C1
36OveCanR-2
36SandSW-1
36WheBB5-3
36WorWidGV-113
37ExhFou-10
37GouFliMR-7A
37GouFliMR-7B
37GouThuMR-7
37KelPepS-BB1
37OPCBatUV-115
37WheBB8-1
38BasTabP-1
38ExhFou-10
39ExhSal-1A
39ExhSal-1B
39GouPreR303A-1
39GouPreR303B-1
39WhiSoxTI-2
39WorWidGTP-1
40WheM4-12
40WhiSoxL-2
41DouPlaR-69
47Exh-6
48BluTin-10
48WhiSoxTI-1
49Bow-175
49Lea-59
50Bow-37
50RoyDes-16
60Fle-27
60Top-461
67TopVen-158
76ChiGre-1
76GalBasGHoF-1
76RowExh-1
76ShaPiz-95
76TayBow4-38
76WhiSoxTAG-1
77BobParHoF-3
77GalGloG-80
77TCMTheWY-12
80PacLeg-22
80PerHaloFP-95
80SSPHOF-95
80WhiSoxGT-4
82DiaCla-25
83ConMar-6
83DonHOFH-8
83TCMPla1942-16
84BraPol-55
85WhiSoxC-1
87HygAllG-3
88ConAmeA-1
88PacLegI-4
89SweBasG-30
89WhiSoxK-6
90PacLeg-3
90SweBasG-18
91SweBasG-3
92ConTSN-475
92ConTSNGI-730
92PacSea-57
93ConTSN-730
93TedWil-26
94ConTSN-1008
94ConTSNB-1008
94UppDecAH-41
94UppDecAH1-41

Aquedo, Vasquez
87Ft.MyeRP-16

Aquino, Geronimo
93HicCraF-1290

Aquino, Julio
94GreFalDSP-2
95SanBerSTI-1
96HudValRB-22

Aquino, Luis
86SyrChiP-2
87Don-655
87OPC-301
87SyrChiP-1937
87SyrChiT-1
87Top-301
87TopTif-301
88BlaYNPRWLU-22
88OmaRoyC-2
88OmaRoyP-1520
89BlaYNPRWL-71
89Don-534
89Fle-275
89FleGlo-275
89Top-266
89TopTif-266
90Don-179
90Fle-101
90FleCan-101
90OPC-707
90PubSti-341
90Sco-432
90Top-707
90TopTif-707
90UppDec-274
90VenSti-15
91Don-718
91Fle-550
91OPC-169
91RoyPol-2
91StaClu-451
91Top-169
91TopDesS-169
91TopMic-169
91TopTif-169
91UppDec-504
92Don-544
92Fle-151
92OPC-412
92Pin-454
92RoyPol-2
92Sco-369
92StaClu-365
92Top-412
92TopGol-412
92TopGolW-412
92TopMic-412
92UppDec-219
93Fle-615
93FleFinE-48
93Lea-509
93MarPub-1
93PacSpa-130
93RoyPol-3
93Top-643
93TopGol-643
93TopInaM-643
93TopMic-643
93TopTra-76T
93Ult-363
93UppDec-711
93UppDecGold-711
94ColC-39
94ColChoGS-39
94ColChoSS-39
94Don-67
94Fle-458
94Pac-233
94Pin-223
94PinArtP-223
94PinMusC-223
94Sco-255
94ScoGolR-255
94StaClu-160
94StaCluFDI-160
94StaCluGR-160
94StaCluMOP-160
94Top-76
94TopGol-76
94TopSpa-76
94Ult-191
95Fle-324
95Pac-165

Aquino, Pedro
87SpoIndP-20
88SpoIndP-1929

Arace, Pasquale
91AugPirC-19
91AugPirP-816
92SalBucC-8
92SalBucF-74

Aracena, Juan
96BurIndB-1

Aracena, Luinis
92MadMusC-14
92MadMusF-1247
93MadMusC-3
93MadMusF-1833
93SouOreAC-2
93SouOreAF-4075

Aragon, Joey
86VisOakP-2
87VisOakP-19
88OrlTwiB-11

Aragon, Reno
76DubPacT-3
77CocAstT-2

Aragon, Steve
82WisRapTF-23
83VisOakF-3
84VisOakT-24
85OrlTwiT-1
86OrlTwiP-1

Arai, Kiyoshi
92SalSpuC-1
92SalSpuF-3761

Araki, Daisuke
87JapPlaB-6

Arango, Fernando
92OneYanC-29

Arangure, Maurillo
85MexCitTT-3

Arano, Eloy
94BriTigC-2
94BriTigF-3508

Aranzamendi, Aloxio
92FroRowDP-72
94KanCouCC-3
94KanCouCF-167
94KanCouCTI-3

Aranzamendi, Jorge
77St.PetCT-12
78ArkTraT-1
79ArkTraT-12
80ArkTraT-3
81ArkTraT-8
82ArkTraT-24
83ArkTraT-24

Aranzullo, Mike
91SalLakTP-3215
91SalLakTSP-7

Arape, Ali
76VenLeaS-155

Araujo, Andy
85DomLeaS-28
86NewBriRSP-1
87PawRedSP-64
87PawRedST-1
88PawRedSC-5
88PawRedSP-446
89PawRedSC-8
89PawRedSP-679
89PawRedSTI-1
93LimRocDWB-114

Araujo, Jesus
76VenLeaS-6

Archdeacon, Flash
94ConTSN-1307
94ConTSNB-1307

Archer, Carl
91PulBraC-4
91PulBraP-4010

Archer, Jim (James William)
61AthJayP-1
61Top-552
62Jel-98
62Pos-98
62PosCan-98
62SalPlaC-75
62ShiPlaC-75
62Top-433
62TopBuc-4
62TopStaI-52
63AthJayP-1

Archer, Jimmy (James Peter)
08AmeCarE-34
09BusBroBPP-1
09ColChiE-11
09MaxPubP-20
09RamT20-3
09SpoNewSM-59

10ChiE-1
10DarChoE-1
10DomDisP-2
10OrnOvaPP-1
10SweCapPP-79A
10SweCapPP-79B
11SpoLifM-165
11T205-3
12ColRedB-11
12ColTinT-11
12HasTriFT-13B
12HasTriFT-13C
12HasTriFT-13D
12HasTriFT-36A
12HasTriFT-36C
12HasTriFT-36D
13PolGroW-1
14CraJacE-64
14FatPlaT-2
14TexTomE-1
15CraJacE-64
15SpoNewM-6
16BF2FP-64
16ColE13-7
16SpoNewM-6
90DodTar-20
93ConTSN-884
Archer, Kurt
90HelBreSP-15
90SanDieSA3-1
91Cla/Bes-223
91StoPorC-8
91StoPorP-3023
92StoPorC-22
92StoPorF-26
93ElPasDF-2940
94ElPasDF-3137
94StoPorC-2
Archibald, Dan
88JamExpP-1920
89JamExpP-2142
90RocExpLC-1
90RocExpP-2684
Archibald, Jaime
86ColMetP-2
87LynMetP-9
Arcia, Jose R.
68Top-258
68TopVen-258
69MilBra-16
69Top-473A
69Top-473B
69TopSta-91
69TopTeaP-12
70Top-587
71MLBOffS-217
71OPC-134
71Top-134
72MilBra-19
73OPC-466
73Top-466
Ard, Johnny
89Bow-153
89BowTif-153
89CalLeaA-13
89VisOakCLC-96
89VisOakP-1427
90Bes-60
90Bow-406
90BowTif-406
90CMC-809
90OrlSunRB-23
90OrlSunRP-1075
90OrlSunRS-1
90ProAaA-39
91Bow-634
91LinDriAAA-385
91PhoFirLD-385
91PhoFirP-58
92PhoFirF-2814
92PhoFirS-376
92ProFS7-342
92SkyAAAF-173
93ClaFS7-41
Ardizola, Rinaldo
46RemBre-20
Ardner, Hoss (Joseph)
87OldJudN-13
Ardoin, Dan
96ModA'sB-3
Arduini, Salvatore
52LavPro-84
Arellanes, Frank J.
09RamT20-4
09T206-8
11SpoLifCW-6
11SpoLifM-1
12PhiCarE-3
Arellano, Carlos
94BurIndC-1
94BurIndF-3783
Arena, Rich
89OneYanP-2120
90GreHorB-29
90GreHorP-2681
90TamYanD-28
92GulCoaYF-3707
93PriWilCC-27
93PriWilCF-673
96TamYanY-2
Arena, Sam
92ForLauYTI-1
Arendas, Dan
87Ft.LauYP-13
88Ft.LauYS-1
Arendas, David
88CapCodPPaLP-100
Arendt, Jim
91PriRedC-29
Arffa, Steve
94PitMetC-3
94PitMetF-3514
95StLucMTI-5
96StLucMTI-30
Arft, Hank (Henry Irven)
49Bow-139
51Bow-173
52Bow-229
52Top-284
53MotCoo-26
79DiaGre-192
83TopRep5-284
Argo, Billy
88BakDodCLC-244
89VerBeaDS-1
Arguelles, Fernando
89SalBucS-2
90SanBerSB-16
90SanBerSCLC-100
90SanBerSP-2636
91JacSunLD-326
91JacSunP-152
91LinDriAA-326
Arguto, Sam
93NiaFalRF-3377
94FayGenC-2
94FayGenF-2138
Arias, Alex
87WytCubP-27
88ChaWheB-9
88SouAtlLAGS-13
89PeoChiTI-17
90ChaKniTI-5
90TopTVCu-36
91ChaKniLD-126
91ChaKniP-1693
91Cla/Bes-10
91LinDriAA-126
92FleUpd-72
92IowCubF-4055
92IowCubS-202
92OPC-551
92ProFS7-202
92SkyAAAF-96
92Top-551
92TopGol-551
92TopGolW-551
92TopMic-551
93ClaGam-6
93Don-4
93Don-254
93Don-780
93Fla-45
93FleFinE-49
93FleMajLP-A16
93Lea-462
93LinVenB-311
93MarPub-2
93MarUSPC-1S
93MarUSPC-7H
93OPCPre-84
93PacSpa-452
93Pin-483
93Pin-612
93Sco-565
93StaClu-741
93StaCluFDI-741
93StaCluMarI-4
93StaCluMOP-741
93Top-516
93TopGol-516
93TopInaM-516
93TopMic-516
93Ult-364
93UppDec-631
93UppDecGold-631
94ColC-401
94ColChoGS-401
94ColChoSS-401
94Don-97
94Fle-459
94Pac-234
94Pin-390
94PinArtP-390
94PinMusC-390
94Sco-199
94ScoGolR-199
94Sel-137
94StaClu-230
94StaCluFDI-230
94StaCluGR-230
94StaCluMOP-230
94StaCluMOP-ST5
94StaCluST-ST5
94StaCluT-85
94StaCluTFDI-85
94Top-104
94TopGol-104
94TopSpa-104
94USPlaCR-2H
95Pac-166
95PacPri-53
95Sco-541
95ScoGolR-541
95ScoPlaTS-541
95StaClu-63
95StaCluFDI-63
95StaCluMOP-63
95StaCluSTWS-63
96ColCho-552
96ColChoGS-552
96ColChoSS-552
96Fle-381
96FleTif-381
96LeaSigEA-4
96Pac-71
96Sco-478
97Fle-324
97FleTif-324
97Pac-295
97PacLigB-295
97PacSil-295
Arias, Alfredo
94St.CatBJC-2
94St.CatBJF-3631
95HagSunF-59
Arias, Amador
91CedRapRC-16
91CedRapRP-2724
91Cla/Bes-340
91EriSaiC-1
91EriSaiP-4074
92ChaWheF-13
92ChaWVWC-20
93LinVenB-120
93WinSpiC-3
93WinSpiF-1575
94WinSpiC-3
94WinSpiF-276
95ChaLooTI-1
95LinVen-85
96CarLeaA1B-17
96CarLeaA2B-17
Arias, Francisco
87PocGiaTB-26
88PocGiaP-2078
Arias, George
94LakElsSC-2
94LakElsSF-1669
94Top-369
94TopGol-369
94TopSpa-369
95Bes-10
95BowBes-B66
95BowBesR-B66
95Exc-17
95MidAngOHP-2
95MidAngTI-2
95SPML-26
95SPMLA-3
95TopTra-122T
95UppDecML-139
96AngMot-12
96Bow-202
96BowBesMI-3
96BowBesMIAR-3
96BowBesMIR-3
96ColCho-426
96ColChoGS-426
96ColChoSS-426
96EmoXL-23
96Exc-21
96ExcAll-4
96ExcSeaTL-1
96Fin-G202
96FinRef-G202
96Fla-33
96FlaWavotF-2
96FleUpd-U19
96FleUpdNH-2
96FleUpdTC-U19
96LeaLimR-10
96LeaLimRG-10
96LeaPre-131
96LeaPreP-131
96LeaSig-111
96LeaSigPPG-111
96LeaSigPPP-111
96Pin-373
96PinAfi-161
96PinAfiAP-161
96PinFoil-373
96Sel-166
96SelArtP-166
96SelCer-115
96SelCerAP-115
96SelCerCB-115
96SelCerCR-115
96SelCerMB-115
96SelCerMG-115
96SelCerMR-115
96SP-2
96Stu-146
96StuPrePB-146
96StuPrePG-146
96StuPrePS-146
96Sum-170
96SumAbo&B-170
96SumArtP-170
96SumFoi-170
96Top-434
96Ult-324
96UltGolM-324
96UppDec-238
96UppDecFSP-FS1
96UppDecPHE-H21
96UppDecPreH-H21
96VanCanB-5
96Zen-107
96ZenArtP-107
97Bow-156
97BowInt-156
97Cir-195
97CirRav-195
97Don-127
97Don-393
97DonEli-72
97DonEliGS-72
97DonPreP-127
97DonPreP-393
97DonPrePGold-127
97DonPrePGold-393
97Fle-35
97FleTif-35
97Lea-4
97LeaFraM-4
97LeaFraMDC-4
97MetUni-37
97Pac-2
97PacLatotML-1
97PacLigB-2
97PacSil-2
97Pin-167
97PinArtP-167
97PinIns-135
97PinInsCE-135
97PinInsDE-135
97PinMusC-167
97Sco-128
97ScoPreS-128
97ScoShoS-128
97ScoShoSAP-128
97SelToootT-15
97SelToootTMB-15
97Stu-152
97StuPrePG-152
97StuPrePS-152
97Top-306
97Ult-23
97UltGolME-23
97UltPlaME-23
97UppDec-293
95UppDecMLFS-139
Arias, German
90MarPhiP-3207
Arias, Jose
90HamRedS-2
90SavCarP-2058
91JohCitCC-27
96MarPhiB-2
Arias, Juan
78SalPirT-1
79BufBisT-11
Arias, Pedro
88BurIndP-1787
Arias, Rogelio
95AshTouTI-18
96AshTouB-6
96PorRocB-6
Arias, Rudy (Rodolfo M.)
59Top-537
Arias, Tony
85MadMusP-3
85MadMusT-6
86MadMusP-2
88ModA'sTI-19
Arias, Wagner
93HelBreF-4084
93HelBreSP-6
94BelBreC-2
94BelBreF-92
Arigoni, Scott
82ArkTraT-1
83SprCarF-9
Ariola, Anthony
88SouOreAP-1696
89MadMusS-2
89Sta-64
90CMC-581
90ProAAAF-131
90TacTigC-4
90TacTigP-84
Aristimuno, Jesus
76VenLeaS-159
Arita, Shuzo
91SalSpuC-27
91SalSpuP-2261
Arito, Michiyo
79TCMJapPB-63
Arland, Mark
90ChaWheB-20
90ChaWheP-2250
91ChaWheC-21
91ChaWheP-2898
Arlett, Buzz (Russell Loris)
20WalMaiW-1
31Exh-11
78HalHalR-15
Arlich, Don (Donald Louis)
77FriOneYW-90
Arlin, Steve (Stephen Ralph)
72OPC-78
72PadTeal-2
72Top-78
73OPC-294
73Top-294
74OPC-406
74Top-406
75OPC-159
75Top-159
77PadSchC-4A
77PadSchC-4B
Arline, James
78RicBraT-2
79RicBraT-23
Armas, Familia
94VenLinU-141
Armas, Julio
93LinVenB-149
94VenLinU-163
Armas, Marcos
89MedAthB-24
90MadMusB-4
91HunStaC-1
91HunStaLD-276
91HunStaP-1807
91LinDriAA-276
91ModA'sP-3093
92ClaFS7-134

92HunStaF-3955
92HunStaS-302
92SkyAA F-127
93Bow-429
93ClaGolF-20
93FleFinE-253
93Lea-478
93LinVenB-175
93TacTigF-3043
93TopTra-100T
94Don-51
94Fle-253
94Pac-444
94Pin-398
94PinArtP-398
94PinMusC-398
94TacTigF-3180
94Top-311
94TopGol-311
94TopSpa-311
94VenLinU-123
94VenLinU-197
95LinVen-169
Armas, Tony (Antonio Rafael)
76VenLeaS-77
76VenLeaS-223
77Top-492
78Top-298
79Top-507
80Top-391
80VenLeaS-99
80VenLeaS-130
81A'sGraG-20
81AllGamPI-46
81Don-239
81Dra-30
81Fle-575
81FleStiC-5
81OPC-151
81Squ-24
81Top-629
81TopScr-6
81TopSti-116
82A'sGraG-1
82Don-365
82Dra-1
82Fle-85
82FleSta-128
82Kel-35
82OPC-60
82PerCreC-17
82PerCreCG-17
82Top-60
82Top-162
82TopSti-4
82TopSti-224
83AllGamPI-46
83Don-71
83Fle-513
83OPC-353
83Top-1
83Top-435
83TopSti-108
83TopSti-191
83TopSti-192
83TopTra-4T
84AllGamPI-136
84Don-294
84Fle-390
84FleSti-21
84FunFooP-24
84Nes792-105
84OPC-105
84Top-105
84TopGloS-20
84TopRubD-1
84TopSti-218
84TopTif-105
85AllGamPI-46
85Don-249
85Dra-1
85Fle-149
85FleStaS-12
85FleStaS-28
85Lea-112
85OPC-394
85Top-707
85Top-785
85TopGaloC-1
85TopGloS-10
85TopRubD-1
85TopSti-95
85TopSti-194
85TopSti-209
85TopSup-10
85TopTif-707
85TopTif-785
86Don-5
86Don-127
86DonSupD-5
86Fle-339
86Lea-5
86OPC-255
86Spo-61
86Spo-145
86Top-255
86TopSti-254
86TopTat-11
86TopTif-255
86Woo-1
87A'sMot-21
87BoaandB-15
87Don-498
87Fle-26
87FleGlo-26
87OPC-174
87Top-535
87TopTif-535
88AngSmo-5
88Fle-484
88FleGlo-484
88Sco-487
88ScoGlo-487
88Top-761
88TopTif-761
89Bow-51
89BowTif-51
89Don-580
89Fle-467
89FleGlo-467
89PanSti-295
89Sco-182
89Top-332
89TopBig-99
89TopTif-332
89UppDec-212
90Don-525
90Fle-126
90FleCan-126
90OPC-603
90PubSti-364
90Sco-378
90Top-603
90TopTif-603
90UppDec-58
90VenSti-16
93LinVenB-281
93LinVenB-282
93LinVenB-283
93LinVenB-284
93LinVenB-285
93LinVenB-286
93LinVenB-287
95LinVen-133
Armbrister, Ed (Edison R.)
72OPC-524
72Top-524
74OPC-601
74Top-601
75OPC-622
75Top-622
76OPC-652
76RedKro-1
76RedPos-1
76SSP-42
76Top-652
77Top-203
78IndIndTI-8
78SSP270-124
78Top-556
Armbruster, Charles
11SpoLifCW-7
Armbruster, Harry (Herman)
09T206-393
Armendariz, Jesse
94WilCubC-1
94WilCubF-3753
Armer, Rick
77WauMetT-2
Armour, Bill
11SpoLifCW-8
Armstead, Al
79WatA'sT-10
Armstrong, Bill
79MemChiT-3
84EvaTriT-20
Armstrong, Eldridge
84IdaFalATI-2
Armstrong, Jack
88NasSouC-1
88NasSouP-484
88NasSouTI-1
88RedKah-40
88ScoRoo-78T
88ScoRooG-78T
88TopTra-6T
88TopTraT-6T
89ClaLigB-97
89Don-493
89PanSti-63
89Sco-462
89ScoHot1R-99
89Top-317
89TopTif-317
89TriA AAC-12
89UppDec-257
90ClaYel-T74
90Don-544
90DonBesN-142
90Fle-412
90FleCan-412
90Lea-374
90OPC-642
90RedKah-1
90ScoYouS2-11
90Top-642
90TopBig-314
90TopTif-642
90TriAAAC-12
90UppDec-684
90USPlaCA-JKO
91BasBesAotM-2
91Bow-679
91ClaGam-6
91Don-439
91Don-571
91Fle-55
91Lea-459
91OPC-175
91PanFreS-165
91PanSti-126
91RedFolS-114
91RedKah-40
91RedPep-1
91Sco-231
91Sco100S-83
91StaClu-510
91Top-175
91TopDesS-175
91TopGloA-21
91TopMic-175
91TopTif-175
91UppDec-373
92Bow-252
92Don-762
92Fle-398
92IndFanC-2
92Lea-247
92OPC-77
92OPCPre-192
92Sco-488
92ScoRoo-58T
92StaClu-791
92StaCluNC-791
92Stu-162
92Top-77
92TopGol-77
92TopGolW-77
92TopMic-77
92TopTra-6T
92TopTraG-6T
92Ult-344
92UppDec-296
92UppDec-789
93Don-69
93Don-777
93Fla-46
93Fle-417
93FleFinE-50
93Lea-235
93MarPub-3
93MarUSPC-2D
93MarUSPC-11S
93PacSpa-453
93Pin-513
93Sco-655
93StaClu-567
93StaCluFDI-567
93StaCluMarI-9
93StaCluMOP-567
93Top-434
93TopGol-434
93TopInaM-434
93TopMic-434
93TopTra-80T
93Ult-365
93UppDec-758
93UppDecGold-758
94ColC-40
94ColC-418
94ColChoGS-40
94ColChoGS-418
94ColChoSS-40
94ColChoSS-418
94Don-466
94Fla-107
94Fle-460
94Lea-226
94Pac-235
94Pin-166
94PinArtP-166
94PinMusC-166
94RanMagM-1
94Sco-410
94ScoGolR-410
94ScoRoo-RT45
94ScoRooGR-RT45
94StaClu-594
94StaCluFDI-594
94StaCluGR-594
94StaCluMOP-594
94StaCluT-256
94StaCluTFDI-256
94Top-551
94TopGol-551
94TopSpa-551
94UppDec-460
94UppDecED-469
95Top-222
Armstrong, Jim
91IdaFalBP-4319
91IdaFalBSP-10
Armstrong, Kevin
85LitFalMT-2
86ColMetP-3
87WicPiIRD-2
88RivRedWCLC-206
89SanAntMB-6
Armstrong, Mike (Michael D.)
79NaSouTI-3
80HawIsIT-16
80VenLeaS-208
81Fle-503
81HawIsIT-11
82OmaRoyT-1
82Roy-2
82Top-731
83Fle-105
83Top-219
84Don-217
84Fle-342
84Nes792-417
84Top-417
84TopTif-417
84TopTra-3T
84TopTraT-3T
85Don-602
85Fle-120
85Top-612
85TopTif-612
86ColCliP-1
86YanTCM-4
87ColCliP-1
87ColCliP-21
92YanWIZ8-4
Armstrong, William
83EvaTriT-23
Arnason, Chuck
72Dia-66
Arndt, Harry J.
09T206-394
11SpoLifCW-9
Arndt, Larry
86MadMusP-3
87HunStaTI-2
89TacTigC-22
89TacTigP-1557
90CMC-600
90ProAAAF-144
90TacTigC-23
90TacTigP-97
90TopDeb89-7
Arner, Michael
90Bes-200
90CMC-479
90GasRanB-19
90GasRanP-2511
90GasRanS-1
90ProAaA-80
90SouAtlLAS-1
90StaFS7-96
91ChaRanC-1
91ChaRanP-1305
92ChaRanC-24
93TulDriF-2726
93TulDriTI-2
Arnerich, Ken
82QuaCitCT-18
Arnett, Curt
74GasRanT-1
75LynRanT-2
Arnett, Jon
58HarSta-21
Arnette, Steve
89TenTecGE-1
Arney, Jeff
82WisRapTF-25
83VisOakF-2
85WatIndT-14
86WatIndP-1
Arnold, Bryan
88WatPirP-14
Arnold, Chris
72OPC-232
72Top-232
73OPC-584
73Top-584
74OPC-432
74Top-432
76SSP 00
77PhoGiaCC-2
77PhoGiaCP-2
77PhoGiaVNB-1
77Top-591
79TCMJapPB-43
Arnold, Gary
87NewOriP-6
88GenCubP-1636
89GenCubP-1858
Arnold, Greg
89PulBraP-1912
Arnold, James
47SmiClo-10
93ClaGolF-110
Arnold, Jamie
92ClaBluBF-BC25
92ClaDraP-16
92ClaDraPFB-BC15
92ClaFS7-407
92UppDecML-12
93ClaFS7-42
93MacBraC-2
93MacBraF-1391
93Pin-455
93Sco-487
93Sel-303
93StaCluM-65
93Top-559
93TopGol-559
93TopInaM-559
93TopMic-559
94CarLeaAF-CAR27
94Cla-135
94ClaGolF-113
94ClaTriF-T1
94DurBulC-2
94DurBulF-319
94DurBulTI-2
94ExcFS7-151
94UppDecML-36
95BreBtaTI-34
95DurBulTI-1
95UppDecML-159
96GreBraB-5
96GreBraTI-46
95UppDecMLFS-159
Arnold, Jay
96OgdRapTI-37
Arnold, Jeff
84NewOriT-25
Arnold, John
77WatIndT-2
96EugEmeB-21
Arnold, Ken
91HunCubC-3
91HunCubP-3339
92PeoChiC-27

92PeoChiTI-2
92ProFS7-212
94BowBayF-2418
96TulDriTI-1
Arnold, Ron
84AlbA'sT-2
84TacTigC-75
Arnold, Scott
86FloStaLAP-5
86St.PetCP-2
87ArkTraP-13
87TexLeaAF-21
88LouRedBTI-8
88TexLeaAGS-20
89LouRedBC-2
89LouRedBP-1248
89LouRedBTI-9
90CMC-101
90LouRedBC-1
90LouRedBLBC-7
90LouRedBP-394
90ProAAAF-508
90SprCarDGB-18
90TopTVCa-38
Arnold, Sheila
88GenCubP-1660
Arnold, Tim
86FloStaLAP-6
86WesPalBEP-2
87JacExpP-430
88VisOakCLC-149
88VisOakP-97
89OrlTwiB-8
89OrlTwiP-1353
Arnold, Tony
84ChaO'sT-26
85ChaO'sT-8
86RocRedWP-1
87OriFreB-57
88AlbDukC-5
88AlbDukP-261
89SanAntMB-5
90YakBeaTI-19
91OriCro-13
91YakBeaP-4265
92TexLon-3
92YakBeaC-26
93WatIndC-30
94WatIndC-29
95KinIndTI-1
96CanIndB-2
Arnovich, Morrie (Morris)
38ExhFou-6
39PlaBal-46
39WorWidGV-1
40PlaBal-97
40WheM4-4
41DouPlaR-139
41Gou-25
41HarHarW-1
41PlaBal-57
92ConTSN-500
Arnsberg, Brad
84GreHorT-10
85AlbYanT-1
86ColCliP-2
86YanTCM-2
87ColCliP-2
87ColCliP-24
87ColCliT-1
87IntLeaAT-3
88Fle-202
88FleGlo-202
88Top-159
88TopTif-159
89RanMot-15
89RanSmo-2
90AlbDecGB-27
90CMC-157
90Lea-495
90OklCit8C-7
90OklCit8P-423
90ProAAAF-669
90Sco100RS-72
90TopTra-3T
90TopTraT-3T
91Bow-279
91Don-633
91Fle-279
91OPC-706
91PacRyaTEI-68
91RanMot-25
91Sco-510
91StaClu-540
91Top-706A
91Top-706B
91TopDesS-706
91TopMic-706
91TopTif-706
91Ult-346
91UppDec-608
92ColSprSSF-742
92Fle-298
92IndFanC-3
92IowCubF-4045
92StaClu-668
92StaCluECN-668
92YanWIZ8-5
93PacSpa-92
93RanKee-54
93TacTigF-3024
95ChaRivTI-28
96ChaRivTI-9603
Arnsberg, Tim
86AshTouP-1
87OscAstP-26
Arntzen, Brian
90NebCor-2
92WatIndC-15
92WatIndF-3237
93ColRedC-2
93ColRedF-600
Arocha, Rene
92LouRedF-1879
92LouRedS-251
92SkyAAAF-122
92TriA AAS-251
92UppDecML-136
93Bow-276
93CarPol-2
93Don-572
93ExcFS7-95
93Fla-119
93FleFinE-123
93LeaGolR-R15
93OPCPre-6
93PacBeiA-29
93PacSpa-628
93Pin-599
93SelRoo-62T
93SelRooAR-9
93SP-73
93StaClu-712
93StaCluCa-2
93StaCluFDI-712
93StaCluMOP-712
93Top-742
93TopGol-742
93TopInaM-742
93TopMic-742
93TopTra-77T
93Toy-78
93Ult-460
93UltAllR-1
93UppDec-3
93UppDecGold-3
94Bow-208
94CarPol-2
94ColC-41
94ColChoGS-41
94ColChoSS-41
94Don-60
94ExtBas-356
94Fin-5
94FinJum-5
94FinRef-5
94Fla-223
94Fle-628
94FleRooS-1
94Lea-228
94OPC-234
94Pac-586
94Pin-107
94PinArtP-107
94PinMusC-107
94Sco-164
94ScoBoyoS-25
94ScoGolR-164
94Sel-300
94StaClu-306
94StaCluFDI-306
94StaCluGR-306
94StaCluMOP-306
94StaCluT-315
94StaCluTFDI-315
94Top-348
94TopGol-348
94TopSpa-348
94Ult-264
94UppDec-191
94UppDecED-191
94USPlaCR-10S
95ColCho-197
95ColChoGS-197
95ColChoSS-197
95Don-2
95DonPreP-2
95Fin-46
95FinRef-46
95Fla-191
95Fle-494
95Lea-166
95Pac-405
95PacPri-130
95Sco-374
95ScoGolR-374
95ScoPlaTS-374
95StaClu-16
95StaCluFDI-16
95StaCluMOP-16
95StaCluSTWS-16
95StaCluVR-10
95Top-24
95TopCyb-20
95Ult-221
95UltGolM-221
95UppDecSE-94
95UppDecSEG-94
95StaCluVRMC-10
Arola, Bruce
88MadMusP-2
89BoiHawP-1996
91SalSpuC-22
91SalSpuP-2234
92SalSpuF-3748
Aronetz, Cam
91GreFalDSP-22
92BakDodCLC-2
93BelBreC-1
93BelBreF-1700
Arp, Ron
76BatTroTI-1
Arrandale, Matt
93GleFalRC-4
93GleFalRF-3993
94SavCarC-3
94SavCarF-496
94SouAtlLAF-SAL46
95ArkTraTI-3
95Exc-260
95Top-316
95UppDecML-44
96LouRedB-6
95UppDecMLFS-44
Arredondo, Hernando
96ButCopKB-9
Arredondo, Joe
90PitMetP-6
91PitMetC-13
91PitMetP-3427
Arredondo, Roberto
90ChaRaiB-9
90ChaRaiP-2045
91MidLeaAP-MWL29
91WatDiaC-14
91WatDiaP-1261
92ClaFS7-10
92HigDesMC-6
92ProFS7-338
Arrevalos, Ryan
95HelBreTI-4
Arriete, Nelson
88MisStaB-1
89MisStaB-3
Arrigo, Jerry (Gerald W.)
64Top-516
65OPC-39
65RedEnq-1
65Top-39
66Top-357
66TopVen-357
67Top-488
68Kah-B7
68Top-302
68TopVen-302
69Kah-B4
69OPC-213
69Top-213
69TopFou-14
69TopSta-22
69TopTeaP-20
70OPC-274
70Top-274
72MilBra-20
78TCM60I-64
78TCM60I-86
91MetWIZ-14
Arrington, Dave
74WicAerODF-122
Arrington, Mike
76AshTouT-13
Arrington, Sam
80WisRapTT-1
82OrlTwiT-23
83VisOakF-4
Arrington, Tom
86BurExpP-1
Arrington, Warren
87WytCubP-26
88PeoChiTI-2
89PeoChiTI-23
Arrollado, Courtney
95ButCopKtI-3
96SpoIndB-4
Arroyd, Freddie
86SanJosBP-1
Arroyo, Bronson
95TopTra-47T
96AugGreB-4
Arroyo, Carlos R.
81OklCit8T-2
86ClePhiP-1
87ClePhiP-15
88ReaPhiP-888
89BlaYNPRWL-197
90BatCliP-3084
91BatCliC-18
91BatCliP-3501
92ReaPhiF-592
92ReaPhiS-550
93ReaPhiF-311
94ReaPhiF-2079
Arroyo, Felipe
80AndBraT-11
Arroyo, Fernando
76OPC-614
76SSP-357
76Top-614
78Top-607
81Top-408
82Don-177
82Fle-546
82Top-18
82Top-396
82TwiPos-1
91LakTigC-17
91LakTigP-283
93EdmTraF-1153
Arroyo, Hector
81ChaRoyT-2
Arroyo, Luis
93WatDiaC-3
94MidLeaAF-MDW55
94SprSulC-2
94SprSulF-2028
95RanCucQT-21
96StLucMTI-6
Arroyo, Luis Enrique
47StaPinP2-2
56Top-64
56TopPin-45
57Top-394
58JetPos-2
61Top-142
61TopStaI-188
61Yan61RL-17
62Jel-12
62Pos-12
62PosCan-12
62Top-455
62YanJayP-1
63Top-569
78TCM60I-258
83YanASFY-2
89BlaYNPRWL-64
91RinPos1Y1-6
92YanWIZ6-3
92YanWIZA-1
Arsenault, Ed
75SanAntBT-2
76WilTomT-2
Arsenault, Pierre
92ExpPos-3
Arst, Matt
90WicStaSGD-3
Arteaga, Edito
76VenLeaS-171
Arteaga, Ivan
93BurBeeC-3
93BurBeeF-148
93LinVenB-5
94NewHavRF-1541
94VenLinU-2
95Bow-97
95LinVen-96
95NewHavRTI-22
95SigRoo-3
95SigRooSig-3
Artiaga, Sal
90CalLeaACLC-28
Arundel, Tug (John Thomas)
87BucN28-36
87OldJudN-14
Arvelo, Thomas
92GulCoaMF-3486
94KinMetC-2
94KinMetF-3829
95PitMetTI-21
Arvesen, Scott
89WelPirP-2
90AugPirP-2455
91AugPirC-2
91AugPirP-795
Arzola, Richard
86St.PetCP-3
Asadoor, Randy
84TulDriTI-18
85LasVegSC-116
86LasVegSP-1
87Don-574
87Fle-650
87FleGlo-650
87LasVegSP-7
87Spo-158
87SpoTeaP-16
Asai, Itsuki
90GatCitPP-3345
90GatCitPSP-2
Asano, Keishi
92SalSpuC-29
92SalSpuF-3774
Asbe, Daryl
86BurExpP-2
Asbell, Frank
40SolHug-2
Asbell, John
79WatIndT-12
80WatIndT-10
81WatIndT-5
Asbill, Darin
88MisStaB-2
89MisStaB-4
Asbjornson, Asby (Robert A.)
94ConTSN-1315
94ConTSNB-1315
Ascencio, Juan
86BenPhiC-152
Asche, Mike
94WelPirC-3
94WelPirF-3501
96HonShaHWB-7
96LynHilB-2
Asche, Scott
91MiaMirC-5
91MiaMirP-399
Aschoff, Jerry
92BelMarC-4
92BelMarF-1432
93AppFoxC-2
93AppFoxF-2451
Asencio, Alex
94GreFalDSP-7
96VerBeaDB-5
Asermely, Bill
93BluOriC-2
93BluOriF-4136
Asgewan, Cecil
94ButCopKSP-14
Ash, Ken (Kenneth Lowther)
92ConTSN-601
Ashburn, Richie (Don Richard)
47Exh-7A
47Exh-7B
47Exh-7C
47PM1StaP1-6
49Bow-214

49EurSta-127
49PhiBul-1
49PhiLumPB-1
50Bow-84
51BerRos-A9
51Bow-186
51R42SmaS-1
51TopBluB-3
52BasPho-1
52BerRos-1
52Bow-53
52DixLid-1
52DixPre-1
52RedMan-NL2
52StaCalL-77A
52StaCalS-89C
52Top-216
53BowC-10
53DixLid-1
53DixPre-1
53NorBreL-2
53RedMan-NL3
54Bow-15
54DixLid-1
54RedHeaF-1
54RedMan-NL1
54Top-45
55Bow-130
55RedMan-NL1
55RobGouS-22
55RobGouW-22
56Top-120
56YelBasP-4
57SwiFra-17
57Top-70
58Hir-10
58PhiJayP-2
58Top-230
59ArmCoi-3
59Baz-2
59Top-300
59Top-317
60Baz-24
60CubJayP-3
60KeyChal-4
60MacSta-2
60RawGloT-2
60Top-305
60TopTat-4
60TopTat-87
61CubJayP-3
61Pos-192A
61Pos-192B
61Top-88
61TopStal-3
62Jel-186
62Pos-186
62PosCan-186
62SalPlaC-171
62ShiPlaC-171
62Top-213
62TopBuc-5
63BasMagM-7
63Jel-197
63Pos-197
63SalMetC-27
63Top-135
63TopStil-3
74MetOriEB-1
77GalGloG-14
79DiaGre-318
79PhiTeal-1
79TCM50-17
80MarExh-2
80PacLeg-94
80PerHaloFP-220
82DiaCla-42
82GSGalAG-23
82MetGal62-2
83PhiPosGM-1
83TopRep5-216
84OCoandSI-59
84OCoandSI-220
84PhiTas-7
86PhiGreT-2
87Phi195T-7
88PacLegI-8
88PhiTas-39
88PhiTopAS-1
88PhiTopAS-2
88PhiTopAS-3
88PhiTopAS-4
88PhiTopAS-5
88PhiTopAS-6
88PhiTopAS-7
88PhiTopAS-8
88PhiTopAS-9
88PhiTopAS-10
88PhiTopAS-11
88PhiTopAS-12
88PhiTopAS-13
89BowInsT-1
89BowRepI-1
89BowTif-R1
89SweBasG-85
90PacLeg-70
90PhiTas-29
90PhiTas-35
91MetWIZ-15
91SweBasG-4
91TopArc1-311
92ActPacA-24
92BazQua5A-5
93TedWil-70
94TopArc1-45
94TopArc1G-45
95Phi-2

Ashby, Alan Dean
76OPC-209
76SSP-514
76Top-209
77Hos-124
77OPC-148
77Top-564
77TopCloS-1
78BluJayP-1
78OPC-76
78Top-319
79AstTeal-2
79Hos-142
79OPC-14
79Top-36
80OPC-105
80Top-187
81AllGamPI-127
81CokTeaS-61
81Don-259
81Fle-64
81OPC-146
81Top-696
82AstAstI-6
82Don-317
82Fle-212
82OPC-184
82Top-433
82TopSti-48
83AllGamPI-127
83Don-144
83Fle-445
83FleSta-4
83FleSti-141
83FleSti-212
83OPC-84
83Top-774
83TopSti-241
84AllGamPI-37
84AstMot-3
84Don-539
84Fle-220
84Nes792-217
84OPC-217
84Top-217
84TopSti-72
84TopTif-217
85AstHouP-5
85AstMot-13
85Don-283
85Fle-343
85OPC-29
85Top-564
85TopTif-564
86AstMilL-1
86AstPol-8
86AstTeal-1
86BasStaB-3
86Don-405
86Fle-292
86OPC-331
86Top-331
86TopTif-331
87AstMot-11
87AstPol-21
87Don-332
87DonOpeD-17
87Fle-50
87FleGlo-50
87Top-112
87TopTif-112
88AstMot-11
88AstPol-4
88Don-163
88DonBasB-8
88Fle-439
88FleGlo-439
88OPC-48
88PanSti-291
88RedFolSB-2
88Sco-73
88ScoGlo-73
88Spo-219
88StaLinAst-3
88Top-48
88TopSti-32
88TopTif-48
89AstMot-10
89AstSmo-3
89Bow-327
89BowTif-327
89Don-88
89Fle-350A
89Fle-350B
89FleGlo-350
89OPC-359
89RedFolSB-4
89Sco-366
89Top-492
89TopDouA-20
89TopTif-492
89UppDec-305
90EliSenL-63
90MLBBasB-39
93UppDecS-1
96KisCobB-1

Ashby, Andy (Andrew)
86BenPhiC-139
87SpaPhiP-13
87UtiBluSP-25
90Bes-46
90CMC-784
90ProAaA-22
90ReaPhiB-7
90ReaPhiP-1211
90ReaPhiS-3
91Bow-485
91FleUpd-105
91LinDriAAA-478
91PhiMed-2
91ScrRedBLD-478
91ScrRedBP-2530
91StaCluMO-2
91UppDecFE-64F
92Bow-286
92Cla1-T6
92ClaGam-200
92Don-11
92Fle-521
92Lea-405
92OPC-497
92PhiMed-3
92Pin-265
92ProFS7-294
92Sco-396
92ScoRoo-18
92StaClu-717
92StaCluECN-717
92Top-497
92TopDeb91-5
92TopGol-497
92TopGolW-497
92TopMic-497
92TriPla-128
92Ult-541
92UppDec-19
92UppDecSR-SR1
93Don-743
93Fle-401
93FleFinE-21
93PacSpa-420
93Pin-572
93RocUSPC-3H
93RocUSPC-10C
93StaClu-700
93StaCluFDI-700
93StaCluMOP-700
93StaCluRoc-18
93Top-794
93TopGol-794
93TopInaM-794
93TopMic-794
93Ult-339
93UppDec-763
93UppDecGold-763
94Don-70
94ExtBas-367
94Fin-255
94FinRef-255
94Fla-433
94Fle-652
94Lea-32
94PadMot-21
94StaClu-524
94StaCluFDI-524
94StaCluGR-524
94StaCluMOP-524
94Top-648
94TopGol-648
94TopSpa-648
94Ult-275
95ColCho-358
95ColChoGS-358
95ColChoSS-358
95Don-86
95DonPreP-86
95DonTopotO-336
95Fla-198
95Fle-553
95Lea-68
95Pac-356
95PadCHP-3
95PadMot-23
95Pin-425
95PinArtP-425
95PinMusC-425
95Sco-175
95ScoGolR-175
95ScoPlaTS-175
95StaClu-228
95StaCluFDI-228
95StaCluMOP-228
95StaCluSTWS-228
95Top-85
95TopCyb-60
95Ult-435
95UltGolM-435
96Cir-183
96CirRav-183
96ColCho-698
96ColChoGS-698
96ColChoSS-698
96Don-450
96DonPreP-450
96EmoXL-273
96Fla-369
96Fle-559
96FleTif-559
96Lea-62
96LeaPrePB-62
96LeaPrePG-62
96LeaPrePS-62
96LeaSigA-10
96LeaSigAG-10
96LeaSigAS-10
96MetUni-231
96MetUniP-231
96Pac-185
96PadMot-21
96PanSti-102
96ProSta-84
96Sco-216
96SP-162
96StaClu-134
96StaClu-246
96StaCluMOP-134
96StaCluMOP-246
96Top-82
96TopGal-61
96TopGalPPI-61
96TopLas-49
96Ult-280
96UltGolM-280
96UppDec-187
97Cir-188
97CirRav-188
97ColCho-449
97Don-313
97DonLim-67
97DonLimLE-67
97DonPre-25
97DonPreCttC-25
97DonPreP-313
97DonPrePGold-313
97Fin-192
97FinRef-192
97Fle-456
97FleTif-456
97Lea-307
97LeaFraM-307
97LeaFraMDC-307
97MetUni-216
97Pac-419
97PacLigB-419
97PacSil-419
97PinX-P-91
97PinX-PMoS-91
97Sco-138
97ScoPreS-138
97ScoShoS-138
97ScoShoSAP-138
97SpoIll-37
97SpoIllEE-37
97SpoIllGS-19
97StaClu-294
97StaCluMOP-294
97Stu-137
97StuPrePG-137
97StuPrePS-137
97Top-15
97Ult-279
97UltGolME-279
97UltPlaME-279
97UppDec-164

Ashby, Christopher
95GreBatTI-2
96TamYanY-3

Ashby, Gary
81HawIsIT-3

Ashford, Emmett
77Spo-7315

Ashford, Tucker (Thomas S.)
78PadFamF-2
78Top-116
79HawIsIC-8
79Top-247
80ChaChaT-16
81ColCliP-12
81ColCliT-2
82ColCliP-12
82ColCliT-2
83TidTidT-26
84Nes792-492
84Top-492
84TopTif-492
87JacMetF-4
88JacMetGS-4
91MetWIZ-16
92YanWIZ8-6
93RanKee-55

Ashkinazy, Alan
85GreHorT-2
86GreHorP-2

Ashley, Billy
90BakDodCLC-260
91Cla/Bes-210
91VerBeaDC-24
91VerBeaDP-785
92AlbDukF-731
92Bow-168
92ClaFS7-243
92DonRoo-5
92SanAntMS-553
92SkyAA F-242
93AlbDukF-1473
93Bow-210
93ClaFS7-123
93Don-56
93FleMajLP-A9
93Lea-100
93Pin-281
93PinTea2-16
93Sco-267
93ScoBoyoS-1
93StaClu-342
93StaCluD-22
93StaCluFDI-342
93StaCluMOP-342
93Top-815
93TopGol-815
93TopInaM-815
93TopMic-815
93Toy-86
93TriAAAGF-13
93UppDec-22
93UppDecGold-22
94BowBes-B32
94BowBesR-B32
94Cla-27
94DodPol-1
94Don-420
94Fle-504

94Lea-111
94LeaLimR-53
94Pin-324
94PinArtP-324
94PinMusC-324
94PinNewG-NG21
94SpoRoo-111
94SpoRooAP-111
94Top-53
94TopGol-53
94TopSpa-53
94TriAAF-AAA24
94TriPla-287
94Ult-513
95ActPac2GF-8G
95ActPacF-18
95ActPacF-69
95Baz-127
95Bow-223
95BowGolF-223
95ColCho-225
95ColChoGS-225
95ColChoSS-225
95DodMot-14
95DodPol-1
95Don-180
95DonPreP-180
95DonTopotO-262
95Fin-278
95FinRef-278
95Fla-150
95Fle-532
95Lea-196
95LeaLim-9
95Pin-31
95Pin-290
95PinArtP-31
95PinArtP-290
95PinMusC-31
95PinMusC-290
95PinNewB-NB8
95PinUps-US29
95ScoAi-AM8
95Sel-71
95Sel-233
95SelArtP-71
95SelArtP-233
95SelCanM-CM6
95SelCer-82
95SelCerMG-82
95SelCerPU-5
95SelCerPU9-5
95SigRooFD-FD1
95SigRooFDS-FD1
95SigRooOJHP-HP1
95SigRooOJHPS-HP1
95SigRooOJSS-5
95SigRooOJSSS-5
95SP-71
95SPCha-62
95SPChaDC-62
95Spo-39
95SpoArtP-39
95SPSil-71
95SPSpeF-41
95StaClu-469
95StaCluCB-CB5
95StaCluMOP-469
95StaCluMOP-CB5
95StaCluSTWS-469
95Stu-127
95Sum-12
95SumNewA-NA5
95SumNthD-12
95Top-489
95TopCyb-280
95UC3-89
95UC3ArtP-89
95UC3CleS-CS6
95Ult-392
95UltGolM-392
95UppDec-75
95UppDecED-75
95UppDecEDG-75
95UppDecSE-169
95UppDecSEG-169
95Zen-8
96ColCho-178
96ColChoGS-178
96ColChoSS-178
96DodMot-13
96DodPol-1
96Don-7
96DonPreP-7
96Fle-425
96FleTif-425
96Lea-117
96LeaPrePB-117
96LeaPrePG-117
96LeaPrePS-117
96Sco-170
96ScoDugC-A96
96ScoDugCAP-A96
96SelCer-79
96SelCerAP-79
96SelCerCB-79
96SelCerCR-79
96SelCerMB-79
96SelCerMG-79
96SelCerMR-79
96Ult-216
96UltGolM-216
97PacPriGotD-GD155
97Sco-409
97ScoHobR-409
97ScoResC-409
97ScoShoS-409
97ScoShoSAP-409

Ashley, Duane
91JamExpC-16
91JamExpP-3534

Ashley, Shon
86BelBreP-1
87BelBreP-4
88CalLeaACLC-14
88StoPorCLC-194
88StoPorP-724
89ElPasDGS-25
89TexLeaAGS-14
90ElPasDGS-4
91ElPasDLD-176
91ElPasDP-2758
91LinDriAA-176
92IndIndF-1871
92IndIndS-176
92ProFS7-85
92SkyAAAF-84

Ashman, Mike
82MadMusF-23
83AlbA'sT-11
84AlbA'sT-21
85TacTigC-136
86NasPirP-1
90AlbDecGB-2

Ashmore, Mitch
82ChaRoyT-7
82OmaRoyT-13
84MemChiT-8

Ashton, Jeff
92PriRedC-3
92PriRedF-3092
93BilMusF-3951

Ashworth, Kym
93GreFalDSP-4
94BakDodC-1
94Bow-157
94BowBes-B74
94BowBesR-B74
94Cla-194
94ClaTriF-T40
95AusFut-22
95AusFutGP-2
95Bow-148
95SigRooOJ-2
95SigRooOJP-2
95SigRooOJPS-2
95SigRooOJS-2
95VerBeaDTI-2
96BesAutS-6

Ashworth, Mike
88BurIndP-1793
89SalLakTTI-28

Asp, Bryan
89EliTwiS-1

Aspray, Mike
87GenCubP-1
88PeoChiTI-3
89WinSpiS-NNO
90VisOakCLC-59
90VisOakP-2151

Aspromonte, Bob (Robert T.)
47Exh-8
58MonRoyF-2
60Top-547
61Top-396
62Baz-9
62Col.45B-2
62Col45'HC-2
62Col45'JP-2
62Top-248
62TopStal-124
63Col45"P-1
63Col45'JP-1
63ExhStaB-3
63Fle-37
63Jel-187
63Pos-187
63Top-45
63TopStil-4
64Col.45JP-1
64Top-467
64TopCoi-84
64TopCoi-163
64TopSta-16
64TopStaU-5
65AstBigLBPP-2
65Baz-19
65OPC-175
65Top-175
65TopEmbl-61
66Baz-24
66Top-273
66Top-352
66TopRubl-6
66TopVen-273
66TopVen-352
67Ast-2
67AstTeal1-1
67AstTeal2-2
67Baz-24
67CokCapAs-2
67DexPre-14
67Top-274
67TopVen-269
68AtlOilPBCC-5
68CokCapA-2
68DexPre-8
68OPC-95
68Top-95
68TopActS-4C
68TopActS-15C
68TopVen-95
69MilBra-17
69MLBOffS-111
69Top-542
69TopSta-31
70MLBOffS-2
70OPC-529
70Top-529
71MLBOffS-146
71OPC-469
71Top-469
72MilBra-21
72Top-659
87AstSer1-1
87AstSer1-29
89AstCol4S-16
90DodTar-21
91MetWIZ-17

Aspromonte, Ken
58Top-405
59SenTealW-1
59Top-424
60Top-114
60TopVen-114
61AngJayP-1
61Pos-65A
61Pos-65B
61Top-176
61TopStal-133
62Jel-19
62SalPlaC-7A
62SalPlaC-7B
62ShiPlaC-7
62Top-563
63Top-464
64Top-252
64TopVen-252
65TopTral-39
72Top-784
73OPC-449
73Top-449A
73Top-449B
74OPC-521
74Top-521

Asselstine, Brian H.
77Top-479
78Top-372
79Top-529
81BraPol-30
81Don-186
81Fle-256
81Top-64
82Don-184
82Fle-428
82Top-214
83PhoGiaBHN-4

Assenmacher, Paul
84DurBulT-20
85DurBulT-1
86BraPol-30
86DonRoo-28
86FleUpd-5
86SpoRoo-24
86TopTra-4T
86TopTraT-4T
87BraSmo-8
87Don-290
87Fle-511
87FleGlo-511
87Lea-164
87SpoTeaP-24
87Top-132
87TopSti-37
87TopTif-132
87ToyRoo-2
88Fle-532
88FleGlo-532
88StaLinBra-2
88Top-266
88TopTif-266
89Bow-265
89BowTif-265
89BraDub-3
89Don-357
89Fle-586
89FleGlo-586
89PanSti-33
89Sco-373
89Top-454
89TopTif-454
89UppDec-566
90CubMar-1
90Don-459
90Fle-25
90FleCan-25
90Lea-493
90OPC-644
90PubSti-107
90Top-644
90TopTif-644
90TopTVCu-7
90UppDec-660
90VenSti-17
91Bow-431
91CubMar-45
91CubVinL-1
91Don-144
91Fle-413
91Lea-53
91OPC-12
91Sco-147
91StaClu-586
91Top-12
91TopDesS-12
91TopMic-12
91TopTif-12
91UppDec-491
92CubMar-45
92Don-159
92Fle-375
92Lea-117
92OPC-753
92Pin-466
92Sco-360
92StaClu-731
92StaCluNC-731
92Top-753
92TopGol-753
92TopGolW-753
92TopMic-753
92Ult-172
92UppDec-590
93CubMar-1
93Don-54
93Fle-17
93PacSpa-375
93StaClu-332
93StaCluCu-13
93StaCluFDI-332
93StaCluMOP-332
93Top-319
93TopGol-319
93TopInaM-319
93TopMic-319
93Ult-14
93UppDec-320
93UppDecGold-320
94Don-57
94Fle-225
94Sco-224
94ScoGolR-224
94StaClu-133
94StaClu-646
94StaCluFDI-133
94StaCluFDI-646
94StaCluGR-133
94StaCluGR-646
94StaCluMOP-133
94StaCluMOP-646
94StaCluT-195
94StaCluTFDI-195
94Top-239
94TopGol-239
94TopSpa-239
94WhiSoxK-2
95Fle-110
95FleUpd-39
96ColCho-523
96ColChoGS-523
96ColChoSS-523
96Fle-81
96FleInd-2
96FleTif-81
96LeaSigEA-5
96Sco-400
97ScoIndU-13
97ScoIndUTC-13

Astacio, Pedro
90VerBeaDS-2
90YakBeaTI-12
91Cla/Bes-280
91SanAntMP-2966
91VerBeaDC-1
91VerBeaDP-762
92AlbDukF-710
92AlbDukS-2
92Bow-689
92DonRoo-6
92Pin-551
92SkyAAAF-1
93Bow-238
93ClaGam-7
93DodMot-26
93DodPol-1
93Don-407
93Fle-57
93FleRooS-RSB2
93Lea-71
93LimRocDWB-60
93OPC-9
93PacSpa-496
93Pin-396
93Sco-231
93Sel-325
93SelChaR-13
93StaClu-511
93StaCluD-12
93StaCluFDI-511
93StaCluMOP-511
93Top-93
93TopGol-93
93TopInaM-93
93TopMic-93
93Toy-44
93TriPla-29
93Ult-49
93UppDec-367
93UppDecGold-367
93USPlaCR-4S
94Bow-294
94ColC-496
94ColChoGS-496
94ColChoSS-496
94DodMot-16
94DodPol-2
94Don-62
94ExtBas-283
94Fin-343
94FinRef-343
94Fla-177
94Fle-505
94Lea-237
94Pac-302
94Pin-454
94PinArtP-454
94PinMusC-454
94Sel-82
94StaClu-343

94StaCluFDI-343
94StaCluGR-343
94StaCluMOP-343
94Top-431
94TopGol-431
94TopSpa-431
94TriPla-81
94Ult-212
94UppDec-158
94UppDecED-158
95ColCho-228
95ColChoGS-228
95ColChoSS-228
95DodMot-11
95DodPol-2
95Don-337
95DonPreP-337
95Fla-151
95Fle-533
95Lea-137
95Pac-212
95Pin-56
95PinArtP-56
95PinMusC-56
95Sco-460
95ScoGolR-460
95ScoPlaTS-460
95StaClu-358
95StaCluMOP-358
95StaCluSTWS-358
95StaCluVR-188
95Top-589
95TopCyb-361
95Ult-393
95UltGolM-393
95UppDec-318
95UppDecED-318
95UppDecEDG-318
96ColCho-582
96ColChoGS-582
96ColChoSS-582
96DodMot-12
96DodPol-2
96LeaSigA-11
96LeaSigAG-11
96LeaSigAS-11
96Pac-105
95StaCluVRMC-188
97Cir-168
97CirRav-168
97ColCho-363
97Fle-667
97FleTif-667
97Pac-325
97PacLigB-325
97PacSil-325
97StaClu-74
97StaCluMOP-74
97Top-51
97Ult-442
97UltGolME-442
97UltPlaME-442
Astacio, Rafael
91EriSaiC-2
91EriSaiP-4075
Astros, Auburn
92AubAstC-30
92AubAstF-1373
Astros, Cedar Rapids
73CedRapAT-26
Astros, Houston
64TopTatI-9
66TopRubI-109
69FleCloS-10
69FleCloS-26
69TopStaA-10
70OPC-448
70Top-448
71OPC-722
71Top-722
71TopTat-102
72OPC-282
72Top-282
73OPC-158
73OPCBTC-10
73Top-158
73TopBluTC-10
74OPC-154
74OPCTC-10
74Top-154
74TopStaA-10
74TopTeaC-10
78Top-112
83FleSta-234
83FleSti-NNO
87AstSer1-31
87AstShoSO-30
87AstShoSO-31
87AstShoSO-32
87AstShoSTw-30
87AstShoSTw-31
87AstShoSTw-32
87AstShowSTh-30
87AstShowSTh-31
87AstShowSTh-32
87FleWaxBC-C9
87SpoTeaL-8
88PanSti-472
88RedFolSB-113
89FleWaxBC-C24
90PubSti-627
90RedFolSB-117
90VenSti-524
94ImpProP-20
94Sco-652
94ScoGolR-652
95PanSti-140
96PanSti-61
Astroth, Joe (Joseph Henry)
49PhiBul-2
51Bow-298
52Bow-170
52Top-290
53BowC-82
53Top-103
54Bow-131
55A'sRodM-1
55Bow-119
56A'sRodM-1
56Top-106
76A'sRodMC-3
79DiaGre-345
83TopRep5-290
91TopArc1-103
Astroth, Jon
74GasRanT-2
75SpoIndC-13
Atchley, Justin
95BilRedTI-2
96Exc-145
Atencio, Enrique
93AppFoxC-3
93AppFoxF-2465
Atha, Jeff
88JamExpP-1901
Atherton, Keith Rowe
79WatA'sT-6
80WesHavWCT-16
81WesHavAT-2
82TacTigT-23
83TacTigT-1
84A'sMot-26
84Don-497
84Fle-437
84Nes792-529
84Top-529
84TopTif-529
85A'sMot-17
85Don-340
85Fle-415
85Top-166
85TopTif-166
86A'sMot-17
86Fle-410
86Top-353
86TopTif-353
87Don-272
87Fle-534
87FleGlo-534
87Top-52
87TopTif-52
88Don-318
88DonBasB-270
88Fle-1
88FleGlo-1
88Sco-613
88ScoGlo-613
88Top-451
88TopTif-451
88TwiTeal-14
89Don-273
89Fle-103
89FleGlo-103
89FleUpd-24
89IndTeal-3
89Sco-381
89Top-698
89TopTif-698
89TopTra-4T
89TopTraT-4T
89UppDec-599
90PubSti-552
90VenSti-18
Athletics, 19th C (Philadelphia)
90KalTeaN-1
Athletics, Kansas City
56Top-236
57Top-204
58Top-174
59Top-172
59TopVen-172
60Top-413
60TopTat-69
61Top-297
61TopMagR-7
62GuyPotCP-9
62Top-384
63Top-397
64Top-151
64TopTatI-10
64TopVen-151
65OPC-151
65Top-151
66Top-492
66TopRubI-110
67Top-262
90FleWaxBC-C9
Athletics, Oakland
68Top-554
69FleCloS-17
69FleCloS-35
69TopStaA-17
70Top-631
71OPC-624
71Top-624
71TopTat-34
72OPC-454
72Top-454
73OPC-500
73OPCBTC-18
73Top-500
73TopBluTC-18
74OPC-246
74OPCTC-18
74Top-246
74TopStaA-18
74TopTeaC-18
76OPC-421
76Top-421
78Top-577
83FleSta-242
83FleSti-NNO
87SpoTeaL-23
87Top-456
87TopTif-456
88PanSti-465
88RedFolSB-120
89FleWaxBC-C5
90FleWorS-12
90PubSti-635
90RedFolSB-127
90VenSti-532
91PanCanT1-134
91PanCanT1-135
93TedWilPC-18
94ImpProP-11
94Sco-327
94ScoGolR-327
95PanSti-154
96PanSti-219
Athletics, Philadelphia
09SpoNewSM-52
13FatT20-6
38BasTabP-28
51TopTea-6
68LauWorS-7
68LauWorS-10
68LauWorS-11
68LauWorS-26
68LauWorS-27
70FleWorS-10
70FleWorS-11
70FleWorS-26
70FleWorS-27
71FleWorS-12
71FleWorS-27
Atilano, Luis
75CliPilT-21
Atkins, Ross
95WatIndTI-3
Atkins, Tommy (Francis M.)
11SpoLifM-85
12ColRedB-12A
12ColRedB-12B
12ColTinT-12A
12ColTinT-12B
Atkinson, Bill (William C.)
72Dia-1
77ExpPos-2
77ExpPos-3
78OPC-144
78Top-43
80OPC-133
80Top-415
81EdmTraRR-12
83AppFoxF-19
Atkinson, Neil
93EugEmeC-3
93EugEmeF-3845
94RocRoyC-2
94RocRoyF-554
95WicWraTI-31
Atlantics, Brooklyn
94OriofB-16
Attardi, Jay
76AppFoxT-1
Attebery, Russ
76SeaRaiC-1
Attell, Abe
11TurRedT-52
88PacEigMO-28
Attreau, Dick (Richard G.)
94ConTSN-1289
94ConTSNB-1289
Atwater, Buck
90GatCitPP-3353
91PocPioP-3787
Atwater, Joe
94PitMetC-4
94PitMetF-3515
96StLucMTI-12
Atwater, Tyrone
90GatCitPSP-3
91PocPioSP-23
Atwell, Gary
75LafDriT-7
Atwell, Toby (Maurice D.)
47Exh-9
50WorWidGV-34
52Top-356
53BowC-112
53Top-23
54Bow-123
55Bow-164
56Top-232
57SeaPop-1
83TopRep5-356
91TopArc1-23
Atwood, Bill (William F.)
40PlaBal-240
93ConTSN-750
Atwood, Derek
91PocPioP-3773
91PocPioSP-13
Atwood, Jason
93PocPosF-4199
Atz, Jacob Henry
09ColChiE-13
09T206-9
12ColRedB-13
12ColTinT-13
Aube, Paul
76DalCon-1
Aube, Richard
83ChaRoyT-14
Aubel, Larry
72CedRapCT-25
Aubel, Mike
92AubAstC-8
92AubAstF-1365
Aubin, Kevin
91PriRedC-1
91PriRedP-3516
Aubin, Yves
52LavPro-101
Aubrey, Harvey H.
11SpoLifCW-10
Auchard, Dan
89KinMetS-1
Aucoin, Derek
90JamExpP-13
91SumFlyC-2
91SumFlyP-2325
92RocExpC-7
92RocExpF-2106
93WesPalBEC-2
93WesPalBEF-1330
96Bow-356
96ExpDis-5
97PacPriGotD-GD166
97Ult-226
97UltGolME-226
97UltPlaME-226
Audain, Miguel
87PenWhiSP-13
Aude, Rich
90AugPirP-2469
90CMC-851
91SalBucC-3
91SalBucP-957
92SalBucC-3
92SalBucF-68
93CarMudF-2059
93CarMudTI-3
94Bow-462
94BufBisF-1842
94ColC-42
94ColChoGS-42
94ColChoSS-42
94FleMajLP-3
94Top-787
94TopGol-787
94TopSpa-787
94TriAAF-AAA26
95Bow-117
95FleUpd-145
95Pin-444
95PinArtP-444
95PinMusC-444
95PirFil-1
95Sel-207
95SelArtP-207
95SigRoo-4
95SigRooSig-4
95Sum-137
95SumNthD-137
96Don-389
96DonPreP-389
96Pac-167
Audley, Jim
90WicStaSGD-4
91KanCouCTI-2
92FreKeyC-2
92FreKeyF-1817
Auerbach, Rick (Frederick)
72OPC-153
72Top-153
73OPC-427
73Top-427
74OPC-289
74Top-289
75OPC-588
75Top-588
76OPC-622
76SSP-74
76Top-622
78Pep-2
78SSP270-126
78Top-646
79Top-174
80RedEnq-23
80Top-354
82Top-72
90DodTar-22
94BreMilB-99
Aufdermauer, Bud
85AncGlaPTI-44
August, Don
85Top-392
85TopTif-392
86TucTorP-3
87DenZepP-17
88DenZepC-8
88DenZepP-1259
88Don-602
88FleUpd-37
88FleUpdG-37
88ScoRoo-104T
88ScoRooG-104T
88TopTra-7T
88TopTraT-7T
89Bow-130
89BowTif-130
89BreGar-15
89BrePol-38
89BreYea-38
89Don-410

89Fle-177
89FleGlo-177
89PanSti-365
89Sco-419
89ScoHot1R-83
89ScoYouS2-28
89Spo-131
89Top-696
89TopBig-33
89TopTif-696
89UppDec-325
90BrePol-38
90ClaBlu-124
90CMC-45
90DenZepC-20
90DenZepP-616
90Don-617
90OPC-192
90ProAAAF-641
90PubSti-488
90Sco-144
90Top-192
90TopTif-192
90UppDec-295
90VenSti-19
91BreMilB-1
91BrePol-1
92Don-140
92LonTigF-623
92Sco-533
92Ult-78
94BreMilB-100

August, Sam
87AshTouP-20
88OscAstS-2
89ColMudP-140
91Cla/Bes-298
91JacGenLD-552
91JacGenP-916
91LinDriAA-552
92JacGenS-327
92SkyAA F-139
94RivPilCLC-28

Augustine, Andy
94BelMarC-3
94BelMarF-3238
96LanJetB-5

Augustine, Dave (David R.)
74OPC-598
74Top-598
75OPC-616
75Top-616
77ColCliT-1
78ChaChaT-1
79ChaChaT-12
80OmaRoyP-1
81PorBeaT-6
82PorBeaT-18

Augustine, Jerry (Gerald Lee)
77BurCheD-82
77Top-577
78Top-133
79Top-357
80Top-243
81Don-445
81Top-596
82BrePol-46
82Don-332
82Fle-133
82Top-46
83BrePol-46
83Fle-26
83Top-424
84BrePol-46
84Fle-194
84Nes792-658
84Top-658
84TopTif-658
85RocRedWT-14
92BreCarT-1
93UppDecS-9
94BreMilB-189

Augustine, Rob
92BurIndC-15
92BurIndF-1644
93WatIndC-2
93WatIndF-3551
94HigDesMC-2
94HigDesMF-2778

Auker, Eldon Leroy
34DiaMatCSB-3
34BatR31-120
35DiaMatCS3T1-3
35GouPreR-4
35TigFreP-1
36NatChiFPR-3
39PlaBal-4
40PlaBal-139
41BroW75-2
41PlaBal-45
76TigOldTS-1
79DiaGre-379
81TigDetN-91
88ConSer3-3

Aulenback, Jim
83AleDukT-13
84PriWilPT-14

Ault, Doug (Douglas Reagan)
75SpoIndC-10
76SacSolC-9
77OPC-202
77Top-477
78BluJayP-2
78OPC-202
78Top-267
79OPC-205
79SyrChiT-15
79SyrChiTI-17
79Top-392
80SyrChiT-2
80SyrChiTI-2
81Fle-424
82SyrChiT-24
82SyrChiTI-2
83KnoBluJT-20
85SyrChiT-21
86SyrChiP-3
87SyrChiP-1934
87SyrChiT-23
88DunBluJS-25
89DunBluJS-26
90St.CatBJP-3482
91St.CatBJC-26
91St.CatBJP-3411
92MyrBeaHC-27
92MyrBeaHF-2213
92Nab-30
93DunBluJFFN-1
93RanKee-56

Aurila, Brad
92JamExpC-15
92JamExpF-1506

Aurilia, Rich
92ButCopKSP-6
93ChaRanC-2
93ChaRanF-1946
93FloStaLAF-1
94Cla-148
94ClaGolF-32
94ExcFS7-130
94TulDriF-248
94TulDriTI-1
96Bow-350
96ColCho-719
96ColChoGS-719
96ColChoSS-719
96Fin-B351
96FinRef-B351
96FleUpd-U202
96FleUpdTC-U202
96PhoFirB-6
97ColCho-226
97Fle-474
97FleTif-474
97Pac-435
97PacLigB-435
97PacSil-435
97StaCluMOP-325
97Top-396
97UppDec-173

Aurilla, Rich
97StaClu-325

Ausanio, Joe
88WatPirP-2
89SalBucS-3
90HarSenP-1186
90ProAaA-12
91Bow-528
91Cla/Bes-186
92BufBisBS-1
92BufBisF-315
92BufBisS-26
92SkyAAAF-12
94ColCliF-2940
94ColCliP-1
94LeaLimR-15
95ColCliP-1
95ColCliTI-1
95Don-501
95DonPreP-501
95Fle-66
95Sco-574
95ScoGolR-574
95ScoPlaTS-574
95SigRoo-5
95SigRooSig-5
95StaClu-301
95StaCluMOP-301
95StaCluSTWS-301
96NorTidB-7

Ausman, Paul
76TacTwiDQ-1
77OrlTwiT-2

Ausmus, Brad
89OneYanP-2110
90PriWilCTI-5
91Cla/Bes-17
91PriWilCC-13
91PriWilCP-1429
92ClaFS7-3
92ColCliF-355
92OPC-58
92ProFS7-120
92Top-58
92TopGol-58
92TopGolW-58
92TopMic-58
93ClaFS7-153
93ColSprSSF-3088
93Don-773
93SelRoo-83T
93StaClu-367
93StaCluFDI-367
93StaCluMOP-367
93StaCluRoc-30
94Bow-504
94ColC-43
94ColChoGS-43
94ColChoSS-43
94Don-100
94ExtBas-368
94Fin-29
94FinRef-29
94Fle-653
94Lea-239
94PadMot-22
94PanSti-251
94Pin-391
94PinArtP-391
94PinMusC-391
94Sco-579
94ScoBoyoS-43
94ScoGolR-579
94Sel-106
94StaClu-412
94StaCluFDI-412
94StaCluGR-412
94StaCluMOP-412
94Stu-129
94Top-127
94TopGol-127
94TopSpa-127
94TriPla-161
94Ult-276
94UppDec-232
94UppDecED-232
95ColCho-357
95ColChoGS-357
95ColChoSS-357
95Don-178
95DonPreP-178
95DonTopotO-337
95Fle-554
95Lea-150
95PadCHP-2
95PadMot-19
95Sco-465
95ScoGolR-465
95ScoPlaTS-465
95StaClu-77
95StaCluFDI-77
95StaCluMOP-77
95StaCluSTWS-77
95Top-595
95TopCyb-367
95Ult-230
95UltGolM-230
96ColCho-291
96ColChoGS-291
96ColChoSS-291
96Don-34
96DonPreP-34
96EmoXL-274
96Fla-370
96Fle-560
96FleTif-560
96Lea-9
96LeaPrePB-9
96LeaPrePG-9
96LeaPrePS-9
96LeaSigA-12
96LeaSigAG-12
96LeaSigAS-12
96MetUni-232
96MetUniP-232
96Pac-188
96PadMot-25
96PanSti-98
96Sco-479
96StaClu-142
96StaCluMOP-142
96Top-208
96Ult-281
96UltGolM-281
96UppDec-191
97ColCho-347
97Don-320
97DonPreP-320
97DonPrePGold-320
97Fle-93
97Fle-552
97FleTif-93
97FleTif-552
97Lea-289
97LeaFraM-289
97LeaFraMDC-289
97Pac-83
97PacLigB-83
97PacSil-83
97Sco-370
97ScoHobR-370
97ScoResC-370
97ScoShoS-370
97ScoShoSAP-370
97Top-402
97Ult-348
97UltGolME-348
97UltPlaME-348

Aust, Dennis Kay
65CarTeal-1
66OPC-179
66Top-179
66TopVen-179

Austelle, Al
86DavLipB-2
92DavLipB-2

Austerman, Carl
75SacSolC-16

Austin, Corey
92SouBenWSC-8
92SouBenWSF-188

Austin, Dero
76LauIndC-2
76LauIndC-13
76LauIndC-28

Austin, Frank
52MotCoo-18
86NegLeaF-74

Austin, Jacob
92WelPirC-1

Austin, Jake
93AugPirC-2
93AugPirF-1549
94SalBucC-3
94SalBucF-2335
95CarMudF-170
95Exc-249

Austin, James Taylor
11T205-4
14FatPlaT-3
20NatCarE-3
23WilChoV-3
86SpoIndC-178
88RivRedWCLC-207
89ElPasDGS-3
90El PasDAGTI-22
90ElPasDGS-5
91DenZepLD-127
91LinDriAAA-127
92BrePol-2
92StaCluD-8
92WesPalBEC-5
93BrePol-1
93PacSpa-507
93StaCluFDI-587
93StaCluMOP-587
93TopGol-449
93TopInaM-449
93TopMic-449
94BreMilB-190
94StaCluT-202
94StaCluTFDI-202

Austin, Jim (James Parker)
87ChaRaiP-7
88WicPilRD-25
91BreMilB-2
91DenZepP-114
91JamExpC-5
91JamExpP-3557
92ClaFS7-301
92DonRoo-7
92FleUpd-33
92ProFS7-274
92Sco-747
92ScoRoo-107T
92StaClu-411
92TopDeb91-6
92WesPalBEF-2098
93Don-659
93FleRooS-RSB3
93Lea-12
93OPC-6
93Sco-331
93Sel-322
93StaClu-587
93Top-449
93Ult-217
93UppDec-787
93UppDecGold-787
93WesPalBEC-3
93WesPalBEF-1352

Austin, Jimmy (James Phillip)
09BriE97-1
09ColChiE-14A
09ColChiE-14B
10DomDisP-3
10JuJuDE-2
10SweCapPP-51A
10SweCapPP-51B
10W555-2
11E94-1
11SpoLifCW-11
11SpoLifM-74
12ColRedB-14A
12ColRedB-14B
12ColTinT-14A
12ColTinT-14B
12HasTriFT-9
12HasTriFT-65
12HasTriFT-75C
12T207-4
12T207-5
14B18B-30A
14B18B-30B
14CraJacE-40
14TexTomE-2
15CraJacE-40
15SpoNewM-7
16ColE13-8
16SpoNewM-7
17HolBreD-2
91ConTSN-236

Austin, Pat
87LakTigP-18
88GleFalTP-914
89TolMudHC-18
89TolMudHP-766
90CMC-123
90HagSunP-1418
90HagSunS-1
90LouRedBC-23
90LouRedBP-406
90ProAAAF-520
90Sco-626

Austin, Paul
89SanDieSAS-1

Austin, Rick
80WisRapTT-13
82OrlTwiT-14
83TolMudHT-11

Austin, Rick Gerald
71MLBOffS-361
71OPC-41
71Top-41
75SacSolC-14

76OPC-269
76SpoIndC-21
76SSP-248
76SSP-249
76Top-269
94BreMilB-191
Austin, Terry
81QuaCitCT-12
Austin, Tracy
82MonNew-1
Auten, Jim
83MemChiT-16
84MidCubT-19
Auterson, Jeff
96GreFalDB-3
96GreFalDTI-27
Auth, Bob
86QuaCitAP-3
Autry, Al (Albert)
75OmaRoyTI-2
78SprRedWK-15
Autry, Bucky
84LitFalMT-18
Autry, Gene
61NuSco-414
85AngStrH-1
92AngPol-2
93AngPol-1
93PacRya2S-246
Autry, Martin Gordon
29ExhFou-20
Avalos, Gilbert
94PeoChiC-2
94PeoChiF-2271
95RocCubTI-2
96DayCubB-2
Aven, Bruce
94WatIndC-1
94WatIndF-3948
95KinIndTI-2
96Bow-354
96CanIndB-4
96Exc-39
97Bow-316
97BowChr-218
97BowChrI-218
97BowChrIR-218
97BowChrR-218
97BowInt-316
Avent, Stephen
90BenBucL-18
91SpaPhiC-13
91SpaPhiP-898
Averill, Earl (Howard Earl)
28PorandAR-A1
28PorandAR-B1
29ExhFou-22
31Exh-22
31W517-51
32OrbPinNP-12
32OrbPinUP-3
33ButCanV-1
33ButCre-1
33DouDisP-3
33ExhFou-11
33GeoCMil-3
33Gou-194
33TatOrb-3
33TatOrbSDR-160
34BatR31-24
34BatR31-113
34ButPreR-1
34DiaStaR-35
34DiaStaR-100
34ExhFou-11
35ExhFou-11
35GouPuzR-1L
35GouPuzR-2E
35GouPuzR-16E
35GouPuzR-17E
36ExhFou-11
36GouWidPPR-A2
36GouWidPPR-C2
36NatChiFPR-4
36OveCanR-3
36R31Pre-G1
36SandSW-2
36WheBB3-1
36WheBB5-12
37ExhFou-11
37OPCBatUV-103
37WheBB8-2
38BasTabP-2
38ExhFou-11
39ExhSal-2
39GouPreR303A-2
39PlaBal-143
39WorWidGTP-2
40PlaBal-46
60Fle-71
61Fle-5
75ShaPiz-4
75TCMAllG-1
76RowExh-5
76ShaPiz-147
76ShaPiz-A
76SSPYanOD-1
77GalGloG-79
77GalGloG-202
77ShaPiz-A
79DiaGre-280
80MarExh-3
80PacLeg-4
80PerHaloFP-147
80SSPHOF-147
81ConTSN-20
82DiaCla-17
82OhiHaloF-23
83ConMar-16
86SpoDecG-15
87SpoCubG-3
88ConAmeA-2
89PacLegI-203
91ConTSN-31
92ConTSN-597
93ConTSN-668
94ConTSN-1089
94ConTSNB-1089
95ConTSN-1377
Averill, Earl (James)
86EveGiaPC-1
Averill, Earl D. Jr.
59Top-301
60Lea-110
60Top-39
60TopVen-39
61Top-358
62AngJayP-1
62Jel-80
62Pos-80
62PosCan-80
62SalPlaC-24A
62SalPlaC-24B
62ShiPlaC-24
62Top-452
63Top-139
Aversa, Joe
90JohCitCS-2
91SprCarC-3
91SprCarP-747
92St.PetCC-14
93ArkTraF-2816
94St.PetCC-2
94St.PetCF-2589
95LouRedF-279
Avery, John
92PulBraC-2
92PulBraF-3169
Avery, Larry
81BurBeeT-29
82BurRanF-2
82BurRanT-27
Avery, Mark
96PriWilCB-4
Avery, Steve
89BasAmeAPB-AA13
89Bow-268
89BowTif-268
89DurBullS-1
89DurBulTI-1
89GreBraB-28
89Sta-67
89Top-784
89TopTif-784
90Bow-9
90BowTif-9
90BraDubS-1
90ClaUpd-T4
90CMC-277
90Don-39
90DonRoo-42
90FleUpd-1
90Lea-481
90ProAAAF-397
90RicBraBC-7
90RicBraC-1
90RicBraP-252
90RicBraTI-1
90ScoRoo-109T
90TopMag-29
90TopTra-4T
90TopTraT-4T
90UppDec-65
91Bow-566
91BraDubP-1
91BraSubS-1
91Cla2-T26
91ClaGam-138
91Don-187
91Fle-681
91Lea-510
91OPC-227
91RedFolS-105
91Sco-80
91Sco100RS-5
91StaClu-48
91Stu-141
91Top-227
91TopDeb90-6
91TopDesS-227
91TopMic-227
91TopRoo-3
91TopTif-227
91ToyRoo-3
91Ult-1
91UppDec-365
92Bow-180
92BraLykP-1
92BraLykS-1
92Cla1-T7
92Cla1-NNO
92Cla2-T12
92ClaGam-188
92Don-81
92DonCraJ1-4
92Fle-349
92FleSmo'nH-S10
92Fre-18
92Hig5-21
92Hig5S-1
92JimDea-5
92KinDis-11
92Lea-59
92LeaGolP-1
92LeaPre-1
92OPC-574
92OPCPre-170
92PanSti-169
92Pin-231
92Pin-585
92Pin-612
92PinTea2-66
92PinTeaP-2
92PolAve-1
92Sco-241
92Sco-797
92Sco100S-34
92ScoImpP-12
92ScoSam-4
92StaAve-1
92StaAve-2
92StaAve-3
92StaAve-4
92StaAve-5
92StaAve-6
92StaAve-7
92StaAve-8
92StaAve-9
92StaAve-10
92StaAve-11
92StaClu-60
92StaClu-594
92StaCluD-9
92StaPro-2
92Stu-1
92Top-574
92TopGol-574
92TopGolW-574
92TopKid-36
92TopMcD-16
92TopMic-574
92TriPla-85
92Ult-157
92UppDec-41
92UppDec-475
92UppDecF-1
92UppDecFG-1
92UppDecTMH-6
93Bow-198
93BraFloA-2
93BraLykP-1
93BraLykS-1
93ClaGam-8
93DiaMar-5
93Don-26
93Fin-160
93FinRef-160
93Fla-1
93Fle-1
93FunPac-62
93HumDumC-26
93KinDis-5
93Lea-121
93LeaFas-13
93OPC-5
93PacSpa-331
93Pin-315
93Sco-169
93Sel-109
93SP-55
93StaClu-626
93StaCluB-10
93StaCluFDI-626
93StaCluMOP-626
93Stu-5
93Top-615
93TopGol-615
93TopInaM-615
93TopMic-615
93Toy-95
93TriPla-30
93Ult-1
93UppDec-246
93UppDec-472
93UppDec-816
93UppDecGold-246
93UppDecGold-472
93UppDecGold-816
93UppDecIC-WI5
93UppDecICJ-WI5
93UppDecSH-HI2
94Bow-189
94BowBes-R20
94BowBes-X109
94BowBesR-R20
94BowBesR-X109
94BraLykP-1
94BraLykS-1
94BraUSPC-6C
94BraUSPC-12H
94CarLeaA-DJ16
94ColC-44
94ColChoGS-44
94ColChoSS-44
94Don-41
94DonDiaK-DK3
94DonSpeE-41
94ExtBas-199
94ExtBasPD-6
94Fin-359
94FinRef-359
94Fla-352
94Fle-350
94FleAllS-26
94FUnPac-33
94Lea-138
94LeaL-81
94OPC-196
94Pac-1
94Pin-8
94PinArtP-8
94PinMusC-8
94PinSam-8
94Sco-166
94ScoGolR-166
94Sel-87
94SP-47
94SPDieC-47
94Spo-60
94StaClu-254
94StaCluFDI-254
94StaCluGR-254
94StaCluMOP-254
94StaCluT-32
94StaCluTFDI-32
94Stu-33
94Top-137
94TopGol-137
94TopSpa-137
94TriPla-41
94Ult-147
94UppDec-41
94UppDec-420
94UppDecAJ-18
94UppDecAJG-18
94UppDecED-41
94UppDecED-420
94USPlaCA-9S
95Baz-99
95Bow-377
95ColCho-161
95ColChoGS-161
95ColChoSE-66
95ColChoSEGS-66
95ColChoSESS-66
95ColChoSS-161
95Don-87
95DonPreP-87
95DonTopotO-181
95Emo-99
95Fin-72
95FinRef-72
95Fla-320
95Fle-299
95Lea-209
95LeaLim-5
95Pac-1
95Pin-185
95PinArtP-185
95PinMusC-185
95Sco-185
95ScoGolR-185
95ScoHaloG-HG92
95ScoPlaTS-185
95Sel-7
95SelArtP-7
95SP-33
95SPSil-33
95StaClu-151
95StaCluFDI-151
95StaCluMOP-151
95StaCluSTDW-B151
95StaCluSTMP 1
95StaCluSTWS-151
95Stu-51
95Top-430
95TopCyb-227
95Ult-345
95UltGolM-345
95UppDec-292
95UppDecED-292
95UppDecEDG-292
95UppDecSE-12
95UppDecSEG-12
96ColCho-453
96ColChoGS-453
96ColChoSS-453
96Don-33
96DonPreP-33
96EmoXL-138
96Fin-B57
96FinRef-B57
96Fla-194
96Fle-285
96FleBra-1
96FleTif-285
96Lea-137
96LeaPrePB-137
96LeaPrePG-137
96LeaPrePS-137
96MetUni-126
96MetUniP-126
96Pac-1
96Pin-82
96Sco-101
96ScoDugC-A73
96ScoDugCAP-A73
96StaClu-275
96StaCluEPB-275
96StaCluEPG-275
96StaCluEPS-275
96StaCluMOP-275
96Top-165
96TopChr-47
96TopChrR-47
96Ult-437
96UltGolM-437
96UppDec-269
97Cir-87
97CirRav-87
97Don-204
97Don-295
97DonPreP-204
97DonPreP-295
97DonPrePGold-204
97DonPrePGold-295
97DonTea-55
97DonTeaSPE-55
97FlaSho-A113
97FlaSho-B113

97FlaSho-C113
97FlaShoLC-113
97FlaShoLC-B113
97FlaShoLC-C113
97FlaShoLCM-A113
97FlaShoLCM-B113
97FlaShoLCM-C113
97Fle-251
97Fle-637
97FleTif-251
97FleTif-637
97PacPriGotD-GD108
97Sco-450
97ScoHobR-450
97ScoResC-450
97ScoShoS-450
97ScoShoSAP-450
97SkyE-X-9
97SkyE-XC-9
97SkyE-XEC-9
97SP-36
97StaClu-72
97StaCluMOP-72
97Top-11
97Ult-390
97UltGolME-390
97UltPlaME-390
Avila, Bobby (Roberto G.)
49IndTeal-1
50IndNumN-1
50IndTeal-1
51Bow-188
52Bow-167
52IndNumN-14
52RedMan-AL2
52Top-257
53BowC-29
53IndPenCBP-1
53RedMan-AL26
54Bow-68
54DanDee-1
54RedMan-AL1
55BigLealS-2
55Bow-19
55DaiQueS-2
55IndGolS-12
55RedMan-AL15
56Top-132
57IndSoh-1
57Top-195
58Hir-33
58Top-276
59Top-363
60Lea-59
60Top-90
60TopVen-90
67TopVen-185
83TopRep5-257
91OriCro-14
Avila, Carlos
76VenLeaS-31
Avila, Edwin
95BoiHawTI-2
Avila, Jesus
76VenLeaS-3
80VenLeaS-3
Avila, Jose
96EriSeaB-5
Avila, Ralph
95DodPol-30
Avila, Rolando
94BluOriC-1
94BluOriF-3573
96HigDesMB-5
Aviles, Brian Keith
84DurBulT-25
85GreBraTI-2
87GreBraB-15
Aviles, Ramon Antonio
78SSP270-163
80Top-682
81Fle-23
81Top-644
82Fle-239
82OklCit8T-4
82Top-152
83PorBeaT-10
86ReaPhiP-1
87SpaPhiP-11
88MaiPhiC-24
88MaiPhiP-302
89BlaYNPRWL-36
89BlaYNPRWLU-43
89ReaPhiB-25
89ReaPhiP-671
89ReaPhiS-26b
90ReaPhiB-6
90ReaPhiP-1236
90ReaPhiS-27
91BatCliC-27
91BatCliP-3500
92BatCliF-3282
Avram, Brian
91JohCitCC-23
91JohCitCP-3968
Avrard, Corey
95Bow-178
96PeoChiB-6
Awkard, H.B.
91GulCoaRSP-29
Awkard, Russell
95NegLeaL2-23
Ayala, Adan
91ChaRaiC-12
91ChaRaiP-97
92ChaRaiC-2
92ChaRaiF-121
Ayala, Benny (Benigno Felix)
75OPC-619
75TidTidTI-1
75Top-619
78SprRedWK-8
80Top-262
81Don-236
81Fle-185
81Top-101
82Don-581
82Fle-157
82Top-331
83Don-331
83Fle-52
83Top-59
84Don-270
84Nes792-443
84OriTeal-2
84Top-443
84TopSti-22
84TopTif-443
85IndPol-12
85ThoMcAD-1
85Top-624
85TopTif-624
85TopTifT-3T
85TopTra-3T
91MetWIZ-18
91OriCro-15
Ayala, Bobby
90CedRapRB-15
90CedRapRP-2314
91ChaLooLD-153
91ChaLooP-1951
91LinDriAA-153
92ChaLooF-3811
92ChaLooS-178
92SkyAA F-79
93Bow-498
93Don-30
93Fle-29
93PacSpa-397
93RedKah-1
93ScoBoyoS-19
94Bow-501
94ColC-572
94ColChoGS-572
94ColChoSS-572
94Don-75
94ExtBas-160
94ExtBasSYS-1
94Fin-409
94FinRef-409
94Fla-335
94Fle-404
94FleUpd-80
94Lea-253
94MarMot-14
94Pin-482
94PinArtP-482
94PinMusC-482
94ScoRoo-RT61
94ScoRooGR-RT61
94StaClu-713
94StaCluFDI-713
94StaCluGR-713
94StaCluMOP-713
94Top-673
94TopGol-673
94TopSpa-673
94TopTra-75T
94Ult-416
94UppDec-506
94UppDecED-506
95ColCho-292
95ColChoGS-292
95ColChoSS-292
95Don-157
95DonPreP-157
95DonTopotO-144
95Fin-67
95FinRef-67
95Fla-78
95Fle-260
95Lea-111
95MarMot-14
95MarPac-19
95Pac-389
95Pin-431
95PinArtP-431
95PinMusC-431
95Sco-442
95ScoGolR-442
95ScoPlaTS-442
95StaClu-13
95StaCluFDI-13
95StaCluMOP-13
95StaCluSTWS-13
95StaCluVR-8
95Top-193
95TopCyb-110
95Ult-324
95UltGolM-324
95UppDec-346
95UppDecED-346
95UppDecEDG-346
95UppDecSE-117
95UppDecSEG-117
96ColCho-311
96ColChoGS-311
96ColChoSS-311
96Don-199
96DonPreP-199
96Fla-155
96Fle-226
96FleTif-226
96LeaSigA-13
96LeaSigAG-13
96LeaSigAS-13
96MarMot-20
95StaCluVRMC-8
96Ult-122
96UltGolM-122
97Fle-616
97FleTif-616
97Pac-181
97PacLigB-181
97PacSil-181
Ayala, Eric
80AndBraT-20
Ayala, Fernando
94GreFalDSP-3
Ayala, Jason
91ButCopKSP-2
Ayala, Julio
96EveAquB-2
Ayala, Moises
92BriTigC-15
92BriTigF-1413
93BriTigC-2
Aybar, Manuel
96ArkTraB-5
Ayer, Jack
82ArkTraT-20
84LouRedR-21
85LouRedR-21
86LouRedTI-4
87LouRedTI-3
Ayers, Bill (William Oscar)
47TipTop-120
Ayers, Jason
93MisStaB-48
Ayers, Jim
75CedRapGT-23
Ayers, Kevin
86VerBeaDP-2
Ayers, Lenny
91EveGiaC-22
Ayers, Scott
86WesPalBEP-3
87JamExpP-2556
Aylmer, Bobby
90St.CatBJP-3465
91MyrBeaHC-1
91MyrBeaHP-2935
Aylward, Dick (Richard John)
57HygMea-1
Aylward, Jim
88QuaCitAGS-22
88RenSilSCLC-280
89QuaCitAB-8
89QuaCitAGS-27
90MidAngGS-14
Ayoub, Sam
71RicBraTI-2
81RicBraT-25
82RicBraT-30
83RicBraT-7
84RicBraT-22
85RicBraT-24
86RicBraP-1
87RicBraC-NNO
87RicBraT-29
88RicBraP-6
89RicBraC-14
89RicBraP-820
90CMC-294
90RicBra2ATI-2
90RicBraC-18
90RicBraTI-2
Ayrault, Bob
89RenSilSCLC-240
90Bes-303
90CMC-800
90EasLeaAP-EL31
90ProAaA-23
90ReaPhiB-2
90ReaPhiP-1212
90ReaPhiS-4
90StaFS7-80
91LinDriAAA-479
91ScrRedBLD-479
91ScrRedBP-2531
92DonRoo-8
92PhiMed-37
92ScrRedBS-477
92SkyAAAF-216
93Don-16
93Fle-484
93PacSpa-574
93PhiMed-4
93Pin-229
93Sco-289
93StaClu-4
93StaCluFDI-4
93StaCluMOP-4
93StaCluP-9
93Top-126
93TopGol-126
93TopInaM-126
93TopMic-126
94ColC-45
94ColChoGS-45
94ColChoSS-45
Ayrault, Joe
91PulBraC-1
91PulBraP-4007
92MacBraC-9
92MacBraF-270
93CarLeaAGF-35
93DurBulC-2
93DurBulF-488
93DurBulTI-33
93SouAtlLAPI-2
94GreBraF-416
94GreBraTI-5
95BreBtaTI-42
96RicBraB-5
96RicBraRC-14
96RicBraUB-2
Ayres, Lenny
90EveGiaB-24
90EveGiaP-3117
91EveGiaP-3905
92CliGiaC-8
92CliGiaF-3588
Azar, Todd
88WauTimGS-15
Azcue, Joe (Jose Joaquin)
62Top-417
63Top-501
64IndJayP-2
64Top-199
64TopCoi-110
64TopVen-199
65Kah-3
65Top-514
66IndTeal-2
66Top-452
67CokCapI-9
67DexPre-15
67Top-336
68Baz-4
68Top-443
69AngJacitB-2
69MilBra-18
69MLBOffS-38
69OPC-176
69Top-176
69TopFou-21
69TopSta-162
69TopTeaP-13
69TraSta-1
70DayDaiNM-101
70MLBOffS-170
70OPC-294
70Top-294
71MLBOffS-338
71OPC-657
71Top-657
72MilBra-22
78TCM60I-36
94BreMilB-283
Azocar, Oscar
88AlbYanP-1347
89AlbYanB-19
89AlbYanP-332
89AlbYanS-1
90CMC-213
90ColCliC-13
90ColCliP-12
90ColCliP-688
90FleUpd-111
90ProAAAF-338
90ScoRoo-71T
90TopTVY-36
91Bow-652
91Cla1-T62
91Don-331
91Fle-655
91LasVegSLD-276
91LasVegSP-247
91LinDriAAA-276
91OPC-659
91PanFreS-329
91PanSti-270
91Sco-72
91Sco100RS-46
91StaClu-450
91Top-659
91TopDeb90-7
91TopDesS-659
91TopMic-659
91TopTif-659
91UppDec-464
92Fle-598
92OPC-112
92PadCarJ-2
92PadMot-12
92PadPolD-1
92PadSmo-2
92Sco-692
92StaClu-552
92Top-112
92TopGol-112
92TopGolW-112
92TopMic-112
93LinVenB-50
93PanSti-263
93StaClu-257
93StaCluFDI-257
93StaCluMOP-257
94VenLinU-12
95LinVen-73
Azuaje, Jesus
93BurIndC-2
93BurIndF-3303
94ColRedC-2
94ColRedF-447
94VenLinU-107
95StLucMTI-6
96BinBeeB-2
B.C., Mascot
96FayGenB-30
Baar, Bryan
89GreFalDSP-19
90BakDodCLC-256
91Cla/Bes-292
91LinDriA-528
91SanAntMLD-528
91SanAntMP-2978

92AlbDukS-3
92SkyAAAF-2
Baase, Michael
92StoPorC-5
Babb, Charlie (Charles Amos)
09ColChiE-15A
09ColChiE-15B
11SpoLifCW-12
12ColRedB-15A
12ColRedB-15B
12ColTinT-15A
12ColTinT-15B
90DodTar-23
Babbitt, Gene
47SunBre-1
Babbitt, Troy
91EugEmeC-5
91EugEmeP-3730
92AppFoxF-989
Babcock, Bill
82AppFoxF-19
Babcock, Bob (Robert E.)
77TucTorC-20
78TucTorC-20
80ChaChaT-17
81Top-41
82Don-565
82Top-567
83SalLakCGT-3
93RanKee-57
Babcock, Tom
74WicAerODF-103B
Babcock, Walter
74WicAerODF-103A
Baber, Larue
90HelBreSP-13
91HelBreSP-9
92BelBreC-21
92BelBreF-417
92ClaFS7-363
93WatDiaC-4
93WatDiaF-1779
94RanCucQC-2
94RanCucQF-1648
Babich, Johnny (John Charles)
34BatR31-167
34DiaStaR-82A
34DiaStaR-82B
35GouPreR-5
36NatChiFPR-86
40PlaBal-191
41DouPlaR-127
41PlaBal-40
43CenFlo-1
44CenFlo-1
48SigOil-1
48SmiClo-22
90DodTar-24
Babik, Bill
52LavPro-72
Babin, Brady
95BreCouMF-251
Babineaux, Darrin
95YakBeaTI-1
Babitt, Shooty (Mack Neal) II
79WatA'sT-11
80OgdA'sT-21
80WesHavWCT-17
82Don-556
82Fle-86
82TacTigT-28
82Top-578
83MemChiT-1
83WicAerDS-3
84IndIndTI-14
Babki, Blake
91JamExpC-2
91JamExpP-3558
92LetMouSP-12
Baby, Jim
75WesPalBES-3
Baca, Mark A.
88PalSprACLC-99
88PalSprAP-1456
Bacciocu, Jack
49SomandK-19
Bach, Jan
78CliDodT-1
Bach, Rich
80BurBeeT-16
Bachman, Kent
86WesPalBEP-4
Backlund, Brett
93Bow-134
93BufBisF-508
93StaCluM-61
94CarMudF-1569
94UppDecML-112
Backman, Les (Lester John)
11SpoLifM-262
Backman, Wally (Walter W.)
79JacMetT-2
80TidTidT-4
81Fle-336
81TidTidT-8
82MetPhoA-2
83Don-618
83Fle-537
83TidTidT-3
83Top-444
84JacMetF-2
85Don-319
85Fle-72
85Lea-79
85MetColP-18
85MetFanC-1
85MetTCM-21
85OPC-162
85Top-677
85TopSti-106
85TopTif-677
86BasStaB-4
86Don-238
86Fle-75
86MetColP-16
86MetFanC-1
86MetTCM-16
86MetWorSC-3
86OPC-191
86Top-191
86TopSti-97
86TopTif-191
87Don-316
87Fle-3
87FleGlo-3
87Lea-59
87MetColP-10
87OPC-48
87Spo-124
87SpoTeaP-2
87Top-48
87TopSti-100
87TopTif-48
88Don-241
88DonTeaBM-241
88Fle-128
88FleGlo-128
88Lea-202
88MetColP-14
88MetKah-6
88OPC-333
88PanSti-340
88Sco-303
88ScoGlo-303
88StaLinMe-2
88Top-333
88TopTif-333
89Bow-159
89BowTif-159
89Don-383
89DonBasB-186
89DonTra-10
89Fle-28
89FleGlo-28
89FleUpd-43
89OPC-72
89Sco-315
89ScoRoo-34T
89Top-508
89TopBig-300
89TopTif-508
89TopTra-5T
89TopTraT-5T
89UppDec-188
89UppDec-732
90Bow-177
90BowTif-177
90Don-155
90DonBesN-130
90Fle-367
90FleCan-367
90FleUpd-47
90Lea-341
90OPC-218
90PirHomC-1
90PubSti-321
90Sco-281
90ScoRoo-37T
90Top-218
90TopBig-233
90TopTif-218
90TopTra-5T
90TopTraT-5T
90UppDec-158
90VenSti-20
91Bow-490
91Don-177
91Fle-29
91FleUpd-106
91Lea-482
91MetWIZ-19
91OPC-722
91PhiMed-4
91RedFolS-5
91Sco-16
91ScoRoo-8T
91StaClu-368
91Top-722
91TopDesS-722
91TopMic-722
91TopTif-722
91TopTra-3T
91TopTraT-3T
91UltUpd-98
91UppDec-185
91UppDec-790
92Don-478
92OPC-434
92PhiMed-4
92Sco-177
92StaClu-4
92Top-434
92TopGol-434
92TopGolW-434
92TopMic-434
92UppDec-350
Backowski, Lance
95YakBeaTI-2
96SavSanB-6
Backs, Jason
89SpaPhiP-1038
89SpaPhiS-1
91LinDriAA-501
91ReaPhiLD-501
91ReaPhiP-1362
Backus, Jerry
88BoiHawP-1618
Bacon, Rick
93EugEmeC-4
93EugEmeF-3846
Bacosa, Al
88IdaFalBP-1848
Bacsik, Mike (Michael James)
74GasRanT-3
75SpoIndC-18
76SacSolC-6
76VenLeaS-82
77Top-103
77TucTorC-52
78TucTorC-45
80Top-453
93RanKee-58
96BurIndB-2
Baczewski, Fred
54Bow-60
55Bow-190
Badacour, Bob
89CarNewE-18
90MarPhiP-3189
Badcock, Tom
73WicAerKSB-2
75WatDodT-1
Badgro, Red (Morris Hiram)
81ConTSN-30
88ConSer4-2
Badorek, Mike
91HamRedC-5
91HamRedP-4026
92MidLeaATI-1
92SprCarC-9
92SprCarF-859
93St.PetCC-2
93St.PetCF-2617
94ArkTraF-3081
94ExcFS7-255
95ArkTraTI-4
96LouRedB-7
Bady, Ed
94VerExpC-3
94VerExpF-3920
96WesPalBEB-28
Baecht, Ed (Edward Joseph)
31CubTeal-1
93ConTSN-971
Baehr, Dave
82IdaFalAT-1
83WisRapTF-25
Baerga, Carlos
83KelCerB-4
86ChaRaiP-1
87ChaRaiP-2
88BlaYNPRWL-131
88TexLeaAGS-32
88WicPilRD-15
89BlaYNPRWL-4
89BlaYNPRWLU-40
89BlaYNPRWLU-47
89LasVegSC-18
89LasVegSP-9
90Bow-339
90BowTif-339
90ClaYel-T35
90DonRoo-19
90FleUpd-90
90IndTeal-3
90Lea-443
90ScoRoo-74T
90ScoYouS2-32
90TopBig-229
90TopMag-97
90TopTra-6T
90TopTraT-6T
90UppDec-737
91Bow-69
91Cla3-T22
91Don-274
91Fle-360
91IndFanC-3
91Lea-225
91OPC-147
91PanFreS-218
91PanSti-180
91Sco-74
91Sco100RS-30
91StaClu-115
91Top-147
91TopDeb90-8
91TopDesS-147
91TopMic-147
91TopRoo-4
91TopTif-147
91ToyRoo-4
91Ult-106
91UppDec-125
92Bow-531
92Cla2-T48
92Don-120
92Fle-104
92Hig5-42
92IndFanC-4
92Lea-202
92LeaBlaG-202
92OPC-33
92PanSti-47
92Pin-3
92PinTea2-56
92Sco-128
92SpollIFK1-244
92StaClu-143
92Stu-163
92Top-33
92TopGol-33
92TopGolW-33
92TopMic-33
92TriPla-235
92Ult-46
92UppDec-231
93Bow-585
93CadDis-2
93ClaGam-9
93DiaMar-6
93Don-405
93DonDiaK-DK13
93DonMVP-16
93DonSpiotG-SG15
93DurPowP1-15
93Fin-57
93FinRef-57
93Fla-191
93Fle-213
93Fle-357
93FleTeaL-AL6
93FunPac-105
93FunPac-107
93Hos-15
93IndWUA-2
93Lea-233
93LeaFas-11
93LeaGolA-R4
93OPC-39
93OPCPre-51
93PacBeiA-5
93PacBeiA-6
93PacSpa-93
93PacSpaGE-12
93PacSpaPI-9
93PanSti-51
93Pin-6
93PinHomRC-39
93PinSlu-29
93PinTea2-7
93PinTeaP-5
93Sco-9
93ScoFra-5
93Sel-122
93SelStaL-8
93SP-119
93StaClu-61
93StaClu-593
93StaCluFDI-61
93StaCluFDI-593
93StaCluM-189
93StaCluMOP-61
93StaCluMOP-603
93StaCluMP-1
93Stu-50
93StuHer-9
93Top-221
93Top-402
93TOPBLAG-25
93TopFulS-14
93TopGol-221
93TopGol-402
93TopInaM-221
93TopInaM-402
93TopMic-221
93TopMic-402
93Toy-51
93ToyMasP-3
93TriPla-80
93TriPlaA-18
93Ult-183
93UltAllS-13
93UppDec-45
93UppDec-174
93UppDecDG-12
93UppDecFA-A8
93UppDecFAJ-A8
93UppDecGold-45
93UppDecGold-174
93UppDecOD-D3
93USPlaCA-4D
94Bow-307
94BowBes-R35
94BowBes-X103
94BowBesR-R35
94BowBesR-X103
94ChuHomS-19
94ChuHomSG-19
94ColC-444
94ColChoGS-444
94ColChoSS-444
94Don-14
94DonSpeE-14
94ExtBas-56
94Fin-231
94FinJum-231
94FinRef-231
94Fla-37
94FlaHotN-2
94Fle-99
94FleAllS-2
94FleGolM-2
94FlePro-4
94FleSun-2
94FleTeaL-5
94FUnPac-109
94FUnPac-201
94Kra-1
94Lea-247
94LeaGolS-9

94LeaL-26
94LeaMVPC-A1
94LeaMVPCG-A1
94OPC-106
94OPCAllR-6
94OPCJumA-6
94Pac-166
94PacPro-P1
94PacSilP-16
94PanSti-54
94Pin-2
94PinArtP-2
94PinMusC-2
94PinPowS-PS12
94PinPowS-PS12P
94PinRunC-RC15
94PinSam-2
94PinTeaP-2
94PinTheN-22
94ProMag-37
94RedFolMI-4
94Sco-53
94ScoCyc-TC4
94ScoDreT-4
94ScoGolR-53
94ScoGolS-38
94Sel-279
94SP-96
94SPDieC-96
94Spo-71
94SpoMov-MM11
94StaClu-169
94StaCluFDI-169
94StaCluGR-169
94StaCluMO-45
94StaCluMOP-169
94StaCluMOP-ST19
94StaCluST-ST19
94Stu-91
94Top-450
94TopBlaG-2
94TopGol-450
94TopSpa-450
94TopSupS-2
94TriPla-112
94TriPlaM-5
94Ult-343
94UltHitM-2
94UltRBIK-6
94UltRisS-1
94UppDec-49
94UppDec-115
94UppDecED-49
94UppDecED-115
94USPlaCA-6D
95Baz-103
95BazRedH-RH20
95Bow-336
95BowBes-R37
95BowBesR-R37
95ClaPhoC-20
95ColCho-56
95ColCho-270
95ColChoGS-56
95ColChoGS-270
95ColChoSE-118
95ColChoSEGS-118
95ColChoSESS-118
95ColChoSS-56
95ColChoSS-270
95Don-326
95DonDom-4
95DonPreP-326
95DonTopotO-57
95Emb-95
95EmbGolI-95
95Emo-31
95Fin-199
95FinRef-199
95Fla-29
95Fle-131
95Lea-158
95Lea300C-9
95LeaLim-123
95LeaLimIBP-13
95Pac-117
95PacLatD-4
95PacPri-37
95PanSti-49
95Pin-200
95Pin-280
95PinArtP-200
95PinArtP-280
95PinMusC-200
95PinMusC-280
95PinRedH-RH25
95PinWhiH-WH25
95RedFol-16
95Sco-51
95Sco-565
95ScoGolR-51
95ScoGolR-565
95ScoHaloG-HG23
95ScoPlaTS-51
95ScoPlaTS-565
95Sel-124
95SelArtP-124
95SelCer-43
95SelCerMG-43
95SP-144
95SPCha-143
95SPChaDC-143
95Spo-64
95SpoArtP-64
95SPSil-144
95SPSpeF-8
95StaClu-36
95StaClu-48
95StaClu-403
95StaCluCT-12
95StaCluFDI-36
95StaCluFDI-48
95StaCluMOP-36
95StaCluMOP-48
95StaCluMOP-403
95StaCluSTDW-I19T
95StaCluSTDW-I36
95StaCluSTMP-11
95StaCluSTWS-36
95StaCluSTWS-48
95StaCluSTWS-403
95StaCluVR-25
95Stu-36
95StuGolS-36
95Sum-100
95SumNthD-100
95Top-385
95Top-596
95TopCyb-368
95TopCybSiR-5
95TopTra-157T
95UC3-43
95UC3-140
95UC3ArtP-43
95UC3ArtP-140
95Ult-278
95UltGolM-278
95UppDec-109
95UppDec-339
95UppDecED-109
95UppDecED-339
95UppDecEDG-109
95UppDecEDG-339
95UppDecSE-27
95UppDecSEG-27
95UppDecSoaD-SD11
95Zen-13
95ZenAllS-14
95ZenZ-18
96Baz-33
96Bow-46
96BowBes-86
96BowBesAR-86
96BowBesP-BBP22
96BowBesPAR-BBP22
96BowBesPR-BBP22
96BowBesR-86
96Cir-154
96CirRav-154
96ColCho-119
96ColCho-337
96ColChoGS-119
96ColChoGS-337
96ColChoSS-119
96ColChoSS-337
96ColChoYMtP-2
96ColChoYMtP-2A
96ColChoYMtPGS-2
96ColChoYMtPGS-2A
96Don-435
96DonHitL-5
96DonPreP-435
96EmoXL-45
96Fin-B282
96Fin-S69
96FinRef-B282
96FinRef-S69
96Fla-63
96Fle-82
96FleInd-3
96FleTif-82
96Lea-157
96LeaLim-32
96LeaLimG-32
96LeaPre-32
96LeaPreP-32
96LeaPrePB-157
96LeaPrePG-157
96LeaPrePS-157
96LeaPreSG-24
96LeaPreSte-24
96LeaSig-146
96LeaSigA-14
96LeaSigAG-14
96LeaSigAS-14
96LeaSigPPG-146
96LeaSigPPP-146
96LeaTotB-10
96MetUni-43
96MetUniP-43
96Pac-300
96PacBaeS-1
96PacEstL-EL3
96PacGolCD-DC22
96PacHom-HP4
96PacOctM-OM1
96PacPri-P93
96PacPriG-P93
96PanSti-181
96Pin-218
96Pin-304
96PinAfi-72
96PinAfiAP-72
96PinAfiFPP-72
96PinArtP-118
96PinArtP-188
96PinChrBC-12
96PinFoil-218
96PinFoil-304
96PinSta-118
96PinSta-188
96SchDis-17
96Sco-15
96Sco-372
96ScoBigB-12
96ScoDiaA-25
96ScoDreT-3
96ScoDugC-A14
96ScoDugC-B97
96ScoDugCAP-A14
96ScoDugCAP-B97
96ScoGolS-28
96ScoRef-8
96Sel-21
96SelArtP-21
96SelCer-58
96SelCerAP-58
96SelCerCB-58
96SelCerCR-58
96SelCerMB-58
96SelCerMG-58
96SelCerMR-58
96SelTeaN-1
96SP-67
96Spo-70
96SpoArtP-70
96StaClu-188
96StaClu-331
96StaCluEPB-331
96StaCluEPG-331
96StaCluEPS-331
96StaCluMM-MM4
96StaCluMO-1
96StaCluMOP-188
96StaCluMOP-331
96StaCluMOP-MM4
95StaCluVRMC-25
96Stu-88
96StuPrePB-88
96StuPrePG-88
96StuPrePS-88
96Sum-98
96SumAbo&B-98
96SumArtP-98
96SumFoi-98
96TeaOut-4
96Top-75
96Top-226
96TopChr-26
96TopChr-86
96TopChrR-26
96TopChrR-86
96TopGal-2
96TopGalE-5
96TopGalPPI-2
96TopLas-98
96TopLasSS-1
96TopPro-AL2
96Ult-45
96UltGolM-45
96UppDec-53
96UppDecPRE-R22
96UppDecPreR-R22
96Zen-82
96ZenArtP-82
96ZenMoz-18
97BowBes-99
97BowBesAR-99
97BowBesR-99
97Cir-155
97CirRav-155
97ColCho-169
97Don-135
97DonEli-114
97DonEliGS-114
97DonLim-39
97DonLim-188
97DonLimLE-39
97DonLimLE-188
97DonPreP-135
97DonPrePGold-135
97Fin-230
97FinRef-230
97Fle-391
97FleTif-391
97Lea-255
97LeaFraM-255
97LeaFraMDC-255
97NewPin-54
97NewPinAP-54
97NewPinMC-54
97NewPinPP-54
97Pac-358
97PacLatotML-33
97PacLigB-358
97PacPri-122
97PacPriLB-122
97PacPriP-122
97PacSil-358
97PinPasttM-14
97Sco-135
97ScoPreS-135
97ScoShoS-135
97ScoShoSAP-135
97SP-117
97StaClu-218
97StaCluMat-218
97StaCluMOP-218
97Top-381
97TopChr-131
97TopChrR-131
97TopGal-113
97TopGalPPI-113
97TopSta-12
97TopStaAM-12
97Ult-236
97UltGolME-236
97UltPlaME-236
97UppDec-436

Baerns, Scott
89TenTecGE-3

Baerwald, Rudolph
09ColChiE-16
12ColRedB-16
12ColTinT-16

Baez, Angel
81BufBisT-17

Baez, Benito
96WesMicWB-6

Baez, Diogenes
92WinHavRSC-6
92WinHavRSF-1790
93LynRedSC-1
93LynRedSF-2528
93UtiBluSC-3
93UtiBluSF-3544
94UtiBluSC-3

Baez, Eddie
76VenLeaS-69

Baez, Francisco
90AppFoxBS-3
90AppFoxP-2087
90EugEmeGS-2
91AppFoxC-1
91AppFoxP-1707
92AppFoxC-11
92AppFoxF-974
93WilBluRC-2
93WilBluRF-1987

Baez, Igor
89GreHorP-408

Baez, Jesse
79LodDodT-9
81WauTimT-13
83WauTimF-17

Baez, Jose Antonio
75WatDodT-2
78Top-311
95ForWayWTI-28
96ForWayWB-29

Baez, Kevin
88LitFalMP-2
89ColMetB-12
89ColMetGS-6
89SouAtlLAGS-19
90JacMetGS-16
91LinDriAAA-551
91MetColP-22
91MetWIZ-20
91TidTidLD-551
91TidTidP-2515
91TopDeb90-9
92DonRoo-9
92SkyAAAF-247
92StaClu-543
92TidTidF-902
92TidTidS-551
93Don-361
93FleFinE-98
93NorTidF-2574
94Don-68
94RocRedWF-1003
94RocRedWTI-3
94StaClu-247
94StaCluFDI-247
94StaCluGR-247
94StaCluMOP-247
95TolMudHTI-6
96TolMudHB-5

Baez, Pedro
88MadMusP-3
89ModA'sC-8
89ModA'sCLC-267

Baez, Raul
94UtiBluSF-3831

Bafia, Bob
86WinSpiP-2
87WinSpiP-8
88PitCubP-1363
89ChaKniTI-22
90CMC-86
90IowCubC-11
90IowCubP-323
90ProAAAF-630
90TopTVCu-37
91HunStaC-2
91HunStaLD-277
91HunStaP-1800
91LinDriAA-277

Bagby, James C.J. Jr.
39PlaBal-40
40PlaBal-32
46RedSoxTI-2
79DiaGre-233
83TCMPla1942-12
93ConTSN-936

Bagby, James C.J. Sr.
16ColE13-9
17HolBreD-4
20NatCarE-4
20WalMaiW-2
21E121So1-3
21E121So8-2
21Exh-3
22AmeCarE-2
22E120-31
22W575-3
23W501-20
23WilChoV-4
61Fle-92
77Ind192T-1
92ConTSN-487
95ConTSN-1364

Baggott, Dave
89SalLakTTI-4
94OgdRapSP-29

Bagialemani, Panther
90IBAWorA-15

Bagiotti, Aldo
81RedPioT-10

Bagley, Lorenzo
96MedHatBJTI-3
Bagnall, Jim
83ButCopKT-16
83ChaRoyT-4
Bagshaw, Lance
87SalLakTTT-7
Bagwell, Bill (William M.)
94ConTSN-1310
94ConTSNB-1310
Bagwell, Jeff
88CapCodPB-4
88CapCodPPaLP-57
90Bes-132
90CMC-739
90EasLeaAP-EL40
90NewBriRSB-7
90NewBriRSP-1324
90NewBriRSS-1
90ProAaA-26
90StaFS7-30
90TopMag-61
91AstMot-8
91Bow-183
91Cla2-T84
91ClaGam-90
91DonRoo-30
91FleUpd-87
91LeaGolR-BC14
91ScoRoo-96T
91StaClu-388
91StaCluMO-11
91Stu-172
91TopTra-4T
91TopTraT-4T
91TopTriH-N13
91UltUpd-79
91UppDec-702
91UppDec-755
92AstMot-8
92Bow-200
92Cla1-T8
92Cla2-T2
92ClaGam-187
92ColBag-1
92ColBag-2
92ColBag-3
92ColBag-4
92ColBag-5
92ColBag-6
92ColBag-7
92ColBag-8
92ColBag-9
92ColBag-10
92ColBag-11
92ColBag-12
92ColPro-2
92Don-358
92DonBonC-BC6
92DonCraJ1-2
92DonDiaK-DK11
92DonMcD-24
92Fle-425
92FleCitTP-19
92FleRooS-4
92Fre-1
92Hig5-36
92Hig5S-2
92JimDea-3
92Lea-28
92LeaGolP-4
92LeaPre-4
92MJBHolB-R1
92MJBHolB-R2
92MJBHolB-R3
92MJBHolB-R4
92MJBHolP-R1
92MooSna-2
92MotBag-1
92MotBag-2
92MotBag-3
92MotBag-4
92OPC-520
92OPCPre-107
92PanSti-152
92Pin-70
92PinSlu-15
92PinTea2-10
92Pos-1
92Sco-576
92Sco-793
92Sco100RS-35
92ScoCokD-3
92ScoImpP-2
92ScoProP-19
92SpoIllFK1-278
92StaBag-1
92StaBag-2
92StaBag-3
92StaBag-4
92StaBag-5
92StaBag-6
92StaBag-7
92StaBag-8
92StaBag-9
92StaBag-10
92StaBag-11
92StaClu-330
92StaClu-606
92StaCluECN-606
92StaPro-3
92Stu-31
92StuHer-BC12
92StuPre-16
92Top-520
92TopDeb91-7
92TopGol-520
92TopGolW-520
92TopKid-44
92TopMcD-34
92TopMic-520
92TriPla-200
92TriPlaG-GS7
92Ult-198
92UltAwaW-3
92UppDec-276
92UppDecF-3
92UppDecFG-3
92UppDecHRH-HR25
92UppDecTMH-7
92UppDecWB-T12
93AstMot-7
93Bow-420
93ClaGam-10
93DiaMar-7
93Don-428
93DonLonBL-LL17
93DonMVP-24
93DonPre-4
93Fin-11
93FinRef-11
93Fla-57
93Fle-46
93FleFruotL-3
93FleTeaL-NL9
93FunPac-42
93FunPac-43
93Hos-19
93HumDumC-32
93Lea-125
93LeaFas-17
93LeaGolA-R3
93OPC-29
93PacJugC-20
93PacSpa-117
93PanSti-170
93Pin-10
93Pin-297
93PinHomRC-28
93PinSlu-14
93PinTea2-9
93Sco-89
93ScoFra-18
93Sel-113
93SP-28
93StaClu-384
93StaCluAs-8
93StaCluFDI-384
93StaCluMOP-384
93Stu-34
93StuSil-3
93TedWil-156
93TedWil-157
93TedWil-158
93TedWil-159
93Top-227
93TopFulS-8
93TopGol-227
93TopInaM-227
93TopMic-227
93Toy-56
93TriPla-43
93TriPlaA-12
93Ult-390
93UppDec-256
93UppDec-452
93UppDec-475
93UppDec-813
93UppDecDG-2
93UppDecGold-256
93UppDecGold-452
93UppDecGold-475
93UppDecGold-813
93UppDecIC-WI2
93UppDecICJ-WI2
94AstMot-3
94Bow-118
94BowBes-R53
94BowBesR-R53
94ChuHomS-6
94ChuHomSG-6
94ColC-329
94ColC-590
94ColChoGS-329
94ColChoGS-590
94ColChoSS-329
94ColChoSS-590
94ColChoT-8
94DenHol-4
94Don-365
94DonDiaK-DK27
94DonMVP-6
94DonSpeE-365
94ExtBas-268
94ExtBasGB-1
94Fin-212
94FinJum-212
94FinRef-212
94Fla-385
94FlaInfP-1
94Fle-483
94FleSun-3
94FleTeaL-20
94FUnPac-152
94Kra-16
94Lea-221
94LeaL-110
94LeaMVPC-N1
94LeaMVPCG-N1
94OPC-212
94OPCAllR-5
94OPCJumA-5
94OscMayR-16
94Pac-257
94PacSilP-24
94PanSti-189
94Pin-290
94PinArtP-290
94PinMusC-290
94PinPowS-PS16
94PinRunC-RC36
94PinTeaP-1
94Pos-29
94ProMag-56
94RedFolMI-2
94Sco-4
94ScoGolR-4
94ScoGolS-8
94ScoSam-4
94ScoSam-4GR
94Sel-234
94SP-27
94SPDieC-27
94SPHol-3
94SPHolDC-3
94Spo-7
94SpoSha-SH3
94SPPre-CR1
94StaClu-108
94StaCluF-F1
94StaCluFDI-108
94StaCluGR-108
94StaCluMOP-108
94StaCluMOP-F1
94Stu-16
94SucSav-16
94TomPiz-1
94Top-40
94TopBlaG-23
94TopGol-40
94TopSpa-40
94TopSupS-3
94TriPla-21
94TriPlaM-4
94Ult-203
94UltRisS-2
94UppDec-272
94UppDec-480
94UppDecAJ-36
94UppDecAJG-36
94UppDecDC-C1
94UppDecED-272
94UppDecED-480
94UppDecMLS-MM1
94UppDecMLSED-MM1
94USPlaCA-5D
95AstMot-2
95Baz-61
95BazRedH-RH13
95Bow-279
95BowBes-R16
95BowBes-X15
95BowBesR-R16
95BowBesR-X15
95ClaPhoC-30
95ColCho-76
95ColCho-528
95ColChoCtG-CG1
95ColChoCtG-CG1B
95ColChoCtG-CG1C
95ColChoCtGE-1
95ColChoCtGG-CG1
95ColChoCtGG-CG1B
95ColChoCtGG-CG1C
95ColChoCtGGE-1
95ColChoGS-76
95ColChoGS-528
95ColChoSE-40
95ColChoSE-138
95ColChoSE-254
95ColChoSEGS-40
95ColChoSEGS-138
95ColChoSEGS-254
95ColChoSESS-40
95ColChoSESS-138
95ColChoSESS-254
95ColChoSS-76
95ColChoSS-528
95D3Zon-3
95DenHol-3
95Don-20
95DonBomS-2
95DonDiaK-DK2
95DonDom-3
95DonEli-49
95DonLonBL-8
95DonPreP-20
95DonTopotO-249
95Emb-118
95EmbGolI-118
95Emo-134
95EmoN-1
95Fin-117
95FinPowK-PK7
95FinRef-117
95Fla-143
95FlaHotN-1
95FlaInfP-1
95FlaTodS-1
95Fle-451
95FleAllS-13
95FleAwaW-2
95FleLeaL-8
95FleLumC-1
95FlePro-3
95FleTeaL-20
95FleUpdDT-1
95FleUpdH-1
95KinDis-2
95Kra-17
95Lea-119
95Lea300C-12
95LeaChe-8
95LeaCor-4
95LeaGolS-1
95LeaGreG-1
95LeaHeaftH-3
95LeaLim-132
95LeaLimG-2
95LeaLimIBP-6
95LeaLimL-10
95LeaOpeD-2
95LeaSli-5A
95LeaSli-5B
95NatPac-18
95Pac-180
95PacGolCDC-10
95PacGolP-16
95PacPri-58
95PanSti-31
95PanSti-110
95PanSti-117
95Pin-1
95Pin-301
95Pin-449
95Pin-450
95PinArtP-1
95PinArtP-301
95PinArtP-449
95PinArtP-450
95PinFan-25
95PinGatA-GA4
95PinMusC-1
95PinMusC-301
95PinMusC-449
95PinMusC-450
95PinPin-5
95PinPinR-5
95PinRedH-RH4
95PinTeaP-TP3
95PinWhiH-WH4
95Pos-2
95PosCan-16
95RedFol-20
95Sco-221
95Sco-554
95ScoDouGC-GC9
95ScoGolR-221
95ScoGolR-554
95ScoHaloG-HG4
95ScoPlaTS-221
95ScoPlaTS-554
95ScoRul-SR4
95ScoRulJ-SR4
95ScoSam-221
95Sel-37
95Sel-249
95Sel-250
95SelArtP-37
95SelArtP-249
95SelArtP-250
95SelBigS-BS8
95SelCer-54
95SelCerC-4
95SelCerGT-4
95SelCerMG-54
95SelSam-37
95SP-60
95SPCha-50
95SPCha-55
95SPChaDC-50
95SPChaDC-55
95Spo-48
95Spo-166
95SpoArtP-48
95SpoArtP-166
95SpoDet-DE1
95SpoDouT-1
95SpoHamT-HT3
95SpoPro-PM4
95SPPlaP-PP1
95SPSil-60
95SPSpeF-38
95StaClu-240
95StaClu-375
95StaClu-501
95StaCluCC-CC15
95StaCluCT-1
95StaCluFDI-240
95StaCluMO-2
95StaCluMOP-240
95StaCluMOP-375
95StaCluMOP-501
95StaCluMOP-CC15
95StaCluMOP-PZ1
95StaCluMOP-RL1
95StaCluMOP-VRE3
95StaCluPZ-PZ1
95StaCluRL-RL1
95StaCluSTWS-240
95StaCluSTWS-375
95StaCluSTWS-501
95StaCluVE-VRE3
95StaCluVR-198
95Stu-2
95StuGolS-2
95StuPlaS-2
95Sum-96
95Sum-177
95Sum-197
95SumBigB-BB4
95SumNthD-96
95SumNthD-177
95SumNthD-197
95TomPiz-4
95Top-384
95Top-405
95TopCyb-206
95TopFin-1
95TopLeaL-LL11

95TopLeaL-LL27
95TopLeaL-LL32
95TopTra-8T
95TopTraPB-8
95UC3-55
95UC3-144
95UC3ArtP-55
95UC3ArtP-144
95UC3CycS-CS3
95Ult-169
95UltAwaW-11
95UltAwaW-20
95UltAwaWGM-11
95UltAwaWGM-20
95UltGolM-169
95UltHitM-1
95UltHitMGM-1
95UltHomRK-7
95UltHomRKGM-7
95UltOnBL-1
95UltOnBLGM-1
95UltPowP-4
95UltPowPGM-4
95UltRBIK-6
95UltRBIKGM-6
95UltRisS-2
95UltRisSGM-2
95UppDec-275
95UppDecED-275
95UppDecEDG-275
95UppDecPAW-H6
95UppDecPAWE-H6
95UppDecPC-MLB7
95UppDecPLL-R6
95UppDecPLL-R16
95UppDecPLL-R26
95UppDecPLLE-R6
95UppDecPLLE-R16
95UppDecPLLE-R26
95UppDecSE-45
95UppDecSEG-45
95UppDecSoaD-SD5
95USPlaCMLA-12C
95USPlaCMLA-13D
95Zen-47
95ZenZ-9
96AstMot-2
96Baz-40
96Bow-77
96BowBes-20
96BowBesAR-20
96BowBesMI-1
96BowBesMIAR-1
96BowBesMIR-1
96BowBesP-BBP16
96BowBesPAR-BBP16
96BowBesPR-BBP16
96BowBesR-20
96Cir-133
96CirAcc-19
96CirBos-37
96CirRav-133
96ColCho-160
96ColCho-402
96ColChoCtG-CG19
96ColChoCtG-CG19B
96ColChoCtG-CG19C
96ColChoCtGE-CR19
96ColChoCtGG-CG19
96ColChoCtGG-CG19B
96ColChoCtGG-CG19C
96ColChoCtGGE-CR19
96ColChoGS-160
96ColChoGS-402
96ColChoSS-160
96ColChoSS-402
96ColChoYMtP-3
96ColChoYMtP-3A
96ColChoYMtPGS-3
96ColChoYMtPGS-3A
96DenHol-6
96DenHolGS-7
96DenHolGSAP-7
96Don-81
96DonHitL-11
96DonPreP-81
96DonRouT-3
96EmoXL-193
96Fin-B299
96Fin-G42
96Fin-S161
96FinBro-3
96FinRef-B299
96FinRef-G42
96FinRef-S161
96Fla-272
96FlaDiaC-1
96Fle-400
96FleTeaL-20
96FleTif-400
96FleUpd-U211
96FleUpdH-2
96FleUpdSS-1
96FleUpdTC-U211
96Kin-4
96Lea-199
96LeaAllGMC-5
96LeaAllGMCG-5
96LeaLim-9
96LeaLimG-9
96LeaLimL-9
96LeaLimLB-9
96LeaPicP-9
96LeaPre-8
96LeaPre-148
96LeaPreP-8
96LeaPreP-148
96LeaPrePB-199
96LeaPrePG-199
96LeaPrePS-199
96LeaPreSG-39
96LeaPreSP-7
96LeaPreSta-11
96LeaPreSte-39
96LeaSig-22
96LeaSigPPG-22
96LeaSigPPP-22
96MetUni-172
96MetUniP-172
96Pac-89
96PacGolCD-DC10
96PacPri-P29
96PacPriG-P29
96PacPriRHS-RH6
96PanSti-59
96Pin-10
96Pin-151
96Pin-197
96Pin-259
96Pin-305B
96PinAfi-73
96PinAfiAP-73
96PinAfiFPP-73
96PinAfiMN-5
96PinAfiR-13
96PinAfiR-14
96PinAfiR-15
96PinAfiR-18
96PinAfiR-20
96PinAfiR-22
96PinAfiSP-9
96PinArtP-7
96PinArtP-78
96PinArtP-159
96PinArtP-190
96PinEssotG-11
96PinFan-5
96PinFoil-259
96PinFoil-305B
96PinPow-11
96PinSky-16
96PinSlu-3
96PinSta-7
96PinSta-78
96PinSta-159
96PinSta-190
96PinTeaP-1
96PinTeaS-7
96Pro-1
96ProMagA-13
96ProSta-13
96Sco-269
96Sco-304
96ScoAll-14
96ScoBigB-4
96ScoDiaA-24
96ScoDugC-B29
96ScoDugCAP-B29
96ScoGolS-16
96ScoNumG-7
96ScoRef-15
96ScoTitT-9
96Sel-12
96Sel-160
96SelArtP-12
96SelArtP-160
96SelCer-54
96SelCerAP-54
96SelCerCB-54
96SelCerCR-54
96SelCerIP-12
96SelCerMB-54
96SelCerMG-54
96SelCerMR-54
96SelClaTF-7
96SelEnF-5
96SelTeaN-26
96SP-95
96SPMarM-MM13
96SPMarMDC-13
96Spo-21
96Spo-115
96SpoArtP-21
96SpoArtP-115
96SpoDouT-12
96SpoHitP-7
96SpoPowS-19
96SpoPro-8
96SPSpeFX-44
96SPSpeFXDC-44
96SPx-29
96SPxGol-29
96StaClu-183
96StaClu-429
96StaCluEPB-429
96StaCluEPG-429
96StaCluEPS-429
96StaCluMet-M1
96StaCluMOP-183
96StaCluMOP-429
96StaCluMOP-M1
95StaCluVRMC-198
96Stu-49
96StuHitP-4
96StuMas-3
96StuPrePB-49
96StuPrePG-49
96StuPrePS-49
96StuStaGS-8
96Sum-7
96SumAbo&B-7
96SumArtP-7
96SumBal-14
96SumBigB-7
96SumBigBM-7
96SumFoi-7
96SumPos-1
96TeaOut-5
96Top-4
96Top-380
96TopChr-4
96TopChr-153
96TopChrR-4
96TopChrR-153
96TopChrWC-WC1
96TopChrWCR-WC1
96TopGal-164
96TopGalPPI-164
96TopLas-34
96TopLasPC-9
96TopMysF-M20
96TopMysFR-M20
96TopPowB-4
96TopPro-NL1
96TopWreC-WC1
96Ult-205
96Ult-574
96UltChe-A1
96UltCheGM-A1
96UltGolM-205
96UltGolM-574
96UltPowP-1
96UltPowPGM-1
96UppDec-80
96UppDecA-3
96UppDecDD-DD21
96UppDecDDG-DD21
96UppDecDDS-DD21
96UppDecPHE-H31
96UppDecPRE-R41
96UppDecPRE-R51
96UppDecPreH-H31
96UppDecPreR-R41
96UppDecPreR-R51
96Zen-24
96ZenArtP-24
96ZenDiaC-7
96ZenDiaCP-7
96ZenMoz-25
97Bow-243
97BowBes-58
97BowBesAR-58
97BowBesBC-BC7
97BowBesBCAR-BC7
97BowBesBCR-BC7
97BowBesMI-MI2
97BowBesMIAR-MI2
97BowBesMIARI-MI2
97BowBesMII-MI2
97BowBesMIR-MI2
97BowBesMIRI-MI2
97BowBesP-10
97BowBesPAR-10
97BowBesPR-10
97BowBesR-58
97BowChr-68
97BowChrI-68
97BowChrIR-68
97BowChrR-68
97BowInt-243
97Cir-102
97CirBos-1
97CirLimA-1
97CirRav-102
97CirSupB-1
97ColCho-125
97ColChoAC-19
97ColChoCtG-18A
97ColChoCtG-18B
97ColChoCtG-18C
97ColChoCtGIW-CG18
97ColChoNF-NF25
97ColChoNF-NF26
97ColChoS-5
97ColChoTBS-24
97ColChoTBSWH-24
97ColChoTotT-T14
97Don-146
97Don-409
97DonDiaK-5
97DonDiaKC-5
97DonEli-17
97DonEli-8
97DonEliGS-17
97DonLim-11
97DonLim-27
97DonLim-70
97DonLimFotG-52
97DonLimFotG-65
97DonLimLE-11
97DonLimLE-27
97DonLimLE-70
97DonLonL-10
97DonPowA-4
97DonPowADC-4
97DonPre-69
97DonPre-177
97DonPreCttC-69
97DonPreCttC-177
97DonPreP-146
97DonPreP-409
97DonPrePGold-146
97DonPrePGold-409
97DonPrePM-13
97DonPreS-8
97DonPreTB-1
97DonPreTBG-1
97DonPreTF-1
97DonPreTP-1
97DonPreTPG-1
97DonRocL-8
97DonTeaSMVP-4
97Fin-10
97Fin-159
97Fin-318
97FinEmb-159
97FinEmb-318
97FinEmbR-159
97FinEmbR-318
97FinPro-159
97FinRef-10
97FinRef-159
97FinRef-318
97FlaSho-A5
97FlaSho-B5
97FlaSho-C5
97FlaShoDC-1
97FlaShoLC-5
97FlaShoLC-B5
97FlaShoLC-C5
97FlaShoLCM-A5
97FlaShoLCM-B5
97FlaShoLCM-C5
97Fle-339
97Fle-697
97Fle-732
97FleHea-1
97FleLumC-2
97FleMilDM-50
97FleTeaL-20
97FleTif-339
97FleTif-697
97FleTif-732
97FleZon-1
97Lea-54
97Lea-352
97LeaBanS-1
97LeaDrefS-7
97LeaFraM-54
97LeaFraM-352
97LeaFraMDC-54
97LeaFraMDC-352
97LeaGet-6
97LeaGolS-6
97LeaKnoG-6
97LeaLeaotN-10
97MetUni-134
97MetUniBF-1
97MetUniMF-2
97MetUniML-2
97MetUniT-1
97NewPin-57
97NewPinAP-57
97NewPinIE-10
97NewPinMC-57
97NewPinPP-57
97NewPinPP-I10B
97Pac-311
97PacCar-28
97PacCarM-28
97PacCerCGT-2
97PacGolCD-28
97PacLigB-311
97PacPri-105
97PacPriGA-GA23
97PacPriLB-105
97PacPriP-105
97PacPriSH-SH10A
97PacPriSL-SL10A
97PacSil-311
97PacTriCD-17
97Pin-76
97PinArtP-76
97PinCar-18
97PinCer-5
97PinCer-145
97PinCerCMGT-2
97PinCerCT-2
97PinCerMBlu-5
97PinCerMBlu-145
97PinCerMG-5
97PinCerMG-145
97PinCerMR-5
97PinCerMR-145
97PinCerR-5
97PinCerR-145
97PinHom-9
97PinHom-10
97PinIns-63
97PinInsC-13
97PinInsCE-63
97PinInsDD-2
97PinInsDE-63
97PinMin-13
97PinMinB-13
97PinMinCB-13
97PinMinCG-13
97PinMinCGR-13
97PinMinCN-13
97PinMinCS-13
97PinMinG-13
97PinMinS-13
97PinMusC-76
97PinTeaP-1
97PinTeaP-10
97PinTotCPB-5
97PinTotCPB-145
97PinTotCPG-5
97PinTotCPG-145
97PinTotCPR-5
97PinTotCPR-145
97PinX-P-78
97PinX-PF&A-5
97PinX-PMoS-78
97PinX-PMW-12
97PinX-PMWG-12
97PinX-PMWS-12
97PinX-PSfF-42
97PinX-PSfFU-42
97ProMag-17

97ProMagML-17
97Sco-1
97Sco-502
97ScoAllF-2
97ScoBla-10
97ScoHigZ-9
97ScoHobR-502
97ScoPreS-1
97ScoResC-502
97ScoShoS-1
97ScoShoS-502
97ScoShoSAP-1
97ScoShoSAP-502
97ScoStaaD-22
97ScoSteS-3
97ScoTitT-8
97Sel-51
97SelArtP-51
97SelRegG-51
97SelToootT-10
97SelToootTMB-10
97SkyE-X-76
97SkyE-XC-76
97SkyE-XEC-76
97SkyE-XHoN-16
97SP-85
97SPInsI-9
97SPMarM-MM12
97SpoIll-101
97SpoIllEE-101
97SPSpeF-9
97SPSpxF-3
97SPSPxFA-3
97SPVinAu-1
97SPVinAu-2
97SPVinAu-3
97SPVinAu-4
97SPx-27
97SPxBoufG-11
97SPxBoufGSS-1
97SPxBro-27
97SPxCorotG-6
97SPxGraF-27
97SPxSil-27
97SPxSte-27
97StaClu-13
97StaClu-382
97StaCluFR-F1
97StaCluMat-13
97StaCluMOP-13
97StaCluMOP-382
97StaCluMOP-FB1
97StaCluMOP-PG14
97StaCluPG-PG14
97Stu-102
97StuMasS-2
97StuMasS8-2
97StuPor8-15
97StuPrePG-102
97StuPrePS-102
97Top-295
97TopChr-100
97TopChrDD-DD5
97TopChrDDR-DD5
97TopChrR-100
97TopGal-126
97TopGalGoH-GH8
97TopGalPPI-126
97TopHobM-HM6
97TopIntF-ILM9
97TopIntFR-ILM9
97TopScr-1
97TopSta-8
97TopSta1AS-AS4
97TopStaAM-8
97TopSweS-SS2
97TopTeaT-TT4
97Ult-204
97UltDiaP-1
97UltDouT-14
97UltFamGam-8
97UltFieC-2
97UltGolME-204
97UltHitM-10
97UltLeaS-7
97UltPlaME-204
97UltPowP-A1
97UltPowP-B9
97UltRBIK-1
97UltThu-4
97UltTop3-13
97UltTop3GM-13
97UppDec-83
97UppDec-370
97UppDecAG-AG14
97UppDecPP-PP7
97UppDecPPJ-PP7
97UppDecRP-RP23
97UppDecU-38
97Zen-3
97Zen8x1-3
97Zen8x1D-3

Baham, Leon
82IdaFalAT-16
87SanBerSP-14
88TamTarS-2

Bahnert, Barrie
95AusFut-13
95AusFut-88
95AusFut-106

Bahns, Ed
78AppFoxT-2
79AppFoxT-4

Bahnsen, Stan (Stanley R.)
67OPC-93
67Top-93
68Top-214
68TopVen-214
69CitMetC-9
69Top-380
69TopSta-201
69TopTeaP-19
70Top-568
70YanCliDP-8
71MilDud-2
71MLBOffS-482
71OPC-184
71Top-184
71YanArcO-2
71YanCliDP-1
72Top-662
72WhiSox-2
72WhiSoxTI1-3
73OPC-20
73Top-20
74OPC-254
74Top-254
74TopSta-152
75OPC-161
75SSP18-15
75Top-161
76OPC-534
76SSP-486
76Top-534
77BurCheD-112
77ExpPos-4
77Top-383
78ExpPos-1
78OPC-54
78Top-97
79ExpPos-2
79OPC-244
79Top-468
80ExpPos-3
80OPC-345
80Top-653
81Don-452
81Fle-156
81OPC-267
81TCM60I-369
81Top-267
82Don-392
82Fle-183
82OPC-131
82Top-131
83PorBeaT-23
89PacSenL-78
89SweBasG-39
89T/MSenL-4
89TopSenL-62
92YanWIZ6-4
92YanWIZ7-9

Bahr, Ed (Edson Garfield)
84TCMPla1-40

Bahrens, Scott
92IdaFalGSP-14

Baich, Dan
57SeaPop-2

Baier, Marty
82CliGiaF-15
83CliGiaF-7

Bailes, Scott
83AleDukT-10
85NasPirT-1
86DonRoo-25
86FleUpd-6
86IndOhH-43
86IndTeal-3
86SpoRoo-9
86TopTra-5T
86TopTraT-5T
87Don-227
87Fle-242
87FleGlo-242
87IndGat-43
87OPC-134
87Top-585
87TopTif-585
87ToyRoo-3
88Don-104
88DonBasB-285
88Fle-600
88FleGlo-600
88IndGat-43
88OPC-107
88PanSti-68
88StaLinI-2
88Top-107
88TopSti-206
88TopTif-107
89Don-202
89Fle-398
89FleGlo-398
89IndTeal-4
89Sco-424
89Top-339
89TopSti-217
89TopTif-339
89UppDec-209
90AngSmo-19
90Don-468
90Fle-484
90FleCan-484
90Lea-380
00OPC 784
90PubSti-553
90RedFolSB-2
90Sco-218
90ScoRoo-64T
90Top-784
90TopTif-784
90VenSti-21
91Bow-205
91Sco-535
91UppDec-190
92Don-357
92Fle-53
92OPC-95
92Sco-331
92StaClu-167
92Top-95
92TopGol-95
92TopGolW-95
92TopMic-95
93PacSpa-40

Bailey, Ben
95BilRedTI-8

Bailey, Bill (William F.)
09AmeCarE-1
09ColChiE-17
09PC7HHB-1
10NadCarE-1
11SpoLifM-106
11T205-5
12ColRedB-17
12ColTinT-17

Bailey, Bob (Robert S.)
63Kah-1
63PirIDL-1
63PirJayP-1
63Top-228
64Kah-2
64PirKDK-2
64Top-91
64TopGia-4
64TopVen-91
65Kah-4
65Top-412
66Kah-4
66PirEasH-7
66Top-485
67CokCapD-2
67CokCapDA-2
67DexPre-16
67OPC-32
67Top-32
68Top-580
69ExpFudP-1
69MLBOffS-154
69Top-399
69TopSta-52
69TopTeaP-10
70ExpPin-2
70ExpPos-6
70MLBOffS-62
70OPC-293
70Top-293
71ExpLaPR-1
71ExpPS-1
71MLBOffS-121
71OPC-157
71Top-157
71TopCoi-59
72MilBra-23
72OPC-493
72ProStaP-1
72Top-493
72Top-526
73OPC-505
73Top-505
74ExpWes-1
74OPC-97
74Top-97
74TopSta-51
75Hos-55
75OPC-365
75Top-365
76OPC-338
76RedKro-2
76RedPos-2
76SSP-333
76Top-338
76TopTra-338T
77Top-221
78PapGinD-20
78SSP270-173
78Top-457
79OPC-282
79Top-549
81TCM60I-310
86ExpGreT-4
86PenWhiSP-4
87HawIsIP-26
90DodTar-25
92Nab-11

Bailey, Brandon
86ColMetP-4
87ColMetP-3
88St.LucMS-1

Bailey, Buddy
80AndBraT-17
82DurBulT-23
86DurBulP-1
87SumBraP-10
88BasAmeAAB-30
88DurBulS-4B
89GreBraB-20
89GreBraP-1178
89GreBraS-25
89SouLeaAJ-23
90GreBraP-1143
90GreBraS-24
91CarLeaAP-CAR21
91LynRedSC-25
91LynRedSP-1215
92LynRedSC-26
93PawRedSDD-2
93PawRedSF-2424
93PawRedSTI-1
94PawRedSDD-2
94PawRedSF-960
95PawRedSDD-2
95PawRedTI-26
96PawRedSDD-1

Bailey, Cory
91ElmPioC-16
91ElmPioP-3261
92LynRedSC-5
92LynRedSF-2898
92ProFS7-25
93ExcFS7-129
93PawRedSDD-3
93PawRedSF-2399
93PawRedSTI-2
94Bow-447
94FleMajLP-4
94LeaLimR-55
94PawRedSDD-3
94PawRedSF-939
94Pin-420
94PinArtP-420
94PinMusC-420
94SpoRoo-30
94SpoRooAP-30
94Top-764
94TopGol-764
94TopSpa-764
95Don-344
95DonPreP-344
95LeaGolR-14
95LouRedF-266
95Sco-596
95ScoGolR-596
95ScoPlaTS-596
95Top-632
96FleUpd-U182
96FleUpdTC-U182

Bailey, Darryl
77BurBeeT-1
78BurBeeT-2
79HolMilT-22

Bailey, Ed (Lonas Edgar)
47Exh-10A
47Exh-10B
53Top-206
54Top-184
55Top-69
55TopDouH-29
56Kah-1
56RedBurB-1
57Kah-2
57RedSoh-1
57SwiFra-5
57Top-128
58Kah-1
58RedEnq-3
58RedJayP-1
58Top-330
58Top-386
58Top-490
59Kah-1
59RedBurBP-1
59RedEnq-2
59RedShiBS-2
59Top-210
60Kah-1
60Top-411
61Baz-21
61Kah-2
61Pos-188A
61Pos-188B
61Raw-2
61RedJayP-1
61Top-418
61TopStaI-13
62GiaJayP-2
62Jel-137
62Pos-137
62PosCan-137
62SalPlaC-113A
62SalPlaC-113B
62ShiPlaC-113
62Top-459
62TopStaI-194
63Top-368
64Top-437
64WheSta-4
65Top-559
66Top-246
66TopVen-246
78TCM60I-37
78TCM60I-173
79TCM50-11
84GiaMot-17
91TopArc1-206
91UppDecS-9
94TopArc1-184
94TopArc1G-184

Bailey, Greg
83TriTriT-21
86TulDriTI-18

Bailey, Howard Lee
82EvaTriT-1
82Top-261
83Tig-3
84Don-212
84EvaTriT-2
84Fle-75
84Nes792-284
84Top-284
84TopTif-284

Bailey, Jay
93MisStaB-48

Bailey, Jim
82IdaFalAT-2
86DavLipB-3

Bailey, Lash
89BelMarL-17
90PenPilS-1

Bailey, Mark (John Mark)

84FleUpd-3
85AstHouP-17
85AstMot-17
85Don-450
85Fle-344
85OPC-64
85Top-64
85TopTif-64
86AstMilL-2
86AstPol-14
86Don-354
86Fle-293
86Top-432
86TopSti-30
86TopTif-432
87AstMot-15
87AstPol-2
87Don-235
87Top-197
87TopTif-197
88AstMot-15
88AstPol-5
88TopBig-248
89TidTidC-29
89TidTidP-1949
90CMC-540
90PhoFirC-13
90PhoFirP-13
90ProAAAF-39
91LinDriAAA-377
91PhoFirLD-377
91PhoFirP-69
92PhoFirF-2823
92PhoFirS-377

Bailey, Mel
56RedBurB-2

Bailey, Mike
91EugEmeC-25
91EugEmeP-3714
94SouBenSHC-2
94SouBenSHF-585

Bailey, Otha
92NegLeaRLI-1

Bailey, Pat
86EugEmeC-31
87AppFoxP-19

Bailey, Phillip
95BelGiaTI-41
96SanJosGB-22

Bailey, Robert
89WelPirP-3
90SalBucS-1
91SalBucC-4
91SalBucP-958
92SalBucC-18
92SalBucF-75

Bailey, Roger
92BenRocC-2
92BenRocF-1466
92ClaDraP-71
92FroRowDP-96
92UppDecML-23
93Bow-120
93CenValRC-4
93CenValRF-2884
93ClaFS7-94
93ExcFS7-31
93StaCluM-120
93StaCluRoc-29
93Top-433
93TopGol-433
93TopInaM-433
93TopMic-433
94NewHavRF-1542
95Fla-342
95FleUpd-164
95TopTra-76T
95UppDecML-91
96ColSprSSTI-2
96Fle-358
96FleTif-358
96LeaSigEA-6
96RocPol-1
96StaClu-340
96StaCluMOP-340
97DonTea-102
97DonTeaSPE-102
97PacPriGotD-GD132
95UppDecMLFS-91

Bailey, Roy
90HamRedB-2
90HamRedS-3
91SavCarC-1
91SavCarP-1642
92St.PetCC-4
92St.PetCF-2017
93St.PetCC-3
93St.PetCF-2618

Bailey, Troy
88WytCubP-2003
89WytCubS-2

Bailey, Vince
79BurBeeT-18

Bailor, Bob (Robert M.)
76SSP-386
77OPC-48
77Top-474
78Hos-148
78Kel-39
78OPC-148
78TasDis-26
78Top-196
79BluJayBY-1
79Hos-105A
79Hos-105B
79OPC-259
79Top-492
80Kel-16
80OPC-304
80Top-581
81Don-389
81Fle-409
81OPC-297
81Top-297
81TopTra-732
82Don-308
82Fle-521
82MetPhoA-3
82Top-79
83Don-506
83Fle-538
83FleSta-5
83FleSti-230
83Top-343
83TopSti-260
84DodPol-21
84Don-595
84Fle-580
84FleUpd-4
84Nes792-654
84Top-654
84TopSti-109
84TopTif-654
84TopTra-4T
84TopTraT-4T
85DodCokP-3
85Don-397
85Fle-367
85Top-728
85TopTif-728
86BluJayGT-2
86Fle-124
86Top-522
86TopTif-522
87DunBluJP-928
88SyrChiC-24
88SyrChiP-817
89SyrChiC-25
89SyrChiMB-25
89SyrChiP-796
90CMC-674
90DodTar-26
90ProAAAF-368
90SyrChiC-26
90SyrChiMB-1
90SyrChiP-588
90TriAllGP-AAA11
91BluJayFS-2
91LinDriAAA-524
91MetWIZ-21
91OriCro-16
91SyrChiLD-524
91SyrChiMB-1
91SyrChiP-2496
92Nab-36
92UppDecS-3
93BluJayFS-2
93UppDecS-1

Bain, Paul
77CliDodT-1
78LodDodT-1
79LodDodT-3

Bain, Tyler
96ButCopKB-10

Baine, David
92EveGiaC-24
92EveGiaF-1676
93CliGiaC-3
93EveGiaF-3758

Baine, Tom (John T.)
86EriCarP-2
87SprCarB-8
88TexLeaAGS-16
89LouRedBC-20
89LouRedBP-1265
89LouRedBTI-10
90SprCarDGB-23

Baines, Harold D.
78KnoKnoST-1
79IowOakP-3
81Fle-346
81OPC-347
81Top-347
82Don-568
82Fle-336
82FleSta-184
82OPC-56
82Top-684
83AllGamPI-47
83Don-143
83Fle-229
83FleSta-6
83FleSti-155
83Kel-16
83OPC-177
83Top-177
83TopSti-52
83WhiSoxTV-3
84AllGamPI-137
84Don-58
84DonActAS-11
84Fle-51
84FleSti-4
84FunFooP-110
84Nes792-434
84OPC-197
84Top-434
84TopRubD-1
84TopSti-242
84TopTif-434
84WhiSoxTV-3
85AllGamPI-47
85Don-58
85DonActA-58
85Dra-2
85Fle-507
85FleStaS-21
85Lea-231
85OPC-249
85SevCoi-G6
85Top-249
85Top-275
85TopGloS-34
85TopRubD-1
85TopSti-234
85TopSup-51
85TopTif-249
85TopTif-275
85WhiSoxC-3
86Don-13
86Don-180
86DonAll-49
86DonSupD-13
86Dra-24
86Fle-198
86FleLimE-3
86FleMin-42
86FleSluBC-M1
86FleStiC-1
86GenMilB-2A
86Lea-13
86MSAJayPCD-1
86OPC-65
86SevCoi-C4
86SevCoi-E4
86SevCoi-S4
86SevCoi-W4
86Spo-7
86Spo-52
86Top-755
86TopMinL-8
86TopSti-288
86TopSup-9
86TopTat-4
86TopTif-755
86WhiSoxC-3
87BoaandB-16
87ClaGam-42
87Don-429
87DonAll-25
87DonOpeD-236
87Dra-22
87Fle-485
87Fle-643
87FleBasA-1
87FleGamW-1
87FleGlo-485
87FleGlo-643
87FleHotS-2
87FleMin-3
87FleStiC-2
87HosSti-21
87KayB-1
87KraFoo-13
87Lea-52
87MandMSL-8
87OPC-309
87RedFolSB-119
87SevCoi-C1
87SmoAmeL-4
87Spo-153
87Spo-171
87SpoTeaP-26
87StuPan-17
87Top-772
87TopCoi-1
87TopGloS-14
87TopSti-284
87TopTif-772
87WhiSoxC-2
88Don-211
88DonAll-12
88DonBasB-11
88Fle-391
88FleExcS-1
88FleGlo-391
88GreBasS-4
88Lea-157
88OPC-35
88PanSti-62
88RedFolSB-3
88Sco-590
88ScoGlo-590
88Spo-33
88StaLinWS-1
88Top-35
88Top-321
88TopBig-224
88TopCoi-5
88TopRitTM-16
88TopSti-293
88TopTif-35
88TopTif-321
88TopUKM-1
88TopUKMT-1
88WhiSoxC-1
88WhiSoxK-5
89Bow-72
89BowTif-72
89CadEllD-1
89Don-148
89DonBasB-81
89Fle-491
89FleExcS-1
89FleGlo-491
89FleSup-2
89K-M-22
89OPC-152
89PanSti-318
89Sco-128
89ScoRoo-62T
89Spo-157
89Top-585
89TopBasT-88
89TopBig-266
89TopCoi-33
89TopHilTM-1
89TopSti-304
89TopTif-585
89TopUKM-2
89TVSpoM-113
89UppDec-211
89UppDec-692
89UppDecS-1
89WhiSoxC-5
89WhiSoxK-4
90Bow-501
90BowTif-501
90ClaBlu-69
90Don-402
90Don-660A
90Don-660B
90Don-660C
90Don-660D
90DonBesA-69
90Fle-290
90FleAll-1
90FleCan-290
90Lea-126
90OPC-345
90PanSti-167
90PanSti-200
90PubSti-275
90PubSti-383
90RanMot-6
90Sco-470
90Spo-125
90Top-345
90TopBig-157
90TopHilHM-30
90TopSti-158
90TopSti-245
90TopTif-345
90UppDec-353
90VenSti-22
90VenSti-23
91A'sMot-14
91A'sSFE-1
91Bow-231
91CadEllD-2
91ClaGam-13
91Don-748
91Fle-2
91Lea-196
91OPC-166
91RedFolS-6
91Sco-291
91StaClu-303
91StuPre-8
91Top-166
91TopDesS-166
91TopMic-166
91TopTif-166
91UltUpd-45
91UppDec-562
91USPlaCA-9D
92A'sUno7P-5
92AthMot-14
92Bow-171
92ClaGam-6
92Don-68
92DonDiaK-DK14
92Fle-249
92Fle-707
92Hig5-101
92KinDis-22
92Lea-126
92OPC-635
92Pin-41
92Sco-137
92ScoProP-13
92StaClu-536
92StaCluD-10
92Stu-221
92Top-635
92TopGol-635
92TopGolW-635
92TopKid-120
92TopMic-635
92TriPla-34
92Ult-109
92UppDec-158
93Bow-281
93CadDis-3
93Don-725
93Fin-153
93FinRef-153
93Fle-659
93FleFinE-156
93Lea-249
93OPC-3
93OPCPre-68
93PacSpa-216
93Pin-111
93Pin-488
93RanKee-59
93Sco-585
93Sel-257
93SelRoo-8T
93StaClu-666
93StaCluFDI-666
93StaCluM-187
93StaCluMOP-666
93Stu-190
93Top-345
93TopGol-345
93TopInaM-345
93TopMic-345
93Ult-492
93UppDec-81

93UppDec-765
93UppDecGold-81
93UppDecGold-765
93UppDecSH-HI3
94Bow-19
94ColC-478
94ColChoGS-478
94ColChoSS-478
94Don-486
94ExtBas-2
94Fin-254
94FinRef-254
94Fla-1
94Fle-2
94Lea-84
94LeaCleC-12
94OPC-221
94OriPro-4
94OriUSPC-2H
94OriUSPC-7H
94OriUSPC-13S
94Pac-26
94PanSti-18
94Pin-408
94PinArtP-408
94PinMusC-408
94Sco-469
94ScoGolR-469
94Sel-31
94StaClu-16
94StaCluFDI-16
94StaCluGR-16
94StaCluMOP-16
94StaCluT-278
94StaCluTFDI-278
94Stu-121
94Top-420
94TopGol-420
94TopSpa-420
94TriPla-152
94TriPlaM-15
94Ult-302
94UppDec-188
94UppDecED-188
95ColCho-338
95ColChoGS-338
95ColChoSS-338
95Don-538
95DonPreP-538
95DonTopotO-2
95Fla-2
95Fle-2
95Lea-309
95LeaLim-154
95Pac-18
95PanSti-93
95Pin-422
95PinArtP-422
95PinMusC-422
95Sco-57
95ScoGolR-57
95ScoPlaTS-57
95Sel-156
95SelArtP-156
95SP-122
95SPSil-122
95StaClu-444
95StaCluMOP-444
95StaCluSTWS-444
95StaCluVR-235
95Stu-197
95Top-232
95TopCyb-130
95Ult-251
95UltGolM-251
95UppDec-128
95UppDecED-128
95UppDecEDG-128
95UppDecSE-183
95UppDecSEG-183
96Cir-25
96CirRav-25
96ColCho-55
96ColCho-510
96ColChoGS-55
96ColChoGS-510
96ColChoSS-55
96ColChoSS-510
96Don-208
96DonPreP-208
96EmoXL-33
96Fin-B205
96FinRef-B205
96Fla-47
96Fle-3
96FleTif-3
96FleUpd-U23
96FleUpdTC-U23
96FleWhiS-2
96LeaSigA-15
96LeaSigAG-15
96LeaSigAS-15
96Pac-232
96Pin-80
96Pin-241
96PinArtP-141
96PinFoil-241
96PinSta-141
96Sco-408
96SP-56
95StaCluVRMC-235
96Top-357
96Ult-330
96UltGolM-330
96UppDec-112
96UppDec-490U
97Bow-38
97BowBes-96
97BowBesAR-96
97BowBesR-96
97BowChr-33
97BowChrI-33
97BowChrIR-33
97BowChrR-33
97BowInt-38
97Cir-343
97CirRav-343
97ColCho-75
97Don-199
97DonPreP-199
97DonPrePGold-199
97DonTea-67
97DonTeaSPE-67
97Fin-126
97FinEmb-126
97FinEmbR-126
97FinRef-126
97Fle-55
97FleTif-55
97MetUni-53
97Pac-50
97PacLigB-50
97PacPri-19
97PacPriLB-19
97PacPriP-19
97PacPriSL-SL2C
97PacSil-50
97Pin-87
97PinArtP-87
97PinMusC-87
97Sco-104
97ScoPreS-104
97ScoShoS-104
97ScoShoSAP-104
97ScoWhiS-5
97ScoWhiSPI-5
97ScoWhiSPr-5
97SP-49
97StaClu-70
97StaCluMOP-70
97Top-46
97TopChr-17
97TopChrR-17
97TopGal-10
97TopGalPPI-10
97TopSta-30
97TopStaAM-30
97Ult-35
97UltDouT-4
97UltGolME-35
97UltPlaME-35
97UppDec-37
Bair, Dennis
96DayCubB-3
Bair, Doug (Charles Douglas)
78OPC-229
78Pep-3
78SSP270-114
78Top-353
79Hos-3
79OPC-58
79Top-126
80OPC-234
80RedEnq-40
80Top-449
81Don-64
81Fle-213
81OPC-73
81Top-73
82Top-262
83Car-2
83Don-372
83Fle-2
83Top-627
83TopTra-5T
84Don-369
84Fle-76
84Nes792-536
84TigWavP-3
84Top-536
84TopTif-536
85Don-369
85Fle-1
85TigCaiD-1
85TigWen-2
85Top-744
85TopTif-744
87Fle-386
87FleGlo-386
87MaiGuiP-2
87PhiTas-58
88SyrChiC-9
88SyrChiP-816
89SyrChiC-1
89SyrChiMB-1
89SyrChiP-807
90PirHomC-2
90Sco-517
Bair, Rich
84NewOriT-9
Bair, Rod
96PorRocB-7
Baird, Allard
89AppFoxP-870
Baird, Chris
85DurBulT-19
Baird, Doug (Howard D.)
16ColE13-10
16SpoNewM-8
90DodTar-894
Baird, Hal
75OmaRoyTI-3
76OmaRoyTT-2
Bajda, Mike
94JamJamC-2
94JamJamF-3956
Bajus, Mark
80BatTroT-3
81BatTroT-1
81WatIndT-6
Bakely, Jersey (Edward Enoch)
88SpoTimM-2
Bakenhaster, Dave (David L.)
64Top-479
Baker, Al (Albert Jones)
75CliPilT-23
Baker, Andy
89BurIndS-2
91ColIndC-8
91ColIndP-1475
92ColRedC-20
92ColRedF-2378
Baker, Bill (William)
41HarHarW-2
49EurSta-177
Baker, Chuck (Charles Joseph)
78PadFamF-3
79HawIsIC-11
79HawIsIT-16
79Top-456
80HawIsIT-1
81Fle-500
82Fle-561
82Top-253
Baker, Curt
78WauMetT-1
Baker, Darnell
78CedRapGT-2
Baker, Dave (David Glen)
54Top-133
79SyrChiT-11
79SyrChiTI-5
80SyrChiT-17
80SyrChiTI-3
81SyrChiT-11
81SyrChiTI-1
82SyrChiT-14
82SyrChiTI-3
83TolMudHT-13
84TolMudHT-20
Baker, Del (Delmar David)
14B18B-10A
14B18B-10B
14B18B-10C
34DiaMatCSB-4
35TigFreP-2
36WorWidGV-31
49SolSunP-1
60Top-456
81TigDetN-58
88ConSer5-2
94ConTSN-1215
94ConTSNB-1215
94TopArc1-133
94TopArc1G-133
Baker, Derek
92GulCoaMF-3470
93KinMetC-3
93KinMetF-3787
94PitMetC-5
94PitMetF-3516
Baker, Derrell
86IndIndTI-13
87WesPalBEP-658
88JacExpB-14
88JacExpP-968
89RocExpLC-2
Baker, Doug (Douglas)
83BirBarT-8
84EvaTriT-13
84TigWavP-4
85NasSouTI-1
85Top-269
85TopTif-269
86NasSouTI-1
87TolMudHP-17
87TolMudHT-20
88PorBeaC-13
88PorBeaP-647
89PorBeaC-14
89PorBeaP-230
90BirBarDGB-4
90CMC-570
90Fle-368
90FleCan-368
90PorBeaC-18
90PorBeaP-182
90ProAAAF-252
90PubSti-322
90VenSti-24
91LinDriAAA-603
91TucTorLD-603
91TucTorP-2217
92DurBulF-1116
92PulBraC-28
92PulBraF-3196
93CedRapKC-29
94CedRapKC-26
Baker, Dusty (Johnny B.)
71OPC-709
71RicBraTI-3
71Top-709
72Top-764
73OPC-215
73Top-215
73TopCanL-3
74BraPhoC-2
74OPC-320
74Top-320
74TopSta-2
75Hos-117
75OPC-33
75Top-33
76OPC-28
76SSP-16
76Top-28
76TopTra-28T
77Top-146
78Hos-56
78RCColC-67
78SSP270-57
78Top-668
79DodBlu-1
79OPC-290
79Top-562
80DodPol-12
80OPC-135
80Top-255
81AllGamPI-136
81Dod-1
81DodPol-12
81Don-179
81Fle-115
81FleStiC-62
81LonBeaPT-5
81PerCreC-27
81Squ-17
81Top-495
81TopScr-71
81TopSti-182
81TopSupHT-43
82DodPol-12
82DodUniOV-1
82DogBuiE-1
82Don-336
82Fle-1
82FleSta-4
82Kel-50
82OPC-375
82Top-311
82Top-375
82TopSti-52
83AllGamPI-136
83DodPol-12
83DodPos-1
83Don-462
83Fle-201
83FleSta-7
83FleSti-121
83FleSti-140
83OPC-220
83SevCoi-6
83Top-220
83TopGloS-22
83TopSti-245
84DodUniOP-8
84Don-226
84DonActAS-47
84Fle-96
84FleUpd-5
84GiaPos-1
84Nes792-40
84OPC-40
84SevCoi-W18
84Top-40
84TopSti-80
84TopTif-40
84TopTra-5T
84TopTraT-5T
85A'sMot-15
85Don-445
85Fle-602
85FleUpd-3
85OPC-165
85Top-165
85TopMin-165
85TopTif-165
85TopTifT-4T
85TopTra-4T
86A'sMot-3
86Don-467
86Fle-411
86Lea-231
86OPC-31
86Top-645
86TopTif-645
87DodSmoA-2
87Fle-387
87FleGlo-387
87Top-565
87TopTif-565
88DodSmo-21
88DodSmo-22
88GiaMot-27
89DodSmoG-93
89GiaMot-28
90DodTar-27
90GiaMot-21
90GiaSmo-1
90PacLeg-71
90RicBra2ATI-3
91DodUno7P-5
91GiaMot-27
92DodStaTA-21
92GiaFanFFB-1
92GiaMot-28
92GiaPacGaE-2
93GiaMot-1
93GiaPos-1
93Top-514
93TopGol-514
93TopInaM-514
93TopMic-514
94GiaAMC-1
94GiaMot-1
94GiaSFC-1

94GiaTeal-1
94GiaTeal-2
95GiaMot-1
96GiaMot-1
Baker, Ernie
89JohCitCS-7
89Sta-162
90SavCarP-2059
91St.PetCC-1
91St.PetCP-2265
92St.PetCC-23
92St.PetCF-2018
Baker, Floyd Wilson
47TipTop-16
48WhiSoxTI-2
49Bow-119
49Lea-153
50Bow-146
51Bow-87
52Top-292
53BowBW-49
53BowC-159
83TopRep5-292
85TCMPla1-12
96Bro194F-29
Baker, Frank Watts
71OPC-213
71OPC-689
71Top-213
71YanArcO-3
71YanCliDP-8
72OPC-409
72Top-409
73OriJohP-15
74OPC-411
74Top-411
91OriCro-17
92YanWIZ7-10
Baker, Gene (Eugene Walter)
47Exh-11
52MotCoo-45
55Bow-7
56Top-142
56YelBasP-5
57Top-176A
57Top-176B
58Hir-65
58Kah-2
58Top-358
59Top-238
60Top-539
61Top-339
79DiaGre-121
79TCM50-48
87NegLeaPD-32
Baker, George F.
92SalLakTSP-25
Baker, Gerald
86QuaCitAP-4
Baker, Greg
81ShrCapT-16
Baker, Home Run (Frank)
08AmeCarE-35
09AmeCarE-2
09ColChiE-18
09SpoNewSM-42
09T206-10
10CouT21-71
10CouT21-72
10CouT21-73
10CouT21-257
10DomDisP-4
10E12AmeCDC-3
10LuxCigPP-1
10NadE1-4
10RedCroT-169
10SweCapPP-40
11A'sFirT20-1
11BasBatEU-1
11DiaGumP-2
11L1L-120
11MecDFT-1
11MecDFT-17
11PloCanE-2
11S74Sil-26
11S81LarS-95
11SpoLifCW-13
11SpoLifM-86
11T205-6
11TurRedT-78
12ColRedB-18
12ColTinT-18
12HasTriFT-6
12HasTriFT-18
12HasTriFT-25B
12HasTriFT-70A
12PhiCarE-4
12T22SeroC-1
13NatGamW-2
13PolGroW-2
14CraJacE-2
14TexTomE-3
15CraJacE-2
15SpoNewM-8
16BF2FP-33
16ColE13-11
16SpoNewM-9
17HolBreD-3
19W514-75
20NatCarE-5
21E121So8-3A
21E121So8-3B
21Exh-4
21KoBreWSI-27
22AmeCarE-3
22E120-61
22W573-5
22W575-4
23W515-15
23WilChoV-5
23W551-1
40PlaBal-177
50CalHOFW-3
60ExhWriH-3
60Fle-41
61Fle-1
61Fle-6
61GolPre-21
69SCFOldT-24
70Top-704
71FleWorS-9
71Top-689
75FlePio-16
76ShaPiz-78
77GalGloG-155
77GalGloG-180
77SerSta-2
80PacLeg-41
80PerHaloFP-74
80SSPHOF-74
81SpoHaloF-11
82DiaCla-19
85UltBasC-5
89PacLegI-146
90PerGreM-76
92ConTSN-565
92YanWIZH-1
92YanWIZH-2
93ConMasC-6
94ConTSNCI-39
96PitPosH-1
Baker, Jack Edward
11BasBatEU-2
Baker, Jared
92ClaDraP-63
92FroRowDP-12
92SpoIndC-1
92SpoIndF-1284
92UppDecML-22
93RanCucQC-2
93RanCucQF-818
94RanCucQC-3
94RanCucQF-1626
95RanCucQT-36
95SigRooOJ-3
95SigRooOJP-3
95SigRooOJPS-3
95SigRooOJS-3
Baker, Jason
92EliTwiC-20
92EliTwiF-3690
93BilMusF-3957
93BilMusSP-21
93EliTwiC-3
93EliTwiF-3425
94ForWayWC-2
94ForWayWF-2020
94MidLeaAF-MDW11
94VerExpC-4
94VerExpF-3898
95ForMyeMTI-1
95GreFalDTI-21
96DelShoB-7
97Bow-366
97BowInt-366
Baker, Jay
88GasRanP-999
Baker, Jim
80UtiBluJT-4
83SyrChiT-4
84SyrChiT-29
Baker, John
83AndBraT-7
Baker, Ken
80NasSouTI-1
89FreStaBS-1
90BirBarDGB-6
Baker, Kenny
79WesHavYT-12
82BirBarT-10
83EvaTriT-17
85OmaRoyT-27
Baker, Kerry
84PriWilPT-32
85NasPirT-2
86NasPirP-2
Baker, Mark
83QuaCitCT-6
85OscAstTI-3
86ColAstP-3
87ColAstP-13
95WatIndTI-4
96WatIndTI-2
Baker, Mike
86ElmPioRSP-1
87GreHorP-21
88WinHavRSS-3
89LynRedSS-1
Baker, R.L.
40WheM4-4
41WheM5-18
Baker, Ricky (Rick)
80WatIndT-26
81ChaLooT-15
82ChaLooT-7
83MidCubT-25
84MidCubT-18
Baker, Sam
90BurIndP-3001
91ColIndC-9
91ColIndP-1476
91WatIndC-1
91WatIndP-3356
92ColRedF-2379
Baker, Scott
90JohCitCS-3
91SavCarP-1643
92St.PetCC-10
92St.PetCF-2019
93HunStaF-2075
93StaCluAt-25
94HunStaF-1323
95EdmTraTI-1
Baker, Steve (Steven Byrne)
80EvaTriT-12
81SyrChiT-1
81SyrChiTI-2
83TopTra-6T
84LouRedR-25
85IndIndTI-6
Baker, Tom (Thomas Calvin)
90DodTar-28
93ConTSN-739
Bakkum, Scott
92Min-2
93LynRedSC-2
93LynRedSF-2508
94SarRedSC-3
94SarRedSF-1941
95TreThuTI-6
Bakley, Jersey (Edward)
87OldJudN-15
Bakner, Brett
94LetMouF-3889
94LetMouSP-1
Bako, Paul
93BilMusF-3948
93BilMusSP-13
94Bow-158
94Cla-192
94ClaTriF-T19
94Top-686
94TopGol-686
94TopSpa-686
94WinSpiC-4
94WinSpiF-273
95SigRooOJ-4
95SigRooOJP-4
95SigRooOJPS-4
95SigRooOJS-4
96ChaLooB-6
Balabon, Anthony
86Ft.LauYP-2
Balabon, Rick
87PriWilYP-9
89SanBerSB-4
89SanBerSCLC-74
90CarLeaA-45
90PenPilS-2
91CalCanLD-52
91CalCanP-508
91LinDriAAA-52
Balance, Dale
92LetMouSP-6
93LetMouF-4142
93LetMouSP-17
94LetMouF-3868
94LetMouSP-6
Balaz, John Lawrence
75SalLakCC-3
76OPC-539
76Top-539
Balboni, Steve (Stephen C.)
80NasSouTI-2
81ColCliP-37
81ColCliT-11
82ColCliP-35
82ColCliT-4
82Top-83
83ColCliT-15
83Don-73
83OPC-8
83Top-8
84FleUpd-6
84Nes792-782
84Top-782
84TopTif-782
84TopTra-6T
84TopTraT-6T
85Don-419
85Fle-196
85Lea-95
85OPC-152
85Top-486
85TopSti-271
85TopTif-486
86BasStaB-5
86Don-222
86Dra-20
86Fle-1
86Lea-98
86OPC-164
86RoyKitCD-17
86RoyNatP-45
86Spo-186
86Top-164
86TopGloS-6
86TopMinL-17
86TopSti-265
86TopTat-21
86TopTif-164
87Don-102
87DonOpeD-199
87Fle-362
87FleGlo-362
87Lea-262
87OPC-240
87RedFolSB-85
87Top-240
87TopSti-263
87TopTif-240
88Don-424
88Fle-251
88FleGlo-251
88Sco-273
88ScoGlo-273
88ScoRoo-46T
88ScoRooG-46T
88StaLinRo-1
88Top-638
88TopTif-638
89Don-143
89DonBasB-188
89DonTra-48
89Fle-538
89FleGlo-538
89FleUpd-45
89OPC-336
89Sco-353
89ScoRoo-27T
89Top-336
89TopSti-222
89TopTif-336
89TopTra-6T
89TopTraT-6T
89UppDec-111
89YanScoNW-17
90Bow-436
90BowTif-436
90Don-315
90Fle-436
90FleCan-436
90Lea-373
90MLBBasB-66
90OPC-716
90PubSti-424
90Sco-327
90Top-716
90TopBig-160
90TopTif-716
90TopTVY-22
90UppDec-497
90VenSti-25
90YanScoNW-25
91Don-650
91Fle-656
91OPC-511
91Sco-159
91StaClu-134
91StaCluP-2
91Top-511
91TopDesS-511
91TopMic-511
91TopTif-511
92OklCit8F-1918
92OklCit8S-302
92YanWIZ8-7
93OklCit8F-1630
93RanKee-394
Balcena, Bobby (Robert R.)
52Par-20
57HygMea-2
Baldrick, Bob
83WauTimF-22
86ChaLooP-2
Baldschun, Jack
62Top-46
62TopStal-164
62TopVen-46
63Top-341
64PhiJayP-2
64PhiPhiB-3
64Top-520
64TopCoi-69
64TopSta-90
64TopStaU-6
65PhiJayP-2
65Top-555
65TopEmbl-34
66Top-272
66TopVen-272
67OPC-114
67Top-114
70OPC-284
70Top-284
78TCM60I-104
Baldwin, Billy (Robert H.)
76SSP-370
77MetDaiPA-3
91MetWIZ-23
Baldwin, Brian
87BelMarTI-19
88WauTimGS-21
89SanBerSB-8
89SanBerSCLC-73
Baldwin, Dave
68Top-231
68TopVen-231
69OPC-132
69SenTeal8-3
69Top-132
69TopFou-17
70Top-613
71MLBOffS-433
71OPC-48
71Top-48
81TCM60I-309
94BreMilB-5
Baldwin, James
92MidLeaATI-2
92SouBenWSF-169
92UppDecML-319
93BirBarF-1185
93Bow-611
93ClaFS7-61

93ClaGolF-204
93ExcFS7-149
94ActPac-31
94ActPac-63
94ActPac2G-9G
94Bow-155
94Bow-370
94BowBes-B4
94BowBesR-B4
94Cla-123
94ClaCreotC-C14
94ColC-652
94ColChoGS-652
94ColChoSS-652
94ExcFS7-34
94ExcLeaLF-1
94ExtBas-41
94ExtBasMLH-1
94NasSouF-1242
94OPC-210
94StaCluT-145
94StaCluTFDI-145
94Top-766
94TopGol-766
94TopSpa-766
94Ult-333
94UppDec-3
94UppDecED-3
94UppDecML-146
94UppDecML-245
94UppDecMLPotYF-PY27
95ActPacF-19
95Bow-196
95BowBes-B77
95BowBesR-B77
95Exc-25
95ExcLeaL-2
95Fle-241
95FleMajLP-2
95FleUpd-33
95NasSouTI-1
95Pin-413
95PinArtP-413
95PinMusC-413
95SelCer-97
95SelCerMG-97
95Sum-146
95SumNthD-146
95Top-49
95UltGolP-1
95UltGolPGM-1
95UppDecML-43
95UppDecMLT1PF-2
95Zen-123
96ColCho-91
96ColChoGS-91
96ColChoSS-91
96NasSouB-7
96Sco-245
97Cir-73
97CirRav-73
97ColCho-299
97Don-176
97DonEli-111
97DonEliGS-111
97DonPre-82
97DonPreCttC-82
97DonPreP-176
97DonPrePGold-176
97DonTea-66
97DonTeaSPE-66
97Fin-54
97FinRef-54
97Fle-56
97FleRooS-2
97FleTif-56
97Lea-138
97LeaFraM-138
97LeaFraMDC-138
97MetUni-54
97MetUniPP-1
97PacPriGotD-GD26
97Pin-85
97PinArtP-85
97PinIns-77
97PinInsCE-77
97PinInsDE-77
97PinMusC-85
97Sco-54
97ScoPreS-54
97ScoShoS-54
97ScoShoSAP-54
97ScoWhiS-2
97ScoWhiSPI-2
97ScoWhiSPr-2
97StaClu-317
97StaCluMOP-317
97Stu-54
97StuPrePG-54
97StuPrePS-54
97Top-310
97TopChr-104
97TopChrR-104
97TopGal-164
97TopGalPPI-164
97Ult-36
97UltGolME-36
97UltPlaME-36
97UltRooR-1
97UppDec-39
95UppDecMLFS-43

Baldwin, Jeff
86AshTouP-2
87OscAstP-10
88OscAstS-3
89ColMudB-13
89ColMudP-135
89ColMudS-3
90CMC-753
90ColMudB-9
90ColMudP-1357
90ColMudS-4
91JacGenLD-553
91JacGenP-930
91LinDriAA-553
91TopDeb90-10
92JacGenF-4011
92JacGenS-328

Baldwin, Johnny
83GreHorT-1
84NasSouTI-1

Baldwin, Kid (Clarence G.)
87OldJudN-16

Baldwin, Kirk
89EugEmeB-3
90AppFoxBS-4
90AppFoxP-2088

Baldwin, Lady (Charles)
87OldJudN-18
88AugBecN-1
88GandBCGCE-2
90DodTar-895

Baldwin, Mark (Marcus E.)
87OldJudN-17
94OriofB-65

Baldwin, Reggie (Reginald C.)
79ChaChaT-4
80TidTidT-13
80Top-678

Baldwin, Rick (Rickey Alan)
75MetSSP-22
76OPC-372
76SSP-552
76Top-372
77Top-587
78SanJosMMC-11
91MetWIZ-22

Baldwin, Scott
93SouOreAC-3
93SouOreAF-4054
94MidLeaAF-MDW30
94WesMicWC-2
94WesMicWF-2287

Baldwin, Tony
88SumBraP-391
89BurBraP-1608
89BurBraS-1
90BurBraB-19
90BurBraP-2361
90BurBraS-2

Bale, John
96StCatSB-4

Balelo, Nesi
87ChaLooB-19
88VerMarP-949

Balentine, Bryant
91PriRedC-24
91PriRedP-3504

Bales, Daniel
95IdaFalBTI-23

Bales, Joe
96BriWhiSB-9

Bales, Lee (Wesley Owen)
67OPC-51
67Top-51
81TCM60I-370

Bales, Tom
88LitFalMP-3

Balfanz, John
88St.PetCS-1
89CalLeaA-37
89RenSilSCLC-261

Balfe, Ryan
94BriTigC-3
94BriTigF-3509
95FayGenTI-1
96LakTigB-6

Balint, Rob
94BriTigC-4
94BriTigF-3505
95FayGenTI-2

Ball, Harry (Harrison)
88CapCodPB-19
88CapCodPPaLP-27
90JohCitCS-4

Ball, Jeff
94JacGenF-221

Ball, Jeff D.
90AubAstB-9
90AubAstP-3408
91OscAstC-16
91OscAstP-690
92JacGenF-4002
92JacGenS-329
93MidLeaAGF-45
93QuaCitRBC-2
93QuaCitRBF-105
95TusTorTI-2
96TusTorB-2

Ball, Jeff G.
87HawRai-17
90BoiHawP-3310

Ball, Jim
77QuaCitAT-1

Ball, Jim (James Chandler)
09RamT20-5

Ball, Neal (Cornelius)
09RamT20-6
09T206-11
09T206-12
10DomDisP-5
10RedCroT-3
10RedCroT-170
10SweCapPP-16
11T205-7
12HasTriFT-21
12T207-6
91ConTSN-203

Ball, Robert
80AshTouT-10
81TulDriT-26
82TulDriT-21

Ball, Thomas
93GenCubC-3
93GenCubF-3165

Balla, Gary
77QuaCitAT-2
78QuaCitAT-1

Ballanfant, Lee
55Bow-295

Ballanger, Mark
77JacSunT-1

Ballara, Juan
92JohCitCC-6
92JohCitCF-3118
94St.PetCC-3
94St.PetCF-2587
95PeoChiTI-15

Ballard, Butch (Glenn)
77SpaPhiT-14
80OrlTwiT-14
80WisRapTT-14

Ballard, Jeff
86HagSunP-1
87IntLeaAT-28
87RocRedWP-25
87RocRedWT-1
88Don-520
88Fle-554
88FleGlo-554
88OriFreB-34
88RocRedWC-1
88RocRedWP-199
88RocRedWTI-1
88Top-782
88TopTif-782
89Bow-7
89BowTif-7
89Don-495
89DonBasB-30
89Fle-607
89FleGlo-607
89OriFreB-29
89PanSti-253
89Sco-551
89Top-69
89TopSti-230
89TopTif-69
89UppDec-595
90Bow-244
90BowTif-244
90ClaBlu-89
90Don-51
90DonBesA-29
90Fle-173
90FleAwaW-1
90FleCan-173
90HagSunDGB-1
90Hot50RS-5
90K-M-27
90Lea-118
90MLBBasB-110
90OPC-296
90OPC-394
90PanSti-13
90PubSti-573
90RedFolSB-3
90Sco-349
90ScoYouSI-25
90Spo-123
90Top-296
90Top-394
90TopBig-278
90TopDou-2
90TopGloS-17
90TopMinL-1
90TopSti-232
90TopStiB-61
90TopTif-296
90TopTif-394
90TopTVA-27
90UppDec-259
90VenSti-26
91Bow-98
91Don-279
91Fle-467
91Lea-522
91OPC-546
91OriCro-18
91Sco-243
91StaClu-283
91StaCluP-3
91Top-546
91TopDesS-546
91TopMic-546
91TopTif-546
91UppDec-260
92Don-74
92LouRedF-1880
92LouRedS-252
92OPC-104
92Sco-129
92StaClu-771
92StaCluECN-771
92Top-104
92TopGol-104
92TopGolW-104
92TopMic-104
94Pac-491

Ballard, Matt
89TenTecGE-2

Ballard, Tim
78GreBraT-2
82ChaRoyT-13

Baller, Jay (Jay Scott)
82ReaPhiT-1
83ChaChaT-1
83IndPos-2
83IndWhe-2
84BufBisT-9
85IowCubT-12
86CubGat-48
86CubUno-1
86Don-613
86FleUpd-7
87IowCubTI-5
88CalCanC-5
88CalCanP-792
88Top-717
88TopTif-717
89IndIndC-7
89IndIndP-1231
90CMC-176
90OmaRoyC-1
92ScrRedBF-2439
92ScrRedBS-478
93Don-356
93LinVenB-16
93LinVenB-277

Ballinger, Mark A.
76OmaRoyTT-3

Ballou, Bill
89UtiBluSP-29
90UtiBluSP-26
91UtiBluSC-22
91UtiBluSP-3258
96AubDouB-25

Ballou, Win
90DodTar-896

Ballwinkle, Mascot
95BinMetTI-NNO
96BinBeeB-3

Balmer, Steve
83QuaCitCT-7

Balsley, Darren
84IdaFalATI-3
86ModA'sC-3
86ModA'sP-3
87DunBluJP-931
88KnoBluJB-10
89KnoBluJB-3
89KnoBluJP-1137
89KnoBluJS-5
90St.CatBJP-3484
91MyrBeaHC-28
91MyrBeaHP-2962
92MyrBeaHC-29
92MyrBeaHF-2214
93HagSunC-27
93HagSunF-1898
94MedHatBJF-3697
94MedHatBJSP-26
96HagSunB-28

Baltes, Nick
89BoiHawP-1978

Balthazar, Doyle
87ChaWheP-28
87LakTigP-8
88LakTigS-2
89LonTigP-1384
90FloStaLAS-25
90LakTigS-2
91LinDriAA-376
91LonTigLD-376
91LonTigP-1880
92SanBerC-14
92SanBerSF-956

Baltz, Nick
76BatRouCT-2

Baltzell, Beau
96AriBlaDB-7

Bamberger, George I.
50RemBre-1
53MotCoo-38
59Top-529
73OPC-136
73Top-136A
73Top-136B
74OPC-306
74Top-306
75Gia195T-1
79Top-577
80Top-659
81TCM60I-307
82MetPhoA-4
83Top-246
85BreGar-1
85BrePol-31
85TopTifT-5T
85TopTra-5T
86BrePol-31
86Top-21
86TopTif-21
87Top-468
87TopTif-468
90PacLeg-11
90SweBasG-23
91OriCro-19

Ban, George
75LynRanT-3

Ban, Mark
86QuaCitAP-5

Ban, Yoshitiro
92NiaFalRC-10
92NiaFalRF-3314

Banach, Joe
81CliGiaT-1

Bananas, Willie P.
89WesPalBES-26
93WesPalBEC-30
Banasiak, Edward
87ElmPio(C-24
88WinHavRSS-4
Bancells, Richard
81RocRedWT-20
83RocRedWT-24
Bancroft, Dave (David James)
09RamT20-7
15SpoNewM-9
16BF2FP-84
16ColE13-12
16FleBreD-6
16SpoNewM-10
19W514-40
20NatCarE-6
20WalMaiW-3
21E121So1-4
21E121So8-4A
21E121So8-4B
21Exh-5
21KoBreWSI-1
21Nei-73
21OxfConE-2
22AmeCarE-4
22E120-181
22W572-4
22W573-6
22W575-5
22WilPatV-38
23W501-64
23W503-25
23W515-4
23W551-2
23WilChoV-6
25Exh-1
26Exh-4
26SpoComoA-4
27AmeCarE-52
27Exh-1
27YorCarE-19
28Exh-5
28StaPlaCE-1
28W502-19
28W512-1
28Yue-19
29ExhFou-4
61Fle-7
75SheGrePG-13
76GrePlaG-13
76RowExh-12
76ShaPiz-119
77GalGloG-122
80PerHaloFP-119
80SSPHOF-119
83PhiPosGPaM-4
89DodSmoG-2
89HOFStiB-20
90DodTar-29
91ConTSN-17
92ConTSN-598
94ConTSN-1065
94ConTSNB-1065
20W516-30
Bando, Chris (Christopher M.)
81ChaChaT-8
81Top-451
82Don-551
82Ind-2
82IndTeal-1
82IndWhe-11
82Top-141
83Don-33
83Fle-400
83IndPos-3
83IndWhe-3
83Top-227
84Don-224
84Fle-534
84Ind-2
84IndWhe-23
84Nes792-431
84Top-431
84TopTif-431
85Don-520
85Fle-438
85Ind-1
85IndPol-23
85Lea-39
85OPC-14
85Top-14
85TopTif-14
86Don-373
86Fle-579
86IndOhH-23
86IndTeal-4
86OPC-211
86Top-594
86TopTif-594
87Don-501
87DonOpeD-105
87Fle-243
87FleGlo-243
87IndGat-23
87Top-322
87TopTif-322
88ChaLooLTI-1
88Don-95
88Fle-601
88FleGlo-601
88IndGat-23
88OPC-51
88PanSti-71
88Sco-172
88ScoGlo-172
88StaLinI-3
88Top-604
88TopSti-209
88TopTif-604
90CalLeaACLC-29
90StoPorB-27
90StoPorCLC-200
90StoPorP-2200
91StoPorC-24
91StoPorP-3047
92ElPasDF-3937
92ElPasDS-224
93NewOrlZF-986
94NewOrlZF-1483
Bando, Sal (Salvatore L.)
67OPC-33
67Top-33
68OPC-146
68Top-146
68TopVen-146
69A'sJacitB-1
69MLBOffS-82
69Top-371
69Top-556
69TopSta-211
69TopTeaP-21
70Kel-51
70MLBOffS-254
70OPC-120
70Top-120
70TopScr-4
70TopSup-2
71MLBOffS-506
71OPC-285
71Top-285
71TopCoi-132
71TopGreM-5
71TopSup-57
71TopTat-1
72'sA'sPos-15
72Kel-52A
72Kel-52B
72MilBra-24
72OPC-348
72Top-348
72Top-650
73A'sPos-40
73LinPor-137
73OPC-155
73Top-155
73TopCanL-4
74A'sPos-51
74Kel-51
74OPC-103
74Top-103
74TopSta-221
75Hos-4
75HosTwi-4
75OPC-380
75SSP42-13
75Top-380
76A'sPos-70
76OPC-90
76SSP-497
76Top-90
77BurCheD-87
77Hos-126
77MSADis-1
77OPC-145
77RCColC-1
77Spo-1409
77Top-498
78Hos-94
78OPC-174
78RCColC-41
78Top-265
78WifBalD-1
79Hos-119
79OPC-283
79Top-550
80OPC-363
80Top-715
81Don-84
81Fle-510
81OPC-276
81Top-623
82Don-592
82Fle-134
86A'sGreT-4
87A'sMot-4
88PacLegI-99
89SweBasG-63
90PacLeg-4
90SweBasG-7
92ActPacA-40
93GleFalRC-5
93GleFalRF-4007
93TedWil-42
93UppDecAH-5
94BreMilB-6
94NewJerCC-1
94NewJerCF-3422
94UppDecAH-88
94UppDecAH1-88
Bandy, Ken
87QuaCitAP-28
Bane, Craig
90MisStaB-4
91MisStaB-4
92MisStaB-4
93MisStaB-3
Bane, Ed (Edward Lee)
74OPC-592
74TacTwiC-5
74Top-592
75IntLeaASB-2
75PacCoaLAB-2
75TacTwiK-13
76SSP-212
77TacTwiDQ-11
77Top-486
Banes, Dave
82NasSouTI-1
Baney, Dick (Richard Lee)
69PilPos-39
70OPC-88
70Top-88
74OPC-608
74Top-608A
74Top-608B
83Pil69G-5
Bangert, Greg
81CliGiaT-10
Bangston, Pat
88KenTwiP-1406
88MidLeaAGS-34
89OrlTwiB-9
89OrlTwiP-1338
90CMC-554
90PorBeaC-2
90PorBeaP-169
90ProAAAF-239
91LinDriAA-476
91OrlSunRLD-476
91OrlSunRP-1842
Banister, Jeff
86WatPirP-3
87MacPirP-4
88HarSenP-855
89EasLeaAP-23
89EasLeaDDP-DD28
89HarSenP-306
89HarSenS-2
90HarSenP-1195
90HarSenS-3
91BufBisLD-26
91BufBisP-544
91LinDriAAA-26
92TopDeb91-8
93CarMudF-2056
94WelPirC-29
94WelPirF-3511
96HonShaHWB-28
96LynHilB-27
Bankhead, Dan (Daniel R.)
51Bow-225
52Par-64
79TCM50-159
86NegLeaF-102
90DodTar-30
91RinPosBD3-6
Bankhead, Sam
78LauLonABS-31
86NegLeaF-97
Bankhead, Scott
85Top-393
85TopTif-393
86DonRoo-36
86FleUpd-8
86OmaRoyP-1
86OmaRoyT-25
86SpoRoo-39
87Fle-363
87FleGlo-363
87FleUpd-1
87FleUpdG-1
87MarMot-13
87SpoTeaP-25
87Top-508
87TopTif-508
87TopTra-2T
87TopTraT-2T
88Don-70
88Fle-368
88FleGlo-368
88MarMot-13
88OPC-246
88PanSti-180
88Sco-238
88ScoGlo-238
88ScoYouS2-37
88Top-738
88TopTif-738
89Bow-203
89BowTif-203
89Don-463
89DonBasB-219
89Fle-539
89FleGlo-539
89MarMot-13
89OPC-79
89PanSti-429
89Sco-341
89ScoYouSI-42
89Top-79
89TopTif-79
89UppDec-316
90Bow-466
90BowTif-466
90Don-261
90DonBesA-40
90Fle-505
90FleCan-505
90Lea-127
90MarMot-24
90OPC-213
90PanSti-147
90PubSti-426
90Sco-555
90Spo-41
90Top-213
90TopSti-222
90TopTif-213
90UppDec-561
90VenSti-27
91Bow-254
91Don-189
91Fle-442
91Lea-345
91MarCouH-11
91OPC-436
91Sco-817
91StaClu-597
91Top-436
91TopDesS-436
91TopMic-436
91TopTif-436
91UppDec-294
92Don-304
92FleUpd-78
92Lea-485
92OPC-155
92OPCPre-18
92Pin-580
92RedKah-25
92Sco-594
92ScoRoo-47T
92StaClu-375
92StaClu-701
92StaCluNC-701
92Top-155
92TopDaiQTU-6
92TopGol-155
92TopGolW-155
92TopMic-155
92TopTra-7T
92TopTraG-7T
92Ult-478
93Don-690
93Fle-386
93FleFinE-169
93OPC-21
93OPCPre-94
93PacSpa-353
93RedSoxWHP-2
93Sco-584
93Sel-265
93SelRoo-122T
93StaClu-145
93StaCluFDI-145
93StaCluMOP-145
93Top-361
93TopGol-361
93TopInaM-361
93TopMic-361
93Ult-505
93UppDec-329
93UppDec-760
93UppDecGold-329
93UppDecGold-760
94Don-429
94Fla-10
94Fle-25
94Pac-48
94Sco-139
94ScoGolR-139
94Top-633
94TopGol-633
94TopSpa-633
Banko, Joe
89AncGlaP-1
Bankowski, Chris
81RedPioT-27
83RedPioT-3
Banks, Brian
93HelBreF-4107
94BelBreC-3
94BelBreF-113
94ExcFS7-77
94MidLeaAF-MDW6
95ElPasDTI-1
95SPML-83
96BesAutSA-3
96Bow-287
96Exc-68
96Top-435
97Bow-352
97BowCerBIA-CA4
97BowCerGIA-CA4
97BowChr-237
97BowChrI-237
97BowChrIR-237
97BowChrR-237
97BowInt-352
97Cir-106
97CirRav-106
97Fle-508
97FleTif-508
97Ult-540
97UltGolME-540
97UltPlaME-540
97UppDec-481
Banks, Darryl
82QuaCitCT-1
83MidCubT-12
84MidCubT-8
Banks, Dave
86AubAstP-2
Banks, Dean
91PocPioP-3788
91PocPioSP-10
Banks, Ernie (Ernest)
47Exh-12A
47Exh-12B
47Exh-12C
54Top-94
55Bow-242
55DonWin-11
55RobGouS-26
55RobGouW-26
55Top-28

55TopDouH-31
56Top-15
56TopPin-5
56YelBasP-6
57Top-55
58HarSta-11
58Top-310
58Top-482
59ArmCoi-4
59Baz-3
59HomRunD-3
59Top-147
59Top-350
59Top-469
59Top-559
59TopVen-147
59WilSpoG-2
60ArmCoi-3
60Baz-1
60CubJayP-4
60KeyChal-5
60NuHi-20
60RawGloT-3
60Top-10
60Top-560
60TopTat-5
60TopVen-10
61Baz-19
61ChePat-1
61CubJayP-4
61NuSco-420
61Pos-191A
61Pos-191B
61SevElev-23
61Top-43
61Top-350
61Top-485
61Top-575
61TopMagR-21
61TopStal-4
62AurRec-2
62Baz-32
62CubJayP-3
62ExhStaB-3
62Jel-188
62Pos-188
62PosCan-188
62SalPlaC-177A
62SalPlaC-177B
62ShiPlaC-177
62Top-25
62TopBuc-6
62TopStal-104
62TopVen-25
63BasMagM-8
63Baz-3
63CubJayP-1
63ExhStaB-4
63Jel-169
63Pos-169
63SalMetC-17
63Top-3
63Top-242
63Top-380
63TopStil-5
64CubJayP-1
64Top-55
64TopCoi-42
64TopSta-25
64TopStaU-7
64TopTatl-24
64TopVen-55
65CubJayP-2
65OldLonC-3
65Top-510
65TopEmbl-58
66CubTeal-3
66OPC-110
66Top-110
66TopRubl-7
66TopVen-110
67CokCapA-21
67CokCapC-2
67CokCapNLA-27
67CubProPS-2
67DexPre-17
67ProPizC-2
67Top-215
67TopVen-275
68AtlOilPBCC-6
68Top-355
68TopActS-6C
68TopVen-355
69CubJewT-3
69CubPho-2
69CubTealC-1
69EquSpoHoF-BB1
69KelPin-2
69MilBra-19
69MLBOffS-118
69MLBPin-34
69OPC-6
69OPC-20
69Top-6
69Top-20
69TopSta-11
69TopTeaP-4
69TraSta-40
70CubDunD-1
70DayDaiNM-18
70Kel-40
70MilBra-3
70MLBOffS-13
70SunPin-1
70Top-630
70TopBoo-14
70TraSta-3C
71AllBasA-3
71Kel-50
71MatMin-3
71MatMin-4
71MilDud-34
71MLBOffS-25
71MLBOffS-555
71OPC-525
71Top-525
71TopGreM-36
72CubChi-1
72CubTeal-1
72MilBra-25
73OPC-81
73Top-81A
73Top-81B
75OPC-196
75OPC-197
75Top-196
75Top-197
76ChiGre-2
76GalBasGHoF-2
76LauDiaJ-2
77BobParHoF-4
77GalGloG-29
77GalGloG-254
77Spo-1207
78TCM60I-255
79BasGre-69
79TCM50-5
80CubGreT-12
80Lau300-27
80MarExh-4
80PacLeg-33
80PerHaloFP-158
80SSPHOF-158
82BasCarN-11
82CraJac-10
83DiaClaS2-56
83KelCerB-11
84CubUno-2
84CubUno-3
84CubUno-4
84CubUno-7
84OCoandSI-46
84SpoDesPW-21
84WilMay-32
85CirK-10
85Woo-3
86BigLeaC-9
86SpoDecG-29
86SpoDesJM-7
86SpoDesJM-19
86TCMSupS-46
87HygAllG-4
87NesDreT-26
88GreBasS-64
88HouSho-6
88PacLegI-36
89HOFStiB-6
89PerCelP-3
89TopBasT-17
90BasWit-19
90Col-11
90PacLeg-5
90PerGreM-21
90SweBasG-95
91Kel3D-4
91KelStaU-2
91LinDri-18
91SweBasG-5
92CubOldS-3
92FroRowBa-1
92FroRowBa-2
92FroRowBa-3
92FroRowBa-4
92FroRowBa-5
92MVP-11
92MVP2H-5
92TVSpoMF5HRC-2
92UppDecS-28
93NabAllA-1
93UppDecS-6
94CubWGN-8
94TopArc1-94
94TopArc1G-94
95NegLeaL2-1
96AriLot-1
96IllLot-1
97St.VinHHS-2

Banks, George Edward
61TwiCloD-2
63Top-564
64Top-223
64TopVen-223
65Top-348
66Top-488

Banks, James
92SouOreAC-20
92SouOreAF-3404
93MadMusC-4
93MadMusF-1814
94ModA'sC-3
94ModA'sF-3056
95Exc-106
95HunStaTI-3

Banks, Lance
90ChaRaiB-2
90ChaRaiP-2032
91WatDiaC-1
91WatDiaP-1248

Banks, Tony
93SouOreAC-4
93SouOreAF-4076
94WesMicWC-3
94WesMicWF-2307
95ModA'sTI-1

Banks, Willie
88KenTwiP-1380
89CalLeaA-4
89VisOakCLC-101
89VisOakP-1426
90Bes-11
90Bow-411
90BowTif-411
90ClaYel-T31
90CMC-808
90OrlSunRB-1
90OrlSunRP-1076
90OrlSunRS-2
90ProAaA-40
90StaFS7-45
91Bow-341
91Cla2-T57
91LeaGolR-BC5
91LinDriAAA-402
91PorBeaLD-402
91PorBeaP-1559
91Ult-373
91UppDec-74
92Bow-553
92ClaGam-160
92Don-760
92Fle-657
92OPC-747
92Pin-575
92PinRool-6
92PorBeaF-2659
92PorBeaS-401
92ScoRoo-39
92SkyAAAF-182
92StaClu-321
92Top-747
92TopDeb91-9
92TopGol-747
92TopGolW-747
92TopMic-747
92Ult-393
92UppDec-14
92UppDecSR-SR2
93Bow-76
93Don-79
93Fle-637
93Lea-351
93PacSpa-518
93PanSti-127
93Sco-235
93Sel-314
93StaClu-170
93StaCluFDI-170
93StaCluMOP-170
93Top-226
93TopGol-226
93TopInaM-226
93TopMic-226
93Toy-54
93Ult-579
93UppDec-686
93UppDecGold-686
94ColC-46
94ColC-522
94ColChoGS-46
94ColChoGS-522
94ColChoSS-46
94ColChoSS-522
94Don-79
94ExtBas-215
94Fin-286
94FinRef-286
94Fla-134
94Fle-199
94FleUpd-106
94Lea-245
94Pac-349
94PanSti-89
94Pin-177
94PinArtP-177
94PinMusC-177
94Sco-185
94ScoGolR-185
94ScoRoo-RT41
94ScoRooGR-RT41
94SpoRoo-84
94SpoRooAP-84
94StaClu-692
94StaCluFDI-692
94StaCluGR-692
94StaCluMOP-692
94StaCluT-334
94StaCluTFDI-334
94Top-14
94TopGol-14
94TopSpa-14
94TopTra-15T
94Ult-83
94Ult-453
94UppDec-434
94UppDecED-434
95ColCho-213
95ColChoGS-213
95ColChoSS-213
95Don-515
95DonPreP-515
95Fle-408
95Lea-201
95Pac-66
95Pin-337
95PinArtP-337
95PinMusC-337
95Sco-191
95ScoGolR-191
95ScoPlaTS-191
95StaClu-127
95StaCluFDI-127
95StaCluMOP-127
95StaCluSTWS-127
95Top-470
95TopCyb-264
95Ult-134
95UltGolM-134
95UppDec-64
95UppDecED-64
95UppDecEDG-64

Banning, Doug
86MidAngP-1
87EdmTraP-2067
87MidAngP-6
90ChaLooGS-4

Banning, Jim (James M.)
87OldJudN-19

Bannister, Alan
77Top-559
77WhiSoxJT-1
78Kel-38
78SSP270-151
78Top-213
79Top-134
80OPC-317
80Top-608
81Top-632
82Don-159
82Fle-359
82Ind-3
82IndTeal-2
82IndWhe-21
82Top-287
83Don-285
83Fle-401
83IndPos-4
83IndWhe-4
83OPC-348
83Top-348
84AstMot-21
84Don-154
84Fle-535
84FleUpd-7
84Nes792-478
84RanJarP-2
84Top-478
84TopSti-257
84TopTif-478
84TopTra-7T
84TopTraT-7T
85Fle-555
85RanPer-5
85Top-76
85TopTif-76
86Don-525
86Fle-556
86Top-784
86TopTif-784
88RocExpLC-1
89JacExpB-2
89JacExpP-151
89PacSenL-14
89T/MSenL-5
89TopSenL-30
91LinDriAAA-400
91PhoFirLD-400
91PhoFirP-84
93RanKee-60

Bannister, Floyd F.
78AstBurK-6
78Top-39
79OPC-154
79Top-306
80OPC-352
80Top-699
81AllGamPI-73
81Don-286
81Fle-599
81MarPol-2
81OPC-166
81Top-166
81TopSti-128
82Don-100
82Fle-504
82Top-468
82TopSti-234
83Don-21
83Don-50
83Fle-471
83FleSta-8
83FleSti-182
83Kel-41
83OPC-203
83Top-545
83Top-706
83TopSti-18
83TopSti-113
83TopTra-7T
83WhiSoxTV-24
84Don-366
84Fle-52
84FleSti-84
84Nes792-280
84OPC-280
84Top-280
84TopSti-247
84TopTif-280
84WhiSoxTV-4
85Don-379
85Don-424A
85Fle-508
85OPC-354
85Top-274
85Top-725
85TopMin-725
85TopTif-274
85TopTif-725
85WhiSoxC-24
86Don-244
86Fle-199

86Lea-118
86OPC-64
86Top-64
86TopMinL-9
86TopTif-64
86WhiSoxC-19
87Don-211
87Fle-486
87FleGlo-486
87FleLimE-1
87FleStiC-3
87OPC-356
87Top-737
87TopSti-286
87TopTif-737
87WhiSoxC-3
88AlaGolAA'TI-18
88Don-383
88DonBasB-7
88Fle-392
88FleGlo-392
88OPC-357
88PanSti-52
88RedFolSB-4
88RoySmo-8
88Sco-622
88ScoGlo-622
88ScoRoo-63T
88ScoRooG-63T
88StaLinWS-2
88Top-357
88TopBig-174
88TopTif-357
88TopTra-8T
88TopTraT-8T
89Bow-112
89BowTif-112
89Don-262
89Fle-276
89FleGlo-276
89OPC-194
89RedFolSB-5
89Sco-249
89Spo-154
89Top-638
89TopSti-269
89TopTif-638
89UppDec-549
90OPC-116
90PubSti-342
90Top-116
90TopTif-116
90UppDec-695
90VenSti-28
91Bow-190
91FleUpd-8
91Lea-439
92RanMot-13
92RanTeal-1
92StaClu-743
92Ult-437
93RanKee-61
93UppDecS-14
Bannister, Tim
77BurBeeT-2
78BurBeeT-3
Bannon, Jimmy (James Henry)
95May-2
98CamPepP-2
Banta, Jack (John Kay)
43ParSpo-73
49EurSta-28
50Bow-224
79TCM50-203
90DodTar-31
91RinPosBD3-2
Banton, Scott
89HamRedS-1
90SavCarP-2079
91SprCarC-4
91SprCarP-753
Baptist, Travis
91MedHatBJP-4089
91MedHatBJSP-10
92MyrBeaHF-2188
93ClaFS7-62
93ExcFS7-237
93ExcLeaLF-1
93KnoSmoF-1240
94SyrChiF-964
94SyrChiTI-2
94UppDecML-71
95SyrChiTI-1
96SigRooOJ-2
96SigRooOJS-2
96SyrChiTI-2
Barajas, Rod
96AriBlaDB-8
97Top-469
Baranoski, Jim
89IdaFalBP-2025
Barba, Doug
84CedRapRT-4
Barba, Michael
82HolMilT-1
83ArkTraT-6
Barbao, Joe
94BatCliC-2
94BatCliF-3436
95PiePhiF-178
96PieBolWB-4
Barbara, Dan (Daniel)
89SanBerSB-7
89SanBerSCLC-76
90PenPilS-3
90StaFS7-77
Barbara, Don
91MidAngOHP-2
91MidLeaAP-MWL24
91QuaCitAC-15
91QuaCitAP-2633
92EdmTraF-3543
92EdmTraS-151
92SkyAAAF-73
94AlbDukF-846
95PawRedSDD-3
95PawRedTI-37
Barbare, Walter L.
21Exh-6
22E120-121
Barbary, Travis
94GreFalDSP-12
Barbe, Yogi (Jim)
78AshTouT-1
79TulDriT-17
Barbeau, Jap (William J.)
08AmeCarE-67
09T206-13
11SpoLifCW-14
Barbein, Joe
92YakBeaC-23
92YakBeaF-3438
Barber, Brian
91Cla/Bes-443
91ClaDraP-18
91FroRowDP-21
91JohCitCC-18
91JohCitCP-3969
92Bow-29
92ClaFS7-268
92OPC-594
92Pin-298
92ProFS7-324
92Sco-803
92SprCarC-4
92SprCarF-860
92St.PetCF-2020
92StaCluD-11
92Top-594
92TopGol-594
92TopGolW-594
92TopMic-594
92UppDecML-178
93ArkTraF-2804
93Bow-136
93ClaFS7-124
93ExcFS7-96
93StaCluCa-29
93Ult-461
94ActPac-21
94Bow-180
94Bow-364
94BowBes-B10
94BowBesR-B10
94Cla-82
94ClaGolF-13
94ExcFS7-256
94LouRedF-2971
94SigRoo-24
94SigRooS-24
94Top-788
94TopGol-788
94TopSpa-788
94Ult-563
94UppDecML-236
95Bow-31
95BowBes-B8
95BowBesR-B8
95LouRedF-267
95Sel-168
95SelArtP-168
96ColCho-24
96ColChoGS-24
96ColChoSS-24
96Don-547
96DonPreP-547
96LouRedB-8
96Pin-167
96Sco-237
96StaClu-409
96StaCluMOP-409
96Top-433
96Ult-270
96UltGolM-270
96UppDecFSP-FS2
97PacPriGotD-GD196
Barber, David
83QuaCitCT-5
Barber, Greg
96SouBenSHS-3
Barber, Red
88RinPosD1-4C
88RinPosD1-5C
Barber, Steve (Stephen David)
47Exh-13
60Top-514
61Pos-74A
61Pos-74B
61Top-125
61TopStal-97
62SalPlaC-11
62ShiPlaC-11
62Top-57
62Top-355
62TopVen-57
63BasMagM-9
63ExhStaB-5
63Fle-1
63Jel-64
63Pos-64
63Top-12
64Baz-3
64OriJayP-2
64Top-450
64TopCoi-8
64TopSta-54
64TopStaU-8
64TopTatl-25
64WheSta-5
64YanReqKP-1
65OPC-113
65Top-113
66Top-477
67OPC-82
67Top-82
68Top-316
68TopVen-316
69MilBra-20
69MLBOffS-92
69PilPos-12
69Top-233
69TopSta-222
69TopTeaP-9
70MLBOffS-265
70OPC-224
70Top-224
72MilBra-26
72OPC-333
72Top-333
73OPC-36
73Top-36
74OPC-631
74Top-631
78TCM60I-57
81Ori6F-4
83Pil69G-26
91OriCro-20
92YanWIZ6-5
Barber, Turner (Tyrus Turner)
20NatCarE-7
21E121So1-5
21Exh-7
22E120-153
22W573-7
23W501-60
23WilChoV-7
Barberich, Frank F.
12ImpTobC-16
Barberie, Bret
88TopTra-9T
88TopTraT-9T
89Sta-32
89TopBig-19
89WesPalBES-2
90JacExpB-3
90JacExpP-1379
91IndIndLD-176
91IndIndP-465
91LinDriAAA-176
91UltUpd-90
91UppDecFE-67F
92Bow-467
92Cla1-T9
92Don-449
92ExpDonD-1
92ExpPos-4
92Fle-472
92Lea-288
92LeaGolP-6
92LeaPre-6
92OPC-224
92OPCPre-36
92Pin-93
92PinTea2-50
92ProFS7-256
92Sco-419
92Sco100RS-14
92StaClu-427
92Stu-51
92Top-224
92TopDaiQTU-16
92TopDeb91-10
92TopGol-224
92TopGolW-224
92TopMic-224
92TriPla-134
92Ult-512
92UppDec-363
93Bow-446
93Don-12
93Don-759
93Fla-47
93Fle-418
93FleFinE-51
93FunPac-118
93Lea-256
93MarFloA-6
93MarPub-4
93MarUSPC-6S
93MarUSPC-11D
93PacSpa-454
93Pin-553
93PinExpOD-4
93Sco-617
93SP-136
93StaClu-481
93StaCluFDI-481
93StaCluMarl-18
93StaCluMOP-481
93TriPla-195
93Ult-366
93UppDec-479
93UppDec-552
93UppDecGold-479
93UppDecGold-552
94Bow-674
94ColC-47
94ColChoGS-47
94ColChoSS-47
94Don-127
94ExtBas-257
94Fin-187
94FinRef-187
94Fla-378
94Fle-461
94FUnPac-61
94Lea-62
94PanSti-179
94Pin-136
94PinArtP-136
94PinMusC-136
94Sco-434
94ScoGolR-434
94Sel-133
94StaClu-415
94StaCluFDI-415
94StaCluGR-415
94StaCluMOP-415
94StaCluT-62
94StaCluTFDI-62
94Stu-106
94Top-132
94TopGol-132
94TopSpa-132
94TriPla-131
94Ult-192
94UppDec-151
94UppDecED-151
95ColCho-341
95ColChoGS-341
95ColChoSE-132
95ColChoSEGS-132
95ColChoSESS-132
95ColChoSS-341
95Don-85
95DonPreP-85
95DonTopotO-3
95Fla-217
95Fle-325
95FleUpd-2
95Lea-382
95Pac-167
95PacPri-54
95Pin-80
95PinArtP-80
95PinMusC-80
95Sco-395
95ScoGolR-395
95ScoPlaTS-395
95StaClu-265
95StaCluFDI-265
95StaCluMOP-265
95StaCluSTWS-265
95StaCluVR-133
95Top-44
95TopCyb-33
95TopTra-136T
95Ult-252
95UltGolM-252
95UppDec-126
95UppDecED-126
95UppDecEDG-126
96IowCubB-6
95StaCluVRMC-133
Barbieri, Jim (James P.)
67OPC-76
67Top-76
90DodTar-32
Barbisan, Vince
76SeaRaiC-2
Barbosa, Rafael
84DurBulT-11
Barboza, Domingo
76VenLeaS-183
80VenLeaS-228
Barboza, James
85CloHSS-2
Barcelo, Lorenzo
95BelGiaTI-14
96BurBeeTI-1
96MidLeaAB-12
Barcelo, Marc
94ClaGolF-183
94NasXprF-377
94Top-747
94TopGol-747
94TopSpa-747
95Bow-155
95Exc-78
95SigRoo-6
95SigRooSig-6
95Top-639
95UppDecML-51
96BesAutS-7
96BesAutSA-4
96PinAfi-189
96PinAfiAP-189
96Sel-176
95UppDecMLFS-51
Barclay, Curt (Curtis C.)
57SeaPop-3
57Top-361
58GiaJayP-2
58GiaSFCB-2
58Hir-70
58Top-21
59Top-307
Barczi, Scott
87WatPirP-7
88AugPirP-368
89SalBucS-4
90HarSenP-1196
90HarSenS-4
Bard, Michael
91BenBucC-26
91BenBucP-3699
Bard, Paul Z.

81VerBeaDT-2
82VerBeaDT-12
84ChaO'sT-21
Barden, Geoff
91BriBanF-8
Barden, Steve
89RicBraP-819
Bardot, Gene
76WauMetT-1
77LynMetT-3
Bare, Ray (Raymond Douglas)
76OPC-507
76SSP-613
76Top-507
77Top-43
78RocRedWT-1
Barefoot, Mike
89MiaMirIS-1
Barfield, Brian
96JohCitCTI-2
Barfield, Jesse Lee
78DunBluJT-1
80KnoBluJT-13
82OPC-203
82Top-203
82TopTra-2T
83Don-595
83Fle-424
83OPC-257
83Top-257
83TopSti-307
84AllGamPI-139
84BluJayFS-4
84Don-193
84Fle-147
84Nes792-488
84OPC-316
84Top-488
84TopSti-372
84TopTif-488
85AllGamPI-48
85BluJayFS-4
85BluJayPLP-1
85Don-195
85Fle-99
85Lea-209
85OPC-24
85OPCPos-20
85Top-24
85TopSti-362
85TopTif-24
86BluJayAF-3
86BluJayFS-3
86Don-193
86Fle-52
86FleMin-12
86FleStiC-2
86GenMilB-3A
86Lea-254
86OPC-234
86SevCoi-E16
86Spo-76
86Top-593
86TopSti-192
86TopTat-2
86TopTif-593
87BluJayFS-1
87ClaGam-58
87Don-121
87DonAll-23
87DonOpeD-34
87Fle-219
87Fle-643
87FleBasA-2
87FleExcS-3
87FleGlo-219
87FleGlo-643
87FleLeaL-1
87FleMin-4
87FleSlu-2
87FleStiC-4
87FleWaxBC-C2
87GenMilB-1A
87HosSti-1
87KayB-2
87KraFoo-41
87Lea-127
87OPC-24
87RedFolSB-3
87Spo-14
87Spo-153
87SpoTeaP-5
87StuPan-27
87Top-106
87Top-655
87TopCoi-2
87TopGaloC-1
87TopGloS-35
87TopMinL-73
87TopSti-184
87TopTif-106
87TopTif-655
87Woo-9
88BluJay5-1
88BluJayFS-1
88Don-442
88DonBasB-216
88Fle-102
88FleGlo-102
88FleRecS-1
88FleStiC-70
88Lea-225
88MSAHosD-19
88OPC-140
88PanSti-223
88Sco-8
88ScoGlo-8
88Spo-13
88StaLinBJ-1
88Top-140
88TopBig-92
88TopGloS-2
88TopSti-192
88TopStiB-46
88TopTif-140
89BluJayFS-1
89Bow-257
89BowTif-257
89ClaLigB-66
89Don-425
89DonBasB-132
89DonGraS-11
89Fle-225
89FleGlo-225
89FleUpd-46
89OPC-325
89PanSti-471
89RedFolSB-6
89Sco-160
89ScoRoo-22T
89Spo-9
89Top-325
89TopAme2C-1
89TopTif-325
89TopTra-7T
89TopTraT-7T
89UppDec-149
89UppDec-702
89YanScoNW-5
90BluJayHS-2
90BluJayHS-5
90Bow-433
90BowTif-433
90ClaBlu-99
90Don-74
90DonBesA-109
90Fle-437
90FleCan-437
90Lea-201
90MLBBasB-61
90OPC-740
90PacLeg-110
90PanSti-120
90PubSti-530
90RedFolSB-4
90Sco-222
90Spo-10
90Top-740
90TopBig-188
90TopHilHM-24
90TopSti-314
90TopTif-740
90TopTVY-29
90UppDec-476
90VenSti-29
90YanScoNW-5
91BasBesHRK-1
91Bow-169
91ClaGam-61
91Don-498
91Fle-657
91Lea-308
91OPC-85
91PanFreS-330
91Sco-148
91Sco-414
91SimandSMLBL-2
91StaClu-103
91StaCluP-4
91Stu-91
91Top-85
91TopDesS-85
91TopMic-85
91TopTif-85
91Ult-228
91UppDec-485
92Bow-295
92Don-316
92Fle-221
92OPC-650
92PanSti-139
92Pin-425
92Sco-565
92StaClu-214
92Top-650
92TopGol-650
92TopGolW-650
92TopMic-650
92Ult-99
92UppDec-139
92UppDec-644
92YanWIZ8-8
93BluJayDM-2
95AstMot-28
97BluJayS-34
Barfield, John D.
87PorChaRP-5
88TexLeaAGS-17
88TulDriTI-14
89BlaYNPRWLU-12
89OklCit8C-2
89OklCit8P-1518
90CMC-159
90OklCit8C-9
90OklCit8P-424
90ProAAAF-670
90TopDeb89-8
91Don-688
91FleUpd-58
91OPC-428
91RanMot-13
91Sco-573
91Top-428
91TopDesS-428
91TopMic-428
91TopTif-428
91UppDec-629
92Don-168
92OklCit8F-1906
92Sco-683
92StaClu-364
92UppDec-691
93RanKee-62
94SanAntMF-2458
94VenLinU-153
Bargar, Greg (Gregory R.)
80MemChiT-5
83MemChiT-20
83WicAerDS-4
84IndIndTI-13
84IndIndTI-18
84Nes792-474
84OPC-292
84Top-474
84TopTif-474
85IndIndTI-13
86CarTeal-3
87LouRedTI-4
88LouRedBTI-9
Bargas, Rob
91WesPalBEC-18
91WesPalBEP-1234
Barger, Bob
76WauMetT-2
Barger, Cy (Eros Bolivar)
09T206-395
10CouT21-74
10DomDisP-6
10SweCapPP-69
11PloCanE-3
11S74Sil-48
11SpoLifCW-15
11SpoLifM-148
11T205-8A
11T205-8B
12HasTriFT-3A
12HasTriFT-61A
12T207-7
14CraJacE-141
14PieStaT-1
15CraJacE-141
Barger, David W.
89CarNewE-26
Barger, Mike
93BelMarC-3
93BelMarF-3221
94AppFoxC-2
94AppFoxF-1065
96PorCitRB-6
Barger, Vince
85DurBulT-2
Bargerhuff, Brian
83CliGiaF-17
86ChaLooP-3
Bargfeldt, John
79QuaCitCT-19
Barillari, Al
52LavPro-50
Bark, Brian
88CapCodPPaLP-114
90PulBraB-1
90PulBraP-3101
91DurBulC-2
91DurBulP-1535
92GreBraF-1147
92GreBraS-227
92SkyAA F-97
93RicBraBB-10
93RicBraF-176
93RicBraP-3
93RicBraRC-12
93RicBraRC-5
94RicBraF-2837
95RicBraRC-1
96NorTidB-8
Barker, Bob
87AlbYanP-3
Barker, Glen
93NiaFalRF-3400
94FayGenC-3
94FayGenF-2159
95JacSunTI-1
96JacSunB-5
Barker, Jeff
78HolMilT-1
94JamJamC-3
94JamJamF-3957
Barker, Kevin
96OgdRapTI-4
Barker, Len (Leonard H.)
74GasRanT-4
76SacSolC-20
76VenLeaS-93
77Top-489
77TucTorC-40
78RanBurK-9
78SSP270-91
78Top-634
79OPC-40
79Top-94
80Top-227
81AllGamPI-74
81Don-320
81Fle-408
81OPC-3
81Top-6
81Top-432
81TopSti-5
81TopSti-72
82Don-6
82Don-137
82Fle-360
82Fle-639
82FleSta-200
82Ind-4
82IndTeal-3
82IndWhe-12
82Kel-37
82OPC-360
82Top-166
82Top-360
82TopSti-12
82TopSti-113
82TopSti-178
83Don-111
83Fle-402
83Fle-642
83FleSta-9
83FleSti-245
83IndPos-5
83IndWhe-5
83Kel-33
83OPC-120
83Top-120
83TopSti-57
84BraPol-39
84Don-443
84Fle-170
84Nes792-614
84OPC-309
84Top-614
84TopTif-614
85BraHos-2
85BraPol-39
85Don-165
85Fle-318
85Top-557
85TopTif-557
86Don-409
86Fle-507
86IndIndTI-20
86Top-24
86TopTif-24
91PacSenL-153
93RanKee-63
94BreMilB-7
Barker, Marvin
91PomBlaBPB-2
Barker, Ray (Raymond H.)
61Top-428
65Top-546
66Top-323
66TopVen-323
67Top-583
81TCM60I-314
91OriCro-21
92YanWIZ6-6
Barker, Richard
94HunCubF-3542
95RocCubTI-27
96DayCubB-4
94HunCubC-2
Barker, Tim (Timothy C.)
86TamTarP-2
87BelBreP-17
88ChaRaiP-1221
89GreFalDSP-14
90BakDodCLC-255
90CalLeaACLC-8
91LinDriAA-529
91SanAntMLD-529
92SanAntMF-3980
92SanAntMS-554
92SkyAA F-243
93OttLynF-2440
94NewOrlZF-1473
96ColCliB-2
Barker, Timothy N..
91SanAntMP-2980
Barkett, Andy
93BazTeaU-3
93TopTra-93T
95ButCopKtI-30
Barkley, Brian
96BesAutS-8
96Bow-240
96TreThuB-5
Barkley, Charles
91UppDecS-2
Barkley, Jeff
83WatIndF-20
84MaiGuiT-15
85IndPol-49
85MaiGuiT-1
86Top-567
86TopTif-567
Barkley, Red
90DodTar-33
Barkley, Sam (Samuel E.)
87BucN28-84
87BucN28-93
87OldJudN-20
Barksdale, Joey
95MicBatCTI-2
96SarRedSB-6
Barley, Ned
90MedHatBJB-12
Barlick, Al
55Bow-265
80PerHaloFP-201
90PerGreM-86
90T/MUmp-71
Barling, Glenn
82CliGiaF-6
Barlok, Todd
95GreFalDTI-29
96VerBeaDB-6
Barlow, Andy
90JamExpP-31

Barlow, Clem
91BelMarC-1
91BelMarP-3678
Barlow, Ethan
96VerExpB-8
Barlow, Mike
76SSP-298
77SalLakCGC-21
78AngFamF-2
78Top-429
80SyrChiT-13
80SyrChiTI-4
80Top-312
81OPC-77
81Top-77
82SyrChiT-1
82SyrChiTI-4
78STLakCGC-21
Barlow, Ricky
86GleFalTP-1
87TolMudHP-9
87TolMudHT-19
Barlow, Stuart
91SydWavF-16
Barna, Babe (Herbert Paul)
78HalHalR-7
Barnard, Alan
90LSUTigA-8
Barnard, Jeff
81AppFoxT-2
Barnard, Steve
85PriWilPT-11
Barnard, Tom
88WatPirP-32
92WelPirC-30
92WelPirF-1341
Barnden, Miles
93AlbPolC-2
93BluOriC-3
93BluOriF-4130
94AlbPolC-3
94AlbPolF-2241
94OriPro-5
Barnes, Alan
80ElmPioRST-1
Barnes, Brian
88CapCodPPaLP-130
90Bes-261
90CMC-660
90JacExpB-14
90JacExpP-1365
90ProAaA-36
91Bow-438
91ClaGam-8
91Don-415
91ExpPos-1
91OPC-211
91OPCPre-4
91Sco-708
91ScoRoo-10
91StaClu-114
91Stu-192
91Top-211
91TopDeb90-11
91TopDesS-211
91TopMic-211
91TopTif-211
91UppDec-12
92Bow-501
92Don-117
92ExpDonD-2B
92Fle-473
92IndIndS-177
92OPC-73
92OPCPre-52
92Sco-715
92Sco100RS-78
92SkyAAAF-85
92StaClu-549
92Top-73
92TopGol-73
92TopGolW-73
92TopMic-73
92UppDec-361
93Don-88
93ExpPosN-3
93Fle-457
93OPC-249
93PacSpa-181
93StaClu-500
93StaCluFDI-500
93StaCluMOP-500
93Top-112
93TopGol-112
93TopInaM-112
93TopMic-112
93UppDec-214
93UppDecGold-214
94Fle-532
94Pac-373
94Sco-289
94ScoGolR-289
94Top-694
94TopGol-694
94TopSpa-694
Barnes, Chris
88CapCodPPaLP-115
Barnes, Colin
91SydWavF-8
Barnes, Craig
75LafDriT-9
Barnes, Donald L.
41BroW75-3
Barnes, Frank
60Top-538
93NegLeaRL2-1
Barnes, Harry
92NegLeaRLI-2
Barnes, Jeff
91MidAngOHP-3
92ModA'sC-12
Barnes, Jesse L.
19W514-120
21KoBreWSI-2
22E120-182
22W572-5
22W573-8
22W575-6
23MapCriV-1
23W503-22
23W515-31
23W551-3
23WilChoV-8
25Exh-2
26SpoComoA-5
90DodTar-34
92ConTSN-355
20W516-12
Barnes, John S.
91HigSchPLS-10
91HigSchPLS-18
92ChaRaiC-18
97Bow-422
97BowChr-282
97BowChrI-282
97BowChrIR-282
97BowChrR-282
97BowInt-422
Barnes, Jon
91ClaDraP-47
91FroRowDP-20
92ChaRaiF-112
92StaCluD-12
93WatDiaC-5
93WatDiaF-1759
94RanCucQC-4
94RanCucQF-1627
Barnes, Keith
94AshTouC-2
94AshTouF-1771
95AshTouUTI-31
95SalAvaTI-4
96SalAvaB-2
Barnes, Kelvin
96RocCubTI-1
Barnes, Larry
94SigRooDP-57
94SigRooDPS-57
94StaCluDP-40
94StaCluDPFDI-40
94TopTra-38T
96CedRapKTI-4
96MidLeaAB-15
96OgdRapTI-43
97Bow-322
97BowChr-221
97BowChrI-221
97BowChrIR-221
97BowChrR-221
97BowInt-322
Barnes, Lute (Luther Owen)
91MetWIZ-24
Barnes, Mike
80BufBisT-1
Barnes, Red (Emile Deering)
28StaPlaCE-2
93ConTSN-984
Barnes, Richard
78KnoKnoST-2
79KnoKnoST-5
80IowOakP-1
81EdmTraRR-10
82EdmTraT-19
84Don-608
84MaiGuiT-6
Barnes, Skeeter (William Henry)
79NaSouTI-4
80WatRedT-15
81IndIndTI-29
82WatRedT-13
83IndIndTI-31
84WicAerRD-16
85Don-530
85ExpPos-1
86IndIndTI-16
88BufBisC-23
88BufBisP-1487
88NasSouTI-2
89NasSouC-13
89NasSouP-1289
89NasSouTI-1
89TriA AAC-6
89TriAAP-AAA15
90CMC-138
90NasSouC-13
90NasSouP-244
90ProAAAF-556
90TriAAAC-6
91LinDriAAA-578
91TolMudHLD-578
91TolMudHP-1942
91TopTra-5T
91TopTraT-5T
92Don-749
92OPC-221
92Pin-218
92Sco-569
92StaClu-585
92Top-221
92TopGol-221
92TopGolW-221
92TopMic-221
92Ult-358
92UppDec-470
93Don-437
93Fle-603
93PacSpa-441
93PanSti-121
93StaClu-389
93StaCluFDI-389
93StaCluMOP-389
93TigGat-2
93Top-26
93TopGol-26
93TopInaM-26
93TopMic-26
94Fle-124
94Pac-210
94Sco-232
94ScoGolR-232
94StaClu-50
94StaCluFDI-50
94StaCluGR-50
94StaCluMOP-50
94TolMudHF-1036
94Top-561
94TopGol-561
94TopSpa-561
95Pac-148
95TolMudHTI-2
96TolMudHB-3
Barnes, Tom
52LavPro-90
Barnes, Virgil
23W515-31
28Exh-17
Barnett, Larry
88T/MUmp-7
89T/MUmp-5
89T/MUmp-60
90T/MUmp-5
Barnett, Marty
95BatCliTI-3
96HicCraB-28
Barnett, Mike
90SouBenWSB-26
90SouBenWSGS-30
91SarWhiSC-28
91SarWhiSP-1130
92SarWhiSCB-29
92SarWhiSF-225
93BirBarF-1208
94BirBarC-28
94BirBarF-638
Barnett, Rick
93BluOriF-4115
Barney, Rex
47HomBon-1
48Bow-41
49Bow-61
49EurSta-29
50Bow-76
51Bow-153
90DodTar-35
91RinPosBD4-8
Barnhart, Clyde Lee
21Exh-8
21Nei-108
22E120-212
27AmeCarE-2
79DiaGre-353
Barnhart, Rick
79WatIndT-11
79WauTimT-13
80WatIndT-13
Barnhill, Dave
78HalHalR-18
86NegLeaF-101
Barnhouse, Scott
83WauTimF-18
Barniak, Jim
90PhiTas-36
Barnicle, George B.
77TCMTheWY-63
Barnicle, Ted
76CedRapGT-3
79KnoKnoST-21
80GleFalWSBT-11
80GleFalWSCT-19
Barnie, Billy (William H.)
87OldJudN-22
90DodTar-36
Barnowski, Ed (Edward A.)
66Top-442
67Top-507
91OriCro-22
Barns, Jeff
88PalSprACLC-100
88PalSprAP-1451
89MidAngGS-5
90MidAngGS-9
90TexLeaAGS-11
91LinDriAA-427
91MidAngLD-427
91MidAngP-438
92ModA'sF-3904
93ModA'sC-2
93ModA'sF-804
94MidAngF-2454
94MidAngOHP-1
95MidAngOHP-3
95MidAngTI-3
96MidAngB-3
96MidAngOHP-2
Barnwell, Rich (Richard)
90Ft.LauYS-1
91Ft.LauYC-24
91Ft.LauYP-2438
92AlbYanF-2236
92AlbYanS-2
93AlbYanF-2173
94ColCliF-2962
Barnwell, Rob
87WatPirP-21
Barojas, Salome
83Don-67
83Fle-230
83FleSti-154
83WhiSoxTV-30
84Don-570
84Fle-53
84WhiSoxTV-5
85Don-605
85Fle-482
85MarMot-19
Baron, Jimmy
93StaCluM-134
93Top-538
93TopGol-538
93TopInaM-538
93TopMic-538
94SprSulC-3
94SprSulF-2029
95IdaFalBTI-20
96HilStaHWB-22
96RanCucQB-6
Baron, Sean
88BurIndP-1778
Barone, Dick (Richard A.)
57JetPos-1
61UniOil-SD1
Barons, Bismarck
93NegLeaRL2-58
Barr, Bob
76WatRoyT-1
Barr, Bob (Robert A.)
90DodTar-897
Barr, Jim (James Leland)
72OPC-232
72Top-232
73OPC-387
73Top-387
74OPC-233
74Top-233
75Hos-13
75HosTwi-13
75OPC-107
75Top-107
76OPC-308
76SSP-92
76Top-308
77BurCheD-103
77Gia-2
77Hos-83
77OPC-119
77Top-609
78OPC-19
78Top-62
79Top-461
80OPC-275
80Top-529
81Don-412
81Fle-287
81Top-717
83Don-398
83Fle-252
83Top-133
84Don-79
84Fle-365
84Nes792-282
84Top-282
84TopTif-282
88AlaGolAA'TI-9
Barr, Steve (Steven Charles)
76OPC-595
76Top-595
76VenLeaS-80
93RanKee-64
Barr, Tim
78GreBraT-3
80OrlTwiT-2
Barragan, Cuno (Facundo A.)
59DarFar-1
62Top-66
62TopVen-66
63Top-557
Barragan, Gerry
87MadMusP-1
87MadMusP-12
88ModA'sCLC-73
Barragan, Jimmy (Jaime)
87UtiBluSP-27
88SpaPhiP-1036
88SpaPhiS-17
89ClePhiS-1
90ClePhiS-1
Barranca, German
75WatRoyT-1A
75WatRoyT-1B
76WatRoyT-2
77JacSunT-2
80OmaRoyP-2
81IndIndTI-25
83EvaTriT-25
84OklCit8T-24
85WatIndT-17
Barranco, Vince
88BurIndP-1777
Barreiro, Efrain
90AshTouC-1
90AubAstB-5
90AubAstP-3413
91AshTouP-559
Barreiro, Fernando
91SprCarC-5

91SprCarP-732
Barrera, Nelson
85BufBisT-7
Barrera, Ruben
95GreFalDTI-34
Barreto, Miguel
76VenLeaS-160
80VenLeaS-147
Barreto, Saul
87GasRanP-6
88BlaYNPRWL-3
Barreto, Simon
76VenLeaS-22
Barrett, Bessie
08AllLadBC-1
Barrett, Bill (William J.)
93ConTSN-977
Barrett, Bob (Robert S.)
90DodTar-37
Barrett, Charles
47TipTop-76
77LodDodT-1
Barrett, Dick
43CubTeal-1
47CenFlo-1
50W720HolS-3
Barrett, Jimmy (James E.)
03BreE10-3
04FanCraAL-2
11MecDFT-32
11SpoLifCW-16
Barrett, Johnny (John Joseph)
77TCMTheWY-37
83TCMPla1944-26
Barrett, Keith
87BolMarL-20
Barrett, Kewpie
47SigOil-74
Barrett, Mark
94SpoIndC-2
94SpoIndF-3313
Barrett, Marty (Martin Glen)
81PawRedST-14
83PawRedST-14
84FleUpd-8
84Nes792-683
84Top-683
84TopTif-683
85AllGamPl-10
85Don-127
85Fle-150
85Lea-229
85Top-298
85TopSti-219
85TopTif-298
86Don-294
86Fle-340
86Lea-169
86OPC-314
86Top-734
86TopSti-250
86TopTif-734
87ClaGam-61
87Don-523
87DonOpeD-188
87Fle-27
87FleAwaW-1
87FleGlo-27
87FleGlo-WS6
87FleLimE-2
87FleStiC-5
87FleWorS-6
87Lea-165
87OPC-39
87RedSoxSAP-1
87SevCoi-M2
87Spo-112
87Spo-182
87SpoTeaP-9
87Top-39
87TopSti-18
87TopTif-39
87Woo-17
88Don-276
88DonBasB-9
88DonTeaBRS-276
88Fle-343
88FleGlo-343
88Lea-141
88OPC-338
88PanSti-28
88Sco-155
88ScoGlo-155
88Spo-157
88StaLinRS-1
88Top-525
88TopBig-54
88TopSti-248
88TopTif-525
89Bow-28
89BowTif-28
89Don-184
89DonBasB-252
89Fle-78
89FleGlo-78
89OPC-155
89PanSti-276
89Sco-63
89Spo-198
89Top-155
89TopBig-278
89TopSti-257
89TopTif-155
89TVSpoM-66
89UppDec-173
90Bow-282
90BowTif-282
90Don-240
90Fle-266
90FleCan-266
90OPC-355
90PanSti-15
90PubSti-446
90RedSoxP-1
90RedSoxP-20
90Sco-15
90Top-355
90TopBig-44
90TopSti-256
90TopTif-355
90TopTVRS-21
90UppDec-133
90VenSti-30
91Bow-648
91Fle-84
91Lea-474
91OPC-496
91PadMag-10
91Sco-228
91Top-496
91TopDesS-496
91TopMic-496
91TopTif-496
91UppDec-90
93LasVegSF-961
94LasVegSF-884
95RanCucQT-17
Barrett, Michael
95Bes-124
95BowBes-X7
95BowBesR-X7
95TopTra-25T
96Bow-249
96DelShoB-8
96HonShaHWB-15
96Top-15
96TopPowB-15
97Bow-122
97BowChr-136
97BowChrI-136
97BowChrIR-136
97BowChrR-136
97BowInt-122
Barrett, Red (Charles H.)
39ExhSal-3
46SeaSLP-2
49Bow-213
49EurSta-4
52Par-14
77TCMTheWY-23
79DiaGre-213
83TCMPla1945-28
95ConTSN-1403
Barrett, Scott
93EveGiaC-3
93EveGiaF-3770
Barrett, Tim
86IndIndTI-34
87IndIndTI-9
88IndIndC-5
88IndIndP-502
89IndIndC-1
89IndIndP-1229
Barrett, Tom
84NasSouTI-2
85ColCliP-1
85ColCliT-13
86AlbYanT-5
87ReaPhiP-7
88BlaYNPRWL-145
88MaiPhiC-16
88MaiPhiP-284
88PhiTas-27
88TriAAC-18
89BlaYNPRWL-57
89ScrRedBC-11
89ScrRedBP-725
89Top-653
89TopBig-177
89TopTif-653
90AlbDecGB-15
90Sco-633A
90Sco-633B
91LinDriAAA-352
91PawRedSDD-2
91PawRedSLD-352
91PawRedSP-44
92PawRedSF-928
92PawRedSS-352
93TucTorF-3063
94NewBriRSF-666
96MicBatCB-1
97DunDonPPS-2
Barretto, Saul M.
88GasRanP-1022
Barrick, Andy
88BatCliP-1687
Barrick, Troy
94NewJerCC-2
94NewJerCF-3404
94SavCarC-4
94SavCarF-497
Barrilleaux, John
89OneYanP-2099
Barringer, Reggie
85PriWilPT-20
86PriWilPP-1
87SalBucP-23
Barrios, Eugene
85GreHorT-24
Barrios, Francisco
77Top-222
77WhiSoxJT-2
78SSP270-144
78Top-552
79Hos-21
79Top-386
80OPC-58
80Top-107
81Fle-352
Barrios, Gregg
86WinHavRSP-3
Barrios, Jose Manuel
76CedRapGT-4
80PhoGiaVNB-17
80VenLeaS-26
81PhoGiaVNB-12
82PhoGiaVNB-24
Barrios, Manuel
94QuaCitRBC-3
94QuaCitRBF-525
95QuaCitRBTI-1
96JacGenB-4
96TexLeaAB-1
Barron, Jose
95AubAstTI-9
96AubDouB-28
Barron, Tony (Anthony)
89Sta-26
89VerBeaDS-2
90StaFS7-18
90VerBeaDS-3
91LinDriAA-530
91SanAntMLD-530
91SanAntMP-2986
92AlbDukF-732
92SanAntMS-555
93AlbDukF-1474
94JacSunF-1423
96HarSenB-5
Barros, Ellie
82DanSunF-17
Barrow, Edward G.
50CalHOFW-4
60Fle-23
76ShaPiz-65
77GalGloG-174
80PerHaloFP-63
80SSPHOF-63
81TigDetN-77
89HOFStiB-94
95ConTSN-1394
Barrow, Mel
75LynRanT-4
76SanAntBTI-1
79TucTorT-22
79TulDriT-21
80TulDriT-11
81TulDriT-6
90TulDriDGB-26
Barrs, Stan
88SavCarP-349
Barry, Dan
90GeoColC-35
Barry, Eric
84ModA'sC-1
Barry, Jack (John Joseph)
08AmeCarE-36
09AmeCarE-3
09ColChiE-19
09SpoNewSM-65
09T206-14
10DomDisP-7
10E101-1
10E12AmeCDC-4
10LuxCigPP-2
10MelMinE-1
10NadCarE-2
10NadE1-5
10PeoT21-1A
10PeoT21-1B
10SweCapPP-41
11A'sFirT20-2
11MecDFT-2
11PloCanE-4
11S74Sil-27
11SpoLifCW-18
11SpoLifM-87
11T205-9
11TurRedT-78
12ColRedB-19
12ColTinT-19
12HasTriFT-18
12HasTriFT-70A
12T207-8
14CraJacE-28
14FatPlaT-4
14PieStaT-2
15AmeCarE-1
15CraJacE-28
15SpoNewM-10
16BF2FP-1
16ColE13-13
16FleBreD-7
16SpoNewM-11
77GalGloG-180
84OCoandSI-180
88ConSer3-4
91ConTSN-139
Barry, Jeff
89AncGlaP-2
89SanDieSAS-2
90JamExpP-7
90SanDieSA3-2
91Cla/Bes-365
91WesPalBEC-24
91WesPalBEP-1239
92St.LucMF-1759
93ClaFS7-95
93St.LucMC-2
94BinMetF-714
95BinMetTI-27
95TopTra-22T
96MemChiB-7
96MetKah-2
93StLucMF-2931
Barry, Joe
85RedWinA-23
86RedWinA-14
Barry, John
69SCFOldT-17
86CliGiaP-1
88FreSunCLC-10
88FreSunP-1227
Barry, Mike
85RedWinA-2
86RedWinA-8
Barry, Shad (John C.)
08RosComP-159
09PC7HHB-2
09T206-396
11SpoLifCW-17
Barry, W.J.M.
88AllandGN-45
Barstad, Scott
93MarPhiC-4
93MarPhiF-3463
Bartee, Kimera
93BluOriC-4
93BluOriF-4137
94CarLeaAF-CAR1
94FreKeyF-2625
94OriPro-6
95AusFut-37
95Bes-30
95Bow-124
95BowBayTI-18
95Exc-1
95RocRedWTI-7
95SPML-88
95UppDecML-42
96BesAutSA-5
96Exc-1
96Fin-S223
96FinRef-S223
96FleUpdTC-U33
96LeaSig-124
96LeaSigPPG-124
96LeaSigPPP-124
96Ult-345
96UltGolM-345
97DonEli-126
97DonEliGS-126
97DonRatR-5
97Fle-94
97FleTif-94
94FreKeyC-1
97Lea-29
97LeaFraM-29
97LeaFraMDC-29
97Pac-84
97PacLigB-84
97PacSil-84
97Pin-63
97PinArtP-63
97PinIns-9
97PinInsCE-9
97PinInsDE-9
97PinMusC-63
97Sco-166
97ScoPreS-166
97ScoShoS-166
97ScoShoSAP-166
97Top-309
97UppDec-74
95UppDecMLFS-42
Bartell, Dick (Richard)
29ExhFou-13
31Exh-12
32OrbPinNP-15
32OrbPinUP-4
32R33So2-424
33DouDisP-4
33ExhFou-6
33GeoCMil-4
33Gou-28
33GouCanV-28
33NatLeaAC-3
33RitCE-4S
33TatOrb-4
33TatOrbSDR-158
34DiaMatCSB-5
34BatR31-4
34ButPreR-2
34DiaStaR-15A
34DiaStaR-15B
34DiaStaR-101
34ExhFou-6
35DiaMatCS3T1-4
35GouPreR-6
35GouPuzR-4A
35GouPuzR-7A
35GouPuzR-12A
36GouWidPPR-A3
36GouWidPPR-A4
36WorWidGV-37
38GouHeaU-248
38GouHeaU-272
39CubTeal-1
41DouPlaR-55
47PM1StaP1-7
55Bow-234
77GalGloG-212
88ConSer4-3
92ConTSN-452
93ConTSN-684
94ConTSN-1243
94ConTSNB-1243

Bartell, Mike
75CliPilT-26
Bartels, Bill
85AncGlaPTI-2
87VerBeaDP-26
88LynRedSS-1
Bartels, Todd
96ForWayWB-3
Barthelson, Bob (Robert E.)
47SunBre-2
Barthol, Blake
96SalAvaB-3
Bartholow, Bud
83ReaPhiT-1
Bartilinski, Al
75WatRoyT-2
Bartirome, Tony (Anthony J.)
52Top-332
53Top-71
58JetPos-3
83TopRep5-332
91TopArc1-71
Bartlett, Bob
40WheM4-9
75TidTidTI-2
Bartley, Bill (William J.)
09ColChiE-20
12ColRedB-20
12ColTinT-20
Bartley, Boyd Owen
90DodTar-898
Bartley, Greg
84ChaLooT-29
86CalCanP-1
87ChaLooB-3
Bartolomucci, Tony
86AppFoxP-1
Barton, Bob (Robert Wilbur)
66Top-511
67CokCapG-10
67Top-462
68Top-351
68TopVen-351
69OPC-41
69Top-41
70OPC-352
70Top-352
71MLBOffS-218
71OPC-589
71Top-589
72MilBra-27
72OPC-39
72OPC-40
72PadTeal-3
72Top-39
72Top-40
73OPC-626
73Top-626
74PadDea-2
77PadSchC-5
Barton, Harry Lamb
11SpoLifCW-19
Barton, Jeff
89SpoIndSP-21
90ChaRaiB-3
90ChaRaiP-2051
Barton, Ken
76CedRapGT-5
77CedRapGT-10
81ChaChaT-10
Barton, Larry
40SolHug-3
47SigOil-22
Barton, Paul
91St.CatBJC-18
91St.CatBJP-3386
Barton, Scott
92HunCubC-11
92HunCubF-3150
Barton, Shawn
86ReaPhiP-2
86SanJosBP-2
87MaiGuiP-6
87MaiGuiT-1
87PhiTas-xx
87SanJosBP-29
88JacMetGS-19
89CalLeaA-42
89RenSilSCLC-260
89TidTidC-8
89TidTidP-1969
90CMC-352
90ProAAAF-265
90RenSilSCLC-272
90TidTidC-1
90TidTidP-534
90TopTVM-35
91JacSunLD-327
91JacSunP-141
91LinDriAA-327
92CalCanS-53
93CalCanF-1156
93Don-53
93Pin-250
93Top-569
93TopGol-569
93TopInaM-569
93TopMic-569
95PhoFirTI-18
96Pac-199
96PhoFirB-7
Bartorillo, John
91BriBanF-1
Barun, Barton
82RedPioT-24
Barwick, Lyall
92BoiHawC-9
92BoiHawF-3641
93BoiHawC-2
93BoiHawF-3926
94CedRapKC-3
94CedRapKF-1111
Barylak, Alex
94WilCubC-2
94WilCubF-3754
Baseball, Seymore
78RicBraT-20
79RicBraT-8
Basey, Marsalis
93AubAstC-2
93AubAstF-3449
Basgall, Matt
85CloHSS-3
Basgall, Monty (Romanus)
49EurSta-152
52Top-12
73OPC-569
73Top-569
74OPC-144
74Top-144
81DodPol-NNO
83DodPol-NNO
83TopRep5-12
84DodPol-NNO
85DodCokP-4
86DodCokP-3
86DodPol-NNO
Basham, Gene
96HudValRB-27
Basinski, Eddie (Edward F.)
47TipTop-136
52MotCoo-6
53MotCoo-32
83TCMPla1945-29
90DodTar-899
Bass, Barry
83BurRanF-9
83BurRanT-1
84TulDriTI-22
85TulDriTI-26
87ElPasDP-27
88ElPasDB-17
Bass, Bart
77CedRapGT-16
Bass, Earl
76TulOilGP-25
76VenLeaS-126
78ArkTraT-2
Bass, Ed
85Ft.MyeRT-1
Bass, Jayson
93BriTigC-3
93BriTigF-3658
94JamJamC-4
94JamJamF-3977
95DanBraTI-3
95FayGenTI-3
96DanBraB-4
96FayGenB-5
Bass, Jerry
78CliDodT-2
79LodDodT-16
82BirBarT-18
Bass, John E.
75WatRoyT-3
Bass, Kevin
77NewCoPT-1
78BurBeeT-4
79HolMilT-5
79Top-708
80HolMilT-13
81VanCanT-24
82BrePol-26
82VanCanT-4
84Don-450
84Fle-221
84Nes792-538
84Top-538
84TopTif-538
85AstHouP-12
85AstMot-22
85Don-136
85Fle-345
85FleStaS-52
85Top-326
85TopTif-326
86AstMilL-3
86AstPol-4
86AstTeal-2
86Don-548
86DonHig-21
86Fle-294
86OPC-52
86Top-458
86TopSti-28
86TopTif-458
87AstMot-9
87AstPol-22
87ClaGam-17
87Don-410
87DonAll-40
87DonOpeD-14
87Dra-17
87Fle-51
87FleGlo-51
87FleHotS-3
87FleMin-5
87FleSlu-1
87FleStiC-6
87GenMilB-6A
87Lea-211
87OPC-85
87Spo-117
87Spo-175
87SpoTeaP-8
87Top-85
87TopGloS-34
87TopMinL-7
87TopSti-34
87TopTif-85
88AstMot-9
88AstPol-6
88Don-286
88DonBasB-38
88Fle-440
88FleExcS-2
88FleGlo-440
88FleMin-77
88FleStiC-85
88Lea-137
88OPC-175
88PanSti-298
88Sco-33
88ScoGlo-33
88Spo-55
88StaLinAst-4
88Top-175
88Top-291
88TopBig-77
88TopSti-29
88TopTif-175
88TopTif-291
89AstLenH-5
89AstMot-8
89AstSmo-4
89Don-325
89Fle-351
89FleGlo-351
89OPC-102
89PanSti-91
89Sco-226
89Spo-11
89Top-646
89TopAme2C-2
89TopBasT-98
89TopBig-187
89TopSti-14
89TopTif-646
89UppDec-425
90Bow-240
90BowTif-240
90Don-589
90DonBesN-36
90DonGraS-10
90Fle-223
90FleCan-223
90FleUpd-60
90GiaMot-24
90Lea-305
90MLBBasB-45
90OPC-281
90PanSti-261
90PubSti-87
90Sco-279
90Sco100S-100
90ScoRoo-2T
90Spo-198
90Top-281
90TopBig-236
90TopSti-17
90TopTif-281
90TopTra-7T
90TopTraT-7T
90UppDec-302
90UppDec-793
90VenSti-31
91Bow-625
91Don-630
91Fle-253
91GiaMot-24
91GiaPacGaE-10
91GiaSFE-1
91Lea-365
91OPC-752
91Sco-616
91SimandSMLBL-3
91StaClu-29
91Top-752
91TopDesS-752
91TopMic-752
91TopTif-752
91Ult-315
91UppDec-287
92Don-373
92Fle-626
92GiaMot-24
92GiaPacGaE-3
92Lea-76
92OPC-513
92PanSti-216
92Pin-53
92Sco-139
92ScoRoo-76T
92StaClu-6
92Stu-111
92Top-513
92TopGol-513
92TopGolW-513
92TopMic-513
92Ult-284
92UppDec-107
93AstMot-16
93Don-745
93Fle-466
93FleFinE-76
93Sco-578
93StaCluAs-18
93Top-672
93TopGol-672
93TopInaM-672
93TopMic-672
93UppDec-679
93UppDecGold-679
94AstMot-21
94BreMilB-8
94ColC-521
94ColChoGS-521
94ColChoSS-521
94Fle-484
94Pac-258
94Sco-128
94ScoGolR-128
94StaClu-590
94StaCluFDI-590
94StaCluGR-590
94StaCluMOP-590
94Top-362
94TopGol-362
94TopSpa-362
95Don-411
95DonPreP-411
95Fle-452
95Pac-181
95Sco-372
95ScoGolR-372
95ScoPlaTS-372
Bass, Norm
61AthJayP-2
62Top-122
62TopVen-122
63AthJayP-2
63Top-461
Bass, Randy William
75TacTwiK-7
76TacTwiDQ-2
77TacTwiDQ-23
79Top-707
82Don-439
82Fle-566
82Top-307
87JapPlaB-7
89TopSenL-50
90EliSenL-49
93RanKee-65
Bass, Regan
86DayBeaIP-2
Basse, Mike
91HelBreSP-25
92CalLeaACL-18
92StoPorF-46
93ElPasDF-2961
94NewOrlZF-1479
Bassett, Charley (Charles E.)
87BucN28-37
87OldJudN-23
88WG1CarG-28
Bassett, Matt
84OmaRoyT-29
85OmaRoyT-2
Bassett, Pepper
86NegLeaF-103
Bassler, Johnny (John Landis)
14B18B-1A
14B18B-1B
20WalMaiW-4
21Exh-9
22E120-46
22W572-6
22W573-9
22W575-7
23MapCriV-10
23WilChoV-9
25Exh-89
26Exh-89
27AmeCarE-55
27Exh-45
92ConTSN-414
93ConTSN-878
Basso, Mike (Michael A.)
86SpoIndC-167
87ChaRaiP-20
88BlaYNPRWL-179
88TexLeaAGS-23
88WicPilRD-16
89WicChaR-10
89WicStaR-9
89WicWraR-16
90CMC-514
90LasVegSC-11
90LasVegSP-126
90ProAAAF-14
91LinDriAA-601
91WicWraLD-601
91WicWraP-2601
91WicWraRD-11
92LasVegSF-2798
93LasVegSF-947
94RanCucQC-5
94RanCucQF-1652
95IdaFalBTI-35
96RanCucQB-2
Bast, Steve (Steven)
86ElmPioRSP-2
87NewBriRSP-11
89NewBriRSP-608
89PawRedSTI-2
90CMC-260
90PawRedSC-9
90PawRedSDD-1
90PawRedSP-452
90ProAAAF-424
90TopTVRS-36
Bastable, John M.
76OklCit8TI-24

76VenLeaS-84
Bastian, Charlie (Charles J.)
87BucN28-75
87OldJudN-24
87OldJudN-25
88WG1CarG-47
90KalBatN-2
Bastian, Jack (John K.)
09T206-476
Bastian, Jose
75WesPalBES-6
79RocRedWT-17
81TolMudHT-3
Bastian, Robert
81RedPioT-1
83NasAngT-1
85EdmTraC-21
86EdmTraP-1
Bastien, Bazz (Aldege)
43ParSpo-2
Baston, Stanley
96MedHatBJTI-4
Batch, Emil Henry
09T206-397
11SpoLifCW-20
11T205-198
12ImpTobC-48
Batchelor, Rich (Richard Anthony)
91Cla/Bes-54
91FloStaLAP-FSL11
91Ft.LauYC-1
91Ft.LauYP-2416
92AlbYanF-2217
92AlbYanS-3
92ProFS7-119
92SkyAA F-1
93AlbYanF-2153
94CarPol-3
94Don-649
94Fin-269
94FinRef-269
94LouRedF-2972
94StaClu-344
94StaCluFDI-344
94StaCluGR-344
94StaCluMOP-344
94StaCluT-327
94StaCluTFDI-327
94Top-788
94TopGol-788
94TopSpa-788
94Ult-265
95LouRedF-268
96LouRedB-9
Bateman, John Alvin
69ExpPin-1
63Col45"P-2
63Top-386
64Top-142
64TopCoi-107
64TopVen-142
65AstBigLBPP-3
65Top-433
66OPC-86
66Top-86
66TopVen-86
67Ast-3
67AstTeal1-2
67AstTeal2-3
67CokCapAs-9
67DexPre-18
67Top-231
68CokCapA-9
68DexPre-9
68Top-592
69ExpFudP-2
69MilBra-21
69MLBOffS-155
69OPC-138
69Top-138
69TopFou-23
69TopSta-53
69TopTeaP-10
70ExpPin-3
70ExpPos-14
70MLBOffS-61
70OPC-417
70Top-417
71ExpPS-2
71MLBOffS-122
71OPC-31
71OPC-628
71Top-628
71TopCoi-19
72MilBra-28
72OPC-5
72Top-5
86ExpGreT-8
87AstSer1-2
87AstShowSTh-2
87AstShowSTh-27
Bates, Benny
36WorWidGV-126
Bates, Billy
86ElPasDP-4
87DenZepP-7
88DenZepC-17
88DenZepP-1271
89BlaYNPRWL-89
89DenZepC-15
89DenZepP-38
89TriAAP-AAA41
90BrePol-34
90El PasDAGTI-1
90IdaFalBP-3265
90Sco-608A
90Sco-608B
90Sco100RS-80
90TopDeb89-9
91LinDriAAA-251
91NasSouLD-251
92IowCubF-4056
92TexLon-4
94BreMilB-101
Bates, Buddy (Hubert Edgar)
36GouWidPPR-D1
Bates, Dick (Richard)
69PilPos-22
83Pil69G-12
Bates, Eric
89BilMusP-2061
Bates, Fletcher
95PitMetTI-39
96Bow-359
Bates, Jason
92AriWilP-1
92BenRocC-6
92BenRocF-1478
93Bow-176
93ClaFS7-168
93ColSprSSF-3090
93ExcFS7-32
93Top-579
93TopGol-579
93TopInaM-579
93TopMic-579
94ColSprSSF-738
94ExcFS7-183
94Top-780
94TopGol-780
94TopSpa-780
94UppDecML-181
95Bow-76
95BowBes-R78
95BowBesR-R78
95ColCho-578T
95DonTopotO-224
95Emo-122
95EmoRoo-2
95Fin-288
95FinRef-288
95Fla-343
95FlaWavotF-1
95FleAllR-M2
95RocPol-1
95SigRooOJ-5
95SigRooOJP-5
95SigRooOJPS-5
95SigRooOJS-5
95SP-47
95SPCha-18
95SPChaDC-18
95SPSil-47
95StaClu-529
95StaCluCB-CB7
95StaCluMOP-529
95StaCluMOP-CB7
95StaCluSTWS-529
95TopTra-67T
95TopTra-100T
95UltGolMR-M3
95UppDec-240
95UppDecED-240
95UppDecEDG-240
95UppDecSE-239
95UppDecSEG-239
95Zen-127
96ColCho-129
96ColChoGS-129
96ColChoSS-129
96Don-2
96DonPreP-2
96EmoXL-171
96Fla-242
96Fle-359
96FleRoc-1
96FleTif-359
96LeaSigA-16
96LeaSigAG-16
96LeaSigAS-16
96Pac-59
96Pin-16
96RocPol-2
96Sco-422
96Top-336
96Ult-185
96UltGolM-185
96UppDec-326
97Pac-278
97PacLigB-278
97PacSil-278
97Sco-427
97ScoHobR-427
97ScoResC-427
97ScoShoS-427
97ScoShoSAP-427
Bates, Johnny (John William)
09ColChiE-21A
09ColChiE-21B
09RamT20-8
09T206-15
10DomDisP-8
10LuxCigPP-3
10NadE1-6
10SweCapPP-94
10W555-3
11E94-2
11PloCanE-5
11S74Sil-97
11SpoLifCW-21
11SpoLifM-224
11T205-10
12ColRedB-21A
12ColRedB-21B
12ColTinT-21A
12ColTinT-21B
12HasTriFT-56
Bates, Kevin
84ShrCapFB-1
Bates, Steve
86AncGlaPTI-1
88ClePhiS-1
Bates, Tommy
91WatIndC-17
91WatIndP-3372
92KinIndC-7
92KinIndF-2480
Batesole, Michael
86BakDodP-2
87VerBeaDP-15
88VerBeaDS-1
Bathe, Bill
82WesHavAT-10
83TacTigT-10
84TacTigC-80
85TacTigC-148
86A'sMot-23
86DonRoo-41
86FleUpd-9
87Don-281
88IowCubC-23
88IowCubP-527
88TriAAAP-16
88TriAAC-1
89PhoFirC-11
89PhoFirP-1495
90Bow-234
90BowTif-234
90Don-680
90GiaMot-22
90UppDec-478A
91OPC-679
91Top-679
91TopDesS-679
91TopMic-679
91TopTif-679
Bathe, Bob
84AlbA'sT-23
85TacTigC-143
86IowCubP-2
Batina, John
87BriYouC-11
Batista, Dario
94BelMarC-4
94BelMarF-3248
Batista, Decartes (Miguel Jerez)
93Bow-564
Batista, Francisco
82SprCarF-24
83ArkTraT-20
83St.PetCT-20
90SprCarDGB-5
Batista, Juan
93JamExpC-3
93JamExpF-3332
94BurBeeC-2
94BurBeeF-1086
Batista, Miguel
86ChaRaiP-2A
86ChaRaiP-2B
88BenBucL-17
92WesPalBEC-9
92WesPalBEF-2078
93HarSenF-260
93LimRocDWB-8
93LimRocDWB-140
94HarSenF-2082
95ChaKniTI-6
96ChaKniB-8
97Pac-296
97PacLigB-296
97PacSil-296
Batista, Tony
94ModA'sC-4
94ModA'sF-3067
95Exc-107
95HunStaTI-4
96Fla-141
96FlaWavotF-3
96FleUpd-U70
96FleUpdNH-3
96FleUpdTC-U70
96Ult-396
96UltGolM-396
96UltGolP-3
96UltGolPHGM-3
97BowBes-136
97BowBesAR-136
97BowBesR-136
97Cir-95
97CirRav-95
97ColCho-411
97Fle-183
97FleTif-183
97MetUni-126
97Pac-164
97PacLigB-164
97PacPri-56
97PacPriLB-56
97PacPriP-56
97PacSil-164
97StaClu-344
97StaCluMOP-344
97Top-344
97Ult-108
97UltGolME-108
97UltPlaME-108
97UppDec-447
Batiste, Chris
89BluOriS-3
Batiste, Darnell
93BurIndC-3
93BurIndF-3304
94BurIndC-2
94BurIndF-3800
Batiste, Kevin
87DunBluJP-941
88KnoBluJB-7
89KnoBluJB-2
89KnoBluJP-1124
89KnoBluJS-7
90GreBraB-18
90GreBraP-1140
90GreBraS-2
90TopDeb89-10
90UppDec-115
Batiste, Kim
87UtiBluSP-4
88SpaPhiP-1035
88SpaPhiS-18
89ClePhiS-2
90Bes-227
90CMC-803
90EasLeaAP-EL20
90ReaPhiB-15
90ReaPhiP-1225
90ReaPhiS-5
90StaFS7-81
91Bow-488
91LinDriAAA-480
91ScrRedBLD-480
91ScrRedBP-2543
92Bow-44
92Cla1-T10
92ClaGam-191
92Don-402
92Fle-522
92Lea-421
92OPC-514
92PhiMed-5
92Pin-266
92PinRoo-18
92PinRooI-9
92PinTea2-69
92ProFS7-293
92Sco-833
92ScoImpP-86
92ScoRoo-37
92StaClu-788
92StaCluECN-788
92Stu-71
92Top-514
92TopDeb91-11
92TopGol-514
92TopGolW-514
92TopMic-514
92Ult-542
92UppDec-422
92UppDecSR-SR3
93Don-148
93Fle-485
93PacSpa-230
93PhiMed-5
93Pin-390
93Sco-191
93Top-679
93TopGol-679
93TopInaM-679
93TopMic-679
93Ult-436
93UppDec-516
93UppDecGold-516
94ColC-48
94ColChoGS-48
94ColChoSS-48
94Don-470
94Fle-583
94Pac-469
94PhiMed-2
94PhiMel-2
94PhiUSPC-3H
94PhiUSPC-11S
94Pin-207
94PinArtP-207
94PinMusC-207
94Sco-540
94ScoGolR-540
94StaClu-303
94StaCluFDI-303
94StaCluGR-303
94StaCluMOP-303
94StaCluT-212
94StaCluTFDI-212
94Top-238
94TopGol-238
94TopSpa-238
94Ult-242
95BowBayTI-13
95Pac-325
95Sco-183
95ScoGolR-183
95ScoPlaTS-183
95Top-173
96GiaMot-26
97Pac-436
97PacLigB-436
97PacSil-436
Batiste, Terrance
88NebCor-10
Battell, Mark
88HamRedP-1725
89HamRedS-2
Batten, Mark
80SanJosMJitB-3
81WauTimT-8

Battey, Earl Jesse
47Exh-14
55DonWin-12
57Top-401
58Top-364
59Top-114
59TopVen-114
60Lea-66
60Top-328
60WhiSoxTS-2
61Baz-28
61Pos-97A
61Pos-97B
61Top-315
61Top-582
61TopDicG-1
61TopStal-177
61TwiCloD-3
61TwiJayP-2
61TwiPetM-22
61TwiUniMC-2
62Baz-4
62Jel-90
62Pos-90
62PosCan-90
62SalPlaC-19
62ShiPlaC-19
62Top-371
62TopBuc-7
62TopStal-74
63BasMagM-10
63ExhStaB-6
63Jel-8
63Pos-8
63SalMetC-44
63Top-306
63Top-410
63TwiJayP-3
64Top-90
64TopCoi-101
64TopCoi-136
64TopSta-71
64TopStaU-9
64TopVen-90
64TwiJayP-2
64WheSta-6
65Top-490
65TopEmbl-70
66Top-240
66TopRubl-8
66TopVen-240
66TwiFaiG-3
67CokCapTw-3
67DexPre-19
67OPC-15
67Top-15
67TopVen-222
78TCM60I-113
78TwiFri-2
86TwiGreT-8
88PacLegI-35
94TedWil-46
Battle, Allen
92ClaFS7-269
92MidLeaATI-3
92SprCarC-6
92SprCarF-880
93ArkTraF-2822
93ClaGolF-182
94LouRedF-2992
94TriAAF-AAA35
95ActPacF-50
95Bow-45
95Exc-261
95ExcLeaL-3
95FleUpd-153
95LouRedF-286
95SigRoo-7
95SigRooSig-7
95Sum-156
95SumNthD-156
95UppDec-304
95UppDecED-304
95UppDecEDG-304
95UppDecML-123
96ColCho-283
96ColChoGS-283
96ColChoSS-283
96Don-22
96DonPreP-22
96EmoXL-100
96Fla-142
96Fle-537
96FleTif-537
96FleUpd-U71
96FleUpdTC-U71
96LeaSigA-17
96LeaSigAG-17
96LeaSigAS-17
96Sco-443
96Ult-397
96UltGolM-397
97PacPriGotD-GD78
95UppDecMLFS-123
Battle, Howard
90MedHatBJB-26
91Cla/Bes-29
91MyrBeaHC-16
91MyrBeaHP-2950
91SouAtlLAGP-SAL36
92Bow-183
92ClaFS7-88
92DunBluJC-5
92DunBluJF-2005
92ProFS7-172
92UppDecML-27
92UppDecML-280
93Bow-195
93ClaFS7-43
93ClaGolF-85
93ExcFS7-238
93KnoSmoF-1256
93LinVenB-119
94Cla-107
94ClaCreotC-C6
94ClaGolF-108
94ExcFS7-138
94SyrChiF-976
94SyrChiTI-3
94TedWil-118
94TedWilDGC-DG5
94UppDecML-144
94VenLinU-105
95Exc-133
95LinVen-170
95SyrChiTI-2
95UppDecML-124
96Fle-491
96FleTif-491
96PhiTeal-1
96Pin-181
96Sco-510
96ScrRedBB-5
96Spo-135
96SpoArtP-135
95UppDecMLFS-124
Battles, Jeff
93JohCitCC-2
93JohCitCF-3668
94SavCarC-5
94SavCarF-498
Batton, Chris
76TusTorCr-10
76VenLeaS-156
77ColCliT-2
77Top-475
Batts, Matt (Matthew Daniel)
47Exh-15
48RedSoxTI-1
49Lea-108
51Bow-129
52Bow-216
52Top-230
53BowBW-22
53TigGle-1
54Bow-183
54Top-88
55Bow-161
76BatRouCT-3
79DiaGre-243
83TopRep5-230
94TopArc1-88
94TopArc1G-88
Batts, Rodney
96BatCliTI-17
Bauer, Alice
52Whe-1A
52Whe-1B
Bauer, Bobby
43ParSpo-3
Bauer, Charles
95HudValRTI-17
Bauer, Chuck
96ChaRivTI-9606
Bauer, Dave
89PenPilS-1
Bauer, Eric
85SpoIndC-1
87WicPilRD-22
88WicPilRD-33
Bauer, Hank (Henry Albert)
47Exh-16A
47Exh-16B
47StaPinP2-3
50Bow-219
51BerRos-A4
51Bow-183
51TopRedB-24
52BerRos-2
52Bow-65
52CokTip-1
52TipTop-1
52Top-215
53BowC-44
53BowC-84
53Bri-29
53Dor-104
53RedMan-AL2
53StaMey-1
54Bow-129
54DanDee-2
54NewYorJA-40
54RedMan-AL23
54StaMey-1
54Top-130
55Bow-246
55RedMan-AL22
55StaMey-1
55Top-166
56Top-177
57Top-240
57YanJayP-1
58Top-9
58YanJayP-1
59HayComBP-1
59Top-240
60A's-1
60A'sJayP-1
60A'sTeal-1
60RawGloT-4
60Top-262
61AthJayP-3
61Pos-90A
61Pos-90B
61Top-119
61Top-398
61TopStal-156
62Top-127
62Top-463
62TopVen-127
64OriJayP-3
64Top-178
64TopVen-178
65Top-323
66Top-229
66TopVen-229
67OPC-1
67Top-1
67Top-534
68LauWorS-55
68Top-513
69A'sJacitB-2
69OPC-124
69Top-124
69TopFou-13
71FleWorS-56
79TCM50-22
81Ori6F-5
83FraBroR-21
83FraBroR-24
83TopRep5-215
83YanASFY-3
84FifNatCT-1
86OriGreT-2
89PacLegI-144
89SweBasG-82
91TopArc1-290
92UppDecS-16
92YanWIZA-2
93UppDecAH-6
94TopArc1-130
94TopArc1G-130
94UppDecAH-93
94UppDecAH1-93
97TopMan-21
97TopManF-21
97TopManFR-21
Bauer, Mark
84ModA'sC-2
85HunStaJ-26
85ModA'sC-19
Bauer, Marlene
52Whe-2A
52Whe-2B
Bauer, Matt
91BriTigC-21
91BriTigP-3595
92LakTigC-15
92NiaFalRF-3315
93FayGenC-2
93FayGenF-120
94TreThuF-2112
Bauer, Pete (Peter)
86LitFalMP-2
87LynMetP-14
88ColMetGS-2
89JacMetGS-23
90OscAstS-3
91JacGenLD-554
91JacGenP-917
91LinDriAA-554
Bauer, Phil
76CliPilT-1
78AppFoxT-3
79AppFoxT-14
Bauer, Ray
57SeaPop-4
Bauer, Theo
87AllandGN-32
88AllandGN-30
Bauers, Russell
40PlaBal-219
52Par-4
Baugh, Darren
96HicCraB-2
Baugh, Gavin
93LetMouF-4155
93LetMouSP-7
93Top-641
93TopGol-641
93TopInaM-641
93TopMic-641
94KanCouCC-4
94KanCouCF-168
94KanCouCTI-4
95BreCouMF-252
Baugh, Sam
38DixLid-1
38DixLidP-1
Baughman, Justin
95BoiHawTI-3
96CedRapKTI-3
Bauldree, Joe
96DanBraB-5
Baum, Jeff
88AppFoxP-158
Bauman, Brad
81ShrCapT-10
Baumann, David
90GreFalDSP-13
91VerBeaDC-2
91VerBeaDP-763
91YakBeaC-21
Baumann, Frank
58Top-167
59Top-161
59TopVen-161
60Top-306
60WhiSoxTS-3
61Pos-34
61Top-46
61Top-550
61WhiSoxTS-2
62Top-161
62TopVen-161
62WhiSoxJP-2
62WhiSoxTS-2
63Top-381
63WhiSoxTS-1
64Top-453
64WhiSoxTS-2
65OPC-161
65Top-161
Baumann, Matt
93EveGiaC-4
93EveGiaF-3759
Baumann, Paddy (Charles John)
12T207-9
14B18B-11A
14B18B-11B
14B18B-11C
Baumer, Jim (James Sloan)
58JetPos-4
61RedJayP-2
61Top-292
Baumgardner, George
14CraJacE-131
14FatPlaT-5
15CraJacE-131
Baumgarner, Jeff
91HagSunLD-226
92HagSunF-2549
Baumgarten, Ross
78AppFoxT-4
79Top-704
80Top-138
81Don-41
81OPC-328
81Top-398
82Don-104
82Fle-337
82OPC-322
82Top-563
82TopTra-3T
83Fle-302
83Top-97
Baumgartner, Stan
81ConTSN-8
94ConTSN-1317
94ConTSNB-1317
Baumholtz, Frank C.
47Exh-17
49Bow-21
51R42SmaS-3
52Bow-195
52Top-225
54Bow-221
54RedHeaF-2
54Top-60
55Bow-227
55Top-172
56Top-274
76BooProC-2
83TopRep5-225
94TopArc1-60
94TopArc1G-60
Baur, Al
89MarPhiS-1
90BatCliP-3056
Bauta, Ed
61UniOil-P1
62Top-344
63Top-336
76Met63 S-1
91MetWIZ-25
Bautista, Antonio
76ForLauYS-12
77WesHavYT-2
Bautista, Benny
85NewOriT-12
87HagSunP-6
Bautista, Danny (Daniel)
90BriTigP-3154
91FayGenC-23
91FayGenP-1182
92FayGenC-13
92FayGenF-2179
93Bow-95
93ClaFS7-167
93LimRocDWB-6
93LonTigF-2319
94Bow-97
94BowBes-B16
94BowBesR-B16
94ColC-557
94ColChoGS-557
94ColChoSS-557
94Don-442
94Fin-435
94FinJum-435
94FinRef-435
94Fla-291
94FleMajLP-5
94FleUpd-39
94LeaGolR-7
94LeaLimR-12
94Pac-211
94Pin-234
94PinArtP-234
94PinMusC-234
94PinNewG-NG24
94Sco-559
94ScoBoyoS-51
94ScoGolR-559
94ScoRoo-RT84
94ScoRooGR-RT84
94Sel-186

94SpoRoo-124
94SpoRooAP-124
94StaClu-155
94StaCluFDI-155
94StaCluGR-155
94StaCluMOP-155
94Top-768
94TopGol-768
94TopSpa-768
95ColCho-466
95ColChoGS-466
95ColChoSS-466
95Don-249
95DonPreP-249
95DonTopotO-70
95Fle-44
95Lea-248
95PacPri-47
95Pin-15
95PinArtP-15
95PinMusC-15
95Sco-496
95ScoGolR-496
95ScoPlaTS-496
95Sel-31
95SelArtP-31
95StaClu-78
95StaCluFDI-78
95StaCluMOP-78
95StaCluSTWS-78
95StaCluVR-48
95Top-557
95TopCyb-242
95Ult-44
95UltGolM-44
96Don-465
96DonPreP-465
96Fle-105
96FleTif-105
96Pac-308
96Sco-390
95StaCluVRMC-48

Bautista, Ed
93SanJosGC-30

Bautista, German
86MiaMarP-1

Bautista, Hector
90WauTimB-25
90WauTimP-2139
90WauTimS-2

Bautista, J.J.
90CMC-321
90RocRedWC-20

Bautista, Jose
85LynMetT-9
87JacMetF-3
87MetColP-24
88DonRoo-41
88FleUpd-1
88FleUpdG-1
88OriFreB-48
88TopTra-10T
88TopTraT-10T
89Bow-3
89BowTif-3
89Don-451
89Fle-608
89FleGlo-608
89OriFreB-48
89Sco-573
89Top-469
89TopSti-229
89TopTif-469
89UppDec-574
90ProAAAF-453
90PubSti-574
90RocRedWGC-28
90RocRedWP-696
90UppDec-8
90VenSti-32
91OriCro-23
92Fle-2
92OmaRoyF-2953
92OmaRoyS-326
93CubMar-2
93FleFinE-6
93LimRocDWB-99
93PacSpa-376
93StaCluCu-30
94ColC-623
94ColChoGS-623
94ColChoSS-623
94Don-458
94Fin-175
94FinRef-175
94Fle-379
94Lea-88
94Pac-94
94Pin-445
94PinArtP-445
94PinMusC-445
94Sco-249
94ScoGolR-249
94StaClu-421
94StaCluFDI-421
94StaCluGR-421
94StaCluMOP-421
94StaCluT-340
94StaCluTFDI-340
94Top-92
94TopGol-92
94TopSpa-92
94Ult-159
94UppDec-108
94UppDecED-108
95Don-243
95DonPreP-243
95Fle-409
95GiaMot-26
95Pac-67
95Top-42
96Pac-204
96PhoFirB-8
97Pac-437
97PacLigB-437
97PacSil-437

Bautista, Juan
93AlbPolC-3
93AlbPolF-2030
93JohCitCC-3
93JohCitCF-3603
94JohCitCC-3
94JohCitCF-3715
94OriPro-7
95PeoChiTI-28
96BowBayB-5

Bautista, Ramon
80CliGiaT-4
82CliGiaF-13
83CliGiaF-8
88WatIndP-676
89KinIndS-2
90KinIndTI-16
91CanIndLD-76
91CanIndP-983
91LinDriAA-76

Bavasi, Buzzie
77PadSchC-6

Baxes, Jim
49W72HolS-1
59Top-547
60Top-318
90DodTar-38

Baxes, Mike (Michael)
58Top-302
59Top-381

Baxter, Bob
90JamExpP-14
91RocExpC-1
91RocExpP-2037
92WesPalBEC-16
92WesPalBEF-2079
94HarSenF-2083

Baxter, Herb
93YakBeaC-2
93YakBeaF-3873
94VerBeaDC-4
94VerBeaDF-61
95ModA'sTI-2

Baxter, Jim
88WatIndP-671
89LakTigS-2
91LinDriAA-402
91MemChiLD-402
91MemChiP-657

Baxter, William
12ImpTobC-80

Bay, Harry Elbert
03BreE10-10
04FanCraAL-3
05IndSouPSoCP-1
08AmeLeaPC-1
09T206-477
10CouT21-1
11SpoLifCW-22

Bayas, Subby (Richard Thomas)
87NegLeaPD-16

Bayer, Chris
86ColMetP-5
88St.LucMS-2

Bayless, Dick (Harry Owen)
09ColChiE-22
12ColRedB-22
12ColTinT-22

Baylor, Don Edward
71OPC-709
71Top-709
72OPC-474
72Top-474
73OPC-384
73OriJohP-25
73Top-384
74OPC-187
74Top-187
74TopSta-121
75OPC-382
75Top-382
76Hos-118
76OPC-125
76SSP-394
76Top-125
77A'sPos-81
77Hos-129
77OPC-133
77Top-462
78AngFamF-3
78OPC-173
78SSP270-208
78Top-48
79Hos-63
79OPC-335
79Top-635
80BurKinPHR-12
80Kel-56
80OPC-150
80Top-203
80Top-285
80TopSup-9
81AllGamPI-47
81Don-413
81Fle-271
81FleStiC-122
81Kel-15
81LonBeaPT-5
81OPC-309
81Top-580
81TopSti-51
81TopSupHT-55
82Don-493
82Fle-451
82FleSta-220
82K-M-35
82OPC-234
82Top-415
82TopSti-158
83Don-493
83Dra-1
83Fle-77
83FleSta-10
83FleSti-33
83Kel-29
83OPC-105
83Top-105
83TopFol-5
83TopSti-40
83TopTra-8T
84AllGamPI-138
84Don-152
84Dra-1
84Fle-119
84FleSti-45
84FunFooP-39
84Nes792-335
84Nes792-486
84OPC-335
84Top-335
84Top-486
84TopRubD-2
84TopSti-320
84TopTif-335
84TopTif-486
85AllGamPI-49
85AngStrH-2
85Don-173
85DonHig-35
85Dra-3
85Fle-121
85FleStaS-49
85Lea-146
85OPC-70
85Top-70
85TopRubD-2
85TopSti-311
85TopTif-70
86BasStaB-6
86Don-347
86Fle-99
86Fle-631
86FleStiC-3
86FleUpd-10
86OPC-184
86Spo-57
86Top-765
86TopSti-300
86TopTif-765
86TopTra-6T
86TopTraT-6T
86Woo-2
87BoaandB-17
87ClaGam-14
87Don-339
87DonOpeD-186
87Fle-28
87FleGamW-2
87FleGlo-28
87FleHotS-4
87FleMin-6
87FleStiC-7
87KayB-3
87Lea-232
87OPC-230
87OPCBoxB-A
87RedSoxSAP-2
87SevCoi-E2
87Spo-163
87SpoTeaP-9
87StuPan-15
87Top-230
87TopGloS-27
87TopSti-252
87TopTif-230
87TopWaxBC-A
88A'sMot-8
88DonTeaBA-NEW
88Fle-2
88FleGlo-2
88FleGlo-WS11
88FleStiWBC-S1
88FleWorS-11
88OPCBoxB-A
88Sco-250
88ScoGlo-250
88ScoRoo-55T
88ScoRooG-55T
88StaLinTw-1
88Top-545
88TopBig-162
88TopSti-10
88TopTif-545
88TopTra-11T
88TopTraT-11T
88TopWaxBC-A
88TwiTeal-12
88Woo-1
88Woo-29
89AngSmo-13
89Fle-1
89FleGlo-1
89Sco-205
89Top-673
89TopAme2C-3
89TopTif-673
89UppDec-601
90BasWit-5
90BreMilB-32
90BrePol-NNO
90PacLeg-6
91BreMilB-32
91BrePol-NNO
91Kel3D-14
91LinDri-14
91OriCro-24
91SweBasG-6
92MDAMVP-13
92MVP-1
92MVP2H-15
92YanWIZ8-9
93TedWil-59
93Top-504
93TopGol-504
93TopInaM-504
93TopMic-504
93UppDecAH-7
94RocPol-1
94UppDecAH-179
94UppDecAH1-179
95RocPol-2
96RocPol-3

Bayne, William
22E120-91

Bazan, Pete
80QuaCitCT-14

Bazydlo, Edward
52LavPro-17

Bazzani, Matt
96SarRedSB-7

Beach, Oarsman
88GooN16-11

Beach, Randy
75TacTwiK-6

Beach, William
87AllandGN-21
88KimN18-1

Beacom, Chris
89St.CatBJP-2085
90DunBluJS-1

Beahan, Scott
83GreHorT-2

Beal, Sally
78NewWayCT-2

Beal, Tony
86NewBriRSP-2

Beale, Charles
96LowSpiB-5

Beall, Bob (Robert Brooks)
76SSP-21
79Top-222
80RicBraT-19
81PorBeaT-7

Beall, Mike
89AppFoxP-864
90BasCitRS-2

Beall, Walter
94ConTSN-1288
94ConTSNB-1288

Beals, Bryan
88GreFalDTI-19
89BakDodCLC-197
90BakDodCLC-257

Beals, Greg
91PitMetC-2
91PitMetP-3425
92ColMetC-7
92ColMetF-298
92ColMetPI-8
93St.LucMC-3
93StLucMF-2923

Beamesderfer, Kurt
86ChaOriW-1
87ChaO'sW-19

Beamon, Charlie (Charles Alon.)
59Top-192
59TopVen-192
60HenHouW-30
75WatRoyT-4
77SanJosMC-9
78SanJosMMC-12
79SpoIndT-6
80SpoIndT-24
80Top-672
81SyrChiT-12
81SyrChiTI-3
82SyrChiT-15
82SyrChiTI-5
91OriCro-25

Beamon, Pepper (Nick)
80WesHavWCT-18A

Beamon, Trey
92ClaDraP-44
92ClaFS7-431
93AugPirC-3
93AugPirF-1557
93Bow-302
93ClaFS7-125
93StaCluM-143
94Bow-518
94BowBes-B64
94BowBesR-B64
94CarMudF-1591
94Cla-11
94ClaGolF-10
94UppDecML-198
95Bes-47
95Bow-272
95BowBes-B75
95BowBesR-B75
95BowGolF-272

95ColCho-36
95ColChoGS-36
95ColChoSS-36
95Exc-250
95ExcAll-6
95PinETA-5
95SigRooOJA-AS1
95SigRooOJAS-AS1
95SPML-6
95SPML-135
95SPMLA-4
95SPMLDtS-DS14
95Top-288
95UppDecML-41
95UppDecMLOP-OP22
96Bow-197
96BowBes-147
96BowBesAR-147
96BowBesR-147
96ColCho-435
96ColChoGS-435
96ColChoSS-435
96LeaSig-140
96LeaSigPPG-140
96LeaSigPPP-140
96Top-439
96UppDec-235
96UppDecFSP-FS3
96UppDecPHE-H52
96UppDecPreH-H52
97Cir-88
97CirRav-88
97Don-376
97DonEli-102
97DonEliGS-102
97DonEliTotC-6
97DonEliTotCDC-6
97DonLim-113
97DonLimLE-113
97DonPreP-376
97DonPrePGold-376
97DonRatR-4
97Fle-424
97FleTif-424
97Lea-172
97LeaFraM-172
97LeaFraMDC-172
97PacPriGotD-GD188
97Pin-200
97PinArtP-200
97PinIns-43
97PinInsCE-43
97PinInsDE-43
97PinMusC-200
97Sco-317
97ScoPreS-317
97ScoShoS-317
97ScoShoSAP-317
97Sel-73
97SelArtP-73
97SelRegG-73
97SelRooR-19
97Stu-159
97StuPrePG-159
97StuPrePS-159
97Top-476
97Ult-259
97UltGolME-259
97UltPlaME-259
97UppDec-457
95UppDecMLFS-41
Beams, Michael
88AshTouP-1054
88AubAstP-1962
89AshTouP-968
90OscAstS-4
91LinDriAA-451
91NewBriRSLD-451
91NewBriRSP-362
92NewBriRSF-444
92NewBriRSS-476
93NewBriRSF-1232
93PawRedSTI-3
Bean, Belve
93ConTSN-974
Bean, Billy
87TolMudHP-26
88TolMudHC-12
88TolMudHP-595
88Top-267
88TopTif-267
89ClaLigB-33
89DodStaSV-7
89ScoHot1R-19
89TolMudHP-772
90AlbDukC-25
90AlbDukP-356
90AlbDukT-1
90CMC-427
90DodTar-39
90ProAAAF-77
91AlbDukLD-1
91AlbDukP-1152
91LinDriAAA-1
91Top-279A
93LasVegSF-949
94Fle-654
94Pac-515
94PadMot-13
94StaClu-669
94StaCluFDI-669
94StaCluGR-669
94StaCluMOP-669
Bean, Kenneth
88MarPhiS-2
89MarPhiS-2
Beanblossom, Brad
88CapCodPPaLP-147
91St.PetCC-17
91St.PetCP-2200
92ArkTraF-1134
92ArkTraS-27
Beane, Billy (William Lamar)
82JacMetT-19
84JacMetT-17
85IntLeaAT-7
85MetTCM-30
85TidTidT-14
86Don-647
86FleUpd-11
86TwiTeal-15
87Fle-535
87FleGlo-535
87PorBeaP-5
87Top-114
87TopTif-114
91MetWIZ-26
Bear, Cubbie
88IowCubP-554
Bear, Smokey
84AngSmo-28
84DodSmo-1
84DodSmo-2
84DodSmo-3
84DodSmo-4
84PadSmo-23
85CloHSS-39
86FreGiaP-29
86FreGiaP-30
86FreGiaP-31
87BraSmo-NNO
87SalSpuP-31
87SmoNatL-13
88CubVanLS-4
88DodSmo-NNO
88RoySmo-27
Beard, Dave
79WatA'sT-24
80OgdA'sT-15
81TacTigT-24
81Top-96
82Fle-87
83A'sGraG-33
83Don-113
83Fle-514
83FleSta-11
83FleSti-187
83Top-102
84AllGamPI-163
84Don-218
84Fle-438
84FleUpd-9
84MarMot-11
84Nes792-513
84OPC-149
84Top-513
84TopSti-336
84TopTif-513
84TopTra-8T
84TopTraT-8T
85Fle-483
85MaiGuiT-2
85Top-232
85TopTif-232
86RicBraP-2
88TolMudHC-1
88TolMudHP-586
89TolMudHC-10
89TolMudHP-777
Beard, Garrett
89SalDodTI-6
90YakBeaTI-1
91BakDodCLC-23
92ModA'sC-7
92ModA'sF-3901
93ModA'sC-3
93ModA'sF-805
93TacTigF-3038
94HunStaF-1334
95HunStaTI-5
Beard, Mike
76OPC-53
76Top-53
Beard, Ollie (Oliver Perry)
87OldJudN-26
Beard, Ralph
55Bow-206
Beard, Ted
81TCM60I-302
Beard, Ted (Cramer T.)
50PirTeal-1
51Bow-308
52Top-150
77SerSta-3
83TopRep5-150
Bearden, Brent
94St.CatBJC-3
94St.CatBJF-3632
Bearden, Doug
96BriWhiSB-10
Bearden, Gene
46RemBre-17
46SpoExcW-1-12
47Exh-18
48IndTeal-1
49Bow-57
49IndTeal-3
49IndVisEI-1
50Bow-93
50IndNumN-2
51Bow-284
52Bow-173
52NatTeaL-1
52Top-229
53ExhCan-3
53IndPenCBP-2
79TCM50-222
83TopRep5-229
Beardman, Larry
84MadMusP-24
Beardsley, Chris
89PalSprACLC-58
Beardsley, Marve
88KimN18-2
Beare, Gary Ray
76SpoIndC-14
76VenLeaS-79
78SpoIndC-27
78Top-516
94BreMilB-102
Bearnarth, Larry
63Top-386
64MetJayP-1
64Top-527
65MetJayP-1
65OPC-258
65Top-258
66Top-464
76ExpRed-2
78TCM60I-61
80MemChiT-8
85ExpPos-2
86ExpProPa-14
87ExpPos-1
89ExpPos-2
90ExpPos-2
91MetWIZ-27
94BreMilB-103
94RocPol-27
Bears, Yakima
90YakBeaTI-NNO
Bearse, Kevin
88CarLeaAS-24
88KinIndS-2
89CanIndB-1
89CanIndP-1306
90Bow-330
90BowTif-330
90FleUpd-91
90IndTeal-4
90UppDec-715
91Fle-361
91IndIndLD-177
91IndIndP-453
91LinDriAAA-177
91TopDeb90-12
Beasley, Andy
90HamRedS-4
91SprCarC-6
91SprCarP-743
92ClaFS7-277
92St.PetCC-3
92St.PetCF-2029
93St.PetCC-4
93St.PetCF-2628
Beasley, Bud
46SunBre-1
47SigOil-58
47SunBre-3
Beasley, Chris
86WatIndP-2
87WilBilP-22
89PalSprAP-488
90CMC-501
90EdmTraC-4
90EdmTraP-509
90ProAAAF-85
91EdmTraP-1508
92EdmTraF-3533
92EdmTraS-152
92Fle-54
92SkyAAAF-74
92StaClu-492
92TopDeb91-12
92UppDec-614
Beasley, Lew (Lewis Paige)
76SacSolC-18
77TucTorC-4
93RanKee-66
Beasley, Ray
96DanBraB-6
Beasley, Tony
89EriOriS-1
90FreKeyTI-4
91CarLeaAP-CAR5
91FreKeyC-16
91FreKeyP-2370
92SalBucC-25
92SalBucF-69
93CarMudF-2060
93CarMudTI-4
95CarMudF-162
96CarMudB-16
Beason-Samuels, Cody
92GulCoaYF-3795
Beatin, Ebenezer
87OldJudN-27
Beattie, Burt
87KenTwiP-8
Beattie, Jim
77Spo-8824
77WesHavYT-3
79ColCliT-8
79OPC-86
79Top-179
79YanBurK-7
79YanPicA-1
80Top-334
81Don-166
81SpoIndT-29
81Top-443
82Don-478
82Top-22
83Don-176
83Fle-472
83FleSta-12
83OPC-191
83Top-675
83Top-711
84Don-191
84Fle-605
84MarMot-12
84Nes792-288
84OPC-288
84Top-288
84TopSti-346
84TopTif-288
85Don-313
85Fle-484
85Lea-85
85MarMot-15
85OPC-303
85Top-505
85TopSti-334
85TopTif-505
86Don-196
86Fle-458
86MarMot-27
86Top-729
86TopTif-729
87Top-117
87TopTif-117
92YanWIZ7-11
Beatty, Blaine
87HagSunP-12
88JacMetGS-15
88TexLeaAGS-18
89MetColP-22
89TidTidC-9
89TidTidP-1964
90Bow-130
90BowTif-130
90Fle-197
90FleCan-197
90HagSunDGB-2
90MetColP-25
90Sco-632
90TopDeb89-11
90TopTVM-7
90UppDec-23
91LinDriAAA-552
91MetColP-23
91MetWIZ-28
91TidTidLD-552
91TidTidP-2500
92IndIndF-1852
92IndIndS-183
92Sco-843
92SkyAAAF-86
93CarMudF-2044
93CarMudTI-12
94ChaLooF-1350
95IndIndF-88
96CarMudB-1
Beatty, Gary
91BatCliC-30
92SpaPhiC-25
Beauchamp, Jim (James E.)
62KahAtl-1
64Top-492
65Top-409
66OPC-84
66Top-84
66TopVen-84
67Top-307
69Top-613
71MLBOffS-266
71OPC-322
71Top-322
72Top-594
73OPC-137
73Top-137
74OPC-424
74Top-424
78ChaChaT-2
79ChaChaT-2
80IndIndTI-2
81IndIndTI-2
82SyrChiT-26
82SyrChiTI-6
83SyrChiT-1
84SyrChiT-1
85GreBraTI-3
86GreBraTI-3
87AstSer1-3
87GreBraB-1
87SouLeaAJ-22
88RicBraC-23
88RicBraP-15
89RicBraBC-1
89RicBraC-25
89RicBraP-822
89RicBraTI-1
89TriAAP-AAA53
90CMC-283
90ProAAAF-419
90RicBra2ATI-4
90RicBraC-7
90RicBraP-274
90RicBraTI-3
91BraSubS-2
91MetWIZ-29
92BraLykS-2
93BraLykS-2
93ColRedC-3
93ColRedF-588
94BraLykP-2

94BraLykS-2
Beauchamp, Kash
86KnoBluJP-1
87SyrChiT-29
88KnoBluJB-9
89RicBraBC-2
89RicBraC-23
89RicBraP-836
89RicBraTI-2
90CMC-544
90PhoFirC-17
90PhoFirP-21
90ProAAAF-47
94AlbDukF-853
94SanAntMF-2480
96WesPalBEB-4
Beaulac, Joe
89SalLakTTI-24
90MiaMirIS-2
Beaumont, Ginger (Clarence H.)
03BreE10-4
06FanCraNL-2
08RosComP-87
09ColChiE-23A
09ColChiE-23B
09ColChiE-23C
09T206-16
11SpoLifCW-23
11SpoLifM-166
12ColRedB-23A
12ColRedB-23B
12ColRedB-23C
12ColTinT-23A
12ColTinT-23B
12ColTinT-23C
Beaumont, Matt
93BazTeaU-18
93TopTra-30T
94SigRooBS-1
94StaCluDP-48
94StaCluDPFDI-48
95Bes-11
95LakElsSTI-3
95SigRooDDS-DD1
95SigRooDDSS-DD1
95SPML-27
96Bow-331
96Exc-22
96ExcSeaC-1
96HilStaHWB-33
96MidAngB-6
96MidAngOHP-3
96TexLeaAB-19
Beaurivage, Ron
77ModA'sC-19
Beavers, Alan
92HamRedC-14
92HamRedF-1579
Beavers, Mark
85AncGlaPTI-3
86MedA'sC-55
86ModA'sC-23
87MadMusP-2
87MadMusP-20
88ModA'sCLC-61
89RivRedWB-2
89RivRedWCLC-23
89RivRedWP-1390
Beazley, Johnny
46SeaSLP-3
79DiaGre-220
84TCMPla1-26
BeBop, Spec
76LauIndC-20
Beck, Boom Boom (Walter)
34DiaMatCSB-6
34Gou-50
40PlaBal-217
43PhiTeal-2
55Bow-281
77TCMTheWY-28
79DiaGre-310
90DodTar-40
93ConTSN-734
Beck, Brian
90ChaRaiB-4
90ChaRaiP-2050
91ChaRaiC-20
91ChaRaiP-106
92AugPirC-21
92AugPirF-249
93WelPirC-2
93WelPirF-3347
Beck, Chris
94BelMarC-5
94BelMarF-3224
96LanJetB-6
Beck, Clyde Eugene
29ExhFou-5
Beck, Dion
85BenPhiC-1
87ReaPhiP-8
91RenSilSCLC-23
Beck, Erve (Ervin Thomas)
03BreE10-5
90DodTar-900
Beck, Fred (Frederick T.)
09T206-17
11S74Sil-42
11SpoLifCW-24
11SpoLifM-135
11T205-11
Beck, Greg
94HelBreF-3604
94HelBreSP-22
95BelBreTI-10
96StoPorB-12
Beck, Johnny
94MarPhiC-3
94MarPhiF-3282
Beck, Rich
66Top-234
66TopVen-234
81TCM60I-476
92YanWIZ6-7
Beck, Rod
88CliGiaP-695
88MidLeaAGS-5
89SanJosGB-2
89SanJosGCLC-209
89SanJosGP-459
89SanJosGS-1
89Sta-82
90ShrCapP-1435
90ShrCapS-2
91LinDriAAA-378
91PhoFirLD-378
91PhoFirP-59
92Don-461
92Fle-627
92GiaMot-14
92GiaPacGaE-4
92OPCPre-197
92Pin-613
92Sco-746
92TopDeb91-13
92TopGol-264
92TopGolW-264
92Ult-586
93Bow-308
93Don-420
93Fla-137
93Fle-150
93GiaMot-12
93GiaPos-2
93Lea-232
93OPC-11
93Pin-398
93Sco-391
93SP-109
93StaClu-81
93StaCluFDI-81
93StaCluG-12
93StaCluMOP-81
93Top-604
93TopGol-604
93TopInaM-604
93TopMic-604
93Ult-126
93UppDec-73
93UppDecGold-73
94Bow-191
94BowBes-R14
94BowBesR-R14
94ColC-49
94ColChoGS-49
94ColChoSS-49
94Don-604
94ExtBas-381
94ExtBasGB-2
94Fin-169
94FinPre-169P
94FinRef-169
94Fla-442
94Fle-680
94FleAllS-27
94FUnPac-95
94GiaAMC-2
94GiaMot-8
94GiaTarBCI-1
94GiaUSPC-6H
94GiaUSPC-13S
94Lea-224
94LeaL-155
94OPC-182
94Pac-538
94PanSti-260
94Pin-118
94PinArtP-118
94PinMusC-118
94Sco-508
94ScoGolR-508
94Sel-328
94SP-89
94SPDieC-89
94Spo-129
94StaClu-436
94StaCluFDI-436
94StaCluGR-436
94StaCluMO-44
94StaCluMOP-436
94StaCluT-30
94StaCluTFDI-30
94Stu-82
94Top-146
94TopGol-146
94TopSpa-146
94TriPla-101
94Ult-285
94UltFir-7
94UppDec-46
94UppDec-142
94UppDecED-46
94UppDecED-142
95Baz-73
95Bow-319
95ColCho-251
95ColChoGS-251
95ColChoSE-112
95ColChoSEGS-112
95ColChoSESS-112
95ColChoSS-251
95Don-113
95DonPreP-113
95DonTopotO-347
95Emb-138
95EmbGolI-138
95Emo-191
95Fin-34
95FinRef-34
95Fla-206
95Fle-572
95FleAllS-23
95FleTeaL-28
95GiaMot-10
95Lea-328
95PacPri-119
95PanSti-3
95Pin-326
95PinArtP-326
95PinMusC-326
95RedFol-33
95Sco-165
95ScoGolR-165
95ScoHaloG-HG53
95ScoPlaTS-165
95SP-112
95SPCha-97
95SPChaDC-97
95SPSil-112
95StaClu-59
95StaCluFDI-59
95StaCluMOP-59
95StaCluSTWS-59
95StaCluVR-36
95Stu-146
95Top-417
95TopCyb-217
95Ult-239
95UltGolM-239
95UppDec-86
95UppDecED-86
95UppDecEDG-86
95UppDecSE-202
95UppDecSEG-202
96Baz-56
96Cir-191
96CirRav-191
96ColCho-715
96ColChoGS-715
96ColChoSS-715
96Don-165
96DonPreP-165
96EmoXL-285
96Fin-B111
96FinRef-B111
96Fla-383
96Fle-581
96FleTif-581
96GiaMot-3
96Lea-204
96LeaPrePB-204
96LeaPrePG-204
96LeaPrePS-204
96MetUni-240
96MetUniP-240
96Pac-209
96PanSti-106
96Pin-292
96PinFoil-292
96Sco-428
96SelTeaN-18
96SP-168
96StaClu-59
96StaClu-270
96StaCluEPB-59
96StaCluEPG-59
96StaCluEPS-59
96StaCluMOP-59
96StaCluMOP-270
95StaCluVRMC-36
96Top-201
96TopChr-68
96TopChrR-68
96TopGal-27
96TopGalPPI-27
96Ult-564
96UltGolM-564
96UppDec-453
97Cir-260
97CirRav-260
97ColCho-453
97Don-329
97DonLim-92
97DonLimLE-92
97DonPreP-329
97DonPrePGold-329
97Fin-263
97FinRef-263
97Fle-475
97FleTif-475
97MetUni-241
97Pac-438
97PacLigB-438
97PacSil-438
97SpoIll-123
97SpoIllEE-123
97StaClu-140
97StaCluMOP-140
97Top-429
97TopChr-152
97TopChrR-152
97TopSta-79
97TopStaAM-79
97Ult-301
97UltGolME-301
97UltPlaME-301
97UppDec-496
Beck, Wynn
90MadMusB-28
90MadMusP-2271
Beck, Zinn Bertram
15SpoNewM-11
16SpoNewM-12
Beckendorf, Heinie (Henry W.)
07TigACDPP-16
09BusBroBPP-2
09TigTaCP-1
10JHDABE-1
11SpoLifCW-25
11SpoLifM-53
Becker, Beals
09ColChiE-24
09T206-18
10CouT21-2
10DomDisP-9
10SweCapPP-107
11S74Sil-80
11T205-12
12ColRedB-24
12ColTinT-24
12HasTriFT-48D
12T207-10
14CraJacE-96
14PieStaT-3
15CraJacE-96
16FleBreD-8
Becker, David
92ClaDraP-106
94MedHatBJF-3686
94MedHatBJSP-10
Becker, Gregory
87St.PetCP-23
88MidLeaAGS-27
88SprCarB-5
89St.PetCS-2
89Sta-47
Becker, Heinz R.
43CubTeal-2
44CubTeal-1
Becker, Joe (Joseph Edward)
52Par-1
55DodGolS-29
56Dod-3
60DodUniO-23
60Top-463
65CarTeal-2
79TCM50-187
Becker, July
52LavPro-105
Becker, Kevin
94UtiBluSC-4
94UtiBluSF-3810
Becker, Rich
90EliTwiS-1
91Cla/Bes-345
91KenTwiC-25
91KenTwiP-2086
92Bow-330
92CalLeaACL-37
92ClaFS7-293
92UppDecML-245
92VisOakC-2
92VisOakF-1025
93Bow-593
93ClaFS7-151
93ClaGolF-41
93ExcFS7-197
93ExcLeaLF-9
93NasXprF-413
93Top-658
93TopGol-658
93TopInaM-658
93TopMic-658
93UppDec-447
93UppDecGold-447
94Bow-216
94Bow-375
94ColC-1
94ColChoGS-1
94ColChoSS-1
94ExtBas-114
94Fla-72
94FleAllR-M2
94FleUpd-59
94FUnPac-9
94LeaGolR-16
94LeaLimR-4
94Pin-529
94PinArtP-529
94PinMusC-529
94ScoRoo-RT94
94ScoRooGR-RT94
94ScoRooSR-SU12
94Sel-390
94SelRooS-RS14
94SP-183
94SPDieC-183
94SpoRoo-102
94SpoRooAP-102
94SpoRooRS-TR17
94SpoRooS-102
94Top-71
94TopGol-71
94TopSpa-71
94Ult-385
94UppDec-4
94UppDecED-4
95Bow-421
95ColCho-491
95ColChoGS-491
95ColChoSS-491
95Don-88
95DonPreP-88
95Fin-310
95FinRef-310
95Fle-197

95Pac-245
95Pin-211
95PinArtP-211
95PinMusC-211
95Sco-296
95ScoGolR-296
95ScoPlaTS-296
95Sel-150
95SelArtP-150
95SP-174
95SPSil-174
95Stu-126
95Ult-72
95UltGolM-72
95UppDecSE-82
95UppDecSEG-82
95Zen-118
96ColCho-608
96ColChoGS-608
96ColChoSS-608
96Don-436
96DonPreP-436
96Fla-111
96Fle-163
96FleTif-163
96LeaSigA-18
96LeaSigAG-18
96LeaSigAS-18
96Pac-364
96Sco-2
96ScoDugC-A2
96ScoDugCAP-A2
96Top-28
96Ult-372
96UltGolM-372
97Cir-54
97CirRav-54
97ColCho-152
97Don-230
97DonLim-66
97DonLimLE-66
97DonPreP-230
97DonPrePGold-230
97Fle-143
97FleTif-143
97Lea-117
97LeaFraM-117
97LeaFraMDC-117
97MetUni-208
97Pac-133
97PacLigB-133
97PacSil-133
97Sco-417
97ScoHobR-417
97ScoResC-417
97ScoShoS-417
97ScoShoSAP-417
97SP-106
97StaClu-282
97StaCluMOP-282
97Top-148
97Ult-409
97UltGolME-409
97UltPlaME-409
97UppDec-409

Becker, Tim
87Ft.LauYP-1
88AlbYanP-1341
89AlbYanB-20
89AlbYanP-315
89AlbYanS-2

Becker, Tom
88LitFalMP-4
96GreBatB-5

Beckerman, Andy
92PitMetC-5
92PitMetF-3286
93CapCitBC-2
93CapCitBF-451
93SouAtlLAGF-34
94BinMetF-696

Beckert, Glenn Alfred
65Top-549
66CubTeal-4
66Top-232
66TopVen-232
67CokCapC-3
67CubProPS-3
67DexPre-20
67ProPizC-3
67Top-296
68OPC-101
68Top-101
68TopVen-101
69CubJewT-4
69CubPho-3
69CubTealC-2
69KelPin-3
69MilBra-22
69MLBOffS-119
69OPC-171
69Top-171
69TopFou-5
69TopSta-12
69TopTeaP-4
70CubDunD-2
70DayDaiNM-102b
70Kel-43
70MLBOffS-14
70OPC-480
70SunPin-2
70Top-480
70TopScr-5
71Kel-71
71MilDud-35
71MLBOffS-26
71OPC-390
71Top-390
71TopCoi-143
71TopSup-50
71TopTat-10
72CubChi-2
72CubTeal-2
72Kel-24
72MilBra-29
72OPC-45
72OPC-46
72OPC-85
72Top-45A
72Top-45B
72Top-46
72Top-85
73OPC-440
73Top-440
74OPC-241
74PadDea-3
74PadMcDD-2
74Top-241A
74Top-241B
74TopSta-11
75Hos-103
75HosTwi-103
75OPC-484
75Top-484
77PadSchC-7
81TCM60I-367
84CubUno-2
84CubUno-7
89PacLegI-142
89SweBasG-116
93UppDecAH-8

Beckett, Dr. (Jim)
85DalNatCC-12

Beckett, Robbie
90ClaDraP-25
91Bow-655
91ChaRaiC-1
91ChaRaiP-87
91Cla/Bes-162
91Sco-673
92Bow-508
92WatDiaC-14
92WatDiaF-2133
93Bow-406
93ClaFS7-154
93RanCucQC-3
93RanCucQF-819
94BowBes-B27
94BowBesR-B27
94Cla-93
94SigRoo-23
94SigRooS-23
94WicWraF-182
95MemChiTI-11
96NewHavRB-5
96PorSeaDB-7

Beckley, Jake (Jacob Peter)
03BreE10-6
06FanCraNL-3
09T206-398
75SheGrePG-7
76GrePlaG-7
76ShaPiz-120
80PerHaloFP-120
80SSPHOF-120
87OldJudN-28
94OriofB-69

Beckman, Bernie
74AlbDukTI-2
83SyrChiT-2

Beckman, Bill
92ConTSN-623

Beckwith, Joe
79AlbDukT-20
80AlbDukT-2
80DodPol-27
80Top-679
81DodPol-27
81Top-231
82AlbDukT-1
83DodPol-27
83Fle-202
84Don-337
84Fle-97
84FleUpd-10
84Nes792-454
84Top-454
84TopTif-454
84TopTra-9T
84TopTraT-9T
85Don-541
85Fle-197
85Top-77
85TopTif-77
86Fle-2
86SyrChiP-4
86Top-562
86TopTif-562
90DodTar-41

Beckwith, John
74LauOldTBS-6
86NegLeaF-67
90NegLeaS-22

Becquer, Julio V.
58Top-458
59SenTealW-2
59Top-93
59TopVen-93
60Lea-43
60SenJayP-2
60Top-271
61AngJayP-2
61Top-329

Bedard, Roger
52LavPro-49

Bedell, Howard W.
61Top-353
62SalPlaC-217
62ShiPlaC-217
62Top-76
62TopVen-76
93BenRocC-27
93BenRocF-3283

Bedell, Jeff
86Ft.MyeRP-3

Bedinger, Doug
95ForWayWTI-2

Bedrosian, Dave
76WauMetT-3

Bedrosian, Steve
79SavBraT-14
81RicBraT-12
82BraBurKL-2
82BraPol-32
82Don-401
82Top-502
82TopTra-4T
83BraPol-32
83Don-173
83Fle-129
83FleSti-89
83OPC-157
83Top-157
84AllGamPI-74
84BraPol-32
84Don-565
84Fle-171
84Nes792-365
84OPC-365
84Top-365
84TopSti-38
84TopTif-365
85AllGamPI-164
85BraHos-3
85BraPol-32
85Don-628
85Fle-319
85Lea-51
85OPC-25
85SevCoi-S6
85Top-25
85TopMin-25
85TopSti-23
85TopTif-25
86Don-199
86Fle-508
86FleUpd-12
86OPC-181
86PhiCIG-11
86PhiTas-40
86Top-648
86TopSti-40
86TopTif-648
86TopTra-7T
86TopTraT-7T
87Don-185
87DonHig-9
87Fle-170
87FleGlo-170
87FleLimE-3
87FleSluBC-M1
87FleStiC-8
87OPC-233
87PhiTas-40
87RedFolSB-98
87SmoNatL-7
87Spo-110
87SpoTeaP-6
87Top-736
87TopMinL-27
87TopSti-124
87TopTif-736
88ClaBlu-222
88Don-62
88DonAll-61
88DonBasB-16
88Fle-298
88Fle-627
88FleAwaW-1
88FleGlo-298
88FleGlo-627
88FleMin-98
88FleStiC-107
88FleSup-1
88Lea-82
88MSAIceTD-18
88Nes-25
88OPC-344
88OPCBoxB-B
88PanSti-351
88PanSti-440
88PhiTas-3
88Sco-161
88Sco-656
88ScoGlo-161
88ScoGlo-656
88Spo-70
88Spo-222
88StaLinPh-2
88Top-407
88Top-440
88TopBig-23
88TopCoi-34
88TopGaloC-1
88TopGloS-28
88TopMinL-64
88TopRevLL-11
88TopSti-6
88TopSti-116
88TopStiB-31
88TopTif-407
88TopTif-440
88TopUKM-2
88TopUKMT-2
88TopWaxBC-B
88Woo-10
89Bow-395
89BowTif-395
89ClaLigB-34
89Don-24
89Don-75
89DonBasB-303
89DonSupD-24
89Fle-562
89FleBasM-1
89FleGlo-562
89MSAIceTD-15
89PanSti-145
89PhiTas-1
89Sco-260
89ScoHot1S-29
89ScoRoo-49T
89Spo-63
89Top-20
89TopBasT-147
89TopBig-137
89TopSti-112
89TopTif-20
89TopTra-8T
89TopTraT-8T
89UppDec-511
90Bow-226
90BowTif-226
90ClaBlu-62
90Don-295
90DonBesN-99
90Fle-50
90FleCan-50
90GiaMot-6
90GiaSmo-2
90Lea-3
90OPC-310
90PanSti-364
90PubSti-232
90Sco-379
90Sco100S-31
90Spo-104
90Top-310
90TopBig-275
90TopSti-86
90TopTif-310
90UppDec-618
90VenSti-33
91Bow-317
91Don-207
91Fle-254
91Lea-505
91OPC-125
91OPCPre-5
91RedFolS-7
91Sco-459
91ScoRoo-14T
91StaClu-531
91Stu-82
91Top-125
91TopDesS-125
91TopMic-125
91TopTif-125
91TopTra-6T
91TopTraT-6T
91UppDec-422
91UppDec-738
92Don-184
92Fle-197
92OPC-267
92Sco-17
92Top-267
92TopGol-267
92TopGolW-267
92TopMic-267
92UppDec-622
93BraLykP-2
93BraLykS-3
93FleFinE-1
93StaClu-708
93StaCluFDI-708
93StaCluMOP-708
93Ult-301
93UppDec-701
93UppDecGold-701
94BraLykP-3
94BraLykS-3
94BraUSPC-6S
94BraUSPC-10D
94Don-479
94Fle-351
94Pac-2
94Sco-247
94ScoGolR-247
94StaClu-64
94StaCluFDI-64
94StaCluGR-64
94StaCluMOP-64
94StaCluT-43
94StaCluTFDI-43
94Top-617
94TopGol-617
94TopSpa-617
94Ult-148
95Fle-300
95Top-523
95TopCyb-345
96DanBraB-2

Bee, Buddy the
95BinMetTI-NNO
96BinBeeB-3

Beebe, Fred
08RosComP-160
09ColChiE-25

09PC7HHB-3
09RamT20-9
10SweCapPP-95
11SpoLifCW-26
11SpoLifM-186
12ColRedB-25
12ColTinT-25
12ImpTobC-54
Beebe, Hans
96PitMetB-5
Beech, Matt
94BatCliC-3
94BatCliF-3437
95ClePhiF-208
95ReaPhiELC-3
96Bow-346
96ReaPhiB-1
97ColCho-16
97Fle-406
97FleTif-406
97UppDec-237
Beecher, Ed (Edward H.)
87BucN28-85
Beecher, Harry Ward
88GooN16-12
Beeckman, Tenni
88GooN16-13
Beecroft, Mike
81BirBarT-25
82BirBarT-6
Beeler, Jodie (Joseph Sam)
76DalCon-2
Beeler, Pete
87TamTarP-27
88CedRapRP-1147
88MidLeaAGS-8
89CedRapRS-25
89ChaLooB-11
89ChaLooGS-4
91ChaLooLD-154
91LinDriAA-154
91NasSouP-2158
91WavRedF-3
92BufBisF-325
92BufBisS-27
Beene, Andy
82ElPasDT-14
84VanCanC-26
94BreMilB-104
Beene, Fred
70OPC-121
70Top-121
71MLBOffS-219
73OPC-573
73Top-573
74OPC-274
74Top-274
75OPC-181
75Top-181
76SSP-504
80TidTidT-14
91OriCro-26
92YanWIZ7-12
Beene, Steve
76WatRoyT-3
77DayBealT-1
Beeney, Ryan
94OneYanC-2
94OneYanF-3797
94StaCluDP-67
94StaCluDPFDI-67
96TamYanY-4
Beer, Darrin
89GenCubP-1863
Beerbrower, Dan
76QuaCitAT-1
Bees, Burlington
96BurBeeTI-31
Beesley, Mascot
96BurBeeTI-30
Beeston, Paul
93BluJayDM-24
Befort, Curt
87ClePhiP-3
Befort, Jay
85RedWinA-22
BeFort, Lyle
86AncGlaPTI-2
Beggs, Joe
41HarHarW-3
47Exh-19
75YanDyn1T-2
79DiaGre-20
Begnaud, Gary
77ReaPhiT-1
Begue, Roger
82LynMetT-18
Behel, Steven A.D.
87OldJudN-29
Behenna, Rick
81DurBulT-15
83BraPol-49
84Don-346
84Ind-3
85Ind-2
85IndPol-32
Behm, Bill
84TigWavP-5
Behney, Mel
72OPC-524
72Top-524
73OPC-602
73Top-602
Behnsch, Bobby
87ClePhiP-7
Behny, Mark
86EriCarP-3
87SavCarP-24
88SavCarP-339
Behr, George
92HelBreF-1719
92HelBreSP-8
92Min-3
Behrend, Mike
83EriCarT-11
84SavCarT-26
Behrens, Scott
91IdaFalBP-4320
91PulBraC-16
91PulBraP-3995
92IdaFalGF-3501
Behrman, Hank (Henry)
49EurSta-101
50RemBre-2
90DodTar-42
91RinPosBD3-7
Beiras, Mike
87BelMarL-26
Beirman, Jim
75ForLauYS-16
Beirne, Kevin
96SouBenSHS-5
Beitey, Dan
75CedRapGT-10
Beja, Aaron
91FayGenC-25
Bejma, Ollie (Aloysius Frank)
34BatR31-55
34BatR31-93
35DiaMatCS3T1-5
35DiaMatCS3T1-6
36R31PasP-26
79DiaGre-138
Bekkedal, Matt
96BriWhiSB-4
Belan, Lance
86PriWilPP-2
Belanger, Lee
82OrlTwiT-2
83VisOakF-1
Belanger, Mark Henry
67Top-558
68CokCapO-14
68DexPre-10
68OPC-118
68Top-118
68TopVen-118
69Top-299
69TopSta-121
69TopTeaP-5
70DayDaiNM-159
70MLBOffS-145
70Ori-1
70Top-615
71MLBOffS-289
71OPC-99
71Ori-1
71Top-99
72OPC-224
72OPC-456
72OriPol-1
72Top-224
72Top-456
73LinPor-7
73OPC-253
73OriJohP-7
73Top-253
74OPC-329
74Top-329
74TopSta-122
75OPC-74
75Top-74
76OPC-505
76Top-505
77BurCheD-38
77Hos-71
77OPC-154
77RCColC-2
77Top-135
78OPC-125
78RCColC-8
78Top-315
79OPC-27
79Top-65
80OPC-217
80Top-425
81AllGamPI-19
81Don-472
81Fle-175
81FleStiC-39
81Top-641
82DodPol-8
82DodUniOV-2
82Fle-158
82FleSta-148
82OPC-42
82Top-776
82TopTra-5T
83Don-514
83FraBroR-26
83Top-273
90DodTar-43
91OriCro-27
96UppDecRCJ-21
Belardi, Wayne (Carroll W.)
55Bow-36
79TCM50-110
90DodTar-44
Belbru, Juan
88BlaYNPRWLU-23
89BlaYNPRWL-138
89SavCarP-356
90HamRedS-5
Belcher, Glenn
87FayGenP-27
88FayGenP-1080
89FayGenP-1568
Belcher, Kevin
88GasRanP-1010
89GasRanP-1004
89GasRanS-2
89SouAtlLAGS-30
89Sta-134
90CMC-744
90ProAaA-67
90TexLeaAGS-26
90TulDriP-1166
90TulDriTI-3
91Don-46
91Fle-280
91LinDriAAA-302
91OklCit8LD-302
91OklCit8P-189
91Sco-714
91ScoRoo-15
91Stu-121
91TopDeb90-13
91UppDec-26
92TulDriF-2706
92TulDriS-602
93BirBarF-1203
93RanKee-67
Belcher, Tim
84MadMusP-9
85HunStaJ-31
85Top-281
85TopTif-281
87TacTigP-21
88DodMot-23
88DodPol-49
88Don-587
88DonBasB-10
88DonRoo-28
88Fle-509
88FleGlo-509
88ScoRoo-101T
88ScoRooG-101T
88TopTra-12T
88TopTraT-12T
89Baz-1
89Bow-336
89BowTif-336
89ClaLigB-57
89DodMot-23
89DodPol-25
89DodStaSV-2
89Don-203
89DonBasB-234
89Fle-54
89FleGlo-54
89FleGlo-WS2
89FleSup-3
89FleWorS-2
89K-M-9
89OPC-177
89PanSti-21
89PanSti-95
89Sco-418
89ScoHot1R-94
89ScoYouSI-36
89Spo-121
89Top-456
89TopBig-145
89TopGloS-30
89TopRoo-3
89TopSti-317
89TopTif-456
89ToyRoo-3
89UppDec-648
89Woo-19
89Woo-29
90Bow-85
90BowTif-85
90DodMot-9
90DodPol-49
90DodTar-45
90Don-79
90DonBesN-17
90Fle-389
90FleAwaW-2
90FleCan-389
90FleLeaL-2
90FleWaxBC-C2
90Lea-200
90OPC-173
90PanSti-281
90PubSti-2
90PubSti-608
90Sco-126
90Top-173
90TopBig-246
90TopCoi-38
90TopMinL-57
90TopTif-173
90UppDec-547
90VenSti-34
90VenSti-35
91BasBesAotM-3
91Bow-605
91DodMot-9
91DodPol-49
91Don-70
91Fle-194
91Lea-508
91OPC-25
91Sco-187
91StaClu-152
91Top-25
91TopDesS-25
91TopMic-25
91TopTif-25
91Ult-159
91UppDec-576
92Bow-319
92Bow-664
92Cla2-T78
92Don-78
92Fle-447
92FleUpd-79
92Lea-417
92OPC-688
92OPCPre-113
92Pin-384
92RedKah-31
92Sco-368
92ScoRoo-65T
92StaClu-842
92StaCluNC-842
92Top-688
92TopGol-688
92TopGolW-688
92TopMic-688
92TopTra-8T
92TopTraG-8T
92Ult-479
92UppDec-668
92UppDec-761
93Bow-118
93Don-82
93Fla-24
93Fle-30
93Lea-243
93OPC-48
93PacSpa-398
93Pin-357
93RedKah-2
93Sco-423
93Sel-191
93SelRoo-3T
93StaClu-9
93StaCluFDI-9
93StaCluMOP-9
93Top-382
93TopGol-382
93TopInaM-382
93TopMic-382
93TriPla-163
93Ult-26
93UppDec-368
93UppDecGold-368
94Bow-677
94ColC-561
94ColChoGS-561
94ColChoSS-561
94Don-56
94Fin-301
94FinRef-301
94Fle-74
94FleUpd-40
94Lea-232
94OPC-70
94Pac-119
94Pin-491
94PinArtP-491
94PinMusC-491
94Sco-470
94ScoGolR-470
94Sel-248
94StaClu-255
94StaClu-582
94StaCluFDI-255
94StaCluFDI-582
94StaCluGR-255
94StaCluGR-582
94StaCluMOP-255
94StaCluMOP-582
94Top-62
94TopGol-62
94TopSpa-62
94TopTra-32T
94Ult-353
94UppDec-364
94UppDecED-364
95Don-339
95DonPreP-339
95IndIndF-89
95MarMot-21
95MarPac-20
95Pac-149
95Sco-484
95ScoGolR-484
95ScoPlaTS-484
95Top-209
95TopCyb-123
96Fle-227
96FleTif-227
96FleUpd-U33
96FleUpd-U38
96FleUpdTC-U38
96RoyPol-2
96StaClu-322
96StaCluMOP-322
96Top-38
97ColCho-129
97Don-223
86HumStaDS-31
97DonPreP-223
97DonPrePGold-223
97Fle-110
97FleTif-110
97Pac-98
97PacLigB-98
97PacSil-98
97Pin-146
97PinArtP-146
97PinMusC-146
97RoyPol-2

97Sco-390
97ScoHobR-390
97ScoResC-390
97ScoShoS-390
97ScoShoSAP-390
97StaClu-266
97StaCluMOP-266
97Top-422
97Ult-505
97UltGolME-505
97UltPlaME-505
97UppDec-87

Belcik, Keith
84LitFalMT-2

Belen, Lance
85PriWilPT-14
87HarSenP-11
88HarSenP-844

Belen, Mattie
89BluOriS-4

Belford, John
89WelPirP-35
95StCatSTI-30

Belfour, Ed
91StaCluCM-42
91StaCluCM-43

Belinda, Stan
87MacPirP-17
88CarLeaAS-3
88SalBucS-2
89HarSenP-305
89HarSenS-3
89TriA AAC-13
90BufBisC-1
90BufBisP-365
90CMC-1
90FleUpd-48
90Lea-486
90OPC-354
90ProAAAF-480
90Sco-634
90Top-354
90TopDeb89-12
90TopTif-354
90TriAAAC-13
90UppDec-759
91Don-699
91Fle-30
91OPC-522
91Sco-296
91Sco100RS-8
91StaClu-453
91Top-522
91TopDesS-522
91TopMic-522
91TopTif-522
91Ult-273
91UppDec-161
92Bow-455
92Don-501
92Fle-548
92Lea-287
92OPC-466
92Pin-370
92PirNatl-1
92Sco-325
92StaClu-75
92Top-466
92TopGol-466
92TopGolW-466
92TopMic-466
92Ult-550
92UppDec-202
93Bow-22
93Don-490
93Fla-109
93Fle-110
93Lea-339
93PacSpa-242
93PanSti-282
93Pin-142
93PirHil-1
93PirNatl-1
93Sco-369
93SP-181
93StaClu-268
93StaCluFDI-268
93StaCluMOP-268
93Top-748
93TopGol-748
93TopInaM-748
93TopMic-748
93Ult-95
93UppDec-359
93UppDecGold-359
94ColC-377
94ColChoGS-377
94ColChoSS-377
94Don-77
94Fla-55
94Fle-148
94Sco-160
94ScoGolR-160
94StaClu-8
94StaCluFDI-8
94StaCluGR-8
94StaCluMOP-8
94Top-247
94TopGol-247
94TopSpa-247
94Ult-360
95FleUpd-8
95Pac-197
95StaClu-222
95StaCluFDI-222
95StaCluMOP-222
95StaCluSTWS-222
95TopTra-153T
96ColCho-477
96ColChoGS-477
96ColChoSS-477
96Don-427
96DonPreP-427
96Fle-23
96FleRedS-1
96FleTif-23
96Sco-203
96Ult-14
96UltGolM-14
96UppDec-24

Belinskas, Dan
86CedRapRT-1

Belinsky, Bo
62Top-592
63AngJayP-1
63Top-33
64Top-315
64TopVen-315
65OPC-225
65Top-225
66Top-506
67Top-447A
67Top-447B
69Top-366
76BooProC-1
81TCM60I-447
85AngStrH-3
87AstShoSTw-28
87AstShoSTw-29
87AstShowSTh-3
89PacLegI-130
89SweBasG-16

Beliveau, Jean
72Dia-67

Belk, Chuck
79WisRapTT-20

Belk, Tim
92BenMusSP-24
92BilMusF-3360
93CarLeaAGF-40
93ClaFS7-271
93ExcFS7-16
93WinSpiC-4
93WinSpiF-1576
94Bow-588
94BowBes-B57
94BowBesR-B57
94ChaLooF-1362
94Cla-38
94ExcFS7-172
95Bow-119
95BowBes-B36
95BowBesR-B36
95IndIndF-99
95Sel-158
95SelArtP-158
95SigRooOJA-AS2
95SigRooOJAS-AS2
95Sum-167
95SumNthD-167
95Top-647
96Bow-366
96IndIndB-6
97Don-257
97DonPreP-257
97DonPrePGold-257
97Ult-173
97UltGolME-173
97UltPlaME-173

Bell, Beau
36R31PasP-41
38ExhFou-15

Bell, Beau (Roy Chester)
35DiaMatCS3T1-7
37OPCBatUV-105
38WheBB10-7
39PlaBal-136
40PlaBal-138
93ConTSN-781

Bell, Bobby
86PalSprAP-5
86PalSprAP-2
87PalSprP-25
88PalSprAP-1459

Bell, Brent
91MarPhiC-14
91MarPhiP-3457
92MarPhiC-18
92MarPhiF-3063
93BatCliC-4
93BatCliF-3156

Bell, Buddy (David Gus)
54RedHeaF-3
54RedMan-NL19B
55RedMan-NL23
55RobGouS-16
55RobGouW-16
57RedSoh-2
60MacSta-3
61Pos-186A
62Pos-120
73LinPor-60
73OPC-31
73Top-31
74Kel-10
74OPC-257
74Top-257
74TopDecE-37
74TopSta-161
75Hos-30
75HosTwi-30
75OPC-38
75Top-38
76Hos-95
76OPC-66
76OPC-358
76Spo-7
76SSP-517
76Top-66
76Top-358
77BurCheD-57
77Hos-69
77MSADis-2
77OPC-86
77PepGloD-11
77Top-590
77TopCloS-2
78Hos-15
78OPC-234
78PapGinD-34
78Pep-26
78TasDis-1
78Top-280
78WifBalD-2
79Hos-147
79Kel-14A
79Kel-14B
79OPC-367
79Top-690
80Kel-53
80OPC-107
80Top-190
80TopSup-47
80WilGloT-1
81AllGamPI-28
81Don-145
81Fle-625
81FleStiC-11
81Kel-64
81MSAMinD-1
81OPC-66
81Top-475
81TopScr-21
81TopSti-130
81TopSupHT-91
81TopSupN-1
82Don-23
82Don-368
82Dra-2
82Fle-313
82FleSta-172
82FleSta-239
82Kel-33
82OPC-50
82Top-50
82TopSti-238
82WilSpoG-1
83AllGamPI-28
83Don-215
83DonActA-40
83Fle-562
83Fle-632
83FleSta-13
83FleSti-148
83FleSti-164
83Kel-12
83OPC-330
83RanAffF-25
83Top-330
83Top-412
83TopGloS-9
83TopSti-119
84AllGamPI-118
84Don-56
84DonActAS-12
84Fle-413
84FunFooP-76
84Nes792-37
84Nes792-665
84OPC-347
84RanJarP-25
84SevCoi-W11
84Top-37
84Top-665
84TopRubD-3
84TopSti-351
84TopTif-37
84TopTif-665
85AllGamPI-28
85Don-56
85DonActA-11
85Fle-556
85FleLimE-1
85FleStaS-7
85GenMilS-13
85Lea-174
85OPC-176
85RanPer-25
85ThoMcAD-2
85Top-131
85Top-745
85TopRubD-3
85TopSti-347
85TopSup-53
85TopTif-131
85TopTif-745
86BasStaB-7
86Don-447
86Fle-172
86FleMin-37
86OPC-285
86RedTexG-25
86SevCoi-S10
86Spo-151
86Top-285
86TopSti-139
86TopTat-15
86TopTif-285
86TruVal-20
87BoaandB-21
87Don-556
87DonOpeD-196
87Fle-193
87FleGlo-193
87Lea-169
87OPC-104
87RedFolSB-38
87RedKah-25
87Spo-141
87SpoTeaP-4
87StuPan-4
87Top-545
87TopSti-143
87TopTif-545
88Don-206
88Fle-227
88FleGlo-227
88Lea-192
88MSAJifPD-1
88Nes-30
88OPC-130
88PacLegI-65
88PanSti-279
88RedFolSB-5
88Sco-99
88ScoGlo-99
88Spo-147
88StaLinAl-1
88StaLinRe-1
88Top-130
88TopSti-138
88TopTif-130
88TopTra-13T
88TopTraT-13T
89Bow-229
89BowTif-229
89Fle-352
89FleGlo-352
89OPC-92
89RanMot-9
89RanSmo-3
89Sco-610
89Top-461
89TopBig-270
89TopSti-18
89TopTif-461
89UppDec-112
90ColSprSSP-55
90PacLeg-74
90ProAAAF-236
90PubSti-404
90VonSti-36
91MetWIZ-30
91SweBasG-7
91TopArc1-118
92BazQua5A-14
93RanKee-68
93TedWil-31
94RanAllP-8
94RanAllP-9
94RanAllP-10
94RanAllP-12
94UppDecAH-183
94UppDecAH1-183

Bell, Cliff
86NegLeaF-100

Bell, Cool Papa (James)
74LauOldTBS-24
75SheGrePG-21
76CooPapB-1
76CooPapB-2
76CooPapB-3
76CooPapB-4
76CooPapB-5
76CooPapB-6
76CooPapB-7
76CooPapB-8
76CooPapB-9
76CooPapB-10
76CooPapB-11
76CooPapB-12
76CooPapB-13
76GrePlaG-21
76ShaPiz-141
80PerHaloFP-141
80SSPHOF-141
83ConMar-49
83DonHOFH-25
86NegLeaF-3
86NegLeaF-90
87LeaSpeO*-H12
87NegLeaPD-24
88ConHar-1
88ConNegA-1
88NegLeaD-14
89KahCoo-1
89PerCelP-4
89RinPosNL1-7
90NegLeaS-28
90PerGreM-51
90PomBlaBNLP-2543
91PomBlaBPB-1
91PomBlaBPB-16
93DiaStaES-N1
93TedWil-97
94PomNegLB-8
94UppDecTAE-49

Bell, Curt
92NiaFalRC-24
92NiaFalRF-3326
93FayGenC-3
93FayGenF-131

Bell, David
90SprCarB-3
91Cla/Bes-104
91ColIndC-22
91ColIndP-1489
92KinIndC-18
92KinIndF-2481
92UppDecML-80

93CanIndF-2844
94ChaKniF-899
94Top-369
94TopGol-369
94TopSpa-369
94UppDecML-105
95ARuFalLS-1
95Bow-179
95Exc-35
95SelCer-119
95SelCerMG-119
95Sum-126
95SumNthD-126
95Top-581
95UppDec-241
95UppDecED-241
95UppDecEDG-241
95UppDecML-16
96ColCho-656
96ColCho-687
96ColChoGS-656
96ColChoGS-687
96ColChoSS-656
96ColChoSS-687
96Don-92
96DonPreP-92
96Fle-538
96FleTif-538
96Lea-70
96LeaPrePB-70
96LeaPrePG-70
96LeaPrePS-70
96LeaSigA-19
96LeaSigAG-19
96LeaSigAS-19
96Pin-193
96StaClu-125
96StaCluMOP-125
96Top-388
96Ult-540
96UltGolM-540
97PacPriGotD-GD197
95UppDecMLFS-16

Bell, Derek

88MyrBeaBJP-1171
88OPC-311
88SouAtlLAGS-20
89KnoBluJB-1
89KnoBluJP-1149
89KnoBluJS-1
90CMC-340
90ProAAAF-362
90ScoRoo-81T
90SyrChiC-14
90SyrChiMB-2
90SyrChiP-582
91BluJayFS-3
91BluJayS-20
91Cla3-T28
91Don-32
91Fle-168
91LinDriAAA-501
91Sco100RS-32
91SyrChiK-1
91SyrChiLD-501
91SyrChiMB-2
91SyrChiP-2491
91TopTra-7T
91TopTraT-7T
91TriA AAGP-AAA42
91UppDecFE-26F
92Bow-237
92Bow-559
92Cla1-T11
92ClaGam-74
92Don-581
92Fle-324
92Lea-243
92OPC-121
92OPCPre-189
92Pin-250
92PinRoo-7
92PinRool-18
92ProFS7-158
92Sco-402
92Sco100RS-64
92ScoHotR-9
92ScoImpP-23
92ScoRoo-3
92SkyAAAF-290
92SkyAAAF-292
92StaClu-555
92Stu-252
92SyrChiTT-2
92Top-121
92TopDeb91-14
92TopGol-121
92TopGolW-121
92TopMcD-36
92TopMic-121
92Ult-448
92UppDec-26
92UppDecSR-SR4
93BluJayD4-3
93BluJayDWS-3
93BluJayDWS-7
93CadDis-4
93DiaMar-8
93Don-557
93Fla-131
93Fle-331
93FleFinE-134
93Lea-179
93OPC-31
93PacSpa-320
93PadMot-12
93PanSti-32
93Pin-171
93PinHomRC-37
93Sco-122
93Sel-286
93SelRoo-132T
93SP-163
93StaClu-504
93StaCluFDI-504
93StaCluMOP-504
93Stu-18
93Top-268
93TopGol-268
93TopInaM-268
93TopMic-268
93TopTra-55T
93Toy-93
93TriPla-255
93Ult-286
93Ult-469
93UppDec-158
93UppDec-696
93UppDecGold-158
93UppDecGold-696
93USPlaCR-5S
94Bow-288
94ColC-490
94ColChoGS-490
94ColChoSS-490
94Don-591
94ExtBas-369
94Fin-114
94FinRef-114
94Fla-231
94Fle-655
94FUnPac-156
94Lea-113
94LeaL-150
94OPC-64
94Pac-517
94PadMot-8
94PanSti-252
94Pin-22
94PinArtP-22
94PinMusC-22
94PinPowS-PS22
94ProMag-116
94Sco-338
94ScoGolR-338
94Sel-146
94SP-128
94SPDieC-128
94StaClu-286
94StaCluFDI-286
94StaCluGR-286
94StaCluMOP-286
94Stu-130
94Top-364
94TopGol-364
94TopSpa-364
94TriPla-162
94Ult-572
94UppDec-495
94UppDecED-495
94VenLinU-101
95AstMot-5
95ColCho-115
95ColChoGS-115
95ColChoSE-165
95ColChoSEGS-165
95ColChoSESS-165
95ColChoSS-115
95Don-364
95DonPreP-364
95DonTopotO-250
95Emo-135
95Fin-290
95FinRef-290
95Fla-357
95Fle-555
95FleUpd-138
95Lea-268
95LeaLim-58
95Pac-357
95PacPri-115
95Pin-362
95PinArtP-362
95PinMusC-362
95Sco-426
95ScoGolR-426
95ScoPlaTS-426
95SelCer-49
95SelCerMG-49
95SP-64
95SPCha-56
95SPChaDC-56
95Spo-136
95SpoArtP-136
95SPSil-64
95StaClu-143
95StaClu-619
95StaCluFDI-143
95StaCluMOP-143
95StaCluMOP-619
95StaCluSTWS-143
95StaCluSTWS-619
95StaCluVR-73
95Stu-128
95Sum-33
95SumNthD-33
95Top-616
95TopCyb-384
95TopTra-27T
95Ult-231
95UltGolM-231
95UppDec-274
95UppDecED-274
95UppDecEDG-274
95UppDecSE-179
95UppDecSEG-179
95Zen-28
96AstMot-4
96Baz-88
96Bow-103
96BowBes-80
96BowBesAR-80
96BowBesR-80
96Cir-134
96CirRav-134
96ColCho-165
96ColCho-358
96ColChoGS-165
96ColChoGS-358
96ColChoSS-165
96ColChoSS-358
96Don-126
96DonDiaK-23
96DonPreP-126
96EmoXL-194
96Fin-B133
96Fin-S328
96FinRef-B133
96FinRef-S328
96Fla-273
96Fle-401
96FleRoaW-1
96FleTif-401
96FleUpd-U212
96FleUpdTC-U212
96Lea-195
96LeaLim-88
96LeaLimG-88
96LeaPre-104
96LeaPreP-104
96LeaPrePB-195
96LeaPrePG-195
96LeaPrePS-195
96LeaPreSG-18
96LeaPreSte-18
96LeaSig-62
96LeaSigPPG-62
96LeaSigPPP-62
96MetUni-173
96MetUniP-173
96Pac-87
96PacPri-P30
96PacPriG-P30
96PanSti-62
96Pin-244
96PinAfi-148
96PinAfiAP-148
96PinArtP-144
96PinFoil-244
96PinSta-144
96ProSta-11
96Sco-110
96ScoBigB-14
96ScoDiaA-19
96ScoDugC-A75
96ScoDugCAP-A75
96ScoNumG-8
96ScoSam-110
96Sel-96
96SelArtP-96
96SelTeaN-26
96SP-91
96Spo-65
96SpoArtP-65
96SPx-30
96SPxGol-30
96StaClu-14
96StaCluEPB-14
96StaCluEPG-14
96StaCluEPS-14
96StaCluMO-2
96StaCluMOP-14
95StaCluVRMC-73
96Stu-107
96StuPrePB-107
96StuPrePG-107
96StuPrePS-107
96Sum-109
96SumAbo&B-109
96SumArtP-109
96SumFoi-109
96Top-160
96TopChr-45
96TopChrR-45
96TopGal-39
96TopGalPPI-39
96TopLas-2
96TopPro-NL2
96TopRoaW-RW1
96Ult-206
96UltGolM-206
96UltRBIK-1
96UltRBIKGM-1
96UppDec-85
96UppDec-420
96UppDecPRE-R52
96UppDecPreR-R52
96Zen-89
96ZenArtP-89
96ZenMoz-25
97BluJayS-34
97Bow-264
97BowBes-92
97BowBesAR-92
97BowBesR-92
97BowInt-264
97Cir-298
97CirRav-298
97ColCho-119
97Don-38
97DonEli-146
97DonEliGS-146
97DonPreP-38
97DonPrePGold-38
97Fin-198
97FinRef-198
97FlaSho-A129
97FlaSho-B129
97FlaSho-C129
97FlaShoLC-129
97FlaShoLC-B129
97FlaShoLC-C129
97FlaShoLCM-A129
97FlaShoLCM-B129
97FlaShoLCM-C129
97Fle-340
97FleTif-340
97Lea-235
97LeaFraM-235
97LeaFraMDC-235
97MetUni-135
97NewPin-109
97NewPinAP-109
97NewPinMC-109
97NewPinPP-109
97Pac-312
97PacLigB-312
97PacPri-106
97PacPriLB-106
97PacPriP-106
97PacPriSL-SL10C
97PacSil-312
97PinIns-124
97PinInsCE-124
97PinInsDE-124
97PinX-PSfF-55
97PinX-PSfFU-55
97ProMag-18
97ProMagML-18
97Sco-271
97ScoPreS-271
97ScoShoS-271
97ScoShoSAP-271
97Sel-96
97SelArtP-96
97SelRegG-96
97SP-82
97SpoIll-102
97SpoIllEE-102
97StaClu-208
97StaCluMat-208
97StaCluMOP-208
97Stu-84
97StuPrePG-84
97StuPrePS-84
97Top-93
97TopChr-37
97TopChrR-37
97TopGal-125
97TopGalPPI-125
97Ult-205
97UltDouT-14
97UltGolME-205
97UltPlaME-205
97UppDec-365

Bell, Eric

84NewOriT-2
86ChaOriW-2
87Don-39
87DonRoo-2
87FleUpd-2
87FleUpdG-2
87Lea-39
87OriFreB-45
87SpoRool-1
87SpoTeaP-21
87TopTra-3T
87TopTraT-3T
88ClaRed-193
88Don-125
88Fle-555
88FleGlo-555
88OPC-383
88PanSti-4
88RocRedWC-2
88RocRedWP-194
88RocRedWTI-2
88Sco-101
88ScoGlo-101
88ScoYouS2-38
88StaLinO-1
88Top-383
88TopSti-224
88TopTif-383
90HagSunDGB-3
90ProAAAF-454
90RocRedWGC-16
90RocRedWP-697
91CanIndLD-77
91CanIndP-971
91LinDriAA-77
91OriCro-28
92ColSprSSF-743
92IndFanC-5
92Lea-379
93AstMot-25
93TucTorF-3051
94TucTorF-752
96TusTorB-3

Bell, Gary

59Kah-2
59Top-327
60Kah-2
60Top-441
61Kah-3
61Pos-58A
61Pos-58B
61Top-274
62IndJayP-1
62Kah-1A

62Kah-1B
62SalPlaC-213
62ShiPlaC-213
62Top-273
63IndJayP-2
63Top-129
64Top-234
64TopVen-234
65Top-424
66Top-525
67CokCapI-7
67DexPre-21
67Top-479
68CokCapRS-3
68DexPre-11
68OPC-43
68Top-43
68TopVen-43
69MilBra-23
69MLBOffS-93
69PilPos-7
69Top-377
69TopSta-223
69TopTeaP-9
81RedSoxBG2S-70
83Pil69G-34
89PacLegI-213

Bell, George (Jorge Antonio)

80CarMudF-13
82Don-54
82Fle-609
82OPC-254
82SyrChiT-20
82SyrChiTI-7
82Top-254
83SyrChiT-21
84BluJayFS-5
84Don-73
84Fle-148
84FunFooP-113
84Nes792-278
84OPC-278
84Top-278
84TopTif-278
85AllGamPI-50
85BluJayFS-5
85DomLeaS-19
85Don-146
85Fle-100
85FleStaS-39
85Lea-248
85OPC-59
85OPCPos-18
85Top-698
85TopSti-360
85TopTif-698
86BasStaB-8
86BluJayAF-4
86BluJayFS-4
86Don-4
86Don-71
86DonSupD-4
86Fle-53
86FleMin-13
86GenMilB-3B
86Lea-4
86OPC-338
86OPCBoxB-A
86SevCoi-E11
86Spo-102
86Top-338
86Top-718
86TopGloS-47
86TopSti-187
86TopSup-10
86TopTat-3
86TopTif-338
86TopTif-718
86TopWaxBC-A
87BluJayFS-2
87ClaGam-56
87Don-271
87DonOpeD-39
87Fle-220
87FleAll-9
87FleAwaW-2
87FleGamW-3
87FleGlo-220
87FleLimE-4
87FleMin-7
87FleSlu-3
87FleStiC-9
87GenMilB-1B
87HosSti-3
87KraFoo-43
87Lea-184
87OPC-12
87Spo-51
87Spo-80
87StuPan-27
87SyrChi1A-10
87Top-106
87Top-612
87Top-681
87TopCoi-3
87TopGloS-45
87TopMinL-74
87TopSti-193
87TopTif-106
87TopTif-612
87TopTif-681
88Baz-1
88BluJay5-2
88BluJayFS-2
88CheBoy-4
88ClaBlu-242
88Don-656
88DonAll-6
88DonBasB-31
88DonBonM-BC19
88DonPop-6
88Dra-22
88Fle-103
88Fle-623
88FleAll-5
88FleAwaW-2
88FleBasA-1
88FleBasM-1
88FleExcS-3
88FleGlo-103
88FleGlo-623
88FleHotS-1
88FleLeaL-1
88FleMin-59
88FleRecS-2
88FleSlu-1
88FleStiC-71
88FleSup-2
88FleTeaL-1
88GreBasS-76
88K-M-1
88KayB-1
88Lea-213
88Lea-214
88Lea-254
88MSAFanSD-7
88MSAHosD-22
88Nes-34
88OPC-173
88PanSti-224
88PanSti-230
88RedFolSB-6
88Sco-540
88ScoBoxC-6
88ScoGlo-540
88Spo-4
88StaBel-1
88StaBel-2
88StaBel-3
88StaBel-4
88StaBel-5
88StaBel-6
88StaBel-7
88StaBel-8
88StaBel-9
88StaBel-10
88StaBel-11
88StaLinAl-2
88StaLinBJ-2
88StaStiGB-1
88StaStiGB-2
88StaStiGB-3
88StaStiGB-4
88StaStiGB-5
88StaStiGB-6
88StaStiGB-7
88StaStiGB-8
88StaStiGB-9
88StaStiGB-10
88Top-390
88Top-590
88Top-729
88TopBig-15
88TopCoi-1
88TopGaloC-2
88TopGloA-6
88TopGloS-31
88TopMinL-37
88TopRevLL-18
88TopRitTM-26
88TopSti-158
88TopSti-188
88TopStiB-47
88TopTif-390
88TopTif-590
88TopTif-729
88TopUKM-3
88TopUKMT-3
88Woo-9
89BluJayFS-2
89Bow-256
89BowTif-256
89ClaLigB-43
89Don-149
89DonBasB-272
89Fle-226
89FleBasA-2
89FleBasM-2
89FleGlo-226
89FleHeroB-1
89K-M-17
89OPC-50
89PanSti-472
89RedFolSB-7
89Sco-347
89ScoHot1S-91
89Spo-25
89Top-1
89Top-50
89TopAme2C-4
89TopBasT-53
89TopBig-318
89TopGloS-27
89TopMinL-75
89TopSti-1
89TopSti-193
89TopTif-1
89TopTif-50
89TopUKM-3
89TVSpoM-79
89UppDec-255
89Woo-7
90BluJayFS-2
90BluJayHS-1
90BluJayHS-2
90BluJayHS-5
90Bow-515
90BowTif-515
90ClaBlu-84
90Don-206
90DonBesA-139
90DOnBonM-BC13
90DonLeaS-25
90Fle-76
90Fle-628
90FleBasM-1
90FleCan-76
90FleCan-628
90FleLeaL-3
90GooHumICBLS-2
90Hot50PS-1
90Lea-185
90MLBBasB-67
90MSAHolD-1
90MSAIceTD-9
90OPC-170
90PanSti-180
90PubSti-276
90PubSti-509
90Sco-286
90Sco100S-27
90ScoMcD-20
90ScoYouSI-19
90Spo-17
90Top-170
90TopAmeA-22
90TopBig-153
90TopCoi-5
90TopDou-3
90TopGloS-24
90TopHilHM-12
90TopMinL-41
90TopSti-192
90TopStiB-46
90TopTif-170
90TopTVA-21
90UppDec-95
90UppDec-127
90USPlaCA-12C
90VenSti-37
90VenSti-38
90VicPos-1
90WinDis-6
91BasBesHM-1
91Bow-418
91Cla2-T30
91ClaGam-104
91CubMar-11
91CubVinL-3
91CubVinL-36
91Don-642
91Fle-169
91FleUpd-77
91Lea-389
91OPC-440
91OPCPre-6
91PanFreS-340
91PanSti-158
91Sco-195
91Sco100S-40
91ScoRoo-13T
91StaClu-504
91StaPro-1
91Stu-151
91Top-440
91TopDesS-440
91TopMic-440
91TopTif-440
91TopTra-8T
91TopTraT-8T
91TopTriH-N2
91Ult-55
91UppDec-532
91UppDec-725
91UppDec-742
91USPlaCA-6S
92Cla2-T86
92ClaGam-26
92Don-127
92DonCraJ2-6
92DonDiaK-DK7
92DonUpd-U12
92Fle-376
92FleUpd-12
92Hig5-26
92Lea-462
92OPC-320
92OPCPre-182
92PanSti-188
92Pin-37
92Sco-45
92Sco100S-88
92ScoProP-7
92ScoProP-14
92ScoRoo-24T
92StaClu-525
92StaClu-840
92StaCluD-13
92StaCluECN-840
92Stu-151
92Top-320
92TopGol-320
92TopGolW-320
92TopKid-3
92TopMic-320
92TopTra-9T
92TopTraG-9T
92TriPla-42
92Ult-173
92Ult-332
92UppDec-236
92UppDec-724
92WhiSoxK-21
93BluJayDM-4
93Bow-639
93CadDis-5
93ClaGam-11
93Don-95
93DonSpiotG-SG6
93Fin-175
93FinRef-175
93Fle-200
93FunPac-198
93Lea-217
93OPC-26
93PacBeiA-3
93PacSpa-67
93PacSpaPI-10
93PanSti-143
93Pin-387
93PinSlu-25
93Sco-387
93Sel-100
93StaClu-330
93StaCluFDI-330
93StaCluMOP-330
93StaCluWS-22
93Stu-28
93Top-790
93TopGol-790
93TopInaM-790
93TopMic-790
93TriPla-247
93Ult-171
93UppDec-345
93UppDecGold-345
93UppDecHRH-HR12
93WhiSoxK-2
94Fle-75
94PanSti-44
94Sco-541
94ScoGolR-541
94Top-214
94TopGol-214
94TopSpa-214
96BluJayOH-1
97BluJayS-34

Bell, George G.

09AmeCarE-4
09ColChiE-26
09RamT20-10
09SpoNewSM-20
09T206-19
09T206-20
10DomDisP-10
10SweCapPP-70A
10SweCapPP-70B
11S74Sil-49
11SpoLifCW-27
11SpoLifM-149
11T205-13
11TurRedT-79
12ColRedB-26
12ColTinT-26
90DodTar-46

Bell, Greg

86WinSpiP-1
87PitCubP-2

Bell, Gus (David Russell)

47PM1StaP1-8
50PirTeal-2
51Bow-40
51TopRedB-17
52Top-170
53BowBW-1
53NorBreL-3
53Top-118
54Bow-124
55Bow-243
55Kah-1
56Kah-2
56Top-162
57Kah-3
57Top-180
58Kah-3
58RedEnq-4
58RedJayP-2
58Top-75
59Kah-3
59RedBurBP-2
59RedShiBS-3
59Top-365
60Kah-3
60KeyChal-6
60RedJayP-1
60Top-235
60Top-352
61Kah-4
61Pos-186B
61RedJayP-3
61Top-25
61Top-215
61TopStal-14
62Jel-120
62MetJayP-1
62PosCan-120
62SalPlaC-158A
62SalPlaC-158B
62ShiPlaC-158
62Top-408
62TopBuc-8
62TopStal-153
63Top-547
64Top-534
74MetOriEB-2
76OPC-66
76Top-66
79TCM50-89
82OhiHaloF-35

83TopRep5-170
85Top-131
85TopTif-131
Bell, Hi (Herman)
34DiaMatCSB-7
34Gou-52
92ConTSN-632
Bell, Jason
96Bow-253
96FtMyeMB-4
96HarCitRCB-7
Bell, Jay
85VisOakT-8
86IndTeal-5
86WatIndP-4
87BufBisP-4
88Don-637
88DonBasB-61
88Fle-602
88FleGlo-602
88IndGat-16
88StaLinI-4
88Top-637
88TopTif-637
89BufBisC-4
89BufBisP-1679
89Don-350
89PirVerFJ-3
89Sco-352
89Top-144
89TopTif-144
89TriAAP-AAA7
89UppDec-489
90Bow-174
90BowTif-174
90Don-488
90DonBesN-136
90Fle-459
90FleCan-459
90Lea-248
90OPC-523
90PanSti-321
90PirHomC-4
90Sco-563
90ScoYouS2-12
90Top-523
90TopTif-523
90UppDec-517
91Bow-522
91Don-289
91Fle-31
91Lea-130
91OPC-293
91PanFreS-118
91PanSti-110
91Sco-323
91StaClu-84
91Stu-221
91Top-293
91TopDesS-293
91TopMic-293
91TopTif-293
91Ult-274
91UppDec-183
92Bow-519
92Cla1-T12
92Don-100
92DonDiaK-DK17
92Fle-549
92HitTheBB-3
92Lea-143
92OPC-779
92PanSti-255
92Pin-34
92PirNatI-2
92Sco-180
92StaClu-507
92Stu-81
92Top-779
92TopGol-779
92TopGolW-779
92TopMic-779
92TriPla-184
92Ult-250
92UppDec-115
93Bow-330
93CadDis-6
93DiaMar-9
93Don-18
93Fin-194
93FinRef-194
93Fla-110
93Fle-111
93FunPac-149
93Lea-116
93OPC-19
93PacSpa-243
93PanSti-283
93Pin-48
93PirNatI-2
93Sco-32
93Sel-81
93SP-182
93StaClu-138
93StaCluFDI-138
93StaCluMOP-138
93Stu-20
93Top-354
93TopGol-354
93TopInaM-354
93TopMic-354
93TriPla-140
93TriPla-261
93Ult-96
93UppDec-103
93UppDec-480
93UppDec-830
93UppDecGold-103
93UppDecGold-480
93UppDecGold-830
94Bow-106
94ChuHomS-20
94ChuHomSG-20
94ColC-497
94ColChoGS-497
94ColChoSS-497
94Don-21
94DonSpeE-21
94ExtBas-343
94Fin-411
94FinRef-411
94Fla-214
94Fle-605
94FleAllS-28
94FleSun-4
94FleTeaL-25
94FUnPac-161
94Lea-12
94LeaL-139
94OPC-222
94Pac-492
94PanSti-233
94Pin-151
94PinArtP-151
94PinMusC-151
94PinRunC-RC37
94PinTeaP-4
94PirBloP-1
94PirQui-1
94ProMag-107
94RedFolMI-3
94Sco-32
94ScoCyc-TC15
94ScoGolR-32
94ScoGolS-12
94Sel-5
94SP-140
94SPDieC-140
94Spo-95
94Spo-188
94StaClu-18
94StaCluFDI-18
94StaCluGR-18
94StaCluMOP-18
94StaCluMOP-ST11
94StaCluST-ST11
94Stu-144
94TomPiz-2
94Top-15
94TopBlaG-24
94TopGol-15
94TopSpa-15
94TriPla-181
94TriPlaM-8
94Ult-254
94UltAllS-14
94UltAwaW-14
94UppDec-177
94UppDec-277
94UppDecAJ-37
94UppDecAJG-37
94UppDecED-177
94UppDecED-277
95Baz-96
95Bow-363
95ColCho-380
95ColChoGS-380
95ColChoSE-175
95ColChoSEGS-175
95ColChoSESS-175
95ColChoSS-380
95Don-206
95DonPreP-206
95DonTopotO-312
95Emb-15
95EmbGolI-15
95Emo-172
95Fin-122
95FinRef-122
95Fla-184
95Fle-472
95FleTeaL-25
95Lea-179
95LeaLim-19
95Pac-340
95PacPri-111
95PanSti-61
95Pin-86
95PinArtP-86
95PinMusC-86
95PirFil-2
95Sco-438
95ScoGolR-438
95ScoHaloG-HG81
95ScoPlaTS-438
95Sel-24
95SelArtP-24
95SelCer-73
95SelCerMG-73
95SP-95
95SPCha-79
95SPCha-82
95SPChaDC-79
95SPChaDC-82
95Spo-43
95SpoArtP-43
95SPSil-95
95StaClu-125
95StaCluCC-CC11
95StaCluFDI-125
95StaCluMOP-125
95StaCluMOP-CC11
95StaCluSTWS-125
95StaCluVR-64
95Stu-119
95Sum-95
95SumNthD-95
95Top-230
95TopCyb-129
95UC3-76
95UC3ArtP-76
95Ult-423
95UltGolM-423
95UppDec-150
95UppDecED-150
95UppDecEDG-150
95UppDecSE-220
95UppDecSEG-220
95Zen-45
96Baz-41
96Bow-52
96Cir-170
96CirAcc-25
96CirBos-44
96CirRav-170
96ColCho-405
96ColCho-675
96ColChoGS-405
96ColChoGS-675
96ColChoSS-405
96ColChoSS-675
96ColChoYMtP-4
96ColChoYMtP-4A
96ColChoYMtPGS-4
96ColChoYMtPGS-4A
96DenHol-28
96Don-21
96DonPreP-21
96EmoXL-252
96Fin-B106
96FinRef-B106
96Fla-343
96Fle-514
96FleTif-514
96Lea-152
96LeaPre-11
96LeaPreP-11
96LeaPrePB-152
96LeaPrePG-152
96LeaPrePS-152
96LeaSig-34
96LeaSigPPG-34
96LeaSigPPP-34
96MetUni-214
96MetUniP-214
96Pac-173
96PacPri-P55
96PacPriG-P55
96PanSti-65
96Pin-64
96PinAfi-2
96PinAfiAP-2
96PinAfiFPP-2
96PinArtP-56
96PinFan-20
96PinSta-56
96ProSta-93
96Sco-300
96ScoDugC-B25
96ScoDugCAP-B25
96Sel-16
96SelArtP-16
96SelCer-9
96SelCerAP-9
96SelCerCB-9
96SelCerCR-9
96SelCerMG-9
96SelCerMR-9
96SelTeaN-3
96SP-150
96Spo-92
96SpoArtP-92
96StaClu-172
96StaCluEPB-172
96StaCluEPG-172
96StaCluEPS-172
96StaCluMOP-172
95StaCluVRMC-64
96Stu-83
96StuPrePB-83
96StuPrePG-83
96StuPrePS-83
96Sum-25
96SumAbo&B-25
96SumArtP-25
96SumFoi-25
96Top-156
96TopLas-18
96Ult-260
96UltGolM-260
96UppDec-435
96Zen-27
96ZenArtP-27
96ZenMoz-23
97Bow-249
97BowChr-73
97BowChrI-73
97BowChrIR-73
97BowChrR-73
97BowInt-249
97Cir-79
97CirRav-79
97Don-124
97DonPreP-124
97DonPrePGold-124
97Fin-178
97FinRef-178
97FlaSho-A145
97FlaSho-B145
97FlaSho-C145
97FlaShoLC-145
97FlaShoLC-B145
97FlaShoLC-C145
97FlaShoLCM-A145
97FlaShoLCM-B145
97FlaShoLCM-C145
97Fle-425
97Fle-541
97FleTif-425
97FleTif-541
97Lea-150
97LeaFraM-150
97LeaFraMDC-150
97NewPin-60
97NewPinAP-60
97NewPinMC-60
97NewPinPP-60
97Pac-390
97PacLigB-390
97PacSil-390
97PinX-PSfF-6
97PinX-PSfFU-6
97RoyPol-3
97Sco-77
97Sco-433
97ScoHobR-433
97ScoPreS-77
97ScoResC-433
97ScoShoS-77
97ScoShoS-433
97ScoShoSAP-77
97ScoShoSAP-433
97SP-89
97SpoIll-154
97SpoIllEE-154
97StaClu-261
97StaCluMOP-261
97Top-259
97Ult-302
97UltGolME-302
97UltPlaME-302
97UppDec-537
Bell, Jerry
72OPC-162
72Top-162
73OPC-92
73Top-92
74CarSalLCA-98
74OPC-261
74Top-261
74TopSta-191
75SanAntBT-3
94BreMilB-105
Bell, Juan
87BakDodP-7
88BasAmeAAB-23
88SanAntMB-24
88TriAAC-44
89Bow-11
89BowTif-11
89ClaTraP-170
89RocRedWC-21
89RocRedWP-1658
89UppDec-20
89UppDec-747
90CMC-312
90OPC-724
90ProAAAF-464
90RocRedWC-13
90RocRedWGC-9
90RocRedWP-707
90Sco-603
90Top-724
90TopDeb89-13
90TopTif-724
91Bow-96
91Fle-468
91Lea-262
91OPCPre-7
91OriCro-29
91Sco100RS-59
91StuPre-1
91UppDecFE-59F
92Don-479
92Fle-3
92FleUpd-108
92OPC-52
92RocRedWS-451
92Sco-646
92StaClu-835
92StaCluNC-835
92Top-52
92TopGol-52
92TopGolW-52
92TopMic-52
93Bow-48
93Don-200
93Fle-98
93FleFinE-222
93Lea-205
93PacSpa-231
93PhiMed-6
93Pin-566
93Sco-588
93StaClu-157
93StaCluFDI-157
93StaCluMOP-157
93TriPla-98
93Ult-84
93UppDec-580
93UppDecGold-580
94BreMilB-106
94Fle-173
94Pac-325
94Sco-282
94ScoGolR-282
94StaClu-236
94StaCluFDI-236
94StaCluGR-236

94StaCluMOP-236
94Top-651
94TopGol-651
94TopSpa-651
94Ult-72
94WesPalBEC-3
94WesPalBEF-46
95Pac-261
95PawRedSDD-4
95PawRedTI-23
95Sco-412
95ScoGolR-412
95ScoPlaTS-412
Bell, Kevin Robert
75AppFoxT-2
77Top-83
78SSP270-150
78Top-463
79IowOakP-4
79Top-662
80OPC-197
80Top-379
81Don-39
81Fle-343
81TacTigT-25
82TacTigT-13
Bell, Lenny
88PeoChiTI-4
89WinSpiS-1
Bell, Les (Lester Rowland)
25Exh-57
26Exh-57
27YorCarE-58B
28W502-58
28W56PlaC-JOK
28Yue-58
30ChiEveAP-1
31CubTeal-2
35GouPreR-7
79DiaGre-151
92ConTSN-651
Bell, Matty (Madison)
40WheM4-5
Bell, Michael Allen
87SumBraP-16
88CarLeaAS-25
88DurBulS-1
89GreBraB-4
89GreBraP-1173
89GreBraS-3
89Sta-34
90GreBraP-1134
90GreBraS-3
90ProAaA-64
90StaFS7-94
91BraSubS-3
91Fle-682
91LinDriAAA-427
91RicBraBC-20
91RicBraLD-427
91RicBraP-2575
91RicBraTI-8
91Sco-375
91TopDeb90-14
91UppDec-644
92Fle-350
92GreBraF-1158
92GreBraS-228
92Sco-249
93BufBisF-522
Bell, Mike
94Bow-350
94ChaRivC-1
94ChaRivF-2679
94Cla-171
94ClaGolF-78
94ClaTriF-T79
94SouAtlLAF-SAL3
94SP-1
94SPDieC-1
94Top-201
94TopGol-201
94TopSpa-201
94UppDec-542
94UppDecAHNIL-1
94UppDecED-542
94UppDecML-218
95Bow-192
95Exc-124
95SPML-158
95UppDecML-26
95UppDecMLMLA-1
96BesAutS-9
96Bow-188
96DelShoB-9
96TulDriTI-2
95UppDecMLFS-26
Bell, Randy
92DavLipB-3
Bell, Robbie
95TopTra-88T
96EugEmeB-2
97Bow-353
97BowChr-238
97BowChrI-238
97BowChrIR-238
97BowChrR-238
97BowInt-353
Bell, Robert
86EugEmeC-34
Bell, Ron
77SanJosMC-20
Bell, Sam
39WorWidGV-2
Bell, Stewart
91ParPatF-15
Bell, Terry
86ChaLooP-4
86MemChiSTOS-1
86MemChiTOS-1
87MemChiB-23
87MemChiP-17
88GreBraB-2
89GreBraB-19
89GreBraP-1162
89GreBraS-4
Bell, Tito
93LimRocDWB-58
Bell, Tom
88FreSunCLC-27
88FreSunP-1248
Bell, William
86NegLeaF-99
Bella, Zeke (John)
59Top-254
60A'sTeal-2
Bellacetin, Juan
85MexCitTT-27
Bellaman, Mike
86WatIndP-3
87WilBilP-10
Belle, Albert (Joey)
87LSUTigP-1
88KinIndS-3
89CanIndS-25
89FleUpd-25
89ScoRoo-106T
89Sta-199
90Bow-333
90BowTif-333
90ClaBlu-100
90Don-390
90Fle-485
90FleCan-485
90Hot50RS-6
90IndTeal-5
90Lea-180
90OPC-283
90Sco-508
90Sco100RS-9
90ScoYouSI-3
90Spo-159
90Top-283
90TopDeb89-14
90TopRoo-2
90TopSti-212
90TopTif-283
90ToyRoo-3
90UppDec-446
91Bow-81
91Cla3-T37
91FleUpd-16
91IndFanC-4
91Lea-239
91OPCPre-8
91StaBelRG-1
91StaBelRG-2
91StaBelRG-3
91StaBelRG-4
91StaBelRG-5
91StaBelRG-6
91StaBelRG-7
91StaBelRG-8
91StaBelRG-9
91StaBelRG-10
91StaBelRG-11
91StaClu-465
91Ult-107
91UppDec-764
92Bow-329
92Cla1-T13
92ClaGam-140
92DenHol-6
92Don-500
92Fle-105
92Hig5-43
92IndFanC-6
92Lea-350
92LeaBlaG-350
92MooSna-1
92OPC-785
92OPCPre-100
92PanSti-51
92Pin-31
92PinTea2-18
92Sco-31
92Sco100S-39
92ScoProP-10
92SpoIllFK1-187
92SpoIllFK1-416
92SpoStaCC-2
92StaBel-1
92StaBel-2
92StaBel-3
92StaBel-4
92StaBel-5
92StaBel-6
92StaBel-7
92StaBel-8
92StaBel-9
92StaBel-10
92StaBel-11
92StaClu-220
92Stu-164
92Top-785
92TopGol-785
92TopGolW-785
92TopKid-73
92TopMic-785
92TriPla-103
92Ult-47
92UppDec-137
92UppDecHRH-HR13
92UppDecTMH-8
92UppDecWB-T13
93Bow-445
93ClaGam-12
93DenHol-12
93DiaMar-10
93Don-435
93DonEliD-17
93DonLonBL-LL3
93Fin-16
93FinRef-16
93Fla-192
93Fle-590
93Fle-712
93FleFruotL-4
93FunPac-108
93IndWUA-3
93Lea-18
93OPC-66
93PacSpa-94
93PanSti-52
93Pin-93
93PinHomRC-5
93PinSlu-11
93Sco-84
93Sel-50
93SP-120
93SPPlaP-PP1
93StaClu-102
93StaCluFDI-102
93StaCluMOP-102
93Stu-95
93Top-635
93TopGol-635
93TopInaM-635
93TopMic-635
93TriPla-94
93Ult-538
93UltHomRK-5
93UppDec-45
93UppDec-586
93UppDec-823
93UppDecGold-45
93UppDecGold-586
93UppDecGold-823
93UppDecHRH-HR5
93UppDecIC-WI12
93UppDecICJ-WI12
93UppDecOD-D4
93USPlaCA-9C
94Bow-411
94BowBes-R41
94BowBes-X98
94BowBesR-R41
94BowBesR-X98
94BowPre-3
94ChuShoS-7
94ColC-314
94ColC-339
94ColC-620
94ColChoGS-314
94ColChoGS-339
94ColChoGS-620
94ColChoHRA-HA6
94ColChoSS-314
94ColChoSS-339
94ColChoSS-620
94ColChoT-9
94DenHol-5
94Don-351
94DonDiaK-DK8
94DonEli-40
94DonMVP-19
94DonSpeE-351
94ExtBas-57
94ExtBasGB-3
94Fin-208
94FinJum-208
94FinRef-208
94Fla-38
94FlaOutP-1
94Fle-100
94FleAllS-3
94FleLeaL-2
94FleLumC-1
94FUnPac-130
94FUnPac-183
94FUnPac-204
94KinDis-9
94Lea-251
94LeaCleC-11
94LeaL-27
94LeaMVPC-A2
94LeaMVPCG-A2
94LeaPowB-10
94OPC-43
94OPCAllR-12
94OPCJumA-12
94Pac-165
94PacGolP-4
94PanSti-7
94PanSti-55
94Pin-15
94PinArtP-15
94PinMusC-15
94PinPowS-PS11
94PinRunC-RC8
94PinTheN-6
94Pos-27
94ProMag-38
94RedFolMI-4
94Sco-7
94ScoCyc-TC20
94ScoGolR-7
94ScoGolS-46
94ScoSam-7
94ScoSam-7GR
94Sel-235
94SP-97
94SPDieC-97
94Spo-10
94SpoRooGGG-GG11
94StaClu-219
94StaClu-258
94StaCluF-F2
94StaCluFDI-219
94StaCluFDI-258
94StaCluGR-219
94StaCluGR-258
94StaCluMO-18
94StaCluMOP-219
94StaCluMOP-258
94StaCluMOP-F2
94StaCluMOP-ST19
94StaCluST-ST19
94Stu-92
94TomPiz-17
94Top-390
94Top-480
94TopBlaG-3
94TopGol-390
94TopGol-480
94TopSpa-390
94TopSpa-480
94TopSupS-4
94TriPla-113
94TriPlaBS-9
94TriPlaM-11
94Ult-41
94UltAllS-6
94UltHomRK-4
94UltRBIK-1
94UltRisS-3
94UppDec-40
94UppDec-131
94UppDec-285
94UppDecAJ-29
94UppDecAJG-29
94UppDecED-40
94UppDecED-131
94UppDecED-285
94UppDecMLS-MM2
94UppDecMLSED-MM2
94USPlaCA-9C
95Baz-116
95BazRedH-RH21
95Bow-276
95BowBes-R50
95BowBesJR-1
95BowBesR-R50
95ClaPhoC-19
95ColCho-83
95ColChoCtA-1
95ColChoCtAG-1
95ColChoCtG-CG2
95ColChoCtG-CG2B
95ColChoCtG-CG2C
95ColChoCtGE-2
95ColChoCtGG-CG2
95ColChoCtGG-CG2B
95ColChoCtGG-CG2C
95ColChoCtGGE-2
95ColChoGS-83
95ColChoSE-120
95ColChoSEGS-120
95ColChoSESS-120
95ColChoSS-83
95D3-7
95DenHol-4
95Don-264
95DonBomS-3
95DonDom-7
95DonEli-60
95DonPreP-264
95DonTopotO-58
95Emb-125
95EmbGolI-125
95Emo-32
95EmoN-2
95Fin-82
95FinPowK-PK11
95FinRef-82
95Fla-30
95FlaHotN-2
95FlaOutP-1
95Fle-132
95FleAllS-17
95FleLumC-2
95FleTeaL-5
95FleUpdDT-2
95FleUpdH-2
95Lea-284
95LeaGolS-2
95LeaLim-147
95LeaLimG-5
95LeaLimIBP-23
95LeaLimL-1
95NatPac2-1
95Pac-118
95PacGolCDC-7
95PacGolP-14
95PacPri-38
95PanSti-90
95Pin-233
95Pin-298
95PinArtP-233
95PinArtP-298
95PinFan-4
95PinGatA-GA8
95PinMusC-233
95PinMusC-298
95PinPer-PP2
95PinPin-16
95PinPinR-16
95PinRedH-RH7
95PinTeaP-TP8
95PinUps-US5

95PinWhiH-WH7
95Pos-13
95RedFol-16
95Sco-223
95Sco-557
95ScoDreT-DG6
95ScoGolR-223
95ScoGolR-557
95ScoHaloG-HG9
95ScoPlaTS-223
95ScoPlaTS-557
95ScoRul-SR6
95ScoRulJ-SR6
95ScoSam-223
95Sel-60
95Sel-244
95SelArtP-60
95SelArtP-244
95SelBigS-BS12
95SelCer-56
95SelCerMG-56
95SP-145
95SPCha-145
95SPChaDC-145
95SPChaDFC-3
95SPChaFCDC-3
95Spo-14
95SpoArtP-14
95SpoDet-DE7
95SpoDouT-10
95SpoHamT-HT6
95SpoPro-PM7
95SPPlaP-PP9
95SPSil-145
95SPSpeF-9
95StaClu-489
95StaClu-514
95StaCluCC-CC16
95StaCluCT-4
95StaCluMO-3
95StaCluMOP-489
95StaCluMOP-514
95StaCluMOP-CC16
95StaCluMOP-PZ2
95StaCluMOP-RL22
95StaCluMOP-VRE4
95StaCluPZ-PZ2
95StaCluRL-RL22
95StaCluSTDW-I19T
95StaCluSTDW-I489
95StaCluSTMP-12
95StaCluSTWS-489
95StaCluSTWS-514
95StaCluVE-VRE4
95StaCluVR-269
95Stu-15
95StuGolS-15
95StuPlaS-15
95Sum-11
95Sum-187
95SumBigB-BB14
95SumNthD-11
95SumNthD-187
95SumSam-11
95Top-389
95Top-503
95TopCyb-293
95TopFin-2
95TopLeaL-LL1
95TopLeaL-LL14
95TopLeaL-LL33
95TopTra-4T
95TopTra-161T
95TopTraPB-4
95UC3-58
95UC3-131
95UC3ArtP-58
95UC3ArtP-131
95UC3CycS-CS12
95UllHomRK-1
95Ult-36
95UltAllS-2
95UltAllSGM-2
95UltGolM-36
95UltHitM-2
95UltHitMGM-2
95UltHomRK-3
95UltHomRKGM-3
95UltOnBL-2
95UltOnBLGM-2
95UltPowP-1
95UltPowPGM-1
95UltRBIK-3
95UltRBIKGM-3
95UltRisS-3
95UltRisSGM-3
95UppDec-340
95UppDecED-340
95UppDecEDG-340
95UppDecPAW-H1
95UppDecPAWE-H1
95UppDecPLL-R1
95UppDecPLL-R11
95UppDecPLL-R59
95UppDecPLLE-R1
95UppDecPLLE-R11
95UppDecPLLE-R59
95UppDecSE-25
95UppDecSEG-25
95USPlaCMLA-9C
95USPlaCMLA-11D
95Zen-1
95ZenAllS-11
95ZenZ-14
96Baz-59
96Bow-92
96BowBes-6
96BowBesAR-6
96BowBesMI-5
96BowBesMIAR-5
96BowBesMIR-5
96BowBesR-6
96Cir-32
96CirAcc-5
96CirBos-8
96CirRav-32
96ColCho-3
96ColCho-4
96ColCho-279
96ColCho-364
96ColCho-530
96ColChoCtG-CG11
96ColChoCtG-CG11B
96ColChoCtG-CG11C
96ColChoCtGE-CR11
96ColChoCtGG-CG11
96ColChoCtGG-CG11B
96ColChoCtGG-CG11C
96ColChoCtGGE-CR11
96ColChoGS-3
96ColChoGS-4
96ColChoGS-279
96ColChoGS-364
96ColChoGS-530
96ColChoSS-3
96ColChoSS-4
96ColChoSS-279
96ColChoSS-364
96ColChoSS-530
96ColChoYMtP-5
96ColChoYMtP-5A
96ColChoYMtPGS-5
96ColChoYMtPGS-5A
96DenHol-4
96DenHolGS-8
96DenHolGSAP-8
96Don-222
96DonFreF-6
96DonPowA-4
96DonPowADC-4
96DonPreP-222
96DonPurP-3
96DonRouT-1
96EmoLegoB-1
96EmoN-1
96EmoXL-46
96Fin-B214
96Fin-G9
96Fin-S188
96FinLan-2
96FinRef-B214
96FinRef-G9
96FinRef-S188
96Fla-64
96FlaDiaC-2
96FlaPow-1
96Fle-83
96FleGolM-1
96FleInd-4
96FleLumC-1
96FleTif-83
96FleUpd-U213
96FleUpdH-3
96FleUpdTC-U213
96FleZon-1
96Kin-9
96Lea-94
96LeaAllGMC-17
96LeaAllGMCG-17
96LeaGolS-10
96LeaHatO-7
96LeaLim-41
96LeaLimG-41
96LeaLimPC-5
96LeaPicP-8
96LeaPre-46
96LeaPreP-46
96LeaPrePB-94
96LeaPrePG-94
96LeaPrePS-94
96LeaPreSG-68
96LeaPreSP-1
96LeaPreSta-9
96LeaPreSte-68
96LeaSig-59
96LeaSigPPG-59
96LeaSigPPP-59
96LeaStaS-7
96LeaTotB-2
96MetUni-44
96MetUniHM-1
96MetUniP-44
96MetUniT-1
96Pac-307
96PacGolCD-DC26
96PacMil-M1
96PacOctM-OM2
96PacPri-P94
96PacPriFB-FB1
96PacPriG-P94
96PacPriRHS-RH11
96PanSti-121
96PanSti-175
96Pin-137
96Pin-207
96Pin-262
96PinAfi-77
96PinAfi-197
96PinAfiAP-77
96PinAfiAP-197
96PinAfiFPP-77
96PinAfiMN-7
96PinAfiP-MN7
96PinAfiSP-8
96PinArtP-64
96PinArtP-107
96PinArtP-162
96PinChrBC-10
96PinEssotG-13
96PinFan-8
96PinFoil-207
96PinFoil-262
96PinPow-13
96PinSky-5
96PinSlu-6
96PinSta-64
96PinSta-107
96PinSta-162
96PinTeaP-7
96PinTeaS-9
96Pro-2
96ProMagA-9
96ProMagDM-10
96ProSta-57
96SchDis-9
96Sco-72
96Sco-275
96Sco-379
96ScoAll-2
96ScoBigB-10
96ScoDiaA-21
96ScoDugC-A59
96ScoDugC-B104
96ScoDugCAP-A59
96ScoDugCAP-B104
96ScoGolS-11
96ScoNumG-13
96ScoPowP-2
96ScoRef-12
96ScoTitT-1
96Sel-36
96Sel-154
96SelArtP-36
96SelArtP-154
96SelCer-22
96SelCer-140
96SelCerAP-22
96SelCerAP-140
96SelCerCB-22
96SelCerCB-140
96SelCerCR-22
96SelCerCR-140
96SelCerIP-24
96SelCerMB-22
96SelCerMB-140
96SelCerMG-22
96SelCerMG-140
96SelCerMR-22
96SelCerMR-140
96SelCerSF-4
96SelClaTF-6
96SelEnF-8
96SelTeaN-1
96SP-70
96SPBasH-83
96SPMarM-MM12
96SPMarMDC-12
96Spo-7
96Spo-101
96SpoArtP-7
96SpoArtP-101
96SpoDouT-8
96SpoHitP-6
96SpoPowS-5
96SpoPro-4
96SPPreF-3
96SPSpeFX-30
96SPSpeFXDC-30
96SPx-19
96SPxGol-19
96StaClu-201
96StaClu-297
96StaCluEPB-297
96StaCluEPG-297
96StaCluEPS-297
96StaCluMM-MM7
96StaCluMO-3
96StaCluMOP-201
96StaCluMOP-297
96StaCluMOP-MM7
96StaCluMOP-PC1
96StaCluMOP-PP1
96StaCluMOP-PS3
96StaCluMOP-TSCA2
96StaCluPC-PC1
96StaCluPP-PP1
96StaCluPS-PS3
96StaCluTA-2
95StaCluVRMC-269
96Stu-143
96StuHitP-8
96StuPrePB-143
96StuPrePG-143
96StuPrePS-143
96StuStaGS-7
96Sum-82
96SumAbo&B-82
96SumArtP-82
96SumBal-2
96SumBigB-3
96SumBigBM-3
96SumFoi-82
96SumHitI-8
96SumPos-7
96TeaOut-6
96TeaOut-C93
96Top-45
96Top-223
96TopBigC-1
96TopChr-17
96TopChr-83
96TopChrR-17
96TopChrR-83
96TopChrWC-WC2
96TopChrWCR-WC2
96TopGal-157
96TopGalE-19
96TopGalPG-PG9
96TopGalPPI-157
96TopLas-99
96TopLasPC-1
96TopMysF-M17
96TopMysFR-M17
96TopPro-AL3
96TopRoaW-RW2
96TopWreC-WC2
96Ult-46
96Ult-575
96UltChe-B1
96UltCheGM-B1
96UltDiaP-1
96UltDiaPGM-1
96UltGolM-46
96UltGolM-575
96UltHitM-1
96UltHitMGM-1
96UltHomRKGM-1
96UltHomRKR-1
96UltRBIK-2
96UltRBIKGM-2
96UltThu-1
96UltThuGM-1
96UppDec-315
96UppDec-371
96UppDecA-4
96UppDecDD-DD16
96UppDecDDG-DD16
96UppDecDDS-DD16
96UppDecG-GF4
96UppDecHC-HC5
96UppDecPD-PD1
96UppDecPHE-H1
96UppDecPRE-R1
96UppDecPRE-R11
96UppDecPreH-H1
96UppDecPreR-R1
96UppDecPreR-R11
96UppDecRunP-RP1
96Zen-95
96Zen-131
96ZenArtP-95
96ZenArtP-131
96ZenDiaC-1
96ZenDiaCP-1
96ZenMoz-18
96ZenZ-2
97Bow-67
97BowBes-3
97BowBesAR-3
97BowBesBC-BC10
97BowBesBCAR-BC10
97BowBesBCR-BC10
97BowBesMI-MI10
97BowBesMIAR-MI10
97BowBesMIARI-MI10
97BowBesMII-MI10
97BowBesMIR-MI10
97BowBesMIRI-MI10
97BowBesR-3
97BowChr-48
97BowChrI-48
97BowChrIR-48
97BowChrR-48
97BowInt-67
97Cir-250
97CirBos-2
97CirLimA-2
97CirRav-250
97CirRavR-1
97CirSupB-2
97ColCho-58
97ColCho-76
97ColCho-329
97ColChoAC-7
97ColChoCtG-9A
97ColChoCtG-9B
97ColChoCtG-9C
97ColChoCtGIW-CG9
97ColChoNF-NF25
97ColChoPP-PP4
97ColChoPPG-PP4
97ColChoS-8
97ColChoTBS-15
97ColChoTBSWH-15
97ColChoTotT-T10
97Don-160
97Don-289
97Don-442
97DonDom-6
97DonEli-9
97DonEliGS-9
97DonLim-51
97DonLim-63
97DonLim-111
97DonLimFotG-13
97DonLimFotG-62
97DonLimLE-51
97DonLimLE-63
97DonLimLE-111
97DonLonL-2
97DonPowA-8
97DonPowADC-8
97DonPre-13
97DonPre-187
97DonPreCttC-13
97DonPreCttC-187
97DonPreP-160
97DonPreP-289
97DonPreP-442
97DonPrePGold-160

97DonPrePGold-289
97DonPrePGold-442
97DonPrePM-4
97DonPreS-12
97DonPreTB-2
97DonPreTBG-2
97DonPreTF-2
97DonPreTP-2
97DonPreTPG-2
97DonPreXP-4A
97DonRocL-2
97DonTea-70
97DonTeaSMVP-11
97DonTeaSPE-70
97Fin-240
97Fin-319
97Fin-347
97FinEmb-319
97FinEmb-347
97FinEmbR-319
97FinEmbR-347
97FinRef-240
97FinRef-319
97FinRef-347
97FlaSho-A48
97FlaSho-B48
97FlaSho-C48
97FlaShoDC-2
97FlaShoLC-48
97FlaShoLC-B48
97FlaShoLC-C48
97FlaShoLCM-A48
97FlaShoLCM-B48
97FlaShoLCM-C48
97Fle-75
97Fle-491
97Fle-600
97FleBleB-1
97FleDiaT-1
97FleHea-2
97FleLumC-3
97FleMilDM-36
97FleSoaS-1
97FleTeaL-5
97FleTif-75
97FleTif-491
97FleTif-600
97FleZon-2
97Lea-190
97Lea-202
97Lea-375
97LeaDrefS-3
97LeaFraM-190
97LeaFraM-202
97LeaFraM-375
97LeaFraMDC-190
97LeaFraMDC-202
97LeaFraMDC-375
97LeaGet-9
97LeaGolS-20
97LeaLeaotN-9
97LeaStaS-1
97LeaWarT-2
97MetUni-55
97MetUniBF-2
97MetUniT-2
97NewPin-12
97NewPin-193
97NewPinAP-12
97NewPinAP-193
97NewPinIE-1
97NewPinMC-12
97NewPinMC-193
97NewPinPP-12
97NewPinPP-193
97NewPinPP-I1A
97NewPinPP-AB1
97NewPinPP-AB2
97NewPinPP-AB3
97NewPinPP-AB4
97NewPinPP-AB5
97NewPinS-AB1
97NewPinS-AB2
97NewPinS-AB3
97NewPinS-AB4
97NewPinS-AB5
97Pac-67
97PacCar-8
97PacCarM-8
97PacCerCGT-15
97PacCraC-3
97PacFirD-6
97PacGolCD-8
97PacLigB-67
97PacPri-25
97PacPriGotD-GD33
97PacPriLB-25
97PacPriP-25
97PacPriSL-SL3A
97PacSil-67
97PacTriCD-5
97Pin-100
97PinArtP-100
97PinCar-6
97PinCer-17
97PinCer-140
97PinCerCMGT-15
97PinCerCT-15
97PinCerMBlu-17
97PinCerMBlu-140
97PinCerMG-17
97PinCerMG-140
97PinCerMR-17
97PinCerMR-140
97PinCerR-17
97PinCerR-140
97PinHom-23
97PinHom-24
97PinIns-35
97PinInsC-9
97PinInsCE-35
97PinInsDD-3
97PinInsDE-35
97PinInsFS-6
97PinMin-8
97PinMinB-8
97PinMinCB-8
97PinMinCG-8
97PinMinCGR-8
97PinMinCN-8
97PinMinCS-8
97PinMinG-8
97PinMinS-8
97PinMusC-100
97PinTeaP-6
97PinTeaP-10
97PinTotCPB-17
97PinTotCPB-140
97PinTotCPG-17
97PinTotCPG-140
97PinTotCPR-17
97PinTotCPR-140
97PinX-P-47
97PinX-PF&A-1
97PinX-PMoS-47
97PinX-PMW-13
97PinX-PMWG-13
97PinX-PMWS-13
97PinX-PSfF-14
97PinX-PSfFU-14
97ProMag-50
97ProMagML-50
97Sco-12
97Sco-428
97Sco-495
97ScoAllF-9
97ScoBla-4
97ScoFra-6
97ScoFraG-6
97ScoHeaotO-5
97ScoHigZ-4
97ScoHobR-428
97ScoHobR-495
97ScoInd-1
97ScoIndPl-1
97ScoIndPr-1
97ScoPreS-12
97ScoResC-428
97ScoResC-495
97ScoShoS-12
97ScoShoS-428
97ScoShoS-495
97ScoShoSAP-12
97ScoShoSAP-428
97ScoShoSAP-495
97ScoSteS-10
97ScoTitT-6
97Sel-17
97SelArtP-17
97SelRegG-17
97SelToootT-5
97SelToootTMB-5
97SkyE-X-12
97SkyE-XACA-4
97SkyE-XC-12
97SkyE-XEC-12
97SkyE-XHoN-14
97SP-45
97SPInsI-15
97SpoIll-149
97SpoIllEE-149
97SpoIllGS-9
97SPSpeF-4
97SPSpxF-2
97SPSPxFA-2
97SPx-18
97SPxBoufG-8
97SPxBro-18
97SPxCorotG-2
97SPxGraF-18
97SPxSil-18
97SPxSte-18
97StaClu-227
97StaClu-379
97StaCluFR-F2
97StaCluI-I14
97StaCluMat-227
97StaCluMOP-227
97StaCluMOP-379
97StaCluMOP-I14
97StaCluMOP-FB2
97StaCluMOP-PG2
97StaCluPG-PG2
97Stu-98
97StuHarH-2
97StuMasS-16
97StuMasS8-16
97StuPor8-9
97StuPrePG-98
97StuPrePS-98
97Top-69
97TopAll-AS11
97TopChr-24
97TopChrAS-AS11
97TopChrDD-DD10
97TopChrDDR-DD10
97TopChrR-24
97TopChrSAR-AS11
97TopChrSB-9
97TopChrSB-12
97TopChrSBR-9
97TopChrSBR-12
97TopGal-82
97TopGalPMS-2
97TopGalPMSSS-3
97TopGalPPI-82
97TopHobM-HM4
97TopIntF-ILM6
97TopIntFR-ILM6
97TopScr-2
97TopSeaB-SB9
97TopSeaB-SB12
97TopSta-39
97TopStaAM-39
97TopSweS-SS3
97TopTeaT-TT14
97Ult-46
97Ult-411
97UltDouT-5
97UltFamGam-10
97UltGolME-46
97UltGolME-411
97UltHitM-8
97UltHRK-1
97UltPlaME-46
97UltPlaME-411
97UltPowP-B7
97UltRBIK-2
97UltSeaC-1
97UltStaR-11
97UltTop3-11
97UltTop3GM-11
97UppDec-50
97UppDec-333
97UppDec-419
97UppDecAG-AG8
97UppDecAWJ-5
97UppDecHC-HC12
97UppDecLDC-LD4
97UppDecP-10
97UppDecPP-PP8
97UppDecPPJ-PP8
97UppDecRP-RP3
97UppDecU-4
97UppDecUMA-MA6
97Zen-7
97Zen8x1-8
97Zen8x1D-8

Bellenger, Butch
96EriSeaB-6

Bellhorn, Mark
96Bow-221
96BowBesMI-4
96BowBesMIAR-4
96BowBesMIR-4
96HunStaTI-3
96Top-22
96TopPowB-22
97Bow-167
97BowChr-163
97BowChrI-163
97BowChrIR-163
97BowChrR-163
97BowInt-167
97Top-487

Belliard, Carlos
93MadMusC-5
93MadMusF-1815
94ModA'sC-5

Belliard, Rafael
83LynPirT-14
85DomLeaS-132
85Pir-2
87Don-538
87DonOpeD-165
87Fle-602
87FleGlo-602
87Top-541
87TopTif-541
88Fle-321
88FleGlo-321
88Sco-453
88ScoGlo-453
88StaLinPi-1
88Top-221
88TopBig-175
88TopTif-221
89Fle-201
89FleGlo-201
89OPC-119
89PirVerFJ-6
89Sco-379
89Top-723
89TopBig-196
89TopSti-133
89TopTif-723
89UppDec-90
90Don-252
90Fle-460
90FleCan-460
90OPC-143
90PirHomC-3
90PubSti-148
90Sco-520
90Top-143
90TopTif-143
90UppDec-208
90VenSti-39
91Bow-578
91BraDubP-2
91BraSubS-4
91Fle-32
91FleUpd-70
91Lea-453
91OPC-487
91ScoRoo-76T
91StaClu-404
91Top-487
91TopDesS-487
91TopMic-487
91TopTif-487
91TopTra-9T
91TopTraT-9T
91UltUpd-65
91UppDec-706
92Bow-75
92BraLykP-2
92BraLykS-3
92Don-107
92Fle-351
92Lea-310
92OPC-367
92PanSti-165
92Pin-357
92Sco-116
92StaClu-105
92Top-367
92TopGol-367
92TopGolW-367
92TopMic-367
92Ult-158
92UppDec-510
93BraLykP-3
93BraLykS-4
93Don-398
93Fle-361
93PacSpa-1
93Pin-494
93Sco-478
93Sel-267
93StaClu-58
93StaCluB-20
93StaCluFDI-58
93StaCluMOP-58
93Top-62
93TopGol-62
93TopInaM-62
93TopMic-62
93TriPla-15
93Ult-2
93UppDec-91
93UppDecGold-91
94BraLykP-4
94BraLykS-4
94BraUSPC-4H
94BraUSPC-10C
94Fle-352
94Sco-303
94ScoGolR-303
94StaClu-426
94StaCluFDI-426
94StaCluGR-426
94StaCluMOP-426
94StaCluT-59
94StaCluTFDI-59
94Top-261
94TopGol-261
94TopSpa-261
95Fle-301
95Pac-2
95Sco-10
95ScoGolR-10
95ScoPlaTS-10
95StaClu-234
95StaCluFDI-234
95StaCluMOP-234
95StaCluSTWS-234
95Top-117
96ColCho-457
96ColChoGS-457
96ColChoSS-457
96Fle-286
96FleTif-286
96LeaSigA-20
96LeaSigAG-20
96LeaSigAS-20
96Pac-11
97Pac-230
97PacLigB-230
97PacSil-230

Belliard, Ron
95BelBreTI-25
96El PasDB-6
96TexLeaAB-20
97Bow-372
97BowChr-248
97BowChrI-248
97BowChrIR-248
97BowChrR-248
97BowInt-372
97Sel-139
97SelArtP-139
97SelRegG-139

Bellinger, Clay
90Bes-33
90CliGiaB-1
90CliGiaP-2558
90CMC-844
91CalLeLA-41
91SanJosGC-4
91SanJosGP-15
92ShrCapF-3877
92ShrCapS-576
92SkyAA F-253
93PhoFirF-1519
94PhoFirF-1524
95PhoFirTI-20
96RocRedWB-5

Bellino, Frank
85NewOriT-25
86HagSunP-2
87HagSunP-21
88FreSunCLC-8
89EasLeaDDP-DD39
89ReaPhiB-18
89ReaPhiP-659
89ReaPhiS-2
90Bes-266
90ReaPhiB-20
90ReaPhiP-1230

90ReaPhiS-6
Bellman, Bill
92KinMetF-1520
Bello, Duben
88FayGenP-1091
Belloir, Bob (Robert E.)
77Top-312
78Top-681
Bellomo, Bill
79CedRapGT-12
Bellomo, Kevin
91EveGiaC-28
91EveGiaP-3926
92ClaFS7-236
93SanJosGC-3
93SanJosGF-23
Bellum, Donnie
92HamRedC-6
92HamRedF-1604
Bellver, Juan
86MiaMarP-2
Belmonte, Nick
91SalLakTP-3227
91SalLakTSP-28
92SalLakTSP-30
Belmonte, Pedro
92KinMetC-19
92KinMetF-1521
93LinVenB-13
95LinVen-24
Belmonte, Phil
80QuaCitCT-25
Belru, Juan
90HamRedB-26
Beltran, Alonso
92MedHatBJF-3201
92MedHatBJSP-7
93St.CatBJC-3
93St.CatBJF-3966
94DunBluJC-2
94DunBluJF-2546
95KnoSmoF-32
Beltran, Angel
89WelPirP-4
Beltran, Carlos
95SPML-111
95TopTra-18T
96BesAutS-10
96LanLugB-5
96SpolndB-5
97Bow-377
97BowBes-176
97BowBesAR-176
97BowBesR-176
97BowInt-377
Beltran, Julio
78DayBeaAT-3
82MiaMarT-13
Beltran, Rigo
91HamRedC-6
91HamRedP-4027
92ClaFS7-367
92SavCarC-17
92SavCarF-652
93ArkTraF-2805
94ArkTraF-3082
94LouRedF-2973
95LouRedF-269
95SigRoo-8
95SigRooSig-8
96LouRedB-10
Beltre, Adrian
96SavSanB-2
96SavSanB-30
97Bow-194
97BowBes-117
97BowBesAR-117
97BowBesMI-MI9
97BowBesMIAR-MI9
97BowBesMIARI-MI9
97BowBesMII-MI9
97BowBesMIR-MI9
97BowBesMIRI-MI9
97BowBesR-117
97BowChr-182
97BowChrI-182
97BowChrIR-182
97BowChrR-182
97BowInt-194
Beltre, Eddy
92KinMetC-17
92KinMetF-1536
94HicCraC-2
94HicCraF-2182
Beltre, Esteban
85UtiBluST-12
86WesPalBEP-5
87JacExpP-439
88JacExpB-17
88JacExpP-991
89RocExpLC-3
90CMC-74
90IndIndC-24
90IndIndP-281
90ProAAAF-564
91DenZepLD-128
91DenZepP-127
91LinDriAAA-128
92Bow-458
92Cla2-T84
92DonRoo-10
92Fle-75
92Pin-535
92Sco-766
92ScoRoo-24
92StaClu-611
92StaCluECN-611
92TopDeb91-15
92Ult-333
93Don-595
93LimRocDWB-106
93NasSouF-573
93StaClu-375
93StaCluFDI-375
93StaCluMOP-375
93Top-13
93TopGol-13
93TopInaM-13
93TopMic-13
94RanMagM-2
94StaCluT-146
94StaCluTFDI-146
95Don-153
95DonPreP-153
95Pac-420
95RanCra-3
95Sco-6
95ScoGolR-6
95ScoPlaTS-6
96Pac-433
97Pac-32
97PacLigB-32
97PacSil-32
Beltre, Sergio
79JacMetT-9
81TidTidT-10
Belyeu, Randy
91HunCubC-4
91HunCubP-3336
Bemis, Gregg
77TacTwiDQ-14
Bemis, Harry Parker
03BreE10-7
05IndSouPSoCP-2
08RosComP-21
09AmeCarE-5
09ColChiE-27A
09ColChiE-27B
10E101-2
10MelMinE-2
10NadCarE-3
10PeoT21-2
11SpoLifCW-28
11SpoLifM-37
12ColRedB-27A
12ColRedB-27B
12ColTinT-27A
12ColTinT-27B
Ben, Elijah
83BurRanF-8
83BurRanT-12
Benard, Marvin
92EveGiaC-4
92EveGiaF-1702
93CliGiaC-4
93CliGiaF-2499
94ShrCapF-1617
95PhoFirTI-4
96ColChoSS-717
96Don-459
96DonPreP-459
96Fle-582
96FleTif-582
96PhoFirB-9
96Sco-502
96Sel-193
96UppDecPHE-H56
96UppDecPreH-H56
97ColCho-217
97Don-183
97Don-387
97DonPreP-183
97DonPreP-387
97DonPrePGold-183
97DonPrePGold-387
97Fle-476
97FleTif-476
97Lea-181
97Lea-336
97LeaFraM-181
97LeaFraM-336
97LeaFraMDC-181
97LeaFraMDC-336
97Pac-439
97PacLigB-439
97PacSil-439
97Pin-174
97PinArtP-174
97PinMusC-174
97Sco-325
97ScoPreS-325
97ScoShoS-325
97ScoShoSAP-325
97StaClu-151
97StaCluMOP-151
97Top-114
Benavente, Ronny
94VenLinU-86
Benavides, Al
92ClaFS7-235
92SanJosGC-25
93FreKeyC-3
93FreKeyF-1016
Benavides, Freddie (Alfredo)
88CedRapRP-1142
89ChaLooB-12
89ChaLooGS-5
89NasSouTI-2
90ChaLooGS-5
91Bow-672
91FleUpd-84
91LinDriAAA-252
91NasSouLD-252
91NasSouP-2161
91RedKah-57
91ScoRoo-98T
91UppDecFE-32F
92Don-573
92Fle-399
92Pin-278
92RedKah-12
92Sco-813
92Sco100RS-53
92StaClu-394
92TopDeb91-16
92TopTra-10T
92TopTraG-10T
92Ult-480
93Bow-472
93Don-746
93Fle-402
93Lea-244
93PacBeiA-22
93PacSpa-421
93Pin-548
93PinExpOD-6
93RocUSPC-4S
93RocUSPC-13D
93Sco-627
93StaClu-456
93StaCluFDI-456
93StaCluMOP-456
93StaCluRoc-21
93Top-356
93TopGol-356
93TopInaM-356
93TopMic-356
93TopTra-7T
93Ult-340
93UppDec-732
93UppDecGold-732
94Don-76
94Fle-432
94Pac-187
94PanSti-170
94Sco-229
94ScoGolR-229
94StaClu-132
94StaCluFDI-132
94StaCluGR-132
94StaCluMOP-132
94Top-553
94TopGol-553
94TopSpa-553
94Ult-180
95IowCubTI-4
95Pac-262
95Top-164
Benbow, Lou
91St.CatBJC-3
91St.CatBJP-3401
92St.CatBJC-12
92St.CatBJF-3391
93HagSunC-2
93HagSunF-1884
94DunBluJC-3
94DunBluJF-2562
94St.LucMC-3
95DurBulTI-2
95StLucMTI-7
96RicBraB-6
96RicBraRC-25
96RicBraUB-3
Bench, Johnny Lee
68Kah-B8
68Top-247
68TopVen-247
69MilBra-24
69MLBOffS-127
69MLBPin-35
69OPC-95
69Top-95
69Top-430
69TopSta-23
69TopTeaP-20
70DayDaiNM-2
70Kel-58
70MLBOffS-25
70OPC-404
70Top-464
70Top-660
70TopPos-11
70TopSup-8
71AllBasA-4
71BazNumT-29
71BazUnn-8
71MilDud-36
71MLBOffS-49
71MLBOffS-556
71OPC-64
71OPC-66
71OPC-250
71Top-64
71Top-66
71Top-250
71TopCoi-149
71TopGreM-13
71TopSup-32
71TopTat-87
71TopTat-88
72Dia-54
72MilBra-30
72OPC-433
72OPC-434
72ProStaP-14
72Top-433
72Top-434
73LinPor-54
73OPC-62
73OPC-63
73OPC-208
73OPC-380
73Top-62
73Top-63
73Top-208
73Top-380
73TopCanL-5
73TopCom-3
73TopPin-3
74Kel-28
74NewYorNTDiS-1
74OPC-10
74OPC-331
74Top-10
74Top-331
74TopDecE-71
74TopPuz-3
74TopSta-21
75BlaBacD-2
75Hos-83
75Kel-7
75OPC-208
75OPC-210
75OPC-260
75OPC-308
75SSP42-29
75SSPPuzB-2
75Top-208
75Top-210
75Top-260
75Top-308
76CraDis-2
76Hos-22
76HosTwi-22
76Kel-36
76LinSup-91
76OPC-195
76OPC-300
76RedIceL-1
76RedKro-3
76RedPos-3
76SafSupLB-1
76SafSupLB-6
76SafSupLB-7
76SafSupLB-8
76SafSupLB-9
76SSP-31
76Top-195
76Top-300
77BurCheD-205
77Hos-6
77MSADis-3
77OPC-100
77PepGloD-44
77RCColC-3
77Spo-422
77Spo-1509
77Spo-3515
77Top-70
77Top-411
77Top-412
77TopCloS-3
78Hos-44
78OPC-50
78Pep-4
78RCColC-65
78SSP270-128
78Top-700
78WifBalD-3
79Hos-128
79OPC-101
79Top-200
79TopCom-21
80Kel-52
80OPC-55
80PerHaloFP-202
80RedEnq-5
80Top-100
80TopSup-3
81AllGamPI-128
81CokTeaS-37
81Don-62
81Don-182
81Fle-196
81FleStiC-37
81Kel-65
81MSAMinD-2
81OPC-286
81PerCreC-1
81Squ-20
81Top-201
81Top-600
81TopScr-64
81TopSti-160
81TopSupHT-31
81TopSupN-2
82Don-400
82Don-628
82Dra-3
82Fle-57
82Fle-634
82FleSta-17
82K-M-18
82K-M-22
82Kel-30
82OPC-18
82OPC-304
82PerCreC-1
82PerCreCG-1
82RedCok-1
82Top-400
82Top-401
82TopSti-35
83Don-22
83Don-500
83DonActA-14
83Fle-584
83FleSta-14
83FleSti-214

83Oco& SSBG-2
83OPC-60
83OPC-61
83RedYea-5
83Top-60
83Top-61
83TopFol-2
83TopSti-7
83TopSti-229
84Don-B
84DonCha-51
84Fle-462
84Fle-640
84FleSti-96
84Nes792-6
84OCoandSI-24
84OCoandSI-85
84OCoandSI-161
84OCoandSI-230
84Top-6
84TopGloA-22
84TopTif-6
85CirK-22
86RedGreT-12
87K-M-12
87NesDreT-30
88GreBasS-1
88PacLegI-110
89KahCoo-2
89PerCelP-5
89TopBasT-14
90BasWit-54
90OPC-664
90PerGreM-49
90Top-664
90TopTif-664
92UppDecBH-37
92UppDecBH-38
92UppDecBH-39
92UppDecBH-42
92UppDecBH-43
92UppDecBH-44
92UppDecBH-AU5
93PMGolB-1
93TedWil-28
93TedWilM-16
93Yoo-1
94CarLeaA-DJ33
96Red76K-2
96Red76K-3

Bencomo, Omar
85KinBluJT-2
87KnoBluJP-1507
88KnoBluJB-17
93LinVenB-124
94VenLinU-203
95LinVen-63

Bender, Chief (Charles A.)
03BreE10-8
03WilCarE-1
04FanCraAL-4
08AmeCarE-1
08AmeCarE-37
08RosComP-55
09AmeCarE-6
09PhiCarE-1
09RamT20-11
09SpoNewSM-54
09T206-21
09T206-22
09T206-23
10CouT21-3
10CouT21-75
10CouT21-76
10CouT21-77
10CouT21-78
10CouT21-79
10CouT21-80
10CouT21-258
10CouT21-259
10DarChoE-2
10DomDisP-11
10E101-3A
10E101-3B
10E102-1
10E12AmeCDC-5
10E98-1
10JuJuDE-3
10MelMinE-3A
10MelMinE-3B
10NadCarE-4A
10NadCarE-4B
10NadE1-7
10PeoT21-3A
10PeoT21-3B
10PeoT21-3C
10PeoT21-3D
10RedCroT-4
10RedCroT-5
10RedCroT-90
10RedCroT-91
10RedCroT-171
10StaCarE-2
10SweCapPP-42A
10SweCapPP-42B
10W555-4
11A'sFirT20-3
11BasBatEU-3
11DiaGumP-3
11L1L-119
11MecDFT-38
11PloCanE-6
11S74Sil-28
11S81LarS-94
11SpoLifCW-29
11SpoLifM-88
11T205-14
11TurRedT-80
12HasTriFT-19
12T207-11
12T22SeroC-2
13NatGamW-3
13TomBarW-2
14CraJacE-19
14TexTomE-4
15AmeCarE-2A
15AmeCarE-2B
15CraJacE-19
15VicT21-1
16BF2FP-85
16SpoNewM-13
40PlaBal-172
50CalHOFW-5
60Fle-7
61Fle-8
61GolPre-18
63BazA-11
69Baz-3
69SCFOldT-36
70FleWorS-7
71FleWorS-3
75SheGrePG-10
76GrePlaG-10
76ShaPiz-66
77BobParHoF-5
77GalGloG-142
80PacLeg-93
80PerHaloFP-64
80SSPHOF-64
83DiaClaS2-105
86ConSer1-39
90PerGreM-90
91ConTSN-20
92ConTSN-335
93ConTSN-774

Bender, Gary
75BreBro-2

Bendix, William
48BabRutS-1
48BabRutS-4
48BabRutS-9
48BabRutS-11
48BabRutS-12
48BabRutS-22
48BabRutS-23
48BabRutS-24
48BabRutS-25
48BabRutS-26
48BabRutS-28

Bendorf, Jerry
82VerBeaDT-17

Bene, Bill
88GreFalDTI-1
89BakDodCLC-184
89Bow-340
89BowTif-340
89SalDodTI-7
89Top-84
89TopTif-84
90VerBeaDS-4
91VerBeaDC-3
91VerBeaDP-764
92SanAntMS-556
92SkyAA F-244
93SanAntMF-2996
94AlbDukF-835

Benedetti, Don
75CedRapGT-26

Benedict, Bruce Edwin
78RicBraT-3
79Top-715
80Top-675
81BraPol-20
81Don-208
81Fle-248
81Top-108
82BraBurKL-1
82BraPol-20
82Don-375
82Fle-429
82OPC-168
82Top-424
82TopSti-21
82TopStiV-21
83AllGamPI-128
83BraPol-20
83Don-299
83Fle-130
83OPC-204
83Top-521
83TopSti-151
83TopSti-152
83TopSti-154
83TopSti-217
84AllGamPI-38
84BraPol-20
84Don-409
84Fle-172
84Nes792-255
84OPC-255
84Top-255
84TopRubD-4
84TopSti-34
84TopTif-255
85BraHos-4
85BraPol-20
85Don-263
85Fle-320
85Lea-196
85OPC-335
85Top-335
85TopRubD-4
85TopSti-31
85TopTif-335
86BraPol-20
86Don-554
86Fle-509
86OPC-78
86Top-78
86TopTif-78
87BraSmo-11
87Don-448
87Fle-512
87FleGlo-512
87StuPan-2
87Top-186
87TopTif-186
88Sco-423
88ScoGlo-423
88Top-652
88TopTif-652
89Bow-271
89BowTif-271
89BraDub-4
89Don-475
89Fle-587
89FleGlo-587
89OPC-353
89Sco-502
89Top-778
89TopBig-83
89TopTif-778
89UppDec-121
90OPC-583
90PubSti-108
90Top-583
90TopTif-583
90VenSti-40
92UppDecS-4
93DanBraC-30
93DanBraF-3637
94GreBraF-428
94GreBraTI-1
95BreBtaTI-20
96NorTidB-3

Benedict, Jim
91ButCopKSP-29
93EriSaiC-29
93EriSaiF-3132

Benedict, Tom
91PacSenL-94

Benes, Adam
95NewJerCTI-1
95SPML-103
96PeoChiB-7

Benes, Alan
94Bow-12
94BowBes-B61
94BowBesR-B61
94Cla-172
94ClaGolF-25
94ClaGolN1PLF-LP1
94ClaGolREF-RE1
94ColC-641
94ColChoGS-641
94ColChoSS-641
94ExcFS7-257
94FloStaLAF-FSL41
94SavCarC-1
94SavCarF-499
94SigRoo-22
94SigRooS-22
94SigRooTPD-T5
94SigRooTPS-T5
94St.PetCC-1
94Top-202
94TopGol-202
94TopSpa-202
94UppDec-529
94UppDecAHNIL-2
94UppDecED-529
94UppDecML-90
95ActPac2GF-11G
95ActPacF-43
95ActPacF-72
95ARuFalLS-2
95Bow-273
95BowBes-B55
95BowBesR-B55
95BowGolF-273
95ColChoSE-11
95ColChoSEGS-11
95ColChoSESS-11
95Exc-262
95ExcAll-10
95FleMajLP-3
95LouRedF-270
95Top-233
95UltGolP-2
95UltGolPGM-2
95UppDec-217
95UppDecED-217
95UppDecEDG-217
95UppDecML-11
95UppDecML-161
95UppDecMLMLA-2
95UppDecMLOP-OP23
95UppDecMLT1PF-8
95UppDecPAW-H16
95UppDecPAWE-H16
95UppDecSE-92
95UppDecSEG-92
96Bow-75
96BowBes-51
96BowBesAR-51
96BowBesP-BBP2
96BowBesPAR-BBP2
96BowBesPR-BBP2
96BowBesR-51
96CarPol-1
96Cir-175
96CirRav-175
96ColCho-654
96ColCho-695
96ColChoGS-654
96ColChoGS-695
96ColChoSS-654
96ColChoSS-695
96EmoXL-261
96Fin-B76
96FinRef-B76
96Fla-354
96FlaWavotF-4
96Fle-539
96FleTif-539
96Lea-212
96LeaPre-128
96LeaPreP-128
96LeaPrePB-212
96LeaPrePG-212
96LeaPrePS-212
96LeaPreSG-67
96LeaPreSte-67
96LeaSig-78
96LeaSigPPG-78
96LeaSigPPP-78
96MLBPin-3
96Pin-379
96PinAfi-179
96PinAfiAP-179
96PinFoil-379
96PinProS-9
96Sel-172
96SelArtP-172
96SelCer-101
96SelCerAP-101
96SelCerCB-101
96SelCerCR-101
96SelCerMB-101
96SelCerMG-101
96SelCerMR-101
96SelCerSF-13
96SigRooOJRS-R5
96SP-10
96SP-152
96StaClu-433
96StaCluMOP-433
96StPetCB-4
96Stu-121
96StuPrePB-121
96StuPrePG-121
96StuPrePS-121
96Sum-155
96Sum-173
96SumAbo&B-155
96SumAbo&B-173
96SumArtP-155
96SumArtP-173
96SumFoi-155
96SumFoi-173
96Top-216
96TopChr-78
96TopChrR-78
96TopLas-50
96TopLasBS-9
96Ult-541
96UltGolM-541
96UppDec-444
96UppDecBCP-BC13
96Zen-102
96ZenArtP-102
97Bow-229
97BowInt-229
97Cir-383
97CirRav-383
97ColCho-204
97Don-184
97DonEli-117
97DonEliGS-117
97DonLim-124
97DonLimLE-124
97DonPreP-184
97DonPrePGold-184
97DonTea-157
97DonTeaSPE-157
97Fin-208
97FinRef-208
97FlaSho-A128
97FlaSho-B128
97FlaSho-C128
97FlaShoLC-128
97FlaShoLC-B128
97FlaShoLC-C128
97FlaShoLCM-A128
97FlaShoLCM-B128
97FlaShoLCM-C128
97Fle-438
97FleRooS-3
97FleTif-438
97Lea-104
97LeaFraM-104
97LeaFraMDC-104
97LeaGet-13
97MetUni-227
97NewPin-88
97NewPinAP-88
97NewPinMC-88
97NewPinPP-88
97Pac-403
97PacLigB-403
97PacSil-403
97Pin-11
97PinArtP-11
97PinCer-6
97PinCerMBlu-6
97PinCerMG-6
97PinCerMR-6
97PinCerR-6
97PinIns-106
97PinInsCE-106

97PinInsDE-106
97PinMusC-11
97PinTotCPB-6
97PinTotCPG-6
97PinTotCPR-6
97Sco-84
97ScoPreS-84
97ScoShoS-84
97ScoShoSAP-84
97Sel-98
97SelArtP-98
97SelRegG-98
97SP-148
97StaClu-86
97StaCluC-CO6
97StaCluM-M11
97StaCluMOP-86
97StaCluMOP-M11
97Stu-18
97StuPrePG-18
97StuPrePS-18
97Top-351
97TopChr-118
97TopChrR-118
97TopGal-176
97TopGalPPI-176
97Ult-268
97UltGolME-268
97UltPlaME-268
97UppDec-466
95UppDecMLFS-11
95UppDecMLFS-161
97UppDecRSF-RS19

Benes, Andy

88TopTra-14T
88TopTraT-14T
89BasAmeAPB-AA24
89Bow-448
89BowTif-448
89Sta-111
89TexLeaAGS-10
89Top-437
89TopBig-114
89TopTif-437
89TriA AAC-43
89WicChaR-19
89WicStaR-8
89WicUpdR-5
89WicUpdR-19
89WicWraR-30
90Bow-207
90BowTif-207
90ClaBlu-120
90Don-41
90DonBesN-47
90Fle-151
90FleCan-151
90Hot50RS-7
90Lea-56
90OPC-193
90PadCok-2
90PadMag-9
90PanSti-382
90Sco-578
90Sco100RS-69
90ScoYouS2-13
90Spo-90
90StaBen-1
90StaBen-2
90StaBen-3
90StaBen-4
90StaBen-5
90StaBen-6
90StaBen-7
90StaBen-8
90StaBen-9
90StaBen-10
90StaBen-11
90Top-193
90TopBig-260
90TopDeb89-15
90TopRoo-3
90TopTif-193
90ToyRoo-4
90TriAAAC-43
90UppDec-55
91Bow-665
91Cla3-T7
91ClaGam-85
91Don-207
91Fle-524
91Lea-275
91OPC-307
91PadMag-18
91PadSmo-3
91PanFreS-99
91PanSti-92
91Sco-538
91StaClu-51
91StaCluP-5
91Stu-242
91Top-307
91TopDesS-307
91TopMic-307
91TopTif-307
91Ult-301
91UppDec-275
92Bow-249
92Bow-599
92Cla1-T14
92ClaGam-150
92Don-524
92Fle-599
92FleSmo'nH-S9
92Lea-74
92LeaGolP-29
92OPC-682
92PadCarJ-3
92PadMot-16
92PadPolD-3
92PadSmo-3
92Pin-74
92PinTea2-12
92Sco-133
92ScoImpP-88
92StaClu-423
92Stu-101
92Top-682
92TopDaiQTU-13
92TopGol-682
92TopGolW-682
92TopMic-682
92TriPla-33
92Ult-274
92UppDec-323
92UppDecTMH-9
93Bow-518
93Don-22
93Fin-19
93FinRef-19
93Fla-132
93Fle-519
93FunPac-137
93Lea-192
93OPC-17
93PacSpa-255
93PadMot-14
93PanSti-265
93Pin-42
93Sco-91
93Sel-117
93SP-164
93StaClu-581
93StaCluFDI-581
93StaCluMOP-581
93Stu-53
93Top-568
93TopComotH-28
93TopGol-568
93TopInaM-568
93TopMic-568
93TriPla-201
93Ult-116
93UppDec-261
93UppDecGold-261
94Bow-392
94ColC-570
94ColChoGS-570
94ColChoSS-570
94Don-332
94DonSpeE-332
94ExtBas-370
94Fin-328
94FinRef-328
94Fla-434
94Fle-656
94FleAllS-29
94FUnPac-40
94Lea-143
94LeaL-151
94OPC-83
94Pac-516
94PadMot-3
94PanSti-253
94Pin-51
94PinArtP-51
94PinMusC-51
94ProMag-117
94RedFolMI-5
94Sco-44
94ScoGolR-44
94Sel-363
94SP-129
94SPDieC-129
94Spo-52
94StaClu-102
94StaCluFDI-102
94StaCluGR-102
94StaCluMOP-102
94Stu-131
94Top-70
94TopGol-70
94TopSpa-70
94TriPla-163
94Ult-573
94UppDec-388
94UppDecED-388
95Baz-111
95Bow-399
95BowBes-R48
95BowBesR-R48
95ColCho-350
95ColChoGS-350
95ColChoSE-162
95ColChoSEGS-162
95ColChoSESS-162
95ColChoSS-350
95D3-12
95Don-336
95DonPreP-336
95DonTopotO-145
95Emb-40
95EmbGolI-40
95Emo-184
95Fin-111
95FinRef-111
95Fla-414
95Fle-556
95FleLeaL-10
95FleTeaL-27
95Lea-227
95LeaLim-185
95MarPac-21
95Pac-358
95PadMot-6
95PanSti-10
95PanSti-119
95Pin-328
95PinArtP-328
95PinMusC-328
95RedFol-32
95Sco-411
95ScoGolR-411
95ScoHaloG-HG98
95ScoPlaTS-411
95Sel-75
95SelArtP-75
95SelCer-25
95SelCerMG-25
95SP-106
95Spo-37
95SpoArtP-37
95SPSil-106
95StaClu-26
95StaCluFDI-26
95StaCluMO-4
95StaCluMOP-26
95StaCluSTWS-26
95StaCluVR-18
95Stu-189
95Sum-14
95SumNthD-14
95Top-449
95TopCyb-245
95TopLeaL-LL22
95UC3-24
95UC3ArtP-24
95Ult-232
95UltGolM-232
95UltLeaL-9
95UltLeaLGM-9
95UltStrK-1
95UltStrKGM-1
95UppDec-134
95UppDec-468T
95UppDecED-134
95UppDecEDG-134
95UppDecSE-133
95UppDecSEG-133
95Zen-3
96CarPol-2
96ColCho-317
96ColCho-786
96ColChoGS-317
96ColChoSS-317
96Don-166
96DonPreP-166
96EmoXL-262
96Fin-B273
96FinRef-B273
96Fla-355
96Fle-228
96FleTif-228
96FleUpd-U183
96FleUpdTC-U183
96LeaSigA-21
96LeaSigAG-21
96LeaSigAS-21
96MetUni-221
96MetUniP-221
96MLBPin-4
96Pac-406
96Pin-7
96Pin-344
96PinAfi-95
96PinAfiAP-95
96PinAfiFPP-95
96PinFoil-344
96Sco-198
96Sco-314
96ScoDugC-B39
96ScoDugCAP-B39
96Sel-132
96SelArtP-132
96SelCerIP-15
96SP-152
96StaClu-116
96StaCluEPB-116
96StaCluEPG-116
96StaCluEPS-116
96StaCluMOP-116
95StaCluVRMC-18
96Sum-64
96Sum-155
96SumAbo&B-64
96SumAbo&B-155
96SumArtP-64
96SumArtP-155
96SumFoi-64
96SumFoi-155
96Top-314
96TopLas-51
96Ult-542
96UltGolM-542
96UppDec-204
96UppDec-508U
97Bow-13
97BowChr-9
97BowChrI-9
97BowChrIR-9
97BowChrR-9
97BowInt-13
97Cir-147
97CirRav-147
97ColCho-437
97Don-40
97DonLim-109
97DonLimLE-109
97DonPre-88
97DonPreCttC-88
97DonPreP-40
97DonPrePGold-40
97DonTea-152
97DonTeaSPE-152
97Fin-34
97FinRef-34
97FlaSho-A140
97FlaSho-B140
97FlaSho-C140
97FlaShoLC-140
97FlaShoLC-B140
97FlaShoLC-C140
97FlaShoLCM-A140
97FlaShoLCM-B140
97FlaShoLCM-C140
97Fle-439
97FleTif-439
97Lea-90
97LeaFraM-90
97LeaFraMDC-90
97MetUni-228
97NewPin-77
97NewPinAP-77
97NewPinMC-77
97NewPinPP-77
97Pac-404
97PacLigB-404
97PacSil-404
97PinCar-12
97PinCer-16
97PinCerMBlu-16
97PinCerMG-16
97PinCerMR-16
97PinCerR-16
97PinTotCPB-16
97PinTotCPG-16
97PinTotCPR-16
97PinX-P-103
97PinX-PMoS-103
97Sco-174
97ScoPreS-174
97ScoShoS-174
97ScoShoSAP-174
97SP-147
97StaClu-120
97StaCluMOP-120
97Top-190
97TopChr-74
97TopChrR-74
97TopChrSB-20
97TopChrSBR-20
97TopGal-85
97TopGalPPI-85
97TopSeaB-SB20
97Ult-342
97UltGolME-342
97UltPlaME-342
97UppDec-372
97UppDec-465

Benes, Joe (Joseph Anthony)

82WauTimF-7

Benge, Brett

91BluOriC-22
91BluOriP-4119

Benge, Ray

29ExhFou-12
33ExhFou-6
33Gou-141
34DiaMatCSB-8
34BatR31-11
34BatR31-99
34Gou-24
34GouCanV-13
34GouCanV-49
35GouPuzR-8A
35GouPuzR-8M
79DiaGre-93
90DodTar-47

Bengoechea, Brandy

93SouOreAC-5
94SouChr-9
94SouOreAC-1
94SouOreAF-3628
95ModA'sTI-3

Bengough, Benny (Bernard O.)

28PorandAR-A2
28PorandAR-B2
29ExhFou-25
31Exh-11
33Gou-1
33GouCanV-1
49EurSta-128
49PhiBul-3
91ConTSN-103
93ConTSN-860
94ConTSNCI-32

Benhardt, Chris

91SpoIndC-24
91SpoIndP-3937
92WatDiaF-2134

Beniquez, Juan Jose

74OPC-647
74Top-647
75OPC-601
75Top-601
76OPC-496
76SSP-406
76Top-496
77BurCheD-27
77Top-81
78RanBurK-18
78SSP270-103
78Top-238
79Top-478
79YanBurK-22
79YanPicA-2
80Top-114
81Don-518
81Fle-596

81LonBeaPT-17
81LonBeaPT-22
81Top-306
81TopTra-733
82Don-587
82Fle-452
82Top-572
83Don-640
83Fle-78
83Top-678
84AngSmo-2
84Don-207
84Fle-508
84Nes792-53
84Top-53
84TopTif-53
85AngSmo-14
85Don-573
85Fle-294
85ThoMcAD-3
85Top-226
85TopTif-226
86Don-352
86Fle-148
86FleStiC-4
86FleUpd-13
86Lea-156
86OPC-325
86Top-325
86TopSti-185
86TopTif-325
86TopTra-8T
86TopTraT-8T
87Don-371
87Fle-462
87FleGlo-462
87FleUpd-3
87FleUpdG-3
87OPC-173
87Top-688
87TopTif-688
87TopTra-4T
87TopTraT-4T
88BlaYNPRWL-162
88BluJayFS-3
88Fle-104
88FleGlo-104
88OPC-77
88OPCBoxB-C
88StaLinBJ-3
88Top-541
88TopSti-12
88TopTif-541
88TopWaxBC-C
89BimBreD-8
89PacSenL-119
89T/MSenL-6
89TopSenL-131
90EliSenL-108
91OriCro-30
92YanWIZ7-13
93RanKee-69

Benitez, Armando
92BluOriC-21
92BluOriF-2352
93AlbPolC-4
93AlbPolF-2017
93LimRocDWB-40
94BowBayF-2405
94Cla-52
94ExcFS7-1
94LeaLimR-74
94OriPro-8
95ActPacF-42
95Bow-429
95BowBes-B65
95BowBesR-B65
95ColCho-4
95ColChoGS-4
95ColChoSE-13
95ColChoSEGS-13
95ColChoSESS-13
95ColChoSS-4
95Don-216
95DonPreP-216
95DonTopotO-4
95Fin-20
95FinRef-20
95Fla-218
95FlaWavotF-2
95FleMajLP-4
95FleUpd-3
95Lea-342
95LeaGolR-4
95Pac-19
95Pin-134
95PinArtP-134
95PinMusC-134
95Sco-299
95ScoGolR-299
95ScoPlaTS-299
95ScoRooDT-RDT11
95Sel-208
95SelArtP-208
95SelCer-100
95SelCerMG-100
95Spo-148
95SpoArtP-148
95StaClu-254
95StaCluFDI-254
95StaCluMOP-254
95StaCluSTWS-254
95Stu-66
95Sum-136
95SumNthD-136
95Top-346
95UC3-102
95UC3ArtP-102
95Ult-253
95UltGolM-253
95UltGolP-3
95UltGolPGM-3
95UppDec-218
95UppDecED-218
95UppDecEDG-218
95UppDecPAW-H11
95UppDecPAWE-H11
95UppDecSE-48
95UppDecSEG-48
95Zen-112
96ColCho-52
96ColChoGS-52
96ColChoSS-52
96Don-513
96DonPreP-513
96Fle-4
96FleOri-3
96FleTif-4
96LeaSigA-22
96LeaSigAG-22
96LeaSigAS-22
96Pac-245
96Sco-152
96StaClu-366
96StaCluMOP-366
96Ult-302
96UltGolM-302
97Cir-77
97CirRav-77
97DonTea-40
97DonTeaSPE-40
97Fle-558
97FleTif-558
97Pac-19
97PacLigB-19
97PacSil-19
97Sco-386
97ScoHobR-386
97ScoResC-386
97ScoShoS-386
97ScoShoSAP-386
97Top-484
97Ult-349
97UltGolME-349
97UltPlaME-349

Benitez, Christian
89BluOriS-5
90WauTimB-22
90WauTimP-2136
90WauTimS-3

Benitez, Eduardo
76VenLeaS-48

Benitez, Fernando
93DanBraC-2
93DanBraF-3620

Benitez, Luis
80VenLeaS-174
89ChaWheB-12
89ChaWheP-1749
89GenCubP-1870
90GenCubP-3050
90GenCubS-1

Benitez, Manuel
86BakDodP-3
87VerBeaDP-12

Benitez, Yamil
92AlbPolC-17
92JamExpC-19
92JamExpF-1511
93BurBeeC-1
93BurBeeF-169
93ExcFS7-57
94HarSenF-2103
95Bow-217
95Emo-149
95Exc-219
95SigRooOJ-6
95SigRooOJP-6
95SigRooOJPS-6
95SigRooOJS-6
95UppDecML-147
96Bow-364
96Cir-148
96CirRav-148
96ColCho-613
96ColChoGS-613
96ColChoSS-613
96Don-486
96DonPreP-486
96EmoXL-219
96Fla-303
96FlaWavotF-5
96Fle-452
96FlePro-1
96FleTif-452
96Lea-186
96LeaPrePB-186
96LeaPrePG-186
96LeaPrePS-186
96MetUni-189
96MetUniMFG-1
96MetUniP-189
96Pac-129
96SelArtP-176
96Spo-131
96SpoArtP-131
96Top-439
96Ult-502
96UltGolM-502
96UltGolP-1
96UltGolPGM-1
96UppDecFSP-FS4
96UppDecPHE-H53
96UppDecPreH-H53
97Don-193
97DonPreP-193
97DonPrePGold-193
97FlaSho-A155
97FlaSho-B155
97FlaSho-C155
97FlaShoLC-155
97FlaShoLC-B155
97FlaShoLC-C155
97FlaShoLCM-A155
97FlaShoLCM-B155
97FlaShoLCM-C155
97Fle-376
97FleTif-376
97Sco-303
97ScoPreS-303
97ScoShoS-303
97ScoShoSAP-303
97Ult-227
97UltGolME-227
97UltPlaME-227
95UppDecMLFS-147

Benjamin, Bobby
88NebCor-11
90NebCor-3
91BelBreC-17
91BelBreP-2114
92SalLakTSP-24
92StoPorC-3

Benjamin, Jerry
86NegLeaF-82

Benjamin, Kyle
83QuaCitCT-5

Benjamin, Mike
88ShrCapP-1283
88TexLeaAGS-11
89PhoFirC-16
89PhoFirP-1500
90CMC-549
90Fle-51
90FleCan-51
90PhoFirC-22
90PhoFirP-15
90ProAAAF-41
90TopDeb89-16
90UppDec-750
91Cla1-T6
91Don-432
91GiaPacGaE-20
91GiaSFE-2
91OPC-791
91Sco-345
91ScoRoo-25
91StaClu-143
91Stu-252
91Top-791
91TopDesS-791
91TopMic-791
91TopTif-791
91UppDec-651
92GiaPacGaE-5
92PhoFirF-2825
92Sco-649
92Sco100RS-7
92StaClu-314
92UppDec-268
93Don-472
93Fle-526
93GiaMot-19
93GiaPos-3
93OPC-377
93PacSpa-606
93Sco-603
93StaClu-405
93StaCluFDI-405
93StaCluMOP-405
93Top-384
93TopGol-384
93TopInaM-384
93TopMic-384
93Ult-127
94Fin-197
94FinRef-197
94Fle-681
94GiaAMC-3
94GiaMot-22
94GiaUSPC-3D
94GiaUSPC-10C
94Sco-273
94ScoGolR-273
94StaClu-318
94StaCluFDI-318
94StaCluGR-318
94StaCluMOP-318
94StaCluT-12
94StaCluTFDI-12
94Top-487
94TopGol-487
94TopSpa-487
95Don-546
95DonPreP-546
95DonTopotO-348
95Fin-325
95FinRef-325
95Fle-573
95GiaMot-23
96PhiTeal-2

Benner, Brian
95ButCopKtl-4

Bennese, Larry
91KinMetC-25
92PitMetC-21
93St.LucMC-28
94St.LucMC-26
95StLucMTI-3

Bennett, Albert
88MarPhiS-3
89BatCliP-1920
91SpaPhiC-21
91SpaPhiP-906
92SpaPhiC-12
92SpaPhiF-1273

Bennett, Bob
89FreStaBS-2
89FreStaBS-3
91FreStaBS-1
92FroRowDP-90
92SouOreAC-2
92SouOreAF-3405
94ModA'sF-3057
94WesMicWC-1
94WesMicWF-2288
95HunStaTI-6
96HunStaTI-2

Bennett, Brad
82SprCarF-23

Bennett, Brian
89AshTouP-954

Bennett, Charlie (Charles W.)
76SSP188WS-16
81TigDetN-2
87AllandGN-2
87BucN28-27
87OldJudN-30
87ScrDC-10
88WG1CarG-19
89N526N7C-1

Bennett, Chris
89WesPalBES-3
90Bes-213
90JacExpB-15
90JacExpP-1366
91IndIndP-454

Bennett, Dave
64Top-561
65Top-521

Bennett, Dennis
63Top-56
64PhiPhiB-4
64Top-396
65OPC-147
65Top-147
66Top-491
67CokCapRS-14
67Top-206
67TopRedSS-1
78TCM60I-93
81RedSoxBG2S-71
91MetWIZ-31

Bennett, Doug
90ArkRaz-1
91YakBeaC-22
91YakBeaP-4237
92StaCluD-14
92YakBeaC-1
92YakBeaF-3439

Bennett, Erik
88CapCodPPaLP-153
89BenBucL-1
90QuaCitAGS-14
92QuaCitRBF-800
93MidAngF-314
94VanCanF-1856
96LeaSigEA-7

Bennett, Gary
90MarPhiP-3190
91MarPhiC-16
91MarPhiP-3454
92BatCliC-4
92BatCliF-3267
93SpaPhiC-5
93SpaPhiF-1057
94ClePhiC-4
94ClePhiF-2529
95ReaPhiELC-4
95ReaPhiTI-17
96ScrRedBB-6

Bennett, Herschel E.
93ConTSN-986

Bennett, Jason
95WatIndTI-5

Bennett, Jim
82WesHavAT-20
83TacTigT-14
84AlbA'sT-1
87MemChiB-7
87MemChiP-25
89WauTimGS-17
90SanBerSB-4
90SanBerSCLC-91
90SanBerSP-2625
92LetMouSP-11
95BoiHawTI-4
96BoiHawB-3

Bennett, Joel
92WinHavRSC-15
92WinHavRSF-1767
93CarLeaAGF-5
93LynRedSC-3
93LynRedSF-2509
94Bow-287
94ExcFS7-18
94ExcLeaLF-2
94NewBriRSF-642
95PawRedSDD-5
95PawRedTI-18

Bennett, Jose
86BelMarC-104
87WauTimP-11

Bennett, Keith
86WatIndP-3
87EriCarP-13
87WilBilP-2
88ColSprSSP-1535
88WatIndP-684

Bennett, Matt
95NewJerCTI-2
Bennett, Pug (Justin Titus)
11SpoLifCW-30
Bennett, Rick
90OklSoo-19
93HicCraC-2
93HicCraF-1269
94SouBenSHC-3
94SouBenSHF-586
Bennett, Ryan
96PitMetB-6
Bennett, Shayne
94Bow-587
95AusFut-68
96BesAutS-11
96Bow-381
96HarSenB-6
Bennington, Jeff
91BurAstC-23
91BurAstP-2803
Benny, Peter
95HelBreTI-26
96BelSnaTI-1
96MidLeaAB-9
Benoit, Dickens
87EveGiaC-28
89SalSpuCLC-137
89SalSpuP-1827
Benoit, Joe
43ParSpo-4
Bensch, Bob
87PanAmTUBI-NNO
Bensching, Bruce
90SpoIndSP-22
91WatDiaC-2
91WatDiaP-1249
92WatDiaC-6
92WatDiaF-2135
Benson, Coach
80WesHavWCT-23A
Benson, Gene
91NegLeaRL-27
91PomBlaBPB-2
92NegLeaRLI-3
93TedWil-99
95NegLeaLI-27
Benson, George
76SeaRaiC-3
77ReaPhiT-2
Benson, Jeremy
94OneYanC-3
94OneYanF-3779
Benson, Kris
97Bow-175
97BowBes-116
97BowBesAR-116
97BowBesMI-MI3
97BowBesMIAR-MI3
97BowBesMIARI-MI3
97BowBesMII-MI3
97BowBesMIR-MI3
97BowBesMIRI-MI3
97BowBesR-116
97BowCerBIA-CA5
97BowCerGIA-CA5
97BowChr-167
97BowChrI-167
97BowChrIR-167
97BowChrR-167
97BowInt-175
97Top-481
97TopSta-103
97TopStaAM-103
Benson, Mark
79CedRapGT-3
Benson, Matt
91HelBreSP-3
Benson, Nate
90KinMetB-18
90KinMetS-2
Benson, Neal
86DavLipB-4
Benson, Randy
76BatRouCT-4
80SyrChiT-18
80SyrChiTI-5
80VenLeaS-52
Benson, Steve
80OrlTwiT-11
83ColAstT-8
Benson, Tom
89EliTwiS-2
90EliTwiS-2
Benson, Vern (Vernon A.)
53Top-205
61UniOil-P2
71CarTeal-2
73OPC-497
73Top-497A
73Top-497B
74OPC-236
74Top-236
78SyrChiT-3
79SyrChiT-2
79SyrChiTI-8
80GiaPol-8
80VenLeaS-46
91TopArc1-205
Bentley, Blake
91PriRedC-20
91PriRedP-3525
Bentley, Jack (John N.)
20WalMaiW-5
22WilPatV-26
23W515-12
26Exh-41
27Exh-17
93ConTSN-919
95ConTSN-1326
Benton, Al (John Alton)
46SpoExcW-1-2
49IndTeal-2
50IndNumN-3
50IndTeal-2
52Top-374
53IndPenCBP-3
53MotCoo-27
81TigDetN-57
81TigSecNP-28
83TopRep5-374
Benton, Butch (Alfred Lee)
76WauMetT-4
77LynMetT-4A
77LynMetT-4B
79TidTidT-8
80TidTidT-8
82IowCubT-1
83WicAerDS-5
85Ind-3
89PacSenL-24
89TopSenL-66
91MetWIZ-32
91PacSenL-145
Benton, Larry (Lawrence)
25Exh-3
26Exh-1
28PorandAR-A3
28PorandAR-B3
28W56PlaC-D9
29ExhFou-9
29PorandAR-3
33ButCanV-2
33Gou-45
33GouCanV-45
34DiaMatCSB-9
34ButPreR-3
35GouPuzR-8L
35GouPuzR-9L
91ConTSN-182
Benton, Rube (John C.)
11L1L-113
11S81LarS-88
14CraJacE-97
14FatPlaT-6
15CraJacE-97
20WalMaiW-6
28W513-69
78HalHalR-17
Benz, Jake
94VerExpC-5
94VerExpF-3899
96Exc-184
96HarSenB-7
Benz, Joseph Louis
11PloCanE-7
12T207-12
14E&SP-1
15CraJacE-175
15SpoNewM-13
16BF2FP-8
16ColE13-14
16SpoNewM-14
75WhiSox1T-1
92Man191BSR-1
Benza, Brett
82TulDriT-26
83SprCarF-10
Benzinger, Todd
86PawRedSP-2
87DonRoo-30
87IntLeaAT-20
87PawRedSP-57
87PawRedST-13
87SpoRoo2-47
88ClaBlu-245
88Don-297
88DonBasB-289
88DonTeaBRS-297
88Fle-344
88Fle-630
88FleGlo-344
88FleGlo-630
88Lea-111
88OPC-96
88Sco-546
88ScoGlo-546
88ScoYouSI-31
88StaLinRS-2
88Top-96
88TopTif-96
88ToyRoo-1
89Bow-312
89BowTif-312
89Don-358
89DonBasB-174
89DonTra-47
89Fle-79
89FleGlo-79
89FleUpd-83
89OPC-188
89PanSti-275
89RedKah-25
89Sco-371
89ScoRoo-15T
89Top-493
89TopTif-493
89TopTra-9T
89TopTraT-9T
89UppDec-184
89UppDec-785
89UppDecS-2
90Bow-55
90BowTif-55
90Don-257
90DonBesN-101
90DonGraS-8
90Fle-413
90FleCan-413
90Lea-15
90OPC-712
90PanSti-250
90PubSti-22
90RedKah-2
90Sco-65
90Spo-56
90Top-712
90TopBig-14
90TopSti-138
90TopTif-712
90UppDec-186
90VenSti-41
91Don-640
91Fle-56
91OPC-334
91PanFreS-127
91RedKah-25
91RedPep-3
91Sco-90
91StaClu-113
91Top-334
91TopDesS-334
91TopMic-334
91TopTif-334
91Ult-87
91UltUpd-25
91UppDec-280
91UppDecFE-41F
92Bow-141
92DodMot-11
92DodPol-36
92DodSmo-5492
92Don-536
92Fle-152
92Lea-257
92OPC-506
92PanSti-94
92Pin-438
92Sco-563
92StaClu-764
92Top-506
92TopGol-506
92TopGolW-506
92TopMic-506
92TopTra-11T
92TopTraG-11T
92Ult-499
92UppDec-518
93Don-562
93Fle-58
93FleFinE-149
93GiaMot-11
93GiaPos-4
93Top-620
93TopGol-620
93TopInaM-620
93TopMic-620
93Ult-481
93UppDec-790
93UppDecGold-790
94ColC-551
94ColChoGS-551
94ColChoSS-551
94ExtBas-382
94Fla-238
94Fle-682
94GiaAMC-4
94GiaMot-20
94GiaUSPC-4S
94GiaUSPC-10D
94Lea-85
94Pac-539
94Pin-39
94PinArtP-39
94PinMusC-39
94Sco-301
94ScoGolR-301
94Sel-365
94StaClu-61
94StaCluFDI-61
94StaCluGR-61
94StaCluMOP-61
94StaCluT-29
94StaCluTFDI-29
94Top-398
94TopGol-398
94TopSpa-398
94Ult-586
94UppDec-163
94UppDecED-163
95ColCho-262
95ColChoGS-262
95ColChoSS-262
95Pac-372
95Pin-307
95PinArtP-307
95PinMusC-307
95Sco-260
95ScoGolR-260
95ScoPlaTS-260
95Top-124
Berardi, Scott
94LSUTig-12
Berardino, Dick
79ElmPioRST-21
80ElmPioRST-29
86PawRedSP-1
87GreHorP-3
90TopTVRS-2
Berardino, Johnny (John)
41BroW75-4
46SeaSLP-4
47TipTop-61
48IndTeal-2
49IndTeal-4
51Bow-245
52Top-253
83TopRep5-253
84TCMPla1-18
Berberet, Lou (Louis J.)
56Top-329
57Top-315
58Top-188
58Top-383
59Top-96
59TopVen-96
60Lea-24
60MacSta-4
60TigJayP-1
60Top-6
60TopVen-6
61Pos-43A
61Pos-43B
Berblinger, Jeff
93GleFalRC-6
93GleFalRF-4008
94ExcFirYPF-3
94ExcFS7-258
94SavCarC-6
94SavCarF-512
94SouAtlLAF-SAL47
95ArkTraTI-5
95Exc-263
96ArkTraB-6
96TexLeaAB-2
Bere, Jason
91SouBenWSC-13
91SouBenWSP-2849
92Bow-358
92ClaFS7-253
92SarWhiSCB-6
92SarWhiSF-198
93Bow-91
93Bow-364
93ClaFS7-157
93ClaGolF-203
93FlaWavotF-1
93FleFinE-192
93Lea-524
93NasSouF-563
93SelRoo-81T
93SP-271
93StaCluWS-25
93TopTra-26T
93Ult-527
93UppDec-453
93UppDecGold-453
93WhiSoxK-3
94Bow-381
94Bow-567
94ColC-50
94ColChoGS-50
94ColChoSS-50
94Don-80
94ExtBas-42
94ExtBasSYS-2
94Fin-12
94FinJum-12
94FinRef-12
94Fla-29
94Fle-76
94FleRooS-2
94FUnPac-50
94Lea-241
94LeaL-20
94OPC-206
94OPCDiaD-13
94Pac-120
94Pin-347
94PinArtP-347
94PinMusC-347
94PinNewG-NG3
94Sco-563
94ScoBoyoS-18
94ScoGolR-563
94Sel-259
94SP-189
94SPDieC-189
94Spo-68
94SpoSha-SH4
94StaClu-212
94StaClu-702
94StaCluFDI-212
94StaCluFDI-702
94StaCluGR-212
94StaCluGR-702
94StaCluMOP-212
94StaCluMOP-702
94StaCluT-144
94StaCluTFDI-144
94Top-118
94TopGol-118
94TopSpa-118
94TriPla-262
94Ult-31
94UltSecYS-1
94UppDec-42
94UppDec-146
94UppDecED-42
94UppDecED-146
94USPlaCR-13S
94WhiSoxK-3
95Baz-5
95Bow-382
95ColCho-504
95ColChoGS-504
95ColChoSE-233
95ColChoSEGS-233
95ColChoSESS-233
95ColChoSS-504

95DenHol-5
95Don-332
95DonMouM-8
95DonPreP-332
95DonTopotO-45
95Emb-8
95EmbGolI-8
95Emo-25
95Fin-101
95FinFlaT-FT1
95FinRef-101
95Fla-24
95FlaTodS-2
95Fle-111
95FleAllS-25
95FleUpdSS-2
95Lea-235
95LeaLim-27
95Pac-83
95PanSti-19
95Pin-334
95PinArtP-334
95PinMusC-334
95PinPer-PP18
95PinUps-US19
95Sco-394
95ScoGolR-394
95ScoHaloG-HG59
95ScoPlaTS-394
95ScoRul-SR22
95ScoRulJ-SR22
95Sel-68
95SelArtP-68
95SelCer-85
95SelCerMG-85
95SP-137
95SPCha-137
95SPChaDC-137
95SPSil-137
95SPSpeF-7
95StaClu-457
95StaCluMOP-457
95StaCluSTWS-457
95StaCluVR-247
95Stu-91
95Sum-84
95SumNthD-84
95Top-444
95TopCyb-240
95UC3-92
95UC3ArtP-92
95Ult-273
95UltGolM-273
95UppDec-202
95UppDecED-202
95UppDecEDG-202
95WhiSoxK-3
96ColCho-506
96ColChoGS-506
96ColChoSS-506
96Don-37
96DonPreP-37
96EmoXL-34
96Fla-48
96Fle-63
96FleTif-63
96FleWhiS-3
96Lea-187
96LeaPrePB-187
96LeaPrePG-187
96LeaPrePS-187
96LeaSigA-23
96LeaSigAG-23
96LeaSigAS-23
96Pin-133
96Sco-409
95StaCluVRMC-247
96Ult-331
96UltGolM-331
96UppDec-301
97Fle-57
97FleTif-57
97Top-378
Berenger, Tom
89MajLeaM-1
89MajLeaM-10
Berenguer, Juan
76VenLeaS-143
78TidTidT-3
79TacTugT-6
79Top-721
80TidTidT-3
80VenLeaS-206
81Top-259
82Don-580
82EvaTriT-2
82OPC-107
82OPCPos-12
82Top-437
83Tig-4
84Don-125
84Fle-77
84Nes792-174
84TigWavP-6
84Top-174
84TopTif-174
85Don-272
85Fle-2
85TigCaiD-2
85TigWen-3
85Top-672
85TopTif-672
86Fle-221
86GiaMot-27
86Top-47
86TopTif-47
86TopTra-9T
86TopTraT-9T
87Don-616
87Fle-265
87FleGlo-265
87FleUpd-4
87FleUpdG-4
87Top-303
87TopTif-303
87TopTra-5T
87TopTraT-5T
88Don-395
88DonBasB-298
88Fle-3
88FleGlo-3
88StaLinTw-2
88Top-526
88TopBig-222
88TopTif-526
88TwiMasBD-3
88TwiTeal-25
89Bow-152
89BowTif-152
89Don-81
89DonBasB-46
89Fle-104
89FleGlo-104
89OPC-294
89Sco-414
89Top-294
89TopBig-117
89TopSti-291
89TopTif-294
89UppDec-232
90Bow-410
90BowTif-410
90Don-301
90Fle-369
90FleCan-369
90Lea-169
90OPC-709
90PubSti-323
90Sco-223
90Top-709
90TopTif-709
90UppDec-440
90VenSti-42
91Bow-572
91BraDubP-3
91BraSubS-5
91Don-340
91Fle-604
91FleUpd-71
91Lea-526
91MetWIZ-33
91OPC-449
91Sco-111
91ScoPro-111
91ScoRoo-73T
91StaClu-460
91Top-449
91TopDesS-449
91TopMic-449
91TopTif-449
91UltUpd-66
91UppDec-411
92BraLykP-3
92BraLykS-4
92Don-205
92Fle-352
92OPC-172
92Pin-515
92Sco-216
92StaClu-44
92Top-172
92TopGol-172
92TopGolW-172
92TopMic-172
92Ult-455
92UppDec-493
Berenyi, Bruce
79IndIndTI-14
80IndIndTI-9
81Top-606
82Fle-58
82RedCok-2
82Top-459
83Don-103
83Fle-585
83OPC-139
83RedYea-38
83Top-139
84Don-487
84Fle-463
84Nes792-297
84OPC-297
84RedEnq-20
84Top-297
84TopTif-297
84TopTra-10T
84TopTraT-10T
85Don-625
85Fle-73
85IndIndTI-32
85MetColP-7
85MetFanC-2
85MetTCM-6
85OPC-27
85Top-27
85TopTif-27
86MetColP-19
86MetTCM-2
86MetWorSC-10
86Top-339
86TopTif-339
87Top-582
87TopTif-582
91MetWIZ-34
Berg, Chris
91WasVia-1
92KinMetF-1522
Berg, Dave
93ElmPioC-2
93ElmPioF-3829
94KanCouCC-5
94KanCouCF-169
94KanCouCTI-5
95BreCouMF-253
96PorSeaDB-8
Berg, Moe (Morris)
29PorandAR-4
30ChiEveAP-11
33Gou-158
33GouCanV-84
34BatR31-149
36NatChiFPR-6
39PlaBal-103
40PlaBal-30
88ConSer5-3
90DodTar-48
91ConTSN-184
93DiaStaES-121
95ConTSN-1350
95ConTSN-1400
Berg, Patty
52Whe-3A
52Whe-3B
Berg, Rich
88ModA'sTI-4
89MadMusS-3
90HunStaB-2
91StoPorC-7
91StoPorP-3024
Berg, Rick
88BurBraP-22
90ProAAAF-423
90RicBraBC-22
90RicBraP-278
90RicBraTI-4
91RicBraBC-42
91RicBraP-2584
Berge, Jordan
84CedRapRT-10
86VerRedP-1
Berge, Lou
86LitFalMP-3
Bergen, Bill (William A.)
06FanCraNL-4
09T206-24
09T206-25
10DomDisP-12
10E-UOraBSC-3
10E101-4
10MelMinE-4
10NadCarE-5
10PeoT21-4
10SweCapPP-71
11MecDFT-3
11PloCanE-8
11S74Sil-50
11SpoLifCW-31
11SpoLifM-150
11T205-15
11TurRedT-2
12HasTriFT-3A
12HasTriFT-3B
12HasTriFT-61A
90DodTar-49
Bergen, Marty (Martin)
98CamPepP-3
Bergendahl, Wray
83WauTimF-28
85LynMetT-7
86JacMetT-3
Berger, Boze (Louis William)
34DiaMatCSB-10
34BatR31-84
35DiaMatCS3T1-8
95ConTSN-1342
Berger, Brandon
96SpoIndB-6
Berger, Heinie (Charles)
08AmeLeaPC-2
09ColChiE-28A
09ColChiE-28B
09T206-26
11SpoLifCW-32
11SpoLifM-38
12ColRedB-28A
12ColRedB-28B
12ColTinT-28A
12ColTinT-28B
Berger, Ken
77SpaPhiT-24
Berger, Mike
84PriWilPT-7
85NasPirT-3
86NasPirP-3
87JacExpP-434
88IndIndC-20
88IndIndP-519
89OklCit8C-11
89OklCit8P-1515
90CMC-160
90OklCit8C-10
90OklCit8P-434
90ProAAAF-680
91OklCit8P-181
92OklCit8F-1931
92OklCit8S-325
93OklCit8F-1640
94OklCit8F-1509
95ChaRivTI-29
Berger, Wally (Walter Anton)
30SchR33-12
31Exh-2
32OrbPinNP-51
32OrbPinUP-5
32USCar-19
33DouDisP-5
33ExhFou-1
33GeoCMil-5
33Gou-98
33NatLeaAC-9
33RitCE-7C
33TatOrb-5
34DiaMatCSB-11
34BatR31-1
34BatR31-172
34ButPreR-4
34DiaStaR-25
34DiaStaR-108
34ExhFou-1
35DiaMatCS2-2
35DiaMatCS3T1-9
35ExhFou-1
35GouPreR-8
35WheBB1-3
36ExhFou-1
36GouBWR-1
36GouWidPPR-A5
36NatChiFPR-7
36OveCanR-4
36WorWidGV-35
37ExhFou-1
37GouFliMR-13A
37GouFliMR-13B
37GouThuMR-13
38CinOraW-1
38OurNatGPP-1
39GouPreR303A-3
39OrcPhoAP-1
39PlaBal-99
39WorWidGTP-3
40PlaBal-81
77GalGloG-220
79DiaGre-201
82DiaCla-10
83ConMar-33
86BraGreT-6
88ConNatA-1
88ConSer3-5
91ConTSN-229
93ConTSN-686
94ConTSN-1098
94ConTSNB-1098
Bergeron, Gilles
87JamExpP-2559
Bergeron, Peter
96YakBeaTI-25
Bergert, Ned
76QuaCitAT-2
77QuaCitAT-3
78QuaCitAT-2
Bergman, Dave (David Bruce)
76SSP-454
78AstBurK-21
78Top-705
79ChaChaT-8
79Top-697
81Don-139
81Fle-76
81Top-253
81TopTra-734
82Don-146
82Top-498
83Don-550
83Fle-253
83GiaMot-18
83Top-32
84Don-624
84Fle-366
84FleUpd-11
84Nes792-522
84TigFarJ-1
84TigWavP-7
84Top-522
84TopTif-522
84TopTra-11T
84TopTraT-11T
85Don-537
85Fle-3
85OPC-368
85TigCaiD-3
85TigWen-4
85Top-368
85TopTif-368
86BasStaB-9
86Don-471
86Fle-222
86TigCaiD-1
86Top-101
86TopTif-101
87Don-420
87Fle-144
87FleGlo-144
87OPC-256
87TigCaiD-4
87TigCok-9
87Top-700
87TopTif-700
88Don-373
88Fle-52
88FleGlo-52
88Sco-217
88ScoGlo-217
88StaLinTi-2
88TigPep-14
88TigPol-3
88Top-289
88TopTif-289

89Don-389
89Fle-129
89FleGlo-129
89Sco-469
89TigMar-14
89TigPol-14
89Top-631
89TopTif-631
89UppDec-266
90Bow-355
90BowTif-355
90Don-445
90Fle-600
90FleCan-600
90Lea-244
90OPC-77
90PanSti-67
90PubSti-468
90Sco-254
90TigCok-2
90Top-77
90TopSti-285
90TopTif-77
90UppDec-381
90VenSti-43
91Don-342
91Fle-331
91Lea-92
91OPC-412
91PanSti-241
91Sco-562
91StaClu-386
91TigCok-14
91TigPol-2
91Top-412
91TopDesS-412
91TopMic-412
91TopTif-412
91Ult-120
91UppDec-599
92OPC-354
92Sco-543
92StaClu-171
92Top-354
92TopGol-354
92TopGolW-354
92TopMic-354
92Ult-56
92YanWIZ7-14
Bergman, Sean
91NiaFalRC-24
91NiaFalRP-3624
92LakTigC-19
92StaCluD-15
93Bow-531
93ClaFS7-164
93TolMudHF-1643
94Bow-41
94TolMudHF-1017
94Top-768
94TopGol-768
94TopSpa-768
94TriAAF-AAA21
95ColCho-467
95ColChoGS-467
95ColChoSS-467
95Fin-306
95FinRef-306
95FleUpd-17
95Lea-254
95Top-636
95UppDec-189
95UppDecED-189
95UppDecEDG-189
96Don-9
96DonPreP-9
96FleUpd-U195
96FleUpdTC-U195
96LeaSigEA-8
96PadMot-13
96PanSti-150
96Sco-120
96StaClu-84
96StaCluMOP-84
96Top-42
96Ult-554
96UltGolM-554
Bergoechea, Brandy
93SouOreAF-4068
Beringer, Carroll
73OPC-486
73Top-486A
73Top-486B
74OPC-119
74Top-119
78PhiSSP-34
78SSP270-34
Beringhele, Vince
85VerBeaDT-17
Berkman, Lance
97Bow-438
97BowChr-298
97BowChrI-298
97BowChrIR-298
97BowChrR-298
97BowInt-438
97TopSta-125
97TopStaAM-125
Berley, John
36WorWidGV-118
Berlin, Mike
92BriTigC-1
92BriTigF-1399
93FayGenC-4
93FayGenF-121
94LakTigC-2
Berlin, Randy
89HamRedS-12
89Sta-104
90SprCarB-4
91FreKeyC-17
91FreKeyP-2371
Berman, Gary
86BenPhiC-150
87ClePhiP-18
88ReaPhiP-873
Bermudez, Manuel
95BelGiaTI-39
96BurBeeTI-2
Bernabe, Sam
84IowCubT-13
85IowCubT-18
Bernal, Manuel
96LanLugB-6
Bernal, Vic
77PadSchC-8
79HawIslC-10
79HawIslT-8
Bernard, Dwight
75TidTidTI-3
78TidTidT-4
79TidTidT-6
79Top-721
81VanCanT-4
82BrePol-47
83BreGar-2
83Don-28
83Fle-27
83Top-244
84TucTorC-55
86MacPirP-4
87KenTwiP-16
88KenTwiP-1381
89OrlTwiB-4
89OrlTwiP-1342
91MetWIZ-35
92BreCarT-2
94BreMilB-107
94EliTwiF-3747
Bernard, Erik
84AlbA'sT-16
85AlbYanT-29
86AlbYanT-12
Bernard, Marvin
96ColCho-717
96ColChoGS-717
96Fin-B326
96FinRef-B326
97UppDec-172
Bernardo, Rick
87PorChaRP-18
88ChaRanS-1
89ChaRanS-2
89MiaMirIS-1
Bernardo, Robert
86WauTimP-1
87SalSpuP-13
Bernazard, Tony (Antonio)
75WesPalBES-29A
75WesPalBES-30
79ExpPos-3
80ExpPos-4
80OPC-351
80Top-680
81Don-449
81Fle-168
81OPC-194
81Top-413
81TopTra-735
82Don-143
82Fle-338
82Top-206
82TopSti-171
82TopStiV-171
83Don-482
83Fle-231
83OPC-369
83Top-698
83TopSti-49
83TopTra-9T
83WhiSoxTV-14
84Don-240
84Fle-606
84FleUpd-12
84Ind-4
84IndWhe-4
84Nes792-41
84OPC-41
84Top-41
84TopSti-340
84TopTif-41
84TopTra-12T
84TopTraT-12T
85Don-102
85Fle-439
85Ind-4
85IndPol-4
85OPC-171
85ThoMcAD-4
85Top-533
85TopSti-252
85TopTif-533
86Don-520
86Fle-580
86IndOhH-4
86IndTeal-6
86Lea-249
86OPC-354
86Top-354
86TopSti-210
86TopTat-14
86TopTif-354
87Don-377
87DonOpeD-110
87Fle-244
87FleGamW-4
87FleGlo-244
87FleMin-8
87IndGat-4
87OPC-394
87RedFolSB-105
87Spo-60
87Spo-112
87SpoTeaP-3
87Top-607
87Top-758
87TopGloS-43
87TopSti-207
87TopTif-607
87TopTif-758
88Don-344
88Fle-275
88FleGlo-275
88OPC-122
88Sco-604
88ScoGlo-604
88StaLinAs-1
88Top-122
88TopTif-122
91Bow-143
Bernhard, David
96AubDouB-11
Bernhard, William H.(Bill)
03BreE10-9
09T206-478
10CouT21-4
04FanCraAL-5
05IndSouPSoCP-3
11SpoLifCW-33
Bernhardt, Cesar
88SouBenWSGS-1
89SouBenWSGS-24
90Bes-80
90BirBarB-6
90BirBarP-1114
90CMC-821
91Bow-360
91LinDriAAA-626
91VanCanLD-626
91VanCanP-1599
92BirBarS-77
92OPC-179
92SkyAA F-37
92Top-179
92TopGol-179
92TopGolW-179
93LimRocDWB-51
Bernhardt, Juan Ramon
77Top-494
78SanJosMMC-13
78Top-698
79OPC-189
79Top-366
92YanWIZ7-15
Bernhardt, Moncho
79SpoIndT-24
Bernhardt, Steven
93BenRocC-2
93BenRocF-3274
94CenValRC-3
94CenValRF-3209
95SalAvaTI-17
96SalAvaB-4
Berni, Denny
91LynRedSC-11
91LynRedSP-1201
92LynRedSC-8
92LynRedSF-2909
Bernier, Carlos R.
53Top-243
54Bow-171
91TopArc1-243
Berninger, Darren
95HelBreTI-8
96BelSnaTI-2
Bernsen, Corbin
89MajLeaM-2
Bernstine, Pookie
83WatIndF-16
84ButBisT-23
86IowCubP-3
87IowCubTI-16
88PeoChiTI-5
89GenCubP-1886
89PeoChiTI-29
96MicBatCB-2
86StaoftFT -12
Berra, Dale Anthony
77ColCliT-3
78ColCliT-1
79Top-723
80Top-292
81Don-253
81Fle-369
81OPC-147
81Top-147
82Don-250
82Fle-476
82Top-588
83Don-185
83Fle-303
83FleSta-15
83FleSti-77
83OPC-271
83Top-433
83TopSti-279
84AllGamPI-19
84Don-430
84Fle-245
84Nes792-18
84OPC-18
84Top-18
84TopSti-136
84TopTif-18
85Don-444
85Fle-461
85FleUpd-4
85OPC-305
85Top-132
85Top-305
85TopSti-133
85TopTif-132
85TopTif-305
85TopTifT-6T
85TopTra-6T
86Don-295
86Fle-100
86OPC-366
86Top-692
86TopTif-692
86YanTCM-21
87TucTorP-8
88RocRedWC-12
88RocRedWGCP-3
88RocRedWP-193
88RocRedWTI-3
92YanWIZ8-10
Berra, Yogi (Lawrence Peter)
46SpoExcW-5-11
47Exh-20A
47Exh-20B
47HomBon-2
47PM1StaP1-9
47PM1StaP1-10
47PM1StaP1-11
47StaPinP2-4
47TipTop-46
48Bow-6
48YanTeal-2
49Bow-60
49MPR302-2-117
50Bow-46
50Dra-24
51BerRos-B4
51Bow-2
51R42SmaS-5
51TopCurA-1
51TopRedB-1
52BerRos-3
52Bow-1
52NatTeaL-2
52RedMan-AL3
52StaCalL-70C
52StaCalS-84B
52TipTop-2
52Top-191
52Whe-4A
52Whe-4B
53BowC-44
53BowC-121
53Dor-102
53RedMan-AL3
53Top-104
54Bow-161
54NewYorJA-41
54RedMan-AL20
54Top-50
55ArmCoi-2
55BigLeaIS-3
55Bow-168
55DaiQueS-3
55RedMan-AL16
55Top-198
56Top-110
56TopPin-27
56YelBasP-7
57Top-2
57Top-407
57YanJayP-2
58HarSta-8
58Top-370
58YanJayP-2
58YooMatBC-1
59Top-180
59TopVen-180
59Yoo-1
60Baz-8
60KeyChal-7
60NuHi-28
60Top-480
60TopTat-6
60YanJayP-1
61ChePat-2
61NuSco-453
61Pos-1A
61Pos-1B
61SevElev-22
61Top-425
61Top-472
61TopMagR-23
61TopStal-189
61Yan61RL-8
61YanJayP-1
62ExhStaB-4
62Jel-7
62Pos-7
62PosCan-7
62SalPlaC-33
62ShiPlaC-33
62Top-88
62Top-360
62TopBuc-9
62TopStal-83
62TopVen-88
62YanJayP-2
63BasMagM-11
63ExhStaB-7
63Jel-17
63Pos-17

63SalMetC-62
63Top-340
63YanJayP-1
64ChatheY-1
64Top-21
64TopVen-21
64YanJayP-1
64YanReqKP-2
65MetJayP-2
65Top-470
67MetTeal-1
67TopVen-179
73HalofFPP-1
73MetAllEB-1
73NewYorN-1
73OPC-257
73Top-257A
73Top-257B
74MetDaiPA-15
74MetJapEB-1
74NewYorNTDiS-1
74NewYorNTDiS-11
74NewYorNTDiS-28
74OPC-179
74Top-179
75MetSSP-19
75OPC-189
75OPC-192
75OPC-193
75OPC-421
75SheGrePG-22
75SSP18-5
75SSP42-40
75Top-189
75Top-192
75Top-193
75Top-421
76GalBasGHoF-3
76GrePlaG-22
76ShaPiz-127
76TayBow4-10
79BasGre-71
79TCM50-2
79YanPicA-3
80PacLeg-67
80PerHaloFP-127
80SSPHOF-127
81Don-351
81TCM60I-382
81TCM60I-407
81TCM60I-474
82BasCarN-4
82Don-387
83ASAJohM-11
83DonHOFH-24
83FraBroR-9
83KelCerB-8
83MLBPin-2
83Oco& SSBG-3
83TopRep5-191
83YanASFY-4
83YanYealT-8
84FifNatCT-2
84OCoandSI-39
84OCoandSI-136
84TopTra-13T
84TopTraT-13T
85CirK-33
85GeoSteM-1
85Top-132
85Top-155
85TopTif-132
85TopTif-155
85Woo-4
86AstPol-26
86SpoDecG-31
86TCM-11
86TCMSupS-9
86TCMSupS-39
87AstMot-27
87AstPol-26
87HygAllG-5
87LeaSpeO*-H2
87NesDreT-19
87Top-531
87TopTif-531
87Yan196T-6
88AstMot-27
88HouSho-11
88PacLegI-53
89AstLenH-14
89AstMot-27
89AstSmo-5
89BowInsT-2
89BowRepI-2
89BowTif-R2
89CMCMan-10
89PerCelP-6
89RinPosM1-35
90AGFA-22
90BasWit-24
90PacLeg-7
90PerGreM-53
90PerMasW-26
90PerMasW-27
90PerMasW-28
90PerMasW-29
90PerMasW-30
90SweBasG-105
91Col-35
91Kel3D-11
91KelStaU-3
91LinDri-7
91MDAA-11
91MetWIZ-36
91RinPos1Y1-1
91SweBasG-8
91TopArc1-104
91UppDecS-8
92ActPacA-1
92ActPacA2-1G
92ActPacAP-1
92BazQua5A-4
92FroRowBe-1
92FroRowBe-2
92FroRowBe-3
92FroRowBe-4
92FroRowBe-5
92MDAMVP-1
92MVP-2
92MVP2H-4
92PinMan-25
92RevLeg1-10
92RevLeg1-11
92RevLeg1-12
92SpollIFK1-212
92YanWIZ6-8
92YanWIZA-3
92YanWIZH-3
92Zip-10
93ActPacAC-1
93MetIma-3
93TedWil-58
93TedWilLC-1
93TedWilPC-21
93UppDecAH-9
93Yoo-2
94Met69CCPP-4
94Met69CS-3
94Met69T-30
94TedWilM-M25
94TopArc1-50
94TopArc1G-50
94UppDecAH-114
94UppDecAH-145
94UppDecAH-158
94UppDecAH1-114
94UppDecAH1-145
94UppDecAH1-158
94UppDecTAE-62
95BalParF-1
95StoPop-1
97JimDea-1
97SpollICC-2
97TopMan-21
97TopMan-23
97TopManF-21
97TopManF-23
97TopManFR-21
97TopManFR-23

Berres, Ray (Raymond F.)
34DiaMatCSB-12
39PlaBal-156
40PlaBal-164
60Top-458
79DiaGre-216
90DodTar-50

Berringer, John
87PeoChiP-10
88WinSpiS-1

Berrios, Harry
92LSUTigM-4
93LSUTigM-10
94AlbPolC-4
94LSUTigMP-8
95Bow-58
95Exc-2
95ExcLeaL-4
96BowBayB-6
94FreKeyC-3

Berrios, Hector
87FayGenP-1
88BlaYNPRWL-132
88GleFalTP-935
89BlaYNPRWL-5
90LakTigS-3
91MidAngOHP-4
91PalSprAP-2007
92AlbDukS-4
92IowCubF-4046

Berrios, Juan
87EugEmeP-2669

Berroa, Ed
79ElmPioRST-22

Berroa, Geronimo
85KinBluJT-21
86VenGulP-1
87KnoBluJP-1508
87SouLeaAJ-3
88Don-659
88SyrChiC-13
88SyrChiP-808
88TriAAAP-36
89Bow-279
89BowTif-279
89DonRoo-19
89FleUpd-72
89Sco-632
89ScoHot1R-30
89ScoYouS2-17
89Spo-225
89TopBig-297
89TopTra-10T
89TopTraT-10T
90ClaBlu-83
90CMC-292
90Don-104
90Fle-575
90FleCan-575
90OPC-617
90ProAAAF-414
90RicBraBC-15
90RicBraC-16
90RicBraP-269
90RicBraTI-5
90Sco-151
90Sco100RS-36
90Top-617
90TopDeb89-17
90TopTif-617
90UppDec-531
91ColSprSSP-2195
92NasSouF-1843
92NasSouS-284
92TriA AAS-284
93Don-214
93EdmTraF-1147
93FleFinE-52
93LimRocDWB-29
93StaCluMarl-23
93TopTra-117T
94A'sMot-13
94ExtBas-144
94Fin-245
94FinRef-245
94Fla-328
94FleUpd-73
94Pin-387
94PinArtP-387
94PinMusC-387
94Sel-374
94SpoRoo-12
94SpoRooAP-12
94StaClu-591
94StaCluFDI-591
94StaCluGR-591
94StaCluMOP-591
94TopTra-86T
95A'sCHP-3
95AthMot-12
95ColCho-131
95ColChoGS-131
95ColChoSS-131
95Don-84
95DonPreP-84
95DonTopotO-132
95Emo-69
95Fin-286
95FinRef-286
95Fla-292
95Fle-239
95Lea-56
95LeaLim-2
95Pac-309
95PacLatD-5
95PacPri-101
95Pin-210
95PinArtP-210
95PinMusC-210
95Sco-502
95ScoGolR-502
95ScoPlaTS-502
95StaClu-296
95StaCluMOP-296
95StaCluSTWS-296
95StaCluVR-154
95Stu-198
95Top-187
95TopCyb-107
95Ult-90
95UltGolM-90
95UppDec-29
95UppDecED-29
95UppDecEDG-29
95UppDecSE-246
95UppDecSEG-246
96A'sMot-14
96Cir-71
96CirRav-71
96ColCho-238
96ColChoGS-238
96ColChoSS-238
96Don-391
96DonPreP-391
96EmoXL-101
96Fla-143
96Fle-203
96FleTif-203
96Lea-158
96LeaPrePB-158
96LeaPrePG-158
96LeaPrePS-158
96LeaSigA-24
96LeaSigAG-24
96LeaSigAS-24
96MetUni-98
96MetUniP-98
96Pac-397
96PacEstL-EL4
96PacPri-P124
96PacPriG-P124
96PanSti-217
96ProSta-10
96Sco-470
96StaClu-225
96StaClu-358
96StaCluEPB-358
96StaCluEPG-358
96StaCluEPS-358
96StaCluMOP-225
96StaCluMOP-358
95StaCluVRMC-154
96Stu-35
96StuPrePB-35
96StuPrePG-35
96StuPrePS-35
96Top-154
96TopGal-57
96TopGalPPI-57
96Ult-110
96UltGolM-110
96UppDec-160
97Bow-41
97BowInt-41
97Cir-178
97CirRav-178
97ColCho-185
97Don-95
97Don-302
97DonLim-170
97DonLimLE-170
97DonPreP-95
97DonPreP-302
97DonPrePGold-95
97DonPrePGold-302
97Fin-189
97FinRef-189
97FlaSho-A92
97FlaSho-B92
97FlaSho-C92
97FlaShoLC-92
97FlaShoLC-B92
97FlaShoLC-C92
97FlaShoLCM-A92
97FlaShoLCM-B92
97FlaShoLCM-C92
97Fle-184
97FleTif-184
97Lea-141
97LeaFraM-141
97LeaFraMDC-141
97MetUni-127
97Pac-165
97PacLatotML-17
97PacLigB-165
97PacPri-57
97PacPriGA-GA12
97PacPriLB-57
97PacPriP-57
97PacPriSL-SL5C
97PacSil-165
97PinX-PSfF-7
97PinX-PSfFU-7
97ProMag-68
97ProMagML-68
97Sco-37
97ScoPreS-37
97ScoShoS-37
97ScoShoSAP-37
97SP-132
97StaClu-243
97StaCluMat-243
97StaCluMOP-243
97Top-169
97TopChr-68
97TopChrR-68
97TopGal-67
97TopGalPPI-67
97Ult-109
97UltGolME-109
97UltPlaME-109
97UppDec-130

Berry, Al
91HigSchPLS-34

Berry, Charlie (Charles F.)
31Exh-17
33CraJacP-1
33ExhFou-9
33ExhFou-10
33Gou-184
34DiaMatCSB-13
35GouPuzR-4C
35GouPuzR-7C
35GouPuzR-12C
36NatChiFPR-8
40PlaBal-190
92ConTSN-398
94ConTSN-1044
36ExhFou-14
94ConTSNB-1044

Berry, Jason
94OneYanC-4
94OneYanF-3780
96HudValRB-18
96WesOahCHWB-34

Berry, Jeff
94SarRedSC-4
94SarRedSF-1953
94UtiBluSC-5
94UtiBluSF-3821

Berry, Joe (Joseph H.)
21KoBreWSI-3
22W575-8

Berry, Ken (Allen Kent)
65Top-368
66OPC-127
66Top-127
66TopVen-127
66WhiSoxTI-3
67CokCapWS-17
67DexPre-22
67OPC-67
67Top-67
67TopVen-250
68Top-485
69MilBra-25
69MLBOffS-29
69Top-494
69TopSta-153
69TopTeaP-11
69WhiSoxTI-3
70MLBOffS-182
70OPC-239
70Top-239
70WhiSoxTI-2
71AngJacitB-2
71MLBOffS-339
71OPC-466
71Top-466
72MilBra-31

72OPC-379
72Top-379
73OPC-445
73Top-445
74OPC-163
74Top-163
75OPC-432
75Top-432
78TCM60I-53
82OneYanT-4
87AppFoxP-24
89BirBarB-20
89BirBarP-89
90BirBarB-28
90BirBarDGB-3
90BirBarP-1397
94BreMilB-9
Berry, Kevin
90BilMusP-3211
91CedRapRC-1
91CedRapRP-2709
Berry, Kirk
86MacPirP-3
Berry, Mark
85CedRapRT-14
86FloStaLAP-7
86TamTarP-3
87NasSouTI-1
87VerRedP-24
88GreHorP-1575
89GreHorP-405
90ChaWheP-2256
91CedRapRC-27
91CedRapRP-2736
92CedRapRC-28
92CedRapRF-1089
93WinSpiC-25
93WinSpiF-1584
94CarLeaAF-CAR44
94WinSpiC-26
94WinSpiF-287
96ChaLooB-1
Berry, Mary
90ChaWheB-25
Berry, Mike
96HigDesMB-6
Berry, Neil (Cornelius John)
49Bow-180
50Bow-241
51Bow-213
52Bow-219
54OriEss-2
91OriCro-31
Berry, Perry
91OscAstC-17
91OscAstP-691
92BurAstC-20
92BurAstF-552
93OscAstC-4
93OscAstF-633
Berry, Sean
86EugEmeC-38
87Ft.MyeRP-7
88BasCitRS-6
89BasCitRS-5
90Bes-86
90MemChiB-6
90MemChiP-1016
90MemChiS-2
90ProAaA-49
91LinDriAAA-326
91OmaRoyLD-326
91OmaRoyP-1039
91Sco-764
91TopDeb90-15
91UppDec-10
92Cla1-T15
92Don-651
92Fle-680
92OmaRoyF-2966
92OmaRoyS-327
92Pin-271
92Sco-678
92SkyAAAF-149
92StaClu-114
93Don-275
93ExpPosN-4
93Fle-458
93Lea-336
93OPC-37
93OPCPre-97
93PacSpa-529
93Pin-212
93Sco-543
93ScoBoyoS-16
93SelRoo-146T
93StaClu-184
93StaCluFDI-184
93StaCluMOP-184
93Top-758
93TopGol-758
93TopInaM-758
93TopMic-758
93Ult-411
93UppDec-644
93UppDecGold-644
94ColC-51
94ColChoGS-51
94ColChoSS-51
94Don-461
94ExtBas-300
94Fin-342
94FinRef-342
94Fla-186
94Fle-533
94Lea-42
94Pac-374
94PanSti-207
94Pin-456
94PinArtP-456
94PinMusC-456
94Sel-373
94StaClu-67
94StaClu-649
94StaCluFDI-67
94StaCluFDI-649
94StaCluGR-67
94StaCluGR-649
94StaCluMOP-67
94StaCluMOP-649
94Stu-75
94Top-344
94TopGol-344
94TopSpa-344
94Ult-223
94UppDec-427
94UppDecED-427
95ColCho-234
95ColChoGS-234
95ColChoSS-234
95Don-293
95DonPreP-293
95DonTopotO-277
95Fle-345
95Lea-291
95Pac-263
95Sco-514
95ScoGolR-514
95ScoPlaTS-514
95StaClu-391
95StaCluMOP-391
95StaCluSTWS-391
95StaCluVR-205
95Top-530
95TopCyb-315
95Ult-187
95UltGolM-187
95UppDec-76
95UppDecED-76
95UppDecEDG-76
96AstMot-6
96ColCho-773
96Don-368
96DonPreP-368
96EmoXL-195
96Fin-S274
96FinRef-S274
96Fla-274
96Fle-453
96FleTif-453
96FleUpd-U137
96FleUpdTC-U137
96MetUni-174
96MetUniP-174
96Pac-120
96Pin-337
96PinFoil-337
96Sco-435
96StaClu-67
96StaCluMOP-67
95StaCluVRMC-205
96Top-113
96Ult-484
96UltGolM-484
96UppDec-134
96UppDec-497U
97Cir-17
97CirRav-17
97ColCho-348
97Fle-341
97FleTif-341
97Pac-313
97PacLigB-313
97PacPri-107
97PacPriLB-107
97PacPriP-107
97PacSil-313
97Sco-41
97ScoPreS-41
97ScoShoS-41
97ScoShoSAP-41
97StaClu-259
97StaCluMOP-259
97Top-248
97Ult-206
97UltGolME-206
97UltPlaME-206
97UppDec-366
Berry, Tony
89GasRanP-1009
89GasRanS-3
Berryhill, Damon
86PitCubP-2
87IowCubTI-15
88CubDavB-9
88Don-639
88DonBasB-261
88DonRoo-31
88DonTeaBC-639
88Fle-642
88FleGlo-642
88FleUpd-75
88FleUpdG-75
88IowCubC-12
88IowCubP-537
88ScoRoo-82T
88ScoRooG-82T
88TopTra-15T
88TopTraT-15T
89Baz-2
89Bow-288
89BowTif-288
89CubMar-9
89Don-275
89Don-491
89DonBasB-116
89Fle-418
89FleGlo-418
89K-M-8
89OPC-6
89PanSti-52
89Sco-336
89ScoHot1R-77
89ScoYouSI-24
89Spo-216
89Top-543
89TopBig-60
89TopGloS-39
89TopRoo-4
89TopSti-51
89TopSti-318
89TopTif-543
89ToyRoo-4
89TVSpoM-22
89UppDec-455
90Bow-33
90BowTif-33
90Don-167
90Fle-26
90FleCan-26
90MLBBasB-52
90OPC-362
90PanSti-234
90PeoChiUTI-U3
90PubSti-190
90Sco-163
90Spo-164
90Top-362
90TopSti-49
90TopTif-362
90TopTVCu-19
90UppDec-322
90VenSti-44
91CubMar-9
91CubVinL-4
91Don-631
91Fle-414
91Lea-156
91OPC-188
91Sco-881
91StaClu-28
91Top-188
91TopDesS-188
91TopMic-188
91TopTif-188
91Ult-56
91UppDec-319
92BraLykP-4
92BraLykS-5
92Don-771
92Lea-423
92OPC-49
92Pin-390
92StaClu-856
92StaCluNC-856
92Top-49
92TopGol-49
92TopGolW-49
92TopMic-49
92Ult-456
92UppDec-706
93BluJayDM-19
93BraLykP-4
93BraLykS-5
93Don-78
93Don-254
93Fle-362
93Lea-196
93OPC-32
93PacSpa-332
93Pin-392
93Sco-373
93StaClu-261
93StaCluB-14
93StaCluFDI-261
93StaCluM-62
93StaCluMOP-261
93Top-306
93TopGol-306
93TopInaM-306
93TopMic-306
93TriPla-113
93Ult-3
93UppDec-606
93UppDecGold-606
93UppDecSH-HI4
94ColC-602
94ColChoGS-602
94ColChoSS-602
94Don-58
94Fla-259
94Fle-353
94FleUpd-9
94Pac-3
94Sco-275
94ScoGolR-275
94Top-289
94TopGol-289
94TopSpa-289
94TopTra-11T
94Ult-149
95Fle-23
95RedKah-2
95Sco-251
95ScoGolR-251
95ScoPlaTS-251
97Ult-454
97UltGolME-454
97UltPlaME-454
Berryman, Robb
93UtiBluSC-4
93UtiBluSF-3525
Bertaina, Frank
65Top-396
66Top-579
68OPC-131
68SenTeal-1
68Top-131
68TopVen-131
69MilBra-26
69Top-554
70Top-638
71MLBOffS-267
71OPC-422
71Top-422
72MilBra-32
81TCM60I-446
91OriCro-32
Bertell, Dick (Richard G.)
61Top-441
62TopStal-105
63CubJayP-2
63Jel-176
63Pos-176
63Top-287
64CubJayP-2
64Top-424
65CubJayP-3
65OPC-27
65Top-27
66Top-587
Berteotti, Jerry
94YakBeaC-1
94YakBeaF-3853
Berthau, Terrell
91ButCopKSP-4
Berthel, Dan
89EriOriS-2
90CarLeaA-6
90FreKeyTI-19
91FreKeyC-22
91FreKeyP-2376
Berthelot, Eric
94LSUTig-15
Berti, Don
83DayBeaAT-14
Bertman, Skip
90LSUTigGM-1
90LSUTigP-1
91LSUTigP-3
92LSUTigM-1
93LSUTigM-2
94LSUTig-1
Bertoia, Reno Peter
54Top-131
55Top-94
57Top-390
58Top-232
59SenTealW-3
59TigGraASP-3
59Top-84
59TopVen-84
60Top-297
61Pos-95A
61Pos-95B
61Top-392
61TopStal-178
61TwiPetM-20
61TwiUniMC-3
94TopArc1-131
94TopArc1G-131
Bertolani, Jerry
86PenWhiSP-5
87DayBeaAP-22
88BirBarB-23
88SouLeaAJ-8
89BirBarB-12
89BirBarP-100
Bertolotti, Fulvio
78St.PetCT-1
79ArkTraT-15
Bertoni, Jeff
78QuaCitAT-3
80SalLakCGT-9
80VenLeaS-112
81SalLakCGT-16
82SpoIndT-13
83EvaTriT-13
Bertotti, Mike
91UtiBluSC-4
91UtiBluSP-3232
92SouBenWSC-11
92SouBenWSF-170
93HicCraC-3
93HicCraF-1270
94BirBarC-3
94PriWilCC-2
94PriWilCF-1912
95Exc-26
96NasSouB-8
92UtiBluSC-25
Bertucio, Charlie
83SanJosBC-3
Berube, Joe Henry
93BelMarC-4
93BelMarF-3211
Berube, Luc (George)
87Ft.LauYP-11
87OneYanP-31
88Ft.LauYS-2
Berumen, Andres
91BasCitRC-1
91BasCitRP-1388
91Cla/Bes-65
92AppFoxC-2
92AppFoxF-975
93HigDesMC-3
93HigDesMF-32
93Top-627

93TopGol-627
93TopInaM-627
93TopMic-627
94Bow-92
94Cla-57
94LasVegSF-862
94UppDecML-61
95Fla-415
95FleUpd-180
95PadMot-25
95Top-657
95UltGolMR-M4
96ColCho-293
96ColChoGS-293
96ColChoSS-293
96LasVegSB-6
97PacPriGotD-GD204
Besana, Fred
91OriCro-33
Bescher, Bob (Robert Henry)
09AmeCarE-7
09ColChiE-29
09SpoNewSM-64
09T206-27
09T206-28
10DarChoE-3
10DomDisP-13
10E101-5
10E102-2
10MelMinE-5
10NadCarE-6
10PeoT21-5A
10PeoT21-5B
10SweCapPP-96
10W555-5
11E94-3
11S74Sil-72
11SpoLifCW-34
11SpoLifM-187
11T205-16
11TurRedT-81
12ColRedB-29
12ColTinT-29
12HasTriFT-56
12T207-13
13NatGamW-4
13TomBarW-3
14CraJacE-110
14TexTomE-5
15AmeCarE-3
15CraJacE-110
15SpoNewM-14
16SpoNewM-15
16TanBraE-1
Besh, Jeff
89GeoColC-1
Bess, Johnny
92PriRedC-10
92PriRedF-3089
93WesVirWC-2
93WesVirWF-2868
94WinSpiC-5
94WinSpiF-274
Bessard, Lloyd
79ElmPioRST-1
Besse, Herman
47SigOil-75
49BowPCL-29
77TCMTheWY-34
Bessent, Don
56Dod-4
56Top-184
57Top-178
58Top-401
59DodTeal-2
59Top-71
59TopVen-71
90DodTar-51
95TopArcBD-154
Best, Bill
81ChaRoyT-21
82ForMyeRT-18
84MemChiT-5
Best, Jayson
89EliTwiS-3
90Bes-225
90KenTwiB-17
90KenTwiP-2286
90KenTwiS-1
90MidLeaASGS-3
91VisOakC-1
91VisOakP-1735
92ClaFS7-334
92Ft.MyeMCB-1
92Ft.MyeMF-2737
93NasXprF-394
Best, Jim
83AppFoxF-6
Best, Karl
80LynSaiT-11
81LynSaiT-1
82LynSaiT-2
83SalLakCGT-5
84SalLakCGC-189
85CalCanC-76
85FleUpd-5
86Don-511
86Fle-459
86MarMot-19
86SevCoi-W16
86Top-61
86TopTif-61
87CalCanP-2318
87Don-198
87Fle-579
87FleGlo-579
87Top-439
87TopTif-439
88PorBeaC-2
88PorBeaP-646
88TriAAC-43
Beswick, Jim (James W.)
79HawIslC-21
79HawIslT-10
79Top-725
80HawIslT-8
81HawIslT-7
83NasAngT-17
Betances, Junior
94HelBreF-3619
94HelBreSP-4
95BelBreTI-19
96StoPorB-25
Betances, Marcos
88BriTigP-1882
89FayGenP-1574
89NiaFalRP-3
90HamRedB-3
90HamRedS-6
90SavCarP-2060
Betancourt, Damaso
93LinVenB-20
95LinVen-34
Betancourt, Jose
93LinVenB-133
Betancourt, Rafael
95LinVen-158
96MicBatCB-5
Betemit, Manuel
77NewCoPT-2
78BurBeeT-5
Bethancourt, Jose
90EliTwiS-3
Bethea, Bill (William Lamar)
60DarFar-4
77FriOneYW-31
92TexLon-5
Bethea, Larry
95GreFalDTI-25
Bethea, Scott
90LSUTigP-10
91LynRedSC-14
91LynRedSP-1204
92NewBriRSF-438
92NewBriRSS-477
93NewBriRSF-1226
94HigDesMC-3
94HigDesMF-2794
Bethea, Steve
89SpoIndSP-25
90RivRedWB-2
90RivRedWCLC-7
90RivRedWP-2612
91Cla/Bes-148
91HigDesMC-18
91HigDesMP-2401
92WicWraF-3660
92WicWraS-626
93LasVegSF-950
Bethke, James
65Top-533
81TCM60I-413
91MetWIZ-37
Bethke, Jamie
91GulCoaRSP-7
92ButCopKSP-5
93ChaRaiC-3
93ChaRaiF-1913
94HigDesMC-4
94HigDesMF-2791
Bethune, Ian
96NewHavRB-31
Betten, Randy
95BoiHawTI-5
96LakElsSB-14
Bettencourt, Justin
94BriTigC-5
94BriTigF-3492
96FayGenB-6
Bettendorf, Dave
86AncGlaPTI-3
88HagSunS-2
89HagSunB-9
89HagSunP-273
89HagSunS-1
89Sta-132
90HagSunDGB-4
90HagSunP-1419
Bettendorf, Jeff
83LynMetT-4
84A'sMot-25
84JacMetT-9
85MetTCM-7
85TidTidT-4
86ColAstP-4
87BirBarB-9
87SouLeaAJ-21
Betti, Richard
96SarRedSB-8
96TreThuB-6
Bettis, Jerome
93StaCluMO-46
Betto, Kaoru
79TCMJapPB-50
Betts, Darrell
95NewJerCTI-3
96NewJerCB-2
Betts, Huck (Walter)
22E120-196
34DiaMatCSB-14
34Gou-36
34GouCanV-83
34TarThoBD-1
79DiaGre-212
Betts, Todd
93BurIndC-4
93BurIndF-3305
94WatIndC-2
94WatIndF-3942
95Exc-36
95KinIndTI-3
96CanIndB-5
Betz, Robert
52Par-80
Betzel, Bruno (Christian)
15SpoNewM-15
16ColE13-15
16SpoNewM-16
Betzsold, Jim
94WatIndC-3
94WatIndF-3949
95Exc-37
95KinIndTI-4
96CanIndB-6
96WesOahCHWB-21
Beuder, John
87SalLakTTT-4
88BakDodCLC-246
Beuder, Mike
83VerBeaDT-1
Beuerlein, Ed
90AshTouP-2751
91OscAstC-14
91OscAstP-867
92AshTouC-5
Beuerlein, John
86StoPorP-1
87DenZepP-14
Bevacqua, Kurt A.
72OPC-193
72Top-193
74OPC-454
74Top-454
74TopTra-454T
76OPC-427
76OPC-564
76SpoIndC-15
76SSP-233
76Top-427
76Top-564
77Top-317
77TucTorC-33
78RanBurK-16
78SSP270-93
78Top-725
79Top-44
80Top-584
81Fle-382A
81Fle-382B
81Top-118
82Fle-477
82Top-267
82TopTra-6T
83Fle-352
83Top-674
84Don-80
84Fle-294
84FleSti-43
84Nes792-346
84PadMot-6
84PadSmo-1
84Top-346
84TopTif-346
85Don-647
85Fle-26
85PadMot-14
85Top-478
85TopSti-16
85TopTif-478
86Don-528
86Fle-315
86Top-789
86TopTif-789
93RanKee-70
94BreMilB-192
Bevan, Hal (Harold Joseph)
53BowBW-43
55A'sRodM-2
55JetPos-1
60HenHouW-10
60UniOil-22
61Top-456
Bevel, Bobby
96AshTouB-7
Bevenour, Keith
89WatIndS-2
Bevens, Bill (Floyd)
46SpoExcW-1-7
47TipTop-47
48Bow-22
60NuHi-3
83TCMPla1945-11
Beverlin, Jason
94SigRooDP-72
94SigRooDPS-72
95WesMicWTI-15
Beverly, Bill
92NegLeaRLI-4
Bevil, Brian
92AppFoxC-9
92AppFoxF-976
92MidLeaATI-4
93Bow-125
93ClaGolF-103
93ExcFS7-172
93WilBluRC-3
93WilBluRF-1988
94ExcFS7-64
94MemChiF-349
94SigRoo-4
94SigRooS-4
94UppDecML-46
96TexLeaAB-21
96WicWraB-17
97Fle-677
97FleTif-677
97UppDec-286
Beville, Monte (Henry Monte)
11SpoLifCW-35
Bevington, Terry
78BurBeeT-6
79HolMilT-2
80VanCanT-6
81BurBeeT-30
82BelBreF-24
84ElPasDT-12
86VanCanP-2
87DenZepP-13
88VanCanP-778
90WhiSoxC-30
91WhiSoxK-NNO
92WhiSoxK-NNO
93WhiSoxK-30
94WhiSoxK-30
95WhiSoxK-4
95WhiSoxK-31
Beyeler, Arnie
87FayGenP-19
88LakTigS-3
89LonTigP-1371
90EasLeaAP-EL7
90LonTigP-1274
91LinDriAAA-579
91TolMudHLD-579
91TolMudHP-1938
Beyers, Tom
87VerBeaDP-22
89SalDodTI-1
90BakDodCLC-244
91CalLeLA-23
92BakDodCLC-30
93AlbDukF-1479
94SanAntMF-2486
Beyna, Terry
94AubAstC-3
94AubAstF-3764
Bezdek, Hugo
19W514-83
92ConTSN-396
Bhagwat, Tom
80ElPasDT-13
Biagini, Greg
86ChaOriW-3
87ChaO'sW-24
87SouLeaAJ-24
88ChaKniTI-23
89RocRedWC-25
89RocRedWP-1660
90CMC-326
90ProAAAF-477
90RocRedWC-25
90RocRedWGC-34
90RocRedWP-720
91LinDriAAA-474
91LinDriAAA-475
91RocRedWLD-474
91RocRedWP-1918
91TriA AAGP-AAA39
96OklCit8B-1
Bialas, Dave
78SprRedWK-7
82SprCarF-2
83SprCarF-22
84ArkTraT-14
86FloStaLAP-8
86St.PetCP-4
87St.PetCP-18
89St.PetCS-27
90ArkTraGS-1
90SprCarDGB-22
91St.PetCC-9
91St.PetCP-2292
92St.PetCC-27
92St.PetCF-2041
93PadMot-28
94PadMot-28
Biancalana, Buddy (Roland A.)
82OmaRoyT-14
83OmaRoyT-13
85Top-387
85TopTif-387
86BasStaB-10
86Don-605
86Fle-3
86RoyKitCD-2
86RoyNatP-1
86Spo-200
86Top-99
86TopSti-21
86TopTif-99
87Don-527
87DonOpeD-202
87Fle-364
87FleGlo-364
87SmoAmeL-7
87Top-554
87TopTif-554
88OmaRoyC-20
88OmaRoyP-1502
88Sco-383
88ScoGlo-383
93UppDecAH-10
Biancamano, John
91SpoIndC-22
91SpoIndP-3953

Bianchi, Ben
86VisOakP-3
87PorBeaP-16
89OrlTwiB-10
89OrlTwiP-1329
Bianchi, Steve
77AshTouT-2
79TucTorT-9
Bianchi, Whitey
90IBAWorA-33
Bianco, Robert
75AppFoxT-3
Bianco, Ron
86SumBraP-3
Bianco, Toby
75SacSolC-5
76SpoIndC-20
Bianco, Tommy (Thomas A.)
74SacSolC-50
76SSP-250
77EvaTriT-3
78RocRedWT-2
79RocRedWT-11
94BreMilB-193
Biasatti, Hank (Henry A.)
49PhiBul-4
50WorWidGV-44
Biasucci, Joe
91WinSpiC-16
91WinSpiP-2833
92PeoChiTI-3
92WinSpiC-19
93MidLeaAGF-48
93SprCarC-2
93SprCarF-1855
94ArkTraF-3093
94Bow-346
94ExcFS7-259
Bibb, Mitch
90WauTimS-29
91FreKeyC-30
95BowBayTI-NNO
96BowBayB-4
Bibby, Edwin
88AllandGN-31
Bibby, Jim
72OPC-316
72Top-316
73LinPor-172
74OPC-11
74Top-11
74TopSta-231
75OPC-155
75SSP18-2
75Top-155
76OPC-324
76Top-324
77Top-501
78OPC-61
78Top-636
79OPC-39
79Top-92
80Top-229
81AllGamPI-165
81CokTeaS-109
81Don-134
81Fle-370
81FleStiC-65
81OPC-93
81Top-430
81TopScr-105
81TopSti-216
81TopSti-260
82Don-171
82Fle-478
82FleSta-78
82FleSta-106
82OPC-170
82Top-170
82TopSti-86
83Top-355
84Fle-246
84Nes792-566
84Top-566
84TopTif-566
85LynMetT-2
86LynMetP-2
87LynMetP-20
89LynRedSS-24
89PacSenL-52
89T/MSenL-7
89TopSenL-128
90LynRedSTI-26
91LynRedSC-26
91LynRedSP-1216
93LynRedSC-27
93LynRedSF-2534
93RanKee-71
94LynRedSC-27
94LynRedSF-1909
95LynHilTI-1
96LynHilB-28
Bibeault, Paul
43ParSpo-5
Biberdorf, Cam
88GreFalDTI-24
89BakDodCLC-190
90FloStaLAS-1
90VerBeaDS-5
91LinDriAA-531
91SanAntMLD-531
Bible, Mike
89SalLakTTI-21
Bice, Justin
96AriBlaDB-9
Bichette, Dante
86PalSprAP-3
88EdmTraC-23
88EdmTraP-576
89ClaTraP-199
89Don-634
89DonRoo-29
89Fle-468
89FleGlo-468
89PanSti-283
89Top-761
89TopTif-761
89UppDec-24
90ClaYel-T11
90Fle-127
90FleCan-127
90Lea-340
90OPC-43
90PubSti-365
90ScoYouS2-10
90Top-43
90TopTif-43
90UppDec-688
90VenSti-45
91Bow-31
91BreMilB-3
91BrePol-2
91Don-303
91Fle-307
91FleUpd-29
91Lea-242
91OPC-564
91PanFreS-186
91PanSti-139
91Sco-463
91ScoRoo-37T
91StaClu-211
91Top-564
91TopDesS-564
91TopMic-564
91TopTif-564
91TopTra-10T
91TopTraT-10T
91UppDec-317
91UppDec-712
92Bow-264
92BrePol-3
92Don-347
92Fle-173
92Lea-134
92OPC-371
92PanSti-39
92Pin-514
92Sco-316
92StaClu-7
92Stu-191
92Top-371
92TopGol-371
92TopGolW-371
92TopMic-371
92Ult-79
92UppDec-378
93Bow-92
93DenHol-23
93DiaMar-11
93Don-45
93Don-783
93Fla-35
93Fle-403
93FleFinE-22
93FunPac-174
93Lea-258
93MetBak-21
93PacSpa-422
93Pin-232
93PinExpOD-9
93RocUSPC-3D
93RocUSPC-11H
93Sco-428
93Sel-114
93SP-217
93StaClu-616
93StaCluFDI-616
93StaCluMOP-616
93StaCluRoc-5
93Stu-24
93Top-644
93TopGol-644
93TopInaM-644
93TopMic-644
93TriPla-154
93Ult-341
93UppDec-478
93UppDec-683
93UppDecGold-478
93UppDecGold-683
94Bow-666
94BowBes-R17
94BowBesR-R17
94BreMilB-194
94ChuHomS-28
94ChuHomSG-28
94ColC-52
94ColChoGS-52
94ColChoSS-52
94Don-418
94ExtBas-242
94Fin-59
94FinPre-59P
94FinRef-59
94Fla-151
94Fle-433
94FUnPac-68
94Lea-81
94LeaL-100
94LeaMVPC-N2
94LeaMVPCG-N2
94OPC-30
94Pac-188
94PanSti-171
94Pin-346
94PinArtP-346
94PinMusC-346
94PinRunC-RC41
94ProMag-41
94RocPol-2
94Sco-110
94ScoCyc-TC9
94ScoGolR-110
94ScoGolS-22
94Sel-147
94SP-164
94SPDieC-164
94Spo-22
94StaClu-366
94StaCluFDI-366
94StaCluGR-366
94StaCluMOP-366
94StaCluT-105
94StaCluTFDI-105
94Stu-175
94Top-468
94TopGol-468
94TopSpa-468
94TriPla-221
94Ult-181
94UppDec-454
94UppDecED-454
95Baz-114
95Bow-384
95BowBes-R24
95BowBesR-R24
95ClaPhoC-24
95ColCho-450
95ColChoGS-450
95ColChoSE-209
95ColChoSE-260
95ColChoSEGS-209
95ColChoSEGS-260
95ColChoSESS-209
95ColChoSESS-260
95ColChoSS-450
95Don-302
95DonDiaK-DK4
95DonPreP-302
95DonTopotO-225
95Emb-83
95EmbGolI-83
95Emo-123
95Fin-68
95FinPowK-PK13
95FinRef-68
95Fla-344
95FlaOutP-2
95Fle-514
95FleAllS-18
95FleTeaL-18
95Lea-135
95LeaLim-23
95LeaLimIBP-24
95Pac-132
95PacPri-43
95PanSti-71
95Pin-336
95PinArtP-336
95PinMusC-336
95RedFol-17
95RocPol-3
95Sco-15
95ScoGolR-15
95ScoHaloG-HG19
95ScoPlaTS-15
95Sel-10
95SelArtP-10
95SelCer-68
95SelCerMG-68
95SP-52
95SPCha-44
95SPChaDC-44
95Spo-125
95SpoArtP-125
95SPSil-52
95SPSpeF-34
95StaClu-326
95StaCluCT-11
95StaCluMO-5
95StaCluMOP-326
95StaCluSTWS-326
95StaCluVR-168
95Stu-71
95Sum-105
95SumNthD-105
95Top-140
95Top-390
95TopCyb-85
95TopFin-6
95TopLeaL-LL38
95UC3-71
95UC3ArtP-71
95UllHomRK-2
95Ult-151
95UltGolM-151
95UltHitM-3
95UltHitMGM-3
95UltRBIK-8
95UltRBIKGM-8
95UppDec-175
95UppDecED-175
95UppDecEDG-175
95UppDecPLL-R49
95UppDecPLLE-R49
95UppDecSE-242
95UppDecSEG-242
95USPlaCMLA-3C
95Zen-20
96Baz-38
96Bow-25
96BowBes-14
96BowBesAR-14
96BowBesR-14
96Cir-120
96CirBos-33
96CirRav-120
96ColCho-3
96ColCho-4
96ColCho-135
96ColCho-278
96ColCho-407
96ColCho-753
96ColChoCtG-CG14
96ColChoCtG-CG14B
96ColChoCtG-CG14C
96ColChoCtGE-CR14
96ColChoCtGG-CG14
96ColChoCtGG-CG14B
96ColChoCtGG-CG14C
96ColChoCtGGE-CR14
96ColChoGS-3
96ColChoGS-4
96ColChoGS-135
96ColChoGS-278
96ColChoGS-407
96ColChoGS-753
96ColChoSS-3
96ColChoSS-4
96ColChoSS-135
96ColChoSS-278
96ColChoSS-407
96ColChoSS-753
96DenHol-19
96Don-224
96DonEli-71
96DonPowA-6
96DonPowADC-6
96DonPreP-224
96DonPurP-6
96DonRouT-10
96EmoXL-172
96Fin-B126
96Fin-G66
96Fin-S289
96FinRef-B126
96FinRef-G66
96FinRef-S289
96Fla-243
96Fle-360
96FleLumC-2
96FleRoc-2
96FleTeaL-18
96FleTif-360
96Kin-3
96Lea-101
96LeaAllGMC-9
96LeaAllGMCG-9
96LeaGolS-2
96LeaLim-48
96LeaLimG-48
96LeaPre-59
96LeaPreP-59
96LeaPrePB-101
96LeaPrePG-101
96LeaPrePS-101
96LeaPreSG-71
96LeaPreSte-71
96LeaSig-47
96LeaSigPPG-47
96LeaSigPPP-47
96MetUni-154
96MetUniP-154
96Pac-53
96PacGolCD-DC29
96PacOctM-OM3
96PacPri-P19
96PacPriFB-FB2
96PacPriG-P19
96PanSti-81
96PanSti-114
96PanSti-115
96Pin-3
96Pin-139
96Pin-272
96PinAfi-31
96PinAfiAP-31
96PinAfiFPP-31
96PinAfiSP-10
96PinArtP-3
96PinArtP-66
96PinArtP-172
96PinFan-11
96PinFoil-272
96PinPow-9
96PinSam-3
96PinSlu-9
96PinSta-3
96PinSta-66
96PinSta-172
96ProMagA-18
96ProMagDM-12
96ProSta-111
96RocPol-4
96Sco-271
96Sco-298
96ScoAll-8
96ScoDugC-B23
96ScoDugCAP-B23
96ScoGolS-23
96ScoPowP-11
96ScoTitT-7
96Sel-62
96SelArtP-62
96SelCer-71
96SelCerAP-71
96SelCerCB-71
96SelCerCR-71

96SelCerMB-71
96SelCerMG-71
96SelCerMR-71
96SelClaTF-16
96SelEnF-18
96SelTeaN-4
96SP-75
96Spo-4
96Spo-103
96SpoArtP-4
96SpoArtP-103
96SpoHitP-11
96SpoPowS-7
96SpoPro-13
96SPSpeFX-26
96SPSpeFXDC-26
96SPx-22
96SPxGol-22
96StaClu-204
96StaClu-336
96StaCluEPB-336
96StaCluEPG-336
96StaCluEPS-336
96StaCluMO-4
96StaCluMOP-204
96StaCluMOP-336
96StaCluMOP-PP15
96StaCluMOP-PS4
96StaCluPP-PP15
96StaCluPS-PS4
95StaCluVRMC-168
96Stu-137
96StuPrePB-137
96StuPrePG-137
96StuPrePS-137
96Sum-11
96SumAbo&B-11
96SumArtP-11
96SumBal-3
96SumBigB-12
96SumBigBM-12
96SumFoi-11
96SumHitI-12
96TeaOut-7
96Top-195
96TopChr-63
96TopChrR-63
96TopGal-3
96TopGalPPI-3
96TopLas-35
96TopMysF-M18
96TopMysFR-M18
96TopPro-NL11
96Ult-186
96UltGolM-186
96UltHomRKGM-2
96UltHomRKR-2
96UltRBIK-3
96UltRBIKGM-3
96UppDec-320
96UppDecA-5
96UppDecDD-DD19
96UppDecDDG-DD19
96UppDecDDS-DD19
96UppDecPHE-H32
96UppDecPRE-R31
96UppDecPRE-R42
96UppDecPRE-R53
96UppDecPreH-H32
96UppDecPreR-R31
96UppDecPreR-R42
96UppDecPreR-R53
96UppDecRunP-RP2
96UppDecVJLS-VJ18
96Zen-13
96ZenArtP-13
96ZenMoz-12
97Bow-241
97BowBes-100
97BowBesAR-100
97BowBesR-100
97BowChr-67
97BowChrI-67
97BowChrIR-67
97BowChrR-67
97BowInt-241
97Cir-172
97CirRav-172
97ColCho-100
97ColChoCtG-14A
97ColChoCtG-14B
97ColChoCtG-14C
97ColChoCtGIW-CG14
97ColChoNF-NF13
97ColChoNF-NF14
97ColChoS-12
97ColChoTBS-21
97ColChoTBSWH-21
97Don-80
97Don-418
97DonEli-60
97DonEliGS-60
97DonLim-140
97DonLim-178
97DonLimLE-140
97DonLimLE-178
97DonPre-48
97DonPreCttC-48
97DonPreP-80
97DonPreP-418
97DonPrePGold-80
97DonPrePGold-418
97DonTea-94
97DonTeaSPE-94
97Fin-5
97Fin-103
97Fin-346
97FinEmb-103
97FinEmb-346
97FinEmbR-103
97FinEmbR-346
97FinRef-5
97FinRef-103
97FinRef-346
97FlaSho-A110
97FlaSho-B110
97FlaSho-C110
97FlaShoLC-110
97FlaShoLC-B110
97FlaShoLC-C110
97FlaShoLCM-A110
97FlaShoLCM-B110
97FlaShoLCM-C110
97Fle-307
97FleTif-307
97Lea-135
97LeaDrefS-5
97LeaFraM-135
97LeaFraMDC-135
97MetUni-71
97NewPin-130
97NewPinAP-130
97NewPinMC-130
97NewPinPP-130
97Pac-279
97PacLigB-279
97PacPri-96
97PacPriLB-96
97PacPriP-96
97PacPriSL-SL9A
97PacSil-279
97PacTriCD-14
97Pin-44
97PinArtP-44
97PinCer-36
97PinCerMBlu-36
97PinCerMG-36
97PinCerMR-36
97PinCerR-36
97PinIns-125
97PinInsCE-125
97PinInsDE-125
97PinMin-20
97PinMinB-20
97PinMinCB-20
97PinMinCG-20
97PinMinCGR-20
97PinMinCN-20
97PinMinCS-20
97PinMinG-20
97PinMinS-20
97PinMusC-44
97PinTotCPB-36
97PinTotCPG-36
97PinTotCPR-36
97PinX-P-28
97PinX-PMoS-28
97PinX-PSfF-41
97PinX-PSfFU-41
97ProMag-11
97ProMagML-11
97Sco-25
97ScoBla-11
97ScoPreS-25
97ScoRoc-1
97ScoRocPl-1
97ScoRocPr-1
97ScoShoS-25
97ScoShoSAP-25
97Sel-86
97SelArtP-86
97SelRegG-86
97SkyE-X-67
97SkyE-XC-67
97SkyE-XEC-67
97SP-64
97SpoIll-110
97SpoIllEE-110
97SPSpxF-1
97SPSPxFA-1
97SPx-23
97SPxBro-23
97SPxGraF-23
97SPxSil-23
97SPxSte-23
97StaClu-30
97StaCluMat-30
97StaCluMOP-30
97StaCluMOP-PG3
97StaCluPG-PG3
97Stu-34
97StuPrePG-34
97StuPrePS-34
97Top-380
97TopChr-130
97TopChrDD-DD9
97TopChrDDR-DD9
97TopChrR-130
97TopGal-58
97TopGalPPI-58
97TopIntF-ILM3
97TopSta-62
97TopStaAM-62
97Ult-183
97UltChe-A1
97UltDouT-13
97UltGolME-183
97UltPlaME-183
97UltRBIK-3
97UltSeaC-2
97UppDec-60
97UppDecP-14
97UppDecRP-RP14

Bickford, Charles
48BabRutS-5

Bickford, Vern
49Bow-1
50Bow-57
51Bow-42
51FisBakL-1
52Bow-48
52Top-252
53BraJohC-3
53BraSpiaS3-3
53Top-161
54Bow-176
79TCM50-114
83ASASpa-4
83TopRep5-252
91OriCro-34
91TopArc1-161

Bickhardt, Eric
89ButCopKSP-5
90GasRanB-14
90GasRanP-2512
90GasRanS-2
91ChaRanC-2
91ChaRanP-1306

Bicknell, Charlie
49EurSta-129
49PhiBul-5

Bicknell, Greg
89St.CatBJP-2090
90MyrBeaBJP-2767
91MyrBeaHC-2
91MyrBeaHP-2936
92PenPilC-20
92PenPilF-2924
93JacSunF-2703
94ElPasDF-3138
94SanBerSF-2750

Bieger, Philip
87AncGlaP-1
89AncGlaP-3

Biehl, Rod
91AubAstC-4
91AubAstP-4267
92BurAstC-12
92BurAstF-536

Bieksha, Steve
87BelMarTI-29
88WauTimGS-18

Bielanin, Ray
89GreFalDSP-11

Bielecki, Mike
82BufBisT-16
83LynPirT-1
84HawIslC-131
85Don-28
85Fle-650
85Pir-3
86Fle-603
86TopTra-10T
86TopTraT-10T
87Don-415
87Fle-603
87FleGlo-603
87Top-394
87TopTif-394
87VanCanP-1598
88Don-484
88DonTeaBC-NEW
88Sco-611
88ScoGlo-611
88Top-436
88TopTif-436
88TriAAAP-18
89CubMar-36
89Don-512
89DonBasB-194
89Fle-419
89FleGlo-419
89Top-668
89TopTif-668
89UppDec-321A
90Bow-22
90BowTif-22
90CubMar-2
90Don-9
90Don-373
90DonBesN-3
90DonSupD-9
90Fle-27
90FleCan-27
90Lea-45
90OPC-114
90PanSti-242
90PubSti-191
90Sco-484
90Top-114
90TopBig-129
90TopMinL-48
90TopSti-54
90TopTif-114
90TopTVCu-8
90UppDec-359
90VenSti-46
91Bow-422
91CubMar-36
91CubVinL-5
91Don-87
91Fle-415
91OPC-501
91Sco-453
91StaClu-109
91Top-501
91TopDesS-501
91TopMic-501
91TopTif-501
91Ult-57
91UppDec-597
92BraLykP-5
92BraLykS-6
92Don-776
92Lea-505
92OPC-26
92Pin-566
92StaClu-656
92Top-26
92TopGol-26
92TopGolW-26
92TopMic-26
92Ult-457
92UppDec-730
93Fle-363
93IndWUA-4
93Lea-270
93OPCPre-112
93Sco-457
93StaClu-721
93StaCluFDI-721
93StaCluMOP-721
93Top-251
93TopGol-251
93TopInaM-251
93TopMic-251
93Ult-539
93UppDec-659
93UppDecGold-659
94BraLykP-5
94BraLykS-5
95AngMot-18
97PacPriGotD-GD109
97Ult-526
97UltGolME-526
97UltPlaME-526

Bielenberg, Bruce
84IowCubT-19
85IowCubT-33
89MiaMirIS-21
90MiaMirIS-30

Bienek, Vince
79AppFoxT-18
80GleFalWSBT-20
80GleFalWSCT-11
81GleFalWST-17
82GleFalWST-1

Bieniek, Carrie
96BelSnaTI-3

Bierbauer, Lou (Louis W.)
87OldJudN-31
87OldJudN-32
90KalBatN-3
90KalBatN-4
98CamPepP-4

Bierbrodt, Nick
96BesAutS1RP-FR16
97Top-249

Biercevicz, Greg
78SanJosMMC-3
79SpoIndT-21
79Top-712
80SpoIndT-3
81SpoIndT-8
81Top-282
82TidTidT-17
83TidTidT-15
85RocRedWT-30

Bierek, Kurt
93OneYanC-4
93OneYanF-3508
94GreBatF-481
95TamYanYI-1
96TamYanY-14
97GreBatC-3

Bierley, Brad
85VisOakT-7
86OrlTwiP-2
87OrlTwiP-14
88PorBeaC-16
88PorBeaP-639
89PorBeaC-18
89PorBeaP-231
90CMC-97
90IowCubC-22
90IowCubP-329
90ProAAAF-636
90TopTVCu-38
91IowCubLD-201
91IowCubP-1073
91LinDriAAA-201
92GenCubC-28
92GenCubF-1576

Bierman, Bernie
40WheM4-3
41WheM5-15

Bierman, Steve
93JohCitCC-4
93JohCitCF-3684
94SavCarC-7
94SavCarF-513
95PeoChiTI-1
96StPetCB-5

Biernat, Joe
93GenCubC-4
93GenCubF-3179
94PeoChiC-3
94PeoChiF-2272

Bierscheid, Gene
87SpaPhiP-3

Bieser, Steve
89BatCliP-1934
90BatCliP-3078
91SpaPhiC-22
91SpaPhiP-907
92ClePhiC-5
92ClePhiF-2058
93ReaPhiF-305
93ScrRedBF-2554
94ScrRedBF-930

95ScrRedBTI-1
Bifone, Pete
94SpoIndC-3
94SpoIndF-3327
Bigbee, Carson Lee
21E121So1-6A
21E121So1-6B
21E121So1-6C
21E121So1-6D
21Exh-10
21Nei-54
22E120-213
22W573-10
22W575-9
23W501-85
23W503-52
25Exh-49
26Exh-49
Bigelow, Elliott A.
94ConTSN-1285
94ConTSNB-1285
Biggers, Allan
89HamRedS-3
89SavCarP-362
Biggers, Brian
91SalLakTP-3216
91SalLakTSP-8
Biggerstaff, Kent
75TidTidTI-4
78HolMilT-2
79VanCanT-22A
80VanCanT-12
81PorBeaT-27
Biggio, Craig
88FleUpd-89
88FleUpdG-89
88ScoRoo-103T
88ScoRooG-103T
88TucTorC-15
88TucTorJP-2
88TucTorP-166
89AstLenH-24
89AstMot-14
89AstSmo-6
89ClaLigB-51
89Don-561
89DonBasB-176
89Fle-353
89FleGlo-353
89PanSti-79
89Sco-237
89ScoHot1R-98
89ScoYouS2-33
89Top-49
89TopTif-49
89UppDec-273
90AstLenH-4
90AstMot-5
90Bow-78
90BowTif-78
90ClaBlu-57
90Don-306
90DonBesN-89
90Fle-224
90FleCan-224
90K-M-8
90Lea-37
90OPC-157
90OPC-404
90PanSti-259
90PubSti-88
90Sco-275
90Spo-22
90SupActM-13
90Top-157
90Top-404
90TopBig-111
90TopCoi-39
90TopGloS-54
90TopHeaU-6
90TopSti-23
90TopStiB-22
90TopTif-157
90TopTif-404
90TopTVA-41
90UppDec-104
90VenSti-47
91AstMot-5
91Bow-556
91CadEllD-3
91Cla3-T2
91ClaGam-7
91DenHol-24
91Don-2
91Don-595
91DonSupD-2
91Fle-499
91JimDea-16
91KinDis-13
91Lea-12
91LeaPre-4
91MooSna-22
91OPC-565
91PanFreS-6
91PanSti-10
91RedFolS-8
91Sco-161
91Sco-872
91Sco100S-55
91SevCoi-T1
91SimandSMLBL-4
91StaClu-176
91Stu-173
91Top-565
91TopDesS-565
91TopMic-565
91TopTif-565
91TopTriH-N4
91Ult-132
91UppDec-158
91USPlaCA-9C
92AstMot-5
92Bow-484
92ClaGam-2
92Don-75
92DonCraJ2-1
92Fle-426
92Hig5-37
92HitTheBB-4
92KinDis-21
92Lea-315
92Mr.Tur3-4
92OPC-715
92OPCPre-135
92PanSti-151
92Pin-140
92Sco-460
92Sco-888
92Sco100S-52
92ScoImpP-22
92SevCoi-12
92SpoIllFK1-478
92StaClu-200
92StaCluD-16
92Stu-32
92Top-393
92Top-715
92TopGol-393
92TopGol-715
92TopGolW-393
92TopGolW-715
92TopKid-43
92TopMic-393
92TopMic-715
92TriPla-150
92Ult-199
92UppDec-31
92UppDec-162
93AstMot-4
93Bow-560
93ClaGam-13
93DiaMar-12
93Don-84
93DonDiaK-DK24
93DurPowP1-7
93Fin-119
93FinRef-119
93Fla-58
93Fle-47
93FleFruotL-5
93FunPac-44
93Lea-223
93LeaGolA-R13
93MilBonSS-20
93OPC-56
93PacSpa-118
93PanSti-171
93Pin-50
93Sco-18
93Sel-25
93SP-29
93StaClu-183
93StaCluAs-14
93StaCluFDI-183
93StaCluM-115
93StaCluMOP-183
93Stu-86
93Top-680
93TopGol-680
93TopInaM-680
93TopMic-680
93TriPla-100
93Ult-37
93UppDec-114
93UppDec-475
93UppDecGold-114
93UppDecGold-475
94AstMot-5
94Bow-390
94ColC-456
94ColChoGS-456
94ColChoSS-456
94Don-12
94DonSpeE-12
94ExtBas-269
94Fin-382
94FinRef-382
94Fla-386
94Fle-485
94FUnPac-158
94FUnPac-218
94Lea-236
94LeaL-111
94OPC-230
94Pac-259
94PanSti-190
94Pin-20
94PinArtP-20
94PinMusC-20
94PinRunC-RC33
94ProMag-59
94Sco-48
94ScoGolR-48
94Sel-296
94SP-28
94SPDieC-28
94StaClu-374
94StaCluFDI-374
94StaCluGR-374
94StaCluMOP-374
94Stu-17
94Top-305
94TopBlaG-25
94TopGol-305
94TopSpa-305
94TriPla-22
94TriPlaM-6
94Ult-499
94UppDec-312
94UppDecAJ-36
94UppDecAJG-36
94UppDecED-312
95AstMot-7
95Baz-33
95Bow-369
95BowBes-R32
95BowBes-X6
95BowBesR-R32
95BowBesR-X6
95ClaPhoC-29
95ColCho-109
95ColChoGS-109
95ColChoSE-38
95ColChoSE-255
95ColChoSEGS-38
95ColChoSEGS-255
95ColChoSESS-38
95ColChoSESS-255
95ColChoSS-109
95Don-456
95DonDom-4
95DonPreP-456
95DonTopotO-251
95Emb-66
95EmbGolI-66
95Emo-136
95Fin-129
95FinRef-129
95Fla-144
95Fle-453
95FleAllS-14
95Lea-126
95LeaLim-68
95Pac-182
95PacPri-59
95PanSti-45
95PanSti-118
95Pin-266
95PinArtP-266
95PinMusC-266
95PinPin-7
95PinPinR-7
95PinTeaP-TP4
95RedFol-20
95Sco-423
95ScoGolR-423
95ScoHaloG-HG68
95ScoPlaTS-423
95Sel-107
95SelArtP-107
95SelCer-69
95SelCerMG-69
95SP-61
95SPCha-52
95SPChaDC-52
95Spo-80
95SpoArtP-80
95SPSil-61
95SPSpeF-39
95StaClu-185
95StaCluFDI-185
95StaCluMO-6
95StaCluMOP-185
95StaCluSTWS-185
95StaCluVR-95
95Stu-50
95StuGolS-50
95Sum-31
95SumNthD-31
95Top-190
95TopCyb-108
95TopLeaL-LL41
95TopTra-157T
95UC3-72
95UC3ArtP-72
95Ult-384
95UltAllS-3
95UltAllSGM-3
95UltAwaW-12
95UltAwaWGM-12
95UltGolM-384
95UltLeaL-7
95UltLeaLGM-7
95UltOnBL-3
95UltOnBLGM-3
95UppDec-25
95UppDecED-25
95UppDecEDG-25
95UppDecSE-181
95UppDecSEG-181
95USPlaCMLA-11H
95Zen-18
96AstMot-3
96Baz-67
96Bow-29
96BowBes-49
96BowBesAR-49
96BowBesMI-2
96BowBesMIAR-2
96BowBesMIR-2
96BowBesR-49
96Cir-135
96CirRav-135
96ColCho-159
96ColCho-274
96ColChoGS-159
96ColChoGS-274
96ColChoSS-159
96ColChoSS-274
96ColChoYMtP-6
96ColChoYMtP-6A
96ColChoYMtPGS-6
96ColChoYMtPGS-6A
96Don-472
96DonPreP-472
96EmoXL-196
96Fin-B238
96Fin-G355
96Fin-S112
96FinRef-B238
96FinRef-G355
96FinRef-S112
96Fla-275
96Fle-402
96FleTif-402
96Lea-207
96LeaLim-63
96LeaLimG-63
96LeaPre-77
96LeaPreP-77
96LeaPrePB-207
96LeaPrePG-207
96LeaPrePS-207
96LeaPreSG-72
96LeaPreSte-72
96LeaSig-29
96LeaSigPPG-29
96LeaSigPPP-29
96MetUni-175
96MetUniP-175
96Pac-94
96PacPri-P31
96PacPriG-P31
96PanSti-57
96Pin-211
96PinAfi-25
96PinAfiAP-25
96PinAfiFPP-25
96PinArtP-111
96PinFirR-10
96PinFoil-211
96PinSta-111
96PinTeaP-9
96ProSta-12
96Sco-88
96ScoDugC-A68
96ScoDugCAP-A68
96ScoRef-20
96Sel-147
96SelArtP-147
96SelCer-33
96SelCerAP-33
96SelCerCB-33
96SelCerCR-33
96SelCerMB-33
96SelCerMG-33
96SelCerMR-33
96SelTeaN-26
96SP-94
96Spo-37
96SpoArtP-37
96SpoDouT-2
96SPSpeFX-12
96SPSpeFXDC-12
96SPx-28
96SPxGol-28
96StaClu-186
96StaClu-298
96StaCluB&B-BB4
96StaCluEPB-298
96StaCluEPG-298
96StaCluEPS-298
96StaCluMM-MM4
96StaCluMO-5
96StaCluMOP-186
96StaCluMOP-298
96StaCluMOP-BB4
96StaCluMOP-MM4
95StaCluVRMC-95
96Stu-41
96StuPrePB-41
96StuPrePG-41
96StuPrePS-41
96Sum-139
96SumAbo&B-139
96SumArtP-139
96SumFoi-139
96SumPos-2
96TeaOut-8
96Top-9
96Top-306
96TopChr-9
96TopChr-122
96TopChrR-9
96TopChrR-122
96TopGal-58
96TopGalPPI-58
96TopLas-19
96TopPowB-9
96TopRoaW-RW3
96Ult-485
96UltGolM-485
96UltPriL-12
96UltPriLGM-12
96UppDec-345
96UppDecA-6
96UppDecPRE-R54
96UppDecPreR-R54
96Zen-71
96ZenArtP-71
96ZenMoz-25
97Bow-24
97BowBes-71
97BowBesAR-71
97BowBesMI-MI8
97BowBesMIAR-MI8
97BowBesMIARI-MI8
97BowBesMII-MI8
97BowBesMIR-MI8
97BowBesMIRI-MI8

97BowBesR-71
97BowChr-20
97BowChrI-20
97BowChrIR-20
97BowChrR-20
97BowInt-24
97Cir-362
97CirRav-362
97ColCho-350
97ColChoAC-20
97ColChoTBS-23
97ColChoTBSWH-23
97Don-14
97DonEli-38
97DonEliGS-38
97DonLim-48
97DonLim-144
97DonLimFotG-58
97DonLimLE-48
97DonLimLE-144
97DonPre-99
97DonPreCttC-99
97DonPreP-14
97DonPrePGold-14
97Fin-128
97Fin-327
97FinEmb-128
97FinEmb-327
97FinEmbR-128
97FinEmbR-327
97FinRef-128
97FinRef-327
97FlaSho-A14
97FlaSho-B14
97FlaSho-C14
97FlaShoLC-14
97FlaShoLC-B14
97FlaShoLC-C14
97FlaShoLCM-A14
97FlaShoLCM-B14
97FlaShoLCM-C14
97Fle-342
97FleTif-342
97Lea-247
97LeaBanS-11
97LeaFraM-247
97LeaFraMDC-247
97MetUni-136
97NewPin-92
97NewPinAP-92
97NewPinMC-92
97NewPinPP-92
97Pac-314
97PacLigB-314
97PacPri-108
97PacPriLB-108
97PacPriP-108
97PacPriSL-SL10B
97PacSil-314
97PinCer-9
97PinCerMBlu-9
97PinCerMG-9
97PinCerMR-9
97PinCerR-9
97PinIns-28
97PinInsCE-28
97PinInsDE-28
97PinTotCPB-9
97PinTotCPG-9
97PinTotCPR-9
97PinX-P-64
97PinX-PMoS-64
97Sco-235
97ScoPreS-235
97ScoShoS-235
97ScoShoSAP-235
97Sel-39
97SelArtP-39
97SelRegG-39
97SkyE-X-77
97SkyE-XC-77
97SkyE-XEC-77
97SP-84
97SpoIll-100
97SpoIllEE-100
97StaClu-252
97StaCluMat-252
97StaCluMOP-252
97StaCluMOP-PL6
97StaCluPL-PL6
97Stu-70
97StuPrePG-70
97StuPrePS-70
97Top-85
97TopChr-32
97TopChrDD-DD5
97TopChrDDR-DD5
97TopChrR-32
97TopGal-46
97TopGalP-PP4
97TopGalPPI-46
97TopSta-46
97TopSta1AS-AS11
97TopStaAM-46
97Ult-343
97UltGolME-343
97UltPlaME-343
97UppDec-143
97UppDec-367

Biggs, Doug
88BriTigP-1864

Biggus, Bengie
80BurBeeT-29

Bigham, Craig
88SpoIndP-1931

Bigham, David
89EliTwiS-4
90EliTwiS-4
91KenTwiC-12
91KenTwiP-2066
92VisOakC-6
92VisOakF-1004
93ForMyeMC-2
93ForMyeMF-2647
94ForMyeMC-2
94ForMyeMF-1158
96FreKeyB-26

Bigham, Scott
89RivRedWB-3
89RivRedWCLC-1
89RivRedWP-1396
90RivRedWB-3
90RivRedWCLC-8
90RivRedWP-2613

Bigler, Jeff
92SpaPhiC-16
92SpaPhiF-1274
93ClePhiC-2
94ClePhiC-5
94ClePhiF-2532
96AugGreB-5

Bigusiak, Mike
76CliPilT-2
86SanJosBP-3

Biittner, Larry David
71SenTealW-2
72OPC-122
72Top-122
73OPC-249
73Top-249
75OPC-543
75Top-543
76OPC-238
76SSP-336
76Top-238
77CubJewT-1
77Top-64
78SSP270-244
78Top-346
79OPC-224
79Top-433
80OPC-334
80Top-639
81Don-515
81Fle-314
81Top-718
81TopTra-736
82Don-43
82Fle-59
82RedCok-3
82Top-159
83Don-440
83Fle-586
83FleSta-16
83FleSti-215
83RanAffF-14
83Top-527
83TopTra-10T
84Don-342
84Fle-414
84Nes792-283
84Top-283
84TopTif-283
93RanKee-2

Biko, Tom
80OrlTwiT-3
82AmaGolST-14

Bilak, Paul
86PalSprAP-4
87PalSprP-6

Bilardello, Dann J.
83TopTra-11T
84Don-408
84Fle-464
84Nes792-424
84RedEnq-14
84Top-424
84TopSti-57
84TopTif-424
85Don-243
85Top-28
85TopTif-28
86BasStaB-11
86ExpPos-1
86ExpProPa-2
86Top-253
86TopTif-253
87Fle-313
87FleGlo-313
87OPC-217
87Top-577
87TopTif-577
87VanCanP-1618
88OmaRoyC-17
88OmaRoyP-1518
89BufBisC-13
89BufBisP-1677
90BufBisC-13
90BufBisP-375
90BufBisTI-2
90CMC-13
90OPC-682
90ProAAAF-490
90Top-682
90TopTif-682
91LasVegSLD-277
91LasVegSP-237
91LinDriAAA-277
91Sco-659
92Lea-348
92PadCarJ-4
92PadMot-13
92PadSmo-4
92Sco-719
92StaClu-254
93NorTidF-2572
93PacSpa-256

Bilbert, Roy
91HagSunLD-230

Bilderback, Tyler
95BoiHawTI-6

Bilello, John
88BoiHawP-1605
88FreSunCLC-18
88FreSunP-1224
89BoiHawP-1997
89RenSilSCLC-241

Bilko, Steve (Steven Thomas)
47Exh-21
51Bow-265
52Top-287
53CarHunW-1
54Bow-206
54CarHunW-2
54Top-116
55Bow-88
55Top-93
55TopDouH-117
58RedEnq-5
58RedJayP-3
58Top-346
59DarFar-2
59Top-43
59TopVen-43
60Lea-106
60Top-396
61AngJayP-3
61Top-184
62AngJayP-2
62Jel-74
62Pos-74
62PosCan-74
62SalPlaC-17A
62SalPlaC-17B
62ShiPlaC-17
62Top-422
62TopStal-63
63Jel-24
63Pos-24
63RocRedWSP-2
79TCM50-177
83TopRep5-287
88LitSunMLL-6
90DodTar-52
94TopArc1-116
94TopArc1G-116

Bill, Bob
79NewCoPT-4
83TriTriT-28
86TulDriTI-26
88WatPirP-33

Bill, Robert
94UtiBluSC-30

Billeci, Craig
91BatCliC-6
91BatCliP-3488

Billingham, Jack
68Top-228
68TopVen-228
69OPC-92
69Top-92
69TopTeaP-10
70Top-701
71MLBOffS-74
71OPC-162
71Top-162
72Top-542
73OPC-89
73Top-89
74OPC-158
74Top-158
74TopSta-22
75OPC-235
75Top-235
76OPC-155
76RedKro-4
76RedPos-4
76SSP-23
76Top-155
77PepGloD-53
77Top-512
78TigBurK-6
78Top-47
79Top-388
80Top-603
85SpoIndGC-2
87AstShoSTw-2
87OscAstP-18
89SweBasG-43
90DodTar-53
90OscAstS-28
91OscAstP-700
92OscAstF-2547
93OscAstC-28
93OscAstF-644
93UppDecAH-11
94OscAstC-27
94OscAstF-1155
96KisCobB-2

Billingham, James
92OscAstC-28

Billings, Dick (Richard A.)
71OPC-729
71SenTealW-3
71Top-729
72OPC-148
72Top-148
73OPC-94
73Top-94
74OPC-466
74Top-466
75TulOil7-24
76SSP-288
86RanGreT-12
93RanKee-3

Billings, Haskell
94ConTSN-1313
94ConTSNB-1313

Billingsley, Marvin
93AshTouC-3
93AshTouF-2267
94OscAstC-3
94OscAstF-1129

Billingsley, Rod
89SpoIndSP-3
90WatDiaB-7
90WatDiaP-2380

Billmeyer, Mickey
86HagSunP-3
87MiaMarP-11
87PorChaRP-16
88MiaMarS-2
89ChaRanS-3
90QuaCitAGS-18
91CalLeLA-15
91MidAngOHP-5
91PalSprAP-2018
92EdmTraF-3541
92EdmTraS-168
92MidAngF-4030
92MidAngS-453
92SkyAA F-192
95AngMot-28
96AngMot-28

Billoni, Mike
87BufBisP-27
89BufBisC-1

Bills, Walter
92MedHatBJF-3202
92MedHatBJSP-14

Biltimier, Mike
93GreFalDSP-6
94BakDodC-2
95VerBeaDTI-3

Bilyeu, Aaron
90NebCor-4

Bingham, Dave
94HicCraC-3
94HicCraF-2179

Bingham, David
92IdaFalGF-3524
92IdaFalGSP-2

Bingham, Mark
82DanSunF-5

Binkley, Brett
93YakBeaC-3
93YakBeaF-3874
94VerBeaDC-5
94VerBeaDF-62
95DurBulTI-3

Binks, George Eugene
50WorWidGV-21
83TCMPla1945-5

Binversie, Brian
94OneYanC-5
94OneYanF-3781
95GreBatTI-4

Biot, Charlie
92NegLeaRLI-5
95NegLeaL2-17

Birch, Brent
90ArkRaz-2

Birch, Brock
86EveGiaC-23
86EveGiaPC-2
87CliGiaP-20

Bird, Bill
90PitMetP-29

Bird, Billy
88LouRedBTI-52
89LouRedBTI-1
91LouRedTI-1
96LouRedB-5

Bird, David
88AlaGolTI-2
89WelPirP-5
90AugPirP-2456
90ProAaA-75
91SalBucC-14
91SalBucP-944
92CarMudF-1172
92CarMudS-126
92SkyAA F-59

Bird, Doug
74OPC-17
74Top-17
75OPC-364
75Top-364
76OPC-96
76SSP-180
76Top-96
77BurCheD-68
77OPC-191
77Top-556
78Roy-1
78SSP270-218
78Top-183
79PhiBurK-12
79Top-664
80Top-421
81Fle-106
81Top-516
81TopTra-737
82CubRedL-47
82Don-504
82Fle-586
82Top-273
83Don-48
83Fle-490

83Top-759
83TopTra-12T
84Fle-391
84Nes792-82
84Top-82
84TopTif-82
89PacSenL-90
90EliSenL-65
92YanWIZ8-11
Bird, Fred
86CarSchM-25
Bird, Larry
94TedWil-LP1
Bird, Oriole
94MasMan-10
Bird, Steven
88KinIndS-4
Birdie, BJ
93FunPacM-4
94MasMan-3
Birdt, Louis
93PocPosF-4200
93PocPosSP-23
Birkbeck, Mike
86VanCanP-3
87BrePol-40
87Don-33
87DonRoo-19
87FleUpd-5
87FleUpdG-5
87Lea-33
87Top-229
87TopTif-229
88BrePol-40
88Don-49
88Sco-369
88ScoGlo-369
88Top-692
88TopTif-692
89Bow-132
89BowTif-132
89BrePol-40
89BreYea-40
89Don-501
89Fle-178
89FleGlo-178
89Sco-596
89Top-491
89TopTif-491
90BrePol-40
90CMC-46
90DenZepC-21
90DenZepP-617
90ProAAAF-642
90PubSti-489
90VenSti-48
91CanIndP-972
92TidTidF-888
92TidTidS-552
93RicBraBB-21
93RicBraF-177
93RicBraP-9
93RicBraRC-6
94BreMilB-195
94RicBraF-2838
95NorTidTI-6
96SigRooOJ-3
96SigRooOJS-3
Birkel, Tony
85RedWinA-12
86RedWinA-24
Birkofer, Ralph
34DiaMatCSB-15
34BatR31-90
35DiaMatCS3T1-10
36NatChiFPR-9
90DodTar-901
Birmingham, Dode (Joseph L.)
08AmeLeaPC-3
08RosComP-22
09BriE97-2
09ColChiE-31
09SpoNewSM-101
09T206-29
10DomDisP-14
10SweCapPP-17
10W555-6
11SpoLifM-39
11T205-17
12ColRedB-31
12ColTinT-31
12HasTriFT-7
12HasTriFT-8
12HasTriFT-72
12T207-14
13NatGamW-5
13TomBarW-4
14CraJacE-106
14PieStaT-4
15CraJacE-106
Birrell, Bob
79ElmPioRST-24
83PawRedST-1
Birrell, Simon
96DanBraB-7
Birrer, Babe (Werner)
56Top-84
58MonRoyF-4
90DodTar-54
91OriCro-35
Birriel, Jose
86NewBriRSP-3
87NewBriRSP-24
88BlaYNPRWL-66
88EasLeaAP-19
88NewBriRSP-902
89BlaYNPRWL-72
89BlaYNPRWLU-25
89LynRedSS-2
Birtsas, Tim
82OneYanT-8
85DomLeaS-191
85FleUpd-6
86A'sMot-25
86Don-462
86Fle-412
86FleStiC-5
86Lea-227
87HunStaTI-3
87TacTigP-23
88FleUpd-82
88FleUpdG-82
88NasSouC-2
88NasSouP-477
88RedKah-48
88Top-501
88TopTif-501
89Fle-152
89FleGlo-152
89RedKah-48
89Sco-454
89Top-103
89TopTif-103
89UppDec-638
90Don-493
90Fle-414
90FleCan-414
90OPC-687
90RedKah-3
90Sco-408
90Top-687
90TopTif-687
90UppDec-137
91OPC-289
91Sco-648
91Top-289
91TopDesS-289
91TopMic-289
91TopTif-289
Biscan, Frank
46SeaSLP-5
Bisceglia, Dave
81WatRedT-20
Bisceglia, James
86SalAngC-90
87QuaCitAP-14
88PalSprAP-1458
89PalSprACLC-52
Bish, Brent
90SpoIndSP-10
91ChaRaiC-15
91ChaRaiP-100
92CalLeaACL-36
92HigDesMC-3
93RanCucQC-4
93RanCucQF-837
Bishop, Charles
52Par-98
53Top-186
55A'sRodM-3
55Top-96
55TopDouH-109
91TopArc1-186
Bishop, Craig
90BakDodCLC-243
90YakBeaTI-27
Bishop, Greg
89CarNewE-16
92MisStaB-50
Bishop, James
83KinBluJTI-1
86KnoBluJP-2
87WilBilP-8
88CedRapRP-1165
89MiaMirIS-2
91SalSpuC-9
91SalSpuP-2249
92BirBarF-2587
92BirBarS-78
92ClaFS7-239
Bishop, Josh
96BelSnaTI-4
96Bow-302
Bishop, Max F.
25Exh-105
26Exh-105
28PorandAR-A4
28PorandAR-B4
28W56PlaC-C4
29ExhFou-28
29PorandAR-5
33Gou-61
33GouCanV-61
33RitCE-13S
33TatOrbSDR-187
34DiaStaR-6
35DiaMatCS3T1-11
35GouPuzR-6E
35GouPuzR-11G
35GouPuzR-13E
35GouPuzR-15E
88ConSer4-4
91ConTSN-183
94ConTSN-1149
94ConTSNB-1149
Bishop, Mike (Michael D.)
77QuaCitAT-4
80ElPasDT-12
81SalLakCGT-14
82SpoIndT-10
83TidTidT-6
87AncGlaP-2
91MetWIZ-38
Bishop, Teddy
94BelMarC-6
94BelMarF-3239
Bishop, Terry
96MarPhiB-3
Bishop, Tim
87OneYanP-28
88PriWilYS-2
Bishop, William
87OldJudN-33
Bison, Buster T.
89BufBisC-12
89BufBisP-1666
92BufBisBS-28
Bisons, Buffalo
88BufBisTI-9
94OriofB-49
Bispo, Randy
86SanJosBP-4
Bissant, John L.
93NegLeaRL2-2
Bissonette, Del
28W56PlaC-S13
29ExhFou-4
29PorandAR-6
31Exh-4
36GouWidPPR-D2
90DodTar-55
Bithorn, Hi
43CubTeal-3
Bitker, Joe
86BeaGolGP-2
87LasVegSP-1
88LasVegSC-1
88LasVegSP-230
89LasVegSC-1
89LasVegSP-4
90CMC-586
90ProAAAF-132
90TacTigC-9
90TacTigP-85
90TriAllGP-AAA47
91Don-624
91Fle-281
91OklCit8P-171
91TopDeb90-16
91UppDec-797
92Sco-743
92Sco100RS-87
93RanKee-72
Bitter, Mike
89SanDieSAS-3
Bittiger, Jeff
82JacMetT-1
83TidTidT-13
84TidTidT-13
85IntLeaAT-20
85MetTCM-37
85TidTidT-8
86PorBeaP-1
87PorBeaP-1
88ScoRoo-66T
88ScoRooG-66T
88VanCanC-1
89Bow-60
89BowTif-60
89Sco-512
89Top-209
89TopTif-209
89UppDec-509
89VanCanC-1
90AlbDukC-2
90AlbDukP-335
90AlbDukT-2
90CMC-404
90ProAAAF-56
91ColSprSSLD-77
91ColSprSSP-2176
91LinDriAAA-77
92HunStaF-3941
92HunStaS-303
Bivens, William E.
87SprCarB-10
88SprCarB-7
88St.PotCC-3
89TexLeaAGS-25
Bivin, Jim
94ConTSN-1299
94ConTSNB-1299
Bjorkman, George A.
80ArkTraT-2
80VenLeaS-79
82LouRedE-1
83ColAstT-1
84IndIndTI-10
84IndIndTI-20
84Nes792-116
84Top-116
84TopTif-116
85IndIndTI-20
85RocRedWT-31
Bjornson, Craig
92AshTouC-18
92AubAstC-22
92AubAstF-1344
93QuaCitRBC-3
93QuaCitRBF-90
Black Barons, Birmingham
92NegLeaRLI-91
92NegLeaRLI-92
92NegLeaRLI-93
93NegLeaRL2-52
93NegLeaRL2-53
93NegLeaRL2-75
93NegLeaRL2-76
93NegLeaRL2-77
93NegLeaRL2-78
93TedWilPC-4
Black Caps, Louisville
93TedWilPC-13
Black Crackers, Atlanta
93TedWilPC-1
Black Yankees, New York
93TedWilPC-16
Black, Allen
82QuaCitCT-2
Black, Bob
89RicBraC-9
Black, Bud (Harry)
80SanJosMJitB-4
81LynSaiT-2
83Don-322
83Fle-107
83Fle-644
83OmaRoyT-2
83Roy-2
83Top-238
84Don-130
84Fle-343
84Nes792-26
84Top-26
84TopSti-283
84TopTif-26
85Don-100
85Fle-198
85Lea-202
85OPC-47
85Top-412
85TopSti-275
85TopTif-412
86BasStaB-12
86Don-374
86Fle-4
86Lea-170
86OPC-319
86RoyKitCD-7
86RoyNatP-40
86Top-697
86TopSti-261
86TopTif-697
87Don-404
87Fle-365
87FleGlo-365
87OPC-315
87Top-669
87TopTif-669
88Don-301
88Fle-252
88FleGlo-252
88OPC-301
88RoySmo-9
88SanDieSAAG-3
88SanDieSAAG-4
88Sco-313
88ScoGlo-313
88ScoRoo-11T
88ScoRooG-11T
88Top-301
88TopTif-301
88TopTra-16T
88TopTraT-16T
89Bow-82
89BowTif-82
89Don-556
89IndTeal-5
89OPC-5
89SanDieSAG-3
89SanDieSAG-4
89Sco-404
89Top-509
89TopSti-209
89TopTif-509
89UppDec-466
90Don-556
90DonBesA-118
90Fle-486
90FleCan-486
90IndTeal-6
90Lea-451
90OPC-144
90PubSti-554
90Sco-197
90Top-144
90TopBig-223
90TopSti-213
90TopTif-144
90UppDec-498
90VenSti-49
91Bow-639
91Don-719
91FleUpd-128
91GiaMot-7
91GiaPacGaE-19
91GiaSFE-3
91Lea-312
91OPC-292
91OPCPre-9
91ScoRoo-46T
91StaClu-302
91Stu-260
91Top-292
91TopDesS-292
91TopMic-292
91TopTif-292
91TopTra-11T
91TopTraT-11T
91UltUpd-115
91UppDec-799
92Bow-692
92Don-93
92Fle-628
92GiaMot-7
92GiaPacGaE-6
92Lea-3
92OPC-774
92Pin-202

92Sco-358
92StaClu-55
92Top-774
92TopGol-774
92TopGolW-774
92TopMic-774
92UppDec-697
93Bow-28
93Don-50
93Fle-151
93GiaMot-22
93GiaPos-5
93Lea-212
93OPC-38
93PacSpa-267
93Pin-181
93Sco-131
93Sel-221
93StaClu-624
93StaCluFDI-624
93StaCluG-24
93StaCluMOP-624
93Top-498
93TopGol-498
93TopInaM-498
93TopMic-498
93Ult-482
93UppDec-229
93UppDecGold-229
94Don-64
94Fle-683
94Pin-140
94PinArtP-140
94PinMusC-140
94Sco-176
94ScoGolR-176
94Top-89
94TopGol-89
94TopSpa-89
95ColCho-263
95ColChoGS-263
95ColChoSS-263
95FleUpd-40
95Sco-115
95ScoGolR-115
95ScoPlaTS-115

Black, Don
47IndTeal-1
47IndVanPP-1
48BluTin-28
48IndTeal-3
53IndPenCBP-4
76TayBow4-66

Black, Joe
47PM1StaP1-12
47PM1StaP1-13
47PM1StaP1-14
52Top-321
53RedMan-NL4
53SpoMagP-1
53Top-81
54NewYorJA-1
54Top-98
55DodGolS-9
55Top-156
56Kah-3
56Top-178
56TopPin-54
79DiaGre-271
79TCM50-160
83TopRep5-321
89PacLegI-177
89SweBasG-69
90DodTar-56
91RinPosBD3-1
91SweBasG-9
91TopArc1-81
92BazQua5A-13
93ActPacA-143
93TedWil-132
93UppDecAH-12
93UppDecAH-154
94TopArc1-98
94TopArc1G-98
94UppDecAH-52
94UppDecAH1-52
95DodROY-3
95TopArcBD-22
95TopArcBD-44
95TopArcBD-71
95TopArcBD-103

Black, Keith
91HamRedC-23
91HamRedP-4043
92HamRedC-24
92HamRedF-1596
93SavCarC-4
93SavCarF-691
93SouAtlLAGF-45
94St.PetCC-4
94St.PetCF-2590

Black, Robbie
89CarNewE-23

Black, Stephen
91MelBusF-18

Blackaby, Ethan Allan
75PhoGiaCK-25
76PheGiaCr-NNO
76PhoGiaCC-2
77PhoGiaCC-3
78PhoGiaC-1
80PhoGiaVNB-24
81PhoGiaVNB-27
83PhoGiaBHN-26
82PhoGiaVNB-11

Blackburn, J.D.
95DavLipB-1

Blackburn, Jackie
85Ft.MyeRT-24

Blackburn, James Ray
49Bow-160
51Bow-287
79TCM50-259

Blackburn, Ron
57JetPos-2
58Top-459
59Top-401
60Top-209

Blackburne, Lena (Russell)
09T206-399
10ChiE-12
11SpoLifCW-36
11SpoLifM-20
11T205-18
12T207-15
91ConTSNP-905
93ConTSN-905

Blackmon, Anthony
87SalLakTTT-22

Blackmon, Tom
80BatTroT-7
83KnoBluJT-1

Blackmun, Ben
85BenPhiC-2

Blackshear, Steve
87ReaPhiP-18

Blackwell, Barry
85AncGlaPTI-4
89KinIndS-3

Blackwell, Eric
90GreFalDSP-14
90YakBeaTI-30
91VerBeaDP-786
91YakBeaC-8
91YakBeaP-4259

Blackwell, Ewell
46SpoExcW-1-6
47Exh-22A
47Exh-22B
47HomBon-3
47PM1StaP1-15
48BluTin-4
48Bow-2
49EurSta-77
49Lea-39
50AmeNut&CCP-1
50Bow-63
50RoyDes-9
51Bow-24
52BerRos-4
52BerRos-20
52RedMan-NL3
52RoyPre-1
52Top-344
53Top-31
76TayBow4-24
79TCM50-119
80MarExh-5
82GSGalAG-22
83TopRep5-344
85TCMPla1-37
89PacLegI-188
91TopArc1-31
92BazQua5A-18

Blackwell, Juan
91Ft.LauYC-19
91Ft.LauYP-2432
92AlbYanF-2230
92AlbYanS-4

Blackwell, Larry
86KenTwiP-2
87OrlTwiP-26
88VisOakCLC-159
88VisOakP-83
89OrlTwiB-11
89OrlTwiP-1340

Blackwell, Orlando
83CliGiaF-11
84ShrCapFB-2

Blackwell, Richie
94WelPirC-4
94WelPirF-3483

Blackwell, Teddy
89BurIndS-29
90WatIndS-26
91CollndC-30
92ColRedC-29
93ColRedC-30
93SouAtlLAGF-10
94KinIndC-26

Blackwell, Tim (Timothy P.)
76SSP-415
77ExpPos-5
78OPC-223
78Top-449
80Top-153
81CokTeaS-13
81Don-559
81Fle-304
81OPC-43
81Top-553
81TopSupHT-22
82Don-99
82ExpHygM-1
82ExpPos-1
82Fle-587
82Top-374
82TopSti-28
82TopTra-7T
83Don-214
83ExpPos-1
83ExpStu-26
83OPC-57
83Top-57
84PhoGiaC-241
86FreGiaP-1
88PhoFirC-25
89PitMetS-24
90FloStaLAS-24
90St.LucMS-28
91ColMetPI-1
91ColMetPPI-7
91SouAtlLAGP-SAL12
92ColMetC-26
92ColMetF-312
92ColMetPI-1
96BowBayB-1

Blackwell, Todd
90RenSilSCLC-268

Blackwell, Tom
88PhoFirP-53

Blades, Ray (Francis R.)
21Exh-11
25Exh-58
26Exh-58
28Exh-30
54Top-243
91ConTSN-130
92ConTSN-646
94TopArc1-243
94TopArc1G-243

Bladow, Dave
92EugEmeC-6
92EugEmeF-3017
93WilBluRF-1989

Bladt, Richard Alan
74OPC-601
74SyrChiTI-2
74Top-601
75SyrChiTI-NNO
76SSP-444
76VenLeaS-103
77RocRedWM-9
92YanWIZ7-16

Blaeholder, George
32OrbPinNP-9
32OrbPinUP-6
33Gou-16
33GouCanV-16
33TatOrb-6
34DiaMatCSB-16
34DiaStaR-13
35DiaMatCS3T1-12
35GouPuzR-5D
35GouPuzR-6D
35GouPuzR-11F
35GouPuzR-13D
36GouWidPPR-A6
93ConTSN-742

Blaine, James
93IdaFalBF-4023
93IdaFalBSP-16

Blaine, Tom
88ArkTraGS-8

Blair, Brian
93EriSaiC-2
93EriSaiF-3127
94ChaRivC-2
94ChaRivF-2680
96TulDriTI-3

Blair, Buddy (Louis Nathan)
83TCMPla1942-23

Blair, Dennis
72Dia-2
75OPC-521
75Top-521
76OPC-642
76SSP-344
76Top-642
77OPC-189
77RocRedWM-23
77Top-593
78Top-466
79HawIsIT-22
80HawIsIT-9

Blair, Dirk
91PulBraC-17
91PulBraP-3996
92MacBraC-2
92MacBraF-258
93CarLeaAGF-36
93DurBulC-3
93DurBulF-477
93DurBulTI-35
94GreBraF-405
94GreBraTI-6
95AusFut-81
95BreBtaTI-43

Blair, Donny
93BelBreC-2
93BelBreF-1701
94StoPorC-3
94StoPorF-1684

Blair, Footsie (Clarence Vick)
31CubTeal-3
79DiaGre-102

Blair, Garnett E.
91NegLeaRL-19
93NegLeaRL2-3
93TedWil-98
95NegLeaLI-19

Blair, Lonnie
91NegLeaRL-18
95NegLeaLI-18

Blair, Paul
65Top-473
66OPC-48
66Top-48
66TopVen-48
67CokCapO-3
67OPC-153
67Top-153
67Top-319
67TopVen-218
68CokCapO-3
68DexPre-12
68OPC-135
68Top-135
68TopVen-135
69MilBra-27
69MLBOffS-1
69Top-506
69TopTeaP-5
70DayDaiNM-157
70MLBOffS-146
70OPC-285
70Top-285
71Kel-35
71MLBOffS-290
71OPC-53
71Top-53
71TopTat-45
72MilBra-33
72OriPol-2
72Top-660
73LinPor-8
73OPC-528
73OriJohP-6
73Top-528
74OPC-92
74Top-92
74TopSta-123
75Hos-12
75HosTwi-12
75OPC-275
75Top-275
76OPC-473
76SSP-395
76Top-473
77BurCheD-39
77Top-313
77YanBurK-21
78SSP270-20
78Top-114
78YanBurK-22
78YanSSPD-20
79OPC-304
79Top-582
80OPC-149
80Top-281
81Ori6F-6
81TCM60I-311
84EveGiaC-19
86OriGreT-5
88CalLeaACLC-4
88SanJosGCLC-117
88SanJosGP-109
89PacSenL-76
89ShrCapP-1834
89T/MSenL-8
90CMC-308
90EliSenL-77
90ProAAAF-479
90RocRedWC-7
90RocRedWP-722
90WinSpiTI-4
91ChaKniLD-127
91ChaKniP-1694
91LinDriAA-127
91OriCro-36
92MCIAmb-8
92YanWIZ7-17
92YanWIZ8-12
93ActPacA-158
93MCIAmb-2
93OriCroASU-9
93UppDecAH-13
94MCIAmb-7
94TedWil-8
94UppDecAH-197
94UppDecAH-211
94UppDecAH1-197
94UppDecAH1-211
95MCIAmb-5

Blair, Walter Allan
09RamT20-12
11MecDFT-4
12HasTriFT-4
14CraJacE-126
14PieStaT-5
15CraJacE-126

Blair, William E.
87OldJudN-34

Blair, Willie
87DunBluJP-944
89SyrChiC-6
89SyrChiMB-2
89SyrChiP-805
90BluJayFS-3
90Bow-504
90BowTif-504
90ClaYel-T52
90DonRoo-29
90FleUpd-126
90Lea-449
90ScoRoo-88T
90TopTra-8T
90TopTraT-8T
91ColSprSSLD-78
91ColSprSSP-2177
91Don-267
91Fle-170
91LinDriAAA-78
91OPC-191
91Sco-57
91Sco100RS-19
91Top-191

91TopDeb90-17
91TopDesS-191
91TopMic-191
91TopTif-191
91UppDec-427
92Fle-106
92Sco-730
92StaClu-813
92TucTorF-478
92TucTorS-601
93Don-740
93Fla-36
93Fle-404
93FleFinE-23
93PacSpa-423
93RocUSPC-8C
93RocUSPC-10H
93TopTra-96T
93Ult-342
93UppDec-720
93UppDecGold-720
94Don-631
94Fle-434
94Pac-189
94RocPol-3
94Sco-118
94ScoGolR-118
94StaClu-348
94StaCluFDI-348
94StaCluGR-348
94StaCluMOP-348
94StaCluT-116
94StaCluTFDI-116
94Top-439
94TopGol-439
94TopSpa-439
94Ult-182
95Don-47
95DonPreP-47
95Fle-515
95PadMot-20
95StaClu-157
95StaCluFDI-157
95StaCluMOP-157
95StaCluSTWS-157
95Top-292
96Fle-561
96FleTif-561
96LeaSigA-25
96LeaSigAG-25
96LeaSigAS-25
96PadMot-26
96Sco-209
96Ult-555
96UltGolM-555
97Ult-496
97UltGolME-496
97UltPlaME-496
Blais, Jean-Marc
52LavPro-111
Blais, Mike
94LynRedSC-3
94LynRedSF-1884
95MicBatCTI-3
96TreThuB-7
Blake, Ben
92WatIndC-8
92WatIndF-3225
Blake, Bob
79WisRapTT-5
Blake, Ed
52Top-144
83TopRep5-144
Blake, Sherriff (John Frederick)
26Exh-18
31CubTeal-4
92ConTSN-478
Blake, Todd
92JohCitCC-25
92JohCitCF-3106
93SprCarC-3
93SprCarF-1841
94SavCarC-8
94SavCarF-500
Blake, Toe
43ParSpo-8
Blakely, Dave
85EveGiaC-1
86CliGiaP-2
87VisOakP-10
Blakely, Link (Lincoln H.)
36GouWidPPR-D3
Blakeman, Todd
90EliTwiS-5
91KenTwiC-3
91KenTwiP-2080
92KenTwiC-8
Blanchard, Doc
74NewYorNTDiS-25
74NewYorNTDiS-33
Blanchard, Johnny (John Edwin)
47StaPinP2-5
59Top-117
59TopVen-117
60Lea-89
60Top-283
61Pos-18
61Top-104
61TopStal-190
61Yan61RL-9
62Jel-11
62Pos-11
62PosCan-11
62Top-93
62TopVen-93
62YanJayP-3
63Jel-21
63Pos-21
63Top-555
64ChatheY-2
64Top-118
64TopVen-118
64YanReqKP-3
65ChaTheY-1
65Top-388
66Top-268
66TopVen-268
78TCM60I-78
81TCM60I-382
81TCM60I-474
89SweBasG-92
91RinPos1Y1-7
92YanWIZ6-9
93UppDecS-11
Blanche, Al (Prosper A.)
34BatR31-83
Blanchette, Bill
92BoiHawC-11
92BoiHawF-3616
93BoiHawC-3
93BoiHawF-3904
Blanco, Alberto
94QuaCitRBC-4
94QuaCitRBF-526
95MidLeaA-3
95QuaCitRBTI-2
96QuaCitRB-8
Blanco, Gil
65Top-566
67Top-303
92YanWIZ6-10
Blanco, Henry
90KisDodD-1
91GreFalDSP-5
92BakDodCLC-3
92UppDecML-201
93LinVenB-159
94SanAntMF-2474
94VenLinU-29
95LinVen-16
95SanAntMTI-48
96SanAntMB-1
Blanco, Ossie (Oswaldo C.)
76VenLeaS-128
80VenLeaS-192
Blanco, Pedro
92EliTwiF-3684
93EliTwiC-4
93EliTwiF-3426
93LinVenB-147
Blanco, Roger
96EveAquB-3
Blanco, Romualdo
73CedRapAT-22
75DubPacT-11
76VenLeaS-119
Bland, Lance
90SanBerSCLC-116
Bland, Nathan
93YakBeaC-4
93YakBeaF-3875
94BakDodC-3
94GreFalDSP-4
95BakBlaTI-11
96VerBeaDB-7
Blandford, Paul
96VerExpB-9
Blanding, Fritz (Fred)
12T207-16
14CraJacE-109
15CraJacE-109
Blanke, Scott
83CliGiaF-26
Blankenship, Bob
89BilMusP-2060
90BenBucL-11
Blankenship, Cliff
09AmeCarE-8
09RamT20-13
Blankenship, Kevin
84AriWilP-1
85DurBulT-3
86GreBraTI-4
87GreBraB-19
88GreBraB-16
88SouLeaAJ-28
89Don-658
89IowCubC-7
89IowCubP-1699
89TriAAP-AAA44
89UppDec-762
90Bow-24
90BowTif-24
90CMC-78
90Fle-28
90FleCan-28
90IowCubC-3
90IowCubP-311
90ProAAAF-618
90Sco-646
90UppDec-47
91BufBisP-533
92OklCit8F-1907
92OklCit8S-303
92SkyAAAF-139
Blankenship, Lance
86MedA'sC-69
86ModA'sC-13
87HunStaTI-4
87ModA'sP-10
88TacTigC-11
88TacTigP-630
88TriAAAP-38
89Don-621
89Fle-2
89FleGlo-2
89Sco-641
89ScoHot1R-20
89TacTigC-12
89TacTigP-1539
89UppDec-15
90A'sMot-21
90Fle-1
90FleCan-1
90Hot50RS-8
90OPC-132
90Sco-536
90Sco100RS-82
90ScoYouS2-36
90Top-132
90TopBig-173
90TopTif-132
90UppDec-687
91A'sMot-21
91Don-701
91Fle-3
91OPC-411
91Sco-303
91StaClu-437
91Top-411
91TopDesS-411
91TopMic-411
91TopTif-411
92AthMot-21
92Don-768
92Fle-250
92Lea-410
92OPC-386
92Sco-279
92StaClu-897
92Ult-418
92UppDec-749
93AthMot-22
93Bow-273
93Don-23
93Fle-290
93Lea-221
93OPC-30
93PacSpa-562
93Pin-338
93StaClu-413
93StaCluAt-2
93StaCluFDI-413
93StaCluMOP-413
93Top-548
93TopGol-548
93TopInaM-548
93TopMic-548
93Ult-253
93UppDec-108
93UppDecGold-108
94Don-401
94Fle-254
94Pac-445
94StaClu-341
94StaCluFDI-341
94StaCluGR-341
94StaCluMOP-341
94Top-17
94TopGol-17
94TopSpa-17
95Top-253
Blankenship, Ted
26Exh-73
27Exh-37
92ConTSN-457
Blanks, Daryl
88IdaFalBP-1834
89BurBraP-1621
89BurBraS-2
90BurBraB-23
90BurBraP-2362
90BurBraS-3
Blanks, Larvell
73OPC-609
73Top 600
75OPC-394
75Top-394
76OPC-127
76SSP-8
76Top-127
76TopTra-127T
77PepGloD-6
77Top-441
78OPC-213
78Top-61
79Top-307
80Top-656
89PacSenL-206
89TopSenL-92
93RanKee-73
Blanton, Cy (Darrell)
34BatR31-88
34DiaStaR-57
35GouPuzR-8K
35GouPuzR-9K
36GouWidPPR-A7
36GouWidPPR-C3
36NatChiFPR-10
36R31PasP-2
36WorWidGV-3
37ExhFou-7
38ExhFou-7
39GouPreR303A-4
39WorWidGTP-4
91ConTSN-134
Blanton, Garrett
91HamRedC-16
91HamRedP-4049
93SavCarC-5
93SavCarF-697
Blaser, Mark
83GreHorT-16
85AlbYanT-14
86WesPalBEP-6
Blasingame, Don (Donald L.)
47Exh-23A
47Exh-23B
56Top-309
57Top-47
58CarJayP-1
58Top-199
59ArmCoi-5
59Top-491
60GiaJayP-2
60Top-397
61GiaJayP-2
61Pos-148A
61Pos-148B
61Top-294
61TopStal-73
62Jel-117
62Pos-117
62PosCan-117
62RedEnq-1
62SalPlaC-103
62ShiPlaC-103
62Top-103
62TopVen-103
63Jel-126
63Kah-2
63Pos-126
63RedEnq-1
63RedFreBC-1
63Top-518
64Top-327
64TopVen-327
65OPC-21
65Top-21
66SenTeal-1
78TCM60I-84
79TCMJapPB-80
Blasingame, Kent
94ClePhiC-6
94ClePhiF-2538
94FloStaLAF-FSL31
95ReaPhiELC-5
95ReaPhiTI-29
Blasingame, Wade
65OPC-44
65Top-44
66Kah-5
66Top-355
66TopVen-355
67Ast-4
67CokCapB-14
67DexPre-23
67OPC-119
67Top-119
68CokCapA-7
68Top-507
69MilBra-28
69Top-308
71AstCok-2
71OPC-79
71Top-79
72Top-581
92YanWIZ7-18
Blasingim, Chad
94DavLipB-1
Blasingim, Joe
95BelGiaTI-37
96BelGiaTI-30
Blaske, Kevin
92ChaRanC-29
Blass, Steve
65OPC-232
65Top-232
66PirEasH-28
66Top-344
66TopVen-344
67CokCapPi-7
67PirTeal-3
67Top-562
67TopPirS-4
68PirKDK-28
68PirTeal-3
68Top-499
69Kah-B5
69OPC-104
69PirGre-3
69Top-104
69TopSta-83
69TopSup-57
69TopTeaP-16
70OPC-396
70PirTeal-1
70Top-396
71MLBOffS-194
71OPC-143
71PirActP-13
71PirArc-2
71Top-143
72Kel-44
72MilBra-34
72OPC-229
72OPC-320
72Top-229
72Top-320
73Kel2D-11
73OPC-95
73Top-95
74OPC-595
74Top-595
84OCoandSI-178
91UppDecS-13

93PirNatl-3
93UppDecAH-14
94UppDecAH-191
94UppDecAH1-191
Blasucci, Tony
85PriWilPT-18
86PriWilPP-3
87DayBeaAP-5
88BirBarB-2
89BirBarB-10
89BirBarP-94
90CalCanC-2
90CalCanP-644
90CMC-429
90ProAAAF-109
Blateric, Steve
73OPC-616
73Top-616
75SalLakCC-19
92YanWIZ7-19
Blatnick, Johnny (John Louis)
49Bow-123
Blatt, Charles P.
88KimN18-3
Blattner, Buddy (Robert G.)
40SolHug-4
47TipTop-121
49EurSta-130
49PhiBul-6
75JohMiz-1
84TCMPla1-45
Blauser, Jeff
86DurBulP-2
87IntLeaAT-33
87RicBraC-2
87RicBraT-11
87SpoRoo2-48
88Don-513
88Fle-533
88FleGlo-533
88RicBraC-22
88RicBraP-18
88Sco-562
88ScoGlo-562
88ScoYouS2-14
88StaLinBra-3
89BraDub-5
89Don-592
89Fle-588
89FleGlo-588
89PanSti-41
89Sco-589
89Top-83
89TopBig-317
89TopTif-83
89UppDec-132
90Bow-15
90BowTif-15
90BraDubP-1
90BraDubS-2
90ClaBlu-123
90Don-271
90DonBesN-74
90Fle-576
90FleCan-576
90Lea-191
90OPC-251
90PanSti-217
90PubSti-109
90Sco-178
90Top-251
90TopBig-180
90TopSti-28
90TopTif-251
90UppDec-406
90VenSti-50
91BraDubP-4
91BraSubS-6
91Don-229
91Fle-683
91Lea-115
91OPC-623
91PanFreS-22
91Sco-52
91StaClu-377
91Top-623
91TopDesS-623
91TopMic-623
91TopTif-623
91Ult-2
91UppDec-382
92BraLykP-6
92BraLykS-7
92Don-228
92Fle-353
92Lea-147
92OPC-199
92Pin-477
92Sco-362
92StaClu-168
92Top-199
92TopGol-199
92TopGolW-199
92TopMic-199
92Ult-159
92UppDec-370
93Bow-142
93BraFloA-3
93BraLykP-5
93BraLykS-6
93Don-134
93Fla-2
93Fle-364
93Lea-86
93OPC-59
93PacSpa-333
93PanSti-183
93Pin-432
93Sco-142
93SP-56
93StaClu-436
93StaCluB-5
93StaCluFDI-436
93StaCluMOP-436
93StuSil-8
93Top-552
93TopGol-552
93TopInaM-552
93TopMic-552
93Ult-302
93UppDec-591
93UppDecGold-591
94Bow-517
94BraLykP-6
94BraLykS-6
94BraUSPC-1S
94BraUSPC-8H
94ColC-53
94ColChoGS-53
94ColChoSS-53
94Don-88
94ExtBas-200
94Fin-27
94FinRef-27
94Fla-124
94Fle-354
94FleAllS-30
94FUnPac-104
94Lea-194
94OPC-214
94Pac-4
94PanSti-143
94Pin-98
94PinArtP-98
94PinMusC-98
94PinRunC-RC29
94Sco-54
94ScoGolR-54
94ScoGolS-5
94Sel-14
94SP-48
94SPDieC-48
94Spo-111
94StaClu-229
94StaCluFDI-229
94StaCluGR-229
94StaCluMOP-229
94StaCluMOP-ST1
94StaCluST-ST1
94StaCluT-60
94StaCluTFDI-60
94Top-318
94Top-387
94TopBlaG-26
94TopGol-318
94TopGol-387
94TopSpa-318
94TopSpa-387
94TriPla-42
94TriPlaM-8
94Ult-150
94UppDec-324
94UppDecED-324
95ColCho-168
95ColChoGS-168
95ColChoSS-168
95Don-363
95DonPreP-363
95DonTopotO-182
95Fla-321
95Fle-302
95Lea-390
95Pac-3
95Pin-241
95PinArtP-241
95PinMusC-241
95Sco-440
95ScoGolR-440
95ScoPlaTS-440
95StaClu-136
95StaCluFDI-136
95StaCluMOP-136
95StaCluSTDW-B1T
95StaCluSTWS-136
95Top-414
95TopCyb-214
95Ult-346
95UltGolM-346
95UppDec-44
95UppDecED-44
95UppDecEDG-44
96ColCho-452
96ColChoGS-452
96ColChoSS-452
96Don-461
96DonPreP-461
96Fla-195
96Fle-287
96FleBra-2
96FleTif-287
96Pac-15
96Pin-89
96Sco-288
96ScoDugC-B13
96ScoDugCAP-B13
96StaClu-438
96StaCluEPB-438
96StaCluEPG-438
96StaCluEPS-438
96StaCluMOP-438
96Top-406
96Ult-152
96UltGolM-152
96UppDec-273
88RicBraBC-6
97Cir-94
97CirRav-94
97ColCho-267
97Don-336
97DonLim-49
97DonLimLE-49
97DonPreP-336
97DonPrePGold-336
97DonTea-27
97DonTeaSPE-27
97Fle-252
97FleTif-252
97Sco-434
97ScoHobR-434
97ScoResC-434
97ScoShoS-434
97ScoShoSAP-434
97StaClu-131
97StaCluMOP-131
97Top-419
97TopSta-45
97TopSta1AS-AS19
97TopStaAM-45
97Ult-546
97UltGolME-546
97UltPlaME-546
Blaylock, Gary
59Top-539
Blaylock, Marv (Marvin E.)
55Bow-292
57Top-224
Blaylock, Robert
59Top-211
64TulOil-1
Blaze, Bakersfield
95BakBlaTI-32
Blazier, Ron
90PriPatD-2
91BatCliC-26
91BatCliP-3475
92SpaPhiC-10
92SpaPhiF-1255
93Bow-244
93ClaFS7-241
93ClePhiC-3
93ClePhiF-2675
93ExcFS7-83
93StaCluP-23
94ClePhiC-7
94ClePhiF-2518
95ReaPhiELC-6
95ReaPhiTI-40
96Cir-163
96CirRav-163
96Exc-195
96ScrRedBB-7
97Fle-407
97FleTif-407
97Pac-373
97PacLigB-373
97PacSil-373
97Top-492
97Ult-247
97UltGolME-247
97UltPlaME-247
Bleaszard, David
96MedHatBJTI-5
Bledsoe, Randy
93JohCitCC-5
93JohCitCF-3669
94NewJerCC-3
94NewJerCF-3405
Blefary, Curt (Curtis LeRoy)
65OPC-49
65Top-49
66Baz-28
66Top-460
66TopRubI-9
67Baz-28
67CokCapO-13
67DexPre-24
67OPC-180
67Top-180
67Top-521
67TopVen-227
68CokCapO-13
68DexPre-13
68Top-312
68TopVen-312
69MilBra-29
69MLBOffS-137
69Top-458
69TopSta-122
69TopSup-44
69TopTeaP-6
70MLBOffS-242
70OPC-297
70Top-297
70YanCliDP-3
71MLBOffS-483
71OPC-131
71Top-131
71YanCliDP-2
72MilBra-35
72Top-691
72Top-692
81Ori6F-7
81TCM60I-412
83FraBroR-23
87AstShoSTw-24
91OriCro-37
92YanWIZ7-20
94CarLeaA-DJ24
Blemker, Ray
77FriOneYW-112
Bleser, Al
96PorRocB-2
97BenRocC-29
Blessitt, Ike (Isiah)
75TucTorC-9
77HolMilT-1
89PacSenL-190
89TopSenL-20
Bleuberg, Jim
91JacSunP-142
Blevins, Brad
83QuaCitCT-8
Blevins, Greg
90ButCopKSP-2
91GasRanC-13
91GasRanP-2690
Blevins, Jeremy
96BesAutS-12
96BesAutSA-6
96BoiHawB-5
Bligh, Ned (Edwin Forrest)
87OldJudN-35
94OriofB-31
Bliss, Bill (William)
91FroRowDP-45
91GenCubC-1
91GenCubP-4207
91PeoChiTI-34
92ClaFS7-218
92PeoChiC-4
92PeoChiTI-4
92StaCluD-17
92UppDecML-159
93PeoChiC-2
93PeoChiF-1075
93PeoChiTI-1
95SalAvaTI-25
Bliss, Elmer Ward
11SpoLifCW-37
Bliss, John J.A.
09AmeCarE-9
09PC7HHB-4
09T206-30
11SpoLifM-263
Blizzard, Kevin
89GeoColC-2
89GeoColC-28
Blizzard, Mascot
96WatIndTI-NNO
Blobaum, Jeff
84PhoGiaC-19
Block, Bruno (James John)
10JuJuDE-4
11SpoLifM-21
12T207-17
Block, Cy (Seymour)
50WorWidGV-9
76TayBow4-111
Block, Richard
79NewCoPT-19
Blocker, Terry
82JacMetT-20
84TidTidT-20
85IntLeaAT-16
85MetColP-17
85MetTCM-28
85TidTidT-19
86MetTCM-36
86TidTidP-2
87MetColP-25
87TidTidP-5
87TidTidT-19
89Fle-589
89FleGlo-589
89RicBraBC-3
89RicBraC-17
89RicBraTI-3
89Sco-605
89Top-76
89TopTif-76
89UppDec-399
91MetWIZ-39
Blohm, Pete
89AugPirP-516
89SouAtlLAGS-45
90DunBluJS-3
90KnoBluJB-3
90KnoBluJP-1246
90KnoBluJS-1
91KnoBluJLD-351
91LinDriAA-351
91SyrChiMB-3
91SyrChiP-2475
92SyrChiF-1959
92SyrChiMB-1
92SyrChiS-501
93SyrChiF-992
Blomberg, Ron (Ronald Mark)
72OPC-203
72Top-203
73LinPor-129
73NewYorN-5
73OPC-462
73SyrChiTI-3
73Top-462
73Yan-1
74Kel-54
74OPC-117
74SyrChiTI-1
74Top-117
74TopDecE-60
74TopSta-211
75OPC-68
75SyrChiTI-1
75Top-68
75YanSSP-4

76Hos-38
76HosTwi-38
76OPC-354
76SSP-450
76Top-354
77Top-543
78Hos-147
78SSP270-157
78Top-506
79OPC-17
79Top-42
88Top-663
88TopTif-663
92YanWIZ6-11
92YanWIZ7-21
94CarLeaA-DJ38
97FleMilDM-39
Blomberg, Steve
76ShrCapT-16
Blomdahl, Ben
91NiaFalRC-19
91NiaFalRP-3625
92ClaFS7-99
92FayGenC-2
92FayGenF-2159
93Bow-207
93ClaFS7-158
93ClaGolF-51
93LonTigF-2297
94TolMudHF-1018
95TolMudHTI-7
96Sco-242
96TolMudHB-6
Blondin, Strongman
88KimN18-4
Blood, Darin
95BelGiaTI-16
96Bow-380
96Exc-240
96SanJosGB-17
97Bow-192
97BowCerBIA-CA6
97BowCerGIA-CA6
97BowChr-180
97BowChrI-180
97BowChrIR-180
97BowChrR-180
97BowInt-192
97Top-493
Bloodworth, Jimmy (James H.)
40PlaBal-189
49EurSta-78
51Bow-185
79DiaGre-386
Bloomfield, Clyde S.
64Top-532
Bloomfield, Jack (Gordon L.)
74PadDea-4
Blosser, Doug
96LanLugB-7
Blosser, Greg
89HigSchPLS-21
90Bow-278
90BowTif-278
90CarLeaA-12
90LynRedSTI-1
90Sco-681
90TopTVRS-37
91Bow-115
91Cla/Bes-226
91LinDriAA-452
91NewBriRSLD-452
91NewBriRSP-363
91UppDec-70
92Bow-251
92ClaFS7-194
92NewBriRSF-445
92NewBriRSS-478
92SkyAA F-203
92UppDecML-260
93Bow-199
93ClaFS7-44
93ClaGolF-27
93ExcFS7-130
93FleFinE-170
93PawRedSDD-4
93PawRedSF-2419
93PawRedSTI-4
93Top-798
93TopGol-798
93TopInaM-798
93TopMic-798
93Ult-506
94ColC-2
94ColChoGS-2
94ColChoSS-2
94Fin-402
94FinRef-402
94LeaLimR-30
94PawRedSDD-4
94Pin-245
94PinArtP-245
94PinMusC-245
94ScoRoo-RT162
94ScoRooGR-RT162
94Sel-190
94StaClu-172
94StaCluFDI-172
94StaCluGR-172
94StaCluMOP-172
94UppDec-5
94UppDecED-5
95PawRedSDD-6
95PawRedTI-33
95Sco-286
95ScoGolR-286
95ScoPlaTS-286
95TreThuTI-27
96RocRedWB-6
Blouin, Gary
86EugEmeC-45
87Ft.MyeRP-3
Blount, Bill
85SpoIndC-2
86ChaRaiP-3
87LasVegSP-16
88RivRedWCLC-230
88RivRedWP-1421
Blowers, Mike (Michael)
86JamExpP-1
87WesPalBEP-664
88JacExpB-16
88JacExpP-975
89IndIndC-14
89IndIndP-1221
90Bow-441
90BowTif-441
90ClaUpd-T5
90Don-656
90DonRoo-26
90Fle-438
90FleCan-438
90Lea-109
90Sco-624
90ScoYouS2-34
90TopDeb89-18
90TopTra-9T
90TopTraT-9T
90TopTVY-23
90UppDec-767
91Don-63
91OPC-691
91Sco-838
91Sco100RS-17
91Top-691
91TopDesS-691
91TopMic-691
91TopTif-691
91UppDec-730
92CalCanF-3739
92CalCanS-54
92SkyAAAF-23
92YanWIZ8-13
93FleFinE-264
93Lea-457
93MarMot-13
93PacSpa-618
93StaClu-144
93StaCluFDI-144
93StaCluMOP-144
94ColC-54
94ColChoGS-54
94ColChoSS-54
94Don-423
94Fin-183
94FinRef-183
94Fle-279
94Lea-218
94MarMot-17
94Pac-562
94Sco-521
94ScoGolR-521
94Sel-66
94StaClu-604
94StaCluFDI-604
94StaCluGR-604
94StaCluMOP-604
94StaCluMOP-ST26
94StaCluST-ST26
94Top-717
94TopGol-717
94TopSpa-717
94TriPla-123
94Ult-117
94UppDec-309
94UppDecED-309
95ColCho-284
95ColChoGS-284
95ColChoSS-284
95Don-46
95DonPreP-46
95DonTopotO-146
95Fla-79
95Fle-261
95Lea-289
95MarMot-10
95MarPac-22
95Pac-390
95Sco-531
95ScoGolR-531
95ScoPlaTS-531
95SP-191
95SPSil-191
95StaClu-494
95StaCluMOP-494
95StaCluSTDW-M26T
95StaCluSTDW-M494
95StaCluSTWS-494
95Top-348
95Ult-325
95UltGolM-325
95UppDecED-347
95UppDecEDG-347
96ColCho-313
96ColCho-586
96ColChoGS-313
96ColChoGS-586
96ColChoSS-313
96ColChoSS-586
96DodMot-10
96DodPol-3
96Don-148
96DonPreP-148
96EmoXL-204
96Fin-B215
96FinRef-B215
96Fla-286
96Fle-426
96FleDod-1
96FleTif-426
96FleUpd-U141
96FleUpdTC-U141
96LeaSigA-26
96LeaSigAG-26
96LeaSigAS-26
96MetUni-181
96MetUniP-181
96Pac-403
96Pin-55
96Pin-350
96PinFoil-350
96Sco-295
96ScoDugC-B20
96ScoDugCAP-B20
96StaClu-192
96StaCluMOP-192
96Top-419
96Ult-123
96Ult-492
96UltGolM-123
96UltGolM-492
96UppDec-359
97Fle-356
97Fle-545
97FleTif-356
97FleTif-545
97Top-192
97Ult-375
97UltGolME-375
97UltPlaME-375
Blue Jays, Dunedin
93DunBluJFFN-30
Blue Jays, Knoxville
82KnoBluJT-1
Blue Jays, St. Catharines
92St.CatBJF-3403
93St.CatBJC-30
Blue Jays, Toronto
78OPC-58
78Top-626
79BluJayS-2
80OPC-300
81OPC-331
83FleSta-250
83FleSti-NNO
85BluJayFS-36
86BluJayFS-36
87SpoTeaL-5
88BluJayFS-35
88PanSti-468
88RedFolSB-118
89BluJayFS-36
90FleWaxBC-C13
90PubSti-645
90RedFolSB-114
90TopMag-99
90VenSti-540
91PanCanT1-133
92BluJayMH-1
92BluJayMH-2
92BluJayMH-3
92BluJayMH-4
92BluJayMH-5
92BluJayMH-6
92BluJayMH-7
92BluJayMH-8
92BluJayMH-9
92BluJayMH-10
92BluJayMH-11
92BluJayMH-12
92BluJayMH-13
92BluJayMH-14
92BluJayMH-15
92BluJayMH-16
92KelFroFBB-1
92OPCBoxB-3
93BluJayDM-23
93BluJayDM-23A
94ImpProP-14
94Sco-330
94ScoGolR-330
95PanSti-151
96PanSti-163
Blue, Lu (Luzerne Atwell)
21Nei-5
22E120-47
22W572-7
22W573-11
23WilChoV-10
26Exh-90
27AmeCarE-54
28Exh-57
28StaPlaCE-3
29ExhFou-30
29PorandAR-7
31Exh-20
31W517-50
33ExhFou-10
46SpoExcW-1-10
81TigDetN-115
81TigSecNP-10
90DodTar-57
94ConTSN-1229
94ConTSNB-1229
Blue, Vida
70OPC-21
70Top-21
71A'sPos-8
71MLBOffS-507
71OPC-544
71Top-544
72'sA'sPos-21
72Kel-9A
72Kel-9B
72OPC-92
72OPC-94
72OPC-96
72OPC-169
72OPC-170
72ProStaP-25
72Top-92
72Top-94
72Top-96
72Top-169
72Top-170
72TopPos-8
73OPC-430
73Top-430
74OPC-290
74Top-290
74TopSta-222
75OPC-209
75OPC-510
75SSP42-12
75Top-209
75Top-510
76CraDis-3
76Hos-20
76HosTwi-20
76Kel-47A
76Kel-47B
76OPC-140
76OPC-200
76SSP-481
76Top-140
76Top-200
77BurCheD-114
77Hos-52
77OPC-75
77RCColC-4
77Spo-6518
77Top-230
77TopCloS-4
78OPC-177
78RCColC-43
78Top-680
78WifBalD-4
79GiaPol-14
79Hos-74
79Kel-23
79OPC-49
79Top-110
79TopCom-33
80BurKinPHR-1
80GiaPol-14
80Kel-42
80OPC-14
80Top-30
80TopSup-59
81AllGamPI-166
81Don-433
81Fle-432
81FleStiC-63
81Kel-23
81OPC-310
81Top-310
81TopScr-108
81TopSti-239
82Don-4
82Don-222
82FBIDis-1
82Fle-384
82FleSta-61
82K-M-19
82Kel-63
82OPC-82
82OPC-267
82Roy-3
82Top-430
82Top-431
82Top-576
82TopSti-111
82TopTra-8T
83Don-34
83Don-648
83Fle-106
83Fle-643
83FleSta-17
83FleSti-96
83OPC-178
83Roy-3
83Top-471
83Top-570
83TopFol-1
84GiaMot-25
84OCoandSI-145
85FleUpd-7
85GiaMot-10
85GiaPos-1
86Don-509
86Fle-533
86GiaMot-10
86Lea-247
86Spo-132
86Spo-142
86SpoDecG-63
86Top-770
86TopTif-770
87A'sMot-7
87Don-362
87Fle-266
87FleGlo-266
87OPC-260
87RedFolSB-128
87Top-260
87TopTif-260
89PacLegI-198
89PacSenL-215

89T/MSenL-9
89TopSenL-48
90EliSenL-50
90EliSenL-121
90PacLeg-8
90SweBasG-89
91PacSenL-81
91SweBasG-10
92A'sUno7P-2
92A'sUno7P-4
92ActPacA-44
92MDAMVP-8
92UppDecHoB-H5
92UppDecHoB-H8
92UppDecHoB-AU5
92UppDecS-27
92UppDecS-33
93MCIAmb-1
93MetIma-2
93TedWil-43
93UppDecS-10
94UppDecAH-71
94UppDecAH1-71
95MCIAmb-1

Blueberg, James
86BelMarC-120
87WauTimP-2
88CalLeaACLC-30
88SanBerSB-15
88SanBerSCLC-47
89SanBerSB-6
90CMC-795
90WilBilB-2
90WilBilP-1049
90WilBilS-1
91JacSunLD-328
91LinDriAA-328

Bluege, Ossie (Oswald Louis)
25Exh-121
26Exh-121
26SpoComoA-6
29ExhFou-31
31Exh-32
31SenTeaIPW-2
33Gou-113
33Gou-159
33GouCanV-83
34BatR31-105
34DiaStaR-71
36ExhFou-16
36NatChiFPR-11
36WorWidGV-87
60SenUniMC-2
61Fle-93
79DiaGre-61
91ConTSN-295

Bluege, Otto Adam
94ConTSN-1305
94ConTSNB-1305

Bluepper,
92PadPolD-2

Bluepper, Mascot
94MasMan-4

Blues, Cleveland
86JosHalC-6

Blues, Kansas City
38BasTabP-30

Bluestone, Brad
86EriCarP-4
87SprCarB-27
88SprCarB-27
90CMC-680
90LouRedBC-29
94St.PetCC-30

Bluewinkle, Rocky
94WilBluRC-27

Bluhm, Bill
87EveGiaC-25
88WatIndP-668
89RenSilSCLC-262

Bluhm, Brandon
91BurIndP-3290
92BurIndC-6
92BurIndF-1645

Blum, Brent
86AlbYanT-30
87AlbYanP-22
88PriWilYS-3

Blum, Geoff
94StaCluDP-65
94StaCluDPFDI-65
94VerExpC-24
94VerExpF-3914
95Bow-245
95BowGolF-245
95Exc-220
95SPML-93
95UppDecML-126
96HarSenB-8
96HonShaHWB-24
95UppDecMLFS-126

Bluma, Jaime
94EugEmeC-1
94EugEmeF-3701
94SigRooDP-65
94SigRooDPS-65
95Bow-239
95BowGolF-239
95Exc-53
95WicWraTI-19
96BesAutSA-7
96Bow-147
96Exc-55
96OmaRoyB-8
96Top-431
97Bow-98
97BowCerBIA-CA7
97BowCerGIA-CA7
97BowChr-120
97BowChrI-120
97BowChrIR-120
97BowChrR-120
97BowInt-98
97Cir-264
97CirRav-264
97Fin-32
97FinRef-32
97Fle-111
97FleTif-111
97RoyPol-4
97SpoIll-2
97SpoIllEE-2
97StaCluM-M35
97StaCluMOP-M35
97TopAweI-AI1
97UppDec-479

Bluma, Jeff
90WicStaSGD-5

Blumberg, Rob
89St.CatBJP-2088
90MyrBeaBJP-2768
90ProAaA-89
90SouAtlLAS-27
91KanCouCC-4
91KanCouCP-2651
92HagSunS-252

Blume, David
81WauTimT-11

Blumenstock, Brad
96SouOreTI-12

Blumeyer, Rich
80WatIndT-33

Blundin, Barry
88BurIndP-1791

Bluthardt, Jay
88WatPirP-15
94SalBucF-2340

Blyleven, Bert
71MLBOffS-458
71OPC-26
71Top-26
72OPC-515
72Top-515
73Kel2D-35
73LinPor-104
73OPC-199
73Top-199
74Kel-46
74OPC-98
74Top-98
74TopDecE-47
74TopSta-201
75Hos-74
75OPC-30
75Top-30
76Hos-116
76Kel-11
76OPC-204
76OPC-235
76SSP-219
76Top-204
76Top-235
77BurCheD-22
77OPC-101
77Spo-4209
77Top-630
77TopCloS-5
78Hos-74
78Kel-53
78OPC-113
78RCColC-68
78Top-131
78WifBalD-5
79Hos-133
79OPC-155
79Top-308
80Kel-5
80OPC-238
80Top-457
81Don-135
81Fle-383
81OPC-294
81Top-554
81TopTra-738
82Don-111
82Fle-361
82FleSta-199
82Ind-5
82IndTeal-4
82IndWhe-1
82OPC-164
82Top-559
82Top-685
82TopSti-173
83AllGamPI-73
83Don-589
83IndPos-6
83IndWhe-6
83OPC-280
83Top-280
83TopFol-1
84AllGamPI-164
84Don-129
84DonActAS-45
84DonCha-42
84Fle-536
84FunFooP-106
84Ind-5
84IndWhe-28
84Nes792-716
84Nes792-789
84OPC-126
84Top-716
84Top-789
84TopSti-261
84TopTif-716
84TopTif-789
85Don-4
85Don-224
85DonSupD-4
85Fle-440
85FleLimE-2
85FleStaS-81
85FleStaS-92
85FleStaS-112
85Ind-5
85IndPol-28
85Lea-4
85OPC-355
85SevCoi-G7
85Top-355
85TopGloS-17
85TopMin-355
85TopSti-247
85TopSup-35
85TopTif-355
86Don-649
86DonAll-52
86DonHig-31
86Fle-386
86FleMin-82
86FleSlu-1
86FleStiC-6
86Lea-88
86OPC-272
86QuaGra-21
86SevCoi-C10
86Spo-64
86Spo-103
86Spo-142
86Top-445
86Top3-D-1
86TopMinL-23
86TopSti-279
86TopSup-11
86TopTat-24
86TopTif-445
86TwiTeal-21
87Don-71
87DonOpeD-226
87Fle-536
87FleAwaW-3
87FleGlo-536
87FleMin-9
87FleStiC-10
87FleStiWBC-S3
87Lea-100
87OPC-25
87RedFolSB-101
87Spo-81
87SpoTeaP-17
87Top-25
87TopMinL-61
87TopSti-278
87TopTif-25
88Don-71
88DonBasB-18
88Fle-4
88FleGlo-4
88FleStiC-41
88Lea-52
88OPC-295
88PanSti-132
88Sco-90
88ScoGlo-90
88Spo-92
88StaLinTw-3
88Top-295
88TopBig-180
88TopSti-20
88TopSti-276
88TopTif-295
88TwiMasBD-1
88TwiSmoC-6
88TwiTeal-19
88Woo-21
89Bow-41
89BowTif-41
89Don-119
89DonBasB-3
89DonTra-35
89Fle-105
89FleGlo-105
89FleUpd-12
89OPC-204
89Sco-215
89ScoRoo-17T
89Top-555
89TopBasT-96
89TopSti-285
89TopTif-555
89TopTra-11T
89TopTraT-11T
89UppDec-225
89UppDec-712
90AngSmo-2
90Bow-285
90BowTif-285
90ClaBlu-142
90Don-331
90DonBesA-4
90Fle-128
90FleAwaW-3
90FleBasM-2
90FleCan-128
90KayB-2
90Lea-63
90MLBBasB-96
90OPC-130
90PanSti-28
90PubSti-366
90RedFolSB-5
90Sco-180
90Sco100S-12
90Spo-193
90Top-130
90TopBig-114
90TopMinL-7
90TopSti-165
90TopTif-130
90UppDec-527
90UppDecS-3
90VenSti-51
90Woo-7
91BasBesRB-1
91Don-453
91Fle-308
91OPC-615
91OPCBoxB-A
91Sco-235
91StaClu-175
91Stu-23
91Top-615
91TopDesS-615
91TopMic-615
91TopTif-615
91TopWaxBC-A
91UppDec-571
91Woo-7
92AngPol-3
92OPC-375
92Top-375
92TopGol-375
92TopGolW-375
92TopMic-375
93Fle-568
93PacSpa-41
93Pin-83
93Pin-296
93RanKee-74
93Sco-577
93Sel-252
93Top-48
93TopGol-48
93TopInaM-48
93TopMic-48
95MCIAmb-9

Blyleven, Joe
78QuaCitAT-4

Blyleven, Todd
94BoiHawC-2
94BoiHawF-3343
95Exc-18
95LakElsSTI-4
95MidAngOHP-4

Blyth, Bert (Robert)
82IowCubT-14

Blythe, Billy
94StaCluDP-44
94StaCluDPFDI-44
95EugEmeTI-4
96MacBraB-2

Blyzka, Mike (Michael)
54OriEss-3
54Top-152
91OriCro-38
94TopArc1-152
94TopArc1G-152

Boag, Jack
78St.PetCT-2

Boak, Chet (Chester Robert)
77FriOneYW-98

Boatman, John
92DavLipB-4
93DavLipB-2
94DavLipB-2
95DavLipB-2

Boatright, Dennis
83ButCopKT-1

Bobb, Jason
92GulCoaDF-3557
93ButCopKSP-18

Bobb, Randy (Mark Randall)
70OPC-429
70Top-429
71OPC-83
71Top-83

Bobbitt, Greg
93HunCubC-2
93HunCubF-3227
94MidLeaAF-MDW46
94PeoChiC-4
94PeoChiF-2258

Bobel, Jay
87SalAngP-3

Bobo, Elgin
91BoiHawC-10
91BoiHawP-3882
92BoiHawC-24
92BoiHawF-3635
92ClaFS7-448
92QuaCitRBC-17
92QuaCitRBF-812

Bobo, Paul
93DavLipB-3
94DavLipB-3

Bocachica, Hiram
94ClaUpdCotC-CC18
94SigRooDP-21
94SigRooDPS-21
95Bes-82
95SPML-91
95UppDecML-155
95UppDecML-224
96Exc-185
96WesPalBEB-21
97Bow-179

97BowBes-182
97BowBesAR-182
97BowBesMI-MI1
97BowBesMIAR-MI1
97BowBesMIARI-MI1
97BowBesMII-MI1
97BowBesMIR-MI1
97BowBesMIRI-MI1
97BowBesR-182
97BowChr-171
97BowChrI-171
97BowChrIR-171
97BowChrR-171
97BowInt-179
95UppDecMLFS-155
95UppDecMLFS-224
Boccabella, John D.
64Top-192
64TopVen-192
66Top-482
67CokCapC-5
67CubProPS-4
67DexPre-25
67Top-578
68Top-542
69MilBra-30
69Top-466
70ExpPos-15
70OPC-19
70Top-19
71ExpLaPR-2
71ExpPS-3
71MLBOffS-123
71OPC-452
71Top-452
72Dia-3
72OPC-159
72ProStaP-2
72Top-159
73OPC-592
73Top-592
74ExpWes-2
74OPC-253
74Top-253
74TopSta-52
75OPC-553
75Top-553
78TCM60I-291
92Nab-35
Bochesa, Greg
86WinHavRSP-4
87NewBriRSP-13
88NewBriRSP-900
Bochte, Bruce Anton
74CarSalLCA-96
75OPC-392
75Top-392
76OPC-637
76SSP-200
76Top-637
77Top-68
78Hos-81
78PapGinD-29
78TasDis-25
78Top-537
79Hos-123
79OPC-231
79Top-443
80Kel-59
80OPC-80
80Top-143
80TopSup-55
81AllGamPI-2
81Don-403
81Dra-25
81Fle-600
81FleStiC-8
81Kel-62
81MSAMinD-3
81OPC-18
81Squ-31
81Top-723
81TopScr-30
81TopSti-123
82Don-505
82Fle-505
82FleSta-222
82OPC-224
82Top-224
82TopSti-232
83Don-127
83Fle-473
83FleSta-18
83FleSti-185
83OPC-28
83Top-28
83Top-711
83TopSti-111
84A'sMot-6
84FleUpd-13
85A'sMot-10
85Don-253
85Fle-416
85OPC-391
85Top-632
85TopSti-331
85TopTif-632
86A'sMot-10
86Don-400
86Fle-413
86FleMin-86
86FleStiC-7
86Lea-183
86OPC-378
86Top-378
86TopSti-170
86TopTat-6
86TopTif-378
87Fle-388
87FleGlo-388
87Top-496
87TopSti-169
87TopTif-496
Bochtler, Doug
90MidLeaASGS-4
90RocExpLC-2
90RocExpP-2694
91WesPalBEC-2
91WesPalBEP-1218
92HarSenF-452
92HarSenS-276
92SkyAA F-117
93Top-523
93TopGol-523
93TopInaM-523
93TopMic-523
94AriFalLS-2
94LasVegSF-863
96LeaSigEA-9
96PadMot-18
97Fle-612
97FleTif-612
Bochy, Bruce Douglas
76DubPacT-4
77CocAstT-3
79Top-718
80Top-289
81Don-20
81Fle-69
81TidTidT-2
82TidTidT-6
84LasVegSC-225
84Nes792-571
84Top-571
84TopTif-571
85Don-505
85PadMot-12
85Top-324
85TopTif-324
86Don-551
86Top-608
86TopTif-608
87Don-311
87Fle-411
87FleGlo-411
87Top-428
87TopTif-428
88LasVegSC-21
88LasVegSP-241
88Sco-469
88ScoGlo-469
88Top-31
88TopTif-31
89PacSenL-194
89RivRedWB-25
89RivRedWCLC-29
89RivRedWP-1405
89SpoIndSP-4
90EliSenL-51
90RivRedWB-22
90RivRedWCLC-24
91HigDesMC-29
91HigDesMP-2412
91MetWIZ-40
92WicWraF-3669
92WicWraS-649
93PadMot-28
94PadMot-28
95PadCHP-16
95PadMot-1
96PadMot-1
Bock, Doug
87EugEmeP-2656
88AppFoxP-157
Bock, Jeff
93DanBraC-3
93DanBraF-3608
94DurBulC-3
94DurBulF-320
94DurBulTI-3
95DurBulTI-4
96GreBraB-6
96GreBraTI-39
Bock, Paul
75AppFoxT-4
77CliDodT-2
Bockewitz, Stan
76WilTomT-3
Bockhorn, Glen
85GreBraTI-4
86BufBisP-1
Bockman, Eddie (Joseph E.)
47IndTeal-2
47IndVanPP-2
49Bow-195
49EurSta-153
Bockus, Randy
84ShrCapFB-3
86PhoFirP-3
87FleUpd-6
87FleUpdG-6
87PhoFirP-3
88FleUpd-127
88FleUpdG-127
88PhoFirC-1
88PhoFirP-55
89BlaYNPRWL-58
89BlaYNPRWLU-65
89Bow-96
89BowTif-96
89TolMudHC-1
89TolMudHP-769
89Top-733
89TopTif-733
91EdmTraLD-155
91LinDriAAA-155
Boddicker, Mike
80RocRedWT-6
81RocRedWT-1
81RocRedWW-23
81Top-399
82RocRedWT-1
83OriPos-2
84AllGamPI-165
84Don-123
84Fle-1
84Fle-645
84FleSti-110
84FunFooP-121
84Nes792-191
84Nes792-426
84OriEng-1
84OriTeal-3
84SevCoi-E9
84Top-191
84Top-426
84TopSti-13
84TopSti-375
84TopTif-191
84TopTif-426
85AllGamPI-74
85Don-291
85Dra-34
85Fle-170
85FleStaS-80
85FleStaS-90
85Lea-109
85OPC-225
85OriHea-2
85SevCoi-E6
85ThoMcAD-5
85Top-225
85Top-709
85Top3-D-26
85TopGloS-4
85TopMin-225
85TopRubD-5
85TopSti-202
85TopSup-16
85TopTif-225
85TopTif-709
86Don-8
86Don-47
86DonSupD-8
86Fle-269
86FleMin-57
86Lea-8
86OPC-367
86SevCoi-E14
86Spo-104
86Spo-149
86Top-575
86TopSti-233
86TopTif-575
87Don-125
87DonOpeD-140
87Fle-463
87FleGlo-463
87FleLeaL-2
87FleStiC-11
87Lea-76
87OPC-149
87OriFreB-52
87RedFolSB-40
87SevCoi-M8
87Spo-56
87SpoTeaP-21
87Top-455
87TopSti-227
87TopTif-455
88AlaGolAA'TI-23
88Don-89
88DonBasB-317
88Fle-556
88FleGlo-556
88FleStiC-1
88FleUpd-5
88FleUpdG-5
88OPC-281
88OriFreB-52
88PanSti-5
88Sco-67
88ScoGlo-67
88Spo-146
88StaLinO-2
88Top-725
88TopSti-231
88TopTif-725
89Bow-21
89BowTif-21
89ClaTraO-139
89Don-612
89DonBasB-297
89Fle-80
89FleGlo-80
89OPC-71
89Sco-549
89Spo-122
89Top-71
89TopBig-296
89TopSti-261
89TopTif-71
89TVSpoM-67
89UppDec-542
90Bow-267
90BowTif-267
90Don-280
90DonBesA-3
90Fle-267
90FleCan-267
90Lea-19
90OPC-652
90PanSti-20
90PubSti-447
90RedSoxP-2
90Sco-31
90Top-652
90TopBig-258
90TopSti-258
90TopTif-652
90TopTVRS-7
90UppDec-652
90VenSti-52
91Bow-296
91Don-680
91Fle-85
91Lea-330
91OPC-303
91OPCPre-10
91OriCro-39
91PanCanT1-108
91RoyPol-3
91Sco-232
91ScoRoo-45T
91StaClu-400
91Stu-61
91Top-303
91TopDesS-303
91TopMic-303
91TopTif-303
91TopTra-12T
91TopTraT-12T
91UppDec-438
91UppDec-719
92Bow-132
92Don-176
92Fle-153
92HitTheBB-5
92Lea-268
92OPC-106
92Pin-142
92RoyPol-3
92Sco-102
92StaClu-39
92Top-106
92TopGol-106
92TopGolW-106
92TopMic-106
92TriPla-12
92Ult-67
92UppDec-213
93CadDis-7
93Don-469
93Fle-616
93PacSpa-132
93RoyPol-4
93StaClu-192
93StaCluFDI-192
93StaCluMOP-192
93Top-239
93TopGol-239
93TopInaM-239
93TopMic-239
93Ult-205
94BreMilB-284
Boddie, Eric
89BakDodCLC-193
90VerBeaDS-6
Boddie, Rod (Rodney)
88JamExpP-1905
89RocExpLC-4
90StaFS7-6
90WesPalBES-1
Bodell, Howard J.
52LavPro-81
Bodenhamer, Don
74GasRanT-5
Bodie, Keith
76WauMetT-5
79JacMetT-11
80ColAstT-18
86AubAstP-3
87AshTouP-4
88FloStaLAS-3
89CliGiaP-898
90SanBerSB-26
90SanBerSCLC-114
90SanBerSP-2649
91CalCanLD-74
91CalCanP-530
91LinDriAAA-74
92CalCanF-3745
92CalCanS-74
93CalCanF-1181
95PhoFirTI-31
Bodie, Ping (Frank Stephan)
09MaxPubP-1
09SpoNewSM-81
12T207-18
14CraJacE-79
14TexTomE-6
14TexTomE-51
15CraJacE-79
16ColE13-16
17HolBreD-7
19W514-66
21E121So8-5
21KoBreWSI-28
22AmeCarE-5
22W575-10
81ConTSN-91
20W516-3
Boeckel, Tony (Norman Doxie)
21Nei-80
22E120-122
22W572-8
22W573-12

23WilChoV-11
Boehler, George
90DodTar-58
Boehling, John Joseph
14CraJacE-72
15CraJacE-72
16ColE13-17
Boehlow, Jason
92HunCubC-3
92HunCubF-3153
Boehmer, Len (Leonard J.)
69Top-519
81TCM60I-355
92YanWIZ6-12
92YanWIZ7-22
Boehringer, Brian
92ClaFS7-258
92SouBenWSC-1
92SouBenWSF-171
93FloStaLAF-21
93SarWhiSC-3
93SarWhiSF-1361
94AbaYanF-1430
94ClaGolF-193
94ExcFS7-35
95ColCliP-2
95ColCliTI-2
95Exc-90
95FleAllR-M3
96ColCliB-3
97Fle-606
97FleTif-606
Boelter, Tarry
79WisRapTT-14
Boemier, Bill
53MotCoo-63
Boermans, Oswald
90IBAWorA-11
Boever, Dan
85CedRapRT-21
88NasSouC-15
88NasSouP-476
88NasSouTI-3
89CalCanC-12
89CalCanP-535
89CanIndB-7
89CanIndP-1325
89CanIndS-3
90CedRapRDGB-33
Boever, Joe
83St.PetCT-1
86LouRedTI-6
87LouRedTI-5
88BlaYNPRWL-146
88Fle-534
88FleGlo-534
88RicBraC-9
88RicBraP-22
88Sco-542
88ScoGlo-542
88Top-627
88TopTif-627
88TriAAAP-34
89BraDub-6
89Don-168
89Top-586
89TopTif-586
90BraDubP-2
90BraDubS-3
90Don-357
90Fle-577
90FleCan-577
90Lea-349
90OPC-410
90PanSti-220
90PubSti-110
90Sco-81
90SprCarDGB-14
90Top-410
90TopSti-34
90TopTif-410
90UppDec-408
90VenSti-53
91Bow-502
91Don-578
91Fle-387
91Lea-68
91OPC-159
91PhiMed-4
91StaClu-462
91Top-159
91TopDesS-159
91TopMic-159
91TopTif-159
91UppDec-430
92AstMot-13
92Don-493
92Fle-523
92Lea-491
92OPC-696
92Sco-647
92StaClu-156
92StaClu-639
92StaCluECN-639
92Top-696
92TopGol-696
92TopGolW-696
92TopMic-696
92TopTra-12T
92TopTraG-12T
92UppDec-402
93AthMot-25
93Don-504
93Fle-48
93PacSpa-119
93PacSpa-563
93StaCluAt-15
93Top-792
93TopGol-792
93TopInaM-792
93TopMic-792
93UppDec-310
93UppDec-810
93UppDecGold-310
93UppDecGold-810
94FleUpd-41
94StaClu-458
94StaCluFDI-458
94StaCluGR-458
94StaCluMOP-458
94Top-467
94TopGol-467
94TopSpa-467
95Don-362
95DonPreP-362
95DonTopotO-71
95Fle-45
95Sco-203
95ScoGolR-203
95ScoPlaTS-203
95Top-457
95TopCyb-252
96ColCho-139
96ColChoGS-139
96ColChoSS-139
96Don-32
96DonPreP-32
96Fle-106
96FleTif-106
88RicBraBC-1
Boffek, Scott
91VerBeaDC-19
Bogar, Tim
87LitFalMP-2397
89JacMetGS-3
90CMC-365
90ProAAAF-280
90TidTidC-14
90TidTidP-549
90TopTVM-36
91LinDriAA-626
91WilBilLD-626
91WilBilP-298
92TidTidF-903
92TidTidS-553
93Bow-326
93FleFinE-99
93Lea-525
93MetColP-26
93MetKah-23
93OPCPre-108
93SelRoo-54T
93SP-145
93StaClu-702
93StaCluFDI-702
93StaCluMOP-702
93TopTra-119T
94ColC-55
94ColChoGS-55
94ColChoSS-55
94Don-316
94Fin-354
94FinRef-354
94Fle-557
94Lea-99
94MetColP-5
94MetShuST-3
94Pac-395
94Sco-557
94ScoGolR-557
94Sel-104
94StaClu-170
94StaCluFDI-170
94StaCluGR-170
94StaCluMOP-170
94Top-509
94TopGol-509
94TopSpa-509
94Ult-234
94UppDec-101
94UppDecED-101
95Pac-276
96ColCho-619
96ColChoGS-619
96ColChoSS-619
96Don-16
96DonPreP-16
96Fle-473
96FleTif-473
96LeaSigEA-10
96MetKah-3
96MetKah-2
97Pac-359
97PacLigB-359
97PacSil-359
Bogardus, A.H.
87AllandGN-38
88GooN16-14
Bogatyrev, Ilya
89EasLeaDDP-DD17
93Top-633
93TopGol-633
93TopInaM-633
93TopMic-633
Bogener, Terry (Terrence W.)
79TulDriT-15
83Don-520
83OklCit8T-3
84WicAerRD-13
86ChaOriW-4
93RanKee-75
Boggess, Dusty
55Bow-297
Boggetto, Brad
91YakBeaC-20
91YakBeaP-4238
Boggs, Robert
96ForWayWB-4
Boggs, Tommy
76SacSolC-8
77Top-328
78Top-518
79RicBraT-22
79Top-384
81BraPol-40
81Don-597
81Fle-261
81Top-132
82BraBurKL-3
82Don-249
82Fle-430
82Top-61
83Don-349
83Fle-131
83Top-649
85OklCit8T-7
93RanKee-76
Boggs, Wade Anthony
81PawRedST-15
83AllGamPI-29
83Don-586
83Fle-179
83FleSta-19
83FleSti-64
83Top-498
83TopSti-308
84AllGamPI-119
84Don-26
84Don-26A
84Don-151
84DonActAS-22
84DonCha-16
84Dra-2
84Fle-392
84Fle-630
84FleSti-11
84FleSti-28
84FleSti-52
84FunFooP-43
84MilBra-1
84Nes792-30
84Nes792-131
84Nes792-786
84OCoandSI-6
84OCoandSI-226
84OPC-30
84RalPur-11
84SevCoi-E10
84Top-30
84Top-131
84Top-786
84TopCer-11
84TopGloS-8
84TopRubD-5
84TopSti-100
84TopSti-216
84TopStiB-7
84TopSup-7
84TopTif-30
84TopTif-131
84TopTif-786
85AllGamPI-29
85Don-172
85DonActA-38
85DonHig-49
85Fle-151
85Fle-160
85FleLimE-3
85FleStaS-6
85Lea-179
85OPC-350
85SevCoi-C8
85SevCoi-E7
85Top-350
85TopRubD-6
85TopSti-210
85TopTif-350
86BasStaB-13
86BurKinA-9
86Don-371
86DonAll-47
86DonAllB-PC7
86DonHig-11
86DonHig-13
86DorChe-18
86Dra-27
86Fle-341
86Fle-634
86Fle-639
86FleLeaL-1
86FleLimE-4
86FleMin-72
86FleSlu-2
86FleStiC-8
86FleStiWBC-S2
86FraGloT-1
86GenMilB-1A
86Lea-168
86MeaGolBB-1
86MeaGolM-1
86MeaGolSB-9
86MSAJifPD-2
86OPC-262
86OPCBoxB-B
86QuaGra-22
86SevCoi-C2
86SevCoi-E2
86SevCoi-S2
86SevCoi-W2
86Spo-3
86Spo-75
86Spo-180
86Spo-183
86Spo-184
86SpoDecG-68
86StaBog-1
86StaBog-2
86StaBog-3
86StaBog-4
86StaBog-5
86StaBog-6
86StaBog-7
86StaBog-8
86StaBog-9
86StaBog-10
86StaBog-11
86StaBog-12
86Top-510
86Top3-D-3
86TopGaloC-1
86TopGloS-26
86TopMinL-3
86TopSti-164
86TopSti-247
86TopSup-12
86TopTat-22
86TopTif-510
86TopWaxBC-B
86TruVal-30
86Woo-3
87BoaandB-31
87BurKinA-1
87ClaGam-60
87ClaUpdY-105
87Don-252
87DonAll-7
87DonHig-14
87DonHig-44
87DonOpeD-181
87DonP-7
87Dra-16
87Fle-29
87Fle-637
87FleBasA-3
87FleExcS-4
87FleGamW-5
87FleGlo-29
87FleGlo-637
87FleGlo-WS2
87FleHea-1
87FleLeaL-3
87FleMin-10
87FleSlu-4
87FleStiC-12
87FleStiWBC-S2
87FleWorS-2
87GenMilB-2A
87HosSti-19
87K-M-23
87KayB-4
87KraFoo-7
87Lea-193
87MandMSL-5
87MSAIceTD-13
87MSAJifPD-20
87OPC-150
87RalPur-3
87RedFolSB-96
87RedSoxSAP-3
87SevCoi-E5
87SevCoi-M6
87Spo-2
87Spo-114
87Spo-197
87SpoDeaP-2
87SpoRea-32
87SpoTeaP-9
87StaAwaW-4
87StaAwaW-5
87StuPan-15
87Top-150
87Top-608
87TopCoi-4
87TopGaloC-2
87TopGloA-15
87TopGloS-18
87TopMinL-41
87TopSti-148
87TopSti-253
87TopTif-150
87TopTif-608
87Woo-10
88ActPacT-1
88Baz-2
88CheBoy-22
88ClaBlu-214
88ClaRed-155
88Don-153
88DonAll-7
88DonAll-31
88DonBasB-65
88DonBonM-BC7
88DonPop-7
88DonTeaBRS-153
88Dra-4
88Fle-345
88FleAll-8
88FleAwaW-3
88FleBasA-2
88FleBasM-2
88FleExcS-4
88FleGlo-345
88FleHotS-2
88FleLeaL-2
88FleMin-4
88FleRecS-3
88FleSlu-2
88FleStiC-5
88FleSup-3

88FleTeaL-2
88GreBasS-5
88K-M-2
88KayB-2
88Lea-65
88MSAFanSD-8
88MSAIceTD-1
88MSAJifPD-2
88Nes-32
88OPC-200
88PanSti-29
88PanSti-228
88Sco-2
88ScoBoxC-4
88ScoGlo-2
88Spo-50
88SpoGam-3
88StaBog-1
88StaBog-2
88StaBog-3
88StaBog-4
88StaBog-5
88StaBog-6
88StaBog-7
88StaBog-8
88StaBog-9
88StaBog-10
88StaBog-11
88StaBog-1
88StaBog-2
88StaBog-3
88StaBog-4
88StaBog-5
88StaBog-6
88StaBog-7
88StaBog-8
88StaBog-9
88StaBog-10
88StaBog-11
88StaBog/G-1
88StaBog/G-2
88StaBog/G-4
88StaBog/G-6
88StaBog/G-8
88StaBog/G-10
88StaLinAl-3
88StaLinRS-3
88Top-21
88Top-200
88Top-388
88TopBig-32
88TopCoi-4
88TopGaloC-3
88TopGloA-4
88TopGloS-51
88TopMinL-1
88TopRevLL-16
88TopRitTM-14
88TopSti-157
88TopSti-244
88TopStiB-40
88TopTif-21
88TopTif-200
88TopTif-388
88TopUKM-4
88TopUKMT-4
88Woo-13
89Baz-3
89Bow-32
89BowTif-32
89CadEllD-2
89ClaLigB-2
89ClaTraO-102
89Don-68
89DonAll-7
89DonBasB-140
89DonPop-7
89Fle-81
89Fle-633
89FleBasA-3
89FleBasM-3
89FleExcS-2
89FleForTR-1
89FleGlo-81
89FleGlo-633
89FleHeroB-2
89FleLeaL-2
89FleSup-4
89FleWaxBC-C2
89K-M-14
89KayB-1
89KinDis-3
89MasBreD-5
89MSAHolD-2
89MSAIceTD-7
89Nis-2
89OPC-184
89PanSti-7
89PanSti-242
89PanSti-245
89PanSti-277
89RedFolSB-8
89Sco-175
89Sco-654A
89Sco-654B
89ScoHot1S-100
89ScoSco-17
89Spo-100
89Spo-221
89SpollIFKI-176
89Top-2
89Top-399
89Top-600
89TopBasT-57
89TopBatL-1
89TopBig-241
89TopCoi-32
89TopDouA-3
89TopGaloC-1
89TopGloA-4
89TopGloS-5
89TopHeaUT-11
89TopHilTM-2
89TopMinL-45
89TopSti-9
89TopSti-147
89TopSti-260
89TopStiB-7
89TopTif-2
89TopTif-399
89TopTif-600
89TopUKM-4
89TVSpoM-64
89TVSpoM-126
89UppDec-389
89UppDec-687
89UppDecS-1
89Woo-8
90AllBasT-3
90Bow-281
90BowTif-281
90ClaBlu-26
90Col-26
90Don-68
90Don-712A
90Don-712B
90DonBesA-86
90DonLeaS-21
90DonPre-11
90Fle-268
90Fle-632
90FleAwaW-4
90FleBasA-1
90FleBasM-3
90FleCan-268
90FleCan-632
90FleLeaL-4
90FleLeaS-5
90GooHumICBLS-3
90Hot50PS-2
90K-M-19
90KayB-3
90KinDis-9
90Lea-51
90MLBBasB-68
90MSAIceTD-7
90OPC-387
90OPC-760
90OPCBoxB-A
90PanSti-19
90PanSti-199
90Pos-17
90PubSti-277
90PubSti-448
90RedFolSB-6
90RedSoxP-3
90Sco-245
90Sco-683A
90Sco-683B
90Sco-704
90Sco100S-80
90Spo-2
90StaLonJS-6
90StaLonJS-17
90StaLonJS-22
90Top-387
90Top-760
90TopAmeA-16
90TopBatL-1
90TopBig-77
90TopCoi-6
90TopDou-4
90TopGloA-15
90TopGloS-22
90TopHilHM-19
90TopMag-23
90TopMinL-3
90TopSti-8
90TopSti-156
90TopSti-253
90TopStiB-40
90TopTif-387
90TopTif-760
90TopTVA-20
90TopTVRS-22
90TopWaxBC-A
90UppDec-555
90UppDecS-4
90USPlaCA-11C
90VenSti-54
90VenSti-55
90WinDis-2
90Woo-8
91BasBesHM-2
91Bow-129
91CadEllD-4
91Cla1-T19
91Cla3-T3
91ClaGam-192
91Col-16
91Don-55
91Don-178
91Fle-86
91FouBal-30
91KinDis-11
91Lea-273
91LeaPre-14
91MajLeaCP-9
91MooSna-11
91OPC-450
91OPCPre-11
91PanCanT1-30
91PanFreS-169
91PanFreS-266
91PanSti-214
91RedFolS-9
91RedFolS-115
91Sco-12
91Sco-393
91Sco-889
91Sco100S-3
91ScoCoo-B1
91Sev3DCN-1
91SevCoi-NE1
91StaClu-170
91StaPinB-3
91Stu-11
91SunSee-2
91Top-450
91TopCraJI-29
91TopDesS-450
91TopGloA-4
91TopMic-450
91TopSta-3
91TopTif-450
91TopTriH-A2
91Ult-27
91UppDec-546
91UppDecFE-84F
91USPlaCA-WCO
92Bow-70
92Cla2-T63
92ClaGam-70
92ColAllG-7
92ColAllP-7
92Don-23
92Don-210
92DonCraJ2-29
92DonDiaK-DK9
92DonEli-9
92DonPre-1
92Fle-32
92Fle-707
92FleCitTP-9
92FleTeaL-13
92Fre-14
92Hig5-6
92Hig5S-3
92KinDis-16
92Lea-286
92New-2
92OPC-10
92OPCPre-1
92PanSti-87
92PanSti-274
92PepDieM-21
92Pin-175
92Pin-282
92Pos-19
92RedSoxDD-2
92Sco-434
92Sco-660
92Sco-885
92Sco100S-30
92ScoProaG-4
92SpollIFK1-178
92SpoStaCC-3
92StaClu-520
92StaCluD-18
92StaCluMO-3
92StaCluMP-1
92Stu-131
92StuHer-BC3
92StuPre-14
92Top-10
92Top-399
92TopGol-10
92TopGol-399
92TopGolW-10
92TopGolW-399
92TopKid-68
92TopMic-10
92TopMic-399
92TopMic-G10
92TriPla-211
92Ult-311
92UltAllS-4
92UppDec-443
92UppDec-646
92UppDecF-13
92UppDecFG-13
92UppDecTMH-10
92UppDecWB-T1
93Bow-399
93CadDis-8
93ColAllG-7
93DiaMar-13
93Don-619
93DonSpiotG-SG7
93Fin-90
93FinJum-90
93FinRef-90
93Fla-245
93Fle-554
93FleFinE-243
93FleFinEDT-1
93FunPac-206
93Lea-285
93LeaGolA-U5
93MetBak-1
93OPC-196
93OPCPre-49
93PacSpa-27
93PacSpa-552
93PanSti-152
93Pin-424
93Pin-476
93PinCoo-13
93PinCooD-13
93Sco-592
93Sel-48
93SelRoo-17T
93SP-2
93StaClu-134
93StaClu-601
93StaCluFDI-134
93StaCluFDI-601
93StaCluM-15
93StaCluMOP-134
93StaCluMOP-601
93StaCluY-5
93Stu-31
93Top-390
93TopGol-390
93TopInaM-390
93TopMic-390
93TopTra-47T
93TriPla-143
93TriPla-258
93TriPlaG-GS3
93Ult-591
93UppDec-556
93UppDecCP-R2
93UppDecGold-556
93UppDecIC-WI20
93UppDecICJ-WI20
93UppDecOD-D5
93UppDecTAN-TN1
94Bow-305
94BowBes-R42
94BowBesR-R42
94ColC-380
94ColChoGS-380
94ColChoSS-380
94Don-36
94DonAnn8-7
94DonSpeE-36
94ExtBas-128
94Fin-173
94FinRef-173
94Fla-319
94Fle-226
94FleAllS-4
94FUnPac-126
94KinDis-5
94Lea-257
94LeaL-54
94LeaLimGA-5
94OPC-193
94Pac-421
94PacSilP-9
94PanSti-99
94Pin-31
94PinArtP-31
94PinMusC-31
94ProMag-87
94Sco-101
94ScoGolR-101
94ScoGolS-50
94Sel-156
94SP-196
94SPDieC-196
94Spo-102
94StaClu-349
94StaCluFDI-349
94StaCluGR-349
94StaCluMOP-349
94StaCluT-204
94StaCluTFDI-204
94Stu-212
94Top-386
94Top-520
94Top-603
94TopGol-386
94TopGol-520
94TopGol-603
94TopPre-390
94TopSpa-386
94TopSpa-520
94TopSpa-603
94TriPla-272
94TriPlaM-9
94Ult-93
94UppDec-112
94UppDecAJ-8
94UppDecAJG-8
94UppDecED-112
95Baz-89
95BazRedH-RH18
95Bow-408
95BowBes-R26
95BowBesR-R26
95ClaPhoC-40
95ColCho-520
95ColChoGS-520
95ColChoSE-245
95ColChoSEGS-245
95ColChoSESS-245
95ColChoSS-520
95Don-355
95DonAll-AL5
95DonPreP-355
95DonTopotO-117
95Emb-49
95EmbGolI-49
95Emo-59
95Fin-100
95FinRef-100
95Fla-63
95Fle-67
95FleAllS-4
95KinDis-3
95Lea-40
95Lea300C-11
95LeaCor-3
95LeaGreG-4
95LeaLim-105
95LeaLimIBP-3
95Pac-293
95PacGolP-6

95PacPri-95
95PanSti-57
95Pin-47
95PinArtP-47
95PinMusC-47
95Pos-1
95Sco-349
95Sco-560
95ScoGolR-349
95ScoGolR-560
95ScoHaloG-HG96
95ScoPlaTS-349
95ScoPlaTS-560
95Sel-16
95SelArtP-16
95SelCer-30
95SelCerMG-30
95SP-25
95SP-180
95SPCha-172
95SPChaDC-172
95Spo-107
95SpoArtP-107
95SpoDouT-4
95SPSil-25
95SPSil-180
95SPSpeF-14
95StaClu-85
95StaCluFDI-85
95StaCluMO-7
95StaCluMOP-85
95StaCluMOP-RL38
95StaCluRL-RL38
95StaCluSTWS-85
95StaCluVR-52
95Stu-46
95StuGolS-46
95Sum-65
95SumNthD-65
95Top-170
95Top-386
95TopCyb-100
95TopLeaL-LL3
95TopTra-158T
95UC3-30
95UC3ArtP-30
95Ult-80
95UltAllS-4
95UltAllSGM-4
95UltAwaW-4
95UltAwaWGM-4
95UltGolM-80
95UltOnBL-4
95UltOnBLGM-4
95UppDec-445
95UppDecED-445
95UppDecEDG-445
95UppDecPLL-R21
95UppDecPLLE-R21
95UppDecSE-10
95UppDecSEG-10
95USPlaCMLA-8D
95Zen-107
96Baz-34
96Bow-26
96BowBes-4
96BowBesAR-4
96BowBesMI-3
96BowBesMIAR-3
96BowBesMIR-3
96BowBesR-4
96Cir-61
96CirBos-15
96CirRav-61
96Cla7/1PC-7
96ColCho-230
96ColCho-420
96ColChoGS-230
96ColChoGS-420
96ColChoSS-230
96ColChoSS-420
96ColChoYMtP-7
96ColChoYMtP-7A
96ColChoYMtPGS-7
96ColChoYMtPGS-7A
96DenHol-14
96Don-355
96Don-440
96DonHitL-14
96DonPreP-355
96DonPreP-440
96EmoXL-87
96Fin-B155
96Fin-B301
96FinRef-B155
96FinRef-B301
96Fla-125
96Fle-180
96FleTif-180
96FleUpd-U214
96FleUpd-1
96FleUpdTC-U214
96Lea-91
96LeaLim-61
96LeaLimG-61
96LeaPre-67
96LeaPreP-67
96LeaPrePB-91
96LeaPrePG-91
96LeaPrePS-91
96LeaPreSG-9
96LeaPreSte-9
96LeaSig-5
96LeaSigA-27
96LeaSigAG-27
96LeaSigAS-27
96LeaSigPPG-5
96LeaSigPPP-5
96MetUni-84
96MetUniP-84
96Pac-378
96PacCraC-CC2
96PacGolCD-DC20
96PacMil-M6
96PacPri-P118
96PacPriG-P118
96PacPriRHS-RH16
96PanSti-153
96Pin-215
96Pin-269
96Pin-334
96PinAfi-19
96PinAfiAP-19
96PinAfiFPP-19
96PinAfiSP-26
96PinArtP-115
96PinArtP-169
96PinArtP-199
96PinFan-13
96PinFoil-215
96PinFoil-269
96PinFoil-334
96PinSky-8
96PinSta-115
96PinSta-169
96PinSta-199
96ProSta-136
96Sco-345
96ScoDugC-B70
96ScoDugCAP-B70
96ScoRef-13
96Sel-1
96SelArtP-1
96SelCer-74
96SelCerAP-74
96SelCerCB-74
96SelCerCR-74
96SelCerIP-10
96SelCerMB-74
96SelCerMG-74
96SelCerMR-74
96SelEnF-15
96SelTeaN-6
96SP-131
96Spo-1
96SpoArtP-1
96SpoHitP-14
96SPSpeFX-18
96SPSpeFXDC-18
96SPx-44
96SPxGol-44
96StaClu-96
96StaCluEPB-96
96StaCluEPG-96
96StaCluEPS-96
96StaCluMM-MM5
96StaCluMO-6
96StaCluMOP-96
96StaCluMOP-MM5
95StaCluVRMC-52
96Stu-46
96StuPrePB-46
96StuPrePG-46
96StuPrePS-46
96Sum-149
96SumAbo&B-149
96SumArtP-149
96SumFoi-149
96SumHitI-7
96TeaOut-9
96Top-225
96Top-323
96TopChr-85
96TopChr-127
96TopChrMotG-11
96TopChrMotGR-11
96TopChrR-85
96TopChrR-127
96TopGal-84
96TopGalPPI-84
96TopLas-36
96TopMasotG-11
96Ult-98
96Ult-576
96UltGolM-98
96UltGolM-576
96UltOn-L-1
96UltOn-LGM-1
96UltPriL-5
96UltPriLGM-5
96UppDec-117
96UppDec-372
96UppDec-410
96UppDecA-7
96UppDecDD-DD27
96UppDecDDG-DD27
96UppDecDDS-DD27
96UppDecPRE-R23
96UppDecPreR-R23
96Zen-58
96ZenArtP-58
96ZenMoz-22
97Bow-58
97BowBes-57
97BowBesAR-57
97BowBesR-57
97BowChr-44
97BowChrI-44
97BowChrIR-44
97BowChrR-44
97BowInt-58
97Cir-27
97CirRav-27
97ColCho-177
97Don-17
97Don-405
97DonEli-47
97DonEliGS-47
97DonLim-32
97DonLim-125
97DonLim-191
97DonLimFotG-8
97DonLimLE-32
97DonLimLE-125
97DonLimLE-191
97DonPre-54
97DonPreCttC-54
97DonPreP-17
97DonPreP-405
97DonPrePGold-17
97DonPrePGold-405
97DonPrePM-11
97DonTea-121
97DonTeaSPE-121
97Fin-62
97FinRef-62
97FlaSho-A163
97FlaSho-B163
97FlaSho-C163
97FlaShoLC-163
97FlaShoLC-B163
97FlaShoLC-C163
97FlaShoLCM-A163
97FlaShoLCM-B163
97FlaShoLCM-C163
97Fle-161
97FleDecoE-1
97FleDecoERT-1
97FleTif-161
97Lea-1
97Lea-380
97LeaFraM-1
97LeaFraM-380
97LeaFraMDC-1
97LeaFraMDC-380
97MetUni-114
97NewPin-47
97NewPinAP-47
97NewPinMC-47
97NewPinPP-47
97Pac-147
97PacCar-12
97PacCarM-12
97PacGolCD-10
97PacLigB-147
97PacPri-49
97PacPriGA-GA8
97PacPriGotD-GD69
97PacPriLB-49
97PacPriP-49
97PacPriSL-SL4C
97PacSil-147
97PinCer-78
97PinCerMBlu-78
97PinCerMG-78
97PinCerMR-78
97PinCerR-78
97PinIns-61
97PinInsCE-61
97PinInsDE-61
97PinTotCPB-78
97PinTotCPG-78
97PinTotCPR-78
97PinX-P-69
97PinX-PMoS-69
97Sco-167
97ScoHeaotO-17
97ScoPitP-13
97ScoPreS-167
97ScoShoS-167
97ScoShoSAP-167
97ScoYan-10
97ScoYanPl-10
97ScoYanPr-10
97Sel-34
97SelArtP-34
97SelRegG-34
97SelToootT-17
97SelToootTMB-17
97SkyE-X-31
97SkyE-XC-31
97SkyE-XEC-31
97SkyE-XHoN-6
97SP-129
97SPSpeF-44
97SPSpxF-9
97SPSPxFA-9
97StaClu-217
97StaCluMat-217
97StaCluMOP-217
97Stu-47
97StuPrePG-47
97StuPrePS-47
97Top-8
97TopChr-4
97TopChrR-4
97TopGal-20
97TopGalPPI-20
97TopSta-57
97TopStaAM-57
97Ult-95
97UltFieC-3
97UltGolME-95
97UltPlaME-95
97UppDec-125

Bogle, Bryan
94HunCubF-3564
96HigDesMB-7
94HunCubC-3

Bogle, Sean
94WilCubF-3755
96RocCubTI-2

Bogott, Kurt
96DunBluJB-2
96DunBluJTI-2
96KnoSmoB-5

Bogues, Muggsy
91GasRanC-29

Bohanon, Brian
88ChaRanS-2
90Bow-489
90BowTif-489
90DonRoo-13
90FleUpd-122
90RanMot-13
90UppDec-731
91Sco100RS-53
91TopDeb90-18
92ClaGam-185
92DonRoo-11
92OklCit8F-1908
92OPC-149
92RanMot-18
92Sco-672
92StaClu-297
92Top-149
92TopGol-149
92TopGolW-149
92TopMic-149
92TulDriF-2686
93Don-27
93RanKee-395
93StaClu-154
93StaCluFDI-154
93StaCluMOP-154
93Top-638
93TopGol-638
93TopInaM-638
93TopMic-638
93UppDec-380
93UppDecGold-380
94Fle-302
94OklCit8F-1488
94StaClu-55
94StaCluFDI-55
94StaCluGR-55
94StaCluMOP-55
94StaCluT-245
94StaCluTFDI-245
96BluJayOH-2
96Pac-317

Bohlke, Scott
88DurBulS-2

Bohman, John
96GreFalDTI-2

Bohmbach, Jay
85RedWinA-5
86RedWinA-4

Bohmbach, Jim
85RedWinA-11
86RedWinA-16

Bohmbach, Kelly
85RedWinA-13
86RedWinA-13

Bohmbach, Lonnie
86RedWinA-23

Bohn, Matt
88CalLeaACLC-23

Bohne, Sammy Arthur
21Exh-12
21Nei-67
22E120-166
23MapCriV-20
90DodTar-59

Bohnenkamp, Dave
89CliGiaP-880

Bohnet, Bob
79WisRapTT-13
80WatIndT-21
82HolMilT-14

Bohnet, John
80WatIndT-9
81ChaLooT-13
82ChaChaT-2
82Ind-6
82IndTeal-5
84BufBisT-14

Bohringer, Helms
91BakDodCLC-24

Bohrofen, Brent
89OklSoo-6
90OklSoo-12
91HamRedC-22
91HamRedP-4050
92SavCarF-674

Boigenzahn, Jeff
85RedWinA-21
86RedWinA-2

Boisclair, Bruce A.
75TidTidTI-5
77MetDaiPA-4
77Top-399
78MetDaiPA-2
78Top-277
79OPC-68
79Top-148
80Top-654
91MetWIZ-41

Boitano, Danny
76OklCit8TI-16
79VanCanT-9
80Top-668
80VanCanT-14
81TidTidT-27
91MetWIZ-42
93RanKee-77
94BreMilB-196

Bojan, Tim
92SouOreAC-19
92SouOreAF-3406

93MadMusC-6
93MadMusF-1816
94WesMicWC-4
94WesMicWF-2289
Bojcun, Pat (Patrick)
91BatCliC-21
91BatCliP-3476
92BatCliC-7
92BatCliF-3255
Boka, Ben
93LetMouF-4151
93LetMouSP-3
94PitMetC-6
94PitMetF-3525
Bokek, Ken
76CliPilT-3
Bokelman, Dick
53Top-204
79TCM50-249
91TopArc1-204
Bokemeier, Matt
94HudValRF-3390
96WesOahCHWB-41
94HudValRC-1
Boken, Bob (Robert A.)
34Gou-74
Boker, John
96OgdRapTI-23
Boker, Mike
91BenBucC-11
91BenBucP-3685
92CliGiaC-4
92CliGiaF-3589
Bolan, Bob
52LavPro-21
Bolanos, Marcos
94VenLinU-173
Bolar, Wendell
86BelMarC-106
87WauTimP-9
88BoiHawP-1607
Bolden, Ed
91PomBlaBPB-23
Bolden, Jim
93NegLeaRL2-4
Boldt, Sean
92MarPhiC-3
92MarPhiF-3046
Bolek, Ken
78WatIndT-2
83ColAstT-23
86AshTouP-3
87OscAstP-6
88WatIndP-687
89KinIndS-25
90CanIndB-4
90CanIndP-1309
90CanIndS-20
91CanIndLD-99
91CanIndP-995
91LinDriAA-99
92IndFanC-30
94DayCubC-27
94DayCubF-2369
Boles, Carl Theodore
63Top-428
Boles, John
83AppFoxF-25
85BufBisT-1
86OmaRoyP-2
86OmaRoyT-23
Boley, Joe (John Peter)
31Exh-27
94ConTSN-1141
94ConTSNB-1141
Bolger, Jim (James Cyril)
55Top-179
57SeaPop-5
57Top-289
58Top-201
59Top-29
59TopVen-29
61UniOil-SD2
Bolick, Frank
76SanAntBTI-2
Bolick, Frank C.
88BelBreGS-4
89BelBreIS-1
89Sta-108
90CalLeaACLC-11
90CMC-713
90ProAaA-152
90StoPorB-7
90StoPorCLC-193
90StoPorP-2192
91Bow-534
91Cla/Bes-381
91JacSunLD-329
91JacSunP-154
91LinDriAA-329
92JacSunF-3712
92JacSunS-351
92OPC-473
92SkyAA F-148
92Top-473
92TopGol-473
92TopGolW-473
92TopMic-473
93Bow-296
93ExpPosN-5
93FleFinE-89
93Lea-231
93OPCPre-72
93PacSpa-530
93Pin-588
93StaClu-724
93StaCluFDI-724
93StaCluMOP-724
93Ult-412
93UppDec-531
93UppDecGold-531
94BufBisF-1843
94Don-63
94Pac-375
Bolin, Bobby
61Top-449
62Top-329
63Top-106
64Top-374
65Top-341
66OPC-61
66Top-61
66TopVen-61
67CokCapG-1
67Top-252
68DexPre-14
68OPC-169
68Top-169
68TopVen-169
69OPC-8
69Top-8
69Top-505A
69Top-505B
69TopSta-101
69TopTeaP-14
70BreMcD-2
70MLBOffS-266
70Top-574
71MLBOffS-314
71OPC-446
71Top-446
72MilBra-36
72OPC-266
72Top-266
73LinPor-15
73OPC-541
73Top-541
74OPC-427
74Top-427
78TCM60I-109
86BirBarTI-20
94BreMilB-197
Bolin, George
91MelBusF-10
Boling, John
86AppFoxP-2
87BirBarB-12
88BirBarB-18
Bolinger, Monte
72CedRapCT-29
Bolivar, Flores
76VenLeaS-101
80VenLeaS-128
80VenLeaS-133
93LinVenB-82
95LinVen-35
Bolke, Ken
93IndWUA-33
Bolling, Frank Elmore
55Bow-48A
55Bow-204A
55Bow-204B
57Top-325
58Top-95
59TigGraASP-4
59Top-280
60TigJayP-2
60Top-482
61Pos-41A
61Pos-41B
61Top-335
61TopStal-145
62BraJayP-3
62Jel-146
62Pos-146
62PosCan-146
62SalPlaC-140
62ShiPlaC-140
62Top-130
62Top-211
62TopStal-145
62TopVen-130
63BraJayP-2
63Fle-44
63Jel-149
63Pos-149
63SalMetC-18
63Top-570
64BraJayP-2
64Top-115
64TopVen-115
65Kah-5
65OPC-269
65Top-269
66Kah-6
78AtlCon-4
78TCM60I-9
81TigDetN-103
Bolling, John Edward
79DiaGre-312
90DodTar-60
Bolling, Milt (Milton J.)
53RedSoxTI-1
53Top-280
54Bow-130
54Top-82
55Bow-48A
55Bow-48B
55Bow-204A
55Top-91
55TopDouH-91
56Top-315
57Top-131
58Top-188
79DiaGre-245
91TopArc1-280
94TopArc1-82
94TopArc1G-82
Bollo, Greg
65Top-541
66Top-301
66TopVen-301
78TCM60I-30
Bollweg, Don (Donald R.)
47PM1StaP1-16
52Top-128
53Dor-120
54Bow-115
55A'sRodM-4
55Bow-54
83TopRep5-128
Bolognese, Keith
94DanBraC-2
94DanBraF-3537
Bolster, Bob
80GleFalWSBT-29
80GleFalWSCT-23
Bolt, James
86SanJosBP-5
Bolt, Michelle
91FreStaLBS-14
Bolton, Cliff (William C.)
31SenTealPW-3
34DiaStaR-47
34Gou-65
36GouWidPPR-A8
36NatChiFPR-12
36R31PasP-27
36WorWidGV-133
79DiaGre-71
92ConTSN-505
Bolton, Jacques
94WilCubC-29
Bolton, Rod
90UtiBluSP-14
91Cla/Bes-56
91FloStaLAP-FSL27
91SarWhiSC-1
91SarWhiSP-1104
92Bow-240
92ProFS7-45
92SkyAAAF-279
92TriA AAS-628
92UppDecML-117
92VanCanF-2713
92VanCanS-628
93Bow-471
93ExcFS7-150
93FleFinE-193
93LeaGolR-R12
93Pin-580
93SelRoo-43T
93StaCluWS-3
93Ult-528
93UppDec-502
93UppDecGold-502
93WhiSoxK-4
94Bow-18
94Don-598
94Fle-77
94NasSouF-1243
94Pac-121
94Pin-130
94PinArtP-130
94PinMusC-130
94Sco-553
94ScoGolR-553
94StaClu-466
94StaCluFDI-466
94StaCluGR-466
94StaCluMOP-466
94StaCluT-131
94StaCluTFDI-131
94Top-766
94TopGol-766
94TopSpa-766
95NasSouTI-2
95Top-634
Bolton, Tom
80ElmPioRST-2
87IntLeaAT-22
87PawRedSP-62
87PawRedST-27
88Fle-346
88FleGlo-346
88PawRedSC-9
88PawRedSP-452
88Top-442
88TopTif-442
89Don-539
89PawRedSC-1
89PawRedSP-680
89PawRedSTI-3
89Sco-531
89Top-269
89TopTif-269
89TriAAP-AAA17
89UppDec-545
90PawRedSDD-2
90PawRedSP-453
90ProAAAF-425
90TopTVRS-38
90UppDec-351
91Bow-114
91Don-609
91Fle-87
91Lea-47
91OPC-37
91RedSoxP-1
91Sco-781
91StaClu-588
91Top-37
91TopDesS-37
91TopMic-37
91TopTif-37
91Ult-28
91UppDec-86
92Fle-33
92OPC-708
92RedSoxDD-3
92Sco-99
92ScoProP-23
92ScoRoo-77T
92StaClu-561
92Top-708
92TopGol-708
92TopGolW-708
92TopMic-708
92UppDec-110
93PacSpa-442
93TigGat-3
93UppDec-633
93UppDecGold-633
94ColC-56
94ColChoGS-56
94ColChoSS-56
94Pac-212
94RocRedWF-990
95NasSouTI-3
Boltz, Brian
90Bes-87
90GreBraB-7
90GreBraP-1122
90GreBraS-4
93GreBraF-341
Bomback, Mark
77HolMilT-2
79VanCanT-7
81Fle-323
81OPC-264
81Top-567
81TopTra-739
82Don-559
82Fle-610
82OPC-307
82Top-707
83SyrChiT-5
84SyrChiT-23
89PacSenL-39
91MetWIZ-43
94BreMilB-198
Bombard, Marc
86FloStaLAP-9
87TamTarP-8
88CedRapRP-1144
88MidLeaAGS-15
89ElPasDGS-1
90CedRapRDGB-28
90EasLeaAP-EL29
90HarSenP-1208
90HarSenS-23
91CarMudLD-124
91CarMudP-1101
91LinDriAA-124
92BufBisBS-2
92BufBisF-338
92BufBisS-49
93IndIndF-1503
93TriAAAGF-7
94IndIndF-1824
95IndIndF-111
Bombard, Rich
82AubAstT-13
83DayBeaAT-3
86ColAstP-5
87CedRapRP-26
88ChaLooB-5
89ChaLooB-8
89ChaLooGS-2
91FayGenC-12
92LakTigC-28
92LakTigF-2294
93LakTigC-28
93LakTigF-1327
94TreThuF-2135
95JacSunTI-2
96LakTigB-2
Bomgardner, Rich
89ColMetB-25
89ColMetGS-3
Bonacquista, Jeff
87AncGlaP-3
Bonanno, Rob
94BoiHawC-3
94BoiHawF-3344
95LakElsSTI-5
95MidAngTI-4
96MidAngOHP-4
Bonaparte, Elijah
77SpaPhiT-17
81OklCit8T-3
82TolMudHT-19
83RocRedWT-19
Bonarigo, Nick
43CenFlo-2
Bonchek, Jeff
88BurIndP-1779
89MiaMirIS-3
Boncore, Steve
82VerBeaDT-13
83VerBeaDT-14
Bond, Daven
86AubAstP-4
87AshTouP-6
88OscAstS-4
89OscAstS-2
90ColMudB-14
90ColMudP-1338
90ColMudS-5
91ColCliLD-102

91ColCliP-2
91ColCliP-589
91LinDriAAA-102
92JacSunS-352
Bond, David
87SpoIndP-16
88ChaRaiP-1196
89ChaRaiP-993
Bond, Doug
88BilMusP-1809
Bond, Jason
96EveAquB-4
Bond, Michael
91BelMarC-11
91BelMarP-3670
92BelMarC-21
92BelMarF-1449
92JacSunF-3713
Bond, Walt (Walter F.)
60Top-552
61Top-334
62SalPlaC-208
62ShiPlaC-208
63Top-493
64Top-339
64TopVen-339
65AstBigLBPP-4
65OPC-109
65Top-109
65TopEmbl-50
65TopTral-4
66Top-431
67AstTeal2-4
67Top-224
87AstSer1-4
87AstSer1-29
Bondra, Peter
93StaCluMO-54
Bonds, Barry
86DonRoo-11
86FleUpd-14
86SpoRoo-13
86TopTra-11T
86TopTraT-11T
87ClaUpdY-113
87Don-361
87DonOpeD-163A
87DonOpeD-163B
87Fle-604
87FleGlo-604
87FleHotS-5
87Lea-219
87OPC-320
87SpoTeaP-18
87Top-320
87TopGloS-30
87TopSti-131
87TopTif-320
87ToyRoo-4
88Don-326
88DonBasB-17
88Fle-322
88FleGlo-322
88FleSup-4
88KinDis-11
88Lea-113
88OPC-267
88PanSti-376
88RedFolSB-7
88Sco-265
88ScoGlo-265
88ScoYouS2-12
88Spo-119
88StaLinPi-2
88Top-231
88Top-450
88TopBig-89
88TopSti-135
88TopTif-231
88TopTif-450
88TopUKM-5
88TopUKMT-5
89Bow-426
89BowTif-426
89ClaTraO-117
89Don-92
89DonBasB-73
89Fle-202
89FleGlo-202
89FleHeroB-3
89OPC-263
89PanSti-172
89PirVerFJ-24
89RedFolSB-9
89Sco-127
89ScoHot1S-31
89Spo-146
89SpoIllFKI-229
89Top-620
89TopAme2C-5
89TopBasT-106
89TopBig-5
89TopSti-127
89TopStiB-46
89TopTif-620
89TopUKM-5
89TVSpoM-12
89UppDec-440
90Bow-181
90BowTif-181
90ClaBlu-82
90ClaYel-T68
90Don-126
90DonBesN-45
90Fle-461
90FleCan-461
90Lea-91
90MLBBasB-37
90OPC-220
90PanSti-322
90PirHomC-5
90PlaPri-1
90PubSti-149
90RedFolSB-7
90Sco-4
90Sco100S-53
90ScoMcD-11
90Spo-143
90SunSee-9
90SupActM-19
90Top-220
90TopBig-128
90TopCoi-40
90TopDou-5
90TopMag-42
90TopMinL-70
90TopSti-9
90TopSti-123
90TopTif-220
90UppDec-227
90USPlaCA-13D
90VenSti-56
91Baz-1
91Bow-380
91Bow-513
91CadElID-5
91Cla1-T81
91Cla2-T78
91ClaGam-195
91Col-26
91ColBon-1
91ColBon-2
91ColBon-3
91ColBon-4
91ColBon-5
91ColBon-6
91ColBon-7
91ColBon-8
91ColBon-9
91ColBon-10
91ColBon-11
91ColBon-12
91ColBon-xx
91Don-4
91Don-495
91Don-762
91DonEli-1
91DonGraS-5
91DonPre-10
91DonSupD-4
91Fle-33
91Fle-710
91FleAll-5
91FlePro-F1
91JimDea-4
91KinDis-21
91Lea-261
91Lea-364
91LeaPre-9
91MajLeaCP-57
91MooSna-3
91OPC-401
91OPC-570
91OPCPre-12
91PanCanT1-12
91PanCanT1-20
91PanCanT1-33
91PanCanT1-43
91PanCanT1-105
91PanFreS-119
91PanSti-114
91PepSup-7
91PetSta-16
91Pos-21
91PosCan-5
91Sco-330
91Sco-668
91Sco-868
91Sco-876
91Sco100S-26
91Sev3DCN-2
91SevCoi-F1
91SevCoi-T2
91SevCoi-NE2
91StaClu-220
91StaCluCM-3
91StaPinB-4
91Stu-222
91Top-401
91Top-570
91TopCraJI-19
91TopDesS-401
91TopDesS-570
91TopGaloC-2
91TopMic-401
91TopMic-570
91TopSta-4
91TopTif-401
91TopTif-570
91TopTriH-N9
91Ult-275
91Ult-391
91UltGol-1
91UppDec-94
91UppDec-154
91UppDecSS-SS5
91Woo-1
92Bow-60
92Bow-590
92Cla1-T16
92Cla1-NNO
92Cla2-T70
92ClaGam-155
92ColAllG-22
92ColAllP-22
92ColPro-3
92DenHol-20
92Don-243
92DonCraJ2-14
92DonPre-2
92Fle-550
92FleAll-3
92FleCitTP-23
92FleLumC-L8
92Fre-7
92Hig5-91
92Hig5S-4
92JimDea-2
92Lea-275
92LeaBlaG-275
92MSABenSHD-18
92OPC-380
92OPCPre-157
92PanSti-258
92PepDieM-29
92Pin-500
92PinSlu-4
92PinTeaP-8
92PirNatI-3
92Pos-15
92PosCan-9
92Sco-555
92Sco-777
92Sco100S-26
92ScoImpP-55
92ScoProaG-15
92SpoIllFK1-157
92SpoIllFK1-562
92SpoStaCC-4
92StaClu-604
92StaClu-620
92StaCluECN-604
92StaCluECN-620
92StaCluMP-2
92Stu-82
92StuPre-15
92Top-380
92Top-390
92TopGol-380
92TopGol-390
92TopGolW-380
92TopGolW-390
92TopKid-21
92TopMcD-12
92TopMic-380
92TopMic-390
92TopMic-G380
92TriPla-116
92Ult-251
92UltAllS-16
92UltAwaW-11
92UppDec-134
92UppDec-711
92UppDec-721
92UppDecF-14
92UppDecFG-14
92UppDecHRH-HR21
92UppDecTMH-11
92UppDecWB-T2
93Ble23KB-1
93Ble23KB-2
93Ble23KB-3
93BlePro-1
93BlePro-2
93BlePro-3
93Bow-140
93Bow-702
93ClaGam-14
93ClaGolF-1
93ClaGolF-AU1
93ColAllG-2
93DiaMar-14
93DiaMarA-2
93Don-678
93DonEli-31
93DonEliD-16
93DonEliS-13
93DonMasotG-14
93DonMVP-25
93DurPowP1-17
93Fin-103
93FinJum-103
93FinRef-103
93Fla-138
93Fle-112
93Fle-350
93FleAll-NL7
93FleAtl-2
93FleFinE-150
93FleFruotL-6
93FunPac-11
93FunPac-99
93FunPac-100
93FunPac-222
93FunPacA-AS7
93GiaMot-4
93GiaPos-6
93GiaPos-7
93HumDumC-49
93JimDea-10
93KinDis-1
93Lea-269
93LeaGolA-R16
93MetBak-2
93OPC-46
93OPCPre-1
93OPCPreSP-14
93OPCPreSPF-14
93PacJugC-21
93PacSpa-607
93PanSti-165
93PanSti-243
93Pin-484
93Pin-504
93PinCoo-15
93PinCooD-15
93PinHomRC-4
93PinSlu-6
93PinTeaP-8
93Pos-15
93Pro22KGB-1
93Sco-482
93Sco-523
93Sco-560
93Sel-1
93SelChaS-7
93SelRoo-23T
93SelStaL-29
93SelStaL-40
93SelStaL-46
93SelStaL-52
93SP-10
93SPPlaP-PP2
93StaClu-51
93StaClu-51A
93StaClu-684
93StaClu-747
93StaCluFDI-51
93StaCluFDI-51A
93StaCluFDI-51B
93StaCluFDI-684
93StaCluFDI-747
93StaCluG-1
93StaCluM-161
93StaCluMO-2
93StaCluMOP-51A
93StaCluMOP-51B
93StaCluMOP-684
93StaCluMOP-747
93StaCluMP-25
93StaCluU-1
93StaCluU-4
93StaCluU-5
93StaCluU-7
93StaCluU-10
93Stu-12
93StuSil-2
93StuSupoC-10
93Top-2
93Top-407
93TOPBLAG-1
93TopFulS-3
93TopGol-2
93TopGol-407
93TopInaM-2
93TopInaM-407
93TopMic-2
93TopMic-407
93TopPre-2
93TopTra-1T
93TriPlaG-GS1
93TriPlaLL-L1
93Ult-483
93UltAllS-6
93UltAwaW-7
93UltAwaW-24
93UltHomRK-6
93UltPer-1
93UppDec-210
93UppDec-471
93UppDec-476
93UppDec-486
93UppDec-567
93UppDecCP-R3
93UppDecDG-11
93UppDecFH-56
93UppDecGold-210
93UppDecGold-471
93UppDecGold-476
93UppDecGold-486
93UppDecGold-567
93UppDecHRH-HR6
93UppDecSH-HI5
93UppDecTriCro-TC1
93USPlaCA-10C
94Bow-135
94BowBes-R59
94BowBes-X97
94BowBesR-R59
94BowBesR-X97
94CarLeaA-DJ13
94ChuShoS-2
94ColC-311
94ColC-313
94ColC-316
94ColC-338
94ColC-610
94ColC-632
94ColChoGS-311
94ColChoGS-313
94ColChoGS-316
94ColChoGS-338
94ColChoGS-610
94ColChoGS-632
94ColChoHRA-HA3
94ColChoSS-311
94ColChoSS-313
94ColChoSS-316
94ColChoSS-338
94ColChoSS-610
94ColChoSS-632
94ColChoT-2
94ColChoT-11
94DenHol-6
94Don-349
94DonAwaWJ-1
94DonAwaWJ-4
94DonDiaK-DK1
94DonDom-A2
94DonDom-B7

94DonEli-44
94DonLonBL-9
94DonMVP-14
94DonPro-1
94DonPro-1SE
94DonSpeE-349
94DonSpiotG-2
94ExtBas-383
94ExtBasGB-4
94Fin-230
94FinJum-230
94FinRef-230
94Fla-239
94FlaHotG-1
94FlaOutP-2
94Fle-684
94FleAllS-31
94FleAwaW-2
94FleLeaL-8
94FleLumC-2
94FleSun-5
94FleUpdDT-1
94FUnPac-25
94FUnPac-190
94FUnPac-194
94FUnPac-199
94FUnPac-212
94FUnPac-225
94FUnPac-226
94FUnPac-237
94GiaAMC-5
94GiaMot-3
94GiaSFC-2
94GiaTeal-3
94GiaTeal-4
94GiaTeal-5
94GiaTeal-6
94GiaTeal-9
94GiaUSPC-1S
94GiaUSPC-7H
94KinDis-24
94Kra-17
94Lea-264
94LeaGam-8
94LeaGolS-2
94LeaL-156
94LeaLimGA-10
94LeaMVPC-N3
94LeaMVPCG-N3
94LeaPowB-3
94LeaSli-6
94LeaStaS-2
94OPC-200
94OPCAllR-3
94OPCJumA-3
94OscMayR-17
94Pac-540
94Pac-655
94PacGolP-11
94PacSilP-28
94PanSti-12
94PanSti-13
94PanSti-261
94Pin-26
94PinArtP-26
94PinMusC-26
94PinRunC-RC23
94PinTeaP-7
94PinTheN-2
94PinTri-TR8
94Pos-11
94PosCan-11
94PosCanG-11
94ProMag-121
94RedFolMI-29
94Sco-1
94Sco-632
94ScoCyc-TC16
94ScoGolR-1
94ScoGolR-632
94ScoGolS-1
94ScoSam-1
94ScoSam-1GR
94Sel-211
94SelCroC-CC6
94SelSki-SK6
94SP-90
94SPDieC-90
94Spo-91
94Spo-190
94SpoFanA-AS6
94SpoRooGGG-GG8
94SPPre-WR1
94StaClu-238
94StaClu-259
94StaClu-532
94StaCluDD-DD6
94StaCluF-F3
94StaCluFDI-238
94StaCluFDI-259
94StaCluFDI-532
94StaCluGR-238
94StaCluGR-259
94StaCluGR-532
94StaCluMO-24
94StaCluMOF-1
94StaCluMOP-238
94StaCluMOP-259
94StaCluMOP-532
94StaCluMOP-F3
94StaCluMOP-DD6
94StaCluP-238
94StaCluT-1
94StaCluTF-2
94StaCluTFDI-1
94Stu-83
94StuEdiC-1
94StuHer-1
94StuSerS-2
94SucSav-19
94TomPiz-3
94Top-390
94Top-605
94Top-700
94TopBlaG-27
94TopGol-390
94TopGol-605
94TopGol-700
94TopPre-2
94TopSpa-390
94TopSpa-605
94TopSpa-700
94TopSupS-5
94TriPla-102
94TriPlaBS-4
94TriPlaM-12
94TriPlaP-3
94Ult-286
94UltAllS-16
94UltAwaW-15
94UltAwaW-20
94UltHitM-3
94UltHomRK-7
94UltOnBL-2
94UltRBIK-7
94UppDec-38
94UppDec-280
94UppDec-400
94UppDecAJ-35
94UppDecAJG-35
94UppDecDC-W1
94UppDecED-38
94UppDecED-280
94UppDecED-400
94UppDecMLS-MM3
94UppDecMLSED-MM3
94USPlaCA-1C
94USPlaCA-11D
95Baz-20
95BazRedH-RH3
95Bow-376
95BowBes-R13
95BowBesR-R13
95ClaFanFPCP-1
95ClaPhoC-47
95ColCho-60
95ColCho-82
95ColCho-86
95ColChoCtA-2
95ColChoCtAG-2
95ColChoCtG-CG3
95ColChoCtG-CG3B
95ColChoCtG-CG3C
95ColChoCtGE-3
95ColChoCtGG-CG3
95ColChoCtGG-CG3B
95ColChoCtGG-CG3C
95ColChoCtGGE-3
95ColChoGS-60
95ColChoGS-82
95ColChoGS-86
95ColChoSE-105
95ColChoSE-259
95ColChoSEGS-105
95ColChoSEGS-259
95ColChoSESS-105
95ColChoSESS-259
95ColChoSS-60
95ColChoSS-82
95ColChoSS-86
95D3-24
95Don-8
95DonAll-NL7
95DonBomS-3
95DonDom-7
95DonEli-56
95DonLonBL-7
95DonPreP-8
95DonTopotO-349
95Emb-120
95EmbGolI-120
95Emo-192
95EmoMas-1
95EmoN-3
95Fin-192
95FinPowK-PK17
95FinRef-192
95Fla-207
95FlaHotG-2
95FlaHotN-3
95FlaOutP-3
95Fle-574
95FleAllF-6
95FleAllS-6
95FleLumC-3
95FleUpdDT-3
95FleUpdH-3
95FleUpdSL-2
95GiaMot-3
95KinDis-4
95Kra-18
95Lea-279
95LeaGolS-5
95LeaGreG-3
95LeaHeaftH-4
95LeaLim-11
95LeaLimG-4
95LeaLimIBP-15
95LeaLimL-2
95LeaOpeD-3
95NatPac-7
95Pac-373
95PacGolCDC-15
95PacGolP-13
95PacPri-120
95PanSti-73
95Pin-272
95Pin-299
95PinArtP-272
95PinArtP-299
95PinFan-24
95PinGatA-GA6
95PinMusC-272
95PinMusC-299
95PinPer-PP3
95PinPin-13
95PinPinR-13
95PinRedH-RH6
95PinTeaP-TP7
95PinWhiH-WH6
95Pos-11
95PosCan-17
95RedFol-1
95Sco-30
95Sco-562
95ScoDouGC-GC3
95ScoGolR-30
95ScoGolR-562
95ScoHaloG-HG16
95ScoPlaTS-30
95ScoPlaTS-562
95ScoRul-SR9
95ScoRulJ-SR9
95Sel-46
95Sel-246
95SelArtP-46
95SelArtP-246
95SelBigS-BS9
95SelCer-1
95SelCerC-6
95SelCerGT-6
95SelCerMG-1
95SP-115
95SPCha-96
95SPChaDC-96
95SPChaDFC-9
95SPChaFCDC-9
95Spo-53
95Spo-170
95SpoArtP-53
95SpoArtP-170
95SpoDet-DE6
95SpoDouT-9
95SpoHamT-HT7
95SpoPro-PM10
95SPPlaP-PP2
95SPSil-115
95StaClu-271
95StaClu-509
95StaCluCC-CC27
95StaCluCT-19
95StaCluMO-8
95StaCluMOP-271
95StaCluMOP-509
95StaCluMOP-CC27
95StaCluMOP-PZ3
95StaCluMOP-RL30
95StaCluMOP-SS2
95StaCluMOP-VRE1
95StaCluPZ-PZ3
95StaCluRL-RL30
95StaCluSS-SS2
95StaCluSTWS-271
95StaCluSTWS-509
95StaCluVE-VRE1
95StaCluVR-136
95Stu-7
95StuGolS-7
95StuPlaS-7
95Sum-9
95Sum-179
95Sum-199
95SumBigB-BB6
95SumNthD-9
95SumNthD-179
95SumNthD-199
95TomPiz-20
95Top-100
95Top-388
95TopCyb-64
95TopCybSiR-1
95TopFin-7
95TopLeaL-LL8
95TopTra-3T
95TopTra-161T
95TopTraPB-3
95UC3-18
95UC3-128
95UC3ArtP-18
95UC3ArtP-128
95UC3CycS-CS5
95UC3InM-IM5
95UllHomRK-3
95Ult-442
95UltAllS-5
95UltAllSGM-5
95UltAwaW-15
95UltAwaWGM-15
95UltGolM-442
95UltHitM-4
95UltHitMGM-4
95UltHomRK-8
95UltHomRKGM-8
95UltOnBL-5
95UltOnBLGM-5
95UltPowP-5
95UltPowPGM-5
95UppDec-103
95UppDec-335
95UppDecED-103
95UppDecED-335
95UppDecEDG-103
95UppDecEDG-335
95UppDecPAW-H7
95UppDecPAWE-H7
95UppDecPC-MLB8
95UppDecPLL-R7
95UppDecPLL-R17
95UppDecPLLE-R7
95UppDecPLLE-R17
95UppDecSE-70
95UppDecSEG-70
95USPlaCMLA-4H
95USPlaCMLA-10C
95Zen-5
95ZenAllS-13
95ZenAllS-18
95ZenZ-6
96Baz-118
96Bow-78
96BowBes-10
96BowBesAR-10
96BowBesMI-6
96BowBesMIAR-6
96BowBesMIR-6
96BowBesP-BBP4
96BowBesPAR-BBP4
96BowBesPR-BBP4
96BowBesR-10
96Cir-192
96Cir-197
96CirAcc-29
96CirBos-49
96CirRav-192
96CirRav-197
96ColCho-108
96ColCho-300
96ColCho-409
96ColChoCtG-CG23
96ColChoCtG-CG23B
96ColChoCtG-CG23C
96ColChoCtGE-CR23
96ColChoCtGG-CG23
96ColChoCtGG-CG23B
96ColChoCtGG-CG23C
96ColChoCtGGE-CR23
96ColChoGS-108
96ColChoGS-300
96ColChoGS-409
96ColChoSS-108
96ColChoSS-300
96ColChoSS-409
96ColChoYMtP-8
96ColChoYMtP-8A
96ColChoYMtPGS-8
96ColChoYMtPGS-8A
96DenHol-8
96DenHolGS-6
96DenHolGSAP-6
96Don-216
96DonDiaK-8
96DonHitL-10
96DonLonBL-1
96DonPowA-2
96DonPowADC-2
96DonPreP-216
96DonPurP-2
96DonRouT-2
96DonSam-2
96DonSho-2
96EmoLegoB-2
96EmoN-2
96EmoXL-286
96EmoXLD-2
96Fin-B146
96Fin-B240
96Fin-G105
96FinRef-B146
96FinRef-B240
96FinRef-G105
96Fla-384
96FlaDiaC-3
96FlaHotG-2
96FlaPow-2
96Fle-583
96FleChe-1
96FleGolM-2
96FleLumC-3
96FleTeaL-28
96FleTif-583
96FleUpd-U215
96FleUpd-U246
96FleUpd-2
96FleUpdH-4
96FleUpdSL-2
96FleUpdSS-2
96FleUpdTC-U215
96FleUpdTC-U246
96FleZon-2
96GiaMot-2
96Kin-23
96Lea-78
96LeaAllGMC-14
96LeaAllGMCG-14
96LeaLim-71
96LeaLimG-71
96LeaLimPC-9
96LeaPicP-12
96LeaPre-94
96LeaPreP-94
96LeaPrePB-78
96LeaPrePG-78
96LeaPrePS-78
96LeaPreSG-6
96LeaPreSP-6
96LeaPreSta-10
96LeaPreSte-6
96LeaSig-89
96LeaSigPPG-89
96LeaSigPPP-89

96LeaTotB-4
96MetUni-241
96MetUniHM-2
96MetUniML-1
96MetUniP-241
96MetUniT-2
96Pac-202
96PacGolCD-DC36
96PacPri-P65
96PacPriFB-FB3
96PacPriG-P65
96PacPriRHS-RH15
96PanSti-107
96Pin-148
96Pin-199
96Pin-208
96Pin-260
96PinAfi-80
96PinAfiAP-80
96PinAfiFPP-80
96PinAfiR-14
96PinAfiR-17
96PinAfiR-19
96PinAfiR-22
96PinAfiR-23
96PinAfiR-24
96PinAfiSP-7
96PinArtP-75
96PinArtP-108
96PinArtP-160
96PinEssotG-18
96PinFan-16
96PinFirR-9
96PinFoil-208
96PinFoil-260
96PinPow-5
96PinSky-10
96PinSlu-4
96PinSta-75
96PinSta-108
96PinSta-160
96PinTeaP-5
96PinTeaS-12
96Pro-3
96ProMagA-14
96ProMagDM-20
96ProSta-52
96SchDis-20
96Sco-340
96ScoAll-7
96ScoBigB-6
96ScoDiaA-6
96ScoDreT-6
96ScoDugC-B65
96ScoDugCAP-B65
96ScoGolS-15
96ScoNumG-5
96ScoPowP-13
96ScoRef-11
96ScoTitT-17
96Sel-101
96Sel-156
96SelArtP-101
96SelArtP-156
96SelCer-31
96SelCerAP-31
96SelCerCB-31
96SelCerCR-31
96SelCerIP-9
96SelCerMB-31
96SelCerMG-31
96SelCerMR-31
96SelCerSF-16
96SelClaTF-18
96SelEnF-6
96SelTeaN-18
96SP-166
96SPBasH-84
96SPMarM-MM8
96SPMarMDC-8
96Spo-5
96Spo-112
96SpoArtP-5
96SpoArtP-112
96SpoDouT-8
96SpoHitP-16
96SpoPowS-16
96SpoPro-16
96SPPreF-5
96SPSpeFX-25
96SPSpeFXDC-25
96SPx-51
96SPxBoufG-3
96SPxGol-51
96StaClu-202
96StaClu-402
96StaCluB&B-BB2
96StaCluEPB-402
96StaCluEPG-402
96StaCluEPS-402
96StaCluEWB-EW7
96StaCluEWG-EW7
96StaCluEWS-EW7
96StaCluMet-M2
96StaCluMM-MM7
96StaCluMO-7
96StaCluMOP-202
96StaCluMOP-402
96StaCluMOP-M2
96StaCluMOP-BB2
96StaCluMOP-MM7
96StaCluMOP-PC2
96StaCluMOP-PS14
96StaCluPC-PC2
96StaCluPS-PS14
95StaCluVRMC-136
96Stu-76
96StuHitP-7
96StuPrePB-76
96StuPrePG-76
96StuPrePS-76
96StuStaGS-10
96Sum-107
96SumAbo&B-107
96SumArtP-107
96SumBal-13
96SumBigB-5
96SumBigBM-5
96SumFoi-107
96SumPos-7
96TeaOut-10
96TeaOut-C94
96Top-10
96Top-300
96TopChr-10
96TopChr-119
96TopChrMotG-18
96TopChrMotGR-18
96TopChrR-10
96TopChrR-119
96TopChrWC-WC3
96TopChrWCR-WC3
96TopClaC-CC6
96TopGal-156
96TopGalPPI-156
96TopLas-37
96TopLasPC-10
96TopLasSS-2
96TopMasotG-18
96TopMysF-M13
96TopMysFR-M13
96TopPowB-10
96TopPro-NL3
96TopRoaW-RW4
96TopWreC-WC3
96Ult-290
96Ult-577
96UltCalttH-1
96UltCalttHGM-1
96UltChe-A2
96UltCheGM-A2
96UltDiaP-2
96UltDiaPGM-2
96UltGolM-290
96UltGolM-577
96UltHitM-2
96UltHitMGM-2
96UltHomRKGM-3
96UltHomRKR-3
96UltOn-L-2
96UltOn-LGM-2
96UltPowP-2
96UltPowPGM-2
96UltPriL-15
96UltPriLGM-15
96UltPro-1
96UltRaw-2
96UltRawGM-2
96UltRBIK-4
96UltRBIKGM-4
96UltSeaC-1
96UltSeaCGM-1
96UltThu-2
96UltThuGM-2
96UppDec-195
96UppDec-373
96UppDecA-8
96UppDecDD-DD33
96UppDecDDG-DD33
96UppDecDDS-DD33
96UppDecG-GF3
96UppDecHC-HC12
96UppDecPD-PD2
96UppDecPHE-H33
96UppDecPRE-R32
96UppDecPRE-R43
96UppDecPRE-R55
96UppDecPreH-H33
96UppDecPreR-R32
96UppDecPreR-R43
96UppDecPreR-R55
96UppDecRCJ-2
96UppDecRipC-2
96UppDecRunP-RP3
96UppDecVJLS-VJ4
96Zen-29
96Zen-144
96ZenArtP-29
96ZenArtP-144
96ZenMoz-4
96ZenZ-14
97Bow-244
97BowBes-73
97BowBesAR-73
97BowBesMI-MI5
97BowBesMIAR-MI5
97BowBesMIARI-MI5
97BowBesMII-MI5
97BowBesMIR-MI5
97BowBesMIRI-MI5
97BowBesP-3
97BowBesPAR-3
97BowBesPR-3
97BowBesR-73
97BowChr-69
97BowChrI-69
97BowChrIR-69
97BowChrR-69
97BowInt-244
97Cir-25
97CirBos-3
97CirLimA-3
97CirRav-25
97CirRavR-2
97CirSupB-3
97ColCho-225
97ColChoAC-24
97ColChoBS-14
97ColChoBSGS-14
97ColChoCtG-26A
97ColChoCtG-26B
97ColChoCtG-26C
97ColChoCtGIW-CG26
97ColChoNF-NF5
97ColChoNF-NF6
97ColChoPP-PP9
97ColChoPPG-PP9
97ColChoS-15
97ColChoTBS-40
97ColChoTBSWH-40
97ColChoTotT-T26
97Don-167
97Don-269
97Don-421
97Don-438
97DonArmaD-10
97DonEli-16
97DonEli-4
97DonEliGS-16
97DonEliLaL-7
97DonFraFea-7
97DonLim-6
97DonLim-89
97DonLim-123
97DonLimFotG-10
97DonLimFotG-40
97DonLimLE-6
97DonLimLE-89
97DonLimLE-123
97DonPowA-16
97DonPowADC-16
97DonPre-94
97DonPre-182
97DonPreCttC-94
97DonPreCttC-182
97DonPreP-167
97DonPreP-269
97DonPreP-421
97DonPreP-438
97DonPrePGold-167
97DonPrePGold-269
97DonPrePGold-421
97DonPrePGold-438
97DonPrePM-17
97DonPreS-11
97DonPreTBG-3
97DonPreTF-3
97DonPreTP-3
97DonRocL-11
97DonTeaSMVP-12
97Fin-1
97Fin-175
97Fin-313
97FinEmb-175
97FinEmb-313
97FinEmbR-175
97FinEmbR-313
97FinPro-1
97FinRef-1
97FinRef-175
97FinRef-313
97FlaSho-A25
97FlaSho-B25
97FlaSho-C25
97FlaShoHG-2
97FlaShoLC-25
97FlaShoLC-B25
97FlaShoLC-C25
97FlaShoLCM-A25
97FlaShoLCM-B25
97FlaShoLCM-C25
97Fle-477
97Fle-698
97Fle-744
97FleBleB-2
97FleDecoE-2
97FleDecoERT-2
97FleDiaT-2
97FleGolM-1
97FleGouG-1
97FleGouGF-1
97FleHea-3
97FleLumC-4
97FleMilDM-4
97FleNig&D-1
97FleSoaS-2
97FleTeaL-28
97FleTif-477
97FleTif-698
97FleTif-744
97FleZon-3
97Lea-65
97Lea-354
97LeaFraM-65
97LeaFraM-354
97LeaFraMDC-65
97LeaFraMDC-354
97LeaGet-8
97LeaGolS-16
97LeaLeaotN-1
97LeaStaS-11
97LeaWarT-3
97MetUni-242
97MetUniBF-3
97MetUniMF-3
97MetUniML-3
97NewPin-117
97NewPin-184
97NewPin-192
97NewPinAP-117
97NewPinAP-184
97NewPinAP-192
97NewPinIE-9
97NewPinKtP-6
97NewPinMC-117
97NewPinMC-184
97NewPinMC-192
97NewPinPP-117
97NewPinPP-184
97NewPinPP-192
97NewPinPP-I9B
97NewPinPP-K6
97Pac-440
97PacCar-36
97PacCarM-36
97PacCerCGT-12
97PacFirD-20
97PacGolCD-36
97PacLigB-440
97PacPri-147
97PacPriGA-GA32
97PacPriGotD-GD213
97PacPriLB-147
97PacPriP-147
97PacSil-440
97PacTriCD-20
97Pin-97
97PinArtP-97
97PinCar-12
97PinCer-1
97PinCerCMGT-12
97PinCerCT-12
97PinCerMBlu-1
97PinCerMG-1
97PinCerMR-1
97PinCerR-1
97PinHom-13
97PinHom-14
97PinIns-60
97PinInsC-6
97PinInsCE-60
97PinInsDD-3
97PinInsDE-60
97PinInsFS-2
97PinMin-18
97PinMinB-18
97PinMinCB-18
97PinMinCG-18
97PinMinCGR-18
97PinMinCN-18
97PinMinCS-18
97PinMinG-18
97PinMinS-18
97PinMusC-97
97PinTeaP-6
97PinTeaP-10
97PinTotCPB-1
97PinTotCPG-1
97PinTotCPR-1
97PinX-P-30
97PinX-PMoS-30
97PinX-PSfF-40
97PinX-PSfFU-40
97ProMag-40
97ProMagML-40
97Sco-91
97Sco-504
97ScoBla-5
97ScoHigZ-6
97ScoHobR-504
97ScoPreS-91
97ScoResC-504
97ScoShoS-91
97ScoShoS-504
97ScoShoSAP-91
97ScoShoSAP-504
97ScoTitT-15
97Sel-26
97SelArtP-26
97SelRegG-26
97SelToootT-9
97SelToootTMB-9
97SkyE-X-95
97SkyE-XACA-9
97SkyE-XC-95
97SkyE-XEC-95
97SkyE-XHoN-11
97SP-160
97SPGamF-GF9
97SPInsI-20
97SPMarM-MM3
97SpoIll-121
97SpoIll-169
97SpoIllEE-121
97SpoIllEE-169
97SpoIllGS-20
97SPSpeF-3
97SPSpxF-4
97SPSPxFA-4
97SPx-43
97SPxBoufG-17
97SPxBro-43
97SPxCorotG-1
97SPxGraF-43
97SPxSil-43
97SPxSte-43
97StaClu-15
97StaClu-386
97StaCluFR-F3
97StaCluI-I5
97StaCluMat-15
97StaCluMOP-15
97StaCluMOP-386
97StaCluMOP-I5
97StaCluMOP-FB3
97StaCluMOP-PG4
97StaCluMOP-PL3
97StaCluPG-PG4
97StaCluPL-PL3
97Stu-59

97StuMasS-4
97StuMasS8-4
97StuPor8-14
97StuPrePG-59
97StuPrePS-59
97Top-1
97Top-465
97TopAll-AS12
97TopChr-1
97TopChrAS-AS12
97TopChrR-1
97TopChrSAR-AS12
97TopGal-42
97TopGalPMS-9
97TopGalPMSSS-4
97TopGalPPI-42
97TopHobM-HM16
97TopIntF-ILM1
97TopIntFR-ILM1
97TopScr-3
97TopSta-42
97TopSta1AS-AS15
97TopStaAM-42
97TopSweS-SS4
97TopTeaT-TT7
97Ult-290
97UltBasR-1
97UltChe-A2
97UltDiaP-2
97UltDouT-20
97UltFamGam-17
97UltFieC-4
97UltGolME-290
97UltHRK-2
97UltPlaME-290
97UltPowP-A2
97UltPowP-B12
97UltRBIK-4
97UltSeaC-3
97UltThu-1
97UltTop3-22
97UltTop3GM-22
97UppDec-152
97UppDec-170
97UppDec-215
97UppDec-323
97UppDecAG-AG17
97UppDecHC-HC11
97UppDecLDC-LD9
97UppDecMM-8
97UppDecP-24
97UppDecPP-PP16
97UppDecPPJ-PP16
97UppDecRP-RP2
97UppDecU-9
97UppDecUMA-MA4
97Zen-14
97Zen8x1-16
97Zen8x1D-16
Bonds, Bobby
92ClaDraP-84
92ClaDraPFB-BC17
93ClaFS7-176
93LeaGolA-U7
93WatDiaC-1
93WatDiaF-1780
94RanCucQC-6
94UppDecML-214
96SanJosGB-10
Bonds, Bobby Lee
69MilBra-31
69Top-630
70Gia-1
70GiaCheB-1
70MLBOffS-121
70OPC-425
70Top-425
71GiaTic-1
71MLBOffS-241
71OPC-295
71Top-295
71TopCoi-13
72MilBra-37
72Top-711
72Top-712
73Kel2D-8
73LinPor-157
73OPC-145
73Top-145
73TopCanL-6
74Kel-39
74LauAllG-73
74OPC-30
74Top-30
74TopDecE-36
74TopPuz-4
74TopSta-101
75Hos-145
75OPC-55
75SSPPuzB-3
75Top-55
75YanSSP-2
76Hos-18
76HosTwi-18
76OPC-2
76OPC-380
76SSP-439
76Top-2
76Top-380
76TopTra-380T
77BurCheD-124
77OPC-173
77RCColC-5
77Spo-8219
77Top-570
78Hos-42
78OPC-206
78RCColC-44
78SSP270-140
78Top-150
78WifBalD-6
79OPC-142
79Top-285
80BurKinPHR-23
80OPC-215
80Top-410
81Don-71A
81Don-71B
81Fle-548
81OPC-223
81Top-635
81TopTra-740
82Fle-588
82OPC-27
82Top-580
84GiaMot-12
84Ind-6
84IndWhe-NNO
85Ind-6
85IndPol-NNO
86IndOhH-NNO
86IndTeal-7
89PacSenL-128
89T/MSenL-10
89T/MSenL-119
89TopSenL-40
90EliSenL-109
90EliSenL-122
91MDAA-7
91SweBasG-11
91UppDecS-12
91UppDecS-19
92ActPacA-62
92UppDecF-53
92UppDecFG-53
92UppDecHH-HI1
92UppDecS-35
92YanWIZ7-23
92YanWIZA-4
93Bow-702
93GiaMot-28
93GiaPos-8
93MetIma-4
93RanKee-78
93StaCluU-3
93StaCluU-5
93TedWil-51
94GiaMot-28
94Yoo-2
95GiaMot-28
96GiaMot-28
Bone, Pat
82OneYanT-10
Bones, Ricky (Ricardo)
86SpoIndC-163
87ChaRaiP-21
88BlaYNPRWL-99
88CalLeaACLC-41
88RivRedWCLC-208
88RivRedWP-1426
89BlaYNPRWL-106
89BlaYNPRWLU-42
89BlaYNPRWLU-54
89BlaYNPRWLU-64
89WicChaR-20
89WicStaR-16
89WicWraR-10
90TexLeaAGS-12
90WicWraRD-2
91Bow-643
91LasVegSLD-278
91LasVegSP-226
91LinDriAAA-278
92BrePol-4
92Cla2-T11
92ClaGam-60
92Don-545
92Fle-600
92Lea-500
92OPC-711
92Sco-758
92StaClu-109
92Stu-192
92Top-711
92TopDeb91-17
92TopGol-711
92TopGolW-711
92TopMic-711
92TopTra-13T
92TopTraG-13T
92Ult-378
92UppDec-623
92UppDec-762
93BrePol-2
93Don-413
93Fle-247
93Lea-122
93OPC-33
93PacBeiA-9
93PacSpa-508
93Pin-393
93Sco-470
93StaClu-225
93StaCluFDI-225
93StaCluMOP-225
93Top-71
93TopGol-71
93TopInaM-71
93TopMic-71
93Ult-568
93UppDec-328
93UppDecGold-328
94BreMilB-199
94BrePol-2
94ColC-57
94ColChoGS-57
94ColChoSS-57
94Don-59
94ExtBas-98
94Fin-293
94FinRef-293
94Fla-63
94Fle-174
94Lea-222
94LeaL-42
94Pac-326
94Pin-123
94PinArtP-123
94PinMusC-123
94Sco-236
94ScoGolR-236
94SP-56
94SPDieC-56
94StaClu-398
94StaClu-564
94StaCluFDI-398
94StaCluFDI-564
94StaCluGR-398
94StaCluGR-564
94StaCluMOP-398
94StaCluMOP-564
94Stu-42
94Top-367
94TopGol-367
94TopSpa-367
94TriPla-51
94Ult-370
95ColCho-185
95ColChoGS-185
95ColChoSE-68
95ColChoSEGS-68
95ColChoSESS-68
95ColChoSS-185
95Don-143
95DonPreP-143
95DonTopotO-95
95Emo-52
95Fin-234
95FinRef-234
95Fla-50
95Fle-174
95FleTeaL-8
95Lea-388
95PacPri-74
95Pin-218
95PinArtP-218
95PinMusC-218
95Sco-98
95ScoGolR-98
95ScoPlaTS-98
95SP-163
95SPCha-163
95SPCha-166
95SPChaDC-163
95SPChaDC-166
95SPSil-163
95StaClu-199
95StaCluFDI-199
95StaCluMOP-199
95StaCluSTWS-199
95StaCluVR-105
95Top-35
95TopCyb-27
95Ult-62
95UltGolM-62
95UppDec-298
95UppDecED-298
95UppDecEDG-298
95UppDecSE-101
95UppDecSEG-101
96Cir-49
96CirRav-49
96ColCho-589
96ColChoGS-589
96ColChoSS-589
96Don-118
96DonPreP-118
96EmoXL-71
96Fin-B55
96FinRef-B55
96Fla-97
96Fle-141
96FleTif-141
96LeaSigA-28
96LeaSigAG-28
96LeaSigAS-28
96MetUni-68
96MetUniP-68
96Pac-345
96PacEstL-EL5
96PacPri-P108
96PacPriG-P108
96PanSti-192
96Sco-63
96StaClu-136
96StaCluMOP-136
95StaCluVRMC-105
96Top-396
96Ult-77
96UltGolM-77
96UppDec-362
97Ult-331
97UltGolME-331
97UltPlaME-331
97UppDec-97
Bonetti, Julio
93ConTSN-965
Bongiovanni, Nino (Anthony)
38CinOraW-2
39OrcPhoAP-2
Bonham, Bill
72OPC-29
72Top-29A
72Top-29B
73LinPor-39
73OPC-328
73Top-328
74OPC-528
74Top-528
75OPC-85
75Top-85
76OPC-151
76SSP-303
76Top-151
77BurCheD-192
77CubJewT-2
77OPC-95
77Top-446
78Pep-5
78SSP270-112
78Top-276
79Kel-31
79OPC-182
79Top-354
80OPC-26
80RedEnq-42
80Top-47
81Fle-215A
81Fle-215B
81IndIndTI-13
81Top-712
86AubAstP-5
Bonham, Tiny (Ernie)
43MPR302-1-1
43YanSta-1
47TipTop-137
49Bow-77
49EurSta-154
85TCMPla1-41
92YanWIZA-5
Boni, Joel
82MadMusF-2
Bonifay, Ken
92AugPirC-18
92SalBucF-70
93CarLeaAGF-45
93SalBucC-1
93SalBucF-437
95LynHilTI-2
96CarMudB-17
Bonifazio, Anthony
93LetMouF-4158
93LetMouSP-8
Bonikowski, Joe
61TwiCloD-4
62Top-592
Bonilla, Bobby
83AleDukT-16
86DonRoo-30
86FleUpd-15
86SpoRoo-26
86TopTra-12T
86TopTraT-12T
86WhiSoxC-26
87Don-558
87DonOpeD-167
87Fle-605
87FleGlo-605
87SpoTeaP-18
87Top-184
87TopTif-184
88ClaBlu-236
88Don-238
88DonBasB-33
88Fle-323
88FleBasA-3
88FleGlo-323
88FleHotS-3
88FleMin-103
88FleSlu-3
88FleStiC-114
88GreBasS-62
88Lea-188
88OPC-189
88PanSti-372
88PanSti-373
88Sco-116
88ScoGlo-116
88ScoYouS2-9
88Spo-131
88StaLinPi-3
88Top-231
88Top-681
88TopBig-25
88TopCoi-37
88TopSti-129
88TopTif-231
88TopTif-681
89Bow-422
89BowTif-422
89CadEllD-3
89Don-2
89Don-151
89DonAll-39
89DonBasB-33
89DonPop-39
89DonSupD-2
89Fle-203
89Fle-637
89FleAll-1
89FleBasA-4
89FleGlo-203
89FleGlo-637
89MSAHolD-15
89Nis-15
89OPC-142
89PanSti-171
89PanSti-234
89PirVerFJ-25

89RedFolSB-10
89Sco-195
89ScoHot1S-42
89Spo-182
89SpoIllFKI-181
89Top-388
89Top-440
89TopBasT-114
89TopBig-159
89TopCoi-5
89TopDouA-15
89TopGloA-15
89TopGloS-24
89TopMinL-30
89TopSti-131
89TopSti-158
89TopStiB-40
89TopTif-388
89TopTif-440
89TopUKM-6
89TVSpoM-10
89UppDec-578
90Bow-169
90BowTif-169
90ClaBlu-143
90ClaYel-T73
90Don-290
90DonBesN-70
90DOnBonM-BC16
90Fle-462
90FleBasA-2
90FleBasM-4
90FleCan-462
90GooHumICBLS-4
90Hot50PS-3
90KinDis-8
90Lea-196
90LeaPre-10
90MLBBasB-38
90MSAIceTD-11
90MSASupS-11
90OPC-273
90PanSti-325
90PirHomC-6
90PubSti-150
90PubSti-253
90Sco-170
90Sco100S-37
90Spo-195
90StaLonJS-5
90StaLonJS-31
90Top-273
90TopBig-208
90TopCoi-41
90TopDou-6
90TopMag-43
90TopMinL-71
90TopSti-129
90TopStiB-7
90TopTif-273
90TopTVA-59
90UppDec-16
90UppDec-366
90USPlaCA-11H
90VenSti-57
90VenSti-58
91Bow-381
91Bow-525
91CadEllD-6
91Cla2-T92
91Cla3-T4
91Cla3-NNO
91ClaGam-144
91DenHol-17
91Don-325
91DonGraS-2
91Fle-34
91Fle-711
91Lea-357
91MLBKeyC-1
91OPC-403
91OPC-750
91PanCanT1-18
91PanCanT1-50
91PanFreS-120
91PanSti-111
91PepSup-15
91Pos-14
91RedFolS-10
91Sco-315
91Sco-402
91Sco-670
91Sco100S-42
91StaClu-139
91StaCluP-6
91StaPinB-5
91StaPro-2
91Stu-223
91SunSee-3
91Top-403
91Top-750
91TopCraJ2-15
91TopDesS-403
91TopDesS-750
91TopMic-403
91TopMic-750
91TopSta-5
91TopTif-403
91TopTif-750
91TopTriH-N9
91Ult-276
91UppDec-152
91UppDecFE-99F
91UppDecSS-SS15
91USPlaCA-JKO
92Bow-235
92Cla2-T47
92ClaGam-176
92Don-427
92Don-610
92DonCraJ2-18
92DonUpd-U20
92Fle-551
92Fle-699
92FleAll-4
92FleTeaL-9
92FleUpd-101
92HitTheBB-6
92JimDea-16
92KinDis-5
92Lea-308
92Lea-463
92MetColP-2
92MetKah-25
92MSABenSHD-20
92OPC-160
92OPCPre-143
92PanSti-256
92Pin-310
92Pin-395
92PinSlu-6
92Pos-21
92RemUltP-P1
92RemUltP-P2
92RemUltP-P3
92RemUltP-P16
92RemUltP-P17
92RemUltP-P18
92Sco-225
92Sco100S-80
92ScoRoo-5T
92SpoIllFK1-68
92SpoStaCC-5
92StaClu-608
92StaClu-780
92StaCluD-19
92StaCluECN-608
92Stu-61
92SunSee-16
92Top-160
92Top-392
92TopGol-160
92TopGol-392
92TopGolW-160
92TopGolW-392
92TopKid-22
92TopMcD-9
92TopMic-160
92TopMic-392
92TopTra-14T
92TopTraG-14T
92TriPlaG-GS1
92Ult-527
92UppDec-225
92UppDec-755
92UppDecF-15
92UppDecFG-15
93Bow-158
93ClaGam-15
93DiaMar-15
93Don-594
93Fin-66
93FinRef-66
93Fla-89
93Fle-84
93FleAtl-3
93FunPac-124
93Hos-3
93HumDumC-43
93Kra-16
93Lea-236
93MetBak-3
93MetColP-22
93MetKah-25
93OPC-15
93PacJugC-22
93PacSpa-192
93PacSpaGE-2
93PanSti-253
93Pin-43
93PinHomRC-41
93Pos-24
93PosCan-12
93Sco-8
93ScoFra-21
93Sel-11
93SP-146
93StaClu-163
93StaCluFDI-163
93StaCluMOP-163
93Stu-16
93Top-52
93TopGol-52
93TopInaM-52
93TopMic-52
93TopPreS-2
93TriPla-173
93TriPlaA-2
93Ult-422
93UppDec-275
93UppDec-484
93UppDec-826
93UppDecGold-275
93UppDecGold-484
93UppDecGold-826
93UppDecHRH-HR23
94Bow-128
94BowBes-R50
94BowBesR-R50
94ColC-58
94ColChoGS-58
94ColChoHRA-HA4
94ColChoSS-58
94DenHol-7
94Don-347
94DonDiaK-DK13
94DonMVP-9
94DonSpeE-347
94ExtBas-315
94Fin-234
94FinJum-234
94FinRef-234
94Fla-407
94Fle-558
94FleAllS-32
94FleTeaL-23
94FUnPac-127
94FUnPac-223
94Kra-18
94Lea-31
94LeaCleC-4
94LeaL-129
94MetColP-2
94MetShuST-4
94OPC-202
94OscMayR-18
94Pac-396
94PacAll-6
94PacGolP-17
94PanSti-215
94Pin-33
94PinArtP-33
94PinMusC-33
94Pos-10
94ProMag-91
94RedFolMI-6
94Sco-378
94ScoGolR-378
94ScoGolS-26
94Sel-238
94SP-115
94SPDieC-115
94Spo-49
94StaClu-59
94StaCluFDI-59
94StaCluGR-59
94StaCluMOP-59
94StaCluMOP-ST9
94StaCluST-ST9
94Stu-113
94SucSav-18
94TomPiz-4
94Top-730
94TopGol-730
94TopSpa-730
94TopSupS-6
94TriPla-141
94Ult-528
94UppDec-275
94UppDec-344
94UppDecAJ-41
94UppDecAJG-41
94UppDecED-275
94UppDecED-344
94USPlaCA-3C
95Baz-36
95Bow-284
95BowBes-R11
95BowBesR-R11
95ColCho-320
95ColChoGS-320
95ColChoSE-145
95ColChoSEGS-145
95ColChoSESS-145
95ColChoSS-320
95D3-22
95Don-308
95DonDiaK-DK8
95DonPreP-308
95DonTopotO-5
95Emb-38
95EmbGolI-38
95Emo-158
95Fin-104
95FinRef-104
95Fla-169
95Fle-365
95FleTeaL-23
95Lea-295
95LeaLim-15
95Pac-277
95PacGolP-23
95PacPri-90
95PanSti-51
95Pin-5
95PinArtP-5
95PinMusC-5
95RedFol-26
95Sco-424
95ScoGolR-424
95ScoHaloG-HG64
95ScoPlaTS-424
95Sel-47
95SelArtP-47
95SelCer-34
95SelCerMG-34
95SP-80
95SPCha-70
95SPChaDC-70
95Spo-18
95SpoArtP-18
95SPSil-80
95StaClu-118
95StaClu-312
95StaClu-504
95StaCluCC-CC7
95StaCluFDI-118
95StaCluMOP-118
95StaCluMOP-312
95StaCluMOP-504
95StaCluMOP-CC7
95StaCluSTWS-118
95StaCluSTWS-312
95StaCluSTWS-504
95StaCluVR-60
95Stu-105
95Sum-76
95SumNthD-76
95Top-502
95TopCyb-292
95UC3-34
95UC3ArtP-34
95UC3CycS-CS15
95Ult-195
95UltGolM-195
95UppDec-360
95UppDec-470T
95UppDecED-360
95UppDecEDG-360
95UppDecSE-60
95UppDecSEG-60
95Zen-9
96Baz-63
96Bow-39
96ColCho-464
96ColChoGS-464
96ColChoSS-464
96ColChoYMtP-9
96ColChoYMtP-9A
96ColChoYMtPGS-9
96ColChoYMtPGS-9A
96Don-225
96DonPreP-225
96EmoXL-3
96Fin-B175
96FinRef-B175
96Fla-3
96Fle-5
96FleOri-4
96FleTif-5
96Lea-120
96LeaPrePB-120
96LeaPrePG-120
96LeaPrePS-120
96LeaPreSG-34
96LeaPreSte-34
96LeaSig-139
96LeaSigPPG-139
96LeaSigPPP-139
96MetKah-4
96MetMod-1
96MetTeal-1
96MetUni-3
96MetUniP-3
96MLBPin-5
96Pac-242
96PacEstL-EL6
96PacPri-P74
96PacPriG-P74
96PanSti-133
96Pin-30
96PinAfi-41
96PinAfiAP-41
96PinAfiFPP-41
96PinArtP-14
96PinSta-14
96ProMagDM-5
96ProSta-77
96Sco-167
96ScoDugC-A95
96ScoDugCAP-A95
96Sel-75
96SelArtP-75
96SelTeaN-20
96SP-32
96Spo-47
96SpoArtP-47
96StaClu-146
96StaCluEPB-146
96StaCluEPG-146
96StaCluEPS-146
96StaCluMOP-146
95StaCluVRMC-60
96Stu-27
96StuPrePB-27
96StuPrePG-27
96StuPrePS-27
96Sum-52
96SumAbo&B-52
96SumArtP-52
96SumFoi-52
96Top-329
96TopChr-131
96TopChrR-131
96TopGal-36
96TopGalPG-PG13
96TopGalPPI-36
96TopLas-20
96Ult-3
96UltGolM-3
96UltThu-3
96UltThuGM-3
96UppDec-279
97Bow-63
97BowInt-63
97Cir-231
97CirRav-231
97Don-102
97DonEli-45
97DonEliGS-45
97DonLim-152
97DonLimFotG-44
97DonLimLE-152
97DonPre-27
97DonPreCttC-27
97DonPreP-102
97DonPrePGold-102
97Fin-199
97FinRef-199
97FlaSho-A88

97FlaSho-B88
97FlaSho-C88
97FlaShoLC-88
97FlaShoLC-B88
97FlaShoLC-C88
97FlaShoLCM-A88
97FlaShoLCM-B88
97FlaShoLCM-C88
97Fle-3
97Fle-536
97FleTif-3
97FleTif-536
97Lea-262
97LeaFraM-262
97LeaFraMDC-262
97MetUni-170
97NewPin-28
97NewPinAP-28
97NewPinMC-28
97NewPinPP-28
97Pac-20
97PacLatotML-4
97PacLigB-20
97PacSil-20
97PinCer-77
97PinCerMBlu-77
97PinCerMG-77
97PinCerMR-77
97PinCerR-77
97PinIns-53
97PinInsCE-53
97PinInsDE-53
97PinTotCPB-77
97PinTotCPG-77
97PinTotCPR-77
97PinX-P-107
97PinX-PMoS-107
97PinX-PSfF-54
97PinX-PSfFU-54
97ProMag-14
97ProMagML-14
97Sco-123
97Sco-347
97ScoHobR-347
97ScoOri-6
97ScoOriPl-6
97ScoOriPr-6
97ScoPreS-123
97ScoResC-347
97ScoShoS-123
97ScoShoS-347
97ScoShoSAP-123
97ScoShoSAP-347
97Sel-65
97SelArtP-65
97SelRegG-65
97SP-80
97Spolll-82
97SpollIEE-82
97StaClu-14
97StaCluMat-14
97StaCluMOP-14
97Stu-75
97StuPrePG-75
97StuPrePS-75
97Top-374
97TopChr-127
97TopChrR-127
97TopGal-16
97TopGalPPI-16
97TopSta-73
97TopStaAM-73
97Ult-360
97UltGolME-360
97UltPlaME-360
97UppDec-535
Bonilla, Denny
96WisTimRB-7
Bonilla, George
85EveGiaC-2A
85EveGiaC-2B
86CliGiaP-3
88ShrCapP-1289
89ShrCapP-1855
90CMC-531
90PhoFirC-4
90PhoFirP-2
90ProAAAF-28
Bonilla, Juan G.
78WatIndT-3
80TacTigT-19
82Don-220
82Fle-567
82Top-464
83AllGamPl-100
83Don-346
83Fle-353
83Top-563
84Don-234
84Fle-295
84Nes792-168
84OPC-168
84Top-168
84TopSti-152
84TopTif-168
85ColCliT-26
85IntLeaAT-26
86TopTra-13T
86TopTraT-13T
87Fle-464
87FleGlo-464
87OPC-131
87Top-668
87TopTif-668
88ChaLooLTI-2
91OriCro-40
92YanWIZ8-14
Bonilla, Miguel
92WelPirC-2
92WelPirF-1314
93AugPirC-4
93AugPirF-1536
93LetMouF-4143
93LetMouSP-9
Bonilla, Welnis
95ButCopKtl-5
Bonin, Greg
88T/MUmp-56
89T/MUmp-54
90T/MUmp-52
Bonine, Eddie
83TucTorT-1
84TucTorC-64
85TucTorC-70
90GatCitPP-3363
90GatCitPSP-22
Bonitio, Arturo
77QuaCitAT-5
Bonitto, Arturo
78QuaCitAT-5
Bonk, Thomas
85GreHorT-5
Bonnano, Robert
96HilStaHWB-21
Bonneau, Britton
93HunCubC-3
93HunCubF-3240
Bonneau, Rob
88WytCubP-1976
Bonnell, Barry (Robert Barry)
78BraCok-1
78Hos-142
78Top-242
79Top-496
80OPC-331
80Top-632
81Don-272
81Fle-413
81OPC-82
81OPCPos-19
81Top-558
82Don-432
82Fle-611
82OPC-99
82Top-99
82TopSti-251
82TopStiV-251
83AllGamPl-48
83Don-430
83Fle-425
83FleSti-109
83OPC-281
83Top-766
83TopSti-133
84Don-559
84Fle-149
84FleUpd-14
84MarMot-2
84Nes792-302
84OPC-302
84Top-302
84TopSti-370
84TopTif-302
84TopTra-14T
84TopTraT-14T
85Don-191
85Fle-485
85Lea-195
85MarMot-10
85OPC-107
85Top-423
85TopSti-342
85TopTif-423
86Fle-460
86MarMot-10
86OPC-119
86Top-119
86TopTif-119
91PacSenL-123
92Nab-6
Bonner, Bob (Robert A.)
80RocRedWT-1
81RocRedWT-2
81RocRedWW-21
82Don-610
82Top-21
83Fle-53
83RocRedWT-14
84RocRedWT-13
91OriCro-41
Bonner, Jeff (Jeffry)
89CliGiaP-892
90CliGiaB-5
90CliGiaP-2560
91Cla/Bes-76
91SanJosGC-9
91SanJosGP-22
Bonner, Mark
82DanSunF-25
83RedPioT-4
85MidAngT-5
Bonnici, James
92BelMarC-18
92BelMarF-1446
93RivPilCLC-4
94RivPilCLC-8
95Bes-42
95PorCitRTI-2
95SPML-149
96Bow-307
96Exc-102
96TacRaiB-5
96Top-425
97Top-202
Bonura, Tony
86SalAngC-93
Bonura, Zeke (Henry John)
34BatR31-37
34BatR31-141
34DiaStaR-65
35DiaMatCS3T1-13
35ExhFou-10
35GouPuzR-8B
35GouPuzR-9B
36ExhFou-10
36GouBWR-2
36GouWidPPR-B3
36GouWidPPR-C4
36NatChiFPR-13
36OveCanR-5
36R31PasP-41
36SandSW-3
36WorWidGV-112
37ExhFou-10
37OPCBatUV-116
37WheBB14-1
37WheBB6-3
37WheBB7-29A
37WheBB9-1
38GouHeaU-252
38GouHeaU-276
38WheBB15-1
39GouPreR303A-5
39PlaBal-144
39WorWidGTP-5
39WorWidGV-3
40PlaBal-131
76ChiGre-3
79DiaGre-139
83DiaClaS2-63
85WhiSoxC-0
88ConSer5-4
91ConTSN-237
93ConTSN-738
Booker, Eric
90ProAaA-168
90SouOreAB-10
90SouOreAP-3429
91Cla/Bes-286
91ModA'sC-16
91ModA'sP-3101
92ClaFS7-34
92MadMusC-11
92MadMusF-1248
92ModA'sC-9
Booker, Greg
83LasVegSBHN-1
84LasVegSC-218
85Fle-27
85PadMot-22
85Top-262
85TopTif-262
86LasVegSP-2
86Top-429
86TopTif-429
87TopTra-6T
87TopTraT-6T
88Don-311
88Fle-577
88FleGlo-577
88PadCok-51
88PadSmo-4
88Sco-447
88ScoGlo-447
88Top-727
88TopTif-727
89Sco-417
89Top-319
89TopBig-194
89TopTif-319
89UppDec-641
90CMC-536
90PhoFirC-9
90PhoFirP-3
90ProAAAF-29
90PubSti-44
90VenSti-59
93CarLeaAGF-26
93KinIndC-29
93KinIndF-2264
93KinIndTI-30
94KinIndC-24
94KinIndF-2661
Booker, Kevin
92HunCubC-8
92HunCubF-3160
93GenCubC-5
93GenCubF-3189
94HicCraC-4
94HicCraF-2187
Booker, Rod
82OrlTwi8SCT-1
82TolMudHT-12
83ArkTraT-19
84LouRedR-12
86ArkTraP-2
86LouRedTI-7
87FleUpd-7
87FleUpdG-7
87LouRedTI-6
88LouRedBTI-10
88StaLinCa-1
88Top-483
88TopTif-483
89LouRedBC-8
89LouRedBP-1264
89LouRedBTI-11
89TopBig-256
89UppDec-644
90PhiTas-2
91Fle-388
91OPC-186
91PhiMed-5
91Top-186
91TopDesS-186
91TopMic-186
91TopTif-186
92TucTorF-493
92TucTorS-602
Boomer, Mascot
95TreThuTI-30
96TreThuB-30
Boone, Aaron
94BilMusF-3674
94BilMusSP-3
94SigRooDP-62
94SigRooDPS-62
94StaCluDP-10
94StaCluDPFDI-10
95Bes-65
95Bow-246
95BowGolF-246
95Exc-172
95ExcFirYP-4
95SPML-40
95SPMLA-5
95SPMLDtS-DS17
95Top-581
95UppDecML-95
96Bow-235
96ChaLooB-7
96Exc-146
97Bow-139
97BowBes-125
97BowBesAR-125
97BowBesR-125
97BowChr-147
97BowChrI-147
97BowChrIR-147
97BowChrR-147
97BowInt-139
97ColCho-467
97Fle-754
97FleTif-754
97SP-7
97Top-204
95UppDecMLFS-95
Boone, Antonio
91HamRedC-13
91HamRedP-4028
92HamRedC-9
92HamRedF-1580
Boone, Bob (Robert Raymond)
73LinPor-142
73OPC-613
73Top-613
74OPC-131
74PhiJohP-8
74Top-131
74TopSta-71
75OPC-351
75Top-351
76OPC-67
76OPC-318
76SSP-471
76Top-67
76Top-318
77BurCheD-164
77OPC-68
77RCColC-6
77Top-545
78Hos-29
78OPC-141
78PhiSSP-33
78RCColC-78
78SSP270-33
78Top-161
79Hos-113
79OPC-38
79PhiBurK-2
79PhiTeal-2
79Top-90
80OPC-246
80PhiBurK-2
80Top-470
81AllGamPl-129
81CokTeaS-97
81Don-262
81Fle-4
81FleStiC-79
81OPC-290
81Top-290
81TopSti-203
81TopSupHT-79
82Don-471
82Fle-240
82OPC-23
82OPC-392
82Top-615
82Top-616
82TopSti-77
82TopStiV-77
82TopTra-9T
83AllGamPl-37
83Don-192
83Fle-79
83FleSta-20
83FleSti-34
83OPC-366
83PhiPosGPaM-3
83Top-765
83TopSti-45
84AllGamPl-127
84AngSmo-3
84Don-158
84Fle-509
84Fle-637
84Nes792-520

84OPC-174
84Top-520
84TopSti-234
84TopTif-520
85AllGamPI-37
85AngSmo-3
85Don-230
85Fle-295
85OPC-348
85Top-133
85Top-348
85TopSti-228
85TopTif-133
85TopTif-348
86AngSmo-3
86Don-17
86Don-230
86DonSupD-17
86Fle-149
86Lea-17
86OPC-62
86Top-62
86TopSti-179
86TopTif-62
87Don-233
87DonHig-41
87Fle-73
87FleAwaW-4
87FleGlo-73
87Lea-202
87OPC-166
87Top-166
87Top-556
87TopSti-180
87TopTif-166
87TopTif-556
88AlaGolAA'TI-10
88AngSmo-9
88Don-305
88DonBasB-3
88Fle-485
88FleGlo-485
88Lea-151
88OPC-158
88OPCBoxB-D
88PanSti-39
88Sco-63
88ScoGlo-63
88Spo-212
88StaLinAn-1
88Top-498
88TopBig-30
88TopSti-5
88TopSti-182
88TopTif-498
88TopUKM-6
88TopUKMT-6
88TopWaxBC-D
89AngSmo-17
89Bow-119
89BowTif-119
89ClaTraP-187
89Don-170
89DonBasB-263
89DonTra-5
89Fle-469
89FleGlo-469
89FleUpd-36
89OPC-243
89PanSti-287
89Sco-233
89ScoHot1S-81
89ScoRoo-74T
89Spo-40
89Top-243
89Top-404
89TopBasT-135
89TopBig-269
89TopSti-175
89TopStiB-22
89TopTif-243
89TopTif-404
89TopTra-12T
89TopTraT-12T
89UppDec-119
89UppDec-767
90Bow-373
90BowTif-373
90Don-326
90DonBesA-50
90Fle-102
90FleAwaW-5
90FleCan-102
90Lea-46
90MLBBasB-107
90OPC-671
90PubSti-278
90PubSti-343
90Sco-60
90Spo-40
90Top-671
90TopBig-268
90TopTif-671
90UppDec-271
90VenSti-60
90VenSti-61
91Don-356
91Fle-551
91UppDec-502
92TacTigS-549
94RedKah-33
94TedWil-72
94Yoo-3
96RoyPol-3
97RoyPol-5

Boone, Bret

88AlaGolTI-3
90TopMag-101
91Bow-261
91JacSunLD-330
91JacSunP-155
91LinDriAA-330
92Bow-511
92CalCanF-3740
92CalCanS-55
92DonRooP-BC2
92FleUpd-54
92LeaGolR-BC12
92ProFS7-142
92ScoRoo-104T
92SkyAAAF-24
92TriA AAS-55
92UppDec-771
93Bow-219
93ClaFS7-63
93Don-188
93Fle-304
93Lea-546
93OPC-13
93PacSpa-280
93Pin-243
93PinRooTP-5
93PinTea2-8
93Sco-335
93ScoProaG-3
93Sel-326
93SelChaR-21
93SelRoo-58T
93StaClu-532
93StaCluFDI-532
93StaCluMari-6
93StaCluMOP-532
93Top-808
93TopGol-808
93TopInaM-808
93TopMic-808
93Toy-35
93TriPla-133
93Ult-266
93UppDec-65
93UppDecGold-65
93UppDecSH-HI6
94Bow-458
94ColC-59
94ColC-544
94ColChoGS-59
94ColChoGS-544
94ColChoSS-59
94ColChoSS-544
94Don-413
94ExtBas-227
94Fin-386
94FinRef-386
94Fla-143
94Fle-280
94FleUpd-114
94FUnPac-105
94Lea-233
94LeaL-94
94OPC-170
94PanSti-116
94Pin-510
94PinArtP-510
94PinMusC-510
94RedKah-1
94Sco-568
94ScoBoyoS-26
94ScoGolR-568
94ScoRoo-RT60
94ScoRooGR-RT60
94Sel-265
94SP-158
94SPDieC-158
94SpoRoo-14
94SpoRooAP-14
94SpoRooS-14
94StaClu-671
94StaCluFDI-671
94StaCluGR-671
94StaCluMOP-671
94Stu-167
94Top-659
94TopGol-659
94TopSpa-659
94TopTra-77T
94Ult-468
94UppDec-448
94UppDecED-448
94USPlaCR-8C
95Baz-49
95ColCho-427
95ColChoGS-427
95ColChoSE-198
95ColChoSEGS-198
95ColChoSESS-198
95ColChoSS-427
95D3-33
95Don-26
95DonPreP-26
95DonTopotO-208
95Emb-18
95EmbGolI-18
95Emo-115
95Fin-54
95FinRef-54
95Fla-119
95Fle-429
95Lea-97
95LeaLim-22
95Pac-99
95PacGolP-29
95PacPri-32
95PanSti-44
95Pin-317
95PinArtP-317
95PinMusC-317
95PinUps-US27
95RedKah-3
95Sco-455
95ScoGolR-455
95ScoHaloG-HG95
95ScoPlaTS-455
95Sel-8
95SelArtP-8
95SP-44
95SPCha-37
95SPChaDC-37
95Spo-47
95SpoArtP-47
95SPSil-44
95SPSpeF-31
95StaClu-252
95StaCluFDI-252
95StaCluMOP-252
95StaCluSTDW-RE252
95StaCluSTWS-252
95StaCluVR-124
95Stu-139
95Sum-59
95SumNthD-59
95Top-113
95Top-385
95TopCyb-73
95Ult-363
95UltGolM-363
95UppDec-165
95UppDecED-165
95UppDecEDG-165
95UppDecPLL-R58
95UppDecPLLE-R58
95UppDecSE-164
95UppDecSEG-164
95UppDecSoaD-SD14
96Baz-47
96Cir-114
96CirRav-114
96ColCho-515
96ColChoGS-515
96ColChoSS-515
96Don-178
96DonPreP-178
96EmoXL-161
96Fin-S65
96FinRef-S65
96Fla-227
96Fle-334
96FleTif-334
96Lea-65
96LeaPrePB-65
96LeaPrePG-65
96LeaPrePS-65
96MetUni-147
96MetUniP-147
96Pac-35
96PacPri-P14
96PacPriG-P14
96PanSti-56
96Pin-235
96PinAfi-110
96PinAfiAP-110
96PinArtP-135
96PinFoil-235
96PinSta-135
96ProSta-105
96Sco-70
96ScoDugC-A58
96ScoDugCAP-A58
96Sel-88
96SelArtP-88
96SelTeaN-25
96SP-62
96StaClu-168
96StaCluEPB-168
96StaCluEPG-168
96StaCluEPS-168
96StaCluMOP-168
95StaCluVRMC-124
96Stu-62
96StuPrePB-62
96StuPrePG-62
96StuPrePS-62
96Sum-133
96SumAbo&B-133
96SumArtP-133
96SumFoi-133
96Top-162
96TopGal-119
96TopGalPG-PG4
96TopGalPPI-119
96Ult-174
96UltGolM-174
96UppDec-50
96UppDecPRE-R56
96UppDecPreR-R56
97Bow-50
97BowInt-50
97Cir-125
97CirRav-125
97ColCho-302
97Don-195
97DonPreP-195
97DonPrePGold-195
97FlaSho-A86
97FlaSho-B86
97FlaSho-C86
97FlaShoLC-86
97FlaShoLC-B86
97FlaShoLC-C86
97FlaShoLCM-A86
97FlaShoLCM-B86
97FlaShoLCM-C86
97Fle-290
97FleTif-290
97Lea-163
97LeaFraM-163
97LeaFraMDC-163
97MetUni-44
97Pac-262
97PacLigB-262
97PacPri-90
97PacPriLB-90
97PacPriP-90
97PacSil-262
97Sco-63
97ScoPreS-63
97ScoShoS-63
97ScoShoSAP-63
97SP-51
97StaClu-170
97StaCluMOP-170
97Top-135
97TopChr-52
97TopChrR-52
97Ult-174
97UltGolME-174
97UltPlaME-174
97UppDec-340

Boone, Danny

79SalLakCGT-23B
82Don-187
82Fle-568
82Top-407
83TucTorT-2
84VanCanC-36
85AncGlaPTI-5
90CMC-689
90El PasDAGTI-38
90ProAAAF-455
90RocRedWC-27
90RocRedWGC-15
90RocRedWP-698
91OriCro-42
91PacSenL-44
91Sco-715

Boone, Ike (Isaac Morgan)

36GouWidPPR-D4
87ConSer2-24
88LitSunMLL-3
90DodTar-61

Boone, Luke (Lute Joseph)

14B18B-20
15SpoNewM-12

Boone, Ray (Raymond Otis)

49IndTeal-5
50IndNumN-4
50IndTeal-3
51Bow-54
51TopRedB-23
52Bow-214
52IndNumN-13
52Top-55
53BowC-79
53IndPenCBP-5
53Top-25
54Top-77
55RedMan-AL1
55RobGouS-11
55RobGouW-11
55Top-65
55TopDouH-113
56Top-6
56TopHocF-A7
56TopHocF-B9
56TopPin-36
57Top-102
58Top-185
59Top-252
60BraLaktL-3
60Top-281
76OPC-67
76Top-67
79TCM50-179
81TigDetN-84
83TigAIKS-15
83TopRep5-55
85Top-133
85TopTif-133
91TopArc1-25
92BazQua5A-6
93TedWil-36
93UppDecAH-15
94TopArc1-77
94TopArc1G-77
94UppDecAH-22
94UppDecAH1-22

Boone, Ron

75lowOakT-2

Bootay, Kevin

86SalRedBP-1
86TulDriTI-16
88TexLeaAGS-9
88TulDriTI-13
89ScrRedBC-24
89ScrRedBP-713

Booth, David

88PocGiaP-2098
89SanJosGB-10
89SanJosGCLC-228
89SanJosGP-440
89SanJosGS-2

Boothby, John

90WauTimS-4
91BriBanF-12
95AusFut-82
95AusFut-95

Booty, Josh

94Cla#1DPMF-DD5
94ClaUpdCotC-CC5
94SigRooDP-1

94SigRooDPS-1
95ActPacF-56
95ElmPioTI-1
95ElmPioUTI-1
95Exc-193
95KanCouCLTI-1
95KanCouCTI-35
95ScoDraP-DP5
95SigRooDDS-DD2
95SigRooDDSS-DD2
95SPML-63
95UppDecML-135
95UppDecML-219
95UppDecMLOP-OP11
96Bow-161
96KanCouCTI-2
96KanCouCUTI-1
96KanCouCUTI-2
96MauStiHWB-22
97Lea-179
97LeaFraM-179
97LeaFraMDC-179
95UppDecMLFS-135
95UppDecMLFS-219
Boozer, John
63Top-29A
63Top-29B
64PhiPhiB-5
64Top-16
64TopVen-16
65OPC-184
65Top-184
66Top-324
66TopVen-324
68OPC-173
68Top-173
68TopVen-173
69Top-599
89ChaLooLIII-3
Boras, Scott
77St.PetCT-17
Borbon, Ernie
82VerBeaDT-2
83AlbDukT-21
84AlbDukC-159
85DomLeaS-54
Borbon, Pedro
70OPC-358
70Top-358
71OPC-613
71Top-613
73OPC-492
73Top-492
74OPC-410
74Top-410
74TopSta-23
75OPC-157
75Top-157
76LinSup-101
76OPC-77
76SSP-24
76Top-77
77PepGloD-54
77Top-581
78OPC-199
78Pep-6
78SSP270-111
78Top-220
79OPC-164
79Top-326
80Top-627
89PacSenL-49
89T/MSenL-11
89TopSenL-77
90EliSenL-93
92UppDecS-14
Borbon, Pedro Jr.
90Bes-31
90BurBraB-1
90BurBraP-2340
90BurBraS-4
90DurBulUTI-2
90MidLeaASGS-58
90ProAaA-124
91DurBulC-10
91DurBulP-1536
92GreBraF-1148
92GreBraS-229
93Bow-226
93LimRocDWB-45
93RicBraBB-11
93RicBraF-178
93RicBraP-5
93RicBraRC-8
93RicBraRC-7
94BraUSPC-5C
94RicBraF-2839
94StaClu-233
94StaCluFDI-233
94StaCluGR-233
94StaCluMOP-233
94StaCluT-42
94StaCluTFDI-42
95FleUpd-89
96ColCho-391T
96ColCho-459
96ColChoGS-459
96ColChoSS-459
96Don-324
96DonPreP-324
96Fle-288
96FleTif-288
96LeaSigEA-12
96MLBPin-6
96Pac-3
97PacPriGotD-GD110
Borcherding, Mark
89BilMusP-2066
90CedRapRB-24
90ChaWheP-2232
91CedRapRC-2
91CedRapRP-2710
91Cla/Bes-372
91MidLeaAP-MWL21
Borchers, Rick
79TacTugT-3
80TacTigT-21
82ChaLooT-20
Borchert, Shane
89CliGiaP-889
90MadMusB-27
91MadMusC-21
92RenSilSCLC-62
Bordagaray, Frenchy (Stanley)
36ExhFou-2
36GouBWR-3
36GouWidPPR-A9
36NatChiFPR-85
36R31PasP-28
38CinOraW-3
39OrcPhoAP-3
39PlaBal-75
42DodTeal-2
43DodTeal-2
90DodTar-62
Borden, Joe
63GadFunC-47
Border, Bob
78QuaCitAT-6
80ElPasDT-10
Border, Mark
82IdaFalAT-3
Borders, Charlie
75SpoIndC-4
76SacSolC-11
Borders, Pat
85KinBluJT-15
86KnoBluJP-3
87KnoBluJP-1513
88BluJayFS-4
88DonRoo-12
88FleUpd-65
88FleUpdG-65
88ScoRoo-99T
88ScoRooG-99T
88TopTra-17T
88TopTraT-17T
89BluJayFS-3
89Don-560
89Fle-227
89FleGlo-227
89OPC-343
89PanSti-464
89Sco-198
89ScoHot1R-91
89ScoYouSI-11
89Top-693
89TopSti-191
89TopTif-693
89UppDec-593
90BluJayFS-4
90Bow-521
90BowTif-521
90ClaYel-T39
90Don-560
90Fle-77
90FleCan-77
90Lea-343
90OPC-191
90PanSti-175
90PubSti-510
90Sco-288
90Spo-45
90Top-191
90TopBig-60
90TopTif-191
90UppDec-113
90VenSti-62
91BluJayFS-3
91BluJayFS-4
91BluJayS-11
91Bow-14
91Don-317
91Fle-171
91Lea-23
91OPC-49
91PanFreS-335
91PanSti-156
91Sco-425
91StaClu-266
91Top-49A
91Top-49B
91TopDesS-49
91TopMic-49
91TopTif-49
91Ult-359
91UppDec-147
92Bow-646
92Don-379
92Fle-325
92Lea-324
92OPC-563
92PanSti-24
92Pin-421
92Sco-288
92StaClu-77
92Stu-253
92Top-563
92TopGol-563
92TopGolW-563
92TopMic-563
92Ult-144
92UppDec-140
93BluJayCP1-2
93BluJayCP1-5
93BluJayD-21
93BluJayD4-4
93BluJayDM-11
93BluJayDM-25
93BluJayDM-34
93BluJayDWS-8
93BluJayFS-3
93Bow-687
93DiaMar-16
93Don-115
93Fin-133
93FinRef-133
93Fla-288
93Fle-332
93HumDumC-23
93Lea-157
93OPC-58
93OPCWorC-2
93OPCWorSH-1
93PacSpa-321
93PanSti-25
93Pin-203
93PosCan-1
93Sco-642
93Sel-369
93SP-46
93StaClu-1
93StaCluFDI-1
93StaCluM-136
93StaCluMOP-1
93Stu-36
93Top-322
93TopGol-322
93TopInaM-322
93TopMic-322
93TriPla-134
93Ult-287
93UltAwaW-21
93UppDec-149
93UppDecGold-149
94BluJayP-2
94BluJayUSPC-4C
94BluJayUSPC-12H
94Bow-441
94ColC-60
94ColChoGS-60
94ColChoSS-60
94Don-54
94ExtBas-187
94Fin-266
94FinRef-266
94Fla-348
94Fle-325
94Lea-179
94OPC-178
94OPCWorC-8
94Pac-633
94PanSti-135
94Pin-477
94PinArtP-477
94PinMusC-477
94PosCan-7
94PosCanG-7
94Sco-343
94ScoGolR-343
94Sel-74
94StaClu-305
94StaCluFDI-305
94StaCluGR-305
94StaCluMOP-305
94StaCluT-165
94StaCluTFDI-165
94Stu-25
94Top-219
94TopGol-219
94TopSpa-219
94Ult-135
94UppDec-417
94UppDecED-417
95BluJayUSPC-5H
95BluJayUSPC-12C
95ColCho-146
95ColChoGS-146
95ColChoSS-146
95Don-499
95DonPreP-499
95Fla-263
95Fle-88
95FleUpd-44
95Lea-396
95Pac-436
95Sco-154
95ScoGolR-154
95ScoPlaTS-154
95StaClu-141
95StaClu-546
95StaCluFDI-141
95StaCluMOP-141
95StaCluMOP-546
95StaCluSTWS-141
95StaCluSTWS-546
95Top-424
95TopCyb-222
95TopTra-151T
95UppDec-417
95UppDecED-417
95UppDecEDG-417
96CarPol-3
96FleUpd-U184
96FleUpdTC-U184
96LeaSigEA-11
97BluJayS-42
97PacPriGotD-GD27
Bordi, Rich
81TacTigT-10
82SalLakCGT-4
82Top-531
83IowCubT-1
84CubChiT-2
84CubSev-42
85Don-289
85Fle-49
85FleUpd-8
85Lea-166
85Top-357
85TopTif-357
85TopTifT-7T
85TopTra-7T
86Don-518
86Fle-101
86FleUpd-16
86Top-94
86TopTif-94
86TopTra-14T
86TopTraT-14T
87ColCliP-3
87ColCliP-18
87ColCliT-2
87Don-213
87Fle-465
87FleGlo-465
87Top-638
87TopTif-638
88TacTigC-1
88TacTigP-627
89TacTigC-1
89TacTigP-1544
90PhoFirP-4
90ProAAAF-30
91OriCro-43
92YanWIZ8-15
Bordick, Mike (Michael)
87ModA'sC-1
87ModA'sP-6
88HunStaTI-1
88SouLeaAJ-4
89TacTigC-23
89TacTigP-1565
90ProAAAF-145
90TacTigP-98
91Cla2-T58
91LinDriAAA-527
91Sco-339
91TacTigLD-527
91TopDeb90-19
92AthMot-20
92Bow-350
92Don-505
92Fle-251
92Lea-364
92OPC-317
92OPCPre-5
92Pin-462
92Sco-681
92StaClu-272
92Top-317
92TopGol-317
92TopGolW-317
92TopMic-317
92Ult-419
92UppDec-727
93AthMot-7
93Bow-401
93ClaGam-16
93Don-83
93Don-264
93DonSpiotG-SG1
93Fla-256
93Fle-291
93Lea-117
93OPC-57
93PacSpa-217
93PanSti-16
93Pin-85
93Sco-100
93Sel-208
93SP-37
93StaClu-80
93StaCluAt-18
93StaCluFDI-80
93StaCluMOP-80
93Top-639
93TopGol-639
93TopInaM-639
93TopMic-639
93Toy-3
93TriPla-45
93TriPla-64
93Ult-254
93UppDec-189
93UppDecGold-189
94A'sMot-5
94Bow-576
94ColC-61
94ColChoGS-61
94ColChoSS-61
94Don-81
94ExtBas-145
94Fin-81
94FinRef-81
94Fla-89
94Fle-255
94Lea-128
94OPC-264
94Pac-446
94PanSti-107
94Pin-463
94PinArtP-463
94PinMusC-463
94Sco-491
94ScoGolR-491
94Sel-176
94StaClu-227
94StaCluFDI-227

94StaCluGR-227
94StaCluMOP-227
94StaCluMOP-ST25
94StaCluST-ST25
94Top-188
94TopGol-188
94TopSpa-188
94TriPla-1
94Ult-105
94UppDec-174
94UppDecED-174
95A'sCHP-6
95AthMot-10
95ColCho-127
95ColChoGS-127
95ColChoSS-127
95Don-148
95DonPreP-148
95DonTopotO-133
95Fin-176
95FinRef-176
95Fle-240
95Lea-81
95Pac-310
95Pin-219
95PinArtP-219
95PinMusC-219
95Sco-72
95ScoGolR-72
95ScoPlaTS-72
95StaClu-245
95StaCluFDI-245
95StaCluMOP-245
95StaCluSTWS-245
95Top-281
95TopCyb-153
95Ult-91
95UltGolM-91
95UppDec-281
95UppDecED-281
95UppDecEDG-281
96A'sMot-5
96ColCho-639
96ColChoGS-639
96ColChoSS-639
96Don-130
96DonPreP-130
96Fla-144
96Fle-204
96FleTif-204
96LeaSigA-29
96LeaSigAG-29
96LeaSigAS-29
96Pac-391
96Pin-358
96PinFoil-358
96SelCer-86
96SelCerAP-86
96SelCerCB-86
96SelCerCR-86
96SelCerMB-86
96SelCerMG-86
96SelCerMR-86
96SelTeaN-5
96StaClu-89
96StaCluMOP-89
96Sum-95
96SumAbo&B-95
96SumArtP-95
96SumFoi-95
96Ult-398
96UltGolM-398
96UppDec-166
96Zen-68
96ZenArtP-68
96ZenMoz-21
97Cir-120
97CirRav-120
97ColCho-274
97DonTea-44
97DonTeaSPE-44
97Fle-185
97Fle-670
97FleTif-185
97FleTif-670
97Lea-297
97LeaFraM-297
97LeaFraMDC-297
97Pac-166
97PacLigB-166
97PacSil-166
97Sco-465
97ScoHobR-465
97ScoResC-465
97ScoShoS-465
97ScoShoSAP-465
97StaClu-115
97StaCluMOP-115
97Top-86
97Ult-370
97UltGolME-370
97UltPlaME-370
97UppDec-308

Bordley, Bill
79PhoGiaVNB-7
80PhoGiaVNB-10

Borel, Jamie
94BriTigC-6
94BriTigF-3515
95FayGenTI-4
96LakTigB-7

Borg, Bjorn
82MonNew-2

Borg, Gary
86VisOakP-4
87OrlTwiP-16
88OrlTwiB-12
89CalLeaA-34
89StoPorB-18
89StoPorCLC-164
89StoPorP-396
89StoPorS-1

Borgatti, Mike
87HagSunP-1
88VirGenS-2
89WatDiaP-1793
89WatDiaS-1
90HagSunB-19
90HagSunP-1402
90HagSunS-2

Borges, Gary
96PitMetB-4

Borges, George
83MidCubT-15
84PriWilPT-33

Borges, Jose
89ButCopKSP-9

Borgese, Jeff
88CapCodPPaLP-20
90MarPhiP-3201
90ProAaA-194

Borgmann, Bennie
40SolHug-5

Borgmann, Glenn D.
73TacTwiC-2
73OPC-284
73Top-284
74OPC-547
74Top-547
75OPC-127
75Top-127
76OPC-498
76SSP-213
76Top-498
77Top-87
78Top-307
78TwiFriP-2
79Top-431
79TwiFriP-2
80Top-634
81Don-159
81Top-716

Borgogno, Mate
88NebCor-19
89AlaGol-17
90CliGiaUTI-U1
90EveGiaB-16
90EveGiaP-3132
91CliGiaC-11
91CliGiaP-839

Borhinger, Helms
90YakBeaTI-4

Boris, Paul
80NasSouTI-3
81ColCliP-31
81ColCliT-7
83TolMudHT-1
83Top-266
84RicBraT-4

Bork, Frank
64PirKDK-3
65Top-592
66OPC-123
66Top-123
66TopVen-123

Borkowski, Bob (Robert V.)
49PorBeaP-1
52Top-328
53Top-7
54Top-138
55Top-74
55TopDouH-63
83TopRep5-328
91TopArc1-7
94TopArc1-138
94TopArc1G-138
95TopArcBD-110

Borkowski, David
96FayGenB-7

Borland, Scott
83AleDukT-4
84PriWilPT-18
85PriWilPT-15

Borland, Toby
88MarPhiS-4
89SpaPhiP-1037
89SpaPhiS-2
90ClePhiS-2
90StaFS7-70
91Cla/Bes-336
91LinDriAA-502
91ReaPhiLD-502
91ReaPhiP-1363
92ScrRedBF-2440
92ScrRedBS-479
92SkyAAAF-217
92UppDecML-239
93ReaPhiF-289
94ScrRedBF-913
94SpoRoo-45
94SpoRooAP-45
94TopTra-5T
95Fla-176
95Fle-386
95Phi-3
95PhiMel-2
95Sel-214
95SelArtP-214
96ColCho-667
96ColChoGS-667
96ColChoSS-667
96Fle-492
96FleTif-492
96LeaSigA-30
96LeaSigAG-30
96LeaSigAS-30
96Pac-152
96PhiTeal-3
96Ult-517
96UltGolM-517
97PacPriGotD-GD181

Borland, Tom
60Lea-26
60Top-117
60TopVen-117
61Top-419
89AstCol4S-6

Bormann, Mike
83DurBulT-16
85DurBulT-4

Borom, Red (Edward Jones)
76DalCon-3

Boros, Julius
68AtlOil-1

Boros, Steve (Stephen)
58Top-81A
58Top-81B
59Top-331
61TigJayP-1
61Top-348
61TopStal-146
62Jel-16
62Pos-16
62PosCan-16
62SalPlaC-50
62ShiPlaC-50
62TigJayP-1
62TigPosCF-2
62Top-62
62Top-72
62TopStal-42
62TopVen-62
62TopVen-72
63Jel-47
63Pos-47
63Top-532
64Top-131
64TopVen-131
65OPC-102
65RedEnq-2
65Top-102
78TCM60I-88
81ExpPos-1
82ExpPos-2
83A'sGraG-14
83TopTra-13T
84A'sMot-1
84Nes792-531
84Top-531
84TopTif-531
86TopTra-15T
86TopTraT-15T
87Top-143
87TopTif-143
93RoyPol-27

Boroski, Stan
83BelBreF-28
86Ft.MyeRP-4
87Ft.MyeRP-2

Borowicz, Ray
88BurIndP-1801

Borowski, Bill
93CenValRC-28
94CenValRC-30
95SalAvaTI-26
96SalAvaB-29

Borowski, Joe
91KanCouCC-2
91KanCouCP-2652
91KanCouCTI-3
92FreKeyC-23
92FreKeyF-1798
93FreKeyC-4
93FreKeyF-1017
94BowBayF-2406
94OriPro-9
95BowBayTI-12
95RocRedWTI-8
96RicBraB-7
96RicBraUB-4
97Fle-542
97FleTif-542
97Ult-530
97UltGolME-530
97UltPlaME-530

Borowski, Rich
83IdaFalAT-20
84MadMusP-23

Borowsky, Erez
83VisOakF-15
84VisOakT-3
85OrlTwiT-2

Borowy, Hank (Henry)
39ExhSal-4
43YanSta-2
49Bow-134
49EurSta-131
49PhiBul-7
49PhiLumPB-2
50Bow-177
51Bow-250
92YanWIZA-6

Borrelli, Dean
88SouOreAP-1705
89MadMusS-4
90ModA'sC-1
90ModA'sCLC-164
90ModA'sP-2214
91HunStaC-3
91HunStaLD-278
91HunStaP-1798
91HunStaTI-2
91LinDriAA-278
92HunStaF-3952
92HunStaS-304
93TacTigF-3034
94TacTigF-3177

Borrero, Richie
93UtiBluSC-5
93UtiBluSF-3535

Borriello, Sebby
82WisRapTF-13

Borrome, Edmundo
85DomLeaS-208

Borruel, Jeff
78CedRapGT-3

Borski, Jeff
91BelMarC-23
91BelMarP-3655
91Cla/Bes-448
92JacSunF-3700
92SanBerC-7
92SanBerSF-944
93RivPilCLC-5

Borucki, Ray
80PenPilBT-19
80PenPilCT-25
81ReaPhiT-18

Boryczewski, Marty
94LetMouF-3881
94LetMouSP-19
96LakTigB-8

Borzello, Aaire
91JohCitCC-3

Borzello, Mike
93GleFalRC-7
93GleFalRF-4005
94SavCarC-9
94SavCarF-507

Bosarge, Scott
91BelMarC-15
91BelMarP-3667

Bosch, Don (Donald John)
68Top-572
69ExpFudP-3
69Top-578
70ExpPos-12
70OPC-527
70Top-527
72MilBra-38
91MetWIZ-44

Bosco, Joseph
90PeoChiTI-37

Bosco, Mike
89RenSilSCLC-253

Bosetti, Rick (Richard Alan)
76OklCit8TI-10
78Top-710
79BluJayBY-2
79OPC-279
79Top-542
80OPC-146
80Top-277
80TopSup-51
81Don-152
81OPC-46
81OPCPos-18
81Top-46
81TopTra-741
82Don-626
82Fle-88
82TacTigT-33
82Top-392
86BluJayGT-6
92Nab-16
92UppDecS-3

Bosio, Chris
83BelBreF-27
86VanCanP-4
87BrePol-29
87Don-478
87DonRoo-20
87Fle-338
87FleGlo-338
87SpoRool-2
87Top-448
87TopTif-448
88BrePol-29
88Don-117
88DonBasB-295
88Fle-156
88FleGlo-156
88OPC-137
88Sco-38
88ScoGlo-38
88ScoYouSI-4
88StaLinBre-1
88Top-137
88TopTif-137
89Bow-134
89BowTif-134
89BrePol-29
89BreYea-29
89Don-412
89DonBasB-109
89Fle-179
89FleGlo-179
89RedFolSB-11
89Sco-243
89Top-311
89TopTif-311
89UppDec-292
90Bow-389
90BowTif-389
90BreMilB-1
90BrePol-29
90ClaYel-T42
90Don-20

90Don-57
90DonBesA-9
90DonSupD-20
90El PasDAGTI-2
90Fle-316
90FleCan-316
90Lea-26
90OPC-597
90PanSti-99
90PubSti-490
90RedFolSB-8
90Sco-283
90Spo-25
90Top-597
90TopBig-139
90TopMinL-19
90TopSti-205
90TopTif-597
90UppDec-293
90VenSti-63
91Bow-43
91BreMilB-4
91BrePol-3
91Don-160
91Fle-576
91Lea-518
91OPC-217
91Sco-43
91StaClu-164
91StaCluP-7
91Top-217
91TopDesS-217
91TopMic-217
91TopTif-217
91UppDec-529
92BrePol-5
92Don-471
92Hig5-66
92Lea-266
92OPC-638
92PanSti-42
92Pin-367
92Sco-37
92StaClu-578
92Top-638
92TopGol-638
92TopGolW-638
92TopMic-638
92Ult-379
92UppDec-615
93Bow-191
93Don-499
93Fin-140
93FinRef-140
93Fla-267
93Fle-628
93FleFinE-265
93Lea-255
93MarDaiQ-3
93MarMot-20
93MSABenSPD-2
93OPC-60
93OPCPre-3
93PacSpa-619
93Pin-440
93Sco-616
93SelRoo-108T
93StaClu-79
93StaCluFDI-79
93StaCluMari-28
93StaCluMO-3
93StaCluMOP-79
93Stu-14
93Top-775
93TopGol-775
93TopInaM-775
93TopMic-775
93TopTra-28T
93Ult-614
93UppDec-588
93UppDecGold-588
94Bow-613
94BreMilB-200
94ColC-391
94ColChoGS-391
94ColChoSS-391
94Don-546
94ExtBas-161
94Fin-252
94FinRef-252
94Fla-99
94Fle-281
94FleGolM-10
94Lea-9
94MarMot-7
94OPC-134
94Pac-563
94Pin-372
94PinArtP-372
94PinMusC-372
94Sco-264
94Sco-316
94ScoGolR-264
94ScoGolR-316
94SP-103
94SPDieC-103
94StaClu-103
94StaCluFDI-103
94StaCluGR-103
94StaCluMOP-103
94Top-60
94TopGol-60
94TopSpa-60
94TriPla-124
94Ult-417
94UppDec-228
94UppDecED-228
95Don-529
95DonPreP-529
95Fle-262
95Lea-330
95MarMot-11
95MarPac-23
95Pac-391
95Pin-13
95PinArtP-13
95PinMusC-13
95StaClu-92
95StaCluFDI-92
95StaCluMOP-92
95StaCluSTDW-M92
95StaCluSTWS-92
95Top-320
95TopCyb-174
95Ult-99
95UltGolM-99
96ColCho-731
96ColChoGS-731
96ColChoSS-731
96Don-250
96DonPreP-250
96EmoXL-109
96Fla-156
96Fle-229
96FleTif-229
96LanJetB-7
96MarMot-11
96Pac-409
96Sco-417
96StaClu-413
96StaCluMOP-413
96Ult-124
96UltGolM-124
96UppDec-461
97Sco-18
97ScoMar-1
97ScoMarPl-1
97ScoMarPr-1
97ScoPreS-18
97ScoShoS-18
97ScoShoSAP-18

Boskie, Shawn
87PeoChiP-8
89ChaKniTI-17
90ClaYel-T43
90CMC-76
90CubMar-3
90DonLeaS-31
90DonRoo-18
90FleUpd-7
90IowCubC-1
90IowCubP-312
90Lea-519
90ProAAAF-619
90ScoRoo-94T
90TopTra-10T
90TopTraT-10T
90TopTVCu-39
90UppDec-722
91CubMar-47
91CubVinL-6
91Don-241
91Fle-416
91Lea-221
91OPC-254
91Sco-59
91Sco100RS-4
91StaClu-521
91Stu-152
91Top-254
91TopDeb90-20
91TopDesS-254
91TopMic-254
91TopTif-254
91UppDec-471
92CubMar-47
92Fle-377
92Lea-162
92OPC-229
92Pin-527
92Sco-713
92StaClu-284
92Top-229
92TopGol-229
92TopGolW-229
92TopMic-229
92TriPla-246
92Ult-466
93Don-500
93Fle-373
93IowCubF-2128
93StaClu-583
93StaCluFDI-583
93StaCluMOP-583
93Top-563
93TopGol-563
93TopInaM-563
93TopMic-563
94Don-61
94Fle-380
94Pac-95
94PhiMel-3
94StaCluT-353
94StaCluTFDI-353
94Top-177
94TopGol-177
94TopSpa-177
94TopTra-53T
95AngMot-19
95FleUpd-65
96AngMot-17
96LeaSigEA-13
97Fle-36
97FleTif-36
97PacPriGotD-GD2

Bosley, Rich
86BelBreP-2

Bosley, Thad (Thaddis)
75QuaCitAT-29
77SalLakCGC-9
78SSP270-141
78Top-619
79Top-127
80Top-412
81Don-162
81Fle-353
82Top-350
83CubThoAV-20
84CubChiT-3
84CubSev-27
84IowCubT-7
84Nes792-657
84Top-657
84TopTif-657
85CubLioP-2
85CubSev-27
85Don-388
85Top-432
85TopTif-432
86CubGat-27
86CubUno-2
86Don-483
86Fle-361
86Top-512
86TopTif-512
87Don-191
87Fle-555
87FleGlo-555
87FleUpd-8
87FleUpdG-8
87Top-58
87TopTif-58
87TopTra-7T
87TopTraT-7T
88Don-348
88Fle-253
88FleGlo-253
88Top-247
88TopTif-247
89UppDec-591
90RanMot-16
93RanKee-79
94BreMilB-201

Bosman, Dick
67Top-459
68Top-442
69SenTeal-2
69SenTeal8-4
69Top-607
70DayDaiNM-47
70MLBOffS-278
70OPC-68
70OPC-175
70SenPolY-1
70Top-68
70Top-175
70TopScr-6
70TopSup-22
71MLBOffS-530
71OPC-60
71SenPolP-1
71SenTealW-4
71Top-60
71TopCoi-70
71TopGreM-49
71TopSup-7
71TopTat-2
72MilBra-39
72OPC-365
72Top-365
73OPC-640
73Top-640
73TopCanL-7
74OPC-465
74Top-465
75Hos-114
75OPC-7
75OPC-354
75Top-7
75Top-354
76A'sPos-75
76OPC-298
76SSP-483
76Top-298
77Top-101
86BufBisP-2
89PacSenL-20
89RocRedWC-24
89RocRedWP-1641
89SweBasG-124
90CMC-681
90EliSenL-3
90ProAAAF-478
90RocRedWC-26
90RocRedWGC-35
90RocRedWP-721
91LinDriAAA-475
91RocRedWLD-475
91RocRedWP-1919
93RanKee-4
95RanCra-4
96RanMot-28

Boss, David
89HamRedS-5
90HamRedB-8
90HamRedS-7

Bossy, Mike
93Pin-299

Bost, Heath
96AshTouB-8

Bostic, Dwain
92ClaDraP-34
92ClaFS7-424
92GulCoaDF-3571
93GreFalDSP-23

Bostic, Jerry
75SpoIndC-17
76SacSolC-19

Bostic, Josh
95DavLipB-3

Bostic, Randy
94DavLipB-4
95DavLipB-4

Bostock, Jim
93SpoIndC-2
93SpoIndF-3597

Bostock, Lyman Sr.
91NegLeaRL-4
93TedWil-100
95NegLeaL2-2
95NegLeaLI-4

Bostock, Lyman W. Jr.
74TacTwiC-23
76OPC-263
76Top-263
77BurCheD-54
77Hos-102
77Kel-16A
77Kel-16B
77OPC-239
77Spo-5503
77Top-531
78AngFamF-4
78Hos-145
78Kel-46
78RCColC-69
78SSP270-195
78Top-655

Boston, D.J.
91MedHatBJP-4105
91MedHatBJSP-1
92St.CatBJC-11
92St.CatBJF-3392
93HagSunC-3
93HagSunF-1885
93SouAtlLAGF-24
94Bow-347
94BowBes-B50
94BowBesR-B50
94Cla-9
94ClaGolF-21
94DunBluJC-1
94DunBluJF-2567
94ExcAllF-9
94ExcFS7-139
94SP-2
94SPDieC-2
94Top-448
94TopGol-448
94TopSpa-448
94UppDecAHNIL-3
94UppDecML-94
94UppDecML-120
94UppDecML-259
95Exc-134
95KnoSmoF-46
95UppDecML-52
96BesAutSA-8
96CarMudB-18
96SyrChiTI-3
95UppDecMLFS-52

Boston, Daryl L.
82AppFoxF-24
83GleFalWST-1
85Don-33
85FleUpd-9
85TopTifT-8T
85TopTra-8T
85WhiSoxC-8
86BufBisP-3
86Don-86
86Top-139
86TopTif-139
86WhiSoxC-8
87Don-137
87Fle-487
87FleGlo-487
87Top-482
87TopTif-482
87WhiSoxC-4
88BlaYNPRWLU-1
88Fle-393
88FleGlo-393
88Sco-582
88ScoGlo-582
88StaLinWS-3
88Top-739
88TopTif-739
88WhiSoxC-2
89Bow-70
89BowTif-70
89Don-455
89Fle-492
89FleGlo-492
89PanSti-311
89Sco-443
89Top-633
89TopTif-633
89UppDec-496
89WhiSoxC-6
90Bow-317
90BowTif-317
90DonBesN-135
90FleUpd-33
90Lea-514
90OPC-524
90PanSti-52
90PubSti-384
90Sco-213
90ScoRoo-47T

90Top-524
90TopBig-54
90TopTif-524
90TopTra-11T
90TopTraT-11T
90UppDec-529
90VenSti-64
91Bow-476
91Don-210
91Fle-140
91Lea-202
91MetColP-7
91MetKah-8
91MetWIZ-45
91OPC-83
91PanFreS-84
91Sco-618
91StaClu-125
91StaCluP-8
91Stu-201
91Top-83
91TopDesS-83
91TopMic-83
91TopTif-83
91Ult-211
91UppDec-159
92Don-612
92Fle-495
92MetColP-11
92MetKah-6
92OPC-227
92Pin-343
92Sco-276
92StaClu-328
92Top-227
92TopGol-227
92TopGolW-227
92TopMic-227
92Ult-227
93Bow-528
93DiaMar-17
93Don-38
93Fle-85
93Lea-281
93PacSpa-193
93PanSti-254
93Pin-545
93RocUSPC-6H
93RocUSPC-9C
93Sco-447
93StaClu-3
93StaClu-498
93StaCluFDI-3
93StaCluFDI-498
93StaCluMOP-3
93StaCluMOP-498
93StaCluRoc-12
93Top-399
93TopGol-399
93TopInaM-399
93TopMic-399
93TopTra-126T
93Ult-343
93UppDec-203
93UppDec-737
93UppDecGold-203
93UppDecGold-737
94ColC-62
94ColChoGS-62
94ColChoSS-62
94Fle-435
94Pac-190
94Sco-396
94ScoGolR-396
94ScoRoo-RT123
94ScoRooGR-RT123
94Top-106
94TopGol-106
94TopSpa-106
94TopTra-114T
95Top-114

Boswell, Dave
67CokCapTw-7
67DexPre-26
67Top-575
68Top-322
68TopVen-322
69Top-459
70MLBOffS-230
70OPC-70
70OPC-325
70Top-70
70Top-325
71MLBOffS-459
71OPC-675
71Top-675
72MilBra-40
78TwiFri-3
81TCM60I-403
91OriCro-44

Boswell, Ken (Kenneth G.)
68DexPre-15
69MetCit-2
69MetNewYDN-2
69Top-402
69TopTeaP-24
70MetTra-22A
70OPC-196
70OPC-214
70Top-196
70Top-214
71MLBOffS-147
71OPC-492
71Top-492
72MilBra-41
72OPC-305
72OPC-306
72Top-305
72Top-306
73OPC-87
73Top-87
74MetDaiPA-16
74OPC-645
74Top-645
75OPC-479
75Top-479
76OPC-379
76SSP-55
76Top-379
77Top-429
81TCM60I-312
87Met196T-9
89RinPosM1-4
91MetWIZ-46
94Met69CCPP-8
94Met69CS-7
94Met69T-17

Boswell, Mike
87GenCubP-12
88PeoChiTI-6

Botelho, Derek
83OmaRoyT-3
84IowCubT-NNO
85IowCubT-13
87OmaRoyP-10
88LouRedBTI-11
90MarPhiP-3209
91ChaWheC-27
91ChaWheP-2903
91PacSenL-38
92ChaWheF-24
93WinSpiC-26
93WinSpiF-1585
94CarLeaAF-CAR45
94WinSpiC-27
94WinSpiF-288

Bothwell, Monte
77ModA'sC-14

Botkin, Alan
88CapCodPPaLP-81
89JohCitCS-3
90HamRedS-8
90SprCarB-5
91SprCarC-7
91SprCarP-733
92St.PetCC-24
92St.PetCF-2021
93St.PetCC-5
93St.PetCF-2619

Botkin, Mike
83DayBeaAT-24

Bottalico, Ricky (Rick)
92ClaFS7-262
92SpaPhiF-1256
93ClePhiC-4
93ClePhiF-2676
94Bow-496
94BowPre-7
94Cla-22
94ColC-653
94ColChoGS-653
94ColChoSS-653
94ExcFS7-243
94ExcLeaLF-3
94ExtBas-329
94ExtBasMLH-2
94LeaLimR-17
94OPC-204
94ScrRedBF-914
94SigRoo-3
94SigRooS-3
94Ult-541
94UppDec-6
94UppDecED-6
94UppDecML-148
94UppDecML-225
95Bow-275
95BowBes-R90
95BowBesR-R90
95ColCho-367
95ColChoGS-367
95ColChoSS-367
95Don-125
95DonPreP-125
95DonTopotO-299
95Emo-163
95Fla-388
95Fle-387
95Lea-327
95LeaGolR-8
95Phi-4
95PhiMel-3
95Pin-143
95PinArtP-143
95PinMusC-143
95Sco-280
95ScoGolR-280
95ScoPlaTS-280
95ScoRooDT-RDT12
95Stu-52
95Top-59
95UppDec-376
95UppDecED-376
95UppDecEDG-376
95UppDecSE-73
95UppDecSEG-73
96Cir-164
96CirRav-164
96ColCho-249
96ColChoGS-249
96ColChoSS-249
96Don-420
96DonPreP-420
96EmoXL-241
96Fla-329
96Fle-493
96FleTif-493
96Lea-61
96LeaPrePB-61
96LeaPrePG-61
96LeaPrePS-61
96LeaSigA-31
96LeaSigAG-31
96LeaSigAS-31
96MetUni-207
96MetUniP-207
96Pac-160
96PacPri-P50
96PacPriG-P50
96PhiTeal-4
96Pin-73
96Sco-445
96StaClu-169
96StaCluMOP-169
96Top-161
96TopGal-97
96TopGalPPI-97
96Ult-249
96UltGolM-249
96UppDec-428
97Bow-20
97BowChr-16
97BowChrI-16
97BowChrIR-16
97BowChrR-16
97BowInt-20
97Cir-230
97CirRav-230
97ColCho-192
97Fin-77
97FinRef-77
97Fle-408
97FleTif-408
97Lea-164
97LeaFraM-164
97LeaFraMDC-164
97MetUni-200
97Pac-374
97PacLigB-374
97PacSil-374
97Pin-152
97PinArtP-152
97PinMusC-152
97Sco-61
97ScoPreS-61
97ScoShoS-61
97ScoShoSAP-61
97SP-136
97SpoIll-92
97SpoIllEE-92
97StaClu-355
97StaCluMOP-355
97Top-14
97TopChr-8
97TopChrR-8
97TopGal-138
97TopGalPPI-138
97Ult-353
97UltGolME-353
97UltPlaME-353
97UppDec-135

Bottenfield, Brian
92Ft.LauYF-2629

Bottenfield, Kent
87BurExpP-1071
88WesPalBES-4
89JacExpB-9
89JacExpP-163
90JacExpB-16
90JacExpP-1367
91IndIndLD-178
91IndIndP-455
91LinDriAAA-178
92Bow-478
92DonRoo-12
92IndIndF-1853
92IndIndS-178
92SkyAAAF-87
93Don-484
93ExpPosN-6
93FleFinE-90
93FleMajLP-B6
93OPCPre-64
93PacSpa-531
93Pin-617
93Sco-312
93StaClu-101
93StaCluFDI-101
93StaCluMOP-101
93Top-695
93TopGol-695
93TopInaM-695
93TopMic-695
93Ult-62
93UppDec-635
93UppDecGold-635
94Don-528
94Fle-436
94RocPol-4
94StaCluT-108
94StaCluTFDI-108
94Top-589
94TopGol-589
94TopSpa-589
94Ult-183
95TolMudHTI-8
96IowCubB-7

Bottenfield, Keven
88BoiHawP-1628

Bottin, Andy
95EveAqaTI-2
96EveAquB-29

Botting, Ralph
75QuaCitAT-2
76QuaCitAT-3
80SalLakCGT-1
80Top-663
80VenLeaS-168
81SalLakCGT-2
81Top-214
82OmaRoyT-2

Bottomley, Jim (James L.)
21Exh-13
23MapCriV-19
25Exh-59
26Exh-59
26SpoComoA-7
27Exh-30
28PorandAR-A5
28PorandAR-B5
28W56PlaC-C5
29ExhFou-15
29PorandAR-8
31Exh-15
33ButCanV-3
33DouDisP-6
33GeoCMil-6
33Gou-44
33GouCanV-44
33RitCE-11S
33TatOrbSDR-205
34DiaMatCSB-17
34BatR31-8
34BatR31-115
34BatR31-179
34ButPreR-5
34DiaStaR-59
34ExhFou-4
35DiaMatCS3T1-14
35ExhFou-4
35GouPuzR-1H
35GouPuzR-3F
35GouPuzR-5B
35GouPuzR-6B
35GouPuzR-11K
35GouPuzR-13B
35GouPuzR-14F
35GouPuzR-15F
36NatChiFPR-100
36R31Pre-G2
36WorWidGV-85
40PlaBal-236
60Fle-45
61Fle-9
69Baz-7
72FleFamF-6
72LauGreF-13
75SheGrePG-12
75TCMAllG-2
76GrePlaG-12
76RowExh-2
76ShaPiz-142
77BobParHoF-6
77GalGloG-67
80PacLeg-64
80PerHaloFP-142
80SSPHOF-142
81DiaStaCD-119
83CarGreT-1
83DiaClaS2-59
90BasWit-83
90HOFStiB-26
90PerGreM-92
91ConTSN-22
91ConTSN-302
92CarMcD-1
92ConTSN-440
92ConTSN-645
92ConTSNCI-1
93ConTSN-909
94ConTSN-1004
94ConTSNB-1004
95ConTSNGJ-8

Bottoms, Derrick
92AubAstC-19
92AubAstF-1345

Botts, Jacob
91GreFalDSP-9

Botts, Jake
90KisDodD-2
93YakBeaC-5
93YakBeaF-3876

Botz, Bob
77FriOneYW-41

Bouchard, Butch (Emile)
43ParSpo-6
43ParSpo-7

Bouchard, Pierre
72Dia-68
72Dia-69

Bouchee, Ed (Edward F.)
57Top-314
59Top-39
59TopVen-39
60PhiJayP-3
60Top-347
61CubJayP-5
61Top-196
61TopStaI-5
62Jel-182
62Pos-182
62PosCan-182
62SalPlaC-116
62ShiPlaC-116
62Top-497
81TCM60I-328
91MetWIZ-47

Boucher, Denis
88MyrBeaBJP-1168
88SouAtlLAGS-23

89DunBluJS-1
90DunBluJS-2
91BluJayFS-4
91Bow-29
91DonRoo-45
91OPCPre-13
91SyrChiMB-4
91UppDec-761
92ColSprSSS-78
92Don-604
92Sco-848
92SkyAAAF-35
92StaClu-773
92StaCluNC-773
92TopDeb91-18
93Don-755
93Fle-405
93LasVegSF-936
93OPC-22
93Top-541
93TopGol-541
93TopInaM-541
93TopMic-541
94ColC-541
94ColChoGS-541
94ColChoSS-541
94Fin-294
94FinRef-294
94OPC-236
94StaClu-545
94StaCluFDI-545
94StaCluGR-545
94StaCluMOP-545
94Top-164
94TopGol-164
94TopSpa-164
Boudreau, Jim
84MidCubT-4
86ChaOriW-5
Boudreau, Lou (Louis P.)
39ExhSal-5
41DouPlaR-131
43MPR302-1-2
46SpoExcW-2-2
47HomBon-4
47IndTeal-3
47IndVanPP-3
47PM1StaP1-17
47PM1StaP1-18
47PM1StaP1-19
48BluTin-22
48IndTeal-4
49Bow-11
49IndTeal-6
49IndVisEl-2
49IndVisEl-3
49IndVisEl-4
49Lea-106
49MPR302-2-100
50Bow-94
50IndNumN-5
50IndTeal-4
51Bow-62
53BowC-57
53IndPenCBP-6
53RedSoxTI-2
55A'sRodM-5
55Bow-89
56A'sRodM-2
60Fle-16
61Fle-94
75TCMAllG-3
76A'sRodMC-4
76RowExh-5
76ShaPiz-115
76TayBow4-25
77GalGloG-19
79DiaGre-291
79TCM50-287
80MarExhH-2
80PacLeg-79
80PerHaloFP-115
80SSPHOF-115
82GSGalAG-8
82OhiHaloF-16
83DiaClaS2-103
83DonHOFH-12
83TCMPla1942-10
83YanYealT-18
86IndGreT-3
86SpoDecG-17
87SpoRea-38
88PacLegI-106
89PacLegI-166
89PerCelP-7
89SweBasG-80
90PacLeg-9
90PerGreM-63
90SweBasG-31
91SweBasG-12
91TopArc1-304
92ActPacA-7
92ActPacA2-7G
92BazQua5A-19
92MVP-3
92MVP2H-11
93ActPacAC-7
93TedWil-32
93UppDecAH-16
93UppDecS-30
94UppDecAH-204
94UppDecAH1-204
95ConTSN-1425
95ConTSNP-1425
Boudreau, Tommy
91BelMarC-3
91BelMarP-3679
Boudreaux, Corey
93Sou-5
Boudreaux, Eric
87ClePhiP-12
89ReaPhiB-19
89ReaPhiP-668
90CMC-227
90ReaPhiB-3
90ReaPhiP-1214
90ReaPhiS-7
90ScrRedBC-1
Boughton, Mike
96AriBlaDB-10
Bouie, Tony
92AriWilP-2
Bouldin, Carl
63Top-496
64Top-518
Boulo, Tyler
96IdaFalB-2
Boulware, Ben
94HicCraC-5
94HicCraF-2183
95Exc-27
96PriWilCB-5
Bourassa, Jocelyne
72Dia-144
Bourbakis, Michael
95GreFalDTI-10
96GreFalDB-4
96GreFalDTI-3
Bourgeois, Steve
93EveGiaC-5
93EveGiaF-3760
94CliLumF-1971
96Bow-230
96GiaMot-27
94CliLumC-5
Bourjos, Chris (Christopher)
77CedRapGT-22
79PhoGiaVNB-16
80PhoGiaVNB-11
80VenLeaS-70
81RocRedWT-21
81RocRedWW-3
81Top-502
83PorBeaT-14
Bourne, Kendrick
86ElmPioRSP-3
87ElmPio(C-6
88WinHavRSS-5
89ClePhiS-3
Bourne, Tim
95StCatSTI-24
Bournigal, Rafael
89Sta-27
89VerBeaDS-3
90SanAntMGS-5
91VerBeaDC-17
91VerBeaDP-778
92AlbDukF-725
92AlbDukS-5
93AlbDukF-1466
93Don-10
93FleMajLP-B7
93Pin-279
93Sco-307
93StaClu-197
93StaCluFDI-197
93StaCluMOP-197
93Top-651
93TopGol-651
93TopInaM-651
93TopMic-651
93Ult-50
94AlbDukF-847
94DodPol-3
94FleUpd-148
94Pac-303
94SpoRoo-138
94SpoRooAP-138
94StaClu-500
94StaCluFDI-500
94StaCluGR-500
94StaCluMOP-500
95ColCho-217
95ColChoGS-217
95ColChoSS-217
95DodPol-3
95Fla-152
95Fle-534
95Sco-472
95ScoGolR-472
95ScoPlaTS-472
95StaClu-116
95StaCluFDI-116
95StaCluMOP-116
95StaCluSTWS-116
95Top-628
95TopCyb-394
95UppDec-319
95UppDecED-319
95UppDecEDG-319
96A'sMot-26
96LeaSigEA-14
97PacPriGotD-GD79
97Pin-148
97PinArtP-148
97PinMusC-148
97Sco-305
97ScoPreS-305
97ScoShoS-305
97ScoShoSAP-305
Bourque, Pat (Patrick D.)
73OPC-605
73Top-605
74OPC-141
74Top-141
75OPC-502
75Top-502
Bourque, Ray
91StaCluCM-44
Bouton, Jim
62Top-592
63Top-401
64ChatheY-3
64Top-4
64Top-219
64Top-470
64TopCoi-4
64TopCoi-138
64TopSta-45
64TopVen-4
64TopVen-219
64WheSta-7
64YanReqKP-4
65ChaTheY-2
65OPC-30
65OPC-137
65Top-30
65Top-137
65TopEmbl-25
65TopTral-5
66Top-276
66TopVen-276
67CokCapYM-V7
67DexPre-27
67Top-393
68Top-562
69PilPos-35
70DayDaiNM-81
76BooProC-3
76BooProC-14
78TCM60I-77
83Pil69G-1
87AstShoSTw-3
88PacLegI-20
89SweBasG-66
90LitSunW-22
91FouBal-36
91SweBasG-123
92YanWIZ6-13
92YanWIZA-7
93TedWil-60
Bouton, Tony
91GasRanC-1
91GasRanP-2678
92ChaRanC-11
92ChaRanF-2218
Bouvrette, Lionel
43ParSpo-9
Bovee, Mike (Michael)
92AppFoxC-18
92AppFoxF-977
92UppDecML-212
93RocRoyC-3
93RocRoyF-704
94CarLeaAF-CAR14
94WilBluRC-1
94WilBluRF-290
95Bow-114
95Exc-54
95WicWraTI-38
96SigRooOJTP-T2
96WicWraB-2
Bovender, Andy
95AubAstTI-5
96QuaCitRB-9
Bowa, Larry (Lawrence Robert)
70OPC-539
70PhiTeal-1
70Top-539
71MLBOffS-169
71OPC-233
71PhiArcO-1
71Top-233
71TopTat-127
72Dia-55
72OPC-520
72Top-520
73LinPor-143
73OPC-119
73Top-119
74OPC-255
74PhiJohP-10
74Top-255
74TopDecE-70
74TopSta-72
75OPC-420
75Top-420
76CraDis-4
76Hos-145
76OPC-145
76SSP-464
76Top-145
77BurCheD-170
77Hos-62
77MSADis-5
77OPC-17
77RCColC-7
77Top-310
78Hos-71
78Kel-26
78OPC-68
78Pep-27
78PhiSSP-49
78RCColC-60
78SSP270-49
78Top-90
79Hos-134
79Kel-44
79OPC-104
79PhiBurK-15
79PhiTeal-3
79Top-210
80Kel-39
80OPC-330
80PhiBurK-7
80Top-630
80TopSup-34
81AllGamPI-109
81CokTeaS-98
81Don-142
81Fle-2
81Fle-645
81Fle-645B
81FleStiC-20
81FleStiC-43
81Kel-43
81OPC-120
81Top-120
81Top-403
81TopSti-201
81TopSupHT-80
82CubRedL-1
82Don-63
82Fle-241
82FleSta-56
82FleSta-107
82OPC-194
82OPC-374
82Top-515
82Top-516
82TopSti-80
82TopTra-10T
83AllGamPI-109
83CubThoAV-1
83Don-435
83Fle-491
83FleSta-21
83FleSti-128
83OPC-305
83PhiPosGPaM-4
83Top-305
83TopFol-5
83TopSti-221
84CubChiT-4
84CubSev-1
84CubUno-7
84Don-239
84Fle-486
84FunFooP-126
84Nes792-705
84Nes792-757
84OPC-346
84Top-705
84Top-757
84TopSti-46
84TopTif-705
84TopTif-757
85AllGamPI-109
85CubLioP-1
85CubSev-1
85Don-361
85DonHig-7
85Fle-50
85OPC-56
85Top-484
85TopSti-45
85TopTif-484
86LasVegSP-3
86PhiGreT-9
87PadBohHB-10
87TopTra-8T
87TopTraT-8T
88PadCok-10
88PhiTas-31
88Top-284
88TopTif-284
89PhiTas-2
90PhiTas-34
91MetWIZ-48
91PhiMed-6
91UppDecS-17
92PhiMed-6
92UppDecS-24
93PhiMed-7
93TedWil-71
94PhiMed-3
95Phi-5
96PhiTeal-5
Bowden, James
84ButCopKT-3
Bowden, Mark
81CedRapRT-22
86ReaPhiP-3
87ReaPhiP-17
88RocRedWC-4
88RocRedWGCP-2
88RocRedWP-208
88RocRedWTI-4
90IowCubP-313
90ProAAAF-620
Bowden, Merritt
89AncGlaP-4
91EliTwiP-4310
Bowden, Steve
85BenPhiC-3
87HagSunP-15
88FreSunCLC-16
Bowen, Joe
94JohCitCC-4
94JohCitCF-3704
Bowen, John
89EriOriS-3
Bowen, Kenny
88MemChiB-5
89MemChiB-8
89MemChiP-1207
89MemChiS-2
Bowen, Mitch

93ElmPioC-3
93ElmPioF-3814
94BreCouMC-2
94BreCouMF-1
95BreCouMF-237
96BreCouMB-6
Bowen, Ryan
87AshTouP-5
88OscAstS-5
89ColMudB-18
89ColMudP-126
89ColMudS-4
90Bes-245
90CMC-603
90ProAAAF-186
90TucTorC-1
90TucTorP-196
91Bow-539
91LinDriAAA-604
91TucTorLD-604
91TucTorP-2205
91UppDecFE-45F
92Bow-401
92Cla1-T17
92ClaGam-117
92Don-671
92Lea-385
92OPC-254
92OPCPre-28
92Pin-473
92ProFS7-225
92Sco-762
92StaClu-101
92Top-254
92TopDeb91-19
92TopGol-254
92TopGolW-254
92TopMic-254
92TucTorF-479
92Ult-488
92UppDec-354
93Don-372
93Fle-419
93FleFinE-53
93MarFloA-3
93MarPub-5
93MarUSPC-3S
93MarUSPC-9D
93PacSpa-455
93Pin-571
93StaClu-350
93StaCluFDI-350
93StaCluMarI-16
93StaCluMOP-350
93TopTra-130T
93Ult-367
93UppDec-780
93UppDecGold-780
94ColC-63
94ColChoGS-63
94ColChoSS-63
94Don-407
94Fin-30
94FinRef-30
94Fle-462
94Lea-238
94Pac-236
94Pin-117
94PinArtP-117
94PinMusC-117
94Sco-142
94ScoGolR-142
94Sel-59
94StaClu-345
94StaCluFDI-345
94StaCluGR-345
94StaCluMOP-345
94StaCluT-72
94StaCluTFDI-72
94Top-494
94TopGol-494
94TopSpa-494
94TriPla-132
94Ult-193
94UppDec-78
94UppDecED-78
95Don-236
95DonPreP-236
95Fle-326
Bowen, Sam (Samuel Thomas)
78PapGinD-6
81PawRedST-18
Bowens, Sam (Samuel Edward)
63RocRedWSP-3
64Top-201
64TopVen-201
65OPC-188
65Top-188
66Top-412
67CokCapO-12
67Top-491
68OPC-82
68Top-82
68TopVen-83
69MilBra-32
81Ori6F-8
81TCM60I-313
91OriCro-45
Bowens, Steve
83IdaFalAT-1
Bowerman, Frank E.
06GiaUllAFS-11
09RamT20-14
09T206-31
11SpoLifCW-38
98CamPepP-5
Bowers, Billy (Grover Bill)
52Par-6
Bowers, Brent
90MedHatBJB-10
91MyrBeaHC-23
91MyrBeaHP-2957
92DunBluJC-6
92DunBluJF-2009
93Bow-407
93ClaFS7-169
93KnoSmoF-1261
94Cla-84
94KnoSmoF-1314
94UppDecML-38
95Bow-3
95SyrChiTI-3
96BowBayB-7
Bowers, Cedric
97Top-470
Bowers, Mickey
80LynSaiT-15
81LynSaiT-25
82LynSaiT-18
83ChaLooT-12
Bowers, R.J.
94QuaCitRBC-5
94QuaCitRBF-546
95MidLeaA-4
95QuaCitRBTI-3
96MidLeaAB-25
96QuaCitRB-10
Bowers, Shane
93EliTwiC-5
93EliTwiF-3408
94ForWayWC-3
94ForWayWF-2000
95Bes-31
95ForMyeMTI-2
95SPML-84
96Exc-76
96HarCitRCB-8
Bowers, Stewart
79RedSoxEF-6
Bowers, Tom
58GiaSFCB-3
Bowie, Jim
86BelMarC-102
87WauTimP-15
88CalLeaACLC-27
88SanBerSB-16
88SanBerSCLC-30
89CalCanC-17
89CalCanP-525
90Bes-258
90CMC-796
90WilBilB-3
90WilBilP-1067
90WilBilS-2
91JacSunLD-331
91JacSunP-156
91LinDriAA-331
92CalCanS-56
92JacSunF-3714
92SkyAA F-291
92SkyAAAF-25
93HunStaF-2087
94ExcFS7-117
94TacTigF-3181
95EdmTraTI-2
95Sco-598
95ScoGolR-598
95ScoPlaTS-598
96SigRooOJ-4
96SigRooOJS-4
Bowie, Micah
95DurBulTI-5
96DurBulBIB-2
Bowlan, Mark
89HamRedS-4
91SprCarC-8
91SprCarP-734
Bowles, Brian
96MedHatBJTI-6
Bowles, John
92HigSchPLS-13
94UtiBluSC-6
94UtiBluSF-3826
95MicBatCTI-4
96SarRedSB-9
Bowles, Justin
96SouOreTI-21
Bowlin, Allan
80ElmPioRST-3
Bowling, Robert
76VenLeaS-102
Bowling, Steve (Stephen S.)
75SacSolC-13
76SpoIndC-18
79IndIndTI-20
94BreMilB-202
Bowman, Billy Joe
39PlaBal-128
40PlaBal-162
90AstMot-27
93AstMot-28
94ConTSN-1224
Bowman, Bob (Robert LeRoy)
47PM1StaP1-20
57Top-332
58PhiJayP-3
58Top-415
59Top-221
Bowman, Ernie (Ernest F.)
61TacBan-2
62Top-231
63Top-61
66Top-302
66TopVen-302
81TCM60I-352
Bowman, General Manager (Don)
88PulBraP-1771
Bowman, Joe (Joseph Emil)
79DiaGre-357
94ConTSNB-1224
Bowman, Michael
89BriTigS-1
Bowman, Paul
94KinMetC-3
94KinMetF-3814
Bowman, Roger
55Bow-115
57SeaPop-6
75Gia195T-2
Bowman, Scotty
72Dia-70
Bowman, William
77St.PetCT-2
Bowness, Brian
96SouBenSHS-6
Bowrosen, Ricky
93SouBenWSC-2
93SouBenWSF-1436
92UtiBluSC-13
Bowser, Robert
95MarPhiTI-3
Bowsfield, Ted (Edward)
59Top-236
60Top-382
61Top-216
62Top-369
62TopStal-64
63Top-339
64Top-447
Box, Newt
80CedRapRT-2
Box, Shawn
96DayCubB-5
Boxberger, Rod
80ColAstT-12
81NasSouTI-1
83NasAngT-2
Boyan, Michael
88CapCodPPaLP-155
Boyce, Bob
82MiaMarT-14
Boyce, Joe
90EriSaiS-1
Boyce, Randy
78NewWayCT-3
79BurBeeT-19
Boyce, Tommy
88SalLakCTTI-10
89KenTwiS-1
89MiaMirIS-2
89Sta-141
90MiaMirIS-3
Boyd, Bert
95PeoChiTI-NNO
96PeoChiB-3
Boyd, Bob
76QuaCitAT-4
77QuaCitAT-6
Boyd, Bob (Robert Richard)
53Top-257
54Bow-118
54Top-113
57Top-26
58Hir-75
58OriJayP-1
58Top-279
59OriJayP-1
59Top-82
59TopVen-82
60Lea-13
60Top-207
61A'sTeal-1
61AthJayP-4
61Top-199
61TopStal-157
86NegLeaF-49
87NegLeaPD-9
91OriCro-46
91TopArc1-257
92NegLeaRLI-6
94TopArc1-113
94TopArc1G-113
94CliLumC-30
Boyd, Daryl
86WatPirP-4
89WesPalBES-4
Boyd, Gary Lee
70OPC-7
70Top-7
Boyd, Greg
90ArkRaz-29
93BenRocC-3
93BenRocF-3275
93Top-621
93TopGol-621
93TopInaM-621
93TopMic-621
Boyd, Jake (Jacob Henry)
87OldJudN-38
Boyd, Jason
94MarPhiC-4
94MarPhiF-3283
95PiePhiF-179
Boyd, Oil Can (Dennis)
80ElmPioRST-4
83PawRedST-2
84Don-457
84Fle-393
85AllGamPI-75
85Don-151
85Fle-152
85Top-116
85TopTif-116
86BasStaB-14
86Don-50
86Fle-342
86FleStiC-9
86Lea-35
86OPC-259
86Spo-152
86Top-605
86TopMinL-4
86TopSti-249
86TopTat-16
86TopTif-605
87ClaGam-85
87Don-51
87Fle-30
87FleBasA-4
87FleExcS-5
87FleGlo-30
87Lea-248
87OPC-285
87RedFolSB-122
87RedSoxSAP-4
87SmoAmeL-2
87Spo-47
87SpoTeaP-9
87Top-285
87TopSti-249
87TopTif-285
88Don-462
88DonTeaBRS-462
88Fle-347
88FleGlo-347
88Lea-252
88PanSti-20
88Sco-121
88ScoGlo-121
88ScoSam-121
88StaLinRS-4
88Top-704
88TopTif-704
89Don-476
89Fle-82
89FleGlo-82
89OPC-326
89PanSti-269
89Sco-238
89Top-326
89TopTif-326
89UppDec-415
90Bow-102
90BowTif-102
90Don-633
90ExpPos-3
90FleUpd-26
90Lea-159
90OPC-544
90PubSti-449
90Sco-137
90ScoRoo-24T
90Top-544
90TopTif-544
90TopTra-12T
90TopTraT-12T
90UppDec-484
90UppDec-749
90VenSti-65
91Bow-456
91ClaGam-9
91Don-194
91Fle-226
91Lea-167
91OPC-48
91PanFreS-147
91Sco-202
91StaClu-142
91Stu-193
91Top-48
91TopDesS-48
91TopMic-48
91TopTif-48
91Ult-197
91UppDec-359
91UppDecFE-51F
92Don-447
92OPC-428
92Sco-531
92StaClu-99
92Top-428
92TopGol-428
92TopGolW-428
92TopMic-428
92UppDec-559
93RanKee-80
Boyd, Quincy
95VerBeaDTI-4
Boyd, Randy
77SanJosMC-16
Boyer, Clete (Leroy)
47StaPinP2-6
57Top-121
59Top-251
60Lea-46
60Top-109
60TopVen-109
61Pos-11
61Raw-3
61Top-19
61TopStal-191
61Yan61RL-6
61YanJayP-2

62Jel-3
62Pos-3
62PosCan-3
62SalPlaC-80
62ShiPlaC-80
62Top-163
62Top-490
62TopStal-84
62TopVen-163
62YanJayP-4
63Jel-14
63Kah-3
63Pos-14
63Top-361
63YanJayP-2
64ChatheY-4
64Top-69
64TopVen-69
64YanJayP-2
64YanReqKP-5
65ChaTheY-3
65Top-475
66OPC-9
66Top-9
66TopVen-9
66YanTeal-1
67BralrvD-1
67CokCapB-13
67DexPre-28
67Top-328
68Baz-1
68CokCapB-13
68DexPre-16
68Kah-A4
68Kah-B9
68Top-518A
68Top-518B
68Top-550
69Top-489
69TopSta-3
69TopTeaP-2
70OPC-206
70Top-206
71MLBOffS-4
71OPC-374
71Top-374
72MilBra-42
78GreBraT-4
81TCM60I-477
84A'sMot-27
85A'sMot-27
87ColCliP-25
87ColCliP-2
87ColCliT-24
88PacLegI-13
89Ft.LauYS-27
89PacSenL-149
89SweBasG-94
89T/MSenL-12
89TopSenL-4
90ColCliC-24
90ColCliP-2
90EliSenL-34
90PacLeg-10
90ProAAAF-343
90SweBasG-102
91ColCliP-NNO
91LinDriAAA-125
91PacSenL-43
91PacSenL-54
91RinPos1Y1-12
91SweBasG-109
92YanWIZ6-14

Boyer, Cloyd
51Bow-228
52Top-280
53BowC-115
53CarHunW-3
53Top-60
55A'sRodM-6
55A'sRodM-7
55Bow-149
76A'sRodMC-5
76VenLeaS-71
83Roy-4
83TopRep5-280
85SyrChiT-30
88PulBraP-1770
89IdaFalBP-2008
90PulBraB-28
90PulBraP-3113
91PulBraC-20
91PulBraP-4023
91TopArc1-60
92PulBraC-29
92PulBraF-3197

Boyer, Dave
78ArkTraT-3

Boyer, Ken (Kenton Lloyd)
47Exh-24
55CarHunW-2
55Top-125
56Top-14
56TopPin-46
57SwiFra-8
57Top-122
58CarJayP-2
58Top-350
59Baz-4
59HomRunD-4
59Top-325
59Top-557
60ArmCoi-4
60Baz-9
60CarJayP-1
60KeyChal-8
60Lea-12
60Top-160
60Top-485
60TopVen-160
61Baz-14
61CarJayP-1
61Pos-171A
61Pos-171B
61SevElev-18
61Top-43
61Top-375
61Top-573
61TopStal-85
62AurRec-4
62Baz-20
62CarJayP-1
62ExhStaB-5
62Jel-159
62Pos-159
62PosCan-159
62SalPlaC-167
62ShiPlaC-167
62Top-52
62Top-370
62Top-392
62TopBuc-10
62TopStal-183
62TopVen-52
63CarJayP-1
63CarJayP-2
63ExhStaB-8
63Fle-60
63Jel-160
63Pos-160
63SalMetC-15
63Top-375
63TopStil-6
64Baz-35
64CarTeal-1
64Raw-1
64Top-11
64Top-160
64TopCoi-25
64TopCoi-145
64TopGia-57
64TopSta-61
64TopStaU-10
64TopTatl-26
64TopVen-11
64TopVen-160
64WheSta-8
65Baz-35
65CarJayP-1
65OldLonC-4
65OPC-6
65OPC-100
65OPC-135
65Top-6
65Top-100
65Top-135
65TopEmbl-47
65TopTral-40
66Top-385
66TopRubl-10
67Baz-33
67CokCapYM-V28
67DexPre-29
67Kah-6A
67Kah-6B
67MetTeal-2
67OPC-105
67Top-105
67TopVen-235
68Top-259
68TopActS-8A
68TopVen-259
69MilBra-33
69Top-379
71CarTeal-3
74LauAllG-56
74SupBlaB-1
75OPC-202
75Top-202
75TulOil7-3
76GrePlaG-37
76TulOilGP-1
77RocRedWM-25
78CarTeal-1
78TCM60I-67
79Car5-1
79Top-192
80Top-244
81TCM60I-414
82K-M-6
83CarGreT-3
88PacLegI-12
90DodTar-63
91MetWIZ-49
92CarMcD-29
93ActPacA-145
97TopMan-28
97TopManF-28
97TopManFR-27

Boyer, Mickey
84IdaFalATI-4
89IdaFalBP-2008

Boyette, Tony
94PriRedC-4
94PriRedF-3263

Boykin, Tyrone
91BoiHawC-5
92QuaCitRBC-23
92QuaCitRBF-821
93PalSprAC-3
93PalSprAF-81
94MidAngF-2443
94MidAngOHP-2
95MidAngOHP-5
95MidAngTI-5
96MidAngB-7
96MidAngOHP-5

Boylan, Brad
84SalLakCGC-193
86TolMudHP-2
87PorBeaP-24
88PorBeaP-648

Boyland, Dorian Scott
77ShrCapT-1
78ColCliT-2
79PorBeaT-7
80PorBeaT-2
80Top-683
81PorBeaT-8
82PhoGiaVNB-15

Boyle, Buzz (Ralph Francis)
34DiaMatCSB-18
34ButPreR-6
90DodTar-64

Boyle, Gary
76QuaCitAT-5

Boyle, Henry J.
87BucN28-38
87OldJudN-40
88WG1CarG-29

Boyle, Jack (John Anthony)
87OldJudN-39

Boyle, Jeff
93PocPosF-4212
93PocPosSP-1

Boyles, John
85CedRapRT-1
86VerRedP-2
89WauTimGS-6

Boyne, Bryan
76CedRapGT-6

Boynewicz, Jim
94BurBeeC-3
94BurBeeF-1072

Boynton, Paul
88KimN18-5

Boyton, Capt (Paul)
88AllandGN-49

Boyzuick, Mike
91GreFalDSP-12
92BakDodCLC-4
92VerBeaDF-2881
93BelBreC-3
93BelBreF-1715

Boze, Marshall
91HelBreSP-5
92BelBreC-6
92BelBreF-395
93Bow-675
93ClaFS7-165
93StoPorC-2
93StoPorF-735
94ActPac-29
94Bow-37
94Cla-139
94ClaGolF-174
94ClaTriF-T43
94ExcFS7-78
94NewOrlZF-1461
94UppDecML-249
94UppDecMLPotYF-PY6
95SigRooOJ-7
95SigRooOJP-7
95SigRooOJPS-7
95SigRooOJS-7

Bozich, Gary
81BirBarT-11

Braase, John
88GreFalDTI-14
90BakDodCLC-241

Braatz, Kim
95ColSilB-1
96ColSilB-2

Brabant, Dan
93BurIndC-5
93BurIndF-3287
94ColRedC-4
94ColRedF-433
95KinIndTI-5
96KenIndB-1

Brabender, Gene
66Top-579
67OPC-22
67Top-22
68OPC-163
68Top-163
68TopVen-163
69Top-393
70BreMcD-3
70BreMil-1
70OPC-289
70Top-289
71MLBOffS-340
71OPC-666
71Top-666
81Ori6F-9
83Pil69G-43
91OriCro-47
94BreMilB-203

Brabinski, Marek
90IdaFalBP-3268

Bracho, Alejandro
96GreBatB-6

Bracho, Jose
52Par-24
95LinVen-282

Brack, Gib (Gilbert Herman)
39PlaBal-127

Bradbury, George
77LynMetT-5

Bradbury, Miah
88AlaGolTI-4
90MiaMirIS-1
91Cla/Bes-110
91MiaMirC-16
91MiaMirP-410
92PenPilC-3
92PenPilF-2935
93ExcFS7-220
93HarSenF-271

Braddy, Junior
96SarRedSB-10

Braddy, Leonard
84VisOakT-9

Bradenburg, Mark
94FloStaLAF-FSL1

Brader, Tim
88BriTigP-1865
89FayGenP-1583

Bradford, Buddy (Charles W.)
68OPC-142
68Top-142
68TopVen-142
69MilBra-34
69OPC-97
69Top-97
69TopTeaP-11
69WhiSoxTI-4
70Ind-1
70MLBOffS-183
70OPC-299
70Top-299
70WhiSoxTI-3
71Ind-1
71MLBOffS-362
71OPC-552
71Top-552
72MilBra-43
74OPC-357
74Top-357
75OPC-504
75Top-504
76OPC-451
76SSP-281
76Top-451

Bradford, Chad
96HicCraB-3

Bradford, Chris
89AncBucTI-23

Bradford, Josh
96StCatSB-5

Bradford, Larry
75LynRanT-5
78RicBraT-4
79RicBraT-17
80Top-675
81BraPol-34
81Don-584
81Fle-265
81Top-542
82Don-553
82Fle-431
82Top-271
83PorBeaT-24
85GreBraTI-5

Bradford, Mark
88BatCliP-1672

Bradford, Tony
94OrlCubF-1377

Bradford, Troy
88CapCodPPaLP-103
90AriWilP-1
90GenCubP-3030
90GenCubS-2
91CarLeaAP-CAR39
91WinSpiC-1
91WinSpiP-2820
92ChaKniF-2764
92PeoChiC-24

Bradford, Vincent
90BriTigP-3169
90BriTigS-2
90HigSchPLS-16
91BriTigC-15
91BriTigP-3617

Bradish, Mike
90UtiBluSP-29
92SalSpuC-23
93SarWhiSC-4
94PriWilCC-3
94PriWilCF-1926

Bradley, Bert
80WesHavWCT-10
81WesHavAT-3
82WesHavAT-2
83TacTigT-2
84TacTigC-92
85ColCliP-2
85ColCliT-2
87MadMusP-1
88MadMusP-4
90MadMusB-26
90MadMusP-2284
91HunStaC-17
91HunStaLD-300
91HunStaP-1812
91HunStaTI-24
91LinDriAA-300
92HunStaF-3965
92HunStaS-325
94TacTigF-3191
95WesMicWTI-17
96WesMicWB-2

Bradley, Bill (William J.)
03BreE10-11
04FanCraAL-6
05IndSouPSoCP-4

08AmeLeaPC-4
08RosComP-23
09AmeCarE-10
09BriE97-3
09T206-32
09T206-33
10CouT21-81
10W555-7
11SpoLifCW-39
11SpoLifCW-40
Bradley, Byron
92GenCubF-1565
94DayCubF-2357
Bradley, David
91WelPirC-23
Bradley, Eric
90MyrBeaBJP-2769
Bradley, Fred
48WhiSoxTI-3
Bradley, Grin (George W.)
87OldJudN-42
90HOFStiB-1
Bradley, Hugh F.
11SpoLifM-40
12T207-19
Bradley, Kenny
92KinMetC-2
92KinMetF-1537
Bradley, Len
80GleFalWSBT-2
80GleFalWSCT-2
81GleFalWST-23
82EdmTraT-17
Bradley, London
92GenCubC-25
93ClaFS7-272
93PeoChiC-3
93PeoChiF-1089
93PeoChiTI-2
94DayCubC-3
Bradley, Mark
77LodDodT-2
82AlbDukT-19
83DodPol-22
84Fle-581
84Nes792-316
84Top-316
84TopTif-316
90DodTar-65
91MetWIZ-50
Bradley, Mike
89AncBucTI-1
90SpoIndSP-18
91ChaRaiC-2
91ChaRaiP-88
Bradley, Milton
97Bow-145
97BowInt-145
Bradley, Nick (J. Nichols)
87OldJudN-41
Bradley, Otis
79CliDodT-7
Bradley, Paul
84ModA'sC-3
85ModA'sC-2
Bradley, Phil (Philip Poole)
83SalLakCGT-11
84FleUpd-15
84MarMot-24
84TopTra-15T
84TopTraT-15T
85Don-631
85Fle-486
85Lea-50
85MarMot-21
85OPC-69
85Top-449
85TopTif-449
86Don-22
86Don-191
86DonAll-41
86DonSupD-22
86Fle-461
86FleLimE-5
86FleMin-96
86FleStiC-10
86GenMilB-2B
86Lea-22
86MarMot-8
86OPC-305
86SevCoi-W11
86Spo-77
86Top-305
86TopGloS-54
86TopSti-217
86TopSup-13
86TopTat-14
86TopTif-305
87Don-270
87DonOpeD-122
87Fle-581
87FleGlo-581
87FleLeaL-4
87FleMin-11
87FleStiC-13
87GenMilB-3A
87HosSti-29
87Lea-200
87MarMot-6
87OPC-170
87Spo-89
87SpoTeaP-25
87StuPan-25
87Top-525
87TopMinL-70
87TopSti-221
87TopTif-525
88Don-243
88DonBasB-47
88Fle-369
88FleGlo-369
88FleUpd-107
88FleUpdG-107
88OPC-55
88PanSti-191
88PhiTas-4
88Sco-66
88ScoGlo-66
88ScoRoo-34T
88ScoRooG-34T
88Spo-93
88StaLinMa-1
88StaLinPh-3
88Top-55
88Top-519
88TopMinL-33
88TopSti-218
88TopTif-55
88TopTif-519
88TopTra-18T
88TopTraT-18T
89Bow-17
89BowTif-17
89Don-369
89DonBasB-198
89DonTra-41
89Fle-563
89FleGlo-563
89FleUpd-1
89OPC-308
89OriFreB-16
89PanSti-154
89Sco-79
89ScoRoo-44T
89Top-608
89TopAme2C-6
89TopSti-113
89TopTif-608
89TopTra-13T
89TopTraT-13T
89UppDec-229
89UppDec-749
90Bow-261
90BowTif-261
90Don-259
90Fle-174
90FleCan-174
90Lea-138
90OPC-163
90PanSti-4
90PubSti-575
90Sco-24
90Sco100S-36
90ScoRoo-44T
90Spo-95
90Top-163
90TopBatL-20
90TopBig-202
90TopMinL-2
90TopSti-241
90TopTif-163
90UppDec-194
90VenSti-66
91Don-646
91Fle-114
91OPC-717
91OriCro-48
91Sco-560
91SimandSMLBL-5
91Top-717
91TopDesS-717
91TopMic-717
91TopTif-717
91UppDec-641
92EdmTraF-3550
92ExpDonD-3B
Bradley, Rick
75PhoGiaC-7
77PhoGiaCC-4
77PhoGiaCP-3
77PhoGiaVNB-2
78PhoGiaC-2
79PhoGiaVNB-14
Bradley, Scott W.
83NasSouTI-1
84ColCliP-2
84ColCliT-11
85Don-37
86BufBisP-4
86Don-396
86Top-481
86TopTif-481
87Don-440
87Fle-580
87FleBasA-5
87FleGlo-580
87MarMot-14
87SpoTeaP-25
87Top-376
87TopSti-217
87TopTif-376
88Don-147
88DonBasB-24
88Fle-370
88FleGlo-370
88Lea-75
88MarMot-14
88OPC-199
88PanSti-183
88RedFolSB-8
88Sco-151
88ScoGlo-151
88StaLinMa-2
88Top-762
88TopSti-222
88TopTif-762
89Bow-209
89BowTif-209
89Don-261
89Fle-540
89FleGlo-540
89MarMot-14
89OPC-279
89PanSti-432
89Sco-324
89Top-279
89TopSti-225
89TopTif-279
89UppDec-226
90Bow-483
90BowTif-483
90Don-581
90Fle-506
90FleCan-506
90Lea-404
90MarMot-25
90OPC-593
90PubSti-427
90Sco-228
90Top-593
90TopBig-181
90TopSti-229
90TopTif-593
90UppDec-383
90VenSti-67
91Bow-239
91Don-287
91Fle-443
91Lea-99
91MarCouH-5
91OPC-38
91Sco-113
91ScoPro-113
91StaClu-252
91Top-38
91TopDesS-38
91TopMic-38
91TopTif-38
91Ult-332
91UppDec-130
92Don-713
92Fle-273
92OPC-608
92Sco-304
92StaClu-146
92Top-608
92TopGol-608
92TopGolW-608
92TopMic-608
92UppDec-390
92YanWIZ8-16
94ColSprSSF-736
Bradley, Tom
71OPC-588
71Top-588
72OPC-248
72Top-248
73OPC-336
73Top-336
74OPC-455
74Top-455
74TopSta-102
75OPC-179
75PhoGiaCK-9
75Top-179
76OPC-644
76Top-644
76TucTorCa-16
76TusTorCr-35
Bradley, Wayne
75CedRapGT-28
Bradshaw, Craig
92IdaFalGF-3502
92IdaFalGSP-28
93DanBraC-4
93DanBraF-3609
Bradshaw, Joe
90DodTar-903
Bradshaw, Kevin
87LakTigP-7
88GleFalTP-934
89TolMudHC-19
89TolMudHP-783
91BriTigC-30
92TolMudHF-1058
92TolMudHS-600
93LakTigC-27
93LakTigF-1328
94BriTigC-28
94TreThuF-2136
Bradshaw, Terry
90HamRedB-23
91Cla/Bes-269
91SavCarC-23
91SavCarP-1664
91SouAtlLAGP-SAL41
92ProFS7-320
93ClaFS7-242
93St.PetCC-6
93St.PetCF-2639
94ArkTraF-3100
94Bow-648
94Cla-58
94ExcFS7-260
95Bow-71
95Exc-264
95FleUpd-154
95LouRedF-287
95Sum-164
95SumNthD-164
95Top-656
95UppDecML-35
96ColCho-282
96ColChoGS-282
96ColChoSS-282
96Don-422
96DonPreP-422
96LouRedB-11
96Sco-255
97Pac-405
97PacLigB-405
97PacSil-405
95UppDecMLFS-35
Brady, Brian
86MidAngP-2
87MidAngP-5
88EdmTraC-16
88EdmTraP-572
90CMC-539
90PhoFirC-12
90PhoFirP-16
90ProAAAF-42
90TopDeb89-19
Brady, Dave
83RedPioT-6
Brady, Doug
91UtiBluSC-2
91UtiBluSP-3244
92ClaFS7-377
92SarWhiSCB-25
92SarWhiSF-211
92SouBenWSC-9
93SarWhiSC-5
93SarWhiSF-1374
94BirBarC-4
94BirBarF-626
95ARuFalLS-3
95NasSouTI-4
96NasSouB-9
Brady, Jim
56Top-126
77SalPirT-2
Brady, Lawrence
86WatPirP-5
Brady, Mike
89MyrBeaBJP-1477
90St.LucMS-1
91St.LucMP-702
91VerBeaDC-4
91VerBeaDP-765
92VerBeaDC-21
Brady, Neil
92StaCluMO-43
Brady, Pat
89SalSpuCLC-138
89SalSpuP-1815
90SanJosGB-4
90SanJosGCLC-31
90SanJosGP-2023
90SanJosGS-1
90SanJosGS-26
91ClePhiC-15
91ClePhiP-1626
91FloStaLAP-FSL6
92ClePhiC-22
92ClePhiF-2068
93ReaPhiF-306
94ScrRedBF-931
Brady, Steve (Stephen A.)
87OldJudN-43
88GandBCGCE-3
Bragan, Bobby (Robert R.)
43DodTeal-3
47TipTop-91
53MotCoo-4
59DarFar-3
60DodTeal-2
60Top-463
63Top-73
64BraJayP-3
64Top-506
65Top-346
66Top-476
79DiaGre-84
81TCM60I-410
85TCMPla1-26
90DodTar-66
Bragan, Jimmy
73ExpPos-1
89ChaLooLITI-4
Bragan, Peter
89JacExpB-23
96JacSunB-1
Bragg, Darren
92ClaFS7-213
92PenPilC-23
92PenPilF-2945
93ExcFS7-221
93JacSunF-2721
94LeaLimR-45
94MarMot-15
94SpoRoo-74
94SpoRooAP-74
94UppDecML-53
95ColCho-556T
95Don-496
95DonPreP-496
95Fla-299
95FleAllR-M4
95LinVen-145
95LinVen-270
95MarMot-15
95MarPac-24
95Sco-589
95ScoGolR-589
95ScoPlaTS-589
95SigRoo-9
95SigRooSig-9
95StaClu-561

95StaCluMOP-561
95StaCluSTWS-561
95TacRaiTI-5
95TopTra-87T
95UltGolMR-M5
95UppDec-238
95UppDecED-238
95UppDecEDG-238
95UppDecPAW-H36
95UppDecPAWE-H36
95UppDecSE-254
95UppDecSEG-254
96ColCho-314
96ColChoGS-314
96ColChoSS-314
96Fle-230
96FleTif-230
96LeaSigA-32
96LeaSigAG-32
96LeaSigAS-32
96MarMot-24
96TacRaiB-6
96Ult-407
96UltGolM-407
97ColCho-51
97Don-250
97DonPreP-250
97DonPrePGold-250
97DonTea-54
97DonTeaSPE-54
97Fle-17
97FleTif-17
97MetUni-18
97Pac-33
97PacLigB-33
97PacSil-33
97Pin-133
97PinArtP-133
97PinMusC-133
97Sco-188
97ScoPreS-188
97ScoRedS-9
97ScoRedSPI-9
97ScoRedSPr-9
97ScoShoS-188
97ScoShoSAP-188
97Top-354
97UppDec-314
Bragga, Matt
94ButCopKSP-25
Braggs, Glenn
86SpoRoo-21
86VanCanP-5
87BrePol-26
87BreTeal-1
87Don-337
87DonOpeD-52
87Fle-339
87FleGlo-339
87SpoTeaP-19
87Top-622
87TopTif-622
88BrePol-26
88Don-240
88DonBasB-15
88Fle-157
88FleGlo-157
88OPC-263
88PanSti-127
88Sco-59
88ScoGlo-59
88ScoYouS2-2
88StaLinBre-2
88Top-263
88Top-639
88TopSti-197
88TopTif-263
88TopTif-639
89Bow-145
89BowTif-145
89BreGar-12
89BrePol-26
89BreYea-26
89ClaTraP-169
89Don-103
89DonBasB-277
89Fle-180
89FleGlo-180
89OPC-271
89PanSti-375
89Sco-147
89Spo-29
89Top-718
89TopBig-204
89TopSti-196
89TopTif-718
89UppDec-504
90Bow-403
90BowTif-403
90BrePol-26
90Don-264
90El PasDAGTI-3
90Fle-317
90FleCan-317
90FleUpd-11
90Lea-466
90OPC-88
90PanSti-97
90PubSti-491
90RedKah-4
90Sco-105
90ScoRoo-56T
90Top-88
90TopBig-10
90TopSti-206
90TopTif-88
90TopTra-13T
90TopTraT-13T
90UppDec-456
90UppDec-714
90VenSti-68
91Bow-669
91Don-253
91Fle-57
91Lea-362
91OPC-444
91RedKah-15
91RedPep-3
91Sco-18
91StaClu-187
91Top-444
91TopDesS-444
91TopMic-444
91TopTif-444
91Ult-88
91UppDec-631
92Don-363
92Fle-400
92OPC-197
92PanSti-268
92Pin-502
92RedKah-15
92Sco-393
92StaClu-13
92Top-197
92TopGol-197
92TopGolW-197
92TopMic-197
92TriPla-61
92Ult-185
92UppDec-341
94BreMilB-204
Brahms, Russ
82QuaCitCT-3
Brain, Dave (David Leonard)
09T206-400
11SpoLifCW-41
Brainard, Matthew
93BatCliC-5
93BatCliF-3152
94SpaPhiF-1725
94SparPhiC-3
Brake, Greg
85MadMusP-4
Brakebill, Mark
89BelMarL-21
90PenPilS-4
91PenPilC-18
91PenPilP-383
92QuaCitRBC-24
92QuaCitRBF-815
93MidAngF-326
97MidAngOHP-2
Brakeley, Bill
89HelBreSP-9
90HelBreSP-27
91BelBreC-1
91BelBreP-2094
Braley, Jeff (Jeffrey)
89BriTigS-2
90FayGenP-2397
90ProAaA-85
90SouAtlLAS-2
91FloStaLAP-FSL19
91LakTigC-1
91LakTigP-257
92LonTigF-624
92LonTigS-401
92SkyAA F-170
93LonTigF-2298
Brame, Erv (Ervin Beckham)
93ConTSN-959
Bramlett, Jeff
95GreFalDTI-27
96GreFalDB-5
96GreFalDTI-20
Brammer, John
96WatIndTI-3
Branca, Ralph
46SpoExcW-1-11
47Exh-25
47HomBon-5
47TipTop-92
49Bow-194
49EurSta-30
50Bow-59
51Bow-56
51FisBakL-2
51R42SmaS-4
51TopBluB-20
52Bow-96
52TipTop-3
52Top-274
53BowBW-52
53ExhCan-8
76SSP-594
76TayBow4-26
79TCM50-32
83TopRep5-274
88RinPosD1-7A
89DodSmoG-51
90DodTar-67
90PacLeg-13
90SweBasG-133
91Bow-410
91SweBasG-14
91TopArc1-293
92ActPacA-41
92BazQua5A-7
93TedWil-8
95TopArcBD-17
95TopArcBD-58
Brancato, Al (Albert)
41DouPlaR-47
41PlaBal-43
79DiaGre-341
83TCMPla1945-22
Branch, Roy
75WatRoyT-5
80SpoIndT-7
89PacSenL-210
91PacSenL-57
Branconier, Paul
89SalDodTI-8
90AshTouC-2
90YakBeaTI-31
91AshTouP-560
Brand, Ron (Ronald George)
69ExpPin-2
64Top-326
64TopVen-326
65AstBigLBPP-5
65OPC-212
65Top-212
66Top-394
67CokCapAs-10
68CokCapA-10
68DexPre-17
68Top-317
68TopVen-317
69Top-549
70ExpPos-16
70MLBOffS-63
70OPC-221
70Top-221
71ExpPS-4
71MLBOffS-124
71OPC-304
71Top-304
72MilBra-44
72Top-773
78TCM60I-41
87AstSer1-5
87AstShowSTh-27
Brandenburg, Mark
92ButCopKSP-8
93ChaRaiC-4
93ChaRaiF-1901
94ChaRanF-2490
95Exc-125
96FleRan-1
96FleUpd-U86
96FleUpdTC-U86
96LeaSigEA-15
96RanMot-21
Brandon, Darrell
66Top-456
67CokCapRS-5
67OPC-117
67Top-117
67TopRedSS-2
68CokCapRS-5
68DexPre-18
68OPC-26
68Top-26
68TopVen-26
69MilBra-35
69PilPos-37
69Top-301
72OPC-283
72Top-283
73OPC-326
73Top-326
89PacSenL-44
Brandon, Jelani
94EugEmeC-2
94EugEmeF-3724
95SprSulTI-2
Brandow, Derek
91OklStaC-1
92OklStaC-1
92St.CatBJC-24
92St.CatBJF-3377
93HagSunC-4
93HagSunF-1870
94DunBluJC-4
94DunBluJF-2547
95KnoSmoF-33
96SyrChiTI-4
Brandt, Dutch/Lefty (Ed)
32USCar-28
33ButCre-2
33DouDisP-7
33Gou-50
33GouCanV-50
34DiaMatCSB-19
34BatR31-2
34BatR31-107
34ExhFou-1
34Gou-5
34GouCanV-62
34TarThoBD-2
35DiaMatCS3T1-15
35ExhFou-1
35GouPuzR-1J
35GouPuzR-3A
35GouPuzR-4E
35GouPuzR-7E
35GouPuzR-12E
35GouPuzR-14A
35GouPuzR-15A
36ExhFou-2
90DodTar-68
91ConTSN-298
Brandt, Jackie (John George)
47Exh-26
59Top-297
60OriJayP-1
60Top-53
60TopVen-53
61Pos-76A
61Pos-76B
61Top-515
61TopMagR-27
61TopStaI-98
62Jel-31
62Pos-31
62PosCan-31
62SalPlaC-53A
62SalPlaC-53B
62ShiPlaC-53
62Top-165
62TopBuc-11
62TopStaI-3
62TopVen-165
63Jel-58
63Pos-58
63Top-65
64OriJayP-4
64Top-399
65OPC-33
65Top-33
66PhiTeal-2
66Top-383
67OPC-142
67Top-142
78TCM60I-33
91OriCro-49
Brandt, Randy
77SalPirT-3
Brandts, Mike
87SalSpuP-5
Branham, Luther H.
93NegLeaRL2-5
Brannan, Ryan
97Bow-332
97BowChr-228
97BowChrI-228
97BowChrIR-228
97BowChrR-228
97BowInt-332
Brannon, Cliff
89HamRedS-6
90SavCarP-2080
91ArkTraLD-27
91ArkTraP-1298
91LinDriAA-27
92ArkTraF-1141
92ArkTraS-28
92SkyAA F-12
Brannon, Paul
92SanBerC-25
92SanBerSF-960
Bransfield, Kitty (William)
08RosComP-135
09AmeCarE-11
09AmeCarE-12
09BriE97-4
09ColChiE-32
09RamT20-15
09T206-34
10NadE1-8
10SweCapPP-124
10W555-8
11SpoLifCW-42
11SpoLifM-225
11T205-19
11TurRedT-82
12ColRedB-32
12ColTinT-32
94ConTSN-1193
94ConTSNB-1193
Branson, Jeff
88TopTra-19T
88TopTraT-19T
89CedRapRB-1
89CedRapRP-928
89CedRapRS-1
89TopBig-69
90Bow-52
90BowTif-52
90CedRapRDGB-20
90ChaLooGS-6
91ChaLooLD-155
91ChaLooP-1965
91LinDriAA-155
92Bow-512
92DonRoo-13
92NasSouF-1836
92Pin-533
92StaClu-716
92StaCluECN-716
93Don-138
93Fle-31
93Lea-481
93PacSpa-399
93RedKah-3
93Sco-308
93StaClu-188
93StaCluFDI-188
93StaCluMOP-188
93Top-784
93TopGol-784
93TopInaM-784
93TopMic-784
93Ult-27
93UppDec-642
93UppDecGold-642
93USPlaCR-6H
94ColC-64
94ColChoGS-64
94ColChoSS-64
94Don-642
94Fin-189
94FinRef-189
94Fle-405

94Pac-141
94RedKah-2
94Sco-225
94ScoGolR-225
94StaClu-20
94StaCluFDI-20
94StaCluGR-20
94StaCluMOP-20
94Top-368
94TopGol-368
94TopSpa-368
95Don-508
95DonPreP-508
95DonTopotO-209
95Fle-430
95RedKah-4
95Sco-535
95ScoGolR-535
95ScoPlaTS-535
95Top-198
96ColCho-516
96ColChoGS-516
96ColChoSS-516
96Don-267
96DonPreP-267
96Fla-228
96Fle-335
96FleTif-335
96LeaSigA-33
96LeaSigAG-33
96LeaSigAS-33
96Pac-46
96Ult-175
96UltGolM-175
96UppDec-52
97Fle-291
97FleTif-291
97Pac-263
97PacLigB-263
97PacSil-263

Brant, Marshall Lee
78TidTidT-5
79TidTidT-13
80ColCliP-33
80ColCliT-20
81ColCliP-33
81ColCliT-13
82ColCliP-33
82ColCliT-6
83ColCliT-16
92YanWIZ8-17

Brantley, Cliff
88ClePhiS-2
89ReaPhiB-11
89ReaPhiP-662
90ClePhiS-3
90ReaPhiS-8
91LinDriAA-503
91ReaPhiLD-503
91ReaPhiP-1364
92Bow-120
92Don-722
92Fle-662
92Lea-434
92OPC-544
92PhiMed-7
92Pin-557
92ProFS7-299
92Sco-854
92StaClu-583
92Top-544
92TopDeb91-20
92TopGol-544
92TopGolW-544
92TopMic-544
92Ult-543
93Don-250
93Fle-486
93ScrRedBF-2538
93ScrRedBTI-3
93StaClu-253
93StaCluFDI-253
93StaCluMOP-253
93Top-773
93TopGol-773
93TopInaM-773
93TopMic-773

Brantley, Jeff
86ShrCapP-1
87PhoFirP-28
87ShrCapP-13
88BlaYNPRWL-79
88PhoFirC-5
88PhoFirP-78
89DonRoo-41
89FleUpd-127
89GiaMot-17
89ScoRoo-101T
89TopTra-14T
89TopTraT-14T
90Don-466
90Fle-52
90FleCan-52
90GiaMot-25
90Hot50RS-9
90Lea-357
90OPC-703
90Sco-371
90Sco100RS-22
90ScoYouSI-24
90Top-703
90TopTif-703
90UppDec-358
90USPlaCA-3H
91Bow-620
91Cla2-T47
91ClaGam-143
91Don-319
91Fle-255
91GiaMot-25
91GiaPacGaE-7
91GiaSFE-4
91Lea-136
91MisStaB-5
91OPC-17
91PanFreS-75
91PanSti-70
91Sco-160
91SimandSMLBL-6
91StaClu-567
91Top-17
91TopDesS-17
91TopMic-17
91TopTif-17
91Ult-316
91UppDec-424
92Don-295
92Fle-629
92GiaMot-25
92GiaPacGaE-7
92Lea-56
92OPC-491
92Pin-470
92Sco-157
92StaClu-294
92Stu-112
92Top-491
92TopGol-491
92TopGolW-491
92TopMic-491
92Ult-285
92UppDec-581
93Don-100
93Fle-152
93GiaMot-17
93GiaPos-9
93Lea-102
93OPC-65
93PacSpa-608
93Pin-512
93Sco-153
93StaClu-260
93StaCluFDI-260
93StaCluG-14
93StaCluMOP-260
93Top-631
93TopGol-631
93TopInaM-631
93TopMic-631
93TriPla-213
93Ult-128
93UppDec-581
93UppDecGold-581
94ColC-607
94ColChoGS-607
94ColChoSS-607
94Don-94
94ExtBas-228
94Fla-365
94Fle-685
94FleUpd-115
94Pac-541
94Pin-198
94PinArtP-198
94PinMusC-198
94RedKah-3
94StaClu-709
94StaCluFDI-709
94StaCluGR-709
94StaCluMOP-709
94Top-116
94TopGol-116
94TopSpa-116
94TopTra-37T
95ColCho-422
95ColChoGS-422
95ColChoSS-422
95Don-523
95DonPreP-523
95DonTopotO-210
95Fle-431
95Pac-100
95RedKah-5
95Top-236
95TopCyb-89
95Ult-142
95UltGolM-142
96ColCho-117
96ColChoGS-117
96ColChoSS-117
96Don-306
96DonPreP-306
96EmoXL-162
96Fla-229
96Fle-336
96FleTif-336
96Pac-39
96Sco-484
96StaClu-74
96StaClu-267
96StaCluMOP-74
96StaCluMOP-267
96Top-271
96Ult-176
96UltGolM-176
96UppDec-48
97Bow-60
97BowInt-60
97Cir-272
97CirRav-272
97ColCho-63
97ColCho-79
97Don-227
97DonPreP-227
97DonPrePGold-227
97Fin-147
97FinEmb-147
97FinEmbR-147
97FinRef-147
97Fle-292
97FleTif-292
97Lea-79
97LeaFraM-79
97LeaFraMDC-79
97MetUni-45
97Pac-264
97PacLigB-264
97PacPri-91
97PacPriLB-91
97PacPriP-91
97PacSil-264
97Pin-62
97PinArtP-62
97PinMusC-62
97Sco-126
97ScoPreS-126
97ScoShoS-126
97ScoShoSAP-126
97StaClu-303
97StaCluMOP-303
97Top-188
97TopGal-65
97TopGalPPI-65
97Ult-175
97UltGolME-175
97UltPlaME-175
97UppDec-336
97UppDecAWJ-16

Brantley, Mickey
84ChaLooT-26
85CalCanC-88
86CalCanP-2
86Fle-651
86SpoRoo-45
87Don-656
87DonRoo-27
87Fle-582
87FleGlo-582
87MarMot-15
87SpoTeaP-25
87Top-347
87TopTif-347
88Don-610
88DonBasB-80
88Fle-371
88FleExcS-5
88FleGlo-371
88FleMin-51
88Lea-258
88MarMot-15
88PanSti-192
88Sco-213
88ScoGlo-213
88ScoYouS2-15
88StaLinMa-3
88Top-687
88TopTif-687
89ChaLooLITI-5
89Don-212
89Fle-541
89FleGlo-541
89MarMot-7
89OPC-369
89PanSti-439
89Sco-89
89Spo-6
89Top-568
89TopBig-38
89TopSti-219
89TopTif-568
89UppDec-550
90CalCanC-15
90CMC-442
90PubSti-428
90VenSti-69
91DenZepLD-129
91DenZepP-133
91LinDriAAA-129
92TucTorS-603
93PhoFirF-1525
95BurBeeTI-34

Branyan, Russell
94BurIndC-3
94BurIndF-3801
96Bow-342
96Exc-40
97Bow-335
97BowBes-199
97BowBesAR-199
97BowBesMI-MI9
97BowBesMIAR-MI9
97BowBesMIARI-MI9
97BowBesMII-MI9
97BowBesMIR-MI9
97BowBesMIRI-MI9
97BowBesR-199
97BowChr-230
97BowChrI-230
97BowChrIR-230
97BowChrR-230
97BowInt-335
97StaClu-190
97StaCluMOP-190

Brashear, Roy Parks
09T206-401

Brasher, Anthony
95AusFut-58

Brassil, Tom
85BeaGolGT-14
86BeaGolGP-3
87WicPilRD-19
88LasVegSC-23
88LasVegSP-238
89SpoIndSP-13

Brassington, Phil
93EugEmeC-5
93EugEmeF-3847

Braswell, Bryan
96AubDouB-1

Brathwaite, Alonso
52LavPro-58

Bratlien, Erik
88BatCliP-1673
89BatCliP-1941
89ReaPhiS-3

Braun, Bart
77ModA'sC-15
79WatA'sT-4
81RedPioT-29

Braun, John Paul
65OPC-82
65Top-82

Braun, Randy
83DayBeaAT-17
86CalCanP-3
87CalCanP-2323
88JacExpB-21
88JacExpP-976
88SouLeaAJ-20
89IndIndC-16
89IndIndP-1213
90CMC-69
90IndIndC-19
90IndIndP-283
90ProAAAF-566

Braun, Steve (Stephen R.)
72OPC-244
72Top-244
73LinPor-105
73OPC-16
73Top-16
74OPC-321
74Top-321
74TopSta-202
75Kel-41
75OPC-273
75Top-273
76Hos-96
76OPC-183
76SSP-221
76Top-183
77Hos-134
77MSADis-6
77OPC-123
77RCColC-8
77Top-606
77TopCloS-6
78RCColC-9
78Roy-2
78Top-422
79Top-502
80Top-9
81Car5x7-1
81Fle-427
82Don-418
82Fle-111
82Top-316
83Car-3
83Fle-3
83Top-734
84Car-3
84Car5x7-3
84Fle-320
84FleSti-42
84Nes792-227
84Top-227
84TopTif-227
85CarTeal-3
85Fle-221
85FleStaS-51
85Top-152
85TopTif-152
86CarKASD-4
86CarTeal-4
86Don-534
86Fle-27
86LouRedTI-5
86Top-631
86TopTif-631
88LouRedBTI-4
90TopTVCa-2
92WinHavRSC-29

Braunecker, Darek
91JamExpC-24
91JamExpP-3535

Brauning, Jeff
90SanJosGB-5
90SanJosGCLC-34
90SanJosGP-2015
90SanJosGS-2

Brave, Homer the
90BraDubS-13
92BraLykS-16
93BraLykS-14
94MasMan-7

Braves, Atlanta
66Top-326
66TopVen-326
67Top-477
68Top-221
68TopVen-221
69FleCloS-1
69FleCloS-27
69TopStaA-1
70OPC-472
70Top-472
71OPC-652
71Top-652
71TopTat-42
72OPC-21

72Top-21
73OPC-521
73OPCBTC-1
73Top-521
73TopBluTC-1
74OPC-483
74OPCTC-1
74Top-483
74TopStaA-1
74TopTeaC-1
78Top-551
83FleSta-225
83FleSti-NNO
87SpoTeaL-24
88PanSti-469
88RedFolSB-105
90PubSti-628
90RedFolSB-130
90VenSti-515
93TedWilPC-2
94ImpProP-15
94Sco-647
94ScoGolR-647
95PanSti-139
95StaCluSTWS-R1L
95StaCluSTWS-R1W
96FleBra-19
96PanSti-6
96TopGalPG-PG15
Braves, Boston
13FatT20-9
36R31Pre-G18
38BasTabP-29
48ExhTea-1
68LauWorS-11
70FleWorS-11
70FleWorS-45
71FleWorS-12
71FleWorS-46
80MarExh-32
86JosHalC-2
90KalTeaN-3
94OriofB-98
Braves, Bourne
88CapCodPB-26
Braves, Idaho Falls
88IdaFalBP-1833
Braves, Milwaukee
55BraGolS-1
56Top-95A
56Top-95B
56Top-95C
57Top-114
58Top-377A
58Top-377B
59Top-419
60Top-381
60TopTat-59
61Top-426
61TopMagR-18
62GuyPotCP-12
62Top-158
62TopVen-158
63GadFunC-58
63Top-503
64Top-132
64TopTatI-12
64TopVen-132
65Top-426
66TopRubI-112
71FleWorS-55
93TedWilPC-17
Braves, Pulaski
90PulBraP-3115
92PulBraC-30
92PulBraF-3199
Braves, Richmond
89RicBraP-818
92RicBraBB-26
93RicBraBB-NNO
Bravo, Angel (Angel Alfonso)
70DayDaiNM-74
70OPC-283
70Top-283
71MLBOffS-50
71OPC-538
71Top-538
76VenLeaS-115
Bravo, Danny
96WesPalBEB-22
Bravo, Dino
72Dia-114
Bravo, Luis
79WisRapTT-17
80VenLeaS-14
83AlbA'sT-17
Braxton, Garland
91ConTSN-248
Braxton, Glenn
86AppFoxP-3
87PenWhiSP-16
89UtiBluSP-2
Bray, Chris
96BluOriB-6
Bray, Frank
96JacSunB-30
Bray, Notorris
95ButCopKtl-26
Bray, Scott
89SalLakTTI-23
Brazeau, Jay
90ColMetGS-29
Brazell, Don
78WauMetT-2
Brazill, Frank (Frank Leo)
23WilChoV-12
Brazle, Alpha
46SeaSLP-6
47TipTop-150
49Bow-126A
49Bow-126B
49EurSta-178
50Bow-126
51Bow-157
52Bow-134
52Top-228
53BowC-140
53CarHunW-2
54Bow-142
54CarHunW-3
55Bow-230
83CarGreT-11
83TopRep5-228
Brazoban, Candido
93BriTigF-3639
94BriTigC-7
94BriTigF-3493
Breadon, Sam
41CarW75-1
Bream, Scott
90ChaRaiP-2049
91ChaRaiC-16
91ChaRaiP-101
91Cla/Bes-184
91SpoIndC-23
91SpoIndP-3954
92WatDiaC-3
92WatDiaF-2148
93RanCucQC-5
93RanCucQF-842
94WicWraF-194
Bream, Sid (Sidney Eugene)
82VerBeaDT-18
83AlbDukT-15
84AlbDukC-149
85Don-470
85Top-253
85TopTif-253
86Don-566
86Fle-604
86Top-589
86TopTif-589
87Don-79
87DonOpeD-168
87Fle-606
87FleExcS-6
87FleGlo-606
87FleMin-12
87FleSlu-5
87FleStiC-14
87Lea-239
87OPC-35
87SpoTeaP-18
87Top-35
87Top-131
87TopSti-126
87TopTif-35
87TopTif-131
88Don-188
88DonBasB-45
88Fle-324
88FleExcS-6
88FleGlo-324
88FleStiC-113
88OPC-304
88PanSti-370
88Sco-260
88ScoGlo-260
88Spo-98
88StaLinPi-4
88Top-478
88TopBig-205
88TopSti-130
88TopTif-478
89Bow-419
89BowTif-419
89Don-252
89DonBasB-89
89Fle-204
89FleGlo-204
89OPC-126
89PanSti-169
89PirVerFJ-5
89Sco-48
89Top-126
89TopBig-106
89TopMinL-31
89TopSti-125
89TopTif-126
89UppDec-556
90Bow-175
90BowTif-175
90DodTar-69
90Don-329
90DonBesN-33
90Fle-463
90FleCan-463
90OPC-622
90PirHomC-7
90PubSti-151
90Sco-423
90Top-622
90TopTif 622
90UppDec-250
90VenSti-70
91Bow-585
91BraDubP-5
91BraSubS-7
91Don-644
91Fle-35
91FleUpd-72
91Lea-379
91OPC-354
91PanFreS-115
91PanSti-119
91Sco-304
91ScoRoo-12T
91StaClu-427
91Stu-142
91Top-354
91TopDesS-354
91TopMic-354
91TopTif-354
91TopTra-13T
91TopTraT-13T
91UppDec-109
91UppDec-710
92Bow-356
92BraLykP-7
92BraLykS-8
92DenHol-7
92Don-202
92Fle-354
92Lea-242
92OPC-770
92PanSti-162
92Pin-446
92Sco-131
92StaClu-478
92Stu-2
92Top-770
92TopGol-770
92TopGolW-770
92TopMic-770
92TriPla-258
92Ult-160
92UppDec-495
93Bow-689
93BraFloA-4
93BraLykP-6
93BraLykS-7
93Don-526
93Fle-2
93Lea-178
93OPC-84
93PacSpa-2
93PanSti-181
93Pin-204
93Sco-396
93Sel-382
93StaClu-151
93StaCluB-15
93StaCluFDI-151
93StaCluMOP-151
93Stu-38
93Top-224
93TopGol-224
93TopInaM-224
93TopMic-224
93Ult-4
93UppDec-104
93UppDecGold-104
94AstMot-10
94Don-118
94Fle-355
94FleUpd-140
94Pac-5
94ScoRoo-RT58
94ScoRooGR-RT58
94StaClu-79
94StaClu-655
94StaCluFDI-79
94StaCluFDI-655
94StaCluGR-79
94StaCluGR-655
94StaCluMOP-79
94StaCluMOP-655
94Top-528
94TopGol-528
94TopSpa-528
95ColCho-55
95ColChoGS-55
95ColChoSS-55
95Sco-240
95ScoGolR-240
95ScoPlaTS-240
95Top-19
Breard, Stan
43ParSpo-74
Breaux, Greg
88MarPhiS-5
Breazeale, Jim (James Leo)
71RicBraTI-4
73OPC-33
73Top-33
79AppFoxT-17
83MiaMarT-25
Brecheen, Harry
46SpoExcW-1-3
47Exh-27
47HomBon-6
49Bow-158
49EurSta-179
49Lea-158
50AmeNut&CCP-2
50Bow-90
51Bow-86
51FisBakL-3
51R42SmaS-8
51TopBluB-28
52Bow-176
52Top-263
53ExhCan-14
54OriEss-4
54Top-203
55OriEss-3
55Top-113
55TopDouH-73
56Top-229
59OklTodML-19
60Lea-132
60Top-455
76TayBow4-27
79TCM50-166
81Ori6F-10
83CarGreT-9
83TopRep5-263
92CarMcD-48
94TopArc1-203
94TopArc1G-203
Brecht, Mike
83PhoGiaBHN-17
Brechtel, Johnny
93Sou-3
Brede, Brent
90EliTwiS-6
91EliTwiP-4311
91KenTwiC-7
91KenTwiP-2087
92ClaFS7-147
92KenTwiC-19
92KenTwiF-615
93FloStaLAF-14
93ForMyeMC-3
93ForMyeMF-2666
94ClaGolF-65
94ForMyeMC-3
94ForMyeMF-1178
95HarCitRCTI-1
97Fle-689
97FleTif-689
97Ult-528
97UltGolME-528
97UltPlaME-528
Bree, Charlie
89PacSenL-217
Breeden, Danny (Daniel R.)
69Top-536
69TopTeaP-12
70OPC-36
70Top-36
71MLBOffS-27
Breeden, Hal (Harold Noel)
72Dia-4
72Top-684
73ExpPos-2
73OPC-173
73Top-173
74OPC-297
74Top-297
75OPC-341
75Top-341
76SSP-329
Breeden, Joe
89MemChiB-25
89MemChiP-1193
90AppFoxBS-5
90AppFoxP-2111
91AppFoxC-26
91AppFoxP-1731
Breeden, Scott
82IowCubT-26
83IowCubT-27
85CedRapRT-32
86RedTexG-NNO
87RedKah-NNO
88RedKah-NNO
89RedKah-xx
93St.CatBJC-27
96DunBluJB-28
96DunBluJTI-3
Breeding, Marv (Marvin E.)
60OriJayP-2
60Top-525
61Pos-77A
61Pos-77B
61Top-321
61TopStaI-99
62Jel-28
62Pos-28
62PosCan-28
62SalPlaC-65A
62SalPlaC-65B
62ShiPlaC-65
62Top-6
62TopVen-6
63Top-149
83FraBroR-7
90DodTar-70
91OriCro-50
Breedlove, Larry R.
87SprCarB-21
Breen, Dick
12ImpTobC-88
Breining, Fred
77ShrCapT-2
78ColCliT-3
79BufBisT-13
80PhoGiaVNB-9
82Don-186
82Fle-385
82Top-144
83Don-503
83Fle-254
83FleSti-51
83GiaMot-7
83Top-747
84Don-387
84ExpPos-2
84ExpStu-35
84Fle-367
84FleUpd-16
84Nes792-428
84Top-428

84TopTif-428
84TopTra-16T
84TopTraT-16T
85Fle-392
85IndIndTI-10
85OPC-36
85Top-36
85TopTif-36
86NasSouTI-2
Breitenbucher, Karl
87PocGiaTB-21
89CliGiaP-888
Breitenstein, Keith
94WelPirC-5
94WelPirF-3484
Breitenstein, Ted
09T206-479
10CouT21-5
98CamPepP-6
Bremer, Bernard
85AlbYanT-28
Bremigan, Nick
88T/MUmp-19
89T/MUmp-15
90T/MUmp-63
Brenizer, Todd
77ReaPhiT-3
Brenly, Bob (Robert Earl)
77CedRapGT-2
80VenLeaS-19
81PhoGiaVNB-4
82Don-574
82Top-171
83Don-377
83Fle-255
83GiaMot-6
83Top-494
84Don-616
84Fle-368
84GiaPos-2
84Nes792-378
84Top-378
84TopSti-174
84TopTif-378
85AllGamPI-127
85Don-26
85Don-187
85DonSupD-26
85Fle-603
85GiaMot-7
85GiaPos-2
85Lea-26
85OPC-215
85Top-215
85TopGloS-3
85TopSti-158
85TopTif-215
86Don-323
86Fle-534
86GiaMot-5
86Lea-194
86OPC-307
86Top-625
86TopSti-92
86TopTat-3
86TopTif-625
87Don-485
87DonOpeD-95
87Fle-267
87FleGlo-267
87GiaMot-4
87OPC-125
87SpoTeaP-10
87Top-125
87Top-231
87TopSti-87
87TopTif-125
87TopTif-231
88Don-189
88Fle-77
88FleGlo-77
88GiaMot-4
88OPC-69
88PanSti-419
88Sco-134A
88Sco-134B
88ScoGlo-134A
88ScoGlo-134B
88StaLinG-2
88Top-703
88TopBig-143
88TopSti-92
88TopTif-703
89BluJayFS-4
89Bow-249
89BowTif-249
89Don-453
89OPC-52
89Sco-395
89Top-52
89TopTif-52
89UppDec-479
92GiaMot-28
92GiaPacGaE-8
93GiaMot-28
93GiaPos-10
94GiaMot-28
95GiaMot-28
Brennaman, Marty
93RedKah-4
Brennan, Addison
14CraJacE-115
15CraJacE-115
Brennan, Bill (William)
85VerBeaDT-15
87AlbDukP-5
88AlbDukC-6
88AlbDukP-250
88TriAAC-41
89AlbDukC-1
89AlbDukP-65
89Don-589
89Sco-622
89ScoHot1R-9
89UppDec-16
90CMC-610
90DodTar-72
90ProAAAF-187
90TucTorC-8
90TucTorP-197
92TolMudHF-1032
92TolMudHS-577
94IowCubF-1270
94TopGol-395
Brennan, James D.
32OrbPinNP-92
34DiaMatCSB-20
34BatR31-178
35DiaMatCS3T1-16
Brennan, Jim (James A.)
87OldJudN-45
Brennan, Shawn
93DanBraC-5
93DanBraF-3629
94IdaFalBF-3573
94IdaFalBSP-7
Brennan, Tom
80WauTimT-1
81ChaChaT-1
81WauTimT-5
83GleFalWST-12
Brennan, Tom (Thomas M.)
75OklCit8TI-5
77WatIndT-3A
77WatIndT-3B
79TacTugT-5
80TacTigT-12
80VenLeaS-229
81Top-451
82IndWhe-13
82Top-141
83Fle-403
83Top-524
84Don-102
84Fle-537
84Nes792-662
84Top-662
84TopTif-662
84WhiSoxTV-6
85DodCokP-5
85DomLeaS-20
90DodTar-71
Brenneman, Jim
77FriOneYW-21
81TCM60I-409
92YanWIZ6-15
Brennen, James
87DayBeaAP-9
Brenner, Jack
52LavPro-11
Brenzel, Bill (William R.)
94ConTSN-1302
94ConTSNB-1302
94TopGol-395
Breslin, Willie
87OldJudN-323
Bresnahan, Dave
86WatIndP-4
87WilBilP-14
Bresnahan, Roger P.
03WilCarE-2
06FanCraNL-5
08AmeCarE-2
08RosComP-124
09AmeCarE-13
09ColChiE-33A
09ColChiE-33B
09MaxPubP-20
09PC7HHB-5
09RamT20-16
09SpoNewSM-1
09T206-35
09T206-36
10CouT21-82
10CouT21-83
10CouT21-260
10DarChoE-4
10DomDisP-15
10E98-2
10JHDABE-2
10PeoT21-6
10RedCroT-92
10SepAnoP-1
10SweCapPP-145A
10SweCapPP-145B
11L1L-129
11MecDFT-5
11PloCanE-9
11S74Sil-117
11S81LarS-104
11SpoLifCW-43
11SpoLifM-264
11T205-20A
11T205-20B
11TurRedT-4
12ColRedB-33A
12ColRedB-33B
12ColTinT-33A
12ColTinT-33B
12HasTriFT-11
12HasTriFT-12
12HasTriFT-48B
12T207-20
13NatGamW-6
13TomBarW-5
14CraJacE-17
14FatPlaT-7
15AmeCarE-4
15CraJacE-17
15SpoNewM-16
15SpoNewP-1
15VicT21-2
16TanBraE-2
36PC7AlbHoF-29
48ExhHoF-2
50CalHOFW-6
60ExhWriH-4
60Fle-8
61Fle-10
75FlePio-7
76ShaPiz-29
77GalGloG-179
80MarExhH-3
80PacLeg-102
80PerHaloFP-29
80SSPHOF-29
81ConTSN-74
84GalHaloFRL-29
89HOFStiB-55
92ConTSN-459
93ConTSN-871
Bressler, Rube (Raymond B.)
19W514-28
20RedWorCP-2
25Exh-25
26Exh-25
27Exh-13
90DodTar-73
91ConTSN-173
94ConTSN-1280
94ConTSNB-1280
Bressoud, Ed (Edward F.)
47PM1StaP1-21
58GiaSFCB-4
58Top-263
59Top-19
59TopVen-19
60GiaJayP-3
60Top-253
61Pos-152A
61Pos-152B
61Top-203
61TopStal-74
62RedSoxJP-1
62SalPlaC-182A
62SalPlaC-182B
62ShiPlaC-182
62Top-504
63Jel-78
63Pos-78
63Top-188
64Top-352
64TopVen-352
65Top-525
66Top-516
67CokCapYM-V29
67DexPre-30
67OPC-121
67Top-121
78TCM60I-39
78TCM60I-164
81RedSoxBG2S-72
91MetWIZ-51
Brester, Jason
95BelGiaTI-26
96BurBeeTI-3
96Top-237
97Bow-217
97BowChr-195
97BowChrI-195
97BowChrIR-195
97BowChrR-195
97BowInt-217
Brett, George Howard
75OPC-228
75Top-228
76Hos-114
76OPC-19
76SSP-167
76SSP-589
76Top-19
77BurCheD-71
77Hos-36
77Kel-6
77MSADis-7
77OPC-1
77OPC-170
77OPC-261
77PepGloD-32
77RCColC-9
77Spo-3809
77Top-1
77Top-231
77Top-580
77Top-631
77TopCloS-7
78Hos-27
78Kel-6
78OPC-215
78PapGinD-36
78Pep-28
78RCColC-23
78Roy-3
78SSP270-217
78TasDis-9
78Top-100
78WifBalD-7
79Hos-68
79Kel-50
79OPC-167
79RoyTeal-2
79Top-330
79TopCom-9
80BurKinPHR-13
80Kel-9
80OPC-235
80Top-450
80TopSup-14
80WilGloT-2
81AllGamPI-29
81CokTeaS-74
81Don-100
81Don-491
81Don-537
81Dra-5
81Fle-28
81Fle-655
81Fle-655B
81FleStiC-116
81FleStiC-127
81GeoBreP-1
81Kel-8
81MSAMinD-4
81OPC-113
81PerAll-10
81PerCreC-3
81RoyPol-2
81Squ-1
81Top-1
81Top-401
81Top-700
81TopScr-1
81TopSti-9
81TopSti-14
81TopSti-82
81TopSti-243
81TopSupN-3
82Don-15
82Don-34
82Dra-4
82Fle-405
82FleSta-202
82FleSta-239
82K-M-38
82Kel-3
82OPC-200
82OPC-201
82OPC-261
82PerAll-9
82PerAllG-9
82PerCreC-19
82PerCreCG-19
82Roy-4
82SpoBre-5
82Squ-3
82Top-96
82Top-200
82Top-201
82Top-549
82TopSti-133
82TopSti-190
82WilSpoG-2
83AllGamPI-30
83Don-338
83DonActA-42
83Fle-108
83FleSta-22
83FleSti-98
83FunBal-1
83Kel-4
83Oco& SSBG-4
83OPC-3
83OPC-388
83PerAll-1
83PerAllG-1
83PerCreC-19
83PerCreCG-19
83Roy-5
83RoyPol-2
83Top-388
83Top-600
83TopFol-3
83TopGloS-31
83TopSti-76
84AllGamPI-120
84Don-53
84DonActAS-55
84DonCha-15
84Dra-3
84Fle-344
84Fle-638
84FleSti-36
84FunFooP-6
84MilBra-2
84Nes792-399
84Nes792-500
84Nes792-710
84NesDreT-3
84OCoandSI-13
84OCoandSI-88
84OPC-212
84OPC-223
84RalPur-13
84SevCoi-C5
84SevCoi-E5
84SevCoi-W5
84StaBre-1
84StaBre-2
84StaBre-3
84StaBre-4
84StaBre-5
84StaBre-6
84StaBre-7
84StaBre-8
84StaBre-9
84StaBre-10
84StaBre-11
84StaBre-12

84StaBre-13
84StaBre-14
84StaBre-15
84StaBre-16
84StaBre-17
84StaBre-18
84StaBre-19
84StaBre-20
84StaBre-21
84StaBre-22
84StaBre-23
84StaBre-24
84Top-399
84Top-500
84Top-710
84TopCer-13
84TopGaloC-1
84TopGloA-4
84TopGloS-12
84TopRubD-6
84TopSti-198
84TopSti-275
84TopSup-13
84TopTif-399
84TopTif-500
84TopTif-710
85AllGamPI-30
85Don-53
85DonActA-26
85DonHig-11
85DonHig-25
85Dra-4
85Fle-199
85FleLimE-4
85GenMilS-14
85Lea-176
85OPC-100
85SevCoi-C2
85SevCoi-E2
85SevCoi-G2
85Top-100
85Top-703
85Top3-D-4
85TopGloA-15
85TopRubD-7
85TopSti-188
85TopSti-268
85TopSup-46
85TopTif-100
85TopTif-703
86BasStaB-15
86BurKinA-20
86Don-53
86DonAll-12
86DonHig-3
86DonPop-12
86DorChe-1
86Dra-14
86Fle-5
86Fle-634
86FleAll-3
86FleLeaL-2
86FleLimE-6
86FleMin-1
86FleSlu-3
86FleStiC-11
86FleWaxBC-C2
86GenMilB-2C
86Lea-42
86MeaGolBB-2
86MeaGolM-2
86MeaGolSB-1
86MSAJifPD-4
86OPC-300
86OPCBoxB-C
86QuaGra-23
86RoyKitCD-20
86RoyNatP-5
86SevCoi-C2
86SevCoi-E2
86SevCoi-S2
86SevCoi-W2
86Spo-1
86Spo-52
86Spo-63
86Spo-179
86Spo-180
86Spo-186
86SpoDecG-64
86SpoIndC-160
86Top-300
86Top-714
86Top3-D-5
86TopGloA-4
86TopGloS-18
86TopMinL-18
86TopSti-3
86TopSti-16
86TopSti-23
86TopSti-157
86TopSti-256
86TopSup-14
86TopTat-6
86TopTif-300
86TopTif-714
86TopWaxBC-C
86TruVal-17
86Woo-4
87BoaandB-13
87ClaGam-47
87Don-15
87Don-54
87DonAll-27
87DonOpeD-206
87DonSupD-15
87Dra-14
87Fle-366
87FleGamW-6
87FleGlo-366
87FleHotS-6
87FleLeaL-5
87FleLimE-5
87FleMin-13
87FleRecS-1
87FleSlu-6
87FleStiC-15
87FleWaxBC-C3
87GenMilB-3B
87HosSti-24
87K-M-24
87KayB-5
87KraFoo-21
87Lea-15
87Lea-96
87MandMSL-14
87MSAJifPD-5
87OPC-126
87RedFolSB-111
87Spo-5
87Spo-114
87Spo-197
87SpoDeaP-4
87SpoSupD-12
87SpoTeaP-13
87StuPan-20
87Top-256
87Top-400
87TopCoi-5
87TopGloS-31
87TopMinL-57
87TopSti-254
87TopTif-256
87TopTif-400
88ClaBlu-248
88Don-102
88DonBasB-39
88Fle-254
88FleBasA-4
88FleGlo-254
88FleHotS-4
88FleStiC-30
88GreBasS-55
88K-M-3
88KinDis-7
88Lea-93
88MSAFanSD-2
88OPC-312
88PanSti-104
88RoySmo-20
88Sco-11
88ScoGlo-11
88Spo-150
88StaLinAl-4
88StaLinRo-2
88Top-141
88Top-700
88TopBig-157
88TopGloS-53
88TopSti-259
88TopStiB-41
88TopTif-141
88TopTif-700
88TopUKM-7
88TopUKMT-7
89Bow-121
89BowTif-121
89CadEllD-4
89CerSup-9
89ClaLigB-47
89Don-204
89DonAll-11
89DonBasB-7
89DonBonM-BC7
89Fle-277
89FleBasM-4
89FleGlo-277
89FleSup-5
89FleWaxBC-C3
89KayB-2
89MasBreD-9
89OPC-200
89OPCBoxB-A
89PanSti-355
89RedFolSB-12
89RoyTasD-1
89Sco-75
89Sco-75A
89ScoHot1S-4
89ScoSco-11
89Spo-64
89SpollIFKI-162
89Top-200
89TopBasT-52
89TopBatL-5
89TopBig-46
89TopCapC-9
89TopCoi-34
89TopGloS-14
89TopHilTM-3
89TopMinL-54
89TopSti-270
89TopStiB-1
89TopTif-200
89TopUKM-7
80TopWaxDC-A
89TVSpoM-105
89UppDec-215
89UppDec-689
90AllBasT-1
90Bow-382
90BowTif-382
90ClaUpd-T6
90Col-21
90Don-144
90DonBesA-35
90DonLeaS-1
90Fle-103
90Fle-621A
90Fle-621B
90FleBasM-5
90FleCan-103
90FleCan-621
90HOFStiB-93
90KayB-4
90Lea-178
90MLBBasB-101
90OPC-60
90OPCBoxB-B
90PanSti-91
90Pos-4
90PubSti-344
90RedFolSB-9
90Sco-140
90Sco100S-76
90ScoMcD-19
90Spo-214
90Top-60
90TopAmeA-2
90TopBatL-5
90TopHilHM-10
90TopMag-88
90TopSti-265
90TopTif-60
90TopWaxBC-B
90UppDec-124
90VenSti-71
90Woo-9
91BasBesHM-3
91Baz-10
91Bow-300
91Cla1-T46
91Cla2-T70
91ClaGam-137
91Col-28
91Don-201
91Don-396
91DonBonC-BC19
91DonEli-2
91Fle-552
91JimDea-12
91Lea-264
91Lea-335
91MajLeaCP-21
91MooSna-19
91OPC-2
91OPC-540
91OPCBoxB-B
91OPCPre-14
91PanCanT1-5
91PanFreS-276
91PanSti-224
91PetSta-13
91Pos-26
91PosCan-29
91RedFolS-11
91RoyPol-4
91Sco-120
91Sco-769
91Sco-853
91Sco100S-85
91ScoCoo-B5
91ScoPro-120
91SevCoi-F2
91SevCoi-M1
91SevCoi-NW1
91StaClu-159
91StaCluCM-2
91StaPinB-6
91Stu-62
91SunSee-4
91Top-2
91Top-540
91TopCraJI-15
91TopDesS-2
91TopDesS-540
91TopGaloC-3
91TopMic-2
91TopMic-540
91TopSta-6
91TopTif-2
91TopTif-540
91TopTriH-A7
91TopWaxBC-B
91Ult-144
91UppDec-525
91Woo-8
92Bow-500
92Cla2-T79
92ClaGam-81
92Don-143
92DonCraJ2-30
92DonMcD-3
92Fle-154
92Hig5-61
92HitTheBB-7
92JimDeaLL-1
92Lea-255
92LeaBlaG-255
92LeaGolP-19
92LeaPre-19
92MooSna-21
92Mr.TurS-5
92New-3
92OPC-620
92OPCPre-114
92PanSti-102
92Pin-60
92Pin-282
92PinRool-3
92Pos-11
92RoyPol-4
92Sco-650
92Sco100S-21
92ScoProP-14
92SevCoi-25
92SpoStaCC-6
92StaClu-150
92StaClu-609
92StaCluECN-609
92StaCluMO-4
92Stu-181
92Top-620
92TopGol-620
92TopGolW-620
92TopKid-105
92TopMcD-6
92TopMic-620
92TriPla-115
92Ult-68
92UppDec-444
92UppDecF-16
92UppDecFG-16
92UppDecTMH-12
93Bow-265
93ClaGam-17
93DiaMar-18
93DonEliD-15
93DonMVP-3
93DonPre-16
93DurPowP2-5
93Fin-63
93FinRef-63
93Fla-213
93Fle-236
93FleFinEDT-2
93FleFruotL-7
93FleGolM-A1
93FunPac-181
93HumDumC-9
93JimDea-15
93KinDis-9
93Kra-4
93Lea-146
93LeaHeaftH-7
93OPC-50
93PacJugC-2
93PacSpa-133
93PanSti-110
93Pin-131
93Pin-294
93PinCoo-2
93PinCooD-2
93PinTri-1
93PinTri-2
93PinTri-3
93PinTri-4
93PinTri-5
93Pos-25
93RoyPol-5
93RoySta2-1
93Sco-57
93Sco-517
93Sel-78
93SP-227
93StaClu-424
93StaCluFDI-424
93StaClul-A2
93StaCluMO-4
93StaCluMOP-424
93StaCluMOP-MA2
93StaCluMP-13
93StaCluRoy-1
93Stu-25
93StuHer-1
93Top-397
93TopGol-397
93TopInaM-397
93TopMagJRC-3
93TopMic-397
93TopMic-P397
93TriPla-64
93TriPla-214
93Ult-206
93UppDec-54
93UppDec-56
93UppDec-SP5
93UppDecDG-24
93UppDecGold-54
93UppDecGold-56
93UppDecIC-WI22
93UppDecICJ-WI22
93UppDecOD-D6
93UppDecSH-HI7
93UppDecTAN-TN2
94ColC-65
94ColChoGS-65
94ColChoSS-65
94Don-107
94DonAnn8-3
94Fle-149
94FleGolM-6
94StaClu-5
94StaCluFDI-5
94StaCluGR-5
94StaCluMOP-5
94Top-180
94TopGol-180
94TopPre-397
94TopSpa-180
94UppDecAH-20
94UppDecAH-123
94UppDecAH1-20
94UppDecAH1-123
94UppDecTAE-80
95ColCho-49
95ColCho-54
95ColChoGS-49
95ColChoGS-54
95ColChoSS-49
95ColChoSS-54

95SP-3
95SPCha-101
95SPChaCP-CP5
95SPChaCPDC-CP5
95SPChaDC-101
95SPSil-3
95UppDec-449
95UppDecED-449
95UppDecEDG-449
95UppDecSE-190
95UppDecSEG-190
96Pro-4

Brett, Ken (Kenneth Alvin)
69Top-476A
69Top-476B
70RedSoxCPPC-3
71MLBOffS-315
71OPC-89
71RedSoxA-2
71Top-89
72MilBra-45
72OPC-517
72Top-517
73LinPor-148
73OPC-444
73Top-444
74OPC-237
74Top-237
75Kel-52
75OPC-250
75Top-250
76OPC-401
76SSP-569
76Top-401
76TopTra-401T
77Hos-65
77OPC-21
77Top-157
77Top-631
78AngFamF-5
78SSP270-192
78Top-682
79Top-557
80DodPol-34
80Top-521
81RedSoxBG2S-73
81Top-47
82Don-364
82Fle-406
82Top-397
85UtiBluST-24
90DodTar-74
90SweBasG-52
92YanWIZ7-24
93UppDecAH-17
94BreMilB-285
94UppDecAH-192
94UppDecAH1-192

Breuer, James
93GreFalDSP-29
94YakBeaC-2

Breuer, Marvin
40PlaBal-183
43YanSta-3
75YanDyn1T-3

Brevell, Bubba (Ron)
86KinEagP-2
88MiaMarS-3

Brewer, Bernie
92BreCarT-xx
94BrePol-1
94MasMan-1

Brewer, Billy
90JamExpP-15
92WesPalBEC-20
92WesPalBEF-2080
93Bow-561
93FleFinE-215
93OPCPre-99
93PacSpa-485
93Pin-606
93SelRoo-143T
93Ult-557
94Don-137
94Fle-150
94Pac-280
94Sco-564
94ScoGolR-564
94StaClu-490
94StaCluFDI-490
94StaCluGR-490
94StaCluMOP-490
94Top-123
94TopGol-123
94TopSpa-123
95ColCho-463
95ColChoGS-463
95ColChoSS-463
95Don-141
95DonPreP-141
95DonTopotO-83
95Fle-153
95Sco-140
95ScoGolR-140
95ScoPlaTS-140
95Top-439
95TopCyb-235
95Ult-54
95UltGolM-54
95UppDec-416
95UppDecED-416
95UppDecEDG-416

Brewer, Brett
94DanBraF-3543
95MacBraTI-1
95MacBraUTI-1

Brewer, Brian
93BluOriC-5
93BluOriF-4116
94AlbPolC-5
94AlbPolF-2228
94OriPro-10
96BowBayB-8

Brewer, Chet
78LauLonABS-23
87NegLeaPD-29

Brewer, Doug
94DanBraC-3

Brewer, Gay
68AtlOil-2

Brewer, Jim
61Top-317
61TopStaI-629
62Top-191
62TopVen-191
63Top-309
64Top-553
65Top-416
66OPC-158
66Top-158
66TopVen-158
67CokCapD-7
67CokCapDA-7
67OPC-31
67Top-31
68Top-298
68TopVen-298
69MilBra-36
69Top-241
70Top-571
71DodTic-3
71MLBOffS-98
71OPC-549
71Top-549
72MilBra-46
72OPC-151
72Top-151
73OPC-126
73Top-126
74Kel-14
74OPC-189
74Top-189
75OPC-163
75Top-163
76OPC-459
76Top-459
77ExpPos-6
77OPC-198
78TCM60I-243
79ExpPos-4
87DodSmoA-3
88DodSmo-14
89DodSmoG-79
90DodTar-75
92DodStaTA-12

Brewer, John H.
48SomandK-2
49BowPCL-8
49SomandK-2

Brewer, Mark
91SalLakTP-3228
91SalLakTSP-26
96GreFalDTI-34

Brewer, Matt
91Cla/Bes-420
91EveGiaC-21
91EveGiaP-3927
92ProFS7-359
92SanJosGC-1

Brewer, Mike
84OmaRoyT-9
85MaiGuiT-26
86OmaRoyP-3
86OmaRoyT-13

Brewer, Mudcat
94BenRocF-3600

Brewer, Nevin
93EugEmeC-6
93EugEmeF-3848
94RocRoyC-3
94RocRoyF-555
95Exc-55
95WilBluRTI-37

Brewer, Omar
88ChaRanS-3

Brewer, Rodney
88SprCarB-19
90CMC-112
90LouRedBC-12
90LouRedBLBC-8
90LouRedBP-407
90ProAAAF-521
90TopTVCa-39
91Cla1-T92
91LinDriAAA-227
91LouRedLD-227
91LouRedP-2925
91LouRedTI-14
91TopDeb90-21
92LouRedF-1897
92LouRedS-253
92Sco-864
92SkyAAAF-123
92TriA AAS-253
93CarPol-3
93FleMajLP-A17
93PacSpa-629
93StaClu-527
93StaCluCa-7
93StaCluFDI-527
93StaCluMOP-527
93Top-566
93TopGol-566
93TopInaM-566
93TopMic-566
93UppDec-381
93UppDecGold-381
94Don-400
94Fle-629
94Sco-297
94ScoGolR-297
94StaCluT-326
94StaCluTFDI-326

Brewer, Tom
47Exh-28
55Bow-178
55Top-83
55TopDouH-127
56Top-34
57Top-112
58RedSoxJP-1
58Top-220
59RedSoxJP-1
59Top-55
59Top-346
59TopVen-55
60RedSoxJP-1
60Top-439
61Pos-50A
61Pos-50B
61Top-434
61TopStaI-108
62SalPlaC-4
62ShiPlaC-4

Brewer, Tony (Anthony Bruce)
83AlbDukT-20
84AlbDukC-161
85AlbDukC-152
85Don-31
87JapPlaB-42
90DodTar-76

Brewer, Woody (Sherwood)
93NegLeaRL2-6

Brewers, Helena
95HelBreTI-32
96HelBreTI-NNO

Brewers, Milwaukee
71OPC-698
71Top-698
71TopTat-61
72OPC-106
72Top-106
73OPC-127
73OPCBTC-13
73Top-127
73TopBluTC-13
74OPC-314
74OPCTC-13
74Top-314
74TopStaA-13
74TopTeaC-13
78Top-328
82BrePol-NNO
83BrePol-NNO
83FleSta-237
83FleSti-NNO
84BrePol-NNO
87BrePol-NNO
87SpoTeaL-19
87Top-56
87TopTif-56
88BrePol-NNO
88PanSti-462
88RedFolSB-115
90PubSti-644
90RedFolSB-123
90VenSti-527
91PanCanT1-126
92BreCarT-xx
94ImpProP-8
94Sco-324
94ScoGolR-324
95PanSti-155
96PanSti-195

Brewers, Minors (Milwaukee)
38BasTabP-31

Brewington, Jamie
92EveGiaC-18
92EveGiaF-1677
93ClaGolF-159
93CliGiaC-5
93CliGiaF-2480
95UltGolMR-M6
96ColCho-38
96ColCho-660
96ColChoGS-38
96ColChoGS-660
96ColChoSS-38
96ColChoSS-660
96Don-495
96DonPreP-495
96Fle-584
96FleTif-584
96PhoFirB-10
96Top-331
96Ult-291
96UltGolM-291
96UppDec-193
96UppDecFSP-FS5

Brewington, Mike (Michael)
89WelPirP-6
90AugPirP-2476
90CMC-725
91SalBucC-10
91SalBucP-964

Brewster, Charlie (Charles L.)
43PhiTeal-3

Brewster, Rich
76QuaCitAT-6
77QuaCitAT-7
80ElPasDT-20

Brian, Braden
87JamExpP-2554

Brice, Alan
77FriOneYW-97

Brickell, Fred (George F.)
33Gou-38
33GouCanV-38
33RitCE-4D
35GouPuzR-6C
35GouPuzR-11E
35GouPuzR-13C
35GouPuzR-15C
93ConTSN-808

Brickell, Fritzie (Fritz D.)
61AngJayP-4
61MapLeaBH-2
61Top-333
81TCM60I-294

Brickey, Josh
89KinMetS-29
90KinMetS-30

Brickhouse, Jack
89PacLegI-209

Brickler, Tim
93MisStaB-4

Brideweser, Jim (James E.)
53BowC-136
55Bow-151
57Top-382
91OriCro-51

Bridge, Eric
89FreStaBS-4

Bridge, Mark
85CloHSS-5

Bridgers, Brandon
93BluOriC-6
93BluOriF-4138
94AlbPolC-6
94AlbPolF-2248
94OriPro-11
94SouAtlLAF-SAL1

Bridges, Jason
88OneYanP-2045
89PriWilCS-1
90PriWilCTI-6

Bridges, Jim
85BurRanT-28

Bridges, Kary
94QuaCitRBC-6
94QuaCitRBF-539
95JacGenTI-19
96JacGenB-5
96TusTorB-4

Bridges, Marshall
58UniOil-1
64ChatheY-5
64YanReqKP-6
78TCM60I-48
92YanWIZ6-16

Bridges, Rocky (Everett L.)
50WorWidGV-1
52Top-239
53BowBW-32
54Bow-156
55Bow-136
56Top-324
57RedSoh-3
57Top-294
58SenJayP-1
58Top-274
59Top-318
60Lea-31
60TigJayP-3
60Top-22
60TopVen-22
61Top-508
62Jel-75
62Pos-75
62PosCan-75
74PhoGiaC-90
75PhoGiaCK-1
76PheGiaCr-26
76PhoGiaCa-6
76PhoGiaCC-3
76PhoGiaVNB-2
77PhoGiaCC-5
77PhoGiaCP-4
77PhoGiaVNB-3
78PhoGiaC-3
79PhoGiaVNB-5
80PhoGiaVNB-22
81PhoGiaVNB-25
83TopRep5-239
84EveGiaC-28
84OCoandSI-117
85GiaMot-27
85GiaPos-3
86PriWilPP-4
87VanCanP-1605
88BufBisC-25
88BufBisP-1478
88BufBisTI-1
89SalBucS-25
90DodTar-77
90WelPirP-33
95TopArcBD-14
82PhoGiaVNB-7

Bridges, Thomas
33ButCanV-4
33Gou-199
33TatOrbSDR-177
34BatR31-9
34BatR31-81

34DiaStaR-5
34Gou-44
34GouCanV-87
35GolMedFR-1
35GouPuzR-1D
35GouPuzR-2D
35GouPuzR-16D
35GouPuzR-17D
35WheBB1-4
36GouWidPPR-A10
36GouWidPPR-C5
36NatChiFPR-14
36WorWidGV-33
37OPCBatUV-133
37WheBB14-2
37WheBB7-29J
37WheBB9-2
38ExhFou-12
39PlaBal-104
41PlaBal-65
48SweSpoT-13
61Fle-95
70FleWorS-32
76TigOldTS-2
81TigDetN-56
81TigSecNP-15
83ConMar-24
83DiaClaS2-77
88ConAmeA-3
91ConTSN-180
93ConTSN-723

Bridges-Clements, Tony
88BasCitRS-9
89MemChiB-7
89MemChiP-1202
89MemChiS-3
91MemChiP-659
92BasCitRF-3850
92ClaFS7-237
92MemChiF-2430
92MemChiS-427
92SkyAA F-179

Bridwell, Al (Albert H.)
08AmeCarE-3
08AmeCarE-38
09AmeCarE-14
09ColChiE-34
09RamT20-17
09T206-37
09T206-38
10CouT21-84
10CouT21-85
10CouT21-261
10DarChoE-5
10DomDisP-16
10E101-6
10E12AmeCDC-6
10E98-3
10MelMinE-6
10NadCarE-7
10NadE1-9
10PeoT21-7A
10PeoT21-7B
10PeoT21-7C
10RedCroT-6
10RedCroT-172
10SepAnoP-2
10SweCapPP-108
11BasBatEU-4
11MecDFT-6
11S74Sil-81
11SpoLifCW-44
11SpoLifM-205
11T205-21
11TurRedT-83
12ColRedB-34
12ColTinT-34
12HasTriFT-20
12HasTriFT-50A
14CraJacE-42
14PieStaT-6
15AmeCarE-5
15CraJacE-42
16TanBraE-3
91ConTSN-170

Brief, Bunny (Anthony V.)
94ConTSN-1290
94ConTSNB-1290

Brier, Coe
83WisRapTF-1

Briggs, Anthony
94IdaFalBF-3574
95MacBraTI-2
96DurBulBlB-4
96DurBulBrB-5
96Exc-122

Briggs, Buttons (Herbert)
98CamPepP-7

Briggs, Dan (Daniel Lee)
74CarSalLCA-100
75SalLakCC-5
76SalLakCGC-20
77Top-592
79Top-77
80Top-352
82OPC-102
82Top-102
82TopTra-11T
84ColCliP-3
84ColCliT-5
85ColCliP-3
85ColCliT-14
85IntLeaAT-33

Briggs, David
88SpoIndP-1938
89ChaRaiP-994

Briggs, John Edward
64PhiPhiB-6
64Top-482
65OPC-163
65Top-163
66Top-359
66TopVen-359
67CokCapPh-3
67DexPre-31
67PhiPol-3
67Top-268
68Top-284
68TopVen-284
69MilBra-37
69MLBOffS-173
69OPC-73
69Top-73
69TopSta-72
70MLBOffS-85
70PhiTeal-2
70Top-564
71MLBOffS-170
71OPC-297
71Top-297
72MilBra-47
72OPC-197
72Top-197
73LinPor-98
73OPC-71
73Top-71
74OPC-218
74Top-218
74TopSta-192
75Kel-16
75OPC-123
75Top-123
76OPC-373
76Top-373
81TCM60I-424
86BreGreT-6
94BreMilB-286

Briggs, John T.
57SeaPop-7
59Top-177
59TopVen-177
60Top-376

Briggs, Ken
91SalSpuC-1
91SalSpuP-2246

Briggs, Kenny
83WauTimF-29

Briggs, Stoney
91MedHatBJP-4113
92MyrBeaHC-16
92MyrBeaHF-2209
93WatDiaC-6
93WatDiaF-1781
94RanCucQC-7
94RanCucQF-1649
95MemChiTI-6
95UppDecML-146
96MemChiB-8
95UppDecMLFS-146

Briggs, Walter O.
81TigDetN-5

Briggs, William
91MedHatBJSP-20

Bright, Brian
91ElmPioC-1
91ElmPioP-3281
92WinHavRSC-23
92WinHavRSF-1791
93FloStaLAF-13
93ForLauRSC-3
93ForLauRSFP-1608
94ClaGolF-64
94SarRedSC-5
94SarRedSF-1964

Bright, Don
74GasRanT-6
75AndRanT-43
76SanAntBTI-3
78TucTorC-21

Bright, Harry James
59Top-523
60Top-277
61Top-447
62Top-551
63Jel-95
63Pos-95
63RedEnq-2
63Top-304
64ChatheY-6
64Top-259
64TopVen-259
65Top-584
76TucTorCa-9
76TusTorCr-23
78TCM60I-214
85DurBulT-14
92YanWIZ6-17

Bright, Tom
77AppFoxT-2

Briles, Nellie (Nelson)
64TulOil-2
65CarTeal-3
65Top-431
66Top-243
66TopVen-243
67Top-404
67TopVen-283
68OPC-153
68Top-153
68Top-540
68TopVen-153
69MilBra-38
69MLBOffS-208
69OPC-60
69Top-60
69TopSta-111
69TopTeaP-18
70MLBOffS-134
70OPC-435
70Top-435
71CarTeal-4
71MLBOffS-195
71OPC-257
71Pir-1
71PirActP-2
71Top-257
72MilBra-48
72OPC-227
72Top-227
72Top-605
73OPC-303
73Top-303
74OPC-123
74Top-123
74TopSta-81
74TopTra-123T
75OPC-495
75Top-495
76OPC-569
76SSP-159
76Top-569
77Top-174
78Top-717
79Top-262
81TCM60I-308
89SweBasG-79
91OriCro-52
93RanKee-81
93UppDecAH-18
94UppDecAH-27
94UppDecAH1-27

Briley, Greg
86BelMarC-107
87ChaLooB-17
88CalCanC-13
88CalCanP-799
88ScoRoo-74T
88ScoRooG-74T
89FleUpd-57
89ScoHot1R-54
89Top-781
89TopBig-247
89TopTif-781
89UppDec-770
90Baz-17
90Bow-482
90BowTif-482
90ClaBlu-54
90Don-463
90Fle-507
90FleCan-507
90Lea-391
90MarMot-14
90OPC-288
90PanSti-148
90Sco-303
90Sco100RS-60
90ScoYouSI-12
90Spo-43
90Top-288
90TopBig-35
90TopGloS-19
90TopRoo-4
90TopSti-226
90TopSti-320
90TopTif-288
90ToyRoo-5
90UppDec-455
91Bow-256
91Don-352
91Fle-444
91Lea-194
91MarCouH-4
91OPC-133
91Sco-494
91StaClu-130
91Top-133
91TopDesS-133
91TopMic-133
91TopTif-133
91UppDec-479
92Don-487
92Fle-274
92Lea-65
92MarMot-15
92OPC-502
92PanSti-61
92Sco-387
92StaClu-228
92Top-502
92TopGol-502
92TopGolW-502
92TopMic-502
92Ult-120
92UppDec-369
93Don-695
93Fle-670
93FleFinE-54
93MarPub-6
93MarUSPC-8S
93PacSpa-281
93StaClu-440
93StaCluFDI-440
93StaCluMOP-440
93Top-14
93TopGol-14
93TopInaM-14
93TopMic-14
93TopTra-35T
93Ult-368
93UppDec-634
93UppDecGold-634
94ChaKniF-906
94VenLinU-48
95IndIndF-106

Briley, Paxton
92BoiHawC-25
92BoiHawF-3617
93StaCluM-158

Brilinski, Tyler
86ModA'sC-5
86ModA'sP-4
87HunStaTI-5
88TacTigC-12
88TacTigP-617
89TacTigC-13
89TacTigP-1561

Brill, Clinton
83AndBraT-26

Brill, Tim
78WatIndT-4
79SavBraT-6

Brill, Todd
88OneYanP-2042

Brimhall, Bradley
90MadMusP-2260
90SouOreAB-22
90SouOreAP-3439
91MadMusC-5
91MadMusP-2122
92KanCouCTI-2

Brimsek, Frank
43ParSpo-10

Brincks, Mark
93HicCraC-4
93HicCraF-1271

Bringhurst, Stewart
78WauMetT-3

Brink, Brad
87ClePhiP-23
88MaiPhiC-5
88MaiPhiP-289
88PhiTas-27
89ScrRedBP-721
92DonRoo-14
92PhiMed-38
92ReaPhiS-527
92ScrRedBS-484
92SkyAA F-227
93Sco-224
93ScrRedBF-2539
93ScrRedBTI-4
93Top-818
93TopGol-818
93TopInaM-818
93TopMic-818
94PhiUSPC-2D
94PhiUSPC-9S
94PhoFirF-1512
95PhoFirTI-10

Brink, Craig
88OneYanP-2051

Brink, Mike
85CloHSS-6

Brinkley, Christie
96PinChrBC-PCB

Brinkley, Darryl
96RanCucQB-7

Brinkley, Josh
96WesPalBEB-17

Brinkman, Chuck (Charles E.)
71OPC-13
71Top-13
72Top-786
73OPC-404
73Top-404
74OPC-641
74Top-641

Brinkman, Ed (Edwin A.)
63Top-479
64Top-46
64TopCoi-108
64TopGia-27
64TopVen-46
65Top-417
66SenTeal-2
66Top-251
66TopVen-251
67CokCapS-3
67DexPre-32
67SenTeal-2
67Top-311
68OPC-49
68SenTeal81/2-1
68Top-49A
68Top-49B
68TopVen-49
69MilBra-39
69MLBOffS-101
69OPC-153
69SenTeal-3
69SenTeal8-5
69SenTeal8-6
69Top-153
69TopFou-16
69TopSta-232
69TopTeaP-23
70MLBOffS-279
70SenPolY-2
70Top-711
71MLBOffS-385
71OPC-389
71Top-389
71TopCoi-46
72MilBra-49
72Top-535
73OPC-5
73TigJew-1
73Top-5

74OPC-138
74Top-138
74TopSta-171
75OPC-439
75Top-439
75YanSSP-3
76SSP-447
81TigDetN-70
82BirBarT-24
84WhiSoxTV-8
92YanWIZ7-25
93RanKee-82
Brinkman, Greg
84ButCopKT-8
87SalSpuP-11
88VerMarP-957
89OrlTwiB-30
89VisOakP-1428
Brinkman, Joe
88T/MUmp-15
89T/MUmp-13
90T/MUmp-13
Brinkopf, Leon C.
77FriOneYW-18
Brinson, Hugh
86VenGulP-2
87DunBluJP-927
88KnoBluJB-24
Briones, Chris
95HudValRTI-15
96ChaRivTI-9607
Brisbin, Steve
75QuaCitAT-30
Brisco, Jamie
83EriCarT-9
84SavCarT-13
86StoPorP-2
87ElPasDP-10
88ElPasDB-4
Briscoe, John
90ModA'sC-2
90ModA'sCLC-150
90ModA'sP-2204
91HunStaLD-279
91LinDriAA-279
91ScoRoo-108T
92DonRoo-15
92SkyAAAF-235
92StaClu-681
92StaCluECN-681
92TacTigF-2495
92TacTigS-539
92TopDeb91-21
93HunStaF-2076
94A'sMot-27
95Fla-70
95Fle-241
95Top-435
95TopCyb-232
96LeaSigEA-16
Briskey, Dick
45CenFlo-2
Brison, Sam
76LauIndC-4
76LauIndC-11
76LauIndC-29
76LauIndC-37
Brissie, Lou
47Exh-29
49Bow-41
49Lea-31
49PhiBul-8
50Bow-48
50Dra-4
50RoyDes-8A
50RoyDes-8B
51Bow-155
51TopBluB-31
52Bow-79
52IndNumN-1
52NatTeaL-3
52RoyPre-2
52TipTop-4
52Top-270
53IndPenCBP-7
83TopRep5-270
Bristol, Dave
67OPC-21
67Top-21
68OPC-148
68Top-148
68TopVen-148
69Top-234
70BreMcD-4
70BreMil-2
70BreTeal-2
70Top-556
71BreTeal-2
71OPC-637
71Top-637
72Dia-5
72Top-602
73OPC-377
73Top-377
74OPC-531
74Top-531
76OPC-631
76Top-631
77Top-442
79GiaPol-1
80GiaPol-1
80Top-499
81Don-436
81Top-686
84PhiTas-9
85PhiTas-3
85PhiTas-8
88PhiTas-29
89RedKah-xx
Bristow, Richie
90KinMetB-21
90KinMetS-3
91ColMetPI-12
91ColMetPPI-2
Brito, Adan
84IdaFalATI-5
Brito, Bernardo
81BatTroT-20
81WatIndT-31
83WatIndF-17
86IndTeal-8
86WatIndP-5
87WilBilP-23
88OrlTwiB-28
88SouLeaAJ-13
89PorBeaC-21
89PorBeaP-212
90CMC-575
90PorBeaC-23
90PorBeaP-190
90ProAAAF-260
91LinDriAAA-403
91PorBeaLD-403
91PorBeaP-1575
92PorBeaF-2677
92PorBeaS-402
92SkyAAAF-183
93LimRocDWB-79
93Pin-274
93PorBeaF-2392
93Sco-306
93TopGol-394
93TriAAAGF-46
94Fle-200
94Pac-350
94SalLakBF-827
94TriAAF-AAA15
Brito, Domingo
94MarPhiC-5
94MarPhiF-3300
95BatCliTI-4
95MarPhiTI-4
Brito, Frank
88BenBucL-6
Brito, Jorge
88ModA'sCLC-68
88ModA'sTI-17
89ModA'sCLC-282
90Bes-180
90HunStaB-13
91HunStaTI-3
91LinDriAAA-528
91TacTigLD-528
91TacTigP-2309
92HunStaF-3953
92TacTigS-527
94NewHavRF-1551
95FleUpd-165
96ColSprSSTI-3
96LeaSigEA-17
Brito, Jose Oscar
80WatRedT-12
81IndIndTI-11
82LouRedE-3
83LouRedR-14
85ChaO'sT-26
85RocRedWT-15
Brito, Luis
89MarPhiS-3
90PriPatD-3
91MarPhiC-13
91MarPhiP-3458
92ClePhiF-2061
92SpaPhiC-17
92SpaPhiF-1267
93SpaPhiC-6
93SpaPhiF-1060
94ClePhiC-8
94ClePhiF-2533
95ClePhiF-221
96DurBulBrB-26
Brito, Mario
87JamExpP-2557
88MidLeaAGS-45
88RocExpLC-2
90CMC-660
90JacExpB-17
90JacExpP-1368
91LinDriAAA-627
91VanCanLD-627
91VanCanP-1586
92HarSenF-453
92HarSenS-277
93HarSenF-261
93LimRocDWB-9
96ChaKniB-9
Brito, Tilson
93ClaFS7-273
93DunBluJC-2
93DunBluJF-1801
93DunBluJFFN-2
94KnoSmoF-1308
96FleUpd-U93
96FleUpdTC-U93
96LeaSigA-34
96LeaSigAG-34
96LeaSigAS-34
96SyrChiTI-5
96Ult-425
96UltGolM-425
97BluJayS-20
97Pac-213
97PacLigB-213
97PacSil-213
Britt, Bob
88SpaPhiP-1046
Britt, Bryan
96NewJerCB-3
Britt, Doug
78ChaPirT-1
81BufBisT-3
82DayBeaAT-10
Britt, Ken
92HamRedC-16
92HamRedF-1581
93GleFalRC-8
93GleFalRF-3994
Britt, Patrick
87ModA'sC-2
87ModA'sP-21
Britt, Stephan
92DavLipB-5
92DavLipB-23
Brittain, Grant
90IdaFalBP-3251
90ProAaA-198
91MacBraC-17
91MacBraP-870
92DurBulC-10
92DurBulTI-9
Brittan, Corey
96PitMetB-7
Britton, James Allan
64Top-94
64TopVen-94
68OPC-76
68Top-76
68TopVen-76
69OPC-154
69Top-154
69TopFou-3
70Top-646
71OPC-699
71Top-699
72MilBra-50
Britton, Jimmy W.
72OPC-351
72Top-351
Brixey, Dustin
95SprSulTI-3
96WilBluRB-23
Brizzolara, Tony
79RicBraT-25
80OPC-86
80RicBraT-7
80Top-156
80VenLeaS-108
81RicBraT-2
82RicBraT-2A
82RicBraT-2B
83RicBraT-2
84RicBraT-9
85IntLeaAT-11
85RicBraT-1
86BufBisP-5
90RicBra2ATI-5
Broaca, Johnny
34BatR31-192
75YanDyn1T-4
92ConTSN-517
94ConTSN-995
94ConTSNB-995
Broach, Donald
93PriRedC-2
93PriRedF-4191
94BilMusF-3681
94BilMusSP-10
96ChaLooB-8
Broadfoot, Scott
87EriCarP-15
88St.PetCS-2
89SprCarB-6
Broas, Rick
77NewCoPT-3
Broberg, Pete
71SenTealW-5
72OPC-64
72Top-64
73Kel2D-41
73OPC-162
73Top-162
74OPC-425
74Top-425
75OPC-542
75Top-542
76BreA&P-2
76Hos-74
76OPC-39
76SSP-245
76Top-39
76VenLeaS-29
77Hos-145
77OPC-55
77Top-409
78Top-722
79OPC-301
79Top-578
89TopSenL-87
93RanKee-5
94BreMilB-287
Brocail, Doug
86SpoIndC-162
87ChaRaiP-23
88ChaRaiP-1211
89WicStaR-13
89WicWraR-28
90WicWraRD-3
91LinDriAA-602
91WicWraLD-602
91WicWraP-2590
91WicWraRD-1
92DonRoo-16
92LasVegSF-2789
92LasVegSS-226
92SkyAAAF-110
93Don-418
93FleFinE-135
93LasVegSF-937
93Top-821
93TopGol-821
93TopInaM-821
93TopMic-821
94Don-615
94Fle-657
94Lea-165
94Pac-518
94PadMot-25
94Top-579
94TopGol-579
94TopSpa-579
94TriPla-164
95AstMot-19
95FleUpd-139
96AstMot-20
96ColCho-358
96ColChoGS-358
96ColChoSS-358
96FleUpd-U138
96FleUpdTC-U138
96LeaSigEA-18
97Fle-556
97FleTif-556
97PacPriGotD-GD149
Brock, Chris
92IdaFalGF-3503
92IdaFalGSP-19
93MacBraC-3
93MacBraF-1392
94ExcFS7-152
94GreBraF-406
94GreBraTI-7
95RicBraRC-2
95RicBraTI-2
96RicBraB-8
96RicBraRC-6
96RicBraUB-5
Brock, Don
88PocGiaP-2073
89SanJosGB-6
89SanJosGCLC-210
89SanJosGP-442
89SanJosGS-3
90SanJosGB-18
90SanJosGCLC-50
90SanJosGP-2004
90SanJosGS-3
Brock, Greg (Gregory Allen)
82AlbDukT-15
83DodPol-17
83DodPos-2
83Don-579
83Fle-203
83SevCoi-12
83TopTra-14T
84DodPol-9
84Don-296
84Fle-98
84Nes792-555
84OPC-242
84Top-555
84TopSti-376
84TopTif-555
85AllGamPI-91
85DodCokP-6
85Fle-368
85OPC-242
85Top-753
85TopMin-753
85TopTif-753
86BasStaB-16
86DodCokP-4
86DodPol-9
86DodUniOP-2
86Don-296
86Fle-125
86OPC-368
86Top-368
86TopSti-67
86TopTif-368
87BrePol-9
87BreTeal-2
87DonOpeD-50
87Fle-437
87FleGlo-437
87FleUpd-9
87FleUpdG-9
87OPC-26
87Top-26
87TopSti-68
87TopTif-26
87TopTra-9T
87TopTraT-9T
88BrePol-9
88Don-337
88DonBasB-71
88Fle-158
88FleGlo-158
88Lea-148
88OPC-212
88PanSti-121
88Sco-234
88ScoGlo-234
88Spo-184
88StaLinBre-3
88Top-212
88TopBig-217
88TopTif-212
89Bow-143
89BowTif-143

89BreGar-11
89BrePol-9
89BreYea-9
89Don-57
89DonBasB-239
89Fle-181
89FleGlo-181
89OPC-163
89PanSti-371
89Sco-307
89Top-517
89TopBig-100
89TopSti-201
89TopTif-517
89UppDec-543
90Bow-395
90BowTif-395
90BreMilB-2
90DodTar-78
90Don-293
90DonBesA-142
90Fle-318
90FleCan-318
90Lea-454
90OPC-139
90PanSti-104
90PubSti-492
90Sco-485
90Top-139
90TopBig-47
90TopSti-208
90TopTif-139
90UppDec-514
90VenSti-72
91Bow-41
91BrePol-4
91Don-572
91Fle-577
91OPC-663
91PanFreS-204
91RedFolS-12
91Sco-522
91StaClu-269
91Top-663
91TopDesS-663
91TopMic-663
91TopTif-663
91Ult-172
91UppDec-289
94BreMilB-288
Brock, Lou (Louis Clark)
62Top-387
63CubJayP-3
63Top-472
64CubJayP-3
64Top-29
64TopCoi-97
64TopVen-29
65CarTeal-4
65Top-540
66CarTeal-1
66OPC-125
66Top-125
66TopVen-125
67OPC-63
67Top-63
67Top-285
67TopVen-307
68AtlOilPBCC-7
68Baz-15
68OPC-151
68Top-151
68Top-372
68Top-520
68TopVen-151
69KelPin-4
69MilBra-40
69MLBOffS-209
69MLBPin-36
69NabTeaF-3
69OPC-85
69OPC-165
69Top-85
69Top-165
69Top-428
69TopFou-4
69TopSta-112
69TopTeaP-18
69TraSta-31
70CarTeal-2
70DayDaiNM-88
70Kel-44
70MilBra-2
70MLBOffS-135
70OPC-330
70Top-330
70TopPos-4
70TopSup-11
71CarTeal-5
71Kel-17
71MilDud-37
71MLBOffS-268
71OPC-625
71Top-625
71TopCoi-87
71TopGreM-27
71TopSup-25
72Kel-48
72MilBra-51
72OPC-200
72Top-200
73Kel2D-40
73LinPor-165
73OPC-64
73OPC-320
73Top-64
73Top-320
73TopCanL-8
74GreHeroBP-2
74GreHeroBP-6
74OPC-60
74OPC-204
74Top-60
74Top-204
74TopDecE-20
74TopSta-111
75Hos-23
75HosTwi-23
75Kel-39
75OPC-2
75OPC-309
75OPC-540
75Top-2
75Top-309
75Top-540
76CooPapB-2
76CraDis-5
76Hos-7
76HosTwi-7
76Kel-40
76LauDiaJ-14
76OPC-10
76OPC-197
76SSP-275
76SSP-590
76Top-10
76Top-197
77BurCheD-15
77Car5-2
77CarTeal-2
77GalGloG-269
77Hos-32
77MSADis-4
77OPC-51
77RCColC-10
77Spo-2416
77Top-355
77TopCloS-8
78CarTeal-2
78Kel-7
78OPC-204
78OPC-236
78TasDis-6
78Top-1
78Top-170
78WifBalD-8
79Car5-2
79OPC-350
79Top-415
79Top-665
80MarExh-6
80PerHaloFP-190
80SSPHOF-195
80Top-1
81TCM60I-341
82BasCarN-9
82BasCarN-12
83KelCerB-13
84OCoandSI-75
85DalNatCC-8
85Woo-5
86SpoDecG-59
86SpoDesJM-2
86TCMSupS-27
87K-M-13
88HouSho-10
89KahCoo-3
89Top-662
89TopBasT-26
89TopTif-662
90HOFStiB-86
90PacLeg-12
90PerGreM-66
90SweBasG-71
91Col-11
91Kel3D-10
91KelStaU-4
91LinDri-24
91SweBasG-13
91UppDec-636
91UppDec-636A
91UppDecHoB5-1
91UppDecS-6
91UppDecS-11
91UppDecS-14
91UppDecS-15
92ActPacA-2
92ActPacA2-2G
92CarMcD-30
92MVP-12
92MVP2H-6
92UppDecF-48
92UppDecFG-48
92UppDecHH-HI2
92UppDecHoB-H6
92UppDecHoB-H8
92UppDecHoB-AU6
92UppDecS-11
92UppDecS-33
92UppDecS-35
93ActPacAC-2
93FroRowB-1
93FroRowB-2
93FroRowB-3
93FroRowB-4
93FroRowB-5
93MetIma-5
93TedWil-86
93TedWilLC-2
93UppDecS-26
93Yoo-3
94UppDecAH-3
94UppDecAH-79
94UppDecAH-176
94UppDecAH-220
94UppDecAH1-3
94UppDecAH1-79
94UppDecAH1-176
94UppDecAH1-220
94UppDecS-2
97SpollICC-3
97St.VinHHS-3
Brock, Norman
86FloStaLAP-10
86OscAstP-1
87ColAstP-24
88ColAstB-27
89CedRapRB-18
89CedRapRP-938
89CedRapRS-2
Brock, Russell
91SouOreAC-10
91SouOreAP-3832
92ProFS7-136
92RenSilSCLC-46
92StaCluD-20
93ModA'sC-4
93ModA'sF-790
94ExcFS7-118
94HunStaF-1324
94TacTigF-3167
95EdmTraTI-3
Brock, Tarrik
91BriTigC-6
91Cla/Bes-407
91FroRowDP-52
91HigSchPLS-8
92Bow-345
92FayGenC-6
92FayGenF-2180
92StaCluD-21
92UppDecML-189
93FayGenC-5
93FayGenF-140
94FloStaLAF-FSL13
94LakTigC-1
94LakTigF-3048
96LakTigB-9
Brocker, Gene (John)
49SomandK-26
Brockett, Lew
09ColChiE-35
12ColRedB-35
12ColTinT-35
12ImpTobC-55
Brocki, Mike
87SanBerSP-16
88SanBerSB-26
88SanBerSCLC-40
89WilBilP-629
91PacSenL-92
Brocklander, Fred
88T/MUmp-38
89T/MUmp-36
90T/MUmp-34
Brockway, Kevin
86TriTriC-188
Broda, Turk
43ParSpo-11
Broderick, Stan
83QuaCitCT-24
Brodie, John
74NewYorNTDiS-38
Brodowski, Dick
52Top-404
53Top-69
54Top-221
55Top-171
56Top-157
59Ind-1
59Kah-4
59Top-371
83TopRep5-404
91TopArc1-69
94TopArc1-221
94TopArc1G-221
Broersma, Eric
82OrlTwi8SCT-13
82OrlTwiT-3
83OrlTwiT-19
83TolMudHT-26
84TolMudHT-17
85TolMudHT-2
86TolMudHP-3
87TacTigP-11
Broglio, Ernie
59Top-296
60Lea-41
60Top-16
60TopVen-16
61Baz-16
61CarJayP-2
61Pos-179A
61Pos-179B
61Top-45
61Top-47
61Top-49
61Top-420
61Top-451
62CarJayP-2
62Jel-164
62Pos-164
62PosCan-164
62SalPlaC-132
62ShiPlaC-132
62Top-507
63CarJayP-3
63CarJayP-4
63Jel-165
63Pos-165
63Top-313
64Top-59
64TopCoi-95
64TopSta-77
64TopStaU-11
64TopVen-59
65CubJayP-4
65Top-565
66CubTeal-5
66Top-423
78TCM60I-18
Brogna, Dennis
81WatIndT-3
83MidCubT-6
84MidCubT-13
92MyrBeaHC-30
93HagSunC-28
94DunBluJC-30
95DunBluJTI-2
96DunBluJB-30
96DunBluJTI-4
Brogna, Rico
88BriTigP-1885
89Bow-102
89BowTif-102
89LakTigS-3
90Bow-351
90BowTif-351
90EasLeaAP-EL4
90LonTigP-1275
90ProAaA-30
91Bow-134
91Cla2-T12
91ClaGam-197
91LeaGolR-BC11
91LinDriAAA-580
91Sco-741
91TolMudHLD-580
91TolMudHP-1939
91UppDec-73
92Bow-256
92DonRoo-17
92FleUpd-19
92OPC-126
92ProFS7-63
92SkyAAAF-258
92TolMudHF-1049
92TolMudHS-578
92Top-126
92TopGol-126
92TopGolW-126
92TopMic-126
92UppDec-74
93ClaFS7-170
93Don-41
93FleMajLP-A15
93Pin-240
93Sco-114
93ScoBoyoS-17
93StaClu-530
93StaCluFDI-530
93StaCluMOP-530
93TolMudHF-1657
93Top-598
93TopGol-598
93TopInaM-598
93TopMic-598
93UppDec-386
93UppDecGold-386
94FleUpd-156
94LeaLimR-2
94NorTidF-2925
95Baz-129
95Bow-414
95ColCho-314
95ColChoGS-314
95ColChoSS-314
95Don-525
95DonPreP-525
95DonTopotO-289
95Emo-159
95Fin-14
95FinRef-14
95Fla-170
95Fle-366
95FleRooS-2
95Lea-83
95LeaLim-162
95Pac-278
95Pin-265
95PinArtP-265
95PinFan-27
95PinMusC-265
95Sel-148
95SelArtP-148
95SelCer-31
95SelCerMG-31
95SigRoo-10
95SigRooSig-10
95SP-79
95Spo-103
95SpoArtP-103
95SPSil-79
95StaClu-170
95StaCluFDI-170
95StaCluMOP-170
95StaCluSTWS-170
95StaCluVR-88
95Stu-156
95Sum-69
95SumNthD-69
95Top-490
95TopCyb-281
95UC3-31
95UC3ArtP-31
95Ult-196
95UltGolM-196
95UppDec-121
95UppDecED-121
95UppDecEDG-121

95Zen-88
96Baz-50
96Bow-107
96ColCho-224
96ColCho-398
96ColChoGS-224
96ColChoGS-398
96ColChoSS-224
96ColChoSS-398
96Don-274
96DonPreP-274
96EmoXL-228
96Fin-B116
96FinRef-B116
96Fla-316
96Fle-474
96FleTeaL-23
96FleTif-474
96Lea-129
96LeaPre-2
96LeaPreP-2
96LeaPrePB-129
96LeaPrePG-129
96LeaPrePS-129
96LeaSig-8
96LeaSigA-35
96LeaSigAG-35
96LeaSigAS-35
96LeaSigPPG-8
96LeaSigPPP-8
96MetKah-5
96MetKah-3
96MetUni-198
96MetUniP-198
96Pac-135
96PacPri-P46
96PacPriG-P46
96PanSti-26
96PinAfi-125
96PinAfiAP-125
96ProSta-74
96Sco-48
96ScoDugC-A41
96ScoDugCAP-A41
96Sel-46
96SelArtP-46
96SelCer-36
96SelCerAP-36
96SelCerCB-36
96SelCerCR-36
96SelCerMB-36
96SelCerMG-36
96SelCerMR-36
96SelTeaN-21
96SP-124
96Spo-32
96SpoArtP-32
96SpoDouT-12
96StaClu-367
96StaCluEPB-367
96StaCluEPG-367
96StaCluEPS-367
96StaCluMOP-367
95StaCluVRMC-88
96Stu-99
96StuPrePB-99
96StuPrePG-99
96StuPrePS-99
96Sum-143
96SumAbo&B-143
96SumArtP-143
96SumFoi-143
96Top-259
96TopChr-103
96TopChrR-103
96TopGal-122
96TopGalPPI-122
96Ult-240
96UltGolM-240
96UppDec-141
96Zen-17
96ZenArtP-17
96ZenMoz-24
97Bow-283
97BowInt-283
97Cir-29
97CirRav-29
97ColCho-420
97Don-153
97DonPreP-153
97DonPrePGold-153
97Fle-599
97FleTif-599
97NewPin-150
97NewPinAP-150
97NewPinMC-150
97NewPinPP-150
97Pac-360
97PacLigB-360
97PacSil-360
97Pin-115
97PinArtP-115
97PinMusC-115
97Sco-60
97Sco-368
97ScoHobR-368
97ScoPreS-60
97ScoResC-368
97ScoShoS-60
97ScoShoS-368
97ScoShoSAP-60
97ScoShoSAP-368
97Top-289
97Ult-382
97UltGolME-382
97UltPlaME-382

Brohamer, Jack (John A.)
73OPC-181
73Top-181
74OPC-586
74Top-586
75OPC-552
75Top-552
76OPC-618
76SSP-518
76Top-618
76TopTra-618T
77BurCheD-78
77Top-293
78PapGinD-3
78SSP270-166
78Top-416
79OPC-25
79Top-63
80Top-349
81Fle-393
81Top-462

Brohawn, Troy
94SigRooDP-80
94SigRooDPS-80
94StaCluDP-56
94StaCluDPFDI-56

Brohm, Jeff
90BurIndP-3019
91WatIndC-24
91WatIndP-3379

Bromby, Scott
88RocExpLC-3
89RocExpLC-5

Bronkey, Jeff
87OrlTwiP-21
88VisOakCLC-166
88VisOakP-95
89OrlTwiB-12
89OrlTwiP-1337
91LinDriAAA-305
91OklCit8LD-305
91OklCit8P-172
92TulDriF-2687
92TulDriS-603
93FleFinE-277
93OklCit8F-1618
93RanKee-396
94BreMilB-289
94BrePol-3
94ExtBas-99
94Fla-64
94FleUpd-52
94Pac-609
94TopGol-396

Bronson, Aaron
93DavLipB-25

Brookens, Andy
91EugEmeC-3
91EugEmeP-3731

Brookens, Tim
75AndRanT-8

Brookens, Tom (Thomas D.)
77EvaTriT-4
80Top-416
81Don-6
81Fle-473
81Top-251
82Don-202
82Fle-263
82OPC-11
82Top-753
83Don-454
83Fle-327A
83Fle-327B
83FleSti-250
83Tig-5
83Top-119
84Don-578
84Fle-78
84Nes792-14
84TigWavP-8
84Top-14
84TopTif-14
85Don-593
85Fle-4
85TigCaiD-4
85TigWen-5
85Top-512
85TopTif-512
86Don-537
86Fle-223
86OPC-286
86TigCaiD-2
86Top-643
86TopTif-643
87Don-296
87Fle-145
87FleGlo-145
87OPC-232
87TigCaiD-1
87TigCok-17
87Top-713
87TopTif-713
88Don-107
88Fle-53
88FleGlo-53
88PanSti-93
88Sco-233
88ScoGlo-233
88StaLinTi-3
88TigPep-16
88TigPol-4
88Top-474
88TopTif-474
89Don-508
89DonTra-53
89Fle-130A
89Fle-130B
89FleGlo-130
89OPC-342
89PanSti-340
89Sco-269
89ScoRoo-73T
89Top-342
89TopSti-278
89TopTif-342
89UppDec-106
89YanScoNW-21
90Fle-439
90FleCan-439
90IndTeal-7
90Sco-297
90UppDec-138
91Don-658
91Fle-362
91OPC-268
91Sco-106
91Top-268
91TopDesS-268
91TopMic-268
91TopTif-268
91UppDec-102
92YanWIZ8-18

Brooks, Antone
95EugEmeTI-12
96DanBraB-8
96MacBraB-3

Brooks, Billy
87BakDodP-6
88BakDodCLC-250

Brooks, Bob
89CalLeaA-54
90CalLeaACLC-33
91CalLeLA-28

Brooks, Bobby (Robert)
70OPC-381
70Top-381
71OPC-633
71Top-633

Brooks, Brian Todd
87ChaRaiP-1
88RivRedWCLC-216
88RivRedWP-1410
89WicUpdR-12
89WicWraR-25

Brooks, Craig
81BriRedST-1

Brooks, Damon
86AubAstP-6
87AubAstP-5

Brooks, Desi
86LynMetP-3
87LynMetP-6

Brooks, Eddie
94SigRooDP-87
94SigRooDPS-87
94StaCluDP-62
94StaCluDPFDI-62
96LynHilB-3

Brooks, Eric
89MyrBeaBJP-1460
91DunBluJC-12
91DunBluJP-208
92DunBluJC-4
92DunBluJF-2002
93DunBluJC-3
93DunBluJF-1798
93DunBluJFFN-3
94KnoSmoF-1305
95SyrChiTI-4

Brooks, Herb
87SpoCubG-1

Brooks, Hubie (Hubert)
79JacMetT-3
80TidTidT-15
81Top-259
81TopTra-742
82Don-476
82Fle-522
82FleSta-81
82Kel-10
82MetPhoA-5
82OPC-266
82Top-246
82Top-494
82TopSti-68
83AllGamPI-118
83Don-49
83Fle-539
83FleSta-23
83OPC-134
83Top-134
83TopSti-261
84Don-607
84Fle-582
84JacMetF-3
84Nes792-368
84OPC-368
84Top-368
84TopSti-103
84TopTif-368
85AllGamPI-110
85Don-197
85ExpPos-3
85Fle-74
85FleUpd-10
85Lea-214
85OPC-222
85OPCPos-5
85Top-222
85TopMin-222
85TopSti-104
85TopTif-222
85TopTifT-9T
85TopTra-9T
86Don-55
86DonHig-15
86ExpProPa-1
86ExpProPo-3
86Fle-244
86FleLimE-7
86FleMin-52
86FleStiC-12
86GenMilB-6A
86Lea-44
86OPC-308
86Spo-187
86Top-555
86TopSti-77
86TopSup-15
86TopTat-13
86TopTif-555
87Don-17
87Don-88
87DonAll-48
87DonOpeD-91
87DonSupD-17
87ExpPos-2
87Fle-314
87FleGamW-7
87FleGlo-314
87FleLeaL-6
87FleMin-14
87FleStiC-16
87GenMilB-4A
87HosSti-4
87KayB-6
87KraFoo-42
87Lea-17
87Lea-142
87OPC-3
87RedFolSB-91
87Spo-18
87Spo-79
87Spo-197
87SpoTeaP-20
87StuPan-8
87Top-650
87TopCoi-27
87TopGloS-46
87TopSti-76
87TopTif-650
88Don-468
88DonAll-45
88DonBasB-12
88ExpPos-1
88Fle-179
88FleGlo-179
88GreBasS-17
88Lea-257
88MSAHosD-5
88OPC-50
88PanSti-328
88Sco-305
88ScoGlo-305
88Spo-187
88StaLinE-1
88Top-50
88Top-111
88TopBig-81
88TopSti-81
88TopStiB-10
88TopTif-50
88TopTif-111
88TopUKM-8
88TopUKMT-8
89Bow-367
89BowTif-367
89Don-220
89DonBasB-292
89ExpPos-3
89Fle-371
89FleBasM-5
89FleGlo-371
89OPC-221
89PanSti-123
89RedFolSB-13
89Sco-53
89Spo-96
89Top-485
89TopBasT-133
89TopBig-301
89TopMinL-21
89TopSti-72
89TopTif-485
89TopUKM-8
89TVSpoM-15
89UppDec-122
90Bow-100
90BowTif-100
90ClaBlu-129
90ClaYel-T75
90DodMot-10
90DodPol-21
90Don-130
90DonBesN-115
90Fle-341
90FleCan-341
90FleUpd-19
90Lea-16
90OPC-745
90PubSti-169
90Sco-299
90ScoRoo-34T
90Top-745
90TopBig-262
90TopSti-77
90TopTif-745
90TopTra-14T
90TopTraT-14T
90UppDec-197
90UppDec-791
90VenSti-73

91BasBesHM-4
91Bow-461
91ClaGam-77
91Don-349
91Fle-195
91FleUpd-100
91Lea-295
91MetColP-12
91MetKah-7
91MetWIZ-52
91OPC-115
91OPCPre-15
91PanFreS-59
91PanSti-56
91RedFolS-13
91Sco-196
91ScoRoo-5T
91StaClu-325
91Top-115
91TopDesS-115
91TopMic-115
91TopTif-115
91TopTra-14T
91TopTraT-14T
91UltUpd-94
91UppDec-217
91UppDec-787
92AngPol-4
92Bow-97
92Don-64
92Fle-496
92Lea-378
92OPC-457
92OPCPre-198
92PanSti-226
92Pin-449
92Sco-107
92ScoRoo-69T
92StaClu-754
92Stu-142
92Top-457
92TopGol-457
92TopGolW-457
92TopMic-457
92TopTra-15T
92TopTraG-15T
92Ult-322
92UppDec-114
92UppDec-709
93CadDis-9
93Don-563
93StaCluRoy-26
93UppDec-680
93UppDecGold-680
94Don-166
94Fle-151
94Sco-125
94ScoGolR-125
94StaClu-647
94StaCluFDI-647
94StaCluGR-647
94StaCluMOP-647

Brooks, Jerry
88GreFalDTI-11
89BakDodCLC-203
89CalLeaA-18
90SanAntMGS-6
91AlbDukLD-2
91AlbDukP-1153
91LinDriAAA-2
91TriA AAGP-AAA1
92AlbDukF-733
92AlbDukS-6
93AlbDukF-1463
94AlbDukF-854
95IndIndF-97
96ChaKniB-10

Brooks, John
25Exh-19

Brooks, Kevin
88VirGenS-3

Brooks, Michael
73TacTwiC-3
75OklCit8TI-22
75SanAntBT-4
76BatRouCT-5
82RedPioT-1

Brooks, Monte
87SpoIndP-12
88ChaRaiP-1204
89RivRedWB-27
89RivRedWCLC-10
89RivRedWP-1417
90ChaRaiP-2048

Brooks, Rae
93RocRoyF-718
94HigDesMC-5
94HigDesMF-2792

Brooks, Ramy
90EugEmeGS-3
91EugEmeC-7
91EugEmeP-3728
92EugEmeC-7
92EugEmeF-3032
93RocRoyC-4
95WilBluRTI-22
96WilBluRB-4

Brooks, Rodney
88HamRedP-1740

Brooks, Trey
83MidCubT-16
84IowCubT-14
85IowCubT-3
86IowCubP-4
86StaoftFT-10

Brooks, Wes
94LynRedSC-4
94LynRedSF-1885
95TreThuTI-7

Broome, Corey
93NiaFalRF-3392
94FayGenF-2148

Broome, Curtis
94HicCraC-6
94HicCraF-2167
96PriWilCB-6

Broome, John
94WilCubC-3
94WilCubF-3756

Broome, Kim
80WelPirP 7

Brophy, E.J.
92MarPhiC-25
92MarPhiF-3057
93SpaPhiC-7
93SpaPhiF-1058
94ClePhiC-9
94ClePhiF-2530
95ScrRedBTI-2

Brosious, Frank
82BurRanF-8
82BurRanT-14

Brosius, Scott
88MadMusP-5
88MidLeaAGS-50
89HunStaB-12
90Bes-74
90HunStaB-15
91LinDriAAA-529
91TacTigLD-529
91TacTigP-2310
92AthMot-27
92Bow-527
92Cla1-T19
92Cla2-T5
92Don-591
92Fle-671
92Pin-274
92Sco-846
92TacTigF-2508
92TopDeb91-22
92Ult-420
92UppDec-312
93Don-419
93PacSpa-218
93StaClu-62
93StaCluAt-27
93StaCluFDI-62
93StaCluMOP-62
93Top-796
93TopGol-796
93TopInaM-796
93TopMic-796
93Ult-603
93UppDec-681
93UppDecGold-681
94A'sMot-26
94ColC-376
94ColChoGS-376
94ColChoSS-376
94Don-630
94ExtBas-146
94Fin-396
94FinRef-396
94Fla-329
94Fle-256
94Lea-208
94StaClu-164
94StaCluFDI-164
94StaCluGR-164
94StaCluMOP-164
94Top-74
94TopGol-74
94TopSpa-74
94UppDec-306
94UppDecED-306
95AthMot-27
95ColCho-126
95ColChoGS-126
95ColChoSS-126
95Don-548
95DonPreP-548
95DonTopotO-134
95Fla-71
95Fle-242
95Lea-204
95Sco-160
95ScoGolR-160
95ScoPlaTS-160
95Top-102
95Ult-315
95UltGolM-315
96A'sMot-7
96ColCho-239
96ColChoGS-239
96ColChoSS-239
96Don-218
96DonPreP-218
96Fla-145
96Fle-205
96FleTif-205
96LeaSigA-36
96LeaSigAG-36
96LeaSigAS-36
96Pac-386
96Sco-490
96SP-139
96StaClu-383
96StaCluMOP-383
96Ult-111
96UltGolM-111
96UppDec-165
96ZenMoz-21
97Cir-269
97CirRav-269
97ColCho-183
97Don-188
97DonPreP-188
97DonPrePGold-188
97FlaSho-A112
97FlaSho-B112
97FlaSho-C112
97FlaShoLC-112
97FlaShoLC-B112
97FlaShoLC-C112
97FlaShoLCM-A112
97FlaShoLCM-B112
97FlaShoLCM-C112
97Fle-186
97FleTif-186
97MetUni-128
97Pac-167
97PacLigB-167
97PacSil-167
97Pin-94
97PinArtP-94
97PinMusC-94
97Sco-97
97ScoPreS-97
97ScoShoS-97
97ScoShoSAP-97
97SpoIll-57
97SpoIllEE-57
97StaClu-142
97StaCluMOP-142
97Top-457
97Ult-361
97UltGolME-361
97UltPlaME-361
97UppDec-127

Brosnan, Jason
89GreFalDSP-10
90BakDodCLC-234
90CalLeaACLC-17
91LinDriAA-532
91SanAntMLD-532
92AlbDukS-7
92VerBeaDF-2866
93VerBeaDC-2
93VerBeaDF-2206
94SanAntMF-2459
96PorCitRB-7

Brosnan, Jim
55Bow-229
57Top-155
58Top-342
59Top-194
59TopVen-194
60Lea-124
60Top-449
61Kah-5
61Top-513
61TopMagR-25
61TopStal-15
62Jel-125
62Kah-2
62Pos-125
62PosCan-125
62RedEnq-2
62RedJayP-1
62Top-2
62TopVen-2
63RedEnq-3
63RedJayP-1
63Top-116
90LitSunW-10

Brosnan, Timothy
87OldJudN-46

Bross, Terry
87LitFalMP-2382
88LitFalMP-15
89MetColP-23
89St.LucMS-2
90Bow-129
90BowTif-129
90Don-502
90JacMetGS-7
90MetColP-26
90TexLeaAGS-32
90TopTVM-37
91Don-34
91MetColP-24
91TidTidP-2501
92Fle-653
92LasVegSS-227
92Sco-763
92ScoRoo-21
92SkyAAAF-111
92TopDeb91-23
92UppDec-531
93PhoFirF-1507
94IndIndF-1801

Brothers, John
91PriRedC-25
91PriRedP-3505
93ClaFS7-159
93WesVirWC-3
93WesVirWF-2856
94WinSpiC-6
94WinSpiF-263

Broughton, Cal (Cecil C.)
87OldJudN-47

Brouhard, Mark Steven
82BrePol-29
82Don-154
82Fle-135
82Top-517
83BreGar-3
83Don-532
83Fle-28
83Top-167
84BreGar-2
84BrePol-29
84Don-211
84Fle-195
84Nes792-528
84Top-528
84TopTif-528
85BreGar-2
85BrePol-29
85Don-149
85Fle-576
85Top-653
85TopTif-653
86OPC-21
86Top-473
86TopTif-473
92BreCarT-3
94BreMilB-290

Brousseau, Fernand
52LavPro-95

Brouthers, Dan (Dennis J.)
36PC7AlbHoF-30
50CalHOFW-7
75FlePio-6
76ShaPiz-30
76SSP188WS-12
77BobParHoF-7
80PerHaloFP-30
80SSPHOF-30
81TigDetN-80
84GalHaloFRL-30
87BucN28-28A
87BucN28-28B
87OldJudN-48
87ScrDC-11
88AugBecN-2
88GooN16-3
88SpoTimM-3
88WG1CarG-20
89DodSmoG-3
89EdgR.WG-2
89HOFStiB-7
89N526N7C-2
90BasWit-102
90DodTar-79
94OriofB-60
95May-3A
95May-3B

Brovia, Joe (Joseph John)
48SomandK-11
52MotCoo-51
53MotCoo-18
77FriOneYW-3

Brow, Dennis
88PriWilYS-4
89PriWilCS-2

Brow, Scott
90St.CatBJP-3458
91DunBluJC-1
91DunBluJP-197
92DunBluJC-3
92DunBluJF-1990
93Bow-435
93FleFinE-286
93KnoSmoF-1241
94BluJayUSPC-8H
94BluJayUSPC-9S
94Pac-634
94ScoRoo-RT115
94ScoRooGR-RT115
94StaCluT-169
94StaCluTFDI-169
94Ult-435
95Pac-437
95SyrChiTI-5
96SyrChiTI-6

Brow, Steve
87Ft.LauYP-28

Browder, Bubba
88WytCubP-1987

Browder, Cameron
93IdaFalBF-4042
93IdaFalBSP-20

Brower, Bob
83BurRanF-11
83BurRanT-13
83TulDriT-13
85OklCit8T-21
86OklCit8P-1
87Don-651
87DonRoo-49
87FleUpd-10
87FleUpdG-10
87RanMot-18
87RanSmo-26
87SpoRooI-3
87TopTra-10T
87TopTraT-10T
88Don-346
88Fle-461
88Fle-462A
88FleGlo-461
88OPC-252
88RanMot-18
88RanSmo-16
88RedFolSB-9
88Sco-236
88ScoGlo-236
88StaLinRa-1
88Top-252
88TopTif-252
88ToyRoo-2
89Bow-182
89BowTif-182
89Don-411
89Fle-514
89FleGlo-514
89Sco-344
89Top-754

89TopTif-754
89UppDec-439
90PubSti-531
90TopTVY-37
90VenSti-74
92OklCit8F-1925
92OklCit8S-305
92YanWIZ8-19
93RanKee-83
Brower, Jim
94HudValRF-3374
95Bow-244
95BowGolF-244
Brown, Adam
88BakDodCLC-242
88CalLeaACLC-48
89SanAntMB-10
90AlbDukC-14
90AlbDukP-347
90AlbDukT-3
90CMC-416
90ProAAAF-68
90SanAntMGS-7
91FloStaLAP-FSL36
91VerBeaDC-14
91VerBeaDP-775
92SanAntMF-3977
92SanAntMS-557
93DayCubC-3
93DayCubF-861
94OrlCubF-1387
95ChaLooTI-2
Brown, Adrian
93LetMouF-4159
93LetMouSP-4
96CarMudB-5
96LynHilB-4
97Fle-759
97FleTif-759
Brown, Alvin
91EliTwiP-4302
91KenTwiC-1
91KenTwiP-2077
93BriTigC-4
93BriTigF-3640
94FayGenC-4
94LakTigF-3027
Brown, Anthony
90WelPirP-10
91AugPirP-817
91Cla/Bes-246
Brown, Armann
93ClaFS7-171
93EliTwiC-6
93EliTwiF-3427
93ForWayWC-2
93ForWayWF-1978
94ForWayWC-4
94ForWayWF-2021
96FtMyeMB-27
Brown, Big Bill (Willard)
87OldJudN-50
89SFHaCN-1
Brown, Bill (William Verna)
88GandBCGCE-4
Brown, Bob
33ButCanV-5
34Gou-81
85UtiBluST-17
94ConTSN-1281
94ConTSNB-1281
Brown, Bobby (Robert W.)
47TipTop-48
48BluTin-9
48YanTeal-3
49Bow-19
50Bow-101
51BerRos-B6
51Bow-110
52BerRos-5
52Bow-105
76TayBow4-110
79DiaGre-18
91SweBasG-15
92UppDecS-16
93TedWil-61
93UppDecAH-19
94UppDecAH-149
94UppDecAH1-149
Brown, Bobby (Rogers Lee)
78LodDodT-2
79ColCliT-27
79YanPicA-4
80Top-670
81Don-469
81Fle-95
81OPC-107
81Top-418
82Don-552
82Fle-30
82Top-791
82TopTra-12T
83LasVegSBHN-2
83Top-287
84Don-478
84Fle-296
84Nes792-261
84PadMot-14
84PadSmo-2
84Top-261
84TopSti-157
84TopTif-261
85Don-383
85Fle-28
85OPC-92
85PadMot-23
85Top-583
85TopTif-583
86Top-182
86TopTif-182
92YanWIZ7-26
92YanWIZ8-20
Brown, Brant
92ClaDraP-58
92FroRowDP-83
92PeoChiTI-5
93Bow-284
93ClaFS7-172
93StaCluM-194
94Bow-494
94Cla-128
94ExcFS7-163
94OrlCubF-1390
94SigRoo-2
94SigRooS-2
94UppDecML-134
94UppDecMLPotYF-PY8
96Cir-108
96CirRav-108
96IowCubB-8
97BowBes-173
97BowBesAR-173
97BowBesR-173
97Cir-128
97CirRav-128
97ColCho-291
97Don-149
97DonLim-118
97DonLimLE-118
97DonPre-145
97DonPreCttC-145
97DonPreP-149
97DonPrePGold-149
97Fin-188
97FinRef-188
97Fle-273
97FleTif-273
97Lea-339
97LeaFraM-339
97LeaFraMDC-339
97MetUni-150
97NewPin-162
97NewPinAP-162
97NewPinMC-162
97NewPinPP-162
95OrlCubF-15
97Pac-246
97PacLigB-246
97PacSil-246
97Pin-156
97PinArtP-156
97PinMusC-156
97Sco-263
97Sco-482
97ScoHobR-482
97ScoPreS-263
97ScoResC-482
97ScoShoS-263
97ScoShoS-482
97ScoShoSAP-263
97ScoShoSAP-482
97StaClu-361
97StaCluM-M9
97StaCluMOP-361
97StaCluMOP-M9
97Ult-163
97UltGolME-163
97UltPlaME-163
97UppDec-241
Brown, Bryan
90LSUTigA-14
92WinHavRSC-18
92WinHavRSF-1792
93ForLauRSC-4
93ForLauRSFP-1609
Brown, Buster (Charles E.)
08RosComP-88
08RosComP-136
09AmeCarE-15
11SpoLifCW-45
11SpoLifM-136
Brown, Carmon
86DavLipB-5
Brown, Chad
92MedHatBJF-3203
92MedHatBJSP-2
93St.CatBJC-4
93St.CatBJF-3967
94DunBluJC-5
94DunBluJF-2548
95KnoSmoF-34
96KnoSmoB-6
96MauStiHWB-23
Brown, Charlie
92GulCoaYF-3780
94OneYanC-6
94OneYanF-3782
95GreBatTI-5
96TamYanY-5
Brown, Chris (John C.)
80CliGiaT-16
84PhoGiaC-23
85FleUpd-11
85GiaMot-18
85GiaPos-4
85TopTifT-10T
85TopTra-10T
86Don-553
86Fle-535
86FleLimE-8
86FleMin-108
86FleStiC-13
86GiaMot-18
86KayB-2
86Lea-215
86OPC-383
86SevCoi-W13
86Spo-78
86Top-383
86TopGloS-10
86TopSti-85
86TopSti-311
86TopTat-18
86TopTif-383
87ClaGam-65
87Don-11
87Don-80
87DonAll-44
87DonOpeD-100
87DonSupD-11
87Fle-268
87FleGlo-268
87FleLeaL-7
87FleMin-15
87FleRecS-2
87FleUpd-11
87FleUpdG-11
87GiaMot-5
87Lea-11
87Lea-236
87OPC-180
87Spo-13
87Spo-115
87SpoTeaP-10
87Top-180
87TopSti-86
87TopTif-180
88Don-483
88DonBasB-77
88Fle-578
88FleGlo-578
88Lea-221
88OPC-112
88PadCok-35
88PadSmo-5
88PanSti-408
88Sco-363
88ScoGlo-363
88Top-568
88TopBig-130
88TopSti-111
88TopTif-568
89Bow-106
89BowTif-106
89Don-183
89DonTra-9
89Fle-301
89FleGlo-301
89Sco-369
89Top-481
89TopSti-103
89TopTif-481
89UppDec-193
89UppDec-784
90PubSti-469
90VenSti-75
Brown, Clinton
34BatR31-82
34BatR31-189
39WhiSoxTI-3
40WhiSoxL-3
91ConTSN-132
Brown, Coach (Paul)
74NewYorNTDiS-40
Brown, Cory
93BluOriC-7
93BluOriF-4117
94AlbPolC-7
94AlbPolF-2229
94OriPro-12
Brown, Craig
83AleDukT-19
84PriWilPT-26
85NasPirT-4
86NasPirP-4
87HarSenP-8
Brown, Curt (Curtis)
81HolMilT-11
Brown, Curt S.
84ColCliP-1
84ColCliT-15
85ColCliP-4
85ColCliT-3
86IndIndTI-25
87IndIndTI-13
88ChaKniTI-24
88RocRedWGCP-4
92YanWIZ8-21
Brown, Dan
89SanDieSAS-4
91MarPhiC-26
91MarPhiP-3444
92ClePhiF-2047
92ProFS7-304
93SpaPhiC-8
93SpaPhiF-1049
94ClePhiC-10
94ClePhiF-2519
Brown, Dana
88CapCodPPaLP-95
89BatCliP-1932
90SpaPhiB-19
90SpaPhiP-2502
90SpaPhiS-2
91LinDriAA-504
91ReaPhiLD-504
91ReaPhiP-1380
Brown, Danny
90ArkRaz-3
Brown, Daren
89St.CatBJP-2073
90MyrBeaBJP-2770
91DunBluJC-2
91DunBluJP-198
92KnoBluJF-2981
92KnoBluJS-376
93KnoSmoF-1242
Brown, Darold
93DanBraC-6
93DanBraF-3610
94IdaFalBF-3575
94IdaFalBSP-8
Brown, Darrell Wayne
80EvaTriT-11
84Fle-556
84MinTwiP-1
84Nes792-193
84Top-193
84TopSti-311
84TopTif-193
84TwiTeal-20
85Don-558
85Fle-270
85NasSouTI-2
85RocRedWT-11
85Top-767
85TopSti-306
85TopTif-767
Brown, Dave
78LauLonABS-27
89EriOriS-4
90NegLeaS-12
Brown, Dermal
96BesAutS1RP-FR4
97Bow-311
97BowChr-215
97BowChrI-215
97BowChrIR-215
97BowChrR-215
97BowInt-311
97Top-272
Brown, Deshon
92GulCoaRSP-7
Brown, Dick (Richard Ernest)
58Top-456
59Top-61
59TopVen-61
60Top-256
61TigJayP-2
61Top-192
62Jel-21
62Pos-21
62PosCan-21
62SalPlaC-37
62ShiPlaC-37
62TigJayP-2
62TigPosCF-3
62Top-438
63Jel-52
63Pos-52
63Top-112
78TCM60I-95
91OriCro-53
Brown, Dickie
90BurIndP-3002
91ColIndC-10
91ColIndP-1477
92ColRedC-2
92ColRedF-2380
92KinIndC-5
93KinIndC-3
93KinIndF-2237
93KinIndTI-2
94HigDesMC-6
94HigDesMF-2779
Brown, Don
87CedRapRP-22
88GreHorP-1572
89CedRapRS-26
89ChaLooB-22
89ChaLooGS-6
Brown, Drew
94LetMouF-3884
94LetMouSP-23
Brown, Duane
90AshTouC-3
91AshTouP-561
92AshTouC-10
93OscAstC-5
93OscAstF-619
Brown, Ed (Edward P.)
27AmeCarE-50
Brown, Eddie (Edward William)
21KoBreWSI-4
22W575-11
27AmeCarE-44
28Exh-1
90DodTar-80
Brown, Elmer
90DodTar-81
Brown, Emil
95MidLeaA-5
95WesMicWTI-32
96ModA'sB-16
97ColCho-433
97FlaShoWotF-20
97Fle-571
97FleTif-571
97SpoIll-3
97SpoIllEE-3
97Ult-486
97UltGolME-486
97UltPlaME-486
Brown, Eric
74CedRapAT-12
82IdaFalAT-4

95GreFalDTI-39
96YakBeaTI-12
Brown, Gates (William James)
64Top-471
65OPC-19
65TigJayP-2
65Top-19
66Top-362
66TopVen-362
67OPC-134
67Top-134
68CokCapT-7
68TigDetFPB-1
68Top-583
69MilBra-41
69Top-256
70OPC-98
70Top-98
71MLBOffS-386
71OPC-503
71Top-503
72MilBra-52
72OPC-187
72Top-187
73OPC-508
73TigJew-2
73Top-508
74OPC-389
74Tig-1
74Top-389
75OPC-371
75Top-371
76SSP-371
80VenLeaS-91
81TigDetN-106
83Tig-6
84TigWavP-9
86TigSpoD-18
88TigDom-1
89PacSenL-199
89T/MSenL-13
Brown, Gavin
96EugEmeB-3
Brown, George
05RotCP-3
06FanCraNL-6
09T206-39
09T206-40
Brown, Greg
78WauMetT-4
91BatCliC-24
91BatCliP-3477
92SpaPhiF-1257
93ClePhiC-5
93ClePhiF-2677
93FloStaLAF-25
94ReaPhiF-2055
Brown, Ike (Isaac)
70OPC-152
70Top-152
71MLBOffS-387
71OPC-669
71Top-669
72OPC-284
72Top-284
72TopCloT-3
73OPC-633
73TigJew-3
73Top-633
74OPC-409
74Top-409
Brown, J.B.
80AppFoxT-6
82GleFalWST-2
83GleFalWST-2
Brown, Jackie G.
57JetPos-3
71MLBOffS-531
71OPC-591
71SenTealW-6
71Top-591
72Dia-6
74OPC-89
74Top-89
75OPC-316
75Top-316
76OPC-301
76Top-301
77ExpPos-7
77OPC-36
77Top-147
78OPC-126
78Top-699
78TucTorC-39
86HawIslP-1
87VanCanP-1599
88BufBisP-1479
89BufBisC-25
89BufBisP-1683
90BufBisP-390
90BufBisTI-3
90ProAAAF-505
91BufBisLD-50
91BufBisP-557
91LinDriAAA-50
92WhiSoxK-NNO
93RanKee-84
93WhiSoxK-30
94WhiSoxK-30
Brown, Jake (Jerald Ray)
75LafDriT-6
78
94StaCluDPFDI-78
95Bow-236
95BowGolF-236
Brown, Jarvis
87KenTwiP-14
88KenTwiP-1390
88MidLeaAGS-33
89VisOakCLC-106
89VisOakP-1437
90OrlSunRB-9
90OrlSunRP-1095
90OrlSunRS-3
91LinDriAAA-404
91PorBeaLD-404
91PorBeaP-1576
92Don-770
92Fle-669
92Pin-644
92ProFS7-92
92Sco-870
92ScoRoo-27
92StaClu-515
92TopDeb91-24
92Ult-394
93LasVegSF-955
94Fle-658
94Pac-519
94RicBraF-2858
94Sco-281
94ScoGolR-281
94StaCluT-36
94StaCluTFDI-36
95BowBayTI-4
Brown, Jeff
85AncGlaPTI-6
85Ft.MyeRT-14
87SanAntDTI-12
87VerBeaDP-16
88BakDodCLC-234
88CalLeaACLC-46
91ChaRaiC-3
91ChaRaiP-89
92BriTigC-2
92BriTigF-1400
92WatDiaC-8
92WatDiaF-2136
93RanCucQC-6
93RanCucQF-820
94ClaGolF-140
Brown, Jim
39PlaBal-132
66AurSpoMK-1
76QuaCitAT-7
Brown, Jimmy
90KisDodD-3
91NiaFalRC-2
91NiaFalRP-3639
Brown, Jimmy (James Roberson)
40PlaBal-112
41CarW75-2
41DouPlaR-145
41PlaBal-12
Brown, John (James Murray)
67OPC-72
67Top-72
76BatTroTI-2
Brown, Jumbo (Walter G.)
33Gou-192
35DiaMatCS3T1-18
39PlaBal-124
40PlaBal-154
75YanDyn1T-5
92ConTSN-454
Brown, Keith
80AppFoxT-15
87CedRapRP-10
88ChaLooB-3
88NasSouTI-4
89ChaLooLITI-6
89Don-115
89Fle-154
89FleGlo-154
89NasSouC-2
89NasSouP-1296
89NasSouTI-3
90CedRapRDGB-32
90CMC-134
90NasSouC-9
90NasSouP-224
90ProAAAF-536
91Fle-58
91LinDriAAA-253
91NasSouLD-253
91NasSouP-2149
92NasSouS-279
93OmaRoyF-1672
93TopGol-823
Brown, Ken
88PriWilYS-5
Brown, Kevin (James Kevin)
87Don-627
88BasAmeAAB-25
88TulDriTI-15
89Don-613
89DonBasB-256
89DonRoo-44
89Fle-641
89FleGlo-641
89FleUpd-63
89RanMot-18
89RanSmo-4
89ScoRoo-89T
89TopTra-15T
89TopTraT-15T
89UppDec-752
90Bow-488
90BowTif-488
90ClaYel-T41
90Don-343
90DonBesA-13
90Fle-291
90FleCan-291
90Lea-47
90OPC-136
90PanSti-168
90ProAAAF-266
90PubSti-405
90RanMot-21
90Sco-210
90Sco100RS-28
90ScoYouSI-29
90Spo-73
90Top-136
90TopBig-261
90TopRoo-5
90TopSti-248
90TopTif-136
90ToyRoo-6
90TulDriDGB-32
90UppDec-123
90VenSti-76
91Bow-274
91Don-314
91Fle-282
91Lea-250
91OPC-584
91PanSti-208
91RanMot-21
91Sco-846
91StaClu-56
91Top-584
91TopDesS-584
91TopMic-584
91TopTif-584
91Ult-347
91UppDec-472
92Bow-191
92Don-55
92Fle-299
92Lea-326
92OPC-297
92Pin-405
92RanMot-21
92RanTeal-2
92Sco-709
92ScoProaG-9
92StaClu-123
92Top-297
92TopGol-297
92TopGolW-297
92TopMic-297
92TriPla-226
92Ult-438
92UppDec-578
93Bow-685
93Don-377
93Fin-134
93FinRef-134
93Fla-277
93Fle-317
93FunPac-154
93Lea-202
93OPC-20
93PacSpa-306
93PanSti-79
93PanSti-156
93Pin-356
93RanKee-397
93Sco-146
93Sel-204
93SelAce-7
93SelStaL-62
93SelStaL-85
93SP-190
93StaClu-396
93StaCluFDI-396
93StaCluM-176
93StaCluMOP-396
93StaCluR-20
93Stu-21
93Top-785
93TopComotH-14
93TopGol-785
93TopInaM-785
93TopMic-785
93TriPla-252
93Ult-276
93UppDec-76
93UppDecGold-76
94Bow-325
94ColC-537
94ColChoGS-537
94ColChoSS-537
94Don-22
94DonSpeE-22
94ExtBas-175
94Fin-257
94FinRef-257
94Fla-343
94Fle-303
94FUnPac-41
94Lea-231
94OPC-205
94Pac-610
94Pin-71
94PinArtP-71
94PinMusC-71
94ProMag-131
94RanAllP-20
94RedFolMI-8
94Sco-99
94ScoGolR-99
94Sel-267
94Spo-132
94StaClu-382
94StaCluFDI-382
94StaCluGR-382
94StaCluMOP-382
94StaCluT-260
94StaCluTFDI-260
94Stu-151
94Top-345
94TopGol-345
94TopSpa-345
94TriPla-191
94TriPlaM-13
94Ult-126
94UppDec-487
94UppDecED-487
95Bow-405
95ColCho-394
95ColCho-562T
95ColChoGS-394
95ColChoSS-394
95Don-207
95DonPreP-207
95Emo-2
95Fin-252
95FinRef-252
95Fla-219
95Fle-280
95FleUpd-4
95Pac-421
95Pin-231
95PinArtP-231
95PinMusC-231
95Sco-199
95ScoGolR-199
95ScoPlaTS-199
95Sel-228
95SelArtP-228
95StaClu-417
95StaClu-626
95StaCluMOP-417
95StaCluMOP-626
95StaCluSTWS-417
95StaCluSTWS-626
95StaCluVR-215
95Top-456
95Top-575
95TopCyb-349
95TopTra-148T
95Ult-332
95UltGolM-332
95UppDec-472T
95UppDec-TC4
95UppDecSE-182
95UppDecSEG-182
96Bow-176
96Cir-126
96CirRav-126
96ColCho-554
96ColChoGS-554
96ColChoSS-554
96Don-399
96DonPreP-399
96EmoXL-182
96Fin-B286
96FinRef-B286
96Fla-257
96Fle-6
96FleTif-6
96FleUpd-U131
96FleUpdTC-U131
96LeaSig-145
96LeaSigPPG-145
96LeaSigPPP-145
96Pac-244
96Sco-183
95StaCluVRMC-215
96TeaOut-11
96Top-376
96TopLas-115
96Ult-478
96UltGolM-478
96UppDec-495U
97Bow-45
97BowChr-36
97BowChrI-36
97BowChrIR-36
97BowChrIR-138
97BowChrR-36
97BowInt-45
97Cir-268
97CirRav-268
97ColCho-62
97ColCho-118
97Don-81
97Don-431
97DonEli-97
97DonEliGS-97
97DonLim-143
97DonLim-152
97DonLimLE-143
97DonLimLE-152
97DonPre-72
97DonPreCttC-72
97DonPreP-81
97DonPreP-431
97DonPrePGold-81
97DonPrePGold-431
97Fin-25
97FinRef-25
97FlaSho-A166
97FlaSho-B166
97FlaSho-C166
97FlaShoLC-166
97FlaShoLC-B166
97FlaShoLC-C166
97FlaShoLCM-A166
97FlaShoLCM-B166
97FlaShoLCM-C166
97Fle-325
97FleTif-325

97Lea-216
97Lea-381
97LeaFraM-216
97LeaFraM-381
97LeaFraMDC-216
97LeaFraMDC-381
97LeaGet-7
97MetUni-171
97NewPin-50
97NewPinAP-50
97NewPinMC-50
97NewPinPP-50
97Pac-297
97PacLigB-297
97PacPri-100
97PacPriLB-100
97PacPriP-100
97PacSil-297
97Pin-80
97PinArtP-80
97PinCar-18
97PinCer-85
97PinCerMBlu-85
97PinCerMG-85
97PinCerMR-85
97PinCerR-85
97PinIns-26
97PinInsCE-26
97PinInsDE-26
97PinMusC-80
97PinTotCPB-85
97PinTotCPG-85
97PinTotCPR-85
97PinX-P-102
97PinX-PMoS-102
97Sco-127
97Sco-532
97ScoHobR-532
97ScoPreS-127
97ScoPreS-324
97ScoResC-532
97ScoShoS-127
97ScoShoS-532
97ScoShoSAP-127
97ScoShoSAP-532
97Sel-16
97SelArtP-16
97SelRegG-16
97SkyE-X-71
97SkyE-XC-71
97SkyE-XEC-71
97SpoIll-32
97SpoIll-79
97SpoIllEE-32
97SpoIllEE-79
97StaClu-235
97StaCluMat-235
97StaCluMOP-235
97Stu-13
97StuPrePG-13
97StuPrePS-13
97Top-115
97TopChr-44
97TopChrR-44
97TopGal-18
97TopGalPPI-18
97TopSta-87
97TopStaAM-87
97Ult-193
97UltGolME-193
97UltPlaME-193
97UppDec-71
97UppDec-76
97UppDecAWJ-14

Brown, Kevin D.
86LynMetP-4
87SumBraP-7
87WicPilRD-21
88St.LucMS-3
88WicPilRD-32
89JacMetGS-26
89MetColP-24
89TidTidP-1962
90Bow-127
90BowTif-127
90CMC-353
90MetColP-27
90St.LucMS-2
90TidTidC-2
90TidTidP-535
90TopTVM-38
91Bow-49
91BreMilB-5
91BrePol-5
91Don-674
91Lea-475
91MetWIZ-53
91TopDeb90-22
92CalCanF-3726
92CalCanS-52
92Fle-174
93PhoFirF-1508
94BreMilB-291

Brown, Kevin L.
94HudValRF-3386
94SigRooDP-48
94SigRooDPS-48
94StaCluDP-79
94StaCluDPFDI-79
94TopTra-129T
95Bow-32
95Exc-126
95SPML-161
96BesAutS-13
96BesAutSA-9
96Bow-176
96Exc-108
96TexLeaAB-3
96TulDriTI-4
97Bow-124
97BowBesMI-MI4
97BowBesMIAR-MI4
97BowBesMIARI-MI4
97BowBesMII-MI4
97BowBesMIR-MI4
97BowBesMIRI-MI4
97BowCerBIA-CA8
97BowCerGIA-CA8
97BowChr-138
97BowChrI-138
97BowChrR-138
97BowInt-124
94HudValRC-2
97ColCho-12
97MetUniMfG-2
97PinIns-145
97PinInsCE-145
97PinInsDE-145
97Sel-129
97SelArtP-129
97SelRegG-129
97Top-205
97UppDec-473

Brown, Knock-out
11TurRedT-66

Brown, Kurt
86AppFoxP-4
87PenWhiSP-26
88SouBenWSGS-13
88TamTarS-3
89SarWhiSS-1
90Bes-189
90BirBarB-2
90BirBarP-1111
91LinDriAAA-628
91VanCanLD-628
91VanCanP-1596

Brown, Larry
78LauLonABS-2
86NegLeaF-26
94TedWil-102

Brown, Larry Lesley
64Top-301
64TopVen-301
65Top-468
66OPC-16
66Top-16
66TopVen-16
67CokCapI-3
67DexPre-33
67OPC-145
67Top-145
67TopVen-219
68Kah-B10
68Top-197
68TopVen-197
69MilBra-42
69MLBOffS-39
69Top-503
69TopSta-163
70Ind-2
70MLBOffS-194
70OPC-391
70Top-391
71MLBOffS-363
71OPC-539
71Top-539
72MilBra-53
72OPC-279
72Top-279
73OriJohP-21
81TCM60I-416
83LasVegSBHN-3
84LasVegSC-238
91OriCro-55
93RanKee-85

Brown, Leon
74PhoGiaC-82
75PhoGiaC-1
75PhoGiaCK-21
80OmaRoyP-3
91MetWIZ-54

Brown, Lindsay (John Lindsay)
90DodTar-82

Brown, Lloyd
31SenTealPW-4
35DiaMatCS3T1-17
90DodTar-83
91ConTSN-181

Brown, Mace
36R31PasP-3
39GouPreR303A-6
39WorWidGTP-6
40PlaBal-220
41DodTeal-1
42RedSoxTI-1
43RedSoxTI-1
46RedSoxTI-3
79DiaGre-359
90DodTar-84

Brown, Mark
81MiaOriT-4
83RocRedWT-2
85TolMudHT-3
86ChaOriW-6
86TolMudHP-4
86Top-451
86TopTif-451
89EriOriS-28
91OriCro-56

Brown, Marty
86CedRapRT-14
87VerRedP-5
88NasSouC-18
88NasSouP-481
88NasSouTI-5
88TriAAAP-26
89Fle-645
89FleGlo-645
89NasSouC-14
89NasSouP-1292
89NasSouTI-4
89ScoHot1R-70
90CedRapRDGB-29
90DonRoo-39
90RocRedWGC-17
91ColSprSSLD-79
91ColSprSSP-2188
91LinDriAAA-79
91OriCro-57

Brown, Matt
90EliTwiS-7
91Cla/Bes-93
91VisOakC-12
91VisOakP-1743
92VisOakC-16
92VisOakF-1017
93ForMyeMC-4
93ForMyeMF-2658

Brown, Michael
96LynHilB-5

Brown, Michael (Mike)
90WelPirP-2
91AugPirC-24
91AugPirP-809
91Cla/Bes-88
92AugPirF-243
93SalBucC-2
93VerBeaDC-3
94CarMudF-1584
94ExcFS7-251

Brown, Mike
77LynMetT-6
86OscAstP-2
87OscAstP-3
89KinIndS-26
91ColIndP-1504
91GreFalDSP-3
93CarLeaAGF-46
93SalBucF-438
93SouAtlLAGF-11
93VerBeaDF-2222
95CarMudF-163

Brown, Mike (Michael C.)
82SpoIndT-19
83TopTra-15T
84Don-42
84EdmTraC-117
84FleUpd-17
84Nes792-643
84Top-643
84TopTif-643
85AngSmo-4
85Don-207
85Fle-296
85Top-258
85TopTif-258
86Don-642
86Fle-605
86FleMin-117
86Lea-256
86PawRedSP-3
86Top-114
86TopTif-114
87Don-168
87Fle-607
87FleGlo-607
87RicBraC-42
87Top-341
87TopTif-341
88TolMudHC-24
88TolMudHP-611
88TolMudHP-NNO
89EdmTraC-18
89EdmTraP-558
92ColCliP-2
92ColCliS-125

Brown, Mike (Michael G.)
81HolMilT-8
84Don-517
84Fle-394
84Nes792-472
84Top-472
84TopTif-472
85Don-614
87CalCanP-2315
87Don-563
87Fle-583
87FleGlo-583
87RicBraT-27
87Top-271
87TopTif-271
88ColSprSSC-2
88ColSprSSP-1526
90PriWilCTI-1
90RenSilSCLC-286
91Ft.LauYC-29
91Ft.LauYP-2444
92ColRedC-27
92ColRedF-2407
92YakBeaF-3452
93ColRedC-27
93ColRedF-614
94CanIndF-3134

Brown, Mordecai
03WilCarE-3
06FanCraNL-7
07CubA.CDPP-1
07CubGFGCP-1
08AmeCarE-4
08AmeCarE-39
08RosComP-100
09AmeCarE-16
09RamT20-18
09SpoNewSM-22
09T206-41
09T206-42
09T206-43
10ChiE-2
10CouT21-86
10CouT21-87
10CouT21-262
10DarChoE-6
10DomDisP-17
10E98-4
10RedCroT-93
10SepAnoP-3
10StaCarE-3
10SweCapPP-80A
10SweCapPP-80B
10W555-9
11BasBatEU-5
11DiaGumP-4
11MecDFT-28
11PloCanE-10
11S74Sil-58
11SpoLifCW-46
11SpoLifM-167
11T205-22
11TurRedT-1
12HasTriFT-70B
12PhiCarE-5
14CraJacE-32
14FatPlaT-8
14PieStaT-7
15CraJacE-32
15SpoNewM-23
16BF2FP-65
16SpoNewM-17
36PC7AlbHoF-56
37KelPepS-BB2
50CalHOFW-8
60ExhWriH-5
60Fle-9
61Fle-11
63BazA-13
67TopVen-173
69SCFOldT-30
75FlePio-23
76ISCHooHA-9
76MotOldT-5
76ShaPiz-57
80PacLeg-71
80PerHaloFP-56
80SSPHOF-56
87Cub190T-2
87HygAllG-6
89HOFStiB-60
90BasWit-89
92ConTSN-555
92CubOldS-4
93ConTSN-883
93CraJac-18
94ConTSNCI-37
94OriofB-90

Brown, Nate
96WesPalBEB-23

Brown, Ollie Lee
66Top-524
67CokCapG-2
67DexPre-34
67OPC-83
67Top-83
68Top-223
68TopVen-223
69MLBOffS-190
69OPC-149
69PadVol-1
69Top-149
69TopFou-8
69TopSta-92
69TopSup-63
69TopTeaP-12
70Kel-55
70MLBOffS-109
70OPC-130
70Top-130
70TopPos-18
70TopSup-36
71MLBOffS-220
71OPC-505
71Top-505
71TopCoi-133
72MilBra-54
72PadTeal-4
72Top-551
72Top-552
73OPC-526
73Top-526
74OPC-625
74Top-625
75OPC-596
75Top-596
76OPC-223
76SSP-466
76Top-223
77PadSchC-9
77Top-84
81TCM60I-368
86PadGreT-6
94BreMilB-292

Brown, Oscar Lee
71MLBOffS-5
71OPC-52
71Top-52
72OPC-516
72Top-516
73OPC-312
73Top-312

Brown, Paul
87ElmPio(C-34
87HawRai-28
88LynRedSS-2
90LynRedSTI-15
91WinHavRSC-2
91WinHavRSP-482
Brown, Paul D.
62Top-181
62TopVen-181
63Top-478
64Top-319
64TopVen-319
Brown, Randy
76WauMetT-6
77LynMetT-7
96TreThuB-20
Brown, Randy J.
90ElmPioP-3
91Cla/Bes-131
91WinHavRSC-15
91WinHavRSP-495
92WinHavRSC-3
92WinHavRSF-1783
93CarLeaAGF-6
93LynRedSC-4
93LynRedSF-2521
94NewBriRSF-654
95PawRedSDD-7
95PawRedTI-25
Brown, Ray
94BilMusF-3675
94BilMusSP-4
94StaCluDP-78
95Exc-173
95ExcFirYP-2
95Top-79
96BesAutS-14
96ChaLooB-9
97Bow-303
97BowCerBIA-CA9
97BowCerGIA-CA9
97BowInt-303
Brown, Reggie
89HelBreSP-3
Brown, Renard
87StoPorP-9
Brown, Rick
86LitFalMP-4
87ColMetP-12
88St.LucMS-4
Brown, Rob
89SanDieSAS-5
90ChaRanS-2
91LinDriAA-576
91TulDriLD-576
91TulDriP-2765
91TulDriTI-2
92TulDriF-2688
92TulDriS-604
93OklCit8F-1619
Brown, Ron
91MisStaB-6
92MisStaB-5
93ElmPioC-4
93ElmPioF-3835
93MisStaB-5
94KanCouCC-6
94KanCouCF-173
94KanCouCTI-6
95BreCouMF-257
96PorSeaDB-9
Brown, Ronnie
89WytCubS-3
Brown, Roosevelt
94IdaFalBF-3596
94IdaFalBSP-1
95EugEmeTI-7
96KanCouCUTI-3
96MacBraB-22
Brown, Sam (Samuel W.)
11SpoLifCW-47
Brown, Scott
79NaSouTI-5
80IndIndTI-17
81IndIndTI-19
82Fle-60
82Roy-5
82Top-351
83OmaRoyT-4
94VenLinU-115
Brown, Shawn
93NiaFalRF-3395
94LakTigC-3
94LakTigF-3042
Brown, Skinny (Hector Harold)
53RedSoxTI-3
53Top-184
54Top-172
55Bow-221
55Top-148
55TopDouH-85
57Top-194
58Hir-18
58Top-381
59Top-487
60Top-89
60TopVen-89
61Pos-78
61Top-46
61Top-218
62Top-488
63Top-289
64Top-56
64TopVen-56
87AstSer1-6
91OriCro-54
91TopArc1-184
92YanWIZ6-18
94TopArc1-172
94TopArc1G-172
Brown, Stacy
89BurIndS-3
Brown, Stanley
41DouPlaR-35
Brown, Steven E.
80ElPasDT-16
81SalLakCGT-3
82SpoIndT-1
05IndIndTI-24
Brown, Tab
89PulBraP-1899
90Bes-62
90CMC-828
90SumBraB-2
90SumBraP-2425
Brown, Terry M.
87BelBreP-15
89KenTwiP-1068
89KenTwiS-2
Brown, Thomas D.
76BatRouCT-6
89PacSenL-139
Brown, Tibor
92FroRowDP-62
Brown, Tim
88St.CatBJP-2007
89MyrBeaBJP-1465
90DunBluJS-4
91DunBluJC-3
91DunBluJP-199
92ClaFS7-158
92KnoBluJF-2982
92KnoBluJS-377
93SyrChiF-993
95SyrChiTI-6
Brown, Todd
86StoPorP-3
87ElPasDP-17
88DenZepC-19
88DenZepP-1278
94BluOriF-3574
Brown, Tom
78SanJosMMC-16
79TacTugT-2
80SyrChiT-8
80SyrChiT-6
80VenLeaS-74
81SyrChiT-2
81SyrChiTI-4
89HagSunB-11
89HagSunP-283
89HagSunS-22
90HagSunB-5
90HagSunP-1432
90HagSunS-27
96OklCit8B-2
Brown, Tom (Thomas Michael)
49Bow-178
49EurSta-31
52Bow-236
52Top-281
53BowC-42
78ReaRem-1
83TopRep5-281
90DodTar-85
91RinPosBD4-3
Brown, Tom (Thomas T.)
87BucN28-86
87OldJudN-49
88WG1CarG-1
89N526N7C-3
Brown, Tom (Thomas William)
64Top-311
64TopVen-311
Brown, Tony
86ReaPhiP-4
87ReaPhiP-2
88EasLeaAP-31
88ReaPhiP-867
89BlaYNPRWLU-1
89TidTidC-27
89TidTidP-1974
90Bes-298
90HunStaB-20
91AugPirC-23
92MidAngF-4036
92MidAngOHP-3
92MidAngS-455
Brown, Vick
94GreBatF-482
94SouAtlLAF-SAL12
95GreBatTI-6
96TamYanY-6
97GreBatC-4
Brown, Willard
93BoiHawC-4
93BoiHawF-3905
94CedRapKC-4
95MidAngOHP-6
95MidAngTI-6
96MidAngOHP-6
Brown, Willard Jessie
90NegLeaS-7
94TedWil-101
Brown, Willie
92EriSaiC-1
92EriSaiF-1635
93LetMouF-4160
93LetMouSP-10
93StaCluM-54
93Top-497
93TopGol-497
93TopInaM-497
93TopMic-497
94CedRapKF-1102
94KanCouCC-7
94KanCouCF-174
94KanCouCTI-7
94MidLeaAF-MDW35
95BreCouMF-258
Brown, Winston
61Top-391
89SprCarB-8
Browne, Byron
92BelBreC-4
92BelBreF-396
93StoPorC-3
93StoPorF-736
95ElPasDTI-2
96Bow-205
Browne, Byron Ellis
66OPC-139
66Top-139
66TopVen-139
67CokCapC-18
67ProPizC-4
67Top-439
68Top-296
68TopVen-296
70OPC-388
70Top-388
71MLBOffS-171
71OPC-659
71Top-659
Browne, George Edward
08AmeCarE-68
11SpoLifCW-48
11TurRedT-84
Browne, Jerry
86TulDriTI-9A
87ClaUpdY-146
87Don-41
87DonOpeD-170
87DonRoo-29
87Fle-647
87FleGlo-647
87FleUpd-12
87FleUpdG-12
87Lea-41
87RanMot-22
87RanSmo-31
87SpoRooI-4
87TopTra-11T
87TopTraT-11T
88Don-408
88Fle-462A
88Fle-462B
88FleGlo-462
88Lea-236
88OPC-139
88PanSti-201
88RanMot-22
88RanSmo-15
88Sco-278
88ScoGlo-278
88ScoYouS2-13
88StaLinRa-2
88Top-139
88TopBig-163
88TopRoo-21
88TopTif-139
88ToyRoo-3
89Bow-85
89BowTif-85
89Don-529
89DonBasB-280
89DonTra-44
89FleUpd-26
89IndTeal-6
89Top-532
89TopBig-236
89TopTif-532
89TopTra-16T
89TopTraT-16T
89UppDec-314
90Bow-332
90BowTif-332
90ClaBlu-53
90Don-138
90Fle-487
90FleCan-487
90IndTeal-8
90Lea-48
90OPC-442
90PanSti-54
90PubSti-555
90Sco-52
90Spo-111
90Top-442
90TopBig-256
90TopCoi-7
90TopSti-210
90TopTif-442
90TulDriDGB-27
90UppDec-426
90VenSti-77
91Bow-71
91Don-162
91Fle-363
91IndFanC-5
91Lea-43
91OPC-76
91PanFreS-217
91Sco-481
91StaClu-25
91Top-76
91TopDesS-76
91TopMic-76
91TopTif-76
91Ult-108
91UppDec-116
92Fle-107
92FleUpd-47
92OPC-219
92Pin-208
92Sco-496
92StaClu-251
92Top-219
92TopGol-219
92TopGolW-219
92TopMic-219
92TopTra-16T
92TopTraG-16T
92TriPla-130
92Ult-48
92UppDec-340
93AthMot-13
93Don-447
93Fle-292
93Lea-150
93OPC-234
93PacSpa-219
93PanSti-18
93Pin-391
93RanKee-86
93Sco-382
93StaClu-509
93StaCluAt-4
93StaCluFDI-509
93StaCluM-167
93StaCluMOP-509
93Top-383
93TopGol-383
93TopInaM-383
93TopMic-383
93Ult-255
93UppDec-129
93UppDecGold-129
94ColC-448
94ColChoGS-448
94ColChoSS-448
94Fla-379
94Fle-257
94FleUpd-133
94Pin-489
94PinArtP-489
94PinMusC-489
94Sco-349
94ScoGolR-349
94ScoRoo-RT47
94ScoRooGR-RT47
94StaClu-683
94StaCluFDI-683
94StaCluGR-683
94StaCluMOP-683
94StaCluT-68
94StaCluTFDI-68
94Top-624
94TopGol-624
94TopSpa-624
94TopTra-16T
95ColCho-301
95ColChoGS-301
95ColChoSS-301
95Don-446
95DonPreP-446
95Fle-327
95Pac-168
95Sco-363
95ScoGolR-363
95ScoPlaTS-363
96ColCho-149
96ColChoGS-149
96ColChoSS-149
96Fle-382
96FleTif-382
Browne, Pidge (Prentice A.)
77FriOneYW-50
89AstCol4S-20
Brownholtz, Joe
92ChaRanF-2219
92GasRanC-8
93ChaRanC-3
93ChaRanF-1931
Browning, Mike
82NasSouTI-2
83NasSouTI-2
84EdmTraC-114
86MiaMarP-3
87MiaMarP-15
88MiaMarS-4
89ColMudB-17
89ColMudP-122
89ColMudS-5
90ColMudB-20
90ColMudP-1339
90ColMudS-6
Browning, Pete (Louis R.)
87OldJudN-51
90DodTar-86
94OriofB-35
Browning, Tom
83TamTarT-5
84WicAerRD-5
85Don-634
85DonHig-43
85FleUpd-12
85TopTifT-11T
85TopTra-11T
86BasStaB-17
86Don-384
86Dra-37
86Fle-173
86FleMin-38
86FleSlu-4

86FleStiC-14
86FleWaxBC-C6
86KayB-3
86Lea-179
86RedTexG-32
86SevCoi-S15
86Spo-79
86Spo-185
86Top-652
86TopGloS-49
86TopMinL-40
86TopSti-141
86TopSti-313
86TopSup-16
86TopTat-10
86TopTif-652
87ClaGam-78
87Don-63
87DonOpeD-194
87Fle-194
87FleGlo-194
87Lea-138
87OPC-65
87RedKah-32
87SpoTeaP-4
87Top-65
87TopSti-137
87TopTif-65
88Don-63
88DonBasB-335
88Fle-228
88FleGlo-228
88RedKah-32
88Sco-132
88ScoGlo-132
88StaLinRe-2
88Top-577
88TopBig-96
88TopTif-577
89Bow-306
89BowTif-306
89ClaTraO-126
89Don-71
89DonBasB-62
89Fle-153
89Fle-629
89FleGlo-153
89FleGlo-629
89OPC-234
89PanSti-4
89PanSti-65
89RedKah-32
89Sco-554
89Sco-658
89ScoHot1S-61
89Spo-180
89Spo-222
89Top-234
89TopBig-14
89TopGloS-46
89TopMinL-6
89TopSti-7
89TopSti-141
89TopStiB-61
89TopTif-234
89TVSpoM-41
89UppDec-617
89UppDecS-3
89Woo-9
90Bow-43
90BowTif-43
90ClaUpd-T7
90Don-308
90DonBesN-27
90DonLeaS-54
90Fle-415
90FleCan-415
90Lea-110
90MLBBasB-20
90OPC-418
90PanSti-247
90PubSti-23
90RedKah-5
90Sco-165
90Sco100S-33
90Spo-91
90Top-418
90TopBig-48
90TopSti-135
90TopTif-418
90UppDec-189
90VenSti-78
91Bow-684
91ClaGam-10
91Don-528
91Fle-59
91Lea-88
91OPC-151
91RedKah-32
91RedPep-4
91Sco-229
91Sco100S-32
91StaClu-235
91Stu-161
91Top-151
91TopDesS-151
91TopMic-151
91TopTif-151
91Ult-89
91UppDec-633
91USPlaCA-5S
92Bow-161
92Don-136
92Fle-401
92Lea-46
92OPC-339
92Pin-101
92RedKah-32
92Sco-642
92StaClu-624
92StaCluD-22
92Top-339
92TopGol-339
92TopGolW-339
92TopMic-339
92Ult-186
92UppDec-461
93Don-190
93Fle-387
93Lea-359
93OPC-74
93PacSpa-79
93Pin-405
93RedKah-5
93Sco-404
93Sel-249
93Top-733
93TopGol-733
93TopInaM-733
93TopMic-733
93TriPla-91
93Ult-325
93UppDec-270
93UppDecGold-270
94ColC-439
94ColChoGS-439
94ColChoSS-439
94ExtBas-229
94Fin-337
94FinRef-337
94Fla-144
94Fle-406
94Pac-142
94PanSti-161
94Pin-335
94PinArtP-335
94PinMusC-335
94RedKah-4
94Sco-168
94ScoGolR-168
94StaClu-433
94StaCluFDI-433
94StaCluGR-433
94StaCluMOP-433
94Top-619
94TopGol-619
94TopSpa-619
94Ult-469
95Sco-197
95ScoGolR-197
95ScoPlaTS-197

Browns, 19th C (St. Louis)
86JosHalC-11

Browns, St. Louis
13FatT20-7
36R31Pre-G27
38BasTabP-32
68LauWorS-41
70FleWorS-41
71FleWorS-42
93TedWilPC-20
96Bro194F-1

Brownson, Mark
95AshTouTI-17
96NewHavRB-6

Broyles, Jason
90KisDodD-4
91YakBeaC-19
91YakBeaP-4239

Brubaker, Bill (Wilbur L.)
36GouBWR-4
36GouWidPPR-A11
39PlaBal-130
40PlaBal-166
94ConTSN-1133
94ConTSNB-1133

Brubaker, Bruce
65Top-493
67Top-276
90DodTar-904
94BreMilB-293

Brubaker, John
89OneYanP-2128
90Ft.LauYS-2

Brucato, Bob
89ChaRaiP-973

Bruce, Andy
91JohCitCC-5
91JohCitCP-3981
92ProFS7-325
92St.PetCF-2033
93MidLeaAGF-49
93SprCarC-4
93SprCarF-1856
94ArkTraF-3094

Bruce, Bob
60Top-118
60TopVen-118
61Top-83
62Col.45B-3
62Col45'JP-3
62Top-419
63Col45"P-3
63Col45'JP-2
63Top-24
64Col.45JP-2
64Top-282
64TopVen-282
65OPC-240
65Top-240
66OPC-64
66Top-64
66TopRubl-11
66TopVen-64
67AstTeal2-5
67CokCapB-11
67DexPre-35
67Top-417A
67Top-417B
87AstSer1-7
89AstCol4S-1

Bruce, Tim
93BelMarC-5
93BelMarF-3197
94AppFoxC-3
94AppFoxF-1044

Bruck, Tom
90BurBraB-5
90BurBraP-2341
90BurBraS-5

Brucker, Earle F. Jr.
49PhiBul-9
79DiaGre-340

Brueggeman, Dean
96PorRocB-8

Brueggemann, Jeff
80TolMudHT-18
83VisOakF-14

Brueggemann, Steve
85LitFalMT-3

Bruehl, Darin
89AubAstP-2179

Bruett, J.T. (Joseph T.)
88CapCodPPaLP-168
89KenTwiP-1074
89KenTwiS-3
90CalLeaACLC-13
90CMC-576
90PorBeaC-24
90ProAaA-154
90VisOakCLC-74
90VisOakP-2165
91LinDriAAA-405
91PorBeaLD-405
91PorBeaP-1577
92Bow-112
92DonRoo-18
92PorBeaF-2678
92PorBeaS-403
92SkyAAAF-184
93FleMajLP-B8
93PacSpa-519
93Pin-241
93Sco-275
93StaClu-397
93StaCluFDI-397
93StaCluMOP-397
93Top-309
93TopGol-309
93TopInaM-309
93TopMic-309
93Ult-229
94SalLakBF-828
95OmaRoyTI-4

Brugo, Dale
91LynRedSC-1

Bruhert, Mike
78MetDaiPA-3
78TidTidT-6
79Top-172
79TucTorT-3
82ColCliP-25
82ColCliT-7
91MetWIZ-55

Brumbaugh, Cliff
95HudValRTI-1
96Bow-156
96ChaRivTI-9608

Brumfield, Harvey
87ClePhiP-9
88ReaPhiP-881
89ReaPhiB-20
89ReaPhiP-667
89ReaPhiS-4

Brumfield, Jacob
87Ft.MyeRP-33
88MemChiB-6
89MemChiB-3
89MemChiP-1188
89MemChiS-4
90BasCitRS-3
90FloStaLAS-26
90StaFS7-43
91LinDriAAA-327
91OmaRoyLD-327
91OmaRoyP-1045
92DonRoo-19
92Lea-499
92NasSouF-1844
92OPC-591
92Pin-553
92Top-591
92TopGol-591
92TopGolW-591
92TopMic-591
92Ult-481
93IndIndF-1499
93PacSpa-80
93RedKah-6
93Sco-292
94Don-473
94Fle-407
94Pac-143
94RedKah-5
94StaClu-166
94StaCluFDI-166
94StaCluGR-166
94StaCluMOP-166
94Top-69
94TopGol-69
94TopSpa-69
95DonTopotO-313
95Fin-262
95FinRef-262
95Fle-473
95Lea-393
95Pac-101
95Pin-308
95PinArtP-308
95PinMusC-308
95PirFil-3
95Sco-93
95ScoGolR-93
95ScoPlaTS-93
95Sel-153
95SelArtP-153
95StaClu-553
95StaCluMOP-553
95StaCluSTWS-553
95TopTra-56T
96ColCho-683
96ColChoGS-683
96ColChoSS-683
96Don-247
96DonPreP-247
96Fle-515
96FleTif-515
96Pac-174
96Sco-151
96StaClu-341
96StaCluMOP-341
96Top-72
96Ult-261
96UltGolM-261
97BluJayS-18
97Cir-117
97CirRav-117
97Fle-234
97FleTif-234
97Pac-214
97PacLigB-214
97PacSil-214

Brumley, Duff
90JohCitCS-5
91HamRedC-10
91HamRedP-4029
92HamRedC-8
92HamRedF-1582
93FloStaLAF-42
93St.PetCC-7
93St.PetCF-2620
94Bow-73
94ExcFS7-261
94ExcLeaLF-5
94OklCit8F-1489
94Top-316
94TopGol-316
94TopSpa-316
94Ult-427
96ScrRedBB-8
96SigRooOJ-5
96SigRooOJS-5

Brumley, Mike (Anthony Michael)
86IowCubP-5
87IowCubTI-13
88Don-609
88LasVegSC-19
88LasVegSP-235
88TriAAAP-21
88TriAAC-35
89Don-302
89DonRoo-39
89Fle-302
89FleGlo-302
89FleUpd-30
89TigMar-12
89TopBig-324
90Don-533
90MarMot-26
90OPC-471
90Sco100RS-88
90Top-471
90TopTif-471
90UppDec-312
91Fle-445
91LinDriAAA-353
91PawRedSLD-353
91PawRedSP-45
91Sco-624
92OPC-407
92PawRedSF-929
92PawRedSS-353
92Sco-363
92TexLon-6
93TucTorF-3064
95TusTorTI-3
96TusTorB-5
86StaoftFT -8
97DunDonPPS-3

Brumley, Mike (Tony Mike)
58MonRoyF-6
60DarFar-19
64TopVen-167
65Top-523
66OPC-29
66SenTeal-3
66Top-29
66TopVen-29

Brummer, Don
63RocRedWSP-4

Brummer, Glenn Edward
78ArkTraT-4
81Car5x7-2
82LouRedE-2
82Top-561
83Car-4
83Don-418
83Fle-4
83Top-311

84Car-4
84Car5x7-4
84Don-138
84Fle-321
84Nes792-152
84Top-152
84TopTif-152
85Don-290
85RanPer-7
86Fle-557
86HawlsIP-2
86Top-616
86TopTif-616
87CubCan-1
93RanKee-87
Brummer, Jeff
90YakBeaTI-7
Brummett, Greg
88AlaGolTI-5
89EveGiaS-26
90CliGiaB-7
90CliGiaP-2546
91CliGiaC-23
92SanJosGC-16
93FleFinE-151
93StaCluG-28
94SalLakBF-808
Brunansky, Tom (Thomas A.)
80ElPasDT-17
81LonBeaPT-19
81SalLakCGT-21
82SpoIndT-20
82Top-653
82TopTra-13T
83AllGamPI-49
83Don-555
83Fle-607
83FleSta-24
83FleSti-138
83OPC-232
83Top-232
83TopSti-90
83TopSti-309
83TwiTeal-17
83TwiTeal-33
84AllGamPI-140
84Don-242
84Fle-557
84FunFooP-130
84MinTwiP-2
84Nes792-447
84OPC-98
84Top-447
84TopRubD-7
84TopSti-304
84TopTif-447
84TwiTeal-18
85AllGamPI-51
85Don-364
85Fle-271
85GenMilS-15
85Lea-36
85OPC-122
85Top-122
85TopGloS-39
85TopRubD-8
85TopSti-299
85TopSup-57
85TopTif-122
85Twi7-7
85TwiTeal-19
86Don-24
86Don-192
86DonAll-44
86DonSupD-24
86Fle-387
86FleLimE-9
86FleMin-83
86FleStiC-15
86KayB-4
86Lea-24
86OPC-392
86SevCoi-C15
86Spo-80
86Top-565
86TopSti-276
86TopTat-18
86TopTif-565
86TwiTeal-17
87Don-194
87DonOpeD-222
87Fle-537
87FleGlo-537
87FleHotS-7
87FleStiC-17
87Lea-244
87OPC-261
87RedFolSB-75
87Spo-134
87SpoTeaP-17
87StuPan-22
87Top-776
87TopSti-280
87TopTif-776
88CarSmo-25
88Don-245
88DonBasB-19
88Fle-5
88FleGlo-5
88FleSlu-4
88FleStiC-42
88FleUpd-117
88FleUpdG-117
88OPC-375
88PanSti-142
88Sco-194
88ScoGlo-194
88ScoRoo-5T
88ScoRooG-5T
88Spo-194
88StaLinTw-4
88Top-375
88TopBig-211
88TopSti-15
88TopSti-275
88TopTif-375
88TopTra-20T
88TopTraT-20T
88TwiMasBD-12
88TwiTeal-15
89Bow-444
89BowTif-444
89CarSmo-1
89ClaTraP-186
89Don-112
89DonBasB-187
89Fle-444
89FleGlo-444
89FleHeroB-4
89OPC-60
89PanSti-187
89RedFolSB-14
89Sco-184
89Spo-161
89Top-60
89Top-261
89TopBasT-152
89TopBig-54
89TopHilTM-4
89TopSti-41
89TopTif-60
89TopTif-261
89TopUKM-9
89TVSpoM-26
89UppDec-272
90Bow-202
90BowTif-202
90ClaBlu-119
90Don-399
90DonBesA-130
90El PasDAGTI-34
90Fle-242
90FleCan-242
90FleUpd-70
90Lea-447
90MLBBasB-31
90OPC-409
90PanSti-344
90PubSti-211
90Sco-72
90ScoRoo-49T
90Top-409
90TopBig-94
90TopSti-45
90TopTif-409
90TopTra-15T
90TopTraT-15T
90TopTVCa-31
90UppDec-257
90UppDec-708
90VenSti-79
91Bow-125
91ClaGam-11
91Don-513
91Fle-88
91Lea-164
91OPC-675
91PanFreS-270
91RedFolS-14
91RedSoxP-2
91Sco-245
91SimandSMLBL-7
91StaClu-297
91Top-675
91TopDesS-675
91TopMic-675
91TopTif-675
91Ult-29
91UppDec-163
92Don-490
92Fle-34
92OPC-296
92PanSti-89
92Pin-314
92RedSoxDD-4
92Sco-46
92StaClu-464
92Top-296
92TopGol-296
92TopGolW-296
92TopMic-296
92Ult-12
92UppDec-543
93BrePol-3
93BreSen5-2
93Don-693
93Fle-555
93FleFinE-223
93Lea-226
93OPC-217
93OPCPre-34
93PacSpa-28
93Pin-534
93Sco-612
93Sel-210
93SelRoo-134T
93StaClu-625
93StaCluFDI-625
93StaCluMOP-625
93Top-532
93TopGol-532
93TopInaM-532
93TopMic-532
93TriPla-217
93Ult-569
93UppDec-806
93UppDecGold-806
93UppDecHRH-HR26
94BreMilB-294
94BrePol-4
94ColC-603
94ColChoGS-603
94ColChoSS-603
94Sco-423
94ScoGolR-423
94ScoRoo-RT127
94ScoRooGR-RT127
94SpoRoo-145
94SpoRooAP-145
94StaClu-661
94StaCluFDI-661
94StaCluGR-661
94StaCluMOP-661
95ColCho-413
95ColChoGS-413
95ColChoSS-413
95Don-359
95DonPreP-359
95Fle-24
95Sco-86
95ScoGolR-86
95ScoPlaTS-86
Brundage, Dave
87ClePhiP-20
88VerMarP-951
89WilBilP-642
89WilBilS-1
90WilBilS-3
91CalCanLD-53
91CalCanP-525
91LinDriAAA-53
92CalCanF-3742
92CalCanS-57
92SkyAAAF-26
93CalCanF-1182
94CalCanF-805
96LanJetB-1
Brune, Jim
88BilMusP-1804
88CedRapRP-1154
Brunelle, Rodney
85BenPhiC-4
87ChaWheP-7
88ClePhiS-3
Brunenkant, Barry
84OklCit8T-15
85TulDriTI-14
86MaiGuiP-1
87BufBisP-5
Bruner, Clayton
96FayGenB-8
Brunet, George
58Top-139
63Top-538
64Top-322
64TopVen-322
65OPC-242
65Top-242
66Top-393
67CokCapDA-31
67OPC-122
67Top-122
68Top-347
68TopVen-347
69MilBra-43
69MLBOffS-19
69MLBPin-3
69SenTeal-4
69Top-645
69TopSta-141
69TopTeaP-17
70MLBOffS-267
70OPC-328
70Top-328
71MLBOffS-269
71OPC-73
71Top-73
72MilBra-55
91OriCro-58
Bruneteau, Eddie
43ParSpo-12
Bruneteau, Modere
43ParSpo-13
Brunk, Brenda
75WatRoyT-6
Brunner, Clayton
97Bow-400
97BowChr-264
97BowChrI-264
97BowChrIR-264
97BowChrR-264
97BowInt-400
Brunner, Mike
95AubAstTI-11
Brunner, Tom
79ElmPioRST-26
Bruno, Joe
80PenPilBT-15
80PenPilCT-21
81ReaPhiT-20
87CedRapRP-12
88ChaLooB-17
88SouLeaAJ-37
89ChaLooB-21
89ChaLooGS-7
89SouLeaAJ-18
90ChaLooGS-7
Bruno, Julio
90ChaRaiB-5
90ChaRaiP-2046
90SpoIndSP-20
91Cla/Bes-367
91WatDiaC-15
91WatDiaP-1262
92ClaFS7-23
92HigDesMC-25
93Bow-546
93ClaFS7-173
93RanCucQC-1
93RanCucQF-838
94Bow-420
94Cla-17
94LasVegSF-876
94UppDecML-119
96LasVegSB-7
96MemChiB-9
Bruno, Paul
91Cla/Bes-343
91KenTwiC-23
91KenTwiP-2078
Bruno, Thomas
76OmaRoyTT-4
77OPC-32
78SprRedWK-16
79Top-724
Bruns, Aaron
94JohCitCC-30
96JohCitCTI-3
Brunsberg, Arlo A.
77FriOneYW-24
Brunson, Bill
92PriRedF-3077
Brunson, Eddie
78NewWayCT-4
80HolMilT-7
Brunson, Matt
94ActPac-5
94Bow-28
94Cla-187
94ClaTriF-T28
94ColC-27
94ColChoGS-27
94ColChoSS-27
94FayGenC-1
94FayGenF-2151
94Pin-433
94PinArtP-433
94PinMusC-433
94Sco-532
94ScoGolR-532
94UppDec-296
94UppDec-547
94UppDecED-296
94UppDecED-547
94UppDecML-182
95Bow-195
95Exc-46
95FayGenTI-5
95UppDecML-39
96BreCouMB-7
95UppDecMLFS-39
Brunson, Will
92PriRedC-14
93WesVirWC-4
93WesVirWF-2857
94CarLeaAF-CAR46
94WinSpiC-7
94WinSpiF-264
95SanBerSTI-2
96SanAntMB-2
Brunswick, Mark
85LitFalMT-13
86ColMetP-6
87LynMetP-25
Brunswick, Tom
77SpaPhiT-2
Bruske, James
87KinIndP-17
88WilBilP-1323
89KinIndS-4
90CanIndB-18
90CanIndP-1285
90CanIndS-1
90StaFS7-12
91CanIndLD-78
91CanIndP-973
91LinDriAA-78
92JacGenF-3992
93JacGenF-2100
93LinVenB-116
94ExcFS7-197
94TucTorF-753
97Sco-209
97ScoDod-9
97ScoDodPI-9
97ScoDodPr-9
97ScoPreS-209
97ScoShoS-209
97ScoShoSAP-209
Brusky, Brad
86CedRapRT-2
87VerRedP-1
88CedRapRP-1156
89WilBilP-644
89WilBilS-2
Brusstar, Warren
78PhiSSP-54
78SSP270-54
78Top-297
79PhiBurK-9
79Top-653
80Top-52
81OklCit8T-4
81Top-426
82Fle-242
82Top-647
83CubThoAV-41
84CubChiT-5
84CubSev-41

84Don-442
84Fle-487
84Nes792-304
84Top-304
84TopTif-304
85CubLioP-3
85CubSev-41
85Don-533
85Fle-51
85Top-189
85TopTif-189
86Don-555
86Fle-362
86Top-564
86TopTif-564
87SanJosBP-21
94SanBerSC-26
94SanBerSF-2775
Brust, Dave
90DurBulTI-20
91DurBulC-8
91DurBulP-1550
Brust, Jerry
76QuaCitAT-8
Brutcher, Lenny
90Bes-28
90MidLeaASGS-5
90SouBenWSB-1
90SouBenWSGS-1
91SarWhiSC-2
91SarWhiSP-1105
91UppDec-75
Bruton, Bill (William Haron)
47Exh-30
47PM1StaP1-22
53BraJohC-22
53BraSpiaS3-4
53BraSpiaS7-2
53Top-214
54Bow-224
54BraJohC-38
54BraSpiaSP-3
54Top-109
55Bow-11
55BraGolS-21
55BraJohC-38
55BraSpiaSD-3
55RobGouS-15
55RobGouW-15
56BraBilaBP-3
56Top-185
56YelBasP-8
57BraSpiaS4-3
57Top-48
58Top-355
59Top-165
59TopVen-165
60BraJayP-2
60BraLaktL-4
60BraSpiaS-3
60Top-37
60TopVen-37
61Pos-109A
61Pos-109B
61TigJayP-3
61Top-251
61TopStal-39
62Jel-18
62PC7HFGSS-2
62Pos-18
62PosCan-18
62SalPlaC-92
62ShiPlaC-92
62Top-335
62TopStal-43
63Jel-49
63Pos-49
63TigJayP-2
63Top-437
64TigJayP-2
64TigLid-2
64Top-98
64TopVen-98
78BraTCC-3
81TigDetN-101
83Bra53F-38
84OCoandSI-112
91TopArc1-214
92BazQua5A-12
94TopArc1-109
94TopArc1G-109
Bryan, Billy (William Ronald)
63Top-236
64A's-1
65AthJayP-1
65OPC-51
65Top-51
66Top-332
66TopVen-332
67Top-601
68Top-498
78TCM60I-47
92YanWIZ6-19
Bryan, Frank
85CloHSS-7
87NewOriP-9
87SanJosBP-9
88FreSunCLC-17
88FreSunP-1222
89PalSprACLC-47
89PalSprAP-487
Bryan, Leonardo
95BoiHawTI-8
Bryan, Rusty
89CarNewE-10
Bryand, Renay
88SpoIndP-1941
89ChaRaiP-996
90RivRedWB-4
90RivRedWCLC-13
90RivRedWP-2597
91HigDesMC-1
91HigDesMP-2384
91WicWraP-2591
92WicWraF-3651
92WicWraS-627
93WicWraF-2970
Bryans, Jason
91EugEmeC-27
91EugEmeP-3715
Bryant, Adam
94BilMusF-3661
94BilMusSP-14
95BilRedTI-11
Bryant, Allen
92NegLeaRLI-7
Bryant, Bobby
77LynMetT-8
79JacMetT-19
79TidTidT-21
Bryant, Chris
87IdaFalBP-12
93HunCubC-4
93HunCubF-3228
96FreKeyB-27
Bryant, Clay
35DiaMatCS3T1-19
36DiaMatCS3T2-1
58MonRoyF-5
74OPC-521
74Top-521
79DiaGre-104
Bryant, Craig
92ClaFS7-246
92SanBerC-13
92SanBerSF-961
93AppFoxC-4
93AppFoxF-2466
Bryant, Derek Roszell
77SanJosMC-4
80OgdA'sT-4
80Top-671
81TacTigT-9
Bryant, Don (Donald Ray)
67CokCapC-9
69Top-499
70OPC-473
70Top-473
74OPC-403
74Top-403
77Top-597
Bryant, Erick
87BelMarL-25
87BelMarTI-2
89WauTimGS-25
Bryant, Erwin
77BriRedST-1
81BriRedST-16
Bryant, Franklin S.
81VerBeaDT-3
Bryant, James
86ChaLooP-5
87ChaLooB-7
Bryant, John
82ChaRoyT-5
83ChaRoyT-15
86CedRapRT-23
87VerRedP-15
Bryant, Keith
89BelMarL-3
Bryant, Mike
80ElmPioRST-25
Bryant, Neil
82AmaGolST-15
83MidCubT-5
Bryant, Patrick
91Cla/Bes-57
91ColIndC-29
91ColIndP-1496
92ClaFS7-85
92ColRedC-3
92ColRedF-2402
92WatIndC-18
92WatIndF-3245
93ColRedC-4
93ColRedF-609
94CanIndF-3129
96CanIndB-7
Bryant, Phil
87GasRanP-7
88ChaRanS-4
89TulDriGS-6
89TulDriTI-4
90CMC-740
90TulDriP-1149
Bryant, Ralph
82VerBeaDT-21
83VerBeaDT-22
85AlbDukC-161
85DomLeaS-183
86AlbDukP-2
87AlbDukP-25
87DodPol-24
87Don-587
87Fle-649
87FleGlo-649
87FleUpd-13
87FleUpdG-13
87SpoTeaP-14
87TopTra-12T
87TopTraT-12T
88Fle-510
88FleGlo-510
90DodTar-87
96MidAngB-8
96MidAngOHP-7
86StaoftFT-17
Bryant, Ron
70OPC-433
70Top-433
71MLBOffS-242
71OPC-621
71Top-621
72OPC-185
72OPC-186
72Top-185
72Top-186
73LinPor-158
73OPC-298
73Top-298
74OPC-104
74OPC-205
74Top-104
74Top-205
74TopDecE-21
74TopSta-103
75OPC-265
75Top-265
Bryant, Scott
90Bes-64
90Bow-59
90BowTif-59
90CedRapRB-1
90CedRapRDGB-30
90CedRapRP-2336
90CMC-877
90ProAaA-129
90Sco-667
91ChaLooLD-156
91ChaLooP-1970
91Cla/Bes-69
91LinDriAA-156
91UppDecFE-5F
92IowCubF-4059
92IowCubS-203
92SkyAAAF-97
93ClaFS7-126
93LinVenB-198
93LinVenB-296
93LinVenB-314
95EdmTraTI-4
Bryant, Shawn
90BurIndP-3003
91KinIndC-2
91KinIndP-314
92ClaFS7-153
92KinIndC-1
92KinIndF-2467
93CanIndF-2832
94SalLakBF-809
Bryden, T.R. (Thomas R.)
82DanSunF-4
83RedPioT-7
85MidAngT-11
87EdmTraP-2081
87Top-387
87TopTif-387
88PorBeaC-3
88PorBeaP-663
Brye, Steve (Stephen Robert)
71OPC-391
71Top-391
72OPC-28
72Top-28
73LinPor-106
73OPC-353
73Top-353
74OPC-232
74Top-232
75OPC-151
75Top-151
76OPC-519
76SSP-215
76Top-519
77Top-424
78Top-673
79HawIsIC-9
79HawIsIT-12
79Top-28
94BreMilB-295
Bryeans, Chris
82ChaRoyT-10
83ChaRoyT-5
Brynan, Charles
87OldJudN-52
Brynt, Chris
96RocCubTI-3
Brzezinski, George
88GenCubP-1657
Brzozoski, Marc
96PorRocB-9
Buba, Mark
77BriRedST-2
Bubalo, Mike
90BenBucL-8
91EveGiaP-3934
Bubear, George
87AllandGN-22
Bubrewicz, Tim
91ElmPioP-3262
Buccheri, James
88SouOreAP-1692
89MadMusS-5
89Sta-65
90ModA'sC-3
90ModA'sCLC-162
90ModA'sP-2217
91HunStaC-5
91HunStaLD-280
91HunStaP-1801
91HunStaTI-4
91LinDriAA-280
92HunStaS-305
92SkyAA F-128
93TacTigF-3044
94TacTigF-3185
Bucci, Carmen
95IdaFalBTI-5
96CliLumKTI-4
Bucci, Mike
76SanAntBTI-4
78TucTorC-15A
79TucTorT-5
80TacTigT-13
81ChaChaT-11
82WauTimF-12
83ChaLooT-9
85BurRanT-10
86SalRedBP-2
87BufBisP-26
88BurIndP-1786
Buccola, Vic
47SigOil-39
48SmiClo-16
Bucha, Johnny (John George)
52Top-19
53TigGle-2
54Bow-215
83TopRep5-19
Buchanan, Bob
81CedRapRT-23
82WatRedT-7
83IndIndTI-28
87MetColP-26
87TidTidP-26
87TidTidT-27
88OmaRoyC-3
88OmaRoyP-1514
89OmaRoyC-1
89OmaRoyP-1724
91LinDriAAA-328
91OmaRoyLD-328
91OmaRoyP-1027
92NasSouS-277
92SkyAAAF-131
Buchanan, Brian
94ClaUpdCotC-CC20
94SigRooDP-23
94SigRooDPS-23
94StaCluDP-18
94StaCluDPFDI-18
95Bow-37
95Exc-91
95GreBatTI-7
95ScoDraP-DP18
95SelSurS-SS8
95SPML-117
95StaClu-111
95StaCluFDI-111
95StaCluMOP-111
95StaCluSTWS-111
95Top-28
95UppDecML-197
96TamYanY-7
96Top-245
95UppDecMLFS-197
Buchanan, Donald
52LavPro-12
Buchanan, Reggie
81BufBisT-25
Buchanan, Rob
88EugEmeB-13
89AppFoxP-868
89EugEmeB-21
Buchanan, Shawn
88NebCor-1
90NebCor-5
91UtiBluSC-5
91UtiBluSP-3252
92SarWhiSCB-17
92SarWhiSF-218
93SanBerSC-3
93SanBerSF-781
93SarWhiSF-1381
94SouBenSHC-4
94SouBenSHF-605
95PriWilCTI-5
Buchek, Jerry (Gerald Peter)
61UniOil-P3
62KahAtl-2
62Top-439
64Top-314
64TopVen-314
65CarTeal-5
65Top-397
66CarTeal-2
66Top-454
67Top-574
68Top-277
68TopVen-277
69MilBra-44
91MetWIZ-56
Bucher, Jim (James Quinter)
35DiaMatCS3T1-20
36NatChiFPR-5
36NatChiFPR-86
90DodTar-88
Buchheister, Bucky (Don)
72CedRapCT-4
73CedRapAT-9
74CedRapAT-28
76CedRapGT-7
77CedRapGT-19
78CedRapGT-5

79CedRapGT-29
80CedRapRT-21
81CedRapRT-20
82CedRapRT-27
83CedRapRT-26
84CedRapRT-19
85CedRapRT-28
86CedRapRT-27
88CedRapRP-1136
89CedRapRB-24
89CedRapRP-931
90CedRapRDGB-34
Buck, Bucky
88BenBucL-34
89BenBucL-30
Buckels, Gary
87SalAngP-2
88MidLeaAGS-25
88QuaCitAGS-28
89MidAngGS-6
90CMC-480
90EdmTraC-3
90EdmTraP-510
90ProAAAF-85
91EdmTraLD-156
91EdmTraP-1509
91LinDriAAA-156
93LouRedF-206
94LouRedF-2974
Buckenberger, Albert
87OldJudN-53
Buckeye, Garland
28StaPlaCE-4
93ConTSN-981
Buckeyes, Cleveland
92NegLeaRLI-95
93NegLeaRL2-89
93TedWilPC-8
Buckholz, Steven
88WatPirP-3
90SalBucS-2
91SalBucP-945
92CarMudF-1173
92CarMudS-127
Buckhorn, Glen
81DurBulT-11
Buckle, Larry
80CedRapRT-5
82WatRedT-2
Buckles, Bucky
94StaCluDP-72
94StaCluDPFDI-72
95Exc-127
95Top-369
Buckles, Matthew
95MarPhiT-5
96MarPhiB-4
Buckley, Brian
81RedPioT-2
82HolMilT-2
84PriWilPT-10
Buckley, Dick (Richard D.)
87OldJudN-54
Buckley, Joe
89SpoIndSP-7
Buckley, Kevin John
82BurRanF-3
82BurRanT-15
83BurRanF-20
83BurRanT-2
83TulDriT-16
84OklCit8T-16
84TulDriTI-27
85MaiGuiT-15
86IndTeal-9
86MaiGuiP-2
87LasVegSP-8
90TulDriDGB-14
93RanKee-88
Buckley, Matt
94BoiHawC-4
94BoiHawF-3360
95AusFut-40
96BilMusTI-2
Buckley, Mike
81QuaCitCT-6
Buckley, Terrell
93ClaFS7-96
93MacBraC-4
93MacBraF-1405
Buckley, Travis
90GasRanB-4
90GasRanP-2513
90GasRanS-3
90ProAaA-78
91ChaRanC-3
91ChaRanP-1307
92HarSenF-454
92HarSenS-278
92SkyAA F-118
93Top-732
93TopGol-732
93TopInaM-732
93TopMic-732
94JacSunF-1404
95IndIndF-90
96ChaLooB-10
Buckley, Troy
88CapCodPPaLP-170
89AncBucTI-11
90CalLeaACLC-15
90CMC-863
90VisOakCLC-75
90VisOakP-2157
91Cla/Bes-203
91VisOakC-13
91VisOakP-1744
92Ft.MyeMCB-19
92Ft.MyeMF-2748
93ClaGolF-64
93WinSpiC-5
93WinSpiF-1572
94ChaLooF-1360
Buckman, Tom
96BriWhiSB-11
Buckmier, Jim
83AleDukT-29
84PriWilPT-2
Buckner, Bill (William J.)
70OPC-286
70Top-286
71MLBOffS-99
71OPC-529
71Top-529
72OPC-114
72Top-114
73LinPor-92
73OPC-368
73Top-368
74OPC-505
74Top-505
74TopSta-41
75Hos-97
75Kel-32
75OPC-244
75Top-244
76LinSup-123
76OPC-253
76SSP-91
76Top-253
77BurCheD-195
77CubJewT-3
77Hos-54
77Top-27
78Hos-46
78OPC-127
78RCColC-70
78SSP270-264
78Top-473
78WifBalD-10
79Hos-27
79OPC-177
79Top-346
80OPC-75
80Top-135
81AllGamPI-91
81CokTeaS-14
81Don-482
81Dra-13
81Fle-292
81FleStiC-29
81MSAMinD-5
81OPC-202
81Squ-6
81Top-1
81Top-625
81TopScr-55
81TopSti-17
81TopSti-153
81TopSupHT-23
82CubRedL-22
82Don-403
82Dra-5
82Fle-589
82FleSta-96
82Kel-2
82OPC-124
82Top-456
82Top-760
82TopSti-29
82TopStiV-29
83AllGamPI-91
83CubThoAV-22
83Don-14
83Don-99
83DonActA-7
83Dra-2
83Fle-492
83FleSta-25
83FleSti-132
83Kel-59
83OPC-250
83PerCreC-1
83PerCreCG-1
83Top-250
83TopGloS-24
83TopSti-223
84AllGamPI-1
84Don-117
84DonActAS-28
84DonCha-18
84Dra-4
84Fle-488
84FleUpd-18
84FunFooP-100
84Nes792-545
84OPC-96
84Top-545
84TopRubD-8
84TopSti-42
84TopSup-14
84TopTif-545
84TopTra-17T
84TopTraT-17T
85AllGamPI-1
85Don-416
85Fle-153
85Lea-254
85OPC-65
85SpoIndGC-3
85ThoMcAD-6
85Top-65
85TopMin-65
85TopRubD-9
85TopSti-214
85TopTif-65
86BasStaB-18
86Don-151
86Dra-17
86Fle-343
86FleStiC-16
86Lea-77
86OPC-239
86Spo-81
86Spo-140
86Top-443
86TopSti-252
86TopSup-17
86TopTat-14
86TopTif-443
86Woo-5
87BoaandB-14
87Don-462
87DonOpeD-183
87Fle-31
87FleGlo-31
87FleLimBC-C2
87Lea-241
87OPC-306
87RedSoxSAP-5
87Spo-70
87Top-764
87TopSti-250
87TopTif-764
88Don-456
88Fle-486
88FleGlo-486
88OPC-147
88Sco-591
88ScoGlo-591
88ScoRoo-36T
88ScoRooG-36T
88StaLinAn-2
88Top-147
88TopTif-147
89Fle-278
89FleGlo-278
89OPCBoxB-B
89Sco-214
89TopWaxBC-B
89UppDec-639
90DodTar-89
90Don-474
90PubSti-345
90RedSoxP-4
90Sco-396
90TopTVRS-23
90UppDec-252
90VenSti-80
92UppDecS-26
93TedWil-20
93UppDecAH-20
94UppDecAH-189
94UppDecAH1-189
Buckner, Jim
79TidTidT-10
79TolMudHT-14
80BufBisT-5
81OmaRoyT-20
Buckner, Rex
89MisStaB-5
90MisStaB-5
91MisStaB-7
92MisStaB-6
93MisStaB-6
Buckthorpe, David
91WavRedF-8
Bucz, Bruce
88VisOakCLC-171
90VisOakCLC-81
Bucz, Joseph
90VisOakCLC-83
Buczkowski, Matthew
96MarPhiB-5
Budaska, Mark David
79OgdA'sT-18
80OgdA'sT-17
81TacTigT-13
82Top-531
Buddie, Mike
92ClaDraP-77
92FroRowDP-13
92OneYanC-2
93ClaFS7-64
93GreHorC-3
93GreHorF-877
94TamYanC-3
94TamYanF-2373
95NorNavTI-36
96NorNavB-5
Buddin, Don (Donald Thomas)
58RedSoxJP-2
58Top-297
59Top-32
59TopVen-32
60RedSoxJP-2
60Top-520
61Pos-53A
61Pos-53B
61Top-99
62Col45'HC-3
62Col45'JP-4
62Jel-59
62Pos-59
62PosCan-59
62SalPlaC-68A
62SalPlaC-68B
62ShiPlaC-68
62Top-332
89AstCol4S-19
Budke, Todd
85VisOakT-17
86OrlTwiP-3
Budner, Scott
90SouOreAB-30
90SouOreAP-3450
91MadMusC-13
91MadMusP-2147
92RenSilSCLC-60
Budnick, Michael
47TipTop-122
Budrewicz, Timothy
91ElmPioC-17
92WinSpiC-25
92WinSpiF-1199
Budz, Ed
94St.CatBJC-4
94St.CatBJF-3633
Budzinski, Mark
95WatIndTI-6
Buechele, Steve
82TulDriT-27
83TulDriT-22
84OklCit8T-13
85OklCit8T-17
86Don-544
86Fle-558
86RanPer-22
86Top-397
86TopTif-397
87Don-180
87DonOpeD-179
87Fle-121
87FleGlo-121
87OPC-176
87RanMot-7
87RanSmo-11
87Top-176
87TopSti-242
87TopTif-176
88Don-224
88DonBasB-312
88Fle-463
88FleGlo-463
88OPC-2
88PanSti-203
88PanSti-204
88RanMot-7
88RanSmo-12
88Sco-306
88ScoGlo-306
88StaLinRa-3
88Top-201
88Top-537
88TopBig-104
88TopSti-235
88TopTif-201
88TopTif-537
89Bow-232
89BowTif-232
89Don-174
89DonBasB-223
89Fle-515
89FleGlo-515
89OPC-83
89PanSti-453
89RanMot-8
89RanSmo-5
89Sco-368
89Top-729
89Top-732
89TopBig-156
89TopSti-250
89TopTif-729
89TopTif-732
89UppDec-418
90Bow-493
90BowTif-493
90Don-107
90Fle-292
90FleCan-292
90Lea-179
90OPC-279
90PanSti-169
90PubSti-406
90RanMot-14
90Sco-221
90Top-279
90TopBig-63
90TopSti-251
90TopTif-279
90TulDriDGB-15
90UppDec-685
90VenSti-81
91Bow-268
91Don-357
91Fle-283
91OPC-464
91PanFreS-254
91PanSti-209
91RanMot-5
91Sco-257
91ScoRoo-77T
91StaClu-337
91Top-464
91TopDesS-464
91TopMic-464
91TopTif-464
91UppDec-650
92Bow-335
92ClaGam-66
92Don-699
92Fle-552
92Lea-91
92OPC-622
92PanSti-254
92Pin-430
92PirNatl-4
92Sco-695

92ScoRoo-21T
92StaClu-405
92Stu-83
92Top-622
92TopGol-622
92TopGolW-622
92TopMic-622
92TriPla-50
92Ult-252
92UppDec-488
93Bow-608
93CubMar-3
93Don-104
93Fla-13
93Fle-18
93Lea-106
93OPC-8
93PacSpa-53
93PanSti-206
93Pin-176
93RanKee-89
93Sco-97
93Sel-129
93SP-82
93StaClu-494
93StaCluCu-7
93StaCluFDI-494
93StaCluMOP-494
93Stu-8
93Top-74
93TopGol-74
93TopInaM-74
93TopMic-74
93TriPla-79
93Ult-15
93UppDec-159
93UppDecGold-159
94Bow-522
94ColC-66
94ColChoGS-66
94ColChoSS-66
94Don-555
94ExtBas-216
94Fin-51
94FinRef-51
94Fla-135
94Fle-381
94Lea-180
94OPC-78
94Pac-96
94Pin-200
94PinArtP-200
94PinMusC-200
94ProMag-21
94Sco-346
94ScoGolR-346
94Sel-166
94StaClu-204
94StaCluFDI-204
94StaCluGR-204
94StaCluMOP-204
94StaCluT-333
94StaCluTFDI-333
94Stu-58
94Top-666
94TopGol-666
94TopSpa-666
94TriPla-71
94Ult-160
94UppDec-136
94UppDecED-136
95ColCho-203
95ColChoGS-203
95ColChoSS-203
95Don-186
95DonPreP-186
95Fla-330
95Fle-410
95Lea-71
95Pin-182
95PinArtP-182
95PinMusC-182
95Sco-389
95ScoGolR-389
95ScoPlaTS-389
95StaClu-181
95StaCluFDI-181
95StaCluMOP-181
95StaCluSTWS-181
95Stu-196
95Top-303
95TopCyb-163
95Ult-135
95UltGolM-135
95UppDec-312
95UppDecED-312
95UppDecEDG-312

Buelow, Fritz (Frederick W.)
03BreE10-12
05IndSouPSoCP-5

Buettemeyer, Kim
80WicAerT-3

Buetter, Bud
79RedSoxEF-6
79RedSoxEF-24

Buffamoyer, John
75BurBeeT-1
77HolMilT-3
78SpoIndC-20
80ChaO'sP-2
80ChaO'sW-2

Buffinton, Charlie (Charles G.)
87OldJudN-55
88GandBCGCE-5
89EdgR.WG-3
90KalBatN-5

Buffolino, Rocco
87PocGiaTB-24
88FreSunCLC-24
88FreSunP-1231

Buford, Bobby
75LynRanT-6
76CliPilT-4

Buford, Damon
91Cla/Bes-198
91FreKeyC-23
91FreKeyP-2377
92Bow-224
92ClaFS7-120
92HagSunF-2567
92HagSunS-253
92SkyAA F-105
92UppDecML-51
92UppDecML-221
93Bow-141
93ExcFS7-122
93FleFinE-157
93Lea-492
93RocRedWF-251
93SelRoo-149T
93StaClu-742
93StaCluFDI-742
93StaCluMOP-742
93Top-576
93TopGol-576
93TopInaM-576
93TopMic-576
93TopTra-63T
93UppDec-691
93UppDecGold-691
94Don-605
94OriPro-13
94OriUSPC-6C
94OriUSPC-11H
94Pac-27
94Pin-423
94PinArtP-423
94PinMusC-423
94RocRedWF-1008
94RocRedWTI-4
94Sco-582
94ScoBoyoS-55
94ScoGolR-582
94SpoRoo-106
94SpoRooAP-106
94StaCluT-283
94StaCluTFDI-283
94Top-61
94TopGol-61
94TopSpa-61
94Ult-303
95Don-540
95DonPreP-540
95Fle-3
95Lea-24
96ColCho-739
96ColChoGS-739
96ColChoSS-739
96Don-544
96DonPreP-544
96Fle-475
96FleRan-2
96FleTif-475
96FleUpd-U87
96FleUpdTC-U87
96LeaSigA-37
96LeaSigAG-37
96LeaSigAS-37
96RanMot-25
96Sco-482
96StaClu-393
96StaCluMOP-393
96Ult-418
96UltGolM-418
97Cir-80
97CirRav-80
97ColCho-487
97Fle-218
97FleTif-218
97NewPin-146
97NewPinAP-146
97NewPinMC-146
97NewPinPP-146
97Sco-444
97ScoHobR-444
97ScoResC-444
97ScoShoS-444
97ScoShoSAP-444
97Stu-20
97StuPrePG-20
97StuPrePS-20
97Ult-308
97UltGolME-308
97UltPlaME-308

Buford, Don
87NewOriP-19
88HagSunS-3
89EasLeaDDP-DD38
89HagSunB-15
89HagSunP-277
89HagSunS-2
90HagSunP-1420
90HagSunS-3
90SouCalS-1

Buford, Don (Donald Alvin)
64Top-368
64TopVen-368
64WhiSoxTS-3
65OPC-81
65Top-81
66Top-465
66WhiSoxTI-4
67CokCapWS-6
67DexPre-36
67OPC-143
67ProPizC-5
67Top-143
67Top-232
67TopVen-258
68DexPre-19
68OPC-194
68Top-194
68TopVen-194
69MilBra-45
69MLBOffS-2
69Top-478
69TopSta-123
70DayDaiNM-151
70MLBOffS-147
70OPC-305
70OPC-428
70Ori-2
70Top-305
70Top-428
71MLBOffS-291
71OPC-29
71OPC-328
71Ori-2
71Top-29
71Top-328
72MilBra-56
72OPC-370
72OriPol-3
72Top-370
73OPC-183
73Top-183
74GreHeroBP-5
77SerSta-4
81TCM60I-299
84GiaPos-3
86IndIndTI-29
88OriFreB-2
91FreKeyP-2382
91OriCro-59
92HagSunF-2570
92HagSunS-274
93BowBayF-2203
93UppDecAH-21

Bug(Mascot), The
89SanBerSCLC-94
90SanBerSB-27
90SanBerSCLC-xxx
93SanBerSC-25
94SanBerSC-29
95SanBerSTI-32
96SanBerSB-30

Bugg, Jason
93IdaFalBF-4037
93IdaFalBSP-24
94HigDesMC-7
94HigDesMF-2795

Buggs, Doc (Ron)
77NewCoPT-4
78NewWayCT-5
79BurBeeT-9

Buggs, Michael J.
82AppFoxF-26

Buhe, Tim
89KinMetS-2
90PitMetP-9

Buheller, Tim
86ElmPioRSP-4
87WinHavRSP-1
88LynRedSS-3
89LynRedSS-3

Buher, Brad
92DavLipB-6
93DavLipB-4
94DavLipB-5

Buhl, Bob
53BraJohC-4
53BraSpiaS3-5
53BraSpiaS7-3
54BraJohC-10
54BraMer-1
54BraSpiaSP-4
54Top-210
55Bow-43
55BraGolS-7
55BraJohC-10
55BraSpiaSD-4
56BraBilaBP-4
56Top-244
57BraSpiaS4-4
57Top-127
58Top-176
59Top-347
60BraLaktL-5
60BraSpiaS-4
60Top-230
60Top-374
61Pos-103A
61Pos-103B
61Top-145
61TopStal-40
62Jel-154
62Pos-154
62PosCan-154
62SalPlaC-117
62ShiPlaC-117
62Top-458A
62Top-458B
63CubJayP-4
63Top-175
64CubJayP-4
64Top-96
64TopVen-96
65CubJayP-5
65OPC-264
65Top-264
66OPC-185
66Top-185
66TopVen-185
67OPC-68
67Top-68
78BraTCC-4
83Bra53F-10
87Bra195T-9
89SweBasG-21
94TopArc1-210
94TopArc1G-210

Buhner, Jay
87ColCliP-4
87ColCliP-15
87ColCliT-19
87IntLeaAT-2
88BlaYNPRWL-22
88ClaBlu-244
88ColCliC-23
88ColCliP-18
88ColCliP-329
88Don-545
88DonReaBY-545
88DonRoo-11
88ScoRoo-95T
88ScoRooG-95T
88Spo-223
88TopTra-21T
88TopTraT-21T
89Baz-4
89Bow-219
89BowTif-219
89CalCanC-13
89CalCanP-544
89Don-581
89DonBasB-136
89Fle-542
89FleGlo-542
89K-M-5
89OPC-223
89PanSti-440
89Sco-530
89ScoYouSI-6
89Spo-89
89Top-223
89TopBig-20
89TopCoi-35
89TopGloS-9
89TopRoo-5
89TopSti-319
89TopTif-223
89TopUKM-10
89ToyRoo-5
89TVSpoM-124
89UppDec-220
90Bow-477
90BowTif-477
90Don-448
90Fle-508
90FleCan-508
90Lea-114
90MarMot-7
90OPC-554
90Sco-521
90Top-554
90TopTif-554
90UppDec-534
91Bow-247
91Don-509
91DonGraS-6
91Fle-446
91Lea-62
91MarCouH-13
91OPC-154
91PanFreS-234
91PanSti-190
91Sco-125
91StaClu-153
91Top-154
91TopDesS-154
91TopMic-154
91TopTif-154
91UltUpd-49
91UppDec-128
92Bow-248
92Cla1-T20
92DenHol-23
92Don-61
92Fle-275
92Hig5-106
92Lea-128
92MarMot-6
92OPC-327
92PanSti-59
92Pin-27
92Pin-305
92Sco-64
92ScoProP-6
92ScoProP-18
92StaClu-213
92Stu-231
92Top-327
92TopGol-327
92TopGolW-327
92TopMic-327
92Ult-121
92UppDec-441
92UppDecHRH-HR18
92YanWIZ8-22
93Bow-23
93Don-111
93Fin-124
93FinRef-124
93Fla-268
93Fle-305
93FunPac-112
93Lea-271
93MarMot-6

93OPC-40
93PacJugC-3
93PacSpa-282
93PanSti-65
93Pin-68
93PinHomRC-36
93Sco-172
93Sel-202
93SP-128
93StaClu-310
93StaCluFDI-310
93StaCluMari-23
93StaCluMO-5
93StaCluMOP-310
93Stu-52
93Top-718
93TopGol-718
93TopInaM-718
93TopMic-718
93TriPla-231
93Ult-267
93UppDec-55
93UppDec-224
93UppDecGold-55
93UppDecGold-224
94Bow-557
94BowBes-R67
94BowBesR-R67
94ColC-424
94ColChoGS-424
94ColChoSS-424
94Don-369
94DonSpeE-369
94ExtBas-162
94Fin-122
94FinRef-122
94Fla-336
94Fle-282
94FUnPac-78
94Lea-131
94LeaL-65
94MarMot-6
94OPC-268
94Pac-564
94PanSti-117
94Pin-343
94PinArtP-343
94PinMusC-343
94PinRunC-RC17
94ProMag-126
94RedFolMI-7
94Sco-353
94ScoGolR-353
94Sel-79
94SP-104
94SPDieC-104
94Spo-18
94StaClu-299
94StaCluFDI-299
94StaCluGR-299
94StaCluMOP-299
94StaCluMOP-ST26
94StaCluST-ST26
94Stu-100
94Top-472
94TopGol-472
94TopSpa-472
94TriPla-125
94Ult-118
94UppDec-61
94UppDecED-61
95Baz-15
95Bow-362
95ColCho-290
95ColChoGS-290
95ColChoSE-124
95ColChoSEGS-124
95ColChoSESS-124
95ColChoSS-290
95Don-471
95DonPreP-471
95DonTopotO-147
95Emb-65
95EmbGolI-65
95Emo-76
95Fin-105
95FinRef-105
95Fla-80
95Fle-263
95Lea-172
95LeaLim-13
95MarMot-6
95MarPac-13
95MarPac-25
95Pac-392
95PacPri-124
95PanSti-84
95Pin-234
95PinArtP-234
95PinMusC-234
95RedFol-34
95Sco-68
95ScoGolR-68
95ScoPlaTS-68
95Sel-38
95SelArtP-38
95SP-192
95SPCha-187
95SPChaDC-187
95SPSil-192
95StaClu-73
95StaCluFDI-73
95StaCluMOP-73
95StaCluMOP-SS3
95StaCluSS-SS3
95StaCluSTDW-M26T
95StaCluSTDW-M73
95StaCluSTWS-73
95StaCluVR-46
95Stu-114
95Top-25
95TopCyb-21
95Ult-326
95UltGolM-326
95UppDec-345
95UppDecED-345
95UppDecEDG-345
95UppDecSE-253
95UppDecSEG-253
96Baz-37
96Bow-9
96BowBes-62
96BowBesAR-62
96BowBesR-62
96Cir-76
96CirBos-19
96CirRav-76
96ColCho-383T
96ColCho-730
96ColChoCtG-CG25
96ColChoCtG-CG25B
96ColChoCtG-CG25C
96ColChoCtGE-CR25
96ColChoCtGG-CG25
96ColChoCtGG-CG25B
96ColChoCtGG-CG25C
96ColChoCtGGE-CR25
96ColChoGS-730
96ColChoSS-730
96DenHol-7
96Don-141
96DonPreP-141
96EmoXL-110
96Fin-B237
96Fin-G164
96Fin-S353
96FinRef-B237
96FinRef-G164
96FinRef-S353
96Fla-157
96Fle-231
96FleTif-231
96Lea-113
96LeaLim-69
96LeaLimG-69
96LeaPre-103
96LeaPreP-103
96LeaPrePB-113
96LeaPrePG-113
96LeaPrePS-113
96LeaSig-86
96LeaSigEA-19
96LeaSigEACM-1
96LeaSigPPG-86
96LeaSigPPP-86
96MarMot-3
96MetUni-104
96MetUniP-104
96Pac-415
96PacPri-P129
96PacPriFB-FB4
96PacPriG-P129
96PanSti-228
96Pin-224
96PinAfi-46
96PinAfiAP-46
96PinAfiFPP-46
96PinArtP-124
96PinFoil-224
96PinSta-124
96ProSta-63
96Sco-323
96ScoDugC-B48
96ScoDugCAP-B48
96ScoPowP-3
96ScoTitT-18
96Sel-86
96SelArtP-86
96SelCer-84
96SelCerAP-84
96SelCerCB-84
96SelCerCR-84
96SelCerIP-9
96SelCerMB-84
96SelCerMG-84
96SelCerMR-84
96SP-173
96Spo-91
96Spo-120
96SpoArtP-91
96SpoArtP-120
96SpoPowS-24
96SPSpeFX-8
96SPSpeFXDC-8
96SPx-54
96SPxGol-54
96StaClu-211
96StaClu-333
96StaCluEPB-333
96StaCluEPG-333
96StaCluEPS-333
96StaCluMO-8
96StaCluMOP-211
96StaCluMOP-333
96StaCluMOP-PP14
96StaCluMOP-PS5
96StaCluPP-PP14
96StaCluPS-PS5
95StaCluVRMC-46
96Stu-98
96StuPrePB-98
96StuPrePG-98
96StuPrePS-98
96Sum-65
96SumAbo&B-65
96SumArtP-65
96SumFoi-65
96TeaOut-12
96Top-270
96TopChr-109
96TopChrR-109
96TopGal-16
96TopGalPPI-16
96TopLas-100
96TopLasPC-2
96TopPro-AL11
96TopRoaW-RW5
96Ult-408
96UltGolM-408
96UppDec-201
96UppDecDD-DD36
96UppDecDDG-DD36
96UppDecDDS-DD36
96UppDecPD-PD3
96UppDecPRE-R2
96UppDecPRE-R12
96UppDecPreR-R2
96UppDecPreR-R12
96UppDecRunP-RP4
96UppDecVJLS-VJ11
96Zen-48
96ZenArtP-48
97Bow-255
97BowBes-17
97BowBesAR-17
97BowBesR-17
97BowChr-78
97BowChrI-78
97BowChrIR-78
97BowChrR-78
97BowInt-255
97Cir-72
97CirRav-72
97ColCho-480
97ColChoBS-17
97ColChoBSGS-17
97ColChoCtG-27A
97ColChoCtG-27B
97ColChoCtG-27C
97ColChoCtGIW-CG27
97ColChoNF-NF13
97ColChoPP-PP7
97ColChoPPG-PP7
97ColChoS-9
97ColChoTBS-42
97ColChoTBSWH-42
97Don-58
97DonEli-41
97DonEliGS-41
97DonLim-170
97DonLim-196
97DonLimLE-170
97DonLimLE-196
97DonLonL-7
97DonPre-63
97DonPreCttC-63
97DonPreP-58
97DonPrePGold-58
97DonTea-138
97DonTeaSPE-138
97Fin-35
97Fin-172
97Fin-282
97FinEmb-172
97FinEmb-282
97FinEmbR-172
97FinEmbR-282
97FinRef-35
97FinRef-172
97FinRef-282
97FlaSho-A119
97FlaSho-B119
97FlaSho-C119
97FlaShoLC-119
97FlaShoLC-B119
97FlaShoLC-C119
97FlaShoLCM-A119
97FlaShoLCM-B119
97FlaShoLCM-C119
97Fle-202
97FleLumC-5
97FleTif-202
97Lea-102
97LeaFraM-102
97LeaFraMDC-102
97MetUni-143
97NewPin-55
97NewPinAP-55
97NewPinMC-55
97NewPinPP-55
97Pac-182
97PacCar-16
97PacCarM-16
97PacLigB-182
97PacPri-61
97PacPriLB-61
97PacPriP-61
97PacPriSL-SL6C
97PacSil-182
97Pin-195
97PinArtP-195
97PinCar-10
97PinCer-82
97PinCerMBlu-82
97PinCerMG-82
97PinCerMR-82
97PinCerR-82
97PinIns-39
97PinInsCE-39
97PinInsDE-39
97PinInsFS-8
97PinMin-30
97PinMinB-30
97PinMinCB-30
97PinMinCG-30
97PinMinCGR-30
97PinMinCN-30
97PinMinCS-30
97PinMinG-30
97PinMinS-30
97PinMusC-195
97PinTotCPB-82
97PinTotCPG-82
97PinTotCPR-82
97PinX-P-36
97PinX-PF&A-13
97PinX-PMoS-36
97PinX-PSfF-20
97PinX-PSfFU-20
97ProMag-70
97ProMagML-70
97Sco-168
97Sco-513
97ScoHeaotO-8
97ScoHobR-513
97ScoMar-7
97ScoMarPl-7
97ScoMarPr-7
97ScoPreS-168
97ScoResC-513
97ScoShoS-168
97ScoShoS-513
97ScoShoSAP-168
97ScoShoSAP-513
97ScoStaaD-7
97ScoTitT-13
97Sel-49
97SelArtP-49
97SelRegG-49
97SkyE-X-39
97SkyE-XC-39
97SkyE-XEC-39
97SP-164
97SpoIll-38
97SpoIllEE-38
97SpoIllGS-21
97SPSpeF-33
97SPSpxF-1
97SPSPxFA-1
97SPVinAu-5
97SPVinAu-6
97SPVinAu-7
97SPx-44
97SPxBro-44
97SPxGraF-44
97SPxSil-44
97SPxSte-44
97StaClu-19
97StaClu-390
97StaCluMat-19
97StaCluMOP-19
97StaCluMOP-390
97StaCluMOP-PG5
97StaCluPG-PG5
97Stu-129
97StuPrePG-129
97StuPrePS-129
97Top-40
97TopChr-15
97TopChrDD-DD3
97TopChrDDR-DD3
97TopChrR-15
97TopGal-50
97TopGalPPI-50
97TopSta-65
97TopStaAM-65
97UltRBIK-5
97UppDec-177
97UppDecLDC-LD7
97UppDecP-25
97UppDecPP-PP4
97UppDecPPJ-PP4
97UppDecRP-RP11
97UppDecU-7
97Zen-38

Buhner, Shawn
94BelMarC-7
94BelMarF-3241
96LanJetB-8

Buice, DeWayne
78CedRapGT-4
81WesHavAT-4
82TacTigT-1
83TacTigT-3
86MidAngP-3
87DonRoo-6
87FleUpd-14
87FleUpdG-14
87SpoRoo2-26
87TopTra-13T
87TopTraT-13T
88AngSmo-7
88Don-58
88Fle-487
88FleGlo-487
88OPC-396
88Sco-376
88ScoGlo-376
88StaLinAn-3
88Top-649
88TopMinL-4
88TopRoo-4
88TopSti-180
88TopTif-649
88ToyRoo-4
88UppDecP-A1
88UppDecP-B1
88UppDecP-C1
89Sco-153
89SyrChiC-8

89SyrChiMB-3
89SyrChiP-811
89Top-147
89TopTif-147
89UppDec-147
Buirley, Matt
96VerExpB-10
Buitimea, Martin
85MexCitTT-5
Buker, Cy
77FriOneYW-7
Buksa, Ken
88WatPirP-16
Bulkeley, Morgan G.
36PC7AlbHoF-6
50CalHOFW-9
76ShaPiz-9
77BobParHoF-8
80PerHaloFP-6
80SSPHOF-6
84GalHaloFRL-9
Bull, Wool E.
95DurBulTI-NNO
96HigDesMB-4
Bullard, Jason
91WelPirC-28
91WelPirP-3563
92CarMudF-1174
92CarMudS-128
96NorTidB-9
Bullard, Rocky (Larry)
76BatTroTI-3
78DunBluJT-2
Bullett, Scott
90WelPirP-11
91AugPirC-25
91AugPirP-818
91Cla/Bes-245
91SouAtlLAGP-SAL3
92Bow-321
92CarMudF-1191
92CarMudS-129
92ClaBluBF-BC4
92ClaFS7-42
92ClaRedB-BC4
92ProFS7-312
92SkyAA F-60
92StaClu-288
92TopDeb91-25
92Ult-551
93Bow-402
93BufBisF-529
93ClaFS7-127
93Lea-497
94Don-431
94lowCubF-1285
94Pac-493
94Top-584
94TopGol-584
94TopSpa-584
96Don-331
96DonPreP-331
96Fle-311
96FleTif-311
96LeaSigEA-20
96SigRooOJ-6
96SigRooOJS-6
96Ult-448
96UltGolM-448
97ColCho-53
97Pac-247
97PacLigB-247
97PacSil-247
Bulling, Bud (Terry C.)
77OrlTwiT-3
78OrlTwiT-1
78Top-432
79SpolndT-23
80SpolndT-10
82Don-612
82Top-98
83Don-226
83Fle-630
83SalLakCGT-15
83Top-519
Bullinger, Jim
86GenCubP-1
87WinSpiP-10
88PitCubP-1367
89ChaKniTI-6
90WinSpiTI-17
91ChaKniLD-128
91ChaKniP-1681
91Cla/Bes-176
91LinDriAA-128
92DonRoo-20
92FleUpd-73
92lowCubS-204
92ScoRoo-101T
92SkyAAAF-98
92StaClu-714
92StaCluECN-714
92TopTra-17T
92TopTraG-17T
93Don-556
93Fle-374
93lowCubF-2129
93Lea-31
93Sco-339
93Sel-285
93StaClu-118
93StaCluCu-26
93StaCluFDI-118
93StaCluMOP-118
93Top-101
93TopGol-101
93ToplnaM-101
93TopMic-101
93Toy-6
93UppDec-379
93UppDecGold-379
94FleUpd-107
94StaCluT-360
94StaCluTFDI-360
94TopGol-713
94TopSpa-713
95Don-239
95DonPreP-239
95DonTopotO-195
95Fla-111
95Fle-411
95Lea-341
95Pin-428
95PinArtP-428
95PinMusC-428
95Top-428
95TopCyb-226
95Ult-357
95UltGolM-357
96ColCho-79
96ColChoGS-79
96ColChoSS-79
96Don-185
96DonPreP-185
96EmoXL-151
96Fla-212
96Fle-312
96FleCub-2
96FleTif-312
96Pac-24
96Sco-128
96StaClu-53
96StaCluMOP-53
96Top-316
96Ult-163
96UltGolM-163
96UppDec-37
97ColCho-385
97Fle-587
97FleTif-587
97Ult-532
97UltGolME-532
97UltPlaME-532
Bullinger, Kirk
92HamRedC-2
92HamRedF-1583
93MidLeaAGF-50
93SprCarC-5
93SprCarF-1842
94ExcFS7-262
94St.PetCC-5
94St.PetCF-2576
94Top-713
95HarSenTI-46
96HarSenB-9
Bullinger, Matt
79WatlndT-1B
81ChaLooT-6
82JacMetT-2
Bullock, Craig
91ChaRaiC-17
91ChaRaiP-102
92ColMetC-18
92ColMetF-301
92ColMetPI-25
93CapCitBC-3
93CapCitBF-452
94St.LucMC-4
94St.LucMF-1186
95StLucMTI-8
96StLucMTI-17
Bullock, Eric
82DayBeaAT-12
83ColAstT-9
85TucTorC-52
87TucTorP-19
88PorBeaC-17
88PorBeaP-640
89Fle-106
89FleGlo-106
89PhiTas-38
90CMC-67
90IndIndC-17
90IndIndP-285
90ProAAAF-568
91Bow-457
91ExpPos-2
91Lea-470
92Don-683
92ExpPos-5
92Fle-474
92IndIndF-1872
92Sco-661
92StaClu-659
93NorTidF-2580
96LasVegSB-4
Bullock, Josh
90NebCor-6
93JamExpC-4
93JamExpF-3318
94BurBeeC-4
94BurBeeF-1073
Bullock, Renaldo
92BelMarC-26
92BelMarF-1455
Bullock, Wynn
75TopPho-104
Bulls, Dave
86PorBeaP-2
Bulls, Durham
90DurBulTI-1
92DurBulTI-NNO
93DurBulTI-5
95DurBulTI-NNO
96DurBulBrB-1
Bumagat, Noel
90IBAWorA-30
Bumbry, Al (Alonza B.)
73LinPor-9
73OPC-614
73OriJohP-1
73Top-614
74OPC-137
74Top-137
75OPC-358
75Top-358
76OPC-307
76SSP-396
76Top-307
77BurCheD-37
77Hos-90
77OPC-192
77Top-626
78Top-188
79Top-517
80OPC-36
80Top-65
81AllGamPI-48
81Don-355
81Fle-172
81FleStiC-30
81OPC-34
81Top-425
81TopScr-29
81TopSti-35
82Don-153
82Fle-159
82FleSta-147
82OPC-265
82Top-265
82TopSti-141
83Don-383
83Fle-54
83FleSta-26
83FleSti-203
83OPC-272
83OriPos-3
83Top-655
83TopFol-5
84Don-210
84Fle-2
84Nes792-319
84OriTeal-4
84Top-319
84TopTif-319
85Don-350
85Fle-171
85FleUpd-13
85PadMot-25
85Top-726
85TopSti-205
85TopTif-726
85TopTifT-12T
85TopTra-12T
86Fle-316
86Top-583
86TopTif-583
87ElmPio(C-29
89PacSenL-47
89T/MSenL-14
89TopSenL-27
90EliSenL-94
90SweBasG-29
90TopTVRS-3
91OriCro-60
92RedSoxDD-5
93TedWil-82
93UppDecAH-22
94BowBayF-2429
94UppDecAH-73
94UppDecAH1-73
Bumgarner, Jeff
86KenTwiP-3
87ColAstP-25
87OrlTwiP-1
88PorBeaC-4
88PorBeaP-659
89JacMetGS-10
90FreKeyTI-27
91HagSunP-2447
91LinDriAA-226
92HagSunS-254
Bumstead, Mark
78St.PetCT-3
Bunch, Melvin
93MidLeaAGF-17
93RocRoyC-5
93RocRoyF-705
94ClaGolF-195
94ExcFS7-65
94WilBluRC-2
94WilBluRF-291
95FleUpd-45
95OmaRoyTI-5
95TopTra-104T
96ColCho-168
96ColChoGS-168
96ColChoSS-168
96Don-164
96DonPreP-164
96OmaRoyB-9
96RoyPol-4
Bundy, Lorenzo
83AleDukT-31
84HawlslC-127
89IndIndC-17
89IndIndP-1223
90JacExpB-27
90JacExpP-1389
91SumFlyC-26
91SumFlyP-2351
92AlbPolC-27
92AlbPolF-2321
93BurBeeC-26
93BurBeeF-173
94BurBeeC-26
94BurBeeF-1097
Bunge, Todd
86AncGlaPTI-4
Bunker, Wally
64Top-201
64TopVen-201
65OPC-9
65Top-9
65Top-290
66Top-499
67CokCapO-15
67DexPre-37
67Top-585
67TopVen-254
68CokCapO-15
68Top-489
69MLBOffS-56
69OPC-137
69RoySol-2
69Top-137
69TopFou-2
69TopSta-182
69TopTeaP-7
70DayDaiNM-23
70Kel-70
70MLBOffS-218
70OPC-266
70RoyTeal-4
70Top-266
70TopBoo-7
71MLBOffS-410
71OPC-528
71Top-528
72MilBra-57
81Ori6F-11
81TCM60I-408
91OriCro-61
Bunkley, Antuan
96ForWayWB-5
Bunning, Jim
47StaPinP2-7
57Top-338
58Top-115
59TigGraASP-5
59Top-149
59TopVen-149
60Lea-144
60TigJayP-4
60Top-502
61Pos-39A
61Pos-39B
61TigJayP-4
61Top-46
61Top-50
61Top-490
61TopStal-147
62Jel-26
62Pos-26
62PosCan-26
62SalPlaC-13
62ShiPlaC-13
62TigJayP-3
62TigPosCF-4
62Top-57
62Top-59
62Top-460
62TopBuc-12
62TopStal-44
62TopVen-57
62TopVen-59
63BasMagM-12
63Jel-53
63Pos-53
63SalMetC-33
63TigJayP-3
63Top-8
63Top-10
63Top-218
63Top-365
63TopStil-7
64PhiJayP-3
64PhiPhiB-7
64PhiTeaS-1
64Top-6
64Top-265
64TopCoi-93
64TopGia-10
64TopVen-6
64TopVen-265
64WheSta-9
65Baz-21
65OldLonC-5
65OPC-20
65PhiJayP-3
65Top-20
65TopEmbl-17
65TopTral-6
66Baz-31
66PhiTeal-3
66Top-435
66TopRubl-12
67AshOil-1
67Baz-31
67CokCapA-15
67CokCapNLA-20
67CokCapPh-16
67DexPre-38
67DexPre-39
67PhiPol-2
67Top-238
67Top-560
67TopVen-274
68AtlOilPBCC-8
68Baz-7

68OPC-7
68OPC-9
68OPC-11
68PirKDK-14
68PirTeal-4
68Top-7
68Top-9
68Top-11
68Top-215
68TopActS-8A
68TopVen-7
68TopVen-9
68TopVen-11
68TopVen-215
69CitMetC-20
69MilBra-46
69MLBOffS-183
69OPC-175
69Top-175
69TopFou-8
69TopSta-84
69TopTeaP-16
70DayDaiNM-77
70MLBOffS-86
70OPC-403
70Top-403
71MLBOffS-172
71OPC-574
71PhiArcO-2
71Top-574
71TopCoi-3
71TopGreM-43
72MilBra-58
74LauAllG-61
76LauDiaJ-10
76OklCit8TI-14
79DiaGre-397
80PerHaloFP-225
81TCM60I-454
81TigDetN-97
83PhiPosGM-4
83PhiPosGPaM-9
83TigAlKS-15
83TigAlKS-24
84OCoandSI-89
86SpoDesJM-14
86TigSpoD-13
88PacLegI-92
89SweBasG-7
90DodTar-90
90PacLeg-76
91UppDecS-17
97FleMilDM-29
97TopStaHRR-2
97TopStaHRRA-2
Buonantony, Rich
82QuaCitCT-4
86LouRedTI-8
87LouRedTI-7
88LouRedBC-7
88LouRedBP-445
88LouRedBTI-12
90ReaPhiS-9
91RenSilSCLC-19
Burba, Dave
88SanBerSB-17
88SanBerSCLC-49
89WilBilP-630
89WilBilS-25
90CalCanC-6
90CalCanP-645
90CMC-433
90ProAAAF-110
91Bow-263
91CalCanLD-54
91CalCanP-509
91DonRoo-12
91Fle-447
91LinDriAAA-54
91Sco-742
91TopDeb90-23
92Bow-190
92Cla1-T21
92Don-566
92GiaMot-26
92GiaPacGaE-9
92Lea-471
92OPC-728
92OPCPre-160
92Pin-529
92Sco-611
92ScoRoo-51T
92StaClu-348
92StaClu-718
92Top-728
92TopGol-728
92TopGolW-728
92TopMic-728
92TopTra-18T
92TopTraG-18T
92Ult-587
93Don-128
93Fle-527
93GiaMot-18
93GiaPos-11
93LinVenB-28
93PacSpa-609
93StaClu-245
93StaCluFDI-245
93StaCluMOP-245
93Ult-484
93UppDec-809
93UppDecGold-809
94ColC-67
94ColChoGS-67
94ColChoSS-67
94Don-124
94Fla-443
94Fle-686
94GiaMot-25
94GiaUSPC-5D
94GiaUSPC-12C
94Pac-542
94Sco-219
94ScoGolR-219
94StaCluT-8
94StaCluTFDI-8
94Top-433
94TopGol-433
94TopSpa-433
94Ult-287
95Don-495
95DonPreP-495
95Fle-575
95GiaMot-25
95StaClu-134
95StaCluFDI-134
95StaCluMOP-134
95StaCluSTWS-134
95Top-304
95Ult-240
95UltGolM-240
95UppDec-488T
96ColCho-521
96ColChoGS-521
96ColChoSS-521
96Don-531
96DonPreP-531
96Fla-230
96Fle-337
96FleTif-337
96LeaSigEA-21
96Pac-45
96Ult-177
96UltGolM-177
96UppDec-311
97ColCho-304
97Fle-630
97FleTif-630
97Pac-265
97PacLigB-265
97PacSil-265
97StaClu-273
97StaCluMOP-273
97Ult-456
97UltGolME-456
97UltPlaME-456
Burbach, Bill
69Top-658
70OPC-167
70Top-167
71MLBOffS-484
71OPC-683
71Top-683
92YanWIZ6-20
92YanWIZ7-27
Burbank, Dennis
88CapCodPB-6
88CapCodPPaLP-151
91OklStaC-2
91OneYanP-4145
92ForLauYTI-2
92Ft.LauYF-2602
Burbrink, Nels (Nelson E.)
49W725AngTI-4
56Top-27
Burch, Al (Albert William)
09ColChiE-37A
09T206-44
09T206-45
10JHDABE-3
11SpoLifM-151
12ColRedB-37A
12ColRedB-37B
12ColTinT-37A
12ColTinT-37B
Burch, Ernest W.
87OldJudN-56
88KimN18-6
Burcham, Tim (Timothy)
86QuaCitAP-6
87PalSprP-21
88MidAngGS-6
89EdmTraC-5
89EdmTraP-553
89MidAngGS-7
90CMC-481
90EdmTraC-4
90EdmTraP-511
90ProAAAF-87
91EdmTraLD-157
91EdmTraP-1510
91LinDriAAA-157
93PalSprAC-4
93PalSprAF-61
Burchart, Kyle
96MedHatBJTI-7
Burchart, Larry
69Top-597
70OPC-412
70Top-412
Burchell, Fred
09RamT20-19
09T206-402
12ImpTobC-14
Burchers, Rick
81ChaLooT-18
Burchett, Kerry D.
81ArkTraT-10
Burckel, Brad
91MisStaB-8
Burda, Bob (Edward Robert)
61UniOil-P4
62KahAtl-3
69Top-392
70OPC-357
70Top-357
71CarTeal-6
71OPC-541
71Top-541
72Top-734
94BreMilB-296
Burden, John
80WauTimT-2
81ChaLooT-2
83ChaLooT-20
86ChaLooP-6
87SalSpuP-29
Burdette, Freddie
64Top-408
Burdette, Lew
47Exh-31A
47Exh-31B
52Bow-244
53BowBW-51
53BraJohC-5
53BraSpiaS3-6
53BraSpiaS7-4
54Bow-192
54BraJohC-33
54BraSpiaSP-5
54RedMan-NL24
55Bow-70
55BraGolS-4
55BraJohC-33
55BraSpiaSD-5
56BraBilaBP-5
56Top-219
57BraSpiaS4-5
57Top-208
58BraJayP-3
58Top-10
58Top-289
59Top-440
60BraLaktL-6
60BraSpiaS-5
60KeyChal-9
60NuHi-35
60Top-70
60Top-230
60TopTat-7
60TopVen-70
61NuSco-408
61NuSco-435
61Pos-102A
61Pos-102B
61SevElev-24
61Top-47
61Top-320
62BraJayP-4
62ExhStaB-6
62Jel-153
62Pos-153
62PosCan-153
62SalPlaC-166
62ShiPlaC-166
62Top-380
62TopBuc-13
62TopStal-146
63BraJayP-3
63ExhStaB-9
63Jel-155
63Pos-155
63Top-429
64Top-523
65CubJayP-6
65OPC-64
65Top-64
66Top-299
66TopVen-299
67CokCapDA-22
67Top-265
68LauWorS-54
70FleWorS-54
73OPC-237
73Top-237A
73Top-237B
78BraTCC-5
78TCM60I-276
83ASASpa-6
83Bra53F-33
87Bra195T-7
88PacLegI-68
91LinDri-15
91SweBasG-16
91TopArc1-310
92BazQua5A-13
93ActPacA-142
93MetIma-6
93TedWil-46
93UppDecAH-23
94UppDecAH-92
94UppDecAH1-92
Burdette, Ricky
77SpaPhiT-11
80AshTouT-24
Burdick, Kevin
87WatPirP-11
88SalBucS-3
89EasLeaDDP-DD22
89HarSenP-297
89HarSenS-4
89Sta-19
90BufBisC-16
90BufBisP-378
90BufBisTI-4
90CMC-16
90ProAAAF-493
91ColSprSSLD-80
91ColSprSSP-2189
91LinDriAAA-80
Burdick, Morgan
94BenRocF-3582
95AshTouTI-21
Burdick, Stacey
87MiaMarP-3
89FreKeyS-1
90Bes-255
90EasLeaAP-EL43
90HagSunB-17
90HagSunP-1403
90HagSunS-4
91HagSunLD-227
91HagSunP-2448
91LinDriAA-227
Burdick, William B.
87OldJudN-57
Burdock, Jack (John Joseph)
87BucN28-5
87OldJudN-58
90DodTar-91
Burdy, Mascot (B.J.)
91BluJayFS-35
Bure, Pavel
91StaCluMO-38
Burgen, Chris
88OklSoo-24
Burger, Rob
96PieBolWB-5
Burgess, Bob
89WelPirP-34
90WelPirP-34
Burgess, Gus
80ElmPioRST-26
83PawRedST-20
84PawRedST-9
85PawRedST-1
Burgess, Kurt
86LakTigP-3
92MacBraC-23
92MacBraF-259
93DurBulC-4
93DurBulF-478
93DurBulTI-12
94HigDesMC-8
94HigDesMF-2780
95DurBulTI-6
Burgess, Smoky (Forrest H.)
49EurSta-52
49W725AngTI-5
51Bow-317
52Bow-112
52Top-357
53BowC-28
53Top-10
54Bow-31
55Bow-209
55RobGouS-12
55RobGouW-12
56Kah-4
56RedBurB-3
56Top-192
57Kah-4
57RedSoh-4
57Top-228
58Kah-4
58RedEnq-6
58RedJayP-4
58Top-49
59Kah-5
59Top-432
60Kah-4
60KeyChal-10
60PirJayP-1
60PirTag-6
60Top-393
61Kah-6
61PirJayP-1
61Pos-138A
61Pos-138B
61Top-461
61TopStal-61
62Kah-3
62Pos-176
62PosCan-176
62SalPlaC-114
62ShiPlaC-114
62Top-389
62TopStal-173
63Fle-55
63Jel-144
63Kah-4
63PirIDL-2
63PirJayP-2
63Pos-144
63Top-18
63Top-425
64PirKDK-4
64Top-37
64TopVen-37
65OPC-198
65Top-198
66Top-354
66TopVen-354
67Top-506
72LauGreF-28
77GalGloG-6
78GreBraT-5
78TCM60I-1
79DiaGre-370
83TopRep5-357
85WhiSoxC-17
87Pir196T-6
88PulBraP-1750
89PacLegI-201
89SweBasG-32
90PacLeg-77

91TopArc1-10
92BazQua5A-9
93ActPacA-141
Burgess, Thomas R.
54CarHunW-4
79RicBraT-15
80ChaChaT-1
81TulDriT-20
82TulDriT-22
83OklCit8T-2
84OklCit8T-3
87GleFalTP-3
90TulDriDGB-28
Burgmeier, Tom
69Top-558
70OPC-108
70RoyTeal-5
70Top-108
71MLBOffS-411
71OPC-431
71Top-431
72OPC-246
72Top-246
73OPC-306
73Top-306
75OPC-478
75Top-478
76OPC-87
76SSP-206
76Top-87
77Top-398
78PapGinD-16
78Top-678
79OPC-272
79Top-524
80Top-128
81CokTeaS-1
81Don-97A
81Don-97B
81Fle-228
81OPC-320
81Top-320
81TopSupHT-1
82Don-361
82Fle-288
82RedSoxC-2
82Top-455
83A'sGraG-39
83Don-235
83Fle-180
83FleSti-59
83OPC-213
83Top-213
83TopFol-4
83TopTra-16T
84A'sMot-18
84Don-522
84Fle-439
84Nes792-33
84OPC-33
84Top-33
84TopTif-33
85Don-400
85Fle-417
93RocRoyC-29
93RocRoyF-732
94RocRoyC-29
94RocRoyF-582
95WilBluRTI-15
96WilBluRB-29
Burgo, Dale
88WinHavRSS-6
89LynRedSS-4
91LynRedSP-1190
Burgos, Carlos
92AppFoxF-986
94EugEmeC-3
94EugEmeF-3715
95SprSulTI-4
Burgos, Enrique
87KnoBluJP-1510
88BlaYNPRWL-100
88SyrChiP-815
89DunBluJS-2
93OmaRoyF-1673
94OmaRoyF-1216
95PhoFirTI-47
Burgos, Francisco
89BlaYNPRWL-107
Burgos, John
87GasRanP-27
88BlaYNPRWL-163
89SavCarP-351
90ArkTraGS-6
91LinDriAA-505
91ReaPhiLD-505
91ReaPhiP-1365
94ChaLooF-1351
95ChaLooTI-3
Burgos, Paco
87SanJosBP-17
88ChaRanS-5
89ChaRanS-4
90TulDriP-1160
90TulDriTI-4
91LinDriAAA-306
91OklCit8LD-306
91OklCit8P-183
91TulDriTI-3
92AppFoxC-12
92MemChiF-2424
92MemChiS-428
92SkyAA F-180
Burguillos, Carlos
91NiaFalRC-17
91NiaFalRP-3644
92ClaFS7-101
92FayGenF-2181
93LakTigC-3
93LakTigF-1321
93LinVenB-211
94LakTigC-4
94LakTigF-3049
94VenLinU-232
95LinVen-51
Burgus, Travis
95ElmPioTI-2
95ElmPioUTI-2
96KanCouCTI-3
Burk, Mack Edwin
57Top-91
58Top-278
Burke, Alan
92BatCliC-10
92BatCliF-3270
93ClaFS7-179
93SpaPhiC-9
93SpaPhiF-1065
94ClaGolF-163
94ClePhiC-11
94ClePhiF-2539
94ExcFS7-244
Burke, Bobby (Robert J.)
31SenTealPW-5
33Gou-71
34GouCanV-25
35GouPuzR-4C
35GouPuzR-7C
35GouPuzR-12C
92ConTSN-362
94ConTSN-1183
94ConTSNB-1183
Burke, Curtis
83DayBeaAT-25
85OscAstTI-22
Burke, Don
86JamExpP-2
87WesPalBEP-663
87WesPalBEP-675
Burke, Eddie (Edward D.)
98CamPepP-8
Burke, Edward
95NewN566-177
Burke, Glenn L.
75WatDodT-3
78SSP270-76
78Top-562
79OPC-78
79Top-163
90DodTar-92
Burke, Jamie
93BoiHawC-5
93BoiHawF-3906
94CedRapKC-5
94CedRapKF-1113
95LakElsSTI-6
96MidAngB-9
96VanCanB-6
Burke, Jimmy (James Timothy)
09T206-403
10JuJuDE-5
11SpoLifCW-49
19W514-89
Burke, Joe
92UppDecS-20
Burke, John C.
92BenRocC-1
92BenRocF-1467
92ClaBluBF-BC29
92ClaDraP-79
92ClaFS7-412
92UppDecML-17
93Bow-388
93CenValRC-5
93CenValRF-2885
93ClaExp#PF-EP1
93ClaFS7-180
93ClaGolF-205
93ExcFS7-33
93StaClu-513
93StaCluFDI-513
93StaCluMOP-513
93UppDec-444
93UppDecGold-444
94Bow-226
94Bow-356
94BowBes-B11
94BowBesR-B11
94Cla-32
94ClaGolF-27
94ColSprSSF-725
94ExcFS7-184
94SigRoo-21
94SigRooHP-S1
94SigRooS-21
94TedWil-119
94Top-780
94TopGol-780
94TopSpa-780
94Ult-477
94UppDecML-200
94UppDecMLPotYF-PY23
95Bow-73
96ColSprSSTI-4
96SalAvaB-23
97DonRatR-29
97Fle-664
97FleTif-664
97ScoPreS-274
97ScoRoc-15
97ScoRocPl-15
97ScoRocPr-15
Burke, Kevin
85NewOriT-24
87HagSunP-20
Burke, Leo Patrick
63Top-249
64Top-557
65OPC-202
65Top-202
91OriCro-62
Burke, Matt
90OklSoo-3
Burke, Mike (Michael E.)
86BakDodP-4
87VerBeaDP-25
Burke, Steve
77JacSunT-3
78Top-709
79SpoIndT-22
Burke, Stoney
94BelBreC-4
94BelBreF-104
96LynHilB-6
Burke, Tim
82BufBisT-15
83ColCliT-7
83NasSouTI-3
84IndIndTI-23
85ExpPos-4
85FleUpd-14
86Don-421
86ExpPos-2
86ExpProPa-17
86Fle-245
86Lea-198
86OPC-258
86SevCoi-E15
86Top-258
86TopTif-258
87Don-222
87ExpPos-3
87Fle-315
87FleGlo-315
87Lea-205
87OPC-132
87SpoTeaP-20
87Top-624
87TopSti-78
87TopTif-624
88Don-98
88DonBasB-34
88ExpPos-2
88Fle-180
88FleGlo-180
88FleMin-87
88FleStiC-95
88Lea-84
88MSAHosD-2
88OPC-14
88Sco-187
88ScoGlo-187
88StaLinE-2
88Top-529
88TopTif-529
89Bow-360
89BowTif-360
89Don-274
89DonBasB-180
89ExpPos-4
89Fle-372
89FleGlo-372
89OPC-48
89PanSti-113
89RedFolSB-15
89Sco-228
89Spo-73
89Top-48
89TopSti-69
89TopTif-48
89UppDec-456
90Bow-103
90BowTif-103
90Don-334
90DonBesN-42
90ExpPos-4
90Fle-342
90FleBasA-3
90FleCan-342
90Lea-28
90OPC-195
90PanSti-294
90PubSti-170
90RedFolSB-10
90Sco-127
90Sco100S-34
90Spo-199
90Top-195
90TopBig-187
90TopMinL-61
90TopSti-72
90TopTif-195
90TopTVA-60
90UppDec-515
90VenSti-82
91Don-125
91Fle-227
91Lea-124
91OPC-715
91PanFreS-148
91RedFolS-15
91Sco-181
91StaClu-514
91Top-715
91TopDesS-715
91TopMic-715
91TopTif-715
91Ult-198
91UltUpd-95
91UppDec-215
91UppDecFE-70F
92Don-366
92Fle-497
92Lea-44
92MetColP-10
92MetKah-44
92OPC-322
92Pin-471
92Sco-651
92StaClu-392
92Stu-62
92Top-322
92TopGol-322
92TopGolW-322
92TopMic-322
92TriPla-14
92Ult-228
92UppDec-433
93Fle-647
93Top-249
93TopGol-249
93TopInaM-249
93TopMic-249
Burke, Todd
87VisOakP-18
Burke, Tom
77ChaPatT-1
Burke, William I.
09ColChiE-38A
09ColChiE-38B
12ColRedB-38A
12ColRedB-38B
12ColTinT-38A
12ColTinT-38B
Burkett, Jesse Cail
09RamT20-20
21KoBreWSI-5
22W575-12
36PC7AlbHoF-39
50CalHOFW-10
76ShaPiz-39
80PerHaloFP-39
80SSPHOF-39
81ConTSN-75
84GalHaloFRL-39
89HOFStiB-33
94OriofB-88
95ConTSN-1388
98CamPepP-9
Burkett, John
85FreGiaP-22
86ShrCapP-2
87ShrCapP-14
87TexLeaAF-33
88Fle-651
88FleGlo-651
88PhoFirC-2
88PhoFirP-76
89PhoFirC-1
89PhoFirP-1483
90ClaYel-T6
90DonBesN-12
90DonRoo-51
90FleUpd-61
90GiaMot-26
90Lea-384
90PhoFirP-5
90ProAAAF-31
90ScoRoo-73T
90TopTra-16T
90TopTraT-16T
90UppDec-735
91Bow-637
91ClaGam-86
91Don-638
91Fle-256
91GiaMot-26
91GiaPacGaE-3
91GiaSFE-5
91Lea-56
91OPC-447
91PanFreS-74
91PanSti-78
91Sco-70
91Sco100RS-7
91SevCoi-NC1
91StaClu-119
91Stu-253
91Top-447
91TopDesS-447
91TopMic-447
91TopRoo-5
91TopTif-447
91Ult-317
91UppDec-577
92Don-257
92Fle-630
92GiaMot-5
92GiaPacGaE-10
92Lea-179
92OPC-762
92Pin-292
92Pin-578
92Sco-522
92SpoIllFK1-190
92StaClu-136
92Stu-113
92Top-762
92TopGol-762
92TopGolW-762
92TopMic-762
92Ult-286
92UppDec-148
93Bow-520
93DiaMar-19
93Don-156
93Fin-44
93FinRef-44
93Fla-139

93Fle-153
93GiaMot-7
93GiaPos-12
93Lea-342
93OPC-89
93PacSpa-268
93Pin-375
93Sco-174
93SP-110
93StaClu-412
93StaCluFDI-412
93StaCluG-10
93StaCluMOP-412
93Stu-44
93Top-66
93TopGol-66
93TopInaM-66
93TopMic-66
93Ult-129
93UppDec-160
93UppDecGold-160
94Bow-463
94BowBes-R28
94BowBesR-R28
94ColC-68
94ColC-306
94ColChoGS-68
94ColChoGS-306
94ColChoSS-68
94ColChoSS-306
94Don-13
94DonSpeE-13
94ExtBas-384
94Fin-295
94FinRef-295
94Fla-240
94Fle-687
94FleAllC-33
94FUnPac-82
94GiaAMC-6
94GiaMot-5
94GiaTarBCI-2
94GiaTeal-7
94GiaUSPC-6D
94GiaUSPC-13C
94Lea-73
94LeaL-157
94OPC-19
94Pac-543
94PacSilP-19
94PanSti-14
94PanSti-262
94Pin-24
94PinArtP-24
94PinMusC-24
94ProMag-122
94Sco-5
94ScoGolR-5
94ScoGolS-21
94ScoSam-5
94ScoSam-5GR
94Sel-341
94SP-91
94SPDieC-91
94Spo-29
94StaClu-88
94StaCluFDI-88
94StaCluGR-88
94StaCluMO-32
94StaCluMOP-88
94StaCluT-28
94StaCluTFDI-28
94Top-213
94TopGol-213
94TopSpa-213
94TriPla-103
94Ult-587
94UppDec-403
94UppDecAJ-6
94UppDecAJG-6
94UppDecED-403
94USPlaCA-5S
95Bow-435
95ColCho-393
95ColCho-557T
95ColChoGS-393
95ColChoSS-393
95Don-233
95DonPreP-233
95DonTopotO-238
95Fin-198
95Fin-285
95FinRef-198
95FinRef-285
95Fla-350
95Fle-576
95FleUpd-94
95Lea-357
95Pac-374
95Pin-361
95PinArtP-361
95PinMusC-361
95SP-54
95SPSil-54
95StaClu-267
95StaClu-567
95StaCluFDI-267
95StaCluMOP-267
95StaCluMOP-567
95StaCluSTWS-267
95StaCluSTWS-567
95Top-491
95TopCyb-282
95TopTra-48T
95Ult-333
95UltGolM-333
95UppDec-353
95UppDecED-353
95UppDecEDG-353
96ColCho-556
96ColChoGS-556
96ColChoSS-556
96Don-116
96DonPreP-116
96EmoXL-183
96Fin-B107
96FinRef-B107
96Fla-258
96Fle-383
96FleTif-383
96MetUni-162
96MetUniP-162
96Pac-77
96PanSti-12
96Sco-427
96StaClu-71
96StaCluMOP-71
96Top-179
96Ult-196
96UltGolM-196
96UppDec-76
97Cir-162
97CirRav-162
97Don-158
97Fin-73
97FinRef-73
97Fle-517
97FleTif-517
97Lea-243
97LeaFraM-243
97LeaFraMDC-243
97Sco-213
97ScoPreS-213
97ScoRan-14
97ScoRanPl-14
97ScoRanPr-14
97ScoShoS-213
97ScoShoSAP-213
97StaClu-312
97StaCluMOP-312
97Top-27
97Ult-332
97UltGolME-332
97UltPlaME-332
97UppDec-507

Burkhart, Ken

46SeaSLP-7
47TipTop-151

Burks, Ellis

86NewBriRSP-4
87DonRoo-5
87FleUpd-15
87FleUpdG-15
87PawRedSP-73
87PawRedST-22
87SpoRooI-5
87TopTra-14T
87TopTraT-14T
88ClaBlu-229
88Don-174
88DonBasB-121
88DonTeaBRS-174
88Fle-348
88Fle-630
88FleGlo-348
88FleGlo-630
88FleSlu-5
88FleStiC-6
88Lea-174
88MSAIceTD-2
88OPC-269
88PanSti-31
88RedFolSB-10
88Sco-472
88ScoGlo-472
88ScoYouSI-37
88Spo-144
88StaLinRS-5
88Top-269
88TopBig-80
88TopGloS-50
88TopRoo-2
88TopSti-250
88TopSti-310
88TopTif-269
88ToyRoo-5
89Bow-36
89BowTif-36
89ClaTraP-152
89ClaTraP-175
89Don-303
89DonBasB-9
89DonGraS-12
89Fle-83
89FleGlo-83
89Nis-3
89OPC-311
89PanSti-278
89Sco-9
89ScoHot1S-43
89ScoSco-25
89Spo-191
89Top-785
89TopAme2C-7
89TopBig-259
89TopHeaUT-12
89TopSti-254
89TopTif-785
89TVSpoM-62
89UppDec-434
90Bow-280
90BowTif-280
90ClaUpd-T8
90Don-23
90Don-228
90DonBesA-30
90DonSupD-23
90Fle-269
90FleCan-269
90Lea-261
90OPC-155
90PanSti-21
90PubSti-450
90PubSti-594
90RedFolSB-11
90RedSoxP-5
90Sco-340
90Sco100S-16
90Spo-80
90Top-155
90TopBig-107
90TopCoi-8
90TopDou-7
90TopSti-259
90TopTif-155
90TopTVRS-28
90UppDec-343
90USPlaCA-7C
90VenSti-83
90VenSti-84
91Bow-109
91Bow-373
91ClaGam-12
91DenHol-1
91Don-235
91Fle-89
91Lea-121
91MajLeaCP-11
91OPC-70
91PanCanT1-114
91PanFreS-269
91PanSti-212
91RedSoxP-3
91Sco-8
91Sco100S-48
91StaClu-108
91StaCluCM-4
91Stu-12
91Top-70
91TopCraJ2-8
91TopDesS-70
91TopMic-70
91TopTif-70
91Ult-30
91UppDec-436
91UppDecSS-SS10
92Bow-570
92ClaGam-71
92Don-234
92Fle-35
92Lea-314
92OPC-416
92PanSti-90
92Pin-26
92RedSoxDD-6
92Sco-270
92Sco100S-83
92ScoImpP-78
92ScoProP-10
92SpoIllFK1-516
92StaClu-399
92Top-416
92TopGol-416
92TopGolW-416
92TopKid-70
92TopMic-416
92Ult-13
92UppDec-94
92UppDec-525
93Bow-231
93Don-33
93Fla-181
93Fle-176
93FleFinE-194
93Lea-252
93OPCPre-93
93PacSpa-29
93PacSpa-386
93PanSti-95
93Pin-46
93Sco-78
93Sel-68
93SelRoo-10T
93StaClu-187
93StaClu-607
93StaCluFDI-187
93StaCluFDI-607
93StaCluMOP-187
93StaCluMOP-607
93StaCluWS-27
93Stu-33
93Top-351
93TopGol-351
93TopInaM-351
93TopMic-351
93TopTra-104T
93Ult-529
93UppDec-265
93UppDec-526
93UppDecGold-265
93UppDecGold-526
93WhiSoxK-5
94Bow-414
94BowBes-R72
94BowBesR-R72
94ColC-554
94ColChoGS-554
94ColChoSS-554
94Don-145
94ExtBas-243
94Fin-275
94FinRef-275
94Fla-152
94Fle-78
94FleUpd-122
94FUnPac-49
94Lea-242
94LeaL-101
94OPC-90
94Pac-122
94PanSti-45
94Pin-496
94PinArtP-496
94PinMusC-496
94ProMag-42
94RocPol-5
94Sco-431
94ScoGolR-431
94ScoRoo-RT4
94ScoRooCP-CP7
94ScoRooGR-RT4
94ScoRooS-RT4
94Sel-287
94SP-165
94SPDieC-165
94SpoRoo-20
94SpoRooAP-20
94SpoRooS-20
94StaClu-622
94StaCluFDI-622
94StaCluGR-622
94StaCluMOP-622
94StaCluT-115
94StaCluTFDI-115
94Stu-176
94Top-538
94TopGol-538
94TopSpa-538
94TopTra-18T
94TriPla-222
94Ult-478
94UppDec-483
94UppDecED-483
95ColCho-447
95ColChoGS-447
95ColChoSS-447
95Don-300
95DonPreP-300
95Fla-127
95Fle-516
95Lea-281
95Pac-133
95Pin-54
95PinArtP-54
95PinMusC-54
95RocPol-4
95Sco-370
95ScoGolR-370
95ScoHaloG-HG63
95ScoPlaTS-370
95Sel-127
95SelArtP-127
95Spo-11
95SpoArtP-11
95StaClu-443
95StaCluMOP-443
95StaCluSTWS-443
95StaCluVR-234
95Stu-153
95Top-235
95TopCyb-132
95Ult-152
95UltGolM-152
95UppDec-174
95UppDecED-174
95UppDecEDG-174
96Cir-121
96CirRav-121
96ColCho-534
96ColChoGS-534
96ColChoSS-534
96Don-70
96Don-71
96DonPreP-70
96EmoXL-173
96Fla-244
96Fle-361
96FleRoc-3
96FleTif-361
96LeaSig-143
96LeaSigPPG-143
96LeaSigPPP-143
96Pac-55
96RocPol-5
96Sco-442
96SP-79
95StaCluVRMC-234
96TeaOut-13
96Top-123
96Ult-187
96UltGolM-187
96UppDec-323
97Bow-222
97BowBes-28
97BowBesAR-28
97BowBesR-28
97BowChr-52
97BowChrI-52
97BowChrIR-52
97BowChrR-52
97BowInt-222
97Cir-234
97CirRav-234
97ColCho-319
97ColChoAC-42
97ColChoPP-PP16
97ColChoPPG-PP16
97Don-185
97DonEli-119
97DonEliGS-119

97DonLim-108
97DonLimLE-108
97DonPre-31
97DonPreCttC-31
97DonPreP-185
97DonPrePGold-185
97DonTea-96
97DonTeaSPE-96
97Fin-75
97Fin-290
97FinEmb-290
97FinEmbR-290
97FinRef-75
97FinRef-290
97FlaSho-A179
97FlaSho-B179
97FlaSho-C179
97FlaShoLC-179
97FlaShoLC-B179
97FlaShoLC-C179
97FlaShoLCM-A179
97FlaShoLCM-B179
97FlaShoLCM-C179
97Fle-308
97FleLumC-6
97FleNig&D-2
97FleTeaL-18
97FleTif-308
97Lea-120
97LeaFraM-120
97LeaFraMDC-120
97MetUni-72
97NewPin-10
97NewPin-189
97NewPinAP-10
97NewPinAP-189
97NewPinMC-10
97NewPinMC-189
97NewPinPP-10
97NewPinPP-189
97Pac-280
97PacLigB-280
97PacPri-95
97PacPriLB-95
97PacPriP-95
97PacSil-280
97PacTriCD-15
97Pin-27
97PinArtP-27
97PinCer-88
97PinCerMBlu-88
97PinCerMG-88
97PinCerMR-88
97PinCerR-88
97PinIns-120
97PinInsCE-120
97PinInsDE-120
97PinInsFS-7
97PinMusC-27
97PinTeaP-7
97PinTeaP-10
97PinTotCPB-88
97PinTotCPG-88
97PinTotCPR-88
97PinX-P-19
97PinX-PMoS-19
97PinX-PSfF-36
97PinX-PSfFU-36
97ProMag-12
97ProMagML-2
97ProMagML-12
97Sco-74
97ScoPreS-74
97ScoRoc-4
97ScoRocPl-4
97ScoRocPr-4
97ScoShoS-74
97ScoShoSAP-74
97Sel-81
97SelArtP-81
97SelRegG-81
97SkyE-X-68
97SkyE-XC-68
97SkyE-XEC-68
97SP-66
97StaClu-199
97StaCluMat-199
97StaCluMOP-199
97Stu-50
97StuPrePG-50
97StuPrePS-50
97Top-146
97TopAll-AS14
97TopChr-56
97TopChrAS-AS14
97TopChrR-56
97TopChrSAR-AS14
97TopChrSB-3
97TopChrSBR-3
97TopGal-32
97TopGalPPI-32
97TopSeaB-SB3
97TopSta-69
97TopStaAM-69
97Ult-184
97UltGolME-184
97UltPlaME-184
97UppDec-349
97UppDecU-12
Burks, Robert E.
87OldJudN-59
Burks, Will
86DavLipB-6
Burleson, Rick (Richard P.)
75OPC-302
75Top-302
76Hos-44
76HosTwi-44
76LinSup-110
76OPC-29
76RedSox-1
76RedSoxSM-1
76SSP-410
76Top-29
77BurCheD-28
77Hos-68
77OPC-237
77Spo-8408
77Top-585
78OPC-37
78PapGinD-7
78SSP270-175
78Top-245
79OPC-57
79Top-125
80OPC-339
80Top-645
81AllGamPI-20
81Don-454
81Fle-225
81FleStiC-33
81Kel-49
81LonBeaPT-3
81OPC-172
81Squ-13
81Top-455
81TopScr-37
81TopSti-52
81TopSupHT-56
81TopTra-743
82Don-342
82Fle-453
82FleSta-219
82Kel-44
82OPC-55
82Top-55
82TopSti-134
82TopSti-157
83Don-318
83Fle-80
83OPC-315
83Top-315
84AngSmo-4
84Fle-510
84Nes792-735
84OPC-376
84Top-735
84TopSti-238
84TopTif-735
86AngSmo-15
86TopTra-16T
86TopTraT-16T
87DonOpeD-134
87Fle-74
87FleGlo-74
87OPC-152
87Top-579
87TopTif-579
91A'sMot-28
91OriCro-63
92RedSoxDD-7
95AngMot-28
96AngMot-28
Burley, Rick
93EugEmeC-7
93EugEmeF-3849
93RocRoyC-6
93RocRoyF-706
94MidLeaAF-MDW20
94RocRoyC-4
94RocRoyF-556
Burley, Tony
82CedRapRT-16
83TamTarT-1
Burley, Travis
90MedHatBJB-4
Burlingame, Ben
91GenCubC-2
91GenCubP-4208
92WinSpiC-24
92WinSpiF-1200
93DayCubC-4
93DayCubF-851
93PeoChiTI-3
94OrlCubF-1378
96IowCubB-9
95OrlCubF-2
Burlingame, Dennis
88SouAtlLAGS-28
88SumBraP-393
89DurBullS-2
89DurBulTI-2
91DurBulC-7
91DurBulP-1537
92GreBraF-1149
92GreBraS-230
92SkyAA F-98
92UppDecML-299
93GreBraF-342
93RicBraP-19
94HigDesMC-9
94HigDesMF-2781
Burlingame, Greg
87HawRai-22
89SanBerSB-5
89SanBerSCLC-70
Burlingame, Mark
77ForLauYS-26
Burmeister, Jerry
46SeaSLP-8
Burnau, Ben
89WauTimGS-10
Burnett, John P.
35DiaMatCS3T1-21
Burnett, Johnny (John H.)
36GouWidPPR-D5
91ConTSN-82
92ConTSN-543
Burnett, Lance
88PocGiaP-2083
Burnett, Mickey
47SigOil-40
47SmiClo-17
Burnett, Ora
46RemBre-9
47RemBre-5
49BowPCL-36
Burnett, Roger
91OneYanP-4160
92PriWilCC-12
92PriWilCF-154
93PriWilCC-2
93PriWilCF-661
94AbaYanF-1446
95NorNavTI-26
Burnette, Wallace
57Top-13
58Top-69
Burney, Wayne
74AlbDukTI-3
75AlbDukC-10
Burnham, Elizabeth
95ColSilB-2
Burnham, George W.
87OldJudN-60
Burnitz, Jeromy
88CapCodPPaLP-145
90ClaDraP-17
90PitMetP-31
91Bow-474
91Cla/Bes-68
91Cla1-T4
91ClaGolB-BC5
91LinDriAA-627
91Sco-380
91WilBilLD-627
91WilBilP-304
92Bow-189
92OPC-591
92ProFS7-280
92SkyAAAF-248
92TidTidF-908
92TidTidS-554
92Top-591
92TopGol-591
92TopGolW-591
92TopMic-591
92UppDec-65
92UppDecML-130
93Bow-622
93Don-787
93ExcFS7-69
93FlaWavotF-2
93FleFinE-100
93Lea-503
93NorTidF-2581
93SelRoo-85T
93SP-147
93Top-658
93TopGol-658
93TopInaM-658
93TopMic-658
93TopTra-110T
93Ult-423
94Bow-512
94ColC-69
94ColChoGS-69
94ColChoSS-69
94Don-575
94Fin-15
94FinJum-15
94FinRef-15
94Fla-195
94Fle-559
94FleRooS-3
94FUnPac-81
94Lea-230
94MetColP-6
94MetShuST-2
94NorTidF-2931
94OPC-110
94Pac-397
94PanSti-216
94Pin-395
94PinArtP-395
94PinMusC-395
94PinNewG-NG23
94ProMag-94
94Sco-570
94ScoBoyoS-5
94ScoGolR-570
94Sel-282
94StaClu-201
94StaCluFDI-201
94StaCluGR-201
94StaCluMOP-201
94Top-122
94TopGol-122
94TopSpa-122
94TriPla-142
94Ult-235
94UppDec-190
94UppDecED-190
94USPlaCR-9C
95ActPacF-35
95ColCho-279
95ColChoGS-279
95ColChoSS-279
95Don-142
95DonPreP-142
95Fle-367
95Pac-279
95PacPri-91
95Pin-370
95Pin-381
95PinArtP-370
95PinArtP-381
95PinMusC-370
95PinMusC-381
95Sco-179
95ScoGolR-179
95ScoPlaTS-179
95Top-366
95TopCyb-194
96MetTeal-7
97ColCho-374
97Fle-125
97FleTif-125
97Pac-114
97PacLigB-114
97PacSil-114
97Sco-191
97ScoPreS-191
97ScoShoS-191
97ScoShoSAP-191
97Top-475
97Ult-309
97UltGolME-309
97UltPlaME-309
Burnos, Jim
83WisRapTF-20
Burns, Britt
79KnoKnoST-6
81AllGamPI-75
81CokTeaS-25
81Don-279
81Fle-342A
81Fle-342B
81OPC-218
81Top-412
81TopSti-63
81TopSupHT-13
82Don-230
82Fle-339
82FleSta-189
82Top-44
83Don-23
83Don-193
83Fle-232
83FleSti-156
83Kel-43
83Top-541
83TopSti-48
83WhiSoxTV-40
84Don-424
84Fle-54
84Nes792-125
84OPC-125
84Top-125
84TopTif-125
84WhiSoxTV-7
85Don-257
85Fle-509
85OPC-338
85Top-338
85TopTif-338
85WhiSoxC-40
86Don-58
86Fle-200
86FleStiC-17
86OPC-174
86Spo-105
86Top-679
86TopMinL-10
86TopSti-292
86TopTif-679
86YanTCM-18
90TopTVY-38
94BreCouMC-25
95BreCouMF-262
96PorSeaDB-2
Burns, Craig
72CedRapCT-23
Burns, Dan
83ElPasDT-1
Burns, Daren
88WytCubP-1985
Burns, Ed (Edward James)
15SpoNewM-17
16ColE13-18
16FleBreD-9
16SpoNewM-18
17HolBreD-8
Burns, George
19W514-24
20WalMaiW-7
21Nei-1
21Nei-70
23W503-39
75ShaPiz-7
80LauFamF-35
Burns, George Henry
16ColE13-19
16SpoNewM-19
17HolBreD-10
20GasAmeMBD-5
20NatCarE-8
21E121So8-6
21Exh-16
21Exh-17
22AmeCarE-6
22E120-1
22W572-9
22W573-13
22W575-13
23WilChoV-13
26Exh-81
27Exh-41
27YorCarE-9

28StaPlaCE-5
28W502-9
28Yue-9
77Ind192T-2
91ConTSN-201
91ConTSN-309
94ConTSN-1153
94ConTSN-1272
94ConTSNB-1153
94ConTSNB-1272
95ConTSN-1359
20W516-10
Burns, George Joseph
14B18B-12A
14B18B-12B
14B18B-12C
14B18B-65
14FatPlaT-9
15SpoNewM-18
16BF2FP-75
16ColE13-20
16FleBreD-10
16SpoNewM-20
17HolBreD-9
20GasAmeMBD-27
20NatCarE-9
21E121So8-7
21Exh-14
21Exh-15
21KoBreWSI-6
22AmeCarE-7
22E120-167
22W573-14
23W515-54
23WilChoV-14
27YorCarE-9
28Yue-9
91ConTSN-158
Burns, Gregory
85MadMusT-7
Burns, Ian
91DaiDolF-11
Burns, J.J.
92ChaRaiC-5
Burns, Jack (John Irving)
32OrbPinNP-64
32OrbPinUP-7
33Gou-198
33TatOrb-7
34DiaMatCSB-21
34BatR31-18
34DiaStaR-75
34ExhFou-15
34TarThoBD-3
35DiaMatCS3T1-22
35ExhFou-15
35GouPuzR-8C
35GouPuzR-9C
37GouFliMR-1A
37GouFliMR-1B
37GouThuMR-1
91ConTSN-131
Burns, James
83St.PetCT-16
Burns, Jerry
92ChaRaiF-113
Burns, Jim (James M.)
87OldJudN-62
Burns, John Joseph
34BatR31-191
Burns, Kerry
83TriTriT-4
Burns, Kevin
96AubDouB-19
Burns, Michael
91BurAstC-24
91BurAstP-2804
92OscAstC-5
92OscAstF-2532
93OscAstC-6
93OscAstF-630
Burns, Oyster (Thomas P.)
87BucN28-1
87BucN28-19
87OldJudN-63
88GandBCGCE-6
88WG1CarG-11
90DodTar-905
Burns, Sleepy (Bill)
09T206-46
11TurRedT-85
88PacEigMO-17
88PacEigMO-18
Burns, Thomas Everett
87OldJudN-64
Burns, Todd
85MadMusP-5
85MadMusT-8
86SouLeaAJ-18
87HunStaTI-6
88FleUpd-52
88FleUpdG-52
88ScoRoo-106T
88ScoRooG-106T
88TacTigC-2
88TacTigP-632
89A'sMot-24
89ClaTraP-171
89Don-564
89Fle-3
89FleGlo-3
89PanSti-411
89Sco-465
89ScoHot1R-100
89ScoYouS2-4
89Spo-87
89Top-174
89TopBig-10
89TopTif-174
89UppDec-718
90A'sMot-20
90Don-446
90Fle-2
90FleCan-2
90Lea-458
90OPC-369
90PubSti-299
90Sco-64
90Top-369
90TopTif-369
90UppDec-689
00VonSti 86
91A'sMot-20
91Bow-221
91Don-479
91Fle-4
91OPC-608
91Sco-41
91StaClu-207
91Top-608
91TopDesS-608
91TopMic-608
91TopTif-608
91Ult-243
91UppDec-405
92OklCit8S-306
92Sco-341
92SkyAAAF-140
93Don-641
93Fle-318
93PacSpa-307
93RanKee-398
93StaClu-210
93StaCluFDI-210
93StaCluMOP-210
93StaCluR-27
93Top-279
93TopGol-279
93TopInaM-279
93TopMic-279
93UppDec-749
93UppDecGold-749
94CalCanF-781
86HumStaDS-21
Burns, Tom
85LynMetT-11
86TidTidP-3
87JacMetF-21
87MetColP-27
Burns, Tom (Thomas E.)
80BatTroT-8
81BatTroT-2
81WatIndT-7
83WauTimF-4
88AugBecN-3A
88AugBecN-3B
Burnside, Adrian
96GreFalDB-6
96GreFalDTI-4
Burnside, Pete
58Top-211
59Top-354
60Top-261
61Pos-46
61SenJayP-1
61Top-507
62Top-207
63Top-19
91OriCro-64
Burnside, Sheldon
80IndIndTI-3
80RedEnq-34
81Fle-220
Burr, Chris
92GulCoaRSP-2
93ChaRaiC-26
93ChaRaiF-1916
93ClaGolF-113
Burrell, Buster (Frank Andrew)
90DodTar-93
Burrell, Kevin
85LynMetT-14
86ShrCapP-3
87PhoFirP-8
88MemChiB-11
88SouLeaAJ-2
89OmaRoyC-10
89OmaRoyP-1733
90OmaRoyP-68
90ProAAAF-603
91LinDriAAA-329
91OmaRoyLD-329
91OmaRoyP-1037
Burrell, Scott
92UppDecML-71
Burress, Andy
95BilRedTI-1
96BilMusTI-3
Burress, Davey
76CliPilT-5
Burright, Larry
62Top-348
63MetJayP-1
63Top-174
01TOM00I-404
90DodTar-94
91MetWIZ-57
Burrill, Casey
93IdaFalBF-4035
93IdaFalBSP-23
Burris, Paul Robert
54BraJohC-29
55JetPos-2
83Bra53F-14
Burris, Pierre
91BilMusP-3765
91BilMusSP-2
Burris, Ray
74OPC-161
74Top-161
75OPC-566
75Top-566
76Hos-60
76HosTwi-60
76OPC-51
76Top-51
77BurCheD-194
77CubJewT-4
77Hos-67
77OPC-197
77Top-190
78SSP270-261
78Top-371
78WifBalD-9
79OPC-43
79Top-98
79YanPicA-5
80Top-364
81Don-524A
81Don-524B
81ExpPos-2
81Fle-328
81OPC-323
81Top-654
81TopTra-744
82Don-414
82ExpHygM-2
82ExpPos-3
82ExpZel-20
82Fle-184
82OPC-227
82Top-227
83Don-36
83ExpStu-16
83Fle-277
83OPC-12
83Top-474
84A'sMot-22
84Don-331
84Fle-270
84FleUpd-19
84Nes792-552
84OPC-319
84Top-552
84TopTif-552
84TopTra-18T
84TopTraT-18T
85BrePol-48
85Don-218
85Fle-418
85FleUpd-15
85Lea-116
85OPC-238
85Top-758
85TopSti-328
85TopTif-758
85TopTifT-13T
85TopTra-13T
86CarTeal-5
86Don-107
86Fle-482
86Top-106
86TopTif-106
89HelBreSP-26
89TopSenL-108
90BreMilB-32
90BrePol-NNO
90EliSenL-18
91BreMilB-32
91BrePol-NNO
91MetWIZ-58
92RanMot-28
92YanWIZ7-28
93RanKee-90
94BreMilB-297
Burritt, Mike
92BurIndC-8
92BurIndF-1646
Burrough, Butch
92EliTwiC-7
92EliTwiF-3691
93ForMyeMF-2667
94AlbPolC-8
94AlbPolF-2249
Burroughs, Darren
80CarMudF-11
81ReaPhiT-4
82OklCit8T-23
83ReaPhiT-2
84LasVegSC-235
86BufBisP-6
88CalCanC-1
88CalCanP-780
Burroughs, Eric
90BilMusP-3233
Burroughs, Jeff (Jeffrey A.)
72OPC-191
72Top-191
73LinPor-173
73OPC-489
73Top-489
74Kel-16
74OPC-223
74Top-223
74TopDecE-48
74TopSta-232
75Hos-94
75Kel-8
75OPC-212
75OPC-308
75OPC-470
75SSP42-27
75SSPPuzB-4
75Top-212
75Top-308
75Top-470
76CraDis-6
76Hos-111
76OPC-360
76Spo-4
76SSP-269
76Top-360
77BurCheD-214
77MSADis-8
77OPC-209
77PepGloD-58
77Spo-4002
77Top-55
78BraCok-2
78Hos-61
78Kel-15
78OPC-134
78Pep-29
78RCColC-25
78TasDis-4
78Top-130
78WifBalD-11
79Hos-20
79Kel-12
79OPC-124
79Top-245
80OPC-283
80Top-545
81Don-66
81Fle-245
81MarPol-1
81Top-20
81TopTra-745
82Don-379
82Fle-506
82FleSta-226
82K-M-25
82OPC-309
82Top-440
82TopSti-231
82TopStiV-231
82TopTra-14T
83Don-323
83Fle-515
83FleSta-27
83FleSti-186
83Top-648
84A'sMot-17
84Don-156
84DonCha-7
84Fle-440
84Nes792-354
84OPC-354
84Top-354
84TopSti-329
84TopTif-354
85BluJayFS-6
85Don-542
85FleUpd-16
85OPC-91
85Top-91
85Top-272
85TopMin-91
85TopTif-91
85TopTif-272
85TopTifT-14T
85TopTra-14T
86Fle-54
86OPC-168
86RanGreT-11
86Top-168
86TopTif-168
91UppDecS-6
92MCIAmb-9
92MDAMVP-9
93RanKee-6
93UppDecAH-24
93UppDecS-2
94RanAllP-2
94TedWil-86
Burroughs, Kenny
89UtiBluSP-3
90YakBeaTI-8
Burrows, John
44CubTeal-2
Burrows, Mike
95EveAqaTI-3
96EveAquB-5
Burrows, Terry
90ButCopKSP-5
91Cla/Bes-265
91GasRanC-2
91GasRanP-2679
92ChaRanC-25
92ClaFS7-65
93Bow-573
93ClaFS7-166
93OklCit8F-1620
94OklCit8F-1490
95FleUpd-81
95LinVen-219
95RanCra-5
Burrus, Daryl
87BelMarTI-25
Burrus, Dick (Maurice L.)
25Exh-4
26Exh-3
94ConTSN-1238
94ConTSNB-1238
Burt, Chris
94HelBreF-3605
94HelBreSP-7
95BelBreTI-14
95MidLeaA-6

96StoPorB-23
Burton, Adam
95AusFut-55
Burton, Bob
89WauTimGS-4
90ColMetGS-27
90SouAtlLAS-48
91ColMetPI-4
92St.LucMCB-29
Burton, Chris
89IdaFalBP-2022
90IdaFalBP-3259
91Cla/Bes-163
91MiaMirC-27
91MiaMirP-420
Burton, Darren
91AppFoxC-22
91AppFoxP-1727
91MidLeaAP-MWL1
92BasCitRC-23
92BasCitRF-3856
92Bow-424
92ClaFS7-20
92UppDecML-303
93Bow-181
93ClaFS7-99
93ClaGolF-81
93WilBluRC-4
93WilBluRF-2009
94Bow-639
94Cla-48
94MemChiF-368
94UppDecML-187
96OmaRoyB-10
Burton, Ellis N.
59Top-231
60Top-446
61MapLeaBH-3
63Top-262
64Top-269
64TopVen-269
Burton, Essex
92SouBenWSC-20
92SouBenWSF-182
93ExcFS7-151
93MidLeaAGF-20
93SouBenWSC-3
93SouBenWSF-1437
94CarLeaAF-CAR6
94PriWilCC-4
94PriWilCF-1927
96ReaPhiB-16
Burton, Jaime
96SpoIndB-7
Burton, Jim
76OPC-471
76SSP-418
76Top-471
78SSP270-168
Burton, Ken
76CedRapGT-8
Burton, Michael
89FreStaBS-5
90Bes-268
90GasRanP-2526
90GasRanS-4
90ProAaA-99
90SouAtlLAS-3
91LinDriAA-577
91TulDriLD-577
91TulDriP-2777
91TulDriTI-4
92ChaRanC-2
92ChaRanF-2229
Burton, Steve
91GulCoaRSP-23
92GasRanC-21
92GasRanF-2258
93ChaRaiC-5
93ChaRaiF-1917
Burton, Terry
89TenTecGE-4
Burtschy, Ed
55A'sRodM-8
55Bow-120
57JetPos-4
Burtt, Dennis
81BriRedST-21
83PawRedST-3
84PawRedST-5
85IntLeaAT-39
85TolMudHT-4
86TwiTeal-12
87AlbDukP-6
88AlbDukC-7
88AlbDukP-276
88BlaYNPRWL-180
89AlbDukC-2
89AlbDukP-68
89BlaYNPRWL-22
90CMC-380
90ProAAAF-372
90TolMudHC-3
90TolMudHP-142
92Ft.MyeMCB-27
92Ft.MyeMF-2762
93NewBriRSF-1238
94NewBriRSF-667
86StaoftFT-24
Burwell, Bill
60Top-467
Burwell, Phil
83EriCarT-17
Busby, Jim (James F.)
51Bow-302
52BerRos-6
52Bow-68
52StaCalL-73F
52StaCalS-87D
52Top-309
53BowC-15
53Bri-1
53NorBreL-4
54Bow-8
54RedMan-AL2
55Bow-166
55DonWin-1
55RedMan-AL2
55RobGouS-8
55RobGouW-8
56Top-330
57IndSoh-2
57Top-309
58Hir-68
58HirTes-2
58OriJayP-2
58Top-28
59Top-185
59TopVen-185
60Lea-11
60Top-232
62SalPlaC-30
62ShiPlaC-30
67AstTeal2-6
73OPC-237
73Top-237A
73Top-237B
74OPC-634
74Top-634
77ShrCapT-3
77Top-597
79TCM50-66
83TopRep5-309
87AstSer1-30
91OriCro-65
Busby, Mike
91HigSchPLS-14
92SavCarF-653
93SavCarC-6
93SavCarF-678
93SouAtlLAGF-46
94ClaGolF-158
94ExcFS7-263
94St.PetCC-6
94St.PetCF-2577
95ArkTraTI-6
96Bow-345
96Exc-226
96FleUpd-U185
96FleUpdTC-U185
96LeaSigA-38
96LeaSigAG-38
96LeaSigAS-38
96LouRedB-12
96Pin-392
96PinAfi-187
96PinAfiAP-187
96PinFoil-392
96Sum-192
96SumAbo&B-192
96SumArtP-192
96SumFoi-192
96Ult-543
96UltGolM-543
Busby, Paul Miller
43PhiTeal-4
Busby, Steve
73OPC-608
73Top-608
74OPC-365
74Top-365
74TopSta-181
75Hos-124
75Kel-24
75OPC-7
75OPC-120
75SSP42-39
75Top-7
75Top-120
76Hos-71
76Kel-33
76LauDiaJ-15
76OPC-260
76Spo-2
76SSP-183
76Top-260
78Top-336
80OmaRoyP-4
80Top-474
81Fle-33
86RoyGreT-9
90SouCalS-2
93RoySta2-2
Busby, Wayne
89SouBenWSGS-23
90SarWhiSS-2
91BirBarLD-52
91BirBarP-1458
91LinDriAA-52
92BirBarF-2588
92BirBarS-79
92SkyAA F-38
Busch, Ed (Edgar John)
83TCMPla1944-16
Busch, Gussie
81TCM60I-362
Busch, Mike
90GreFalDSP-3
91BakDodCLC-25
92ClaFS7-346
92SanAntMS-558
93AlbDukF-1467
94AlbDukF-848
94Bow-650
94ExcFS7-210
94ExcLeaLF-4
95SigRoo-11
95SigRooSig-11
96DodPol-4
Buschorn, Don
65Top-577
Bush, Chuck
91HelBreSP-26
92StoPorC-2
92StoPorF-27
Bush, Craig
92ElmPioC-5
92ElmPioF-1374
93UtiBluSC-6
93UtiBluSF-3526
94UtiBluSC-7
94UtiBluSF-3811
95MicBatCTI-5
Bush, Donie (Owen Joseph)
07TigACDPP-17
09AmeCarE-17
09BusBroBPP-3
09ColChiE-40
09SpoNewSM-25
09T206-47
09TigMorPenWBPP-1
09TigTaCP-2
10JuJuDE-6
10PeoT21-8
11DiaGumP-5
11PloCanE-11
11SpoLifM-54
12ColRedB-40
12ColTinT-40
12HasTriFT-9
14CraJacE-122
14TexTomE-7
15AmeCarE-6
15CraJacE-122
15SpoNewM-20
16BF2FP-25
16ColE13-22
16SpoNewM-22
17HolBreD-11
19W514-30
21E121So8-8
21Exh-19
22AmeCarE-8
22W575-14
30ChiEveAP-12
61Fle-96
76ISCHooHA-19
81TigDetN-38
81TigSecNP-5
86IndIndTI-2
94ConTSN-1234
94ConTSNB-1234
Bush, George W.
80PerHaloFP-F
92MegRut-149
92MegRutP-134
Bush, Guy T.
28StaPlaCE-6
28W56PlaC-S11
29PorandAR-9
31CubTeal-5
32CubTeal-1
32OrbPinNP-16
32OrbPinUP-8
33ButCre-3
33Gou-67
33GouCanV-67
33TatOrb-8
33TatOrbSDR-189
34DiaMatCSB-22
34BatR31-158
35ExhFou-7
35GouPuzR-1E
35GouPuzR-3C
35GouPuzR-5C
35GouPuzR-14C
36ExhFou-7
79DiaGre-356
83ConMar-44
83DiaClaS2-84
88ConNatA-2
91ConTSN-196
Bush, Homer
92ChaRaiC-16
92ChaRaiF-124
92ClaFS7-52
93MidLeaAGF-55
93WatDiaC-7
93WatDiaF-1772
94Bow-8
94ExcFS7-277
94RanCucQC-8
94RanCucQF-1643
95ActPacF-46
95AusFut-109
95Bow-174
95Exc-279
95MemChiTI-24
95SPML-138
95UppDecML-151
96BesAutS-15
96BesAutSA-10
96Bow-320
96LasVegSB-8
97Bow-157
97BowCerBIA-CA10
97BowCerGIA-CA10
97BowInt-157
97Top-203
95UppDecMLFS-151
Bush, Joe (Leslie Ambrose)
14FatPlaT-10
15CraJacE-166
15SpoNewM-19
16ColE13-21
16SpoNewM-21
20NatCarE-10
20WalMaiW-8
21E121So1-7
21Exh-18
21Nei-4
22E120-62
22W572-10
22W575-15
22WilPatV-5
23W501-34
23W503-1
23W515-27
27AmeCarE-3
69SCFOldT-12
92ConTSN-345
93CraJac-24
94ConTSN-1279
94ConTSNB-1279
Bush, Kalani
89GenCubP-1872
Bush, Randy (Robert Randall)
80TolMudHT-8
82OrlTwi8SCT-2
82TolMudHT-20
83TopTra-17T
83TwiTeal-18
84Don-513
84Fle-558
84MinTwiP-3
84Nes792-429
84OPC-84
84Top-429
84TopSti-314
84TopTif-429
84TwiTeal-19
85Don-633
85Fle-272
85Top-692
85TopTif-692
85TwiTeal-20
86Fle-388
86OPC-214
86Top-214
86TopTif-214
86TwiTeal-18
87Don-441
87Fle-538
87FleGlo-538
87Top-364
87TopTif-364
88Don-272
88Fle-6
88FleGlo-6
88FleGlo-WS2
88FleWorS-2
88PanSti-450
88Sco-292
88ScoGlo-292
88StaLinTw-5
88Top-73
88TopTif-73
88TwiMasBD-7
88TwiSmoC-9
88TwiTeal-16
89Bow-164
89BowTif-164
89Don-537
89DonBasB-214
89Fle-107
89FleGlo-107
89OPC-288
89PanSti-391
89Sco-212
89Top-577
89TopBig-282
89TopTif-577
89UppDec-158
90Bow-416
90BowTif-416
90Don-199
90Fle-370
90FleCan-370
90Lea-83
90OPC-747
90PanSti-109
90PubSti-324
90Sco-278
90Top-747
90TopBig-92
90TopSti-294
90TopTif-747
90UppDec-493
90VenSti-86
91Don-382
91Fle-605
91Lea-26
91OPC-124
91Sco-574
91Top-124
91TopDesS-124
91TopMic-124
91TopTif-124
91UltUpd-34
92Don-728
92Fle-198
92Lea-467
92OPC-476
92Sco-377
92StaClu-84
92Top-476
92TopGol-476

92TopGolW-476
92TopMic-476
93Don-781
93Fle-638
93StaClu-645
93StaCluFDI-645
93StaCluMOP-645
Bush, Ricky
92MarPhiC-10
92MarPhiF-3058
Bush, Todd
91MiaHurBB-3
Busha, Rodney
90ButCopKSP-1
Bushart, John
95CedRapKTI-33
Bushell, James
91AdeGiaF-6
Bushelman, Jack (John)
12T207-21
Bushing, Chris
89PenPilS-2
90ProAaA-111
90RocExpLC-3
90RocExpP-2695
91WesPalBEC-3
91WesPalBEP-1219
92ReaPhiF-566
92ReaPhiS-528
93ChaLooF-2353
94NasSouF-1244
Bushong, Doc (Albert John)
76SSP188WS-13
87BucN28-94
87LonJacN-1
87OldJudN-65A
87OldJudN-65B
87ScrDC-1
88SpoTimM-4
90DodTar-95
94OriofB-27
Busick, Warren
86DayBealP-3
Buskey, Tom (Michael T.)
74SyrChiTI-3
75OPC-403
75Top-403
76OklCit8TI-7
76OPC-178
76SSP-505
76Top-178
77Top-236
79BluJayBY-3
79SyrChiTI-29
80OPC-265
80Top-506
81Don-270
92YanWIZ7-29
Buss, Scott
86ChaLooP-7
87KinIndP-5
Bussa, Todd
92FayGenC-11
92FayGenF-2160
93FayGenC-6
93FayGenF-122
94LakTigC-5
95KanCouCTI-39
95MidLeaA-7
Busse, Ray (Raymond Edward)
72OPC-101
72Top-101
73OPC-607
73Top-607
75IowOakT-3
Bustabad, Juan
83PawRedST-15
84PawRedST-25
85PawRedST-2
87SanAntDTI-9
88SanAntMB-12
89AlbDukC-20
89AlbDukP-78
90YakBeaTI-5
93LetMouF-4165
93LetMouSP-24
Bustamante, Eddie
89FreStaBS-6
Bustamante, Rafael
87UtiBluSP-3
90Bes-201
90ChaWheB-14
90ChaWheP-2245
91ChaWheC-15
91ChaWheP-2892
Bustillos, Albert
89Sta-28
89VerBeaDS-4
91BakDodCLC-26
92AlbDukF-711
92SanAntMS-559
93AlbDukF-1452
94SanAntMF-2460
96ColSprSSTI-5
Bustos, Saul
94WilCubC-4
94WilCubF-3770
95RocCubTI-11
96DayCubB-6
Buszka, John
76BatTroTI-4
77WatIndT-4
78WatIndT-5
Butcher, Arthur
89BelBreIS-2
90BelBreB-20
90BelBreS-2
92SalSpuC-17
Butcher, Gary
81SanDieSC-1
81SanDieSC-20
Butcher, Hank (Henry Joseph)
12T207-22
Butcher, Jason
92GreFalDSP-22
94YakBeaC-3
94YakBeaF-3839
Butcher, John
78AshTouT-2
79TulDriT-16
80ChaChaT-13
81Fle-635
81Top-41
82Top-418
83Don-37
83Fle-563
83RanAffF-29
83Top-534
84Don-220
84Fle-415
84FleUpd-20
84MinTwiP-4
84Nes792-299
84Top-299
84TopTif-299
84TopTra-19T
84TopTraT-19T
84TwiTeal-23
85Don-314
85Fle-273
85Lea-71
85OPC-356
85Top-741
85TopSti-305
85TopTif-741
85Twi7-5
85TwiTeal-22
86Don-120
86Fle-389
86Top-638
86TopTif-638
86TwiTeal-23
87Fle-245
87FleGlo-245
87Top-107
87TopTif-107
93RanKee-91
Butcher, Matthew
84VisOakT-17
Butcher, Max (A. Maxwell)
40PlaBal-222
90DodTar-96
93ConTSN-756
94ConTSN-1073
94ConTSNB-1073
Butcher, Mike
86EugEmeC-40
87AppFoxP-10
88BasCitRS-7
89MidAngGS-8
90MidAngGS-15
91LinDriAA-428
91MidAngLD-428
91MidAngOHP-6
91MidAngP-427
92EdmTraF-3534
92EdmTraS-153
92FleUpd-7
92SkyAAAF-75
93Don-665
93Fle-569
93PacSpa-364
93Pin-262
93Sco-277
93StaClu-407
93StaCluFDI-407
93StaCluMOP-407
93Top-104
93TopGol-104
93TopInaM-104
93TopMic-104
94AngLAT-15
94AngMot-21
94ColC-436
94ColChoGS-436
94ColChoSS-436
94Don-52
94Fle-48
94Pac-71
94StaClu-78
94StaCluFDI-78
94StaCluGR-78
94StaCluMOP-78
94Top-236
94TopGol-236
94TopSpa-236
94Ult-20
95AngMot-21
95DonTopotO-31
95Top-368
96TacRaiB-7
Butcher, Ryan
90GeoColC-1
Butcher, The
88BufBisP-1477
Buteaux, Shane
96SouBenSHS-7
Butera, Brian
80ElmPioRST-36
Butera, Sal (Salvatore P.)
77TacTwiDQ-5
79TolMudHT-8
80VenLeaS-35
81Don-530
81Fle-570
81Top-243
82Don-532
82Fle-548
82Top-676
82TwiPos-2
83Tig-2
83Top-67
84IndIndTI-5
84IndIndTI-10
85ExpPos-5
85IndIndTI-15
86BasStaB-19
86OPC-261
86RedTexG-22
86Top-407
86TopTif-407
87Fle-195
87FleGlo-195
87Top-358
87TopTif-358
88Sco-361
88ScoGlo-361
88SyrChiC-16
88SyrChiP-826
88Top-772
88TopTif-772
88TwiTeal-22
89BluJayFS-5
89PacSenL-209
89SyrChiC-11
89SyrChiMB-4
89SyrChiP-802
89T/MSenL-15
89TopSenL-42
90OscAstS-27
91OscAstC-26
91OscAstP-700
92OscAstC-26
92OscAstF-2545
93JacGenF-2123
94JacGenF-231
95HarCitRCTI-2
Butkus, Stan
76TulOilGP-4
Butland, Bill
42RedSoxTI-2
Butler, Adam
95EugEmeTI-22
96GreBraB-7
96GreBraTI-58
Butler, Art (Arthur Edward)
15SpoNewM-21
16SpoNewM-23
Butler, Bill (W. J.)
69Top-619
70MLBOffS-219
70OPC-377
70RoyTeal-6
70Top-377
71MLBOffS-412
71OPC-681
71Top-681
72MilBra-59
75OPC-549
75Top-549
76OPC-619
76SSP-207
76TacTwiDQ-3
76Top-619
76VenLeaS-26
77TacTwiDQ-24A
78SSP270-61
Butler, Brent
96AppLeaAB-19
96HilStaHWB-11
96JohCitCTI-4
97Bow-409
97BowChr-271
97BowChrI-271
97BowChrIR-271
97BowChrR-271
97BowInt-409
Butler, Brett Morgan
80AndBraT-26
81RicBraT-8
82BraBurKL-4
82BraPol-22
82Don-275
82Top-502
83BraPol-22
83Don-636
83Fle-132
83Top-364
84Don-141
84Fle-173
84FleUpd-21
84Ind-7
84IndWhe-2
84Nes792-77
84Top-77
84TopTif-77
84TopTra-20T
84TopTraT-20T
85AllGamPI-52
85Don-216
85DonActA-23
85Fle-441
85FleStaS-56
85Ind-7
85IndPol-2
85Lea-186
85OPC-241
85Top-637
85TopSti-246
85TopTif-637
86Don-12
86Don-102
86DonSupD-12
86Fle-581
86FleMin-114
86FleStiC-18
86IndOhH-2
86IndTeal-10
86Lea-12
86OPC-149
86SevCoi-C14
86Spo-26
86Top-149
86TopGloS-52
86TopMinL-12
86TopSti-206
86TopSup-18
86TopTat-9
86TopTif-149
87ClaGam-36
87Don-219
87DonOpeD-113
87Fle-246
87FleGlo-246
87FleHotS-8
87IndGat-2
87Lea-183
87OPC-197
87RedFolSB-79
87Spo-69
87SpoTeaP-3
87Top-723
87TopTif-723
88Don-279
88DonBasB-23
88Fle-603
88FleGlo-603
88FleUpd-128
88FleUpdG-128
88GiaMot-14
88OPC-202
88PanSti-78
88Sco-122
88ScoGlo-122
88ScoRoo-3T
88ScoRooG-3T
88Spo-153
88StaLinG-3
88StaLinI-5
88Top-479
88TopBig-166
88TopSti-212
88TopTif-479
88TopTra-22T
88TopTraT-22T
89Bow-480
89BowTif-480
89ClaLigB-38
89Don-217
89DonBasB-274
89Fle-324
89FleGlo-324
89GiaMot-5
89OPC-241
89PanSti-220
89Sco-216
89Spo-31
89Top-241
89TopBasT-155
89TopBig-62
89TopCoi-6
89TopMinL-40
89TopSti-85
89TopTif-241
89TopUKM-11
89UppDec-218
90Bow-237
90BowTif-237
90Don-249
90DonBesN-139
90Fle-53
90FleCan-53
90GiaMot-7
90Lea-251
90MLBBasB-27
90OPC-571
90PanSti-365
90PubSti-64
90RedFolSB-12
90RicBra2ATI-6
90Sco-236
90Sco100S-47
90Spo-136
90Top-571
90TopBig-259
90TopMinL-83
90TopSti-87
90TopTif-571
90UppDec-119
90VenSti-87
91Bow-597
91ClaGam-4
91DodMot-6
91DodPol-22
91Don-143
91Fle-257
91FleUpd-91
91Lea-411
91OPC-325
91OPCBoxB-C
91OPCPre-16
91PanCanT1-25
91PanCanT1-44
91PanCanT1-51
91PanFreS-72
91PanSti-75
91Sco-455

91ScoRoo-23T
91StaClu-389
91Stu-181
91Top-325
91TopDesS-325
91TopMic-325
91TopTif-325
91TopTra-15T
91TopTraT-15T
91TopWaxBC-C
91UltUpd-85
91UppDec-270
91UppDec-732
91USPlaCA-8S
92Bow-597
92ClaGam-32
92DodMot-2
92DodPol-22
92DodSmo-4292
92DodStaTA-30
92Don-369
92DonCraJ1-9
92DonDiaK-DK18
92Fle-448
92Fle-702
92Hig5-51
92HitTheBB-8
92Lea-186
92OPC-655
92OPCPre-145
92PanSti-197
92Pin-133
92Pin-619
92PinTeaP-9
92PosCan-8
92Sco-465
92Sco-778
92ScoCokD-4
92StaClu-292
92StaCluD-23
92Stu-41
92StuPre-19
92SunSee-21
92Top-655
92TopGol-655
92TopGolPS-655
92TopGolW-655
92TopKid-49
92TopMic-655
92TopPreS-325
92TriPla-59
92TriPla-243
92Ult-209
92UppDec-307
93Bow-422
93DiaMar-20
93DodMot-3
93DodPol-2
93Don-86
93Fin-6
93FinRef-6
93Fla-68
93Fle-59
93FleFruotL-8
93FunPac-87
93FunPac-210
93Hos-20
93KinDis-16
93Lea-230
93MilBonSS-17
93OPC-36
93PacSpa-143
93PanSti-218
93Pin-91
93Pin-487
93Sco-20
93ScoFra-19
93Sel-115
93SelStaL-54
93SP-91
93StaClu-216
93StaCluD-14
93StaCluFDI-216
93StaCluMOP-216
93Stu-9
93Top-65
93TopGol-65
93TopInaM-65
93TopMic-65
93TriPla-136
93Ult-51
93UppDec-259
93UppDecGold-259
94Bow-382
94Bow-622
94BowBes-R48
94BowBesR-R48
94ColC-70
94ColChoGS-70
94ColChoSS-70
94DodMot-6
94DodPol-4
94Don-543
94ExtBas-284
94Fin-367
94FinRef-367
94Fla-393
94Fle-506
94Fle-711
94FUnPac-72
94Lea-187
94LeaL-116
94OPC-215
94Pac-304
94PanSti-197
94Pin-369
94PinArtP-369
94PinMusC-369
94PinRunC-RC43
94Sco-46
94ScoCyc-TC1
94ScoCyc-TC14
94ScoGolR-46
94ScoGolS-28
94Sel-258
94SP-75
94SPDieC-75
94StaClu-121
94StaCluFDI-121
94StaCluGR-121
94StaCluMOP-121
94Stu-66
94Top-172
94TopGol-172
94TopSpa-172
94TriPla-82
94Ult-213
94UppDec-183
94UppDecED-183
94USPlaCA-2H
95Baz-80
95Bow-287
95ColCho-230
95ColCho-561T
95ColChoGS-230
95ColChoSE-87
95ColChoSEGS-87
95ColChoSESS-87
95ColChoSS-230
95Don-160
95Don-390
95DonPreP-160
95DonPreP-390
95DonTopotO-290
95Fin-32
95Fin-272
95FinRef-32
95FinRef-272
95Fla-381
95Fle-535
95FleUpd-110
95Lea-362
95LeaLim-42
95Pac-213
95PacPri-68
95Pin-401
95PinArtP-401
95PinMusC-401
95Sco-344
95ScoGolR-344
95ScoHaloG-HG103
95ScoPlaTS-344
95ScoYouTE-344T
95Sel-125
95SelArtP-125
95SP-82
95SPSil-82
95StaClu-242
95StaClu-629
95StaCluFDI-242
95StaCluMO-9
95StaCluMOP-242
95StaCluMOP-629
95StaCluSTDW-D242
95StaCluSTWS-242
95StaCluSTWS-629
95StaCluVR-121
95Stu-67
95Top-610
95TopCyb-378
95TopTra-41T
95Ult-394
95UltGolM-394
95UppDec-69
95UppDec-364
95UppDecED-69
95UppDecED-364
95UppDecEDG-69
95UppDecEDG-364
95UppDecSE-192
95UppDecSEG-192
96Cir-140
96CirRav-140
96ColCho-584
96ColChoGS-584
96ColChoSS-584
96DodMot-8
96DodPol-5
96Don-515
96DonPreP-515
96Fla-287
96Fle-427
96FleDod-2
96FleTif-427
96Lea-180
96LeaPrePB-180
96LeaPrePG-180
96LeaPrePS-180
96LeaSig-147
96LeaSigPPG-147
96LeaSigPPP-147
96MetKah-6
96Pac-112
96Sco-91
96StaClu-126
96StaCluEPB-126
96StaCluEPG-126
96StaCluEPS-126
96StaCluMOP-126
95StaCluVRMC-121
96Top-277
96TopChr-112
96TopChrR-112
96Ult-217
96UltGolM-217
96UppDec-357
97Cir-59
97CirRav-59
97ColCho-137
97Don-191
97DonEli-103
97DonEliGS-103
97DonLim-91
97DonLimLE-91
97DonPreP-191
97DonPrePGold-191
97DonTea-112
97DonTeaSPE-112
97Fin-197
97FinRef-197
97FlaSho-A175
97FlaSho-B175
97FlaSho-C175
97FlaShoLC-175
97FlaShoLC-B175
97FlaShoLC-C175
97FlaShoLCM-A175
97FlaShoLCM-B175
97FlaShoLCM-C175
97Fle-357
97FleTif-357
97Pac-326
97PacLigB-326
97PacSil-326
97Pin-70
97PinArtP-70
97PinIns-47
97PinInsCE-47
97PinInsDE-47
97PinMusC-70
97Sco-102
97ScoDod-13
97ScoDodPI-13
97ScoDodPr-13
97ScoPreS-102
97ScoShoS-102
97ScoShoSAP-102
97Top-324
97TopChr-109
97TopChrR-109
97Ult-417
97UltGolME-417
97UltPlaME-417
97UppDec-90

Butler, Cecil
62Top-239
63Top-201

Butler, Chris
89KinMetS-3
89Sta-181

Butler, Jason
91PulBraC-21
91PulBraP-3997
92MacBraC-15
92MacBraF-260
93MacBraC-5
93MacBraF-1393
94DurBulC-4
94DurBulF-321

Butler, John
90PeoChiTI-3

Butler, John Albert
09AmeCarE-18
90DodTar-97
90DodTar-906

Butler, Johnny (John S.)
09T206-404
11MecDFT-7
12ImpTobC-46

Butler, Johnny (John Stephen)
26Exh-9
27Exh-5

Butler, Mark
83SanJosBC-11

Butler, Mick
86PalSprAP-17
86PalSprAP-5

Butler, Mike
92BoiHawC-20
92BoiHawF-3618
93PalSprAC-5
93PalSprAF-62
94LakElsSC-3
94LakElsSF-1655
95MidAngOHP-7
95MidAngTI-7

Butler, Rich
92MyrBeaHC-12
92MyrBeaHF-2210
93DunBluJC-4
93DunBluJF-1807
93DunBluJFFN-4
93FloStaLAF-7
94ClaGolF-54
94ExcFS7-140
94KnoSmoF-1315
95SigRooOJ-8
95SigRooOJP-8
95SigRooOJPS-8
95SigRooOJS-8
95SyrChiTI-7

Butler, Rob (Robert Frank John)
91St.CatBJC-8
91St.CatBJP-3406
92Bow-603
92ClaFS7-89
92DunBluJC-7
92DunBluJF-2010
92ProFS7-174
92UppDecML-315
93Bow-547
93ClaFisN-3
93ClaFS7-45
93ClaGolF-86
93ExcFS7-239
93ExcLeaLF-3
93SyrChiF-1009
93TopTra-15T
94BluJayUSPC-3D
94BluJayUSPC-11S
94ColC-71
94ColChoGS-71
94ColChoSS-71
94Don-558
94Fin-313
94FinRef-313
94Lea-17
94OPC-232
94Pac-635
94Pin-397
94PinArtP-397
94PinMusC-397
94ScoRoo-RT112
94ScoRooGR-RT112
94Sel-412
94SpoRoo-85
94SpoRooAP-85
94StaCluT-178
94StaCluTFDI-178
94SyrChiF-982
94SyrChiTI-4
94Top-361
94TopGol-361
94TopSpa-361
94UppDec-176
94UppDecED-176
95LinVen-166
95Pac-438
95ScrRedBTI-3
95Top-116
96ScrRedBB-9

Butler, Todd
88BurIndP-1782
88OklSoo-17

Butterfield, Brian J.
82NasSouTI-3
86ColCliP-25
87OneYanP-14
89OneYanP-2098
90GreHorB-27
90GreHorP-2679
90GreHorS-26
92ForLauYC-23
92ForLauYTI-3
93AlbYanF-2178

Butterfield, Chris
89PitMetS-1
89Sta-157
90St.LucMS-3
91St.LucMC-10
91St.LucMP-715
92BinMetF-522
92BinMetS-52
92SkyAA F-22
93BinMetF-2345
95SanAntMTI-41

Butters, Dave
85PriWilPT-28

Butters, Tom
63Top-299
64PirKDK-5
64Top-74
64TopVen-74
65OPC-246
65Top-246

Butterworth, Gary
91MisStaB-9

Button, Dick
51BerRos-B17

Butts, David
87SumBraP-29
88DurBulS-3
89DurBullS-3
89DurBulTI-3

Butts, Randy
86EriCarP-5
87St.PetCP-24
88HamRedP-1735

Butts, Tom
82IowCubT-29

Butts, Tommy
78LauLonABS-11

Butz, Bryan
96LynHilB-30

Buxbaum, Danny
95BoiHawTI-7
96Bow-272
96Exc-23
96LakElsSB-15
97Bow-392
97BowChr-259
97BowChrI-259
97BowChrIR-259
97BowChrR-259
97BowInt-392

Buxowatz, Jack
52LavPro-92

Buxton, Buck (Ralph)
46RemBre-21
47RemBre-6
47SigOil-41
47SmiClo-11
48SigOil-2
48SmiClo-11
49RemBre-1

Buzard, Brian
90WicStaSGD-6
91WatIndC-2

91WatIndP-3357
92ColRedC-25
Buzas, Joe (Joseph John)
47CenFlo-2
Buzhardt, John
59Top-118
59TopVen-118
60Top-549
61Top-3
61TopStaI-49
62Jel-200
62Pos-200
62PosCan-200
62SalPlaC-129A
62SalPlaC-129B
62ShiPlaC-129
62Top-555
62WhiSoxTS-3
63Top-35
63WhiSoxTS-2
64Top-323
64TopVen-323
64WhiSoxTS-4
65Top-458
66Top-245
66TopVen-245
67Ast-5
67CokCapWS-7
67OPC-178
67Top-178
68Top-403
81TCM60I-361
91OriCro-66
Buzzard, Buddy
87KenTwiP-7
Buzzard, Dale
89JamExpP-2130
Buzzell, Ron
95AubAstTI-2
96AubDouB-27
Byam, George
50WorWidGV-47
Byerly, Bud (Eldred)
52Top-161
58Top-72
60Top-371
61TacBan-3
83TopRep5-161
Byerly, Jim
92SouOreAC-18
92SouOreAF-3407
Byerly, Rod (Rodney)
89AugPirP-518
89WelPirP-8
90BurBraB-26
90BurBraP-2342
90BurBraS-6
90DurBulUTI-5
Byers, Bill (James W.)
09ColChiE-41
Byers, John William
12ColRedB-41
12ColTinT-41
12ImpTobC-74
Byers, MacGregor
96SouOreTI-8
Byers, Randell
86BeaGolGP-4
87LasVegSP-14
88Don-605
88Fle-653
88FleGlo-653
88LasVegSC-13
88LasVegSP-224
89LasVegSC-12
89LasVegSP-6
89LouRedBC-23
89LouRedBP-1245
89LouRedBTI-12
Byers, Scott
96BoiHawB-6
Byington, Jimmie
93EugEmeC-8
93EugEmeF-3866
94RocRoyC-5
94RocRoyF-570
95WilBluRTI-9
96WilBluRB-13
Byington, John
88CapCodPPaLP-21
89BelBreIS-3
90BelBreB-15
90BelBreS-3
90Bes-254
90MidLeaASGS-6
91Cla/Bes-356
91ElPasDLD-177
91ElPasDP-2752
91LinDriAA-177
92ClaFS7-336
92ElPasDF-3926
92ElPasDS-201
92SkyAA F-90
92UppDecML-86
93ExcFS7-181
93NewOrlZF-977
94NewOrlZF-1474
Byrd, Anthony
92KenTwiF-616
93ForWayWC-3
93ForWayWF-1979
93MidLeaAGF-5
94ExcFS7-91
94NasXprF-397
95HarCitRCTI-3
96HarCitRCB-9
Byrd, Bill
86NegLeaF-52
Byrd, Felan
76CliPilT-6
Byrd, Harry
53BowC-38
53Top-131
54Bow-49
54NewYorJA-42
55Bow-159
55OriEss-4
58Top-154
79TCM50-172
91OriCro-67
91TopArc1-131
Byrd, Isaac
96JohCitCTI-5
Byrd, James
90CarLeaA-13
90LynRedSTI-5
91LynRedSC-15
95TulDriTI-1
Byrd, Jeff
75AndRanT-29
76SanAntBTI-5
78OPC-211
78SyrChiT-4
78Top-667
Byrd, Jim
89Sta-10
89WinHavRSS-2
91LynRedSP-1205
92PawRedSF-930
92WinHavRSC-9
93FleFinE-171
93PawRedSDD-5
93PawRedSF-2412
93PawRedSTI-5
94NewBriRSF-655
Byrd, Leland
77VisOakT-2
Byrd, Matt
93DanBraC-7
93DanBraF-3611
94DurBulC-5
94DurBulF-322
94DurBulTI-4
95DurBulTI-7
96Exc-123
96GreBraB-8
96GreBraTI-34
Byrd, Paul
90LSUTigA-3
90LSUTigP-4
91LSUTigP-14
92Bow-349
92CanIndF-682
92CanIndS-102
92ClaFS7-37
92SkyAA F-47
92UppDecML-242
93Bow-233
93ChaKniF-535
93ClaFS7-156
93ExcFS7-158
94CanIndF-3107
95NorTidTI-7
96Fle-476
96FleTif-476
96MetKah-4
97PacPriGotD-GD172
Byrd, Sammy (Samuel D.)
32OrbPinNP-96
33Gou-157
33GouCanV-86
34BatR31-56
34DiaStaR-84
35GouPuzR-4F
35GouPuzR-7F
35GouPuzR-12F
36GouWidPPR-A12
36NatChiFPR-15
91ConTSN-281
Byrdak, Tim
94EugEmeC-4
94EugEmeF-3702
94SigRooDP-88
94SigRooDPS-88
95Bes-25
95WilBluRTI-12
96Exc-56
96WicWraB-4
Byrne, Bobby (Robert M.)
08RosComP-161
09ColChiE-42
09PC7HHB-6
09RamT20-21
09SpoNewSM-61
09T206-48
10CouT21-6
10CouT21-88
10CouT21-263
10DomDisP-18
10E12AmeCDC-7
10PirHerP-3
10PirTipTD-13
10RedCroT-7
10RedCroT-94
10RedCroT-173
10SweCapPP-133
10W555-10
11E94-4
11MecDFT-8
11PloCanE-12
11S74Sil-106
11SpoLifM-245
11T205-23
12ColRedB-42
12ColTinT-42
12HasTriFT-25A
12T207-23
14TexTomE-8
15SpoNewM-22
16ColE13-23
16FleBreD-11
16SpoNewM-24
Byrne, Clayton
92KanCouCC-25
92KanCouCF-103
92KanCouCTI-3
93AlbPolC-5
93AlbPolF-2036
93SouAtlLAGF-1
94ClaGolF-4
94FreKeyF-2626
94OriPro-14
94FreKeyC-4
Byrne, Earl
95RocCubTI-6
Byrne, T.J.
81HolMilT-4
Byrne, Tommy (Thomas Joseph)
43YanSta-4
47TipTop-49
51BerRos-D4
51Bow-73
51TopBluB-35
52Bow-61
52BroPenCB-1
52DixLid-2
52DixPre-2
52Top-241
53Bri-2
53Top-123
55Bow-300
56Top-215
57Top-108
79TCM50-198
83TopRep5-241
83YanASFY-5
91TopArc1-123
92YanWIZA-8
Byrnes, Chris
87OneYanP-20
Byrnes, Milt (Milton John)
96Bro194F-3
Byron, Bill
73FleWilD-20
93ConTSN-731
Byron, Tim
82OneYanT-11
85AlbYanT-2
Bystrom, Marty
77SpaPhiT-3
81Top-526
82Don-93
82Top-416
83Don-93
83Fle-154
83PhiTas-3
83Top-199
84Don-259
84Fle-24
84Nes792-511
84PhiTas-15
84Top-511
84TopTif-511
85Fle-122
85Top-284
85TopTif-284
86Don-591
86Fle-102
86Top-723
86TopTif-723
86YanTCM-5
87Ft.LauYP-18
88MaiPhiC-1
88MaiPhiP-292
92YanWIZ8-23
Caballero, Ed
87GenCubP-18
88PeoChiTI-7
89WinSpiS-2
90WinSpiTI-18
91WinSpiC-2
91WinSpiP-2821
Caballero, Jose
82MiaMarT-8
Caballero, Putsy (Ralph J.)
49EurSta-132
49PhiBul-10
91JesHSA-4
Cabana, Gerry
52LavPro-37
Cabassa, Carlos
80PenPilBT-3
80PenPilCT-3
81ReaPhiT-9
Cabbage, Wayne
89CarNewE-5
Cabell, Billy
83CliGiaF-4
Cabell, Enos Milton
73OPC-605
73Top-605
75OPC-247
75Top-247
76OPC-404
76SSP-61
76Top-404
77BurCheD-2
77Hos-94
77Top-567
78AstBurK-14
78Hos-9
78OPC-44
78Top-132
79AstTeal-3
79Hos-70
79OPC-269
79Top-515
80BurKinPHR-24
80OPC-201
80Top-385
81AllGamPI-92
81Don-138
81Fle-58
81FleStiC-36
81OPC-45
81Top-45
81TopTra-746
82Don-272
82Fle-386
82FleSta-64
82OPC-311
82Top-627
82TopSti-105
82TopStiV-105
82TopTra-15T
83Don-202
83Fle-328
83FleSta-28
83OPC-225
83Tig-7
83Top-225
84AstMot-11
84Don-456
84Fle-79
84FleUpd-22
84Nes792-482
84Top-482
84TopSti-273
84TopTif-482
84TopTra-21T
84TopTraT-21T
85AllGamPI-92
85AstHouP-4
85AstMot-10
85Don-110
85Fle-346
85Lea-161
85Top-786
85TopSti-61
85TopTif-786
86DodCokP-5
86DodPol-23
86DodUniOP-3
86Don-418
86Fle-126
86Top-197
86TopTif-197
87Fle-438
87FleGlo-438
87Top-509
87TopTif-509
90DodTar-98
91OriCro-68
94TedWil-35
Cabella, Jim
89BurIndS-27
Cabello, Bobby
86SalAngC-83
Cabral, Irene
91EriSaiC-3
91EriSaiP-4080
Cabral, Joaquin
91HunCubC-5
91HunCubP-3340
Cabreja, Alexis
95NorNavTI-23
Cabrera, Alex
93GenCubC-6
93GenCubF-3180
94PeoChiC-5
94PeoChiF-2273
95Exc-161
95LinVen-225
Cabrera, Basilio
87FayGenP-5
88LakTigS-4
89LakTigS-4
90LonTigP-1278
91LinDriAA-377
91LonTigLD-377
91LonTigP-1888
92LonTigF-643
92LonTigS-402
93BriTigC-28
94FayGenC-29
95FayGenTI-6
96LakTigB-3
Cabrera, Carlos
80UtiBluJT-3
80VenLeaS-55
93DunBluJF-1802
94HagSunC-3
94HagSunF-2736
94St.CatBJC-5
94St.CatBJF-3649
Cabrera, Francisco
86VenGulP-3
87MyrBeaBJP-1462
88BasAmeAAB-20
88DunBluJS-1
88SouLeaAJ-22
89FleUpd-68
89SyrChiC-20
89SyrChiMB-5
89SyrChiP-791
89TriA AAC-16
89TriAAP-AAA16
90BraDubP-3
90BraDubS-4

90CMC-289
90Don-646
90FleUpd-2
90OPC-254
90ProAAAF-409
90RicBraC-13
90RicBraP-264
90RicBraTI-6
90ScoRoo-67T
90Top-254
90TopDeb89-20
90TopTif-254
90TriAAAC-16
90UppDec-64
91BraDubP-6
91BraSubS-8
91Don-341
91Fle-684
91OPC-693
91Sco-63
91Sco100RS-33
91Top-693
91TopDesS-693
91TopMic-693
91TopTif-693
91Ult-3
91UppDec-439
92BraLykP-8
92BraLykS-9
92Don-482
92Fle-355
92RicBraBB-21
92RicBraF-379
92RicBraRC-1
92Sco-581
92StaClu-797
92StaCluNC-797
93BraLykP-7
93BraLykS-8
93Don-184
93Fle-365
93LimRocDWB-46
93OPC-383
93PacSpa-3
93PacSpaPI-1
93Sco-472
93StaCluB-8
93StaCluM-172
93Top-769
93TopGol-769
93TopInaM-769
93TopMic-769
93Ult-303
93UppDec-611
93UppDecGold-611
93UppDecSH-HI8
94Fle-356
94Pac-6
94Sco-222
94ScoGolR-222
97RicBraBC-14

Cabrera, Fremio
86WauTimP-2

Cabrera, Jairo
94BluOriC-2
94BluOriF-3565

Cabrera, Jolbert
91SumFlyP-2340
92AlbPolC-7
92AlbPolF-2312
93BurBeeC-4
93BurBeeF-164
93MidLeaAGF-29
94WesPalBEC-4
94WesPalBEF-47
96HarSenB-10

Cabrera, Jose
92BurIndC-9
92BurIndF-1647
93ClaGolF-107
93ColRedC-5
93ColRedF-589
94KinIndC-2
94KinIndF-2634

Cabrera, Juan
91BelBreC-13
91BelBreP-2107
91SouOreAP-3852

Cabrera, Miguel
91AubAstP-4284
92AshTouC-17

Cabrera, Nasusel
88MadMusP-6

Cabrera, Orlando
96DelShoB-10
97Bow-351
97BowChr-236
97BowChrI-236
97BowChrIR-236
97BowChrR-236
97BowInt-351
97FlaShoWotF-13
97Fle-675
97FleTif-675
97Ult-491
97UltGolME-491
97UltPlaME-491

Cabrera, Ruben
76VenLeaS-169
80VenLeaS-113

Cabrera, Tony (Antonio)
84IdaFalATI-6
85ModA'sC-3
86MadMusP-4
93BelMarC-6
93BelMarF-3214

Cabrera, Victor
86ChaRaiP-4

Cacanindin, Lance
96HilStaHWB-NNO

Cacciatore, Frank
88AubAstP-1967
89TucTorC-24
89TucTorJP-2
89TucTorP-202
90AshTouC-26
90AshTouP-2764
91AshTouP-584
92OscAstC-29
92OscAstF-2546
93CliGiaC-27
93CliGiaF-2505
94ShrCapF-1623

Cacciatore, Paul
76WauMetT-7
77WauMetT-3
79JacMetT-10

Cacek, Craig Thomas
78ChaChaT-3
79PorBeaT-18
80PorBeaT-3
81PorBeaT-9
82SpoIndT-14

Caceres, Edgar
86WesPalBEP-7
87JacExpP-437
89SarWhiSS-2
90Bes-206
90BirBarB-7
90BirBarP-1395
92ElPasDF-3927
92ElPasDS-202
93ExcFS7-182
93LinVenB-167
93NewOrlZF-978
94OmaRoyF-1228
94VenLinU-49
95LinVen-19

Caci, Bob
86BelBreP-3

Cacini, Ron
91AubAstP-4279
92AshTouC-13

Cadahia, Ben
81ChaRoyT-15
82ForMyeRT-4

Cadahia, Chino
80OrlTwiT-13
81TolMudHT-11
82OrlTwi8SCT-3
82OrlTwiT-15
83OrlTwiT-10
86DayBeaIP-4
86TulDriTI-12
91GulCoaRSP-30
92GulCoaRSP-30

Cadania, Aurelio
87GasRanP-3

Cadaret, Greg
84ModA'sC-4
85HunStaJ-34
88A'sMot-26
88Don-528
88DonTeaBA-528
88ModA'sTI-35
88Top-328
88TopTif-328
89A'sMot-20
89Don-479
89Fle-4
89FleGlo-4
89Sco-340
89ScoRoo-69T
89Top-552
89TopTif-552
90Don-545
90Fle-440
90FleCan-440
90OPC-659
90PubSti-300
90Top-659
90TopTif-659
90TopTVY-7
90UppDec-549
90VenSti-88
90YanScoNW-19
91Bow-157
91Don-236
91Fle-658
91Lea-415
91OPC-187
91Sco-188
91StaClu-536
91Top-187
91TopDesS-187
91TopMic-187
91TopTif-187
91Ult-229
91UppDec-343
92Bow-231
92Don-628
92Fle-222
92Lea-24
92OPC-18
92Pin-402
92Sco-454
92StaClu-176
92Top-18
92TopGol-18
92TopGolW-18
92TopMic-18
92Ult-404
92UppDec-412
92YanWIZ8-24
93Don-610
93FleFinE-14
93PacSpa-204
93RedKah-7
93Top-478
93TopGol-478
93TopInaM-478
93TopMic-478
94StaClu-585
94StaCluFDI-585
94StaCluGR-585
94StaCluMOP-585
94StaCluT-166
94StaCluTFDI-166
94Top-303
94TopGol-303
94TopSpa-303
96BufBisB-3
86HumStaDS-34

Caddell, Carl
96AppLeaAB-28

Cade, Jerry
58RedEnq-7

Cadian, Larry
89PorBeaC-7

Cadore, Leon
20NatCarE-11
21Exh-20
21Nei-97
22E120-136
22W572-11
23W503-35
23WilChoV-15
61Top-403
72FleFamF-19
72LauGreF-37
90DodTar-99
90HOFStiB-22

Cady, Hick (Forrest LeRoy)
11T205-191
12RedSoxBASP-1
12RedSoxBDASP-1
14CraJacE-87
15CraJacE-87
16BF2FP-2
16ColE13-24
16SpoNewM-25

Cady, Todd
94ElmPioF-3477
94SigRooDP-58
94SigRooDPS-58
95KanCouCTI-25
95MidLeaA-8
96BreCouMB-8
94ElmPioC-2

Cafaro, Cio
96HelBreTI-2

Cafaro, Rocco
94AlbPolC-9
94AlbPolF-2230
94OriPro-15
96BowBayB-9

Cafferty, Jason
96BatCliTI-13

Caffie, Joe (Joseph C.)
58Top-182

Caffrey, Bob
85Top-394
85TopTif-394
87WesPalBEP-661
88JacExpB-25
88JacExpP-979
88SouLeaAJ-19

Caffrey, Marty
76ForLauYS-16

Cage, Wayne Levell
76WilTomT-4
78Top-706
79OPC-70
79TacTugT-26
79Top-150
80TacTigT-4
80Top-208

Cahill, Mark
80WauTimT-3
81LynSaiT-3
83ChaLooT-21

Cahill, Patsy (John F.P.)
87BucN28-39
87OldJudN-66

Cain, Aaron
82HawIslT-9

Cain, Bob
50Bow-236
51Bow-197
52Bow-19
52Top-349
53BowC-56
53Top-266
54Bow-195
54Top-61
79DiaGre-197
83TopRep5-349
91TopArc1-266
94TopArc1-61
94TopArc1G-61

Cain, Cal
86CedRapRT-19
87CedRapRP-18

Cain, Chance
93GleFalRC-9
93GleFalRF-3995
94MadHatC-3
94MadHatF-122
94MidLeaAF-MDW42

Cain, Jerald
83VerBeaDT-23

Cain, John
88RocExpLC-4
90RocExpLC-4

Cain, Les
69Top-324
71Kel-29
71MLBOffS-388
71OPC-101
71Top-101
72Top-783
73TigJew-4

Cain, Sugar (Merritt)
33RitCE-7D
35DiaMatCS3T1-23
93ConTSN-952

Cain, Tim
91BenBucC-2
91BenBucP-3686
95TreThuTI-8

Cain, Travis
94DanBraC-4
94DanBraF-3522
95MacBraTI-3
96HudValRB-17
96WesOahCHWB-28

Caines, Art (Arturo)
89BriTigS-3
90FayGenP-2419

Cairncross, Cameron
91BriBanF-11
91ChaRaiC-4
91ChaRaiP-90
92WatDiaC-12
92WatDiaF-2137
93Bow-658
93RanCucQC-7
93RanCucQF-821
94Bow-644
94RanCucQC-9
94RanCucQF-1628
95AusFutGP-6

Cairo, Miguel
92GulCoaDF-3572
93VerBeaDC-4
93VerBeaDF-2224
94BakDodC-4
94VenLinU-47
95LinVen-9
95SanAntMTI-30
95Top-540
96SyrChiTI-7
97Pac-215
97PacLigB-215
97PacSil-215

Cairo, Sergio
89BluOriS-6
90WauTimB-14
90WauTimP-2142
90WauTimS-5
91CarLeaAP-CAR6
91FreKeyC-24
91FreKeyP-2378
92HagSunF-2568
92HagSunS-255
93BirBarF-1204
93LimRocDWB-53
94TulDriF-254
94TulDriTI-2

Cajide, Al
76BatTroTI-5
78DayBeaAT-4

Cakora, Matt (Matthew)
87WytCubP-25
88ChaWheB-17
89ChaKniTI-20
89ChaWheB-22
89ChaWheP-1770
90MiaMirIS-2

Cala, Craig A.
88CapCodPPaLP-92
90SanJosGB-6
90SanJosGCLC-35
90SanJosGP-2022
90SanJosGS-4

Calarco, John
92SalLakTSP-23

Calcagno, Dan
91EveGiaP-3916
92CliGiaF-3600
92SanJosGC-11
93SanJosGC-4
93SanJosGF-12
94ElPasDF-3148

Calcaterra, Jeff
92GulCoaYF-3781

Calder, Joe
92AugPirC-23
92AugPirF-244
92UppDecML-101
93SalBucC-3
93SalBucF-439

Caldera, Jose V.
76VenLeaS-97
77BriRedST-3
80VenLeaS-262

Calderon, Ivan
81WauTimT-26
82WauTimF-10
83ChaLooT-27
84SalLakCGC-173
85FleUpd-17
85MarMot-26
86Don-435
86Fle-462
86Lea-204
86MarMot-15
86OPC-382
86SevCoi-W13
86Top-382

86TopTif-382
87DonOpeD-230
87Fle-488
87FleGlo-488
87FleSlu-7
87TopTra-15T
87TopTraT-15T
87WhiSoxC-5
88Don-25
88Don-182
88DonBasB-25
88DonBonM-BC5
88DonSupD-25
88Fle-394
88FleBasM-4
88FleGlo-394
88FleLeaL-3
88FleMin-14
88FleStiC-14
88Lea-25
88Lea-175
88OPC-184
88PanSti-63
88Sco-607
88ScoGlo-607
88ScoYouS2-22
88Spo-166
88StaLinWS-4
88Top-184
88TopBig-63
88TopCoi-6
88TopMinL-7
88TopSti-285
88TopTif-184
88TopUKM-9
88TopUKMT-9
88WhiSoxC-3
88WhiSoxK-4
89BlaYNPRWL-108
89Bow-68
89BowTif-68
89Don-371
89DonBasB-193
89Fle-493
89FleGlo-493
89OPC-101
89RedFolSB-16
89Sco-331
89Top-656
89TopBig-289
89TopSti-297
89TopTif-656
89UppDec-650
89WhiSoxC-7
90Bow-316
90BowTif-316
90Don-294
90DonBesA-141
90Fle-529
90FleCan-529
90Lea-89
90OPC-569
90PanSti-47
90PubSti-385
90RedFolSB-13
90Sco-94
90Spo-167
90Top-569
90TopBig-80
90TopCoi-9
90TopMinL-11
90TopSti-297
90TopTif-569
90UppDec-503
90VenSti-89
90WhiSoxC-1
91Bow-440
91Cla3-T5
91Don-203
91ExpPos-3
91Fle-115
91FleUpd-97
91Lea-338
91OPC-93
91OPCPre-17
91PanFreS-318
91PanSti-258
91Sco-254
91ScoRoo-6T
91StaClu-383
91Stu-194
91Top-93
91TopDesS-93
91TopMic-93
91TopTif-93
91TopTra-16T
91TopTraT-16T
91Ult-199
91UppDec-285
91UppDec-786
91UppDecFE-96F
91USPlaCA-13C
92Bow-179
92Don-48
92Don-431
92DonCraJ2-9
92ExpDonD-4
92ExpPos-7
92Fle-475
92Hig5-56
92Lea-283
92OPC-775
92PanSti-208
92PanSti-287
92Pin-58
92Sco-83
92Sco100S-61
92ScoProP-11
92ScoProP-22
92SevCoi-4
92StaClu-73
92StaCluD-24
92Stu-52
92Top-775
92TopGol-775
92TopGolW-775
92TopKid-7
92TopMic-775
92TriPla-196
92Ult-513
92UppDec-226
92UppDecHRH-HR24
92UppDecTMH-13
93Bow-663
93Don-196
93Fin-55
93FinRef-55
93Fle-71
93FleFinE-172
93Lea-242
93OPC-88
93OPCPre-105
93PacSpa-354
93PanSti-98
93Pin-150
93Sco-95
93Sel-125
93SelRoo-118T
93StaClu-119
93StaClu-647
93StaCluFDI-119
93StaCluFDI-647
93StaCluMOP-119
93StaCluMOP-647
93Top-540
93TopGol-540
93TopInaM-540
93TopMic-540
93Ult-507
93UppDec-751
93UppDecGold-751
94Pin-192
94PinArtP-192
94PinMusC-192
97ScoIndPr-4
Calderon, Jose
81BufBisT-16
84PorBeaC-207
85MaiGuiT-3
87ArkTraP-4
87LouRedTI-8
88BlaYNPRWL-164
89BlaYNPRWL-139
Calderon, Ricardo
95BelGiaTI-44
96BelGiaTI-17
Calderone, Jeff
90BurBraB-10
90BurBraP-2343
90BurBraS-7
Calderone, Sammy (Samuel F.)
50JJKCopP-2
53Top-260
54BraJohC-42
54Top-68
79TCM50-236
91TopArc1-260
94TopArc1-68
94TopArc1G-68
Caldwell, Bruce
90DodTar-100
Caldwell, David
94BurIndC-4
94BurIndF-3784
96KenIndB-2
Caldwell, Earl W.
39WorWidGV-4
47TipTop-17
48WhiSoxTI-4
84TCMPla1-15
Caldwell, Mike (Ralph M.)
72PadTeal-5
73OPC-182
73Top-182
74OPC-344
74Top-344
75Gia-1
75OPC-347
75Top-347
76OPC-157
76SSP-93
76Top-157
77Top-452
78Top-212
79Hos-14
79OPC-356
79Top-651
80OPC-269
80Top-515
81Don-86
81Fle-512
81OPC-85
81Top-85
81TopSti-97
82BrePol-48
82Don-330
82Fle-136
82OPC-378
82Top-378
83BreGar-4
83BrePol-48
83Don-154
83Fle-29
83FleSti-21
83OPC-142
83Top-142
83TopSti-184
83TopSti-185
84AllGamPI-166
84BreGar-3
84BrePol-48
84Don-237
84Fle-196
84Nes792-605
84OPC-326
84Top-605
84TopTif-605
85Don-490
85Fle-577
85Top-419
85TopSti-289
85TopTif-419
86BreGreT-10
92BreCarT-4
92HelBreF-1733
92HelBreSP-24
93HelBreF-4113
93HelBreSP-28
94BreMilB-205
94HelBreF-3629
94HelBreSP-26
95BelBreTI-30
96El PasDB-2
Caldwell, Ray (Raymond B.)
14CraJacE-129
15CraJacE-129
15SpoNewM-25
16FleBreD-12
16SpoNewM-27
77Ind192T-3
93ConTSN-705
Caldwell, Rich
84NewOriT-17
85ChaO'sT-19
Calero, Enrique
96SpoIndB-8
Calhoon, Greg
92StoPorC-25
Calhoun, Brad
77AppFoxT-3
Calhoun, Gary
90HelBreSP-29
91NiaFalRC-29
91NiaFalRP-3650
Calhoun, Jeff
83ColAstT-13
85AstMot-24
85FleUpd-18
86AstPol-19
86Don-426
86Fle-295
86Top-534
86TopTif-534
87Don-578
87Fle-52
87FleGlo-52
87MaiGuiP-14
87MaiGuiT-2
87Top-282
87TopTif-282
87TopTra-16T
87TopTraT-16T
88Don-509
88Fle-299
88FleGlo-299
88PhiTas-5
88StaLinPh-4
88Top-38
88TopTif-38
89UppDec-33
Calhoun, Ray
89GreFalDSP-30
90VerBeaDS-7
91FloStaLAP-FSL37
91VerBeaDC-5
91VerBeaDP-766
92SanAntMF-3968
92SanAntMS-560
Calini, Ron
91AubAstC-11
Calise, Mike (Michael S.)
78ArkTraT-5
80ArkTraT-6
82LouRedE-4
83LouRedR-21
84RocRedWT-5
85TucTorC-63
Call, Keith
82MadMusF-26
83MadMusF-14
Call, Michael
93MidLeaAGF-21
93SouBenWSC-4
93SouBenWSF-1421
94CarLeaAF-CAR7
94PriWilCC-5
94PriWilCF-1913
95PriWilCTI-16
Callaghan, Marty (Martin F.)
21Nei-66
22E120-154
22W573-15
Callahan, Ben
82NasSouTI-4
83ColCliT-14
83NasSouTI-4
84NasSouTI-3
Callahan, Brian
88AriWilP-1
Callahan, Damon
94PriRedC-5
94PriRedF-3254
95BilRedTI-16
95Exc-174
Callahan, Harry
75TopPho-18
Callahan, Leo
90DodTar-107A
Callahan, Mike
83DayBeaAT-4
Callahan, Nixey (James J.)
03BreE10-13
09ColChiE-43
09SpoNewSM-77
10DomDisP-19
10SweCapPP-8
11PloCanE-13
11SpoLifCW-50
12ColRedB-43
12ColTinT-43
12T207-24
13NatGamW-7
13TomBarW-6
14CraJacE-111
14TexTomE-9
15SpoNewM-24
16FleBreD-13
16SpoNewM-26
95ConTSN-1351
Callahan, Pat (Patrick H.)
77ForLauYS-1
79WesHavYT-6
80NasSouTI-4
81ColCliP-23
81ColCliT-4
81NasSouTI-2
82NasSouTI-5
Callahan, Steve
89EveGiaS-3
89Sta-196
90CliGiaB-2
90CliGiaP-2545
91SanJosGC-14
91SanJosGP-2
92ModA'sC-13
92ModA'sF-3891
Callan, Brett
93AubAstC-3
93AubAstF-3446
94OscAstC-4
94OscAstF-1140
Callari, Ray
91Cla/Bes-316
91RocExpC-17
91RocExpP-2052
Callas, Pete
87ChaWheP-6
88ClePhiS-4
Callaway, Frank B.
22E120-76
Callaway, Mickey
96ButCopKB-11
Calley, Robert
85VisOakT-10
86VisOakP-5
Callihan, John
92YakBeaC-20
92YakBeaF-3456
Callis, Al
75CliPilT-27
Callison, Johnny (John W.)
47Exh-32
47StaPinP2-8
59OklTodML-18
59Top-119
59TopVen-119
60Lea-118
60PhiJayP-4
60Top-17
60TopVen-17
61Pos-123A
61Pos-123B
61Top-468
61TopStal-50
62Baz-18
62SalPlaC-204
62ShiPlaC-204
62Top-17
62TopStal-165
62TopVen-17
63Baz-15
63ExhStaB-10
63Fle-51
63Jel-179
63Pos-179
63SalMetC-26
63Top-434
63TopStil-8
64Baz-15
64PhiJayP-4
64PhiPhiB-8
64Top-135
64TopCoi-50
64TopGia-36
64TopSta-80
64TopStaU-12
64TopTatl-27
64TopVen-135
65Baz-15
65OPC-4
65PhiJayP-4
65Top-4
65Top-310
65TopEmbl-32
65TopTral-41
66Baz-12
66OPC-52

66PhiTeal-4
66Top-52
66Top-230
66TopRubI-13
66TopVen-52
66TopVen-230
67Baz-12
67CokCapPh-4
67DexPre-40
67OPC-85
67OPCPapI-14
67PhiPol-4
67Top-85
67Top-309
67TopPos-14
67TopTesF-2
67TopVen-299
68AtlOilPBCC-9
68Top-415
68TopActS-4C
68TopActS-15C
69MilBra-47
69MLBOffS-174
69MLBPin-37
69OPC-133
69PhiTeal-2
69Top-133
69TopFou-6
69TopSta-73
69TopTeaP-8
69TraSta-59
70DayDaiNM-130
70MLBOffS-15
70OPC-375
70Top-375
71MLBOffS-28
71OPC-12
71Top-12
72MilBra-60
72OPC-364
72Top-364
72TopCloT-4
73OPC-535
73SyrChiTI-4
73Top-535
74LauAllG-64
78TCM60I-29
83PhiPosGM-6
83PhiPosGPaM-1
92YanWIZ7-30
93ActPacA-146
93UppDecAH-25
94UppDecAH-198
94UppDecAH1-198

Callistro, Robby
91PocPioP-3774
91PocPioSP-2

Calmus, Dick
64Top-231
64TopVen-231
68Top-427
90DodTar-101

Calmus, Lance
96WatIndTI-4

Calufetti, Larry
76WauMetT-8

Calui, Mark
92BelMarF-1447

Calvert, Art
87PriWilYP-8
88Ft.LauYS-3
89St.PetCS-4
89Sta-48

Calvert, Chris
85VisOakT-12
87VisOakP-13
88ClePhiS-5
88ReaPhiP-886
89EasLeaDDP-DD34
89ReaPhiB-21
89ReaPhiP-664
89ReaPhiS-5

Calvert, Mark
81PhoGiaVNB-9
83PhoGiaBHN-2
84PhoGiaC-2
85MaiGuiT-4

Calvert, Steve
92Min-4

Calvey, Jack
46SunBre-2

Calvi, Mark
92BelMarC-19

Calvin, Derrick
93BenRocC-4
93BenRocF-3257

Calzado, Francis
84EveGiaC-23

Calzado, Johnny
89JohCitCS-4
90SavCarP-2081
91Cla/Bes-79
91SprCarC-9
91SprCarP-754

Calzado, Lorenzo
89SavCarP-360

Camacho, Adulfo
85MexCitTT-18

Camacho, Dan
93GreFalDSP-22
94BakDodC-5
95SanBerSTI-3
96VerBeaDB-8

Camacho, Ernie
77ModA'sC-8
81Top-96
84Ind-8
84IndWhe-13
85Don-129
85Fle-442
85Ind-8
85IndPol-13
85Top-739
85TopSti-253
85TopTif-739
86Fle-582
86IndOhH-13
86IndTeal-11
86Top-509
86TopTif-509
87Don-350
87Fle-247
87FleGlo-247
87IndGat-13
87OPC-353
87Top-353
87TopSti-209
87TopTif-353
88AstMot-16
88TucTorP-189
89PhoFirC-6
89PhoFirP-1494
90Bow-229
90BowTif-229
90GiaMot-27
90LouRedBLBC-9
90TopTVCa-51
91PacSenL-132

Camacho, Joe
93RanKee-40

Camarena, Miguel
90HunCubP-3272
91HunCubC-6
91HunCubP-3326

Cambria, Fred
71OPC-27
71Top-27
72OPC-392
72Top-392
92SpoIndC-28
92SpoIndF-1311

Camelli, Hank (Henry R.)
47TipTop-77

Camelo, Pete
86JacExpT-6
87JacExpP-432

Cameron, Ken
95NewJerCTI-4
96NewJerCB-4

Cameron, Mike
93SouBenWSC-5
93SouBenWSF-1442
94PriWilCC-6
94PriWilCF-1932
96BirBarB-2
96Bow-264
96ColCho-507
96ColChoGS-507
96ColChoSS-507
96Don-378
96DonPreP-378
96FleUpd-U24
96FleUpdTC-U24
96UltGolP-4
96UltGolPHGM-4
97Bow-378
97BowBes-127
97BowBesAR-127
97BowBesR-127
97BowCerBIA-CA11
97BowCerGIA-CA11
97BowChr-251
97BowChrI-251
97BowChrIR-251
97BowChrR-251
97BowInt-378
97Cir-123
97CirRav-123
97ColCho-74
97Don-234
97DonLim-126
97DonLimLE-126
97DonPre-144
97DonPreCttC-144
97DonPreP-234
97DonPrePGold-234
97DonTea-69
97DonTeaSPE-69
97Fle-58
97FleTif-58
97Lea-187
97LeaFraM-187
97LeaFraMDC-187
97MetUni-56
97PacPriGotD-GD28
97Pin-166
97PinArtP-166
97PinMusC-166
97ScoPreS-326
97ScoWhiS-15
97ScoWhiSPI-15
97ScoWhiSPr-15
97Sel-112
97SelArtP-112
97SelRegG-112
97SkyE-X-13
97SkyE-XC-13
97SkyE-XEC-13
97Top-201
97Ult-37
97UltGolME-37
97UltPlaME-37
97UppDec-238
92UtiBluSC-6

Cameron, Paul
84ChaO'sT-5
85ChaO'sT-30
86ChaOriW-7
87ChaO'sW-NNO

Cameron, Stanton
89PitMetS-2
90ColMetGS-25
90ColMetPPI-4
91St.LucMC-4
91St.LucMP-722
92FreKeyC-8
92FreKeyF-1818
93BowBayF-2199
93ClaGolF-62
93ExcFS7-123
94CarMudF-1592
94ExcFS7-2
94Top-79
94TopGol-79
94TopSpa-79
94UppDecML-84

Cameron, Tony
77ForLauYS-30

Cameron, Troy
97Bow-436
97BowChr-296
97BowChrI-296
97BowChrIR-296
97BowChrR-296
97BowInt-436
97TopSta-121
97TopStaAM-121

Camfield, Eric
96GreBatB-7
96TamYanY-8

Camilli, Dolph (Adolf Louis)
34DiaMatCSB-23
34BatR31-150
34Gou-91
36ExhFou-6
36GouBWR-5
36GouWidPPR-A13
36NatChiFPR-16
36NatChiFPR-101
36R31PasP-4
36SandSW-4
37ExhFou-6
37WheBB14-3
38ExhFou-2
38WheBB10-16
39ExhSal-6A
39ExhSal-6B
39PlaBal-86
40DodTeal-1
40PlaBal-68
40WheM4-11
41DouPlaR-19
41PlaBal-51
42DodTeal-3
43DodTeal-4
43MPR302-1-3
47PM1StaP1-23
61Fle-97
77TCMTheWY-64
79DiaGre-301
83TCMPla1943-31
89DodSmoG-42
90DodTar-102
91RinPosBD3-5

Camilli, Doug (Douglass J.)
61UnIOil-SP1
62Top-594
63Top-196
64Top-249
64TopVen-249
65OPC-77
65Top-77
66Top-593
67Top-551
69SenTeal8-7
73OPC-131
73Top-131A
73Top-131B
85GreHorT-1
86GreHorP-3
87WinHavRSP-24
89WinHavRSS-28
90DodTar-103
90WinHavRSS-27

Camilli, Jason
94SigRooDP-39
94SigRooDPS-39
94StaCluDP-27
94StaCluDPFDI-27
95Top-540
96DelShoB-11

Camilli, Kevin
86GreHorP-4
88FayGenP-1099

Camilli, Lou (Louis Steven)
71MLBOffS-364
71OPC-612
71Top-612

Caminiti, Ken
85OscAstTI-17
86ColAstP-6
87SouLeaAJ-10
87SpoRoo2-37
88BlaYNPRWL-80
88ClaBlu-228
88Don-308
88Fle-441
88FleGlo-441
88OPC-64
88Sco-164
88ScoGlo-164
88ScoYouSI-29
88Spo-124
88StaLinAst-5
88Top-64
88TopSti-33
88TopTif-64
88ToyRoo-6
88TucTorC-11
88TucTorJP-3
88TucTorP-182
89AstLenH-21
89AstMot-25
89AstSmo-7
89Don-542
89DonBasB-262
89Top-369
89TopBig-210
89TopTif-369
89UppDec-141
90AstLenH-5
90AstMot-6
90Bow-73
90BowTif-73
90Don-424
90DonBesN-126
90Fle-225
90FleCan-225
90Lea-253
90MLBBasB-42
90OPC-531
90PanSti-260
90PubSti-89
90Sco-76
90Spo-209
90Top-531
90TopBig-170
90TopSti-20
90TopTif-531
90TopTVA-37
90UppDec-122
90VenSti-90
91AstMot-6
91Bow-543
91Don-221
91Fle-500
91Lea-502
91OPC-174
91PanFreS-9
91PanSti-17
91Sco-186
91Sco-415
91SimandSMLBL-8
91StaClu-520
91Stu-174
91Top-174
91TopDesS-174
91TopMic-174
91TopTif-174
91TopTriH-N4
91Ult-133
91UppDec-180
92AstMot-6
92Bow-538
92DenHol-2
92Don-66
92Fle-427
92Hig5-38
92Lea-140
92OPC-740
92PanSti-154
92Pin-43
92Sco-69
92ScoProP-20
92StaClu-142
92Stu-33
92Top-740
92TopGol-740
92TopGolW-740
92TopKid-45
92TopMic-740
92TriPla-78
92Ult-200
92UppDec-279
93AstMot-9
93Bow-504
93DiaMar-21
93Don-140
93Fin-131
93FinRef-131
93Fla-59
93Fle-432
93FunPac-45
93Kra-17
93Lea-261
93MilBonSS-6
93OPC-81
93PanSti-173
93Pin-59
93Sco-40
93Sel-47
93SP-30
93StaClu-464
93StaCluAs-4
93StaCluFDI-464
93StaCluMOP-464
93Stu-143
93Top-448
93TopGol-448
93TopInaM-448
93TopMic-448
93TriPla-61
93TriPla-149
93Ult-38
93UppDec-305
93UppDecGold-305
94AstMot-7

94Bow-230
94ColC-72
94ColChoGS-72
94ColChoSS-72
94Don-53
94ExtBas-270
94Fin-191
94FinRef-191
94Fla-387
94Fle-486
94FUnPac-137
94Lea-244
94LeaL-112
94Pac-260
94PanSti-191
94Pin-193
94PinArtP-193
94PinMusC-193
94Sco-342
94ScoGolR-342
94Sel-359
94SP-29
94SPDieC-29
94StaClu-322
94StaCluFDI-322
94StaCluGR-322
94StaCluMOP-322
94Stu-18
94SucSav-2
94Top-646
94TopGol-646
94TopSpa-646
94TriPla-23
94Ult-500
94UppDec-409
94UppDecED-409
95ColCho-354
95ColChoGS-354
95ColChoSE-39
95ColChoSEGS-39
95ColChoSESS-39
95ColChoSS-354
95Don-472
95DonPreP-472
95DonTopotO-338
95Emo-185
95Fin-182
95FinRef-182
95Fla-416
95Fle-454
95FleAllS-11
95FleUpd-181
95Lea-312
95LeaCor-4
95LeaLim-17
95PadCHP-10
95PadMot-3
95PanSti-55
95Pin-82
95PinArtP-82
95PinMusC-82
95Sco-56
95ScoGolR-56
95ScoHaloG-HG55
95ScoPlaTS-56
95Sel-225
95SelArtP-225
95SP-107
95SPCha-89
95SPChaDC-89
95Spo-132
95SpoArtP-132
95SPSil-107
95StaClu-91
95StaClu-621
95StaCluFDI-91
95StaCluMOP-91
95StaCluMOP-621
95StaCluSTWS-91
95StaCluSTWS-621
95StaCluVR-57
95Stu-115
95Top-105
95TopCyb-68
95TopTra-85T
95UC3-32
95UC3ArtP-32
95Ult-170
95UltGolM-170
95UppDec-370
95UppDecED-370
95UppDecEDG-370
95UppDecSE-267
95UppDecSEG-267
95Zen-60
96Baz-30
96Bow-73
96BowBes-11
96BowBesAR-11
96BowBesR-11
96Cir-184
96CirRav-184
96ColCho-294
96ColCho-358
96ColCho-363
96ColChoCtG-CG22
96ColChoCtG-CG22B
96ColChoCtG-CG22C
96ColChoCtGE-CR22
96ColChoCtGG-CG22
96ColChoCtGG-CG22B
96ColChoCtGG-CG22C
96ColChoCtGGE-CR22
96ColChoGS-294
96ColChoGS-358
96ColChoGS-363
96ColChoSS-294
96ColChoSS-358
96ColChoSS-363
96Don-310
96DonPreP-310
96EmoXL-275
96Fin-B12
96FinRef-B12
96Fla-371
96Fle-562
96FleTif-562
96Lea-121
96LeaPre-75
96LeaPreP-75
96LeaPrePB-121
96LeaPrePG-121
96LeaPrePS-121
96LeaSig-106
96LeaSigEA-22
96LeaSigEACM-2
96LeaSigPPG-106
96LeaSigPPP-106
96MetUni-233
96MetUniP-233
96Pac-196
96PadMot-5
96PanSti-100
96Pin-106
96PinAfi-23
96PinAfiAP-23
96PinAfiFPP-23
96PinArtP-31
96PinSta-31
96ProSta-82
96Sco-338
96ScoDugC-B63
96ScoDugCAP-B63
96Sel-17
96SelArtP-17
96SelTeaN-22
96SP-158
96SPx-50
96SPxGol-50
96StaClu-77
96StaCluEPB-77
96StaCluEPG-77
96StaCluEPS-77
96StaCluEWB-EW5
96StaCluEWG-EW5
96StaCluEWS-EW5
96StaCluMOP-77
96StaCluVRMO-57
96Stu-129
96StuPrePB-129
96StuPrePG-129
96StuPrePS-129
96Sum-45
96SumAbo&B-45
96SumArtP-45
96SumFoi-45
96TeaOut-14
96Top-182
96TopChr-54
96TopChrR-54
96TopGal-34
96TopGalPPI-34
96TopLas-21
96Ult-282
96UltGolM-282
96UppDec-190
96UppDec-423
96UppDecVJLS-VJ8
97Bow-56
97BowBes-34
97BowBesAR-34
97BowBesBC-BC9
97BowBesBCAR-BC9
97BowBesBCR-BC9
97BowBesR-34
97BowChr-43
97BowChrI-43
97BowChrIR-43
97BowChrR-43
97BowInt-56
97Cir-385
97CirBos-4
97CirRav-385
97CirSupB-4
97ColCho-450
97ColChoAC-21
97ColChoBS-12
97ColChoBSGS-12
97ColChoCtG-25A
97ColChoCtG-25B
97ColChoCtG-25C
97ColChoCtGIW-CG25
97ColChoNF-NF7
97ColChoNF-NF8
97ColChoPP-PP14
97ColChoPPG-PP14
97ColChoS-29
97ColChoTotT-T24
97Don-173
97Don-446
97DonDom-19
97DonEli-83
97DonEliGS-83
97DonLim-50
97DonLim-132
97DonLimFotG-38
97DonLimLE-50
97DonLimLE-132
97DonPowA-12
97DonPowADC-12
97DonPre-81
97DonPre-181
97DonPreCttC-81
97DonPreCttC-181
97DonPreP-173
97DonPreP-446
97DonPrePGold-173
97DonPrePGold-446
97DonPrePM-14
97DonPreS-15
97DonPreXP-10B
97Fin-115
97Fin-161
97Fin-266
97FinEmb-115
97FinEmb-161
97FinEmbR-115
97FinEmbR-161
97FinRef-115
97FinRef-161
97FinRef-266
97FlaSho-A40
97FlaSho-B40
97FlaSho-C40
97FlaShoDC-3
97FlaShoLC-40
97FlaShoLC-B40
97FlaShoLC-C40
97FlaShoLCM-A40
97FlaShoLCM-B40
97FlaShoLCM-C40
97Fle-457
97Fle-699
97FleHea-4
97FleMilDM-30
97FleTif-457
97FleTif-699
97FleZon-4
97Lea-57
97Lea-392
97LeaBanS-10
97LeaDrefS-10
97LeaFraM-57
97LeaFraM-392
97LeaFraMDC-57
97LeaFraMDC-392
97LeaGet-16
97LeaLeaotN-3
97LeaStaS-13
97MetUni-217
97NewPin-52
97NewPinAP-52
97NewPinMC-52
97NewPinPP-52
97Pac-420
97PacCar-34
97PacCarM-34
97PacCerCGT-6
97PacGolCD-34
97PacLigB-420
97PacPri-142
97PacPriGA-GA30
97PacPriGotD-GD205
97PacPriLB-142
97PacPriP-142
97PacPriSL-SL12B
97PacSil-420
97PacTriCD-19
97Pin-84
97PinArtP-84
97PinCar-2
97PinCer-21
97PinCerCMGT-6
97PinCerCT-6
97PinCerMBlu-21
97PinCerMG-21
97PinCerMR-21
97PinCerR-21
97PinIns-83
97PinIns-150
97PinInsC-21
97PinInsCE-83
97PinInsCE-150
97PinInsDD-2
97PinInsDE-83
97PinInsDE-150
97PinInsFS-3
97PinMin-22
97PinMinB-22
97PinMinCB-22
97PinMinCG-22
97PinMinCGR-22
97PinMinCN-22
97PinMinCS-22
97PinMinG-22
97PinMinS-22
97PinMusC-84
97PinTeaP-3
97PinTeaP-10
97PinTotCPB-21
97PinTotCPG-21
97PinTotCPR-21
97PinX-P-56
97PinX-PF&A-15
97PinX-PMoS-56
97PinX-PSfF-43
97PinX-PSfFU-43
97ProMag-37
97ProMagML-37
97Sco-21
97Sco-505
97ScoAllF-8
97ScoBla-14
97ScoHeaotO-27
97ScoHobR-505
97ScoPreS-21
97ScoResC-505
97ScoShoS-21
97ScoShoS-505
97ScoShoSAP-21
97ScoShoSAP-505
97Sel-36
97Sel-143
97SelArtP-36
97SelArtP-143
97SelRegG-36
97SelRegG-143
97SkyE-X-92
97SkyE-XC-92
97SkyE-XEC-92
97SP-154
97SPInsI-21
97SpoIll-35
97SpoIll-118
97SpoIllEE-35
97SpoIllEE-118
97SPSpeF-25
97SPSpxF-3
97SPSPxFA-3
97SPx-41
97SPxBoufG-16
97SPxBro-41
97SPxGraF-41
97SPxSil-41
97SPxSte-41
97StaClu-60
97StaClu-389
97StaCluI-I9
97StaCluI-I18
97StaCluMat-60
97StaCluMOP-60
97StaCluMOP-389
97StaCluMOP-I9
97StaCluMOP-I18
97StaCluMOP-PG12
97StaCluMOP-PL2
97StaCluPG-PG12
97StaCluPL-PL2
97Stu-10
97StuPrePG-10
97StuPrePS-10
97Top-262
97TopChr-93
97TopChrR-93
97TopGal-38
97TopGalPMS-3
97TopGalPMSSS-6
97TopGalPPI-38
97TopHobM-HM15
97TopSta-28
97TopSta1AS-AS8
97TopStaAM-28
97TopTeaT-TT2
97Ult-426
97UltGolME-426
97UltHitM-18
97UltLeaS-10
97UltPlaME-426
97UltTop3-24
97UltTop3GM-24
97UppDec-144
97UppDec-216
97UppDec-244
97UppDec-377
97UppDec-490
97UppDecAWJ-21
97UppDecLDC-LD17
97UppDecP-22
97UppDecRP-RP22
97UppDecU-13
97UppDecUSS-1
97Zen-25
97Zen8x1-7
97Zen8x1D-7

Camnitz, Howard (Samuel H.)
08RosComP-148
09AmeCarE-19
09BriE97-5
09ColChiE-44
09T206-49
09T206-50
09T206-51
10CouT21-89
10CouT21-90
10CouT21-91
10DomDisP-20
10PirHerP-4
10PirTipTD-8
10RedCroT-8
10RedCroT-95
10RedCroT-174
10SweCapPP-134A
10SweCapPP-134B
11L1L-124
11S74Sil-107
11S81LarS-99
11SpoLifCW-51
11SpoLifM-246
11T205-24
11TurRedT-7
12ColRedB-44
12ColTinT-44
12HasTriFT-30A
12T207-25
14CraJacE-16
14PieStaT-8
14TexTomE-10
15CraJacE-16
15VicT21-3

Camp, Jered
95HelBreTI-3
96BelSnaTI-5
96WatIndTI-5

Camp, Rick
77Top-475
78BraCok-3
78Top-349
79RicBraT-21
79Top-105

81BraPol-37
81Don-197
81Fle-246
81OPC-87
81Top-87
81TopSti-150
82BraBurKL-5
82BraPol-37
82Don-223
82Fle-432
82OPC-138
82Top-637
82TopSti-24
83AllGamPI-164
83BraPol-37
83Don-149
83Fle-133
83FleSti-82
83Top-207
84BraPol-37
84Don-165
84Fle-174
84Nes792-597
84OPC-136
84Top-597
84TopTif-597
85BraHos-5
85BraPol-37
85Don-409
85Fle-321
85Lea-130
85OPC-167
85Top-491
85TopMin-491
85TopTif-491
86Don-385
86Fle-510
86Top-319
86TopTif-319
Camp, Scott
86OscAstP-3
Campa, Eric
90MadMusB-5
Campagno, Steve
82OneYanT-9
Campanella, Roy
47Exh-33
47PM1StaP1-24
47PM1StaP1-25
47PM1StaP1-26
47PM1StaP1-27
49Bow-84
49EurSta-32
50Bow-75
50Dra-6
51Bow-31
51R42SmaS-12
52BerRos-7
52Bow-44
52StaCalL-79C
52StaCalS-91B
52TipTop-5
52Top-314
52Whe-5A
52Whe-5B
53BowC-46
53Dor-125
53ExhCan-20
53RedMan-NL5
53StaMey-2
53Top-27
54Bow-90
54NewYorJA-2
54RedMan-NL13
54Wil-1
55BigLeaIS-4
55Bow-22
55DaiQueS-4
55DodGolS-12
56Dod-5
56Top-101
57Top-210
57Top-400
58DodBelB-1
58DodJayP-2
59DodVol-2
59Top-550
60NuHi-29
61NuSco-429
61Top-480
63BasMagM-13
67TopVen-180
69EquSpoHoF-BB2
73HalofFPP-2
75OPC-189
75OPC-191
75OPC-193
75Top-189
75Top-191
75Top-193
76GalBasGHoF-4
76ShaPiz-111
77BobParHoF-9
77GalGloG-5
77GalGloG-251
77Spo-6906
78HalHalR-6
79TCM50-8
79TCM50-43
80DodGreT-11
80MarExhH-4
80PacLeg-90
80PerHaloFP-111
80SSPHOF-111
82BasCarN-13
82BasCarN-16
82DiaCla-4
83DonHOFH-39
83MLBPin-20
83Oco& SSBG-5
83TopRep5-314
84DodUniOP-2
84OCoandSI-185
84OCoandSI-241
84SpoDesPW-22
86SpoDecG-33
86TCMSupS-35
87Dod195T-2
87HygAllG-7
87LeaSpeO*-H3
88PacLegI-47
88RinPosD1-9A
89DodSmoG-4
89HOFStiB-54
89PerCelP-8
90BasWit-30
90DodTar-104
90PerGreM-7
91PomBlaBPB-2
91TopArc1-27
92BazQua5A-20
92FroRowAH-2
93FroRowC-1
93FroRowC-2
93FroRowC-3
93FroRowC-4
93FroRowC-5
93FroRowCGS-1
93FroRowCGS-2
93FroRowCH-1
93TedWil-9
93TedWil-133
93TedWil-141
93TedWilM-1
93TedWilPC-21
93TedWilPC-22
93UppDecS-17
94UppDecAH-11
94UppDecAH-147
94UppDecAH-159
94UppDecAH1-11
94UppDecAH1-147
94UppDecAH1-159
95TopArcBD-19
95TopArcBD-40
95TopArcBD-84
95TopArcBD-122
95TopArcBD-149
97St.VinHHS-4
Campaneris, Bert (Blanco D.)
65OPC-266
65Top-266
66Baz-44
66OPC-175
66Top-175
66TopRubI-14
66TopVen-175
67Baz-44
67CokCapAt-2
67DexPre-41
67OPCPapI-2
67Top-515
67TopPos-2
67TopTesF-3
67TopVen-197
68AtlOilPBCC-10
68Baz-3
68OPC-109
68Top-109
68TopActS-5A
68TopVen-109
69A'sJacitB-3
69MilBra-48
69MLBOffS-83
69Top-423
69Top-495
69Top-556
69TopSta-212
69TopSup-29
69TopTeaP-21
70DayDaiNM-48
70Kel-39
70MLBOffS-255
70OPC-205
70Top-205
70TopPos-23
71BazNumT-31
71BazUnn-4
71MLBOffS-508
71OPC-440
71Top-440
71TopCoi-64
71TopGreM-6
71TopSup-31
71TopTat-54
72MilBra-61
72OPC-75
72Top-75
73A'sPos-38
73LinPor-138
73OPC-64
73OPC-209
73OPC-295
73Top-64
73Top-209
73Top-295
74GreHeroBP-5
74Kel-4
74OPC-155
74OPC-335
74OPC-474
74OPC-478
74Top-155
74Top-335
74Top-474
74Top-478
74TopDecE-46
74TopSta-223
75Hos-28
75HosTwi-28
75OPC-170
75SSP42-14
75Top-170
76A'sPos-76
76Hos-61
76OPC-580
76SSP-492
76Top-580
77BurCheD-19
77Hos-149
77Kel-2
77MSADis-9
77OPC-74
77RCColC-11
77Spo-6810
77Top-373
78RanBurK-14
78RCColC-52
78SSP270-101
78Top-260
78TopZes-2
78WifBalD-12
79OPC-326
79Top-620
80OPC-264
80Top-505
81Don-50
81Fle-280
81LonBeaPT-20
81Top-410
82Don-593
82Fle-454
82Top-772
83ColCliT-17
83TopTra-18T
84Fle-120
84Nes792-139
84Nes792-711
84Nes792-714
84Top-139
84Top-711
84Top-714
84TopTif-139
84TopTif-711
84TopTif-714
86A'sGreT-3
87A'sMot-1
89PacLegI-157
89PacSenL-63
89T/MSenL-16
89TopSenL-32
90EliSenL-78
90HOFStiB-67
90PacLeg-15
90SweBasG-121
91KelLey-1
91SweBasG-110
92ActPacA-42
92MCIAmb-4
92UppDecS-27
92UppDecS-30
92YanWIZ8-25
93RanKee-92
93TedWil-44
93UppDecAH-26
94RanAllP-5
94UppDecAH-129
94UppDecAH-214
94UppDecAH1-129
94UppDecAH1-214
95MCIAmb-2
95SonGre-1
Campanis, Al (Alexander)
90DodTar-105
91FouBal-12
Campanis, Jim
88TopTra-23T
88TopTraT-23T
89SanBerSB-1
89SanBerSCLC-85
90PenPilS-5
91JacSunLD-332
91JacSunP-153
91LinDriAA-332
92Bow-144
92ClaFS7-328
92Don-647
92JacSunF-3709
92JacSunS-353
92OPC-58
92ProFS7-143
92SkyAA F-149
92Top-58
92TopGol-58
92TopGolW-58
92TopMic-58
92UppDecML-223
93ClaFS7-295
93JacSunF-2714
Campanis, Jim (James A.)
67OPC-12
67Top-12
68Top-281
68TopVen-281
69RoyTeal-2
69Top-396
70RoyTeal-7
70Top-671
71MLBOffS-196
74OPC-513
74Top-513
90DodTar-106
Campas, Mike
89HamRedS-7
89Sta-105
90SprCarB-6
91St.PetCC-18
91St.PetCP-2281
Campau, Count (Charles C.)
87OldJudN-67
Campbell, Bill
73TacTwiC-4
74OPC-26
74Top-26
75OPC-226
75Top-226
76OPC-288
76SSP-208
76Top-288
77OPC-8
77OPC-12
77RCColC-12
77Top-8
77Top-166
78Hos-107
78OPC-8
78OPC-87
78PapGinD-22
78RCColC-16
78SSP270-169
78Top-208
78Top-545
79OPC-195
79RedSoxTI-1
79Top-375
80Top-15
81Fle-240
81OPC-256
81Top-396
82CubRedL-39
82Don-487
82Fle-289
82Top-619
82TopTra-16T
83CubThoAV-39
83Don-504
83Fle-493
83FleSti-127
83Top-436
83TopFol-4
84Don-555
84Fle-489
84FleUpd-23
84Nes792-787
84PhiTas-16
84Top-787
84TopTif-787
84TopTra-22T
84TopTraT-22T
85CarTeal-4
85Don-163
85Fle-245
85FleUpd-19
85OPC-209
85PhiTas-9
85Top-209
85TopMin-209
85TopTif-209
85TopTifT-15T
85TopTra-15T
86CarTeal-6
86Don-571
86Fle-28
86FleUpd-17
86Top-112
86TopTif-112
86TopTra-17T
86TopTraT-17T
87Fle-146
87FleGlo-146
87OPC-362
87Top-674
87TopTif-674
89PacLegI-191
89PacSenL-34
89T/MSenL-17
89TopSenL-106
90EliSenL-95
91PacSenL-125
92DenZepF-2656
93NewOrlZF-987
94NewOrlZF-1484
96BelSnaTI-6
Campbell, Bruce D.
32OrbPinNP-34
32OrbPinUP-9
33TatOrb-9
34BatR31-152
34TarThoBD-4
35GouPuzR-8D
35GouPuzR-9D
36NatChiFPR-17
41PlaBal-37
79DiaGre-278
92ConTSN-539
93ConTSN-881
94ConTSN-1228
94ConTSNB-1228
Campbell, Camp
93BurIndC-6
93BurIndF-3288
94BurIndF-3785
94ColRedC-4
94ColRedF-434
Campbell, D.C
90DurBulTI-8
Campbell, Darrin
89SarWhiSS-3

90SarWhiSS-3
91BirBarLD-53
91BirBarP-1456
91LinDriAA-53
93RocRedWF-242
Campbell, Dave (David Alan)
78Top-402
79Top-9
Campbell, Dave (David W.)
69Top-324
70MLBOffS-110
70Top-639
71MLBOffS-221
71OPC-46
71Top-46
72OPC-384
72PadTeal-6
72Top-384
73OPC-488
73Top-488
74OPC-556
74Top-556
77PadSchC-10A
77PadSchC-10B
78PadFamF-4
84PadSmo-3
Campbell, Donovan
88IdaFalBP-1845
89BurBraP-1620
89BurBraS-3
92St.PetCC-7
Campbell, Gilly (William G.)
34BatR31-164
90DodTar-107B
Campbell, Greg
82BurRanF-26
83BurRanF-25
83BurRanT-28
84TulDriTI-NNO
85OklCit8T-14
86OklCit8P-2
Campbell, Jim (James A.)
81TigDetN-130
83TigAlKS-22
83TigAlKS-44
83TigAlKS-54
Campbell, Jim (James Marcus)
87EugEmeP-2654
88MemChiB-10
89Fle-646
89FleGlo-646
89MemChiB-17
89MemChiP-1194
89MemChiS-5
90Bes-311
90MemChiB-22
90MemChiP-1002
90MemChiS-3
90ProAaA-15
91SpoIndC-3
91SpoIndP-3938
91TopDeb90-24
92ClaFS7-267
92OmaRoyF-2954
93OmaRoyF-1674
Campbell, Jim (James R.)
62Col.45B-4
63Col45"P-4
63Top-373
64Top-303
64TopVen-303
89AstCol4S-13
Campbell, Keiver
91St.CatBJC-2
91St.CatBJP-3407
92St.CatBJC-14
92St.CatBJF-3397
Campbell, Kevin
87VerBeaDP-17
88VerBeaDS-2
89BakDodCLC-182
90SanAntMGS-8
90TexLeaAGS-16
91LinDriAAA-530
91TacTigLD-530
91TacTigP-2296
91TriA AAGP-AAA45
92DonRoo-21
92FleUpd-48
92Sco-855
92SkyAAAF-236
92StaClu-647
92StaCluECN-647
92TacTigS-528
92TopDeb91-26
92TopTra-19T
92TopTraG-19T
93Don-155
93Fle-660
93StaClu-235
93StaCluFDI-235
93StaCluMOP-235
93TacTigF-3025
93Top-236
93TopGol-236
93TopInaM-236
93TopMic-236
94SalLakBF-810
Campbell, Mark
82DayBeaAT-17
Campbell, Mike
86CedRapRT-4
87CalCanP-2322
87TamTarP-21
88BlaYNPRWLU-2
88Don-30
88DonBasB-163
88DonRoo-2
88Fle-372
88FleGlo-372
88Lea-30
88MarMot-18
88StaLinMa-4
88Top-246
88TopTif-246
89Don-497
89Fle-543
89FleGlo-543
89MarMot-18
89Sco-568
89ScoHot1R-86
89ScoYouS2-30
89Top-143
89TopTif-143
89UppDec-337
90CMC-634
90ProAAAF-160
90VanCanC-7
90VanCanP-482
91TulDriTI-5
92OklCit8F-1909
92OklCit8S-307
93RanKee-93
94LasVegSF-864
95IowCubTI-5
96IowCubB-10
Campbell, Paul M.
42RedSoxTI-3
Campbell, Ron (Ronald T.)
67CokCapC-6
67Top-497
Campbell, Scott
90OklSoo-8
91JamExpC-8
91JamExpP-3550
92WesPalBEC-10
92WesPalBEF-2093
Campbell, Soup (Clarence)
40PlaBal-200
41DouPlaR-131
Campbell, Steve
82IdaFalAT-23
Campbell, Tedde
96EriSeaB-7
Campbell, Tim
95IdaFalBTI-29
96CliLumKTI-5
Campbell, Vin (Arthur V.)
09ColChiE-45
10PirTipTD-16
11SpoLifM-247
12ColRedB-45
12ColTinT-45
15CraJacE-168
Campbell, William J.
08RosComP-112
09T206-52
10CouT21-7
10CouT21-92
Campbell, Wylie
96BilMusTI-4
Campeau, Jean Claude
43ParSpo-14
43ParSpo-15
Camper, Cardell
76ArkTraT-1
78Top-711
91PacSenL-96
93HelBreSP-4
94HelBreF-3616
94NewOrlZF-1471
96StoPorB-24
Campillo, Robert
92JamExpC-8
92JamExpF-1505
93HelBreF-4097
94HelBreSP-13
Campisi, Sal
70Top-716
71OPC-568
71Top-568
Campos, Frank
87WytCubP-24
88ChaWheB-24
89ChaWheB-23
89ChaWheP-1767
90SouBenWSGS-23
90UtiBluSP-15
91SouBenWSC-14
91SouBenWSP-2850
92BirBarF-2574
92SarWhiSCB-18
92UppDecML-180
93BirBarF-1186
93LinVenB-12
94VenLinU-70
95LinVen-234
Campos, Frank (Francisco J.)
52Top-307
53Top-51
83TopRep5-307
91TopArc1-51
Campos, Jesus
93JamExpC-5
93JamExpF-3337
94BurBeeF-1093
Campos, Marcos
80VenLeaS-238
Campos, Rafael
89AshTouP-949
Campos, Tony
52LavPro-103
Campusano, Aribal
92LetMouSP-5
Campusano, Carlos
96BelSnaTI-7
Campusano, Genaro
90WelPirP-3
91AugPirC-29
91AugPirP-810
92SalBucC-9
Campusano, Sil (Silvestre)
86KnoBluJP-4
87IntLeaAT-24
87SyrChiP-1928
87SyrChiT-18
88BluJayFS-5
88DonRoo-42
88FleUpd-66
88FleUpdG-66
88ScoRoo-93T
88ScoRooG-93T
88TopTra-24T
88TopTraT-24T
89BluJayFS-6
89ClaTra0-137
89Don-584
89OPC-191
89Sco-473
89SyrChiC-21
89SyrChiMB-6
89SyrChiP-808
89Top-191
89TopTif-191
89UppDec-45
90ClaYel-T66
90PhiTas-3
91Fle-389
91OPC-618
91PhiMed-7
91Sco-847
91ScrRedBP-2549
91StaClu-484
91Top-618
91TopDesS-618
91TopMic-618
91TopTif-618
91UppDec-469
93LimRocDWB-81
Campusano, Teo
89AubAstP-2162
Cana, Nelson
96StoPorB-21
Canadiens, Montreal
43ParSpo-72
Canady, Chuckie
82BurRanF-16
82BurRanT-16
83TulDriT-14
84OklCit8T-17
85OklCit8T-29
90TulDriDGB-2
Canale, George
87StoPorP-18
88ElPasDB-5
89BlaYNPRWL-59
89DenZepC-19
89DenZepP-35
90Bow-392
90BowTif-392
90CMC-42
90DenZepC-17
90DenZepP-630
90Don-699
90El PasDAGTI-28
90Fle-641
90FleCan-641
90OPC-344
90OPC-538
90ProAAAF-655
90Sco-656
90Top-344
90Top-538
90TopDeb89-21
90TopTif-344
90UppDec-59
91DenZepLD-130
91DenZepP-128
91Fle-578
91LinDriAAA-130
91Sco100RS-27
93ChaKniF-548
94BreMilB-10
94MemChiF-362
95CarMudF-164
Canan, Dick
86PeoChiP-2
87PeoChiP-5
89WinSpiS-3
90ChaKniTI-3
91ChaKniLD-129
91ChaKniP-1695
91LinDriAA-129
Canas, Nelson
76VenLeaS-60
95LinVen-212
Canate, William
90WatIndS-2
91KinIndC-23
91KinIndP-335
92ClaFS7-86
92ColRedC-4
92ColRedF-2403
93ClaGolF-11
93ExcFS7-159
93FleFinE-287
93LinVenB-188
93LinVenB-279
93LinVenB-342
93PacSpa-650
93SouAtlLAIPI-15
93SouAtlLAPI-3
94BluJayUSPC-10C
94StaCluT-163
94StaCluTFDI-163
94SyrChiF-983
94SyrChiTI-5
94Top-124
94TopGol-124
94TopSpa-124
94VenLinU-102
95LinVen-177
95SyrChiTI-8
Canavan, Jimmy (James Edward)
87OldJudN-68
90DodTar-108
Cancel, Danny
91PeoChiP-1353
Cancel, David
96SouBenSHS-8
Cancel, Robinson
95HelBreTI-25
96BelSnaTI-8
Cancel, Victor
88WytCubP-1980
89WytCubS-4
90GenCubP-3034
90GenCubS-3
90PeoChiTI-15
91PeoChiC-18
91PeoChiTI-23
Cancini, Ron
93QuaCitRBF-106
Candaele, Casey
85IndIndTI-25
86IndIndTI-33
87ClaUpdY-128
87Don-549
87DonRoo-33
87ExpPos-4
87FleUpd-16
87FleUpdG-16
87Spo-158
87SpoRool-6
87SpoTeaP-20
87TopTra-17T
87TopTraT-17T
88Don-179
88DonBasB-68
88ExpPos-3
88Fle-181
88FleGlo-181
88Lea-199
88MSAHosD-12
88OPC-87
88PanSti-329
88RedFolSB-11
88Sco-97
88ScoGlo-97
88ScoYouSI-34
88Spo-140
88StaLinE-3
88Top-431
88TopGloS-60
88TopRoo-11
88TopSti-77
88TopSti-305
88TopTif-431
88ToyRoo-7
89AstSmo-8
89TucTorC-16
89TucTorJP-3
89TucTorP-197
89UppDec-58
90AstLenH-6
90AstMot-25
90TopTra-17T
90TopTraT-17T
91AstMot-25
91Bow-559
91Don-324
91Fle-501
91Lea-114
91OPC-602
91PanFreS-8
91Sco-577
91StaClu-434
91Top-602
91TopDesS-602
91TopMic-602
91TopTif-602
91Ult-134
91UppDec-511
92AstMot-25
92Don-150
92Fle-428
92OPC-161
92PanSti-153
92Sco-147
92StaClu-178
92Top-161
92TopGol-161
92TopGolW-161
92TopMic-161
92Ult-489
92UppDec-387
93AstMot-24
93Don-536
93Fle-49
93Lea-15
93OPC-105
93PacSpa-120
93PanSti-177
93StaClu-70

93StaCluAs-28
93StaCluFDI-70
93StaCluMOP-70
93Top-584
93TopGol-584
93TopInaM-584
93TopMic-584
93UppDec-294
93UppDecGold-294
94IndIndF-1820
94Sco-285
94ScoGolR-285
96BufBisB-4

Candelari, Rick
87BelMarL-1
89WauTimGS-21

Candelaria, Al
83AndBraT-9
85FreGiaP-20

Candelaria, Ben
93MedHatBJF-3748
93MedHatBJSP-13
94St.CatBJC-6
94St.CatBJF-3656
95DunBluJTI-3
96KnoSmoB-7

Candelaria, John
75Pir-1
76CraDis-7
76Hos-92
76OPC-317
76SSP-563
76Top-317
77BurCheD-188
77Hos-80
77Kel-7
77MSADis-10
77OPC-59
77PepGloD-63
77PirPosP-1
77Spo-3504
77Top-510
78Hos-104
78Kel-18
78OPC-7
78OPC-221
78RCColC-72
78Top-190
78Top-207
79Hos-86
79Kel-34
79OPC-29
79Top-70
80OPC-332
80Top-635
81CokTeaS-110
81Don-374
81Fle-375
81OPC-265
81Top-265
82Don-297
82Fle-479
82OPC-3
82Top-425
83Don-549
83Fle-304
83FleSti-70
83OPC-127
83Top-291
83Top-755
83TopSti-282
84AllGamPI-75
84Don-357
84Fle-247
84FleSti-57
84FunFooP-50
84Nes792-330
84OPC-330
84Top-330
84TopSti-127
84TopTif-330
85AllGamPI-165
85Don-430
85Fle-462
85FleStaS-98
85Lea-157
85OPC-50
85Pir-4
85Top-50
85TopSti-123
85TopTif-50
86AngSmo-16
86Don-499
86Fle-150
86OPC-140
86Spo-129
86Top-140
86TopTat-5
86TopTif-140
87AngSmo-1
87Don-551
87Fle-75
87FleAwaW-5
87FleGlo-75
87FleLimBC-C3
87Lea-242
87OPC-313
87SmoAmeL-3
87Spo-148
87SpoTeaP-11
87Top-630
87TopTif-630
88Don-608
88DonBasB-20
88DonReaBY-NEW
88FleUpd-46
88FleUpdG-46
88Sco-293
88ScoGlo-293
88ScoRoo-40T
88ScoRooG-40T
88Top-546
88TopTif-546
88TopTra-25T
88TopTraT-25T
89Bow-171
89BowTif-171
89Don-192
89Fle-251
89FleGlo-251
89OPC-285
89PanSti-397
89Sco-246
89Spo-202
89Top-285
89TopSti-306
89TopTif-285
89UppDec-248
89YanScoNW-8
90KayB-5
90Lea-492
90OPC-485
90PubSti-532
90ScoRoo-54T
90Top-485
90TopTif-485
90TopTra-18T
90TopTraT-18T
90UppDec-720
90VenSti-91
91DodMot-22
91DodPol-54
91FleUpd-92
91Lea-324
91MetWIZ-59
91OPC-777
91Sco-791
91ScoRoo-32T
91StaClu-538
91Top-777
91TopDesS-777
91TopMic-777
91TopTif-777
91TopTra-17T
91TopTraT-17T
91UppDecFE-40F
92DodMot-12
92DodPol-54
92DodSmo-5592
92Don-125
92Fle-449
92OPC-363
92Sco-350
92StaClu-164
92Top-363
92TopGol-363
92TopGolW-363
92TopMic-363
92Ult-500
92UppDec-482
92YanWIZ8-26
93Fle-443
93PacSpa-584
93PirHil-2
93PirNatI-4
93Sco-448
93Top-682
93TopGol-682
93TopInaM-682
93TopMic-682
93UppDec-690
93UppDecGold-690
94CarLeaA-DJ3

Candelaria, Jorge
88BlaYNPRWL-4
88OneYanP-2055
89BlaYNPRWL-171
89BoiHawP-1998
89RenSilSCLC-242

Candini, Mario
47SenGunBP-7
49RemBre-2
51Bow-255

Candiotti, Tom
81ElPasDT-22
84Don-393
84Fle-197
84Nes792-262
84Top-262
84TopTif-262
84VanCanC-32
86FleUpd-18
86IndOhH-49
86IndTeal-12
86TopTra-18T
86TopTraT-18T
87Don-342
87DonOpeD-104
87Fle-248
87FleGlo-248
87FleMin-16
87FleStiC-18
87IndGat-49
87Lea-81
87OPC-296
87SpoTeaP-3
87Top-463
87TopMinL-50
87TopSti-211
87TopTif-463
88Don-377
88DonBasB-112
88Fle-604
88FleGlo-604
88IndGat-49
88OPC-123
88PanSti-69
88Sco-595
88ScoGlo-595
88Spo-37
88StaLinI-6
88Top-123
88TopBig-93
88TopTif-123
89Bow-80
89BowTif-80
89Don-256
89DonBasB-117
89Fle-399
89FleGlo-399
89IndTeal-7
89PanSti-317
89RedFolSB-17
89Sco-239
89Top-599
89TopBig-267
89TopSti-211
89TopTif-599
89UppDec-470
90Bow-324
90BowTif-324
90Don-256
90DonBesA-89
90El PasDAGTI-32
90Fle-488
90FleCan-488
90IndTeal-9
90Lea-55
90OPC-743
90PanSti-57
90PubSti-556
90Sco-269
90Spo-126
90Top-743
90TopCoi-10
90TopSti-216
90TopTif-743
90UppDec-388
90VenSti-92
91BluJayS-28
91Bow-62
91ClaGam-54
91Don-115
91Fle-364
91FleUpd-64
91IndFanC-6
91Lea-79
91OPC-624
91PanFreS-223
91PanSti-174
91RedFolS-16
91Sco-488
91Sco100S-36
91ScoRoo-31T
91StaClu-405
91Stu-132
91Top-624
91TopDesS-624
91TopMic-624
91TopTif-624
91TopTra-18T
91TopTraT-18T
91Ult-109
91UltUpd-59
91UppDec-218
91UppDecFE-49F
92Bow-606
92DodMot-3
92DodPol-49
92DodSmo-4792
92Don-459
92Fle-326
92FleUpd-89
92Lea-409
92OPC-38
92OPCPre-142
92Pin-459
92Pin-610
92Sco-575
92ScoRoo-68T
92StaClu-113
92StaClu-875
92StaCluNC-875
92Stu-42
92Top-38
92TopGol-38
92TopGolW-38
92TopMic-38
92TopTra-20T
92TopTraG-20T
92Ult-501
92UppDec-447
92UppDec-760
93Bow-322
93DodMot-11
93DodPol-3
93Don-142
93Fin-132
93FinRef-132
93Fle-60
93Lea-487
93OPC-63
93PacSpa-497
93Pin-147
93Sco-175
93Sel-143
93StaClu-325
93StaCluD-19
93StaCluFDI-325
93StaCluMOP-325
93Top-365
93TopComotH-22
93TopGol-365
93TopInaM-365
93TopMic-365
93Ult-52
93UppDec-98
93UppDecGold-98
94Bow-126
94BreMilB-11
94ColC-402
94ColChoGS-402
94ColChoSS-402
94DodMot-15
94DodPol-5
94Don-521
94ExtBas-285
94Fin-107
94FinRef-107
94Fla-394
94Fle-507
94Lea-72
94Pac-305
94PanSti-198
94Pin-115
94PinArtP-115
94PinMusC-115
94ProMag-67
94Sco-203
94ScoGolR-203
94StaClu-32
94StaCluFDI-32
94StaCluGR-32
94StaCluMOP-32
94Top-211
94TopGol-211
94TopSpa-211
94Ult-514
94UppDec-260
94UppDecED-260
94USPlaCA-2S
95BluJayUSPC-9C
95ColCho-222
95ColChoGS-222
95ColChoSS-222
95DodMot-21
95DodPol-4
95Don-116
95DonPreP-116
95DonTopotO-263
95Emb-84
95EmbGolI-84
95Fin-94
95FinRef-94
95Fle-536
95Lea-234
95Pin-441
95PinArtP-441
95PinMusC-441
95Sco-511
95ScoGolR-511
95ScoPlaTS-511
95StaClu-456
95StaCluMOP-456
95StaCluSTDW-D456
95StaCluSTWS-456
95StaCluVR-246
95Top-416
95TopCyb-216
95Ult-178
95UltGolM-178
96ColCho-179
96ColChoGS-179
96ColChoSS-179
96DodMot-14
96DodPol-6
96Don-94
96DonPreP-94
96EmoXL-205
96Fla-288
96Fle-428
96FleDod-3
96FleTif-428
96LeaSigA-39
96LeaSigAG-39
96LeaSigAS-39
96Pac-102
96StaClu-392
96StaCluEPB-392
96StaCluEPG-392
96StaCluEPS-392
96StaCluMOP-392
95StaCluVRMC-246
96Top-153
96Ult-493
96UltGolM-493
97Cir-321
97CirRav-321
97PacPriGotD-GD156
97StaClu-341
97StaCluMOP-341
97Top-91

Canefires, West Oahu
96WesOahCHWB-NNO

Caneira, John
75QuaCitAT-34
77SalLakCGC-18
78STLakCGC-18

Caneman, Mascot
96WesOahCHWB-NNO

Canepa, Vincent
52LavPro-52

Canestro, Art
88OneYanP-2060
89OneYanP-2104
90PriWilCTI-7
91Ft.LauYC-2
91Ft.LauYP-2417
92SalLakTSP-28

Cangelosi, John

83AppFoxF-13
86DonHig-51
86DonRoo-51
86FleUpd-19
86SpoRoo-31
86TopTra-19T
86TopTraT-19T
86WhiSoxC-44
87Don-162
87Fle-489
87FleGlo-489
87Lea-251
87OPC-201
87SevCoi-C3
87Spo-157
87SpoTeaP-26
87Top-201
87TopMinL-49
87TopRoo-2
87TopSti-293
87TopTif-201
87TopTra-18T
87TopTraT-18T
88BlaYNPRWLU-24
88Don-435
88Fle-325
88FleGlo-325
88OPC-328
88PanSti-377
88Sco-418
88ScoGlo-418
88StaLinPi-5
88Top-506
88TopTif-506
89PirVerFJ-44
89Sco-601
89Top-592
89TopTif-592
89UppDec-67
90Don-565
90OPC-29
90PirHomC-8
90Sco-367
90Top-29
90TopTif-29
90UppDec-370
91LinDriAAA-629
91VanCanLD-629
91VanCanP-1605
92Bow-442
92RanMot-27
92RanTeal-3
92Ult-439
93RanKee-94
94MetColP-7
96AstMot-22
96Fle-403
96FleTif-403
96LeaSigEA-23

Cangemi, Jamie
87BelBreP-7
89BelBreIS-4
89StoPorB-6
89StoPorCLC-150
89StoPorP-389
89StoPorS-13
90StoPorB-21
90StoPorCLC-182
90StoPorP-2182
91StoPorC-1
91StoPorP-3025

Caniglia, Pete
52LavPro-45

Canino, Carlos
87WytCubP-23
88GenCubP-1655

Canizaro, Jay
92OklStaC-2
94SanJosGC-2
94SanJosGF-2822
95Bow-215
95SPML-146
96BesAutS-16
96BesAutSA-11
96Bow-126
96ColCho-448
96ColChoGS-448
96ColChoSS-448
96Exc-241
96PhoFirB-11
96UppDec-247
97Bow-381
97BowCerBIA-CA12
97BowCerGIA-CA12
97BowInt-381
97ColCho-227
97Fle-478
97FleTif-478
97PacPriGotD-GD214
97Ult-291
97UltGolME-291
97UltPlaME-291
97UppDec-174

Cannaday, Aaron
92WelPirC-3
92WelPirF-1325
93WelPirC-3
93WelPirF-3359
94AugGreC-2
94AugGreF-3011

Cannell, Rip (Virgin Wirt)
11SpoLifCW-52

Cannizzaro, Chris
82RedPioT-25
86PawRedSP-4
87PawRedSP-77
87PawRedST-2
88PawRedSC-15
88PawRedSP-451
89PawRedSC-11
89PawRedSP-686
89PawRedSTI-4

Cannizzaro, Chris John
61Top-118
62Top-26
62TopVen-26
65MetJayP-3
65OPC-61
65Top-61
66Top-497
69OPC-131
69Top-131
69TopFou-24
70DayDaiNM-91
70OPC-329
70Top-329
71MLBOffS-222
71OPC-426
71Top-426
71TopCoi-109
71TopTat-46
72Top-759
75OPC-355
75Top-355
81RedPioT-28
82MetGal62-6
90DodTar-109
91MetWIZ-60

Cannon, J.D.
95IndIndF-115

Cannon, J.J. (Joseph Jerome)
75DubPacT-15
78ChaChaT-4
79SyrChiT-7
79SyrChiTI-23
80OPC-118
80Top-221
81SyrChiT-17
81SyrChiTI-5
82KnoBluJT-18
83KinBluJTI-2
86KnoBluJP-5
87KnoBluJP-1519
89KnoBluJB-25
89KnoBluJP-1129
89KnoBluJS-24
90KnoBluJB-10
90KnoBluJP-1260
90KnoBluJS-25
91MedHatBJP-4117
91MedHatBJSP-26
92St.CatBJC-27
92St.CatBJF-3401
93St.CatBJC-25
93St.CatBJF-3989
94St.CatBJC-27
94St.CatBJF-3659
95StCatSTI-26
96HagSunB-27

Cannon, Kevan
96MicBatCB-6

Cannon, Robby
91BoiHawP-3894

Cannon, Scott
86KinEagP-3

Cannon, Stan
79WisRapTT-16

Cannon, Tim
83MiaMarT-22

Cannons, Prince William
90PriWilCTI-30

Cano, Felix
90IBAWorA-31

Cano, Jose
83AndBraT-8
84DurBulT-22
87OscAstP-27
88TucTorC-7
88TucTorJP-4
88TucTorP-171
89ColMudB-25
90AstLenH-7
90Bow-68
90BowTif-68
90ColMudB-25
90ColMudP-1340
90TopDeb89-22
90UppDec-43
93LimRocDWB-116

Canseco, Jose
83MadMusF-13
84ModA'sC-5
84TopPewB-4
84TopPewB-6
85HunStaJ-44
86A'sMot-9
86Don-39
86DonHig-55
86DonRoo-22
86Fle-649
86FleLeaL-3
86FleMin-87
86FleSlu-5
86FleStiC-19
86FleUpd-20
86SouLeaAJ-14
86Spo-178
86SpoRoo-11
86StaCan-1
86StaCan-2
86StaCan-3
86StaCan-4
86StaCan-5
86StaCan-6
86StaCan-7
86StaCan-8
86StaCan-9
86StaCan-10
86StaCan-11
86StaCan-12
86StaCan-13
86StaCan-14
86StaCan-15
86StaStiC-1
86StaStiC-2
86StaStiC-3
86StaStiC-4
86StaStiC-5
86StaStiC-6
86StaStiC-7
86StaStiC-8
86StaStiC-9
86StaStiC-10
86StaStiC-11
86StaStiC-12
86StaStiC-13
86StaStiC-14
86StaStiC-15
86TopTra-20T
86TopTraT-20T
87A'sMot-26
87A'sMot-27
87A'sSmoC-2
87ClaGam-46
87ClaUpdY-125
87Don-6
87Don-97
87DonAll-21
87DonHig-40
87DonOpeD-24
87DonSupD-6
87DonWaxBC-PC12
87Dra-4
87Fle-389
87Fle-625
87Fle-628
87Fle-633
87FleAwaW-6
87FleBasA-6
87FleExcS-7
87FleGamW-8
87FleGlo-389
87FleGlo-625
87FleGlo-628
87FleGlo-633
87FleHea-2
87FleHotS-9
87FleLeaL-8
87FleLimE-6
87FleMin-17
87FleRecS-3
87FleSlu-8
87FleStiC-19
87FleStiC-131
87GenMilB-3C
87HosSti-28
87KayB-7
87KraFoo-35
87Lea-6
87Lea-151
87MandMSL-10
87MSAIceTD-17
87OPC-247
87RedFolSB-63
87SmoAmeL-1
87Spo-80
87Spo-90
87SpoTeaP-23
87StaAwaW-1
87StaAwaW-2
87StaAwaW-3
87StuPan-24
87Top-620
87TopCoi-6
87TopGaloC-3
87TopGloS-59
87TopMinL-68
87TopRoo-3
87TopSti-164
87TopSti-304
87TopTif-620
87ToyRoo-5
87Woo-12
88A'sMot-7
88A'sMot-28
88Baz-3
88ClaRed-165
88ClaRed-197
88Don-302
88DonBasB-22
88DonTeaBA-302
88Fle-276
88Fle-624
88FleAwaW-4
88FleBasA-5
88FleBasM-3
88FleExcS-7
88FleGlo-276
88FleGlo-624
88FleHotS-5
88FleLeaL-4
88FleMin-45
88FleRecS-4
88FleSlu-6
88FleStiC-54
88FleSup-5
88FleTeaL-3
88K-M-4
88KayB-3
88Lea-138
88Nes-37
88OPC-370
88PanSti-173
88Sco-45
88ScoGlo-45
88ScoYouSI-30
88Spo-201
88StaCan-1
88StaCan-2
88StaCan-3
88StaCan-4
88StaCan-5
88StaCan-6
88StaCan-7
88StaCan-8
88StaCan-9
88StaCan-10
88StaCan-11
88StaLinAs-2
88Top-370
88Top-759
88TopBig-13
88TopCoi-7
88TopGloS-55
88TopMinL-30
88TopSti-173
88TopStiB-48
88TopTif-370
88TopTif-759
88TopUKM-10
88TopUKMT-10
89A'sMot-7
89A'sMot-28
89A'sMotR-1
89A'sMotR-4
89Baz-5
89Bow-201
89BowTif-201
89CadEllD-5
89CerSup-12
89ClaLigB-3
89ClaTraO-103
89CMCCan-1
89CMCCan-2
89CMCCan-3
89CMCCan-4
89CMCCan-5
89CMCCan-6
89CMCCan-7
89CMCCan-8
89CMCCan-9
89CMCCan-10
89CMCCan-11
89CMCCan-12
89CMCCan-13
89CMCCan-14
89CMCCan-15
89CMCCan-16
89CMCCan-17
89CMCCan-18
89CMCCan-19
89CMCCan-20
89CMCCan-P1
89Don-91
89Don-643
89DonAll-2
89DonAll-30
89DonBasB-57
89DonBonM-BC5
89DonGraS-1
89DonPop-2
89Fle-5
89Fle-628
89Fle-634
89FleAll-2
89FleBasA-5
89FleBasM-6
89FleExcS-3
89FleGlo-5
89FleGlo-628
89FleGlo-634
89FleGlo-WS3
89FleHeroB-5
89FleLeaL-3
89FleSup-6
89FleWaxBC-C4
89FleWorS-3
89K-M-18
89KayB-3
89KinDis-17
89MasBreD-10
89ModA'sC-34
89MotCan-1
89MotCan-2
89MotCan-3
89MotCan-4
89MSAHolD-5
89MSAIceTD-18
89Nis-5
89OPC-389
89PanSti-8
89PanSti-238
89PanSti-246
89PanSti-422
89PanSti-477
89PanSti-480
89RedFolSB-18
89Sco-1
89Sco-582
89Sco-655
89ScoHot1S-1
89ScoSco-40
89Spo-1
89Spo-221
89SpoIllFKI-11
89TacTigP-1536
89Top-401
89Top-500
89TopAme2C-8

89TopBasT-60
89TopBig-190
89TopCapC-1
89TopCoi-29
89TopDouA-5
89TopGaloC-2
89TopGloA-6
89TopGloS-12
89TopHeaUT-18
89TopHilTM-5
89TopMinL-68
89TopSti-11
89TopSti-148
89TopSti-171
89TopStiB-13
89TopTif-401
89TopTif-500
89TopUKM-12
89TVSpoM-93
89TVSpoM-125
89TVSpoM-133
89UppDec-371
89UppDec-659A
89UppDec-659B
89UppDec-670
89Woo-1
89Woo-23
90A'sMot-6
90AllBasT-15
90BasWit-11
90Bow-460
90BowTif-460
90ClaBlu-22
90ClaYel-T32
90Col-25
90ColCan-1
90ColCan-2
90ColCan-3
90ColCan-4
90ColCan-5
90ColCan-6
90ColCan-7
90ColCan-8
90ColCan-9
90ColCan-10
90ColCan-11
90ColCan-12
90Don-125
90DonBesA-81
90DonLeaS-6
90Fle-3
90Fle-629
90FleAwaW-6
90FleBasA-4
90FleBasM-6
90FleCan-3
90FleCan-629
90FleLeaL-5
90FleLeaS-4
90FleWorS-5
90FleWorS-10
90GooHumICBLS-5
90HOFStiB-95
90Hot50PS-4
90K-M-21
90Lea-108
90MLBBasB-78
90MotCan-1
90MotCan-2
90MotCan-3
90MotCan-4
90MSAIceTD-4
90OPC-250
90PanSti-142
90PepCan-1
90PepCan-2
90PepCan-3
90PepCan-4
90PepCan-5
90PepCan-6
90PepCan-7
90PepCan-8
90PepCan-9
90PepCan-10
90Pos-16
90PubSti-279
90PubSti-301
90RedFolSB-14
90Sco-375
90Sco-702
90Sco100S-5
90Spo-23
90SupActM-2
90Top-250
90TopAmeA-29
90TopBig-270
90TopDou-8
90TopGloS-31
90TopHeaU-18
90TopHilHM-7
90TopMag-21
90TopSti-177
90TopStiB-47
90TopTif-250
90TopTVA-11
90UppDec-66
90USPlaCA-WCO
90VenSti-93
90VenSti-94
90WinDis-8
90WonBreS-14
91A'sMot-6
91A'sSFE-2
91BasBesHRK-2
91BasBesRB-2
91Bow-227
91Bow-372
91CadEllD-7
91Cla2-T19
91Cla3-T6
91ClaGam-135
91Col-13
91Don-50A
91Don-50B
91Don-536
91DonEli-3
91DonGraS-4
91DonPre-11
91Fle-5
91FleAll-8
91FlePro-6
91FleWorS-3
91JimDea-19
91Lea-182
91MajLeaCP-38
91MooSna-1
91OPC-390
91OPC-700
91OPCPre-18
91PanCanT1-15
91PanCanT1-24
91PanCanT1-39
91PanFreS-173
91PanFreS-198
91PanSti-149
91PepSup-17
91PerGamC-1
91Pos-4
91RedFolS-17
91RedFolS-116
91Sco-1
91Sco-398
91Sco-441
91Sco-690
91Sco100S-1
91SevCoi-A6
91SevCoi-T3
91SevCoi-NC2
91SevCoi-NW2
91SevCoi-SC2
91SpoNSP-1
91StaClu-155
91StaCluMO-29
91StaPinB-7
91Stu-101
91Top-390
91Top-700
91TopCraJI-10
91TopDesS-390
91TopDesS-700
91TopGloA-8
91TopMic-390
91TopMic-700
91TopSta-7
91TopTif-390
91TopTif-700
91TopTriH-A11
91Ult-244
91UppDec-146
91UppDec-155
91UppDecSS-SS4
92A'sUno7P-1
92A'sUno7P-2
92AthMot-6
92Bow-600
92Cla1-T22
92Cla2-T3
92Cla2-NNO
92ClaGam-110
92ColAllG-21
92ColAllP-21
92ColPro-4
92DenHol-22
92Don-548
92DonCraJ1-25
92DonMcD-13
92Fle-252
92Fle-688
92FleAll-24
92FleCitTP-13
92FleLumC-L5
92FleTeaL-19
92FleUpd-59
92Fre-4
92Hig5-102
92Hig5S-5
92Lea-267
92LeaGolP-23
92LeaPre-23
92MSABenSHD-12
92OPC-100
92OPCPre-24
92PanSti-19
92PanSti-144
92PepDieM-24
92Pin-130
92PinSlu-3
92Pos-25
92PosCan-16
92RemUltP-P4
92RemUltP-P5
92RemUltP-P6
92RemUltP-P19
92Sco-500
92Sco100S-67
92ScoImpP-52
92ScoProaG-8
92ScoRoo-9T
92SevCoi-21
92SpoStaCC-7
92StaClu-370
92StaClu-597
92StaCluMP-3
92Stu-222
92StuHer-BC4
92SunSee-18
92Top-100
92Top-314
92Top-401
92TopGol-100
92TopGol-314
92TopGol-401
92TopGolW-100
92TopGolW-314
92TopGolW-401
92TopKid-115
92TopMcD-22
92TopMic-100
92TopMic-314
92TopMic-401
92TopMic-G100
92TriPla-214
92Ult-110
92Ult-133
92UppDec-196
92UppDec-333
92UppDec-640
92UppDec-649
92UppDecF-17
92UppDecFG-17
92UppDecHRH-HR1
92UppDecTMH-14
92UppDecWB-T3
93Bow-545
93CadDis-10
93ClaGam-18
93DiaMar-22
93Don-159
93DonLonBL-LL6
93DonMasotG-7
93DonPre-21
93DonSpiotG-SG5
93DurPowP2-19
93Fin-99
93FinJum-99
93FinRef-99
93Fla-278
93Fle-319
93FleFruotL-9
93FunPac-12
93FunPac-155
93Hos-10
93Lea-241
93LeaGolA-R9
93MetBak-22
93OPC-47
93OPCPre-81
93PacBeiA-14
93PacBeiA-15
93PacBeiA-27
93PacSpa-308
93PacSpaGE-13
93PacSpaPI-11
93PanSti-85
93Pin-49
93PinHomRC-10
93PinSlu-24
93RanKee-399
93Sco-13
93Sel-364
93SP-191
93StaClu-499
93StaCluFDI-499
93StaCluMOP-499
93StaCluMP-14
93StaCluR-28
93Stu-47
93StuSupoC-2
93Top-500
93TopGol-500
93TopInaM-500
93TopMic-500
93TriPla-243
93Ult-627
93UppDec-52
93UppDec-365
93UppDecCP-R4
93UppDecGold-52
93UppDecGold-365
93UppDecOD-D7
93UppDecTriCro-TC2
94Bow-600
94BowBes-R24
94BowBesR-R24
94ColC-560
94ColChoGS-560
94ColChoSS-560
94Don-372
94DonDom-A7
94DonSpeE-372
94ExtBas-176
94ExtBasGB-5
94Fin-222
94FinJum-222
94FinRef-222
94Fla-344
94Fle-304
94FUnPac-133
94FUnPac-209
94Lea-249
94LeaL-70
94LeaMVPC-A3
94LeaMVPCG-A3
94OPC-169
94Pac-611
94PacAll-15
94PanSti-125
94Pin-306
94PinArtP-306
94PinMusC-306
94ProMag-132
94RedFolMI-8
94Sco-61
94ScoGolR-61
94Sel-276
94SP-146
94SPDieC-146
94SPHol-4
94SPHolDC-4
94Spo-141
94StaClu-171
94StaCluFDI-171
94StaCluGR-171
94StaCluMOP-171
94StaCluMOP-ST27
94StaCluST-ST27
94StaCluT-250
94StaCluTFDI-250
94Stu-152
94Top-80
94TopGol-80
94TopSpa-80
94TopSupS-7
94TriPla-192
94Ult-428
94UppDec-140
94UppDecAJ-34
94UppDecAJG-34
94UppDecED-140
94UppDecMLS-MM4
94UppDecMLSED-MM4
95Baz-42
95BazRedH-RH9
95Bow-417
95BowBes-R29
95BowBesR-R29
95ClaPhoC-7
95ColCho-415
95ColChoCtG-CG4
95ColChoCtG-CG4B
95ColChoCtG-CG4C
95ColChoCtGE-4
95ColChoCtGG-CG4
95ColChoCtGG-CG4B
95ColChoCtGG-CG4C
95ColChoCtGGE-4
95ColChoGS-415
95ColChoSE-185
95ColChoSEGS-185
95ColChoSESS-185
95ColChoSS-415
95Don-350
95DonBomS-4
95DonEli-59
95DonLonBL-6
95DonPreP-350
95DonTopotO-18
95Emo-9
95Fin-170
95FinRef-170
95Fla-226
95FlaOutP-4
95Fle-281
95FleLumC-4
95FleTeaL-13
95FleUpd-9
95FleUpdH-4
95Lea-391
95LeaGolS-12
95LeaLim-21
95LeaLimG-9
95LeaLimL-12
95LeaOpeD-7
95NatPac-9
95Pac-33
95PacGolCDC-5
95PacGolP-1
95PacLatD-6
95PacPri-134
95PanSti-92
95Pin-49
95PinArtP-49
95PinMusC-49
95RedFol-35
95Sco-4
95ScoGolR-4
95ScoHaloG-HG13
95ScoPlaTS-4
95ScoRul-SR11
95ScoRulJ-SR11
95ScoSam-4
95Sel-231
95SelArtP-231
95SelCerGT-12
95SP-130
95SPCha-127
95SPChaDC-127
95Spo-127
95SpoArtP-127
95SpoPro-PM8
95SPSil-130
95SPSpeF-1
95StaClu-214
95StaClu-347
95StaClu-630
95StaCluCC-CC10
95StaCluCT-6
95StaCluFDI-214
95StaCluMO-10
95StaCluMOP-214
95StaCluMOP-347
95StaCluMOP-630
95StaCluMOP-CC10
95StaCluMOP-RL8
95StaCluRL-RL8
95StaCluSTDW-RS347
95StaCluSTWS-214
95StaCluSTWS-347
95StaCluSTWS-630
95StaCluVR-183

95Stu-9
95StuGolS-9
95StuPlaS-9
95Sum-19
95Sum-185
95SumBigB-BB12
95SumNthD-19
95SumNthD-185
95SumSam-BB12
95Top-300
95TopCyb-161
95TopCybSiR-2
95TopFin-14
95TopLeaL-LL10
95TopTra-72T
95UC3-60
95UC3ArtP-60
95UC3CycS-CS9
95UllHomRK-4
95Ult-260
95UltGolM-260
95UltHitM-5
95UltHitMGM-5
95UltHomRK-4
95UltHomRKGM-4
95UppDec-158
95UppDecED-158
95UppDecEDG-158
95UppDecPAW-H30
95UppDecPAWE-H30
95UppDecPLL-R2
95UppDecPLL-R42
95UppDecPLLE-R2
95UppDecPLLE-R42
95UppDecSE-213
95UppDecSEG-213
95UppDecCooD CD10
95USPlaCMLA-7C
95Zen-56
96Baz-108
96Bow-23
96BowBes-57
96BowBesAR-57
96BowBesR-57
96Cir-9
96CirBos-3
96CirRav-9
96ColCho-101
96ColCho-327
96ColCho-475
96ColChoCtG-CG5
96ColChoCtG-CG5B
96ColChoCtG-CG5C
96ColChoCtGE-CR5
96ColChoCtGG-CG5
96ColChoCtGG-CG5B
96ColChoCtGG-CG5C
96ColChoCtGGE-CR5
96ColChoGS-101
96ColChoGS-327
96ColChoGS-475
96ColChoSS-101
96ColChoSS-327
96ColChoSS-475
96ColChoYMtP-10
96ColChoYMtP-10A
96ColChoYMtPGS-10
96ColChoYMtPGS-10A
96Don-266
96DonPreP-266
96EmoN-3
96EmoXL-11
96Fin-B221
96Fin-G117
96FinRef-B221
96FinRef-G117
96Fla-15
96Fle-24
96FleRedS-2
96FleTif-24
96FleUpd-U216
96FleUpdTC-U216
96Lea-64
96LeaPre-86
96LeaPreP-86
96LeaPrePB-64
96LeaPrePG-64
96LeaPrePS-64
96LeaPreSG-47
96LeaPreSte-47
96LeaSig-105
96LeaSigPPG-105
96LeaSigPPP-105
96MetUni-12
96MetUniP-12
96Pac-246
96PacEstL-EL7
96PacGolCD-DC17
96PacHom-HP12
96PacMil-M4
96PacOctM-OM4
96PacPri-P78
96PacPriFB-FB5
96PacPriG-P78
96PacPriRHS-RH2
96PanSti-135
96Pin-36
96PinAfi-37
96PinAfiAP-37
96PinAfiFPP-37
96PinArtP-17
96PinSta-17
96ProMagA-2
96ProSta-107
96Sco-303
96ScoDugC-B28
96ScoDugCAP-B28
96Sel-91
96SelArtP-91
96SelCer-98
96SelCerAP-98
96SelCerCB-98
96SelCerCR-98
96SelCerMB-98
96SelCerMG-98
96SelCerMR-98
96SelTeaN-8
96SP-38
96Spo-94
96SpoArtP-94
96SPSpeFX-32
96SPSpeFXDC-32
96SPx-8
96SPxGol-8
96StaClu-223
96StaClu-342
96StaCluEPB-342
96StaCluEPG-342
96StaCluEPS-342
96StaCluMet-M3
96StaCluMOP-223
96StaCluMOP-342
96StaCluMOP-M3
96StaCluMOP-PP3
96StaCluPP-PP3
95StaCluVRMC-183
96Stu-53
96StuPrePB-53
96StuPrePG-53
96StuPrePS-53
96Sum-23
96SumAbo&B-23
96SumArtP-23
96SumFoi-23
96Top-362
96TopChr-146
96TopChrR-146
96TopChrWC-WC4
96TopChrWCR-WC4
96TopGal-33
96TopGalE-14
96TopGalPPI-33
96TopLas-38
96TopLasPC-11
96TopWreC-WC4
96Ult-15
96UltGolM-15
96UltHomRKGM-4
96UltHomRKR-4
96UltThu-4
96UltThuGM-4
96UppDec-285
96UppDecPD-PD4
96UppDecRunP-RP5
96UppDecVJLS-VJ7
97Bow-254
97BowBes-72
97BowBesAR-72
97BowBesR-72
97BowChr-77
97BowChrI-77
97BowChrIR-77
97BowChrR-77
97BowInt-254
97Cir-119
97CirRav-119
97ColCho-45
97ColCho-410
97ColChoCtG-23A
97ColChoCtG-23B
97ColChoCtG-23C
97ColChoCtGIW-CG23
97ColChoNF-NF3
97ColChoTBS-9
97ColChoTBSWH-9
97Don-54
97Don-277
97DonEli-52
97DonEliGS-52
97DonLim-17
97DonLim-168
97DonLimLE-17
97DonLimLE-168
97DonLonL-15
97DonPre-30
97DonPreCttC-30
97DonPreP-54
97DonPreP-277
97DonPrePGold-54
97DonPrePGold-277
97Fin-101
97Fin-284
97FinEmb-101
97FinEmb-284
97FinEmbR-101
97FinEmbR-284
97FinRef-101
97FinRef-284
97FlaSho-A109
97FlaSho-B109
97FlaSho-C109
97FlaShoLC-109
97FlaShoLC-B109
97FlaShoLC-C109
97FlaShoLCM-A109
97FlaShoLCM-B109
97FlaShoLCM-C109
97Fle-18
97Fle-535
97FleTif-18
97FleTif-535
97Lea-195
97Lea-206
97LeaFraM-195
97LeaFraM-206
97LeaFraMDC-195
97LeaFraMDC-206
97MetUni-19
97NewPin-15
97NewPinAP-15
97NewPinMC-15
97NewPinPP-15
97Pac-34
97PacCar-5
97PacCarM-5
97PacGolCD-6
97PacLatotML-5
97PacLigB-34
97PacPri-13
97PacPriLB-13
97PacPriP-13
97PacPriSH-SH2A
97PacSil-34
97Pin-25
97PinArtP-25
97PinCer-90
97PinCerMBlu-90
97PinCerMG-90
97PinCerMR-90
97PinCerR-90
97PinIns-79
97PinInsCE-79
97PinInsDE-79
97PinMusC-25
97PinTotCPB-90
97PinTotCPG-90
97PinTotCPR-90
97PinX-P-12
97PinX-PMoS-12
97PinX-PSfF-11
97PinX-PSfFU-11
97Sco-170
97Sco-360
97ScoHobR-360
97ScoPreS-170
97ScoRedS-7
97ScoRedSPl-7
97ScoRedSPr-7
97ScoResC-360
97ScoShoS-170
97ScoShoS-360
97ScoShoSAP-170
97ScoShoSAP-360
97Sel-5
97SelArtP-5
97SelRegG-5
97SkyE-X-37
97SkyE-XC-37
97SkyE-XEC-37
97SP-131
97SpoIll-166
97SpoIllEE-166
97SPSpeF-39
97SPSpxF-4
97SPSPxFA-4
97SPx-37
97SPxBro-37
97SPxGraF-37
97SPxSil-37
97SPxSte-37
97StaClu-234
97StaCluMat-234
97StaCluMOP-234
97Stu-35
97StuPrePG-35
97StuPrePS-35
97Top-246
97TopChr-87
97TopChrR-87
97TopGal-8
97TopGalPPI-8
97TopSta-19
97TopStaAM-19
97Ult-12
97Ult-376
97UltDouT-2
97UltGolME-12
97UltGolME-376
97UltPlaME-12
97UltPlaME-376
97UppDec-24
97UppDecPP-PP18
97UppDecPPJ-PP18

Canseco, Ozzie
83GreHorT-3
87MadMusP-3
87MadMusP-6
88MadMusP-7
88MidLeaAGS-51
89HunStaB-28
89UppDec-756
90Bes-162
90FleUpd-117
90HunStaB-21
90Lea-516
91MajLeaCP-41
91OPC-162
91Sco-346
91Top-162
91TopDeb90-25
91TopDesS-162
91TopMic-162
91TopTif-162
91UppDec-146
92LouRedF-1898
92LouRedS-254
92SkyAAAF-124
93Bow-164
93CarPol-4
93ClaFS7-128
93Don-336
93LouRedF-226
93PacBeiA-27
93PacSpa-630
93Pin-272
93Sco-241
93ScoBoyoS-25
93StaClu-634
93StaCluCa-14
93StaCluFDI-634
93StaCluMOP-634
94NewOrlZF-1480

Cantillon, Pongo (Joe)
11SpoLifCW-53

Canton, Michael
92ElmPioC-4
92ElmPioF-1387

Cantrell, Dave
89SalSpuCLC-129
89SalSpuP-1826

Cantrell, Derrick
92ClaDraP-111

Cantrell, Guy
90DodTar-110

Cantrelle, Lee
91OklStaC-3

Cantres, Jorge
90YakBeaTI-35

Cantu, Mike
91HamRedC-19
91HamRedP-4044
92St.PetCF-2034
93FloStaLAF-43
93St.PetCC-8
93St.PetCF-2632
94ClaGolF-169
94St.PetCC-7
94St.PetCF-2591

Cantwell, Ben
30SchR33-25
33Gou-139
33TatOrbSDR-168
34DiaMatCSB-24
34BatR31-96
34GouCanV-14
35DiaMatCS3T1-24
35GouPuzR-8L
35GouPuzR-9L
36SandSW-5
90DodTar-111
91ConTSN-211

Cantwell, Rob
88SpoIndP-1924
89WatDiaP-1780
89WatDiaS-2

Cantz, Bart (Bartholomew L.)
87OldJudN-69

Canzeroni, Tony
28W513-97

Capel, Mike
84MidCubT-10
86PitCubP-3
87IowCubTI-4
88DonRoo-46
88IowCubC-1
88IowCubP-547
89Fle-643
89FleGlo-643
89IowCubC-1
89IowCubP-1706
89Top-767
89TopTif-767
90CMC-30
90DenZepC-5
90DenZepP-618
90ProAAAF-643
91LinDriAAA-605
91TucTorLD-605
91TucTorP-2206
92Fle-429
92Sco-687
92TexLon-7
92TucTorF-480
92TucTorS-604
93TucTorF-3052
94BreMilB-12

Capellan, Carlos
88KenTwiP-1396
89CalLeaA-6
89VisOakCLC-112
89VisOakP-1441
90CalLeaACLC-9
90VisOakCLC-71
90VisOakP-2159
91LinDriAA-477
91OrlSunRLD-477
91OrlSunRP-1854
93LimRocDWB-132

Capello, Pete
87AppFoxP-4
88VirGenS-4
89AppFoxP-865

Capilla, Doug
76TulOilGP-7
76VenLeaS-25
78OPC-11
78SSP270-127
78Top-477
80Top-628
81Don-587
81Fle-309
81Top-136
82Top-537
82WicAerTI-3
89PacSenL-172

Caple, Kyle
92KenTwiF-607

Caplinger, Roger
91HelBreSP-28

93HelBreSP-26
Capowski, Jim
78AshTouT-3
79TulDriT-4
Cappadona, Pete
86NewBriRSP-5
Cappuccio, Carmine
93SarWhiSC-6
93SarWhiSF-1382
93SouBenWSC-6
94PriWilCC-7
94PriWilCF-1933
95NasSouTI-5
96NasSouB-10
92UtiBluSC-5
Cappuzzello, George
77EvaTriT-5
78IndIndTI-15
79IndIndTI-16
81EvaTriT-2
82AstAstI-10
82Fle-264
82Top-137
82TucTorT-20
83Top-422
84ColCliP-4
84ColCliT-7
Capra, Buzz (Lee)
72OPC-141
72Top-141
75OPC-105
75OPC-311
75Top-105
75Top-311
76Hos-85
76OPC-153
76SSP-1
76Top-153
77Top-432
78Top-578
83AndBraT-6
86AppFoxP-5
87BurExpP-1087
88SpaPhiP-1047
88SpaPhiS-7
90SpaPhiB-26
90SpaPhiS-27
91MetWIZ-61
91SpaPhiC-29
91SpaPhiP-914
92SpaPhiC-24
92SpaPhiF-1281
93SpaPhiC-27
93SpaPhiF-1072
94SpaPhiF-1739
94SparPhiC-26
95PitMetTI-38
96PitMetB-2
Capra, Nick Lee
79TulDriT-20
80TulDriT-8
83OklCit8T-4
84OklCit8T-11
85OklCit8T-25
86BufBisP-7
87OklCit8P-23
88OmaRoyC-12
88OmaRoyP-1499
89Fle-279
89FleGlo-279
89OmaRoyC-19
89OmaRoyP-1742
90CMC-166
90OklCit8C-16
90OklCit8P-443
90ProAAAF-689
91LinDriAAA-307
91OklCit8LD-307
91OklCit8P-190
92NasSouF-1845
92NasSouS-280
93EdmTraF-1148
93RanKee-95
94EdmTraF-2884
95ChaKniTI-7
96BriWhiSB-1
Capriati, Jeff
91PacSenL-76
Caprillo, Matias
85MexCitTT-25
Capriotti, Jeff
96MemChiB-4
Captains, Shreveport
76ShrCapT-NNO
86ShrCapP-28
Capusano, Genaro
91Cla/Bes-161
Caraballo, Felix
88MadMusP-8
88ModA'sTI-5
90RenSilSCLC-281
Caraballo, Gary
90AppFoxBS-6
90AppFoxP-2100
91AppFoxC-15
91AppFoxP-1721
91Cla/Bes-211
91MidLeaAP-MWL2
92BasCitRC-19
92Bow-54
92UppDecML-289
93WilBluRC-5
93WilBluRF-2002
94MemChiF-363
95ForMyeMTI-3
96HarCitRCB-10
Caraballo, Ramon
85PhiTas-41
86PhiTas-xx
87ClePhiP-11
88ClePhiS-6
90Bes-260
90BurBraB-4
90BurBraP-2360
90BurBraS-8
90MidLeaASGS-27
90ProAaA-131
91Bow-584
91Cla/Bes-376
91DurBulC-24
91DurBulP-1551
92DonRooP-BC13
92GreBraS-231
92ProFS7-187
92RicBraBB-11
92SkyAA F-99
92UppDecML-210
93RicBraBB-2
93RicBraF-189
93RicBraP-12
93RicBraRC-2
93RicBraRC-8
93StaCluB-30
93Top-451
93TopGol-451
93TopInaM-451
93TopMic-451
94BraUSPC-10S
94Cla-133
94GreBraTI-8
94Pac-7
94Pin-260
94PinArtP-260
94PinMusC-260
94RicBraF-2851
94StaCluT-44
94StaCluTFDI-44
95LouRedF-280
97RicBraBC-13
Caraballo, Wilmer
85LynMetT-21
86LynMetP-5
87BirBarB-6
Carabba, Robbie
92AlbPolC-10
92AlbPolF-2313
Carabello, Nelson
89WelPirP-9
Caradonna, Brett
97Bow-425
97BowChr-285
97BowChrI-285
97BowChrIR-285
97BowChrR-285
97BowInt-425
97TopSta-117
97TopStaAM-117
Caranza, Pedro
93PocPosF-4213
Caravelli, Michael
96BreCouMB-9
Caray, Harry
88PeoChiTI-8
Carballo, Gary
92ClaFS7-176
Carballo, Jay
90EugEmeGS-4
Carballo, Lee
88SalLakCTTI-28
88VirGenS-5
Carbo, Bernie (Bernardo)
70DayDaiNM-50
70OPC-36
70Top-36
71CarTeal-7
71MLBOffS-51
71OPC-478
71Top-478
72OPC-463
72Top-463
73LinPor-166
73OPC-171
73Top-171
74OPC-621
74Top-621
75OPC-379
75Top-379
76OPC-278
76SSP-411
76Top-278
77Top-159
78SSP270-185
78Top-524
79Car5-3
79Top-38
80Top-266
89PacSenL-45
89T/MSenL-18
89TopSenL-13
90EliSenL-96
92UppDecS-14
94BreMilB-108
94TedWil-2
94TedWilM-M33
Carbonneau, Guy
91StaCluMO-39
Carbonnet, Mark
92ColRedF-2395
Carcione, Tom (Thomas)
88SouOreAP-1699
89MadMusS-6
89ModA'sC-19
90ModA'sC-4
90ModA'sCLC-167
90ModA'sP-2215
91HunStaC-6
91HunStaLD-281
91HunStaP-1799
91LinDriAA-281
92HunStaS-306
92ModA'sC-24
92ModA'sF-3902
Cardenal, Jose
65Top-374
66Top-505
66TopRubI-15
67CokCapDA-29
67OPC-193
67Top-193
67TopVen-203
68OPC-102
68Top-102
68TopVen-102
69MilBra-49
69MLBOffS-40
69Top-325
69TopSta-164
69TopSup-15
69TopTeaP-13
69TraSta-5
70CarTeal-3
70DayDaiNM-93
70DayDaiNM-125
70MLBOffS-136
70Top-675
71Kel-26
71MLBOffS-270
71OPC-435
71Top-435
72MilBra-62
72OPC-12
72Top-12
72Top-757
73LinPor-40
73OPC-393
73Top-393
74GreHeroBP-6
74OPC-185
74Top-185
74TopDecE-55
74TopSta-12
75Hos-65
75HosTwi-65
75Kel-29
75OPC-15
75Top-15
76CraDis-8
76Hos-37
76HosTwi-37
76OPC-430
76SSP-310
76Top-430
76VenLeaS-117
76VenLeaS-241
77BurCheD-197
77Hos-85
77MSADis-11
77OPC-127
77RCColC-13
77Top-610
77TopCloS-9
78Top-210
79PhiBurK-18
79Top-317
80Top-512
81Top-473
89PacLegI-149
89SweBasG-61
91MetWIZ-62
93RedKah-8
94BreMilB-109
Cardenas, Daniel
90YakBeaTI-10
91BakDodCLC-22
Cardenas, Epi
92WatIndC-14
92WatIndF-3240
93ColRedC-6
93ColRedF-602
93SouAtlLAGF-12
94KinIndC-3
94KinIndF-2650
Cardenas, Johnny
93BelMarC-7
93BelMarF-3212
94RivPilCLC-22
95PorCitRTI-3
96OklCit8B-5
96PorCitRB-8
Cardenas, Leo (Leonardo L.)
60Top-119
60TopVen-119
61Top-244
61TopStal-16
62Kah-4
62RedEnq-3
62RedJayP-2
62Top-381
63Jel-127
63Kah-5
63Pos-127
63RedEnq-4
63RedFreBC-2
63Top-203
64Kah-3
64RedJayP-1
64Top-72
64TopVen-72
65Kah-6
65RedEnq-3
65Top-437
66Kah-7
66Top-370
66TopVen-370
67CokCapR-2
67DexPre-42
67Kah-7
67OPCPapI-10
67Top-325
67TopPos-10
67TopTesF-4
67TopVen-310
68Kah-A5
68Kah-B11
68OPC-23
68Top-23
68Top-480
68TopVen-23
69MilBra-50
69Top-265
69TopTeaP-15
69TwiTealC-2
70DayDaiNM-119
70MLBOffS-231
70OPC-245
70Top-245
71MLBOffS-460
71OPC-405
71Top-405
71TopCoi-148
71TopTat-62
72Kel-30
72MilBra-63
72Top-561
72Top-562
73OPC-522
73Top-522
75OPC-518
75Top-518
76OPC-587
76SSP-261
76Top-587
78TCM60I-69
78TwiFri-27
83WisRapTF-15
86RedGreT-7
91UppDecS-9
93RanKee-96
Cardieri, Ron
82MiaMarT-9
Cardiff, Patsy
88KimN18-7
Cardin, Mark
95DavLipB-5
Cardinal, Randy (Conrad)
63Top-562
Cardinals, Orleans
88CapCodPB-22
Cardinals, St Louis
13FatT20-16
36R31Pre-G28
38BasTabP-33
46SpoExcW-11-3
51TopTea-8
56Top-134
57Top-243
58Top-216
59Top-223
60Top-242
60TopTat-62
61Top-347
61TopMagR-16
62GuyPotCP-18
62Top-61
62TopVen-61
63Top-524
64Top-87
64TopTatI-18
64TopVen-87
65OPC-57
65Top-57
66Top-379
66TopRubI-119
67OPC-173
67Top-173
68LauWorS-27
68LauWorS-39
68LauWorS-41
68Top-497
69FleCloS-20
69FleCloS-28
69TopStaA-20
70FleWorS-27
70FleWorS-31
70FleWorS-39
70FleWorS-40
70FleWorS-41
70FleWorS-64
70FleWorS-65
70Top-549
71FleWorS-32
71FleWorS-40
71FleWorS-41
71FleWorS-42
71FleWorS-62
71FleWorS-65
71FleWorS-66
71OPC-308
71Top-308
71TopTat-126
72Top-688
73OPC-219
73OPCBTC-23
73Top-219
73TopBluTC-23
74Car193T-31
74OPC-36
74OPCTC-23
74Top-36

74TopStaA-23
74TopTeaC-23
78Top-479
83FleSta-245
83FleSti-NNO
86FleWaxBC-C5
87CarSmo-NNO
87SpoTeaL-12
87Top-181
87TopTif-181
88FleSupBC-C6
88FleWaxBC-C1
88PanSti-478
88RedFolSB-116
90FleWaxBC-C18
90PubSti-633
90RedFolSB-118
90VenSti-535
94ImpProP-26
94Sco-658
94ScoGolR-658
95PanSti-141
96PanSti-77
Cardinals, St. Petersburg
89St.PetCS-29
Cardona, Al
89AncBucTI-2
Cardona, Isbel
91MedHatBJP-4090
91MedHatBJSP-11
94CliLumF-1972
94EveGiaC-2
94EveGiaF-3641
95LinVen-181
94CliLumC-6
Cardona, James
91WelPirC-6
91WelPirP-3585
Cardona, Javier
95FayGenTI-7
96FayGenB-9
Cardona, Jose
90ButCopKSP-9
91GasRanC-3
91GasRanP-2680
93LinVenB-10
94VenLinU-77
Cardona, Ruben
95NewJerCTI-5
Cardoz, Don
78RocRedWT-3
Cardwell, Buddy
77WauMetT-4
Cardwell, Don
57Top-374
58Top-372
59Top-314
60Top-384
61NuSco-410
61Pos-194A
61Pos-194B
61Top-393
61Top-564
62CubJayP-4
62Top-495
62TopBuc-14
62TopStal-106
63PirIDL-3
63Top-575
64PirKDK-6
64Top-417
65Top-502
66PirEasH-43
66Top-235
66TopVen-235
67CokCapYM-V23
67MetTeal-3
67Top-555
68Top-437
69MetNewYDN-3
69MilBra-51
69OPC-193
69Top-193
69TopFou-2
70OPC-83
70Top-83
72MilBra-64
78TCM60I-89
79DiaGre-374
89RinPosM1-6
90SweBasG-72
91MetWIZ-63
94Met69CCPP-9
94Met69CS-8
94Met69T-26
Cardwood, Alfredo
85OrlTwiT-15
86VisOakP-6
87WesPalBEP-655
Carew, Jeff
91GulCoaRSP-17
92ButCopKSP-3
93ButCopKSP-16
Carew, Rod (Rodney Cline)
67Top-569
68Baz-13
68DexPre-20
68OPC-80
68Top-80
68Top-363
68TopActS-7C
68TopGamI-29
68TopVen-80
68TopVen-363
69MilBra-52
69MLBOffS-65
69MLBPin-4
69OPCDec-3
69Top-419
69Top-510
69TopDec-12
69TopSta-192
69TopTeaP-15
69TwiTealC-3
70DayDaiNM-62
70Kel-47
70MilBra-4
70MLBOffS-232
70OPC-62
70OPC-290
70OPC-453
70Top-62
70Top-290
70Top-453
70TopPos-16
71MLBOffS-461
71OPC-210
71Top-210
71TopCoi-24
71TopTat-119
72EssCoi-2
72MilBra-65
72Top-695
72Top-696
73Kel2D-51
73LinPor-107
73OPC-61
73OPC-330
73Top-61
73Top-330
73TopCanL-9
74GreHeroBP-3
74GreHeroBP-5
74Kel-30
74OPC-50
74OPC-201
74OPC-333
74Top-50
74Top-201
74Top-333
74TopDecE-32
74TopSta-203
75Hos-56
75Kel-33
75OPC-306
75OPC-600
75SSP42-32
75SSPPuzB-5
75Top-306
75Top-600
76CraDis-9
76Hos-33
76HosTwi-33
76Kel-48
76OPC-192
76OPC-400
76SSP-214
76Top-192
76Top-400
77BurCheD-51
77Hos-9
77Kel-53
77MSADis-12
77OPC-143
77PepGloD-2
77RCColC-14
77Spo-1007
77Spo-3101
77Top-120
77TopCloS-10
78Hos-140
78Kel-29
78OPC-1
78OPC-230
78PapGinD-35
78Pep-30
78RCColC-48
78TasDis-8
78Top-201
78Top-580
78TwiFriP-3
78WifBalD-13
79Hos-38
79Kel-13
79OPC-151
79Top-1
79Top-300
79TopCom-11
80BurKinPHR-14
80Kel-60
80OPC-353
80PerHaloFP-207
80Top-700
80TopSup-12
81AllGamPI-3
81Don-49
81Don-169
81Don-537
81Dra-2
81Fle-268
81FleStiC-40
81Kel-26
81LonBeaPT-1
81MSAMinD-6
81OPC-100
81PerAll-11
81PerCreC-22
81Squ-9
81Top-100
81TopScr-18
81TopSti-49
81TopSupHT-57
81TopSupN-4
82Don-8
82Don-216
82Dra-6
82FBIDis-2
82Fle-455
82FleSta-217
82K-M-31
82Kel-51
82OPC-36
82OPC-187
82OPC-363
82PerCreC-21
82PerCreCG-21
82Top-276
82Top-500
82Top-501
82Top-547
82TopSti-131
82TopSti-160
83AllGamPI-2
83Don-90
83DonActA-38
83Dra-3
83Fle-81
83FleSta-29
83FleSti-26
83Kel-1
83Oco& SSBG-6
83OPC-200
83OPC-201
83OPC-386
83PerAll-7
83PerAllG-2
83PerCreC-20
83PerCreCG-20
83SevCoi-1
83Top-200
83Top-201
83Top-386
83Top-651
83TopFol-3
83TopFol-5
83TopGloS-29
83TopSti-39
84AllGamPI-91
84AngSmo-5
84Don-352
84DonCha-21
84Dra-5
84Fle-511
84Fle-629
84FleSti-12
84FleSti-54
84FleSti-103
84FunFooP-35
84MilBra-3
84Nes792-276
84Nes792-600
84Nes792-710
84Nes792-711
84OCoandSI-15
84OCoandSI-73
84OPC-26
84RalPur-17
84SevCoi-W8
84Top-276
84Top-600
84Top-710
84Top-711
84TopCer-17
84TopGaloC-2
84TopGloA-2
84TopGloS-26
84TopRubD-9
84TopSti-227
84TopStiB-11
84TopTif-276
84TopTif-600
84TopTif-710
84TopTif-711
85AllGamPI-2
85AngSmo-5
85AngStrH-4
85Don-85
85DonHig-31
85Fle-297
85FleLimE-5
85Lea-132
85OPC-300
85SevCoi-W6
85ThoMcAD-7
85Top-300
85TopGloA-13
85TopRubD-5
85TopSti-184
85TopSti-223
85TopTif-300
86AngGreT-1
86Don-280
86Fle-151
86Fle-629
86FleFutHoF-4
86FleLeaL-4
86FleStiC-20
86OPC-371
86SevCoi-W10
86Spo-69
86Spo-74
86Spo-106
86Spo-146
86Spo-180
86Spo-182
86Top-400
86TopGloS-16
86TopSti-4
86TopSti-176
86TopTif-400
86TwiGreT-2
86Woo-6
87K-M-14
87NesDreT-12
88GreBasS-48
88HouSho-7
89AngSmo-10
89TopBasT-25
90AGFA-7
90PacLeg-17
90PerGreM-77
90SweBasG-4
91Bow-1
91Bow-2
91Bow-3
91Bow-4
91Bow-5
91KelLey-2
91SweBasG-103
91TopRut-8
92KelAll-4
92MDAMVP-11
92Pin-584
93ActPacA-128
93ActPacA2-62G
93AngMot-28
93AngPol-4
93MetIma-7
93PacRya2S-242
93Yoo-4
94AngMot-28
94CarLeaA-DJ34
94TedWil-47
94TopSpa-L4
95AngMot-28
95JimDeaAG-1
96AngMot-28
97SpoIllCC-4
97St.VinHHS-5
Carey, Andy (Andrew Arthur)
47StaPinP2-9
53Top-188
54NewYorJA-43
54Top-105
55Top-20
55TopDouH-35
56Top-12
57Top-290
58Top-333
59Top-45
59TopVen-45
60Top-196
60TopVen-196
60YanJayP-2
61A'sTeal-2
61Top-518
61TopStal-158
62Jel-52
62Pos-52
62PosCan-52
62SalPlaC-86A
62SalPlaC-86B
62ShiPlaC-86
62Top-418
79DiaGre-22
79TCM50-243
90DodTar-112
91TopArc1-188
92YanWIZ6-21
94TopArc1-105
94TopArc1G-105
Carey, Brooks M.
80ChaO'sP-3
80ChaO'sW-3
81RocRedWT-3
81RocRedWW-22
82IndIndTI-9
Carey, Frank
90Bes-67
90CliGiaB-4
90CliGiaP-2555
90MidLeaASGS-28
91LinDriAA-301
91ShrCapLD-301
91ShrCapP-1826
Carey, Jeff
82WesHavAT-3
Carey, Max George
10CouT21-8
12T207-26
14B18B-75A
14B18B-75B
14CraJacE-73
15CraJacE-73
15SpoNewM-26
16BF2FP-92
16ColE13-25
16SpoNewM-28
17HolBreD-12
19W514-22
20NatCarE-12
21E121So1-8
21E121So8-9A
21E121So8-9B
21Exh-21
21Nei-71
21OxfConE-3
22AmeCarE-9
22E120-214
22W573-16
22W575-16
22WilPatV-28
23W501-86
23W503-53
23WilChoV-16
25Exh-50
26Exh-50
26SpoComoA-8
27AmeCarE-32

27YorCarE-32
28Exh-6
28W502-32
28Yue-32
40PlaBal-178
61Fle-12
72LauGreF-9
76RowExh-11
76ShaPiz-85
77GalGloG-103
77GalGloG-214
80LauFamF-12
80PerHaloFP-85
80SSPHOF-85
89DodSmoG-5
89HOFStiB-38
90BasWit-88
90DodTar-113
90PerGreM-50
91ConTSN-24
93ConTSN-797
94ConTSN-1232
94ConTSNB-1232
Carey, P.J.
87BelMarL-28
89BelMarL-30
91BilMusP-3770
91BilMusSP-28
92ChaWheF-23
92ChaWVWC-23
93CenValRF-2909
93SouAtlLAPI-4
94NewHavRF-1566
96AshTouB-2
96MauStiHWB-32
Carey, Paul
90MiaMirIS-3
91Cla/Bes-190
91HagSunLD-228
91HagSunP-2466
91LinDriAA-228
92ClaFS7-392
92FreKeyC-1
92RocRedWF-1949
93ClaFS7-65
93FleFinE-158
93RocRedWF-246
94Don-465
94OriPro-16
94OriUSPC-3C
94Pac-28
94Pin-403
94PinArtP-403
94PinMusC-403
94RocRedWTI-5
94StaCluT-275
94StaCluTFDI-275
94Top-4
94TopGol-4
94TopSpa-4
95RocRedWTI-9
94FreKeyC-5
Carey, Pete
86Ft.MyeRP-5
87TamTarP-2
Carey, Scoops (George C.)
03BreE10-14
09T206-480
Carey, Tim
93LynRedSC-5
93LynRedSF-2518
Carey, Todd
92ElmPioC-9
92ElmPioF-1388
93ForLauRSC-5
93ForLauRSFP-1602
94LynRedSC-5
94LynRedSF-1897
95TreThuTI-28
96TreThuB-21
Carey, Tom (Thomas Francis)
34BatR31-89
35DiaMatCS2-3
35DiaMatCS3T1-25
35DiaMatCS3T1-28
36DiaMatCS4-1
39PlaBal-62
40PlaBal-39
42RedSoxTI-4
93ConTSN-698
Carger, Ed
08AmeCarE-69
Caribaldo, Chris
89AppFoxP-862
Caridad, Rolando
90UtiBluSP-16
91SouBenWSC-15
91SouBenWSP-2851
92SarWhiSCB-11
92SarWhiSF-199
94VenLinU-142
Caridad, Ron
90HigSchPLS-11
91EliTwiP-4293
92EliTwiC-21
92EliTwiF-3672
93ForWayWC-4
93ForWayWF-1959
94ForMyeMC-4
94ForMyeMF-1159
94VenLinU-145
Cariel, Rafael
76ShrCapT-20
76VenLeaS-150
Carillo, Matias
94ScoRoo-RT138
Carisen, Robert
91MadMusC-25
Carista, Mike
85ElmPioT-3
86WinHavRSP-5
87GreHorP-5
88EasLeaAP-20
88NewBriRSP-909
89NewBriRSP-605
90NewBriRSB-12
90NewBriRSP-1311
90NewBriRSS-2
Carl, Jeff
83MemChiT-5
Carl, Todd
94BreCouMC-3
94ElmPioF-3465
95BreCouMF-238
96DayCubB-7
94ElmPioC-3
Carlesen, Donald
49W725AngTI-6
Carleton, Tex (James)
34DiaMatCSB-25
34ButPreR-7
34Gou-48
34GouCanV-90
34TarThoBD-5
35DiaMatCS3T1-26
35GouPuzR-1A
35GouPuzR-2A
35GouPuzR-16A
35GouPuzR-17A
36DiaMatCS3T2-2
40DodTeal-2
74Car193T-1
87Car193T-8
90DodTar-114
92ConTSN-378
Carley, David
86AriWilP-1
87BelBreP-19
Carlin, Mike
89SpaPhiP-1035
89SpaPhiS-3
Carlisle, Matthew
86NegLeaF-85
Carlos, Cisco
68Top-287
68TopVen-287
69OPC-54
69Top-54
70OPC-487
70Top-487
72MilBra-66
Carlos, Gil
84IowCubT-20
Carlsen, Robert
91MadMusP-2137
92ChaWheF-14
Carlson, Bill
87CliGiaP-11
87PocGiaTB-13
88CliGiaP-700
89SanJosGB-9
89SanJosGCLC-229
89SanJosGP-439
89SanJosGS-4
90SalSpuCLC-131
90SalSpuP-2730
91SalSpuC-30
91SalSpuP-2250
Carlson, Bob
91EliTwiP-4294
92KenTwiC-21
92ProFS7-103
Carlson, Brad
80WisRapTT-21
Carlson, Dan
90EveGiaB-3
90EveGiaP-3119
91CliGiaC-1
91CliGiaP-826
92ClaFS7-183
92ShrCapF-3864
92ShrCapS-577
92SkyAA F-254
93ClaFS7-45
93ExcFS7-113
93PhoFirF-1509
93StaCluG-26
94Bow-331
94PhoFirF-1513
95PhoFirTI-19
95Top-658
96PhoFirB-12
97Fle-654
97FleTif-654
Carlson, Garret
96BriWhiSB-12
Carlson, Hal
23WilChoV-17
28W513-75
29PorandAR-10
94ConTSN-1116
94ConTSNB-1116
Carlson, Lynn
90WelPirP-19
91AugPirC-3
91AugPirP-796
Carlson, Tom
76CliPilT-7
Carlton, Andy
90St.CatBJP-3476
91MyrBeaHC-17
91MyrBeaHP-2951
Carlton, Scott
91SpaPhiC-1
91SpaPhiP-886
Carlton, Steve
65CarTeal-6
65Top-477
67OPC-146
67Top-146
68Top-408
69Top-255
70MLBOffS-137
70OPC-67
70OPC-220
70Top-67
70Top-220
71CarTeal-8
71CarTeal-9
71MLBOffS-271
71OPC-55
71Top-55
71TopCoi-115
72Dia-56
72MilBra-67
72OPC-93
72OPC-420
72Top-93
72Top-420
72Top-751
73Kel2D-7
73LinPor-144
73OPC-65
73OPC-66
73OPC-67
73OPC-300
73Top-65
73Top-66
73Top-67
73Top-300
73TopCanL-10
73TopCom-4
73TopPin-4
74OPC-95
74PhiJohP-32
74Top-95
74TopDecE-5
74TopSta-73
75Hos-63
75OPC-185
75OPC-312
75Top-185
75Top-312
76CraDis-10
76OPC-355
76SSP-459
76Top-355
77BurCheD-171
77Hos-117
77Kel-57
77MSADis-13
77OPC-93
77Spo-2702
77Top-110
77TopCloS-11
78Hos-49
78Kel-1
78OPC-5
78OPC-170
78PhiSSP-29
78RCColC-71
78SSP270-29
78Top-205
78Top-540
78WifBalD-14
79Hos-71
79Kel-18
79OPC-9
79PhiBurK-4
79Top-25
80BurKinPHR-2
80Kel-14
80OPC-113
80PerHaloFP-217
80PhiBurK-15
80Top-210
81AllGamPI-167
81CokTeaS-99
81Don-33
81Don-481
81Fle-6
81Fle-6B
81Fle-6C
81Fle-660
81Fle-660B
81FleStiC-85
81Kel-50
81MSAMinD-7
81OPC-203
81PerCreC-16
81Top-5
81Top-6
81Top-202
81Top-630
81TopScr-104
81TopSti-25
81TopSti-28
81TopSti-29
81TopSti-206
81TopSti-261
81TopSupHT-81
82Don-42
82FBIDis-3
82Fle-243
82Fle-632
82Fle-641
82FleSta-54
82FleSta-240
82FleSta-241
82Kel-27
82OPC-68
82OPC-122
82PerCreC-10
82PerCreCG-10
82Top-1
82Top-480
82Top-481
82Top-636
82TopSti-75
82TopSti-129
83AllGamPI-165
83Don-16
83Don-219
83DonActA-24
83Fle-155
83FleSta-30
83FleSti-176
83Kel-45
83KelCerB-12
83OPC-70
83OPC-71
83OPC-384
83PerCreC-2
83PerCreCG-2
83PhiPosGM-9
83PhiPosGPaM-2
83PhiTas-4
83Top-70
83Top-71
83Top-229
83Top-406
83Top-705
83Top-706
83TopFol-1
83TopGloS-36
83TopLeaS-5
83TopSti-176
83TopSti-203
83TopSti-204
83TopSti-267
83TopTraBP-1
84Don-111
84DonActAS-24
84DonCha-38
84Fle-25
84Fle-642
84FleSti-78
84FleSti-101
84FunFooP-30
84MilBra-4
84Nes792-1
84Nes792-4
84Nes792-136
84Nes792-395
84Nes792-706
84Nes792-707
84Nes792-708
84Nes792-780
84NesDreT-21
84OCoandSI-18
84OPC-214
84OPC-395
84PhiTas-5
84PhiTas-17
84RalPur-16
84SevCoi-E12
84StaCar-1
84StaCar-2
84StaCar-3
84StaCar-4
84StaCar-5
84StaCar-6
84StaCar-7
84StaCar-8
84StaCar-9
84StaCar-10
84StaCar-11
84StaCar-12
84StaCar-13
84StaCar-14
84StaCar-15
84StaCar-16
84StaCar-17
84StaCar-18
84StaCar-19
84StaCar-20
84StaCar-21
84StaCar-22
84StaCar-23
84StaCar-24
84Top-1
84Top-4
84Top-136
84Top-395
84Top-706
84Top-707
84Top-708
84Top-780
84TopCer-16
84TopGaloC-3
84TopGloS-27
84TopRubD-10
84TopSti-1
84TopSti-2
84TopSti-15
84TopSti-119
84TopSti-184
84TopSup-16
84TopTif-1
84TopTif-4
84TopTif-136
84TopTif-395
84TopTif-706
84TopTif-707
84TopTif-708
84TopTif-780
85Don-305
85DonActA-55
85Dra-35

85Fle-246
85FleLimE-6
85KASDis-1
85KitCloD-1
85Lea-113
85OPC-360
85PhiCIG-12
85PhiTas-9
85PhiTas-14
85SevCoi-E3
85SevCoi-S2
85ThoMcAD-25
85Top-360
85Top3-D-25
85TopMin-360
85TopRubD-10
85TopSti-112
85TopSup-24
85TopTif-360
85Woo-6
86BurKinA-6
86Don-183
86DonHig-35
86Fle-435
86FleFutHoF-2
86FleMin-91
86FleSluBC-M2
86FleStiC-21
86Lea-117
86MeaGolM-3
86OPC-120
86PhiKel-1
86PhiTas-32
86SevCoi-C8
86SevCoi-E8
86SevCoi-S8
86SovCoi-W8
86Spo-27
86Spo-70
86SpoDecG-54
86Top-120
86Top-246
86TopSti-116
86TopTat-3
86TopTif-120
86TopTif-246
87Don-617
87Fle-490
87Fle-635
87FleExcS-8
87FleGlo-490
87FleGlo-635
87FleUpd-17
87FleUpdG-17
87K-M-15
87OPC-271
87OPCBoxB-B
87Spo-200
87Top-718
87TopTif-718
87TopTra-19T
87TopTraT-19T
87TopWaxBC-B
87Woo-1
88Fle-7
88FleGlo-7
89SweBasG-95
89TopBasT-37
90AGFA-15
90BasWit-43
90HOFStiB-78
90PacLeg-16
90PhiTas-30
90SweBasG-110
91Kel3D-8
91KelStaU-5
91LinDri-9
91MDAA-1
91SweBasG-17
92MVP-13
92MVP2H-7
92UppDecS-24
93TedWil-72
94Met69T-53
94UppDecAH-70
94UppDecAH-124
94UppDecAH-155
94UppDecAH1-70
94UppDecAH1-124
94UppDecAH1-155
94Yoo-4
96FanCar-1
96FanCar-2
96FanCar-3
96FanCar-4
96FanCar-5
96PinFan-31

Carlucci, Dave
86BakDodP-5

Carlucci, Rich
81WatRedT-1
82IndIndTI-19
83IndIndTI-16
84RocRedWT-2
86SyrChiP-6

Carlucci, Tony
83TriTriT-14

Carlyle, Kenny
92FayGenF-2161
92FroRowDP-6
93Bow-151
93ClaFS7-162
93ClaGolF-207
93LonTigF-2299
93StaCluM-116
94TreThuF-2113
95TolMudHTI-9
96JacSunB-6

Carman, Don
80PenPilBT-11
80PenPilCT-5
81ReaPhiT-8
82OklCit8T-24
83ReaPhiT-3
84PhiTas-41
84PorBeaC-204
85FleUpd-20
85PhiTas-9
85PhiTas-15
85TopTifT-16T
85TopTra-16T
86Don-427
86Fle-436
86FleStiC-22
86Lea-200
86PhiCIG-2
86PhiTas-42
86Top-532
86TopTif-532
87Don-432
87Fle-171
87FleGlo-171
87Lea-174
87OPC-355
87PhiTas-42
87Spo-108
87SpoTeaP-6
87Top-355
87TopSti-122
87TopTif-355
88Don-385
88DonBasB-72
88Fle-300
88FleGlo-300
88PhiTas-6
88Sco-401
88ScoGlo-401
88StaLinPh-5
88Top-415
88TopTif-415
89Bow-392
89BowTif-392
89Don-396
89Fle-564
89FleGlo-564
89OPC-154
89PanSti-146
89PhiTas-3
89Sco-222
89Top-154
89TopSti-121
89TopTif-154
89UppDec-409
90Don-604
90Fle-552
90FleCan-552
90OPC-731
90PhiTas-4
90PubSti-233
90Top-731
90TopTif-731
90UppDec-420
90VenSti-95
91Don-377
91Fle-390
91OPC-282
91RedKah-36
91Sco-237
91Top-282
91TopDesS-282
91TopMic-282
91TopTif-282
91UppDec-288
92OklCit8F-1910
92TulDriF-2689
92TulDriS-616
93RanKee-97
94ScrRedBF-915

Carmel, Duke (Leon James)
60Top-120
60TopVen-120
61UniOil-P5
63Top-544
64MetJayP-2
64Top-44
64TopCoi-81
64TopVen-44
65ChaTheY-4
65OPC-261
65Top-261
76Met63 S-2
91MetWIZ-64
92YanWIZ6-22

Carmichael, Al
85LynMetT-15
86LynMetP-6
87JacMetF-12

Carmody, Kevin
89BelBreIS-2
89BelBreIS-5
90StoPorB-20
90StoPorCLC-181
90StoPorP-2181

Carmona, Cesarin
96CliLumKTI-6

Carmona, Greg
89St.PetCS-5
90ArkTraGS-7
90TopTVCa-40
91ArkTraLD-28
91ArkTraP-1291
91Bow-392
91LinDriAA-28
91LouRedP-2920
91LouRedTI-21
92LouRedF-1892
92LouRedS-255
93LimRocDWB-74
93StoPorC-4

Carmona, Rafael
93BelMarC-8
93BelMarF-3198
94RivPilCLC-17
95MarMot-19
95MarPac-26
96Bow-258
96MarMot-14
97Pac-183
97PacLigB-183
97PacSil-183

Carmona, William
89MarPhiS-4
90MarPhiP-3181
91PocPioP-3795
91PocPioSP-27
92MarPhiC-21
92MarPhiF-3068
93SpaPhiC-10
94PriRedC-6
94PriRedF-3255

Carmuso, Mike
72CedRapCT-11

Carnelius, Brian
92LonTigS-403

Carnera, Primo
47HomBon-7

Carnes, Scott
77QuaCitAT-8
80ElPasDT-3
81SalLakCGT-17
82SpoIndT-15

Carnett, Eddie (Edwin E.)
43CenFlo-3
77TCMTheWY-63

Carnevale, Anthony
89AncGlaP-5

Carnevale, Dan
70RoyTeal-8

Carney, Jack (John Joseph)
87AllandGN-11
87OldJudN-70

Carney, Pat (Patrick J.)
11SpoLifCW-54

Carney, Ron
78AshTouT-4
79TulDriT-18
80AshTouT-14
81TulDriT-10

Caro, Joe
91BoiHawP-3900

Caro, Jorge
91BriTigC-2
91BriTigP-3611

Caroland, Kevin
89TenTecGE-6

Carone, Rick
94HicCraC-7
94HicCraF-2180
96PriWilCB-30

Carosielli, Marc
88WytCubP-1999

Carothers, Ron
91WavRedF-12
95AusFut-5
95AusFut-86

Carpenter, Brian
93ClaFS7-129
93GreFalDSP-27
93SavCarC-7
93SavCarF-679
94BakDodC-6
94St.PetCC-8
94St.PetCF-2578
96ArkTraB-7

Carpenter, Bubba
90ArkRaz-4
92AlbYanF-2237
92AlbYanS-5
93AlbYanF-2167
94AbaYanF-1452
95ColCliMCTI-23
95ColCliP-3
95ColCliTI-3
96ColCliB-4

Carpenter, Chris
94MedHatBJF-3673
94MedHatBJSP-13
95Bes-49
95Bow-83
95BowBes-B74
95BowBesR-B74
95DunBluJTI-4
95Exc-135
95UppDecML-133
96Bow-185
96BowBes-129
96BowBesAR-129
96BowBesR-129
96KnoSmoB-8
97BluJayS-60
97Bow-158
97BowBes-184
97BowBesAR-184
97BowBesR-184
97BowChr-156
97BowChrI-156
97BowChrIR-156
97BowChrR-156
97BowInt-158
97Lea-329
97LeaFraM-329
97LeaFraMDC-329
95UppDecMLFS-133

Carpenter, Cris
87PanAmTURB-19
88DonRoo-50
88LouRedBC-8
88LouRedBP-428
88LouRedBTI-13
89ClaTraP-185
89Don-39
89DonRoo-40
89FleUpd-117
89LouRedBTI-13
89ScoRoo-81T
89ScoYouS2-37
89Top-282
89TopBig-307
89TopTif-282
89UppDec-8
90CMC-103
90Don-634
90Fle-243
90FleCan-243
90Hot50RS-10
90LouRedBC-3
90LouRedBLBC-10
90LouRedBP-395
90OPC-443
90ProAAAF-509
90PubSti-212
90Sco100RS-74
90Top-443
90TopTif-443
90TopTVCa-7
90UppDec-523
90VenSti-96
91Fle-628
91Lea-507
91OPC-518
91StaClu-499
91Top-518
91TopDesS-518
91TopMic-518
91TopTif-518
91UltUpd-105
92CarPol-2
92Don-79
92Fle-575
92OPC-147
92Sco-160
92StaClu-429
92Top-147
92TopGol-147
92TopGolW-147
92TopMic-147
92Ult-563
92UppDec-686
93Don-734
93Fle-420
93FleFinE-55
93MarUSPC-3C
93MarUSPC-13D
93PacSpa-456
93Pin-562
93RanKee-400
93Sco-633
93StaClu-706
93StaCluFDI-706
93StaCluMarI-11
93StaCluMOP-706
93Top-629
93TopGol-629
93TopInaM-629
93TopMic-629
93Ult-369
93UppDec-726
93UppDecGold-726
94ColC-73
94ColChoGS-73
94ColChoSS-73
94FleUpd-89
94Lea-261
94RanMagM-3
94StaClu-239
94StaCluFDI-239
94StaCluGR-239
94StaCluMOP-239
94StaCluT-259
94StaCluTFDI-259
94Top-317
94TopGol-317
94TopSpa-317
95Don-493
95DonPreP-493
95Fle-282
95LouRedF-271
95Pac-422
95Top-99
95Ult-107
95UltGolM-107
96LeaSigEA-24
87PanAmTUBI-34A
87PanAmTUBI-34B

Carpenter, Danny
87WytCubP-22

Carpenter, Doug
84GreHorT-9
85AlbYanT-20
86Ft.LauYP-3
87MiaMarP-7
89RenSilSCLC-254
90LakTigS-27
91LakTigC-10
91LakTigP-284

Carpenter, Glenn
83DayBeaAT-18
86TucTorP-4

87TucTorP-2
88TucTorC-12
88TucTorJP-5
88TucTorP-173
Carpenter, Hick (Warren W.)
87OldJudN-71
89EdgR.WG-4
Carpenter, Jay
90ArkRaz-5
Carpenter, Jerry
94BoiHawC-5
94BoiHawF-3357
Carpenter, John
45CenFlo-3
Carpenter, Kevin
90JohCitCS-6
Carpenter, Matt
91MisStaB-10
92MisStaB-7
93MisStaB-7
95WatIndTI-7
97BenRocC-2
Carpenter, Mike
85RedWinA-25
86RedWinA-12
Carpenter, Paul
44CenFlo-2
47CenFlo-3
Carpenter, Rob
90KinMetB-10
90KinMetS-4
91ColMetPI-26
Carpenter, Terry
91FreStaLBS-1
Carpentier, Boxer (Georges)
28W512-47
Carpentier, Edouard
72Dia-115
Carpentier, Georges
52LaPat-2
52LavPro-54
Carpentier, Mike
95YakBeaTI-3
96SanBerSB-6
96VerBeaDB-9
Carpentier, Rob
91ColMetPPI-1
92St.LucMCB-12
92St.LucMF-1737
93St.LucMC-4
93StLucMF-2912
Carper, Mark
88CapCodPPaLP-172
91FreKeyC-1
91FreKeyP-2355
92AlbYanF-2218
92HagSunS-256
93AlbYanF-2154
94ColCliF-2941
94ColCliP-2
95ColCliMCTI-7
95ColCliP-4
95ColCliTI-4
96ColCliB-5
Carpin, Frank
66OPC-71
66Top-71
66TopVen-71
Carpine, Bill
91CliGiaC-16
92CliGiaC-29
95PhoFirTI-NNO
96PhoFirB-5
Carpio, Jorge
82QuaCitCT-5
84MidCubT-6
Carr, Bobby
92GulCoaMF-3471
93KinMetC-4
93KinMetF-3788
Carr, Charlie (Charles Carbitt)
03BreE10-15
05IndSouPSoCP-6
09ColChiE-46A
09ColChiE-46B
09ColChiE-46C
09T206-405
11SpoLifCW-55
12ColRedB-46A
12ColRedB-46B
12ColRedB-46C
12ColTinT-46A
12ColTinT-46B
12ColTinT-46C
Carr, Chuck
84Top-244
87BelMarTI-9
88MidLeaAGS-56
88WauTimGS-8
89JacMetGS-2
89TexLeaAGS-28
90FleUpd-34
90JacMetGS-24
91Fle-141
91MetColP-25
91MetWIZ-65
91TidTidP-2521
91TopDeb90-26
91UppDec-514
92ArkTraS-29
92LouRedF-1899
92Sco-857
92SkyAA F-13
92SpoIllFK1-266
93Bow-474
93Don-124
93Don-762
93Fla-48
93Fle-421
93FleFinE-56
93Lea-541
93MarPub-7
93MarUSPC-6H
93MarUSPC-12D
93PacSpa-457
93Pin-618
93Sco-545
93SelRoo-37T
93SP-137
93StaClu-564
93StaCluFDI-564
93StaCluMarI-25
93StaCluMOP-564
93Top-722
93TopGol-722
93TopInaM-722
93TopMic-722
93Ult-370
93UppDec-590
93UppDecGold-590
94Bow-66
94BowBes-R66
94BowBesR-R66
94ColC-404
94ColChoGS-404
94ColChoSS-404
94Don-509
94ExtBas-258
94ExtBasSYS-3
94Fin-8
94FinJum-8
94FinRef-8
94Fla-380
94Fle-463
94FleLeaL-10
94FleRooS-4
94FUnPac-87
94FUnPac-198
94Lea-408
94LeaL-105
94OPC-220
94Pac-237
94PanSti-180
94Pin-195
94PinArtP-195
94PinMusC-195
94Sco-512
94ScoBoyoS-31
94ScoGolR-512
94Sel-11
94SP-108
94SPDieC-108
94StaClu-29
94StaCluFDI-29
94StaCluGR-29
94StaCluMO-25
94StaCluMOP-29
94StaCluT-84
94StaCluTFDI-84
94Stu-107
94Top-653
94TopGol-653
94TopSpa-653
94TriPla-133
94Ult-194
94UltLeaL-8
94UltSecYS-6
94UppDec-202
94UppDecED-202
94USPlaCA-13H
94USPlaCR-1D
95Baz-69
95Bow-294
95ColCho-299
95ColChoGS-299
95ColChoSE-133
95ColChoSEGS-133
95ColChoSESS-133
95ColChoSS-299
95D3-52
95Don-192
95DonPreP-192
95DonTopotO-239
95Emb-16
95EmbGolI-16
95Fin-70
95FinRef-70
95Fla-351
95Fle-328
95Lea-213
95Pac-169
95Pin-30
95PinArtP-30
95PinMusC-30
95Sco-224
95ScoGolR-224
95ScoPlaTS-224
95ScoSam-224
95StaClu-357
95StaClu-409
95StaCluMOP-357
95StaCluMOP-409
95StaCluMOP-SS4
95StaCluSS-SS4
95StaCluSTWS-357
95StaCluSTWS-409
95StaCluVR-187
95Stu-72
95Top-96
95TopCyb-63
95TopLeaL-LL20
95Ult-161
95UltGolM-161
95UppDec-352
95UppDecED-352
95UppDecEDG-352
95UppDecSE-116
95UppDecSEG-116
95USPlaCMLA-7H
96ColCho-593
96ColChoGS-593
96ColChoSS-593
96Don-236
96DonPreP-236
96EmoXL-72
96Fla-98
96Fle-142
96FleTif-142
96FleUpd-U45
96FleUpdTC-U45
96LeaSigEA-25
96Pac-70
96Sco-118
95StaCluVRMC-187
96Ult-362
96UltGolM-362
97Pac-115
97PacLigB-115
97PacSil-115
97Sco-436
97ScoHobR-436
97ScoResC-436
97ScoShoS-436
97ScoShoSAP-436
97Ult-427
97UltGolME-427
97UltPlaME-427
Carr, Ernie
88GreFalDTI-4
89BakDodCLC-200
90SanAntMGS-9
Carr, Jeff
96WisTimRB-4
Carr, Jeremy
93EugEmeC-9
93EugEmeF-3860
94RocRoyC-6
94RocRoyF-571
95BakBlaTI-6
96HonShaHWB-11
96TexLeaAB-22
96WicWraB-6
Carr, Taylor
95FayGenTI-30
Carr, Terence
86SalAngC-95
87QuaCitAP-1
88QuaCitAGS-9
89RenSilSCLC-255
90PalSprACLC-203
90PalSprAP-2589
Carrano, Rick
86MiaMarP-4
Carranza, Javier
83St.PetCT-2
Carranza, Pedro
94AshTouC-3
94AshTouF-1787
95AshTouTI-23
Carrara, Giovanni
91St.CatBJC-13
91St.CatBJP-3387
92DunBluJC-17
92MyrBeaHC-25
92ProFS7-175
93DunBluJC-5
93DunBluJF-1787
93DunBluJFFN-5
93LinVenB-21
93SouAtlLAPI-5
94KnoSmoF-1295
94VenLinU-124
95LinVen-186
95SyrChiTI-9
96FleUpd-U94
96FleUpdTC-U94
96SyrChiTI-8
96Ult-426
96UltGolM-426
Carrasco, Carlos
88BakDodCLC-251
89RenSilSCLC-243
90SalSpuCLC-127
90SalSpuP-2718
91SalSpuC-23
91SalSpuP-2235
Carrasco, Claudio
86WatIndP-5
87WatIndP-26
88WilBilP-1320
89QuaCitAB-23
89QuaCitAGS-29
89RenSilSCLC-259
Carrasco, Ernie
83EriCarT-22
84SavCarT-15
86ArkTraP-3
Carrasco, Hector
89KinMetS-4
90KinMetB-16
90KinMetS-5
91PitMetC-21
91PitMetP-3415
92AshTouC-24
93Bow-262
93ClaFS7-97
93KanCouCC-2
93KanCouCF-907
94Bow-130
94BowBes-R89
94BowBesR-R89
94ExtBas-230
94ExtBasRS-3
94Fin-316
94FinRef-316
94Fla-145
94FleUpd-116
94LeaGolR-20
94LeaLimR-8
94RedKah-6
94ScoRoo-RT80
94ScoRooGR-RT80
94Sel-385
94SpoRoo-128
94SpoRooAP-128
94StaClu-552
94StaClu-634
94StaCluFDI-552
94StaCluFDI-634
94StaCluGR-552
94StaCluGR-634
94StaCluMOP-552
94StaCluMOP-634
94TopTra-91T
94Ult-470
94UppDec-511
94UppDecED-511
95Don-101
95DonPreP-101
95DonTopotO-211
95Fin-28
95FinRef-28
95Fla-337
95Fle-432
95FleRooS-3
95KanCouCLTI-2
95Lea-306
95Pac-102
95PacLatD-7
95Pin-26
95PinArtP-26
95PinMusC-26
95RedKah-6
95Sco-13
95ScoGolR-13
95ScoPlaTS-13
95StaClu-392
95StaCluMOP-392
95StaCluSTDW-RE392
95StaCluSTWS-392
95Top-447
95TopCyb-243
95Ult-143
95UltGolM-143
95UppDec-166
95UppDecED-166
95UppDecEDG-166
96Don-112
96DonPreP-112
96Fle-338
96FleTif-338
96IndIndB-7
96Pac-34
93KanCouCTI-1
97Pac-266
97PacLigB-266
97PacSil-266
Carrasco, Jose
94BoiHawC-6
94BoiHawF-3345
Carrasco, Norman
82DanSunF-28
83RedPioT-5
85EdmTraC-22
86EdmTraP-2
87EdmTraP-2079
88MidAngGS-25
89TolMudHC-20
89TolMudHP-768
Carrasco, Troy
93EliTwiC-7
93EliTwiF-3409
94ForWayWC-5
94ForWayWF-2001
95ForMyeMTI-5
95SPML-86
96BesAutS-17
96HarCitRCB-11
Carrasquel, Alex
67TopVen-176
93ConTSN-956
Carrasquel, Chico (Alfonso)
47Exh-34A
47Exh-34B
47PM1StaP1-28
51Bow-60
51FisBakL-4
51R42SmaS-9
51TopBluB-26
52BerRos-8
52Bow-41
52DixLid-3
52DixPre-3
52StaCalL-73D
52StaCalS-87B
52Top-251
53BowC-54
53DixLid-2
53DixPre-2
53Dor-122
53ExhCan-4
54Bow-54
54RedMan-AL19
55Bow-173
55RedMan-AL23
55RobGouS-4

55RobGouW-4
56Top-230
57IndSoh-3
57Top-67
58Hir-11
58Top-55
59OriJayP-2
59Top-264
67TopVen-181
76VenLeaS-74
79TCM50-74
80VenLeaS-92
80VenLeaS-132
83TopRep5-251
85WhiSoxC-5
91OriCro-69
94TopSpa-L5
Carrasquel, Domingo
94HelBreF-3620
94HelBreSP-3
94VenLinU-110
95LinVen-172
96BelSnaTI-9
Carrasquel, Emilio
80VenLeaS-117
82BirBarT-22
Carrasquillo, Angel
88BenBucL-1
Carraway, Rod
82WatIndF-9
82WatIndT-14
Carreno, Amalio
87PriWilYP-19
88AlbYanP-1329
89ReaPhiS-6
90Bes-140
90ReaPhiB-5
90ReaPhiP-1213
90ReaPhiS-11
91LinDriAAA-481
91ScrRedBLD-481
91ScrRedBP-2532
92Sco-867
92TopDeb91-27
93LinVenB-71
Carreon, Cam (Camilo G.)
60Lea-88
60Top-121
60TopVen-121
61Top-509
61WhiSoxTS-3
62Top-178
62TopStaI-23
62TopVen-178
62WhiSoxTS-4
63Top-308
63WhiSoxJP-1
63WhiSoxTS-3
64Top-421
64WhiSoxTS-5
65Top-578
66Top-513
91OriCro-70
Carreon, Mark
83LynMetT-14A
84JacMetT-20
85TidTidT-25
86TidTidP-4
87IntLeaAT-12
87MetColP-28
87TidTidP-21
87TidTidT-20
88Fle-129
88FleGlo-129
88MetColP-15
88TidTidCa-14
88TidTidCM-22
88TidTidP-1588
88TriAAAP-39
88TriAAC-23
89Bow-389
89BowTif-389
89ClaLigB-84
89DonRoo-18
89Fle-29
89FleGlo-29
89MetColP-25
89MetKah-3
89ScoHot1R-16
89ScoRoo-108T
89TidTidC-14
89TidTidC-24
90ClaBlu-112
90Don-454
90Fle-198
90FleCan-198
90Hot50RS-11
90Lea-488
90MetColP-28
90MetKah-45
90OPC-434
90Sco-363
90Sco100RS-67
90ScoYouSI-17
90Top-434
90TopRoo-6
90TopTif-434
90TopTVM-30
90ToyRoo-7
90UppDec-135
91Don-731
91Fle-142
91MetColP-13
91MetKah-45
91MetWIZ-66
91OPC-764
91Sco-165
91StaClu-196
91Top-764
91TopDesS-764
91TopMic-764
91TopTif-764
92Bow-111
92Don-465
92Fle-498
92Lea-259
92OPC-111
92OPCPre-88
92Pin-441
92Sco-19
92ScoProP-3
92ScoRoo-37T
92StaClu-678
92StaCluNC-678
92Top-111
92TopGol-111
92TopGolW-111
92TopMic-111
92TopTra-21T
92TopTraG-21T
92Ult-359
92UppDec-398
92UppDec-739
93Don-71
93Fle-604
93FleFinE-152
93GiaMot-15
93GiaPos-13
93PacSpa-104
93Pin-136
93Sco-366
93StaClu-680
93StaCluFDI-680
93StaCluG-23
93StaCluMOP-680
93Top-567
93TopGol-567
93TopInaM-567
93TopMic-567
93UppDec-570
93UppDecGold-570
94Fle-688
94GiaAMC-7
94GiaMot-27
94GiaUSPC-4D
94GiaUSPC-11C
94Sco-132
94ScoGolR-132
94StaCluT-13
94StaCluTFDI-13
94Top-327
94TopGol-327
94TopSpa-327
94Ult-288
95Fle-577
95GiaMot-27
95Pac-375
95Sco-248
95ScoGolR-248
95ScoPlaTS-248
95Top-361
96ColCho-302
96ColChoGS-302
96ColChoSS-302
96Don-316
96DonPreP-316
96EmoXL-287
96Fla-385
96Fle-585
96FleTif-585
96GiaMot-8
96Pac-206
96Pin-317
96PinFoil-317
96Sco-147
96StaClu-318
96StaCluMOP-318
96Top-74
96Ult-292
96UltGolM-292
96UppDec-197
97Fle-76
97FleTif-76
97Sco-211
97ScoInd-12
97ScoIndPl-12
97ScoIndPr-12
97ScoPreS-211
97ScoShoS-211
97ScoShoSAP-211
97Top-391
97Ult-47
97UltGolME-47
97UltPlaME-47
Carrera, Mahaly
93LinVenB-126
95LinVen-230
Carrick, William
03BreE10-16
Carrier, Brent
89TenTecGE-5
89TenTecGE-35
Carrigan, Bill (William F.)
09BriE97-6
09PhiCarE-2
09RamT20-22
09SpoNewSM-44
09T206-53
10DomDisP-21
10E-UOraBSC-4
10E12AmeCDC-8
10SweCapPP-1A
10SweCapPP-1B
11BasBatEU-6
11DiaGumP-6
11S74Sil-1
11SpoLifCW-56
11SpoLifM-2
11T205-25
11TurRedT-86
12HasTriFT-10A
12HasTriFT-10B
12HasTriFT-24
12T207-27
12T207-28
13TomBarW-7
14CraJacE-27
14PieStaT-9
15CraJacE-27
16FleBreD-14
93ConTSN-828
94ConTSN-1056
94ConTSNB-1056
Carriger, Rick
87HagSunP-18
88JacExpB-1
88JacExpP-988
89JacExpB-19
89JacExpP-168
Carrigg, Mike
94OgdRapF-3740
94OgdRapSP-2
Carrillo, Joe
92JohCitCC-24
92JohCitCF-3107
93SavCarC-8
93SavCarF-680
Carrillo, Matias
86NasPirP-5
87SalBucP-10
88ElPasDB-12
89DenZepC-22
89DenZepP-49
91DenZepLD-131
91DenZepP-134
91LinDriAAA-131
92TopDeb91-28
93LinVenB-304
94BreMilB-110
94Pac-238
94ScoRooGR-RT138
94SpoRoo-108
94SpoRooAP-108
94StaClu-235
94StaCluFDI-235
94StaCluGR-235
94StaCluMOP-235
94Ult-490
95Don-255
95DonPreP-255
95Fle-329
95Pac-170
95Sco-159
95ScoGolR-159
95ScoPlaTS-159
Carrillo, Paul
85CloHSS-8
Carrion, German
92ChaRaiC-15
92ChaRaiF-125
93WatDiaC-8
Carrion, Jesus
86OscAstP-4
Carrion, Jorge
97Bow-421
97BowChr-281
97BowChrI-281
97BowChrIR-281
97BowChrR-281
97BowInt-421
Carrion, Leonel
76VenLeaS-199
80MemChiT-12
80VenLeaS-235
83MemChiT-15
84IndIndTI-3
86JacExpT-9
88ExpPos-4
93LinVenB-222
Carrithers, Don
71MLBOffS-243
72Dia-7
72OPC-76
72Top-76
73OPC-651
73Top-651
74OPC-361
74Top-361
75OPC-438
75Top-438
76ExpRed-3
76OPC-312
76SSP-348
76Top-312
77OPC-18
77Top-579
78PhoGiaC-4
78Top-113
79PhoGiaVNB-11
Carrol, Jamey
96VerExpB-11
Carroll, Bob
75AndRanT-37
76AshTouT-5
77VisOakT-3
Carroll, Carson
83OrlTwiT-25
83WisRapTF-7
84VisOakT-15
86AlbYanT-3
87AlbYanP-14
Carroll, Chris
86Ft.LauYP-4
87Ft.LauYP-5
Carroll, Clay
65Top-461
66Top-307
66TopVen-307
67Top-219
68DexPre-21
68Top-412
69Kah-B6
69OPC-26
69Top-26
70DayDaiNM-71
70OPC-133
70Top-133
71MLBOffS-52
71OPC-394
71Top-394
72MilBra-68
72OPC-311
72OPC-312
72Top-311
72Top-312
73OPC-68
73OPC-195
73Top-68
73Top-195
74OPC-111
74Top-111
75OPC-345
75Top-345
76Kel-6A
76Kel-6B
76OPC-211
76SSP-25
76Top-211
76TopTra-211T
77Car5-3
77CarTeal-3
77Top-497
78Top-615
79VanCanT-14
86RedGreT-1
Carroll, Cliff (Samuel C.)
87BucN28-107
87OldJudN-72
Carroll, David
94MadHatC-4
94MadHatF-123
95PeoChiTI-25
Carroll, Don
88GreFalDTI-12
89SalDodTI-9
90KisDodD-5
91BakDodCLC-27
91YakBeaC-18
91YakBeaP-4240
Carroll, Ed
78HolMilT-3
79HolMilT-4
00HolMilT-19
Carroll, Fred (Frederick H.)
87BucN28-87
87OldJudN-74
88WG1CarG-55
89EdgR.WG-4
Carroll, James
86MedA'sC-71
87MadMusP-4
87MadMusP-21
88MadMusP-9
88ModA'sTI-6
89ClePhiS-4
Carroll, Joe
78AshTouT-5
Carroll, Kevin
90ColMetGS-23
90ColMetPPI-2
91St.LucMC-12
91St.LucMP-713
92LynRedSC-17
92LynRedSF-2910
93NewBriRSF-1224
Carroll, Owen
28StaPlaCE-7
29PorandAR-11
33ButCanV-6
33DouDisP-8
33Gou-72
34DiaMatCSB-26
34ButPreR-8
34GouCanV-46
90DodTar-115
92ConTSN-496
Carroll, Scrappy (John E.)
87AllandGN-12
87OldJudN-73
Carroll, Shadow
12ImpTobC-39
Carroll, Steve
83IowCubT-24
85IowCubT-30
Carroll, Thomas M.
75OPC-507
75Top-507
76IndIndTI-12
76OPC-561
76Top-561
Carroll, Tim
80AppFoxT-22
Carroll, Tommy (Thomas E.)
55Top-158
56Top-139
57Top-164
59Top-513
Carruth, Jason
94LetMouF-3869

94LetMouSP-7
Carruth, Jim
76BatRouCT-7
Carruthers, Robert
87BucN28-95
89EdgR.WG-3
94OriofB-39
Carse, Bob
43ParSpo-16
Carsey, Kid (Wilfred)
90DodTar-908
Carsley, Jeff
78DunBluJT-3
Carson, Henry
83St.PetCT-3
86St.PetCP-5
Carson, Kit (Walter Lloyd)
36NatChiFPR-18
Carson, Paul
89MarPhiS-5
Carson, Ted
84SavCarT-23
Carstensen, Chris
77NewCoPT-5
78BurBeeT-7
Carswell, Frank W.
53TigGle-3
Cartagena, Jesus
90IBAWorA-35
Cartaya, Joel
86SalRedBP-3
87PorChaRP-21
88TulDriTI-16
89ChaRanS-5
93LinVenB-131
Cartaya, Luis
95LinVen-229
Carte, Nick
72Dia-116
Cartelli, Doc (John)
85ModA'sC-28
86ModA'sC-26
86ModA'sP-5
87ModA'sC-25
87ModA'sP-22
Carter, Andy
88SouAtlLAGS-27
88SpaPhiS-19
89ClePhiS-5
90ClePhiS-4
91LinDriAA-506
91ReaPhiLD-506
91ReaPhiP-1366
92ClePhiF-2048
92ReaPhiS-529
92SkyAA F-228
95ScrRedBTI-4
96PhoFirB-13
Carter, Bart
89MisStaB-6
Carter, Bruce
86ClePhiP-2
86TriTriC-189
Carter, Bubba
92MisStaB-8
Carter, Cale
96LakElsSB-23
Carter, Chris
93HelBreF-4098
93HelBreSP-20
Carter, Cliff
91PomBlaBPB-23
Carter, Dale
92StaCluMO-38
Carter, David
90GatCitPP-3361
90GatCitPSP-4
91EriSaiC-14
91EriSaiP-4060
Carter, Dell
85ElmPioT-4
Carter, Dennis
87ArkTraP-1
88St.PetCS-3
89ArkTraGS-4
90CMC-110
90LouRedBC-10
90LouRedBP-414
90ProAAAF-528
Carter, Dick
60Top-466
Carter, Don
83MemChiT-7
84BufBisT-21
Carter, Dwight
75CliPilT-3
Carter, E.C.
88AllandGN-37
Carter, Ed
90St.PetCS-1
Carter, Eddie
87EriCarP-7
88SavCarP-354
89SavCarP-358
Carter, Fred
87Ft.LauYP-29
88RenSilSCLC-290
89PalSprACLC-45
89PalSprAP-479
Carter, Gary Edmund
75IntLeaAT-21
75OPC-620
75Top-620
76ExpRed-4
76Hos-62
76Kel-34
76OPC-441
76SSP-334
76Top-441
77BurCheD-154
77ExpPos-8
77Hos-41
77OPC-45
77Top-295
78ExpPos-2
78Hos-146
78OPC-135
78Top-120
79Hos-24
79OPC-270
79Top-520
80ExpPos-5
80OPC-37
80Top-70
80TopSup-52
81AllGamPI-130
81Don-90
81Dra-23
81Fle-142
81FleStiC-73
81OPC-6
81OPCPos-8
81PerAll-1
81PerCreC-32
81Top-660
81TopScr-66
81TopSti-184
81TopSti-259
82Don-2
82Don-114
82Dra-7
82ExpHygM-3
82ExpPos-4
82ExpZel-1
82ExpZel-6
82ExpZel-13
82ExpZel-16
82ExpZel-19
82FBIDis-4
82Fle-185
82Fle-635
82Fle-638
82FleSta-39
82Kel-24
82OPC-244
82OPC-344
82OPCPos-16
82PerAll-10
82PerAllG-10
82PerCreC-4
82PerCreCG-4
82Squ-19
82Top-344
82Top-730
82TopSti-61
82TopSti-128
82TopSti-253
82TopStiV-61
83AllGamPI-129
83Don-340
83DonActA-58
83Dra-4
83ExpPos-2
83ExpStu-8
83Fle-278
83Fle-637
83Fle-638
83FleSta-31
83FleSti-262
83Kel-55
83OPC-314
83OPC-370
83PerAll-10
83PerAllG-10
83PerCreC-3
83PerCreCG-3
83Top-370
83Top-404
83TopGloS-20
83TopSti-178
83TopSti-255
83TopStiB-2
84AllGamPI-39
84Don-55
84DonCha-58
84Dra-6
84ExpPos-3
84ExpStu-15
84ExpStu-36
84Fle-271
84FunFooP-3
84MilBra-5
84Nes792-393
84Nes792-450
84OCoandSI-52
84OPC-366
84OPC-393
84RalPur-28
84SevCoi-C15
84Top-393
84Top-450
84TopCer-28
84TopGloA-20
84TopGloS-9
84TopRubD-11
84TopSti-90
84TopSti-183
84TopSup-18
84TopTif-393
84TopTif-450
85AllGamPI-128
85Don-55
85DonActA-57
85DonHig-21
85DonHig-47
85Dra-5
85Fle-393
85Fle-631
85Fle-632
85FleStaS-16
85FleStaS-26
85FleStaS-35
85FleUpd-21
85GenMilS-1
85Lea-241
85MetColP-23
85MetFanC-3
85MetTCM-18
85OPC-230
85PolMet-M2
85SevCoi-C9
85Top-230
85Top-719
85Top3-D-15
85TopGloA-9
85TopGloS-36
85TopMin-230
85TopRubD-11
85TopSti-83
85TopSti-180
85TopSti-192
85TopSup-13
85TopTif-230
85TopTif-719
85TopTifT-17T
85TopTra-17T
86BasStaB-20
86Don-68
86DorChe-3
86Dra-1
86Fle-76
86FleAll-4
86FleLeaL-5
86FleLimE-10
86FleMin-17
86FleSluBC-M3
86FleStiC-23
86FleWaxBC-C7
86GenMilB-4A
86Lea-63
86MetColP-3
86MetFanC-2
86MetTCM-13
86MetWorSC-2
86MSAJifPD-19
86OPC-170
86QuaGra-4
86SevCoi-E16
86Spo-28
86Spo-126
86Spo-137
86SpoDecG-72
86Top-170
86Top-708
86Top3-D-2
86TopGloS-23
86TopMinL-50
86TopSti-96
86TopSup-19
86TopTat-20
86TopTif-170
86TopTif-708
86TruVal-16
86Woo-7
87BoaandB-11
87BurKinA-2
87ClaGam-5
87Don-69
87DonAll-19
87DonOpeD-130
87DonP-19
87Dra-20
87Fle-4
87Fle-629
87Fle-634
87FleAll-2
87FleAwaW-7
87FleBasA-7
87FleExcS-9
87FleGamW-9
87FleGlo-4
87FleGlo-629
87FleGlo-634
87FleGlo-WS4
87FleMin-18
87FleStiC-20
87FleWorS-4
87GenMilB-5A
87HosSti-12
87K-M-25
87KayB-8
87Lea-109
87MandMSL-12
87MetColP-2
87MetFanC-1
87MSAIceTD-8
87OPC-20
87RalPur-9
87RedFolSB-110
87SevCoi-E1
87SevCoi-M1
87Spo-50
87Spo-151
87SpoSupD-9
87SpoTeaP-2
87StaGarC-1
87StaGarC-2
87StaGarC-3
87StaGarC-4
87StaGarC-5
87StaGarC-6
87StaGarC-7
87StaGarC-8
87StaGarC-9
87StaGarC-10
87StaGarC-11
87StaGarC-12
87StaGarC-13
87StaGarC-14
87StuPan-1
87Top-20
87Top-331
87Top-602
87TopCoi-28
87TopGloA-9
87TopGloS-11
87TopMinL-20
87TopSti-14
87TopSti-22
87TopSti-101
87TopSti-158
87TopTif-20
87TopTif-331
87TopTif-602
87Woo-25
88CheBoy-10
88Don-199
88DonAll-41
88DonBasB-14
88DonPop-19
88DonTeaBM-199
88Dra-10
88Fle-130
88Fle-636
88FleGlo-130
88FleGlo-636
88FleStiWBC-S2
88GreBasS-37
88Lea-156
88MetColP-1
88MetFanC-8
88MetKah-8
88MSAJifPD-3
88Nes-26
88OPC-157
88PanSti-232
88PanSti-338
88Sco-325
88ScoBoxC-10
88ScoGlo-325
88Spo-28
88SpoGam-14
88StaGarC-1
88StaGarC-2
88StaGarC-3
88StaGarC-4
88StaGarC-5
88StaGarC-6
88StaGarC-7
88StaGarC-8
88StaGarC-9
88StaGarC-10
88StaGarC-11
88StaLinAl-5
88StaLinMe-3
88Top-530
88Top-579
88TopBig-37
88TopGloA-20
88TopGloS-7
88TopSti-105
88TopSti-152
88TopStiB-22
88TopTif-530
88TopTif-579
88TopUKM-11
88TopUKMT-11
89Bow-379
89BowTif-379
89CadEllD-6
89ClaLigB-64
89Don-53
89DonAll-41
89DonBasB-182
89DonPop-41
89Fle-30
89FleGlo-30
89FleSup-7
89KayB-4
89MetColP-3
89MetFanC-8
89MetKah-4
89OPC-324
89PanSti-136
89PanSti-228
89PAORelT-1
89RedFolSB-19
89Sco-240
89Spo-155
89Top-3
89Top-393
89Top-680
89TopBasT-76
89TopBig-325
89TopDouM-4
89TopGloA-20
89TopGloS-17
89TopSti-2
89TopSti-94
89TopSti-160
89TopStiB-55
89TopTif-3
89TopTif-393
89TopTif-680
89UppDec-390
89Woo-10
90BasWit-32
90Bow-236
90BowTif-236
90Don-147

90DonBesN-48
90DonLeaS-5
90Fle-199
90FleCan-199
90FleUpd-62
90GiaMot-3
90GiaSmo-3
90KayB-6
90Lea-134
90MLBBasB-17
90OPC-790
90PubSti-128
90Sco-416
90ScoRoo-35T
90Top-790
90TopTif-790
90TopTra-19T
90TopTraT-19T
90UppDec-168
90UppDec-774
90VenSti-97
91BasBesRB-3
91Bow-598
91DodMot-16
91DodPol-12
91Don-151
91DonBonC-BC8
91Fle-258
91FleUpd-93
91Lea-457
91MetWIZ-67
91OPC-310
91OPCPre-19
91Sco-215
91ScoRoo-26T
91StaClu-424
91Stu-182
91Top-310
91TopDesS-310
91TopMic-310
91TopTif-310
91TopTra-19T
91TopTraT-19T
91UltUpd-86
91UppDec-176
91UppDec-758
92Bow-385
92Don-36
92DonUpd-U19
92ExpDonD-5
92ExpPos-6
92Fle-450
92Lea-442
92OPC-45
92OPC-387
92OPC-389
92OPC-399
92OPC-402
92OPCPre-29
92PepDieM-12
92Pin-321
92Sco-489
92ScoRoo-59T
92StaClu-845
92StaCluMO-5
92StaCluNC-845
92Stu-53
92Top-45
92TopGol-45
92TopGolW-45
92TopMic-45
92TopTra-22T
92TopTraG-22T
92TriPla-26
92TriPlaP-5
92Ult-514
92UppDec-267
92UppDec-767
93Don-122
93ExpDonM-12
93Sel-55
93Top-205
93TopGol-205
93TopInaM-205
93TopMic-205
93TopPreS-3
93UppDec-219
93UppDecGold-219
93UppDecS-27
94TedWil-50
94TedWil-136
95StoPop-2
95UppDecSHoB-8
Carter, Glenn
88BenBucL-21
89QuaCitAB-1
89QuaCitAGS-8
90MidAngGS-18
91Cla/Bes-305
91LinDriAA-429
91MidAngLD-429
91MidAngP-428
93ElPasDF-2941
94NewBriRSF-643
94PawRedSDD-5
Carter, Herbert
82WisRapTF-10
Carter, Jeff
85EveGialC-1
86CliGiaP-4
87JamExpP-2564
88RocExpLC-5
88ShrCapP-1291
89ShrCapP-1846
89TexLeaAGS-29
89WesPalBES-5
90Bes-316
90CMC-545
90JacExpB-18
90JacExpP-1369
90PhoFirC-18
90PhoFirP-17
90ProAaA-38
90ProAAAF-43
91LinDriAAA-379
91LinDriAAA-630
91PhoFirLD-379
91PhoFirP-71
91VanCanLD-630
91VanCanP-1587
92SkyAAAF-237
92TacTigF-2509
92TacTigS-529
92VanCanF-2714
92VanCanS-630
93NasSouF-564
94SalLakBF-821
94VenLinU-267
95ChaKniTI-8
96ColSprSSTI-6
Carter, Jeffrey A.
91Bow-348
92Pin-280
92Sco-770
92StaClu-381
92TopDeb91-29
Carter, Joe
83CubThoAV-33
83IowCubT-20
84Don-41
84IndWhe-30
84IowCubT-25
85Don-616
85Fle-443
85Ind-9
85IndPol-30
85Top-694
85TopTif-694
86Don-224
86DonHig-42
86Fle-583
86IndOhH-30
86IndTeal-13
86OPC-377
86Top-377
86TopSti-213
86TopTat-15
86TopTif-377
86WilGloT-1
87ClaUpdY-127
87Don-156
87DonOpeD-109
87Fle-249
87FleAwaW-8
87FleBasA-8
87FleGlo-249
87FleLeaL-9
87FleLimE-7
87FleMin-19
87FleStiC-21
87IndGat-30
87KayB-9
87KraFoo-15
87Lea-133
87MandMSL-16
87OPC-220
87RedFolSB-27
87SmoAmeL-5
87Spo-176
87SpoSupD-1
87SpoTeaP-3
87StuPan-18
87Top-220
87TopCoi-7
87TopGaloC-4
87TopGloS-16
87TopMinL-51
87TopSti-208
87TopTif-220
88Don-254
88DonBasB-56
88DonBonM-BC9
88Fle-605
88FleGlo-605
88FleMin-18
88FleSlu-7
88FleStiC-18
88FleSup-6
88GreBasS-56
88IndGat-30
88KayB-4
88Lea-184
88Nes-36
88OPC-75
88OPCBoxB-I
88PanSti-72
88Sco-80
88ScoGlo-80
88Spo-5
88StaLinI-7
88Top-75
88Top-789
88TopBig-71
88TopCoi-8
88TopGloS-44
88TopRitTM-17
88TopSti-213
88TopStiB-49
88TopTif-75
88TopTif-789
88TopUKM-12
88TopUKMT-12
88TopWaxBC-I
89Bow-91
89BowTif-91
89CadEllD-7
89ClaLigB-11
89Don-83
89DonBasB-56
89DonBonM-BC3
89Fle-400
89FleExcS-4
89FleGlo-400
89FleHeroB-6
89IndTeal-8
89KinDis-8
89OPC-164
89PanSti-327
89RedFolSB-20
89Sco-213
89ScoHot1S-55
89ScoSco-34
89Spo-104
89Top-420
89TopAme2C-9
89TopBasT-104
89TopBig-155
89TopCoi-36
89TopGloS-3
89TopHilTM-6
89TopSti-216
89TopStiB-14
89TopTif-420
89TopUKM-13
89TVSpoM-85
89UppDec-190
90Bow-220
90BowTif-220
90ClaBlu-138
90ClaUpd-T9
90Don-114
90DonBesN-72
90Fle-489
90FleCan-489
90FleUpd-55
90Hot50PS-5
90Lea-379
90LeaPre-2
90OPC-580
90PadCok-3
90PadMag-27
90PanSti-65
90Pos-30
90PubSti-280
90PubSti-557
90RedFolSB-15
90Sco-319
90Sco100S-59
90ScoRoo-19T
90Spo-120
90Top-580
90TopAmeA-27
90TopBig-245
90TopCoi-42
90TopDou-9
90TopGloS-33
90TopHilHM-28
90TopMag-58
90TopMinL-13
90TopSti-209
90TopStiB-48
90TopTif-580
90TopTra-20T
90TopTraT-20T
90TopTVA-43
90UppDec-53
90UppDec-375
90UppDec-754
90VenSti-98
90VenSti-99
90WicStaSGD-7
91BluJayFS-5
91BluJayS-1
91BluJayS-37
91Bow-11
91Cla1-T21
91Cla2-T98
91ClaGam-91
91ColJoeC-1
91ColJoeC-2
91ColJoeC-3
91ColJoeC-4
91ColJoeC-5
91ColJoeC-6
91ColJoeC-7
91ColJoeC-8
91ColJoeC-9
91ColJoeC-10
91ColJoeC-11
91ColJoeC-12
91ColJoeC-xx
91Don-298
91Don-409
91DonGraS-1
91Fle-525
91FleUpd-65
91Lea-353
91OPC-120
91OPCPre-20
91PanCanT1-19
91PanFreS-95
91PanSti-90
91Sco-9
91Sco100S-81
91ScoRoo-11T
91SpoNSP-1
91StaClu-513
91Stu-133
91Top-120
91TopDesS-120
91TopMic-120
91TopTif-120
91TopTra-20T
91TopTraT-20T
91TopTriH-A14
91Ult-360
91UppDec-226
91UppDec-765
91USPlaCA-4H
92Bow-573
92Bow-667
92ClaGam-11
92ColAllG-12
92ColAllP-12
92ColPro-5A
92ColPro-5B
92DenHol-26
92Don-677
92Don-693
92DonCraJ2-21
92DonDiaK-DK3
92DonEli-10
92DonMcD-G2
92Fle-327
92Fle-685
92Fle-703
92FleAll-21
92FleTeaL-14
92Fre-16
92Hig5-117
92Hig5S-6
92HitTheBB-9
92KinDis-24
92Lea-375
92LeaGolP-26
92LeaPre-26
92MSABenSHD-2
92OPC-790
92OPCPre-194
92PanSti-29
92PepDieM-25
92Pin-148
92Pos-12
92Sco-90
92Sco-435
92Sco100S-35
92SpoIllFK1-254
92StaClu-10
92StaCluD-25
92Stu-254
92SunSee-12
92Top-402
92Top-790
92TopGol-402
92TopGol-790
92TopGolW-402
92TopGolW-790
92TopKid-89
92TopMcD-29
92TopMic-402
92TopMic-790
92TriPla-108
92Ult-145
92UppDec-224
92UppDecHRH-HR6
93BluJayCP1-3
93BluJayCP1-6
93BluJayD-6
93BluJayD4-5
93BluJayDM-22
93BluJayDM-32
93BluJayDWS-2
93BluJayFS-4
93Bow-575
93ClaGam-19
93ColAllG-19
93DenHol-4
93DiaMar-23
93Don-615
93Fin-94
93FinJum-94
93FinRef-94
93Fla-289
93Fle-333
93Fle-713
93FleAll-AL8
93FleFruotL-10
93FunPac-56
93HumDumC-20
93KinDis-13
93Lea-228
93LeaGolA-R8
93LeaGolA-U9
93MetBak-4
93OPC-83
93OPCPreSP-13
93OPCPreSPF-13
93OPCWorC-3
93PacSpa-322
93PanSti-31
93Pin-427
93PinCoo-21
93PinCooD-21
93PinHomRC-7
93PinSlu-4
93PinTeaP-10
93PosCan-4
93Sco-506
93Sco-575
93Sel-96
93SelChaS-20
93SelDufIP-1
93SelStaL-32
93SP-3
93SPPlaP-PP3
93StaClu-279
93StaClu-749
93StaCluFDI-279
93StaCluFDI-749
93StaCluM-74

93StaCluMO-6
93StaCluMO-7
93StaCluMOP-279
93StaCluMOP-749
93Stu-87
93StuSupoC-5
93Top-350
93Top-407
93TOPBLAG-26
93TopGol-350
93TopGol-407
93TopInaM-350
93TopInaM-407
93TopMic-350
93TopMic-407
93TriPla-123
93TriPlaA-30
93Ult-288
93UltHomRK-7
93UppDec-41
93UppDec-42
93UppDec-223
93UppDecCP-R5
93UppDecGold-41
93UppDecGold-42
93UppDecGold-223
93UppDecHRH-HR7
93USPlaCA-8C
94BluJayP-3
94BluJayUSPC-1H
94BluJayUSPC-6C
94BluJayUSPC-8S
94Bow-1
94BowBes-R16
94BowBesR-R16
94ChuShoS-8
94ColC-455
94ColChoGS-455
94ColChoSS-455
94Don-366
94DonAnn8-1
94DonDom-A5
94DonSpeE-366
94ExtBas-188
94ExtBasGB-6
94Fin-207
94FinJum-207
94FinRef-207
94Fla-116
94FlaOutP-3
94Fle-326
94FleAllS-5
94FleSun-6
94FleUpdDT-2
94FUnPac-29
94FUnPac-227
94Lea-193
94LeaCleC-8
94LeaL-76
94LeaLimGA-13
94LeaMVPC-A4
94LeaMVPCG-A4
94LeaPowB-9
94LeaStaS-7
94OPC-145
94OPCAllR-23
94OPCJumA-23
94OPCWorC-4
94Pac-636
94PacGolP-6
94PacPro-P2
94PanSti-136
94Pin-345
94PinArtP-345
94PinMusC-345
94PosCan-1
94PosCan-NNO
94PosCanG-1
94PosCanG-NNO
94ProMag-137
94ProMag-AU137
94RedFolMI-30
94Sco-73
94Sco-625
94ScoGolR-73
94ScoGolR-625
94ScoGolS-31
94Sel-12
94SP-40
94SPDieC-40
94Spo-12
94Spo-183
94SpoMov-MM10
94SpoRooGGG-GG12
94StaClu-300
94StaClu-527
94StaCluFDI-300
94StaCluFDI-527
94StaCluGR-300
94StaCluGR-527
94StaCluMO-11
94StaCluMOP-300
94StaCluMOP-527
94StaCluT-151
94StaCluTFDI-151
94Stu-26
94StuHer-3
94StuSerS-5
94SucSav-5
94Top-645
94TopBlaG-4
94TopGol-645
94TopSpa-645
94TopSupS-8
94TriPla-32
94TriPlaN-4
94Ult-136
94UltCarA-1
94UltHomRK-6
94UltRBIK-3
94UppDec-91
94UppDecAJ-24
94UppDecAJG-24
94UppDecED-91
94UppDecMLS-MM5
94UppDecMLSED-MM5
95Baz-76
95BluJayP-2
95BluJayUSPC-1D
95BluJayUSPC-6C
95Bow-297
95BowBes-R2
95BowBesR-R2
95ClaPhoC-56
95ColCho-59
95ColCho-150
95ColCho-529
95ColChoCtG-CG5
95ColChoCtG-CG5B
95ColChoCtG-CG5C
95ColChoCtGE-5
95ColChoCtGG-CG5
95ColChoCtGG-CG5B
95ColChoCtGG-CG5C
95ColChoCtGGE-5
95ColChoGS-59
95ColChoGS-150
95ColChoGS-529
95ColChoSE-54
95ColChoSEGS-54
95ColChoSESS-54
95ColChoSS-59
95ColChoSS-150
95ColChoSS-529
95D3-55
95Don-490
95Don-522
95DonAll-AL7
95DonBomS-6
95DonDiaK-DK9
95DonPreP-490
95DonPreP-522
95DonTopotO-172
95Emb-133
95EmbGolI-133
95Emo-91
95Fin-163
95FinRef-163
95Fla-95
95FlaOutP-5
95Fle-89
95FleAllS-6
95FleLumC-5
95FleTeaL-14
95FleUpdH-5
95KinDis-5
95Kra-2
95Lea-10
95LeaGolS-8
95LeaLim-31
95LeaStaS-1
95Pac-439
95PacGolP-4
95PacPri-139
95PanSti-85
95Pin-52
95PinArtP-52
95PinMusC-52
95PinRedH-RH16
95PinWhiH-WH16
95PosCan-8
95RedFol-2
95Sco-357
95ScoGolR-357
95ScoHaloG-HG60
95ScoPlaTS-357
95Sel-80
95SelArtP-80
95SelCer-74
95SelCerMG-74
95SP-205
95SPCha-102
95SPCha-200
95SPChaCP-CP4
95SPChaCPDC-CP4
95SPChaDC-102
95SPChaDC-200
95Spo-120
95SpoArtP-120
95SPSil-205
95SPSpeF-24
95StaClu-215
95StaClu-281
95StaClu-523
95StaCluCC-CC26
95StaCluCT-8
95StaCluFDI-215
95StaCluMO-11
95StaCluMOP-215
95StaCluMOP-281
95StaCluMOP-523
95StaCluMOP-CC26
95StaCluMOP-PZ4
95StaCluMOP-RL25
95StaCluPZ-PZ4
95StaCluRL-RL25
95StaCluSTWS-215
95StaCluSTWS-281
95StaCluSTWS-523
95StaCluVR-144
95Stu-14
95StuGolS-14
95StuPlaS-14
95Sum-74
95Sum-188
95SumBigB-BB15
95SumNthD-74
95SumNthD-188
95Top-240
95TopCyb-133
95TopLeaL-LL37
95UC3-77
95UC3-146
95UC3ArtP-77
95UC3ArtP-146
95UC3CycS-CS20
95Ult-337
95UltGolM-337
95UltRBIK-2
95UltRBIKGM-2
95UppDec-39
95UppDecED-39
95UppDecEDG-39
95UppDecPLL-R12
95UppDecPLL-R31
95UppDecPLLE-R12
95UppDecPLLE-R31
95UppDecSE-200
95UppDecSEG-200
95UppDecSoaD-SD6
95USPlaCMLA-2C
95Zen-53
96Baz-91
96BluJayB-1
96BluJayOH-3
96Bow-81
96BowBes-28
96BowBesAR-28
96BowBesR-28
96Cir-93
96CirBos-24
96CirRav-93
96ColCho-350
96ColCho-423
96ColChoCtG-CG30
96ColChoCtG-CG30B
96ColChoCtG-CG30C
96ColChoCtGG-CG30
96ColChoCtGG-CG30B
96ColChoCtGG-CG30C
96ColChoGS-350
96ColChoGS-423
96ColChoSS-350
96ColChoSS-423
96ColChoYMtP-11
96ColChoYMtP-11A
96ColChoYMtPGS-11
96ColChoYMtPGS-11A
96DenHol-23
96Don-192
96DonPreP-192
96EmoXL-129
96Fin-B315
96Fin-S143
96FinRef-B315
96FinRef-S143
96Fla-181
96Fle-268
96FleTeaL-14
96FleTif-268
96Lea-118
96LeaLim-76
96LeaLimG-76
96LeaPre-56
96LeaPreP-56
96LeaPrePB-118
96LeaPrePG-118
96LeaPrePS-118
96LeaPreSG-59
96LeaPreSte-59
96LeaSig-21
96LeaSigPPG-21
96LeaSigPPP-21
96LeaTotB-6
96MetUni-118
96MetUniP-118
96Pac-445
96PacPri-P141
96PacPriG-P141
96PanSti-162
96Pin-33
96Pin-162
96PinAfi-15
96PinAfiAP-15
96PinAfiFPP-15
96PinArtP-15
96PinArtP-89
96PinFan-29
96PinPow-15
96PinSta-15
96PinSta-89
96ProMagDM-25
96ProSta-18
96Sco-308
96ScoDugC-B33
96ScoDugCAP-B33
96Sel-47
96SelArtP-47
96SelCer-5
96SelCerAP-5
96SelCerCB-5
96SelCerCR-5
96SelCerMB-5
96SelCerMG-5
96SelCerMR-5
96SelTeaN-7
96SP-185
96Spo-85
96SpoArtP-85
96SPx-59
96SPxGol-59
96StaClu-129
96StaCluEPB-129
96StaCluEPG-129
96StaCluEPS-129
96StaCluMOP-129
95StaCluVRMC-144
96Stu-86
96StuPrePB-86
96StuPrePG-86
96StuPrePS-86
96Sum-130
96SumAbo&B-130
96SumArtP-130
96SumFoi-130
96TeaOut-15
96Top-115
96TopChr-31
96TopChrMotG-16
96TopChrMotGR-16
96TopChrR-31
96TopChrWC-WC5
96TopChrWCR-WC5
96TopGal-165
96TopGalPPI-165
96TopLas-3
96TopMasotG-16
96TopWreC-WC5
96Ult-143
96UltGolM-143
96UltRes-1
96UltResGM-1
96UltThu-5
96UltThuGM-5
96UppDec-215
96UppDecDD-DD40
96UppDecDDG-DD40
96UppDecDDS-DD40
96Zen-40
96ZenArtP-40
96ZenMoz-15
97BluJayS-3
97BluJayS-40
97Bow-271
97BowBes-90
97BowBesAR-90
97BowBesR-90
97BowChr-88
97BowChrI-88
97BowChrIR-88
97BowChrR-88
97BowInt-271
97Cir-273
97CirRav-273
97ColCho-505
97Don-5
97DonEli-61
97DonEliGS-61
97DonLim-96
97DonLim-183
97DonLimFotG-68
97DonLimLE-96
97DonLimLE-183
97DonPre-29
97DonPreCttC-29
97DonPreP-5
97DonPrePGold-5
97Fin-127
97Fin-338
97FinEmb-127
97FinEmb-338
97FinEmbR-127
97FinEmbR-338
97FinRef-127
97FinRef-338
97FlaSho-A29
97FlaSho-B29
97FlaSho-C29
97FlaShoLC-29
97FlaShoLC-B29
97FlaShoLC-C29
97FlaShoLCM-A29
97FlaShoLCM-B29
97FlaShoLCM-C29
97Fle-235
97Fle-748
97FleMilDM-20
97FleTif-235
97FleTif-748
97Lea-11
97LeaFraM-11
97LeaFraMDC-11
97MetUni-181
97NewPin-72
97NewPinAP-72
97NewPinMC-72
97NewPinPP-72
97Pac-216
97PacLigB-216
97PacPri-72
97PacPriLB-72
97PacPriP-72
97PacSil-216
97Pin-24
97PinArtP-24
97PinCer-40
97PinCerMBlu-40
97PinCerMG-40
97PinCerMR-40
97PinCerR-40
97PinIns-3
97PinInsCE-3
97PinInsDE-3
97PinMusC-24
97PinTotCPB-40
97PinTotCPG-40
97PinTotCPR-40
97PinX-P-115
97PinX-PMoS-115
97PinX-PSfF-29

97PinX-PSfFU-29
97ProMag-77
97ProMagML-77
97Sco-247
97ScoPitP-9
97ScoPreS-247
97ScoShoS-247
97ScoShoSAP-247
97Sel-21
97SelArtP-21
97SelRegG-21
97SkyE-X-48
97SkyE-XC-48
97SkyE-XEC-48
97SP-177
97SpoIll-39
97SpoIllEE-39
97StaClu-197
97StaCluMat-197
97StaCluMOP-197
97Stu-96
97StuPrePG-96
97StuPrePS-96
97Top-238
97TopChr-83
97TopChrR-83
97TopGal-31
97TopGalPPI-31
97TopIntF-ILM11
97TopIntFR-ILM11
97TopSta-58
97TopStaAM-58
97Ult-141
97UltGolME-141
97UltPlaME-141
97UppDec-515
97UppDecPP-PP2
97UppDecPPJ-PP2
Carter, John
92WelPirC-4
92WelPirF-1315
93ColRedC-7
93ColRedF-590
94Bow-663
94BowBes-B47
94BowBesR-B47
94CanIndF-3108
95Bow-190
95SigRooOJ-9
95SigRooOJP-9
95SigRooOJPS-9
95SigRooOJS-9
Carter, Lance
94EugEmeC-5
94EugEmeF-3703
95SprSulTI-6
96WilBluRB-18
Carter, Larry G.
89SalSpuCLC-126
89SalSpuP-1816
91ShrCapLD-302
91ShrCapP-1814
Carter, Larry L.
89BelBrelS-6
90BelBreB-4
90BelBreS-4
91BelBreC-2
91BelBreP-2095
91LinDriAA-302
91MidLeaAP-MWL32
92PhoFirF-2815
92PhoFirS-378
92ProFS7-347
92SkyAA F-294
92SkyAAAF-174
92StoPorC-1
93Bow-168
93Don-76
93PhoFirF-1510
93Sco-300
93ScoBoyoS-18
Carter, Marlin
86NegLeaF-50
92NegLeaRLI-8
93TedWil-101
Carter, Michael
91BelBreC-22
91BelBreP-2108
91Cla/Bes-214
92Bow-243
92ElPasDF-3933
92UppDecML-270
93ElPasDF-2962
95AusFut-9
Carter, Mike
90HelBreSP-24
91MidLeaAP-MWL33
92StoPorF-47
94IowCubF-1286
95IowCubTI-6
96IowCubB-11
Carter, Nick (Paul Warren)
19W514-45
Carter, Paul
91PomBlaBPB-23
Carter, Richard
87LakTigP-13
88LakTigS-6
89SanBerSB-3
89SanBerSCLC-68
Carter, Richie
86PalSprAP-14
86PalSprAP-6
Carter, Ron
86MadMusP-5
87SanBerSP-8
Carter, Steve
87WatPirP-10
88AugPirP-385
89BufBisP-1665
89DonRoo-8
90Bow-179
90BowTif-179
90BufBisC-22
90BufBisP-385
90BufBisTI-5
90CMC-22
90OPC-482
90ProAAAF-500
90Top-482
90TopDeb89-23
90TopTif-482
90TriAllGP-AAA17
90UppDec-368
91Don-418
91IowCubLD-202
91IowCubP-1074
91LakTigC-8
91LinDriAAA-202
91Ult-374
92SkyAAAF-259
92TolMudHF-1053
92TolMudHS-579
93IndIndF-1500
94VenLinU-265
Carter, Tim
90HelBreSP-1
91BelBreC-14
91BelBreP-2109
92StoPorC-6
92StoPorF-38
Carter, Tom
92ForLauYC-9
92ForLauYTI-4
92Ft.LauYF-2603
93PriWilCF-647
94AbaYanF-1431
Carter, Tommy
93PriWilCC-3
95NorNavTI-53
Cartwright, Alan
84ElPasDT-19
86ElPasDP-5
87DenZepP-19
88ElPasDB-13
Cartwright, Alexander J.
36PC7AlbHoF-15
50CalHOFW-11
76ShaPiz-15
77BobParHoF-10
80PerHaloFP-15
80SSPHOF-15
84GalHaloFRL-15
89HOFStiB-90
90BasWit-96
94OriofB-6
94UppDecTAE-2
94UppDecTAELD-LD2
Cartwright, Ed (Edward C.)
87OldJudN-75
95May-30
Cartwright, Mark
83VisOakF-16
Carty, Jorge
77ChaPatT-2
Carty, Rico (Ricardo Adolfo)
64Top-476
65Kah-7
65OPC-2
65Top-2
65Top-305
65TopTral-7
66OPC-153
66Top-153
66TopVen-153
67CokCapB-17
67Kah-8
67OPC-35
67Top-35
67Top-240
67TopVen-271
68CokCapB-17
68DexPre-22
68Top-455
69MLBOffS-112
69Top-590
69TopTeaP-2
70DayDaiNM-40
70MLBOffS-3
70OPC-145
70Top-145
71AllBasA-5
71BazNumT-28
71BazUnn-7
71MilDud-38
71MLBOffS-6
71MLBOffS-557
71OPC-62
71OPC-270
71Top-62
71Top-270
71TopCoi-113
71TopGreM-3
71TopSup-29
71TopTat-89
72EssCoi-3
72Top-740
73OPC-435
73Top-435
75OPC-655
75Top-655
76OPC-156
76SSP-519
76Top-156
77OPC-114
77PepGloD-9
77Top-465
78BluJayP-3
78Top-305
79BluJayBY-4
79OPC-291
79Top-565
80OPC-25
80Top-46
91KelLey-3
91SweBasG-18
91UppDecS-6
92ActPacA-74
93RanKee-98
93UppDecAH-27
94TedWil-41
94UppDecAH-202
94UppDecAH-221
94UppDecAH1-202
94UppDecAH1-221
Caruso, Gene
93PocPosF-4201
93PocPosSP-3
94StoPorC-4
94StoPorF-1685
95ElPasDTI-3
Caruso, Joe
92LynRedSC-20
92LynRedSF-2899
92StaCluD-26
92UppDecML-111
93ClaFS7-47
93ExcFS7-131
93ExcLeaLF-15
93PawRedSDD-6
93PawRedSF-2400
93PawRedSTI-6
94NewBriRSF-644
Caruso, Mike
96BelGiaTI-16
97Bow-304
97BowChr-211
97BowChrI-211
97BowChrIR-211
97BowChrR-211
97BowInt-304
Caruthers, Bob (Robert Lee)
76SSP188WS-1
87AllandGN-3
87LonJacN-2
87OldJudN-76A
87OldJudN-76B
87ScrDC-2
88GooN16-4
90DodTar-116
Caruthers, Clay
94BilMusF-3662
94BilMusSP-15
94SigRooDP-86
94SigRooDPS-86
94StaCluDP-58
94StaCluDPFDI-58
95Bow-54
Carvajal, Jhonny
93PriRedC-1
93PriRedF-4184
94ChaWheC-4
94ChaWheF-2709
95LinVen-41
96WesPalBEB-24
Carvajal, Jovina
90OneYanP-3375
91FloStaLAP-FSL12
91Ft.LauYC-25
91Ft.LauYP-2439
92ClaFS7-110
92ForLauYC-2
92ForLauYTI-5
92Ft.LauYF-2624
93PriWilCC-4
93PriWilCF-667
94CedRapKC-6
94CedRapKF-1120
95MidAngOHP-8
95MidAngTI-8
96Exc-24
Carver, Billy Paul
87AubAstP-6
88AshTouP-1049
88SouAtlLAGS-4
89ColMudB-23
89OscAstS-3
Carver, Steve
95BatCliTI-5
96Exc-196
Carver, W.F.
87AllandGN-39
Carveth, Joe
43ParSpo-17
Cary, Chuck
82BirBarT-9
83BirBarT-14
85NasSouTI-3
86FleUpd-21
86NasSouTI-3
87Don-461
87Fle-147
87FleGlo-147
87RicBraBC-1
87RicBraC-47
87RicBraT-1
87Top-171
87TopTif-171
88BlaYNPRWL-52
89ColCliC-7
89ColCliP-1
89ColCliP-745
89TopTra-17T
89TopTraT-17T
89UppDec-396
89YanScoNW-27
90ClaBlu-125
90Don-429
90Lea-50
90OPC-691
90PanSti-123
90Sco-393
90Top-691
90TopSti-315
90TopTif-691
90TopTVY-8
90UppDec-528
90YanScoNW-15
91Bow-176
91Don-179
91Fle-659
91Lea-66
91OPC-359
91PanFreS-331
91Sco-566
91StaClu-40
91StaCluP-9
91Top-359
91TopDesS-359
91TopMic-359
91TopTif-359
91UppDec-409
92YanWIZ8-27
93WhiSoxK-6
Cary, Jeff
80LynSaiT-12
81WauTimT-15
82MadMusF-31
Cary, Scott
47SenGunBP-2
Casado, Cancio
89MarPhiS-6
Casagrande, ,Tom
55Top-167
Casale, Jerry
59Top-456
60MacSta-5
60RedSoxJP-3
60Top-38
60TopVen-38
61Top-195
61TopStal-169
Casano, Andy
88WatIndP-666
89KinIndS-5
Casanova, Paul (Ortiz P.)
67CokCapA-9
67CokCapAAm-35
67CokCapS-9
67DexPre-43
67OPC-115
67SenTeal-3
67Top-115
67TopVen-231
68Baz-1
68SenTeal-2
68Top-560
68TopActS-3C
68TopActS-14C
69MilBra-53
69MLBOffS-102
69NabTeaF-4
69SenTeal-5
69Top-486A
69Top-486B
69TopSta-233
69TopTeaP-23
70MLBOffS-280
70OPC-84
70SenPolY-3
70Top-84
71MLBOffS-532
71OPC-139
71SenPolP-2
71SenTealW-7
71Top-139
71TopCoi-146
72MilBra-69
72Top-591
73OPC-452
73Top-452
74OPC-272
74Top-272
75OPC-633
75Top-633
76LauIndC-24
89PacSenL-58
93HicCraC-27
94HicCraC-29
94HicCraF-2193
Casanova, Raul
92ColMetC-19
92ColMetF-299
92KinMetC-10
92KinMetF-1533
93WatDiaC-9
93WatDiaF-1770
94RanCucQC-10
94RanCucQF-1641
95Bow-91
95BowBes-B67
95BowBesR-B67
95ColCho-33
95ColChoGS-33
95ColChoSS-33
95Exc-280
95ExcAll-1
95MemChiTI-22

95Sel-197
95SelArtP-197
95SP-20
95SPML-141
95SPMLA-6
95SPSil-20
95UppDec-11
95UppDecED-11
95UppDecEDG-11
95UppDecML-20
95UppDecMLOP-OP24
95UppDecSE-131
95UppDecSEG-131
96BesAutS-18
96Bow-352
96Exc-234
96LeaPre-143
96LeaPreP-143
96LeaSig-64
96LeaSigPPG-64
96LeaSigPPP-64
96TolMudHB-7
96Zen-122
96ZenArtP-122
97Bow-399
97BowInt-399
97Cir-139
97CirRav-139
97Don-392
97DonEli-91
97DonEliGS-91
97DonLim-179
97DonLimLE-179
97DonPreP-392
97DonPrePGold-392
97DonRatR-16
97Fle-95
97FleTif-95
97Lea-53
97LeaFraM-53
97LeaFraMDC-53
97Pac-85
97PacLigB-85
97PacPri-29
97PacPriLB-29
97PacPriP-29
97PacSil-85
97PinCer-122
97PinCerMBlu-122
97PinCerMG-122
97PinCerMR-122
97PinCerR-122
97PinInsCE-138
97PinInsDE-138
97PinTotCPB-122
97PinTotCPG-122
97PinTotCPR-122
97Sco-28
97ScoPreS-28
97ScoShoS-28
97ScoShoSAP-28
97Sel-111
97SelArtP-111
97SelRegG-111
97StaClu-96
97StaCluMOP-96
97Ult-57
97UltGolME-57
97UltPlaME-57
97UppDec-474
95UppDecMLFS-20
Casarotti, Rich
88BurBraP-21
88MidLeaAGS-17
89DurBullS-4
89DurBulTI-4
89Sta-68
90GreBraB-10
90GreBraP-1135
90GreBraS-5
91GreBraC-14
91GreBraLD-201
91GreBraP-3008
91LinDriAA-201
91RicBraBC-28
92ChaKniF-2776
Casavant, Denys
43ParSpo-18
Cascarella, Joe
34BatR31-162
35DiaMatCS3T1-27
38CinOraW-4
Case, Christopher
96MacBraB-4
Case, George W.
39GouPreR303A-7
39GouPreR303B-2
39PlaBal-138
39WorWidGTP-7
40PlaBal-15
41DouPlaR-75
41DouPlaR-87
41Gou-16
41PlaBal-69
46SpoExcW-1-9
47Exh-35
83DiaClaS2-75
83TCMPla1942-20
Case, Mike
92BenRocC-8
92BenRocF-1484
93CenValRC-6
93CenValRF-2903
93TopInaM-661
93TopMic-661
94NewHavRF-1553
95NewHavRTI-24
Casey, Dan
87BucN28-76
87OldJudN-77
88WG1CarG-48
90KalBatN-6
Casey, Doc (James Peter)
03BreE10-17
06FanCraNL-8
09T206-406
10E101-7
10MelMinE-7
10PeoT21-9
11SpoLifCW-57
90DodTar-117
Casey, Hugh
39PlaBal-151
40DodTeaI-3
40PlaBal-148
42DodTeaI-4
46SpoExcW-2-7
47Exh-36
47TipTop-93
49Bow-179
49EurSta-155
80DodGreT-8
80LauFamF-27
90DodTar-118
Casey, Joe (Joseph Felix)
10NadCarE-8
Casey, Joie
88SalLakCTTI-NNO
Casey, Keith
90GatCitPP-3338
90GatCitPSP-5
Casey, Kim
87SalLakTTT-NNO
Casey, Mascot
95OmaRoyTI-29
96OmaRoyB-5
Casey, Mickey
91PomBlaBPB-23
Casey, Pat
83BeaGolGT-16
84BeaGolGT-16
85CalCanC-86
86CalCanP-4
87PorBeaP-7
Casey, Philip
88KimN18-8
Casey, Ryan
94HunCubF-3543
95RocCubTI-19
94HunCubC-4
Casey, Sean
95WatIndTI-8
96CarLeaA1B-22
96CarLeaA2B-22
96KenIndB-3
96Top-25
96TopPowB-25
97Bow-367
97BowChr-245
97BowChrI-245
97BowChrIR-245
97BowChrR-245
97BowInt-367
97Top-202
Casey, Tim (Timothy)
86StoPorP-4
87ElPasDP-13
89HunStaB-14
90CMC-589
90ProAAAF-151
90TacTigC-12
90TacTigP-104
Cash, Bill
86NegLeaF-57
91NegLeaRL-2
92NegLeaRLI-9
95NegLeaLI-2
Cash, Dave (David)
69PirJacitB-2
70OPC-141
70Top-141
71MLBOffS-197
71OPC-582
71Pir-2
71PirActP-3
71Top-582
72OPC-125
72Top-125
73LinPor-145
73OPC-397
73Top-397
74OPC-198
74PhiJohP-16
74Top-198
75Hos-93
75Kel-48
75OPC-22
75SSPPuzB-6
75Top-22
76CraDis-11
76Hos-40
76HosTwi-40
76Kel-16
76OPC-295
76Spo-8
76SSP-465
76Top-295
77BurCheD-162
77ExpPos-9
77Hos-133
77MSADis-14
77OPC-180
77PepGloD-66
77RCColC-15
77Top-649
77TopCloS-12
78Hos-23
78OPC-18
78RCColC-6
78TasDis-17
78Top-495
78WifBalD-15
79ExpPos-5
79OPC-207
79Top-395
80OPC-3
80Top-14
81Don-121
81Fle-492
81Top-707
86ExpGreT-2
88BatCliP-1663
89PacSenL-192
89ScrRedBC-6
89T/MSenL-19
89TopSenL-64
91PacSenL-58
91PacSenL-80
93ExpDonM-13
93ScrRedBF-2559
93ScrRedBTI-5
93UppDecAH-28
94ScrRedBF-936
95ScrRedBTI-5
96PhiTeal-6
Cash, Earl
85OscAstTI-4
86OscAstP-5
87ColAstP-19
Cash, Johnny
86DurBulP-3
Cash, Mike
75CedRapGT-15
78PhoGiaC-5
Cash, Norm (Norman Dalton)
47Exh-37
55DonWin-13
59Top-509
60Top-488
61Pos-40A
61Pos-40B
61TigJayP-5
61Top-95
61TopStal-148
62Baz-35
62ExhStaB-7
62Jel-14
62Pos-14A
62Pos-14B
62PosCan-14
62SalPlaC-72
62ShiPlaC-72
62TigJayP-4
62Top-51
62Top-250
62Top-466
62TopBuc-15
62TopStal-45
62TopVen-51
63ExhStaB-11
63Jel-46
63Pos-46
63TigJayP-4
63Top-4
63Top-445
64Baz-20
64TigJayP-3
64TigLid-3
64Top-331
64Top-425
64TopCoi-79
64TopSta-49
64TopStaU-13
64TopTatI-28
64TopVen-331
65OPC-153
65TigJayP-3
65Top-153
66Top-218
66Top-315
66TopVen-218
66TopVen-315
67CokCapTi-2
67DexPre-44
67TigDexP-1
67Top-216
67Top-540
67TopVen-198
68AtlOilPBCC-11
68CokCapT-2
68TigDetFPB-2
68Top-256
68TopVen-256
69MilBra-54
69MLBOffS-46
69OPC-80
69TigTeal-1
69TigTealC-1
69Top-80
69TopSta-171
69TopTeaP-1
70MLBOffS-205
70Top-611
71MLBOffS-389
71OPC-599
71Top-599
72MilBra-70
72OPC-90
72OPC-150
72Top-90
72Top-150
73LinPor-68
73OPC-485
73TigJew-5
73Top-485
74OPC-367
74Top-367
74TopSta-172
75SSP42-38
78TCM60I-49
78TigDeaCS-13
81TigDetN-73A
81TigDetN-73B
83MLBPin-3
83TigAIKS-19
83TigAIKS-22
83TigAIKS-24
85CirK-25
86TigSpoD-14
88TigDom-2
91FouBal-19
93ActPacA-147
94TedWil-29
94TedWilM-M29
97TopMan-36
97TopManF-36
97TopManFR-36
Cash, Ron (Ronald Forrest)
74OPC-600
74Tig-2
74Top-600
Cash, Timothy
88VerBeaDS-3
Cash, Todd
86CliGiaP-5
Cashen, Frank
92TopCas-1
Cashion, Jay Carl
09ColChiE-47
12ColRedB-47
12ColTinT-47
14CraJacE-62
Cashman, Joseph
59FleWil-32
Casian, Larry
88OrlTwiB-20
88SouLeaAJ-29
89PorBeaP-223
90CMC-555
90PorBeaC-3
90PorBeaP-170
90ProAAAF-240
91Bow-325
91Lea-481
91OPC-374
91Top-374
91TopDeb90-27
91TopDesS-374
91TopMic-374
91TopTif-374
92Fle-199
92PorBeaF-2660
92PorBeaS-404
92Sco100RS-94
92SkyAAAF-185
92TriA AAS-404
93Don-343
93FleFinE-233
93Lea-498
94Don-109
94Fle-201
94StaClu-479
94StaCluFDI-479
94StaCluGR-479
94StaCluMOP-479
94Top-543
94TopGol-543
94TopSpa-543
94Ult-84
96Fle-313
96FleTif-313
96LeaSigEA-26
Casillas, Adam
88GreHorP-1562
89CedRapRB-14
89CedRapRP-922
89CedRapRS-3
89Sta-198
90CedRapRDGB-18
91LinDriAAA-254
91NasSouLD-254
91NasSouP-2168
92MemChiS-430
92OmaRoyF-2973
92SkyAA F-181
93MemChiF-385
Casimiro, Carlos
96AppLeaAB-2
96BluOriB-7
Caskill, Derrick
95HelBreTI-21
Casper, Tim
91EveGiaC-13
91EveGiaP-3920
93SanJosGC-5
93SanJosGF-15
Cassel, Grahame
91ParPatF-9
Cassels, Chris
88BelBreGS-23
89StoPorB-19
89StoPorCLC-163
89StoPorP-392
89StoPorS-14
90CalLeaACLC-41
90StoPorB-14
90StoPorCLC-199
90StoPorP-2199

91HarSenLD-251
91HarSenP-638
91LinDriAA-251
Cassidy, Dave (David)
89HamRedS-9
91St.PetCP-2266
92ArkTraF-1121
Cassidy, Hop (Howard)
79ColCliT-25
92ColCliP-2
94ColCliP-3
Cassidy, Mike
91St.PetCC-2
Cassidy, Pete (Peter F.)
09T206-407
90DodTar-909
Cassidy, Reid
79WatIndT-15
Cassillas, Adam
90ChaLooGS-8
Cassini, Jack Dempsey
76BatTroTI-6
78HalHalR-12
Castaigne, Arcilio
80AndBraT-2
Castain, Maurice
83IdaFalAT-26
84MadMusP-22
Castaldo, Eric
96DanBraB-9
Castaldo, Gregg
92KanCouCTI-4
93FreKeyF-1031
94FreKeyF-2619
95BowBayTI-23
94FreKeyC-6
Castaldo, Joe
91HamRedC-1
91HamRedP-4030
Castaldo, Vince
90HelBreSP-16
91Cla/Bes-264
91StoPorC-19
91StoPorP-3036
92ElPasDF-3934
92ElPasDS-203
93OttLynF-2441
Castaneda, Hector
93BluOriC-8
93BluOriF-4127
94AlbPolC-10
94AlbPolF-2239
95BowBayTI-27
Castaneda, Michael
90IBAWorA-24
Castaneda, Nick
82AleDukT-13
83AleDukT-5
84PriWilPT-31
85MexCitTT-23
89OmaRoyC-13
89OmaRoyP-1722
91LinDriAAA-228
91LouRedLD-228
91LouRedP-2921
Castaneda, Robbie
91BenBucP-3687
Casteel, Brent
86WinSpiP-3
Castellano, Miguel
90ButCopKSP-3
91GasRanC-16
92ChaRanC-14
93ClaFS7-177
93TulDriF-2737
Castellano, Pedro
89Sta-163
89WytCubS-5
90MidLeaASGS-29
90PeoChiTI-8
90PeoChiTI-9
91CarLeaAP-CAR40
91Cla/Bes-173
91WinSpiC-17
91WinSpiP-2834
92Bow-271
92Bow-649
92DonRoo-22
92IowCubF-4057
92IowCubS-205
92ProFS7-204
92SkyAAAF-99
92UppDecML-133
93Bow-232
93ColSprSSF-3091
93Don-761
93ExcFS7-7
93FleFinE-24
93LinVenB-26
93TopTra-69T
94ColSprSSF-739
94Don-449
94Pac-191
94Pin-229
94PinArtP-229
94PinMusC-229
94StaCluT-97
94StaCluTFDI-97
94VenLinU-225
95LinVen-48
96ColSprSSTI-7
96FleUpd-U127
96FleUpdTC-U127
Castellanos, Miquel
91GasRanP-2693
92ChaRanF-2230
93LinVenB-118
94VenLinU-94
95LinVen-231
93TulDriTI-3
Castello, Brian
89SalSpuCLC-149
Caster, George
35DiaMatCS3T1-29
41BroW75-5
96Bro194F-31
Castiglione, Pete (Peter P.)
49EurSta-156
50Bow-201
50PirTeal-3
51Bow-17
52Bow-47
52DixLid-4
52DixPre-4
52Top-260
54Bow-174
83TopRep5-260
Castilla, Vinny (Vinicio)
90Bes-278
90CMC-727
90SouAtlLAS-28
90SumBraB-28
90SumBraP-2439
91GreBraC-15
91GreBraLD-202
91GreBraP-3009
91LinDriAA-202
91RicBraBC-29
92Fle-666
92ProFS7-183
92RicBraBB-2
92RicBraF-382
92RicBraRC-2
92RicBraS-427
92Sco-860
92SkyAAAF-195
92TopDeb91-30
93Bow-556
93Don-102
93Don-770
93Fle-406
93FleFinE-25
93JimDeaR-2
93Lea-495
93OPCPre-65
93PacJugC-23
93PacSpa-424
93RocUSPC-4H
93RocUSPC-13C
93StaClu-547
93StaCluFDI-547
93StaCluMOP-547
93StaCluRoc-23
93Stu-212
93TopTra-33T
93Ult-344
93UppDec-560
93UppDecGold-560
94ColC-74
94ColChoGS-74
94ColChoSS-74
94Don-549
94Fle-437
94Lea-214
94Pac-192
94PanSti-172
94Pin-191
94PinArtP-191
94PinMusC-191
94RocPol-6
94Sco-305
94ScoGolR-305
94StaClu-244
94StaCluFDI-244
94StaCluGR-244
94StaCluMOP-244
94StaCluMOP-ST4
94StaCluST-ST4
94StaCluT-92
94StaCluTFDI-92
94Top-163
94TopGol-163
94TopSpa-163
94USPlaCR-2C
95Don-181
95DonPreP-181
95DonTopotO-226
95Emo-124
95Fin-277
95FinRef-277
95Fla-128
95FleUpd-166
95Lea-230
95LeaLim-171
95Pac-134
95RocPol-5
95Sco-483
95ScoGolR-483
95ScoPlaTS-483
95SP-51
95SPCha-43
95SPChaDC-43
95SPSil-51
95StaClu-476
95StaCluMOP-476
95StaCluSTWS-476
95Top-552
95TopCyb-331
95UppDec-491T
95Zen-106
96Baz-71
96Bow-60
96BowBes-67
96BowBesAR-67
96BowBesR-67
96Cir-122
96CirRav-122
96ColCho-136
96ColCho-753
96ColChoCtG-CG15
96ColChoCtG-CG15B
96ColChoCtG-CG15C
96ColChoCtGE-CR15
96ColChoCtGG-CG15
96ColChoCtGG-CG15B
96ColChoCtGG-CG15C
96ColChoCtGGE-CR15
96ColChoGS-136
96ColChoGS-753
96ColChoSS-136
96ColChoSS-753
96Don-305
96DonPreP-305
96EmoXL-174
96Fin-S99
96FinRef-S99
96Fla-245
96Fle-362
96FleRoc-4
96FleTif-362
96Lea-138
96LeaPrePB-138
96LeaPrePG-138
96LeaPrePS-138
96LeaPreSG-43
96LeaPreSte-43
96MetUni-155
96MetUniP-155
96Pac-58
96PacEstL-EL8
96PacGolCD-DC27
96PacHom-HP14
96PacPri-P20
96PacPriG-P20
96PanSti-88
96Pin-245
96PinAfi-81
96PinAfiAP-81
96PinAfiFPP-81
96PinArtP-145
96PinFoil-245
96PinSta-145
96ProSta-112
96RocPol-6
96Sco-74
96ScoDugC-A60
96ScoDugCAP-A60
96Sel-87
96SelArtP-87
96SP-76
96SPx-24
96SPxGol-24
96StaClu-5
96StaCluEPB-5
96StaCluEPG-5
96StaCluEPS-5
96StaCluMM-MM5
96StaCluMO-9
96StaCluMOP-5
96StaCluMOP-MM5
96Stu-16
96StuPrePB-16
96StuPrePG-16
96StuPrePS-16
96Sum-129
96SumAbo&B-129
96SumArtP-129
96SumFoi-129
96TeaOut-16
96Top-188
96TopChr-58
96TopChrR-58
96TopGal-113
96TopGalPPI-113
96TopLas-39
96Ult-188
96UltGolM-188
96UppDec-62
97Bow-28
97BowBes-80
97BowBesAR-80
97BowBesR-80
97BowChr-24
97BowChrI-24
97BowChrIR-24
97BowChrR-24
97BowInt-28
97BowIntB-BBI8
97BowIntBAR-BBI8
97BowIntBR-BBI8
97Cir-32
97CirRav-32
97ColCho-95
97ColChoAC-39
97ColChoCtG-15A
97ColChoCtG-15B
97ColChoCtG-15C
97ColChoCtGIW-CG15
97ColChoPP-PP15
97ColChoPPG-PP15
97Don-78
97DonLim-14
97DonLimLE-14
97DonPre-61
97DonPreCttC-61
97DonPreP-78
97DonPrePGold-78
97DonTea-93
97DonTeaSPE-93
97Fin-125
97Fin-213
97FinEmb-125
97FinEmbR-125
97FinRef-125
97FinRef-213
97FlaSho-A165
97FlaSho-B165
97FlaSho-C165
97FlaShoLC-165
97FlaShoLC-B165
97FlaShoLC-C165
97FlaShoLCM-A165
97FlaShoLCM-B165
97FlaShoLCM-C165
97Fle-309
97FleTif-309
97Lea-155
97LeaFraM-155
97LeaFraMDC-155
97MetUni-73
97Pac-281
97PacLatotML-26
97PacLigB-281
97PacPri-97
97PacPriLB-97
97PacPriP-97
97PacPriSL-SL9C
97PacSil-281
97Pin-68
97PinArtP-68
97PinInsFS-10
97PinMusC-68
97PinX-P-21
97PinX-PMoS-21
97PinX-PSfF-34
97PinX-PSfFU-34
97RicBraBC-4
97Sco-183
97ScoPreS-183
97ScoRoc-9
97ScoRocPl-9
97ScoRocPr-9
97ScoShoS-183
97ScoShoSAP-183
97SP-63
97SpoIll-109
97SpoIllEE-109
97SpoIllGS-13
97StaClu-221
97StaCluMat-221
97StaCluMOP-221
97Top-398
97TopChr-139
97TopChrR-139
97TopGal-107
97TopGalPG-PG12
97TopGalPPI-107
97TopSta-40
97TopStaAM-40
97Ult-443
97UltGolME-443
97UltPlaME-443
97UppDec-197
97UppDec-351
97UppDecU-14
Castillo, Ace
75QuaCitAT-27
Castillo, Albert
80VenLeaS-57
89KinMetS-5
Castillo, Alberto
90ColMetGS-19
90ColMetPPI-2
90PitMetP-23
91ColMetPI-10
91ColMetPPI-7
92St.LucMCB-15
92St.LucMF-1748
93St.LucMC-5
94BinMetF-706
94Bow-23
94EveGiaC-3
94EveGiaF-3657
94StaCluDP-6
94StaCluDPFDI-6
95BelGiaTI-33
95NorTidTI-8
96NorTidB-10
96Pac-142
96UltGolP-2
96UltGolPGM-2
93StLucMF-2924
97PacPriGotD-GD173
Castillo, Axel
88BurIndP-1781
Castillo, Benny (Ben)
88BriTigP-1892
89FayGenP-1580
91SalLakTP-3222
91SalLakTSP-16
92ChaRanC-3
92ChaRanF-2236
93TulDriF-2745
93TulDriTI-4
Castillo, Roberto
81Fle-137
82Don-236
82Fle-2
83Don-102
90QuaCitAGS-8
93LinVenB-176
94VenLinU-190
95LinVen-139
Castillo, Bobby
79AlbDukT-22
79Top-641
80DodPol-37
81DodPol-37
81Don-298

81LonBeaPT-14
81Top-146
82Top-48
82TopTra-17T
82TwiPos-3
83Fle-608
83FleSta-32
83FleSti-139
83Top-327
83Top-771
83TwiTeal-23
84Don-436
84Fle-559
84MinTwiP-5
84Nes792-491
84OPC-329
84Top-491
84TopTif-491
84TwiTeal-24
85DodCokP-7
85DomLeaS-80
85Fle-274
85FleUpd-22
85Top-588
85TopTif-588
85TopTifT-18T
85TopTra-18T
86Fle-127
86Top-252
86TopTif-252
90DodTar-119
Castillo, Braulio
89BakDodCLC-202
89CalLeaA-9
90SanAntMGS-10
91Cla/Bes-307
91Cla2-T85
91LinDriAA-533
91SanAntMLD-533
91SanAntMP-2987
92Bow-104
92Don-753
92OPC-353
92ProFS7-245
92Sco-824
92ScoRoo-32
92ScrRedBF-2458
92ScrRedBS-480
92SkyAAAF-218
92StaClu-124
92Top-353
92TopDeb91-31
92TopGol-353
92TopGolW-353
92TopMic-353
92UppDec-21
93Don-386
93Fle-407
93LimRocDWB-80
93RocUSPC-5C
93RocUSPC-8S
93Sco-629
93Sel-340
93TucTorF-3072
Castillo, Carlos
91YakBeaC-23
91YakBeaP-4241
92BakDodCLC-5
92VisOakF-1005
95LakElsSTI-7
96LakElsSB-1
96MidAngB-10
96MidLeaAB-49
96SouBenSHS-9
97Fle-645
97FleTif-645
97Ult-503
97UltGolME-503
97UltPlaME-503
Castillo, Carmen (M. Carmelo)
79WatIndT-19
80WatIndT-27
81ChaLooT-16
82ChaChaT-19
82Ind-7
82IndTeal-6
83Fle-404
83IndPos-7
84Ind-9
84IndWhe-8
85DomLeaS-129
85Don-590
Fle-444
85Ind-10
85IndPol-8
85OPC-184
85Top-184
85TopSti-255
85TopTif-184
86Don-460
86Fle-584
86IndOhH-8
86IndTeal-14
86TopTra-21T
86TopTraT-21T
87Don-588
87Fle-250
87FleGlo-250
87IndGat-8
87Top-513
87TopTif-513
88Don-403
88Fle-606
88FleGlo-606
88IndGat-8
88Sco-581
88ScoGlo-581
88StaLinI-8
88Top-341
88TopTif-341
89Don-374
89Fle-401
89FleGlo-401
89Sco-497
89ScoRoo-23T
89Top-637
89TopBig-91
89TopTif-637
89TopTra-18T
89TopTraT-18T
89UppDec-487
90Don-554
90Fle-371
90FleCan-371
90OPC-427
90Sco-123
90Top-427
90TopTif-427
90UppDec-281
91Fle-606
91OPC-266
91Sco-608
91Top-266
91TopDesS-266
91TopMic-266
91TopTif-266
93LimRocDWB-93
Castillo, Felipe
87GasRanP-1
88GasRanP-1008
89ChaRanS-6
89TulDriGS-7
89TulDriTI-5
90CMC-741
90TulDriP-1150
90TulDriTI-5
Castillo, Frank
87WytCubP-21
89WinSpiS-4
90ChaKniTI-20
91DonRoo-20
91IowCubLD-203
91LinDriAAA-203
91UppDecFE-27F
92CubMar-49
92Don-492
92Fle-378
92Lea-290
92OPC-196
92OPCPre-159
92Pin-504
92Sco-399
92Sco100RS-61
92StaClu-65
92Top-196
92TopDeb91-32
92TopGol-196
92TopGolW-196
92TopMic-196
92Ult-467
92UppDec-526
93CubMar-4
93Don-400
93Fle-375
93Lea-141
93PacBeiA-17
93PacSpa-54
93Pin-208
93Sco-462
93StaClu-346
93StaCluCu-21
93StaCluFDI-346
93StaCluMOP-346
93Top-533
93TopGol-533
93TopInaM-533
93TopMic-533
93Ult-16
93UppDec-408
93UppDecGold-408
94ColC-454
94ColChoGS-454
94ColChoSS-454
94Don-91
94Fle-382
94Lea-217
94Pac-97
94StaClu-337
94StaCluFDI-337
94StaCluGR-337
94StaCluMOP-337
94StaCluT-341
94StaCluTFDI-341
94Top-399
94TopGol-399
94TopSpa-399
94UppDec-464
94UppDecED-464
95Fin-314
95FinRef-314
95FleUpd-125
95Top-358
96ColCho-494
96ColChoGS-494
96ColChoSS-494
96Don-319
96DonPreP-319
96EmoXL-152
96Fla-213
96Fle-314
96FleCub-3
96FleTif-314
96LeaSigA-40
96LeaSigAG-40
96LeaSigAS-40
96MetUni-138
96MetUniP-138
96Pac-28
96PacPri-P8
96PacPriG-P8
96Sco-217
96StaClu-252
96StaCluMOP-252
96Top-146
96TopGal-88
96TopGalPPI-88
96Ult-164
96UltGolM-164
96UppDec-299
97ColCho-67
97UppDec-327
Castillo, Jeff
88GreFalDTI-8
Castillo, Juan Brayas
80BurBeeT-22
80UtiBluJT-13
81BurBeeT-20
83ElPasDT-10
84ElPasDT-16
85VanCanC-205
86BrePol-3
86FleUpd-22
87BrePol-3
87Don-249
87FleUpd-18
87FleUpdG-18
87TopTra-20T
87TopTraT-20T
88BrePol-3
88Don-363
88Fle-159
88FleGlo-159
88OPC-362
88Sco-429
88ScoGlo-429
88StaLinBre-4
88Top-362
88TopBig-117
88TopTif-362
89Don-530
89Top-538
89TopBig-9
89TopTif-538
89UppDec-522
90ColSprSSP-41
90PitMetP-20
90ProAAAF-222
91ColMetPI-14
91ColMetPPI-3
91DenZepLD-132
91DenZepP-129
91LinDriAAA-132
91SouAtlLAGP-SAL13
92St.LucMCB-13
92St.LucMF-1738
93BinMetF-2326
93Bow-538
94BreMilB-111
95ColCho-17
95ColChoGS-17
95ColChoSS-17
95StaClu-389
95StaCluMOP-389
95StaCluSTWS-389
95UppDec-119
95UppDecED-119
95UppDecEDG-119
Castillo, Juan F.
93LinVenB-15
94BinMetF-697
94VenLinU-17
95LinVen-99
95SigRoo-12
95SigRooSig-12
96TulDriTI-5
Castillo, Luis Antonio
95KanCouCLTI-3
95KanCouCTI-4
96BesAutS-19
96BesAutSA-12
96Bow-189
96BowBes-154
96BowBesAR-154
96BowBesMI-2
96BowBesMIAR-2
96BowBesMIR-2
96BowBesR-154
96PorSeaDB-10
97Bow-150
97BowBes-138
97BowBesAR-138
97BowBesR-138
97BowCerBIA-CA13
97BowCerGIA-CA13
97BowInt-150
97Cir-358
97CirRav-358
97ColCho-26
97Don-316
97DonLim-21
97DonLimLE-21
97DonPre-137
97DonPreCttC-137
97DonPreP-316
97DonPrePGold-316
97DonRatR-18
97Fin-46
97FinRef-46
97Fle-326
97FleTif-326
97Lea-182
97LeaFraM-182
97LeaFraMDC-182
97Pac-298
97PacLigB-298
97PacSil-298
97Pin-160
97PinArtP-160
97PinMusC-160
97Sco-273
97ScoShoS-273
97ScoShoSAP-273
97SP-12
97StaClu-119
97StaCluM-M7
97StaCluMOP-119
97StaCluMOP-M7
97Top-267
97TopChr-95
97TopChrR-95
97TopGal-143
97TopGalPPI-143
97Ult-194
97UltGolME-194
97UltPlaME-194
97UppDec-223
97UppDecU-44
97UppDecUGN-GN3
Castillo, Luis T.
82WauTimF-16
87StoPorP-17
88ElPasDB-8
Castillo, Manny (Esteban M.)
76ArkTraT-2
78SprRedWK-9
80OmaRoyP-5
81OmaRoyT-15
81Top-66
83Don-253
83Fle-474
83Top-258
84Fle-607
84Nes792-562
84SyrChiT-24
84Top-562
84TopTif-562
Castillo, Marino
93CliGiaC-6
93CliGiaF-2481
94SanJosGC-3
94SanJosGF-2808
Castillo, Marty (Martin H.)
80EvaTriT-19
81EvaTriT-11
82EvaTriT-11
82Fle-265
82Top-261
83EvaTriT-11
84Don-247
84Nes792-303
84TigWavP-10
84Top-303
84TopTif-303
85Don-394
85Fle-5
85TigCaiD-5
85TigWen-6
85Top-461
85TopTif-461
86Top-788
86TopTif-788
89PacSenL-88
89TopSenL-10
90EliSenL-66
91PacSenL-2
Castillo, Neldy
76VenLeaS-105
Castillo, Tomas
80UtiBluJT-12
Castillo, Tony (Anthony)
79HawIsIC-27
79HawIsIT-24
80HawIsIT-21
81HawIsIT-6
85KinBluJT-3
Castillo, Tony (Antonio Jose)
85IowCubT-1
87DunBluJP-934
88DunBluJS-2
89Bow-244
89BowTif-244
89DonRoo-12
90BraDubP-4
90Don-592
90OPC-620
90Top-620
90TopTif-620
90UppDec-551
91Fle-685
91LinDriAAA-428
91OPC-353
91RicBraBC-7
91RicBraLD-428
91RicBraP-2560
91RicBraTI-6
91Sco-582
91Top-353
91TopTif-353
91TopDesS-353
91TopMic-353
91UppDec-458
92Don-739
92Fle-499
92Sco-682
92TolMudHF-1033
92TolMudHS-580
93FleFinE-288

93LinVenB-2
94BluJayUSPC-4D
94BluJayUSPC-12S
94Don-601
94Fle-327
94Pac-637
94Sco-177
94ScoGolR-177
94StaClu-470
94StaCluFDI-470
94StaCluGR-470
94StaCluMOP-470
94StaCluT-167
94StaCluTFDI-167
94VenLinU-127
95Don-235
95DonPreP-235
95Fla-96
95Fle-90
95LinVen-185
95LinVen-273
95Pac-440
95Sco-219
95ScoGolR-219
95ScoPlaTS-219
96BluJayOH-4
96Don-347
96DonPreP-347
96Fle-269
96Pac-448
96Top-109
96Ult-144
96UltGolM-144
96ColCho-749
96ColChoGS-749
96ColChoSS-749
96FleTif-269
96LeaSigEA-27
97PacPriGotD-GD29
Castillo, William
76VenLeaS-27
Castino, John A.
77OrlTwiT-4
78OrlTwiT-2
79TwiFriP-3
80OPC-76
80Top-137
81AllGamPI-30
81Don-488
81Dra-29
81Fle-554
81FleStiC-112
81OPC-304
81Squ-29
81Top-304
81TopScr-33
81TopSti-99
82Don-256
82Fle-549
82FleSta-230
82Kel-29
82OPC-73
82Top-396
82Top-644
82TopSti-209
82TwiPos-4
83Don-303
83Fle-609
83OPC-93
83Top-93
83TopSti-89
83TwiTeal-1
84AllGamPI-121
84Don-4
84Don-4A
84Don-120
84DonActAS-7
84Fle-560
84MinTwiP-6
84Nes792-237
84OPC-237
84Top-237
84TopSti-307
84TopTif-237
84TwiTeal-1
85OPC-298
85Top-452
85TopMin-452
85TopTif-452
Castle, Don (Donald Hardy)
74SpoIndC-35
77WesHavYT-4
93RanKee-99
Castleberry, Kevin
88CapCodPPaLP-111
88OklSoo-8
89OklSoo-7
90DurBulTI-6
91MiaMirC-18
91MiaMirP-412
92BirBarF-2589
92SarWhiSCB-8
93ElPasDF-2954
Castleman, Clydell
36GouBWR-6
36GouWidPPR-A14
36GouWidPPR-A15
36WorWidGV-36
79DiaGre-47
Castleman, Foster E.
55GiaGolS-27
56Top-271
57Top-237
58Top-416
79TCM50-225
91OriCro-71
Castner, Rodger
87WatPirP-2
88WatPirP-4
Castor, John
91OklStaC-4
Castro, Antionio
85MexCitTT-24
93CedRapKC-2
93CedRapKF-1744
96KanCouCTI-4
Castro, Bill
76OPC-293
76Top-293
77Top-528
78Top-448
79Top-133
80Top-303
81Don-578
81Fle-517
81Top-271
82TacTigT-4
83Fle-109
92BrePol-30
92YanWIZ8-28
94BreMilB-112
Castro, Dennis
96BreCouMB-10
Castro, Earnest
89WauTimGS-3
Castro, Edgar
82MiaMarT-15
88BlaYNPRWL-101
89BlaYNPRWL-109
Castro, Fidel
88LitSunMLL-11
Castro, Francisco
94GreFalDSP-8
Castro, Frank
85BeaGolGT-15
86BeaGolGP-5
Castro, Genaro
86LitFalMP-5
Castro, Guillermo
82DayBeaAT-1
83DayBeaAT-5
Castro, Jose
80CarMudF-2
82EdmTraT-2
85BufBisT-8
86SyrChiP-7
87SyrChiP-1945
87SyrChiT-12
88OmaRoyC-24
88OmaRoyP-1509
89OmaRoyC-14
89OmaRoyP-1731
90CMC-73
90IndIndC-23
90IndIndP-287
90JamExpP-29
90ProAAAF-570
91RocExpC-13
91RocExpP-2063
92EriSaiF-1643
93KanCouCC-27
93KanCouCF-932
94PorSeaDF-693
94PorSeaDTI-5
95BreCouMF-263
96BreCouMB-2
93KanCouCTI-2
Castro, Juan
91GreFalDSP-26
92BakDodCLC-6
93SanAntMF-3010
94SanAntMF-2475
95Exc-209
95WesMicWTI-4
96ColCho-21
96Fle-429
96FleTif-429
96Pac-113
97Pac-327
97PacLigB-327
97PacSil-327
Castro, Liliano
87FayGenP-21
88FayGenP-1101
Castro, Nelson
90KisDodD-6
91GreFalDSP-4
92BakDodCLC-7
93BakDodCLC-3
94BakDodC-7
94SanAntMF-2461
95SanAntMTI-27
Castro, Pablo
88St.CatBJP-2012
Castro, Ramon
94ClaUpdCotC-CC15
94SigRooDP-17
94SigRooDPS-17
94StaCluDP-21
94StaCluDPFDI-21
95AubAstTI-30
95SelSurS-SS6
95SPML-66
95StaClu-115
95StaCluFDI-115
95StaCluMOP-115
95StaCluSTWS-115
95Top-313
95UppDecML-198
96BesAutS-20
96Bow-115
96Exc-170
96MidLeaAB-26
96QuaCitRB-11
95UppDecMLFS-198
Castro, Ruben
94EliTwiC-4
94EliTwiF-3738
Castro, Tony
91EugEmeC-1
91EugEmeP-3737
Cat, Rally
96MicBatCB-30
Catalanotto, Frank
93BriTigC-5
93BriTigF-3657
94FayGenC-5
94FayGenF-2152
94SouAtlLAF-SAL11
95JacSunTI-3
95UppDecML-157
96JacSunB-7
96SigRooOJ-7
96SigRooOJS-7
95UppDecMLFS-157
Cataline, Dan
81QuaCitCT-16
83VerBeaDT-24
Cater, Danny Anderson
64PhiPhiB-9
64Top-482
65OPC-253
65Top-253
66Top-398
67CokCapAt-17
67DexPre-45
67OPC-157
67Top-157
68Top-535
69A'sJacitB-4
69MilBra-55
69MLBOffS-84
69OPC-1
69OPC-44
69Top-1
69Top-44
69Top-556
69TopSta-213
69TopTeaP-21
69TraSta-12
70MLBOffS-243
70OPC-437
70Top-437
70YanCliDP-5
71Kel-30
71MilDud-3
71MLBOffS-485
71OPC-358
71Top-358
71TopCoi-14
71YanArcO-4
71YanCliDP-3
72MilBra-71
72Top-676
73LinPor-16
73OPC-317
73Top-317
74OPC-543
74Top-543
75OPC-645
75Top-645
92YanWIZ7-31
Cater, Michael
92StoPorC-19
Cates, Tim
83MemChiT-11
85IndIndTI-8
Cathcart, Gary
86Ft.LauYP-5
87AlbYanP-9
88AlbYanP-1335
Cather, Mike
94ChaRanF-2491
95TulDriTI-3
96GreBraB-9
96GreBraTI-24
Cather, Ted (Theodore P.)
15CraJacE-145
Catlett, David
93IdaFalBF-4038
93IdaFalBSP-29
94Bow-665
94IdaFalBF-3591
94IdaFalBSP-16
94MacBraC-2
94MacBraF-2211
96RocCubTI-5
Cato, Keefe
81WatRedT-2
82WatRedT-3
83WatRedT-1
84WicAerRD-14
85LasVegSC-118
85Top-367
85TopTif-367
86OmaRoyP-4
Cato, Wayne
76CedRapGT-9
79CedRapGT-15
80CliGiaT-26
Catterson, Tom (Thomas H.)
90DodTar-910
Caudill, Bill
76ArkTraT-3
78SSP270-262
80Top-103
81Don-586
81Fle-306
81OPC-346
81Top-574
81TopSti-152
82Don-426
82Fle-590
82Top-303
82TopTra-18T
83AllGamPI-74
83Don-302
83Fle-475
83FleSta-33
83FleSti-179
83MarNal-1
83OPC-78
83Top-78
83TopSti-118
84A'sMot-12
84AllGamPI-167
84Don-118
84Fle-608
84FleSti-76
84FleUpd-24
84Nes792-769
84OPC-299
84Top-769
84TopSti-345
84TopTif-769
84TopTra-23T
84TopTraT-23T
85BluJayFS-7
85BluJayPLP-2
85Don-96
85Fle-419
85FleStaS-100
85FleUpd-23
85Lea-154
85OPC-275
85OPCPos-23
85Top-685
85TopMin-685
85TopSti-322
85TopTif-685
85TopTifT-19T
85TopTra-19T
86BluJayAF-5
86BluJayFS-5
86Don-317
86Fle-55
86GenMilB-3C
86OPC-207
86Top-435
86TopTif-435
87A'sMot-24
87Fle-221
87FleGlo-221
87OPC-156
87Top-733
87TopTif-733
Caughey, Wayne
77OrlTwiT-5
77TacTwiDQ-2A
79TolMudHT-11
80AlbDukT-18
81AlbDukT-14
82PorBeaT-12
Cauley, Chris
88TamTarS-4
89SarWhiSS-4
Caulfield, Tom
83EriCarT-23
Causey, Red (Cecil)
20GasAmeMBD-28
21E121So1-9
21E121So8-10
21KoBreWSI-7
22AmeCarE-10
23W501-65
Causey, Wayne (James Wayne)
61A'sTeal-3
61AthJayP-5
62SalPlaC-100
62ShiPlaC-100
62Top-496
63AthJayP-3
63Top-539
64A's-3
64AthJayP-1
64Top-75
64TopCoi-102
64TopCoi-161A
64TopCoi-161B
64TopGia-45
64TopSta-87
64TopStaU-14
64TopTatl-29
64TopVen-75
65AthJayP-2
65Top-425
65TopEmbl-21
65TopTral-8
66Top-366
66TopVen-366
67CokCapWS-8
67Top-286
68Top-522
69OPC-33
69Top-33
78TCM60I-8
91OriCro-72
Causion, Bill
58JetPos-5
Cavalier, Kevin
87JamExpP-2563
88WesPalBES-5
Cavalli, Brian
90OklSoo-2
92OklStaC-3
93BoiHawC-6
93BoiHawF-3919

Cavallo, Gary
74SacSolC-51
Cavallo, Pablo
77NewCoPT-6
78NewWayCT-6
Cavanagh, Michael
92EveGiaC-21
92EveGiaF-1692
93CliGiaC-7
93CliGiaF-2491
94CliLumF-1982
94CliLumC-7
Cavanaugh, Marty
14B18B-13A
14B18B-13B
14B18B-13C
Cavarretta, Phil
34BatR31-101
35DiaMatCS3T1-30
36DiaMatCS3T2-3
36GouWidPPR-A16
36OveCanR-6
36R31PasP-29
36R31PasP-31
36SandSW-6
36WorWidGV-54
38BasTabP-3
39CubTeal-2
39ExhSal-7
41CubTeal-1
41DouPlaR-103
43CubTeal-4
44CubTeal-3
46SpoExcW-1-1A
47PM1StaP1-29
47TipTop-105
48KelPep*-BB1
49Bow-6
49EurSta-53
49Lea-168
50AmeNut&CCP-3
50Bow-195
51Bow-138
51R42SmaS-13
52Bow-150
52StaCalL-80F
52StaCalS-92A
52TipTop-6
52Top-295
53BowC-30
54Top-55
55Bow-282
62TigPosCF-5
74LauAllG-44
76ChiGre-4
76SSP-617
76TayBow4-41
81DiaStaCD-111
83TCMPla1943-35
83TopRep5-295
84CubUno-3
89PacLegI-131
91TopArc1-295
92CubOldS-5
94TopArc1-55
94TopArc1G-55
94UppDecAH-46
94UppDecAH1-46
Cavazzoni, Ken
91PriRedC-5
91PriRedP-3519
Caveney, Ike (James C.)
21Exh-22
21Nei-116
22E120-168
22W573-17
Cavers, Mike
89FreKeyS-2
90HagSunB-25
90HagSunP-1404
90HagSunS-5
Cawhorn, Gerald
93WatIndC-3
93WatIndF-3567
94ColRedC-5
94ColRedF-448
94SouAtlLAF-SAL6
95KinIndTI-6
96KenIndB-4
Cayson, Tony
87BelMarL-3
87BelMarTI-20
89BelMarL-25
Cebuhar, John
88HamRedP-1721
89HamRedS-8
Ceccarelli, Art
55A'sRodM-9
58Top-191
59Top-226
60Top-156
60TopVen-156
76A'sRodMC-6
91OriCro-73
Cecchetti, George
80WatIndT-20
81ChaLooT-14
82ChaLooT-14
83BufBisT-22
84BufBisT-2
85WatIndT-20
86MaiGuiP-3
Cecchini, Jim
86JacExpT-3
Cecena, Jose
86ReaPhiP-5
88DonRoo-6
88FleUpd-62
88FleUpdG-62
88RanMot-12
88TopTra-26T
88TopTraT-26T
89Fle-516
89FleGlo-516
89ScoHot1R-35
89Top-683
89TopTif-683
89UppDec-560
93CarMudF-2045
93CarMudTI-15
93RanKee-100
Cecere, Mike
93EveGiaC-6
93EveGiaF-3771
Ceci, Sam
74TacTwiC-15
76SpoIndC-3
Cecil, Rex
47CenFlo-4
49RemBre-3
Cecil, Timothy
90ChaWheB-12
90ChaWheP-2233
90CMC-708
91ChaWheC-1
91ChaWheP-2878
91Cla/Bes-262
Cedeno, Andujar
89AshTouP-952
90Bes-72
90Bow-77
90BowTif-77
90CMC-811
90ColMudB-3
90ColMudP-1351
90ColMudS-7
90ProAaA-58
91Bow-563
91Cla1-T43
91ClaGam-200
91Fle-502
91LeaGolR-BC20
91LinDriAAA-606
91MajLeaCP-45
91OPC-646
91Sco-753
91ScoRoo-40
91StaClu-476
91StuPre-12
91Top-646
91TopDeb90-28
91TopDesS-646
91TopMic-646
91TopTif-646
91TucTorLD-606
91TucTorP-2218
91Ult-135
91UppDec-23
92AstMot-9
92Bow-9
92Cla1-T23
92Don-549
92Fle-430
92Lea-341
92OPC-288
92OPCPre-156
92PanSti-155
92Pin-84
92PinTea2-33
92ProFS7-224
92Sco-599
92Sco100RS-65
92StaClu-310
92Stu-34
92Top-288
92TopGol-288
92TopGolW-288
92TopMic-288
92TriPla-68
92TucTorF-494
92Ult-201
92Ult-490
92UppDec-257
93AstMot-10
93Bow-672
93Don-456
93Fla-60
93Fle-433
93Lea-108
93LimRocDWB-136
93LinVenB-277
93LinVenB-300
93LinVenB-319
93OPC-129
93PacBeiA-24
93PacJugC-24
93PacSpa-121
93PanSti-172
93Pin-32
93Sco-127
93SP-31
93StaClu-207
93StaCluAs-20
93StaCluFDI-207
93StaCluMOP-207
93Top-553
93TopGol-553
93TopInaM-553
93TopMic-553
93Ult-391
93UppDec-562
93UppDecGold-562
94AstMot-18
94Bow-558
94ColC-75
94ColChoGS-75
94ColChoSS-75
94Don-519
94ExtBas-271
94Fin-97
94FinRef-97
94Fla-168
94Fle-487
94Lea-260
94LeaL-113
94OPC-10
94Pac-261
94PanSti-192
94Pin-292
94PinArtP-292
94PinMusC-292
94ProMag-58
94Sco-104
94ScoGolR-104
94Sel-308
94StaClu-138
94StaCluFDI-138
94StaCluGR-138
94StaCluMOP-138
94Stu-19
94Top-11
94TopGol-11
94TopSpa-11
94TriPla-24
94Ult-204
94UppDec-354
94UppDecED-354
94VenLinU-57
95ColCho-351
95ColChoGS-351
95ColChoSS-351
95Don-530
95DonPreP-530
95DonTopotO-339
95Fin-231
95FinRef-231
95Fla-417
95Fle-455
95FleUpd-182
95Lea-373
95LeaLim-44
95Pac-183
95PadCHP-12
95PadMot-5
95Pin-366
95PinArtP-366
95PinMusC-366
95Sco-477
95ScoGolR-477
95ScoPlaTS-477
95Sel-229
95SelArtP-229
95StaClu-468
95StaClu-539
95StaCluMOP-468
95StaCluMOP-539
95StaCluSTWS-468
95StaCluSTWS-539
95StaCluVR-256
95Stu-130
95Top-464
95TopCyb-259
95TopTra-57T
95Ult-436
95UltGolM-436
95UppDec-373
95UppDecED-373
95UppDecEDG-373
95UppDecSE-268
95UppDecSEG-268
96ColCho-358
96ColCho-712
96ColChoGS-358
96ColChoGS-712
96ColChoSS-358
96ColChoSS-712
96Don-508
96DonPreP-508
96Fla-372
96Fle-563
96FleTif-563
96LeaSigA-41
96LeaSigAG-41
96LeaSigAS-41
96Pac-194
96PacPri-P60
96PacPriG-P60
96PadMot-12
96ProSta-83
96Sco-121
96StaClu-334
96StaCluMOP-334
95StaCluVRMC-256
96Top-29
96Ult-556
96UltGolM-556
96UppDec-448
97Pin-145
97PinArtP-145
97PinMusC-145
Cedeno, Blas
91BriTigC-19
91BriTigP-3596
92BriTigC-3
92BriTigF-1401
93FayGenC-7
93FayGenF-123
93LinVenB-173
94LakTigF-3028
94TreThuF-2114
94VenLinU-229
95JacSunTI-4
95LinVen-62
96JacSunB-8
96LakTigB-10
Cedeno, Cesar
71AstCok-3
71OPC-237
71Top-237
71TopSup-15
72EssCoi-4
72OPC-65
72Top-65
73Kel2D-13
73LinPor-80
73OPC-290
73Top-290
74AstFouTIP-3
74OPC-200
74OPC-337
74Top-200
74Top-337
74TopSta-31
75Hos-17
75HosTwi-17
75OPC-590
75SSP42-26
75SSPPuzB-7
75Top-590
76CraDis-12
76Hos-47
76HosTwi-47
76OPC-460
76Raw-1
76SSP-63
76Top-460
77BurCheD-7
77Hos-58
77OPC-131
77RCColC-16
77Top-90
77TopCloS-13
78AstBurK-18
78Hos-50
78OPC-226
78RCColC-51
78Top-650
78WifBalD-16
79AstTeal-4
79Hos-91
79OPC-294
79Top-570
80BurKinPHR-25
80Kel-36
80OPC-193
80Top-370
80TopSup-56
81AllGamPI-137
81CokTeaS-62
81Don-263
81Dra-20
81Fle-59
81FleStiC-35
81Kel-14
81MSAMinD-8
81OPC-190
81PerCreC-25
81Top-190
81TopScr-77
81TopSti-167
81TopSti-258
81TopSupHT-97
82Don-118
82Fle-213
82FleSta-41
82OPC-48
82RedCok-4
82Top-640
82TopSti-47
82TopTra-19T
83AllGamPI-137
83Don-43
83Fle-587
83FleSta-34
83FleSti-221
83OPC-238
83RedYea-28
83Top-351
83Top-475
83TopFol-5
83TopSti-231
84Don-306
84Fle-465
84FunFooP-42
84Nes792-705
84Nes792-725
84OPC-191
84RedEnq-13
84Top-705
84Top-725
84TopSti-54
84TopTif-705
84TopTif-725
85Don-447
85Fle-531
85Lea-87
85OPC-54
85RedYea-1
85ThoMcAD-26
85Top-54
85TopSti-55
85TopTif-54
86AstGreT-6
86AstMot-11
86DodCokP-6
86Don-648
86Fle-29
86OPC-224
86Top-224
86TopTif-224

87AstShoSO-1
87AstShoSTw-21
87AstShoSTw-26
87AstShoSTw-27
89PacSenL-62
89T/MSenL-20
89T/MSenL-118
89TopSenL-69
90DodTar-120
90EliSenL-79
90SweBasG-41
91KelLey-4
91LinDri-36
91PacSenL-40
91PacSenL-53
91SweBasG-104
91UppDecS-15
92ActPacA-29
92UppDecS-14
93QuaCitRBC-26
93QuaCitRBF-116
93TedWil-41
93UppDecAH-29
94QuaCitRBC-27
94QuaCitRBF-551
94UppDecAH-89
94UppDecAH1-89
Cedeno, Domingo
89MyrBeaBJP-1456
90DunBluJS-5
91KnoBluJLD-352
91KnoBluJP-1773
91LinDriAA-352
92KnoBluJF-2995
92KnoBluJS-378
93FleFinE-289
93Lea-486
93LimRocDWB-133
93SyrChiF-1002
94Don-455
94ScoRoo-RT105
94ScoRooGR-RT105
94SpoRoo-72
94SpoRooAP-72
94StaCluT-164
94StaCluTFDI-164
94Top-776
94TopGol-776
94TopSpa-776
94Ult-436
95Pac-441
95Sco-7
95ScoGolR-7
95ScoPlaTS-7
95Top-89
96BluJayOH-5
96ColCho-348
96ColChoGS-348
96ColChoSS-348
96Don-134
96DonPreP-134
96Fle-270
96FleTif-270
96LeaSigA-42
96LeaSigAG-42
96LeaSigAS-42
96Pac-439
96StaClu-295
96StaCluMOP-295
96Ult-427
96UltGolM-427
97PacPriGotD-GD30
Cedeno, Eduardo
93AshTouC-4
93AshTouF-2281
93AubAstC-4
93AubAstF-3450
94EugEmeC-26
94EugEmeF-3718
94RocRoyC-7
94RocRoyF-572
95SprSulTI-6
96WilBluRB-12
Cedeno, Ramon
88AshTouP-1053
89OscAstS-4
90VisOakCLC-68
90VisOakP-2166
Cedeno, Roger
92GreFalDSP-19
93Bow-534
93ClaFS7-130
93LinVenB-218
93LinVenB-278
93SanAntMF-3015
93SP-272
93StaCluD-24
94AlbDukF-855
94Bow-238
94BowBes-B17
94BowBesR-B17
94Cla-142
94ExcFS7-211
94UppDecML-25
94UppDecML-257
94UppDecMLPotYF-PY9
94UppDecMLT1PJF-TP1
94UppDecMLT1PMF-1
94VenLinU-53
95ActPacF-23
95Bow-104
95BowBes-B54
95BowBesR-B54
95Exc-210
95LinVen-1
95Sel-155
95SelArtP-155
95SelCer-93
95SelCerMG-93
95SP-67
95SPCha-2
95SPChaDC-2
95SPSil-67
95Sum-169
95SumNthD-169
95Top-651
95UppDec-228
95UppDecED-228
95UppDecEDG-228
95UppDecML-13
95UppDecML-107
95UppDecMLT1PF-7
95UppDecSE-170
95UppDecSEG-170
96Bow-80
96BowBes-115
96BowBesAR-115
96BowBesR-115
96ColCho-12
96ColChoGS-12
96ColChoSS-12
96DodMot-27
96DodPol-7
96Don-337
96DonPreP-337
96Fin-B283
96FinRef-B283
96Fla-289
96FleDod-4
96FlePro-2
96FleUpd-U142
96FleUpdTC-U142
96Lea-216
96LeaPrePB-216
96LeaPrePG-216
96LeaPrePS-216
96LeaSigA-43
96LeaSigAG-43
96LeaSigAS-43
96MetUni-182
96MetUniP-182
96PanSti-90
96Pin-176
96PinAfi-182
96PinAfiAP-182
96Sco-233
96Spo-124
96SpoArtP-124
96StaClu-313
96StaCluMOP-313
96Stu-3
96StuPrePB-3
96StuPrePG-3
96StuPrePS-3
96Top-436
96TopGal-142
96TopGalPPI-142
96Ult-494
96UltGolM-494
96UltGolP-3
96UltGolPGM-3
96UppDecBCP-BC14
96UppDecPHE-H54
96UppDecPreH-H54
97Don-74
97DonPreP-74
97DonPrePGold-74
97DonTea-108
97DonTeaSPE-108
97Fle-358
97FleTif-358
97Pac-328
97PacLigB-328
97PacSil-328
97Pin-46
97PinArtP-46
97PinMusC-46
97Sco-186
97ScoDod-6
97ScoDodPl-6
97ScoDodPr-6
97ScoPreS-186
97ScoShoS-186
97ScoShoSAP-186
97StaClu-268
97StaCluMOP-268
97Top-126
97Ult-214
97UltGolME-214
97UltPlaME-214
95UppDecMLFS-13
95UppDecMLFS-107
Cedeno, Vinicio
86MidAngP-4
87MidAngP-8
88MidAngGS-4
89MidAngGS-9
Cederblad, Brett
91DaiDolF-6
96TreThuB-8
Celis, Lucio
76VenLeaS-39
80VenLeaS-47
Censale, Silvio
93BatCliC-6
93BatCliF-3136
95PiePhiF-180
Centala, Scott
88CapCodPPaLP-123
89EugEmeB-7
90Bes-29
90CMC-748
90MemChiB-14
90MemChiP-1001
90MemChiS-4
90StaFS7-83
Centeno, Henry
92AshTouC-3
93LinVenB-146
93QuaCitRBC-4
93QuaCitRBF-107
94OscAstC-5
94OscAstF-1143
95JacGenTI-20
95LinVen-153
Centeno, Jose
75CliPilT-24
93AshTouC-5
93AshTouF-2268
93LinVenB-256
94VenLinU-30
94VerExpC-6
94VerExpF-3900
95LinVen-22
96DelShoB-12
96WesPalBEB-5
Cento, Tony
86AppFoxP-6
87PenWhiSP-28
Cepeda, Jose
96Bow-347
96LanLugB-8
96MidLeaAB-36
Cepeda, Malcom
93EugEmeC-10
94EugEmeC-6
94EugEmeF-3719
96BurBeeTI-15
Cepeda, Octavio
86MacPirP-5
87SalBucP-5
Cepeda, Orlando M.
47Exh-38A
47Exh-38B
47PM1StaP1-30
47PM1StaP1-31
58GiaSFCB-5
58Top-343
59Baz-5
59Top-390
59Top-553
60Baz-10
60GiaJayP-4
60Lea-128
60Top-450
60TopTat-8
61GiaJayP-3
61Pos-144A
61Pos-144B
61SevElev-20
61Top-435
61TopStal-75
62Baz-7
62ExhStaB-8
62GiaJayP-3
62Jel-136
62Pos-136
62PosCan-136
62SalPlaC-175
62ShiPlaC-175
62Top-40
62Top-54
62Top-390
62Top-401
62TopBuc-16
62TopStal-195
62TopVen-40
62TopVen-54
63BasMagM-15
63Baz-22
63ExhStaB-12
63Fle-64
63GiaJayP-2
63Jel-101
63Pos-101
63SalMetC-13
63Top-3
63Top-520
63TopStil-10
64GiaJayP-1
64Top-9
64Top-306
64Top-390
64TopCoi-63
64TopCoi-142
64TopGia-55
64TopSta-50
64TopStaU-15
64TopTatl-30
64TopVen-9
64TopVen-306
64WheSta-10
65OldLonC-6
65OPC-4
65Top-4
65Top-360
65TopEmbl-45
65TopTral-9
66OPC-132
66Top-132
66TopVen-132
67OPC-20
67OPCPapl-9
67Top-20
67TopGiaSU-13
67TopPos-9
67TopTesF-5
67TopVen-291
68AtlOilPBCC-12
68Baz-6
68OPC-3
68Top-3
68Top-200
68Top-278
68Top-362
68TopActS-1A
68TopActS-9B
68TopActS-14A
68TopGamI-32
68TopPla-15
68TopPos-12
68TopVen-3
68TopVen-200
68TopVen-278
68TopVen-362
69MilBra-56
69MLBOffS-113
69MLBPin-38
69Top-385
69TopSta-113
69TopTeaP-18
70MLBOffS-4
70Top-555
70TopBoo-13
71BazNumT-33
71BazUnn-6
71MilDud-39
71MLBOffS-7
71OPC-605
71Top-605
71TopCoi-61
71TopGreM-26
71TopTat-17
72EssCoi-5
72MilBra-72
72OPC-195
72Top-195
73LinPor-17
73OPC-545
73Top-545
74Kel-24
74OPC-83
74Top-83
74TopSta-132
75OPC-205
75Top-205
78AtlCon-5
78TCM60I-50
80GleFalWSBT-26
80GleFalWSCT-25
80VenLeaS-245
82K-M-12
83MLBPin-21
83TigAlKS-51
84GiaMot-11
84OCoandSI-162
85CirK-24
86SpoDecG-48
88PacLegI-94
89SweBasG-8
90PacLeg-65
90SweBasG-28
91KelLey-5
91SweBasG-105
92ActPacA-66
92CarMcD-26
92GiaFanFFB-2
92KodCelD-1
92MDAMVP-5
92MVP-14
92MVP2H-13
92UppDecS-7
93TedWil-87
93UppDecS-7
93UppDecS-22
93UppDecS-28
94TopSpa-L6
94UppDecAH-136
94UppDecAH-215
94UppDecAH1-136
94UppDecAH1-215
Cepeda, Rafael
80VenLeaS-237
Cephas, Ruben
93HelBreF-4108
93HelBreSP-3
Cepicky, Scott
90Bes-173
90MidLeaASGS-7
90SouBenWSB-2
90SouBenWSGS-2
91Cla/Bes-86
91FloStaLAP-FSL28
91SarWhiSC-15
91SarWhiSP-1118
92BirBarF-2590
92BirBarS-80
92Bow-297
92Bow-614
92ClaFS7-30
92ProFS7-44
92SkyAA F-39
92UppDecML-304
93ExcFS7-152
93LinVenB-63
93NasSouF-574
Cerame, Mike
89PulBraP-1903
90PulBraB-29
91PulBraC-30
94OscAstC-29
Ceravolo, Steve
93Sou-6
Cerdan, Marcel
47HomBon-8
Cerefin, Mike
85OscAstTI-5
Cerio, Steve
92SprCarC-25
92SprCarF-871

93St.PetCC-9
93St.PetCF-2629
94St.PetCC-9
94St.PetCF-2597
Cerny, Chris
88BakDodCLC-252
89BoiHawP-1999
Cerny, Mark
89BilMusP-2054
90EriSaiS-2
Cerny, Marty
87PorChaRP-7
88GasRanP-1016
89MiaMirIS-4
89MiaMirIS-3
Cerny, Scott
86SalAngC-86
87QuaCitAP-24
88CalLeaACLC-33
88PalSprACLC-101
88PalSprAP-1440
89MidAngGS-10
90MidAngGS-8
Cerone, Rick (Richard Aldo)
76SSP-516
77OPC-76
77Top-476
78OPC-129
78Top-469
79BluJayBY-5
79OPC-72
79Top-152
80OPC-311
80Top-591
81AllGamPI-37
81Don-346
81Fle-83
81FleStiC-88
81OPC-335
81Top-335
81TopScr-28
81TopSti-109
81TopSti-248
81TopSupHT-61
82Don-199
82Fle-31
82FleSta-118
82FleSta-238
82OPC-45
82Top-45
82TopSti-218
83AllGamPI-38
83Don-577
83Fle-376
83FleSta-35
83FleSti-43
83OPC-254
83Top-254
83YanRoyRD-1
84Don-492
84Fle-121
84Nes792-617
84OPC-228
84Top-617
84TopTif-617
85BraHos-6
85BraPol-5
85Don-274
85Fle-123
85FleUpd-24
85OPC-337
85Top-429
85TopTif-429
85TopTifT-20T
85TopTra-20T
86BluJayGT-8
86BrePol-11
86Don-310
86Fle-511
86FleUpd-23
86OPC-203
86Top-747
86TopTif-747
86TopTra-22T
86TopTraT-22T
87Fle-340
87FleGlo-340
87Top-129
87TopTif-129
87TopTra-21T
87TopTraT-21T
88Don-351
88DonBasB-332
88DonTeaBRS-NEW
88Fle-203
88FleGlo-203
88FleUpd-6
88FleUpdG-6
88PanSti-151
88Sco-486
88ScoGlo-486
88ScoRoo-21T
88ScoRooG-21T
88StaLinY-1
88Top-561
88TopTif-561
88TopTra-27T
88TopTraT-27T
89Don-398
89DonBasB-308
89Fle-84
89FleGlo-84
89OPC-96
89Sco-396
89Top-96
89TopBig-119
89TopTif-96
89UppDec-152
90Bow-435
90BowTif-435
90Don-305
90Fle-270
90FleCan-270
90OPC-303
90PubSti-451
90Sco-139
90ScoRoo-63T
90Top-303
90TopSti-1
90TopTif-303
90TopTra-21T
90TopTraT-21T
90TopTVY-20
90UppDec-405
90VenSti-100
90YanScoNW-28
91Bow-468
91Fle-660
91FleUpd-101
91Lea-493
91MetColP-26
91MetKah-13
91OPC-237
91Sco-580
91ScoRoo-41T
91StaClu-511
91Top-237
91TopDesS-237
91TopMic-237
91TopTif-237
91TopTra-21T
91TopTraT-21T
91UltUpd-96
92Don-335
92ExpPos-8
92Lea-523
92OPC-643
92OPCPre-90
92PanSti-221
92StaClu-705
92StaCluNC-705
92Top-643
92TopGol-643
92TopGolW-643
92TopMic-643
92YanWIZ8-29
94BreMilB-113
Cerqueira, Jeff
88CapCodPPaLP-83
Cerrud, Roberto
80UtiBluJT-14
Cerutti, John
83KnoBluJT-3
84SyrChiT-31
85SyrChiT-27
86DonRoo-20
86FleUpd-24
86SpoRoo-36
86SyrChiP-8
86TopTra-23T
86TopTraT-23T
87BluJayFS-3
87Don-442
87Fle-222
87FleGlo-222
87Lea-210
87OPC-282
87SpoTeaP-5
87SyrChi1A-9
87Top-557
87TopTif-557
87ToyRoo-6
88BluJayFS-6
88Don-321
88Fle-105
88FleGlo-105
88Lea-152
88OPC-191
88Sco-98
88ScoGlo-98
88Top-191
88TopTif-191
89BluJayFS-7
89Bow-247
89BowTif-247
89Don-467
89Fle-228
89FleGlo-228
89OPC-347
89Sco-304
89Top-347
89TopTif-347
89UppDec-129
90BluJayFS-5
90Bow-507
90BowTif-507
90Don-645
90Fle-78
90FleCan-78
90Lea-27
90OPC-211
90PanSti-177
90PubSti-511
90Sco-429
90Spo-86
90Top-211
90TopSti-195
90TopTif-211
90UppDec-485
90VenSti-101
91Bow-139
91Don-467
91Fle-172
91FleUpd-22
91Lea-270
91OPC-687
91Sco-786
91ScoRoo-40T
91StaClu-445
91TigCok-55
91Top-687A
91Top-687B
91TopDesS-687
91TopMic-687B
91TopTif-687
91UppDec-585
92Don-709
92Fle-129
92OPC-487
92PawRedSF-915
92PawRedSS-354
92Sco-179
92StaClu-71
92Top-487
92TopGol-487
92TopGolW-487
92TopMic-487
92UppDec-487
97DunDonPPS-4
Cerv, Bob (Robert Henry)
47Exh-39A
47Exh-39B
53Top-210
55Bow-306
56Top-288
57Top-269
58JayPubA-3
58Top-329
59ArmCoi-6
59Baz-6
59HomRunD-5
59Top-100
59TopVen-100
60A'sTeal-3
60Baz-15
60Top-415
61AngJayP-5
61Pos-13
61Top-563
61TopStaI-170
61Yan61RL-19
62Top-169
62TopVen-169
79TCM50-162
91RinPos1Y3-6
91TopArc1-210
92YanWIZ6-23
Cervantes, Manny
92ClaFS7-151
92SanBerC-16
92SanBerSF-962
93ClaGolF-142
93RivPilCLC-30
94RivPilCLC-31
Cervantes, Pedro
95YakBeaTI-4
96GreFalDTI-5
Cervantes, Raymond
92EriSaiC-22
92EriSaiF-1629
94SanBerSC-2
94SanBerSF-2764
Cesar, Dionys
96SouOreTI-26
Cesari, Jeff
89GenCubP-1868
Cesarlo, Jim
83TriTriT-23
Cespedes, Angel
96PorRocB-10
Cespedes, Teodoro
89EveGiaS-4
Cey, Ron (Ronald Charles)
72Top-761
73OPC-615
73Top-615
74OPC-315
74Top-315
74TopSta-42
75Hos-61
75HosTwi-61
75OPC-390
75Top-390
76CraDis-13
76Hos-63
76LinSup-117
76OPC-370
76SSP-75
76Top-370
77BurCheD-153
77Hos-89
77Kel-18
77MSADis-15
77OPC-199
77RCColC-17
77Spo-3016
77Top-50
77TopCloS-14
78Hos-93
78Kel-24
78OPC-130
78RCColC-19
78SSP270-62
78Top-630
78WifBalD-17
79DodBlu-2
79Hos-28
79OPC-94
79Top-190
80DodPol-10
80Kel-19
80OPC-267
80Top-510
81AllGamPI-118
81Dod-2
81DodPol-10
81Don-296
81Fle-126A
81Fle-126B
81FleStiC-3
81LonBeaPT-4
81OPC-260
81Top-260
81TopScr-73
81TopSti-177
81TopSupHT-44
82DodPol-10
82DodUniOV-3
82DogBuiE-2
82Don-210
82Fle-3
82FleSta-3
82Kel-46
82OPC-216
82OPC-367
82Top-410
82Top-411
82TopSti-51
83AllGamPI-119
83CubThoAV-11
83Don-84
83DonActA-21
83Fle-204
83FleSta-36
83FleSti-122
83OPC-15
83Top-15
83TopFol-2
83TopSti-244
83TopTra-19T
84AllGamPI-28
84CubChiT-6
84CubSev-11
84CubUno-7
84DodUniOP-8
84Don-361
84Dra-7
84Fle-490
84FunFooP-89
84Nes792-357
84OPC-357
84Top-357
84TopRubD-12
84TopSti-41
84TopTif-357
85AllGamPI-118
85CubLioP-4
85CubSev-11
85Don-320
85Dra-6
85Fle-52
85FleStaS-19
85Lea-84
85OPC-366
85Top-768
85TopSti-42
85TopTif-768
86CubGat-11
86CubUno-3
86Don-198
86Fle-363
86OPC-194
86Spo-130
86Top-669
86TopTif-669
87DodSmoA-4
87Fle-556
87FleGlo-556
87OPC-322
87OPCBoxB-C
87Top-581
87Top-767
87TopTif-581
87TopTif-767
87TopTra-22T
87TopTraT-22T
87TopWaxBC-C
88DodSmo-15
88DodSmo-21
88DodSmo-27
89DodSmoG-82
90DodTar-121
91DodUno7P-1
91DodUno7P-5
92DodStaTA-14
92UppDecS-15
93ActPacA-163
93Pin-480
93TedWil-10
93UppDecS-24
94UppDecAH-77
94UppDecAH1-77
Chacon, Elio R.
60Top-543
62MetJayP-2
62Top-256
62TopVen-199
82MetGal62-5
91MetWIZ-68
Chacon, Shawn
97Bow-349
97BowInt-349
Chacon, Troy
88CapCodPPaLP-183
Chadwick, Henry
36PC7AlbHoF-16
50CalHOFW-12
76ShaPiz-16
77BobParHoF-11

80PerHaloFP-16
80SSPHOF-16
84GalHaloFRL-16
90LitSunW-2
94OriofB-11
94UppDecTAE-3
Chadwick, Ray
86EdmTraP-3
87Don-505
88BirBarB-4
90CMC-177
90OmaRoyC-2
90OmaRoyP-58
90ProAAAF-593
Chadwick, Robert
86NewBriRSP-6
87NewBriRSP-9
87UtiBluSP-14
88NewBriRSP-893
Chafin, John
88UtiBluSP-14
91ElmPioC-23
91ElmPioP-3263
Chagnon, Leon
36GouWidPPR-D6
Chajin, David
91JohCitCP-3970
Chakales, Bob
52IndNumN-9
52Top-120
55Bow-148
57Top-261
60MapLeaSF-2
61MapLeaBH-4
83TopRep5-120
91OriCro-74
Chalk, Dave (David Lee)
74OPC-507
74Top-597
75Hos-46
75HosTwi-46
75OPC-64
75Top-64
76Hos-59
76HosTwi-59
76OPC-65
76SSP-194
76Top-52
77BurCheD-119
77Top-315
78AngFamF-6
78SSP270-198
78Top-178
79OPC-362
79Top-682
80OPC-137
80Top-261
81Don-101
81Fle-35
82Don-590
82Fle-407
82Top-462
86AngGreT-4
93RanKee-101
Challinor, John
94YakBeaC-4
94YakBeaF-3840
95VerBeaDTI-5
Chalmers, George
12T207-29
14FatPlaT-11
15SpoNewM-27
16SpoNewM-29
Chamberlain, Bill
78WauMetT-5
Chamberlain, Craig
80OmaRoyP-6
80Top-417
81OmaRoyT-4
81Top-274
83PhoGiaBHN-23
88ChaKniTI-12
82PhoGiaVNB-12
Chamberlain, Elton
87OldJudN-78
Chamberlain, Matt
93LSUTigM-11
93WelPirF-3348
94LSUTigMP-9
94SalBucC-4
94SalBucF-2316
Chamberlain, Murph
43ParSpo-19
Chamberlain, Tom
78St.PetCT-4
79ArkTraT-19A
Chamberlain, Wes (Wesley)
86AncGlaPTI-5
87WatPirP-12
88AugPirP-359
89BasAmeAPB-AA1
89EasLeaAP-5
89HarSenP-296
89HarSenS-5
89Sta-171
90BufBisC-23
90BufBisP-386
90BufBisTI-6
90CMC-23
90ProAAAF-501
91Bow-505
91Cla1-T80
91Cla3-T8
91ClaGam-92
91Don-423
91DonRoo-3
91Fle-391
91Lea-178
91OPC-603
91PhiMed-8
91Sco-713
91ScoRoo-14
91ScrRedBP-2550
91StaClu-317
91Stu-211
91Top-603A
91Top-603B
91TopDeb90-29
91TopDesS-603
91TopMic-603
91TopTif-603
91Ult-258
91UppDec-626
92Bow-412
92Cla2-T55
92ClaGam-63
92Don-384
92DonCraJ1-18
92Fle-524
92FleRooS-16
92Hig5-76
92JimDea-17
92Lea-453
92OPC-14
92PhiMed-8
92Pin-36
92ProFS7-295
92Sco-384
92Sco100RS-25
92ScoImpP-11
92ScoProP-8
92ScrRedBF-2459
92StaClu-396
92Stu-72
92Top-14
92TopGol-14
92TopGolW-14
92TopMic-14
92Ult-239
92UppDec-347
93Bow-456
93Don-304
93Fle-99
93Lea-338
93OPC-45
93PacSpa-232
93PanSti-275
93PhiMed-8
93Pin-328
93Sco-168
93Sel-217
93StaClu-34
93StaCluFDI-34
93StaCluMOP-34
93StaCluP-13
93Stu-19
93Top-154
93TopGol-154
93TopInaM-154
93TopMic-154
93Ult-85
93UppDec-267
93UppDecGold-267
94ColC-76
94ColChoGS-76
94ColChoSS-76
94Don-101
94ExtBas-15
94Fin-123
94FinRef-123
94Fla-260
94Fle-584
94FleUpd-10
94Lea-243
94OPC-27
94Pac-470
94PhiMed-4
94PhiUSPC-6S
94PhiUSPC-10D
94Pin-201
94PinArtP-201
94PinMusC-201
94Sco-438
94ScoGolR-438
94ScoRoo-RT25
94ScoRooGR-RT25
94Sel-67
94SpoRoo-81
94SpoRooAP-81
94StaClu-432
94StaCluFDI-432
94StaCluGR-432
94StaCluMOP-432
94StaCluT-238
94StaCluTFDI-238
94Top-419
94TopGol-419
94TopSpa-419
94Ult-542
94UppDec-148
94UppDecED-148
95Don-316
95DonPreP-316
95Fle-25
95Lea-82
95Pin-309
95PinArtP-309
95PinMusC-309
95Sco-510
95ScoGolR-510
95ScoPlaTS-510
95StaClu-458
95StaCluMOP-458
95StaCluSTWS-458
95StaCluVR-248
95Top-606
95TopCyb-376
95Ult-9
95UltGolM-9
95StaCluVRMC-248
96SyrChiTI-9
Chamberlain, Wilt
74NewYorNTDiS-36
Chamberlin, Buck
79TolMudHT-13
80TolMudHT-14
81TolMudHT-2
82TolMudHT-24
Chambers, Al (Albert E.)
81LynSaiT-20
82SalLakCGT-5
83Don-649
83SalLakCGT-21
84SalLakCGC-188
85CalCanC-80
85Don-389
85Top-277
85TopTif-277
87ColAstP-1
Chambers, Carl
87WatIndP-17
Chambers, Cliff
47SigOil-23
49EurSta-157
50Bow-202
50PirTeal-4
51Bow-131
51FisBakL-5
51TopRedB-25
52Bow-14
52RedMan-NL4
52StaCalL-81C
52StaCalS-93C
52Top-68
53CarHunW-4
54Bow-126
79DiaGre-118
83TopRep5-68
Chambers, Jeff
89EliTwiS-31
Chambers, Mark
91PulBraC-11
91PulBraP-4017
92PulBraC-5
92PulBraF-3189
93BurIndC-7
93BurIndF-3306
93MacBraC-6
93MacBraF-1412
94BurIndC-5
94BurIndF-3802
Chambers, Scott
95YakBeaTI-5
96VerBeaDB-10
Chambers, Travis
86ClePhiP-3
87IntLeaAT-37
87MaiGuiP-19
87MaiGuiT-3
88MaiPhiC-2
88MaiPhiP-283
89JacExpB-10
89JacExpP-162
90CMC-54
90IndIndC-4
90IndIndP-282
90ProAAAF-565
Chamblee, Jim
96MicBatCB-7
Chambliss, Chris (Carroll C.)
72OPC-142
72Top-142
73LinPor-61
73OPC-11
73Top-11
74OPC-384
74Top-384
74TopDecE-15
74TopSta-162
75OPC-585
75Top-585
75YanSSP-14
76Hos-58
76HosTwi-58
76OPC-65
76SSP-434
76Top-65
77BurCheD-173
77Hos-98
77Kel-52
77OPC-49
77RCColC-18
77Top-220
77Top-276
77YanBurK-12
78Hos-98
78Kel-13
78OPC-145
78RCColC-20
78SSP270-7
78Top-485
78WifBalD-18
78YanBurK-12
78YanSSPD-7
79Kel-37
79OPC-171
79Top-335
79YanBurK-12
79YanPicA-6
80OPC-328
80Top-625
81AllGamPI-93
81BraPol-10
81Don-219
81Fle-252
81FleStiC-81
81OPC-155
81Top-155
81TopSti-147
82BraBurKL-6
82BraPol-10
82Don-47
82Fle-433
82FleSta-70
82Kel-52
82OPC-320
82OPC-321
82Top-320
82Top-321
82TopSti-17
82TopStiV-17
83AllGamPI-92
83BraPol-10
83Don-123
83Fle-134
83FleSta-37
83FleSti-86
83OPC-11
83Top-792
83TopSti-212
84AllGamPI-2
84BraPol-10
84Don-537
84DonActAS-29
84Fle-175
84FunFooP-123
84Nes792-50
84OPC-50
84Top-50
84TopRubD-13
84TopSti-28
84TopTif-50
85BraHos-7
85BraPol-10
85Don-287
85Fle-322
85Lea-168
85OPC-187
85Top-518
85TopSti-29
85TopTif-518
86BraPol-10
86Don-618
86Fle-512
86Top-293
86TopTif-293
87Fle-513
87FleGlo-513
87OPC-204
87Top-777
87TopTif-777
89LonTigP-1378
91GreBraC-25
91GreBraLD-224
91GreBraP-3018
91LinDriAA-224
91UppDecS-6
92ActPacA-55
92RicBraBB-5
92RicBraF-391
92RicBraRC-3
92RicBraS-449
92YanWIZ7-32
92YanWIZ8-30
92YanWIZA-9
97FleMilDM-37
97RicBraBC-26
Champ, Jeff
89PenPilS-3
Champ, Mascot
96NasSouB-29
Champagne, Andre
89OklSoo-8
90OklSoo-4
Champagne, Boo
86EugEmeC-44
87Ft.MyeRP-8
Champion, Billy
70OPC-149
70Top-149
71MLBOffS-173
71OPC-323
71Top-323
72Top-599
73OPC-74
73Top-74
74OPC-391
74Top-391
75Hos-118
75OPC-256
75Top-256
76OPC-501
76Top-501
93BenRocC-29
93BenRocF-3284
94BreMilB-206
94NewHavRF-1567
95SalAvaTI-28
96SalAvaB-27
Champion, Brian
88BurBraP-10
89DurBullS-5
89DurBulTI-5
89Sta-69
90CarLeaA-31
90DurBulTI-3
90GreBraB-3
91Cla/Bes-177

91GreBraC-16
91GreBraLD-203
91GreBraP-3010
91LinDriAA-203
Champion, Jim
95ForMyeMTI-6
Champion, Keith
88SavCarP-337
89SavCarP-344
90SprCarB-26
92WatDiaC-26
92WatDiaF-2156
93RanCucQC-27
93RanCucQF-847
94WicWraF-205
Champion, Kirk
89SouBenWSGS-5
90SouBenWSB-27
90SouBenWSGS-28
91SouBenWSC-26
91SouBenWSP-2874
92SarWhiSCB-28
92SarWhiSF-226
93BirBarF-1209
94BirBarC-27
94BirBarF-639
Champion, Mike (Robert M.)
76HawIslC-21
77PadSchC-11
77PadSchC-12
77Top-494
78PadFamF-5
78Top-683
79TacTugT-14
80TacTigT-16
Champion, Randall
83St.PetCT-14
87ArkTraP-8
Champlin, Kelly
91FreStaBS-2
Chance, Bob (Robert)
64Top-146
64TopVen-146
65Baz-18
65OPC-224
65Top-224
66SenTeal-4
66Top-564
67Top-349
69Top-523
69TopTeaP-17
78TCM60I-82
Chance, Dean
47Exh-40
62Top-194
62TopVen-194
63AngJayP-2
63AngJayP-3
63ExhStaB-13
63Jel-32
63Pos-32
63Top-6
63Top-355
64Top-32
64TopCoi-67
64TopGia-16
64TopVen-32
65Baz-5
65OldLonC-22
65OPC-7
65OPC-9
65OPC-11
65OPC-140
65Top-7
65Top-9
65Top-11
65Top-140
65TopEmbl-66
65TopTral-10
65TopTral-42
66AngDexP-1
66Baz-25
66Top-340
66TopRubl-16
66TopVen-340
67Baz-25
67CokCapTw-14
67DexPre-46
67Top-380
67TopGiaSU-12
67TopVen-217
68AtlOilPBCC-13
68Baz-10
68DexPre-23
68OPC-10
68OPC-12
68Top-10A
68Top-10B
68Top-12
68Top-255
68TopActS-4A
68TopActS-13A
68TopGamI-16
68TopPla-2
68TopPos-1
68TopVen-10
68TopVen-12
68TopVen-255
69MilBra-57
69MLBOffS-66
69MLBPin-5
69Top-620
69TopSta-193
69TopSup-21
69TopTeaP-15
69TwiTealC-4
70Kel-67
70MLBOffS-195
70Top-625
71MLBOffS-148
71OPC-36
71Top-36
72MilBra-73
78TCM60I-66
78TwiFri-4
80MarExh-7
82OhiHaloF-4
85AngStrH-5
86AngGreT-9
89AngSmo-2
89SweBasG-89
91MetWIZ-69
94SnaDeaC-1
94TedWil-14
Chance, Frank Leroy
03BreE10-18
03WilCarE-4
06FanCraNL-9
07CubA.CDPP-2
07CubGFGCP-2
08AmeCarE-5
08AmeCarE-40
08CubPos-1
08RosComP-101
09AmeCarE-20
09ColChiE-48A
09ColChiE-48B
09MaxPubP-2
09PhiCarE-3
09RamT20-23
09SpoNewSM-8
09T206-54
09T206-55
09T206-56
09TigHMTP-8
10ChiE-3
10CouT21-9
10CouT21-93
10CouT21-94
10CouT21-95
10CouT21-96
10CouT21-264
10CouT21-265
10DomDisP-22
10E101-8
10E98-5
10JHDABE-4
10JuJuDE-7
10MelMinE-8
10NadCarE-9
10OrnOvaPP-2
10PeoT21-10
10RedCroT-9
10RedCroT-96
10RedCroT-175
10SepAnoP-6
10StaCarE-4
10SweCapPP-81A
10SweCapPP-81B
10W555-11
11BasBatEU-7
11DiaGumP-7
11E94-5
11MecDFT-9
11S74Sil-59
11SpoLifCW-58
11SpoLifM-168
11T205-26
11TurRedT-47
12ColRedB-48A
12ColRedB-48B
12ColTinT-48A
12ColTinT-48B
12HasTriFT-13A
12HasTriFT-13B
12HasTriFT-13C
12HasTriFT-13D
12HasTriFT-13E
12HasTriFT-36B
12HasTriFT-36E
12T207-30
13LawSemC-1
13NatGamW-8
13PolGroW-3
13TomBarW-8
14B18B-21
14CraJacE-99
14FatPlaT-12
14PieStaT-10
14TexTomE-11
15SpoNewM-28
36PC7AlbHoF-40
40PlaBal-234
48ExhHoF-3
50CalHOFW-13
60ExhWriH-6
60Fle-50
61Fle-98
63BazA-25
68LauWorS-5
69Baz-5
69Baz-11
70FleWorS-5
73FleWilD-2
76MotOldT-11
76ShaPiz-40
77GalGloG-161
80MarExhH-5
80PacLeg-84
80PerHaloFP-40
80SSPHOF-40
81ConTSN-12
84CubUno-7
84CubUno-8
84GalHaloFRL-40
87Cub190T-8
90PerGreM-40
92CubOldS-6
92YanWIZH-4
93ConTSN-819
93UppDecAH-30
93UppDecAH-148
94ConTSN-1166
94ConTSNB-1166
94OriofB-89
93UppDecTR-9
96PitPosH-2
Chance, Tony
86MacPirP-6
86PriWilPP-5
87SalBucP-25
88HarSenP-854
89UppDec-3
90CMC-319
90ProAAAF-470
90RocRedWC-19
90RocRedWGC-19
90RocRedWP-713
91LinDriAAA-451
91RocRedWLD-451
91RocRedWP-1913
92IowCubF-4060
92IowCubS-206
93IowCubF-2144
Chandler, Bob
90PadMag-16
91PadCok-1
Chandler, Chris
92St.CatBJC-21
92St.CatBJF-3393
Chandler, Ed
52MotCoo-63
90DodTar-122
Chandler, George
85CloHSS-9
Chandler, Happy (A.B.)
49EurSta-1
50CalHOFW-14
75JohMiz-5
76TayBow4-80
80PerHaloFP-178
80SSPHOF-179
89HOFStiB-97
89PerCelP-9
Chandler, Jason
93PriRedC-3
93PriRedF-4168
Chandler, Ken
81WisRapTT-13
Chandler, Spud
40PlaBal-181
43YanSta-5
46SpoExcW-3-2
47Exh-41
75YanDyn1T-6
77TCMTheWY-55
79DiaGre-9
83TCMPla1943-1
83YanASFY-6
89PacLegI-136
92YanWIZA-10
93ConTSN-763
94ConTSN-1068
94ConTSNB-1068
Chandler, Steve
93OneYanF-3521
Chaney, Bruce
81BirBarT-16
Chaney, Darrel Lee
69Top-624
70DayDaiNM-133
70OPC-3
70Top-3
71MLBOffS-53
71OPC-632
71Top-632
72OPC-136
72Top-136
73OPC-507
73Top-507
74OPC-559
74Top-559
75OPC-581
75Top-581
76OPC-259
76SSP-33
76Top-259
76TopTra-259T
77BurCheD-216
77Hos-57
77OPC-134
77Top-384
78Top-443
79OPC-91
79Top-184
Chaney, Keith
91PulBraC-5
91PulBraP-4011
Chaney, Michael
96EriSeaB-8
Chang, Soon-Jo
90IBAWorA-3
Chant, Charlie (Charles J.)
75IntLeaASB-3
75PacCoaLAB-3
75TucTorC-8
75TucTorTI-2
76TulOilGP-20
Chanye, Bruce
80WatIndT-18
83MidCubT-10
Chapa, Javier
95GreFalDTI-9
Chapin, Darrin
88Ft.LauYS-4
89AlbYanP-340
89AlbYanS-3
89ColCliC-30
90AlbYanP-1029
90AlbYanS-1
90CMC-220
90ColCliC-20
90ColCliP-668
90ProAaA-19
90ProAAAF-318
90StaFS7-51
91ColCliLD-103
91ColCliP-3
91ColCliP-590
91LinDriAAA-103
92Don-745
92ScrRedBF-2441
92ScrRedBS-481
92SkyAAAF-219
92TopDeb91-33
93LinVenB-264
94EdmTraF-2867
Chaplin, Tiny
94ConTSN-1308
94ConTSNB-1308
Chapman, Dan
88StoPorCLC-205
88StoPorP-751
89StoPorB-28
89StoPorCLC-174
89StoPorP-398
89StoPorS-23
Chapman, Ben (William B.)
30SchR33-40
32OrbPinNP-99
33Gou-191
34BatR31-62
34BatR31-188
34ButPreR-9
34DiaStaR-38
34Gou-9
34GouCanV-51
36GouWidPPR-B4
36NatChiFPR-19
36NatChiFPR-87
36OveCanR-7
36WorWidGV-90
37OPCBatUV-130
39GouPreR303A-8
39GouPreR303B-3
39WorWidGTP-8
41DouPlaR-73
46SpoExcW-2-12
52Top-391
75YanDyn1T-7
77GalGloG-197
79DiaGre-2
83ConMar-12
83TopRep5-391
83YanASFY-7
88ConAmeA-4
88ConSer3-6
90DodTar-123
92YanWIZA-11
93ConTSN-688
94ConTSN-1081
94ConTSNB-1081
Chapman, Dave
79AshTouT-7
Chapman, Eric
93WatIndC-4
93WatIndF-3574
Chapman, Glenn J.
90DodTar-911
Chapman, Jake
96SpoIndB-9
Chapman, Jim
92MegRut-160
Chapman, Kelvin Keith
77WauMetT-5
79TidTidT-18
80TidTidT-18
81SyrChiT-13
81SyrChiTI-6
82TidTidT-2
83TidTidT-7
84TidTidT-27
85Don-626
85Fle-75
85MetColP-24
85MetTCM-22
85Top-751
85TopTif-751
86Top-492
86TopTif-492
91MetWIZ-70
Chapman, Ken
92YakBeaC-12
92YakBeaF-3457
Chapman, Mark
88BelBreGS-10
88MidLeaAGS-59
89ElPasDGS-4
90ElPasDGS-6
91ElPasDLD-178
91ElPasDP-2739
91LinDriAA-178
92HarSenF-455
92HarSenS-279
Chapman, Nathan
76ForLauYS-11
79ColCliT-22
80NasSouTI-5

81NasSouTI-3
82NasSouTI-6
Chapman, Ray (Raymond J.)
14B18B-2A
14B18B-2B
15SpoNewM-29
16BF2FP-22
16ColE13-26
16SpoNewM-30
77Ind192T-4
81ConTSN-52
94UppDecTAE-32
95ConTSNP-1464
Chapman, Ron
85AlbYanT-15
91WavRedF-13
Chapman, Sam (Samuel Blake)
40PlaBal-194
41DouPlaR-125
41PlaBal-44
46SpoExcW-3-7
49Bow-112
49Lea-26
49OlmStu-1
49PhiBul-11
50Bow-104
51Bow-9
51TopBluB-52
52MotCoo-33
52NatTeaL-4
52Top-391
76TayBow4-30
83TopRep5-391
85TCMPla1-20
Chapman, Walker
95ForWayWTI-3
Chappas, Harry (Harold Perry)
78AppFoxT-5
79IowOakP-5
80Top-347
Chappelle, William
09T206-408
10CouT21-97
10CouT21-98
Charboneau, Joe (Joseph)
81AllGamPI-49
81Don-82A
81Don-82B
81Dra-21
81Fle-397
81Kel-54
81OPC-13
81Squ-32
81Top-13
81TopScr-12
81TopSti-66
82ChaSupJ-1
82ChaSupJ-2
82Don-363
82Fle-362
82FleSta-192
82Ind-8
82IndTeal-7
82IndWhe-2
82OPC-211
82Top-630
83BufBisT-23
84PriWilPT-15
88ChaLooLTI-3
93MCIAmb-6
93UppDecAH-31
94UppDecAH-141
94UppDecAH1-141
Charbonneau, Marc
95GreFalDTI-13
96SavSanB-3
Charbonnet, Mark
89BurIndS-4
90RenSilSCLC-269
90WatIndS-3
91ColIndC-7
91ColIndP-1497
92ColRedC-13
93KinIndC-4
93KinIndF-2258
93KinIndTI-3
94WesPalBEC-5
94WesPalBEF-53
95HarSenTI-27
Charland, Colin
86SalAngC-76
87PalSprP-9
88CalLeaACLC-31
88PalSprACLC-85
88PalSprAP-1447
89EdmTraC-6
89EdmTraP-565
90Fle-640
90FleCan-640
90IndTeal-10
92CanIndF-683
92CanIndS-110
92SkyAA F-48
97MidAngOHP-3
Charles, Chappy (Raymond)
09PC7HHB-7
09T206-57
10CouT21-10
11SpoLifM-188
Charles, Curtis
96BluOriB-8
Charles, Domingo
93JohCitCC-6
93JohCitCF-3670
94JohCitCC-5
94JohCitCF-3689
Charles, Ed (Edwin)
52LavPro-19
62Top-595
63Jel-89
63Pos-89
63Top-67
64A's-2
64AthJayP-2
64Top-475
64TopCoi-117
64TopSta-1
64TopStaU-16
65AthJayP-3
65OPC-35
65Top-35
66Top-422
66TopRubI-17
67CokCapA-35
67CokCapAAm-25
67CokCapAt-3
67DexPre-47
67OPC-182
67Top-182
68Top-563
69MilBra-58
69MLBOffS-164
69Top-245
69TopSta-62
69TopTeaP-24
70OPC-310
78TCM60I-25
89RinPosM1-5
90SweBasG-123
91MetWIZ-71
94Met69CCPP-10
94Met69CS-9
94Met69T-18
94UppDecAH-62
94UppDecAH1-62
96Met69Y-1
Charles, Ezzard
51BerRos-A13
74NewYorNTDiS-5
Charles, Frank
91EveGiaC-11
91EveGiaP-3917
92ProFS7-357
94ChaRanF-2499
95TulDriTI-4
96TulDriTI-6
Charles, Justin
94ElmPioF-3481
94ElmPioC-4
Charles, Steve
96StCatSB-6
Charleston, Oscar
74LauOldTBS-34
76LauIndC-30
76ShaPiz-152
80PerHaloFP-152
80SSPHOF-152
83ConMar-50
86NegLeaF-4
86NegLeaF-8
86NegLeaF-24
88ConNegA-2
88NegLeaD-7
90NegLeaS-36
91PomBlaBPB-9
91PomBlaBPB-18
93TedWil-102
94PomNegLB-10
Charleston, Porter
91PomBlaBPB-23
Charlton, Aaron
95BurBeeTI-25
Charlton, Norm
86VerRedP-3
87NasSouTI-2
88NasSouC-3
88NasSouP-488
88NasSouTI-6
88TriAAC-12
89Don-544
89Fle-155
89FleGlo-155
89RedKah-37
89Sco-646
89ScoYouS2-15
89Top-737
89TopTif-737
89UppDec-783
90Don-426
90Fle-416
90FleCan-416
90Lea-334
90OPC-289
90PubSti-24
90RedKah-6
90Sco-248
90Top-289
90TopTif-289
90UppDec-566
90VenSti-102
91Bow-690
91Don-384
91Fle-60
91Lea-414
91OPC-309
91RedKah-37
91RedPep-5
91Sco-530
91StaClu-305
91Top-309
91TopDesS-309
91TopMic-309
91TopTif-309
91Ult-89
91Ult-90
91UppDec-394
92Don-102
92Fle-402
92Lea-120
92OPC-649
92Pin-216
92RedKah-37
92Sco-267
92StaClu-530
92Stu-21
92Top-649
92TopGol-649
92TopGolW-649
92TopMic-649
92TriPla-163
92Ult-482
92UppDec-677
93Bow-655
93Don-238
93Fin-178
93FinRef-178
93Fla-269
93Fle-32
93FleFinE-266
93Lea-287
93MarMot-10
93OPC-98
93OPCPre-50
93PacSpa-620
93Pin-439
93Sco-375
93Sel-207
93SelRoo-96T
93SP-129
93StaClu-659
93StaCluFDI-659
93StaCluM-144
93StaCluMari-13
93StaCluMOP-659
93Top-57
93TopGol-57
93TopInaM-57
93TopMic-57
93TopTra-123T
93Ult-615
93UppDec-663
93UppDecGold-663
94ColC-559
94ColChoGS-559
94ColChoSS-559
94Don-96
94Fle-283
94Pac-565
94PhiMed-5
94Pin-216
94PinArtP-216
94PinMusC-216
94Sco-549
94ScoGolR-549
95FleUpd-118
95Lea-359
95MarPac-27
95Phi-6
95PhiMel-4
96Cir-77
96CirRav-77
96ColCho-726
96ColChoGS-726
96ColChoSS-726
96Don-529
96DonPreP-529
96Fle-232
96FleTif-232
96LeaSigA-44
96LeaSigAG-44
96LeaSigAS-44
96MarMot-16
96Pac-402
96StaClu-423
96StaCluEPB-423
96StaCluEPG-423
96StaCluEPS-423
96StaCluMOP-423
96Top-392
96Ult-409
96UltGolM-409
96UppDec-203
97Cir-190
97CirRav-190
97ColCho-234
97Fle-203
97FleTif-203
97Pac-184
97PacLigB-184
97PacSil-184
97Sco-331
97ScoHobR-331
97ScoResC-331
97ScoShoS-331
97ScoShoSAP-331
97StaClu-278
97StaCluMOP-278
97Top-199
97Ult-119
97UltGolME-119
97UltPlaME-119
Charno, Joe
88AshTouP-1055
89AshTouP-962
Charpia, Billie Jo
95ColSilB-3
Charpia, Reed
89HelBreSP-16
Charry, Stephen
83MadMusF-2
Chartak, Mike (Michael G.)
96Bro194F-25
Charton, Pete (Frank)
64Top-459
66Top-329
66TopVen-329
Chase, Dave
80AndBraT-12
Chase, Hal (Harold Homer)
03WilCarE-5
08RosComP-43
09AmeCarE-21
09ColChiE-49
09SpoNewSM-23
09T206-58
09T206-59
09T206-60
09T206-61
09T206-62
10CouT21-11
10CouT21-12
10CouT21-99
10CouT21-100
10CouT21-101
10CouT21-102
10CouT21-103
10CouT21-104
10CouT21-266
10CouT21-267
10CouT21-268
10DomDisP-23
10E-UOraBSC-5
10E101-9
10E102-3
10E98-6
10MelMinE-9
10NadCarE-10
10PeoT21-11A
10PeoT21-11B
10PeoT21-11C
10RedCroT-10
10RedCroT-176
10SepAnoP-7
10StaCarE-5
10SweCapPP-32A
10SweCapPP-32B
10W555-12
11BasBatEU-8
11DiaGumP-8
11MecDFT-46
11PloCanE-14
11S74Sil-20
11SpoLifCW-59
11SpoLifM-75
11T205-27A
11T205-27B
11TurRedT-6
12ColRedB-49
12ColTinT-49
12HasTriFT-14A
12HasTriFT-14B
12HasTriFT-14C
12HasTriFT-15A
12HasTriFT-15B
12HasTriFT-16A
12HasTriFT-16B
12HasTriFT-16C
12HasTriFT-17
12HasTriFT-18
12HasTriFT-41A
12HasTriFT-41B
12HasTriFT-61B
13NatGamW-9
13TomBarW-9
14PieStaT-11
14TexTomE-12
15AmeCarE-7A
15AmeCarE-7B
15CraJacE-99
16TanBraE-4
19W514-114
69SCFOldT-34
75FlePio-22
75ShaPiz-13
77GalGloG-146
88ConSer4-5
91ConTSN-160
Chase, Ken
39PlaBal-59
40PlaBal-19
42RedSoxTI-5
43RedSoxTI-2
79DiaGre-59
Chase, Scott
89OneYanP-2107
Chasey, Mark
88UtiBluSP-4
89SouBenWSGS-21
90SarWhiSS-4
91BirBarLD-54
91BirBarP-1459
91LinDriAA-54
Chasin, David
91JohCitCC-22
Chasteen, Steve
83IdaFalAT-2
Chataing, Blanco
91PomBlaBPB-2
Chatham, Buster (Charles L.)
94ConTSN-1287
94ConTSNB-1287
Chatman, Karl
96VerExpB-12
Chatterton, Christopher
92BluOriC-14

92BluOriF-2353
93AlbPolC-6
93AlbPolF-2018
Chauncey, Keathel
75AndRanT-9
76SanAntBTI-6
77TucTorC-12
78TucTorC-12
79TucTorT-19
80WesHavWCT-21A
81TolMudHT-19
Chavarria, David
92ButCopKSP-17
94HudValRF-3375
95ChaRivTI-18
Chavarria, Ossie (Oswaldo Q.)
67CokCapAt-6
67DexPre-48
67Top-344
Chavera, Arnie
96QuaCitRB-12
Chaves, Rafael
86ChaRaiP-5
92HigDesMC-23
93BowBayF-2182
93ClaGolF-56
94PorSeaDF-670
95LynHilTI-3
Chavez, Anthony
77RocRedWM-11
92BoiHawC-19
92BoiHawF-3619
93CedRapKC-3
93CedRapKF-1730
93MidLeaAGF-34
94LakElsSC-4
94LakElsSF-1656
95LakElsSTI-8
Chavez, Carlos
92BluOriC-22
92BluOriF-2354
93AlbPolC-7
93AlbPolF-2019
93BluOriC-9
93BluOriF-4118
94AlbPolC-11
94BluOriC-3
94BluOriF-3552
94OriPro-17
96BowBayB-10
96Exc-2
Chavez, Devin
91HunCubC-7
91HunCubP-3341
Chavez, Eric
97Bow-210
97BowChr-192
97BowChrI-192
97BowChrIR-192
97BowChrR-192
97BowInt-210
97Top-479
Chavez, Eric O's
92BluOriF-2364
93AlbPolC-8
93AlbPolF-2031
93SouAtlLAGF-2
94ClaGolF-5
94ExcFS7-3
94FreKeyF-2620
94OriPro-18
96FreKeyB-3
94FreKeyC-7
Chavez, Harold P.
20WalMaiW-9
Chavez, Joe
86BeaGolGP-6
88WicPilRD-NNO
89WicWraR-NNO
Chavez, Mark
96AriBlaDB-11
Chavez, Pedro
80VenLeaS-116
83BirBarT-21
86NasSouTI-4
87GleFalTP-21
88TolMudHC-17
88TolMudHP-601
93LinVenB-3
94VenLinU-160
95LinVen-157
Chavez, Rafael
88BlaYNPRWL-102
88CalLeaACLC-42
88RivRedWCLC-209
88RivRedWP-1429
89BlaYNPRWL-110
89WicStaR-25
89WicWraR-14
90WicWraRD-4
91LinDriAA-603
91WicWraLD-603
91WicWraP-2592
91WicWraRD-2
94PorSeaDTI-9
Chavez, Raul
91BurAstC-13
91BurAstP-2807
92AshTouC-8
93LinVenB-263
93OscAstC-7
93OscAstF-631
94JacGenF-219
94VenLinU-5
95JacGenTI-13
95LinVen-87
97PacPriGotD-GD167
Chavez, Sam (Samuel)
88CedRapRP-1160
89SouBenWSGS-9
90HunStaB-3
Chavez, Steve
96IdaFalB-3
97Bow-327
97BowInt-327
Chech, Charles
08AmeCarE-70
09RamT20-24
Checo, Pedro
89BriTigS-4
Checo, Robinson
97Fle-518
97FleTif-518
Cheek, Carey
86PriWilPP-6
Cheek, Harry (Harry G.)
10JuJuDE-8
Cheek, Jeff
93St.CatBJC-5
93St.CatBJF-3968
94St.CatBJF-3634
Cheek, Patrick
90PriPatD-4
91BatCliC-7
91BatCliP-3489
Cheetham, Sean
90HigSchPLS-5
90HunCubP-3273
90ProAaA-185
91Bow-414
91Cla/Bes-231
91WinSpiC-3
91WinSpiP-2822
92ClaFS7-315
92WinSpiC-6
92WinSpiF-1201
Cheeves, Chief (Virgil)
21Nei-84
22E120-155
22W572-12
27AmeCarE-23
Cheff, Tyler
94BurIndC-6
94BurIndF-3797
Chelette, Mark
80SanJosMJitB-5
81WauTimT-23
Chelini, Dan
83ButCopKT-2
Chelini, Italo
34BatR31-114
Chen, Bruce
95DanBraTI-4
96EugEmeB-4
97Bow-212
97BowChr-194
97BowChrI-194
97BowChrIR-194
97BowChrR-194
97BowInt-212
Chenevey, Jim
88MadMusP-10
88MidLeaAGS-53
Cheney, Larry
13PolGroW-4
14CraJacE-89
15CraJacE-89
15SpoNewM-30
16ColE13-27
16FleBreD-15
16SpoNewM-31
90DodTar-124
Cheney, Tom
47Exh-42
57Top-359
61Top-494
63ExhStaB-14
63Fle-27
63Jel-99
63Pos-99
64ChatheY-27
78TCM60I-85
Chergey, Dan
93ElmPioC-5
93ElmPioF-3815
94FloStaLAF-FSL26
96ChaKniB-11
94BreCouMC-4
94BreCouMF-2
95PorSeaDTI-2
Cherry, Gus
85OmaRoyT-6
Cherry, Joe
76LauIndC-15
76LauIndC-32
Cherry, Lamar
90HigSchPLS-3
91MarPhiC-12
91MarPhiP-3459
92BatCliC-5
92BatCliF-3271
92SpaPhiC-15
92SpaPhiF-1275
Cherry, Michael
85VerBeaDT-23
86VerBeaDP-3
Cherry, Paul
83SprCarF-3
86ArkTraP-4
87LouRedTI-9
88TolMudHC-9
88TolMudHP-591
Chervinko, Paul
90DodTar-912
Chesbro, Jack
03BreE10-19
04FanCraAL-7
05RotCP-2
08RosComP-44
09T206-63
11SpoLifCW-60
36PC7AlbHoF-41
48ExhHoF-4
50CalHOFW-15
61Fle-13
61Top-407
63BazA-3
69Baz-9
69SCFOldT-10
72FleFamF-39
72LauGreF-12
76ShaPiz-41
79Top-416
80PerHaloFP-41
80SSPHOF-41
84GalHaloFRL-41
85Woo-7
92YanWIZH-5
94OriofB-92
Cheshire, Donnie
78St.PetCT-5
Chesnes, Bob
49Bow-13
50Bow-70
Cheso, Reno
49SomandK-11
53MotCoo-33
Chestnut, Troy
87KnoBluJP-1500
Chevalier, Bonel
89BelMarL-23
90BenBucL-7
Chevalier, Virgil
96Exc-11
96HilStaHWB-32
96MicBatCB-8
96MidLeaAB-42
Chevez, Tony
78RocRedWT-4
79RocRedWT-19
91OriCro-75
Chevolek, Tom
80ElPasDT-5
Chew, Greg
94WelPirC-6
94WelPirF-3485
Chiamparino, Scott
88HunStaTI-2
88ModA'sCLC-64
88ModA'sTI-8
90CMC-580
90ProAAAF-133
90ScoRoo-108T
90TacTigC-3
90TacTigP-86
90TriAllGP-AAA49
91Bow-282
91Cla1-T84
91ClaGam-183
91Don-42
91DonPre-3
91Lea-401
91MajLeaCP-37
91OPC-676
91RanMot-14
91Sco-352A
91Sco-352B
91Sco100RS-14
91ScoRoo-29
91StaClu-384
91Stu-122
91Top-676
91TopDeb90-30
91TopDesS-676
91TopMic-676
91TopTif-676
91Ult-375
91UppDec-8
92OPC-277
92RanMot-14
92RanTeal-4
92Sco-688
92StaClu-896
92Top-277
92TopGol-277
92TopGolW-277
92TopMic-277
93Don-738
93Fle-422
93RanKee-102
93Sco-386
93StaCluMarl-7
93Top-64
93Top-711
93TopGol-64
93TopGol-711
93TopInaM-64
93TopInaM-711
93TopMic-64
93TopMic-711
93TriPla-63
94LasVegSF-865
Chick, Bruce
91CarLeaAP-CAR22
91Cla/Bes-13
91LynRedSC-20
91LynRedSP-1210
92NewBriRSF-446
92NewBriRSS-480
92SkyAA F-204
94NewBriRSF-661
Chickasaw, Chief
96MemChiB-5
Chicken, Chano
85MexCitTT-29
Chicken, Famous (San Diego)
82Don-531A
82Don-531B
83Don-645
84Don-651
84PadSmo-4
85DalNatCC-7
92TriPla-138
Chicken, Nashua Angel
83NasAngT-27
Chiefs, Peoria
89PeoChiTI-14
Chiefs, Syracuse
87IntLeaAT-42
92SyrChiMB-31
Chiffer, Floyd
81HawIslT-18
83Don-44
83Fle-354
83Top-298
85TolMudHT-32
87RicBraBC-2
87RicBraC-28
87RicBraT-2
Chikida, Honen
89SalSpuP-1812
Childers, Bob
88AlaGolTI-6
Childers, Chabon
92OklStaC-4
Childers, Jeffrey
85BeaGolGT-1
88ModA'sTI-7
88WicPilRD-30
Childers, Terry
93PitMetC-3
93PitMetF-3712
Childress, Billy
92HunCubF-3137
93HunCubC-5
93HunCubF-3229
Childress, Chip
83DurBulT-1
84DurBulT-13
85DurBulT-20
86GreBraTI-5
Childress, Rocky
85PhiTas-45
85PorBeaC-31
86PhiTas-50
87TucTorP-10
88Don-554
88Fle-442
88FleGlo-442
88Top-643
88TopTif-643
88TucTorC-8
88TucTorJP-6
88TucTorP-181
89TucTorC-1
89TucTorJP-4
89TucTorP-194
90CMC-354
90ProAAAF-267
90TidTidC-3
90TidTidP-536
Childress, Willie J.
87GreBraB-11
Childs, Cupid (Clarence A.)
87OldJudN-79
98CamPepP-10
Childs, Mike
79AshTouT-20
Chiles, Barry
90PulBraB-2
90PulBraP-3100
91MacBraC-1
91MacBraP-855
92DurBulC-20
92DurBulF-1092
92DurBulTI-34
93DurBulC-5
93DurBulF-479
93DurBulTI-34
Chiles, Bill
74HawIslC-107
Chiles, Rich (Richard F.)
72OPC-56
72Top-56
73OPC-617
73Top-617
78Top-193
78TwiFriP-4
79TacTugT-20
79Top-498
91MetWIZ-72
92CarMudF-1196
92CarMudS-150
Chimelis, Joel
88SouOreAP-1703
89ModA'sC-22
89ModA'sCLC-279
90ModA'sC-5
90RenSilSCLC-267
91HunStaC-7
91HunStaLD-282
91HunStaP-1802
91HunStaTI-5
91LinDriAA-282
92ClaFS7-446
92ShrCapF-3878
92ShrCapS-578

93Bow-464
93ClaFS7-161
93ExcFS7-114
93PhoFirF-1520
94ShrCapF-1611
95PhoFirTI-11
95Top-581
Chin, Chien Wei
90IBAWorA-13
Ching, Darcie
91HawWomS-1
Ching, Mo (Maurice)
83GreHorT-17
84GreHorT-22
86AlbYanT-18
Chiozza, Lou (Louis Peo)
34DiaMatCSB-27
34DiaStaR-80
35DiaMatCS2-4
35DiaMatCS3T1-31
38OurNatGPP-2
39PlaBal-58
40PlaBal-157
41Gou-3
94ConTSN-1074
94ConTSNB-1074
Chipman, Bob (Robert)
47TipTop-106
49Bow-184
49EurSta-54
50Bow-192
52Bow-228
52Top-388
83TCMPla1944-33
83TopRep5-388
90DodTar-125
Chireno, Manny
87BelBreP-24
Chirinos, Dario
76VenLeaS-195
80VenLeaS-232
Chism, Tom (Thomas R.)
78RocRedWT-5
79RocRedWT-18
81RocRedWT-4
81RocRedWW-24
82RocRedWT-21
83RocRedWT-23
91OriCro-76
Chisum, Dave
91BurIndP-3306
92WatIndC-16
92WatIndF-3246
Chitford, Erie
93StoPorF-755
Chiti, Dom
79SavBraT-1
85ChaO'sT-13
86RocRedWP-2
87RocRedWP-15
87RocRedWT-25
88RocRedWGCP-28
88RocRedWP-212
88RocRedWTI-5
92IndFanC-30
93IndWUA-33
Chiti, Harry Dominick
53BowC-7
55Bow-304
56Top-179
58Top-119
59Top-79
59TopVen-79
60Top-339
61Top-269
61TopStal-149
62Top-253
79DiaGre-119
91MetWIZ-73
Chitren, Steve (Stephen)
86AncGlaPTI-6
87AncGlaP-4
89MedAthB-20
90Bes-279
90HunStaB-4
91A'sMot-27
91Bow-214
91Don-431
91Lea-486
91Sco-760
91TopDeb90-31
91Ult-376
91UppDec-753
92Bow-506
92Don-385
92Fle-253
92FleRooS-14
92Lea-32
92OPC-379
92Pin-236
92Sco-202
92SkyAAAF-238
92StaClu-518
92TacTigF-2496
92TacTigS-530
92Top-379
92TopGol-379
92TopGolW-379
92TopMic-379
92UppDec-471
93HunStaF-2077
94BowBayF-2407
94OriPro-19
95RocRedWTI-10
Chittum, Nelson
60Top-296
63RocRedWSP-5
Chiyomaru, Akihiko
90GatCitPP-3339
90GatCitPSP-6
Chlan, Greg
75OmaRoyTI-4
Chlupsa, Bob
71OPC-594
71Top-594
Chmil, Steve
83DurBulT-2
Choate, Don
60TacBan-3
61UniOil-P6
77FriOneYW-64
Choate, John
94WatIndC-4
94WatIndF-3950
95WatIndTI-9
Choate, Mark
90MedHatBJB-6
91MyrBeaHC-18
91MyrBeaHP-2952
92St.CatBJC-13
92St.CatBJF-3394
Choi, Ray
95BoiHawTI-9
Cholowsky, Dan
91ClaDraP-35
91FroRowDP-5
92ClaFS7-370
92SavCarC-18
92SavCarF-667
92StaCluD-27
93Bow-488
93ClaGolF-95
93SouAtlLAIPI-8
93SouAtlLAPI-6
93St.PetCC-10
93St.PetCF-2633
94ArkTraF-3095
94UppDecML-42
95ArkTraTI-7
Chorley, Dave
74CarSalLCA-94
Chouinard, Bobby
92KanCouCC-20
92KanCouCF-82
92KanCouCTI-5
92MidLeaATI-5
93ClaFS7-48
93ModA'sC-5
93ModA'sF-791
94ModA'sC-6
94ModA'sF-3058
95HunStaTI-7
96A'sMot-16
96BowBes-176
96BowBesAR-176
96BowBesR-176
97Fle-187
97FleTif-187
97Top-237
97Ult-110
97UltGolME-110
97UltPlaME-110
97UppDec-283
Chourio, Joe
76VenLeaS-211
Chris, Mike
80EvaTriT-5
80Top-666
81EvaTriT-3
85TacTigC-149
82PhoGiaVNB-2
Chrisley, Neil (Barbra O.)
57Top-320
58Top-303
59Top-189
59TopVen-189
60Lea-117
60Top-273
62Top-308
Chrisman, Jim
91AppFoxC-2
91AppFoxP-1708
92BasCitRC-10
92BasCitRF-3837
93WilBluRC-6
93WilBluRF-1990
Chrismon, Thad
95EugEmeTI-21
Christ, Michael
87ChaLooB-11
88CalCanC-6
Christenbury, Lloyd
23WilChoV-18
Christensen, Bruce R.
74PhoGiaC-86
75PhoGiaC-10
75PhoGiaCK-15
76PheGiaCr-17
76PhoGiaCa-2
76PhoGiaCC-5
76PhoGiaVNB-3
Christensen, Jim
80WisRapTT-15
82TolMudHT-13
83TacTigT-30A
Christensen, John L.
84TidTidT-4
85MetColP-12
85MetTCM-31
86Don-360
86PawRedSP-5
86PawRedSP-6
86Top-287
86TopTif-287
87MarMot-27
87TopTra-23T
87TopTraT-23T
88CalCanC-17
88CalCanP-794
88Sco-419A
88Sco-419B
88ScoGlo-419A
88ScoGlo-419B
88Top-413
88TopTif-413
89Fle-108
89FleGlo-108
89PorBeaC-19
89PorBeaP-214
91MetWIZ-74
Christensen, McKay
94SigRooDP-6
94SigRooDPS-6
95Pin-167
95PinArtP-167
95PinMusC-167
95ScoDraP-DP1
95ScoSam-DP8
95SelSurS-SS7
95Top-473
Christenson, Gary
81OmaRoyT-5
Christenson, Kim
83AppFoxF-4
84PriWilPT-25
85NasPirT-5
Christenson, Larry
74OPC-587
74Top-587
75OPC-551
75Top-551
76OPC-634
76SSP-460
76Top-634
77OPC-194
77Top-59
78OPC-17
78PhiSSP-47
78SSP270-47
78Top-247
79OPC-260
79PhiBurK-5
79Top-493
80OPC-89
80PhiBurK-16
80Top-161
81Fle-8
81Top-346
82Don-219
82Fle-244
82Top-544
83Don-345
83Fle-156
83FleSta-38
83OPC-286
83PhiTas-5
83Top-668
84Nes792-252
84Top-252
84TopTif-252
Christian, Eddie
92FroRowDP-46
93KanCouCC-3
93KanCouCF-927
93Top-683
93TopGol-683
93TopInaM-683
93TopMic-683
94PorSeaDF-689
94PorSeaDTI-10
96MidAngOHP-8
93KanCouCTI-3
Christian, Rick
86EriCarP-6
87EriCarP-1
88HamRedP-1724
89St.PetCS-6
90ArkTraGS-8
91ArkTraLD-29
91ArkTraP-1299
91LinDriAA-29
92LouRedS-256
Christian, Robert
69OPC-173
69Top-173
69TopFou-21
70OPC-51
70Top-51
Christiansen, Clay
82NasSouTI-7
83ColCliT-9
84ColCliP-5
84ColCliT-12
85ColCliP-5
85ColCliT-4
85Don-396
85Top-211
85TopTif-211
86AlbYanT-28
86ColCliP-3
88TucTorP-179
92YanWIZ8-31
Christiansen, Jason
92AugPirC-7
92SalBucC-11
92SalBucF-55
93CarLeaAGF-47
93SalBucC-4
93SalBucF-422
94CarMudF-1570
95Fla-397
95FleUpd-146
95PirFil-4
95StaClu-596
95StaCluMOP-596
95StaCluSTWS-596
95UltGolMR-M7
96Fle-516
96FleTif-516
96LeaSigEA-28
96Pac-168
96PacPri-P56
96PacPriG-P56
97Pac-391
97PacLigB-391
97PacPriGotD-GD189
97PacSil-391
Christiansen, Jeff
89AncGlaP-6
Christianson, Alex
79WauTimT-19
Christie, Steve
93StaCluMO-47
Christman, Mark J.
46SeaSLP-9
46SpoExcW-2-8
49Bow-121
83TCMPla1944-2
96Bro194F-26
Christman, Scott
94Bow-211
94Cla-164
94ClaGolF-153
94ClaGolN1PLF-LP2
94Pin-266
94PinArtP-266
94PinMusC-266
94PriWilCC-8
94PriWilCF-1914
94Sco-548
94ScoGolR-548
95Bow-9
Christman, Tim
96PorRocB-11
Christmas, Maurice
93ClaGolF-148
93DanBraC-8
93DanBraF-3612
94MacBraC-3
94MacBraF-2196
95DurBulTI-8
96MacBraB-5
Christmas, Steve (Stephen R.)
80WatRedT-3
81WatRedT-12
82IndIndTI-22
83TucTorT-12
85BufBisT-4
86CubGat-18
86IowCubP-6
Christmon, Drew
93BriTigC-6
93BriTigF-3659
94FayGenC-6
94FayGenF-2160
Christofferson, Bob
83TacTigT-25B
Christoperson, Dave
85RedWinA-7
86RedWinA-10
Christopher, Chris
93JohCitCC-7
93JohCitCF-3694
94SavCarC-10
94SavCarF-519
94SouAtlLAF-SAL48
Christopher, Fred
86BenPhiC-143
87SpaPhiP-27
88ClePhiS-7
89ClePhiS-6
89ReaPhiS-7
90ReaPhiP-1215
Christopher, Joe
61Top-82
63Top-217
64Top-546
65Baz-20
65ChaTheY-25
65Top-495
65TopEmbl-52
65TopTral-43
66Top-343
66TopVen-343
76Met63 S-3
78TCM60I-7
82MetGal62-17
91MetWIZ-75
Christopher, Lloyd
43CenFlo-4
44CenFlo-3
47SigOil-24
47TipTop-18
48SigOil-3
48SmiClo-5
49RemBre-4
50RemBre-3
Christopher, Mike
86Ft.LauYP-6
87Ft.LauYP-8
88AlbYanP-1337
89AlbYanB-22
89AlbYanP-321
89AlbYanS-4
90AlbDukC-1
90AlbDukP-336
90AlbDukT-4
90CMC-403
90ProAAAF-57

91AlbDukLD-3
91AlbDukP-1134
91LinDriAAA-3
92Bow-374
92ColSprSSF-744
92ColSprSSS-80
92DonRoo-23
92Fle-654
92SkyAAAF-36
92StaClu-612
92StaCluECN-612
92TopDeb91-34
93IndWUA-5
93OPCPre-11
93PacSpa-408
93StaClu-308
93StaCluFDI-308
93StaCluMOP-308
93Top-786
93TopGol-786
93TopInaM-786
93TopMic-786
94TolMudHF-1019
95TolMudHTI-10
Christopher, Russ
48IndTeal-5
Christopher, Terry
92BelBreC-3
92BelBreF-397
Christopher, Tyron
92GulCoaYF-3782
Christopherson, Eric
89AncGlaP-7
89SanDieSAS-6
90ClaDraP-19
90ClaYel-T87
90EveGiaB-13
90EveGiaP-3129
90ProAaA-170
90SanDieSA3-3
91Bow-635
91Cla/Bes-320
91CliGiaC-14
91CliGiaP-836
91MidLeaAP-MWL3
91Sco-672
92Bow-38
92ClaFS7-254
92ProFS7-354
92ShrCapF-3874
92ShrCapS-579
92SkyAA F-255
92UppDecML-128
93ExcFS7-115
94ShrCapF-1609
95PhoFirTI-16
Christopherson, Gary
91BurAstC-14
91BurAstP-2808
92OscAstC-8
92OscAstF-2535
Christy, Al
83PeoSunF-19
Christy, Claude
53MotCoo-47
Chue, Jose
79CedRapGT-18
80CliGiaT-3
81CliGiaT-7
Chueden, Chris
82MonNew-4
Chumas, Steve
83IdaFalAT-18
Chun, Bo
92VerBeaDF-2894
Chung, Lo-Kuo
90IBAWorA-34
Church, Bubba (Emory)
47Exh-43
51Bow-149
52Bow-40
52Top-323
53BowC-138
53Top-47
55Bow-273
83TopRep5-323
91TopArc1-47
Church, Dan
80AndBraT-1
Church, Donald
86BenPhiC-138
Church, Len
77FriOneYW-71
Churchill, James
82AleDukT-16
Churchill, Norman
77WatIndT-5
79QuaCitCT-27
80QuaCitCT-12
Churchill, Tim
88MarPhiS-6
89BatCliP-1919
89SpaPhiP-1053
89SpaPhiS-4
90SpaPhiB-14
90SpaPhiP-2496
90SpaPhiS-3
Churn, Chuck
59DarFar-4
60DarFar-13
90DodTar-126
Chylak, Nestar
55Bow-283
Ciaglo, Paul
88CapCodPPaLP-6
89JamExpP-2135
90WesPalBES-2
Ciammachilli, Franco
77ReaPhiT-4
Ciampa, Mike
80ElmPioRST-27
Cianfrocco, Archi
87JamExpP-2539
88RocExpLC-6
89JacExpB-11
89JacExpP-160
90JacExpB-4
90JacExpP-1380
91HarSenLD-252
91HarSenP-632
91LinDriAA-252
92Bow-450
92DonRoo-24
92ExpPos-9
92Lea-493
92Pin-510
92ScoRoo-99T
92StaClu-802
92StaCluECN-802
92TopTra-23T
92TopTraG-23T
92Ult-515
92UltAllR-4
92UppDec-772
92UppDecSR-SR5
93Don-246
93ExpColP7-2
93Fle-72
93OPC-112
93PacSpa-182
93Pin-349
93Sco-340
93SP-165
93StaClu-388
93StaCluFDI-388
93StaCluMOP-388
93Top-151
93TopGol-151
93TopInaM-151
93TopMic-151
93Ult-63
93UppDec-736
93UppDecGold-736
94Bow-672
94ColC-77
94ColChoGS-77
94ColChoSS-77
94Don-493
94ExtBas-371
94Fin-144
94FinRef-144
94Fla-232
94Fle-659
94Lea-79
94PadMot-7
94Pin-331
94PinArtP-331
94PinMusC-331
94Sel-138
94StaClu-221
94StaCluFDI-221
94StaCluGR-221
94StaCluMOP-221
94Top-704
94TopGol-704
94TopSpa-704
94TriPla-165
94Ult-574
94UppDec-75
94UppDecED-75
96FleUpd-U196
96FleUpdTC-U196
96LeaSigEA-29
96PadMot-19
97ColCho-206
97Fle-458
97FleTif-458
97Pac-421
97PacLigB-421
97PacSil-421
97UppDec-167
Ciardi, Mark
86VanCanP-6
87BrePol-34
88DenZepC-9
88DenZepP-1272
88Top-417
88TopTif-417
94BreMilB-207
Cias, Darryl
80WesHavWCT-14
81WesHavAT-5
82TacTigT-11
83TacTigT-9
84Nes792-159
84Top-159
84TopTif-159
86SanJosBP-6
Ciccarella, Joe
89AlaGol-4
92ClaFS7-185
92UppDecML-99
92WinHavRSC-2
92WinHavRSF-1768
93Bow-551
93PawRedSDD-7
93PawRedSF-2401
93PawRedSTI-7
94NewBriRSF-645
95PawRedSDD-8
95PawRedTI-32
95SigRoo-13
95SigRooSig-13
95TreThuTI-16
96OrlCubB-5
Cicione, Mike
84EveGiaC-3
Cicotte, Al
57Top-398
58Top-382
59Top-57
59TopVen-57
60MapLeaSF-3
60Top-473
61Top-241
62Col45'HC-4
62Top-126
62TopVen-126
89AstCol4S-2
Cicotte, Eddie
09ColChiE-50
09PhiCarE-4
09RamT20-25
09T206-64
10DarChoE-7
10DomDisP-24
10E12AmeCDC-9
10JuJuDE-9
10SweCapPP-2
10W555-13
11BasBatEU-9
11E94-6
11MecDFT-47
11S74Sil-2
11SpoLifCW-61
11SpoLifM-3
11T205-28
12ColRedB-50
12ColTinT-50
12HasTriFT-46
12T207-31
14CraJacE-94
15CraJacE-94
15SpoNewM-31
16ColE13-28
16SpoNewM-32
17HolBreD-14
19W514-82
75WhiSox1T-2
77GalGloG-175
77SerSta-5
87ConSer2-29
87SpoCubG-3
88PacEigMO-6
88PacEigMO-14
88PacEigMO-19
88PacEigMO-22
88PacEigMO-38
88PacEigMO-58
88PacEigMO-59
88PacEigMO-104
92Man191BSR-2
94ConTSN-1034
94ConTSN-1041
94ConTSNB-1034
94ConTSNB-1041
20W516-21
Cicotte, Greg
80BurBeeT-17
Ciczczon, Steve
89ColSprSSC-25
Cienscyzk, Frank
86A'sMot-26
90A'sMot-28
93AthMot-28
Ciesla, Theodore
90JamExpP-1
91RocExpC-18
91RocExpP-2053
Cieslak, Mark
85CedRapRT-2
Cifarelli, Gerard
89ChaRaiP-980
Cihocki, Al (Albert J.)
50WorWidGV-4
Cihocki, Ed (Edward J.)
33RitCE-8S
35DiaMatCS3T1-32
Cijntje, Sherwin
85NewOriT-13
86HagSunP-4
87ChaO'sW-2
88ChaKniTI-25
88RocRedWC-20
88RocRedWP-198
88RocRedWTI-6
89HagSunB-7
89HagSunS-3
89RocRedWC-15
89RocRedWP-1632
Cimino, Pete
66Top-563
67OPC-34
67Top-34
68OPC-143
68Top-143
68TopVen-143
Cimo, Matt
87ChaO'sW-15
88RocRedWC-11
88RocRedWGCP-5
88RocRedWP-203
88RocRedWTI-7
89ScrRedBC-14
89ScrRedBP-730
Cimoli, Gino Nicholas
50WorWidGV-22
52Par-70
57Top-319
58DodBelB-2
58DodJayP-3
58Hir-63
58Top-286
59Top-418
60Kah-5
60KeyChal-11
60Lea-142
60PirJayP-2
60Top-58
60TopVen-58
61Kah-7
61Pos-136A
61Pos-136B
61Top-165
61Top-309
62Jel-150
62Pos-150
62PosCan-150
62SalPlaC-148
62ShiPlaC-148
62Top-402
63Jel-88
63Pos-88
63Top-321
64Top-26
64TopVen-26
65Top-569
89DodSmoG-62
90DodTar-127
91OriCro-77
91RinPosBD3-4
Cimorelli, Frank
89JohCitCS-5
90SprCarB-23
91SprCarC-10
91SprCarP-735
92MidLeaATI-6
92SprCarC-23
92SprCarF-861
93ArkTraF-2806
94Bow-223
94LouRedF-2975
Cina, Randy
88LynRedSS-4
Cindrich, Jeff
92GulCoaYF-3783
93GreHorC-4
93GreHorF-878
94TamYanC-4
94TamYanF-2374
95TamYanYI-2
Cinnella, Doug
87HagSunP-29
88FloStaLAS-4
88WesPalBES-6
89WesPalBGS-6
90JacMetGS-15
91LinDriAAA-553
91TidTidLD-553
91TidTidP-2502
Cintron, Jose
94BoiHawC-7
94BoiHawF-3346
95CedRapKTI-10
96CedRapKTI-5
96MidLeaAB-16
Ciocca, Eric
91SpoIndC-1
91SpoIndP-3939
92ChaRaiF-114
Cipaula, Julio
85DomLeaS-182
Cipolloni, Joe
86PhiTas-xx
86PorBeaP-3
87MaiGuiP-18
87MaiGuiT-8
87PhiTas-23
Cipot, Ed
76WauMetT-9
78TidTidT-7
79TidTidT-14
80TidTidT-7
81TolMudHT-20
82GleFalWST-3
Cipres, Mark
83TriTriT-6
Ciprian, Francis
88ModA'sCLC-78
88ModA'sTI-18
Cipriani, Frank D.
61AthJayP-6
62Top-333
Cirbo, Dennis
78St.PetCT-6
Cirillo, Jeff
91HelBreSP-12
92BelBreC-25
92BelBreF-409
92MidLeaATI-7
93ElPasDF-2955
93ExcFS7-183
94BreMilB-298
94ExcFS7-79
94NewOrlZF-1475
94StaClu-699
94StaCluFDI-699
94StaCluGR-699
94StaCluMOP-699
95ColCho-173
95ColChoGS-173
95ColChoSS-173
95Fla-269
95Fle-175
95Pac-228
95Pin-165
95PinArtP-165
95PinMusC-165
95Sco-599
95ScoGolR-599

95ScoPlaTS-599
95Sel-176
95SelArtP-176
95SelCer-131
95SelCerMG-131
95SigRooOJ-10
95SigRooOJP-10
95SigRooOJPS-10
95SigRooOJS-10
95StaClu-390
95StaCluMOP-390
95StaCluSTWS-390
95StaCluVR-249
95Sum-104
95SumNthD-104
95Top-544
95TopCyb-325
95UC3-105
95UC3ArtP-105
95Ult-294
95UltGolM-294
95UppDec-52
95UppDecED-52
95UppDecEDG-52
96Cir-50
96CirRav-50
96ColCho-188
96ColChoGS-188
96ColChoSS-188
96Don-326
96DonPreP-326
96Fla-99
96Fle-143
96FleTif-143
96LeaSig-27
96LeaSigA-45
96LeaSigAG-45
96LeaSigAS-45
96LeaSigPPG-27
96LeaSigPPP-27
96MetUni-69
96MetUniP-69
96Pac-341
96Pin-83
96Sco-397
96StaClu-65
96StaCluMOP-65
95StaCluVRMC-249
96TeaOut-17
96Top-282
96TopGal-121
96TopGalPPI-121
96Ult-78
96UltGolM-78
96UppDec-366
97Bow-31
97BowChr-27
97BowChrI-27
97BowChrIR-27
97BowChrR-27
97BowInt-31
97Cir-228
97CirRav-228
97ColCho-149
97Don-92
97DonLim-176
97DonLimLE-176
97DonPre-36
97DonPreCttC-36
97DonPreP-92
97DonPrePGold-92
97Fin-216
97FinRef-216
97FlaSho-A126
97FlaSho-B126
97FlaSho-C126
97FlaShoLC-126
97FlaShoLC-B126
97FlaShoLC-C126
97FlaShoLCM-A126
97FlaShoLCM-B126
97FlaShoLCM-C126
97Fle-126
97Fle-735
97FleTif-126
97FleTif-735
97Lea-115
97LeaFraM-115
97LeaFraMDC-115
97MetUni-63
97Pac-116
97PacLigB-116
97PacPri-40
97PacPriLB-40
97PacPriP-40
97PacSil-116
97Pin-101
97PinArtP-101
97PinMusC-101
97PinX-P-48
97PinX-PMoS-48
97Sco-88
97ScoPreS-88
97ScoShoS-88
97ScoShoSAP-88
97SkyE-X-26
97SkyE-XC-26
97SkyE-XEC-26
97SP-102
97SpoIll-152
97SpoIllEE-152
97StaClu-132
97StaCluMOP-132
97Stu-77
97StuPrePG-77
97StuPrePS-77
97Top-49
97TopChr-18
97TopChrR-18
97TopGal-136
97TopGalPPI-136
97TopSta-92
97TopStaAM-92
97Ult-74
97UltGolME-74
97UltPlaME-74
97UppDec-96
Cisar, George Joseph
90DodTar-913
Cisarik, Brian
88CpoIndP-1940
89WicChaR-8
89WicStaR-5
89WicWraR-32
90WicWraRD-5
91LinDriAA-604
91WicWraLD-604
91WicWraP-2609
91WicWraRD-19
Cisco, Galen
61UniOil-S1
62Top-301
63Top-93
64Top-202
64TopGia-47
64TopVen-202
65MetJayP-4
65Top-364
67Top-596
69OPC-211
69Top-211
73OPC-593
73Top-593
74Top-166
80ExpPos-6
82ExpPos-5
83ExpPos-3
83ExpStu-13
84ExpPos-4
84ExpStu-4
84ExpStu-38
88SyrChiC-25
88SyrChiP-818
89SyrChiC-24
89SyrChiP-799
90BluJayFS-6
91BluJayFS-6
91MetWIZ-76
93BluJayFS-5
96LasVegSB-3
Cisco, Jeff
86ChaRaiP-6
Cissell, Bill (Chalmer W.)
28Exh-37
28PorandAR-C1
28PorandAR-D1
28StaPlaCE-8
29ExhFou-19
29PorandAR-12
30ChiEveAP-13
31Exh-19
31W517-5
32OrbPinNP-23
32OrbPinUP-10
33CraJacP-2
33Gou-26
33GouCanV-26
33TatOrb-10
34BatR31-13
34ExhFou-9
35GouPuzR-6E
35GouPuzR-11G
35GouPuzR-13E
35GouPuzR-15E
92ConTSN-411
Ciszczon, Steve
80TacTigT-26
83ChaChaT-21
85MaiGuiT-31
86MaiGuiP-4
88ColSprSSP-1539
89ColSprSSP-250
Ciszkowski, Jeff
84LitFalMT-16
86LynMetP-7
87LynMetP-13
88St.LucMS-5
89StoPorB-11
89StoPorCLC-154
89StoPorP-399
89StoPorS-17
Citarella, Ralph A.
81ArkTraT-18
82LouRedE-5
83LouRedR-16
84Car-5
84LouRedR-16
85Don-504
85PhiTas-46
85PorBeaC-44
86LouRedTI-9
86TacTigP-2
87HawIslP-6
Citari, Joe
86OmaRoyP-5
86OmaRoyT-14
87OmaRoyP-9
88OmaRoyC-21
88OmaRoyP-1519
89ReaPhiS-8
Citronnelli, Ed
87SalLakTTT-13
Civit, Xavier
94VerExpC-7
94VerExpF-3901
96DelShoB-13
Clabaugh, Moose (John W.)
90DodTar-128
Clack, Marvin
82AleDukT-12
83AleDukT-7
Clancey, Bill (William E.)
09T206-409
Clancy, Bill
12ColRedB-51
Clancy, Bud (John William)
28PorandAR-D2
29ExhFou-19
33Gou-32
33GouCanV-32
90DodTar-129
94ConTSN-1131
94ConTSNB-1131
Clancy, Jim
75AndRanT-32
76SanAntBTI-7
78BluJayP-4
78OPC-103
78Top-496
79BluJayBY-6
79OPC-61
79Top-131
80OPC-132
80Top-249
81Fle-412
81OPC-19
81OPCPos-21
81Top-19
81TopSti-143
82Don-227
82Fle-612
82OPC-28
82Top-665
83Don-101
83Fle-426
83FleSta-39
83FleSti-108
83OPC-345
83Top-345
83TopSti-132
84BluJayFS-6
84Don-19
84Don-19A
84Don-119
84DonActAS-49
84Fle-150
84Nes792-575
84OPC-337
84Top-575
84TopSti-367
84TopTif-575
85BluJayFS-8
85Don-439
85Fle-101
85OPC-188
85Top-746
85TopTif-746
86BluJayAF-6
86BluJayFS-6
86Don-268
86Fle-56
86Lea-141
86OPC-213
86Top-96
86Top-412
86TopTif-96
86TopTif-412
87BluJayFS-5
87Don-639
87DonHig-11
87Fle-223
87FleGlo-223
87Lea-90
87OPC-122
87Spo-189
87Top-122
87TopSti-189
87TopTif-122
88BluJay5-3
88BluJayFS-7
88Don-74
88DonBasB-48
88Fle-106
88FleGlo-106
88Lea-73
88MSAHosD-13
88OPC-54
88Sco-530
88ScoGlo-530
88Spo-215
88StaLinBJ-4
88Top-54
88TopBig-258
88TopSti-184
88TopTif-54
89AstLenH-7
89AstMot-15
89AstSmo-9
89Bow-324
89BowTif-324
89Don-267
89DonBasB-206
89DonTra-32
89Fle-229
89FleGlo-229
89FleUpd-88
89OPC-219
89Sco-538
89ScoRoo-42T
89Top-219
89TopTif-219
89TopTra-19T
89TopTraT-19T
89UppDec-282
90AstLenH-8
90AstMot-23
90BluJayHS-4
90Don-69
90Fle-226
90FleCan-226
90OPC-648
90PubSti-90
90Sco-424
90Top-648
90TopTif-648
90UppDec-203
90VenSti-103
91AstMot-23
91Bow-554
91BraSubS-9
91UppDec-682
92Don-639
92OPC-279
92Sco-627
92Top-279
92TopGol-279
92TopGolW-279
92TopMic-279
Clapham, Mark
78OrlTwiT-3
Clapinski, Chris
93KanCouCC-4
93KanCouCF-921
94BreCouMC-5
94BreCouMF-18
95PorSeaDTI-3
96PorSeaDB-11
93KanCouCTI-4
Clapp, Steve
89TenTecGE-7
Clapp, Stubby
96JohCitCTI-6
Clarey, Doug (Douglas W.)
77HolMilT-4
Clark, Al
88T/MUmp-24
89T/MUmp-22
90T/MUmp-21
Clark, Allie (Alfred A.)
48IndTeal-6
49Bow-150
49IndTeal-7
50Bow-233
50IndNumN-6
50IndTeal-5
51Bow-29
52Bow-130
52Top-278
53BowC-155
53IndPenCBP-8
83TopRep5-278
Clark, Bob (Robert Cale)
76QuaCitAT-9
79SalLakCGT-12
80SalLakCGT-23
84Nes792-626
84TopTif-626
84TopTraT-24T
85TopTif-553
86TopTif-452
90DodTar-130
Clark, Bob (Robert H.)
87OldJudN-82
Clark, Bobby (Robert Cale)
80Top-663
81Don-572
81Top-288
82Don-318
82Fle-456
82Top-74
83Don-444
83Fle-82
83Top-184
84BreGar-4
84BrePol-25
84Don-524
84Fle-512
84FleUpd-25
84Top-626
84TopTra-24T
85BreGar-3
85Don-481
85Fle-578
85Top-553
85VanCanC-204
86EdmTraP-4
86OPC-352
86Top-452
87TacTigP-4
94BreMilB-208
94BreMilB-299
Clark, Brian
92MisStaB-9
93GreFalDSP-5
93MisStaB-8
Clark, Bryan Donald
77SalPirT-4
78ChaPirT-2
80SpoIndT-8
80VenLeaS-161
82Don-596
82Fle-507
82SalLakCGT-6
82Top-632
83Don-603
83Fle-476
83Top-789
84BluJayFS-7

84Don-562
84Fle-609
84FleUpd-26
84Nes792-22
84Top-22
84TopTif-22
84TopTra-25T
84TopTraT-25T
85IndPol-43
85MaiGuiT-5
85OPC-217
85Top-489
85TopMin-489
85TopTif-489
85TopTifT-21T
85TopTra-21T
86BufBisP-8
86MarGreT-11
89TacTigC-7
89TacTigP-1563
89TriA AAC-41
89TriAAP-AAA39
90TriAAAC-41
96NewJerCB-5

Clark, Casey
77SalPirT-5
78ChaPirT-3

Clark, Chris
81HolMilT-9
82HolMilT-19
84EdmTraC-108
85EdmTraC-18
96CliLumKTI-7

Clark, Dan
21Exh-23
84ButCopKT-4

Clark, Dave
85WatIndT-15
86IndTeal-15
86MaiGuiP-5
87BufBisP-6
87Don-623
87Fle-644
87FleGlo-644
87IndGat-12
87Spo-118
88BlaYNPRWLU-47
88Don-473
88IndGat-25
88RocExpLC-7
88Sco-633
88ScoGlo-633
88StaLinI-9
88Top-49
88TopTif-49
89Don-585
89Fle-402
89FleGlo-402
89IndTeal-9
89Top-574
89TopTif-574
89UppDec-517
90CubMar-4
90Don-492
90Fle-490
90FleCan-490
90OPC-339
90PubSti-558
90Sco-141
90Top-339
90TopTif-339
90TopTVCu-29
90UppDec-449
90VenSti-104
91Don-616
91Fle-417
91OPC-241
91Sco-542
91Top-241
91TopDesS-241
91TopMic-241
91TopTif-241
91UppDec-314
92BufBisBS-3
92BufBisF-332
92BufBisS-28
92Sco-657
93PirNatl-5
94ColC-78
94ColChoGS-78
94ColChoSS-78
94Fle-606
94Pac-494
94PirQui-2
94Sco-267
94ScoGolR-267
94StaClu-498
94StaCluFDI-498
94StaCluGR-498
94StaCluMOP-498
94TopTra-6T
95ColCho-386
95ColChoGS-386
95ColChoSS-386
95Don-265
95DonPreP-265
95DonTopotO-314
95Fin-52
95FinRef-52
95Fle-474
95Pac-341
95Pin-101
95PinArtP-101
95PinMusC-101
95PirFil-5
95Sco-161
95ScoGolR-161
95ScoPlaTS-161
95SP-97
95SPSil-97
95Top-585
95TopCyb-358
95Ult-212
95UltGolM-212
95UppDec-388
95UppDecED-388
95UppDecEDG-388
96ColCho-677
96ColChoGS-677
96ColChoSS-677
96Fle-517
96FleTif-517
96Pin-21

Clark, Dera
88BasCitRS-8
89MemChiB-18
89MemChiP-1199
89MemChiS-6
89Sta-40
90CMC-178
90OmaRoyC-3
90OmaRoyP-59
90ProAAAF-594
92OmaRoyF-2955
93OmaRoyF-1675
94RicBraF-2840
96MemChiB-10

Clark, Doug
90ArkRaz-26

Clark, Dutch (Earl)
40WheM4-4

Clark, Earl (Bailey Earl)
33Gou-57
34GouCanV-41

Clark, Fred (Alfred Robert)
12PhiCarE-6

Clark, Garry
87ClePhiP-13
87SpaPhiP-7
88ClePhiS-8
90RenSilSCLC-284

Clark, Geoff
89SalDodTI-4
91YakBeaC-30

Clark, Glen Ester
77FriOneYW-67

Clark, Howie
93AlbPolC-9
93BluOriC-10
93BluOriF-4131
94AlbPolC-12
94AlbPolF-2242
96BowBayB-11

Clark, Isaiah
86BelBreP-4
87StoPorP-11
88ModA'sTI-20
89RivRedWB-29
89RivRedWCLC-9
89RivRedWP-1404
90Bes-196
90CMC-720
90SanBerSB-7
90SanBerSCLC-103
90SanBerSP-2638

Clark, Jack Anthony
75LafDriT-13
76PheGiaCr-22
76PhoGiaCa-19
76PhoGiaCC-6
76PhoGiaVNB-4
77Gia-3
77Top-488
78Top-384
79GiaPol-22
79Hos-116
79Kel-40
79OPC-268
79Top-512
79TopCom-32
80GiaPol-22
80Kel-57
80OPC-93
80Top-167
80TopSup-54
81AllGamPI-138
81Don-315
81Dra-15
81Fle-433
81FleStiC-52
81MSAMinD-9
81OPC-30
81Squ-18
81Top-30
81TopScr-70
81TopSti-234
82Don-46
82Dra-8
82Fle-387
82FleSta-65
82Top-460
82TopSti-106
83AllGamPI-138
83Don-222
83DonActA-29
83Dra-5
83Fle-256
83FleSta-40
83FleSti-48
83GiaMot-2
83Kel-48
83OPC-210
83Top-210
83TopGloS-32
83TopSti-162
83TopSti-300
84AllGamPI-46
84Don-7
84Don-7A
84Don-65
84DonActAS-31
84Fle-369
84FunFooP-19
84GiaMot-7
84GiaPos-4
84Nes792-690
84OPC-381
84Top-690
84TopRubD-14
84TopSti-167
84TopTif-690
85AllGamPI-136
85CarTeal-5
85Don-65
85DonActA-30
85Fle-604
85FleUpd-25
85KASDis-2
85KitCloD-2
85Lea-207
85OPC-208
85Top-740
85TopRubD-12
85TopSti-160
85TopTif-740
85TopTifT-22T
85TopTra-22T
86BasStaB-21
86CarIGAS-1
86CarKASD-9
86CarSchM-1
86CarTeal-7
86Don-168
86DonAll-23
86Fle-30
86FleLeaL-6
86FleMin-6
86FleStiC-24
86GenMilB-4B
86Lea-96
86OPC-350
86QuaGra-5
86SevCoi-S13
86Spo-107
86Top-350
86TopGloS-4
86TopMinL-59
86TopSti-50
86TopTat-19
86TopTif-350
87BoaandB-25
87CarSmo-13
87ClaUpdY-148
87Don-111
87DonOpeD-67
87Fle-289
87FleGlo-289
87FleLimBC-C4
87FleSlu-9
87OPC-331
87SpoTeaP-12
87StuPan-11
87Top-520
87TopSti-52
87TopTif-520
88ClaBlu-205
88Don-15
88Don-183
88DonAll-33
88DonBasB-49
88DonPop-11
88DonReaBY-NEW
88DonSupD-15
88Fle-26
88FleAll-11
88FleBasA-6
88FleExcS-8
88FleGlo-26
88FleMin-39
88FleRecS-5
88FleSup-7
88FleUpd-47
88FleUpdG-47
88K-M-5
88KayB-5
88Lea-15
88Lea-181
88MSAJifPD-4
88Nes-17
88OPC-100
88PanSti-232
88PanSti-388
88RedFolSB-12
88Sco-100
88Sco-650
88ScoBoxC-11
88ScoGlo-100
88ScoGlo-650
88ScoRoo-1T
88ScoRooG-1T
88Spo-18
88SpoGam-25
88StaLinAl-6
88StaLinCa-2
88StaLinY-2
88Top-100
88Top-397
88TopBig-262
88TopCoi-9
88TopGaloC-4
88TopGloA-13
88TopGloS-41
88TopMinL-69
88TopRevLL-4
88TopRitTM-10
88TopSti-46
88TopSti-150
88TopStiB-1
88TopTif-100
88TopTif-397
88TopTra-28T
88TopTraT-28T
88TopUKM-13
88TopUKMT-13
89Bow-456
89BowTif-456
89ClaTraP-158
89Don-311
89DonBasB-98
89DonTra-2
89Fle-252
89FleGlo-252
89FleUpd-123
89KayB-5
89OPC-3
89PadCok-2
89PadMag-6
89RedFolSB-21
89Sco-25
89ScoHot1S-27
89ScoRoo-3T
89Spo-26
89Top-410
89TopBasT-65
89TopBig-240
89TopCapC-14
89TopCoi-7
89TopGloS-56
89TopMinL-65
89TopSti-308
89TopTif-410
89TopTra-20T
89TopTraT-20T
89TopUKM-14
89UppDec-346
89UppDec-773
90Bow-214
90BowTif-214
90Don-128
90DonBesN-109
90DonGraS-11
90Fle-152
90FleAwaW-8
90FleCan-152
90Lea-287
90MLBBasB-56
90OPC-90
90PadCok-4
90PadMag-18
90PanSti-348
90PubSti-45
90RedFolSB-16
90Sco-20
90Spo-28
90Top-90
90TopAmeA-12
90TopBig-39
90TopHilHM-18
90TopMinL-78
90TopSti-104
90TopTif-90
90TopTVA-44
90UppDec-342
90VenSti-105
91Bow-122
91Cla2-T99
91ClaGam-154
91Don-618
91Fle-526
91FleUpd-4
91Lea-201
91OPC-650
91OPCPre-21
91PanFreS-91
91PanSti-98
91RedFolS-18
91RedSoxP-4
91Sco-523
91ScoRoo-4T
91StaClu-500
91Stu-13
91Top-650
91TopDesS-650
91TopMic-650
91TopTif-650
91TopTra-22T
91TopTraT-22T
91UltUpd-5
91UppDec-331
91UppDec-735
92Bow-233
92DenHol-5
92Don-169
92Fle-36
92Lea-366
92OPC-207
92Pin-85
92RedSoxDD-8
92Sco-318
92ScoProP-12
92StaClu-186
92Top-207
92TopGol-207
92TopGolW-207
92TopMic-207
92Ult-14
92UppDec-521
92UppDecHRH-HR14
92YanWIZ8-32
93Don-63

93Fle-556
93OPC-240
93Pin-221
93RedSoxWHP-7
93Sel-188
93StaClu-20
93StaCluFDI-20
93StaCluMOP-20
93Top-781
93TopGol-781
93TopInaM-781
93TopMic-781
93Ult-148
Clark, Jeff
89PulBraP-1910
90BurBraB-16
90BurBraP-2363
90BurBraS-9
91DurBulC-20
91DurBulP-1558
Clark, Jerald
85SpoIndC-3
87WicPilRD-24
88LasVegSC-12
88LasVegSP-229
89Bow-462
89BowTif-462
89Don-599
89Fle-642
89FleGlo-642
89LasVegSC-13
89LasVegSP-10
89Sco-644
89Spo-179
89TriA AAC-37
89TriAAP-AAA49
89UppDec-30
90ClaUpd-T10
90Don-593
90DonRoo-48
90Lea-510
90PubSti-46
90Sco-660
90ScoYouS2-41
90TriAAAC-37
90UppDec-624
90VenSti-106
91Bow-658
91Don-74
91FleUpd-121
91Lea-265
91OPC-513
91PadMag-7
91PadMag-15B
91PadSmo-4
91Sco-242
91StaClu-468
91Top-513
91TopDesS-513
91TopMic-513
91TopTif-513
91UltUpd-110
91UppDec-624
92Bow-323
92Don-144
92Fle-601
92Lea-55
92OPC-749
92PadCarJ-5
92PadMot-9
92PadPolD-4
92PadSmo-5
92Pin-48
92Sco-257
92StaClu-149
92Stu-102
92Top-749
92TopGol-749
92TopGolW-749
92TopMic-749
92Ult-275
92UppDec-292
93Bow-612
93Don-74
93Don-790
93Fla-37
93Fle-137
93FleFinE-26
93FunPac-175
93Lea-290
93OPC-44
93OPCPre-91
93PacSpa-425
93Pin-234
93PinExpOD-7
93RocUSPC-7C
93RocUSPC-12H
93Sco-405
93SP-218
93StaClu-671
93StaCluFDI-671
93StaCluMOP-671
93StaCluRoc-13
93Stu-41
93Top-194
93Top-565
93TopGol-194
93TopGol-565
93TopInaM-194
93TopInaM-565
93TopMic-194
93TopMic-565
93TriPla-126
93Ult-345
93UppDec-140
93UppDec-797
93UppDecGold-140
93UppDecGold-797
94ColC-79
94ColChoGS-79
94ColChoSS-79
94Don-136
94Fle-438
94Pac-193
94PanSti-173
94Pin-103
94PinArtP-103
94PinMusC-103
94Sco-362
94ScoGolR-362
94StaClu-98
94StaCluFDI-98
94StaCluGR-98
94StaCluMOP-98
94Top-77
94TopGol-77
94TopSpa-77
94Ult-184
95FleUpd-58
95StaClu-579
95StaCluMOP-579
95StaCluSTWS-579
95TopTra-118T
Clark, John
96PorRocB-12
Clark, Kevin
94UtiBluSC-8
94UtiBluSF-3822
96MicBatCB-9
96MidLeaAB-43
Clark, Kirby
96BatCliTI-8
Clark, Lefty (William Watson)
28W56PlaC-H1
32OrbPinNP-8
32OrbPinUP-11
32R33So2-407
33DouDisP-9
33Gou-17
33GouCanV-17
33TatOrb-11
34DiaMatCSB-28
35GouPuzR-1G
35GouPuzR-3E
35GouPuzR-5E
35GouPuzR-14E
36WorWidGV-86
90DodTar-131
Clark, Leroy
76DubPacT-5
Clark, Marcus
79WatIndT-18
Clark, Mark
87SumBraP-11
88HamRedP-1736
89SavCarP-370
90St.PetCS-2
90TopTVCa-41
91LouRedTI-2
92Bow-109
92DonRoo-25
92FleUpd-118
92LouRedS-257
92SkyAAAF-125
92TopDeb91-35
92Ult-564
92UppDec-702
92UppDec-773
93Don-152
93Fle-508
93IndWUA-6
93Lea-172
93Sco-320
93Sel-301
93StaClu-60
93StaCluFDI-60
93StaCluMOP-60
93Top-339
93TopGol-339
93TopInaM-339
93TopMic-339
93UppDec-629
93UppDecGold-629
94ColC-538
94ColChoGS-538
94ColChoSS-538
94Don-656
94ExtBas-58
94Fla-39
94Fle-101
94Pac-167
94StaClu-207
94StaCluFDI-207
94StaCluGR-207
94StaCluMOP-207
94Top-696
94TopGol-696
94TopSpa-696
95ColCho-266
95ColChoGS-266
95ColChoSE-121
95ColChoSEGS-121
95ColChoSESS-121
95ColChoSS-266
95Don-156
95DonPreP-156
95Fle-133
95Lea-317
95Pin-183
95PinArtP-183
95PinMusC-183
95Sco-132
95ScoGolR-132
95ScoPlaTS-132
95StaClu-54
95StaCluFDI-54
95StaCluMOP-54
95StaCluSTWS-54
95Top-463
95TopCyb-258
95Ult-37
95UltGolM-37
95UppDec-93
95UppDecED-93
95UppDecEDG-93
96ColCho-529
96ColChoGS-529
96ColChoSS-529
96Don-510
96DonPreP-510
96Fin-B339
96FinRef-B339
96Fle-84
96FleTif-84
96FleUpd-U155
96FleUpdTC-U155
96LeaSigEA-30
96MetKah-5
97Cir-90
97CirRav-90
97ColCho-393
97Fin-68
97FinRef-68
97Fle-392
97FleTif-392
97Lea-310
97LeaFraM-310
97LeaFraMDC-310
97MetUni-191
97PacPriGotD-GD174
97Sco-364
97ScoHobR-364
97ScoResC-364
97ScoShoS-364
97ScoShoSAP-364
97StaClu-71
97StaCluMOP-71
97Top-5
97UppDec-431
Clark, Mel (Melvin Earl)
53BowC-67
54Bow-175
55Bow-41
Clark, Mike J.
53CarHunW-5
53Top-193
91TopArc1-193
Clark, Pepper (Joshua B.)
09T206-410
Clark, Phil
58Top-423
59Top-454
87FayGenP-23
88FloStaLAS-31
88LakTigS-7
89LonTigP-1383
90CMC-400
90ProAAAF-382
90TolMudHC-23
90TolMudHP-152
91Fle-332
91LinDriAAA-581
91Sco-756
91ScoRoo-7
91TolMudHLD-581
91TolMudHP-1934
92TolMudHS-581
92TopTra-24T
92TopTraG-24T
93Don-391
93FleFinE-136
93PadMot-21
93Pin-287
93Sel-335
93Top-802
93TopGol-802
93TopInaM-802
93TopMic-802
93Ult-470
94ColC-426
94ColChoGS-426
94ColChoSS-426
94Don-130
94Fle-660
94Pac-520
94PadMot-5
94PanSti-254
94Pin-167
94PinArtP-167
94PinMusC-167
94Sco-241
94ScoGolR-241
94Sel-153
94StaClu-399
94StaCluFDI-399
94StaCluGR-399
94StaCluMOP-399
94Top-408
94TopGol-408
94TopSpa-408
94Ult-277
95Fle-557
95Pac-359
95PadMot-7
95Top-298
96Pac-187
96PawRedSDD-2
Clark, Randy
79QuaCitCT-14
Clark, Rickey
70Top-586
71OPC-697
71Top-697
72OPC-462
72Top-462
73OPC-636
73Top-636
Clark, Rob
83TulDriT-4
84OklCit8T-2
85TulDriTI-27
86OklCit8P-3
90TulDriDGB-33
Clark, Rodney
85UtiBluST-13
Clark, Ron
96IowCubB-2
Clark, Ron (Ronald Bruce)
67OPC-137
67Top-137
68Top-589
69Top-561
70OPC-531
70Top-531
71MLBOffS-509
75IntLeaAT-13
76OklCit8TI-3
80CarMudF-17
80VenLeaS-260
81ReaPhiT-23
82OklCit8T-6
83KinBluJTI-3
83Pil69G-40
86ClePhiP-4
90WhiSoxC-30
92IndFanC-30
93IndWUA-33
94BreMilB-209
95IowCubTI-7
Clark, Roy
79TulDriT-24
80LynSaiT-20
81SpoIndT-6
82SalLakCGT-7
Clark, Russell
76WauMetT-10
77LynMetT-9
79JacMetT-20
79TidTidT-22
Clark, Skip
81MiaOriT-12
Clark, Spider (Owen F.)
87OldJudN-80
87OldJudN-81
Clark, Stephen C.
80PerHaloFP-B
Clark, Terry
83ArkTraT-3
84LouRedR-24
86MidAngP-5
87EdmTraP-2082
88EdmTraC-1
88EdmTraP-569
89Don-607
89Fle-470
89FleGlo-470
89OPC-129
89Sco-566
89ScoHot1R-89
89Top-129
89TopTif-129
89TriAAP-AAA27
89UppDec-234
90CMC-605
90ProAAAF-188
90TucTorC-3
90TucTorP-198
91LinDriAAA-607
91TucTorLD-607
91TucTorP-2207
92ColSprSF-745
92ColSprSS-81
94RicBraF-2841
94TriAAF-AAA41
94VenLinU-34
95LinVen-32
96LeaSigEA-31
96RoyPol-5
Clark, Tim
90BelBreS-5
90LSUTigP-14
91StoPorC-23
91StoPorP-3042
92SalLakTSP-8
93Bow-699
93HigDesMC-4
93HigDesMF-53
94ActPac-39
94Bow-343
94Bow-562
94BowBes-B51
94BowBesR-B51
94ClaGolF-94
94ExcFS7-189
94PorSeaDF-684
94PorSeaDTI-11
94Top-79
94TopGol-79
94TopSpa-79
94UppDecML-98
94UppDecML-106
95PorSeaDTI-4
Clark, Tom
90LitSunW-18
Clark, Tony
86DayBealP-5
90BriTigP-3173
90BriTigS-3
90ProAaA-189

91NiaFalRC-13
91NiaFalRP-3645
92NiaFalRC-1
92NiaFalRF-3336
92UppDecML-182
94AriFalLS-3
94Bow-209
94BowBes-B62
94BowBesR-B62
94BowPre-8
94Cla-196
94TreThuF-2124
94UppDecML-57
95ActPacF-8
95Bow-253
95BowBes-B20
95BowBesR-B20
95BowGolF-253
95ColCho-16
95ColChoGS-16
95ColChoSS-16
95Exc-47
95ExcAll-2
95SP-16
95SPSil-16
95TolMudHTI-11
95Top-153
95UppDec-227
95UppDecED-227
95UppDecEDG-227
95UppDecML-70
95UppDecMLOP-OP10
96Bow-164
96ColCho-543
96ColChoGS-543
96ColChoSS-543
96Don-407
96DonPreP-407
96Fin-B356
96FinRef-B356
96FlePro-3
96Lea-30
96LeaPre-114
96LeaPreP-114
96LeaPrePB-30
96LeaPrePG-30
96LeaPrePS-30
96LeaSig-87
96LeaSigPPG-87
96LeaSigPPP-87
96Pin-166
96PinArtP-93
96PinSam-166
96PinSta-93
96Sco-229
96Spo-123
96SpoArtP-123
96StaClu-42
96StaCluMOP-42
96TolMudHB-8
96Top-337
96TopGal-138
96TopGalPPI-138
96UppDec-327
96UppDecFSP-FS6
96UppDecPHE-H23
96UppDecPreH-H23
96Zen-106
96ZenArtP-106
97Bow-8
97BowBes-26
97BowBesAR-26
97BowBesR-26
97BowChr-6
97BowChrI-6
97BowChrIR-6
97BowChrR-6
97BowInt-8
97Cir-244
97CirRav-244
97ColCho-104
97Don-341
97DonEli-120
97DonEliGS-120
97DonEliTotC-9
97DonEliTotCDC-9
97DonFraFea-10
97DonLim-78
97DonLim-106
97DonLimFotG-14
97DonLimLE-78
97DonLimLE-106
97DonPre-110
97DonPreCttC-110
97DonPreP-341
97DonPrePGold-341
97DonRatR-13
97Fin-129
97Fin-245
97FinEmb-129
97FinEmbR-129
97FinRef-129
97FinRef-245
97FlaSho-A173
97FlaSho-B173
97FlaSho-C173
97FlaShoLC-173
97FlaShoLC-B173
97FlaShoLC-C173
97FlaShoLCM-A173
97FlaShoLCM-B173
97FlaShoLCM-C173
97Fle-96
97Fle-730
97FleTif-96
97FleTif-730
97Lea-42
97LeaFraM-42
97LeaFraMDC-42
97LeaGolS-28
97LeaLeaotN-15
97MetUni-108
97Pac-86
97PacLigB-86
97PacPri-30
97PacPriLB-30
97PacPriP-30
97PacSil-86
97Pin-110
97PinArtP-110
97PinCer-18
97PinCerMBlu-18
97PinCerMG-18
97PinCerMR-18
97PinCerR-18
97PinIns-143
97PinInsCE-143
97PinInsDE-143
97PinMusC-110
97PinTotCPB-18
97PinTotCPG-18
97PinTotCPR-18
97PinX-P-39
97PinX-P-145
97PinX-PMoS-39
97PinX-PMoS-145
97PinX-PSfF-2
97PinX-PSfFU-2
97Sco-142
97ScoPreS-142
97ScoShoS-142
97ScoShoSAP-142
97SkyE-X-20
97SkyE-XC-20
97SkyE-XEC-20
97SkyE-XSD2-14
97SP-71
97SpoIII-58
97SpoIII-137
97SpoIIIEE-58
97SpoIIIEE-137
97StaClu-263
97StaCluM-M5
97StaCluMOP-263
97StaCluMOP-M5
97Stu-100
97StuPrePG-100
97StuPrePS-100
97Top-406
97TopAwel-AI2
97TopChr-143
97TopChrR-143
97TopGal-166
97TopGalPPI-166
97TopStaFAS-FAS8
97Ult-58
97UltGolME-58
97UltPlaME-58
97UppDec-62
95UppDecMLFS-70
97Zen-10

Clark, Will

84OCoandSI-208
86DonHig-1
86DonRoo-32
86FleSlu-6
86FleUpd-25
86GiaMot-7
86SpoRoo-6
86StaCan-13
86TopTra-24T
86TopTraT-24T
87BurKinA-3
87Don-66
87DonOpeD-96
87Fle-269
87FleExcS-10
87FleGlo-269
87FleLimE-8
87FleSluBC-M2
87FleStiC-22
87GiaMot-2
87Lea-144
87OPC-361
87RedFolSB-50
87Spo-95
87Spo-195
87SpoTeaP-10
87Top-420
87TopRoo-4
87TopSti-88
87TopTif-420
87ToyRoo-7
88ClaBlu-225
88Don-21
88Don-204
88DonBasB-79
88DonBonM-BC24
88DonSupD-21
88Dra-27
88Fle-78
88FleAwaW-5
88FleBasA-7
88FleBasM-5
88FleExcS-9
88FleGlo-78
88FleHotS-6
88FleLeaL-5
88FleMin-116
88FleRecS-6
88FleSlu-8
88FleStiC-126
88FleSup-8
88FleTeaL-4
88GiaMot-2
88K-M-6
88Lea-21
88Lea-170
88MotWilC-1
88MotWilC-2
88MotWilC-3
88MotWilC-4
88MSAFanSD-12
88MSAIceTD-10
88MSAJifPD-5
88Nes-14
88OPC-350
88PanSti-420
88PanSti-421
88Sco-27
88Sco-78
88Sco-84
88ScoGlo-27
88ScoGlo-78
88ScoGlo-84
88ScoYouSI-25
88Spo-9
88SpoGam-4
88StaCla-1
88StaCla-2
88StaCla-3
88StaCla-4
88StaCla-5
88StaCla-6
88StaCla-7
88StaCla-8
88StaCla-9
88StaCla-10
88StaCla-11
88StaLinG-4
88Top-350
88TopBig-9
88TopCoi-38
88TopRitTM-12
88TopSti-87
88TopTif-350
88TopUKM-14
88TopUKMT-14
89Bow-476
89BowTif-476
89CadEIID-25
89ClaLigB-18
89ClaTraO-150
89ClaTraP-180
89Don-249
89DonAll-33
89DonBasB-23
89DonBonM-BC22
89DonPop-33
89Fle-325
89Fle-631
89Fle-632
89FleAll-3
89FleBasA-6
89FleBasM-7
89FleExcS-5
89FleGlo-325
89FleGlo-631
89FleGlo-632
89FleHeroB-7
89FleLeaL-4
89FleSup-8
89FleWaxBC-C6
89GiaMot-2
89K-M-23
89KayB-6
89KinDis-22
89MotWilC-1
89MotWilC-2
89MotWilC-3
89MotWilC-4
89MSAIceTD-4
89OPC-321
89PanSti-212
89PanSti-232
89RedFolSB-22
89Sco-450
89ScoHot1S-85
89ScoSco-10
89Spo-170
89SpoIIIFKI-70
89StaMit/C-1
89StaMit/C-3
89StaMit/C-5
89StaMit/C-7
89StaMit/C-9
89StaMit/C-11
89Top-660
89TopBasT-47
89TopBig-146
89TopCapC-19
89TopCoi-8
89TopDouA-13
89TopGaloC-3
89TopGloA-13
89TopGloS-11
89TopHeaUT-2
89TopHilTM-7
89TopMinL-41
89TopSti-88
89TopSti-159
89TopStiB-34
89TopTif-660
89TopUKM-15
89TVSpoM-49
89TVSpoM-131
89UppDec-155
89UppDec-678
89UppDecS-1
90AllBasT-18
90Bow-231
90BowIns-1
90BowInsT-1
90BowTif-231
90BowTif-A1
90ClaBlu-6
90ClaBlu-87A
90ClaBlu-87B
90ClaBlu-150A
90ClaBlu-150B
90ClaUpd-T11
90ClaYel-T7
90Col-4
90ColPosWC-1
90ColPosWC-2
90ColPosWC-3
90ColPosWC-4
90ColPosWC-5
90ColPosWC-6
90ColPosWC-7
90ColPosWC-8
90ColWilC-1
90ColWilC-2
90ColWilC-3
90ColWilC-4
90ColWilC-5
90ColWilC-6
90ColWilC-7
90ColWilC-8
90ColWilC-9
90ColWilC-10
90ColWilC-11
90ColWilC-12
90Don-230
90Don-707A
90Don-707B
90DonBesN-24
90DonLeaS-23
90DonPre-4
90Fle-54
90Fle-630A
90Fle-630B
90Fle-637
90FleAll-2
90FleAwaW-7
90FleBasA-5
90FleBasM-7
90FleCan-54
90FleCan-630
90FleCan-637
90FleLeaL-6
90FleWorS-4
90FleWorS-10
90GiaMot-2
90GiaSmo-4
90GooHumICBLS-6
90Hot50PS-6
90K-M-1
90Lea-172
90Lea-444
90MLBBasB-28
90MotWilC-1
90MotWilC-2
90MotWilC-3
90MotWilC-4
90MSAHolD-11
90MSAIceTD-1
90OPC-100
90OPC-397
90PanSti-207
90PanSti-363
90Pos-7
90PubSti-65
90PubSti-254
90RedFolSB-17
90Sco-300
90Sco-684
90Sco-699
90Sco100S-30
90ScoMcD-1
90Spo-5
90StaCla-1
90StaCla-2
90StaCla-4
90StaCla-6
90StaCla-8
90StaCla-10
90SunSee-17
90Top-100
90Top-397
90TopAmeA-31
90TopBig-224
90TopCoi-43
90TopDou-10
90TopGloA-2
90TopGloS-52
90TopHeaU-2
90TopHilHM-2
90TopMag-11
90TopMinL-84
90TopSti-85
90TopSti-147
90TopStiB-1
90TopTif-100
90TopTif-397
90TopTVA-34
90UppDec-50
90UppDec-556
90USPlaCA-12D
90VenSti-107
90VenSti-108
90WonBreS-19
90Woo-24
91BasBesHM-5
91Bow-616
91CadEIID-8
91Cla2-T94
91Cla3-T9
91Cla3-NNO

91ClaGam-48
91DenHol-3
91Don-86
91Don-441
91Fle-259
91FlePro-2
91GiaMot-2
91GiaPacGaE-14
91GiaSFE-6
91JesHSA-8
91JimDea-1
91KinDis-15
91Lea-238
91LeaPre-12
91MajLeaCP-63
91MisStaB-11
91OPC-500
91OPCPre-22
91PanFreS-67
91PanFreS-158
91PanSti-79
91PetSta-20
91PlaWilC-21
91PlaWilC-22
91PlaWilC-23
91PlaWilC-24
91PlaWilC-25
91PlaWilC-39
91PlaWilC-40
91PlaWilC-41
91PlaWilC-42
91PlaWilC-43
91Pos-3
91PosCan-9
91RedFolS-19
91RedFolS-117
91Sco-7
91Sco-664
91Sco-871
91Sco-886
91Sco100S-4
91ScoCoo-B6
91SevCoi-NC3
91SilHol-5
91SimandSMLBL-9
91StaClu-5
91StaPinB-8
91Stu-254
91Top-500
91TopCraJI-35
91TopDesS-500
91TopGloA-13
91TopMic-500
91TopSta-8
91TopTif-500
91TopTriH-N11
91Ult-318
91UltGol-2
91UppDec-445
91UppDecFE-92F
91USPlaCA-WCO
92Bow-260
92Bow-673
92Cla1-T24
92Cla2-T37
92ClaGam-136
92ColAllG-2
92ColAllP-2
92ColPro-6
92DenHol-24
92Don-214
92Don-428
92DonCraJ1-14
92DonDiaK-DK2
92DonEli-11
92DonMcD-18
92DonPre-3
92Fle-631
92Fle-699
92FleAll-13
92FleCitTP-22
92FleTeaL-8
92Fre-11
92GiaMot-2
92GiaPacGaE-11
92GiaPacGaE-12
92Hig5-126
92Hig5S-7
92Hig5S-31
92HitTheBB-10
92JimDea-7
92Lea-241
92LeaGolP-12
92LeaPre-12
92MooSna-8
92Mr.TurS-6
92MSABenSHD-17
92New-4
92OPC-330
92OPCPre-146
92PanSti-212
92PanSti-281
92PepDieM-14
92Pin-122
92PinSlu-12
92PinTeaP-4
92Pos-14
92PosCan-3
92Sco-3
92Sco-773
92Sco-883
92Sco100S-24
92ScoImpP-51
92ScoProP-2
92SevCoi-20
92SpoIllFK1-86
92SpoStaCC-8
92StaClu-460
92StaClu-598
92StaCluD-28
92StaCluMP-4
92StaWilC-1
92StaWilC-2
92StaWilC-3
92StaWilC-4
92StaWilC-5
92StaWilC-6
92StaWilC-7
92StaWilC-8
92StaWilC-9
92StaWilC-10
92StaWilC-11
92Stu-114
92StuHer-BC8
92StuPre-11
92SunSee-8
92Top-330
92Top-386
92TopDaiQTU-2
92TopGol-330
92TopGol-386
92TopGolW-330
92TopGolW-386
92TopKid-58
92TopMcD-18
92TopMic-330
92TopMic-386
92TriPla-155
92Ult-287
92UltAllS-11
92UltAwaW-14
92UppDec-175
92UppDec-718
92UppDecF-18
92UppDecFG-18
92UppDecTMH-15
92UppDecWB-T4
93Bow-252
93DenHol-11
93DiaMar-24
93DiaMarP-2
93Don-446
93DonEli-S3
93DonMasotG-9
93DonMVP-13
93DonPre-11
93DonSpiotG-SG8
93DurPowP1-22
93Fin-108
93FinJum-108
93FinRef-108
93Fla-140
93FlaPro-1
93Fle-154
93FleAtl-4
93FleFruotL-11
93FleTeaL-NL1
93FunPac-13
93FunPac-101
93FunPacA-AS3
93GiaMot-2
93GiaPos-14
93GiaPos-15
93Hos-17
93Kra-18
93Lea-247
93LeaGolA-R11
93MetBak-23
93MilBonSS-7
93OPC-113
93OPCPreSP-12
93OPCPreSPF-12
93PacSpa-269
93PanSti-236
93Pin-16
93PinCoo-16
93PinCooD-16
93PinHomRC-38
93PinSlu-20
93Pos-2
93Sco-22
93ScoFra-26
93Sel-3
93SelStaL-17
93SP-111
93SPPlaP-PP4
93StaClu-562
93StaCluFDI-562
93StaCluG-9
93StaCluI-B1
93StaCluM-139
93StaCluMOP-562
93StaCluMOP-MB1
93StaCluMP-15
93Stu-48
93Top-10
93TOPBLAG-2
93TopGol-10
93TopInaM-10
93TopMic-10
93TriPla-107
93TriPlaA-11
93TriPlaN-4
93Ult-130
93UltAllS-2
93UppDec-315
93UppDec-471
93UppDec-476
93UppDec-576
93UppDecCP-R6
93UppDecGold-315
93UppDecGold-471
93UppDecGold-476
93UppDecGold-576
93UppDecIC-WI11
93UppDecICJ-WI11
93UppDecOD-D8
93UppDecTriCro-TC3
94BalParF-1
94Bow-485
94BowBes-R79
94BowBesR-R79
94ColC-540
94ColChoGS-540
94ColChoSS-540
94Don-38
94DonSpeE-38
94ExtBas-177
94Fin-238
94FinJum-238
94FinRef-238
94Fla-108
94FlaHotG-2
94FlaHotN-3
94FlaInfP-2
94Fle-689
94FleTeaL-28
94FleUpd-90
94FleUpdDT-3
94FUnPac-22
94GiaTeal-9
94KelRusSWC-1
94Lea-404
94LeaGam-10
94LeaL-71
94LeaMVPC-A5
94LeaMVPCG-A5
94OPC-187
94Pac-544
94PanSti-263
94Pin-513
94PinArtP-513
94PinMusC-513
94Pos-22
94ProMag-134
94RanAllP-22
94RedFolMI-9
94Sco-10
94ScoGolR-10
94ScoRoo-RT1
94ScoRooCP-CP1
94ScoRooGR-RT1
94ScoRooS-RT1
94Sel-319
94SP-147
94SPDieC-147
94Spo-146
94SpoRoo-1
94SpoRooAP-1
94SpoRooS-1
94StaClu-203
94StaClu-666
94StaCluFDI-203
94StaCluFDI-666
94StaCluGR-203
94StaCluGR-666
94StaCluMOP-203
94StaCluMOP-666
94StaCluT-258
94StaCluTFDI-258
94Stu-153
94Top-240
94TopGol-240
94TopSpa-240
94TopSupS-9
94TopTra-115T
94TriPla-193
94Ult-429
94UppDec-350
94UppDecAJ-22
94UppDecAJG-22
94UppDecED-350
95Baz-32
95Bow-403
95BowBes-R22
95BowBesR-R22
95ClaFanFPCP-2
95ClaPhoC-54
95ColCho-400
95ColChoGS-400
95ColChoSE-184
95ColChoSEGS-184
95ColChoSESS-184
95ColChoSS-400
95D3-21
95Don-128
95DonDiaK-DK17
95DonPreP-128
95DonTopotO-157
95Emb-22
95EmbGolI-22
95Emo-83
95Fin-123
95FinRef-123
95Fla-86
95Fle-283
95FleAllS-12
95FleUpdH-6
95Lea-167
95Lea300C-6
95LeaCor-5
95LeaLim-20
95LeaLimG-8
95LeaLimIBP-11
95LeaSli-6A
95LeaSli-6B
95NatPac-13
95Pac-423
95PacGolP-22
95PacPri-135
95PanSti-36
95Pin-269
95Pin-288
95PinArtP-269
95PinArtP-288
95PinFan-8
95PinGatA-GA11
95PinMusC-269
95PinMusC-288
95PinPer-PP11
95PinRedH-RH17
95PinWhiH-WH17
95Pos-16
95RanCra-6
95RedFol-35
95Sco-37
95Sco-570
95ScoGolR-37
95ScoGolR-570
95ScoHaloG-HG20
95ScoPlaTS-37
95ScoPlaTS-570
95ScoRulJ-SR19
95ScoRulJ-SR19
95Sel-99
95SelArtP-99
95SelBigS-BS6
95SelCer-11
95SelCerGT-9
95SelCerMG-11
95SP-200
95SPCha-103
95SPCha-189
95SPCha-194
95SPChaDC-103
95SPChaDC-189
95SPChaDC-194
95Spo-119
95SpoArtP-119
95SpoDouT-2
95SpoHamT-HT9
95SpoPro-PM11
95SPSil-200
95SPSpeF-21
95StaClu-131
95StaClu-522
95StaCluCT-15
95StaCluFDI-131
95StaCluMOP-131
95StaCluMOP-522
95StaCluMOP-RL18
95StaCluRL-RL18
95StaCluSTWS-131
95StaCluSTWS-522
95StaCluVR-67
95Stu-12
95StuGolS-12
95StuPlaS-12
95Sum-85
95Sum-182
95SumBigB-BB9
95SumNthD-85
95SumNthD-182
95Top-558
95TopCyb-334
95UC3-7
95UC3-132
95UC3ArtP-7
95UC3ArtP-132
95UC3CycS-CS10
95UC3InM-IM10
95Ult-108
95UltGolM-108
95UltOnBL-6
95UltOnBLGM-6
95UppDec-390
95UppDecED-390
95UppDecEDG-390
95UppDecPAW-H25
95UppDecPAWE-H25
95UppDecPLL-R43
95UppDecPLL-R51
95UppDecPLLE-R43
95UppDecPLLE-R51
95UppDecSE-39
95UppDecSEG-39
95USPlaCMLA-4D
95Zen-110
95ZenZ-13
96Baz-43
96Bow-108
96BowBes-77
96BowBesAR-77
96BowBesR-77
96Cir-84
96CirBos-22
96CirRav-84
96ColCho-320
96ColChoGS-320
96ColChoSS-320
96Don-20
96DonHitL-3
96DonPreP-20
96EmoXL-120
96Fin-B149
96Fin-B193
96Fin-S62
96FinRef-B149
96FinRef-B193
96FinRef-S62
96Fla-167
96FlaHotG-3
96Fle-247
96FleRan-3
96FleTif-247
96FleUpdSL-3
96Lea-147
96LeaLim-68
96LeaLimG-68
96LeaPre-76

96LeaPreP-76
96LeaPrePB-147
96LeaPrePG-147
96LeaPrePS-147
96LeaPreSG-16
96LeaPreSte-16
96LeaSig-72
96LeaSigA-46
96LeaSigAG-46
96LeaSigAS-46
96LeaSigPPG-72
96LeaSigPPP-72
96MetUni-112
96MetUniP-112
96Pac-424
96PacGolCD-DC2
96PacPri-P135
96PacPriG-P135
96PanSti-231
96Pin-156
96Pin-213
96Pin-270
96Pin-302
96PinAfi-26
96PinAfiAP-26
96PinAfiFPP-26
96PinArtP-83
96PinArtP-113
96PinArtP-170
96PinArtP-186
96PinEssotG-16
96PinFirR-17
96PinFoil-213
96PinFoil-270
96PinFoil-302
96PinSky-9
96PinSta-83
96PinSta-113
96PinSta-170
96PinSta-186
96ProMagDM-23
96ProSta-97
96RanMot-2
96Sco-1
96Sco-371
96ScoDugC-A1
96ScoDugC-B96
96ScoDugCAP-A1
96ScoDugCAP-B96
96ScoNumG-28
96ScoRef-15
96Sel-97
96SelArtP-97
96SelCer-11
96SelCerAP-11
96SelCerCB-11
96SelCerCR-11
96SelCerIP-12
96SelCerMB-11
96SelCerMG-11
96SelCerMR-11
96SelTeaN-14
96SP-177
96Spo-3
96SpoArtP-3
96StaClu-181
96StaClu-274
96StaCluEPB-274
96StaCluEPG-274
96StaCluEPS-274
96StaCluMeg-MH5
96StaCluMOP-181
96StaCluMOP-274
96StaCluMOP-MH5
95StaCluVRMC-67
96Stu-42
96StuPrePB-42
96StuPrePG-42
96StuPrePS-42
96Sum-105
96SumAbo&B-105
96SumArtP-105
96SumFoi-105
96TeaOut-18
96Top-299
96TopChr-118
96TopChrR-118
96TopGal-149
96TopGalPPI-149
96TopLas-40
96TopLasSS-9
96Ult-132
96UltGolM-132
96UltPriL-2
96UltPriLGM-2
96UltThu-6
96UltThuGM-6
96UppDec-207
96Zen-54
96ZenArtP-54
96ZenMoz-2
97Bow-36
97BowBes-48
97BowBesAR-48
97BowBesR-48
97BowChr-31
97BowChrI-31
97BowChrIR-31
97BowChrR-31
97BowInt-36
97Cir-328
97CirRav-328
97ColCho-241
97Don-137
97DonEli-37
97DonEliGS-37
97DonLim-90
97DonLim-194
97DonLimLE-90
97DonLimLE-194
97DonPre-114
97DonPreCttC-114
97DonPreP-137
97DonPrePGold-137
97Fin-44
97FinRef-44
97Fle-219
97FleTif-219
97Lea-7
97LeaFraM-7
97LeaFraMDC-7
97MetUni-161
97NewPin-107
97NewPinAP-107
97NewPinMC-107
97NewPinPP-107
97Pac-197
97PacLigB-197
97PacPri-67
97PacPriLB-67
97PacPriP-67
97PacSil-197
97PinCer-97
97PinCerMBlu-97
97PinCerMG-97
97PinCerMR-97
97PinCerR-97
97PinIns-24
97PinInsCE-24
97PinInsDD-14
97PinInsDE-24
97PinTotCPB-97
97PinTotCPG-97
97PinTotCPR-97
97PinX-P-65
97PinX-PMoS-65
97ProMag-74
97ProMagML-74
97Sco-6
97Sco-539
97ScoHeaotO-1
97ScoHobR-539
97ScoPitP-11
97ScoPreS-6
97ScoRan-2
97ScoRanPI-2
97ScoRanPr-2
97ScoResC-539
97ScoShoS-6
97ScoShoS-539
97ScoShoSAP-6
97ScoShoSAP-539
97Sel-94
97SelArtP-94
97SelRegG-94
97SkyE-X-45
97SkyE-XC-45
97SkyE-XEC-45
97SP-172
97SpoIll-161
97SpoIll-175
97SpoIllEE-161
97SpoIllEE-175
97StaClu-49
97StaCluMat-49
97StaCluMOP-49
97Stu-93
97StuPrePG-93
97StuPrePS-93
97Top-387
97TopChr-133
97TopChrR-133
97TopGal-17
97TopGalPPI-17
97TopSta-66
97TopStaAM-66
97Ult-130
97UltDouT-10
97UltGolME-130
97UltPlaME-130
97UppDec-505

Clark, Willie (William Otis)
75WatRoyT-7

Clarke, Boileryard (William Jones)
03BreE10-20
98CamPepP-12

Clarke, C.W.V.
88AllandGN-35

Clarke, Fred C.
03BreE10-21
06FanCraNL-10
08AmeCarE-71
08RosComP-149
09AmeCarE-22
09AmeCarE-23
09ColChiE-53
09SpoNewSM-13
09T206-65
09T206-66
10DarChoE-8
10DomDisP-25
10E-UOraBSC-6
10E12AmeCDC-10
10E98-7
10NadE1-10
10PirAmeCE-2
10PirHerP-5
10PirTipTD-3
10StaCarE-9
10SweCapPP-135A
10SweCapPP-135B
10W555-14
11BasBatEU-10
11MecDFT-8
11PloCanE-15
11S74Sil-108
11SpoLifCW-62
11SpoLifM-248
11T205-29
11TurRedT-8
12ColRedB-52
12ColTinT-52
12ColTinT-54
12HasTriFT-14B
12HasTriFT-16B
12HasTriFT-20
12HasTriFT-25A
12HasTriFT-62
13NatGamW-10
13TomBarW-10
14CraJacE-70
14PieStaT-12
15CraJacE-70
36PC7AlbHoF-31
48ExhHoF-5
50CalHOFW-16
63BazA-26
73FleWilD-21
75SheGrePG-11
75TCMAllG-4
76GrePlaG-11
76ShaPiz-31
77GalGloG-164
80PerHaloFP-31
80SSPHOF-31
84GalHaloFRL-31
86ConSer1-53
93CraJac-13
94OriofB-85
96PitPosH-3

Clarke, Horace M.
66Top-547
67CokCapYM-V6
67DexPre-49
67OPC-169
67Top-169
68Top-263
68TopVen-263
69MilBra-59
69MLBOffS-73
69OPC-87
69Top-87
69TopSta-202
69TopTeaP-19
70MLBOffS-244
70Top-623
70YanCliDP-6
71MLBOffS-486
71OPC-715
71Top-715
71YanArcO-5
71YanCliDP-4
72MilBra-74
72OPC-387
72Top-387
73NewYorN-7
73OPC-198
73SyrChiTI-5
73Top-198
74OPC-529
74Top-529
92YanWIZ6-24
92YanWIZ7-33

Clarke, Jeff
91AppFoxC-16
91AppFoxP-1722
92AppFoxC-13
92AppFoxF-990

Clarke, Josh (Joshua B.)
08RosComP-24
09T206-67

Clarke, Nig (Jay Austin)
09ColChiE-52
11SpoLifCW-63
11SpoLifM-41
12ColRedB-54

Clarke, Stan
83KnoBluJT-2
84BluJayFS-8
84SyrChiT-19
85SyrChiT-4
86SyrChiP-5
87CalCanP-2326
88TolMudHC-2
88TolMudHP-607
88Top-556
88TopTif-556
89BlaYNPRWL-90
89OmaRoyC-2
89OmaRoyP-1737
90CMC-104
90LouRedBC-4
90LouRedBLBC-11
90LouRedBP-396
90ProAAAF-510
90TopTVCa-42
91LinDriAAA-229
91LouRedLD-229
86STaoftFT-28

Clarke, Tim
82QuaCitCT-6

Clarke, Tommy (Thomas A.)
11MecDFT-10
11SpoLifCW-64
11SpoLifM-189
12ColRedB-53
12ColTinT-53
12T207-32
15SpoNewM-32
16ColE13-29
16FleBreD-16
16SpoNewM-33

Clarke, William H.
87OldJudN-83
95NewN566-201
98CamPepP-11

Clarkin, Mike
86WinHavRSP-6
87NewBriRSP-1
88NewBriRSP-891

Clarkson, Buster
86NegLeaF-44

Clarkson, David
91WavRedF-14
95AusFut-62

Clarkson, John Gibson
69SCFOldT-4
75FlePio-26
76ShaPiz-91
77BobParHoF-12
80PerHaloFP-91
80SSPHOF-91
87AllandGN-4
87BucN28-20A
87BucN28-20B
87FouBasHN-2
87OldJudN-84
88AugBecN-4A
88AugBecN-4B
88GandBCGCE-7
88WG1CarG-2
89EdgR.WG-7
89N526N7C-4
94OriofB-47
95May-4

Clarkson, Walter
08AmeLeaPC-5
11SpoLifCW-65

Clary, Doug
76TulOilGP-5

Clary, Ellis
60Top-470
88ChaLooLTI-5
96Bro194F-20

Clary, Marty
85RicBraT-2
86Don-36
87IntLeaAT-34
87RicBraBC-3
87RicBraC-34
87RicBraT-3
88Fle-535
88FleGlo-535
88RicBraC-10
88RicBraP-11
89BraDub-8
89RicBraC-1
89RicBraP-826
89RicBraTI-4
90BraDubP-5
90Don-381
90Fle-578
90FleCan-578
90OPC-304
90Top-304
90TopTif-304
90UppDec-779
91Fle-686
91LinDriAAA-230
91LouRedLD-230
91LouRedP-2906
91OPC-582
91Top-582
91TopDesS-582
91TopMic-582
91TopTif-582
91UppDec-478
88RicBraBC-11

Clatterbuck, Don
79NewCoPT-9

Claudio, Patricio
92BurIndC-21
92BurIndF-1668
93ColRedC-8
93ColRedF-610
93LimRocDWB-91
94KinIndC-4
94KinIndF-2655
96KenIndB-5

Claus, Marc
92KenTwiF-609
93ForWayWC-5
93ForWayWF-1973
94ForMyeMC-5
94ForMyeMF-1172

Claus, Todd
91BoiHawC-1
91BoiHawP-3885
92ClaFS7-226
92QuaCitRBC-2
92QuaCitRBF-816
93PalSprAC-6
93PalSprAF-75
95BoiHawTI-10
96BoiHawB-2
97MidAngOHP-4

Claussen, Phil
87CubCan-2

Clawson, Chris
86AshTouP-4

Clawson, Ken
87PorChaRP-1

Clay, Billy
79NewCoPT-17

Clay, Danny
83WisRapTF-16
85OrlTwiT-16

86TolMudHP-5
87PorBeaP-11
88BlaYNPRWL-53
88FleUpd-108
88FleUpdG-108
88MaiPhiP-297
89BlaYNPRWLU-13
89ScrRedBP-706
90CMC-52
90IndIndC-2
90IndIndP-284
90ProAAAF-567
90TopTVCu-40
Clay, Dave
82CedRapRT-26
82DurBulT-14
83DurBulT-17
85RicBraT-3
86ElPasDP-6
87DenZepP-1
Clay, Jeff
81CedRapRT-21
86SalRedBP-4
Clay, Ken
78SSP270-16
78Top-89
78YanSSPD-16
79OPC-225
79Top-434
79YanPicA-7
80ColCliP-36
80Top-159
81Fle-633
81MarPol-8
81Top-305
81TopTra-747
82Fle-508
82Top-649
89PacSenL-72
92YanWIZ7-34
93RanKee-103
Claybrook, Steve
95BilRedTI-19
Clayton, Craig
91BelMarC-13
91BelMarP-3671
92ClaFS7-114
92SanBerC-21
92SanBerSF-963
93RivPilCLC-6
94Bow-74
94JacSunF-1405
94RivPilCLC-2
96CliLumKTI-8
Clayton, Kenny
82BelBreF-14
82IdaFalAT-22
Clayton, Royal
88CarLeaAS-4
88PriWilYS-6
89AlbYanB-6
89AlbYanP-318
89AlbYanS-5
89Sta-96
90AlbDecGB-10
90AlbYanB-23
90AlbYanP-1030
90AlbYanS-2
90Bes-287
90CMC-785
90EasLeaAP-EL13
90StaFS7-50
91ColCliLD-104
91ColCliP-4
91ColCliP-591
91LinDriAAA-104
92ColCliF-343
92ColCliP-3
92ColCliS-101
92SkyAAAF-44
93ColCliF-1102
93ColCliP-1
94ColCliF-2942
94ColCliP-4
Clayton, Royce
89Bow-472
89BowTif-472
89CliGiaP-895
90Bes-114
90CalLeaACLC-49
90CMC-855
90ProAaA-156
90SanJosGB-7
90SanJosGCLC-36
90SanJosGP-2018
90SanJosGS-5
90TopMag-73
91Bow-641
91Cla/Bes-251
91Cla3-T10
91ClaGolB-BC12
91ShrCapLD-303
91ShrCapP-1827
91UppDec-61
91UppDecFE-4F
92Bow-212
92Cla1-T25
92Cla2-T35
92ClaGam-179
92DEL-AU6
92Don-397
92DonCraJ2-10
92Fle-632
92GiaMot-4
92GiaPacGaE-13
92Lea-272
92OPC-786
92OPCPre-39
92Pin-268
92PinRoo-26
92PinRool-15
92PinTea2-34
92ProFS7-343
92Sco-841
92ScoHotR-2
92ScoImpP-24
92ScoRoo-12
92StaClu-630
92StaCluNC-630
92Stu-115
92Top-786
92TopDeb91-36
92TopGol-786
92TopGolW-786
92TopMcD-38
92TopMic-786
92TriPla-123
92Ult-288
92UppDec-2
92UppDecF-5
92UppDecFG-5
92UppDecSR-SR6
93Bow-548
93ClaGam-20
93Don-208
93Fla-141
93Fle-155
93GiaMot-6
93GiaPos-16
93Lea-176
93OPC-138
93PacSpa-270
93PanSti-238
93Pin-321
93PinTea2-11
93Sco-157
93Sel-400
93SP-112
93StaClu-39
93StaCluFDI-39
93StaCluG-4
93StaCluMOP-39
93Stu-94
93Top-542
93TopGol-542
93TopInaM-542
93TopMic-542
93Toy-16
93TriPla-39
93Ult-131
93UppDec-151
93UppDecGold-151
93USPlaCR-10S
94Bow-519
94ColC-80
94ColChoGS-80
94ColChoSS-80
94Don-153
94ExtBas-385
94Fin-28
94FinRef-28
94Fla-241
94Fle-690
94GiaAMC-8
94GiaMot-4
94GiaTarBCI-3
94GiaUSPC-7C
94GiaUSPC-13H
94Lea-381
94LeaL-158
94OPC-164
94Pac-545
94PanSti-264
94Pin-111
94PinArtP-111
94PinMusC-111
94Sco-448
94ScoGolR-448
94Sel-278
94SP-92
94SPDieC-92
94Spo-86
94StaClu-39
94StaCluFDI-39
94StaCluGR-39
94StaCluMOP-39
94StaCluT-2
94StaCluTFDI-2
94Stu-84
94Top-267
94TopGol-267
94TopSpa-267
94TriPla-104
94Ult-289
94UppDec-221
94UppDecED-221
95Bow-398
95ColCho-254
95ColChoGS-254
95ColChoSS-254
95Don-285
95DonPreP-285
95DonTopotO-350
95Emb-31
95EmbGolI-31
95Emo-193
95Fin-134
95FinRef-134
95Fla-208
95Fle-578
95GiaMot-4
95Lea-33
95LeaLim-38
95Pac-376
95PanSti-65
95Pin-221
95PinArtP-221
95PinMusC-221
95Sco-413
95ScoGolR-413
95ScoPlaTS-413
95Sel-105
95SelArtP-105
95SelCer-81
95SelCerMG-81
95Spo-7
95SpoArtP-7
95StaClu-126
95StaCluFDI-126
95StaCluMOP-126
95StaCluSTWS-126
95Stu-194
95Sum-87
95SumNthD-87
95Top-67
95TopCyb-49
95UC3-88
95UC3ArtP-88
95Ult-443
95UltGolM-443
95UppDec-333
95UppDecED-333
95UppDecEDG-333
95UppDecSE-72
95UppDecSEG-72
95Zen-94
96CarPol-4
96Cir-176
96CirBos-45
96CirRav-176
96ColCho-303
96ColCho-787
96ColChoGS-303
96ColChoSS-303
96Don-235
96DonPreP-235
96EmoXL-263
96Fin-B306
96FinRef-B306
96Fla-356
96Fle-586
96FleTif-586
96FleUpd-U186
96FleUpdTC-U186
96MetUni-222
96MetUniP-222
96Pac-210
96PanSti-111
96Pin-329
96PinAfi-139
96PinAfiAP-139
96PinFoil-329
96Sco-386
96Sel-106
96SelArtP-106
96StaClu-141
96StaCluEPB-141
96StaCluEPG-141
96StaCluEPS-141
96StaCluMOP-141
96Sum-24
96SumAbo&B-24
96SumArtP-24
96SumFoi-24
96Top-61
96Ult-293
96Ult-544
96UltGolM-293
96UltGolM-544
96UppDec-198
96UppDec-507U
97Cir-256
97CirRav-256
97ColCho-439
97Don-217
97DonPreP-217
97DonPrePGold-217
97DonTea-159
97DonTeaSPE-159
97Fin-56
97FinRef-56
97FlaSho-A135
97FlaSho-B135
97FlaSho-C135
97FlaShoLC-135
97FlaShoLC-B135
97FlaShoLC-C135
97FlaShoLCM-A135
97FlaShoLCM-B135
97FlaShoLCM-C135
97Fle-440
97FleTif-440
97Lea-51
97LeaFraM-51
97LeaFraMDC-51
97NewPin-103
97NewPinAP-103
97NewPinMC-103
97NewPinPP-103
97Pac-406
97PacLigB-406
97PacSil-406
97Sco-291
97ScoPreS-291
97ScoShoS-291
97ScoShoSAP-291
97StaClu-128
97StaCluMOP-128
97Top-18
97Ult-333
97UltGolME-333
97UltPlaME-333
97UppDec-467
Clear, Bob
78AngFamF-7
Clear, Mark
76QuaCitAT-10
77QuaCitAT-9
80Top-638
81Don-291
81Top-12
81TopTra-748
82Don-452
82Fle-290
82OPC-169
82RedSoxC-3
82Top-421
82TopSti-154
83Don-361
83Fle-181
83Fle-629
83FleSta-41
83FleSti-61
83OPC-162
83Top-162
83TopSti-36
84Don-611
84Fle-395
84Nes792-577
84OPC-148
84Top-577
84TopTif-577
85Don-538
85Fle-154
85Lea-32
85Top-207
85TopTif-207
86BrePol-25
86Don-493
86Fle-344
86FleUpd-26
86Top-349
86TopTif-349
86TopTra-25T
86TopTraT-25T
87BrePol-25
87BreTeal-3
87Don-355
87Fle-341
87FleBasA-9
87FleGlo-341
87FleStiC-23
87OPC-244
87Top-640
87TopSti-195
87TopTif-640
88BrePol-25
88Don-372
88Fle-160
88FleGlo-160
88Sco-446
88ScoGlo-446
88Top-742
88TopTif-742
89Don-528
89Fle-182
89FleGlo-182
89Sco-430
89Top-63
89TopTif-63
90El PasDAGTI-37
94BreMilB-210
Cleary, Tony
79ElmPioRST-16
86PawRedSP-7
87PawRedSP-65
88PawRedSC-14
88PawRedSP-467
89PawRedSP-683
89PawRedSTI-5
Clelland, Rick
92AlbPolC-14
92AlbPolF-2297
92ClaFS7-378
93BurBeeC-5
93BurBeeF-149
94BurBeeC-5
94BurBeeF-1074
Clem, Brad
92EriSaiC-23
92EriSaiF-1636
Clem, Brian
85CloHSS-10
Clem, John
86WauTimP-3
87SalSpuP-9
Clemens, Doug (Douglas H.)
67CokCapPh-5
67Top-489
78ReaRem-2
Clemens, Roger
84FleUpd-27
84OCoandSI-242
84PawRedST-22
85Don-273
85Fle-155
85FleStaS-123
85Lea-99
85Top-181
85TopTif-181
86Don-172
86DonHig-5
86DonHig-6
86DonHig-17
86DonHig-18
86DonHig-26
86Fle-345
86FleMin-73
86FleSlu-7

86OPC-98
86Top-661
86TopTif-661
87BurKinA-4
87ClaGam-84
87ClaUpdY-114
87Don-2
87Don-276
87DonAll-8
87DonAllB-PC14
87DonP-8
87DonSupD-2
87Dra-31
87Fle-32
87Fle-634
87Fle-640
87FleAll-11
87FleAwaW-9
87FleBasA-10
87FleExcS-11
87FleGamW-10
87FleGlo-32
87FleGlo-634
87FleGlo-640
87FleGlo-WS3
87FleHotS-10
87FleLeaL-10
87FleLimE-9
87FleMin-20
87FleRecS-4
87FleSlu-10
87FleStiC-24
87FleWorS-3
87GenMilB-2B
87KayB-10
87KraFoo-45
87Lea-2
87Lea-190
87MandMSL-7
87MSAIceTD-2
87MSAJifPD-12
87OPC-340
87RalPur-10
87RedFolSB-70
87RedSoxSAP-6
87SevCoi-E8
87SevCoi-M10
87Spo-10
87Spo-111
87Spo-159
87Spo-196
87SpoDeaP-1
87SpoRea-12
87SpoTeaP-9
87StaCle-1
87StaCle-2
87StaCle-3
87StaCle-4
87StaCle-5
87StaCle-6
87StaCle-7
87StaCle-8
87StaCle-9
87StaCle-10
87StaCle-11
87StaCle-12
87StaCle2-1
87StaCle2-2
87StaCle2-3
87StaCle2-4
87StaCle2-5
87StuPan-15
87Top-1
87Top-340
87Top-614
87TopCoi-8
87TopGaloC-5
87TopGloA-21
87TopGloS-5
87TopMinL-42
87TopSti-2
87TopSti-3
87TopSti-154
87TopSti-244
87TopTif-1
87TopTif-340
87TopTif-614
87Woo-7
88Baz-4
88CheBoy-23
88ClaBlu-217
88ClaRed-158
88Don-51
88DonBasB-57
88DonTeaBRS-51
88Dra-30
88Fle-349
88FleAll-4
88FleAwaW-6
88FleBasA-8
88FleBasM-6
88FleExcS-10
88FleGlo-349
88FleHotS-7
88FleLeaL-6
88FleMin-5
88FleRecS-7
88FleSlu-9
88FleStiC-7
88FleSup-9
88FleTeaL-5
88GreBasS-47
88HouSho-13
88K-M-7
88KinDis-20
88Lea-56
88MSAIceTD-9
88MSAJifPD-6
88Nes-1
88OPC-70
88PanSti-21
88RedFolSB-13
88Sco-110
88ScoGlo-110
88ScoYouS2-23
88Spo-207
88SpoGam-20
88StaCle-1
88StaCle-2
88StaCle-4
88StaCle-6
88StaCle-8
88StaCle-10
88StaLinAl-7
88StaLinRS-6
88Top-70
88Top-394
88TopBig-118
88TopCoi-2
88TopGaloC-5
88TopGloS-13
88TopMinL-2
88TopRevLL-28
88TopSti-251
88TopStiB-58
88TopTif-70
88TopTif-394
88TopUKM-15
88TopUKMT-15
88Woo-11
89Bow-26
89BowTif-26
89CadEllD-9
89CerSup-7
89ClaTraO-119
89Don-280
89DonAll-14
89DonBasB-65
89Fle-85
89FleBasA-7
89FleBasM-8
89FleExcS-6
89FleForTR-2
89FleGlo-85
89FleHeroB-8
89FleLeaL-5
89FleSup-9
89K-M-20
89KayB-7
89MSAHolD-16
89MSAIceTD-8
89Nis-16
89OPC-121
89PanSti-249
89PanSti-270
89RedFolSB-23
89Sco-350A
89Sco-350B
89ScoHot1S-90
89ScoSco-20
89Spo-3
89SpollIFKI-60
89Top-405
89Top-450
89TopBasT-58
89TopBig-42
89TopCapC-18
89TopCoi-37
89TopDouA-9
89TopGloS-23
89TopHilTM-8
89TopMinL-46
89TopSti-259
89TopStiB-25
89TopTif-405
89TopTif-450
89TopUKM-16
89TVSpoM-63
89UppDec-195
90AllBasT-8
90Bow-268
90BowTif-268
90ClaBlu-51
90Col-19
90Don-184
90DonBesA-58
90Fle-271
90Fle-627
90FleBasM-8
90FleCan-271
90FleCan-627
90FleWaxBC-C3
90Hot50PS-7
90Lea-12
90MLBBasB-69
90OPC-245
90PanSti-24
90Pos-2
90PubSti-281
90PubSti-452
90RedFolSB-18
90RedSoxP-6
90Sco-310
90Sco100S-79
90ScoMcD-18
90Spo-149
90SunSee-18
90Top-245
90TopBig-22
90TopDou-11
90TopMag-26
90TopMinL-4
90TopSti-255
90TopTif-245
90TopTVA-25
90TopTVRS-8
90UppDec-57
90UppDec-323
90USPlaCA-1S
90VenSti-109
90VenSti-110
90WinDis-3
90WonBreS-2
91BasBesAotM-4
91Bow-118
91CadEllD-9
91Cla1-T18
91Cla2-T65
91Cla2-T97
91ClaGam-149
91Col-1
91Don-9
91Don-81
91Don-395
91DonSupD-9
91Fle-90
91FleAll-10
91FlePro-9
91JimDea-18
91Lea-174
91Lea-488
91MajLeaCP-8
91MSAHolD-13
91OPC-530
91OPCPre-23
91PanCanT1-63
91PanCanT1-69
91PanCanT1-80
91PanCanT1-94
91PanFreS-271
91PanSti-215
91PepSup-6
91PetSta-3
91Pos-12
91PosCan-18
91RedFolS-20
91RedSoxP-5
91Sco-399
91Sco-655
91Sco-684
91Sco-850
91Sco100S-50
91Sev3DCN-3
91SevCoi-F3
91SevCoi-T4
91SevCoi-NE3
91SilHol-6
91StaClu-309
91StaCluMO-12
91StaPinB-9
91StaPro-3
91Stu-14
91StuPre-2
91Top-530
91TopCraJl-22
91TopDesS-530
91TopMic-530
91TopSta-9
91TopTif-530
91TopTriH-A2
91Ult-31
91UppDec-655
91USPlaCA-10H
92Bow-691
92Cla1-T26
92Cla1-NNO
92Cla2-T61
92ClaGam-189
92ColAllG-19
92ColAllP-19
92Don-244
92DonBonC-BC3
92DonCraJ1-17
92DonMcD-10
92Fle-37
92FleCitTP-6
92FleCle-1
92FleCle-2
92FleCle-3
92FleCle-4
92FleCle-5
92FleCle-6
92FleCle-7
92FleCle-8
92FleCle-9
92FleCle-10
92FleCle-11
92FleCle-12
92FleCle-13
92FleCle-14
92FleCle-15
92FleCle-AU0
92FleCle-NNO
92FleSmo'nH-S4
92Fre-2
92Hig5-7
92Hig5S-8
92JimDea-10
92KinDis-9
92Lea-19
92LeaBlaG-19
92MooSna-4
92Mr.TurS-7
92OPC-150
92OPCPre-105
92PacRyaTEI-200
92PanSti-92
92PanSti-146
92PepDieM-1
92Pin-95
92PinRool-4
92PinTeaP-1
92Pos-16
92PosCan-10
92RedSoxDD-9
92Sco-21
92Sco-790
92Sco100S-74
92ScoCokD-5
92ScoImpP-57
92SevCoi-3
92SpollIFK1-36
92SpoStaCC-9
92StaClu-80
92StaClu-593
92StaCluD-29
92StaCluMO-11
92Stu-132
92TexLon-8
92Top-150
92Top-405
92TopGol-150
92TopGol-405
92TopGolW-150
92TopGolW-405
92TopKid-67
92TopMcD-10
92TopMic-150
92TopMic-405
92TriPla-216
92Ult-15
92UltAwaW-6
92UppDec-545
92UppDec-641
92UppDecF-19
92UppDecFG-19
92UppDecTMH-16
93Bow-635
93CadDis-11
93ClaGam-21
93DiaMar-25
93Don-119
93DonDiaK-DK3
93DonMVP-15
93DonPre-13
93DurPowP1-1
93Fin-104
93FinJum-104
93FinRef-104
93Fla-160
93Fle-177
93Fle-348
93Fle-717
93FleAtl-5
93FleFruotL-12
93FleTeaL-AL4
93FunPac-14
93FunPac-23
93FunPac-29
93FunPac-161
93FunPac-162
93Hos-27
93HumDumC-3
93JimDea-7
93KinDis-21
93Kra-5
93Lea-279
93LeaGolA-R20
93LeaHeaftH-6
93MetBak-5
93MSABenSPD-12
93OPC-259
93OPCPreSP-18
93OPCPreSPF-18
93PacJugC-4
93PacSpa-30
93PanSti-90
93Pin-25
93PinCoo-18
93PinCooD-18
93Pos-4
93PosCan-3
93RedSoxWHP-8
93Sco-7
93ScoFra-2
93Sel-14
93SelAce-1
93SelChaS-21
93SelDufIP-2
93SelStaL-62
93SelStaL-75
93SelStaL-79
93SelStaL-87
93SP-199
93StaClu-220
93StaClu-748
93StaCluFDI-220
93StaCluFDI-748
93StaCluM-97
93StaCluMOP-220
93StaCluMOP-748
93Stu-22
93StuHer-3
93Top-4
93Top-409
93TOPBLAG-27
93TopComotH-3
93TopFulS-15
93TopGol-4
93TopGol-409
93TopInaM-4
93TopInaM-409
93TopMic-4
93TopMic-409
93TriPla-118
93TriPlaA-14
93TriPlaN-2
93Ult-508
93UltStrK-1
93UppDec-48

93UppDec-135
93UppDec-630
93UppDecCP-R7
93UppDecDG-21
93UppDecFH-57
93UppDecGold-48
93UppDecGold-135
93UppDecGold-630
93UppDecOD-D9
93USPlaCA-11S
94Bow-475
94BowBes-R37
94BowBes-X100
94BowBesR-R37
94BowBesR-X100
94ChuHomS-13
94ChuHomSG-13
94ColC-322
94ColC-348
94ColC-550
94ColChoGS-322
94ColChoGS-348
94ColChoGS-550
94ColChoSS-322
94ColChoSS-348
94ColChoSS-550
94ColChoT-3
94Don-356
94Don-600
94DonSpeE-356
94ExtBas-16
94ExtBasGB-7
94ExtBasPD-1
94Fin-217
94FinJum-217
94FinRef-217
94Fla-261
94Fle-26
94FleSmo'nH-1
94FleSun-7
94FleUpdDT-4
94FUnPac-21
94FUnPac-207
94Lea-255
94LeaL-7
94OPC-67
94OPCAllR-18
94OPCJumA-18
94OscMayR-3
94Pac-49
94PanSti-26
94Pin-25
94PinArtP-25
94PinMusC-25
94PinTheN-25
94ProMag-11
94RedFolMI-31
94Sco-25
94ScoGolR-25
94Sel-61
94SelCroC-CC3
94SP-152
94SPDieC-152
94SPHol-5
94SPHolDC-5
94Spo-15
94StaClu-534
94StaClu-650
94StaCluFDI-534
94StaCluFDI-650
94StaCluGR-534
94StaCluGR-650
94StaCluMOP-534
94StaCluMOP-650
94Stu-159
94SucSav-20
94Top-720
94TopGol-720
94TopSpa-720
94TopSupS-10
94TriPla-201
94Ult-11
94UppDec-450
94UppDecAJ-21
94UppDecAJG-21
94UppDecDC-E2
94UppDecED-450
95Baz-9
95Bow-293
95BowBes-R23
95BowBesR-R23
95ClaPhoC-9
95ColCho-410
95ColChoGS-410
95ColChoSE-190
95ColChoSEGS-190
95ColChoSESS-190
95ColChoSS-410
95D3-9
95DenHol-6
95Don-427
95DonPreP-427
95DonTopotO-19
95Emb-106
95EmbGolI-106
95Emo-10
95Fin-185
95FinFlaT-FT2
95FinRef-185
95Fla-10
95Fle-26
95FleTeaL-2
95FleUpdH-7
95Lea-255
95LeaLim-48
95Pac-34
95PacPri-12
95PanSti-14
95Pin-2
95PinArtP-2
95PinFan-2
95PinGatA-GA13
95PinMusC-2
95PinRedH-RH18
95PinWhiH-WH18
95RedFol-3
95Sco-118
95ScoDouGC-GC7
95ScoGolR-118
95ScoHaloG-HG15
95ScoPlaTS-118
95Sel-72
95SelArtP-72
95SelCer-88
95SelCerMG-88
95SP-127
95SPCha-122
95SPChaDC-122
95Spo-51
95SpoArtP-51
95SPSil-127
95SPSpeF-2
95StaClu-10
95StaCluFDI-10
95StaCluMOP-10
95StaCluMOP-RL32
95StaCluRL-RL32
95StaCluSTDW-RS10
95StaCluSTWS-10
95StaCluVR-5
95Stu-16
95StuGolS-16
95StuPlaS-16
95Sum-41
95Sum-190
95SumNthD-41
95SumNthD-190
95Top-360
95TopCyb-192
95TopLeaL-LL23
95UC3-95
95UC3-141
95UC3ArtP-95
95UC3ArtP-141
95Ult-10
95UltGolM-10
95UltStrK-2
95UltStrKGM-2
95UppDec-159
95UppDec-J159
95UppDecA-1
95UppDecED-159
95UppDecEDG-159
95UppDecPC-MLB9
95UppDecSE-212
95UppDecSEG-212
95USPlaCMLA-10S
95Zen-91
96Baz-62
96Bow-89
96BowBes-33
96BowBesAR-33
96BowBesR-33
96Cir-10
96CirRav-10
96ColCho-60
96ColCho-419
96ColChoGS-60
96ColChoGS-419
96ColChoSS-60
96ColChoSS-419
96Don-539
96DonPreP-539
96DonSho-4
96EmoXL-12
96Fin-S46
96FinRef-S46
96Fla-16
96Fle-25
96FleRedS-3
96FleSmo'H-2
96FleTif-25
96Kin-1
96Lea-69
96LeaLim-2
96LeaLimG-2
96LeaPre-19
96LeaPreP-19
96LeaPrePB-69
96LeaPrePG-69
96LeaPrePS-69
96LeaPreSG-63
96LeaPreSte-63
96LeaSig-28
96LeaSigEA-32
96LeaSigEACM-3
96LeaSigPPG-28
96LeaSigPPP-28
96MetUni-13
96MetUniP-13
96Pac-258
96PacPri-P79
96PacPriFT-FT3
96PacPriG-P79
96PanSti-136
96Pin-247
96PinAfi-9
96PinAfiAP-9
96PinAfiFPP-9
96PinAfiP-9
96PinArtP-147
96PinFoil-247
96PinSta-147
96Pro-5
96ProSta-110
96Sco-333
96ScoDugC-B58
96ScoDugCAP-B58
96Sel-20
96SelArtP-20
96SelCer-8
96SelCerAP-8
96SelCerCB-8
96SelCerCR-8
96SelCerIP-5
96SelCerMB-8
96SelCerMG-8
96SelCerMR-8
96SelTeaN-8
96SP-39
96SPMarM-MM19
96SPMarMDC-19
96Spo-58
96SpoArtP-58
96SPSpeFX-38
96SPSpeFXDC-38
96SPx-9
96SPxGol-9
96StaClu-25
96StaCluEPB-25
96StaCluEPG-25
96StaCluEPS-25
96StaCluMeg-MH8
96StaCluMet-M4
96StaCluMOP-25
96StaCluMOP-M4
96StaCluMOP-MH8
95StaCluVRMC-5
96Stu-11
96StuPrePB-11
96StuPrePG-11
96StuPrePS-11
96Sum-101
96Sum-152
96SumAbo&B-101
96SumAbo&B-152
96SumArtP-101
96SumArtP-152
96SumFoi-101
96SumFoi-152
96Top-197
96TopChr-65
96TopChrMotG-17
96TopChrMotGR-17
96TopChrR-65
96TopClaC-CC13
96TopGal-174
96TopGalPG-PG8
96TopGalPPI-174
96TopLas-52
96TopLasSS-10
96TopMasotG-17
96Ult-16
96UltGolM-16
96UppDec-20
96UppDec-374
96UppDecDD-DD11
96UppDecDDG-DD11
96UppDecDDS-DD11
96UppDecPHE-H11
96UppDecPreH-H11
96UppDecVJLS-VJ13
96Zen-83
96ZenArtP-83
96ZenMoz-9
97BluJayS-6
97BluJayS-31
97Bow-64
97BowBes-86
97BowBesAR-86
97BowBesR-86
97BowChr-46
97BowChrI-46
97BowChrIR-46
97BowChrR-46
97BowInt-64
97Cir-21
97CirRav-21
97ColCho-61
97ColCho-500
97ColChoNF-NF17
97ColChoTBS-10
97ColChoTBSWH-10
97ColChoTotT-T30
97Don-27
97Don-273
97Don-428
97DonDom-11
97DonEli-40
97DonEliGS-40
97DonLim-110
97DonLim-124
97DonLim-165
97DonLimLE-110
97DonLimLE-124
97DonLimLE-165
97DonPre-52
97DonPreCttC-52
97DonPreP-27
97DonPreP-273
97DonPreP-428
97DonPrePGold-27
97DonPrePGold-273
97DonPrePGold-428
97DonPreTB-4
97DonPreTBG-4
97DonPreTF-4
97DonPreTP-4
97DonPreTPG-4
97DonTeaSMVP-17
97Fin-233
97Fin-344
97FinEmb-344
97FinEmbR-344
97FinRef-233
97FinRef-344
97FlaSho-A21
97FlaSho-B21
97FlaSho-C21
97FlaShoLC-21
97FlaShoLC-B21
97FlaShoLC-C21
97FlaShoLCM-A21
97FlaShoLCM-B21
97FlaShoLCM-C21
97Fle-19
97Fle-569
97FleDecoE-3
97FleDecoERT-3
97FleMilDM-12
97FleTif-19
97FleTif-569
97Lea-208
97Lea-366
97LeaFraM-208
97LeaFraM-366
97LeaFraMDC-208
97LeaFraMDC-366
97LeaGet-11
97LeaGolS-13
97MetUni-20
97NewPin-21
97NewPinAP-21
97NewPinKtP-10
97NewPinMC-21
97NewPinPP-21
97NewPinPP-K10
97Pac-35
97PacLigB-35
97PacPri-14
97PacPriGotD-GD18
97PacPriLB-14
97PacPriP-14
97PacPriSH-SH2B
97PacSil-35
97Pin-55
97PinArtP-55
97PinCar-13
97PinCer-39
97PinCer-138
97PinCerLI-11
97PinCerMBlu-39
97PinCerMBlu-138
97PinCerMG-39
97PinCerMG-138
97PinCerMR-39
97PinCerMR-138
97PinCerR-39
97PinCerR-138
97PinIns-36
97PinInsCE-36
97PinInsDD-15
97PinInsDE-36
97PinMusC-55
97PinTotCPB-39
97PinTotCPB-138
97PinTotCPG-39
97PinTotCPG-138
97PinTotCPR-39
97PinTotCPR-138
97PinX-P-54
97PinX-P-148
97PinX-PMoS-54
97PinX-PMoS-148
97PinX-PMW-20
97PinX-PMWG-20
97PinX-PMWS-20
97Sco-181
97Sco-430
97Sco-525
97ScoHobR-430
97ScoHobR-525
97ScoPreS-181
97ScoRedS-8
97ScoRedSPI-8
97ScoRedSPr-8
97ScoResC-430
97ScoResC-525
97ScoShoS-181
97ScoShoS-430
97ScoShoS-525
97ScoShoSAP-181
97ScoShoSAP-430
97ScoShoSAP-525
97Sel-24
97SelArtP-24
97SelRegG-24
97SelToootT-22
97SelToootTMB-22
97SkyE-X-49
97SkyE-XC-49
97SkyE-XEC-49
97SkyE-XHoN-7
97SP-180
97SPInsI-24
97SpoIll-30
97SpoIll-133
97SpoIll-171
97SpoIllEE-30
97SpoIllEE-133
97SpoIllEE-171
97SPSpeF-24
97SPSPxFA-5
97SPx-50
97SPxBro-50
97SPxGraF-50
97SPxSil-50
97SPxSte-50
97StaClu-209
97StaClul-I4

97StaCluMat-209
97StaCluMOP-209
97StaCluMOP-I4
97Stu-17
97StuPrePG-17
97StuPrePS-17
97Top-370
97TopChr-126
97TopChrR-126
97TopGal-41
97TopGalPPI-41
97TopSta-50
97TopStaAM-50
97Ult-13
97Ult-377
97UltGolME-13
97UltGolME-377
97UltPlaME-13
97UltPlaME-377
97UppDec-26
97UppDec-520
97UppDecAWJ-11
97UppDecP-30
97UppDecU-21
97Zen-19
97Zen Z-Z-9
97Zen8x1-12
97Zen8x1D-12

Clemens, Troy
90SprCarB-7
91RenSilSCLC-17
92SanJosGC-13
93SanJosGC-6
93SanJosGF-13
94SanJosGC-4
94SanJosGF-2819

Clement, Matt
95IdaFalBTI-31
95RanCucQT-31
96CliLumKTI-9
96MidLeaAB-18
97Bow-207
97BowChr-190
97BowChrI-190
97BowChrIR-190
97BowChrR-190
97BowInt-207

Clement, Wally (Wallace Oaks)
09AmeCarE-24
90DodTar-914

Clemente, Joe
93MisStaB-9

Clemente, Roberto W.
47Exh-44
47PM1StaP1-32
55Top-164
56Top-33
57Kah-5
57Top-76
58Kah-5
58Top-52A
58Top-52B
59Kah-6
59Top-478
59Top-543
60Baz-7
60Kah-6
60PirJayP-3
60PirTag-21
60Top-326
61Kah-8
61PirJayP-2
61PirRigF-1
61Pos-132A
61Pos-132B
61Top-41
61Top-388
62Baz-11
62ExhStaB-9
62Jel-173
62Kah-5
62Pos-173A
62Pos-173B
62PosCan-173
62SalPlaC-150
62ShiPlaC-150
62Top-10
62Top-52
62TopBuc-17
62TopStal-174
62TopVen-10
62TopVen-52
63Baz-14
63ExhStaB-15
63Fle-56
63Jel-143
63Kah-6
63PirIDL-4
63PirJayP-3
63Pos-143
63SalMetC-23
63Top-18
63Top-540
63TopStil-9
64Baz-14
64Kah-4
64PirKDK-7
64Top-7
64Top-440
64TopCoi-55
64TopCoi-150
64TopGia-11
64TopSta-27
64TopStaU-17
64TopVen-7
64WheSta-11
65Baz-14
65MacSta-1
65OPC-2
65OPC-160
65Top-2
65Top-160
65TopEmbl-19
65TopTral-44
66Baz-26
66Kah-8
66PirEasH-21
66Top-215
66Top-300
66TopRubl-18
66TopVen-215
66TopVen-300
67Baz-26
67CokCapPi-18
67DexPre-50
67DexPre-51
67OPCPapl-11
67PirTeal-4
67Top-242
67Top-361
67Top-400
67TopGiaSU-7
67TopPirS-6
67TopPirS-27
67TopPos-11
67TopTesF-6
67TopVen-278
68AtlOilPBCC-14
68Baz-12
68DexPre-24
68OPC-1
68OPC-3
68OPC-150
68PirKDK-21
68PirTeal-5
68Top-1
68Top-3
68Top-150
68Top-374
68Top-480
68Top3-D-1
68TopActS-9C
68TopActS-12B
68TopGamI-6
68TopPla-16
68TopPos-6
68TopVen-1
68TopVen-3
68TopVen-150
69MilBra-60
69MLBOffS-184
69MLBPin-39
69NabTeaF-5
69OPC-50
69OPCDec-4
69PirGre-4
69Top-50
69TopDec-27
69TopDecl-6
69TopSta-85
69TopSup-58
69TopTeaP-16
69TraSta-56
70DayDaiNM-32
70Kel-27
70MilBra-5
70MLBOffS-99
70OPC-61
70OPC-350
70PirTeal-2
70Top-61
70Top-350
70TopPos-21
70TopSup-12
70TraSta-5B
71AllBasA-6
71BazNumT-38
71BazUnn-11
71Kel-5
71MilDud-40
71MLBOffS-198
71MLBOffS-558
71OPC-630
71Pir-3
71PirActP-4
71PirArc-3
71Top-630
71TopCoi-71
71TopSup-37
71TopTat-79
72Dia-57
72Kel-49
72MilBra-75
72OPC-226
72OPC-309
72OPC-310
72ProStaP-15
72Top-226
72Top-309
72Top-310
72TopCloT-6
72TopPos-23
73OPC-50
73PicCle-1
73PicCle-2
73PicCle-3
73PicCle-4
73PicCle-5
73PicCle-6
73PicCle-7
73PicCle-8
73PicCle-9
73PicCle-10
73PicCle-11
73PicCle-12
73Top-50
74LauAllG-62
75OPC-204
75TCMAllG-5
75Top-204
76GalBasGHoF-5
76ShaPiz-135
76Spo-C
77GalGloG-41
77GalGloG-252
77SerSta-6
77Spo-3201
77Spo-6116
78TCM60I-13
79TCM50-23
80LauFamF-21
80PacLeg-50
80PerHaloFP-135
80SSPHOF-135
82BasCarN-10
82BHCRSpoL-8
82K-M-10
83DiaClaS2-74
83DonHOFH-17
83KelCerB-7
83MLBPin-22
83Oco& SSBG-7
84OCoandSI-60
84OCoandSI-77
84OCoandSI-129
84SpoDesPW-3
84WilMay-19
86ChaRaiP-7
86PirGreT-7
86SpoDecG-43
86SpoDesJM-18
86TCM-1
86TCMSupS-6
87Don-612
87DonAllB-PUZ
87DonSupD-NNO
87DonWaxBC-PUZ
87HygAllG-8
87K-M-2
87Lea-163
87NesDreT-27
87Pir196T-4
87SpoRea-27
87Top-313
87TopTif-313
88GreBasS-73
89CMCBasG-1
89HOFStiB-46
89PacLegI-135
89SweBasG-125
89TopBasT-38
89USPLegSC-1
90AGFA-8
90Col-35
90PerGreM-32
90RinPosC-1
90RinPosC-2
90RinPosC-3
90RinPosC-4
90RinPosC-5
90RinPosC-6
90RinPosC-7
90RinPosC-8
90RinPosC-9
90RinPosC-10
90RinPosC-11
90RinPosC-12
90SweBasG-20
91CadEllD-10
91HomCooC-7
91KelLey-6
91LinDri-39
91SweBasG-132
91USGamSBL-11C
91USGamSBL-11D
91USGamSBL-11H
91USGamSBL-11S
92PMGol-3
92RevLeg1-7
92RevLeg1-8
92RevLeg1-9
93ActPacA-119
93ActPacA2-53G
93CadDis-12
93CitPriC-1
93CitPriC-2
93CitPriC-3
93CitPriC-4
93CitPriC-5
93CitPriC-6
93LegFoi-1
93TedWilM-11
93TedWilRC-1
93TedWilRC-2
93TedWilRC-3
93TedWilRC-4
93TedWilRC-5
93TedWilRC-6
93TedWilRC-7
93TedWilRC-8
93TedWilRC-9
93TedWilRC-10
93ZCle-1
93ZCle-2
93ZCle-3
93ZCle-4
93ZCle-5
93ZCle-6
93ZCle-7
93ZCle-8
93ZCle-9
93ZCle-10
94ActPac-67
94ActPac-68
94ActPac-69
94ActPac-70
94ActPac-71
94FanCle-1
94FanCle-2
94FanCle-3
94FanCle-4
94FanCle-5
94KelCle-1
94KelCle-2
94KelCle-3
94TopArc1-251
94TopArc1G-251
94UppDecTAE-72
94UppDecTAEGM-2
94WenCle-1
94Yoo-5
95TopArcBD-82
95TopLegot6M-8
97St.VinHHS-6

Clements, Dave
83SprCarF-2
84ArkTraT-2
85LouRedR-14
86ArkTraP-5

Clements, Ed (Edward)
89PacSenL-54

Clements, Jack (John T.)
87BucN28-77
87OldJudN-85
88SpoTimM-5
88WG1CarG-49
90KalBatN-7
98CamPepP-13

Clements, Pat
85AngSmo-22
85FleUpd-26
85TopTifT-23T
85TopTra-23T
86Don-600
86Fle-606
86OPC-283
86Top-754
86TopTif-754
87Don-390
87Fle-608
87FleGlo-608
87Top-16
87TopTif-16
88ColCliC-1
88ColCliP-1
88ColCliP-318
88Don-52
88Fle-204
88FleGlo-204
88Sco-389
88ScoGlo-389
88StaLinY-3
88Top-484
88TopTif-484
89Bow-452
89BowTif-452
89LasVegSP-15
89Top-159
89TopTif-159
90Fle-153
90FleCan-153
90OPC-548
90Top-548
90TopTif-548
91LasVegSP-227
91PadSmo-5
92Bow-533
92Fle-602
92PadMot-23
92PadSmo-6
92Sco-714
92YanWIZ8-33
93RocRedWF-232

Clements, Tony
87EugEmeP-2667
91LinDriAA-403
91MemChiLD-403

Clements, Wes
83TucTorT-14
84TucTorC-53
85BelBreT-14
87GleFalTP-5
89PacSenL-176

Clemo, Scott
86JamExpP-3
87IndIndTI-28
88WesPalBES-7

Clemons, Chris
94SigRooDP-31
94SigRooDPS-31
95PriWilCTI-17
95Top-551
96PriWilCB-7
97Bow-330
97BowChr-226
97BowChrI-226
97BowChrIR-226
97BowChrR-226
97BowInt-330

Clemons, Lance
72OPC-372
72Top-372

Clemons, Mark
85KinBluJT-1
86OrlTwiP-4
87OrlTwiP-10
88JacExpB-8
88JacExpP-977

Clemons, Robert

12ColRedB-55
12ColTinT-55
Clemons, Verne
21Nei-85
22E120-227
23WilChoV-19
Clemons, Verne James
22W573-18
Clendenon, Donn Alvin
62Top-86
62TopVen-86
63Kah-7
63PirIDL-5
63PirJayP-4
63Top-477
64Kah-5
64PirKDK-8
64Top-163
64TopCoi-15
64TopSta-76
64TopStaU-18
64TopVen-163
65Kah-8
65Top-325
65TopEmbl-9
66OPC-99
66PirEasH-17
66Top-99
66Top-375
66TopVen-99
67CokCapPi-3
67DexPre-52
67PirTeal-5
67Top-266
67Top-535
67TopPirS-7
67TopPirS-30
68PirKDK-17
68PirTeal-6
68Top-344
68TopVen-344
69MetNewYDN-4
69MilBra-61
69OPC-208
69Top-208A
69Top-208B
69TopDecl-7
69TopFou-3
69TopSta-54
69TopTeaP-6
70DayDaiNM-142
70MetTra-25C
70MLBOffS-74
70OPC-280
70OPC-306
70Top-280
70Top-306
71CarTeal-10
71MLBOffS-149
71OPC-115
71Top-115
71TopCoi-151
71TopSup-4
71TopTat-47
72MilBra-76
72Top-671
78TCM60I-237
89Met196C-2
89RinPosM1-7
90SweBasG-82
91MetWIZ-77
91UppDecS-8
94Met69CCPP-11
94Met69CS-10
94Met69T-10
94Met69T-38
96Met69Y-2
Cleveland, Elmer E.
87OldJudN-86
Cleveland, Reggie
70Top-716
71CarTeal-11
71OPC-216
71Top-216
72OPC-375
72Top-375
73OPC-104
73Top-104
74OPC-175
74Top-175
74TopSta-112
74TopTra-175T
75OPC-32
75Top-32
76OPC-419
76RedSoxSM-2
76Top-419
77OPC-111
77Top-613
78RanBurK-10
78SSP270-165
78Top-105
79OPC-103
79Top-209
80Top-394
81Don-206
81Fle-523
81Top-576
82Don-456
82Fle-137
82Top-122
82Top-737
91PacSenL-61
91PacSenL-79
92St.CatBJC-28
93RanKee-104
93St.CatBJC-28
94BreMilB-211
94HagSunC-27
94HagSunF-2747
95HagSunF-85
Clevenger, Tex
58SenJayP-2
58Top-31
59SenTealW-4
59Top-298
60SenJayP-3
60Top-392
61Top-291
61Yan61RL-18
63Top-457
92YanWIZ6-25
Cleverly, Gary
75SanAntBT-5
Cliburn, Stan (Stanley Gene)
75QuaCitAT-5
76QuaCitAT-11
82PorBeaT-10
83LynPirT-11
84HawIslC-132
85HawIslC-242
86EdmTraP-5
86EdmTraP-6
87RicBraC-29
87RicBraT-28
88BufBisC-24
88BufBisP-1480
88WatPirP-31
89AugPirP-514
89PacSenL-150
89SouAtlLAGS-1
89TopSenL-54
90SalBucS-25
91PacSenL-30
91PacSenL-51
91SalBucC-25
91SalBucP-968
92GasRanC-26
92GasRanF-2269
93TulDriF-2749
94TulDriF-258
94TulDriTI-26
78STLakCGC-14
93TulDriTI-5
Cliburn, Stewart
77SalPirT-6
79BufBisT-2
80PorBeaT-13
80VenLeaS-126
81BufBisT-9
83NasAngT-3
84EdmTraC-113
85DomLeaS-59
85EdmTraC-19
85FleUpd-27
86Don-301
86EdmTraP-7
86Fle-152
86SevCoi-W16
86Spo-177
86Top-179
86TopTif-179
87Don-530
88AngSmo-19
89Don-462
89EdmTraC-7
89EdmTraP-566
89Fle-471
89FleGlo-471
89Sco-445
89Top-649
89TopTif-649
89UppDec-483
91PacSenL-29
91PacSenL-51
91PalSprAP-2034
92CalLeaACL-51
92PalSprAC-30
92PalSprAF-856
93EliTwiC-23
93EliTwiF-3431
94ForWayWC-27
94ForWayWF-2026
95ForWayWTI-27
96ForWayWB-28
Clifford, Eric
95EveAqaTI-4
Clifford, James
92BelMarC-22
92BelMarF-1450
93BelMarC-9
93BelMarF-3215
94AppFoxC-4
94AppFoxF-1059
96LanJetB-9
Clifford, Jeff
90SouOreAB-13
90SouOreAP-3440
Clifford, John
96AshTouB-9
Clift, Harland Benton
36ExhFou-15
36NatChiFPR-115
36OveCanR-8
37ExhFou-15
37OPCBatUV-104
37WheBB9-3
38ExhFou-15
39ExhSal-8
41BroW75-6
41DouPlaR-147
41Gou-2
41PlaBal-66
77TCMTheWY-8
77TCMTheWY-60
79DiaGre-58
83DiaClaS2-109
83TCMPla1943-15
93DiaStaES-122
94ConTSN-1124
94ConTSNB-1124
Clifton, Flea (Herman Earl)
35DiaMatCS3T1-33
36GouWidPPR-B5
36WorWidGV-32
39WorWidGV-5
76TigOldTS-3
Clinatis, Mike
76CedRapGT-10
Cline, Monk (John)
87OldJudN-87
Cline, Pat
93HunCubC-6
93HunCubF-3237
95MidLeaA-9
95RocCubTI-23
96Bow-257
96DayCubB-8
96Exc-136
97Bow-164
97BowBes-123
97BowBesAR-123
97BowBesR-123
97BowChr-160
97BowChrI-160
97BowChrIR-160
97BowChrR-160
97BowInt-164
97ColCho-473
97FlaShoWotF-5
97Fle-674
97FleTif-674
97Ult-544
97UltGolME-544
97UltPlaME-544
Cline, Steve
75CedRapGT-3
81CliGiaT-3
82CliGiaF-3
84ShrCapFB-4
88ShrCapP-1286
89ShrCapP-1837
90CliGiaB-10
90CliGiaP-2566
91CliGiaC-27
91CliGiaP-853
92ShrCapF-3888
93ShrCapF-2776
94ShrCapF-1624
95PhoFirTI-32
96OgdRapTI-32
Cline, Ty (Tyrone A.)
61Top-421
62Kah-6
62Top-362
62TopStal-32
63Jel-74
63Pos-74
63Top-414
64Top-171
64TopVen-171
65OPC-63
65Top-63
66Top-306
66TopVen-306
67CokCapB-2
67DexPre-53
67Top-591
68Top-469
69MilBra-62
69MLBOffS-156
69Top-442
70DayDaiNM-99
70MLBOffS-64
70OPC-164
70Top-164
71MLBOffS-54
71OPC-199
71OPC-201
71OPC-319
71Top-199
71Top-201
71Top-319
72MilBra-77
78AtlCon-6
78TCM60I-149
78TCM60I-191
Clines, Gene (Eugene)
71OPC-27
71PirActP-14
71Top-27
72OPC-152
72Top-152
73OPC-333
73Top-333
74OPC-172
74Top-172
75MetSSP-17
75OPC-575
75Top-575
76OPC-417
76SSP-543
76Top-417
77CubJewT-5
77Top-237
78SSP270-253
78Top-639
79Top-171
88AstMot-27
89MarMot-27
89PacSenL-146
89T/MSenL-21
90MarMot-27
91MetWIZ-78
92MarMot-27
93RanKee-105
Clinkscales, Sherard
92ClaDraP-22
92ClaFS7-414
92EugEmeC-1
92EugEmeF-3018
92FroRowDP-3
93ClaGolF-184
93RocRoyC-7
93RocRoyF-707
93StaCluM-6
93Top-706
93TopGol-706
93TopInaM-706
93TopMic-706
94ClaGolF-146
Clinton, Barry
86ColCliP-21
Clinton, Bill
93TriPla-32
94UppDecTAE-78
Clinton, Jim (James)
89ButCopKSP-11
90GasRanB-24
90GasRanP-2527
90GasRanS-5
91ChaRanP-1320
92ChaRanC-15
92ChaRanF-2231
93ChaRanC-4
93TulDriF-2738
94TulDriF-249
94TulDriTI-3
95TulDriTI-5
Clinton, Lu (Luciean L.)
60Top-533
61UniOil-S2
62Top-457
63Fle-6
63Jel-82
63Pos-82
63Top-96
64Top-526
65OPC-229
65Top-229
67Top-426
81RedSoxBG2S-74
92YanWIZ6-26
Clipper, Chipper the
91BatCliC-29
Clippers, Columbus
87IntLeaAT-39
88ColCliP-330
91ColCliP-613
Clisanchez, Gilberto
93LinVenB-44
94VenLinU-116
Cloherty, John
78DayBeaAT-5
Cloninger, Darin
85AlbYanT-3
Cloninger, Greg
88SumBraP-406
89BurBraP-1601
89BurBraS-4
Cloninger, Todd
86GenCubP-2
87WinSpiP-3
Cloninger, Tom
87OneYanP-33
Cloninger, Tony
62Top-63
62TopVen-63
63Jel-157
63Pos-157
63Top-367
64BraJayP-4
64Top-575
65Kah-9
65Top-520
66Baz-27
66Kah-9
66OPC-10
66Top-10
66Top-223
66TopRubl-19
66TopVen-10
66TopVen-223
67Baz-27
67CokCapB-5
67DexPre-54
67Kah-9
67Top-396
67Top-490
68CokCapB-5
68DexPre-25
68OPC-93
68Top-93
68TopVen-93
69Kah-B7
69MLBOffS-128
69Top-492
70DayDaiNM-97
70MLBOffS-26
70Top-705
71CarTeal-12
71MLBOffS-55
71OPC-218
71Top-218
72Top-779
78AtlCon-7
78TCM60I-20
88AlbYanP-1353
90HOFStiB-70

91PacSenL-31
Clontz, Brad
92PulBraC-13
92PulBraF-3170
93ClaFS7-2
93DurBulC-6
93DurBulF-480
93DurBulTI-14
94Bow-641
94GreBraF-407
94GreBraTI-9
95Exc-148
95ExcLeaL-5
95Fin-247
95FinRef-247
95Fla-322
95FleAllR-M5
95Lea-319
95SigRooOJHP-HP2
95SigRooOJHPS-HP2
95StaClu-568
95StaCluMOP-568
95StaCluSTWS-568
95Sum-151
95SumNthD-151
95Top-369
95TopTra-132T
95UltGolMR-M8
95UppDec-245
95UppDecED-245
95UppDecEDG-245
96ColCho-454
96ColChoGS-454
96ColChoSS-454
96Don-288
96DonPreP-288
96Fla-196
96Fle-289
96FleBra-3
96FleTif-289
96Ult-153
96UltGolM-153
96UppDec-274
97Fle-253
97FleTif-253
97Top-224
Close, Casey
88ColCliC-21
88ColCliP-19
88ColCliP-325
90CalCanC-19
90CalCanP-661
90CMC-446
90ProAAAF-126
Clossen, Bill
86DurBulP-4
87PriWilYP-15
Closter, Alan
66Top-549
69OPC-114
69Top-114
69TopFou-24
72OPC-124
72Top-124
73OPC-634
73SyrChiTI-6
73Top-634
92YanWIZ7-35
Clothery, John
76DubPacT-6
Cloud, David
95DavLipB-6
Cloud, Tony
96BilMusTI-5
Cloude, Ken
96LanJetB-10
97Bow-396
97BowBes-162
97BowBesAR-162
97BowBesR-162
97BowChr-262
97BowChrI-262
97BowChrIR-262
97BowChrR-262
97BowInt-396
Clougherty, Pat
93BazTeaU-8
93TopTra-34T
Clowns, Indianapolis
92NegLeaRLI-76
92NegLeaRLI-99
93NegLeaRL2-92
93NegLeaRL2-93
Cluck, Bob
74CedRapAT-22
75DubPacT-10
76DubPacT-7
81TucTorT-5
84LasVegSC-239
85LasVegSC-110
90AstMot-27
91AstMot-28
92AstMot-27
93AstMot-28
96A'sMot-28
Cluff, Paul
87BriYouC-14
89BoiHawP-2006
Clutterbuck, Bryan
82BelBreF-20
83ElPasDT-15
84ElPasDT-5
85VanCanC-222
86VanCanP-7
87DenZepP-23
87Don-397
87Fle-342
87FleGlo-342
87Top-562
87TopTif-562
89BrePol-48
89TopTra-21T
89TopTraT-21T
90OPC-264
90Top-264
90TopTif-264
90UppDec-239
94BreMilB-212
Clyburn, Danny
92ClaDraP-32
92ClaFS7-422
92FroRowDP-18
93AugPirC-5
93AugPirF-1558
93Bow-542
93ClaFS7-98
93ClaGolF-194
93SouAtlLAGF-32
93StaCluM-12
94Bow-406
94CarLeaAF-CAR37
94Cla-12
94SalBucC-1
94SalBucF-2336
94UppDecML-76
94UppDecMLPotYF-PY19
95Exc-251
95SPML-16
95UppDecML-33
96BowBayB-12
96MauStiHWB-20
97Bow-315
97BowChr-217
97BowChrI-217
97BowChrIR-217
97BowChrR-217
97BowInt-315
95UppDecMLFS-33
Clyde, David
73LinPor-174
74OPC-133
74Top-133
74TopSta-233
75OPC-12
75Top-12
76LauDiaJ-19
76SacSolC-21
77TucTorC-32
79Top-399
80Top-697
93RanKee-106
Clymer, Otis Edgar
08RosComP-76
09ColChiE-56
09MaxPubP-21
09RamT20-26
09SenBarP-1
11SpoLifCW-66
12ColRedB-56
12ColTinT-56
Clymer, William J.
09T206-411
Coach, Calvin
94JohCitCC-6
94JohCitCF-3716
Coachman, Pete
86PalSprAP-22
86PalSprAP-7
87EdmTraP-2073
88EdmTraC-13
88EdmTraP-578
89EdmTraC-12
89EdmTraP-563
90CMC-497
90EdmTraC-20
90EdmTraP-522
90ProAAAF-98
91LinDriAAA-531
91Sco-344
91TacTigLD-531
91TacTigP-2311
91TopDeb90-32
Coakley, Andrew
08RosComP-113
08RosComP-178
09RamT20-27
11SpoLifCW-67
Coan, Gil (Gilbert F.)
47SenGunBP-11
49Bow-90
49MPR302-2-114
50Bow-54
51Bow-18
52Bow-51
52RedMan-AL4
52Top-291
53BowC-34
53Bri-3
53Top-133
54Bow-40
54OriEss-5
55Bow-78
55OriEss-5
79DiaGre-74
83TopRep5-291
88ChaLooLTI-6
91OriCro-78
91TopArc1-133
Coates, Jim
55DonWin-14
59Top-525
60Lea-35
60Top-51
60TopVen-51
61Pos-17
61Top-531
61Yan61RL-16
62Top-553
63Top-237
67Top-401
78TCM60I-217
78TCM60I-267
83YanASFY-8
91RinPos1Y1-5
92YanWIZ6-27
92YanWIZA-12
Coates, Thomas
91IdaFalBP-4339
91IdaFalBSP-6
92PulBraC-7
92PulBraF-3190
93DurBulC-7
93DurBulF-496
93DurBulTI-19
Coatney, Rick
81DurBulT-16
82DurBulT-15
Coats, Nathan
96WatIndTI-6
Cobb, Mark
87UtiBluSP-13
88SpaPhiS-20
89ClePhiS-7
89Sta-11
Cobb, Marvin
88OklSoo-16
89BenBucL-2
89OklSoo-9
90PalSprACLC-219
90PalSprAP-2570
91LinDriAA-430
91MidAngLD-430
91MidAngOHP-7
91MidAngP-429
92MidAngF-4019
92MidAngS-456
92SkyAA F-193
Cobb, Mickey
75OmaRoyTI-5
Cobb, Paul
75McCCob-11
Cobb, Trevor
93EliTwiC-8
93EliTwiF-3410
94EliTwiC-5
94EliTwiF-3722
95Exc-79
96FtMyeMB-28
Cobb, Ty (Tyrus Raymond)
03WilCarE-6
07TigACDPP-1
07TigACDPP-18
08AmeLeaPC-6
08RosComP-31
09AmeCarE-25
09BusBroBPP-4
09ColChiE-57A
09ColChiE-57B
09MaxPubP-3
09PhiCarE-5
09SpoNewSM-5
09SpoNewSM-36
09T206-68
09T206-69
09T206-70
09T206-71
09TigHMTP-1
09TigMorPenWBPP-2
09TigTaCP-3
09WolNewDTPP-1
09WolNewDTPP-2
09WWSmiP-1
10CouT21-13
10CouT21-105
10CouT21-106
10CouT21-269
10CouT21-270
10DarChoE-9
10DomDisP-26A
10DomDisP-26B
10E-UOraBSC-7
10E101-10
10E102-4
10E98-8
10JuJuDE-10
10MelMinE-10
10NadCarE-11
10OrnOvaPP-3
10PeoT21-12A
10PeoT21-12B
10PeoT21-12C
10RedCroT-11
10RedCroT-97
10SepAnoP-4
10SepAnoP-5
10StaCarE-6
10SweCapPP-22A
10SweCapPP-22B
10W555-15
11BasBatEU-11
11DiaGumP-9
11E94-7
11L1L-127
11MecDFT-11
11PloCanE-16
11S74Sil-13
11S81LarS-102
11SpoLifCW-68
11SpoLifM-55
11T205-30
11TurRedT-9
12ColRedB-57A
12ColRedB-57B
12ColTinT-57A
12ColTinT-57B
12HasTriFT-2
12HasTriFT-37
12HasTriFT-39
12HasTriFT-75A
12HasTriFT-75B
12HasTriFT-75C
12SenVasS-1
12T22SeroC-3
13NatGamW-11
13PolGroW-5
13TomBarW-11
14B18B-14A
14B18B-14B
14B18B-14C
14CraJacE-30
14E&SP-2
14PieStaT-13
14TexTomE-13
15AmeCarE-8A
15AmeCarE-8B
15CraJacE-30
15SpoNewP-2
15VicT21-4
16BF2FP-26
16ColE13-30
16FleBreD-17
16SpoNewM-38
16TanBraE-5
17HolBreD-15
19W514-43
20NatCarE-13
21E121So1-10A
21E121So1-10B
21E121So8-11A
21E121So8-11B
21Exh-24
21Nei-30
21OxfConE-4
22AmeCarE-11
22E120-48
22W572-13
22W573-19
22W575-17
22WilPatV-46
23MapCriV-22
23W501-8
23W515-10
23W551-4
23WilChoV-20
24MrsShePP-2
25Exh-90
26Exh-91
26SpoComoA-9
27AmeCarE-17
27Exh-53
27YorCarE-27
28StaPlaCE-9
28W502-27
28W512-3
28Yue-27
32USCar-14
33SpoKin-1
36PC7AlbHoF-1
48ExhHoF-6
50CalHOFW-17
51R42SmaS-14
60ExhWriH-7
60Fle-42
60NuHi-43
61Fle-1
61Fle-14
61GolPre-25
61NuSco-443
63BasMagM-16
63BazA-35
63GadFunC-11
63GadFunC-32
63HalofFB-1
67TopVen-146
68LauWorS-6
68SpoMemAG-10
69Baz-7
69Baz-8
69SCFOldT-9
70FleWorS-6
71FleWorS-6
72FleFamF-15
72KelATG-15
72LauGreF-35
73FleWilD-35
73HalofFPP-3
73OPC-471
73OPC-475
73Top-471
73Top-475
75FlePio-14
75McCCob-1
75McCCob-2
75McCCob-3
75McCCob-4
75McCCob-5
75McCCob-6
75McCCob-7
75McCCob-8
75McCCob-9
75McCCob-10
75McCCob-11
75McCCob-12
75McCCob-13
75McCCob-15
75McCCob-16
75McCCob-17
75McCCob-18
75McCCob-19
75McCCob-20

75TCMAllG-6
76MotOldT-3
76OPC-346
76RowExh-7
76ShaPiz-1
76TayBow4-113
76Top-346
77BobParHoF-13
77GalGloG-100
77GalGloG-136
77ShaPiz-19
79Pew-1
79Top-411
79Top-414
80Lau300-4
80LauFamF-28
80MarExhH-6
80PacLeg-31
80PerHaloFP-1
80SSPHOF-2
80TigGreT-3
81ConTSN-1
81SpoHaloF-5
81TigDetN-17
81TigSecNP-1
82BHCRSpoL-1
82DiaCla-39
83Don-653
83DonHOFH-1
84DonCha-26
84GalHaloFRL-1
84OCoandSI-86
84SpoDesPW-8
85FegMurCG-2
85UltBasC-1
85Woo-8
86ConSer1-2
86ConSor1 6
86ConSer1-24
86ConSer1-41
86TCM-5
86TigSpoD-1
87ConSer2-5
87HygAllG-9
87NesDreT-7
87SpoCubG-2
88ConHar-2
88ConSer4-6
88FriBasCM-3
88GreBasS-40
89CMCBasG-2
89HOFStiB-37
89PacLegI-117
89SpoIllFKI-321
89SweBasG-2
89TopBasT-22
90BasWit-56
90HOFStiB-19
90PerGreM-12
90SweBasG-15
91CadEllD-11
91ConTSN-250
91ConTSNP-13
91ConTSNP-250
91ConTSNP-500
91FouBal-7
91HomCooC-4
91LinDri-48
91SweBasG-127
91USGamSBL-1C
91USGamSBL-1D
91USGamSBL-1H
91USGamSBL-1S
92ConTSN-425
92ConTSN-525
92ConTSNCI-10
92ConTSNGI-1000G
92MegRut-125
92Sco-878
92St.VinHHS-1
92WhiLegtL-1
92WhiPro-1
93ActPacA-88
93ActPacA2-22G
93CadDis-13
93CokCasI-TC1
93ConMasB-7
93ConTSN-796
93ConTSN-838
93CraJac-1
93Hoy-1
93SpeHOFI-2
93TedWil-125
93UppDecAH-32
93UppDecAH-145
93UppDecAH-146
93UppDecAH-160
94ConTSN-1000
94ConTSN-1011
94ConTSNB-1000
94ConTSNB-1011
94TedWil-30
94TedWilLC-LC11
94UppDecAH-30
94UppDecAH-106
94UppDecAH-174
94UppDecAH1-30
94UppDecAH1-106
94UppDecAH1-174
94UppDecAJ-44
94UppDecAJG-44
94UppDecTAE-11
94UppDecTAEGM-3
95ConTSNGJ-3
95UppDecSHoB-19
93UppDecTR-2
93UppDecTR-6
93UppDecTR-7
93UppDecTR-8
96ColCho-501
96ColChoGS-501
96ColChoSS-501
20W516-6
Coble, Drew
88T/MUmp-45
89T/MUmp-43
90T/MUmp-41
Coble, Tony
90HelBreSP-4
Cobleigh, Mike
89ModA'sC-5
Coburn, Todd
96PieBolWB-6
Coca, Mark
95OdgRapTI-3
Cocanower, Jaime
81VanCanT-1
82VanCanT-20
84BrePol-47
84FleUpd-28
84TopTra-26T
84TopTraT-26T
85BreGar-4
85BrePol-47
85Don-455
85Fle-579
85Top-576
85TopSti-288
85TopTif-576
85VanCanC-210
86BrePol-47
86Don-393
86Fle-483
86Top-277
86TopTif-277
87AlbDukP-7
87Top-423
87TopTif-423
94BreMilB-213
Coccia, Dan
88MarPhiS-7
Cochran, Andrew
95DanBraTI-5
96EugEmeB-5
Cochran, Arnold
81BatTroT-12
81WatIndT-20
Cochran, Dave
84JacMetT-21
Cochran, Greg
79ColCliT-17
80ColCliP-27
80ColCliT-21
81ColCliP-27
81ColCliT-12
82ColCliP-27
82ColCliT-8
Cochran, Jamie
91JohCitCC-17
91JohCitCP-3971
92HamRedC-5
92HamRedF-1584
92ProFS7-327
93ExcFS7-97
93SavCarC-9
93SavCarF-681
93SouAtlLAGF-47
94ExcFS7-264
94ExcLeaLF-6
Cochrane, Chris
94SouOreAC-2
94SouOreAF-3612
95WesMicWTI-36
96ModA'sB-9
Cochrane, Dave
83LynMetT-14B
86BirBarTI-11
87HawIslP-13
87SevCoi-C5
87Spo-158
87SpoTeaP-26
88CalCanC-14
88CalCanP-785
89CalCanC-14
89CalCanP-542
90CalCanC-11
90CMC-438
90OPC-491
90Top-491
90TopTif-491
91CalCanLD-55
91CalCanP-518
91LinDriAAA-55
92Don-539
92Lea-398
92MarMot-14
92Sco-461
92Sco100RS-70
92StaClu-69
92Ult-431
93Don-481
93Fle-671
93Top-288
93TopGol-288
93TopInaM-288
93TopMic-288
Cochrane, Mickey (Gordon S.)
26SpoComoA-10
28Exh-53
28StaPlaCE-10
28W56PlaC-JOK
29ExhFou-27
30SchR33-32
30W554-1
31Exh-28
31W517-37
31W517-54
32OrbPinNP-28
32OrbPinUP-12
32USCar-12
33ButCanV-7
33ButCre-4
33DelR33-6
33DouDisP-10
33ExhFou-14
33Gou-76
33GouCanV-69
33TatOrb-12
33TatOrbSDR-155
33TatOrbSDR-186
34BatR31-25
34ButPreR-10
34DiaStaR-9
34ExhFou-12
34ExhFou-14
34Gou-2
34GouCanV-59
35AlDemDCR3-23
35AlDemDCR3-24
35ExhFou-12
35GolMedFR-2
35GouPreR-9
35GouPuzR-1D
35GouPuzR-2D
35GouPuzR-5A
35GouPuzR-6A
35GouPuzR-11J
35GouPuzR-13A
35GouPuzR-16D
35GouPuzR-17D
35TigFreP-3
35WheBB1-5A
35WheBB1-5B
36ExhFou-12
36GouBWR-7
36GouWidPPR-A17
36NatChiFPR-90
36PC7AlbHoF-50
36R31PasP-5
36R31Pre-G3
36WheBB3-2
36WorWidGV-45
37ExhFou-12
40PlaBal-180
46SpoExcW-2-11
48ExhHoF-7
49LeaPre-2
50CalHOFW-18A
50CalHOFW-18B
51TopConMA-2
60Fle-24
60NuHi-19
61Fle-15
61GolPre-12
61NuSco-419
63BazA-34
67TopVen-153
68SpoMemAG-7
69Baz-5
69Baz-8
69SCFOldT-22
71FleWorS-33
72KelATG-4
74Car193T-30
76OPC-348
76RowExh-13
76ShaPiz-50
76TigOldTS-4
76Top-348
77GalGloG-61
77GalGloG-238
77ShaPiz-8
78TigDeaCS-14
80MarExhH-7
80PacLeg-38
80PerHaloFP-50
80SSPHOF-50
80TigGreT-11
81SpoHaloF-20
81TigDetN-3
81TigSecNP-22
83ConMar-7
86ConSer1-7
86SpoDecG-13
86TigSpoD-5
87HygAllG-10
87NesDreT-8
88ConAmeA-5
88ConSer3-7
89HOFStiB-56
89PacLegI-151
90SweBasG-3
91ConTSN-51
91ConTSN-266
91LinDri-49
91SweBasG-142
92ConTSN-432
92ConTSN-551
93ActPacA-98
93ActPacA2-32G
93ConMasB-5
93ConTSN-866
94ConTSN-1087
94ConTSN-1146
94ConTSNB-1087
94ConTSNB-1146
94TedWil-65
95MegRut-24
Cock, J.R.
91BenBucC-1
91BenBucP-3688
Cockburn, J.C.
88KimN18-9
Cockrell, Alan
86ShrCapP-4
87PhoFirP-15
88PhoFirC-19
88PhoFirP-68
89PorBeaC-20
89PorBeaP-224
90CMC-475
90ColSprSSC-23
90ColSprSSP-49
90ProAAAF-230
90TriAllGP-AAA50
91CalCanLD-56
91CalCanP-526
91LinDriAAA-56
92ColSprSSF-753
92ColSprSSS-82
92OPC-591
92Top-591
92TopGol-591
92TopGolW-591
92TopMic-591
93ChaKniF-555
94NewHavRF-1554
96ColSprSSTI-8
Codd, Tim
95HudValRTI-14
96ChaRivTI-9609
Codinach, Antonio
84VisOakT-19
Codiroli, Chris
82WesHavAT-4
83TopTra-20T
84A'sMot-10
84Don-345
84Fle-441
84Nes792-61
84OPC-61
84Top-61
84TopSti-330
84TopTif-61
85A'sMot-9
85Don-462
85Fle-420
85Top-552
85TopSti-327
85TopTif-552
86A'sMot-15
86Don-278
86Fle-414
86Lea-151
86OPC-388
86Top-433
86TopSti-173
86TopTat-9
86TopTif-433
87Don-226
87Fle-390
87FleGlo-390
87Top-217
87TopTif-217
89Top-6
Cody, Buffalo (Bill)
87AllandGN-40
88GooN16-15
Cody, Ron
92BelMarC-8
93AppFoxC-5
93AppFoxF-2452
Cody, William
92BelMarF-1433
Coe, Keith
94BoiHawC-8
94BoiHawF-3347
95BoiHawTI-11
Coe, Ryan
96MidLeaAB-27
96QuaCitRB-13
Coentopp, Kevin
86SpoIndC-175
Cofer, Brian
90WatIndS-4
91ColIndC-11
91ColIndP-1478
92KinIndC-3
92KinIndF-2468
Coffee, Gary
96BesAutS-21
96Bow-225
96Exc-57
96LanLugB-9
Coffey, Mike
85CedRapRT-3
86ElmPioRSP-5
87WinHavRSP-11
Coffey, Paul
91StaCluCM-45
91StaCluMO-40
Coffey, Stephen
90GenCubP-3047
90GenCubS-4
91PeoChiP-1346
Coffman, Dick (Samuel R.)
28StaPlaCE-11
33Gou-101
34BatR31-92
34GouCanV-23
34TarThoBD-6
35DiaMatCS3T1-34
35GouPuzR-5D
35GouPuzR-6D
35GouPuzR-11F
35GouPuzR-13D
39PlaBal-24
40PlaBal-55
40PlaBal-140

91ConTSN-321
Coffman, George David
39PlaBal-147
41Gou-32
Coffman, Jim
82AmaGolST-12
Coffman, Kevin
85DurBulT-5
86DurBulP-5
87GreBraB-20
87SouLeaAJ-19
88BlaYNPRWL-54
88DonRoo-49
88Fle-536
88FleGlo-536
88TopTra-29T
88TopTraT-29T
89Bow-282
89BowTif-282
89OPC-44
89Top-488
89TopTif-488
91JacGenLD-555
91JacGenP-918
91LinDriAA-555
92GreBraS-232
92RicBraF-370
93CalCanF-1157
88RicBraBC-21
97RicBraBC-23
Coggin, David
95MarPhiTI-6
96BesAutSA-13
96Bow-298
96PieBolWB-7
96Top-431
97Bow-174
97BowCerBIA-CA14
97BowCerGIA-CA14
97BowInt-174
Coggins, Franklin
68OPC-96
68SenTeal-3
68Top-96
68TopVen-96
Coggins, Rich (Richard A.)
73OPC-611
73OriJohP-2
73Top-611
74OPC-353
74Top-353
75OPC-167
75Top-167
76OPC-572
76SSP-446
76Top-572
91OriCro-79
92YanWIZ7-36
Coghen, Al
77WauMetT-6
78WauMetT-6
Coghill, Dave
80AndBraT-7
Cohea, Dave
77CliDodT-3
82AlbDukT-25
83AlbDukT-24
Cohen, Alta (Albert)
90DodTar-132
Cohen, Andy (Andrew Howard)
28W56PlaC-H13
33Gou-52
33GouCanV-52
60Top-466
95ConTSN-1334
Cohen, Jim
92NegLeaK-13
92NegLeaRLI-10
95NegLeaL2-15
Cohen, John
88MisStaB-3
89MisStaB-7
90MisStaB-6
91Cla/Bes-78
91VisOakC-20
91VisOakP-1752
Cohen, Tony
87MacPirP-23
88AugPirP-380
Cohick, Emmitt
91QuaCitAC-23
91QuaCitAP-2642
92PalSprAC-21
92PalSprAF-852
93MidAngF-331
94MidAngF-2450
94MidAngOHP-3
95MidAngOHP-9
95MidAngTI-9
97MidAngOHP-5
Cohoon, Don
86WauTimP-4
88ChaWheB-18
89WinSpiS-5
Coin, Mike
85BelBreT-5
Coker, Jimmie Goodwin
60PhiJayP-5
60Top-438
61Top-144
63Top-456
64Top-211
64TopVen-211
65OPC-192
65RedEnq-4
65Top-192
66Top-292
66TopVen-292
67OPC-158
67Top-158
Coker, Kerry
92DavLipB-7
93DavLipB-5
Coker, Kyle
92DavLipB-8
92DavLipB-23
Coker, Larry
88FayGenP-1084
Colarusso, Sam
88CapCodPPaLP-105
89AncGlaP-8
Colavito, Rocky (Rocco D.)
47Exh-45A
47Exh-45B
55DonWin-15
57IndSoh-4
57SwiFra-18
57Top-212
58HarSta-14
58Top-368
59Baz-7
59HomRunD-6
59Ind-2
59Kah-7
59Top-166
59Top-420
59Top-462
59TopVen-166
60ArmCoi-5
60Baz-30
60NuHi-68
60TigJayP-5
60Top-260
60Top-400
60TopTat-9
60TopTat-88
61Baz-17
61NuSco-468
61Pos-36A
61Pos-36B
61TigJayP-6
61Top-44
61Top-330
62AurRec-4
62Baz-42
62ExhStaB-10
62Pos-19
62PosCan-19
62SalPlaC-28
62ShiPlaC-28
62TigJayP-5
62TigPosCF-6
62Top-20
62Top-314
62Top-472
62TopBuc-18
62TopStal-46
62TopVen-20
63BasMagM-17
63Baz-33
63ExhStaB-16
63Jel-50
63Pos-50
63SalMetC-58
63TigJayP-5
63Top-4
63Top-240
63TopStil-11
64Baz-33
64Top-320
64TopCoi-46
64TopGia-9
64TopSta-65
64TopStaU-19
64TopTatl-31
64TopVen-320
65Baz-33
65OldLonC-23
65Top-380
65TopEmbl-46
65TopTral-45
66Baz-15
66IndTeal-3
66OPC-150
66Top-150
66Top-220
66TopRubl-20
66TopVen-150
66TopVen-220
67Baz-15
67CokCapl-4
67DexPre-55
67OPC-109
67Top-109
67Top-580
68OPC-99
68Top-99
68TopVen-99
73OPC-449
73Top-449A
73Top-449B
78TigDeaCS-1
79TCM50-216
81TigDetN-99
82OhiHaloF-36
83Roy-6
83TigAlKS-19
84OCoandSI-12
84OCoandSI-181
85CirK-27
89SweBasG-126
90DodTar-133
90PacLeg-18
90SweBasG-119
91SweBasG-116
92ActPacA-65
92UppDecS-23
92YanWIZ6-28
93MetIma-8
93TedWil-33
94TedWil-146
Colavito, Steve
88WatIndP-679
Colbern, Mike (Michael M.)
79IowOakP-6
79Top-704
80IowOakP-2A
80IowOakP-2B
80Top-664
81EdmTraRR-19
81Top-522
82RicBraT-22
Colbert, Craig
88CliGiaP-707
89ShrCapP-1844
89TexLeaAGS-30
90CMC-543
90PhoFirC-16
90PhoFirP-18
90ProAAAF-44
91LinDriAAA-380
91PhoFirLD-380
91PhoFirP-70
92DonRoo-26
92PhoFirF-2826
92StaClu-891
92StaCluECN-891
92Ult-588
93Fle-528
93GiaMot-21
93GiaPos-18
93PacSpa-610
93Sco-255
93Sel-338
93StaCluG-27
93Top-91
93TopGol-91
93TopInaM-91
93TopMic-91
94ChaKniF-897
96LasVegSB-9
Colbert, Nate (Nathan)
66Top-596
69MilBra-63
69Top-408
70DayDaiNM-41
70MLBOffS-111
70OPC-11
70Top-11
70TopScr-7
71Kel-72
71MLBOffS-223
71OPC-235
71Top-235
71TopCoi-77
71TopGreM-28
71TopSup-22
71TopTat-3
72Kel-41
72MilBra-78
72PadTeal-7
72Top-571
72Top-572
73Kel2D-33
73LinPor-154
73OPC-340
73Top-340
73TopCanL-11
73TopCom-5
73TopPin-5
74Kel-19
74OPC-125
74PadDea-5
74PadMcDD-3
74Top-125A
74Top-125B
74TopDecE-34
74TopSta-91
75Hos-76
75OPC-599
75Top-599
76LauDiaJ-16
76OPC-495
76SSP-330
76Top-495
77PadSchC-13A
77PadSchC-13B
77PadSchC-14
77PadSchC-28
77Top-433
86PadGreT-1
87AstShowSTh-4
87WicPilRD-6
88WicPilRD-17
89PadMag-12
89RivRedWB-24
89RivRedWCLC-27
89RivRedWP-1391
90HOFStiB-80
90RivRedWB-19
90RivRedWCLC-26
90RivRedWP-2622
93UppDecS-13
94TedWil-85
Colbert, Rick
81BriRedST-10
85TucTorC-59
87LouRedTI-10
88ArkTraGS-1
89SprCarB-27
90SavCarP-2084
91HamRedC-29
91HamRedP-4056
92SprCarC-27
92SprCarF-885
93CanIndF-2853
Colbert, Vince
71MLBOffS-365
71OPC-231
71Top-231
72OPC-84
72Top-84
Colborn, Jim
71MLBOffS-29
71OPC-38
71Top-38
72OPC-386
72Top-386
73LinPor-99
73OPC-408
73Top-408
74OPC-75
74Top-75
74TopDecE-49
74TopSta-193
75OPC-305
75Top-305
76BreA&P-3
76OPC-521
76SSP-226
76Top-521
77Top-331
78OPC-116
78SSP270-238
78Top-129
79OPC-137
79Top-276
85IowCubT-29
86BreGreT-9
86IowCubP-7
94BreMilB-214
94WesMicWC-26
94WesMicWF-2312
95WesMicWTI-48
96ModA'sB-27
Colbrunn, Greg
88MidLeaAGS-42
88RocExpLC-8
89WesPalBES-7
90Bes-5
90JacExpB-1
90JacExpP-1377
90ProAaA-53
91Bow-449
91Don-425
91OPC-91
91StaClu-215
91Top-91
91TopDesS-91
91TopMic-91
91TopTif-91
91UppDec-15
92Don-557
92FleUpd-96
92IndIndF-1864
93ClaGam-22
93Don-328
93ExpPosN-7
93Fla-79
93FleFinE-91
93FleMajLP-B3
93Lea-55
93OPC-137
93PanSti-225
93Pin-538
93Sco-271
93Sel-295
93StaClu-522
93StaCluFDI-522
93StaCluMOP-522
93Top-464
93TopGol-464
93TopInaM-464
93TopMic-464
93Toy-74
93Ult-64
93UppDec-342
93UppDecGold-342
93USPlaCR-3H
94Don-93
94Fla-381
94Fle-534
94FleUpd-134
94Pin-474
94PinArtP-474
94PinMusC-474
94ScoRoo-RT92
94ScoRooGR-RT92
94Sel-387
94SpoRoo-146
94SpoRooAP-146
94Top-134
94TopGol-134
94TopSpa-134
94TopTra-47T
95ColCho-312
95ColChoGS-312
95ColChoSS-312
95Don-463
95DonPreP-463
95DonTopotO-240
95Emo-127
95Fla-136
95Fle-330
95Lea-116
95LeaLim-163
95Pac-171
95Pin-206

95PinArtP-206
95PinMusC-206
95Sco-97
95ScoGolR-97
95ScoPlaTS-97
95Sel-137
95SelArtP-137
95Spo-72
95SpoArtP-72
95StaClu-459
95StaCluMOP-459
95StaCluSTWS-459
95Sum-29
95SumNthD-29
95Top-476
95TopCyb-269
95Ult-378
95UltGolM-378
95UppDec-357
95UppDecED-357
95UppDecEDG-357
96Cir-127
96CirRav-127
96ColCho-152
96ColChoGS-152
96ColChoSS-152
96Don-133
96DonPreP-133
96EmoXL-184
96Fin-B176
96FinRef-B176
96Fla-259
96Fle-384
96FleTif-384
96Lea-40
96LeaPrePB-40
96LeaPrePG-40
96LeaPrePS-40
96MetUni-163
96MetUniP-163
96Pac-76
96PanSti-16
96Pin-66
96PinAfi-102
96PinAfiAP-102
96ProSta-70
96Sco-347
96ScoDugC-B72
96ScoDugCAP-B72
96Sel-138
96SelArtP-138
96SP-90
96StaClu-19
96StaCluMOP-19
96Sum-14
96SumAbo&B-14
96SumArtP-14
96SumFoi-14
96Top-408
96TopGal-77
96TopGalPPI-77
96Ult-197
96UltGolM-197
96UppDec-77
97Fin-269
97FinRef-269
97Fle-327
97Fle-621
97FleTif-327
97FleTif-621
97MetUni-172
97Pac-299
97PacLigB-299
97PacSil-299
97Sco-69
97Sco-357
97ScoHobR-357
97ScoPreS-69
97ScoResC-357
97ScoShoS-69
97ScoShoS-357
97ScoShoSAP-69
97ScoShoSAP-357
97StaClu-353
97StaCluMOP-353
97Top-294
97Ult-334
97UltGolME-334
97UltPlaME-334
Cole, Abdul
95KanCouCTI-20
Cole, Alex
86FloStaLAP-11
86St.PetCP-6
87ArkTraP-20
88LouRedBC-11
88LouRedBP-438
88LouRedBTI-14
89LouRedBC-21
89LouRedBP-1266
89LouRedBTI-14
89St.PetCS-7
89TriA AAC-14
90CMC-519
90Fle-244
90FleCan-244
90LasVegSC-16
90LasVegSP-133
90ProAAAF-21
90TriAAAC-14
90UppDec-751
91Bow-64
91Cla1-T36
91Don-383
91Fle-365
91IndFanC-7
91Lea-108
91OPC-421
91OPCPre-24
91PanCanT1-48
91PanFreS-222
91Sco-555
91Sco100RS-13
91StaClu-392
91Top-421
91TopDeb90-33
91TopDesS-421
91TopMic-421
91TopRoo-6
91TopTif-421
91TopTriH-A5
91ToyRoo-6
91Ult-110
91UppDec-654
92Bow-173
92Don-220
92Fle-108
92Hig5-44
92IndFanC-7
92Lea-307
92OPC-170
92PanSti-50
92Pin-66
92Sco-463
92ScoProP-20
92StaClu-437
92Stu-165
92Top-170
92TopGol-170
92TopGolW-170
92TopMic-170
92TriPla-49
92Ult-345
92UppDec-197
93Bow-36
93CadDis-14
93Don-70
93Don-786
93Fin-12
93FinRef-12
93Fla-38
93Fle-408
93FleFinE-27
93Lea-312
93PacSpa-426
93Pin-556
93PinExpOD-8
93RocUSPC-7H
93RocUSPC-12C
93Sco-400
93SP-219
93StaClu-458
93StaCluFDI-458
93StaCluMOP-458
93StaCluRoc-6
93Stu-106
93Top-591
93TopGol-591
93TopInaM-591
93TopMic-591
93TopPos-2
93TopPos-3
93Ult-346
93UppDec-538
93UppDecGold-538
94ExtBas-115
94Fin-292
94FinRef-292
94Fla-312
94Fle-439
94FleUpd-60
94Pac-194
94Pin-467
94PinArtP-467
94PinMusC-467
94Sco-336
94ScoGolR-336
94ScoRoo-RT50
94ScoRooGR-RT50
94SpoRoo-142
94SpoRooAP-142
94StaClu-584
94StaCluFDI-584
94StaCluGR-584
94StaCluMOP-584
94TopTra-12T
94Ult-386
95ColCho-492
95ColChoGS-492
95ColChoSS-492
95Don-304
95DonPreP-304
95DonTopotO-107
95Fin-139
95FinRef-139
95Fle-198
95Lea-361
95Pin-190
95PinArtP-190
95PinMusC-190
95Sco-404
95ScoGolR-404
95ScoPlaTS-404
95StaClu-207
95StaCluFDI-207
95StaCluMOP-207
95StaCluSTWS-207
95StaCluVR-108
95Top-331
95TopCyb-168
95Ult-73
95UltGolM-73
95USPlaCMLA-3H
96PawRedSDD-3
95StaCluVRMC-108
Cole, Bert
21Nei-28
22E120-49
22W573-20
23WilChoV-21
Cole, Butch
91AppFoxC-23
91AppFoxP-1728
92BasCitRC-15
92BasCitRF-3857
93MemChiF-386
Cole, Chris
89BurIndS-5
Cole, David
52Bow-132
53BowBW-38
53BraJohC-6
83Bra53F-30
Cole, Dick (Richard Roy)
52MotCoo-35
53BraSpiaS3-7
54Bow-27
54Top-84
55Bow-28
57Top-234
58UniOil-2
94TopArc1-84
94TopArc1G-84
Cole, Doc
80ChaO'sP-4
80ChaO'sW-4
Cole, Eric
96AubDouB-21
Cole, Howard
90RenSilSCLC-283
Cole, Jason
94VerExpC-8
94VerExpF-3902
96DelShoB-14
96WesPalBEB-6
Cole, Jim
93HelBreF-4085
93HelBreSP-19
94BelBreC-5
94BelBreF-93
94MidLeaAF-MDW7
95Bow-187
95Exc-69
95SPML-79
95UppDecML-182
96Bow-195
95UppDecMLFS-182
Cole, Joey
79QuaCitCT-13
Cole, King (Leonard)
09SpoNewSM-50
10ChiE-4
10DarChoE-10
10JuJuDE-11
11BasBatEU-12
11MecDFT-12
11PloCanE-17
12T207-33
14B18B-22
Cole, Mark
88OklSoo-10
89OklSoo-10
90LakTigS-4
92StoPorC-20
92StoPorF-39
93StoPorF-749
Cole, Marvin
88WytCubP-1982
90PeoChiUTI-U5
91WinSpiC-18
91WinSpiP-2835
Cole, Michael
81WisRapTT-15
Cole, Popeye (Robert)
88SumBraP-392
89BurBraP-1627
89BurBraS-5
90CarLeaA-30
90DurBulTI-12
91GreBraC-20
91GreBraLD-204
91GreBraP-3014
91LinDriAA-204
Cole, Rodger
85PhiTas-42
85PorBeaC-45
86IndIndTI-17
Cole, Stu (Stewart)
87EugEmeP-2652
89MemChiB-9
89MemChiP-1184
89MemChiS-7
89Sta-41
90MemChiB-4
90MemChiP-1014
90MemChiS-5
90StaFS7-84
91LinDriAAA-330
91OmaRoyLD-330
91OmaRoyP-1040
92OmaRoyF-2967
92OmaRoyS-328
92SkyAAAF-150
92StaClu-553
92TopDeb91-37
93ColSprSSF-3092
94ColSprSSF-740
96AshTouB-3
Cole, Terry
95AshTouTI-NNO
Cole, Tim
78GreBraT-6
79SavBraT-20
82RicBraT-3
83DurBulT-18
Cole, Victor
89MemChiB-19
89MemChiP-1185
89MemChiS-8
90CMC-830
90MemChiB-20
90MemChiP-1006
90MemChiS-6
91LinDriAAA-331
91OmaRoyLD-331
91OmaRoyP-1028
92Bow-239
92BufBisF-316
92BufBisS-29
92DonRoo-27
92FleUpd-113
92SkyAAAF-13
93BufBisF-509
93Don-120
93Top-453
93TopGol-453
93TopInaM-453
93TopMic-453
Cole, Winston
76BatRouCT-8
77SalPirT-7
Coleman, Billy
91OneYanP-4146
92GreHorC-14
92GreHorF-770
93GreHorC-5
93GreHorF-879
94AbaYanF-1432
94TamYanC-5
94TamYanF-2375
95NorNavTI-52
Coleman, Choo Choo (Clarence)
47Exh-46
61Top-502
63ExhStaB-17
63Top-27
64MetJayP-3
64Top-251
64TopVen-251
66Top-561
76Met63 S-4
81TCM60I-298
82MetGal62-25
89TidTidC-5
91MetWIZ-79
Coleman, Dale
90SanAntMGS-11
91SanAntMP-2967
91VerBeaDC-6
91VerBeaDP-767
Coleman, Dave (David Lee)
79TolMudHT-17
80ColCliP-17
80ColCliT-19
81ColCliP-17
81ColCliT-18
Coleman, DeWayne
86VisOakP-7
87WinSpiP-25
88ChaWheB-19
Coleman, Ed (Parke Edward)
34Gou-28
34GouCanV-76
35DiaMatCS3T1-35
35GouPuzR-8J
35GouPuzR-9J
93ConTSN-921
Coleman, Elliot
92NegLeaRLI-11
Coleman, Georgia
37DixLid-1
37DixPre-1
Coleman, Glenn
91BluOriC-14
91BluOriP-4139
Coleman, Gordy (Gordon C.)
47Exh-47
56RedBurB-4
59RedBurBP-3
60HenHouW-5
60Top-257
60UniOil-19
61Kah-9
61RedJayP-4
61Top-194
62Jel-116
62Kah-7
62Pos-116
62PosCan-116
62RedEnq-4
62RedJayP-3
62SalPlaC-110
62ShiPlaC-110
62Top-508
62TopStal-113
63Jel-125
63Kah-8
63Pos-125
63RedEnq-5
63RedFreBC-3
63RedJayP-2
63Top-90
64RedJayP-2
64Top-577
65Kah-10
65RedEnq-5

65Top-289
66Top-494
67CokCapR-3
67DexPre-56
67OPC-61
67Top-61
93UppDecS-8
Coleman, Guy
52LavPro-46
Coleman, Hampton
52LaPat-3
53ExhCan-52
Coleman, Hampton (Solomon)
52Par-65
Coleman, J. Dale
89VerBeaDS-5
Coleman, Jeff
85CloHSS-11
Coleman, Jerry (Gerald F.)
47Exh-48
47PM1StaP1-33
47StaPinP2-10
49Bow-225
50Bow-47
50Dra-26
51BerRos-A6
51Bow-49
51R42SmaS-10
51TopRedB-18
52BerRos-9
52Bow-73
52StaCalL-70E
52StaCalS-84C
52Top-237
53Dor-126
54Bow-81
54NewYorJA-44
55Bow-99
55RobGouS-25
55RobGouW-25
56Top-316
57Top-192
77PadSchC-15
78PadFamF-6
79TCM50-36
80Top-356
83TopRep5-237
84PadSmo-5
90PadMag-8
91PadCok-2
91SweBasG-19
92YanWIZA-13
93UppDecAH-33
94UppDecAH-57
94UppDecAH1-57
Coleman, Joe H.
66TopVen-333
67OPC-167
67Top-167
68Top-573
69MilBra-64
69MLBOffS-103
69SenTeal-6
69SenTeal8-8
69Top-246
69TopSta-234
69TopTeaP-23
70MLBOffS-281
70OPC-127
70Top-127
71MLBOffS-390
71OPC-403
71Top-403
72Kel-18A
72Kel-18B
72MilBra-79
72OPC-96
72Top-96
72Top-640
73Kel2D-48
73OPC-120
73TigJew-6
73Top-120
74Kel-3
74OPC-240
74Tig-3
74Top-240
74TopDecE-53
74TopSta-173
75Hos-60
75OPC-42
75Top-42
76Hos-89
76OPC-68
76OPC-456
76SSP-358
76Top-68
76Top-456
77Top-219
78Top-554
79OPC-166
79PorBeaT-11
79Top-329
80SpoIndT-5
80Top-542
81SpoIndT-19
81TigDetN-126
82SpoIndT-25
83PeoSunF-29
89PacSenL-109
Coleman, Joe P.
49PhiBul-12
50Bow-141
51Bow-120
53Top-279
54OriEss-6
54Top-156
55Bow-3
55OriEss-6
55RedMan-AL17
55RobGouS-20
55RobGouW-20
55Top-162
76OPC-68
76Top-68
91OriCro-80
91TopArc1-279
94TopArc1-156
94TopArc1G-156
Coleman, John Francis
87BucN28-88
87OldJudN-89
88GandBCGCE-8
88WG1CarG-56
Coleman, Ken
89UtiBluSP-4
92SarWhiSCB-2
92SarWhiSF-212
93SarWhiSC-7
94BirBarC-5
94BirBarF-627
95OrlCubF-16
Coleman, Matthew
89BriTigS-5
Coleman, Michael
95MicBatCTI-6
96HilStaHWB-17
96SarRedSB-11
96Top-438
Coleman, Paul
89HigSchPLS-10
89JohCitCS-6
90Bow-199
90BowTif-199
90CMC-842
90OPC-654
90SavCarP-2082
90Sco-662
90Top-654
90TopTif-654
90TopTVCa-43
91Bow-385
91SprCarP-755
Coleman, Ray (Raymond L.)
50Bow-250
51Bow-136
52Bow-201
52Top-211
52WhiSoxH-1
79DiaGre-194
83TopRep5-211
Coleman, Rickey
85BeaGolGT-2
Coleman, Rico
89SpoIndSP-24
90ChaRaiB-6
90ChaRaiP-2053
Coleman, Ronnie
91BurIndP-3314
92BurIndC-26
92BurIndF-1669
93BurIndC-8
93BurIndF-3310
Coleman, Scott
91MarPhiC-25
91MarPhiP-3445
92MarPhiC-13
92MarPhiF-3047
Coleman, Ty
80BurBeeT-14
Coleman, Vince
84LouRedR-20
85CarTeal-6
85DonHig-29
85DonHig-54
85FleUpd-28
85LouRedR-5
85TopTifT-24T
85TopTra-24T
86BasStaB-22
86CarIGAS-2
86CarKASD-1
86CarSchM-2
86CarTeal-8
86Don-181
86Don-651
86Fle-31
86Fle-636
86Fle-637
86FleLeaL-7
86FleLimE-11
86FleMin-7
86FleSluBC-M4
86FleStiC-25
86KayB-5
86Lea-115
86Lea-225
86OPC-370
86OPCBoxB-D
86QuaGra-3
86SevCoi-S9
86Spo-24
86Spo-136
86Spo-176
86Top-201
86Top-370
86TopGaloC-2
86TopGloS-21
86TopMinL-60
86TopSti-5
86TopSti-47
86TopSti-306
86TopSup-8
86TopTat-16
86TopTif-201
86TopTif-370
86TopWaxBC-D
87CarSmo-24
87ClaGam-30
87Don-263
87DonHig-36
87DonOpeD-60
87Fle-290
87FleGlo-290
87FleLeaL-11
87FleLimE-10
87FleMin-21
87FleSluBC-M3
87FleStiC-25
87KayB-11
87KraFoo-18
87Lea-194
87OPC-119
87RedFolSB-8
87Spo-65
87Spo-152
87Spo-199
87SpoTeaP-12
87StuPan-11
87Top-590
87TopCoi-29
87TopGloS-38
87TopMinL-32
87TopSti-50
87TopTif-590
88Baz-5
88CarSmo-19
88ClaBlu-223
88Don-293
88DonBasB-44
88Fle-27
88Fle-634
88FleBasM-7
88FleExcS-11
88FleGlo-27
88FleGlo-634
88FleGlo-WS6
88FleLeaL-7
88FleMin-106
88FleStiC-117
88FleWorS-6
88K-M-8
88Lea-128
88MSAIceTD-11
88MSAJifPD-7
88OPC-260
88PanSti-394
88Sco-68
88Sco-652
88ScoGlo-68
88ScoGlo-652
88ScoYouS2-24
88Spo-67
88Spo-221
88StaLinCa-3
88Top-1
88Top-260
88TopBig-5
88TopMinL-70
88TopRevLL-3
88TopSti-4
88TopSti-47
88TopTif-1
88TopTif-260
88TopUKM-16
88TopUKMT-16
88Woo-2
89Baz-6
89Bow-443
89BowTif-443
89CadEllD-10
89CarSmo-2
89Don-19
89Don-181
89DonAll-38
89DonBasB-19
89DonPop-38
89DonSupD-19
89Fle-445
89FleBasA-8
89FleExcS-7
89FleGlo-445
89FleLeaL-6
89OPC-90
89PanSti-188
89PanSti-229
89Sco-155
89ScoHot1S-86
89ScoSco-35
89Spo-113
89Top-90
89TopBasT-141
89TopBig-124
89TopGloA-17
89TopMinL-34
89TopSti-43
89TopSti-154
89TopTif-90
89TVSpoM-28
89TVSpoM-132
89UppDec-253
90BasWit-45
90Baz-8
90Bow-198
90BowTif-198
90CarSmo-1
90ClaBlu-105
90Don-279
90DonBesN-138
90Fle-245
90FleAwaW-9
90FleCan-245
90HOFStiB-100
90KayB-7
90Lea-90
90MLBBasB-35
90MSAHolD-15
90OPC-6
90OPC-660
90PanSti-216
90PanSti-336
90PanSti-383
90PubSti-213
90PubSti-609
90RedFolSB-19
90Sco-260
90Sco100S-73
90Spo-142
90SprCarDGB-31
90Top-6
90Top-660
90TopBig-184
90TopDou-12
90TopMinL-73
90TopSti-4
90TopSti-39
90TopTif-6
90TopTif-660
90TopTVCa-32
90UppDec-68
90UppDec-223
90VenSti-111
90VenSti-112
90Woo-10
91BasBesRB-4
91Baz-12
91Bow-471
91CadEllD-12
91Cla1-T91
91ClaGam-93
91Don-487
91Fle-629
91FleUpd-102
91Lea-427
91MetCol8-3
91MetColP-8
91MetKah-1
91OPC-160
91OPCPre-25
91PanCanT1-41
91PanFreS-35
91PanSti-35
91Pos-5
91RedFolS-21
91Sco-450
91ScoRoo-57T
91SimandSMLBL-10
91StaClu-498
91Stu-202
91Top-160
91TopDesS-160
91TopMic-160
91TopTif-160
91TopTra-23T
91TopTraT-23T
91TopTriH-N7
91Ult-212
91UppDec-461
91UppDec-768
92Bow-613
92CarMcD-42
92ClaGam-52
92Don-218
92Fle-500
92Lea-42
92MetColP-12
92MetKah-1
92OPC-500
92PanSti-227
92Pin-39
92Sco-95
92Sco100S-79
92ScoProP-24
92StaClu-40
92Stu-63
92Top-500
92TopGol-500
92TopGolW-500
92TopMic-500
92TriPla-208
92Ult-229
92UppDec-131
93Bow-186
93Don-618
93Fla-90
93Fle-467
93Lea-57
93MetColP-27
93MetKah-11
93PacSpa-194
93PanSti-252
93Pin-69
93Sco-650
93Sel-175
93SP-148
93StaClu-195
93StaCluFDI-195
93StaCluMOP-195
93Stu-56
93Top-765
93TopGol-765
93TopInaM-765
93TopMic-765
93TriPla-14
93Ult-424
93UppDec-748
93UppDecGold-748
94Bow-499

94ColC-601
94ColChoGS-601
94ColChoSS-601
94ExtBas-84
94Fin-326
94FinRef-326
94Fla-56
94FleUpd-47
94Lea-240
94ScoRoo-RT12
94ScoRooGR-RT12
94Sel-369
94SpoRoo-24
94SpoRooAP-24
94StaClu-570
94StaCluFDI-570
94StaCluGR-570
94StaCluMOP-570
94TopTra-106T
94Ult-361
94UppDec-376
94UppDecED-376
95ColCho-458
95ColChoGS-458
95ColChoSS-458
95Don-118
95DonPreP-118
95DonTopotO-84
95Fle-154
95Lea-318
95MarPac-2
95MarPac-28
95Pac-198
95Sco-261
95ScoGolR-261
95ScoPlaTS-261
95StaClu-68
95StaCluFDI-68
95StaCluMO-12
95StaCluMOP-68
95StaCluSTWS-68
95StaCluVR-42
95Top-419
95TopCyb-219
95TopLeaL-LL42
95UppDecSE-52
95UppDecSEG-52
95USPlaCMLA-13H
96Don-496
96DonPreP-496
96EmoXL-163
96Fla-231
96Fle-233
96FleTif-233
96FleUpd-U117
96FleUpdTC-U117
96MetMod-2
96MetUni-105
96MetUniP-105
96Pac-413
96PanSti-229
96Sco-441
95StaCluVRMC-42
96Top-263
96Ult-458
96UltGolM-458
96VanCanB-7
97Ult-499
97UltGolME-499
97UltPlaME-499
Coleman, W. Rip
57Top-354
59Top-51
59TopVen-51
60MapLeaSF-4
60Top-179
60TopVen-179
61MapLeaBH-5
91OriCro-81
Coles, Cad (Cadwallader R.)
09T206-481
Coles, Chuck (Charles Edward)
59RedEnq-3
59Top-120
59TopVen-120
Coles, Darnell
81WauTimT-19
83ChaLooT-1
84Don-630
84MarMot-26
84SalLakCGC-190
85CalCanC-96
85DomLeaS-26
85Don-118
85Top-108
85TopTif-108
86Don-557
86FleUpd-27
86Top-337
86TopTif-337
86TopTra-26T
86TopTraT-26T
87Don-47
87Don-230
87DonOpeD-215
87Fle-148
87FleGlo-148
87OPC-388
87SevCoi-D1
87SpoTeaP-15
87TigCaiD-2
87TigCok-14
87Top-411
87TopSti-271
87TopTif-411
88Don-572
88DonBasB-185
88OPC-46
88Sco-554
88ScoGlo-554
88StaLinPi-6
88Top-46
88TopBig-255
88TopTif-46
89Bow-217
89BowTif-217
89Don-566
89DonBasB-163
89Fle-544
89FleGlo-544
89MarMot-23
89Sco-83
89Top-738
89TopBig-133
89TopTif-738
89UppDec-339
90Bow-480
90BowTif-480
90Don-212
90Fle-509
90FleCan-509
90MarMot-22
90OPC-232
90PanSti-145
90PubSti-429
90Sco-62
90Top-232
90TopSti-227
90TopTif-232
90UppDec-311
90VenSti-113
91Fle-333
91LinDriAAA-381
91OPC-506
91PhoFirLD-381
91PhoFirP-79
91Sco-629
91Top-506
91TopDesS-506
91TopMic-506
91TopTif-506
92Bow-382
92NasSouS-281
92RedKah-26
93BluJayD-16
93BluJayFS-6
93Fle-388
93FleFinE-290
93PacSpa-651
93Sco-416
93SelRoo-105T
93UppDec-721
93UppDecGold-721
94BluJayUSPC-5S
94BluJayUSPC-12D
94Fle-328
94Sco-537
94ScoGolR-537
94StaCluT-162
94StaCluTFDI-162
94Ult-137
95Sco-35
95ScoGolR-35
95ScoPlaTS-35
Colescott, Rob
85LitFalMT-15
86LitFalMP-6
87ColMetP-27
88SavCarP-335
88SouAtlLAGS-24
89SprCarB-5
Coletta, Chris
75IntLeaAT-12
75IntLeaAT-27
Coletti, John
91BilMusSP-13
Coletti, Mike
91BilMusP-3745
Colina, Victor
76VenLeaS-140
80VenLeaS-202
Collazo, Alfonso
76VenLeaS-161
Collett, Mike
93BelMarC-1
93BelMarF-3199
94BelMarC-8
94BelMarF-3225
Colletti, Manny
80WisRapTT-16
82OmaRoyT-15
82OrlTwi8SCT-4
Colley, Jay
88RocRedWP-220
Collie, Tim
96AugGreB-6
Collier, Anthony
89GreFalDSP-22
90StaFS7-20
90VerBeaDS-8
91BakDodCLC-20
91CalLeLA-17
92ClaFS7-204
92VerBeaDC-11
92VerBeaDF-2888
93SanAntMF-3016
Collier, Dan
92ElmPioC-2
92ElmPioF-1394
93UtiBluSC-1
93UtiBluSF-3545
94LynRedSC-6
94LynRedSF-1903
96TreThuB-23
Collier, Ervin
92KinMetC-20
92KinMetF-1523
93KinMetF-3789
Collier, Lou
93WelPirC-4
93WelPirF-3362
94AugGreC-1
94AugGreF-3014
94SouAtlLAF-SAL33
95Bow-5
95Exc-252
95LynHilTI-4
95SPML-134
96Bow-158
96CarMudB-19
97ColCho-425
97DonLim-22
97DonLimLE-22
Collier, Slick
93KinMetC-5
Collins, Allen
86WesPalBEP-8
87WesPalBEP-666
88WesPalBES-8
90CanIndB-25
90CanIndP-1286
90CanIndS-2
Collins, Bill (William S.)
12ImpTobC-34
90DodTar-960
Collins, Chris
86QuaCitAP-7
87MidAngP-4
88MidAngGS-7
Collins, Dave (David S.)
75SalLakCC-2
76OPC-363
76SalLakCGC-19
76SSP-191
76Top-363
77OPC-248
77Top-431
78Pep-7
78SSP270-135
78Top-254
79Top-622
80RedEnq-29
80Top-73
81AllGamPI-139
81CokTeaS-38
81Don-185
81Fle-201
81OPC-175
81Top-175
81TopScr-84
81TopSti-162
81TopSupHT-32
82Don-169
82Fle-61
82FleSta-14
82OPC-349
82Top-595
82TopSti-33
82TopStiV-33
82TopTra-20T
83Don-234
83Fle-377
83FleSti-42
83MadMusF-3
83OPC-359
83Top-359
83TopTra-21T
84BluJayFS-9
84Don-650
84Fle-151
84Nes792-733
84OPC-38
84Top-733
84TopTif-733
85A'sMot-14
85AllGamPI-53
85Don-241
85Fle-102
85FleStaS-55
85FleUpd-29
85Lea-172
85OPC-164
85Top-463
85TopSti-363
85TopTif-463
85TopTifT-25T
85TopTra-25T
86Don-218
86Fle-415
86FleUpd-28
86OPC-271
86TigCaiD-3
86Top-271
86TopSti-172
86TopTif-271
86TopTra-27T
86TopTraT-27T
87Don-215
87Fle-149
87FleGlo-149
87SpoTeaP-20
87Top-148
87TopTif-148
88RedKah-22
88Sco-371
88ScoGlo-371
88StaLinRe-3
89Sco-267
89T/MSenL-22
89UppDec-351
90BluJayHS-5
90CarSmo-2
90TopTVCa-33
92YanWIZ8-34
Collins, Don
80TacTigT-5
82SprCarF-18
Collins, Eddie (Edw.T.) Sr.
03WilCarE-7
08AmeCarE-41
09AmeCarE-26
09ColChiE-58
09PhiCarE-6
09RamT20-28
09SpoNewSM-16
09T206-72
10CouT21-107
10CouT21-108
10CouT21-109
10CouT21-271
10DarChoE-11
10DomDisP-27
10E101-11
10E102-5
10E12AmeCDC-11
10E98-9
10LuxCigPP-4
10MelMinE-11
10NadCarE-12
10NadE1-11
10PeoT21-13A
10PeoT21-13B
10PeoT21-13C
10RedCroT-12
10RedCroT-98
10RedCroT-177
10SepAnoP-8
10StaCarE-7
10SweCapPP-43A
10SweCapPP-43B
10W555-16
10W555-17
11A'sFirT20-4
11DiaGumP-10
11L1L-125
11MecDFT-1
11PloCanE-18
11S74Sil-29
11S81LarS-100
11SpoLifCW-69
11SpoLifM-89
11T205-31A
11T205-31B
11TurRedT-87
12ColRedB-58
12ColTinT-58
12HasTriFT-6
12HasTriFT-25A
12HasTriFT-25B
12HasTriFT-26C
12T207-34
13PolGroW-6
14CraJacE-7
14PieStaT-14
15AmeCarE-9
15CraJacE-7
15SpoNewM-33
15SpoNewP-3
16BF2FP-9
16ColE13-31
16SpoNewM-34
16TanBraE-6
17HolBreD-16
19W514-25
20NatCarE-14
21E121So1-11
21E121So8-12
21Exh-25
21Nei-29
21OxfConE-5
22AmeCarE-12
22E120-16
22W572-14
22W573-21
22W575-18
22WilPatV-35
23MapCriV-4
23W501-38
23W515-58
25Exh-73
26Exh-74
26SpoComoA-11
27AmeCarE-16
27Exh-54
27YorCarE-47
28StaPlaCE-12
31W517-52
32USCar-1
33Gou-42
33GouCanV-42
36PC7AlbHoF-18
48ExhHoF-8
50CalHOFW-19
51TopConMA-3
59FleWil-9
59FleWil-39
59FleWil-75
60ExhWriH-8
60Fle-20
61Fle-16
61GolPre-28
63BazA-41
63GadFunC-57
63HalofFB-23
69Baz-7
69Baz-8
71FleWorS-8
72FleFamF-18

72KelATG-10
72LauGreF-43
75FlePio-20
75WhiSox1T-3
76RowExh-13
76ShaPiz-17
76WhiSoxTAG-2
77BobParHoF-14
77GalGloG-111
77GalGloG-180
77GalGloG-182
77ShaPiz-16
79RedSoxEF-16
80LauFamF-32
80PacLeg-26
80PerHaloFP-18
80SSPHOF-18
80WhiSoxGT-2
81ConTSN-39
81SpoHaloF-7
82DiaCla-29
84GalHaloFRL-17
85WhiSoxC-44
87ConSer2-27
87HygAllG-11
88ConSer5-5
88PacEigMO-8
88PacEigMO-99
89WhiSoxK-2
90BasWit-76
90PerGreM-45
91ConTSN-21
91ConTSN-312
92ConTSN-582
92Man191BSR-3
93ActPacA-89
93ActPacA2-23G
93CraJac-17
94ConTSN-1040
94ConTSN-1142
94ConTSNB-1040
94ConTSNB-1142
94TedWil-19
95ConTSN-1332
96PitPosH-4
20W516-23

Collins, Edward
95HelBreTI-20
96BelSnaTI-10

Collins, Hub (George H.)
87OldJudN-91

Collins, Jimmy (James Joseph)
03BreE10-22
04FanCraAL-8
04RedSoxUP-1
08AmeCarE-6
08RosComP-56
09RamT20-29
09T206-412
11SpoLifCW-70
11T205-196
34ButPreR-11
36PC7AlbHoF-32
36R31PasP-42
50CalHOFW-20
51TopConMA-4
60ExhWriH-9
60Fle-25
61Fle-99
63BazA-23
67TopVen-155
69SCFOldT-15
76ShaPiz-32
77BobParHoF-15
80PerHaloFP-32
80SSPHOF-32
84GalHaloFRL-32
89HOFStiB-23
94OriofB-70

Collins, Joe (Joseph E.)
47StaPinP2-11
52BerRos-10
52Bow-181
52Top-202
53Dor-105
53Dor-105A
53Top-9
54NewYorJA-45
54Top-83
55Top-63
55TopDouH-65
56Top-21
56TopPin-28
57Top-295
79TCM50-21
83TopRep5-202
84FifNatC-6
91TopArc1-9
94TopArc1-83
94TopArc1G-83

Collins, Kenneth
95DanBraTI-6

Collins, Kevin M.
65Top-581
69OPC-127
69Top-127
69TopFou-13
70Top-707
71OPC-553
71Top-553
91MetWIZ-80

Collins, Mike
92BenMusSP-14
92BilMusF-3361
94ButCopKSP-26
95SanBerSTI-28
96SanAntMB-27

Collins, Mrs. (Eddie)
79RedSoxEF-2

Collins, Pat (Tharon L.)
21Nei-35
22E120-92
22W573-22
27AmeCarE-35
28Exh-49
29ExhFou-1
91ConTSN-118

Collins, Patrick T.
26Exh-97

Collins, Phil
32OrbPinNP-22
32OrbPinUP-13
33Gou-21
33GouCanV-21
33RitCE-13D
33TatOrb-13
34DiaMatCSB-30
35ExhFou-6
93ConTSN-785

Collins, Ray
11SpoLifM-4
12RedSoxBDASP-2
15CraJacE-169
16FleBreD-18

Collins, Rip (Harry W.)
20GasAmeMBD-7
21E121So8-13
21KoBreWSI-29
22W575-19
94ConTSN-1261

Collins, Rip (James A.)
34DiaMatCSB-29
34BatR31-78
34BatR31-146
34Gou-51
35DiaMatCS3T1-36
35WheBB1-6
36DiaMatCS3T2-4
36NatChiFPR-20
36R31PasP-6
36SandSW-7
36WorWidGV-18
74Car193T-2
81DiaStaCD-116
83ConMar-34
87Car193T-4
88ConNatA-3
92CarMcD-2
92ConTSN-656
94ConTSN-1237
94ConTSNB-1237
94ConTSNB-1261

Collins, Ron
88EugEmeB-18
89EugEmeB-20

Collins, Scott
81BatTroT-19

Collins, Sean
89EugEmeB-24
90BasCitRS-4

Collins, Shano (John Francis)
11BasBatEU-13
15SpoNewM-34
16BF2FP-10
16ColE13-32
16SpoNewM-35
20NatCarE-15
21Exh-26
22E120-2
22W572-15
23WilChoV-22
75WhiSox1T-4
79RedSoxEF-22
88PacEigMO-98
92Man191BSR-4
93ConTSN-745
94ConTSN-1042
94ConTSNB-1042

Collins, Sherman
89VerBeaDS-6

Collins, Stacey
91RocExpC-3
91RocExpP-2038

Collins, Terry
75AlbDukC-8
80AlbDukT-19
82VerBeaDT-26
84AlbDukC-167
85AlbDukC-156
85DomLeaS-43
86AlbDukP-3
87AlbDukP-1
88AlbDukC-25
88AlbDukP-270
88TriAAAP-47
89BufBisC-24
89BufBisP-1668
90BufBisC-3
90BufBisP-389
90BufBisTI-7
90CMC-3
90ProAAAF-504
90TriAllGP-AAA36
91BufBisLD-49
91BufBisP-556
91LinDriAAA-49
92PirNatl-5
93PirNatl-6
94AstMot-1
95AstMot-1
96AstMot-1

Collins, Tim
85BenPhiC-5

Collins, Tony
86GenCubP-3
86PeoChiP-3

Collins, Zach
94IdaFalBF-3576
94IdaFalBSP-9

Collum, Gary
93PitMetC-4
93PitMetF-3723
94CapCitBC-2
94CapCitBF-1762

Collum, Jack
50WorWidGV-30
54Bow-204
55Bow-189
57Top-268
90DodTar-134

Colman, Frank Lloyd
52Par-9

Colmenares, Carlos
92MedHatBJF-3212
92MedHatBJSP-18
93MedHatBJF-3742
93MedHatBJSP-1

Colmenares, Luis
95AshTouTI-19
95LinVen-122
96SalAvaB-5

Colombino, Carlo
86AshTouP-5
87OscAstP-4
88ColAstB-19
88SouLeaAJ-10
89TucTorC-21
89TucTorJP-5
89TucTorP-206
91LinDriAAA-608
91TucTorLD-608
91TucTorP-2219
92CanIndF-695
92CanIndS-103
93ReaPhiF-299
96KenIndB-30

Colombino, Chris
90OscAstS-5

Colon, Angel
92WelPirC-6
92WelPirF-1328

Colon, Bartolo
94BurIndF-3786
95Bes-16
95Bow-22
95BowBes-B73
95BowBesR-B73
95KinIndTI-7
95SPML-45
95SPMLA-7
96BesAutSA-14
96Bow-312
96BowBes-100
96BowBesAR-100
96BowBesMI-9
96BowBesMIAR-9
96BowBesMIR-9
96BowBesR-100
96BowMinLP-8
96CanIndB-8
96Exc-41
96ExcSeaC-2
96Top-428
97Bow-94
97BowBes-111
97BowBesAR-111
97BowBesP-19
97BowBesPAR-19
97BowBesPR-19
97BowBesR-111
97BowCerBIA-CA15
97BowCerGIA-CA15
97BowChr-118
97BowChrI-118
97BowChrIR-118
97BowChrR-118
97BowInt-94
97ColCho-464
97Don-354
97DonLim-147
97DonLimLE-147
97DonPre-161
97DonPreCttC-161
97DonPreP-354
97DonPrePGold-354
97DonRooDK-5
97DonRooDKC-5
97DonTea-90
97DonTeaSPE-90
97Fin-275
97FinRef-275
97Fle-561
97FleTif-561
97Lea-326
97LeaFraM-326
97LeaFraMDC-326
97PinCer-131
97PinCerMBlu-131
97PinCerMG-131
97PinCerMR-131
97PinCerR-131
97PinTotCPB-131
97PinTotCPG-131
97PinTotCPR-131
97Sel-113
97SelArtP-113
97SelRegG-113
97SP-8
97StaClu-192
97StaCluM-M24
97StaCluMOP-192
97StaCluMOP-M24
97Stu-146
97StuPrePG-146
97StuPrePS-146
97Top-386
97Ult-550
97UltGolME-550
97UltPlaME-550
97UppDec-529

Colon, Charlie
88NebCor-2
90NebCor-7

Colon, Cris
87PorChaRP-22
88GasRanP-1005
89GasRanP-1014
89GasRanS-4
90ChaRanS-3
90SouAtlLAS-4
91ChaRanC-17
91ChaRanP-1321
91Cla/Bes-183
92Bow-405
92SkyAA F-266
92TulDriF-2700
92TulDriS-605
93Don-353
93LinVenB-150
93LinVenB-301
93LinVenB-319
93RanKee-107
93Sco-314
93Top-809
93TopGol-809
93TopInaM-809
93TopMic-809
93TulDriF-2739
93UppDec-14
93UppDecGold-14
94ClaGolF-180
94IowCubF-1280
94UppDecML-197
94VenLinU-227
95IowCubTI-8
95LinVen-43
93TulDriTI-6

Colon, David
88BlaYNPRWL-103
88SumBraP-411
89BlaYNPRWL-111
90CMC-702
90WatDiaB-2
90WatDiaP-2389
91PalSprAP-2027
92PalSprAC-24
92PalSprAF-853

Colon, Dennis
92BurAstC-19
92BurAstF-553
93OscAstC-8
93OscAstF-634
94JacGenF-222
95JacGenTI-21
96JacGenB-6

Colon, Felix
90WinHavRSS-2
91ElmPioC-2
91ElmPioP-3275
92WinHavRSF-1784
93LynRedSC-6
93LynRedSF-2522
94ExcFS7-19
94NewBriRSF-656

Colon, Hector
91JohCitCC-14
91JohCitCP-3988
92JohCitCC-22
92JohCitCF-3129
93SavCarC-10
93SavCarF-698
94MadHatC-5
94MadHatF-138

Colon, Jose
91BurIndP-3291

Colon, Julio
94GreFalDSP-5
95SanBerSTI-4
96VerBeaDB-11

Colon, Roque
92HunCubC-7
92HunCubF-3161

Colon, Tony
88BlaYNPRWLU-48
89GenCubP-1875

Colonels, Louisville
38BasTabP-34
86JosHalC-9

Colonials, Georgia
89GeoColC-33

Colpaert, Dick
73OPC-608
73Top-608

Colpitt, Mike
87SpaPhiP-28

Colschen, Donna
76CliPilT-37

Colson, Brent
92YakBeaF-3440
93BakDodCLC-4

Colson, Bruce
88CedRapRP-1145

Colson, Loyd
71OPC-111
71Top-111
92YanWIZ7-37

Colston, Frank
87MiaMarP-16

87SalLakTTT-18
88WauTimGS-24
Colt 45s, Houston
62GuyPotCP-8
63Top-312
89AstCol4S-29
93TedWilPC-10
Colton, Lawrence
68Top-348
68TopVen-348
69Top-454A
69Top-454B
Coluccio, Bob (Robert P.)
74OPC-124
74Top-124
74TopSta-194
75OPC-456
75Top-456
76OPC-333
76SSP-150
76Top-333
78ChaChaT-5
94BreMilB-300
Columna, Jose
93DanBraC-9
93DanBraF-3623
94MacBraC-4
94MacBraF-2212
Colvard, Ben (Benny)
88BilMusP-1830
89CedRapRB-19
89CedRapRP-916
89CedRapRS-4
89Sta-197
90ChaLooGS-9
91ChaLooP-1971
92ChaLooP-3029
92ChaLooS-179
92ClaFS7-69
Colvin, Jeff
92DavLipB-9
Colzie, Rick
79WatIndT-20
80BatTroT-22
81WatIndT-2
Combe, Geoff
79IndIndTI-19
79NaSouTI-6
80IndIndTI-7
81IndIndTI-3
81Top-606
82EdmTraT-23
82Fle-62
82Top-351
Combs, Bobby
75AppFoxT-5
77AppFoxT-4
Combs, Earle Bryan
26Exh-98
28W502-21
28W513-86
28Yue-21
29ExhFou-25
29PorandAR-13
30SchR33-28
31Exh-25
31W517-1
32OrbPinNP-111
32USCar-5
33Gou-103
34GouCanV-21
36GouWidPPR-A18
40PlaBal-124
43YanSta-6
46SpoExcW-3-8
54Top-183
61Fle-17
75YanDyn1T-8
76RowExh-2
76ShaPiz-116
77GalGloG-109
80PacLeg-105
80PerHaloFP-116
80SSPHOF-116
87Yan192T-6
91ConTSN-105
91ConTSN-262
92ConTSN-466
92ConTSN-583
92YanWIZH-6
93ConTSN-732
94TopArc1-183
94TopArc1G-183
Combs, Mark
87SanBerSP-9
88FreSunCLC-2
Combs, Merrill R.
48SigOil-4
48SmiClo-23
52Top-18
83TopRep5-18
93RanKee-108
Combs, Pat
87PanAmTURB-5
88TopTra-30T
88TopTraT-30T
89BasAmeAPB-AA10
89Bow-398
89BowTif-398
89ClePhiS-8
89ReaPhiP-676
89ReaPhiS-9
89Sta-12
89TopBig-227
90Bow-148
90BowTif-148
90ClaUpd-T12
90Don-44
90DonBesN-49
90DonRoo-3
90Fle-553
90FleCan-553
90Lea-78
90OPC-384
90PhiTas-5
90Sco-623
90ScoRooDT-B2
90ScoYouS2-4
90Top-384
90TopBig-136
90TopDeb89-24
90TopTif-384
90UppDec-763
90UppDecS-1
91Bow-498
91Cla2-T41
91ClaGam-94
91Don-60
91Fle-392
91Lea-32
91OPC-571
91PhiMed-9
91Sco-440
91Sco100RS-72
91StaClu-36
91StaCluP-10
91Top-571
91TopDesS-571
91TopMic-571
91TopRoo-7
91TopTif-571
91ToyRoo-6
91Ult-259
91UppDec-537
92Don-76
92Fle-525
92OPC-456
92PhiMed-39
92Sco-106
92ScrRedBF-2442
92ScrRedBS-482
92StaClu-443
92Top-456
92TopGol-456
92TopGolW-456
92TopMic-456
92TriPla-170
92UppDec-442
93ScrRedBF-2540
93ScrRedBTI-6
94ScrRedBF-916
87PanAmTUBI-25
Comeau, Drew
88CapCodPPaLP-124
Comeaux, Eddie
94HudValRF-3397
95ChaRivTI-25
94HudValRC-3
Comer, H. Wayne
69PilPos-13
69Top-346
70BreMcD-5
70BreMil-3
70MLBOffS-268
70OPC-323
70Top-323
83Pil69G-42
88TigDom-3
94BreMilB-301
Comer, Steve
79Top-463
80Top-144
81Top-592
82Don-341
82Fle-314
82FleSta-177
82Top-16
82TopSti-242
83Don-163
83Fle-564
83Top-353
84IndWhe-31
85Top-788
85TopTif-788
86MaiGuiP-6
88OrlTwiB-7
93RanKee-109
Comimbre, Pancho (Francisco)
87NegLeaPD-38
Comiskey, Charlie (Charles A.)
09SpoNewSM-15
14CraJacE-23
15CraJacE-23
15SpoNewM-35
16BF2FP-11
16SpoNewM-36
36PC7AlbHoF-19
50CalHOFW-21
61Fle-18
76ShaPiz-22
76SSP188WS-14
77BobParHoF-16
80PerHaloFP-20
80SSPHOF-19
84GalHaloFRL-22
87AllandGN-5
87BucN28-96
87ConSer2-26
87LonJacN-3
87OldJudN-92A
87OldJudN-92B
87ScrDC-3
88GandBCGCE-9
88PacEigMO-24
88PacEigMO-80
88SpoTimM-6
89EdgR.WG-5
92Man191BSR-5
94OriofB-71
95ConTSN-1397
95ConTSNP-1397
Commodores, Falmouth
88CapCodPB-27
Como, George
82HolMilT-25
83NasAngT-26
85NasPirT-28
Comoletti, Glenn
78St.PetCT-7
Comorosky, Adam A.
31Exh-13
33Gou-77
33GouCanV-70
34BatR31-44
34Gou-85
35GouPuzR-1H
35GouPuzR-3F
35GouPuzR-5B
35GouPuzR-6B
35GouPuzR-11K
35GouPuzR-13B
35GouPuzR-14F
35GouPuzR-15F
91ConTSN-73
Compres, Fidel
87WatIndP-1
90ChaRanS-4
91ArkTraP-1276
91LinDriAAA-231
91LouRedLD-231
92ArkTraF-1122
92ArkTraS-30
92ClaFS7-331
92SkyAA F-14
93LimRocDWB-7
93LouRedF-207
94LasVegSF-866
Compton, Bruce
80QuaCitCT-20
Compton, Clint
92ChaRaiC-17
93RanCucQC-8
93RanCucQF-822
Compton, Clint (Robert Clinton)
73WicAerKSB-3
Compton, Council
89PulBraP-1891
Compton, Kenny
86FreGiaP-27
Compton, Mike (Michael Lynn)
71MLBOffS-174
71OPC-77
71Top-77
77SpaPhiT-19
80WatRedT-10
Compton, Scott
93YakBeaC-6
93YakBeaF-3894
Comstock, Brad
87EveGiaC-27
88FreSunCLC-25
88FreSunP-1226
Comstock, Keith
77QuaCitAT-10
80WesHavWCT-19B
81WesHavAT-6
82TacTigT-39
82WesHavAT-5
83BirBarT-22
84MinTwiP-7
84TolMudHT-16
84TwiTeal-16
88Fle-579
88FleGlo-579
88LasVegSC-2
88LasVegSP-246
88Sco-438
88ScoGlo-438
88Top-778A
88Top-778B
88TopTif-778
89LasVegSC-2
89LasVegSP-14
90BirBarDGB-5
90Bow-467
90BowTif-467
90Fle-510
90FleCan-510
90Lea-522
90MarMot-23
91Don-246
91MarCouH-20
91OPC-337
91Sco-502
91StaClu-556
91Top-337A
91Top-337B
91TopDesS-337
91TopMic-337
91TopTif-337
94EveGiaC-29
95BurBeeTI-33
96BurBeeTI-28
Conaster, Clint
50W720HolS-5
Conatser, Clint (Clinton A.)
49EurSta-5
Concello, Antoinette
40WheM4-11
41WheM5-17
Concepcion, Carlos
84ChaO'sT-6
Concepcion, Dave (David E.)
70DayDaiNM-59
71MLBOffS-56
71OPC-14
71Top-14
72OPC-267
72Top-267
72TopCloT-7
73OPC-554
73Top-554
74OPC-435
74Top-435
74TopSta-24
75Hos-47
75OPC-17
75Top-17
76Hos-128
76LinSup-98
76OPC-48
76RedIceL-2
76RedKro-5
76RedPos-5
76SSP-34
76Top-48
76VenLeaS-5
76VenLeaS-227
77BurCheD-200
77Hos-95
77MSADis-16
77OPC-258
77PepGloD-47
77RCColC-19
77Top-560
78Hos-108
78OPC-220
78Pep-8
78RCColC-47
78SSP270-133
78Top-180
78WifBalD-19
79Hos-85
79OPC-234
79Top-450
80OPC-117
80RedEnq-13
80Top-220
81AllGamPI-110
81CokTeaS-39
81Don-181
81Fle-197
81FleStiC-101
81Kel-28
81OPC-83
81PerAll-2
81Top-375
81TopScr-95
81TopSti-161
81TopSupHT-33
82Don-421
82Fle-63
82Fle-630
82FleSta-15
82FleSta-109
82Kel-22
82OPC-86
82OPC-221
82OPC-340
82PerAll-11
82PerAllG-11
82RedCok-5
82Squ-15
82Top-340
82Top-660
82Top-661
82TopSti-37
82TopSti-124
82TopStiV-37
83AllGamPI-110
83Don-148
83DonActA-47
83Fle-588
83Fle-631
83FleSta-42
83FleSti-219
83Kel-57
83OPC-32
83OPC-102
83RedYea-13
83Top-400
83Top-720
83TopFol-5
83TopGloS-34
83TopSti-227
84AllGamPI-20
84Don-2
84Don-2A
84Don-121
84Fle-466
84FunFooP-23
84MilBra-6
84Nes792-55
84OCoandSI-55
84OPC-55
84RalPur-20
84RedEnq-5
84Top-55
84TopCer-20
84TopRubD-15
84TopSti-56
84TopTif-55
85AllGamPI-111
85Don-203
85DonHig-8

85Fle-532
85Lea-131
85OPC-21
85RedYea-2
85Top-515
85TopMin-515
85TopRubD-13
85TopSti-48
85TopTif-515
86BasStaB-23
86Don-243
86Fle-174
86GenMilB-5A
86OPC-195
86RedTexG-13
86Spo-131
86Spo-153
86Top-195
86Top-366
86TopSti-137
86TopTat-22
86TopTif-195
86TopTif-366
87Fle-196
87FleGlo-196
87OPC-193
87RedFolSB-12
87RedKah-13
87Top-731
87TopTif-731
88Don-329
88Fle-229
88FleGlo-229
88OPC-336
88PanSti-275
88RedKah-13
88Sco-210
88ScoGlo-210
88Spo-218
88StaLinRe-4
88Top-422
88TopBig-144
88TopTif-422
89Fle-156
89FleGlo-156
89Sco-166
89UppDec-196
91MDAA-6
93Pin-482
96Red76K-4

Concepcion, Onix

81OmaRoyT-16
82Roy-6
83Don-516
83Fle-110
83Roy-7
83Top-52
84Don-95
84Fle-345
84Nes792-247
84Top-247
84TopTif-247
85AllGamPI-19
85Don-155
85Fle-200
85ThoMcAD-8
85Top-697
85TopTif-697
86Don-252
86Fle-6
86OPC-163
86RoyKitCD-5
86Top-596
86TopTif-596

Concepcion, Yamil

91PriRedC-19
91PriRedP-3520
92PriRedC-6
92PriRedF-3078
93PriRedC-4
93PriRedF-4185

Conde, Argenis

88SouBenWSGS-18
93LinVenB-18
94VenLinU-154
95LinVen-123

Conde, Ramon Luis

60DarFar-14
61UniOil-SP2
89BlaYNPRWL-30

Cone, David

82ChaRoyT-20
84MemChiT-25
85OmaRoyT-25
86OmaRoyP-6
86OmaRoyT-16
87Don-502
87DonRoo-35
87SpoRoo2-39
87TopTra-24T
87TopTraT-24T
88Don-653
88DonBasB-40
88DonTeaBM-653
88Fle-131
88FleGlo-131
88MetColP-16
88MetKah-44
88Sco-49
88ScoGlo-49
88StaCon-1
88StaCon-2
88StaCon-3
88StaCon-4
88StaCon-5
88StaCon-6
88StaCon-7
88StaCon-8
88StaCon-9
88StaCon-10
88StaCon-11
88StaLinMe-4
88Top-181
88TopTif-181
88ToyRoo-8
89Bow-375
89BowTif-375
89CadEllD-11
89ClaLigB-100
89ClaTraO-125
89Don-9
89Don-388
89DonAll-44
89DonBasB-96
89DonSupD-9
89Fle-31
89Fle-636
89FleBasA-9
89FleExcS-8
89FleGlo-31
89FleGlo-636
89FleHeroB-9
89FleLeaL-7
89FleWaxBC-C7
89MetColP-4
89MetFanC-44
89MetKah-5
89MSAHolD-19
89MSAIceTD-2
89Nis-19
89OPC-384
89PanSti-129
89RedFolSB-24
89Sco-221
89ScoHot1S-2
89ScoYouSI-9
89Spo-51
89Top-710
89TopDouM-6
89TopGloS-6
89TopHilTM-9
89TopMinL-24
89TopSti-96
89TopStiB-58
89TopTif-710
89TopUKM-17
89TVSpoM-6
89UppDec-584
90Bow-125
90BowTif-125
90Don-265
90DonBesN-43
90Fle-200
90FleCan-200
90FleLeaL-7
90Lea-40
90MetColP-12
90MetFanC-44
90MetKah-44
90MLBBasB-11
90OPC-30
90PanSti-301
90PubSti-129
90Sco-430
90Spo-201
90Top-30
90TopBig-11
90TopMinL-65
90TopSti-93
90TopTif-30
90TopTVM-8
90UppDec-224
90VenSti-114
91Bow-460
91Don-154
91Fle-143
91Lea-253
91MetCol8-6
91MetColP-14
91MetKah-17
91MetTro-1
91MetWIZ-81
91OPC-680
91PanCanT1-73
91PanSti-80
91Sco-409
91Sco-549
91SimandSMLBL-11
91StaClu-367
91StaCluMO-13
91Top-680
91TopDesS-680
91TopMic-680
91TopTif-680
91Ult-213
91UppDec-366
92Bow-238
92Cla1-T27
92Cla2-T45
92ClaGam-143
92Don-97
92Fle-501
92Fle-687
92FleSmo'nH-S3
92FleUpd-63
92Hig5-71
92Lea-92
92MetColP-6
92MetKah-17
92OPC-195
92OPCPre-175
92Pin-450
92Pin-590
92Pin-611
92Sco-680
92Sco-795
92Sco100S-16
92ScoImpP-90
92ScoRoo-27T
92SpoIllFK1-381
92StaClu-17
92Top-195
92TopGol-195
92TopGolW-195
92TopKid-16
92TopMic-195
92TriPla-35
92TriPla-64
92TriPlaP-8
92Ult-230
92UltAllS-19
92UppDec-364
92UppDecTMH-17
93BluJayD4-15
93Bow-97
93ClaGam-23
93Don-712
93Fin-115
93FinJum-115
93FinRef-115
93Fla-214
93Fle-691
93FleFinE-216
93FunPac-179
93FunPac-182
93Lea-250
93OPC-107
93OPCPre-92
93OPCWorC-4
93PacSpa-486
93Pin-489
93Pin-544
93RoyPol-6
93Sco-654
93Sel-361
93SelRoo-18T
93SelStaL-77
93SP-228
93StaClu-703
93StaCluFDI-703
93StaCluM-154
93StaCluMOP-703
93StaCluRoy-17
93Top-720
93TopGol-720
93TopInaM-720
93TopMic-720
93TopTra-125T
93Ult-558
93UppDec-335
93UppDec-534
93UppDecGold-335
93UppDecGold-534
94Bow-593
94BowBes-R46
94BowBesR-R46
94ColC-81
94ColChoGS-81
94ColChoSS-81
94Don-194
94ExtBas-85
94ExtBasPD-3
94Fin-52
94FinPre-52P
94FinRef-52
94Fla-297
94Fle-152
94FleSmo'nH-2
94Lea-274
94LeaL-36
94OPC-260
94Pac-281
94Pin-325
94PinArtP-325
94PinMusC-325
94ProMag-63
94RedFolMI-19
94Sco-405
94ScoGolR-405
94Sel-76
94SP-171
94SPDieC-171
94Spo-39
94StaClu-292
94StaCluFDI-292
94StaCluGR-292
94StaCluMOP-292
94Stu-182
94Top-510
94TopGol-510
94TopSpa-510
94TriPla-232
94Ult-362
94UppDec-413
94UppDecED-413
95Baz-57
95BazRedH-RH12
95BluJayUSPC-9S
95Bow-407
95BowBes-R31
95BowBesR-R31
95ColCho-66
95ColCho-536T
95ColCho-TC2
95ColChoGS-66
95ColChoSE-210
95ColChoSEGS-210
95ColChoSESS-210
95ColChoSS-66
95Don-289
95DonDiaK-DK25
95DonDom-1
95DonMouM-2
95DonPreP-289
95DonTopotO-118
95Emb-98
95EmbGolI-98
95Emo-92
95Fin-99
95FinRef-99
95Fla-43
95Fla-313
95Fle-155
95FleAllS-19
95FleAwaW-3
95FleTeaL-7
95FleUpd-29
95FleUpdDT-4
95Lea-339
95LeaChe-2
95LeaLim-59
95Pac-199
95PacPri-63
95PanSti-18
95PanSti-112
95Pin-270
95PinArtP-270
95PinMusC-270
95PosCan-12
95RedFol-21
95Sco-443
95ScoGolR-443
95ScoHaloG-HG93
95ScoHaloGYTE-HG93T
95ScoPlaTS-443
95ScoYouTE-443T
95Sel-111
95SelArtP-111
95SelCer-16
95SelCerMG-16
95SP-202
95SPCha-197
95SPChaDC-197
95Spo-26
95SpoArtP-26
95SPSil-202
95StaClu-204
95StaClu-216
95StaClu-620
95StaCluFDI-204
95StaCluFDI-216
95StaCluMOP-204
95StaCluMOP-216
95StaCluMOP-620
95StaCluSTWS-204
95StaCluSTWS-216
95StaCluSTWS-620
95StaCluVR-106
95Stu-33
95StuGolS-33
95Sum-80
95Sum-191
95SumNthD-80
95SumNthD-191
95SumSam-80
95TomPiz-2
95Top-5
95Top-392
95TopCyb-4
95TopTra-110T
95UC3-13
95UC3ArtP-13
95Ult-55
95UltAllS-6
95UltAllSGM-6
95UltAwaW-21
95UltAwaWGM-21
95UltGolM-55
95UppDec-178
95UppDec-288
95UppDec-495T
95UppDecED-178
95UppDecED-288
95UppDecEDG-178
95UppDecEDG-288
95UppDecSE-198
95UppDecSEG-198
95USPlaCMLA-9S
95Zen-24
96Baz-58
96Bow-57
96Cir-62
96CirRav-62
96ColCho-235
96ColChoGS-235
96ColChoSS-235
96Don-39
96DonPreP-39
96EmoXL-88
96Fin-B120
96FinRef-B120
96Fla-126
96Fle-181
96FleSmo'H-3
96FleTif-181
96Lea-154
96LeaLim-28
96LeaLimG-28
96LeaPre-26
96LeaPreP-26
96LeaPrePB-154
96LeaPrePG-154
96LeaPrePS-154
96LeaSig-103
96LeaSigPPG-103
96LeaSigPPP-103
96MetMod-3
96MetUni-85
96MetUniP-85
96Pac-374

96PacPriFT-FT8
96PanSti-158
96Pin-212
96PinAfi-12
96PinAfiAP-12
96PinAfiFPP-12
96PinArtP-112
96PinFoil-212
96PinSta-112
96ProSta-139
96Sco-176
96Sco-196
96Sco-364
96ScoDugC-A99
96ScoDugC-B89
96ScoDugCAP-A99
96ScoDugCAP-B89
96ScoRef-14
96Sel-66
96SelArtP-66
96SelCer-64
96SelCerAP-64
96SelCerCB-64
96SelCerCR-64
96SelCerIP-11
96SelCerMB-64
96SelCerMG-64
96SelCerMR-64
96SelTeaN-6
96SP-129
96Spo-24
96SpoArtP-24
96StaClu-151
96StaCluEPB-151
96StaCluEPG-151
96StaCluEPS-151
96StaCluMOP-3
96StaCluMOP-151
95StaCluVRMC-106
96Stu-58
96StuPrePB-58
96StuPrePG-58
96StuPrePS-58
96Sum-48
96SumAbo&B-48
96SumArtP-48
96SumFoi-48
96Top-124
96TopChr-33
96TopChrR-33
96TopGal-178
96TopGalPPI-178
96TopLas-116
96Ult-381
96UltGolM-381
96UppDec-405
96UppDecPHE-H12
96UppDecPreH-H12
96Zen-96
96ZenArtP-96
97Bow-253
97BowChr-76
97BowChrI-76
97BowChrIR-76
97BowChrR-76
97BowInt-253
97Cir-382
97CirRav-382
97ColCho-400
97Don-70
97Don-435
97DonEli-124
97DonEliGS-124
97DonLim-2
97DonLimLE-2
97DonPre-15
97DonPreCttC-15
97DonPreP-70
97DonPreP-435
97DonPrePGold-70
97DonPrePGold-435
97DonTea-125
97DonTeaSPE-125
97Fin-145
97FinEmb-145
97FinEmbR-145
97FinRef-145
97FlaSho-A63
97FlaSho-B63
97FlaSho-C63
97FlaShoLC-63
97FlaShoLC-B63
97FlaShoLC-C63
97FlaShoLCM-A63
97FlaShoLCM-B63
97FlaShoLCM-C63
97Fle-162
97FleTif-162
97Lea-234
97LeaFraM-234
97LeaFraMDC-234
97MetUni-115
97NewPin-14
97NewPinAP-14
97NewPinMC-14
97NewPinPP-14
97Pac-148
97PacLigB-148
97PacSil-148
97PinCar-10
97PinCer-34
97PinCerMBlu-34
97PinCerMG-34
97PinCerMR-34
97PinCerR-34
97PinIns-1
97PinInsCE-1
97PinInsDE-1
97PinTotCPB-34
97PinTotCPG-34
97PinTotCPR-34
97PinX-P-60
97PinX-PMoS-60
97Sco-178
97ScoPreS-178
97ScoShoS-178
97ScoShoSAP-178
97ScoYan-12
97ScoYanPI-12
97ScoYanPr-12
97Sel-6
97SelArtP-6
97SelRegG-6
97SP-123
97SpoIll-131
97SpoIllEE-131
97StaClu-231
97StaCluMat-231
97StaCluMOP-231
97Stu-25
97StuPrePG-25
97StuPrePS-25
97Top-360
97TopChr-123
97TopChrR-123
97TopGal-39
97TopGalPPI-39
97TopSta-75
97TopStaAM-75
97Ult-391
97UltGolME-391
97UltPlaME-391
97UppDec-264
97UppDec-382
97UppDec-438

Confreda, Gene
83BeaGolGT-23
87AshTouP-3
88AshTouP-1076
90OscAstS-30

Congalton, Bunk (William M.)
09ColChiE-59A
09ColChiE-59B
09ColChiE-59C
09T206-413
11SpoLifCW-71
12ColRedB-59A
12ColRedB-59B
12ColRedB-59C
12ColTinT-59A
12ColTinT-59B
12ColTinT-59C

Conger, Jeff
92AugPirC-24
92AugPirF-250
92ClaFS7-16
93SalBucC-5
93SalBucF-444
94SalBucC-5
94SalBucF-2337
95LynHilTI-5
96CarMudB-23

Conigliaro, Billy (William)
69Top-628
70DayDaiNM-118
70OPC-317
70RedSoxCPPC-4
70Top-317
71MLBOffS-316
71OPC-114
71RedSoxA-3
71RedSoxTI-2
71Top-114
72MilBra-80
72OPC-481
72Top-481
74OPC-545
74Top-545
81RedSoxBG2S-67
81RedSoxBG2S-76
94BreMilB-302

Conigliaro, Tony (Anthony)
47PM1StaP1-34
47PM1StaP1-35
64Top-287
64TopVen-287
65OPC-55
65Top-55
65TopTral-11
66Baz-6
66Top-218
66Top-380
66TopRubI-21
66TopVen-218
67Baz-6
67Top-280
67TopRedSS-3
67TopRedSS-30
67TopVen-245
68Baz-4
68OPC-140
68Top-140
68TopActS-8C
68TopVen-140
69RedSoxAO-2
69RedSoxTI-2
69Top-330
69TopTeaP-3
70DayDaiNM-96
70OPC-340
70RedSoxCPPC-5
70Top-340
71AngJacitB-3
71BazNumT-45
71MLBOffS-342
71OPC-63
71OPC-105
71Top-63
71Top-105
71TopCoi-142
71TopTat-80
76BooProC-4
78TCM60I-206
81RedSoxBG2S-67
81RedSoxBG2S-75
92UppDecS-6
94TedWil-137

Conine, Jeff
88BasCitRS-10
89BasCitRS-6
90Bes-156
90CMC-743
90MemChiB-8
90MemChiP-1017
90MemChiS-7
90ProAaA-48
90StaFS7-85
91Bow-184
91Cla1-T47
91ClaGam-96
91Don-427
91Fle-553
91LinDriAAA-332
91OmaRoyLD-332
91OmaRoyP-1041
91OPCPre-26
91Sco-722
91ScoHotR-5
91ScoRoo-19
91StaClu-578
91Stu-63
91TopDeb90-34
91Ult-145
91UppDec-27
92DonRooP-BC3
92OmaRoyF-2968
92OmaRoyS-329
92Sco100RS-21
92SkyAAAF-151
92SpoIllFK1-462
92StaClu-683
92TriA AAS-329
93Bow-670
93CadDis-15
93Don-101
93Don-765
93Fin-54
93FinRef-54
93Fla-49
93Fle-423
93FleFinE-57
93FunPac-119
93JimDeaR-3
93Lea-288
93MarFloA-8
93MarPub-8
93MarUSPC-5S
93MarUSPC-9C
93MarUSPC-11H
93OPCPre-119
93PacSpa-458
93Pin-479
93Pin-601
93PinExpOD-7
93Sco-402
93Sel-321
93SelChaR-12
93SelRooAR-1
93SP-138
93StaClu-340
93StaCluFDI-340
93StaCluMarI-13
93StaCluMOP-340
93Stu-54
93Top-789
93TopGol-789
93TopInaM-789
93TopMic-789
93TriPla-93
93Ult-371
93UltAllR-2
93UppDec-479
93UppDec-754
93UppDecGold-479
93UppDecGold-754
94Bow-383
94Bow-394
94BowBes-R34
94BowBesR-R34
94ColC-63
94ColChoGS-82
94ColChoSS-82
94Don-156
94ExtBas-259
94ExtBasSYS-4
94Fin-4
94FinJum-4
94FinRef-4
94Fla-161
94Fle-464
94FleRooS-5
94FUnPac-117
94Lea-41
94LeaL-106
94OPC-238
94OPCDiaD-12
94OscMayR-19
94Pac-239
94PacSilP-23
94PanSti-181
94Pin-30
94PinArtP-30
94PinMusC-30
94ProMag-51
94Sco-484
94ScoBoyoS-1
94ScoGolR-484
94ScoGolS-30
94Sel-26
94SP-109
94SPDieC-109
94Spo-62
94StaClu-406
94StaCluFDI-406
94StaCluGR-406
94StaCluMO-50
94StaCluMOP-406
94StaCluT-90
94StaCluTFDI-90
94Stu-108
94Top-466
94TopGol-466
94TopSpa-466
94TriPla-134
94Ult-491
94UltSecYS-7
94UppDec-162
94UppDecED-162
94USPlaCR-7C
94USPlaCR-12H
95Baz-60
95Bow-390
95BowBes-R38
95BowBesR-R38
95ClaPhoC-28
95ColCho-305
95ColChoGS-305
95ColChoSE-134
95ColChoSEGS-134
95ColChoSESS-134
95ColChoSS-305
95D3-25
95Don-392
95DonDiaK-DK6
95DonPreP-392
95DonTopotO-241
95Emb-86
95EmbGolI-86
95Emo-128
95Fin-148
95FinRef-148
95Fla-137
95Fle-331
95FleTeaL-19
95FleUpdSS-3
95Kra-19
95Lea-293
95LeaLim-41
95Pac-172
95PacGolP-28
95PacPri-55
95Pin-11
95PinArtP-11
95PinMusC-11
95Sco-54
95Sco-573
95ScoGolR-54
95ScoGolR-573
95ScoHaloG-HG28
95ScoPlaTS-54
95ScoPlaTS-573
95Sel-119
95SelArtP-119
95SelCer-58
95SelCerMG-58
95SP-53
95SPCha-45
95SPCha-49
95SPChaDC-45
95SPChaDC-49
95Spo-118
95SpoArtP-118
95SPSil-53
95StaClu-193
95StaClu-401
95StaCluFDI-193
95StaCluMO-13
95StaCluMOP-193
95StaCluMOP-401
95StaCluSTWS-193
95StaCluSTWS-401
95StaCluVR-101
95Stu-135
95Sum-25
95SumNthD-25
95TomPiz-21
95Top-130
95TopCyb-81
95TopFin-15
95Ult-379
95UltGolM-379
95UppDec-115
95UppDecED-115
95UppDecEDG-115
95UppDecSE-251
95UppDecSEG-251
95Zen-46
95ZenAllS-16
96Baz-53
96Bow-14
96BowBes-31
96BowBesAR-31
96BowBesR-31
96Cir-128
96CirRav-128
96Cla7/1PC-4
96ColCho-555
96ColChoGS-555
96ColChoSS-555

96Don-463
96DonDiaK-21
96DonPreP-463
96EmoXL-185
96Fin-B265
96Fin-G100
96FinRef-B265
96FinRef-G100
96Fla-260
96Fle-385
96FleTeaL-19
96FleTif-385
96Lea-125
96LeaPrePB-125
96LeaPrePG-125
96LeaPrePS-125
96LeaPreSG-5
96LeaPreSte-5
96LeaSig-112
96LeaSigA-47
96LeaSigAG-47
96LeaSigAS-47
96LeaSigPPG-112
96LeaSigPPP-112
96MetUni-164
96MetUniP-164
96Pac-82
96PacPri-P24
96PacPriG-P24
96PanSti-14
96Pin-226
96Pin-300
96PinAfi-42
96PinAfiAP-42
96PinAfiFPP-42
96PinArtP-126
96PinArtP-184
96PinFoil-226
96PinFoil-300
96PinSta-126
96PinSta-184
96ProSta-67
96Sco-9
96ScoDugC-A9
96ScoDugCAP-A9
96Sel-76
96SelArtP-76
96SP-89
96Spo-96
96SpoArtP-96
96StaClu-205
96StaClu-280
96StaCluEPB-280
96StaCluEPG-280
96StaCluEPS-280
96StaCluMO-10
96StaCluMOP-205
96StaCluMOP-280
96StaCluMOP-TSCA4
96StaCluTA-4
95StaCluVRMC-101
96Stu-8
96StuPrePB-8
96StuPrePG-8
96StuPrePS-8
96Sum-111
96SumAbo&B-111
96SumArtP-111
96SumFoi-111
96TeaOut-19
96Top-422
96TopChr-165
96TopChrR-165
96TopGal-15
96TopGalPG-PG6
96TopGalPPI-15
96TopLas-4
96Ult-198
96UltGolM-198
96UppDec-75
96UppDecPRE-R44
96UppDecPreR-R44
96ZenMoz-16
97Bow-265
97BowBes-18
97BowBesAR-18
97BowBesR-18
97BowInt-265
97Cir-110
97CirRav-110
97ColCho-113
97Don-265
97Don-445
97DonEli-48
97DonEliGS-48
97DonLim-90
97DonLimLE-90
97DonPre-117
97DonPreCttC-117
97DonPreP-265
97DonPreP-445
97DonPrePGold-265
97DonPrePGold-445
97Fin-164
97FinEmb-164
97FinEmbR-164
97FinRef-164
97FlaSho-A159
97FlaSho-B159
97FlaSho-C159
97FlaShoLC-159
97FlaShoLC-B159
97FlaShoLC-C159
97FlaShoLCM-A159
97FlaShoLCM-B159
97FlaShoLCM-C159
97Fle-328
97FleTif-328
97Lea-251
97LeaFraM-251
97LeaFraMDC-251
97MetUni-173
97Pac-300
97PacLigB-300
97PacPri-101
97PacPriLB-101
97PacPriP-101
97PacSil-300
97Pin-117
97PinArtP-117
97PinIns-64
97PinInsCE-64
97PinInsDE-64
97PinMusC-117
97PinPreP-1
97PinX-P-89
97PinX-PMoS-89
97ProMag-15
97ProMagML-15
97Sco-4
97ScoPreS-4
97ScoShoS-4
97ScoShoSAP-4
97SP-74
97StaClu-9
97StaCluMat-9
97StaCluMOP-9
97Stu-33
97StuPrePG-33
97StuPrePS-33
97Top-159
97TopChr-62
97TopChrR-62
97TopGal-114
97TopGalPPI-114
97TopSta-47
97TopStaAM-47
97TopStaASGM-ASM2
97Ult-195
97UltGolME-195
97UltPlaME-195
97UppDec-359
Conklin, Chip
82WauTimF-28
83WauTimF-11
84ModA'sC-6
85HunStaJ-17
Conkright, Dan
88BirBarB-21
Conlan, Jocko (John Bertrand)
35DiaMatCS3T1-37
55Bow-303
75SheGrePG-3
75TCMAllG-7
76GrePlaG-3
76ShaPiz-143
77GalGloG-87
80PacLeg-59
80PerHaloFP-143
80SSPHOF-143
88T/MUmp-63
89HOFStiB-98
89PerCelP-10
94ConTSN-1196
94ConTSNB-1196
Conley, Bob
78WatIndT-6
Conley, Bob (Robert Burns)
59Top-121
59TopVen-121
Conley, Curt
93BenRocC-5
93BenRocF-3258
94CenValRC-4
94CenValRF-3194
95SalAvaTI-12
Conley, Gene (D. Eugene)
53Top-215
54BraJohC-22
54BraSpiaSP-6
54Top-59
55BraGolS-6
55BraJohC-22
55BraSpiaSD-6
55Top-81
55TopDouH-33
56BraBilaBP-6
56Top-17
56TopPin-17
57BraSpiaS4-6
57Top-28
58Top-431
59Top-492
60ArmCoi-6
60Top-293
61Pos-124A
61Pos-124B
61Top-193
61TopStal-119
62RedSoxJP-2
62Top-187
62TopVen-187
63Top-216
64Top-571
81RedSoxBG2S-77
90PacLeg-79
91TopArc1-215
94TopArc1-59
94TopArc1G-59
Conley, Greg
88SpoIndP-1922
89ChaRaiP-974
90WatDiaB-22
90WatDiaP-2381
91HigDesMC-15
91HigDesMP-2398
Conley, Matt
91SumFlyC-3
91SumFlyP-2326
92AlbPolC-18
92AlbPolF-2298
Conley, Virgil
83TamTarT-2
84CedRapRT-8
85CedRapRT-4
86PenWhiSP-6
87PenWhiSP-27
88JacMetGS-11
Conlon, Charles M.
86ConSer1-59
86ConSer1-60
91ConTSN-327
94ConTSN-1266
94ConTSNB-1266
Conlon, Margie
86ConSer1-60
Conn, Gary
75BurBeeT-2
76BurBeeT-2
77HolMilT-5
Connally, Fritzie Lee
81QuaCitCT-5
83IowCubT-13
84LasVegSC-224
85FleUpd-30
91OriCro-82
Connally, Sarge (George)
32R33So2-406
33Gou-27
33GouCanV-27
34TarThoBD-7
91ConTSN-247
Connell, Lino
92BoiHawC-14
92BoiHawF-3636
93CedRapKC-4
93CedRapKF-1745
93LinVenB-206
95LinVen-50
Connell, Monty
89GeoColC-3
Connell, Pete (Peter J.)
87OldJudN-93
Connelly, Bill
53Top-126
79TCM50-60
91TopArc1-126
Connelly, Daron
86TriTriC-196
87CliGiaP-24
88SanJosGCLC-130
88SanJosGP-135
Connelly, David
86TriTriC-197
Connelly, Steve
96ModA'sB-24
Conner, Decomba
94PriRedC-1
94PriRedF-3275
95Bow-234
95BowGolF-234
95Exc-175
95ExcFirYP-6
96BesAutS-22
96Bow-215
Conner, Greg
88SanJosGCLC-118
88SanJosGP-129
89ShrCapP-1839
Conner, Jeff
78QuaCitAT-7
81HolMilT-12
82HolMilT-3
83NasAngT-4
84EvaTriT-18
85NasSouTI-4
86NasSouTI-5
Conner, John
90AppFoxBS-7
90AppFoxP-2089
91BasCitRC-2
91BasCitRP-1389
91Cla/Bes-71
Conner, Scott
93AlbPolC-10
93AlbPolF-2020
94FreKeyF-2605
95BowBayTI-32
96FreKeyB-4
94FreKeyC-8
Connolly, Chris
91EugEmeC-29
91EugEmeP-3716
92AppFoxF-978
93RocRoyC-8
93RocRoyF-708
94WilBluRC-3
94WilBluRF-292
95WilBluRTI-30
Connolly, Craig
90SouOreAB-20
90SouOreAP-3441
91MadMusC-6
91MadMusP-2123
92RenSilSCLC-37
93ModA'sC-6
93ModA'sF-792
Connolly, Ed (Edward J.)
65Top-543
Connolly, Edward Joseph Sr.
34DiaMatCSB-31
Connolly, Joe (Joseph A.)
14B18B-47A
14B18B-47B
15CraJacE-155
15SpoNewM-36
16SpoNewM-37
Connolly, Matt
91EriSaiC-16
91EriSaiP-4061
92VisOakC-4
92VisOakF-1006
93WesPalBEF-1331
96OrlCubB-6
Connolly, Sean
96BriWhiSB-13
Connolly, Steve
87PocGiaTB-4
88CliGiaP-696
88MidLeaAGS-6
89ShrCapP-1830
90ShrCapP-1437
90ShrCapS-3
Connolly, Thomas H.
50CalHOFW-22
76ShaPiz-67
77GalGloG-149
80PerHaloFP-65
80SSPHOF-65
89T/MUmp-63
92ConTSN-469
94ConTSN-1186
94ConTSNB-1186
94OriofB-72
Connor, Mark
84ColCliP-25
84ColCliT-21
90TopTVY-2
94KnoSmoF-1320
95KnoSmoF-56
Connor, Roger
76ShaPiz-153
80PerHaloFP-153
80SSPHOF-153
86OldJudN-1
87BucN28-64A
87BucN28-64B
87OldJudN-94A
87OldJudN-94B
88GandBCGCE-10
88WG1CarG-37
89EdgR.WG-5
89HOFStiB-9
89SFHaCN-2
90KalBatN-8
94OriofB-33
Connors, Billy
67ProPizC-6
67Top-272
82CubRedL-NNO
83CubThoAV-NNO
84CubChiT-7
84CubSev-NNO
85CubSev-NNO
86CubGat-NNO
87MarMot-28
90TopTVY-3
91CubMar-NNO
91MetWIZ-82
92CubMar-NNO
93CubMar-5
Connors, Chad
93BilMusF-3935
93BilMusSP-1
94ChaWheC-5
94ChaWheF-2693
Connors, Chuck (Kevin Joseph)
50WorWidGV-2
52MotCoo-4
77FriOneYW-2
80PacLeg-28
88PacLegI-71
88RinPosD1-9B
90DodTar-135
Connors, Jimmy (James Scott)
82MonNew-3
Conquest, Tom
82IdaFalAT-5
83MadMusF-12
Conrad, Phil
48BabRutS-6
Conro, Pam
96ColSilB-3
Conroy, Bill (William G.)
42RedSoxTI-6
43RedSoxTI-3
46SunBre-4
Conroy, Brian
90CarLeaA-9
90LynRedSTI-16
91LinDriAA-453
91NewBriRSLD-453
91NewBriRSP-344
92NewBriRSF-425
92PawRedSS-355
92SkyAAAF-160
93Bow-579
93PawRedSDD-8
93PawRedSF-2402
93PawRedSTI-8
94PawRedSF-940
97DunDonPPS-5
Conroy, Daniel
96IdaFalB-4
Conroy, Mike

88StoPorP-752
89StoPorB-31
89StoPorS-28
Conroy, Tim
79WatA'sT-22
80WesHavWCT-22B
81WesHavAT-7
84A'sMot-24
84Don-340
84Fle-442
84Nes792-156
84Nes792-189
84Top-156
84Top-189
84TopTif-156
84TopTif-189
85A'sMot-16
85DomLeaS-12
85Don-156
85Fle-421
85Top-503
85TopTif-503
86CarSchM-3
86CarTeal-9
86FleUpd-29
86TopTra-28T
86TopTraT-28T
87Fle-291
87FleGlo-291
87Top-338
87TopTif-338
88LouRedBC-5
88LouRedBTI-15
88Sco-384
88ScoGlo-384
88Top-658
88TopTif-658
89HarSenP-288
89HarSenS-6
93ButCopKSP-24
94HigDesMC-28
94HigDesMF-2805
Conroy, Wid (William E.)
08AmeCarE-72
08RosComP-45
09ColChiE-60
09RamT20-30
09SenBarP-2
09T206-73
09T206-74
10DarChoE-12
10JHDABE-5
10RedCroT-13
10SenWasT-1
11SpoLifCW-72
11SpoLifM-121
12ColRedB-60
12ColTinT-60
Consolo, Billy (William A.)
53RedSoxTI-4
54Top-195
55Top-207
57Top-399
58Top-148
59SenTealW-5
59Top-112
59TopVen-112
60SenJayP-4
60Top-508
61Pos-100A
61Pos-100B
61Top-504
61TwiPetM-26
83Tig-8
84TigWavP-11
88TigPep-NNO
89TigMar-NNO
90TigCok-28
91TigCok-NNO
94TopArc1-195
94TopArc1G-195
Constable, Jimmy
59Top-451
63Top-411
Constant, Andres
89FreKeyS-3
90FreKeyTI-25
91FreKeyC-2
91FreKeyP-2356
Constantinides, Nick
94BriTigC-8
94BriTigF-3494
Constantino, Kraig
92SpoIndC-16
92SpoIndF-1298
Consuegra, Sandy
51Bow-96
52Bow-143
53BowC-89
54Bow-166
55Bow-116
55RedMan-AL25
56Top-265
79TCM50-170
91OriCro-83
Conte, Mike (Michael)
89MedAthB-1
90MadMusP-2276
90ModA'sC-6
91HunStaC-4
91HunStaP-1808
91HunStaTI-6
92HunStaF-3959
92HunStaS-307
93SanBerSC-4
93SanBerSF-764
93SouOreAC-6
93SouOreAF-4055
Conti, Guy
86WatPirP-6
88BakDodCLC-263
89BakDodCLC-207
89CalLeaA-24
90GreFalDSP-29
92GreFalDSP-30
93BakDodCLC-29
94BakDodC-28
Conti, Jason
96AriBlaDB-12
96HonShaHWB-6
97BowBes-196
97BowBesAR-196
97BowBesR-196
97Top-468
Conti, Joe
88CapCodPPaLP-15
Contreras, Efrain
94NewJerCC-4
94NewJerCF-3429
95PeoChiTI-11
96StPetCB-6
Contreras, Frank
82MiaMarT-21
Contreras, Henry
81BurBeeT-15
93LinVenB-110
95LinVen-35
Contreras, Joaquin
85LitFalMT-22
86ColMetP-7
87JacMetF-15
87TexLeaAF-16
88JacMetGS-20
88MetColP-17
88TidTidCa-15
88TidTidCM-17
89BlaYNPRWL-23
89TidTidC-16
89TidTidP-1960
90ProAAAF-476
90RocRedWGC-25
90RocRedWP-719
91LinDriAAA-452
91RocRedWLD-452
96WisTimRB-3
Contreras, Nardi
75TidTidTI-6
77ReaPhiT-5
80IowOakP-3
81EdmTraRR-4
82EdmTraT-14
85BufBisT-2
87RicBraC-43
87RicBraT-22
88JacExpB-23
88JacExpP-969
88SouLeaAJ-40
89JacExpB-26
89JacExpP-173
89PacSenL-26
90JacExpB-26
90JacExpP-1392
91IndIndP-478
94ColCliF-2968
94ColCliP-3
Contreras, Rafael
77ReaPhiT-6
Converse, Jim
90HigSchPLS-22
91PenPilC-2
92JacSunF-3701
92JacSunS-354
92SkyAA F-150
92UppDecML-259
93Bow-543
93CalCanF-1158
93ExcFS7-222
93FleFinE-267
93StaClu-683
93StaCluFDI-683
93StaCluMOP-683
93TopTra-40T
93Ult-616
94CalCanF-782
94Pac-566
94SpoRoo-54
94SpoRooAP-54
95Pac-393
95StaClu-324
95StaCluMOP-324
95StaCluSTWS-324
95TacRaiTI-6
96LeaSigEA-33
96RoyPol-6
Converse, Mike
86CedRapRT-3
87TamTarP-3
Convertino, Phil
77ReaPhiT-7
Conway, Jack
92TexLon-9
Conway, Jack Clements
47IndTeal-4
47IndVanPP-4
Conway, James P.
87OldJudN-97
Conway, Jeff
94SpoIndC-4
94SpoIndF-3334
Conway, John
52Par-96
Conway, Keith
94MadHatC-6
94MadHatF-124
96StPetCB-7
Conway, Pete (Peter J.)
87OldJudN-96
Conway, Rip (Richard D.)
87OldJudN-95
Coogan, Dale Roger
50Bow-244
50PirTeal-5
52Top-87
83TopRep5-87
Cook, Alan
95OdgRapTI-4
Cook, Andy
88OneYanP-2041
89PriWilCS-3
90AlbYanB-2
90AlbYanP-1031
90AlbYanS-3
90CMC-731
91AlbYanLD-1
91AlbYanP-999
91LinDriAA-1
92ColCliF-342
93Bow-124
93ColCliF-1103
93ColCliP-2
93FleFinE-244
94ColCliF-2943
94ColCliP-5
94Pin-257
94PinArtP-257
94PinMusC-257
94SalLakBF-811
95ColCliMCTI-18
95ColCliP-5
95ColCliTI-5
Cook, Brian
90ArkRaz-6
Cook, Cliff (Raymond C.)
61Top-399
62RedEnq-5
62Top-41
62TopVen-41
63Top-566
81TCM60I-296
82MetGal62-4
91MetWIZ-83
Cook, Dennis
86FreGiaP-16
87ShrCapP-4
88PhoFirC-3
88PhoFirP-80
89Don-646
89DonBasB-327
89Fle-652
89FleGlo-652
89FleUpd-104
89PanSti-207
89PhiTas-39
89PhoFirC-3
89PhoFirP-1482
89UppDec-779
90ClaBlu-80
90Don-193
90DonBesN-93
90Fle-554
90FleCan-554
90Hot50RS-12
90Lea-342
90OPC-633
90PanSti-320
90PhiTas-6
90Sco-545
90Sco100RS-75
90Top-633
90TopTif-633
90UppDec-71
91AlbDukLD-4
91DodPol-25
91Don-657
91Fle-196
91Lea-257
91LinDriAAA-4
91OPC-467
91StaClu-411
91Top-467
91TopDesS-467
91TopMic-467
91TopTif-467
91UppDec-612
92Bow-497
92Fle-451
92IndFanC-8
92Lea-503
92Pin-493
92StaClu-887
92StaCluNC-887
92TexLon-10
92Ult-346
93Don-625
93Fle-214
93IndWUA-7
93Lea-193
93PacSpa-409
93StaClu-153
93StaCluFDI-153
93StaCluMOP-153
93Top-141
93TopGol-141
93TopInaM-141
93TopMic-141
93UppDec-202
93UppDecGold-202
94FleUpd-23
94WhiSoxK-4
95Fle-112
96LeaSigEA-34
96RanMot-24
Cook, Doc (Luther Almus)
15SpoNewM-37
Cook, Doug
81ChaRoyT-12
83ChaRoyT-16
84MemChiT-12
91IdaFalBP-4321
Cook, Glen
82BurRanF-23
82BurRanT-17
83BurRanF-12
83BurRanT-3
83TulDriT-2
84OklCit8T-22
85DomLeaS-128
85OklCit8T-8
86OklCit8P-4
86Top-502
86TopTif-502
87OklCit8P-14
93RanKee-110
Cook, Hayward
95KanCouCTI-42
96BreCouMB-11
Cook, Jake
95MicBatCTI-7
Cook, James
86KenTwiP-4
Cook, Jason
94AppFoxC-26
94AppFoxF-1060
96LanJetB-11
Cook, Jeff
86PriWilPP-7
87HarSenP-10
88EasLeaAP-13
88HarSenP-835
89HarSenP-304
89HarSenS-7
90BufBisC-24
90BufBisP-387
90CMC-24
90ProAAAF-502
Cook, John
96AubDouB-17
Cook, Kenny
92GulCoaDF-3558
93YakBeaC-7
93YakBeaF-3877
94BakDodC-8
Cook, Kerry
83SanJosBC-13
86WesPalBEP-9
Cook, Kyle
93MisStaB-10
Cook, Larry
86PalSprAP-11
86PalSprAP-8
Cook, Mike
86MidAngP-6
88EdmTraC-2
88EdmTraP-567
89Fle-472
89FleGlo-472
90CMC-556
90PorBeaC-4
90PorBeaP-171
90ProAAAF-241
90TriAllGP-AAA21
91CalCanLD-57
91LinDriAAA-57
92LouRedF-1881
92LouRedS-258
93LinVenB-307
93RocRedWF-233
94OriPro-20
94OriUSPC-2C
94StaCluT-289
94StaCluTFDI-289
94TopGol-791
Cook, Mitch
83QuaCitCT-9
86ColAstP-2
87ColAstP-9
Cook, Paul
87OldJudN-98
Cook, Rodney
95ChaRivTI-4
Cook, Ron
88FayGenP-1096
89LakTigS-5
90LakTigS-5
90StaFS7-33
91LinDriAA-378
91LonTigLD-378
Cook, Ron W.
71MLBOffS-75
71OPC-583
71Top-583
72OPC-339
72Top-339
72TopCloT-8
Cook, Scott
94EveGiaC-5
94EveGiaF-3642
Cook, Stan
89BoiHawP-1982
90EriSaiS-3
Cook, Steve
93ButCopKSP-9
94CedRapKC-7
94CedRapKF-1114
Cook, Tim
79HolMilT-12
81ElPasDT-20
82VanCanT-12
83LasVegSBHN-4
84BeaGolGT-12

Cooke, Dusty (Allan Lindsey)
34BatR31-148
38CinOraW-5
39OrcPhoAP-27
49PhiBul-13
92ConTSN-418
Cooke, Mitch
82QuaCitCT-7
Cooke, Scott
89MisStaB-8
Cooke, Steve
90WelPirP-20
91AugPirC-4
91AugPirP-797
92Bow-274
92BufBisBS-4
92CarMudS-130
92ClaFS7-43
92DonRoo-28
92SkyAA F-61
93Bow-514
93Don-150
93Fla-111
93FleMajLP-B16
93Lea-240
93OPCPre-19
93PacSpa-585
93Pin-260
93PirHil-3
93PirNatI-7
93Sco-296
93SelRoo-69T
93SP-183
93StaClu-726
93StaCluFDI-726
93StaCluMOP-726
93Top-716
93TopGol-716
93TopInaM-716
93TopMic-716
93Ult-449
93UppDec-599
93UppDecGold-599
94Bow-434
94ColC-83
94ColChoGS-83
94ColChoSS-83
94Don-72
94ExtBas-344
94ExtBasSYS-5
94Fin-19
94FinJum-19
94FinRef-19
94Fla-215
94Fle-607
94FleRooS-6
94Lea-169
94OPC-85
94Pac-495
94PanSti-234
94Pin-93
94PinArtP-93
94PinMusC-93
94PirQui-3
94Sco-186
94ScoGolR-186
94Sel-130
94StaClu-47
94StaCluFDI-47
94StaCluGR-47
94StaCluMOP-47
94Top-72
94TopGol-72
94TopSpa-72
94TriPla-182
94Ult-255
94UppDec-132
94UppDecED-132
94USPlaCR-7S
95ColCho-378
95ColChoGS-378
95ColChoSS-378
95Don-196
95DonPreP-196
95Fla-185
95Fle-475
95Lea-77
95Pac-342
95Pin-194
95PinArtP-194
95PinMusC-194
95PirFil-6
95Sco-522
95ScoGolR-522
95ScoPlaTS-522
95StaClu-58
95StaCluFDI-58
95StaCluMOP-58
95StaCluSTWS-58
95Stu-144
95Top-197
95TopCyb-113
95Ult-213
95UltGolM-213
95UppDec-148
95UppDecED-148
95UppDecEDG-148
96LeaSigA-48
96LeaSigAG-48
96LeaSigAS-48
97ColCho-432
Cookie, Mascot
89WicStaR-29
90WicWraRD-28
Cookson, Brent
91SouOreAC-11
91SouOreAP-3860
92CliGiaC-5
93SanJosGC-7
93SanJosGF-24
94ShrCapF-1618
94UppDecML-41
95OmaRoyTI-6
95PhoFirTI-12
96Pac-334
96PawRedSDD-4
Coolbaugh, Mike
90MedHatBJB-1
91St.CatBJC-7
91St.CatBJP-3402
92St.CatBJC-3
92St.CatBJF-3395
93HagSunC-5
93HagSunF-1886
94DunBluJC-6
94DunBluJF-2563
95KnoSmoF-47
Coolbaugh, Scott
88TexLeaAGS-12
88TulDriTI-18
89OklCit8C-21
89OklCit8P-1512
89TriA AAC-5
89TriAAP-AAA26
90Bow-494
90BowTif-494
90ClaYel-T24
90Don-43
90DonRoo-32
90Fle-293
90FleCan-293
90FleSoaS-5
90Hot50RS-13
90Lea-363
90Sco-612
90Sco100RS-79
90Spo-180
90TopDeb89-25
90TopTra-22T
90TopTraT-22T
90TriAAAC-5
90TulDriDGB-1
90UppDec-42
91Bow-649
91FleUpd-122
91LasVegSLD-280
91LasVegSP-241
91Lea-397
91LinDriAAA-280
91OPC-277
91PadSmo-6
91Sco100RS-36
91StaClu-493
91Top-277
91TopDesS-277
91TopMic-277
91TopTif-277
91TopTra-24T
91TopTraT-24T
91UppDec-451
91UppDecFE-37F
92LasVegSS-228
92Sco-205
92SkyAAAF-112
92TexLon-11
93RanKee-111
93RocRedWF-247
94LouRedF-2985
94TriAAF-AAA36
Cooley, Chad
94LSUTig-11
94LSUTigMP-10
Cooley, Duff (Dick Gordon)
03BreE10-23
11SpoLifCW-73
Cooley, Fred
89MedAthB-9
90MadMusB-6
90MadMusP-2275
90MidLeaASGS-8
90ProAaA-126
91Cla/Bes-228
91HunStaC-8
91HunStaLD-283
91HunStaP-1803
91LinDriAA-283
91ModA'sP-3094
92OrlSunRS-502
Cooley, Jack
91PacSenL-90
Cooley, Shannon
96BatCliTI-11
Coombes, Melissa
94ColSilBC-1
95ColSilB-4
95ColSilB9-6
96ColSilB-4
Coombs, Bobby (Raymond)
34DiaMatCSB-32
Coombs, Daniel
65Top-553
66Top-414
67Ast-6
67AstTeal2-7
67Top-464
68Top-547
69Top-389
71OPC-126
71Top-126
71TopCoi-49
72OPC-91
72Top-91
87AstShoSO-2
87AstShoSTw-29
Coombs, Glenn
91WelPirC-25
91WelPirP-3564
92AugPirF-229
Coombs, Jack (John W.)
08RosComP-57
09ColChiE-62
09RamT20-31
09SpoNewSM-46
10E98-10
10JHDABE-6
10JuJuDE-12
10LuxCigPP-5
11MecDFT-13
11PloCanE-19
11SpoLifCW-74
11SpoLifM-90
12ColRedB-62
12ColTinT-62
14TexTomE-14
15SpoNewM-38
16FleBreD-19
27YorCarE-31
70FleWorS-7
86ConSer1-40
90DodTar-136
Coombs, Mike
90HelBreSP-28
Coomer, Ron (Ronald)
88CalLeaACLC-9
88ModA'sCLC-72
88ModA'sTI-21
90HunStaB-16
91BirBarLD-55
91BirBarP-1460
91LinDriAA-55
92SkyAAAF-280
92VanCanF-2727
92VanCanS-631
93BirBarF-1197
94AlbDukF-849
94ExcFS7-36
94TriAAF-AAA25
95DodPol-5
95Exc-211
95ExcAll-4
95Top-651
96Cir-54
96CirRav-54
96ColCho-602
96ColChoGS-602
96ColChoSS-602
96Don-526
96DonPreP-526
96Fin-B349
96FinRef-B349
96Fle-164
96FleTif-164
96Pin-177
96UppDec-128
97Cir-140
97CirRav-140
97ColCho-379
97Don-283
97DonLim-58
97DonLimLE-58
97DonPreP-283
97DonPrePGold-283
97Fle-144
97FleTif-144
97Lea-159
97LeaFraM-159
97LeaFraMDC-159
97Pac-134
97PacLigB-134
97PacSil-134
97Top-186
Coonan, Bill
86MedA'sC-58
Cooney, Ed
88CapCodPPaLP-14
Cooney, James E.
26Exh-19
Cooney, Jim
95ChaRivTI-24
Cooney, Jimmy (James Edward)
87OldJudN-99
Cooney, Johnny (John Walter)
36OveCanR-9
36OveCanR-10
39PlaBal-85
40PlaBal-60
41DouPlaR-41
41PlaBal-50
43DodTeal-5
54BraJohC-28
55BraGolS-29
55BraJohC-28
60Top-458
79DiaGre-205
83Bra53F-28
90DodTar-137
91ConTSN-94
Cooney, Kyle
94GreFalDSP-13
95VerBeaDTI-6
96MauStiHWB-21
96SanBerSB-7
Cooney, Terry
88T/MUmp-21
89T/MUmp-19
90T/MUmp-18
Cooper, Arley Wilbur
16FleBreD-20
21E121So1-12
22W572-16
Cooper, Army (Alfred)
87NegLeaPD-11
Cooper, Bill
86LakTigP-4
87GleFalTP-8
88GleFalTP-933
Cooper, Brian
96LakElsSB-2
Cooper, Cecil C.
72OPC-79
72Top-79
74OPC-523
74Top-523
75OPC-489
75Top-489
76OPC-78
76RedSoxSM-3
76SSP-404
76Top-78
77OPC-102
77Top-235
78Hos-119
78Kel-41
78OPC-71
78Top-154
79Hos-36
79OPC-163
79Top-325
80OPC-52
80Top-95
80TopSup-33
81AllGamPI-4
81Don-83
81Dra-16
81Fle-639
81FleStiC-16
81Kel-32
81MSAMinD-10
81OPC-356
81PerCreC-15
81Squ-30
81Top-3
81Top-555
81TopScr-2
81TopSti-10
81TopSti-13
81TopSti-93
81TopSti-241
81TopSupN-5
82BrePol-15
82Don-258
82Dra-9
82Fle-138
82FleSta-140
82Kel-60
82OPC-167
82PerAll-2
82PerAllG-2
82PerCreC-18
82PerCreCG-18
82Squ-1
82Top-675
82Top-703
82TopSti-199
83AllGamPI-3
83BreGar-5
83BrePol-15
83Don-106
83DonActA-19
83Dra-6
83Fle-30
83FleSta-43
83FleSti-23
83Kel-28
83OPC-190
83PerCreC-21
83PerCreCG-21
83Top-190
83TopFol-3
83TopGloS-15
83TopSti-80
83TopSti-173
83TopSti-181
84AllGamPI-92
84BreGar-5
84BrePol-15
84Don-351
84DonCha-24
84Dra-8
84Fle-198
84FleSti-31
84FunFooP-48
84MilBra-7
84Nes792-133
84Nes792-420
84Nes792-710
84OPC-43
84RalPur-27
84SevCoi-C8
84Top-133
84Top-420
84Top-710
84TopCer-27
84TopGloS-34
84TopRubD-15
84TopSti-200A
84TopSti-291
84TopTif-133
84TopTif-420
84TopTif-710
85AllGamPI-3
85BreGar-5
85BrePol-15
85Don-170
85Fle-580
85Lea-246
85OPC-290

85ThoMcAD-9
85Top-290
85TopRubD-13
85TopSti-287
85TopTif-290
86BrePol-15
86Don-7
86Don-170
86DonAll-54
86DonAllB-PC9
86DonSupD-7
86Fle-484
86FleLimE-12
86FleMin-100
86FleStiC-26
86Lea-7
86MSAJayPCD-2
86OPC-385
86SevCoi-C15
86Spo-29
86Spo-145
86Spo-180
86Top-385
86TopSti-196
86TopSup-20
86TopTat-6
86TopTif-385
86Woo-8
87BoaandB-6
87BrePol-15
87BreTeal-4
87Don-363
87Fle-343
87FleAwaW-10
87FleGlo-343
87FleMin-22
87Lea-230
87OPC-10
87OPCBoxB-D
87RedFolSB-48
87Spo-169
87StuPan-21
87Top-10
87TopSti-198
87TopTif-10
87TopWaxBC-D
87Woo-2
88Fle-161
88FleGlo-161
88Sco-169
88ScoGlo-169
88Top-769
88TopTif-769
89PacSenL-42
89T/MSenL-23
91UppDecS-10
92BreCarT-5
92UppDecS-9
93ActPacA-164
93TedWil-49
93UppDecAH-34
93UppDecS-9
94BreMilB-215
94BreMilB-303
94UppDecAH-21
94UppDecAH1-21

Cooper, Chris
87BriYouC-5

Cooper, Craig
86SpoIndC-168
88WicPilRD-24
89WicUpdR-8
89WicWraR-34
90ElPasDGS-7
92CanIndS-104

Cooper, Darren
90MarPhiP-3200

Cooper, Dave
84AriWilP-2
87LakTigP-23
88TolMudHC-8
88TolMudHP-608
89LonTigP-1362
95EveAqaTI-5

Cooper, David
94Top-761
94TopGol-761
94TopSpa-761

Cooper, Don
79WesHavYT-3
80NasSouTI-6
82Fle-550
82TolMudHT-1
82Top-409
83SyrChiT-6
84ColCliP-6
84ColCliT-17
85ColCliP-6
85ColCliT-5
86SyrChiP-9
88SouBenWSGS-14
89SarWhiSS-25
90SarWhiSS-27
91PacSenL-22
91SarWhiSC-16
91SarWhiSP-1131
92BirBarF-2600
92BirBarS-100
92YanWIZ8-35
95WhiSoxK-31
96NasSouB-2

Cooper, Gary Clifton
86AubAstP-7
87OscAstP-21
88ColAstB-21
89TucTorC-22
89TucTorJP-6
89TucTorP-184
90CMC-612
90HamRedB-19
90HamRedS-9
90ProAAAF-203
90TucTorC-10
90TucTorP-213
91LinDriAAA-609
91TriA AAGP-AAA51
91TucTorLD-609
91TucTorP-2224
92Don-774
92PinRool-3
92Sco-840
92ScoImpP-25
92ScoRoo-28
92SkyAAAF-270
92TopDeb91-38
92TriA AAS-605
92TucTorF-495
92TucTorS-605
93BufBisF-523
93ExcFS7-40
94IndIndF-1815
95JacSunTI-5

Cooper, Gary N.
74GasRanT-7
79SavBraT-2
81DurBulT-6

Cooper, Jamie
87EveGiaC-9
88CliGiaP-715
88MidLeaAGS-4
89SanJosGB-3
89SanJosGCLC-230
89SanJosGP-458
89SanJosGS-5
89Sta-83
90ShrCapP-1457
90ShrCapS-4
91ShrCapP-1833
92PhoFirS-380
92SkyAAAF-179

Cooper, Jeff
91SalLakTP-3217

Cooper, Kent
84EveGiaC-7

Cooper, Mark
85KinBluJT-12

Cooper, Mort (Morton)
39PlaBal-131
40PlaBal-113
41CarW75-3
43MPR302-1-4
47Exh-49
47PM1StaP1-36
76TayBow4-78
83TCMPla1943-25
84TCMPla1-34
87SpoRea-24
91ConTSN-301
92CarMcD-19
92ConTSN-624

Cooper, Neal
76DubPacT-8

Cooper, Paul
78DayBeaAT-6

Cooper, Scott
86ElmPioRSP-6
87GreHorP-10
88CarLeaAS-5
88LynRedSS-5
89BasAmeAPB-AA9
89NewBriRSP-609
89NewBriRSS-3
89Sta-126
90Bow-277
90BowTif-277
90ClaUpd-T13
90CMC-265
90PawRedSC-14
90PawRedSDD-3
90PawRedSP-467
90ProAAAF-439
90Sco-651
90TopTVRS-39
91Don-496
91Fle-91
91LinDriAAA-354
91PawRedSDD-3
91PawRedSLD-354
91PawRedSP-46
91TopDeb90-35
91TriA AAGP-AAA29
91UppDec-22
92Bow-129
92Cla1-T28
92ClaGam-142
92Don-570
92Lea-182
92OPC-488
92Pin-252
92PinRoo-2
92ProFS7-16
92Sco-876
92Sco100RS-88
92ScoHotR-5
92ScoImpP-26
92ScoRoo-13
92StaClu-377
92Top-488
92TopGol-488
92TopGolW-488
92TopMic-488
92TriPla-180
92Ult-312
92UppDec-541
93Bow-467
93Don-135
93Fin-7
93FinRef-7
93Fla-161
93Fle-178
93Lea-175
93OPC-385
93OPCPre-13
93PacSpa-355
93PanSti-93
93Pin-330
93RedSoxWHP-9
93Sco-198
93Sel-302
93SP-200
93StaClu-368
93StaCluFDI-368
93StaCluMOP-368
93Stu-45
93Top-655
93TopGol-655
93TopInaM-655
93TopMic-655
93Toy-29
93TriPla-25
93Ult-149
93UppDec-57
93UppDecGold-57
93USPlaCR-11D
94Bow-203
94ColC-84
94ColChoGS-84
94ColChoSS-84
94Don-417
94ExtBas-17
94Fin-168
94FinPre-168P
94FinRef-168
94Fla-11
94Fle-27
94FleAllS-6
94Lea-75
94LeaL-8
94OPC-4
94Pac-50
94PanSti-27
94Pin-72
94PinArtP-72
94PinMusC-72
94Sco-388
94ScoGolR-388
94Sel-39
94SP-153
94SPDieC-153
94StaClu-396
94StaCluFDI-396
94StaCluGR-396
94StaCluMOP-396
94Stu-160
94Top-235
94TopGol-235
94TopSpa-235
94TriPla-202
94Ult-313
94UppDec-502
94UppDecED-502
95ColCho-408
95ColCho-540T
95ColChoGS-408
95ColChoSE-192
95ColChoSEGS-192
95ColChoSESS-192
95ColChoSS-408
95Don-413
95DonDiaK-DK15
95DonPreP-413
95DonTopotO-325
95Fin-145
95Fin-244
95FinRef-145
95FinRef-244
95Fla-11
95Fla-406
95Fle-27
95FleAllS-11
95FleUpd-155
95Lea-155
95LeaLim-7
95Pac-35
95PacPri-13
95PanSti-58
95Pin-67
95PinArtP-67
95PinMusC-67
95Sco-427
95ScoGolR-427
95ScoPlaTS-427
95ScoYouTE-427T
95SP-99
95SPSil-99
95StaClu-328
95StaClu-614
95StaCluMOP-328
95StaCluMOP-614
95StaCluMOP-SS16
95StaCluSS-SS16
95StaCluSTWS-328
95StaCluSTWS-614
95Stu-169
95Sum-86
95SumNthD-86
95Top-4
95TopTra-138T
95Ult-261
95UltGolM-261
95UppDec-454T
95UppDecSE-77
95UppDecSE-228
95UppDecSEG-77
95UppDecSEG-228
96ColCho-286
96ColChoGS-286
96ColChoSS-286
96Don-480
96DonPreP-480
96Fle-540
96FleTif-540
96Pac-215
96PanSti-79
96Sco-430
96StaClu-291
96StaCluMOP-291
96Top-371
96Ult-271
96UltGolM-271
97Ult-392
97UltGolME-392
97UltPlaME-392

Cooper, Tim
90TamYanD-1
91GreHorP-3064
92GreHorC-21
92GreHorF-785
93SanBerSC-5
93SanBerSF-777
94ClaGolF-148
94TamYanC-6
94TamYanF-2389
95TamYanYI-3

Cooper, Virgil
88UtiBluSP-15
89SouBenWSGS-10

Cooper, Walker (William W.)
41CarW75-4
43MPR302-1-5
46SpoExcW-2-1A
47Exh-50
48Bow-9
49Bow-117
49EurSta-79
50Bow-111
51Bow-135
51R42SmaS-11
52Bow-208
52DixLid-5
52DixPre-5
52Top-294
53BowBW-30
53BraJohC-14
53BraSpiaS3-8
53ExhCan-58
54DanDee-3
56Top-273
57Top-380
60Top-462
76TayBow4-44
79DiaGre-168
79TCM50-69
83Bra53F-39
83TCMPla1943-24
83TopRep5-294
87SpoRea-24
92CarMcD-14
92ConTSN-633

Cooper, Wilbur
19W514-42
20NatCarE-16
21Exh-27
21Nei-57
22E120-215
22W573-23
23W501-80
77GalGloG-166
86PirGreT-10
20W516-19

Cope, Gary
91KisDodP-4175
92GreFalDSP-5

Cope, Robin
94AppFoxC-6
94AppFoxF-1045

Copeland, Mark
90AubAstB-24

Coplon, Mitch
82DayBeaAT-2

Copp, Bill
86WatPirP-7
87SalBucP-19
88HarSenP-853

Coppell, Shannon
89CliGiaP-902

Coppenbarger, Frank
77QuaCitAT-11

Copper Kings, Butte
95ButCopKtI-31

Copper, Jeff
91SalLakTSP-22

Coppeta, Greg
90NiaFalRP-16
91FayGenC-1
91FayGenP-1161
92LakTigC-12
93LakTigC-4
93LakTigF-1300

Coppinger, Rocky
94BluOriC-4
94BluOriF-3553
95Bes-1
95BesFra-F3
95BowBayTI-45
95SPML-18
96Bow-145
96BowBes-126
96BowBesAR-126

96BowBesR-126
96Cir-3
96CirRav-3
96Exc-3
96ExcCli-2
96LeaPre-120
96LeaPreP-120
96RocRedWB-8
96Zen-119
96ZenArtP-119
97BowCerBIA-CA16
97BowCerGIA-CA16
97Cir-291
97CirRav-291
97ColCho-2
97Don-145
97DonPre-138
97DonPreCttC-138
97DonPreP-145
97DonPrePGold-145
97DonTea-36
97DonTeaSPE-36
97Fin-4
97FinRef-4
97FlaSho-A108
97FlaSho-B108
97FlaSho-C108
97FlaShoLC-108
97FlaShoLC-B108
97FlaShoLC-C108
97FlaShoLCM-A108
97FlaShoLCM-B108
97FlaShoLCM-C108
97Fle-4
97FleTif-4
97MetUni-3
97Pac-21
97PacLigB-21
97PacSil-21
97Pin-175
97PinArtP-175
97PinMusC-175
97Sco-87
97ScoOri-4
97ScoOriPl-4
97ScoOriPr-4
97ScoPreS-87
97ScoShoS-87
97ScoShoSAP-87
97SP-33
97StaClu-299
97StaCluMOP-299
97Top-311
97TopChr-105
97TopChrR-105
97TopGal-155
97TopGalPPI-155
97Ult-3
97UltGolME-3
97UltPlaME-3
97UppDec-225
97UppDecBCP-BC6
97UppDecTTS-TS16
97UppDecU-57
97UppDecUGN-GN11
Coppock, Mark
90ArkRaz-30
Coppol, Carmen
77LynMetT-10
Coquillette, Trace
94BurBeeF-1087
94VerExpC-9
94VerExpF-3915
96WesPalBEB-25
Cora, Joey
85SpoIndC-4
86BeaGolGP-7
87DonOpeD-147
87PadBohHB-4
88BlaYNPRWL-104
88Fle-580
88FleGlo-580
88LasVegSC-18
88LasVegSP-234
88Sco-420
88ScoGlo-420
88Top-91
88TopTif-91
88TriAAAP-22
89BlaYNPRWL-112
89BlaYNPRWLU-49
89LasVegSC-14
89LasVegSP-23
89TriA AAC-33
90Bow-211
90BowTif-211
90Don-538
90Fle-154
90FleCan-154
90Lea-366
90ScoYouS2-14
90TriAAAC-33
90UppDec-601
91Fle-527
91FleUpd-11
91Lea-375
91Sco-253
91UppDec-291
91WhiSoxK-21
92Don-108
92Fle-76
92OPC-302
92PanSti-126
92Sco-326
92StaClu-535
92Top-302
92TopGol-302
92TopGolW-302
92TopMic-302
92Ult-334
92UppDec-359
92WhiSoxK-28
93Don-697
93Fla-182
93Fle-580
93Lea-461
93PacSpa-68
93Sco-454
93StaClu-54
93StaCluFDI-54
93StaCluMOP-54
93StaCluWS-6
93Top-122
93TopGol-122
93TopInaM-122
93TopMic-122
93Ult-172
93UppDec-742
93UppDecGold-742
93WhiSoxK-7
94ColC-85
94ColChoGS-85
94ColChoSS-85
94Don-447
94ExtBas-43
94Fin-146
94FinRef-146
94Fla-275
94Fle-79
94Lea-175
94Pac-123
94PanSti-46
94Pin-318
94PinArtP-318
94PinMusC-318
94Sco-485
94ScoCyc-TC12
94ScoGolR-485
94Sel-132
94StaClu-100
94StaCluFDI-100
94StaCluGR-100
94StaCluMOP-100
94StaCluST-ST18
94StaCluT-143
94StaCluTFDI-143
94Top-478
94TopGol-478
94TopSpa-478
94Ult-32
94UppDec-371
94UppDecED-371
94WhiSoxK-5
95Don-33
95DonPreP-33
95DonTopotO-148
95Fin-311
95FinRef-311
95Fla-300
95Fle-113
95FleUpd-74
95MarMot-8
95MarPac-16
95MarPac-29
95Pac-84
95Sco-454
95ScoGolR-454
95ScoPlaTS-454
95StaClu-33
95StaClu-536
95StaCluFDI-33
95StaCluMOP-33
95StaCluMOP-536
95StaCluSTDW-M536
95StaCluSTWS-33
95StaCluSTWS-536
95StaCluVR-22
95Top-545
95TopCyb-326
95TopTra-125T
95Ult-27
95UltGolM-27
96ColCho-312
96ColChoGS-312
96ColChoSS-312
96Don-259
96DonPreP-259
96EmoXL-111
96Fla-158
96Fle-234
96FleTif-234
96LeaSigA-49
96LeaSigAG-49
96LeaSigAS-49
96MarMot-8
96MetUni-106
96MetUniP-106
96Pac-417
96PacPri-P130
96PacPriG-P130
96Sco-162
96StaClu-374
96StaCluMOP-374
95StaCluVRMC-22
96TeaOut-20
96Top-304
96Ult-125
96UltGolM-125
96UppDec-199
97Cir-390
97CirRav-390
97ColCho-233
97Don-132
97DonPreP-132
97DonPrePGold-132
97DonTea-142
97DonTeaSPE-142
97Fle-204
97FleTif-204
97Lea-81
97LeaFraM-81
97LeaFraMDC-81
97Pac-185
97PacLatotML-18
97PacLigB-185
97PacPri-62
97PacPriLB-62
97PacPriP-62
97PacSil-185
97Pin-137
97PinArtP-137
97PinMusC-137
97Sco-201
97ScoMar-10
97ScoMarPl-10
97ScoMarPr-10
97ScoPreS-201
97ScoShoS-201
97ScoShoSAP-201
97StaClu-149
97StaCluMOP-149
97Top-35
97TopSta-85
97TopStaAM-85
97Ult-120
97UltGolME-120
97UltPlaME-120
97UppDec-499
Cora, Manny
92ChaRaiC-1
92ChaRaiF-126
92ClaFS7-53
92UppDecML-203
93SouAtlLAIPI-12
93SouAtlLAPI-7
93WatDiaF-1773
94RivPilCLC-4
95PorCitRTI-4
Corbell, Charlie
85FreGiaP-17
86ShrCapP-5
87MetColP-29
87PhoFirP-6
88TacTigC-3
88TacTigP-636
Corbell, Eric
91KinMetC-17
91KinMetP-3804
Corbett, Doug
79IndIndTI-12
81Don-546
81Fle-555
81OPC-162
81Top-162
81TopSti-106
82Don-53
82Fle-551
82FleSta-227
82OPC-157
82Top-560
82TopSti-210
82TopTra-21T
82TwiPos-5
83Fle-83
83Top-27
84EdmTraC-111
85AngSmo-18
85Don-474
85Fle-298
85Top-682
85TopTif-682
86AngSmo-8
86Top-234
86TopTif-234
87Don-333
87Fle-76
87FleGlo-76
87Top-359
87TopTif-359
89PacSenL-193
89T/MSenL-24
89TopSenL-114
90EliSenL-52
91OriCro-84
Corbett, Gene (Eugene Louis)
46SunBre-3
79DiaGre-305
Corbett, Ray
81CedRapRT-8
82WatRedT-11
83IndIndTI-15
85RocRedWT-1
90CedRapRDGB-25
Corbett, Sherman
86MidAngP-7
87EdmTraP-2078
88BlaYNPRWL-147
88FleUpd-11
88FleUpdG-11
89Don-407
89EdmTraC-8
89EdmTraP-547
89Fle-473
89FleGlo-473
89Top-99
89TopTif-99
89ToyRoo-6
89UppDec-464
90CMC-482
90EdmTraC-5
90EdmTraP-512
90ProAAAF-88
91LinDriAA-431
91MidAngLD-431
91MidAngOHP-8
91MidAngP-430
92LonTigF-625
93TolMudHF-1644
Corbin, A. Ray
72OPC-66
72Top-66
73OPC-411
73Top-411
74OPC-296
74Top-296
74TopSta-204
75OPC-78
75Top-78
76OPC-474
76SSP-209
76Top-474
78TwiFri-28
Corbin, Archie
89ColMetB-5
89ColMetGS-7
90St.LucMS-4
91Cla/Bes-293
91LinDriAA-404
91MemChiLD-404
91MemChiP-646
92ClaFS7-180
92Don-400
92MemChiF-2410
92MemChiS-431
92ProFS7-75
92SkyAA F-182
92StaClu-473
92TopDeb91-39
93ClaGolF-125
93HarSenF-262
94BufBisF-1828
96RocRedWB-9
Corbin, Ted
92ClaDraP-97
92FroRowDP-8
92Ft.MyeMCB-2
92Ft.MyeMF-2751
93ForMyeMC-5
93ForMyeMF-2660
94NasXprF-391
Corbitt, Claude E.
47RoyMon-1
Corbitt, Cord
91SpoIndC-19
91SpoIndP-3940
Corcino, Luis
86BurExpP-3
87Ft.MyeRP-22
88VirGenS-6
Corcoran, Larry (Lawrence J.)
86OldJudN-2
87OldJudN-100
88AugBecN-5
90KalBatN-9
Corcoran, Lori
83GleFalWST-23
Corcoran, Mickey (Michael J.)
12ColTinT-63
12ImpTobC-49
Corcoran, Tim (Timothy M.)
77EvaTriT-6
78TigBurK-20
78Top-515
79Top-272
80VenLeaS-31
81Don-367
81EvaTriT-18
81Fle-479
81Top-448
82OklCit8T-3
83PorBeaT-11
84PhiTas-34
85Don-381
85Fle-247
85PhiCIG-6
85PhiTas-12
85PhiTas-34
85Top-302
85TopTif-302
86Don-381
86Fle-437
86MetColP-21
86MetTCM-43
86TidTidP-5
86Top-664
86TopTif-664
87MaiGuiT-24
88ReaPhiP-887
91MetWIZ-84
Corcoran, Tommy (Thomas W.)
03BreE10-24
06FanCraNL-11
12ColRedB-63
90DodTar-138
95May-5
98CamPepP-15
Cordani, Richard
88CapCodPPaLP-8
90LSUTigP-6
91LSUTigP-8
Cordeiro, Richard
52LavPro-6
Corder, Daniel
74WicAerODF-108
Cordero, Edward

93BriTigC-7
93BriTigF-3650
96DurBulBlB-26
96DurBulBrB-27

Cordero, Pablo
95BurBeeTI-26
96BurBeeTI-23

Cordero, Wilfredo (Wil)
88BlaYNPRWLU-15
88JamExpP-1895
89WesPalBES-8
90Bes-128
90CMC-682
90JacExpB-5
90JacExpP-1381
90TopMag-103
91Bow-436
91Cla2-T2
91IndIndLD-179
91IndIndP-466
91LeaGolR-BC3
91LinDriAAA-179
91UppDec-60
92Bow-194
92Don-2
92DonRooP-BC20
92FleUpd-97
92IndIndF-1865
92IndIndS-179
92OPC-551
92ProFS7-254
92ScoRoo-110T
92SkyAAAF-88
92Top-551
92TopGol-551
92TopGolW-551
92TopMic-551
92TriPla-179
92UppDec-16
93Bow-508
93Don-432
93ExpColP7-3
93ExpPosN-8
93Fin-123
93FinRef-123
93Fla-80
93Fle-73
93FunPac-1
93HumDumC-36
93Lea-37
93LeaGolR-R2
93OPC-161
93OPCPre-29
93PacBeiA-25
93PacBeiA-26
93PacSpa-532
93PanSti-227
93Pin-280
93PinRooTP-7
93PinTea2-1
93Sco-334
93ScoProaG-1
93Sel-336
93SelChaR-18
93SelRoo-150T
93SP-101
93StaClu-361
93StaCluFDI-361
93StaCluMOP-361
93Stu-93
93Top-256
93TopGol-256
93TopInaM-256
93TopMic-256
93Toy-90
93TriPla-27
93Ult-65
93UppDec-60
93UppDecDG-32
93UppDecGold-60
93USPlaCR-3S
94Bow-153
94ColC-395
94ColChoGS-395
94ColChoSS-395
94Don-545
94ExtBas-301
94ExtBasSYS-6
94Fin-20
94FinJum-20
94FinRef-20
94Fla-187
94FleUpd-152
94Lea-103
94OPC-252
94OPCDiaD-10
94Pac-376
94PanSti-208
94Pin-89
94PinArtP-89
94PinMusC-89
94PinNewG-NG7
94ProMag-82
94Sco-412
94ScoGolR-412
94Sel-81
94Spo-36
94StaClu-393
94StaCluFDI-393
94StaCluGR-393
94StaCluMO-46
94StaCluMOP-393
94Stu-76
94Top-21
94TopGol-21
94TopSpa-21
94TriPla-92
94Ult-224
94UppDec-97
94UppDecED-97
94USPlaCR-3C
94USPlaCR-6D
95Baz-95
95Bow-337
95ColCho-245
95ColChoGS-245
95ColChoSE-97
95ColChoSE-257
95ColChoSEGS-97
95ColChoSEGS-257
95ColChoSESS-97
95ColChoSESS-257
95ColChoSS-245
95D3-50
95Don-150
95DonDom-6
95DonPreP-150
95DonTopotO-278
95Emb-85
95EmbGolI-85
95Emo-150
95Fin-40
95FinRef-40
95Fla-373
95Fle-346
95FleAllS-10
95Lea-128
95LeaLim-10
95Pac-264
95PacLatD-8
95PacPri-85
95PanSti-64
95Pin-346
95PinArtP-346
95PinFan-30
95PinMusC-346
95PinSam-US22
95PinUps-US22
95Sco-386
95ScoGolR-386
95ScoHaloG-HG105
95ScoPlaTS-386
95Sel-93
95SelArtP-93
95SelCer-6
95SelCerMG-6
95SP-74
95Spo-56
95SpoArtP-56
95SpoDouT-6
95SPSil-74
95StaClu-255
95StaCluFDI-255
95StaCluMOP-255
95StaCluSTWS-255
95StaCluVR-125
95Stu-186
95Sum-67
95SumNthD-67
95Top-108
95Top-387
95TopCyb-70
95UC3-2
95UC3ArtP-2
95Ult-188
95UltGolM-188
95UppDec-324
95UppDecED-324
95UppDecEDG-324
95UppDecSE-2
95UppDecSEG-2
95Zen-109
96ColCho-765
96Don-256
96DonPreP-256
96EmoXL-13
96Fla-17
96Fle-454
96FleRedS-4
96FleTif-454
96FleUpd-U11
96FleUpdTC-U11
96MetUni-14
96MetUniP-14
96Pac-131
96PacPri-P41
96PacPriG-P41
96PanSti-24
96Pin-11
96Pin-339
96PinAfi-121
96PinAfiAP-121
96PinArtP-8
96PinFoil-339
96PinSta-8
96ProSta-46
96Sco-344
96ScoDugC-B69
96ScoDugCAP-B69
96StaClu-327
96StaCluEPB-327
96StaCluEPG-327
96StaCluEPS-327
96StaCluMOP-327
96StaCluVRMC-125
96Sum-125
96SumAbo&B-125
96SumArtP-125
96SumFoi-125
96Top-413
96Ult-229
96Ult-312
96UltGolM-229
96UltGolM-312
96UppDec-282
97ColCho-52
97Fle-20
97FleTif-20
97NewPin-106
97NewPinAP-106
97NewPinMC-106
97NewPinPP-106
97Pac-36
97PacLigB-36
97PacSil-36
97ProMag-24
97ProMagML-24
97Sco-57
97ScoPreS-57
97ScoRedS-1
97ScoRedSPl-1
97ScoRedSPr-1
97ScoShoS-57
97ScoShoSAP-57
97StaClu-332
97StaCluMOP-332
97Top-394
97Ult-431
97UltGolME-431
97UltPlaME-431

Cordner, Steve
83QuaCitCT-19

Cordoba, Wilfrido
82AleDukT-9
83LynPirT-2
84PriWilPT-13

Cordona, Javier
94JamJamC-5
94JamJamF-3966

Cordova, Antonio
80VenLeaS-190
82QuaCitCT-21
84MidCubT-2

Cordova, Francisco
96Fin-B343
96FinRef-B343
96FleUpd-U174
96FleUpdTC-U174
96LeaSigEA-35
97Cir-265
97CirRav-265
97ColCho-427
97Don-300
97DonLim-119
97DonLimLE-119
97DonPreP-300
97DonPrePGold-300
97Fle-426
97FleTif-426
97MetUni-237
97Pac-392
97PacLigB-392
97PacPri-133
97PacPriLB-133
97PacPriP-133
97PacSil-392
97StaClu-289
97StaCluMOP-289
97Top-118
97UppDec-158

Cordova, Luis
92EriSaiC-25
92EriSaiF-1637
93LetMouF-4161
93LetMouSP-14

Cordova, Marty
89EliTwiS-5
92CalLeaACL-32
92UppDecML-115
92UppDecMLPotY-PY24
92VisOakC-14
92VisOakF-1026
93Bow-345
93ClaGolF-42
93ClaMVPF-3
93ExcFS7-198
93ExcLeaLF-4
93NasXprF-414
94AriFalLS-4
94Bow-544
94ExcFS7-92
94FleMajLP-6
94UppDecML-73
95Bow-183
95BowBes-R74
95BowBesR-R74
95ColCho-582T
95DonTopotO-108
95Emo-56
95EmoRoo-3
95Exc-80
95Fin-235
95FinRef-235
95Fla-278
95FlaWavotF-3
95Fle-199
95Lea-358
95LeaLim-26
95Sel-159
95SelArtP-159
95SelCer-114
95SelCerMG-114
95SigRooMR-MR1
95SigRooMRS-MR1
95SigRooOJSS-9
95SigRooOJSSS-9
95SP-23
95SPCha-8
95SPChaDC-8
95SPSil-23
95StaClu-538
95StaCluCB-CB9
95StaCluMOP-538
95StaCluMOP-CB9
95StaCluSTWS-538
95Sum-148
95SumNthD-148
95Top-639
95TopTra-45T
95UC3-118
95UC3ArtP-118
95UltGolMR-M9
95UppDec-250
95UppDecED-250
95UppDecEDG-250
95UppDecPAW-H40
95UppDecPAWE-H40
95UppDecSE-215
95UppDecSEG-215
95Zen-116
95ZenRooRC-12
96Baz-54
96Bow-91
96BowBes-44
96BowBesAR-44
96BowBesR-44
96Cir-55
96CirRav-55
96ColCho-199
96ColCho-704
96ColCho-755
96ColChoGS-199
96ColChoGS-704
96ColChoGS-755
96ColChoSS-199
96ColChoSS-704
96ColChoSS-755
96Don-353
96DonPreP-353
96EmoRarB-2
96EmoXL-80
96Fin-B184
96Fin-B206
96Fin-G4
96FinRef-B184
96FinRef-B206
96FinRef-G4
96Fla-112
96Fle-165
96FleRooS-2
96FleTif-165
96FleUpd-U217
96FleUpdTC-U217
96Lea-31
96LeaLim-39
96LeaLimG-39
96LeaPre-54
96LeaPreP-54
96LeaPrePB-31
96LeaPrePG-31
96LeaPrePS-31
96LeaPreSG-70
96LeaPreSte-70
96LeaSig-141
96LeaSigA-50
96LeaSigAG-50
96LeaSigAS-50
96LeaSigPPG-141
96LeaSigPPP-141
96MetUni-75
96MetUniMFG-2
96MetUniP-75
96MetUniPP-2
96Pac-361
96Pac-368
96PacMil-M5
96PacPri-P113
96PacPriG-P113
96PanSti-201
96PanSti-246
96Pin-121
96PinAfi-141
96PinAfiAP-141
96PinArtP-30
96PinSta-30
96ProSta-128
96Sco-299
96Sco-511
96ScoDugC-B24
96ScoDugCAP-B24
96ScoFutF-11
96Sel-35
96SelArtP-35
96SelCer-43
96SelCerAP-43
96SelCerCB-43
96SelCerCR-43
96SelCerMB-43
96SelCerMG-43
96SelCerMR-43
96SelTeaN-19
96SigRooOJMC-RY1
96SigRooOJMC-RY2
96SigRooOJMC-RY3
96SigRooOJMC-RY4
96SigRooOJMC-RY5
96SP-113
96Spo-12
96SpoArtP-12
96SPx-38
96SPxGol-38
96StaClu-131
96StaClu-228
96StaCluEPB-131
96StaCluEPG-131
96StaCluEPS-131
96StaCluMO-47
96StaCluMOP-131
96StaCluMOP-228
96Stu-68

96StuPrePB-68
96StuPrePG-68
96StuPrePS-68
96Sum-90
96SumAbo&B-90
96SumArtP-90
96SumFoi-90
96TeaOut-21
96Top-187
96TopBroLL-6
96TopChr-57
96TopChrR-57
96TopGal-91
96TopGalPPI-91
96TopLas-41
96TopLasBS-10
96TopMysF-M5
96TopMysFR-M5
96TopPro-AL12
96Ult-88
96Ult-593
96UltFreF-2
96UltFreFGM-2
96UltGolM-88
96UltGolM-593
96UltRisS-2
96UltRisSGM-2
96UppDec-390
96UppDecBCP-BC5
96Zen-25
96ZenArtP-25
97Bow-269
97BowChr-87
97BowChrI-87
97BowChrIR-87
97BowChrR-87
97BowInt-269
97Cir-271
97CirRav-271
97ColCho-154
97Don-68
97DonEli-99
97DonEliGS-99
97DonLim-33
97DonLimLE-33
97DonPre-130
97DonPreCttC-130
97DonPreP-68
97DonPrePGold-68
97Fin-61
97FinRef-61
97FlaSho-A102
97FlaSho-B102
97FlaSho-C102
97FlaShoLC-102
97FlaShoLC-B102
97FlaShoLC-C102
97FlaShoLCM-A102
97FlaShoLCM-B102
97FlaShoLCM-C102
97Fle-145
97FleTif-145
97Lea-63
97LeaFraM-63
97LeaFraMDC-63
97MetUni-209
97NewPin-138
97NewPinAP-138
97NewPinMC-138
97NewPinPP-138
97Pac-135
97PacLatotML-11
97PacLigB-135
97PacPri-44
97PacPriLB-44
97PacPriP-44
97PacSil-135
97Pin-149
97PinArtP-149
97PinIns-34
97PinInsCE-34
97PinInsDE-34
97PinMusC-149
97PinX-P-59
97PinX-PMoS-59
97ProMag-61
97ProMagML-61
97Sco-34
97ScoPreS-34
97ScoShoS-34
97ScoShoSAP-34
97Sel-10
97SelArtP-10
97SelRegG-10
97SP-108
97SpoIII-147
97SpoIIIEE-147
97StaClu-58
97StaCluC-CO9
97StaCluM-M16
97StaCluMat-58
97StaCluMOP-58
97StaCluMOP-M16
97Stu-61
97StuPrePG-61
97StuPrePS-61
97Top-435
97TopChr-154
97TopChrR-154
97TopGal-165
97TopGalPPI-165
97Ult-86
97UltDouT-6
97UltGolME-86
97UltPlaME-86
97UppDec-104

Cordova, Rocky
78CliDodT-5
79LodDodT-7

Corey, Bryan
93BriTigF-3651
94JamJamC-6
94JamJamF-3970
96Exc-49
96FayGenB-10

Corey, Mark M.
79RocRedWT-15
79Top-701
80RocRedWT-5
80Top-661
81Fle-193
81RocRedWW-4
81Top-399
82EvaTriT-23
86JacExpT-20
87IndIndTI-30
89PacSenL-195
91OriCro-85

Corgan, Chuck (Charles H.)
90DodTar-916

Corkhill, Pop (John S.)
87OldJudN-101
89EdgR.WG-6
90DodTar-139

Corkins, Mike
70Top-573
71MLBOffS-224
71OPC-179
71Top-179
72PadTeal-8
72Top-608
73OPC-461
73Top-461
74OPC-546
74PadDea-6
74Top-546

Cormack, Terry
83DurBulT-3
84DurBulT-6
85DurBulT-21

Corman, Dave
85BeaGolGT-20
90HagSunDGB-5

Cormier, Eric
93UtiBluSC-7
93UtiBluSF-3527

Cormier, Rheal
89St.PetCS-8
90ArkTraGS-9
90LouRedBLBC-12
91Bow-396
91LouRedP-2907
91LouRedTI-5
92Bow-473
92Don-712
92FleUpd-119
92Lea-469
92OPC-346
92ProFS7-315
92Sco-851
92StaClu-506
92Top-346
92TopDeb91-40
92TopGol-346
92TopGolW-346
92TopMic-346
92UppDec-574
93Bow-80
93CarPol-5
93Don-228
93Fle-124
93Lea-209
93MSABenSPD-20
93OPC-34
93PacSpa-631
93Pin-360
93Sco-371
93StaClu-15
93StaCluCa-18
93StaCluFDI-15
93StaCluMOP-15
93Top-149
93TopGol-149
93TopInaM-149
93TopMic-149
93Toy-21
93Ult-462
93UppDec-79
93UppDecGold-79
94CarPol-4
94ColC-481
94ColChoGS-481
94ColChoSS-481
94Don-622
94ExtBas-357
94Fin-248
94FinRef-248
94Fla-224
94Fle-630
94Lea-110
94Pac-587
94StaClu-437
94StaCluFDI-437
94StaCluGR-437
94StaCluMOP-437
94StaCluT-303
94StaCluTFDI-303
94Top-594
94TopGol-594
94TopSpa-594
94UppDec-422
94UppDecED-422
95ColCho-572T
95Don-352
95DonPreP-352
95Fle-495
95Lea-304
95Top-138
95TopTra-33T
96ColCho-61
96ColChoGS-61
96ColChoSS-61
96Don-97
96DonPreP-97
96ExpDis-6
96LeaSigA-51
96LeaSigAG-51
96LeaSigAS-51
97Fle-555
97FleTif-555
97Top-467
97Ult-371
97UltGolME-371
97UltPlaME-371

Cormier, Russ
89MedAthB-21
90ModA'sC-7
91HunStaC-9
91HunStaLD-284
91HunStaP-1788
91LinDriAA-284

Corn, Chris
94OneYanF-3783
95GreBatTI-8
96Exc-84
96TamYanY-9

Cornejo, Mardie
78MetDaiPA-4
78TidTidT-8
91MetWIZ-85

Cornelius, Brian
89NiaFalRP-4
90FayGenP-2420
91Cla/Bes-15
91FloStaLAP-FSL20
91LakTigC-23
91LakTigP-277
92LonTigF-644
92SkyAA F-171
93LonTigF-2320

Cornelius, Jon
95BatCliTI-7
96PieBolWB-8

Cornelius, Reid
89RocExpLC-6
90WesPalBES-3
91Bow-458
91Cla/Bes-52
91FloStaLAP-FSL42
91WesPalBEC-4
91WesPalBEP-1220
92ClaFS7-124
92HarSenS-280
92ProFS7-264
92SkyAA F-119
93HarSenF-263
94ExcFS7-223
94OttLynF-2894
95FleUpd-104
95NorTidTI-9
96BufBisB-5

Cornelius, Willie
78LauLonABS-17

Cornell, Daren
90BelBreB-16

Cornell, David
92EugEmeF-3041

Cornell, Jeff
83PhoGiaBHN-7
84PhoGiaC-12
85PhoGiaC-200
85Top-514
85TopTif-514
86IowCubP-8

Cornett, Brad
92St.CatBJC-22
92St.CatBJF-3378
93HagSunC-6
93HagSunF-1871
93SouAtlLAGF-25
94ClaGolF-88
94ExcFS7-141
94KnoSmoF-1296
94SyrChiTI-6
95AusFut-107
95Fle-91
95Pac-442
95Ult-117
95UltGolM-117

Cornish, Tim
92MarPhiC-14
92MarPhiF-3069
93MarPhiC-5
93MarPhiF-3482
95OdgRapTI-5

Cornutt, Terry
75LafDriT-23
76PheGiaCr-38
76PhoGiaCa-9
76PhoGiaCC-4
76PhoGiaVNB-5
77Gia-4
77PhoGiaVNB-4
78PhoGiaC-6
79PhoGiaVNB-15
80PhoGiaVNB-8

Corominas, Mike
95AubAstTI-18

Corona, John
90SprCarB-22
91St.PetCC-3
91St.PetCP-2267
93St.PetCC-11
93St.PetCF-2621
94ArkTraF-3083

Coronado, Osvaldo
95PitMetTI-27

Corps, Edwin
94SanJosGC-5
94SanJosGF-2809
96Exc-242

Corps, Erick
94MidLeaAF-MDW56
94SprSulC-4
94SprSulF-2041
95RanCucQT-5

Corrado, Gary
77WauMetT-7

Corral, Ruben
96HagSunB-1

Corrales, Pat (Patrick)
65OPC-107
65Top-107
66OPC-137
66Top-137
66TopVen-137
67OPC-78
67Top-78
69Top-382
70DayDaiNM-46
70OPC-507
70Top-507
71MLBOffS-57
71OPC-293
71Top-293
72Top-705
72Top-706
73OPC-542
73Top-542
74HawIslC-105
74OPC-498
74Top-498
76VenLeaS-73
79Top-499
80Top-41
81Fle-623
83Don-626
83PhiTas-6
83Top-637
84Ind-10
84IndWhe-18
84Nes792-141
84Top-141
84TopTif-141
85Ind-11
85IndPol-18
85Top-119
85TopTif-119
86IndOhH-7
86IndTeal-16
86Top-699
86TopTif-699
87IndGat-7
87IndGat-NNO
87Top-268
87TopTif-268
88ChaLooLTI-4
88TolMudHC-25
88TolMudHP-590
90BraDubS-5
91BraSubS-10
92BraLykS-10
93BraLykS-9
93RanKee-112
94BraLykS-7

Correa, Amilcar
89WytCubS-6
90GenCubP-3051
90GenCubS-5
91PeoChiC-3
91PeoChiP-1334
91PeoChiTI-5
92WinSpiC-16
92WinSpiF-1202

Correa, Antonio
76VenLeaS-121

Correa, Edwin
83AppFoxF-17
86DonRoo-4
86FleUpd-30
86RanPer-18
86SpoRoo-2
87ClaUpdY-143
87Don-57
87Fle-122
87FleGlo-122
87Lea-145
87OPC-334
87RanMot-19
87RanSmo-22
87Top-334
87TopTif-334
88Don-57
88Fle-464
88FleGlo-464
88PanSti-196
88RanSmo-18
88Sco-523
88ScoGlo-523
88Top-227
88TopTif-227
89RedFolSB-25
89UppDec-598
90VerBeaDS-9
93RanKee-113
93VerBeaDF-2207
95GreFalDTI-36
96SavSanB-1

Correa, Elvis

96GreFalDB-7
96GreFalDTI-6
Correa, Jorge
92AubAstC-26
92AubAstF-1346
Correa, Jose
92EliTwiC-16
92EliTwiF-3673
93ForWayWC-6
93ForWayWF-1960
94ForMyeMC-6
94ForMyeMF-1160
94VenLinU-177
Correa, Mickey
96DurBulBrB-12
Correa, Miguel
92IdaFalGF-3525
92IdaFalGSP-16
93MacBraC-7
93MacBraF-1413
93SouAtlLAGF-36
94GreBraF-424
95DurBulTI-9
Correa, Ramser
89HelBreSP-15
90BelBreB-1
90Bes-24
92StoPorF-28
93StoPorC-5
94CanIndF-3109
95SanAntMTI-50
96SanAntMB-3
Correia, Rod
88SouOreAP-1702
89ModA'sC-23
89ModA'sCLC-277
90ModA'sC-0
90ModA'sCLC-163
90ModA'sP-2218
91HunStaTI-7
91TacTigP-2312
92MidAngF-4032
92MidAngOHP-4
92MidAngS-457
93ExcFS7-140
93FleFinE-179
93SelRoo-142T
93StaCluAn-10
93VanCanF-2603
94AngMot-10-
94Fle-49
94Pac-72
94Sco-594
94ScoGolR-594
94StaClu-352
94StaCluFDI-352
94StaCluGR-352
94StaCluMOP-352
94Top-532
94TopGol-532
94TopSpa-532
94Ult-21
94VanCanF-1868
95Pac-52
96HunStaTI-4
96Pac-263
Correll, Vic (Victor C.)
75OPC-177
75Top-177
76OPC-608
76SSP-14
76Top-608
76VenLeaS-43
77Top-364
78IndIndTI-19
78Top-527
79Top-281
80RedEnq-9
80Top-419
81Top-628
Correnti, Chris
91BurAstC-28
92BurAstC-29
94LynRedSC-29
95TreThuTI-4
Corriden, John M. Jr.
43DodTeal-6
90DodTar-140
Corriden, John M. Sr.
32CubTeal-2
39CubTeal-3
48BluTin-17
48YanTeal-4
Corridon, Frank
08RosComP-137
09AmeCarE-27
09PC7HHB-8
11SpoLifCW-75
11SpoLifM-265
11T205-32
12ImpTobC-17
Corrigan, Cory
93JohCitCC-8
93JohCitCF-3671
94SavCarC-11
94SavCarF-501
95PeoChiTI-23
Corrigan, Larry
75WatDodT-4
Corry, DeLynn
92HamRedC-29
92HamRedF-1585
Corsaro, Robby
89BatCliP-1945
Corsi, Jim (James)
83GreHorT-4
85GreHorT-16
86NewBriRSP-7
87HunStaTI-7
87ModA'sC-3
87ModA'sP-25
88TacTigC-7
88TacTigP-625
89Fle-649
89FleGlo-649
89ScoHot1R-36
89TacTigC-2
89TacTigP-1560
89Top-292
89TopTif-292
90Don-422
90Fle-4
90FleCan-4
90OPC-623
90Sco-553
90Top-623
90TopTif-623
90UppDec-521
91AstMot-21
91UltUpd-80
92Don-467
92Fle-431
92Sco-524
92TacTigS-531
93Don-741
93Fle-424
93FleFinE-58
93MarUSPC-8D
93MarUSPC-10H
93Top-753
93TopGol-753
93TopInaM-753
93TopMic-753
94BreCouMF-3
95AthMot-25
95FleUpd-70
96A'sMot-18
96FleUpd-U72
96FleUpdTC-U72
96LeaSigEA-36
97Fle-188
97FleTif-188
Cort, Barry
75BurBeeT-3
78SpoIndC-18
79HolMilT-26
80HolMilT-4
94BreMilB-304
Cortes, Hernan
89BlaYNPRWL-172
89PenPilS-4
90Ft.LauYS-3
90StaFS7-39
91LinDriAA-628
91WilBilLD-628
91WilBilP-299
Cortez, Conde (Argenis)
87DayBeaAP-12
91BirBarLD-56
91BirBarP-1447
91LinDriAA-56
Cortez, Dave
87WicPilRD-18
Corujo, Rey
95BelGiaTI-10
96SanJosGB-7
Corwin, Al (Elmer)
52Bow-121
53BowC-126
53BowC-149
54Bow-137
55Bow-122
55GiaGolS-10
75Gia195T-3
79TCM50-232
Cosby, Bill
84WilMay-46
Cosby, Darin
88OklSoo-15
89OklSoo-11
Cosby, Rob
84EveGiaC-13A
Coscarart, Joe (Joseph M.)
36GouBWR-8
36GouWidPPR-A19
Coscarart, Pete (Peter J.)
39PlaBal-141
40DodTeal-4
40PlaBal-63
41DodTeal-2
49BowPCL-21
79DiaGre-365
83TCMPla1945-33
89DodSmoG-46
90DodTar-141
Cosenza, Vincent
52LavPro-40
Cosey, Ray (Donald Ray)
79OgdA'sT-16
80OgdA'sT-2
Cosgrove, Mike
74AstFouTIP-4
75IowOakT-4
75OPC-96
75Top-96
76Hos-131
76OPC-122
76Top-122
77Top-589
Cosio, Raymundo
78CedRapGT-6
79CedRapGT-27
Cosman, Jeff
93PitMetC-5
93PitMetF-3699
94CapCitBC-3
94CapCitBF-1742
95StLucMTI-9
Cosman, Jim
67Top-384
70OPC-429
70Top-429
89MarPhiS-7
Coss, Mike
91BluOriC-10
91BluOriP-4133
92FreKeyF-1810
Cossins, Tim
93EriSaiC-3
93EriSaiF-3119
94HudValRF-3387
95ChaRivUTIS-38
Costa, Tim
92MarPhiF-3048
Costa, Tony
92MarPhiC-6
93BatCliC-7
93BatCliF-3137
94SpaPhiF-1712
94SparPhiC-4
95ClePhiF-209
96ReaPhiB-2
Costas, Bob
89ChaLooLITI-7
Costell, Arnie
75DubPacT-28
Costello, Bob
83WisRapTF-14
Costello, Brian
89SalSpuP-1828
90CliGiaB-12
92SanJosGC-29
93MarPhiC-6
93MarPhiF-3487
94SpaPhiF-1734
94SparPhiC-5
95ClePhiF-227
Costello, Bubba
93BakDodCLC-5
94VerBeaDF-63
Costello, Chris
92GulCoaDF-3559
93GreFalDSP-26
94VerBeaDC-6
Costello, Dan (Daniel F.)
15SpoNewM-39
Costello, Fred
88AshTouP-1063
89ColMudB-16
89ColMudP-129
89ColMudS-6
90Bes-218
90ColMudB-16
90ColMudP-1341
90ColMudS-8
91OscAstC-1
91OscAstP-673
92JacGenF-3993
92OscAstC-11
93JacGenF-2101
94PhoFirF-1514
Costello, John
83EriCarT-18
84SavCarT-4
85SprCarT-5
86St.PetCP-7
87ArkTraP-25
88FleUpd-118
88FleUpdG-118
88LouRedBC-1
88LouRedBP-440
88LouRedBTI-16
88ScoRoo-107T
88ScoRooG-107T
89CarSmo-3
89ClaTraO-142
89Don-518
89Fle-446
89FleGlo-446
89PanSti-176
89Sco-534
89ScoHot1R-75
89Top-184
89TopTif-184
89UppDec-625
90Don-555
90ExpPos-5
90Fle-246
90FleCan-246
90OPC-36
90PubSti-214
90Sco-347
90SprCarDGB-10
90Top-36
90TopTif-36
90TopTVCa-8
90UppDec-486
90VenSti-115
91LasVegSLD-281
91LasVegSP-228
91LinDriAAA-281
91PadSmo-7
92Sco-614
Costello, Lou
93ActPacA-168
93ActPacA2-65G
Costello, Mike
86BeaGolGP-8
87WicPilRD-15
88WicPilRD-26
89DenZepC-5
89DenZepP-45
89ElPasDGS-5
Costello, T.J.
96SouOreTI-16
Costello, Tim
77VisOakT-4
Costic, Tim
91FreStaBS-3
92EliTwiC-5
92EliTwiF-3692
93ForWayWC-7
93ForWayWF-1980
94ForWayWC-6
94ForWayWF-2014
Costner, Kevin
88BulDurM-1
88DurBulS-9B
88DurBulS-NNO
89DurBullS-29
Costo, Tim
90ClaDraP-8
90KinIndTI-NNO
91Bow-79
91CanIndLD-79
91CanIndP-984
91Cla/Bes-389
91Cla/Bes-438
91Cla1-T38
91ClaGam-58
91LeaGolR-BC18
91LinDriAA-79
91LinDriP-79
91OPC-103
91Sco-680
91Top-103
91TopDesS-103
91TopMic-103
91TopTif-103
91UppDec-62
92Bow-489
92ChaLooF-3824
92ChaLooS-180
92ClaFS7-70
92DonRoo-29
92ProFS7-51
92SkyAA F-80
93Bow-314
93ClaFS7-160
93Don-270
93FleMajLP-A3
93IndIndF-1493
93Lea-529
93Pin-582
93Sco-265
93StaClu-390
93StaCluFDI-390
93StaCluMOP-390
93Top-577
93TopGol-577
93TopInaM-577
93TopMic-577
93Toy-25
93Ult-326
93UppDec-11
93UppDecGold-11
94Bow-416
94ColC-86
94ColChoGS-86
94ColChoSS-86
94Don-561
94Fle-408
94Lea-53
94Pac-144
94Sco-552
94ScoBoyoS-48
94ScoGolR-552
94StaClu-119
94StaCluFDI-119
94StaCluGR-119
94StaCluMOP-119
94Top-513
94TopGol-513
94TopSpa-513
94UppDec-168
94UppDecED-168
96BufBisB-6
Cota, Chris
85MexCitTT-11
87DayBeaAP-20
89BenBucL-3
Cota, Francisco
83MiaMarT-4
Cota, Tim
87VisOakP-4
Cote, Brice
80ElmPioRST-5
Cote, Gerard
43ParSpo-84
Cotes, Eugenio
77SalPirT-8
79PorBeaT-10
79Top-723
85DomLeaS-168
Cotner, Andrew
91KinMetC-28
91KinMetP-3805
92KinMetC-22
92KinMetF-1524
93KinMetC-6
93KinMetF-3790
93StLucMF-2913
Cottier, Chuck (Charles K.)
55DonWin-16
60BraLaktL-7
60BraSpiaS-6
60Lea-138
60Top-417
61Pos-113
61SenJayP-2

61TigJayP-7
61Top-13
62Jel-66
62Pos-66
62PosCan-66
62SalPlaC-20
62ShiPlaC-20
62Top-27
62TopBuc-19
62TopStal-93
62TopVen-27
63Fle-28
63Jel-98
63Pos-98
63Top-219
64Top-397
69Top-252
77QuaCitAT-12
78TCM60I-189
84MarMot-27
85MarMot-1
85Top-656
85TopTif-656
86Top-141
86TopTif-141
88CubDavB-NNO
89CubMar-NNO
90CubMar-28
90TopTVCu-3
91CubMar-NNO
91CubVinL-7
92CubMar-NNO
93CubMar-6

Cotto, Hector
88MiaMarS-5

Cotto, Henry
81QuaCitCT-15
83IowCubT-21
84CubChiT-8
84CubSev-28
85Don-411
85Fle-53
85FleUpd-31
85Top-267
85TopTif-267
86YanTCM-31
87ColCliP-16
87ColCliT-20
87Top-174
87TopTif-174
88BlaYNPRWL-35
88DonBasB-51
88Fle-205
88FleGlo-205
88FleUpd-58
88FleUpdG-58
88MarMot-6
88OPC-172
88Sco-368
88ScoGlo-368
88ScoRoo-48T
88ScoRooG-48T
88StaLinMa-5
88Top-766
88TopBig-125
88TopTif-766
88TopTra-31T
88TopTraT-31T
89BlaYNPRWL-37
89BlaYNPRWLU-51
89BlaYNPRWLU-59
89Don-109
89Fle-545
89FleGlo-545
89MarMot-6
89OPC-207
89PanSti-441
89Sco-209
89Top-468
89TopBig-160
89TopSti-218
89TopTif-468
89UppDec-134
90Bow-476
90BowTif-476
90Don-644
90Fle-511
90FleCan-511
90MarMot-9
90OPC-31
90PubSti-430
90Sco-161
90Top-31
90TopBig-156
90TopTif-31
90UppDec-207
90VenSti-116
91Bow-244
91Don-343
91Fle-448
91Lea-113
91MarCouH-18
91OPC-634
91PanFreS-232
91Sco-282
91StaClu-525
91Top-634
91TopDesS-634
91TopMic-634
91TopTif-634
91Ult-333
91UppDec-110
92Don-356
92Fle-276
92Lea-472
92MarMot-9
92OPC-311
92Pin-342
92Sco-390
92StaClu-14
92Top-311
92TopGol-311
92TopGolW-311
92TopMic-311
92Ult-432
92UppDec-616
92YanWIZ8-36
93Don-705
93Fle-672
93MarMot-5
93MarPub-9
93PacSpa-283
93PanSti-64
93Pin-323
93StaClu-565
93StaCluFDI-565
93StaCluMOP-565
93Top-206
93TopGol-206
93TopInaM-206
93TopMic-206
93TopTra-121T
93UppDec-411
93UppDecGold-411
94Don-184
94Fle-465
94Pac-240
94Sco-161
94ScoGolR-161
94Top-522
94TopGol-522
94TopSpa-522
96PorCitRB-2

Cotton, Joe
96BatCliTI-9

Cotton, John
89BurIndS-6
90WatIndS-5
91ColIndC-23
91ColIndP-1490
92KinIndC-16
92KinIndF-2482
92UppDecML-321
93CarLeaAGF-27
93KinIndC-5
93KinIndF-2259
93KinIndTI-4
94SprSulF-2048
95MemChiTI-7
96JacSunB-9
96TolMudHB-9

Cottrell, Steve
84EveGiaC-8

Couch, Johnny
94ConTSN-1297
94ConTSNB-1297

Couch, Richard
76AshTouT-12
77AshTouT-3

Couchee, Mike
82AmaGolST-16
85ChaO'sT-31
85LasVegSC-123
86TulDriTI-4
88QuaCitAGS-2
88SanDieSAAG-5
89SanDieSAG-5

Cougar, Ozzie
93KanCouCC-30
93KanCouCTI-30

Coughenour, Cara
95ColSilB-5
96ColSilB-5

Coughlin, Bill (William P.)
03BreE10-25
07TigACDPP-2
08RosComP-32
09TigHMTP-2
09WolNewDTPP-3
11SpoLifCW-76

Coughlin, Kevin
90UtiBluSP-1
91SouBenWSC-9
91SouBenWSP-2868
92SarWhiSCB-19
93SarWhiSC-8
93SarWhiSF-1375
94BirBarC-6
94BirBarF-631
94ClaGolF-154
95UppDecML-105
96BesAutS-23
96BirBarB-24
96Exc-31
96ExcSeaTL-2
96TreThuB-24
95UppDecMLFS-105

Coughlin, Red
85SyrChiT-24
86SyrChiP-10
87SyrChiT-33
88SyrChiP-819

Coughlin, Roscoe (William Edward)
87OldJudN-102

Coughlon, Kevin
82MadMusF-7
84MadMusP-21
85ModA'sC-12

Coughtry, Marlan (James M.)
61UniOil-S3
62Top-595

Coulon, Johnny
11TurRedT-54

Coulson, Robert
12T207-35

Coulson, Steven
77WesHavYT-5

Coulter, Chris
91BurIndP-3292

Coulter, Darrell
87UtiBluSP-19
88SpaPhiP-1029
88SpaPhiS-21
89SpaPhiP-1042
89SpaPhiS-5

Coulter, Roy
75AppFoxT-6
76AppFoxT-2
78AppFoxT-6

Coulter, Shannon
94EugEmeC-7
94EugEmeF-3720

Coumbe, Fritz (Fred)
16ColE13-33

Counsell, Craig
92BenRocC-9
92BenRocF-1479
93CenValRC-7
93CenValRF-2897
94NewHavRF-1555
96Bow-194
96ColSprSSTI-9

Counts, Rick
78DunBluJT-4

Cournoyer, Yvan
72Dia-71
72Dia-72

Courtney, Bill
93SouOreAC-30

Courtney, Clint (Clinton D.)
53BowC-70
53NorBreL-5
53Top-127
54Bow-69
54DixLid-2
54OriEss-7
55Bow-34
56Top-159
57Top-51
58SenJayP-3
58Top-92A
58Top-92B
59SenTealW-6
59Top-483
60Top-344
61A'sTeal-4
61SevElev-13
61Top-342
79TCM50-169
87AstSer1-30
91OriCro-86
91TopArc1-127

Courtney, Ernie (Ernest E.)
09ColChiE-64
11SpoLifCW-77
12ColRedB-64
12ColTinT-64

Courtney, Harry
22E120-106

Courtright, John
91BilMusP-3746
91BilMusSP-15
92ChaWheF-1
92ChaWVWC-14
93ChaLooF-2354
93SouAtlLAPI-8
94Bow-570
94ChaLooF-1352
95FleUpd-131

Cousins, Derryl
88T/MUmp-40
89T/MUmp-38
90T/MUmp-36

Cousy, Bob
51BerRos-A11
53SpoMagP-2
60Pos-1

Couture, Mike
90HelBreSP-11
91StoPorC-15
91StoPorP-3043
92BelBreC-10
92BelBreF-418
92MidLeaATI-8
93StoPorC-6
93StoPorF-756

Coveleski, Harry
09ColChiE-65A
09T206-75
10W555-18
11SpoLifM-280
11TurRedT-88
12ColRedB-65A
12ColTinT-65A
12ColTinT-65B
14B18B-15A
14B18B-15B
14B18B-15C
15SpoNewM-40
16BF2FP-27
16ColE13-34
16SpoNewM-39
81TigDetN-39
81TigSecNP-12
94ConTSN-1172
94ConTSNB-1172

Coveleski, Stan
09ColChiE-65B
10StaCarE-8
12ColRedB-65B
20NatCarE-17
21E121So1-13
21Exh-28
22E120-32
22W572-17
22W575-20
23W501-21
23W503-64
23WilChoV-23
25Exh-122
26Exh-122
26SpoComoA-12
27YorCarE-57
28StaPlaCE-13
28W502-57
28Yue-57
61Fle-100
70FleWorS-17
76ShaPiz-113
77GalGloG-118
77Ind192T-5
79DiaGre-276
80PerHaloFP-112
80SSPHOF-112
82OhiHaloF-24
83DiaClaS2-57
88SouBenWSGS-28
92ConTSN-462
92YanWIZH-7
93ConTSN-707
94ConTSN-1172
94ConTSNB-1172
95ConTSN-1362

Coveney, Jim
89AshTouP-961
93AshTouC-26
93AshTouF-2295

Coveney, Patrick
84AriWilP-3
86ClePhiP-5
87DayBeaAP-13

Covert, Dave
77LynMetT-11

Covington, Tex (William)
12T207-36

Covington, Wes (John W.)
56BraBilaBP-7
57BraSpiaS4-7
57Top-283
58BraJayP-4
58Top-140
59Top-290
59Top-565
60BraJayP-3
60BraLaktL-8
60Top-158
60TopVen-158
61Pos-108A
61Pos-108B
61Top-296
61TopStal-41
62SalPlaC-105
62ShiPlaC-105
62Top-157
62TopVen-157
63Jel-182
63Pos-182
63Top-529
64PhiPhiB-10
64Top-208
64TopVen-208
65Top-583
66OPC-52
66Top-52
66Top-484
66TopVen-52
78BraTCC-6
78TCM60I-132
87Bra195T-6
90DodTar-142

Cowan, Billy Roland
64Top-192
64TopVen-192
65OPC-186
65Top-186
69Top-643
71MLBOffS-341
71OPC-614
71Top-614
72OPC-19
72Top-19
78TCM60I-282
91MetWIZ-86
92YanWIZ6-29

Cowan, Ed
77DayBealT-2

Cowan, Jed
96OgdRapTI-NNO

Cowan, Johnnie
92NegLeaRLI-12

Cowboys, Kansas City
86JosHalC-8

Cowens, Al (Alfred Edward)
75OPC-437
75Top-437
76Hos-28
76HosTwi-28
76OPC-648
76SSP-175
76SSP-589
76Top-648
77Top-262
78Hos-67
78Kel-5
78OPC-143
78RCColC-74
78Roy-4

78SSP270-240
78Top-46
79OPC-258
79Top-490
80OPC-174
80Top-330
81CokTeaS-50
81Don-369
81Fle-471
81OPC-123
81Top-123
82Don-207
82Fle-266
82OPC-103
82Top-575
82TopSti-182
82TopTra-22T
83AllGamPI-50
83Don-554
83Fle-477
83FleSti-184
83MarNal-2
83OPC-193
83Top-763
83TopSti-115
84Don-511
84Fle-610
84MarMot-19
84Nes792-622
84Top-622
84TopSti-344
84TopTif-622
85Don-196
85Fle-487
85Lea-239
85MarMot-6
85OPC-224
85ThoMcAD-10
85Top-224
85TopSti-333
85TopTif-224
86Don-389
86Fle-463
86Lea-184
86MarMot-6
86OPC-92
86Top-92
86TopTif-92
89PacSenL-145
89T/MSenL-25
93RoySta2-3

Cowger, Tracy
79AshTouT-2
80TulDriT-18
81TulDriT-2
82TulDriT-12
83OklCit8T-5
83TulDriT-17

Cowley, Bill
43ParSpo-20

Cowley, Joe
78GreBraT-7
79SavBraT-15
82BraPol-38
83RicBraT-3
83Top-288
84ColCliP-7
84ColCliT-13
85Don-613
85Fle-124
85Lea-58
85Top-769
85TopSti-318
85TopTif-769
86BufBisP-9
86Don-608
86DonHig-44
86Fle-103
86FleUpd-31
86Top-427
86TopTif-427
86TopTra-29T
86TopTraT-29T
86WhiSoxC-40
87Don-552
87Fle-491
87FleGlo-491
87FleLeaL-12
87Lea-240
87PhiTas-39A
87Spo-196
87SpoTeaP-26
87Top-27
87TopSti-290
87TopTif-27
92YanWIZ8-37

Cowsill, Brendon
96BoiHawB-7

Cox, Billy (William Richard)
47PM1StaP1-37
47PM1StaP1-38
47TipTop-138
49Bow-73
49EurSta-33
50Bow-194
51Bow-224
51TopBluB-48
52Bow-152
52DixLid-6
52DixPre-6
52Top-232
53BowBW-60
53DixLid-3
53DixPre-3
53NorBreL-6
54Bow-26
54NewYorJA-3
54RedHeaF-4
54RedMan-NL2
55Bow-56
55OriEss-7
79TCM50-83
83TopRep5-232
84TCMPla1-41
90DodTar-143
91OriCro-87
91RinPosBD2-11
95TopArcBD-13
95TopArcBD-64
95TopArcBD-85

Cox, Bobby (Robert Joe)
69MilBra-65
69Top-237
69TopTeaP-19
75SyrChiTI-2
76VenLeaS-37
78Top-93
79Top-302
80Top-192
81BraPol-6
81Don-426
81Fle-247
81Top-675
83OPC-34
83Top-606
84BluJayFS-10
84Fle-653
84Nes792-202
84OPC-202
84Top-202
84TopTif-202
85BluJayFS-9
85OPC-135
85Top-411
85TopTif-411
86BluJayGT-12
86OPC-359
86Top-471
86TopTif-471
90BraDubS-6
90TopTra-23T
90TopTraT-23T
91BraDubP-7
91BraSubS-11
91OPC-759
91Top-759
91TopDesS-759
91TopMic-759
91TopTif-759
92BraLykP-9
92BraLykS-11
92OPC-489
92Top-489
92TopGol-489
92TopGolW-489
92TopMic-489
92YanWIZ6-30
93BluJayDM-15
93BraLykP-8
93BraLykS-10
93Top-501
93TopGol-501
93TopInaM-501
93TopMic-501
94BraLykP-7
94BraLykS-8
96UppDec-477

Cox, Boyce
89BriTigS-31
90BriTigS-30
96BriWhiSB-7

Cox, Carl
47SigOil-2
86VerBeaDP-4

Cox, Carter
76Top-595
87BriYouC-16

Cox, Chris
93DanBraC-10
93DanBraF-3624

Cox, Chuck
95BatCliTI-8
96PieBolWB-9

Cox, Danny
82SprCarF-12
83St.PetCT-4
84Car-6
84Car5x7-5
84Don-449
85CarTeal-7
85Don-571
85Fle-222
85Top-499
85TopTif-499
86BasStaB-24
86CarIGAS-3
86CarKASD-5
86CarSchM-4
86CarTeal-10
86Don-382
86Fle-32
86Lea-177
86OPC-294
86Spo-108
86Top-294
86TopMinL-61
86TopSti-48
86TopTif-294
87CarSmo-6
87Don-553
87Fle-292
87FleExcS-12
87FleGlo-292
87Lea-160
87OPC-202
87SpoTeaP-12
87Top-621
87TopMinL-33
87TopTif-621
88CarSmo-2
88Don-60
88DonBasB-75
88Fle-28
88FleGlo-28
88Lea-72
88LouRedBTI-17
88OPC-59
88PanSti-383
88Sco-415
88ScoGlo-415
88Spo-84
88StaLinCa-4
88Top-59
88TopBig-111
88TopTif-59
88Woo-27
89Don-348
89Fle-447
89FleGlo-447
89OPC-158
89Sco-613
89Top-562
89TopTif-562
89UppDec-535
90CarSmo-3
90LouRedBLBC-13
90OPC-184
90PubSti-215
90SprCarDGB-9
90Top-184
90TopTif-184
90TopTVCa-9
90VenSti-117
91Lea-350
91PhiMed-10
91TopTra-25T
91TopTraT-25T
92BufBisBS-5
92Don-614
92Fle-526
92OPC-791
92PhiMed-9
92Sco-568
92StaClu-351
92Top-791
92TopGol-791
92TopGolW-791
92TopMic-791
93BluJayD-3
93BluJayFS-7
93Don-466
93Fle-499
93FleFinE-291
94BluJayUSPC-3H
94BluJayUSPC-11C
94Don-114
94Fle-329
94Lea-87
94Sco-242
94ScoGolR-242
94StaCluT-152
94StaCluTFDI-152
94Top-582
94TopGol-582
94TopSpa-582
95BluJayUSPC-9H

Cox, Darren
87IdaFalBP-21

Cox, Darron
88CapCodPPaLP-97
88OklSoo-12
89BilMusP-2067
89OklSoo-12
90Bes-20
90ChaWheB-1
90ChaWheP-2243
90CMC-840
90SouAtlLAS-5
91CedRapRC-13
91CedRapRP-2720
92ChaLooF-3822
92ChaLooS-181
93ChaLooF-2363
94IowCubF-1278
95Top-646
96RicBraB-9
96RicBraRC-21
95OrlCubF-13

Cox, Dick (Elmer Joseph)
22E120-17
22W573-24
27AmeCarE-5
90DodTar-917

Cox, Doug
87BakDodP-13
88VerBeaDS-4

Cox, J. Casey
66Top-549
67CokCapS-7
67Top-414
68OPC-66
68Top-66A
68Top-66B
68TopVen-66
69SenTeal8-9
69Top-383
70OPC-281
70Top-281
71MLBOffS-533
71OPC-82
71SenTealW-8
71Top-82
72MilBra-81
72OPC-231
72Top-231
73OPC-419
73Top-419
92YanWIZ7-38
93RanKee-7

Cox, Jeff (Jeffrey Linden)
79OgdA'sT-12
80OgdA'sT-19
81Don-230
81TacTigT-19
81Top-133
82EvaTriT-14
83OmaRoyT-14
86VerRedP-4
87VanCanP-1600
87WatPirP-30
88AugPirP-382
88ChaLooLTI-7
89MemChiB-24
89MemChiP-1195
89MemChiS-24
90MemChiB-26
90MemChiP-1025
90MemChiS-26
91LinDriAA-424
91MemChiLD-424
91MemChiP-669
92OmaRoyF-2977
92OmaRoyS-349
93OmaRoyF-1696
93TriAAAGF-41
94OmaRoyF-1238
94VenLinU-99
96GreBraB-1
96GreBraTI-43

Cox, Jim
85ElmPioT-5

Cox, Jim (James Charles)
72Dia-8
74OPC-600
74Top-600
76SSP-325

Cox, John
86HumStaDS-41

Cox, Larry Eugene
76SSP-596
76TacTwiDQ-4
77Top-379
78SSP270-258
78Top-541
79Top-489
80OPC-63
80Top-116
81Don-285
81Fle-604
81Top-249
81TopTra 740
83QuaCitCT-2
85IowCubT-28
86IowCubP-9
87IowCubTI-22
88CubDavB-NNO
89CubMar-NNO
93RanKee-114

Cox, Robbie
76BatRouCT-9

Cox, Stan
86DavLipB-7

Cox, Steve
92ClaDraP-85
92FroRowDP-98
93Bow-653
93SouOreAC-1
93SouOreAF-4069
94WesMicWC-5
94WesMicWF-2302
95Bes-38
95ModA'sTI-4
95SPML-126
96ColCho-434
96ColChoGS-434
96ColChoSS-434
96Exc-97
96ExcAll-2
96Fla-146
96FlaWavotF-6
96FleUpd-U73
96FleUpdNH-4
96FleUpdTC-U73
96HunStaTI-5
96Top-424
96Ult-399
96UltGolM-399
96UltGolP-5
96UltGolPHGM-5
96UppDec-237
96UppDecFSP-FS7
97Bow-338
97BowInt-338

Cox, Ted
91PeoChiTI-30

Cox, Ted (William Ted)
78Top-706
79Top-79
80Top-252
80VenLeaS-215
81Don-283
81Fle-602
81SpoIndT-16

Cox, Terry
71OPC-559
71Top-559

Coyle, Bryan
94GreFalDSP-6
95YakBeaTI-6

Coyle, Rocky (Joseph)
84ModA'sC-8
87KnoBluJP-1499
87SyrChiT-27
86HumStaDS-15
Cozzi, Dante
52LavPro-73
Cozzolino, Paul
82VerBeaDT-3
Crabbe, Bruce
86PitCubP-4
87IowCubTI-12
88IowCubC-13
88IowCubP-550
89IowCubC-14
89IowCubP-1714
90CMC-290
90ProAAAF-410
90RicBraBC-5
90RicBraC-14
90RicBraP-265
90RicBraTI-7
91LinDriAAA-429
91RicBraBC-2
91RicBraLD-429
91RicBraP-2576
91RicBraTI-21
92SyrChiF-1973
92SyrChiMB-2
92SyrChiS-502
94ButCopKSP-27
95ColSilB-6
96ColSilB-6
Crable, George
90DodTar-918
Crabtree, Chris
91YakBeaC-24
91YakBeaP-4242
Crabtree, Estel C.
36WorWidGV-134
41CarW75-5
82OhiHaloF-45
Crabtree, Robert
96BelGiaTI-29
Crabtree, Tim
92ClaDraP-45
92ClaFS7-432
92FroRowDP-9
92St.CatBJC-23
92St.CatBJF-3379
93ClaFS7-66
93ClaGolF-208
93ExcFS7-240
93KnoSmoF-1243
93StaCluM-29
93Top-742
93TopGol-742
93TopInaM-742
93TopMic-742
94SyrChiF-965
94SyrChiTI-7
95LinVen-182
95SyrChiTI-10
96BluJayOH-6
96Fle-271
96FleTif-271
96LeaSigEA-37
96Top-351
97BluJayS-22
97Fle-236
97FleTif-236
97Top-129
Craddock, Walt
59Top-281
Cradle, Cobi
93PriRedC-5
93PriRedF-4192
94ChaWheC-6
94ChaWheF-2715
94SouAtlLAF-SAL39
95StLucMTI-10
Cradle, Rickey
92MedHatBJF-3218
92MedHatBJSP-15
93HagSunC-7
93HagSunF-1890
94DunBluJC-7
94DunBluJF-2568
95KnoSmoF-50
96KnoSmoB-9
Craft, Harry Francis
38CinOraW-6
39OrcPhoAP-4
39PlaBal-65
40PlaBal-79
41HarHarW-4
55A'sRodM-21
58A'sJayP-1
62Col.45B-5
62Col45'JP-5
62Top-12
62TopVen-12
63Col45'JP-3
63Top-491
64Col.45JP-3
64Top-298
64TopVen-298
76A'sRodMC-7
78TCM60I-244
79DiaGre-258
89AstCol4S-27
Craft, Mark
90SouOreAB-16
90SouOreAP-3442
Crafton, Kevin
96NewJerCB-6
Craig, Dale
89WytCubS-7
90WinSpiTI-8
91GenCubC-3
91GenCubP-4220
Craig, Dean
78CliDodT-6
79WauTimT-18
82NasSouTI-8
Craig, Morris
90HunCubP-3287
91GenCubC-4
91PeoChiP-1347
92PeoChiC-23
Craig, Pete
65Top-466
66OPC-11
66Top-11
66TopVen-11
67Top-459
Craig, Rodney Paul
79SpoIndT-5
80Top-672
81ChaChaT-19
81Don-288
81Fle-597
81Top-282
82Ind-9
82IndTeal-8
82IndWhe-14
83ChaChaT-15
83Don-515
84MaiGuiT-19
Craig, Roger
47Exh-51
56Dod-6
56Top-63
57Top-173
58Top-194
59DodTeal-3
60DodBelB-15
60DodJayP-1
60DodMor-2
60DodPos-2
60DodTeal-3
60DodUniO-2
60Lea-8
60Top-62
60TopVen-62
61DodBelB-38
61DodUniO-2
61Top-543
62MetJayP-3
62SalPlaC-189
62ShiPlaC-189
62Top-183
62TopBuc-20
62TopStal-154
62TopVen-183
63ExhStaB-18
63Fle-47
63Jel-200
63MetJayP-2
63Pos-200
63Top-197
64Top-295
64TopVen-295
65RedEnq-6
65Top-411
66Top-543
72PadTeal-9
74MetOriEB-3
74OPC-31
74Top-31
76SSP-628
77PadSchC-16
78PadFamF-7
78TCM60I-201
79Top-479
80MarExh-8
81TCM60I-482
82MetGal62-22
83Tig-9
84TigWavP-12
86GiaMot-1
86Top-111
86TopTif-111
87GiaMot-1
87Top-193
87TopTif-193
88GiaMot-1
88RinPosD1-3B
88Top-654
88TopTif-654
89GiaMot-1
89PacLegI-145
89Top-744
89TopBasT-102
89TopTif-744
90DodTar-144
90GiaMot-1
90GiaSmo-5
90K-M-33
90OPC-351
90Top-351
90TopTif-351
90TopTVA-66
91GiaMot-1
91GiaPacGaE-6
91MetWIZ-87
91OPC-579
91Top-579
91TopDesS-579
91TopGloA-12
91TopMic-579
91TopTif-579
92GiaMot-1
92GiaPacGaE-14
92OPC-109
92Top-109
92TopGol-109
92TopGolW-109
92TopMic-109
95TopArcBD-111
95TopArcBD-145
Craig, Tom
82SyrChiT-25
83SyrChiT-3
84SyrChiT-3
Crain, Gregg
91CedRapRC-29
Crall, Jim
75AndRanT-18
Cram, Jerry
71OPC-247
71Top-247
75TidTidTI-7
76OmaRoyTT-5
76SSP-559
80OmaRoyP-7
81OmaRoyT-2
82OmaRoyT-26
83OmaRoyT-25
84OmaRoyT-13
91MetWIZ-88
Cramer, Bill
90RocExpLC-5
90RocExpP-2698
91WesPalBEC-15
91WesPalBEP-1231
Cramer, Doc (Roger Maxwell)
33ButCanV-8
33RitCE-1C
34DiaMatCSB-33
34BatR31-53
34Gou-25
34GouCanV-74
35DiaMatCS3T1-38
35GouPuzR-8J
35GouPuzR-9J
36GouWidPPR-B6
39PlaBal-101
40PlaBal-29
77GalGloG-71
79DiaGre-57
81DiaStaCD-114
81TigDetN-24
83DiaClaS2-61
83TCMPla1943-12
89PacLegI-181
92ConTSN-451
93ConTSN-903
94ConTSN-1154
94ConTSNB-1154
Cramer, George
35ExhFou-14
Cramer, Mike (Michael J.)
75PhoGiaCK-26
Cramer, Rob
86VisOakP-8
Crandall, Bob
80ElmPioRST-33
Crandall, Del (Delmar W.)
47Exh-52
47StaPinP2-12
50Bow-56
50JJKCopP-3
51Bow-20
52Top-162
53BraJohC-15
53BraSpiaS3-9
53BraSpiaS7-5
53Top-197
54Bow-32
54BraJohC-1
54BraSpiaSP-7
54RedMan-NL3
54Top-12
55ArmCoi-3
55Bow-217
55BraGolS-15
55BraJohC-1
55BraSpiaSD-7
55RedMan-NL2
56BraBilaBP-8
56Top-175
57BraSpiaS4-8
57Top-133
58BraJayP-5
58JayPubA-4
58Top-351
58Top-390
59ArmCoi-7
59Baz-8
59Top-425
59Top-567
60ArmCoi-7
60Baz-36
60BraLaktL-9
60BraSpiaS-7A
60BraSpiaS-7B
60KeyChal-12
60MacSta-6
60Top-170
60Top-568
60TopVen-170
61Pos-110A
61Pos-110B
61Top-390
61Top-583
61TopDicG-2
61TopStal-42
62BraJayP-5
62Top-351
62Top-443
62TopStal-147
63BraJayP-4
63Jel-153
63Pos-153
63SalMetC-11
63Top-460
64ChatheY-28
64GiaJayP-2
64Top-169
64TopVen-169
65OPC-68
65Top-68
66Top-339
66TopVen-339
73OPC-646
73Top-646
74Top-99
75OPC-384
75Top-384
78AtlCon-5
78BraTCC-7
78TCM60I-144
79DiaGre-223
79TCM50-68
80AlbDukT-23
81AlbDukT-25
82AlbDukT-24
83AlbDukT-23
83Bra53F-1
83TopRep5-162
84Don-632
84MarMot-1
84Nes792-721
84Top-721
84TopTif-721
86BraGreT-8
88PacLegI-98
89SweBasG-132
91TopArc1-197
92BazQua5A-4
94TopArc1-12
94TopArc1G-12
96SanBerSB-1
Crandall, Doc (James Otis)
09ColChiE-66
09RamT20-32
09T206-76
09T206-77
10CouT21-110
10CouT21-111
10DomDisP-28
10NadE1-12
10RedCroT-14
10RedCroT-99
10RedCroT-178
10SweCapPP-109
11S74Sil-82
11SpoLifCW-78
11SpoLifM-206
11T205-33
12ColRedB-66
12ColTinT-66
12HasTriFT-48C
12HasTriFT-74B
12T207-37
14CraJacE-67
15CraJacE-67
76ISCHooHA-17
Crandall, Ducky
75LafDriT-29
Crane, Cannonball (Edward N.)
87OldJudN-103
89SFHaCN-3
Crane, Gordy
75SacSolC-18
Crane, John
96BatCliTI-24
Crane, Rich
89FreStaBS-7
89GreFalDSP-3
90BakDodCLC-235
Crane, Sam (Samuel Byren)
22E120-137
90DodTar-919
Crane, Sam (Samuel N.)
87BucN28-109
87OldJudN-104
Crane, Todd
95BatCliTI-9
96BatCliTI-3
96PieBolWB-10
Cranford, Jay
93AugPirC-6
93AugPirF-1550
94CarLeaAF-CAR38
94SalBucC-6
94SalBucF-2328
95Bow-64
95CarMudF-165
96CarMudB-20
Cranford, John
92WelPirC-5
92WelPirF-1329
Cranston, William
09T206-482
10CouT21-14
Cravath, Gavvy (Clifford C.)
09ColChiE-67
09T206-414
12ColRedB-67
12ColTinT-67
14CraJacE-82
15CraJacE-82
15SpoNewM-41
16BF2FP-86

16ColE13-35
16SpoNewM-40
17HolBreD-19
19W514-11
83PhiPosGPaM-5
91ConTSN-277
93ConTSN-803
Craven, Britt
91QuaCitAC-2
91QuaCitAP-2619
Crawford, Carlos
91BurIndP-3293
92ColRedC-6
92ColRedF-2381
93KinIndC-6
93KinIndF-2238
93KinIndTI-5
94CanIndF-3110
96PhiTeal-7
96ScrRedBB-10
Crawford, Glenn M.
47RemBre-25
Crawford, Jack
82DanSunF-8
83PeoSunF-15
Crawford, Jerry
88T/MUmp-28
89T/MUmp-26
90T/MUmp-25
Crawford, Jim
74OPC-279
74Top-279
76OPC-428
76SSP-47
76Top-428
76TopTra-428T
77Top-69
89GasRanP-1015
Crawford, Joe
91KinMetC-16
91KinMetP-3806
92ColMetPI-39
92ProFS7-290
92St.LucMCB-5
92St.LucMF-1739
93St.LucMC-6
94BinMetF-698
94St.LucMC-5
95BinMetTI-43
96BinBeeB-4
96NorTidB-11
93StLucMF-2914
Crawford, Johnny
77ForLauYS-3
Crawford, Marty
96BatCliTI-19
Crawford, Pat
94ConTSN-1293
94ConTSNB-1293
34DiaMatCSB-34
74Car193T-3
Crawford, Paxton
96MicBatCB-10
Crawford, Rufus
55Bow-121
Crawford, Sam (Samuel Earl)
03WilCarE-8
04FanCraAL-9
07TigACDPP-3
08RosComP-33
09AmeCarE-28
09BusBroBPP-5
09ColChiE-68
09PhiCarE-7
09SpoNewSM-31
09T206-78
09T206-79
09TigHMTP-3
09TigMorPenWBPP-3
09TigTaCP-4
09WolNewDTPP-4
09WolNewDTPP-5
10CouT21-112
10CouT21-272
10DarChoE-13
10E-UOraBSC-8
10E101-12
10E102-6
10MelMinE-12
10NadCarE-13
10NadE1-13
10PeoT21-13
10RedCroT-15
10RedCroT-179
10SepAnoP-9
10W555-19
11BasBatEU-14
11E94-8
11MecDFT-11
11SpoLifCW-79
11SpoLifM-56
11TurRedT-5
12ColRedB-68
12ColTinT-68
12HasTriFT-5
12HasTriFT-26
12SenVasS-2
13NatGamW-12
13TomBarW-12
14CraJacE-14
14TexTomE-15
15AmeCarE-10
15CraJacE-14
15SpoNewM-42
16BF2FP-28
16ColE13-36
16SpoNewM-41
16TanBraE-7
19W514-95
63GadFunC-40
72FleFamF-27
75ShaPiz-9
76ShaPiz-82
77BobParHoF-17
77GalGloG-140
77GalGloG-267
80PacLeg-55
80PerHaloFP-82
80SSPHOF-82
81ConTSN-98
81TigDotN 121
81TigSecNP-9
82DiaCla-27
85Woo-9
87ConSer2-30
87HygAllG-12
89HOFStiB-50
90BasWit-78
94ConTSN-1221
94ConTSNB-1221
96PitPosH-5
Crawford, Shag
89PacLegI-199
Crawford, Steve
82Don-564
82Fle-291
82RedSoxC-4
82Top-157
83PawRedST-4
83Top-419
84PawRedST-14
85Don-395
85Fle-156
85Top-661
85TopTif-661
86Don-416
86Fle-346
86Lea-193
86Top-91
86TopTif-91
87Don-399
87Fle-33
87FleGlo-33
87Top-589
87TopTif-589
88Fle-350
88FleGlo-350
88Sco-289
88ScoGlo-289
88Top-299
88TopTif-299
90Lea-494
91Fle-554
91OPC-718
91RoyPol-5
91Sco-287
91Top-718
91TopDesS-718
91TopMic-718
91TopTif-718
92Sco-349
Crawford, Willie M.
65Top-453
68Top-417
69Top-327
69TopTeaP-22
70Kel-26
70OPC-34
70Top-34
71DodTic-4
71MLBOffS-100
71OPC-519
71Top-519
72Top-669
73LinPor-93
73OPC-639
73Top-639
74OPC-480
74Top-480
74TopSta-43
75OPC-186
75Top-186
76OPC-76
76SSP-84
76Top-76
77BurCheD-107
77Top-642
78TCM60I-157
78Top-507
85SpoIndGC-4
90DodTar-146
Crawfords, Pittsburgh
88NegLeaD-4
90PomBlaBNLP-2546
91PomBlaBPB-7
92NegLeaRLI-84
93NegLeaRL2-45
93NegLeaRL2-46
93NegLeaRL2-61
93NegLeaRL2-62
93NegLeaRL2-63
Creamer, Gerry
94SarRedSC-6
94SarRedSF-1942
Creamer, Robert
90LitSunW-14
Crede, Brad
96BatCliTI-26
Credeur, Todd
85AncGlaPTI-7
86AshTouP-6
87OscAstP-28
88OscAstS-6
89ColMudB-26
89OscAstS-5
90ColMudB-17
90ColMudP-1342
90ColMudS-9
Cree, Birdie (William F.)
09T206-80
10CouT21-15
10CouT21-113
10DomDisP-29
10RedCroT-16
10RedCroT-100
10RedCroT-180
10SweCapPP-33
11SpoLifM-76
12HasTriFT-27
14TexTomE-16
15VicT21-5
Creech, Ed
90GatCitPSP-24
91JamExpC-28
91JamExpP-3561
Creed, Bennett
90MiaMirIS-30
Creek, Doug
91HamRedP-4031
93ArkTraF-2807
94Bow-3
94LouRedF-2976
95ArkTraTI-8
96FleUpd-U203
96FleUpdTC-U203
96GiaMot-17
96LeaSigEA-38
96Ult-565
96UltGolM-565
97PacPriGotD-GD215
Creek, Ryan
94QuaCitRBC-7
94QuaCitRBF-527
95JacGenTI-1
96JacGenB-7
Creekmore, Niles
87SalLakTTT-17
Creel, Keith
82OmaRoyT-3
83Don-574
83OmaRoyT-5
83Roy-8
84Fle-346
84OmaRoyT-15
85MaiGuiT-6
86IndTeal-17
86MaiGuiP-7
87OklCit8P-7
93RanKee-115
Creger, Bernie (Bernard Odell)
47TipTop-152
Creighton, James
94OriofB-17
Crema, Pat
92MedHatBJF-3204
92MedHatBJSP-4
Crenshaw, Ken
89PriPirS-28
Crespi, Creepy (Frank A.)
41CarW75-6
41DouPlaR-145
79DiaGre-159
Crespo, Felipe
91MedHatBJP-4106
91MedHatBJSP-22
92Bow-77
92MyrBeaHC-19
92MyrBeaHF-2202
93ClaFS7-274
93DunBluJC-6
93DunBluJF-1803
93DunBluJFFN-6
93FloStaLAF-8
94ClaGolF-55
94KnoSmoF-1309
95SPML-162
95SyrChiTI-11
96BluJayOH-7
96Bow-305
96Fin-B217
96FinRef-B217
96Fla-182
96FleUpd-U95
96FleUpdTC-U95
96LeaSigA-52
96LeaSigAG-52
96LeaSigAS-52
96PinAfi-175
96PinAfiAP-175
96Sel-187
96SelArtP-187
96SelCer-130
96SelCerAP-130
96SelCerCB-130
96SelCerCR-130
96SelCerMB-130
96SelCerMG-130
96SelCerMR-130
96Sum-182
96SumAbo&B-182
96SumArtP-182
96SumFoi-182
96SyrChiTI-10
96Ult-428
96UltGolM-428
97BluJayS-55
97Fle-507
97FleTif-507
97Pac-217
97PacLigB-217
97PacSil-217
97Sco-426
97ScoHobR-426
97ScoResC-426
97ScoShoS-426
97ScoShoSAP-426
97Top-203
97UppDec-275
Crespo, Michael
91ButCopKSP-7
91GasRanC-14
91GasRanP-2691
92GasRanC-3
92GasRanF-2255
93ChaRanC-5
93ChaRanF-1943
Cress, Missy
95ColSilB-7
96ColSilB-7
Cresse, Mark
81DodPol-NNO
83DodPol-NNO
84DodPol-NNO
85DodCokP-8
86DodCokP-7
86DodPol-NNO
87DodMot-27
87DodPol-29
88DodMot-28
89DodMot-27
89DodPol-1
90DodMot-28
90DodPol-NNO
91DodMot-28
91DodPol-NNO
92DodMot-28
92DodPol-NNO
93DodMot-28
93DodPol-30
94DodMot-28
94DodPol-30
95DodMot-28
95DodPol-30
96DodMot-28
96DodPol-8
Crew, Ken
86MemChiSTOS-2
86MemChiTOS-2
87MemChiB-8
87MemChiP-20
88ColAstB-6
Crews, Jason
96AriBlaDB-13
Crews, Larry
82CliGiaF-19
84ShrCapFB-5
85PhoGiaC-178
Crews, Tim
81BurBeeT-10
83ElPasDT-17
84ElPasDT-10
86ElPasDP-7
87AlbDukP-8
88AlbDukC-8
88AlbDukP-264
88DodPol-27
88Don-464
88DonRoo-20
88Fle-511
88FleGlo-511
88Sco-641
88ScoGlo-641
88Spo-224
88Top-57
88TopTif-57
89DodMot-24
89DodPol-27
89DodStaSV-2
89Don-486
89PanSti-96
89Sco-505
89Top-22
89TopTif-22
89UppDec-611
90DodMot-26
90DodPol-52
90DodTar-147
90Don-550
90El PasDAGTI-29
90Fle-390
90FleCan-390
90OPC-551
90Sco-164
90Top-551
90TopTif-551
90UppDec-670
91DodMot-26
91DodPol-52
91Don-294
91Fle-197
91Lea-141
91OPC-737
91Sco-302
91StaClu-375
91Top-737
91TopDesS-737
91TopMic-737
91TopTif-737
91UltUpd-87
91UppDec-596
92DodMot-13
92DodPol-52
92DodSmo-5692
92Don-437
92Fle-452
92OPC-642
92Sco-238
92StaClu-349

92Top-642
92TopGol-642
92TopGolW-642
92TopMic-642
92Ult-502
92UppDec-687
93Fle-444
93Pin-554
Cribb, Buddy
89AlaGol-19
Crider, Jerry
69Top-491A
69Top-491B
71OPC-113
71Top-113
Criger, Louis
03BreE10-26
04FanCraAL-10
04RedSoxUP-2
09AmeCarE-29
09PC7HHB-10
09RamT20-33
09SpoNewSM-2
09T206-81
10E-UOraBSC-9
11BasBatEU-15
11SpoLifCW-80
11SpoLifM-77
11T205-34
11TurRedT-89
Crills, Brad
94BluOriC-5
94BluOriF-3554
96HigDesMB-8
Crim, Chuck
83BelBreF-22
84ElPasDT-6
85VanCanC-220
86VanCanP-8
87BrePol-32
87DonRoo-18
87FleUpd-19
87FleUpdG-19
87TopTra-25T
87TopTraT-25T
88BrePol-32
88Don-355
88Fle-162
88FleGlo-162
88Sco-402
88ScoGlo-402
88StaLinBre-5
88Top-286
88TopTif-286
89Bow-136
89BowTif-136
89BrePol-32
89BreYea-32
89Don-617
89DonBasB-127
89Fle-183
89FleGlo-183
89OPC-99
89Sco-272
89Top-466
89TopTif-466
89UppDec-501
90BreMilB-3
90BrePol-32
90Don-221
90El PasDAGTI-7
90Fle-319
90FleCan-319
90Lea-58
90OPC-768
90PanSti-103
90PubSti-493
90Sco-108
90Top-768
90TopTif-768
90UppDec-511
90VenSti-118
91Bow-51
91BreMilB-6
91BrePol-6
91Don-684
91Fle-579
91Lea-28
91OPC-644
91Sco-99
91StaClu-112
91Top-644
91TopDesS-644
91TopMic-644
91TopTif-644
91Ult-173
91UppDec-391
92Don-103
92Fle-175
92Lea-312
92OPC-169
92Sco-22
92ScoProP-6
92ScoRoo-53T
92StaClu-823
92Top-169
92TopGol-169
92TopGolW-169
92TopMic-169
92UppDec-496
93AngMot-20
93Don-649
93Fle-570
93PacSpa-365
93Sco-455
93StaClu-327
93StaCluAn-2
93StaCluFDI-327
93StaCluMOP-327
93Top-499
93TopGol-499
93TopInaM-499
93TopMic-499
94BreMilB-305
94FleUpd-108
95Fle-412
Crimian, Jack
53CarHunW-6
56Top-319
57Top-297
Criminger, John
92BelBreF-398
93StoPorC-7
93StoPorF-737
Crimmins, John
92ElmPioC-8
92ElmPioF-1384
Cripe, Dave (David Gordon)
76OmaRoyTT-6
83DayBeaAT-1
85OscAstTI-1
86ColAstP-8
Cripps, Bobby
96GreFalDB-8
96GreFalDTI-17
Criscione, Dave G.
74SpoIndC-33
75SpoIndC-12
76SacSolC-1
77RocRedWM-1
78RocRedWT-6
91OriCro-88
Criscola, Tony (Anthony P.)
47CenFlo-5
Crisler, Joel
77QuaCitAT-13
79SalLakCGT-15
80ElPasDT-11
Crisler, Thomas
81RedPioT-3
Crispin, Carlos
93AubAstC-5
93AubAstF-3451
Criss, Dode
09ColChiE-69
09PC7HHB-9
09T206-82
11SpoLifCW-81
11SpoLifM-107
12ColRedB-69
12ColTinT-69
Criss, Matt
90WicStaSGD-8
Crist, Clark
81LynSaiT-28
81WauTimT-21
82LynSaiT-10
84ChaLooT-6
91AubAstC-24
91AubAstP-4291
92AubAstC-28
92AubAstF-1372
Crist, Jack
71RicBraTI-5
Crist, W.E.
88AllandGN-18
Cristelli, Pat
76SalLakCGC-10
77SalLakCGC-10
78STLakCGC-10
Cristopher, Carlos
93BenRocC-6
93BenRocF-3276
Criswell, Brian
85MadMusP-6
85MadMusT-9
86MadMusP-6
87HunStaTI-8
88HunStaTI-3
Criswell, Tim
86DurBulP-6
87DurBulP-7
Critz, Hughie (Hugh Melville)
20WalMaiW-10
25Exh-26
26Exh-26
28Exh-13
28StaPlaCE-14
28W56PlaC-H2
29ExhFou-7
29PorandAR-14
30SchR33-46
31Exh-9
31W517-25
33ExhFou-5
33Gou-3
33Gou-238
33GouCanV-3
33RitCE-6C
34DiaMatCSB-35
34Gou-17
34GouCanV-72
35DiaMatCS3T1-39
35ExhFou-5
35GouPuzR-4A
35GouPuzR-7A
35GouPuzR-12A
61Fle-101
87ConSer2-10
88ConSer5-6
91ConTSN-290
Crnich, Jeff
89BelMarL-36
Croak, David
90MarPhiP-3188
Crocker, H.G.
88AllandGN-19
Crockett, Claude
77St.PetCT-18
Crockett, Rusty
88PeoChiTI-9
89WinSpiS-6
90ChaKniTI-21
90TopTVCu-41
91ChaKniLD-130
91ChaKniP-1696
91LinDriAA-130
92ChaKniF-2777
92ChaKniS-151
Crofford, Kenny
93QuaCitRBC-28
94QuaCitRBC-28
Croft, Paul
78WisRapTT-2
90HagSunDGB-6
Crogan, Jack
87OldJudN-105
Croghan, Andrew
92GreHorC-5
94AbaYanF-1433
95Exc-92
Croghan, Andy
89AlaGol-10
91OneYanP-4147
92GreHorF-771
93PriWilCC-5
93PriWilCF-648
Cromartie, Warren L.
76VenLeaS-86
77ExpPos-10
78OPC-117
78Top-468
79ExpPos-6
79OPC-32
79Top-76
80ExpPos-7
80OPC-102
80Top-180
81AllGamPI-140
81Don-332
81Fle-144
81FleStiC-92
81OPC-345
81OPCPos-5
81Top-345
81TopScr-78
81TopSti-188
82Don-340
82ExpHygM-4
82ExpPos-6
82ExpPos-7
82ExpZel-7
82ExpZel-18
82FBIDis-5
82Fle-186
82FleSta-33
82OPC-61
82OPC-94
82OPCPos-13
82Top-526
82Top-695
82TopSti-60
83AllGamPI-139
83Don-466
83ExpStu-18
83Fle-279
83FleSta-44
83FleSti-261
83OPC-351
83Top-495
84Fle-272
84Nes792-287
84OPC-287
84Top-287
84TopTif-287
87JapPlaB-27
91Bow-315
91FleUpd-25
91Lea-458
91Stu-64
92Sco-637
93ExpDonM-14
93UppDecS-27
Crombie, Kevin
92NiaFalRC-19
92NiaFalRF-3316
93FayGenC-8
93FayGenF-124
Cromer, Brandon
92ClaDraP-25
92ClaFS7-416
92FroRowDP-36
92UppDecML-18
93ClaGolF-173
93St.CatBJC-6
93St.CatBJF-3979
93StaCluM-190
94HagSunC-4
94HagSunF-2737
95DunBluJTI-5
96KnoSmoB-10
Cromer, Burke
92IdaFalGF-3504
92IdaFalGSP-21
93DanBraC-11
93DanBraF-3613
Cromer, D.T.
92SouOreAF-3431
93MadMusC-7
94WesMicWC-6
94WesMicWF-2308
95ModA'sTI-5
96ModA'sB-7
97Bow-177
97BowChr-169
97BowChrI-169
97BowChrIR-169
97BowChrR-169
97BowInt-177
Cromer, David T.
92SouOreAC-7
93MadMusF-1834
Cromer, Tripp
89HamRedS-10
90St.PetCS-3
91St.PetCC-19
91St.PetCP-2282
92ArkTraF-1135
92ArkTraS-31
92SkyAA F-15
93Bow-52
93LouRedF-220
93TriAAAGF-22
94Cla-56
94Don-419
94FleMajLP-7
94LouRedF-2986
94Pac-588
94Pin-425
94PinArtP-425
94PinMusC-425
94StaCluT-328
94StaCluTFDI-328
94Top-139
94TopGol-139
94TopSpa-139
94UppDec-113
94UppDecED-113
95FleUpd-156
95StaClu-602
95StaCluMOP-602
95StaCluSTWS-602
96ColCho-287
96ColChoGS-287
96ColChoSS-287
96Don-153
96DonPreP-153
96Fle-541
96FleTif-541
96LouRedB-13
96Pac-223
96Top-41
96Ult-272
96UltGolM-272
Crompton, Herb (Herbert B.)
52LavPro-80
Cromwell, Brian
94DavLipB-6
95DavLipB-7
Cromwell, Nate
88MyrBeaBJP-1174
89DunBluJS-3
90CMC-816
90KnoBluJB-27
90KnoBluJP-1238
90KnoBluJS-2
91Cla/Bes-91
91KnoBluJLD-353
91KnoBluJP-1760
91LinDriAA-353
92KnoBluJF-2983
92KnoBluJS-379
93KnoSmoF-1244
93WicWraF-2971
94WicWraF-183
Cron, Chris
86DurBulP-7
87QuaCitAP-23
88CalLeaACLC-34
88PalSprACLC-102
88PalSprAP-1441
89MidAngGS-11
89TexLeaAGS-2
90CMC-498
90EdmTraC-21
90EdmTraP-523
90ProAAAF-99
91EdmTraLD-158
91EdmTraP-1521
91LinDriAAA-158
92Cla1-T29
92Don-698
92Fle-656
92Sco-847
92SkyAAAF-281
92TopDeb91-41
92VanCanF-2728
92VanCanS-632
93Fle-581
93NasSouF-575
94ChaKniF-900
96HicCraB-28
Crone, Bill
81LynSaiT-16
82LynSaiT-11
83SalLakCGT-18
84SalLakCGC-172
85CalCanC-93
86CalCanP-5
87TucTorP-4
Crone, Ray
54BraJohC-20
54BraSpiaSP-8
54Top-206
55BraGolS-14
55BraJohC-12

55Top-149
56Top-76
57BraSpiaS4-9
57Top-68
58GiaArmT-1
58GiaSFCB-6
58Top-272
85NewOriT-18
94TopArc1G-206
Crone, Raymond H.
94TopArc1-206
Cronin, Chuck
47SunBre-4
Cronin, James John
90DodTar-148
94ConTSN-1158
94ConTSNB-1158
Cronin, Jeff
91DurBulC-5
91DurBulP-1538
Cronin, Joe (Joseph Edward)
30SchR33-37
31Exh-31
31SenTealPW-6
32USCar-7
33ButCanV-9
33ButCre-5
33DouDisP-11
33GeoCMil-7
33Gou-63
33Gou-109
33Gou-189
33GouCanV-63
33RitCE-7H
33TatOrbSDR-176
34BatR31-32
34BatR31-183
34ButPreR-12
34ExhFou-16
35ExhFou-9
35GouPuzR-6E
35GouPuzR-11G
35GouPuzR-13E
35GouPuzR-15E
36ExhFou-9
36GouWidPPR-A20
36GouWidPPR-B7
36NatChiFPR-21
36R31PasP-32
36R31Pre-G4
36SandSW-8
36WorWidGV-46
37ExhFou-9
37OPCBatUV-124
38ExhFou-9
38OurNatGPP-3
39GouPreR303A-9
39GouPreR303B-4
39WorWidGTP-9
40PlaBal-134
40WheM4-7A
40WheM4-7B
41DouPlaR-59
41DouPlaR-81
41PlaBal-15
42RedSoxTI-7
43MPR302-1-6
43RedSoxTI-4
46RedSoxTI-4
59FleWil-39
59FleWil-55
60SenUniMC-3
61GolPre-14
67TopVen-164
73HalofFPP-4
75ShaPiz-6
76RowExh-16
76ShaPiz-80
77GalGloG-65
77GalGloG-198
79RedSoxEF-6
79RedSoxEF-24
80PacLeg-39
80PerHaloFP-80
80SSPHOF-80
81ConTSN-65
81SanDieSC-19
82DiaCla-51
83ConMar-14
83DonHOFH-20
86ConSer1-9
86RedSoxGT-6
86SpoDecG-7
87HygAllG-13
87RedSox1T-1
88ConAmeA-6
89CMCMan-8
89HOFStiB-19
89PacLegI-167
91ConTSN-50
91ConTSN-314
92ConTSN-600
93ConTSN-676
93ConTSN-843
93DiaStaES-123
94ConTSN-1085
94ConTSNB-1085
Cronin, John J.
11SpoLifCW-82
Cronk, Doug
89GasRanP-1013
89GasRanS-5
89SouAtlLAGS-29
89Sta-135
90ChaRanS-5
Cronkright, Dan
86PenWhiSP-7
Cronkright, Dave
87DayBeaAP-24
Crooks, John Charles
87OldJudN-106
Crosby, Ed (Edward C.)
71CarTeal-13
71OPC-672
71Top-672
73OPC-599
73Top-599
76OPC-457
76SSP-520
76Top-457
76TulOilGP-9
78SanJosMMC-5
79SpoIndT-1
Crosby, Ken
75TulOil7-6
76OPC-593
76SSP-602
76Top-593
Crosby, Mike
92ColRedC-9
92ColRedF-2393
93Bow-177
93KinIndC-7
93KinIndF-2250
93KinIndTI-6
94CanIndF-3120
Crosby, Pat
86LitFalMP-7
Crosby, Todd
87SpaPhiP-15
88ClePhiS-9
89St.PetCS-9
89Sta-49
90CMC-124
90LouRedBC-24
90LouRedBLBC-14
90LouRedBP-408
90ProAAAF-522
90TopTVCa-44
91LinDriAAA-232
91LouRedLD-232
91LouRedP-2922
91LouRedTI-18
92ShrCapF-3879
92ShrCapS-580
Crosetti, Frankie (Frank P.)
33Gou-217
34BatR31-182
34DiaStaR-86
36GouBWR-9
36GouWidPPR-A21
36NatChiFPR-22
36NatChiFPR-107
36R31Pre-L12
36SandSW-9
36WorWidGV-91
38OurNatGPP-4
39GouPreR303A-10
39WorWidGTP-10
39WorWidGV-6
41DouPlaR-113
43YanSta-7
47TipTop-50
48BluTin-24
48YanTeal-5
51R42SmaS-17
52Bow-252
52Top-384
53Dor-136
60Top-465
61Yan61RL-33
68Baz-13
69PilPos-21
75YanDyn1T-9
75YanDyn1T-51
75YanDyn1T-52
81TCM60I-481
83Pil69G-20
83TCMPla1943-2
83TopRep5-384
88ConSer3-8
90PacLeg-19
90SweBasG-48
91SweBasG-20
92ActPacA-45
92YanWIZA-14
93UppDecAH-35
94UppDecAH-37
94UppDecAH1-37
Crosnoe, Cory
91PulBraC-6
91PulBraP-4012
92MacBraC-11
92MacBraF-272
Cross, Adam
95DanBraTI-7
96EugEmeB-6
Cross, Bob
79NewCoPT-16
Cross, Jeff (Joffre)
46SeaSLP-10
47TipTop-153
Cross, Jesse
89MyrBeaBJP-1474
90DunBluJS-6
90FloStaLAS-27
90StaFS7-63
91KnoBluJLD-354
91KnoBluJP-1761
91LinDriAA-354
92KnoBluJF-2984
92SyrChiS-503
93SyrChiF-994
94ExcFS7-142
94SyrChiF-966
94SyrChiTI-8
Cross, Lave (LaFayette N.)
03BreE10-27
04FanCraAL-11
11SpoLifCW-83
87OldJudN-107
90DodTar-149
95May-6
98CamPepP-16
Cross, Leach
11TurRedT-69
Cross, Mike
92FreKeyC-4
Cross, Monte (Montford M.)
03BreE10-28
04FanCraAL-12
09T206-415
11SpoLifCW-84
Crossan, Clay
96AriBlaDB-14
Crossley, Chad
95BoiHawTI-12
Crossley, William
87OldJudN-108
Croteau, Julie
92SpoIllFK1-268
94ColSilBC-2
95ColSilB9-3
Crotty, Joe (Joseph P.)
87OldJudN-109A
87OldJudN-109B
Crouch, Bill
41CarW75-7
90DodTar-150
Crouch, Matt
86BurExpP-4
88MemChiB-8
89OmaRoyC-5
89OmaRoyP-1717
Crouch, Zach
85GreHorT-9
87NewBriRSP-2
88PawRedSC-6
88PawRedSP-457
89NewBriRSP-612
89NewBriRSS-4
90TopTVRS-40
Crough, Bill
41Gou-27
Crouse, Buck (Clyde E.)
92ConTSN-509
Croushore, Rich
93GleFalRC-10
93GleFalRF-3996
94MadHatC-7
94MadHatF-125
96ArkTraB-8
Crouwel, Michael
92MarPhiC-2
92MarPhiF-3059
Crow, Bill
93EliTwiC-25
Crow, Dean
93BelMarC-10
93BelMarF-3200
96PorCitRB-9
97Bow-365
97BowBes-146
97BowBesAR-146
97BowBesR-146
97BowInt-365
Crow, Don (Donald Leroy)
80AlbDukT-27
81AlbDukT-13
82AlbDukT-12
90DodTar-151
Crow, Gabby (Roger)
79QuaCitCT-4
80QuaCitCT-32
81QuaCitCT-32
82QuaCitCT-12
83QuaCitCT-1
Crowder, General (Alvin)
31SenTealPW-7
33ButCanV-10
33Gou-95
33Gou-122
33GouCanV-71
33TatOrbSDR-185
34DiaMatCSB-36
34BatR31-161
34ButPreR-13
34DiaStaR-93
34ExhFou-16
34Gou-15
34GouCanV-65
35DiaMatCS3T1-40
35GouPuzR-5F
35GouPuzR-6F
35GouPuzR-11H
35GouPuzR-13F
36R31PasP-46
60SenUniMC-4
61Fle-102
76TigOldTS-5
77GalGloG-187
83ConMar-19
88ConAmeA-7
91ConTSN-257
93ConTSN-682
94ConTSN-1277
94ConTSNB-1277
Crowe, George Daniel
52Top-360
53BraJohC-18
53BraSpiaS3-10
53Top-3
55BraJohC-39
56Top-254
57Kah-6
57Top-73
58Kah-6
58RedEnq-8
58RedJayP-5
58Top-12
59Top-337
60Top-419
61Top-52
83Bra53F-37
83TopRep5-360
91TopArc1-3
Crowe, Ron
88NebCor-3
89EveGiaS-5
89Sta-195
90Bes-170
90CliGiaB-21
90CliGiaP-2557
91SanJosGC-5
91SanJosGP-16
92ShrCapF-3875
92ShrCapS-581
93CliGiaC-8
93CliGiaF-2482
Crowell, James
95WatIndTI-10
Crowell, William
87OldJudN-110
Crowley, Brian
89ButCopKSP-8
Crowley, Jim
91ElmPioC-3
91ElmPioP-3276
92LynRedSC-18
92LynRedSF-2912
93NewBriRSF-1227
94LynRedSC-7
94LynRedSF-1898
Crowley, Ray
78MemChiBC-2
79MemChiT-16
80MemChiT-11
Crowley, Terry
88SalBucS-4
89SalBucS-5
90CMC-762
90HarSenP-1198
90HarSenS-5
91CarMudLD-104
91CarMudP-1091
91LinDriAA-104
92CanIndF-696
Crowley, Terry (Terrence M.)
70OPC-121
70Top-121
71MLBOffS-292
71OPC-453
71Top-453
72Top-628
73OPC-302
73OriJohP-11
73Top-302
74OPC-648
74Top-648
74TopTra-648T
75OPC-447
75Top-447
76OPC-491
76SSP-35
76Top-491
77RocRedWM-10
79Top-91
80Top-188
81Don-507
81Fle-190
81OPC-342
81Top-543
82Don-383
82Fle-160
82Top-232
83Don-457
83ExpPos-4
83Fle-55
83Top-372
83TopTra-22T
84Nes792-732
84OPC-246
84Top-732
84TopTif-732
87OriFreB-10
88OriFreB-10
91OriCro-89
93OriCroASU-10
Crowley, William M.
87BucN28-49
Crownover, Derek
86DavLipB-8
Crowther, Brent
94BenRocF-3583
95AshTouTI-31
95Bes-68
96Exc-151
96ExcCli-3
96NewHavRB-7
96SalAvaB-6
97BenRocC-3
Crowther, John
94SigRooDP-53
94SigRooDPS-53
94St.CatBJC-7
94St.CatBJF-3635

94StaCluDP-33
94StaCluDPFDI-33
95HagSunF-60
95StCatSTI-5
96HagSunB-2

Cruise, Mark
94JohCitCC-7
94JohCitCF-3690

Cruise, Walt (Walton Edwin)
20NatCarE-18
21Exh-29
22E120-123
22W572-18
23WilChoV-24
95ConTSN-1410

Crum, George
83BurRanF-4
83BurRanT-14
85TulDriTI-4
86WatIndP-6

Crump, Jamie
90PulBraB-15
90PulBraP-3095

Crump, Jody
94JohCitCC-8
94JohCitCF-3691

Crutcher, Dave
79TulDriT-19
80TulDriT-2
81TulDriT-15

Crutchfield, Jimmie (Jim)
78LauLonABS-35
86NegLeaF-29
91NegLeaRL-8
92NegLeaK-6
92NegLeaRLI-13
95NegLeaLI-8

Cruz, Andres
90MemChiB-23
90MemChiP-1003
90MemChiS-8
91LinDriAA-405
91MemChiLD-405
91MemChiP-647

Cruz, Arcadio
77ChaPatT-3

Cruz, Bernardo
88SouBenWSGS-12

Cruz, Brian
94MacBraC-5
94MacBraF-2208

Cruz, Charlie
95EugEmeTI-5
96MacBraB-6

Cruz, Cirilo
96EveAquB-6

Cruz, Daniel
90BriTigP-3162
90BriTigS-4

Cruz, Deivi
95BelGiaTI-7
96BurBeeTI-16
97Bow-346
97BowInt-346
97ColCho-338
97Don-388
97DonPre-166
97DonPreCttC-166
97DonPreP-388
97DonPrePGold-388
97Fle-591
97FleTif-591
97Lea-341
97LeaFraM-341
97LeaFraMDC-341
97PinX-P-136
97PinX-PMoS-136
97Sco-488
97ScoHobR-488
97ScoResC-488
97ScoShoS-488
97ScoShoSAP-488
97Ult-512
97UltGolME-512
97UltPlaME-512

Cruz, Fausto
91ModA'sP-3095
92CalLeaACL-9
92RenSilSCLC-38
92UppDecML-157
93LimRocDWB-18
93LimRocDWB-141
93ModA'sC-7
93ModA'sF-806
94Bow-436
94Cla-45
94ExcFS7-119
94SpoRoo-112
94SpoRooAP-112
94TacTigF-3182
94Ult-406
95ColCho-128
95ColChoGS-128
95ColChoSS-128
95EdmTraTI-5
95Pin-146
95PinArtP-146
95PinMusC-146
95Sco-583
95ScoGolR-583
95ScoPlaTS-583
95Sel-216
95SelArtP-216
96ColCho-641
96ColChoGS-641
96ColChoSS-641
96TolMudHB-10
97PacPriGotD-GD40

Cruz, Georgie
83MemChiT-2

Cruz, Heity (Hector Dilan)
75TulOil7-1
76OPC-598
76Top-598
77Car5-4
77CarTeal-4
77Top-624
78SSP270-248
78Top-257
79GiaPol-9
79Top-436
80RedEnq-7
80Top-516
81Fle-206
81Top-52
81TopTra-750
82Don-57
82Fle-591
82OPC-364
82Top-663
91PacSenL-60

Cruz, Henry Acosta
74AlbDukTI-64
74AlbDukTI-4
76OPC-590
76SSP-85
76Top-590
78SSP270-152
78Top-316
80IowOakP-4
90DodTar-152

Cruz, Ismael
89MarPhiS-8
90BatCliP-3071

Cruz, Ivan
89NiaFalRP-5b
90FloStaLAS-28
90LakTigS-6
90StaFS7-34
91Bow-153
91Cla/Bes-18
91LinDriAA-379
91LonTigLD-379
91LonTigP-1882
92Bow-170
92ClaFS7-171
92LonTigF-638
92LonTigS-404
92SkyAA F-172
92UppDecML-241
92UppDecMLPotY-PY23
93Bow-319
93ClaFS7-181
93ExcFS7-170
93TolMudHF-1658
93Top-423
93TopGol-423
93TopInaM-423
93TopMic-423
94TolMudHF-1030
95JacSunTI-6
96ColCliB-6

Cruz, J.J.
91EriSaiC-4
91EriSaiP-4071
92BatCliC-6
92BatCliF-3268

Cruz, Jacob
94SigRooDP-30
94SigRooDPS-30
94StaCluDP-19
94StaCluDPFDI-19
95BowBes-B85
95BowBesR-B85
95SPML-144
95Top-521
96BesAutS-24
96BesAutSA-15
96Bow-273
96Exc-243
96PhoFirB-14
96Top-438
97Bow-110
97BowCerBIA-CA17
97BowCerGIA-CA17
97BowChr-130
97BowChrI-130
97BowChrIR-130
97BowChrR-130
97BowInt-110
97ColCho-9
97PacPri-148
97PacPriGotD-GD216
97PacPriLB-148
97PacPriP-148
97StaClu-280
97StaCluM-M3
97StaCluMOP-280
97StaCluMOP-M3
97Top-220
97Ult-292
97UltGolME-292
97UltPlaME-292
97UppDec-232

Cruz, Javier
85MexCitTT-26

Cruz, Jesus
79CedRapGT-2

Cruz, Jose Dilan
71CarTeal-14
72OPC-107
72Top-107
73OPC-292
73Top-292
74OPC-464
74Top-464
74TopSta-113
75OPC-514
75Top-514
76OPC-321
76SSP-62
76Top-321
77BurCheD-9
77Hos-75
77Kel-50
77OPC-147
77Top-42
78AstBurK-17
78Hos-72
78Kel-16
78OPC-131
78Top-625
79AstTeal-5
79Hos-111
79OPC-143
79Top-289
80OPC-367
80Top-722
81AllGamPI-141
81CokTeaS-63
81Don-383
81Fle-60
81FleStiC-78
81OPC-105
81Top-105
81TopScr-83
81TopSti-169
81TopSupHT-98
82AstAstI-8
82Don-244
82Dra-10
82Fle-214
82FleSta-50
82OPC-325
82Top-325
82TopSti-44
83AllGamPI-140
83Don-41
83Fle-446
83FleSta-45
83FleSti-206
83OPC-327
83Top-585
83TopFol-5
83TopSti-242
84AllGamPI-47
84AstMot-8
84Don-182
84Fle-222
84FleSti-8
84FleSti-24
84FunFooP-129
84Nes792-66
84Nes792-422
84OCoandSI-198
84OPC-189
84SevCoi-W19
84Top-66
84Top-422
84TopRubD-16
84TopSti-65
84TopStiB-13
84TopTif-66
84TopTif-422
85AllGamPI-137
85AstHouP-2
85AstMot-4
85Don-20
85Don-304
85DonSupD-20
85Dra-7
85Fle-347
85Lea-20
85OPC-95
85SevCoi-C10
85ThoMcAD-27
85Top-95
85TopGloS-20
85TopMin-95
85TopRubD-14
85TopSti-59
85TopSup-34
85TopTif-95
86AstMilL-4
86AstMot-20
86AstPol-12
86AstTeal-3
86BasStaB-25
86Don-60
86DonAll-19
86Fle-296
86FleLeaL-8
86FleLimE-13
86FleMin-62
86FleStiC-27
86Lea-49
86OPC-96
86SevCoi-S13
86Spo-30
86Top-186
86Top-640
86TopSti-26
86TopTat-11
86TopTif-186
86TopTif-640
87AstMot-3
87AstPol-3
87Don-85
87DonOpeD-13
87Fle-53
87FleBasA-11
87FleGlo-53
87FleStiC-26
87FleStiWBC-S4
87Lea-116
87OPC-343
87RedFolSB-95
87Spo-42
87Spo-152
87SpoTeaP-8
87Top-670
87TopSti-29
87TopTif-670
88DonReaBY-NEW
88Fle-443
88FleGlo-443
88GreBasS-10
88HouSho-14
88PanSti-299
88Sco-28
88ScoGlo-28
88StaLinAst-6
88Top-278
88TopTif-278
89PacSenL-188
89T/MSenL-26
89TopSenL-78
90EliSenL-53
90KisDodD-7
91PacSenL-36
92UppDecS-8
92YanWIZ8-38

Cruz, Jose Jr.
95Bes-129
95EveAqaTI-6
95SPML-110
95SPMLDtS-DS9
96Exc-103
96ExcFirYP-2
96LanJetB-12
96SigRooOJPP-P2
97Bow-100
97BowBes-188
97BowBesA-188
97BowBesAAR-188
97BowBesAR-188
97BowBesBC-BC11
97BowBesBCAR-BC11
97BowBesBCR-BC11
97BowBesMI-MI5
97BowBesMIAR-MI5
97BowBesMIARI-MI5
97BowBesMII-MI5
97BowBesMIR-MI5
97BowBesMIRI-MI5
97BowBesR-188
97BowCerBIA-CA18
97BowCerGIA-CA18
97BowChr-122
97BowChrI-122
97BowChrIR-122
97BowChrR-122
97BowChrSHR-SHR10
97BowChrSHRR-SHR10
97BowInt-100
97BowIntB-BBI19
97BowIntBAR-BBI19
97BowIntBR-BBI19
97BowScoHR-10
97Don-396
97DonLim-18
97DonLim-196
97DonLimFotG-30
97DonLimLE-18
97DonLimLE-196
97DonPreP-396
97DonPrePGold-396
97DonTea-148
97DonTeaSPE-148
97Fin-337
97FinEmb-337
97FinEmbR-337
97FinRef-337
97FlaShoWotF-WF2
97Fle-589
97FleNewH-2
97FleTif-589
97Lea-330
97LeaFraM-330
97LeaFraMDC-330
97PinCer-NNO
97PinTotCPB-NNO
97SP-15
97SpoIll-4
97SpoIllEE-4
97SPx-47
97SPxBro-47
97SPxGraF-47
97SPxSil-47
97SPxSte-47
97TopStaFAS-FAS6
97Ult-551
97UltGolME-551
97UltPlaME-551
97UppDec-547
97Zen-47

Cruz, Juan-1
83MadMusF-21
84ModA'sC-14
85MidAngT-23

Cruz, Juan-2
92ChaRaiC-11
92SpoIndC-25
92SpoIndF-1305

Cruz, Julio
96TulDriT-7

Cruz, Julio Luis
75QuaCitAT-8
78Top-687

79Hos-58
79OPC-305
79Top-583
80BurKinPHR-26
80OPC-16
80Top-32
81AllGamPI-10
81Don-163
81Fle-601
81MarPol-6
81OPC-121
81Top-397
81TopSti-126
82Don-50
82Fle-509
82FleSta-225
82OPC-130
82Top-130
82TopSti-114
82TopSti-235
83Don-379
83Fle-478
83OPC-113
83Top-414
83TopFol-5
83TopSti-112
83TopTra-23T
84AllGamPI-100
84Don-379
84Fle-55
84FleSti-95
84Nes792-257
84OPC-257
84Top-257
84TopSti-248
84TopTif-257
84WhiSoxTV-9
85AllGamPI-11
85Don-452
85Fle-510
85OPC-71
85Top-749
85TopSti-239
85TopTif-749
85WhiSoxC-12
86Don-257
86Fle-201
86OPC-14
86Top-14
86TopTif-14
86WhiSoxC-12
87Fle-492
87FleGlo-492
87OPC-53
87Top-790
87TopTif-790
89StoPorCLC-179
90SweBasG-88
91LinDri-32
91SweBasG-21
93UppDecS-14
Cruz, Luis
83WisRapTF-19
86PitCubP-5
87WinSpiP-9
88BlaYNPRWL-5
88CarLeaAS-26
88WinSpiS-2
89BlaYNPRWL-173
89ChaKniTI-8
89IowCubC-15
89IowCubP-1692
Cruz, Nandi
90SarWhiSS-5
91DunBluJC-16
91DunBluJP-213
Cruz, Pablo
77SalPirT-9A
77SalPirT-9B
78SalPirT-2
Cruz, Rafael
86DayBealP-6
87GasRanP-13
Cruz, Ricardo
93GenCubC-7
93GenCubF-3176
Cruz, Ruben
91BurAstC-19
91BurAstP-2813
92OscAstC-22
92OscAstF-2541
93OscAstC-9
93OscAstF-635
Cruz, Todd Ruben
77ReaPhiT-8
80Top-492
80VenLeaS-258
81CokTeaS-26
81Fle-341
81Top-571
83AllGamPI-19
83Don-505
83Fle-479
83MarNal-3
83OPC-132
83OriPos-4
83Top-132
84Don-148
84Fle-3
84Nes792-773
84OriTeal-5
84Top-773
84TopTif-773
85Fle-172
85Top-366
85TopTif-366
86MarGreT-3
87SanBerSP-20
91OriCro-90
91PacSenL-147
91SalSpuC-5
91SalSpuP-2251
Cruz, Tommy
75IntLeaASB-4
75SpoIndC-8
76SacSolC-7
79ColCliT-13
Cruz, Tommy (Cirilio Dilan)
75PacCoaLAB-4
78TacYanC-44
92PenPilC-28
92PenPilF-2949
94AppFoxC-24
Cruz, Victor
78SyrChiT-5
79Top-714
80OPC-54
80Top-99
81Don-321
81Fle-407
81OPC-252
81Top-252
81TopTra-751
82Fle-480
82Top-263
83OklCit8T-6
84OklCit8T-20
85DomLeaS-16
88PocGiaP-2089
93RanKee-116
Csefalvay, John
83ColAstT-3
84NasSouTI-4
Cub, Casey the
95RocCubTI-NNO
96RocCubTI-4
Cubanich, Creighton
91SouOreAC-23
Cubans, New York
93NegLeaRL2-94
93TedWilPC-4
Cubbage, Mike (Michael Lee)
74SpoIndC-39
75OPC-617
75SpoIndC-14
75Top-617
76OPC-615
76Top-615
77BurCheD-50
77Top-149
78Top-219
78TwiFriP-5
79OPC-187
79Top-362
79TwiFriP-4
80OPC-262
80Top-503
81Don-492
81Fle-566
81Top-657
81TopTra-752
82Fle-523
82TidTidT-26
82Top-43
85LynMetT-1
86JacMetT-24
87TidTidP-12
87TidTidT-23
88TidTidCa-3
88TidTidCM-24
88TidTidP-1586
88TriAAAP-54
89TidTidC-21
89TidTidP-1947
90MetColP-29
90MetKah-4
90TopTVM-2
91MetColP-27
91MetKah-4
91MetWIZ-89
92MetColP-33
92MetKah-4
93RanKee-117
96MetKah-7
96MetKah-6
Cubbie, Mascot
96IowCubB-29
Cubee, Rich
89OmaRoyC-25
Cubillan, Darwin
95LinVen-128
Cubs, Chicago
09MaxPubP-23
09SpoNewSM-53
13FatT20-11
36R31Pre-G24
36R31Pre-L15
38BasTabP-35
56Top-11A
56Top-11B
56Top-11C
57Top-183
58Top-327
59Top-304
60Top-513
60TopTat-56
61Top-122
61TopMagR-17
62GuyPotCP-3
62Top-552
63Top-222
64Top-237
64TopTatI-4
64TopVen-237
65OPC-91
65Top-91
66Top-204
66TopRubI-104
66TopVen-204
67Top-354
68LauWorS-3
68LauWorS-4
68LauWorS-7
68LauWorS-15
68LauWorS-26
68LauWorS-32
68LauWorS-35
69FleCloS-5
69FleCloS-29
69TopStaA-5
70FleWorS-3
70FleWorS-4
70FleWorS-15
70FleWorS-26
70Top-593
71FleWorS-4
71FleWorS-5
71FleWorS-27
71FleWorS-36
71OPC-502
71Top-502
71TopTat-51
72OPC-192
72Top-192
73FleWilD-1
73OPC-464
73OPCBTC-5
73Top-464
73TopBluTC-5
74OPC-211
74OPCTC-5
74Top-211
74TopStaA-5
74TopTeaC-5
78Top-302
82CubRedL-NNO
83CubThoAV-NNO
83FleSta-229
83FleSti-NNO
85Fle-642
86JosHalC-4
87SpoTeaL-22
88PanSti-470
88RedFolSB-121
90FleWaxBC-C6
90PubSti-632
90RedFolSB-122
90VenSti-519
91PanCanT1-120
93TedWilPC-5
94ImpProP-16
94Sco-648
94ScoGolR-648
95PanSti-142
96FleCub-19
96PanSti-45
Cubs, Wytheville
87WytCubP-31
88WytCubP-2004
Cuccinello, Al (Alfred E.)
94ConTSN-1171
94ConTSNB-1171
Cuccinello, Tony (Anthony)
33Gou-99
33NatLeaAC-5
34DiaMatCSB-37
34BatR31-79
34DiaStaR-55
35DiaMatCS3T1-41
35ExhFou-2
36DiaMatCS4-2
36GouWidPPR-A22
38ExhFou-1
39ExhSal-9
39PlaBal-61
40PlaBal-61
49EurSta-80
55IndGolS-30
60Top-458
68TigDetFPB-3
77GalGloG-223
79DiaGre-208
89DodSmoG-37
89PacLegI-170
90DodTar-153
94ConTSN-1171
94ConTSNB-1171
95ConTSN-1391
Cucjen, Romy
85FreGiaP-13
87ShrCapP-9
88ShrCapP-1293
89LouRedBC-15
89LouRedBP-1257
89LouRedBTI-15
90CMC-72
90IndIndC-22
90IndIndP-289
90ProAAAF-572
Cudjo, Lavell
89GreHorP-406
89SouAtlLAGS-34
90CedRapRB-9
90CedRapRP-2332
92LetMouSP-20
Cudworth, Jim (James A.)
87OldJudN-111
Cuellar, Bobby
75LynRanT-7
76SanAntBTI-8
77TucTorC-53
78TucTorC-46
79TacTugT-7
80TacTigT-6
80Top-665
81ChaChaT-2
84SalLakCGC-192
85CalCanC-84
86WauTimP-5
87WauTimP-1
88SanBerSB-27
88SanBerSCLC-54
89WilBilP-627
89WilBilS-3
90WilBilB-26
90WilBilP-1073
90WilBilS-26
91JacSunLD-350
91JacSunP-167
91LinDriAA-350
93RanKee-118
94CalCanF-806
95MarMot-28
96MarMot-28
Cuellar, Jose
94AppFoxC-7
94AppFoxF-1056
Cuellar, Mike
80KnoBluJT-12
Cuellar, Mike Angel
59Top-518
60Top-398
65Top-337
66Top-566
67Ast-7
67AstTeal1-3
67CokCapAs-14
67OPC-97
67Top-97
67Top-234
67TopVen-318
68CokCapA-14
68DexPre-26
68Top-274
68TopActS-8C
68TopVen-274
69MilBra-66
69Top-453
69Top-532
70DayDaiNM-56
70MLBOffS-148
70OPC-68
70OPC-70
70OPC-199
70Ori-3
70Top-70
70Top-199
70Top-590
70TopBoo-1
71Kel-49
71MLBOffS-293
71OPC-69
71OPC-170
71Ori-3
71Top-69
71Top-170
71TopCoi-150
71TopTat-128
72EssCoi-6
72Kel-27A
72Kel-27B
72MilBra-82
72OPC-70
72OriPol-4
72Top-70
73Kel2D-47
73OPC-470
73OriJohP-35
73Top-470
74OPC-560
74Top-560
75Hos-42
75OPC-410
75SSP42-24
75Top-410
76Hos-121
76OPC-285
76OriEngCL-1
76SSP-375
76Top-285
77Top-162
86AstMot-5
87AstShoSO-3
87AstShoSTw-29
89PacSenL-46
89T/MSenL-27
91KelLey-7
91OriCro-91
Cuen, Eleno
73CedRapAT-24
75DubPacT-13
81PorBeaT-26
82BufBisT-14
Cuervo, Ed
78WauMetT-7
83ColAstT-2
Cuesta, Jamie
88BurBraP-17
89DurBullS-6
89DurBulTI-6
Cuevas, Angelo
86LynMetP-8
88BlaYNPRWL-36
88JacMetGS-21
88TexLeaAGS-10
89BlaYNPRWL-38
89JacMetGS-14
Cuevas, Eduardo

94SprSulC-5
94SprSulF-2042
95RanCucQT-19
96CliLumKTI-10
Cuevas, Johnny
86SumBraP-4
87DurBulP-8
88SumBraP-397
89BurBraP-1597
89BurBraS-6
90DurBulTI-16
91GreBraC-11
91GreBraLD-205
91GreBraP-3005
91LinDriAA-205
92DurBulC-2
92DurBulF-1103
92DurBulTI-28
Cuevas, Rafael
78NewWayCT-7
Cuevas, Trent
95YakBeaTI-7
96GreFalDB-9
96GreFalDTI-21
Culberson, Calvain
88PulBraP-1760
89SumBraP-1101
92CedRapRC-24
92CedRapRF-1061
93ChaLooF-2355
94ChaLooF-1353
Culberson, Charles
85FreGiaP-3
86FreGiaP-25
87Ft.MyeRP-15
88MemChiB-17
91UtiBluSC-24
91UtiBluSP-3259
Culberson, Delbert Leon
46RedSoxTI-5
47TipTop-1
Culberson, Don
92SouBenWSC-2
92SouBenWSF-172
93SouBenWSC-7
93SouBenWSF-1422
Culkar, Steve
87NewOriP-11
88VirGenS-7
89HagSunB-8
89HagSunP-276
89HagSunS-4
90HagSunB-16
90HagSunP-1405
90HagSunS-6
91HagSunP-2449
Cullen, Jack (John)
63Top-54A
63Top-54B
66OPC-31
66Top-31
66TopVen-31
92YanWIZ6-31
Cullen, Mike
85KinBluJT-4
Cullen, Tim
67OPC-167
67Top-167
68Top-209
68TopVen-209
69Top-586
70Kel-30
70OPC-49
70Top-49
71MLBOffS-534
71OPC-566
71SenPolP-3
71SenTealW-9
71Top-566
72OPC-461
72Top-461
Cullenbine, Roy
41BroW75-7
79DiaGre-185
81TigDetN-43
83TCMPla1945-3
90DodTar-154
93ConTSN-849
Culler, Dick
47TipTop-78
83TCMPla1945-38
Cullers, Steve
85BurRanT-5
Cullop, Glen
92PriRedC-27
92PriRedF-2685
94ChaLooF-1354
Cullop, Henry Nick
19W514-59
29ExhFou-3
31Exh-7
82OhiHaloF-3
87ConSer2-11
88ConSer4-7
90DodTar-156
Culmer, Will
80PenPilBT-8
80PenPilCT-19
81ReaPhiT-21
82OklCit8T-25
83ChaChaT-16
83IndPos-8
83IndWhe-7
84MaiGuiT-14
Culmo, Kevin
96YakBeaTI-19
Culp, Bennie
43PhiTeal-5
Culp, Brian
95SalAvaTI-13
96SalAvaB-7
Culp, Matt
95WatIndTI-11
Culp, Ray
60Lea-75
63Top-29A
63Top-29B
64PhiPhiB-11
64Top-412
64TopCoi-35
64TopSta-96
64TopStaU-20
64TopTatI-32
64WheSta-12
65Top-505
66OPC-4
66PhiTeal-5
66Top-4
66TopVen-4
67CokCapC-7
67DexPre-57
67OPC-168
67Top-168
68CokCapRS-7
68Top-272
68TopVen-272
69MilBra-67
69MLBOffS-11
69RedSoxAO-3
69Top-391
69TopSta-132
69TopSup-6
69TopTeaP-3
70Kel-35
70MLBOffS-158
70OPC-144
70RedSoxCPPC-6
70Top-144
71MilDud-4
71MLBOffS-317
71OPC-660
71RedSoxA-4
71RedSoxTI-3
71Top-660
71TopTat-103
72MilBra-83
72OPC-2
72Top-2
78TCM60I-197
81RedSoxBG2S-78
Culp, Wes
94DanBraC-5
94DanBraF-3523
95MacBraTI-4
Culpepper, Kevin
92KinMetC-25
93KinMetC-27
94KinMetC-28
Culver, George
65OPC-166
65Top-166
67Top-499
68Top-319
68TopVen-319
69Kah-B8
69Top-635
70OPC-92
70Top-92
71MLBOffS-76
71OPC-291
71Top-291
72MilBra-84
72Top-732
73OPC-242
73Top-242
74OPC-632
74Top-632
81ReaPhiT-24
83PorBeaT-12
84PorBeaC-215
86ReaPhiP-6
87AstShoSTw-4
87ReaPhiT-21
88MaiPhiC-23
88MaiPhiP-300
89ReaPhiS-26b
89ScrRedBP-724
90DodTar-155
90ReaPhiB-25
90ReaPhiP-1235
90ReaPhiS-28
93ScrRedBF-2558
93ScrRedBTI-7
93TriAAAGF-19
Culver, Lanell C.
83TamTarT-3
84CedRapRT-16
Cumberbatch, Abdiel
90TamYanD-2
92OneYanC-4
93GreHorC-6
93GreHorF-897
93OneYanC-5
93OneYanF-3515
94SanBerSF-2770
Cumberland, Chris
93OneYanC-6
93OneYanF-3495
94GreBatF-464
94SouAtlLAF-SAL13
95Bow-193
95Exc-93
96Bow-324
96ColCliB-7
96SigRooOJ-8
96SigRooOJS-8
97GreBatC-5
Cumberland, John
69OPC-114
69Top-114
69TopFou-24
71MLBOffS-244
71OPC-108
71Top-108
72OPC-403
72Top-403
83LynMetT-13
85TidTidT-26
86TidTidP-6
87TidTidP-18
87TidTidT-24
88TidTidCa-2
88TidTidCM-25
88TidTidP-1579
90CMC-685
90ProAAAF-292
90TidTidC-28
90TidTidP-561
91LinDriAA-625
91WicWraLD-625
91WicWraP-2615
91WicWraRD-25
92YanWIZ6-32
92YanWIZ7-39
93LasVegSF-962
96PawRedSDD-5
Cummings, Audelle
89GreFalDSP-8
Cummings, Bob
79CedRapGT-32
80CliGiaT-24
84ShrCapFB-6
85PhoGiaC-197
Cummings, Brian
88BatCliP-1689
88BurBraP-12
89BatCliP-1943
89BurBraP-1618
89BurBraS-7
90DurBulTI-19
Cummings, Candy (William)
36PC7AlbHoF-20
50CalHOFW-23
76ShaPiz-23
80PerHaloFP-19
80SSPHOF-20
84GalHaloFRL-23
89HOFStiB-64
90BasWit-60
94OriofB-23
Cummings, Dick
84IowCubT-21
85IowCubT-25
92GenCubC-29
Cummings, John
89AncGlaP-9
91SanBerSC-1
91SanBerSP-1977
92PenPilC-17
92PenPilF-2925
92UppDecML-179
93Bow-135
93ClaGolF-33
93ExcFS7-223
93ExcLeaLF-19
93FleFinE-268
93Lea-303
93MarMot-26
93OPCPre-69
93PacSpa-621
93Pin-595
93StaCluMari-21
93TopTra-129T
93Ult-617
93UppDec-503
93UppDecGold-503
94Don-126
94MarMot-18
94Top-443
94TopGol-443
94TopSpa-443
95Fle-264
96DodPol-9
96Fle-430
96FleTif-430
96LeaSigEA-39
97Fle-97
97FleTif-97
Cummings, Midre
91Cla/Bes-318
91KenTwiC-24
91KenTwiP-2088
92ClaBluBF-BC13
92ClaFS7-240
92ClaRedB-BC13
92ProFS7-98
92SalBucC-1
92SalBucF-76
92UppDecML-41
92UppDecML-277
92UppDecMLPotY-PY18
92UppDecMLTPHF-TP1
93Bow-357
93Bow-598
93CarMudF-2066
93CarMudTI-22
93ClaFisN-12
93ClaGolF-76
93ClaYouG-YG1
93ExcFS7-90
93Top-616
93TopGol-616
93TopInaM-616
93TopMic-616
93UppDec-440
93UppDecGold-440
94ActPac-12
94Bow-363
94Bow-630
94BowBes-B7
94BowBesR-B7
94BufBisF-1848
94Cla-87
94ClaCreotC-C22
94ColC-3
94ColChoGS-3
94ColChoSS-3
94Don-608
94FleMajLP-8
94LeaGolR-4
94LeaLimRP-3
94Pac-496
94SigRooDP-90
94SigRooDPS-90
94Top-787
94TopGol-787
94TopSpa-787
94TriPla-292
94UppDec-7
94UppDecED-7
95ColCho-384
95ColChoGS-384
95ColChoSS-384
95Don-193
95DonPreP-193
95Fla-398
95Fle-476
95Lea-171
95Pin-421
95PinArtP-421
95PinMusC-421
95PirFil-7
95Sel-165
95Sel-237
95SelArtP-165
95SelArtP-237
95SelCerPU-7
95SelCerPU9-7
95Spo-145
95SpoArtP-145
95StaClu-229
95StaCluFDI-229
95StaCluMOP-229
95StaCluSTWS-229
95StaCluVR-116
95Stu-178
95Sum-15
95SumNthD-15
95Top-78
95TopCyb-55
95UC3-117
95UC3ArtP-117
95Ult-214
95UltGolM-214
95UppDec-382
95UppDecED-382
95UppDecEDG-382
95UppDecSE-88
95UppDecSEG-88
95Zen-139
96ColCho-259
96ColCho-342
96ColChoGS-259
96ColChoGS-342
96ColChoSS-259
96ColChoSS-342
96Don-308
96DonPreP-308
96Fle-518
96FleTif-518
96Pac-181
96Sco-391
96StaClu-155
96StaCluMOP-155
95StaCluSTWS-116
95StaCluVRMC-116
97Sco-389
97ScoHobR-389
97ScoResC-389
97ScoShoS-389
97ScoShoSAP-389
97UppDec-207
97UppDec-458
Cummings, Ron
84ModA'sC-7
Cummings, Steve
87DunBluJP-924
88KnoBluJB-20
88SouLeaAJ-27
89SyrChiC-7
89SyrChiMB-7
89SyrChiP-803
90CMC-329
90Don-698
90OPC-374
90ScoRoo-78T
90SyrChiC-3
90SyrChiMB-3
90Top-374
90TopDeb89-26
90TopTif-374
91ColSprSSLD-81
91ColSprSSP-2178
91LinDriAAA-81
92SkyAAAF-260
92TolMudHF-1034
92TolMudHS-582
Cummings, William
88AllandGN-38
Cunha, Steve

91SalLakTP-3223
91SalLakTSP-11
Cunnane, Will
94KanCouCC-8
94KanCouCF-153
94KanCouCTI-8
95Bow-61
95Exc-194
95ExcLeaL-6
95KanCouCLTI-4
95PorSeaDTI-5
95SPML-59
95UppDecML-116
96Bow-239
96PorSeaDB-12
97Fle-515
97FleTif-515
95UppDecMLFS-116
Cunningham, Bill
86WesPalBEP-10
87JacExpP-445
Cunningham, Bill Aloysius
21KoBreWSI-8
21Nei-112
22E120-183
22W573-25
22W575-21
23W503-9
23W515-1
Cunningham, Chip
85PriWilPT-5
Cunningham, Dave
88AshTouP-1075
89WatDiaP-1795
89WatDiaS-3
Cunningham, Earl
89HigSchPLS-2
89WytCubS-8
90Bow-34
90BowTif-34
90OPC-134
90PeoChiCTI-1
90PeoChiCTI-2
90PeoChiCTI-3
90PeoChiCTI-4
90PeoChiTI-1
90PeoChiTI-2
90PeoChiTI-9
90Sco-670
90StaFS7-23
90Top-134
90TopTif-134
90TopTVCu-42
91Bow-420
91Cla/Bes-435
91PeoChiC-8
91PeoChiP-1354
91PeoChiTI-24
92Bow-81
92ClaFS7-316
92PeoChiC-1
92PeoChiTI-6
92ProFS7-208
92WinSpiC-2
93PeoChiTI-4
94LakElsSC-5
94LakElsSF-1675
95LakElsSTI-9
96AshTouB-10
Cunningham, Ellsworth
87OldJudN-112
Cunningham, Everett
88ButCopKSP-27
89GasRanP-1000
89GasRanS-6
89SouAtlLAGS-43
90ChaRanS-6
90FloStaLAS-29
90TulDriTI-6
91LinDriAA-578
91TulDriLD-578
91TulDriP-2766
91TulDriTI-6
Cunningham, Glen
51BerRos-D16
Cunningham, Joe (Joseph R.)
47Exh-53A
47Exh-53B
55Top-37
55TopDouH-37
57Top-304
58CarJayP-3
58Top-168
59Top-285
60Baz-27
60CarJayP-2
60Top-40
60Top-562
60TopTat-10
60TopVen-40
61CarJayP-3
61Pos-172A
61Pos-172B
61SevElev-19
61Top-520
62Jel-160
62Pos-160
62PosCan-160
62SalPlaC-173A
62SalPlaC-173B
62ShiPlaC-173
62Top-195
62TopVen-195
62WhiSoxTS-5
63ExhStaB-19
63Jel-35
63Pos-35
63Top-100
63WhiSoxJP-2
63WhiSoxTS-4
64Top-340
64TopVen-340
64WhiSoxTS-6
65Top-496
65TopEmbl-63
66Top-531
79DiaGre-175
79TCM50-105
Cunningham, Joseph
87St.PetCP-8
90JohCitCS-20
91JohCitCC-30
91JohCitCP-4172
92CarMcD-33
93JohCitCC-30
94MadHatC-27
94MadHatF-149
95LouRedF-292
96LouRedB-2
88St.PetCS-4
89HamRedS-28
Cunningham, Kenn
89LakTigS-27
90BriTigP-3174
90BriTigS-27
Cunningham, O'Brian
91HigSchPLS-13
92LetMouSP-21
Cunningham, Randall
91StaCluCM-35
Cunningham, Scott
91OklStaC-5
92OklStaC-6
94NewJerCC-5
94NewJerCF-3406
Cunningham, Sean
87BurExpP-1091
88RocExpLC-9
89JacExpB-22
89JacExpP-158
90WesPalBES-31
91WesPalBEC-30
Cunningham, Shawn
88BenBucL-3
88BenBucL-33
Cunningham, Troy
89SpoIndSP-17
90ChaRaiB-7
90ChaRaiP-2034
Cunningham, Wm. J.
12T207-38
20NatCarE-19
Cuomo, Mario
94UppDecTAE-60
Cupit, Wayne
92AubAstC-23
92AubAstF-1347
Cupples, Michael
84IdaFalATI-7
85MadMusP-7
85MadMusT-10
86MadMusP-7
87MadMusP-5
87MadMusP-16
Cuppy, Nig (George)
98CamPepP-17
Curbelo, Jorge
82MiaMarT-10
Curl, John
96DunBluJB-3
96DunBluJTI-5
96Exc-114
Curley, Tim
89PriPirS-3
Curnal, Jim
78TacYanC-19
Curnow, Robert
88SpoIndP-1939
89WatDiaP-1777
89WatDiaS-4
90ChaRaiB-8
90ChaRaiP-2042
Curran, Bud
79CedRapGT-14
88CedRapRP-1161
Curran, Dave
80HolMilT-22
Curran, Mike
75WesPalBES-15
Curran, Pat
75WatRoyT-8
Curran, Shawn
91ClaDraP-48
91FroRowDP-27
91HigSchPLS-25
92StaCluD-30
94OriPro-21
Curran, Tighe
94JohCitCC-9
94JohCitCF-3692
95PeoChiTI-9
Currence, Lafayette (Delaney)
76SSP-251
04DrcMilD-000
Current, Matt
88MarPhiS-8
89MarPhiS-9
89Sta-143
90SpaPhiB-13
90SpaPhiP-2494
90SpaPhiS-4
91ClePhiC-13
91ClePhiP-1624
Currie, Brian
89BoiHawP-2000
90EriSaiS-4
Currie, Clarence
11SpoLifCW-85
Currier, Bryan
92EugEmeC-8
92EugEmeF-3019
93RocRoyC-9
93RocRoyF-709
Currier, Lenny
86AlbDukP-4
87AlbDukP-4
88AlbDukP-272
Currin, Wes
88SumBraP-395
89DurBullS-7
89DurBulTI-7
89Sta-70
Curron, Bud
85CedRapRT-30
Curry, Clinton
83TriTriT-25
Curry, Dell
91GasRanC-27
Curry, Floyd
43ParSpo-21
Curry, G. Tony
60Top-541
61Pos-120A
61Pos-120B
61Top-262
61TopStal-51
81TCM60I-452
Curry, Steve
80CarMudF-24
81RicBraT-17
86GreBraTI-6
86RicBraP-3
89BurBraP-1613
89BurBraS-29
90IdaFalBP-3262
91IdaFalBP-4344
91RicBraBC-43
92BurAstC-26
92BurAstF-563
Curry, Steve (Stephen T.)
86NewBriRSP-8
87PawRedSP-53
87PawRedST-3
88PawRedSC-7
88PawRedSP-468
88ScoRoo-81T
88ScoRooG-81T
88TriAAAP-31
89Fle-86
89FleGlo-86
89PanSti-267
89PawRedSC-2
89PawRedSP-691
89PawRedSTI-6
89ScoHot1R-53
89Top-471
89TopTif-471
90PawRedSDD-4
90PawRedSP-454
90ProAAAF-426
90TopTVRS-41
92MemChiF-2411
92MemChiS-432
Curtis, Chad
90MidLeaASGS-30
90QuaCitAGS-21
91EdmTraLD-159
91EdmTraP-1522
91LinDriAAA-159
91TriA AAGP-AAA13
92AngPol-5
92Bow-627
92Cla2-T96
92DonRoo-30
92DonUpd-U5
92FleUpd-8
92LeaGolR-BC1
92Pin-523
92PinRoo-29
92PinRool-17
92PinTea2-40
92ProFS7-29
92ScoRoo-87T
92Stu-143
92TopTra-25T
92TopTraG-25T
92Ult-323
92UltAllR-6
92UppDec-774
93AngAdoFD-1
93AngMot-12
93AngPol-7
93Bow-313
93DiaMar-26
93Don-93
93Fin-146
93FinRef-146
93Fla-170
93Fle-571
93FleRooS-RSB4
93Lea-227
93OPC-28
93OPCPre-2
93PacSpa-42
93PanSti-10
93Pin-411
93Sco-354
93Sel-290
93SelChaR-9
93SP-19
93StaClu-543
93StaCluAn-23
93StaCluFDI-543
93StaCluMOP-543
93Stu-2
93Top-699
93TopGol-699
93TopInaM-699
93TopMic-699
93Toy-2
93TriPla-70
93TriPlaA-26
93Ult-159
93UppDec-235
93UppDecGold-235
93USPlaCA-2H
93USPlaCR-13S
94AngLAT-2
94AngMot-4
94Bow-179
94ColC-87
94ColChoGS-87
94ColChoSS-87
94Don-11
94DonSpeE-11
94ExtBas-30
94Fin-358
94FinRef-358
94Fla-267
94Fle-50
94FUnPac-114
94Lea-19
94LeaL-14
94OPC-98
94Pac-73
94PanSti-35
94Pin-282
94PinArtP-282
94PinMusC-282
94ProMag-16
94Sco-95
94ScoGolR-95
94ScoGolS-56
94Sel-345
94SP-22
94SPDieC-22
94Spo-119
94StaClu-295
94StaCluFDI-295
94StaCluGR-295
94StaCluMOP-295
94Stu-8
94Top-56
94TopGol-56
94TopSpa-56
94TriPla-11
94Ult-323
94UppDec-82
94UppDecED-82
94USPlaCA-8H
95Bow-340
95BowBes-R64
95BowBesR-R64
95ColCho-99
95ColCho-580T
95ColChoGS-99
95ColChoSE-32
95ColChoSEGS-32
95ColChoSESS-32
95ColChoSS-99
95Don-99
95DonPreP-99
95DonTopotO-72
95Emo-41
95Fin-179
95Fin-263
95FinRef-179
95FinRef-263
95Fla-16
95Fla-255
95Fle-219
95FleUpd-18
95Lea-297
95LeaLim-25
95Pac-53
95Pin-220
95PinArtP-220
95PinMusC-220
95Sco-392
95ScoGolR-392
95ScoPlaTS-392
95ScoYouTE-392T
95Sel-184
95SelArtP-184
95SP-152
95Spo-100
95SpoArtP-100
95SPSil-152
95StaClu-169
95StaClu-547
95StaCluFDI-169
95StaCluMOP-169
95StaCluMOP-547
95StaCluSTWS-169
95StaCluSTWS-547
95Stu-70
95Top-154
95TopCyb-92
95TopTra-21T
95Ult-266
95UltGolM-266
95UppDec-424
95UppDecED-424
95UppDecEDG-424
95UppDecSE-229
95UppDecSEG-229
96Baz-77
96ColCho-147

96ColChoGS-147
96ColChoSS-147
96Don-135
96DonDiaK-18
96DonPreP-135
96EmoXL-58
96Fin-B172
96FinRef-B172
96Fla-78
96Fle-107
96FleTif-107
96Lea-67
96LeaPrePB-67
96LeaPrePG-67
96LeaPrePS-67
96LeaSigA-53
96LeaSigAG-53
96LeaSigAS-53
96MetUni-56
96MetUniP-56
96Pac-313
96PacPri-P100
96PacPriG-P100
96PanSti-144
96Pin-118
96ProSta-121
96Sco-11
96ScoDugC-A11
96ScoDugCAP-A11
96SP-84
96StaClu-21
96StaCluB&B-BB9
96StaCluEPB-21
96StaCluEPG-21
96StaCluEPS-21
96StaCluMOP-21
96StaCluMOP-BB9
96Stu-95
96StuPrePB-95
96StuPrePG-95
96StuPrePS-95
96Sum-97
96SumAbo&B-97
96SumArtP-97
96SumFoi-97
96Top-202
96TopGal-85
96TopGalPPI-85
96Ult-57
96UltGolM-57
96UppDec-67
97Cir-326
97CirRav-326
97ColCho-314
97Fle-359
97FleTif-359
97Sco-239
97Sco-349
97ScoDod-11
97ScoDodPl-11
97ScoDodPr-11
97ScoHobR-349
97ScoPreS-239
97ScoResC-349
97ScoShoS-239
97ScoShoS-349
97ScoShoSAP-239
97ScoShoSAP-349
97Top-449
97Ult-452
97UltGolME-452
97UltPlaME-452
97UppDec-344

Curtis, Chris
91ButCopKSP-10
92ClaFS7-327
92GasRanC-19
92GasRanF-2243
92StaCluD-31
93ChaRanC-6
94TulDriF-235
94TulDriTI-4
96OklCit8B-6

Curtis, Cliff (Clinton)
11SpoLifM-137
90DodTar-920

Curtis, Craig
90AshTouP-2753
91OscAstC-22
91OscAstP-696
92BurAstC-18
92BurAstF-554

Curtis, Ed
12ImpTobC-90

Curtis, Jack P.
61Top-533
62CubJayP-5
62Top-372

Curtis, John D.
72Top-724
73LinPor-18
73OPC-143
73Top-143
74OPC-373
74Top-373
74TopTra-373T
75OPC-381
75Top-381
76OPC-239
76Top-239
77Top-324
78Top-486
79GiaPol-40
79Top-649
80Top-12
81Fle-491
81OPC-158
81Top-531
81TopSti-231
82Fle-569
82Top-219
83Don-170
83Fle-84
83Top-777
84AngSmo-6
84Fle-513
84Nes792-158
84Top-158
84TopTif-158
89PriPirS-4
90WelPirP-12

Curtis, Kevin
94OriPro-22
96BowBayB-13

Curtis, Matt
96BoiHawB-8

Curtis, Mike
86GenCubP-4
87WinSpiP-27
88HarSenP-843
90Bes-119
90CanIndB-26
90CanIndP-1287
90CanIndS-3
90CMC-733
90EasLeaAP-EL38
91CanIndLD-80
91CanIndP-974
91LinDriAA-80

Curtis, Randy
91PitMetC-6
91PitMetP-3434
92ClaFS7-80
92ColMetC-24
92ColMetF-307
92ColMetPI-13
92ColMetPI-31
93ClaFS7-131
93FloStaLAF-39
93St.LucMC-7
94Bow-345
94ClaGolF-167
94ExcFS7-233
94LasVegSF-879
94UppDecML-65
94UppDecML-99
95SigRooOJ-11
95SigRooOJP-11
95SigRooOJPS-11
95SigRooOJS-11
96RanCucQB-8
93StLucMF-2932

Curtis, Tacks
87OldJudN-113

Curtwright, Guy
47Exh-54

Cusack, John
88PacEigMO-12

Cusack, Rocky
87LakTigP-12
88ChaKniTI-13

Cusey, Lee
92MadMusC-13
92MadMusF-1226
93AlbPolF-2021

Cushing, Steve
81BatTroT-4
81WatIndT-32
82WatIndF-15
82WatIndT-1

Cushman, Ed
87BucN28-56
87OldJudN-114A
87OldJudN-114B
90KalBatN-10

Cusick, Anthony
87OldJudN-115

Cusick, Jack
52Bow-192

Cusson, Mario
82MonNew-5

Cutchins, Todd
96PitMetB-8

Cutler, Brad
75TacTwiK-16

Cutshall, Bill
86JacExpT-24
87NasSouTI-3
88OrlTwiB-27

Cutshaw, George
14B18B-56
16ColE13-37
16FleBreD-21
17HolBreD-20
20NatCarE-20
21Exh-30
22E120-50
22W573-26
23WilChoV-25
90DodTar-157

Cutty, Fran
81ChaRoyT-11
82ForMyeRT-15

Cuyler, KiKi (Hazen)
25Exh-51
26Exh-51
26SpoComoA-13
26SpoNewSM-1
27Exh-25
28StaPlaCE-15
28W56PlaC-C1
29ExhFou-6
30ChiEveAP-2
30SchR33-3
30SchR33-29
31Exh-6
31W517-19
32CubTeal-3
32OrbPinNP-6
32OrbPinUP-14
33CraJacP-3
33DelR33-8
33Gou-23
33GouCanV-23
33RitCE-5C
33TatOrb-14
33TatOrbSDR-152
34DiaMatCSB-38
34DiaStaR-31A
34DiaStaR-31B
34Gou-90
35DiaMatCS3T1-42
35GouPuzR-1F
35GouPuzR-3D
35GouPuzR-14D
35GouPuzR-15D
36GouBWR-10
36GouWidPPR-A23
36NatChiFPR-91
36R31PasP-7
36R31PasP-37
36SandSW-10
36WorWidGV-55
37WheBB9-4
43CubTeal-25
60Fle-75
61Fle-19
71FleWorS-23
73FleWilD-14
76RowExh-9
76ShaPiz-109
77GalGloG-72
80CubGreT-8
80PacLeg-92
80PerHaloFP-108
80SSPHOF-108
82DiaCla-54
89DodSmoG-6
90DodTar-158
91ConTSN-12
92ConTSN-587
92CubOldS-7
93ConTSN-741
94ConTSN-1096
94ConTSNB-1096

Cuyler, Milt
87FayGenP-8
88FloStaLAS-32
88LakTigS-8
89TolMudHC-21
89TolMudHP-787
90Bow-358
90BowTif-358
90CMC-398
90ProAAAF-390
90Sco-583A
90Sco-583B
90Sco100RS-84
90TolMudHC-21
90TolMudHP-160
91Bow-141
91Cla1-T42
91ClaGam-191
91Don-40
91DonRoo-6
91Fle-334
91Lea-251
91OPC-684
91OPCPre-27
91StaClu-470
91Stu-51
91TigCok-22
91Top-684
91TopDeb90-36
91TopDesS-684
91TopMic-684
91TopTif-684
91UltUpd-22
91UppDec-556
92Bow-196
92ClaGam-87
92Don-232
92Fle-130
92FleRooS-7
92Lea-75
92OPC-522
92PanSti-110
92Pin-174
92PinTea2-44
92Sco-26
92Sco100RS-1
92ScoImpP-4
92StaClu-5
92Stu-171
92Top-522
92TopGol-522
92TopGolW-522
92TopMic-522
92TriPla-100
92Ult-57
92UppDec-536
93Don-173
93Fle-224
93Lea-38
93PacSpa-105
93Pin-193
93Sco-82
93Sel-166
93StaClu-156
93StaCluFDI-156
93StaCluMOP-156
93TigGat-4
93Top-429
93TopGol-429
93TopInaM-429
93TopMic-429
93TriPla-44
93Ult-194
93UppDec-162
93UppDecGold-162
94Don-475
94Fle-125
94Pin-359
94PinArtP-359
94PinMusC-359
94Sco-79
95Don-274
95DonPreP-274
95Fle-46
95Pin-130
95PinArtP-130
95PinMusC-130
95Sco-259
95ScoGolR-259
95ScoPlaTS-259
95TolMudHTI-12
95Top-182

Cvejdlik, Kent
76WatRoyT-4
80OmaRoyP-8

Cyburt, Phil
78SalPirT-3

Cypret, Greg
80ColAstT-1
81TucTorT-1
82TucTorT-6
83TucTorT-15
84TucTorC-54

Czajkowski, Jim
87SumBraP-19
88DurBulS-4A
89DurBullS-8
89DurBulTI-8
90HarSenP-1187
90HarSenS-6
91ElPasDLD-179
91ElPasDP-2740
91LinDriAA-179
92ElPasDF-3913
92ElPasDS-204
94ColSprSSF-726
96SyrChiTI-11

Czanstkowski, Tom
93AubAstC-6
93AubAstF-3433
94QuaCitRBC-8
94QuaCitRBF-528

Czarkowski, Mark
92JacSunF-3702
93CalCanF-1159

Czarnik, Chris
89BurBraP-1617
89BurBraS-8
89Sta-110
90DurBulTI-9

D'Acquisto, John (John F.)
74OPC-608
74Top-608A
74Top-608B
75OPC-372
75Top-372
76OPC-628
76SSP-94
76Top-628
77PadSchC-17
77Top-19
78PadFamF-8
79PadFamF-1
79Top-506
80Top-339
81Fle-163
81LonBeaPT-23
81OPC-204
81Top-427
82RicBraT-4
82Top-58
83Fle-516
89PacSenL-121
89TopSenL-31

D'Alessandro, Sal
85DurBulT-22
86GreBraTI-7
87RicBraBC-4
87RicBraC-10
88GreBraB-3

D'Alexander, Greg
90ArkRaz-10
90MiaMirIS-4
91MiaMirC-19
91MiaMirP-413

D'Allessandro, Marc
96AshTouB-11

D'Amato, Brian
92ChaRaiC-8
92ChaRaiF-115
93WatDiaC-10
93WatDiaF-1760
94HigDesMC-10
94HigDesMF-2782

D'Ambrosia, Mark
94HunCubF-3557
94HunCubC-5

D'Amico, Jeff
95WesMicWTI-30
96ModA'sB-18

D'Amico, Jeff Charles
94Bow-205
94Bow-374
94BrePol-5
94Cla-173

94ClaGolF-2
94ClaGolN1PLF-LP3
94ClaGolREF-RE3
94SigRoo-30
94SigRooS-30
94Top-759
94TopGol-759
94TopSpa-759
95BelBreTI-9
95Bow-74
95BowBes-B47
95BowBesR-B47
95MidLeaA-11
95SPML-80
95Top-282
96BesAutS-25
96Bow-165
96BowBes-95
96BowBesAR-95
96BowBesR-95
96El PasDB-7
96Exc-69
96Top-429
97Bow-55
97BowBes-113
97BowBesAR-113
97BowBesR-113
97BowCerBIA-CA19
97BowCerGIA-CA19
97BowInt-55
97Cir-345
97CirRav-345
97ColCho-3
97DonRatR-7
97Fin-39
97FinRef-39
97Fle-127
97FleTif-127
97Lea-3
97LeaFraM-3
97LeaFraMDC-3
97MetUni-64
97Pin-159
97PinArtP-159
97PinMusC-159
97Sco-269
97ScoPreS-269
97ScoShoS-269
97ScoShoSAP-269
97SP-103
97StaClu-286
97StaCluM-M32
97StaCluMOP-286
97StaCluMOP-M32
97Top-39
97TopChr-14
97TopChrR-14
97TopGal-145
97TopGalPPI-145
97Ult-75
97UltGolME-75
97UltPlaME-75
97UppDec-227
97UppDecBCP-BC14
97UppDecTTS-TS17
D'Amore, Louis
81CliGiaT-14
D'Andrea, Mike (Michael)
92PulBraC-25
92PulBraF-3171
93ExcFS7-1
93MacBraC-8
93MacBraF-1394
94DurBulC-6
94DurBulF-323
94DurBulTI-5
95BreBtaTI-46
D'Aquila, Tom
94BluOriC-7
94BluOriF-3575
96FreKeyB-5
D'Onofrio, Gary
83DayBeaAT-20
D'Oro, Pool
88GooN16-18
D'Vincenzo, Mark
86LitFalMP-8
Daal, Omar
92AlbDukF-712
92SanAntMS-561
93AlbDukF-1453
93Bow-42
93DodMot-15
93FleFinE-81
93LinVenB-37
94DodMot-19
94Fle-508
94Pac-306
94Top-29
94TopGol-29
94TopSpa-29
94Ult-214
94VenLinU-35
95DodMot-17
95DodPol-6
95Fle-537
95LinVen-21
95Pac-214
95Top-518
95TopCyb-239
95Ult-179
95UltGolM-179
96FleUpd-U147
96FleUpdTC-U147
96LeaSigEA-40
96Pac-115
97Pac-342
97PacLigB-342
97PacSil-342
Dabney, Fred
88UtiBluSP-16
89SouBenWSGS-11
90SarWhiSS-6
91SarWhiSC-3
91SarWhiSP-1106
92BirBarF-2575
92BirBarS-81
93NasSouF-565
94CanIndF-3111
95IowCubTI-9
Dabney, Ty
85EveGiaC-3
86FreGiaP-19
87ShrCapP-3
87TexLeaAF-32
88PhoFirC-22
88PhoFirP-72
Daboll, Dennis
65Top-561
Dace, Derek
96AubDouB-15
Dacko, Mark
81BirBarT-7
82EvaTriT-3
83EvaTriT-1
84EvaTriT-6
Dacosta, Bill
87OneYanP-11
88PriWilYS-7
Dacus, Barry
86PalSprAP-19
86PalSprAP-9
87MidAngP-28
88EdmTraC-10
88EdmTraP-568
Dade, Paul (Lonnie Paul)
74CarSalLCA-99
76SalLakCGC-18
78Kel-14
78OPC-86
78Top-662
79OPC-3
79Top-13
80OPC-134
80Top-254
81Top-496
Dafforn, Mike
88MarPhiS-9
89MarPhiS-10
Dafun, Kekoa
95BoiHawTI-13
Dagres, Angie (Angelo George)
91OriCro-92
Dahl, Greg
80ColAstT-11
Dahl, Jay
77FriOneYW-117
Dahle, Dave
52MotCoo-15
Dahlen, Bill (William F.)
03BreE10-29
05RotCP-4
06FanCraNL-12
08RosComP-89
09ColChiE-70
09T206-83
09T206-84
10DarChoE-14
10DomDisP-30
10E98-11
10JuJuDE-13
10SweCapPP-72
11PloCanE-20
11S74Sil-51
11SpoLifCW-86
11SpoLifM-152
11T205-35
11TurRedT-11
12ColRedB-70
12ColTinT-70
12HasTriFT-43
12HasTriFT-76
13NatGamW-13
14PieStaT-15
90DodTar-159
95May-31
Dahlgren, Babe (Ellsworth)
39PlaBal-81
40PlaBal-3
41PlaBal-49
43PhiTeal-6
46SeaSLP-11
75YanDyn1T-10
79DiaGre-8
90DodTar-160
Dahse, David
84NewOriT-4
Daigle, Tim
94BluOriC-6
94BluOriF-3555
Dailey, Jason
93DanBraC-12
93DanBraF-3630
94IdaFalBF-3507
94IdaFalBSP-2
Dailey, Steve
91OklStaC-6
92OklStaC-7
Dailey, William G.
63Top-391
63TwiJayP-4
63TwiVol-3
64Top-156
64TopVen-156
Daily, Con (Cornelius F.)
87OldJudN-119
90DodTar-922
Daily, Ed (Edward M.)
87BucN28-110
87OldJudN-117
88GandBCGCE-11
Dakin, Brian
90EveGiaB-17
90EveGiaP-3133
Dal Canton, Bruce (John B.)
69Top-468A
69Top-468B
70OPC-52
70Top-52
71MLBOffS-413
71OPC-168
71Top-168
72Top-717
73OPC-487
73Top-487
74OPC-308
74Top-308
75OPC-472
75Top-472
76OPC-486
76Top-486
77Top-114
79KnoKnoST-18
82DurBulT-22
85IntLeaAT-23
85RicBraT-23
86RicBraP-4
89BraDub-7
91LinDriAAA-450
91RicBraBC-40
91RicBraLD-450
91RicBraP-2585
92RicBraF-392
92RicBraRC-4
92RicBraS-450
93RicBraF-202
93RicBraRC-2
94GreBraF-429
94GreBraTI-2
95BreBtaTI-39
96DurBulBIB-20
Dale, Carl
94NewJerCC-6
94NewJerCF-3407
94SigRooDP-46
94SigRooDPS-46
94StaCluDP-30
94StaCluDPFDI-30
95MidLeaA-10
95PeoChiTI-40
96ModA'sB-6
Dale, Gene (Emmett Eugene)
15SpoNewM-43
16SpoNewM-42
Dale, Phil
86TamTarP-4
87CedRapRP-2
88ChaLooB-18
89GreHorP-427
90CedRapRDGB-22
91IdaFalBP-4345
91WavRedF-xx
95AusFut-93
95AusFutSFP-SFFP9
Dale, Ron
93RanCucQF-823
Dalena, Pete
83NasSouTI-5
84ColCliP-8
84ColCliT-18
84NasSouTI-5
85ColCliP-7
85ColCliT-15
86ColCliP-4
87ColCliP-5
87ColCliP-7
87ColCliT-12
88ColCliC-16
88ColCliP-14
88ColCliP-321
89ColSprSSC-12
89ColSprSSP-235
89TriAAP-AAA36
90CMC-641
90ProAAAF-172
90TopDeb89-27
90VanCanC-14
90VanCanP-494
91HarSenP-643
91LinDriAA-275
93BurBeeC-27
Dalesandro, Mark
90BoiHawP-3324
90ProAaA-166
91Cla/Bes-259
91MidLeaAP-MWL25
91QuaCitAC-16
91QuaCitAP-2634
92CalLeaACL-38
92PalSprAC-20
92PalSprAF-846
93PalSprAC-7
93PalSprAF-72
94Sel-198
94TopTra-34T
94VanCanF-1866
95AngMot-10
95Pac-54
95Sco-278
95ScoGolR-278
95ScoPlaTS-278
96ColCliB-8
97MidAngOHP-6
Daley, Bill (William)
87BucN28-6
87OldJudN-118
Daley, Buddy (Leavitt Leo)
47Exh-55
58Top-222
59Top-263
60A'sJayP-2
60A'sTeal-4
60ArmCoi-8
60Baz-2
60Top-8
60TopTat-11
60TopVen-8
61A'sTeal-5
61AthJayP-7
61Baz-4
61Pos-83A
61Pos-83B
61Top-48
61Top-422
61TopStal-159
61TopStal-201
61Yan61RL-14
62SalPlaC-203
62ShiPlaC-203
62Top-376
62YanJayP-5
63Top-38
64Top-164
64TopVen-164
65OPC-262
65Top-262
78TCM60I-257
91RinPos1Y3-11
92YanWIZ6-33
Daley, Jud
90DodTar-923
Daley, Pete (Peter Harvey)
55Top-206
57Top-388
58Top-73
59Top-276
60Top-108
60TopVen-108
61Top-158
62TopStal-94
Dalkowski, Steve
63Top-496
Dallard, Eggie
91PomBlaBPB-23
Dallas, Gershon
90AshTouP-2759
91OscAstC-23
91OscAstP-697
92ColRedC-14
92ColRedF-2404
Dallessandro, Dom
41CubTeal-2
41DouPlaR-101
43CubTeal-5
44CubTeal-4
49BowPCL-9
77SerSta-7
78ReaRem-3
79DiaGre-109
83TCMPla1944-32
Dallimore, Brian
96AubDouB-6
Dalrymple, Abner (Abner F.)
87OldJudN-120
88WG1CarG-57
Dalrymple, Clay (Clayton E.)
47StaPinP2-13
60Lea-143
60Top-523
61Top-299
61TopStal-52
62Jel-197
62Pos-197
62PosCan-197
62SalPlaC-141
62ShiPlaC-141
62Top-434
62TopStal-166
63Fle-52
63Jel-184
63Pos-184
63Top-192
64PhiJayP-5
64PhiPhiB-12
64PhiTeaS-2
64Top-191
64TopVen-191
65PhiJayP-5
65Top-372
66PhiTeal-6
66Top-202
66TopVen-202
67CokCapPh-9
67DexPre-58
67OPC-53
67PhiPol-5
67Top-53
68Top-567
69MilBra-68
69OPC-151
69Top-151A
69Top-151B
69TopFou-12
69TopSta-74
70OPC-319

70Ori-4
70Top-319
71MLBOffS-294
71OPC-617
71Top-617
78TCM60I-203
91OriCro-93
Dalson, Kevin
89WytCubS-9
Dalton, Brian
94HelBreF-3606
94HelBreSP-10
95BelBreTI-5
Dalton, Dee
93JohCitCC-1
93JohCitCF-3685
94MadHatC-8
94MadHatF-139
96ArkTraB-9
Dalton, Harry
82BrePol-NNO
Dalton, Jack
90DodTar-161
Dalton, Jed
95BoiHawTI-14
96CedRapKTI-6
Dalton, Mike
86PawRedSP-8
87PawRedSP-66
87PawRedST-4
88NewBriRSP-896
89NewBriRSP-607
89PawRedSTI-7
90CMC-275
90PawRedSC-24
90PawRedSDD-5
90PawRedSP-455
90ProAAAF-427
90TopTVRS-42
91LinDriAAA-582
91TolMudHLD-582
91TolMudHP-1923
92BufBisBS-6
92BufBisF-317
92BufBisS-30
92Fle-131
92Sco100RS-95
92TopDeb91-42
93BufBisF-510
Dalton, Rich
78OrlTwiT-4
Daly, Billiards
88GooN16-16
Daly, Bob
92GulCoaMF-3487
93KinMetC-7
93KinMetF-3800
95PitMetTI-17
Daly, J.C.
88AllandGN-15
Daly, Mark
81TidTidT-25
Daly, Maurice
87AllandGN-43
Daly, Sun (James J.)
87OldJudN-122
Daly, Tom (Thomas Peter)
03BreE10-30
79RedSoxEF-15
87FouBasHN-1
87OldJudN-121
88AugBecN-6
90DodTar-162
95May-32
Dalzachio, Paul
91ButCopKSP-6
Damascus, Horse
68AtlOil-5
Damaska, Jack
77FriOneYW-60
Damato, Joseph
49W725AngTI-7
Damian, Len (Leonard)
86PeoChiP-4
87PitCubP-13
88IowCubC-2
88IowCubP-544
89IowCubC-2
89IowCubP-1705
90TopTVCu-43
Dammann, Bill
98CamPepP-18
Damon, John
83MemChiT-4
Damon, Johnny David
92ClaFS7-417
92UppDecML-1
92UppDecML-19
93ClaFS7-182
93ClaGolF-201
93RocRoyC-1
93RocRoyF-727
93SP-273
94ActPac-18
94Bow-373
94BowBes-B41
94BowBes-X96
94BowBesR-B41
94BowBesR-X96
94CarLeaAF-CAR15
94Cla-25
94ClaCreotC-C5
94ClaTriF-T37
94ColC-642
94ColChoGS-642
94ColChoSS-642
94ExcAllF-6
94ExcFS7-66
94SPDieC-3
94UppDec-546
94UppDecAHNIL-4
94UppDecED-546
94UppDecML-125
94UppDecML-252
94UppDecMLT1PJF-TP2
94UppDecMLT1PMF-2
94WilBluRC-4
94WilBluRF-311
95ActPacF-22
95Bow-254
95BowBes-B45
95BowBesR-B45
95BowGolF-254
95Exc-56
95ExcAll-7
95PinETA-4
95SigRooOP-OP2
95SigRooOPS-OP2
95Top-599
95UltGolMR-M10
95UppDecML-6
95UppDecML-162
95UppDecMLMLA-3
95UppDecMLOP-OP13
95UppDecMLT1PF-3
95WicWraTI-18
96Baz-125
96Bow-166
96BowBes-56
96BowBesAR-56
96BowBesR-56
96Cir-44
96CirRav-44
96ColCho-10
96ColCho-411
96ColCho-650
96ColChoGS-10
96ColChoGS-411
96ColChoGS-650
96ColChoSS-10
96ColChoSS-411
96ColChoSS-650
96Don-60
96DonPreP-60
96EmoXL-65
96Fin-G102
96FinRef-G102
96Fla-87
96Fle-124
96FleRooS-3
96FleTif-124
96Lea-82
96LeaLim-24
96LeaLimG-24
96LeaPre-30
96LeaPreP-30
96LeaPrePB-82
96LeaPrePG-82
96LeaPrePS-82
96LeaPreSG-65
96LeaPreSte-65
96LeaSig-32
96LeaSigA-54
96LeaSigAG-54
96LeaSigAS-54
96LeaSigPPG-32
96LeaSigPPP-32
96MetUni-63
96MetUniP-63
96Pac-326
96PacGolCD-DC3
96PacPri-P105
96PacPriG-P105
96PanSti-190
96Pin-170
96Pin-277
96PinAfi-128
96PinAfiAP-128
96PinAfiSP-19
96PinArtP-96
96PinArtP-177
96PinFoil-277
96PinProS-4
96PinSta-96
96PinSta-177
96PinTeaS-11
96PinTeaT-2
96RoyPol-7
96Sco-29
96Sco-223
96Sco-382
96ScoDiaA-29
96ScoDugC-A103
96ScoDugC-B107
96ScoDugCAP-A103
96ScoDugCAP-B107
96ScoFutF-7
96Sel-37
96SelArtP-37
96SelCer-27
96SelCerAP-27
96SelCerCB-27
96SelCerCR-27
96SelCerIP-7
96SelCerMB-27
96SelCerMG-27
96SelCerMR-27
96SelCerSF-18
96SelClaTF-15
96SelEnF-23
96SelTeaN-17
96SigRooOJMR-M2
96SP-100
96Spo-15
96Spo-118
96SpoArtP-15
96SpoArtP-118
96SpoPowS-22
96SPSpeFX-22
96SPSpeFXDC-22
96SPx-31
96SPxGol-31
96StaClu-148
96StaClu-259
96StaCluEPB-148
96StaCluEPG-148
96StaCluEPS-148
96StaCluMOP-148
96StaCluMOP-259
96Stu-125
96StuPrePB-125
96StuPrePG-125
96StuPrePS-125
96Sum-124
96Sum-158
96SumAbo&B-124
96SumAbo&B-158
96SumArtP-124
96SumArtP-158
96SumBal-12
96SumFoi-124
96SumFoi-158
96SumPos-8
96Top-215
96TopChr-77
96TopChrR-77
96TopGal-93
96TopGalPG-PG7
96TopGalPPI-93
96TopLas-101
96Ult-352
96UltGolM-352
96UltGolP-4
96UltGolPGM-4
96UppDec-90
96UppDecBCP-BC2
96UppDecHC-HC8
96Zen-31
96ZenArtP-31
97Bow-287
97BowInt-287
97Cir-111
97CirRav-111
97ColCho-360
97Don-98
97DonLim-186
97DonLimLE-186
97DonPre-102
97DonPreCttC-102
97DonPreP-98
97DonPrePGold-98
97Fin-122
97FinEmb-122
97FinEmbR-122
97FinRef-122
97FlaSho-A22
97FlaSho-B22
97FlaSho-C22
97FlaShoLC-22
97FlaShoLC-B22
97FlaShoLC-C22
97FlaShoLCM-A22
97FlaShoLCM-B22
97FlaShoLCM-C22
97Fle-112
97FleTif-112
97Lea-229
97LeaFraM-229
97LeaFraMDC-229
97MetUni-91
97NewPin-97
97NewPinAP-97
97NewPinMC-97
97NewPinPP-97
97Pac-99
97PacLigB-99
97PacPri-35
97PacPriLB-35
97PacPriP-35
97PacSil-99
97PinCer-104
97PinCerMBlu-104
97PinCerMG-104
97PinCerMR-104
97PinCerR-104
97PinTotCPB-104
97PinTotCPG-104
97PinTotCPR-104
97ProMag-57
97ProMagML-57
97RoyPol-6
97Sco-3
97ScoPreS-3
97ScoShoS-3
97ScoShoSAP-3
97SkyE-X-24
97SkyE-XC-24
97SkyE-XEC-24
97SP-90
97StaClu-333
97StaCluMOP-333
97Top-196
97TopChr-76
97TopChrR-76
97TopGal-169
97TopGalPPI-169
97TopIntF-ILM7
97TopIntFR-ILM7
97Ult-66
97UltGolME-66
97UltPlaME-66
97UppDec-390
95UppDecMLFS-6
95UppDecMLFS-162
97UppDecRSF-RS6
97UppDecTTS-TS18
Dana, Derek
91EveGiaC-12
91EveGiaP-3918
92CliGiaC-14
92CliGiaF-3601
Danapilis, Eric
93NiaFalRF-3401
94ExcFS7-52
94FayGenC-7
94FayGenF-2153
95JacSunTI-7
Dancer, Faye
94TedWil-93
Dancy, Bill
76VenLeaS-207
80PenPilBT-27
80PenPilCT-12
83ReaPhiT-23
85PorBeaC-35
87MaiGuiT-23
89ScrRedBC-25
89ScrRedBP-1208
90CMC-244
90ScrRedBC-18
90TriAllGP-AAA27
91LinDriAAA-499
91ScrRedBLD-499
91ScrRedBP-2555
92ClePhiF-2073
93ClePhiC-26
93ClePhiF-2699
94ReaPhiF-2078
95ReaPhiELC-7
96RicBraB-1
96RicBraRC-24
Dando, Patrick
90ProAaA-191
90PulBraB-16
90PulBraP-3096
91DurBulC-18
91DurBulP-1552
92BasCitRC-3
92BasCitRF-3851
93WilBluRC-7
93WilBluRF-2003
Dandos, Mike
85EveGialC-2
Dandridge, Brad
93SpoIndC-3
94OgdRapF-3746
94OgdRapSP-15
95SanBerSTI-5
96SanAntMB-4
Dandridge, Hooks (Ray)
74LauOldTBS-26
78HalHalR-2
80PerHaloFP-197
80SSPHOF-199
86NegLeaF-7
87DonHig-18
88NegLeaD-17
89HOFStiB-26
89PerCelP-11
90NegLeaS-14
90PerGreM-34
91NegLeaRL-5
91PomBlaBPB-24
92FroRowD-1
92FroRowD-2
92FroRowD-3
92FroRowD-4
92FroRowD-5
92NegLeaPL-4
93TedWil-103
93UppDecS-17
94PomNegLB-7
95NegLeaLI-5
Danek, Bill
86PeoChiP-5
87WinSpiP-5
Danforth, Dave (David C.)
12T207-39
21E121So1-14
21Exh-31
21Nei-26
22E120-93
22W572-19
22W573-27
23W501-102
75WhiSox1T-5
92Man191BSR-6
93ConTSN-719
Danforth, Perry
76SpoIndC-11
77SpoIndC-7
Daniel, Chuck
88MisStaB-4
89MisStaB-9
90MisStaB-7
91MisStaB-12
92GenCubC-23
92GenCubF-1551
92MisStaB-10
93PeoChiC-4
93PeoChiF-1076
Daniel, Clay
85CedRapRT-5
86VerRedP-5
88HarSenP-860
90MiaMirIS-5
Daniel, Dave
82VerBeaDT-4
Daniel, Jake
90DodTar-924

Daniel, Jim
86ChaRaiP-8
86MemChiSTOS-3
86MemChiTOS-3
87ChaO'sW-11
88ChaKniTI-16
88RivRedWCLC-231
88RivRedWP-1412
89RivRedWB-28
89RivRedWP-1407
90RivRedWB-21
93RanCucQC-29
94RanCucQC-28
95RanCucQT-NNO
96RanCucQB-5
Daniel, Keith
90KisDodD-8
Daniel, Lee
90MedHatBJB-21
Daniel, Michael
91JamExpC-6
91JamExpP-3548
91OklStaC-7
92ClaFS7-302
92ProFS7-273
92WesPalBEC-23
92WesPalBEF-2090
93WesPalBEC-4
93WesPalBEF-1343
95LynHilTI-6
Daniel, Scott
91JamExpC-29
Daniel, Steve
85BurRanT-25
Daniels, B.A.
94ConTSN-1268
94ConTSNB-1268
Daniels, Bennie
55DonWin-17
58Top-392
59Top-122
59TopVen-122
60Lea-7
60Top-91
60TopVen-91
61SenJayP-3
61Top-368
62SalPlaC-42
62ShiPlaC-42
62Top-378
62TopBuc-21
62TopStaI-95
63BasMagM-18
63Top-497
64Top-587
65OPC-129
65Top-129
66SenTeal-5
78TCM60I-145
Daniels, Bert (Bernard E.)
09ColChiE-71
10JuJuDE-14
11PloCanE-21
12ColRedB-71
12ColTinT-71
12T207-40
Daniels, Dave
78AppFoxT-7
79AppFoxT-11
80AppFoxT-23
Daniels, David
96AugGreB-7
96EriSeaB-9
Daniels, Gary
90EriSaiS-5
Daniels, Greg
87MiaMarP-19
Daniels, Jack (Harold Jack)
53BowC-83
Daniels, Jerry
87EriCarP-23
88St.PetCS-5
Daniels, Jim
89RivRedWCLC-28
Daniels, John
94BelMarC-9
94BelMarF-3226
96LanJetB-13
Daniels, Kal
83CedRapRF-17
83CedRapRT-22
86Don-27
86Fle-646
86RedTexG-28
86SpoRoo-43
87ClaUpdY-130
87Don-142
87DonOpeD-192
87Fle-197
87FleGlo-197
87FleLeaL-13
87RedKah-28
87SpoTeaP-4
87Top-466
87TopTif-466
87ToyRoo-8
88ClaRed-161
88Don-14
88Don-289
88DonBasB-6
88DonSupD-14
88Fle-230
88FleAwaW-7
88FleGlo-230
88FleMin-72
88FleStiC-82
88Lea-14
88Lea-150
88OPC-53
88PanSti-281
88RedFolSB-14
88RedKah-28
88Sco-86
88ScoGlo-86
88ScoYouSI-39
88Spo-112
88StaLinRe-5
88Top-622
88TopBig-48
88TopSti-139
88TopTif-622
89Bow-314
89BowTif-314
89ClaLigB-74
89DodStaSV-4
89Don-198
89DonBasB-118
89DonBonM-BC18
89Fle-157
89FleGlo-157
89FleLeaL-8
89FleSup-10
89OPC-45
89PanSti-75
89RedFolSB-26
89RedKah-28
89Sco-7
89ScoRoo-48T
89Spo-52
89Top-45
89TopAme2C-10
89TopBasT-97
89TopBig-323
89TopMinL-7
89TopSti-144
89TopTif-45
89TVSpoM-42
89UppDec-160
90Bow-99
90BowTif-99
90CedRapRDGB-2
90ClaYel-T64
90DodMot-3
90DodPol-28
90DodTar-925
90Don-432
90DonBesN-127
90FleUpd-20
90Lea-313
90OPC-585
90PanSti-280
90PubSti-25
90PubSti-610
90Sco-490
90Top-585
90TopBig-238
90TopTif-585
90UppDec-603
90VenSti-119
90VenSti-120
91Bow-600
91ClaGam-14
91DodMot-3
91DodPol-28
91Don-336
91DonGraS-3
91Fle-198
91Lea-112
91MooSna-7
91OPC-245
91PanFreS-60
91PanSti-58
91RedFolS-22
91Sco-20
91Sco100S-53
91StaClu-116
91SunSee-5
91Top-245
91TopDesS-245
91TopMic-245
91TopTif-245
91Ult-160
91UppDec-166
92Bow-487
92ClaGam-125
92DenHol-14
92DodMot-14
92DodPol-28
92DodSmo-5792
92Don-343
92Fle-453
92OPC-767
92PanSti-198
92Pin-374
92Sco-110
92ScoRoo-70T
92StaClu-514
92Top-767
92TopGol-767
92TopGolW-767
92TopKid-51
92TopMic-767
92Ult-210
92UppDec-284
93PanSti-207
93Sel-181
93Top-128
93TopGol-128
93TopInaM-128
93TopMic-128
Daniels, Lance
89BriTigS-6
Daniels, Law (Lawrence L.)
87OldJudN-123
Daniels, Lee
91MedHatBJP-4114
91MedHatBJSP-14
92St.CatBJC-9
92St.CatBJF-3380
94Bow-197
94DunBluJC-8
94DunBluJF-2549
94FloStaLAF-FSL5
96BowBes-117
96BowBesAR-117
96BowBesR-117
96GreBraB-10
96GreBraTI-10
Daniels, Moe
93CedRapKC-5
93CedRapKF-1750
94LakElsSC-6
94LakElsSF-1676
95LakElsSTI-10
95MidAngOHP-10
Daniels, Steve
80CedRapRT-24
Danies, Franklin
90IBAWorA-16
Dann, Tom
79NewCoPT-1
Danner, Deon
91WelPirC-18
91WelPirP-3565
92AugPirC-8
92AugPirF-230
Danning, Harry (Harry)
36WorWidGV-22
39PlaBal-18
39WorWidGV-7
40PlaBal-93
41DouPlaR-25
41DouPlaR-91
41PlaBal-7
43MPR302-1-7
Danson, Roger
76BurBeeT-3
Dantonio, Fats
90DodTar-921
91JesHSA-1
Dantzler, Eric
95BurBeeTI-27
Dantzler, Shawn
86ClePhiP-6
87ClePhiP-10
88ClePhiS-10
Dapper, Cliff
50W720HolS-6
90DodTar-163
Darby, Mike
86WauTimP-6
87SalSpuP-17
Darcuiel, Faruq
96WisTimRB-8
Darcy, Pat (Patrick L.)
75OPC-615
75Top-615
76OPC-538
76SSP-26
76Top-538
Darden, Tony
94ElmPioF-3482
95KanCouCTI-8
96BreCouMB-12
94ElmPioC-5
Dare, Brian
89AncBucTI-3
90IdaFalBP-3241
Darensbourg, Vic
93KanCouCC-5
93KanCouCF-908
94Bow-234
94Cla-15
94ExcFS7-190
94PorSeaDF-671
94PorSeaDTI-12
94SigRooDP-100
94SigRooDPS-100
95KanCouCLTI-5
95Top-649
93KanCouCTI-5
Dares, Darrin
90LSUTigA-15
Dark, Alvin (Alvin Ralph)
47Exh-56A
47Exh-56B
47Exh-56C
47PM1StaP1-39
49Bow-67
49EurSta-6
49Lea-51
49MPR302-2-116
50Bow-64
50Dra-20
50RoyDes-18
51Bow-14
51R42SmaS-20
52BerRos-11
52Bow-34
52RoyPre-3
52StaCalL-78B
52StaCalS-90C
52Top-351
53BowC-19
53Top-109
54Bow-41
54NewYorJA-21
54RedHeaF-5
55Bow-2
55GiaGolS-19
56Top-148
57Top-98
58Top-125
59OklTodML-17
59Top-502
60PhiJayP-6
60Top-472
61GiaJayP-4
61Top-220
62Top-322
63GiaJayP-3
63Top-258
64GiaJayP-3
64Top-529
66Top-433
67Top-389
68Top-237
68TopVen-237
69OPC-91
69Top-91
70Ind-3
70OPC-524
70Top-524
71Ind-2
71OPC-397
71Top-397
75Gia195T-4
75OPC-561
75Top-561
76GalBasGHoF-6
76SSP-488
78Top-467
79TCM50-25
80GiaGreT-8
80PacLeg-80
82GSGalAG-2
83TopRep5-351
84FifNatCT-3
86A'sGreT-12
87A'sMot-13
88PacLegI-28
89SweBasG-77
90PacLeg-69
91LinDri-23
91SweBasG-22
91TopArc1-109
92BazQua5A-15
93TedWil-52
93UppDecAH-36
Dark, David
92GenCubC-22
92GenCubF-1552
Darkis, Willie
83ReaPhiT-18
84PorBeaC-211
86GleFalTP-2
Darley, Ned
91MedHatBJP-4091
91MedHatBJSP-19
92St.CatBJC-8
92St.CatBJF-3381
93HagSunC-8
93HagSunF-1872
96HigDesMB-9
Darling, Dell (Dell Conrad)
87OldJudN-124
88KimN18-10
Darling, Gary
89T/MUmp-58
90T/MUmp-56
Darling, Ron (Ronald M.)
81TulDriT-18
82TidTidT-13
83TidTidT-1
84Don-30A
84Don-30B
84FleUpd-29
84MetFanC-2
84TopTra-27T
84TopTraT-27T
85Don-434
85Fle-76
85FleStaS-117
85Lea-256
85MetColP-20
85MetTCM-8
85OPC-138
85Top-415
85TopMin-415
85TopSti-105
85TopTif-415
86BasStaB-26
86Don-563
86DonAll-37
86Fle-77
86FleMin-18
86FleStiC-28
86KayB-6
86Lea-221
86MetColP-13
86MetFanC-3
86MetTCM-3
86MetWorSC-22
86OPC-225
86SevCoi-E14
86Spo-109
86Top-225
86TopSti-98
86TopTat-10
86TopTif-225
87BurKinA-6
87Don-192
87Dra-28
87Fle-5
87FleGlo-5
87FleGlo-WS5
87FleHotS-11
87FleLimBC-C1

87FleMin-23
87FleStiC-27
87FleWorS-5
87KraFoo-28
87Lea-85
87MetColP-11
87MetFanC-2
87MSAlceTD-3
87OPC-75
87Spo-53
87SpoTeaP-2
87Top-75
87TopMinL-21
87TopSti-105
87TopTif-75
87Woo-26
88Don-6
88Don-76
88DonBasB-41
88DonSupD-6
88DonTeaBM-76
88Fle-132
88FleGlo-132
88FleSluBC-C1
88FleStiC-100
88Lea-6
88Lea-78
88MetColP-2
88MetKah-12
88OPC-38
88PanSti-335
88Sco-141
88ScoGlo-141
88Spo-73
88StaLinMe-5
88Top-685
88TopBig-85
88TopSti-98
88TopTif-685
89Bow-372
89BowTif-372
89Don-171
89DonBasB-41
89Fle-32
89FleGlo-32
89MetColP-5
89MetKah-6
89OPC-105
89PanSti-130
89Sco-180
89ScoHot1S-71
89Spo-32
89Top-105
89TopBasT-86
89TopBig-166
89TopDouM-7
89TopSti-100
89TopTif-105
89TVSpoM-2
89UppDec-159
90Don-289
90DonLeaS-29
90Fle-201
90FleCan-201
90Lea-304
90MetColP-13
90MetKah-15
90MLBBasB-14
90OPC-330
90PanSti-295
90PubSti-130
90Sco-446
90Top-330
90TopBig-113
90TopSti-98
90TopTif-330
90TopTVM-9
90TulDriDGB-18
90UppDec-241
90VenSti-121
91Bow-483
91Don-472
91Fle-144
91Lea-378
91MetColP-28
91MetKah-15
91MetWIZ-90
91OPC-735
91Sco-456
91StaClu-60
91Top-735
91TopDesS-735
91TopMic-735
91TopTif-735
91Ult-214
91UppDec-198
91UppDecFE-69F
92AthMot-24
92Bow-30
92Don-723
92Fle-254
92Lea-447
92OPC-259
92Pin-378
92Sco-710
92StaClu-685
92StaCluECN-685
92Top-259
92TopGol-259
92TopGolW-259
92TopMic-259
92Ult-111
92UppDec-669
93AthMot-12
93Bow-189
93Don-700
93Fle-661
93Lea-182
93OPC-82
93PacSpa-220
93PanSti-22
93Pin-199
93Sco-619
93Sel-10
93StaClu-305
93StaCluAt-14
93StaCluFDI-305
93StaCluMOP-305
93Top-182
93TopGol-182
93TopInaM-182
93TopMic-182
93Ult-256
93UppDec-168
93UppDecGold-168
94A'sMot-16
94ColC-88
94ColChoGS-88
94ColChoSS-88
94Don-452
94ExtBas-147
94Fin-243
94FinRef-243
94Fla-90
94Fle-258
94Lea-57
94Pac-447
94Pin-90
94PinArtP-90
94PinMusC-90
94Sco-159
94ScoGolR-159
94StaClu-428
94StaCluFDI-428
94StaCluGR-428
94StaCluMOP-428
94Top-549
94TopGol-549
94TopSpa-549
94Ult-106
94UppDec-498
94UppDecED-498
95AthMot-6
95ColCho-136
95ColChoGS-136
95ColChoSS-136
95Don-13
95DonPreP-13
95Fla-72
95Fle-243
95Lea-112
95Pin-389
95PinArtP-389
95PinMusC-389
95Sco-381
95ScoGolR-381
95ScoPlaTS-381
95StaClu-142
95StaCluFDI-142
95StaCluMOP-142
95StaCluSTWS-142
95Top-16
95TopCyb-14
95Ult-92
95UltGolM-92
95UppDec-282
95UppDecED-282
95UppDecEDG-282

Darnbrough, William
87OldJudN-125

Darnell, Bob (Robert Jack)
55Bow-39
79TCM50-257
90DodTar-164
95TopArcBD-124

Darnell, Steve
76WauMetT-11

Darr, Mike
94BriTigF-3516
94SigRooDP-45
94SigRooDPS-45
94StaCluDP-25
94StaCluDPFDI-25
95FayGenTI-8
96Bow-247
96LakTigB-11

Darr, Mike (Michael Edward)
78SyrChiT-6

Darrell, Tommy
96BoiHawB-9

Darretta, Dave
85BurRanT-9

Darrow, Darrell
75SalLakCC-9
76SalLakCGC-1
79SalLakCGT-17B

Darrow, George (George Oliver)
34Gou-87

Darula, Bobby
96OgdRapTI-36

Darwin, Bobby (Arthur B.)
69Top-641
73LinPor-108
73OPC-228
73Top-228
74OPC-527
74Top-527
74TopSta-205
75Hos-98
75OPC-346
75Top-346
76Hos-31
76HosTwi-31
76OPC-63
76SSP-247
76Top-63
76VenLeaS-213
77Top-617
90DodTar-165
94BreMilB-13

Darwin, Brian
94SouOreAC-3
94SouOreAF-3635

Darwin, Danny Wayne
78TucTorC-28
79Top-713
80Top-498
81Don-147
81Fle-632
81OPC-22
81Top-22
81TopSti-136
82Don-321
82Fle-315
82Top-298
82TopSti-237
83Don-289
83Fle-565
83FleSta-46
83FleSti-161
83RanAffF-44
83Top-609
83TopSti-121
84AllGamPI-168
84Don-544
84Fle-416
84Nes792-377
84RanJarP-44
84Top-377
84TopSti-359
84TopTif-377
85AllGamPI-76
85BrePol-18
85Don-98
85Fle-557
85FleUpd-32
85OPC-227
85Top-227
85TopSti-352
85TopTif-227
85TopTifT-26T
85TopTra-26T
86BrePol-18
86Don-149
86Fle-485
86Lea-75
86OPC-206
86Top-519
86TopSti-205
86TopTif-519
87AstMot-14
87AstPol-4
87Don-508
87Fle-54
87FleGlo-54
87OPC-157
87Top-157
87TopTif-157
88AstMot-14
88AstPol-7
88Don-358
88Fle-444
88FleGlo-444
88Sco-184
88ScoGlo-184
88StaLinAst-7
88Top-461
88TopTif-461
89AstLenH-13
89AstMot-13
89AstSmo-10
89Don-390
89Fle-354
89FleGlo-354
89Sco-553
89Top-719
89TopTif-719
89UppDec-97
90AstLenH-9
90AstMot-15
90Bow-66
90BowTif-66
90Don-561
90DonBesN-53
90Fle-227
90FleCan-227
90Lea-346
90OPC-64
90PubSti-91
90Sco-402
90Spo-83
90Top-64
90TopSti-14
90TopTif-64
90UppDec-305
90VenSti-122
91Bow-111
91Cla1-T44
91ClaGam-170
91Don-165
91Don-401
91Fle-503
91FleUpd-5
91Lea-405
91OPC-666
91OPCPre-28
91PanCanT1-65
91PanFreS-15
91PanSti-18
91RedSoxP-6
91Sco-51
91ScoRoo-24T
91StaClu-394
91Top-666
91TopDesS-666
91TopMic-666
91TopTif-666
91TopTra-26T
91TopTraT-26T
91UppDec-586
91UppDec-705
92Don-87
92Fle-38
92OPC-324
92RedSoxDD-10
92Sco-138
92StaClu-539
92Top-324
92TopGol-324
92TopGolW-324
92TopMic-324
92UppDec-678
93Don-647
93Fle-179
93Lea-455
93PacSpa-356
93RanKee-119
93RedSoxWHP-3
93StaClu-484
93StaCluFDI-484
93StaCluMOP-484
93Top-214
93TopGol-214
93TopInaM-214
93TopMic-214
93Ult-150
93UppDec-220
93UppDecGold-220
94BreMilB-14
94ColC-89
94ColChoGS-89
94ColChoSS-89
94Don-469
94ExtBas-18
94Fin-58
94FinRef-58
94Fla-12
94Fle-28
94Lea-114
94Pac-51
94Pin-303
94PinArtP-303
94PinMusC-303
94Sco-192
94ScoGolR-192
94Sel-110
94StaClu-251
94StaCluFDI-251
94StaCluGR-251
94StaCluMOP-251
94Top-292
94TopGol-292
94TopSpa-292
94Ult-12
94UppDec-123
94UppDecED-123
95Sco-208
95ScoGolR-208
95ScoPlaTS-208
95StaClu-534
95StaCluMOP-534
95StaCluSTWS-534
96FleUpd-U175
96FleUpdTC-U175
97PacPriGotD-GD150

Darwin, Jeff
89BelMarL-4
90PenPilS-6
91Cla/Bes-51
91SanBerSC-2
91SanBerSP-1978
92PenPilC-16
92PenPilF-2926
93Bow-627
93JacSunF-2704
94CalCanF-783
95TacRaiTI-7
96NasSouB-11
96SigRooOJRS-R4
97Don-258
97DonPreP-258
97DonPrePGold-258
97Sco-314
97ScoPreS-314
97ScoShoS-314
97ScoShoSAP-314
97ScoShoSAP-315
97ScoWhiS-4
97ScoWhiSPl-4
97ScoWhiSPr-4

Dascenzo, Doug
86WinSpiP-4
87PitCubP-23
88BlaYNPRWL-148
88IowCubC-19
88IowCubP-528
89Don-491
89Fle-420
89FleGlo-420
89IowCubC-20
89IowCubP-1702
89PanSti-47
89Sco-621
89ScoHot1R-4
89Spo-42
89Top-149
89TopTif-149
89UppDec-10

90CubMar-5
90OPC-762
90ScoYouS2-40
90Top-762
90TopTif-762
90TopTVCu-30
90UppDec-211
91CubMar-29
91CubVinL-8
91Don-749
91Fle-418
91Lea-483
91OPC-437
91Sco-209
91Top-437
91TopDesS-437
91TopMic-437
91TopTif-437
91Ult-60
92Bow-287
92CubMar-29
92Don-38
92Lea-51
92OPC-509
92Pin-160
92Sco-319
92StaClu-252
92Stu-11
92Top-509
92TopGol-509
92TopGolW-509
92TopMic-509
92UppDec-239
93Bow-193
93Don-212
93Fle-376
93PacSpa-55
93PanSti-210
93Pin-555
93RanKee-401
93Sco-446
93StaClu-664
93StaCluFDI-664
93StaCluMOP-664
93StaCluR-15
93Top-211
93TopGol-211
93TopInaM-211
93TopMic-211
93UppDec-64
93UppDec-739
93UppDecGold-64
93UppDecGold-739
94Pac-612
96LasVegSB-10

Dascoli, Frank
55Bow-291

DaSilva, Fernando
93BurBeeC-6
93BurBeeF-150
93ClaGolF-112
93JamExpC-6
93JamExpF-3319
94BurBeeC-6
94BurBeeF-1075
96WesPalBEB-7

DaSilva, Manny
94SouOreAC-4
94SouOreAF-3625
95WesMicWTI-25

Daspit, Jamie
92VerBeaDC-18
93SanAntMF-2997
93VerBeaDF-2208
94JacGenF-208
95TusTorTI-4

Daspit, Jim (James)
90GreFalDSP-5
91BakDodCLC-21
92VerBeaDF-2867
95Exc-200

Dasso, Frank (Francis J.)
47SigOil-3
47SigOil-59
49SolSunP-2

Dattola, Kevin
90SouOreAB-4
91Cla/Bes-115
91HunStaTI-8
91ModA'sC-25
91ModA'sP-3102
92HunStaF-3960
92HunStaS-308
93HunStaF-2093
93TacTigF-3045

Datz, Jeff
82AubAstT-11
83DayBeaAT-15
86ColAstP-9
87ColAstP-2
88TucTorC-9
88TucTorJP-7
88TucTorP-187
89TolMudHC-11
89TolMudHP-761
90CMC-507
90ColCliC-19
90ColCliP-678
90ProAAAF-328
90TopDeb89-28
94WatIndC-28
94WatIndF-3954
96CanIndB-1
96WesOahCHWB-45

Daub, Dan
90DodTar-926

Daubach, Brian
91KinMetC-6
91KinMetP-3818
92PitMetC-15
92PitMetF-3302
94St.LucMC-6
94St.LucMF-1200
95BinMetTI-8
96BinBeeB-5

Daubert, Jake (Jacob E.)
09ColChiE-72A
09ColChiE-72B
09SpoNewSM-94
11MecDFT-14
11S74Sil-52
11T205-36
12ColRedB-72A
12ColRedB-72B
12ColTinT-72A
12ColTinT-72B
12HasTriFT-27
12T207-41
13NatGamW-14
13TomBarW-13
14B18B-57
14CraJacE-143
14PieStaT-16
15CraJacE-143
15SpoNewM-44
16BF2FP-59
16ColE13-38
16FleBreD-22
16SpoNewM-43
17HolBreD-21
19W514-68
20NatCarE-21
20RedWorCP-3
20WalMaiW-11
21E121So1-15
21E121So8-14
21Exh-32
21Nei-99
22AmeCarE-13
22E120-169
22W572-20
22W575-22
22WilPatV-48
23W501-52
23W503-57
23WilChoV-26
75FlePio-24
87ConSer2-12
88PacEigMO-95
90DodTar-166
91ConTSN-307
93ConTSN-805
94ConTSN-1019
94ConTSNB-1019

Dauer, Edward
50W720HolS-27

Dauer, Rich (Richard F.)
76VenLeaS-136
77Top-477
78Top-237
79Top-666
80OPC-56
80Top-102
81AllGamPI-11
81Don-232
81Fle-182
81OPC-314
81Top-314
81TopSti-36
82Don-257
82Fle-161
82OPC-8
82Top-8
82TopSti-147
83AllGamPI-10
83Don-455
83Fle-57
83FleSta-47
83FleSti-196
83OPC-192
83OriPos-5
83Top-579
83TopSti-27
84AllGamPI-101
84Don-350
84Fle-4
84Nes792-723
84OPC-374
84OriEng-2
84OriTeal-6
84Top-723
84TopSti-214
84TopTif-723
85Don-106
85Fle-173
85OPC-58
85Top-494
85TopSti-203
85TopTif-494
86Fle-270
86OPC-251
86Top-251
86TopTif-251
87SanBerSP-7
89ColSprSSC-21
89ColSprSSP-242
89SanBerSB-28
90IndTeal-11
90SouCalS-3
91IndFanC-30
91OriCro-94
91PacSenL-105
92KanCouCTI-6
93OmaRoyF-1698

Daugherty, Jack
86JacExpT-25
87IndIndTI-10
88BlaYNPRWLU-16
88IndIndC-21
88IndIndP-521
89OklCit8C-13
89OklCit8P-1525
90Bow-503
90BowTif-503
90Don-461
90Fle-294
90FleCan-294
90Lea-521
90OPC-52
90RanMot-11
90Sco-564
90Sco100RS-61
90Top-52
90TopTif-52
90UppDec-614
91Bow-277
91Don-576
91Fle-284
91Lea-17
91OPC-622
91RanMot-11
91Sco-309
91StaClu-276
91Top-622
91TopDesS-622
91TopMic-622
91TopTif-622
91UppDec-284
92Don-569
92Fle-300
92OPC-344
92RanMot-11
92RanTeal-5
92Sco-622
92StaClu-634
92StaCluNC-634
92Top-344
92TopGol-344
92TopGolW-344
92TopMic-344
93Fle-682
93RanKee-120
93TucTorF-3065
94Sco-146
94ScoGolR-146
94SyrChiF-977
94SyrChiTI-9

Daugherty, Jim
90AshTouC-4
91AshTouP-562
91SouAtlLAGP-SAL1
92ProFS7-235

Daugherty, Keith
95DanBraTI-9
96MacBraB-16

Daugherty, Pat
90JamExpP-27

Daughterty, Mike
83SanJosBC-19

Daughtry, Dorian
87BelMarL-2
87BelMarTI-4
89SanBerSB-2
89SanBerSCLC-88

Dault, Donnie
93AubAstF-3434
96KisCobB-5

Dault, Raymond
93AubAstC-7

Daulton, Darren
83ReaPhiT-11
84PorBeaC-198
85FleUpd-33
85PhiTas-10
85PhiTas-24
85PorBeaC-42
86Don-477
86Fle-438
86PhiCIG-7
86PhiTas-10
86Top-264
86TopTif-264
87Don-262
87Fle-172
87FleGlo-172
87MaiGuiT-21
87OPC-57
87PhiTas-10
87Top-636
87TopTif-636
88Don-309
88PhiTas-7
88Sco-473
88ScoGlo-473
88StaLinPh-6
88Top-468
88TopTif-468
89Don-549
89DonBasB-128
89PhiTas-4
89Sco-413
89Top-187
89TopTif-187
89UppDec-448
90Bow-158
90BowTif-158
90Don-194
90DonBesN-20
90Fle-555
90FleCan-555
90Lea-369
90OPC-542
90PhiTas-7
90PubSti-234
90Sco-389
90Top-542
90TopTif-542
90UppDec-418
90VenSti-123
91Bow-507
91ClaGam-81
91ClaGam-187
91Don-316
91Fle-393
91Lea-192
91OPC-89
91PanFreS-102
91PanSti-109
91PhiMed-11
91Sco-246
91StaClu-4
91Stu-212
91Top-89
91TopDesS-89
91TopMic-89
91TopTif-89
91Ult-260
91UppDec-408
92Bow-440
92Don-198
92Fle-527
92Lea-335
92OPC-244
92PanSti-241
92PhiMed-10
92Pin-241
92Sco-506
92StaClu-529
92Stu-73
92StuHer-BC13
92Top-244
92TopGol-244
92TopGolW-244
92TopMic-244
92TriPla-143
92Ult-240
92UppDec-429
93Bow-160
93ClaGam-24
93ColAllG-6
93DiaMar-27
93Don-92
93DonDiaK-DK17
93DonEli-29
93DonEliS-11
93DonMVP-11
93DonPre-8
93Fin-171
93FinRef-171
93Fla-97
93FlaPro-2
93Fle-100
93Fle-352
93Fle-705
93Fle-715
93FleAll-NL9
93FleAtl-6
93FleFruotL-13
93FunPac-142
93FunPac-143
93FunPacA-AS2
93JimDea-5
93KinDis-10
93Kra-19
93Lea-95
93LeaGolA-R1
93LeaGolA-U2
93OPC-71
93OPCPre-12
93PacSpa-233
93PanSti-269
93PhiMed-9
93Pin-99
93PinHomRC-9
93PinTeaP-3
93Pos-18
93PosCan-10
93Sco-10
93Sco-526
93ScoFra-22
93Sel-13
93SelChaS-5
93SelDufIP-3
93SelStaL-34
93SP-11
93SPPlaP-PP5
93StaClu-313
93StaCluFDI-313
93StaCluM-91
93StaCluMOP-313
93StaCluP-1
93Stu-51
93StuSupoC-7
93Top-180
93Top-408
93TOPBLAG-3
93TopFulS-13
93TopGol-180
93TopGol-408
93TopInaM-180
93TopInaM-408
93TopMic-180
93TopMic-408
93TriPla-7
93TriPla-229
93TriPlaA-5
93TriPlaLL-L5
93TriPlaP-7
93Ult-86
93UltAllS-1

93UltHomRK-9
93UppDec-137
93UppDec-485
93UppDec-498
93UppDec-829
93UppDecGold-137
93UppDecGold-485
93UppDecGold-498
93UppDecGold-829
93UppDecHRH-HR8
93UppDecIC-WI17
93UppDecICJ-WI17
93USPlaCA-3C
94Bow-140
94Bow-384
94BowBes-R11
94BowBesR-R11
94ColC-358
94ColChoGS-358
94ColChoSS-358
94Don-333
94DonPro-2
94DonSpeE-333
94ExtBas-330
94ExtBasGB-8
94Fin-220
94FinJum-220
94FinRef-220
94Fla-204
94FlaInfP-3
94Fle-585
94FleAllS-34
94FlePro-1
94FleSun-8
94FUnPac-140
94KinDis-4
94Lea-170
94LeaL-134
94LeaMVPC-N4
94LeaMVPCG-N4
94LeaPro-2
94LeaSli-3
94OPC-123
94Pac-471
94PacSilP-31
94PanSti-224
94PhiMed-6
94PhiMel-4
94PhiUSPC-8C
94PhiUSPC-13H
94Pin-91
94PinArtP-91
94PinMusC-91
94PinRunC-RC31
94Pos-9
94ProMag-101
94Sco-34
94ScoGolR-34
94ScoGolS-4
94Sel-9
94SP-134
94SPDieC-134
94Spo-128
94StaClu-450
94StaCluDD-DD12
94StaCluFDI-450
94StaCluGR-450
94StaCluMOP-450
94StaCluMOP-DD12
94StaCluT-237
94StaCluTFDI-237
94Stu-136
94Top-380
94Top-608
94TopBlaG-28
94TopGol-380
94TopGol-608
94TopSpa-380
94TopSpa-608
94TopSupS-11
94TriPla-171
94TriPlaM-2
94Ult-243
94Ult-P243
94UltPhiF-1
94UltPhiF-2
94UltPhiF-3
94UltPhiF-4
94UltPhiF-5
94UltPhiF-11
94UltPhiF-12
94UltPhiF-13
94UltPhiF-14
94UltPhiF-15
94UltPhiF-M1
94UltPhiF-M3
94UltPhiF-AU1
94UltRBIK-12
94UppDec-65
94UppDecAJ-7
94UppDecAJG-7
94UppDecED-65
95Baz-105
95Bow-326
95BowBes-R9
95BowBesR-R9
95ClaPhoC-43
95ColCho-370
95ColChoGS-370
95ColChoSE-171
95ColChoSEGS-171
95ColChoSESS-171
95ColChoSS-370
95DenHol-7
95Don-497
95DonDom-2
95DonPreP-497
95DonTopotO-300
95Emb-61
95EmbGolI-61
95Emo-164
95Fin-164
95FinRef-164
95Fla-177
95FlaInfP-2
95Fle-388
95FleTeaL-24
95Lea-274
95LeaLim-99
95NatPac2-2
95Pac-326
95PacPri-105
95PanSti-21
95Phi-7
95PhiMel-5
95Pin-205
95PinArtP-205
95PinMusC-205
95Sco-432
95ScoGolR-432
95ScoHaloG-HG94
95ScoPlaTS-432
95Sel-44
95SelArtP-44
95SelCer-57
95SelCerMG-57
95SP-90
95SPCha-73
95SPCha-74
95SPChaDC-73
95SPChaDC-74
95Spo-27
95SpoArtP-27
95SPSil-90
95StaClu-237
95StaClu-263
95StaClu-505
95StaCluFDI-237
95StaCluFDI-263
95StaCluMOP-237
95StaCluMOP-263
95StaCluMOP-505
95StaCluMOP-RL19
95StaCluRL-RL19
95StaCluSTWS-237
95StaCluSTWS-263
95StaCluSTWS-505
95StaCluVR-131
95Stu-159
95Sum-70
95SumNthD-70
95Top-477
95TopCyb-270
95UC3-59
95UC3ArtP-59
95Ult-417
95UltGolM-417
95UppDec-380
95UppDecED-380
95UppDecEDG-380
95UppDecPLL-R50
95UppDecPLLE-R50
95UppDecSE-75
95UppDecSEG-75
95Zen-21
96Baz-39
96ColCho-397
96ColCho-671
96ColChoGS-397
96ColChoGS-671
96ColChoSS-397
96ColChoSS-671
96ColChoYMtP-12
96ColChoYMtP-12A
96ColChoYMtPGS-12
96ColChoYMtPGS-12A
96DenHol-27
96Don-395
96DonPreP-395
96EmoXL-242
96Fin-B136
96FinRef-B136
96Fla-330
96Fle-494
96FleTeaL-24
96FleTif-494
96Lea-196
96LeaPrePB-196
96LeaPrePG-196
96LeaPrePS-196
96LeaPreSG-36
96LeaPreSte-36
96MetUni-208
96MetUniP-208
96Pac-151
96PacPri-P51
96PacPriG-P51
96PanSti-36
96PhiTeal-8
96Pin-217
96PinAfi-32
96PinAfiAP-32
96PinAfiFPP-32
96PinArtP-117
96PinFan-30
96PinFoil-217
96PinSta-117
96ProSta-90
96Sco-12
96ScoDugC-A12
96ScoDugCAP-A12
96ScoGolS-21
96Sel-69
96SelArtP-69
96SelTeaN-10
96Spo-89
96SpoArtP-89
96StaClu-106
96StaCluEPB-106
96StaCluEPG-106
96StaCluEPS-106
96StaCluMOP-106
95StaCluVRMC-131
96Stu-52
96StuPrePB-52
96StuPrePG-52
96StuPrePS-52
96Sum-128
96SumAbo&B-128
96SumArtP-128
96SumFoi-128
96Top-85
96TopGal-148
96TopGalPPI-148
96TopLas-5
96Ult-250
96UltGolM-250
96UppDec-169
97Cir-143
97CirRav-143
97ColCho-193
97Don-287
97DonPreP-287
97DonPrePGold-287
97FlaSho-A160
97FlaSho-B160
97FlaSho-C160
97FlaShoLC-160
97FlaShoLC-B160
97FlaShoLC-C160
97FlaShoLCM-A160
97FlaShoLCM-B160
97FlaShoLCM-C160
97Fle-669
97FleTif-669
97Lea-263
97LeaFraM-263
97LeaFraMDC-263
97Sco-20
97ScoPreS-20
97ScoShoS-20
97ScoShoSAP-20
97SpoIll-40
97SpoIllEE-40
97SpoIllGS-18
97Ult-365
97UltGolME-365
97UltPlaME-365
97UppDec-455

Daunic, Willie

93MedHatBJF-3743
93MedHatBJSP-7
94St.CatBJC-8
94St.CatBJF-3650

Dauphin, Phil

90GenCubP-3036
90GenCubS-6
91MidLeaAP-MWL7
91PeoChiP-1355
91PeoChiTI-25
92ChaKniF-2782
92ChaKniS-152
92ClaFS7-60
92ProFS7-209
92SkyAA F-70
92UppDecML-305
93ClaFS7-3
93OrlCubF-2796
95HarSenTI-22

Dauphin, Philip J.

91PeoChiC-25
92Bow-169
93StaCluCu-25

Dauss, Hooks (George August)

16ColE13-39
17HolBreD-22
21E121So1-16
21E121So8-15
21Exh-33
21Nei-18
22AmeCarE-14
22E120-51
22W573-28
22W575-23
23MapCriV-11
23W501-111
23WilChoV-27
25Exh-91
26Exh-92
27Exh-46
76ISCHooHA-7
81TigDetN-74
88ConSer5-7
94ConTSN-1070
94ConTSNB-1070

Davalillo, David

95CedRapKTI-4
95LinVen-4
96CedRapKTI-7
96MidLeaAB-17

Davalillo, Pompeyo

76VenLeaS-109
80VenLeaS-182
93LinVenB-245
93LinVenB-316
94VenLinU-236
95LinVen-36

Davalillo, Vic (Victor J.)

63IndJayP-3
63Top-324
64IndJayP-3
64Kah-6
64Top-435
64TopCoi-86
64TopSta-100
64TopTatI-33
65ChaTheY-26
65Kah-11
65OldLonC-24
65OPC-128
65Top-128
66IndTeal-4
66Kah-10
66Top-216
66Top-325
66TopRubI-22
66TopVen-216
66TopVen-325
67CokCapI-17
67DexPre-59
67OPC-69
67Top-69
67TopVen-190
68Top-397
69MilBra-70
69MLBOffS-20
69Top-275
69TopSta-142
69TopSup-9
69TopTeaP-17
70CarTeal-4
70MLBOffS-138
70OPC-256
70Top-256
71MLBOffS-199
71OPC-4
71PirActP-15
71Top-4
72MilBra-86
72Top-785
73OPC-163
73Top-163
74OPC-444
74Top-444
76VenLeaS-8
76VenLeaS-242
78SSP270-66
78Top-539
79Top-228
80VenLeaS-33
81Fle-132
90DodTar-167
95LinVen-280

DaVanon, Jeff

96WesMicWB-7

DaVanon, Jerry (Frank G.)

69Top-637
71OPC-32
71Top-32
75IowOakT-5
76OPC-551
76Top-551
77Top-283
91OriCro-95

Davenport, Adell

87AncGlaP-5
89CliGiaP-882
90Bes-58
90CalLeaACLC-47
90CMC-715
90SanJosGB-8
90SanJosGCLC-39
90SanJosGP-2019
90SanJosGS-6
91CalLeLA-29
91SanJosGC-6
91SanJosGP-17
92ClaFS7-435
92ShrCapF-3880
92ShrCapS-582
92SkyAA F-256
93Bow-408
93ClaFS7-49
93ClaGolF-211
93ExcFS7-116
93PhoFirF-1521
93ShrCapF-2764
93StaCluG-17
93Top-494
93TopGol-494
93TopInaM-494
93TopMic-494
94NasXprF-392

Davenport, Dave (Arthur D.)

17HolBreD-23

Davenport, Gary

86FreGiaP-2

Davenport, Jim (James H.)

47PM1StaP1-40
58GiaSFCB-7
58Top-413
59Baz-9
59Top-198
60GiaJayP-5
60Top-154
60TopVen-154
61GiaJayP-5
61Pos-149A
61Pos-149B
61Top-55
61TopDicG-3
61TopStal-76
62GiaJayP-4
62Jel-134
62Pos-134
62PosCan-134
62SalPlaC-169
62ShiPlaC-169

62Top-9
62TopStaI-196
62TopVen-9
63Fle-65
63GiaJayP-4
63Jel-104
63Pos-104
63SalMetC-19
63Top-388
64GiaJayP-4
64Top-82
64TopSta-63
64TopVen-82
65GiaTeal-1
65OPC-213
65Top-213
66OPC-176
66Top-176
66TopVen-176
67CokCapG-3
67DexPre-60
67Top-441
67TopVen-326
68DexPre-27
68Top-525
69MilBra-69
69OPC-102
69Top-102
69TopSta-102
69TopTeaP-14
70MLBOffS-122
70OPC-378
70Top-378
72MilBra-85
74PadDea-7
76SSP-626
78TCM60I-131
79GiaPol-12
79TCM50-288
80GiaPol-12
84GiaMot-6
85GiaMot-1
85GiaPos-5
85TopTifT-27T
85TopTra-27T
86PhiTas-2
87PhiTas-xx0
89IndTeal-28
89PacLegI-118
91HamRedC-24
91HamRedP-4051
91TigCok-NNO
92UppDecS-7
93SanJosGC-27
93SanJosGF-28
93UppDecS-7
94SanJosGC-29
94SanJosGF-2834
96GiaMot-28
Davenport, Joe
95HagSunF-61
96StCatSB-7
Davenport, Neal
86CedRapRT-26
87TamTarP-23
Davenport, Scott
86AncGlaPTI-7
Daves, Eddie
78SprRedWK-11
Davey, Mike (Michael Gerard)
79SpoIndT-14
80PorBeaT-19
Davey, Tom
94MedHatBJF-3674
94MedHatBJSP-14
95StCatSTI-1
96HagSunB-3
Daviault, Ray
61TacBan-4
77FriOneYW-105
91MetWIZ-91
David, Andre
82OrlTwi8SCT-5
82OrlTwiT-16
83TolMudHT-19
84TolMudHT-19
85TolMudHT-20
85Top-43
85TopTif-43
85TwiTeal-16
86TolMudHP-7
87Don-519
87TidTidP-24
87TidTidT-12
88MetColP-18
88TidTidCa-7
88TidTidCM-18
88TidTidP-1596
89ElPasDGS-26
91KinMetC-24
91KinMetP-3829
92KinMetC-23
92KinMetF-1547
94St.LucMC-29
94St.LucMF-1212
86STaoftFT-23
David, Armin
86HumStaDS-10
David, Brian
83WauTimF-6
86ChaLooP-8
87ChaLooB-23
David, Gerald
92ElmPioC-15
David, Greg
87DunBluJP-942
88MyrBeaBJP-1176
89MyrBeaBJP-1454
90TexLeaAGS-3
90WicWraRD-6
91LinDriAA-605
91WicWraLD-605
91WicWraP-2603
91WicWraRD-13
92MemChiF-2421
92MemChiS-433
David, House of
93NegLeaRL2-96
94UppDecTAE-39
Davidsmeier, Dan
82ElPasDT-5
84VanCanC-29
85VanCanC-201
86VanCanP-9
87DenZepP-22
Davidson, Archer
63GadFunC-72
Davidson, Bob
86AlbYanT-31
87PriWilYP-3
88T/MUmp-44
89AlbYanB-3
89T/MUmp-42
90CMC-226
90ColCliC-26
90ColCliP-10
90ColCliP-669
90ProAAAF-319
90T/MUmp-40
90TopTVY-39
91LinDriAAA-233
91LouRedLD-233
91LouRedP-2908
Davidson, Bobby
88AlbYanP-1334
89AlbYanP-327
89AlbYanS-6
89Sta-97
90TopDeb89-29
92YanWIZ8-39
Davidson, Cletus
94SigRooDP-37
94SigRooDPS-37
96ForWayWB-6
Davidson, Grady
91WatIndC-3
91WatIndP-3358
Davidson, Harley
78HalHalR-11
Davidson, Jackie
86PitCubP-6
87IowCubTI-3
88PitCubP-1375
89ChaKniTI-19
Davidson, John
91KisDodP-4176
Davidson, Mark
85OrlTwiT-3
86TolMudHP-6
86TwiTeal-20
87DonOpeD-225
87DonRoo-22
87FleUpd-20
87FleUpdG-20
88Don-519
88Fle-8
88FleGlo-8
88Sco-570
88ScoGlo-570
88StaLinTw-6
88Top-19
88TopTif-19
88TwiTeal-18
89Fle-109
89FleGlo-109
89PorBeaC-22
89PorBeaP-227
89Sco-107
89Top-451
89TopBig-320
89TopTif-451
89UppDec-577
90AstLenH-10
90AstMot-11
90OPC-267
90Top-267
90TopTif-267
91AstMot-11
91Don-540
91Fle-504
91Lea-143
91OPC-678
91StaClu-584
91Top-678
91TopDesS-678
91TopMic-678
91TopTif-678
91Ult-136
92ColSprSSF-763
92ColSprSSS-83
92Fle-432
92Sco-289
92TopGol-86
93ChaKniF-556
Davidson, Mike
88BriTigP-1871
89FayGenP-1593
Davidson, Paul
09T206-416
Davidson, Randy
78IndIndTI-24
79IndIndTI-13
81CedRapRT-19
82CedRapRT-25
Davidson, Rodney
93LetMouF-4144
93LetMouSP-2
Davidson, Scott
93MisStaB-11
Davidson, Ted (Thomas E.)
65OPC-243
65Top-243
66OPC-89
66Top-89
66TopVen-89
67Top-519
68OPC-48
68Top-48
68TopVen-48
Davidson, William J.
11SpoLifM-153
Davie, Jerry (Gerald Lee)
59Top-256
60Top-301
Davies, Bob
52Whe-6A
52Whe-6B
Davies, Dan
85MiaHur-1
Davila, Jose (J.D.)
91SpoIndC-18
91SpoIndP-3941
92WatDiaC-10
92WatDiaF-2138
Davila, Vic
83ButCopKT-17
94HagSunC-5
94HagSunF-2738
95DunBluJTI-6
96DunBluJB-4
96DunBluJTI-6
Davin, D.
87OldJudN-126
Davino, Mike
89UtiBluSP-5
90SarWhiSS-7
91BirBarLD-57
91BirBarP-1448
91LinDriAA-57
Davins, Jim
86MacPirP-7
87KenTwiP-1
88PorBeaC-10
88PorBeaP-660
89PorBeaC-1
89PorBeaP-211
90CMC-61
90IndIndC-11
90IndIndP-286
90ProAAAF-569
91DenZepLD-133
91DenZepP-115
91LinDriAAA-133
Davis, Alvin
83ChaLooT-8
84FleUpd-30
84FunFooP-37
84MarMot-23
84TopTra-28T
84TopTraT-28T
85AllGamPI-4
85Don-18
85Don-69
85DonActA-16
85DonSupD-18
85Dra-8
85Fle-488
85FleLimE-7
85FleStaS-15
85GenMilS-16
85Lea-18
85MarMot-2
85OPC-145
85SevCoi-W7
85Top-145
85TopGaloC-2
85TopGloS-8
85TopRubD-15
85TopSti-332
85TopSti-368
85TopSup-6
85TopTif-145
86Don-69
86Fle-464
86FleLeaL-9
86FleMin-97
86FleSlu-8
86FleStiC-29
86KayB-7
86Lea-65
86MarMot-2
86OPC-309
86Spo-31
86Spo-74
86Top-440
86TopSti-218
86TopTat-12
86TopTif-440
86TruVal-21
87Don-75
87DonOpeD-115
87Fle-584
87FleExcS-13
87FleGlo-584
87FleMin-24
87FleRecS-5
87FleStiC-28
87KraFoo-37
87Lea-118
87MarMot-2
87OPC-235
87RedFolSB-71
87Spo-21
87SpoTeaP-25
87StuPan-25
87Top-235
87TopCoi-9
87TopSti-220
87TopTif-235
88Don-193
88DonBasB-107
88DonBonM-BC25
88Fle-373
88FleGlo-373
88FleRecS-8
88FleStiC-59
88FleSup-10
88GreBasS-78
88KayB-6
88KinDis-17
88Lea-196
88MarMot-2
88OPC-349
88PanSti-185
88Sco-83
88ScoGlo-83
88Spo-52
88StaLinMa-6
88Top-785
88TopBig-64
88TopCoi-10
88TopRitTM-24
88TopSti-219
88TopTif-785
88TopUKM-17
88TopUKMT-17
89Bow-215
89BowTif-215
89ChaLooLITI-8
89ClaLigB-81
89Don-345
89DonBasB-24
89DonBonM-BC25
89Fle-546
89FleGlo-546
89MarMot-2
89OPC-57
89PanSti-435
89PAORelT-2
89RedFolSB-27
89Sco-51
89ScoHot1S-78
89Spo-33
89Top-687
89TopBasT-59
89TopBig-218
89TopCoi-38
89TopMinL-72
89TopSti-227
89TopTif-687
89TopUKM-18
89TVSpoM-122
89UppDec-105
89UppDec-680
90Bow-479
90BowTif-479
90ClaBlu-136
90Don-109
90DonBesA-26
90DOnBonM-BC9
90Fle-512
90FleCan-512
90Hot50PS-8
90Lea-35
90MarMot-2
90MLBBasB-116
90OPC-373
90PanSti-149
90PubSti-431
90Sco-205
90Sco100S-26
90Spo-112
90Top-373
90TopAmeA-26
90TopBig-315
90TopCoi-11
90TopDou-13
90TopHilHM-26
90TopMinL-33
90TopSti-220
90TopTif-373
90UppDec-364
90VenSti-124
91Bow-258
91DenHol-19
91Don-482
91Fle-449
91Lea-429
91MarCouH-14
91OPC-515
91PanSti-185
91Sco-482
91SevCoi-NW3
91SimandSMLBL-12
91StaClu-82
91Stu-111
91Top-515
91TopDesS-515
91TopMic-515
91TopTif-515
91Ult-334
91UppDec-457
92AngPol-6
92Bow-341
92Don-124
92Fle-277
92Lea-168
92OPC-130
92OPCPre-183

92Pin-467
92Sco-76
92StaClu-90
92StaClu-617
92StaCluNC-617
92Top-130
92TopGol-130
92TopGolW-130
92TopMic-130
92Ult-324
92UppDec-386
Davis, Anthony
91PacSenL-95
Davis, Ben
95Bes-111
95BowBes-X1
95BowBesR-X1
95IdaFalBTI-13
95IdaFalBTI-NNO
95TopTra-74T
96Bow-260
96BowBes-102
96BowBesAR-102
96BowBesMI-8
96BowBesMIAR-8
96BowBesMIR-8
96BowBesR-102
96Exc-235
96ExcFirYP-3
96RanCucQB-10
96SigRooOJPP-P10
96Top-16
96TopPowB-16
97Bow-193
97BowBes-110
97BowBesAR-110
97BowBesR-110
97BowCerBIA-CA20
97BowCerGIA-CA20
97BowChr-181
97BowChrI-181
97BowChrIR-181
97BowChrR-181
97BowInt-193
97Top-205
Davis, Bill
82IdaFalAT-17
Davis, Bill (Arthur W.)
65Top-546
66OPC-44
66Top-44
66TopVen-44
67Top-253
68Top-432
69Top-304
69TopTeaP-12
Davis, Bo (Allen)
89BluOriS-7
90WauTimB-26
90WauTimP-2140
90WauTimS-6
91KanCouCC-21
91KanCouCP-2668
Davis, Bob (Robert Edward)
61Top-246
75HawIslC-3
75IntLeaASB-5
75PacCoaLAB-5
76OPC-472
76Top-472
76VenLeaS-107
77PadSchC-18
77Top-78
78PadFamF-9
78Top-713
80OPC-185
80Top-351
81Don-30
81Fle-428
81OPC-221
81SalLakCGT-26
81Top-221
86Ft.MyeRP-6
Davis, Brad
85Ft.MyeRT-3
Davis, Brad Earnest
85DalNatCC-12
Davis, Braz
87WytCubP-20
88ChaWheB-20
89PeoChiTI-2
Davis, Brent
92Min-5
Davis, Bret
85AncGlaPTI-8
86WauTimP-7
88JamExpP-1897
89RocExpLC-7
90WesPalBES-4
Davis, Brian
88TamTarS-5
89UtiBluSP-6
90ColMetGS-12
90ColMetPPI-5
90SouAtlLAS-29
91St.LucMP-723
Davis, Brock (Bryshear B.)
63Top-553
71OPC-576
71Top-576
72OPC-161
72Top-161
73OPC-366
73Top-366
94BreMilB-15
Davis, Butch (Wallace M.)
84Don-277
85OmaRoyT-12
85Top-49
85TopTif-49
87VanCanP-1614
88ChaKniTI-3
89RocRedWC-22
89RocRedWP-1652
89TriA AAC-21
90AlbDukC-22
90AlbDukP-357
90AlbDukT-5
90CMC-424
90ProAAAF-78
90TriAAAC-21
91AlbDukLD-5
91AlbDukP-1154
91LinDriAAA-5
91OriCro-96
92SkyAAAF-224
92SyrChiF-1980
92SyrChiMB-3
92SyrChiS-504
92TriA AAS-503
93RanKee-402
93StaCluR-8
94OklCit8F-1502
94Pac-613
95RocRedWTI-43
96RocRedWB-4
Davis, Chili (Charles T.)
78CedRapGT-7
82Top-171
82TopTra-23T
83AllGamPI-141
83Don-348
83Fle-257
83FleSti-53
83GiaMot-3
83OPC-115
83Top-115
83TopSti-319
84AllGamPI-48
84Don-114
84Fle-370
84FunFooP-38
84GiaPos-5
84Nes792-494
84OPC-367
84Top-494
84TopSti-171
84TopTif-494
85AllGamPI-138
85Don-480
85Dra-9
85Fle-605
85FleStaS-10
85GiaMot-2
85GiaPos-6
85Lea-66
85OPC-245
85Top-245
85TopSti-162
85TopSup-40
85TopTif-245
86BasStaB-27
86Don-6
86Don-65
86DonSupD-6
86Fle-536
86FleMin-109
86GiaMot-2
86Lea-6
86Spo-82
87Don-268
87DonAll-38
87DonOpeD-97
87Fle-270
87FleBasA-12
87FleGlo-270
87FleMin-25
87FleStiC-29
87GiaMot-3
87KraFoo-46
87Lea-208
87OPC-162
87RedFolSB-76
87Spo-45
87SpoTeaP-10
87StuPan-13
87Top-672
87TopSti-95
87TopTif-672
88AngSmo-10
88Don-313
88Fle-79
88FleGlo-79
88FleUpd-12
88FleUpdG-12
88OPC-15
88Sco-605
88ScoGlo-605
88ScoRoo-28T
88ScoRooG-28T
88Spo-172
88StaLinAn-4
88StaLinG-5
88Top-15
88TopBig-235
88TopTif-15
88TopTra-32T
88TopTraT-32T
89Bow-50
89BowTif-50
89ClaLigB-80
89Don-449
89DonBasB-115
89Fle-474
89FleGlo-474
89FleLeaL-9
89OPC-103
89PanSti-296
89RedFolSB-28
89Sco-54
89Spo-129
89Top-525
89TopBasT-134
89TopBig-294
89TopSti-177
89TopTif-525
89UppDec-126
90AngSmo-3
90Bow-301
90BowTif-301
90Don-136
90DOnBonM-BC20
90Fle-129
90FleCan-129
90Lea-288
90OPC-765
90PanSti-39
90PubSti-367
90Sco-326
90Spo-21
90Top-765
90TopBig-280
90TopCoi-12
90TopSti-173
90TopTif-765
90UppDec-38
90VenSti-125
91Bow-331
91Cla3-T12
91Don-580
91Fle-309
91FleUpd-36
91Lea-374
91OPC-355
91PanSti-134
91Sco-803
91ScoRoo-70T
91StaClu-329
91Top-355
91TopDesS-355
91TopMic-355
91TopTif-355
91TopTra-27T
91TopTraT-27T
91UltUpd-35
91UppDec-339
91UppDec-722
92Bow-195
92ClaGam-92
92Don-115
92Fle-200
92Lea-395
92OPC-118
92Pin-46
92Sco-94
92ScoCokD-6
92ScoProP-15
92ScoProP-25
92StaClu-18
92StaCluD-32
92Top-118
92TopGol-118
92TopGolW-118
92TopKid-113
92TopMic-118
92TriPla-27
92Ult-89
92UppDec-126
92UppDecHRH-HR12
93AngMot-6
93AngPol-6
93Bow-553
93DenHol-1
93Don-679
93Fla-171
93Fle-262
93FleFinE-180
93FunPac-38
93Lea-254
93OPC-52
93OPCPre-24
93PacSpa-366
93PanSti-131
93Pin-536
93Sco-583
93Sel-238
93SelRoo-124T
93SP-20
93StaClu-222
93StaClu-611
93StaCluAn-3
93StaCluFDI-222
93StaCluFDI-611
93StaCluMOP-222
93StaCluMOP-611
93Stu-32
93Top-455
93TopGol-455
93TopInaM-455
93TopMic-455
93Ult-518
93UppDec-239
93UppDec-794
93UppDecGold-239
93UppDecGold-794
94AngLAT-1
94AngMot-14
94Bow-451
94ColC-491
94ColChoGS-491
94ColChoSS-491
94Don-82
94ExtBas-31
94Fin-112
94FinRef-112
94Fla-268
94Fle-51
94Lea-258
94LeaL-15
94OPC-143
94Pac-74
94Pin-458
94PinArtP-458
94PinMusC-458
94Sco-345
94ScoGolR-345
94Sel-283
94SP-23
94SPDieC-23
94StaClu-173
94StaCluFDI-173
94StaCluGR-173
94StaCluMOP-173
94Stu-9
94Top-265
94TopGol-265
94TopSpa-265
94TriPla-12
94Ult-324
94UppDec-74
94UppDecED-74
95AngCHP-8
95AngMot-5
95AngTeal-2
95Baz-87
95Bow-387
95BowBes-R3
95BowBesR-R3
95ColCho-101
95ColChoGS-101
95ColChoSE-31
95ColChoSEGS-31
95ColChoSESS-31
95ColChoSS-101
95Don-452
95Don-550
95DonDiaK-DK3
95DonPreP-452
95DonPreP-545
95DonPreP-550
95DonTopotO-32
95Emb-20
95EmbGolI-20
95Emo-18
95Fin-149
95FinRef-149
95Fla-234
95Fle-220
95Lea-93
95LeaLim-134
95Pac-55
95PacPri-17
95PanSti-95
95Sco-14
95ScoGolR-14
95ScoHaloG-HG100
95ScoPlaTS-14
95Sel-117
95SelArtP-117
95SelCer-12
95SelCerMG-12
95SP-133
95SPCha-129
95SPCha-133
95SPChaDC-129
95SPChaDC-133
95Spo-111
95SpoArtP-111
95SPSil-133
95StaClu-133
95StaCluCC-CC8
95StaCluFDI-133
95StaCluMOP-133
95StaCluMOP-CC8
95StaCluSTWS-133
95StaCluVR-69
95Stu-158
95Sum-20
95SumNthD-20
95TomPiz-7
95Top-335
95TopCyb-182
95UC3-8
95UC3ArtP-8
95Ult-19
95UltGolM-19
95UppDec-17
95UppDecED-17
95UppDecEDG-17
95UppDecSE-263
95UppDecSEG-263
95Zen-16
96AngMot-2
96ColCho-70
96ColCho-331
96ColChoGS-70
96ColChoGS-331
96ColChoSS-70
96ColChoSS-331
96Don-122
96DonPreP-122
96EmoXL-24
96Fin-B123
96FinRef-B123
96Fla-34
96Fle-43
96FleTif-43
96Lea-27
96LeaPrePB-27

96LeaPrePG-27
96LeaPrePS-27
96MetUni-24
96MetUniP-24
96Pac-276
96PanSti-208
96Pin-32
96PinAfi-13
96PinAfiAP-13
96PinAfiFPP-13
96PinArtP-58
96PinSta-58
96ProSta-5
96Sco-332
96ScoDugC-B57
96ScoDugCAP-B57
96Sel-93
96SelArtP-93
96SP-43
96Spo-46
96SpoArtP-46
96StaClu-222
96StaClu-311
96StaCluMOP-222
96StaCluMOP-311
95StaCluVRMC-69
96Stu-102
96StuPrePB-102
96StuPrePG-102
96StuPrePS-102
96Sum-22
96SumAbo&B-22
96SumArtP-22
96SumFoi-22
96Top-280
96TopChr-113
96TopChrMotG-10
96TopChrMotGR-10
96TopChrR-113
96TopGal-171
96TopGalPPI-171
96TopLas-102
96TopMasotG-10
96Ult-26
96UltGolM-26
96UppDec-293
97BowBes-56
97BowBesAR-56
97BowBesR-56
97Cir-248
97CirRav-248
97ColCho-358
97Don-88
97Don-282
97DonLim-17
97DonLimLE-17
97DonPreP-88
97DonPreP-282
97DonPrePGold-88
97DonPrePGold-282
97Fin-250
97FinRef-250
97FlaSho-A104
97FlaSho-B104
97FlaSho-C104
97FlaShoLC-104
97FlaShoLC-B104
97FlaShoLC-C104
97FlaShoLCM-A104
97FlaShoLCM-B104
97FlaShoLCM-C104
97Fle-37
97Fle-602
97FleTif-37
97FleTif-602
97Lea-207
97LeaFraM-207
97LeaFraMDC-207
97MetUni-92
97NewPin-7
97NewPinAP-7
97NewPinMC-7
97NewPinPP-7
97Pac-3
97PacLigB-3
97PacPri-1
97PacPriLB-1
97PacPriP-1
97PacSil-3
97RoyPol-7
97Sco-11
97Sco-338
97ScoHobR-338
97ScoPitP-8
97ScoPreS-11
97ScoResC-338
97ScoShoS-11
97ScoShoS-338
97ScoShoSAP-11
97ScoShoSAP-338
97SP-87
97StaClu-85
97StaCluMOP-85
97Top-365
97TopChr-125
97TopChrR-125
97TopGal-9
97TopGalPPI-9
97TopSta-63
97TopStaAM-63
97Ult-24
97Ult-432
97UltGolME-24
97UltGolME-432
97UltPlaME-24
97UltPlaME-432
97UppDec-538
Davis, Chris
78St.PetCT-8
79ArkTraT-17
90ElmPioP-15
91ElmPioC-18
91ElmPioP-3264
92ProFS7-24
92WinHavRSC-1
93ForLauRSC-6
93ForLauRSFP-1588
Davis, Chuck
86NewBriRSP-9
87PawRedSP-74
87PawRedST-5
Davis, Clint
92SavCarC-7
92SavCarF-654
93FloStaLAF-44
93St.PetCC-12
93St.PetCF-2622
94Bow-564
94ClaGolF-170
94ExcFS7-265
94Ult-564
Davis, Corbin
90MisStaB-8
91MisStaB-13
Davis, Courtney
90CliGiaUTI-U2
90EveGiaB-22
90EveGiaP-3138
91CliGiaP-845
Davis, Crash
89BluDurOS-1
Davis, Curt (Curtis Benton)
34BatR31-97
36DiaMatCS3T2-5
36ExhFou-6
36GouWidPPR-A24
36WheBB4-1
40DodTeal-5
42DodTeal-5
43DodTeal-7
90DodTar-168
91ConTSN-282
Davis, Darwin
91KinMetC-3
91KinMetP-3819
Davis, Dick (Richard Earl)
77SpoIndC-21
79Top-474
80Top-553
81Don-528
81Fle-527
81Top-183
81TopTra-753
82Don-147
82Fle-245
82Top-352
82TopTra-24T
83Don-647
83Fle-305
83PorBeaT-16
83Top-667
87JapPlaB-18
94BreMilB-16
Davis, Dixie (Frank)
19W514-48
21E121So1-17
21Nei-36
22E120-94
22W573-29
22W575-24
23W501-3
23WilChoV-28
Davis, Doc (Dennis)
77SalPirT-10
Davis, Doug (Douglas)
82BurRanF-22
82BurRanT-18
85MidAngT-14
86MidAngP-8
87MidAngP-10
88EdmTraC-18
88EdmTraP-559
89BelMarL-18
89EdmTraC-15
89EdmTraP-551
90CMC-495
90EdmTraC-18
90EdmTraP-519
90ProAAAF-95
91EdmTraLD-160
91EdmTraP-1518
91LinDriAAA-160
92Bow-490
92DonRoo-31
92OklCit8F-1916
92OklCit8S-308
92StaClu-692
92StaCluECN-692
93OklCit8F-1628
93RanKee-121
94OklCit8F-1496
96PitMetB-1
Davis, Eddie
94Top-237
94TopGol-237
94TopSpa-237
95YakBeaTI-8
96SanBerSB-8
Davis, Eric (Eric Keith)
82CedRapRT-20
83WatRedT-15
84RedBor-44
84RedEnq-26
84WicAerRD-15
85Don-325
85Fle-533
85RedYea-3
85Top-627
85TopTif-627
86Don-164
86DonHig-30
86Fle-175
86OPC-85
86RedTexG-44
86SevCoi-S9
86Top-28
86Top-85
86TopTif-28
86TopTif-85
87ClaGam-21
87ClaUpdY-102
87ClaUpdY-150
87Don-22A
87Don-22B
87Don-265
87DonHig-3
87DonHig-8
87DonOpeD-197
87DonSupD-22
87Fle-198
87FleAwaW-11
87FleExcS-14
87FleGamW-11
87FleGlo-198
87FleHotS-12
87FleMin-26
87FleSlu-11
87FleStiC-30
87FleStiC-132
87GenMilB-6B
87HosSti-9
87KraFoo-10
87Lea-22
87Lea-179
87MSAIceTD-7
87OPC-228
87RedKah-44
87Spo-22
87Spo-155
87Spo-199
87SpoSupD-18
87SpoTeaP-4
87StuPan-4
87Top-412
87TopCoi-30
87TopGloS-44
87TopMinL-4
87TopSti-136
87TopTif-412
88Baz-6
88CheBoy-2
88ClaBlu-201
88ClaBlu-213
88ClaRed-154
88Don-369
88DonAll-38
88DonBasB-62
88DonBonM-BC2
88DonPop-16
88Dra-24
88Fle-231
88Fle-637
88FleAll-7
88FleAwaW-8
88FleBasA-9
88FleBasM-8
88FleExcS-12
88FleGlo-231
88FleGlo-637
88FleHotS-8
88FleLeaL-8
88FleMin-73
88FleRecS-9
88FleSlu-10
88FleStiC-83
88FleStiWBC-S6
88FleSup-11
88FleTeaL-6
88GreBasS-32
88KayB-7
88KinDis-22
88Lea-149
88MSAFanSD-14
88MSAIceTD-12
88Nes-3
88OPC-150
88OPCBoxB-J
88PanSti-235
88PanSti-282
88RedFolSB-15
88RedKah-44
88Sco-10
88Sco-649
88ScoBoxC-15
88ScoGlo-10
88ScoGlo-649
88ScoYouS2-10
88Spo-10
88SpoGam-5
88StaDav-1
88StaDav-2
88StaDav-4
88StaDav-6
88StaDav-8
88StaDav-10
88StaEriD-1
88StaEriD-2
88StaEriD-3
88StaEriD-4
88StaEriD-5
88StaEriD-6
88StaEriD-7
88StaEriD-8
88StaEriD-9
88StaEriD-10
88StaEriD-11
88StaEriD-12
88StaLinAl-8
88StaLinRe-6
88Top-150
88TopBig-20
88TopCoi-39
88TopGloA-17
88TopGloS-16
88TopMinL-46
88TopRitTM-3
88TopSti-141
88TopSti-146
88TopStiB-14
88TopTif-150
88TopUKM-18
88TopUKMT-18
88TopWaxBC-J
89Bow-316
89BowTif-316
89CadEllD-12
89ClaLigB-9
89ClaTraO-109
89Don-80
89DonBasB-6
89Fle-158
89Fle-639
89FleBasM-9
89FleExcS-9
89FleGlo-158
89FleGlo-639
89FleHeroB-10
89FleLeaL-10
89FleSup-11
89KayB-8
89MSAHolD-7
89MSAIceTD-11
89Nis-7
89OPC-330
89PanSti-76
89RedFolSB-29
89RedKah-44
89Sco-109
89ScoHot1S-58
89ScoSco-18
89Spo-69
89SpoIllFKI-140
89Top-111
89Top-330
89TopAme2C-11
89TopBasT-51
89TopBig-273
89TopCapC-13
89TopCoi-9
89TopGloS-2
89TopHeaUT-21
89TopMinL-6
89TopSti-138
89TopStiB-47
89TopTif-111
89TopTif-330
89TopUKM-19
89TVSpoM-37
89UppDec-410
89UppDec-688
90Bow-58
90BowTif-58
90CedRapRDGB-1
90ClaBlu-11
90Col-28
90Don-233
90Don-695A
90Don-695B
90DonBesN-1
90DOnBonM-BC23
90Fle-417
90FleAwaW-10
90FleBasA-6
90FleBasM-9
90FleCan-417
90FleLeaL-8
90FleWaxBC-C4
90GooHumICBLS-7
90Hot50PS-9
90Lea-189
90MLBBasB-22
90OPC-260
90OPC-402
90PanSti-209
90PanSti-246
90Pos-24
90PubSti-26
90PubSti-255
90RedFolSB-20
90RedKah-7
90Sco-185
90Sco100S-95
90Spo-97
90StaLonJS-3
90StaLonJS-38
90SunSee-21
90Top-260
90Top-402
90TopAmeA-28
90TopBig-72
90TopCoi-44
90TopDou-14
90TopGloA-7
90TopGloS-25
90TopHilHM-1
90TopMag-18
90TopMinL-53
90TopSti-134
90TopSti-149
90TopStiB-13

90TopTif-260
90TopTif-402
90TopTVA-38
90UppDec-116
90VenSti-126
90VenSti-127
91BasBesHRK-3
91Bow-686
91CadEllD-13
91Cla1-T34
91Cla3-T13
91ClaGam-136
91DenHol-4
91Don-84
91Fle-61
91FlePro-10
91FleWorS-1
91Lea-37
91MajLeaCP-70
91MSAHolD-2
91OPC-550
91OPCPre-29
91PanFreS-131
91PanSti-124
91PetSta-6
91RedKah-44
91RedPep-6
91Sco-137
91Sco-403
91Sco-669
91Sco-696
91Sco-863
91Sco100S-9
91SevCoi-SC6
91StaClu-37
91StaCluCM-5
91StaPinB-10
91Stu-162
91StuPre-11
91Top-550
91TopCraJI-16
91TopDesS-550
91TopMic-550
91TopSta-10
91TopTif-550
91TopTriH-N3
91Ult-91
91UppDec-355
91Woo-25
92Bow-671
92Cla2-T25
92ClaGam-161
92DodMot-4
92DodPol-33
92DodSmo-4392
92Don-503
92DonCraJ2-8
92Fle-403
92FleUpd-90
92Hig5-31
92Lea-430
92New-5
92OPC-610
92OPCPre-129
92PanSti-267
92Pin-323
92Pin-602
92PinRool-1
92Sco-44
92Sco100S-44
92ScoProP-13
92ScoRoo-62T
92SpoStaCC-10
92StaClu-660
92StaCluNC-660
92Stu-43
92Top-610
92TopGol-610
92TopGolW-610
92TopKid-38
92TopMic-610
92TopTra-26T
92TopTraG-26T
92Ult-503
92UppDec-125
92UppDec-756
92UppDecF-20
92UppDecFG-20
93Bow-450
93DiaMar-28
93DodMot-7
93DodPol-4
93Don-482
93Fin-126
93FinRef-126
93Fle-445
93Lea-267
93OPC-87
93PacSpa-144
93PanSti-221
93Pin-429
93Sco-570
93Sel-91
93SelRoo-92T
93SP-92
93StaClu-381
93StaCluD-20
93StaCluFDI-381
93StaCluMOP-381
93Top-745
93TopGol-745
93TopInaM-745
93TopMic-745
93TriPla-112
93Ult-53
93UppDec-477
93UppDec-595
93UppDecGold-477
93UppDecGold-595
94Bow-293
94ColC-563
94ColChoGS-563
94ColChoSS-563
94Don-618
94ExtBas-71
94Fin-80
94FinRef-80
94Fla-46
94Fle-126
94Lea-256
94OPC-226
94Pac-213
94PanSti-62
94Pin-388
94PinArtP-388
94PinMusC-388
94Sco-504
94ScoGolR-504
94Sel-273
94Spo-124
94StaClu-209
94StaCluFDI-209
94StaCluGR-209
94StaCluMOP-209
94Stu-189
94Top-488
94TopGol-488
94TopSpa-488
94TriPla-241
94Ult-354
94UppDec-261
94UppDecED-261
95Pin-338
95PinArtP-338
95PinMusC-338
95Sco-406
95ScoGolR-406
95ScoPlaTS-406
96Cir-115
96CirRav-115
96Fin-B222
96FinRef-B222
96FleUpd-U118
96FleUpdTC-U118
96TeaOut-22
96Ult-459
96UltGolM-459
96UppDec-491U
97Cir-175
97CirRav-175
97ColCho-276
97Don-190
97Don-292
97DonLim-162
97DonLimLE-162
97DonPreP-190
97DonPreP-292
97DonPrePGold-190
97DonPrePGold-292
97DonTea-39
97DonTeaSPE-39
97Fin-260
97FinRef-260
97Fle-293
97Fle-642
97FleTif-293
97FleTif-642
97Lea-313
97LeaFraM-313
97LeaFraMDC-313
97MetUni-46
97NewPin-143
97NewPinAP-143
97NewPinMC-143
97NewPinPP-143
97Pac-267
97PacLigB-267
97PacPri-92
97PacPriLB-92
97PacPriP-92
97PacSil-267
97Pin-6
97PinArtP-6
97PinMusC-6
97Sco-280
97Sco-356
97ScoHobR-356
97ScoPreS-280
97ScoResC-356
97ScoShoS-280
97ScoShoS-356
97ScoShoSAP-280
97ScoShoSAP-356
97StaClu-180
97StaCluMOP-180
97Top-218
97Ult-176
97Ult-383
97UltGolME-176
97UltGolME-383
97UltPlaME-176
97UltPlaME-383
97UppDec-44
97UppDec-306

Davis, Freddie
87SalAngP-28
89LynRedSS-5
90CarLeaA-10
90LynRedSTI-17
90WinHavRSS-3
91Cla/Bes-123
91LinDriAA-454
91NewBriRSLD-454
91NewBriRSP-345

Davis, Geff
86BurExpP-5
87WesPalBEP-678

Davis, George
76CliPilT-8
94ConTSN-1235
94ConTSNB-1235

Davis, George (George Allen)
15SpoNewM-45
33Gou-236

Davis, George (George Stacey)
03BreE10-31
07WhiSoxGWH-2
09AmeCarE-31
09ColChiE-74
09T206-85
10JuJuDE-15
11PloCanE-22
11SpoLifCW-87
12ColRedB-74
94DukCabN-1

Davis, Gerald
92ElmPioF-1395

Davis, Gerrod
90KinMetB-3
92St.LucMCB-19

Davis, Gerry
82AmaGolST-5
83LasVegSBHN-5
88T/MUmp-52
89T/MUmp-50
90T/MUmp-48

Davis, Glenn
52Whe-7A
52Whe-7B
74NewYorNTDiS-25
97Bow-434
97BowChr-294
97BowChrI-294
97BowChrIR-294
97BowChrR-294
97BowInt-434
97TopSta-120
97TopStaAM-120

Davis, Glenn (Glenn Earle)
82DayBeaAT-20
83ColAstT-11
84TucTorC-62
85AstHouP-20
85Fle-652
85TucTorC-65
86AstMilL-5
86AstPol-22
86AstTeal-4
86BasStaB-28
86Don-380
86Fle-297
86FleMin-63
86Lea-175
86OPC-389
86Spo-188
86Top-389
86TopGloS-59
86TopSti-29
86TopSti-314
86TopTat-18
86TopTif-389
87AstMot-10
87AstPol-23
87ClaGam-28
87ClaUpdY-107
87Don-61
87DonAll-42
87DonOpeD-16
87Fle-55
87Fle-636
87FleGamW-12
87FleGlo-55
87FleGlo-636
87FleLeaL-14
87FleLimE-11
87FleMin-27
87FleStiC-31
87FleStiWBC-S5
87KayB-12
87KraFoo-36
87Lea-115
87OPC-56
87RedFolSB-43
87Spo-17
87Spo-195
87SpoTeaP-8
87StuPan-5
87Top-560
87TopCoi-31
87TopGloS-4
87TopMinL-8
87TopSti-26
87TopTif-560
88AstMot-10
88AstPol-8
88ClaRed-182
88Don-184
88DonBasB-64
88Fle-445
88FleGlo-445
88FleMin-78
88FleSlu-11
88FleStiC-86
88FleSup-12
88HouSho-17
88Lea-186
88OPC-159
88PanSti-292
88Sco-460
88ScoGlo-460
88Spo-102
88StaLinAst-8
88Top-430
88TopBig-192
88TopSti-35
88TopTif-430
88TopUKM-19
88TopUKMT-19
89AstLenH-26
89AstMot-9
89AstSmo-11
89Bow-331
89BowTif-331
89CadEllD-13
89ClaLigB-17
89ClaTraP-168
89Don-25
89Don-236
89DonBasB-8
89DonSupD-25
89Fle-355
89FleBasM-10
89FleExcS-10
89FleGlo-355
89FleHeroB-11
89FleLeaL-11
89OPC-378
89PanSti-88
89RedFolSB-30
89Sco-164
89ScoHot1S-46
89Spo-137
89Top-579
89Top-765
89TopBasT-99
89TopBig-89
89TopCoi-10
89TopGloS-32
89TopHilTM-10
89TopSti-21
89TopStiB-35
89TopTif-579
89TopTif-765
89TopUKM-20
89TVSpoM-54
89UppDec-443
90AstLenH-11
90AstMot-2
90Bow-80
90BowTif-80
90ClaBlu-71
90Don-118
90DonBesN-65
90DOnBonM-BC21
90DonLeaS-22
90Fle-228
90FleBasA-7
90FleBasM-10
90FleCan-228
90FleLeaL-9
90FleWaxBC-C5
90Hot50PS-10
90Lea-30
90MLBBasB-41
90OPC-50
90PanSti-258
90PubSti-92
90RedFolSB-21
90Sco-272
90Sco100S-52
90Spo-19
90StaLonJS-15
90StaLonJS-30
90Top-50
90TopBig-122
90TopCoi-45
90TopDou-15
90TopGloS-3
90TopHilHM-22
90TopMinL-55
90TopSti-13
90TopStiB-2
90TopTif-50
90TopTVA-45
90UppDec-245
90VenSti-128
91BasBesHRK-4
91Bow-83
91CadEllD-14
91Cla2-T6
91ClaGam-169
91Don-474
91Fle-505
91FleUpd-1
91Lea-398
91OPC-350
91OPCPre-30
91OriCro-496
91PanFreS-7
91PanSti-19
91PosCan-14
91RedFolS-23
91Sco-405
91Sco-830
91ScoRoo-7T
91SevCoi-A1
91SevCoi-F4
91SevCoi-T5
91StaClu-391
91StaPinB-11
91Stu-1
91SunSee-6
91Top-350
91TopDesS-350
91TopMic-350
91TopTif-350
91TopTra-28T
91TopTraT-28T

91Ult-14
91UppDec-81
91UppDec-535
91UppDec-757
92Bow-428
92ClaGam-174
92Don-597
92Fle-4
92Lea-316
92OPC-190
92Pin-138
92Sco-615
92StaClu-808
92StaCluNC-808
92Stu-122
92Top-190
92TopGol-190
92TopGolW-190
92TopKid-65
92TopMic-190
92TriPla-60
92Ult-1
92UppDec-654
93Bow-1
93Don-163
93Fin-41
93FinRef-41
93Fle-164
93Lea-45
93OPC-69
93PacSpa-15
93Pin-217
93Sco-383
93Sel-378
93StaClu-326
93StaCluFDI-326
93StaCluMOP-326
93Top-485
93TopGol-485
93TopInaM-485
93TopMic-485
93TriPla-73
93Ult-139
93UppDec-353
93UppDec-827
93UppDecGold-353
93UppDecGold-827
94OmaRoyF-1229
Davis, Grant
93MisStaB-12
Davis, Greg
90KisDodD-9
91GreFalDSP-15
Davis, Harry
84EveGiaC-5
86FreGiaP-26
88ShrCapP-1299
89WilBilP-641
89WilBilS-4
Davis, Harry (Harry H.)
03BreE10-32
03WilCarE-9
04FanCraAL-13
08AmeCarE-7
08AmeCarE-42
08RosComP-58
09BriE97-7
09ColChiE-73
09RamT20-34
09SpoNewSM-58
09T206-86
09T206-87
10CouT21-114
10CouT21-115
10CouT21-273
10E101-13
10E12AmeCDC-12
10E98-12
10LuxCigPP-6
10MelMinE-13
10NadCarE-14
10NadE1-14
10PeoT21-14
10RedCroT-17
10RedCroT-101
10RedCroT-181
10W555-20
11A'sFirT20-5
11BasBatEU-16
11DiaGumP-11
11E94-9
11SpoLifCW-88
11SpoLifM-91
12ColRedB-73
12ColTinT-73
12PhiCarE-7
12T207-42
Davis, I.M.
25Exh-77
Davis, J.J.
97Bow-437
97BowChr-297
97BowChrI-297
97BowChrIR-297
97BowChrR-297
97BowInt-437
97TopSta-122
97TopStaAM-122
Davis, Jacke (Jacke S.)
62Top-521
63Top-117
Davis, Jasper
09AmeCarE-30
Davis, Jay
90KinMetS-6
91ColMetPI-24
91ColMetPPI-1
91SouAtlLAGP-SAL14
92St.LucMF-1760
93BinMetF-2346
93ExcFS7-70
94BinMetF-715
95BinMetTI-22
96TusTorB-20
Davis, Jeff
93EriSaiC-4
93EriSaiF-3105
94ChaRivC-3
94ChaRivF-2664
95Bes-46
95SPML-159
96Exc-109
96TulDriTI-8
Davis, Jerry
90JohCitCS-7
Davis, Jerry (Gerald Edward)
84LasVegSC-222
85Don-162
85FleUpd-34
85PadMot-26
85TopTifT-28T
85TopTra-28T
86Don-429
86Fle-317
86Top-323
86TopTif-323
87TolMudHP-30
87TolMudHT-24
Davis, Jim (James Bennett)
52MotCoo-2
53MotCoo-46
55Top-68
55TopDouH-27
55TopTesS-1
56Top-102
57Top-273
Davis, Jody (Jody Richard)
79JacMetT-7
82CubRedL-7
82Don-225
82Fle-592
82Top-508
83AllGamPI-130
83CubThoAV-7
83Don-183
83Fle-494
83Top-542
83TopSti-226
84AllGamPI-40
84CubChiT-9
84CubSev-7
84CubUno-6
84Don-433
84Fle-491
84FunFooP-51
84JacMetF-4
84Nes792-73
84OPC-73
84Top-73
84TopSti-43
84TopTif-73
85AllGamPI-129
85CubLioP-5
85CubSev-7
85Don-76
85DonActA-54
85Fle-54
85Lea-180
85OPC-384
85Top-384
85TopSti-37
85TopTif-384
86BasStaB-29
86CubGat-7
86CubUno-4
86Don-289
86Fle-364
86FleStiC-30
86MSAJayPCD-3
86OPC-176
86Top-767
86TopSti-58
86TopTat-13
86TopTif-767
87CubCan-3
87CubDavB-7
87Don-269
87DonAll-50
87DonOpeD-72
87Fle-557
87FleBasA-13
87FleGlo-557
87FleLeaL-15
87KraFoo-6
87Lea-48
87OPC-270
87RedFolSB-68
87SevCoi-C2
87SevCoi-M3
87SmoNatL-3A
87SmoNatL-3B
87Spo-170
87SpoTeaP-22
87StuPan-3
87Top-270
87TopSti-64
87TopTif-270
88CubDavB-7
88Don-119
88DonTeaBC-119
88Fle-414
88Fle-425A
88FleGlo-414
88Lea-69
88OPC-376
88PanSti-258
88PanSti-262
88Sco-551
88ScoGlo-551
88Spo-60
88StaLinAl-9
88Top-615
88TopSti-60
88TopStiB-23
88TopTif-615
89Bow-270
89BowTif-270
89BraDub-9
89Don-650
89DonBasB-58
89Fle-421
89FleGlo-421
89OPC-115
89RedFolSB-31
89Sco-173
89ScoRoo-64T
89Spo-187
89Top-115
89TopBig-3
89TopTif-115
89TopTra-22T
89TopTraT-22T
89TVSpoM-60
89UppDec-148
89UppDec-795
90Fle-579
90FleCan-579
90OPC-453
90PubSti-111
90Sco-328
90Top-453
90TopBig-26
90TopTif-453
90UppDec-429
90VenSti-129
Davis, Joe
89AncGlaP-10
Davis, Joel
86Don-623
86Fle-202
86TopTra-30T
86TopTraT-30T
86WhiSoxC-52
87Don-124
87Top-299
87TopTif-299
87WhiSoxC-6
88BlaYNPRWL-149
88Top-511
88TopTif-511
88VanCanC-2
88VanCanP-763
89ColSprSSC-7
89ColSprSSP-237
Davis, John
75OklCit8TI-23
88CapCodPPaLP-56
91LinDriAAA-430
91PeoChiTI-28
95GreFalDTI-4
96SavSanB-15
Davis, John (John Humphrey)
52MotCoo-27
Davis, John Kirk
83ChaRoyT-17
86MemChiSTOS-4
86MemChiTOS-4
87OmaRoyP-19
88Don-594
88DonRoo-48
88Fle-255
88FleGlo-255
88FleUpd-15
88FleUpdG-15
88Sco-636
88ScoGlo-636
88Spo-224
88Top-672
88TopTif-672
88WhiSoxC-5
89Sco-608
89Top-162
89TopTif-162
89UppDec-548
89VanCanC-9
89VanCanP-582
91RicBraBC-6
91RicBraLD-430
91RicBraTI-22
Davis, Johnny
86NegLeaF-95
Davis, Joshua
96IdaFalB-5
Davis, Jumbo (James J.)
87OldJudN-127
Davis, Kane
94WelPirC-7
94WelPirF-3486
96LynHilB-7
Davis, Keith
94SpoIndC-5
94SpoIndF-3314
96RanCucQB-9
Davis, Kelvin
88EugEmeB-17
Davis, Kenny
87VisOakP-15
88VisOakCLC-145
88VisOakP-81
Davis, Kevin
83PeoSunF-3
83RedPioT-8
85MidAngT-18
87SalBucP-30
88EasLeaAP-14
88HarSenP-837
89BirBarB-6
89BirBarP-98
91LinDriAA-432
91MidAngLD-432
91MidAngOHP-9
91MidAngP-439
92SalSpuF-3762
93MidAngF-327
94MemChiF-364
97MidAngOHP-7
Davis, Kiddo (George Willis)
33RitCE-5D
36WorWidGV-17
92ConTSN-502
Davis, Lance
96BilMusTI-6
Davis, Larry
75TucTorTI-22
81TacTigT-1
82TacTigT-20
83TacTigT-22
86A'sMot-26
90A'sMot-28
94CarLeaA-DJ22
Davis, Lefty
90DodTar-1102
Davis, Mark (Mark Anthony)
84LitFalMT-22
86KenTwiP-5
87PenWhiSP-1
87SavCarP-12
88BirBarB-14
88BlaYNPRWL-23
88SumBraP-396
89BurBraP-1599
89BurBraS-9
89VanCanC-22
89VanCanP-585
90MidAngGS-10
91EdmTraLD-161
91EdmTraP-1527
91LinDriAAA-161
92TopDeb91-43
Davis, Mark (Mark William)
80CarMudF-4
81OklCit8T-6
82OklCit8T-12
82Top-231
83PhoGiaBHN-20
84Don-201
84Fle-371
84GiaPos-6
84Nes792-343
84Top-343
84TopTif-343
85Don-553
85Fle-606
85GiaMot-20
85GiaPos-7
85Top-541
85TopTif-541
86Don-265
86Fle-537
86GiaMot-20
86Top-138
86TopSti-91
86TopTif-138
87Don-313
87Fle-271
87FleGlo-271
87FleUpd-21
87FleUpdG-21
87GiaMot-14
87Top-21
87TopTif-21
88Don-64
88DonBasB-98
88Fle-581
88FleGlo-581
88PadCok-48
88PadSmo-6
88Sco-391
88ScoGlo-391
88StaLinPa-2
88Top-482
88TopTif-482
89Bow-447
89BowTif-447
89Don-65
89DonAll-46
89DonBasB-133
89Fle-303
89Fle-635
89FleBasA-10
89FleGlo-303
89FleGlo-635
89FleUpd-18
89OPC-59
89PadCok-3
89PadMag-13
89PanSti-193
89RedFolSB-32
89Sco-490
89ScoHot1S-62
89Spo-74
89Top-59
89TopAwaW-1
89TopSti-110

89TopStiB-64
89TopTif-59
89UppDec-268
90aSab-1
90aSab-3
90aSab-5
90aSab-7
90aSab-9
90aSab-11
90Baz-3
90Bow-369
90BowIns-2
90BowInsT-2
90BowTif-369
90BowTif-A2
90ClaUpd-T14
90ClaUpd-NNO
90Don-302
90DonBesA-8
90Fle-155
90Fle-631
90FleAll-3
90FleCan-155
90FleCan-631
90FleUpd-101
90Hot50PS-11
90K-M-14
90Lea-468
90MSAHolD-6
90OPC-205
90OPC-407
90PanSti-215
90PanSti-352
90PubSti-47
90RedFolSB-22
90Sco-259
90Sco100S-51
90ScoRoo-26T
90Spo-62
90Top-205
90Top-407
90TopBig-312
90TopCoi-34
90TopDou-16
90TopGaloC-1
90TopGloS-58
90TopMinL-79
90TopSti-102
90TopStiB-31
90TopTif-205
90TopTif-407
90TopTra-24T
90TopTraT-24T
90TopTVA-12
90UppDec-431
90UppDec-710
90VenSti-130
90Woo-4
91BasBesRB-5
91Bow-306
91ClaGam-15
91Don-560
91Fle-555
91Lea-16
91OPC-116
91RedFolS-24
91RoyPol-6
91Sco-136
91StaClu-136
91Top-116
91TopDesS-116
91TopMic-116
91TopTif-116
91UppDec-589
92Don-54
92Lea-163
92OPC-766
92Pin-359
92RoyPol-5
92Sco-718
92SpoStaCC-11
92StaClu-212
92Top-766
92TopGol-766
92TopGolW-766
92TopMic-766
92TriPla-247
92Ult-369
92UppDec-607
93Don-52
93Pin-425
93StaClu-371
93StaCluFDI-371
93StaCluMOP-371
93Ult-437
94Don-657
94Fle-661
94Pac-521
94PadMot-10
94StaClu-497
94StaCluFDI-497
94StaCluGR-497
94StaCluMOP-497

Davis, Marty
91GulCoaRSP-18

Davis, Matt
91CliGiaC-12
91CliGiaP-840
92CalLeaACL-14
92SanJosGC-23
93ShrCapF-2765
94ElPasDF-3151

Davis, Melvin
93EveGiaC-7
93EveGiaF-3782
94CliLumF-1993
94CliLumC-8

Davis, Michael
82TacTigT-34
86TidTidP-7

Davis, Mike (Michael Dwayne)
79WatA'sT-15
81Don-470
81Fle-586
81SyrChiT-14
81TacTigT-11
81Top-364
82TidTidT-3
82Top-671
83A'sGraG-16
83PawRedST-16
83TopTra-24T
84A'sMot-5
84Don-298
84Fle-443
84Nes792-558
84PawRedST-7
84PawRedST-26
84Top-558
84TopSti-338
84TopTif-558
85A'sMot-7
85Don-223
85DonHig-3
85Fle-422
85TidTidT-23
85Top-778
85TopTif-778
86A'sMot-7
86Don-14
86Don-96
86DonSupD-14
86Fle-416
86FleLimE-14
86FleMin-88
86FleStiC-31
86Lea-14
86OPC-165
86Spo-83
86Top-165
86TopSti-166
86TopTat-4
86TopTif-165
87A'sSmoC-3
87Don-133
87DonOpeD-21
87Fle-391
87FleGlo-391
87FleLimE-12
87FleMin-28
87FleStiC-32
87SpoTeaP-23
87Top-83
87TopSti-168
87TopTif-83
88DodMot-12
88DodPol-37
88Don-281
88DonBasB-36
88Fle-277
88FleGlo-277
88OPC-217
88PanSti-174
88RedFolSB-16
88Sco-211
88ScoGlo-211
88ScoRoo-53T
88ScoRooG-53T
88Spo-206
88StaLinAs-3
88StaLinD-2
88Top-448
88TopBig-154
88TopSti-171
88TopTif-448
88TopTra-33T
88TopTraT-33T
89Bow-352
89BowTif-352
89BurIndS-7
89DodMot-12
89DodPol-11
89DodStaSV-5
89Don-316
89Fle-55
89FleGlo-55
89OPC-277
89PanSti-24
89Sco-376
89Top-277
89TopAme2C-12
89TopBig-225
89TopTif-277
89UppDec-146
89Woo-32
90DodTar-169
90Don-552
90Fle-391
90FleCan-391
90OPC-697
90PubSti-3
90Sco-437
90Top-697
90TopTif-697
90UppDec-258
90VenSti-131
90WatIndS-6
91IndIndLD-180
91IndIndP-472
91LinDriAAA-180

Davis, Nick
89KinMetS-6
90ColMetGS-5
90ColMetPPI-6
91AshTouP-573
91Cla/Bes-49

Davis, Nicky
90AshTouC-12
90PitMetP-11

Davis, Odie (Odie Ernest)
79TucTorT-18
80ChaChaT-15
81ChaChaT-16
93RanKee-122

Davis, Pamela
95ColSilB-8
96ColSilB-8

Davis, Peaches (Ray)
38CinOraW-7
39OrcPhoAP-5
39PlaBal-123

Davis, Pepper (Lavonne)
93TedWil-118

Davis, Piper (Lorenzo)
53MotCoo-54
86NegLeaF-12
86NegLeaF-47
87NegLeaPD-37
92NegLeaRLI-15
93UppDecS-17

Davis, Ray
93SavCarC-11
93SavCarF-682
94MadHatC-9
94MadHatF-126
94MidLeaAF-MDW43
95ArkTraTI-9
96ArkTraB-10

Davis, Red
60TacBan-4
61TacBan-5
61UniOil-T10
76WilTomT-5

Davis, Reggie
96AriBlaDB-15

Davis, Rick
89SpoIndSP-11
90Bes-78
90RivRedWB-5
90RivRedWCLC-14
90RivRedWP-2598
91LinDriAA-606
91WicWraLD-606
91WicWraP-2593
91WicWraRD-3
92LasVegSF-2790
92LasVegSS-229
92SkyAAAF-113
93LasVegSF-938

Davis, Robert
89BriTigS-7

Davis, Ron (Ronald E.)
67Ast-8
67CokCapAs-3
67DexPre-61
67Top-298
68CokCapA-3
68DexPre-28
68OPC-21
68Top-21
68TopVen-21
69MilBra-71
69MLBOffS-185
69Top-553
69TopTeaP-12
70MLBOffS-100
87AstShoSTw-5

Davis, Ron (Ronald Gene)
79ColCliT-14
79YanPicA-8
80OPC-101
80Top-179
81Don-467
81Fle-86
81OPC-16
81Top-16
82Don-451
82Fle-32
82FleSta-117
82FleSta-242
82OPC-283
82Top-2
82Top-635
82TopTra-25T
82TwiPos-6
83Don-228
83Fle-610
83FleSta-48
83FleSti-133
83OPC-380
83Top-380
83TopSti-94
83TwiTeal-25
84AllGamPI-169
84Don-269
84Fle-561
84FleSti-75
84FunFooP-112
84MinTwiP-8
84Nes792-519
84OPC-101
84Top-519
84TopRubD-17
84TopSti-309
84TopTif-519
84TwiTeal-26
85Don-120
85Fle-275
85FleStaS-103
85OPC-78
85Top-430
85TopRubD-16
85TopSti-297
85TopTif-430
85Twi7-8
85TwiTeal-29
86Don-364
86Fle-390
86OPC-265
86Top-265
86TopSti-281
86TopTat-18
86TopTif-265
86TwiTeal-27
87CubCan-4
87CubDavB-39
87Don-438
87Fle-558
87FleGlo-558
87OPC-383
87Top-383
87TopTif-383
89PhoFirP-1505
90ColCliP-9
90DodTar-170
91PacSenL-115
92YanWIZ7-40
92YanWIZ8-40
92YanWIZA-15

Davis, Russ (Russell Stuart)
89Ft.LauYS-2
89OneYanP-2109
90CarLeaA-18
90PriWilCTI-8
91AlbYanLD-2
91AlbYanP-1014
91Cla/Bes-182
91LinDriAA-2
92AlbYanF-2231
92AlbYanS-6
92ClaFS7-115
92SkyAA F-2
92UppDecML-132
93Bow-342
93ClaMVPF-9
93ColCliF-1115
93ColCliP-13
93ExcFS7-205
93ExcLeaLF-18
93FlaWavotF-3
93FleFinE-245
93SP-274
93Ult-592
94ActPac-13
94ActPacP-3
94Bow-109
94BowBes-B39
94BowBesR-B39
94Cla-143
94ColCliF-2956
94ColCliP-6
94ExcAllF-4
94ExcFS7-100
94Fle-227
94LeaGolR-8
94LeaLimR-5
94SigRoo-1
94SigRooHP-S2
94SigRooS-1
94StaCluT-194
94StaCluTFDI-194
94Top-772
94TopGol-772
94TopSpa-772
94UppDecML-130
94UppDecML-155
95ActPac2GF-13G
95ActPacF-9
95ActPacF-74
95Bow-428
95ColCho-524
95ColChoGS-524
95ColChoSE-18
95ColChoSEGS-18
95ColChoSESS-18
95ColChoSS-524
95ColCliMCTI-15
95Don-545
95Lea-300
95Pac-294
95Pin-414
95PinArtP-414
95PinMusC-414
95Sco-601
95ScoAi-AM6
95ScoGolR-601
95ScoPlaTS-601
95Sel-160
95SelArtP-160
95SelCer-104
95SelCerMG-104
95Spo-152
95SpoArtP-152
95SpoSam-152
95StaClu-359
95StaCluMOP-359
95StaCluSTWS-359
95Sum-162
95SumNthD-162
95Top-536
95UC3-110
95UC3ArtP-110
95UppDec-204
95UppDecED-204
95UppDecEDG-204
95Zen-132
96ColCho-723
96ColChoGS-723

96ColChoSS-723
96Don-241
96DonPreP-241
96EmoXL-112
96Fin-S295
96FinRef-S295
96Fla-159
96Fle-235
96FleTif-235
96FleUpd-U78
96FleUpdTC-U78
96LeaSigA-55
96LeaSigAG-55
96LeaSigAS-55
96MarMot-27
96Pin-349
96PinAfi-137
96PinAfiAP-137
96PinFoil-349
96Sco-129
96ScoDugC-A80
96ScoDugCAP-A80
96Sel-127
96SelArtP-127
96SP-174
96Stu-66
96StuPrePB-66
96StuPrePG-66
96StuPrePS-66
96Sum-30
96SumAbo&B-30
96SumArtP-30
96SumFoi-30
96Ult-99
96Ult-410
96UltGolM-99
96UltGolM-410
96UppDec-458
97Cir-159
97CirRav-159
97ColCho-484
97Don-210
97DonLim-32
97DonLimLE-32
97DonPreP-210
97DonPrePGold-210
97Fle-205
97FleTif-205
97Lea-162
97LeaFraM-162
97LeaFraMDC-162
97Sco-437
97ScoHobR-437
97ScoResC-437
97ScoShoS-437
97ScoShoSAP-437
97StaClu-362
97StaCluMOP-362
97Top-193
97Ult-321
97UltGolME-321
97UltPlaME-321

Davis, Sammy
78WatIndT-7
79WatIndT-10

Davis, Saul
92NegLeaRLI-14

Davis, Scott
90EugEmeGS-5

Davis, Spud (Virgil L.)
33Gou-210
33RitCE-9H
34DiaMatCSB-39
35DiaMatCS3T1-43
36GouWidPPR-A25
36SandSW-11
36WorWidGV-12
39PlaBal-37
40PlaBal-163
74Car193T-4
83ConMar-26
83DiaClaS2-64
86PhiGreT-4
87Car193T-9
88ConNatA-4
91ConTSN-269
93ConTSN-863
94ConTSN-1072
94ConTSNB-1072

Davis, Stan
77NewCoPT-7
78NewWayCT-8
79BurBeeT-21
81ElPasDT-6
82VanCanT-9
83ElPasDT-6
84ElPasDT-14

Davis, Steven K.
86BluJayAF-7
86BluJayFS-7
87SyrChiT-2
88BlaYNPRWL-81
88BlaYNPRWLU-49
88SyrChiC-1
88SyrChiP-814
89ColSprSSC-1
89ColSprSSP-249
90AlbDukC-4
90AlbDukP-337
90AlbDukT-6
90CMC-406
90JacMetGS-28
90OPC-428
90ProAAAF-58
90Sco-187
90Top-428
90TopTif-428
91GenCubC-5
91GenCubP-4209
91LinDriAA-629
94BirBarC-30

Davis, Steven Michael
80SyrChiTI-7
81SyrChiTI-7
87SyrChiP-1948
87TamTarP-19
88CedRapRP-1150
90SarWhiSS-29
91WilBilLD-629
91WilBilP-305

Davis, Storm (George)
83Don-619
83Fle-56
83OriPos-6
83Top-268
83TopSti-310
84Don-585
84Fle-5
84FunFooP-120
84Nes792-140
84OPC-140
84OriEng-3
84OriTeal-7
84Top-140
84TopTif-140
85Don-454
85Fle-174
85Lea-81
85OPC-73
85OriHea-3
85Top-599
85TopTif-599
86Don-169
86Fle-271
86Lea-99
86OPC-179
86Top-469
86TopSti-231
86TopTif-469
87Don-273
87Fle-466
87FleGlo-466
87FleUpd-22
87FleUpdG-22
87OPC-349
87PadBohHB-34
87Top-349
87TopSti-230
87TopTif-349
87TopTra-26T
87TopTraT-26T
88A'sMot-19
88Don-595
88DonBasB-282
88DonTeaBA-595
88Fle-278
88FleGlo-278
88Top-248
88TopTif-248
89A'sMot-18
89Bow-192
89BowTif-192
89Don-210
89Fle-6
89FleGlo-6
89PanSti-413
89Sco-248
89Top-701
89TopBig-121
89TopTif-701
89UppDec-153
90Bow-368
90BowTif-368
90ClaUpd-T15
90Don-479
90Fle-5
90FleCan-5
90FleUpd-102
90Lea-362
90OPC-606
90PubSti-302
90Sco-266
90ScoRoo-21T
90Top-606
90TopMinL-26
90TopTif-606
90TopTra-25T
90TopTraT-25T
90UppDec-292
90UppDec-712
90VenSti-132
91Bow-293
91ClaGam-16
91Don-185
91Fle-556
91Lea-161
91OPC-22
91OriCro-97
91RoyPol-7
91Sco-511
91StaClu-67
91Stu-65
91Top-22
91TopDesS-22
91TopMic-22
91TopTif-22
91UltUpd-26
91UppDec-639
92Don-529
92Fle-155
92Lea-465
92OPC-556
92Pin-312
92Sco-264
92ScoRoo-34T
92StaClu-728
92Top-556
92TopGol-556
92TopGolW-556
92TopMic-556
92UppDec-499
93AthMot-18
93Don-769
93Fle-541
93Lea-259
93PacSpa-564
93Sco-449
93StaClu-174
93StaCluAt-6
93StaCluFDI-174
93StaCluMOP-174
93Ult-604
93UppDec-746
93UppDecGold-746
94FleUpd-42
94Pac-214
94Top-682
94TopGol-682
94TopSpa-682
95Fle-47

Davis, Ted
78AshTouT-6
79WauTimT-20
80TulDriT-4
81TulDriT-8
82JacMetT-3
83BirBarT-18

Davis, Tim
90ElmPioP-4
92TopTra-27T
92TopTraG-27T
93AppFoxC-6
93AppFoxF-2453
93ForLauRSC-7
93ForLauRSFP-1603
93MidLeaAGF-1
93StaCluM-103
94Bow-257
94ClaGolF-12
94ExcFS7-125
94ExtBas-163
94ExtBasRS-4
94Fla-100
94FleUpd-81
94LeaLimR-56
94MarMot-23
94SpoRoo-117
94SpoRooAP-117
94Top-167
94TopGol-167
94TopSpa-167
94Ult-418
94UppDec-512
94UppDecED-512
94UppDecML-224
95ColCho-281
95ColChoGS-281
95ColChoSS-281
95Don-179
95DonPreP-179
95Fle-265
95MarMot-9
95Pac-394
95Pin-142
95PinArtP-142
95PinMusC-142
95Sco-61
95ScoGolR-61
95ScoPlaTS-61
95StaClu-60
95StaCluFDI-60
95StaCluMOP-60
95StaCluSTWS-60
95Top-83
95TopCyb-59
95UppDec-344
95UppDecED-344
95UppDecEDG-344
96TopRaiB-8

Davis, Tod (Thomas Oscar)
47SigOil-4
49PhiBul-14

Davis, Tom
76ForLauYS-6

Davis, Tommy
94SigRooDP-47
94SigRooDPS-47
94StaCluDP-22
94StaCluDPFDI-22
95Bow-115
95BowBes-B72
95BowBesR-B72
95Exc-3
95SPML-19
95Top-555
96BesAutS-26
96Bow-375
96BowBayB-14
96Exc-4

Davis, Tommy (Herman Thomas)
59DarFar-5
60DodUniO-3
60Top-509
61DodBelB-12
61DodMor-1
61DodUniO-3
61Pos-165
61Raw-4
61Top-168
61TopStal-25
62DodBelB-12
62Jel-105
62Pos-105
62PosCan-105
62SalPlaC-154A
62SalPlaC-154B
62ShiPlaC-154
62Top-358
63Baz-36
63DodJayP-2
63Fle-40
63Jel-117
63Pos-117
63Top-1
63Top-310
63TopStil-12
64Baz-36
64DodHea-1
64Top-7
64Top-137
64Top-180
64TopCoi-57
64TopCoi-153
64TopGia-43
64TopSta-64
64TopStaU-21
64TopVen-7
64TopVen-137
64TopVen-180
64WheSta-13
65Baz-36
65DodJayP-2
65DodTeal-2
65Top-370
65TopEmbl-49
65TopTral-46
66OPC-75
66Top-75
66TopVen-75
67Baz-37
67CokCapYM-V30
67DexPre-62
67Kah-10
67MetTeal-4
67Top-370
67TopVen-332
68AtlOilPBCC-15
68Baz-10
68Top-265
68TopGaml-10
68TopPla-17
68TopVen-265
69MilBra-72
69MLBOffS-94
69OPC-135
69PilPos-6
69Top-135
69TopDec-15
69TopDecl-8
69TopFou-4
69TopSta-224
69TopSup-32
69TopTeaP-9
70AstTeal-1
70MilBra-6
70MLBOffS-38
70Top-559
71OPC-151
71Top-151
72MilBra-87
72OPC-41
72OPC-42
72Top-41
72Top-42
73OriJohP-12
74Kel-43
74OPC-396
74Top-396
74TopSta-124
75OPC-564
75SSP42-7
75Top-564
76OPC-149
76SSP-398
76Top-149
77Top-362
78TCM60I-87
82Don-648
83Pil69G-14
87AstShowSTh-5
87DodSmoA-5
88BakDodCLC-265
88DodSmo-8
88PacLegl-83
89DodSmoG-70
90DodTar-171
91MetWIZ-92
91OriCro-98
92DodStaTA-2
93TedWil-11
93TedWilM-7
93TedWilPC-25
93UppDecAH-37
94UppDecAH-188
94UppDecAH1-188

Davis, Trench
82PorBeaT-19
84HawIslC-139
85HawIslC-238
86HawIslP-3
87RicBraBC-5
87RicBraC-32
87RicBraT-17

Davis, Wayne
87MyrBeaBJP-1454
88DunBluJS-3

Davis, Willie (Willie Henry)
60DarFar-8

61DodBelB-3
61DodUniO-4
61Top-506
62DodBelB-3
62Jel-106
62Pos-106
62PosCan-106
62SalPlaC-161
62ShiPlaC-161
62Top-108
62TopVen-108
63DodJayP-3
63Jel-119
63Pos-119
63SalMetC-21
63Top-229
64DodHea-2
64Raw-2
64Top-68
64TopVen-68
65DodJayP-3
65DodTeal-3
65OldLonC-7
65Top-435
66Top-535
66TopRubI-23
67CokCapD-17
67CokCapDA-17
67DexPre-63
67DexPre-64
67OPC-160
67Top-160
67TopVen-319
68Top-208
68Top3-D-2
68TopVen-208
69MilBra-73
69MLBOffS-145
69MLBPin-40
69OPC-65
69Top-65
69TopSta-41
69TopSup-45
69TopTeaP-22
69TraSta-45
70MLBOffS-49
70OPC-390
70Top-390
70TopPos-3
70TopSup-39
70TraSta-2B
71DodTic-5
71Kel-16
71MilDud-41
71MLBOffS-101
71OPC-585
71Top-585
71TopCoi-93
72Dia-9
72Dia-58
72Kel-3A
72Kel-3B
72MilBra-88
72OPC-390
72Top-390
72TopCloT-9
72TopPos-12
73Kel2D-43
73OPC-35
73Top-35
73TopCanL-12
73TopCom-6
73TopPin-6
74Kel-45
74OPC-165
74Top-165
74TopDecE-42
74TopSta-44
74TopTra-165T
75OPC-10
75SSP18-11
75Top-10
76OPC-265
76SSP-279
76Top-265
77PadSchC-19
77Top-603
78TCM60I-24
84DodUniOP-3
87DodSmoA-6
88DodSmo-12
89DodSmoG-77
90DodTar-172
92DodStaTA-10
92Pin-591
93RanKee-123

Davison, Mike (Michael Lynn)
71MLBOffS-245
71OPC-276
71Top-276

Davison, Nathan
91AdeGiaF-5

Davison, Scott
89JamExpP-2145
90RocExpLC-6
90RocExpP-2699
91WesPalBEC-19
91WesPalBEP-1235
94BelMarC-10
94BelMarF-3227
95Exc-114
95PorCitRTI-5
96TacRaiB-9

Davisson, Jay
83ReaPhiT-4
84PorBeaC-213
85PorBeaC-41

Dawes, Scott
95AusFut-33

Dawkins, Walter
95BatCliTI-10

Dawley, Bill
79NaSouTI-7
80IndIndTI-25
81IndIndTI-28
82IndIndTI-7
84AstMot-22
84Don-328
84Fle-223
84FleSti-108
84Nes792-248
84OPC-248
84Top-248
84TopSti-71
84TopTif-248
85AstMot-16
85Don-354
85Fle-348
85OPC-363
85Top-634
85TopMin-634
85TopTif-634
86AstMot-25
86Don-283
86Fle-298
86FleUpd-32
86Top-376
86TopTif-376
87CarSmo-9
87Don-628
87Fle-493
87FleGlo-493
87FleUpd-23
87FleUpdG-23
87Top-54
87TopTif-54
88Don-331
88Fle-29
88FleGlo-29
88Sco-328
88ScoGlo-328
88Top-509
88TopTif-509
89TacTigC-5
89TacTigP-1555

Dawley, Joey
93BluOriC-11
93BluOriF-4119
94BluOriC-8
94BluOriF-3556
94OriPro-23

Dawsey, Jason
95HelBreTI-16
96BelSnaTI-11

Dawson, Andre (Andre Nolan)
77ExpPos-11
77ExpPos-12
77Top-473
78ExpPos-3
78OPC-180
78RCColC-73
78Top-72
79ExpPos-7
79OPC-179
79Top-348
80ExpPos-8
80OPC-124
80Top-235
81AllGamPI-142
81Don-212
81Fle-145
81FleStiC-123
81OPC-125
81OPCPos-6
81PerAll-3
81Top-125
81TopScr-90
81TopSti-187
82Don-88
82ExpHygM-5
82ExpPos-8
82ExpZel-4
82ExpZel-10
82ExpZel-14
82FBIDis-6
82Fle-187
82FleSta-35
82OPC-341
82OPC-379
82OPCPos-18
82PerAll-12
82PerAllG-12
82Squ-17
82Top-341
82Top-540
82TopSti-57
82TopSti-125
82TopStiV-57
83AllGamPI-142
83Don-518
83DonActA-9
83ExpStu-4
83Fle-280
83FleSta-49
83FleSti-264
83OPC-173
83OPC-303
83PerAll-11
83PerAllG-11
83PerCreC-4
83PerCreCG-4
83Top-402
83Top-680
83TopSti-164
83TopSti-252
84AllGamPI-49
84Don-97
84DonActAS-18
84Dra-9
84ExpPos-5
84ExpStu-11
84ExpStu-36
84ExpStu-37
84Fle-273
84FleSti-18
84FleSti-25
84FleSti-33
84FunFooP-22
84MilBra-8
84Nes792-200
84Nes792-392
84NesDreT-16
84OPC-200
84OPC-392
84RalPur-6
84SevCoi-C1
84SevCoi-E1
84SevCoi-W1
84Top-200
84Top-392
84TopCer-6
84TopGloA-18
84TopGloS-35
84TopRubD-6
84TopSti-92
84TopSti-181
84TopSup-20
84TopTif-200
84TopTif-392
85AllGamPI-139
85Don-421
85DonHig-41
85ExpPos-6
85Fle-394
85FleLimE-8
85GenMilS-2
85Lea-133
85OPC-133
85OPCPos-9
85SevCoi-S7
85Top-420
85TopRubD-7
85TopSti-86
85TopTif-420
86Don-25
86Don-87
86DonSupD-25
86ExpProPa-9
86ExpProPo-9
86Fle-246
86FleMin-53
86FleStiC-32
86GenMilB-6B
86Lea-25
86OPC-256
86SevCoi-E13
86Spo-66
86Spo-110
86Top-576
86Top-760
86TopSti-74
86TopTat-20
86TopTif-576
86TopTif-760
86TruVal-29
87BoaandB-10
87ClaUpdY-124
87CubCan-5
87CubDavB-8
87Don-458
87DonHig-28
87DonHig-30
87DonOpeD-70
87Fle-316
87FleGlo-316
87FleHotS-13
87FleSlu-12
87FleStiC-33
87FleUpd-24
87FleUpdG-24
87Lea-212
87OPC-345
87RedFolSB-13
87Spo-139
87StuPan-3
87Top-345
87TopSti-77
87TopTif-345
87TopTra-27T
87TopTraT-27T
88ActPacT-2
88CheBoy-18
88ClaBlu-216
88ClaRed-157
88CubDavB-8
88Don-9
88Don-269
88DonAll-36
88DonBasB-225
88DonBonM-BC10
88DonPop-14
88DonSupD-9
88DonTeaBC-269
88Dra-16
88Fle-415
88FleAll-6
88FleAwaW-9
88FleBasA-10
88FleBasM-9
88FleExcS-13
88FleGlo-415
88FleHotS-9
88FleLeaL-9
88FleMin-67
88FleRecS-10
88FleSlu-12
88FleStiC-79
88FleSup-13
88FleTeaL-7
88GreBasS-41
88K-M-9
88KayB-8
88KinDis-14
88Lea-9
88Lea-126
88MSAFanSD-15
88MSAJifPD-8
88Nes-9
88OPC-247
88PanSti-236
88PanSti-265
88RedFolSB-17
88Sco-4
88ScoBoxC-16
88ScoGlo-4
88Spo-3
88StaDaw-1
88StaDaw-2
88StaDaw-3
88StaDaw-4
88StaDaw-5
88StaDaw-6
88StaDaw-7
88StaDaw-8
88StaDaw-9
88StaDaw-10
88StaDaw-11
88StaLinAl-10
88StaLinCu-1
88Top-401
88Top-500
88TopBig-153
88TopCoi-33
88TopGaloC-6
88TopGloA-18
88TopGloS-1
88TopMinL-43
88TopRevLL-2
88TopRitTM-2
88TopSti-56
88TopSti-148
88TopStiB-13
88TopTif-401
88TopTif-500
88TopUKM-20
88TopUKMT-20
88Woo-8
89Bow-298
89BowTif-298
89CadEIID-14
89CerSup-2
89ClaLigB-37
89ColPosD-1
89ColPosD-2
89ColPosD-3
89ColPosD-4
89ColPosD-5
89ColPosD-6
89ColPosD-7
89ColPosD-8
89CubMar-8
89Don-167
89DonAll-36
89DonBasB-4
89DonBonM-BC8
89DonPop-36
89Fle-422
89FleBasA-11
89FleBasM-11
89FleExcS-11
89FleGlo-422
89FleHeroB-12
89FleLeaL-12
89FleSup-12
89KayB-9
89MSAIceTD-14
89OPC-10
89PanSti-59
89PanSti-230
89RedFolSB-33
89Sco-2
89ScoHot1S-80
89ScoSco-28
89Spo-95
89SpollIFKI-52
89Top-4
89Top-10
89Top-391
89TopAme2C-13
89TopBasT-78
89TopBig-120
89TopCapC-10
89TopCoi-11
89TopDouA-17
89TopGloA-18
89TopHilTM-11
89TopMinL-3
89TopSti-5
89TopSti-54
89TopSti-156
89TopStiB-48
89TopTif-4
89TopTif-10
89TopTif-391
89TopUKM-21
89TVSpoM-21
89UppDec-205
89UppDecS-3

89Woo-11
90AllBasT-24
90Bow-39
90BowTif-39
90ClaBlu-85
90CubMar-6
90Don-223
90DonBesN-97
90DonLeaS-52
90Fle-29
90FleCan-29
90HOFStiB-96
90KayB-8
90Lea-177
90MLBBasB-54
90OPC-140
90OPCBoxB-C
90PanSti-240
90PubSti-192
90PubSti-256
90RedFolSB-23
90Sco-265
90Sco100S-74
90ScoMcD-10
90Spo-108
90Top-140
90TopAmeA-9
90TopBig-91
90TopDou-17
90TopGloS-41
90TopHilHM-15
90TopMag-65
90TopSti-47
90TopStiB-14
90TopTif-140
90TopTVCu-31
90TopWaxBC-C
90UppDec-73
90UppDec-357
90USPlaCA-9H
90VenSti-133
90VenSti-134
90Woo-11
91BasBesHRK-5
91Bow-429
91CadEllD-15
91Cla3-T14
91ClaGam-26
91CubMar-8
91CubVinL-9
91CubVinL-36
91DenHol-14
91Don-129
91Don-435
91DonEli-4
91Fle-419A
91Fle-419B
91Fle-713
91Lea-400
91MajLeaCP-67
91OPC-640
91OPCBoxB-D
91OPCPre-31
91PanFreS-49
91PanSti-41
91PepSup-2
91PosCan-7
91RedFolS-25
91RedFolS-118
91Sco-445
91Sco100S-87
91SevCoi-M2
91SimandSMLBL-13
91StaClu-310
91StaPinB-12
91Stu-153
91SunSee-14
91Top-640
91TopCraJ2-7
91TopDesS-640
91TopGloA-19
91TopMic-640
91TopSta-11
91TopTif-640
91TopWaxBC-D
91Ult-58
91UppDec-454
91UppDec-725
91UppDecFE-98F
91USPlaCA-11C
91Woo-9
92Bow-625
92Cla2-T24
92ClaGam-27
92CubMar-8
92Don-119
92Don-422
92DonPre-4
92Fle-379
92FleTeaL-20
92Hig5-27
92HitTheBB-12
92Lea-183
92MooSna-15
92OPC-460
92OPCPre-45
92PanSti-186
92PanSti-285
92Pin-115
92Sco-75
92Sco100S-48
92ScoCokD-7
92ScoProP-19
92SpoStaCC-12
92StaClu-810
92StaCluD-33
92Stu-12
92StuHer-BC9
92Top-460
92TopGol-460
92TopGolW-460
92TopKid-2
92TopMcD-31
92TopMic-460
92TopMic-G460
92TriPla-113
92TriPla-174
92Ult-468
92UppDec-124
92UppDecHRH-HR9
93Bow-495
93CadDis-16
93DiaMar-29
93Don-632
93DurPowP1-3
93ExpDonM-2
93Fin-84
93FinJum-84
93FinRef-84
93Fla-162
93Fle-377
93FleFinE-173
93FleFinEDT-3
93FleFruotL-14
93FunPac-163
93Lea-310
93OPC-35
93OPCPre-18
93PacSpa-56
93PanSti-97
93Pin-497
93PinCoo-11
93PinCooD-11
93PinHomRC-16
93PinSlu-26
93RedSoxWHP-4
93Sco-552
93Sel-9
93SelRoo-11T
93SP-201
93StaClu-203
93StaClu-655
93StaCluFDI-203
93StaCluFDI-655
93StaCluMOP-203
93StaCluMOP-655
93Stu-104
93Top-265
93TOPBLAG-4
93TopGol-265
93TopInaM-265
93TopMic-265
93TopPreS-4
93TopTra-92T
93TriPlaG-GS2
93Ult-509
93UppDec-308
93UppDec-777
93UppDec-832
93UppDecGold-308
93UppDecGold-777
93UppDecGold-832
94Bow-531
94ColC-412
94ColChoGS-412
94ColChoSS-412
94Don-448
94ExtBas-19
94Fin-50
94FinRef-50
94Fla-13
94Fle-29
94FUnPac-100
94Lea-142
94LeaL-9
94OPC-138
94Pac-52
94PanSti-28
94Pin-320
94PinArtP-320
94PinMusC-320
94ProMag-12
94Sco-471
94ScoGolR-471
94Sel-93
94SP-154
94SPDieC-154
94Spo-79
94StaClu-371
94StaCluFDI-371
94StaCluGR-371
94StaCluMOP-371
94Stu-161
94Top-595
94TopGol-595
94TopSpa-595
94TriPla-203
94Ult-13
94UppDec-96
94UppDecAJ-12
94UppDecAJG-12
94UppDecED-96
95ColCho-420
95ColCho-560T
95ColChoGS-420
95ColChoSE-195
95ColChoSEGS-195
95ColChoSESS-195
95ColChoSS-420
95Don-487
95DonPreP-487
95DonTopotO-242
95Emo-129
95Fin-330
95FinRef-330
95Fla-352
95Fle-28
95FleUpd-95
95Lea-316
95Pac-36
95Pin-318
95PinArtP-318
95PinMusC-318
95Sco-333
95ScoGolR-333
95ScoPlaTS-333
95ScoYouTE-333T
95SP-56
95SPCha-48
95SPChaDC-48
95SPSil-56
95StaClu-146
95StaClu-578
95StaCluFDI-146
95StaCluMOP-146
95StaCluMOP-578
95StaCluMOP-RL10
95StaCluRL-RL10
95StaCluSTWS-146
95StaCluSTWS-578
95StaCluVR-75
95TopTra-155T
95Ult-262
95UltGolM-262
95UppDec-160
95UppDec-350
95UppDecED-160
95UppDecED-350
95UppDecEDG-160
95UppDecEDG-350
95UppDecSE-250
95UppDecSEG-250
96ColCho-150
96ColChoGS-150
96ColChoSS-150
96Don-260
96DonPreP-260
96Fla-261
96Fle-386
96FleTif-386
96LeaLim-75
96LeaLimG-75
96LeaPre-100
96LeaPreP-100
96LeaSig-127
96LeaSigA-56
96LeaSigAG-56
96LeaSigAS-56
96LeaSigPPG-127
96LeaSigPPP-127
96Pac-75
96PacPri-P25
96PacPriG-P25
96Pin-86
96PinAfi-54
96PinAfiAP-54
96PinAfiFPP-54
96PinArtP-48
96PinSta-48
96Sco-51
96ScoDugC-A44
96ScoDugCAP-A44
96ScoRef-9
96Sel-79
96SelArtP-79
96SelCer-96
96SelCerAP-96
96SelCerCB-96
96SelCerCR-96
96SelCerMB-96
96SelCerMG-96
96SelCerMR-96
96SelTeaN-16
96SP-88
95StaCluVRMC-75
96Sum-148
96SumAbo&B-148
96SumArtP-148
96SumFoi-148
96Top-275
96Ult-199
96UltGolM-199
96UltThu-7
96UltThuGM-7
96UppDec-102
96UppDec-335
96Zen-44
96ZenArtP-44
97ColCho-115
97Don-142
97DonEli-109
97DonEliGS-109
97DonPreP-142
97DonPrePGold-142
97Fle-329
97FleTif-329
97PacPriGotD-GD140
97Pin-15
97PinArtP-15
97PinMusC-15
97Ult-196
97UltGolME-196
97UltPlaME-196
97UppDec-80
97UppDec-214

Dawson, Charlie
94IdaFalBF-3587
94IdaFalBSP-14
95MacBraTI-5

Dawson, David
89BakDodCLC-180

Dawson, Dwayne
92AubAstC-20
92AubAstF-1348
93QuaCitRBC-5
93QuaCitRBF-91

Dawson, Gary
83MadMusF-24

Dawson, Joe
94ConTSN-1311
94ConTSNB-1311

Dawson, Larry
88AppFoxP-164

Dawson, Red (Lowell)
40WheM4-10
41WheM5-16

Day, Boots (Charles F.)
70ExpPin-4
70Top-654
71ExpPS-5
71MLBOffS-125
71OPC-42
71Top-42
72OPC-254
72ProStaP-3
72Top-254
73OPC-307
73Top-307
74ExpWes-3
74OPC-589
74Top-589
77EvaTriT-7

Day, Dexter
83WatRedT-16
84CedRapRT-13

Day, George
91AppFoxC-17
91AppFoxP-1723

Day, Kevin
89AshTouP-943

Day, Leon
78LauLonABS-5
80PerHaloFP-221
90NegLeaS-13
91NegLeaRL-6
92NegLeaK-1
92NegLeaRLI-16
93LeoDayCC-1
93UppDecS-17
94TedWil-103
94TedWil-NNO
95NegLeaL2-4
95NegLeaLI-6

Day, Mike
86WesPalBEP-11

Day, Ned
52Whe-8A
52Whe-8B

Day, Paul
88AugPirP-388

Day, Pea (Clyde Henry)
78HalHalR-13
90DodTar-173

Day, Randy
86PhiTas-xx
86PorBeaP-4
87SyrChiT-31

Day, Steve
77NewCoPT-8
93EveGiaC-8
93EveGiaF-3761
94CliLumF-1973
94ExcFS7-287
94CliLumC-9

Day, Tim
91AdeGiaF-4

Dayett, Brian (Brian Kelly)
79WesHavYT-4
80NasSouTI-7
81NasSouTI-4
82NasSouTI-9
83ColCliT-26
84ColCliP-9
84ColCliT-4
84Don-45
85CubLioP-6
85CubSev-24
85DomLeaS-185
85Don-152
85Fle-125
85FleUpd-35
85IowCubT-8
85Top-534
85TopTif-534
85TopTifT-29T
85TopTra-29T
86Top-284
86TopTif-284
87CubCan-6
87CubDavB-24
87DonOpeD-73
87FleUpd-25
87FleUpdG-25
87Top-369
87TopTif-369
88Don-416
88Fle-416
88FleGlo-416
88OPC-136
88Sco-205
88ScoGlo-205
88Top-136
88TopTif-136
92YanWIZ8-41

Dayle, Snookie
94TedWil-94

Dayley, Ken (Kenneth Grant)
81RicBraT-19
82BraBurKL-7

82Don-501
82RicBraT-25
83Don-375
83Fle-135
83RicBraT-4
83Top-314
84Don-199
84Fle-176
84Nes792-104
84Top-104
84TopTif-104
84TopTra-29T
84TopTraT-29T
85CarTeal-8
86CarKASD-2
86CarSchM-5
86CarTeal-11
86Don-303
86Fle-33
86OPC-202
86Top-607
86TopTif-607
87Don-357
87Fle-293
87FleGlo-293
87Top-59
87TopTif-59
88CarSmo-3
88Don-357
88DonBasB-299
88Fle-30
88FleGlo-30
88Sco-517
88ScoGlo-517
88StaLinCa-5
88Top-234
88TopTif-234
89Bow-428
89BowTif-428
89CarSmo-4
89Don-299
89DonBasB-268
89Fle-448
89FleGlo-448
89OPC-396
89Top-409
89TopTif-409
89UppDec-114
90Bow-191
90BowTif-191
90CarSmo-4
90Don-281
90DonBesN-22
90Fle-247
90FleCan-247
90Lea-275
90OPC-561
90PubSti-216
90RicBra2ATI-7
90Sco-556
90Top-561
90TopSti-36
90TopTif-561
90TopTVCa-10
90UppDec-280
90VenSti-135
91BluJayFS-7
91BluJayS-27
91Bow-27
91Don-735
91Fle-630
91OPC-41
91OPCPre-32
91Sco-607
91StaClu-552
91Stu-134
91Top-41
91TopDesS-41
91TopMic-41
91TopTif-41
91UppDec-628
91UppDec-781
92OPC-717
92Sco-685
92StaClu-137
92Top-717
92TopGol-717
92TopGolW-717
92TopMic-717
93BluJayD4-30
93BluJayFS-8
De Barr, Dennis
79WatA'sT-1
De La Cruz, Miguel
85DomLeaS-206
De Leon, Erasmo
85DomLeaS-126
De Los Santos, Pintacora
85DomLeaS-31
De Los Santos, Valerio
96BelSnaTI-12
96MidLeaAB-10
97Bow-319
97BowBes-179
97BowBesAR-179
97BowBesR-179
97BowInt-319
De Wyre, Mike
85RedWinA-15
86RedWinA-22
Deabenderfer, Blaine
87MadMusP-6
87MadMusP-22
Deak, Brian
87SumBraP-26
88BurBraP-27
88MidLeaAGS-16
89DurBullS-9
89DurBulTI-9
89Sta-71
90DurBulTI-4
91GreBraC-12
91GreBraLD-206
91GreBraP-3006
91LinDriAA-206
92RicBraBB-13
92RicBraF-380
92RicBraRC-5
92RicBraS-428
93CalCanF-1168
93StaCluMari-5
94LasVegSF-873
95LouRedF-277
97RicBraBC-8
Deak, Darrel
88AlaGolTI-7
89AlaGol-12
91JohCitCC-6
91JohCitCP-3982
92SprCarC-18
93ArkTraF-2817
93StaCluCa-11
94Bow-620
94LouRedF-2987
95Exc-265
95LouRedF-281
95SigRoo-14
95SigRooSig-14
96LouRedB-14
Deakman, Josh
95BoiHawTI-15
96LakElsSB-3
Deal, Charlie (Charles Albert)
15SpoNewM-46
16ColE13-40
16SpoNewM-44
19W514-18
20GasAmeMBD-24
20NatCarE-22
21E121So8-16A
21E121So8-16B
21Exh-34
22AmeCarE-15
22W575-25
23WilChoV-29
Deal, Cot (Ellis Fergason)
54CarHunW-5
54Top-192
60Top-459
78ColCliT-4
81OklCit8T-22
82OklCit8T-5
84AstMot-27
85AstMot-27
94TopArc1-192
94TopArc1G-192
Deal, Jamon
92BelMarC-7
92BelMarF-1434
93AppFoxC-7
93AppFoxF-2454
Deal, Lindsay
90DodTar-927
Dealey, Pat (Patrick E.)
87OldJudN-128
Dean, Bob
73CedRapAT-5
75DubPacT-7
Dean, Brian
89CarNewE-3
Dean, Chris
92HigSchPLS-10
94BelMarC-12
94BelMarF-3242
95Exc-115
95ExcFirYP-3
96WisTimRB-9
Dean, Chubby (Alfred Lovill)
40PlaBal-193
Dean, Daffy (Paul Dee)
34DiaMatCSB-41
34BatR31-143
35ExhFou-8
35GolMedFR-4
35WheBB1-8
35WheBB1-9
36ExhFou-8
39PlaBal-19
40PlaBal-156
59OklTodML-14
60NuHi-14
61NuSco-476
68LauWorS-31
74Car193T-5
74Car193T-6
74NewYorNTDiS-29
76TulOilGP-24
77Spo-7013
81ConTSN-22
87Car193T-2
87SpoRea-17
88ConSer3-9
88WilMulP-3
92ConTSN-363
92ConTSN-631
93ConTSNP-1170
93DiaStaES-125
94ConTSN-1170
94ConTSNB-1170
Dean, Dizzy (Jay Hanna)
30SchR33-31
30SchR33-35
32OrbPinNP-14
32OrbPinUP-15
33ButCanV-11
33CraJacP-4
33GeoCMil-8
33Gou-223
33TatOrb-15
33TatOrbSDR-202
34DiaMatCSB-40
34BatR31-64
34ButPreR-14
34Gou-6
34GouCanV-55
34WarBakSP-1
35DiaMatCS2-5
35DiaMatCS3T1-44
35ExhFou-8
35GolMedFR-3
35GouPuzR-1A
35GouPuzR-2A
35GouPuzR-16A
35GouPuzR-17A
35WheBB1-7
35WheBB1-8
36DiaMatCS3T2-6
36ExhFou-8
36R31Pre-G5
36WorWidGV-19
37ExhFou-8
38BasTabP-4
38ExhFou-3
38OurNatGPP-5
38WheBB10-13
39CubTeal-4
39ExhSal-10
39WorWidGV-8
41CubTeal-25
46SpoExcW-3-11
47PM1StaP1-41
50CalHOFW-24
51R42SmaS-21
59OklTodML-15
60KeyChal-13
60NuHi-14
61GolPre-8
61NuSco-476
63BasMagM-19
66CarCoi-1
68LauWorS-31
73HalofFPP-5
74Car193T-7
74Car193T-28
74LauAllG-36
74NewYorNTDiS-9
74NewYorNTDiS-29
75SpoHobBG-1
76RowExh-3
76ShaPiz-63
77BobParHoF-18
77GalGloG-52
80LauFamF-5
80MarExhH-8
80PacLeg-12
80PerHaloFP-66
80SSPHOF-66
81ConTSN-21
82DiaCla-12
83ConMar-45
83DonHOFH-29
84OCoandSI-126
85FegMurCG-3
86ConSer1-10
86SpoDecG-14
87Car193T-1
87SpoRea-17
88ConNatA-5
88ConSer4-8
88GreBasS-27
88WilMulP-3
90BasWit-71
90PerGreM-18
90SweBasG-6
91ConTSN-3
91ConTSNP-34
91HomCooC-8
91LinDri-50
91SweBasG-138
91TopArc1-326
92CarMcD-15
92ConTSN-428
92ConTSN-635
92ConTSNCI-19
92St.VinHHS-2
93ActPacA-106
93ActPacA2-40G
93ConTSN-928
93ConTSNP-1170
93DiaStaES-124
93Hoy-2
93LegFoi-2
93SpeHOFI-5
93UppDecAH-38
94ConTSN-1109
94ConTSN-1170
94ConTSNB-1109
94ConTSNB-1170
94TedWil-82
94UppDecTAE-45
95MegRut-24
96NoiSatP-3
Dean, Greg
96HigDesMB-10
Dean, Jeff
83MiaMarT-11
Dean, Jimmy
93NegLeaRL2-7
Dean, John
77SalPirT-11A
77SalPirT-11B
Dean, Kevin
87WesPalBEP-660
88JacExpB-13
88JacExpP-984
89IndIndC-21
89IndIndP-1225
90CMC-625
90GreBraS-6
90ProAAAF-204
90TucTorC-23
90TucTorP-214
91JacGenLD-556
91JacGenP-936
91LinDriAA-556
92JacGenS-330
Dean, Mark
93GleFalRC-11
93GleFalRF-4009
94NewJerCF-3423
95PeoChiTI-5
Dean, Roger
85UtiBluST-9
Dean, Steve
90OklSoo-10
Dean, Tommy (Tommy Douglas)
69PadVol-2
69Top-641
70OPC-234
70Top-234
71MLBOffS-225
71OPC-364
71Top-364
90DodTar-174
DeAngelis, Steve
86ReaPhiP-7
87MaiGuiP-13
88PhiTas-27
88ReaPhiP-877
89QuaCitAB-29
89QuaCitAGS-26
90MidAngGS-3
Deares, Greg
93GleFalRC-12
93GleFalRF-4017
DeArmas, Roly
80CarMudF-18
87ClePhiP-19
88MarPhiS-10
89MarPhiS-35
91MarPhiC-29
92MarPhiC-30
92MarPhiF-3075
93ClePhiC-27
94WhiSoxK-30
95WhiSoxK-31
Dease, Don'l
90IdaFalBP-3247
Deasley, Pat (Thomas H.)
86OldJudN-3
87BucN28-65
87FouBasHN-3
87OldJudN-129
88AugBecN-7
88GandBCGCE-12
90KalBatN-11
DeBattista, Dan
77SalPirT-12
Debee, Rich
87MemChiP-11
89OmaRoyP-1739
90OmaRoyC-23
DeBerry, Hank (John Herman)
21Nei-101
22E120-138
22W572-21
22W573-30
25Exh-9
26SpoComoA-14
27AmeCarE-30
29ExhFou-4
29PorandAR-15
90DodTar-175
DeBerry, Joe
91BilMusP-3759
91BilMusSP-14
91FroRowDP-30
92CedRapRC-14
92CedRapRF-1076
92ClaFS7-46
92StaCluD-34
92UppDecML-126
93AlbYanF-2168
94AbaYanF-1453
95NorNavTI-17
95TamYanYI-4
96NorNavB-6
96StoPorB-13
DeBoer, Rob
94SouOreAC-5
94SouOreAF-3626
95WesMicWTI-18
96HunStaTI-6
96ModA'sB-8
DeBoever, William
86JamExpP-4
DeBold, Rusty
85MiaHur-2
DeBord, Bob
83ChaRoyT-18
DeBottis, Marc
88SyrChiP-828
DeBrand, Genaro
90NiaFalRP-12
Debrand, Juan
93UtiBluSC-8

93UtiBluSF-3539
Debrand, Rafael
93St.CatBJC-7
93St.CatBJF-3985
Debrino, Rob
94ForWayWC-7
94ForWayWF-2002
95ForMyeMTI-8
DeBryn, Norm
90ArkRaz-28
DeBruhl, Randy
93PriRedC-6
93PriRedF-4181
94ChaWheC-7
94ChaWheF-2705
Debus, John Eric
81VerBeaDT-4
84AlbDukC-164
86AlbDukP-5
92GreFalDSP-29
87AlbDukP-15
88AlbDukC-15
88AlbDukP-269
89AlbDukC-12
89AlbDukP-76
90SanAntMGS-3
91VerBeaDP-792
93GreFalDSP-30
94VerBeaDC-27
94VerBeaDF-90
95VerBeaDTI-30
96MauStiHWB-31
96VerBeaDB-1
DeBusschere, Dave (David A.)
63Top-54A
63Top-54B
63WhiSoxTS-5
64Top-247
64TopVen-247
64WhiSoxTS-7
65Top-297
78TCM60I-246
DeButch, Mike
86BeaGolGP-9
87TexLeaAF-1
87WicPilRD-1
88WicPilRD-10
89JacMetGS-19
89TidTidP-1959
90CMC-366
90ProAAAF-281
90TidTidC-15
90TidTidP-550
90TopTVM-39
92LonTigF-639
92LonTigS-405
Decatur, Art (A.R.)
25Exh-10
27Exh-21
90DodTar-176
DeCelle, Mike
96ButCopKB-12
97Top-472
DeChavez, Oscar
83IdaFalAT-3
84ModA'sC-9
85ModA'sC-5
Decillis, Dean
88LakTigS-9
89LonTigP-1372
90CMC-397
90ProAAAF-384
90TolMudHC-20
90TolMudHP-154
91LinDriAA-380
91LonTigLD-380
91LonTigP-1883
92TolMudHF-1050
92TolMudHS-583
94TreThuF-2125
DeCinces, Doug (Douglas V.)
75OPC-617
75Top-617
76OPC-438
76SSP-387
76Top-438
77BurCheD-44
77Hos-15
77OPC-228
77Top-216
78Hos-10
78OPC-192
78Top-9
79Hos-54
79OPC-217
79Top-421
80OPC-322
80Top-615
81AllGamPI-31
81Don-352
81Fle-173
81Fle-195
81FleStiC-90
81OPC-188
81Top-188
82Don-279
82Fle-162
82FleSta-142
82OPC-174
82Top-564
82TopSti-142
82TopTra-26T
83AllGamPI-31
83Don-216
83Fle-85
83FleSta-50
83FleSti-30
83FraBroR-37
83OPC-341
83PerCreC-22
83PerCreCG-22
83SevCoi-7
83Top-341
83TopSti-46
83TopSti-155
83TopSti-171
84AllGamPI-122
84AngSmo-7
84Don-230
84DonActAS-6
84Fle-514
84FunFooP-73
84Nes792-790
84OPC-82
84Top-790
84TopSti-229
84TopTif-790
85AllGamPI-31
85AngSmo-6
85Don-2
85Don-179
85DonActA-51
85DonSupD-2
85Fle-299
85Lea-2
85OPC-111
85Top-111
85TopSti-222
85TopTif-111
86AngSmo-6
86Don-57
86DonHig-39
86DonWaxBC-PC6
86Fle-153
86OPC-257
86Spo-173
86Top-257
86TopSti-178
86TopTat-12
86TopTif-257
87AngSmo-17
87Don-356
87DonOpeD-1
87Fle-77
87FleGlo-77
87FleHotS-14
87FleMin-29
87FleStiC-34
87OPC-22
87SevCoi-W1
87Spo-106
87SpoTeaP-11
87StuPan-16
87Top-22
87TopGloS-52
87TopSti-182
87TopTif-22
88Fle-31
88FleGlo-31
88OPC-141
88Sco-239
88ScoGlo-239
88Spo-185
88Top-446
88TopTif-446
89AngSmo-16
91LinDri-19
91OriCro-99
91SweBasG-23
93UppDecAH-39
94TedWil-15
DeCinces, Tim
96BluOriB-9
Deck, Billy
96AppLeaAB-20
96JohCitCTI-7
Deck, Todd
85CloHSS-12
Decker, Edward
87OldJudN-130
Decker, Joe (George Henry)
71MLBOffS-30
71OPC-98
71Top-98
72Top-612
73OPC-311
73Top-311
74OPC-469
74Top-469
74TopSta-206
75Hos-96
75OPC-102
75Top-102
76OPC-636
76SSP-210
76Top-636
78SanJosMMC-6
78TwiFri-29
79SpolndT-12
82SalLakCGT-25
83SalLakCGT-10
89TopSenL-112
90NiaFalRP-29
91PacSenL-101
Decker, Marty (Dee Martin)
82OklCit8T-22
83PorBeaT-18
84LasVegSC-226
85LasVegSC-107
Decker, Steve
89SanJosGB-11
89SanJosGCLC-227
89SanJosGP-446
89SanJosGS-6
89Sta-84
90ProAaA-72
90ShrCapP-1445
90ShrCapS-5
90TexLeaAGS-24
90TopMag-55
91Bow-622
91Cla1-T7
91Cla2-T64
91Cla2-T100
91ClaGam-198
91Don-428
91Fle-260
91GiaMot-3
91GiaPacGaE-13
91GiaSFE-7
91Lea-441
91OPCPre-33
91Sco-710
91ScoAllF-2
91ScoHotR-8
91ScoRoo-12
91SevCoi-NC4
91StaClu-569
91Stu-260
91StuPre-16
91TopDeb90-37
91TopTra-29T
91TopTraT-29T
91Ult-319
91UppDec-25
92Don-389
92Fle-633
92OPC-593
92PanSti-211
92PhoFirF-2824
92PhoFirS-381
92Pin-63
92Sco-317
92Sco100RS-56
92SkyAAAF-175
92StaClu-417
92Top-593
92TopGol-593
92TopGolW-593
92TopMic-593
92TriA AAS-381
92Ult-289
92UppDec-173
93Don-260
93Don-768
93Fle-425
93MarUSPC-4S
93MarUSPC-8C
93PacSpa-459
93Pin-233
93Sco-653
93StaClu-692
93StaCluFDI-692
93StaCluMarl-15
93StaCluMOP-692
93Top-544
93TopGol-544
93TopInaM-544
93TopMic-544
93Ult-372
93UppDec-744
93UppDecGold-744
96GiaMot-24
Decksen, Robert
90BelBreB-26
DeClue, Jon
96MidAngB-11
96MidAngOHP-9
DeCordova, David
87St.PetCP-14
DeCosta, Bob
83VisOakF-8
DeDario, Joe
90NiaFalRP-31
Dede, Artie
90DodTar-928
Dedeaux, Rod (Raoul)
85Top-389
85TopTif-389
90DodTar-177
90SouCalS-4
Dedmon, Jeff (Jeffrey L.)
81DurBulT-17
82DurBulT-16
84TopTra-30T
84TopTraT-30T
85Don-554
85Fle-323
85RicBraT-4
85Top-602
85TopTif-602
86BraPol-49
86Don-443
86Fle-513
86Top-129
86TopTif-129
87BraSmo-7
87Don-314
87Fle-514
87FleGlo-514
87Top-373
87TopTif-373
88Don-325
88Fle-537
88FleGlo-537
88IndGat-50
88Sco-498
88ScoGlo-498
88StaLinBra-4
88Top-469
88TopTif-469
89IndIndP-1214
Dedos, Felix
87WinHavRSP-2
89BlaYNPRWL-113
89WinHavRSS-3
Dedrick, James
91KanCouCC-5
91KanCouCP-2653
91KanCouCTI-4
92FreKeyC-15
93BowBayF-2183
94OriPro-24
94RocRedWF-991
94RocRedWTI-6
95BowBayTI-28
95RocRedWTI-11
96RocRedWB-10
Dedrick, Tim
92FreKeyF-1799
Deeble, Jon
95AusFut-21
95AusFut-89
Deer, Rob (Robert George)
79CedRapGT-28
80CliGiaT-20
84PhoGiaC-4
85Fle-648
85GiaMot-25
85GiaPos-8
86BrePol-45
86Fle-538
86FleUpd-33
86Top-249
86TopTif-249
86TopTra-31T
86TopTraT-31T
87BrePol-45
87BreTeal-5
87ClaGam-43
87ClaUpdY-141
87Don-274
87DonOpeD-57
87Fle-344
87FleBasA-14
87FleExcS-15
87FleGlo-344
87FleMin-30
87OPC-188
87Spo-172
87SpoTeaP-19
87Top-547
87TopCoi-10
87TopGloS-22
87TopMinL-59
87TopSti-194
87TopTif-547
88BrePol-45
88Don-274
88DonBasB-109
88Fle-163
88FleGlo-163
88FleStiC-36
88OPC-33
88PanSti-128
88RedFolSB-18
88Sco-95
88ScoGlo-95
88Spo-183
88StaLinBre-6
88Top-33
88TopBig-151
88TopSti-198
88TopTif-33
89Bow-146
89BowTif-146
89BreGar-4
89BrePol-45
89BreYea-45
89ClaLigB-39
89Don-173
89DonBasB-71
89Fle-184
89FleGlo-184
89OPC-364
89PanSti-376
89RedFolSB-34
89Sco-72
89Spo-111
89Top-364
89Top-759
89TopBig-78
89TopSti-202
89TopTif-364
89TopTif-759
89UppDec-442
90Bow-401
90BowTif-401
90BreMilB-4
90BrePol-45
90Don-55
90Fle-320
90FleCan-320
90Lea-322
90MLBBasB-80
90OPC-615
90PanSti-102
90PubSti-494
90RedFolSB-24
90Sco-390
90Spo-137
90Top-615
90TopBig-74
90TopSti-204
90TopTif-615
90UppDec-176

90VenSti-136
91Bow-132
91Don-729
91Fle-580
91FleUpd-23
91Lea-237
91OPC-192
91PanFreS-209
91RedFolS-26
91Sco-248
91ScoRoo-47T
91StaClu-539
91Stu-52
91TigCok-44
91Top-192
91TopDesS-192
91TopMic-192
91TopTif-192
91TopTra-30T
91TopTraT-30T
91UppDec-272
91UppDec-726
92Bow-363
92Don-532
92Fle-132
92Lea-193
92OPC-441
92PanSti-109
92Pin-348
92Sco-56
92StaClu-92
92Stu-172
92Top-441
92TopGol-441
92TopGolW-441
92TopMic-441
92Ult-58
92UppDec-294
93Bow-332
93Don-231
93DonLonBL-LL1
93DonSpiotG-SG10
93Fle-225
93Lea-246
93PacSpa-106
93PanSti-119
93Pin-167
93PinHomRC-15
93Sco-636
93Sel-186
93SelRoo-2T
93SP-235
93StaClu-357
93StaCluFDI-357
93StaCluMOP-357
93Stu-26
93TigGat-5
93Top-243
93TopGol-243
93TopInaM-243
93TopMic-243
93TriPla-137
93Ult-195
93UppDec-217
93UppDecGold-217
93USPlaCA-5C
94BreMilB-114
94ColC-90
94ColChoGS-90
94ColChoSS-90
94Don-74
94Fle-30
94Sco-475
94ScoGolR-475
94StaClu-139
94StaCluFDI-139
94StaCluGR-139
94StaCluMOP-139
94Top-531
94TopGol-531
94TopSpa-531
96LasVegSB-11
Dees, Charlie (Charles Henry)
63AngJayP-4
64Top-159
64TopVen-159
Defelice, Mike
95ArkTraTI-10
96LouRedB-15
DeFillippis, Art
75SpoIndC-20
76OPC-595
76SacSolC-12
77TacTwiDQ-19
DeFord, Logan
92MisStaB-11
DeFrancesco, Anthony
85GreHorT-25
86WinHavRSP-7
87NewBriRSP-15
88ChaLooB-7
88NasSouTI-7
89ChaLooB-3
89ChaLooGS-8
90ChaLooGS-10
90NasSouP-235
90ProAAAF-547
91LinDriAAA-255
91NasSouLD-255
91NasSouP-2159
92RenSilSCLC-39
92SouOreAC-30
93SouOreAF-4082
DeFreites, Art (Arturo S.)
76IndIndTI-4
77IndIndTI-20
78IndIndTI-22
80Top-677
85DomLeaS-155
91PacSenL-77
DeGerick, Mike
77FriOneYW-116
Degifico, Vince (Vincent)
87ElmPio(C-16
89Sta-119
89WinHavRSS-4
90NewBriRSB-16
90NewBriRSP-1325
90NewBriRSS-3
DeGrasse, Tim
91HamRedC-2
91HamRedP-4032
92HamRedC-15
92HamRedF-1586
93SprCarC-6
93SprCarF-1843
Deguero, Jerry
86ModA'sP-6
DeHart, Greg
78NewWayCT-9
79BurBeeT-20
80BurBeeT-6
83SanJosBC-25
DeHart, Rick
87BirBarB-28
92AlbPolC-15
92AlbPolF-2299
93SanBerSC-6
93SanBerSF-765
94FloStaLAF-FSL51
94WesPalBEC-6
94WesPalBEF-31
95HarSenTI-33
96HarSenB-11
Dehdashtion, Derek
92RocExpC-14
92RocExpF-2118
Deidel, Jim
92YanWIZ7-41
Deiley, Lou
87AshTouP-23
88OscAstS-7
Deisel, Pat
90DodTar-929
Deitz, Tim
86CedRapRT-5
88ChaLooB-15
89GreBraB-12
89GreBraP-1175
89GreBraS-5
Dejak, Tom
78DunBluJT-5
80KnoBluJT-16
DeJardin, Bobby (Bob)
88OneYanP-2044
89PriWilCS-4
90AlbYanB-14
90AlbYanP-1039
90Bes-212
91AlbYanLD-3
91AlbYanP-1015
91LinDriAA-3
92ColCliF-358
92ColCliP-16
92ColCliS-102
92OPC-179
92SkyAAAF-45
92Top-179
92TopGol-179
92TopGolW-179
92TopMic-179
93ColCliF-1116
94ColCliF-2957
94ColCliP-7
95RocRedWTI-12
DeJardin, Brad
88AlaGolTI-8
91KinIndP-336
91SydWavF-13
Dejarld, John
90GreFalDSP-24
DeJean, Mike
92OneYanC-18
93ClaFS7-174
93GreHorC-7
93GreHorF-880
94FloStaLAF-FSL18
94TamYanC-7
94TamYanF-2376
95NorNavTI-33
96ColSprSSTI-10
96NewHavRB-8
DeJesus, Ivan
74AlbDukTI-68
74AlbDukTI-5
76SSP-76
77CubJewT-6
78OPC-158
78SSP270-256
78Top-152
79Hos-88
79OPC-209
79Top-398
80OPC-349
80Top-691
81AllGamPI-111
81CokTeaS-15
81Don-483A
81Don-483B
81Fle-297
81OPC-54
81Top-54
81TopScr-94
81TopSti-156
81TopSupHT-24
82Don-14
82Don-48
82Fle-593
82FleSta-95
82OPC-313
82Top-484
82TopSti-32
82TopTra-27T
83AllGamPI-111
83Don-399
83Fle-157
83FleSta-51
83FleSti-169
83OPC-233
83PhiTas-7
83Top-587
83TopSti-271
84AllGamPI-21
84Don-427
84Fle-26
84Nes792-279
84OPC-279
84PhiTas-29
84Top-279
84TopSti-121
84TopTif-279
85AllGamPI-112
85CarTeal-9
85Don-204
85Fle-248
85PhiTas-11
85ThoMcAD-28
85Top-791
85TopTif-791
85TopTifT-30T
85TopTra-30T
86CarTeal-12
86Don-449
86Fle-34
86Top-178
86TopTif-178
88BlaYNPRWL-165
89BlaYNPRWL-140
89TolMudHP-774
89UppDec-355
90DodTar-178
90EliSenL-4
90KisDodD-29
92SanBerC-27
92SanBerSF-228
92YanWIZ8-42
94OscAstC-28
94OscAstF-1156
96KisCobB-3
DeJesus, Javier
93EliTwiC-9
93EliTwiF-3411
94ForWayWC-8
94ForWayWF-2003
94MidLeaAF-MDW12
95Exc-81
DeJesus, Jorge
78NewWayCT-10
80BurBeeT-21
DeJesus, Jose
85Ft.MyeRT-12
85MexCitTT-19
86Ft.MyeRP-7
87MemChiB-9
87MemChiP-5
88BasAmeAAB-14
88BlaYNPRWL-37
88MemChiB-18
89BlaYNPRWL-39
89Don-558
89Fle-280
89FleGlo-280
89OmaRoyC-6
89OmaRoyP-1735
89UppDec-769
90Fle-104
90FleCan-104
90FleUpd-42
90Lea-415
90OPC-596
90ProAAAF-294
90Sco-587
90Sco100RS-95
90ScrRedBP-592
90Spo-131
90Top-596
90TopTif-596
90UppDec-255
91Don-596
91Fle-394
91Lea-200
91OPC-232
91PhiMed-12
91Sco-623
91Sco100RS-16
91StaClu-104
91Top-232
91TopDesS-232
91TopMic-232
91TopTif-232
91Ult-261
91UppDec-486
92Don-300
92Fle-528
92OPC-471
92Pin-172
92Sco-380
92Top-471
92TopGol-471
92TopGolW-471
92TopMic-471
92UppDec-631
94OmaRoyF-1217
95OmaRoyTI-7
DeJesus, Malvin
92NiaFalRC-4
92NiaFalRF-3329
93FayGenC-9
93FayGenF-134
93NiaFalRF-3396
94FayGenC-8
94FayGenF-2154
DeJohn, Mark (Mark Stephen)
75TidTidTI-8
80EvaTriT-2
80VenLeaS-114
81EvaTriT-13
83EvaTriT-24
87SavCarP-26
88SprCarB-26
89JohCitCS-24
90JohCitCS-28
91LinDriAAA-249
91LouRedLD-249
91LouRedP-2932
91LouRedTI-30
92LonTigF-648
92LonTigS-424
DeJonghe, Emile
39WorWidGV-9
Dejulio, Frank
80CedRapRT-15
DeKneef, Mike
91Cla/Bes-171
91WinHavRSC-17
91WinHavRSP-496
92NewBriRSF-440
92NewBriRSS-481
DeKraai, Brad
81BurBeeT-21
82BelBreF-22
Del Guercio, Ted
55JetPos-3
Del Juego, Antes
80VenLeaS-218
Dela Cuesta, Clara
91HawWomS-2
DeLa Maza, Roland
93WatIndC-5
93WatIndF-3552
94ColRedC-6
94ColRedF-435
95KinIndTI-8
96CanIndB-9
Dela, Fernando
96CedRapKTI-8
DelaCruz, Anthony
89BurIndS-8
89Sta-177
DeLaCruz, Carlos
87DayBeaAP-6
88UtiBluSP-17
89SouBenWSGS-12
90BirBarB-14
90BirBarP-1102
93LimRocDWB-32
96FayGenB-11
Delacruz, Fernando
96BoiHawB-10
DeLaCruz, Francisco
87SpoIndP-15
DeLaCruz, Gerry
77CliDodT-4
DeLaCruz, Hector
87DunBluJP-938
88KnoBluJB-8
89SyrChiC-18
89SyrChiMB-8
89SyrChiP-816
90CMC-346
90ProAAAF-363
90SyrChiC-20
90SyrChiMB-4
90SyrChiP-583
DeLaCruz, Lorenzo
93MedHatBJF-3749
93MedHatBJSP-20
94HagSunC-6
94HagSunF-2742
95KnoSmoF-51
96KnoSmoB-11
DeLaCruz, Marcelino
92ChaRaiC-9
92SpoIndC-26
92SpoIndF-1299
Delacruz, Narcisco
94MedHatBJF-3675
94MedHatBJSP-15
95StCatSTI-10
Delafield, Glenn
92GulCoaYF-3701
Delafield, Wil
94GreBatF-487
95GreBatTI-9
97GreBatC-6
Delahanty, Ed (Edward J.)
03BreE10-33
36PC7AlbHoF-33
50CalHOFW-25
63GadFunC-36
72FleFamF-38
72LauGreF-10
75FlePio-10
76ShaPiz-33
80PerHaloFP-33
80SSPHOF-33
83PhiPosGPaM-5
84GalHaloFRL-33

87OldJudN-131
89HOFStiB-31
90BasWit-70
94DukCabN-2
94OriofB-74
95May-33
Delahanty, Frank (Frank G.)
09T206-417
Delahanty, Jim (James C.)
07TigACDPP-19
08AmeCarE-73
08RosComP-77
09ColChiE-75
09T206-88
09TigTaCP-5
10DomDisP-31
10NadE1-15
10StaCarE-10
10SweCapPP-23
10W555-21
11BasBatEU-17
11PloCanE-23
11S74Sil-14
11SpoLifCW-89
11SpoLifM-57
11T205-37
12ColRedB-75
12ColTinT-75
12HasTriFT-28
12HasTriFT-47
12PhiCarE-8
12T207-43
14CraJacE-81
15CraJacE-81
Delahanty, Joseph
08RosComP-162
09PC7HHB-11
12ImpTobC-67
DeLaHoya, Javier
89HigSchPLS-13
90VerBeaDS-10
90YakBeaTI-2
91BakDodCLC-18
92VerBeaDC-22
92VerBeaDF-2868
93SanAntMF-2998
94Bow-178
94PorSeaDF-672
94PorSeaDTI-13
DeLaHoz, Mike (Miguel A.)
61Top-191
62Top-123
62TopVen-123
63IndJayP-4
63Top-561
64Top-216
64TopVen-216
65OPC-182
65Top-182
66Top-346
66TopVen-346
67Top-372
DeLaMata, Fred
87MiaMarP-21
Delancer, Julio
86KenTwiP-7
DeLancey, Bill (William P.)
34DiaStaR-81
35WheBB1-10
36WorWidGV-15
74Car193T-8
92ConTSN-625
Delaney, Donovan
94EugEmeC-8
94EugEmeF-3725
95WilBluRTI-40
96HonShaHWB-30
96WilBluRB-9
Delaney, Jack
28W513-90
Delaney, Sean
92AppFoxF-3105
93RocRoyC-10
93RocRoyF-719
95SprSulTI-7
96WicWraB-15
DeLaNuez, Rex
89EliTwiS-24
90Bes-118
90KenTwiB-2
90KenTwiP-2305
90KenTwiS-8
91Cla/Bes-147
91VisOakC-21
91VisOakP-1753
92ClaFS7-199
92OrlSunRF-2857
92OrlSunRS-503
92SkyAA F-216
93NasXprF-415
95JacSunTI-8
Delany, Dennis
79ArkTraT-16
81ArkTraT-4
DeLao, Mike
85DurBulT-17
88FayGenP-1105
89LonTigP-1367
90EasLeaAP-EL48
91FayGenC-30
DeLaRosa, Benny
77ChaPatT-4
81BufBisT-6
DeLaRosa, Cesar
87SpaPhiP-24
88QuaCitAGS-23
89PalSprACLC-43
89PalSprAP-475
DeLaRosa, Domingo
87PocGiaTB-11
89CliGiaP-905
DeLaRosa, Elvis
94BriTigC-9
94BriTigF-3506
DeLaRosa, Francisco
89FreKeyS-4
90CMC-764
90HagSunB-23
90HagSunP-1406
90HagSunS-7
90ProAaA-3
90RocRedWGC-29
91LinDriAAA-453
91RocRedWLD-453
91RocRedWP-1895
92ColCliF-344
92ColCliP-4
92ColCliS-103
92StaClu-61
92TopDeb91-44
93ColCliF-1104
93ColCliP-3
93LimRocDWB-39
95LouRedF-272
DeLaRosa, Jesus
75IowOakT-10
80KnoBluJT-20
89PacSenL-57
DeLaRosa, Juan
88MyrBeaBJP-1175
89MyrBeaBJP-1458
90DunBluJS-7
91KnoBluJLD-355
91KnoBluJP-1779
91LinDriAA-355
92ClaFS7-436
92KnoBluJF-3002
92KnoBluJS-380
92UppDecML-73
93Bow-519
93ClaFS7-50
93ClaGolF-92
93ExcFS7-241
93LimRocDWB-28
93SyrChiF-1010
94SalLakBF-829
DeLaRosa, Maximo
86DurBulP-8
92BurIndC-30
92BurIndF-1670
93BurIndC-9
93BurIndF-3289
94ColRedC-7
94ColRedF-436
94SouAtlLAF-SAL7
95KinIndTI-9
96CanIndB-10
DeLaRosa, Miguel
96ChaRivTI-9610
DeLaRosa, Nelson
82AleDukT-25
83AleDukT-23
85NasPirT-6
Delarwelle, Chris
90Bes-229
91VisOakC-14
91VisOakP-1746
92OrlSunRF-2852
92ProFS7-96
Delas, Mickey
88BriTigP-1883
89FayGenP-1590
Delbianco, Ronnie
52LavPro-29
DeLeeuw, Karel
75WatRoyT-9
76WatRoyT-5
DeLeon, Elcilio
93LetMouF-4145
93LetMouSP-5
94WelPirC-8
94WelPirF-3487
DeLeon, Gerbacio
90MadMusB-14
DeLeon, Huascar
90BasCitRS-5
91BasCitRC-13
92BasCitRC-11
DeLeon, Jesus
87Ft.MyeRP-11
88AppFoxP-155
88MidLeaAGS-39
DeLeon, John
81MiaOriT-7
DeLeon, Jose
94BelMarC-11
94BelMarF-3249
96JohCitCTI-8
DeLeon, Jose Chestaro
81BufBisT-4
82PorBeaT-1
84Don-628
84Fle-218
84Nes792-581
84Top-581
84TopTif-581
85AllGamPI-166
85Don-308
85Fle-463
85OPC-385
85Pir-5
85Top-385
85TopTif-385
86Don-235
86Fle-607
86OPC-75
86Top-75
86TopTat-3
86TopTif-75
87Don-457
87Fle-494
87FleGlo-494
87Top-421
87TopTif-421
87WhiSoxC-7
88CarSmo-4
88Don-59
88Fle-395
88FleGlo-395
88FleStiC-15
88FleUpd-119
88FleUpdG-119
88OPC-23
88Sco-508
88ScoGlo-508
88ScoRoo-7T
88ScoRooG-7T
88StaLinWS-5
88Top-634
88TopBig-194
88TopTif-634
88TopTra-34T
88TopTraT-34T
89Bow-431
89BowTif-431
89CarSmo-5
89Don-437
89Fle-449
89FleGlo-449
89OPC-107
89PanSti-177
89RedFolSB-35
89Sco-115
89Top-107
89TopMinL-35
89TopTif-107
89UppDec-293
90Bow-186
90BowTif-186
90CarSmo-6
90Don-536
90DonBesN-59
90Fle-248
90FleAwaW-11
90FleCan-248
90Lea-485
90OPC-257
90PanSti-334
90PubSti-217
90RedFolSB-25
90Sco-309
90Spo-76
90Top-257
90TopBig-31
90TopGaloC-2
90TopMinL-74
90TopSti-38
90TopTif-257
90TopTVCa-11
90UppDec-697
90VenSti-137
91Bow-400
91CarPol-48
91Don-128
91Fle-631A
91Fle-631B
91Lea-190
91OPC-711
91Sco-221
91StaClu-455
91Top-711
91TopDesS-711
91TopMic-711
91TopTif-711
91Ult-288
91UppDec-220
92Bow-265
92CarPol-3
92Don-246
92Fle-576
92Lea-227
92OPC-85
92PanSti-178
92Pin-341
92Sco-81
92StaClu-67
92Top-85
92TopGol-85
92TopGolW-85
92TopKid-30
92TopMic-85
92Ult-565
92UppDec-458
93Don-464
93Fle-487
93PacSpa-575
93PhiMed-10
93StaCluP-25
93Ult-438
94FleUpd-24
94StaCluT-130
94StaCluTFDI-130
94WhiSoxK-6
95Don-126
95DonPreP-126
95Fle-114
95Pac-85
95WhiSoxK-5
DeLeon, Julio
87PorChaRP-20
DeLeon, Luis (Luis Antonio)
80ArkTraT-7
80TacTigT-27
81ChaLooT-4
82ChaChaT-14
82Don-588
82Top-561
83ChaChaT-9
83Don-296
83Fle-355
83FleSta-52
83FleSti-224
83OPC-323
83Top-323
84Don-162
84Fle-297
84Nes792-38
84PadMot-17
84PadSmo-6
84Top-38
84TopTif-38
85Don-406
85Fle-29
85PadMot-11
85ThoMcAD-29
85Top-689
85TopTif-689
86Fle-318
86Top-286
86TopTif-286
87RocRedWP-16
87RocRedWT-2
88BlaYNPRWL-67
88TucTorC-10
88TucTorJP-8
88TucTorP-174
89BlaYNPRWL-73
89CalCanC-1
91OriCro-100
DeLeon, Paulo
73CedRapAT-13
74CedRapAT-27
75DubPacT-20
DeLeon, Pedro
86AshTouP-7
88OscAstS-8
89PriWilCS-5
89Sta-88
DeLeon, Pichy
84MaiGuiT-11
DeLeon, Rafael
86Ft.MyeRP-8
DeLeon, Reymundo
95EugEmeTI-19
DeLeon, Roberto
89SumBraP-1113
90Bes-166
90BurBraB-11
90BurBraP-2351
90DurBraG-10
92SpoIndC-12
92SpoIndF-1300
93WatDiaC-11
93WatDiaF-1774
94RanCucQC-11
94RanCucQF-1644
95MemChiTI-25
Deleon, Santos
94BelMarC-13
94BelMarF-3250
DeLeon, Yobanne
92AppFoxC-16
92AppFoxF-987
92BasCitRF-3848
Delgado, Alex
90WinHavRSS-4
91LynRedSC-16
91LynRedSP-1206
92WinHavRSF-1779
93ForLauRSC-8
93ForLauRSFP-1599
93LinVenB-121
94VenLinU-215
95LinVen-47
95PawRedSDD-9
95PawRedTI-20
96TreThuB-16
96Ult-313
96UltGolM-313
97Pac-37
97PacLigB-37
97PacSil-37
Delgado, Carlos
89St.CatBJP-2077
90ProAaA-184
90St.CatBJP-3454
91Cla/Bes-63
91MyrBeaHC-12
91MyrBeaHP-2946
91SouAtlLAGP-SAL37
92Bow-127
92ClaBluBF-BC6
92ClaFS7-90
92ClaRedB-BC6
92DunBluJC-20
92DunBluJF-2003
92ProFS7-170
92SyrChiMB-4
92UppDecML-50
92UppDecML-53
92UppDecML-264
92UppDecMLPotY-PY4
93Bow-379
93Bow-693
93ClaFisN-4
93ClaFS7-AU1
93ClaGolF-87

93ClaGolLF-5
93ClaMVPF-10
93ClaPla&MotYF-PM1
93ClaPro-2
93ClaYouG-YG2
93ExcAllF-6
93ExcFS7-242
93KnoSmoF-1252
93SP-275
93StaClu-520
93StaCluFDI-520
93StaCluMOP-520
93Top-701
93TopGol-701
93TopInaM-701
93TopMic-701
93UppDec-425
93UppDecGold-425
94BluJayP-4
94BluJayUSPC-8D
94Bow-341
94Bow-637
94BowBes-R83
94BowBes-X105
94BowBesR-R83
94BowBesR-X105
94ColC-4
94ColChoGS-4
94ColChoSS-4
94Don-568
94ExtBas-189
94ExtBasRS-5
94Fin-423
94FinJum-423
94FinRef-423
94Fla-117
94FlaWavotF-A2
94FleAllR-M3
94FleMajLP-9
94FleUpd-96
94FUnPac-4
94LeaGolR-10
94LeaL-77
94LeaLimRP-4
94OPC-100
94OPCHotP-5
94Pin-413
94Pin-SR1
94PinArtP-413
94PinMusC-413
94PinNewG-NG18
94PinRooTP-1
94Sco-614
94ScoBoyoS-45
94ScoGolR-614
94ScoRoo-RT102
94ScoRooGR-RT102
94ScoRooS-RT102
94ScoRooSR-SU1
94Sel-193
94Sel-RY1
94SelRooS-RS4
94SP-41
94SPDieC-41
94SPHol-6
94SPHolDC-6
94SpoRoo-132
94SpoRooAP-132
94SpoRooRS-TR4
94StaClu-600
94StaClu-629
94StaCluFDI-600
94StaCluFDI-629
94StaCluGR-600
94StaCluGR-629
94StaCluMOP-600
94StaCluMOP-629
94StaCluT-168
94StaCluTFDI-168
94Stu-27
94Top-686
94TopGol-686
94TopSpa-686
94TriPla-296
94Ult-437
94UltAllR-2
94UltAllRJ-2
94UppDec-8
94UppDecED-8
94UppDecMLS-MM6
94UppDecMLSED-MM6
94UppDecNG-2
94UppDecNGED-2
95ActPac2GF-4G
95ActPacF-6
95ActPacF-65
95Baz-124
95BluJayUSPC-8C
95Bow-431
95ColCho-147
95ColChoGS-147
95ColChoSE-52
95ColChoSEGS-52
95ColChoSESS-52
95ColChoSS-147
95Don-37
95DonPreP-37
95Fin-16
95FinPowK-PK4
95FinRef-16
95Fla-314
95Fle-92
95Lea-326
95Pac-443
95PacGolCDC-20
95PacGolP-12
95PacLatD-9
95PacPri-140
95Pin-277
95Pin-390
95PinArtP-277
95PinArtP-390
95PinMusC-277
95PinMusC-390
95PinNewB-NB7
95PinPin-4
95PinPinR-4
95PinTeaP-TP2
95PinUps-US6
95Sco-214
95ScoAi-AM12
95ScoGolR-214
95ScoHaloG-HG72
95ScoPlaTS-214
95ScoRul-SR29
95ScoRulJ-SR29
95Sel-56
95SelArtP-56
95SelCanM-CM8
95SelCerF-8
95SelCerPU-18
95SelCerPU9-18
95Spo-104
95SpoArtP-104
95SpoDouT-7
95StaClu-17
95StaCluFDI-17
95StaCluMOP-17
95StaCluSTWS-17
95StaCluVR-10
95StaCluVR-11
95Stu-43
95StuGolS-43
95Sum-28
95SumNewA-NA9
95SumNthD-28
95SyrChiTI-12
95Top-469
95TopCyb-263
95UC3-104
95UC3ArtP-104
95UC3CleS-CS7
95Ult-118
95UltGolM-118
95UppDec-38
95UppDecED-38
95UppDecEDG-38
95UppDecSE-199
95UppDecSEG-199
95Zen-14
96BluJayOH-8
96BowBes-63
96BowBesAR-63
96BowBesR-63
96Cir-94
96CirRav-94
96ColCho-352
96ColChoGS-352
96ColChoSS-352
96Don-360
96DonPreP-360
96EmoXL-130
96Fin-B30
96FinRef-B30
96Fle-272
96FleTif-272
96Lea-156
96LeaLim-16
96LeaLimG-16
96LeaPre-90
96LeaPreP-90
96LeaPrePB-156
96LeaPrePG-156
96LeaPrePS-156
96LeaPreSG-46
96LeaPreSte-46
96LeaSig-63
96LeaSigA-57
96LeaSigAG-57
96LeaSigAS-57
96LeaSigPPG-63
96LeaSigPPP-63
96Pac-436
96PacPri-P142
96PacPriG-P142
96PinAfi-143
96PinAfiAP-143
96ProSta-20
96Sco-139
96ScoDugC-A87
96ScoDugCAP-A87
96Sel-135
96SelArtP-135
96SelCer-77
96SelCerAP-77
96SelCerCB-77
96SelCerCR-77
96SelCerIP-18
96SelCerMB-77
96SelCerMG-77
96SelCerMR-77
96SP-181
96SPx-60
96SPxGol-60
96StaClu-346
96StaCluMOP-346
95StaCluVRMC-11
96Stu-57
96StuPrePB-57
96StuPrePG-57
96StuPrePS-57
96Sum-38
96SumAbo&B-38
96SumArtP-38
96SumFoi-38
96Ult-429
96UltGolM-429
96UppDec-470
96UppDecFSP-FS8
96Zen-62
96ZenArtP-62
96ZenMoz-15
97BluJayS-10
97Bow-23
97BowBes-70
97BowBesAR-70
97BowBesR-70
97BowChr-19
97BowChrI-19
97BowChrIR-19
97BowChrR-19
97BowInt-23
97Cir-208
97CirRav-208
97ColCho-498
97ColChoNF-NF33
97Don-46
97DonEli-85
97DonEliGS-85
97DonLim-110
97DonLim-185
97DonLimLE-110
97DonLimLE-185
97DonPre-35
97DonPreCttC-35
97DonPreP-46
97DonPrePGold-46
97Fin-57
97FinRef-57
97FlaSho-A64
97FlaSho-B64
97FlaSho-C64
97FlaShoLC-64
97FlaShoLC-B64
97FlaShoLC-C64
97FlaShoLCM-A64
97FlaShoLCM-B64
97FlaShoLCM-C64
97Fle-237
97FleTif-237
97Lea-25
97LeaFraM-25
97LeaFraMDC-25
97MetUni-182
97NewPin-119
97NewPinAP-119
97NewPinMC-119
97NewPinPP-119
97Pac-218
97PacLigB-218
97PacPri-73
97PacPriLB-73
97PacPriP-73
97PacSil-218
97Pin-32
97PinArtP-32
97PinIns-90
97PinInsCE-90
97PinInsDE-90
97PinMusC-32
97PinX-PSfF-25
97PinX-PSfFU-25
97ProMag-78
97ProMagML-78
97Sco-92
97ScoPreS-92
97ScoShoS-92
97ScoShoSAP-92
97Sel-76
97SelArtP-76
97SelRegG-76
97SP-179
97SpoIll-59
97SpoIllEE-59
97StaClu-204
97StaCluM-M8
97StaCluMat-204
97StaCluMOP-204
97StaCluMOP-M8
97Stu-49
97StuPrePG-49
97StuPrePS-49
97Top-92
97TopGal-149
97TopGalPPI-149
97Ult-142
97UltGolME-142
97UltPlaME-142
97UppDec-204
97UppDec-512
97UppDecRSF-RS17
97UppDecTTS-TS15

Delgado, Ernesto
96HagSunB-4

Delgado, Eugenio
92KanCouCTI-7

Delgado, Geno
93AlbPolC-11
93AlbPolF-2032

Delgado, Jesus
93LinVenB-254
95LinVen-188

Delgado, Jose
94DanBraC-6
94DanBraF-3538
95MacBraTI-6
96MacBraB-17

Delgado, Juan
83DayBeaAT-19
85DomLeaS-86
86ColAstP-10
87OscAstP-22

Delgado, Luis (Luis Felipe)
78SanJosMMC-14

Delgado, Pablo
89GenCubP-1879
90HunCubP-3296

Delgado, Richard
91ElmPioC-19
91ElmPioP-3265
91WinHavRSC-29
93LinVenB-40

Delgado, Roberto
92CliGiaC-7
93LimRocDWB-130

Delgado, Tim
90GenCubP-3045
90MiaMirIS-4
91PeoChiC-4
91PeoChiP-1335
91PeoChiTI-6
92WinSpiC-14
92WinSpiF-1203
93DayCubC-5
93DayCubF-852
93FloStaLAF-30
93OrlCubF-2778
94ClaGolF-49

Delgado, Wilson
95BurBeeTI-1
96Bow-208
96SanJosGB-4
97ColCho-454

Delgatti, Scott
75ForLauYS-27
77ForLauYS-22

DelGreco, Bobby (Robert G.)
52Top-353
53Top-48
57Top-94
60Top-486
61Top-154
61TopStal-53
62SalPlaC-16
62ShiPlaC-16
62Top-548
63Jel-91
63Pos-91
63Top-282
78TCM60I-259
83TopRep5-353
91TopArc1-48

DeLima, Rafael
86KenTwiP-8
87KenTwiP-6
88BasAmeAAB-15
88OrlTwiB-22
88SouLeaAJ-11
89PorBeaC-23
89PorBeaP-222
90CMC-574
90PorBeaC-22
90PorBeaP-191
90ProAAAF-261
91LinDriAA-478
91OrlSunRLD-478
91OrlSunRP-1861
92OrlSunRS-504
93LinVenB-140
94VenLinU-187
95LinVen-105

Deliza, Juan
77ShrCapT-4

Delker, Edward
33ButCanV-12
34DiaMatCSB-42

Delkus, Pete
88KenTwiP-1398
88MidLeaAGS-35
89OrlTwiB-13
89OrlTwiP-1331
90CMC-557
90PorBeaC-5
90PorBeaP-172
90ProAAAF-242
91OrlSunRP-1843

Dell, Tim
88BatCliP-1674
89SpaPhiP-1052
89SpaPhiS-6
89Sta-54
90ClePhiS-5
91StoPorP-3026
92ElPasDF-3914
92ElPasDS-205
93ElPasDF-2942

Dell, Wheezer (William George)
16ColE13-41
16FleBreD-23
20WalMaiW-12

Dellaero, Jason
97Bow-440
97BowChr-300
97BowChrI-300
97BowChrIR-300
97BowChrR-300
97BowInt-440
97TopSta-123
97TopStaAM-123

Dellamano, Anthony
96HudValRB-23

DellaRatta, Pete
96SouOreTI-18

Deller, Bob
90OneYanP-3388
91GreHorP-3071
92Ft.LauYF-2625

93PriWilCC-6
93PriWilCF-668
Deller, Tom
87AncGlaP-6
89WelPirP-10
90SalBucS-3
Delli Carri, Joe
90JacMetGS-9
91LinDriAA-630
91WilBilLD-630
92BinMetS-53
93NorTidF-2575
95BinMetTI-25
88CapCodPPaLP-16
89PitMetS-3
90St.LucMS-5
91WilBilP-300
92BinMetF-523
94TreThuF-2126
Dellucci, David
96FreKeyB-6
Delmas, Bert
90DodTar-930
Delmonico, Rod
95TenVolW-1
DeLoach, Bobby
87SavCarP-1
89SavCarP-346
90FloStaLAS-2
90St.PetCS-4
90StaFS7-62
91KnoBluJLD-356
91KnoBluJP-1780
91LinDriAA-356
DeLoach, Lee
89GreFalDSP-16
DeLoach, Rich
80QuaCitCT-27
Delock, Ike (Ivan Martin)
52Bow-250
52Top-329
55Bow-276
56Top-284
57Top-63
58Top-328
59Top-437
60RedSoxJP-4
60Top-336
61Top-268
61TopStal-110
62Top-201
63Top-136
79DiaGre-241
83TopRep5-329
91OriCro-101
DelOrbe, Chico
75LafDriT-1
85DomLeaS-211
DeLosSantos, Alberto
89PriPirS-5
91Cla/Bes-152
91SalBucC-6
91SalBucP-959
92CarMudF-1192
92CarMudS-131
92SkyAA F-62
93CarMudF-2067
93CarMudTI-24
93ClaFS7-132
93LimRocDWB-138
DeLosSantos, German
75CedRapGT-5
76CedRapGT-25
DeLosSantos, Luis
85Ft.MyeRT-28
86MemChiSTOS-5
86MemChiTOS-5
86SouLeaAJ-9
87OmaRoyP-25
88OmaRoyC-22
88OmaRoyP-1506
88TriAAAP-30
88TriAAC-2
89Don-562
89DonRoo-33
89Fle-646
89FleGlo-646
89FleUpd-37
89OmaRoyP-1729
89PanSti-347
89Sco-648
89ScoHot1R-52
89TriA AAC-2
89UppDec-12
90ClaBlu-9
90CMC-186
90Fle-105
90FleCan-105
90Hot50RS-14
90OmaRoyC-11
90OmaRoyP-70
90OPC-452
90ProAAAF-605
90Sco-659
90Sco100RS-100
90ScoRooDT-B4
90Top-452
90TopTif-452
90TriAAAC-2
91Bow-152
93EdmTraF-1142
93LimRocDWB-19
DeLosSantos, Mariano
92AugPirC-14
92AugPirF-231
93CarLeaAGF-48
93LimRocDWB-10
93SalBucC-6
93SalBucF-423
94CarMudF-1571
95UppDecML-149
96CarMudB-2
95UppDecMLFS-149
DeLosSantos, Pedro
89AshTouP-951
DeLosSantos, Ramon
75IowOakT-11
84TacTigC-76
DeLosSantos, Reynoldo
91MarPhiC-5
91MarPhiP-3466
92BatCliC-8
92BatCliF-3276
93SpaPhiC-11
93SpaPhiF-1066
Delpiano, Marc
89BurIndS-9
90WatIndS-7
93EriSaiC-28
93EriSaiF-3133
94HudValRC-27
DelPozo, Roberto
90SanBerSB-10
90SanBerSCLC-104
90SanBerSP-2643
91PenPilC-23
91PenPilP-388
DelRosario, Manny
83MiaMarT-18
DelRosario, Maximo
85DurBulT-6
87GreBraB-18
88GreBraB-17
89GreBraB-11
89GreBraP-1161
89GreBraS-6
90GreBraP-1123
90GreBraS-7
DelRosario, Sergio
83MiaMarT-6
Delsing, Jim (James Henry)
47SigOil-5
51Bow-279
52Bow-157
52Top-271
53BowBW-44
53TigGle-4
53Top-239
54Bow-55
54RedMan-AL24
54Top-111
55Bow-274
55Top-192
56Top-338
59Top-386
83TopRep5-271
91TopArc1-239
94TopArc1-111
94TopArc1G-111
DeLuca, Kurt
85LitFalMT-16
86ColMetP-8
Delucchi, Ron
86PriWilPP-8
DeLucia, Chris
95GreBatTI-31
96GreBatB-4
97GreBatC-30
DeLucia, Rich (Richard)
86BelMarC-121
88SanBerSB-8
88SanBerSCLC-50
89WilBilP-649
89WilBilS-5
90Bes-228
90ProAaA-134
90SanBerSB-2
90SanBerSCLC-88
90SanBerSP-2626
90StaFS7-48
90WilBilS-4
91Bow-242
91Don-426
91DonRoo-2
91FleUpd-52
91Lea-222
91MarCouH-27
91Sco-728
91ScoRoo-37
91TopDeb90-38
91TopTra-31T
91TopTraT-31T
91UltUpd-50
91UppDec-727
92Bow-665
92Don-118
92Fle-278
92FleRooS-11
92Lea-155
92OPC-686
92OPCPre-171
92Pin-388
92Sco-135
92Sco100RS-61
92ScoImpP-6
92StaClu-511
92Top-686
92TopGol-686
92TopGolW-686
92TopMic-686
92Ult-122
92UppDec-637
93Don-185
93Fle-673
93MarMot-18
93PacSpa-284
93StaClu-402
93StaCluFDI-402
93StaCluMOP-402
93Top-152
93TopGol-152
93TopInaM-152
93TopMic-152
94IndIndF-1802
94Pac-567
96GiaMot-25
96LeaSigEA-41
DelVecchio, Jim
77CliDodT-5
DelVecchio, Nick
92OneYanC-19
93ClaFS7-175
93GreHorC-8
93GreHorF-890
93SouAtlLAGF-19
94ClaGolF-82
94ExcFS7-101
94TamYanC-8
94TamYanF-2390
95Bes-33
95NorNagUTI-47
95NorNavTI-47
95SPML-118
96ColCliB-9
96Exc-85
96SigRooOJTP-T7
Delyon, Gene
77HolMilT-6
Delzer, Ed
85MidAngT-22
86KinEagP-4
Delzine, Domingo
92GulCoaRSP-16
94ChaRivC-4
94ChaRivF-2665
DeMaestri, Joe (Joseph P.)
52Top-286
54Bow-147
55A'sRodM-10
55A'sRodM-11
55Bow-176
56A'sRodM-3
56Top-161
57Top-44
58A'sJayP-2
58Top-62
59Top-64
59TopVen-64
60Lea-139
60Top-358
61Top-116
61Yan61RL-22
76A'sRodMC-8
79DiaGre-350
83TopRep5-286
91RinPos1Y3-12
92YanWIZ6-34
Deman, Lou
95NewJerCTI-6
96NewJerCB-7
DeMar, Clarence
28W512-35
Demaree, Al (Albert W.)
09SpoNewSM-98
10OrnOvaPP-4
14CraJacE-92
14FatPlaT-13
14TexTomE-17
15CraJacE-92
94ConTSN-1216
94ConTSNB-1216
Demaree, Frank (Joseph F.)
15SpoNewM-47
16SpoNewM-45
32CubTeal-4
33Gou 224
34BatR31-166
36DiaMatCS3T2-7
36R31PasP-31
36SandSW-12
37WheBB14-4
37WheBB7-29C
38GouHeaU-244
38GouHeaU-268
38OurNatGPP-6
39PlaBal-34
40PlaBal-90
41PlaBal-58
91ConTSN-212
96Bro194F-10
DeMars, Billy (William L.)
50Bow-252
51Bow-43
52Par-8
73OPC-486
73Top-486A
73Top-486B
74OPC-119
74Top-119
78PhiSSP-45
78SSP270-45
82ExpPos-9
82ExpZel-9
83ExpPos-5
83ExpStu-11
84ExpPos-6
84ExpStu-3
84ExpStu-38
86RedTexG-NNO
87RedKah-NNO
Dembowski, Steve
79NewCoPT-7
Dembrowski, Steve
77Spo-8718
DeMeo, Bob M.
77ReaPhiT-9
81OklCit8T-21
DeMerit, John (John Stephen)
61Top-501
62SalPlaC-192
62ShiPlaC-192
62Top-4
62TopVen-4
78TCM60I-129
91MetWIZ-93
DeMerit, Thomas
88VerBeaDS-5
DeMerritt, Martin
75BurBeeT-4
76DubPacT-9
88PhoFirC-25
88PhoFirP-67
89PhoFirC-7
89PhoFirP-1486
92EriSaiF-1643
93HigDesMC-27
93HigDesMF-58
94PorSeaDF-694
94PorSeaDTI-4
96OrlCubB-2
95OrlCubF-26
Demers, Tony
43ParSpo-22
Demerson, Tim
90TamYanD-3
92ForLauYC-21
92ForLauYTI-6
92GreHorF-791
93SanBerSC-7
93SanBerSF-782
Demery, Larry (Lawrence C.)
75OPC-433
75Top-433
76OPC-563
76SSP-564
76Top-563
77PirPosP-2
77Top-607
78Top-138
Demeter, Don (Donald Lee)
58Top-244
59OklTodML-16
59Top-324
60DodBelB-14
60DodJayP-2
60DodTeal-4
00DodUniO-4
60Top-234
61DodBelB-16
61Top-23
62Jel-195
62Pos-195
62PosCan-195
62SalPlaC-170
62ShiPlaC-170
62Top-146
62TopBuc-22
62TopStal-167
62TopVen-146
63Fle-53
63Jel-180
63Pos-180
63Top-268
64TigLid-4
64Top-58
64TopCoi-116
64TopVen-58
65TigJayP-4
65Top-429
66OPC-98
66Top-98
66TopVen-98
67CokCapRS-3
67DexPre-65
67Top-572
67TopRedSS-4
78TCM60I-198
79DiaGre-324
79TCM50-237
90DodTar-179
Demeter, Steve (Stephen)
60MapLeaSF-5
61MapLeaBH-6
77FriOneYW-94
77SalPirT-13
79BufBisT-7
80BufBisT-16
87SalBucP-29
Demeter, Todd
85SprCarT-6
Demetral, Chris
91YakBeaC-7
91YakBeaP-4252
92BakDodCLC-8
93FloStaLAF-46
93VerBeaDC-1
93VerBeaDF-2225
94ClaGolF-184
94ExcFS7-212
94SanAntMF-2476
Demetral, Scott
95OdgRapTI-6
Demetre, Doug
90OneYanP-3383

Demmitt, Ray (Charles R.)
09AmeCarE-32
09ColChiE-76A
09ColChiE-76B
09ColChiE-76C
09T206-89
09T206-90
10CouT21-116
10PeoT21-15
11SpoLifM-266
12ColRedB-76A
12ColRedB-76B
12ColRedB-76C
12ColTinT-76A
12ColTinT-76B
12ColTinT-76C
12ImpTobC-11
14B18B-16A
14B18B-16B
14B18B-16C
15AmeCarE-11
15VicT21-6
16TanBraE-10
DeMola, Don (Donald John)
72Dia-10
75OPC-391
75Top-391
76OPC-571
76Top-571
DeMontreville, Eugene
03BreE10-34
90DodTar-180
Demoran, Joe
43CenFlo-5
44CenFlo-4
45CenFlo-4
DeMorejon, Pete
96BriWhiSB-14
DeMoss, Bingo
74LauOldTBS-4
86NegLeaF-66
90NegLeaS-6
DeMoss, Dave
92GenCubC-21
92GenCubF-1571
Dempsay, Adam
87LakTigP-24
88GleFalTP-932
Dempsey, Con (Cornelius F.)
48SomandK-3
49SomandK-4
52Top-44
83TopRep5-44
Dempsey, Dalton
93WatIndC-6
Dempsey, Jack
28W512-41
32USCar-22
66AurSpoMK-2
87AllandGN-13
87SpoCubG-2
88GooN16-17
88KimN18-11
Dempsey, John
76BurBeeT-4
90JohCitCS-8
91JohCitCC-2
91JohCitCP-3979
91SprCarC-12
91SprCarP-744
92SavCarC-13
93WilBluRC-8
93WilBluRF-1999
94WilBluRC-5
94WilBluRF-302
Dempsey, Mark (Mark S.)
81ShrCapT-11
83PhoGiaBHN-21
82PhoGiaVNB-14
Dempsey, Mike
77BurBeeT-4
78HolMilT-4
Dempsey, Pat
77ModA'sC-9
79OgdA'sT-20
80OgdA'sT-22
80VenLeaS-159
81TacTigT-7
81Top-96
82TacTigT-26
84NasSouTI-6
85MaiGuiT-14
86TolMudHP-8
87PorBeaP-2
Dempsey, Pete
82SyrChiTI-8
Dempsey, Rick (John Rikard)
72Top-778
74OPC-569
74SyrChiTI-4
74Top-569
75OPC-451
75SyrChiTI-3
75Top-451
75YanSSP-12
76OPC-272
76SSP-438
76Top-272
77Top-189
78Top-367
79Hos-73
79OPC-312
79Top-593
80OPC-51
80Top-91
81AllGamPI-38
81Don-113
81Fle-177A
81Fle-177B
81OPC-132
81Top-615
81TopSti-38
82Don-77
82Fle-163
82FleSta-146
82OPC-262
82Top-489
83AllGamPI-39
83Don-329
83Fle-58
83OPC-138
83OriPos-7
83Top-138
83TopSti-30
84AllGamPI-128
84Don-413
84Fle-6
84Fle-644
84FleSti-115
84Nes792-272
84OPC-272
84OriEng-4
84OriTeal-8
84SevCoi-E21
84Top-272
84TopRubD-5
84TopSti-23
84TopSti-213
84TopTif-272
85AllGamPI-38
85Don-332
85Fle-175
85OPC-94
85OriHea-4
85Top-521
85TopRubD-6
85TopSti-199
85TopTif-521
86Don-106
86Fle-272
86OPC-358
86Spo-147
86Top-358
86Top-726
86TopSti-232
86TopTat-5
86TopTif-358
86TopTif-726
87Don-294
87Fle-467
87FleGlo-467
87FleUpd-26
87FleUpdG-26
87IndGat-24
87OPC-28
87RedFolSB-92
87Top-28
87TopSti-225
87TopTif-28
87TopTra-28T
87TopTraT-28T
88DodMot-15
88Sco-262
88ScoGlo-262
88ScoRoo-32T
88ScoRooG-32T
89Bow-343
89BowTif-343
89DodMot-15
89DodPol-10
89DodStaSV-12
89Don-432
89Sco-556
89Top-606
89TopBig-108
89TopTif-606
89UppDec-713
90DodMot-16
90DodPol-17
90DodTar-181
90Don-557
90DonLeaS-15
90Fle-392
90FleCan-392
90OPC-736
90PubSti-4
90Sco-414
90Top-736
90TopTif-736
90VenSti-138
91BreMilB-7
91BrePol-7
91Lea-484
91OPC-427
91OriCro-102
91Sco-816
91StaClu-553
91Top-427
91TopDesS-427
91TopMic-427
91TopTif-427
92YanWIZ7-42
93BakDodCLC-28
93OriCroASU-1
94AlbDukF-858
94BreMilB-115
Dempsey, Steve
93PocPosF-4202
93PocPosSP-4
93WatIndF-3553
Dempster, Kurt
88BilMusP-1828
89BilMusP-2053
89GreHorP-426
Dempster, Ryan
96Bow-140
96ChaRivTI-9611
96KanCouCUTI-4
Demus, Joe
90ElmPioP-13
91WinHavRSC-11
91WinHavRSP-491
92NewBriRSF-436
92NewBriRSS-482
92WinHavRSF-1780
DeMuth, Dana
88T/MUmp-53
89T/MUmp-51
90T/MUmp-49
DeMuth, Don
89SpaPhiP-1056
Demyan, Kirk
93BelBreC-4
93BelBreF-1702
94CapCitBC-4
94CapCitBF-1743
Denbo, Gary
84CedRapRT-26
85CedRapRT-16
86VerRedP-6
87TamTarP-1
88CedRapRP-1143
89GreHorP-404
90CarLeaA-19
90PriWilCTI-2
91ColCliLD-125
91LinDriAAA-125
92GulCoaYF-3706
93GreHorF-904
94AbaYanF-1458
96NorNavB-2
Denbow, Don
94EveGiaC-6
94EveGiaF-3666
95BurBeeTI-2
96BurBeeTI-24
96MidLeaAB-13
97Bow-291
97BowChr-199
97BowChrI-199
97BowChrIR-199
97BowChrR-199
97BowInt-291
Denby, Darryl
83LynMetT-6
84JacMetT-19
86GreBraTI-8
Denehy, Bill (William F.)
67Top-581
68Top-526
91MetWIZ-94
Denevi, Mike
77JacSunT-4
Denkenberger, Ralph
88WatPirP-17
Denkinger, Don
88T/MUmp-8
89T/MUmp-6
90T/MUmp-6
Denman, Brian (Brian John)
81BriRedST-7
83PawRedST-5
84PawRedST-24
85NasSouTI-5
86NasSouTI-6
Denman, John
80ChaO'sP-5
80ChaO'sW-5
Denman, Ralph
93IdaFalBF-4043
93IdaFalBSP-14
94DanBraC-7
94DanBraF-3539
Denning, Wes
96DelShoB-15
Dennis, Brian
94WilCubC-5
94WilCubF-3767
95RocCubTI-24
Dennis, Don (Donald Ray)
65CarTeal-7
66OPC-142
66Top-142
66TopVen-142
67Top-259
Dennis, Eddie (Ed)
78DunBluJT-6
80KnoBluJT-14
82KnoBluJT-16
83KnoBluJT-16
86KnoBluJP-6
88St.CatBJP-2014
91PacSenL-71
Dennis, Les
96GreBatB-8
Dennis, Michael
91SydWavF-7
Dennis, Shane
94SpoIndC-6
94SpoIndF-3315
96MemChiB-11
96RanCucQB-11
Dennison, Brian
90ArkRaz-30
91HelBreSP-15
92BelBreC-12
92BelBreF-399
94BelBreC-6
94BelBreF-94
Dennison, Jim
90ElmPioP-16
90WinHavRSS-5
91LynRedSC-2
91LynRedSP-1191
92LynRedSC-24
92LynRedSF-2900
Dennison, Scott
91JamExpC-10
91JamExpP-3551
92RocExpC-2
92RocExpF-2121
Denny, Jerry (Jeremiah D.)
87BucN28-40A
87BucN28-40B
87OldJudN-132
88SpoTimM-8
88WG1CarG-30
89EdgR.WG-8
Denny, John (John Allen)
75OPC-621
75Top-621
76OPC-339
76SSP-295
76Top-339
77BurCheD-14
77Car5-5
77CarTeal-5
77Hos-42
77OPC-7
77OPC-109
77Top-7
77Top-541
78CarTeal-3
78Hos-129
78RCColC-64
78Top-609
79Car5-4
79Hos-1
79Top-59
80OPC-242
80Top-464
81Top-122
82Don-572
82Fle-363
82FleSta-194
82Ind-10
82IndTeal-9
82IndWhe-22
82Top-773
83Don-237
83Fle-158
83PhiTas-8
83Top-211
84AllGamPI-76
84Don-407
84Fle-27
84FleSti-56
84FunFooP-49
84Nes792-17
84Nes792-135
84Nes792-637
84NesDreT-20
84PhiTas-18
84SevCoi-E19
84Top-17
84Top-135
84Top-637
84TopRubD-18
84TopSti-19
84TopSti-122
84TopSti-177
84TopSup-4
84TopTif-17
84TopTif-135
84TopTif-637
85AllGamPI-167
85Don-111
85Fle-249
85Lea-228
85OPC-325
85PhiCIG-13
85PhiTas-9
85PhiTas-16
85Top-325
85TopMin-325
85TopRubD-17
85TopSti-119
85TopTif-325
86BasStaB-30
86Don-204
86Fle-439
86FleUpd-34
86OPC-268
86RedTexG-40
86Spo-64
86Spo-132
86Spo-134
86Top-556
86TopTif-556
86TopTra-32T
86TopTraT-32T
87Don-329
87Fle-199
87FleGlo-199
87OPC-139
87Top-644
87TopTif-644
90SweBasG-116
93UppDecS-12
Denson, Drew (Andrew)
86DurBulP-9
87GreBraB-7
88GreBraB-9
88SouLeaAJ-17
89RicBraBC-4
89RicBraC-18

89RicBraP-847
89RicBraTI-5
90CMC-287
90ProAAAF-411
90RicBraC-11
90RicBraP-266
90RicBraTI-8
90TopDeb89-30
92VanCanF-2729
92VanCanS-637
93NasSouF-576
93TriAAAGF-34
94NasSouF-1255
94Pin-241
94PinArtP-241
94PinMusC-241
94TriAAF-AAA5
95IndIndF-100
Dent, Bucky (Russell Earl)
74OPC-582
74Top-582
75OPC-299
75SSPPuzB-8
75Top-299
76Hos-119
76OPC-154
76SSP-143
76Top-154
77BurCheD-81
77Hos-91
77OPC-122
77Top-29
77YanBurK-14
78Kel-2
78OPC-164
78SSP270-24
78Top-335
78YanBurK-15
78YanSSPD-24
79Hos-131
79OPC-254
79Top-485
79YanBurK-14
79YanPicA-9
80OPC-33
80Top-60
81AllGamPI-21
81Don-465
81Fle-80
81FleStiC-110
81Kel-7
81MSAMinD-11
81OPC-164
81PerAll-12
81Top-650
81TopSti-110
81TopSupHT-62
82Don-209
82Fle-33
82Fle-629
82OPC-240
82OPC-241
82OPC-298
82Top-240
82Top-241
82Top-550
83Fle-566
83OPC-279
83RanAffF-7
83Top-565
83TopSti-122
84Don-300
84Fle-417
84Nes792-331
84OPC-331
84Top-331
84TopSti-362
84TopTif-331
87ColCliP-6
87ColCliP-1
87ColCliT-23
88ColCliC-25
88ColCliP-25
88ColCliP-306
89ColCliC-25
89ColCliP-25
89ColCliP-755
89ColCliP-757
89SweBasG-72
89TriAAP-AAA21
90OPC-519
90Top-519
90TopTif-519
90TopTVY-1
92YanWIZ7-43
92YanWIZ8-43
92YanWIZA-16
93RanKee-124
93UppDecAH-40
94UppDecAH-18
94UppDecAH-28
94UppDecAH1-18
94UppDecAH1-28
95RanCra-7
96RanMot-28
97FleMilDM-43
Dent, Darrell
96AppLeaAB-3
96BluOriB-10
Dent, Eddie
90DodTar-182
Dente, Sam (Samuel Joseph)
50Bow-107
51Bow-133
52Top-304
52WhiSoxH-2
53BowC-137
55IndGolS-23
79DiaGre-299
83TopRep5-304
DePalo, Jim
79TCM50-82
DePaolo, Jimmy
77ForLauYS-25
DePastino, Joe
93UtiBluSC-9
93UtiBluSF-3540
94UtiBluSC-9
94UtiBluSF-3823
95MicBatCTI-8
96SarRedSB-12
DePastino, Rich
87MyrBeaBJP-1456
88DunBluJS-5
89MyrBeaBJP-1628
90DunBluJS-8
DePaula, Sean
96BurIndB-3
DePew, Daren
88BoiHawP-1627
DePrimo, John
85GreHorT-28
Derdivannis, Kent
93PirNatI-8
DeRicco, John
90GenCubP-3043
90GenCubS-8
Deriso, Phil
81BatTroT-8
Derksen, Rob
85BelBreT-25
86StoPorP-5
87StoPorP-2
88CalLeaACLC-18
88StoPorCLC-201
88StoPorP-721
89StoPorB-30
89StoPorCLC-177
89StoPorP-385
89StoPorS-25
90BelBreS-25
91BelBreC-27
91BelBreP-2119
92ElPasDF-3938
92ElPasDS-225
93ElPasDF-2967
94ElPasDF-3162
95ElPasDTI-4
Dermendziev, Tony
94AshTouC-4
94AshTouF-1793
Dernier, Bob (Robert E.)
80CarMudF-15
80VenLeaS-256
81OklCit8T-5
82Top-231
82TopTra-28T
83Don-189
83Fle-159
83OPC-43
83PhiTas-9
83Top-43
83TopSti-320
84CubChiT-10
84CubSev-20
84CubUno-2
84Don-541
84Fle-28
84FleUpd-31
84FunFooP-127
84Nes792-358
84OPC-358
84Top-358
84TopTif-358
84TopTra-31T
84TopTraT-31T
85AllGamPI-140
85CubLioP-7
85CubSev-20
85Don-510
85Fle-55
85Lea-57
85OPC-334
85Top-589
85TopMin-589
85TopSti-38
85TopTif-589
86BasStaB-31
86CubGat-20
86CubUno-5
86Don-266
86Fle-365
86Lea-139
86MSAJayPCD-4
86OPC-188
86Top-188
86TopSti-63
86TopTif-188
87CubCan-7
87CubDavB-20
87Don-146
87DonOpeD-68
87Fle-559
87FleGlo-559
87OPC-138
87Top-715
87TopTif-715
88Don-392
88Fle-417
88FleGlo-417
88OPC-183
88PhiTas-8
88Sco-451
88ScoGlo-451
88ScoRoo-45T
88ScoRooG-45T
88StaLinCu-2
88StaLinPh-7
88Top-642
88TopTif-642
89Don-430
89Fle-565
89FleGlo-565
89PanSti-155
89PhiTas-5
89Sco-357
89Top-418
89TopBig-265
89TopTif-418
89UppDec-340
90OPC-204
90PubSti-235
90Top-204
90TopTif-204
90VenSti-139
93MCIAmb-12
Derosa, Jeff
93ButCopKSP-5
DeRosa, Mark
96EugEmeB-7
DeRosa, Tom
77NewCoPT-9
78BurBeeT-8
DeRosa, Tony
75ForLauYS-9
80SyrChiTI-8
81SyrChiT-24
DeRosso, Tony
95MicBatCTI-9
96HilStaHWB-25
96SarRedSB-13
Derotal, Francisco
94SpoIndC-7
94SpoIndF-3335
95RanCucQT-12
Derr, Jason
90GreFalDSP-15
Derrick, Claud (Claud Lester)
12T207-44
Derringer, Paul
34DiaMatCSB-43
34BatR31-190
34ButPreR-15
34Gou-84
35DiaMatCS3T1-45
35ExhFou-4
36ExhFou-4
36GouBWR-11
36GouWidPPR-A26
36NatChiFPR-23
36R31Pre-L1
36SandSW-13
36WorWidGV-66
37ExhFou-4
37GouFliMR-9A
37GouFliMR-9B
37GouThuMR-9
38BasTabP-5
38CinOraW-8
38ExhFou-4
39ExhSal-11
39GouPreR303A-11
39OrcPhoAP-6
39PlaBal-15
39WorWidGTP-11
39WorWidGV-10
40PlaBal-74
40WheM4-7C
40WheM4-8B
41DouPlaR-7
41HarHarW-5
41PlaBal-4
43CubTeal-6
44CubTeal-5
60Fle-43
61Fle-20
77GalGloG-74
80PacLeg-113
82OhiHaloF-55
83TCMPla1945-23
86RedGreT-3
86SpoDecG-14
91ConTSN-213
Derrington, Jim (Chas. J.)
58Top-129
Derryberry, Tim
82RocRedWT-9
Dersin, Eric
86AlbYanT-14
Dertli, Chuck
87WinSpiP-21
DeSa, Joe (Joseph)
79ArkTraT-10
82LouRedE-6
83LouRedR-7
85WhiSoxC-20
86BufBisP-10
86DeSCom-1
86Don-546
86Top-313
86TopTif-313
Desabrais, Mark D.
96IdaFalB-6
DeSalvo, Steve
85Ft.MyeRT-22
96GreBraTI-GM
DeSantis, Dominic
91MarPhiC-24
91MarPhiP-3446
92SpaPhiC-9
92SpaPhiF-1258
93ClePhiC-6
93ClePhiF-2678
94ClePhiF-2520
DeSanto, Tom
79ElmPioRST-27
DeSapio, Jim
88AubAstP-1968
89AubAstP-2172
Desautels, Gene (Eugene A.)
34DiaMatCSB-44
39PlaBal-116
40PlaBal-28
53MotCoo-60
79DiaGre-387
Deschenes, Marc
95WatIndTI-12
DeSensi, Craig
95ButCopKtI-28
Desert, Harry
52Par-92
Deshaies, Jim
85ColCliP-8
85ColCliT-23
85IntLeaAT-34
86AstMilL-6
86AstPol-24
86DonHig-45
86DonRoo-34
86FleUpd-35
86SpoRoo-15
87AstMot-23
87AstPol-19
87ClaUpdY-137
87Don-184
87Fle-56
87FleGlo-56
87FleMin-31
87Lea-255
87Spo-156
87SpoTeaP-8
87Top-2
87Top-167
87TopGloS-20
87TopSti-1
87TopTif-2
87TopTif-167
87ToyRoo-9
88AstMot-23
88AstPol-9
88Don-85
88DonBasB-94
88Fle-446
88FleGlo-446
88Lea-96
88OPC-24
88PanSti-287
88Sco-354
88ScoGlo-354
88Spo-190
88Top-24
88TopSti-27
88TopTif-24
89AstLenH-11
89AstMot-22
89AstSmo-12
89Bow-320
89BowTif-320
89Don-241
89DonBasB-120
89Fle-356
89FleGlo-356
89OPC-341
89Sco-546
89Top-341
89TopBig-29
89TopTif-341
89UppDec-76
90AstLenH-12
90AstMot-12
90Bow-70
90BowTif-70
90Don-7
90Don-187
90DonBesN-4
90DonSupD-7
90Fle-229
90FleCan-229
90Lea-168
90OPC-225
90PanSti-267
90PubSti-93
90RedFolSB-26
90Sco-154
90Spo-32
90Top-225
90TopBig-212
90TopSti-21
90TopTif-225
90UppDec-221
90VenSti-140
91AstMot-9
91Bow-541
91Don-652
91Fle-506
91Lea-49
91OPC-782
91PanSti-11
91Sco-193
91StaClu-262
91Stu-175
91Top-782
91TopDesS-782
91TopMic-782
91TopTif-782
91Ult-137
91UppDec-208

92Don-515
92LasVegSF-2791
92OPC-415
92PadPolD-5
92Sco-364
92Top-415
92TopGol-415
92TopGolW-415
92TopMic-415
92UppDec-297
92YanWIZ8-44
93Fla-234
93Fle-520
93FleFinE-234
93Lea-522
93Ult-580
93UppDec-648
93UppDecGold-648
94ColC-91
94ColC-437
94ColChoGS-91
94ColChoGS-437
94ColChoSS-91
94ColChoSS-437
94Fin-190
94FinRef-190
94Pin-301
94PinArtP-301
94PinMusC-301
95Pac-246
95ScrRedBTI-6

DeShields, Delino
88MidLeaAGS-44
88OPC-88
88RocExpLC-10
89BasAmeAPB-AA15
89JacExpB-15
89JacExpP-152
89SouLeaAJ-5
90Bow-119
90BowTif-119
90ClaBlu-55
90ClaYel-T95
90Don-42
90DonBesN-116
90DonLeaS-47
90DonRoo-6
90ExpPos-6
90Fle-653
90FleCan-653
90FleUpd-27
90Lea-193
90OPC-224
90Sco-645
90ScoYouS2-3
90Top-224
90TopBig-231
90TopMag-22
90TopTif-224
90UppDec-702
90UppDec-746
90UppDecS-2
91Baz-14
91Bow-445
91CadEllD-16
91Cla1-T61
91Cla2-T71
91ClaGam-134
91Don-11
91Don-555
91DonBonC-BC16
91DonSupD-11
91Fle-228
91Lea-139
91MajLeaCP-78
91OPC-432
91OPCPre-34
91PanFreS-140
91PanSti-69
91PosCan-1
91RedFolS-27
91Sco-545
91Sco100RS-55
91StaClu-194
91StaCluCM-6
91StaCluP-11
91StaPinB-13
91Stu-195
91Top-432
91TopCraJ2-35
91TopDeb90-39
91TopDesS-432
91TopMic-432
91TopRoo-8
91TopTif-432
91TopTriH-N6
91ToyRoo-7
91Ult-200
91UppDec-364
92Bow-47
92Cla2-T34
92ClaGam-38
92Don-277
92ExpDonD-6
92ExpPos-10
92Fle-476
92Hig5-57
92Lea-138
92OPC-515
92OPCPre-163
92PanSti-203
92Pin-24
92PinTea2-22
92Sco-16
92ScoCokD-8
92StaClu-505
92Stu-54
92Top-515
92TopGol-515
92TopGolW-515
92TopKid-9
92TopMic-515
92TriPla-209
92Ult-220
92UppDec-36
92UppDec-167
92UppDecF-4
92UppDecFG-4
93Bow-424
93ClaGam-25
93DiaMar-30
93Don-564
93DurPowP2-22
93ExpColP7-4
93ExpDonM-3
93Fin-168
93FinRef-168
93Fla-81
93Fle-74
93FleAll-NL2
93FleFruotL-15
93FunPac-94
93HumDumC-35
93Kra-21
93Lea-268
93LeaGolA-R5
93OPC-183
93OPCPre-7
93PacSpa-183
93PanSti-226
93Pin-121
93Pin-302
93PinTea2-12
93PinTeaP-5
93Sco-145
93Sel-43
93SelStaL-59
93SP-102
93StaClu-78
93StaCluFDI-78
93StaCluMOP-78
93StaCluMP-2
93Stu-150
93Top-368
93TOPBLAG-5
93TopGol-368
93TopInaM-368
93TopMic-368
93Toy-61
93TriPla-102
93Ult-66
93UppDec-142
93UppDec-454
93UppDec-481
93UppDecGold-142
93UppDecGold-454
93UppDecGold-481
93UppDecIC-WI10
93UppDecICJ-WI10
93USPlaCA-7H
94Bow-454
94BowBes-R39
94BowBesR-R39
94ColC-92
94ColC-524
94ColChoGS-92
94ColChoGS-524
94ColChoSS-92
94ColChoSS-524
94DodMot-3
94DodPol-6
94Don-350
94DonSpeE-350
94ExtBas-286
94Fin-270
94FinRef-270
94Fla-395
94Fle-535
94FleUpd-149
94FUnPac-94
94Kra-19
94Lea-277
94LeaL-117
94OPC-59
94Pac-377
94PanSti-209
94Pin-147
94PinArtP-147
94PinMusC-147
94ProMag-68
94Sco-38
94ScoGolR-38
94ScoRoo-RT6
94ScoRooCP-CP9
94ScoRooGR-RT6
94ScoRooS-RT6
94Sel-227
94SP-76
94SPDieC-76
94SpoRoo-6
94SpoRooAP-6
94StaClu-549
94StaCluFDI-549
94StaCluGR-549
94StaCluMOP-549
94Stu-67
94Top-109
94TopGol-109
94TopSpa-109
94TopTra-42T
94TriPla-83
94Ult-515
94UppDec-465
94UppDecED-465
94USPlaCA-4H
95Baz-39
95Bow-332
95ColCho-218
95ColChoGS-218
95ColChoSE-88
95ColChoSEGS-88
95ColChoSESS-88
95ColChoSS-218
95DodMot-9
95DodPol-7
95Don-71
95DonPreP-71
95DonTopotO-264
95Emb-53
95EmbGolI-53
95Fin-74
95FinRef-74
95Fla-153
95Fle-538
95Lea-154
95LeaLim-161
95Pac-215
95PanSti-42
95Pin-102
95PinArtP-102
95PinMusC-102
95Sco-99
95ScoGolR-99
95ScoHaloG-HG39
95ScoPlaTS-99
95Sel-30
95SelArtP-30
95SP-68
95Spo-17
95SpoArtP-17
95SPSil-68
95StaClu-467
95StaCluMOP-467
95StaCluSTDW-D467
95StaCluSTWS-467
95StaCluVR-255
95Stu-90
95Top-9
95TopCyb-7
95Ult-395
95UltGolM-395
95UppDec-72
95UppDecED-72
95UppDecEDG-72
96ColCho-581
96ColChoGS-581
96ColChoSS-581
96DodMot-6
96DodPol-10
96Don-255
96DonPreP-255
96EmoXL-206
96Fin-B96
96FinRef-B96
96Fla-290
96Fle-431
96FleDod-5
96FleTif-431
96Lea-3
96LeaPrePB-3
96LeaPrePG-3
96LeaPrePS-3
96Pac-101
96ProSta-44
96Sco-446
96StaClu-50
96StaCluEPB-50
96StaCluEPG-50
96StaCluEPS-50
96StaCluMOP-50
95StaCluVRMC-255
96Stu-133
96StuPrePB-133
96StuPrePG-133
96StuPrePS-133
96Top-312
96Ult-495
96UltGolM-495
96UppDec-356
97Cir-56
97CirRav-56
97ColCho-438
97Don-130
97Don-285
97DonPreP-130
97DonPreP-285
97DonPrePGold-130
97DonPrePGold-285
97DonTea-163
97DonTeaSPE-163
97Fin-304
97FinEmb-304
97FinEmbR-304
97FinRef-304
97Fle-360
97Fle-636
97FleTif-360
97FleTif-636
97Lea-239
97LeaFraM-239
97LeaFraMDC-239
97Pac-329
97PacLigB-329
97PacSil-329
97Pin-95
97PinArtP-95
97PinMusC-95
97Sco-132
97Sco-343
97ScoDod-4
97ScoDodPl-4
97ScoDodPr-4
97ScoHobR-343
97ScoPreS-132
97ScoResC-343
97ScoShoS-132
97ScoShoS-343
97ScoShoSAP-132
97ScoShoSAP-343
97StaClu-114
97StaCluMOP-114
97Top-285
97Ult-322
97UltGolME-322
97UltPlaME-322

Deshong, Jimmie (James B.)
34Gou-96
35DiaMatCS3T1-46
35GouPuzR-8E
35GouPuzR-9E
39PlaBal-10
79DiaGre-63

DeSilva, John
87BriYouC-6
89NiaFalRP-6
90FloStaLAS-30
90LakTigS-8
91Bow-148
91LinDriAA-381
91LonTigLD-381
91LonTigP-1869
92Bow-229
92SkyAAAF-269
92TolMudHF-1035
92TolMudHS-598
92UppDecML-137
93TolMudHF-1645
94AlbDukF-836
95LinVen-23
95RocRedWTI-13
96PawRedSDD-6

DeSimone, Jerry
82HawIsIT-7
83LasVegSBHN-6
84LasVegSC-223

Desimone, Ray
93EriSaiC-5
93EriSaiF-3122

DesJardins, Brad
89WatIndS-29

Desjarlais, Keith
81AppFoxT-3
82EdmTraT-7
83GleFalWST-13

Deskins, Casey
96YakBeaTI-50

DeSonnaville, Erik
89CalLeaA-53

Desrosiers, Erik
96PriWilCB-8

Dessau, Rube (Frank Rolland)
09T206-418
11SpoLifM-154
12ImpTobC-61
90DodTar-931

Dessellier, Chris
93ClaGolF-144

Dessens, Elmer
95Bes-93
95CarMudF-148
97PacPriGotD-GD190

Destrade, Orestes
82OneYanT-1
85AlbYanT-16
86ColCliP-5
87ColCliP-7
87ColCliP-8
87ColCliT-13
87IntLeaAT-23
88BufBisC-20
88BufBisP-1486
88ScoRoo-110T
88ScoRooG-110T
89BufBisP-1687
89Top-27A
89Top-27B
89TopTif-27
90AlbDecGB-21
92YanWIZ8-45
93Bow-418
93DiaMar-31
93Fin-144
93FinRef-144
93Fla-50
93FleFinE-59
93Lea-304
93MarPub-10
93MarUSPC-7S
93MarUSPC-10D
93MarUSPC-11C
93OPCPre-32
93PacJugC-25
93PacSpa-460
93Pin-526
93PinExpOD-3
93SP-139
93StaClu-554
93StaCluFDI-554
93StaCluMarI-29
93StaCluMOP-554
93Stu-97
93TopTra-11T
93Ult-373
93UppDec-479
93UppDec-524
93UppDecGold-479
93UppDecGold-524
94Bow-506

94ColC-397
94ColChoGS-397
94ColChoSS-397
94Don-212
94Fin-272
94FinRef-272
94Fla-162
94Fle-466
94Lea-191
94OPC-23
94Pac-241
94PacSilP-22
94PanSti-182
94Pin-373
94PinArtP-373
94PinMusC-373
94Sco-372
94ScoGolR-372
94Sel-150
94StaClu-387
94StaCluFDI-387
94StaCluGR-387
94StaCluMOP-387
94StaCluT-70
94StaCluTFDI-70
94Top-710
94TopGol-710
94TopSpa-710
94TriPla-135
94Ult-195
94UppDec-304
94UppDecED-304
86STaoftFT-5

Detherage, Bob (Robert W.)
75WatDodT-5
80OmaRoyP-9
81OmaRoyT-21

Detmers, Kris
96ArkTraB-11
96Bow-160
97Bow-342
97BowCerBIA-CA30
97BowCerGIA-CA30
97BowInt-342

Dettmer, John
91TopTra-32T
91TopTraT-32T
92GasRanF-2244
92StaCluD-35
92TopDaiQTU-19
93ChaRanC-7
93ChaRanF-1932
94Bow-129
94BowBes-B68
94BowBesR-B68
94ExcFS7-131
94ExcLeaLF-7
94SigRooDP-91
94SigRooDPS-91
94TopTra-72T
94TulDriF-236
94TulDriTI-5
94UppDecML-235
95ColCho-403
95ColChoGS-403
95ColChoSS-403
95Lea-355
95StaClu-488
95StaCluMOP-488
95StaCluSTWS-488
95StaCluVR-268
95UppDec-152
95UppDecED-152
95UppDecEDG-152
96GreBraB-11
96RicBraUB-6
95StaCluVRMC-268

Dettola, Kevin
92SkyAA F-129

Dettore, Tom (Thomas A.)
74WicAerODF-106
75OPC-469
75Top-469
76OPC-126
76Top-126
89PriPirS-27
91SalBucP-969
93BufBisF-533
94BufBisF-1853

Deutsch, John
89GreFalDSP-17
90BakDodCLC-249
90CalLeaACLC-3
91VerBeaDC-18
91VerBeaDP-779
92SanAntMF-3981
92SanAntMS-562
92SkyAA F-245
93PeoChiC-5
93PeoChiF-1090

Deutsch, Melvin
46RedSoxTI-6
92TexLon-12

Deutsch, Mike
89FreKeyS-5
90FreKeyTI-5

Devares, Cesar
89BluOriS-8
90Bes-133
90WauTimB-17
90WauTimP-2130
90WauTimS-7
91CarLeaAP-CAR7
91FreKeyC-12
91FreKeyP-2366
92HagSunF-2559
92HagSunS-257
92SkyAA F-106
93FreKeyC-5
93FreKeyF-1028
93LimRocDWB-48
94BowBayF-2415
94OriPro-25
95Exc-4
95RocRedWTI-14
95UppDecML-160
96ColCho-466
96ColChoGS-466
96ColChoSS-466
96RocRodWB 11
96Sco-264
97Fle-5
97FleTif-5
97PacPriGotD-GD10
95UppDecMLFS-160

DeVaughan, Jeff
92SalLakTSP-4

Devens, Charlie
94ConTSN-1284
94ConTSNB-1284

Devereaux, Mike
87SanAntDTI-10
87TexLeaAF-28
88AlbDukC-18
88AlbDukP-252
88BlaYNPRWL-181
88DodMot-27
88Don-546
88Fle-512
88FleGlo-512
88Sco-637
88ScoGlo-637
88TriAAAP-1
88TriAAC-36
89ClaTraP-181
89Don-603
89DonBasB-326
89DonRoo-51
89DonTra-30
89Fle-56
89FleGlo-56
89FleUpd-2
89OriFreB-12
89ScoHot1R-11
89ScoYouS2-22
89TopTra-23T
89TopTraT-23T
89UppDec-68
90Bow-260
90BowTif-260
90DodTar-183
90Don-282
90Fle-175
90FleCan-175
90Lea-223
90OPC-127
90PanSti-12
90PubSti-576
90Sco-232A
90Sco-232B
90Sco100RS-90
90Spo-114
90Top-127
90TopBig-178
90TopRoo-7
90TopTif-127
90ToyRoo-8
90UppDec-681
90VenSti-141
91Bow-93
91Don-444
91Fle-469A
91Fle-469B
91Lea-138
91OPC-758
91OriCro-103
91PanFreS-245
91PanSti-196
91Sco-258
91StaClu-555
91Top-758
91TopDesS-758
91TopMic-758
91TopTif-758
91Ult-15
91UppDec-308
92Bow-688
92Don-354
92Fle-5
92Hig5-1
92Lea-79
92OPC-492
92PanSti-70
92Pin-165
92Sco-36
92StaClu-199
92Stu-123
92Top-492
92TopGol-492
92TopGolW-492
92TopMic-492
92Ult-2
92UppDec-209
93Dow-005
93Don-455
93Fin-74
93FinRef-74
93Fla-150
93Fle-165
93FunPac-132
93Lea-67
93OPC-93
93PacSpa-16
93PanSti-75
93Pin-400
93Sco-170
93Sel-170
93SelStaL-20
93SP-155
93StaClu-56
93StaCluFDI-56
93StaCluMOP-56
93Stu-55
93Top-741
93TOPBLAG-28
93TopGol-741
93TopInaM-741
93TopMic-741
93Toy-8
93TriPla-34
93Ult-493
93UppDec-167
93UppDecGold-167
93UppDecHRH-HR14
94Bow-403
94ColC-502
94ColChoGS-502
94ColChoSS-502
94Don-69
94ExtBas-3
94Fin-117
94FinRef-117
94Fla-252
94Fle-3
94Lea-154
94OPC-203
94OriPro-26
94OriUSPC-7S
94OriUSPC-12D
94Pac-29
94PanSti-19
94Pin-13
94PinArtP-13
94PinMusC-13
94Sco-386
94ScoGolR-386
94Sel-131
94StaClu-424
94StaCluFDI-424
94StaCluGR-424
94StaCluMOP-424
94StaCluT-299
94StaCluTFDI-299
94Stu-122
94Top-534
94TopGol-534
94TopSpa-534
94TriPla-153
94Ult-304
94UppDec-356
94UppDecED-356
95ColCho-583T
95Don-368
95DonPreP-368
95DonTopotO-46
95Fin-284
95FinRef-284
95Fla-242
95Fle-4
95FleUpd-34
95Lea-360
95Pac-20
95Pin-399
95PinArtP-399
95PinMusC-399
95Sco-476
95ScoGolR-476
95ScoPlaTS-476
95StaClu-282
95StaCluMOP-282
95StaCluSTWS-282
95StaCluVR-145
95Top-23
95TopCyb-19
95TopPre-PP7
95TopTra-32T
95Ult-254
95UltGolM-254
95WhiSoxK-6
96ColCho-379T
96ColCho-468
96ColChoGS-468
96ColChoSS-468
96Don-468
96DonPreP-468
96Fle-290
96FleTif-290
96FleUpd-U2
96FleUpdTC-U2
96MLBPin-7
96Sco-205
95StaCluVRMC-145
96Ult-303
96UltGolM-303
96UppDec-221
97Sco-451
97ScoHobR-451
97ScoResC-451
97ScoShoS-451
97ScoShoSAP-451
97Ult-459
97UltGolME-459
97UltPlaME-459

Devereaux, Todd
88AriWilP-2
90Ft.LauYS-4

Devereux, Charles
93AlbPolC-12
94FreKeyF-2606
94FreKeyC-9

Devers, Edgar
93SouBenWSC-8
93SouBenWSF-1443

Devich, John
83ButCopKT-24

Devil Rays, Tampa Bay
97Fle-750
97FleTif-750

Deville, Dan
89SpoIndSP-10
90RivRedWB-6
90RivRedWCLC-15
90RivRedWP-2599
91HigDesMC-2
91HigDesMP-2385

Devincenzo, John
80CarMudF-14

DeVincenzo, Rich
83AppFoxF-7
86BirBarTI-27

Devine, Adrian (Paul Adrian)
74OPC-614
74Top-614
76VenLeaS-141
77Top-339
78Top-92
79Top-257
80Top-528
81Top-464
93RanKee-125

Devine, Kevin
86VerBeaDP-5
87VerBeaDP-23

Devito, Fred
80WesHavWCT-13

DeViveiros, Bernie
94ConTSN-1282
94ConTSNB-1282

Devlin, Art (Arthur M.)
03WilCarE-10
08AmeCarE-8
08AmeCarE-43
08RosComP-125
09ColChiE-77
09PhiCarE-8
09RamT20-35
09T206-91
10DomDisP-32
10E101-14
10E12AmeCDC-13
10MelMinE-14
10NadCarE-15
10SepAnoP-11
10SweCapPP-110
10W555-22
11BasBatEU-18
11E94-10
11S74Sil-83
11SpoLifCW-90
11SpoLifM-207
11T205-38
11TurRedT-10
12ColRedB-77
12ColTinT-77
12HasTriFT-29A
12HasTriFT-29B
12HasTriFT-29C
12HasTriFT-29D
12HasTriFT-74A
12HasTriFT-74B
12HasTriFT-74C
12HasTriFT-74D
12HasTriFT-74E
12HasTriFT-74F
12T207-45
93UppDecTR-1

Devlin, Bob
84GreHorT-21
86WesPalBEP-12
87JacExpP-446

Devlin, Paul
88LynRedSS-6
89LynRedSS-6

Devlin, Steven
91BriBanF-4

Devlin, Tim (James H.)
87OldJudN-133
90KalBatN-12

Devoe, Dan
91KinIndC-29
92KinIndC-29
93CarLeaAGF-28
93KinIndC-30
93KinIndTI-29
96CanIndB-30

Devore, Josh (Joshua)
09BriE97-8
09ColChiE-78A
09ColChiE-78B
09T206-92
10CouT21-117
10CouT21-118
10DomDisP-33
10E12AmeCDC-14
10RedCroT-18
10RedCroT-102
10RedCroT-182
10SweCapPP-111
10W555-23
11BasBatEU-19
11E94-11
11PloCanE-24
11S74Sil-84
11SpoLifM-208
11T205-39
12ColRedB-78A
12ColRedB-78B
12ColTinT-78A

12ColTinT-78B
12HasTriFT-48D
12T207-46
14CraJacE-47
14PieStaT-17
15CraJacE-47
16BF2FP-87
16SpoNewM-46
Devore, Ted
91ChaRaiC-5
91ChaRaiP-91
92HigDesMC-14
DeVormer, Al (Albert E.)
21E121So1-18
21KoBreWSI-30
22E120-63
22W572-22
22W573-31
22W575-26
23W501-106
23W503-14
28W513-80
Devries, Andy
94HunCubF-3544
94HunCubC-6
Dewechter, Pat
85GreHorT-14
Deweerdt, Dan
88RocExpLC-11
Deweese, Brent
92MisStaB-13
93MisStaB-13
Dewett, Martin
94AshTouC-5
94AshTouF-1772
Dewey, Mark
87EveGiaC-32
88CliGiaP-711
89CalLeaA-43
89SanJosGB-7
89SanJosGCLC-211
89SanJosGP-448
89SanJosGS-7
89Sta-85
90ProAaA-65
90ShrCapP-1436
90ShrCapS-6
91LinDriAAA-382
91PhoFirLD-382
91PhoFirP-60
91Sco-371
91TidTidP-2503
91TopDeb90-40
92StaClu-817
92StaCluECN-817
92TidTidF-889
92TidTidS-564
93Fle-468
93MetColP-28
94ColC-584
94ColChoGS-584
94ColChoSS-584
94Don-102
94Fin-298
94FinRef-298
94Fla-216
94FleUpd-172
94Lea-82
94Pac-497
94PirQui-4
94Top-101
94TopGol-101
94TopSpa-101
95Don-129
95DonPreP-129
95Fle-477
95FleUpd-192
95GiaMot-19
95Sco-24
95ScoGolR-24
95ScoPlaTS-24
95Top-378
96GiaMot-19
96LeaSigEA-42
Dewey, Todd Alan
86DurBulP-10
87GreBraB-10
88RicBraC-11
88RicBraP-4
89DurBullS-10
89DurBulTI-10
90DurBulTI-25
88RicBraBC-6
DeWillis, Jeff
88Sco-583
88ScoGlo-583
DeWitt, Matt
96JohCitCTI-9
DeWitt, Scott
96KanCouCTI-5
DeWitt, William O.
41BroW75-8
63RedFreBC-4
DeWolf, Rob
85BelBreT-7
86StoPorP-6
87ElPasDP-6
88ElPasDB-14
89WicChaR-2
89WicChaR-8
89WicChaR-17
89WicUpdR-15
89WicUpdR-17
89WicWraR-9
DeWright, Wayne
78DunBluJT-7
Dews, Bobby (Robert)
64TulOil-3
82DurBulT-25
85BraPol-53
DeYoung, Rob
86AncGlaPTI-8
87BurExpP-1094
88WesPalBES-9
89WesPalBES-9
Diagostino, Gary
89GeoColC-4
Dial, Bryan
85BurRanT-20
86SalRedBP-5
Dials, Lou
86NegLeaF-14
86NegLeaF-20
89RinPosNL1-9
92NegLeaRLI-17
Diamond Dog, Jake the
96KanCouCTI-14
Diamondbacks, Arizona
97Fle-749
97FleTif-749
Diar, Einar
93BurIndF-3300
Diaz, Alberto
89KinMetS-7
90ColMetGS-14
90ColMetPPI-2
91St.LucMC-9
Diaz, Alex
88BlaYNPRWL-68
88ColMetGS-14
89BlaYNPRWL-74
89BlaYNPRWLU-41
89St.LucMS-3
90CMC-374
90ProAAAF-286
90TidTidC-23
90TidTidP-555
90TopTVM-40
91IndIndLD-181
91IndIndP-473
91LinDriAAA-181
91St.LucMP-716
92DenZepF-2645
92DenZepS-126
93BrePol-4
93PacSpa-509
94BreMilB-116
94ExtBas-100
94Fla-65
94FleUpd-53
94Lea-250
94Pac-327
94Pin-416
94PinArtP-416
94PinMusC-416
94ScoRoo-RT119
94ScoRooGR-RT119
94SpoRoo-73
94SpoRooAP-73
94Top-519
94TopGol-519
94TopSpa-519
95DonTopotO-149
95Fle-176
95MarMot-26
95MarPac-30
95Pac-229
95Sco-533
95ScoGolR-533
95ScoPlaTS-533
95Top-216
96Don-314
96DonPreP-314
96Fle-236
96FleTif-236
96LeaSigEA-43
96MarMot-21
96Pac-407
96TacRaiB-10
96Top-94
97PacPriGotD-GD85
Diaz, Alfredo
95LakElsSTI-11
96VanCanB-8
Diaz, Andres
90KisDodD-10
Diaz, Angel
89HelBreSP-2
Diaz, Armando
52LavPro-76
Diaz, Bo (Baudilio Jose)
76VenLeaS-78
78Top-708
79Top-61
80Top-483
80VenLeaS-95
81Don-517
81Fle-404
81Top-362
82Don-263
82Fle-364
82Fle-639
82FleSta-197
82OPC-258
82Top-258
82TopSti-176
82TopStiV-176
82TopTra-29T
83AllGamPI-131
83Don-147
83Fle-160
83Fle-637
83FleSta-53
83FleSti-177
83OPC-175
83PhiPosGPaM-3
83PhiTas-10
83Top-175
83Top-229
83TopSti-273
84AllGamPI-41
84Don-137
84Fle-29
84FleSti-118
84Nes792-535
84OPC-131
84PhiTas-25
84Top-535
84TopSti-120
84TopTif-535
85Fle-250
85OPC-219
85PhiTas-10
85PhiTas-25
85Top-737
85TopTif-737
86BasStaB-32
86Don-530
86Fle-176
86Lea-258
86OPC-253
86RedTexG-6
86Top-639
86TopTif-639
87Don-246
87DonHig-21
87DonOpeD-190
87Fle-200
87FleGlo-200
87FleMin-32
87OPC-41
87RedKah-6
87Top-41
87Top-281
87TopSti-142
87TopTif-41
88Don-186
88DonAll-47
88DonBasB-110
88Fle-232
88FleGlo-232
88Lea-191
88OPC-265
88PanSti-273
88RedKah-6
88Sco-206
88ScoGlo-206
88Spo-117
88StaLinRe-7
88Top-265
88TopSti-143
88TopTif-265
89Bow-307
89BowTif-307
89Don-242
89DonBasB-293
89Fle-159
89FleGlo-159
89OPC-201
89PanSti-71
89RedFolSB-36
89RedKah-6
89Sco-187
89Top-422
89TopSti-135
89TopTif-422
89UppDec-169
90Don-139
90PubSti-27
90Sco-434
90UppDec-664
90VenSti-142
Diaz, Carlos (Carlos Antonio)
80SpolndT-4
81RicBraT-13
82RicBraT-5
83Don-562
83Fle-540
84DodPol-27
84Don-600
84Fle-583
84FleUpd-32
84Nes792-524
84Top-524
84TopTif-524
84TopTra-32T
84TopTraT-32T
85DodCokP-9
85Fle-369
85Top-159
85TopTif-159
86DodCokP-9
86DodPol-27
86DodUniOP-4
86Don-348
86Fle-128
86Top-343
86TopTif-343
90DodTar-184
91MetWIZ-96
Diaz, Carlos Francisco
87DunBluJP-923
88KnoBluJB-12
89KnoBluJB-4
89KnoBluJP-1125
89KnoBluJS-2
90CMC-336
90SyrChiC-10
90SyrChiMB-5
91BriTigC-18
91BriTigP-3612
91DenZepLD-134
91DenZepP-124
91LinDriAAA-134
91TopDeb90-41
92MemChiF-2422
92MemChiS-434
92OmaRoyF-2963
93MemChiF-378
94MemChiF-360
Diaz, Cesar
91KinMetC-27
91KinMetP-3815
92ColMetPI-11
92PitMetC-11
92PitMetF-3298
93ExcFS7-71
93KinMetC-8
93KinMetF-3798
94CapCitBC-5
94CapCitBF-1753
94SouAtlLAF-SAL36
95LinVen-89
95StLucMTI-11
96StLucMTI-23
Diaz, Derek
85BelBreT-23
86ElPasDP-8
87ElPasDP-16
Diaz, Ed
86VanCanP-10
92SanBerC-20
92SanBerSF-964
94ClaGolF-79
95Top-480
95Top-642
Diaz, Eddie
83WatIndF-4
91Sco-576
Diaz, Eddy
91BelMarC-5
91BelMarP-3672
93AppFoxF-2467
93JacSunF-2716
93LinVenB-138
93MidLeaAGF-2
94ClaGolF-101
94JacSunF-1416
94VenLinU-15
95LinVen-78
95PorCitRTI-6
96TacRaiB-11
Diaz, Edwin
94ChaRivC-5
94ChaRivF-2681
95Bow-129
96BesAutS-27
96Bow-233
96Exc-110
96TexLeaAB-4
96TulDriTI-9
97Bow-201
97BowChr-187
97BowChrI-187
97BowChrIR-187
97BowChrR-187
97BowInt-201
Diaz, Einar
92BurIndC-28
92BurIndF-1662
93BurIndC-10
94ColRedC-8
94ColRedF-445
94SouAtlLAF-SAL8
95Exc-38
95KinIndTI-10
95UppDecML-53
96BesAutS-28
96BowBes-177
96BowBesAR-177
96BowBesR-177
96CanIndB-11
96Exc-42
97UppDec-483
95UppDecMLFS-53
Diaz, Enrique
80WauTimT-15
81WauTimT-16
Diaz, Freddy
93BoiHawC-7
93BoiHawF-3921
94LakElsSC-7
94LakElsSF-1670
95MidAngOHP-11
Diaz, German
90GenCubP-3039
90GenCubS-9
91PeoChiC-16
91PeoChiP-1348
91PeoChiTI-16
92ClaFS7-219
92GenCubC-20
92GenCubF-1566
92PeoChiC-10
93WatIndC-7
93WatIndF-3554
Diaz, Jairo
96RocCubTI-6
Diaz, Javier
94AshTouF-1788
Diaz, Johnny
87ElmPio(C-22
88WinHavRSS-7
89ElmPioP-2
Diaz, Jorge
83MadMusF-8
Diaz, Jose
87MyrBeaBJP-1437
88DunBluJS-4

88FloStaLAS-33
89KnoBluJB-5
89KnoBluJS-3
Diaz, Kiki
92ChaLooS-182
93OmaRoyF-1683
93OmaRoyF-1693
Diaz, Kiki (Edgar)
83BelBreF-23
87BrePol-2
88BlaYNPRWL-38
88DenZepC-18
88DenZepP-1256
89BlaYNPRWL-40
89DenZepC-12
89DenZepP-47
90BreMilB-5
90BrePol-2
90El PasDAGTI-16
90FleUpd-105
90Lea-335
90TopTra-26T
90TopTraT-26T
91Don-197
91Fle-581
91OPC-164
91Top-164
91TopDesS-164
91TopMic-164
91TopTif-164
91UppDec-286
92NasSouS-288
94BreMilB-216
94BreMilB-307
97PacPriGotD-GD34
Diaz, Lino
93EugEmeC-11
93EugEmeF-3861
93MarPhiC-7
93MarPhiF-3488
94MarPhiC-6
94MarPhiF-3307
94MidLeaAF-MDW21
94RocRoyC-8
94RocRoyF-573
95Bes-24
95Exc-57
95Top-581
96BesAutSA-16
96Exc-58
96OmaRoyB-11
Diaz, Mario
96ColCliB-10
Diaz, Mario Rafael
80WauTimT-14
81LynSaiT-17
82LynSaiT-12
84ChaLooT-25
86CalCanP-6
87CalCanP-2319
88BlaYNPRWL-39
88CalCanP-804
88Fle-649
88FleGlo-649
88FleUpd-59
88FleUpdG-59
88MarMot-21
89BlaYNPRWL-41
89Fle-547
89FleGlo-547
89MarMot-21
89PanSti-427
89Top-309
89TopTif-309
89UppDec-318
90CalCanP-655
90OPC-781
90ProAAAF-120
90PubSti-432
90Top-781
90TopTif-781
90VenSti-143
91Lea-363
91MetWIZ-97
91RanMot-24
92CalCanS-58
92Don-149
92Fle-301
92OklCit8F-1919
93Lea-470
93OklCit8F-1631
93RanKee-126
94Don-73
94Fle-305
94Pac-614
94Sco-169
94ScoGolR-169
94StaCluT-71
94StaCluTFDI-71
95Sco-230
95ScoGolR-230
95ScoPlaTS-230
96Pac-69
Diaz, Mike
80QuaCitCT-13
83IowCubT-11
85PhiTas-41
85PorBeaC-50
86SpoRoo-50
87Don-267
87Fle-609
87FleGlo-609
87SpoTeaP-18
87Top-469
87TopTif-469
88BlaYNPRWL-133
88Don-267
88Fle-326
88FleGlo-326
88OPC-239
88PanSti-378
88Sco-143
88ScoGlo-143
88StaLinPi-7
88Top-567
88TopTif-567
89Don-655
89Fle-494
89FleGlo-494
89Sco-603
89Top-142
89TopTif-142
89UppDec-606
Diaz, Rafael
90JamExpP-16
91RocExpC-4
91RocExpP-2039
92WesPalBEC-14
92WesPalBEF-2081
93PocPosF-4203
93PocPosSP-5
Diaz, Ralph
93HarSenF-264
94OttLynF-2895
Diaz, Remigio
90StoPorB-6
90StoPorCLC-192
90StoPorP-2191
91StoPorC-13
91StoPorP-3036
Diaz, Rich
83WatIndF-25
Diaz, Roberto
78NewWayCT-11
79BurBeeT-16
Diaz, Sandy
89EliTwiS-6
90EliTwiS-8
90KenTwiB-18
90KenTwiP-2287
90KenTwiS-2
91EliTwiP-4295
92KenTwiF-595
92ProFS7-104
Diaz, Steve
89BelBreIS-7
90StoPorB-3
90StoPorCLC-188
90StoPorP-2187
91BelBreC-11
91BelBreP-2105
Diaz, Tony
84ButCopKT-9
88MiaMarS-6
89St.LucMS-4
Diaz, Victor
72CedRapCT-9
87MyrBeaBJP-1457
89BirBarB-4
89BirBarP-101
Diaz, William
86WauTimP-8
87SalSpuP-6
88SanBerSB-9
88SanBerSCLC-37
89WilBilP-640
89WilBilS-6
DiBartolomeo, Steve
90CarLeaA-52
90WinSpiTI-16
91ChaKniLD-131
91ChaKniP-1682
91LinDriAA-131
Dibble, Rob
85CedRapRT-6
86VerRedP-7
87NasSouTI-4
88BlaYNPRWL-55
88FleUpd-83
88FleUpdG-83
88NasSouC-4
88NasSouP-493
88NasSouTI-8
88ScoRoo-86T
88ScoRooG-86T
89Bow-305
89BowTif-305
89ClaLigB-76
89Don-426
89DonBasB-334
89Fle-160
89FleGlo-160
89RedKah-49
89Sco-618
89Top-264
89TopTif-264
89UppDec-375
90Bow-42
90BowTif-42
90CedRapRDGB-16
90ClaBlu-43
90Don-189
90DonBesN-76
90Fle-418
90FleCan-418
90Lea-57
90OPC-46
90PanSti-249
90PubSti-28
90RedKah-8
90Sco-277
90ScoYouS2-15
90Top-46
90TopTif-46
90UppDec-586
90USPlaCA-WCO
90VenSti-144
91Bow-667
91Cla1-T23
91Cla3-T15
91ClaGam-168
91Don-321
91Fle-62
91Lea-282
91OPC-662
91PanSti-128
91RedFolS-4
91RedKah-49
91RedPep-7
91Sco-17
91Sco-407
91StaClu-131
91Stu-163
91Top-662
91TopDesS-662
91TopMic-662
91TopTif-662
91Ult-92
91UppDec-635
91USPlaCA-10S
91Woo-23
92Bow-242
92Cla2-T76
92ClaGam-75
92Don-139
92Fle-404
92Lea-69
92New-6
92OPC-757
92OPCPre-53
92Pin-180
92PinTeaP-11
92RedKah-49
92Sco-455
92Sco-891
92Sco100S-41
92ScoImpP-71
92StaClu-548
92StaCluD-36
92Stu-22
92StuPre-12
92Top-757
92TopGol-757
92TopGolPS-757
92TopGolW-757
92TopKid-40
92TopMic-757
92TopPreS-131
92TriPla-257
92Ult-187
92UppDec-30
92UppDec-142
92UppDecF-21
92UppDecFG-21
93Bow-526
93ClaGam-26
93Don-322
93Fin-180
93FinRef-180
93Fla-25
93Fle-389
93FleFruotL-16
93FunPac-168
93Lea-280
93LeaGolA-R10
93MilBonSS-16
93OPC-122
93PacSpa-81
93PanSti-297
93Pin-101
93PinTeaP-B11
93RedKah-9
93Sco-651
93Sel-65
93SelSam-65
93SP-208
93StaClu-369
93StaCluFDI-369
93StaCluMOP-369
93Top-470
93TopGol-470
93TopInaM-470
93TopMic-470
93TriPla-52
93Ult-327
93UppDec-473
93UppDec-675
93UppDecGold-473
93UppDecGold-675
94ColC-93
94ColChoGS-93
94ColChoSS-93
94Don-451
94ExtBas-231
94Fin-88
94FinRef-88
94Fle-409
94Lea-166
94OPC-224
94Pac-145
94Pin-41
94PinArtP-41
94PinMusC-41
94RedKah-7
94Sco-114
94ScoGolR-114
94Sel-340
94Spo-14
94StaClu-202
94StaCluFDI-202
94StaCluGR-202
94StaCluMOP-202
94Top-183
94TopGol-183
94TopSpa-183
94TriPla-211
94Ult-471
94UppDec-308
94UppDecED-308
95Sco-530
95ScoGolR-530
95ScoPlaTS-530
95ScoYouTE-530T
95WhiSoxK-7
DiCeglio, Tom
85VisOakT-11
86KenTwiP-6
Dick, Bill
76BurBeeT-5
77BurBeeT-5
77HolMilT-7
78BurBeeT-9
78HolMilT-5
Dick, Ed
79TCM50-81
Dick, Ralph
88SanBerSB-14
88SanBerSCLC-53
89SanBerSB-11
89SanBerSCLC-90
Dicken, Rongie
92JohCitCC-5
92JohCitCF-3122
93JohCitCC-9
93JohCitCF-3686
Dickens, John
92EugEmeC-9
92EugEmeF-3020
93RocRoyC-11
93RocRoyF-710
94WilBluRC-6
94WilBluRF-293
95WilBluRTI-25
Dickerman, Leo
90DodTar-932
Dickerson, Bobby (Bob)
87OneYanP-27
88Ft.LauYS-5
89AlbYanB-16
89AlbYanP-319
89AlbYanS-7
90AlbYanB-15
90AlbYanP-1040
90AlbYanS-4
91HagSunLD-229
91HagSunP-2461
91LinDriAA-229
92RocRedWF-1944
92RocRedWS-452
93RocRedWF-248
94FayGenC-9
94FayGenF-2161
90BluOriB-1
Dickerson, Jim
86PitCubP-7
Dickerson, Robert
92NiaFalRC-9
92NiaFalRF-3337
93NiaFalRF-3402
Dickey, Bill (William M.)
30SchR33-11
31Exh-25
32USCar-6
33ButCanV-13
33ExhFou-13
33GeoCMil-9
33Gou-19
33GouCanV-19
33TatOrbSDR-161
34BatR31-30
34BatR31-117
34ButPreR-16
34DiaStaR-11
34DiaStaR-103
34ExhFou-13
35ExhFou-13
35GouPuzR-4D
35GouPuzR-7D
35GouPuzR-12D
36GouWidPPR-A27
36NatChiFPR-109
36R31PasP-8
36SandSW-14
36WheBB5-9
36WorWidGV-34
37OPCBatUV-119
37WheBB6-1
38BasTabP-6
38ExhFou-13
39ExhSal-12A
39ExhSal-12B
39GouPreR303A-12
39GouPreR303B-5
39PlaBal-30
39WorWidGTP-12
40PlaBal-7
40WheM4-3
41DouPlaR-65
41PlaBal-70
43MPR302-1-8
43YanSta-8
46SpoExcW-1-1B
47PM1StaP1-42
48SweSpoT-6
50CalHOFW-26
51Bow-290
51R42SmaS-22
52Top-400
60NuHi-34
60Top-465

61GolPre-27
61NuSco-434
63BazA-40
67TopVen-140
68SpoMemAG-8
69SCFOldT-7
75YanDyn1T-12
75YanDyn1T-51
76RowExh-4
76ShaPiz-71
77GalGloG-68
77GalGloG-188
77ShaPiz-9
77TCMTheWY-55
80MarExhH-9
80PacLeg-44
80PerHaloFP-71
80SSPHOF-71
80YanGreT-8
81SanDieSC-18
81SanDieSC-19
82DiaCla-23
83ConMar-9
83DonHOFH-26
83TCMPla1942-3
83TopRep5-400
83YanASFY-9
83YanYealT-10
85FegMurCG-4
86SpoDecG-13
86TCM-16
87HygAllG-14
88ConAmeA-8
89PerCelP-12
90PerGreM-37
90RinPosYMP-7
92ConTSN-474
92MegRut-158
92YanWIZA-17
92YanWIZH-8
93ConTSN-755
93ConTSN-869
94ConTSN-1086
94ConTSNB-1086
94ConTSNCI-36
95ConTSNP-1475
95MegRut-5

Dickey, Chad
85CloHSS-13

Dickey, George W.
47TipTop-19
85TCMPla1-14

Dickey, R.A.
97Bow-81
97BowChr-108
97BowChrI-108
97BowChrIR-108
97BowChrR-108
97BowInt-81

Dickman, Dave
89PulBraP-1888
89SumBraP-1100

Dickman, Geo. Emerson
39PlaBal-17
40PlaBal-37
41Gou-6
79DiaGre-228
94ConTSN-1167
94ConTSNB-1167

Dickman, Mark
85KinBluJT-5
86VenGulP-4

Dickshot, Johnny
79DiaGre-364
83TCMPla1945-16
94ConTSN-1286
94ConTSNB-1286

Dickson, Jason
95CedRapKTI-29
95SPML-28
96Bow-219
96MidAngB-12
96VanCanB-9
97Bow-79
97BowBes-105
97BowBesAR-105
97BowBesR-105
97BowChr-106
97BowChrI-106
97BowChrIR-106
97BowChrR-106
97BowInt-79
97ColCho-254
97Don-371
97DonLim-52
97DonLim-198
97DonLimLE-52
97DonLimLE-198
97DonPre-158
97DonPreCttC-158
97DonPreP-371
97DonPrePGold-371
97DonTea-11
97DonTeaSPE-11
97Fle-38
97FleTif-38
97Lea-338
97LeaFraM-338
97LeaFraMDC-338
97NewPin-158
97NewPinAP-158
97NewPinMC-158
97NewPinPP-158
97Pin-134
97PinArtP-134
97PinCer-124
97PinCerMBlu-124
97PinCerMG-124
97PinCerMR-124
97PinCerR-124
97PinMusC-134
97PinTotCPB-124
97PinTotCPG-124
97PinTotCPR-124
97PinX-P-130
97PinX-PMoS-130
97Sco-475
97ScoHobR-475
97ScoResC-475
97ScoShoS-475
97ScoShoSAP-475
97Sel-117
97SelArtP-117
97SelRegG-117
97SP-13
97SpollI-5
97SpollIEE-5
97TopSta-91
97TopStaAM-91
97Ult-451
97UltGolME-451
97UltGolP-7
97UltPlaME-451
97UppDec-522

Dickson, Jim (James Edward)
64Top-524
65Top-286
66Top-201
66TopVen-201

Dickson, Ken
87AubAstP-21
88AshTouP-1050

Dickson, Lance
90AriWilP-2
90ChaKniTI-1
90ClaDraP-23
90ClaYel-T85
90GenCubP-3029
90GenCubS-10
90PeoChiUTI-U1
90ProAaA-173
91Bow-411
91Cla2-T55
91Don-424
91IowCubLD-204
91IowCubP-1053
91LinDriAAA-204
91OPC-114
91OPCPre-35
91Sco-385
91ScoRoo-24
91StaClu-44
91Stu-154
91Top-114
91TopDeb90-42
91TopDesS-114
91TopMic-114
91TopTif-114
91UppDec-9
91UppDecFE-3F
92Bow-316
92Don-421
92DonCraJ1-7
92IowCubS-207
92Pin-272
92ProFS7-199
92Sco100RS-96
92ScoImpP-85
92SkyAAAF-100
92StaClu-836
92StaCluNC-836
92TriPla-97
92UppDecML-74
93DayCubC-6
93DayCubF-853
93StaCluCu-15
94IowCubF-1271
94StaCluT-352
94StaCluTFDI-352

Dickson, Murry (Murry Monroe)
46SeaSLP-12
47Exh-57
49Bow-8
49EurSta-158
50Bow-34
50PirTeal-6
51Bow-167
51R42SmaS-23
51TopBluB-16
52Bow-59
52RedMan-NL5
52TipTop-7
52Top-266
53RedMan-NL22
54Bow-111
55Bow-236
56Top-211
57Top-71
58Top-349
59Top-23
59TopVen-23
79DiaGre-320
83TopRep5-266

Dickson, Walt (Walter R.)
11T205-40

Didier, Bob (Robert Daniel)
69Top-611
70MLBOffS-5
70OPC-232
70Top-232
71MLBOffS-8
71OPC-432
71Top-432
73OPC-574
73Top-574
74OPC-482
74Top-482
75IowOakT-6
80VanCanT-11
81WesHavAT-1
82WesHavAT-26
83TacTigT-18
84A'sMot-27
85A'sMot-27
86A'sMot-27
87TucTorP-24
88TucTorC-24
88TucTorJP-9
88TucTorP-190
89MarMot-27
90MarMot-27
94SyrChiF-986
94SyrChiTI-10

Didion, Kristopher
96SpoIndB-10

Dieguez, Mike
94HunCubF-3558
95PitMetTI-43
94HunCubC-7

Diehl, Charles
52Whe-9A
52Whe-9B

Diehl, Greg
75ForLauYS-8
76ForLauYS-20

Diemido, Chet
87PenWhiSP-3
91SarWhiSP-1132

Dierderger, George
78WisRapTT-3
79WisRapTT-4

Diering, Bob
79WatIndT-22

Diering, Chuck (Charles E.)
47TipTop-154
49EurSta-180
50Bow-179
51Bow-158
52Bow-198
52NatTeaL-5
52Top-265
54OriEss-8
55OriEss-8
55Top-105
55TopDouH-1
56Top-19
56TopPin-1
57SeaPop-8
79TCM50-51
83TopRep5-265
91OriCro-104

Dierker, Larry (Lawrence E.)
65Top-409
66Top-228
66TopVen-228
67Ast-9
67AstTeal1-4
67AstTeal2-8
67CokCapAs-15
67DexPre-66
67Top-498
68CokCapA-15
68Top-565
69MLBOffS-138
69Top-411
69TopSta-32
69TopTeaP-6
70AstTeal-2
70DayDaiNM-17
70MLBOffS-39
70OPC-15
70Top-15
70TopPos-15
70TopSup-6
71AstCok-4
71BazNumT-24
71BazUnn-33
71Kel-48
71MLBOffS-77
71OPC-540
71Top-540
71TopCoi-141
71TopGreM-32
71TopSup-30
71TopTat-48
72MilBra-89
72OPC-155
72Top-155
73Kel2D-53
73OPC-375
73Top-375
73TopCanL-13
74AstFouTIP-2
74OPC-660
74Top-660
75OPC-49
75Top-49
76AstPosD-1
76Hos-25
76HosTwi-25
76OPC-75
76Top-75
77Car5-6
77CarTeal-6
77Top-350
78Top-195
81Car5x7-3
82AstAstI-1
86AstMot-8
87AstSer1-8
87AstShoSO-4
87AstShowSTh-24
87AstShowSTh-26
87AstShowSTh-28
89SweBasG-78
93UppDecAH-41

Dietrich, Bill (William J.)
34DiaMatCSB-45
35DiaMatCS3T1-47
36NatChiFPR-24
36OveCanR-11
36OveCanR-12
39WhiSoxTI-4
40WhiSoxL-4
41Gou-9
83TCMPla1944-19
91ConTSN-133
92ConTSN-366

Dietrich, Jason
94BenRocF-3584
96AshTouB-12
97BenRocC-4

Dietrick, Pat (Patrick J.)
85MadMusP-9
85MadMusT-12
86MadMusP-8
86ModA'sC-6
87HunStaTI-9
88HunStaTI-4
89TacTigC-24
89TacTigP-1553
90CMC-590
90ProAAAF-152
90TacTigC-13
90TacTigP-105

Dietz, Dick (Richard Allen)
62KahAtl-4
67Top-341
68OPC-104
68Top-104
68TopVen-104
69Top-293
69TopSta-103
69TopTeaP-14
70DayDaiNM-58
70Gia-2
70MLBOffS-123
70OPC-135
70Top-135
71GiaTic-2
71Kel-42
71MilDud-42
71MLBOffS-246
71OPC-545
71Top-545
71TopCoi-33
71TopTat-26
72MilBra-90
72OPC-295
72OPC-296
72Top-295
72Top-296
73OPC-442
73Top-442
84GiaMot-21
90DodTar-185
90SanJosGB-28
90SanJosGP-2027
90SanJosGS-28
91SanJosGC-25
91SanJosGP-28
92ShrCapF-3889
92ShrCapS-600
93SanJosGC-26
93SanJosGF-27
94SanJosGC-27
94SanJosGF-2833

Dietz, Don
87VerRedP-11

Dietz, Jim
89SanDieSAS-7

Dietz, Lloyd
43PhiTeal-7

Dietz, Steve
94FayGenC-10
94FayGenF-2155

Dietzman, Steve
93CliGiaC-29
94CliLumF-1998
94CliLumC-29

Diez, Scott
87MiaMarP-14
88FloStaLAS-5
88MiaMarS-7
90DurBulUTI-3

DiFelice, Mike
91HamRedC-15
91HamRedP-4041
92HamRedC-23
92HamRedF-1593
93SprCarC-7
93SprCarF-1853
94ArkTraF-3091

DiFilippo, John
94PriRedC-7
94PriRedF-3267

Diggle, Ron
75TidTidTI-9
77SpoIndC-16
78SpoIndC-3
79RocRedWT-14

Diggs, Tony
89HelBreSP-8
90HelBreSP-9
91BelBreC-18

91BelBreP-2115
92ElPasDF-3935
92ElPasDS-206
92SkyAA F-91
93StoPorC-8
94ArkTraF-3101
96ArkTraB-12
96LouRedB-16
DiGiacomo, Kevin
92WatIndC-25
92WatIndF-3241
DiGioia, John
85SprCarT-7
86PalSprAP-7
86PalSprAP-10
DiGiovanna, Charlie
55DodGolS-31
Digirolama, Dave
83ButCopKT-3
Digrace, Jack
52LavPro-87
DiGrandi, Vince
90NebCor-8
DiHigo, Martin
74LauOldTBS-29
80PerHaloFP-159
80SSPHOF-159
83ConMar-60
86NegLeaF-19
88ConNegA-3
88NegLeaD-10
89HOFStiB-63
89RinPosNL1-2
90NegLeaS-23
91PomBlaBPB-14
95NegLeaL2-5
DiLauro, Jack (Jack Edward)
70OPC-382
70Top-382
71MLBOffS-78
71OPC-677
71Top-677
87AstShowSTh-6
89RinPosM1-8
91MetWIZ-95
94Met69CCPP-12
94Met69CS-11
94Met69T-21
Dileso, Anthony
93IdaFalBF-4044
93IdaFalBSP-25
Dilks, Darren
84IndIndTI-27
Dill, Chip (Walter)
84AriWilP-4
Dillard, Don (David Donald)
57SeaPop-9
59Top-123
59TopVen-123
60MapLeaSF-6
60Top-122
60TopVen-122
61Top-172
63Top-298
Dillard, Gordon
87HagSunP-25
88ChaKniTI-20
88RocRedWGCP-6
89ScrRedBC-7
89ScrRedBP-714
90BufBisC-2
90BufBisP-366
90CMC-2
90ProAAAF-481
91OriCro-105
Dillard, Harrison
51BerRos-D18
Dillard, Jay
75LafDriT-18
76PhoGiaVNB-6
Dillard, Mike
87ElmPio(C-32
Dillard, Ron
81MiaOriT-1
82TulDriT-18
83BurRanF-14
83BurRanT-15
Dillard, Stephen B.
75IntLeaAT-22
76VenLeaS-151
77Top-142
78TigBurK-16
78Top-597
79Top-217
80Top-452
81Don-502
81Fle-298
81Top-78
82Don-174
82EdmTraT-4
82Fle-594
82Top-324
88SouBenWSGS-15
89PacSenL-140
90EliSenL-35
91AubAstC-26
91AubAstP-4289
92AubAstC-27
92AubAstF-1370
93QuaCitRBC-25
93QuaCitRBF-115
94QuaCitRBC-25
94QuaCitRBF-550
95RocCubTI-NNO
Dillhoefer, Pickles (William)
19W514-71
Dillinger, Bob (Robert B.)
46SeaSLP-13
46SpoExcW-2-11
47Exh-58
48BluTin-14
49Bow-143A
49Bow-143B
49Lea-144
50Bow-105
51Bow-63
53MotCoo-61
76TayBow4-103
79DiaGre-195
Dillinger, John
92FroRowDP-51
93ClaGolF-198
93LetMouF-4146
93LetMouSP-6
94AugGreC-3
94AugGreF-3000
95LynHilTI-7
96LynHilB-8
Dillingham, Dan
94EugEmeC-9
94EugEmeF-3726
Dillman, Bill (William H.)
67Top-558
68Top-466
69OPC-141
69Top-141
69TopFou-9
70OPC-386
70Top-386
91OriCro-106
Dillmore, Phillip
87KinIndP-6
Dillon, Chad
95ButCopKtI-7
Dillon, Jim (James)
90SouOreAB-11
90SouOreAP-3443
91MadMusC-7
91MadMusP-2124
91MidLeaAP-MWL40
92ModA'sC-21
92ModA'sF-3892
Dillon, Pop (Frank Edward)
03BreE10-35
03BreE10-36
11SpoLifCW-91
90DodTar-186
Dillon, Steve (Stephen E.)
64Top-556
76Met63 S-5
91MetWIZ-98
Dilone, Juan
93SouOreAC-7
93SouOreAF-4070
94WesMicWC-7
94WesMicWF-2303
96ModA'sB-5
Dilone, Miguel (Miguel Angel)
77PirPosP-3
78Top-705
79Hos-118
79OPC-256
79Top-487
80Top-541
81AllGamPI-50
81Don-441
81Fle-391
81FleStiC-86
81OPC-141
81Top-141
81TopSti-67
82Don-515
82Fle-365
82FleSta-196
82Ind-11
82IndTeal-10
82IndWhe-23
82OPC-77
82Top-77
83Don-85
83Fle-405
83IndPos-9
83IndWhe-8
83Top-303
84ExpPos-7
84ExpStu-25
85DomLeaS-62
85Don-453
85Fle-395
85Lea-135
85OPC-178
85Top-178
85TopMin-178
85TopTif-178
93LimRocDWB-94
Dilorenzo, Joe
52LavPro-30
DiMaggio, Dom (Dominic P.)
41DouPlaR-107
41PlaBal-63
42RedSoxTI-8
46RedSoxTI-7
46SpoExcW-2-3
47Exh-59
47HomBon-9
47PM1StaP1-43
47PM1StaP1-44
47TipTop-2
48RedSoxTI-2
49Bow-64
49Lea-75
50Bow-3
50Dra-33
50RoyDes-4
51BerRos-A8
51R42SmaS-24
51TopRedB-20
52BerRos-12
52NatTeaL-6
52RedMan-AL5
52RoyPre-4
52StaCalL-71F
52StaCalS-85B
52Top-22
53ExhCan-23
53RedMan-AL22
53RedSoxTI-5
53Top-149
76TayBow4-28
79DiaGre-227
82DiaCla-33
82GSGalAG-4
84TCMPla1-1
87RedSox1T-5
91TopArc1-149
91UppDecS-4
DiMaggio, Joe (Joseph Paul)
36GouWidPPR-A117
36GouWidPPR-C6
36NatChiFPR-105
36OveCanR-13
36R31PasP-9
36R31Pre-L12
36WorWidGV-51
37ExhFou-13
37GouFliMR-4A
37GouFliMR-4B
37GouThuMR-4
37OPCBatUV-118
37WheBB14-5
37WheBB6-11
37WheBB7-29I
37WheBB8-3
37WheBB9-5
38BasTabP-7
38ExhFou-13
38GouHeaU-250
38GouHeaU-274
38OurNatGPP-7
38WheBB10-11
38WheBB15-2
39ExhSal-13
39GouPreR303A-13
39GouPreR303B-6
39OrcPhoAP-7
39PlaBal-26
39WorWidGTP-13
39WorWidGV-11
40PlaBal-1
40WheM4-2A
40WheM4-2B
41DouPlaR-63
41PlaBal-71
41WheM5-17
43MPR302-1-9
46SpoExcW-4-7
47HomBon-10
47PM1StaP1-45
47PM1StaP1-46
47PM1StaP1-47
47PM1StaP1-48
47PM1StaP1-49
47PM1StaP1-50
48BluTin-16
48SweSpoT-15
48YanTeal-6
49Lea-1
49MPR302-2-105
50CalHOFW-27
51BerRos-B5
51R42SmaS-25
52BerRos-13
53ExhCan-28
60NuHi-7
60NuHi-38
60RawGloT-5
61GolPre-9
61NuSco-438
61NuSco-467
63BasMagM-20
63GadFunC-33
63HalofFB-5
67TopVen-145
68LauWorS-36
69A'sJacitB-5
70YanCliDP-13
72BowBanD-1
72LauGreF-1
73HalofFPP-6
73SyrChiTI-7
74LauAllG-39
74SyrChiTI-5
75McCCob-15
75ShaPiz-1
75SpoHobBG-2
75YanDyn1T-11
75YanDyn1T-51
75YanDyn1T-53
76GalBasGHoF-7
76LauDiaJ-25
76RowExh-4
76ShaPiz-74
76SSPYanOD-2
76TayBow4-4
76TayBow4-49
77BobParHoF-19
77GalGloG-1
77GalGloG-235
77ShaPiz-24
77Spo-208
79DiaGre-1
79TCM50-1
80MarExhH-10
80PacLeg-5
80PerHaloFP-75
80SSPHOF-75
80YanGreT-7
81SanDieSC-14
81SanDieSC-19
81SpoHaloF-14
82BasCarN-8
82BasCarN-18
82DiaCla-1
82GSGalAG-6
83MLBPin-4
83TCMPla1942-2
83YanASFY-10
83YanYealT-1
84OCoandSI-50
84SpoDesPW-5
84WilMay-44
85SpoPro-1
85UltBasC-9
86SpoDecG-20
86SpoDesJM-11
86TCM-8
86TCMSupS-9
86TCMSupS-18
86TCMSupS-25
87HygAllG-15
88PacLegI-100
88WilMulP-4
89CMCMan-15
89HOFStiB-39
90BasWit-49
90HOFStiB-39
90RinPosYMP-12
92ScoDiM-1
92ScoDiM-2
92ScoDiM-3
92ScoDiM-4
92ScoDiM-5
92ScoDiM-AU0
92ScoFacI-B12
92ScoFacI-B13
92ScoFacI-B14
92YanWIZA-18
92YanWIZH-9
93DiaStaES-126
93PinDiM-1
93PinDiM-2
93PinDiM-3
93PinDiM-4
93PinDiM-5
93PinDiM-6
93PinDiM-7
93PinDiM-8
93PinDiM-9
93PinDiM-10
93PinDiM-11
93PinDiM-12
93PinDiM-13
93PinDiM-14
93PinDiM-15
93PinDiM-16
93PinDiM-17
93PinDiM-18
93PinDiM-19
93PinDiM-20
93PinDiM-21
93PinDiM-22
93PinDiM-23
93PinDiM-24
93PinDiM-25
93PinDiM-26
93PinDiM-27
93PinDiM-28
93PinDiM-29
93PinDiM-30
93PinDiMA-1
93PinDiMA-2
93PinDiMA-3
93PinDiMA-4
93PinDiMA-5
95SigRooOJ-JD1
95SigRooOJS-JD1
DiMaggio, Vince (Vincent P.)
38ExhFou-1
39WorWidGV-12
41PlaBal-61
47SigOil-42
79DiaGre-211
83DiaClaS2-58
83TCMPla1942-38
DiMarco, Steven
91EriSaiC-5
91EriSaiP-4077
91KanCouCC-15
91KanCouCP-2662
DiMare, Gino
91MiaHurBB-4
93ForLauRSC-9
93ForLauRSFP-1610
Dimartino, John
52LavPro-43
Dimas, Rodolfo
85MexCitTT-7
DiMascio, Dan
87GleFalTP-22
88EasLeaAP-6
88GleFalTP-931
89TolMudHC-17
89TolMudHP-788

Dimeda, Jose
91MacBraC-21
DiMichele, Frank
86QuaCitAP-8
87PalSprP-27
88EdmTraP-565
88MidAngGS-8
89BlaYNPRWLU-5
89MidAngGS-12
90MidAngGS-22
Dimmel, Mike (Michael Wayne)
75WatDodT-6
78RocRedWT-7
80ArkTraT-8
91OriCro-107
Dimuro, Ray
91CalLeLA-53
Dineen, Bill (William H.)
04FanCraAL-14
04RedSoxUP-3
09PC7HHB-12
09RamT20-36
09T206-93
11SpoLifCW-92
92ConTSN-374
94ConTSN-1200
94ConTSNB-1200
Dineen, Kerry (Kerry Michael)
76SSP-452
92YanWIZ7-44
Dinger, David
86DavLipB-9
Dinger, Mascot
94MasMan-5
Dinges, Vance
79DiaGre-307
Dinkelmeyer, John
75CliPilT-12
Dinneen, Bill (William H.)
03BreE10-37
Dinnen, Kevin
93BurIndC-11
93BurIndF-3290
Dinyar, Eric
94JamJamC-7
94JamJamF-3958
95FayGenTI-9
96LakTigB-12
Dinzey, Amado
75LynRanT-8
Dion, Connie
43ParSpo-23
Dion, Jos.
87AllandGN-44
Diorio, Mike
93AubAstC-8
93AubAstF-3435
95QuaCitRBTI-4
96KisCobB-6
Diorio, Ron (Ronald M.)
74OPC-599
74Top-599A
74Top-599B
74Top-599C
DiPietro, Fred
76CliPilT-9
DiPino, Frank M.
78BurBeeT-10
80HolMilT-12
81VanCanT-17
82Top-333
82VanCanT-16
83TopTra-25T
84AstMot-17
84Don-502
84Fle-224
84FleSti-72
84Nes792-172
84Top-172
84TopSti-74
84TopTif-172
85AstHouP-21
85AstMot-11
85Don-232
85Fle-349
85OPC-376
85Top-532
85TopSti-66
85TopTif-532
86AstMilL-7
86AstPol-25
86Don-304
86Fle-299
86Top-26
86TopTif-26
87CubCan-8
87CubDavB-33
87Don-416
87Fle-560
87FleGlo-560
87OPC-297
87Top-662
87TopTif-662
88CubDavB-33
88Don-570
88DonBasB-205
88DonTeaBC-570
88Fle-418
88FleGlo-418
88Sco-413
88ScoGlo-413
88StaLinCu-3
88Top-211
88TopTif-211
89Bow-434
89BowTif-434
89CarSmo-6
89Don-393
89Fle-423
89FleGlo-423
89FleUpd-118
89Sco-146
89Top-439
89TopTif-439
89TopTra-24T
89TopTraT-24T
89UppDec-61
90Bow-187
90BowTif-187
90CarSmo-5
90Don-518
90Fle-249
90FleCan-249
90Lea-103
90OPC-788
90PubSti-218
90Sco-462
90Top-788
90TopTif-788
90TopTVCa-12
90UppDec-202
90VenSti-145
91CarPol-35
91Don-360
91Fle-632
91OPC-112
91Sco-553
91StaClu-439
91Top-112
91TopDesS-112
91TopMic-112
91TopTif-112
91UppDec-350
92StaClu-886
92StaCluECN-886
94BreMilB-217
DiPino, Paul
90IdaFalBP-3254
DiPoto, Jerry
89WatIndS-3
90CarLeaA-36
90KinIndTI-1
91CanIndLD-81
91CanIndP-975
91LinDriAA-81
92Bow-92
92ColSprSSF-746
92ColSprSSS-84
92SkyAAAF-39
93ChaKniF-536
93FleFinE-199
93TriAAAGF-36
94Fle-102
94Sco-278
94ScoGolR-278
94StaClu-380
94StaCluFDI-380
94StaCluGR-380
94StaCluMOP-380
94Top-767
94TopGol-767
94TopSpa-767
96Don-261
96DonPreP-261
96MetKah-8
96MetKah-7
Dirit, Nidio
76VenLeaS-209
Disabato, Pat
87LitFalMP-2383
DiSalvo, Pio
77EvaTriT-8
84TigWavP-13
DiSarcina, Gary
88BenBucL-7
89BasAmeAPB-AA30
89MidAngGS-13
89TexLeaAGS-4
90Bow-290
90BowTif-290
90CMC-496
90EdmTraC-19
90EdmTraP-524
90ProAAAF-100
90ScoRoo-68T
90TopDeb89-31
90UppDec-761
91EdmTraLD-162
91EdmTraP-1523
91LinDriAAA-162
91Sco-768
91Sco100RS-26
92AngPol-7
92Bow-159
92Cla2-T8
92Don-497
92DonRoo-32
92Fle-664
92Lea-48
92LeaGolP-30
92LeaGolR-BC21
92Pin-52
92PinRoo-8
92PinTea2-38
92ScoRoo-25
92StaClu-458
92Stu-144
92TopTra-28T
92TopTraG-28T
92TriPla-251
92Ult-24
92UltAllR-3
92UppDec-726
92UppDecSR-SR7
93AngMot-2
93AngPol-17
93Bow-145
93DiaMar-32
93Don-121
93Fla-172
93Fle-188
93FleRooS-RSB5
93Lea-260
93OPC-80
93PacSpa-43
93PanSti-6
93Pin-337
93Sco-374
93Sel-281
93SP-21
93StaClu-196
93StaCluAn-27
93StaCluFDI-196
93StaCluMOP-196
93Stu-85
93Top-157
93TopGol-157
93TopInaM-157
93TopMic-157
93TriPla-58
93Ult-160
93UppDec-230
93UppDecGold-230
93USPlaCR-13H
94AngAdoF-1
94AngLAT-4
94AngMot-6
94Bow-507
94ColC-94
94ColChoGS-94
94ColChoSS-94
94Don-478
94ExtBas-32
94Fin-171
94FinRef-171
94Fla-20
94Fle-52
94Lea-173
94LeaL-16
94Pac-75
94PanSti-36
94Pin-97
94PinArtP-97
94PinMusC-97
94Sco-377
94ScoGolR-377
94Sel-226
94StaClu-213
94StaCluFDI-213
94StaCluGR-213
94StaCluMOP-213
94Stu-10
94Top-351
94TopGol-351
94TopSpa-351
94TriPla-13
94Ult-325
94UppDec-165
94UppDecED-165
95AngCHP-4
95AngMot-6
95ColCho-97
95ColChoGS-97
95ColChoSS-97
95Don-256
95DonPreP-256
95DonTopotO-33
95Emo-19
95Fla-17
95Fle-221
95Lea-367
95Pac-56
95PanSti-70
95Pin-232
95PinArtP-232
95PinMusC-232
95Sco-448
95ScoGolR-448
95ScoPlaTS-448
95StaClu-338
95StaCluMOP-338
95StaCluSTWS-338
95StaCluVR-177
95Stu-116
95Top-12
95TopCyb-10
95Ult-267
95UltGolM-267
95UppDec-19
95UppDecED-19
95UppDecEDG-19
96AngMot-7
96ColCho-482
96ColChoGS-482
96ColChoSS-482
96Don-31
96DonPreP-31
96Fla-35
96Fle-44
96FleTif-44
96Lea-134
96LeaPrePB-134
96LeaPrePG-134
96LeaPrePS-134
96MetUni-25
96MetUniP-25
96Pac-271
96Pin-320
96PinFoil-320
96ProSta-1
96Sco-64
96ScoDugC-A55
96ScoDugCAP-A55
96StaClu-36
96StaCluMOP-36
95StaCluVRMC-177
96Sum-114
96SumAbo&B-114
96SumArtP-114
96SumFoi-114
96Top-296
96Ult-27
96UltGolM-27
96UppDec-27
97Cir-309
97CirRav-309
97ColCho-263
97DonTea-15
97DonTeaSPE-15
97Fle-39
97FleTif-39
97MetUni-38
97Pac-4
97PacLigB-4
97PacPriGotD-GD3
97PacSil-4
97Sco-423
97ScoHobR-423
97ScoResC-423
97ScoShoS-423
97ScoShoSAP-423
97StaClu-93
97StaCluMOP-93
97Top-59
97UppDec-294
DiSarcina, Glenn
91UtiBluSC-16
91UtiBluSP-3245
92ClaFS7-259
92SouBenWSC-15
92SouBenWSF-183
93FloStaLAF-22
93SarWhiSC-1
93SarWhiSF-1376
94BirBarC-7
94BirBarF-628
94Bow-99
94ClaGolF-194
94UppDecML-247
96BirBarB-8
96NasSouB-12
Disher, Dan
87WauTimP-4
88SanBerSB-10
88SanBerSCLC-31
Disher, David
86BelMarC-122
Dishington, Nate
94ClaGolF-104
96PeoChiB-8
Dishman, Glenn
93SpoIndC-1
93SpoIndF-3581
94ExcFS7-278
94WicWraF-184
95Bow-214
95BowBes-B84
95BowBesR-B84
95Exc-281
95ExcLeaL-7
95SPCha-16
95SPChaDC-16
95TopTra-107T
95UppDec-473T
96ColCho-27
96ColChoGS-27
96ColChoSS-27
96Don-263
96DonPreP-263
96Fle-564
96FleTif-564
96LasVegSB-12
96StaClu-401
96StaCluMOP-401
96Top-410
96Ult-283
96UltGolM-283
96UppDec-186
Dishon, Chris
89PulBraP-1891
Dismuke, Jamie
91CedRapRC-17
91CedRapRP-2725
91Cla/Bes-368
92ChaWheF-15
92ChaWVWC-16
92ClaFS7-57
93ChaLooF-2365
93ClaGolF-185
93ExcFS7-17
94ExcFS7-173
94IndIndF-1816
94UppDecML-74
94VenLinU-266
95ChaLooTI-4
Dismukes, Dizzy (William)
87NegLeaPD-15
93NegLeaRL2-48
Distaso, Alec (Alec John)
69Top-602
Distefano, Benny
83LynPirT-19
84HawIslC-144
85Don-166
85HawIslC-231
85Top-162
85TopTif-162
86Don-78

86HawIslP-4
87Don-514
87Top-651
87TopTif-651
88BlaYNPRWL-150
88BufBisC-11
88BufBisP-1489
88BufBisTI-6
88TriAAAP-4
89BufBisC-11
89BufBisP-1682
89Fle-205
89FleGlo-205
89PirVerFJ-30
89TopTra-25T
89TopTraT-25T
90Fle-464
90FleCan-464
90PubSti-152
90VenSti-146
91LinDriAAA-454
91RocRedWLD-454
91RocRedWP-1907
92AstMot-14
92Bow-414
92TucTorS-606
93OklCit8F-1636

Ditmar, Art (Arthur J.)
55A'sRodM-12
55Bow-90
56A'sRodM-4
56Top-258
57Top-132
58Top-354
59Top-374
60Lea-78
60MacSta-7
60Top-430
61Pos-16
61Top-46
61Top-48
61Top-510
61TopStaI-192
61Yan61RL-20
61YanJayP-3
62Jel-100
62Pos-100
62PosCan-100
62SalPlaC-202
62ShiPlaC-202
62Top-246
76A'sRodMC-9
79TCM50-220
91RinPos1Y2-9
92YanWIZ6-35

Dittmer, Jack (John D.)
53BraJohC-19
53BraSpiaS3-11
53BraSpiaS7-6
53Top-212
54Bow-48
54BraJohC-6
54BraSpiaSP-9
54Top-53
55Bow-212
55BraGolS-17
55BraJohC-6
55BraSpiaSD-8
57Top-282
83Bra53F-6
91TopArc1-212
94TopArc1-53
94TopArc1G-53

Ditton, Julian
76CliPilT-10
77OrlTwiT-6

Divison, Julio
75LafDriT-20
91St.CatBJC-25
91St.CatBJP-3412

Dixon, Andrew
86EveGiaC-11
86EveGiaPC-3
88ShrCapP-1287

Dixon, Bryan
88St.CatBJP-2030

Dixon, Bubba
94SpoIndC-1
94SpoIndF-3316
95RanCucQT-16
96Exc-236
96MemChiB-12

Dixon, Colin
90WinHavRSS-6
91LinDriAA-455
91NewBriRSLD-455
91NewBriRSP-356
92NewBriRSF-439
92NewBriRSS-483
92SkyAA F-205
93NewBriRSF-1228
94SanBerSC-1
94SanBerSF-2765
95SalAvaTI-2
97DunDonPPS-6

Dixon, Dan
79AshTouT-23
79TulDriT-7

Dixon, Dee
87CliGiaP-15
89ShrCapP-1836
90ElPasDGS-8
90TexLeaAGS-9

Dixon, Dickie
91KenTwiC-13
91KenTwiP-2067
92VisOakC-3
92VisOakF-1007
93ForMyeMC-6
93ForMyeMF-2648

Dixon, Eddie
86WesPalBEP-13
87WesPalBEP-672
88JacExpB-6
88JacExpP-967
89JacExpB-5
89JacExpP-159
90CMC-60
90IndIndC-10
90IndIndP-288
90ProAAAF-571
91IndIndLD-182
91IndIndP-456
91LinDriAAA-182
92BufBisRF-318
92BufBisS-31
93TucTorF-3053
94ChaLooF-1355

Dixon, Gary
95Exc-282

Dixon, Hal
55Bow-309

Dixon, Jim
94HicCraC-8
94HicCraF-2168
96PriWilCB-9

Dixon, John
55A'sRodM-13

Dixon, Ken
84ChaO'sT-17
85Don-270
85FleUpd-36
85OriHea-5
85TopTifT-31T
85TopTra-31T
86Don-148
86Fle-273
86Top-198
86TopTif-198
87Don-171
87Fle-468
87FleGlo-468
87OriFreB-39
87Top-528
87TopTif-528
88Don-48
88Fle-557
88FleGlo-557
88Sco-411
88ScoGlo-411
88Top-676
88TopTif-676
91OriCro-108

Dixon, Mason
90ColMudS-28

Dixon, Mike
81WatIndT-8

Dixon, Rap
74LauOldTBS-2
86NegLeaF-78
91PomBlaBPB-23

Dixon, Roger
90EliTwiS-9

Dixon, Ronn
82WauTimF-14
83WauTimF-7

Dixon, Seanelle
91HawWomS-3

Dixon, Sonny (John Craig)
53Bri-4
55Bow-211
88ChaLooLTI-8

Dixon, Steve
89JohCitCS-8
90SavCarP-2061
91St.PetCC-4
91St.PetCP-2268
92ArkTraF-1123
92ArkTraS-32
92ClaFS7-13
93Bow-192
93ClaFS7-133
93LouRedF-208
94LouRedF-2977
94StaCluT-314
94StaCluTFDI-314
94Top-168
94TopGol-168
94TopSpa-168
94TriAAF-AAA37
95IowCubTI-10
96RocRedWB-12

Dixon, Tim
96WesPalBEB-8

Dixon, Tom (Thomas Earl)
75DubPacT-19
79OPC-186
79Top-361
80TidTidT-12
80Top-513
80VenLeaS-110
81TidTidT-14
82SyrChiT-2
82SyrChiTI-9
83WicAerDS-6

Dixon, Troy
83BirBarT-23

Dixon, Tyrone
93NiaFalRF-3403

Dixon, Xavier
76SeaRaiC-4

Djakonow, Paul
75ShrCapT-1
76ShrCapT-9
77ShrCapT-5
79BufBisT-21
80BufBisT-10
82EvaTriT-15

Doak, Bill (William L.)
14B18B-83A
14B18B-83B
15SpoNewM-48
16ColE13-42
16SpoNewM-47
19W514-51
20NatCarE-23
21E121So1-19
21E121So8-17
21Exh-35
21Exh-36
21Nei-65
22AmeCarE-16
22E120-228
22W572-23
22W573-32
22W575-27
23W501-78
23WilChoV-30
90DodTar-187

Dobbek, Dan (Daniel John)
55DonWin-18
59Top-124
59TopVen-124
60SenJayP-5
60Top-123
60TopVen-123
61Top-108
61TwiPetM-24
62Top-267

Dobbins, Joe
43CenFlo-6
44CenFlo-5
45CenFlo-5

Dobbs, Gary
78WisRapTT-4
79WisRapTT-15

Dobbs, John
11SpoLifCW-93
90DodTar-188

Doberenz, Mark
82IdaFalAT-32
83IdaFalAT-33
84ModA'sC-25

Dobernic, Jess (Andrew J.)
49Bow-200
49EurSta-81

Dobie, Reggie
85LynMetT-5
86JacMetT-2
87MetColP-30
87TidTidP-3
87TidTidT-1
88BlaYNPRWLU-3
88MetColP-19
88TidTidP-1590
89CalCanC-5
89CalCanP-528

Dobrolsky, Bill
92BelBreC-19
92BelBreF-407
92HelBreF-1717
92HelBreSP-5
93StoPorC-9
93StoPorF-746
94BelBreC-7
94BelBreF-105
96El PasDB-8

Dobson, Chuck (Charles T.)
66Top-588
67CokCapAt-14
67Top-438
68OPC-62
68Top-62
68TopVen-62
69A'sJacitB-6
69MilBra-74
69Top-397
70MLBOffS-256
70OPC-331
70Top-331
71Kel-32
71MLBOffS-510
71OPC-238
71Top-238
72MilBra-91
72OPC-523
72Top-523
75OPC-635
75Top-635
77SalLakCGC-6

Dobson, Joe (Joseph Gordon)
42RedSoxTI-9
43RedSoxTI-5
46RedSoxTI-8
47Exh-60
47TipTop-3
48RedSoxTI-3
49Bow-7
50Bow-44
51Bow-36
52Top-254
52WhiSoxH-3
53BowC-88
53RedMan-AL15
53Top-5
79DiaGre-284
82Bow195E-262
83TopRep5-254
91TopArc1-5

Dobson, Pat (Patrick E.)
67Top-526
68OPC-22
68TigDetFPB-4
68Top-22
68TopVen-22
69TigTealC-2
69Top-231
70MLBOffS-112
70OPC-421
70Top-421
71MLBOffS-295
71OPC-547
71Top-547
72MilBra-92
72OPC-140
72Top-140
73OPC-34
73Top-34
74OPC-463
74SyrChiTI-6
74Top-463
75OPC-44
75SyrChiTI-4
75Top-44
75YanSSP-16
76OPC-296
76SSP-431
76Top-296
76TopTra-296T
77PepGloD-8
77Top-618
78Top-575
80NasSouTI-8
83BrePol-NNO
84BrePol-NNO
88PadSmo-7
88TigDom-4
89PacSenL-87
89PacSenL-219
89T/MSenL-28
89TopSenL-96
90EliSenL-64
90PadMag-22
91OriCro-109
91PacSenL-9
92BreCarT-xx
92YanWIZ7-45

Doby, Larry (Lawrence Eugene)
47Exh-61
47IndTeal-5
47PM1StaP1-51
47PM1StaP1-52
47PM1StaP1-53
48IndTeal-7
49Bow-233
49IndTeal-8
49IndVisEI-5
49Lea-138
49MPR302-2-124
50Bow-39
50IndNumN-7
50IndTeal-6
51Bow-151
51R42SmaS-18
51TopCurA-2
52BerRos-14
52Bow-115
52IndNumN-18
52RedMan-AL6
52StaCalL-74A
52StaCalS-88B
52Top-243
53BowC-40
53ExhCan-11
53IndPenCBP-9
54Bow-84
54DanDee-4
54Top-70
55ArmCoi-4
55BigLeaIS-5
55DaiQueS-5
55Ind-1
55IndGolS-15
55RedMan-AL18
56Top-250
56YelBasP-9
57Top-85
58Hir-17
58Top-424
59Top-166
59Top-455
59TopVen-166
72Dia-11
73ExpPos-3
73OPC-377
73Top-377
74OPC-531
74Top-531
76ExpRed-5
78SSP270-153
79TCM50-27
80AppFoxT-26
82CraJac-1
83TopRep5-243
84FifNatC-7
84OCoandSI-42
84OCoandSI-206
86IndGreT-7
88PacLegI-102
89SweBasG-115
90PacLeg-20
90SweBasG-43
91SweBasG-24
91TopArc1-333
92ActPacA-27
92MVP-4
92MVP2H-12

92UppDecS-18
93TedWil-134
93UppDecAH-42
93UppDecAH-153
94TopArc1-70
94TopArc1G-70
94UppDecAH-47
94UppDecAH1-47
Dockins, George
90DodTar-189
Dodd, Bill
88CedRapRP-1138
88MidLeaAGS-11
89ChaLooB-14
89ChaLooGS-9
90ChaLooGS-11
91ChaLooLD-157
91ChaLooP-1952
91LinDriAA-157
Dodd, Daniel
88St.CatBJP-2018
89MyrBeaBJP-1472
Dodd, Lance
82AleDukT-8
Dodd, Mike
75CedRapGT-22
Dodd, Rob
90ArkRaz-7
91BoiHawC-26
91BoiHawP-3869
Dodd, Robert
95ClePhiF-210
95ReaPhiELC-8
96ReaPhiB-3
Dodd, Scott
91BilMusP-3747
91BilMusSP-11
92CedRapRF-1062
Dodd, Tim
83TamTarT-7
84CedRapRT-11
Dodd, Tom
86ChaOriW-8
86SouLeaAJ-12
87ChaO'sW-8
87SouLeaAJ-6
88OmaRoyC-19
88OmaRoyP-1505
89OmaRoyC-11
89OmaRoyP-1727
90CalCanC-16
90CalCanP-662
90CMC-443
90ProAAAF-127
91OriCro-110
Dodd, Tommie
82NasSouTI-10
Dodge, Tom
91QuaCitAC-12
91QuaCitAP-2630
92PalSprAC-19
92PalSprAF-842
93PalSprAC-8
93PalSprAF-76
Dodgers, Brooklyn
13FatT20-10
36R31Pre-G20
38BasTabP-36
48ExhTea-3
48ExhTea-9
48ExhTea-13
48ExhTea-15
51TopTea-2
56Top-166
57Top-324
58Top-71
70FleWorS-38
70FleWorS-53
70OPC-411
71FleWorS-14
71FleWorS-39
71FleWorS-51
71FleWorS-54
71FleWorS-64
73Top-91
86JosHalC-3
93TedWilPC-20
95TopArcBD-152
Dodgers, Great Falls
96GreFalDTI-NNO
Dodgers, Los Angeles
59Top-457
60Top-18
60TopTat-58
60TopVen-18
61Top-86
61TopMagR-13
62GuyPotCP-11
62Top-43
62TopVen-43
63Top-337
64Top-531
64TopTatI-11
65OPC-126
65Top-126
66Top-238
66TopRubI-111
66TopVen-238
67Top-503
68LauWorS-63
68OPC-168
68Top-168
68TopVen-168
69FleCloS-12
69FleCloS-30
69TopStaA-12
70FleWorS-62
70FleWorS-63
70Top-411
71FleWorS-61
71FleWorS-63
71FleWorS-64
71OPC-402
71Top-402
71TopTat-43
72OPC-522
72Top-522
73OPC-91
73OPCBTC-12
73TopBluTC-12
74OPC-643
74OPCTC-12
74Top-643
74TopStaA-12
74TopTeaC-12
78Top-259
80DodPol-NNO
81DodPol-NNO
82TopSti-255
82TopSti-256
83FleSta-235
83FleSti-NNO
86DodPol-NNO
87SpoTeaL-14
87Top-431
87TopTif-431
88PanSti-473
88RedFolSB-124
89FleGlo-WS12
89FleWaxBC-C9
89FleWorS-12
90PubSti-623
90RedFolSB-111
90VenSti-526
94ImpProP-21
94Sco-653
94ScoGolR-653
95PanSti-132
96FleDod-19
96PanSti-93
Dodgers, Newark
93NegLeaRL2-80
Dodig, Jeff
87IdaFalBP-25
88DurBulS-5
Dodson, Bo
89HelBreSP-17
89HigSchPLS-11
90CalLeaACLC-38
90ProAaA-150
90StoPorB-26
90StoPorCLC-190
90StoPorP-2189
91Bow-38
91CalLeLA-55
91Cla/Bes-358
91StoPorC-20
91StoPorP-3038
92ElPasDF-3928
92ElPasDS-207
92ProFS7-87
92SkyAA F-92
92UppDecML-311
93ElPasDF-2956
94ExcFS7-80
94NewOrlZF-1476
95ElPasDTI-5
96PawRedSDD-7
Dodson, Dan
94SanJosGC-30
Dodson, Pat
84PawRedST-19
85PawRedST-3
86PawRedSP-9
87ClaGam-8
87Don-44
87Lea-44
87PawRedST-24
87SevCoi-E11
87Spo-118
87SpoTeaP-9
87Top-449
87TopTif-449
88PawRedSC-16
88PawRedSP-466
88Sco-352
88ScoGlo-352
90OklCit8P-437
90ProAAAF-683
91RoyPol-25
Doerr, Bobby (Robert P.)
36GouWidPPR-C7
38GouHeaU-258
38GouHeaU-282
39PlaBal-7
40PlaBal-38
41DouPlaR-105
41PlaBal-64
42RedSoxTI-10
43RedSoxTI-6
46RedSoxTI-9
46SpoExcW-2-1B
47Exh-62
47HomBon-11
47TipTop-4
48RedSoxTI-4
49Bow-23
49Lea-83
50AmeNut&CCP-4
50Bow-43
50Dra-13
51TopBluB-37
52BerRos-15
53ExhCan-24
60RawGloT-6
67TopVen-169
74LauAllG-43
75ShaPiz-14
76TayBow4-1
79BluJayBY-7
79DiaGre-229
80PerHaloFP-194
80SSPHOF-192
83MLBPin-5
85TCMPla1-3
86DonHig-32
86RedSoxGT-5
87RedSox1T-3
88PacLegI-73
89HOFStiB-11
89PacLegI-150
89PerCelP-13
89SweBasG-110
89TopGloA-11
90PacLeg-21
90PerGreM-36
90SweBasG-96
91SweBasG-25
91UppDecS-4
91UppDecS-19
92ActPacA-8
92ActPacA2-8G
92ConTSN-467
93ActPacAC-8
93ConTSN-913
94TedWil-3
Doerr, Tim
76CliPilT-11
Doescher, Edward
12ImpTobC-50
Doezie, Troy
94OgdRapSP-10
94OgdRapSP-28
95NewJerCTI-7
Doffek, Scott
90YakBeaTI-15
91VerBeaDP-780
92SanAntMF-3982
92SanAntMS-563
Doggett, George
85LynMetT-26
Doggett, Jerry
59DodVol-14
60DodUniO-22
60DodUniO-23
61DodUniO-24
71DodTic-20
Doheny, Ed
11SpoLifCW-94
Doherty, John Harold
89NiaFalRP-7
90LakTigS-7
91LinDriAA-382
91LonTigLD-382
91LonTigP-1870
92Bow-518
92Cla2-T99
92DonRoo-33
92FleUpd-20
92LeaGolR-BC24
92Pin-513
92PinRoo-4
92ScoRoo-81T
92Ult-360
93Don-277
93Fla-200
93Fle-226
93Lea-534
93Pin-407
93Sco-353
93Sel-298
93TigGat-6
93Top-713
93TopGol-713
93TopInaM-713
93TopMic-713
93Ult-196
93UppDec-757
93UppDecGold-757
93USPlaCR-7D
94ColC-442
94ColChoGS-442
94ColChoSS-442
94Don-78
94ExtBas-72
94Fin-277
94FinRef-277
94Fla-47
94Fle-127
94Lea-371
94Pac-219
94Pin-96
94PinArtP-96
94PinMusC-96
94Sco-531
94ScoGolR-531
94Sel-335
94StaClu-184
94StaCluFDI-184
94StaCluGR-184
94StaCluMOP-184
94Top-371
94TopGol-371
94TopSpa-371
94TriPla-242
94Ult-51
94UppDec-247
94UppDecED-247
95ColCho-477
95ColChoGS-477
95ColChoSS-477
95Don-312
95DonPreP-312
95Fla-37
95Fle-48
95Lea-9
95Sco-231
95ScoGolR-231
95ScoPlaTS-231
95StaClu-460
95StaCluMOP-460
95StaCluSTWS-460
95Stu-191
95Top-125
95Ult-284
95UltGolM-284
95UppDec-423
95UppDecED-423
95UppDecEDG-423
96Don-303
96DonPreP-303
96Fle-108
96FleTif-108
96PawRedSDD-8
96TreThuB-9
Doherty, John Michael
75OPC-524
75SalLakCC-6
75Top-524
Dohne, Heriberto
88ModA'sCLC-76
Doi, Masahiro
79TCMJapPB-15
Doiron, Serge
91GenCubC-6
91GenCubP-4221
Dolan, Brett
96BelSnaTI-13
Dolan, Cozy
11SpoLifCW-95
14B18B-84A
14B18B-84B
23MapCriV-9
81ConTSN-41
90DodTar-190
98CamPepP-14
Dolan, John
88ElmPioC-7
89LynRedSS-7
Dolan, Tom (Thomas J.)
87OldJudN-134
Dold, John
93PriRedC-7
93PriRedF-4193
Dolejsi, Brad
91OklStaC-8
Dolejsi, Dale
94BriTigC-10
94BriTigF-3495
Dolf, Mike
76WilTomT-11
Doljack, Frank
34DiaMatCSB-46
35TigFreP-4
76TigOldTS-6
Doll, Chris
87BelMarL-24
88WauTimGS-4
Dollar, Toby
96GreFalDB-10
96GreFalDTI-7
Dolson, Andrew
91MedHatBJP-4092
91MedHatBJSP-17
92MedHatBJF-3205
92MedHatBJSP-8
93HagSunF-1873
94DunBluJC-9
94DunBluJF-2550
Doman, Roger
92St.CatBJC-7
92St.CatBJF-3382
93HagSunC-9
93HagSunF-1874
94DunBluJC-10
94DunBluJF-2551
95KnoSmoF-35
96DunBluJB-5
96DunBluJTI-7
Dombrowski, Robert
89BilMusP-2055
90CedRapRP-2328
Domecq, Ray
90MarPhiP-3192
91SpaPhiP-887
Domenichelli, Dom
59DarFar-6
Domenico, Brian
94SouOreAC-6
94SouOreAF-3613
Domingo, Placido
92PacSea-61
Domingo, Tyrone
92HigSchPLS-28
Dominguez, Frank
85MiaHur-3
89RenSilSCLC-256
90PalSprACLC-209
90PalSprAP-2580
91PalSprAP-2019
Dominguez, Johnny
93ElmPioC-6
Dominguez, Jose
85VisOakT-22
86OrlTwiP-5
88ShrCapP-1281
88TexLeaAGS-19
89ShrCapP-1854
Dominguez, Ken
90OneYanP-3390

92PriWilCC-28
92PriWilCF-165
93GreHorC-28
93OneYanC-27
93OneYanF-3520
94OneYanC-26
94OneYanF-3808
87PanAmTUBI-NNO
Dominico, Ron
84LitFalMT-26
85LitFalMT-4
Domino, Robert
93PriRedC-8
93PriRedF-4182
94BilMusF-3673
94BilMusSP-2
Dominow, Eric
93EriSaiC-6
93EriSaiF-3123
Donaghue, Ray
77St.PetCT-15
78ArkTraT-6
Donahue, Chuck
86TamTarP-5
Donahue, Jack
87OldJudN-135
Donahue, Jiggs (John Augustus)
03BreE10-38
08AmeCarE-74
11SpoLifCW-96
90KalBatN-13
Donahue, Jim (James A.)
87OldJudN-136A
87OldJudN-136B
Donahue, Margaret
31CubTeal-6
Donahue, Matt
92EriSaiC-27
92EriSaiF-1611
93KanCouCC-6
93KanCouCF-909
93KanCouCTI-6
Donahue, Pat (Patrick W.)
09RamT20-37
11SpoLifM-5
Donahue, Red (Francis Rostell)
05IndSouPSoCP-7
Donahue, Tim
90RenSilSCLC-270
91CollndC-24
91CollndP-1491
92KinIndC-11
92KinIndF-2483
98CamPepP-19
Donald, Atley (Richard Atley)
40PlaBal-121
41PlaBal-38
43YanSta-9
75YanDyn1T-13
79DiaGre-12
95ConTSN-1413
Donald, Skip
95PitMetTI-NNO
Donald, Tremayne
90JohCitCS-9
92St.PetCC-19
92St.PetCF-2038
Donaldson, James
91SydWavF-20
Donaldson, John
78LauLonABS-28
86NegLeaF-77
90NegLeaS-8
94TedWil-104
Donaldson, John (John David)
68Top-244
68TopVen-244
69MilBra-75
69MLBOffS-85
69OPC-217
69Top-217
70MLBOffS-269
70OPC-418
70Top-418
72MilBra-93
83Pil69G-32
Donatelli, Andy
85UtiBluST-18
Donatelli, Augie
55Bow-313
Donati, John
92StaCluD-37
93BoiHawC-8
93BoiHawF-3922
94BoiHawC-9
94BoiHawF-3361
95Bow-233
95BowGolF-233
95CedRapKTI-25
95Exc-19
95MidLeaA-12
Donato, Dan
95GreBatTI-3
96BowBes-121
96BowBesAR-121
96BowBesR-121
96Exc-86
96NorNavB-7
Done, Johnny
94WatIndC-5
94WatIndF-3926
96AriBlaDB-16
Donecq, Ray
91SpaPhiC-2
Donkey-Hokey, Mascot
96ButCopKB-8
Donlin, Mike (Michael J.)
03BreE10-39
06FanCraNL-13
06GiaUllAFS-2
08AmeCarE-9
08AmeCarE-44
08RosComP-126
09AmeCarE-33
09RamT20-38
09T206-94
09T206-95
09T206-96
10CouT21-119
10CouT21-120
10CouT21-274
10RedCroT-19
10RedCroT-103
10RedCroT-183
11SpoLifCW-97
12ColRedB-79
12ColTinT-79
12HasTriFT-30A
12HasTriFT-30B
12HasTriFT-30C
12HasTriFT-30D
12HasTriFT-30E
12T207-47
75FlePio-25
92ConTSN-450
94ConTSN-1051
94ConTSNB-1051
Donnelly, Blix (Sylvester)
49Bow-145
49EurSta-133
49PhiBul-15
50Bow-176
50PhiPhil-1
51Bow-208
76TayBow4-71
Donnelly, Brendan
93GenCubC-8
93GenCubF-3166
96ChaLooB-11
Donnelly, Ed (Edward)
12T207-48
Donnelly, Jim (James B.)
87BucN28-111
87OldJudN-137
88WG1CarG-64
Donnelly, Rich
74GasRanT-8
76SacSolC-22
77TucTorC-14
78TucTorC-42
79TucTorT-8
83RanAffF-NNO
84RanJarP-NNO
85RanPer-NNO
89PirVerFJ-39
90PirHomC-9
92PirNatl-6
93PirNatl-9
93RanKee-127
94PirQui-5
78TucTorC-42
Donnelly, Robert
95NewJerCTI-8
96PeoChiB-9
Donnels, Chris
88ColMetGS-26
88St.LucMS-6
89St.LucMS-5
89Sta-116
90JacMetGS-12
90MetColP-30
90TopTVM-41
91Bow-465
91Cla3-T16
91Lea-447
91LinDriAAA-554
91MetColP-29
91ScoRoo-104T
91TidTidLD-554
91TidTidP-2516
91TriA AAGP-AAA47
91UppDecFE-61F
92Don-619
92MetColP-21
92OPC-376
92Pin-168
92ProFS7-275
92Sco-212
92Sco100RS-79
92ScoRoo-29
92SkyAAAF-249
92StaClu-353
92TidTidF-904
92TidTidS-555
92Top-376
92TopDeb91-45
92TopGol-376
92TopGolW-376
92TopMic-376
92UppDec-44
93AstMot-22
93Don-747
93Fle-426
93PacSpa-475
93StaCluAs-23
93Top-238
93TopGol-238
93ToplnaM-238
93TopMic-238
94AstMot-16
94Fle-488
94Pac-262
94Sco-172
94ScoGolR-172
94StaClu-334
94StaCluFDI-334
94StaCluGR-334
94StaCluMOP-334
94Top-153
94TopGol-153
94TopSpa-153
95ColCho-107
95ColChoGS-107
95ColChoSS-107
Donofrio, Larry
80AshTouT-22
81AppFoxT-13
82GleFalWST-4
Donohue, J.A.
08AmeCarE-75
Donohue, Jiggs (John F.)
07WhiSoxGWH-3
08RosComP-13
09T206-97
11T205-41
Donohue, Jim (James A.)
87BucN28-57
Donohue, Jim (James T.)
60Top-124
60TopVen-124
61Top-151
62Top-498
Donohue, Pat
93JohCitCC-10
93JohCitCF-3687
Donohue, Pete (Peter J.)
21Nei-77
22E120-170
22W572-24
25Exh-27
26Exh-27
29PorandAR-16
31W517-26
91ConTSN-322
Donohue, Steve
79WesHavYT-19
84ColCliT-21
Donohue, Tom (Thomas J.)
77SalLakCGC-8
80Top-454
81Don-51A
81Don-51B
81Fle-281
81Top-621
78STLakCGC-8
Donovan, Bret
88CapCodPPaLP-165
92ClaFS7-322
92ElmPioC-3
92ElmPioF-1375
92WinHavRSC-22
93LynRedSC-7
93LynRedSF-2510
Donovan, Dick (Richard E.)
47Exh-63A
47Exh-63B
55Top-146
56Top-18
56TopPin-32
57Top-181
58Top-290
58WhiSoxJP-2
59Top-5
59TopVen-5
60Lea-72
60Top-199
60WhiSoxTS-4
61Baz-10
61Top-414
61TopStal-202
62IndJayP-2
62Jel-73
62Kah-8
62Pos-73
62PosCan-73
62Top-15
62Top-55
62TopStal-33
62TopVen-15
62TopVen-55
63Baz-10
63Fle-11
63IndJayP-5
63Jel-75
63Pos-75
63SalMetC-34
63Top-8
63Top-370
63TopStil-13
64IndJayP-4
64Kah-7
79TCM50-34
83Bra53F-20
Donovan, Gary
77BurBeeT-6
Donovan, Jack
81TucTorT-25
Donovan, Mike (Michael B.)
80BurBeeT-3
Donovan, Patsy (Patrick J.)
03BreE10-40
04FanCraAL-15
11BasBatEU-20
11SpoLifCW-98
11SpoLifM-6
90DodTar-191
98CamPepP-21
Donovan, Scot
94WatIndC-6
94WatIndF-3927
96KenIndB-6
Donovan, Wild Bill (William E.)
03WilCarE-11
07TigACDPP-4
07TigACDPP-20
08RosComP-34
08TigFreGWP-1
09AmeCarE-34
09BusBroBPP-6
09ColChiE-80
09RamT20-39
09T206-98
09T206-99
09TigHMTP-5
09TigHMTP-6
09TigHMTP-8
09TigMorPenWBPP-4
09TigTaCP-6
09WolNewDTPP-6
09WolNewDTPP-19
10CouT21-16
10CouT21-121
10CouT21-275
10DarChoE-15
10E101-15
10E102-7
10MelMinE-15
10NadCarE-16
10PeoT21-17A
10PeoT21-17B
10StaCarE-11
10SweCapPP-24
10W555-24
11MecDFT-45
11PloCanE-25
11SpoLifCW-99
11SpoLifM-58
11TurRedT-12
12ColRedB-80
12ColTinT-80
12PhiCarE-9
15AmeCarE-12
15SpoNewM-49
16ColE13-43
16FleBreD-24
16SpoNewM-48
21E121So8-18
22AmeCarE-17
22W575-28
23WilChoV-31
69SCFOldT-27
81TigDetN-29
81TigSecNP-7
87ConSer2-13
90DodTar-192
Doody, Tom
96BatCliTI-32
Dooin, Red (Charles S.)
03WilCarE-12
06FanCraNL-14
08RosComP-138
09AmeCarE-35
09ColChiE-79
09ColChiE-81
09SpoNewSM-43
09T206-100
10DomDisP-34
10E101-16
10E102-8
10E98-13
10LuxCigPP-7
10MelMinE-16
10NadCarE-17
10PeoT21-18A
10PeoT21-18B
10SepAnoP-12
10StaCarE-12
10SweCapPP-125A
10SweCapPP-125B
10W555-25
11DiaGumP-12
11L1L-126
11MecDFT-16
11PloCanE-26
11S74Sil-98
11S81LarS-101
11SpoLifCW-100
11SpoLifM-226
11T205-42
11TurRedT-14
12ColRedB-81
12ColTinT-81
12HasTriFT-30D
12HasTriFT-31A
12HasTriFT-31B
12HasTriFT-31C
12HasTriFT-51
12PhiCarE-10
12T207-49
13NatGamW-15
13TomBarW-14
14CraJacE-38
14TexTomE-18
15AmeCarE-13
15CraJacE-38
15SpoNewM-50
16BF2FP-76
16SpoNewM-49
16TanBraE-8
16TanBraE-14
Doolan, Blake
92BatCliC-25
92BatCliF-3256

93SpaPhiC-12
93SpaPhiF-1050
94ClePhiC-12
94ClePhiF-2521
95ReaPhiELC-9
95ReaPhiTI-10
96Exc-197
96ScrRedBB-11

Doolan, Mickey (Michael J.)
06FanCraNL-15
08RosComP-139
09BriE97-9
09ColChiE-82
09T206-101
09T206-102
09T206-103
10CouT21-17
10CouT21-122
10CouT21-123
10CouT21-124
10CouT21-125
10CouT21-276
10CouT21-277
10DomDisP-35
10E-UOraBSC-10
10E101-17
10LuxCigPP-8
10MelMinE-17
10NadCarE-18
10PeoT21-19A
10PeoT21-19B
10RedCroT-20
10RedCroT-104
10RedCroT-105
10RedCroT-184
10RedCroT-185
10SweCapPP-126A
10SweCapPP-126B
10W555-26
11E94-12
11S74Sil-99
11SpoLifCW-101
11SpoLifM-227
11T205-43
11TurRedT-90
12ColRedB-82
12ColTinT-82
12HasTriFT-31A
14CraJacE-120
15AmeCarE-14
15CraJacE-120
15SpoNewM-51
15VicT21-7
16SpoNewM-50
90DodTar-193

Dooley, Chris
96JohCitCTI-10

Dooley, Marvin
89PriPirS-6

Dooner, Glenn
82TolMudHT-2

Doornenweerd, Dave
92Bow-146
92StaCluD-38
94SalBucC-7
94SalBucF-2317
96LakElsSB-4
96MidAngB-13

Dophied, Tracy
82AubAstT-12

Doprante, Luis
93ForLauRSC-28

Dopson, John
86IndIndTI-12
88DonRoo-43
88ExpPos-5
88FleUpd-99
88FleUpdG-99
88ScoRoo-88T
88ScoRooG-88T
89Bow-24
89BowTif-24
89ClaTraP-161
89Don-392
89DonBasB-177
89DonTra-7
89Fle-373
89FleGlo-373
89FleUpd-8
89OPC-251
89Sco-466
89ScoRoo-40T
89Top-251
89TopTif-251
89TopTra-26T
89TopTraT-26T
89UppDec-57
90Don-162
90Fle-272
90FleCan-272
90Lea-130
90OPC-733
90PanSti-18
90RedSoxP-7
90Sco-331
90ScoYouSI-26
90Top-733
90TopSti-260
90TopTif-733
90TopTVRS-9
90UppDec-671
91Don-193
91Fle-92
91OPC-94
91Sco-772
91Top-94
91TopDesS-94
91TopMic-94
91TopTif-94
91UppDec-88
92OPC-400
92PawRedSS-360
92StaClu-287
93Fle-557
93PacSpa-31
93RedSoxWHP-10
93StaClu-41
93StaCluFDI-41
93StaCluMOP-41
93Top-187
93TopGol-187
93TopInaM-187
93TopMic-187
93Ult-151
93UppDec-409
93UppDecGold-409
94AngLAT-3
94AngMot-27
94ColC-443
94ColChoGS-443
94ColChoSS-443
94Don-104
94Fle-31
94Pac-53
94Sco-113
94ScoGolR-113
94StaClu-641
94StaCluFDI-641
94StaCluGR-641
94StaCluMOP-641
94Top-321
94TopGol-321
94TopSpa-321
97DunDonPPS-7

Doran, Bill
82TucTorT-7
83TopTra-26T
84AllGamPI-10
84AstMot-4
84Don-580
84Fle-225
84Nes792-198
84OPC-198
84Top-198
84TopSti-377
84TopTif-198
85AllGamPI-100
85AstHouP-1
85AstMot-8
85Don-84
85Fle-350
85OPC-299
85Top-684
85TopSti-68
85TopTif-684
86AstMilL-8
86AstPol-5
86AstTeal-5
86BasStaB-33
86Don-10
86Don-110
86DonSupD-10
86Fle-300
86Lea-10
86OPC-57
86SevCoi-S14
86Top-57
86TopSti-25
86TopTat-19
86TopTif-57
87AstMot-4
87AstPol-5
87Don-286
87DonOpeD-11
87Fle-57
87FleGlo-57
87GenMilB-6C
87Lea-197
87OPC-243
87RedFolSB-69
87Spo-116
87Spo-162
87SpoTeaP-8
87Top-472
87TopMinL-9
87TopSti-31
87TopTif-472
88AstMot-4
88AstPol-10
88Don-235
88DonBasB-120
88Fle-447
88FleGlo-447
88FleLeaL-10
88FleStiC-87
88Lea-183
88Nes-19
88OPC-166
88PanSti-295
88Sco-52
88ScoGlo-52
88Spo-48
88StaLinAst-9
88Top-745
88TopBig-51
88TopSti-34
88TopTif-745
89AstLenH-8
89AstMot-4
89AstSmo-13
89Bow-329
89BowTif-329
89Don-306
89DonBasB-38
89Fle-357
89FleGlo-357
89OPC-226
89PanSti-89
89RedFolSB-37
89Sco-21
89Spo-57
89Top-226
89TopBig-168
89TopSti-16
89TopTif-226
89TopUKM-22
89UppDec-101
90AstLenH-13
90AstMot-7
90Bow-76
90BowTif-76
90Don-236
90DonBesN-102
90Fle-230
90FleCan-230
90Lea-161
90MLBBasB-44
90OPC-368
90PanSti-268
90PubSti-94
90PubSti-257
90Sco-182
90Sco100S-8
90Top-368
90TopBig-159
90TopSti-15
90TopTif-368
90UppDec-198
90UppDecS-1
90VenSti-147
90VenSti-148
91Bow-682
91Don-756
91Fle-63
91Lea-197
91OPC-577
91RedKah-19
91RedPep-8
91Sco-775
91SimandSMLBL-14
91StaClu-148
91Top-577
91TopDesS-577
91TopMic-577
91TopTif-577
91Ult-93
91UppDec-398
92Bow-234
92Don-293
92Fle-405
92Lea-231
92OPC-136
92PanSti-263
92Pin-47
92RedKah-19
92Sco-77
92ScoProP-11
92StaClu-38
92Top-136
92TopGol-136
92TopGolW-136
92TopMic-136
92Ult-188
92UppDec-280
93BrePol-5
93Don-370
93Fle-390
93PacSpa-82
93Top-608
93TopGol-608
93TopInaM-608
93TopMic-608
93Ult-28
93UppDec-107
93UppDecGold-107
94BreMilB-308

Doran, John (John F.)
87OldJudN-139

Doran, Mark
86PalSprAP-11
87MidAngP-21
88EdmTraC-24
88EdmTraP-570
89MidAngGS-14

Doran, Tom
11SpoLifCW-102

Dorante, Luis
87ElmPio(C-14
88ElmPioC-12
89ElmPioP-3
90LynRedSTI-11
91WinHavRSC-12
91WinHavRSP-492
93ForLauRSFP-1614
93LinVenB-52
94VenLinU-75

Dorencz, Mark
94QuaCitRBC-9
94QuaCitRBF-540

Dorgan, Charles
77CliDodT-6

Dorgan, Mike (Michael C.)
86OldJudN-4
87BucN28-66A
87BucN28-66B
87OldJudN-140
88AugBecN-8
90KalBatN-14

Dorish, Harry
48RedSoxTI-5
51Bow-266
52Top-303
53Top-145
54Bow-86
54Top-110
55Bow-248
56Top-167
79BufBisT-12
79DiaGre-240
80PorBeaT-14
83TopRep5-303
91OriCro-111
91TopArc1-145
94TopArc1-110
94TopArc1G-110

Dorlarque, Aaron
89AncBucTI-4
92EugEmeC-10
92EugEmeF-3021
93RocRoyC-12
93RocRoyF-711
94MemChiF-350
95WicWraTI-17

Dorn, Chris
89PitMetS-4
90ColMetGS-20
90ColMetPPI-5
91St.LucMC-22
91St.LucMP-703
92BinMetF-508
92BinMetS-54
93BinMetF-2327

Dorner, Gus (Augustus)
09RamT20-40
09T206-419
11SpoLifCW-103

Dorsett, Brian
84ModA'sC-10
85HunStaJ-22
85MadMusP-8
85MadMusT-11
86TacTigP-3
87TacTigP-22
88Fle-607
88FleGlo-607
89ColCliC-14
89ColCliP-12
89ColCliP-759
90ColCliP-18
90ColCliP-679
90ProAAAF-329
90TopTVY-40
90TriAllGP-AAA14
91LasVegSLD-279
91LasVegSP-238
91LinDriAAA-279
91PadSmo-8
92BufBisBS-7
92BufBisF-326
92BufBisS-32
92YanWIZ8-46
93IndIndF-1492
93TriAAAGF-8
94Pac-146
94RedKah-8
94Top-688
94TopGol-688
94TopSpa-688
95Don-549
95DonPreP-549
95Fla-120
95Fle-433
95IndIndF-98
95Pac-103
95Sco-252
95ScoGolR-252
95ScoPlaTS-252
95Ult-364
95UltGolM-364
97PacPriGotD-GD117

Dorsett, Cal
94ConTSN-1295
94ConTSNB-1295

Dorsey, Jim (James Edward)
75QuaCitAT-7
79SalLakCGT-14
80SalLakCGT-16
80VenLeaS-169
81PawRedST-9
81Top-214
83PawRedST-6
84PawRedST-6
85DomLeaS-127
93KinMetC-9
93KinMetF-3808
94PitMetC-7
94PitMetF-3533

Dorsey, Lee
90UtiBluSP-30

Doscher, Jack
90DodTar-194

Doss, Dennis
76BatTroTI-7
77WatIndT-6

Doss, Greg
88SavCarP-357

Doss, Jason
88WytCubP-1998
89ChaWheB-20
89ChaWheP-1765
90PeoChiTI-19
91PeoChiC-5
91PeoChiP-1336
91PeoChiTI-7
92WinSpiC-9
92WinSpiF-1204

Doss, Larry
87JamExpP-2546

Doss, Raymond
89WelPirP-11
Doss, Rick
79CedRapGT-10
Dostal, Bruce
88BakDodCLC-247
89VerBeaDS-7
90FloStaLAS-3
90VerBeaDS-11
91LinDriAA-507
91ReaPhiLD-507
91ReaPhiP-1381
92ReaPhiF-586
92ScrRedBS-483
92SkyAAAF-220
93ScrRedBTI-8
94RocRedWF-1009
94RocRedWTI-7
Doster, David
94ClePhiC-1
94ClePhiF-2534
94FloStaLAF-FSL32
95Exc-241
95ReaPhiELC-10
95ReaPhiTI-3
96BesAutS-29
96Bow-316
96ColCho-444
96ColChoGS-444
96ColChoSS-444
96Exc-198
96Fla-311
96FlaWavotF-7
96FleUpd-U163
96FleUpdTC-U163
96ScrRedBB-12
96Ult-518
96UltGolM-518
96UppDec-265
97ColCho-194
97Don-162
97DonPreP-162
97DonPrePGold-162
97Pac-375
97PacLigB-375
97PacSil-375
97Ult-248
97UltGolME-248
97UltPlaME-248
Doster, Zach
87FayGenP-7
88FayGenP-1090
89MiaMirIS-5
Dotel, Angel
92BakDodCLC-9
93VerBeaDC-5
93VerBeaDF-2226
Dotel, Mariano
91MyrBeaHC-19
91MyrBeaHP-2953
92DunBluJC-12
92DunBluJF-2006
93HagSunC-10
93HagSunF-1887
Dotel, Octavio
97Bow-364
97BowChr-244
97BowChrI-244
97BowChrIR-244
97BowChrR-244
97BowInt-364
Dotelson, Angel
91KisDodP-4200
Dotolo, C.L.
92CliGiaC-25
92CliGiaF-3603
93SanJosGF-16
94SanJosGC-6
94SanJosGF-2823
Dotson, Gene (J.)
78ArkTraT-7
79ArkTraT-8
83LouRedR-15
Dotson, Larry
81WatIndT-25
Dotson, Rich (Richard E.)
78KnoKnoST-3
79KnoKnoST-8
81AllGamPI-76
81CokTeaS-27
81Don-280
81Fle-356
81OPC-138
81Top-138
81TopSti-62
81TopSupHT-14
82Don-356
82Fle-340
82FleSta-186
82OPC-257
82Top-461
82TopSti-166
82TopStiV-166
83AllGamPI-75
83Don-319
83Fle-233
83OPC-46
83Top-46
83WhiSoxTV-34
84AllGamPI-170
84Don-180
84Fle-56
84FleSti-62
84Nes792-216
84Nes792-759
84OPC-24
84Top-216
84Top-759
84TopSti-241
84TopTif-216
84TopTif-759
84WhiSoxTV-10
85Don-3
85Don-302
85DonSupD-3
85Fle-511
85Lea-3
85OPC-364
85Top-364
85TopSti-233
85TopTif-364
85WhiSoxC-34
86Don-160
86Fle-203
86MSAJayPCD-5
86OPC-233
86Spo-133
86Top-156
86Top-612
86TopTif-156
86TopTif-612
86WhiSoxC-34
87Don-383
87DonOpeD-238
87Fle-495
87FleGlo-495
87FleMin-33
87OPC-211
87Top-720
87TopTif-720
87WhiSoxC-8
88Don-124
88DonBasB-52
88DonReaBY-NEW
88Fle-396
88FleGlo-396
88FleUpd-48
88FleUpdG-48
88OPC-209
88PanSti-53
88Sco-480
88ScoGlo-480
88ScoRoo-60T
88ScoRooG-60T
88StaLinWS-6
88Top-209
88TopSti-291
88TopTif-209
88TopTra-35T
88TopTraT-35T
89Don-277
89Fle-253
89FleGlo-253
89OPC-357
89PanSti-398
89Sco-278
89ScoRoo-80T
89Spo-194
89Top-511
89TopDouM-22
89TopSti-316
89TopTif-511
89UppDec-80
89YanScoNW-23
90OPC-169
90PubSti-533
90Sco-19
90Top-169
90TopTif-169
90VenSti-149
92YanWIZ8-47
93UppDecS-14
Dotter, Gary (Gary Richard)
65Top-421
Dotterer, Dutch (Henry John)
58RedEnq-9
58Top-396
59RedEnq-4
59RedShiBS-4
59Top-288
60RedJayP-2
60Top-21
60TopVen-21
61Top-332
61TopMagR-24
Dotterer, Tommy
61Top-332
Doty, Derrin
91WasVia-2
93BoiHawC-9
93BoiHawF-3927
94CedRapKC-8
94CedRapKF-1121
94MidLeaAF-MDW36
95AusFut-36
95LakElsSTI-12
96MidAngB-14
Doty, Sean
89BilMusP-2052
90BilMusP-3212
91ChaWheC-2
91ChaWheP-2879
92CedRapRC-25
92CedRapRF-1063
Dotzler, Mike
86DayBealP-7
87SalBucP-12
88OrlTwiB-21
89VisOakCLC-105
89VisOakP-1438
Doubleday, Abner
80PerHaloFP-A
90BasWit-108
94OriofB-1
Doucet, Eric
89BoiHawP-1983
Doucette, Darren
92HamRedC-22
92HamRedF-1598
93SavCarC-12
93SavCarF-692
94MadHatC-10
94MadHatF-140
Dougherty, Jim (James)
88CapCodPPaLP-55
92ClaFS7-351
92OscAstC-17
92OscAstF-2521
93ClaGolF-65
93ExcFS7-41
93JacGenF-2102
94ExcFS7-198
94TriAAF-AAA45
94TucTorF-754
94UppDecML-121
95AstMot-25
95Emo-137
95Fla-358
95FleAllR-M6
95StaClu-598
95StaCluMOP-598
95StaCluSTWS-598
96ColCho-561
96ColChoGS-561
96ColChoSS-561
96Fle-404
96FleTif-404
96Sco-232
96Top-76
96TusTorB-6
96Ult-486
96UltGolM-486
Dougherty, Mark
83EriCarT-7
86ArkTraP-6
87LouRedTI-11
88LouRedBC-23
88LouRedBP-444
88LouRedBTI-18
Dougherty, Pat
04FanCraAL-16
07WhiSoxGWH-4
86BurExpP-6
Dougherty, Patsy (Patrick H.)
03BreE10-41
04RedSoxUP-4
09AmeCarE-36
09ColChiE-83
09T206-104
09T206-105
10ChiE-13
10DarChoE-16
10DomDisP-36
10E101-18
10E102-9
10MelMinE-18
10NadCarE-19
10PeoT21-20
10RedCroT-21
10RedCroT-106
10RedCroT-186
10SweCapPP-9
11E94-13
11MecDFT-15
11SpoLifCW-104
11SpoLifM-22
11T205-44A
11T205-44B
12ColRedB-83
12ColTinT-83
Dougherty, Tony
94WatIndC-7
94WatIndF-3928
96WesOahCHWB-32
Doughty, Brian
93BelMarC-11
93BelMarF-3201
94AppFoxC-8
94AppFoxF-1046
Doughty, Jamie
85TulDriTI-9
86TulDriTI-11
Douglas, Charles
88BoiHawP-1624
Douglas, Dave
87HarSenP-16
Douglas, John
88OklSoo-7
89OklSoo-13
Douglas, John Franklin
90DodTar-933
Douglas, Klondike (William B.)
03BreE10-42
Douglas, Murray
93Sou-7
Douglas, Phil (Phillip B.)
19W514-5
21E121So1-20
21E121So8-19
21KoBreWSI-9
22E120-184
22W575-29
23W501-74
90DodTar-195
91FouBal-9
Douglas, Preston
88UtiBluSP-27
Douglas, Steve
82OrlTwi8SCT-6
82OrlTwiT-17
Douglas, Whammy (Charles)
57JetPos-5
58JetPos-6
58Top-306
59Top-431
Douma, Todd
90PitMetP-13
91FloStaLAP-FSL30
91St.LucMC-24
91St.LucMP-704
92BinMetF-509
92BinMetS-55
92ProFS7-286
92SkyAA F-23
93BinMetF-2328
93ExcFS7-72
Dour, Brian
88CapCodPPaLP-64
89EveGiaS-6
90Bes-253
90SanJosGB-21
90SanJosGCLC-42
90SanJosGP-2009
90SanJosGS-7
91SanJosGC-15
91SanJosGP-3
93SanJosGC-10
93SanJosGF-1
Douris, John D.
91WelPirC-21
91WelPirP-3566
Douthit, Taylor (Taylor Lee)
28W56PlaC-C7
29ExhFou-16
29PorandAR-17
31Exh-16
33ExhFou-4
33Gou-40
33GouCanV-40
79DiaGre-152
91ConTSN-264
94ConTSN-1214
94ConTSNB-1214
Dovalis, Alex
79WisRapTT-6
Dovey, Troy
89AshTouP-956
90AshTouP-2739
90OscAstS-6
91BurAstC-2
91BurAstP-2793
92OscAstF-2522
Dowd, Charlie
95NewHavRTI-NNO
96NewHavRB-30
Dowd, Snooks
90DodTar-196
Dowell, Ken
83ReaPhiT-13
84PorBeaC-210
85PorBeaC-46
86PorBeaP-5
87FleUpd-27
87FleUpdG-27
87MaiGuiP-16
87MaiGuiT-10
88MetColP-20
88TidTidCa-8
88TidTidCM-14
88TidTidP-1595
89TidTidC-11
89TidTidP-1963
90CMC-298
90ProAAAF-412
90RicBraC-22
90RicBraP-267
90RicBraTI-9
Dowhower, Deron
93EliTwiF-3412
94EliTwiC-6
94EliTwiF-3723
95ForWayWTI-4
96FtMyeMB-29
Dowies, Butch
82DanSunF-10
Dowler, Dee
93GenCubC-9
93GenCubF-3181
94DayCubC-4
94DayCubF-2364
96OrlCubB-7
Dowless, Mike
81WatRedT-3
82IndIndTI-16
83IndIndTI-23
84CedRapRT-24
Dowling, Dave (David B.)
65OPC-116
65Top-116
66Top-482
67Top-272
88AlaGolAA'TI-12
Down, Rick
90AlbYanP-1180
90AlbYanS-24
91ColCliLD-124
91ColCliP-614
91LinDriAAA-124
92ColCliF-367
92ColCliS-124
94VenLinU-198
Downey, Charles
90ArkRaz-8
Downey, Red (Alexander

C.)
90DodTar-934
Downey, Tom (Thomas E.)
09ColChiE-84
09T206-106
09T206-107
10CouT21-126
10DomDisP-37
10SweCapPP-97A
10SweCapPP-97B
11MecDFT-17
11S74Sil-73
11SpoLifCW-105
11SpoLifM-190
11T205-45
11TurRedT-91
12ColRedB-84
12ColTinT-84
12T207-50
14CraJacE-107
14PieStaT-18
15CraJacE-107
15VicT21-8
Downhower, Deron
93EliTwiC-10
Downing, Al (Alphonso E.)
61Yan61RL-35
62Top-219
64ChatheY-7
64Top-86
64Top-219
64TopCoi-109
64TopVen-86
64TopVen-219
64YanJayP-3
65ChaTheY-5
65MacSta-2
65OPC-11
65Top-11
65Top-598
66Top-384
66YanTeal-2
67CokCapYM-V14
67DexPre-67
67Top-308
67TopVen-221
68Baz-12
68OPC-105
68Top-105
68TopActS-5A
68TopVen-105
69MilBra-76
69Top-292
70Top-584
71MLBOffS-102
71OPC-182
71Top-182
72MilBra-94
72OPC-93
72OPC-460
72Top-93
72Top-460
73OPC-324
73Top-324
74OPC-620
74Top-620
75OPC-498
75Top-498
76OPC-605
76SSP-66
76Top-605
81TCM60I-450
83YanASFY-11
90DodTar-197
91RinPos1Y1-4
92YanWIZ6-36
92YanWIZA-19
94BreMilB-309
Downing, Brian (Brian Jay)
74OPC-601
74Top-601
75OPC-422
75Top-422
76OPC-23
76SSP-141
76Top-23
77Hos-138
77OPC-246
77Top-344
78AngFamF-8
78Top-519
79Top-71
80OPC-315
80Top-602
80TopSup-49
81AllGamPI-39
81Don-410
81Fle-282
81LonBeaPT-8
81OPC-263
81Top-263
81TopSti-50
82Don-115
82Fle-457
82FleSta-215
82OPC-158
82Top-158
83AllGamPI-51
83Don-367
83Fle-86
83FleSta-54
83FleSti-35
83OPC-298
83Top-442
84AllGamPI-141
84AngSmo-8
84Don-423
84Fle-515
84Nes792-574
84OPC-135
84Top-574
84TopSti-236
84TopTif-574
85AllGamPI-54
85AngSmo-7
85Don-158
85Fle-300
85Lea-223
85OPC-374
85Top-374
85TopSti-224
85TopTif-374
86AngSmo-7
86BasStaB-34
86Don-108
86Fle-154
86Lea-39
86OPC-205
86Spo-154
86Top-772
86TopSti-183
86TopTat-14
86TopTif-772
87AngSmo-19
87Don-86
87DonHig-5
87DonOpeD-9
87Fle-78
87FleBasA-15
87FleExcS-16
87FleGlo-78
87FleMin-34
87FleStiC-35
87OPC-88
87Spo-161
87SpoTeaP-11
87Top-782
87TopSti-178
87TopTif-782
88AngSmo-18
88Don-258
88DonBasB-27
88Fle-488
88FleGlo-488
88FleMin-10
88FleStiC-11
88Lea-203
88OPC-331
88PanSti-46
88RedFolSB-19
88Sco-44
88ScoGlo-44
88Spo-181
88StaLinAn-5
88Top-331
88TopBig-78
88TopMinL-5
88TopRevLL-23
88TopSti-181
88TopTif-331
89AngSmo-12
89Bow-53
89BowTif-53
89Don-254
89DonBasB-321
89Fle-475
89FleGlo-475
89OPC-17
89PanSti-288
89Sco-76
89Spo-117
89Top-17
89TopSti-178
89TopTif-17
89UppDec-485
90AngSmo-4
90Bow-294
90BowTif-294
90Don-10A
90Don-10B
90Don-352
90DonSupD-10
90Fle-130
90FleCan-130
90OPC-635
90PanSti-27
90PubSti-368
90Sco-26
90Sco100S-46
90Spo-77
90Top-635
90TopSti-169
90TopTif-635
90UppDec-146
90VenSti-150
91Fle-310
91Lea-269
91OPC-255
91RanMot-17
91Sco-104
91ScoRoo-30T
91StaClu-348
91Top-255
91TopDesS-255
91TopMic-255
91TopTif-255
91TopTra-33T
91TopTraT-33T
91UltUpd-54
91UppDec-231A
91UppDec-231B
91UppDec-770
92Don-167
92Fle-302
92Lea-440
92OPC-173
92Pin-368
92RanMot-17
92RanTeal-7
92Sco-579
92StaClu-494
92Top-173
92TopGol-173
92TopGolW-173
92TopMic-173
92Ult-440
92UppDec-483
93PanSti-88
93RanKee-128
Downs, Brian
96HicCraB-4
Downs, Dorley
84PriWilPT-12
85NasPirT-7
86MacPirP-8
Downs, John
91EugEmeC-22
91EugEmeP-3717
94WilBluRC-7
94WilBluRF-294
Downs, Kelly
82OklCit8T-21
83PorBeaT-9
84PorBeaC-201
85PhoGiaC-189
86PhoFirP-4
87Don-573
87Fle-272
87FleGlo-272
87GiaMot-17
87SpoTeaP-10
87Top-438
87TopTif-438
88ClaRed-194
88Don-145
88DonBasB-106
88Fle-80
88FleGlo-80
88GiaMot-17
88OPC-187
88PanSti-415
88Sco-27
88ScoGlo-27
88ScoYouSI-19
88Spo-203
88Top-629
88TopRoo-19
88TopTif-629
88ToyRoo-9
89Bow-465
89BowTif-465
89Don-367
89DonBasB-247
89Fle-326
89FleGlo-326
89GiaMot-4
89OPC-361
89PanSti-209
89Sco-124
89Spo-39
89Top-361
89TopBig-112
89TopSti-81
89TopTif-361
89UppDec-476
90Don-177
90Fle-55
90FleCan-55
90GiaMot-4
90GiaSmo-6
90OPC-17
90PubSti-66
90Sco-534
90Top-17
90TopTif-17
90UppDec-699
90VenSti-151
91Bow-633
91Don-738
91Fle-261
91GiaMot-4
91GiaPacGaE-4
91OPC-733
91Sco-654
91StaClu-193
91Top-733
91TopDesS-733
91TopMic-733
91TopTif-733
91UltUpd-116
91UppDec-441
92Bow-343
92Don-303
92Fle-634
92GiaMot-21
92GiaPacGaE-15
92OPC-573
92Pin-492
92Sco-191
92StaClu-517
92Top-573
92TopGol-573
92TopGolW-573
92TopMic-573
92Ult-290
92UppDec-583
93AthMot-20
93Fle-662
93PacSpa-565
93UppDec-636
93UppDecGold-636
94Fle-259
Downs, Kirk
80BurBeeT-24
Downs, Red (Jerome Willis)
07TigACDPP-5
09T206-420
09WolNewDTPP-7
11MecDFT-37
11SpoLifCW-106
90DodTar-198
Downs, Ron
88AugPirP-378
88SouAtlLAGS-5
89SalBucS-6
Doxtator, Melvil
52LavPro-74
Doyel, Dan
89SavCarP-347
90ArkTraGS-3
91St.PetCC-30
92St.PetCC-29
Doyle, Blake
77RocRedWM-8
78RocRedWT-8
79RocRedWT-4
80IndIndTI-20
Doyle, Brian (Brian Reed)
75LynRanT-9
78TacYanC-39A
79Top-710
79YanPicA-10
80ColCliP-2
80ColCliT-13
80Top-582
81Fle-104
81Top-159
81TopTra-754
82SyrChiT-16
82SyrChiTI-10
92YanWIZ7-46
92YanWIZ8-48
Doyle, Carl
36NatChiFPR-25
90DodTar-935
Doyle, Denny (Robert Dennis)
70OPC-539
70PhiTeal-3
70Top-539
71MLBOffS-175
71OPC-352
71Top-352
72Top-768
73OPC-424
73Top-424
74OPC-552
74Top-552
75OPC-187
75SSP18-17
75Top-187
76Hos-107
76LinSup-107
76OPC-381
76RedSox-2
76RedSoxSM-4
76SSP-407
76Top-381
77AshTouT-4
77Top-336
78OPC-111
78Top-642
Doyle, Ian
91BurIndP-3294
92ColRedC-18
92ColRedF-2382
93CarLeaAGF-29
93ClaGolF-15
93KinIndC-8
93KinIndF-2239
93KinIndTI-7
93SouAtlLAPI-9
94CanIndF-3112
94ExcFS7-42
Doyle, Jack (John Joseph)
03BreE10-43
03BreE10-44
11SpoLifCW-108
90DodTar-199
95NewN566-178
Doyle, James
11SpoLifCW-107
11SpoLifM-191
Doyle, Jeff (Jeffrey D.)
81ArkTraT-7
82LouRedE-7
83LouRedR-11
Doyle, Larry (Lawrence J.)
03WilCarE-13
08AmeCarE-45
08RosComP-127
09ColChiE-85
09PhiCarE-9
09SpoNewSM-68
09T206-108A
09T206-108B
09T206-109
09T206-110
09T206-111
10CouT21-127
10CouT21-128
10CouT21-278
10CouT21-279
10DomDisP-38
10E101-19A
10E101-19B
10E102-10A
10E102-10B
10E12AmeCDC-15

10JuJuDE-16
10MelMinE-19A
10MelMinE-19B
10NadCarE-20A
10NadCarE-20B
10NadE1-16
10PeoT21-21A
10PeoT21-21B
10PeoT21-21C
10RedCroT-22
10RedCroT-23
10RedCroT-107
10RedCroT-108
10RedCroT-187
10RedCroT-188
10SweCapPP-112A
10SweCapPP-112B
11BasBatEU-21
11DiaGumP-13
11MecDFT-35
11S74Sil-85
11SpoLifCW-109
11SpoLifM-209
11T205-46
11TurRedT-13
12ColRedB-85
12ColTinT-85
12HasTriFT-30B
12HasTriFT-32
12T207-51
13PolGroW-7
14B18B-66
14CraJacE-4
14PieStaT-19
14TexTomE-19
14TexTomE-52
15AmeCarE-15
15CraJacE-4
15SpoNewM-52
16BF2FP-77
16ColE13-44
16FleBreD-25
16SpoNewM-51
19W514-81
77GalGloG-157
91ConTSN-317
20W516-13
Doyle, Paul (Paul S.)
70OPC-277
70Top-277
72Top-629
Doyle, Rich
82WatIndF-23
82WatIndT-2
83BufBisT-3
84BufBisT-11
85WatIndT-6
86BeaGolGP-10
88SanBerSB-24
88SanBerSCLC-52
89CalCanC-7
89CalCanP-541
89EasLeaDDP-DD32
Doyle, Slow (Judd Bruce)
88FriBasCM-2
Doyle, Tim
91SouOreAC-4
91SouOreAP-3833
Doyle, Tom
86ColMetP-9
87ColMetP-23
88JacMetGS-7
88MarPhiS-11
90WatDiaB-26
90WatDiaP-2383
91ChaRaiC-18
91ChaRaiP-103
92JamExpC-3
92Min-6
93BurBeeC-7
93BurBeeF-165
93SpoIndC-4
93SpoIndF-3582
96ChaLooB-12
Dozier, D.J.
90FloStaLAS-4
90ScoRoo-97T
90St.LucMS-6
90StaFS7-9
90TopMag-47
91Bow-478
91Cla/Bes-387
91Cla2-T4
91ClaGam-89
91LinDriAA-631
91MetColP-30
91UppDec-3
91WilBilLD-631
91WilBilP-306
92Bow-219
92Don-20
92MetColP-22
92OPC-591
92ProFS7-282
92SkyAAAF-250
92TidTidF-909
92TidTidS-556
92Top-591
92TopGol-591
92TopGolW-591
92TopMic-591
93Don-90
93LasVegSF-956
Dozier, Tom
82SprCarF-15
83St.PetCT-5
84AlbA'sT-11
85HunStaJ-15
85TacTigC-145
86TacTigP-4
87TacTigP-1
88GreBraB-18
90SprCarDGB-8
Drabek, Doug
85AlbYanT-4
86ColCliP-6
86DonRoo-31
86FleUpd-36
86YanTCM-6
87Don-251
87DonHig-32
87Fle-96
87FleGlo-96
87Top-283
87TopTif-283
87TopTra-29T
87TopTraT-29T
88Don-79
88DonBasB-73
88Fle-327
88FleGlo-327
88Lea-88
88OPC-143
88RedFolSB-20
88Sco-51
88ScoGlo-51
88StaLinPi-8
88Top-591
88TopBig-124
88TopSti-134
88TopTif-591
89Bow-416
89BowTif-416
89Don-211
89DonBasB-17
89Fle-206
89FleGlo-206
89OPC-37
89PanSti-161
89PirVerFJ-15
89Sco-117
89ScoHot1S-87
89ScoYouSI-21
89Spo-27
89SpoIllFKI-266
89Top-478
89TopTif-478
89TVSpoM-11
89UppDec-597
90AlbDecGB-22
90Bow-164
90BowTif-164
90Don-92
90DonBesN-9
90Fle-465
90FleCan-465
90Lea-296
90OPC-197
90PanSti-332
90PirHomC-10
90PubSti-153
90RedFolSB-27
90Sco-505
90Top-197
90TopBig-185
90TopMag-87
90TopSti-130
90TopTif-197
90UppDec-422
90VenSti-152
91BasBesAotM-5
91Baz-4
91Bow-515
91Cla1-T82
91Cla2-T79
91ClaGam-167
91Col-29
91Don-269
91Don-411
91Don-750
91DonEli-5
91DonPre-2
91Fle-36
91Lea-516
91MajLeaCP-59
91MSAHolD-7
91OPC-405
91OPC-685
91PanCanT1-57
91PanCanT1-92
91PanFreS-122
91PanSti-116
91RedFolS-28
91Sco-472
91Sco-661
91Sco-878
91Sco100S-6
91StaClu-202
91StaCluCM-7
91StaPinB-14
91Stu-224
91StuPre-15
91Top-405
91Top-685
91TopCraJI-12
91TopDesS-405
91TopDesS-685
91TopGaloC-4
91TopMic-405
91TopMic-685
91TopTif-405
91TopTif-685
91Ult-277
91UltGol-3
91UppDec-278
91Woo-3
92Bow-465
92Cla2-T68
92ClaGam-67
92Don-209
92DonCraJ1-34
92Fle-553
92Hig5-92
92Lea-11
92New-7
92OPC-440
92OPCPre-32
92PanSti-259
92Pin-96
92PirNatl-7
92Sco-115
92Sco100S-53
92ScoProP-23
92StaClu-170
92Stu-84
92Top-440
92TopGol-440
92TopGolW-440
92TopKid-24
92TopMic-440
92TriPla-106
92Ult-253
92UppDec-39
92UppDec-221
92UppDecTMH-18
92YanWIZ8-49
93AstMot-5
93Bow-208
93Don-622
93DurPowP1-12
93Fin-127
93FinRef-127
93Fla-61
93Fle-500
93FleFinE-77
93FleFruotL-17
93FunPac-46
93JimDea-19
93KinDis-23
93Kra-20
93Lea-293
93LeaGolA-R20
93MetBak-6
93MSABenSPD-7
93OPC-72
93OPCPre-73
93PacSpa-476
93Pin-423
93Pin-485
93Sco-580
93Sel-153
93SelAce-16
93SelRoo-97T
93SelStaL-65
93SP-32
93StaClu-167
93StaClu-672
93StaCluAs-1
93StaCluFDI-167
93StaCluFDI-672
93StaCluMOP-167
93StaCluMOP-672
93Stu-194
93Top-190
93TopComotH-26
93TopGol-190
93TopInaM-190
93TopMic-190
93TopTra-94T
93TriPla-232
93Ult-392
93UppDec-475
93UppDec-664
93UppDecGold-475
93UppDecGold-664
94AstMot-14
94Bow-174
94ColC-95
94ColChoGS-95
94ColChoSS-95
94Don-632
94ExtBas-272
94ExtBasPD-10
94Fin-345
94FinRef-345
94Fla-388
94Fle-489
94FUnPac-138
94Lea-271
94LeaL-114
94OPC-248
94Pac-263
94PanSti-193
94Pin-104
94PinArtP-104
94PinMusC-104
94ProMag-60
94RedFolMI-2
94Sco-426
94ScoGolR-426
94Sel-349
94SP-30
94SPDieC-30
94Spo-17
94StaClu-408
94StaCluFDI-408
94StaCluGR-408
94StaCluMOP-408
94Stu-20
94Top-220
94TopGol-220
94TopSpa-220
94TriPla-25
94Ult-501
94UppDec-452
94UppDecED-452
95AstMot-11
95Baz-107
95Bow-307
95ColCho-116
95ColChoGS-116
95ColChoSE-37
95ColChoSEGS-37
95ColChoSESS-37
95ColChoSS-116
95D3-44
95Don-532
95DonMouM-6
95DonPreP-532
95DonTopotO-252
95Emb-104
95EmbGolI-104
95Fin-135
95FinRef-135
95Fla-359
95Fle-456
95FleAllS-20
95FleTeaL-20
95Lea-321
95LeaLim-183
95Pac-184
95PacPri-60
95PanSti-2
95Pin-72
95PinArtP-72
95PinMusC-72
95Sco-378
95ScoGolR-378
95ScoHaloG-HG97
95ScoPlaTS-378
95Sel-129
95SelArtP-129
95SP-63
95SPCha-54
95SPChaDC-54
95Spo-15
95SpoArtP-15
95SPSil-63
95StaClu-224
95StaCluFDI-224
95StaCluMOP-224
95StaCluSTWS-224
95StaCluVR-113
95Stu-143
95Top-75
95TopCyb-52
95Ult-171
95UltGolM-171
95UppDec-26
95UppDecED-26
95UppDecEDG-26
95UppDecSE-180
95UppDecSEG-180
95USPlaCMLA-11S
96AstMot-7
96Baz-126
96Cir-136
96CirRav-136
96ColCho-565
96ColChoGS-565
96ColChoSS-565
96Don-142
96DonPreP-142
96EmoXL-197
96Fin-B181
96FinRef-B181
96Fla-276
96Fle-405
96FleTif-405
96Lea-161
96LeaPrePB-161
96LeaPrePG-161
96LeaPrePS-161
96LeaSigA-58
96LeaSigAG-58
96LeaSigAS-58
96MetUni-176
96MetUniP-176
96Pac-97
96PanSti-63
96ProSta-14
96Sco-109
96SP-93
96StaClu-127
96StaCluEPB-127
96StaCluEPG-127
96StaCluEPS-127
96StaCluMOP-127
95StaCluVRMC-113
96Top-105
96TopGal-18
96TopGalPPI-18
96TopLas-53
96Ult-207
96UltGolM-207
96UppDec-342
86STaoftFT-3
97Cir-305
97CirRav-305
97DonTea-68
97DonTeaSPE-68
97Fin-203
97FinRef-203
97FlaSho-A178
97FlaSho-B178
97FlaSho-C178
97FlaShoLC-178
97FlaShoLC-B178
97FlaShoLC-C178
97FlaShoLCM-A178

97FlaShoLCM-B178
97FlaShoLCM-C178
97Fle-343
97Fle-534
97FleTif-343
97FleTif-534
97Pac-315
97PacLigB-315
97PacSil-315
97Sco-463
97ScoHobR-463
97ScoResC-463
97ScoShoS-463
97ScoShoSAP-463
97StaClu-107
97StaCluMOP-107
97Top-143
97Ult-444
97UltGolME-444
97UltPlaME-444

Drabinski, Marek
91MacBraC-14
91MacBraP-867

Drabowsky, Moe (Myron W.)
57Top-84
58Top-135
59Top-407
60CubJayP-5
60Lea-68
60Top-349
61Top-364
62RedEnq-6
62Top-331
64A's-4
64AthJayP-3
64Top-42
64TopSta-82
64TopTatl-34
64TopVen-42
65Top-439
66Top-291
66TopVen-291
67CokCapO-16
67OPC-125
67OPC-151
67Top-125
67Top-151
68CokCapO-16
68DexPre-29
68Top-242
68TopVen-242
69MilBra-77
69MLBOffS-57
69RoySol-3
69RoyTeal-3
69Top-508
69TopSta-183
70MLBOffS-220
70RoyTeal-9
70Top-653
71CarTeal-15
71CarTeal-16
71MLBOffS-272
71OPC-685
71Top-685
72MilBra-95
72Top-627
78TCM60I-121
81Ori6F-12
87BirBarB-3
88BirBarB-7
89PacLegI-215
89SweBasG-103
89VanCanC-25
89VanCanP-581
90CMC-175
90ProAAAF-184
90VanCanC-26
90VanCanP-506
91LinDriAAA-650
91OriCro-112
91VanCanP-1610
92HagSunF-2572
92HagSunS-275
93UppDecAH-43
93UppDecS-4

Draeger, Mark
95HudValRTI-26
96ChaRivTI-9612
96HudValRB-4

Drago, Dick (Richard A.)
69RoySol-4
69Top-662
70OPC-37
70RoyTeal-10
70Top-37
71MLBOffS-414
71OPC-752
71Top-752
72Kel-40A
72Kel-40B
72OPC-205
72Top-205
73OPC-392
73Top-392
74OPC-113
74Top-113
75OPC-333
75Top-333
76OPC-142
76SSP-422
76Top-142
77Top-426
78PapGinD-11
78SSP270-171
78Top-567
79OPC-2
79Top-12
80Top-271
81Don-336
81Fle-239
81OPC-332
81Top-647
81TopTra-755
82Fle-510
82Top-742
89T/MSenL-29
89TopSenL-17
91OriCro-113
93UppDecS-4

Dragon, Homer the
96ChaKniB-5

Drahman, Brian
87BelBreP-10
88StoPorCLC-186
88StoPorP-734
89ElPasDGS-6
90BirBarB-15
90BirBarP-1103
91Bow-363
91ScoRoo-81T
91WhiSoxK-50
92Fle-77
92OPC-231
92Sco-734
92Sco100RS-55
92StaClu-744
92StaCluNC-744
92Top-231
92TopDeb91-46
92TopGol-231
92TopGolW-231
92TopMic-231
92VanCanS-633
93Don-672
93NasSouF-566
93TriAAAGF-35
94EdmTraF-2868
94StaCluT-82
94StaCluTFDI-82
95ChaKniTI-9

Drake, Delos (Delos Daniel)
12ColRedB-86
12ColTinT-86
12T207-52

Drake, H.P.
78LodDodT-3

Drake, Kevin
74CedRapAT-19
75DubPacT-29

Drake, Plunk (William)
78LauLonABS-8
86NegLeaF-69
87NegLeaPD-10

Drake, Sam
88CapCodPPaLP-131
89HelBreSP-22
90BelBreB-6
90BelBreS-6
91StoPorC-9
91StoPorP-3027

Drake, Sammy (Samuel H.)
62Top-162
62TopVen-162
91MetWIZ-99

Drake, Solly (Solomon L.)
57Top-159
59Top-406
90DodTar-200

Drake, Tex
85KinBluJT-26
86KinEagP-5
89RicBraP-819

Drake, Tom
90DodTar-201

Dramer, Tommy
90KinIndTI-2

Dransfeldt, Kelly
96HudValRB-2

Draper, Mike
88OneYanP-2059
89PriWilCS-6
90Ft.LauYS-5
91AlbYanLD-4
91AlbYanP-1000
91LinDriAA-4
92ColCliF-345
92ColCliP-5
92ColCliS-104
92DonRoo-34
92SkyAAAF-46
92TriA AAS-104
93Bow-482
93ExcFS7-206
93FleFinE-101
93LinVenB-248
93MetColP-29
93MetKah-47
93PacSpa-540
93StaClu-732
93StaCluFDI-732
93StaCluMOP-732
93Ult-425
94LasVegSF-867
94Pac-398

Dravecky, Dave (David F.)
79BufBisT-1
80BufBisT-4
82HawIslT-20
83Fle-356
83Top-384
84Don-8
84Don-8A
84Don-551
84Fle-298
84Nes792-290
84Nes792-366
84OPC-290
84PadMot-11
84PadSmo-7
84Top-290
84Top-366
84TopSti-155
84TopTif-290
84TopTif-366
85Don-112
85Fle-30
85OPC-32
85PadMot-8
85Top-530
85TopMin-530
85TopSti-154
85TopTif-530
86Don-162
86Fle-319
86Lea-92
86OPC-276
86Top-735
86TopTif-735
87Don-187
87Fle-412
87FleGlo-412
87FleUpd-28
87FleUpdG-28
87OPC-62
87PadBohHB-43
87PadFirPTB-1
87Top-470
87TopSti-107
87TopTif-470
88Don-485
88DonBasB-135
88Fle-81
88FleBasM-10
88FleGlo-81
88FleStiC-127
88GiaMot-9
88Sco-564
88ScoGlo-564
88StaLinG-6
88Top-68
88TopTif-68
89Fle-327
89FleGlo-327
89GiaMot-9
89Top-601
89TopTif-601
89UppDec-39
90OPC-124
90PacLeg-80
90PanSti-360
90PanSti-386
90Sco-550
90Top-124
90TopTif-124
90UppDec-679
92SteDra-1
92SteDra-2
92SteDra-3
92SteDra-4
92SteDra-5
92SteDra-6
92SteDra-7
92SteDra-8
92SteDra-9
92SteDra-10
92SteDra-11
92SteDra-12
93TedWil-53
93UppDecAH-44
94UppDecAH-84
94UppDecAH1-84

Drawdy, Duke
76ForLauYS-2
77WesHavYT-6

Drees, Tom
86PenWhiSP-8
87DayBeaAP-4
88BirBarB-3
88SouLeaAJ-34
89TriAAP-AAA29
89VanCanC-10
89VanCanP-588
90BirBarDGB-7
90CMC-630
90Fle-644
90FleCan-644
90ProAAAF-161
90TriAllGP-AAA38
90UppDec-3
90VanCanC-3
90VanCanP-483
91LinDriAAA-631
91VanCanLD-631
91VanCanP-1588
92OklCit8S-309
92SkyAAAF-141
92TopDeb91-47
93PorBeaF-2378

Dreifort, Darren
91TopGolS-4
91TopTra-34T
91TopTraT-34T
92StaCluD-39
92TopTra-29T
92TopTraG-29T
93StaCluM-13
94DodMot-24
94DodPol-7
94LeaLimR-59
94Pin-540
94PinArtP-540
94PinMusC-540
94SP-3
95ColCho-226
95ColChoGS-226
95ColChoSE-6
95ColChoSEGS-6
95ColChoSESS-6
95ColChoSS-226
95Don-131
95DonPreP-131
95Fle-539
95LeaGolR-5
95Pac-216
95Sco-300
95ScoGolR-300
95ScoPlaTS-300
95Ult-180
95UltGolM-180
95UppDec-73
95UppDecED-73
95UppDecEDG-73
96LeaSigA-59
96LeaSigAG-59
96LeaSigAS-59
97DonRatR-28
97DonTea-120
97DonTeaSPE-120
97Fle-564
97FleTif-564
97Lea-303
97LeaFraM-303
97LeaFraMDC-303
97PacPriGotD-GD157
97Pin-50
97PinArtP-50
97PinMusC-50
97Sco-206
97ScoDod-8
97ScoDodPI-8
97ScoDodPr-8
97ScoPreS-206
97ScoShoS-206
97ScoShoSAP-206
97Ult-464
97UltGolME-464
97UltPlaME-464

Dreifort, Todd
90WicStaSGD-9
92JamExpC-7
92JamExpF-1512

Dreisbach, Bill
91PriRedC-12
91PriRedP-3517
92BenMusSP-22
92BilMusF-3357

Drell, Tom
88CapCodPB-1
88CapCodPPaLP-18
89AncGlaP-11
90NiaFalRP-17
91LakTigC-2
91LakTigP-258
92LakTigC-21

Drent, Brian
96SouBenSHS-10

Dresch, Michael
96BilMusTI-7

Dressen, Chuck (Charles W.)
25Exh-28
26Exh-28
28StaPlaCE-16
29PorandAR-18
36NatChiFPR-95
36R31PasP-10
40PlaBal-72
48BluTin-8
48YanTeal-7
49RemBre-6
50RemBre-4
51Bow-259
52Bow-188
52Top-377
53BowC-124
53RedMan-NL1
53Top-50
55DonWin-2
56BraBilaBP-9
59DodTeal-4
60BraJayP-4
60BraLaktL-10
60BraSpiaS-8
60Top-213
61Top-137
64TigJayP-4
64TigLid-5
64Top-443
65TigJayP-5
65Top-538
66OPC-187
66Top-187
66TopVen-187
79TCM50-56
83TigAlKS-29
83TopRep5-377
87ConSer2-31
88ConSer4-9
89DodSmoG-59
90DodTar-202
91RinPosBD2-1
91TopArc1-50
92ConTSN-400
93ConTSN-832
94ConTSN-1120
94ConTSNB-1120

95TopArcBD-28
95TopArcBD-42
Dressendorfer, Kirk
88CapCodPPaLP-134
90ProAaA-163
90SouOreAB-3
90SouOreAP-3425
90TopMag-53
91A'sMot-19
91Bow-235
91Cla1-T77
91Cla2-T20
91ClaGam-159
91DonRoo-24
91FleUpd-50
91LeaGolR-BC13
91OPCPre-39
91ScoRoo-97T
91TopTra-35T
91TopTraT-35T
91UppDec-756
92Bow-91
92ClaGam-7
92Don-594
92OPC-716
92Pin-270
92Sco-728
92Sco100RS-37
92StaClu-806
92StaCluECN-806
92TexLon-13
92Top-716
92TopDeb91-48
92TopGol-716
92TopGolW-716
92TopMic-716
92TriPla-177
92UppDec-632
95ModA'sTI-6
Dressler, Rob (Robert Alan)
75IntLeaASB-6
75LafDriT-16
75PacCoaLAB-6
75PhoGiaC-14
75PhoGiaCK-11
76OPC-599
76PheGiaCr-37
76PhoGiaCC-7
76Top-599
77Gia-5
77PhoGiaCC-6
77PhoGiaCP-5
77PhoGiaVNB-5
77Top-11
78PhoGiaC-7
79SpoIndT-19
80Top-366
81Don-406
81OPC-163
81Top-508
Drew, Bob
74WicAerODF-126
75LafDriT-25
Drew, Cameron
86AshTouP-8
87ColAstP-7
87SouLeaAJ-7
88TriAAAP-44
88TriAAC-37
88TucTorC-14
88TucTorJP-10
88TucTorP-188
89Bow-334
89BowTif-334
89ClaTraO-135
89Don-30
89Fle-640
89FleGlo-640
89Sco-643
89ScoHot1R-3
89Spo-225
Drewien, Dan
93SpoIndC-5
93SpoIndF-3583
94MidLeaAF-MDW57
94SprSulC-6
94SprSulF-2030
95RanCucQT-NNO
Drews, Karl (Karl August)
48YanTeal-8
49Bow-188
52Top-352
53BowC-113
53Top-59
54Bow-191
83TopRep5-352
91TopArc1-59
Drews, Matt
94Bow-53
94ColC-30
94ColChoGS-30
94ColChoSS-30
94OneYanC-1
94OneYanF-3784
94Pin-265
94PinArtP-265
94PinMusC-265
94Sco-506
94ScoGolR-506
94SigRoo-29
94SigRooS-29
94UppDecML-107
95Bes-35
95BesFra-F4
95Bow-21
95BowBes-B68
95BowBesR-B68
95Exc-94
95SPML-120
95SPMLDtS-DS18
95TamYanYI-5
95UppDecML-54
96Bow-183
96BowBes-131
96BowBesAR-131
96BowBesR-131
96ColCliB-11
96Exc-87
96ExcSeaC-3
96Top-430
95UppDecMLFS-54
Dreyer, Darren
92GenCubC-19
92GenCubF-1553
94OrlCubF-1379
Dreyer, Steve
90ButCopKSP-10
91GasRanC-4
91GasRanP-2681
91SouAtlLAGP-SAL22
92ChaRanC-23
92ChaRanF-2220
92UppDecML-129
93RanKee-403
93TulDriF-2727
94ColC-5
94ColChoGS-5
94ColChoSS-5
94FleMajLP-10
94OklCit8F-1491
94RanMagM-4
94SpoRoo-77
94SpoRooAP-77
94StaCluT-244
94StaCluTFDI-244
94Top-193
94TopGol-193
94TopSpa-193
94Ult-430
94UppDec-9
94UppDecED-9
95Don-271
95DonPreP-271
95StaClu-477
95StaCluMOP-477
95StaCluSTWS-477
96OklCit8B-7
93TulDriTI-7
Dreyfuss, Barney
10PirTipTD-1
Drezek, Karl
88AppFoxP-148
88EugEmeB-21
Driessen, Dan (Daniel)
74OPC-341
74Top-341
74TopSta-25
75OPC-133
75Top-133
76LinSup-100
76OPC-514
76RedKro-6
76RedPos-6
76SSP-36
76Top-514
77BurCheD-199
77OPC-31
77PepGloD-45
77Top-23
78Hos-64
78OPC-84
78Pep-9
78RCColC-76
78SSP270-123
78Top-246
79Kel-26
79OPC-247
79Top-475
80OPC-173
80RedEnq-22
80Top-325
81AllGamPI-94
81CokTeaS-40
81Don-301
81Fle-205
81FleStiC-22
81OPC-14
81Top-655
81TopSti-164
81TopSupHT-34
82Don-248
82Fle-64
82Fle-630
82OPC-373
82RedCok-6
82Top-785
83AllGamPI-93
83Don-274
83Fle-589
83FleSta-55
83FleSti-217
83OPC-165
83RedYea-22
83Top-165
83TopSti-228
84AllGamPI-3
84Don-243
84Fle-467
84Nes792-585
84OPC-44
84RedEnq-2
84Top-585
84TopSti-55
84TopTif-585
85AllGamPI-93
85Don-619
85ExpPos-7
85Fle-396
85Lea-255
85OPC-285
85OPCPos-2
85Top-285
85TopSti-92
85TopTif-285
86Don-641
86Fle-539
86GiaMot-14
86Lea-255
86Top-65
86TopSti-89
86TopTat-14
86TopTif-65
87LouRedTI-12
88FleGlo-WS7
88FleWorS-7
89PacSenL-102
89PacSenL-105
89T/MSenL-30
89TopSenL-46
90EliSenL-67
91PacSenL-1
Driggers, Lee
90AugPirP-2480
91WelPirP-3591
Drill, Lew (Lewis L.)
03BreE10-45
Drilling, Robert
49SomandK-20
Drinkwater, Sean
92SpoIndC-15
92SpoIndF-1301
93RanCucQC-9
93RanCucQF-839
94ExcFS7-279
94WicWraF-195
95MemChiTI-26
Driscoll, Jem
11TurRedT-51
Driscoll, Jim (James B.)
71OPC-317
71Top-317
85WatIndT-19
86WatIndP-7
93RanKee-8
Driscoll, Mary Ellen
85FreGiaP-31
Driskell, Jeff
94JamJamC-8
94JamJamF-3967
Driskill, Travis
93WatIndC-8
93WatIndF-3555
94ColRedC-9
94ColRedF-437
95Exc-39
96CanIndB-12
96SigRooOJ-9
96SigRooOJS-9
Driver, Ron
77NewCoPT-10
78HolMilT-6
79HolMilT-11
Drizmala, Tom
83ChaRoyT-19
Drizos, Justin
96AshTouB-13
Drohan, Bill
88EugEmeB-5
89AppFoxP-854
90BasCitRS-6
Droll, Jeff
92HelBreF-1708
92HelBreSP-9
93BelBreC-5
93BelBreF-1703
93HelBreF-4086
94HicCraC-1
94HicCraF-2169
Dromerhauser, Rob
85NewOriT-17
88MetColP-21
89MetColP-26
90MetColP-31
91MetColP-31
Droogsma, Tim
85RedWinA-4
Dropo, Walt (Walter)
47Exh-64
49SolSunP-3
50Bow-246
51R42SmaS-19
51TopCurA-3
52Bow-169
52Top-235
53BowC-45
53RedMan-AL4
53TigGle-5
53Top-121
54Bow-7
54Top-18
55Bow-285
56Top-238
57Top-257
58Top-338
59RedEnq-5
59RedShiBS-5
59Top-158
59TopVen-158
60Top-79
60TopVen-79
61Top-489
79TCM50-116
80LauFamF-36
83FraBroR-8
83TopRep5-235
89SweBasG-108
90PacLeg-22
90SweBasG-57
91OriCro-114
91SweBasG-111
91TopArc1-121
92BazQua5A-20
94TopArc1-18
94TopArc1G-18
Droschak, Dave
83SprCarF-5
Drott, Dick (Richard Fred)
58Top-80
59Top-15
59TopVen-15
60Lea-76
60Top-27
60TopVen-27
61Top-231
79TCM50-64
Drucke, Louis
10DomDisP-39
10SweCapPP-113
Drumheller, Albert
93OneYanC-7
93OneYanF-3496
94GreBatF-465
95TamYanYI-6
96TamYanY-10
97GreBatC-7
Drumm, Doug
93EveGiaC-9
93EveGiaF-3762
Drummond, Tim
86PriWilPP-9
87VanCanP-1610
88TidTidCa-18
88TidTidCM-4
88TidTidP-1593
89MetColP-27
89TidTidC-1
89TidTidP-1952
90Don-510
90DonRoo-50
90FleUpd-107
90OPC-713
90ScoRoo-103T
90Top-713
90TopTif-713
91Don-694
91Fle-607
91LinDriAAA-406
91OPC-46
91PorBeaLD-406
91PorBeaP-1560
91Sco-76
91Sco100RS-95
91Top-46
91TopDesS-46
91TopMic-46
91TopTif-46
91UppDec-698
92HagSunF-2550
Drumright, Keith A.
78ChaChaT-6
79ChaChaT-1
80OmaRoyP-10
81TacTigT-17
82Don-616
82Fle-89
82TacTigT-29
82Top-673
Drumright, Mike
95Bes-119
96Exc-50
96JacSunB-10
97Bow-119
97BowBes-166
97BowBesAR-166
97BowBesR-166
97BowCerBIA-CA21
97BowCerGIA-CA21
97BowChr-135
97BowChrI-135
97BowChrIR-135
97BowChrR-135
97BowInt-119
Druna, Roland
82ChaRoyT-17
Drury, Scott
88BatCliP-1668
Dryden, Ken
72Dia-73
Drysdale, Brooks
94CedRapKC-9
94CedRapKF-1103
94MidLeaAF-MDW37
96StoPorB-26
Drysdale, Don (Donald S.)
47Exh-65A
47Exh-65B
56Dod-7
57Top-18
58DodBelB-3
58DodJayP-4
58HarSta-13
58Hir-55
58Top-25
59Baz-10
59DodMor-1
59DodTeal-5
59DodVol-3
59Top-262
59Top-387

60ArmCoi-9
60DodJayP-3
60DodMor-3
60DodPos-3
60DodTeal-5
60DodUniO-5
60KeyChal-14
60Pos-2
60Top-475
60Top-570
60TopTat-12
61Baz-26
61DodJayP-2
61DodMor-2
61DodUniO-5
61Pos-160A
61Pos-160B
61Top-45
61Top-49
61Top-260
61TopDicG-4
61TopStal-26
62AurRec-5
62DodBelB-53
62DodJayP-2
62Jel-110
62Pos-110
62PosCan-110
62Top-60
62Top-340
62Top-398
62TopBuc-23
62TopStal-133
62TopVen-60
63BasMagM-21
63Baz-17
63DodJayP-4
63ExhStaB-20
63Fle-41
63Jel-123
63Pos-123
63SalMetC-1
63Top-5
63Top-7
63Top-9
63Top-360
63Top-412
63TopStil-14
64DodHea-3
64Top-5
64Top-120
64TopCoi-34
64TopSta-79
64TopStaU-22
64TopVen-5
64TopVen-120
65DodJayP-4
65DodTeal-4
65OPC-8
65OPC-12
65OPC-260
65Top-8
65Top-12
65Top-260
65TopEmbl-15
65TopTral-47
66Baz-42
66Top-223
66Top-430
66TopRubl-24
66TopVen-223
67Baz-42
67OPC-55
67OPCPapl-16
67Top-55
67TopGiaSU-11
67TopPos-16
67TopVen-295
68Baz-6
68Baz-15
68OPC-145
68Top-145
68TopActS-2C
68TopActS-11B
68TopActS-13C
68TopPla-18
68TopPos-7
68TopVen-145
69MLBPin-41
69Top-314
69Top-400
69TopDecl-9
69TopSta-42
69TopSup-46
69TopTeaP-22
72LauGreF-38
74SupBlaB-2
76BooProC-5
77GalGloG-246
77Spo-7213
78TCM60I-3
79DiaGre-96
80PerHaloFP-186
80SSPHOF-187
82K-M-42
83MLBPin-23
84DodUniOP-4
84SpoDesPW-9
84WilMay-35
86TCMSupS-22
87AstShoSO-26
87DodSmoA-7
88DodSmo-11
88GreBasS-45
88RinPosD1-8A
89CalLeaA-28
89DodSmoG-7
89TopBasT-39
90DodTar-203
90HOFStIB-73
90PacLeg-29
90SweBasG-62
90TopGloA-11
91Col-10
91DodUno7P-3
91LinDri-1
91SweBasG-26
92DodStaTA-3
93ActPacA-121
93ActPacA2-55G
93NabAllA-2
93TedWil-12
93TedWilM-6
95StoPop-3
95TopArcBD-112
95TopLegot6M-4

Drzayich, Emil
80CedRapRT-4

Duant, Rich
86LitFalMP-9

Duany, Claro
95NegLeaL2-22

Duarte, Luis
80BatTroT-16
81WatIndT-17

Duarte, Rene
90IBAWorA-22

Dube, Greg
85OscAstTI-6
87WilBilP-19

DuBeau, Jack
78WatIndT-8

Dubee, Rich
76WatRoyT-6
77DayBeaIT-3
84MemChiT-2
85OmaRoyT-11
86MemChiSTOS-6
86MemChiTOS-6
87MemChiB-3
88OmaRoyC-23
88OmaRoyP-1494
90OmaRoyP-82
90ProAAAF-617
91RocExpC-16
91RocExpP-2064
92IndIndF-1876
93WesPalBEC-27
93WesPalBEF-1358
94EdmTraF-2891

Dubiel, Monk (Walter John)
47CenFlo-6
49EurSta-55
51Bow-283
52Top-164
83TopRep5-164

DuBois, Brian
86HagSunP-5
87HagSunP-4
88CarLeaAS-6
88VirGenS-8
89HagSunB-13
89HagSunP-274
89HagSunS-5
90Bow-349
90BowTif-349
90ClaUpd-T17
90Don-38
90DonRoo-4
90Fle-601
90FleCan-601
90HagSunDGB-7
90Lea-266
90OPC-413
90Sco-657
90TigCok-3
90Top-413
90TopBig-272
90TopDeb89-32
90TopTif-413
90UppDec-78
91Sco100RS-85
93FreKeyC-1
93FreKeyF-1018
94OriPro-27
94RocRedWF-992
95ScrRedBTI-7

DuBose, Brian
90BriTigP-3163
90BriTigS-5
91NiaFalRC-10
91NiaFalRP-3640
92ClaFS7-103
92FayGenC-5
92FayGenF-2174
93LakTigC-5
93LakTigF-1316
94TedWil-120
94TreThuF-2130
94UppDecML-142
94UppDecMLPotYF-PY25

Dubuc, Jean (Jean J.)
09T206-112
10CouT21-18
10CouT21-129
10CouT21-280
10RedCroT-109
10RedCroT-189
15CraJacE-156
15SpoNewM-53
16BF2FP-29
16SpoNewM-52

Ducey, Rob
86VenGulP-5
87BluJayFS-6
87DonHig-39
87IntLeaAT-26
87SyrChiP-1943
87SyrChiT-19
88BluJayFS-8
88Fle-107
88FleGlo-107
88OPC-106
88Sco-629
88ScoGlo-629
88SyrChiC-14
88SyrChiP-825
88Top-438
88TopTif-438
89BluJayFS-8
89OPC-203
89PanSti-459
89ScoHot1R-7
89Top-203
89TopBig-280
89TopTif-203
89UppDec-721
90CMC-347
90OPC-619
90ProAAAF-364
90PubSti-512
90ScoYouSI-34
90SyrChiC-21
90SyrChiMB-6
90SyrChiP-584
90Top-619
90TopTif-619
90UppDec-464
90VenSti-153
91BluJayFS-8
91BluJayS-22
91Don-705
91LinDriAAA-502
91OPC-101
91Sco-821
91StaClu-374
91SyrChiLD-502
91SyrChiMB-5
91SyrChiP-2492
91Top-101
91TopDesS-101
91TopMic-101
91TopTif-101
91TriA AAGP-AAA43
92Don-466
92Fle-328
92OPC-739
92ProFS7-163
92Sco-609
92StaClu-422
92Top-739
92TopGol-739
92TopGolW-739
92TopMic-739
93BluJayD4-40
93Don-489
93OPC-55
93RanKee-404
93StaClu-69
93StaCluFDI-69
93StaCluMOP-69
93Top-293
93TopGol-293
93TopInaM-293
93TopMic-293
93TriAAAGF-53
94OklCit8F-1503
94RanMagM-5
94StaCluT-257
94StaCluTFDI-257
94Top-618
94TopGol-618
94TopSpa-618
94TriAAF-AAA9

Duchin, David
90LynRedSTI-25
91LynRedSC-27
92LynRedSC-27
93LynRedSC-28

Duck, Daffy
91UppDecCBP-1

Duck, Diamond
91RicBraTI-27

Duck, Dinger
90NiaFalRP-33

Duckett, Mahlon
86NegLeaF-40
91NegLeaRL-11
92NegLeaRLI-18
93TedWil-104
95NegLeaLI-11

Duckhorn, Steve
79CedRapGT-1

Duckworth, Jim (James R.)
78TCM60I-23
78TCM60I-151

Duda, Steve
93HelBreF-4087
94StoPorC-5
94StoPorF-1686

Dudeck, Dave
94LetMouF-3870
94LetMouSP-8

Dudek, Steve
91JohCitCC-9
91JohCitCP-3983
92JohCitCC-4
92JohCitCF-3123
93SavCarC-13
93SavCarF-699

Dudley, Clise
90DodTar-204

Duenas, Vernon
88ChaWheB-11

Duensing, Larry
80HawIsIT-3
81HawIsIT-20
82HawIsIT-25
84LasVegSC-244

Dues, Hal (Hal Joseph)
75WesPalBES-10
78ExpPos-4
79OPC-373
79Top-699
81OPC-71
81Top-71

Duey, Kody
86JamExpP-5

Duey, Kyle
90MedHatBJB-5
91MyrBeaHC-3
91MyrBeaHP-2937
92DunBluJC-22
92DunBluJF-1991
93KnoSmoF-1255
94SyrChiF-967
94SyrChiTI-11

Duezabou, Mel
47RemBre-20
47SigOil-43
47SmiClo-23
48SigOil-5
48SmiClo-14
49RemBre-5
50RemBre-5

Dufault, Monte
92KenTwiC-20
92KenTwiF-610

Duff, Dave
82JacMetT-12

Duff, Scott
90BilMusP-3213
91ChaWheC-3
91ChaWheP-2880
92CedRapRC-23
92CedRapRF-1064
93WinSpiC-6
93WinSpiF-1563

Duffalo, Jim
62Top-578
63Top-567
64Top-573
65OPC-159
65Top-159
78TCM60I-204
78TCM60I-248
80PhoGiaVNB-23
81ShrCapT-13

Duffee, Charlie (Charles E.)
87OldJudN-142

Dufficy, Pat
96ColSilB-9

Duffie, John
77FriOneYW-29
90DodTar-936

Duffy, Allen
86GleFalTP-3

Duffy, Darrin
86MedA'sC-72
87HunStaTI-10
88ModA'sTI-22
89WinSpiS-7
90ChaKniTI-4
90TopTVCu-44
91PeoChiTI-33
92ChaKniS-153
92IowCubF-4058

Duffy, Frank (Frank Thomas)
71OPC-164
71Top-164
72Top-607
73OPC-376
73Top-376
74OPC-81
74Top-81
74TopSta-163
75OPC-448
75Top-448
76Hos-115
76OPC-232
76SSP-521
76Top-232
77BurCheD-63
77OPC-253
77PepGloD-18
77Top-542
78PapGinD-17
78SSP270-184
78Top-511
79OPC-47
79Top-106

Duffy, Hugh
06FanCraNL-16
09AmeCarE-37
09T206-113
10SweCapPP-10A
10SweCapPP-10B
11S74Sil-5
11SpoLifCW-110
11SpoLifM-23
11T205-47
23WilChoV-32
36PC7AlbHoF-34
48ExhHoF-9
50CalHOFW-28
63BazA-33
63GadFunC-49

69Baz-4
75TCMAllG-8
76ShaPiz-34
77GalGloG-147
80PerHaloFP-34
80SSPHOF-34
81ConTSN-18
84GalHaloFRL-34
87ConSer2-33
87OldJudN-143
90BasWit-67
90HOFStiB-8
92ConTSN-532
94ConTSN-1014
94ConTSNB-1014
94OriofB-75
95May-7
Duffy, John
87GleFalTP-23
88TolMudHC-10
88TolMudHP-596
89MemChiB-2
89MemChiP-1181
89MemChiS-9
96LowSpiB-6
Duffy, Patsy
88AllandGN-7
Duffy, Ryan
96AriBlaDB-17
Duffy, Tom
83VerBeaDT-2
Dugan, Joe (Joseph Anthony)
20NatCarE-24
20WalMaiW-13
21Exh-37
21Exh-38
21Exh-39
22E120-3
22W573-33
22W575-30
23W503-17
23W515-30
23WilChoV-33
27YorCarE-3A
27YorCarE-3B
28StaPlaCE-17
28W502-3
28W513-66
28Yue-3
29ExhFou-1
61Fle-103
79DiaGre-3
88ConSer5-8
91ConTSN-112
94ConTSN-1059
94ConTSNB-1059
Dugan, Ken
86DavLipB-10
92DavLipB-10
93DavLipB-6
94DavLipB-7
95DavLipB-8
Dugan, Kurt
92DavLipB-11
93DavLipB-7
94DavLipB-8
95DavLipB-9
Dugan, Mike
86DavLipB-11
Dugas, Gus (Augustin J.)
36GouWidPPR-D7
Dugas, Shanie
81WatIndT-21
82ChaLooT-13
83BufBisT-15
84MaiGuiT-23
85MaiGuiT-17
87AlbDukP-18
88AlbDukC-22
88AlbDukP-266
89AlbDukC-13
89AlbDukP-85
Dugdale, Dan (Daniel E.)
87OldJudN-144
Duge, Don
40WheM4-2A
Dugey, Oscar (Oscar Joseph)
15CraJacE-60
15SpoNewM-54
16SpoNewM-53
Duggan, Tom
83WauTimF-21
86SalRedBP-6
Dugger, Bart
93BakDodCLC-31
94BakDodC-30
Dugger, Keith
91SpoIndC-30
93BenRocC-30
96ColSprSSTI-11
Dugger, Lonnie
81HolMilT-13
82HolMilT-4
Duggleby, Bill
11SpoLifCW-111
Dukart, Derek
94OneYanC-7
94OneYanF-3798
94StaCluDP-68
94StaCluDPFDI-68
95GreBatTI-10
96TamYanY-11
Duke, Andy
89BilMusP-2056
Duke, Darrick
93SpoIndC-6
93SpoIndF-3602
94SprSulC-7
94SprSulF-2049
Duke, Doug
87BurExpP-1073
88JacExpB-22
88JacExpP-970
89JacExpB-6
89JacExpP-167
Duke, Ed
86ColAstP-11
Duke, Jerome
86JamExpP-6
Duke, Kyle
90PenPilS-7
91BenBucC-4
91BenBucP-3689
92SanBerC-4
92SanBerSF-945
94NewHavRF-1543
Duke, Martin F.
87OldJudN-146
Duke, Marvin
36WorWidGV-116
Duke, Richard
87IdaFalBP-6
Dukes, Jan (Jan Noble)
70OPC-154
70Top-154
93RanKee-9
Dukes, Kevin
82LynSaiT-3
83ChaLooT-19
Dukes, Tom (Thomas Earl)
68OPC-128
68Top-128
68TopVen-128
69Top-223
71OPC-106
71Top-106
91OriCro-115
Dukes, Willie
90ElmPioP-9
90WinHavRSS-7
91WinHavRSC-13
91WinHavRSP-493
Duliba, Bob (Robert John)
60Lea-77
60Top-401
62KahAtl-5
62Top-149
62TopVen-149
63Top-97
64Top-441
66OPC-53
66Top-53
66TopVen-53
67Top-599
Dulin, Tim
86MiaMarP-5
87HagSunP-10
88ChaKniTI-5
88SouLeaAJ-9
89RocRedWC-20
89RocRedWP-1646
90CMC-316
90ProAAAF-465
90RocRedWC-16
90RocRedWGC-5
90RocRedWP-708
Dull, Darrell
83IdaFalAT-19
Dull, Mike
87BurExpP-1075
88WesPalBES-10
89JacExpB-7
89JacExpP-164
Dulom, Kirk
90Ft.LauYS-6
Dumart, Woody
43ParSpo-3
Dumas, Don
87SavCarP-21
Dumas, Michael
93BelBreC-6
93BelBreF-1716
94BelBreC-8
94BelBreF-106
Dume, Mike
55JetPos-8
Dummies, Crash
94TulDriTI-30
95TulDriTI-30
96OklCit8B-25
96OklCit8B-26
96TulDriTI-29
Dumont, Serge
72Dia-117
Dumouchelle, Pat
81MiaOriT-8
84ChaO'sT-13
90HagSunDGB-8
Dumoulin, Dan
77IndIndTI-13
78IndIndTI-7
79IndIndTI-26
Dunavan, Chad
93BelMarC-12
93BelMarF-3222
94AppFoxF-1066
Dunbar, Matt
88CapCodPPaLP-65
90OneYanP-3382
91GreHorP-3050
92PriWilCC-9
92PriWilCF-139
93CarLeaAGF-19
93PriWilCC-7
93PriWilCF-649
94AbaYanF-1434
94ColCliF-2944
94VenLinU-172
95ColCliP-6
95ColCliTI-6
95FleUpd-96
96NorNavB-8
Dunbar, Tommy (Thomas Jerome)
82TulDriT-10
83OklCit8T-7
84Don-28
84OklCit8T-18
84RanJarP-13
85Don-159
85FleUpd-37
85RanPer-13
85Top-102
85TopTif-102
86Don-221
86OklCit8P-5
86Top-559
86TopTif-559
87VanCanP-1603
88GreBraB-21
89GreBraB-26
89GreBraP-1179
89GreBraS-7
90MemChiB-11
90MemChiP-1023
90MemChiS-9
90TulDriDGB-24
91LinDriAAA-333
91OmaRoyLD-333
91OmaRoyP-1046
93RanKee-129
94ChaLooF-1375
88RicBraBC-22
Duncan, Andres
91Cla/Bes-322
91CliGiaC-13
91CliGiaP-841
92SanJosGC-10
92UppDecML-215
93ShrCapF-2766
94NasXprF-393
95HarCitRCTI-4
Duncan, Chip
87WatPirP-6
88SalBucS-5
89SalBucS-7
90SalBucS-4
91CarMudLD-105
91CarMudP-1079
91LinDriAA-105
91ParPatF-18
92MemChiF-2412
95TulDriTI-6
Duncan, Dave (David Edwin)
64Top-528
68Top-261
68TopVen-261
69OPC-68
69Top-68
69TopSta-214
70Top-678
71MLBOffS-511
71OPC-178
71Top-178
72OPC-17
72Top-17
73OPC-337
73Top-337
74OPC-284
74Top-284
74TopSta-164
75OPC-238
75OPC-626
75Top-238
75Top-626
76OPC-40
76SSP-383
76Top-49
77Top-338
84WhiSoxTV-8
86A'sGreT-8
87A'sMot-8
87ModA'sC-A3
88A'sMot-27
89A'sMot-27
90A'sMot-27
91A'sMot-28
91OriCro-116
92AthMot-28
93AthMot-27
94A'sMot-28
95AthMot-28
Duncan, Devohn
94SpoIndC-8
94SpoIndF-3317
95Exc-283
Duncan, Doug
76SanAntBTI-9
77VisOakT-5
Duncan, Duke (C.)
78NewWayCT-12
79HolMilT-27
Duncan, Dunk (Frank)
86NegLeaF-118
87NegLeaPD-45
93NegLeaRL2-8
Duncan, Jeff
92MadMusC-3
92MadMusF-1240
Duncan, John
83WauTimF-26
Duncan, Lindy
81TulDriT-25
Duncan, Mariano
83VerBeaDT-16
85DodCokP-10
85DomLeaS-36
85FleUpd-38
85TopTifT-32T
85TopTra-32T
86DodCokP-8
86DodPol-25
86DodUniOP-5
86Don-128
86Fle-129
86FleLeaL-10
86FleMin-27
86FleStiC-33
86KayB-8
86Lea-50
86OPC-296
86SevCoi-W13
86Top-602
86TopTif-602
87DodMot-7
87DodPol-12
87Don-253
87DonOpeD-84
87Fle-439
87FleGlo-439
87OPC-199
87SevCoi-W2
87SpoTeaP-14
87Top-199
87TopMinL-13
87TopSti-74
87TopTif-199
88AlbDukC-23
88AlbDukP-255
88DodPol-25
88Don-155
88Fle-513
88FleGlo-513
88OPC-181
88Sco-321
88ScoGlo-321
88StaLinD-3
88Top-481
88TopTif-481
89DodMot-26
89DodPol-15
90DodTar-205
90Don-684
90DonBesN-113
90FleUpd-12
90Lea-202
90OPC-234
90RedKah-9
90Sco-506
90Top-234
90TopBig-243
90TopTif-234
90UppDec-430
91Bow-675
91Don-309
91Fle-64
91Lea-494
91OPC-13
91PanFreS-128
91PanSti-123
91RedKah-7
91RedPep-9
91Sco-479
91StaClu-251
91Stu-164
91Top-13
91TopDesS-13
91TopMic-13
91TopTif-13
91Ult-94
91UppDec-112
92Don-540
92Fle-406
92FleUpd-109
92Lea-311
92OPC-589
92PhiMed-11
92Pin-377
92Sco-352
92ScoRoo-54T
92StaClu-614
92Stu-74
92Top-589
92TopGol-589
92TopGolW-589
92TopMic-589
92TopTra-30T
92TopTraG-30T
92Ult-544
92UppDec-659
92UppDec-792
93Don-382
93Fla-98
93Fle-101
93Lea-187
93OPC-95
93PacSpa-234
93PanSti-272
93PhiMed-11
93Pin-218
93Sco-201
93Sel-151
93SelStaL-17
93SP-172
93StaClu-276
93StaCluFDI-276
93StaCluMOP-276

93StaCluP-21
93Top-371
93TopGol-371
93TopInaM-371
93TopMic-371
93Ult-87
93UppDec-201
93UppDecGold-201
94Bow-196
94ColC-429
94ColChoGS-429
94ColChoSS-429
94Don-614
94ExtBas-331
94Fin-352
94FinRef-352
94Fla-411
94Fle-586
94Lea-11
94LeaL-135
94LeaLimGA-4
94Pac-472
94PacAll-8
94PanSti-225
94PhiMed-7
94PhiMel-5
94PhiUSPC-4D
94PhiUSPC-11C
94Pin-479
94PinArtP-479
94PinMusC-479
94Sco-490
94ScoGolR-490
94Sel-271
94StaClu-54
94StaCluFDI-54
94StaCluGR-54
94StaCluMOP-54
94StaCluT-217
94StaCluTFDI-217
94Stu-137
94Top-663
94TopGol-663
94TopSpa-663
94TriPla-172
94Ult-543
94UppDec-181
94UppDecED-181
95ColCho-361
95ColChoGS-361
95ColChoSE-169
95ColChoSEGS-169
95ColChoSESS-169
95ColChoSS-361
95Don-341
95DonAll-NL4
95DonPreP-341
95DonTopotO-301
95Fle-389
95FleAllS-3
95KinDis-6
95Lea-266
95Pac-327
95PacPri-106
95Phi-8
95PhiMel-6
95Sco-350
95ScoGolR-350
95ScoPlaTS-350
95StaClu-27
95StaCluFDI-27
95StaCluMOP-27
95StaCluSTWS-27
95Top-103
95TopCyb-66
95Ult-418
95UltGolM-418
95UppDec-141
95UppDecED-141
95UppDecEDG-141
96Fle-339
96FleTif-339
96FleUpd-U58
96FleUpdTC-U58
96Pac-41
96Ult-382
96UltGolM-382
97Cir-179
97CirRav-179
97ColCho-406
97Fle-163
97FleTif-163
97Lea-311
97LeaFraM-311
97LeaFraMDC-311
97Pac-149
97PacLigB-149
97PacSil-149
97StaClu-117
97StaCluMOP-117
97Top-45
97Ult-433
97UltGolME-433
97UltPlaME-433
97UppDec-437

Duncan, Mark
94LetMouF-3885
94LetMouSP-24

Duncan, Michael
86ModA'sC-7
86ModA'sP-7
87ModA'sP-4

Duncan, Pat (Louis Baird)
20RedWorCP-4
20WalMaiW-14
21Exh-40
21Nei-109
22E120-171
22W572-25
23WilChoV-34
88PacEigMO-94
94ConTSN-1026
94ConTSNB-1026

Duncan, Rick
78OrlTwiT-5
79NaSouTI-8

Duncan, Robert
95DanBraTI-8

Duncan, Sean
96SouBenSHS-11

Duncan, Taylor M.
77RocRedWM-5
79Top-658
89PacSenL-70

Duncan, Tim
80ElmPioRST-20

Dunckel, Bill
92BoiHawC-23
92BoiHawF-3642

Dunckel, Keith
93WatDiaC-12

Duncun, John
86ChaLooP-9

Dundee, Johnny
28W512-43

Dundik, Alexander
89EasLeaDDP-DD10

Dundon, Gus
11SpoLifCW-112

Dunegan, James W. Jr.
71OPC-121
71Top-121

Dunham, Jim
72CedRapCT-10

Dunivan, Kevin
92GulCoaRSP-4

Dunlap, Fred (Frederick C.)
76SSP188WS-6
87BucN28-29
87OldJudN-147
87ScrDC-12
88GooN16-5
88WG1CarG-58
94OriofB-56

Dunlap, Joe
86CedRapRT-15
87VerRedP-10
89CalCanC-18
89CalCanP-529
89EasLeaDDP-DD30

Dunlap, Paul
36WorWidGV-125

Dunlap, Travis
90PulBraB-3
90PulBraP-3099
91IdaFalBSP-11
92MacBraC-10
92MacBraF-261
94WilBluRC-8
94WilBluRF-295

Dunleavy, John E.
06FanCraNL-17
11SpoLifCW-113

Dunlop, Harry
70RoyTeal-11
73OPC-593
73Top-593
74Top-166
80RedEnq-4
83LasVegSBHN-7
84PadMot-27
84PadSmo-8
85PadMot-27
91HelBreSP-30
92HelBreF-1732
92HelBreSP-26
93HelBreF-4112

Dunn, Alan
93GenCubF-3194
94PeoChiC-27
94PeoChiF-2284
95RocCubTI-NNO
96RocCubTI-7

Dunn, Brian
89SanDieSAS-8
90PitMetP-12
91ColMetPI-19
91ColMetPPI-7

Dunn, Bubba
91BasCitRC-3
91BasCitRP-1390

Dunn, Geoff
91WavRedF-1

Dunn, Greg
82SprCarF-13
83SprCarF-14
85SprCarT-8
86LouRedTI-10

Dunn, Jack (John Joseph)
03BreE10-46
09ColChiE-87
09T206-421
10CouT21-130
10CouT21-281
11SpoLifCW-114
11T205-188
12ColRedB-87
12ColTinT-87
12ImpTobC-19
90DodTar-206

Dunn, Jim (James William)
81ShrCapT-3

Dunn, Joe (Joseph Edward)
09RamT20-41
09T206-114
10CouT21-19

Dunn, Michael
95AusFut-50

Dunn, Nathan
92GreFalDSP-3
93YakBeaF-3888

Dunn, Ron (Ronald Ray)
74WicAerODF-119
76SSP-322

Dunn, Steve
88QuaCitAGS-10
90PalSprACLC-220
90PalSprAP-2571

Dunn, Steve Robert
89EliTwiS-7
89KenTwiP-1073
89KenTwiS-4
89Sta-147
90Bes-12
90KenTwiB-1
90KenTwiP-2299
90KenTwiS-3
90MidLeaASGS-9
90StaFS7-55
91Cla/Bes-241
91VisOakC-15
91VisOakP-1747
92UppDecML-216
92VisOakC-19
92VisOakF-1019
93Bow-17
93ClaFS7-155
93ExcFS7-199
93NasXprF-407
94ExcFS7-93
94FleMajLP-11
94LeaLimR-14
94SalLakBF-822
94SpoRoo-43
94SpoRooAP-43
94Ult-387
94UppDecML-169
95ColCho-484
95ColChoGS-484
95ColChoSE-23
95ColChoSEGS-23
95ColChoSESS-23
95ColChoSS-484
95Don-106
95DonPreP-106
95Fle-200
95Pac-247
95Pin-157
95PinArtP-157
95PinMusC-157
95Sco-595
95ScoGolR-595
95ScoPlaTS-595
95Sel-157
95SelArtP-157
95SigRoo-15
95SigRooSig-15
95Spo-144
95SpoArtP-144
96BufBisB-7

Dunn, Todd
93BazTeaU-19
93TopTra-67T
94BelBreC-9
94BelBreF-114
94Bow-657
94UppDec-528
94UppDecED-528
95Bow-189
95SPML-82
95UppDecML-141
96BesAutSA-17
96Bow-333
96El PasDB-9
97Bow-101
97BowChr-123
97BowChrI-123
97BowChrIR-123
97BowChrR-123
97BowInt-101
97Sel-115
97SelArtP-115
97SelRegG-115
97UppDec-476
95UppDecMLFS-141

Dunn, Yvon
58MonRoyF-7

Dunne, Brian
95MarPhiTI-7

Dunne, Mike
85Top-395
85TopTif-395
86LouRedTI-11
87DonRoo-38
87FleUpd-29
87FleUpdG-29
87SpoRoo2-40
87TopTra-30T
87TopTraT-30T
87VanCanP-1612
88ClaBlu-237
88Don-390
88DonBasB-89
88Fle-328
88FleAwaW-10
88FleBasM-11
88FleGlo-328
88FleMin-104
88FleRecS-11
88FleStiC-115
88Lea-235
88OPC-224
88PanSti-367
88Sco-432
88ScoGlo-432
88ScoYouSI-26
88Spo-171
88StaLinPi-9
88Top-619
88TopBig-236
88TopCoi-40
88TopGloS-19
88TopMinL-68
88TopRitTM-9
88TopRoo-16
88TopSti-132
88TopSti-307
88TopTif-619
88TopUKM-21
88TopUKMT-21
88ToyRoo-10
89Don-269
89Fle-207
89FleGlo-207
89OPC-165
89PanSti-162
89PirVerFJ-41
89Sco-285
89Top-165
89TopSti-130
89TopTif-165
89UppDec-518
90Lea-418
90OPC-522
90PadMag-19
90Top-522
90TopTif-522
91OPC-238
91Top-238
91TopDesS-238
91TopMic-238
91TopTif-238
92VanCanF-2715
92VanCanS-634
94ScrRedBF-917

Dunnegan, Steve
82DayBeaAT-11

Dunner, Mike
82CliCiaF-14

Dunning, Steve (Stephen John)
71Ind-3
71OPC-294
71Top-294
72Top-658
73OPC-53
73Top-53
74SpoIndC-28
76ExpRed-6
78Top-647
93RanKee-130

Dunnum, Rick
88AubAstP-1969
89AshTouP-964
90OscAstS-7
91LinDriAA-508
91ReaPhiLD-508
91ReaPhiP-1367

Dunster, Don
86OscAstP-6
87OscAstP-19
88ColAstB-2

Dunston, Shawon
83QuaCitCT-20
84MidCubT-22
85CubLioP-8
85Don-39
85Fle-649
85Top-280
85TopTif-280
86BasStaB-35
86CubGat-12
86CubUno-6
86Don-311
86Fle-366
86FleMin-77
86FleStiC-34
86KayB-9
86Lea-181
86MSAJayPCD-6
86SevCoi-C13
86Spo-155
86Top-72
86TopTat-2
86TopTif-72
87CubCan-9
87CubDavB-12
87Don-119
87DonOpeD-76
87Fle-561
87FleGamW-13
87FleGlo-561
87FleMin-35
87FleRecS-6
87FleStiC-36
87Lea-128
87OPC-346
87RedFolSB-94
87SevCoi-C4
87Spo-79
87Spo-98
87SpoTeaP-22
87Top-346
87TopSti-59
87TopTif-346
88CubDavB-12
88Don-146

88DonBasB-37
88DonTeaBC-146
88Fle-419
88FleGlo-419
88Lea-70
88OPC-277
88PanSti-264
88Sco-529
88ScoGlo-529
88ScoYouS2-18
88Spo-163
88Top-171
88Top-695
88TopBig-225
88TopSti-65
88TopStiB-11
88TopTif-171
88TopTif-695
89Bow-294
89BowTif-294
89CadEllD-15
89CubMar-12
89Don-137
89DonAll-43
89DonBasB-93
89Fle-424
89FleGlo-424
89K-M-26
89OPC-140
89PanSti-58
89RedFolSB-38
89Sco-235
89Spo-190
89Top-140
89TopBig-233
89TopSti-49
89TopStiB-43
89TopTif-140
89TVSpoM-19
89UppDec-107
90Bow-38
90BowTif-38
90CubMar-7
90Don-49
90DonBesN-112
90Fle-30
90FleCan-30
90Lea-229
90MLBBasB-46
90OPC-415
90PanSti-236
90PubSti-193
90Sco-169
90Top-415
90TopBig-62
90TopDou-18
90TopGloS-45
90TopSti-53
90TopStiB-10
90TopTif-415
90TopTVCu-22
90UppDec-231
90USPlaCA-10D
90VenSti-154
91Bow-424
91CadEllD-17
91ClaGam-27
91CubMar-12
91CubVinL-10
91Don-686
91Fle-420
91Lea-25
91OPC-765
91OPCPre-37
91PanFreS-46
91PanSti-47
91RedFolS-29
91Sco-201
91Sco-413
91Sco100S-45
91StaClu-3
91StaCluP-12
91StaPinB-15
91Stu-155
91Top-765
91TopCraJ2-23
91TopDesS-765
91TopMic-765
91TopTif-765
91Ult-59
91UppDec-111
92ClaGam-28
92CubMar-12
92Don-613
92Fle-380
92Lea-249
92OPC-370
92OPCPre-125
92PanSti-185
92Pin-244
92Sco-634
92ScoImpP-70
92StaClu-540
92Top-370
92TopGol-370
92TopGolPS-370
92TopGolW-370
92TopKid-5
92TopMic-370
92TopPreS-3
92TriPla-160
92Ult-174
92UppDec-35
92UppDec-122
92UppDec-714
93CadDis-17
93Don-268
93Fle-19
93MetBak-24
93OPC-62
93PacSpa-57
93PanSti-205
93Pin-89
93Sco-26
93Sel-121
93StaClu-393
93StaCluCu-9
93StaCluFDI-393
93StaCluMOP-393
93Top-595
93TopGol-595
93TopInaM-595
93TopMic-595
93TriPla-40
93Ult-17
93UppDec-101
93UppDecGold-101
94ColC-363
94ColChoGS-363
94ColChoSS-363
94Don-490
94ExtBas-217
94Fin-368
94FinRef-368
94Fla-136
94FleUpd-109
94Lea-316
94LeaL-89
94PanSti-152
94Pin-523
94PinArtP-523
94PinMusC-523
94ProMag-25
94Sel-136
94StaClu-576
94StaCluFDI-576
94StaCluGR-576
94StaCluMOP-576
94StaCluT-354
94StaCluTFDI-354
94Stu-59
94TopTra-46T
94Ult-454
94UppDec-477
94UppDecED-477
95Baz-34
95ColCho-204
95ColChoGS-204
95ColChoSE-82
95ColChoSEGS-82
95ColChoSESS-82
95ColChoSS-204
95Don-39
95DonPreP-39
95DonTopotO-196
95Emb-70
95EmbGolI-70
95Emo-109
95Fin-140
95FinRef-140
95Fla-112
95Fle-413
95Lea-30
95LeaLim-120
95Pac-68
95Pin-4
95PinArtP-4
95PinMusC-4
95Sco-89
95ScoGolR-89
95ScoPlaTS-89
95Spo-89
95SpoArtP-89
95StaClu-29
95StaCluFDI-29
95StaCluMOP-29
95StaCluSTWS-29
95StaCluVR-19
95Stu-62
95Top-214
95TopCyb-122
95Ult-358
95UltGolM-358
95Zen-99
96Cir-193
96CirRav-193
96Don-429
96DonPreP-429
96EmoXL-288
96Fin-B219
96FinRef-B219
96Fla-386
96Fle-315
96FleTif-315
96FleUpd-U204
96FleUpdTC-U204
96GiaMot-11
96LeaSigA-60
96LeaSigAG-60
96LeaSigAS-60
96MetUni-139
96MetUniP-139
96Pac-26
96PanSti-44
96Pin-72
96Pin-354
96PinAfi-85
96PinAfiAP-85
96PinAfiFPP-85
96PinArtP-27
96PinFoil-354
96PinSta-27
96ProSta-37
96Sco-280
96ScoDugC-B5
96ScoDugCAP-B5
96Sel-129
96SelArtP-129
96StaClu-137
96StaCluEPB-137
96StaCluEPG-137
96StaCluEPS-137
96StaCluMOP-137
95StaCluVRMC-19
96Sum-63
96SumAbo&B-63
96SumArtP-63
96SumFoi-63
96Top-399
96TopChr-160
96TopChrR-160
96TopLas-22
96Ult-165
96Ult-566
96UltGolM-165
96UltGolM-566
96UppDec-457
97Cir-213
97CirRav-213
97ColCho-287
97Don-255
97DonPreP-255
97DonPrePGold-255
97Fle-479
97Fle-538
97FleTif-479
97FleTif-538
97Pac-441
97PacLigB-441
97PacSil-441
97Pin-51
97PinArtP-51
97PinMusC-51
97StaClu-306
97StaCluMOP-306
97Top-172
97Ult-293
97Ult-303
97UltGolME-293
97UltGolME-303
97UltPlaME-293
97UltPlaME-303
97UppDec-328

Dunton, Kevin
86WesPalBEP-14

Dunwoody, Todd
95KanCouCTI-37
95MidLeaA-13
96BowBes-139
96BowBesAR-139
96BowBesR-139
96Exc-161
96PorSeaDB-13
97Bow-90
97BowChr-114
97BowChrI-114
97BowChrIR-114
97BowChrR-114
97BowInt-90
97Don-390
97DonLim-174
97DonLimLE-174
97DonPreP-390
97DonPrePGold-390
97Fle-652
97FleTif-652
97Lea-347
97LeaFraM-347
97LeaFraMDC-347
97Ult-552
97UltGolME-552
97UltPlaME-552

DuPlessis, Dave
92SalSpuC-21
92SalSpuF-3763
94WesPalBEC-7
94WesPalBEF-48

Dupont, Margaret
51BerRos-D13

Dupree, Mike (Michael D.)
77Top-491
79HawIslT-19

Dupuy, Jerry
93MisStaB-14

Duquette, Bryan
83ElPasDT-5
84ElPasDT-11
85VanCanC-212
86VanCanP-11

Duquette, Chuck
88FayGenP-1089

Duran, Dan (Daniel James)
74GasRanT-9
75LynRanT-10
76SanAntBTI-10
80ChaChaT-12
93RanKee-131

Duran, Felipe
91BurIndP-3307
92ColRedC-24
92ColRedF-2396
93ColRedC-9
93ColRedF-603

Duran, Ignacio
90SavCarP-2072
91Cla/Bes-283
91SprCarC-13
91SprCarP-748
92SavCarF-668
93WatDiaC-13
93WatDiaF-1775
94SprSulC-8

Duran, Dave
81HolMilT-14
82HolMilT-5

Duran, Rick
79HolMilT-14

Duran, Roberto
92GulCoaDF-3560
93VerBeaDF-2209
93YakBeaC-8
93YakBeaF-3878
94BakDodC-9
95VerBeaDTI-7
96DunBluJB-6
96DunBluJTI-8
96Exc-174

Durant, Mike
91ClaDraP-42
91FroRowDP-17
92CalLeaACL-47
92ClaFS7-294
92StaCluD-40
92UppDecML-288
92VisOakC-21
92VisOakF-1018
93ClaFS7-152
93ClaGolF-43
93ExcFS7-200
93NasXprF-405
94SalLakBF-819
94UppDecML-161
96FleUpd-U51
96FleUpdTC-U51

Durant, Richard
87ColMetP-25
88ColMetGS-3
89StoPorB-7
89StoPorCLC-155
89StoPorP-388
89StoPorS-19

Duren, Ryne (Rinold George)
58Top-296
59Top-485
60Lea-22
60Top-204
60TopTat-13
61Pos-14
61Top-356
61Yan61RL-37
62AngJayP-3
62Jel-81
62Pos-81
62PosCan-81
62SalPlaC-46A
62SalPlaC-46B
62ShiPlaC-46
62Top-388
63BasMagM-22
63Top-17
63Top-231
64Top-173
64TopVen-173
65RedEnq-7
65Top-339
79TCM50-135
83YanASFY-12
89PacLegI-141
91OriCro-117
91RinPos1Y3-8
92YanWIZ6-37
92YanWIZA-20

Durham, Bull (Edward Fant)
09BriE97-10
09T206-115
10W555-27
34DiaMatCSB-47
34Gou-79
90DodTar-207

Durham, Don (Donald Gary)
73OPC-548
73Top-548
93RanKee-132

Durham, Joe (Joseph Vann)
58Top-96
90HagSunB-6
90HagSunP-1433
90HagSunS-28
91HagSunLD-250
91HagSunP-2472
91LinDriAA-250
91OriCro-118
92HagSunF-2571
93FreKeyC-27
93FreKeyF-1043
94FreKeyF-2631
94FreKeyC-27

Durham, Leon
78ArkTraT-8
81CokTeaS-16
81Don-427
81Fle-540
81OPC-321
81Top-321
81TopSupHT-25
81TopTra-756
82CubRedL-10
82Don-151
82Fle-595
82FleSta-94
82OPC-206
82Top-607
82TopSti-25
82TopStiV-25
83AllGamPI-143

83CubThoAV-10
83Don-477
83DonActA-55
83Fle-495
83FleSta-56
83FleSti-131
83Kel-27
83OPC-125
83Top-51
83Top-125
83TopSti-219
84AllGamPI-50
84CubSev-10
84CubUno-7
84Don-5
84Don-5A
84Don-67
84Fle-492
84FunFooP-107
84Nes792-565
84OPC-209
84Top-565
84TopRubD-19
84TopSti-40
84TopTif-565
85AllGamPI-94
85CubLioP-9
85CubSev-10
85Don-189
85DonActA-46
85Fle-56
85Lea-238
85OPC-330
85SevCoi-G8
85Top-330
85TopGloS-11
85TopMin-330
85TopRubD-18
85TopSti-36
85TopTif-330
86BasStaB-36
86CubGat-10
86CubUno-7
86Don-320
86Fle-367
86FleLeaL-11
86FleMin-78
86FleStiC-35
86Lea-190
86OPC-58
86Spo-111
86Top-460
86TopSti-60
86TopTat-4
86TopTif-460
87BoaandB-26
87CubCan-10
87CubDavB-10
87Don-242
87DonOpeD-74
87Fle-562
87FleGlo-562
87FleHotS-15
87Lea-125
87OPC-290
87RedFolSB-120
87SevCoi-C6
87Spo-185
87SpoTeaP-22
87StuPan-3
87Top-290
87TopSti-57
87TopTif-290
88Don-191
88DonTeaBC-191
88Fle-420
88FleGlo-420
88OPC-65
88PanSti-259
88RedKah-10
88Sco-378
88ScoGlo-378
88StaLinCu-4
88Top-65
88TopBig-42
88TopSti-63
88TopTif-65
89LouRedBC-16
89LouRedBP-1260
89LouRedBTI-16
89UppDec-354
96LakElsSB-28
Durham, Ray
91UtiBluSC-6
91UtiBluSP-3246
92SarWhiSF-219
93BirBarF-1198
94Cla-83
94ExcFS7-37
94ExtBas-44
94ExtBasMLH-3
94NasSouF-1256
94TriAAF-AAA6
94Ult-334
94UppDecML-59
95ActPac2GF-3G
95ActPacF-32
95ActPacF-64
95Bow-251
95BowBes-R80
95BowBesR-R80
95BowGolF-251
95ColCho-3
95ColChoGS-3
95ColChoSS-3
95DonTopotO-47
95Emo-26
95EmoRoo-4
95Exc-28
95ExcAll-3
95Fin-292
95FinRef-292
95Fla-243
95FlaWavotF-4
95FleMajLP-5
95FleUpd-35
95FleUpdRU-2
95LeaLim-54
95Pin-416
95PinArtP-416
95PinMusC-416
95Sel-172
95SelArtP-172
95SelCer-110
95SelCerF-7
95SelCerMG-110
95SelCerPU-15
95SelCerPU9-15
95SelCerS-110
95SigRooOJSS-8
95SigRooOJSSS-8
95SigRooOP-OP3
95SigRooOPS-OP3
95SP-8
95SPCha-12
95SPChaDC-12
95SPSil-8
95StaClu-548
95StaCluCB-CB3
95StaCluMOP-548
95StaCluMOP-CB3
95StaCluSTWS-548
95Sum-165
95SumNewA-NA15
95SumNthD-165
95TopTra-11T
95TopTra-28T
95UC3-114
95UC3ArtP-114
95UltGolP-4
95UltGolPGM-4
95UppDec-235
95UppDecED-235
95UppDecEDG-235
95UppDecML-89
95UppDecPAW-H31
95UppDecPAWE-H31
95UppDecSE-153
95UppDecSEG-153
95WhiSoxK-8
95Zen-119
95ZenRooRC-8
96Baz-49
96Bow-2
96BowBes-68
96BowBesAR-68
96BowBesR-68
96Cir-26
96CirRav-26
96ColCho-92
96ColChoGS-92
96ColChoSS-92
96Don-242
96DonPreP-242
96EmoXL-35
96Fin-S121
96FinRef-S121
96Fla-49
96Fle-64
96FleRooS-4
96FleTif-64
96FleWhiS-4
96Lea-51
96LeaLim-72
96LeaLimG-72
96LeaPre-107
96LeaPreP-107
96LeaPrePB-51
96LeaPrePG-51
96LeaPrePS-51
96LeaSigA-61
96LeaSigAG-61
96LeaSigAS-61
96MetUni-35
96MetUniP-35
96Pac-290
96PanSti-168
96Pin-299
96PinAfi-116
96PinAfiAP-116
96PinFoil-299
96Sco-37
96ScoDiaA-3
96ScoDugC-A35
96ScoDugCAP-A35
96Sel-89
96SelArtP-89
96SelCer-97
96SelCerAP-97
96SelCerCB-97
96SelCerCR-97
96SelCerMB-97
96SelCerMG-97
96SelCerMR-97
96SP-61
96Spo-49
96SpoArtP-49
96StaClu-7
96StaClu-232
96StaCluEPB-7
96StaCluEPG-7
96StaCluEPS-7
96StaCluMOP-7
96StaCluMOP-232
96Stu-87
96StuPrePB-87
96StuPrePG-87
96StuPrePS-87
96Sum-5
96SumAbo&B-5
96SumArtP-5
96SumFoi-5
96TeaOut-23
96Top-173
96TopGal-96
96TopGalPPI-96
96TopLas-103
96Ult-36
96UltGolM-36
96UppDec-40
96Zen-46
96ZenArtP-46
96ZenMoz-3
97Bow-270
97BowInt-270
97Cir-2
97CirRav-2
97ColCho-295
97Don-156
97DonEli-73
97DonEliGS-73
97DonLim-12
97DonLimLE-12
97DonPre-67
97DonPreCttC-67
97DonPreP-156
97DonPrePGold-156
97DonTea-65
97DonTeaSPE-65
97Fin-301
97FinEmb-301
97FinEmbR-301
97FinRef-301
97FlaSho-A148
97FlaSho-B148
97FlaSho-C148
97FlaShoLC-148
97FlaShoLC-B148
97FlaShoLC-C148
97FlaShoLCM-A148
97FlaShoLCM-B148
97FlaShoLCM-C148
97Fle-59
97FleTif-59
97Lea-114
97LeaFraM-114
97LeaFraMDC-114
97MetUni-57
97Pac-51
97PacLigB-51
97PacSil-51
97Pin-108
97PinArtP-108
97PinIns-46
97PinInsCE-46
97PinInsDE-46
97PinMusC-108
97PinX-P-62
97PinX-PMoS-62
97Sco-158
97ScoPreS-158
97ScoShoS-158
97ScoShoSAP-158
97ScoWhiS-7
97ScoWhiSPI-7
97ScoWhiSPr-7
97SkyE-X-14
97SkyE-XC-14
97SkyE-XEC-14
97SP-48
97StaClu-293
97StaCluM-M4
97StaCluMOP-293
97StaCluMOP-M4
97Stu-22
97StuPrePG-22
97StuPrePS-22
97Top-215
97TopChr-80
97TopChrR-80
97TopGal-163
97TopGalPPI-163
97Ult-38
97UltGolME-38
97UltPlaME-38
97UppDec-329
95UppDecMLFS-89
Durham, Shane
87AncGlaP-7
Durkin, Chris
91AubAstC-19
91AubAstP-4285
91Cla/Bes-410
91FroRowDP-8
92AshTouC-21
92ClaFS7-15
92StaCluD-41
92UppDecML-177
93QuaCitRBC-6
93QuaCitRBF-111
94OscAstC-6
94OscAstF-1149
96VerBeaDB-12
Durkin, Marty (Martin)
88CapCodPPaLP-128
89WatIndS-4
90MiaMirIS-6
90MiaMirIS-5
91WesPalBEC-25
91WesPalBEP-1240
92WinHavRSF-1785
93ForLauRSC-10
93ForLauRSFP-1604
Durkovic, Peter
96FayGenB-12
Durnan, Bill
43ParSpo-24
51BerRos-A17
Durney, Bill
88PalSprACLC-115
88PalSprAP-1462
89BenBucL-29
Durning, Dick
90DodTar-937
Durocher, Francois
86OscAstP-7
Durocher, Jayson
94VerExpF-3903
96WesPalBEB-9
Durocher, Leo (Leo Ernest)
29ExhFou-26
31Exh-7
33Gou-147
33GouCanV-74
34DiaMatCSB-48
34BatR31-156
34ButPreR-17
34Gou-7
34GouCanV-69
35DiaMatCS3T1-48
36WorWidGV-25
37KelPepS-BB3
38ExhFou-2
39PlaBal-6
40DodTeal-6
40WheM4-1B
41DouPlaR-141
42DodTeal-6
43DodTeal-8
48BluTin-2A
48BluTin-2B
49EurSta-102
50Bow-220
51Bow-233
52Bow-146
52RedMan-NL1
52Top-315
53BowC-55
55GiaGolS-2
66CubTeal-6
67Top-481
68Top-321
68TopVen-321
69CubPho-4
69OPC-147
69Top-147
69TopFou-12
70OPC-291
70Top-291
71OPC-609
71Top-609
72Top-576
73OPC-624
73Top-624
74Car193T-9
74Car193T-28
74Car193T-29
75Gia195T-33
75Gia195T-34
79DiaGre-85
79TCM50-201
80PacLeg-40
80PerHaloFP-218
83TopRep5-315
84CubUno-8
84OCoandSI-187
84WilMay-4
86ConSer1-11
87AstShoSTw-21
87Car193T-6
88ConSer3-10
88PacLegI-27
88RinPosD1-4C
88RinPosD1-6C
89DodSmoG-39
90DodTar-208
91TopArc1-309
92BazQua5A-5
93DiaStaES-127
Duross, Gabe
93GenCubC-10
93GenCubF-3182
94MidLeaAF-MDW47
94PeoChiC-6
94PeoChiF-2274
95Exc-162
96OrlCubB-8
95OrlCubF-17
Durrett, Red
43ParSpo-75
90DodTar-938
Durrington, Trent
95AusFut-53
95BoiHawTI-16
96BoiHawB-11
Durrman, Jim
81WesHavAT-8
83AlbA'sT-9
Durrwacher, Doug
93BilMusF-3954
94BilMusF-3676
94BilMusSP-5
Durso, Joe
93St.CatBJC-8
93St.CatBJF-3977
94HagSunC-7
94HagSunF-2733
95PriWilCTI-13
Durst, Cedric
91ConTSN-108

DuRussel, Scott
91NiaFalRP-3626
92NiaFalRC-18
92NiaFalRF-3317
Duryea, Jesse (James Whitney)
87OldJudN-149
Dusak, Erv (Ervin Frank)
46SeaSLP-14
47TipTop-155
51Bow-310
52Top-183
79TCM50-122
83TopRep5-183
85TCMPla1-23
Dusan, Gene
75OklCit8TI-21
77WatIndT-7
79TacTugT-24
80TacTigT-23
82JacMetT-22
84WicAerRD-22
86CedRapRT-25
90BenBucL-2
Dusan, John
92BenRocC-28
Duser, Carl
55JetPos-4
Dussault, Normand
43ParSpo-25
Dustal, Bob (Robert Andrew)
63Top-299
Dutch, John
95MicBatCTI-10
Duty, Darrell
89AncGlaP-12
Duva, Brian
94WatIndC-8
94WatIndF-3951
Duval, Mickey (Michael)
79IndIndTI-27
82MadMusF-34
DuVall, Brad
88HamRedP-1722
89Bow-430
89BowTif-430
89SprCarB-4
90St.PetCS-5
90TopTVCa-45
Duvall, Michael
96KanCouCTI-6
Duverge, Salvador
96AshTouB-14
Dwight, James
88AllandGN-26
88GooN16-19
Dwight, Pee Wee (Edward Joseph)
87NegLeaPD-4
Dworak, John
52LavPro-61
Dwyer, Frank (John Francis)
87OldJudN-150
98CamPepP-22
Dwyer, Jim (James Edward)
75OPC-429
75Top-429
76ExpRed-7
76OPC-94
76SSP-341
76Top-94
78CarTeal-4
78Top-644
79Top-236
80Top-576
81Don-577
81Fle-235
81OPC-184
81Top-184
81TopTra-757
82Don-611
82Fle-164
82Top-359
83Don-583
83Fle-59
83OriPos-8
83Top-718
84Don-454
84Fle-7
84FleSti-117
84Nes792-473
84OriTeal-9
84Top-473
84TopTif-473
85Fle-176
85OriHea-6
85Top-56
85TopTif-56
86Don-413
86Fle-274
86OPC-339
86Top-653
86TopTif-653
87Don-418
87Fle-469
87FleGlo-469
87OriFreB-9
87Top-246
87TopTif-246
88Don-459
88Fle-558
88FleGlo-558
88OriFreB-9
88Sco-229
88ScoGlo-229
88StaLinO-3
88Top-521
88TopTif-521
89DonBasB-311
90Don-484
90PubSti-325
90VenSti-155
91LinDriAAA-425
91MetWIZ-100
91OriCro-119
91PacSenL-118
91PorBeaLD-425
91PorBeaP-1582
92KenTwiC-25
92KenTwiF-620
93ForWayWC-26
93ForWayWF-1984
94ForWayWC-26
94ForWayWF-2025
95HarCitRCTI-5
96HarCitRCB-3
Dwyer, Scott
79WatIndT-16
Dybzinski, Jerry (Jerome M.)
78WatIndT-9
79TacTugT-13
81Don-438
81Fle-399
81OPC-198
81Top-198
82Don-647
82Fle-366
82Ind-12
82IndTeal-11
82IndWhe-3
82Top-512
83Don-576
83Fle-406
83IndPos-10
83Top-289
83TopTra-27T
84Don-160
84Fle-57
84Nes792-619
84Top-619
84TopTif-619
84WhiSoxTV-11
85Fle-512
85HawIslC-250
85Top-52
85TopTif-52
86CalCanP-7
Dyce, George
89NasSouTI-27
Dyck, Jim (James Robert)
53BowC-111
53NorBreL-7
53Top-177
54Bow-85
56Top-303
57HygMea-3
57SeaPop-10
91OriCro-120
91TopArc1-177
Dye, Jermaine
94Bow-433
94MacBraC-6
94MacBraF-2217
94SouAtlLAF-SAL43
95Bes-52
95Bow-206
95BowBes-B21
95BowBesR-B21
95BreBtaTI-24
95Exc-149
95SPML-11
95SPMLA-8
95UppDecML-93
96BesAutSA-18
96Bow-132
96BowBes-127
96BowBesAR-127
96BowBesR-127
96Cir-98
96CirRav-98
96ColCho-437
96ColChoGS-437
96ColChoSS-437
96EmoXL-139
96Exc-124
96Fin-G324
96FinRef-G324
96Fla-197
96FlaWavotF-8
96FleUpd-U104
96FleUpdNH-5
96FleUpdTC-U104
96LeaLimR-5
96LeaLimRG-5
96LeaPre-123
96LeaPreP-123
96LeaSig-88
96LeaSigEA-44
96LeaSigEACM-4
96LeaSigPPG-88
96LeaSigPPP-88
96MLBPin-8
96Pin-375
96PinAfi-178
96PinAfiAP-178
96PinFoil-375
96PinProS-15
96RicBraB-10
96RicBraRC-9
96RicBraUB-7
96Sel-188
96SelArtP-188
96SelCer-107
96SelCerAP-107
96SelCerCB-107
96SelCerCR-107
96SelCerMB-107
96SelCerMG-107
96SelCerMR-107
96SigRooOJRS-R1
96SP-19
96Sum-191
96SumAbo&B-191
96SumArtP-191
96SumFoi-191
96Top-439
96Ult-438
96UltGolM-438
96UltGolP-6
96UltGolPHGM-6
96UppDec-249
96Zen-108
96ZenArtP-108
96ZenDiaC-6
96ZenDiaCP-6
97BowBes-89
97BowBesAR-89
97BowBesR-89
97Cir-225
97CirRav-225
97ColCho-28
97Don-111
97DonEli-26
97DonEliGS-26
97DonLim-186
97DonLimLE-186
97DonPre-83
97DonPreCttC-83
97DonPreP-111
97DonPrePGold-111
97Fin-16
97FinRef-16
97FlaSho-A41
97FlaSho-B41
97FlaSho-C41
97FlaShoLC-41
97FlaShoLC-B41
97FlaShoLC-C41
97FlaShoLCM-A41
97FlaShoLCM-B41
97FlaShoLCM-C41
97Fle-254
97Fle-525
97FleRooS-4
97FleTif-254
97FleTif-525
97Lea-211
97LeaFraM-211
97LeaFraMDC-211
97MetUni-27
97MetUniPP-2
97NewPin-144
97NewPinAP-144
97NewPinMC-144
97NewPinPP-144
97Pac-231
97PacLigB-231
97PacPri-77
97PacPriLB-77
97PacPriP-77
97PacSil-231
97Pin-86
97PinArtP-86
97PinCer-15
97PinCerMBlu-15
97PinCerMG-15
97PinCerMR-15
97PinCerR-15
97PinIns-100
97PinInsCE-100
97PinInsDE-100
97PinMusC-86
97PinTotCPB-15
97PinTotCPG-15
97PinTotCPR-15
97PinX-P-63
97PinX-PMoS-63
97Sco-141
97ScoBra-7
97ScoBraPI-7
97ScoBraPr-7
97ScoPreS-141
97ScoShoS-141
97ScoShoSAP-141
97Sel-70
97SelArtP-70
97SelRegG-70
97SelRooR-8
97SelToootT-8
97SelToootTMB-8
97SkyE-X-25
97SkyE-XC-25
97SkyE-XEC-25
97SkyE-XSD2-9
97SpoIll-60
97SpoIllEE-60
97StaClu-351
97StaCluC-CO3
97StaCluMOP-351
97Stu-119
97StuHarH-14
97StuPrePG-119
97StuPrePS-119
97Top-239
97TopAwel-AI3
97TopChr-84
97TopChrR-84
97TopGal-170
97TopGalPPI-170
97Ult-151
97Ult-324
97UltGolME-151
97UltGolME-324
97UltPlaME-151
97UltPlaME-324
97UltRooR-2
97UppDec-12
97UppDecBCP-BC9
95UppDecMLFS-93
97UppDecTTS-TS2
97UppDecU-59
97UppDecUGN-GN9
Dye, Mark
82IdaFalAT-18
Dye, Scott
80WatRedT-8
81TidTidT-15
82JacMetT-4
83TidTidT-14
Dye, Steve
89ModA'sC-9
89ModA'sCLC-269
Dyer, Duffy (Don Robert)
69Top-624
70Top-692
71MLBOffS-150
71OPC-136
71Top-136
72Dia-12
72OPC-127
72Top-127
73LinPor-110
73OPC-493
73Top-493
74MetDaiPA-5
74OPC-536
74Top-536
75OPC-538
75Pir-2
75Top-538
76OPC-88
76SSP-581
76Top-88
77BurCheD-185
77PirPosP-4
77Top-318
78Top-637
79ExpPos-8
79Top-286
80OPC-232
80Top-446
81Don-7A
81Don-7B
81Top-196
83CubThoAV-NNO
86ElPasDP-9
87ElPasDP-14
88BlaYNPRWLU-31
88DenZepC-25
88DenZepP-1264
89BrePol-NNO
89RinPosM1-9
90BreMilB-32
90BrePol-NNO
90El PasDAGTI-20
91BreMilB-32
91BrePol-NNO
91MetWIZ-101
92BrePol-30
94Met69CCPP-13
94Met69CS-12
94Met69T-22
96A'sMot-28
Dyer, Eddie
46SeaSLP-15
46SpoExcW-1-5
49EurSta-181
84OCoandSI-148
92ConTSN-618
Dyer, Hal
87ChaWheP-14
93MedHatBJF-3753
93MedHatBJSP-24
94MedHatBJF-3698
94MedHatBJSP-28
Dyer, John
78GreBraT-8
Dyer, Linton
88AppFoxP-143
89AppFoxP-867
90BasCitRS-7
Dyer, Mike
87KenTwiP-11
88OrlTwiB-9
89PorBeaC-8
89PorBeaP-228
90CMC-558
90Don-642
90Fle-372
90FleCan-372
90OPC-576
90PorBeaC-6
90PorBeaP-173
90ProAAAF-243
90Sco-571
90Top-576
90TopDeb89-33
90TopTif-576
90UppDec-374
93IowCubF-2130
94BufBisF-1829
95PirFil-8
95Top-136
Dyes, Andy
76VenLeaS-193
78SyrChiT-7

79HawIslC-28
79HawIslT-5
80HawIslT-24

Dyess, Todd
96FreKeyB-7

Dygert, Jimmy (James Henry)
08RosComP-59
09AmeCarE-38
09BriE97-11
09T206-116
10LuxCigPP-9
10NadE1-17
10SweCapPP-44
10W555-28
11A'sFirT20-6
11MecDFT-18
11S74Sil-30
11SpoLifCW-115
11SpoLifM-92
11T205-48
11TurRedT-92
12ImpTobC-45

Dyke, Bill
89KnoBluJP-1120

Dykes, Jimmy (James Joseph)
20NatCarE-25A
20NatCarE-25B
21Exh-41
22E120-77
22W572-26
23WilChoV-35
25Exh-106
26Exh-107
27YorCarE-51
29ExhFou-28
29PorandAR-19
31Exh-27
31W517-22
32OrbPinNP-11
32OrbPinUP-16
32R33So2-410
33DelR33-18
33DouDisP-12
33GeoCMil-10
33Gou-6
33GouCanV-6
33RitCE-5H
33TatOrb-16
33TatOrbSDR-167
34BatR31-29
34BatR31-159
34DiaStaR-42
34WarBakSP-2
35AlDemDCR3-17
35ExhFou-10
35GouPuzR-1I
35GouPuzR-2F
35GouPuzR-16F
35GouPuzR-17F
36ExhFou-10
36GouBWR-12
36GouWidPPR-A28
36GouWidPPR-B8
36GouWidPPR-C8
36NatChiFPR-99
36NatChiFPR-107
36R31Pre-G6
36WorWidGV-1
37ExhFou-10
40PlaBal-187
40WhiSoxL-5
47SigOil-6
49PhiBul-16
51Bow-226
52Bow-98
53BowC-31
54OriEss-9
58RedEnq-10
60Top-214
61Kah-10
61Top-222
76ChiGre-5
77GalGloG-120
77GalGloG-201
78TCM60I-224
82GSGalAG-12
87ConSer2-37
88ConSer4-10
91ConTSN-92
91TopArc1-281
93ConTSN-678
93ConTSN-848
94ConTSN-1150
94ConTSNB-1150

Dykhoff, Radhames
96FreKeyB-8

Dykstra, Kevin
90CalLeaACLC-32

Dykstra, Lenny (Len)
83LynMetT-15
84JacMetT-18
85MetTCM-32
85TidTidT-20
86BasStaB-37
86Don-482
86Fle-78
86MetColP-15
86MetTCM-24
86MetWorSC-4
86OPC-53
86Top-53
86TopTif-53
87ClaGam-2
87Don-611
87Fle-6
87FleGlo-6
87FleLimE-13
87Lea-88
87MetColP-3
87MetFanC-3
87OPC-295
87SevCoi-E4
87SevCoi-M5
87Spo-58
87SpoTeaP-2
87Top-295
87TopSti-13
87TopSti-21
87TopSti-98
87TopTif-295
87Woo-23
88Don-364
88DonBasB-264
88DonTeaBM-364
88Fle-133
88FleGlo-133
88Lea-135
88MetColP-3
88MetKah-4
88OPC-299
88PanSti-345
88Sco-370
88ScoGlo-370
88ScoYouS2-19
88Spo-106
88StaLinMe-6
88Top-655
88TopBig-203
88TopMinL-59
88TopTif-655
89ClaLigB-36
89Don-353
89DonBasB-159
89Fle-33
89FleGlo-33
89FleUpd-105
89MetColP-6
89OPC-349
89PanSti-138
89PhiTas-40
89Sco-84
89ScoRoo-28T
89Spo-123
89Top-435
89TopBig-41
89TopDouM-12
89TopSti-90
89TopTif-435
89TopTra-27T
89TopTraT-27T
89UppDec-369
90Bow-152
90BowTif-152
90ClaUpd-T18
90Don-313
90DonBesN-118
90Fle-556
90FleCan-556
90Lea-262
90MLBBasB-5
90OPC-515
90PanSti-313
90PhiTas-8
90PubSti-131
90RedFolSB-28
90Sco-427
90ScoMcD-14
90Spo-156
90SupActM-18
90Top-515
90TopBig-300
90TopMag-32
90TopSti-118
90TopTif-515
90UppDec-472
90USPlaCA-9D
90VenSti-156
91BasBesHM-6
91Bow-501
91Cla1-T78
91ClaGam-133
91Col-8
91Don-7
91Don-410
91Don-434
91Don-523
91Don-744
91DonSupD-7
91Fle-395A
91Fle-395B
91Lea-163
91LeaPre-8
91MajLeaCP-60
91MetWIZ-102
91MooSna-18
91OPC-345
91PanCanT1-4
91PanCanT1-26
91PanFreS-108
91PanFreS-163
91PanSti-103
91PepSup-16
91PhiMed-13
91Pos-8
91PosCan-6
91RedFolS-30
91RedFolS-119
91Sco-250
91Sco-867
91Sco100S-11
91Sev3DCN-4
91SevCoi-NE4
91StaClu-150
91StaPinB-16
91Stu-213
91SunSee-9
91Top-345
91TopCraJI-21
91TopDesS-345
91TopGloA-18
91TopMic-345
91TopSta-12
91TopTif-345
91TopTriH-N8
91Ult-262
91UppDec-97
91UppDec-267
92Bow-635
92Cla1-T30
92Cla2-T51
92ClaGam-152
92Don-57
92DonCraJ2-13
92DonMcD-8
92Fle-529
92FleTeaL-10
92Hig5-77
92Lea-504
92OPC-200
92OPCPre-184
92PanSti-247
92PhiMed-12
92Pin-12
92Sco-560
92Sco100S-86
92ScoImpP-74
92SevCoi-8
92SpoIllFK1-236
92SpoStaCC-13
92StaClu-470
92Stu-75
92Top-200
92TopGol-200
92TopGolW-200
92TopKid-18
92TopMic-200
92TriPla-94
92Ult-241
92UppDec-246
93Bow-300
93CadDis-18
93DiaMar-33
93Don-544
93Fin-177
93FinRef-177
93Fla-99
93Fle-488
93FunPac-144
93HumDumC-44
93Lea-59
93OPC-119
93PacSpa-235
93PanSti-274
93PhiMed-12
93Pin-45
93Pin-477
93Sco-30
93Sel-59
93SP-173
93StaClu-477
93StaCluFDI-477
93StaCluMOP-477
93StaCluP-15
93Stu-101
93Top-740
93TopGol-740
93TopInaM-740
93TopMic-740
93TriPla-185
93Ult-439
93UppDec-69
93UppDec-485
93UppDecGold-69
93UppDecGold-485
94Bow-440
94BowBes-R47
94BowBesR-R47
94CarLeaA-DJ8
94ChuHomS-8
94ChuHomSG-8
94ColC-345
94ColC-369
94ColChoGS-345
94ColChoGS-369
94ColChoSS-345
94ColChoSS-369
94ColChoT-4
94DenHol-8
94Don-373
94DonDom-B9
94DonMVP-10
94DonSpeE-373
94DonSpiotG-10
94ExtBas-332
94ExtBasGB-9
94Fin-237
94FinJum-237
94FinRef-237
94Fla-205
94FlaOutP-4
94Fle-587
94FleLeaL-9
94FleSun-9
94FleTeaL-24
94FUnPac-69
94FUnPac-191
94KinDis-15
94Kra-20
94Lea-97
94LeaGam-2
94LeaGolS-5
94LeaL-136
94OPC-168
94OscMayR-20
94Pac-473
94PacSilP-33
94PanSti-226
94PhiMed-8
94PhiMel-6
94PhiUSPC-1H
94PhiUSPC-2C
94PhiUSPC-5S
94Pin-34
94PinArtP-34
94PinMusC-34
94PinRunC-RC24
94PinTeaP-6
94PinTheN-17
94PinTri-TR6
94Pos-20
94PosCan-16
94PosCanG-16
94ProMag-102
94Sco-60
94Sco-624
94ScoCyc-TC8
94ScoGolR-60
94ScoGolR-624
94ScoGolS-17
94Sel-89
94SelCroC-CC1
94SelSam-CC1
94SelSki-SK3
94SP-135
94SPDieC-135
94Spo-1
94Spo-191
94SpoFanA-AS7
94SpoMov-MM12
94SpoSam-1
94StaClu-165
94StaCluFDI-165
94StaCluGR-165
94StaCluMO-13
94StaCluMOP-165
94StaCluT-211
94StaCluTF-3
94StaCluTFDI-211
94Stu-138
94Top-388
94Top-635
94TopBlaG-29
94TopGol-388
94TopGol-635
94TopSpa-388
94TopSpa-635
94TopSupS-12
94TriPla-173
94TriPlaM-12
94TriPlaP-8
94Ult-544
94UltAllS-17
94UltLeaL-7
94UltOnBL-3
94UppDec-172
94UppDecDC-E3
94UppDecED-172
95Baz-90
95Bow-366
95BowBes-R41
95BowBesR-R41
95ClaPhoC-44
95ColCho-365
95ColChoGS-365
95ColChoSE-170
95ColChoSEGS-170
95ColChoSESS-170
95ColChoSS-365
95D3-56
95Don-209
95DonDiaK-DK18
95DonPreP-209
95DonTopotO-302
95Emb-131
95EmbGolI-131
95Emo-165
95Fin-92
95FinRef-92
95Fla-178
95Fle-390
95FleUpdH-8
95KinDis-7
95Kra-20
95Lea-141
95LeaLim-180
95Pac-328
95PacPri-107
95PanSti-72
95Phi-9
95PhiMel-7
95Pin-246
95PinArtP-246
95PinFan-26
95PinMusC-246
95Pos-15
95RedFol-29
95Sco-22
95ScoGolR-22
95ScoHaloG-HG21
95ScoPlaTS-22
95Sel-92
95SelArtP-92
95SelCer-60
95SelCerMG-60
95SP-87
95SPCha-78
95SPChaDC-78
95Spo-42

95SpoArtP-42
95SPSil-87
95StaClu-317
95StaClu-442
95StaCluCC-CC25
95StaCluMOP-317
95StaCluMOP-442
95StaCluMOP-CC25
95StaCluSTWS-317
95StaCluSTWS-442
95StaCluVR-233
95Stu-44
95StuGolS-44
95Sum-34
95SumNthD-34
95TomPiz-22
95Top-120
95TopCyb-76
95TopTra-162T
95UC3-63
95UC3ArtP-63
95Ult-203
95UltGolM-203
95UppDec-140
95UppDecED-140
95UppDecEDG-140
95UppDecSE-206
95UppDecSEG-206
95Zen-68
96Baz-10
96Bow-61
96BowBes-82
96BowBesAR-82
96BowBesR-82
96ColCho-251
96ColChoGS-251
96ColChoSS-251
96Don-167
96DonPreP-167
96EmoXL-243
96Fin-B50
96FinRef-B50
96Fla-332
96Fle-495
96FleTif-495
96Lea-54
96LeaPre-82
96LeaPreP-82
96LeaPrePB-54
96LeaPrePG-54
96LeaPrePS-54
96LeaPreSG-30
96LeaPreSte-30
96LeaSig-97
96LeaSigPPG-97
96LeaSigPPP-97
96MetUni-209
96MetUniP-209
96Pac-161
96PacPri-P52
96PacPriG-P52
96PanSti-33
96PhiTeal-9
96Pin-232
96PinAfi-53
96PinAfiAP-53
96PinAfiFPP-53
96PinArtP-132
96PinFoil-232
96PinSta-132
96Sco-67
96ScoDugC-A57
96ScoDugCAP-A57
96Sel-144
96SelArtP-144
96SelCer-72
96SelCerAP-72
96SelCerCB-72
96SelCerCR-72
96SelCerMB-72
96SelCerMG-72
96SelCerMR-72
96SelTeaN-10
96SP-141
96Spo-17
96SpoArtP-17
96StaClu-17
96StaCluEPB-17
96StaCluEPG-17
96StaCluEPS-17
96StaCluMM-MM8
96StaCluMOP-17
96StaCluMOP-MM8
95StaCluVRMC-233
96Stu-126
96StuPrePB-126
96StuPrePG-126
96StuPrePS-126
96Sum-92
96SumAbo&B-92
96SumArtP-92
96SumFoi-92
96Top-261
96TopChr-104
96TopChrR-104
96TopGal-30
96TopGalPPI-30
96TopLas-104
96Ult-519
96UltGolM-519
96UppDec-430
96Zen-43
96ZenArtP-43
97ColCho-196
97Fle-409
97FleTif-409
97Pac-376
97PacLigB-376
97PacPri-128
97PacPriLB-128
97PacPriP-128
97PacSil-376
97Pin-66
97PinArtP-66
97PinMusC-66
97Sco-435
97ScoHobR-435
97ScoResC-435
97ScoShoS-435
97ScoShoSAP-435
97Top-413
97UppDec-453
Dyson, Ted (Theodore Timothy)
88PalSprACLC-103
88PalSprAP-1453
Dzafic, Bernie
88ElmPioC-5
89LynRedSS-27
89WinHavRSS-5
92WinHavRSF-1769
93NewBriRSF-1212
94LynRedSC-8
94LynRedSF-1886
Dziadkowiec, Andy
87MyrBeaBJP-1461
89DunBluJS-4
90CMC-351
90KnoBluJB-17
90KnoBluJS-3
90ProAAAF-353
90SyrChiC-25
90SyrChiP-573
91MiaMirC-17
91MiaMirP-411
92BinMetF-519
92BinMetS-56
93BinMetF-2336
Eaddy, Brad
94GreFalDSP-22
95BakBlaTI-17
Eaddy, Don
77FriOneYW-54
Eaddy, Keith
92BluOriC-13
92BluOriF-2370
93AlbPolC-13
93AlbPolF-2037
94FreKeyF-2627
94OriPro-28
Eagan, Truck (Charles)
09ColChiE-88
12ColTinT-88
Eagar, Brad
87AncGlaP-8
87BriYouC-18
89MedAthB-7
Eagar, Steve
86LakTigP-5
Eagelston, Chris
86HagSunP-6
Eagen, Charles
12ColRedB-88
Eagle, War (Johnny)
72Dia-118
Eagles, Brooklyn
93NegLeaRL2-81
Eagles, Carson Newman
89CarNewE-NNO
Eagles, Newark
91PomBlaBPB-4
92NegLeaRLI-97
93NegLeaRL2-82
Eaglin, Mike
93IdaFalBF-4039
93IdaFalBSP-7
94MacBraC-7
94MacBraF-2213
95MacBraTI-7
96CarLeaA1B-13
96CarLeaA2B-13
96DurBulBIB-29
96DurBulBrB-29
Eakes, Steven
82RedPioT-2
83RedPioT-9
Eakle, Jim
77PadSchC-20
Ealy, Tom (Thomas)
85EveGiaC-4
86CliGiaP-6
86TriTriC-200
87CliGiaP-12
88CliGiaP-718
89SanJosGB-14
89SanJosGCLC-231
89SanJosGP-434
89SanJosGS-8
90ShrCapP-1454
90ShrCapS-7
91LinDriAA-304
91ShrCapLD-304
91ShrCapP-1834
92LakTigC-23
92LakTigF-2290
Ealy, Tracey
90JohCitCS-10
91SavCarC-24
91SavCarP-1665
92EugEmeC-11
92EugEmeF-3042
93CliGiaC-9
93CliGiaF-2500
94SanJosGC-7
94SanJosGF-2828
Eaman, Bob
89LonTigP-1359
Earl, Scottie
83BirBarT-17
84EvaTriT-14
85Don-491
85NasSouTI-6
86NasSouTI-7
87TolMudHP-1
87TolMudHT-10
88NasSouC-19
88NasSouP-471
88NasSouTI-9
90BirBarDGB-8
Earle, Billy (William)
87OldJudN-151
90DodTar-209
Earley, Arnie (Arnold Carl)
67Top-388
78TCM60I-209
Earley, Bill
83IowCubT-2
84IowCubT-2
85OklCit8T-30
86LouRedTI-12
87LouRedTI-13
88WytCubP-1989
89ChaWheB-24
89ChaWheP-1754
90WinSpiTI-28
91WinSpiC-21
91WinSpiP-2846
92ChaKniF-2787
92ChaKniS-175
93IowCubF-2149
94IowCubF-1291
95IowCubTI-11
96IowCubB-4
Early, Jake (Jacob Willard)
46SpoExcW-2-9
49Bow-106
49Lea-61
93ConTSN-749
Earnshaw, George (George L.)
30SchR33-13
31W517-8
32OrbPinNP-38
32OrbPinUP-17
32USCar-29
33ButCre-6
33DouDisP-13
33RitCE-3H
33TatOrb-17
33TatOrbSDR-169
34ButPreR-18
34ExhFou-10
34Gou-41
34GouCanV-93
35DiaMatCS3T1-49
35GouPuzR-11
35GouPuzR-2F
35GouPuzR-16F
35GouPuzR-17F
36NatChiFPR-85
36R31PasP-28
40PlaBal-233
90DodTar-210
91ConTSN-88
94ConTSN-1137
94ConTSNB-1137
95ConTSN-1338
Easler, Mike (Michael A.)
75IowOakT-7
76TulOilGP-6
77ColCliT-4
78ColCliT-5
78Top-710
80Top-194
80VenLeaS-259
81AllGamPI-143
81CokTeaS-111
81Don-256
81Fle-372
81OPC-92
81Top-92
81TopScr-81
81TopSti-212
82Don-221
82Fle-481
82FleSta-74
82Kel-49
82OPC-235
82Top-235
82TopSti-84
83AllGamPI-144
83Don-221
83Fle-306
83FleSta-57
83FleSti-80
83OPC-385
83Top-385
84Don-444
84Fle-249
84FleUpd-33
84Nes792-589
84OPC-353
84Top-589
84TopSti-137
84TopTif-589
84TopTra-33T
84TopTraT-33T
85AllGamPI-55
85Don-213
85Fle-157
85FleStaS-46
85Lea-206
85OPC-349
85Top-686
85TopSti-213
85TopTif-686
86Don-395
86Fle-347
86FleUpd-37
86Top-477
86TopSti-255
86TopTat-21
86TopTif-477
86TopTra-33T
86TopTraT-33T
86YanTCM-45
87AstShowSTh-7
87Don-277
87DonOpeD-155
87Fle-97
87FleAll-7
87FleGlo-97
87Lea-192
87OPC-135
87PhiTas-34
87Spo-92
87Top-135
87TopSti-295
87TopTif-135
88Fle-206
88FleGlo-206
88OPC-9
88Sco-220
88ScoGlo-220
88StaLinY-4
88Top-741
88TopTif-741
89TopSenL-80
90EliSenL-19
90MiaMirIS-28
90MiaMirIS-26
92BrePol-30
92YanWIZ8-50
Easley, Damion
89BenBucL-16
90MidLeaASGS-31
90QuaCitAGS-24
91Cla/Bes-121
91LinDriAA-433
91MidAngLD-433
91MidAngOHP-10
91MidAngP-440
92Bow-672
92EdmTraF-3544
92EdmTraS-154
92FleUpd-9
92SkyAAAF-76
93AngAdoFD-2
93AngMot-26
93AngPol-13
93Bow-257
93Don-457
93Fla-173
93Fle-189
93Lea-286
93OPC-104
93PacSpa-367
93PanSti-7
93Pin-227
93Sco-222
93Sel-328
93SP-22
93StaClu-6
93StaCluAn-21
93StaCluFDI-6
93StaCluMOP-6
93Stu-142
93Top-184
93TopGol-184
93TopInaM-184
93TopMic-184
93Toy-43
93TriPla-103
93Ult-161
93UppDec-377
93UppDecGold-377
94AngLAT-18
94Bow-563
94ColC-505
94ColChoGS-505
94ColChoSS-505
94Don-112
94ExtBas-33
94Fin-332
94FinRef-332
94Fla-269
94Fle-53
94Lea-86
94OPC-9
94Pac-76
94PanSti-37
94Pin-340
94PinArtP-340
94PinMusC-340
94Sco-17
94ScoGolR-17
94Sel-222
94StaClu-124
94StaCluFDI-124
94StaCluGR-124
94StaCluMOP-124
94Stu-11
94Top-418
94TopGol-418
94TopSpa-418
94TriPla-14
94Ult-326
94UppDec-66

94UppDecED-66
95AngCHP-5
95AngMot-20
95ColCho-96
95ColChoGS-96
95ColChoSS-96
95Don-7
95DonPreP-7
95DonTopotO-34
95Fle-222
95Lea-4
95Pac-57
95PacLatD-10
95Sco-447
95ScoGolR-447
95ScoPlaTS-447
95StaClu-325
95StaCluMOP-325
95StaCluSTWS-325
95Top-306
95Ult-20
95UltGolM-20
96Don-403
96DonPreP-403
96Fle-45
96FleTif-45
96Pac-272
96PacPri-P84
96PacPriG-P84
97ColCho-339
97Fle-672
97FleTif-672
97Sco-439
97ScoHobR-439
97ScoResC-439
97ScoShoS-439
97ScoShoSAP-439
97Ult-330
97UltGolME-330
97UltPlaME-330

Easley, Logan
83GreHorT-5
85AlbYanT-5
86AlbYanT-17
86AlbYanT-32
88BufBisC-1
88BufBisP-1490
90AlbDecGB-5
90DenZepP-619
90ProAAAF-644

Easley, Mike
90RenSilSCLC-266
91CarLeaAP-CAR12
91KinIndC-15
91KinIndP-327
92ShrCapF-3881
92ShrCapS-583

Eason, Greg
80AshTouT-26

Eason, Mal
90DodTar-939
92ConTSN-375

Eason, Samuel
95ReaPhiTI-13

Eason, Tommy
91BatCliC-3
91BatCliP-3485
92ClaFS7-263
92SpaPhiF-1265
93ClaGolF-135
93ExcFS7-84
94ClePhiC-13
94ClePhiF-2535
95ReaPhiELC-11
96Exc-199

East, William G.
88AllandGN-46

Easter, Dick
84IowCubT-4

Easter, Luke (Luscious Luke)
47Exh-66
47PM1StaP1-54
50IndNumN-8
50IndTeal-7
51Bow-258
51TopRedB-26
52Bow-95
52IndNumN-12
52Top-24
53BowC-104
53ExhCan-2
53IndPenCBP-10
53Top-2
54Bow-116
54DanDee-5
54Top-23
63RocRedWSP-6
79TCM50-80
83TopRep5-24
86NegLeaF-83
88LitSunMLL-5
91TopArc1-2
92BazQua5A-6
94TopArc1-23
94TopArc1G-23

Easterly, Jamie (James M.)
75OPC-618
75Top-618
76OPC-511
76Top-511
76VenLeaS-179
78Top-264
79RicBraT-11
79Top-684
82BrePol-28
82Don-623
82Fle-139
82Top-122
83BrePol-28
83Don-280
83Fle-31
83Top-528
83TopTra-28T
84Fle-538
84Ind-11
84IndWhe-36
84Nes792-367
84Top-367
84TopSti-258
84TopTif-367
85Fle-445
85Ind-12
85IndPol-36
85Top-764
85TopTif-764
86Don-582
86Fle-585
86IndOhH-36
86IndTeal-18
86Top-31
86TopTif-31
87IndGat-11
89PacSenL-189
89T/MSenL-31
90EliSenL-54
94BreMilB-17

Easterly, Ted (Theodore H.)
09T206-117
12T207-53
14CraJacE-117
15CraJacE-117

Easterwood, Roy
44CubTeal-6

Eastman, Doug
88CedRapRP-1153
89CedRapRB-20
89CedRapRP-923
89CedRapRS-5

Eastwick, Rawly (Rawlins J.)
75OPC-621
75Top-621
76OPC-469
76RedIceL-3
76RedKro-7
76RedPos-7
77Car5-7
77OPC-8
77OPC-140
77PepGloD-55
78Top-405
78YanBurK-11
79Top-271
80Top-692
82Fle-596
92YanWIZ7-47

Eatinger, Michael
76Top-469
77Top-8
77Top-45
82Top-117
90Bes-222
90MidLeaASGS-10
90SouBenWSB-18
90SouBenWSGS-3
92SarWhiSCB-9
92SarWhiSF-213

Eaton, Adam
97Bow-363
97BowChr-243
97BowChrI-243
97BowChrIR-243
97BowChrR-243
97BowInt-363
97Top-479

Eaton, Craig
76WatRoyT-7
77DayBealT-4
80SalLakCGT-3
80VenLeaS-125
81SalLakCGT-4
82SpoIndT-2
83EvaTriT-2
84IndIndTI-8

Eaton, Dann
91SprCarC-14
91SprCarP-736

Eaton, Mark
93StaCluMO-30

Eaton, Tommy
00ChaO'sP-6
80ChaO'sW-6
81RocRedWT-5
81RocRedWW-19

Eave, Gary
87DurBulP-19
88RicBraC-5
88RicBraP-26
89RicBraBC-5
89RicBraC-2
89RicBraP-828
89RicBraTI-6
90Bow-471
90BowTif-471
90Don-713
90Sco-621
91JacSunLD-333
91JacSunP-143
91LinDriAA-333
97BobCamRB-18

Eaves, Dan
97FreKeyC-28

Ebanks, Weddison
90EugEmeGS-6

Ebbert, Chad
96CliLumKTI-11
96IdaFalB-7

Ebbetts, Charlie
90DodTar-940

Ebel, Brian
89HagSunB-16
89HagSunP-284

Ebel, Dino
89VerBeaDS-8
90VerBeaDS-12
91AdeGiaF-7
91BakDodCLC-19
91SanAntMP-2981
92BakDodCLC-31
93BakDodCLC-30
94BakDodC-29
95SanBerSTI-29
96SanAntMB-28

Eberle, Greg
89PeoChiTI-27

Eberle, Mike
87NewOriP-24
88CarLeaAS-7
88HagSunS-4
89HagSunB-12
89HagSunP-270
89HagSunS-6
90Bes-199
90HagSunB-4
90HagSunP-1415
90HagSunS-8
91LinDriAAA-455
91RocRedWLD-455
91RocRedWP-1905

Eberly, Ryan
90TamYanD-4

Ebersberger, Randy
82CliGiaF-24

Ebert, Derrin
95MacBraTI-8
95MacBraUTI-2
96BesAutS-30
96DurBulBIB-6
96DurBulBrB-7
96Exc-125

Ebert, Scott
88PocGiaP-2080
89EveGiaS-7
90CliGiaUTI-U3
90EveGiaP-3118

Ebright, Chris
88CapCodPPaLP-33
88OklSoo-3
89GenCubP-1876
89OklSoo-14
90PeoChiTI-16
91CarLeaAP-CAR41
91WinSpiC-23
91WinSpiP-3840
92ChaKniF-2778
92ChaKniS-154
92SkyAA F-71
93OrlCubF-2790

Ebright, Hi (Hiram C.)
87OldJudN-152

Eby, Michael
96FayGenB-13

Eccles, John
85AncGlaPTI-9
87OrlTwiP-4
88CalLeaACLC-38
88VisOakCLC-150
88VisOakP-84
89OrlTwiP-1351
90OrlSunRB-2
90OrlSunRP-1086
90OrlSunRS-4

Eccleston, Tom
86WauTimP-9
87SalSpuP-14

Echemendia, Bert (Idaiberto)
88JamExpP-1906
89Sta-33
89WesPalBES-10

Echenique, O.
80VenLeaS-194

Echevarria, Angel
92BenRocC-10
92BenRocF-1485
93CenValRC-8
93CenValRF-2904
94Bow-610
94CenValRC-5
94CenValRF-3214
95NewHavRTI-29
96ColSprSSTI-12
96Exc-152
96Top-439
97DonLim-59
97DonLimLE-59
97Lea-169
97LeaFraM-169
97LeaFraMDC-169
97StaClu-194
97StaCluMOP-194

Echevarria, Francisco
84EveGiaC-17

Echevarria, Robert
87ElmPio(C-7

Echeverria, Phil
90AriWilP-3
92AriWilP-3

Echols, Mandell
95HudValRTI-8

Echols, Tony
76WauMetT-12

Echols, Tracy
89MisStaB-10
90MisStaB-9

Eckard, Paul
91EveGiaC-29

Eckersley, Dennis (Dennis Lee)
76Hos-137
76Kel-19
76OPC-98
76OPC-202
76SSP-506
76Top-98
76Top-202
77BurCheD-58
77Hos-106
77MSADis-17
77OPC-15
77PepGloD-13
77Spo-5007
77Spo-8415
77Top-525
78Hos-78
78OPC-138
78PapGinD-5
78SSP270-178
78Top-122
78WifBalD-20
79Hos-145
79Kel-9
79OPC-16
79RedSoxTI-2
79Top-40
80OPC-169
80Top-320
81AllGamPI-77
81CokTeaS-2
81Don-96
81Fle-226
81FleStiC-34
81OPC-109
81Top-620
81TopSti-48
81TopSupHT-2
82Don-30
82Fle-292
82FleSta-165
82OPC-287
82PerAll-1
82PerAllG-1
82RedSoxC-5
82Top-490
83AllGamPI-76
83Don-487
83Fle-182
83Fle-629
83FleSta-58
83FleSti-63
83OPC-270
83Top-270
83TopSti-34
84CubChiT-11
84CubSev-43
84Don-639
84Fle-396
84FleUpd-34
84Nes792-745
84OPC-218
84Top-745
84TopSti-224
84TopTif-745
84TopTra-34T
84TopTraT-34T
85AllGamPI-168
85CubLioP-10
85CubSev-43
85Don-442
85Fle-57
85OPC-163
85Top-163
85TopTif-163
86BasStaB-38
86CubGat-43
86CubUno-8
86Don-239
86Fle-368
86Lea-113
86OPC-199
86Spo-129
86Top-538
86TopSti-62
86TopTat-2
86TopTif-538
87Don-365
87Fle-563
87FleGlo-563
87FleUpd-30
87FleUpdG-30
87OPC-381
87SevCoi-C8
87SpoTeaP-22
87Top-459
87TopSti-63
87TopTif-459
87TopTra-31T
87TopTraT-31T
88A'sMot-10
88Don-349
88DonBasB-43
88DonTeaBA-349
88Fle-279
88FleGlo-279
88FleSlu-13
88OPC-72
88Sco-104

88ScoGlo-104
88StaLinAs-4
88Top-72
88TopSti-170
88TopTif-72
89A'sMot-10
89Bow-190
89BowTif-190
89CadEllD-16
89ClaLigB-90
89Don-67
89DonAll-16
89DonBasB-134
89Fle-7
89FleAll-4
89FleBasA-12
89FleGlo-7
89FleHeroB-13
89OPC-370
89PanSti-12
89PanSti-414
89RedFolSB-39
89Sco-276
89ScoHot1S-16
89Spo-101
89Spo-222
89SpoIllFKI-197
89Top-370
89TopBasT-128
89TopDouA-11
89TopGaloC-4
89TopGloS-16
89TopHilTM-12
89TopMinL-69
89TopSti-167
89TopStiB-31
89TopTif-370
89TopUKM-23
89TVSpoM-96
89UppDec-289
89UppDec-664
89Woo-20
90A'sMot-7
90Bow-451
90BowTif-451
90Don-210
90DonBesA-12
90Fle-6
90FleCan-6
90FleLeaL-11
90K-M-29
90KayB-9
90Lea-29
90LeaPre-3
90MLBBasB-75
90OPC-670
90PanSti-137
90PubSti-282
90PubSti-303
90RedFolSB-29
90Sco-315
90Spo-170
90Top-670
90TopBig-50
90TopDou-19
90TopGloS-53
90TopHeaU-4
90TopMinL-27
90TopSti-182
90TopStiB-64
90TopTif-670
90TopTVA-13
90UppDec-513
90USPlaCA-8C
90VenSti-157
90VenSti-158
91A'sMot-7
91A'sSFE-3
91BasBesAotM-6
91Bow-237
91Cla2-T18
91ClaGam-126
91Don-270
91Fle-6
91Lea-285
91OPC-250
91OPCPre-38
91PanCanT1-86
91PanFreS-200
91PanSti-148
91RedFolS-31
91Sco-485
91Sco100S-73
91SevCoi-NC5
91StaClu-332
91Stu-102
91Top-250
91TopDesS-250
91TopMic-250
91TopTif-250
91Ult-245
91UppDec-172
91USPlaCA-10D
92AthMot-7
92Bow-431
92ClaGam-8
92ColAllG-17
92ColAllP-17
92Don-147
92DonCraJ1-1
92DonPre-5
92Fle-255
92Hig5-103
92Hig5S-9
92Lea-100
92OPC-738
92OPCPre-188
92PanSti-22
92PepDieM-7
92Pin-25
92PinTeaP-11
92Sco-190
92Sco100S-56
92SpoIllFK1-152
92StaClu-190
92StaCluD-42
92StaCluMO-13
92Stu-223
92Top-738
92TopGol-738
92TopGolW-738
92TopKid-119
92TopMic-738
92TriPla-195
92Ult-421
92UppDec-331
92UppDecTMH-19
93AthMot-4
93Bow-485
93ClaGam-27
93DiaMar-34
93DiaMarP-3
93Don-215
93Don-396
93DonEli-25
93DonEliS-7
93DonPre-19
93DonSpiotG-SG4
93DurPowP2-23
93Fin-100
93FinJum-100
93FinRef-100
93Fla-257
93Fle-293
93Fle-717
93FleAtl-7
93FleFruotL-18
93FleGolM-B1
93FlePro-A2
93FunPac-49
93Hos-11
93Kra-6
93Lea-72
93LeaGolA-R10
93MetBak-25
93MSABenSPD-1
93OPC-106
93OPCPreSP-22
93OPCPreSPF-22
93PacSpa-221
93PanSti-13
93PanSti-157
93PanSti-161
93PanSti-162
93Pin-100
93Pin-474
93PinCoo-6
93PinCooD-6
93Sco-21
93Sco-481
93Sco-483
93Sco-509
93Sco-513
93Sco-540
93ScoFra-11
93ScoGolDT-9
93Sel-38
93SelChaS-24
93SelDufIP-4
93SelStaL-67
93SP-38
93StaClu-291
93StaClu-461
93StaCluAt-1
93StaCluFDI-291
93StaCluFDI-461
93StaCluM-179
93StaCluMOP-291
93StaCluMOP-461
93Stu-1
93Top-155
93Top-411
93TOPBLAG-29
93TopComotH-1
93TopGol-155
93TopGol-411
93TopInaM-155
93TopInaM-411
93TopMagJRC-1
93TopMic-155
93TopMic-411
93TopMic-P155
93TriPla-9
93TriPlaLL-L1
93TriPlaLL-L2
93TriPlaP-9
93Ult-257
93UltAwaW-23
93UltEck-1
93UltEck-2
93UltEck-3
93UltEck-4
93UltEck-5
93UltEck-6
93UltEck-7
93UltEck-8
93UltEck-9
93UltEck-10
93UltEck-11
93UltEck-12
93UltEck-P1
93UltEck-AU0
93UppDec-271
93UppDec-487
93UppDec-489
93UppDec-814
93UppDecCP-R8
93UppDecGold-271
93UppDecGold-487
93UppDecGold-489
93UppDecGold-814
93UppDecOD-D10
93UppDecTAN-TN10
94A'sMot-4
94Bow-520
94ColC-495
94ColChoGS-495
94ColChoSS-495
94Don-16
94DonSpeE-16
94ExtBas-148
94Fin-206
94FinJum-206
94FinRef-206
94Fla-91
94Fle-260
94FUnPac-43
94KinDis-8
94Kra-2
94Lea-234
94LeaL-59
94OPC-144
94Pac-448
94PanSti-108
94Pin-32
94PinArtP-32
94PinMusC-32
94ProMag-96
94RedFolMI-18
94Sco-109
94ScoGolR-109
94Sel-245
94Spo-50
94StaClu-125
94StaCluFDI-125
94StaCluGR-125
94StaCluMOP-125
94StaCluP-125
94Stu-1
94Top-465
94TopGol-465
94TopSpa-465
94TriPla-2
94Ult-407
94UltFir-5
94UppDec-365
94UppDecED-365
95AthMot-4
95Baz-21
95Bow-426
95BowBes-R58
95BowBesR-R58
95ColCho-134
95ColChoGS-134
95ColChoSE-44
95ColChoSEGS-44
95ColChoSESS-44
95ColChoSS-134
95D3-11
95Don-511
95DonPreP-511
95DonTopotO-135
95Emo-70
95Fin-155
95FinRef-155
95Fla-293
95Fle-244
95FleTeaL-11
95FleUpdDT-5
95Lea-352
95LeaLim-109
95Pac-311
95Pin-251
95PinArtP-251
95PinMusC-251
95RedFol-28
95Sco-408
95ScoGolR-408
95ScoHaloG-HG87
95ScoPlaTS-408
95Sel-140
95SelArtP-140
95SP-187
95SPCha-104
95SPCha-182
95SPChaDC-104
95SPChaDC-182
95Spo-116
95SpoArtP-116
95SPSil-187
95StaClu-72
95StaCluFDI-72
95StaCluMOP-72
95StaCluMOP-RL16
95StaCluRL-RL16
95StaCluSTWS-72
95StaCluVR-45
95Stu-129
95Sum-99
95SumNthD-99
95Top-45
95TopCyb-34
95UC3-52
95UC3ArtP-52
95Ult-316
95UltGolM-316
95UppDec-34
95UppDecED-34
95UppDecEDG-34
95UppDecSE-243
95UppDecSEG-243
95UppDecSoaD-SD9
95Zen-27
96Baz-42
96Bow-64
96CarPol-5
96ColCho-245
96ColChoGS-245
96ColChoSS-245
96Don-406
96DonPreP-406
96EmoXL-264
96Fin-G198
96Fin-S54
96FinRef-G198
96FinRef-S54
96Fla-357
96Fle-206
96FleTif-206
96FleUpd-U187
96FleUpdTC-U187
96Lea-2
96LeaPrePB-2
96LeaPrePG-2
96LeaPrePS-2
96LeaPreSG-56
96LeaPreSte-56
96LeaSig-144
96LeaSigPPG-144
96LeaSigPPP-144
96MetUni-99
96MetUniP-99
96MLBPin-9
96Pac-393
96PanSti-215
96Pin-210
96PinAfi-55
96PinAfiAP-55
96PinAfiFPP-55
96PinArtP-110
96PinFoil-210
96PinSta-110
96Sco-324
96ScoDugC-B49
96ScoDugCAP-B49
96Sel-111
96SelArtP-111
96SP-153
96StaClu-130
96StaClu-261
96StaCluEPB-130
96StaCluEPG-130
96StaCluEPS-130
96StaCluMet-M5
96StaCluMOP-130
96StaCluMOP-261
96StaCluMOP-M5
95StaCluVRMC-45
96Stu-32
96StuPrePB-32
96StuPrePG-32
96StuPrePS-32
96Top-368
96TopChr-150
96TopChrMotG-1
96TopChrMotGR-1
96TopChrR-150
96TopGal-176
96TopGalPPI-176
96TopLas-54
96TopMasotG-1
96Ult-112
96Ult-545
96UltGolM-112
96UltGolM-545
96UppDec-101
96UppDec-375
96UppDec-416
96UppDec-442
97Bow-46
97BowBes-60
97BowBesAR-60
97BowBesR-60
97BowChr-37
97BowChrI-37
97BowChrIR-37
97BowChrR-37
97BowInt-46
97Cir-240
97CirRav-240
97ColCho-201
97Don-214
97DonLim-86
97DonLimLE-86
97DonPreP-214
97DonPrePGold-214
97DonTea-158
97DonTeaSPE-158
97Fin-163
97FinEmb-163
97FinEmbR-163
97FinRef-163
97FlaSho-A167
97FlaSho-B167
97FlaSho-C167
97FlaShoLC-167
97FlaShoLC-B167
97FlaShoLC-C167
97FlaShoLCM-A167
97FlaShoLCM-B167
97FlaShoLCM-C167
97Fle-441
97FleTif-441
97Lea-288
97LeaFraM-288
97LeaFraMDC-288
97MetUni-229
97Pac-407
97PacCar-33
97PacCarM-33

97PacLigB-407
97PacPri-137
97PacPriLB-137
97PacPriP-137
97PacSil-407
97Sco-98
97ScoPreS-98
97ScoShoS-98
97ScoShoSAP-98
97SkyE-X-97
97SkyE-XC-97
97SkyE-XEC-97
97SkyE-XHoN-17
97SP-151
97StaClu-239
97StaCluMat-239
97StaCluMOP-239
97Stu-74
97StuPrePG-74
97StuPrePS-74
97Top-388
97TopChr-134
97TopChrR-134
97TopGal-43
97TopGalPPI-43
97TopSta-34
97TopStaAM-34
97Ult-269
97UltGolME-269
97UltPlaME-269
97UppDec-159

Eckfords, Brooklyn
94OriofB-9

Eckhardt, Ox
90DodTar-211

Eckhardt, Tom
89IdaFalBP-2030

Eckstrom, Wayne
85RedWinA-3

Economy, Scott
88BilMusP-1814
89CedRapRB-9
89CedRapRP-921
89CedRapRS-6
90CedRapRP-2317

Eddie, Steve
93BilMusF-3952
93BilMusSP-7
94ChaWheC-8
94ChaWheF-2710

Eddings, Jay
87WytCubP-19
88ChaWheB-12
89ChaWheB-21
89ChaWheP-1766
89PeoChiTI-6
90PeoChiTI-21

Eddings, Jeff
94GreFalDSP-23

Eddins, Glenn
79ElmPioRST-6
81BriRedST-18

Eddolls, Frank
43ParSpo-26

Eddy, Chris
92ClaDraP-57
92EugEmeC-12
92EugEmeF-3022
92FroRowDP-56
93Bow-477
93ClaFS7-109
93StaCluM-82
93StaCluRoy-27
93WilBluRC-9
93WilBluRF-1991
94ExcFS7-67
94MemChiF-351
94UppDecML-58
95OmaRoyTI-8
96WicWraB-23

Eddy, Don (Donald Eugene)
72OPC-413
72Top-413

Eddy, Jim
90RocExpLC-7
90RocExpP-2691
91WesPalBEC-5
91WesPalBEP-1221

Eddy, Martin
88BurIndP-1775

Eddy, Steve (Steven Allen)
76QuaCitAT-12
80SalLakCGT-17

Edelen, Joe (Benny Joe)
77St.PetCT-24
78ArkTraT-9
80ArkTraT-1
82Fle-65
83IndIndTI-8

Eden, Bill
94BenRocF-3585
95AshTouUTI-16
96NewHavRB-9
97BenRocC-5

Eden, Mike (Edward Michael)
75PhoGiaC-11
75PhoGiaCK-16
76PheGiaCr-19
76PhoGiaCa-14
76PhoGiaCC-8
78SSP270-136
79RocRedWT-9
80RocRedWT-12

Edenfield, Ken
90BoiHawP-3308
91Cla/Bes-260
91QuaCitAC-3
91QuaCitAP-2620
92MidAngF-4020
92MidAngOHP-5
92PalSprAC-13
93MidAngF-315
94VanCanF-1857
96LeaSigEA-45
97MidAngOHP-8

Edens, Larry
94WilCubC-6
94WilCubF-3776

Edens, Tom
83ButCopKT-4
86JacMetT-4
87TidTidP-9
87TidTidT-2
88TidTidCa-19
88TidTidCM-5
88TidTidP-1581
89TidTidC-2
89TidTidP-1956
90BreMilB-6
90CMC-29
90DenZepC-4
90DenZepP-620
90ProAAAF-645
91Don-590
91Fle-582
91LinDriAAA-407
91MetWIZ-103
91OPC-118
91PorBeaLD-407
91PorBeaP-1561
91Sco-78
91Sco100RS-2
91Top-118
91TopDesS-118
91TopMic-118
91TopTif-118
91TriA AAGP-AAA35
91UppDec-616
92FleUpd-39
92Sco-720
92StaClu-662
92StaCluNC-662
93AstMot-27
93Don-729
93Fle-434
93FleFinE-78
93Sco-450
94AstMot-12
94BreMilB-18
94BreMilB-310
94Don-456
94Fla-169
94FleUpd-141
94Pac-264
94Top-427
94TopGol-427
94TopSpa-427
96RocRedWB-13

Edgar, Dwaine
94OneYanC-8
94OneYanF-3785

Edge, Alvin
76BurBeeT-6
78BurBeeT-11

Edge, Butch (Claude Lee) Jr.
75BurBeeT-5
76BurBeeT-7
78SyrChiT-8
79SyrChiT-9
79SyrChiTI-19
80OPC-329
80RicBraT-3
80Top-674
81RicBraT-11
82PorBeaT-2

Edge, Greg
86ClePhiP-7
87ReaPhiP-4
88EasLeaAP-32
88ReaPhiP-880
89ElPasDGS-21
89ReaPhiB-16
89ReaPhiP-666
90ElPasDGS-9
91CarMudLD-106
91CarMudP-1092
91LinDriAA-106
92CarMudS-132

Edge, Tim
90WelPirP-16
91SalBucC-1
91SalBucP-955
92SalBucC-19
92SalBucF-66
93CarMudF-2057
93CarMudTI-1
94CarMudF-1582
95CarMudF-159
96CarMudB-13

Edgerton, Bill
83Pil69G-3

Ediger, Lance
78NewWayCT-13

Edison, Thomas Alva
75McCCob-12

Edler, Dave (David Delmar)
80SpoIndT-15
81Fle-610
81MarPol-7
82OmaRoyT-16
82Top-711
83Top-622

Edmendsen, Chris
92LetMouSP-7

Edmonds, Bobby Joe
89ReaPhiB-17
89ReaPhiP-673
89ReaPhiS-10

Edmonds, Jim
88BenBucL-10
89QuaCitAB-27
89QuaCitAGS-6
90CalLeaACLC-6
91PalSprAP-2028
92ClaFS7-343
92MidAngF-4037
92MidAngOHP-6
92MidAngS-458
92SkyAA F-194
93ExcFS7-141
93FlaWavotF-4
93FleFinE-181
93Top-799
93TopGol-799
93TopInaM-799
93TopMic-799
93Ult-519
93VanCanF-2609
94AngLAT-5
94AngMot-16
94Bow-423
94ColC-517
94ColChoGS-517
94ColChoSS-517
94ExtBas-34
94Fla-21
94Fle-54
94LeaLimR-49
94Pin-394
94PinArtP-394
94PinMusC-394
94ScoRoo-RT160
94ScoRooGR-RT160
94ScoRooSR-SU18
94Sel-198
94SpoRoo-104
94SpoRooAP-104
94StaClu-603
94StaCluFDI-603
94StaCluGR-603
94StaCluMOP-603
94Top-404
94TopGol-404
94TopSpa-404
94Ult-327
95AngCHP-9
95AngMot-8
95ColCho-98
95ColChoGS-98
95ColChoSS-98
95D3-29
95Don-223
95DonPreP-223
95DonTopotO-35
95Fin-17
95FinRef-17
95Fla-235
95Fle-223
95Lea-26
95LeaLim-178
95Pac-58
95PacPri-18
95Pin-65
95PinArtP-65
95PinMusC-65
95Sco-253
95ScoGolR-253
95ScoHaloG-HG52
95ScoPlaTS-253
95Sel-40
95SelArtP-40
95SelCer-51
95SelCerMG-51
95SPCha-131
95SPChaDC-131
95StaClu-40
95StaCluFDI-40
95StaCluMOP-40
95StaCluSTWS-40
95StaCluVR-29
95Top-183
95TopCyb-104
95Ult-21
95UltGolM-21
95UppDec-268
95UppDecED-268
95UppDecEDG-268
95Zen-73
96AngMot-6
96Baz-83
96Bow-99
96BowBes-22
96BowBesAR-22
96BowBesR-22
96Cir-18
96CirRav-18
96ColCho-71
96ColChoCtG-CG7
96ColChoCtG-CG7B
96ColChoCtG-CG7C
96ColChoCtGE-CR7
96ColChoCtGG-CG7
96ColChoCtGG-CG7B
96ColChoCtGG-CG7C
96ColChoCtGGE-CR7
96ColChoGS-71
96ColChoSS-71
96Don-227
96DonPowA-8
96DonPowADC-8
96DonPreP-227
96EmoXL-25
96Fin-B216
96Fin-G83
96FinRef-B216
96FinRef-G83
96Fla-36
96Fle-46
96FleTeaL-3
96FleTif-46
96FleTomL-2
96FleUpd-U218
96FleUpdTC-U218
96Lea-89
96LeaLim-58
96LeaLimG-58
96LeaPre-70
96LeaPreP-70
96LeaPrePB-89
96LeaPrePG-89
96LeaPrePS-89
96LeaPreSG-44
96LeaPreSte-44
96LeaSig-46
96LeaSigA-62
96LeaSigAG-62
96LeaSigAS-62
96LeaSigPPG-46
96LeaSigPPP-46
96MetUni-26
96MetUniML-2
96MetUniP-26
96MetUniPP-3
96Pac-262
96PacPri-P85
96PacPriG-P85
96PanSti-212
96Pin-145
96Pin-221
96PinAfi-123
96PinAfiAP-123
96PinArtP-72
96PinArtP-121
96PinFoil-221
96PinPow-8
96PinSta-72
96PinSta-121
96Sco-4
96Sco-359
96ScoDiaA-20
96ScoDugC-A4
96ScoDugC-B84
96ScoDugCAP-A4
96ScoDugCAP-B84
96ScoNumG-15
96ScoSam-4
96Sel-65
96SelArtP-65
96SelCer-75
96SelCerAP-75
96SelCerCB-75
96SelCerCR-75
96SelCerIP-4
96SelCerMB-75
96SelCerMG-75
96SelCerMR-75
96SelTeaN-23
96SP-50
96Spo-22
96SpoArtP-22
96SPSpeFX-6
96SPSpeFXDC-6
96SPx-11
96SPxGol-11
96StaClu-206
96StaClu-276
96StaCluEPB-276
96StaCluEPG-276
96StaCluEPS-276
96StaCluMO-11
96StaCluMOP-206
96StaCluMOP-276
96StaCluMOP-PS15
96StaCluPS-PS15
95StaCluVRMC-29
96Stu-75
96StuPrePB-75
96StuPrePG-75
96StuPrePS-75
96Sum-55
96SumAbo&B-55
96SumArtP-55
96SumFoi-55
96SumPos-8
96TeaOut-24
96Top-171
96TopChr-50
96TopChrR-50
96TopGal-109
96TopGalPPI-109
96TopLas-6
96TopMysF-M11
96TopMysFR-M11
96TopPro-AL13
96TopRoaW-RW6
96Ult-28
96Ult-594
96UltFreF-3
96UltFreFGM-3
96UltGolM-28
96UltGolM-594
96UltRBIK-5
96UltRBIKGM-5
96UltRisS-3
96UltRisSGM-3
96UppDec-30

96UppDecPRE-R13
96UppDecPreR-R13
96UppDecVJLS-VJ16
96Zen-26
96Zen-146
96ZenArtP-26
96ZenArtP-146
96ZenMoz-7
96ZenZ-16
97Bow-251
97BowBes-19
97BowBesAR-19
97BowBesR-19
97BowChr-74
97BowChrI-74
97BowChrIR-74
97BowChrR-74
97BowInt-251
97Cir-97
97CirRav-97
97ColCho-255
97ColChoTBS-12
97ColChoTBSWH-12
97Don-2
97Don-419
97DonEli-28
97DonEliGS-28
97DonLim-138
97DonLim-180
97DonLimLE-138
97DonLimLE-180
97DonPre-116
97DonPreCttC-116
97DonPreP-2
97DonPreP-419
97DonPrePGold-2
97DonPrePGold-419
97DonPreXP-6B
97DonTea-1
97DonTeaSPE-1
97Fin-165
97FinEmb-165
97FinEmbR-165
97FinRef-165
97FlaSho-A125
97FlaSho-B125
97FlaSho-C125
97FlaShoLC-125
97FlaShoLC-B125
97FlaShoLC-C125
97FlaShoLCM-A125
97FlaShoLCM-B125
97FlaShoLCM-C125
97Fle-40
97FleTeaL-3
97FleTif-40
97Lea-231
97Lea-396
97LeaFraM-231
97LeaFraM-396
97LeaFraMDC-231
97LeaFraMDC-396
97LeaWarT-18
97MetUni-39
97NewPin-122
97NewPinAP-122
97NewPinMC-122
97NewPinPP-122
97Pac-5
97PacLigB-5
97PacPri-2
97PacPriGotD-GD4
97PacPriLB-2
97PacPriP-2
97PacSil-5
97PinCer-100
97PinCerMBlu-100
97PinCerMG-100
97PinCerMR-100
97PinCerR-100
97PinIns-115
97PinInsCE-115
97PinInsDE-115
97PinTotCPB-100
97PinTotCPG-100
97PinTotCPR-100
97PinX-P-81
97PinX-PMoS-81
97PinX-PSfF-30
97PinX-PSfFU-30
97Sco-402
97ScoHeatO-33
97ScoHobR-402
97ScoResC-402
97ScoShoS-402
97ScoShoSAP-402
97Sel-84
97SelArtP-84
97SelRegG-84
97SkyE-X-1
97SkyE-XC-1
97SkyE-XEC-1
97SP-19
97SpoIll-164
97SpoIllEE-164
97StaClu-226
97StaCluMat-226
97StaCluMOP-226
97Stu-126
97StuPrePG-126
97StuPrePS-126
97Top-75
97TopChr-28
97TopChrR-28
97TopGal-93
97TopGalPPI-93
97TopSta-18
97TopStaAM-18
97Ult-25
97UltDouT-3
97UltGolME-25
97UltPlaME-25
97UppDec-291

Edmonds, Stan
82WauTimF-4

Edmondson, Bobby
75WatRoyT-10

Edmondson, Brian
91BriTigC-26
91BriTigP-3597
92FayGenC-3
92FayGenF-2162
92StaCluD-43
93Bow-291
93FloStaLAF-17
93LakTigC-6
93LakTigF-1301
94Bow-265
94ExcFS7-53
94TreThuF-2115
96BinBeeB-6

Edmondson, Gavin
92GulCoaDF-3568
93BakDodCLC-6
95AusFut-60

Edmondson, Paul (Paul M.)
70OPC-414
70Top-414

Edsell, Geoff
93BoiHawC-10
93BoiHawF-3907
94CedRapKC-10
94CedRapKF-1104
94MidLeaAF-MDW38
95LakElsSTI-13
96Exc-25
96MidAngB-15
96MidAngOHP-10
96VanCanB-10

Eduardo, Hector
77St.PetCT-21
78St.PetCT-9
79ArkTraT-19B
81EdmTraRR-13

Edwards, Allen
82MadMusF-17
83AlbA'sT-2

Edwards, Billy
88AllandGN-8

Edwards, Bobby
88SalLakCTTI-11

Edwards, Bruce (Charles B.)
46SpoExcW-2-10
47Exh-67
47HomBon-12
47TipTop-94
48BluTin-26
48Bow-43
49Bow-206
49EurSta-34
50Bow-165
51Bow-116
51TopBluB-42
52Bow-88
52Top-224
76TayBow4-29
83TopRep5-224
89DodSmoG-52
90DodTar-212
91RinPosBD4-6

Edwards, Chuck
89JohCitCS-9

Edwards, Dave (David L.)
77TacTwiDQ-3
79TwiFriP-5
80Top-657
81Don-595A
81Don-595B
81Fle-568
81Top-386
81TopTra-758
82Don-247
82Top-151
83Don-565
83Fle-357
83Top-94
87PocGiaTB-17
88PocGiaP-2084
90EveGiaB-28

Edwards, Doc (Howard R.)
62Top-594
63Top-296
64A's-5
64AthJayP-4
64Top-174
64TopVen-174
65AthJayP-4
65OPC-239
65Top-239
79RocRedWT-10
80RocRedWT-13
81RocRedWT-22
81RocRedWW-5
81TCM60I-426
82ChaChaT-23
83ChaChaT-22
84MaiGuiT-10
85IntLeaAT-24
85MaiGuiT-29
86IndOhH-NNO
86IndTeal-19
87IndGat-NNO
88IndGat-32
88Top-374
88TopTif-374
89IndTeal-10
89Top-534
89TopTif-534
90MetColP-32
90MetKah-32
90TopTVM-3
91MetColP-32
91MetKah-32
92BufBisBS-8
92BufBisF-339
92BufBisS-50
92YanWIZ6-38
94BufBisF-1852

Edwards, Glenn
85WatIndT-5

Edwards, Hank (Henry Albert)
47IndTeal-6
47IndVanPP-5
48IndTeal-8
49Bow-136
49EurSta-56
49Lea-72
50Bow-169
52Bow-141
52NatTeaL-7
52Top-176
53Top-90
79DiaGre-296
83TCMPla1943-7
83TopRep5-176
90DodTar-213
91TopArc1-90

Edwards, Jay
93ClePhiF-2694
94ReaPhiF-2074

Edwards, Jeff
86AshTouP-9
86AubAstP-8
87AlbDukP-9
87AshTouP-25
87SanBerSP-3
88ColAstB-16
89CanIndP-1316
89CanIndS-4
89EasLeaDDP-DD41
90CMC-458
90ColSprSSC-6
92GulCoaMF-3499
93PitMetC-26
93PitMetF-3727

Edwards, Jerome
90PriPatD-5
91BatCliC-12
91BatCliP-3495
92SpaPhiC-2
92SpaPhiF-1276
93ClePhiC-7

Edwards, Jim
93ConTSN-985

Edwards, Johnny (John Alban)
56RedBurB-5
62Kah-9
62RedEnq-7
62SalPlaC-191
62ShiPlaC-191
62Top-302
62TopStal-114
63Jel-132
63Kah-9
63Pos-132
63RedEnq-6
63RedFreBC-5
63Top-178
64Kah-8
64Top-507
64WheSta-14
65Kah-12
65MacSta-3
65RedEnq-8
65Top-418
66Kah-11
66Top-507
67CokCapR-10
67DexPre-68
67Kah-11
67Top-202
68Top-558
69MLBOffS-139
69OPC-186
69Top-186
69TopFou-22
69TopSta-33
69TopTeaP-6
70AstTeal-3
70MLBOffS-40
70OPC-339
70Top-339
71AstCok-5
71MLBOffS-79
71OPC-44
71Top-44
72MilBra-96
72OPC-416
72Top-416
73OPC-519
73Top-519
74AstFouTIP-2
74OPC-635
74Top-635
82AstAstI-1
84OCoandSI-183
86AstGreT-8
87AstShoSO-5
87AstShoSTw-27
87AstShowSTh-29
91UppDecS-9

Edwards, Jon
96WatIndTI-7

Edwards, Jovon
86BakDodP-6
87SalSpuP-16
88St.LucMS-7

Edwards, Lamont
96MarPhiB-6

Edwards, Larry
77BurBeeT-7
78BurBeeT-12
79BurBeeT-1
80AndBraT-5
81GleFalWST-24
82GleFalWST-16

Edwards, Marshall L.
78HolMilT-7
79VanCanT-4
80VanCanT-19
82Fle-140
82Top-333
83BreGar-6
83BrePol-16
83Don-406
83Fle-32
83Top-582
84Don-490
84Nes792-167
84Top-167
84TopTif-167
84VanCanC-47
92BreCarT-6
94BreMilB-19

Edwards, Mel
91SpoIndP-3955

Edwards, Mike
91ButCopKSP-9
92ClaFS7-310
92GasRanC-12
92GasRanF-2259
93ChaRanC-8
93ChaRanF-1947
94TulDriF-250
94TulDriTI-6
95TulDriTI-7
96BurIndB-19

Edwards, Mike (Michael L.)
75ShrCapT-2
76ShrCapT-11
77ColCliT-5
79Top-201
79Top-613
80OPC-158
80Top-301
81Don-497

Edwards, Otis
91WatIndC-25
91WatIndP-3380

Edwards, Randy
94AshTouC-6
94AshTouF-1794

Edwards, Ryan
90BilMusP-3223
91CedRapRC-3
91CedRapRP-2711
92CedRapRC-27
92CedRapRF-1065

Edwards, Samuel
90PriPatD-6
91MarPhiC-23
91MarPhiP-3447
92MarPhiC-23
92MarPhiF-3049

Edwards, Todd
86MiaMarP-6
90HelBreSP-19
91BelBreC-19
91BelBreP-2116
91SalLakTP-3224
91SalLakTSP-4
92GenCubC-18
92GenCubF-1554

Edwards, Wayne
86PenWhiSP-9
87DayBeaAP-15
88BirBarB-1
88BlaYNPRWL-24
89BasAmeAPB-AA22
89BirBarB-21
89BirBarP-110
89SouLeaAJ-16
90BirBarDGB-9
90Bow-309
90BowTif-309
90DonRoo-17
90Fle-652
90FleCan-652
90FleUpd-83
90Lea-352
90ScoRoo-85T
90TopDeb89-34
90TopTra-27T
90TopTraT-27T
90UppDec-762
90WhiSoxC-2
90WhiSoxC-28
91Bow-364
91Don-327
91Fle-116
91Lea-454
91OPC-751
91Sco-66
91Sco100RS-10
91StaClu-129

91Top-751
91TopDesS-751
91TopMic-751
91TopTif-751
91UppDec-697
91WhiSoxK-45
92OPC-404
92StaClu-674
92SyrChiF-1960
92SyrChiMB-5
92SyrChiS-505
94TolMudHF-1020
95BakBlaTI-13
Eenhoorn, Robert
90OneYanP-3384
90ProAaA-182
91Bow-172
91PriWilCC-16
91PriWilCP-1432
91UppDecFE-16F
92Bow-278
92ClaFS7-229
92ForLauYC-4
92ForLauYTI-7
92Ft.LauYF-2617
92ProF37-121
92UppDecML-326
93AlbYanF-2169
93Bow-567
93ClaFS7-68
93StaCluY-25
94Bow-277
94ClaGolF-9
94ColCliF-2958
94ColCliP-8
94ExcFS7-102
94ScoRoo-RT103
94ScoRooGR-RT103
94SpoRoo-78
94SpoRooAP-78
94UppDec-514
94UppDecED-514
94UppDecML-143
95ColCliP-7
95ColCliTI-7
95Don-34
95DonPreP-34
95Pin-152
95PinArtP-152
95PinMusC-152
95Sco-281
95ScoGolR-281
95ScoPlaTS-281
96ColCho-228
96ColCho-330
96ColChoGS-228
96ColChoGS-330
96ColChoSS-228
96ColChoSS-330
96ColCliB-12
97UppDec-190
Effrig, Mark
83ElPasDT-7
84ElPasDT-1
Egan, Dick (Richard Wallis)
63Top-169
64Top-572
66Top-536
67Top-539
81TCM60I-434
89RanMot-27
89RanSmo-6
90CMC-172
90DodTar-214
90OklCit8C-22
90OklCit8P-449
91ButCopKSP-30
93RanKee-133
Egan, Jack
94ConTSN-1185
94ConTSNB-1185
Egan, Joe (Richard Joseph)
09T206-118
11SpoLifCW-116
11T205-49
11SpoLifM-192
12HasTriFT-15A
12HasTriFT-71
14PieStaT-20
16FleBreD-26
Egan, Tom (Thomas Patrick)
65Top-486
66Top-263
66TopVen-263
67OPC-147
67Top-147
69Top-407
70MLBOffS-171
70OPC-4
70Top-4
71OPC-537
71Top-537
72MilBra-97
72OPC-207
72Top-207
73OPC-648
73Top-648
75OPC-88
75Top-88
77WauMetT-24
Egawa, Suguru
87JapPlaB-25
Eggert, David
92JamExpC-25
92JamExpF-1492
93BurBeeC-8
93BurBeeF-151
94WesPalBEC-8
94WesPalBEF-32
Eggertsen, Todd
86PalSprAP-16
86PalSprAP-12
87PalSprP-29
88MidAngGS-9
Eggleston, Darren
87WytCubP-18
88ChaWheB-10
Eggleston, Scott
91SpoIndC-17
91SpoIndP-3942
92SpoIndC-20
92SpoIndF-1285
93BatCliC-8
93BatCliF-3138
94SpaPhiF-1713
94SparPhiC-6
Eggleston, Skip
88GenCubP-1639
Eggleston, Wayne
92ButCopKSP-24
93ChaRaiC-6
93ChaRaiF-1918
Egins, Paul C. III
88BurBraP-30
89BurBraP-1625
Egloff, Bruce
87WatIndP-15
89WatIndS-5
90Bes-251
90CanIndB-20
90CanIndP-1288
90ProAaA-11
91Bow-78
91IndFanC-8
92ColSprSSF-747
92Sco-751
92StaClu-503
92TopDeb91-49
Ehardt, Rube
90DodTar-941
Ehler, Dan
94KanCouCC-9
94KanCouCF-154
94KanCouCTI-9
94Top-751
94TopGol-751
94TopSpa-751
95BreCouMF-239
96BreCouMB-13
Ehmann, Kurt
92ClaDraP-83
92EveGiaC-23
93SanJosGC-11
93SanJosGF-17
93StaCluM-70
94ClaGolF-150
94ExcFS7-288
94ShrCapF-1612
94UppDecML-141
95PhoFirTI-6
96PhoFirB-15
Ehmig, Greg
88SalLakCTTI-14
Ehmke, Howard (Howard J.)
20WalMaiW-15
21Exh-42
21Exh-43
22E120-52
22W573-34
23WilChoV-36
25Exh-65
28Exh-54
29PorandAR-20
61Fle-21
88ConSer5-9
92ConTSN-357
93ConTSN-759
94ConTSN-1135
94ConTSNB-1135
Ehret, Red (Philip S.)
87OldJudN-153
Ehrhard, Jim
88Ft.LauYS-6
Ehrhard, Rod
87OneYanP-23
88OneYanP-2072
89PriWilCS-7
90Ft.LauYS-7
Eibey, Scott
96AppLeaAB-4
96BluOriB-11
Eichelberger, Juan T.
79HawIslC-13
79HawIslT-21
80HawIslT-4
80VenLeaS-193
81AllGamPI-168
81Top-478
82Don-422A
82Don-422B
82Fle-570
82Top-366
82Top-614
82TopSti-97
82TopStiV-97
83Don-247
83Don-422
83Fle-358
83IndPos-12
83IndWhe-9
83OPC-168
83Top-168
83TopTra-29T
84Don-398
84Fle-539
84Nes792-226
84Top-226
84TopTif-226
86RicBraP-5
87RicBraBC-6
87RicBraC-15
87RicBraT-4
88RicBraC-6
88RicBraP-10
89PacSenL-175
89T/MSenL-32
89TopSenL-123
90EliSenL-20
91PacSenL-119
94AppFoxC-23
94AppFoxF-1070
96LanJetB-3
Eicher, Mike
92SprCarC-17
92SprCarF-881
93SprCarC-8
93SprCarF-1862
Eichhorn, Dave
86AlbDukP-6
87SanAntDTI-20
88SanAntMB-13
89AlbDukC-6
89AlbDukP-61
Eichhorn, Mark A.
82SyrChiT-3
82SyrChiTI-11
83SyrChiT-7
84SyrChiT-18
86BluJayFS-8
86DonRoo-13
86FleUpd-38
86SpoRoo-38
86TopTra-34T
86TopTraT-34T
87BluJayFS-7
87Don-321
87Fle-224
87FleGamW-14
87FleGlo-224
87FleHotS-16
87FleMin-36
87FleStiC-37
87Lea-173
87Lea-229
87OPC-371
87Spo-194
87SpoTeaP-5
87SyrChi1A-11
87Top-371
87TopGloS-49
87TopRoo-5
87TopSti-187
87TopTif-371
87ToyRoo-10
88BluJay5-4
88BluJayFS-9
88Don-121
88Fle-108
88FleGlo-108
88FleMin-60
88Lea-74
88MSAHosD-18
88OPC-116
88PanSti-212
88Sco-198
88ScoGlo-198
88Spo-210
88StaLinBJ-5
88Top-749
88TopBig-208
88TopRevLL-30
88TopTif-749
89BraDub-10
89Fle-230
89FleGlo-230
89OPC-274
89RicBraP-825
89Sco-152
89Top-274
89TopBig-188
89TopTif-274
89TriA AAC-26
90Fle-580
90FleCan-580
90FleUpd-77
90Lea-472
90OPC-513
90Top-513
90TopTif-513
90TopTra-28T
90TopTraT-28T
90TriAAAC-26
91AngSmo-16
91Don-318
91Fle-311
91OPC-129
91Sco-504
91Top-129
91TopDesS-129
91TopMic-129
91TopTif-129
91UppDec-519
92Don-181
92Fle-55
92Lea-97
92OPC-435
92Pin-353
92Sco-221
92StaClu-857
92StaCluNC-857
92Top-435
92TopGol-435
92TopGolW-435
92TopMic-435
92UppDec-287
93BluJayD-15
93BluJayD4-16
93BluJayFS-9
93FleFinE-292
93StaClu-617
93StaCluFDI-617
93StaCluMOP-617
94Don-144
94Fle-330
94FleUpd-1
94OriPro-29
94Pac-638
94Pin-511
94PinArtP-511
94PinMusC-511
94Sco-266
94ScoGolR-266
94StaCluT-282
94StaCluTFDI-282
95BluJayUSPC-7C
95Don-475
95DonPreP-475
95Fle-5
95Sco-532
95ScoGolR-532
95ScoPlaTS-532
95Top-563
95TopCyb-339
96AngMot-18
96LeaSigEA-46
Eierman, John
91ElmPioC-4
91ElmPioP-3282
92LynRedSC-2
92LynRedSF-2918
93LynRedSC-8
93LynRedSF-2529
94LynRedSC-9
94LynRedSF-1904
Eiffert, Michael
92BenRocC-11
92BenRocF-1468
93BenRocC-7
93BenRocF-3259
93CenValRC-9
93CenValRF-2886
Eiland, Dave
87OneYanP-17
88AlbYanP-1336
88EasLeaAP-1
89ColCliC-8
89ColCliP-2
89ColCliP-750
89Don-481
89Top-8
89TopTif-8
90AlbDecGB-26
90CMC-202
90ColCliC-2
90ColCliP-13
90ColCliP-670
90ProAAAF-320
90Sco-652
90TopTVY-41
91Don-354
91Fle-661
91Lea-184
91OPC-611
91Sco-826
91StaClu-477
91Top-611
91TopDesS-611
91TopMic-611
91TopTif-611
92Fle-223
92Lea-488
92OPC-406
92PadMot-10
92PadPolD-6
92PadSmo-7
92Sco-679
92StaClu-133
92StaClu-879
92StaCluMO-6
92StaCluMO-14
92StaCluNC-879
92Ult-575
92YanWIZ8-51
93PadMot-7
93UppDec-709
93UppDecGold-709
94ColCliF-2945
94ColCliP-9
95ColCliP-8
95ColCliTI-8
96LouRedB-17
Eilers, Dave (David Louis)
66Top-534
78TCM60I-245
91MetWIZ-104
Einerston, Darrell
96GreBatB-9
Einstein, Charles
90LitSunW-11
Einterfeldt, Todd
81TidTidT-7
Eischen, Joey (Joe)
89ButCopKSP-13
90GasRanB-6
90GasRanP-2514
90GasRanS-6

91ChaRanC-4
91ChaRanP-1308
92ClaFS7-303
92WesPalBEC-18
92WesPalBEF-2082
93Bow-240
93ClaFS7-134
93HarSenF-265
94Bow-528
94BowBes-B77
94BowBesR-B77
94Cla-96
94ClaGolF-137
94ColC-656
94ColChoGS-656
94ColChoSS-656
94ExcFS7-224
94ExcLeaLF-8
94ExtBas-302
94ExtBasMLH-4
94OttLynF-2896
94SigRoo-10
94SigRooS-10
94Ult-522
94UppDec-10
94UppDecED-10
94UppDecML-77
94UppDecML-152
95ColCho-241
95ColChoGS-241
95ColChoSS-241
95DodMot-25
95Don-115
95DonPreP-115
95Fle-347
95Pin-162
95PinArtP-162
95PinMusC-162
95Sel-211
95SelArtP-211
96DodMot-16
96DodPol-11
96Fle-432
96FleTif-432
96LeaSigA-63
96LeaSigAG-63
96LeaSigAS-63
97PacPriGotD-GD41
Eisenhower, Dwight D.
94UppDecTAE-59
Eisenreich, Charlie
87AppFoxP-15
Eisenreich, Jim (James M.)
81WisRapTT-21
82TwiPos-7
83Top-197
83TwiTeal-2
83TwiTeal-31
84MinTwiP-9
84TwiTeal-2
87MemChiB-21
87MemChiP-27
88Don-343
88OPC-348
88RoySmo-26
88Sco-456
88ScoGlo-456
88StaLinRo-3
88Top-348
88TopTif-348
89DonBasB-306
89FleUpd-38
89Sco-594
89TopTra-28T
89TopTraT-28T
89UppDec-44
90Bow-374
90BowTif-374
90Don-238
90DonBesA-120
90Fle-106
90FleCan-106
90Lea-278
90OPC-246
90PanSti-80
90PubSti-346
90Sco-179
90Spo-166
90Top-246
90TopBig-234
90TopSti-271
90TopTif-246
90UppDec-294
90VenSti-159
91Bow-304
91Don-448
91Fle-557
91OPC-707
91PanFreS-280
91PanSti-229
91RoyPol-8
91Sco-154
91StaClu-373
91Top-707
91TopDesS-707
91TopMic-707
91TopTif-707
91Ult-146
91UppDec-658
92Don-297
92Fle-156
92Hig5-62
92Lea-295
92OPC-469
92Pin-468
92RoyPol-6
92Sco-158
92StaClu-409
92Top-469
92TopGol-469
92TopGolW-469
92TopMic-469
92TriPla-140
92Ult-69
92UppDec-539
93Don-722
93Fla-100
93Fle-617
93FleFinE-109
93Lea-507
93PacSpa-576
93PanSti-104
93PhiMed-13
93Sco-551
93Sel-241
93StaClu-224
93StaCluFDI-224
93StaCluMOP-224
93StaCluP-7
93Top-22
93TopGol-22
93TopInaM-22
93TopMic-22
93Ult-440
93UppDec-800
93UppDecGold-800
94ColC-388
94ColChoGS-388
94ColChoSS-388
94Don-548
94Fla-206
94Fle-588
94Lea-176
94Pac-474
94PanSti-227
94PhiMed-9
94PhiMel-7
94PhiUSPC-6D
94PhiUSPC-11D
94PhiUSPC-13S
94Pin-149
94PinArtP-149
94PinMusC-149
94Sel-213
94StaClu-27
94StaCluFDI-27
94StaCluGR-27
94StaCluMOP-27
94StaCluT-224
94StaCluTFDI-224
94Top-504
94TopGol-504
94TopSpa-504
94Ult-545
94UppDec-157
94UppDecED-157
95ColCho-366
95ColChoGS-366
95ColChoSS-366
95Don-211
95DonPreP-211
95DonTopotO-303
95Fla-179
95Fle-391
95Lea-149
95Pac-329
95Phi-10
95PhiMel-8
95Sco-362
95ScoGolR-362
95ScoPlaTS-362
95StaClu-209
95StaCluFDI-209
95StaCluMOP-209
95StaCluSTWS-209
95StaCluVR-110
95Top-326
95Ult-204
95UltGolM-204
96Cir-165
96CirRav-165
96ColCho-649
96ColChoGS-649
96ColChoSS-649
96Don-470
96DonPreP-470
96EmoXL-244
96Fla-333
96Fle-496
96FleTif-496
96LeaSigA-64
96LeaSigAG-64
96LeaSigAS-64
96MetUni-210
96MetUniP-210
96Pac-164
96PanSti-40
96PhiTeal-10
96ProSta-86
96Sco-125
96StaClu-281
96StaCluMOP-281
95StaCluVRMC-110
96Top-66
96Ult-251
96UltGolM-251
96UppDec-171
97ColCho-191
97ColCho-342
97Don-180
97DonPreP-180
97DonPrePGold-180
97Fle-410
97Fle-604
97FleTif-410
97FleTif-604
97MetUni-174
97Pac-377
97PacLigB-377
97PacSil-377
97Pin-23
97PinArtP-23
97PinMusC-23
97Sco-452
97ScoHobR-452
97ScoResC-452
97ScoShoS-452
97ScoShoSAP-452
97Top-161
97Ult-249
97Ult-367
97UltGolME-249
97UltGolME-367
97UltPlaME-249
97UltPlaME-367
97UppDec-133
Eisenstat, Harry
40PlaBal-204
90DodTar-215
Eisinger, John
77ModA'sC-21
Eissens, Simon
91PerHeaF-1
95AusFut-57
Eiterman, Tom
90CalLeaACLC-39
90RenSilSCLC-263
91CarLeaAP-CAR13
91KinIndC-25
91KinIndP-337
92CanIndF-700
92CanIndS-105
Eklund, Troy
89ButCopKSP-16
90GasRanB-12
90GasRanP-2532
90GasRanS-7
Ekman, Rich
91PocPioP-3775
91PocPioSP-9
el Himmo, Oyendo
80VenLeaS-135
Elam, Brett
96AshTouB-15
Elam, Scott
82KnoBluJT-2
83KinBluJTI-4
Elam, Todd
88BatCliP-1682
89SpaPhiP-1028
89SpaPhiS-7
90ClePhiS-6
Elarton, Scott
94SigRooDP-24
94SigRooDPS-24
95Bow-242
95BowBes-B37
95BowBesR-B37
95BowGolF-242
95ColCho-32
95ColChoGS-32
95ColChoSS-32
95Exc-201
95Pin-171
95PinArtP-171
95PinMusC-171
95QuaCitRBTI-5
95ScoDraP-DP8
95SPML-67
95StaClu-108
95StaCluFDI-108
95StaCluMOP-108
95StaCluSTWS-108
95Top-510
96Bow-281
96BowBes-112
96BowBesAR-112
96BowBesR-112
96KisCobB-7
97Bow-355
97BowCerBIA-CA22
97BowCerGIA-CA22
97BowChr-240
97BowChrI-240
97BowChrIR-240
97BowChrR-240
97BowInt-355
Elberfeld, Kid (Norman A.)
03BreE10-47
03BreE10-48
04FanCraAL-17
08RosComP-46
09ColChiE-89A
09ColChiE-89B
09ColChiE-89C
09RamT20-42
09T206-119
09T206-120
09T206-121
10CouT21-131
10CouT21-132
10CouT21-282
10DarChoE-17
10RedCroT-24
10RedCroT-110
10RedCroT-190
10SweCapPP-57A
10SweCapPP-57B
11MecDFT-19
11S74Sil-38
11SpoLifCW-117
11SpoLifM-122
11T205-50
11TurRedT-15
12ColRedB-89A
12ColRedB-89B
12ColRedB-89C
12ColTinT-89A
12ColTinT-89B
12ColTinT-89C
12HasTriFT-33
12HasTriFT-34
15VicT21-9
89ChaLooLITI-9
90DodTar-216
92ConTSN-557
Elder, Isaac
89JamExpP-2147
90RocExpLC-8
90RocExpP-2706
Elders, Mike
76CliPilT-12
Eldred, Cal (Calvin)
89BelBreIS-8
90Bes-61
90Bow-387
90BowTif-387
90CMC-866
90ElPasDGS-10
90ProAaA-138
90Sco-669
90StoPorB-1
90StoPorCLC-174
90StoPorP-2178
91Bow-56
91DenZepLD-135
91DenZepP-116
91LinDriAAA-135
92Bow-299
92Cla1-T31
92ClaGam-126
92DenZepF-2631
92DenZepS-127
92Don-718
92Fle-679
92Lea-2
92OPC-433
92Pin-249
92PinTea2-36
92ProFS7-81
92Sco-834
92ScoHotR-1
92ScoImpP-89
92ScoRoo-33
92SkyAAAF-61
92StaClu-327
92Top-433
92TopDeb91-50
92TopGol-433
92TopGolW-433
92TopMic-433
92TriPla-213
92Ult-380
92UppDec-477
93Bow-127
93BrePol-6
93ClaGam-28
93Don-131
93Fin-147
93FinRef-147
93Fla-223
93Fle-248
93FleRooS-RSA2
93FunPac-70
93HumDumC-10
93Lea-34
93LeaFas-16
93OPC-85
93OPCPre-4
93Pin-2
93PinTea2-2
93Sco-368
93Sel-296
93SelAce-21
93SelChaR-15
93SP-64
93StaClu-475
93StaCluFDI-475
93StaCluMOP-475
93Stu-6
93Top-590
93TopGol-590
93TopInaM-590
93TopMic-590
93Toy-80
93TriPla-18
93Ult-218
93UppDec-375
93UppDecGold-375
93USPlaCR-13C
94Bow-393
94BreMilB-20
94BrePol-6
94ColC-606
94ColChoGS-606
94ColChoSS-606
94DenHol-9
94Don-89
94ExtBas-101
94Fin-288
94FinRef-288
94Fla-66
94Fle-175
94FUnPac-166
94Lea-267
94OPC-179
94Pac-328
94Pin-19
94PinArtP-19

94PinMusC-19
94RedFolMI-28
94Sco-449
94ScoGolR-449
94Sel-347
94SP-57
94SPDieC-57
94Spo-107
94StaClu-329
94StaCluFDI-329
94StaCluGR-329
94StaCluMOP-329
94StaCluMOP-ST22
94StaCluST-ST22
94Top-45
94TopGol-45
94TopSpa-45
94TriPla-52
94Ult-73
94UppDec-431
94UppDecED-431
95Bow-361
95ColCho-175
95ColChoGS-175
95ColChoSE-69
95ColChoSEGS-69
95ColChoSESS-69
95ColChoSS-175
95D3-10
95Don-536
95DonPreP-536
95Emb-29
95EmbGolI-29
95Emo-53
95Fin-63
95FinRef-63
95Fla-51
95Fle-177
95Lea-34
95Pac-230
95Pin-377
95PinArtP-377
95PinMusC-377
95RedFol-23
95Sco-393
95ScoGolR-393
95ScoPlaTS-393
95Sel-149
95SelArtP-149
95SP-164
95SPSil-164
95StaClu-20
95StaCluFDI-20
95StaCluMOP-20
95StaCluSTWS-20
95StaCluVR-14
95Stu-174
95Top-580
95TopCyb-354
95Ult-295
95UltGolM-295
95UppDec-53
95UppDecED-53
95UppDecEDG-53
95UppDecSE-235
95UppDecSEG-235
96ColCho-592
96ColChoGS-592
96ColChoSS-592
96Don-333
96DonPreP-333
96StaClu-312
96StaCluMOP-312
95StaCluVRMC-14
96Top-335
97Cir-70
97CirRav-70
97ColCho-143
97Fle-578
97FleTif-578
97PacPriGotD-GD54
97Sco-404
97ScoHobR-404
97ScoResC-404
97ScoShoS-404
97ScoShoSAP-404
97StaClu-318
97StaCluMOP-318
97Top-424
97Ult-315
97UltGolME-315
97UltPlaME-315
97UppDec-408

Eldredge, Ted
87BelMarL-23
88SanBerSB-11
88SanBerSCLC-41
89WauTimGS-9

Eldridge, Brian
89AncGlaP-13
90AriWilP-4
93MadMusC-8
93MadMusF-1826
94ModA'sC-7
94ModA'sF-3068

Eldridge, Rodney
90HamRedB-20
90HamRedS-10
91Cla/Bes-180
91SavCarC-16
91SavCarP-1657
92St.PetCC-15

Elenes, Larry
74CedRapAT-23

Elerman, John
92ClaFS7-388

Elguezabal, Jose
78SanJosMMC-7

Elia, Lee (Lee Constantine)
66Top-529
67Top-406
68Top-561
69Top-312
75IntLeaAT-8
75IntLeaAT-26
77ReaPhiT-10
81TCM60I-428
82CubRedL-4
83CubThoAV-NNO
83Don-614
83Top-456
84PorBeaC-200
85PhiTas-4
85PhiTas-8
86PhiTas-4
87PhiTas-xx0
87TopTra-32T
87TopTraT-32T
88ChaLooLTI-9
88PhiTas-9A
88PhiTas-9B
88PhiTas-32
88Top-254
88TopTif-254
90ClePhiS-26
91ClePhiC-18
91ClePhiP-1638
92ScrRedBF-2462
92ScrRedBS-499
93MarMot-28
94MarMot-28
95MarMot-28
96MarMot-28

Elick, Jason
90VisOakCLC-84

Elite Giants, Baltimore
92NegLeaRLI-98
93NegLeaRL2-51
93NegLeaRL2-87
93NegLeaRL2-88
93TedWilPC-1

Elite Giants, Nashville
93NegLeaRL2-50
93NegLeaRL2-86

Elizabeth, Queen
84WilMay-39

Elkin, Rick
80BatTroT-15
81BatTroT-11

Elkins, Mark
89TenTecGE-8

Ellam, Roy
09ColChiE-90
09T206-483
10CouT21-20
12ColRedB-90
12ColTinT-90

Eller, Hod (Horace Owen)
19W514-38
20RedWorCP-5
88PacEigMO-93
92ConTSN-352
94ConTSN-1027
94ConTSNB-1027

Ellerbe, Frank (Francis R.)
21Nei-51
22E120-95
22W573-35
23WilChoV-37

Elli, Rocky
88ColMetGS-4
90JacMetGS-22
91LinDriAAA-482
91ScrRedBLD-482
91ScrRedBP-2533
92ClePhiF-2049
94SarRedSC-7
94SarRedSF-1943

Ellingsen, H. Bruce
75OklCit8TI-6
75OPC-288
75Top-288

Elliot, Corey
84VisOakT-7

Elliot, David
96BelSnaTI-14

Elliot, Greg
92AubAstC-2
92AubAstF-1359

Elliot, Larry (Lawrence L.)
63Top-407
64Top-536
67OPC-23
67Top-23
91MetWIZ-105

Elliot, Paul
91ParPatF-2

Elliot, Rowdy
90DodTar-942

Elliot, Terry
86AncGlaPTI-9
88St.PetCS-6
89St.PetCS-10

Elliott, Bob (Robert I.)
39ExhSal-14
47HomBon-13
48BluTin-38
48Bow-1
49Bow-58
49EurSta-7
49Lea-65
50AmeNut&CCP-5
50Bow-20
50Dra-35
51Bow-66
51R42SmaS-28
51TopBluB-32
52BerRos-16
52Top-14
53ExhCan-26
60A's-3
60A'sJayP-3
60Top-215
76TayBow4-22
83TCMPla1942-37
83TopRep5-14

Elliott, Claude
11SpoLifCW-118

Elliott, Clay
79SavBraT-11

Elliott, Dave
95HelBreTI-5

Elliott, Donnie
88MarPhiS-12
89BatCliP-1925
90SpaPhiB-16
90SpaPhiP-2482
90SpaPhiS-5
91SpaPhiC-3
91SpaPhiP-888
92ClaFS7-369
92GreBraF-1150
93Bow-58
93RicBraBB-18
93RicBraF-179
93RicBraP-8
93RicBraRC-11
93RicBraRC-9
94Bow-255
94ColC-655
94ColChoGS-655
94ColChoSS-655
94Fla-435
94FleUpd-184
94SpoRoo-53
94SpoRooAP-53
94TopTra-17T
95Don-104
95DonPreP-104
95Fla-199
95Fle-558
95Pac-360
95Ult-437
95UltGolM-437
96ScrRedBB-13

Elliott, Glenn
43CenFlo-7
44CenFlo-6
45CenFlo-6
49EurSta-8

Elliott, Greg
93AshTouC-6
93AshTouF-2282
93ClaGolF-155
93SouAtlLAGF-29
94OscAstC-7
94OscAstF-1144

Elliott, Harry (Harry Lewis)
55CarHunW-3
55Top-137

Elliott, Jim
33Gou-132
34DiaMatCSB-49
34GouCanV-6
90SpoIndSP-11

Elliott, John
86AshTouP-10
87OscAstP-17
88ColAstB-13

Elliott, Jumbo (James Thomas)
28W513-64
33RitCE-11C
90DodTar-217

Elliott, Mark
78CliDodT-7
79CliDodT-1

Elliott, Paul
96HagSunB-29

Elliott, Randy (Randy Lee)
75HawIsIC-4
78Top-719

Elliott, Zach
95MarPhiTI-8
96Exc-200
96PieBolWB-11

Ellis, Bruce
87BriYouC-20

Ellis, Bull
91UtiBluSP-3233

Ellis, Dock (Dock Phillip)
69PirJacitB-3
69Top-286
70PirTeal-3
70Top-551
71MLBOffS-200
71OPC-2
71PirActP-5
71Top-2
71TopCoi-99
72OPC-179
72OPC-180
72Top-179
72Top-180
73OPC-575
73Top-575
74OPC-145
74Top-145
74TopSta-82
75OPC-385
75Top-385
76OPC-528
76Top-528
76TopTra-528T
77Kel-4
77Kel-16A
77OPC-146
77Top-71
78RanBurK-6
78SSP270-96
78Top-209
79Top-691
80OPC-64
80Top-117
89PacSenL-15
89T/MSenL-33
89TopSenL-116
90EliSenL-5
91FouBal-21
91MetWIZ-106
92YanWIZ7-48
93RanKee-134
94TedWil-76

Ellis, Doug
87MacPirP-15

Ellis, Jim
77FriOneYW-28
91MisStaB-14
92MisStaB-12

Ellis, John
96HudValRB-6

Ellis, John (John Charles)
70OPC-516
70Top-516
70YanCliDP-10
71MLBOffS-487
71OPC-263
71Top-263
71YanArcO-6
71YanCliDP-5
72OPC-47
72OPC-48
72Top-47
72Top-48
73LinPor-62
73OPC-656
73Top-656
74OPC-128
74Top-128
74TopSta-165
75Hos-54
75OPC-605
75Top-605
76Hos-27
76HosTwi-27
76OPC-383
76SSP-515
76Top-383
76TopTra-383T
77Top-36
78RanBurK-3
78SSP270-100
78Top-438
79Top-539
80Top-283
81Don-26A
81Don-26B
81Top-339
82Don-642
82Fle-316
82Top-177
92YanWIZ6-39
92YanWIZ7-49
93RanKee-135

Ellis, K.J.
93HunCubF-3241

Ellis, Kevin
93HunCubC-1
94PeoChiC-7
94PeoChiF-2275
96DayCubB-9

Ellis, Paul
90HamRedB-13
90HamRedS-11
91Cla/Bes-81
91FloStaLAP-FSL34
91St.PetCC-15
91St.PetCP-2278
92ClaFS7-278
92St.PetCC-5
92St.PetCF-2030
93ArkTraF-2814
93Bow-336
93ClaFS7-69
93ClaGolF-97
94ArkTraF-3092
95ArkTraTI-12
96ArkTraB-13

Ellis, Rob (Robert Walter)
74SacSolC-61
75SacSolC-11
76SpoIndC-6
76SSP-240
77SpoIndC-24
79TacTugT-23
80PorBeaT-5
94BreMilB-21

Ellis, Robert
89AncGlaP-14
91EveGiaP-3933
91UtiBluSC-7
92SouBenWSC-3
93FloStaLAF-23
93SarWhiSC-9
93SarWhiSF-1364
94ActPac-51
94Bow-183
94Cla-29
94ExcFS7-38

94NasSouF-1245
94UppDec-25
94UppDecML-139
96NasSouB-13
96VanCanB-11

Ellis, Rube (George W.)
09AmeCarE-39
09ColChiE-92
10JuJuDE-17
11SpoLifCW-119
11SpoLifM-267
12ColRedB-92
12ColTinT-92
12T207-54

Ellis, Rufus
86FloStaLAP-12
86Ft.MyeRP-9
87Ft.MyeRP-18
88ChaRanS-6

Ellis, Sammy (Samuel Joseph)
63RedEnq-7
63Top-29A
63Top-29B
64Top-33
64TopVen-33
65Kah-13
65RedEnq-9
65Top-507
66Kah-12
66Top-250
66TopRubl-25
66TopVen-250
67Kah-12A
67Kah-12B
67OPC-176
67Top-176
67TopVen-279
68Top-453
69OPC-32
69Top-32
77ForLauYS-17
78TCM60I-293
80ColCliP-NNO
80ColCliT-14
81ColCliP-NNO
81ColCliT-26
82ColCliP-NNO
82ColCliT-24
86YanTCM-40
90WhiSoxC-30
91WhiSoxK-NNO
92CubMar-NNO
93MarMot-28
94MarMot-28

Ellis, Terry
88MisStaB-5

Ellis, Tim
88GenCubP-1643
90KinIndTI-26
90WatIndS-8

Ellison, Darold
80BatTroT-18

Ellison, Jeff
76DubPacT-10
77CocAstT-5

Ellison, Paul
88SpaPhiS-22
89SpaPhiP-1041
89SpaPhiS-8

Ellison, Skeeter
96DanBraB-10

Ellsworth, Ben
90JohCitCS-11
91HamRedC-25
91HamRedP-4045
92SavCarC-5
92SavCarF-669
93SprCarC-9
93SprCarF-1857
94SavCarC-12
94SavCarF-514

Ellsworth, Dick (Richard C.)
60Top-125
60TopVen-125
61CubJayP-6
61Top-427
61TopStal-7
61WilSpoGH828-1-1
62Top-264
62TopStal-107
63Top-399
64Baz-28
64CubJayP-5
64Top-1
64Top-220
64TopCoi-56
64TopGia-17
64TopSta-5
64TopStaU-23
64TopTatl-35
64TopVen-1
64TopVen-220
65CubJayP-7
65OPC-165
65Top-165
65TopEmbl-67
66CubTeal-7
66Top-447
66TopRubl-26
67CokCapPh-7
67PhiPol-6
67ProPizC-7
67Top-359
68CokCapRS-14
68DexPre-30
68Top-406
69MilBra-78
69MLBOffS-12
69Top-605
70MLBOffS-196
70OPC-59
70Top-59
71MLBOffS-435
71OPC-309
71Top-309
72MilBra-98
81RedSoxBG2S-79
94BreMilB-117

Ellsworth, Steve
86NewBriRSP-10
87PawRedSP-67
87PawRedST-6
88DonRoo-54
88DonTeaBRS-NEW
88ScoRoo-83T
88ScoRooG-83T
89PawRedSC-7
89PawRedSP-704
89PawRedSTI-8
89Top-299
89TopTif-299

Elmore, Jason
96EriSeaB-10

Elmore, Mike
87NewOriP-16

Elpin, Ralph
81WatIndT-33
82WatIndF-12
82WatIndT-3

Elrod, Greg
85CloHSS-14

Elsbecker, Andy
92HunCubC-16
92HunCubF-3138

Elsbernd, David
93HicCraC-5
93HicCraF-1272
94HicCraC-9
94HicCraF-2170
92UtiBluSC-23

Elsea, Dottie
89KinMetS-30
90KinMetS-29

Elster, Kevin
84LitFalMT-19
85LynMetT-19
86JacMetT-13
86MetWorSC-18
87Don-635
87Fle-7
87FleGlo-7
87IntLeaAT-6
87MetColP-31
87TidTidP-32
87TidTidT-13
88ClaRed-190
88Don-37
88DonBasB-70
88DonRoo-34
88DonTeaBM-37
88FleUpd-104
88FleUpdG-104
88Lea-37
88MetColP-22
88MetFanC-21
88MetKah-21
88Sco-624
88ScoGlo-624
88ScoYouS2-40
88SpoGam-24
88Top-8
88TopTif-8
89Bow-383
89BowTif-383
89ClaLigB-75
89Don-289
89DonBasB-97
89Fle-34
89FleGlo-34
89MetColP-7
89MetKah-7
89PanSti-127
89Sco-130
89Spo-71
89TidTidC-15
89Top-356
89TopBig-16
89TopRoo-6
89TopTif-356
89ToyRoo-7
89UppDec-269
90Bow-137
90BowTif-137
90Don-152
90DonBesN-31
90Fle-202
90FleCan-202
90Lea-8
90MetColP-7
90MetFanC-21
90MetKah-21
90MLBBasB-12
90OPC-734
90PanSti-296
90PubSti-132
90Sco-443
90Spo-118
90Top-734
90TopBig-143
90TopSti-2
90TopSti-97
90TopTif-734
90TopTVM-23
90UppDec-187
90VenSti-160
91Bow-469
91Don-304
91Fle-145
91Lea-305
91MetColP-15
91MetKah-21
91MetWIZ-107
91OPC-134
91PanFreS-82
91RedFolS-32
91Sco-633
91StaClu-149
91Top-134
91TopDesS-134
91TopMic-134
91TopTif-134
91Ult-215
91UppDec-101
92Don-307
92Fle-502
92MetColP-13
92MetKah-15
92OPC-251
92PanSti-225
92Pin-89
92Sco-103
92StaClu-201
92Top-251
92TopGol-251
92TopGolW-251
92TopMic-251
92TriPla-66
92Ult-231
92UppDec-385
93Fle-469
93PacSpa-195
96Cir-85
96CirRav-85
96FleRan-4
96FleUpd-U88
96FleUpdTC-U88
96RanMot-12
97Cir-34
97CirRav-34
97ColCho-238
97ColCho-426
97Don-150
97Don-333
97DonPreP-150
97DonPreP-333
97DonPrePGold-150
97DonPrePGold-333
97Fin-225
97FinRef-225
97Fle-220
97Fle-660
97FleTif-220
97FleTif-660
97Lea-106
97Lea-213
97LeaFraM-106
97LeaFraM-213
97LeaFraMDC-106
97LeaFraMDC-213
97NewPin-156
97NewPinAP-156
97NewPinMC-156
97NewPinPP-156
97Pac-198
97PacLigB-198
97PacSil-198
97Pin-67
97PinArtP-67
97PinMusC-67
97Sco-73
97Sco-346
97ScoHobR-346
97ScoPreS-73
97ScoRan-5
97ScoRanPl-5
97ScoRanPr-5
97ScoResC-346
97ScoShoS-73
97ScoShoS-346
97ScoShoSAP-73
97ScoShoSAP-346
97SP-141
97SpoIll-107
97SpoIllEE-107
97StaClu-138
97StaCluMOP-138
97Top-61
97Ult-131
97Ult-394
97UltGolME-131
97UltGolME-394
97UltPlaME-131
97UltPlaME-394
97UppDec-461

Elston, Carey
89BurIndS-10

Elston, Curt
12ImpTobC-23

Elston, Don (Donald Ray)
57Top-376
58Top-363
59Top-520
60CubJayP-6
60Top-233
61CubJayP-7
61Pos-200A
61Pos-200B
61Top-169
61TopStal-8
62CubJayP-6
62Jel-190
62Pos-190
62PosCan-190
62SalPlaC-101
62ShiPlaC-101
62Top-446
63CubJayP-5
63Top-515
64Top-111
64TopVen-111
65Top-436
78TCM60I-143
84CubUno-9
90DodTar-218

Elston, Guy
82NasSouTI-11
83ColCliT-13
84MaiGuiT-13

Elvira, Narciso
88StoPorCLC-183
88StoPorP-748
89StoPorS-6
91Bow-47
91DenZepLD-136
91DenZepP-117
91LinDriAAA-136
91TopDeb90-43
91UppDec-13
92OklCit8F-1911
92OklCit8S-323
94BreMilB-118

Elway, John
82OneYanT-13

Ely, Bones
90DodTar-943
98CamPepP-23

Embree, Alan
90BurIndP-3004
91ColIndC-12
91ColIndP-1479
92Bow-387
92KinIndC-17
92KinIndF-2469
93Bow-389
93Don-333
93FleMajLP-A5
93Pin-593
93ScoBoyoS-20
93StaClu-379
93StaCluFDI-379
93StaCluMOP-379
93Top-742
93TopGol-742
93TopInaM-742
93TopMic-742
93Toy-59
93UppDec-12
93UppDecGold-12
94CanIndF-3113
94UppDecML-22
95Bow-110
96ColCho-526
96ColChoGS-526
96ColChoSS-526
96Fle-85
96FleTif-85
96Sco-246
97ColCho-268
97Fle-676
97FleTif-676
97PacPriGotD-GD35
97Ult-445
97UltGolME-445
97UltPlaME-445

Embree, Red (Charles W.)
47IndTeal-7
47IndVanPP-6
48YanTeal-9
52MotCoo-22
79DiaGre-289

Embry, Todd
90WatDiaB-4
90WatDiaP-2370

Embser, Rich
85SprCarT-2
86ArkTraP-7

Emeralds, Eugene
92EugEmeC-30
92EugEmeF-3649

Emerick, Chris
90GatCitPP-3357
90GatCitPSP-7

Emerson, Scott
92BluOriC-15
92BluOriF-2355
93AlbPolC-14
93AlbPolF-2022
94FreKeyF-2607
94OriPro-30
97FreKeyC-10

Emery, Cal (Calvin Wayne)
77FriOneYW-73
79WatIndT-24
80WatIndT-30
81ChaChaT-24
89VanCanC-21
89VanCanP-572

Emiliano, James
96AshTouB-16

Emm, Art
90ColMetGS-17
90ColMetPPI-1

Emmerich, William P.
49W725AngTI-8

Emmerke, R.
87OldJudN-154

Emmett, John
94HelBreSP-28

Emoto, Kouichi
90SalSpuCLC-121
90SalSpuP-2715
Emoto, Takenori
79TCMJapPB-87
Empting, Mike
83CliGiaF-15
Emslie, Bob
94ConTSN-1203
94ConTSNB-1203
Enard, Tony
95ElmPioTI-3
95ElmPioUTI-3
96BreCouMB-14
96KanCouCTI-7
Enatsu, Yutaka
79TCMJapPB-27
Encarcion, Miguel
76BurBeeT-8
Encarnacion, Angelo
91WelPirC-10
91WelPirP-3574
92AugPirF-241
93CarLeaAGF-49
93SalBucC-8
93SalBucF-434
94CarMudF-1583
95PirFil-9
96ColCho-681
96ColChoGS-681
96ColChoSS-681
96Don-5
96DonPreP-5
96Fle-519
96FleTif-519
96Pac-179
96Ult-262
96UltGolM-262
97PacPriGotD-GD191
Encarnacion, Anito
93RanCucQC-10
93RanCucQF-834
95CedRapKTI-26
Encarnacion, Juan
90AshTouP-2760
94BriTigC-11
94BriTigF-3517
94FayGenC-11
94FayGenF-2162
95Bes-20
95BowBes-B49
95BowBesR-B49
95FayGenTI-10
95SPML-53
96Bow-268
96Exc-51
96LakTigB-13
97Bow-406
97BowChr-269
97BowChrI-269
97BowChrIR-269
97BowChrR-269
97BowInt-406
97Sel-133
97SelArtP-133
97SelRegG-133
97TopSta-101
97TopStaAM-101
Encarnacion, Luis
86WatIndP-8
87WilBilP-5
88MemChiB-12
89MemChiB-20
89MemChiP-1187
89MemChiS-10
89SouLeaAJ-22
90CMC-179
90OmaRoyC-4
90OmaRoyP-60
90ProAAAF-595
91LinDriAAA-334
91OmaRoyLD-334
91OmaRoyP-1029
91TopDeb90-44
93LimRocDWB-1
Encarnacion, Mario
96WesMicWB-8
Endebrock, Kurt
91SouOreAC-25
91SouOreAP-3853
92SouOreAC-27
92SouOreAF-3432
Ender, Scott
81CedRapRT-24
Endicott, Bill
46SeaSLP-16
Engel, Bob
88T/MUmp-5
89T/MUmp-3
90T/MUmp-3
Engel, Joe
88ChaLooLTI-10
Engel, Steve
86Don-510
86IowCubP-10
88ArkTraGS-3
Engelkin, Gary
88JacExpB-28
88JacExpP-990
89JamExpP-2149
Engelmeyer, Bob
77DayBealT-5
Engeln, William
55Bow-301
England, Dave
82ArkTraT-23
83ArkTraT-25
92HelBreF-1709
92HelBreSP-4
Engle, Dave (Ralph David)
79TolMudHT-7
80TolMudHT-15
80VenLeaS-10
81Top-328
82Don-102
82Fle-552
82Top-738
82TwiPos-8
83Don-646
83Top-294
83TwiTeal-14
83TwiTeal-32
84Don-598
84Fle-562
84MinTwiP-10
84Nes792-463
84Top-463
84TopSti-313
84TopTif-463
84TwiTeal-15
85Don-72
85Fle-276
85Lea-173
85OPC-199
85Top-667
85TopSti-298
85TopTif-667
85TwiTeal-15
86Don-438
86Fle-391
86FleUpd-39
86Top-43
86TopTif-43
87ExpPos-5
88OPC-196
88Sco-617
88ScoGlo-617
88Top-196
88TopTif-196
89BrePol-25
90OklCit8P-435
90ProAAAF-681
91LinDriAAA-625
91TucTorLD-625
91TucTorP-2229
92TucTorF-505
93TucTorF-3077
94BreMilB-218
94TucTorF-778
96JacGenB-1
Engle, Eleanor
91TopArc1-332
Engle, Hack (Arthur Clyde)
09AmeCarE-40
09ColChiE-94A
09ColChiE-94B
09T206-122
10CouT21-21
10DomDisP-40
10PeoT21-22
10SweCapPP-3A
10SweCapPP-3B
11SpoLifM-7
11T205-51
12ColRedB-94A
12ColRedB-94B
12ColTinT-94A
12ColTinT-94B
12HasTriFT-35
12HasTriFT-64
12T207-55
14PieStaT-21
15AmeCarE-16
86ConSer1-14
Engle, Rick
79MemChiT-14
Engle, Scott
84AriWilP-5
Engle, Tom
89HigSchPLS-3
89KinMetS-8
90KinMetB-22
90KinMetS-7
91ColMetPI-5
91ColMetPI-31
91ColMetPPI-5
92ColMetPI-29
93CapCitBC-4
93CapCitBF-453
93PitMetC-6
93PitMetF-3700
94Bow-70
94CapCitBC-6
94CapCitBF-1744
95BinMetTI-46
Englehart, Bill
84GreHorT-26
Englehart, Scott
92EriSaiC-12
92EriSaiF-1612
Engleka, Matt
96FayGenB-14
English, Gil
90DodTar-219
English, Jim
80AppFoxT-16
English, Maddy
94TedWil-95
English, Woody (Elwood G.)
28Exh-9
28StaPlaCE-18
29ExhFou-6
29PorandAR-21
30ChiEveAP-3
30SchR33-18
31CubTeal-7
31Exh-6
32CubTeal-5
32OrbPinNP-32A
32OrbPinNP-32B
32OrbPinUP-18
33ExhFou-3
33Gou-135
33NatLeaAC-2
33TatOrb-18
33TatOrbSDR-156
33TatOrbSDR-193
34DiaMatCSB-50
34DiaMatCSB-51
34ExhFou-3
34Gou-4
34GouCanV-11
34GouCanV-50
35DiaMatCS3T1-50
35GouPuzR-1F
35GouPuzR-3D
35GouPuzR-14D
35GouPuzR-15D
36SandSW-15
37ExhFou-2
77GalGloG-210
79DiaGre-86
90DodTar-944
93ConTSN-689
94ConTSN-1240
94ConTSNB-1240
Englishby, Steve
73CedRapAT-18
78DayBeaAT-7
Englund, Tim
86KnoBluJP-7
87KnoBluJP-1501
Engram, Duane
86PenWhiSP-10
Engram, Graylyn
87DayBeaAP-21
Ennen, Chuck
85CloHSS-15
Ennis, Alan
84NewOriT-8
Ennis, Del (Delmar)
46SpoExcW-3-3
47Exh-68
47HomBon-14
47PM1StaP1-55
49EurSta-134
49Lea-49
49MPR302-2-109
49PhiBul-17
49PhiLumPB-3
50Bow-31
50Dra-21
50JJKCopP-4
50PhiPhil-2
51BerRos-A10
51Bow-4
51R42SmaS-29
51TopBluB-4
52BerRos-17
52Bow-76
52NatTeaL-8
52Top-223
53BowC-103
53ExhCan-60
53RedMan-NL17
54Bow-127
54Wil-2
55BigLealS-6
55Bow-17
55DaiQueS-6
56Top-220
57Top-260
58CarJayP-4
58Top-60A
58Top-60B
59RedEnq-6
59RedShiBS-6
59Top-255
76TayBow4-14
79TCM50-18
83PhiPosGM-2
83PhiPosGPaM-6
83TopRep5-223
84TCMPla1-36
86PhiGreT-3
87Phi195T-6
89PacLegI-121
89SweBasG-19
93UppDecAH-45
94TedWil-73
94UppDecAH-32
94UppDecAH1-32
Ennis, Wayne
94PriRedC-8
94PriRedF-3268
Enno, Clayton
89SalDodTI-10
Enos, Dave
82ReaPhiT-13
Enos, Eric
88BatCliP-1671
Enright, George (George A.)
82QuaCitCT-26
84MidCubT-15
Enriquez, Graciano
91BelBreC-20
91BelBreP-2117
92BelBreC-17
92BelBreF-419
Enriquez, Martin
82WauTimF-15
83WauTimF-5
Ens, Jewel
92ConTSN-499
Enyart, Terry (Terry Gene)
79OgdA'sT-1
80OgdA'sT-8
Enzmann, Johnny
90DodTar-220
Ephan, Larry
94ChaRivC-6
94ChaRivF-2676
Epley, Daren
89KinIndS-6
90CanIndB-5
90CanIndP-1296
90CanIndS-4
91CanIndLD-82
91CanIndP-985
91LinDriAA-82
92CloSprSSS-85
92SkyAAAF-37
93TulDriF-2746
93TulDriTI-8
Eppard, Jim
84AlbA'sT-24
85ModA'sC-13
86TacTigP-5
87EdmTraP-2061
88EdmTraC-21
88EdmTraP-558
88Fle-645
88FleGlo-645
88FleUpd-13
88FleUpdG-13
89EdmTraC-14
89EdmTraP-548
89Fle-476
89FleGlo-476
89Sco-607
89Top-42
89TopTif-42
89UppDec-614
90CMC-339
90ProAAAF-356
90SyrChiC-13
90SyrChiMB-7
90SyrChiP-576
92IndIndF-1873
92IndIndS-180
94CenValRC-29
94CenValRF-3219
Epperly, Al
79DiaGre-110
90DodTar-221
Epperly, Tom
76TacTwiDQ-5
77OrlTwiT-7
Epperson, Chad
92GulCoaMF-3483
93KinMetC-10
93KinMetF-3799
94St.LucMC-7
94St.LucMF-1197
95StLucMTI-12
Epple, Tom
82SprCarF-8
83St.PetCT-6
Epps, Hal
96Bro194F-35
Epps, Riley
86SalRedBP-7
Epps, Scott
90ArkRaz-9
93PriWilCF-658
94TamYanC-9
94TamYanF-2385
95NorNavTI-11
Epstein, Mike (Michael P.)
67Top-204
68SenTeal-4
68Top-358
68TopVen-358
69MilBra-79
69MLBOffS-104
69SenTeal-7
69SenTeal8-10
69Top-461A
69Top-461B
69Top-539
69TopSta-235
69TopTeaP-23
69TraSta-25
70DayDaiNM-98
70Kel-24
70MLBOffS-282
70OPC-235
70SenPolY-4
70Top-235
70TopBoo-12
71Kel-34
71MLBOffS-535
71OPC-655
71Top-655
71TopCoi-126
72MilBra-99
72Top-715
73OPC-38
73Top-38
73TopCanL-14
74OPC-650
74Top-650
74TopSta-142
78TCM60I-261
91OriCro-121
93HelBreSP-27
93RanKee-136
Erardi, Joe (Joseph G.)

77HolMilT-8
Erautt, Eddie (Edward L.S.)
49EurSta-82
52Top-171
53Top-226
57SeaPop-11
83TopRep5-171
91TopArc1-226
Erautt, Joe (Joseph M.)
52MotCoo-43
Erb, Gerry
77NewCoPT-11
Erb, Mike
87SalAngP-24
88PalSprACLC-86
88PalSprAP-1443
89QuaCitAB-10
89QuaCitAGS-14
90CMC-483
90EdmTraC-6
90EdmTraP-513
90ProAAAF-89
91EdmTraLD-154
91EdmTraP-1511
91LinDriAAA-154
92JacSunS-369
Erdahl, Jay Michael
82WauTimF-21
Erdman, Brad
90GenCubP-3033
90GenCubS-11
90PeoChiTI-4
91MidLeaAP-MWL8
91PeoChiC-10
91PeoChiP-1344
91PeoChiTI-14
92ClaFS7-317
92WinSpiC-11
92WinSpiF-1210
93OrlCubF-2787
93PeoChiF-1087
94DayCubC-5
94DayCubF-2355
94FloStaLAF-FSL33
96IowCubB-12
Erdos, Todd
93SpoIndC-7
93SpoIndF-3584
93WatDiaC-14
93WatDiaF-1761
95IdaFalBTI-25
96RanCucQB-12
Ereu, William
80VenLeaS-61
93LinVenB-102
Erhard, Barney
91BelMarC-9
91BelMarP-3673
92BelMarC-23
92BelMarF-1451
Erhardt, Herb
88OneYanP-2046
89Ft.LauYS-3
90PriWilCTI-9
91ChaWheC-16
91ChaWheP-2893
Ericks, John
89Bow-433
89BowTif-433
89SavCarP-371
89SouAtlLAGS-36
90ArkTraGS-10
90Bow-190
90BowTif-190
90St.PetCS-6
90TopTVCa-46
91ArkTraLD-30
91ArkTraP-1277
91Bow-393
91Cla/Bes-287
91LinDriAA-30
91UppDec-57
92ArkTraF-1124
92ArkTraS-33
92Bow-48
92ClaFS7-332
92SkyAA F-16
94SalBucC-8
94SalBucF-2318
96Don-265
96DonPreP-265
96Fla-344
96Fle-520
96FleTif-520
96LeaSigEA-47
96StaClu-355
96StaCluMOP-355
96Ult-263
96UltGolM-263
97Cir-376
97CirRav-376
97Fle-539
97FleTif-539
97Ult-325
97UltGolME-325
97UltPlaME-325
Erickson, Corey
96PitMetB-9
97Bow-380
97BowInt-380
Erickson, Don
89BelBreIS-3
Erickson, Eric G.
23WilChoV-38
82CliGiaF-22
86FreGiaP-14
87LynMetP-7
Erickson, Greg
92ForLauYTI-8
93CarLeaAGF-20
93PriWilCC-8
93PriWilCF-662
94AbaYanF-1447
94TamYanC-10
94TamYanF-2391
Erickson, Hal (Harold J.)
53TigGle-6
Erickson, Hank (Henry Nels)
36GouWidPPR-D8
Erickson, Paul
41CubTeal-3
43CubTeal-7
44CubTeal-7
Erickson, Roger F.
78TwiFriP-6
79Hos-94
79OPC-34
79Top-81
79TwiFriP-6
80Top-256
81Don-549
81Fle-561
81OPC-80
81Top-434
81TopSti-105
82Don-303
82Fle-553
82Top-153
82TopSti-211
82TopStiV-211
82TopTra-30T
82TwiPos-9
83Fle-378
83Top-539
87SanJosBP-23
89LouRedBC-3
89LouRedBP-1242
89LouRedBTI-17
90SprCarB-27
91PacSenL-98
91SprCarC-29
91SprCarP-760
91TopTriH-A9
92YanWIZ8-52
Erickson, Scott
90Bes-106
90ButCopKSP-13
90OrlSunRB-16
90OrlSunRP-1077
90OrlSunRS-5
90ProAaA-41
90TopMag-62
90TopTra-29T
90TopTraT-29T
91Bow-335
91Cla2-T16
91Cla3-T17
91Cla3-NNO
91ClaGam-160
91Don-767
91Fle-608
91GasRanC-5
91GasRanP-2682
91Lea-527
91OPC-234
91Sco-812
91StaClu-560
91Stu-83
91Top-234
91TopDeb90-45
91TopDesS-234
91TopMic-234
91TopTif-234
91UltUpd-36
91UppDec-522
92Bow-53
92ClaGam-93
92Don-463
92DonCraJ2-33
92DonDiaK-DK21
92Fle-201
92Fle-693
92FleAll-10
92FleSmo'nH-S6
92Fre-5
92Hig5-82
92Hig5S-10
92KinDis-23
92Lea-166
92LeaGolP-21
92LeaPre-21
92OPC-605
92Pin-106
92PinTea2-60
92Pos-18
92RemUltP-P10
92RemUltP-P11
92RemUltP-P12
92Sco-60
92Sco-438
92Sco-889
92Sco100S-2
92ScoImpP-13
92StaClu-110
92Stu-202
92SunSee-23
92Top-605
92TopGol-605
92TopGolW-605
92TopKid-110
92TopMic-605
92TriPla-3
92Ult-90
92UppDec-89
92UppDec-146
92UppDecTMH-20
93Bow-425
93ClaGam-29
93Don-211
93Fin-142
93FinRef-142
93Fle-263
93FunPac-192
93Lea-142
93OPC-77
93PacSpa-169
93PanSti-123
93Pin-163
93Sco-206
93Sel-253
93SP-245
93StaClu-443
93StaCluFDI-443
93StaCluMOP-443
93Top-90
93TopGol-90
93TopInaM-90
93TopMic-90
93TriPla-33
93Ult-230
93UppDec-397
93UppDecGold-397
94ColC-96
94ColChoGS-96
94ColChoSS-96
94Don-437
94ExtBas-116
94Fin-166
94FinPre-166P
94FinRef-166
94Fla-73
94Fle-202
94Lea-227
94Pac-351
94Pin-361
94PinArtP-361
94PinMusC-361
94Sco-461
94ScoGolR-461
94Sel-171
94SP-184
94SPDieC-184
94StaClu-637
94StaCluFDI-637
94StaCluGR-637
94StaCluMOP-637
94Top-365
94TopGol-365
94TopSpa-365
94TriPla-252
94Ult-85
94UppDec-503
94UppDecED-503
95ColCho-483
95ColChoGS-483
95ColChoSE-225
95ColChoSEGS-225
95ColChoSESS-225
95ColChoSS-483
95Don-161
95DonPreP-161
95DonTopotO-6
95Fla-279
95Fle-201
95Lea-287
95Pac-248
95Pin-335
95PinArtP-335
95PinMusC-335
95Sco-27
95ScoGolR-27
95ScoPlaTS-27
95StaClu-429
95StaCluMOP-429
95StaCluSTWS-429
95StaCluVR-225
95Stu-166
95Top-617
95TopCyb-385
95Ult-301
95UltGolM-301
95UppDec-428
95UppDec-471T
95UppDecED-428
95UppDecEDG-428
95UppDecSE-83
95UppDecSEG-83
96ColCho-57
96ColChoGS-57
96ColChoSS-57
96Don-311
96DonPreP-311
96Fla-4
96Fle-7
96FleOri-5
96FleTif-7
96Pac-231
96Sco-401
96StaClu-51
96StaCluMOP-51
95StaCluVRMC-225
96Ult-4
96UltGolM-4
96UppDec-13
97Cir-245
97CirRav-245
97ColCho-37
97Fle-6
97FleTif-6
97Pac-22
97PacLigB-22
97PacSil-22
97Sco-400
97ScoHobR-400
97ScoResC-400
97ScoShoS-400
97ScoShoSAP-400
97StaClu-291
97StaCluMOP-291
97Top-347
97UppDec-307
Erickson, Steve
87OneYanP-8
88Ft.LauYS-7
89Ft.LauYS-4
Erickson, Tim
87WauTimP-28
Ericson, Mark
88KenTwiP-1394
Ericson, Mike
89AncGlaP-15
90MiaMirIS-7
91MiaMirC-6
91MiaMirP-400
92VisOakC-8
92VisOakF-1008
93CenValRC-10
93CenValRF-2887
94NewHavRF-1544
Erikson, Greg
92Ft.LauYF-2618
Ermer, Cal (Calvin C.)
68Top-206
68TopVen-206
70BreMcD-6
70BreMil-4
74TacTwiC-4
75TacTwiK-10
76TacTwiDQ-6
79TolMudHT-3
80TolMudHT-3
81TolMudHT-1
82TolMudHT-23
83TolMudHT-23
84TolMudHT-6
85TolMudHT-26
88ChaLooLTI-12
Ermis, Chris
91MedHatBJP-4093
91MedHatBJSP-5
Erskine, Carl (Carl Daniel)
47PM1StaP1-56
51Bow-260
52Bow-70
52Top-250
53BowC-12
53Bri-30
53Dor-124
54Bow-10
54NewYorJA-4
54RedHeaF-6
54RedMan-NL4
54StaMey-2
54Wil-3
55Bow-170
55DodGolS-3
55RedMan-NL14
55StaMey-2
56Dod-8
56Top-233
57Top-252
58Top-258
59DodTeal-6
59DodVol-4
59Top-217
60NuHi-69
61NuSco-469
70FleWorS-50
76SSP-594
77SerSta-8
79DiaGre-99
79TCM50-146
81SanDieSC-7
83TopRep5-250
84FifNatCT-4
84OCoandSI-74
86TCMSupS-1
87Dod195T-9
88PacLegI-75
88RinPosD1-1C
88RinPosD1-11B
89DodSmoG-60
89SweBasG-44
90DodTar-222
90PacLeg-14
90SweBasG-36
91SweBasG-27
91TopArc1-308
92ActPacA-54
92BazQua5A-11
93TedWil-13
93UppDecAH-46
94UppDecAH-187
94UppDecAH1-187
95TopArcBD-15
95TopArcBD-61
95TopArcBD-86
95TopArcBD-133
95TopArcBD-157
Erstad, Darin
95ARuFalLS-4
95Bes-128
95BesFra-F1
95LakElsSTI-14
95SPML-25
95SPML-100
95SPMLDtS-DS11
96Cir-19

96CirRav-19
96Exc-26
96ExcFirYP-4
96LeaLimR-2
96LeaLimRG-2
96LeaSig-94
96LeaSigEA-48
96LeaSigEACM-5
96LeaSigPPG-94
96LeaSigPPP-94
96SigRooOJPP-P1
96SP-4
96UppDecDD-DD12
96UppDecDDG-DD12
96UppDecDDS-DD12
96VanCanB-12
96Zen-130
96ZenArtP-130
96ZenDiaC-16
96ZenDiaCP-16
97Bow-92
97BowBes-115
97BowBesAR-115
97BowBesBC-BC13
97BowBesBCAR-BC13
97BowBesBCR-BC13
97BowBesR-115
97BowCerBIA-CA23
97BowCerGIA-CA23
97BowChr-116
97BowChrI-116
97BowChrIR-116
97BowChrR-116
97BowChrSHR-SHR8
97BowChrSHRR-SHR8
97BowInt-92
97BowScoHR-8
97Cir-241
97CirEmeA-241
97CirEmeAR-AU1
97CirRav-241
97ColCho-5
97Don-356
97DonEli-58
97DonEliGS-58
97DonEliTotC-8
97DonEliTotCDC-8
97DonFraFea-2
97DonLim-27
97DonLim-71
97DonLim-198
97DonLimFotG-26
97DonLimLE-27
97DonLimLE-71
97DonLimLE-198
97DonPre-133
97DonPreCttC-133
97DonPreP-356
97DonPrePGold-356
97DonRatR-24
97DonRooDK-8
97DonRooDKC-8
97DonTea-10
97DonTeaSPE-10
97Fin-37
97Fin-276
97FinEmb-276
97FinEmbR-276
97FinRef-37
97FinRef-276
97FlaSho-A39
97FlaSho-B39
97FlaSho-C39
97FlaShoLC-39
97FlaShoLC-B39
97FlaShoLC-C39
97FlaShoLCM-A39
97FlaShoLCM-B39
97FlaShoLCM-C39
97Fle-41
97FleNewH-3
97FleRooS-5
97FleTif-41
97Lea-149
97Lea-399
97LeaFraM-149
97LeaFraM-399
97LeaFraMDC-149
97LeaFraMDC-399
97LeaGolS-25
97LeaLeaotN-14
97MetUni-40
97MetUniEAR-AU1
97NewPin-115
97NewPinAP-115
97NewPinMC-115
97NewPinPP-115
97Pac-6
97PacLigB-6
97PacPri-3
97PacPriLB-3
97PacPriP-3
97PacSil-6
97Pin-161
97Pin-199
97PinArtP-161
97PinArtP-199
97PinCar-16
97PinCer-31
97PinCerMBlu-31
97PinCerMG-31
97PinCerMR-31
97PinCerR-31
97PinIns-110
97PinInsCE-110
97PinInsDD-19
97PinInsDE-110
97PinMusC-161
97PinMusC-199
97PinTotCPB-31
97PinTotCPG-31
97PinTotCPR-31
97PinX-P-82
97PinX-PF&A-12
97PinX-PMoS-82
97Sco-24
97Sco-506
97ScoHeaotO-31
97ScoHobR-506
97ScoPreS-24
97ScoResC-506
97ScoShoS-24
97ScoShoS-506
97ScoShoSAP-24
97ScoShoSAP-506
97Sel-100
97SelArtP-100
97SelRegG-100
97SelRooR-16
97SelToootT-11
97SelToootTMB-11
97SkyE-X-2
97SkyE-XC-2
97SkyE-XEAR-AU1
97SkyE-XEC-2
97SkyE-XSD2-6
97SP-17
97SpoIll-61
97SpoIllEE-61
97SPSpeF-42
97SPx-2
97SPxBro-2
97SPxGraF-2
97SPxSil-2
97SPxSte-2
97StaClu-248
97StaCluMat-248
97StaCluMOP-248
97Stu-162
97StuHarH-23
97StuPrePG-162
97StuPrePS-162
97TopGal-147
97TopGalPPI-147
97TopStaFAS-FAS7
97Ult-26
97UltAutE-4
97UltGolME-26
97UltPlaME-26
97UltRooR-3
97UppDec-230
97UppDecBCP-BC8
97UppDecRSF-RS4
97UppDecTTS-TS9
97UppDecU-45
97UppDecUGN-GN6
97Zen-36

Ervin, Chris
91BelBreC-21

Ervin, Kent
96IdaFalB-8

Erwin, Mat
95ElmPioTI-4
95ElmPioUTI-4

Erwin, Scott
88CapCodPPaLP-78
89MedAthB-5
90ModA'sC-9
90ModA'sCLC-149
90ModA'sP-2205
91ModA'sP-3079
92ClaFS7-135
92HunStaF-3942
92HunStaS-309
92SkyAA F-130
92UppDecML-92

Erwin, Terry
75BurBeeT-6

Erwin, Tex (Ross Emil)
09AmeCarE-54
10DomDisP-41
10SweCapPP-73
11SpoLifM-155
12T207-56
90DodTar-223

Esasky, Nick (Nicholas A.)
80WatRedT-21
81IndIndTI-15
82IndIndTI-4
83IndIndTI-5
84Don-602
84Fle-468
84Nes792-192
84OPC-192
84RedEnq-7
84Top-192
84TopSti-378
84TopTif-192
85Don-121
85Fle-534
85IndIndTI-35
85OPC-253
85RedYea-4
85Top-779
85TopSti-51
85TopTif-779
86BasStaB-39
86Don-286
86Fle-177
86Lea-162
86OPC-201
86RedTexG-12
86Top-677
86TopTif-677
87Don-166
87Fle-201
87FleGlo-201
87OPC-13
87RedKah-12
87Top-13
87TopTif-13
88Don-413
88DonBasB-118
88Fle-233
88FleGlo-233
88Lea-240
88OPC-364
88PanSti-274
88RedKah-12
88Sco-163
88ScoGlo-163
88StaLinRe-8
88Top-364
88TopBig-167
88TopSti-137
88TopTif-364
89Bow-31
89BowTif-31
89Don-189
89DonBasB-284
89DonTra-18
89Fle-161
89FleGlo-161
89FleUpd-9
89OPC-262
89PanSti-72
89Sco-64
89ScoRoo-37T
89Top-554
89TopBig-316
89TopSti-134
89TopTif-554
89TopTra-29T
89TopTraT-29T
89UppDec-299
89UppDec-757
90Bow-20
90BowTif-20
90BraDubP-6
90BraDubS-7
90Don-303
90DonBesN-13
90Fle-273
90FleCan-273
90FleLeaL-10
90FleUpd-3
90Lea-164
90OPC-206
90PanSti-26
90PubSti-453
90Sco-91
90ScoRoo-3T
90Spo-72
90Top-206
90TopBig-251
90TopMinL-5
90TopSti-263
90TopTif-206
90TopTra-30T
90TopTraT-30T
90UppDec-463
90UppDec-758
90VenSti-161
91BraDubP-8
91BraSubS-12
91Fle-687
91OPC-418
91SimandSMLBL-15
91Stu-143
91Top-418
91TopDesS-418
91TopMic-418
91TopTif-418
92BraLykP-10
92OPC-405
92StaClu-497
97RicBraBC-24

Escalera, Carlos
86BelBreP-5
86EugEmeC-30
87AppFoxP-6
88BasCitRS-11
88BlaYNPRWL-69
88FloStaLAS-34
89BlaYNPRWLU-34
89MemChiB-10
89MemChiP-1182
89MemChiS-11

Escalera, Nino
77FriOneYW-10

Escalera, Ruben
87StoPorP-14
88BlaYNPRWL-134
88CalLeaACLC-17
88StoPorCLC-200
88StoPorP-735
89BlaYNPRWL-6
89ElPasDGS-27
90CMC-49
90DenZepC-24
90DenZepP-637
90ElPasDGS-11
90ProAAAF-662
91ElPasDLD-180
91ElPasDP-2759
91LinDriAA-180
92NasSouS-283

Escalet, Roberto
94HelBreF-3621
94HelBreSP-1

Escamilla, Jaime
94HudValRF-3376
95ChaRivTI-9
95Exc-128
94HudValRC-4

Escamilla, Roman
96SpoIndB-11

Escandon, Emiliano
95SpoIndTI-4
96LanLugB-10

Escarrega, Acosta (Ernesto)
83Don-291
83Fle-234

Eschen, Jim
77EvaTriT-9
89KinMetS-26
90PitMetP-25
91LinDriAA-650
91WilBilLD-650
91WilBilP-310

Escobar, Angel
85FreGiaP-4
86ShrCapP-7
87PhoFirP-7
88PhoFirC-14
88PhoFirP-63
89HunStaB-25
93LinVenB-115
94VenLinU-218

Escobar, John
88MarPhiS-13
89BatCliP-1940
90SpaPhiB-15
90SpaPhiP-2497
90SpaPhiS-6
91ClePhiC-16
91ClePhiP-1627
92ReaPhiF-580
92ReaPhiS-530
93ReaPhiF-300

Escobar, Jose
80UtiBluJT-15
80VenLeaS-51
83KinBluJTI-5
87SyrChiP-1944
87SyrChiT-13
88KnoBluJB-13
89SyrChiMB-9
90CMC-341
90ProAAAF-357
90SyrChiC-15
90SyrChiMB-8
90SyrChiP-577
91Bow-74
91IndFanC-9
92TopDeb91-51

Escobar, Kelvim
95LinVen-189
96DunBluJB-7
96DunBluJTI-9
96DunBluJUTI-1
97Bow-394
97BowChr-260
97BowChrI-260
97BowChrIR-260
97BowChrR-260
97BowInt-394

Escobar, Oscar
86VenGulP-6
87MyrBeaBJP-1436
88SalBucS-6
93LinVenB-137

Escobar, Rodney
90WicStaSGD-10

Escribano, Eddie
83MadMusF-17

Eshelman, Vaughn
91BluOriC-7
91BluOriP-4120
91KanCouCTI-5
92Bow-318
92StaCluD-44
93FreKeyC-6
93FreKeyF-1019
94Bow-431
94BowBayF-2408
94OriPro-31
95BowBes-R76
95BowBesR-R76
95ColCho-573T
95Emo-11
95Fin-254
95FinRef-254
95Fla-227
95FlaWavotF-5
95FleUpd-10
95SelCer-113
95SelCerMG-113
95SigRoo-16
95SigRooOJSS-7
95SigRooOJSSS-7
95SigRooSig-16
95StaClu-623
95StaCluMOP-623
95StaCluSTWS-623
95Sum-113
95SumNthD-113
95TopTra-92T
95UC3-108
95UC3ArtP-108
95UltGolMR-M11
95UppDec-481T
95Zen-115
96ColCho-62
96ColChoGS-62
96ColChoSS-62
96Don-29
96DonPreP-29
96Fle-26

96FleRedS-5
96FleTif-26
96Pac-250
96Sco-472
97PacPriGotD-GD19
Eskew, Dan
88SouOreAP-1711
89ModA'sC-10
90Bes-51
90HunStaB-5
91HunStaTI-9
91LinDriAAA-532
91TacTigLD-532
91TacTigP-2297
Eskins, Mark
88IdaFalBP-1856
Esmond, Jimmy (James J.)
09ColChiE-95
12ColRedB-95
12ColTinT-95
Espada, Angel
95DanBraTI-10
96EugEmeB-8
Espada, Joe
96SouOreTI-28
Espinal, Josue
88SouOreAP-1700
Espinal, Juan
94SprSulC-9
94SprSulF-2043
Espinal, Mendy
87CedRapRP-9
Espinal, Sergio
86GenCubP-5
87PeoChiP-4
88PeoChiTI-10
Espinal, Willie (Bill)
89JohCitCS-11
90ProAaA-76
90SavCarP-2062
91SprCarC-15
91SprCarP-737
Espino, Francisco
87WytCubP-17
88GenCubP-1648
89GenCubP-1860
89PeoChiTI-3
Espino, Juan
76ForLauYS-29
77ForLauYS-29
79WesHavYT-24
80ColCliT-28
81ColCliP-29
81ColCliT-15
82ColCliP-29
82ColCliT-23
83ColCliT-3
84Don-92
84MaiGuiT-17
85ColCliP-9
85ColCliT-11
85DomLeaS-161
85IntLeaAT-32
86ColCliP-7
87ColCliP-8
87ColCliP-4
87ColCliT-10
87Top-239
87TopTif-239
88RicBraC-20
88RicBraP-7
92YanWIZ8-53
86STaoftFT-4
97BobCamRB-9
Espinosa, Nino (Anulfo A.)
75TidTidTI-10
77MetDaiPA-5
77Top-376
78MetDaiPA-5
78Top-197
79OPC-292
79PhiBurK-11
79Top-566
80OPC-233
80PhiBurK-17
80Top-447
81Fle-20
81Top-405
85DomLeaS-49
89TidTidC-7
91MetWIZ-108
Espinosa, Philip
87AncGlaP-9
Espinosa, Ramon
92WelPirC-7
92WelPirF-1336
93AugPirC-7
93AugPirF-1559
94CarMudF-1593
95CarMudF-171
Espinosa, Santiago
86SalAngC-98
87QuaCitAP-4
87SalAngP-18
Espinosa, Wendee
96ColSilB-10
Espinoza, Alvaro
80VenLeaS-24
82WisRapTF-7
83VisOakF-23
84TolMudHT-3
85TolMudHT-15
85TwiTeal-1
86TolMudHP-9
87PorBeaP-14
87Top-529
87TopTif-529
88ColCliC-15
88ColCliP-15
88ColCliP-320
89DonBasB-161
89FleUpd-47
89TopTra-30T
89TopTraT-30T
89YanScoNW-3
90Bow-431
90BowTif-431
90Don-245
90DonBesA-123
90Fle-441
90FleCan-441
90Lea-240
90OPC-791
90PanSti-121
90Sco-101
90Top-791
90TopBig-8
90TopSti-311
90TopTif-791
90TopTVY-24
90UppDec-163
90YanScoNW-4
91Bow-163
91Don-226
91Fle-662
91Lea-198
91OPC-28
91PanFreS-327
91PanSti-269
91Sco-127
91StaClu-242
91StaCluP-13
91Top-28
91TopDesS-28
91TopMic-28
91TopTif-28
91Ult-230
91UppDec-204
92ColSprSSF-757
92ColSprSSS-86
92Don-474
92Fle-224
92OPC-243
92PanSti-138
92Sco-41
92StaClu-527
92Top-243
92TopGol-243
92TopGolW-243
92TopMic-243
92Ult-100
92UppDec-119
92UppDecS-1
92YanWIZ8-54
93FleFinE-200
93IndWUA-8
93LinVenB-276
93PacBeiA-6
93PacSpa-410
94Fle-103
94Pac-168
94Sco-141
94ScoGolR-141
94StaClu-461
94StaCluFDI-461
94StaCluGR-461
94StaCluMOP-461
94Top-726
94TopGol-726
94TopSpa-726
94VenLinU-26
95Don-303
95DonPreP-303
95Fle-134
95LinVen-79
95Pac-119
96Fle-86
96FleTif-86
96LeaSigEA-49
96Pac-305
97Fle-393
97FleTif-393
97Pac-361
97PacLigB-361
97PacSil-361
97StaClu-314
97StaCluMOP-314
Espinoza, Andres
85LitFalMT-17
86QuaCitAP-10
87PalSprP-31
93LinVenB-154
94VenLinU-14
95LinVen-83
Espinoza, Carlos
90GatCitPP-3343
Espinoza, Jose
92GulCoaMF-3488
Espinoza, Roberto
80VenLeaS-9
93LinVenB-191
Espinoza-Watson, Laura
96ColSilB-11
Espinsosa, Santiago
86QuaCitAP-9
Esposito, Nick
83TriTriT-9
Esposito, Sammy (Samuel)
57Top-301
58Top-425
59Top-438
60Top-31
60TopVen-31
61Top-323
61WhiSoxTS-4
62Top-586
63Top-181
79DiaGre-145
Epstein, Ian
95WesMicWTI-29
Espy, Cecil (Cecil Edward)
81AppFoxT-14
82VerBeaDT-22
86HawIsIP-5
87OklCit8P-16
88BlaYNPRWL-56
88DonRoo-9
88Fle-465
88FleGlo-465
88RanMot-13
88ScoRoo-73T
88ScoRooG-73T
88TopTra-36T
88TopTraT-36T
89Baz-7
89Bow-236
89BowTif-236
89ClaTraO-143
89Don-292
89DonBasB-335
89Fle-517
89FleGlo-517
89K-M-6
89PanSti-443
89RanMot-12
89RanSmo-7
89Sco-401
89ScoYouS2-10
89Top-221
89TopBig-36
89TopGloS-59
89TopRoo-7
89TopSti-240
89TopSti-320
89TopTif-221
89ToyRoo-8
89UppDec-92
90Bow-502
90BowTif-502
90DodTar-224
90Don-260
90Fle-295
90FleCan-295
90OPC-496
90PubSti-407
90RanMot-25
90Sco-69
90Top-496
90TopBig-37
90TopMinL-36
90TopSti-249
90TopTif-496
90UppDec-371
90VenSti-162
91BufBisLD-27
91BufBisP-551
91LinDriAAA-27
92Don-678
92PirNatl-8
92Sco-673
92StaClu-95
92Ult-552
93RanKee-137
Espy, Duane
75SacSolC-7
77SpoIndC-1
78SpoIndC-1
79BurBeeT-17
80BurBeeT-10
84ShrCapFB-7
86PhoFirP-5
87PhoFirP-22
88SanJosGCLC-141
88SanJosGP-125
89CalLeaA-49
89SanJosGB-28
89SanJosGCLC-235
89SanJosGP-453
89SanJosGS-27
90CMC-551
90PhoFirC-24
90PhoFirP-27
90ProAAAF-53
91LinDriAAA-399
91PhoFirLD-399
91PhoFirP-83
93PhoFirF-1533
94PhoFirF-1536
Esquer, Dave (David)
87NewOriP-1
89QuaCitAB-7
89QuaCitAGS-25
90PalSprACLC-204
90PalSprAP-2583
Esquer, Mercedes
83KnoBluJT-4
Essegian, Chuck (Charles A.)
58Top-460
59Top-278
60DodBelB-11
60DodTeal-6
60DodUniO-6
60Top-166
60TopVen-166
61Top-384
62Jel-45
62Pos-45
62PosCan-45
62Top-379
63Jel-71
63Pos-71
63Top-103
70FleWorS-56
90DodTar-225
91OriCro-122
Esser, Mark (Mark Gerald)
78AppFoxT-8
80GleFalWSBT-14
80GleFalWSCT-5
Essian, Jim (James Sarkis)
76SSP-142
77Top-529
77WhiSoxJT-3
78Top-98
79OPC-239
79Top-458
80OPC-179
80Top-341
81CokTeaS-28
81Don-503
81Fle-593
81Top-178
81TopTra-759
82Don-369
82Fle-341
82Top-269
82TopTra-31T
83Don-478
83IndPos-11
83IndWhe-10
83Top-646
83TopSti-117
83TopTra-30T
84A'sMot-19
84Don-629
84Fle-540
84FleUpd-35
84Nes792-737
84Top-737
84TopTif-737
84TopTra-35T
84TopTraT-35T
85Fle-423
85Top-472
85TopTif-472
86WinSpiP-7
87PitCubP-4
88BlaYNPRWL-97
88EasLeaAP-47
88PitCubP-1360
89ChaKniTI-2
90CMC-99
90IowCubC-24
90IowCubP-333
90ProAAAF-640
91CubMar-41
91IowCubLD-224
91IowCubP-1076
91LinDriAAA-224
91TopTra-36T
91TopTraT-36T
96NorNavB-1
Estalella, Bobby
93MarPhiC-8
93MarPhiF-3476
94SpaPhiF-1726
94SparPhiC-7
95ClePhiF-218
95ReaPhiELC-12
96BesAutS-31
96BesAutSA-19
96Bow-248
96Exc-201
96ReaPhiB-13
97Bow-375
97BowBes-163
97BowBesAR-163
97BowBesR-163
97BowCerBIA-CA24
97BowCerGIA-CA24
97BowChr-249
97BowChrI-249
97BowChrIR-249
97BowChrR-249
97BowInt-375
97Cir-367
97CirRav-367
97Fle-411
97FleTif-411
97Lea-328
97LeaFraM-328
97LeaFraMDC-328
97Pac-378
97PacLigB-378
97PacSil-378
97Top-205
97UppDec-287
Estalella, Bobby (Roberto M.)
41BroW75-9
Estavil, Mauricio
95PiePhiF-181
Esteban, Felipe
87VerBeaDP-21
88VerBeaDS-6
Estelle, Dick (Richard H.)
65OPC-282
65Top-282
66Top-373
Estep, Chad
93DavLipB-8
94DavLipB-9
95DavLipB-10
Estep, Chris
87AncGlaP-10
88WatPirP-18
89AugPirP-499
90CarLeaA-25
90SalBucS-5

91CarMudLD-107
91CarMudP-1097
91LinDriAA-107
92CarMudS-133
92CedRapRF-1082
92ChaLooF-3830
Estep, Richie
95DavLipB-11
Estepa, Ramon
80SanJosMJitB-6
81LynSaiT-21
82LynSaiT-14
83ChaLooT-5
84ChaLooT-2
Estepan, Rafael
80CliGiaT-18
Esterbrook, Dude (Thomas J.)
86OldJudN-5
87BucN28-58
87OldJudN-155
88GandBCGCE-13
88SpoTimM-10
88WG1CarG-31
90DodTar-226
90KalBatN-15
94OriofB-64
Esterday, Henry
87OldJudN-156
Estes, Doc (Frank)
77OrlTwiT-8
78OrlTwiT-6
80OrlTwiT-9
81TolMudHT-21
85IntLeaAT-8
85RicBraT-18
86RicBraP-6
87SyrChiP-1949
87SyrChiT-22
Estes, Joel
84AriWilP-6
86AriWilP-2
86AubAstP-9
87OscAstP-20
89ColMudP-128
89ColMudS-7
90Bes-97
90SanJosGB-17
90SanJosGCLC-45
90SanJosGP-2007
90SanJosGS-8
Estes, Marc
86MiaMarP-7
Estes, Mark
89GeoColC-5
90GeoColC-2
Estes, Shawn
91BelMarC-29
91BelMarP-3656
91Cla/Bes-429
91ClaDraP-8
91HigSchPLS-11
92BelMarC-1
92BelMarF-1435
92Bow-151
92OPC-624
92ProFS7-146
92StaCluD-45
92Top-624
92TopGol-624
92TopGolW-624
92TopMic-624
92UppDecML-164
93AppFoxC-1
93AppFoxF-2455
93Bow-275
93ClaFS7-70
93ClaGolF-191
93ExcFS7-224
93StaCluMari-30
94Bow-473
95ARuFalLS-5
95Bow-205
96Bow-173
96ColCho-722
96ColChoGS-722
96ColChoSS-722
96Fle-587
96FleTif-587
96PhoFirB-16
96Sco-496
96Spo-134
96SpoArtP-134
97Cir-142
97CirRav-142
97Don-140
97DonLim-80
97DonLimLE-80
97DonPreP-140
97DonPrePGold-140
97Fle-480
97FleTif-480
97Lea-50
97LeaFraM-50
97LeaFraMDC-50
97MetUni-243
97Pac-442
97PacLigB-442
97PacSil-442
97Sco-270
97ScoPreS-270
97ScoShoS-270
97ScoShoSAP-270
97StaClu-370
97StaCluMOP-370
97TopSta-32
97TopStaAM-32
97Ult-294
97UltGolME-294
97UltPlaME-294
Estevez, Bernado
76ForLauYS-7
Estevez, Carlos
92Ft.MyeMCB-13
92Ft.MyeMF-2752
92KenTwiC-6
Estevez, Juan
88BriTigP-1866
Estrada, Asdrubal
93LinVenB-145
94VenLinU-106
95LinVen-196
Estrada, Chuck (Charles L.)
60Top-126
60TopVen-126
61Baz-13
61Pos-73
61Top-48
61Top-395
61TopStal-100
62Jel-36
62Pos-36
62PosCan-36
62SalPlaC-212
62ShiPlaC-212
62Top-560
62TopBuc-24
62TopStal-4
63Top-465
64OriJayP-5
64Top-263
64TopVen-263
65Top-378
67Top-537
73OPC-549
73Top-549
78PadFamF-10
82ChaChaT-24
85TacTigC-129
86TacTigP-6
87TacTigP-12
88TacTigP-623
89TacTigC-9
89TacTigP-1564
90ProAAAF-158
90TacTigP-111
91MetWIZ-109
91OriCro-123
93RanKee-138
93SanBerSC-23
93SanBerSF-787
94CenValRC-27
94CenValRF-3220
95NewHavRTI-23
Estrada, Eduardo
86NewBriRSP-11
87NewBriRSP-25
88EasLeaAP-21
88NewBriRSP-903
89NewBriRSS-1
89PawRedSC-23
89PawRedSP-698
Estrada, Francisco
91MetWIZ-110
Estrada, Jay
87SpoIndP-5
88ChaRaiP-1213
89RivRedWB-4
89RivRedWCLC-21
89RivRedWP-1409
90RivRedWB-7
90RivRedWCLC-16
90RivRedWP-2600
91HigDesMC-3
91HigDesMP-2386
Estrada, Josue
94BurBeeC-7
94BurBeeF-1094
94ClaGolF-71
94Top-741
94TopGol-741
94TopSpa-741
Estrada, Luis
79AppFoxT-16
80AppFoxT-1
81GleFalWST-1
Estrada, Manny (Manuel)
78SanJosMMC-22
79SpoIndT-25
80LynSaiT-13
81SpoIndT-2
82SalLakCGT-23
83SalLakCGT-25
84ButCopKT-1
Estrada, Osmani
94ChaRanF-2502
95TulDriTI-8
96OklCit8B-8
Estrada, Pete (Peter)
88ElmPioC-8
89WinHavRSS-6
90LynRedSTI-18
91LinDriAA-456
91NewBriRSLD-456
91NewBriRSP-346
92LynRedSC-3
92LynRedSF-2901
Estrella, Luis
96BelGiaTI-28
Etchandy, Curt
76AppFoxT-3
Etchebarren, Andy
66OPC-27
66Top-27
66TopVen-27
67CokCapO-9
67DexPre-69
67Top-457
68AtlOilPBCC-16
68CokCapO-9
68DexPre-31
68Top-204
68TopVen-204
69MilBra-80
69MLBOffS-3
69Top-634
70DayDaiNM-158
70MLBOffS-149
70OPC-201
70OPC-213
70Ori-5
70Top-201
70Top-213
71MLBOffS-296
71OPC-501
71Ori-4
71Top-501
72MilBra-100
72OPC-26
72Top-26
73OPC-618
73OriJohP-8
73Top-618
74OPC-488
74Top-488
75OPC-583
75Top-583
76OPC-129
76Top-129
77Top-454
78Top-313
81Ori6F-13
84BrePol-NNO
85BrePol-NNO
86BrePol-8
87BrePol-NNO
88BrePol-NNO
89BrePol-NNO
90BreMilB-32
90BrePol-NNO
91BreMilB-32
91BrePol-NNO
91OriCro-124
93BluOriC-12
94BluOriC-23
94BluOriF-3578
94BreMilB-311
94TedWil-9
Etchebarren, Ray
84BeaGolGT-24
Etheredge, Jeff
89BatCliP-1917
Etheridge, Bobby (Bobby L.)
68OPC-126
68Top-126
68TopVen-126
69Top-604
70OPC-107
70Top-107
Etheridge, Haden
90ArkRaz-12
Etheridge, Roger
92PriRedC-9
92PriRedF-3079
93PriRedC-9
93PriRedF-4169
93WesVirWC-5
93WesVirWF-2858
94ChaWheC-9
94ChaWheF-2694
95BreBtaTI-18
96GreBraB-12
96GreBraTI-43
Ethifier, Edouard
72Dia-119
Ethiopian Clowns, Miami
93NegLeaRL2-91
Etler, Todd
92ClaDraP-54
92FroRowDP-63
92HigSchPLS-7
92PriRedC-1
92PriRedF-3080
93BilMusF-3936
93BilMusSP-5
93StaCluM-68
94ChaWheC-10
94ChaWheF-2695
94SouAtlLAF-SAL40
Etohandy, Curt
78AppFoxT-9
Etten, Nick (Nicholas R.)
41DouPlaR-123
43YanSta-10
48SigOil-6
48SmiClo-4
77TCMTheWY-55
79DiaGre-337
Ettles, Mark
89NiaFalRP-8
90LakTigS-9
91LakTigC-3
91LakTigP-259
92WicWraF-3652
92WicWraS-628
93FleFinE-137
93LasVegSF-939
95AusFut-16
95AusFutSFP-SFFP7
Etzweiler, Dan
88MyrBeaBJP-1177
Eubanks, Craig
91ChaRaiC-6
91ChaRaiP-92
Eubanks, Larry
76DubPacT-11
77CocAstT-6
Eufemia, Frank
83VisOakF-11
85TolMudHT-6
86Don-513
86Fle-392
86TolMudHP-10
86Top-236
86TopTif-236
86TwiTeal-19
Eusebio, Ralph
93HunCubC-7
93HunCubF-3248
Eusebio, Tony
88OscAstS-9
89ColMudB-15
89ColMudP-125
89ColMudS-8
90Bes-112
90ColMudB-5
90ColMudP-1350
90ColMudS-10
90StaFS7-15
91JacGenLD-557
91JacGenP-928
91LinDriAA-557
92ClaFS7-338
92JacGenS-331
92Sco-858
92SkyAA F-140
92StaClu-546
92TopDeb91-52
93ExcFS7-42
93LimRocDWB-16
93StaCluAs-29
93TucTorF-3061
94AstMot-24
94ExcFS7-199
94FleUpd-142
94LeaLimR-51
94Pin-537
94PinArtP-537
94PinMusC-537
94ScoRoo-RT116
94ScoRooGR-RT116
94Sel-192
94SpoRoo-93
94SpoRooAP-93
94StaClu-690
94StaCluFDI-690
94StaCluGR-690
94StaCluMOP-690
94Ult-502
95AstMot-12
95ColCho-114
95ColChoGS-114
95ColChoSS-114
95Don-445
95DonPreP-445
95DonTopotO-253
95Fla-145
95Fle-457
95Pac-185
95PacLatD-11
95PacPri-61
95Sco-133
95ScoGolR-133
95ScoPlaTS-133
95Top-454
95TopCyb-250
95Ult-385
95UltGolM-385
95UppDec-24
95UppDecED-24
95UppDecEDG-24
96AstMot-18
96ColCho-563
96ColChoGS-563
96ColChoSS-563
96Don-200
96DonPreP-200
96EmoXL-198
96Fla-277
96Fle-406
96FleTif-406
96MetUni-177
96MetUniP-177
96Pac-93
96PacPri-P32
96PacPriG-P32
96Sco-102
96StaClu-218
96StaClu-347
96StaCluEPB-347
96StaCluEPG-347
96StaCluEPS-347
96StaCluMOP-218
96StaCluMOP-347
96Top-46
96Ult-208
96UltGolM-208
96UppDec-344
97Fle-344
97FleTif-344
97Pac-316
97PacLigB-316
97PacSil-316
97Ult-335
97UltGolME-335
97UltPlaME-335
Evangelista, Alberto
93IdaFalBF-4024

93IdaFalBSP-1
94DanBraC-8
94DanBraF-3524
95MacBraTI-9
Evangelista, George
91GulCoaRSP-19
92ClaFS7-84
92Ft.MyeMCB-3
92Ft.MyeMF-2753
93ChaRanC-9
93ChaRanF-1948
Evans, Al (Alfred Hubert)
46SpoExcW-4-3
47Exh-69
47SenGunBP-2
49Bow-132A
49Bow-132B
49Lea-22
50Bow-144
51Bow-38
52Top-152
83TopRep5-152
84TCMPla1-11
Evans, Barry (Barry Steven)
81Fle-499
81OPC-72
81Top-72
82Don-271
82Fle-571
82Top-541
83ColCliT-19
85MaiGuiT-18
86MaiGuiP-8
92YanWIZ8-55
Evans, Bart
92EugEmeC-13
92EugEmeF-3023
93RocRoyC-13
93RocRoyF-712
94CarLeaAF-CAR16
94WilBluRC-9
94WilBluRF-296
95Bow-35
95Exc-58
95SigRoo-17
95SigRooSig-17
95UppDecML-56
95WicWraTI-37
95WilBluRTI-19
96WicWraB-24
95UppDecMLFS-56
Evans, Billy (William L.)
09SpoNewSM-38
21Exh-44
61Fle-22
76ShaPiz-136
77GalGloG-134
80PerHaloFP-136
80SSPHOF-136
89HOFStiB-100
92ConTSN-472
94ConTSN-1210
94ConTSNB-1210
Evans, Brad
96JohCitCTI-11
Evans, Brent
92ButCopKSP-10
Evans, Brian
89ChaRanS-7
90GasRanB-13
90GasRanP-2515
90GasRanS-8
90ProAaA-81
Evans, Bubba (Rick)
76AppFoxT-4
77ChaPatT-5
79BufBisT-9
80BufBisT-8
89GeoColC-6
Evans, Darrell
70Top-621
72OPC-171
72OPC-172
72Top-171
72Top-172
73LinPor-2
73OPC-374
73Top-374
74BraPhoC-3
74OPC-140
74Top-140
74TopDecE-2
74TopSta-3
75Hos-3
75HosTwi-3
75OPC-475
75Top-475
76Hos-24
76HosTwi-24
76OPC-81
76SSP-9
76Top-81
77Gia-6
77Top-571
78Hos-54
78Top-215
79GiaPol-41
79Hos-33
79OPC-215
79Top-410
80GiaPol-41
80OPC-81
80Top-145
81AllGamPI-119
81Don-192
81Fle-436A
81Fle-436B
81OPC-69
81Top-648
81TopSti-235
82Don-398
82Fle-388
82OPC-17
82Top-17
82TopSti-112
83Don-251
83Fle-258
83GiaMot-9
83OPC-329
83Top-448
83TopFol-2
83TopSti-305
84AllGamPI-93
84Don-431
84Fle-372
84FleSti-3
84FleUpd-36
84FunFooP-117
84GiaMot-27
84Nes792-325
84OPC-325
84TigFarJ-2
84TigWavP-14
84Top-325
84TopGloS-11
84TopSti-163
84TopTif-325
84TopTra-36T
84TopTraT-36T
85AllGamPI-32
85Don-227
85DonHig-51
85Fle-6
85Lea-215
85OPC-319
85SevCoi-D3
85TigCaiD-6
85TigWen-7
85Top-792
85TopTif-792
86Don-369
86Fle-224
86FleStiC-36
86OPC-103
86QuaGra-24
86SevCoi-C15
86Spo-183
86Spo-189
86TigCaiD-4
86Top-515
86Top3-D-7
86TopGaloC-3
86TopGloS-60
86TopMinL-13
86TopSti-165
86TopSti-269
86TopSup-21
86TopTat-4
86TopTif-515
86Woo-9
87Don-398
87DonOpeD-210
87Fle-150
87FleGlo-150
87FleLeaL-16
87OPC-265
87SevCoi-D2
87Spo-132
87SpoTeaP-15
87TigCaiD-6
87TigCok-13
87Top-265
87TopSti-264
87TopTif-265
88Don-250
88DonBasB-35
88Fle-54
88FleGlo-54
88KayB-9
88KinDis-12
88Lea-173
88OPC-390
88OPCBoxB-E
88PanSti-89
88PanSti-90
88PanSti-441
88Sco-75
88ScoGlo-75
88Spo-188
88StaLinTi-4
88TigPep-41
88TigPol-5
88Top-630
88TopBig-82
88TopMinL-10
88TopSti-8
88TopSti-265
88TopTif-630
88TopWaxBC-E
88Woo-3
89Bow-275
89BowTif-275
89Don-533
89OPCBoxB-C
89Sco-171
89ScoRoo-65T
89TopTra-31T
89TopTraT-31T
89TopWaxBC-C
89UppDec-394
90Fle-581
90FleCan-581
90KayB-10
90OPC-55
90OPCBoxB-D
90PubSti-112
90RicBra2ATI-8
90Sco-302
90Top-55
90TopSti-31
90TopTif-55
90TopWaxBC-D
90UppDec-143
90VenSti-163
91UppDecS-6
92SanAntMF-3989
92UppDecS-4
93TedWil-37
94UppDecAH-196
94UppDecAH1-196
Evans, Dave
90CMC-839
90SanBerSB-5
90SanBerSCLC-97
90SanBerSP-2627
91JacSunLD-334
91JacSunP-144
91LinDriAA-334
94JacSunF-1406
95JacGenTI-2
96TusTorB-7
Evans, Dickie
49W725AngTI-31
Evans, Dr. (Richard)
82IowCubT-32
Evans, Duane
82LynMetT-13
Evans, Dwight (Dwight Michael)
73LinPor-19
73OPC-614
73Top-614
74OPC-351
74Top-351
75Hos-18
75HosTwi-18
75Kel-38
75OPC-255
75Top-255
76Hos-87
76LinSup-104
76OPC-575
76RedSox-3
76RedSoxSM-5
76SSP-408
76Top-575
77BurCheD-30
77Hos-21
77OPC-259
77Top-25
78PapGinD-24
78SSP270-181
78Top-695
79Hos-64
79Kel-41
79OPC-73
79Top-155
80OPC-210
80Top-405
81CokTeaS-3
81Don-458
81Fle-232
81OPC-275
81Top-275
81TopSupHT-3
82Don-7
82Don-109
82Dra-11
82Fle-293
82Fle-642
82FleSta-167
82Kel-45
82OPC-355
82RedSoxC-6
82Top-162
82Top-355
82TopSti-4
82TopSti-135
82TopSti-153
83AllGamPI-52
83Don-452
83DonActA-2
83Dra-7
83Fle-183
83FleSta-59
83FleSti-69
83OPC-135
83Top-135
83TopSti-38
84AllGamPI-142
84Don-395
84Fle-397
84FunFooP-62
84Nes792-720
84OCoandSI-57
84OPC-244
84Top-720
84TopRubD-13
84TopSti-219
84TopTif-720
85AllGamPI-56
85Don-294
85DonActA-15
85Dra-10
85Fle-158
85FleStaS-40
85Lea-150
85OPC-271
85SevCoi-E8
85Top-580
85TopMin-580
85TopRubD-19
85TopSti-212
85TopSup-33
85TopTif-580
86Don-249
86Dra-2
86Fle-348
86FleMin-74
86Lea-127
86OPC-60
86SevCoi-E13
86Spo-32
86Top-60
86Top-396
86TopMinL-5
86TopSti-251
86TopSup-22
86TopTat-13
86TopTif-60
86TopTif-396
86Woo-10
87BoaandB-7
87Don-129
87DonHig-33
87DonOpeD-184
87Fle-34
87FleGlo-34
87FleGlo-WS9
87FleLeaL-17
87FleMin-37
87FleStiC-38
87FleWorS-9
87Lea-57
87OPC-368
87RedSoxSAP-7
87Spo-128
87SpoTeaP-9
87Top-3
87Top-645
87TopSti-4
87TopSti-20
87TopSti-251
87TopTif-3
87TopTif-645
87Woo-21
88Don-16
88Don-216
88DonAll-23
88DonBasB-84
88DonSupD-16
88DonTeaBRS-216
88Dra-9
88Fle-351
88FleAwaW-11
88FleBasM-12
88FleGlo-351
88FleLeaL-11
88FleMin-6
88FleStiC-8
88FleWaxBC-C2
88KayB-10
88Lea-16
88Lea-171
88OPC-221
88PanSti-25
88RedFolSB-21
88Sco-65
88ScoGlo-65
88Spo-137
88StaLinRS-7
88Top-470
88TopBig-6
88TopCoi-11
88TopCoi-42
88TopGloS-21
88TopMinL-3
88TopRevLL-24
88TopSti-245
88TopStiB-50
88TopTif-470
88TopUKM-22
88TopUKMT-22
89Bow-35
89BowTif-35
89ClaLigB-44
89Don-240
89DonBasB-121
89Fle-87
89FleExcS-12
89FleGlo-87
89KayB-10
89OPC-205
89PanSti-279
89RedFolSB-40
89Sco-193
89ScoHot1S-8
89Spo-204
89SpoIllFKI-288
89Top-205
89TopBasT-109
89TopBig-193
89TopGloS-36
89TopMinL-47
89TopSti-252
89TopStiB-15
89TopTif-205
89TopUKM-24
89TVSpoM-65
89UppDec-366
90Bow-279
90BowTif-279
90ClaBlu-77
90Don-122
90DonBesA-102
90DonGraS-5
90Fle-274
90FleCan-274
90KayB-11

90Lea-235
90OPC-375
90PanSti-17
90PubSti-454
90RedSoxP-8
90Sco-3
90Sco100S-54
90Spo-217
90Top-375
90TopAmeA-4
90TopBig-1
90TopHilHM-23
90TopSti-257
90TopTif-375
90TopTVA-28
90TopTVRS-29
90UppDec-112
90VenSti-164
90Woo-12
91BasBesHRK-6
91Bow-103
91Don-122
91Fle-93
91FleUpd-2
91Lea-266
91OPC-155
91OPCBoxB-E
91OPCPre-39
91OriCro-497
91PanSti-213
91Sco-225
91Sco100S-99
91ScoRoo-62T
91SevCoi-A2
91StaClu-351
91Stu-2
91Top-155A
91Top-155B
91TopDesS-155
91TopMic-155
91TopTif-155
91TopTra-37T
91TopTraT-37T
91TopWaxBC-E
91UltUpd-1
91UppDec-549
91UppDec-776
91Woo-10
92Don-502
92Fle-6
92OPC-705
92PanSti-69
92Sco-150
92StaClu-463
92Top-705
92TopGol-705
92TopGolW-705
92TopMic-705
92TriPla-67
92Ult-3
92UppDec-248
93Pin-303
94RocPol-27

Evans, Felix
92NegLeaRLI-19

Evans, Frank
85LouRedR-3
91NegLeaRL-23
95NegLeaLI-23

Evans, Freeman
75AndRanT-42
76CliPilT-13

Evans, Gary
82BelBreF-17

Evans, Glenn
92EliTwiC-19
92EliTwiF-3693
92KenTwiC-5

Evans, Godfrey
75WesPalBES-12
78MemChiBC-3
79MemChiT-24

Evans, Jamie
91AubAstC-7
91AubAstP-4268
92AshTouC-12
93QuaCitRBC-7
93QuaCitRBF-92
94OscAstC-8
94OscAstF-1130

Evans, Jason
93HicCraC-6
93HicCraF-1283
94MidLeaAF-MDW26
94SouBenSHC-5
94SouBenSHF-606
96PriWilCB-10
92UtiBluSC-11

Evans, Jim
77CliDodT-7
88T/MUmp-13
89T/MUmp-11
90T/MUmp-11

Evans, Joe
77Ind192T-6
93ConTSN-949

Evans, John
79BurBeeT-15
80BurBeeT-25
81ElPasDT-21
82TacTigT-16

Evans, Kyle
95HudValRTI-3

Evans, Matt
92BriTigC-18
92BriTigF-1417
93FayGenC-10
93FayGenF-135
94LakTigC-6
94LakTigF-3043

Evans, Michael
91SouOreAC-18
91SouOreAP-3834
95WilBluRTI-21
96WilBluRB-3

Evans, Mike
82WauTimF-22
84ChaLooT-1A
87EriCarP-17
88HamRedP-1734
89HamRedS-29
90SprCarB-28
91SprCarC-30
92SprCarC-29
93EugEmeC-12
93EugEmeF-3867
93SprCarC-30

Evans, Park
90MisStaB-10
91MisStaB-15
92MisStaB-14

Evans, Pat
94WatIndC-9
94WatIndF-3939
96KenIndB-7

Evans, Phil
89SalLakTTI-25

Evans, Randy
80GleFalWSBT-4
80GleFalWSCT-15
81GleFalWST-2

Evans, Red (Russell Edison)
39PlaBal-159
90DodTar-227

Evans, Rickey
78SalPirT-4

Evans, Rob
87TidTidP-29

Evans, Roy
90DodTar-945

Evans, Scott
87MiaMarP-4
87NewOriP-23
88HagSunS-5

Evans, Sean
92AugPirC-10
92SalBucF-56
93SalBucC-9
93SalBucF-425
94CarLeaAF-CAR39
94SalBucC-9
95CarMudF-149

Evans, Stanley
92MarPhiC-29
92MarPhiF-3070
93SouAtlLAGF-52
93SpaPhiC-13
93SpaPhiF-1067
94ClaGolF-35
94ClePhiC-14
94ClePhiF-2540
95ClePhiF-228

Evans, Steve (Louis Richard)
09ColChiE-96
09PC7HHB-13
09T206-123
10CouT21-133
10DomDisP-42
10RedCroT-191
10SweCapPP-146
11S74Sil-118
11SpoLifM-268
11T205-52
12ColRedB-96
12ColTinT-96
12HasTriFT-67A
12T207-57
14CraJacE-128
15CraJacE-128

Evans, Tim
92OscAstF-2536
93MidLeaAGF-46
93QuaCitRBC-8
93QuaCitRBF-112
94JacGenF-228

Evans, Tom
92ClaDraP-108
92HigSchPLS-24
92MedHatBJSP-24
93HagSunC-11
93HagSunF-1888
93StaCluM-79
95Bow-52
95DunBluJTI-7
96Bow-171
96KnoSmoB-12

Evans, Tony
83TamTarT-4

Evans, Tory
89SanBerSCLC-65

Evans, Van
85PriWilPT-25
86KinEagP-6

Evaschuk, Brad
88St.CatBJP-2010

Eveline, Billy (William)
86AppFoxP-7
87DayBeaAP-18
88TamTarS-6
89QuaCitAB-26
89QuaCitAGS-30

Evenhus, Jason
94OgdRapF-3729
94OgdRapSP-5

Everett, Carl
90ClaDraP-10
90HigSchPLS-13
90TamYanD-5
91Bow-156
91GreHorP-3072
91OPC-113
91Sco-386
91SouAtlLAGP-SAL25
91Top-113
91TopDesS-113
91TopMic-113
91TopTif-113
92Bow-258
92ForLauYTI-9
92Ft.LauYF-2626
92ProFS7-124
92UppDecML-56
92UppDecML-155
93Bow-94
93ClaFS7-183
93ExcFS7-207
93HigDesMC-1
93HigDesMF-54
93SP-276
93StaCluMarl-30
93TopTra-74T
94Bow-318
94BowBes-B56
94BowBesR-B56
94ColC-6
94ColChoGS-6
94ColChoSS-6
94Don-241
94EdmTraF-2885
94LeaLimR-31
94Pin-252
94PinArtP-252
94PinMusC-252
94Sco-601
94ScoGolR-601
94Sel-393
94SP-110
94SPDieC-110
94Spo-168
94StaCluT-73
94StaCluTFDI-73
94Top-781
94TopGol-781
94TopSpa-781
94TriAAF-AAA29
94UppDec-11
94UppDecED-11
95Bow-20
95ColCho-318
95ColChoGS-318
95ColChoSS-318
95Fla-382
95FlaWavotF-6
95FleUpd-111
95Lea-397
95NorTidTI-10
95Pac-173
95Pin-368
95PinArtP-368
95PinMusC-368
95Sel-142
95SelArtP-142
95Sum-73
95SumNthD-73
96ColCho-219
96ColChoGS-219
96ColChoSS-219
96Don-312
96DonPreP-312
96EmoXL-229
96Fla-317
96Fle-477
96FleRooS-5
96FleTif-477
96Lea-136
96LeaPrePB-136
96LeaPrePG-136
96LeaPrePS-136
96MetKah-8
96MetUni-199
96MetUniP-199
96Pac-139
96PanSti-31
96Pin-77
96Sco-188
96StaClu-58
96StaCluMOP-58
96Top-281
96Ult-241
96UltGolM-241
96UppDec-137
97Fle-623
97FleTif-623
97Lea-300
97LeaFraM-300
97LeaFraMDC-300
97Pac-362
97PacLigB-362
97PacSil-362
97Sco-438
97ScoHobR-438
97ScoResC-438
97ScoShoS-438
97ScoShoSAP-438

Everett, Conrad
80WisRapTT-10

Everett, Smokey
81WisRapTT-3
82OrlTwiT-4

Everingham, Matt
91SydWavF-3
95AusFut-38

Evers, Bill
83GreHorT-28
86CliGiaP-7
87CliGiaP-17
88CliGiaP-712
89ShrCapP-1838
90ShrCapP-1458
90ShrCapS-25
90TexLeaAGS-37
91LinDriAA-324
91ShrCapLD-324
91ShrCapP-1838
92PhoFirF-2837
92PhoFirS-399
93GreHorC-27
93GreHorF-903
93SouAtlLAGF-20
94AbaYanF-1457
95ColCliMCTI-1
95ColCliP-9
95ColCliTI-9

Evers, Hoot (Walter Arthur)
47Exh-70
47TipTop-31
49Bow-42
49Lea-78
49MPR302-2-123
50Bow-41
51Bow-23
51FisBakL-6
51TopCurA-4
52Bow-111
52StaCalL-71H
52StaCalL-72C
52StaCalS-86B
52Top-222
53BowC-25
53RedSoxTI-6
54Bow-18
55OriEss-9
76TayBow4-55
79TCM50-264
81TigDetN-44
83TopRep5-222
91OriCro-125
91TopArc1-291

Evers, Johnny (John Joseph)
07CubA.CDPP-3
07CubGFGCP-3
08AmeCarE-10
08AmeCarE-46
08RosComP-102
09ColChiE-97
09MaxPubP-4
09MaxPubP-20
09PhiCarE-10
09RamT20-43
09SpoNewSM-26
09T206-124
09T206-125
09T206-126
10ChiE-5
10CouT21-22
10CouT21-134
10CouT21-283
10DarChoE-18
10DomDisP-43
10E101-20
10E102-11
10E98-14
10MelMinE-20
10NadCarE-21
10OrnOvaPP-5
10PeoT21-23A
10PeoT21-23B
10RedCroT-111
10RedCroT-192
10SepAnoP-10
10StaCarE-13
10SweCapPP-82
10W555-29
11BasBatEU-22
11DiaGumP-14
11E94-14
11L1L-134
11MecDFT-9
11PloCanE-27
11S74Sil-60
11S81LarS-109
11SpoLifCW-120
11SpoLifM-169
11T205-53
11TurRedT-16
12ColRedB-97
12ColTinT-97
12HasTriFT-36A
12HasTriFT-36B
12HasTriFT-36C
12HasTriFT-36D
12HasTriFT-36E
13NatGamW-16
13TomBarW-15
14CraJacE-18
14TexTomE-20
15AmeCarE-17
15CraJacE-18
15SpoNewM-55
16BF2FP-51
16ColE13-45
16FleBreD-27
16SpoNewM-54
16TanBraE-9
17HolBreD-27
21E121So8-20A
21E121So8-20B

22AmeCarE-18
22W575-31
23WilChoV-39
36PC7AlbHoF-42
37KelPepS-BB4
40PlaBal-174
48ExhHoF-10
50CalHOFW-29
60ExhWriH-10
60Fle-57
61Fle-23
63HalofFB-24
68LauWorS-5
69Baz-6
69Baz-7
69EquSpoHoF-BB3
69SCFOldT-6
70FleWorS-5
72FleFamF-7
75FlePio-17
76ShaPiz-42
77GalGloG-159
80MarExhH-11
80PerHaloFP-42
80SSPHOF-42
81ConTSN-13
84CubUno-7
84GalHaloFRL-42
87Cub190T-9
90PerGreM-40
91ConTSN-15
92CubOldS-8
93ConTSN-818
93ConTSN-892
93CraJac-11
93UppDecAH-47
93UppDecAH-147
93UppDecAH-148
94ConTSN-1165
94ConTSNB-1165
94UppDecTAE-27
96PitPosH-6
Evers, Troy
87Ft.LauYP-4
88AlbYanP-1340
90WilBilB-4
90WilBilP-1050
90WilBilS-5
Eversgerd, Bryan
89JohCitCS-10
91SavCarC-3
91SavCarP-1644
92ProFS7-321
92St.PetCC-12
92St.PetCF-2022
93ArkTraF-2808
94Bow-244
94Fla-427
94FleUpd-178
94ScoRoo-RT141
94ScoRooGR-RT141
94SpoRoo-121
94SpoRooAP-121
94TopTra-71T
95Don-317
95DonPreP-317
95Fle-496
95StaClu-411
95StaCluMOP-411
95StaCluSTWS-411
95StaCluVR-210
95Top-481
95TopCyb-273
96OklCit8B-9
95StaCluVRMC-210
Everson, Greg (Gregory)
88FloStaLAS-35
88LakTigS-10
89LonTigP-1380
90MemChiB-15
90MemChiP-1005
90MemChiS-10
91LinDriAAA-335
91OmaRoyLD-335
91OmaRoyP-1030
Ewart, Ron
86WinSpiP-8
Ewell, Doc
88AstMot-28
89AstMot-28
90AstMot-28
92AstMot-28
Ewell, Jim
60A'sTeal-5
Ewell, Mark
75WesPalBES-5
Ewing, Bill
76QuaCitAT-13
79SalLakCGT-13
Ewing, Buck (William)
36PC7AlbHoF-21
50CalHOFW-30
75FlePio-3
76ShaPiz-24
77BobParHoF-20
80PerHaloFP-21
80SSPHOF-21
84GalHaloFRL-24
86OldJudN-6
87BucN28-67A
87BucN28-67B
87OldJudN-158
87OldJudN-159
88AllandGN-1
88AugBecN-9
88GandBCGCE-14
88SpoTimM-9
88WG1CarG-38
89EdgR.WG-1
89HOFStiB-57
89SFHaCN-4
90BasWit-68
90KalBatN-16
94OriofB-76
95May-8A
95May-8B
98CamPepP-24
Ewing, Jim
84EveGiaC-10B
Ewing, Justin
90MisStaB-11
93MisStaB-15
Ewing, Long Bob (George L.)
06FanCraNL-18
08RosComP-114
09RamT20-44
09T206-127
11S74Sil-100
11SpoLifCW-121
11SpoLifM-228
11T205-54
87OldJudN-157
Ewing, Long John (John)
03WilCarE-14
Ewing, Patrick
93StaCluMO-31
Ewing, Sam (Samuel James)
77OPC-221
78BluJayP-5
78OPC-112
78SyrChiT-9
78Top-344
79OPC-271
79TCMJapPB-34
79Top-521
81AppFoxT-28
Excelsiors, Brooklyn
94OriofB-12
Expos, Burlington
86BurExpP-28
Expos, Jacksonville
87JacExpP-457
88JacExpP-993
89JacExpB-29
89JacExpP-178
90JacExpB-30
90JacExpP-1390
Expos, Montreal
69FleCloS-14
69FleCloS-31
70OPC-509
70Top-509
71OPC-674
71Top-674
71TopTat-8
72Top-582
73OPC-576
73OPCBTC-15
73Top-576
73TopBluTC-15
74OPC-508
74OPCTC-15
74Top-508
74TopStaA-15
74TopTeaC-15
78OPC-207
78Top-244
80OPC-249
81OPC-268
83FleSta-239
83FleSti-NNO
84ExpStu-39
87SpoTeaL-20
87Top-381
87TopTif-381
88PanSti-474
88RedFolSB-128
90PubSti-631
90RedFolSB-115
90VenSti-529
91PanCanT1-121
91PanCanT1-129
93TedWilPC-15
94ImpProP-22
94Sco-654
94ScoGolR-654
94VerExpC-29B
95PanSti-130
95UppDecC-1A
96PanSti-21
Expos, Rockford
90RocExpLC-30
Expos, West Palm Beach
75WesPalBES-4A
Eyre, Scott
92ButCopKSP-18
93Bow-277
93ChaRaiC-1
93ChaRaiF-1902
93ClaFS7-100
93SouAtlLAGF-6
94ClaGolF-29
94ExcFS7-132
94UppDecML-48
95UppDecML-137
96BirBarB-14
95UppDecMLFS-137
Eyrich, George
43PhiTeal-8
78ReaRem-4
Ezell, Glenn
73TacTwiC-5
74PhoGiaC-89
82AmaGolST-23
83RanAffF-NNO
84RanJarP-NNO
85RanPer-NNO
86VenGulP-7
87KnoBluJP-1516
88OmaRoyC-25
88OmaRoyP-1503
91RoyPol-26
92RoyPol-27
93RanKee-139
93RoyPol-27
95ModA'sTI-7
Faatz, Jay
87OldJudN-160
88SpoTimM-11
Fabbro, Arthur
52Par-55
53ExhCan-45
Faber, Dick
52MotCoo-28
Faber, Red (Urban)
15SpoNewM-56
16BF2FP-12
16ColE13-46
16SpoNewM-55
17HolBreD-28
19W514-69
20NatCarE-26
21E121So1-21
21E121So8-21A
21E121So8-21B
21Exh-45
21Nei-14
22AmeCarE-19
22E120-18
22W572-27
22W573-36
22W575-32
23W501-48
23W515-60
23WilChoV-40
27AmeCarE-6
27YorCarE-4
28W502-4
28Yue-4
29PorandAR-22
30ChiEveAP-14
33Gou-79
33GouCanV-54
40PlaBal-230
48WhiSoxTI-5
61Fle-24
69SCFOldT-28
71FleWorS-15
75SheGrePG-20
75TCMAllG-9
75WhiSox1T-6
76ChiGre-12
76GrePlaG-20
76RowExh-1
76ShaPiz-96
77GalGloG-121
80PerHaloFP-96
80SSPHOF-96
85WhiSoxC-24
88PacEigMO-96
89HOFStiB-61
91ConTSN-41
91ConTSNP-710
92ConTSN-483
92Man191BSR-7
93ConTSN-710
94ConTSN-1251
94ConTSNB-1251
94ConTSNCI-26
Fabregas, Jorge
91ClaDraP-30
91MiaHurBB-5
92Bow-8
92ClaFS7-359
92PalSprAC-18
92PalSprAF-843
92StaCluD-46
92UppDecML-329
93Bow-5
93ClaFS7-184
93ClaGolF-31
93MidAngF-324
93StaCluAn-8
94AngMot-26
94Bow-171
94ExcFS7-24
94Fla-270
94FleAllR-M4
94FleUpd-16
94LeaLimR-72
94ScoRoo-RT110
94ScoRooGR-RT110
94Sel-398
94SpoRoo-58
94SpoRooAP-58
94TopTra-62T
94UppDec-515
94UppDecED-515
94UppDecML-14
94VanCanF-1867
95ColCho-91
95ColChoGS-91
95ColChoSS-91
95Don-276
95DonPreP-276
95Pac-59
95PacPri-19
95Pin-136
95PinArtP-136
95PinMusC-136
95Sco-288
95ScoGolR-288
95ScoPlaTS-288
95ScoSam-288
95Top-493
95TopCyb-283
95UppDec-269
95UppDecED-269
95UppDecEDG-269
95UppDecSE-128
96AngMot-16
96ColCho-483
96ColChoGS-483
96ColChoSS-483
96Don-452
96DonPreP-452
96FleUpd-U20
96FleUpdTC-U20
96LeaSigEA-50
96Pac-267
96Sco-185
96Ult-29
96UltGolM-29
97Fle-42
97FleTif-42
97MidAngOHP-9
97Pac-7
97PacLigB-7
97PacSil-7
97Top-47
Fabri, Isidro
86NegLeaF-73
89RinPosNL1-6
Fabrique, Bunny
90DodTar-228
Fabrizio, Kurt
80ChaO'sP-7
80ChaO'sW-7
Faccio, John
89BelBreIS-4
89Sta-4
Faccio, Luis
85BenPhiC-6
88PriWilYS-8
89BlaYNPRWL-75
89SprCarB-7
90SavCarP-2063
91St.PetCC-6
91St.PetCP-2269
93ArkTraF-2809
Face, Elroy
53Top-246
54Top-87
56Top-13
57Kah-7
57Top-166
58Hir-59
58Kah-7
58Top-74
59Kah-8
59Top-339
59Top-428
60Kah-7
60KeyChal-15
60Lea-16
60PirJayP-4
60PirTag-26
60Top-20
60Top-115
60TopTat-14
60TopTat-89
60TopVen-20
60TopVen-115
61Kah-11
61PirJayP-3
61Pos-133
61Top-250
61Top-310
61Top-370
61TopStal-62
62Jel-177
62Pos-177
62PosCan-177
62SalPlaC-174
62ShiPlaC-174
62Top-210
62Top-423
62TopStal-175
63BasMagM-23
63Fle-57
63Jel-147
63PirIDL-6
63PirJayP-5
63Pos-147
63Top-409
64PirKDK-9
64Top-539
65Top-347
66PirEasH-26
66Top-461
67CokCapPi-14
67OPC-49
67PirTeal-6
67Top-49
67TopPirS-8
67TopVen-336
68PirKDK-26
68PirTeal-7
68Top-198
68TopVen-198
69OPC-207
69Top-207
69TopFou-16
70ExpPos-1
72LauGreF-26
74NewYorNTDiS-21
78TCM60I-5
86PirGreT-11

87McDCoi-1
87Pir196T-7
89PacLegI-178
89SweBasG-51
90HOFStiB-58
91SweBasG-28
91TopArc1-246
92ActPacA-26
92BazQua5A-19
92UppDecS-19
93UppDecAH-48
94TedWil-77
94TopArc1-87
94TopArc1G-87
94UppDecAH-59
94UppDecAH1-59
Facione, Chris
93BriTigC-8
93BriTigF-3660
94FayGenC-12
94FayGenF-2163
Faedo, Len
80OrlTwiT-10
81ChaChaT-12
82Top-766
82TwiPos-10
83Fle-611
83Top-671
83TwiTeal-8
84EvaTriT-10
84Fle-563
84MinTwiP-11
84Nes792-84
84Top-84
84TopSti-310
84TopTif-84
84TwiTeal-9
Fagan, Pete
87St.PetCP-26
91SavCarC-4
92SavCarC-25
93St.PetCC-30
95ArkTraTI-11
96ArkTraB-4
Fagan, William
87OldJudN-161
Faggett, Ethan
95MicBatCTI-11
95MidLeaA-14
96SarRedSB-14
Fagley, Dan
96BreCouMB-15
Fagnano, Phil
87UtiBluSP-29
88SpaPhiP-1032
Fagnant, Ray
90WinHavRSS-8
91LinDriAA-457
91NewBriRSLD-457
91NewBriRSP-354
Faherty, Sean
83AleDukT-18
84PriWilPT-3
Fahey, Bill
72OPC-334
72Top-334
73OPC-186
73Top-186
74SpoIndC-34
74OPC-558
74Top-558
75OPC-644
75Top-644
76OPC-436
76SSP-259
76Top-436
77Top-511
78SSP270-97
78Top-388
78TucTorC-14
80OPC-23
80Top-44
81Don-361
81Fle-490
81Top-653
81TopTra-760
82Top-286
83Don-281
83Tig-10
83Top-196
85TulDriTI-28
86GiaMot-28
87GiaMot-27
88GiaMot-27
89GiaMot-28
89Top-351
89TopTif-351
90GiaMot-21
90GiaSmo-7
91GiaMot-27
93RanKee-10
Fahr, Gerald
52Par-23
Fahrow, Bryant
75QuaCitAT-4
Failla, Paul
94SigRooDP-59
94SigRooDPS-59
94StaCluDP-36
94StaCluDPFDI-36
95CedRapKTI-13
95MidLeaA-15
96LakElsSB-16
Fain, Ferris
47Exh-71A
47Exh-71B
47PM1StaP1-57
48Bow-21
49Bow-9
49MPR302-2-107
49OlmStu-2
49PhiBul-18
50Bow-13
50RoyDes-24
51TopRedB-3
52BerRos-18
52Bow-154
52DixLid-7
52DixPre-7
52NatTeaL-9
52RedMan-AL7
52RoyPre-5
52StaCalL-76B
52StaCalS-89B
52TipTop-8
52Top-21
53DixLid-4
53DixPre-4
53Top-24
54Bow-214
54RedHeaF-7
54RedMan-AL22
54Top-27
54Wil-4
55Top-11
55TopDouH-115
83TopRep5-21
85TCMPla1-22
91TopArc1-24
92BazQua5A-3
94TopArc1-27
94TopArc1G-27
Faino, Jeff
92ClaDraP-109
92ElmPioF-1376
93LynRedSC-9
93LynRedSF-2511
94LynRedSC-10
94LynRedSF-1887
95BowBayTI-29
Fairchild, Glenn
86WatIndP-6
87WatIndP-25
88KinIndS-5
Faircloth, Kevin
94YakBeaC-5
94YakBeaF-3856
95SanBerSTI-6
Faircloth, Wayne
93HicCraC-7
93HicCraF-1280
94SouBenSHF-596
Fairey, Jim
68Top-228
68TopVen-228
69MLBOffS-157
69OPC-117
69Top-117
69TopFou-22
71ExpPS-6
71MLBOffS-126
71OPC-474
71Top-474
72Dia-13
72ProStaP-4
72Top-653
73OPC-429
73Top-429
74TacTwiC-24
75HawIslC-7
76HawIslC-15
81TCM60I-334
85SpoIndGC-5
90DodTar-229
Fairfax, Kenny
93WelPirC-5
93WelPirF-3349
Fairley, Craig
90NebCor-9
Fairly, Pat
92GenCubC-17
92GenCubF-1567
Fairly, Ron
69ExpPin-3
59Top-125
59TopVen-125
60DarFar-21
60DodJayP-4
60Top-321
61DodUniO-7
61Top-492
62DodBelB-6
62DodJayP-3
62Top-375
62TopStal-134
63DodJayP-5
63Jel-116
63Pos-116
63Top-105
64DodHea-4
64Top-138
64Top-490
64TopCoi-54
64TopVen-138
65DodJayP-5
65DodTeal-5
65OldLonC-8
65OPC-196
65Top-196
65TopEmbl-2
66Baz-20
66Top-330
66TopRubl-27
66TopVen-330
67Baz-20
67CokCapD-3
67CokCapDA-3
67DexPre-70
67OPC-94
67Top-94
68AtlOilPBCC-17
68Top-510
68Top3-D-3
69MilBra-81
69MLBOffS-146
69MLBPin-42
69OPC-122
69Top-122
69TopFou-5
69TopSta-43
69TopTeaP-22
70ExpPin-5
70MLBOffS-65
70Top-690
70TopPos-10
71ExpLaPR-3
71ExpPS-7
71MLBOffS-127
71OPC-315
71Top-315
71TopCoi-83
72Dia-14
72MilBra-101
72OPC-405
72Top-405
73ExpPos-4
73OPC-125
73Top-125
74Kel-27
74OPC-146
74Top-146
74TopSta-53
75OPC-270
75Top-270
76OPC-375
76SSP-276
76Top-375
77Top-127
78AngFamF-9
78OPC-40
78SSP270-205
78Top-85
79Top-580
81TCM60I-324
86ExpGreT-1
90DodTar-230
90SouCalS-5
92Nab-19
Fairman, Andy
91HelBreSP-16
92BelBreC-20
92BelBreF-410
93StoPorC-10
93StoPorF-750
94StoPorC-6
94StoPorF-1699
Fajardo, Hector
91AugPirC-5
91AugPirP-798
91SouAtlLAGP-SAL4
92Bow-22
92Cla1-T32
92Don-419
92Pin-573
92PinRooI-2
92ProFS7-311
92Sco-842
92ScoRoo-23
92TopDeb91-53
93PacSpa-309
93RanKee-140
93StaClu-430
93StaCluFDI-430
93StaCluMOP-430
94ScoRoo-RT132
94ScoRooGR-RT132
94SpoRoo-37
94SpoRooAP-37
95Don-244
95DonPreP-244
95Pac-424
95PacLatD-12
95Pin-437
95PinArtP-437
95RanCra-8
95StaClu-374
95StaCluMOP-374
95StaCluSTWS-374
95StaCluVR-197
95Top-184
95StaCluVRMC-197
Falciglia, Tony
96NewJerCB-8
Falco, Chris
91FreStaBS-4
91JamExpC-9
91JamExpP-3552
92RocExpC-23
92RocExpF-2122
Falcon, Edwin
96GreFalDTI-18
Falcone, Dave
84ChaO'sT-16
85RocRedWT-4
86ChaOriW-9
87ChaO'sW-36
87SouLeaAJ-1
90HagSunDGB-9
Falcone, Pete
75Gia-2
76OPC-524
76Top-524
76TopTra-524T
77BurCheD-12
77Car5-8
77CarTeal-7
77Hos-24
77OPC-177
77Top-205
78CarTeal-5
78Top-669
79OPC-36
79Top-87
80Top-401
81Don-395
81Fle-327
81OPC-117
81Top-117
82Don-380
82Fle-524
82MetPhoA-6
82Top-326
83BraPol-33
83Don-182
83Fle-541
83Top-764
83TopTra-31T
84BraPol-33
84Don-385
84Fle-177
84Nes792-521
84OPC-51
84Top-521
84TopTif-521
85Top-618
85TopTif-618
89PacSenL-208
89TopSenL-56
90EliSenL-55
91MetWIZ-111
91PacSenL-110
Falk, Bibb A.
21E121So1-22
21Exh-46
21Nei-15
22E120-19
22W572-28
22W573-37
22W575-33
23W501-41
23WilChoV-41
25Exh-74
26Exh-75
27YorCarE-39
28Exh-38
28StaPlaCE-19
28W502-39
28Yue-39
29ExhFou-22
31Exh-22
61Fle-104
92ConTSN-518
Falkenburg, Cy (Frederick)
11MecDFT-20
11SpoLifCW-122
11SpoLifM-42
14CraJacE-20
15CraJacE-20
Falkner, Richard
88BurIndP-1773
89KinIndS-7
89Sta-75
90KinIndTI-18
Fallon, George
49W72HolS-2
50W720HolS-7
90DodTar-231
Fallon, Robert
80AppFoxT-2
81GleFalWST-3
82GleFalWST-17
85BufBisT-17
85FleUpd-39
Falls, Bobby
86ColAstP-12
Falls, Curtis
94LetMouF-3871
94LetMouSP-9
Falteisek, Steven
92JamExpF-1493
94WesPalBEC-9
94WesPalBEF-33
95HarSenTI-17
Falzone, Jim
87MiaMarP-2
Fana, Alberto
95BatCliTI-11
Fancher, Terry
89MisStaB-11
Fancher, Tim
89MisStaB-12
Fandozzi, Mike
52LavPro-15
Faneyte, Ricky (Rikkert)
90IBAWorA-39
90IBAWorA-47
91CliGiaC-22
92SanJosGC-7
92UppDecML-116
93PhoFirF-1526
94Bow-51
94Cla-125
94ColC-97
94ColChoGS-97
94ColChoSS-97
94LeaLimR-40
94PhoFirF-1531
94ScoRoo-RT111
94ScoRooGR-RT111
94Sel-401

94SpoRoo-125
94SpoRooAP-125
94Top-790
94TopGol-790
94TopSpa-790
95ColChoGS-260
95ColChoSS-260
95PhoFirTI-39
95Pin-138
95PinArtP-138
95PinMusC-138
95Sco-282
95ScoGolR-282
95ScoPlaTS-282
95Sel-33
95SelArtP-33
95SigRoo-18
95SigRooSig-18
95Spo-158
95SpoArtP-158
96OklCit8B-10
96Pac-201
96Sco-36
Fang, Wild
95RocRedWTI-47
Fanio, Jeff
92ElmPioC-21
Fannin, Cliff
47TipTop-62
49Bow-120
49Lea-123
50Bow-106
51Bow-244
51TopBluB-36
52Top-285
53Top-203
83TopRep5-285
91TopArc1-203
Fanning, Jim
82Don-492
82ExpHygM-6
82ExpPos-10
85OPC-267
85Top-759
85TopTif-759
86ExpGreT-12
Fanning, Steve
88HamRedP-1739
89SavCarP-363
90ArkTraGS-11
91ArkTraLD-31
91ArkTraP-1292
91LinDriAA-31
92ArkTraF-1136
92ArkTraS-34
93ArkTraF-2818
94LouRedF-2988
Fanok, Harry
62KahAtl-6
63Top-54A
63Top-54B
64Top-262
64TopVen-262
Fanovich, Frank
49EurSta-83
52Par-84
54OriEss-10
Fansler, Stan
85NasPirT-8
86HawIslP-7
87VanCanP-1604
88BufBisC-2
88BufBisP-1469
91CarMudLD-102
91CarMudP-1080
91LinDriAA-102
92CarMudF-1175
92CarMudS-134
92SkyAA F-63
96VerExpB-2
Fantauzzi, John
93ClaFS7-185
93WatDiaC-15
93WatDiaF-1776
94MidLeaAF-MDW58
94SprSulC-1
94SprSulF-2044
95AshTouTI-29
96SalAvaB-8
Fanucchi, Paul
90NebCor-10
Fanzone, Carmen
73OPC-139
73Top-139
74OPC-484
74Top-484
75OPC-363
75Top-363
Farfan, David
95BoiHawTI-17
Fargas, Hector
93SpoIndC-8
93SpoIndF-3585
94SprSulC-10
Faria, Joe
47SmiClo-25
Farias, Tom
77BriRedST-4
Faries, Paul
87SpoIndP-17
88CalLeaACLC-43
88RivRedWCLC-217
88RivRedWP-1422
89TexLeaAGS-7
89WicChaR-5
89WicStaR-18
89WicUpdR-3
89WicWraR-22
90CMC-517
90LasVegSC-14
90LasVegSP-128
90ProAAAF-16
90TriAllGP-AAA8
91Bow-664
91DonRoo-16
91Fle-528
91MajLeaCP-55
91PadCok-3
91PadMag-20
91PadSmo-9
91Sco-711
91StaClu-557
91Stu-243
91TopDeb90-46
91Ult-302
91UppDec-751
92Fle-603
92LasVegSF-2799
92LasVegSS-230
92OPC-162
92Pin-332
92Sco-509
92Sco100RS-22
92StaClu-513
92Top-162
92TopGol-162
92TopGolW-162
92TopMic-162
92TriA AAS-230
92UppDec-310
93PhoFirF-1522
93TriAAAGF-26
94GiaUSPC-2H
94GiaUSPC-9S
94PhoFirF-1525
94TriAAF-AAA40
95EdmTraTI-6
96IowCubB-13
Fariss, Monty
88ButCopKSP-22
88TulDriTI-3
89Bow-233
89BowTif-233
89Top-177
89TopTif-177
89TulDriGS-8
89TulDriTI-6
90Bow-500
90BowTif-500
90CMC-799
90TulDriP-1161
90TulDriTI-7
91Bow-285
91Cla3-T18
91Don-455
91LinDriAAA-308
91OklCit8LD-308
91OklCit8P-184
91TriA AAGP-AAA25
92ClaGam-107
92DonRoo-35
92Fle-668
92Lea-354
92OklCit8F-1926
92OPC-138
92Pin-560
92PinRoo-14
92PinTea2-74
92ProFS7-152
92RanMot-24
92Sco-772
92ScoRoo-30
92StaClu-803
92StaCluNC-803
92Top-138
92TopDeb91-54
92TopGol-138
92TopGolW-138
92TopMic-138
92Ult-441
92UppDec-462
93Don-245
93Don-753
93Fle-427
93Lea-320
93MarUSPC-3H
93MarUSPC-13C
93PacSpa-461
93RanKee-141
93Sco-432
93StaClu-535
93StaCluFDI-535
93StaCluMarl-19
93StaCluMOP-535
93Top-575
93TopGol-575
93TopInaM-575
93TopMic-575
93TopTra-111T
93Ult-374
93UppDec-717
93UppDecGold-717
93USPlaCR-7H
94EdmTraF-2886
Farkas, Ron
78SprRedWK-2
82IndIndTI-24
Farley, Bob
60TacBan-5
61TacBan-6
61UniOil-T34
62Top-426
62WhiSoxTS-6
Farley, Brian
83EriCarT-10
87SprCarB-20
Farley, Cordell
96JohCitCTI-12
Farley, Joe
96BriWhiSB-15
96HicCraB-5
Farlow, Kevin
90SpoIndSP-23
91WatDiaC-16
91WatDiaP-1263
92WatDiaC-1
92WatDiaF-2149
Farmar, Damon
83QuaCitCT-25
85ModA'sC-20
87MidAngP-14
86HumStaDS-18
Farmer, Al
86SalRedBP-8
Farmer, Billy
70OPC-444
70Top-444
Farmer, Bryan Pierce
87GreBraB-16
88GreBraB-13
89RicBraBC-6
89RicBraC-8
89RicBraP-834
89RicBraTI-7
Farmer, Craig
94LetMouF-3872
94LetMouSP-10
Farmer, Ed
72OPC-116
72Top-116
73OPC-272
73Top-272
74OPC-506
74Top-506
77RocRedWM-18
78SpoIndC-22
80Top-702
81CokTeaS-29
81Don-40
81Fle-339
81FleStiC-114
81OPC-36
81Top-36
81TopScr-54
81TopSti-64
81TopSupHT-15
82Don-482
82Fle-342
82OPC-328
82Top-328
82TopTra-32T
83Don-471
83Fle-161
83PhiTas-11
83Top-459
83TopFol-4
84TacTigC-247
86HawIslP-8
91OriCro-126
93RanKee-142
94BreMilB-22
Farmer, Gordon
88AubAstP-1970
89AshTouP-953
91OscAstC-2
91OscAstP-674
Farmer, Howard
87JamExpP-2561
88MidLeaAGS-46
88RocExpLC-12
89BasAmeAPB-AA20
89JacExpB-12
89JacExpP-155
90Bow-107
90BowTif-107
90CMC-53
90IndIndC-3
90IndIndP-290
90ProAAAF-573
90ScoRoo-91T
90UppDec-753
91Don-734
91MajLeaCP-79
91OPCPre-40
91Sco-718
91Sco100RS-20
91TopDeb90-47
91UppDec-362
92Don-779
92IndIndF-1854
92IndIndS-181
92StaClu-367
Farmer, Jon
95KanCouCTI-41
Farmer, Ken
86LitFalMP-10
Farmer, Kevin
87SpoIndP-14
88RivRedWCLC-218
88RivRedWP-1408
89RivRedWB-5
89RivRedWCLC-7
89RivRedWP-1412
Farmer, Michael
91SouAtlLAGP-SAL43
91SpaPhiC-23
91SpaPhiP-908
92ClePhiC-8
93Bow-624
94UppDecML-37
Farmer, Mike
90MarPhiP-3182
92ClaFS7-75
92ClePhiF-2069
93ClaFS7-186
93ReaPhiF-290
94CenValRC-6
94CenValRF-3195
95NewHavRTI-27
Farmer, Randy
91KinMetC-13
91KinMetP-3820
92ColMetC-14
92ColMetF-302
92ColMetPI-6
Farmer, Reggie
87SpoIndP-11
88ChaRaiP-1216
89WatDiaP-1796
89WatDiaS-5
90RivRedWB-8
90RivRedWCLC-9
90RivRedWP-2618
91HigDesMC-24
91HigDesMP-2407
Farmer, William
87OldJudN-162
Farner, Matt
94ClaGolF-68
94Top-203
94TopGol-203
94TopSpa-203
Farnsworth, Jeff
96EveAquB-7
97Bow-186
97BowInt-186
Farnsworth, Kyle
96RocCubTI-8
Farnsworth, Mark
82ChaRoyT-23
83ChaRoyT-26
85Ft.MyeRT-21
86Ft.MyeRP-10
87Ft.MyeRP-31
90BasCitRS-31
95OmaRoyTI-9
96OmaRoyB-4
Farnsworth, Ross
90KisDodD-11
91GreFalDSP-11
92BakDodCLC-10
Faron, Robert J.
87SprCarB-11
88ArkTraGS-9
90SprCarDGB-21
Farr, Jim
79AshTouT-6
80TulDriT-7
83OklCit8T-22
84PhoGiaC-9
93RanKee-143
Farr, Mark
95ElmPioTI-5
95ElmPioUTI-5
Farr, Michael
86WatIndP-7
87KinIndP-15
88WilBilP-1307
Farr, Steve
78ChaPirT-4
80BufBisT-7
81BufBisT-18
82BufBisT-13
84IndWhe-27
84MaiGuiT-4
85Don-653
85Fle-446
85Top-664
85TopTif-664
86Don-588
86Fle-7
86RoyNatP-26
86TopTra-35T
86TopTraT-35T
87Don-301
87Fle-367
87FleGlo-367
87OPC-216
87Top-473
87TopSti-255
87TopTif-473
88Don-378
88Fle-256
88FleGlo-256
88RoySmo-10
88Sco-466
88ScoGlo-466
88Top-222
88TopTif-222
89Bow-114
89BowTif-114
89Don-356
89DonBasB-151
89Fle-281
89FleGlo-281
89OPC-356
89PanSti-349
89RoyTasD-12
89Sco-183
89Top-507
89TopSti-272
89TopTif-507
89UppDec-308
90Bow-366
90BowTif-366
90Don-356
90Fle-107
90FleCan-107
90OPC-149
90PubSti-347

90RedFolSB-30
90Sco-356
90Top-149
90TopSti-270
90TopTif-149
90UppDec-680
90VenSti-165
91Bow-168
91Don-365
91Fle-558
91Lea-348
91OPC-301
91Sco-172
91ScoRoo-21T
91StaClu-419
91Stu-92
91Top-301
91TopDesS-301
91TopMic-301
91TopTif-301
91TopTra-38T
91TopTraT-38T
91UppDec-660
91UppDec-717
92Bow-622
92Don-735
92Fle-225
92Lea-20
92OPC-46
92Pin-206
92Sco-47
92StaClu-793
92StaCluNC-793
92Top-46
92TopGol-46
92TopGolW-46
92TopMic-46
92Ult-405
92UppDec-48
93Bow-539
93Don-21
93Fle-276
93Lea-504
93OPC-27
93PacSpa-553
93Pin-196
93Sco-162
93Sel-172
93SP-263
93StaClu-176
93StaCluFDI-176
93StaCluMOP-176
93StaCluY-7
93Top-717
93TopGol-717
93TopInaM-717
93TopMic-717
93Ult-593
93UppDec-410
93UppDecGold-410
94ColC-514
94ColChoGS-514
94ColChoSS-514
94Don-531
94Fin-348
94FinRef-348
94Fle-228
94Lea-270
94Sco-535
94ScoGolR-535
94ScoRoo-RT70
94ScoRooGR-RT70
94StaClu-593
94StaCluFDI-593
94StaCluGR-593
94StaCluMOP-593
94Top-641
94TopGol-641
94TopSpa-641
94UppDec-467
94UppDecED-467
95ColCho-414
95ColChoGS-414
95ColChoSS-414
95Sco-186
95ScoGolR-186
95ScoPlaTS-186

Farraez, Jesus
96AubDouB-7

Farrar, Sid
87BucN28-78
87OldJudN-163
88WG1CarG-50
90KalBatN-17

Farrar, Terry
91BluOriC-4
91BluOriP-4121
91KanCouCTI-6
92FreKeyC-18
92FreKeyF-1800
93BowBayF-2184
94Bow-78

Farrell, Doc (Edward S.)
26Exh-33
29ExhFou-1
33Gou-148
33GouCanV-73
91ConTSN-324

Farrell, Duke (Charles A.)
03BreE10-49
04RedSoxUP-5
87OldJudN-165
90DodTar-233

Farrell, Jim
95MicBatCTI-12

Farrell, John A.
87BucN28-112A
87BucN28-112B
87OldJudN-164
94OriofB-54

Farrell, John Edward
85WatIndT-21
86WatIndP-9
87BufBisP-15
88ClaBlu-239
88Don-42
88DonBasB-117
88Fle-608
88FleGlo-608
88IndGat-52
88Lea-42
88Sco-620
88ScoBoxC-T6
88ScoGlo-620
88ScoYouSI-33
88Spo-132
88StaLinI-10
88Top-533
88TopBig-213
88TopTif-533
89Bow-74
89BowTif-74
89Don-320
89DonBasB-285
89Fle-403
89FleGlo-403
89IndTeal-11
89OPC-227
89PanSti-318
89Sco-266
89Spo-37
89Top-227
89TopBig-135
89TopSti-214
89TopTif-227
89UppDec-468
90Don-232
90DonBesA-19
90Fle-491
90FleCan-491
90IndTeal-12
90Lea-22
90OPC-32
90PanSti-53
90PubSti-559
90Sco-103
90Top-32
90TopBig-237
90TopSti-217
90TopTif-32
90UppDec-570
90VenSti-166
91Bow-82
91Don-106
91Fle-366
91IndFanC-12
91OPC-664
91Sco-50
91StaClu-185
91Stu-42
91Top-664
91TopDesS-664
91TopMic-664
91TopTif-664
91Ult-111
91UppDec-692
92AugPirC-1
92ClaFS7-17
92StaClu-693
92StaCluECN-693
93AngMot-21
93StaCluAn-20
93UppDec-689
93UppDecGold-689
94Pac-77
94VanCanF-1858

Farrell, John Sebastian
11SpoLifCW-123

Farrell, Jon
88CapCodPPaLP-76
91Cla/Bes-422
91ClaDraP-20
91FroRowDP-12
91FroRowDPP-1
91WelPirC-1
91WelPirP-3575
92AugPirF-251
92Bow-393
92OPC-9
92Pin-299
92ProFS7-313
92Sco-804
92StaCluD-47
92Top-9
92TopGol-9
92TopGolW-9
92TopMic-9
92UppDec-69
92UppDecML-108
93ExcFS7-91
93SalBucC-10
93SalBucF-445
94SalBucC-10
94SalBucF-2338
94UppDecML-171
95CarMudF-172
96CarMudB-22

Farrell, Kerby
73TacTwiC-6

Farrell, Mike
76AppFoxT-5
92CalLeaACL-15
92ElPasDF-3915
92GulCoaMF-3489
92StoPorC-21
92StoPorF-29
93Bow-211
93ClaFS7-187
93ExcFS7-184
93KinMetC-11
93KinMetF-3801
93NewOrlZF-964
94St.LucMC-8
94St.LucMF-1201

Farrell, Turk (Dick)
47Exh-72
58Hir-43
58PhiJayP-4
58Top-76A
58Top-76B
59Top-175
59TopVen-175
60PhiJayP-7
60Top-103
60TopVen-103
61DodUniO-6
61Pos-115A
61Pos-115B
61Top-522
61TopStal-54
62Col.45B-6
62Col45'HC-5
62Col45'JP-6
62SalPlaC-184
62ShiPlaC-184
62Top-304
62TopBuc-25
62TopStal-125
63Baz-8
63Col45"P-5
63Col45'JP-4
63ExhStaB-21
63Fle-38
63Jel-192
63Pos-192
63SalMetC-2
63Top-9
63Top-277
63TopStil-15
64Baz-8
64Col.45JP-4
64Top-560
64TopCoi-91
64TopGia-22
64TopSta-98
64TopStaU-24
65OldLonC-9
65OPC-80
65Top-80
66Top-377
66TopRubl-28
67AstTeal2-9
67CokCapAs-16
67DexPre-71
67OPC-190
67Top-190
68Top-217
68TopVen-217
69MilBra-82
69Top-531
78TCM60I-202
78TCM60I-256
82AstAstI-1
86AstMot-1
87AstSer1-9
87AstSer1-27
87AstShoSO-6
89AstCol43-8
90DodTar-232

Farris, Mark
94ClaUpdCotC-CC10
94SigRooDP-11
94SigRooDPS-11
94StaCluDP-85
94StaCluDPFDI-85
94TopTra-87T
94WelPirC-1
94WelPirF-3502
95Bow-125
95ColCho-41
95ColChoGS-41
95ColChoSS-41
95Exc-253
95SelSurS-SS3
95StaClu-106
95StaCluFDI-106
95StaCluMOP-106
95StaCluSTWS-106
95Top-363
96AugGreB-8
96HonShaHWB-10

Farrish, Keoki
90GreFalDSP-8
91YakBeaC-9
91YakBeaP-4260
92VerBeaDC-2
92VerBeaDF-2890

Farrow, Doug
82IdaFalAT-6

Farrow, James
93GenCubC-11
93GenCubF-3167
96AugGreB-9

Farsaci, Dave
91EugEmeC-17
91EugEmeP-3718

Farson, Bryan
94StaCluDP-54
94StaCluDPFDI-54
95LynHilTI-8

Farson, George
78HolMilT-8
79HolMilT-8
80PenPilCT-11

Farwell, Fred
87BakDodP-20

Fasano, Sal
93EugEmeC-13
93EugEmeF-3858
94MidLeaAF-MDW22
94RocRoyC-1
94RocRoyF-567
95Bow-230
95BowGolF-230
95Exc-59
95SigRooOJ-12
95SigRooOJP-12
95SigRooOJPS-12
95SigRooOJS-12
95SPML-71
95UppDecML-145
95WicWraTI-33
96Bow-308
96Exc-59
96Fin-B307
96FinRef-B307
96FleUpd-U39
96FleUpdTC-U39
96LeaSigA-65
96LeaSigAG-65
96LeaSigAS-65
96Pin-370
96PinAfi-166
96PinAfiAP-166
96PinFoil-370
96Sel-177
96SelArtP-177
96SelCer-105
96Sum-169
96SumAbo&B-169
96SumArtP-169
96SumFoi-169
96Ult-353
96UltGolM-353
96UppDec-260
97Sco-70
97ScoPreS-70
97ScoShoS-70
97ScoShoSAP-70
95UppDecMLFS-145

Fascher, Stan
06AshTouP-11
87OscAstP-11

Fassero, Jeff
85SprCarT-9
86FloStaLAP-13
86St.PetCP-8
87ArkTraP-6
88ArkTraGS-5
88BlaYNPRWL-82
89LouRedBC-4
89LouRedBP-1246
89LouRedBTI-18
90CanIndB-19
90CanIndP-1289
90CanIndS-5
91DonRoo-28
91IndIndLD-183
91IndIndP-457
91LinDriAAA-183
91TopTra-39T
91TopTraT-39T
92Don-717
92ExpDonD-7
92ExpPos-11
92Fle-477
92FleRooS-5
92OPC-423
92OPCPre-119
92Sco-738
92StaClu-469
92Top-423
92TopDeb91-55
92TopGol-423
92TopGolW-423
92TopMic-423
92Ult-516
92UppDec-685
93Don-642
93ExpPosN-9
93Fla-82
93Fle-459
93Lea-91
93OPC-192
93PacSpa-533
93Top-178
93TopGol-178
93TopInaM-178
93TopMic-178
93UppDec-609
93UppDecGold-609
94ColC-98
94ColChoGS-98
94ColChoSS-98
94Don-123
94ExtBas-303
94Fin-250
94FinRef-250
94Fla-401
94Fle-536
94Lea-181
94Pac-378
94Sco-261
94ScoGolR-261
94Sel-124
94StaClu-379
94StaCluFDI-379
94StaCluGR-379
94StaCluMOP-379
94Top-554

94TopGol-554
94TopSpa-554
94TriPla-93
94Ult-225
94UppDec-192
94UppDecED-192
95ColCho-246
95ColChoGS-246
95ColChoSS-246
95Don-310
95DonPreP-310
95DonTopotO-279
95Emo-151
95Fin-291
95FinRef-291
95Fla-374
95Fle-348
95Lea-53
95Pac-265
95Pin-99
95PinArtP-99
95PinMusC-99
95Sco-101
95ScoGolR-101
95ScoPlaTS-101
95SP-72
95SPCha-64
95SPChaDC-64
95SPSil-72
95StaClu-117
95StaCluFDI-117
95StaCluMOP-117
95StaCluSTWS-117
95Top-603
95TopCyb-374
95Ult-189
95UltGolM-189
95UppDec-327
95UppDecED-327
95UppDecEDG-327
95USPlaCMLA-8S
96Don-492
96DonPreP-492
96EmoXL-220
96ExpDis-7
96Fla-304
96Fle-455
96FleTif-455
96LeaSigA-66
96LeaSigAG-66
96LeaSigAS-66
96Pac-132
96Sco-411
96SP-123
96StaClu-296
96StaCluEPB-296
96StaCluEPG-296
96StaCluEPS-296
96StaCluMOP-296
96Top-269
96Ult-230
96UltGolM-230
96UppDec-397
97Cir-323
97CirRav-323
97ColCho-482
97Don-305
97Don-436
97DonLim-159
97DonLimLE-159
97DonPreP-305
97DonPreP-436
97DonPrePGold-305
97DonPrePGold-436
97DonTea-146
97DonTeaSPE-146
97Fle-377
97Fle-682
97FleTif-377
97FleTif-682
97Lea-256
97LeaFraM-256
97LeaFraMDC-256
97MetUni-144
97NewPin-124
97NewPinAP-124
97NewPinMC-124
97NewPinPP-124
97Pac-343
97PacLigB-343
97PacSil-343
97Pin-10
97PinArtP-10
97PinIns-41
97PinInsCE-41
97PinInsDE-41
97PinMusC-10
97PinX-P-100
97PinX-PMoS-100
97Sco-414
97ScoHobR-414
97ScoResC-414
97ScoShoS-414
97ScoShoSAP-414
97SpoIll-41
97SpoIllEE-41
97StaClu-100
97StaCluMOP-100
97Stu-80
97StuPrePG-80
97StuPrePS-80
97Top-335
97Ult-228
97Ult-326
97UltGolME-228
97UltGolME-326
97UltPlaME-228
97UltPlaME-326

Fast, Darcy
72OPC-457
72Top-457

Faszholz, John
55CarHunW-4

Faul, Bill
63Top-558
64Top-236
64TopVen-236
66Top-322
66TopVen-322

Faulk, Jim (James)
88RocExpLC-13
90FloStaLAS-5
90StaFS7-7
90WesPalBES-5

Faulk, Kelly
80PenPilBT-6
80PenPilCT-13
81ReaPhiT-2
82ReaPhiT-2
85ColCliP-10
85ColCliT-6
86ColCliP-8
87IndIndTI-24

Faulk, Paul
94OneYanC-28

Faulkner, Craig
87LSUTigP-2
88HagSunS-6
89HagSunB-14
89HagSunP-266
89HagSunS-7
90CMC-742
90HagSunB-10
90HagSunP-1421
90HagSunS-9
90LSUTigGM-6
91ElPasDLD-181
91ElPasDP-2750
91LinDriAA-181
92ElPasDF-3924
92ElPasDS-208
92SkyAA F-93
93ArkTraF-2819
94OriPro-32
94RocRedWF-1000
94RocRedWTI-8
95BowBayTI-47

Faulkner, Jim
90DodTar-234

Faulkner, Neil
94HunCubF-3545
95RocCubTI-34
94HunCubC-8

Faurot, Adam
96OgdRapTI-2

Faurot, Scott
90YakBeaTI-21

Fauske, Josh
96HicCraB-6

Faust, Nancy
84WhiSoxTV-12
85WhiSoxC-NNO
86WhiSoxC-NNO
87WhiSoxC-9
88WhiSoxC-6
89WhiSoxC-29

Fava, Andres
85AncGlaPTI-10

Faw, Brian
90TamYanD-6
91GreHorP-3051
92ForLauYC-19
92ForLauYTI-10
92Ft.LauYF-2604
93AlbYanF-2155
94AbaYanF-1435
95NorNavTI-22

Fay, May
08AllLadBC-2

Fayne, Jeff
89JohCitCS-13
90HamRedS-12
91SprCarC-16
91SprCarP-756

Fazekas, Robert
88CapCodPPaLP-160
90NiaFalRP-18
91FayGenC-9
91FayGenP-1162

Fazio, Ernie
63Col45"P-6
63Col45"P-17
78TCM60I-215

Fazzini, Frank
86BelBreP-6

Fazzio, Daryl
80WatIndT-14

Fears, Tom
52Whe-10A
52Whe-10B

Febles, Carlos
96LanLugB-11

Feder, Mike
76WauMetT-25

Federici, Rick
78ChaPirT-5
80BufBisT-3

Federico, Gustavo
89HelBreSP-14

Federico, Joe
87AncGlaP-11
88HamRedP-1738
88NebCor-20
89St.PetCS-11
90Bes-93
90SprCarB-8
91St.PetCC-20
91St.PetCP-2283

Federoff, Al
53MotCoo-62

Fedor, Chris
84GreHorT-11

Fedor, Fritz
82BelBreF-9
83BelBreF-24
86BurExpP-7
87KinIndP-10

Feeley, James
82MadMusF-20

Feeley, Peter
91NiaFalRC-16
91NiaFalRP-3646
92NiaFalRC-5
92NiaFalRF-3330
93FayGenC-11
93FayGenF-136

Fehrenbach, Todd
95BilRedTI-10

Feinburg, Ken
77CedRapGT-5
78CedRapGT-8

Feist, Ken
91EveGiaC-9
91EveGiaP-3928
92CliGiaC-6
92CliGiaF-3608

Felch, Jim
94DanBraC-9
94DanBraF-3544

Felda, Brian
75CedRapGT-13

Felden, Keith
88UtiBluSP-18
89MiaMirIS-6

Felder, Kenny
92ClaDraP-9
92ClaDraPFB-BC9
92HelBreF-1726
92HelBreSP-2
93BelBreC-7
93BelBreF-1722
93Bow-563
93ClaFS7-275
93ExcFS7-185
93StaCluM-99
93Top-723
93TopGol-723
93TopInaM-723
93TopMic-723
94Bow-421
94Cla-127
94StoPorC-7
94StoPorF-1705
95ElPasDTI-6
95SigRoo-19
95SigRooSig-19
95UppDecML-121
95UppDecMLFS-121

Felder, Mike
83ElPasDT-9
84ElPasDT-23
85VanCanC-211
86BrePol-16
86Don-634
87BrePol-16
87Don-295
87Top-352
87TopTif-352
88BlaYNPRWL-117
88BrePol-16
88Don-397
88Fle-164
88FleGlo-164
88Sco-388
88ScoGlo-388
88StaLinBre-7
88Top-718
88TopTif-718
89BrePol-16
89Top-263
89TopTif-263
89UppDec-252
90BreMilB-7
90BrePol-16
90Don-609
90El PasDAGTI-12
90Fle-321
90FleCan-321
90Lea-480
90OPC-159
90PubSti-495
90Sco-268
90Top-159
90TopTif-159
90UppDec-178
90VenSti-167
91Don-535
91Fle-583
91FleUpd-129
91GiaMot-15
91GiaPacGaE-28
91Lea-445
91OPC-44
91Sco-97
91StaClu-307
91Top-44
91TopDesS-44
91TopMic-44
91TopTif-44
91UltUpd-117
91UppDec-395
92Bow-93
92Don-182
92Fle-635
92GiaMot-15
92GiaPacGaE-16
92OPC-697
92Pin-311
92Sco-251
92StaClu-194
92Top-697
92TopGol-697
92TopGolW-697
92TopMic-697
92Ult-291
92UppDec-288
93Bow-247
93Fle-529
93FleFinE-269
93Lea-248
93MarMot-9
93PacSpa-622
93Pin-148
93Sco-621
93SelRoo-106T
93StaClu-675
93StaCluFDI-675
93StaCluMari-29
93StaCluMOP-675
93Top-466
93TopGol-466
93TopInaM-466
93TopMic-466
93Ult-618
93UppDec-186
93UppDec-714
93UppDecGold-186
93UppDecGold-714
94AstMot-11
94BreMilB-23
94ColC-361
94ColChoGS-361
94ColChoSS-361
94Don-155
94Fle-284
94Lea-348
94Pac-568
94Pin-352
94PinArtP-352
94PinMusC-352
94Sco-411
94ScoGolR-411
94StaClu-555
94StaCluFDI-555
94StaCluGR-555
94StaCluMOP-555
94Top-569
94TopGol-569
94TopSpa-569
95Fle-458

Feledyk, Kristian
95AusFutSFP-SFFP8

Felioc, Jason
83TamTarT-8
86JacMetT-20
87TidTidP-7

Feliciano, Felix
80UtiBluJT-5

Feliciano, Pedro
95GreFalDTI-2
96GreFalDB-11
96GreFalDTI-8

Felitz, Bill
89JohCitCS-12

Felix, Albert
92ChaRanC-9

Felix, Antonio
89AugPirP-510
90SalBucS-6

Felix, Chris
94HigDesMC-30

Felix, Gus
90DodTar-946

Felix, Junior
87MyrBeaBJP-1455
88KnoBluJB-2
88SouLeaAJ-24
89DonBasB-199
89DonRoo-55
89FleUpd-69
89ScoRoo-83T
89SyrChiC-19
89SyrChiMB-10
89SyrChiP-810
89TopTra-32T
89TopTraT-32T
89UppDec-743
89UppDecS-2
90BluJayFS-7
90BluJayHS-5
90BluJayHS-6
90Bow-522
90BowTif-522
90ClaBlu-50
90Don-70
90DonBesA-70
90Fle-79
90FleCan-79
90FleSoaS-9
90Hot50RS-15
90Lea-422
90OPC-347
90PanSti-377
90Sco-258
90Sco100RS-18
90ScoYouSI-9
90Spo-186
90Top-347
90TopBig-210
90TopDeb89-35

90TopRoo-8
90TopSti-188
90TopTif-347
90ToyRoo-9
90UppDec-106
91AngSmo-2
91Bow-201
91Cla2-T48
91ClaGam-190
91Don-323
91Fle-173
91Lea-435
91OPC-543
91OPCPre-41
91PanFreS-342
91Sco-203
91ScoRoo-20T
91StaClu-457
91Top-543
91TopDesS-543
91TopMic-543
91TopTif-543
91TopTra-40T
91TopTraT-40T
91UppDec-563
91UppDec-711
92AngPol-8
92Bow-404
92Don-217
92Lea-118
92OPC-189
92PanSti-9
92Pin-220
92Sco-519
92StaClu-141
92Top-189
92TopGol-189
92TopGolW-189
92TopMic-189
92TriPla-168
92Ult-325
92UppDec-303
93Bow-122
93ClaGam-30
93Don-197
93Don-771
93Fin-173
93FinRef-173
93Fle-190
93FleFinE-60
93Lea-333
93MarUSPC-6C
93MarUSPC-9H
93MarUSPC-12S
93OPC-128
93PacSpa-462
93Pin-515
93PinExpOD-9
93Sco-425
93Sel-28
93StaClu-457
93StaCluFDI-457
93StaCluMarl-8
93StaCluMOP-457
93Stu-181
93Top-77
93TopGol-77
93TopInaM-77
93TopMic-77
93Ult-375
93UppDec-157
93UppDec-771
93UppDecGold-157
93UppDecGold-771
94ColC-364
94ColChoGS-364
94ColChoSS-364
94Fla-48
94FleUpd-43
94ScoRoo-RT44
94ScoRooGR-RT44
94StaClu-660
94StaCluFDI-660
94StaCluGR-660
94StaCluMOP-660
94TopTra-89T
95Don-309
95DonPreP-309
95Fle-49
95Pac-150
95Pin-42
95PinArtP-42
95PinMusC-42
95Sco-18
95ScoGolR-18
95ScoPlaTS-18
95StaClu-154
95StaCluFDI-154
95StaCluMOP-154
95StaCluSTWS-154
95StaCluVR-80
95Top-68
95TopCyb-135
95Ult-45
95UltGolM-45
95UppDecSE-98
95UppDecSEG-98
95StaCluVRMC-80
Felix, Lauro
93ModA'sC-8
93ModA'sF-807
94ModA'sC-8
94ModA'sF-3069
95ElPasDTI-7
96El PasDB-10
Felix, Nathanael
90TamYanD-7
Felix, Nick
87BelMarL-22
89WauTimGS-16
90SanBerSCLC-92
91ChaRanC-5
91ChaRanP-1309
93WicWraF-2972
Felix, Paul
83WisRapTF-6
85OrlTwiT-4
86GleFalTP-4
87GleFalTP-19
88TolMudHC-20
88TolMudHP-600
Felix, Pedro
95BelGiaTI-3
96BurBeeTI-20
Felix, Ruben
95BelBreTI-11
Feliz, Adolfo
81WatRedT-13
82CedRapRT-15
83TamTarT-9
83WatRedT-11
Feliz, Bienvenido
96WatIndTI-8
Feliz, Janiero
90WelPirP-5
Feller, Bob (Robert)
36GouWidPPR-C9
37ExhFou-11
37GouFliMR-8A
37GouFliMR-8B
37GouThuMR-8
37OPCBatUV-120
37WheBB8-4
37WheBB9-6
38BasTabP-8
38DixLid-2
38DixLidP-2
38ExhFou-11
38GouHeaU-264
38GouHeaU-288
38OurNatGPP-8
38WheBB10-1
39ExhSal-15A
39ExhSal-15B
39GouPreR303A-14
39GouPreR303B-7
39WorWidGTP-14
40WheM4-1A
40WheM4-6B
41DouPlaR-77
41WheM5-15
43MPR302-1-10
46SpoExcW-3-1B
47HomBon-15
47IndTeal-8
47IndVanPP-7A
47IndVanPP-7B
47PM1StaP1-58
47PM1StaP1-59
48BluTin-43
48Bow-5
48IndTeal-9
48SweSpoT-19
48ThoMcAF-1
49Bow-27
49IndTeal-9
49IndVisEl-6
49Lea-93
49MPR302-2-103
50Bow-6
50IndNumN-9
50IndTeal-8
51Bow-30
51R42SmaS-31
51TopRedB-22
51Whe-1
52BerRos-19
52Bow-43
52DixLid-8
52DixPre-8
52IndNumN-5
52RedMan-AL8
52StaCalL-74E
52StaCalS-88B
52Top-88
52Whe-11A
52Whe-11B
53BowC-114
53ExhCan-17
53IndPenCBP-11
53Top-54
54Bow-132
54DanDee-6
54Wil-5
55Bow-134
55IndCarBL-1
55IndGolS-5
56Top-200
60Fle-26
60NuHi-60
61Fle-25
61NuSco-460
63BasMagM-24
63GadFunC-61
67TopVen-160
68LauWorS-45
69EquSpoHoF-BB4
72LauGreF-44
73HalofFPP-7
75SheGrePG-1
75SpoHobBG-3
76GalBasGHoF-8
76GrePlaG-1
76RowExh-5
76ShaPiz-87
76TayBow4-11
77BobParHoF-21
77GalGloG-12
79BasGre-74
79DiaGre-285
79TCM50-28
80PacLeg-53
80PerHaloFP-87
80SSPHOF-87
81SpoHaloF-22
81WatIndT-34
82BasCarN-8
82BasCarN-15
82CraJac-2
82DiaCla-47
82OhiHaloF-5
83DonHOFH-36
83MLBPin-6
83TopRep5-88
84OCoandSI-53
84SpoDesPW-10
84TCMPla1-17
86SpoDecG-16
87HygAllG-16
87NesDreT-20
88GreBasS-75
88PacLegI-101
89HOFStiB-62
89PacLegI-156
89SweBasG-75
90BasWit-13
90Col-36
90PacLeg-85
90PerGreM-83
90SweBasG-60
91ConTSN-35
91HomCooC-6
91LinDri-43
91SweBasG-145
91TopArc1-54
92BazQua5A-7
92ConTSN-370
92ConTSNCI-23
92MCIAmb-14
92PacRyaTEI-135
92St.VinHHS-3
92UppDecS-17
93ActPacA-110
93ActPacA2-44G
93ConTSN-933
93DiaStaES-128
93MCIAmb-5
93PinDiM-11
93UppDecS-3
93UppDecS-30
93Yoo-5
94TedWil-25
94TedWilLC-LC12
94UppDecTAE-48
95ConTSN-1337
95ConTSNCMP-1435
95ConTSNP-1337
95MrTurBG-1
95StoPop-4
97FleMilDM-13
97TopStaHRR-3
97TopStaHRRA-3
Fellows, Mark
82MadMusF-14
83AlbA'sT-3
Felsch, Happy (Oscar)
15SpoNewM-57
16ColE13-47
16SpoNewM-56
16TanBraE-10
17HolBreD-29
19W514-3
75WhiSox1T-7
88PacEigMO-10
88PacEigMO-41
88PacEigMO-55
88PacEigMO-76
88PacEigMO-109
92Man191BSR-8
94ConTSN-1042
94ConTSNB-1042
Felske, John
73OPC-45
73OPC-332
73Top-45
73Top-332
77SpoIndC-26
78SpoIndC-26
79VanCanT-20
82ReaPhiT-22
83PorBeaT-13
84PhiTas-10
85PhiTas-2
85PhiTas-8
85TopTifT-33T
85TopTra-33T
86PhiTas-7
86Top-621
86TopTif-621
87PhiTas-7
87Top-443
87TopTif-443
94BreMilB-24
Felt, Jim
82AleDukT-24
83AleDukT-22
84PriWilPT-5
Felt, Rich
82VerBeaDT-5
83VerBeaDT-3
Felton, Fred
88BatCliP-1686
Felton, Terry
77OrlTwiT-9A
77OrlTwiT-9B
79TolMudHT-9
80TolMudHT-7
81TolMudHT-4
82TwiPos-11
83Don-354
83Fle-612
83TolMudHT-2
83Top-181
Felton, Todd
88SpaPhiP-1043
Fendrick, Dave
74GasRanT-10
Fenn, Harry
57SeaPop-12
Fennell, Mike
82OneYanT-14
83GreHorT-18
85AlbYanT-26
89TopTra-37T
89TopTraT-37T
Fennelly, Francis
87OldJudN-166
Feno, Quinn
92ElmPioC-11
92ElmPioF-1396
Fenton, Cary
94VerExpC-10
94VerExpF-3916
Fenus, Justin
96MarPhiB-7
Fenwick, Bob
72Top-679
73OPC-567
73Top-567
Feola, Larry (Lawrence)
75CliPilT-13
87SanJosBP-22
Ferens, Stan
46SeaSLP-17
Ferguson, Alex
21KoBreWSI-31
22W575-34
27AmeCarE-40
90DodTar-235
93ConTSN-793
Ferguson, Bruce
78WauMetT-8
Ferguson, Charles
87BucN28-79
87OldJudN-167
88GandBCGCE-15
90KalBatN-18
Ferguson, Fergy
83TamTarT-10
Ferguson, George Cecil
06GiaUllAFS-3
08RosComP-90
09ColChiE-98
09RamT20-45
09T206-128
10DomDisP-44
10JuJuDE-18
10SweCapPP-66
11SpoLifCW-124
11SpoLifM-138
11T205-55
12ColRedB-98
12ColTinT-98
Ferguson, Greg
88SouOreAP-1708
Ferguson, Jeff
96HarCitRCB-12
Ferguson, Jim (James)
82OneYanT-15
87SalLakTTT-6
88SavCarP-348
89SavCarP-354
90SavCarP-2075
91JamExpC-23
91JamExpP-3536
92AlbPolC-2
92JamExpC-10
92JamExpF-1494
Ferguson, Joe
72Top-616
73LinPor-94
73OPC-621
73Top-621
74OPC-86
74Top-86
74TopDecE-67
74TopSta-45
75OPC-115
75Top-115
76LinSup-121
76OPC-329
76SSP-81
76Top-329
77BurCheD-8
77OPC-107
77Top-573
78AstBurK-2
78Hos-109
78Top-226
79Top-671
80DodPol-13
80OPC-29
80Top-51
81DodPol-13
81Don-177
81Fle-124
81LonBeaPT-21
81Top-711
82Top-514
83Don-604

83Fle-87
83Top-416
86RanPer-NNO
87RanMot-28
87RanSmo-24
88DodMot-28
89DodMot-27
89DodPol-1
90DodMot-28
90DodPol-NNO
90DodTar-236
91DodMot-28
91DodPol-NNO
92DodMot-28
92DodPol-NNO
93DodMot-28
93DodPol-30
93RanKee-144
94DodMot-28
94DodPol-30
96HigDesMB-1
Ferguson, Mark
83AlbA'sT-4
84GreHorT-19
84ModA'sC-11
85AlbYanT-6
Ferguson, Mike
82CedRapRT-8
Ferguson, Ryan
96MarPhiB-8
Ferguson, Shane
92GulCoaYF-3784
Ferlenda, Greg
86SalRedBP-9
86TulDriTI-15
88KinIndS-6
89CanIndB-14
89CanIndS-5
89KinIndS-8
90CarLeaA-35
90KinIndTI-19
92WatIndC-27
92WatIndF-3251
Ferm, Ed
88BriTigP-1886
90LakTigS-10
91Cla/Bes-289
91LakTigC-4
91LakTigP-260
Fermaint, Mike
91PenPilC-19
91PenPilP-384
Fermin, Carlos
90BriTigP-3149
90BriTigS-6
91Cla/Bes-374
91FayGenC-18
91FayGenP-1177
92NiaFalRC-17
92NiaFalRF-3331
93LakTigC-7
93LakTigF-1317
93LimRocDWB-108
94LakTigC-7
95JacSunTI-9
Fermin, Felix
84PriWilPT-16
85NasPirT-9
86HawIslP-9
87HarSenP-6
88BufBisC-21
88BufBisP-1465
88Don-144
88Fle-643
88FleGlo-643
88StaLinPi-10
88Top-547
88TopTif-547
88TriAAC-5
89Don-565
89DonBasB-229
89DonTra-33
89Fle-208
89FleGlo-208
89FleUpd-27
89IndTeal-12
89Sco-620
89ScoRoo-78T
89Top-303
89TopTif-303
89TopTra-33T
89TopTraT-33T
89UppDec-88
90Bow-334
90BowTif-334
90Don-191
90Fle-492
90FleCan-492
90IndTeal-13
90OPC-722
90PanSti-60
90PubSti-560
90Sco-256
90ScoYouSI-6
90Top-722
90TopTif-722
90UppDec-409
90VenSti-168
91Don-537
91Fle-367
91IndFanC-10
91Lea-137
91OPC-193
91PanFreS-219
91Sco-139
91StaClu-238
91Top-193
91TopDesS-193
91TopMic-193
91TopTif-193
91Ult-112
91UppDec-104
92Don-242
92Fle-109
92IndFanC-9
92OPC-632
92PanSti-48
92Pin-152
92Sco-148
92StaClu-102
92Top-632
92TopGol-632
92TopGolW-632
92TopMic-632
92Ult-49
92UppDec-160
93Don-597
93Fle-591
93IndWUA-9
93Lea-215
93LimRocDWB-107
93LinVenB-309
93OPC-90
93PacBeiA-6
93PacSpa-95
93PanSti-50
93Pin-331
93Sel-256
93StaClu-139
93StaCluFDI-139
93StaCluMOP-139
93Top-462
93TopGol-462
93TopInaM-462
93TopMic-462
93Ult-184
93UppDec-615
93UppDecGold-615
94ColC-387
94ColChoGS-387
94ColChoSS-387
94Don-573
94ExtBas-164
94Fin-271
94FinRef-271
94Fla-101
94Fle-104
94FleUpd-82
94MarMot-5
94Pac-169
94PanSti-56
94Pin-102
94PinArtP-102
94PinMusC-102
94Sco-107
94ScoGolR-107
94ScoRoo-RT37
94ScoRooGR-RT37
94Sel-324
94StaClu-81
94StaClu-675
94StaCluFDI-81
94StaCluFDI-675
94StaCluGR-81
94StaCluGR-675
94StaCluMOP-81
94StaCluMOP-675
94Top-36
94TopGol-36
94TopSpa-36
94TopTra-99T
94Ult-42
94UppDec-389
94UppDecED-389
95ColCho-289
95ColChoGS-289
95ColChoSS-289
95Don-409
95DonPreP-409
95Fle-266
95Lea-146
95MarMot-24
95MarPac-31
95Pac-395
95PacPri-125
95Sco-106
95ScoGolR-106
95ScoPlaTS-106
95StaClu-421
95StaCluMOP-421
95StaCluSTDW-M421
95StaCluSTWS-421
95StaCluVR-219
95Top-234
95TopCyb-131
95Ult-327
95UltGolM-327
96Fle-237
96FleTif-237
95StaCluVRMC-219
96Top-67
Fermin, Miguel
93CedRapKC-6
93CedRapKF-1731
93LimRocDWB-97
Fermin, Pompilio
76CliPilT-14
Fermin, Ramon
92MadMusC-2
92MadMusF-1227
93ModA'sC-9
93ModA'sF-793
94ModA'sC-9
94ModA'sF-3059
95Bow-123
95HunStaTI-8
96JacSunB-11
Fernandes, Eddie
47SunBre-5
Fernandes, Jamie
95ButCopKtI-8
Fernandez, Alex
90Bes-250
90Bes-321
90ClaDraP-4
90ClaYel-T99
90FleUpd-84
90TopMag-40
91Baz-5
91Bow-351
91Cla2-T7
91ClaGam-184
91Don-59
91Fle-117
91Lea-296
91OPC-278
91OPCPre-42
91Sco-382
91Sco100RS-66
91SevCoi-F5
91SevCoi-M9
91StaClu-147
91Stu-31
91Top-278
91TopCraJ2-36
91TopDeb90-48
91TopDesS-278
91TopGolS-1
91TopMic-278
91TopTif-278
91UltUpd-14
91UppDec-645
91WhiSoxK-32
91WhiSoxK-NNO
91Woo-11
92Bow-201
92ClaGam-95
92Don-191
92Fle-78
92Lea-85
92OPC-755
92Pin-30
92Sco-82
92ScoProP-9
92ScoProP-21
92StaClu-467
92Stu-152
92Top-755
92TopGol-755
92TopGolW-755
92TopMic-755
92TriPla-74
92Ult-335
92UppDec-551
92WhiSoxK-32
93Don-139
93Fin-27
93FinRef-27
93Fla-183
93Fle-201
93Lea-41
93OPC-53
93PacSpa-69
93PacSpaPI-12
93Pin-383
93Sco-412
93SP-253
93StaClu-552
93StaCluFDI-552
93StaCluMOP-552
93StaCluWS-23
93Top-41
93TopGol-41
93TopInaM-41
93TopMic-41
93Ult-173
93UppDec-362
93UppDecGold-362
93WhiSoxK-8
94Bow-239
94ColC-99
94ColChoGS-99
94ColChoSS-99
94Don-582
94ExtBas-45
94Fin-26
94FinPre-26P
94FinRef-26
94Fla-30
94Fle-80
94FUnPac-54
94Lea-268
94OPC-6
94Pac-124
94PacAll-19
94Pin-289
94PinArtP-289
94PinMusC-289
94Sco-153
94ScoGolR-153
94Sel-311
94SP-190
94SPDieC-190
94Spo-3
94StaClu-583
94StaCluFDI-583
94StaCluGR-583
94StaCluMOP-583
94StaCluT-142
94StaCluTFDI-142
94Stu-204
94Top-599
94TopGol-599
94TopSpa-599
94TriPla-263
94Ult-33
94UppDec-43
94UppDec-231
94UppDecED-43
94UppDecED-231
94WhiSoxK-7
95Baz-72
95Bow-313
95ColCho-506
95ColChoGS-506
95ColChoSE-234
95ColChoSEGS-234
95ColChoSESS-234
95ColChoSS-506
95Don-259
95DonPreP-259
95DonTopotO-48
95Emb-45
95EmbGolI-45
95Fin-125
95FinRef-125
95Fla-244
95Fle-115
95Lea-69
95Pac-86
95Pin-359
95PinArtP-359
95PinMusC-359
95Sel-115
95SelArtP-115
95SP-141
95SPCha-141
95SPChaDC-141
95Spo-35
95SpoArtP-35
95SPSil-141
95StaClu-272
95StaCluMOP-272
95StaCluSTWS-272
95StaCluVR-137
95Stu-76
95Sum-2
95SumNthD-2
95Top-163
95TopCyb-98
95TopPre-PP9
95UC3-17
95UC3ArtP-17
95Ult-28
95UltGolM-28
95UppDec-434
95UppDecED-434
95UppDecEDG-434
95UppDecSE-19
95UppDecSEG-19
95WhiSoxK-9
95Zen-2
96Cir-27
96CirRav-27
96ColCho-93
96ColChoGS-93
96ColChoSS-93
96Don-504
96DonPreP-504
96EmoXL-36
96Fin-B154
96FinRef-B154
96Fla-50
96Fle-65
96FleTif-65
96FleWhiS-5
96Lea-39
96LeaPre-65
96LeaPreP-65
96LeaPrePB-39
96LeaPrePG-39
96LeaPrePS-39
96LeaSigAG-67
96LeaSigAS-67
96MetUni-36
96MetUniP-36
96Pac-278
96PacPri-P88
96PacPriG-P88
96PanSti-167
96Pin-40
96PinAfi-84
96PinAfiAP-84
96PinAfiFPP-84
96ProSta-135
96Sco-286
96ScoDugC-B11
96ScoDugCAP-B11
96Sel-100
96SelArtP-100
96SelTeaN-27
96SP-59
96StaClu-304
96StaCluEPB-304
96StaCluEPG-304
96StaCluEPS-304
96StaCluMOP-304
95StaCluVRMC-137
96Sum-147
96SumAbo&B-147
96SumArtP-147
96SumFoi-147
96Top-194
96TopChr-62
96TopChrR-62
96TopGal-23
96TopGalPPI-23
96TopLas-117
96Ult-37

96UltGolM-37
96UppDec-42
97Bow-278
97BowBes-41
97BowBesAR-41
97BowBesR-41
97BowInt-278
97Cir-392
97CirRav-392
97ColCho-344
97Don-32
97Don-433
97DonEli-142
97DonEliGS-142
97DonLim-80
97DonLimLE-80
97DonPre-19
97DonPreCttC-19
97DonPreP-32
97DonPreP-433
97DonPrePGold-32
97DonPrePGold-433
97Fin-285
97FinEmb-285
97FinEmbR-285
97FinRef-285
97FlaSho-A133
97FlaSho-B133
97FlaSho-C133
97FlaShoLC-133
97FlaShoLC-B133
97FlaShoLC-C133
97FlaShoLCM-A133
97FlaShoLCM-B133
97FlaShoLCM-C133
97Fle-60
97Fle-563
97FleTif-60
97FleTif-563
97Lea-245
97LeaFraM-245
97LeaFraMDC-245
97MetUni-58
97NewPin-141
97NewPinAP-141
97NewPinMC-141
97NewPinPP-141
97Pac-52
97PacLigB-52
97PacPri-20
97PacPriLB-20
97PacPriP-20
97PacSil-52
97Pin-13
97PinArtP-13
97PinIns-118
97PinInsCE-118
97PinInsDE-118
97PinMusC-13
97PinX-P-75
97PinX-PMoS-75
97Sco-232
97Sco-341
97Sco-531
97ScoHobR-341
97ScoHobR-531
97ScoPreS-232
97ScoResC-341
97ScoResC-531
97ScoShoS-232
97ScoShoS-341
97ScoShoS-531
97ScoShoSAP-232
97ScoShoSAP-341
97ScoShoSAP-531
97ScoWhiS-11
97ScoWhiSPl-11
97ScoWhiSPr-11
97Sel-91
97SelArtP-91
97SelRegG-91
97SP-78
97SpoIll-80
97SpoIllEE-80
97StaClu-228
97StaCluMat-228
97StaCluMOP-228
97Stu-52
97StuPrePG-52
97StuPrePS-52
97Top-355
97TopChr-120
97TopChrR-120
97TopGal-60
97TopGalPPI-60
97Ult-358
97UltGolME-358
97UltPlaME-358
97UppDec-536
Fernandez, Antonio
94SpoIndC-9
94SpoIndF-3328
96HilStaHWB-8
96RanCucQB-13
Fernandez, Chico (Humberto)
55Bow-270
56Dod-9
57Top-305
58Hir-16
58HirTes-3
58PhiJayP-5
58Top-348
59Top-452
60Top-314
61Top-112
61TopStal-150
62Jel-17
62Pos-17
62PosCan-17
62SalPlaC-3
62ShiPlaC-3
62TigJayP-6
62Top-173
62TopVen-173
63TigJayP-6
63Top-278
79TCM50-274
88CedRapRP-1141
90DodTar-237
91MetWIZ-113
91OriCro-127
95TopArcBD-138
Fernandez, Chris
87TamTarP-22
Fernandez, Dan
89SanJosGB-8
89SanJosGCLC-232
89SanJosGP-441
89SanJosGS-9
90SanJosGB-12
90SanJosGCLC-40
90SanJosGP-2012
90SanJosGS-9
91SanJosGC-1
91SanJosGP-12
92ShrCapF-3876
92ShrCapS-584
93ShrCapF-2763
94PhoFirF-1522
Fernandez, Daniel
95JacSunTI-10
Fernandez, Fernando
94BenRocF-3586
97BenRocC-6
Fernandez, Frank
66Top-584
68Top-214
68TopVen-214
69Top-557
70OPC-82
70Top-82
71MLBOffS-512
71OPC-468
71Top-468
72MilBra-102
92YanWIZ6-40
Fernandez, James
88St.PetCS-7
Fernandez, Jared
94UtiBluSC-10
96TreThuB-10
Fernandez, Jose
89HamRedS-11
89St.PetCS-12
90ArkTraGS-12
90St.PetCS-7
91ArkTraLD-32
91ArkTraLD-33
91ArkTraP-1288
91ArkTraP-1293
91HunCubC-8
91HunCubP-3346
91LinDriAA-32
91LinDriAA-33
91LouRedP-2926
91LouRedTI-15
92ArkTraF-1132
92LouRedS-260
92LouRedS-261
92SkyAAAF-126
93ReaPhiF-297
94LouRedF-2983
96DelShoB-16
Fernandez, Jose Maria
86NegLeaF-72
89RinPosNL1-12
Fernandez, Julio
89CliGiaP-900
91BelMarC-17
91BelMarP-3680
92SanBerC-19
Fernandez, Luis
93PriRedC-10
93PriRedF-4170
Fernandez, Mike
91EliTwiP-4305
92KenTwiC-24
92KenTwiF-611
93ForMyeMC-7
93ForMyeMF-2661
94NasXprF-394
Fernandez, Nanny (Frollan)
47TipTop-79
50PirTeal-7
50RoyDes-23
Fernandez, Omar
95GreFalDTI-7
Fernandez, Osvaldo
94RivPilCLC-12
95Bes-43
95PorCitRTI-7
96ColCho-424
96ColChoGS-424
96ColChoSS-424
96EmoXL-289
96Exc-104
96Fla-387
96FlaWavotF-9
96FleUpd-U205
96FleUpdTC-U205
96GiaMot-9
96LeaPre-132
96LeaPreP-132
96Pin-382
96PinAfi-183
96PinAfiAP-183
96PinFoil-382
96Sel-175
96SelArtP-175
96SelCer-116
96SelCerAP-116
96SelCerCB-116
96SelCerCR-116
96SelCerMB-116
96SelCerMG-116
96SelCerMR-116
96SP-3
96SPSpeFX-47
96SPSpeFXDC-47
96SPx-53
96SPxGol-53
96Stu-123
96StuPrePB-123
96StuPrePG-123
96StuPrePS-123
96Ult-567
96UltGolM-567
96UppDec-243
96UppDecPHE-H41
96UppDecPreH-H41
96ZenMoz-4
97Cir-183
97CirRav-183
97ColCho-214
97Don-30
97DonPreP-30
97DonPrePGold-30
97Fle-549
97FleTif-549
97Lea-154
97LeaFraM-154
97LeaFraMDC-154
97Pac-443
97PacLatotML-36
97PacLigB-443
97PacPri-149
97PacPriLB-149
97PacPriP-149
97PacSil-443
97Pin-150
97PinArtP-150
97PinMusC-150
97Sco-300
97ScoPreS-300
97ScoShoS-300
97ScoShoSAP-300
97UppDec-186
97UppDec-497
Fernandez, Ramon
96OgdRapTI-38
Fernandez, Reynaldo
88OneYanP-2053
88PriWilYS-9
Fernandez, Rolando
90HunCubP-3297
91PeoChiC-19
91PeoChiP-1356
91PeoChiTI-26
92WinSpiC-12
92WinSpiF-1218
Fernandez, Rudy
92NegLeaRLI-20
95NegLeaL2-12
Fernandez, Sid
82VerBeaDT-6
84Don-44
84TidTidT-2
85Don-563
85Fle-77
85MetColP-6
85MetTCM-9
85OPC-390
85TidTidT-3
85Top-649
85TopTif-649
86BasStaB-40
86Don-625
86Fle-79
86KayB-10
86Lea-242
86MetColP-20
86MetTCM-4
86MetWorSC-24
86Top-104
86TopMinL-51
86TopTif-104
87ClaGam-74
87Don-323
87DonAll-26
87DonHig-4
87Fle-8
87Fle-629
87FleBasA-16
87FleGlo-8
87FleGlo-629
87FleSlu-13
87Lea-93
87MetColP-12
87OPC-337
87Spo-63
87SpoTeaP-2
87Top-570
87TopMinL-22
87TopSti-97
87TopTif-570
88Don-118
88DonAll-58
88DonTeaBM-118
88Fle-134
88FleBasM-13
88FleGlo-134
88FleStiC-101
88Lea-63
88MetColP-23
88MetFanC-50
88MetKah-50
88OPC-30
88PanSti-336
88RedFolSB-22
88Sco-615
88ScoGlo-615
88Spo-177
88StaLinMe-7
88Top-30
88TopSti-103
88TopStiB-28
88TopTif-30
89Bow-377
89BowTif-377
89Don-471
89Fle-35
89FleGlo-35
89MetColP-28
89MetKah-8
89OPC-34
89Sco-268
89Top-790
89TopBig-276
89TopMinL-25
89TopTif-790
89UppDec-168
90Bow-131
90BowTif-131
90DodTar-238
90Don-572
90DonBesN-105
90Fle-203
90FleCan-203
90K-M-11
90Lea-66
90MetColP-14
90MetFanC-50
90MetKah-50
90OPC-480
90PanSti-299
90PubSti-133
90Sco-18
90Spo-113
90Top-480
90TopBig-155
90TopCoi-46
90TopDou-20
90TopMinL-66
90TopSti-92
90TopStiB-28
90TopTif-480
90TopTVA-61
90TopTVM-10
90UppDec-261
90VenSti-169
91Bow-462
91Don-97
91Fle-146
91MetColP-16
91MetKah-50
91MetWIZ-112
91OPC-230
91PepSidF-1
91PepSidF-2
91Sco-180
91StaClu-225
91StaCluP-14
91Top-230
91TopDesS-230
91TopMic-230
91TopTif-230
91Ult-216
91UppDec-242
92Bow-296
92Don-719
92Fle-503
92Lea-519
92MetColP-14
92MetKah-50
92OPC-382
92Pin-509
92Sco-675
92StaClu-655
92Top-382
92TopGol-382
92TopGolW-382
92TopMic-382
92Ult-528
92UppDec-671
93Bow-214
93Don-566
93Fin-5
93FinRef-5
93Fle-86
93Lea-2
93MetColP-30
93MetKah-50
93OPC-42
93PacSpa-196
93PanSti-248
93Pin-500
93Sco-556
93Sel-243
93StaClu-351
93StaCluFDI-351
93StaCluMOP-351
93Top-188
93TopComotH-24
93TopGol-188
93TopInaM-188
93TopMic-188
93Ult-72
93UppDec-361

93UppDecGold-361
93USPlaCA-3S
94Bow-571
94ColC-511
94ColChoGS-511
94ColChoSS-511
94Don-396
94ElSidPog-1
94ElSidPog-2
94ElSidPog-3
94ElSidPog-4
94ElSidPog-5
94ExtBas-4
94Fin-379
94FinRef-379
94Fla-253
94Fle-560
94FleUpd-2
94Lea-246
94OPC-63
94OriPro-33
94OriUSPC-4H
94Pac-399
94Pin-483
94PinArtP-483
94PinMusC-483
94Sco-182
94ScoGolR-182
94ScoRoo-RT51
94ScoRooGR-RT51
94Sel-353
94SpoRoo-2
94SpoRooAP-2
94StaClu-579
94StaCluFDI-579
94StaCluGR-579
94StaCluMOP-579
94StaCluT-273
94StaCluTFDI-273
94Top-615
94TopGol-615
94TopSpa-615
94TopTra-28T
94Ult-305
94UppDec-433
94UppDecED-433
95ColCho-344
95ColChoGS-344
95ColChoSS-344
95Don-270
95DonPreP-270
95Fla-220
95Fle-6
95Lea-353
95Pin-88
95PinArtP-88
95PinMusC-88
95Sco-182
95ScoGolR-182
95ScoPlaTS-182
95StaClu-188
95StaCluFDI-188
95StaCluMOP-188
95StaCluSTWS-188
95Top-507
95TopCyb-296
95Ult-2
95UltGolM-2
96ColCho-648
96ColChoGS-648
96ColChoSS-648
96EmoXL-245
96Fla-334
96Fle-497
96FleTif-497
96Pac-155
96PhiTeal-11
96Sco-215
96StaClu-122
96StaCluMOP-122
96Ult-520
96UltGolM-520
96UppDec-427
97Fle-666
97FleTif-666
97StaClu-319
97StaCluMOP-319
97Top-299
97Ult-525
97UltGolME-525
97UltPlaME-525

Fernandez, Tony

82SyrChiT-17
82SyrChiTI-12
83SyrChiT-16
84BluJayFS-11
84Don-32
84Fle-152
84SyrChiT-9
85AllGamPl-20
85BluJayFS-10
85Don-390
85Fle-103
85Lea-91
85OPC-48
85OPCPos-16
85Top-48
85TopTif-48
86BluJayAF-8
86BluJayFS-9
86Don-119
86Fle-57
86FleMin-14
86FleStiC-37
86GenMilB-3D
86KayB-11
86Lea-45
86OPC-241
86Spo-112
86Top-241
86TopSti-194
86TopTat-15
86TopTif-241
87BluJayFS-8
87ClaGam-57
87Don-72
87DonAll-35
87DonOpeD-35
87Fle-225
87FleAll-3
87FleAwaW-12
87FleGlo-225
87FleMin-38
87FleRecS-7
87FleStiC-39
87GenMilB-1C
87Lea-106
87OPC-329
87RedFolSB-29
87Spo-113
87Spo-187
87SpoTeaP-5
87StuPan-27
87SyrChi1A-12
87Top-485
87TopMinL-75
87TopSti-191
87TopTif-485
88Baz-7
88BluJay5-5
88BluJayFS-10
88Don-12
88Don-319
88DonAll-25
88DonBasB-87
88DonSupD-12
88Fle-109
88Fle-635
88FleBasM-14
88FleGlo-109
88FleGlo-635
88FleHotS-10
88FleMin-61
88FleStiC-72
88FleSupBC-C3
88Lea-12
88Lea-133
88MSAHosD-21
88OPC-290
88PanSti-222
88Sco-20
88Sco-651
88ScoGlo-20
88ScoGlo-651
88ScoYouS2-6
88Spo-26
88StaLinBJ-6
88Top-290
88TopBig-187
88TopCoi-12
88TopGloS-15
88TopSti-193
88TopStiB-43
88TopTif-290
88TopUKM-23
88TopUKMT-23
89BluJayFS-9
89Bow-254
89BowTif-254
89ClaTraO-115
89Don-206
89DonBasB-48
89Fle-231
89FleGlo-231
89FleSup-13
89OPC-170
89PanSti-470
89RedFolSB-41
89Sco-57
89ScoHot1S-53
89Spo-93
89Top-170
89TopBasT-146
89TopBig-157
89TopCoi-39
89TopGloS-52
89TopMinL-76
89TopSti-189
89TopStiB-10
89TopTif-170
89TopUKM-25
89TVSpoM-80
89UppDec-139
90BluJayFS-8
90BluJayHS-5
90Bow-524
90BowTif-524
90Don-149
90DonBesA-113
90Fle-80
90Fle-634
90FleAwaW-12
90FleBasA-9
90FleBasM-11
90FleCan-80
90FleCan-634
90Lea-53
90OPC-685
90PanSti-176
90PubSti-283
90PubSti-513
90RedFolSB-31
90Sco-89
90Spo-6
90Top-685
90TopBatL-16
90TopBig-165
90TopDou-21
90TopMinL-42
90TopSti-11
90TopSti-194
90TopStiB-43
90TopTif-685
90UppDec-130
90VenSti-170
90VenSti-171
91Bow-642
91CadEllD-19
91Cla2-T45
91ClaGam-161
91Don-524
91Fle-174
91FleUpd-123
91Lea-315
91OPC-320
91OPCPre-43
91PadMag-27
91PadSmo-10
91PanFreS-339
91PanSti-152
91RedFolS-33
91Sco-432
91ScoRoo-66T
91StaClu-515
91Stu-244
91Top-320
91TopDesS-320
91TopMic-320
91TopTif-320
91TopTra-41T
91TopTraT-41T
91UltUpd-111
91UppDec-126
91UppDec-754
92Bow-293
92ColAllG-24
92ColAllP-24
92Don-362
92Fle-604
92Hig5-121
92Lea-187
92OPC-60
92PadCarJ-6
92PadMot-8
92PadPolD-7
92PadPolD-30
92PadSmo-8
92PanSti-235
92Pin-137
92Sco-645
92StaClu-203
92Stu-103
92Top-60
92TopGol-60
92TopGolW-60
92TopKid-57
92TopMic-60
92TriPla-102
92TriPla-165
92Ult-276
92UppDec-272
93Bow-18
93ClaGam-31
93Don-674
93Fin-36
93FinRef-36
93Fle-470
93FleFinE-293
93FunPac-125
93Lea-273
93MetColP-31
93MetKah-1
93OPC-70
93OPCPre-20
93PacSpa-541
93PacSpaGE-3
93PanSti-249
93Pin-533
93Sco-572
93Sel-93
93SelRoo-19T
93SP-47
93StaClu-644
93StaCluFDI-644
93StaCluM-32
93StaCluMOP-644
93Stu-98
93Top-465
93TopGol-465
93TopInaM-465
93TopMic-465
93TopTra-9T
93Ult-426
93UppDec-672
93UppDecGold-672
94ColC-619
94ColChoGS-619
94ColChoSS-619
94Don-172
94Fla-366
94Fle-331
94FleUpd-117
94Lea-266
94OPCWorC-9
94Pac-639
94PanSti-137
94Pin-427
94PinArtP-427
94PinMusC-427
94RedKah-9
94Sco-62
94ScoCyc-TC13
94ScoGolR-62
94ScoRoo-RT39
94ScoRooGR-RT39
94Sel-310
94SpoRoo-44
94SpoRooAP-44
94StaClu-214
94StaCluFDI-214
94StaCluGR-214
94StaCluMOP-214
94Top-702
94TopGol-702
94TopSpa-702
94TopTra-127T
94TriPlaM-7
94UppDec-437
94UppDecED-437
95BluJayUSPC-4D
95BluJayUSPC-11C
95ColCho-514
95ColChoGS-514
95ColChoSS-514
95DonTopotO-119
95Fin-283
95FinRef-283
95Fla-283
95Fle-434
95FleUpd-25
95Lea-340
95Pac-104
95Sco-123
95ScoGolR-123
95ScoPlaTS-123
95Sel-188
95SelArtP-188
95StaClu-221
95StaClu-544
95StaCluFDI-221
95StaCluMOP-221
95StaCluMOP-544
95StaCluSTWS-221
95StaCluSTWS-544
95TopTra-70T
95Ult-308
95UltGolM-308
95UppDec-441
95UppDecED-441
95UppDecEDG-441
96ColCho-232
96ColChoGS-232
96ColChoSS-232
96Don-51
96DonPreP-51
96Fle-182
96FleTif-182
96Pac-380
96StaClu-427
96StaCluMOP-427
96Top-27
97BluJayS-45
97ColCho-309
97Lea-308
97LeaFraM-308
97LeaFraMDC-308
97PacPriGotD-GD70
97Sco-462
97ScoHobR-462
97ScoResC-462
97ScoShoS-462
97ScoShoSAP-462

Ferran, Alex

89WatIndS-6
90RenSilSCLC-265

Ferran, George

86ShrCapP-8
87PhoFirP-4

Ferrand, Ray

93Sou-8

Ferrand, Thomas

96MarPhiB-9

Ferrante, Joe

82DayBeaAT-3

Ferrara, Al

64Top-337
64TopVen-337
65Top-331
66Top-487
67CokCapD-18
67CokCapDA-18
67Top-557
68OPC-34
68Top-34
68TopVen-34
69MLBOffS-191
69NabTeaF-6
69PadVol-3
69Top-452A
69Top-452B
69TopDec-30
69TopSta-93
70MLBOffS-113
70OPC-345
70Top-345
70TopBoo-23
71MLBOffS-226
71OPC-214
71Top-214
71TopCoi-25
72MilBra-103
81TCM60I-330
90DodTar-239

Ferrarese, Don

55Top-185
56Top-266
57Top-146
58Top-469
59Top-247
60Top-477

61Top-558
62Top-547
91OriCro-128
Ferraro, Carl
86ChaRaiP-9
Ferraro, Mike
68Top-539
69OPC-83
69PilPos-17
69Top-83
72Top-613
75ForLauYS-2
76ForLauYS-17
77WesHavYT-7
78TacYanC-1
79YanPicA-11
81TCM60I-436
83IndPos-13
83IndWhe-11
83Pil69G-36
83TopTra-32T
90TopTVY-4
92YanWIZ6-41
94BreMilB-25
Ferraro, Vincent
84VisOakT-5
Ferre, Andre The Giant (Jean)
72Dia-120
Ferrebee, Anthony
87IdaFalBP-2
Ferreira, Jose (Arturo J.)
84IdaFalATI-8
85MadMusP-10
85MadMusT-13
Ferreira, Marcos
95LinVen-33
Ferreira, Tony
82ForMyeRT-11
84OmaRoyT-3
85OmaRoyT-10
86TidTidP-8
87CalCanP-2328
88AlbYanP-1339
90CMC-183
90OmaRoyC-8
90OmaRoyP-61
90ProAAAF-596
92WinHavRSC-7
92WinHavRSF-1786
93ForLauRSC-11
93ForLauRSFP-1605
86STaoftFT-35
Ferreiras, Sal
86PriWilPP-10
Ferrell, Della
88KimN18-12
Ferrell, Frank
75CedRapGT-21
Ferrell, Rick
31Exh-30
33ButCanV-14
33ExhFou-15
33Gou-197
34DiaMatCSB-52
34BatR31-10
34BatR31-126
34ButPreR-19
34DiaStaR-48
34ExhFou-9
35ExhFou-9
35GouPuzR-8G
35GouPuzR-9G
36ExhFou-9
36GouBWR-13
36GouWidPPR-A29
36GouWidPPR-A118
36NatChiFPR-97
36R31PasP-50
36SandSW-17
37ExhFou-9
37KelPepS-BB5
37OPCBatUV-132
38ExhFou-16
39PlaBal-39
40PlaBal-21
41BroW75-10
47SenGunBP-6
61Fle-105
77GalGloG-199
79DiaGre-179
80PerHaloFP-187
80SSPHOF-189
81ConTSN-49
83TCMPla1944-20
89PerCelP-14
90PacLeg-23
90PerGreM-70
90SweBasG-86
91SweBasG-29
92ConTSN-471
93ConTSN-674
93ConTSN-861
93FroRowRF-1
93FroRowRF-2
93FroRowRF-3
93FroRowRF-4
93FroRowRF-5
93TedWil-2
93UppDecAH-49
94ConTSN-994
94ConTSN-1169
94ConTSNB-994
94ConTSNB-1169
94UppDecAH-142
94UppDecAH1-142
Ferrell, Wes
30SchR33-21
31Exh-21
33ButCre-7
33CraJacP-5
33DouDisP-14
33ExhFou-11
33GeoCMil-11
33Gou-218
33TatOrbSDR-162
34DiaMatCSB-53
34BatR31-12
34BatR31-174
34DiaStaR-94
34ExhFou-11
35GouPuzR-8G
35GouPuzR-9G
36GouWidPPR-A30
36GouWidPPR-A118
36NatChiFPR-97
36R31Pre-L2
36WorWidGV-40
37OPCBatUV-138
38ExhFou-16
61Fle-26
75YanDyn1T-14
77GalGloG-189
79RedSoxEF-4
81ConTSN-50
88ConSer3-11
90DodTar-240
90HOFStiB-30
91ConTSN-198
92ConTSN-361
92ConTSN-446
92MegRut-148
94ConTSN-1169
94ConTSNB-1169
Ferrer, Eduardo
96BoiHawB-12
Ferrer, Gavriel
80VenLeaS-198
Ferrer, Sergio
74TacTwiC-17
76OklCit8TI-2
78MetDaiPA-27
78TidTidT-9
79Top-397
80TidTidT-5
80Top-619
81IndIndTI-31
89PacSenL-2
90EliSenL-110
91MetWIZ-114
Ferretti, Sam
88WatIndP-680
89CanIndP-1307
89KinIndS-9
90Bes-309
90CanIndB-7
90CanIndP-1297
90CanIndS-6
91CanIndLD-83
91CanIndP-986
91LinDriAA-83
92HagSunF-2561
92HagSunS-258
93BowBayF-2194
Ferreyra, Raul
77IndIndTI-19
78IndIndTI-21
78SSP270-130
79NaSouTI-9
Ferrick, Tom
47SenGunBP-3
51Bow-182
58RedEnq-11
60Top-461
79DiaGre-330
Ferrier, Ross
94PitMetC-8
94PitMetF-3534
95StLucMTI-13
Ferris, Bob
76QuaCitAT-14
79SalLakCGT-10
80SalLakCGT-24
81SalLakCGT-5
78STLakCGC-19
Ferris, Boo (David)
39ExhSal-16
46RedSoxTI-10
46SpoExcW-3-1A
47TipTop-5
48RedSoxTI-6
49Bow-211
50AmeNut&CCP-6
76TayBow4-101
84TCMPla1-2
87RedSox1T-7
Ferris, Hobe (Albert)
03BreE10-50
04FanCraAL-18
04RedSoxUP-6
08RosComP-67
09ColChiE-99
09RamT20-46
09T206-129
11SpoLifCW-125
12ColRedB-99
12ColTinT-99
Ferro, Bob
83WisRapTF-11
Ferroni, Frank
81MiaOriT-14
Ferry, John
12T207-58
Ferry, Mike
90BilMusP-3214
90ProAaA-195
91CedRapRC-4
91CedRapRP-2712
92CedRapRC-7
92CedRapRF-1066
92MidLeaATI-9
93ChaLooF-2356
94Bow-486
94ExcFS7-174
94IndIndF-1803
95ChaLooTI-5
Ferson, Alexander
87OldJudN-168
Ferst, Larry
78CliDodT-8
79CliDodT-28
Ferullo, Matt
95PitMetTI-47
96PitMetB-10
Fesh, Sean
93AshTouC-7
93AshTouF-2269
94OscAstC-9
94OscAstF-1131
96RanCucQB-14
Fessenden, Wallace
87OldJudN-169
Festa, Chris
96LowSpiB-7
Fette, Lou
38BasTabP-9
38WheBB10-10
38WheBB11-1
79DiaGre-210
90DodTar-241
Fetters, Mike (Michael Lee)
86SalAngC-97
87PalSprP-26
88MidAngGS-10
89EdmTraC-9
90Bow-286
90BowTif-286
90CMC-484
90Don-35
90EdmTraC-7
90EdmTraP-514
90Fle-131
90FleCan-131
90OPC-14
90ProAAAF-90
90Top-14
90TopDeb89-36
90TopTif-14
90UppDec-742
91Don-565
91EdmTraLD-163
91EdmTraP-1512
91Fle-312
91LinDriAAA-163
91OPC-477
91Sco-497
91Sco100RS-74
91StaClu-228
91Top-477
91TopDesS-477
91TopMic-477
91TopTif-477
91UppDec-696
92BrePol-6
92Don-491
92Fle-56
92Lea-460
92OPC-602
92Sco-606
92Sco100RS-38
92StaClu-696
92Top-602
92TopGol-602
92TopGolW-602
92TopMic-602
93BrePol-7
93Don-573
93Fle-249
93OPC-109
93PacSpa-510
93Sco-420
93Sel-174
93StaClu-633
93StaCluFDI-633
93StaCluMOP-633
93Top-527
93TopGol-527
93TopInaM-527
93TopMic-527
93UppDec-193
93UppDecGold-193
94BreMilB-26
94BrePol-7
94Don-603
94Fla-303
94Fle-176
94Sco-200
94ScoGolR-200
94Top-159
94TopGol-159
94TopSpa-159
95ColCho-183
95ColChoGS-183
95ColChoSS-183
95Don-503
95DonPreP-503
95DonTopotO-96
95Fle-178
95Pac-231
95Top-339
95Ult-63
95UltGolM-63
96ColCho-191
96ColChoGS-191
96ColChoSS-191
96Don-173
96DonPreP-173
96Fin-B29
96FinRef-B29
96Fla-100
96Fle-144
96FleTif-144
96LeaSigEA-51
96StaClu-47
96StaCluMOP-47
96Top-142
96Ult-79
96UltGolM-79
97Cir-285
97CirRav-285
97ColCho-146
97Fin-184
97FinRef-184
97Fle-128
97FleTif-128
97Pac-117
97PacLigB-117
97PacSil-117
97Pin-69
97PinArtP-69
97PinMusC-69
97StaClu-143
97StaCluMOP-143
97Top-84
97Ult-438
97UltGolME-438
97UltPlaME-438
97UppDec-403
Fetty, Pat
92BelBreC-23
92BelBreF-400
93StoPorC-11
93StoPorF-738
Fetzer, John E.
81TigDetN-81
83TigAlKS-39
83TigAlKS-44
Feuerstein, David
96AshTouB-17
Fewster, Chick (Wilson)
20GasAmeMBD-8
20NatCarE-27A
20NatCarE-27B
21E121So1-23
21E121So8-22
21KoBreWSI-32
22W575-35
22WilPatV-29
23W501-120
25Exh-81
26Exh-12
27Exh-6
90DodTar-242
95ConTSN-1424
Fiacco, Charlie
90GenCubP-3035
90GenCubS-12
Fiala, Mike
86BakDodP-7
93SanBerSF-774
Fiala, Neil
78St.PetCT-10
79ArkTraT-13
82IndIndTI-29
Fiala, Walter
52LaPat-4
52Par-67
53ExhCan-48
Fichman, Mal
79NewCoPT-6
88BoiHawP-1632
90EriSaiS-29
91RenSilSCLC-29
Fichter, Bob
75TopPho-128
Fick, Barry
85CedRapRT-7
Fick, Chris
96ArkTraB-14
Fick, Chuck
82WesHavAT-11
90EliSenL-111
91PacSenL-93
Ficklin, Winston
81WatIndT-29
82WatIndF-19
82WatIndT-15
83WatIndF-18
85WatIndT-4
86WatIndP-10
87WilBilP-3
88PorBeaC-18
88PorBeaP-652
89IowCubC-21
89IowCubP-1711
Fidge, Darren
94EliTwiC-7
94EliTwiF-3724
95Exc-82
95ForWayWTI-5
Fidler, Andy
89KinMetS-9
90PitMetP-19
91ColMetPPI-1
Fidrych, Mark
77BurCheD-92
77Hos-46
77Kel-26
77MSADis-18

77OPC-7
77OPC-115
77PepGloD-30
77RCColC-20
77Spo-1811
77TigBurK-1
77Top-7
77Top-265
77TopCloS-15
78OPC-235
78PapGinD-32
78TasDis-22
78TigBurK-4
78Top-45
78WifBalD-21
79Hos-77
79OPC-329
79Top-625
80EvaTriT-6
80OPC-231
80Top-445
81Don-8
81EvaTriT-4
81Fle-462
81OPC-150
81TigDetN-6
81Top-150
83PawRedST-7
84OCoandSI-192
88PacLegI-62
90SweBasG-122
91UppDecS-5
92ActPacA-25
92UppDecS-8
93UppDecAH-50
93UppDecS-9
93UppDecS-24
94TedWil-31
94UppDecAH-178
94UppDecAH1-178
Fiedler, Dick
57SeaPop-13
Fiedler, Mark
86LitFalMP-11
Fiegel, Todd
91KinMetC-15
91KinMetP-3807
92ColMetC-11
92ColMetF-288
92ColMetPI-18
92ColMetPI-30
92ProFS7-291
93St.LucMC-8
94St.LucMF-1187
93StLucMF-2915
Field, Greg
77OrlTwiT-10
79PorBeaT-3
83RicBraT-5
84TolMudHT-18
Field, James
09ColChiE-100
12ColRedB-100
12ColTinT-100
Fieldbinder, Mick
96HelBreTI-3
Fielder, Cecil
84OCoandSI-209
86BluJayAF-9
86BluJayFS-10
86Don-512
86Fle-653
86OPC-386
86Top-386
86TopTif-386
87BluJayFS-9
87FleUpd-31
87FleUpdG-31
87OPC-178
87Top-178
87TopTif-178
88BluJayFS-11
88Don-565
88Fle-110
88FleGlo-110
88OPC-21
88Sco-399
88ScoGlo-399
88StaLinBJ-7
88Top-618
88TopTif-618
89Don-442
89Fle-232
89FleGlo-232
89OPC-224
89Sco-120
89SpoIllFKI-205
89Top-541
89TopTif-541
89UppDec-364
90Bow-357
90BowTif-357
90ClaYel-T94
90DonBesA-133
90DonLeaS-26
90FleUpd-95
90Lea-165
90ScoMcD-16
90ScoRoo-9T
90StaFie-1
90StaFie-2
90StaFie-3
90StaFie-4
90StaFie-5
90StaFie-6
90StaFie-7
90StaFie-8
90StaFie-9
90StaFie-10
90StaFie-11
90SupActM-7
90TigCok-4
90TopBig-313
90TopMag-28
90TopTra-31T
90TopTraT-31T
90UppDec-786
90UppDecS-2
90USPlaCA-13S
90WinDis-4
91BasBesHRK-7
91Baz-8
91Bow-136
91Bow-367
91CadEllD-18
91Cla1-T41
91Cla2-T69
91ClaGam-127
91Col-14
91DenHol-2
91Don-3
91Don-397
91Don-451
91DonBonC-BC5
91DonEli-6
91DonGraS-7
91DonSupD-3
91Fle-335
91Fle-709
91FleAll-4
91JimDea-21
91KinDis-14
91Lea-106
91LeaPre-18
91MajLeaCP-32
91MooSna-24
91MSAHolD-17
91OPC-386
91OPC-720
91OPCPre-44
91PanCanT1-13
91PanCanT1-21
91PanCanT1-37
91PanCanT1-54
91PanFreS-288
91PanSti-232
91PepSup-10
91PetSta-11
91Pos-23
91PosCan-19
91RedFolS-34
91Sco-168
91Sco-395
91Sco-693
91Sco-770
91Sco100S-88
91SevCoi-F6
91SevCoi-M3
91SpoNSP-1
91StaClu-186
91StaCluCM-8
91StaCluMO-29
91StaPinB-17
91Stu-53
91SunSee-8
91TigCok-45
91TigPol-3
91Top-386
91Top-720
91TopCraJI-31
91TopDesS-386
91TopDesS-720
91TopGaloC-5
91TopMic-386
91TopMic-720
91TopSta-13
91TopTif-386
91TopTif-720
91TopTriH-A6
91Ult-121
91Ult-392
91UppDec-83
91UppDec-244
91UppDecFE-82F
91UppDecSS-SS12
91USPlaCA-12D
92Bow-90
92Cla1-T33
92Cla2-T73
92ClaGam-129
92DenHol-13
92Don-27
92Don-206
92DonCraJ1-22
92DonMcD-20
92Fle-133
92Fle-692
92Fle-705
92FleCitTP-7
92FleLumC-L1
92FleTeaL-6
92FleUpdH-4
92Hig5-46
92Hig5S-11
92HitTheBB-13
92JimDea-15
92KinDis-17
92Lea-153
92LeaGolP-18
92LeaPre-18
92MooSna-10
92Mr.TurS-8
92MSABenSHD-1
92OPC-425
92OPCPre-70
92PanSti-105
92PanSti-144
92PanSti-272
92PepDieM-13
92Pin-4
92PinSlu-1
92Pos-13
92PosCan-12
92Sco-50
92Sco-431
92Sco100S-66
92ScoImpP-60
92SevCoi-19
92SpoStaCC-14
92StaClu-250
92StaClu-599
92StaCluD-48
92StaCluMP-5
92Stu-173
92Top-397
92Top-425
92TopGol-397
92TopGol-425
92TopGolW-397
92TopGolW-425
92TopKid-76
92TopMcD-1
92TopMic-397
92TopMic-425
92TopMic-G397
92TriPla-29
92Ult-59
92UppDec-96
92UppDec-255
92UppDec-647
92UppDecF-22
92UppDecFG-22
92UppDecHRH-HR2
92UppDecTMH-21
92UppDecWB-T5
93Bow-475
93ClaGam-32
93DenHol-25
93DiaMar-35
93Don-541
93DonDiaK-DK15
93DonEli-34
93DonEliS-16
93DonLonBL-LL13
93DonMVP-17
93DonPre-15
93DonSpiotG-SG10
93DurPowP1-23
93Fin-111
93FinJum-111
93FinRef-111
93Fla-201
93Fle-227
93Fle-345
93Fle-711
93Fle-714
93FleAll-AL5
93FleAtl-8
93FleFruotL-19
93FlePro-B3
93FunPac-185
93FunPac-186
93Hos-16
93HumDumC-8
93JimDea-12
93KinDis-11
93Kra-7
93Lea-283
93LeaGolA-R3
93MetBak-7
93OPC-51
93OPCPre-96
93PacSpa-107
93PanSti-114
93Pin-26
93PinCoo-28
93PinCooD-28
93PinHomRC-3
93PinSlu-3
93Pos-10
93Sco-31
93ScoFra-6
93Sel-20
93SelChaS-13
93SelDufIP-5
93SelStaL-27
93SelStaL-31
93SP-236
93SPPlaP-PP6
93StaClu-503
93StaCluFDI-503
93StaCluMOP-503
93Stu-37
93TigGat-7
93Top-80
93TOPBLAG-30
93TopGol-80
93TopInaM-80
93TopMic-80
93TriPla-5
93TriPlaA-15
93TriPlaLL-L5
93TriPlaP-5
93Ult-548
93UltHomRK-3
93UppDec-46
93UppDec-499
93UppDec-564
93UppDecCP-R9
93UppDecGold-46
93UppDecGold-499
93UppDecGold-564
93UppDecHRH-HR3
93UppDecIC-WI23
93UppDecICJ-WI23
93UppDecOD-D11
93USPlaCA-12C
94Bow-69
94BowBes-R32
94BowBesR-R32
94CarLeaA-DJ2
94ChuShoS-9
94ColC-100
94ColC-352
94ColChoGS-100
94ColChoGS-352
94ColChoHRA-HA5
94ColChoSS-100
94ColChoSS-352
94ColChoT-13
94DenHol-10
94Don-27
94DonDiaK-DK22
94DonDom-A1
94DonLonBL-1
94DonMVP-20
94DonSpeE-27
94ExtBas-73
94ExtBasGB-10
94Fin-219
94FinJum-219
94FinRef-219
94Fla-49
94Fle-128
94FleAllS-7
94FleSun-10
94FleTeaL-6
94FUnPac-45
94Kra-3
94Lea-50
94LeaCleC-5
94LeaL-31
94LeaMVPC-A6
94LeaMVPCG-A6
94LeaPowB-7
94OPC-126
94OPCAllR-20
94OPCJumA-20
94OscMayR-4
94Pac-215
94PacSilP-18
94PanSti-63
94Pin-10
94PinArtP-10
94PinMusC-10
94PinSam-10
94Pos-17
94ProMag-46
94RedFolMI-10
94Sco-393
94ScoGolR-393
94ScoGolS-40
94Sol-233
94SP-176
94SPDieC-176
94SPHol-7
94SPHolDC-7
94Spo-78
94SpoMov-MM3
94SpoRooGGG-GG10
94StaClu-25
94StaClu-535
94StaCluFDI-25
94StaCluFDI-535
94StaCluGR-25
94StaCluGR-535
94StaCluMO-34
94StaCluMOP-25
94StaCluMOP-535
94Stu-190
94SucSav-14
94TomPiz-18
94Top-190
94TopBlaG-5
94TopGol-190
94TopSpa-190
94TopSupS-13
94TriPla-243
94TriPlaBS-2
94TriPlaN-1
94Ult-52
94UltRBIK-5
94UppDec-220
94UppDec-286
94UppDecAJ-23
94UppDecAJG-23
94UppDecDC-E4
94UppDecED-220
94UppDecED-286
94UppDecMLS-MM7
94UppDecMLSED-MM7
95Baz-12
95BluJayUSPC-4C
95BluJayUSPC-13H
95Bow-416
95BowBes-R28
95BowBesR-R28
95ClaPhoC-26
95ColCho-51
95ColCho-470
95ColChoCtG-CG6
95ColChoCtG-CG6B
95ColChoCtG-CG6C
95ColChoCtGE-6
95ColChoCtGG-CG6
95ColChoCtGG-CG6B
95ColChoCtGG-CG6C
95ColChoCtGGE-6
95ColChoGS-51
95ColChoGS-470

95ColChoSE-220
95ColChoSEGS-220
95ColChoSESS-220
95ColChoSS-51
95ColChoSS-470
95DenHol-8
95Don-109
95DonBomS-5
95DonPreP-109
95DonTopotO-73
95Emb-76
95EmbGolI-76
95Emo-42
95EmoN-4
95Fin-124
95FinPowK-PK18
95FinRef-124
95Fla-38
95FlaInfP-3
95Fle-50
95FleTeaL-6
95FleUpdH-9
95Kra-3
95Lea-63
95LeaCor-2
95LeaLim-139
95LeaLimL-15
95Pac-151
95PacGolP-31
95PacPri-48
95PanSti-40
95Pin-184
95PinArtP-184
95PinFan-6
95PinMusC-184
95RedFol-18
95Sco-398
95ScoGolR-398
95ScoHaloG-HG82
95ScoPlaTS-398
95Sel-96
95SelArtP-96
95SelCer-47
95SelCerMG-47
95SP-155
95SPCha-151
95SPCha-155
95SPChaDC-151
95SPChaDC-155
95Spo-82
95SpoArtP-82
95SPPlaP-PP10
95SPSil-155
95StaClu-309
95StaClu-515
95StaCluCC-CC28
95StaCluMO-14
95StaCluMOP-309
95StaCluMOP-515
95StaCluMOP-CC28
95StaCluMOP-PZ5
95StaCluMOP-RL31
95StaCluPZ-PZ5
95StaCluRL-RL31
95StaCluSTWS-309
95StaCluSTWS-515
95StaCluVR-164
95Stu-45
95StuGolS-45
95Sum-57
95SumNthD-57
95TomPiz-8
95Top-220
95TopCyb-124
95TopLeaL-LL35
95UC3-47
95UC3ArtP-47
95Ult-46
95UltGolM-46
95UltHomRK-5
95UltHomRKGM-5
95UppDec-425
95UppDecC-1B
95UppDecED-425
95UppDecEDG-425
95UppDecPC-MLB5
95UppDecPLL-R13
95UppDecPLL-R32
95UppDecPLLE-R13
95UppDecPLLE-R32
95UppDecSE-95
95UppDecSEG-95
95UppDecSoaD-SD12
95USPlaCMLA-4C
95Zen-15
96Baz-93
96Bow-100
96BowBes-5
96BowBesAR-5
96BowBesR-5
96Cir-63
96CirRav-63
96ColCho-103
96ColCho-140
96ColCho-422
96ColChoCtG-CG17
96ColChoCtG-CG17B
96ColChoCtG-CG17C
96ColChoCtGE-CR17
96ColChoCtGG-CG17
96ColChoCtGG-CG17B
96ColChoCtGG-CG17C
96ColChoCtGGE-CR17
96ColChoGS-103
96ColChoGS-140
96ColChoGS-422
96ColChoSS-103
96ColChoSS-140
96ColChoSS-422
96ColChoYMtP-13
96ColChoYMtP-13A
96ColChoYMtPGS-13
96ColChoYMtPGS-13A
96DenHol-18
96Don-434
96DonLonBL-5
96DonPreP-434
96EmoXL-59
96Fin-B344
96Fin-G290
96Fin-S84
96FinRef-B344
96FinRef-G290
96FinRef-S84
96Fla-79
96Fle-109
96FleTif-109
96FleUpd-U219
96FleUpdH-5
96FleUpdTC-U219
96Lea-6
96LeaLim-45
96LeaLimG-45
96LeaPre-85
96LeaPreP-85
96LeaPrePB-6
96LeaPrePG-6
96LeaPrePS-6
96LeaPreSG-76
96LeaPreSte-76
96LeaSig-12
96LeaSigPPG-12
96LeaSigPPP-12
96MetUni-57
96MetUniP-57
96Pac-321
96PacGolCD-DC32
96PacPri-P101
96PacPriG-P101
96PanSti-146
96Pin-144
96Pin-246
96PinAfi-11
96PinAfiAP-11
96PinAfiFPP-11
96PinArtP-71
96PinArtP-146
96PinFan-23
96PinFoil-246
96PinPow-18
96PinSlu-18
96PinSta-71
96PinSta-146
96ProMagDM-14
96ProSta-125
96Sco-76
96Sco-357
96ScoDugC-A62
96ScoDugC-B82
96ScoDugCAP-A62
96ScoDugCAP-B82
96ScoRef-16
96ScoTitT-12
96Sel-39
96SelArtP-39
96SelCer-63
96SelCerAP-63
96SelCerCB-63
96SelCerCR-63
96SelCerIP-19
96SelCerMB-63
96SelCerMG-63
96SelCerMR-63
96SelTeaN-13
96SP-81
96Spo-55
96SpoArtP-55
96SPx-26
96SPxGol-26
96StaClu-95
96StaCluEPB-95
96StaCluEPG-95
96StaCluEPS-95
96StaCluMOP-95
96StaCluMOP-PP8
96StaCluPP-PP8
95StaCluVRMC-164
96Stu-54
96StuPrePB-54
96StuPrePG-54
96StuPrePS-54
96Sum-49
96SumAbo&B-49
96SumArtP-49
96SumFoi-49
96TeaOut-25
96Top-393
96TopChr-157
96TopChrR-157
96TopChrWC-WC6
96TopChrWCR-WC6
96TopGal-160
96TopGalPPI-160
96TopLas-105
96TopLasPC-12
96TopPro-AL4
96TopWreC-WC6
96Ult-58
96UltChe-B2
96UltCheGM-B2
96UltGolM-58
96UltThu-8
96UltThuGM-8
96UppDec-70
96UppDecPD-PD5
96UppDecPRE-R14
96UppDecPreR-R14
96Zen-36
96ZenArtP-36
97Bow-276
97BowBes-2
97BowBesAR-2
97BowBesR-2
97BowInt-276
97Cir-243
97CirRav-243
97ColCho-408
97ColChoCtG-22A
97ColChoCtG-22B
97ColChoCtG-22C
97ColChoCtGIW-CG22
97ColChoNF-NF37
97Don-157
97DonEli-54
97DonEliGS-54
97DonEliPtT-7
97DonEliPtT-9
97DonEliPtTA-7
97DonEliPtTA-9
97DonLim-47
97DonLimLE-47
97DonLonL-13
97DonPre-3
97DonPreCttC-3
97DonPreP-157
97DonPrePGold-157
97DonTea-130
97DonTeaSPE-130
97Fin-322
97Fin-340
97FinEmb-322
97FinEmb-340
97FinEmbR-322
97FinEmbR-340
97FinRef-322
97FinRef-340
97FlaSho-A176
97FlaSho-B176
97FlaSho-C176
97FlaShoLC-176
97FlaShoLC-B176
97FlaShoLC-C176
97FlaShoLCM-A176
97FlaShoLCM-B176
97FlaShoLCM-C176
97Fle-164
97FleTif-164
97Lea-64
97LeaFraM-64
97LeaFraMDC-64
97MetUni-116
97NewPin-30
97NewPinAP-30
97NewPinMC-30
97NewPinPP-30
97Pac-150
97PacLigB-150
97PacPri-50
97PacPriLB-50
97PacPriP-50
97PacSil-150
97PacTriCD-7
97Pin-1
97PinArtP-1
97PinIns-86
97PinInsCE-86
97PinInsDE-86
97PinMusC-1
97PinX-P-11
97PinX-PMoS-11
97PinX-PSfF-19
97PinX-PSfFU-19
97Sco-8
97ScoPreS-8
97ScoShoS-8
97ScoShoSAP-8
97ScoTitT-18
97ScoYan-2
97ScoYanPI-2
97ScoYanPr-2
97Sel-52
97SelArtP-52
97SelRegG-52
97SkyE-X-32
97SkyE-XC-32
97SkyE-XEC-32
97SP-124
97SPSpxF-2
97SPSPxFA-2
97StaClu-211
97StaCluMat-211
97StaCluMOP-211
97Stu-132
97StuPrePG-132
97StuPrePS-132
97Top-411
97TopChr-146
97TopChrR-146
97TopGal-14
97TopGalPPI-14
97TopSta-29
97TopStaAM-29
97Ult-96
97UltGolME-96
97UltPlaME-96
97UppDec-252
97UppDec-445

Fields, Bruce

82BirBarT-11
83SanJosBC-14
86NasSouTI-8
87Don-47
87IntLeaAT-14
87Lea-47
87TolMudHP-14
87TolMudHT-9
88MarMot-16
89CalCanC-19
89CalCanP-534
89ScoHot1R-43
89Top-556
89TopTif-556
89TriA AAC-36
89UppDec-238
90BirBarDGB-10
90CMC-591
90ProAAAF-153
90TacTigC-14
90TacTigP-106
90TriAAAC-36
91RicBraBC-24
91RicBraP-2580
91RicBraTI-5
92LonTigF-649
92LonTigS-425
93TolMudHF-1668
94TolMudHF-1041

Fields, John James

87OldJudN-170

Fields, Red (Wilmer)

52Par-21
91NegLeaRL-17
93NegLeaRL2-9
95NegLeaL2-8
95NegLeaLI-17

Fiene, Lou

09T206-130
09T206-131

Fiepke, Scott

86NasPirP-6

Fier, Mike

90GatCitPP-3350
90GatCitPSP-9

Fierbaugh, Randy

79HawIslC-22

Fierro, John

80PenPilBT-24
80PenPilCT-10
86PeoChiP-6
87CubCan-11

Fife, Dan

73TacTwiC-7
74OPC-421
74TacTwiC-6
74Top-421

Figga, Michael

90TamYanD-8
91PriWilCC-14
91PriWilCP-1430
92ForLauYC-10
92ForLauYTI-11
92Ft.LauYF-2614
93SanBerSC-8
94FloStaLAF-FSL19
94TamYanC-11
94TamYanF-2386
95AusFut-17
95Bes-34
95NorNavTI-46
96ColCliB-13
96Exc-88
96NorNavB-9
96Top-432

Figueroa, Alexis

89WatDiaP-1774
89WatDiaS-6

Figueroa, Bien (Bienvenido)

86EriCarP-7
87SprCarB-22
88ArkTraGS-6
89LouRedBC-17
89LouRedBP-1262
89LouRedBTI-19
90CMC-117
90LouRedBC-17
90LouRedBLBC-15
90LouRedBP-409
90ProAAAF-523
90TopTVCa-47
91LinDriAAA-234
91LouRedLD-234
91LouRedP-2923
91LouRedTI-20
92DonRoo-36
92LouRedF-1893
92LouRedS-262
93LimRocDWB-5
93LouRedF-221
93Pin-263
93Sco-281
93StaClu-304
93StaCluFDI-304
93StaCluMOP-304
93Top-690
93TopGol-690
93TopInaM-690
93TopMic-690
94OttLynF-2903

Figueroa, Danny

93Top-704
93TopGol-704
93TopInaM-704
93TopMic-704
94AshTouC-7
94AshTouF-1789
95AshTouTI-3

Figueroa, Ed

75OPC-476
75Top-476

76OPC-27
76SSP-190
76Top-27
76TopTra-27T
77Kel-42
77OPC-164
77Top-195
77YanBurK-5
78SSP270-9
78Top-365
78TopZes-3
78YanBurK-5
78YanSSPD-9
79OPC-13
79Top-35
79YanBurK-11
79YanPicA-12
80OPC-288
80Top-555
81Fle-624
81TacTigT-32
81Top-245
82TacTigT-10
89PacSenL-75
89T/MSenL-34
89TopSenL-43
90EliSenL-80
91KelLey-8
92YanWIZ7-50
92YanWIZ8-56
93RanKee-145
Figueroa, Fernando
87PriWilYP-22
88BlaYNPRWL-6
88Ft.LauYS-8
89BlaYNPRWL-174
89MiaMirIS-4
90WilBilB-5
90WilBilP-1051
90WilBilS-6
91JacSunLD-335
91JacSunP-145
91LinDriAA-335
92JacSunF-3703
92JacSunS-355
Figueroa, Jesus
75ForLauYS-22
76ForLauYS-1
77WesHavYT-8
80WicAerT-9
81Don-556A
81Don-556B
81Top-533
85DomLeaS-210
87PocGiaTB-25
Figueroa, Julio
96VerExpB-13
Figueroa, Matt
90AriWilP-5
91JamExpC-22
91JamExpP-3537
Figueroa, Nelson
97Bow-178
97BowCerBIA-CA90
97BowCerGIA-CA90
97BowChr-170
97BowChrI-170
97BowChrIR-170
97BowChrR-170
97BowInt-178
97StaClu-184
97StaCluMOP-184
97Top-494
Figueroa, Ray
88GenCubP-1637
Figueroa, Rich
80CliGiaT-23
81CliGiaT-28
Figueroa, Vic
86ModA'sP-8
Filbeck, Ryan
93ElmPioC-7
93ElmPioF-3816
94KanCouCC-10
94KanCouCF-155
94KanCouCTI-10
Filchner, Duane
96MidLeaAB-57
96WesMicWB-9
Filer, Thomas
79WesHavYT-11
80NasSouTI-9
81ColCliT-24
82IowCubT-15
83IowCubT-3
83Top-508
84IowCubT-28
85DomLeaS-152
85SyrChiT-6
86BluJayFS-11
86Don-439
86Fle-58
86Lea-211
86OPC-312
86Top-312
86TopTif-312
88DenZepC-10
88DenZepP-1257
88TopTra-37T
88TopTraT-37T
89Fle-185
89FleGlo-185
89Top-419
89TopTif-419
90Bow-385
90BowTif-385
90BreMilB-8
90BrePol-28
90BreYea-1
90Don-687
90Fle-322
90FleCan-322
92TidTidF-890
93NorTidF-2562
94BreMilB-119
Filippi, James
86AppFoxP-8
87SanBerSP-10
Filkins, Les
80VenLeaS-131
81EvaTriT-19
82EvaTriT-19
Fillingim, Dana
21Exh-47
22E120-124
Fillion, Bob
43ParSpo-28
Fillmore, Joe
86NegLeaF-59
92NegLeaRLI-21
Filosa, Brian
92SouBenWSC-14
92SouBenWSF-184
92UtiBluSC-12
Filotei, Bobby
90BilMusP-3227
91CedRapRP-2726
Filson, Matt
92YakBeaC-22
92YakBeaF-3461
93BakDodCLC-7
Filson, Pete
82ColCliP-30
82ColCliT-9
82TolMudHT-26
83TwiTeal-16
84Don-194
84Fle-564
84MinTwiP-12
84Nes792-568
84Top-568
84TopTif-568
84TwiTeal-17
85Don-607
85Fle-277
85Top-97
85TopTif-97
85TwiTeal-18
86BufBisP-11
86Don-436
86Fle-393
86Top-122
86TopTif-122
86TwiTeal-16
87ColCliP-9
87ColCliP-25
87ColCliT-3
90CMC-184
90OmaRoyC-9
90OmaRoyP-62
90ProAAAF-597
90TriAllGP-AAA23
91BasCitRC-30
91BasCitRP-1414
92BasCitRC-26
92BasCitRF-3862
92YanWIZ8-57
95GreBatTI-28
96PorRocB-3
Filter, Rusty
89SanDieSAS-9
90SanDieSA3-4
90St.CatBJP-3468
Fimple, Jack
81WatIndT-18
82VerBeaDT-14
83AlbDukT-11
84AlbDukC-146
84DodPol-31
84Don-372
84Fle-99
84HawIslC-146
84Nes792-263
84Top-263
84TopTif-263
85AlbDukC-163
86AlbDukP-7
87EdmTraP-2083
90DodTar-243
Finch, Joel
77BriRedST-6
79Top-702
80Top-662
81PawRedST-1
Finch, Steve
77AshTouT-5
79TulDriT-6
81SpoIndT-11
82SalLakCGT-8
84EdmTraC-106
85MidAngT-13
86EdmTraP-8
Fincher, Matt
89GeoColC-7
90GeoColC-3
Findlay, Bill
88GasRanP-997
Fine, Andrea
87SalSpuP-7
Fine, Tom
89PenPilS-5
90VisOakCLC-61
90VisOakP-2147
Fine, Tommy
48SomandK-4
Fingers, Bob
87ModA'sC-26
87ModA'sP-18
Fingers, Rollie
69Top-597
70OPC-502
70Top-502
71MLBOffS-513
71OPC-384
71Top-384
72OPC-241
72Top-241
73A'sPos-36
73LinPor-139
73OPC-84
73Top-84
74OPC-212
74Top-212
75A'sPos-60
75Hos-52
75HosTwi-52
75Kel-55
75OPC-21
75OPC-463
75SSPPuzB-9
75Top-21
75Top-463
76Hos-104
76OPC-405
76SSP-480
76Top-405
77A'sPos-85
77BurCheD-133
77Hos-137
77Kel-51
77MSADis-19
77OPC-52
77PadSchC-21A
77PadSchC-21B
77RCColC-21
77Spo-1409
77Top-523
78Hos-144
78OPC-8
78OPC-201
78PadFamF-11
78RCColC-34
78Top-140
78Top-208
78WifBalD-22
79OPC-203
79Top-8
79Top-390
80BurKinPHR-3
80OPC-343
80PerHaloFP-212
80Top-651
81AllGamPI-78
81Don-2
81Fle-485
81FleStiC-47
81OPC-229
81Top-8
81Top-229
81TopSti-31
81TopTra-761
82BrePol-34
82Don-28
82Fle-141
82Fle-644
82FleSta-132
82K-M-40
82Kel-7
82OPC-44
82OPC-176
82PerCreC-16
82PerCreCG-16
82Squ-11
82Top-168
82Top-585
82Top-586
82TopSti-16
82TopSti-198
83BreGar-7
83BrePol-34
83Don-2
83Don-78
83DonActA-33
83Fle-33
83FleSta-60
83FleSti-13
83Kel-2
83OPC-35
83OPC-36
83PerCreC-23
83PerCreCG-23
83Top-35
83Top-36
83TopFol-4
83TopSti-79
83TopStiB-6
84BreGar-6
84BrePol-34
84Don-A
84DonCha-45
84Fle-199
84FunFooP-10
84Nes792-495
84Nes792-717
84Nes792-718
84OCoandSI-72
84OCoandSI-188
84OPC-283
84Top-495
84Top-717
84Top-718
84TopGaloC-4
84TopTif-495
84TopTif-717
84TopTif-718
85BreGar-6
85BrePol-34
85Don-292
85DonActA-36
85DonHig-2
85Fle-581
85Lea-190
85OPC-182
85Top-750
85TopSti-285
85TopTif-750
85Woo-10
86A'sGreT-11
86BreGreT-11
86Don-229
86Fle-486
86OPC-185
86PadGreT-11
86SevCoi-C11
86Spo-65
86Spo-130
86Spo-146
86Top-185
86TopSti-198
86TopTif-185
87A'sMot-10
88PacLegI-103
89PacSenL-161
89PadMag-8
89T/MSenL-35
89TopSenL-65
90AGFA-18
90BasWit-51
90EliSenL-21
90EliSenL-123
90PerGreM-74
91Kel3D-7
91PacSenL-126
91SweBasG-30
91UppDecS-10
92BreCarT-7
92LegSpoF-RF1
92LegSpoF-RF2
92LegSpoF-RF3
92MDAMVP-15
92PhoFilHoF-1
92UppDecF-45
92UppDecFG-45
92UppDecHH-HI3
92UppDecHoB-H7
92UppDecHoB-H8
92UppDecHoB-AU7
92UppDecS-17
92UppDecS-18
92UppDecS-25
92UppDecS-27
92UppDecS-33
92UppDecS-34
92Zip-3
93ActPacA-130
93ActPacA2-64G
93FroRowF-1
93FroRowF-2
93FroRowF-3
93FroRowF-4
93FroRowF-5
94BreMilB-120
94BreMilB-312
94BreSen-2
94TedWil-66
94UppDecS-3
97TopStaHRR-4
97TopStaHRRA-4
Finigan, Jim
55A'sRodM-14
55ArmCoi-5
55RobGouS-17
55RobGouW-17
55Top-14
55TopDouH-49
56A'sRodM-5
56Top-22
56TopPin-12
57Top-248
58Top-136
59Top-47
59TopVen-47
76A'sRodMC-10
79TCM50-128
91OriCro-129
Finigan, Kevin
87BurExpP-1079
88JamExpP-1915
Fink, Eric
84PriWilPT-11
Fink, Mark
96HelBreTI-4
Finken, Steve
88GreFalDTI-15
89BakDodCLC-205
89CalLeaA-22
90SanAntMGS-12
91LinDriAA-534
91SanAntMLD-534
91SanAntMP-2982
92ShrCapS-592
92SkyAA F-257
Finlayson, Mike
75WesPalBES-23
79MemChiT-12
Finley, Bob
45CenFlo-7
83TCMPla1944-45
Finley, Brian
83BelBreF-18

86ElPasDP-10
88ChaLooB-13
90ChaLooGS-12
Finley, Charles
91FouBal-17
Finley, Chris
93Sou-9
Finley, Chuck
86QuaCitAP-11
87AngSmo-6
87Don-407
87Fle-79
87FleGlo-79
87Top-446
87TopTif-446
88AngSmo-15
88Don-530
88DonBasB-283
88Fle-489
88FleGlo-489
88StaLinAn-6
88Top-99
88TopBig-254
88TopTif-99
89Bow-37
89BowTif-37
89Don-226
89DonBasB-333
89Fle-477
89FleGlo-477
89Sco-503
89Top-708
89TopBig-76
89TopTif-708
89UppDec-632
90AngSmo-5
90Bow-289
90BowTif-289
90Don-344
90DonBesA-103
90Fle-132
90FleCan-132
90K-M-28
90Lea-162
90OPC-147
90PanSti-32
90PubSti-369
90Sco-380
90Sco100S-24
90Spo-172
90Top-147
90TopBig-319
90TopCoi-13
90TopDou-22
90TopMinL-8
90TopSti-177
90TopStiB-62
90TopTif-147
90TopTVA-14
90UppDec-667
90USPlaCA-9S
90VenSti-172
90WinDis-5
91AngSmo-9
91BasBesAotM-7
91Bow-196
91Cla1-T95
91Cla3-T20
91Don-26
91Don-692
91DonSupD-26
91Fle-313
91Lea-45
91LeaPre-15
91OPC-395
91OPC-505
91PanCanT1-70
91PanFreS-187
91PanSti-135
91RedFolS-35
91Sco-100
91Sco100S-90
91StaClu-81
91Stu-24
91SunSee-7
91Top-395
91Top-505
91TopCraJ2-12
91TopDesS-395
91TopDesS-505
91TopMic-395
91TopMic-505
91TopTif-395
91TopTif-505
91TopTriH-A3
91Ult-44
91UppDec-31
91UppDec-437
92AngPol-9
92Bow-32
92ClaGam-1
92Don-255
92Fle-57
92Hig5-12
92Lea-450
92OPC-247
92OPCPre-155
92Pin-42
92Sco-585
92Sco100S-6
92SpollIFK1-72
92StaClu-315
92Stu-145
92Top-247
92TopGol-247
92TopGolW-247
92TopKid-94
92TopMic-247
92TriPla-91
92Ult-25
92UppDec-244
93AngMot-3
93AngPol-19
93Bow-385
93Don-225
93Fin-72
93FinRef-72
93Fla-174
93Fle-191
93FunPac-39
93HumDumC-4
93Lea-292
93OPC-153
93PacSpa-44
93Pin-201
93Sco-158
93Sel-198
93SP-23
93StaClu-301
93StaCluAn-16
93StaCluFDI-301
93StaCluMOP-301
93Top-605
93TopGol-605
93TopInaM-605
93TopMic-605
93TriPla-169
93Ult-162
93UppDec-53
93UppDec-77
93UppDecGold-53
93UppDecGold-77
94AngLAT-11
94AngMot-9
94Bow-67
94ColC-515
94ColChoGS-515
94ColChoSS-515
94Don-363
94DonSpeE-363
94ExtBas-35
94ExtBasPD-5
94Fin-143
94FinRef-143
94Fla-22
94Fle-55
94Lea-394
94OPC-158
94Pac-78
94Pin-38
94PinArtP-38
94PinMusC-38
94ProMag-19
94Sco-151
94ScoGolR-151
94Sel-291
94Spo-21
94StaClu-211
94StaCluFDI-211
94StaCluGR-211
94StaCluMOP-211
94Top-381
94TopGol-381
94TopSpa-381
94TriPla-15
94Ult-328
94UppDec-314
94UppDecED-314
95AngCHP-2
95AngMot-9
95Baz-19
95Bow-298
95ColCho-102
95ColChoGS-102
95ColChoSE-34
95ColChoSEGS-34
95ColChoSESS-34
95ColChoSS-102
95Don-477
95DonPreP-477
95DonTopotO-36
95Emb-48
95EmbGolI-48
95Emo-20
95Fin-87
95FinRef-87
95Fla-18
95Fle-224
95FleTeaL-3
95Lea-67
95LeaLim-111
95Pac-60
95Pin-17
95PinArtP-17
95PinMusC-17
95RedFol-12
95Sco-134
95ScoGolR-134
95ScoPlaTS-134
95SP-134
95SPCha-132
95SPChaDC-132
95SPSil-134
95SPSpeF-5
95StaClu-441
95StaCluMOP-441
95StaCluSTWS-441
95StaCluVR-232
95Stu-132
95Top-455
95TopCyb-251
95TopLeaL-LL48
95Ult-268
95UltGolM-268
95UppDec-21
95UppDecED-21
95UppDecEDG-21
95UppDecSE-264
95UppDecSEG-264
96AngMot-9
96Baz-103
96Cir-20
96CirRav-20
96ColCho-485
96ColChoGS-485
96ColChoSS-485
96Don-147
96DonPreP-147
96EmoXL-26
96Fin-B89
96FinRef-B89
96Fla-37
96Fle-47
96FleSmo'H-4
96FleTif-47
96Lea-5
96LeaPrePB-5
96LeaPrePG-5
96LeaPrePS-5
96MetUni-27
96MetUniP-27
96Pac-275
96PanSti-213
96Sco-410
96SP-46
96StaClu-120
96StaCluEPB-120
96StaCluEPG-120
96StaCluEPS-120
96StaCluMOP-120
95StaCluVRMC-232
96Top-192
96TopGal-25
96TopGalPPI-25
96TopLas-118
96Ult-30
96UltGolM-30
96UppDec-291
96UppDecPHE-H15
96UppDecPreH-H15
97Cir-393
97CirRav-393
97ColCho-256
97Don-260
97DonPreP-260
97DonPrePGold-260
97DonTea-7
97DonTeaSPE-7
97Fin-53
97FinRef-53
97Fle-43
97FleTif-43
97Lea-87
97LeaFraM-87
97LeaFraMDC-87
97MetUni-41
97NewPin-134
97NewPinAP-134
97NewPinMC-134
97NewPinPP-134
97Pac-8
97PacLigB-8
97PacSil-8
97Sco-75
97ScoPreS-75
97ScoShoS-75
97ScoShoSAP-75
97SP-21
97StaClu-102
97StaCluMOP-102
97Top-336
97Ult-27
97UltGolME-27
97UltPlaME-27
97UppDec-295
Finley, David
88ModA'sCLC-70
88ModA'sTI-23
Finley, Steve
87NewOriP-21
88BlaYNPRWL-83
88HagSunS-7
88RocRedWGCP-7
88TriAAAP-29
88TriAAC-21
89Bow-15
89BowTif-15
89DonRoo-47
89FleUpd-3
89OriFreB-10
89RocRedWP-1639
89ScoRoo-95T
89UppDec-742
90Don-215
90Fle-176
90FleCan-176
90HagSunDGB-10
90Lea-329
90OPC-349
90Sco-339
90Sco100RS-58
90ScoYouSI-11
90Top-349
90TopDeb89-37
90TopTif-349
90UppDec-602
91AstMot-2
91Bow-561
91Don-355
91Fle-470
91FleUpd-88
91Lea-231
91OPC-212
91OriCro-130
91PanFreS-244
91Sco-266
91StaClu-376
91Stu-176
91Top-212
91TopDesS-212
91TopMic-212
91TopTif-212
91TopTra-42T
91TopTraT-42T
91UltUpd-81
91UppDec-330
91UppDec-794
92AstMot-2
92Bow-574
92Don-197
92Fle-433
92Lea-66
92OPC-86
92PanSti-157
92Pin-19
92Sco-176
92StaClu-29
92Stu-35
92Top-86
92TopGol-86
92TopGolW-86
92TopKid-46
92TopMic-86
92TriPla-26
92TriPla-43
92TriPlaP-5
92Ult-202
92UppDec-368
93AstMot-2
93Bow-96
93ClaGam-33
93Don-192
93Fin-9
93FinRef-9
93Fla-62
93Fle-50
93FunPac-47
93Lea-325
93OPC-154
93PacSpa-122
93PanSti-174
93Pin-172
93Sco-65
93Sel-88
93SelStaL-23
93SelStaL-60
93SP-33
93StaClu-556
93StaCluAs-10
93StaCluFDI-556
93StaCluMOP-556
93Top-148
93TopGol-148
93TopInaM-148
93TopMic-148
93TriPla-203
93Ult-39
93UppDec-231
93UppDecGold-231
93USPlaCA-5H
94AstMot-8
94Bow-502
94ColC-523
94ColChoGS-523
94ColChoSS-523
94Don-402
94ExtBas-273
94Fin-31
94FinPre-31P
94FinRef-31
94Fla-389
94Fle-490
94FUnPac-91
94Lea-383
94OPC-129
94Pac-265
94PanSti-194
94Pin-351
94PinArtP-351
94PinMusC-351
94Sco-364
94ScoCyc-TC12
94ScoGolR-364
94Sel-362
94Spo-135
94StaClu-308
94StaCluFDI-308
94StaCluGR-308
94StaCluMOP-308
94StaCluMOP-ST6
94StaCluST-ST6
94Stu-21
94Top-580
94TopGol-580
94TopSpa-580
94TriPla-26
94Ult-503
94UppDec-346
94UppDecED-346
95ColCho-349
95ColChoGS-349
95ColChoSS-349
95Don-25
95DonPreP-25
95DonTopotO-340
95Emo-186
95Fin-194
95FinRef-194
95Fla-418
95Fle-459

95FleUpd-183
95Lea-320
95LeaLim-164
95Pac-186
95PadCHP-11
95PadMot-14
95Pin-114
95PinArtP-114
95PinMusC-114
95Sco-397
95ScoGolR-397
95ScoPlaTS-397
95SP-108
95SPSil-108
95StaClu-18
95StaClu-551
95StaCluFDI-18
95StaCluMOP-18
95StaCluMOP-551
95StaCluSTWS-18
95StaCluSTWS-551
95StaCluVR-12
95Stu-133
95Top-626
95TopCyb-393
95TopTra-91T
95Ult-172
95UltGolM-172
95UppDec-371
95UppDecED-371
95UppDecEDG-371
95UppDecSE-269
95UppDecSEG-269
96Baz-66
96Cir-185
96CirRav-185
96ColCho-358
96ColCho-696
96ColChoGS-358
96ColChoGS-696
96ColChoSS-358
96ColChoSS-696
96Don-66
96DonPreP-66
96EmoXL-276
96Fin-S160
96FinRef-S160
96Fla-373
96Fle-565
96FleTif-565
96Lea-12
96LeaPrePB-12
96LeaPrePG-12
96LeaPrePS-12
96MetUni-234
96MetUniP-234
96Pac-192
96PadMot-7
96PanSti-103
96Pin-6
96Sco-287
96ScoDugC-B12
96ScoDugCAP-B12
96SP-163
96StaClu-378
96StaCluEPB-378
96StaCluEPG-378
96StaCluEPS-378
96StaCluMO-12
96StaCluMOP-378
95StaCluVRMC-12
96Top-139
96TopChr-38
96TopChrR-38
96TopGal-9
96TopGalPPI-9
96Ult-557
96UltGolM-557
96UppDec-449
97BowBes-15
97BowBesAR-15
97BowBesR-15
97Cir-254
97CirRav-254
97ColCho-209
97ColChoAC-33
97Don-60
97DonEli-144
97DonEliGS-144
97DonLim-66
97DonLimLE-66
97DonPre-65
97DonPreCttC-65
97DonPreP-60
97DonPrePGold-60
97Fin-314
97FinEmb-314
97FinEmbR-314
97FinRef-314
97FlaSho-A96
97FlaSho-B96
97FlaSho-C96
97FlaShoLC-96
97FlaShoLC-B96
97FlaShoLC-C96
97FlaShoLCM-A96
97FlaShoLCM-B96
97FlaShoLCM-C96
97Fle-459
97FleTif-459
97Lea-100
97LeaFraM-100
97LeaFraMDC-100
97MetUni-218
97NewPin-58
97NewPinAP-58
97NewPinMC-58
97NewPinPP-58
97Pac-422
97PacLigB-422
97PacPri-143
97PacPriLB-143
97PacPriP-143
97PacSil-422
97PinIns-121
97PinInsCE-121
97PinInsDE-121
97PinX-P-50
97PinX-PMoS-50
97Sco-279
97ScoPreS-279
97ScoShoS-279
97ScoShoSAP-279
97Sel-90
97SelArtP-90
97SelRegG-90
97SP-156
97SpoIll-120
97SpoIllEE-120
97StaClu-24
97StaCluMat-24
97StaCluMOP-24
97Top-189
97TopChr-73
97TopChrR-73
97TopGal-76
97TopGalPPI-76
97Ult-280
97UltGolME-280
97UltPlaME-280
97UppDec-165
97UppDec-376
Finley, Tom
91PomBlaBPB-23
Finn, John
89BelBreIS-9
90StoPorB-11
90StoPorCLC-196
90StoPorP-2196
91CalLeLA-30
91StoPorC-18
91StoPorP-3044
92ClaFS7-96
92ElPasDF-3929
92ElPasDS-209
92UppDecML-141
93NewOrlZF-979
Finn, Mickey (Neal)
33DouDisP-15
90DodTar-244
Finnerty, Keith
96NewJerCB-9
Finney, Lou
33RitCE-8H
35DiaMatCS3T1-51
36GouWidPPR-A31
36WorWidGV-64
40PlaBal-197
41PlaBal-30
42RedSoxTI-11
92ConTSN-512
Finney, Mark
91BenBucC-5
91BenBucP-3690
Finnieston, Adam R.
96LanLugB-12
Finnvold, Gar
90ElmPioP-17
91Cla/Bes-192
91LynRedSC-3
91LynRedSP-1192
92ClaFS7-195
92NewBriRSF-426
92NewBriRSS-484
92SkyAA F-206
93PawRedSDD-9
93PawRedSF-2403
93PawRedSTI-9
94Bow-231
94Fla-262
94FleUpd-11
94LeaLimR-68
94PawRedSDD-6
94PawRedSF-941
94SigRooDP-92
94SigRooDPS-92
94TopTra-96T
95Don-283
95DonPreP-283
95Fle-29
95Lea-130
95PawRedSDD-10
95PawRedTI-NNO
95Sco-580
95ScoGolR-580
95ScoPlaTS-580
95Top-92
96PawRedSDD-9
Finzer, Kory
91AubAstC-27
Fiore, Mike
85MiaHur-4
87PanAmTURB-6
88TopTra-38T
88TopTraT-38T
89SprCarB-1
89TopBig-8
90St.PetCS-8
91ArkTraLD-34
91ArkTraP-1294
91LinDriAA-34
87PanAmTUBI-20
Fiore, Mike Gary Joseph
69RoyTeal-4
69Top-376
69TopTeaP-7
70RoyTeal-12
70Top-709
71MLBOffS-318
71OPC-287
71Top-287
72MilBra-104
72OPC-199
72Top-199
77RocRedWM-16
78ColCliT-6
91OriCro-131
Fiore, Tom
86KenTwiP-9
Fiore, Tony
92MarPhiC-22
92MarPhiF-3050
93BatCliC-9
93BatCliF-3139
94SpaPhiF-1714
94SparPhiC-8
95ClePhiF-211
Fiorillo, Nicholas
80WatRedT-1
82WatRedT-10
83TamTarT-27
Firebird, Phineas T.
95PhoFirTI-0
96PhoFirB-29
Firebirds, Phoenix
95PhoFirTI-NNO
96PhoFirB-1
Fireovid, Steve
81HawIsIT-12
82HawIsIT-13
83LasVegSBHN-8
84PorBeaC-214
85BufBisT-18
86CalCanP-8
87Fle-653
87SpoTeaP-25
87SyrChiP-1933
87SyrChiT-30
87Top-357
87TopTif-357
88OmaRoyC-4
88OmaRoyP-1513
89OmaRoyC-3
89OmaRoyP-1718
90CMC-51
90IndIndC-1
90IndIndP-292
90ProAAAF-575
91BufBisLD-28
91BufBisP-534
91LinDriAAA-28
92Bow-334
92OklCit8F-1912
93OklCit8F-1621
93RanKee-146
Firova, Dan
80SpoIndT-22
86CalCanP-9
89UppDec-32
Firpo, Luis
28W512-46
Firsich, Steve
91BluOriC-20
91BluOriP-4122
92KanCouCC-24
92KanCouCF-83
92KanCouCTI-8
Fischback, Bruce
86KinEagP-7
Fischer, Bill (William Charles)
15SpoNewM-58
16ColE13-48
16SpoNewM-57
19W514-27
59SenTealW-7
60TopVen-76
63AthJayP-7
67DexPre-72
72LauGreF-47
80RedEnq-6
90DodTar-947
90HOFStiB-64
94RicBraF-2863
95RicBraTI-27
96RicBraB-2
Fischer, Brad
82MadMusF-19
83MadMusF-31
84MadMusP-1
85HunStaJ-25
87HunStaTI-11
88TacTigP-622
89TacTigC-25
89TacTigP-1551
90ProAAAF-157
90TacTigP-110
96A'sMot-28
86HumStaDS-25
Fischer, Carl
31SenTealPW-9
34DiaMatCSB-54
35DiaMatCS3T1-52
35TigFreP-5
43CenFlo-8
44CenFlo-7
45CenFlo-8
76TigOldTS-7
92ConTSN-409
93DiaStaES-129
Fischer, Dan
80OmaRoyP-11
81OmaRoyT-7
82OmaRoyT-4
Fischer, Hank
63Top-554
64Top-218
64TopVen-218
65Top-585
66Top-381
67CokCapRS-15
67Top-342
67TopRedSS-5
Fischer, Jeff
86FloStaLAP-14
86WesPalBEP-15
87IndIndTI-15
88IndIndC-6
88IndIndP-503
89AlbDukC-3
89AlbDukP-86
90AlbDukC-3
90AlbDukP-338
90AlbDukT-7
90CMC-405
90DodTar-948
90ProAAAF-59
90Sco-654
93BurBeeC-28
93BurBeeF-174
94BurBeeC-27
94BurBeeF-1099
96WesPalBEB-3
Fischer, Todd
82IdaFalAT-7
83MadMusF-4
84AlbA'sT-12
86EdmTraP-9
Fischer, Tom
89Bow-20
89BowTif-20
89LynRedSS-8
90CMC-806
90NewBriRSB-2
90NewBriRSP-1312
90NewBriRSS-4
91Cla/Bes-306
91LinDriAA-458
91NewBriRSLD-458
91NewBriRSP-347
92PawRedSF-916
92PawRedSS-356
93NewBriRSF-1213
97DunDonPPS-8
Fischer, William C.
58Top-56
59Top-230
60Top-76
61Top-553
63Top-301
64Top-409
90TopTVRS-4
Fischetti, Art
75WatDodT-7
Fischlin, Mike
78ChaChaT-7
79ChaChaT-6
79Top-718
80TucTorT-17
81ChaChaT-13
82IndWhe-15
83Don-489
83Fle-407
83IndPos-14
83IndWhe-12
83Top-182
84Fle-541
84Ind-12
84IndWhe-22
84Nes792-689
84Top-689
84TopTif-689
85Don-495
85Fle-447
85Ind-13
85IndPol-22
85Top-41
85TopTif-41
86FleUpd-40
86Top-283
86TopTif-283
86YanTCM-23
87Fle-98
87FleGlo-98
87RicBraBC-7
87RicBraC-18
87RicBraT-12
87Top-434
87TopTif-434
88GreBraB-23
89MyrBeaBJP-1466
90MyrBeaBJP-2792
90SouAtlLAS-47
92YanWIZ8-58
97BobCamRB-12
Fishel, John
86FloStaLAP-15
86OscAstP-8
87ColAstP-12
88FleUpd-88
88FleUpdG-88
88TucTorC-19
88TucTorJP-11
88TucTorP-178
89ColCliC-18
89ColCliP-20
89ColCliP-735
89Don-443
89Fle-358
89FleGlo-358

89PanSti-80
89ScoHot1R-42
90CMC-214
90ColCliC-14
90ColCliP-6
90ColCliP-689
90ProAAAF-339
90TopTVY-42
Fisher, Brian
77NewCoPT-12
Fisher, Brian K.
82DurBulT-17
84RicBraT-20
85ColCliP-11
85ColCliT-7
85FleUpd-40
86Don-492
86Fle-104
86KayB-12
86SevCoi-E15
86Spo-177
86Top-584
86TopGloS-30
86TopSti-312
86TopTat-2
86TopTif-584
86YanTCM-7
87Don-340
87Fle-99
87FleGlo-99
87FleUpd-32
87FleUpdG-32
87OPC-316
87SpoTeaP-18
87Top-316
87TopTif-316
87TopTra-33T
87TopTraT-33T
88Don-415
88DonBasB-101
88Fle-329
88FleGlo-329
88Lea-244
88OPC-193
88PanSti-368
88Sco-130
88ScoGlo-130
88StaLinPi-11
88Top-193
88TopBig-159
88TopTif-193
89Bow-415
89BowTif-415
89Don-126
89Fle-209
89FleGlo-209
89OPC-303
89PirVerFJ-54
89RedFolSB-42
89Sco-24
89Top-423
89TopTif-423
89UppDec-69
90CMC-626
90OPC-666
90ProAAAF-189
90PubSti-154
90Sco-547
90Top-666
90TopTif-666
90TucTorC-24
90TucTorP-199
90UppDec-97
90VenSti-173
91DenZepLD-137
91DenZepP-118
91LinDriAAA-137
92NasSouF-1826
92NasSouS-278
92YanWIZ8-59
93Fle-674
93PhoFirF-1511
Fisher, Chauncey
90DodTar-949
Fisher, Curt
77LynMetT-12
Fisher, David
92MarPhiC-20
92MarPhiF-3064
93ClePhiC-8
93ClePhiF-2688
94ReaPhiF-2067
95ReaPhiELC-13
95ReaPhiTI-6
96ReaPhiB-17
96ScrRedBB-14
Fisher, Eddie
60TacBan-6
60Top-23
60TopVen-23
61Top-161
61Top-366
62WhiSoxTS-7
63Top-6
63Top-223
63WhiSoxTS-6
64Top-66
64TopVen-66
64WhiSoxTS-8
65Top-328
66Baz-47
66OPC-85
66Top-85
66Top-222
66TopRubI-29
66TopVen-85
66TopVen-222
67CokCapO-14
67DexPre-73
67Top-434
68Top-418
69Top-315
69TopSta-143
70OPC-156
70Top-156
71MLBOffS-343
71OPC-631
71Top-631
72Top-689
73OPC-439
73Top-439
81Ori6F-14
91OriCro-132
Fisher, Fritz (Frederick)
64Top-312
64TopVen-312
66Top-209
66TopVen-209
Fisher, Glen
77BriRedST-5
79CedRapGT-13
81ShrCapT-6
82RedPioT-20
Fisher, Jack H.
60OriJayP-3
60Top-46
60Top-399
60TopVen-46
61SevElev-5
61Top-463
62Top-203
63Top-474
64Top-422
65MetJayP-5
65OPC-93
65Top-93
66Top-316
66TopRubI-30
66TopVen-316
67CokCapYM-V32
67DexPre-74
67Kah-13
67MetTeal-5
67Top-533
68Top-444
69Top-318
70Top-684
81TCM60I-478
89ColMetB-23
89ColMetGS-2
90ColMetGS-2
90ColMetPPI-6
91MetWIZ-115
91OriCro-133
Fisher, Kyle
89AugPirP-521
Fisher, Louis
96BluOriB-12
Fisher, Ray
11T205-56
12ColRedB-101
12ColTinT-101
12T207-59
12T207-60
14CraJacE-102
15CraJacE-102
15SpoNewM-59
16ColE13-49
16FleBreD-28
16SpoNewM-58
20RedWorCP-6
88PacEigMO-92
93ConTSN-702
Fisher, Robert
12ImpTobC-43
90DodTar-245
Fisher, Ryan
96AugGreB-10
Fisher, Tom
11SpoLifCW-126
77FriOneYW-37
91OriCro-134
Fisk, Carlton
72OPC-79
72Top-79
73Kel2D-27
73LinPor-20
73OPC-193
73Top-193
73TopCanL-15
74Kel-5
74OPC-105
74OPC-331
74Top-105
74Top-331
74TopDecE-64
74TopSta-133
75Hos-143
75OPC-80
75Top-80
76CraDis-14
76Hos-64
76LinSup-109
76OPC-365
76RedSox-4
76RedSoxSM-6
76SSP-403
76Top-365
77BurCheD-33
77Hos-104
77MSADis-20
77OPC-137
77PepGloD-22
77Spo-5613
77Top-640
78OPC-210
78PapGinD-25
78SSP270-180
78Top-270
78WifBalD-23
79Hos-106
79OPC-360
79Top-680
80Kel-41
80OPC-20
80Top-40
81AllGamPI-40
81Don-335
81Dra-32
81Fle-224
81FleStiC-58
81MSAMinD-12
81OPC-116
81PerAll-13
81Top-480
81TopSti-46
81TopSupHT-4
81TopTra-762
82Don-20
82Don-495
82Dra-12
82Fle-343
82Fle-632
82FleSta-183
82Kel-25
82OPC-58
82OPC-110
82OPC-111
82PerAll-3
82PerAllG-3
82Squ-8
82Top-110
82Top-111
82Top-554
82TopSti-138
82TopSti-170
83AllGamPI-40
83Don-104
83DonActA-43
83Fle-235
83Fle-638
83FleSta-61
83FleSti-148
83FleSti-153
83Kel-56
83OPC-20
83OPC-393
83Top-20
83Top-393
83TopGloS-17
83TopSti-54
83TopSti-177
83WhiSoxTV-72
84AllGamPI-129
84Don-302
84DonCha-52
84Fle-58
84FleSti-39
84FunFooP-72
84MilBra-9
84Nes792-216
84Nes792-560
84OCoandSI-47
84OPC-127
84RalPur-33
84SevCoi-C12
84Top-216
84Top-560
84TopCer-33
84TopGloS-40
84TopRubD-9
84TopSti-243
84TopSup-15
84TopTif-216
84TopTif-560
84WhiSoxTV-13
85AllGamPI-39
85Don-208
85Fle-513
85GenMilS-17
85Lea-155
85OPC-49
85Top-1
85Top-770
85TopRubD-5
85TopSti-243
85TopTif-1
85TopTif-770
85WhiSoxC-72
86BasStaB-41
86Don-366
86DonAll-17
86DonPop-17
86Fle-204
86Fle-643
86FleLeaL-12
86FleLimE-15
86FleMin-43
86FleStiC-38
86FleWaxBC-C8
86GenMilB-2D
86Lea-163
86MeaGolBB-3
86MeaGolSB-13
86MSAJayPCD-7
86OPC-290
86OPCBoxB-E
86SevCoi-C12
86Spo-67
86Spo-125
86SpoDecG-62
86Top-290
86Top-719
86TopGloA-9
86TopGloS-28
86TopMinL-11
86TopSti-162
86TopSti-286
86TopSup-23
86TopTat-23
86TopTif-290
86TopTif-719
86TopWaxBC-E
86WhiSoxC-72
87ClaGam-41
87Don-247
87DonOpeD-232
87Fle-496
87FleGlo-496
87FleRecS-8
87GenMilB-3D
87Lea-199
87OPC-164
87RedFolSB-41
87SevCoi-C7
87Spo-140
87SpoTeaP-26
87StuPan-17
87Top-756
87TopSti-288
87TopTif-756
87WhiSoxC-10
88Don-260
88DonBasB-67
88Fle-397
88FleAwaW-12
88FleGlo-397
88KinDis-18
88Lea-208
88Nes-38
88OPC-385
88PanSti-55
88PanSti-91
88RedFolSB-23
88Sco-592
88ScoGlo-592
88Spo-43
88StaLinAl-11
88StaLinWS-7
88Top-321
88Top-385
88TopBig-197
88TopMinL-8
88TopSti-290
88TopTif-321
88TopTif-385
88WhiSoxC-8
88WhiSoxK-2
89Bow-62
89BowTif-62
89CadEllD-17
89Don-7
89Don-101
89DonBasB-11
89DonSupD-7
89Fle-495
89FleGlo-495
89KayB-11
89OPC-46
89PanSti-304
89RedFolSB-43
89Sco-449
89ScoHot1S-39
89ScoSco-9
89Spo-219
89SpoIllFKI-171
89Top-695
89TopBasT-151
89TopBig-24
89TopCoi-40
89TopDouA-8
89TopSti-299
89TopStiB-23
89TopTif-695
89TopUKM-26
89UppDec-609
89WhiSoxC-8
89WhiSoxK-3
90AllBasT-21
90Bow-314
90BowTif-314
90ClaBlu-116
90Don-58
90DonBesA-5
90DOnBonM-BC19
90DonLeaS-49
90Fle-530
90FleAwaW-13
90FleCan-530
90GooHumICBLS-8
90Hot50PS-12
90KayB-12
90Lea-10
90Lea-174
90OPC-392
90OPC-420
90PanSti-44
90PubSti-284
90PubSti-386
90RedFolSB-32
90Sco-290
90Sco100S-70
90ScoMcD-4
90Spo-204
90Top-392
90Top-420
90TopBig-176
90TopDou-23
90TopGloS-46
90TopHilHM-29

90TopMag-41
90TopSti-303
90TopStiB-55
90TopTif-392
90TopTif-420
90TopTVA-8
90UppDec-367
90VenSti-174
90VenSti-175
90WhiSoxC-3
90WhiSoxC-29
90WhiSoxK-1
90Woo-13
91BasBesRB-6
91Bow-345
91CadElID-20
91Cla3-T21
91ClaGam-51
91Don-108
91DonBonC-BC6
91Fle-118
91KinDis-22
91Lea-384
91LeaPre-16
91MajLeaCP-14
91OPC-3
91OPC-170
91OPC-393
91OPCBoxB-F
91OPCPre-45
91PanFreS-311
91PanSti-255
91PetSta-7
91RedFolS-36
91Sco-265
91Sco-421
91Sco100S-41
91SevCoi-M4
91StaClu-180
91StaCluCM-9
91StaCluMO-14
91StaPinB-18
91Stu-32
91Top-3
91Top-170
91Top-393
91TopCraJ2-2
91TopDesS-3
91TopDesS-170
91TopDesS-393
91TopMic-3
91TopMic-170
91TopMic-393
91TopSta-14
91TopTif-3
91TopTif-170
91TopTif-393
91TopTriH-A4
91TopWaxBC-F
91Ult-72
91UppDec-29
91UppDec-643
91UppDec-677
91USPlaCA-2D
91WhiSoxK-72
91WhiSoxK-NNO0
91Woo-12
92Bow-585
92ClaGam-96
92Don-543
92Fle-79
92FleTeaL-4
92Hig5-16
92JimDeaLL-2
92Lea-303
92Mr.TurS-9
92OPC-630
92OPCPre-86
92PacSea-60
92PanSti-124
92PepDieM-11
92Pin-361
92Sco-72
92Sco100S-72
92ScoFacI-B8
92ScoProP-17
92SpoStaCC-15
92StaClu-480
92StaCluD-49
92StuHer-BC2
92Top-630
92TopGol-630
92TopGolW-630
92TopMcD-15
92TopMic-630
92TriPla-149
92Ult-33
92UppDec-571
92WhiSoxK-72
93Bow-175
93CadDis-19
93Don-519
93Fin-125
93FinRef-125
93Fle-582
93FleFinEDT-4
93Lea-284
93MetBak-26
93OPC-78
93PacSpa-70
93PanSti-135
93Pin-301
93Pin-421
93Pin-475
93PinCoo-4
93PinCooD-4
93Sco-579
93Sel-76
93StaClu-221
93StaCluFDI-221
93StaCluMO-8
93StaCluMOP-221
93StaCluWS-16
93Top-230
93TopGol-230
93TopInaM-230
93TopMic-230
93TopPre-230
93Ult-530
93UppDec-272
93UppDecGold-272
96IllLot-2
97FleMilDM-41
Fisk, Don
77ForLauYS-23
Fister, Corby
90IdaFalBP-3256
Fithian, Grant
95GreBatTI-11
96NorNavB-10
Fitterer, Scott
95StCatSTI-12
96DunBluJB-8
96DunBluJTI-10
96HagSunB-5
Fittipaldi, Emerson
72Dia-140
Fitzer, Doug
91Cla/Bes-362
91SanBerSC-3
91SanBerSP-1979
92PenPilC-11
92PenPilF-2927
94RivPilCLC-27
Fitzgerald, Barry
93MarPhiC-9
93MarPhiF-3477
Fitzgerald, Brian
96EveAquB-8
Fitzgerald, Dave
89BelBreIS-5
89BelBreIS-10
90CalLeaACLC-54
90StoPorB-17
90StoPorCLC-178
90StoPorP-2177
91HelBreSP-18
91StoPorC-11
92ElPasDS-210
Fitzgerald, Ed
47SigOil-60
47SunBre-6
49Bow-109A
49Bow-109B
49EurSta-159
50Bow-178
52Bow-180
52Top-236
53Bri-5
54Bow-168
55Bow-208
55DonWin-3
56Top-198
57Top-22
57Top-367
58Top-236
59Top-33
59TopVen-33
60Top-423
83TopRep5-236
Fitzgerald, Kevin
86EveGiaC-1
86EveGiaPC-4
Fitzgerald, Matthew
06GiaUllAFS-4
09ColChiE-102
12ColRedB-102
12ColTinT-102
Fitzgerald, Mike P.
85SprCarT-11
87ArkTraP-21
87TexLeaAF-26
88LouRedBC-18
88LouRedBP-427
88LouRedBTI-19
89LouRedBC-18
89LouRedBP-1259
89LouRedBTI-20
90ArkTraGS-13
90SprCarDGB-34
Fitzgerald, Mike R.
82TidTidT-4
83TidTidT-2
84Don-482
84FleUpd-37
84TopTra-37T
84TopTraT-37T
85AllGamPI-130
85Don-238
85ExpPos-8
85Fle-78
85FleUpd-41
85OPC-104
85OPCPos-1
85Top-104
85TopSti-108
85TopSti-372
85TopTif-104
85TopTifT-34T
85TopTra-34T
86Don-97
86ExpPos-3
86ExpProPa-26
86ExpProPo-7
86Fle-247
86GenMilB-6C
86Lea-32
86OPC-313
86Top-503
86TopTif-503
87Don-345
87ExpPos-6
87Fle-317
87FleGlo-317
87GenMilB-4B
87Lea-222
87OPC-212
87SmoNatL-14
87SpoTeaP-20
87Top-212
87TopTif-212
88Don-159
88ExpPos-6
88Fle-182
88FleGlo-182
88Lea-81
88MSAHosD-6
88OPC-92
88PanSti-322
88Sco-318
88ScoGlo-318
88StaLinE-4
88Top-674
88TopSti-78
88TopTif-674
89Don-456
89ExpPos-5
89Fle-374
89FleGlo-374
89OPC-23
89Sco-511
89Top-23
89TopTif-23
89UppDec-133
90Don-392
90ExpPos-7
90Fle-343
90FleCan-343
90OPC-484
90PubSti-171
90Sco-361
90Top-484
90TopBig-84
90TopTif-484
90UppDec-558
90VenSti-176
91Bow-453
91Don-82
91ExpPos-4
91Fle-229
91MetWIZ-116
91OPC-317
91PanFreS-138
91Sco-198
91StaClu-128
91Stu-196
91Top-317
91TopDesS-317
91TopMic-317
91TopTif-317
91Ult-201
91UppDec-516
92Bow-186
92Fle-478
92Lea-371
92OPC-761
92Sco-667
92StaClu-844
92StaCluNC-844
92Top-761
92TopGol-761
92TopGolW-761
92TopMic-761
92TopTra-31T
92TopTraG-31T
92UppDec-210
93Don-757
93NewOrlZF-975
93PacSpa-45
Fitzgerald, Patrick
88AllandGN-42
Fitzgerald, Pedestrian
88GooN16-20
Fitzgerald, Richard
52LavPro-100
Fitzmaurice, Shaun
71RicBraTI-6
77FriOneYW-113
91MetWIZ-117
Fitzmorris, Al
70OPC-241
70RoyTeal-13
70Top-241
71OPC-564
71Top-564
72OPC-349
72Top-349
72TopCloT-10
73OPC-643
73Top-643
74OPC-191
74Top-191
75OPC-24
75Top-24
76Hos-8
76HosTwi-8
76OPC-144
76SSP-160
76Top-144
77Top-449
78Top-227
79HawIsIC-19
79HawIsIT-17
79Top-638
Fitzpatrick, Dan
84NewOriT-7
86BelBreP-7
87StoPorP-6
88CalLeaACLC-11
88StoPorCLC-187
88StoPorP-745
89StoPorB-12
89StoPorCLC-151
89StoPorP-395
Fitzpatrick, David
91KisDodP-4177
92GreFalDSP-16
93HicCraC-8
93HicCraF-1273
94SouBenSHC-6
94SouBenSHF-587
Fitzpatrick, Edward
11MecDFT-21
12ImpTobC-70
Fitzpatrick, Gary
83LynPirT-27
Fitzpatrick, John
49W72HolS-3
50W720HolS-8
54Top-213
94TopArc1-213
94TopArc1G-213
Fitzpatrick, Ken
94RocRoyC-9
94RocRoyF-557
95SprSulTI-8
Fitzpatrick, Mike
89EasLeaDDP-DD48
Fitzpatrick, Rob (Robert)
90JamExpP-2
91Cla/Bes-254
91RocExpC-14
91RocExpP-2049
92WesPalBEC-4
92WesPalBEF-2091
93HarSenF-272
94Bow-256
94HarSenF-2095
95HarSenTI-14
Fitzpatrick, Will
93PocPosF-4214
93PocPosSP-8
94BelBreC-10
94BelBreF-107
94MidLeaAF-MDW8
Fitzsimmons, Freddie (Fred)
28PorandAR-A6
28PorandAR-B6
28W56PlaC-D13
29PorandAR-23
31Exh-10
33ExhFou-5
33Gou-130
33Gou-235
34DiaMatCSB-55
34BatR31-72
34GouCanV-20
35DiaMatCS3T1-53
35GouPuzR-8A
35GouPuzR-8M
36DiaMatCS4-3
36SandSW-16
36WorWidGV-14
39PlaBal-110
40DodTeal-7
40PlaBal-65
41DouPlaR-143
43DodTeal-9
52Bow-234
60Top-462
75Gia195T-33
77GalGloG-75
79DiaGre-29
90DodTar-246
91ConTSN-260
94ConTSN-1117
94ConTSNB-1117
Fitzsimmons, Tom
90DodTar-950
Fix, Greg
86SalAngC-91
87QuaCitAP-17
Flach, Jason
96EugEmeB-23
Flack, Max
15SpoNewM-60
16SpoNewM-59
21E121So1-24
22E120-156
22W573-38
23W501-118
23WilChoV-42
25Exh-60
Flacon, Bobby
75WatRoyT-11
Flagg, Paul
92GulCoaDF-3578
Flagstead, Ira
19W514-1
20NatCarE-28
21E121So1-25
21Exh-48
22E120-53
22W573-39
23W501-7
25Exh-66
26Exh-65
27Exh-33
27YorCarE-21

28Exh-33
28StaPlaCE-20
87ConSer2-34
91ConTSN-291
Flaherty, Bernie
93ElmPioC-28
93ElmPioF-3840
Flaherty, John F.
55Bow-272
Flaherty, John Timothy
88ElmPioC-13
89WinHavRSS-7
90CMC-262
90PawRedSC-11
90PawRedSDD-6
90PawRedSP-464
90ProAAAF-436
90TopTVRS-43
91LinDriAA-459
91NewBriRSLD-459
91NewBriRSP-355
91PawRedSDD-4
92DonRoo-37
92Lea-439
92TopTra-32T
92TopTraG-32T
92Ult-313
93Don-561
93PacSpa-32
93PawRedSDD-10
93PawRedSF-2410
93PawRedSTI-10
93Sco-278
94Don-596
94Pin-443
94PinArtP-443
94PinMusC-443
94Sco-313
94ScoGolR-313
94TolMudHF-1028
94Top-197
94TopGol-197
94TopSpa-197
95DonTopotO-74
95FleUpd-19
95Top-334
96ColCho-141
96ColChoGS-141
96ColChoSS-141
96Don-300
96DonPreP-300
96Fle-110
96FleTif-110
96LeaSigEA-52
96MetUni-58
96MetUniP-58
96Pac-314
96PanSti-148
96Sco-424
96StaClu-397
96StaCluMOP-397
96Top-291
96Ult-59
96UltGolM-59
97Cir-83
97CirRav-83
97ColCho-446
97Fle-460
97FleTif-460
97Pin-141
97PinArtP-141
97PinMusC-141
97StaClu-348
97StaCluMOP-348
97Top-412
97Ult-281
97UltGolME-281
97UltPlaME-281
97UppDec-491
Flaherty, Patrick
09ColChiE-103A
09ColChiE-103B
11SpoLifCW-127
12ColRedB-103A
12ColRedB-103B
12ColTinT-103A
12ColTinT-103B
Flammang, Chris
80SanJosMJitB-7
81SpoIndT-1
Flanagan, Dan
90CliGiaUTI-U4
90EveGiaB-4
90EveGiaP-3120
91CliGiaC-2
91CliGiaP-827
92CalLeaACL-7
92SanJosGC-12
Flanagan, James
09T206-422
Flanagan, Mike
76OPC-589
76Top-589
77Spo-10201
77Top-106
78Hos-134
78OPC-231
78Top-341
79Kel-48
79OPC-76
79Top-160
80Kel-3
80OPC-335
80Top-205
80Top-640
81AllGamPI-79
81Don-234
81Fle-171
81FleStiC-56
81Kel-60
81OPC-10
81Top-10
82Don-329
82Fle-165
82FleSta-145
82OPC-153
82Top-520
82TopSti-148
82TopStiV-148
83AllGamPI-77
83Don-105
83Fle-60
83FleSta-62
83FleSti-193
83OPC-172
83OriPos-9
83Top-445
83TopSti-25
84Don-169
84Fle-8
84FleSti-63
84Nes792-295
84OPC-295
84OriEng-5
84OriTeal-10
84Top-295
84TopSti-12
84TopSti-210
84TopTif-295
85Don-88
85Fle-177
85Lea-175
85OPC-46
85OriHea-7
85Top-780
85TopMin-780
85TopSti-207
85TopTif-780
86Don-576
86Fle-275
86Spo-59
86Top-365
86TopTif-365
87Don-459
87Fle-470
87FleGlo-470
87OPC-112
87OriFreB-46
87Top-748
87TopTif-748
88BluJayFS-12
88Don-636
88DonBasB-272
88FleUpd-67
88FleUpdG-67
88OPC-164
88Sco-427
88ScoGlo-427
88Top-623
88TopTif-623
89BluJayFS-10
89Bow-241
89BowTif-241
89Don-324
89DonBasB-316
89Fle-233
89FleGlo-233
89OPC-139
89RedFolSB-44
89Sco-475
89Top-139
89TopBasT-108
89TopBig-243
89TopSti-190
89TopTif-139
89UppDec-385
90Don-324
90Fle-81
90FleCan-81
90OPC-78
90PubSti-514
90Sco-67
90Top-78
90TopTif-78
90UppDec-483
90VenSti-177
91Lea-479
91OriCro-135
91ScoRoo-2T
91StaCluMO-10
92Don-196
92Fle-7
92OPC-218
92Pin-475
92Sco-333
92Sco-427
92StaClu-30
92Top-218
92TopGol-218
92TopGolW-218
92TopMic-218
92UppDec-380
93StaClu-123
93StaCluFDI-123
93StaCluMOP-123
93Top-381
93TopGol-381
93TopInaM-381
93TopMic-381
Flanders, Craig
75WatRoyT-12
Flanigan, Steve
96AugGreB-11
Flanigan, Thomas
87OldJudN-172
Flannelly, Tim
91OneYanP-4161
92GreHorC-3
92GreHorF-786
92ProFS7-128
92StaCluD-50
93PriWilCC-9
93PriWilCF-663
Flannery, John
76QuaCitAT-15
79KnoKnoST-10
81EdmTraRR-11
82BirBarT-15
Flannery, Kevin
81AppFoxT-4
82AppFoxF-21
83TolMudHT-3
Flannery, Tim
80HawIsIT-19
80Top-685
81Fle-493A
81Fle-493B
81HawIsIT-1
81Top-579
82Don-61
82Fle-572
82Top-249
83Don-472
83Fle-359
83FleSti-226
83Top-38
84Don-202
84Fle-299
84Nes792-674
84PadMot-12
84PadSmo-9
84Top-674
84TopTif-674
85Don-551
85Fle-31
85PadMot-20
85Top-182
85TopTif-182
86Don-383
86Fle-320
86OPC-387
86Top-413
86TopSti-112
86TopTif-413
87Don-287
87Fle-413
87FleGlo-413
87OPC-52
87PadBohHB-11
87PadFirPTB-2
87Top-763
87TopSti-114
87TopTif-763
88Don-328
88Fle-582
88FleGlo-582
88OPC-262
88PadCok-11
88PadSmo-8
88PanSti-404
88Sco-483
88ScoGlo-483
88Top-513
88TopSti-108
88TopTif-513
89Bow-457
89BowTif-457
89Don-364
89PadCok-4
89PadMag-15
89Sco-513
89Top-379
89TopBig-174
89TopTif-379
89UppDec-603
90PubSti-48
90VenSti-178
93SpoIndC-28
93SpoIndF-3606
94RanCucQC-26
94RanCucQF-1651
96PadMot-28
Flater, John
09ColChiE-104
12ColRedB-104
12ColTinT-104
Flath, Daniel
90SarWhiSS-30
Flavin, John
77FriOneYW-61
Fleet, Joe
91WatIndC-4
91WatIndP-3359
93KinIndC-9
93KinIndF-2240
93KinIndTI-8
Fleet, Kenyatta
92ColRedC-26
92ColRedF-2383
Fleetham, Ben
94VerExpF-3904
96DelShoB-17
96WesPalBEB-10
Fleetwood, Tony
96WatIndTI-9
Fleischer, Herb
52LavPro-47
Fleita, Oneri
89FreKeyS-6
90WauTimP-2145
91KanCouCC-28
91KanCouCP-2675
92FreKeyC-28
92FreKeyF-1823
Fleming, Bill
43CubTeal-8
44CubTeal-8
91PacSenL-84
Fleming, Carlton
92ClaDraP-98
92OneYanC-5
93CarLeaAGF-21
93PriWilCC-10
93PriWilCF-664
94AbaYanF-1448
95NorNavTI-19
96NorNavB-11
Fleming, Dave
90Bes-57
90TopMag-92
91Bow-249
91Cla/Bes-284
91JacSunLD-336
91JacSunP-146
91LinDriAA-336
92Bow-624
92Cla1-T34
92ClaGam-163
92Don-404
92DonRooP-BC4
92FleUpd-55
92JimDeaRS-6
92Lea-494
92MarMot-17
92OPC-192
92Pin-275
92PinRoo-13
92PinRooI-14
92ProFS7-141
92ScoRoo-85T
92StaClu-814
92StaCluECN-814
92Top-192
92TopDeb91-56
92TopGol-192
92TopGolW-192
92TopMic-192
92UppDec-4
92UppDecSR-SR8
93Bow-487
93ClaGam-34
93Don-243
93Fin-196
93FinRef-196
93Fle-306
93FleAll-AL11
93FleRooS-RSA5
93FunPac-113
93MarMot-2
93OPC-67
93PacSpa-285
93PanSti-57
93Pin-5
93PinTea2-23
93Pos-1
93Sco-356
93Sel-271
93SelAce-23
93SelChaR-20
93SelChaS-22
93SP-130
93StaClu-358
93StaCluFDI-358
93StaCluMari-8
93StaCluMOP-358
93Top-45
93Top-410
93TopComotH-13
93TopGol-45
93TopGol-410
93TopInaM-45
93TopInaM-410
93TopMic-45
93TopMic-410
93TopPreS-5
93Toy-77
93TriPla-99
93Ult-268
93UppDec-141
93UppDecGold-141
93USPlaCR-1D
94Bow-117
94ColC-101
94ColChoGS-101
94ColChoSS-101
94Don-183
94ExtBas-165
94Fin-172
94FinRef-172
94Fla-102
94Fle-285
94FUnPac-135
94Lea-149
94MarMot-10
94OPC-183
94Pac-569
94Pin-158
94PinArtP-158
94PinMusC-158
94Sco-135
94ScoGolR-135
94Sel-173
94StaClu-409
94StaCluFDI-409
94StaCluGR-409
94StaCluMOP-409
94Top-415
94TopGol-415
94TopSpa-415
94TriPla-126

94Ult-119
94UppDec-246
94UppDecED-246
95ColCho-293
95ColChoGS-293
95ColChoSS-293
95Don-373
95DonPreP-373
95Fle-267
95Lea-37
95MarMot-3
95Pac-396
95Sco-212
95ScoGolR-212
95ScoPlaTS-212
95StaClu-487
95StaCluMOP-487
95StaCluSTWS-487
95StaCluVR-267
95Top-482
95TopCyb-274
95Ult-100
95UltGolM-100
95UppDec-348
95UppDecED-348
95UppDecEDG-348
95StaCluVRMC-267

Fleming, Hap
91MisStaB-16
92MisStaB-15
93MisStaB-16

Fleming, Henry
87WytCubP-15

Fleming, Jack
77DayBealT-6
80TucTorT-7

Fleming, Jim
88OklSoo-4
89OklSoo-3
91JamExpP-3561
92JamExpC-27
92JamExpF-1517

Fleming, Keith
87StoPorP-20
88StoPorCLC-185
88StoPorP-725
89ElPasDGS-7
90BelBreB-25
90BelBreS-7

Fleming, Les
47IndTeal-9
47IndVanPP-8
49EurSta-160
76TayBow4-67

Fleming, Paul
82WisRapTF-8

Fleming, Ricky
86EveGiaPC-5

Flener, Huck
90St.CatBJP-3470
91MyrBeaHC-4
91MyrBeaHP-2938
92DunBluJC-24
92DunBluJF-1992
92ProFS7-173
93KnoSmoF-1246
94Pac-640
94StaCluT-177
94StaCluTFDI-177
94SyrChiF-968
94SyrChiTI-12
94Top-39
94TopGol-39
94TopSpa-39
94VenLinU-128
95SyrChiTI-13
96SyrChiTI-12
97BluJayS-52
97Fle-238
97FleTif-238

Flesher, Jay
89GeoColC-8

Fleshman, Richard
75ForLauYS-10
77WesHavYT-9

Fletcher, Arthur
09SpoNewSM-99
09T206-132
10CouT21-23
11S74Sil-86
11SpoLifM-210
11T205-57
12HasTriFT-29C
12HasTriFT-48E
12T207-61
13PolGroW-8
14B18B-67
14FatPlaT-14
15SpoNewM-61
16ColE13-50
16SpoNewM-60
17HolBreD-30
19W514-14
20NatCarE-29
21Exh-49
21Nei-107
22E120-197
22W573-40
23W503-30
40PlaBal-125
43YanSta-11
61Fle-106
75YanDyn1T-15
77GalGloG-183
87ConSer2-32
88ConSer4-11
91ConTSN-117
92ConTSN-490
20W516-14

Fletcher, Bob
89GreFalDSP-27
89SarWhiSS-5
90VerBeaDS-13

Fletcher, Darrin
88SanAntMB-15
89AlbDukC-18
89AlbDukP-58
90AlbDukC-15
90AlbDukP-348
90AlbDukT-8
90CMC-417
90DodTar-951
90ProAAAF-69
90Sco-622
90TopDeb89-38
90TriAllGP-AAA44
91Bow-496
91Cla2-T5
91Don-47
91FleUpd-107
91LinDriAAA-483
91OPC-9
91PhiMed-14
91ScrRedBLD-483
91ScrRedBP-2541
91Top-9
91TopDesS-9
91TopMic-9
91TopTif-9
91Ult-377
91UppDec-428
92Bow-609
92Don-319
92ExpDonD-8
92ExpPos-12
92Fle-530
92IndIndF-1861
92Lea-264
92OPC-159
92OPCPre-41
92Sco-193
92ScoRoo-64T
92Top-159
92TopGol-159
92TopGolW-159
92TopMic-159
92TopTra-33T
92TopTraG-33T
92Ult-517
92UppDec-108
93Bow-620
93CadDis-20
93Don-378
93ExpPosN-10
93Fle-460
93Lea-165
93OPC-64
93PacSpa-184
93PanSti-224
93Sco-216
93SP-103
93StaClu-272
93StaCluFDI-272
93StaCluMOP-272
93Top-665
93TopGol-665
93TopInaM-665
93TopMic-665
93Ult-67
93UppDec-614
93UppDecGold-614
94Bow-612
94ColC-102
94ColChoGS-102
94ColChoSS-102
94Don-152
94ExtBas-304
94Fin-137
94FinRef-137
94Fla-188
94Fle-537
94Lea-118
94Pac-379
94Pin-205
94PinArtP-205
94PinMusC-205
94Sco-436
94ScoGolR-436
94Sel-168
94StaClu-42
94StaCluFDI-42
94StaCluGR-42
94StaCluMOP-42
94Top-412
94TopGol-412
94TopSpa-412
94TriPla-94
94Ult-226
94UppDec-459
94UppDecED-459
95ColCho-243
95ColChoGS-243
95ColChoSS-243
95Don-40
95DonPreP-40
95DonTopotO-280
95Fin-156
95FinRef-156
95Fla-375
95Fle-349
95Lea-133
95Pac-266
95PanSti-22
95Sco-387
95ScoGolR-387
95ScoPlaTS-387
95StaClu-192
95StaCluFDI-192
95StaCluMOP-192
95StaCluSTWS-192
95StaCluVR-100
95Top-255
95TopCyb-140
95Ult-190
95UltGolM-190
96ColCho-614
96ColChoGS-614
96ColChoSS-614
96Don-58
96DonPreP-58
96EmoXL-221
96ExpDis-8
96Fin-B94
96FinRef-B94
96Fla-305
96Fle-456
96FleTif-456
96LeaSigA-68
96LeaSigAG-68
96LeaSigAS-68
96MetUni-190
96MetUniP-190
96ProSta-47
96Sco-97
96StaClu-345
96StaCluEPB-345
96StaCluEPG-345
96StaCluEPS-345
96StaCluMOP-345
95StaCluVRMC-100
96Top-127
96Ult-231
96UltGolM-231
96UppDec-391
97Cir-145
97CirRav-145
97ColCho-387
97Fin-187
97FinRef-187
97Fle-378
97FleTif-378
97MetUni-153
97PacPriGotD-GD168
97Pin-135
97PinArtP-135
97PinMusC-135
97StaClu-360
97StaCluMOP-360
97Top-265
97Ult-229
97UltGolME-229
97UltPlaME-229
97UppDec-426

Fletcher, David
90MedHatBJB-17

Fletcher, Dennis
90ProAaA-77
90SavCarP-2064
91SprCarC-17
91SprCarP-738
92St.PetCC-2
92St.PetCF-2023

Fletcher, Don
76CliPilT-15
91PacSenL-103

Fletcher, Elburt
36GouWidPPR-C10
39PlaBal-69
40PlaBal-103
41DouPlaR-149
41Gou-26
41PlaBal-62
47TipTop-139
49EurSta-9
76TayBow4-72
79DiaGre-361
83TCMPla1943-32
95ConTSN-1373

Fletcher, Guy (Van)
46SunBre-5
47SigOil-61
47SigOil-76
47SunBre-7

Fletcher, Mitch
80TulDriT-26

Fletcher, Paul
92EugEmeC-14
92EugEmeF-3024
92ReaPhiF-567
92ReaPhiS-535
93ScrRedBF-2541
93ScrRedBTI-9
94ScrRedBF-918
95ScrRedBTI-8

Fletcher, Paul (Edward Paul)
46SpoExcW-3-10
88MarPhiS-14
89BatCliP-1921
90SpaPhiB-2
90SpaPhiP-2483
90SpaPhiS-7
91Cla/Bes-111
91ClePhiC-2
91ClePhiP-1613
93Bow-272
93ClaFS7-79

Fletcher, Rob
90WesPalBES-6
91ModA'sC-4
91ModA'sP-3096

Fletcher, Scott
80VenLeaS-158
82Don-554
82IowCubT-2
83WhiSoxTV-1
84Don-452
84Fle-59
84Nes792-364
84Top-364
84TopSti-250
84TopTif-364
84WhiSoxTV-14
85Don-330
85Fle-514
85Top-78
85TopSti-240
85TopTif-78
85WhiSoxC-1
86BasStaB-42
86Don-282
86DonHig-28
86Fle-205
86FleUpd-41
86OPC-187
86RanPer-1
86Top-187
86TopTif-187
86TopTra-36T
86TopTraT-36T
87ClaUpdY-118
87Don-304
87DonOpeD-171
87Fle-123
87FleAwaW-13
87FleGlo-123
87Lea-226
87RanMot-6
87RanSmo-13
87Spo-113
87Spo-136
87SpoTeaP-1
87Top-462
87TopSti-237
87TopTif-462
88Don-11
88Don-180
88DonBasB-32
88DonSupD-11
88Fle-466
88FleGlo-466
88FleMin-54
88FleStiC-63
88Lea-11
88Lea-155
88OPC-345
88PanSti-154
88PanSti-206
88RanMot-6
88RanSmo-10
88RedFolSB-24
88Sco-251
88ScoGlo-251
88Spo-77
88StaLinRa-4
88Top-345
88TopBig-19
88TopSti-241
88TopTif-345
89Bow-230
89BowTif-230
89CadEllD-18
89Don-142
89DonBasB-167
89Fle-518
89FleGlo-518
89FleSup-14
89OPC-295
89PanSti-454
89RanMot-13
89RanSmo-8
89Sco-78
89ScoRoo-47T
89Spo-185
89Top-295
89TopBig-205
89TopSti-246
89TopTif-295
89TVSpoM-120
89UppDec-420
90Bow-319
90BowTif-319
90Don-455
90DonBesA-88
90Fle-531
90FleCan-531
90Lea-141
90OPC-565
90PanSti-43
90PubSti-408
90Sco-58
90Spo-220
90Top-565
90TopBig-207
90TopSti-307
90TopTif-565
90UppDec-310
90VenSti-179
90WhiSoxC-4
90WhiSoxK-5
91Bow-359
91Don-276
91Fle-119
91Lea-306
91OPC-785
91PanFreS-313
91Sco-36
91StaClu-30
91Stu-33
91Top-785

91TopDesS-785
91TopMic-785
91TopTif-785
91Ult-73
91UppDec-321
91WhiSoxK-7
92Bow-7
92BrePol-7
92Fle-80
92FleUpd-34
92Lea-234
92OPC-648
92Sco-203
92StaClu-116
92StaClu-792
92StaCluNC-792
92Stu-193
92Top-648
92TopGol-648
92TopGolW-648
92TopMic-648
92TopTra-34T
92TopTraG-34T
92Ult-381
92UppDec-186
93Bow-383
93Don-631
93Fla-163
93Fle-629
93FleFinE-174
93Lea-344
93OPC-133
93OPCPre-48
93PacSpa-357
93Pin-495
93RanKee-147
93RedSoxWHP-5
93Sco-632
93Sel-140
93SelRoo-98T
93StaClu-112
93StaClu-623
93StaCluFDI-112
93StaCluFDI-623
93StaCluMOP-112
93StaCluMOP-623
93Top-97
93TopGol-97
93TopInaM-97
93TopMic-97
93Ult-510
93UppDec-523
93UppDecGold-523
94Bow-503
94BreMilB-121
94ColC-103
94ColChoGS-103
94ColChoSS-103
94Don-134
94Fin-181
94FinRef-181
94Fle-32
94Lea-422
94Pac-54
94PanSti-29
94Pin-146
94PinArtP-146
94PinMusC-146
94Sco-367
94ScoGolR-367
94StaClu-198
94StaCluFDI-198
94StaCluGR-198
94StaCluMOP-198
94Top-169
94TopGol-169
94TopSpa-169
94Ult-14
95Don-449
95DonPreP-449
95Sco-166
95ScoGolR-166
95ScoPlaTS-166

Fletcher, Tom
77FriOneYW-84

Flick, Elmer
03BreE10-51
04FanCraAL-19
05IndSouPSoCP-8
08AmeLeaPC-7
09ColChiE-105A
09ColChiE-105B
09T206-133
11SpoLifM-43
12ColRedB-105A
12ColRedB-105B
12ColTinT-105A
12ColTinT-105B
76ShaPiz-92
80PerHaloFP-92
80SSPHOF-92
84OCoandSI-168
89HOFStiB-53

Flick, Lew
63GadFunC-25

Flinn, Geoff
89ButCopKSP-15

Flinn, John
77RocRedWM-12
79Top-701
81Top-659
81VanCanT-21
82RocRedWT-2
83RocRedWT-3
85ChaO'sT-24
86ChaOriW-10
87ChaO'sW-25
91OriCro-136
94BreMilB-122

Flinn, Mike
82MadMusF-4

Flint, Frank S.
87BucN28-21
87OldJudN-173
88AugBecN-10
88GandBCGCE-16
88WG1CarG-12

Floethe, Chris
72OPC-268
72Top-268

Flood, Curt
58Top-464
59Top-353
60CarJayP-3
60Lea-141
60Top-275
61CarJayP-4
61Pos-178A
61Pos-178B
61Top-438
61TopStal-86
62CarJayP-3
62Jel-166
62Pos-166
62PosCan-166
62SalPlaC-139
62ShiPlaC-139
62Top-590
63CarJayP-5
63CarJayP-6
63Jel-162
63Pos-162
63Top-505
64CarTeal-2
64Top-103
64TopCoi-65
64TopSta-28
64TopTatl-36
64TopVen-103
65CarJayP-2
65CarTeal-8
65Top-415
66CarTeal-3
66OPC-60
66Top-60
66TopRubl-31
66TopVen-60
67OPC-63
67Top-63
67Top-245
67TopVen-276
68Baz-11
68OPC-180
68Top-180
68Top3-D-4
68TopVen-180
69KelPin-5
69MilBra-83
69MLBOffS-210
69MLBPin-43
69OPCDec-5
69Top-164
69Top-426
69Top-540
69TopDec-28
69TopSta-114
69TopSup-59
69TopTeaP-18
70Kel-48
70MLBOffS-87
70OPC-360
70Top-360
71MLBOffS-536
71OPC-535
71Top-535
71TopSup-41
72MilBra-105
78TCM60I-240
84OCoandSI-169
89PacSenL-220
89T/MSenL-1
90EliSenL-1
92ActPacA-72
92CarMcD-32
93TedWil-88
93UppDecAH-51
93UppDecS-26
94UppDecTAE-71
94UppDecTAELD-LD14

Flood, Thomas J.
87OldJudN-174

Flood, Tim
90DodTar-247
98CamPepP-26

Flora, Kevin
87SalAngP-22
88QuaCitAGS-5
89QuaCitAB-6
89QuaCitAGS-11
90MidAngGS-24
91Cla/Bes-19
91LinDriAA-434
91MidAngLD-434
91MidAngOHP-11
91MidAngP-441
92Bow-283
92EdmTraF-3545
92EdmTraS-156
92ProFS7-33
92SkyAAAF-77
92TopDeb91-57
92UppDecML-96
93ClaFS7-4
93Top-521
93TopGol-521
93TopInaM-521
93TopMic-521
94Cla-144
95Sel-171
95SelArtP-171
96NorTidB-12

Florence, Dan
95NorTidTI-11

Florence, Donald
88WinHavRSS-8
89WinHavRSS-8
90NewBriRSB-10
90NewBriRSP-1313
90NewBriRSS-5
91LinDriAA-460
91NewBriRSLD-460
91NewBriRSP-348
92NewBriRSF-427
92NewBriRSS-485
93PawRedSDD-11
93PawRedSF-2404
93PawRedSTI-11
93TriAAAGF-31
94PawRedSDD-7
94PawRedSF-942
96RocRedWB-14

Florence, Paul
36WorWidGV-117

Flores, Adalberto
76BurBeeT-9
77NewCoPT-13

Flores, Alex
87GreHorP-18

Flores, Bert (Norberto)
77BurBeeT-8
85VerBeaDT-12
86BakDodP-8

Flores, Eric
95GreFalDTI-26
96YakBeaTI-23

Flores, Gil
76SalLakCGC-22
77SalLakCGC-5
78AngFamF-10
78SSP270-209
78Top-268
80TidTidT-6
80Top-478
81TidTidT-11
82TidTidT-7
83TidTidT-22
84TidTidT-7
91MetWIZ-118
78STLakCGC-6

Flores, Jesse
80KnoBluJT-8
87SalAngP-31

Flores, Jesse (Sandoval)
50IndTeal-9

Flores, Joe
92KinMetF-1538
93CapCitBC-5

Flores, Jose
85GreHorT-23
86GreHorP-5
90AshTouC-13
90AubAstB-6
90AubAstP-3411
91AshTouP-574
92AshTouC-2
92KinMetC-21
92PitMetF-3303
93CapCitBF-465
93OscAstC-10
93OscAstF-636
94BatCliC-4
94BatCliF-3452
94JacGenF-223
95ClePhiF-222
95GreFalDTI-3

Flores, Juan
90HelBreSP-3
91StoPorC-22
91StoPorP-3034

Flores, Miguel
90BurIndP-3013
91CarLeaAP-CAR14
91KinIndC-16
91KinIndP-328
92CanIndF-697
92CanIndS-106
92ProFS7-55
92SkyAA F-49
92UppDecML-140
93CanIndF-2845
94ChaKniF-901

Flores, Pedro
96GreFalDB-12
96GreFalDTI-9

Flores, Willi
80VenLeaS-38
82WisRapTF-21

Florez, Tim
91EveGiaC-10
91EveGiaP-3921
92CliGiaC-22
93ShrCapF-2767
94ShrCapF-1613

Florie, Bryce
89ChaRaiP-983
90Bes-130
90WatDiaB-3
90WatDiaP-2371
91WatDiaC-3
91WatDiaP-1250
92HigDesMC-20
93WicWraF-2973
94Bow-316
94ExcFS7-280
94LasVegSF-868
95Bow-93
95Fla-200
95FleUpd-184
95PadMot-27
95Pin-147
95PinArtP-147
95PinMusC-147
95Top-657
95Ult-438
95UltGolM-438
96ColCho-292
96ColChoGS-292
96ColChoSS-292
96Don-86
96DonPreP-86
96Fle-566
96FleTif-566
96LeaSigEA-53
96PadMot-27

Flower, George
86WesPalBEP-16

Flowers, Bennett
53RedSoxTI-7
55Bow-254

Flowers, Doug
91KanCouCC-29

Flowers, Jake (D'Arcy)
29ExhFou-3
31Exh-3
33Gou-151
33GouCanV-81
90DodTar-248

Flowers, Kim
85EveGiaC-5A
85EveGiaC-5B
87CliGiaP-16
88FreSunCLC-11
88FreSunP-1223

Flowers, Larry
90GeoColC-4

Flowers, Perry
86CliGiaP-8

Flowers, Wes
90DodTar-952

Flowers, Willie
78NewWayCT-14

Floyd, Bobby (Robert)
69Top-597
70OPC-101
70Top-101
71MLBOffS-415
71OPC-646
71Top-646
72OPC-273
72Top-273
72TopCloT-11
74OPC-41
74Top-41
75OmaRoyTI-6
80LynSaiT-4
81LynSaiT-24
82SalLakCGT-24
83SalLakCGT-24
84SalLakCGC-191
85CalCanC-78
86LynMetP-9
91OriCro-137

Floyd, Chris
88MyrBeaBJP-1173

Floyd, Cliff
91ClaDraP-11
91FroRowDP-49
91HigSchPLS-19
92AlbPolC-22
92AlbPolF-2314
92Bow-678
92ClaBluBF-BC19
92ClaFS7-380
92ClaRedB-BC19
92OPC-186
92Pin-296
92Sco-801
92StaCluD-51
92Top-186
92TopGol-186
92TopGolW-186
92TopMic-186
92UppDecML-63
92UppDecML-267
92UppDecMLPotY-PY10
92UppDecMLTPHF-TP2
93Bow-128
93Bow-354
93ClaFisN-17
93ClaFS7-AU2
93ClaGolF-72
93ClaYouG-YG3
93ExcFS7-58
93ExcLeaLF-7
93FlaWavotF-5
93FleFinE-92
93HarSenF-274
93SouAtlLAIPI-1
93SouAtlLAIPI-18
93SouAtlLAPI-10
93SP-277
93Top-576
93TopGol-576
93TopInaM-576
93TopMic-576
93Ult-413
93UppDec-431
93UppDecGold-431
94Bow-200
94Bow-340

94BowBes-R87
94BowBesR-R87
94BowPre-5
94ColC-7
94ColC-337
94ColChoGS-7
94ColChoGS-337
94ColChoSS-7
94ColChoSS-337
94ColChoT-15
94Don-651
94ExtBas-305
94ExtBasRS-6
94Fin-427
94FinJum-427
94FinRef-427
94Fla-189
94Fle-538
94FleRooS-7
94FUnPac-2
94FUnPac-205
94LeaGolR-18
94LeaL-124
94LeaLimRP-5
94OPC-223
94OPCHotP-1
94Pac-380
94Pin-392
94PinArtP-392
94PinMusC-392
94PinNewG-NG10
94PinNewG-PNG10
94PinPowS-PS19
94PinRooTP-7
94Sco-587
94ScoBoyoS-60
94ScoGolR-587
94ScoRoo-RT76
94ScoRooGR-RT76
94ScoRooSR-SU8
94Sel-185
94SelRooS-RS1
94SelSam-RS1
94SigRooCF-B1
94SigRooCF-B2
94SigRooCF-B3
94SigRooCF-B4
94SigRooCF-B5
94SP-83
94SPDieC-83
94SPHol-8
94SPHolDC-8
94Spo-173
94Spo-NNO0
94SpoRooRS-TR12
94SPPre-ER2
94StaClu-127
94StaCluFDI-127
94StaCluGR-127
94StaCluMOP-127
94Stu-77
94TedWil-154
94TedWil-155
94TedWil-156
94TedWil-157
94Top-259
94TopGol-259
94TopSpa-259
94TopSupS-14
94TriPla-289
94Ult-227
94UltAllR-3
94UltAllRJ-3
94UltRisS-4
94UppDec-12
94UppDecDC-E5
94UppDecED-12
94UppDecMLS-MM8
94UppDecMLSED-MM8
94UppDecNG-3
94UppDecNGED-3
95Baz-125
95Bow-394
95ColCho-240
95ColChoGS-240
95ColChoSE-100
95ColChoSEGS-100
95ColChoSESS-100
95ColChoSS-240
95Don-212
95DonPreP-212
95Emb-4
95EmbGolI-4
95Emo-152
95Fin-23
95FinRef-23
95Fla-161
95FlaTodS-3
95Fle-350
95FleUpdSS-4
95Lea-184
95Pac-267
95PacPri-86
95PanSti-101
95Pin-8
95Pin-281
95PinArtP-8
95PinArtP-281
95PinGatA-GA18
95PinMusC-8
95PinMusC-281
95PinRedH-RH24
95PinWhiH-WH24
95Sco-401
95ScoAi-AM11
95ScoGolR-401
95ScoHaloG-HG83
95ScoPlaTS-401
95ScoRul-SR17
95ScoRulJ-SR17
95Sel-58
95SelArtP-58
95SelCanM-CM1
95SelCer-79
95SelCerMG-79
95SelCerPU-1
95SelCerPU9-1
95Spo-19
95SpoArtP-19
95SpoDet-DE8
95StaClu-164
95StaCluFDI-164
95StaCluMOP-164
95StaCluSTWS-164
95StaCluVR-87
95Stu-26
95StuGolS-26
95Sum-52
95SumNewA-NA1
95SumNthD-52
95Top-462
95TopCyb-257
95UC3CleS-CS8
95UC3CleS-PCS8
95Ult-402
95UltAllR-1
95UltAllRGM-1
95UltGolM-402
95UltSecYS-1
95UltSecYSGM-1
95UppDec-80
95UppDecED-80
95UppDecEDG-80
95UppDecSE-1
95UppDecSEG-1
96ColCho-211
96ColChoGS-211
96ColChoSS-211
96Don-388
96DonPreP-388
96EmoXL-222
96Fla-306
96Fle-457
96FleTif-457
96Lea-4
96LeaPrePB-4
96LeaPrePG-4
96LeaPrePS-4
96MetUni-191
96MetUniP-191
96Pac-126
96Pin-91
96PinAfi-145
96PinAfiAP-145
96PinArtP-34
96PinSta-34
96Sco-89
96ScoDugC-A69
96ScoDugCAP-A69
96SelTeaN-24
95StaCluVRMC-87
96Top-334
96Ult-503
96Ult-595
96UltGolM-503
96UltGolM-595
96UltRisS-4
96UltRisSGM-4
96UppDec-146
96UppDec-392
97Cir-209
97CirRav-209
97Fle-379
97Fle-679
97FleTif-379
97FleTif-679
97Lea-250
97LeaFraM-250
97LeaFraMDC-250
97MetUni-154
97NewPin-11
97NewPinAP-11
97NewPinMC-11
97NewPinPP-11
97Pac-344
97PacLigB-344
97PacSil-344
97Sco-14
97ScoPreS-14
97ScoShoS-14
97ScoShoSAP-14
97SkyE-X-72
97SkyE-XC-72
97SkyE-XEC-72
97Top-444
97Ult-372
97UltGolME-372
97UltPlaME-372
97UppDec-427

Floyd, D.J.

90EriSaiS-6

Floyd, Spanky

94HelBreF-3623

Floyd, Stan

77ChaPatT-6

Floyd, Tony

88SouOreAP-1707

Flury, Pat

93EugEmeC-14
93EugEmeF-3850
94RocRoyC-10
94RocRoyF-558
95SprSulTI-9
96HonShaHWB-34
96WilBluRB-19

Flynn, Bob

75AppFoxT-7
76AppFoxT-6

Flynn, David

88CapCodPPaLP-13

Flynn, Errol

88PulBraP-1758

Flynn, John Anthony

10E12AmeCDC-16
10PirTipTD-22
10SweCapPP-136
11BasBatEU-23
11S74Sil-109
11SpoLifCW-128
11SpoLifM-249
11T205-58

Flynn, R. Doug

76OPC-518
76SSP-37
76Top-518
77Top-186
78MetDaiPA-6
78Top-453
79Hos-81
79OPC-116
79Top-229
80OPC-32
80Top-58
81AllGamPI-100
81CokTeaS-86
81Don-394
81Fle-330
81OPC-311
81Top-634
81TopScr-93
81TopSti-192
81TopSupHT-74
82Don-427
82ExpPos-11
82Fle-525
82FleSta-87
82OPC-302
82Top-302
82TopSti-70
82TopTra-33T
83AllGamPI-101
83Don-240
83ExpStu-7
83Fle-282
83OPC-169
83Top-169
84Don-254
84ExpPos-8
84ExpStu-29
84Fle-274
84Nes792-749
84OPC-262
84Top-749
84TopSti-97
84TopTif-749
85Don-463
85Fle-397
85Lea-257
85OPC-112
85Top-554
85TopMin-554
85TopSti-93
85TopTif-554
86TigCaiD-5
86Top-436
86TopTif-436
91MetWIZ-119
92MCIAmb-3
93RanKee-148
94MCIAmb-10
94MCIAmb-S1
95MCIAmb-4

Fobbs, Larry

78LodDodT-4
81AlbDukT-15
82AlbDukT-16

Foderaro, Kevin

94JohCitCC-10
94JohCitCF-3693
96PeoChiB-10

Fodge, Gene

58Top-449

Fogarty, James

87BucN28-80
87OldJudN-176
88AllandGN-2
88WG1CarG-51
89EdgR.WG-6
90KalBatN-19
90KalBatN-20

Fogg, Kevin

76BatRouCT-10

Foggie, Cornell

89WatIndS-7

Fogler, Seth

89MiaMirIS-21
90MiaMirIS-29

Fohl, Lee

23MapCriV-5
23WilChoV-43

Foiles, Hank

52Par-85
53Top-252
55IndGolS-20
57Top-104
58Hir-71
58Kah-8
58Top-4
59Top-294
60Top-77
60TopVen-77
61Top-277
62Top-112
62TopVen-112
63RedEnq-8
63Top-326
64Top-554
91OriCro-138
91TopArc1-252

Foit, Jim

83TulDriT-20

Fojas, Francisco

79CedRapGT-9

Foldman, Hal (Harry)

49SomandK-29

Foley, Bill

77NewCoPT-14
78BurBeeT-13
79HolMilT-3
82ElPasDT-6

Foley, Jack

83TamTarT-11

Foley, Jim

87AncGlaP-12
88ModA'sTI-9
89MadMusS-8
90CliGiaP-2549

Foley, Keith

86WesPalBEP-17
87SalSpuP-1
88VerMarP-948

Foley, Mark

87PenWhiSP-4

Foley, Martin

87SpaPhiP-17
88SpaPhiP-1038
88SpaPhiS-23
89ReaPhiB-15
89ReaPhiP-672
89ReaPhiS-11
90ReaPhiB-16
90ReaPhiP-1226
90ReaPhiS-12

Foley, Marv

77AppFoxT-5
78KnoKnoST-4
81Don-399
81EdmTraRR-18
81Top-646
83Don-652
83Top-409
84RanJarP-30
85Don-500
85Top-621
85TopTif-621
86BirBarTI-23
88BlaYNPRWL-1
88TamTarS-10B
89VanCanC-23
89VanCanP-573
90CMC-632
90ProAAAF-183
90TriAllGP-AAA39
90VanCanC-5
90VanCanP-505
91LinDriAAA-649
91PacSenL-23
91VanCanLD-649
91VanCanP-1609
92ChaKniF-2786
92ChaKniS-174
93IowCubF-2148
93RanKee-149
95RocRedWTI-41
96RocRedWB-2

Foley, Rick

79SalLakCGT-18B
80SalLakCGT-15
81HolMilT-15
82SpoIndT-3

Foley, Tom (Thomas)

80WatRedT-19
81IndIndTI-7
82IndIndTI-20
84Don-81
84Nes792-632
84RedEnq-6
84Top-632
84TopTif-632
85Don-569
85Fle-535
85RedYea-5
85Top-107
85TopTif-107
86Don-549
86Fle-440
86PhiTas-11
86Top-466
86TopTif-466
87Don-504
87ExpPos-7
87Fle-318
87FleGlo-318
87OPC-78
87Top-78
87TopTif-78
88Don-303
88Fle-183
88FleGlo-183
88Lea-143
88MSAHosD-3
88OPC-251
88Sco-159
88ScoGlo-159
88StaLinE-5
88Top-251
88TopTif-251
89Don-342
89DonBasB-314
89ExpPos-6

89Fle-375
89FleGlo-375
89OPC-159
89PanSti-121
89Sco-405
89Top-529
89TopBig-261
89TopTif-529
89UppDec-441
90Bow-120
90BowTif-120
90Don-274
90ExpPos-8
90Fle-344
90FleCan-344
90Lea-292
90OPC-341
90PanSti-292
90PubSti-172
90Sco-32
90Top-341
90TopBig-58
90TopTif-341
90UppDec-489
90VenSti-180
91Don-180
91ExpPos-5
91Fle-230
91OPC-773
91Sco-526
91StuPre-13
91Top-773
91TopDesS-773
91TopMic-773
91TopTif-773
91UppDec-381
92Don-538
92ExpPos-13
92Lea-372
92OPC-666
92Sco-486
92StaClu-19
92Top-666
92TopGol-666
92TopGolW-666
92TopMic-666
92TriPla-2
92Ult-221
92UppDec-492
93Don-727
93MilBonSS-13
93PacSpa-586
93PirNatI-10
94Don-132
94Fle-608
94Lea-335
94PirQui-6
94StaClu-142
94StaCluFDI-142
94StaCluGR-142
94StaCluMOP-142
95Fle-478
96ButCopKB-3

Folga, Mike
85PriWilPT-12
87PeoChiP-26

Folger, Ken
92SalLakTSP-16

Foli, Tim
71OPC-83
71Top-83
72Dia-15
72ProStaP-5
72Top-707
72Top-708
73OPC-19
73Top-19
73TopCanL-16
74ExpWes-4
74OPC-217
74Top-217
74TopDecE-19
74TopSta-54
75Hos-9
75HosTwi-9
75OPC-149
75Top-149
76ExpRed-8
76OPC-397
76SSP-328
76Top-397
77BurCheD-156
77OPC-162
77Top-76
78MetDaiPA-7
78OPC-169
78Top-167
79OPC-213
79Top-403
80OPC-131
80Top-246
81AllGamPI-112
81CokTeaS-112
81Don-13
81Fle-379
81OPC-38
81Top-501
82Don-376
82Fle-482
82FleSta-75
82OPC-97
82Top-618
82TopSti-88
82TopTra-34T
83AllGamPI-20
83Don-342
83Fle-88
83OPC-319
83Top-738
84AllGamPI-109
84Don-474
84Fle-516
84FleUpd-38
84Nes792-342
84OPC-342
84Top-342
84TopTif-342
84TopTra-38T
84TopTraT-38T
85Fle-126
85Pir-6
85Top-271
85Top-456
85TopTif-271
85TopTif-456
86ExpGreT-3
86RanLit-1
86RanPer-NNO
87RanMot-28
87RanSmo-29
91MetWIZ-120
92BrePol-30
92YanWIZ8-60
93RanKee-150

Folkers, Rich
71OPC-648
71Top-648
73OPC-649
73Top-649
74OPC-417
74Top-417
75OPC-98
75PadDea-1
75Top-98
76OPC-611
76SSP-114
76Top-611
77SpoIndC-28
77Top-372
91MetWIZ-121
93St.PetCC-28
93St.PetCF-2645
94BreMilB-123
94St.PetCC-29
94St.PetCF-2603
96StPetCB-2

Followell, Vern
81EvaTriT-14
82EvaTriT-18
85TucTorC-57

Fonceca, Chad
96BilMusTI-8

Fondy, Dee
52Bow-231
52Top-359
53BowBW-5
54Bow-173
54RedHeaF-8
55Bow-224
56Top-112
57SeaPop-14
57Top-42
58Kah-9
58RedEnq-12
58Top-157
79TCM50-47
83TopRep5-359

Fong, Steve
87SalLakTTT-21

Fonseca, Angel
82WauTimF-25

Fonseca, Dave
80CliGiaT-13

Fonseca, Lew
20WalMaiW-16
29ExhFou-21
29PorandAR-24
30W554-2
31Exh-22
31W517-48
32OrbPinNP-20
32OrbPinUP-19
33ButCanV-15
33DouDisP-16
33Gou-43
33GouCanV-43
33TatOrb-19
33TatOrbSDR-184
34DiaMatCSB-56
34ButPreR-20
34DiaStaR-7
37KelPepS-BB6
61Fle-27
82OhiHaloF-61
91ConTSN-283

Fontenot, Joe
95BelGiaTI-12
95Bes-118
96Exc-244
96SanJosGB-16
97Bow-202
97BowBes-155
97BowBesAR-155
97BowBesR-155
97BowCerBIA-CA25
97BowCerGIA-CA25
97BowChr-188
97BowChrI-188
97BowChrIR-188
97BowChrR-188
97BowInt-202

Fontenot, Ray
82NasSouTI-12
83ColCliT-5
84Don-370
84Fle-122
84Nes792-19
84Top-19
84TopTif-19
85CubLioP-11
85CubSev-31
85Don-248
85Fle-127
85FleUpd-42
85Top-507
85TopTif-507
85TopTifT-35T
85TopTra-35T
86CubGat-31
86CubUno-9
86Don-361
86Fle-369
86Top-308
86TopTif-308
87Top-124
87TopTif-124
87TucTorP-12
92YanWIZ8-61

Fontes, Brad
88ButCopKSP-24
89KenTwiP-1062
89KenTwiS-5

Fontes, Brian
93BoiHawC-11
93BoiHawF-3908

Fonville, Chad
92ClaFS7-449
92EveGiaC-28
92EveGiaF-1695
93ClaGolF-160
93CliGiaF-2495
93MidLeaAGF-38
94ClaGolF-41
94ExcFS7-289
95ARuFalLS-6
95FleUpd-105
95TopTra-82T
95UltGolMR-M12
95UppDec-462T
96ColCho-181
96ColCho-655
96ColChoGS-181
96ColChoGS-655
96ColChoSS-181
96ColChoSS-655
96DodMot-23
96DodPol-12
96Don-289
96DonPreP-289
96Fin-B140
96FinRef-B140
96Fle-433
96FleDod-6
96FleTif-433
96LeaSigA-69
96LeaSigAG-69
96LeaSigAS-69
96Pac-106
96PanSti-91
96Sco-213
96StaClu-31
96StaCluEPB-31
96StaCluEPG-31
96StaCluEPS-31
96StaCluMOP-31
96Top-402
96Ult-218
96UltGolM-218
96UppDec-93
96UppDecFSP-FS9

Fonville, Charlie
84ButCopKT-10

Foor, Jim
72OPC-257
72Top-257
75TulOil7-20

Foote, Barry
72Dia-16
72Dia-17
74OPC-603
74Top-603
75Hos-39
75OPC-229
75Top-229
76ExpRed-9
76OPC-42
76Top-42
77BurCheD-157
77ExpPos-13
77OPC-207
77Top-612
78PhiSSP-40
78SSP270-40
78Top-513
79Top-161
80OPC-208
80Top-398
81Don-558
81Fle-313
81OPC-305
81Top-492
81TopSti-154
81TopTra-763
82Don-83
82Fle-34
82Top-706
83Top-697
85AlbYanT-23
86ColCliP-21
86ColCliP-9
87MyrBeaBJP-1441
89KnoBluJB-28
89KnoBluJP-1128
89SouLeaAJ-24
90WhiSoxC-30
91WhiSoxK-NNO
92MetColP-34
92MetKah-26
92YanWIZ8-62
86STaoftFT-2

Foote, Derek
94DanBraC-10
94DanBraF-3534
96MacBraB-13

Foran, John
96FayGenB-15

Forbes, Andre
78GreBraT-9

Forbes, P.J.
90BoiHawP-3320
90WicStaSGD-11
91PalSprAP-2022
92ClaFS7-376
92QuaCitRBC-18
92QuaCitRBF-817
93MidAngF-328
94ExcFS7-25
94VanCanF-1869
96VanCanB-13
97MidAngOHP-10

Forbes, Willie
88ChaRaiP-1193

Ford, Allen
91MedHatBJP-4094

Ford, Ben
96Exc-89
96GreBatB-10

Ford, Brian
95BatCliTI-12
96PieBolWB-12

Ford, Calvin
89WytCubS-15
90HunCubP-3298

Ford, Curt
83SprCarF-6
84ArkTraT-16
85LouRedR-13
86Fle-648
86LouRedTI-13
87CarSmo-21
87Don-454
87Fle-294
87FleGlo-294
87Top-399
87TopTif-399
88CarSmo-20
88Don-417
88Fle-32
88FleGlo-32
88PanSti-395
88Sco-288
88ScoGlo-288
88StaLinCa-6
88Top-612
88TopSti-23
88TopTif-612
88Woo-28
89Bow-408
89BowTif-408
89Fle-450
89FleGlo-450
89PhiTas-6
89Top-132
89TopTif-132
89UppDec-309
90Don-694
90Fle-557
90FleCan-557
90OPC-39
90PhiTas-9
90Sco-183
90SprCarDGB-30
90Top-39
90TopTif-39
90UppDec-490
91LinDriAAA-583
91TolMudHLD-583
91TolMudHP-1943
92LouRedF-1900
95ChaKniTI-10

Ford, Dale
88T/MUmp-23
89T/MUmp-21
89T/MUmp-60
90T/MUmp-20

Ford, Dan (Darnell)
76OPC-313
76SSP-216
76Top-313
77BurCheD-48
77Hos-121
77OPC-104
77Top-555
77TopCloS-16
78Hos-18
78OPC-34
78Top-275
78TwiFriP-7
79OPC-201
79Top-385
80OPC-7
80Top-20
81AllGamPI-51
81Don-54
81Fle-273
81LonBeaPT-7
81OPC-303
81Top-422
82Don-468
82Fle-458

82FleSta-216
82OPC-134
82Top-134
82TopSti-163
82TopTra-35T
83Don-509
83Fle-61
83OPC-357
83OriPos-10
83Top-683
84Don-367
84Fle-9
84Nes792-530
84OPC-349
84OriTeal-11
84Top-530
84TopSti-212
84TopTif-530
85Don-489
85Fle-178
85Top-252
85TopTif-252
86Top-753
86TopTif-753
91OriCro-139
Ford, Dave
77RocRedWM-6
79RocRedWT-20
80Top-661
81Don-552
81Fle-192
81Top-706
82Don-597
82Fle-166
82Top-174
83RocRedWT-4
84TacTigC-94
91OriCro-140
Ford, Doug
47CenFlo-7
Ford, Eric
94UtiBluSC-11
94UtiBluSF-3832
Ford, Gervise
85DalNatCC-12
Ford, Hod (Horace E.)
21Nei-111
22E120-125
22W573-41
27AmeCarE-57
29ExhFou-8
29PorandAR-25
31Exh-8
33Gou-24
33GouCanV-24
90DodTar-249
93ConTSN-923
Ford, Jack
96PriWilCB-11
Ford, Jason
96PorRocB-13
Ford, Ken
82AleDukT-23
83LynPirT-20
85NasPirT-10
86NasPirP-7
Ford, M.W.
88AllandGN-16
Ford, Ondra
86EugEmeC-33
89AppFoxP-859
Ford, Randy
82KnoBluJT-3
Ford, Rick
76BurBeeT-10
77BurBeeT-9
77HolMilT-9
78CliDodT-9
Ford, Russ
09ColChiE-106
09SpoNewSM-49
09T206-134
10CouT21-135
10DomDisP-45
10E98-15
10JuJuDE-19
10RedCroT-25
10RedCroT-112
10RedCroT-193
10SweCapPP-34A
10SweCapPP-34B
10W555-30
11L1L-115
11MecDFT-30
11PloCanE-28
11S74Sil-21
11S81LarS-90
11SpoLifM-78
11T205-59A
11T205-59B
12ColRedB-106
12ColTinT-106
12HasTriFT-38A
12HasTriFT-38B
12HasTriFT-67B
12HasTriFT-68A
12HasTriFT-68B
14CraJacE-83
14PieStaT-22
15CraJacE-83
15VicT21-10
95ConTSN-1369
Ford, Rusty
86BeaGolGP-11
87LasVegSP-9
88WicPilRD-41
Ford, Scott
86DavLipB-12
Ford, Steve
90YakBeaTI-20
Ford, Stewart
90PulBraB-4
90PulBraP-3098
91PulBraC-18
91PulBraP-3998
92IdaFalGF-3505
92IdaFalGSP-25
Ford, Ted
71OPC-612
71Top-612
72OPC-24
72Top-24
73OPC-299
73Top-299
74OPC-617
74Top-617
93RanKee-11
Ford, Whitey (Edward C.)
47Exh-73A
47Exh-73B
47Exh-73C
47PM1StaP1-60
47StaPinP2-14
51BerRos-D5
51Bow-1
53BowC-153
53Dor-115
53Top-207
54Bow-177
54NewYorJA-46
54RedMan-AL16
54Top-37
55ArmCoi-6
55Bow-59
55RedMan-AL3
56Top-240
57Top-25
57YanJayP-3
58JayPubA-5
58Top-320
58YanJayP-3
59ArmCoi-8
59Top-430
59Yoo-2
60ArmCoi-10
60Top-35
60TopTat-15
60TopVen-35
60YanJayP-3
61Pos-6A
61Pos-6B
61Top-160
61Top-311
61Top-586
61TopStal-193
61Yan61RL-11
61YanJayP-4
62AurRec-6
62Baz-41
62ExhStaB-11
62Jel-9
62Pos-9
62PosCan-9A
62PosCan-9B
62SalPlaC-8
62ShiPlaC-8
62Top-57
62Top-59
62Top-235
62Top-310
62Top-315
62Top-475
62TopBuc-26
62TopStal-85
62TopVen-57
62TopVen-59
62YanJayP-6
63BasMagM-25
63ExhStaB-22
63Jel-19
63Pos-19
63Top-6
63Top-142
63Top-446
63YanJayP-3
64ChatheY-8
64Top-4
64Top-380
64TopCoi-139
64TopGia-7
64TopVen-4
64WheSta-15
64YanJayP-4
64YanReqKP-7
65ChaTheY-6
65Top-330
66DexPre-1
66OPC-160
66Top-160
66TopRubI-32
66TopVen-160
66YanTeal-3
67NasHeaF-1
67OPC-5
67Top-5
67TopVen-178
68LauWorS-58
70FleWorS-58
71FleWorS-59
74NewYorNTDiS-18
74SupBlaB-3
74SyrChiTI-30
75SSP42-33
75SyrChiTI-5
75TCMAllG-10
76GalBasGHoF-9
76ShaPiz-144
77GalGloG-25
78TCM60I-21
79BasGre-73
80PerHaloFP-144
80SSPHOF-144
80YanGreT-10
81TCM60I-450
82CraJac-3
83DiaClaS2-83
83MLBPin-7
83TigAlKS-16
83YanASFY-13
83YanASFY-14
83YanYealT-17
84FifNatCT-6
84OCoandSI-5
84WilMay-24
85GeoSteM-3
85Woo-11
86SpoDecG-44
86SpoDesJM-24
86TCMSupS-9
87HygAllG-17
87NesDreT-21
87Yan196T-7
89BowInsT-3
89BowRepl-3
89BowTif-R3
89HOFStiB-70
89KahCoo-4
89PacLegI-210
89SweBasG-50
89TopBasT-31
89YanCitAG-1
90AGFA-16
90PerGreM-5
90SweBasG-8
91MDAA-10
91RinPos1Y3-10
91TopArc1-207
92BazQua5A-12
92FroRowF-1
92FroRowF-2
92FroRowF-3
92FroRowF-4
92FroRowF-5
92PinMan-25
92St.VinHHS-4
92YanWIZ6-42
92YanWIZA-21
92YanWIZH-10
93ActPacA-116
93ActPacA2-50G
93TedWil-62
93UppDecAH-52
93UppDecAH-140
93UppDecAH-152
93UppDecAH-158
93Yoo-6
94TopArc1-37
94TopArc1G-37
94UppDecAH-146
94UppDecAH-157
94UppDecAH1-146
94UppDecAH1-157
95EagBalL-6
95SPCha-105
95SPChaDC-105
95UppDecSHoB-1
Fordham, Tom
93SarWhiSF-1362
94HicCraC-10
94HicCraF-2171
94SouAtlLAF-SAL21
95Bes-13
95BowBes-B79
95BowBesR-B79
95PriWilCTI-18
95SPML-37
96BesAutSA-20
96BirBarB-13
96Bow-292
96Exc-32
97Bow-117
97BowCerBIA-CA26
97BowCerGIA-CA26
97BowInt-117
Fordyce, Brook
89KinMetS-10
89Sta-191
90ColMetGS-22
90ColMetPPI-4
90SouAtlLAS-30
91Cla/Bes-220
91ClaGolB-BC10
91ColMetPPI-7
91FloStaLAP-FSL31
91St.LucMC-11
91St.LucMP-714
91UppDec-64
92BinMetF-520
92BinMetS-57
92Bow-56
92ClaFS7-25
92ProFS7-285
92SkyAA F-24
92UppDecML-287
93Bow-333
93ClaFS7-135
93ExcFS7-73
93NorTidF-2573
93Top-701
93TopGol-701
93TopInaM-701
94Bow-540
94Cla-193
94NorTidF-2923
94SigRoo-9
94SigRooS-9
94Top-785
94TopGol-785
94TopSpa-785
94UppDecML-19
96IndIndB-8
Fore, Chuck L.
78SyrChiT-10
79SyrChiT-14
80KnoBluJT-1
81SyrChiT-3
81SyrChiTI-8
83RicBraT-6
Foreman, Dave
87AncGlaP-40
Foreman, Francis
87OldJudN-177
Foreman, Toby
91BelMarC-21
91BelMarP-3657
Forer, Daniel Lynn
81VerBeaDT-5
Forgeur, Freddy
79QuaCitCT-21
Forgione, Chris
85VisOakT-9
86VisOakP-9
87KenTwiP-22
88OrlTwiB-16
Forkerway, Trey
96DayCubB-10
Forkner, Tim
93AubAstC-9
93AubAstF-3452
94MidLeaAF-MDW51
94QuaCitRBC-10
94QuaCitRBF-541
96JacGenB-8
96TexLeaAB-5
Fornasiere, Bob
92Min-20
Forney, Jeff
87TamTarP-25
88CedRapRP-1151
88MidLeaAGS-10
90ChaLooGS-13
Forney, Rick
92KanCouCC-22
92KanCouCF-84
92KanCouCTI-9
92MidLeaATI-10
93CarLeaAGF-1
93FreKeyC-7
93FreKeyF-1020
94Bow-327
94BowBayF-2409
94Cla-55
94ExcFS7-4
94OriPro-34
95BowBayTI-43
95RocRedWTI-15
Fornieles, Mike
54Top-154
55Bow-266
57Top-116
58Top-361
59Top-473
60Top-54
60TopVen-54
61Top-113
62Top-512
62TopStal-12
63Top-28
79TCM50-132
91OriCro-141
94TopArc1-154
94TopArc1G-154
Forrest, Chris
87St.PetCP-15
89BoiHawP-2001
Forrest, Joel
87MacPirP-3
88AugPirP-381
88WatPirP-5
Forrester, Gary
89SalDodTI-11
90BakDodCLC-251
91QuaCitAP-2635
Forrester, Tom
86BirBarTI-15
87HawIslP-7
88BirBarB-12
89VanCanC-20
89VanCanP-597
90BirBarDGB-11
90SouBenWSB-19
90SouBenWSGS-4
Forry, Dewey
75WatDodT-8
Forsch, Ken
71OPC-102
71Top-102
72OPC-394
72Top-394
73OPC-589
73Top-589
74OPC-91
74Top-91
75OPC-357
75Top-357
76OPC-357
76SSP-48
76Top-357
77BurCheD-4
77OPC-78

77Spo-7423
77Top-21
77Top-632
78AstBurK-8
78Kel-50
78Top-181
79AstTeal-6
79Hos-51
79OPC-276
79Top-534
80OPC-337
80Top-642
81AllGamPI-80
81Don-141
81Don-261A
81Fle-52
81LonBeaPT-12
81OPC-269
81Top-269
81TopTra-764
82Don-393
82Fle-459
82FleSta-221
82OPC-385
82Top-276
82Top-385
82TopSti-159
83AllGamPI-78
83Don-164
83Fle-89
83FleSta-64
83FleSti-28
83OPC-346
83Top-625
84AngSmo-9
84Don-280
84Fle-517
84Nes792-765
84OPC-193
84Top-765
84TopSti-237
84TopTif-765
85AngSmo-8
85Fle-301
85OPC-141
85Top-442
85TopTif-442
86AstMot-14
86Fle-155
87AstShoSO-7
87AstShowSTh-26
90SweBasG-37

Forsch, Robert
75OPC-51
75Top-51
76OPC-426
76SSP-294
76Top-426
77Car5-9
77CarTeal-8
77Spo-7423
77Top-381
77Top-632
78CarTeal-6
78Hos-3
78OPC-83
78Top-58
79Car5-5
79Kel-38
79OPC-117
79Top-230
80OPC-279
80Top-535
81Car5x7-4
81CokTeaS-121
81Don-69
81Fle-537
81OPC-140
81Top-140
82Don-91
82Fle-112
82FleSta-22
82OPC-34
82Top-186
82Top-775
82TopSti-90
83Car-5
83Don-64
83Fle-5
83FleSta-63
83FleSti-11
83OPC-197
83Top-415
83TopSti-289
84Car-7
84Car5x7-6
84Don-168
84Fle-322
84Fle-639
84Nes792-5
84Nes792-75
84OPC-75
84Top-5
84Top-75
84TopSti-288A
84TopTif-5
84TopTif-75
85CarTeal-10
85Fle-223
85OPC-137
85Top-631
85TopTif-631
86CarIGAS-4
86CarKASD-6
86CarSchM-6
86CarTeal-13
86Don-353
86Fle-35
86Spo-129
86Top-66
86Top-322
86TopTif-66
86TopTif-322
87CarSmo-7
87Don-540
87Fle-295
87FleAwaW-14
87FleGlo-295
87FleStiC-40
87Lea-161
87OPC-257
87Spo-191
87SpoTeaP-12
87Top-257
87TopSti-47
87TopTif-257
88CarSmo-5
88Don-111
88Fle-33
88FleGlo-33
88PanSti-384
88Sco-264
88ScoGlo-264
88Spo-199
88Top-586
88TopTif-586
89AstLenH-23
89AstMot-11
89AstSmo-14
89Don-118
89Sco-525
89Top-163
89TopTif-163
90Fle-231
90FleCan-231
90PubSti-95
90Sco-219
90VenSti-181
92CarMcD-51

Forster, Guillermo
73CedRapAT-4
74CedRapAT-20

Forster, Scott
94StaCluDP-46
94StaCluDPFDI-46
94VerExpF-3905
96HarSenB-12

Forster, Terry
72Top-539
72WhiSox-3
72WhiSoxTI1-4
73OPC-129
73Top-129
74OPC-310
74Top-310
74TopSta-153
75OPC-137
75OPC-313
75Top-137
75Top-313
76Hos-14
76HosTwi-14
76OPC-437
76SSP-157
76Top-437
77PirPosP-5
77Top-271
78SSP270-68
78Top-347
79DodBlu-3
79OPC-7
79Top-23
80DodPol-51
80Top-605
81Dod-3
81DodPol-51
81Fle-119
81LonBeaPT-16
81Top-104
82DodPol-51
82DodPos-1
82DodUniOV-4
82Don-362
82Fle-4
82Top-444
83BraPol-51
83Don-453
83Fle-205
83Top-583
83TopFol-4
83TopTra-33T
84BraPol-51
84Fle-178
84Nes792-791
84OPC-109
84Top-791
84TopTif-791
85BraHos-8
85BraPol-51
85Fle-324
85OPC-248
85Top-248
85TopMin-248
85TopTif-248
86AngSmo-23
86Don-432
86Fle-514
86FleUpd-42
86Lea-202
86Top-363
86TopTif-363
86TopTra-37T
86TopTraT-37T
87Fle-80
87FleGlo-80
87Top-652
87TopTif-652
90DodTar-250

Forster, Tom
87BucN28-52
87OldJudN-178
87OldJudN-180

Fortaleza, Ray
84GreHorT-2

Fortenberry, Jim
86ClePhiP-8
86FloStaLAP-16
87ReaPhiP-21

Fortin, Blaine
96StCatSB-8

Fortin, Troy
94EliTwiC-8
94EliTwiF-3735
95Exc-83
95ForWayWTI-13
96FtMyeMB-30

Fortinberry, Bill
80PorBeaT-12

Fortugno, Tim
86BelMarC-115
87SalSpuP-26
88ReaPhiP-876
89RenSilSCLC-244
89StoPorS-7
90BelBreB-7
90BelBreS-8
91ElPasDLD-182
91ElPasDP-2741
91LinDriAA-182
92DonRoo-38
92EdmTraF-3535
92EdmTraS-157
92SkyAAAF-78
93Don-299
93Fle-572
93OttLynF-2429
93Sco-262
93StaClu-231
93StaCluFDI-231
93StaCluMOP-231
93Top-320
93TopGol-320
93TopInaM-320
93TopMic-320
93Ult-163
94ChaLooF-1356
94FleUpd-118
94RedKah-10
95Fle-435
95FleUpd-36
95WhiSoxK-10

Fortuna, Mike
89SalBucS-8
89WelPirP-12

Fortune, Grehsam
94ButCopKSP-19

Fortune, Steve
79ElmPioRST-9

Fosnow, Gerald
65Top-529

Foss, Larry
77FriOneYW-106
91MetWIZ-122

Fossa, Dick
88CalLeaACLC-24

Fossas, Tony
80AshTouT-7
81TulDriT-16A
83TulDriT-3
84OklCit8T-12
85OklCit8T-10
86EdmTraP-10
87EdmTraP-2080
88OklCit8C-9
88OklCit8P-34
89DenZepC-3
89DenZepP-55
90BrePol-36
90Don-457
90Fle-323
90FleCan-323
90OPC-34
90Sco-567
90Top-34
90TopTif-34
91Lea-276
91OPC-747
91Sco-634
91Top-747
91TopDesS-747
91TopMic-747
91TopTif-747
92Don-645
92OPC-249
92RedSoxDD-11
92Sco-389
92StaClu-144
92Top-249
92TopGol-249
92TopGolW-249
92TopMic-249
92UppDec-503
93Don-195
93Fle-180
93PacSpa-358
93RanKee-151
93StaClu-247
93StaCluFDI-247
93StaCluMOP-247
94BreMilB-124
94Pac-55
94StaClu-26
94StaCluFDI-26
94StaCluGR-26
94StaCluMOP-26
94Top-378
94TopGol-378
94TopSpa-378
95Fle-30
95Pac-37
95Top-119
96CarPol-6
96Fle-542
96FleTif-542
96LeaSigEA-54
96Pac-220
97PacPriGotD-GD198
97StaClu-367
97StaCluMOP-367

Fosse, Ray
69Top-244
70DayDaiNM-102a
70Ind-4
70OPC-184
70Top-184
71Ind-4
71Kel-39
71MilDud-5
71MLBOffS-366
71OPC-125
71Top-125
71TopCoi-42
71TopSup-51
71TopTat-129
72OPC-470
72Top-470
72TopPos-4
73A'sPos-30
73Kel2D-18
73OPC-226
73Top-226
73TopCanL-17
74A'sPos-46
74OPC-420
74Top-420
75OPC-486
75Top-486
76OPC-554
76SSP-500
76Top-554
76TopTra-554T
77BurCheD-62
77Hos-122
77OPC-39
77PepGloD-17
77Top-267
78Hos-57
78Top-415
79Top-51
80Top-327
86TopRos-68
86TopRos-69
91UppDecS-5
94BreMilB-219

Foster, Alan
69Top-266
70OPC-369
70Top-369
71MLBOffS-367
71OPC-207
71Top-207
72OPC-521
72Top-521
73OPC-543
73Top-543
74OPC-442
74Top-442
75OPC-296
75Top-296
76OPC-266
76SSP-115
76Top-266
77Top-108
81TCM60I-465
85SpoIndGC-6
90DodTar-251

Foster, Bob
79LodDodT-17

Foster, Bryan
88BelBreGS-12
89StoPorB-21
89StoPorCLC-171
89StoPorP-393
89StoPorS-20

Foster, Bud
46RemBre-15
47RemBre-9
47SigOil-44
48SigOil-7
49RemBre-7

Foster, Clifton
92SouOreAC-24
92SouOreAF-3408
93MadMusC-9
93MadMusF-1817

Foster, Doug
78CliDodT-10

Foster, Edward Lee
09T206-484
11MecDFT-49

Foster, Elmer
87OldJudN-179A
87OldJudN-179B
88WG1CarG-39
89SFHaCN-5
90KalBatN-21

Foster, George
71OPC-276
71Top-276
72OPC-256

72Top-256
73OPC-202
73OPC-399
73Top-202
73Top-399
74OPC-646
74Top-646
75OPC-87
75Top-87
76Hos-106
76LinSup-95
76OPC-179
76RedIceL-4
76RedKro-8
76RedPos-8
76SSP-44
76Top-179
77BurCheD-201
77Hos-40
77Kel-1
77MSADis-21
77OPC-3
77OPC-120
77PepGloD-48
77RCColC-22
77Spo-4517
77Top-3
77Top-347
78Hos-2
78Kel-10
78OPC-2
78OPC-3
78OPC-70
78Pep-10
78RCColC-13
78SSP270-113
78Top-202
78Top-203
78Top-500
78WifBalD-24
79Hos-107
79Kel-32
79OPC-316
79Top-2
79Top-3
79Top-600
80BurKinPHR-15
80Kel-50
80OPC-209
80RedEnq-15
80Top-400
80TopSup-24
81AllGamPI-144
81CokTeaS-41
81Don-65
81Dra-18
81Fle-202A
81Fle-202B
81Fle-216
81FleStiC-41
81Kel-1
81OPC-200
81PerAll-4
81PerCreC-9
81Squ-2
81Top-200
81TopScr-65
81TopSti-159
81TopSupHT-35
82Don-274
82Dra-13
82Fle-66
82Fle-630
82FleSta-12
82K-M-32
82Kel-56
82MetPhoA-7
82OPC-177
82OPC-336
82OPC-342
82RegGloT-1
82Squ-18
82Top-342A
82Top-342B
82Top-700
82Top-701
82TopSti-40
82TopSti-126
82TopTra-36T
83AllGamPI-145
83Don-6
83Don-427
83Dra-8
83Fle-542
83FleSta-65
83FleSti-239
83Kel-22
83OPC-80
83Top-80
83TopFol-2
83TopSti-263
84AllGamPI-51
84Don-312
84DonCha-2
84Fle-584
84FunFooP-46
84MetFanC-3
84Nes792-350
84OCoandSI-193
84OPC-350
84Top-350
84TopRubD-20
84TopSti-105
84TopTif-350
85AllGamPI-141
85Don-603
85Fle-79
85Lea-42
85MetColP-26
85MetFanC-4
85MetTCM-33
85OPC-170
85PolMet-M1
85Top-170
85TopMin-170
85TopRubD-20
85TopSti-99
85TopTif-170
86Don-116
86Fle-80
86GenMilB-4C
86MetColP-12
86MetTCM-25
86OPC-69
86Spo-68
86Spo-126
86Spo-131
86Spo-139
86Top-680
86TopSti-100
86TopTif-680
86Woo-11
89PacLegI-173
89PacSenL-114
89T/MSenL-36
89T/MSenL-119
89TopSenL-1
90EliSenL-112
90EliSenL-124
90PacLeg-72
90SweBasG-97
91LinDri-37
91MDAA-8
91MetWIZ-123
91SweBasG-112
91UppDecS-12
92ActPacA-61
92MDAMVP-10
92UppDecS-14
93MetIma-9
93TedWil-29
93TedWilM-17
93TedWilPC-25
93UppDecAH-53
93UppDecS-15
93UppDecS-22
93UppDecS-24
94UppDecAH-182
94UppDecAH1-182
95MCIAmb-16
95SonGre-2
96Red76K-5

Foster, Jeff
94BurBeeC-8

Foster, Jim
93BluOriC-13
93BluOriF-4128
94AlbPolC-1
94AlbPolF-2240
94ExcFirYPF-1
94ExcFS7-5
94OriPro-35
94SouAtlLAF-SAL2
96FreKeyB-10

Foster, John
82WisRapTF-19

Foster, Julio
92UtiBluSC-9

Foster, Ken
81WisRapTT-16
82OrlTwiT-18
83OrlTwiT-11
86SanJosBP-7

Foster, Kevin
89RocExpLC-8
90WesPalBES-7
91SumFlyC-4
91SumFlyP-2327
92WesPalBEF-2083
93JacSunF-2705
94LeaLimR-19
94PhiUSPC-8H
94StaCluT-236
94StaCluTFDI-236
94Top-786
94TopGol-786
94TopSpa-786
94TopTra-79T
95ColCho-214
95ColChoGS-214
95ColChoSS-214
95Don-296
95DonPreP-296
95DonTopotO-197
95Fin-24
95FinRef-24
95Fla-331
95Fle-414
95FleRooS-4
95Lea-45
95Pac-69
95Pin-393
95PinArtP-393
95PinMusC-393
95StaClu-461
95StaCluMOP-461
95StaCluSTWS-461
95StaCluVR-250
95Top-412
95TopCyb-212
95Ult-136
95UltGolM-136
95UppDec-314
95UppDecED-314
95UppDecEDG-314
95UppDecSE-121
95UppDecSEG-121
96ColCho-82
96ColChoGS-82
96ColChoSS-82
96Don-294
96DonPreP-294
96EmoXL-153
96Fla-214
96Fle-316
96FleCub-4
96FleTif-316
96LeaSigA-70
96LeaSigAG-70
96LeaSigAS-70
96Pac-22
96Sco-92
96StaClu-326
96StaCluMOP-326
95StaCluVRMC-250
96Top-62
96Ult-166
96UltGolM-166
96UppDec-34
97ColCho-288

Foster, Kid (Edward C.)
11SpoLifM-123
14B18B-39
15SpoNewM-62
16BF2FP-45
16ColE13-51
16SpoNewM-61
21E121So8-23
22AmeCarE-20
22W575-36

Foster, Kris
95YakBeaTI-9
96SanBerSB-9

Foster, Lamar
89MarPhiS-11
90MarPhiP-3179
91BatCliC-8
91BatCliP-3490

Foster, Larry
77FriOneYW-86

Foster, Leo
74OPC-607
74Top-607
75OPC-418
75TidTidTI-11
75Top-418
77MetDaiPA-1
77Top-458
78Top-229
91MetWIZ-124

Foster, Lindsay
87MyrBeaBJP-1449
88DunBluJS-6
89CanIndB-15
89CanIndP-1304
89CanIndS-6
90KinIndTI-14
91BirBarLD-58
91BirBarP-1461
91LinDriAA-58
92BirBarF-2591
92BirBarS-82

Foster, Mark
93MarPhiC-10
93MarPhiF-3464
94SpaPhiF-1715
94SparPhiC-9
95ReaPhiTI-12
96ReaPhiB-4

Foster, Otis
77BriRedST-7

Foster, Paul
87FayGenP-16
88LakTigS-11

Foster, Randy
87OneYanP-21
88PriWilYS-10

Foster, Roy
71MLBOffS-368
71OPC-107
71Top-107
72OPC-329
72Top-329
72TopCloT-12
89TidTidC-2

Foster, Rube (Andrew)
74LauOldTBS-35
80PerHaloFP-174
80SSPHOF-175
83ConMar-55
84OCoandSI-139
86NegLeaF-18
87NegLeaPD-25
88ConNegA-4
88NegLeaD-1
90NegLeaS-16
91ConTSN-138
91PomBlaBPB-27
94TedWil-105
94UppDecTAE-31

Foster, Rube (George)
09ColChiE-107
12ColRedB-107
12ColTinT-107
17HolBreD-31

Foster, Russ
91PacSenL-75

Foster, Steve (Stephen)
88BilMusP-1818
89CedRapRB-2
89CedRapRP-936
89CedRapRS-7
89Sta-194
90ChaLooGS-14
91ChaLooLD-158
91ChaLooP-1953
91LinDriAA-158
92Cla1-T35
92Don-420
92FleUpd-80
92NasSouF-1827
92OPC-528
92ProFS7-216
92StaClu-826
92StaCluECN-826
92Top-528
92TopDeb91-58
92TopGol-528
92TopGolW-528
92TopMic-528
93Don-666
93Fle-33
93Sco-284
93Top-193
93TopGol-193
93TopInaM-193
93TopMic-193
93Ult-328
94Pac-147
94RedKah-11

Foster, Willie
74LauOldTBS-5
80PerHaloFP-226
90NegLeaS-24

Fothergill, Bob (Robert)
28Exh-45
28StaPlaCE-21
79RedSoxEF-9
81TigDetN-85
81TigSecNP-11
91ConTSN-72

Foucault, Steve
74OPC-294
74Top-294
75OPC-283
75Top-283
76OPC-303
76SSP-252
76Top-303
77Top-459
78TigBurK-10
78Top-68
92BelBreC-29
92BelBreF-423
93BelBreC-27
93BelBreF-1727
93RanKee-152
94BelBreC-28
94BelBreF-119
95HudValRTI-29

Foulk, Leon
52Par-15

Foulke, Keith
94EveGiaC-7
94EveGiaF-3643
96TexLeaAB-6
97Bow-317
97BowChr-219
97BowChrI-219
97BowChrIR-219
97BowChrR-219
97BowInt-317
97Fle-760
97FleTif-760

Foulks, Brian
96GreFalDB-13
96GreFalDTI-28

Fournier, Bruce
79WatA'sT-19
80OgdA'sT-16
80WesHavWCT-5
81WesHavAT-10

Fournier, Jacques F.
12T207-62
15SpoNewM-63
16ColE13-52
16SpoNewM-62
17HolBreD-32
21Exh-50
21Exh-51
22E120-229
22W573-42
23WilChoV-44
25Exh-11
26Exh-10
26SpoComoA-15
90DodTar-252
92ConTSN-541
95ConTSN-1381

Foussianes, George
83BirBarT-11
85TulDriTI-6
90BirBarDGB-12

Foutz, Dave
76SSP188WS-2
87BucN28-97
87LonJacN-4
87OldJudN-181A
87OldJudN-181B
87ScrDC-4
89EdgR.WG-9
90DodTar-253
95May-9
95NewN566-181

Fowble, Greg
87AriWilP-2
88AriWilP-3

Fowler, Ben
96DanBraB-11

Fowler, Dick

47Exh-74
49Bow-171
49OlmStu-3
49PhiBul-19
50Bow-214
52Bow-190
52Top-210
83TopRep5-210
Fowler, Don
80CarMudF-5
81TacTigT-14
82TacTigT-2
84ColCliP-10
84ColCliT-6
84NasSouTI-7
89WatDiaP-1792
89WatDiaS-7
Fowler, Dwayne
91PulBraC-19
91PulBraP-3999
Fowler, Eddie
89WytCubS-10
Fowler, J. Art
55Top-3
55TopDouH-79
56Kah-5
56Top-47
56TopPin-55
57Top-233
59Top-508
62Top-128
62TopVen-128
63Top-454A
63Top-454B
64Top-349
64TopVen-349
73OPC-323
73Top-323
74OPC-379
74Top-379
79YanPicA-13
90DodTar-254
93RanKee-153
Fowler, John
89BluOriS-9
90WauTimB-21
90WauTimP-2134
90WauTimS-8
94TedWil-106
Fowler, Maleke
96BluOriB-13
Fowler, Mike
88DurBulS-6
89DurBulIS-11
89DurBulTI-11
Fowler, Yale
89GreFalDSP-13
90YakBeaTI-32
Fowlkes, Alan Kim
81ShrCapT-7
83Don-46
83Fle-259
83Top-543
84PhoGiaC-16
86EdmTraP-11
88RenSilSCLC-268
Fowlkes, David
76BatTroTI-8
77WatIndT-8
Fox, Andy
89HigSchPLS-8
90Bes-263
90CMC-825
90GreHorB-16
90GreHorP-2668
90GreHorS-1
90SouAtlLAS-6
90TopTVY-43
91CarLeaAP-CAR30
91Cla/Bes-132
91PriWilCC-17
91PriWilCP-1433
92PriWilCC-2
92PriWilCF-155
93AlbYanF-2170
93ClaFS7-71
94AbaYanF-1449
94AlbYanTI-1
94AriFalLS-5
95ColCliP-10
95ColCliTI-10
95NorNavTI-51
96Bow-275
96Fin-S272
96FinRef-S272
96FleUpd-U59
96FleUpdNH-6
96FleUpdTC-U59
96Sel-194
96SelArtP-194
96Ult-383
96UltGolM-383
97PacPriGotD-GD71
97Sco-250
97ScoPreS-250
97ScoShoS-250
97ScoShoSAP-250
97ScoYan-15
97ScoYanPI-15
97ScoYanPr-15
Fox, Blane
87LakTigP-22
88FloStaLAS-36
88LakTigS-12
89ColMudB-14
89ColMudP-143
89ColMudS-9
91LinDriAA-461
91NewBriRSLD-461
91NewBrIRSP-364
Fox, Chad
92ClaDraP-100
92PriRedC-13
92PriRedF-3081
93ClaFS7-101
93ExcFS7-18
93WesVirWC-1
93WesVirWF-2859
94CarLeaAF-CAR47
94WinSpiC-8
94WinSpiF-265
95ChaLooTI-6
95UppDecML-138
96RicBraB-11
96RicBraRC-7
95UppDecMLFS-138
Fox, Charlie
70Gia-3
71GiaTic-3
71OPC-517
71Top-517
72OPC-129
72Top-129
73OPC-252
73Top-252A
73Top-252B
74OPC-78
74Top-78
Fox, Dan
89KenTwiP-1085
89KenTwiS-26
90KenTwiB-29
90KenTwiS-27
91KenTwiC-21
92KenTwiC-27
93ForWaySoxWC-28
94ForWayWC-30
Fox, Eric
85AncGlaPTI-11
87ChaLooB-16
88VerMarP-945
89HunStaB-9
90CMC-592
90ProAAAF-154
90TacTigC-15
90TacTigP-107
91LinDriAAA-533
91TacTigLD-533
91TacTigP-2317
92DonRoo-39
92HunStaF-3961
92ScoRoo-88T
92TacTigS-532
93Don-287
93Fle-663
93PacSpa-566
93Pin-567
93Sco-352
93Sel-313
93StaClu-131
93StaCluFDI-131
93StaCluMOP-131
93TacTigF-3046
93Top-46
93TopGol-46
93TopInaM-46
93TopMic-46
93Ult-605
93UppDec-781
93UppDecGold-781
93USPlaCR-2C
94TacTigF-3186
Fox, Howie (Howard)
49EurSta-84
50Bow-80
51Bow-180
51Bow-232
52Bow-125
52NatTeaL-10
52Top-209
53BowC-158
53Top-22
54OriEss-11
54Top-246
83TCMPla1945-41
83TopRep5-209
91OriCro-142
91TopArc1-22
94TopArc1-246
94TopArc1G-246
Fox, Kenneth
86JamExpP-7
Fox, Mike
87St.PetCP-11
89ArkTraGS-5
Fox, Nellie (Jacob Nelson)
47Exh-75
47PM1StaP1-61
49PhiBul-20
52BasPho-2
52BerRos-4
52BerRos-20
52Bow-21
52DixLid-9
52DixPre-9
52RedMan-AL9
52StaCalL-73G
52StaCalS-87C
52WhiSoxH-4
53BowC-18
53DixLid-5
53DixPre-5
53NorBreL-8
53RedMan-AL5
54Bow-6
54RedHeaF-9
54RedMan-AL3
54Wil-6
55Bow-33
55DonWin-19
55RedMan-AL4
56Top-118
56YelBasP-11
57SwiFra-7
57Top-38
58HarSta-10
58JayPubA-6
58Top-400
58Top-479
58WhiSoxJP-3
59ArmCoi-9
59Baz-11
59Top-30
59Top-408
59Top-556
59TopVen-30
59WilSpoG-3
60ArmCoi-11
60Baz-25
60KeyChal-16
60NuHi-72
60Top-100
60Top-429
60Top-555
60TopTat-16
60TopVen-100
60WhiSoxJP-2
60WhiSoxTS-5
61ChePat-3
61NuSco-472
61Pos-20A
61Pos-20B
61Top-30
61Top-477
61Top-570
61WhiSoxTS-5
62ExhStaB-12
62Jel-47
62Pos-47
62PosCan-47
62SalPlaC-12
62ShiPlaC-12
62Top-73
62TopBuc-27
62TopStal-24
62TopVen-73
62WhiSoxJP-3
62WhiSoxTS-8
63BasMagM-26
63ExhStaB-23
63Jel-36
63Pos-36
63Top-525
63WhiSoxTS-7
64Top-81
64Top-205
64TopGia-13
64TopVen-81
64TopVen-205
64WheSta-16
65AstBigLBPP-6
65Top-485
67AstTeal2-11
69SenTeal8-11
74LauAllG-58
75OPC-197
75Top-197
76ChiGre-6
76LauDiaJ-24
77SerSta-9
79TCM50-15
80LauFamF-7
80PacLeg-68
82GSGalAG-13
83MLBPin-8
83TigAIKS-20
84OCoandSI-78
84OCoandSI-231
85WhiSoxC-12
86SpoDecG-37
87AstSer1-10
87AstSer1-25
87AstSer1-27
87AstShoSTw-6
87NesDreT-13
88GreBasS-25
88PacLegI-57
89WhiSoxK-2
91TopArc1-331
92BazQua5A-17
92Zip-9
93ActPacA-139
93RanKee-41
94TedWil-20
Fox, Nickie
94TedWil-96
Fox, Pete (Ervin)
34BatR31-175
34Gou-70
35AlDemDCR3-25
35GouPreR-10
35GouPuzR-8F
35GouPuzR-9F
35TigFreP-6
36GouWidPPR-A32
36GouWidPPR-B9
36GouWidPPR-C11
36NatChiFPR-26
36R31PasP-30
36SandSW-18
36WorWidGV-30
38GouHeaU-242
38GouHeaU-266
39PlaBal-80
40PlaBal-43
42RedSoxTI-12
43RedSoxTI-7
76ISCHooHA-15
76TigOldTS-8
78TigDeaCS-2
81DiaStaCD-110
81TigDetN-110
81TigSecNP-27
91ConTSN-197
Fox, Terry
61Top-459
62TigPosCF-7
62Top-196
62TopVen-196
63Top-44
64Top-387
65Top-576
66Top-472
67OPC-181
67Top-181
Foxen, Bill
11S74Sil-61
11SpoLifCW-129
11SpoLifM-229
11T205-60
12HasTriFT-13A
Foxes, Appleton
83AppFoxF-15
83AppFoxF-16
88AppFoxP-165
Foxover, David
91DaiDolF-4
Foxx, Jimmie (James Emory)
28PorandAR-A7
28PorandAR-B7
28W56PlaC-JOK
29ExhFou-27
29PorandAR-26
30W554-3
31Exh-28
31W517-21
32OrbPinNP-18
32OrbPinUP-20
32R33So2-xx
32USCar-23
33BulCanV-16A
33ButCanV-16B
33ButCre-8
33DelR33-21
33DouDisP-17
33ExhFou-14
33GeoCMil-12
33Gou-29
33Gou-154
33GouCanV-29
33GouCanV-85
33RitCE-10S
33TatOrb-20
33TatOrbSDR-153
34BatR31-28
34BatR31-144
34ButPreR-21A
34ButPreR-21B
34DiaStaR-64
34ExhFou-14
34Gou-1
34GouCanV-58
34WarBakSP-3
35ExhFou-14
35GouPuzR-1B
35GouPuzR-2B
35GouPuzR-16B
35GouPuzR-17B
35WheBB1-11
36ExhFou-9
36GouWidPPR-B10
36NatChiFPR-90
36OveCanR-14
36PC7AlbHoF-59
36R31PasP-43
36R31Pre-G7
36SandSW-19
36WheBB3-3
36WheBB5-4
36WorWidGV-47
37ExhFou-9
37GouFliMR-12A
37GouFliMR-12B
37GouThuMR-12
37OPCBatUV-106
38BasTabP-10
38DixLid-3
38DixLidP-3
38ExhFou-9
38GouHeaU-249
38GouHeaU-273
38OurNatGPP-9
38WheBB11-2
39ExhSal-17
39GouPreR303A-15
39GouPreR303B-8
39WheBB12-5
39WorWidGTP-15
40PlaBal-133
40WheM4-3
41DouPlaR-59
41PlaBal-13
41WheM5-14
42RedSoxTI-13
43MPR302-1-11
44CubTeal-9
46SpoExcW-1-4
50CalHOFW-31

59FleWil-11
60Fle-53
61Fle-28
61GolPre-22
61SevElev-27
63HalofFB-7
67TopVen-163
71FleWorS-28
72FleFamF-16
72LauGreF-19
73FleWilD-41
74LauAllG-35
75SpoHobBG-4
75TCMAllG-11
76GalBasGHoF-10
76RowExh-6
76ShaPiz-59
76TayBow4-48
77GalGloG-57
77GalGloG-184
77ShaPiz-13
79RedSoxEF-11
79RedSoxEF-18
79RedSoxEF-20
80Lau300-21
80LauFamF-23
80MarExhH-12
80PacLeg-16
80PerHaloFP-59
80SSPHOF-59
81ConTSN-80
81SpoHaloF-10
82BHCRSpoL-4
83ConMar-1
83DiaClaS2-85
83DonHOFH-13
84OCoandSI-142
85CirK-7
85FegMurCG-5
86BigLeaC-7
86ConSer1-12
86RedSoxGT-4
86SpoDecG-2
87HygAllG-18
87NesDreT-11
88ConAmeA-9
88ConSer5-10
90BasWit-61
90SweBasG-101
91ConTSN-2
91ConTSN-303
91LinDri-44
91SweBasG-143
91USGamSBL-6C
91USGamSBL-6D
91USGamSBL-6H
91USGamSBL-6S
92ConTSN-526
92ConTSN-560
92ConTSNCI-16
92TVSpoMF5HRC-3
93ActPacA-100
93ActPacA2-34G
93ConTSN-917
93TedWil-123
93UppDecAH-54
94ConTSN-1083
94ConTSN-1152
94ConTSNB-1083
94ConTSNB-1152
94TedWil5C-5
94UppDecAH-58
94UppDecAH-169
94UppDecAH1-58
94UppDecAH1-169
94UppDecTAE-42
95ConTSNGJ-4
95MegRut-3
Foy, Joe
66Top-456
67CokCapRS-6
67DexPre-75
67Top-331
67TopRedSS-6
67TopVen-208
68CokCapRS-6
68DexPre-32
68Top-387
69MilBra-84
69MLBOffS-58
69OPC-93
69RoySol-5
69RoyTeal-5
69Top-93
69TopDec-22B
69TopDecl-10
69TopSta-184
69TopSup-22
69TopTeaP-7
70DayDaiNM-136
70MLBOffS-75
70OPC-138
70Top-138
71MLBOffS-537
71OPC-706
71SenPolP-4
71Top-706
72MilBra-106
81RedSoxBG2S-80
81TCM60I-321
91MetWIZ-125
Foytack, Paul
53TigGle-7
57Top-77
58Top-282
59TigGraASP-6
59Top-233
60TigJayP-6
60Top-364
61Pos-62A
61Pos-62B
61Top-171
62Top-349
63TigJayP-7
63Top-327
64Top-149
64TopVen-149
81TCM60I-323
Frace, Ryan
96BatCliTI-21
Fragasso, Jerry
94SpoIndC-27
Frailing, Ken
74OPC-605
74Top-605
75OPC-436
75Top-436
76SSP-305
78KnoKnoST-5
Fralick, Bob
90MiaMirIS-28
90MiaMirIS-27
91MiaMirC-30
91MiaMirP-424
Frame, Mike (Michael)
89GreFalDSP-2
90BakDodCLC-236
France, Aaron
94WelPirC-9
94WelPirF-3488
96LynHilB-9
France, Todd
86StoPorP-7
87StoPorP-5
Franceschi, Sean
90EugEmeGS-7
Franchi, Kevin
86MacPirP-9
87SalBucP-1
Franchuk, Orv
90BoiHawP-3332
91BoiHawP-3901
93BoiHawC-28
93BoiHawF-3933
95EdmTraTI-7
Francia, David
96BatCliTI-23
Francingues, Ken
80WisRapTT-9
Francis, Earl
61Top-54
62Top-252
63PirIDL-7
63Top-303
64Top-117
64TopVen-117
78TCM60I-226
Francis, Harry
81RedPioT-13
82HolMilT-20
83NasAngT-12
Francis, Scott
91PulBraC-22
91PulBraP-4000
92MacBraF-262
Francis, Todd
83WauTimF-14
Francis, Tommy
83MiaMarT-23
Francisco, David
93MadMusC-10
93MadMusF-1835
93MidLeaAGF-12
94ModA'sC-10
94ModA'sF-3070
95HunStaTI-9
96HunStaTI-7
Francisco, Rene
89GenCubP-1862
90PeoChiTI-17
Francisco, Vicente
91SouOreAC-22
91SouOreAP-3854
92MadMusC-25
92MadMusF-1241
93MadMusC-11
93MadMusF-1827
94WesMicWC-8
94WesMicWF-2304
95WesMicWTI-13
Franco, John
82AlbDukT-2
84FleUpd-39
84RedEnq-24
84WicAerRD-19
85Don-164
85Fle-536
85FleStaS-120
85RedYea-6
85Top-417
85TopTif-417
86Don-487
86Fle-178
86FleStiC-39
86KayB-13
86Lea-240
86OPC-54
86RedTexG-31
86Spo-156
86Top-54
86TopSti-142
86TopTat-7
86TopTif-54
87ClaGam-100
87Don-289
87DonAll-22
87Fle-202
87Fle-631
87FleBasA-17
87FleGlo-202
87FleGlo-631
87FleLeaL-18
87FleLimE-14
87FleSlu-14
87FleStiC-41
87Lea-178
87OPC-305
87RedFolSB-116
87RedKah-31
87Spo-192
87SpoTeaP-4
87Top-305
87TopMinL-5
87TopSti-138
87TopTif-305
88Don-123
88DonAll-53
88DonBasB-54
88Fle-234
88Fle-627
88FleGlo-234
88FleGlo-627
88FleMin-74
88FleRecS-12
88FleStiC-84
88Lea-79
88Nes-8
88OPC-341
88PanSti-271
88RedKah-31
88Sco-535
88ScoGlo-535
88Spo-195
88StaLinRe-9
88Top-81
88Top-730
88TopBig-232
88TopCoi-41
88TopMinL-47
88TopSti-142
88TopStiB-32
88TopTif-81
88TopTif-730
88TopUKM-24
88TopUKMT-24
89Bow-301
89BowTif-301
89CadEllD-19
89Don-233
89DonBasB-166
89Fle-162
89FleGlo-162
89FleHeroB-14
89FleLeaL-13
89OPC-290
89PanSti-66
89RedFolSB-45
89RedKah-31
89Sco-575
89ScoHot1S-97
89Spo-176
89SpoIllFKI-64
89Top-290
89TopBasT-130
89TopCoi-12
89TopDouA-23
89TopGaloC-5
89TopMinL-9
89TopSti-4
89TopSti-136
89TopStiB-65
89TopTif-290
89TopUKM-27
89TVSpoM-43
89UppDec-407
89Woo-12
90Bow-128
90BowTif-128
90ClaBlu-86
90ClaUpd-T19
90Don-14
90Don-124
90DonBesN-92
90DonSupD-14
90Fle-419
90FleCan-419
90FleUpd-35
90FleWaxBC-C7
90Hot50PS-13
90Lea-356
90MetColP-2
90MetKah-31
90OPC-120
90PanSti-244
90PubSti-29
90PubSti-258
90RedFolSB-33
90Sco-273
90Sco100S-49
90ScoMcD-7
90ScoRoo-15T
90Spo-138
90Top-120
90TopBig-264
90TopHeaU-11
90TopMinL-54
90TopSti-144
90TopTif-120
90TopTra-32T
90TopTraT-32T
90TopTVM-11
90UppDec-139
90UppDec-709
90USPlaCA-7H
90VenSti-182
90VenSti-183
91Bow-475
91Cla1-T65
91ClaGam-125
91Don-322
91Fle-147
91Fle-712
91Lea-437
91MetCol8-4
91MetColP-3
91MetKah-31
91MetTro-2
91MetWIZ-126
91OPC-407
91OPC-510
91PanCanT1-81
91PanSti-87
91Sco-14
91Sco100S-29
91StaClu-22
91Stu-203
91Top-407
91Top-510
91TopDesS-407
91TopDesS-510
91TopGaloC-6
91TopMic-407
91TopMic-510
91TopTif-407
91TopTif-510
91Ult-217
91UppDec-290
92Bow-546
92Don-186
92Fle-504
92Lea-174
92MetColP-15
92MetKah-31
92OPC-690
92OPCPre-73
92Pin-64
92PinTeaP-12
92Sco-605
92Sco100S-57
92ScoImpP-61
92StaClu-565
92Stu-64
92Top-690
92TopGol-690
92TopGolW-690
92TopKid-13
92TopMic-690
92TriPla-64
92TriPla-182
92TriPlaP-8
92Ult-529
92UppDec-514
93Dow-290
93Don-146
93Fin-191
93FinRef-191
93Fle-471
93Lea-112
93MetColP-32
93MetKah-31
93OPC-68
93PacSpa-197
93Pin-216
93Pin-310
93Sco-139
93Sel-167
93SelChaS-11
93StaClu-316
93StaCluFDI-316
93StaCluMOP-316
93Stu-70
93Top-25
93TopGol-25
93TopInaM-25
93TopMic-25
93TriPla-90
93Ult-73
93UppDec-321
93UppDecGold-321
94Bow-184
94ColC-414
94ColChoGS-414
94ColChoSS-414
94Don-98
94ExtBas-316
94Fin-170
94FinRef-170
94Fla-196
94Fle-561
94Lea-144
94LeaL-130
94MetColP-8
94MetShuST-4
94OPC-256
94Pac-400
94Pin-368
94PinArtP-368
94PinMusC-368
94Sco-122
94ScoGolR-122
94StaClu-339
94StaCluFDI-339
94StaCluGR-339
94StaCluMOP-339
94Top-481
94TopGol-481
94TopSpa-481
94UppDec-323
94UppDecED-323
95Baz-48

95ColCho-329
95ColChoGS-329
95ColChoSE-151
95ColChoSEGS-151
95ColChoSESS-151
95ColChoSS-329
95Don-346
95DonPreP-346
95DonTopotO-291
95Fin-131
95FinRef-131
95Fla-383
95Fle-368
95Lea-225
95Pac-280
95PacPri-92
95PanSti-121
95Pin-402
95PinArtP-402
95PinMusC-402
95Sco-457
95ScoGolR-457
95ScoPlaTS-457
95StaClu-189
95StaCluFDI-189
95StaCluMO-15
95StaCluMOP-189
95StaCluSTWS-189
95StaCluVR-98
95Top-280
95Top-394
95TopCyb-152
95Ult-411
95UltGolM-411
95UltLeaL-10
95UltLeaLGM-10
95UppDec-122
95UppDecED-122
95UppDecEDG-122
96Cir-155
96CirRav-155
96ColCho-220
96ColChoGS-220
96ColChoSS-220
96Don-128
96DonPreP-128
96EmoXL-230
96Fin-S174
96FinRef-S174
96Fla-318
96Fle-478
96FleTif-478
96LeaSigA-71
96LeaSigAG-71
96LeaSigAS-71
96MetKah-9
96MetTeal-3
96Pac-134
96PacPri-P47
96PacPriG-P47
96Sco-290
96ScoDugC-B15
96ScoDugCAP-B15
96StaClu-114
96StaClu-266
96StaCluEPB-114
96StaCluEPG-114
96StaCluEPS-114
96StaCluMOP-114
96StaCluMOP-266
95StaCluVRMC-98
96Top-155
96TopGal-48
96TopGalPPI-48
96Ult-511
96UltGolM-511
96UppDec-400
97Cir-281
97CirRav-281
97ColCho-171
97DonLim-30
97DonLimLE-30
97Fin-288
97FinEmb-288
97FinEmbR-288
97FinRef-288
97Fle-394
97FleTif-394
97MetUni-192
97Pac-363
97PacLigB-363
97PacSil-363
97SP-121
97StaClu-373
97StaCluMOP-373
97Top-227
97TopGal-35
97TopGalPPI-35
97TopSta-86
97TopStaAM-86
97Ult-237
97UltGolME-237
97UltPlaME-237
97UppDec-119

Franco, Julio

80PenPilBT-21
80PenPilCT-17
81ReaPhiT-17
82OklCit8T-11
83Don-525
83IndPos-15
83IndWhe-13
83TopTra-34T
84AllGamPI-110
84Don-216
84Fle-542
84FleSti-111
84Ind-13
84IndWhe-14
84Nes792-48
84OPC-48
84Top-48
84TopRubD-13
84TopSti-379
84TopTif-48
85AllGamPI-21
85Don-94
85Fle-448
85Ind-14
85IndPol-14
85Lea-213
85OPC-237
85Top-237
85TopMin-237
85TopRubD-19
85TopSti-245
85TopTif-237
86Don-216
86Fle-586
86FleLeaL-13
86FleLimE-16
86FleMin-115
86FleSlu-9
86FleStiC-40
86IndOhH-14
86IndTeal-20
86KayB-14
86Lea-93
86OPC-391
86Spo-33
86Top-391
86TopSti-211
86TopTat-1
86TopTif-391
87Don-131
87DonOpeD-111
87Fle-251
87FleGlo-251
87FleLeaL-19
87FleLimE-15
87FleMin-37
87FleStiC-42
87IndGat-14
87Lea-131
87OPC-160
87RedFolSB-1
87Spo-84
87SpoTeaP-3
87StuPan-18
87Top-160
87TopSti-210
87TopTif-160
88ClaRed-187
88Don-10
88Don-156
88DonBasB-168
88DonSupD-10
88Fle-609
88FleAwaW-13
88FleBasA-11
88FleBasM-15
88FleExcS-14
88FleGlo-609
88FleHotS-11
88FleLeaL-12
88FleMin-19
88FleRecS-13
88FleStiC-19
88FleTeaL-8
88GreBasS-66
88IndGat-14
88Lea-10
88Lea-71
88MSAFanSD-10
88OPC-49
88PanSti-77
88RedFolSB-25
88Sco-60
88ScoGlo-60
88ScoYouS2-7
88Spo-58
88StaLinI-11
88Top-683
88TopBig-135
88TopSti-207
88TopTif-683
89Bow-228
89BowTif-228
89CadEllD-20
89Don-310
89DonBasB-32
89DonTra-31
89Fle-404
89FleAll-5
89FleGlo-404
89FleUpd-64
89MasBreD-11
89OPC-55
89PanSti-325
89RanMot-3
89RanSmo-9
89Sco-11
89ScoHot1S-36
89ScoRoo-35T
89ScoSco-29
89Spo-149
89Top-55
89Top-398
89TopBatL-14
89TopBig-288
89TopDouA-2
89TopSti-208
89TopStiB-4
89TopTif-55
89TopTif-398
89TopTra-34T
89TopTraT-34T
89UppDec-186
89UppDec-793
90Bow-497
90BowTif-497
90ClaBlu-67
90Don-142
90Don-701A
90Don-701B
90DonBesA-112
90DOnBonM-BC14
90DonLeaS-17
90Fle-296
90FleBasA-8
90FleCan-296
90K-M-18
90Lea-205
90OPC-386
90OPC-550
90PanSti-163
90PanSti-201
90PubSti-285
90PubSti-409
90RanMot-10
90RedFolSB-34
90Sco-160
90Sco100S-84
90ScoMcD-3
90Spo-158
90Top-386
90Top-550
90TopAmeA-21
90TopBatL-11
90TopBig-205
90TopDou-24
90TopGloA-14
90TopGloS-35
90TopMag-70
90TopMinL-37
90TopSti-159
90TopSti-243
90TopStiB-37
90TopTif-386
90TopTif-550
90TopTVA-2
90UppDec-82
90UppDec-103
90USPlaCA-JKO
90VenSti-184
90VenSti-185
90WinDis-6
91Bow-265
91Bow-368
91CadEllD-21
91Don-192
91Fle-285
91Lea-228
91OPC-387
91OPC-775
91PanFreS-253
91PanSti-210
91RanMot-10
91Sco-392
91Sco-493
91Sco100S-84
91SevCoi-T6
91StaClu-173
91StaCluMO-15
91Stu-123
91Top-387
91Top-775
91TopDesS-387
91TopDesS-775
91TopMic-387
91TopMic-775
91TopTif-387
91TopTif-775
91TopTriH-A13
91Ult-348
91UppDec-227
91UppDecSS-SS1
91USPlaCA-6H
92Bow-206
92Cla1-T36
92ClaGam-157
92Don-741
92DonCraJ2-27
92DonDiaK-DK4
92Fle-303
92Fle-690
92FleAll-18
92Fre-3
92Hig5-111
92Hig5S-12
92Lea-119
92MSABenSHD-9
92New-8
92OPC-490
92OPCPre-15
92PanSti-76
92PanSti-145
92Pin-150
92PinRool-5
92RanMot-10
92RanTeal-6
92Sco-108
92Sco-432
92Sco100S-38
92StaClu-440
92StaCluD-52
92Stu-241
92Top-398
92Top-490
92TopGol-398
92TopGol-490
92TopGolW-398
92TopGolW-490
92TopKid-129
92TopMcD-27
92TopMic-398
92TopMic-490
92TriPla-83
92Ult-131
92UppDec-241
93Bow-657
93Don-451
93Fin-161
93FinRef-161
93Fla-279
93Fle-320
93Lea-27
93LinVenB-22
93OPC-73
93PacBeiA-3
93PacBeiA-13
93PacBeiA-14
93PacSpa-310
93PacSpaPl-13
93PanSti-82
93Pin-104
93RanKee-405
93Sco-394
93Sel-58
93SP-192
93StaClu-651
93StaCluFDI-651
93StaCluMOP-651
93StaCluR-25
93Stu-103
93Top-670
93TopGol-670
93TopInaM-670
93TopMic-670
93TriPla-148
93Ult-277
93UppDec-656
93UppDecGold-656
94Bow-399
94BowBes-R74
94BowBesR-R74
94ColC-415
94ColChoGS-415
94ColChoSS-415
94Don-481
94ExtBas-46
94Fin-278
94FinRef-278
94Fla-276
94Fle-306
94FleUpd-25
94Lea-364
94LeaL-21
94OPC-142
94Pac-615
94PanSti-126
94Pin-520
94PinArtP-520
94PinMusC-520
94ProMag-30
94RanAllP-17
94RanAllP-18
94RanAllP-19
94Sco-413
94ScoGolR-413
94ScoRoo-RT29
94ScoRooGR-RT29
94Sel-288
94SP-191
94SPDieC-191
94SpoRoo-41
94SpoRooAP-41
94StaClu-680
94StaCluFDI-680
94StaCluGR-680
94StaCluMOP-680
94StaCluT-147
94StaCluTFDI-147
94Stu-205
94Top-260
94TopGol-260
94TopSpa-260
94TopTra-25T
94Ult-335
94UppDec-57
94UppDecED-57
94VenLinU-158
94WhiSoxK-8
95ColChoSE-231
95ColChoSEGS-231
95ColChoSESS-231
95Don-328
95DonPreP-328
95Fle-116
95Pac-87
95PacPri-28
95Sco-70
95ScoGolR-70
95ScoHaloG-HG42
95ScoPlaTS-70
95StaClu-248
95StaCluCT-5
95StaCluFDI-248
95StaCluMO-16
95StaCluMOP-248
95StaCluMOP-RL21
95StaCluRL-RL21
95StaCluSTWS-248
95StaCluVR-122
95Top-135
95TopCyb-83
95TopLeaL-LL13
95UltRBIK-5
95UltRBIKGM-5
96ColCho-770

96EmoXL-47
96Fin-B314
96FinRef-B314
96Fla-65
96FleUpd-U31
96FleUpdTC-U31
96LeaSigA-72
96LeaSigAG-72
96LeaSigAS-72
96Pin-347
96PinAfi-60
96PinAfiAP-60
96PinAfiFPP-60
96PinChrBC-15
96PinFoil-347
96Sel-120
96SelArtP-120
95StaCluVRMC-122
96Stu-82
96StuPrePB-82
96StuPrePG-82
96StuPrePS-82
96Ult-341
96UltGolM-341
96UppDec-492U
97Cir-101
97CirRav-101
97ColCho-87
97Don-330
97DonPreP-330
97DonPrePGold-330
97DonTea-89
97DonTeaSPE-89
97Fin-291
97FinEmb-291
97FinEmbR-291
97FinRef-291
97Fle-77
97FleTif-77
97Lea-236
97LeaFraM-236
97LeaFraMDC-236
97MetUni-80
97Pac-68
97PacLatotML-8
97PacLigB-68
97PacSil-68
97Sco-139
97ScoInd-5
97ScoIndPl-5
97ScoIndPr-5
97ScoIndU-5
97ScoIndUTC-5
97ScoPreS-139
97ScoShoS-139
97ScoShoSAP-139
97StaClu-65
97StaCluMOP-65
97Stu-131
97StuPrePG-131
97StuPrePS-131
97Top-241
97TopChr-85
97TopChrR-85
97TopGal-40
97TopGalPPI-40
97Ult-48
97UltGolME-48
97UltPlaME-48
97UppDec-51
Franco, Matt (Matthew)
87WytCubP-16
89ChaWheB-11
89ChaWheP-1748
89SouAtlLAGS-14
90PeoChiTI-11
91Cla/Bes-134
91WinSpiC-19
91WinSpiP-2836
92ChaKniF-2779
92ChaKniS-155
93OrlCubF-2791
94ActPac-46
94Cla-141
94ClaTriF-T13
94ExcFS7-164
94IowCubF-1281
94UppDecML-242
95IowCubTI-12
96ColCho-492
96ColChoGS-492
96ColChoSS-492
96Fle-317
96FleTif-317
96NorTidB-13
Francois, Manny
85VerBeaDT-5
87VerBeaDP-11
88SanAntMB-14
89SanAntMB-2
90CanIndB-8
90CanIndP-1298
Francona, Terry
80MemChiT-13
82Don-627
82ExpHygM-7
82ExpPos-12
82ExpZel-5
82ExpZel-11
82Fle-188
82OPC-118
82OPCPos-19
82Top-118
83Don-592
83ExpPos-6
83ExpStu-14
83Fle-281
83OPC-267
83Top-267
83TopSti-321
84Don-463
84ExpPos-9
84ExpStu-18
84Fle-275
84Nes792-496
84OPC-89
84Top-496
84TopTif-496
85Don-132
85Fle-398
85Lea-215
85OPC-258
85Top-134
85Top-578
85TopSti-88
85TopTif-134
85TopTif-578
86CubGat-16
86Don-401
86Fle-248
86FleUpd-43
86IowCubP-11
86Lea-191
86OPC-374
86Top-374
86TopSti-80
86TopTif-374
86TopTra-38T
86TopTraT-38T
87DonOpeD-193
87Fle-564
87FleGlo-564
87OPC-294
87RedKah-10
87Top-785
87TopTif-785
87TopTra-34T
87TopTraT-34T
88ColSprSSC-20
88ColSprSSP-1541
88Sco-297A
88Sco-297B
88ScoGlo-297A
88ScoGlo-297B
88StaLinRe-10
88Top-686
88TopTif-686
89BlaYNPRWL-125
89BlaYNPRWLU-46
89BrePol-30
89Sco-597
89Top-31
89TopTif-31
89TopTra-35T
89TopTraT-35T
89UppDec-536
90BrePol-30
90LouRedBLBC-16
90OPC-214
90Sco-216
90Top-214
90TopTif-214
90TopTVCa-48
90UppDec-180
92SouBenWSC-24
92SouBenWSF-193
93BirBarF-1207
93LinVenB-273
94BirBarC-26
94BirBarF-637
94BreMilB-220
96BirBarB-30
Francona, Tito (John)
47Exh-76
57Top-184
58Top-316
58WhiSoxJP-4
59Top-268
60IndJayP-1
60Kah-8
60Top-30
60Top-260
60TopTat-17
60TopVen-30
61Kah-12
61Pos-64A
61Pos-64B
61Top-503
61TopStal-134
62ExhStaB-13
62IndJayP-3
62Jel-40
62Kah-10
62Pos-40
62PosCan-40
62SalPlaC-15
62ShiPlaC-15
62Top-97
62TopBuc-28
62TopStal-34
62TopVen-97
63BasMagM-27
63ExhStaB-24
63Fle-12
63IndJayP-5
63Jel-67
63Pos-67
63Top-248
63Top-392
64ChatheY-29
64IndJayP-5
64Top-583
65CarTeal-10
65OPC-256
65Top-256
66OPC-163
66Top-163
66TopVen-163
67Top-443
68CokCapB-2
68Top-527
69MilBra-85
69Top-398
69TopSta-4
69TopTeaP-2
70MLBOffS-257
70Top-663
72MilBra-107
78TCM60I-205
78TCM60I-231
85Top-134
85TopTif-134
89PacLegI-133
89SweBasG-76
91OriCro-143
94BreMilB-221
Franek, Ken
88CalLeaACLC-49
Franek, Tom
93BatCliC-1
93BatCliF-3140
94SpaPhiF-1716
94SparPhiC-10
Franjul, Miguel
78CliDodT-11
79LodDodT-15
Frankhouse, Fred
33Gou-131
34DiaMatCSB-57
34BatR31-75
34DiaStaR-62
34GouCanV-19
35GouPuzR-4E
35GouPuzR-7E
35GouPuzR-12E
39PlaBal-70
79DiaGre-79
90DodTar-255
92ConTSN-498
93ConTSN-725
94ConTSN-1110
94ConTSNB-1110
Franklin, Ben
96PinFan-BF1
Franklin, Bo
94IdaFalBF-3598
Franklin, Elliott
76BurBeeT-11
Franklin, Glen
80MemChiT-10
82WatRedT-17
83IndIndTI-24
Franklin, James
93EriSaiC-7
93EriSaiF-3106
95DanBraTI-11
Franklin, Jay
89ButCopKSP-17
90GasRanB-11
90GasRanP-2516
90GasRanS-9
92GasRanF-2245
93DayCubC-7
93DayCubF-854
94DayCubC-6
94DayCubF-2344
Franklin, Jeff
78WauMetT-9
Franklin, Joel
93PriRedC-11
93PriRedF-4171
94BilMusF-3663
94BilMusSP-16
Franklin, Micah
90KinMetB-7
90KinMetS-8
91PitMetC-12
91PitMetP-3428
92BilMusSP-10
92BilMusF-3367
93ExcFS7-19
93WesVirWC-6
93WesVirWF-2876
94WinSpiC-1
94WinSpiF-283
95Bes-92
95Bow-39
95Emo-173
95SigRoo-20
95SigRooSig-20
95SPML-136
95UppDecML-57
96Exc-216
96FlePro-4
96TolMudHB-11
96UltGolP-5
96UltGolPGM-5
95UppDecMLFS-57
Franklin, Murray
50W720HolS-9
Franklin, Ryan
93BelMarC-13
93BelMarF-3202
94AppFoxC-9
94AppFoxF-1047
94RivPilCLC-21
95PorCitRTI-8
96PorCitRB-10
Franklin, Tony
76IndIndTI-23
79RocRedWT-7
89SarWhiSS-25
90SarWhiSS-26
91BirBarLD-74
91BirBarP-1469
91LinDriAA-74
92BirBarF-2598
92BirBarS-99
93SouBenWSF-1446
Franklin, Wayne
96YakBeaTI-16
Franko, Kris
93EveGiaC-10
93EveGiaF-3763
94ExcFS7-290
94SanJosGC-8
94SanJosGF-2810
Franko, Phil
82WisRapTF-18
83VisOakF-5
Franks, Herman
40DodTeal-8
43ParSpo-76
52Top-385
60RawGloT-7
65GiaTeal-2
65OPC-32
65Top-32
66Top-537
67OPC-116
67Top-116
68Top-267
68TopVen-267
75Gia195T-33
77TCMTheWY-46
77Top-518
78SSP270-268
78Top-234
79Top-551
83TopRep5-385
90DodTar-256
Franz, Rodney
51BerRos-C15
Fraraccio, Dan
93SouBenWSF-1438
94PriWilCC-9
94PriWilCF-1928
95PriWilCTI-6
96PriWilCB-12
Frascatore, John
91HamRedC-3
91HamRedP-4033
92SavCarC-8
92SavCarF-655
93SprCarC-10
93SprCarF-1844
94ArkTraF-3084
94BowBes-B81
94BowBesR-B81
95FleUpd-157
95LouRedF-273
95Top-656
96Bow-206
96ColCho-692
96ColChoGS-692
96ColChoSS-692
96LouRedB-18
96Sco-267
96SigRooOJ-10
96SigRooOJS-10
96Top-298
Frascatore, Steve
94NewJerCC-7
94NewJerCF-3408
95NewJerCTI-9
Fraser, Chick
06FanCraNL-19
11SpoLifCW-130
Fraser, Gretchen
52Whe-12A
52Whe-12B
Fraser, Joe
96ForWayWB-7
Fraser, Ron
85MiaHur-5
91MiaHurBB-6
92TopDaiQTU-33
92TopTra-35T
92TopTraG-35T
87PanAmTUBI-NNO
Fraser, Willie (Will)
86PalSprAP-9
86PalSprAP-13
87AngSmo-7
87Don-40
87DonRoo-9
87Fle-646
87FleGlo-646
87FleUpd-33
87FleUpdG-33
87Lea-40
87SpoRoo2-27
87TopTra-35T
87TopTraT-35T
88AngSmo-14
88Don-135
88Fle-490
88FleGlo-490
88OPC-363
88Sco-394
88ScoGlo-394
88StaLinAn-7
88Top-363
88TopBig-183
88TopTif-363
89Don-567
89Fle-478
89FleGlo-478
89Sco-157
89Top-679

89TopBig-272
89TopTif-679
89UppDec-613
90AngSmo-6
90Don-587
90Fle-133
90FleCan-133
90OPC-477
90PubSti-370
90Sco-358
90Top-477
90TopTif-477
90UppDec-85
90VenSti-186
91Bow-6
91Don-379
91Fle-314
91OPC-784
91OPCPre-46
91Sco-96
91StaClu-496
91Top-784
91TopDesS-784
91TopMic-784
91TopTif-784
91UppDec-699
92Don-755
92EdmTraF-3536
92EdmTraS-158
92Sco-721
92StaClu-33
93TolMudHF-1646
94EdmTraF-2869

Frash, Roger
82LynMetT-12

Frasier, Brad
94DavLipB-10
95DavLipB-12

Frasier, Vic
93ConTSN-982

Frassa, Bob
88BriTigP-1867

Fraticelli, Carl
90VisOakCLC-66
90VisOakP-2160

Frattare, Lanny
93PirNatI-11

Frauenhoffer, Mike
90GreFalDSP-21

Frazee, Harry
87SpoCubG-2

Frazier, Boxer (Joe)
92PhiDaiN-9

Frazier, Brad
92EriSaiC-3
92EriSaiF-1613
93KanCouCC-7
93KanCouCF-910
93KanCouCTI-7

Frazier, Fred
74SyrChiTI-7
75IntLeaAT-15
75IntLeaAT-20
77SalLakCGC-2
78KnoKnoST-6
79IowOakP-7
80IowOakP-5

Frazier, George
76BurBeeT-12
77HolMilT-10
78SprRedWK-23
79Car5-6
79Top-724
80Top-684
81Don-310
82Don-584
82Fle-35
82Top-349
83Don-535
83Fle-379
83Top-123
84CubChiT-12
84CubSev-39
84Don-591
84Fle-123
84FleUpd-40
84Ind-14
84Nes792-539
84OPC-139
84Top-539
84TopTif-539
84TopTra-39T
84TopTraT-39T
85CubLioP-12
85CubSev-39
85Don-167
85Fle-58
85OPC-19
85Top-19
85TopTif-19
86CubGat-39
86CubUno-10
86Don-411
86Fle-370
86Top-431
86TopTif-431
87Don-564
87Fle-539
87FleGlo-539
87Top-207
87TopTif-207
88Don-443
88Fle-9
88FleGlo-9
88Sco-332
88ScoGlo-332
88Top-709
88TopTif-709
88TwiTeal-13
92YanWIZ8-63

Frazier, Joe (Joseph F.)
55CarHunW-5
55Top-89
55TopDouH-83
56Top-141
60DarFar-22
75TidTidTI-12
76OPC-531
76SSP-610
76Top-531
77Top-259
82LouRedE-8
91OriCro-144

Frazier, Keith
45CenFlo-9

Frazier, Ken
81CliGiaT-18

Frazier, Lou
87AshTouP-7
88OscAstS-10
89ColMudB-12
89ColMudP-145
89ColMudS-10
90LonTigP-1276
91LinDriAA-383
91LonTigLD-383
91LonTigP-1889
92LonTigF-645
92LonTigS-406
92SkyAA F-173
93ExcFS7-171
93ExpPosN-11
93FleFinE-93
93Lea-515
93SelRoo-49T
94Don-524
94Fle-539
94Pac-381
94Sco-577
94ScoGolR-577
94Sel-263
94StaClu-517
94StaCluFDI-517
94StaCluGR-517
94StaCluMOP-517
94Top-192
94TopGol-192
94TopSpa-192
94USPlaCR-9D
95ColCho-242
95ColChoGS-242
95ColChoSS-242
95Don-388
95DonPreP-388
95Sco-135
95ScoGolR-135
95ScoPlaTS-135
95StaClu-15
95StaCluFDI-15
95StaCluMOP-15
95StaCluSTWS-15
95Top-441
95TopCyb-237
96ColCho-742
96ColChoGS-742
96ColChoSS-742
96LeaSigEA-55

Frazier, Ron
88CapCodPPaLP-90
90OneYanP-3376
91GreHorP-3052
92PriWilCC-21
92PriWilCF-140
93CarLeaAGF-22
93PriWilCC-11
93PriWilCF-650
94Bow-541
94ColCliF-2946
94ColCliP-10
94ExcFS7-103
95ColCliP-11
95ColCliTI-11
96ChaLooB-13

Frazier, Shawn
86SumBraP-5

Frazier, Terance
89FreStaBS-8
92SouOreAC-8
92SouOreAF-3423
93ModA'sC-10
93ModA'sF-811
94ModA'sC-11
94ModA'sF-3074

Frazier, Tyrone
95SpoIndTI-5

Fredbird, Mascot
93FunPacM-3
94MasMan-6
96CarPol-7

Frederick, Charlie
84ChaO'sT-3
85ChaO'sT-29
86ChaOriW-11
87ChaO'sW-NNO

Frederick, Chuck
90EugEmeGS-8

Frederick, Jim
89GeoColC-9

Frederick, John
28PorandAR-A8
28PorandAR-B8
34DiaMatCSB-58
34Gou-47
34GouCanV-85
83ConMar-38
85Woo-12
88ConNatA-6
90DodTar-257
90HOFStiB-34

Frederiksen, Kelly
90GatCitPP-3359
90GatCitPSP-10

Fredlund, Jay
79ElmPioRST-2
81BriRedST-15

Fredrickson, Scott
90SpoIndSP-16
91WatDiaC-4
91WatDiaP-1251
92SkyAA F-278
92WicWraF-3653
92WicWraS-629
93FleFinE-28
93Top-489
93TopGol-489
93TopInaM-489
93TopMic-489
96ColSprSSTI-13

Fredymond, Juan
85DurBulT-23
86DurBulP-11
87DurBulP-21
88SumBraP-409

Freeberger, George
92BluOriC-20
92BluOriF-2362

Freeburg, Larry
82CedRapRT-11

Freeburg, Ryan
92BenRocC-4
92BenRocF-1486
93SanBerSC-9
93SanBerSF-778
93StaCluM-46
93Top-616
93TopGol-616
93TopInaM-616
93TopMic-616
94CenValRC-7
94CenValRF-3206

Freed, Dan (Daniel)
88JamExpP-1899
89RocExpLC-9
90FloStaLAS-6
90StaFS7-8
90WesPalBES-8
91HarSenLD-253
91HarSenP-617
91LinDriAA-253
92LonTigF-626
92LonTigS-407

Freed, Roger
70OPC-477
70Top-477
71MLBOffS-176
71OPC-362
71PhiArcO-3
71Top-362
72OPC-69
72Top-69
77Car5-10
77CarTeal-9
78CarTeal-7
78Top-504
79Car5-7
79Top-111
80Top-418
91OrlCro-145
93UppDecS-11

Freehan, Bill
63Top-466
64TigJayP-5
64TigLid-6
64Top-407
64TopCoi-87
64TopGia-30
64TopSta-68
64TopTatI-37
65ChaTheY-27
65TigJayP-6
65Top-390
65TopEmbI-41
65TopTraI-12
66OPC-145
66Top-145
66TopRubI-33
66TopVen-145
67CokCapTi-9
67DexPre-76
67OPC-48
67TigDexP-2
67Top-48
67TopVen-212
68AtlOilPBCC-18
68Baz-2
68CokCapT-9
68DexPre-33
68Kah-A6
68Kah-B12
68TigDetFPB-5
68Top-375
68Top-470
68TopActS-11A
68TopGamI-11
69MilBra-86
69MLBOffS-47
69MLBPin-6
69NabTeaF-7
69OPCDec-6
69TigTeal-2
69TigTealC-3
69Top-390
69Top-431
69TopDec-10
69TopSta-172
69TopSup-18
69TopTeaP-1
70Kel-57
70MilBra-7
70MLBOffS-206
70OPC-335
70OPC-465
70Top-335
70Top-465
70TopBoo-6
70TopSup-7
71BazNumT-37
71BazUnn-10
71MilDud-6
71MLBOffS-391
71OPC-575
71Top-575
71TopCoi-38
71TopGreM-22
71TopSup-12
71TopTat-95
72Kel-31A
72Kel-31B
72MilBra-108
72OPC-120
72Top-120
73LinPor-69
73OPC-460
73TigJew-7
73Top-460
73TopCanL-18
73TopCom-7
73TopPin-7
74OPC-162
74Tig-4
74Top-162
74TopSta-174
75Hos-120
75OPC-397
75Top-397
76Hos-6
76HosTwi-6
76OPC-540
76Top-540
77BurCheD-94
77Top-22
78TCM60I-285
78TigDeaCS-16
81TigDetN-72
83TigAlKS-33
86SpoDecG-49
86TigSpoD-17
88PacLegI-93
88TigDom-5
89SweBasG-106
91UppDecS-22
93ActPacA-150

Freehill, Mike
94BoiHawC-10
94BoiHawF-3348
95CedRapKTI-23
95MidLeaA-16
96MidAngB-16
96MidAngOHP-11
96TexLeaAB-23

Freehling, Rick
92EriSaiC-21
92EriSaiF-1638
93SanBerSF-783

Freel, Ryan
95StCatSTI-17
96DunBluJB-9
96DunBluJTI-11

Freeland, Dean
85BelBreT-15
86CliGiaP-9
87ShrCapP-5
88ShrCapP-1285
89ShrCapP-1852
90ElPasDGS-12
91JacGenLD-558
91LinDriAA-558
91TucTorP-2208

Freeman, Buck (James J.)
03BreE10-52
04FanCraAL-20
04RedSoxUP-7
08RosComP-79
09RamT20-47
09T206-423
12ColRedB-109
12ColTinT-109

Freeman, Chris
95KnoSmoF-36
95TenVolW-2
96KnoSmoB-13

Freeman, Clarence
88KimN18-13

Freeman, Clem
82WatRedT-6
83TamTarT-12

Freeman, Hersh (Herschel)
53RedSoxTI-8
55Bow-290
56Kah-6
56Top-242
57Kah-8
57RedSoh-5
57Top-32
58RedEnq-13
58Top-27
79TCM50-120

Freeman, Jimmy
73OPC-610
73Top-610

76TulOilGP-10
Freeman, Julius
87OldJudN-182
Freeman, LaVell
86ElPasDP-11
87ElPasDP-1
87TexLeaAF-25
88DenZepC-20
88DenZepP-1277
88TriAAAP-12
88TriAAC-10
89DenZepC-14
89DenZepP-48
89UppDec-788
90CMC-394
90El PasDAGTI-31
90ProAAAF-391
90TolMudHC-17
90TolMudHP-161
90TopDeb89-39
94BreMilB-222
Freeman, Mark
59Top-532
79TCM50-265
Freeman, Marty
86GleFalTP-5
Freeman, Marvin
86ReaPhiP-8
87Don-576
87Fle-651
87FleGlo-651
87MaiGuiP-12
87MaiGuiT-4
87PhiTas-48
87SpoRooP-4
87SpoTeaP-6
88BlaYNPRWL-118
88MaiPhiC-4
88MaiPhiP-279
89Don-631
89Fle-566
89FleGlo-566
89ScoHot1R-34
89ScrRedBC-1
89Top-634
89TopTif-634
90CMC-228
90OPC-103
90ProAAAF-295
90PubSti-236
90ScrRedBC-2
90ScrRedBP-593
90Top-103
90TopTif-103
90VenSti-187
91BraDubP-9
91BraSubS-13
91Don-619
91FleUpd-73
92BraLykP-11
92BraLykS-12
92Don-603
92Fle-356
92Lea-110
92OPC-68
92Sco-307
92StaClu-264
92Top-68
92TopGol-68
92TopGolW-68
92TopMic-68
92Ult-458
92UppDec-491
93BraLykP-9
93BraLykS-11
93Don-662
93Fle-366
93Lea-11
93PacSpa-4
93StaClu-309
93StaCluB-24
93StaCluFDI-309
93StaCluMOP-309
93Top-583
93TopGol-583
93TopInaM-583
93TopMic-583
93Ult-304
93UppDec-519
93UppDecGold-519
94ColC-618
94ColChoGS-618
94ColChoSS-618
94Fin-327
94FinRef-327
94Fla-372
94Fle-357
94FleUpd-123
94RocPol-7
94ScoRoo-RT48
94ScoRooGR-RT48
94StaClu-701
94StaCluFDI-701
94StaCluGR-701
94StaCluMOP-701
94StaCluT-106
94StaCluTFDI-106
94Top-374
94TopGol-374
94TopSpa-374
94TopTra-49T
94Ult-479
95ColCho-444
95ColChoGS-444
95ColChoSE-204
95ColChoSEGS-204
95ColChoSESS-204
95ColChoSS-444
95Don-226
95DonPreP-226
95Fin-31
95FinRef-31
95Fla-129
95Fle-517
95Lea-259
95Pac-135
95PacPri-44
95PanSti-9
95Pin-432
95PinArtP-432
95PinMusC-432
95Sco-407
95ScoGolR-407
95ScoPlaTS-407
95StaClu-388
95StaCluMOP-388
95StaCluSTWS-388
95StaCluVR-204
95Top-465
95TopCyb-260
95Ult-373
95UltGolM-373
95UppDec-176
95UppDecED-176
95UppDecEDG-176
95UppDecSE-238
95UppDecSEG-238
96LeaSigA-73
96LeaSigAG-73
96LeaSigAS-73
96RocPol-7
95StaCluVRMC-204
96Top-93
Freeman, Pete
87WatPirP-9
88AugPirP-367
90MarPhiP-3193
Freeman, Rick
89EliTwiS-8
Freeman, Ricky
94HunCubF-3559
95RocCubTI-31
96DayCubB-11
94HunCubC-9
Freeman, Scott
90YakBeaTI-28
91Cla/Bes-357
91VerBeaDC-7
91VerBeaDP-768
92BakDodCLC-11
93VerBeaDF-2210
Freeman, Sean
94JamJamC-9
94JamJamF-3971
96JacSunB-12
Freeman, Terrance
96SouOreTI-22
Freer, Mike
91OscAstC-27
92OscAstC-27
93OscAstC-29
95JacGenTI-27
96JacGenB-27
Freese, Gene
55Top-205
56RedBurB-6
56Top-46
58Top-293
59RedBurBP-4
59Top-472
60Lea-140
60MacSta-8
60Top-435
60TopTat-18
60WhiSoxJP-3
60WhiSoxTS-6
61Kah-13
61Pos-30A
61Pos-30B
61Top-175
61TopStaI-17
62Jel-118
62Kah-11
62Pos-118
62PosCan-118
62RedEnq-8
62SalPlaC-137
62ShiPlaC-137
62Top-205
62TopStaI-115
63Fle-33
63Kah-10
63RedEnq-9
63Top-133
64PirKDK-10
64Top-266
64TopVen-266
65Top-492
66Top-319
66TopVen-319
79DiaGre-322
81TCM60I-304
Freese, George
55Bow-84
Fregin, Doug
82TolMudHT-27
Fregosi, Jim
85SprCarT-3
86St.PetCP-9
87ArkTraP-11
88ArkTraGS-16
89WesPalBES-11
91BenBucC-12
91BenBucP-3711
Fregosi, Jim Louis
62Top-209
63AngJayP-5
63Top-167
64Baz-22
64Top-97
64TopCoi-98
64TopCoi-128
64TopGia-18
64TopSta-60
64TopStaU-25
64TopTatI-38
64TopVen-97
65Baz-22
65OldLonC-25
65OPC-210
65Top-210
65TopEmbI-39
65TopTraI-13
66Baz-19
66OPC-5
66Top-5
66TopRubI-34
66TopVen-5
67Baz-19
67CokCapA-8
67CokCapAAm-24
67CokCapDA-30
67Top-385
67TopGiaSU-9
67TopVen-244
68AtlOilPBCC-19
68Baz-9
68DexPre-34
68OPC-170
68Top-170
68Top-367
68TopActS-9A
68TopGamI-33
68TopPla-3
68TopPos-4
68TopVen-170
68TopVen-367
69AngJacitB-3
69CitMetC-7
69MilBra-87
69MLBOffS-21
69MLBPin-7
69NabTeaF-8
69Top-365
69TopDec-5
69TopDecI-11
69TopSta-144
69TopSup-7
69TopTeaP-17
69TraSta-14
70DayDaiNM-94
70Kel-36
70MilBra-8
70MLBOffS-172
70Top-570
70TopSup-30
70TraSta-14B
71AngJacitB-4
71BazNumT-25
71BazUnn-13
71Kel-64A
71Kel-64B
71Kel-64C
71Kel-64D
71MilDud-7
71MLBOffS-344
71OPC-360
71Top-360
71TopCoi-136
71TopGreM-16
71TopTat-18
71TopTat-19
72MilBra-109
72OPC-115
72OPC-346
72Top-115
72Top-346
72Top-755
72TopCloT-13
73LinPor-175
73NewYorN-11
73OPC-525
73Top-525
74Top-196
74TopSta-234
75OPC-339
75Top-339
76OPC-635
76SSP-262
76Top-635
77PirPosP-6
78TCM60I-170
78Top-323
79Top-424
80Top-214
81Don-414
81Fle-274
81LonBeaPT-26
81Top-663
83LouRedR-1
84LouRedR-1
85AngStrH-6
85LouRedR-1
86AngGreT-3
86LouRedTI-1
86TopTra-39T
86TopTraT-39T
87Top-318
87TopTif-318
87WhiSoxC-11
88Top-714
88TopTif-714
88WhiSoxC-7
89AngSmo-3
89Top-414
89TopTif-414
91MDAA-15
91MetWIZ-127
91TopTra-43T
91TopTraT-43T
92OPC-669
92PhiMed-13
92Top-669
92TopGol-669
92TopGolW-669
92TopMic-669
93PhiMed-14
93RanKee-154
93TedWil-18
93Top-510
93TopGol-510
93TopInaM-510
93TopMic-510
93UppDecAH-55
94PhiMed-10
95Phi-11
96PhiTeaI-12
Fregoso, Dan
92BluOriC-4
92BluOriF-2356
Freigau, Howard
21Exh-52
25Exh-20
26Exh-20
90DodTar-953
Freiling, Howard
88VerBeaDS-7
89JacMetGS-18
90JacMetGS-11
91ColMetPI-3
92PitMetC-20
92PitMetF-3311
93PitMetC-25
93PitMetF-3726
94PitMetC-25
94PitMetF-3538
Freire, Alejandro
95MidLeaA-17
95QuaCitRBTI-6
96KisCobB-8
Freisleben, Dave
74OPC-599
74PadDea-8
74Top-599A
74Top-599B
74Top-599C
75OPC-37
75Top-37
76HawIslC-16
76OPC-217
76SSP-116
76Top-217
77PadSchC-22A
77PadSchC-22B
77Top-407
78PadFamF-12
78Top-594
79BluJayBY-8
79Top-168
80OPC-199
80Top-382
89ButCopKSP-30
Freitag, Dusty
92RocExpC-26
92RocExpF-2119
Freitas, Antonio
36GouWidPPR-A33
40SolHug-6
46SunBre-6
47SigOil-62
47SunBre-8
49BowPCL-11
79DiaGre-255
Freitas, Joe
96NewJerCB-10
Freitas, Mike
90PitMetP-24
91ColMetPI-23
91ColMetPPI-2
92St.LucMCB-7
92St.LucMF-1740
93ClaGolF-170
95MemChiTI-12
96MemChiB-13
French, Anton
95PeoChiTI-18
96DurBulBIB-15
96Top-437
French, Charlie
12ImpTobC-25
French, Jim
69TopFou-6
71RicBraTI-7
French, Kevin
90NebCor-11
French, Larry
34BatR31-132
34Gou-29
34GouCanV-79
36DiaMatCS3T2-8
36SandSW-20
39CubTeaI-5
41CubTeaI-4
41DouPlaR-1
42DodTeaI-7
76ChiGre-7
79DiaGre-360
80CubGreT-4
83ConMar-47
83TCMPla1942-30

88ConNatA-7
90DodTar-258
92ConTSN-416
95ConTSN-1340
French, Lee
89CarNewE-6
French, Ray
20WalMaiW-17
French, Richard J.
66Top-333
66TopVen-333
69OPC-199
69Top-199
70Top-617
71MLBOffS-538
71OPC-399
71Top-399
French, Ron
90JohCitCS-12
91HamRedC-27
91HamRedP-4052
92HamRedC-7
92HamRedF-1605
93SavCarC-14
93SavCarF-700
French, Steve
84ButCopKT-11
French, Walter
33Gou-177
79DiaGre-329
92ConTSN-397
94ConTSN-1143
94ConTSNB-1143
Frew, Mike
85BelBreT-16
86StoPorP-8
87StoPorP-15
Frey, Al
87AllandGN-49
Frey, Benjamin R.
34DiaMatCSB-59
34ButPreR-22
36R31PasP-11
81DiaStaCD-109
92ConTSN-381
Frey, Eric
77NewCoPT-15
Frey, Jim
73OPC-136
73Top-136A
73Top-136B
74OPC-306
74Top-306
80Top-66
81Don-464
81Top-667
82MetPhoA-28
84CubChiT-13
84CubSev-NNO
84CubUno-8
84CubUno-10
84CubUno-12
84Nes792-51
84Top-51
84TopTif-51
85CubLioP-13
85CubSev-NNO
85Top-241
85TopTif-241
86RoyGreT-12
86Top-231
86TopTif-231
Frey, Lonny (Linus R.)
34DiaMatCSB-60
34Gou-89
35DiaMatCS3T1-54
35GouPuzR-1G
35GouPuzR-3E
35GouPuzR-5E
35GouPuzR-14E
36DiaMatCS3T2-9
36GouWidPPR-A34
38CinOraW-9
39OrcPhoAP-8
39OrcPhoAP-28
39PlaBal-161
40PlaBal-76
41DouPlaR-5
41HarHarW-6
79DiaGre-81
81DiaStaCD-117
83TCMPla1942-36
90DodTar-259
93ConTSN-812
Frey, Steve
85AlbYanT-7
87AlbYanP-23
87Ft.LauYP-3
88MetColP-24
88TidTidCa-20
88TidTidCM-6
88TidTidP-1602
89ExpPos-7
89IndIndC-3
89IndIndP-1218
89MetColP-29
90ExpPos-9
90Fle-649
90FleCan-649
90FleUpd-28
90OPC-91
90Top-91
90TopDeb89-40
90TopTif-91
91Bow-451
91Don-292
91ExpPos-6
91Fle-231
91Lea-153
91OPC-462
91PanFreS-154
91Sco-436
91Top-462
91TopDesS-462
91TopMic-462
91TopTif-462
91Ult-202
91UppDec-397
92Don-660
92Fle-479
92Lea-418
92OPC-174
92StaClu-572
92Top-174
92TopGol-174
92TopGolW-174
92TopMic-174
92Ult-222
93AngMot-22
93Don-533
93Fle-573
93Lea-488
93PacSpa-368
93StaCluAn-12
93Top-728
93TopGol-728
93TopInaM-728
93TopMic-728
93UppDec-750
93UppDecGold-750
94Don-142
94Fle-56
94FleUpd-192
94GiaAMC-9
94GiaMot-18
94Pin-185
94PinArtP-185
94PinMusC-185
94Sco-250
94ScoGolR-250
94StaCluT-26
94StaCluTFDI-26
94Top-503
94TopGol-503
94TopSpa-503
94Ult-22
95Fle-579
95MarMot-22
95Top-201
96PhiTeal-13
Frias, Hanley
92GulCoaRSP-12
93ChaRaiC-7
93ChaRaiF-1919
94HigDesMC-11
94HigDesMF-2796
96TulDriTI-10
Frias, Israel
89BluOriS-10
90BenBucL-25
Frias, Joe
91SpoIndC-27
91SpoIndP-3956
Frias, Pepe (Jesus M.)
72Dia-18
73OPC-607
73Top-607
74OPC-468
74Top-468
75OPC-496
75Top-496
76ExpRed-10
76OPC-544
76SSP-331
76Top-544
77ExpPos-14
77OPC-225
77Top-199
78OPC-171
78Top-654
79OPC-146
79Top-294
80OPC-48
80Top-87
81DodPol-36
81Fle-134
81LonBeaPT-25
89PacSenL-106
90DodTar-260
91CliGiaC-18
92SanJosGC-21
93RanKee-155
Friberg, Barney (A. Bernhardt)
26Exh-42
29ExhFou-11
31Exh-12
33Gou-105
34GouCanV-10
91ConTSN-297
Fric, Sean
93HunCubC-8
93HunCubF-3249
94PeoChiC-8
94PeoChiF-2278
94WilCubC-7
94WilCubF-3777
Fricano, Marion
53Top-199
54Bow-3
54Top-124
55A'sRodM-15
55Bow-316
57HygMea-4
91TopArc1-199
94TopArc1-124
94TopArc1G-124
Frick, Ford
49EurSta-2
59FleWil-48
59Top-1
59TopVen-1
60Fle-74
61Fle-29
76ShaPiz-117
80PerHaloFP-117
80SSPHOF-117
95ConTSN-1395
Frick, James
11T205-192
Frick, Tod
91SouOreAP-3848
Fricke, Dave
90KinMetB-28
90KinMetS-28
92ColMetC-29
92ColMetPI-32
Fridley, Jim
52Top-399
53Top-187
54OriEss-12
59RedEnq-7
72TopTes5-4
83TopRep5-399
91OriCro-146
91TopArc1-187
Fridman, Jason
91ElmPioC-5
Friedel, Chuck
84LitFalMT-5
Friederich, Mike
85OscAstTI-7
86ColAstP-13
Friedland, Michael
90JamExpP-12
91RocExpC-19
91RocExpP-2054
Friedman, Jason
90ElmPioP-5
90WinHavRSS-9
91ElmPioP-3277
92LynRedSC-6
92LynRedSF-2913
93ExcFS7-132
94FloStaLAF-FSL17
94SarRedSC-8
94SarRedSF-1955
95BowBayTI-39
96PorCitRB-11
Friedrich, Steve
96MidLeaAB-50
96SouBenSHS-12
Friel, Bill
03BreE10-53
09ColChiE-110
11SpoLifCW-131
12ColRedB-110
12ColTinT-110
Friend, Bob
47Exh-77
52Bow-191
52Top-233
53BowC-16
54Bow-43
54DanDee-7
55Bow-57
56Top-221
56YelBasP-10
57Kah-9
57Top-150
58Hir-24
58HirTes-4
58JayPubA-7
58Kah-10
58Top-315
58Top-334
58Top-492
59Kah-9
59Top-428
59Top-460
59Top-569
60Kah-9
60KeyChal-17
60Lea-53
60PirJayP-5
60PirTag-19
60Top-437
61Kah-14
61PirJayP-4
61PirRigF-2
61Pos-125A
61Pos-125B
61Top-45
61Top-270
61Top-585
62Jel-178
62Kah-12
62Pos-178
62PosCan-178
62SalPlaC-157
62ShiPlaC-157
62Top-520
62TopBuc-29
62TopStal-176
63BasMagM-28
63Jel-145
63Kah-11
63PirIDL-8
63PirJayP-6
63Pos-145
63Top-450
64Baz-6
64Kah-9
64PirKDK-11
64Top-1
64Top-20
64TopCoi-77
64TopGia-28
64TopSta-66
64TopStaU-26
64TopTatl-39
64TopVen-1
64TopVen-20
65Kah-14
65OldLonC-10
65Top-392
66Top-519
78TCM60I-160
79DiaGre-375
83TopRep5-233
84OCoandSI-224
87Pir196T-8
88PacLegI-78
89SweBasG-86
91MetWIZ-128
91TopArc1-298
92BazQua5A-22
92YanWIZ6-43
Friend, Owen
50Bow-189
51Bow-101
52Top-160
53TigGle-8
54Bow-212
55Bow-256
57SeaPop-15
83TopRep5-160
Frierson, John
83MiaMarT-19
Frierson, Mike
80WauTimT-19
Friesen, Rob
87FayGenP-26
Frill, John E.
09ColChiE-111
09T206-135
11SpoLifM-282
12ColRedB-111
12ColTinT-111
Frink, Keith
88WauTimGS-7
Frisch, Frankie (Frank)
20NatCarE-30
21E121So1-26
21E121So8-24
21Exh-53
21KoBreWSI-10
21Nei-62
21OxfConE-6
22E120-185
22W572-29
22W573-43
22W575-37
22WilPatV-24
23W501-62
23W501-105
23W503-21
23W515-14
23WilChoV-45
25Exh-33
26Exh-34
27YorCarE-50
28Exh-31
28PorandAR-A9
28PorandAR-B9
28StaPlaCE-22
28W502-50
28W512-8
28Yue-50
29ExhFou-15
29PorandAR-27
30SchR33-4
31Exh-15
31W517-16
32R33So2-419
32USCar-30
33ButCre-9
33CraJacP-6
33DouDisP-18
33ExhFou-8
33GeoCMil-13
33Gou-49
33GouCanV-49
33NatLeaAC-11
33RitCE-3S
33RitCE-7S
34DiaMatCSB-61
34BatR31-33
34BatR31-173
34ButPreR-23
34DiaStaR-17
34ExhFou-8
34Gou-13
34GouCanV-64
34WarBakSP-4
35DiaMatCS2-6
35DiaMatCS3T1-55
35ExhFou-8
35GolMedFR-5
35GouPuzR-1A
35GouPuzR-2A
35GouPuzR-16A
35GouPuzR-17A
35WheBB1-12
36DiaMatCS4-4
36ExhFou-8
36GouWidPPR-A35
36NatChiFPR-27
36PC7AlbHoF-51
36R31Pre-G8

36SandSW-21
36WorWidGV-107
40PlaBal-167
46SpoExcW-2-4
48ExhHoF-11
50Bow-229
50CalHOFW-32
51Bow-282
51R42SmaS-32
61Fle-30
61GolPre-19
66CarCoi-7
67TopVen-165
68LauWorS-19
74Car193T-10
76MotOldT-7
76RowExh-3
76ShaPiz-51
77GalGloG-53
77GalGloG-207
80GiaGreT-6
80PacLeg-46
80PerHaloFP-51
80SSPHOF-51
81ConTSN-23
81SpoHaloF-16
82DiaCla-14
83ConMar-41
83TCMPla1945-34
85FegMurCG-6
85Woo-13
86ConSer1-14
87Car193T-5
87HygAllG-19
88ConNatA-8
88ConSer5-11
89HOFStiB-13
89PacLegI-113
90PerGreM-57
91ConTSN-11
91ConTSN-305
91ConTSNP-664
92CarMcD-7
92ConTSN-634
92ConTSNAP-664G
93ConTSN-664
93ConTSN-835
94ConTSN-1091
94ConTSN-1233
94ConTSNB-1091
94ConTSNB-1233
95MegRut-24

Frisella, Danny (Dan)
68OPC-191
68Top-191
68TopVen-191
69Top-343
71MLBOffS-151
71OPC-104
71Top-104
72OPC-293
72OPC-294
72Top-293
72Top-294
72TopCloT-14
73OPC-432
73Top-432
74OPC-71
74Top-71
75OPC-343
75Top-343
76OPC-32
76SSP-117
76Top-32
77Top-278
81TCM60I-470
89TidTidC-1
91MetWIZ-129
94BreMilB-27

Frisz, Paul
76ISCHooHA-26

Fritsch, Ted Sr.
77FriOneYW-8

Fritz, Charles
09T206-485
10CouT21-24
94IdaFalBF-3577
94IdaFalBSP-10

Fritz, Greg
91UtiBluSC-19
91UtiBluSP-3234
92SalSpuC-2
93SouBenWSC-9
93SouBenWSF-1423

Fritz, John
88BenBucL-20
88PalSprACLC-87
88PalSprAP-1445
90PalSprACLC-221
90PalSprAP-2572
91MelBusF-7
91MiaMirC-7
91MiaMirP-401
92QuaCitRBC-10
92QuaCitRBF-801
93ExcFS7-142
93ExcLeaLF-5
93MidAngF-316
94ExcFS7-26
94MidAngOHP-4
94VanCanF-1859
97MidAngOHP-11

Frobel, Doug
78ChaPirT-6
81BufBisT-22
82PorBeaT-20
84Don-38
84Nes792-264
84Top-264
84TopTif-264
85Fle-464
85Top-587
85TopSti-128
85TopTif-587
86BasStaB-43
86TidTidP-9
87BufBisP-7
89BirBarB-7
89BirBarP-105

Frock, Sam
10SepAnoP-13
11SpoLifM-139
12ImpTobC-13

Froemming, Bruce
88T/MUmp-11
89T/MUmp-9
90T/MUmp-9

Frohwirth, Todd
86ClePhiP-9
87PhiTas-52
87ReaPhiP-19
88DonRoo-3
88Fle-301
88FleGlo-301
88MaiPhiC-10
88MaiPhiP-296
88PhiTas-10
88Top-378
88TopTif-378
89Don-587
89Fle-567
89FleGlo-567
89PhiTas-7
89Sco-647
89ScoHot1R-14
89Top-542
89TopTif-542
90CMC-250
90Don-631
90OPC-69
90ProAAAF-296
90ScrRedBC-24
90ScrRedBP-594
90Top-69
90TopTif-69
90UppDec-443
91LinDriAAA-456
91RocRedWLD-456
91RocRedWP-1896
92Don-317
92FleUpd-1
92OPC-158
92Pin-411
92ProFS7-3
92Sco-534
92StaClu-358
92Top-158
92TopGol-158
92TopGolW-158
92TopMic-158
92TopPreS-18
92Ult-302
92UppDec-318
93Don-513
93Fle-166
93PacSpa-342
93StaClu-445
93StaCluFDI-445
93StaCluMOP-445
93Top-415
93TopGol-415
93TopInaM-415
93TopMic-415
93Ult-494
93UppDec-191
93UppDecGold-191
94Fle-4
94Pac-30
94PawRedSF-943
94Sco-226
94ScoGolR-226
94StaClu-248
94StaCluFDI-248
94StaCluGR-248
94StaCluMOP-248
94Top-242
94TopGol-242
94TopSpa-242

Frohwith, Tod
94Don-389

Frolin, Darrel
75AndRanT-67

Fromme, Art
09AmeCarE-41
09ColChiE-112
09RamT20-48
09T206-136
10CouT21-136
10DomDisP-46
10PeoT21-24
10RedCroT-26
10RedCroT-113
10RedCroT-194
10SweCapPP-98
11S74Sil-74
11SpoLifCW-132
11SpoLifM-193
11T205-61
11TurRedT-93
12ColRedB-112
12ColTinT-112
12HasTriFT-73A
12T207-63
14PieStaT-23
15AmeCarE-18
15VicT21-11

Froning, Tom
93BelBreC-8
93BelBreF-1704

Fronio, Jason
91WatIndC-5
91WatIndP-3360
92WatIndC-3
92WatIndF-3226
93CarLeaAGF-30
93KinIndC-10
93KinIndF-2241
93KinIndTI-9
94CanIndF-3114
94ExcFS7-43
94KinIndC-5
94KinIndF-2635

Frontera, Chad
94EveGiaC-8
94EveGiaF-3644
95Bow-51

Froschaner, Trevor
93AubAstC-10
93AubAstF-3447

Frost, Brady
94VerExpC-11
94VerExpF-3906

Frost, C. David
76VenLeaS-189
78AngFamF-11
79Top-703
80Top-423
81Don-52
81Fle-275
81SalLakCGT-6
81Top-286
82Don-290
82Fle-460A
82Fle-460B
82Roy-7
82Top-24
82TopTra-37T
83Fle-111
83Top-656
78STLakCGC-25

Frost, Jerald
87SumBraP-1
88BurBraP-8
89DurBullS-12
89DurBulTI-12

Frostad, Mike
96StCatSB-3

Fruge, Chris
90UtiBluSP-17

Fruge, Jeff
82QuaCitCT-8
83QuaCitCT-10

Fry, Brian
89BilMusP-2051
90BilMusP-3215

Fry, Dave
84ModA'sC-27

Fry, Jerry
75WesPalBES-13
79Top-720

Fry, W.J.
87OldJudN-183

Frye, Dan
92PriRedC-23
92PriRedF-3093
93Bow-698
93ClaGolF-212
93ClaMVPF-8
93ExcFS7-20
93WesVirWC-7
93WesVirWF-2870
94WinSpiC-9
94WinSpiF-277

Frye, Jeff
88ButCopKSP-14
89GasRanP-1023
89GasRanS-7
89SouAtlLAGS-27
89Sta-137
90ChaRanS-7
91LinDriAA-579
91TulDriLD-579
91TulDriP-2778
91TulDriTI-7
92DonRoo-40
92FleUpd-60
92OklCit8F-1920
92OklCit8S-310
92SkyAAAF-142
93Don-724
93Fle-321
93LinVenB-195
93Pin-496
93RanKee-406
93Sco-274
93StaClu-133
93StaCluFDI-133
93StaCluMOP-133
93Top-197
93TopGol-197
93TopInaM-197
93TopMic-197
93Ult-278
93UppDec-371
93UppDecGold-371
93USPlaCR-7C
94FleUpd-91
94StaCluT-261
94StaCluTFDI-261
94VenLinU-164
95ColCho-401
95ColChoGS-401
95ColChoSS-401
95D3-31
95Don-297
95DonPreP-297
95DonTopotO-158
95Fla-87
95Fle-284
95Lea-147
95Pac-425
95Pin-92
95PinArtP-92
95PinMusC-92
95RanCra-9
95Sco-269
95ScoGolR-269
95ScoPlaTS-269
95Sel-4
95SelArtP-4
95StaClu-230
95StaCluFDI-230
95StaCluMOP-230
95StaCluSTWS-230
95Top-591
95TopCyb-363
95Ult-334
95UltGolM-334
95UppDec-393
95UppDecED-393
95UppDecEDG-393
96ColCho-321
96ColChoGS-321
96ColChoSS-321
96Don-473
96DonPreP-473
96Fle-248
96FleTif-248
96Pin-13
96Sco-405
96StaClu-361
96StaCluMOP-361
96Ult-133
96UltGolM-133
97Don-241
97DonPreP-241
97DonPrePGold-241
97DonTea-53
97DonTeaSPE-53
97Fle-21
97FleTif-21
97Pac-38
97PacLigB-38
97PacSil-38
97Pin-7
97PinArtP-7
97PinMusC-7
97Sco-200
97ScoPreS-200
97ScoRedS-10
97ScoRedSPl-10
97ScoRedSPr-10
97ScoShoS-200
97ScoShoSAP-200
97Ult-484
97UltGolME-484
97UltPlaME-484

Frye, Paul
86JamExpP-8
87WesPalBEP-654
88RocExpLC-14

Frye, Walter
94CarLeaA-DJ21

Fryer, Paul
82ReaPhiT-14

Fryhoff, John
83TriTriT-10

Fryman, Travis
88FayGenP-1094
89BasAmeAPB-AA2
89EasLeaAP-4
89LonTigP-1366
90Bow-360
90BowTif-360
90CMC-395
90FleUpd-96
90ProAAAF-385
90TolMudHC-18
90TolMudHP-155
90TopTra-33T
90TopTraT-33T
90TriAllGP-AAA30
91Bow-145
91Cla1-T40
91ClaGam-124
91Don-768
91Fle-336
91Lea-149
91MajLeaCP-34
91OPC-128
91RedFolS-106
91Sco-570
91Sco100RS-68
91SevCoi-M5
91StaClu-355
91Stu-54
91TigCok-24
91TigPol-4
91Top-128
91TopDeb90-49
91TopDesS-128
91TopMic-128
91TopRoo-9
91TopTif-128
91ToyRoo-8
91Ult-122
91UppDec-225
92Bow-37
92ClaGam-88
92Don-349

92DonCraJ1-11
92Fle-134
92Hig5-47
92Lea-304
92LeaBlaG-304
92OPC-750
92OPCPre-56
92PanSti-107
92Pin-110
92PinTea2-4
92Sco-65
92ScoImpP-47
92ScoProP-19
92StaClu-59
92Stu-174
92Top-750
92TopGol-750
92TopGolW-750
92TopKid-78
92TopMic-750
92TriPla-86
92Ult-60
92UppDec-466
92UppDec-643
93Bow-67
93ClaGam-35
93Don-127
93Fin-135
93FinRef-135
93Fla-202
93Fle-228
93FleFruotL-20
93FunPac-187
93Lea-16
93LeaFas-19
93OPC-76
93OPCPre-102
93PacSpa-108
93PanSti-117
93Pin-79
93PinHomRC-48
93PinSlu-30
93PinTea2-10
93Sco-11
93Sel-44
93SP-237
93StaClu-298
93StaClu-448
93StaCluFDI-298
93StaCluFDI-448
93StaCluM-168
93StaCluMO-9
93StaCluMOP-298
93StaCluMOP-448
93StaCluMP-16
93Stu-108
93StuSil-5
93TigGat-8
93Top-392
93Top-404
93TOPBLAG-31
93TopGol-392
93TopGol-404
93TopInaM-392
93TopInaM-404
93TopMic-392
93TopMic-404
93Toy-87
93TriPla-59
93Ult-197
93UppDec-364
93UppDec-455
93UppDec-836
93UppDecDG-25
93UppDecGold-364
93UppDecGold-455
93UppDecGold-836
94Bow-621
94BowBes-R61
94BowBes-X108
94BowBesR-R61
94BowBesR-X108
94ChuHomS-15
94ChuHomSG-15
94ColC-375
94ColChoGS-375
94ColChoSS-375
94Don-378
94DonSpeE-378
94ExtBas-74
94Fin-228
94FinJum-228
94FinRef-228
94Fla-292
94Fle-129
94FleAllS-8
94FUnPac-80
94FUnPac-179
94KinDis-10
94Lea-405
94LeaL-32
94OPC-209
94Pac-216
94PanSti-64
94Pin-183
94PinArtP-183
94PinMusC-183
94PinPowS-PS14
94PinRunC-RC9
94PinTheN-21
94ProMag-50
94Sco-11
94ScoGolR-11
94ScoGolS-48
94Sel-295
94SelSki-SK10
94SP-177
94SPDieC-177
94SPHol-9
94SPHolDC-9
94Spo-16
94Spo-178
94SpoFanA-AS3
94StaClu-309
94StaCluFDI-309
94StaCluGR-309
94StaCluMOP-309
94Stu-191
94Top-285
94TopBlaG-6
94TopGol-285
94TopSpa-285
94TriPla-244
94TriPlaM-9
94Ult-53
94UltRisS-5
94UppDec-37
94UppDec-51
94UppDec-345
94UppDecAJ-23
94UppDecAJG-23
94UppDecED-37
94UppDecED-51
94UppDecED-345
95Baz-59
95Bow-302
95BowBes-R70
95BowBes-X7
95BowBesR-R70
95BowBesR-X7
95ClaPhoC-27
95ColCho-465
95ColChoGS-465
95ColChoSE-222
95ColChoSEGS-222
95ColChoSESS-222
95ColChoSS-465
95D3-51
95Don-82
95DonDiaK-DK21
95DonDom-5
95DonPreP-82
95DonTopotO-75
95Emb-50
95EmbGolI-50
95Emo-43
95Fin-42
95FinRef-42
95Fla-39
95Fle-51
95FleAllS-14
95Lea-207
95LeaCor-2
95LeaLim-52
95Pac-152
95PacPri-49
95PanSti-59
95Pin-124
95PinArtP-124
95PinMusC-124
95PinPin-12
95PinPinR-12
95PinTeaP-TP6
95RedFol-18
95Sco-341
95ScoGolR-341
95ScoHaloG-HG79
95ScoPlaTS-341
95Sel-132
95SelArtP-132
95SelCer-40
95SelCerMG-40
95Spo-90
95SpoArtP-90
95StaClu-6
95StaCluCT-18
95StaCluFDI-6
95StaCluMO-17
95StaCluMOP-6
95StaCluSTWS-6
95StaCluVR-2
95Stu-27
95StuGolS-27
95Sum-91
95SumNthD-91
95Top-40
95TopCyb-32
95TopPre-PP5
95UC3-40
95UC3ArtP-40
95Ult-285
95UltGolM-285
95UppDec-185
95UppDecED-185
95UppDecEDG-185
95UppDecSE-232
95UppDecSEG-232
95Zen-105
96Baz-19
96Bow-106
96BowBes-69
96BowBesAR-69
96BowBesR-69
96Cir-39
96CirRav-39
96ColCho-550
96ColChoGS-550
96ColChoSS-550
96Don-176
96DonPreP-176
96EmoXL-60
96Fin-B152
96FinRef-B152
96Fla-80
96Fle-111
96FleTeaL-6
96FleTif-111
96Lea-68
96LeaLim-26
96LeaLimG-26
96LeaPre-14
96LeaPreP-14
96LeaPrePB-68
96LeaPrePG-68
96LeaPrePS-68
96LeaPreSG-4
96LeaPreSte-4
96LeaSigA-74
96LeaSigAG-74
96LeaSigAS-74
96MetUni-59
96MetUniP-59
96Pac-315
96PanSti-143
96Pin-14
96PinAfi-86
96PinAfiAP-86
96PinAfiFPP-86
96PinArtP-9
96PinSta-9
96ProSta-123
96Sco-309
96ScoDugC-B34
96ScoDugCAP-B34
96Sel-13
96SelArtP-13
96SelCer-40
96SelCerAP-40
96SelCerCB-40
96SelCerCR-40
96SelCerMB-40
96SelCerMG-40
96SelCerMR-40
96SelTeaN-13
96SP-83
96Spo-68
96SpoArtP-68
96StaClu-431
96StaCluEPB-431
96StaCluEPG-431
96StaCluEPS-431
96StaCluMOP-431
95StaCluVRMC-2
96Stu-113
96StuPrePB-113
96StuPrePG-113
96StuPrePS-113
96Sum-26
96SumAbo&B-26
96SumArtP-26
96SumFoi-26
96TeaOut-26
96Top-190
96TopChr-60
96TopChrR-60
96TopGal-32
96TopGalPPI-32
96TopLas-81
96Ult-60
96UltGolM-60
96UppDec-328
96Zen-9
96ZenArtP-9
97Bow-259
97BowBes-81
97BowBesAR-81
97BowBesR-81
97BowChr-81
97BowChrI-81
97BowChrIR-81
97BowChrR-81
97BowInt-259
97Cir-187
97CirRav-187
97ColCho-110
97Don-8
97DonEli-96
97DonEliGS-96
97DonLim-31
97DonLimLE-31
97DonPre-55
97DonPreCttC-55
97DonPreP-8
97DonPrePGold-8
97Fin-18
97FinRef-18
97FlaSho-A124
97FlaSho-B124
97FlaSho-C124
97FlaShoLC-124
97FlaShoLC-B124
97FlaShoLC-C124
97FlaShoLCM-A124
97FlaShoLCM-B124
97FlaShoLCM-C124
97Fle-98
97FleTif-98
97Lea-222
97LeaFraM-222
97LeaFraMDC-222
97MetUni-109
97NewPin-112
97NewPinAP-112
97NewPinMC-112
97NewPinPP-112
97Pac-87
97PacLigB-87
97PacPri-31
97PacPriGotD-GD42
97PacPriLB-31
97PacPriP-31
97PacSil-87
97PinIns-22
97PinInsCE-22
97PinInsDE-22
97PinX-P-77
97PinX-PMoS-77
97ProMag-55
97ProMagML-55
97Sco-195
97ScoPreS-195
97ScoShoS-195
97ScoShoSAP-195
97Sel-62
97SelArtP-62
97SelRegG-62
97SkyE-X-21
97SkyE-XC-21
97SkyE-XEC-21
97SP-70
97SpoIll-138
97SpoIllEE-138
97StaClu-245
97StaCluMat-245
97StaCluMOP-245
97Stu-12
97StuPrePG-12
97StuPrePS-12
97Top-120
97TopChr-46
97TopChrR-46
97TopGal-62
97TopGalPPI-62
97TopIntF-ILM14
97TopIntFR-ILM14
97TopSta-67
97TopStaAM-67
97Ult-59
97UltGolME-59
97UltPlaME-59
97UppDec-63

Fryman, Troy

91UtiBluSC-27
91UtiBluSP-3247
92SouBenWSC-21
92SouBenWSF-185
93MidLeaAGF-22
93SarWhiSF-1377
93SouBenWSC-1
93SouBenWSF-1439
94BirBarC-8
94DirDarF-620
94ClaGolF-155
96BirBarB-3

Fryman, Woodie

66PirEasH-22
66Top-498
67CokCapPi-15
67DexPre-77
67PirTeal-7
67Top-221
67TopPirS-9
68OPC-112
68Top-112
68TopVen-112
69MilBra-88
69MLBOffS-175
69OPC-51
69PhiTeal-3
69Top-51
69TopSta-75
69TopTeaP-8
70MLBOffS-88
70Top-677
71MLBOffS-177
71OPC-414
71Top-414
72MilBra-110
72OPC-357
72Top-357
72TopCloT-15
73OPC-146
73Top-146
74OPC-555
74Top-555
75OPC-166
75Top-166
76ExpRed-11
76OPC-467
76SSP-345
76Top-467
77OPC-126
77Top-28
78SSP270-249
78TigDeaCS-8
78Top-585
79ExpPos-9
79OPC-135
79Top-269
80ExpPos-9
80OPC-316
80Top-607
81Don-331
81Fle-159
81OPC-170
81OPCPos-10
81Top-394
82Don-68
82ExpHygM-8
82ExpPos-13
82ExpZel-12
82Fle-189
82OPC-181
82Top-788
83Don-162
83ExpPos-7
83ExpStu-2
83Fle-283
83FleSti-258
83OPC-137

83Top-137
86ExpGreT-10
93ExpDonM-22
Fu, Kuo-Lee Chien
90IBAWorA-9
Fucci, Dom
80GleFalWSBT-19
80GleFalWSCT-14
81GleFalWST-11
82EdmTraT-18
82GleFalWST-5
Fuccillo, Joe
93PriRedC-12
93PriRedF-4172
Fuchs, Charlie
43PhiTeal-9
90DodTar-261
Fuduric, Tony
93BriTigF-3641
94BriTigC-12
94BriTigF-3496
94ExcFS7-54
94Top-757
94TopGol-757
94TopSpa-757
Fuentes, Brian
96EveAquB-9
Fuentes, Javier
96LowSpiB-8
Fuentes, Miguel
70OPC-88
70Top-88
83Pil69G-11
Fuentes, Mike
83WicAerDS-7
84Don-40
84ExpPos-10
84ExpStu-32
84IndIndTI-12
84IndIndTI-15
85IndIndTI-7
87MemChiB-25
87MemChiP-1
Fuentes, Roberto
85ElmPioT-6
86WinHavRSP-8
Fuentes, Tito
66Top-511
67CokCapG-4
67DexPre-78
67OPC-177
67Top-177
70OPC-42
70Top-42
71GiaTic-4
71MLBOffS-247
71OPC-378
71Top-378
72OPC-427
72OPC-428
72Top-427
72Top-428
73OPC-236
73Top-236
74OPC-305
74Top-305
74TopSta-104
75Hos-108
75OPC-425
75Top-425
76CraDis-15
76OPC-8
76SSP-124
76Top-8
77Top-63
78Top-385
86PadGreT-2
Fuhrman, Ollie (Alfred)
22E120-78
22W573-44
Fujimoto, Kenji
89VisOakCLC-116
89VisOakP-1432
Fujiwara, Mitsuru
79TCMJapPB-71
Fukushima, Akihiro
89SalLakTTI-12
Fulcar, Manuel
93LimRocDWB-101
Fulcher, John
96OgdRapTI-33
Fulgencio, Elvin
85CedRapRT-22
Fulgham, John
77St.PetCT-6
78ArkTraT-10
79Car5-9
80Top-152
81Don-70
81Top-523
82LouRedE-9
83LouRedR-20
Fuller, Aaron
94SarRedSC-9
94SarRedSF-1965
96SarRedSB-15
Fuller, Brian
96FayGenB-16
Fuller, Harry
88AubAstP-1956
89AshTouP-957
Fuller, Jim (James H.)
74OPC-606
74Top-606
75OPC-594
75Top-594
78ColCliT-7
91OriCro-147
Fuller, Jon
90ChaWheP-2244
91CedRapRC-14
91CedRapRP-2721
92CedRapRC-12
92CedRapRF-1074
92MidLeaATI-11
93ChaLooF-2364
94ChaLooF-1361
Fuller, Mark
92PitMetC-14
92PitMetF-3287
93St.LucMC-9
94BinMetF-699
94St.LucMC-9
95BinMetTI-29
96BinBeeB-7
93StLucMF-2916
Fuller, Nig (Charles F.)
90DodTar-954
Fuller, Paul
88UtiBluSP-5
89SarWhiSS-6
89Sta-58
Fuller, Scott
88UtiBluSP-19
Fuller, Steve
95AubAstTI-24
96AubDouB-5
Fuller, Tom
80AndBraT-4
Fuller, Vern
68OPC-71
68Top-71
68TopVen-71
69Top-291
69TopTeaP-13
70MLBOffS-197
70Top-558
72MilBra-111
Fuller, Wayne
88BatCliP-1669
96BatCliTI-30
Fuller, William B.
87OldJudN-185
87OldJudN-186
95NewN566-179
Fullerton, Darren
91SydWavF-9
Fullerton, Hugh
88PacEigMO-29
88PacEigMO-35
88PacEigMO-42
88PacEigMO-64
Fullis, Chick (Charles)
33ButCanV-17
33DouDisP-19
33TatOrbSDR-166
34DiaMatCSB-62
34BatR31-74
74Car193T-11
83ConMar-36
88ConNatA-9
92ConTSN-514
Fullmer, Brad
94Bow-76
94BowBes-B55
94BowBesR-B55
94ColC-643
94ColChoGS-643
94ColChoSS-643
94SP-4
94SPDieC-4
94UppDec-532
94UppDecAHNIL-5
94UppDecED-532
95Bes-81
95SigRoo-21
95SigRooSig-21
95SPML-92
95UppDecML-90
96Bow-369
96BowBes-143
96BowBesAR-143
96BowBesR-143
96Exc-186
96HonShaHWB-20
96WesPalBEB-29
97Bow-171
97BowBes-175
97BowBesAR-175
97BowBesR-175
97BowCerBIA-CA27
97BowCerGIA-CA27
97BowChr-166
97BowChrI-166
97BowChrIR-166
97BowChrR-166
97BowInt-171
97TopSta-102
97TopStaAM-102
95UppDecMLFS-90
Fully, Edward
90KinMetB-11
90KinMetS-9
91ColMetPI-11
91ColMetPPI-3
91SouAtlLAGP-SAL15
92St.LucMCB-20
92St.LucMF-1761
93St.LucMC-10
94BinMetF-716
95BinMetTI-28
93StLucMF-2933
Fulmer, Chris
87BucN28-2
87OldJudN-187
87OldJudN-188
Fulmer, Mike
84MadMusP-20
85ModA'sC-10
86StoPorP-9
Fulton, Bill
84GreHorT-12
86AlbYanT-26
87ColCliP-10
87ColCliP-27
87ColCliT-4
88ColCliC-4
88ColCliP-2
88ColCliP-312
89BlaYNPRWLU-14
89ColCliC-1
89ColCliP-3
89ColCliP-746
92YanWIZ8-64
Fulton, Ed
88SprCarB-24
89St.PetCS-13
90ArkTraGS-14
90LouRedBLBC-17
90TopTVCa-49
91LinDriAAA-235
91LouRedLD-235
91LouRedP-2916
91LouRedTI-28
92LouRedF-1889
93LouRedF-217
94TolMudHF-1029
Fulton, Greg
87ChaLooB-18
88VerMarP-942
89CalCanP-524
89WilBilP-648
90CalCanC-9
90CalCanP-656
90CMC-436
90ProAAAF-121
91HarSenLD-254
91HarSenP-629
91LinDriAA-254
92HarSenS-281
92IndIndF-1866
93HarSenF-283
Fults, Nathan
90IdaFalBP-3260
Fultz, Aaron
93ClaGolF-169
93CliGiaC-10
93CliGiaF-2483
93MidLeaAGF-39
94ExcFS7-291
94ForMyeMF-1161
95ForMyeMTI-7
95SigRooOJ-13
95SigRooOJP-13
95SigRooOJPS-13
95SigRooOJS-13
96SanJosGB-18
96WesOahCHWB-18
Fultz, Bill
82LynMetT-20
83LynMetT-5
84JacMetT-7
Fultz, David
03BreE10-54
11SpoLifCW-133
Fultz, Vince
92AlbPolC-16
92RocExpF-2107
Funaro, Joe
95ElmPioTI-6
95ElmPioUTI-6
96KanCouCTI-8
Funderburk, Mark
78WisRapTT-5
80OrlTwiT-19
82OrlTwiT-7
83OmaRoyT-15
85OrlTwiT-5
86Don-630
86Fle-652
86Spo-178
86TolMudHP-11
87OrlTwiP-25
88OrlTwiB-5
89OrlTwiB-3
89OrlTwiP-1344
90OrlSunRB-29
90OrlSunRP-1099
90OrlSunRS-25
91LinDriAA-500
91OrlSunRLD-500
91OrlSunRP-1866
92OrlSunRF-2863
92OrlSunRS-526
93NasXprF-419
94NasXprF-403
Funk, Art
36GouWidPPR-D9
Funk, Brian
83WatRedT-2
84CedRapRT-6
Funk, E.
31Exh-24
Funk, Frank
60MapLeaSF-7
61Top-362
62Top-587
63Top-476
64Top-289
64TopVen-289
77Gia-7
80PenPilBT-26
84MarMot-27
86OmaRoyP-7
86OmaRoyT-24
87OmaRoyP-1
88RoySmo-2
91CedRapRC-26
91CedRapRP-2735
92NasSouF-1849
92NasSouS-300
93ColSprSSF-3102
94ColSprSSF-749
Funk, Tom
86ColAstP-14
87TucTorP-25
88ColAstB-18
Fuqua, David
75LafDriT-22
Furcal, Lorenzo
89MadMusS-9
89MedAthB-17
Furcal, Manuel
90SanBerSB-11
90SanBerSCLC-98
90SanBerSP-2628
91PenPilC-4
91PenPilP-370
Furch, John
89UtiBluSP-7
Furillo, Carl
46SpoExcW-3-9
47Exh-78
47HomBon-16
47PM1StaP1-62
47PM1StaP1-63
47PM1StaP1-64
47PM1StaP1-65
48SweSpoT-20
49Bow-70
49EurSta-35
50Bow-58
50Dra-18
51Bow-81
52Bow-24
52CokTip-2
52TipTop-9
53BowC-78
53Dor-128
54Bow-122
54NewYorJA-5
55Bow-169
55DodGolS-18
55DodGolS-30
56Dod-10
56Top-190
57Top-45
57Top-400
58DodJayP-5
58Top-417
59DodMor-2
59DodTeal-7
59DodVol-5
59Top-206
60DodBelB-8
60DodMor-4
60NuHi-32
60Top-387
60Top-408
61NuSco-432
72TopTes5-3
77GalGloG-11
78ReaRem-5
79TCM50-43
82GSGalAG-5
84FifNatCT-5
84OCoandSI-146
84TCMPla1-29
87Dod195T-4
88RinPosD1-2B
89DodSmoG-58
90DodTar-262
91TopArc1-305
92BazQua5A-2
95TopArcBD-35
95TopArcBD-60
95TopArcBD-87
95TopArcBD-132
95TopArcBD-155
Furman, Jon
83BirBarT-20
Furmanik, Dan
89ColMetB-6
89ColMetGS-8
90St.LucMS-7
91SalLakTP-3203
91SalLakTSP-2
Fursato, Yasutara
93BriTigF-3642
Furtado, Tim
93RivPilCLC-7
Furtak, Mark
87HawRai-16
Furuta, Atsuya
93GolCar-3
Furuya, Hideo
87JapPlaB-32
Fusco, Thomas
90HamRedB-5
90HamRedS-13
91SavCarP-1645
92SavCarC-20
92SavCarF-656
Fuson, Grady
82IdaFalAT-31
83IdaFalAT-31
89MedAthB-18
90SouOreAB-30
90SouOreAP-3449
91SouOreAP-3866

Fuson, Robin
78WatIndT-10
82ChaLooT-18
83BufBisT-1
84BufBisT-24
85PawRedST-13
Fussell, Chris
96Bow-263
96BowBes-163
96BowBesAR-163
96BowBesR-163
96CarLeaA1B-1
96CarLeaA2B-1
96FreKeyB-9
96MauStiHWB-28
97Bow-95
97BowCerBIA-CA28
97BowCerGIA-CA28
97BowInt-95
Fussell, Denny
92PriRedC-15
92PriRedF-3082
93BilMusF-3937
93BilMusSP-10
94BilMusF-3677
94BilMusSP-6
Fusselman, Les
52Top-378
53CarHunW-7
53Top-218
83TopRep5-378
91TopArc1-218
Futrell, Mark
90WelPirP-21
91AugPirC-6
91AugPirP-799
Fye, Chris
89CliGiaP-885
90Bes-159
90SanJosGB-16
90SanJosGCLC-43
90SanJosGP-2002
90SanJosGP-2172
90SanJosGS-10
Fyhrie, Mike
92BasCitRC-21
92BasCitRF-3838
93WilBluRC-10
94OmaRoyF-1218
95WicWraTI-25
96NorTidB-14
Fynan, Kevin
88ClePhiS-11
89ClePhiS-9
90ClePhiS-7
Fyock, Wade
90HigSchPLS-23
91AppFoxC-3
91AppFoxP-1709
91Cla/Bes-249
Fzelykovskyi, Andrei
89EasLeaDDP-DD13
Gabbani, Mike
90HunCubP-3284
91SydWavF-18
91WinSpiC-13
91WinSpiP-2831
92WinSpiC-20
92WinSpiF-1211
Gabbard, John
43ParSpo-77
Gabella, Jim
90WatIndS-24
91ColSprSSP-2202
91LinDriAAA-100
92CanIndF-707
93BurIndC-30
93BurIndF-3316
94BurIndC-29
Gabler, Frank
34BatR31-91
92ConTSN-606
Gabler, John
60Lea-62
92YanWIZ6-44
Gables, Kenneth
48SomandK-5
49SomandK-3
Gabriel, Denio
96FreKeyB-28
Gabriele, Dan
85ElmPioT-7
86GreHorP-6
87WinHavRSP-10
88NewBriRSP-898
89EasLeaAP-13
89NewBriRSP-604
89NewBriRSS-6
Gabriele, Mike
90SumBraB-3
90SumBraP-2426
Gabrielson, Len
47PM1StaP1-66
63Top-253
64Top-198
64TopVen-198
65OPC-14
65Top-14
66Top-395
67CokCapDA-19
67Top-469
68Top-357
68TopVen-357
69MilBra-89
69MLBOffS-147
69Top-615
69TopSta-44
70MLBOffS-50
70OPC-204
70Top-204
90DodTar-263
Gabrielson, Leonard
43CenFlo-9
Gaddie, Mike
90JohCitCS-30
92JohCitCC-28
Gaddy, John Wilson
90DodTar-955
Gaddy, Robert
89BatCliP-1928
90ProAaA-95
90SouAtlLAS-7
90SpaPhiB-3
90SpaPhiP-2484
90SpaPhiS-8
91ClePhiC-3
91ClePhiP-1614
92ClePhiC-4
92ClePhiF-2050
93ReaPhiF-291
94ScrRedBF-919
95ScrRedBTI-9
Gades, Rene
96HudValRB-28
Gaeckle, Chris
86GreHorP-7
87GreHorP-25
Gaedel, Eddie
60NuHi-26
61NuSco-426
73FleWilD-4
77FriOneYW-1
87SpoCubG-2
87SpoRea-3
91FouBal-34
Gaeta, Chris
85NewOriT-19
Gaeta, Frank
52LavPro-25
Gaetti, Gary
80WisRapTT-17
82OrlTwi8SCT-7
82TwiPos-12
83AllGamPI-32
83Don-53
83Fle-613
83Top-431
83TopSti-87
83TwiTeal-5
83TwiTeal-33
84Don-314
84Fle-565
84FunFooP-131
84MinTwiP-13
84Nes792-157
84OPC-157
84Top-157
84TopRubD-20
84TopSti-306
84TopTif-157
84TwiTeal-5
85AllGamPI-33
85Don-242
85Fle-278
85Lea-145
85OPC-304
85Top-304
85TopRubD-20
85TopSti-302
85TopTif-304
85Twi7-9
85TwiTeal-5
86Don-314
86Fle-394
86OPC-97
86Top-97
86TopSti-283
86TopTif-97
86TwiTeal-5
87ClaGam-54
87Don-122
87DonOpeD-219
87Fle-540
87FleGamW-15
87FleGlo-540
87FleMin-40
87FleRecS-9
87FleStiC-43
87Lea-245
87OPC-179
87Spo-64
87Spo-114
87SpoTeaP-17
87Top-710
87TopGloS-3
87TopMinL-62
87TopSti-279
87TopTif-710
88ClaBlu-233
88Don-19
88Don-194
88DonBasB-46
88DonSupD-19
88Fle-10
88FleGlo-10
88FleHotS-12
88FleLeaL-13
88FleMin-34
88FleStiC-43
88GreBasS-24
88KayB-11
88Lea-19
88Lea-200
88Nes-4
88OPC-257
88PanSti-140
88PanSti-445
88RedFolSB-26
88Sco-62
88ScoGlo-62
88Spo-154
88StaLinTw-7
88Top-578
88Top-609
88TopBig-127
88TopCoi-13
88TopRitTM-31
88TopSti-17
88TopSti-277
88TopTif-578
88TopTif-609
88TopUKM-25
88TopUKMT-25
88TwiMasBD-9
88TwiSmoC-2
88TwiTeal-5
88Woo-18
88Woo-22
89Bow-158
89BowTif-158
89CadEllD-21
89ClaLigB-41
89Don-64
89DonAll-13
89DonBasB-102
89Fle-110
89FleGlo-110
89FleHeroB-15
89MasBreD-3
89OPC-220
89PanSti-389
89RedFolSB-46
89Sco-8
89ScoHot1S-21
89ScoSco-16
89Spo-48
89Top-220
89TopBasT-91
89TopBig-264
89TopGloS-33
89TopMinL-61
89TopSti-289
89TopStiB-8
89TopTif-220
89TVSpoM-104
89UppDec-203
89UppDecS-3
90Bow-417
90BowTif-417
90Don-151
90DonBesA-10
90Fle-373
90FleBasA-10
90FleCan-373
90Hot50PS-14
90Lea-97
90LeaPre-11
90MLBBasB-100
90OPC-630
90PanSti-106
90PubSti-286
90PubSti-326
90Sco-145
90Sco100S-22
90Spo-51
90Top-630
90TopBig-254
90TopCoi-14
90TopDou-25
90TopGloS-28
90TopSti-288
90TopStiB-41
90TopTif-630
90UppDec-454
90VenSti-188
90VenSti-189
91AngSmo-13
91Bow-207
91CadEllD-22
91ClaGam-49
91Don-547
91Fle-609
91FleUpd-9
91Lea-303
91OPC-430
91OPCPre-47
91PanFreS-302
91PanSti-250
91Sco-325
91ScoRoo-39T
91StaClu-353
91Stu-25
91Top-430
91TopDesS-430
91TopMic-430
91TopTif-430
91TopTra-44T
91TopTraT-44T
91UltUpd-8
91UppDec-34
91UppDec-233
91UppDec-731
92AngPol-10
92Bow-564
92Don-96
92Fle-58
92Lea-107
92OPC-70
92PanSti-7
92Pin-81
92Sco-39
92ScoProP-8
92ScoProP-23
92StaClu-436
92Top-70
92TopGol-70
92TopGolW-70
92TopMic-70
92TriPla-223
92Ult-26
92UppDec-321
93AngMot-5
93CadDis-21
93Don-517
93DonSpiotG-SG15
93Fle-574
93Lea-514
93PacSpa-46
93PanSti-4
93Pin-112
93Sco-644
93Sel-262
93SelRoo-95T
93StaClu-512
93StaCluFDI-512
93StaCluMOP-512
93Top-139
93TopGol-139
93TopInaM-139
93TopMic-139
93Ult-520
93UppDec-370
93UppDecGold-370
93UppDecHRH-HR28
94ColC-566
94ColChoGS-566
94ColChoSS-566
94Don-502
94ExtBas-86
94Fin-394
94FinRef-394
94Fla-298
94Fle-153
94Lea-427
94LeaL-37
94Sco-300
94ScoGolR-300
94StaClu-485
94StaCluFDI-485
94StaCluGR-485
94StaCluMOP-485
94Stu-183
94Top-403
94TopGol-403
94TopSpa-403
94Ult-363
94UppDec-466
94UppDecED-466
95ColCho-456
95ColChoGS-456
95ColChoSS-456
95DonTopotO-85
95Emo-49
95Fin-245
95FinRef-245
95Fla-44
95Fle-156
95Lea-315
95LeaLim-177
95Pac-200
95Pin-380
95PinArtP-380
95PinMusC-380
95Sco-343
95ScoGolR-343
95ScoPlaTS-343
95SPCha-161
95SPChaDC-161
95StaClu-9
95StaCluFDI-9
95StaCluMOP-9
95StaCluSTWS-9
95StaCluVR-4
95Top-353
95TopCyb-190
95Ult-288
95UltGolM-288
95UppDec-420
95UppDecED-420
95UppDecEDG-420
95Zen-36
96Baz-99
96CarPol-9
96ColCho-173
96ColCho-785
96ColChoGS-173
96ColChoSS-173
96Don-117
96DonPreP-117
96EmoXL-265
96Fin-B278
96FinRef-B278
96Fla-358
96Fle-125
96FleTeaL-7
96FleTif-125
96FleUpd-U188
96FleUpdTC-U188
96LeaSigA-75
96LeaSigAG-75
96LeaSigAS-75
96MetUni-223
96MetUniP-223
96MLBPin-10
96Pac-332
96PacPri-P106
96PacPriG-P106
96PanSti-183
96Pin-110
96PinArtP-43

96PinSta-43
96Sco-346
96ScoDugC-B71
96ScoDugCAP-B71
96SP-154
96Spo-40
96SpoArtP-40
96StaClu-109
96StaCluMOP-109
96StaCluMOP-PS12
96StaCluPS-PS12
95StaCluVRMC-4
96Sum-151
96SumAbo&B-151
96SumArtP-151
96SumFoi-151
96Top-204
96TopRoaW-RW7
96Ult-68
96Ult-546
96UltGolM-68
96UltGolM-546
96UppDec-153
96UppDec-506U
97Cir-93
97CirRav-93
97ColCho-442
97Don-248
97DonPreP-248
97DonPrePGold-248
97DonTea-161
97DonTeaSPE-161
97Fle-442
97FleTif-442
97Lea-277
97LeaFraM-277
97LeaFraMDC-277
97Pac-408
97PacLigB-408
97PacSil-408
97Pin-136
97PinArtP-136
97PinMusC-136
97Sco-295
97ScoPreS-295
97ScoShoS-295
97ScoShoSAP-295
97SP-149
97StaClu-144
97StaCluMOP-144
97Top-222
97TopGal-15
97TopGalPPI-15
97Ult-316
97UltGolME-316
97UltPlaME-316
97UppDec-256
97UppDec-373
97UppDec-468

Gaff, Brent
78WauMetT-10
79WauTimT-1
81TidTidT-17
82TidTidT-20
83Don-553
83TidTidT-16
84TidTidT-8
85Fle-80
85MetColP-9
85MetTCM-10
85Top-546
85TopTif-546
86Top-18
86TopTif-18
91MetWIZ-130

Gaffke, Fabian
78HalHalR-4
79DiaGre-235
94ConTSN-1306
94ConTSNB-1306

Gaffney, Bill
80SanJosMJitB-8

Gaffney, John H.
87OldJudN-189

Gagliano, Manny
91OklStaC-9
92OklStaC-8
92SpoIndC-17
92SpoIndF-1302
94SanBerSC-3
94SanBerSF-2766

Gagliano, Phil
61UniOil-P7
62KahAtl-7
64Top-568
65CarTeal-11
65Top-503
66CarTeal-4
66Top-418
67Top-304
68Top-479
69Top-609
70OPC-143
70Top-143
71OPC-302
71Top-302
72MilBra-112
72OPC-472
72Top-472
73OPC-69
73Top-69
74OPC-622
74Top-622

Gagliano, Ralph
65Top-501

Gagliardi, Joe
88CalLeaACLC-25
89CalLeaA-56
90CalLeaACLC-27
91CalLeLA-26

Gagne, Eric
96SavSanB-12

Gagne, Greg
82OrlTwiT-8
83TolMudHT-14
84Don-39
85FleUpd-43
85TopTifT-36T
85TopTra-36T
85TwiTeal-21
86Don-550
86Fle-395
86Top-162
86TopTif-162
86TwiTeal-22
87Don-395
87DonOpeD-223
87Fle-541
87FleGlo-541
87SpoTeaP-17
87Top-558
87TopSti-283
87TopTif-558
88Don-441
88DonBasB-74
88Fle-11
88FleGlo-11
88OPC-343
88PanSti-141
88Sco-214
88ScoGlo-214
88StaLinTw-8
88Top-343
88TopBig-58
88TopTif-343
88TwiMasBD-11
88TwiSmoC-8
88TwiTeal-4
88Woo-32
89Bow-161
89BowTif-161
89Don-318
89DonBasB-158
89Fle-111
89FleGlo-111
89OPC-19
89PanSti-390
89Sco-159
89Top-19
89Top-429
89TopBig-186
89TopSti-288
89TopTif-19
89TopTif-429
89UppDec-166
90Bow-414
90BowTif-414
90Don-237
90DonBesA-135
90Fle-374
90FleCan-374
90Lea-302
90MLBBasB-99
90OPC-448
90PanSti-115
90PubSti-327
90Sco-102
90Top-448
90TopBig-78
90TopSti-295
90TopTif-448
90UppDec-217
90VenSti-190
91Bow-338
91Don-284
91Fle-610
91Lea-426
91OPC-216
91PanFreS-303
91PanSti-245
91RedFolS-37
91Sco-211
91StaClu-277
91Stu-84
91Top-216
91TopDesS-216
91TopMic-216
91TopTif-216
91Ult-186
91UppDec-415
92Bow-660
92Don-204
92Fle-202
92Lea-146
92OPC-663
92PanSti-118
92Pin-262
92Sco-182
92ScoFacl-B1
92StaClu-376
92StaCluD-53
92Stu-203
92Top-663
92TopGol-663
92TopGolW-663
92TopMic-663
92TriPla-230
92Ult-395
92UppDec-168
93Bow-449
93CadDis-22
93Don-633
93DonSpiotG-SG13
93Fle-264
93FleFinE-217
93Lea-282
93OPC-101
93OPCPre-117
93PacSpa-487
93PanSti-105
93Pin-510
93RoyPol-7
93Sco-555
93Sel-178
93SelRoo-28T
93StaClu-631
93StaCluFDI-631
93StaCluMOP-631
93StaCluRoy-16
93Stu-39
93Top-715
93TopGol-715
93TopInaM-715
93TopMic-715
93Ult-559
93UppDec-708
93UppDecGold-708
94Bow-283
94ColC-406
94ColChoGS-406
94ColChoSS-406
94Don-595
94ExtBas-87
94Fin-276
94FinRef-276
94Fla-57
94Fle-154
94Lea-122
94LeaL-38
94OPC-141
94Pac-282
94PanSti-72
94Pin-354
94PinArtP-354
94PinMusC-354
94Sco-91
94ScoGolR-91
94Sel-270
94StaClu-159
94StaCluFDI-159
94StaCluGR-159
94StaCluMOP-159
94Stu-184
94Top-151
94TopGol-151
94TopSpa-151
94TriPla-233
94Ult-62
94UppDec-79
94UppDecED-79
95ColCho-457
95ColChoGS-457
95ColChoSS-457
95D3-PB1
95Don-195
95DonPreP-195
95DonTopotO-86
95Fin-174
95FinRef-174
95Fle-157
95Lea-144
95LeaLim-129
95Pac-201
95Pin-217
95PinArtP-217
95PinMusC-217
95Sco-47
95ScoGolR-47
95ScoPlaTS-47
95SP-162
95SPCha-162
95SPChaDC-162
95SPSil-162
95StaClu-294
95StaCluMOP-294
95StaCluSTWS-294
95StaCluVR-152
95Stu-110
95Top-494
95TopCyb-284
95Ult-56
95UltGolM-56
95UppDec-179
95UppDecED-179
95UppDecEDG-179
96ColCho-172
96ColCho-579
96ColChoGS-172
96ColChoGS-579
96ColChoSS-172
96ColChoSS-579
96DodMot-7
96DodPol-13
96Don-447
96DonPreP-447
96EmoXL-207
96Fin-B209
96FinRef-B209
96Fla-291
96Fle-434
96FleDod-7
96FleTif-434
96FleUpd-U143
96FleUpdTC-U143
96Pac-337
96Pin-362
96PinAfi-20
96PinAfiAP-20
96PinAfiFPP-20
96PinFoil-362
96Sco-159
96ScoDugC-A93
96ScoDugCAP-A93
96Sel-123
96SelArtP-123
95StaCluVRMC-152
96Top-56
96Ult-496
96UltGolM-496
96UppDec-97
97Cir-40
97CirRav-40
97ColCho-366
97DonTea-119
97DonTeaSPE-119
97Fin-48
97FinRef-48
97Fle-361
97FleTif-361
97PacPriGotD-GD158
97Sco-220
97ScoDod-10
97ScoDodPl-10
97ScoDodPr-10
97ScoPreS-220
97ScoShoS-220
97ScoShoSAP-220
97StaClu-311
97StaCluMOP-311
97Top-236
97Ult-215
97UltGolME-215
97UltPlaME-215
97UppDec-396

Gagnon, Clint
93IdaFalBF-4025
93IdaFalBSP-22

Gagnon, Johnny
43ParSpo-27
43ParSpo-29

Gahbrielson, Rick
86BakDodP-9

Gaiko, Rob
92OklStaC-9
95BatCliTI-13

Gaillard, Eddy
93NiaFalRF-3378
94LakTigC-8
94LakTigF-3029
95Bes-21
96JacSunB-13

Gainer, Chris
93DavLipB-9
94DavLipB-11
95DavLipB-13

Gainer, Delos C.
09SpoNewSM-75
11PloCanE-29
12T207-64
14B18B-17A
14B18B-17B
15SpoNewM-64
16BF2FP-3
16ColE13-53
16SpoNewM-63
22WilPatV-3

Gainer, Jay
90SpoIndSP-12
91CalLeLA-7
91Cla/Bes-230
91HigDesMC-19
91HigDesMP-2402
92ClaFS7-312
92ProFS7-336
92SkyAA F-279
92WicWraF-3661
92WicWraS-630
93Bow-444
93ColSprSSF-3093
93ExcFS7-109
93FleFinE-29
93TopTra-10T
94ColSprSSF-741
96ColSprSSTI-14

Gainer, Keith
79NewCoPT-18

Gaines, A. Joe
62RedEnq-9
62Top-414
63Top-319
64Top-364
64TopVen-364
65Top-594
66OPC-122
66Top-122
66TopVen-122
67AstTeal2-11
91OriCro-148

Gaines, Jerry
76AshTouT-14
77AshTouT-6

Gainey, Bob
72Dia-74

Gainey, Bryon
94SigRooDP-54
94SigRooDPS-54
96Bow-154

Gainey, Ty
82DayBeaAT-13
83ColAstT-10
85TucTorC-69
86Don-31
86TucTorP-5
87Don-533
87Spo-118
87SpoTeaP-8
87TucTorP-23
88Don-578
88Fle-448
88FleGlo-448

89ColSprSSC-22
89ColSprSSP-258
90CMC-463
90ColSprSSC-11
90ColSprSSP-50
90ProAAAF-231

Gainous, Trey
87EugEmeP-2662
88AppFoxP-151

Gaither, Horace
90SarWhiSS-8
91SouBenWSC-2
91SouBenWSP-2862

Gajkowski, Steve
90BurIndP-3005
91CollndC-13
91CollndP-1480
91WatIndC-6
91WatIndP-3361
93SarWhiSC-10
93SarWhiSF-1363
94BirBarC-9
94BirBarF-615
96NasSouB-14
92UtiBluSC-22

Gakeler, Dan
85GreHorT-20
86GreHorP-8
87NewBriRSP-19
88NewBriRSP-904
89JacExpB-24
89JacExpP-157
90CMC-56
90IndIndC-6
90IndIndP-294
90ProAAAF-577
90WesPalBES-9
91Bow-144
91LinDriAAA-584
91TolMudHLD-584
91TolMudHP-1924
92Fle-135
92OPC-621
92Sco-831
92StaClu-276
92Top-621
92TopDeb91-59
92TopGol-621
92TopGolW-621
92TopMic-621
94NewBriRSF-646
96LowSpiB-2

Galan, Augie
34DiaMatCSB-63
34BatR31-135
35DiaMatCS3T1-56
36DiaMatCS3T2-10
36ExhFou-3
36GouWidPPR-A36
36GouWidPPR-C12
36R31PasP-31
36R31PasP-45
36SandSW-22
36WorWidGV-106
37ExhFou-3
38ExhFou-3
39CubTeal-6
41CubTeal-5
41DouPlaR-101
42DodTeal-8
43DodTeal-10
46SpoExcW-4-9
47Exh-79
48Bow-39
49Bow-230
49EurSta-103
50RemBre-6
53MotCoo-7
54Top-233
76TayBow4-58
83TCMPla1944-42
89DodSmoG-48
90DodTar-264
91RinPosBD2-9
94TopArc1-233
94TopArc1G-233
95ConTSN-1416

Galante, Joe
79BufBisT-4

Galante, Matt
75BurBeeT-7
76BurBeeT-13
77HolMilT-11
80ColAstT-10
83TucTorT-23
84TucTorC-50
85AstMot-27
86AstPol-26
87AstMot-27
87AstPol-26
88AstMot-27
89AstLenH-14
89AstMot-27
89AstSmo-15
90AstMot-27
91AstMot-28
92AstMot-27
93AstMot-28
94AstMot-27
95AstMot-28
96AstMot-28

Galarraga, Andres
80VenLeaS-107
85IndIndTI-3
86Don-33
86Don-33B
86DonRoo-7
86ExpPos-4
86ExpProPa-10
86Fle-647
86FleUpd-44
86Lea-27
86SpoRoo-27
86TopTra-40T
86TopTraT-40T
87ClaGam-71
87Don-303
87DonOpeD-90
87ExpPos-8
87Fle-319
87FleBasA-18
87FleGlo-319
87FleMin-41
87GenMilB-4C
87Lea-221
87OPC-272
87SpoTeaP-20
87Top-272
87TopSti-84
87TopTif-272
88Don-282
88DonBasB-90
88ExpPos-7
88Fle-184
88FleGlo-184
88FleLeaL-14
88FleMin-88
88FleSlu-14
88FleStiC-96
88FleTeaL-9
88FleWaxBC-C3
88Lea-121
88MSAHosD-8
88OPC-25
88PanSti-323
88Sco-19
88ScoGlo-19
88ScoYouS2-8
88Spo-182
88StaLinE-6
88Top-25
88TopBig-55
88TopGloS-58
88TopMinL-56
88TopSti-79
88TopStiB-2
88TopTif-25
89Bow-365
89BowTif-365
89CadEllD-22
89ClaLigB-46
89Don-14
89Don-130
89DonAll-45
89DonBasB-12
89DonBonM-BC16
89DonSupD-14
89ExpPos-8
89Fle-376
89Fle-638
89FleBasA-13
89FleBasM-12
89FleExcS-13
89FleForTR-3
89FleGlo-376
89FleGlo-638
89FleHeroB-16
89FleLeaL-14
89FleSup-15
89FleWaxBC-C8
89KayB-12
89OPC-93
89PanSti-119
89PanSti-224
89RedFolSB-47
89Sco-144
89ScoHot1S-74
89ScoSco-33
89Spo-139
89SpoIllFKI-63
89Top-386
89Top-590
89TopBasT-122
89TopBig-173
89TopCoi-13
89TopGloS-44
89TopHilTM-13
89TopMinL-22
89TopSti-76
89TopStiB-36
89TopTif-386
89TopTif-590
89TopUKM-28
89TVSpoM-14
89UppDec-115
89UppDec-677
89UppDecS-3
90Bow-113
90BowTif-113
90ClaBlu-115
90Don-97
90DonBesN-67
90ExpPos-10
90Fle-345
90FleCan-345
90Hot50PS-15
90Lea-450
90MSAHolD-4
90OPC-720
90PanSti-284
90PubSti-173
90PubSti-611
90RedFolSB-35
90Sco-25
90Sco100S-14
90Spo-148
90Top-720
90TopBig-108
90TopHilHM-31
90TopSti-75
90TopTif-720
90TopTVA-62
90UppDec-356
90VenSti-191
90VenSti-192
91Bow-446
91ClaGam-75
91Don-68
91DonGraS-9
91ExpPos-7
91Fle-232
91Lea-110
91OPC-610
91OPCPre-48
91PanCanT1-100
91PanFreS-139
91PosCan-3
91Sco-443
91StaClu-69
91Stu-197
91Top-610
91TopDesS-610
91TopMic-610
91TopTif-610
91Ult-203
91UppDec-456
92Bow-320
92CarPol-4
92Don-355
92Fle-480
92Lea-449
92Mr.TurS-10
92OPC-240
92OPCPre-191
92PanSti-202
92Pin-381
92Sco-35
92ScoProP-9
92ScoRoo-60T
92SpoIllFK1-274
92StaClu-652
92StaCluNC-652
92Top-240
92TopGol-240
92TopGolW-240
92TopMic-240
92TopTra-36T
92TopTraG-36T
92UppDec-474
92UppDec-758
93Bow-204
93DiaMar-36
93Don-764
93ExpDonM-4
93Fin-130
93FinRef-130
93Fla-39
93FlaPro-3
93Fle-409
93FleFinE-30
93FunPac-173
93FunPac-176
93Hos-18
93Lea-322
93LinVenB-276
93LinVenB-280
93LinVenB-344
93MetBak-27
93OPCPre-58
93PacBeiA-22
93PacJugC-26
93PacSpa-427
93Pin-434
93PinExpOD-3
93RocUSPC-1D
93RocUSPC-2S
93Sco-649
93SelRoo-102T
93SP-220
93StaClu-454
93StaCluFDI-454
93StaCluMOP-454
93StaCluRoc-11
93Stu-163
93StuSupoC-9
93Top-173
93TopFulS-20
93TopGol-173
93TopInaM-173
93TopMic-173
93TopTra-31T
93Ult-347
93UppDec-478
93UppDec-593
93UppDecGold-478
93UppDecGold-593
94Bow-526
94BowBes-R43
94BowBesR-R43
94ColC-312
94ColC-350
94ColC-360
94ColChoGS-312
94ColChoGS-350
94ColChoGS-360
94ColChoSS-312
94ColChoSS-350
94ColChoSS-360
94ColChoT-5
94DenHol-11
94Don-346
94DonDiaK-DK7
94DonEli-48
94DonLonBL-3
94DonMVP-4
94DonSpeE-346
94ExtBas-244
94Fin-35
94FinPre-35P
94FinRef-35
94Fla-373
94Fle-440
94FleAllS-35
94FleLeaL-7
94FleTeaL-18
94FUnPac-14
94KinDis-16
94Kra-21
94Lea-156
94LeaCleC-2
94LeaGolS-7
94LeaL-102
94LeaMVPC-N5
94LeaMVPCG-N5
94OPC-69
94OscMayR-21
94Pac-195
94PacAll-3
94PacSilP-20
94PanSti-11
94PanSti-174
94Pin-446
94PinArtP-446
94PinMusC-446
94PinRunC-RC30
94Pos-23
94ProMag-43
94RedFolMI-12
94RocPol-8
94RocPol-9
94Sco-8
94ScoGolR-8
94ScoGolS-11
94ScoSam-8
94ScoSam-8GR
94Sel-63
94SP-166
94SPDieC-166
94SPHol-10
94SPHolDC-10
94Spo-55
94SpoMov-MM6
94StaClu-454
94StaCluFDI-454
94StaCluGR-454
94StaCluMO-15
94StaCluMOP-454
94StaCluT-91
94StaCluTF-4
94StaCluTFDI-91
94Stu-177
94StuEdiC-4
94TomPiz-5
94Top-525
94TopBlaG-30
94TopGol-525
94TopSpa-525
94TopSupS-15
94TriPla-223
94Ult-480
94UltHitM-4
94UltLeaL-6
94UltOnBL-4
94UppDec-270
94UppDec-315
94UppDecAJ-39
94UppDecAJG-39
94UppDecDC-W2
94UppDecED-270
94UppDecED-315
94USPlaCA-1D
94VenLinU-41
95Baz-83
95Bow-355
95BowBes-R71
95BowBesR-R71
95ClaPhoC-23
95ColCho-440
95ColChoGS-440
95ColChoSE-205
95ColChoSEGS-205
95ColChoSESS-205
95ColChoSS-440
95D3-14
95DenHol-9
95Don-342
95DonBomS-5
95DonPreP-342
95DonTopotO-227
95Emb-90
95EmbGolI-90
95Emo-125
95Fin-69
95FinRef-69
95Fla-130
95FlaInfP-4
95Fle-518
95KinDis-8
95Kra-21
95Lea-276
95LeaGreG-5
95LeaLim-141
95LinVen-14
95LinVen-274
95LinVen-275
95Pac-136
95PacGolCDC-9
95PacGolP-35
95PacLatD-13
95PacPri-45

95PanSti-34
95Pin-240
95PinArtP-240
95PinMusC-240
95PinPer-PP5
95RedFol-17
95RocPol-6
95Sco-338
95ScoGolR-338
95ScoHaloG-HG62
95ScoPlaTS-338
95Sel-85
95SelArtP-85
95SelCer-20
95SelCerMG-20
95SP-48
95SPCha-40
95SPChaDC-40
95Spo-96
95SpoArtP-96
95SPSil-48
95SPSpeF-35
95StaClu-32
95StaClu-313
95StaClu-499
95StaCluCC-CC23
95StaCluFDI-32
95StaCluMO-18
95StaCluMOP-32
95StaCluMOP-313
95StaCluMOP-499
95StaCluMOP-CC23
95StaCluMOP-PZ6
95StaCluMOP-RL40
95StaCluPZ-PZ6
95StaCluRL-RL40
95StaCluSTWS-32
95StaCluSTWS-313
95StaCluSTWS-499
95Stu-42
95StuGolS-42
95Sum-42
95SumNthD-42
95TomPiz-23
95Top-446
95TopFin-9
95TopLeaL-LL6
95UC3-19
95UC3ArtP-19
95Ult-374
95UltGolM-374
95UltHomRK-10
95UltHomRKGM-10
95UppDec-410
95UppDecED-410
95UppDecEDG-410
95UppDecPAW-H29
95UppDecPAWE-H29
95UppDecPLL-R38
95UppDecPLLE-R38
95UppDecSE-105
95UppDecSEG-105
95USPlaCMLA-6C
96Baz-89
96Bow-12
96BowBes-36
96BowBesAR-36
96BowBesR-36
96Cir-123
96CirBos-34
96CirRav-123
96ColCho-131
96ColCho-341
96ColCho-753
96ColCho-758
96ColChoGS-131
96ColChoGS-341
96ColChoGS-753
96ColChoGS-758
96ColChoSS-131
96ColChoSS-341
96ColChoSS-753
96ColChoSS-758
96Don-332
96DonPreP-332
96EmoXL-175
96Fin-B139
96Fin-B254
96Fin-S345
96FinRef-B139
96FinRef-B254
96FinRef-S345
96Fla-246
96Fle-363
96FleRoc-5
96FleTif-363
96FleUpd-U220
96FleUpdTC-U220
96Kin-13
96Lea-135
96LeaLim-18
96LeaLimG-18
96LeaPre-29
96LeaPreP-29
96LeaPrePB-135
96LeaPrePG-135
96LeaPrePS-135
96LeaPreSG-64
96LeaPreSte-64
96LeaSig-18
96LeaSigPPG-18
96LeaSigPPP-18
96MetUni-156
96MetUniP-156
96Pac-64
96PacEstL-EL11
96PacGolCD-DC11
96PacHom-HP8
96PacPri-P21
96PacPriG-P21
96PanSti-84
96Pin-93
96Pin-153
96PinAfi-14
96PinAfiAP-14
96PinAfiFPP-14
96PinArtP-35
96PinArtP-80
96PinSta-35
96PinSta-80
96ProMagDM-13
96ProSta-113
96RocPol-8
96Sco-329
96ScoDugC-B54
96ScoDugCAP-B54
96Sel-3
96SelArtP-3
96SelCer-14
96SelCerAP-14
96SelCerCB-14
96SelCerCR-14
96SelCerMB-14
96SelCerMG-14
96SelCerMR-14
96SelTeaN-4
96SP-77
96Spo-66
96SpoArtP-66
96SPx-25
96SPxGol-25
96StaClu-150
96StaCluEPB-150
96StaCluEPG-150
96StaCluEPS-150
96StaCluEWB-EW3
96StaCluEWG-EW3
96StaCluEWS-EW3
96StaCluMeg-MH7
96StaCluMO-13
96StaCluMOP-150
96StaCluMOP-MH7
96StaCluMOP-PP12
96StaCluPP-PP12
96Stu-124
96StuPrePB-124
96StuPrePG-124
96StuPrePS-124
96Sum-115
96SumAbo&B-115
96SumArtP-115
96SumFoi-115
96Top-249
96TopChr-96
96TopChrR-96
96TopClaC-CC8
96TopGal-44
96TopGalE-18
96TopGalPPI-44
96TopLas-106
96TopLasSS-3
96TopPro-NL12
96Ult-189
96UltGolM-189
96UltThu-9
96UltThuGM-9
96UppDec-65
96UppDecPRE-R45
96UppDecPreR-R45
96Zen-87
96ZenArtP-87
96ZenMoz-12
97Bow-59
97BowBes-88
97BowBesAR-88
97BowBesR-88
97BowChr-45
97BowChrI-45
97BowChrIR-45
97BowChrR-45
97BowInt-59
97Cir-307
97CirRav-307
97ColCho-57
97ColCho-58
97ColCho-320
97ColChoAC-28
97ColChoCtG-16A
97ColChoCtG-16B
97ColChoCtG-16C
97ColChoCtGIW-CG16
97ColChoNF-NF11
97ColChoNF-NF12
97ColChoPP-PP6
97ColChoPPG-PP6
97ColChoS-14
97Don-4
97Don-439
97DonEli-98
97DonEliGS-98
97DonLim-64
97DonLim-140
97DonLimFotG-32
97DonLimLE-64
97DonLimLE-140
97DonPre-17
97DonPreCttC-17
97DonPreP-4
97DonPreP-439
97DonPrePGold-4
97DonPrePGold-439
97DonTea-91
97DonTeaSPE-91
97Fin-170
97Fin-223
97Fin-321
97FinEmb-170
97FinEmb-321
97FinEmbR-170
97FinEmbR-321
97FinRef-170
97FinRef-223
97FinRef-321
97FlaSho-A114
97FlaSho-B114
97FlaSho-C114
97FlaShoLC-114
97FlaShoLC-B114
97FlaShoLC-C114
97FlaShoLCM-A114
97FlaShoLCM-B114
97FlaShoLCM-C114
97Fle-310
97Fle-729
97FleLumC-7
97FleTif-310
97FleTif-729
97FleZon-5
97Lea-241
97LeaFraM-241
97LeaFraMDC-241
97MetUni-74
97MetUniBF-4
97NewPin-18
97NewPin-181
97NewPinAP-18
97NewPinAP-181
97NewPinMC-18
97NewPinMC-181
97NewPinPP-18
97NewPinPP-181
97Pac-282
97PacCar-26
97PacCarM-26
97PacGolCD-26
97PacLatotML-27
97PacLigB-282
97PacPri-98
97PacPriGA-GA22
97PacPriGotD-GD133
97PacPriLB-98
97PacPriP-98
97PacPriSL-SL9B
97PacSil-282
97PacTriCD-16
97Pin-187
97PinArtP-187
97PinCer-48
97PinCerMBlu-48
97PinCerMG-48
97PinCerMR-48
97PinCerR-48
97PinIns-30
97PinInsCE-30
97PinInsDE-30
97PinInsFS-14
97PinMusC-187
97PinTotCPB-48
97PinTotCPG-48
97PinTotCPR-48
97PinX-P-8
97PinX-PMoS-8
97PinX-PSfF-48
97PinX-PSfFU-48
97ProMag-13
97ProMagML-13
97Sco-155
97ScoPreS-155
97ScoRoc-6
97ScoRocPl-6
97ScoRocPr-6
97ScoShoS-155
97ScoShoSAP-155
97Sel-56
97SelArtP-56
97SelRegG-56
97SkyE-X-69
97SkyE-XC-69
97SkyE-XEC-69
97SP-65
97SPMarM-MM2
97SpoIll-42
97SpoIllEE-42
97SpoIllGS-13
97SPSpxF-1
97SPSPxFA-1
97SPx-24
97SPxBro-24
97SPxGraF-24
97SPxSil-24
97SPxSte-24
97StaClu-59
97StaClu-380
97StaCluFR-F4
97StaCluMat-59
97StaCluMOP-59
97StaCluMOP-380
97StaCluMOP-FB4
97StaCluMOP-PG20
97StaCluMOP-PL7
97StaCluPG-PG20
97StaCluPL-PL7
97Stu-15
97StuPrePG-15
97StuPrePS-15
97Top-10
97TopAll-AS4
97TopChr-5
97TopChrAS-AS4
97TopChrDD-DD9
97TopChrDDR-DD9
97TopChrR-5
97TopChrSAR-AS4
97TopChrSB-10
97TopChrSB-11
97TopChrSBR-10
97TopChrSBR-11
97TopGal-3
97TopGalPG-PG13
97TopGalPPI-3
97TopHobM-HM20
97TopScr-4
97TopSeaB-SB10
97TopSeaB-SB11
97TopSta-26
97TopStaAM-26
97TopTeaT-TT6
97Ult-185
97UltDouT-13
97UltGolME-185
97UltPlaME-185
97UppDec-205
97UppDec-350
97UppDecAWJ-4
97UppDecAWJ-6
97UppDecLDC-LD6
97UppDecP-15
97UppDecRP-RP8
97UppDecU-5

Galarza, Edgar
87WytCubP-14

Galarza, Joel
96SanJosGB-12

Galasso, Bob
76VenLeaS-164
78SpoIndC-21
80Top-711
80VanCanT-20
81SpoIndT-9
82Top-598
84RicBraT-16
89PacSenL-200
89TopSenL-100
90EliSenL-56
91PacSenL-114
94BreMilB-28

Galatzer, Milt
34DiaMatCSB-64
35DiaMatCS3T1-57
36NatChiFPR-28

Galbato, Chan
86JamExpP-9

Galbraith, Moe
89TenTecGE-9

Galbreath, John W.
82OhiHaloF-56

Gale, Bill
91St.PetCP-2287

Gale, Rich
76WatRoyT-8
77JacSunT-5
78Roy-5
78SSP270-235
79OPC-149
79Top-298
80Top-433
81Don-462
81Fle-40
81OPC-363
81RoyPol-3
81Top-544
82Don-138
82Fle-408
82OPC-67
82Top-67
82TopTra-38T
83Don-172
83Fle-260
83OPC-243
83RedYea-32
83Top-719
83TopTra-35T
84Don-140
84Fle-469
84FleUpd-41
84Nes792-142
84PawRedST-23
84Top-142
84TopTif-142
84TopTra-40T
84TopTraT-40T
85Top-606
85TopTif-606
89EasLeaDDP-DD43
89NewBriRSP-602
89NewBriRSS-24
89PacSenL-95
90NewBriRSB-26
90NewBriRSP-1335
90NewBriRSS-26
91LinDriAAA-375
91PacSenL-19
91PawRedSDD-5
91PawRedSLD-375
91PawRedSP-55
92RedSoxDD-12
95PorSeaDTI-6

Galehouse, Dennis
34DiaMatCSB-65
35DiaMatCS3T1-58
40PlaBal-198
41BroW75-11
46SeaSLP-18
47TipTop-63
48RedSoxTI-7
61Fle-107
79DiaGre-190
83TCMPla1942-9
96Bro194F-16

Galiffa, Arnold

51BerRos-D14
Galinas, Marck
79BufBisT-10
Galindez, Luis
89BlaYNPRWL-114
89WatDiaP-1789
89WatDiaS-8
90Bes-171
90MidLeaASGS-32
90WatDiaB-5
90WatDiaP-2372
91Cla/Bes-179
91HigDesMC-4
91HigDesMP-2387
92ClaFS7-129
92HigDesMC-16
93RanCucQC-11
93RanCucQF-824
94RanCucQC-12
94RanCucQF-1629
Galindo, Luis
88LakTigS-5
89LakTigS-6
90LonTigP-1277
91LinDriAA-384
91LonTigLD-384
91LonTigP-1884
95LinVen-148
Gallagher, Alan
71OPC-224
71Top-224
72Top-693
72Top-694
78GreBraT-10
81DurBulT-14
82ChaLooT-23
83BufBisT-24
Gallagher, Allen
92BurIndC-17
92BurIndF-1648
Gallagher, Bob
74OPC-21
74Top-21
75OPC-406
75Top-406
76PheGiaCr-18
76PhoGiaCa-13
76PhoGiaCC-9
76PhoGiaVNB-7
76SSP-608
91MetWIZ-131
Gallagher, Dave
80BatTroT-25
81WatIndT-26
82ChaLooT-17
82WatIndF-11
83BufBisT-19
84MaiGuiT-7
85IntLeaAT-35
85MaiGuiT-27
86MaiGuiP-9
87CalCanP-2330
88DonRoo-7
88FleUpd-16
88FleUpdG-16
88ScoRoo-89T
88ScoRooG-89T
88VanCanC-24
88VanCanP-771
89Baz-8
89Bow-71
89BowTif-71
89ChaLooLITI-10
89Don-384
89DonBasB-67
89Fle-496
89FleGlo-496
89K-M-7
89PanSti-299
89Sco-455
89ScoHot1R-96
89ScoYouSI-4
89Spo-88
89Top-156
89TopBig-310
89TopGloS-49
89TopRoo-8
89TopSti-295
89TopSti-321
89TopTif-156
89ToyRoo-9
89UppDec-164
89WhiSoxC-9
90ClaBlu-49
90Don-219
90Fle-532
90FleCan-532
90OPC-612
90PanSti-46
90PubSti-387
90Sco-115
90Sco100S-56
90Spo-105
90Top-612
90TopSti-305
90TopTif-612
90UppDec-328
90VenSti-193
90WhiSoxC-5
91Fle-471
91OPC-349
91OriCro-498
91StaClu-563
91Top-349
91TopDesS-349
91TopMic-349
91TopTif-349
91UltUpd-9
91UppDec-508
92Don-377
92Fle-59
92Lea-224
92MetColP-23
92MetKah-8
92OPC-552
92OPCPre-128
92Sco-239
92ScoRoo-55T
92StaClu-841
92StaCluECN-841
92Top-552
92TopGol-552
92TopGolW-552
92TopMic-552
92TopTra-37T
92TopTraG-37T
92Ult-530
92UppDec-289
93Don-170
93Fle-472
93Lea-479
93MetColP-33
93MetKah-8
93StaClu-476
93StaCluFDI-476
93StaCluMOP-476
93Top-471
93TopGol-471
93TopInaM-471
93TopMic-471
93Ult-74
94BraLykP-8
94BraLykS-9
94BraUSPC-9C
94Don-626
94Fle-562
94Pac-401
94Sco-235
94ScoGolR-235
94StaCluT-37
94StaCluTFDI-37
94Top-274
94TopGol-274
94TopSpa-274
94TopTra-8T
95Fle-303
95Phi-12
95PhiMel-9
95Sco-390
95ScoGolR-390
95ScoPlaTS-390
95TopTra-90T
Gallagher, Doug
77FriOneYW-52
Gallagher, Joe
40DodTeal-9
90DodTar-265
Gallagher, Keith
96NewJerCB-11
Gallagher, Sean
85CloHSS-16
Gallagher, Shawn
96Bow-150
96ChaRivTI-9613
Gallagher, William
90KalBatN-4
Gallaher, Kevin
92BurAstF-537
93OscAstC-11
93OscAstF-620
94Bow-202
94Cla-16
94ExcFS7-200
94JacGenF-209
95Bow-142
95Exc-202
96TusTorB-8
Gallardo, Luis
87QuaCitAP-31
87SalAngP-25
90OneYanP-3366
91GreHorP-3065
92ForLauYC-11
92ForLauYTI-12
92Ft.LauYF-2619
94VenLinU-131
94VenLinU-183
94VenLinU-263
Galle, Mike
89GreFalDSP-28
90YakBeaTI-26
91BakDodCLC-16
Gallego, Mike
82TacTigT-30
82WesHavAT-12
84TacTigC-81
85A'sMot-24
86Don-156
86TacTigP-7
86Top-304
86TopTif-304
88A'sMot-22
88Don-379
88DonTeaBA-379
88ModA'sTI-33
88Sco-428
88ScoGlo-428
88StaLinAs-5
88Top-702
88TopBig-103
88TopTif-702
89A'sMot-23
89Don-422
89Fle-8
89FleGlo-8
89Sco-537
89Top-102
89TopTif-102
89UppDec-583A
89UppDec-583B
90A'sMot-25
90Bow-459
90BowTif-459
90Don-361
90Fle-7
90FleCan-7
90Lea-121
90OPC-293
90PubSti-304
90Sco-323
90Top-293
90TopBig-73
90TopTif-293
90UppDec-230
90VenSti-194
91A'sMot-25
91A'sSFE-4
91Bow-219
91Don-158
91Fle-7
91Lea-78
91OPC-686
91Sco-476
91StaClu-151
91Top-686
91TopDesS-686
91TopMic-686
91TopTif-686
91Ult-246
91UppDec-151
92Bow-273
92Don-314
92Fle-256
92Lea-236
92OPC-76
92OPCPre-131
92PanSti-16
92Pin-387
92Sco-43
92ScoProP-12
92ScoRoo-30T
92StaClu-106
92StaClu-627
92StaCluNC-627
92Stu-211
92Top-76
92TopGol-76
92TopGolW-76
92TopMic-76
92TopTra-38T
92TopTraG-38T
92Ult-112
92Ult-406
92UppDec-193
92UppDec-750
93CadDis-23
93Don-81
93Fle-648
93Lea-96
93Pin-388
93Sel-220
93StaClu-126
93StaCluFDI-126
93StaCluMOP-126
93StaCluY-11
93Top-287
93TopGol-287
93TopInaM-287
93TopMic-287
93TriPla-226
93Ult-240
93UppDec-600
93UppDecGold-600
94ColC-104
94ColChoGS-104
94ColChoSS-104
94Don-495
94ExtBas-129
94Fin-75
94FinRef-75
94Fla-80
94Fle-229
94Lea-136
94Pac-422
94PanSti-100
94Pin-451
94PinArtP-451
94PinMusC-451
94Sco-244
94ScoGolR-244
94Sel-53
94StaClu-388
94StaCluFDI-388
94StaCluGR-388
94StaCluMOP-388
94StaCluT-183
94StaCluTFDI-183
94Top-432
94TopGol-432
94TopSpa-432
94TriPla-273
94Ult-398
94UppDec-412
94UppDecED-412
95AthMot-19
95ColCho-533T
95Don-277
95DonPreP-277
95Fle-68
95Pac-295
95Sco-180
95ScoGolR-180
95ScoPlaTS-180
95StaClu-179
95StaCluFDI-179
95StaCluMOP-179
95StaCluSTWS-179
95Top-531
95TopCyb-316
96CarPol-10
96ColCho-242
96ColChoGS-242
96ColChoSS-242
96LeaSigEA-56
96Pac-399
97Pac-409
97PacLigB-409
97PacSil-409
Gallegos, Matt
83NasSouTI-6
Gallia, Bert (Melvin)
16ColE13-54
19W514-76
Galligani, Marcel
92FroRowDP-67
92SouOreAC-3
92SouOreAF-3424
93SouOreAC-8
93SouOreAF-4071
94WesMicWC-9
94WesMicWF-2309
Galliher, Marve
75HawIslC-9
Gallivan, Phil
90DodTar-266
Gallo, Ben
81CliGiaT-6
90RenSilSCLC-287
Gallo, Raymond
81BurBeeT-6
83ElPasDT-14
Gallone, Santy
94SpaPhiF-1729
94SparPhiC-11
95ClePhiF-223
Galloway, Chick (Clarence E.)
21Exh-54
22E120-79
22W572-30
22W573-45
23WilChoV-46
27AmeCarE-15
27YorCarE-58A
61Fle-108
93ConTSN-967
Galloway, Gill
89BilMusP-2065
Galloway, Ike
87UtiBluSP-31
88BatCliP-1680
Galloway, Joseph
26Exh-106
Galloway, Paul
96BelGiaTI-15
Galloway, Troy
85VisOakT-24
86OrlTwiP-6
87VisOakP-9
Galvan, Mike
88UtiBluSP-20
89UtiBluSP-8
90SarWhiSS-9
90StaFS7-58
91SarWhiSC-4
91SarWhiSP-1107
Galvez, Balvino
85DomLeaS-30
86AlbDukP-8
89ColCliC-10
89ColCliP-4
89ColCliP-748
90DodTar-267
90IndIndP-296
90ProAAAF-579
92SanAntMF-3969
92SanAntMS-564
93LimRocDWB-61
86STaoftFT-19
Galvez, Ricardo
94OrlCubF-1388
Galvez, Roberto
78DunBluJT-8
Galvin, Pud (James)
75FlePio-11
76MotOldT-8
76ShaPiz-102
80PerHaloFP-102
80SSPHOF-102
87OldJudN-190
88AugBecN-11
88SpoTimM-12
88WG1CarG-59
89EdgR.WG-10
89HOFStiB-80
94OriofB-30
Gama, Ricky
95IdaFalBTI-1
96RanCucQB-15
Gamba, Tom J.
87WatIndP-8
88WatIndP-673
Gambee, Brad
86EveGiaC-4
86EveGiaPC-6
87EveGiaC-29
Gambeski, Mike
83SprCarF-23
Gambill, Chad
94BenRocF-3606

95AshTouTI-24
96SalAvaB-9
97BenRocC-7
Gamble, Billy
88WytCubP-2000
Gamble, Freddie
89BriTigS-8
92EriSaiC-4
92EriSaiF-1630
93KanCouCC-8
93KanCouCF-922
93KanCouCTI-8
Gamble, John
74OPC-597
74Top-597
Gamble, Lee
38CinOraW-10
39OrcPhoAP-9
40PlaBal-208
Gamble, Oscar
70Top-654
71MLBOffS-178
71OPC-23
71Top-23
72OPC-423
72Top-423
73OPC-372
73Top-372
74OPC-152
74Top-152
74TopSta-166
75Hos-147
75OPC-213
75Top-213
76OPC-74
76SSP-526
76Top-74
76TopTra-74T
77Top-505
77WhiSoxJT-4
78Hos-100
78PadFamF-13
78Top-390
79OPC-132
79Top-263
80Top-698
81Don-229
81Fle-98
81OPC-139
81Top-139
82Don-360
82Fle-36
82OPC-229
82Top-472
83Don-461
83Fle-380
83OPC-19
83Top-19
84Fle-124
84Nes792-512
84OPC-13
84Top-512
84TopTif-512
85FleUpd-44
85OPC-93
85Top-724
85TopTif-724
85TopTifT-37T
85TopTra-37T
85WhiSoxC-0
89PacSenL-116
89T/MSenL-37
92YanWIZ7-51
92YanWIZ8-65
93RanKee-156
Gamble, Robert
87OldJudN-32
87OldJudN-191
Gamboa, Javier
94EugEmeC-10
94EugEmeF-3704
95MidLeaA-18
95SprSulTI-10
96WilBluRB-7
Gamboa, Tom
88BlaYNPRWL-65
90CMC-691
90ProAAAF-394
90TolMudHC-22
90TolMudHP-164
Gambrell, Glen
91MelBusF-19
Gambs, Chris
92ClaFS7-320
92CliGiaC-13
92CliGiaF-3590
92StaCluD-54
93Bow-280
93CliGiaC-11
93CliGiaF-2484
94CliLumF-1974
95BatCliTI-14
96DayCubB-12
94CliLumC-10
Gamby, Steve
75CliPilT-6
Gamez, Bobby
91QuaCitAC-4
91QuaCitAP-2621
92PalSprAC-8
92PalSprAF-830
93MidAngF-317
94PhoFirF-1515
95PhoFirTI-22
97MidAngOHP-12
Gamez, Francisco
91BelBreC-3
91BelBreP-2096
92ClaFS7-283
92StoPorC-16
92StoPorF-30
93Bow-267
93ElPasDF-2943
94ElPasDF-3139
95ElPasDTI-8
Gamez, Rene
95OdgRapTI-7
Gammage, Mark
82BurRanF-17
82BurRanT-19
Gammill, Jimmy
88MisStaB-6
89MisStaB-13
90MisStaB-12
91MisStaB-17
Gammon, James
89MajLeaM-3
Ganch, Tim
78ChaPirT-7
Ganci, Lou
79WatIndT-2B
Gandarillas, Gus
92ClaDraP-118
92EliTwiF-3674
93ForWayWC-8
93ForWayWF-1961
93MidLeaAGF-6
93StaCluM-138
93Top-786
93TopGol-786
93TopInaM-786
93TopMic-786
94ExcFS7-94
94FloStaLAF-FSL8
94ForMyeMC-7
94ForMyeMF-1162
95Bow-198
95Exc-84
95HarCitRCTI-6
95UppDecML-143
95UppDecMLFS-143
Gandil, Chick (Charles)
09T206-137
10ChiE-14
10CouT21-137
10CouT21-138
10CouT21-284
12ImpTobC-65
14B18B-40
14CraJacE-39
15CraJacE-39
16BF2FP-23
16ColE13-55
16SpoNewM-64
19W514-31
75WhiSox1T-8
88PacEigMO-9
88PacEigMO-22
88PacEigMO-25
88PacEigMO-46
88PacEigMO-48
88PacEigMO-106
92Man191BSR-9
94ConTSN-1031
94ConTSNB-1031
Gandolph, David
91GulCoaRSP-4
92GasRanC-16
92GasRanF-2246
93ChaRanC-10
93ChaRanF-1933
94JacGenF-210
Gandy, Chris
79CliDodT-13
Ganley, Robert
08AmeCarE-47
08RosComP-78
09RamT20-49
09SenBarP-3
09T206-138
11SpoLifCW-134
Gann, Chuck
94IdaFalBF-3578
94IdaFalBSP-11
Gann, Jamie
96AriBlaDB-18
Gann, Steve
93BilMusF-3953
93BilMusSP-18
94ChaWheC-1
94ChaWheF-2711
94SouAtlLAF-SAL41
Gannon, James
89MajLeaM-11
Ganote, Joe
90St.CatBJP-3461
91MyrBeaHC-5
91MyrBeaHP-2939
91SouAtlLAGP-SAL38
92DunBluJF-1993
93KnoSmoF-1247
94KnoSmoF-1297
Gant, Ron (Ronald Edwin)
86DurBulP-12
87GreBraB-13
87SouLeaAJ-13
88BlaYNPRWL-57
88Don-654
88DonBasB-2
88DonRoo-47
88Fle-538
88FleGlo-538
88RicBraC-12
88RicBraP-3
88Sco-647
88ScoGlo-647
88StaLinBra-5
88TopBig-249
88TopTra-39T
88TopTraT-39T
89Baz-9
89Bow-274
89BowTif-274
89BraDub-11
89ClaLigB-35
89Don-50
89Fle-590
89FleGlo-590
89K-M-2
89OPC-196
89PanSti-42
89Sco-372
89ScoHot1R-87
89ScoYouSI-16
89Spo-28
89SpoIllFKI-251
89Top-296
89TopBig-43
89TopGloS-10
89TopRoo-9
89TopSti-34
89TopSti-322
89TopTif-296
89TopUKM-29
89ToyRoo-10
89TVSpoM-59
89UppDec-378
90BraDubP-7
90BraDubS-8
90Don-475
90DonBesN-111
90Fle-582
90FleCan-582
90Lea-376
90OPC-567
90PubSti-113
90PubSti-612
90SupActM-11
90Top-567
90TopBig-66
90TopTif-567
90UppDec-232
90VenSti-195
90VenSti-196
91Bow-583
91BraDubP-10
91BraSubS-14
91Cla1-T5
91Cla3-T23
91Cla3-T24
91ClaGam-123
91Don-10
91Don-507
91DonSupD-10
91Fle-688
91Lea-129
91MajLeaCP-47
91OPC-725
91OPCPre-49
91PanCanT1-36
91PanCanT1-52
91PanFreS-23
91PanSti-27
91RedFolS-38
91Sco-448
91Sco100S-14
91StaClu-454
91StaPinB-19
91Stu-144
91Top-725
91TopCraJ2-19
91TopDesS-725
91TopMic-725
91TopTif-725
91TopTriH-N1
91Ult-4
91UppDec-82
91UppDec-361
92Bow-534
92BraLykP-12
92BraLykS-13
92Cla2-T19
92ClaGam-15
92Don-284
92Fle-357
92FleLumC-L9
92Hig5-22
92Hig5S-16
92Lea-15
92OPC-25
92OPCPre-4
92PanSti-167
92Pin-128
92PinSlu-8
92Sco-25
92Sco100S-76
92ScoCokD-9
92ScoImpP-65
92ScoProP-9
92StaClu-730
92StaCluD-55
92StaCluNC-730
92StaGan-1
92StaGan-2
92StaGan-3
92StaGan-4
92StaGan-5
92StaGan-6
92StaGan-7
92StaGan-8
92StaGan-9
92StaGan-10
92StaGan-11
92Stu-3
92Top-25
92Top-391
92TopGol-25
92TopGol-391
92TopGolW-25
92TopGolW-391
92TopKid-32
92TopMcD-14
92TopMic-25
92TopMic-391
92TriPla-126
92Ult-161
92UppDec-345
92UppDecHRH-HR7
93Bow-382
93BraLykP-10
93BraLykS-12
93DiaMar-37
93Don-210
93DonEliD-4
93Fin-68
93FinRef-68
93Fla-3
93Fle-3
93Lea-225
93OPC-108
93PacSpa-5
93PanSti-185
93Pin-445
93PinHomRC-20
93Sco-220
93Sel-133
93SP-57
93SPPlaP-PP7
93StaClu-28
93StaCluB-6
93StaCluFDI-28
93StaCluM-98
93StaCluMOP-28
93Stu-88
93Top-393
93TopGol-393
93TopInaM-393
93TopMic-393
93TriPla-199
93Ult-5
93UppDec-264
93UppDecGold-264
94BraUSPC-1C
94BraUSPC-2D
94BraUSPC-8D
94CarLeaA-DJ6
94Don-34
94DonDom-A8
94DonSpeE-34
94Fin-165
94FinRef-165
94Fle-358
94Fle-706
94FleLumC-3
94Pac-8
94PacGolP-15
94PanSti-144
94RedKah-12
94Sco-332
94ScoGolR-332
94ScoGolS-14
94Spo-90
94StaClu-111
94StaClu-123
94StaClu-260
94StaCluFDI-111
94StaCluFDI-123
94StaCluFDI-260
94StaCluGR-111
94StaCluGR-123
94StaCluGR-260
94StaCluMO-26
94StaCluMOP-111
94StaCluMOP-123
94StaCluMOP-260
94StaCluP-123
94StaCluT-41
94StaCluTFDI-41
94Top-166
94TopBlaG-31
94TopGol-166
94TopSpa-166
94TopTra-55T
94TriPla-43
94TriPlaBS-7
94UltHomRK-11
94UltRBIK-9
94USPlaCA-5C
95BowBes-R62
95BowBesR-R62
95ClaPhoC-17
95ColCho-429
95ColChoGS-429
95ColChoSE-196
95ColChoSEGS-196
95ColChoSESS-196
95ColChoSS-429
95DonTopotO-212
95Emo-116
95EmoN-5
95Fin-230
95FinRef-230
95Fla-338
95FleUpd-132
95Lea-324
95LeaLim-182
95Pin-228
95PinArtP-228
95PinMusC-228
95RedKah-7

95Sel-141
95SelArtP-141
95SP-42
95SPCha-33
95SPCha-35
95SPChaDC-33
95SPChaDC-35
95SPPlaP-PP3
95SPSil-42
95StaClu-528
95StaCluMOP-528
95StaCluSTDW-RE528
95StaCluSTWS-528
95Top-627
95Ult-365
95UltGolM-365
95UppDec-489T
95UppDecSE-166
95UppDecSEG-166
95Zen-92
96Baz-72
96Bow-31
96BowBes-12
96BowBesAR-12
96BowBesR-12
96CarPol-8
96ColCho-110
96ColCho-711
96ColCho-784
96ColChoCtG-CG27
96ColChoCtG-CG27B
96ColChoCtG-CG27C
96ColChoCtGE-CR27
96ColChoCtGG-CG27
96ColChoCtGG-CG27B
96ColChoCtGG-CG27C
96ColChoCtGGE-CR27
96ColChoGS-110
96ColChoGS-711
96ColChoSS-110
96ColChoSS-711
96ColChoYMtP-14
96ColChoYMtP-14A
96ColChoYMtPGS-14
96ColChoYMtPGS-14A
96Don-415
96DonPreP-415
96EmoXL-266
96Fin-B244
96Fin-G308
96FinRef-B244
96FinRef-G308
96Fla-359
96Fle-340
96FleTif-340
96FleUpd-U189
96FleUpdTC-U189
96LeaPreSG-45
96LeaPreSte-45
96LeaSig-108
96LeaSigPPG-108
96LeaSigPPP-108
96MetUni-224
96MetUniP-224
96MLBPin-11
96Pac-48
96PacPri-P15
96PacPriG-P15
96PanSti-55
96Pin-152
96Pin-333
96PinAfi-27
96PinAfiAP-27
96PinAfiFPP-27
96PinArtP-79
96PinFoil-333
96PinSta-79
96Sco-337
96ScoDugC-B62
96ScoDugCAP-B62
96SP-156
96SPSpeFX-17
96SPSpeFXDC-17
96SPx-47
96SPxGol-47
96StaClu-203
96StaClu-364
96StaCluB&B-BB6
96StaCluEPB-364
96StaCluEPG-364
96StaCluEPS-364
96StaCluMM-MM10
96StaCluMOP-203
96StaCluMOP-364
96StaCluMOP-BB6
96StaCluMOP-MM10
96StaCluMOP-PP5
96StaCluPP-PP5
96Stu-89
96StuPrePB-89
96StuPrePG-89
96StuPrePS-89
96Sum-8
96SumAbo&B-8
96SumArtP-8
96SumFoi-8
96Top-70
96TopChr-25
96TopChrR-25
96TopChrWC-WC7
96TopChrWCR-WC7
96TopGal-68
96TopGalPPI-68
96TopLas-7
96TopPro-NL13
96TopRoaW-RW8
96TopWreC-WC7
96Ult-178
96Ult-547
96UltGolM-178
96UltGolM-547
96UppDec-152
96UppDec-443
96UppDecPRE-R33
96UppDecPreR-R33
97Bow-252
97BowBes-12
97BowBesAR-12
97BowBesR-12
97BowChr-75
97BowChrI-75
97BowChrIR-75
97BowChrR-75
97BowInt-252
97Cir-310
97CirRav-310
97ColCho-205
97Don-174
97DonEli-135
97DonEliGS-135
97DonLim-24
97DonLimLE-24
97DonPre-73
97DonPreCttC-73
97DonPreP-174
97DonPrePGold-174
97DonTea-156
97DonTeaSPE-156
97Fin-130
97Fin-333
97FinEmb-130
97FinEmb-333
97FinEmbR-130
97FinEmbR-333
97FinRef-130
97FinRef-333
97FlaSho-A28
97FlaSho-B28
97FlaSho-C28
97FlaShoLC-28
97FlaShoLC-B28
97FlaShoLC-C28
97FlaShoLCM-A28
97FlaShoLCM-B28
97FlaShoLCM-C28
97Fle-443
97FleTif-443
97Lea-226
97LeaFraM-226
97LeaFraMDC-226
97MetUni-230
97NewPin-69
97NewPinAP-69
97NewPinMC-69
97NewPinPP-69
97Pac-410
97PacLigB-410
97PacPri-138
97PacPriLB-138
97PacPriP-138
97PacSil-410
97Pin-81
97PinArtP-81
97PinCer-65
97PinCerMBlu-65
97PinCerMG-65
97PinCerMR-65
97PinCerR-65
97PinIns-108
97PinInsCE-108
97PinInsDE-108
97PinMusC-81
97PinTotCPB-65
97PinTotCPG-65
97PinTotCPR-65
97PinX-P-110
97PinX-PMoS-110
97PinX-PSfF-45
97PinX-PSfFU-45
97Sco-268
97ScoHeaotO-29
97ScoPreS-268
97ScoShoS-268
97ScoShoSAP-268
97Sel-80
97SelArtP-80
97SelRegG-80
97SkyE-X-98
97SkyE-XC-98
97SkyE-XEC-98
97SP-150
97SpoIll-105
97SpoIllEE-105
97SPx-40
97SPxBro-40
97SPxGraF-40
97SPxSil-40
97SPxSte-40
97StaClu-242
97StaCluMat-242
97StaCluMOP-242
97Stu-4
97StuPrePG-4
97StuPrePS-4
97Top-127
97TopChr-48
97TopChrR-48
97TopGal-59
97TopGalPPI-59
97TopSta-9
97TopStaAM-9
97Ult-270
97UltDouT-18
97UltGolME-270
97UltPlaME-270
97UppDec-160
97UppDec-257
97UppDec-371
97UppDecU-24

Gantner, Jim

76VenLeaS-216
77SpoIndC-4
77Top-494
79Top-154
80Top-374
81Don-204
81Fle-522
81OPC-122
81Top-482
82BrePol-17
82Don-406
82Fle-142
82FleSta-133
82OPC-207
82Top-613
83AllGamPI-11
83BreGar-8
83BrePol-17
83Don-232
83Fle-34
83FleSti-12
83OPC-88
83Top-88
84AllGamPI-102
84BreGar-7
84BrePol-17
84Don-115
84Fle-200
84Nes792-298
84OPC-298
84Top-298
84TopSti-298
84TopTif-298
85AllGamPI-12
85BreGar-7
85BrePol-17
85Don-229
85DonActA-2
85Fle-582
85Lea-217
85OPC-216
85Top-781
85TopSti-295
85TopTif-781
86BrePol-17
86Don-115
86Fle-487
86Lea-43
86MSAJayPCD-8
86OPC-51
86Top-582
86TopSti-202
86TopTat-9
86TopTif-582
87BrePol-17
87BreTeal-6
87Don-172
87DonOpeD-53
87Fle-345
87FleGlo-345
87OPC-108
87SmoAmeL-15
87Top-108
87TopSti-197
87TopTif-108
88BrePol-17
88Don-214
88DonBasB-53
88Fle-165
88FleGlo-165
88Lea-161
88OPC-337
88PanSti-123
88PanSti-124
88Sco-197
88ScoGlo-197
88Spo-130
88StaLinBre-8
88Top-337
88TopSti-195
88TopTif-337
89Bow-141
89BowTif-141
89BreGar-3
89BrePol-17
89BreYea-17
89Don-264
89DonBasB-295
89Fle-186
89FleGlo-186
89OPC-134
89PanSti-372
89Sco-313
89Top-671
89TopBig-184
89TopSti-203
89TopTif-671
89TVSpoM-76
89UppDec-274
90Bow-400
90BowTif-400
90BreMilB-9
90BrePol-17
90Don-291
90Fle-324
90FleCan-324
90MLBBasB-81
90OPC-417
90PanSti-94
90PubSti-496
90Sco-382
90Top-417
90TopBig-124
90TopSti-207
90TopTif-417
90UppDec-218
90VenSti-197
91Bow-48
91BreMilB-8
91BrePol-8
91Don-703
91Fle-584
91Lea-145
91OPC-23
91Sco-532
91StaClu-183
91Top-23
91TopDesS-23
91TopMic-23
91TopTif-23
91Ult-174
91UppDec-618
92Bow-301
92BreCarT-8
92BrePol-8
92Don-574
92Fle-176
92OPC-248
92PanSti-37
92Pin-71
92Sco-246
92ScoProP-20
92StaClu-502
92Top-248
92TopGol-248
92TopGolW-248
92TopMic-248
92Ult-382
92UppDec-360
93Fle-630
93PacSpa-156
93Pin-207
94BreMilB-29
94BreMilB-313

Ganzel, Babe (Foster Pirie)

28StaPlaCE-23

Ganzel, Charles

87OldJudN-192
89N526N7C-5
95May-10
98CamPepP-28

Ganzel, John Henry

08RosComP-115
09T206-424
11SpoLifCW-135
12ImpTobC-26

Gapski, Mark

94WatIndC-10
94WatIndF-3929

Garagiola, Joe

47TipTop-156
49EurSta-182
51Bow-122
52Bow-27
52Top-227
53BowC-21
54Bow-141
79DiaGre-162
79TCM50-262
80PacLeg-76
82DiaCla-34
83TopRep5-227
85TCMPla1-24
90PacLeg-24
90SweBasG-14
91SweBasG-31
91TopArc1-314
92ActPacA-43
92BazQua5A-21
93TedWil-89
94UppDecAH-19
94UppDecAH1-19

Garagozzo, Keith

91OneYanP-4148
92ClaFS7-290
92GreHorC-2
92GreHorF-772
93PriWilCC-12
93PriWilCF-651
94Bow-656
94ColCliF-2947
94Fla-74
94Ult-388

Garbark, Bob

36DiaMatCS3T2-11
39CubTeal-7
93ConTSN-946

Garbark, Mike

83TCMPla1944-8

Garber, Gene

74OPC-431
74Top-431
75OPC-444
75Top-444
76OPC-14
76SSP-458
76Top-14
77Top-289
78BraCok-4
78PhiSSP-38
78SSP270-38
78Top-177
79OPC-331
79Top-629
80OPC-263
80Top-504
81BraPol-26
81Don-77
81Fle-249
81OPC-307

81Top-307
82BraBurKL-8
82BraPol-26
82Don-123
82Fle-434
82Top-32
83BraPol-26
83Don-223
83Fle-136
83FleSta-66
83FleSti-87
83OPC-255
83OPC-256
83Top-255
83Top-256
83TopFol-4
83TopSti-213
84BraPol-26
84Don-287
84Fle-179
84Nes792-466
84Nes792-709
84OPC-167
84Top-466
84Top-709
84TopSti-35
84TopTif-466
84TopTif-709
85BraHos-9
85BraPol-26
85Fle-325
85Top-129
85TopTif-129
86BraPol-26
86Fle-515
86Top-776
86TopTif-776
87BraSmo-9
87Don-414
87Fle-515
87FleExcS-17
87FleGlo-515
87FleRecS-10
87FleStiC-44
87Lea-172
87SpoTeaP-24
87Top-351
87TopSti-40
87TopTif-351
88Don-618
88DonBasB-63
88Fle-257
88FleGlo-257
88OPC-289
88RoySmo-11
88Sco-565
88ScoGlo-565
88Spo-88
88StaLinRo-4
88Top-597
88TopTif-597

Garber, Jeff
88EugEmeB-16
89AppFoxP-863
90BasCitRS-8
91LinDriAA-406
91MemChiLD-406
91MemChiP-660
92MemChiF-2425
92MemChiS-435
93MemChiF-380
94MemChiF-365
96SpoIndB-2

Garber, Joel
96HicCraB-7
96SouBenSHS-13

Garbey, Barbaro
81BirBarT-22
82BirBarT-2
83EvaTriT-18
84FleUpd-42
84TigFarJ-3
84TigWavP-15
84TopTra-41T
84TopTraT-41T
85Don-456
85Fle-7
85FleStaS-121
85Lea-121
85OPC-243
85TigCaiD-7
85TigWen-8
85Top-243
85TopSti-263
85TopTif-243
86Don-349
86Fle-225
86OPC-88
86Top-609
86TopTif-609
88OklCit8C-16
88OklCit8P-45
90BirBarDGB-13
93RanKee-157

Garbould, Bob
44CenFlo-8

Garbozo, Toribio
76VenLeaS-81
80VenLeaS-244

Garces, Jesus
90PriPatD-7
91BatCliC-9
91BatCliP-3491
92SpaPhiC-5
92SpaPhiF-1268
93LinVenB-97
94VenLinU-178
95LinVen-110

Garces, Maduro
89HagSunB-6

Garces, Rich (Richard)
89KenTwiP-1076
89KenTwiS-6
89Sta-51
90CalLeaACLC-18
90ProAaA-140
90VisOakCLC-62
90VisOakP-2148
91Bow-324
91Cla1-T59
91Don-420
91LinDriAAA-408
91OPC-594
91PorBeaLD-408
91PorBeaP-1562
91StaClu-370
91Top-594
91TopDeb90-50
91TopDesS-594
91TopMic-594
91TopTif-594
91Ult-378
91UppDec-741
92Don-516
92OrlSunRF-2840
92OrlSunRS-505
92SkyAA F-217
93LinVenB-214
93PorBeaF-2379
94NasXprF-378
94VenLinU-196
95LinVen-120
95LinVen-283
95LinVen-287
96Pac-73
97PacPriGotD-GD20

Garces, Robinson
87LakTigP-21
88FayGenP-1087
89HagSunP-281
89HagSunS-8
90ElPasDGS-13
93LinVenB-31
94VenLinU-208
95LinVen-66

Garcia, Adrian
92PulBraC-11
92PulBraF-3180
93MacBraC-9
93MacBraF-1402
94DurBulC-7
94DurBulF-330
94DurBulTI-6

Garcia, Alfredo
94HunCubF-3546
95RocCubTI-21
96DayCubB-13
94HunCubC-10

Garcia, Amadeo
89EliTwiS-26

Garcia, Amaury
95ElmPioTI-7
95ElmPioUTI-7
96KanCouCTI-9
96KanCouCUTI-5
96MidLeaAB-32

Garcia, Anastacio
90MedHatBJB-13
91DunBluJC-13
91DunBluJP-209
92MyrBeaHC-5
92MyrBeaHF-2199
93KnoSmoF-1253

Garcia, Anthony
89SalDodTI-3
90BakDodCLC-245

Garcia, Antonio
76VenLeaS-208
80VenLeaS-234

Garcia, Apolinar
89MadMusS-10
90ModA'sC-10
90ModA'sP-2206
91HunStaTI-10
91LinDriAAA-534
91TacTigLD-534
91TacTigP-2298
92Ft.MyeMCB-5
92Ft.MyeMF-2738
93CanIndF-2833
93LimRocDWB-98
94CanIndF-3115

Garcia, Apostol
94BriTigC-13
94BriTigF-3510
96FayGenB-17

Garcia, Ariel
93SouBenWSC-10
93SouBenWSF-1424
95MidLeaA-19
96SouBenSHS-14

Garcia, Butch
90ChaKniTI-10

Garcia, Butch (Victor)
86IndTeal-21
87ColMetP-16
87PeoChiP-2
87PeoChiPW-1
88CarLeaAS-27
88PriWilYS-11
88WinSpiS-3
89BlaYNPRWL-175
89ChaKniTI-7
89Ft.LauYS-5
89GreHorP-407
89IowCubC-11
89IowCubP-1693
90CedRapRB-16
90CedRapRP-2315
90Ft.LauYS-8
90MidLeaASGS-33
90ProAaA-122
91AlbYanLD-5
91AlbYanP-1001
91ChaLooLD-159
91ChaLooP-1954
91LinDriAA-5
91LinDriAA-159
92CanIndF-684
92CanIndS-107
93ChaLooF-2357
93LimRocDWB-102
94AshTouC-1

Garcia, Cano (Efrain)
90IBAWorA-6

Garcia, Carlos Jesus
88AugPirP-365
89SalBucS-9
90CMC-761
90EasLeaAP-EL25
90HarSenP-1199
90HarSenS-7
90ProAaA-28
91Bow-531
91BufBisLD-29
91BufBisP-546
91Fle-37
91LinDriAAA-29
91TopDeb90-51
91Ult-278
92Bow-576
92BufBisBS-9
92BufBisF-327
92BufBisS-33
92Cla1-T37
92Don-14
92Pin-264
92ProFS7-305
92Sco-821
92SkyAAAF-14
92TriA AAS-33
92UppDec-665
93Bow-626
93Don-598
93Fin-4
93FinRef-4
93Fla-112
93Fle-501
93Lea-277
93LinVenB-200
93OPCPre-111
93PacSpa-244
93Pin-558
93PirNatI-12
93Sco-246
93ScoBoyoS-14
93Sel-403
93SelRoo-40T
93SP-184
93StaClu-545
93StaCluFDI-545
93StaCluMOP-545
93Stu-49
93Top-27
93TopGol-27
93TopInaM-27
93TopMic-27
93Toy-70
93TriPla-65
93Ult-450
93UppDec-334
93UppDecGold-334
94Bow-218
94ColC-105
94ColChoGS-105
94ColChoSS-105
94Don-161
94ExtBas-345
94ExtBasSYS-7
94Fin-57
94FinRef-57
94Fla-420
94Fle-609
94FUnPac-168
94Lea-248
94OPC-112
94OPCDiaD-18
94Pac-498
94PanSti-235
94Pin-108
94PinArtP-108
94PinMusC-108
94PirQui-7
94ProMag-106
94Sco-520
94ScoGolR-520
94Sel-119
94SP-141
94SPDieC-141
94StaClu-206
94StaCluFDI-206
94StaCluGR-206
94StaCluMOP-206
94Stu-145
94Top-309
94TopGol-309
94TopSpa-309
94TriPla-183
94Ult-555
94UppDec-198
94UppDecED-198
94USPlaCR-3H
94USPlaCR-6C
94USPlaCR-10D
94VenLinU-1
95Bow-373
95ColCho-376
95ColChoGS-376
95ColChoSE-178
95ColChoSEGS-178
95ColChoSESS-178
95ColChoSS-376
95D3-17
95Don-91
95DonPreP-91
95DonTopotO-315
95Emb-74
95EmbGolI-74
95Fin-110
95FinRef-110
95Fla-399
95Fle-479
95FleAllS-12
95ForWayWTI-16
95Lea-2
95LeaLim-146
95LinVen-80
95LinVen-266
95Pac-343
95PacLatD-14
95PacPri-112
95PanSti-43
95Pin-116
95PinArtP-116
95PinMusC-116
95PirFil-10
95Sco-236
95ScoGolR-236
95ScoHaloG-HG51
95ScoPlaTS-236
95Sel-114
95SelArtP-114
95SP-93
95Spo-59
95SpoArtP-59
95SPSil-93
95StaClu-11
95StaCluFDI-11
95StaCluMOP-11
95StaCluSTWS-11
95StaCluVR-6
95Stu-54
95Top-515
95TopCyb-303
95Ult-215
95UltGolM-215
95UppDec-151
95UppDecED-151
95UppDecEDG-151
95UppDecSE-221
95UppDecSEG-221
96ColCho-685
96ColChoGS-685
96ColChoSS-685
96Don-457
96DonPreP-457
96EmoXL-253
96Fin-B187
96FinRef-B187
96Fla-345
96Fle-521
96FleTif-521
96ForWayWB-8
96Lea-81
96LeaPrePB-81
96LeaPrePG-81
96LeaPrePS-81
96LeaSigA-76
96LeaSigAG-76
96LeaSigAS-76
96MetUni-215
96MetUniP-215
96Pac-177
96PacPri-P57
96PacPriG-P57
96PanSti-69
96Pin-285
96PinFoil-285
96ProSta-92
96Sco-14
96SP-149
96StaClu-153
96StaCluMOP-153
95StaCluVRMC-6
96Top-415
96TopGal-80
96TopGalPPI-80
96Ult-531
96UltGolM-531
96UppDec-179
97BluJayS-7
97Cir-371
97CirRav-371
97ColCho-497
97Don-243
97DonPreP-243
97DonPrePGold-243
97Fin-217
97FinRef-217
97Fle-427
97Fle-553
97FleTif-427
97FleTif-553
97Lea-275
97LeaFraM-275
97LeaFraMDC-275
97NewPin-153
97NewPinAP-153
97NewPinMC-153
97NewPinPP-153

97PacPri-134
97PacPriGotD-GD192
97PacPriLB-134
97PacPriP-134
97Pin-34
97PinArtP-34
97PinMusC-34
97Sco-297
97Sco-353
97ScoHobR-353
97ScoPreS-297
97ScoResC-353
97ScoShoS-297
97ScoShoS-353
97ScoShoSAP-297
97ScoShoSAP-353
97StaClu-156
97StaCluMOP-156
97Stu-115
97StuPrePG-115
97StuPrePS-115
97Top-34
97Ult-260
97Ult-418
97UltGolME-260
97UltGolME-418
97UltPlaME-260
97UltPlaME-418
Garcia, Cheo
89KenTwiP-1083
89KenTwiS-7
91LinDriAA-480
91OrlSunRLD-480
91OrlSunRP-1855
92OrlSunRF-2853
92OrlSunRS-501
92ProFS7-94
93PawRedSDD-12
93PawRedSF-2413
93PawRedSTI-12
Garcia, Chico (Vinicio U.)
54OriEss-13
91OriCro-149
Garcia, Chidez (Cornelio)
86AppFoxP-9
88FloStaLAS-37
88TamTarS-7
89BirBarB-9
89BirBarP-102
90BirBarB-9
90BirBarP-1117
Garcia, Damaso
76ForLauYS-15
77WesHavYT-10
78TacYanC-42
79ColCliT-4
81AllGamPI-12
81Don-269
81Fle-415
81OPC-233
81OPCPos-14
81Top-488
81TopScr-42
81TopSti-137
82Don-479
82Fle-613
82FleSta-234
82OPC-293
82OPCPos-2
82Top-596
82TopSti-245
83AllGamPI-12
83Don-54
83DonActA-17
83Fle-427
83FleSta-67
83FleSti-105
83OPC-202
83OPC-222
83PerCreC-24
83PerCreCG-24
83Top-202
83Top-222
83TopSti-134
84AllGamPI-103
84BluJayFS-12
84Don-241
84Fle-153
84Nes792-124
84OPC-124
84Top-124
84TopRubD-14
84TopSti-364
84TopTif-124
85AllGamPI-13
85BluJayFS-11
85Don-315
85DonActA-6
85Fle-104
85Lea-65
85OPC-353
85OPCPos-15
85Top-645
85Top-702
85TopRubD-12
85TopSti-357
85TopTif-645
85TopTif-702
86BluJayAF-10
86BluJayFS-12
86Don-241
86DonAll-40
86Fle-59
86FleLimE-17
86FleMin-15
86FleStiC-41
86GenMilB-3E
86Lea-116
86OPC-45
86Spo-34
86Top-45
86Top-713
86TopSti-190
86TopTat-24
86TopTif-45
86TopTif-713
87BraSmo-22
87Don-614
87Fle-226
87FleGlo-226
87Lea-92
87OPC-395
87Spo-183
87Top-395
87TopSti-188
87TopTif-395
88Don-414
88Top-241
88TopTif-241
89ExpPos-9
89TopBig-275
90BluJayHS-1
90Fle-346
90FleCan-346
90OPC-432
90Top-432
90TopTif-432
90UppDec-649
92Nab-20
92YanWIZ7-52
97BluJayS-44
Garcia, Danny
76WatRoyT-9
80OmaRoyP-12
80VenLeaS-225
91SpoIndC-28
91SpoIndP-3966
92WicWraF-3670
Garcia, Dave
73OPC-12
73Top-12A
73Top-12B
78AngFamF-12
78SSP270-193
78Top-656
80Top-451
81Don-442
81Top-665
82Don-337
82Ind-13
82IndBurK-1
82IndBurK-2
82IndTeal-12
82IndWhe-4
83BrePol-NNO
83Top-546
84BrePol-NNO
Garcia, Eduardo
92GulCoaDF-3579
94HunCubF-3565
94PriRedC-9
94PriRedF-3256
95BilRedTI-20
94HunCubC-11
Garcia, Fermin
91PriRedC-27
91PriRedP-3506
92BenMusSP-23
92BilMusF-3347
92ChaWheF-2
92ChaWVWC-4
93WesVirWC-8
93WesVirWF-2860
Garcia, Francisco
90AppFoxBS-8
90AppFoxP-2107
Garcia, Frank
80AshTouT-23
80TulDriT-12
83St.PetCT-17
96StPetCB-8
Garcia, Freddy
93MedHatBJF-3744
93MedHatBJSP-14
94St.CatBJC-9
94St.CatBJF-3651
95Bow-213
95Exc-136
95FleUpd-147
95PirFil-11
95SP-18
95SPSil-18
95UppDec-261
95UppDecED-261
95UppDecEDG-261
95UppDecSE-222
95UppDecSEG-222
96Bow-129
96ColCho-261
96ColChoGS-261
96ColChoSS-261
96LynHilB-10
96QuaCitRB-14
97Bow-135
97BowChr-144
97BowChrI-144
97BowChrIR-144
97BowChrR-144
97BowInt-135
Garcia, Guillermo
91KinMetC-14
91KinMetP-3821
92PitMetC-6
92PitMetF-3299
93CapCitBC-6
93CapCitBF-462
93SouAtlLAGF-35
94FloStaLAF-FSL38
94St.LucMC-10
94St.LucMF-1198
Garcia, Jaime
92SouBenWSC-26
92SouBenWSF-194
93SouBenWSC-28
93SouBenWSF-1447
94SouBenSHC-26
94SouBenSHF-611
95PriWilCTI-30
96DelShoB-18
96PriWilCB-2
Garcia, Jason
94DanBraC-11
94DanBraF-3540
Garcia, Jesse
94OriPro-36
96HigDesMB-11
Garcia, Joe
75SanAntBT-6
Garcia, Jose Cheo
94VenLinU-260
95LinVen-106
Garcia, Jose Luis
90CalLeaACLC-4
90CMC-714
90VisOakCLC-78
90VisOakP-2161
93BakDodCLC-8
93LimRocDWB-55
93LinVenB-56
93YakBeaC-9
93YakBeaF-3879
94VerBeaDF-64
95EugEmeTI-11
95SanAntMTI-26
96HelBreTI-5
96MacBraB-7
Garcia, Julio
89PriPirS-26
89SalBucS-NNO
91AugPirC-1
91AugPirP-823
92AugPirC-26
92WelPirC-29
92WelPirF-1342
93WelPirC-30
94BufBisF-1854
94OneYanF-3799
96FreKeyB-24
Garcia, Karim
93BakDodCLC-9
94Cla-167
94FloStaLAF-FSL46
94UppDecML-103
94VerBeaDC-7
94VerBeaDF-86
95Bow-92
95BowBes-B56
95BowBes-X13
95BowBesR-B56
95BowBesR-X13
95ColCho-39
95ColChoGS-39
95ColChoSS-39
95Exc-212
95SigRooOJ-14
95SigRooOJP-14
95SigRooOJPS-14
95SigRooOJS-14
95Top-237
95UppDec-9
95UppDecED-9
95UppDecEDG-9
95UppDecML-14
95UppDecSE-33
95UppDecSEG-33
96BesAutSA-21
96Bow-340
96BowBes-101
96BowBesAR-101
96BowBesMI-5
96BowBesMIAR-5
96BowBesMIR-5
96BowBesP-BBP29
96BowBesPAR-BBP29
96BowBesPR-BBP29
96BowBesR-101
96BowMinLP-7
96ColCho-35
96ColChoGS-35
96ColChoSS-35
96DodPol-14
96Don-474
96DonPreP-474
96EmoXL-208
96Fin-G20
96FinRef-G20
96Fla-292
96FlaWavotF-10
96FleDod-8
96FlePro-5
96FleUpd-U144
96FleUpdTC-U144
96Lea-220
96LeaPrePB-220
96LeaPrePG-220
96LeaPrePS-220
96LeaSig-149
96LeaSigEA-57
96LeaSigEACM-6
96LeaSigPPG-149
96LeaSigPPP-149
96PacPri-P33
96PacPriG-P33
96Pin-368
96PinAfi-154
96PinAfi-173
96PinAfiAP-154
96PinAfiAP-173
96PinFoil-368
96PinProS-3
96PinTeaT-10
96SanAntMB-5
96Sco-220
96Sco-383
96ScoDugC-A102
96ScoDugC-B108
96ScoDugCAP-A102
96ScoDugCAP-B108
96ScoFutF-9
96Sel-192
96SelArtP-192
96SelCer-102
96SelCerAP-102
96SelCerCB-102
96SelCerCR-102
96SelCerMB-102
96SelCerMG-102
96SelCerMR-102
96SigRooOJMR-M3
96SP-15
96StaClu-255
96StaCluMOP-255
96Sum-159
96Sum-196
96SumAbo&B-159
96SumAbo&B-196
96SumArtP-159
96SumArtP-196
96SumFoi-159
96SumFoi-196
96Top-217
96TopChr-79
96TopChrR-79
96TopGal-131
96TopGalPPI-131
96Ult-497
96UltGolM-497
96UppDec-223
96UppDecBCP-BC8
96Zen-101
96ZenArtP-101
96ZenDiaC-19
96ZenDiaCP-19
97Bow-136
97Bow98ROY-ROY2
97BowBes-147
97BowBesAR-147
97BowBesR-147
97BowCerBIA-CA29
97BowCerGIA-CA29
97BowChr-145
97BowChr1RC-ROY2
97BowChr1RCR-ROY2
97BowChrI-145
97BowChrIR-145
97BowChrR-145
97BowInt-136
97BowIntB-BBI17
97BowIntBAR-BBI17
97BowIntBR-BBI17
97ColCho-138
97Don-360
97DonEli-64
97DonEliGS-64
97DonLim-111
97DonLimLE-111
97DonPre-149
97DonPreCttC-149
97DonPreP-360
97DonPrePGold-360
97DonRatR-15
97DonTea-118
97DonTeaSPE-118
97Fin-309
97FinEmb-309
97FinEmbR-309
97FinRef-309
97Fle-362
97FleTif-362
97Lea-337
97LeaFraM-337
97LeaFraMDC-337
97Pac-330
97PacLigB-330
97PacPri-110
97PacPriLB-110
97PacPriP-110
97PacPriSL-SL11C
97PacSil-330
97PinIns-134
97PinInsCE-134
97PinInsDD-20
97PinInsDE-134
97Sco-316
97ScoPreS-316
97ScoShoS-316
97Sel-108
97SelArtP-108
97SelRegG-108
97SelRooR-20
97SelToootT-5
97SelToootTMB-5
97StaClu-237
97StaCluC-CO10
97StaCluM-M18
97StaCluMat-237
97StaCluMOP-237
97StaCluMOP-M18
97Stu-150
97StuHarH-21

97StuPrePG-150
97StuPrePS-150
97Top-363
97TopChr-124
97TopChrR-124
97Ult-216
97UltGolME-216
97UltGolP-4
97UltPlaME-216
97UppDec-398
97UppDecBCP-BC13
95UppDecMLFS-14
97UppDecTTS-TS13
Garcia, Ken
86AncGlaPTI-10
Garcia, Kiko (Alfonso)
77Top-474
78Top-287
79Top-543
80Top-37
81Don-514
81Fle-191
81OPC-192
81Top-688
81TopTra-765
82AstAstI-9
82Don-470
82Fle-215
82Top-377
83Don-569
83Fle-447
83PorBeaT-25
83Top-198
83TopTra-36T
84Don-545
84Fle-30
84Nes792-458
84PhiTas-30
84Top-458
84TopTif-458
85PhiTas-29
85Top-763
85TopTif-763
91OriCro-150
Garcia, Leo
81AppFoxT-15
82AppFoxF-3
83WatRedT-17
84WicAerRD-4
87NasSouTI-5
89TolMudHC-16
89TolMudHP-767
90CMC-140
90NasSouC-15
90NasSouP-245
90ProAAAF-557
91LinDriAAA-256
91NasSouLD-256
91NasSouP-2169
92OmaRoyF-2974
92OmaRoyS-330
Garcia, Leonard
77SalLakCGC-NNO
79SalLakCGT-23A
80SalLakCGT-19
81SalLakCGT-1
82SpoIndT-26
86EdmTraP-12
78STLakCGC-NNO
Garcia, Librado
89BelBreIS-6
89BelBreIS-11
90MiaMirIS-8
Garcia, Longo
87PanAmTURB-14
89MiaMirIS-7
89MiaMirIS-5
87PanAmTUBI-21
Garcia, Luis
90LSUTigP-13
92GulCoaRSP-15
92KenTwiC-16
92KenTwiF-596
93BriTigC-9
93BriTigF-3652
93ForMyeMC-8
93ForMyeMF-2649
93IdaFalBSP-18
94JamJamC-10
94JamJamF-3972
96Bow-138
96JacSunB-14
Garcia, Manny
89ButCopKSP-19
91KanCouCC-16
91KanCouCP-2663
91KanCouCTI-7
Garcia, Marcelino
92SpoIndC-11
92SpoIndF-1296
Garcia, Marcos
90PenPilS-8
91CalLeLA-22
91SanBerSC-4
91SanBerSP-1980
92JacSunS-356
Garcia, Mario
90PriPatD-8
91HunCubC-9
91HunCubP-3327
92HunCubF-3139
Garcia, Michael
89BufBisC-7
89BufBisP-1686
90FayGenP-2398
Garcia, Miguel
75BurBeeT-8
76CliPilT-16
86PalSprAP-8
86PalSprAP-14
87MidAngP-1
89Don-622
89Fle-647
89FleGlo-647
90HarSenP-1188
90HarSenS-8
90UppDec-538
Garcia, Miguel A.
93LimRocDWB-92
93LinVenB-34
94VenLinU-186
94WatIndC-11
94WatIndF-3952
95GreFalDTI-37
95LinVen-121
96GreFalDB-14
96GreFalDTI-10
Garcia, Mike (Edward M.)
49IndTeal-10
50Bow-147
50IndNumN-10
50IndTeal-10
51Bow-150
51TopRedB-40
52Bow-7
52IndNumN-7
52Top-272
53BowC-43
53IndPenCBP-12
53Top-75
54Bow-100
54DanDee-8
55Bow-128
55Ind-2
55IndCarBL-2
55IndGolS-4
56Top-210
57IndSoh-5
57Top-300
58Top-196
59Ind-3
59Top-516
60Top-532
80AndBraT-22
81DurBulT-2
82DurBulT-1
83TopRep5-272
89AncBucTI-22
89BriTigS-9
90ProAaA-84
90SouAtlLAS-8
91LakTigC-5
91LakTigP-261
91TopArc1-75
92LonTigF-627
92LonTigS-408
93LonTigF-2300
94TedWil-26
Garcia, Neil
94JamJamF-3968
95FayGenTI-11
Garcia, Nelson Jose
75OklCit8TI-19
76VenLeaS-62
78ArkTraT-11
80ArkTraT-17
80VenLeaS-82
Garcia, Omar
90KinMetB-13
90KinMetS-10
91ColMetPI-9
91ColMetPI-30
91ColMetPPI-6
92ClaFS7-337
92ColMetC-21
92ColMetF-303
92ColMetPI-7
92ColMetPIISPI-8
93ClaFS7-188
93ClaGolF-157
93SouAtlLAPI-11
93St.LucMC-11
94BinMetF-709
94ExcFS7-234
95NorTidTI-12
96RicBraB-12
96RicBraRC-10
93StLucMF-2927
Garcia, Orlando
93PocPosF-4215
93PocPosSP-12
Garcia, Oscar
89St.CatBJP-2075
Garcia, Ossie
93GleFalRC-13
93GleFalRF-4018
94NewJerCC-8
94NewJerCF-3430
96PeoChiB-11
Garcia, Pedro
73LinPor-100
73OPC-609
73Top-609
74OPC-142
74Top-142
74TopSta-195
75OPC-147
75Top-147
76OPC-187
76SSP-234
76Top-187
77OPC-166
77Top-453
77WatIndT-9
86BreGreT-2
94BreMilB-30
Garcia, Ralph
73OPC-602
73Top-602
Garcia, Ramon
90SarWhiSS-10
91BirBarLD-59
91BirBarP-1449
91DonRoo-13
91LinDriAA-59
92ClaGam-97
92Don-658
92DonRoo-41
92OPC-176
92ProFS7-42
92Sco-745
92SkyAAAF-282
92StaClu-866
92Top-176
92TopDeb91-60
92TopGol-176
92TopGolW-176
92TopMic-176
92VanCanF-2716
92VanCanS-635
93LinVenB-30
93NasSouF-567
94WelPirC-10
94WelPirF-3489
95LinVen-95
97PacPriGotD-GD55
Garcia, Raphael
90MedHatBJB-25
91MyrBeaHC-6
91MyrBeaHP-2940
92DunBluJC-14
92MyrBeaHF-2189
Garcia, Ray
85UtiBluST-19
Garcia, Reggie
88MarPhiS-15
89SpaPhiP-1039
89SpaPhiS-9
Garcia, Rene
86BakDodP-10
87VerBeaDP-27
Garcia, Rich
88T/MUmp-22
89T/MUmp-20
90T/MUmp-19
Garcia, Ricky
95ElmPioTI-8
95ElmPioUTI-8
96KanCouCTI-10
Garcia, Santiago
88VanCanC-13
88VanCanP-764
Garcia, Steve
83BeaGolGT-12
84BeaGolGT-18
85LasVegSC-115
86LasVegSP-4
87LasVegSP-20
88AlbDukC-24
88AlbDukP-249
Garcia, Vincente
94AshTouF-1790
95LinVen-206
95SalAvaTI-18
Garcia-Luna, Frank
92WelPirC-8
92WelPirF-1316
94AugGreC-4
Garciaparra, Nomar
92TopTra-39T
92TopTraG-39T
93StaCluM-93
94ClaUpdCotC-CC11
94SigRooDP-12
94SigRooDPS-12
94StaCluDP-69
94StaCluDPFDI-69
95ActPacF-60
95Bes-3
95BesFra-F2
95Bow-249
95BowBes-B29
95BowBesR-B29
95BowGolF-249
95ColCho-29
95ColChoGS-29
95ColChoSS-29
95Exc-10
95SPML-3
95SPML-20
95SPMLA-9
95SPMLDtS-DS15
95StaClu-97
95StaCluFDI-97
95StaCluMOP-97
95StaCluSTWS-97
95Top-587
95TreThuTI-19
95UppDec-10
95UppDecED-10
95UppDecEDG-10
95UppDecML-205
95UppDecMLOP-OP3
95UppDecSE-78
95UppDecSEG-78
96Bow-181
96BowBes-92
96BowBesAR-92
96BowBesP-BBP27
96BowBesPAR-BBP27
96BowBesPR-BBP27
96BowBesR-92
96Exc-12
96Top-211
96TopChr-73
96TopChrR-73
97Bow-328
97BowBes-177
97BowBesAR-177
97BowBesBC-BC20
97BowBesBCAR-BC20
97BowBesBCR-BC20
97BowBesMI-MI1
97BowBesMIAR-MI1
97BowBesMIARI-MI1
97BowBesMII-MI1
97BowBesMIR-MI1
97BowBesMIRI-MI1
97BowBesP-16
97BowBesPAR-16
97BowBesPR-16
97BowBesR-177
97BowChr-224
97BowChrI-224
97BowChrIR-224
97BowChrR-224
97BowChrSHR-SHR15
97BowChrSHRR-SHR15
97BowInt-328
97BowIntB-BBI11
97BowIntBAR-BBI11
97BowIntBR-BBI11
97BowScoHR-15
97Cir-148
97CirRav-148
97ColCho-25
97ColChoBS-2
97ColChoBSGS-2
97Don-362
97DonFraFea-3
97DonLim-40
97DonLim-69
97DonLimFotG-18
97DonLimLE-40
97DonLimLE-69
97DonPre-147
97DonPre-200
97DonPreCttC-147
97DonPreCttC-200
97DonPreP-362
97DonPrePGold-362
97DonRooDK-7
97DonRooDKC-7
97DonTea-60
97DonTeaSPE-60
97Fin-41
97FinRef-41
97FlaSho-A26
97FlaSho-B26
97FlaSho-C26
97FlaShoLC-26
97FlaShoLC-B26
97FlaShoLC-C26
97FlaShoLCM-A26
97FlaShoLCM-B26
97FlaShoLCM-C26
97Fle-22
97FleNewH-4
97FleRooS-13
97FleTif-22
97Lea-185
97Lea-400
97LeaFraM-185
97LeaFraM-400
97LeaFraMDC-185
97LeaFraMDC-400
97LeaGolS-30
97MetUni-21
97MetUniMfG-3
97NewPin-170
97NewPinAP-170
97NewPinMC-170
97NewPinPP-170
97Pac-39
97PacLigB-39
97PacPri-15
97PacPriLB-15
97PacPriP-15
97PacSil-39
97Pin-172
97PinArtP-172
97PinCer-114
97PinCerMBlu-114
97PinCerMG-114
97PinCerMR-114
97PinCerR-114
97PinIns-146
97PinInsCE-146
97PinInsDE-146
97PinMusC-172
97PinTotCPB-114
97PinTotCPG-114
97PinTotCPR-114
97PinX-P-117
97PinX-PMoS-117
97PinX-PMP-14
97PinX-PMW-15
97PinX-PMWG-15
97PinX-PMWS-15
97Sco-473
97ScoHobR-473
97ScoResC-473
97ScoShoS-473
97ScoShoSAP-473
97Sel-106
97SelArtP-106
97SelRegG-106
97SelRooR-14
97SelToootT-25
97SelToootTMB-25

97SkyE-X-10
97SkyE-XC-10
97SkyE-XEC-10
97SP-3
97SpollI-6
97SpollIEE-6
97SPx-13
97SPxBro-13
97SPxGraF-13
97SPxSil-13
97SPxSte-13
97StaClu-157
97StaClu-188
97StaCluC-CO8
97StaCluM-M37
97StaCluMOP-157
97StaCluMOP-188
97StaCluMOP-M37
97Stu-160
97StuPrePG-160
97StuPrePS-160
97Top-293
97TopAwel-AI4
97TopChr-99
97TopChrR-99
97TopGal-151
97TopGalPPI-151
97TopScr-5
97TopSta-93
97TopStaAM-93
97Ult-327
97UltGolME-327
97UltPlaME-327
97UppDec-234
97UppDecBCP-BC7
95UppDecMLFS-205
97UppDecU-46
97UppDecUGN-GN18
97Zen-44
97Zen8x1-22
97Zen8x1D-22

Garczyk, Eddie (Ed)
89SalLakTTI-9
90MiaMirIS-6

Gardella, Danny
83TCMPla1945-36

Gardella, Mike
88CapCodPPaLP-69
89OneYanP-2103
90CarLeaA-15
90PriWilCTI-10
91AlbYanLD-6
91AlbYanP-1002
91Cla/Bes-46
91LinDriAA-6
92AlbYanS-7
92Bow-52
92CanIndF-685
92ClaFS7-4
93CanIndF-2834
94ShrCapF-1597

Gardenhire, Ron
81TidTidT-5
82Don-649
82MetPhoA-8
82Top-623
82TopTra-39T
83Don-175
83Fle-543
83TidTidT-20
83Top-469
85Don-360
85Fle-81
85MetColP-8
85MetTCM-23
85Top-144
85TopTif-144
86MetTCM-17
86TidTidP-10
86Top-274
86TopTif-274
87PorBeaP-25
88KenTwiP-1402
88MidLeaAGS-36
89OrlTwiB-5
89OrlTwiP-1355
90OrlSunRB-28
90OrlSunRP-1098
90OrlSunRS-24
91MetWIZ-132
92TexLon-14

Gardey, Rudy
88IdaFalBP-1855
90SalSpuCLC-123

Gardiner, Michelle
91FreStaLBS-2

Gardiner, Mike
89WauTimGS-28
90Bes-262
90EasLeaAP-EL17
90ProAaA-16
90StaFS7-49
90WilBilB-6
90WilBilP-1052
90WilBilS-7
91Cla3-T25
91Don-417
91DonRoo-46
91LinDriAAA-355
91PawRedSDD-6
91PawRedSLD-355
91PawRedSP-31
91Sco-721
91TopDeb90-52
91UppDec-14
92Don-290
92Lea-482
92OPC-694
92Pin-505
92ProFS7-17
92RedSoxDD-13
92Sco-694
92StaClu-732
92StaCluNC-732
92Top-694
92TopGol-694
92TopGolW-694
92TopMic-694
92UppDec-588
93Don-515
93Fle-558
93FleFinE-94
93Top-241
93TopGol-241
93TopInaM-241
93TopMic-241
93Ult-414
93UppDec-640
93UppDecGold-640
94FleUpd-44
94StaClu-474
94StaCluFDI-474
94StaCluGR-474
94StaCluMOP-474
95Fle-52
95Top-97
96NorTidB-15

Gardiver, Jimmie
87ChaWheP-20

Gardner, Art
73CedRapAT-7
75IowOakT-8
78PhoGiaC-8
86TulDriTI-5
87GasRanP-24

Gardner, Billy
88EugEmeB-19
90PitMetP-27
91PitMetC-27
91PitMetP-3439
92St.LucMCB-27
92St.LucMF-1764
93ButCopKSP-23
94HigDesMC-29
94HigDesMF-2806
95ButCopKtI-22
96LowSpiB-1

Gardner, Billy F.
55Bow-249
55GiaGolS-26
55Top-27
55TopDouH-61
57Top-17
58Hir-37
58OriJayP-3
58Top-105
59OriJayP-3
59Top-89
59TopVen-89
60SenJayP-6
60Top-106
60TopVen-106
61Pos-96A
61Pos-96B
61Top-123
61TopStaI-179
61TwiCloD-5
61TwiPetM-14
61TwiUniMC-4
61Yan61RL-15
62SalPlaC-211
62ShiPlaC-211
62Top-163
62Top-338
62TopVen-163
63Top-408
77ExpPos-15
77OPC-198
79MemChiT-21
82Don-591
82TwiPos-13
83Top-11
83TwiTeal-27
83TwiTeal-34
84MinTwiP-14
84Nes792-771
84Top-771
84TopTif-771
84TwiTeal-28
85Top-213
85TopTif-213
85TwiTeal-31
87TopTra-36T
87TopTraT-36T
91OriCro-151
91RinPos1Y2-5
92YanWIZ6-45

Gardner, Bob
52Par-88

Gardner, Chris
90AshTouP-2741
91JacGenP-919
92Bow-457
92Don-413
92Lea-8
92Pin-599
92ProFS7-227
92SkyAAAF-271
92TopDeb91-61
92TucTorF-481
92TucTorS-607
94JacGenF-211
95TusTorTI-5

Gardner, Chuck
77CliDodT-8

Gardner, Damon
90MisStaB-13
91MisStaB-18

Gardner, Earl M.
11SpoLifM-79
11T205-62

Gardner, Franklin W.
87OldJudN-193
87OldJudN-194

Gardner, Glen
88PulBraP-1756
89SouAtlLAGS-42
89SumBraP-1097
90Bes-217
90BurBraB-3
90BurBraP-2355
90BurBraS-11

Gardner, Harry R.
16FleBreD-29
22E120-33

Gardner, Jeff
86LynMetP-10
87JacMetF-9
87TexLeaAF-7
88JacMetGS-10
89TidTidC-20
89TidTidP-1966
90CMC-367
90ProAAAF-282
90TidTidC-16
90TidTidP-551
90TopTVM-42
91LinDriAAA-555
91TidTidLD-555
91TidTidP-2517
91TriA AAGP-AAA48
92Fle-675A
92Fle-675B
92LasVegSF-2800
92LasVegSS-231
92ProFS7-279
92Sco-869
92SkyAAAF-114
92TopDeb91-62
93Don-470
93FleFinE-138
93Lea-238
93PadMot-22
93SelRoo-140T
93Top-663
93TopGol-663
93TopInaM-663
93TopMic-663
93UppDec-639
93UppDecGold-639
94ColC-106
94ColChoGS-106
94ColChoSS-106
94Don-406
94Fin-196
94FinRef-196
94Fle-662
94Pac-522
94PanSti-255
94Pin-296
94PinArtP-296
94PinMusC-296
94Sco-478
94ScoGolR-478
94StaClu-58
94StaCluFDI-58
94StaCluGR-58
94StaCluMOP-58
94Top-544
94TopGol-544
94TopSpa-544
94Ult-278

Gardner, Jelly (Floyd)
74LauOldTBS-7

Gardner, Jimmie
11TurRedT-62
86GenCubP-6

Gardner, John
86PeoChiP-7
87WytCubP-13
88ChaWheB-15
89ChaWheB-19
89ChaWheP-1769
90WinSpiTI-6
91ChaKniLD-132
91ChaKniP-1683
91LinDriAA-132
92IowCubF-4047
92IowCubS-208
92SkyAAAF-101

Gardner, Larry (William L.)
09ColChiE-113A
09ColChiE-113B
11MecDFT-22
11SpoLifM-8
12ColRedB-113A
12ColRedB-113B
12ColTinT-113A
12ColTinT-113B
12T207-65
15SpoNewM-65
16ColE13-56
16SpoNewM-65
17HolBreD-33
20GasAmeMBD-6
20NatCarE-31
21E121So1-27
21E121So8-25
21Exh-55
22AmeCarE-21
22W575-38
23W501-24
23WilChoV-47
77Ind192T-7
91ConTSN-147
95ConTSN-1355

Gardner, Mark
86JacExpT-15
87IndIndTI-19
88JacExpB-7
88JacExpP-987
89IndIndC-8
89IndIndP-1224
89TriA AAC-10
89TriAAP-AAA10
90Bow-106
90BowTif-106
90ClaYel-T4
90Don-40
90DonRoo-20
90ExpPos-11
90Fle-646
90FleCan-646
90FleUpd-29
90Hot50RS-16
90Lea-371
90OPC-284
90Sco-639
90Sco100RS-66
90Top-284
90TopDeb89-41
90TopTif-284
90ToyRoo-10
90TriAAAC-10
90UppDec-743
91Don-443
91ExpPos-8
91Fle-233
91OPC-757
91PanCanT1-91
91PanSti-67
91Sco-518
91Sco100RS-71
91StaClu-592
91Top-757
91TopDesS-757
91TopMic-757
91TopTif-757
91UppDec-663
92Bow-562
92Don-238
92ExpDonD-9
92ExpPos-14
92Fle-481
92Lea-512
92OPC-119
92Pin-215
92Sco-586
92Sco-785
92StaClu-42
92Top-119
92TopGol-119
92TopGolW-119
92TopMic-119
92UppDec-557
93Bow-421
93Don-64
93ExpPosN-12
93Fle-75
93FleFinE-218
93Lea-313
93OPCPre-21
93RoyPol-8
93Sco-390
93Sel-185
93StaClu-159
93StaClu-663
93StaCluFDI-159
93StaCluFDI-663
93StaCluMOP-159
93StaCluMOP-663
93StaCluRoy-24
93Top-314
93TopGol-314
93TopInaM-314
93TopMic-314
93Ult-560
93UppDec-348
93UppDec-641
93UppDecGold-348
93UppDecGold-641
94StaClu-546
94StaCluFDI-546
94StaCluGR-546
94StaCluMOP-546
94StaCluT-83
94StaCluTFDI-83
95Fle-332
96FleUpd-U206
96FleUpdTC-U206
96GiaMot-20
97Cir-66
97CirRav-66
97ColCho-457
97Fle-481
97FleTif-481
97MetUni-244
97Top-52
97Ult-295
97UltGolME-295
97UltPlaME-295

Gardner, Mike
88WauTimGS-25

Gardner, Myron
86WatIndP-8
88SalLakCTTI-20

Gardner, Rob
66Top-534
67Top-217

68Top-219
68TopVen-219
71OPC-734
71Top-734
72OPC-22
72Top-22
73OPC-222
73Top-222
91MetWIZ-133
92YanWIZ7-53
94BreMilB-31
Gardner, Scott
82DayBeaAT-4
83MiaMarT-3
90HunCubP-3274
91HunCubC-10
91HunCubP-3328
92GenCubC-16
92GenCubF-1555
93PeoChiF-1077
93PeoChiTI-5
95FayGenTI-12
96StoPorB-16
Gardner, Vassie
81ChaChaT-20
82KnoBluJT-19
Gardner, Wes
83LynMetT-23
84TidTidT-3
85IntLeaAT-21
85MetTCM-11
85TidTidT-9
88Don-634
88DonTeaBRS-634
88Fle-352
88FleGlo-352
88StaLinRS-8
88Top-109
88TopTif-189
89Bow-23
89BowTif-23
89Don-541
89Fle-88
89FleGlo-88
89Sco-412
89Top-526
89TopTif-526
90Bow-266
90BowTif-266
90Don-541
90Fle-275
90FleCan-275
90Lea-407
90OPC-38
90PubSti-455
90RedSoxP-9
90Sco-348
90Top-38
90TopTif-38
90TopTVRS-10
90VenSti-198
91Bow-653
91Fle-94
91MetWIZ-134
91OPC-629
91PadMag-19A
91Sco-592
91Top-629
91TopDesS-629
91TopMic-629
91TopTif-629
91UppDec-214
Gardner, Willie
90HunCubP-3299
91GenCubC-7
91GenCubP-4229
91PeoChiC-20
91PeoChiP-1357
92ClaFS7-220
92PeoChiTI-7
Gargiulo, Jimmy
96JohCitCTI-13
Gargiulo, Mike
94BluOriC-9
94BluOriF-3566
96FreKeyB-11
Garguilo, Mike
94OriPro-37
Garham, John
91AubAstC-29
Garia, Mike
92BazQua5A-14
Garibaldi, Art
40SolHug-7
Garibaldi, Bob
70Top-681
71OPC-701
71Top-701
Garibaldo, Chris
90BasCitRS-9
Gariglio, Robert
80WatIndT-32
81ChaLooT-1
Garland, Chaon
90SouOreAB-14
90SouOreAP-3428
91ModA'sC-5
91ModA'sP-3080
92ModA'sC-11
92ModA'sF-3893
Garland, Jon
97Bow-427
97BowChr-287
97BowChrI-287
97BowChrIR-287
97BowChrR-287
97BowInt-427
Garland, Mike
92BenRocF-1481
Garland, Nookie (Tim)
90GreHorB-21
90GreHorP-2673
90GreHorS-2
91Ft.LauYP-2440
91Ft.LauYC-26
92ClaFS7-222
92PriWilCC-15
92PriWilCF-160
96SanJosGB-8
Garland, Wayne
74OPC-596
74Top-590
76OPC-414
76SSP-376
76Top-414
77BurCheD-59
77Hos-144
77Kel-21A
77Kel-21B
77MSADis-22
77OPC-138
77PepGloD-14
77RCColC-23
77Top-33
77TopCloS-17
78Hos-137
78OPC-15
78RCColC-37
78Top-174
78WifBalD-25
79Top-636
80Top-361
81Don-440
81Fle-394
81OPC-272
81Top-511
82Don-489
82Fle-367
82Top-446
87NasSouTI-6
88NasSouC-24
88NasSouP-494
89MetColP-30
89PacSenL-100
89T/MSenL-38
90EliSenL-68
91OriCro-152
93AugPirC-27
93AugPirF-1561
94CarMudF-1595
Garlick, Gene
85CloHSS-17
Garman, Mike
71OPC-512
71Top-512
72OPC-79
72Top-79
73OPC-616
73Top-616
75OPC-584
75Top-584
76OPC-34
76SSP-293
76Top-34
77Top-302
78SSP270-70
78Top-417
79ExpPos-10
79OPC-88
79PorBeaT-15
79Top-181
90DodTar-268
Garman, Pat
88GasRanP-1014
89ChaRanS-8
90CMC-162
90OklCit8C-12
90OklCit8P-438
90ProAAAF-684
91LinDriAA-580
91TulDriLD-580
91TulDriP-2779
Garman, Sean
94NewJerCC-9
94NewJerCF-3424
95NewJerCTI-10
Garms, Debs
35DiaMatCS3T1-59
39PlaBal-72
40PlaBal-161
41DouPlaR-149
41Gou-29
41PlaBal-11
79DiaGre-176
91ConTSN-296
Garner, Darrin
86DayBeaIP-8
87GasRanP-22
88ChaRanS-7
88FloStaLAS-38
89TulDriGS-9
89TulDriTI-7
90TulDriP-1162
90TulDriTI-8
91LinDriAAA-309
91OklCit8LD-309
91OklCit8P-185
92GulCoaRSP-28
93ChaRanC-27
93ChaRanF-1956
94ChaRanF-2513
95PorCitRTI-9
Garner, Kevin
88RivRedWCLC-220
88RivRedWP-1431
89WicStaR-17
89WicWraR-33
91BirBarLD-60
91BirBarP-1462
91BriBanF-19
91LinDriAA-60
92BirBarF-2592
92ChaLooF-3825
Garner, Mike
87VerBeaDP-13
88RenSilSCLC-277
Garner, Phil
75OPC-623
75Top-623
76OPC-57
76SSP-495
76Top-57
77A'sPos-92
77BurCheD-109
77Hos-11
77OPC-34
77PirPosP-7
77Top-261
78Hos-52
78OPC-203
78Top-53
79Hos-75
79OPC-200
79Top-383
80OPC-65
80Top-118
81AllGamPI-101
81CokTeaS-113
81Don-372
81Fle-364
81FleStiC-71
81Kel-44
81OPC-99
81Top-573
81TopScr-102
81TopSti-209
81TopSti-253
82AstAstI-4
82Don-544A
82Don-544B
82Fle-216
82Squ-13
82Top-683
83AllGamPI-120
83Don-270
83Fle-448
83FleSta-68
83FleSti-205
83OPC-128
83Top-478
83TopSti-170
83TopSti-237
84AllGamPI-29
84AstMot-5
84Don-354
84Fle-226
84Nes792-752
84OPC-119
84Top-752
84TopRubD-11
84TopSti-63
84TopTif-752
85AllGamPI-119
85AstHouP-10
85AstMot-3
85Don-161
85Fle-351
85OPC-206
85Top-206
85TopRubD-11
85TopSti-64
85TopTif-206
86AstMilL-9
86AstPol-9
86AstTeaI-6
86BasStaB-44
86Don-527
86Fle-301
86FleMin-64
86OPC-83
86Top-83
86TopSti-32
86TopTif-83
87A'sMot-16
87AstMot-6
87AstPol-24
87Don-358
87DonOpeD-12
87Fle-58
87FleGlo-58
87OPC-304
87Top-304
87TopSti-30
87TopTif-304
88GiaMot-25
88Sco-431
88ScoGlo-431
88Top-174
88TopTif-174
89AstLenH-14
89AstMot-27
89AstSmo-16
90AstMot-27
90DodTar-269
91AstMot-28
91SweBasG-113
92BrePol-9
92OPC-291
92Top-291
92TopGol-291
92TopGolW-291
92TopMic-291
93BrePol-8
93Top-508
93TopGol-508
93TopInaM-508
93TopMic-508
93UppDecAH-56
94BrePol-8
94TedWil-78
Garner, Willie
92PeoChiC-14
Garnett, Brad
82AleDukT-11
Garr, Ralph
70OPC-172
70Top-172
71MLBOffS-9
71OPC-494
71Top-494
72Kel-21
72OPC-85
72OPC-260
72Top-85
72Top-260
73Kel2D-37
73LinPor-3
73OPC-15
73Top-15
74OPC-570
74Top-570
74TopSta-4
75Hos-87
75Kel-35
75OPC-306
75OPC-550
75Top-306
75Top-550
76OPC-410
76SSP-17
76Top-410
76TopTra-410T
77BurCheD-80
77Hos-108
77Kel-13
77MSADis-23
77OPC-77
77PepGloD-26
77RCColC-24
77Top-133
77TopCloS-18
77WhiSoxJT-5
78Kel-37
78OPC-195
78PapGinD-37
78RCColC-21
78SSP270-155
78TasDis-21
78Top-628
78WifBalD-26
79OPC-156
79Top-309
80OPC-142
80Top-272
90PacLeg-25
90RicBra2ATI-9
90SweBasG-46
92IdaFalGF-3526
92IdaFalGSP-15
93UppDecAH-57
93UppDecS-2
94TedWil-42
94UppDecAH-184
94UppDecAH1-184
Garrelts, Scott
80CliGiaT-10
81ShrCapT-20
83PhoGiaBHN-3
84Don-646
84PhoGiaC-5
85GiaMot-23
85GiaPos-9
85TopTifT-38T
85TopTra-38T
86Don-309
86DonAll-35
86Fle-540
86FleLeaL-14
86FleMin-110
86FleStiC-42
86GiaMot-19
86Lea-180
86OPC-395
86Spo-157
86Top-395
86TopSti-86
86TopTat-16
86TopTif-395
87Don-116
87Fle-273
87FleGlo-273
87FleHotS-17
87FleMin-42
87FleStiC-45
87GiaMot-11
87Lea-75
87OPC-37
87RedFolSB-24
87Spo-68
87SpoTeaP-10
87Top-475
87TopSti-89
87TopTif-475
88Don-80
88DonBasB-162
88Fle-82
88FleGlo-82
88GiaMot-11
88OPC-97
88PanSti-416

88Sco-533
88ScoGlo-533
88Spo-44
88StaLinG-7
88Top-97
88TopBig-240
88TopSti-90
88TopTif-97
89Bow-467
89BowTif-467
89Don-295
89DonBasB-218
89Fle-328
89FleGlo-328
89GiaMot-11
89OPC-214
89RedFolSB-48
89Sco-258
89Top-703
89TopTif-703
89UppDec-50
90Bow-228
90BowTif-228
90Don-217A
90Don-217B
90DonBesN-110
90Fle-56
90FleAwaW-14
90FleBasA-11
90FleCan-56
90GiaMot-16
90GiaSmo-8
90Lea-41
90OPC-602
90PanSti-367
90PubSti-67
90Sco-246
90Spo-39
90Top-602
90TopBig-51
90TopMinL-85
90TopSti-82
90TopTif-602
90UppDec-478A
90UppDec-478B
90VenSti-199
91Bow-626
91Don-311
91Fle-262
91GiaMot-16
91GiaPacGaE-29
91GiaSFE-8
91Lea-5
91OPC-361
91Sco-541
91StaClu-182
91Stu-255
91Top-361
91TopDesS-361
91TopMic-361
91TopTif-361
91Ult-320
91UppDec-443
92Fle-636
92GiaPacGaE-17
92OPC-558
92Sco-117
92StaClu-832
92StaCluECN-832
92Top-558
92TopGol-558
92TopGolW-558
92TopMic-558
Garrett, Bobby
81WesHavAT-9
Garrett, Bryan
93WatIndC-9
93WatIndF-3575
94ColRedC-10
94ColRedF-454
Garrett, Clifton
90BoiHawP-3330
91Cla/Bes-248
91MidLeaAP-MWL26
91QuaCitAC-24
91QuaCitAP-2643
92Bow-51
92ClaFS7-210
92PalSprAC-25
92PalSprAF-854
92UppDecML-314
93CedRapKC-1
93ClaGolF-131
Garrett, Eric
83IdaFalAT-15
84MadMusP-19
84ModA'sC-12
85ModA'sC-6
Garrett, Greg
70Top-642
71MLBOffS-58
71OPC-377
71Top-377
Garrett, Hal
94SprSulC-11
94SprSulF-2031
96CliLumKTI-12
Garrett, Jason
95ElmPioTI-9
95ElmPioUTI-9
Garrett, Jeff
94OgdRapF-3730
94OgdRapSP-6
Garrett, Josh
96BesAutS1RP-FR12
97Bow-405
97BowChr-268
97BowChrI-268
97BowChrIR-268
97BowChrR-268
97BowInt-405
97Top-273
Garrett, Lee
80WatRedT-9
81WatRedT-23
82IndIndTI-31
83IndIndTI-32
85IndIndTI-26
86IndIndTI-36
Garrett, Lynn
79WatIndT-1A
81WesHavAT-11
82WesHavAT-21
83TacTigT-15
Garrett, Neil
93Top-579
93TopGol-579
93TopInaM-579
93TopMic-579
94AshTouC-8
94AshTouF-1773
96AshTouB-18
Garrett, Pat (H. Adrian)
66Top-553
71OPC-576
71Top-576
74OPC-656
74Top-656
76OPC-562
76Top-562
76VenLeaS-106
79TCMJapPB-31
82AppFoxF-31
83GleFalWST-22
87OmaRoyP-16
88RoySmo-2
91RoyPol-25
92RoyPol-27
93EdmTraF-1154
94EdmTraF-2892
Garrett, R. Wayne
69MetNewYDN-5
70OPC-198
70Top-198
70Top-628
71MLBOffS-152
71OPC-228
71Top-228
72Dia-19
72OPC-518
72Top-518
73LinPor-111
73OPC-562
73Top-562
74MetDaiPA-20
74MetJapEB-2
74OPC-510
74Top-510
74TopSta-61
75MetSSP-5
75OPC-111
75Top-111
76ExpRed-12
76OPC-222
76SSP-539
76Top-222
77ExpPos-16
77OPC-117
77Top-417
78OPC-198
78Top-679
79TCMJapPB-77
79Top-319
86MetGreT-4
89Met196C-3
89PacSenL-156
89RinPosM1-10
89T/MSenL-39
91MetWIZ-135
93UppDecS-10
94Met69CCPP-14
94Met69CS-13
94Met69T-23
Garrett, Scott
96BilMusTI-9
Garrett, Smokey
95ChaKniTI-2
Garrett, Steve
80ElmPioRST-6
Garrick, Darren
86SanJosBP-8
88SalLakCTTI-3
89SalLakTTI-3
Garrido, Gil
61TacBan-7
61UniOil-T17
64Top-452
69Top-331
70OPC-48
70Top-48
71MLBOffS-10
71OPC-173
71Top-173
72Top-758
88BurBraP-26
89SumBraP-1094
90BurBraP-2366
90BurBraS-28
91DurBulP-1677
Garrigan, Pat
92SanBerC-3
92SanBerSF-965
Garriott, Cece
47SigOil-25
49W725AngTI-9
Garrison, Ford
43RedSoxTI-8
83TCMPla1944-14
Garrison, Jim
87WatPirP-18
88AugPirP-369
Garrison, Jockey
88GooN16-21
Garrison, Marv
77LodDodT-3
78LodDodT-5
Garrison, Venoy
75CliPilT-29
Garrison, Webster
85KinBluJT-16
87DunBluJP-937
88SouLeaAJ-23
89KnoBluJB-6
89KnoBluJP-1131
89KnoBluJS-4
90CMC-342
90ProAAAF-358
90SyrChiC-16
90SyrChiMB-9
90SyrChiP-578
91LinDriAAA-535
91TacTigLD-535
91TacTigP-2313
92HunStaF-3956
92TacTigS-533
93TacTigF-3039
94ClaGolF-178
94ColSprSSF-742
Garrity, Pat
90LSUTigP-3
91LSUTigP-4
Garrow, David
92KenTwiC-17
92KenTwiF-612
93ForMyeMC-9
93ForMyeMF-2662
94ForMyeMC-8
94ForMyeMF-1179
Garside, Russ
90Bes-35
90ChaRaiB-1
90ChaRaiP-2038
90SpoIndSP-7
Garsky, Brian
96VerExpB-14
Gartner, Mike
91StaCluMO-41
91StaCluMO-42
92StaCluMO-44
93StaCluMO-55
Garver, Ned
47PM1StaP1-67
49Bow-15
50Bow-51
51Bow-172
51FisBakL-7
51TopBluB-18
52BerRos-21
52Bow-29
52StaCalL-75A
52StaCalS-89A
52TipTop-10
52Top-212
53BowC-47
53TigGle-9
53Top-112
54Bow-39
54Top-44
55Bow-188
56Top-189
57Top-285
58A'sJayP-3
58Top-292
59Top-245
60A'sJayP-4
60Top-471
61AngJayP-6
61Top-331
61TopStal-171
83TopRep5-212
89PacLegI-183
91TopArc1-112
94TopArc1-44
94TopArc1G-44
Garvey, Don
91WelPirC-4
91WelPirP-3577
92AugPirF-245
93SalBucC-11
93SalBucF-440
Garvey, Steve
71DodTic-6
71MLBOffS-103
71OPC-341
71Top-341
72Top-686
73OPC-213
73Top-213
74OPC-575
74Top-575
75Hos-49
75HosTwi-49
75Kel-17
75OPC-140
75OPC-212
75OPC-460
75SSPPuzB-10
75Top-140
75Top-212
75Top-460
76CraDis-16
76Hos-19
76HosTwi-19
76Kel-54
76LinSup-115
76OPC-150
76SSP-77
76Top-150
77BurCheD-150
77Hos-35
77Kel-14
77OPC-255
77PepGloD-61
77RCColC-25
77Spo-3419
77Spo-6701
77Top-400
77TopCloS-19
78OPC-190
78Pep-31
78SSP270-71
78TasDis-3
78Top-350
78WifBalD-27
79DodBlu-4
79Hos-8
79OPC-21
79PosGarT-1
79PosGarT-2
79PosGarT-3
79PosGarT-4
79PosGarT-5
79PosGarT-6
79PosGarT-7
79PosGarT-8
79PosGarT-9
79PosGarT-10
79PosGarT-11
79PosGarT-12
79Top-50
79TopCom-24
80DodPol-6
80Kel-31
80OPC-152
80Top-290
80TopSup-13
81AllGamPI-95
81Dod-4
81DodPol-6
81Don-56A
81Don-56B
81Don-176
81Dra-11
81Fle-110
81Fle-606
81FleStiC-1
81Kel-10
81LonBeaPT-1
81MSAMinD-13
81OPC-251
81PerCreC-12
81Squ-4
81Top-530
81TopScr-56
81TopSti-176
81TopSti-252
81TopSupHT-45
81TopSupN-6
82DodPol-6
82DodPos-2
82DodUniOV-5
82DogBuiE-3
82Don-3
82Don-84
82Dra-14
82FBIDis-7
82Fle-5
82FleSta-9
82K-M-26
82Kel-47
82LouSlu-1
82MonNew-6
82OPC-179
82OPC-180
82PerCreC-11
82PerCreCG-11
82Top-179
82Top-180
82TopSti-54
82TopSti-258
83AllGamPI-94
83Don-488
83Fle-206
83FleSta-69
83FleSti-113
83OPC-198
83Top-610
83TopFol-3
83TopSti-243
83TopTra-37T
84AllGamPI-4
84DodUniOP-8
84Don-63
84DonActAS-38
84DonCha-56
84Dra-10
84Fle-300
84Fle-628
84FunFooP-9
84McGCloT-1
84MilBra-10
84Nes792-380
84NesDreT-12
84OCoandSI-43
84OPC-380
84PadMot-7
84PadSmo-10
84RalPur-18
84SevCoi-W7
84StaGar-1

84StaGar-2
84StaGar-3
84StaGar-4
84StaGar-5
84StaGar-6
84StaGar-7
84StaGar-8
84StaGar-9
84StaGar-10
84StaGar-11
84StaGar-12
84StaGar-13
84StaGar-14
84StaGar-15
84StaGar-16
84StaGar-17
84StaGar-18
84StaGar-19
84StaGar-20
84StaGar-21
84StaGar-22
84StaGar-23
84StaGar-24
84StaGar-25
84StaGar-26
84StaGar-27
84StaGar-28
84StaGar-29
84StaGar-30
84StaGar-31
84StaGar-32
84StaGar-33
84StaGar-34
84StaGar-35
84StaGar-36
84Top-380
84TopCer-18
84TopGaloC-5
84TopRubD-21
84TopSti-156
84TopSup-22
84TopTif-380
85AllGamPI-95
85Don-307
85Dra-11
85Fle-32
85Fle-631
85Fle-633
85FleLimE-9
85GenMilS-3
85Lea-94
85OPC-177
85PadMot-6
85SevCoi-W8
85SpoIndGC-7
85Top-2
85Top-450
85TopGloA-2
85TopMin-450
85TopRubD-21
85TopSti-1
85TopSti-2
85TopSti-13
85TopSti-14
85TopSti-149
85TopSti-176
85TopSup-26
85TopTif-2
85TopTif-450
86BasStaB-45
86BurKinA-18
86Don-63
86DonAll-3
86DonPop-3
86Fle-321
86Fle-640
86FleLeaL-15
86FleMin-67
86FleStiC-43
86FleStiWBC-S3
86Lea-56
86MeaGolBB-4
86MeaGolSB-15
86MSAJifPD-18
86OPC-4
86QuaGra-6
86SevCoi-W14
86Spo-35
86Spo-51
86Spo-137
86SpoDecG-61
86Top-660
86TopGloA-13
86TopGloS-38
86TopSti-104
86TopSti-148
86TopSup-24
86TopTat-5
86TopTif-660
86TruVal-2
87BoaandB-18
87BurKinA-5
87ClaGam-27
87DodSmoA-8
87Don-81
87DonOpeD-143
87Fle-414
87FleExcS-18
87FleGamW-16
87FleGlo-414
87FleLimE-16
87FleMin-43
87FleStiC-46
87KraFoo-20
87Lea-114
87MandMSL-20
87OPC-100
87PadBohHB-6
87RalPur-2
87RedFolSB-61
87SmoNatL-10
87Spo-40
87SpoTeaP-16
87StuPan-12
87Top-100
87TopCoi-32
87TopSti-115
87TopTif-100
88DodSmo-15
88DodSmo-17
88DodSmo-21
88Sco-225
88ScoGlo-225
89DodSmoG-83
89PadMag-20
90BasWit-26
90DodTar-270
90PacLeg-27
90SweBasG-103
91DodUno7P-1
91DodUno7P-5
91LinDri-8
91SweBasG-32
92ActPacA-64
92DodStaTA-16
92MCIAmb-2
92UppDecS-15
92UppDecS-17
92UppDecS-18
93TedWil-14
93UppDecS-13
93UppDecS-20
93Yoo-7
94UppDecAH-185
94UppDecAH-213
94UppDecAH1-185
94UppDecAH1-213
94UppDecS-5
95MCIAmb-8
95SonGre-3
95SPCha-106
95SPChaCP-CP10
95SPChaCPDC-CP10
95SPChaDC-106
Garvin, Jerry (Theodore)
78BluJayP-6
78OPC-49
78Top-419
79OPC-145
79SyrChiTI-25
79Top-293
80OPC-320
80Top-611
81Don-150
81Fle-429
81OPC-124
81Top-124
82Don-430
82Fle-614
82OPC-264
82Top-768
83Don-227
83Fle-428
83Top-358
92Nab-14
Garvin, Ned
03BreE10-55
11SpoLifCW-136
90DodTar-271
Garza, Alberto
96BurIndB-4
Garza, Alejandro
93CarMudF-2046
93CarMudTI-7
Garza, Armando
90NebCor-12
Garza, Lonnie
83RedPioT-10
Garza, Mark
85CloHSS-18
Garza, Roberto
92BurIndC-16
92BurIndF-1649
93WatIndC-10
93WatIndF-3556
Garza, Willie
88WatIndP-670
Gasgue, Ed
57SeaPop-16
Gash, Darius
90SpoIndSP-24
91WatDiaC-20
91WatDiaP-1267
92ClaFS7-2
92HigDesMC-27
93WicWraF-2988
Gaskill, Derek
94HelBreF-3607
94HelBreSP-20
96StCatSB-9
Gaspar, Cade
94ClaUpdCotC-CC16
94SigRooDP-18
94SigRooDPS-18
94StaCluDP-13
94StaCluDPFDI-13
95Bow-78
95Exc-48
95SPML-54
95StaClu-105
95StaCluFDI-105
95StaCluMOP-105
95StaCluSTWS-105
95Top-492
95UppDecML-154
96RanCucQB-16
95UppDecMLFS-154
Gaspar, Harry
09ColChiE-114
09T206-139
10DomDisP-47
10SweCapPP-99
11MecDFT-10
11SpoLifCW-137
11SpoLifM-194
11T205-63
12ColRedB-114
12ColTinT-114
12HasTriFT-10A
12HasTriFT-73B
Gaspar, Rod
70OPC-371
70Top-371
71MLBOffS-227
71OPC-383
71Top-383
75HawIsIC-6
76HawIsIC-18
89RinPosM1-12
91MetWIZ-136
94Met69CCPP-15
94Met69CS-14
94Met69T-25
Gass, Jeff
83EriCarT-16
Gassaway, Charles
46RemBre-7
47RemBre-4
47SigOil-45
47SmiClo-8
48SigOil-8
48SmiClo-10
49BowPCL-10
49RemBre-8
50RemBre-7
Gasser, Steve
86KenTwiP-10
87OrlTwiP-11
87SouLeaAJ-18
88OrlTwiB-23
89PitMetS-5
Gast, Joe
87NewOriP-14
89PenPilS-6
Gast, John
91PriRedC-4
91PriRedP-3521
Gastall, Tommy
91OriCro-153
Gastelum, Macario
87BakDodP-3
89BakDodCLC-185
Gastfield, Ed
87OldJudN-195
Gaston, Alex
21E121So1-28
21E121So8-26
21KoBreWSI-11
22W575-39
23W501-112
81ConTSN-69
Gaston, Cito (Clarence)
69MilBra-90
69PadVol-4
69Top-304
70DayDaiNM-73
70Top-604
71BazNumT-12
71BazUnn-30
71Kel-41
71MLBOffS-228
71OPC-25
71Top-25
71TopCoi-1
71TopSup-52
71TopTat-27
72MilBra-113
72OPC-431
72OPC-432
72PadTeal-10
72Top-431
72Top-432
73OPC-159
73PadDea-1
73Top-159
74OPC-364
74PadDea-9
74Top-364A
74Top-364B
75OPC-427
75Top-427
76OPC-558
76SSP-18
76Top-558
76VenLeaS-122
77PadSchC-23A
77PadSchC-23B
77Top-192
78Top-716
79Top-208
84BluJayFS-13
85BluJayFS-12
86BluJayFS-13
86PadGreT-7
87BluJayFS-10
88BluJayFS-13
89BluJayFS-11
89TopTra-36T
89TopTraT-36T
90BluJayFS-9
90OPC-201
90Top-201
90TopTif-201
90TopTVA-33
91BluJayFS-9
91BluJayS-36
91OPC-81
91Top-81
91TopDesS-81
91TopMic-81
91TopTif-81
92OPC-699
92Top-699
92TopGol-699
92TopGolW-699
92TopMic-699
93BluJayD-13
93BluJayD4-28
93BluJayDM-15
93BluJayDM-24
93BluJayFS-10
93OPCWorC-18
93Top-514
93TopGol-514
93TopInaM-514
93TopMic-514
96BluJayOH-9
97BluJayS-24
Gaston, John
77TCMTheWY-4
83GreHorT-6
Gaston, Milt
33Gou-65
33GouCanV-65
34DiaMatCSB-66
79DiaGre-128
81ConTSN-70
Gaston, Russell
90SavCarP-2065
91JohCitCC-19
91SavCarC-5
91SavCarP-1646
Gaston, Welcome
90DodTar-956
Gastreich, Henry
87OldJudN-196
Gastright, Hank
90DodTar-272
Gate, Bill
91St.PetCC-24
Gateman, Wareham
88CapCodPB-25
Gates, Brent
91Cla/Bes-414
91ClaDraP-22
91FroRowDP-22
91SouOreAC-24
91SouOreAP-3855
92CalLeaACL-1
92ClaFS7-187
92DonRoo-42
92LeaGolR-BC2
92ModA'sC-15
92ModA'sF-3905
92OPC-216
92ProFS7-133
92Sco-805
92StaCluD-56
92Top-216
92TopGol-216
92TopGolW-216
92TopMic-216
92UppDecML-145
93AthMot-17
93Bow-457
93ClaFisN-9
93ClaFS7-189
93ClaGolF-74
93ExcAllF-8
93ExcFS7-216
93Fla-258
93FleFinE-254
93FunPac-2
93JimDeaR-4
93Lea-536
93SelRoo-61T
93SelRooAR-2
93SP-39
93StaCluAt-19
93TacTigF-3040
93Top-451
93TopGol-451
93TopInaM-451
93TopMic-451
93TopTra-91T
93UppDec-500
93UppDec-504
93UppDecGold-500
93UppDecGold-504
94A'sMot-21
94Bow-304
94ColC-107
94ColChoGS-107
94ColChoSS-107
94Don-111
94ExtBas-149
94ExtBasSYS-8
94Fin-7
94FinJum-7
94FinRef-7
94Fla-330
94Fle-261
94FUnPac-13
94FUnPac-221
94Lea-161
94OPC-231
94OPCDiaD-15
94Pac-449
94Pin-299
94PinArtP-299

94PinMusC-299
94Sco-187
94ScoBoyoS-19
94ScoGolR-187
94Sel-281
94SP-33
94SPDieC-33
94StaClu-65
94StaCluFDI-65
94StaCluGR-65
94StaCluMOP-65
94StaCluMOP-ST25
94StaCluST-ST25
94Stu-2
94Top-586
94TopGol-586
94TopSpa-586
94TriPla-3
94Ult-107
94UltSecYS-2
94UppDec-110
94UppDecED-110
94USPlaCR-5D
94USPlaCR-9H
95A'sCHP-1
95AthMot-21
95ColCho-124
95ColChoGS-124
95ColChoSE-46
95ColChoSEGS-46
95ColChoSESS-46
95ColChoSS-124
95Don-329
95DonPreP-329
95DonTopotO-136
95Emb-17
95EmbGolI-17
95Fla-73
95Fle-245
95Lea-290
95Pin-191
95PinArtP-191
95PinMusC-191
95PinUps-US7
95Sco-241
95ScoGolR-241
95ScoPlaTS-241
95Sel-133
95SelArtP-133
95Spo-101
95SpoArtP-101
95StaClu-323
95StaCluMOP-323
95StaCluSTWS-323
95StaCluVR-166
95Sum-53
95Sum-163
95SumNthD-53
95Top-129
95TopCyb-80
95Ult-317
95UltGolM-317
95UppDec-283
95UppDecED-283
95UppDecEDG-283
95UppDecSE-108
95UppDecSEG-108
96A'sMot-6
96ColCho-645
96ColChoGS-645
96ColChoSS-645
96Don-76
96DonPreP-76
96EmoXL-102
96Fla-147
96Fle-207
96FleTif-207
96MetUni-100
96MetUniP-100
96Pac-389
96PanSti-220
96Sco-394
96StaClu-39
96StaCluMOP-39
95StaCluVRMC-166
96Top-31
96Ult-113
96UltGolM-113
96UppDec-424
97Fle-189
97FleTif-189
97Pac-168
97PacLigB-168
97PacSil-168
97Top-296
97Ult-111
97Ult-488
97UltGolME-111
97UltGolME-488
97UltPlaME-111
97UltPlaME-488
97UppDec-448

Gates, Bryan
86AncGlaPTI-38
87AncGlaP-34

Gates, Eddie
81EvaTriT-20
82EvaTriT-20

Gates, Joe
75WatRoyT-13
77JacSunT-6
78KnoKnoST-7
80IowOakP-6
81EdmTraRR-16

Gates, Mathew
91BriBanF-6

Gates, Michael
80MemChiT-9
82WicAerTI-4
83Don-114
83OPC-195
83Top-657
83WicAerDS-8
84IndIndTI-29

Gates, Todd
91ButCopKSP-13
92ButCopKSP-7

Gatewood, Aubrey
64Top-127
64TopVen-127
65Top-422
66OPC-42
66Top-42
66TopVen-42

Gatewood, Henry
85VerBeaDT-11
86VisOakP-10
87OrlTwiP-5
88WinSpiS-4

Gatins, Frank
90DodTar-957

Gatlin, Mike
77OrlTwiT-11
82OneYanT-16

Gaton, Frank
75BurBeeT-9
76BurBeeT-14

Gatti, Dom
93ButCopKSP-1
94HudValRF-3398
95ChaRivTI-23
94HudValRC-5

Gattis, Jim
89MiaMirIS-25
89MiaMirIS-6

Gaube, Gerry
77ForLauYS-9

Gaudaub, Jacob
87AllandGN-23

Gaudaur, Oarsman
88GooN16-22

Gaudet, Jim
77JacSunT-7
79Top-707
80EvaTriT-3
80OmaRoyP-13
81OmaRoyT-13
82SyrChiT-11
91JesHSA-7

Gaudreault, Armand
43ParSpo-30

Gaughan, Hank
82ChaLooT-25

Gault, Raymond
76BatTroTI-9
77WatIndT-10

Gause, Ernie
80CarMudF-10

Gausepohl, Dan
82HawIsIT-8

Gauthier, Fernand
43ParSpo-31
43ParSpo-32

Gautreau, Doc
92ConTSN-545

Gautreau, Mike
94NewJerCC-10
94NewJerCF-3409
95PeoChiTI-31

Gautreaux, Sid
90DodTar-273

Gavaghan, Sean
92KenTwiF-597
93ForWayWC-9
93ForWayWF-1962
94NasXprF-379
96HarCitRCB-13

Gavello, Tim
94OgdRapF-3747
94OgdRapSP-16

Gavin, Dave
87ModA'sC-4
88MadMusP-11
89ModA'sC-28
89WatDiaP-1776
89WatDiaS-9

Gavin, Tom
90EliTwiS-10
91VisOakC-22
91VisOakP-1754

Gavlick, Daryle
92HunCubC-26
92HunCubF-3140
93PeoChiC-6
93PeoChiF-1078
93PeoChiTI-7
94DayCubC-7
94DayCubF-2345

Gay, Brad
93BelBreC-9
93BelBreF-1712
93HelBreF-4099
94StoPorC-8
94StoPorF-1696

Gay, Chris
93HicCraC-9

Gay, Jeff
86SalAngC-78
87QuaCitAP-26
89PalSprACLC-34
89PalSprAP-466
90QuaCitAGS-16
91BirBarLD-61
91BirBarP-1457
91LinDriAA-61

Gay, Scott
87Ft.LauYP-17
88Ft.LauYS-9
89SalSpuP-1823

Gay, Steve
86LynMetP-11
94OgdRapF-3731
94OgdRapSP-7

Gaylor, Bobby
86JamExpP-10
87BurExpP-1084
88WesPalBES-11

Gaynor, John
91ParPatF-10

Gaynor, Richard Kent
83ReaPhiT-5
84PorBeaC-212
87BirBarB-11
88BirBarB-17

Gazarek, Marty
94WilCubC-8
94WilCubF-3778
95RocCubTI-33
96DayCubB-14
96WesOahCHWB-15

Gazella, Mike
91ConTSN-121

Gazzilli, Dan
85UtiBluST-26

Gbur, Paul
79AppFoxT-25

Gebhard, Bob
72OPC-28
72Top-28
73TacTwiC-8
75IntLeaAT-29
82ExpPos-14

Geck, Joseph
93HicCraC-30
94HicCraC-30
94SouAtlLAF-SAL22

Geddes, Jim
73OPC-561
73Top-561

Gedeon, Elmer Joe
15SpoNewM-66
16BF2FP-34
16ColE13-57
16FleBreD-30
16SpoNewM-66
17HolBreD-34
19W514-39

Gedman, Rich
81PawRedST-24
82Don-512
82Fle-294
82RedSoxC-7
82Top-59
83Don-156
83Fle-184
83Top-602
84Don-579
84Fle-398
84Nes792-498
84OPC-296
84Top-498
84TopSti-222
84TopTif-498
85AllGamPI-40
85Don-457
85Fle-159
85OPC-18
85Top-529
85TopSti-217
85TopTif-529
86Don-273
86DonAll-56
86Fle-349
86Fle-643
86FleLimE-18
86FleMin-75
86FleStiC-44
86Lea-145
86OPC-375
86Spo-84
86Top-375
86TopSti-248
86TopTat-17
86TopTif-375
87ClaGam-49
87Don-153
87DonAll-39
87Fle-35
87FleGlo-35
87FleGlo-WS9
87FleRecS-11
87FleWorS-9
87Lea-254
87OPC-137
87Spo-149
87Spo-154
87Top-306
87Top-740
87TopSti-247
87TopTif-306
87TopTif-740
88Don-129
88DonBasB-140
88DonTeaBRS-129
88Fle-353
88FleGlo-353
88OPC-245
88PanSti-24
88Sco-241
88ScoGlo-241
88StaLinRS-9
88Top-245
88TopBig-152
88TopSti-252
88TopTif-245
89Bow-27
89BowTif-27
89Don-162
89Fle-89
89FleGlo-89
89OPC-178
89Sco-345
89Top-652
89TopBig-72
89TopSti-253
89TopTif-652
89UppDec-368
90Don-346
90Fle-276
90FleCan-276
90Lea-478
90MLBBasB-72
90OPC-123
90PubSti-456
90RedSoxP-10
90Sco-173
90Top-123
90TopTif-123
90TopTVRS-18
90UppDec-402
90VenSti-200
91CarPol-29
91Lea-418
91UppDec-588
92CarPol-5
92Don-553
92Fle-577
92Sco-689
92StaClu-58
92Ult-566
94OriPro-38

Geeve, Dave
92ChaRanC-18
92ChaRanF-2221
93ChaRanC-11
93ChaRanF-1934
94ExcFS7-133
94TulDriF-237
94TulDriTI-7
96TulDriTI-11

Geffner, Glenn
95RocRedWTI-45

Gegan, Fred
87VerBeaDP-9

Gehrig, Lou (Henry Louis)
25Exh-97
26Exh-99
27Exh-49
28Exh-50
28PorandAR-A10
28PorandAR-B10
28StaPlaCE-24
28W502-26
28W56PlaC-C3
28Yue-26
29ExhFou-26
29PorandAR-28
30SchR33-20
30W554-4
31Exh-26
31W517-35
32USCar-26
33ButCanV-18
33CraJacP-7
33DelR33-7
33Gou-92
33Gou-160
33GouCanV-55
34ButPreR-24
34ExhFou-13
34Gou-37
34Gou-61
34GouCanV-92
35ExhFou-13
35WheBB1-13
36ExhFou-13
36OveCanR-15
36PC7AlbHoF-22
36WheBB3-4
36WheBB4-2
36WorWidGV-96
37ExhFou-13
38BasTabP-11
38ExhFou-13
38OurNatGPP-11
39ExhSal-18
46SpoExcW-3-4
47PM1StaP1-68
47PM1StaP1-69
48BluTin-29
48ExhHoF-12
48SweSpoT-14
49LeaPre-3
50CalHOFW-33
51R42SmaS-35
51TopConMA-5
60ExhWriH-11
60Fle-28
60KeyChal-18
60NuHi-24
60RawGloT-8
61Fle-31
61GolPre-16
61NuSco-424
61Top-405
62Top-140
62TopVen-140
63BasMagM-29
63BazA-15
63GadFunC-5

63GadFunC-43
63HalofFB-8
67TopVen-141
68LauWorS-25
68SpoMemAG-12
69Baz-4
69Baz-5
69Baz-7
69EquSpoHoF-BB5
70FleWorS-25
70FleWorS-29
70FleWorS-35
71FleWorS-26
72FleFamF-5
72KelATG-13
72LauGreF-8
73HalofFPP-8
73OPC-472
73SyrChiTI-8
73Top-472
74FleBasF-5
74NewYorNTDiS-20
74SyrChiTI-8
75SpoHobBG-5
75YanDyn1T-16
75YanDyn1T-51
75YanDyn1T-52
75YanDyn1T-53
75YanDyn1T-54
76GalBasGHoF-11
76LauDiaJ-28
76OPC-341
76RowExh-4
76ShaPiz-18
76Top-341
77BobParHoF-22
77GalGloG-46
77GalGloG-181
77GalGloG-236
77SerSta-10
77ShaPiz-10
79Pew-2
80Lau300-29
80LauFamF-10
80MarExh-9
80PacLeg-13
80PerHaloFP-22
80SSPHOF-22
80YanGreT-1
81ConTSN-5
81SanDieSC-17
81SanDieSC-18
81SanDieSC-19
81SpoHaloF-6
81TigDetN-50
82BHCRSpoL-3
82DiaCla-35
83ConMar-3
83YanASFY-15
84GalHaloFRL-18
84OCoandSI-98
84OCoandSI-174
85CirK-14
85Don-635
85DonHOFS-3
85DonWaxBC-PUZ
85FegMurCG-7
85GeoSteM-2
85Lea-635
85UltBasC-4
85Woo-14
86ConSer1-1
86ConSer1-17
86ConSer1-52
86ConSer1-57
86SpoDecG-10
86TCM-17
86TCMSupS-9
86TCMSupS-28
87ConSer2-1
87HygAllG-20
87NesDreT-1
87SpoCubG-2
87SpoRea-28
87Yan192T-8
88ConAmeA-10
88ConHar-3
88ConSer5-12
88GreBasS-30
89CMCBasG-3
89HOFStiB-1
89PacLegI-174
89RinPosG-1
89RinPosG-2
89RinPosG-3
89RinPosG-4
89RinPosG-5
89RinPosG-6
89RinPosG-7
89RinPosG-8
89RinPosG-9
89RinPosG-10
89SweBasG-25
89TopBasT-21
89USPLegSC-2
89YanCitAG-2
90BasWit-73
90Col-34
90HOFStiB-38
90PerGreM-4
90RinPosYMP-1
90SweBasG-25
91CadEllD-23
91ConTSN-111
91ConTSN-310
91ConTSNP-111
91DenBal-4
91HomCooC-9
91SweBasG-125
91USGamSBL-3C
91USGamSBL-3D
91USGamSBL-3H
91USGamSBL-3S
92ConTSN-529
92ConTSNCI-3
92ConTSNCI-8
92MegRut-81
92MegRut-122
92MegRutP-154
92OPC-40
92Pin-286
92Sco-881
92SpoIllFK1-108
92St.VinHHS-5
92Top-40
92TopGol-40
92TopGolPS-40
92TopGolW-40
92TopMic-40
92WhiLegtL-2
92WhiPro-2
92YanWIZA-22
92YanWIZH-11
93ActPacA-97
93ActPacA2-31G
93CadDis-24
93ConMasB-3
93ConTSN-673
93DiaStaES-130
93Hoy-3
93LegFoi-3
93SpeHOF2-1
93TedWil-63
93TedWil-122
93TedWilPC-23
93TedWilPC-24
93UppDecAH-58
93UppDecAH-131
93UppDecAH-133
94ConTSN-1082
94ConTSN-1249
94ConTSNB-1082
94ConTSNB-1249
94ConTSNCI-31
94MegRutS-3
94TedWil-147
94TedWilLC-LC13
94TedWilTfB-T5
94UppDecAH-4
94UppDecAH-40
94UppDecAH-112
94UppDecAH-160
94UppDecAH1-4
94UppDecAH1-40
94UppDecAH1-112
94UppDecAH1-160
94UppDecTAE-37
95ConTSN-1421
95ConTSNGJ-2
95ConTSNP-1421
95MegRut-3
95MegRut-6
95MegRut-12
95MegRut-13
95UppDecSHoB-4
Gehringer, Charlie (Charles)
26Exh-95
27Exh-47
28StaPlaCE-25
29ExhFou-23
29PorandAR-29
31Exh-23
33ButCanV-19
33DelR33-5
33DouDisP-20
33ExhFou-12
33GeoCMil-14
33Gou-222
33TatOrbSDR-183
34DiaMatCSB-67
34BatR31-42
34BatR31-130
34ButPreR-25
34DiaStaR-77
34ExhFou-12
34Gou-23
34GouCanV-57
34WarBakSP-5
35ExhFou-12
35GouPuzR-1D
35GouPuzR-2D
35GouPuzR-16D
35GouPuzR-17D
35TigFreP-7
36ExhFou-12
36GouWidPPR-A37
36GouWidPPR-C13
36NatChiFPR-29
36OveCanR-16
36PC7AlbHoF-57
36R31Pre-L4
36SandSW-23
36WheBB4-3
36WheBB5-6
36WorWidGV-42
37DixLid-2
37DixPre-2
37ExhFou-12
37OPCBatUV-112
37WheBB6-4
37WheBB8-5
38ExhFou-12
38GouHeaU-241
38GouHeaU-265
38OurNatGPP-10
38WheBB10-14
38WheBB11-3
38WheBB15-3A
38WheBB15-3B
39ExhSal-19
39GouPreR303A-16
39PlaBal-50
39WorWidGTP-16
39WorWidGV-13
40PlaBal-41
41DouPlaR-53
41PlaBal-19
50CalHOFW-34
60Fle-58
61Fle-32
61GolPre-10
63HalofFB-28
70FleWorS-32
76GalBasGHoF-12
76RowExh-7
76ShaPiz-56
76TigOldTS-9
77GalGloG-200
78TigDeaCS-17
79DiaGre-378
80PerHaloFP-57
80SSPHOF-57
80TigGreT-6
81ConTSN-78
81TigDetN-14
81TigSecNP-14
82DiaCla-5
83ConMar-5
83DonHOFH-28
83TigAIKS-33
83TigAIKS-39
84OCoandSI-96
84SpoDesPW-16
85FegMurCG-8
86ConSer1-43
86SpoDecG-12
86TigSpoD-4
87HygAllG-21
88ConAmeA-11
88ConSer5-13
89PerCelP-15
90PacLeg-81
90PerGreM-31
90PerMasW-1
90PerMasW-2
90PerMasW-3
90PerMasW-4
90PerMasW-5
92ConTSN-461
92ConTSN-553
92ConTSNGI-667
93ConTSN-667
94ConTSN-1076
94ConTSN-1122
94ConTSNB-1076
94ConTSNB-1122
94ConTSNCI-34
Geier, Phil
11SpoLifCW-138
Geiger, Burt
82AlbDukT-3
83AlbDukT-2
Geiger, Gary
87EveGiaC-24
88FreSunCLC-23
88FreSunP-1229
Geiger, Gary Merle
58Top-462
59Top-521
60Top-184
60TopVen-184
61Top-33
61TopStal-111
62Jel-60
62Pos-60
62PosCan-60
62RedSoxJP-3
62SalPlaC-38A
62SalPlaC-38B
62ShiPlaC-38
62Top-117
62TopStal-13
62TopVen-117
63Jel-81
63Pos-81
63Top-513
64Top-93
64TopVen-93
65Top-452
66Top-286
66TopVen-286
67CokCapB-1
67Top-566
69Top-278
72CedRapCT-17
77EvaTriT-10
Geis, Jason
92SouOreAC-13
92SouOreAF-3433
Geisel, Harry
94ConTSN-1205
94ConTSNB-1205
Geisel, J. Dave
79Top-716
80Top-676
82Don-633
82SyrChiT-13
84Don-645
84Fle-154
84Nes792-256
84OPC-256
84SalLakCGC-175
84Top-256
84TopTif-256
85MarMot-22
86OklCit8P-6
Geisel, Mark
82SyrChiT-4
Geishert, Vern
70Top-683
Geiske, Mark
90RivRedWCLC-10
Geisler, Phil
91MarPhiC-11
91MarPhiP-3460
92ClePhiC-18
92ClePhiF-2062
93ClePhiC-9
93ClePhiF-2695
94Bow-336
94Cla-19
94ExcFS7-245
94ScrRedBF-932
94Ult-546
94UppDecML-239
95ScrRedBTI-10
95UppDecML-132
96BinBeeB-8
95UppDecMLFS-132
Geiss, Emil
87OldJudN-197
Geist, Pete
86FloStaLAP-17
86VerBeaDP-6
87VerBeaDP-6
88DunBluJS-7
Geivett, Billy
86PalSprAP-23
86PalSprAP-15
87MidAngP-3
Gelatt, Dave
85LitFalMT-18
86ColMetP-10
87LynMetP-18
88St.LucMS-8
Gelb, Jac
89WytCubS-11
90PeoChiTI-22
Gelbert, Charlie (Charles M.)
31Exh-16
33ButCre-10
33ExhFou-8
36GouWidPPR-A38
36NatChiFPR-30
36NatChiFPR-100
36WorWidGV-49
39PlaBal-93
40PlaBal-18
91ConTSN-70
95ConTSN-1428
Gelfarb, Steve
81WesHavAT-12
82WesHavAT-13
Gelinas, Marc
78SalPirT-5
Gellinger, Mike
87DayBeaAP-25
89UtiBluSP-30
90BirBarB-24
90BirBarP-1400
91UtiBluSC-23
91UtiBluSP-3257
94SouBenSHC-25
94SouBenSHF-610
Gelnar, John
65OPC-143
65Top-143
67Top-472
70BreMcD-7
70OPC-393
70Top-393
71MLBOffS-436
71OPC-604
71Top-604
83Pil69G-18
94BreMilB-32
Genao, Huascar
92BurIndC-23
92BurIndF-1663
Gendron, Bob
84ShrCapFB-8
Gendron, Jonnie
92ClaDraP-104
94WelPirC-11
94WelPirF-3490
Generals, Fayetteville
90FayGenP-2422
Genewich, Joe (Joseph)
21Exh-56
25Exh-5
26Exh-5
27Exh-2
92ConTSN-573
Genins, C. Frank
87OldJudN-198
Genke, Todd
93MarPhiC-11
93MarPhiF-3465
94SpaPhiF-1717
94SparPhiC-12
95BatCliTI-15
96SalAvaB-10
Gennaro, Brad
93RanCucQC-12
93RanCucQF-843
94WicWraF-201
95MemChiTI-8
Genovese, George

49W72HolS-4
91HigSchPLS-35
Gentile, Gene
78ChaPirT-8
81BriRedST-4
83PawRedST-21
84AlbA'sT-3
86KinEagP-8
87HarSenP-21
88HarSenP-856
Gentile, Jim
47Exh-80
55DonWin-20
60Top-448
61NuSco-401
61Pos-68A
61Pos-68B
61Top-559
61TopStal-101
62AurRec-7
62Baz-17
62ExhStaB-14
62Jel-27
62Pos-27A
62Pos-27B
62PosCan-27
62SalPlaC-1
62ShiPlaC-1
62Top-53
62Top-290
62TopBuc-30
62TopStal-5
62TopVen-53
63BasMagM-30
63Baz-11
63ExhStaB-25
63Jel-57
63Pos-57
63SalMetC-47
63Top-4
63Top-260
63TopStil-16
64A's-6
64AthJayP-5
64Baz-11
64Top-196
64TopGia-15
64TopSta-75
64TopStaU-27
64TopVen-196
65AthJayP-5
65ChaTheY-28
65Top-365
66OPC-45
66Top-45
66TopVen-45
74SupBlaB-4
78TCM60I-4
83FraBroR-7
83FraBroR-12
85Woo-15
87AstShowSTh-8
90DodTar-274
91OriCro-154
Gentile, Randy
89EliTwiS-9
90KenTwiB-3
90KenTwiP-2300
90KenTwiS-4
Gentile, Scott
92ClaDraP-74
92FroRowDP-43
92JamExpC-17
92JamExpF-1495
93ClaGolF-122
93StaCluM-52
93WesPalBEC-5
93WesPalBEF-1332
94HarSenF-2084
95Bow-170
95Exc-221
95HarSenTI-18
95Top-369
Gentle, Mike
83VerBeaDT-4
Gentleman, Jean (J.P.)
88HamRedP-1743
88SavCarP-356
Gentry, Andry
90GeoColC-5
Gentry, Gary
69MetCit-3
69MetNewYDN-6
69OPC-31
69Top-31
70DayDaiNM-60
70MetTra-23B
70OPC-153
70Top-153
71MLBOffS-153
71OPC-725
71Top-725
72OPC-105
72Top-105
73OPC-288
73Top-288
74OPC-415
74Top-415
75OPC-393
75Top-393
86MetGreT-9
87Met196T-5
89RinPosM1-13
91MetWIZ-137
94Met69CCPP-16
94Met69CS-15
94Met69T-16
Genzale, Henry
88MarMot-28
89MarMot-28
90MarMot-28
George, Andre
88PocGiaP-2075
George, Bill
58MonRoyF-8
George, Chris
89CalLeaA-38
89MisStaB-14
89StoPorB-2
89StoPorCLC-153
89StoPorP-391
89StoPorS-8
90El PasDAGTI-21
90ElPasDGS-14
90MisStaB-14
90TexLeaAGS-17
91Bow-35
91Cla2-T50
91DenZepLD-138
91DenZepP-119
91LinDriAAA-138
91MisStaB-19
91PitMetC-23
91PitMetP-3416
92Bow-213
92ClaGam-20
92DenZepF-2632
92DenZepS-128
92Don-746
92PitMetC-16
92PitMetF-3288
92Sco-835
92ScoRoo-9
92SkyAAAF-62
92St.LucMCB-25
92StaClu-354
92TopDeb91-63
92UppDec-9
93Top-744
93TopGol-744
93TopInaM-744
93TopMic-744
94BreMilB-125
94ElPasDF-3140
George, Curtis
92WatIndC-22
92WatIndF-3242
George, Frankie
74CarSalLCA-93
75SalLakCC-7
76SalLakCGC-4
77SalLakCGC-14
George, Greek
41CubTeal-6
90DodTar-275
George, Lefty (Thomas)
12T207-66
George, Leo
82QuaCitCT-14
George, Louis
88KimN18-14
George, Nattie
84GreHorT-7
George, Phil
83ButCopKT-5
85Ft.MyeRT-11
86Ft.MyeRP-11
86MemChiSTOS-7
86MemChiTOS-7
87MemChiB-11
87MemChiP-2
George, Steve
83GreHorT-7
84GreHorT-18
86AlbYanT-29
88Top-18A
George, W.G.
88AllandGN-39
88KimN18-15
George, Will
80ChaO'sP-8
80ChaO'sW-8
82MiaMarT-1
83MiaMarT-1
87HagSunP-3
89KinIndS-27
90CanIndB-2
90CanIndP-1363
91CanIndP-996
George, William
87OldJudN-199
89SFHaCN-6
Georger, Joe
80LynSaiT-17
81LynSaiT-4
82LynSaiT-4
86WauTimP-10
87BelMarTI-12
89QuaCitAB-3
89QuaCitAGS-3
90QuaCitAGS-2
91QuaCitAC-28
91QuaCitAP-2646
92QuaCitRBC-29
92QuaCitRBF-827
93CedRapKC-28
93CedRapKF-1755
94CedRapKC-24
94CedRapKF-1125
Gerace, Joanne
88UtiBluSP-29
89UtiBluSP-32
Geraghty, Ben
90DodTar-276
Gerald, Dwayne
91HigSchPLS-23
92StaCluD-57
93EugEmeC-15
93EugEmeF-3862
Gerald, Ed (Edward)
89HigSchPLS-19
91AppFoxC-24
91AppFoxP-1729
92AppFoxC-25
92AppFoxF-996
93St.PetCC-13
93St.PetCF-2640
94NasXprF-398
Gerard, Alfonzo
52LavPro-88
Gerber, Craig
82RedPioT-3
83NasAngT-13
84EdmTraC-105
86Don-545
86EdmTraP-13
86Fle-156
86Top-222
86TopTif-222
88EdmTraP-583
88MidAngGS-24
Gerber, Wally (Walter)
20NatCarE-32
21Exh-57
21Nei-49
22E120-96
22W573-46
22W575-40
25Exh-113
26Exh-117
92ConTSN-501
Gerberman, George
77FriOneYW-91
Gerdes, Rob
90LSUTigA-13
Geren, Bob
83SprCarF-13
84ArkTraT-11
87AlbYanP-5
88BlaYNPRWL-25
88ColCliC-11
88ColCliP-12
88ColCliP-303
88TriAAAP-9
88TriAAC-16
89ColCliC-11
89ColCliP-13
89ColCliP-758
89DonRoo-11
89FleUpd-48
89ScoHot1R-66
89ScoRoo-93T
89TopTra-37T
89TopTraT-37T
89YanScoNW-25
90AlbDecGB-4
90Baz-20
90Bow-438
90BowTif-438
90ClaBlu-25
90Don-395
90Fle-442
90FleCan-442
90Lea-182
90OPC-536
90PanSti-128
90Sco-464
90Sco100RS-50
90Spo-205
90SprCarDGB-28
90Top-536
90TopBig-209
90TopGloS-40
90TopRoo-9
90TopSti-316
90TopSti-321
90TopTif-536
90TopTVY-21
90ToyRoo-11
90UppDec-608
90YanScoNW-9
91Don-114
91Fle-663
91OPC-716
91PanFreS-323
91PanSti-265
91Sco-435
91StaClu-171
91StaCluP-15
91Top-716
91TopDesS-716
91TopMic-716
91TopTif-716
91Ult-231
91UppDec-202
92Fle-226
92OPC-341
92PawRedSF-925
92Sco-170
92Top-341
92TopGol-341
92TopGolW-341
92TopMic-341
92YanWIZ8-66
93PadMot-13
97DunDonPPS-9
Gergen, Bob
83BurRanF-13
83BurRanT-16
84TulDriTI-26
85TulDriTI-25
86TulDriTI-14
Gerhardt, Allen
83BeaGolGT-22
87GasRanP-10
Gerhardt, Bill
83MiaMarT-7
Gerhardt, Joe
86OldJudN-7
87BucN28-59
87OldJudN-200
89SFHaCN-7
Gerhardt, Rusty
84OklCit8T-5
85OklCit8T-24
86OklCit8P-7
89ChaRanS-27
Gerhart, Bert
91GulCoaRSP-21
92GasRanC-4
93EriSaiC-8
93EriSaiF-3107
94ChaRivC-7
94ChaRivF-2666
94SouAtlLAF-SAL4
Gerhart, Ken
84ChaO'sT-22
85ChaO'sT-1
86RocRedWP-3
87Don-30
87DonOpeD-141
87DonRoo-24
87FleUpd-34
87FleUpdG-34
87Lea-30
87OriFreB-38
87SpoRool-7
87TopTra-37T
87TopTraT-37T
88BlaYNPRWL-84
88Don-213
88Fle-559
88FleGlo-559
88OPC-271
88OriFreB-38
88PanSti-14
88RedFolSB-27
88Sco-58
88ScoGlo-58
88StaLinO-4
88Top-271
88TopTif-271
88ToyRoo-11
89Fle-609
89FleGlo-609
89OPC-192
89PhoFirC-20
89PhoFirP-1499
89Sco-506
89Top-598
89TopTif-598
89UppDec-426
90HagSunDGB-11
91OriCro-155
Gerheauser, Al
43PhiTeal-10
Gering, Scott
79ElmPioRST-13
Gerken, George
28StaPlaCE-26
Gerlach, Jim
81QuaCitCT-27
83MidCubT-21
Gerland, Greg
95EugEmeTI-23
German, Rene
83QuaCitCT-11
Germann, Mark
86CedRapRT-16
87VerRedP-20
88ChaLooB-10
89NasSouC-15
89NasSouP-1275
Germer, Glen
81DurBulT-18
Gernentz, Keith
85RedWinA-19
86RedWinA-6
Gerner, Ed
20RedWorCP-7
Gernert, Dick
52StaCalL-71G
52Top-343
53BowBW-11
53RedSoxTI-9
54Bow-146
57Top-202
58RedSoxJP-3
58Top-38
59RedSoxJP-2
59Top-13
59Top-519
59TopVen-13
60Top-86
60TopVen-86
61TigJayP-8
61Top-284
61TopStal-151
62Col45'HC-6
62Top-536
62TopBuc-31
78ReaRem-6
79DiaGre-249
83TopRep5-343
89AstCol4S-18
93RanKee-158
Geronimo, Cesar
71OPC-447
71Top-447
72Top-719

73LinPor-55
73OPC-156
73Top-156
74OPC-181
74Top-181
74TopSta-26
75Hos-121
75Kel-50
75OPC-41
75Top-41
76Hos-150
76LinSup-99
76OPC-24
76RedIceL-5
76RedKro-9
76SSP-45
76Top-24
77BurCheD-202
77Hos-76
77Kel-40
77MSADis-24
77OPC-160
77PepGloD-49
77Top-535
78OPC-32
78Pep-11
78SSP270-115
78Top-354
79OPC-111
79Top-220
80OPC-247
80RedEnq-20
80Top-475
81Don-305
81Top-390
81TopTra-766
82Don-322
82Fle-409
82Roy-8
82Top-693
83Don-448
83Fle-112
83Roy-9
83Top-194
84Don-252
84Nes792-544
84Top-544
84TopTif-544
85DomLeaS-21
87AstShoSTw-7
96Red76K-6
Gershberg, Howie
88BenBucL-28
89BenBucL-27
90BoiHawP-3333
91BoiHawP-3902
92BoiHawF-3647
93PalSprAC-28
93PalSprAF-87
94LakElsSC-27
94LakElsSF-1681
96HilStaHWB-13
96LakElsSB-29
Gerstein, Ron
91SumFlyC-5
91SumFlyP-2328
92RocExpC-8
92RocExpF-2108
93StoPorF-739
94ElPasDF-3141
95ElPasDTI-9
Gerteisen, Aaron
93JohCitCC-11
93JohCitCF-3695
94MadHatC-11
94MadHatF-145
94NewJerCC-11
94NewJerCF-3431
Gertz, Mike
82WatIndF-14
82WatIndT-16
83WatIndF-22
Gessler, Doc (Harry)
09RamT20-50
11SpoLifCW-139
11SpoLifM-124
14CraJacE-59
15CraJacE-59
Gettel, Allen
47IndTeal-10
47IndVanPP-9
50RemBre-8
51Bow-304
52MotCoo-3
75Gia195T-5
Getter, Kerry
75AndRanT-23
76CliPilT-17
Gettler, Chris
88BakDodCLC-253
Gettman, Jake
12ImpTobC-40
Getz, Gus (Gustave)
09ColChiE-115A
09ColChiE-115B
12ColRedB-115A
12ColRedB-115B
12ColTinT-115A
12ColTinT-115B
15SpoNewM-67
16ColE13-58
16SpoNewM-67
90DodTar-277
Getz, Rod
96KanCouCTI-11
Getzein, Charles
76SSP188WS-4
87BucN28-30
87OldJudN-201
87ScrDC-13
88AllandGN-3
88GandBCGCE-17
88WG1CarG-21
89SFHaCN-8
Gewecke, Steve
90SprCarB-21
Geyer, Rube (Jacob)
09PC7HHB-14
09T206-140
10CouT21-139
15VicT21-12
Gharrity, Patsy (Edward P.)
19W514-109
20WalMaiW-18
21E121So1-29
21Nei-50
22E120-107
22W572-31
22W573-47
22W575-41
23W501-12
23WilChoV-48
31SenTealPW-10
34DiaMatCSB-68
Ghelfi, Tony (Andrew)
84PhiTas-19
85PhiTas-17
85PorBeaC-40
86WatIndP-9
87KinIndP-16
88WilBilP-1308
88WilBilP-1314
89LasVegSC-5
89LasVegSP-1
Gholston, Rico
92WelPirC-9
92WelPirF-1330
93AugPirC-8
93AugPirF-1551
Ghostlaw, Derek
91HelBreSP-2
Giallella, Brian
95ButCopKtl-29
Giallombardo, Bob
59DarFar-7
59Top-321A
59Top-321B
60DarFar-9
61UniOil-SP3
90DodTar-278
Giamatti, A.Bartlett
89WicChaR-6
90Don-716
90OPC-396
90ScoRooDT-B1
90T/MUmp-65
90Top-396
90TopTif-396
Giambi, Jason
91TopTra-45T
91TopTraT-45T
92ClaDraP-42
92FroRowDP-40
92FroRowDPPS-40
92StaCluD-58
92TopDaiQTU-31
92TopTra-40T
92TopTraG-40T
92UppDecML-20
93ClaFS7-190
93ModA'sC-11
93ModA'sF-808
93StaCluM-156
93StaCluM-200
94ClaGolF-125
94ColC-657
94ColChoGS-657
94ColChoSS-657
94ExcFS7-120
94HunStaF-1336
94TedWil-123
94Top-369
94TopGol-369
94TopSpa-369
94UppDec-525
94UppDecED-525
94UppDecML-145
95A'sCHP-4
95Bow-13
95EdmTraTI-8
95Sum-163
95SumNthD-163
95UppDec-222
95UppDecED-222
95UppDecEDG-222
95UppDecML-9
95UppDecMLMLA-4
95UppDecSE-109
95UppDecSEG-109
96A'sMot-3
96Bow-97
96BowBes-29
96BowBesAR-29
96BowBesR-29
96Cir-72
96CirRav-72
96ColCho-243
96ColChoGS-243
96ColChoSS-243
96Don-47
96DonPreP-47
96Fin-B159
96Fin-G330
96FinRef-B159
96FinRef-G330
96Fla-148
96Fle-208
96FleTif-208
96LeaLim-56
96LeaLimG-56
96LeaPre-87
96LeaPreP-87
96LeaSig-39
96LeaSigA-77
96LeaSigAG-77
96LeaSigAS-77
96LeaSigEA-58
96LeaSigEACM-7
96LeaSigPPG-39
96LeaSigPPP-39
96Pin-126
96Sco-44
96ScoDugC-A39
96ScoDugCAP-A39
96StaClu-61
96StaCluMOP-61
96Stu-13
96StuPrePB-13
96StuPrePG-13
96StuPrePS-13
96TeaOut-27
96Top-210
96TopChr-72
96TopChrR-72
96Ult-400
96UltGolM-400
96UltGolP-6
96UltGolPGM-6
96UppDec-412
97Bow-6
97BowBes-87
97BowBesAR-87
97BowBesR-87
97BowInt-6
97Cir-368
97CirRav-368
97ColCho-184
97Don-47
97Don-446
97DonEli-39
97DonEliGS-39
97DonEliTotC-11
97DonEliTotCDC-11
97DonLim-168
97DonLimLE-168
97DonPre-86
97DonPreCttC-86
97DonPreP-47
97DonPreP-446
97DonPrePGold-47
97DonPrePGold-446
97DonRocL-14
97Fin-118
97FinEmb-118
97FinEmbR-118
97FinRef-118
97FlaSho-A171
97FlaSho-B171
97FlaSho-C171
97FlaShoLC-171
97FlaShoLC-B171
97FlaShoLC-C171
97FlaShoLCM-A171
97FlaShoLCM-B171
97FlaShoLCM-C171
97Fle-190
97FleTif-190
97Lea-137
97LeaFraM-137
97LeaFraMDC-137
97MetUni-129
97NewPin-74
97NewPinAP-74
97NewPinMC-74
97NewPinPP-74
97Pac-169
97PacLigB-169
97PacPri-58
97PacPriLB-58
97PacPriP-58
97PacPriSL-SL5B
97PacSil-169
97PinCer-101
97PinCerMBlu-101
97PinCerMG-101
97PinCerMR-101
97PinCerR-101
97PinIns-32
97PinInsCE-32
97PinInsDE-32
97PinTotCPB-101
97PinTotCPG-101
97PinTotCPR-101
97PinX-P-87
97PinX-PMoS-87
97Sco-241
97Sco-544
97ScoHobR-544
97ScoPreS-241
97ScoResC-544
97ScoShoS-241
97ScoShoS-544
97ScoShoSAP-241
97ScoShoSAP-544
97Sel-72
97SelArtP-72
97SelRegG-72
97SelToootT-10
97SelToootTMB-10
97SP-133
97SpoIll-167
97SpoIllEE-167
97StaClu-336
97StaCluMOP-336
97Stu-89
97StuHarH-15
97StuPrePG-89
97StuPrePS-89
97Top-209
97TopChr-77
97TopChrR-77
97TopGal-177
97TopGalPPI-177
97Ult-112
97UltDouT-8
97UltGolME-112
97UltPlaME-112
97UppDec-131
95UppDecMLFS-9
Giambi, Jeremy
96SpoIndB-12
Giannelli, Ray
89MyrBeaBJP-1470
89SouAtlLAGS-35
90DunBluJS-9
90StaFS7-64
91BluJayS-33
91Cla/Bes-26
91KnoBluJLD-357
91KnoBluJP-1774
91LinDriAA-357
92SkyAAAF-225
92SyrChiF-1974
92SyrChiMB-6
92SyrChiS-506
92TopDeb91-64
93SyrChiF-1003
94SyrChiF-978
94SyrChiTI-13
95LouRedF-288
96ColSprSSTI-15
Giannotta, Go
80EvaTriT-13
Giansanti, Ralph
83AndBraT-21
Giants, Bismarck
93NegLeaRL2-98
Giants, Cedar Rapids
76CedRapGT-37
Giants, Clinton
86CliGiaP-29
87CliGiaP-29
92CliGiaF-3615
Giants, New York
09MaxPubP-25
09SpoNewSM-83
13FatT20-13
38BasTabP-37
48ExhTea-7
48ExhTea-11
51TopTea-5
55GiaGolS-1
56Top-226
57Top-317
58Top-19
60NuHi-56
61NuSco-456
68LauWorS-9
68LauWorS-10
68LauWorS-14
68LauWorS-21
68LauWorS-33
68LauWorS-48
70FleWorS-9
70FleWorS-10
70FleWorS-14
70FleWorS-19
70FleWorS-33
70FleWorS-48
70FleWorS-59
71FleWorS-10
71FleWorS-20
71FleWorS-52
73FleWilD-29
74NewYorNTDiS-37
93TedWilPC-17
Giants, Phoenix
83PhoGiaBHN-27
82PhoGiaVNB-1
Giants, San Francisco
58GiaFalBTP-1
58GiaFalBTP-2
58GiaFalBTP-3
58GiaFalBTP-4
59Top-69
59TopVen-69
60Top-151
60TopTat-63
60TopVen-151
61Top-167
61TopMagR-12
62GuyPotCP-17
62Top-226
63Top-417
64Top-257
64TopTatI-19
64TopVen-257
65GiaTeal-10
65Top-379
66OPC-19
66Top-19
66TopRubI-118
66TopVen-19
67Top-516
68LauWorS-59
69FleCloS-21
69FleCloS-32
69TopStaA-22
70FleWorS-59

70Top-696
71FleWorS-60
71OPC-563
71Top-563
71TopTat-9
72Top-771
73OPC-434
73OPCBTC-22
73Top-434
73TopBluTC-22
74OPC-281
74OPCTC-22
74Top-281
74TopStaA-22
74TopTeaC-22
76OPC-443
76Top-443
78Top-82
83FleSta-247
83FleSti-NNO
87SpoTeaL-10
88FleStiWBC-S7
88FleWaxBC-C9
88PanSti-480
88RedFolSB-108
88Top-261
88TopTif-261
90FleWaxBC-C1
90PubSti-626
90RedFolSB-125
90VenSti-537
92GiaATaTTP-1
92GiaATaTTP-2
92GiaATaTTP-3
92GiaATaTTP-4
92GiaATaTTP-5
92GiaATaTTP-6
92GiaATaTTP-7
92GiaATaTTP-8
92GiaATaTTP-9
92GiaATaTTP-10
92GiaATaTTP-11
92GiaATaTTP-12
92GiaATaTTP-13
92GiaATaTTP-14
92GiaATaTTP-15
92GiaATaTTP-16
92GiaATaTTP-17
92GiaATaTTP-18
92GiaATaTTP-19
92GiaATaTTP-20
92GiaATaTTP-21
92GiaATaTTP-22
92GiaATaTTP-23
92GiaATaTTP-24
92GiaATaTTP-25
92GiaATaTTP-26
92GiaATaTTP-27
92GiaATaTTP-28
92GiaATaTTP-29
92GiaATaTTP-30
92GiaATaTTP-31
92GiaATaTTP-32
92GiaATaTTP-33
92GiaATaTTP-34
92GiaATaTTP-35
93GiaPos-35
94ImpProP-28
94Sco-660
94ScoGolR-660
95PanSti-129
96PanSti-109
Gianukakis, John
86BenPhiC-146
Giard, Joe
91ConTSN-119
Giard, Ken
92IdaFalGF-3506
92IdaFalGSP-5
93MacBraC-10
93MacBraF-1395
94DurBulC-8
94DurBulF-324
94DurBulTI-7
95EugEmeTI-3
96DurBulBIB-3
96DurBulBrB-4
Giardi, Mike
94EveGiaC-9
94EveGiaF-3658
95GreBatTI-12
96GreBatB-11
96WesPalBEB-26
Giaudrone, Charlie
90WicStaSGD-12
Gibbon, Joe
58JetPos-7
60KeyChal-19
60Top-512
61Top-523
62Kah-13
62Top-448
63Kah-12
63PirIDL-9
63Top-101
64PirKDK-12
64Top-307
64TopVen-307
65OPC-54
65Top-54
66Top-457
67Top-541
68OPC-32
68Top-32
68TopVen-32
69OPC-158
69Top-158
69TopFou-2
70OPC-517
70Top-517
72OPC-382
72Top-382
78TCM60I-219
Gibbons, Bill
89CliGiaP-907
Gibbons, John
82BelBreF-8
85Don-116
85IntLeaAT-15
85MetTCM-19
85TidTidT-15
86ElPasDP-12
86MetTCM-14
86TidTidP-11
87ChaLooB-22
87Don-626
87MetColP-32
87TidTidP-16
87TidTidT-10
88AlbDukC-20
88AlbDukP-260
88VerMarP-950
89OklCit8C-12
89OklCit8P-1531
90CMC-236
90ProAAAF-304
90ScrRedBC-10
90ScrRedBP-602
91MetWIZ-138
94CapCitBC-28
94CapCitBF-1768
96HilStaHWB-26
96StLucMTI-1
86STaoftFT-33
Gibbons, Michael
88SalLakCTTI-15
89RocExpLC-10
Gibbs, Jake
62Top-281
64ChatheY-9
64Top-281
64TopVen-281
65ChaTheY-7
65OPC-226
65Top-226
66OPC-117
66Top-117
66TopVen-117
67CokCapYM-V3
67Top-375
68OPC-89
68Top-89
68TopVen-89
69MilBra-91
69MLBOffS-74
69Top-401
69TopSta-203
69TopTeaP-19
70MLBOffS-245
70Top-594
71MLBOffS-488
71OPC-382
71Top-382
71YanCliDP-6
72MilBra-114
92YanWIZ6-46
92YanWIZ7-54
94TamYanF-2402
95TamYanYI-7
Gibbs, Jim (James)
88SprCarB-9
89MedAthB-4
90BenBucL-30
90MadMusB-15
Gibbs, Kevin
95YakBeaTI-10
96VerBeaDB-13
Gibbs, Paul
92WatIndC-2
92WatIndF-3227
93ColRedC-10
93ColRedF-591
Giberti, Dave
91ButCopKSP-8
92Ft.MyeMCB-15
92Ft.MyeMF-2739
93ChaRanC-12
93ChaRanF-1935
94ClaGolF-33
94TulDriF-238
94TulDriTI-8
Gibralter, David
94SarRedSC-10
94SarRedSF-1956
94UtiBluSC-12
94UtiBluSF-3827
95MicBatCTI-13
96SarRedSB-16
Gibralter, Steve
91ChaWheC-22
91ChaWheP-2899
91SouAtlLAGP-SAL7
92CedRapRC-17
92CedRapRF-1083
92ClaFS7-47
92MidLeaATI-12
92UppDecML-69
92UppDecML-284
92UppDecMLPotY-PY21
93Bow-694
93ChaLooF-2370
93ClaFisN-6
93ClaGolF-214
93ClaMVPF-5
93ExcFS7-21
93ExcLeaLF-14
94ChaLooF-1369
94Cla-112
94UppDecML-190
95Bes-62
95Bow-161
95IndIndF-107
96Bow-128
96BowBes-167
96BowBesAR-167
96BowBesR-167
96Cir-116
96CirRav-116
96ColCho-514
96ColChoGS-514
96ColChoSS-514
96EmoXL-164
96Fin-B303
96FinRef-B303
96Fla-232
96FlaWavotF-11
96FleUpd-U119
96FleUpdTC-U119
96IndIndB-9
96LeaPre-122
96LeaPreP-122
96LeaSig-133
96LeaSigPPG-133
96LeaSigPPP-133
96Pin-374
96PinAfi-177
96PinAfiAP-177
96PinFoil-374
96Sel-167
96SelArtP-167
96SelCer-106
96SelCerAP-106
96SelCerCB-106
96SelCerCR-106
96SelCerMB-106
96SelCerMG-106
96SelCerMR-106
96Sum-165
96SumAbo&B-165
96SumArtP-165
96SumFoi-165
96Top-101
96Ult-460
96UltGolM-460
96UppDec-228
97DonRatR-11
97Lea-18
97LeaFraM-18
97LeaFraMDC-18
97Pin-164
97PinArtP-164
97PinIns-139
97PinInsCE-139
97PinInsDE-139
97PinMusC-164
97Sco-112
97ScoPreS-112
97ScoShoS-112
97ScoShoSAP-112
Gibree, Bob
86WauTimP-11
87SalSpuP-20
Gibson, Bob (Robert L.)
79BurBeeT-14
82ElPasDT-21
83BrePol-40
84Don-246
84Fle-201
84Nes792-349
84Top-349
84TopTif-349
84VanCanC-40
85BrePol-40
85Don-393
85TopTifT-39T
85TopTra-39T
86Don-271
86Fle-488
86Top-499
86TopTif-499
86VanCanP-12
87TidTidP-33
87TidTidT-3
88RocRedWC-5
88RocRedWP-196
88RocRedWTI-8
91MetWIZ-139
94BreMilB-126
Gibson, Bob (Robert)
59Top-514
60Top-73
60TopVen-73
61Top-211
62CarJayP-4
62Top-530
63CarJayP-7
63CarJayP-8
63Fle-61
63Jel-166
63Pos-166
63SalMetC-3
63Top-5
63Top-9
63Top-415
64Top-460
64TopCoi-59
64TopGia-41
65Baz-23
65CarJayP-3
65CarTeal-9
65OPC-12
65OPC-138
65Top-12
65Top-138
65Top-320
65TopEmbl-69
65TopTral-14
66Baz-21
66CarTeal-5
66Top-225
66Top-320
66TopRubl-35
66TopVen-225
66TopVen-320
67Baz-21
67Top-210
67Top-236
67TopVen-267
68AtlOilPBCC-20
68Baz-9
68LauWorS-64
68OPC-100
68OPC-154
68Top-100
68Top-154
68Top-378
68TopActS-10C
68TopVen-100
68TopVen-154
69KelPin-6
69MLBOffS-211
69MLBPin-44
69NabTeaF-9
69OPC-8
69OPC-10
69OPC-12
69OPC-107
69OPC-162
69OPC-168
69OPC-200
69OPCDec-7
69Top-8
69Top-10
69Top-12
69Top-107A
69Top-107B
69Top-162
69Top-168
69Top-200
69Top-432
69TopDec-29
69TopDecl-12
69TopFou-7
69TopFou-14
69TopFou-18
69TopSta-115
69TopSup-60
69TopTeaP-18
69TraSta-33
70CarTeal-5
70DayDaiNM-16
70Kel-71A
70Kel-71B
70MLBOffS-139
70OPC-67
70OPC-71
70OPC-530
70Top-67
70Top-68
70Top-71
70Top-530
70TopBoo-22
70TopSup-33
70TraSta-5A
71AllBasA-7
71BazNumT-41
71BazUnn-35
71CarTeal-17
71CarTeal-18
71Kel-51
71MilDud-43
71MLBOffS-273
71MLBOffS-559
71OPC-70
71OPC-72
71OPC-450
71Top-70
71Top-72
71Top-450
71TopCoi-63
71TopGreM-24
71TopSup-48
71TopTat-120
71TopTat-121
72Dia-59
72Kel-26A
72Kel-26B
72OPC-130
72Top-130
73Kel2D-14
73LinPor-167
73OPC-190
73Top-190
73TopCanL-19
74Kel-1
74OPC-350
74Top-350
74TopDecE-3
74TopPuz-5
74TopSta-114
75Hos-119
75OPC-3
75OPC-150
75OPC-206
75Top-3
75Top-150
75Top-206
76GrePlaG-40
77Spo-4705
78TCM60I-60

80PerHaloFP-175
80SSPHOF-174
82BraPol-45
82K-M-14
83BraPol-45
83CarGreT-8
83KelCerB-10
83Oco& SSBG-8
84BraPol-45
84OCoandSI-16
85DalNatCC-3
86SpoDecG-42
86TCMSupS-15
87K-M-3
87NesDreT-31
87SpoRea-9
88Top-664
88TopTif-664
89KahCoo-5
89TopBasT-23
90BasWit-31
90HOFStiB-74
90PacLeg-28
90SweBasG-120
91Col-23
91Kel3D-5
91KelStaU-6
91LinDri-3
91SweBasG-33
91UppDecS-11
91UppDecS-14
91UppDecS-19
92ActPacA-3
92ActPacA2-3G
92ActPacAP-2
92CarMcD-46
92UppDecF-52
92UppDecFG-52
92UppDecHH-HI4
92UppDecS-11
92UppDecS-29
92UppDecS-35
92Zip-2
93ActPacAC-3
93MetIma-10
93TedWil-90
93TedWil-142
94NabAllA-1
94UppDecAH-119
94UppDecAH-130
94UppDecAH-156
94UppDecAH-219
94UppDecAH1-119
94UppDecAH1-130
94UppDecAH1-156
94UppDecAH1-219
94UppDecS-2
94UppDecTAE-69
94UppDecTAELD-LD13
94Yoo-6
95EagBalL-9
95TopLegot6M-3
95UppDecSHoB-11
97FleMilDM-31
97St.VinHHS-7

Gibson, Dave
80KnoBluJT-19

Gibson, Derrick
94BenRocF-3607
95AshTouTI-34
95AshTouUTI-34
95Bes-67
95Bes-108
95BesFra-F8
95Bow-157
95Exc-186
95SPML-50
95SPMLDtS-DS19
96Bow-285
96BowBes-94
96BowBesAR-94
96BowBesP-BBP23
96BowBesPAR-BBP23
96BowBesPR-BBP23
96BowBesR-94
96BowMinLP-2
96Exc-153
96ExcSeaC-4
96MauStiHWB-34
96NewHavRB-10
96NewHavRUSTI-34
96Top-436
97Bow-191
97BowBes-165
97BowBesAR-165
97BowBesR-165
97BowChr-179
97BowChrI-179
97BowChrIR-179
97BowChrR-179
97BowInt-191
97BenRocC-8
97ColCho-470
97Don-391
97DonPreP-391
97DonPrePGold-391
97SP-6
97StaCluM-M30
97StaCluMOP-M30
97Top-290

Gibson, Frank
25Exh-6

Gibson, Hoot
81DurBulT-19

Gibson, J. Russ
67Top-547
68Top-297
68TopVen-297
69MilBra-92
69OPC-89
69RedSoxAO-4
69RedSoxTI-3
69Top-89
69TopSta-133
69TopTeaP-3
70OPC-237
70Top-237
71MLBOffS-248
71OPC-738
71Top-738
72MilBra-115
72Top-643
81RedSoxBG2S-81

Gibson, Joel
65Top-368
78TCM60I-208

Gibson, Josh
91NegLeaRC-24

Gibson, Josh Sr.
74LauOldTBS-8
76ShaPiz-128
80PerHaloFP-128
80SSPHOF-128
83ConMar-51
83DonHOFH-4
85UltBasC-11
86NegLeaF-4
86NegLeaF-9
86NegLeaF-23
86NegLeaF-30
86NegLeaF-31
86NegLeaFS-30
87NegLeaPD-6
87SpoCubG-2
88ConNegA-5
88NegLeaD-12
89RinPosNL1-8
90NegLeaS-2
90PomBlaBNLP-2544
91PomBlaBPB-5
91PomBlaBPB-6
91PomBlaBPB-22
91PomBlaBPB-30
92NegLeaK-17
92NegLeaPL-3
93DiaStaES-N2
93TedWil-105
94PomNegLB-5
94UppDecTAE-44
95NegLeaL2-3
96NoiSatP-1
76CooPapB-13
91NegLeaRL-24
94TedWilLC-LC14
95NegLeaL2-3
95NegLeaLI-24

Gibson, Kirk
81CokTeaS-59
81Fle-481
81OPC-315
81TigDetN-20
81Top-315
81TopSti-78
82Don-407
82Dra-15
82Fle-267
82FleSta-161
82Kel-40
82OPC-105
82PerCreC-24
82PerCreCG-24
82Squ-6
82Top-105
82TopSti-184
83AllGamPI-53
83Don-459
83Fle-329
83OPC-321
83Tig-11
83Top-430
83TopSti-67
84Don-593
84Fle-80
84FunFooP-21
84Nes792-65
84OPC-65
84TigFarJ-4
84TigFliJ-10
84TigWavP-16
84Top-65
84TopSti-272
84TopTif-65
85AllGamPI-57
85Don-471
85Dra-12
85Fle-8
85FleStaS-22
85Lea-103
85OPC-372
85SevCoi-D13
85SevCoi-S8
85TigCaiD-8
85TigWen-9
85Top-565
85TopRubD-22
85TopSti-11
85TopSti-19
85TopSti-267
85TopSup-27
85TopTif-565
86BasStaB-46
86BurKinA-13
86Don-1
86Don-125
86DonSupD-1
86DonWaxBC-PC4
86Dra-28
86Fle-226
86FleLimE-19
86FleMin-47
86FleSlu-10
86FleStiC-45
86GenMilB-1B
86Lea-1
86OPC-295
86SevCoi-C16
86Spo-21
86TigCaiD-6
86Top-295
86TopGloS-29
86TopSti-266
86TopSup-25
86TopTat-22
86TopTif-295
86TruVal-8
86WilGloT-1
87BoaandB-29
87ClaGam-9
87Don-50
87Fle-151
87FleGamW-17
87FleGlo-151
87FleLimE-17
87FleMin-44
87FleStiC-47
87GenMilB-2C
87KraFoo-19
87Lea-104
87OPC-386
87RedFolSB-10
87SevCoi-D3
87Spo-48
87SpoTeaP-15
87StuPan-19
87TigCaiD-9
87TigCok-1
87TolMudHP-28
87Top-765
87TopCoi-11
87TopMinL-53
87TopSti-273
87TopTif-765
88DodMot-8
88DodPol-23
88Don-275
88DonBasB-66
88Fle-55
88FleGlo-55
88FleMin-82
88FleStiC-24
88FleUpd-93
88FleUpdG-93
88Lea-136
88OPC-201
88PanSti-95
88Sco-525
88ScoGlo-525
88ScoRoo-10T
88ScoRooG-10T
88Spo-111
88StaLinD-4
88StaLinTi-5
88Top-429
88Top-605
88TopBig-191
88TopSti-267
88TopTif-429
88TopTif-605
88TopTra-40T
88TopTraT-40T
88TopUKM-26
88TopUKMT-26
89Baz-10
89Bow-351
89BowTif-351
89CadEllD-23
89ClaTraO-120
89DodMot-8
89DodPol-14
89DodStaSV-5
89Don-15
89Don-132
89DonBasB-10
89DonSupD-15
89Fle-57
89FleBasA-14
89FleBasM-13
89FleExcS-14
89FleForTR-4
89FleGlo-57
89FleGlo-WS5
89FleHeroB-17
89FleLeaL-15
89FleSup-16
89FleWaxBC-C10
89FleWorS-5
89KayB-13
89KinDis-1
89MSAHolD-20
89OPC-340
89OPC-382
89PanSti-16
89PanSti-17
89PanSti-107
89PanSti-479
89RedFolSB-49
89Sco-210
89Sco-582
89ScoHot1S-30
89Spo-65
89Top-340
89Top-396
89TopAme2C-14
89TopBasT-67
89TopBig-299
89TopCapC-2
89TopCoi-1
89TopDouA-24
89TopGaloC-6
89TopGloS-55
89TopHilTM-14
89TopMinL-17
89TopSti-66
89TopStiB-49
89TopTif-340
89TopTif-396
89TopUKM-30
89TVSpoM-33
89TVSpoM-136
89UppDec-633
89UppDec-662
89UppDec-666
89UppDec-676
89Woo-2
89Woo-24
90Bow-97
90BowTif-97
90ClaUpd-T20
90DodMot-13
90DodPol-23
90DodTar-279
90Don-368
90DonBesN-41
90Fle-393
90FleCan-393
90GooHumICBLS-9
90KinDis-5
90Lea-173
90MLBBasB-6
90OPC-150
90PanSti-271
90PubSti-5
90PubSti-259
90Sco-487
90Top-150
90TopAmeA-20
90TopBig-326
90TopHilHM-25
90TopSti-60
90TopTif-150
90UppDec-264
90VenSti-201
90VenSti-202
91Bow-302
91CadEllD-24
91ClaGam-57
91Don-445
91Fle-199
91FleUpd-26
91Lea-249
91OPC-490
91OPCPre-50
91RoyPol-9
91Sco-800
91ScoRoo-18T
91StaClu-344
91Stu-66
91Top-490
91TopDesS-490
91TopMic-490
91TopTif-490
91TopTra-46T
91TopTraT-46T
91UltUpd-27
91UppDec-634
91UppDec-737
92Don-39
92Fle-157
92OPC-720
92PanSti-100
92Pin-481
92RoyPol-7
92Sco-520
92SpoIllFK1-185
92StaClu-495
92StaClu-784
92StaCluECN-784
92Top-720
92TopGol-720
92TopGolW-720
92TopMic-720
92UppDec-180
93CadDis-25
93Fla-203
93FleFinE-209
93Lea-314
93MetBak-28
93PacJugC-5
93PacSpa-443
93StaClu-673
93StaCluFDI-673
93StaCluMOP-673
93Stu-165
93TigGat-9
93TopTra-8T
93Ult-549
93UppDec-766
93UppDecGold-766
94ColC-403
94ColChoGS-403
94ColChoSS-403
94Don-108
94ExtBas-75
94Fla-50
94Fle-130
94Lea-342
94Pac-217
94Pin-453
94PinArtP-453
94PinMusC-453

94ProMag-47
94Sco-421
94ScoGolR-421
94Sel-266
94Top-228
94TopGol-228
94TopSpa-228
94Ult-355
95ColCho-472
95ColChoGS-472
95ColChoSE-217
95ColChoSEGS-217
95ColChoSESS-217
95ColChoSS-472
95Don-257
95DonPreP-257
95DonTopotO-76
95Emo-44
95Fla-256
95Fle-53
95Lea-78
95Pac-153
95PanSti-94
95Pin-349
95PinArtP-349
95PinMusC-349
95Sco-94
95ScoGolR-94
95ScoPlaTS-94
95Sel-25
95SelArtP-25
95SelCer-45
95SelCerMG-45
95SP-156
95SPCha-107
95SPCha-154
95SPChaCP-CP3
95SPChaCPDC-CP3
95SPChaDC-107
95SPChaDC-154
95Spo-34
95SpoArtP-34
95SPSil-156
95Sum-109
95SumNthD-109
95Top-519
95TopCyb-306
95UC3-45
95UC3ArtP-45
95Ult-286
95UltGolM-286
95UppDec-186
95UppDecED-186
95UppDecEDG-186
95UppDecSE-231
95UppDecSEG-231
95Zen-66
96ColCho-142
96ColChoGS-142
96ColChoSS-142
Gibson, Leighton
87OldJudN-202
90KalBatN-22
Gibson, Michael
93GenCubC-12
93GenCubF-3190
Gibson, Monty
91PocPioP-3776
91PocPioSP-18
Gibson, Moon (George)
03WilCarE-15
08AmeCarE-76
08RosComP-150
09AmeCarE-42
09AmeCarE-43
09ColChiE-116
09SpoNewSM-35
09T206-141
10DomDisP-48
10E-UOraBSC-11
10E101-21
10E12AmeCDC-17
10JHDABE-7
10MelMinE-21
10NadCarE-22
10NadE1-18
10PeoT21-25A
10PeoT21-25B
10PeoT21-25C
10PeoT21-25D
10PirAmeCE-3
10PirHerP-6
10PirTipTD-6
10SepAnoP-14
10StaCarE-14
10SweCapPP-137
10W555-31
11MecDFT-23
11S74Sil-110
11SpoLifCW-140
11SpoLifM-250
11T205-64
11TurRedT-94
12ColRedB-116
12ColTinT-116
12HasTriFT-14B
12HasTriFT-14C
12HasTriFT-16B
12HasTriFT-16C
12HasTriFT-30A
12HasTriFT-30E
12PhiCarE-11
14B18B-76A
14B18B-76B
15AmeCarE-19A
15AmeCarE-19B
15SpoNewM-68
16SpoNewM-68
19W514-63
21E121So1-30
23W501-89
23WilChoV-49
34DiaMatCSB-69
69SCFOldT-11
92ConTSN-516
93ConTSN-825
Gibson, Norwood
04RedSoxUP-8
11SpoLifCW-141
Gibson, Paul
80CedRapRT-18
82BirBarT-23
83OrlTwiT-20
86GleFalTP-6
86NasSouTI-9
87TolMudHP-10
87TolMudHT-17
88DonRoo-19
88FleUpd-26
88FleUpdG-26
88TigPep-48
89Baz-11
89Bow-99
89BowTif-99
89ClaTraO-140
89Don-445
89Fle-131
89FleGlo-131
89K-M-10
89PanSti-331
89Sco-595A
89Sco-595B
89TigMar-48
89Top-583
89TopBig-230
89TopGloS-20
89TopRoo-10
89TopSti-323
89TopTif-583
89ToyRoo-11
89UppDec-47
90BirBarDGB-14
90Don-657
90Fle-602
90FleCan-602
90Lea-298
90OPC-11
90PubSti-470
90Sco-261
90TigCok-5
90Top-11
90TopTif-11
90UppDec-496
90VenSti-203
91Don-353
91Fle-337
91Lea-55
91OPC-431
91Sco-152
91TigCok-48
91TigPol-5
91Top-431
91TopDesS-431
91TopMic-431
91TopTif-431
91UltUpd-23
91UppDec-579
92Don-375
92Fle-136
92Lea-461
92MetColP-24
92MetKah-45
92OPC-143
92OPCPre-174
92Sco-261
92StaClu-223
92StaClu-694
92Top-143
92TopGol-143
92TopGolW-143
92TopMic-143
92Ult-531
92UppDec-489
93Fle-473
93MetColP-34
93NorTidF-2563
93StaClu-29
93StaCluFDI-29
93StaCluMOP-29
94Fle-230
94StaCluT-185
94StaCluTFDI-185
96ColCliB-14
Gibson, Sam
93ConTSN-962
Gibson, Scott
82AppFoxF-22
84VisOakT-21
Gibson, Steve
78NewWayCT-15
79BurBeeT-13
80BurBeeT-1
81BurBeeT-11
Gibson, Thomas
91NiaFalRC-4
Giddens, Ron
84CedRapRT-20
86MacPirP-10
Giddings, Wayne
83IdaFalAT-4
84MadMusP-18
85HunStaJ-42
Gideon, Brett
86PriWilPP-11
87HarSenP-18
88BufBisC-3
88BufBisP-1492
88Fle-330
88FleGlo-330
89ExpPos-10
89IndIndC-5
89IndIndP-1230
90Bow-105
90BowTif-105
90ExpPos-12
92CanIndF-686
Gideon, Jim
76SacSolC-15
76TacTwiDQ-7
77TacTwiDQ-20
77Top-478
82TulDriT-9
89PacSenL-81
89TopSenL-26
92TexLon-15
93RanKee-159
Gideon, Ron
86LynMetP-12
87LynMetP-8
88JacMetGS-1
89St.LucMS-7
90JacMetGS-23
91St.LucMC-27
91St.LucMP-728
92BinMetF-533
93KinMetC-25
93KinMetF-3811
94KinMetC-25
94KinMetF-3839
95PitMetTI-13
96PorRocB-1
Giebell, Floyd
81TigDetN-88
Giegling, Matt
91CedRapRC-15
91CedRapRP-2722
92CedRapRC-6
92CedRapRF-1075
Giel, Paul
55Bow-125
55GiaGolS-9
58GiaJayP-3
58GiaSFCB-8
58Top-308
59Top-9
59TopVen-9
60Top-526
61Top-374
61TwiCloD-6
61TwiPetM-19
Gienger, Craig
92SouOreAC-14
92SouOreAF-3409
93SouOreAC-9
Gierger, Craig
93SouOreAF-4056
Gierhan, Sam
78NewWayCT-16
79BurBeeT-5
Gies, Chris
90ButCopKSP-22
91Cla/Bes-191
91GasRanC-6
91GasRanP-2683
92ChaRanC-10
92ClaFS7-66
93TulDriF-2728
93TulDriTI-9
Giesdal, Brent
82OneYanT-3
Giesecke, Bob
79CliDodT-21
Giesecke, Doc (Rob)
82VerBeaDT-27
83VerBeaDT-27
86VerBeaDP-7
87VerBeaDP-18
90SanAntMGS-4
90TexLeaAGS-19
94VerBeaDC-30
95VerBeaDTI-8
96VerBeaDB-4
Gieseke, Mark
89WatDiaS-29
90RivRedWP-2614
91CalLeLA-20
91HigDesMC-20
91HigDesMP-2403
92WicWraF-3662
93WicWraF-2982
Giesen, Dan
87ReaPhiP-6
88ReaPhiP-874
Gietzen, Peter
92GreHorC-16
92GreHorF-773
Gifford, Frank
60Pos-3
Giggie, Bob
60BraJayP-5
60BraLaktL-11
Gigon, Norm
67Top-576
Gil, Benji
91ClaDraP-15
91FroRowDP-50
91HigSchPLS-27
92Bow-339
92ClaFS7-309
92GasRanC-1
92GasRanF-2260
92OPC-534
92Pin-302
92Sco-808
92StaCluD-59
92Top-534
92TopGol-534
92TopGolW-534
92TopMic-534
92UppDecML-174
93Bow-629
93ClaGolF-50
93ExcFS7-234
93FleFinE-278
93FunPac-3
93LeaGolR-R18
93OPCPre-27
93PacBeiA-16
93PacSpa-639
93Pin-597
93RanKee-407
93SelRoo-42T
93SouAtlLAIPI-5
93SouAtlLAPI-12
93SP-193
93StaClu-697
93StaCluFDI-697
93StaCluMOP-697
93StaCluR-9
93Top-529
93TopGol-529
93TopInaM-529
93TopMic-529
93TopTra-60T
93TulDriF-2740
93Ult-628
93UppDec-441
93UppDecGold-441
94ActPac-48
94Bow-185
94Bow-379
94Cla-126
94ClaTriF-T79
94ColC-108
94ColChoGS-108
94ColChoSS-108
94Don-103
94OklCit8F-1498
94Pac-616
94Pin-194
94PinArtP-194
94PinMusC-194
94Sco-606
94ScoGolR-606
94StaCluT-246
94StaCluTFDI-246
94Top-231
94TopGol-231
94TopSpa-231
94UppDec-135
94UppDecED-135
95Bow-33
95BowBes-R88
95BowBesR-R88
95ColCho-568T
95DonTopotO-159
95Emo-84
95Fin-222
95FinRef-222
95Fla-305
95Lea-253
95LeaLim-47
95RanCra-10
95SelCer-76
95SelCerMG-76
95SigRooMR-MR2
95SigRooMRS-MR2
95SigRooOJSS-6
95SigRooOJSSS-6
95SP-196
95SPCha-191
95SPChaDC-191
95SPSil-196
95StaClu-573
95StaCluCB-CB8
95StaCluMOP-573
95StaCluMOP-CB8
95StaCluSTWS-573
95Sum-112
95SumNewA-NA10
95SumNthD-112
95Top-336
95UppDec-392
95UppDecED-392
95UppDecEDG-392
95Zen-144
95ZenRooRC-18
96ColCho-322
96ColCho-333
96ColChoGS-322
96ColChoGS-333
96ColChoSS-322
96ColChoSS-333
96Don-223
96DonPreP-223
96Fin-B82
96FinRef-B82
96Fla-168
96Fle-249
96FleRan-5
96FleTif-249
96Lea-95
96LeaPrePB-95
96LeaPrePG-95
96LeaPrePS-95
96LeaSigA-78
96LeaSigAG-78
96LeaSigAS-78
96Pac-429
96Pin-288

96PinAfi-113
96PinAfiAP-113
96PinFoil-288
96ProSta-96
96RanMot-26
96Sco-158
96ScoDugC-A92
96ScoDugCAP-A92
96Sel-82
96SelArtP-82
96SelCer-73
96SelCerAP-73
96SelCerCB-73
96SelCerCR-73
96SelCerMB-73
96SelCerMG-73
96SelCerMR-73
96StaClu-81
96StaCluMOP-81
96Sum-59
96SumAbo&B-59
96SumArtP-59
96SumFoi-59
96Top-152
96Ult-134
96UltGolM-134
96UppDec-464
96Zen-78
96ZenArtP-78
97ColCho-492
97Don-317
97DonPreP-317
97DonPrePGold-317
97Fle-565
97FleTif-565
97Lea-287
97LeaFraM-287
97LeaFraMDC-287
97PacPriGotD-GD94
97Sco-384
97ScoHobR-384
97ScoResC-384
97ScoShoS-384
97ScoShoSAP-384
93TulDriTI-29
97Ult-428
97UltGolME-428
97UltPlaME-428
Gil, Carlos
80QuaCitCT-8
80VenLeaS-152
83MidCubT-7
Gil, Danny
90BoiHawP-3336
91PalSprAP-2020
94HunCubF-3566
94PeoChiC-9
94PeoChiF-2279
94HunCubC-12
Gil, Geronimo
96SavSanB-10
Gil, Jose
82WisRapTF-15
93LinVenB-163
94VenLinU-214
94VenLinU-262
95LinVen-53
Gil, T. Gus
67Top-253
69PilPos-31
69Top-651
75HawIslC-1
76VenLeaS-157
76VenLeaS-225
77ForLauYS-27
80VenLeaS-226
82DanSunF-2
94BreMilB-127
Gilbert, Andy (Andrew)
73OPC-252
73Top-252A
73Top-252B
74OPC-78
74Top-78
Gilbert, Angelo
80BatTroT-1
82IdaFalAT-8
Gilbert, Billy (William O.)
03BreE10-56
06GiaUllAFS-5
08RosComP-163
09PC7HHB-15
09T206-142
11SpoLifCW-142
Gilbert, Brent
90TamYanD-9
91PriWilCC-1
91PriWilCP-1417
Gilbert, Buddy (Drew E.)
58RedEnq-14
59RedEnq-8
60HenHouW-16
60Top-359
60UniOil-6
Gilbert, Charlie (Charles M.)
29ExhFou-16
40DodTeal-10
41CubTeal-7
90DodTar-280
91JesHSA-2
Gilbert, Dennis
80ElPasDT-2
81HolMilT-10
82HolMilT-21
83RedPioT-11
Gilbert, Donald
92KanCouCC-4
92KanCouCF-97
92KanCouCTI-10
Gilbert, Greg
84EveGiaC-6A
85FreGiaP-10
86FreGiaP-7
87AncGlaP-13
87IdaFalBP-15
88SumBraP-405
Gilbert, Jeff
83SanJosBC-21
84ChaO'sT-18
85ChaO'sT-20
Gilbert, Larry (Lawrence W.)
16FleBreD-31
Gilbert, Mark
79QuaCitCT-12
80WatRedT-14
81WatRedT-19
82WatRedT-18
83IndIndTI-22
84WicAerRD-12
85BufBisT-13
Gilbert, Pat
86MedA'sC-59
87MadMusP-7
88ModA'sCLC-79
88ModA'sTI-26
89HunStaB-21
Gilbert, Pete
90DodTar-958
Gilbert, Robbie
86MedA'sC-62
Gilbert, Roy
89FreKeyS-7
90FreKeyTI-14
91FreKeyP-2379
91LinDriAA-230
Gilbert, Shawn
86AncGlaPTI-11
88MidLeaAGS-32
88VisOakCLC-151
88VisOakP-91
89VisOakCLC-104
89VisOakP-1439
90Bes-88
90CMC-750
90OrlSunRB-4
90OrlSunRP-1089
90OrlSunRS-6
91LinDriAA-481
91OrlSunRLD-481
91OrlSunRP-1856
92PorBeaF-2672
92PorBeaS-406
92SkyAAAF-186
93NasSouF-577
93StaCluWS-30
94ScrRedBF-924
95ScrRedBTI-11
96NorTidB-16
Gilbert, Tookie (Harold)
50Bow-235
52MotCoo-31
52Top-61
83TopRep5-61
91JesHSA-5
Gilbert, Wally (Walter John)
90DodTar-959
92ConTSN-404
Gilbreath, Rod
74OPC-93
74Top-93
75OPC-431
75Top-431
76OPC-306
76SSP-10
76Top-306
77Top-126
78BraCok-5
78Top-217
79OPC-296
79PorBeaT-24
79Top-572
80PorBeaT-22
87IdaFalBP-9
Gilchrist, John
88EugEmeB-24
89EugEmeB-22
90AppFoxBS-9
90AppFoxP-2108
91BasCitRC-24
91BasCitRP-1410
Gilcrease, Doug
84MemChiT-19
85Ft.MyeRT-17
86MemChiSTOS-8
86MemChiTOS-8
Gilday, Bill (William)
52LavPro-75
Gile, Don
61Top-236
62Top-244
Gile, Mark
83TriTriT-16
85TulDriTI-10
Giles, Brian Jeffrey
81TidTidT-4
82MetPhoA-27
82TidTidT-8
83Fle-544
83Top-548
83TopSti-322
84Don-563
84Fle-585
84JacMetF-5
84Nes792-676
84OPC-324
84TidTidT-24
84Top-676
84TopSti-111
84TopTif-676
85BrePol-26
87HawIslP-8
88CalCanC-15
88CalCanP-784
89BlaYNPRWL-190
89ColSprSSC-13
89ColSprSSP-253
91MetWIZ-140
94BreMilB-223
Giles, Brian Stephen
90WatIndS-9
91CarLeaAP-CAR15
91Cla/Bes-16
91KinIndC-26
91KinIndP-338
92CanIndF-701
92CanIndS-108
92ClaFS7-38
92ProFS7-56
92SkyAA F-50
93CanIndF-2848
94ChaKniF-907
94UppDecML-27
95UppDecML-120
96BufBisB-8
96SigRooOJ-11
96SigRooOJS-11
97Cir-173
97CirRav-173
97ColCho-27
97Don-166
97DonLim-174
97DonLimLE-174
97DonPre-156
97DonPreCttC-156
97DonPreP-166
97DonPrePGold-166
97DonTea-80
97DonTeaSPE-80
97Fin-206
97FinRef-206
97FlaSho-A65
97FlaSho-B65
97FlaSho-C65
97FlaShoLC-65
97FlaShoLC-B65
97FlaShoLC-C65
97FlaShoLCM-A65
97FlaShoLCM-B65
97FlaShoLCM-C65
97Fle-78
97FleTif-78
97Lea-173
97LeaFraM-173
97LeaFraMDC-173
97NewPin-176
97NewPinAP-176
97NewPinMC-176
97NewPinPP-176
97Pac-69
97PacLigB-69
97PacSil-69
97PinCer-109
97PinCerMBlu-109
97PinCerMG-109
97PinCerMR-109
97PinCerR-109
97PinTotCPB-109
97PinTotCPG-109
97PinTotCPR-109
97PinX-P-129
97PinX-PMoS-129
97Sco-309
97ScoInd-15
97ScoIndPl-15
97ScoIndPr-15
97ScoIndU-15
97ScoIndUTC-15
97ScoPreS-309
97ScoShoS-309
97ScoShoSAP-309
97StaClu-139
97StaCluMOP-139
97Stu-145
97StuPrePG-145
97StuPrePS-145
97Ult-354
97UltGolME-354
97UltGolP-6
97UltPlaME-354
97UppDec-236
95UppDecMLFS-120
Giles, George
86NegLeaF-51
87NegLeaPD-44
89RinPosNL1-5
91NegLeaRL-1
92NegLeaRLI-22
95NegLeaLI-1
Giles, Tim
96MedHatBJTI-8
Giles, Troy
87QuaCitAP-2
87SalAngP-4
88QuaCitAGS-15
89PalSprACLC-32
89PalSprAP-473
Giles, Warren
56Top-2
57Top-100
58Top-300
59Top-200
60Fle-73
61Fle-33
80PerHaloFP-167
80SSPHOF-167
82OhiHaloF-17
84WilMay-27
89HOFStiB-92
Gilevich, Darryl
90LSUTigA-12
Gilhooley, Frank
16ColE13-59
16FleBreD-32
Gilkey, Bernard (Otis Bernard)
87SprCarB-25
88SprCarB-13
89ArkTraGS-6
90CMC-109
90Lea-353
90LouRedBC-9
90LouRedBLBC-2
90LouRedBLBC-18
90LouRedBP-415
90ProAAAF-529
90ScoRoo-106T
90TopTVCa-50
90TriAllGP-AAA19
91Bow-408
91CarPol-23
91Cla1-T93
91ClaGam-165
91Don-30
91Fle-633
91Lea-286
91LouRedTI-23
91OPC-126
91OPCPre-51
91Sco-709
91ScoRoo-11
91StaClu-402
91Stu-231
91Top-126
91TopDeb90-53
91TopDesS-126
91TopMic-126
91TopTif-126
91UppDec-16
92Bow-403
92CarPol-6
92Don-376
92Fle-578
92Lea-502
92OPC-746
92Pin-88
92Sco-544
92Sco100RS-24
92ScoProP-22
92StaClu-234
92Top-746
92TopGol-746
92TopGolW-746
92TopMic-746
92Ult-567
92UppDec-552
93Bow-684
93CarPol-6
93Don-284
93Fla-120
93Fle-125
93Lea-99
93OPC-61
93PacSpa-294
93PanSti-197
93Pin-88
93Pin-304
93Sco-81
93Sel-173
93SP-74
93StaClu-230
93StaCluCa-3
93StaCluFDI-230
93StaCluMOP-230
93Stu-7
93Top-203
93TopGol-203
93TopInaM-203
93TopMic-203
93Toy-81
93TriPla-208
93Ult-106
93UppDec-394
93UppDec-482
93UppDecGold-394
93UppDecGold-482
94Bow-592
94CarPol-5
94ColC-109
94ColChoGS-109
94ColChoSS-109
94Don-90
94ExtBas-358
94Fin-111
94FinRef-111
94Fla-428
94Fle-631
94Lea-152
94LeaL-144
94Pac-589
94PanSti-242
94Pin-79
94PinArtP-79
94PinMusC-79
94PinRunC-RC42
94Sco-420
94ScoGolR-420
94Sel-20

94SP-62
94SPDieC-62
94Spo-140
94StaClu-231
94StaCluFDI-231
94StaCluGR-231
94StaCluMOP-231
94StaCluT-316
94StaCluTFDI-316
94Stu-50
94Top-377
94TopGol-377
94TopSpa-377
94TriPla-61
94Ult-565
94UppDec-406
94UppDecED-406
95ColCho-191
95ColChoGS-191
95ColChoSE-76
95ColChoSEGS-76
95ColChoSESS-76
95ColChoSS-191
95Don-379
95DonPreP-379
95DonTopotO-326
95Emo-179
95Fin-318
95FinRef-318
95Fla-192
95Fle-497
95Lea-239
95LeaLim-187
95Pac-406
95Pin-62
95PinArtP-62
95PinMusC-62
95Sco-485
95ScoGolR-485
95ScoPlaTS-485
95Sel-13
95SelArtP-13
95SelCer-15
95SelCerMG-15
95SP-98
95SPCha-86
95SPChaDC-86
95Spo-12
95SpoArtP-12
95SPSil-98
95StaClu-190
95StaCluFDI-190
95StaCluMOP-190
95StaCluSTWS-190
95Stu-68
95Sum-81
95SumNthD-81
95Top-547
95TopCyb-328
95Ult-222
95UltGolM-222
95UppDec-303
95UppDecED-303
95UppDecEDG-303
95UppDecSE-89
95UppDecSEG-89
95Zen-7
96Cir-156
96CirRav-156
96ColCho-288
96ColCho-620
96ColChoGS-288
96ColChoGS-620
96ColChoSS-288
96ColChoSS-620
96Don-49
96DonPreP-49
96EmoXL-231
96Fin-S231
96FinRef-S231
96Fla-319
96Fle-543
96FleTif-543
96FleUpd-U156
96FleUpdTC-U156
96LeaPre-108
96LeaPreP-108
96MetKah-10
96MetUni-225
96MetUniP-225
96Pac-216
96PacPri-P69
96PacPriG-P69
96PanSti-75
96Pin-346
96PinAfi-76
96PinAfiAP-76
96PinAfiFPP-76
96PinFoil-346
96ProSta-34
96Sco-32
96ScoDugC-A31
96ScoDugCAP-A31
96Sel-143
96SelArtP-143
96SP-127
96StaClu-32
96StaCluEPB-32
96StaCluEPG-32
96StaCluEPS-32
96StaCluMOP-32
96Stu-19
96StuPrePB-19
96StuPrePG-19
96StuPrePS-19
96Sum-132
96SumAbo&B-132
96SumArtP-132
96SumFoi-132
96TeaOut-28
96Top-256
96TopChr-101
96TopChrR-101
96Ult-273
96Ult-512
96UltGolM-273
96UltGolM-512
96UppDec-183
96UppDec-402
97Bow-11
97BowBes-47
97BowBesAR-47
97BowBesR-47
97BowInt-11
97Cir-317
97CirRav-317
97ColCho-170
97ColChoAC-43
97Don-96
97DonLim-42
97DonLimLE-42
97DonPre-16
97DonPreCttC-16
97DonPreP-96
97DonPrePGold-96
97Fin-226
97FinRef-226
97FlaSho-A83
97FlaSho-B83
97FlaSho-C83
97FlaShoLC-83
97FlaShoLC-B83
97FlaShoLC-C83
97FlaShoLCM-A83
97FlaShoLCM-B83
97FlaShoLCM-C83
97Fle-395
97FleTif-395
97Lea-113
97LeaFraM-113
97LeaFraMDC-113
97MetUni-193
97NewPin-17
97NewPinAP-17
97NewPinMC-17
97NewPinPP-17
97Pac-364
97PacLigB-364
97PacPri-123
97PacPriLB-123
97PacPriP-123
97PacSil-364
97PinCer-20
97PinCerMBlu-20
97PinCerMG-20
97PinCerMR-20
97PinCerR-20
97PinTotCPB-20
97PinTotCPG-20
97PinTotCPR-20
97PinX-P-67
97PinX-PMoS-67
97PinX-PSfF-52
97PinX-PSfFU-52
97Sco-109
97ScoPreS-109
97ScoShoS-109
97ScoShoSAP-109
97SP-119
97SpollI-89
97SpollIEE-89
97StaClu-26
97StaCluMat-26
97StaCluMOP-26
97Top-160
97TopChr-63
97TopChrR-63
97TopGal-66
97TopGalPPI-66
97Ult-238
97UltGolME-238
97UltPlaME-238
97UppDec-115

Gilks, Robert
87OldJudN-203

Gill, Chris
89BilMusP-2046
90Bes-141
90ChaWheB-15
90ChaWheP-2246
91ChaWheC-17
91ChaWheP-2894

Gill, John
36SandSW-24
45CenFlo-10

Gill, Ken
73TacTwiC-9

Gill, Ron
77LynMetT-13

Gill, Shawn
82IdaFalAT-14
83MadMusF-11
84MadMusP-17

Gill, Sheldon
75ForLauYS-20

Gill, Steve
90AriWilP-6
91WatDiaC-21
91WatDiaP-1268
92HigDesMC-2
93ElPasDF-2963
94WesPalBEC-10
94WesPalBEF-54

Gill, Turner
87WilBilP-25
88WilBilP-1312

Gillaspie, Mark
83BeaGolGT-15
84BeaGolGT-5
85IowCubT-22
88MemChiB-13

Gilleaudeau, Joseph
94ConTSN-1112
94ConTSNB-1112

Gilleaudeau, Mrs. (Joseph)
94ConTSN-1112
94ConTSNB-1112

Gillen, Kevin
76WatRoyT-10
77JacSunT-8

Gillenwater, Carden
50WorWidGV-32
90DodTar-960

Gilles, Bob
83VerBeaDT-15

Gilles, Mark
87KinIndP-3
88KinIndS-7
89CanIndB-13
89CanIndP-1323
89CanIndS-7

Gilles, Tom
87AppFoxP-16
88KenTwiP-1387
89KnoBluJB-7
89KnoBluJP-1143
90CMC-330
90ProAAAF-344
90SyrChiC-4
90SyrChiMB-10
90SyrChiP-564
91RenSilSCLC-16
91TopDeb90-54

Gilles, Wayne
87AriWilP-3

Gillespie, Don
89WytCubS-12

Gillespie, Eric
96BoiHawB-13

Gillespie, John
22E120-172

Gillespie, Mark
84IdaFalATI-9

Gillespie, Paul
47SmiClo-20

Gillespie, Pete
86OldJudN-8
87BucN28-68A
87BucN28-68B
87FouBasHN-4
87OldJudN-204
88AugBecN-12
90KalBatN-23

Gillespie, Robert
48WhiSoxTI-6
49SolSunP-5
52MotCoo-21

Gillette, Mike
90FayGenP-2409
91LakTigC-15
91LakTigP-269
92LonTigF-636
92LonTigS-409

Gilliam, Bo
86DavLipB-13
92ForLauYC-18
92ForLauYTI-13
92Ft.LauYF-2627
93SanBerSC-10

Gilliam, Darryl
86BakDodP-11
86TriTriC-199

Gilliam, Ed
78BurBeeT-14

Gilliam, Junior (James)
47PM1StaP1-70
47PM1StaP1-71
47StaPinP2-15
52LaPat-5
52Par-68
53Top-258
54Bow-74
54NewYorJA-6
54RedHeaF-10
54RedMan-NL14
54Top-35
55ArmCoi-7
55BigLeaIS-7
55Bow-98
55DaiQueS-7
55DodGolS-14
55Top-5
55TopDouH-129
56Dod-11
56Top-280
57SwiFra-10
57Top-115
58DodBelB-4
58PacBel-3
58Top-215
59DodMor-3
59DodTeal-8
59DodVol-6
59Top-306
60DodBelB-4
60DodJayP-5
60DodTeal-7
60DodUniO-7
60KeyChal-20
60Lea-18
60MacSta-9
60Top-255
60TopTat-19
61DodBelB-19
61DodJayP-3
61DodUniO-8
61Pos-158A
61Pos-158B
61Top-238
62DodBelB-19
62DodJayP-4
62Jel-112
62Pos-112
62PosCan-112
62SalPlaC-201
62ShiPlaC-201
62Top-486
63DodJayP-6
63Jel-114
63Pos-114
63Top-80
64Top-310
64TopVen-310
64WheSta-18
73OPC-569
73Top-569
74OPC-144
74Top-144
78TCM60I-45
79TCM50-290
80DodGreT-2
84OCoandSI-118
86NegLeaF-76
87Dod195T-6
88PacLegI-44
88WilMulP-14
90DodTar-281
91RinPosBD3-10
91TopArc1-258
92BazQua5A-8
93TedWil-135
93TedWil-149
93TedWilM-2
94TopArc1-35
94TopArc1G-35
95DodROY-4
95TopArcBD-55
95TopArcBD-69
95TopArcBD-91
95TopArcBD-128
95TopArcBD-161

Gilliam, Keith
83KinBluJTI-6
85SyrChiT-7
86KnoBluJP-8
87KnoBluJP-1506

Gilliam, Melvin
80AshTouT-4

Gilliam, Sean
90CMC-705
90GreHorB-22
90GreHorP-2674
90GreHorS-3
91GreHorP-3073
93SanBerSF-784

Gilliford, Paul
77FriOneYW-40
91OriCro-156

Gilligan, Barney
87BucN28-113
87OldJudN-205

Gilligan, Jim
87SalLakTTT-11

Gilligan, John
90MedHatBJB-19
91SalLakTP-3204
91SalLakTSP-12
92SalLakTSP-7

Gilligan, Larry
91JohCitCC-7
91JohCitCP-3984
92HamRedC-18
92HamRedF-1599

Gillis, Grant
28StaPlaCE-27

Gillis, Jack
91OneYanP-4168
92OneYanC-27

Gillis, Louis
92NegLeaRLI-23

Gillis, Tim
90Bes-134
90BurBraB-13
90BurBraP-2356
90BurBraS-12
91CarLeaAP-CAR1
91DurBulC-17
91DurBulP-1553
92DurBulC-11
92DurBulF-1107
92DurBulTI-18
93GreBraF-356
94GreBraF-418
94GreBraTI-10

Gills, Amy
85AncGlaPTI-35
86AncGlaPTI-12
87AncGlaP-14

Gills, Jack
87OneYanP-32

Gillum, Kenneth (K.C.)
89BilMusP-2042
90BilMusP-3237
90ChaWheP-2251
90ProAaA-196
91CedRapRC-25
91CedRapRP-2731
91Cla/Bes-369
92ChaWheF-19

92ChaWVWC-15
92ClaFS7-58
93ChaLooF-2371
93ClaFS7-191
93SouAtlLAIPI-17
93SouAtlLAPI-13
Gilmartin, Dan
78NewWayCT-17
79BurBeeT-10
82BelBreF-18
Gilmartin, Kevin
76SeaRaiC-5
Gilmartin, Paul
76SeaRaiC-6
Gilmore, Bill
87AppFoxP-2
Gilmore, Frank T.
87OldJudN-206
Gilmore, Joel
91MarPhiP-3448
92ClaFS7-264
92ClePhiF-2051
93ClePhiC-10
93ClePhiF-2679
95ReaPhiTI-38
Gilmore, Kale
94ButCopKSP-16
Gilmore, Lenny
88BurIndP-1774
Gilmore, Matt
90BurIndP-3014
Gilmore, Quincy Jordan
87NegLeaPD-23
Gilmore, Terry
87SpoIndP-19
88TexLeaAGS-29
88WicPilRD-20
09LasVegSC-4
89LasVegSP-16
90CMC-506
90LasVegSC-4
90LasVegSP-113
90ProAAAF-1
90TriAllGP-AAA18
91LasVegSLD-282
91LasVegSP-229
91LinDriAAA-282
Gilmore, Tony
80UtiBluJT-16
90AubAstP-3397
Gilmore, Tony R.
90ArkRaz-13
91BurAstC-25
91BurAstP-2805
91Cla/Bes-325
91MidLeaAP-MWL15
92OscAstC-2
92OscAstF-2533
93JacGenF-2110
94JacGenF-220
95JacGenTI-14
Gilson, Bob
89LonTigP-1358
Gilson, Hal
68OPC-162
68Top-162
68TopVen-162
69OPC-156
69Top-156
69TopFou-2
Giminez, Issac
75CliPilT-9
Giminez, Ray
75CliPilT-10
Ging, Adam
85SpoIndC-5
87ColMetP-8
88St.LucMS-9
Gingrich, Gary
75WesPalBES-2
76BurBeeT-15
77BurBeeT-10
Gingrich, Jeff
79MemChiT-18
Ginsberg, Joe (Myron)
52Top-192
53BowC-6
53TigGle-10
54Bow-52
57Top-236
58Top-67
59Top-66
59TopVen-66
60Top-304
61Top-79
79TCM50-52
83TopRep5-192
91MetWIZ-141
91OriCro-157
Gioia, Joe
86TriTriC-194
Gionfriddo, Al
48SweSpoT-9
50WorWidGV-24
68LauWorS-44
70FleWorS-44
90DodTar-282
91RinPosBD4-9
Giordano, Marc
89PriPirS-7
90MiaMirIS-9
90MiaMirIS-7
91MiaMirC-20
91MiaMirP-414
Giordano, Mike
83OrlTwiT-21
Giovanola, Ed
89AncBucTI-13
90IdaFalBP-3269
91DurBulC-14
91DurBulP-1554
92GreBraF-1159
92GreBraS-233
93GreBraF-357
94GreBraF-419
95ARuFalLS-7
95RicBraRC-3
95RicBraTI-3
96LeaSigEA-59
96RicBraB-13
96RicBraRC-12
96RicBraUB-8
97PacPriGotD-GD111
Gipner, Marcus
92GulCoaYF-3793
92StaCluD-60
94GreBatF-478
94OneYanC-9
94OneYanF-3793
97GreBatC-8
Gipson, Charles
93AppFoxC-8
93AppFoxF-2468
94RivPilCLC-10
95PorCitRTI-10
96PorCitRB-12
Girardi, Joe
87WinSpiP-17
88BasAmeAAB-8
88EasLeaAP-25
88PitCubP-1359
89CubMar-7
89DonRoo-23
89Fle-644
89FleGlo-644
89ScoRoo-84T
89UppDec-776
90CubMar-8
90Don-404
90DonBesN-87
90Fle-31
90FleCan-31
90Lea-289
90OPC-12
90Sco-535
90Sco100RS-33
90ScoYouS2-29
90Top-12
90TopDeb89-42
90TopTif-12
90TopTVCu-20
90UppDec-304
91Bow-415
91CubMar-7
91CubVinL-11
91Don-184
91Fle-421
91Lea-258
91OPC-214
91PanFreS-42
91PanSti-49
91Sco-585
91StaClu-247
91Stu-156
91Top-214
91TopDesS-214
91TopMic-214
91TopTif-214
91Ult-60
91UppDec-113
92Bow-636
92CubMar-7
92Don-175
92Lea-72
92OPC-529
92Pin-498
92Sco-701
92StaClu-132
92Stu-13
92Top-529
92TopGol-529
92TopGolW-529
92TopMic-529
92TriPla-151
92Ult-469
92UppDec-351
93Bow-668
93Don-736
93Fla-40
93Fle-410
93FleFinE-31
93Lea-332
93MilBonSS-18
93PacSpa-428
93Pin-236
93PinExpOD-2
93RocUSPC-4D
93RocUSPC-13S
93Sco-419
93Sel-53
93SP-221
93StaClu-620
93StaCluFDI-620
93StaCluMOP-620
93StaCluRoc-10
93Stu-188
93Top-425
93TopGol-425
93TopInaM-425
93TopMic-425
93TriPla-237
93Ult-348
93UppDec-571
93UppDecGold-571
94Bow-30
94ColC-396
94ColChoGS-396
94ColChoSS-396
94Don-165
94ExtBas-245
94Fin-72
94FinRef-72
94Fla-153
94Fle-441
94Lea-3
94LeaL-103
94Pac-196
94Pin-74
94PinArtP-74
94PinMusC-74
94RocPol-10
94Sco-76
94ScoGolR-76
94Sel-70
94StaClu-323
94StaCluFDI-323
94StaCluGR-323
94StaCluMOP-323
94StaCluT-107
94StaCluTFDI-107
94Stu-178
94Top-372
94TopGol-372
94TopSpa-372
94TriPla-224
94Ult-185
94UppDec-76
94UppDecED-76
95ColCho-448
95ColChoGS-448
95ColChoSS-448
95Don-367
95DonPreP-367
95DonTopotO-228
95Fin-193
95FinRef-193
95Fla-345
95Fle-519
95Lea-159
95LeaLim-50
95Pac-137
95Pin-357
95PinArtP-357
95PinMusC-357
95RocPol-7
95Sco-95
95ScoGolR-95
95ScoPlaTS-95
95StaClu-184
95StaCluFDI-184
95StaCluMOP-184
95StaCluSTWS-184
95StaCluVR-94
95Stu-149
95Top-539
95TopCyb-321
95Ult-153
95UltGolM-153
95UppDec-409
95UppDecED-409
95UppDecEDG-409
96ColCho-132
96ColCho-632
96ColChoGS-132
96ColChoGS-632
96ColChoSS-132
96ColChoSS-632
96Don-12
96DonPreP-12
96Fin-B311
96FinRef-B311
96Fla-127
96Fle-183
96FleTif-183
96FleUpd-U60
96FleUpdTC-U60
96MetUni-86
96MetUniP-86
96MLBPin-12
96Pac-66
96Sco-104
96StaClu-83
96StaCluEPB-83
96StaCluEPG-83
96StaCluEPS-83
96StaCluMOP-83
95StaCluVRMC-94
96Top-36
96Ult-384
96UltGolM-384
96UppDec-157
97Cir-78
97CirRav-78
97ColCho-402
97Don-334
97DonPreP-334
97DonPrePGold-334
97DonTea-133
97DonTeaSPE-133
97Fin-86
97FinRef-86
97Fle-165
97FleTif-165
97PacPriGotD-GD72
97Sco-464
97ScoHobR-464
97ScoResC-464
97ScoShoS-464
97ScoShoSAP-464
97StaClu-298
97StaCluMOP-298
97Top-291
97Ult-97
97UltGolME-97
97UltPlaME-97
97UppDec-441
Giron, Emiliano
94PriRedC-10
94PriRedF-3257
95Exc-176
Giron, Tomas
85DomLeaS-137
Giron, Ysidro
86Ft.LauYP-7
87PriWilYP-17
Girouard, Mike
88SouBenWSGS-19
Girt, Bob
89AncBucTI-29
Gissell, Chris
97Bow-162
97BowInt-162
Gisselman, Bob
82WauTimF-31
Githens, John
86WatIndP-10
87WatIndP-13
88KinIndS-8
89HagSunB-2
89HagSunP-262
89HagSunS-9
Giudice, John
93BenRocC-8
93BenRocF-3280
94AshTouC-9
94AshTouF-1795
94SouAtlLAF-SAL29
95SalAvaTI-6
96SalAvaB-11
Giuliani, Tony
35DiaMatCS3T1-60
90DodTar-283
Giuliano, Joe
94SigRooDP-70
94SigRooDPS-70
94StaCluDP-34
94StaCluDPFDI-34
95DanBraTI-12
96EugEmeB-9
Giusti, Dave
62Col.45B-7
62Top-509
63Top-189
64Top-354
64TopVen-354
65Top-524
66Top-258
66TopVen-258
67Ast-10
67AstTeal1-5
67AstTeal2-12
67CokCapAs-1
67DexPro-70
67Top-318
68CokCapA-1
68DexPre-36
68OPC-182
68Top-182
68TopVen-182
69MilBra-93
69OPC-98
69PirJacitB-4
69Top-98
69TopSta-95
70OPC-372
70Top-372
71MLBOffS-202
71OPC-562
71PirActP-16
71PirArc-4
71Top-562
72MilBra-116
72OPC-190
72Top-190
73LinPor-149
73OPC-465
73Top-465
74OPC-82
74Top-82
74TopSta-83
75OPC-53
75Top-53
76OPC-352
76SSP-565
76Top-352
77Top-154
87AstSer1-11
87AstShoSO-8
89AstCol4S-3
89SweBasG-58
Giustino, Gerard
89SalLakTTI-26
Givens, Brian
85LitFalMT-5
86ColMetP-11A
86ColMetP-11B
87LynMetP-28
87MetColP-33
88JacMetGS-14
89JacMetGS-27
89MetColP-31
90CMC-355
90ProAAAF-268
90TidTidC-4
90TidTidP-537
93MemChiF-369
94BirBarC-10
94BirBarF-616
96Top-102
Givens, James

91BriTigC-1
91BriTigP-3613
92ClaFS7-165
92LakTigC-22
92LakTigF-2285
93ClaGolF-162
93LonTigF-2314
94TolMudHF-1031
95TolMudHTI-13
Givins, Steve
93IdaFalBF-4051
Givler, Doug
87ChaLooB-9
88ColAstB-7
89ColMudB-11
89ColMudP-124
89ColMudS-11
Gjesdal, Brent
86BeaGolGP-12
Glabman, Barry
76DubPacT-12
Gladd, Jim
52MotCoo-54
53MotCoo-29
Gladden, Danny (Dan)
81ShrCapT-9
83PhoGiaBHN-8
84PhoGiaC-17
85Don-567
85Fle-607
85FleStaS-118
85GiaMot-3
85GiaPos-10
85Lea-30
85Top-386
85TopSti-166
85TopSti-374
85TopTif-386
86BasStaB-47
86Don-187
86Fle-541
86GiaMot-3
86OPC-336
86Top-678
86TopSti-90
86TopTif-678
87Don-189
87DonOpeD-224
87Fle-274
87FleGlo-274
87FleUpd-36
87FleUpdG-36
87OPC-46
87Top-46
87TopSti-93
87TopTif-46
87TopTra-38T
87TopTraT-38T
88Don-491
88DonBasB-130
88Fle-12
88FleGlo-12
88FleGlo-WS1
88FleWorS-1
88OPC-206
88PanSti-143
88Sco-324
88ScoGlo-324
88StaLinTw-9
88Top-502
88TopSti-19
88TopSti-281
88TopTif-502
88TwiSmoC-10
88TwiTeal-21
88Woo-20
89Bow-163
89BowTif-163
89Don-391
89DonBasB-298
89Fle-112
89FleGlo-112
89OPC-387
89PanSti-392
89RedFolSB-50
89Sco-62
89Top-426
89TopSti-286
89TopTif-426
89UppDec-400
90Bow-420
90BowTif-420
90ClaBlu-148
90Don-22
90Don-182
90DonBesA-108
90DonSupD-22
90Fle-375
90FleCan-375
90Lea-254
90OPC-298
90PanSti-111
90PubSti-328
90Sco-61
90Spo-190
90Top-298
90TopBig-147
90TopSti-292
90TopTif-298
90UppDec-238
90VenSti-204
91Bow-318
91Don-228
91Fle-611
91Lea-76
91OPC-778
91PanFreS-304
91Sco-163
91StaClu-54
91Stu-85
91Top-778
91TopDesS-778
91TopMic-778
91TopTif-778
91Ult-187
91UppDec-659
92Don-585
92Fle-203
92FleUpd-21
92Lea-239
92OPC-177
92OPCPre-11
92PanSti-121
92Pin-318
92Sco-28
92ScoRoo-28T
92StaClu-801
92StaCluD-61
92StaCluNC-801
92Top-177
92TopGol-177
92TopGolW-177
92TopMic-177
92TopTra-41T
92TopTraG-41T
92Ult-361
92UppDec-332
92UppDec-737
93Don-467
93Fle-605
93Lea-60
93OPC-100
93PacSpa-109
93PanSti-118
93Pin-333
93Sco-207
93Sel-244
93StaClu-191
93StaCluFDI-191
93StaCluMOP-191
93TigGat-10
93Top-626
93TopGol-626
93TopInaM-626
93TopMic-626
93Ult-198
93UppDec-251
93UppDecGold-251
94Don-138
94Fle-131
94Pac-218
94Sco-215
94ScoGolR-215
94Top-342
94TopGol-342
94TopSpa-342
82PhoGiaVNB-22
Gladden, Jeff
81ChaRoyT-17
82ForMyeRT-13
83CliGiaF-28
Gladding, Fred
64Top-312
64TopVen-312
65OPC-37
65Top-37
66Top-337
66TopVen-337
67Ast-11
67CokCapTi-7
67OPC-192
67Top-192
68CokCapA-5
68Top-423
69OPC-58
69Top-58
70AstTeal-4
70MLBOffS-41
70OPC-208
70Top-208
71MLBOffS-80
71OPC-381
71Top-381
72MilBra-117
72OPC-507
72Top-507
73OPC-17
73Top-17
78TCM60I-158
79TacTugT-25
86AshTouP-12
86AstGreT-11
87AstShoSO-9
87ColAstP-3
88ColAstB-20
89ColMudB-10
89ColMudP-139
90KinIndTI-27
91KinIndC-17
91KinIndP-341
92ColRedF-2408
93ColRedC-29
93ColRedF-615
94ColRedC-27
94ColRedF-461
Glade, Fred
04FanCraAL-21
08RosComP-47
11SpoLifCW-143
Gladu, Jean-Paul
43ParSpo-33
Gladu, Mike
88WytCubP-1993
Gladu, Roland
43ParSpo-78
Glanville, Doug
91Cla/Bes-402
91ClaDraP-9
91GenCubC-24
91GenCubP-4230
92ClaDraP-92
92ProFS7-210
92UppDecML-173
92WinSpiC-1
92WinSpiF-1219
93ClaFS7-5
93ClaGolF-39
93DayCubC-8
93DayCubF-868
93ExcFS7-8
94Bow-177
94Cla-116
94OrlCubF-1396
94UppDecML-85
95Bow-86
95IowCubTI-13
95Top-646
95UppDecML-129
96IowCubB-14
97Fle-594
97FleTif-594
97PacPriGotD-GD118
97Sco-470
97ScoHobR-470
97ScoResC-470
97ScoShoS-470
97ScoShoSAP-470
97StaClu-92
97StaCluMOP-92
97Ult-534
97UltGolME-534
97UltPlaME-534
95UppDecMLFS-129
Glanz, Scott
83PeoSunF-4
Glaser, Gordy
81ChaChaT-3
82ChaChaT-3
82Ind-14
82IndTeal-13
83BufBisT-4
Glaser, Kris
91EugEmeC-28
91EugEmeP-3719
Glasker, Stephen
86SalRedBP-10
87PorChaRP-15
89ChaRanS-9
Glass, Bobby
77JacSunT-9
Glass, Chip
94WatIndC-12
94WatIndF-3953
96CarLeaA1B-21
96CarLeaA2B-21
96KenIndB-8
Glass, Steve
87IdaFalBP-22
88BurBraP-9
89BurBraP-1607
89BurBraS-10
90SumBraB-29
90SumBraP-2452
Glass, Tim
76BatTroTI-10
78WatIndT-11
79WatIndT-2A
80WatIndT-5
81ChaLooT-11
82ChaLooT-6
83BufBisT-11
84BufBisT-3
85WatIndT-18
Glassco, Craig
74SacSolC-55
Glasscock, Jack (John)
75FlePio-21
86IndIndTI-5
87AllandGN-6
87BucN28-41A
87BucN28-41B
87OldJudN-207
88GooN16-6
88SpoTimM-13
88WG1CarG-32
89EdgR.WG-11
94OriofB-67
95May-11A
95May-11B
Glasscock, Larry
83MemChiT-18
Glassey, Josh
96YakBeaTI-45
Glauber, Keith
94NewJerCC-12
94NewJerCF-3410
96PeoChiB-12
Glaviano, Tommy (Thomas)
49EurSta-183
51Bow-301
51TopRedB-47
52Top-56
53Top-140
83TopRep5-56
91TopArc1-140
Glavine, Mike
96Exc-43
Glavine, Tom
86GreBraTI-9
86SouLeaAJ-23
87IntLeaAT-32
87RicBraBC-8
87RicBraC-14
87RicBraT-5
87SpoTeaP-24
88Don-644
88Fle-539
88FleGlo-539
88Sco-638
88ScoGlo-638
88StaLinBra-6
88Top-779
88TopSti-44
88TopTif-779
89Bow-267
89BowTif-267
89BraDub-12
89ClaTraP-159
89Don-381
89DonBasB-2
89Fle-591
89FleGlo-591
89PanSti-34
89Sco-442
89ScoYouS2-23
89Top-157
89TopTif-157
89UppDec-360
90Bow-2
90BowTif-2
90BraDubP-8
90BraDubS-9
90ClaBlu-36
90Don-145
90DonBesN-2
90DOnBonM-BC12A
90DonLeaS-53
90Fle-583
90FleCan-583
90Lea-13
90OPC-506
90PanSti-219
90RedFolSB-36
90Sco-481
90Spo-34
90Top-506
90TopBig-99
90TopMag-74
90TopSti-26
90TopTif-506
90UppDec-571
91Bow-576
91BraDubP-11
91BraSubS-15
91Cla3-T26
91ClaGam-17
91Don-132
91Fle-689
91Lea-172
91OPC-82
91RedFolS-39
91Sco-206
91StaClu-558
91StaCluMO-16
91Stu-145
91Top-82
91TopDesS-82
91TopMic-82
91TopTif-82
91TopTriH-N1
91Ult-5
91UppDec-480
91UppDecFE-90F
91USPlaCA-1S
92Bow-699
92BraLykP-13
92BraLykS-14
92Cla1-T38
92Cla2-T17
92ClaGam-124
92Don-426
92Don-629
92DonBonC-BC4
92DonCraJ2-2
92Fle-358
92Fle-694
92FleAll-6
92FleCitTP-20
92FleSmo'nH-S7
92FleTeaL-11
92Fre-2
92Hig5-23
92Hig5S-13
92Lea-279
92MooSna-22
92OPC-305
92OPCPre-49
92PanSti-288
92PepDieM-5
92Pin-75
92Pin-594
92Sco-450
92Sco-791
92Sco-890
92Sco100S-15
92ScoCokD-10
92ScoImpP-49
92ScoProaG-18
92SpoIllFK1-40
92SpoIllFK1-451
92StaClu-395
92StaCluD-62
92Stu-4
92SunSee-19
92Top-305
92Top-395
92TopGol-305
92TopGol-395
92TopGolW-305

92TopGolW-395
92TopKid-34
92TopMic-305
92TopMic-395
92TriPla-7
92Ult-162
92UltAllS-20
92UltAwaW-7
92UppDec-342
92UppDec-713
93Bow-410
93BraFloA-5
93BraLykP-11
93BraLykS-13
93CadDis-26
93ClaGam-36
93ColAllG-14
93DiaMar-38
93Don-554
93DonDiaK-DK19
93DonEliD-14
93DonPre-1
93DurPowP1-21
93Fin-87
93FinJum-87
93FinRef-87
93Fla-4
93Fle-4
93FleAll-NL11
93FleAtl-9
93FleFruotL-21
93FleGla-1
93FleGla-1B
93FleGla-2
93FleGla-2B
93FleGla-3
93FleGla-3B
93FleGla-4
93FleGla-4B
93FleGla-5
93FleGla-6
93FleGla-7
93FleGla-7B
93FleGla-8
93FleGla-8B
93FleGla-9
93FleGla-9B
93FleGla-10
93FleGla-10B
93FleGla-11
93FleGla-12
93FleGla-13
93FleGla-14
93FleGla-15
93FleGla-AU0
93FlePro-B2
93FunPac-61
93FunPac-63
93Hos-22
93JimDea-14
93KinDis-19
93Kra-22
93Lea-295
93LeaGolA-R18
93MilBonSS-2
93MSABenSPD-6
93OPC-132
93OPCPreSP-21
93OPCPreSPF-21
93PacSpa-6
93PanSti-159
93PanSti-179
93Pin-90
93PinTeaP-2
93Pos-21
93Sco-15
93Sco-539
93ScoGolDT-8
93Sel-7
93SelAce-2
93SelChaS-10
93SelDufIP-6
93SelStaL-88
93SP-58
93StaClu-296
93StaClu-650
93StaCluB-1
93StaCluFDI-296
93StaCluFDI-650
93StaCluM-106
93StaCluMMP-2
93StaCluMOP-296
93StaCluMOP-650
93Stu-145
93Top-280
93Top-410
93TOPBLAG-6
93TopComotH-18
93TopFulS-19
93TopGol-280
93TopGol-410
93TopInaM-280
93TopInaM-410
93TopMic-280
93TopMic-410
93TriPla-117
93TriPla-209
93Ult-6
93UppDec-75
93UppDec-472
93UppDecGold-75
93UppDecGold-472
93USPlaCA-2S
94Bow-21
94BowBes-R12
94BowBesR-R12
94BraLykP-9
94BraLykS-10
94BraUSPC-6H
94BraUSPC-13S
94ColC-306
94ColC-430
94ColChoGS-306
94ColChoGS-430
94ColChoSS-306
94ColChoSS-430
94Don-364
94DonSpeE-364
94ExtBas-201
94ExtBasGB-11
94ExtBasPD-9
94Fin-267
94FinRef-267
94Fla-125
94Fle-359
94FleAllS-36
94FleLeaL-11
94FleSun-11
94FUnPac-47
94Kra-22
94Lea-235
94LeaL-82
94OPC-250
94Pac-9
94PanSti-14
94PanSti-145
94Pin-284
94PinArtP-284
94PinMusC-284
94Pos-16
94RedFolMI-16
94Sco-30
94ScoDreT-2
94ScoGolR-30
94ScoGolS-16
94Sel-250
94SP-49
94SPDieC-49
94Spo-80
94StaClu-538
94StaClu-574
94StaCluFDI-538
94StaCluFDI-574
94StaCluGR-538
94StaCluGR-574
94StaCluMO-23
94StaCluMOP-538
94StaCluMOP-574
94StaCluT-56
94StaCluTFDI-56
94Stu-34
94Top-393
94Top-475
94TopBlaG-32
94TopGol-393
94TopGol-475
94TopSpa-393
94TopSpa-475
94TopSupS-16
94TriPla-44
94Ult-151
94UltAllS-19
94UltLeaL-9
94UppDec-144
94UppDecAJ-11
94UppDecAJG-11
94UppDecED-144
94USPlaCA-6S
95Baz-97
95Bow-286
95ColCho-165
95ColChoGS-165
95ColChoSE-59
95ColChoSEGS-59
95ColChoSESS-59
95ColChoSS-165
95D3-28
95Don-248
95DonPreP-248
95DonTopotO-183
95Emb-111
95EmbGolI-111
95Emo-100
95Fin-64
95FinRef-64
95Fla-323
95Fle-304
95Lea-250
95LeaLim-32
95Pac-4
95PanSti-1
95Pin-264
95PinArtP-264
95PinMusC-264
95Sco-434
95ScoGolR-434
95ScoHaloG-HG65
95ScoPlaTS-434
95Sel-55
95SelArtP-55
95SP-32
95SPCha-24
95SPChaDC-24
95Spo-114
95SpoArtP-114
95SPSil-32
95StaClu-183
95StaCluFDI-183
95StaCluMOP-183
95StaCluSTDW-B183
95StaCluSTMP-2
95StaCluSTWS-183
95StaCluVR-93
95Stu-182
95Sum-23
95SumNthD-23
95Top-175
95TopCyb-101
95UC3-81
95UC3ArtP-81
95Ult-125
95UltGolM-125
95UppDec-46
95UppDecED-46
95UppDecEDG-46
95UppDecSE-147
95UppDecSEG-147
96Baz-44
96Bow-86
96BowBesMI-10
96BowBesMIAR-10
96BowBesMIR-10
96Cir-99
96CirBos-25
96CirRav-99
96ColCho-395T
96ColCho-455
96ColChoGS-455
96ColChoSS-455
96Don-292
96DonPreP-292
96EmoXL-140
96Fin-S72
96FinRef-S72
96Fla-198
96Fle-291
96FleBra-4
96FlePosG-1
96FleTif-291
96Kin-11
96Lea-87
96LeaLim-57
96LeaLimG-57
96LeaPre-74
96LeaPreP-74
96LeaPrePB-87
96LeaPrePG-87
96LeaPrePS-87
96LeaSig-134
96LeaSigEA-60
96LeaSigEACM-8
96LeaSigPPG-134
96LeaSigPPP-134
96MetUni-127
96MetUniP-127
96Pac-13
96PacOctM-OM5
96PacPri-P1
96PacPriFT-FT4
96PacPriG-P1
96PanSti-2
96Pin-230
96PinAfi-35
96PinAfiAP-35
96PinAfiFPP-35
96PinArtP-130
96PinChrBC-4
96PinFoil-230
96PinSta-130
96ProSta-25
96Sco-327
96Sco-517
96ScoDugC-B52
96ScoDugCAP-B52
96Sel-94
96SelArtP-94
96SelCer-42
96SelCerAP-42
96SelCerCB-42
96SelCerCR-42
96SelCerIP-14
96SelCerMB-42
96SelCerMG-42
96SelCerMR-42
96SP-32
96Spo-25
96SpoArtP-25
96SPSpeFX-36
96SPSpeFXDC-36
96SPx-4
96SPxGol-4
96StaClu-49
96StaClu-237
96StaCluEPB-49
96StaCluEPG-49
96StaCluEPS-49
96StaCluMOP-49
96StaCluMOP-237
96StaCluMOP-TSCA3
96StaCluTA-3
95StaCluVRMC-93
96Stu-12
96StuPrePB-12
96StuPrePG-12
96StuPrePS-12
96Sum-106
96SumAbo&B-106
96SumArtP-106
96SumFoi-106
96TeaOut-29
96Top-8
96Top-262
96TopChr-8
96TopChr-105
96TopChrR-8
96TopChrR-105
96TopClaC-CC14
96TopGal-1
96TopGalPPI-1
96TopLas-55
96TopPowB-8
96TopPro-NL14
96Ult-154
96UltGolM-154
96UppDec-9
96UppDec-222
96UppDecPHE-H42
96UppDecPreH-H42
96Zen-98
96ZenArtP-98
97Bow-236
97BowBes-50
97BowBesAR-50
97BowBesR-50
97BowChr-63
97BowChrI-63
97BowChrIR-63
97BowChrR-63
97BowInt-236
97Cir-69
97CirRav-69
97ColCho-35
97Don-86
97Don-429
97DonEli-46
97DonEliGS-46
97DonLim-67
97DonLim-115
97DonLim-189
97DonLimLE-67
97DonLimLE-115
97DonLimLE-189
97DonPre-59
97DonPreCttC-59
97DonPreP-86
97DonPreP-429
97DonPrePGold-86
97DonPrePGold-429
97DonTea-19
97DonTeaSPE-19
97Fin-317
97FinEmb-317
97FinEmbR-317
97FinRef-317
97FlaSho-A74
97FlaSho-B74
97FlaSho-C74
97FlaShoLC-74
97FlaShoLC-B74
97FlaShoLC-C74
97FlaShoLCM-A74
97FlaShoLCM-B74
97FlaShoLCM-C74
97Fle-255
97FleTif-255
97Lea-40
97Lea-382
97LeaFraM-40
97LeaFraM-382
97LeaFraMDC-40
97LeaFraMDC-382
97LeaGet-5
97MetUni-28
97NewPin-154
97NewPinAP-154
97NewPinMC-154
97NewPinPP-154
97Pac-232
97PacLigB-232
97PacSil-232
97Pin-61
97PinArtP-61
97PinCar-2
97PinIns-57
97PinInsCE-57
97PinInsDE-57
97PinMusC-61
97PinX-P-109
97PinX-PMoS-109
97Sco-89
97Sco-528
97ScoBra-4
97ScoBraPI-4
97ScoBraPr-4
97ScoHobR-528
97ScoPreS-89
97ScoResC-528
97ScoShoS-89
97ScoShoS-528
97ScoShoSAP-89
97ScoShoSAP-528
97Sel-99
97SelArtP-99
97SelRegG-99
97SkyE-X-52
97SkyE-XC-52
97SkyE-XEC-52
97SpoIll-74
97SpoIllEE-74
97StaClu-54
97StaCluMat-54
97StaCluMOP-54
97Stu-130
97StuPrePG-130
97StuPrePS-130
97Top-50
97TopAll-AS18
97TopChr-19
97TopChrAS-AS18
97TopChrR-19
97TopChrSAR-AS18
97TopGal-19
97TopGalPPI-19
97TopSta-33
97TopStaAM-33
97Ult-152
97UltGolME-152
97UltPlaME-152
97UppDec-16
97UppDec-66

97UppDec-261
Glaze, Gettys
92ElmPioC-20
92ElmPioF-1377
93Bow-311
93LynRedSC-10
93LynRedSF-2512
94LynRedSC-11
94LynRedSF-1888
Glaze, Ralph
08RosComP-1
Glaze, Randy
96SouOreTI-14
Glazner, Whitey (Charles)
20NatCarE-33
21E121So1-31
22E120-216
22W572-32
22W573-48
22W575-42
23W501-87
Gleason, Harry
03BreE10-57
11SpoLifCW-144
Gleason, Jackie
92Pin-590
Gleason, Kid (William J.)
03BreE10-58
03BreE10-59
17HolBreD-35
19W514-112
20GasAmeMBD-1
21E121So1-32
21E121So8-27
22AmeCarE-22
22W575-43
23W501-39
23W503-31
23WilChoV-50
23WilChoV-51
75WhiSox1T-9
76SSP188WS-9
87OldJudN-208
88ConSer5-14
88GandBCGCE-18
88PacEigMO-23
88PacEigMO-35
88PacEigMO-59
88PacEigMO-73
88PacEigMO-102
92Man191BSR-10
94ConTSN-1038
94ConTSNB-1038
Gleason, Roy
77FriOneYW-44
90DodTar-961
Gleason, William G.
87BucN28-98
87LonJacN-5
87OldJudN-209A
87OldJudN-209B
87OldJudN-538
87ScrDC-5
94OriofB-36
Gleason, William P.
16ColE13-60
Gleaton, Jerry Don
80Top-673
80TulDriT-1
81Top-41
82Top-371
83SalLakCGT-2
84SalLakCGC-186
85BufBisT-19
85Top-216
85TopTif-216
86BufBisP-12
86Top-447
86TopTif-447
88Don-547
88Fle-258
88FleGlo-258
88OmaRoyC-5
88OmaRoyP-1497
88RoySmo-7
88Sco-343
88ScoGlo-343
88StaLinRo-5
88Top-116
88TopTif-116
89Don-444
89Fle-282
89FleGlo-282
89Sco-423
89Top-724
89TopTif-724
90TigCok-6
90TulDriDGB-17
91Don-661
91Fle-338
91Lea-135
91OPC-597
91Sco-316
91StaClu-574
91TigCok-19
91TigPol-6
91Top-597
91TopDesS-597
91TopMic-597
91TopTif-597
92Don-607
92OPC-272
92Sco-375
92TexLon-16
92Top-272
92TopGol-272
92TopGolW-272
92TopMic-272
92UppDec-601
93EdmTraF-1130
93RanKee-160
93StaCluMarl-14
Gleckel, Scott
82OrlTwi8SCT-14
Gledhill, Chance
91BoiHawC-4
91BoiHawP-3870
92QuaCitRBC-14
92QuaCitRBF-802
93MidAngF-318
97MidAngOHP-13
Gleeson, Jim
39CubTeal-8
94ConTSN-1291
94ConTSNB-1291
Gleissner, James
82ForMyeRT-17
Glendenning, Mike
96BelGiaTI-14
Glenn, Darrin
95BurBeeTI-3
96SanJosGB-26
Glenn, Joe
34BatR31-87
36NatChiFPR-108
75YanDyn1T-17
92ConTSN-510
Glenn, John
62KahAtl-8
77FriOneYW-62
Glenn, Leon
90BelBreB-17
90BelBreS-9
90Bes-271
91BelBreC-24
91BelBreP-2110
91BenBucC-25
91BenBucP-3700
91Cla/Bes-215
92ClaFS7-284
92StoPorC-12
92StoPorF-40
93StoPorC-12
93StoPorF-751
94ElPasDF-3157
94UppDecML-206
95AusFut-102
95MidAngOHP-12
95MidAngTI-10
96MidAngOHP-12
Glenn, Mouse
87OldJudN-210
Glenn, Simon
80ElmPioRST-28
Glenn, Stanley
92NegLeaRLI-24
95NegLeaL2-32
Glesecke, Rob
85VerBeaDT-24
Gliatto, Sal
76DalCon-4
Glick, David
96OgdRapTI-20
Glick, Tom
90JamExpP-31
Glinatsis, George
92CalLeaACL-28
92ClaFS7-394
92SanBerC-15
92SanBerSF-946
93ClaGolF-143
93JacSunF-2706
94RivPilCLC-5
95PorCitRTI-11
Glinatsis, Mike
82MiaMarT-2
Glinton, James
91ChaRanC-16
Glisson, Robert
86EriCarP-8
87SprCarB-18
88SprCarB-1
Globetrotters, Harlem
92NegLeaRLI-94
93NegLeaRL2-56
93NegLeaRL2-57
93NegLeaRL2-95
Globig, Dave
76BurBeeT-16
Glossop, Al (Alban)
43DodTeal-11
47SigOil-26
49BowPCL-17
49W725AngTI-10
90DodTar-284
Glover, Gary
96MedHatBJTI-9
Glover, Jason
96OgdRapTI-26
Glover, Jeff
86MedA'sC-68
87MadMusP-8
87MadMusP-17
88ModA'sCLC-60
88ModA'sTI-10
Glover, Reggie
88RenSilSCLC-271
Glover, Terence
88SalLakCTTI-23
Glowzenski, Len
76AshTouT-22
Glynn, Bill (William V.)
50WorWidGV-42
52MotCoo-56
53Top-171
54Top-178
55Top-39
55TopDouH-59
57HygMea-5
91TopArc1-171
94TopArc1-178
94TopArc1G-178
Glynn, Dennis
86JacMetT-14
Glynn, Ed
77EvaTriT-11
77Top-487
79Top-343
80Top-509
81ChaChaT-4
81Top-93
82ChaChaT-4
82Ind-15
82IndTeal-14
83ChaChaT-19
83Don-537
83Fle-408
83IndPos-16
83IndWhe-14
83Top-614
84MaiGuiT-22
86TidTidP-12
87TidTidP-15
87TidTidT-4
89PacSenL-129
91MetWIZ-142
91PacSenL-82
Glynn, Gene
83WicAerDS-9
84IndIndTI-22
85IndIndTI-26
85UtiBluST-25
86WesPalBEP-18
87JamExpP-2553
88RocExpLC-15
89JacExpB-27
89JacExpP-174
90SpoIndSP-26
90WatDiaB-23
90WatDiaP-2395
91SpoIndC-29
91SpoIndP-3965
92BenRocC-24
92BenRocF-1488
94RocPol-27
Glynn, Ryan
95HudValRTI-23
Gmitter, Joe
91HelBreSP-10
Gnacinski, Paul
84PawRedST-8
86GreBraTI-10
Goar, Jot
98CamPepP-29
Gobbo, Michael
85BelBreT-8
86StoPorP-10
87ElPasDP-26
Gobel, Donnie
91AugPirC-7
91AugPirP-800
Gobert, Chris
94DanBraC-12
94DanBraF-3525
95DanBraTI-13
Gochnaur, John
03BreE10-60
90DodTar-285
Godfrey, Tyson
90HunCubP-3275
91Cla/Bes-432
91PeoChiC-12
91PeoChiP-1337
91PeoChiTI-8
92PeoChiC-17
92PeoChiTI-8
Godin, Steve
91KanCouCC-22
91KanCouCP-2669
91KanCouCTI-8
92FreKeyC-13
92FreKeyF-1819
Godwin, Glenn
83MadMusF-25
Goedde, Mike
85CedRapRT-8
89BilMusP-2049
Goedde, Roger
94SigRooDP-40
94SigRooDPS-40
Goedhart, Darrell
89MarPhiS-12
90SpaPhiB-4
90SpaPhiP-2485
90SpaPhiS-9
91ClePhiC-4
91ClePhiP-1615
92ClePhiC-3
92ReaPhiF-568
93ReaPhiF-292
Goergen, Todd
89BatCliP-1927
90SpaPhiB-5
90SpaPhiP-2486
90SpaPhiS-10
91SpaPhiC-4
91SpaPhiP-889
92ClePhiF-2052
93ReaPhiF-293
Goettsch, Jeff
87SalAngP-30
Goetz, Barry
91ChaRanC-6
91ChaRanP-1310
92ChaRanC-20
92ChaRanF-2222
93TulDriF-2729
94OklCit8F-1492
93TulDriTI-10
Goetz, Geoff
97Bow-429
97BowChr-289
97BowChrI-289
97BowChrIR-289
97BowChrR-289
97BowInt-429
97TopSta-112
97TopStaAM-112
Goetz, Jack
75DubPacT-31
Goetz, John
61TacBan-8
Goetz, Lawrence
55Bow-311
Goff, Jerry L.
86BelMarC-110
87WauTimP-17
88SanBerSB-12
88SanBerSCLC-33
89WilBilP-631
89WilBilS-7
90Bow-112
90BowTif-112
90CMC-63
90IndIndC-13
90IndIndP-291
90Lea-476
90ProAAAF-574
91Don-499
91IndIndLD-184
91IndIndP-467
91LinDriAAA-184
91PanFreS-153
91Sco-834
91TopDeb90-55
92IndIndF-1867
92IndIndS-182
92SkyAAAF-89
93BufBisF-520
94Top-463
94TopGol-463
94TopSpa-463
95TusTorTI-6
96TusTorB-9
Goff, Mike
86GreHorP-9
87BelMarTI-18
88MidLeaAGS-57
88WauTimGS-27
89CalLeaA-14
89SanBerSB-24
89SanBerSCLC-72
90WilBilB-7
90WilBilP-1053
90WilBilS-8
94BelMarF-3233
96WisTimRB-1
Goff, Tim
86EugEmeC-32
87Ft.MyeRP-17
Goff, Wally
79WauTimT-8
80PenPilBT-7
80PenPilCT-14
81ReaPhiT-10
Gogas, Keith
91MelBusF-3
Goggin, Chuck
74OPC-457
74Top-457
Gogolewski, Bill
71MLBOffS-539
71OPC-559
71SenTealW-10
71Top-559
72OPC-424
72Top-424
73OPC-27
73Top-27
74OPC-242
74Top-242
76SSP-134
93RanKee-12
Gogolewski, Chris
95ChaRivTI-10
Gogolewski, Gogo (Doug)
87OneYanP-10
88Ft.LauYS-10
89Ft.LauYS-6
90AlbYanP-1032
90AlbYanS-5
90CMC-730
92ForLauYC-3
92ForLauYTI-14
92Ft.LauYF-2605
93AlbYanF-2156
94ShrCapF-1598
Gogolin, Elton
96SouOreTI-19
Gogos, Keith
95AusFut-49
Goguen, Phil
88NebCor-21
Gohl, Lefty
52Par-78
Gohmann, Ken
86LakTigP-6
87LakTigP-26
88GleFalTP-930
89SarWhiSS-7

Gohr, Greg
90Bow-347
90BowTif-347
90LakTigS-11
90Sco-679
91Bow-142
91LinDriAA-385
91LonTigLD-385
91LonTigP-1871
91TolMudHP-1925
92Bow-453
92ProFS7-65
92SkyAAAF-261
92TolMudHF-1036
92TolMudHS-584
92UppDecML-195
93Bow-671
93Don-605
93FleFinE-210
93LeaGolR-R6
93OPCPre-17
93Pin-615
93StaClu-685
93StaCluFDI-685
93StaCluMOP-685
93Ult-550
93UppDec-685
93UppDecGold-685
94Don-167
94Fla-293
94Fle-132
94SpoRoo-42
94SpoRooAP-42
94TolMudHF-1021
94Top-711
94TopGol-711
94TopSpa-711
95ColCho-478
95ColChoGS-478
95ColChoSS-478
95Lea-139
95UppDec-421
95UppDecED-421
95UppDecEDG-421
96LeaSigA-79
96LeaSigAG-79
96LeaSigAS-79
Goike, Bryan
92FayGenC-27
93LakTigC-29
94LakTigC-30
95JacSunTI-11
Goins, Scott
87EveGiaC-3
89SanJosGB-27
89SanJosGCLC-233
89SanJosGP-438
89SanJosGS-10
Goins, Tim
92WatDiaC-15
92WatDiaF-2143
Gokey, Steve
87ModA'sP-8
88ModA'sTI-30
89ModA'sC-6
89ModA'sCLC-289
Gold, Bret
81MiaOriT-20
Gold, Mark
87WauTimP-23
Gold, Steve
94HelBreF-3608
94HelBreSP-5
Goldberg, Lonnie
93EriSaiC-9
93EriSaiF-3124
95ChaRivTI-5
Goldberg, Marc
90St.LucMS-31
91St.LucMC-29
92WesPalBEC-27
Golden Eagles, Tennessee Tech
89TenTecGE-36
Golden, Brian
89HamRedS-16
90EriSaiS-7
Golden, Ike
81AppFoxT-16
Golden, Jim
61Top-298
62Col.45B-8
62Col45'HC-7
62Top-568
63Top-297
64WhiSoxTS-9
89AstCol4S-4
90DodTar-286
Golden, Matt
94NewJerCC-13
94NewJerCF-3411
96StPetCB-9
Golden, Roy
12T207-67
Goldetsky, Larry
78MemChiBC-4
79MemChiT-6
80MemChiT-7
83MemChiT-6
Goldgrabe, Curt
85FreGiaP-30
Goldman, J.
31Exh-21
Goldpanners, Alaska
89AlaGol-1
Goldsberry, Gordon
52Top-46
53Top-200
83TopRep5-46
91TopArc1-200
Goldsby, Walt
87OldJudN-211
Goldsmith, Gary
93NiaFalRF-3379
94LakTigC-9
94LakTigF-3030
95JacSunTI-12
Goldstein, Abe
28W512-49
Goldstein, David R.
80WesHavWCT-20B
Goldstein, Ike
87VisOakP-12
Goldstein, Isidore
34DiaMatCSB-70
Goldthorn, Burk
82AleDukT-15
83LynPirT-12
85PriWilPT-30
86HawIsIP-10
Goldy, Purnal
62TigPosCF-8
63Top-516
Golenbock, Peter
90LitSunW-21
Goliat, Mike
50Bow-205
51BerRos-B10
51Bow-77
58MonRoyF-9
61UniOil-SP4
Goligoski, Jason
94HicCraC-11
94HicCraF-2184
94SouAtlLAF-SAL23
95PriWilCTI-7
96NewHavRB-11
Gollehon, Chris
88BriTigP-1875
89SpoIndSP-20
Golmont, Van
89MadMusS-29
90EriSaiS-8
Golston, Toriano
94ButCopKSP-15
Goltz, Dave
73OPC-148
73Top-148
74OPC-636
74Top-636
75OPC-419
75Top-419
76OPC-136
76SSP-218
76Top-136
77BurCheD-47
77Hos-48
77OPC-73
77Top-321
78Hos-96
78Kel-35
78OPC-5
78OPC-142
78Top-205
78Top-249
78TwiFriP-8
79Hos-16
79OPC-10
79Top-27
79TwiFriP-7
80DodPol-38
80OPC-108
80Top-193
81DodPol-38
81Fle-127
81LonBeaPT-23
81OPC-289
81Top-548
82DodPol-38
82Don-604
82Fle-6
82Top-674
83Fle-90
83Top-468
90DodTar-287
Gomes, Wayne
94ActPac-6
94Bow-608
94BowBes-B66
94BowBesR-B66
94Cla-175
94ClaGolF-36
94ClaGolN1PLF-LP4
94ClaGolREF-RE4
94ClaTriF-T61
94ClePhiC-15
94ClePhiF-2522
94ColC-22
94ColChoGS-22
94ColChoSS-22
94Pin-434
94PinArtP-434
94PinMusC-434
94Sco-494
94ScoGolR-494
94SigRoo-28
94SigRooS-28
94Top-742
94TopGol-742
94TopSpa-742
94Ult-547
94UppDec-540
94UppDecAHNIL-17
94UppDecED-540
94UppDecML-63
95Bes-87
95Bow-149
95Exc-242
95ReaPhiELC-14
95ReaPhiTI-21
95SPML-128
95Top-654
96Bow-193
96ReaPhiB-5
Gomez, Art
81CliGiaT-8
Gomez, Augustine
94HicCraC-12
94HicCraF-2172
94VenLinU-140
95LinVen-135
Gomez, Chris
92ClaDraP-62
92FroRowDP-34
93Bow-39
93ClaFS7-192
93SelRoo-80T
93StaCluM-133
93TolMudHF-1659
94Bow-321
94ColC-110
94ColChoGS-110
94ColChoSS-110
94Don-628
94Fla-294
94FlaWavotF-B2
94Fle-133
94LeaLimR-35
94OPCDiaD-5
94Pac-220
94Pin-414
94PinArtP-414
94PinMusC-414
94Sco-309
94ScoGolR-309
94ScoRoo-RT95
94ScoRooGR-RT95
94Sel-194
94SpoRoo-103
94SpoRooAP-103
94StaClu-73
94StaCluFDI-73
94StaCluGR-73
94StaCluMOP-73
94Top-626
94TopGol-626
94TopSpa-626
94Ult-54
94UppDec-93
94UppDecED-93
95Bow-375
95ColCho-476
95ColChoGS-476
95ColChoSE-219
95ColChoSEGS-219
95ColChoSESS-219
95ColChoSS-476
95D3-59
95Don-172
95DonPreP-172
95DonTopotO-77
95Emb-42
95EmbGolI-42
95Fin-3
95FinRef-3
95Fla-40
95Fle-54
95FleRooS-5
95Lea-35
95Pac-154
95PacLatD-15
95PanSti-66
95PanSti-108
95Pin-69
95PinArtP-69
95PinMusC-69
95Sco-116
95ScoGolR-116
95ScoPlaTS-116
95StaClu-383
95StaCluMOP-383
95StaCluSTWS-383
95StaCluVR-202
95Stu-53
95Top-277
95TopCyb-150
95Ult-47
95UltAllR-2
95UltAllRGM-2
95UltGolM-47
95UltSecYS-2
95UltSecYSGM-2
95UppDec-184
95UppDecED-184
95UppDecEDG-184
96ColCho-549
96ColChoGS-549
96ColChoSS-549
96Don-362
96DonPreP-362
96EmoXL-61
96Fla-81
96Fle-112
96FleTif-112
96LeaSigA-80
96LeaSigAG-80
96LeaSigAS-80
96MetUni-60
96MetUniP-60
96Pac-309
96PanSti-149
96Sco-142
96StaClu-145
96StaCluEPB-145
96StaCluEPG-145
96StaCluEPS-145
96StaCluMOP-145
95StaCluVRMC-202
96Top-134
96TopGal-123
96TopGalPPI-123
96Ult-61
96UltGolM-61
96UppDec-72
97Cir-378
97CirRav-378
97ColCho-447
97Fle-461
97FleTif-461
97Pac-423
97PacLigB-423
97PacSil-423
97StaClu-84
97StaCluMOP-84
97Top-301
97Ult-282
97UltGolME-282
97UltPlaME-282
97UppDec-489
Gomez, Dana
87WinHavRSP-30
Gomez, Dennys
94EveGiaC-10
94EveGiaF-3645
96SanJosGB-15
Gomez, Ernesto
80VenLeaS-156
93LinVenB-187
94VenLinU-184
Gomez, Fabio
88BurIndP-1788
89Sta-180
89WatIndS-8
90KinIndTI-7
91ColIndC-27
91KinIndP-329
92CalLeaACL-2
92RenSilSCLC-40
93HunStaF-2088
94NewHavRF-1556
Gomez, Henry
87GenCubP-17
88ChaWheB-14
90PeoChiTI-23
91ChaKniLD-133
91ChaKniP-1684
91LinDriAA-133
93LinVenB-49
93LonTigF-2301
94VenLinU-205
Gomez, Javier
96AriBlaDB-19
Gomez, Jorge
80AshTouT-3
82BurRanF-12
82BurRanT-20
83TulDriT-1
84TulDriTI-4
Gomez, Jose
83MiaMarT-14
85DomLeaS-196
Gomez, Jose Luis
36NatChiFPR-31
36OveCanR-17
77Top-13
78BluJayP-7
78Top-573
79Top-254
80OPC-95
80Top-169
81BraPol-9
81Don-88
81Fle-253
81Top-477
82Top-372
89PacSenL-17
89TopSenL-16
91PacSenL-143
Gomez, Juan A.
75TucTorC-12
75TucTorTI-3
76TusTorCr-33
77ModA'sC-22
Gomez, Lefty (Vernon)
32OrbPinNP-120
32USCar-31
33ButCanV-20
33CraJacP-8
33DelR33-14
33Gou-216
33TatOrbSDR-151
34BatR31-23
34BatR31-86
34ButPreR-26
34ExhFou-13
35ExhFou-13
35GouPreR-11
36ExhFou-13
36GouBWR-14
36GouWidPPR-A39
36NatChiFPR-32
36NatChiFPR-92
36OveCanR-18
36R31PasP-34
36WheBB5-1
36WorWidGV-56
37ExhFou-13
38BasTabP-12
38ExhFou-13
38OurNatGPP-12

39ExhSal-20
39GouPreR303A-17
39GouPreR303B-9
39PlaBal-48
39WheBB12-3
39WorWidGTP-17
40PlaBal-6
41DouPlaR-61
41PlaBal-72
42GilRazL-1
47PM1StaP1-72
48BabRutS-24
60Fle-54
61Fle-34
72LauGreF-18
75ShaPiz-3
75YanDyn1T-18
76RowExh-4
76ShaPiz-129
77GalGloG-76
77GalGloG-185
77GalGloG-265
79DiaGre-11
80MarExhH-13
80PacLeg-117
80PerHaloFP-129
80SSPHOF-129
81ConTSN-44
81DiaStaCD-118
83ConMar-22
83YanASFY-16
86ConSer1-45
86SpoDecG-9
87ConSer2-2
88ConAmeA-12
88ConSer5-15
89HOFStiB-76
89PerCelP-16
89YanCitAG-3
90PerGreM-44
90RinPosYMP-8
90SweBasG-84
91ConTSN-67
91ConTSNP-662
91HomCooC-3
91SweBasG-129
92ConTSN-536
92ConTSNAP-662G
92YanWIZA-23
92YanWIZH-12
93ActPacA-105
93ActPacA2-39G
93ConTSN-662
94ConTSN-1063
94ConTSN-1088
94ConTSNB-1063
94ConTSNB-1088
96NoiSatP-12

Gomez, Leo
87HagSunP-5
89BlaYNPRWL-76
89EasLeaAP-3
89HagSunB-1
89HagSunP-280
89HagSunS-10
90Bow-262
90BowTif-262
90CMC-311
90HagSunDGB-12
90ProAAAF-466
90RocRedWC-10
90RocRedWGC-6
90RocRedWP-709
90TriAllGP-AAA10
91Bow-88
91Cla1-T12
91Cla3-T31
91ClaGam-164
91Don-35
91Fle-472
91Lea-35
91LeaPre-13
91OPCPre-52
91OriCro-158
91Sco-725
91ScoRoo-20
91SevCoi-A3
91Stu-3
91TopDeb90-56
91TopTra-47T
91TopTraT-47T
91Ult-16
91UppDec-6
92Bow-344
92Cla2-T58
92ClaGam-58
92Don-199
92Fle-8
92Lea-87
92OPC-84
92OPCPre-161
92PanSti-67
92Pin-356
92PinTea2-52
92Sco-240
92Sco100RS-66
92ScoImpP-16
92StaClu-664
92Top-84
92TopGol-84
92TopGolW-84
92TopMic-84
92TriPla-131
92Ult-4
92UppDec-161
93Bow-381
93Don-31
93Fle-167
93Lea-155
93OPC-117
93PacSpa-17
93PanSti-74
93Pin-351
93Sco-104
93Sel-66
93StaClu-536
93StaCluFDI-536
93StaCluMOP-536
93Stu-99
93Top-164
93TopGol-164
93TopInaM-164
93TopMic-164
93Ult-140
93UppDec-132
93UppDecGold-132
94ColC-615
94ColChoGS-615
94ColChoSS-615
94Don-576
94Fla-254
94FleUpd-3
94OriPro-39
94OriUSPC-5S
94OriUSPC-10D
94Pac-31
94Pin-180
94PinArtP-180
94PinMusC-180
94Sco-55
94ScoGolR-55
94Sel-338
94Top-506
94TopGol-506
94TopSpa-506
95ColCho-332
95ColChoGS-332
95ColChoSS-332
95Don-41
95DonPreP-41
95DonTopotO-7
95Fla-3
95Fle-7
95Lea-19
95Pac-21
95Pin-103
95PinArtP-103
95PinMusC-103
95Sco-31
95ScoGolR-31
95ScoPlaTS-31
95StaClu-373
95StaCluMOP-373
95StaCluSTWS-373
95StaCluVR-196
95Top-408
95TopCyb-208
95Ult-255
95UltGolM-255
95UppDec-367
95UppDecED-367
95UppDecEDG-367
96FleCub-5
96FleUpd-U109
96FleUpdTC-U109
96LeaSigA-81
96LeaSigAG-81
96LeaSigAS-81
95StaCluVRMC-196
97Fle-274
97FleTif-274
97Pac-248
97PacLigB-248
97PacSil-248
97Sco-137
97ScoPreS-137
97ScoShoS-137
97ScoShoSAP-137

Gomez, Luis
77TacTwiDQ-2B
78OPC-121
79BluJayBY-9
79OPC-128
86BluJayGT-3

Gomez, Marcos
82BelBreF-10

Gomez, Miguel
78DunBluJT-9
96DunBluJUTI-2

Gomez, Mike
92BatCliC-18
92BatCliF-3272
93ClePhiC-11
93ClePhiF-2689
94ReaPhiF-2068

Gomez, Orlando
82TulDriT-23
83BurRanF-27
83BurRanT-26
84TulDriTI-23
85TulDriTI-23
86WatIndP-11
87BufBisP-25
88GasRanP-1009
89GasRanP-1017
89GasRanS-NNO
89SouAtlLAGS-2
90GasRanB-25
90GasRanP-2536
90GasRanS-26
90SouAtlLAS-24
91RanMot-28
92RanMot-28
93AppFoxC-27
93AppFoxF-2477
93RanKee-161
95EveAqaTI-7
96PorCitRB-1

Gomez, Pat
87PeoChiP-13
87PeoChiPW-2
88ChaWheB-13
89BlaYNPRWL-60
89WinSpiS-8
90Bes-49
90GreBraB-4
91GreBraC-1
91GreBraLD-207
91GreBraP-2995
91HunStaC-26
91LinDriAA-207
91RicBraBC-34
92RicBraBB-15
92RicBraF-371
92RicBraRC-6
92RicBraS-429
92SkyAAAF-196
93Bow-82
93Don-266
93FleFinE-139
93PacSpa-595
93Pin-610
93Sco-310
93Ult-471
94Fle-663
94FleUpd-193
94GiaMot-24
94Pac-523
95GiaMot-22
95Pac-377
97RicBraBC-9

Gomez, Paul
96StLucMTI-2

Gomez, Phil
93ElmPioC-8
93ElmPioF-3817

Gomez, Pierre
90MiaMirIS-8

Gomez, Preston (Pedro)
60DarFar-10
61UniOil-SP5
69OPC-74
69PadVol-5
69Top-74
70OPC-513
70Top-513
71OPC-737
71Top-737
72Top-637
73OPC-624
73Top-624
74AstFouTIP-1
74OPC-31
74Top-31
75OPC-487
75SSP18-6
75Top-487
80Top-381
86PadGreT-12
87AstShowSTh-9

Gomez, Ramon
96HicCraB-8

Gomez, Randy
84PhoGiaC-20
85DomLeaS-81
85PhoGiaC-179
86PhoFirP-6
87HawIslP-24

Gomez, Ruben
47PM1StaP1-73
47StaPinP2-16
54NewYorJA-23
54Top-220
55GiaGolS-5
55Top-71
55TopDouH-89
56Top-9
56TopPin-39
57Top-58
58GiaJayP-4
58GiaSFCB-9
58Top-335
59Top-535
60Top-82
60TopVen-82
61Top-377
67Top-427A
67Top-427B
79TCM50-98
94TopArc1-220
94TopArc1G-220

Gomez, Rudy
91GenCubC-8
91GenCubP-4223
92WinSpiC-18
92WinSpiF-1213
93DayCubC-9
94OrlCubF-1391
95OrlCubF-18

Gomez, Steve
86OrlTwiP-7
87OrlTwiP-13

Gonder, Jesse
59RedEnq-9
61Yan61RL-40
62RedEnq-10
62RedJayP-4
63RedEnq-10
63RedFreBC-6
63Top-29A
63Top-29B
64MetJayP-4
64Top-457
64TopCoi-43
64TopSta-30
64TopStaU-28
65Top-423
66PirEasH-20
66Top-528
67CokCapPi-10
67PirTeal-8
67Top-301
67TopPirS-10
69Top-617
76Met63 S-6
78TCM60I-122
78TCM60I-238
91MetWIZ-143
91RinPos1Y2-2
92YanWIZ6-47

Gongora, Christopher
94DanBraC-13
94DanBraF-3526

Gonring, Doug
87AshTouP-8

Gonsalves, Dennis
83MadMusF-7
84MadMusP-16

Gontkosky, Rob
93KinMetC-12
93KinMetF-3791
94CapCitBC-7
94CapCitBF-1745

Gonzales, Ben (Benjamin)
89AubAstP-2171
90AshTouP-2740
91BurAstC-3
91BurAstP-2794
92ClaFS7-437
92OscAstC-16
92OscAstF-2523
93JacGenF-2103

Gonzales, Dan
77EvaTriT-12
80EvaTriT-20

Gonzales, Eddie
87SanJosBP-25

Gonzales, Frank
90FayGenP-2399
91LakTigC-6
91LakTigP-262
92ClaFS7-172
92LonTigF-628
93TolMudHF-1647
94TolMudHF-1022
95TolMudHTI-14

Gonzales, Javier
96HelBreTI-32

Gonzales, John
90AshTouC-21
91AshTouP-579

Gonzales, Johnny
95AshTouTI-12

Gonzales, Jose
80ChaO'sP-9
80ChaO'sW-9
82ArkTraT-13
87SpoTeaP-14
88AlbDukP-258
89AlbDukC-17
89DodStaSV-10

Gonzales, Larry
87HawRai-7
87PanAmTURB-10
89QuaCitAB-21
89QuaCitAGS-28
89SalDodTI-12
90QuaCitAGS-17
91MelBusF-4
91MidAngLD-435
91MidAngOHP-12
91MidAngP-436
92EdmTraS-159
92SkyAAAF-79
93VanCanF-2601
94MidAngOHP-5
87PanAmTUBI-18

Gonzales, Luis
72CedRapCT-14

Gonzales, Rene C.
83MemChiT-3
84IndIndTI-25
84IndIndTI-26
85IndIndTI-11
86IndIndTI-10
88Don-582
88Fle-560
88FleGlo-560
88OriFreB-88
88StaLinO-5
88Top-98
88TopBig-209
88TopTif-98
89Don-377
89OPC-213
89OriFreB-88
89Sco-585
89Top-213
89TopBig-87
89TopSti-234
89TopTif-213
90Don-401
90OPC-787
90Sco-118
90Top-787
90TopTif-787
91BluJayFS-10
91BluJayS-14
91Bow-25
91Fle-473

91Lea-490
91OPC-377
91OPCPre-53
91OriCro-159
91Sco-638
91StaClu-406
91Top-377
91TopDesS-377
91TopMic-377
91TopTif-377
92AngPol-11
92Don-274
92OPC-681
92Sco-582
92ScoRoo-75T
92StaClu-704
92StaCluECN-704
92Top-681
92TopGol-681
92TopGolW-681
92TopMic-681
92TopTra-42T
92TopTraG-42T
92UppDec-729
93AngMot-14
93AngPol-11
93Don-785
93FleFinE-182
93Lea-345
93OPC-184
93PacSpa-47
93PanSti-11
93Pin-55
93Sco-604
93Sel-379
93StaClu-121
93StaCluAn-15
93StaCluFDI-121
93StaCluMOP-121
93Top-266
93TopGol-266
93TopInaM-266
93TopMic-266
93Ult-164
93UppDec-188
93UppDecGold-188
94ChaKniF-902
94Don-640
94Fle-57
94OriPro-40
94Pin-364
94PinArtP-364
94PinMusC-364
94Sco-455
94ScoGolR-455
94Top-141
94TopGol-141
94TopSpa-141
95Pac-120
97Pac-199
97PacLigB-199
97PacSil-199

Gonzales, Todd
87WatIndP-11
88KinIndS-9
89CanIndB-16
89CanIndP-1320
89CanIndS-8

Gonzales, Tommy
80PhoGiaVNB-25
81PhoGiaVNB-26

Gonzalez, Alex
96KanCouCUTI-6
97Bow-298
97BowBes-104
97BowBesAR-104
97BowBesR-104
97BowChr-206
97BowChrI-206
97BowChrIR-206
97BowChrR-206
97BowInt-298

Gonzalez, Alex Scott
92Bow-596
92MyrBeaHC-11
92MyrBeaHF-2203
92UppDecML-60
92UppDecML-317
93Bow-374
93Bow-603
93ClaFS7-51
93ClaFS7-72
93ClaGolF-128
93ExcFS7-243
93KnoSmoF-1257
93SP-278
93UppDec-456
93UppDecGold-456
94ActPacP-2
94Bow-380
94Bow-469
94BowPre-6
94ColC-8
94ColChoGS-8
94ColChoSS-8
94ExcAllF-5
94ExcFS7-143
94Fin-433
94FinJum-433
94FinRef-433
94FleUpd-97
94FUnPac-139
94LeaLimR-46
94OPC-258
94OPCHotP-8
94Pin-505
94PinArtP-505
94PinMusC-505
94ScoRoo-RT145
94ScoRooGR-RT145
94Sel-178
94SelRooS-RS16
94SP-42
94SPDieC-42
94SpoRoo-76
94SpoRooAP-76
94SpoRooRS-TR6
94StaClu-695
94StaCluFDI-695
94StaCluGR-695
94StaCluMOP-695
94SyrChiTI-14
94TedWil-121
94Top-67
94TopGol-67
94TopSpa-67
94TriAAF-AAA18
94UppDec-13
94UppDecED-13
94UppDecML-1
94UppDecML-97
94UppDecML-150
94UppDecMLPotYF-PY4
94UppDecMLT1PJF-TP3
94UppDecMLT1PMF-3
94UppDecNG-4
94UppDecNGED-4
94VenLinU-119
95ActPac2GF-5G
95ActPacF-11
95ActPacF-66
95Baz-126
95Bow-430
95BowBes-R85
95BowBesR-R85
95ColCho-138
95ColChoGS-138
95ColChoSE-53
95ColChoSEGS-53
95ColChoSESS-53
95ColChoSS-138
95Don-69
95DonPreP-69
95DonTopotO-173
95Emo-93
95EmoRoo-5
95Fin-251
95FinRef-251
95Fla-315
95Fle-93
95Lea-206
95LeaGolR-15
95LeaLim-71
95Pac-444
95PacLatD-16
95PacPri-141
95Pin-193
95PinArtP-193
95PinMusC-193
95Sco-597
95ScoGolR-597
95ScoHaloG-HG73
95ScoPlaTS-597
95ScoRooDT-RDT2
95Sel-95
95SelArtP-95
95SelCanM-CM7
95SelCer-112
95SelCerMG-112
95SelCerPU-6
95SelCerPU9-6
95SP-206
95Spo-161
95SpoArtP-161
95SPSil-206
95SPSpeF-25
95StaClu-526
95StaCluMOP-526
95StaCluSTWS-526
95Sum-125
95SumNewA-NA6
95SumNthD-125
95SumSam-125
95Top-267
95UC3-116
95UC3ArtP-116
95UC3CleS-CS10
95Ult-119
95UltGolM-119
95UppDec-212
95UppDecED-212
95UppDecEDG-212
95UppDecPAW-H12
95UppDecPAWE-H12
95UppDecSE-67
95UppDecSEG-67
95Zen-148
96BesAutS-32
96BluJayOH-10
96Bow-19
96ColCho-353
96ColChoGS-353
96ColChoSS-353
96Don-52
96DonPreP-52
96EmoXL-131
96Fin-B128
96FinRef-B128
96Fla-183
96Fle-273
96FleTif-273
96Lea-141
96LeaPrePB-141
96LeaPrePG-141
96LeaPrePS-141
96MetUni-119
96MetUniP-119
96Pac-449
96PacPri-P143
96PacPriG-P143
96PanSti-164
96Pin-204
96PinAfi-142
96PinAfiAP-142
96PinArtP-104
96PinFoil-204
96PinSta-104
96Sco-156
96ScoDugC-A91
96ScoDugCAP-A91
96Sel-112
96SelArtP-112
96SelTeaN-7
96SP-182
96StaClu-233
96StaCluMOP-233
96Stu-2
96StuPrePB-2
96StuPrePG-2
96StuPrePS-2
96Sum-67
96SumAbo&B-67
96SumArtP-67
96SumFoi-67
96Top-404
96TopChr-162
96TopChrR-162
96TopGal-114
96TopGalPPI-114
96Ult-145
96UltGolM-145
96UppDec-214
96ZenMoz-15
97BluJayS-1
97BluJayS-51
97Cir-89
97CirRav-89
97ColCho-506
97Don-202
97DonEli-90
97DonEliGS-90
97DonPreP-202
97DonPrePGold-202
97Fle-239
97FleTif-239
97Lea-89
97LeaFraM-89
97LeaFraMDC-89
97MetUni-183
97NewPin-49
97NewPinAP-49
97NewPinMC-49
97NewPinPP-49
97Pac-219
97PacLigB-219
97PacSil-219
97Pin-114
97PinArtP-114
97PinMusC-114
97Sco-40
97ScoPreS-40
97ScoShoS-40
97ScoShoSAP-40
97StaClu-122
97StaCluMOP-122
97Stu-135
97StuPrePG-135
97StuPrePS-135
97Top-155
97TopGal-99
97TopGalPPI-99
97Ult-143
97UltGolME-143
97UltPlaME-143
97UppDec-513

Gonzalez, Angel
86WinHavRSP-9
87NewBriRSP-4
88NewBriRSP-910
88PawRedSC-17
88PawRedSP-462
89PawRedSC-22
89PawRedSP-684
89PawRedSTI-9
90CMC-266
90PawRedSC-15
90PawRedSDD-7
90PawRedSP-468
90ProAAAF-440
90TopTVRS-44
91LinDriAAA-257
91NasSouLD-257
91NasSouP-2162

Gonzalez, Arturo
73CedRapAT-1
74CedRapAT-4
85PorBeaC-33
86PhiTas-xx
86PorBeaP-6

Gonzalez, Carlos
86Ft.MyeRP-12
87AppFoxP-14
88BasCitRS-12
89BasCitRS-7

Gonzalez, Cecilio
90JohCitCS-13
91JohCitCC-26
91JohCitCP-3972

Gonzalez, Chris
85CloHSS-19

Gonzalez, Cliff
85LitFalMT-23
86LitFalMP-12
87ColMetP-4
89SarWhiSS-8
90SarWhiSS-11
91CalLeLA-46
91RenSilSCLC-12
92SalSpuC-20
92SalSpuF-3767

Gonzalez, David
91LinDriAA-407
91MemChiLD-407
91MemChiP-661

Gonzalez, Denny (Denio)
82PorBeaT-13
84HawIslC-130
85Don-600
85HawIslC-229
86Don-410
86Fle-608
86Top-746
86TopTif-746
88BufBisC-15
88BufBisP-1473
89ColSprSSC-14
89ColSprSSP-248
90CMC-368
90ProAAAF-283
90TidTidC-17
90TidTidP-552
90TopTVM-43
91LinDriAAA-258
91NasSouLD-258
91NasSouP-2163
93LimRocDP-P2
93LimRocDWB-137
93LimRocDWB-P2

Gonzalez, Eddie
90WesPalBES-10

Gonzalez, Efrain
92ButCopKSP-28

Gonzalez, Enrique
76VenLeaS-40
80VenLeaS-48

Gonzalez, Felipe
86FreGiaP-5
87CliGiaP-7

Gonzalez, Ferdi
83GreHorT-14
84GreHorT-6
86AlbYanT-6
87AlbYanP-20
90MiaMirIS-28
91MiaMirC-1
91MiaMirP-423
92EriSaiC-30
92EriSaiF-1640
93HigDesMC-26
93HigDesMF-57
94BreCouMF-29
95BreCouMF-261
96BreCouMB-1
86Ft.LauYP-8
90VerBeaDS-14
91LinDriAA-535
91SanAntMLD-535
92SanAntMS-565
92VerBeaDF-2889
93LimRocDWB-75
93LinVenB-185
94BreCouMC-24

Gonzalez, Fernando (Jose Fern.)
74OPC-649
74Top-649
74TopTra-649T
77PirPosP-8
78ColCliT-8
78PadFamF-14
78Top-433
79Top-531
80SalLakCGT-25
80Top-171
81SalLakCGT-18
82AleDukT-7
83LynPirT-3
89BlaYNPRWL-169
92YanWIZ7-55

Gonzalez, Frank
92LonTigS-410
92SkyAA F-174
94VenLinU-207
95LinVen-60

Gonzalez, Freddy (Fred)

Gonzalez, Gabe
96BreCouMB-16

Gonzalez, Generoso
94BriTigC-14
94BriTigF-3497
96FayGenB-18

Gonzalez, German
87KenTwiP-26
88BasAmeAAB-18
88OrlTwiB-17
88SouLeaAJ-30
89Don-590
89DonRoo-24
89Fle-113
89FleGlo-113
89PanSti-379
89ScoHot1R-49
89Top-746
89TopTif-746
90Fle-376
90FleCan-376
90Hot50RS-17
90OPC-266
90Sco-133
90Sco100RS-81

90Top-266
90TopTif-266
90UppDec-352
91KisDodP-4193
92GreFalDSP-26
94VenLinU-188
Gonzalez, Gilberto
80ElmPioRST-32
Gonzalez, Henry
84NewOriT-18
85NewOriT-10
Gonzalez, Jamie
91Cla/Bes-449
Gonzalez, Javier
87LitFalMP-2395
88ColMetGS-12
89BlaYNPRWL-176
90JacMetGS-13
91LinDriAA-632
91WilBilLD-632
91WilBilP-296
92TidTidF-899
92TidTidS-560
93BinMetF-2337
94NewBriRSF-652
Gonzalez, Jeremi
93HunCubC-9
93HunCubF-3230
94PeoChiC-10
94PeoChiF-2259
94VenLinU-213
94WilCubC-9
94WilCubF-3757
95LinVen-58
95RocCubTI-20
96OrlCubB-9
97Bow-309
97BowChr-213
97BowChrI-213
97BowChrIR-213
97BowChrR-213
97BowInt-309
97Fle-752
97FleTif-752
97TopStaFAS-FAS14
Gonzalez, Jess
94LetMouF-3873
94LetMouSP-11
Gonzalez, Jesus
91BurIndP-3295
93LinVenB-127
94VenLinU-132
95LinVen-176
Gonzalez, Jim
92BurAstC-22
92BurAstF-549
Gonzalez, Jimmy
91ClaDraP-36
91FroRowDP-32
92OPC-564
92StaCluD-63
92Top-564
92TopGol-564
92TopGolW-564
92TopMic-564
93Bow-292
93QuaCitRBC-9
93QuaCitRBF-102
94OscAstC-10
94OscAstF-1141
95QuaCitRBTI-7
96KisCobB-9
Gonzalez, John
84IdaFalATI-10
Gonzalez, Johnny
80VenLeaS-154
94VenLinU-246
95LinVen-217
Gonzalez, Jose
83LouRedR-13
84Car5x7-7
84LouRedR-13
Gonzalez, Jose Rafael
86AlbDukP-9
87AlbDukP-26
87DodPol-25
87Don-525
87Fle-649
87FleGlo-649
88AlbDukC-19
88Don-341
88Sco-364
88ScoGlo-364
89AlbDukP-80
89DonBasB-260
89DonBasB-275
89ScoHot1R-29
89UppDec-626
90ClaBlu-96
90DodMot-11
90DodPol-38
90DodTar-288
90Don-314
90Fle-394
90FleCan-394
90OPC-98
90Sco-368
90ScoYouSI-16
90Top-98
90TopTif-98
90UppDec-666
91DodMot-11
91DodPol-38
91Don-543
91OPC-279
91Sco-614
91StaClu-208
91Top-279B
91TopDesS-279
91TopMic-279
91TopTif-279
92EdmTraS-160
92Sco-733
92StaClu-774
92StaCluECN-774
93LimRocDWB-83
95LinVen-218
Gonzalez, Juan
76CliPilT-18
76VenLeaS-99
94HelBreF-3609
94HelBreSP-23
95BelBreTI-18
96BreCouMB-17
Gonzalez, Juan A.
87GasRanP-4
88BlaYNPRWL-105
88ChaRanS-8
89BasAmeAPB-AA26
89BlaYNPRWL-42
89BlaYNPRWLU-52
89TexLeaAGS-34
89TulDriGS-10
89TulDriTI-8
90Bow-492
90BowTif-492
90ClaUpd-T21
90CMC-167
90Don-33A
90Don-33B
90Fle-297
90FleCan-297
90OklCit8C-17
90OklCit8P-444
90OPC-331
90ProAAAF-690
90Sco-637
90Top-331
90TopDeb89-43
90TopMag-84
90TopTif-331
90TriAllGP-AAA12
90TulDriDGB-25
90UppDec-72
91Bow-180
91Cla1-T70
91Cla2-T74
91ClaGam-122
91Don-371
91Fle-286
91Lea-119
91MajLeaCP-36
91OPC-224
91OPCPre-54
91RanMot-4
91RedFolS-107
91Sco-805
91Sco100RS-41
91ScoHotR-9
91SevCoi-T7
91StaClu-237
91StaGonRG-1
91StaGonRG-2
91StaGonRG-3
91StaGonRG-4
91StaGonRG-5
91StaGonRG-6
91StaGonRG-7
91StaGonRG-8
91StaGonRG-9
91StaGonRG-10
91StaGonRG-11
91Stu-124
91Top-224
91TopDesS-224
91TopMic-224
91TopTif-224
91TopTriH-A13
91TulDriTI-30
91UltUpd-55
91UppDec-646
92Bow-84
92ClaGam-158
92Don-393
92Fle-304
92Hig5-112
92Hig5S-14
92JimDea-14
92Lea-62
92LeaBlaG-62
92OPC-27
92PanSti-81
92Pin-127
92PinTea2-26
92RanMot-4
92RanTeal-8
92Sco-11
92Sco100S-69
92ScoImpP-27
92SpoIllFK1-121
92SpoStaCC-16
92StaClu-240
92Stu-242
92Top-27
92TopGol-27
92TopGolW-27
92TopKid-131
92TopMic-27
92TriPla-112
92Ult-132
92UppDec-243
92UppDecF-9
92UppDecFG-9
92UppDecHRH-HR19
92UppDecWB-T14
93Bow-305
93ClaGam-37
93ColAllG-15
93DenHol-20
93DiaMar-40
93DiaMarP-4
93Don-555
93DonDiaK-DK7
93DonEli-36
93DonEliD-11
93DonEliD-AU11
93DonEliS-18
93DonLonBL-LL14
93DonMasotG-11
93DonMVP-21
93DonSpiotG-SG5
93Fin-116
93FinJum-116
93FinRef-116
93Fla-280
93Fle-322
93Fle-709
93FleAll-AL6
93FleAtl-10
93FleFruotL-22
93FleGolM-B3
93FleTeaL-AL8
93FunPac-15
93FunPac-153
93FunPac-156
93FunPac-223
93FunPacA-AS7
93JimDea-8
93Lea-170
93LeaFas-5
93LeaGolA-R16
93OPC-97
93OPCPreSP-7
93OPCPreSPF-7
93PacBeiA-12
93PacBeiA-15
93PacJugC-6
93PacSpa-311
93PacSpaGE-14
93PacSpaPI-14
93PanSti-86
93Pin-191
93PinCoo-25
93PinCooD-25
93PinHomRC-1
93PinSlu-1
93PinTea2-13
93PinTeaP-8
93Pos-23
93RanKee-408
93Sco-51
93ScoFra-13
93Sel-40
93SelStaL-25
93SP-194
93SPPlaP-PP8
93StaClu-297
93StaClu-540
93StaCluFDI-297
93StaCluFDI-540
93StaCluMOP-297
93StaCluMOP-540
93StaCluR-21
93Stu-160
93StuHer-2
93StuSil-4
93TedWil-151
93TedWil-152
93TedWil-153
93TedWil-154
93TedWil-AU151
93TedWil-AU152
93TedWil-AU153
93TedWil-AU154
93TedWilP-160
93Top-34
93TOPBLAG-32
93TopFulS-4
93TopGol-34
93TopInaM-34
93TopMic-34
93Toy-85
93TriPla-221
93TriPlaA-22
93TriPlaLL-L4
93Ult-279
93UltAllS-16
93UltHomRK-1
93UltPer-2
93UppDec-52
93UppDec-497
93UppDec-755
93UppDec-831
93UppDecCP-R10
93UppDecDG-20
93UppDecFA-A6
93UppDecFAJ-A6
93UppDecFH-58
93UppDecGold-52
93UppDecGold-497
93UppDecGold-755
93UppDecGold-831
93UppDecHRH-HR1
93UppDecOD-D12
93UppDecS-19
93USPlaCA-1C
94Bow-45
94BowBes-R19
94BowBesR-R19
94ChuShoS-1
94ColC-313
94ColC-323
94ColC-347
94ColC-630
94ColC-633
94ColChoGS-313
94ColChoGS-323
94ColChoGS-347
94ColChoGS-630
94ColChoGS-633
94ColChoHRA-HA1
94ColChoSS-313
94ColChoSS-323
94ColChoSS-347
94ColChoSS-630
94ColChoSS-633
94ColChoT-7
94DenHol-13
94Don-49
94DonAwaWJ-9
94DonDom-A6
94DonEli-42
94DonLonBL-10
94DonMVP-27
94DonSpeE-49
94DonSpiotG-5
94ExtBas-178
94ExtBasGB-12
94Fin-211
94FinJum-211
94FinRef-211
94Fla-109
94FlaOutP-5
94Fle-307
94Fle-710
94FleAllS-9
94FleLumC-4
94FlePro-6
94FleSun-12
94FleTeaL-13
94FUnPac-19
94FUnPac-181
94FUnPac-196
94FUnPac-199
94FUnPac-215
94FUnPac-240
94Kra-4
94Lea-418
94LeaCleC-7
94LeaGam-3
94LeaGolS-13
94LeaL-72
94LeaMVPC-A7
94LeaMVPCG-A7
94LeaPowB-4
94LeaSli-7
94LeaStaS-3
94OPC-28
94OPCAllR-4
94OPCJumA-4
94OscMayR-5
94Pac-617
94PacAll-14
94PacGolP-1
94PacPro-P3
94PacSilP-2
94PanSti-6
94PanSti-127
94Pin-350
94PinArtP-350
94PinMusC-350
94PinPowS-PS24
94PinRunC-RC7
94PinTeaP-7
94PinTheN-4
94PinTri-TR15
94Pos-3
94PosCan-15
94PosCanG-15
94ProMag-133
94RanAllP-21
94RedFolMI-32
94Sco-27
94ScoCyc-TC16
94ScoDreT-7
94ScoGolR-27
94ScoGolS-33
94Sel-212
94SelCroC-CC7
94SelSki-SK5
94SP-148
94SPDieC-148
94SPHol-11
94SPHolDC-11
94Spo-35
94Spo-182
94SpoFanA-AS6
94SpoRooGGG-GG3
94SPPre-WR2
94StaClu-112
94StaClu-261
94StaClu-568
94StaCluF-F4
94StaCluFDI-112
94StaCluFDI-261
94StaCluFDI-568
94StaCluGR-112
94StaCluGR-261
94StaCluGR-568
94StaCluMO-1
94StaCluMOP-112
94StaCluMOP-261
94StaCluMOP-568
94StaCluMOP-F4
94StaCluMOP-ST27
94StaCluST-ST27
94StaCluT-241
94StaCluTF-5
94StaCluTFDI-241
94Stu-154

94StuEdiC-5
94StuSerS-9
94TomPiz-19
94Top-389
94Top-685
94TopBlaG-7
94TopGol-389
94TopGol-685
94TopPre-34
94TopSpa-389
94TopSpa-685
94TopSupS-17
94TriPla-194
94TriPlaBS-3
94TriPlaP-1
94Ult-127
94UltAllS-7
94UltHitM-5
94UltHomRK-1
94UltRBIK-4
94UppDec-52
94UppDec-155
94UppDec-293
94UppDecAJ-25
94UppDecAJG-25
94UppDecDC-W3
94UppDecED-52
94UppDecED-155
94UppDecED-293
94UppDecMLS-MM9
94UppDecMLSED-MM9
94UppDecNG-5
94UppDecNGED-5
94USPlaCA-13C
95Baz-68
95Bow-323
95BowBes-R30
95BowBes-X5
95BowBesR-R30
95BowBesR-X5
95ClaFanFPCP-3
95ClaPhoC-53
95ColCho-84
95ColCho-90
95ColChoCtG-CG7
95ColChoCtG-CG7B
95ColChoCtG-CG7C
95ColChoCtGE-7
95ColChoCtGG-CG7
95ColChoCtGG-CG7B
95ColChoCtGG-CG7C
95ColChoCtGGE-7
95ColChoGS-84
95ColChoGS-90
95ColChoSE-186
95ColChoSEGS-186
95ColChoSESS-186
95ColChoSS-84
95ColChoSS-90
95DenHol-10
95Don-42
95DonPreP-42
95DonTopotO-160
95Emb-30
95EmbGolI-30
95Emo-85
95EmoMas-2
95Fin-158
95FinRef-158
95Fla-88
95FlaOutP-6
95Fle-285
95FleUpdH-10
95Kra-4
95Lea-202
95LeaLim-176
95LeaLimL-3
95NatPac-3
95Pac-426
95PacGolCDC-18
95PacGolP-11
95PacLatD-17
95PacPri-136
95PanSti-83
95Pin-227
95Pin-278
95PinArtP-227
95PinArtP-278
95PinFan-9
95PinMusC-227
95PinMusC-278
95PinPer-PP4
95PinUps-US10
95RanCra-11
95RedFol-4
95Sco-439
95ScoGolR-439
95ScoHaloG-HG58
95ScoPlaTS-439
95ScoRul-SR16
95ScoRulJ-SR16
95Sel-86
95SelArtP-86
95SP-195
95SPCha-190
95SPChaDC-190
95Spo-73
95SpoArtP-73
95SpoDet-DE9
95SpoHamT-HT15
95SPPlaP-PP11
95SPSil-195
95SPSpeF-22
95StaClu-145
95StaClu-406
95StaCluFDI-145
95StaCluMOP-145
95StaCluMOP-406
95StaCluMOP-RL23
95StaCluRL-RL23
95StaCluSTWS-145
95StaCluSTWS-406
95StaCluVR-74
95Stu-21
95StuGolS-21
95StuPlaS-21
95Sum-90
95SumNthD-90
95Top-70
95TopCyb-50
95TopCybSiR-3
95UC3-74
95UC3ArtP-74
95UllHomRK-5
95Ult-109
95UltGolM-109
95UltRisS-4
95UltRisSGM-4
95UppDec-104
95UppDec-395
95UppDecED-104
95UppDecED-395
95UppDecEDG-104
95UppDecEDG-395
95UppDecPAW-H2
95UppDecPAWE-H2
95UppDecPLL-R3
95UppDecPLL-R41
95UppDecPLLE-R3
95UppDecPLLE-R41
95UppDecSE-40
95UppDecSEG-40
95Zen-59
96Baz-73
96Bow-95
96BowBes-58
96BowBesAR-58
96BowBesR-58
96Cir-86
96CirBos-23
96CirRav-86
96ColCho-338
96ColCho-417
96ColCho-740
96ColChoCtG-CG28
96ColChoCtG-CG28B
96ColChoCtG-CG28C
96ColChoCtGE-CR28
96ColChoCtGG-CG28
96ColChoCtGG-CG28B
96ColChoCtGG-CG28C
96ColChoCtGGE-CR28
96ColChoGS-338
96ColChoGS-417
96ColChoGS-740
96ColChoSS-338
96ColChoSS-417
96ColChoSS-740
96ColChoYMtP-15
96ColChoYMtP-15A
96ColChoYMtPGS-15
96ColChoYMtPGS-15A
96Don-375
96DonDiaK-5
96DonPreP-375
96EmoLegoB-3
96EmoXL-121
96Fin-B253
96Fin-G354
96Fin-S115
96FinRef-B253
96FinRef-G354
96FinRef-S115
96Fla-169
96FlaDiaC-4
96FlaPow-3
96Fle-250
96FleRan-6
96FleTeaL-13
96FleTif-250
96FleUpd-U221
96FleUpdH-6
96FleUpdSS-3
96FleUpdTC-U221
96Lea-107
96LeaLim-34
96LeaLimG-34
96LeaLimPC-1
96LeaPre-43
96LeaPreP-43
96LeaPrePB-107
96LeaPrePG-107
96LeaPrePS-107
96LeaPreSG-20
96LeaPreSte-20
96LeaSig-2
96LeaSigEA-61
96LeaSigEACM-9
96LeaSigPPG-2
96LeaSigPPP-2
96LeaTotB-11
96MetUni-113
96MetUniHM-3
96MetUniP-113
96Pac-423
96PacEstL-EL12
96PacPri-P136
96PacPriG-P136
96PanSti-232
96Pin-38
96Pin-163
96PinAfi-99
96PinAfiAP-99
96PinAfiFPP-99
96PinAfiSP-27
96PinArtP-57
96PinArtP-90
96PinPow-20
96PinSlu-15
96PinSta-57
96PinSta-90
96ProMagDM-24
96ProSta-98
96RanMot-3
96Sco-348
96ScoDugC-B73
96ScoDugCAP-B73
96ScoNumG-21
96Sel-56
96SelArtP-56
96SelCer-56
96SelCerAP-56
96SelCerCB-56
96SelCerCR-56
96SelCerMB-56
96SelCerMG-56
96SelCerMR-56
96SelTeaN-14
96SP-175
96SPMarM-MM14
96SPMarMDC-14
96Spo-95
96SpoArtP-95
96SPSpeFX-29
96SPSpeFXDC-29
96SPx-58
96SPxGol-58
96StaClu-9
96StaCluEPB-9
96StaCluEPG-9
96StaCluEPS-9
96StaCluMOP-9
96StaCluMOP-PP11
96StaCluPP-PP11
95StaCluVRMC-74
96Stu-105
96StuPrePB-105
96StuPrePG-105
96StuPrePS-105
96Sum-60
96SumAbo&B-60
96SumArtP-60
96SumBal-7
96SumFoi-60
96TeaOut-30
96Top-325
96TopBigC-2
96TopChr-129
96TopChrR-129
96TopChrWC-WC8
96TopChrWCR-WC8
96TopGal-163
96TopGalPPI-163
96TopLas-8
96TopLasPC-13
96TopPro-AL14
96TopWreC-WC8
96Ult-135
96Ult-578
96UltChe-A3
96UltCheGM-A3
96UltGolM-135
96UltGolM-578
96UltHitM-3
96UltHitMGM-3
96UltHomRKGM-5
96UltHomRKR-5
96UltThu-10
96UltThuGM-10
96UppDec-206
96UppDecDD-DD39
96UppDecDDG-DD39
96UppDecDDS-DD39
96UppDecPD-PD6
96UppDecPRE-R3
96UppDecPreR-R3
96UppDecRunP-RP6
96Zen-61
96ZenArtP-61
96ZenMoz-2
97Bow-29
97BowBes-74
97BowBesAR-74
97BowBesMI-MI6
97BowBesMIAR-MI6
97BowBesMIARI-MI6
97BowBesMII-MI6
97BowBesMIR-MI6
97BowBesMIRI-MI6
97BowBesR-74
97BowChr-25
97BowChrI-25
97BowChrIR-25
97BowChrR-25
97BowInt-29
97BowIntB-BBI3
97BowIntBAR-BBI3
97BowIntBR-BBI3
97Cir-373
97CirBos-5
97CirIco-1
97CirLimA-4
97CirRav-373
97CirRavR-3
97CirSupB-5
97ColCho-218
97ColCho-240
97ColCho-333
97ColChoAC-14
97ColChoCtG-30A
97ColChoCtG-30B
97ColChoCtG-30C
97ColChoCtGIW-CG30
97ColChoNF-NF7
97ColChoPP-PP5
97ColChoPPG-PP5
97ColChoS-22
97ColChoTBS-45
97ColChoTBSWH-45
97ColChoTotT-T29
97Don-1
97Don-406
97DonDom-8
97DonEli-1
97DonEli-12
97DonEliGS-1
97DonFraFea-5
97DonLim-77
97DonLim-88
97DonLim-118
97DonLimFotG-17
97DonLimLE-77
97DonLimLE-88
97DonLimLE-118
97DonLonL-8
97DonPowA-11
97DonPowADC-11
97DonPre-22
97DonPre-173
97DonPreCttC-22
97DonPreCttC-173
97DonPreP-1
97DonPreP-406
97DonPrePGold-1
97DonPrePGold-406
97DonPrePM-5
97DonPreS-6
97DonPreTB-5
97DonPreTBG-5
97DonPreTF-5
97DonPreTP-5
97DonPreTPG-5
97DonPreXP-3B
97DonRocL-6
97DonTeaSMVP-15
97Fin-150
97Fin-212
97Fin-332
97FinEmb-150
97FinEmb-332
97FinEmbR-150
97FinEmbR-332
97FinRef-150
97FinRef-212
97FinRef-332
97FlaSho-A19
97FlaSho-B19
97FlaSho-C19
97FlaShoDC-4
97FlaShoHG-3
97FlaShoLC-19
97FlaShoLC-B19
97FlaShoLC-C19
97FlaShoLCM-A19
97FlaShoLCM-B19
97FlaShoLCM-C19
97Fle-221
97Fle-700
97Fle-747
97FleBleB-3
97FleDiaT-3
97FleHea-5
97FleLumC-8
97FleMilDM-38
97FleNig&D-3
97FleSoaS-3
97FleTeaL-13
97FleTif-221
97FleTif-700
97FleTif-747
97FleZon-6
97Lea-101
97Lea-353
97LeaBanS-3
97LeaDrefS-13
97LeaFraM-101
97LeaFraM-353
97LeaFraMDC-101
97LeaFraMDC-353
97LeaGet-7
97LeaGolS-10
97LeaLeaotN-1
97LeaStaS-2
97LeaWarT-11
97MetUni-162
97MetUniBF-5
97NewPin-68
97NewPin-195
97NewPinAP-68
97NewPinAP-195
97NewPinIE-9
97NewPinKtP-1
97NewPinMC-68
97NewPinMC-195
97NewPinPP-68
97NewPinPP-195
97NewPinPP-I9A
97NewPinPP-K1
97Pac-200
97PacCar-19
97PacCarM-19
97PacCerCGT-11
97PacFirD-13
97PacGolCD-19
97PacLatotML-21
97PacLigB-200
97PacPri-68
97PacPriGA-GA16
97PacPriGotD-GD95
97PacPriLB-68

97PacPriP-68
97PacPriSL-SL7A
97PacSil-200
97PacTriCD-11
97Pin-18
97PinArtP-18
97PinCar-5
97PinCer-69
97PinCer-142
97PinCerCMGT-11
97PinCerCT-11
97PinCerMBlu-69
97PinCerMBlu-142
97PinCerMG-69
97PinCerMG-142
97PinCerMR-69
97PinCerMR-142
97PinCerR-69
97PinCerR-142
97PinIns-4
97PinIns-150
97PinInsC-11
97PinInsCE-4
97PinInsCE-150
97PinInsDD-13
97PinInsDE-4
97PinInsDE-150
97PinInsFS-1
97PinMin-6
97PinMinB-6
97PinMinCB-6
97PinMinCG-6
97PinMinCGR-6
97PinMinCN-6
97PinMinCS-6
97PinMinG-6
97PinMinS-6
97PinMusC-18
97PinPasttM-13
97PinSha-2
97PinTeaP-8
97PinTeaP-10
97PinTotCPB-69
97PinTotCPB-142
97PinTotCPG-69
97PinTotCPG-142
97PinTotCPR-69
97PinTotCPR-142
97PinX-P-4
97PinX-PF&A-6
97PinX-PMoS-4
97PinX-PMP-9
97PinX-PMW-9
97PinX-PMWG-9
97PinX-PMWS-9
97PinX-PSfF-9
97PinX-PSfFU-9
97ProMag-75
97ProMagML-75
97Sco-198
97Sco-498
97ScoAllF-13
97ScoBla-3
97ScoHeaotO-3
97ScoHobR-498
97ScoPreS-198
97ScoRan-11
97ScoRanPl-11
97ScoRanPr-11
97ScoResC-498
97ScoShoS-198
97ScoShoS-498
97ScoShoSAP-198
97ScoShoSAP-498
97ScoStaaD-21
97ScoSteS-1
97ScoTitT-4
97Sel-1
97Sel-142
97SelArtP-1
97SelArtP-142
97SelRegG-1
97SelRegG-142
97SelToootT-7
97SelToootTMB-7
97SkyE-X-46
97SkyE-XACA-5
97SkyE-XC-46
97SkyE-XEC-46
97SkyE-XHoN-13
97SP-175
97SPInsI-23
97SpoIll-160
97SpoIllEE-160
97SpoIllGS-24
97SPSpeF-13
97SPSpxF-8
97SPSPxFA-8
97SPx-48
97SPxBoufG-20
97SPxBro-48
97SPxGraF-48
97SPxSil-48
97SPxSte-48
97StaClu-20
97StaClu-387
97StaCluFR-F12
97StaCluI-I12
97StaCluMat-20
97StaCluMOP-20
97StaCluMOP-387
97StaCluMOP-I12
97StaCluMOP-FB12
97StaCluMOP-PG11
97StaCluPG-PG11
97Stu-55
97StuHarH-20
97StuMasS-23
97StuMasS8-23
97StuPor8-11
97StuPrePG-55
97StuPrePS-55
97Top-124
97TopAll-AS15
97TopChr-47
97TopChrAS-AS15
97TopChrDD-DD6
97TopChrDDR-DD6
97TopChrR-47
97TopChrSAR-AS15
97TopChrSB-13
97TopChrSBR-13
97TopGal-73
97TopGalPPI-73
97TopHobM-HM9
97TopIntF-ILM4
97TopIntFR-ILM4
97TopScr-6
97TopSeaB-SB13
97TopSta-37
97TopStaAM-37
97TopTeaT-TT10
97Ult-132
97UltChe-B10
97UltDouT-10
97UltFamGam-9
97UltGolME-132
97UltHRK-3
97UltLeaS-5
97UltPlaME-132
97UltPowP-A3
97UltPowP-B8
97UltRBIK-6
97UltStaR-10
97UltThu-5
97UltTop3-10
97UltTop3GM-10
97UppDec-200
97UppDec-219
97UppDec-247
97UppDec-423
97UppDec-510
97UppDecAWJ-20
97UppDecHC-HC7
97UppDecLDC-LD5
97UppDecP-28
97UppDecPP-PP19
97UppDecPPJ-PP19
97UppDecRP-RP6
97UppDecU-6
97UppDecUMA-MA3
97Zen-13
97Zen8x1-15
97Zen8x1D-15

Gonzalez, Julian
83PeoSunF-23
85DomLeaS-40
85MidAngT-25
87SanJosBP-24
88SouBenWSGS-20

Gonzalez, Julio C.
78AstBurK-13
78Top-389
79Top-268
80Top-696
81Car5x7-5
81Fle-73
82Don-645
82Top-503
83EvaTriT-14
83Top-74

Gonzalez, Laril
91LinDriAA-435
92EdmTraF-3542
96AshTouB-19

Gonzalez, Luis
75WatRoyT-14
78AshTouT-7
79AshTouT-1
80TulDriT-14
95PacPri-62
95Top-162
95TopCyb-97
96EriSeaB-11

Gonzalez, Luis E.
88AubAstP-1973
89OscAstS-6
89Sta-15
90Bes-95
90CMC-760
90ColMudB-4
90ColMudP-1352
90ColMudS-11
90ProAaA-59
90StaFS7-16
91AstMot-13
91Bow-550
91Cla2-T91
91Don-690
91DonRoo-17
91Fle-507
91LeaGolR-BC2
91ScoRoo-99T
91StaClu-576
91TopDeb90-57
91TopTra-48T
91TopTraT-48T
91UltUpd-82
91UppDec-567
91UppDec-702
92Bow-145
92ClaGam-3
92Don-270
92Fle-434
92Hig5-39
92Lea-160
92OPC-12
92OPCPre-103
92PanSti-158
92Pin-163
92PinTea2-68
92Sco-210
92Sco100RS-6
92StaClu-227
92Top-12
92TopGol-12
92TopGolW-12
92TopMic-12
92TriPla-210
92Ult-203
92UppDec-372
93AstMot-15
93Bow-40
93DiaMar-39
93Don-404
93Fin-195
93FinRef-195
93Fla-63
93Fle-51
93Lea-90
93LinVenB-43
93LinVenB-210
93OPC-178
93PacBeiA-24
93PacSpa-123
93PanSti-175
93Pin-312
93Sco-151
93Sel-205
93SP-34
93StaClu-302
93StaCluAs-26
93StaCluFDI-302
93StaCluMOP-302
93Stu-171
93Top-362
93TopGol-362
93TopInaM-362
93TopMic-362
93Ult-40
93UppDec-572
93UppDecGold-572
94AstMot-4
94Bow-62
94ColC-111
94ColChoGS-111
94ColChoSS-111
94Don-83
94ExtBas-274
94Fin-290
94FinRef-290
94Fla-170
94Fle-491
94Lea-292
94LeaL-115
94OPC-263
94Pac-266
94PacAll-4
94Pin-323
94PinArtP-323
94PinMusC-323
94ProMag-57
94Sco-474
94ScoGolR-474
94Sel-348
94StaClu-35
94StaCluFDI-35
94StaCluGR-35
94StaCluMOP-35
94Stu-22
94Top-484
94TopGol-484
94TopSpa-484
94TriPla-27
94Ult-205
94UppDec-396
94UppDecED-396
94VenLinU-68
95AstMot-3
95ColCho-110
95ColChoGS-110
95ColChoSS-110
95Don-145
95DonPreP-145
95DonTopotO-198
95Emb-58
95EmbGolI-58
95Fin-150
95FinRef-150
95Fla-146
95Fle-460
95Lea-216
95LeaLim-77
95LinVen-90
95Pac-187
95PacLatD-18
95Pin-33
95PinArtP-33
95PinMusC-33
95Sco-79
95ScoGolR-79
95ScoPlaTS-79
95StaClu-257
95StaCluFDI-257
95StaCluMOP-257
95StaCluSTWS-257
95StaCluVR-126
95Stu-95
95Ult-386
95UltGolM-386
95UppDec-276
95UppDec-458T
95UppDecED-276
95UppDecEDG-276
95UppDecSE-44
95UppDecSEG-44
96ColCho-87
96ColChoGS-87
96ColChoSS-87
96Don-358
96DonPreP-358
96EmoXL-154
96Fla-215
96Fle-318
96FleCub-6
96FleTif-318
96Lea-128
96LeaPrePB-128
96LeaPrePG-128
96LeaPrePS-128
96MetUni-140
96MetUniP-140
96Pac-33
96PacPri-P9
96PacPriG-P9
96PanSti-42
96Sco-146
96StaClu-101
96StaCluEPB-101
96StaCluEPG-101
96StaCluEPS-101
96StaCluMOP-101
95StaCluVRMC-126
96Top-278
96Ult-167
96UltGolM-167
96UppDec-38
97Cir-68
97CirRav-68
97ColCho-352
97Don-237
97DonPreP-237
97DonPrePGold-237
97Fle-275
97Fle-531
97FleTif-275
97FleTif-531
97Pac-249
97PacLigB-249
97PacPri-85
97PacPriLB-85
97PacPriP-85
97PacSil-249
97StaClu-331
97StaCluMOP-331
97Top-142
97Ult-504
97UltGolME-504
97UltPlaME-504
97UppDec-364

Gonzalez, Manny
95GreFalDTI-23
96SanBerSB-10

Gonzalez, Manuel
80VenLeaS-94
93LinVenB-272
96SavSanB-4

Gonzalez, Marcos
82MiaMarT-3
87FayGenP-20

Gonzalez, Mario
92GulCoaRSP-17
93LinVenB-135
94ChaRivC-8
94ChaRivF-2682
94VenLinU-91
95LinVen-247

Gonzalez, Maurico
93CenValRC-11
93CenValRF-2898
94CenValRC-8
94CenValRF-3210
95NewHavRTI-4

Gonzalez, Melvin
91ElmPioC-21
91ElmPioP-3266
93ForLauRSC-12
93ForLauRSFP-1589

Gonzalez, Miguel
16ColE13-61
21Exh-58
22W575-44
27YorCarE-34
28StaPlaCE-28
28W502-34
28Yue-34
46SeaSLP-19
92ConTSN-655

Gonzalez, Mike
21E121So8-28
21KoBreWSI-12
40PlaBal-115
41CarW75-8
74Car193T-12
75ShrCapT-3
76ShrCapT-6
86ConSer1-14
89BurIndS-11
90WatIndS-10
95ConTSN-1380

Gonzalez, Orlando
75OklCit8TI-13
76VenLeaS-47
77Top-477
80BurBeeT-7
81Fle-585
83TamTarT-13
87NasSouTI-7
88MiaMarS-8
89PacSenL-82

89TopSenL-83
91PacSenL-35
Gonzalez, Otto
82BurRanF-27
82BurRanT-21
83BurRanF-17
83BurRanT-17
85TulDriTI-35
86DayBeaIP-9
86FloStaLAP-18
88BlaYNPRWL-40
88OklCit8C-12
88OklCit8P-47
89BlaYNPRWL-115
89MidAngGS-15
Gonzalez, Paul
91Cla/Bes-82
91HigDesMC-21
91HigDesMP-2404
92SkyAA F-280
92WicWraF-3663
92WicWraS-632
93WicWraF-2983
94WicWraF-196
95PriWilCTI-8
Gonzalez, Pedro
63Top-537
64ChatheY-10
64Top-581
65ChaTheY-8
65OPC-97
65Top-97
66Kah-13
66Top-266
66TopVen-266
67CokCapI-6
67DexPre-80
67Top-424
91VerBeaDC-15
91VerBeaDP-776
92FayGenC-20
92LakTigF-2281
92TolMudHF-1045
92YanWIZ6-48
93LakTigC-8
96ColSprSSTI-16
Gonzalez, Pete (Pedro)
90VerBeaDS-15
93LakTigF-1313
Gonzalez, Pitcher (Mike)
76VenLeaS-147
Gonzalez, Raul
92AppFoxC-19
92AppFoxF-997
93CarLeaAGF-11
93WilBluRC-11
93WilBluRF-2010
94UppDecML-127
94WilBluRC-10
94WilBluRF-312
95WilBluRTI-14
96WicWraB-26
Gonzalez, Rich
91St.PetCC-25
91St.PetCP-2288
94ChaWheC-11
95WatIndTI-13
Gonzalez, Ruben
87BelMarTI-23
88WauTimGS-6
89CalLeaA-12
89SanBerSB-23
89SanBerSCLC-82
90Bes-198
90CMC-797
90WilBilB-8
90WilBilP-1062
91Cla/Bes-28
91JacSunLD-337
91JacSunP-157
91LinDriAA-337
Gonzalez, Tommy
83PhoGiaBHN-28
Gonzalez, Tony
47Exh-81
60Top-518
61Top-93
61TopStaI-55
62Top-534
62TopStaI-168
63ExhStaB-26
63Jel-181
63Pos-181
63Top-32
64PhiPhiB-13
64PhiTeaS-3
64Top-379
64TopCoi-58
64TopGia-14
64TopSta-58
64TopStaU-29
65OPC-72
65Top-72
66PhiTeaI-7
66Top-478
67CokCapPh-17
67PhiPol-7
67Top-548
67TopVen-265
68Baz-8
68OPC-1
68Top-1
68Top-245
68TopActS-7C
68TopGamI-20
68TopVen-1
68TopVen-245
69MilBra-94
69MLBOffS-192
69Top-501A
69Top-501B
69TopDecI-13
69TopSta-94
69TopTeaP-12
70MLBOffS-6
70OPC-105
70Top-105
71MLBOffS-345
71OPC-256
71Top-256
72MilBra-118
75PhoGiaC-19
75PhoGiaCK-5
77SpaPhiT-15
82DanSunF-13
83PhiPosGPaM-12
Gonzalez, Wallace
89BlaYNPRWL-177
90PulBraB-13
90PulBraP-3093
91MacBraC-15
91MacBraP-868
Gonzalez, Wiklenman
95LinVen-5
96AugGreB-12
Gooch, Arnold
95AshTouTI-15
96Bow-254
96StLucMTI-3
97Bow-334
97BowInt-334
Gooch, Johnny (John B.)
22E120-217
27AmeCarE-1
31Exh-8
79RedSoxEF-5
90DodTar-289
91ConTSN-244
Gooch, Ron
79TucTorT-7
79TulDriT-11
80TulDriT-17
81TulDriT-28
Good, Thomathon
92LetMouSP-8
93EugEmeF-3868
Good, Wilbur
09MaxPubP-21
09T206-143
11T205-65
15SpoNewM-69
16SpoNewM-69
Gooda, David
95HelBreTI-22
Goodale, Jeff
89NiaFalRP-9
90LakTigS-12
91LakTigC-24
91LakTigP-278
Goodale, Wes
75AndRanT-28
Goodchild, Chris
80CliGiaT-6
Goode, William
14PieStaT-24
Goodell, Steve
95ElmPioTI-10
95ElmPioUTI-10
96KanCouCTI-12
Gooden, Doc (Dwight)
83LynMetT-10
84AllGamPI-77
84FleUpd-43
84FunFooP-27
84OCoandSI-107
84OCoandSI-239
84TopPewB-2
84TopTra-42T
84TopTraT-42T
85AllGamPI-169
85Don-190
85DonActA-47
85DonHig-32
85DonHig-33
85DonHig-48
85DonWaxBC-PC1
85Dra-36
85Fle-82
85Fle-634
85FleStaS-87
85FleStaS-95
85FleStaS-113
85Lea-234
85MetColP-19
85MetFanC-5
85MetTCM-12
85OPC-41
85PolMet-M3
85SevCoi-E9
85Top-3
85Top-620
85Top3-D-19
85TopGaloC-3
85TopGloS-38
85TopRubD-19
85TopSti-3
85TopSti-4
85TopSti-107
85TopSti-280
85TopSti-371
85TopSup-7
85TopTif-3
85TopTif-620
85Woo-16
86BurKinA-17
86Don-26
86Don-75
86DonAll-28
86DonHig-8
86DonSupD-26
86DorChe-5
86Dra-35
86Fle-81
86Fle-626
86Fle-638
86Fle-641
86FleAll-10
86FleLeaL-16
86FleLimE-20
86FleMin-19A
86FleMin-19B
86FleSlu-11
86FleStiC-46
86FleStiC-132
86GenMilB-4D
86KayB-15
86Lea-26
86MeaGolBB-5
86MeaGolM-4
86MeaGolSB-3
86MetColP-2
86MetFanC-4
86MetTCM-5
86MetWorSC-12
86MSAJifPD-20
86OPC-250
86OPCBoxB-F
86QuaGra-2
86SevCoi-C1
86SevCoi-E1
86SevCoi-S1
86SevCoi-W1
86Spo-100
86Spo-136
86Spo-143
86Spo-176
86Spo-184
86Spo-185
86SpoDecG-75
86SpoDecGS-1
86SpoRoo-47
86Top-202
86Top-250
86Top-709
86Top3-D-4
86TopGaloC-4
86TopGloS-41
86TopMinL-52
86TopSti-6
86TopSti-94
86TopSup-4
86TopTat-20
86TopTif-202
86TopTif-250
86TopTif-709
86TopWaxBC-F
87ClaGam-72
87Don-199
87DonAll-18
87DonP-18
87Dra-26
87Fle-9
87Fle-629
87Fle-640
87FleAwaW-15
87FleBasA-19
87FleExcS-19
87FleGamW-18
87FleGlo-9
87FleGlo-629
87FleGlo-640
87FleGlo-WS7
87FleHea-3
87FleHotS-18
87FleLeaL-20
87FleLimE-18
87FleMin-45
87FleRecS-12
87FleSlu-15
87FleStiC-48
87FleWaxBC-C4
87FleWorS-7
87GenMilB-5B
87K-M-26
87KayB-13
87Lea-84
87MetColP-4
87MSAJifPD-9
87OPC-130
87RedFolSB-6
87SevCoi-E7
87SevCoi-M9
87Spo-100
87Spo-120
87Spo-159
87SpoDeaP-4
87SpoRea-13
87SpoTeaP-2
87TidTidP-31
87TidTidT-30
87Top-130
87Top-603A
87Top-603B
87TopCoi-33
87TopGloA-10
87TopGloS-51
87TopMinL-23
87TopSti-5
87TopSti-6
87TopSti-96
87TopSti-163
87TopTif-130
87TopTif-603A
87TopTif-603B
88ActPacT-3
88Baz-8
88ClaRed-171
88Don-69
88DonBasB-96
88DonTeaBM-69
88Dra-28
88Fle-135
88FleAwaW-14
88FleBasA-12
88FleBasM-16
88FleExcS-15
88FleGlo-135
88FleHea-5
88FleHotS-13
88FleLeaL-15
88FleMin-92
88FleRecS-14
88FleSlu-15
88FleStiC-102
88FleSup-14
88FleTeaL-10
88GreBasS-20
88K-M-10
88Lea-48
88MetColP-4
88MetFanC-16
88MetKah-16
88MSAIceTD-19
88Nes-21
88OPC-287
88PanSti-337
88Sco-350
88ScoGlo-350
88ScoYouS2-3
88Spo-200
88SpoGam-9
88StaCle-1
88StaCle-3
88StaCle-5
88StaCle-7
88StaCle-9
88StaCle-11
88StaGoo-1
88StaGoo-2
88StaGoo-3
88StaGoo-4
88StaGoo-5
88StaGoo-6
88StaGoo-7
88StaGoo-8
88StaGoo-9
88StaGoo-10
88StaGoo-11
88StaGooB-1
88StaGooB-2
88StaGooB-3
88StaGooB-4
88StaGooB-5
88StaGooB-6
88StaGooB-7
88StaGooB-8
88StaGooB-9
88StaGooB-10
88StaGooB-11
88StaGooB-12
88StaLinAl-12
88StaLinMe-8
88Top-405
88Top-480
88TopBig-11
88TopGloS-54
88TopMinL-60
88TopSti-101
88TopStiB-25
88TopTif-405
88TopTif-480
88TopUKM-27
88TopUKMT-27
89Bow-376
89BowTif-376
89ClaLigB-7
89ClaTraO-107
89ClaTraP-189
89Don-270
89DonAll-40
89DonBasB-14
89DonPop-40
89Fle-36
89Fle-635
89FleBasA-15
89FleBasM-14
89FleExcS-15
89FleGlo-36
89FleGlo-635
89FleHeroB-18
89FleLeaL-16
89FleSup-17
89K-M-31
89KayB-14
89MetCol8-31
89MetCol8-83
89MetColP-8
89MetFanC-16
89MetKah-9
89MSAIceTD-6
89OPC-30
89PanSti-131
89PanSti-227
89RedFolSB-51
89Sco-200
89ScoHot1S-15
89ScoSco-26
89Spo-140
89SpoIllFKI-151
89Top-30

89Top-661
89TopBasT-63
89TopBig-304
89TopCapC-17
89TopCoi-14
89TopDouM-5
89TopGloA-21
89TopGloS-37
89TopHeaUT-3
89TopMinL-26
89TopSti-99
89TopSti-162
89TopStiB-59
89TopTif-30
89TopTif-661
89TopUKM-31
89TVSpoM-3
89UppDec-565
89UppDecS-1
90AllBasT-6
90BasWit-35
90Bow-126
90BowIns-3
90BowInsT-3
90BowTif-126
90BowTif-A3
90ClaBlu-58
90Col-2
90Don-171
90DonBesN-7
90DonLeaS-10
90Fle-204
90FleBasM-12
90FleCan-204
90GooHumICBLS-10
90HOFStiB-98
90Hot50PS-16
90K-M-10
90Lea-139
90MetColP-3
90MetFanC-16
90MetKah-16
90MLBBasB-9
90MSAIceTD-10
90OPC-510
90OPCBoxB-E
90PanSti-297
90Pos-29
90PubSti-134
90PubSti-260
90RedFolSB-37
90Sco-313
90Sco100S-99
90Spo-145
90Top-510
90TopBig-174
90TopDou-26
90TopGloS-23
90TopHeaU-3
90TopMag-51
90TopSti-96
90TopStiB-25
90TopTif-510
90TopTVA-58
90TopTVM-12
90TopWaxBC-E
90UppDec-62
90UppDec-114
90VenSti-205
90VenSti-206
91BasBesAotM-8
91Bow-472
91Cla1-T99
91Cla2-T39
91ClaGam-121
91Col-17
91ColGoo-1
91ColGoo-2
91ColGoo-3
91ColGoo-4
91ColGoo-5
91ColGoo-6
91ColGoo-7
91ColGoo-8
91ColGoo-9
91ColGoo-10
91ColGoo-11
91ColGoo-12
91ColGoo-xx
91DoctheV-1
91Don-266
91DonPre-8
91Fle-148
91FlePro-7
91JimDea-25
91KinDis-8
91Lea-165
91LeaPre-7
91MajLeaCP-74
91MetCol8-1
91MetColP-4
91MetKah-16
91MetTro-3
91MetWIZ-144
91OPC-330
91OPCPre-55
91PanCanT1-60
91PanCanT1-74
91PanFreS-86
91PanSti-89
91PepSup-1
91PetSta-12
91RedFolS-40
91Sco-540
91Sco-685
91Sco-866
91Sco100S-65
91Sev3DCN-5
91SevCoi-F8
91SevCoi-NE5
91SimandSMLBL-16
91StaClu-100
91StaPinB-20
91Stu-204
91StuPre-14
91SunSee-10
91Top-330
91TopCraJI-28
91TopDesS-330
91TopMic-330
91TopSta-15
91TopTif-330
91TopTriH-N7
91Ult-218
91UppDec-224
92Bow-480
92Cla2-T43
92ClaGam-53
92ColPro-7
92Don-446
92DonCraJ1-23
92DonDiaK-DK15
92DonEli-12
92Fle-505
92FleSmo'nH-S8
92Hig5-72
92Hig5S-15
92Lea-112
92MetColP-3
92MetKah-16
92MooSna-18
92Mr.TurS-11
92OPC-725
92OPCPre-47
92PepDieM-2
92Pin-111
92PinRool-6
92Pos-5
92Sco-10
92Sco100S-25
92ScoImpP-54
92SevCoi-1
92SpoStaCC-17
92StaClu-455
92StaClu-602
92StaCluECN-602
92StaCluMO-12
92StaCluMO-28
92StaCluMP-6
92Stu-65
92StuPre-7
92Top-725
92TopGol-725
92TopGolW-725
92TopKid-11
92TopMcD-32
92TopMic-725
92TopMic-G725
92TriPla-167
92Ult-232
92UppDec-84
92UppDec-135
92UppDecF-23
92UppDecFG-23
93Bow-242
93DiaMar-41
93Don-462
93DurPowP1-13
93Fin-113
93FinJum-113
93FinRef-113
93Fla-91
93Fle-474
93FleFruotL-23
93FunPac-123
93FunPac-126
93KinDis-14
93Lea-203
93MetBak-8
93MetColP-23
93MetKah-16
93OPC-92
93PacSpa-198
93PanSti-245
93Pin-96
93PinCoo-19
93PinCooD-19
93Sco-53
93Sel-57
93SelAce-8
93SP-149
93StaClu-514
93StaCluFDI-514
93StaClul B2
93StaCluMOP-514
93StaCluMOP-MB2
93StaCluMP-17
93Stu-155
93Top-640
93TopGol-640
93TopInaM-640
93TopMic-640
93TriPla-146
93TriPlaN-6
93Ult-427
93UppDec-665
93UppDecDG-15
93UppDecGold-665
94Bow-400
94CarLeaA-DJ27
94ChuHomS-2
94ChuHomSG-2
94ColC-342
94ColC-519
94ColChoGS-342
94ColChoGS-519
94ColChoSS-342
94ColChoSS-519
94ColChoT-6
94Don-17
94DonSpeE-17
94ExtBas-317
94Fin-82
94FinPre-82P
94FinRef-82
94Fla-197
94Fle-563
94FUnPac-16
94Lea-10
94MetColP-9
94MetShuST-1
94OPC-24
94Pac-402
94PanSti-217
94Pin-62
94PinArtP-62
94PinMusC-62
94ProMag-93
94RedFolMI-6
94Sco-22
94ScoGolR-22
94Sel-54
94SP-116
94SPDieC-116
94Spo-94
94StaClu-220
94StaCluFDI-220
94StaCluGR-220
94StaCluMOP-220
94Stu-114
94Top-150
94TopGol-150
94TopSpa-150
94TriPla-143
94Ult-236
94UppDec-205
94UppDecAJ-38
94UppDecAJG-38
94UppDecDC-E6
94UppDecED-205
95Fle-369
96Cir-64
96CirBos-16
96CirRav-64
96EmoXL-89
96Fin-S291
96FinRef-S291
96Fla-128
96FleUpd-U61
96FleUpdTC-U61
96LeaPre-92
96LeaPreP-92
96LeaSig-130
96LeaSigPPG-130
96LeaSigPPP-130
96MetMod-4
96MetTeal-2
96Ult-385
96UltGolM-385
97Cir-270
97CirRav-270
97ColCho-175
97ColCho-176
97Don-154
97DonEli-122
97DonEli-148
97DonEliGS-122
97DonEliGS-148
97DonLim-139
97DonLimLE-139
97DonPre-74
97DonPreCttC-74
97DonPreP-154
97DonPrePGold-154
97DonTea-129
97DonTeaSPE-129
97Fin-51
97FinRef-51
97FlaSho-A111
97FlaSho-B111
97FlaSho-C111
97FlaShoLC-111
97FlaShoLC-B111
97FlaShoLC-C111
97FlaShoLCM-A111
97FlaShoLCM-B111
97FlaShoLCM-C111
97Fle-166
97FleGolM-2
97FleTif-166
97Lea-98
97LeaFraM-98
97LeaFraMDC-98
97MetUni-117
97Pac-151
97PacLigB-151
97PacSil-151
97Pin-82
97PinArtP-82
97PinCar-15
97PinCer-94
97PinCerMBlu-94
97PinCerMG-94
97PinCerMR-94
97PinCerR-94
97PinIns-89
97PinInsCE-89
97PinInsDE-89
97PinMusC-82
97PinPreP-2
97PinTotCPB-94
97PinTotCPG-94
97PinTotCPR-94
97Sco-171
97ScoPreS-171
97ScoShoS-171
97ScoShoSAP-171
97ScoYan-11
97ScoYanPl-11
97ScoYanPr-11
97StaClu-105
97StaCluMOP-105
97Stu-76
97StuPrePG-76
97StuPrePS-76
97Top-100
97Top-175
97Ult-98
97UltGolME-98
97UltPlaME-98
97UppDec-120

Gooden, Maury
85LitFalMT-24

Goodenough, Randy
86EugEmeC-39
87Ft.MyeRP-23

Goodfarm, Scott
77LynMetT-14

Goodfellow, Michael
87OldJudN-212

Goodhart, Steve
95BilRedTI-17
96Exc-147

Goodin, Craig
83ChaRoyT-6

Goodin, Rich (Rick)
83ChaRoyT-20
86MemChiSTOS-9
86MemChiTOS-9

Goodlow, Sebastian
89SalDodTI-13

Goodman, Billy
47Exh-82A
47Exh-82B
47PM1StaP1-74
48RedSoxTI-8
49Bow-39
49Lea-30
50Bow-99
51BerRos-C2
51Bow-237
51FisBakL-8
51R42SmaS-33
51TopRedB-46
52Bow-81
52StaCalL-71E
52StaCalS-85C
52Top-23
53BowC-148
53ExhCan-63
53RedSoxFNSMS-1
53RedSoxTI-10
54Bow-82
55Bow-126
56Top-245
57Top-303
58Top-225
58WhiSoxJP-5
59Top-103
59TopVen-103
60Top-69
60TopVen-69
60WhiSoxTS-7
61Top-247
77GalGloG-21
79TCM50-96
80AshTouT-1
83TopRep5-23
91OriCro-160
91TopArc1-334

Goodman, Douglas
92JohCitCC-3
92JohCitCF-3108
93SavCarC-15
93SavCarF-683

Goodman, Herbert
95BilRedTI-9

Goodman, Ival
34BatR31-127
35GouPuzR-8D
35GouPuzR-9D
38CinOraW-11
38ExhFou-4
39GouPreR303A-18
39GouPreR303B-10
39OrcPhoAP-10
39WorWidGTP-18
41DouPlaR-115
41HarHarW-7
44CubTeal-10
79DiaGre-266
93ConTSN-854

Goodman, John
90TopMag-77

Goodrich, Jon
93BenRocC-9
93BenRocF-3260
93Top-704
93TopGol-704
93TopInaM-704
93TopMic-704

Goodson, J. Ed
73OPC-197
73Top-197
74Kel-18
74OPC-494
74Top-494
74TopSta-105
75OPC-322
75Top-322

76OPC-386
76SSP-588
76Top-386
77Top-584
78SSP270-65
78Top-586
90DodTar-290
Goodson, Kirk
91HunCubC-11
91HunCubP-3329
Goodwin, Curtis
92KanCouCC-5
92KanCouCF-104
92KanCouCTI-11
93CarLeaAGF-2
93FreKeyC-8
93FreKeyF-1039
94ActPac-10
94Bow-487
94BowBayF-2423
94BowBes-B38
94BowBesR-B38
94Cla-37
94ExcFS7-6
94OriPro-41
94UppDecML-32
94UppDecML-253
95ActPacF-25
95AusFut-105
95Bow-66
95BowBes-B34
95BowBes-X10
95BowBesR-B34
95BowBesR-X10
95ColCho-37
95ColChoGS-37
95ColChoSS-37
95DonTopotO-8
95Emo-3
95Exc-5
95Fin-273
95FinRef-273
95LeaLim-116
95LinVen-2
95RocRedWTI-16
95SelCer-124
95SelCerF-2
95SelCerMG-124
95SelCerPU-12
95SelCerPU9-12
95SP-11
95SPCha-3
95SPChaDC-3
95SPSil-11
95Sum-123
95SumNthD-123
95Top-599
95TopTra-109T
95UltGolMR-M13
95UppDec-4
95UppDecED-4
95UppDecEDG-4
95UppDecML-58
95UppDecSE-51
95UppDecSEG-51
95Zen-113
95ZenRooRC-9
96Bow-144
96ColCho-50
96ColCho-769
96ColChoGS-50
96ColChoSS-50
96Don-42
96DonPreP-42
96Fle-8
96FleTif-8
96FleUpd-U120
96FleUpdTC-U120
96IndIndB-10
96MetUni-148
96MetUniP-148
96Pac-241
96Pin-111
96Sco-26
96ScoDugC-A25
96ScoDugCAP-A25
96StaClu-174
96StaCluMOP-174
96Top-121
96Ult-5
96UltGolM-5
96UppDec-12
96UppDecFSP-FS11
97DonLim-158
97DonLimLE-158
97Lea-343
97LeaFraM-343
97LeaFraMDC-343
97PacPriGotD-GD125
95UppDecMLFS-58
Goodwin, Danny
77SalLakCGC-7
78SSP270-204
79OgdA'sT-15
79Top-322
80Top-362
81Don-494
81Top-527
82Don-305
82Fle-554
82TacTigT-14
82Top-123
83TacTigT-25A
84TacTigC-91
85TacTigC-134
Goodwin, David
88GenCubP-1641
89ChaWheB-18
89ChaWheP-1768
Goodwin, Jim
48WhiSoxTI-7
Goodwin, Joey
95HudValRTI-9
96ChaRivTI-9614
Goodwin, Keith
96MicBatCB-11
Goodwin, Mike
86PriWilPP-12
Goodwin, Tom
89FreStaBS-9
89FreStaBS-10
89GreFalDSP-1
90BakDodCLC-261
90Bow-96
90BowTif-96
90SanAntMGS-13
90Sco-668
91AlbDukLD-6
91AlbDukP-1155
91Bow-608
91Cla3-T32
91LinDriAAA-6
91UppDecFE-9F
92AlbDukF-734
92AlbDukS-8
92Cla1-T39
92DonRoo-43
92Fle-652
92ProFS7-243
92Sco-830
92ScoRoo-34
92SkyAAAF-3
92StaClu-322
92TopDeb91-65
92UppDec-20
93DodPol-5
93Don-640
93Fle-446
93PacSpa-498
93Sel-349
93StaClu-446
93StaCluFDI-446
93StaCluMOP-446
93Top-228
93TopGol-228
93TopInaM-228
93TopMic-228
93Ult-398
94OmaRoyF-1234
95DonTopotO-87
95Fin-307
95FinRef-307
95FleUpd-46
95Lea-383
95TopTra-86T
96ColCho-171
96ColChoGS-171
96ColChoSS-171
96Don-109
96DonPreP-109
96EmoXL-66
96Fin-B118
96FinRef-B118
96Fla-88
96Fle-126
96FleTif-126
96LeaSigA-82
96LeaSigAG-82
96LeaSigAS-82
96MetUni-64
96MetUniP-64
96Pac-325
96PanSti-184
96ProSta-116
96RoyPol-8
96Sco-140
96StaClu-133
96StaCluMOP-133
96Top-39
96TopGal-118
96TopGalPPI-118
96Ult-69
96UltGolM-69
96UppDec-351
97Cir-295
97CirRav-295
97ColCho-356
97Don-122
97DonEli-134
97DonEliGS-134
97DonPreP-122
97DonPrePGold-122
97Fin-98
97FinRef-98
97Fle-113
97FleTif-113
97Lea-295
97LeaFraM-295
97LeaFraMDC-295
97MetUni-93
97NewPin-41
97NewPinAP-41
97NewPinMC-41
97NewPinPP-41
97Pac-100
97PacLigB-100
97PacPri-36
97PacPriLB-36
97PacPriP-36
97PacSil-100
97PinIns-107
97PinInsCE-107
97PinInsDE-107
97RoyPol-8
97Sco-222
97ScoPreS-222
97ScoShoS-222
97ScoShoSAP-222
97Sel-93
97SelArtP-93
97SelRegG-93
97StaClu-176
97StaCluMOP-176
97Top-122
97TopChrSB-22
97TopChrSBR-22
97TopSeaB-SB22
97Ult-395
97UltGolME-395
97UltPlaME-395
97UppDec-86
Goossen, Greg
67Top-287
68Top-386
70BreMcD-8
70BreMil-5
70OPC-271
70Top-271
83Pil69G-33
91MetWIZ-145
94BreMilB-314
Gorbans, Glen
63GadFunC-9
Gorbould, Bob
45CenFlo-11
Gorbous, Glen
56Top-174
Gordon, Adrian
94EliTwiC-9
94EliTwiF-3742
95Exc-85
95ForWayWTI-22
96ForWayWB-9
96MidLeaAB-30
Gordon, Alan
94LakElsSC-30
Gordon, Andrew
96NewJerCB-12
Gordon, Anthony
89BelMarL-5
90PenPilS-9
92BasCitRC-16
92SarWhiSCB-24
Gordon, Beebop (Harold)
93NegLeaRL2-10
Gordon, Don
83BirBarT-2
85SyrChiT-13
86BluJayAF-11
86BluJayFS-14
87IntLeaAT-10
87RocRedWT-29
87SyrChiP-1932
87SyrChiT-4
87SyrChiT-26
88ColSprSSC-3
88ColSprSSP-1538
88ScoRoo-92T
88ScoRooG-92T
88Top-144
88TopTif-144
89ColSprSSC-2
89ColSprSSP-260
89Fle-405
89FleGlo-405
89Sco-547
90CMC-43
90DenZepC-18
90DenZepP-621
90ProAAAF-646
91ElPasDLD-183
91ElPasDP-2742
91LinDriAA-183
Gordon, Herman
96DunBluJB-10
96DunBluJTI-12
96HagSunB-6
Gordon, Joe
36OveCanR-19
39ExhSal-21A
39ExhSal-21B
39GouPreR303A-19
39GouPreR303B-11
39WorWidGTP-19
41DouPlaR-67
41DouPlaR-83
41WheM5-21
43YanSta-12
46SpoExcW-4-10
47HomBon-17
47IndTeal-11
47IndVanPP-10
47PM1StaP1-75
48IndTeal-10
49Bow-210
49IndTeal-11
49IndVisEI-7
49IndVisEI-15
49Lea-117
50AmeNut&CCP-7
50Bow-129
50IndNumN-11
50IndTeal-11
50RoyDes-13
51R42SmaS-36
52MotCoo-19
53IndPenCBP-13
59Ind-4
59Kah-10
60Top-216
61A'sTeal-6
61AthJayP-8
61Top-224
61TopMagR-30
69RoySol-6
69RoyTeal-6
69Top-484
75YanDyn1T-19
77TCMTheWY-55
83TCMPla1942-1
86SpoDecG-24
92YanWIZA-24
93ActPacA-133
Gordon, Keith
90BilMusP-3228
91ChaWheC-23
92CedRapRC-1
92CedRapRF-1084
92UppDecML-204
93Bow-174
93ChaLooF-2372
95IndIndF-108
Gordon, Kevin
85PriWilPT-21
86NasPirP-8
Gordon, Mike
92GulCoaYF-3785
94GreBatF-466
95TamYanYI-8
96DunBluJB-11
96DunBluJTI-13
Gordon, Mike W.
78SSP270-251
Gordon, Oliver
96AubDouB-29
Gordon, Sid
47HomBon-18
47TipTop-123
48Bow-27
49Bow-101
49EurSta-104
49Lea-131
50Bow-109
50Dra-16
51Bow-19
51TopRedB-2
52Bow-60
52NatTeaL-11
52RedMan-NL6
52TipTop-11
52Top-267
53BowC-5
53BraJohC-23
53BraSpiaS3-12
53DixLid-6A
53DixLid-6B
53DixPre-6
53NorBreL-9
53Top-117
54Bow-11
54DanDee-9
54DixLid-3
55Bow-163
55RobGouS-24
55RobGouW-24
75JohMiz-1
76TayBow4-12
76TayBow4-112
79TCM50-67
83Bra53F-4
83TCMPla1943-45
83TopRep5-267
91TopArc1-117
Gordon, Tommy (Tom)
87EugEmeP-2673
87Ft.MyeRP-25
88AppFoxP-149
88MidLeaAGS-40
89Bow-115
89BowTif-115
89ClaTraP-182
89Don-45
89DonBasB-287
89DonRoo-4
89Fle-284
89FleGlo-284
89Sco-634
89ScoHot1R-68
89ScoSco-7
89ScoYouS2-2
89StaGor-1
89StaGor-2
89StaGor-3
89StaGor-4
89StaGor-5
89StaGor-6
89StaGor-7
89StaGor-8
89StaGor-9
89StaGor-10
89StaGor-11
89TopTra-38T
89TopTraT-38T
89UppDec-736
90Baz-21
90Bow-365
90BowTif-365
90ClaBlu-4
90Don-297
90Fle-108
90FleAwaW-15
90FleCan-108
90FleSoaS-7
90Hot50RS-18
90Lea-14
90OPC-752
90PanSti-89
90PubSti-348
90Sco-472
90Sco100RS-1

90Spo-30
90Top-752
90TopBig-252
90TopCoi-15
90TopGloS-30
90TopHeaU-21
90TopMinL-15
90TopRoo-10
90TopSti-268
90TopSti-322
90TopTif-752
90ToyRoo-12
90UppDec-365
90UppDecS-5
90VenSti-207
91Bow-311
91Don-242
91Fle-559
91Lea-132
91OPC-248
91PanFreS-284
91PanSti-231
91RoyPol-10
91Sco-197
91SimandSMLBL-17
91StaClu-254
91Top-248
91TopDesS-248
91TopMic-248
91TopTif-248
91Ult-147
91UppDec-431
92Bow-477
92ClaGam-82
92Don-250
92Fle-158
92Lea-68
92OPC-431
92Pin-238
92PinTea2-58
92RoyPol-8
92Sco-130
92ScoImpP-69
92StaClu-388
92Stu-182
92Top-431
92TopGol-431
92TopGolW-431
92TopMic-431
92Ult-370
92UppDec-476
93Don-497
93Fla-215
93Fle-237
93Lea-211
93OPC-75
93PacSpa-134
93Pin-105
93RoyPol-9
93Sco-184
93StaClu-523
93StaCluFDI-523
93StaCluMOP-523
93StaCluRoy-3
93Top-611
93TopGol-611
93TopInaM-611
93TopMic-611
93Ult-207
93UppDec-221
93UppDecGold-221
94ColC-112
94ColChoGS-112
94ColChoSS-112
94Don-450
94ExtBas-88
94Fin-397
94FinRef-397
94Fla-299
94Fle-155
94Lea-389
94Pac-283
94PanSti-73
94Pin-317
94PinArtP-317
94PinMusC-317
94ProMag-61
94Sco-234
94ScoGolR-234
94Sel-118
94Top-66
94TopGol-66
94TopSpa-66
94TriPla-234
94Ult-364
94UppDec-474
94UppDecED-474
95ColCho-461
95ColChoGS-461
95ColChoSS-461
95Don-494
95DonPreP-494
95DonTopotO-88
95Fla-264
95Fle-158
95Lea-249
95Pin-411
95PinArtP-411
95PinMusC-411
95Sco-464
95ScoGolR-464
95ScoPlaTS-464
95StaClu-455
95StaCluMOP-455
95StaCluSTWS-455
95StaCluVR-245
95Top-475
95TopCyb-268
95Ult-289
95UltGolM-289
95UppDec-418
95UppDecED-418
95UppDecEDG-418
95UppDecSE-53
95UppDecSEG-53
96ColCho-169
96ColCho-763
96ColChoGS-169
96ColChoSS-169
96Don-494
96DonPreP-494
96Fla-18
96Fle-127
96FleRedS-6
96FleTif-127
96FleUpd-U12
96FleUpdTC-U12
96MetUni-15
96MetUniP-15
96Pac-335
96Pin-9
96Pin-330
96PinFoil-330
96Sco-453
95StaCluVRMC-245
96Ult-70
96Ult-314
96UltGolM-70
96UltGolM-314
96UppDec-286
97Cir-361
97CirRav-361
97ColCho-48
97Fle-23
97FleTif-23
97MetUni-22
97Pac-40
97PacLigB-40
97PacSil-40
97Sco-119
97ScoPreS-119
97ScoRedS-5
97ScoRedSPl-5
97ScoRedSPr-5
97ScoShoS-119
97ScoShoSAP-119
97SP-37
97Ult-14
97UltGolME-14
97UltPlaME-14
97UppDec-311

Gordon, Tony
92SarWhiSF-200
93SarWhiSC-11
94ElPasDF-3142

Gore, Arthur
55Bow-289

Gore, Brad
91OklStaC-10
92OklStaC-10

Gore, Bryan
90ChaRanS-8
91LinDriAA-581
91TulDriLD-581
91TulDriP-2767
91TulDriTI-8
92TulDriF-2690
92TulDriS-606

Gore, George
87BucN28-69
87OldJudN-213
88WG1CarG-40
89SFHaCN-9
90HOFStiB-6

Gore, Kevin
89GenCubP-1865

Gore, Ricky
89IdaFalBP-2017

Gorecki, Rick
91GreFalDSP-24
91HigSchPLS-20
92BakDodCLC-12
92UppDecML-109
93Bow-266
93ClaFS7-136
93SanAntMF-2999
94AlbDukF-837
94Bow-482
94BowBes-B40
94BowBesR-B40
94Cla-145
94ExcFS7-213
94UppDecML-163
95Bow-80

Gorecki, Ryan
95HudValRTI-7

Gorey, Steve
86ModA'sP-9

Gorham, Bobby
92EveGiaC-25
92EveGiaF-1678

Gorin, Charles
54BraJohC-15
55BraGolS-13
55BraJohC-15
92TexLon-17

Gorinski, Bob
75TacTwiK-9
76TacTwiDQ-8
78Top-386
79TidTidT-24

Gorman, Bill
82OmaRoyT-24
83OmaRoyT-23
84OmaRoyT-14
85OmaRoyT-1
95OmaRoyTI-10
96OmaRoyB-7

Gorman, Dave
89UtiBluSP-9
90UtiBluSP-18

Gorman, Dirk
90KisDodD-12

Gorman, Hubert
49W72HolS-5
50W720HolS-10

Gorman, Mike
84ModA'sC-13
86GleFalTP-7

Gorman, Paul
91DaiDolF-14
95AusFut-8
95AusFut-92

Gorman, Tom (Thomas A.)
53BowBW-61
53Dor-134
54Bow-17
55A'sRodM-16
56Top-246
57Top-87
58Top-235
59Top-449
76A'sRodMC-11

Gorman, Tom (Thomas D.)
55Bow-293
84FifNatC-1

Gorman, Tom (Thomas P.)
80MemChiT-4
82WicAerTI-5
83TidTidT-11
84Nes792-774
84TidTidT-14
84Top-774
84TopTif-774
85Fle-83
85MetColP-31
85MetTCM-13
85Top-53
85TopTif-53
86Fle-82
86MetTCM-6
86PorBeaP-7
86Top-414
86TopTif-414
91MetWIZ-146

Gorsica, John
47TipTop-32
79DiaGre-384

Gorski, Gary
86SalAngC-82
88ModA'sCLC-62
88ModA'sTI-11
89ModA'sC-12

Gorton, Chris
89HamRedS-15
90Bes-181
90SprCarB-20
91St.PetCC-7
91St.PetCP-2270

Goryl, John
58Top-384
59Top-77
59TopVen-77
61TwiCloD-7
62Top-558
63Top-314
64Top-194
64TopVen-194
77OrlTwiT-12
78OrlTwiT-7
78TwiFri-30
79TwiFriP-8
81Don-527
81Top-669
82Ind-16
82IndBurK-3
82IndBurK-4
82IndTeal-15
82IndWhe-16
83IndWhe-15
84Ind-15
84IndWhe-NNO
85Ind-15
85IndPol-NNO
86IndOhH-NNO
86IndTeal-22
87IndGat-NNO
88IndGat-45

Goselin, Scott
88PulBraP-1751
89SumBraP-1107

Gosger, Jim
63Top-553
66OPC-114
66Top-114
66TopVen-114
67CokCapAt-18
67OPC-17
67Top-17
68Top-343
68TopVen-343
69MilBra-95
69PilPos-16
69Top-482A
69Top-482B
69TopTeaP-9
70ExpPin-6
70Top-651
71ExpLaPR-4
71ExpPS-8
71MLBOffS-128
71OPC-284
71Top-284
72MilBra-119
74MetDaiPA-7
81RedSoxBG2S-82
83Pil69G-7
91MetWIZ-147

Goshay, Henry Lee
88VerBeaDS-8
89DunBluJS-5

Goshgarian, Dee Marge
91SalSpuC-28

Goslin, Goose (Leon)
21Nei-8
22E120-108
22W573-49
25Exh-123
26Exh-123
26SpoComoA-16
27Exh-61
27YorCarE-49
28Exh-61
28PorandAR-A11
28PorandAR-B11
28W502-49
28W56PlaC-C10
28Yue-49
29ExhFou-31
29PorandAR-30
30SchR33-27
31Exh-29
31W517-47
33CraJacP-9
33DelR33-24
33DouDisP-21
33ExhFou-15
33GeoCMil-15
33Gou-110
33Gou-168
33TatOrbSDR-173
34BatR31-85
34ExhFou-12
35ExhFou-12
35GolMedFR-6
35GouPreR-10
35GouPuzR-5F
35GouPuzR-6F
35GouPuzR-11H
35GouPuzR-13F
35TigFreP-8
35WheBB1-14
36ExhFou-12
36GouWidPPR-A40
36NatChiFPR-33
36NatChiFPR-120
36R31PasP-30
36WorWidGV-43
37ExhFou-12
37OPCBatUV-111
40PlaBal-232
48SweSpoT-13
60SenUniMC-5
61Fle-35
76RowExh-7
76ShaPiz-110
76TigOldTS-10
77BobParHoF-23
77GalGloG-60
78TigDeaCS-5
80PacLeg-104
80PerHaloFP-109
80SSPHOF-109
81DiaStaCD-112
81TigDetN-124
81TigSecNP-18
84OCoandSI-217
87ConSer2-38
90PerGreM-78
91ConTSN-62
91ConTSNP-520
92ConTSN-437
93ConTSN-907
95ConTSN-1385

Gosnell, Mark
93Sou-4

Goss, Howie
57JetPos-6
58JetPos-8
62Top-598
63Top-364

Gossage, Goose (Rich)
73OPC-174
73Top-174
74OPC-542
74Top-542
75OPC-554
75Top-554
76Hos-77
76OPC-180
76OPC-205
76SSP-156
76Top-180
76Top-205
77Hos-128
77PirPosP-9
77Spo-7524
77Top-319
78Kel-8
78RCColC-50
78Top-70
78YanBurK-10
79Hos-48
79OPC-114
79Top-8
79Top-225
79YanBurK-10
79YanPicA-14
80OPC-77
80Top-140

81AllGamPI-81
81Don-347
81Fle-89
81FleStiC-118
81Kel-41
81MSAMinD-14
81OPC-48
81Top-460
81TopSti-8
81TopSti-113
81TopSti-251
81TopSupHT-63
81TopSupN-7
82Don-283
82FBIDis-8
82Fle-37
82FleSta-116
82Kel-32
82OPC-117
82OPC-286
82OPC-396
82Top-557
82Top-770
82Top-771
82TopSti-140
82TopSti-217
83Don-157
83Fle-381
83FleSta-70
83FleSti-36
83Kel-10
83OPC-240
83OPC-241
83Top-240
83Top-241
83TopFol-4
83TopGloS-11
83TopSti-100
83YanRoyRD-2
84AllGamPI-78
84Don-396
84Fle-125
84FleUpd-44
84FunFooP-85
84Nes792-670
84Nes792-718
84OPC-121
84PadMot-2
84SevCoi-E22
84Top-670
84Top-718
84TopRubD-8
84TopSti-316
84TopTif-670
84TopTif-718
84TopTra-43T
84TopTraT-43T
85AllGamPI-170
85Don-185
85DonActA-14
85Fle-33
85Fle-633
85FleLimE-10
85FleStaS-108
85KASDis-3
85KitCloD-3
85Lea-204
85OPC-90
85PadMot-5
85SevCoi-W9
85ThoMcAD-30
85Top-90
85Top3-D-27
85TopGloS-19
85TopRubD-22
85TopSti-147
85TopSup-49
85TopTif-90
86BasStaB-48
86Don-2
86Don-185
86DonAll-31
86DonSupD-2
86Fle-322
86FleMin-68
86FleSlu-12
86Lea-2
86MeaGolSB-20
86OPC-100
86SevCoi-C7
86SevCoi-E7
86SevCoi-S7
86SevCoi-W7
86Spo-55
86Spo-190
86Top-530
86Top3-D-6
86TopGloS-56
86TopSti-107
86TopSup-26
86TopTat-1
86TopTif-530
87ClaGam-96
87Don-483
87Fle-415
87FleGlo-415
87FleLeaL-21
87OPC-380
87PadBohHB-54
87RedFolSB-9
87Top-380
87TopSti-109
87TopTif-380
88CubDavB-54
88Don-434
88DonBasB-26
88DonTeaBC-NEW
88Fle-583
88FleGlo-583
88FleUpd-76
88FleUpdG-76
88OPC-170
88Sco-331
88ScoGlo-331
88ScoRoo-14T
88ScoRooG-14T
88StaLinPa-3
88Top-170
88TopTif-170
88TopTra-41T
88TopTraT-41T
89Don-158
89Fle-425
89FleGlo-425
89GiaMot-27
89OPC-162
89OPCBoxB-D
89Sco-223
89Top-415
89TopBasT-101
89TopTif-415
89TopWaxBC-D
89UppDec-452
90Don-678
90PubSti-68
90VenSti-208
91Bow-271
91Cla3-T98
91FleUpd-59
91Lea-236
91RanMot-16
91Stu-125
92AthMot-12
92Don-555
92Fle-305
92Lea-474
92OPC-215
92PacRyaTEI-198
92Sco-538
92StaClu-719
92Top-215
92TopGol-215
92TopGolW-215
92TopMic-215
92YanWIZ7-56
92YanWIZ8-67
92YanWIZA-25
93AthMot-16
93Fla-259
93FleFinE-255
93PacSpa-567
93RanKee-162
93StaClu-17
93StaCluFDI-17
93StaCluMOP-17
93Ult-606
94Fle-262
94MarMot-12
94Pac-450
94Sco-260
94ScoGolR-260
94StaClu-191
94StaCluFDI-191
94StaCluGR-191
94StaCluMOP-191
95ColCho-285
95ColChoGS-285
95ColChoSE-126
95ColChoSE-262
95ColChoSEGS-126
95ColChoSEGS-262
95ColChoSESS-126
95ColChoSESS-262
95ColChoSS-285
95Fle-268
95Pac-397
95Sco-74
95ScoGolR-74
95ScoPlaTS-74
95UppDec-98
95UppDecED-98
95UppDecEDG-98

Gosse, John
80WesHavWCT-19A

Gosselin, Pat
93WelPirF-3363

Gotay, Julio
62CarJayP-4
62Top-489
63Jel-161
63PirIDL-10
63Pos-161
63Top-122
64PirKDK-13
65Top-552
67Ast-12
68CokCapA-4
68DexPre-35
68OPC-41
68Top-41
68TopVen-41
69MilBra-96
87AstShoSTw-8

Gotay, Ruben
83ArkTraT-2

Gott, Jim (James)
81ArkTraT-17
83Don-353
83OPC-62
83Top-506
84BluJayFS-14
84Don-268
84Fle-155
84Nes792-9
84OPC-9
84Top-9
84TopTif-9
85Don-632
85Fle-105
85FleUpd-45
85GiaMot-21
85GiaPos-11
85Lea-136
85OPC-311
85Top-311
85TopTif-311
85TopTifT-40T
85TopTra-40T
86Don-358
86Fle-542
86GiaMot-21
86OPC-106
86Top-463
86TopTif-463
87FleUpd-35
87FleUpdG-35
87GiaMot-19
87Top-231
87TopTif-231
87TopTra-39T
87TopTraT-39T
88Don-606
88DonBasB-213
88FleUpd-112
88FleUpdG-112
88Lea-253
88Sco-320
88ScoGlo-320
88StaLinPi-12
88Top-127
88TopTif-127
89Bow-411
89BowTif-411
89Don-362
89Fle-210
89FleExcS-16
89FleGlo-210
89FleSup-18
89OPC-172
89PanSti-163
89PirVerFJ-35
89Sco-257
89ScoHot1S-98
89Spo-83
89Top-752
89TopMinL-32
89TopTif-752
89UppDec-539
90DodMot-24
90DodPol-35
90Don-605
90Fle-466
90FleCan-466
90OPC-292
90PubSti-155
90Sco-515
90Top-292
90TopTif-292
90UppDec-89A
90UppDec-89B
90UppDec-701
90VenSti-209
91DodMot-24
91DodPol-35
91Don-601
91Fle-200
91Lea-229
91OPC-606
91Sco-621
91Top-606
91TopDesS-606
91TopMic-606
91TopTif-606
91UppDec-690
92DodMot-15
92DodPol-35
92DodSmo-4892
92Don-601
92Fle-454
92OPC-517
92Pin-228
92Pin-596
92Sco-172
92StaClu-483
92Top-517
92TopGol-517
92TopGolW-517
92TopMic-517
92Ult-504
93DodMot-17
93DodPol-6
93Don-670
93Fla-69
93Fle-447
93Lea-511
93PacSpa-499
93Pin-435
93Sco-422
93StaClu-487
93StaCluD-7
93StaCluFDI-487
93StaCluMOP-487
93Top-418
93TopGol-418
93TopInaM-418
93TopMic-418
93UppDec-666
93UppDecGold-666
94ColC-113
94ColChoGS-113
94ColChoSS-113
94DodMot-18
94DodPol-8
94Don-92
94Fin-49
94FinRef-49
94Fle-509
94Lea-205
94Pac-307
94Pin-307
94PinArtP-307
94PinMusC-307
94Sco-402
94ScoGolR-402
94Top-87
94TopGol-87
94TopSpa-87
94Ult-215
94UppDec-336
94UppDecED-336
95FleUpd-148
95PirFil-12
95Sco-268
95ScoGolR-268
95ScoPlaTS-268
95Top-332

Gottsch, J.J.
94ButCopKSP-20

Goucher, Steve
89SanDieSAS-10
91BenBucC-6
91BenBucP-3691

Goughan, Bob
88RocRedWGCP-32

Gould, Bob
85MadMusP-11
85MadMusT-14
86MadMusP-9
87ModA'sC-5
87ModA'sP-11

Gould, Clint
96LanJetB-14

Gould, Frank
90EveGiaB-5
90EveGiaP-3121

Goulding, Rich
77CliDodT-9
78LodDodT-6

Gouldrup, Gary
85ElmPioT-8

Goulet, Michel
91StaCluMO-43

Gourdin, Tom
94ForWayWC-9
94ForWayWF-2004
95ForWayWTI-6
96FtMyeMB-21

Goure, Samuel
96MedHatBJTI-10

Gourlay, Matthew
96MedHatBJTI-11

Gousha, Sean
92EriSaiC-18
92EriSaiF-1626
93HigDesMC-5
93HigDesMF-44
94PorSeaDF-680
94PorSeaDTI-14

Gouthro, Laurie
95ColSilB-9

Gowdy, Hank
12T207-68
14B18B-48A
14B18B-48B
14B18B-48C
14CraJacE-138
15CraJacE-138
15SpoNewM-70
16BF2FP-52
16ColE13-62
16FleBreD-33
16SpoNewM-70
17HolBreD-36
19W514-67
20NatCarE-34
21E121So1-33
21E121So8-29
21Exh-59
21Exh-60
22AmeCarE-23
22E120-126
22W572-33
22W573-50
22W575-45
23W501-91
23W503-62
23WilChoV-52
34DiaMatCSB-71
36NatChiFPR-34
38CinOraW-12
39OrcPhoAP-11
40PlaBal-82
41HarHarW-8
72FleFamF-33
81ConTSN-26
87ConSer2-39
88ConSer3-12
91ConTSN-209
95ConTSN-1325
20W516-22

Gowell, Larry
73SyrChiTI-9
92YanWIZ7-57

Gozzo, Goose (Mauro)
84LitFalMT-21
86LynMetP-13
87MemChiB-20
87MemChiP-3
88MemChiB-16
89KnoBluJB-8

89KnoBluJP-1145
89KnoBluJS-6
89Sta-121
90CMC-328
90Don-655
90Fle-82
90FleCan-82
90OPC-274
90ProAAAF-345
90Sco-610
90Sco100RS-48
90Spo-168
90SyrChiC-2
90SyrChiMB-11
90SyrChiP-565
90Top-274
90TopDeb89-44
90TopTif-274
91ColSprSSLD-82
91ColSprSSP-2179
91LinDriAAA-82
91MajLeaCP-19
91Sco-843
92PorBeaF-2661
92PorBeaS-407
93NorTidF-2564
94NorTidF-2913

Grabarkewitz, Bill
70DayDaiNM-57
70OPC-446
70Top-446
71DodTic-7
71Kel-56
71MilDud-44
71MLBOffS-104
71OPC-85
71Top-85
71TopCoi-21
71TopTat-35
72Top-578
73OPC-301
73Top-301
74OPC-214
74Top-214
74TopSta-74
75OPC-233
75Top-233
75TucTorC-1
75TucTorTI-4
87DodSmoA-9
89DodSmoG-76
90DodTar-291
92DodStaTA-9

Graber, Red
61UniOil-SP6

Grable, Rob
91NiaFalRC-14
91NiaFalRP-3641
92FayGenC-18
92ProFS7-69
93ClePhiC-12
93ClePhiF-2690
93FloStaLAF-26
94ClaGolF-37
94ReaPhiF-2069
95ReaPhiELC-15
95ReaPhiTI-34
95TopTra-107T
96Exc-202

Grabowski, Johnny
91ConTSN-124

Grabowski, Mike
75WesPalBES-19

Grabowski, Ray
34ButPreR-27

Grace, Earl
34DiaMatCSB-72
34BatR31-69
34DiaStaR-69
34Gou-58
35DiaMatCS3T1-61
36GouWidPPR-A41
36WorWidGV-103
93ConTSN-938

Grace, Joe
41BroW75-12
46SeaSLP-20
49SolSunP-4
52MotCoo-5

Grace, Mark
86PeoChiP-8
87PitCubP-10
88CubDavB-17
88Don-40
88DonBasB-4
88DonRoo-1
88DonTeaBC-40
88Fle-641
88FleGlo-641
88FleMin-68
88FleUpd-77
88FleUpdG-77
88IowCubC-14
88IowCubP-539
88Lea-40
88PeoChiTI-11
88PeoChiTI-34
88SanDieSAAG-6
88ScoRoo-80T
88ScoRooG-80T
88TopTra-42T
88TopTraT-42T
89Baz-12
89Bow-291
89BowTif-291
89ClaLigB-13
89ClaTraP-155
89CubMar-17
89Don-17
89Don-255
89DonSupD-17
89Fle-426
89FleBasM-15
89FleExcS-17
89FleGlo-426
89FleLeaL-17
89FleSup-19
89K-M-1
89MSAHolD-12
89Nis-12A
89Nis-12B
89OPC-297
89PanSti-55
89Sco-362
89ScoHot1R-78
89ScoSco-22
89ScoYouSI-3
89Spo-15
89SpoIllFKI-283
89Top-465
89TopBig-189
89TopCoi-15
89TopGloS-29
89TopHeaUT-15
89TopRoo-11
89TopSti-50
89TopSti-324
89TopTif-465
89ToyRoo-12
89TVSpoM-17
89UppDec-140
89UppDecS-1
90Bow-29
90BowTif-29
90ClaBlu-8
90Col-31
90ColPosG-1
90ColPosG-2
90ColPosG-3
90ColPosG-4
90ColPosG-5
90ColPosG-6
90ColPosG-7
90ColPosG-8
90CubMar-9
90Don-577
90DonBesN-51
90Fle-32
90FleBasA-12
90FleCan-32
90FleLeaL-12
90FleLeaS-6
90Hot50PS-17
90Lea-137
90MLBBasB-51
90NikMin-1
90OPC-240
90PanSti-241
90Pos-19
90PubSti-194
90PubSti-613
90RedFolSB-38
90Sco-150
90Sco100S-60
90Spo-15
90StaCla-3
90StaCla-5
90StaCla-7
90StaCla-9
90StaCla-11
90StaLonJS-2
90StaLonJS-16
90StaLonJS-40
90Top-240
90TopBig-19
90TopDou-27
90TopGloS-12
90TopMinL-49
90TopSti-56
90TopTif-240
90TopTVA-63
90TopTVCu-23
90UppDec-128
90VenSti-210
90VenSti-211
90W/RMarG-1
90W/RMarG-2
90W/RMarG-3
90W/RMarG-4
90W/RMarG-5
90W/RMarG-6
90W/RMarG-7
90W/RMarG-8
90W/RMarG-9
91Bow-433
91CadElID-25
91Cla1-T27
91ClaGam-105
91Col-20
91CubMar-17
91CubVinL-12
91Don-199
91Fle-422
91Lea-170
91MajLeaCP-66
91OPC-520
91PanFreS-43
91PanSti-48
91Pos-22
91Sco-175
91Sco100S-91
91SevCoi-M6
91StaClu-290
91Stu-157
91Top-520
91TopCraJI-24
91TopDesS-520
91TopMic-520
91TopSta-16
91TopTif-520
91TopTriH-N2
91Ult-61
91UppDec-99
91UppDec-134
92Bow-580
92ClaGam-29
92CubMar-17
92Don-281
92DonCraJ2-5
92Fle-381
92Hig5-28
92Lea-26
92OPC-140
92PanSti-182
92Pin-136
92Sco-445
92Sco100S-20
92SpoIllFK1-430
92SpoStaCC-18
92StaClu-174
92Stu-14
92Top-140
92TopGol-140
92TopGolW-140
92TopKid-4
92TopMic-140
92TriPla-114
92Ult-175
92UppDec-143
93Bow-440
93CadDis-27
93CubMar-7
93DiaMar-42
93Don-532
93Fin-73
93FinRef-73
93Fla-14
93Fle-20
93FleFruotL-24
93FunPac-81
93HumDumC-28
93Lea-198
93LeaGolA-R12
93LeaGolA-U10
93MetBak-29
93OPC-86
93PacJugC-27
93PacSpa-58
93PanSti-203
93Pin-34
93Sco-50
93Sel-73
93SelStaL-12
93SP-83
93StaClu-419
93StaCluCu-8
93StaCluFDI-419
93StaCluMO-10
93StaCluMOP-419
93StaCluMP-18
93Stu-42
93StuHer-5
93StuSupoC-8
93Top-630
93TopGol-630
93TopInaM-630
93TopMic-630
93TriPla-11
93TriPla-211
93TriPlaP-11
93Ult-18
93UltAwaW-3
93UppDec-483
93UppDec-573
93UppDecGold-483
93UppDecGold-573
93UppDecIC-WI8
93UppDecICJ-WI8
94Bow-410
94BowBes-R9
94BowBesR-R9
94ColC-114
94ColChoGS-114
94ColChoSS-114
94Don-358
94DonMVP-2
94DonSpeE-358
94ExtBas-218
94ExtBasGB-13
94Fin-390
94FinRef-390
94Fla-360
94Fle-383
94FleAllS-37
94FUnPac-17
94Kra-23
94Lea-43
94LeaGam-6
94LeaL-90
94OPC-146
94Pac-98
94PacSilP-25
94PanSti-153
94Pin-336
94PinArtP-336
94PinMusC-336
94PinRunC-RC34
94Pos-14
94ProMag-22
94RedFolMI-11
94Sco-42
94ScoGolR-42
94ScoGolS-3
94Sel-230
94SP-69
94SPDieC-69
94Spo-120
94StaClu-403
94StaCluFDI-403
94StaCluGR-403
94StaCluMO-10
94StaCluMOP-403
94StaCluT-339
94StaCluTFDI-339
94Stu-60
94TomPiz-6
94Top-360
94TopBlaG-33
94TopGol-360
94TopSpa-360
94TopSupS-18
94TriPla-72
94TriPlaM-4
94Ult-455
94UltAwaW-11
94UltOnBL-5
94UppDec-440
94UppDecAJ-30
94UppDecAJG-30
94UppDecED-440
94USPlaCA-7D
95Baz-71
95BowBes-R19
95BowBesR-R19
95ClaPhoC-11
95ColCho-205
95ColChoGS-205
95ColChoSE-83
95ColChoSEGS-83
95ColChoSESS-83
95ColChoSS-205
95D3-35
95Don-519
95DonPreP-519
95DonTopotO-199
95Emo-110
95Fin-65
95FinRef-65
95Fla-332
95Fle-415
95Lea-277
95Lea300C-16
95LeaLim-8
95LeaLimIBP-8
95Pac-70
95PacPri-22
95PanSti-32
95Pin-371
95PinArtP-371
95PinMusC-371
95RedFol-13
95Sco-364
95ScoGolR-364
95ScoHaloG-HG86
95ScoPlaTS-364
95Sel-221
95SelArtP-221
95SelCer-90
95SelCerMG-90
95SP-38
95SPCha-29
95SPChaDC-29
95Spo-135
95SpoArtP-135
95SPSil-38
95StaClu-213
95StaClu-393
95StaCluFDI-213
95StaCluMOP-213
95StaCluMOP-393
95StaCluSTWS-213
95StaCluSTWS-393
95StaCluVR-206
95Stu-177
95Sum-26
95SumNthD-26
95Top-90
95TopCyb-61
95UC3-87
95UC3ArtP-87
95Ult-359
95UltGolM-359
95UppDec-65
95UppDecED-65
95UppDecEDG-65
95UppDecSE-257
95UppDecSEG-257
95Zen-70
96Baz-48
96Bow-35
96BowBes-89
96BowBesAR-89
96BowBesR-89
96Cir-109
96CirRav-109
96ColCho-80
96ColChoGS-80
96ColChoSS-80
96Don-189
96DonDiaK-14
96DonHitL-7
96DonPreP-189
96EmoXL-155
96EmoXLD-3
96Fin-B267
96Fin-S189
96Fin-S341
96FinRef-B267
96FinRef-S189
96FinRef-S341

96Fla-216
96Fle-319
96FleCub-7
96FleTif-319
96FleUpd-U222
96FleUpdTC-U222
96Lea-126
96LeaLim-54
96LeaLimG-54
96LeaPre-51
96LeaPreP-51
96LeaPrePB-126
96LeaPrePG-126
96LeaPrePS-126
96LeaPreSG-54
96LeaPreSte-54
96LeaSig-49
96LeaSigPPG-49
96LeaSigPPP-49
96MetUni-141
96MetUniP-141
96Pac-31
96PacPri-P10
96PacPriG-P10
96PanSti-47
96Pin-243
96Pin-306
96PinAfi-52
96PinAfiAP-52
96PinAfiFPP-52
96PinArtP-143
96PinArtP-191
96PinFoil-243
96PinFoil-306
96PinSta-143
96PinSta-191
96ProSta-36
96Sco-19
96ScoDugC-A18
96ScoDugCAP-A18
96Sel-81
96SelArtP-81
96SelCer-94
96SelCerAP-94
96SelCerCB-94
96SelCerCR-94
96SelCerMB-94
96SelCerMG-94
96SelCerMR-94
96SelTeaN-15
96SP-54
96Spo-82
96SpoArtP-82
96SPx-15
96SPxGol-15
96StaClu-160
96StaCluEPB-160
96StaCluEPG-160
96StaCluEPS-160
96StaCluMO-14
96StaCluMOP-160
95StaCluVRMC-206
96Stu-140
96StuPrePB-140
96StuPrePG-140
96StuPrePS-140
96Sum-145
96SumAbo&B-145
96SumArtP-145
96SumFoi-145
96TeaOut-31
96Top-55
96TopChr-20
96TopChrR-20
96TopGal-180
96TopGalPPI-180
96TopLas-23
96Ult-168
96UltGolM-168
96UltPriL-11
96UltPriLGM-11
96UltRaw-3
96UltRawGM-3
96UppDec-295
96Zen-73
96ZenArtP-73
96ZenMoz-6
97Bow-237
97BowBes-16
97BowBesAR-16
97BowBesR-16
97BowChr-64
97BowChrI-64
97BowChrIR-64
97BowChrR-64
97BowInt-237
97Cir-316
97CirRav-316
97ColCho-290
97Don-120
97DonEli-86
97DonEliGS-86
97DonLim-71
97DonLim-156
97DonLimFotG-66
97DonLimLE-71
97DonLimLE-156
97DonPre-84
97DonPreCttC-84
97DonPreP-120
97DonPrePGold-120
97Fin-141
97Fin-262
97FinEmb-141
97FinEmbR-141
97FinRef-141
97FinRef-262
97FlaSho-A172
97FlaSho-B172
97FlaSho-C172
97FlaShoLC-172
97FlaShoLC-B172
97FlaShoLC-C172
97FlaShoLCM-A172
97FlaShoLCM-B172
97FlaShoLCM-C172
97Fle-276
97FleTeaL-16
97FleTif-276
97Lea-13
97Lea-305
97LeaFraM-13
97LeaFraM-395
97LeaFraMDC-13
97LeaFraMDC-395
97MetUni-141
97NewPin-39
97NewPinAP-39
97NewPinMC-39
97NewPinPP-39
97Pac-250
97PacLigB-250
97PacPri-84
97PacPriLB-84
97PacPriP-84
97PacSil-250
97Pin-106
97PinArtP-106
97PinIns-96
97PinInsCE-96
97PinInsDE-96
97PinMusC-106
97PinX-P-71
97PinX-PMoS-71
97Sco-179
97ScoPreS-179
97ScoShoS-179
97ScoShoSAP-179
97Sel-37
97SelArtP-37
97SelRegG-37
97SkyE-X-61
97SkyE-XC-61
97SkyE-XEC-61
97SP-44
97SpoIll-96
97SpoIllEE-96
97StaClu-53
97StaCluMat-53
97StaCluMOP-53
97StaCluMOP-PL10
97StaCluPL-PL10
97Stu-66
97StuPrePG-66
97StuPrePS-66
97Top-37
97TopChr-13
97TopChrR-13
97TopGal-48
97TopGalPPI-48
97TopSta-49
97TopStaAM-49
97TopSweS-SS5
97Ult-164
97UltDouT-12
97UltFieC-5
97UltGolME-164
97UltPlaME-164
97UppDec-35
97UppDec-141

Grace, Michael
80VenLeaS-173
87AncGlaP-15
90RocExpLC-9
90RocExpP-2702
95ReaPhiTI-35

Grace, Mike
77IndIndTI-12
78IndIndTI-16
79IndIndTI-18
80IndIndTI-4
83ColAstT-4
89SalLakTTI-14
91BatCliC-22
91BatCliP-3478
91Cla/Bes-431
91WinSpiC-20
91WinSpiP-2837
92ChaKniF-2780
92ChaKniS-156
92SkyAA F-72
92UppDecML-217
93OrlCubF-2792
95ReaPhiELC-16
96Bow-341
96BowBes-43
96BowBesAR-43
96BowBesR-43
96Fin-S317
96FinRef-S317
96FleUpd-U164
96FleUpdNH-7
96FleUpdTC-U164
96LeaLimR-7
96LeaLimRG-7
96LeaPre-125
96LeaPreP-125
96LeaSigA-83
96LeaSigAG-83
96LeaSigAS-83
96PhiTeal-14
96PinAfi-172
96PinAfiAP-172
96Sel-178
96SelArtP-178
96SelCer-109
96SelCerAP-109
96SelCerCB-109
96SelCerCR-109
96SelCerMB-109
96SelCerMG-109
96SelCerMR-109
96SP-13
96Sum-186
96SumAbo&B-186
96SumArtP-186
96SumFoi-186
96Ult-521
96UltGolM-521
96UppDec-246
96Zen-114
96ZenArtP-114
97Fle-412
97FleTif-412
97Lea-69
97LeaFraM-69
97LeaFraMDC-69
97Sco-292
97ScoPreS-292
97ScoShoS-292
97ScoShoSAP-292
97StaClu-137
97StaCluMOP-137
97Top-242
97Ult-250
97UltGolME-250
97UltPlaME-250

Grace, Willie
92NegLeaRLI-25
95NegLeaL2-29

Grachen, Tim
83QuaCitCT-12

Grady, Pat
80BatTroT-26

Graff, Milt
57Top-369
58Top-192
59Top-182
59TopVen-182

Graff, Stephen
86EriCarP-9

Graffanino, Tony (Anthony)
91IdaFalBP-4335
91IdaFalBSP-5
92ClaFS7-372
92MacBraC-1
92MacBraF-273
92ProFS7-195
93CarLeaAGF-37
93DurBulC-8
93DurBulF-490
93DurBulTI-22
94Bow-601
94ExcFS7-153
94GreBraF-420
94GreBraTI-11
94UppDecML-166
95Exc-150
95RicBraTI-4
95Top-645
95UppDec-251
95UppDecED-251
95UppDecEDG-251
95UppDecML-46
96MLBPin-13
96RicBraB-14
96RicBraRC-4
96RicBraUB-9
97Bow-388
97BowInt-388
97Don-382
97DonPreP-382
97DonPrePGold-382
97DonTea-29
97DonTeaSPE-29
97FlaSho-A130
97FlaSho-B130
97FlaSho-C130
97FlaShoLC-130
97FlaShoLC-B130
97FlaShoLC-C130
97FlaShoLCM-A130
97FlaShoLCM-B130
97FlaShoLCM-C130
97Fle-617
97FleTif-617
97ScoPreS-311
97Ult-489
97UltGolME-489
97UltPlaME-489
95UppDecMLFS-46

Graham, Bert
09PC7HHB-16
11SpoLifM-108

Graham, Bill
09T206-144
77FriOneYW-46
91MetWIZ-148

Graham, Brian
83MadMusF-28
84AlbA'sT-6
85HunStaJ-14
87KinIndP-11
88EasLeaAP-51
88WilBilP-1313
89WatIndS-11
90CarLeaA-32
90KinIndTI-28
91CarLeaAP-CAR16
91KinIndC-28
91KinIndP-340
92CanIndF-706
92CanIndS-124
93CanIndF-2852
94ChaKniF-909
96BufBisB-1

Graham, Bruce
85EveGialC-3
86EveGiaPC-7
87EveGiaC-33
89PhoFirP-1488

Graham, Dan
77TacTwiDQ-25
79TolMudHT-6
80Top-669
80VenLeaS-188
81Don-233
81Fle-189
81OPC-161
81Top-161
82Don-455
82Fle-167
82RocRedWT-10
82Top-37
91OriCro-161

Graham, Derrick
91BilMusP-3766
91BilMusSP-9
92BenMusSP-20
92BilMusF-3362

Graham, Everett
82CliGiaF-10
86PhoFirP-7
87ShrCapP-1
88PhoFirC-20
88PhoFirP-60
89MidAngGS-16

Graham, Gordie
91BluOriC-2
91BluOriP-4134

Graham, Greg
91WinHavRSC-18
91WinHavRSP-497
92NewBriRSF-441
92NewBriRSS-486
94BinMetF-710
95NorTidTI-13
93StLucMF-2928

Graham, Jack
50Bow-145
90DodTar-292

Graham, Jeffrey L.
87SprCarB-9

Graham, Jeremy
93DavLipB-10

Graham, Johnny (John)
88AubAstP-1971
89AubAstP-2177
90AubAstB-20

Graham, Lee
81PawRedST-19
83PawRedST-22
84PawRedST-2
85RicBraT-19
86RicBraP-7

Graham, Lew
84LitFalMT-23

Graham, Lindsey
74GasRanT-11

Graham, Mark
93PocPosF-4204
93PocPosSP-6

Graham, Moonlight (Archibald)
93MooGra-1
93MooGra-2
93MooGra-3
93MooGra-4

Graham, Nancy
92WesPalBEC-28

Graham, Otto
52Whe-13A
52Whe-13B
74NewYorNTDiS-40

Graham, Peaches (George)
09AmeCarE-44
09RamT20-51
09T206-145
11MecDFT-24
11S74Sil-43
11S74Sil-62
11SpoLifM-140
11T205-66A
11T205-66B
11TurRedT-95
12ColRedB-117
12HasTriFT-70B
12T207-69

Graham, Randy
83GreHorT-8
84NasSouTI-8
85AlbYanT-8
86ColCliP-9
86ColCliP-10
87ColCliP-11
87ColCliP-19
87ColCliT-5

Graham, Rich
92BelMarC-5
92BelMarF-1436
93AppFoxC-9
93AppFoxF-2456
96SarRedSB-17

Graham, Steve
88HamRedP-1745
89HamRedS-13
90St.PetCS-9
94DanBraC-14

Graham, Tim
90ElmPioP-1

91ElmPioC-6
91ElmPioP-3283
92LynRedSC-12
92LynRedSF-2919
94HigDesMC-12
94HigDesMF-2799
Graham, Wayne
77FriOneYW-107
91MetWIZ-149
92TexLon-18
Graham, William
12ColTinT-117
Grahe, Joe
90MidAngGS-12
91Cla3-T27
91ClaGam-50
91Don-737
91EdmTraLD-164
91EdmTraP-1513
91LinDriAAA-164
91OPC-426
91Sco-367
91Top-426
91TopDeb90-58
91TopDesS-426
91TopMic-426
91TopTif-426
91UppDec-657
92ClaGam-68
92Don-445
92Lea-137
92OPC-496
92OPCPre-158
92Pin-371
92Sco-674
92Sco100RS-97
92StaClu-579
92Top-496
92TopGol-496
92TopGolW-496
92TopMic-496
92UppDec-542
93AngMot-27
93Bow-201
93Don-401
93Fle-192
93Lea-372
93OPC-199
93PacSpa-369
93Pin-412
93Sco-188
93Sel-374
93StaClu-262
93StaCluAn-18
93StaCluFDI-262
93StaCluMOP-262
93Top-129
93TopGol-129
93TopInaM-129
93TopMic-129
93TriPla-256
93Ult-165
93UppDec-290
93UppDecGold-290
94AngLAT-6
94AngMot-25
94ColC-467
94ColChoGS-467
94ColChoSS-467
94Don-454
94Fin-193
94FinRef-193
94Fle-58
94Lea-69
94Pac-79
94Sco-202
94ScoGolR-202
94Top-691
94TopGol-691
94TopSpa-691
94TriPla-16
94Ult-329
94UppDec-401
94UppDecED-401
95Fle-225
95Top-278
Grahek, Larry
81ChaRoyT-22
Grahovac, Mike
89EveGiaS-8
90CliGiaUTI-U5
91CliGiaP-837
Grain, Gregg
90ChaLooGS-3
Grajeda, Billy
92AriWilP-4
Gralewski, Bob
88CapCodPB-5
88CapCodPPaLP-154
Gramly, Tom
77FriOneYW-56
Grammas, Alex
54CarHunW-6
54Top-151
55Bow-186
55CarHunW-6
55Top-21
55TopDouH-107
55TopTesS-2
56Top-37
57RedSoh-6
57Top-222
58Top-254
59Top-6
59TopVen-6
60Top-168
60TopVen-168
61Pos-177A
61Pos-177B
61Top-64
61TopStal-87
62Jel-168
62Pos-168
62PosCan-168
62SalPlaC-197
62ShiPlaC-197
62Top-223
63Top-416
73OPC-296
73Top-296
74OPC-326
74Top-326
76OPC-606
76SSP-620
76Top-606
77Top-51
79DiaGre-174
83Tig-12
84TigWavP-17
88TigPep-NNO
89TigMar-NNO
90TigCok-28
91TigCok-NNO
94TopArc1-151
94TopArc1G-151
Granata, Chris
94WatIndC-13
94WatIndF-3930
96KenIndB-9
Granco, Julio
86SalAngC-79
Grandas, Bob
79OgdA'sT-25
79WatA'sT-20
80OgdA'sT-11
81TacTigT-27
82TacTigT-35
83EvaTriT-19
Grande, Marc
93EveGiaC-11
93EveGiaF-3764
Grandizio, Steve
95PeoChiTI-36
Grandquist, Ken
82IowCubT-27
83IowCubT-29
84IowCubT-5
85IowCubT-26
Grandy, Jack
92WatDiaC-29
Graney, Jack
12T207-70
14B18B-3A
14B18B-3B
15SpoNewM-71
16ColE13-63
16SpoNewM-71
17HolBreD-37
20NatCarE-35
21E121So1-34
21E121So8-30
22AmeCarE-24
22E120-34
22W573-51
22W575-46
23W501-113
77Ind192T-8
92ConTSN-481
94ConTSN-1247
94ConTSNB-1247
95ConTSN-1366
Granger, George
36GouWidPPR-D10
Granger, Greg
93BriTigF-3643
94FayGenC-13
94FayGenF-2139
Granger, Jeff
91TopTra-49T
91TopTraT-49T
92StaCluD-64
92TopDaiQTU-18
92TopTra-43T
92TopTraG-43T
93StaCluM-22
94ActPac-16
94Bow-527
94BowBes-R90
94BowBesR-R90
94ColC-23
94ColChoGS-23
94ColChoSS-23
94ExtBas-89
94FleMajLP-12
94MemChiF-352
94OPC-51
94Pin-269
94PinArtP-269
94PinMusC-269
94PinSam-269
94PinSam-NNO
94Sco-574
94ScoBoyoS-59
94ScoGolR-574
94Sel-399
94SP-172
94SPDieC-172
94Top-204
94TopGol-204
94TopSpa-204
94UppDec-14
94UppDecED-14
95ActPacF-20
95Bow-424
95ColCho-452
95ColChoGS-452
95ColChoSS-452
95Pin-443
95PinArtP-443
95PinMusC-443
95Sco-577
95ScoGolR-577
95ScoPlaTS-577
95Sel-143
95SelArtP-143
95Top-241
95WicWraTI-34
96OmaRoyB-12
97Fle-625
97FleTif-625
97PacPriGotD-GD47
Granger, Lee
82MiaMarT-19
83SanJosBC-4
84RocRedWT-7
85ChaO'sT-2
86ChaOriW-12
Granger, Wayne
69Top-551
70DayDaiNM-42
70MLBOffS-27
70OPC-73
70Top-73
71MLBOffS-59
71OPC-379
71Top-379
72Top-545
73OPC-523
73Top-523
74OPC-644
74Top-644
76ExpRed-13
76OPC-516
76Top-516
76VenLeaS-148
89PacSenL-202
92YanWIZ7-58
Grant, Bob
77LynMetT-15
77WauMetT-8
Grant, Brian
93MedHatBJF-3730
93MedHatBJSP-5
94St.CatBJC-10
94St.CatBJF-3636
Grant, Charles
52Par-10
Grant, Charlie
74LauOldTBS-23
86NegLeaF-70
Grant, Ed
08RosComP-140
09AmeCarE-45
09ColChiE-118A
09ColChiE-118B
10DomDisP-49
10LuxCigPP-10
10NadE1-19
10SweCapPP-100
11E94-15
11MecDFT-33
11S74Sil-75
11SpoLifCW-145
11SpoLifM-230
11T205-67
12ColRedB-118A
12ColRedB-118B
12ColTinT-118A
12ColTinT-118B
12HasTriFT-40
14B18B-68
95ConTSN-1323
Grant, Frank
74LauOldTBS-17
Grant, George
93ConTSN-957
Grant, Ken
86QuaCitAP-12
87PalSprP-7
88QuaCitAGS-21
88VisOakCLC-152
88VisOakP-86
Grant, Larry
90ElmPioP-6
91WinHavRSC-19
91WinHavRSP-498
Grant, Mark
82CliGiaF-23
84PhoGiaC-3
85DomLeaS-89
85Don-601
85PhoGiaC-199
86PhoFirP-8
87Don-644
87GiaMot-26
87SpoTeaP-10
88Don-511
88DonBasB-133
88Fle-584
88FleGlo-584
88PadCok-55
88PadSmo-9
88StaLinPa-4
88Top-752
88TopTif-752
89Fle-304
89FleGlo-304
89PadCok-5
89Sco-349
89ScoYouSI-12
89Top-178
89TopBig-154
89TopTif-178
89UppDec-622
90BraDubS-10
90Don-441
90Fle-156
90FleCan-156
90OPC-537
90PadCok-5
90PadMag-20
90PubSti-49
90Sco-466
90Top-537
90TopTif-537
90UppDec-412
90VenSti-212
91BraDubP-12
91BraSubS-16
91Don-361
91Fle-690
91OPC-287
91Sco-824
91Top-287
91TopDesS-287
91TopMic-287
91TopTif-287
91UppDec-301
92CalCanF-3727
92OPC-392
93AstMot-26
93Fle-675
95IowCubTI-14
86STaoftFT-40
Grant, Mudcat (Jim)
58Top-394
59Ind-5
59Kah-11
59Top-186
59TopVen-186
60IndJayP-2
60Kah-10
60Lea-25A
60Lea-25B
60Top-14
60TopVen-14
61Kah-15
61Pos-60A
61Pos-60B
61Top-18
61TopStal-135
62IndJayP-4
62Kah-14
62SalPlaC-26
62ShiPlaC-26
62Top-307
63IndJayP-7
63Top-227
64IndJayP-6
64Kah-10
64Top-133
64TopCoi-99
64TopSta-37
64TopVen-133
64TwiJayP-3
64WheSta-19
65Top-432
66Baz-37
66OPC-40
66Top-40
66Top-224
66TopRubI-36
66TopVen-40
66TopVen-224
66TwiFaiG-4
67CokCapTw-15
67DexPre-81
67Top-545
67TopVen-251
68Top-398
69ExpFudP-4
69MLBOffS-158
69Top-306
69TopSta-55
69TopTeaP-10
71MLBOffS-201
71OPC-509
71PirActP-6
71Top-509
72MilBra-120
72OPC-111
72Top-111
78TCM60I-200
78TwiFri-5
85DurBulT-15
89PacLegI-186
89SweBasG-84
90DodTar-293
91SweBasG-34
92UppDecS-29
93MCIAmb-3
93TedWil-34
94UppDecAH-31
94UppDecAH1-31
Grant, Sam
95AusFut-63
Grant, Tom
82IowCubT-3
83IowCubT-22
84IowCubT-30
85IowCubT-9
Grantham, George
25Exh-52
26Exh-52
28W513-76
29PorandAR-31
31Exh-14
33CraJacP-10
33ExhFou-4
33Gou-66

33GouCanV-66
91ConTSN-292
Granzow, Judd
95YakBeaTI-11
Grapenthien, Dan
92StaCluD-65
93AshTouF-2283
93AubAstC-11
93AubAstF-3453
Grapenthin, Dick
83WicAerDS-10
84IndIndTI-16
84IndIndTI-21
86LasVegSP-5
87LouRedTI-14
88LouRedBC-2
88LouRedBP-426
88LouRedBTI-20
88TriAAAP-24
89ColCliC-23
89ColCliP-5
89ColCliP-747
Graser, Rick
80SanJosMJitB-9
80WauTimT-18
Grass, Darren
93BazTeaU-13
93TopTra-101T
94SpoIndC-10
94SpoIndF-3325
95RanCucQT-35
Grasser, Craig
93GleFalRC-14
93GleFalRF-3997
94SavCarC-13
94SavCarF-502
94SouAtlLAF-SAL49
95Exc-266
Grasso, Mickey (Newton M.)
49BowPCL-6
51Bow-205
52Bow-174
52Top-90
53BowC-77
53Bri-6
53Top-148
54Bow-184
83TopRep5-90
91TopArc1-148
Grate, Don
88ChaLooLTI-13
Grater, Mark
87SavCarP-11
88SprCarB-2
89St.PetCS-14
90ArkTraGS-15
90CMC-121
90LouRedBC-21
90LouRedBP-397
90ProAAAF-511
91LinDriAAA-236
91LouRedLD-236
91LouRedP-2909
91LouRedTI-7
92LouRedF-1882
92LouRedS-263
92TopDeb91-66
93TolMudHF-1648
Graterol, Beiker
96StCatSB-10
Graterol, Jose
94VenLinU-256
95LinVen-201
Graupmann, Tim
83WisRapTF-9
84VisOakT-16
Graus, Mike
96MacBraB-29
Gravelle, Leo
43ParSpo-34
Graven, Tim
79SavBraT-7
Graves, Bryan
95BoiHawTI-18
96CedRapKTI-9
Graves, Chris
87QuaCitAP-22
88QuaCitAGS-27
89PalSprACLC-40
89PalSprAP-483
Graves, Danny
93BazTeaU-9
93TopTra-97T
95KinIndTI-11
96Bow-153
96BowBes-120
96BowBesAR-120
96BowBesR-120
96BufBisB-9
97Cir-238
97CirRav-238
97Don-164
97DonPreP-164
97DonPrePGold-164
97Pac-70
97PacLigB-70
97PacSil-70
97Sco-255
97ScoInd-14
97ScoIndPl-14
97ScoIndPr-14
97ScoPreS-255
97ScoShoS-255
97ScoShoSAP-255
97StaClu-275
97StaCluMOP-275
97Top-286
97UppDec-276
Graves, Frank M.
87OldJudN-214
Graves, Joe
83LynMetT-20
84JacMetT-8
86JacExpT-11
Graves, John
89ButCopKSP-21
90GasRanB-23
90GasRanP-2517
90GasRanS-10
90ProAaA-82
90SouAtlLAS-9
92YakBeaC-2
92YakBeaF-3441
Graves, Kenley
85BenPhiC-7
Graves, Kenny
90St.LucMS-8
90TopTVM-44
Graves, Pamela
96BelSnaTI-15
Graves, Randy
90KisDodD-13
91GreFalDSP-16
Gray, Dan
90GreFalDSP-2
91YakBeaC-10
91YakBeaP-4250
92VerBeaDC-20
92YakBeaC-4
92YakBeaF-3453
Gray, Dave
64Top-572
Gray, David
88LynRedSS-7
89LynRedSS-9
Gray, Dennis
89AlaGol-16
91St.CatBJC-16
91St.CatBJP-3388
92MyrBeaHC-7
92MyrBeaHF-2190
92StaCluD-66
93DunBluJC-7
93DunBluJF-1788
93DunBluJFFN-7
94KnoSmoF-1298
96HarSenB-13
Gray, Dick
58Top-146
60Top-24
60TopVen-24
90DodTar-294
Gray, Dolly (William)
09AmeCarE-46
09SenBarP-4
09T206-146
10SweCapPP-58
11T205-68
12HasTriFT-44
Gray, Elliott
89MarPhiS-13
90BatCliP-3057
91Cla/Bes-141
91ClePhiC-1
91ClePhiP-1616
92ClePhiC-12
92ClePhiF-2053
92ProFS7-301
Gray, Gary
75AndRanT-15
76SanAntBTI-11
77TucTorC-19
78TucTorC-27
79TucTorT-1
80TacTigT-17
81Fle-402
81TopTra-767
82Fle-511
82OPC-78
82SalLakCGT-9
82Top-523
82TopSti-233
83Don-637
83Fle-480
83Top-313
93RanKee-163
Gray, Jeff
86VerRedP-8
87NasSouTI-8
88BlaYNPRWLU-25
88NasSouC-5
88NasSouP-478
88NasSouTI-10
89BlaYNPRWL-91
89NasSouC-3
89NasSouP-1288
89NasSouTI-5
90CMC-276
90PawRedSC-25
90PawRedSDD-8
90PawRedSP-456
90ProAAAF-428
91Don-721
91Fle-95
91Lea-356
91OPC-731
91RedSoxP-7
91Sco-586
91StaClu-271
91Top-731
91TopDesS-731
91TopMic-731
91TopTif-731
91UppDec-685
92Don-122
92Sco-187
92StaClu-222
96SarRedSB-2
Gray, John L.
55A'sRodM-17
55Top-101
55TopDouH-47
58MonRoyF-10
Gray, Lorenzo
77AppFoxT-6
78AppFoxT-10
79AppFoxT-9
80GleFalWSBT-22
80GleFalWSCT-26
82EdmTraT-10
84MaiGuiT-12
84Nes792-163
84Top-163
84TopTif-163
86SanJosBP-9
Gray, Pete
77FriOneYW-6
77GalGloG-229
87SpoRea-6
88LitSunMLL-2
Gray, Samuel
25Exh-107
28StaPlaCE-29
28W56PlaC-H10
29ExhFou-29
31Exh-30
33ExhFou-15
91ConTSN-75
Gray, Scott
86AubAstP-10
Gray, Stanley
43CenFlo-10
44CenFlo-9
Gray, Steve
89CliGiaP-899
89SalSpuP-1802
Gray, Ted
49Bow-10
50Bow-210
51Bow-178
52Bow-199
52Top-86
53BowC-72
53TigGle-11
53Top-52
54Bow-71
55Bow-86
59Top-244
81TigDetN-131
83TopRep5-86
91OriCro-162
91TopArc1-52
Gray, Terry
77St.PetCT-10
Graybill, Dave
87JacExpP-443
89PalSprACLC-59
Grayner, Paul
82NasSouTI-13
83NasSouTI-7
Grays, Homestead
88NegLeaD-2
91PomBlaBPB-10
92NegLeaRLI-68
92NegLeaRLI-74
92NegLeaRLI-82
92NegLeaRLI-83
93NegLeaRL2-44
93NegLeaRL2-64
93NegLeaRL2-65
93NegLeaRL2-66
93NegLeaRL2-67
93NegLeaRL2-68
93TedWilPC-16
Grayson, Mike
89BelBreIS-7
Grayston, Joe
85BurRanT-1
Grayum, Richie
88MisStaB-7
89GenCubP-1871
89MisStaB-15
90ChaKniTI-23
91WinSpiC-24
91WinSpiP-2841
92ChaKniF-2783
92ChaKniS-157
93OrlCubF-2797
94OrlCubF-1397
Graziano, Andy
92GasRanC-27
93ChaRaiC-30
Grba, Eli
60Top-183
60TopVen-183
61Top-121
62AngJayP-4
62Top-96
62TopVen-96
63Top-231
82VanCanT-23
88VanCanP-769
89RenSilSCLC-265
90PriPatD-28
91MarPhiP-3471
92YanWIZ6-49
Greason, Bill
93NegLeaRL2-11
Grebe, Brett
90PulBraB-5
90PulBraP-3103
Grebeck, Brian
90BoiHawP-3321
90SanDieSA3-5
91QuaCitAC-17
91QuaCitAP-2636
92PalSprAC-11
92PalSprAF-847
93Bow-33
93ExcFS7-143
93MidAngF-329
94MidAngF-2444
94MidAngOHP-6
96VanCanB-14
97MidAngOHP-14
Grebeck, Craig
87PenWhiSP-10
88BirBarB-24
89BirBarB-17
89BirBarP-111
90BirBarDGB-15
90Bow-318
90BowTif-318
90DonRoo-9
90FleUpd-85
90ScoRoo-105T
90UppDec-721
90WhiSoxC-6
90WhiSoxC-28
91Don-378
91Fle-120
91OPC-446
91Sco-69
91Sco100RS-35
91StaClu-559
91Top-446
91TopDeb90-59
91TopDesS-446
91TopMic-446
91TopTif-446
91UltUpd-15
91WhiSoxK-14
92Don-546
92Fle-81
92Lea-344
92OPC-273
92Pin-334
92Sco-561
92StaClu-145
92Top-273
92TopGol-273
92TopGolW-273
92TopMic-273
92Ult-34
92UppDec-603
92WhiSoxK-14
93Don-199
93Fle-202
93PacSpa-71
93Pin-362
93Sco-126
93Sel-389
93StaClu-136
93StaCluFDI-136
93StaCluMOP-136
93StaCluWS-14
93Top-259
93TopGol-259
93TopInaM-259
93TopMic-259
93Ult-531
93UppDec-738
93UppDecGold-738
93WhiSoxK-9
94Fle-81
94Pac-126
94StaClu-225
94StaCluFDI-225
94StaCluGR-225
94StaCluMOP-225
94StaCluT-133
94StaCluTFDI-133
94Top-176
94TopGol-176
94TopSpa-176
94Ult-336
94WhiSoxK-9
95Don-535
95DonPreP-535
95Fle-117
95Sco-136
95ScoGolR-136
95ScoPlaTS-136
95Top-343
95WhiSoxK-11
96LeaSigEA-62
97PacPriGotD-GD141
97Ult-468
97UltGolME-468
97UltPlaME-468
Greco, George
80ElmPioRST-7
Greely, Jim
93LSUTigM-3
94BoiHawC-11
94BoiHawF-3367
94LSUTigMP-6
Green, Bert
94JohCitCC-11
94JohCitCF-3708
Green, Bob
86Ft.LauYP-9
87Ft.LauYP-6
88AlbYanP-1331
89AlbYanB-10
89ColCliC-20
89ColCliP-21
89ColCliP-734
Green, Chad

96BesAutS1RP-FR1
97Bow-80
97BowChr-107
97BowChrI-107
97BowChrIR-107
97BowChrR-107
97BowInt-80
Green, Charlie
87WatPirP-29
Green, Chris
94BelMarC-14
94BelMarF-3228
Green, Christopher
82AleDukT-6
85HawIslC-240
86EdmTraP-14
87RocRedWT-22
Green, Danny (Edward)
03BreE10-61
11SpoLifCW-146
Green, Daryl
86SalAngC-88
87QuaCitAP-10
88QuaCitAGS-13
89ModA'sC-11
89ModA'sCLC-271
90HunStaB-6
91St.PetCC-8
91St.PetCP-2271
Green, David A.
80HolMilT-14
82LouRedE-10
83Car-6
83Don-166
83Fle-6
83Top-578
83TopSti-323
84AllGamPI-5
84Car-8
84Car5x7-8
84Don-425
84Don-625
84Fle-323
84Nes792-362
84OPC-362
84Top-362
84TopSti-149
84TopTif-362
85AllGamPI-96
85Don-303
85Fle-224
85FleUpd-46
85GiaMotS-17
85GiaPos-12
85Lea-191
85OPC-87
85Top-87
85TopSti-145
85TopTif-87
85TopTifT-41T
85TopTra-41T
86Don-114
86Fle-543
86OPC-122
86Top-727
86TopTif-727
87LouRedTI-15
88Fle-34
88FleGlo-34
88LouRedBC-14
88LouRedBP-421
88LouRedBTI-21
91LinDriAA-582
91TulDriLD-582
91TulDriP-2784
91TulDriTI-9
Green, Dick (Richard)
64A's-7
64Top-466
65AthJayP-6
65OPC-168
65Top-168
66Top-545
67CokCapAt-8
67DexPre-82
67OPC-54
67Top-54
67TopVen-215
68Top-303
68TopVen-303
69A'sJacitB-7
69MilBra-97
69Top-515
69TopSta-215
69TopTeaP-21
70MLBOffS-258
70OPC-311
70Top-311
71MLBOffS-514
71OPC-258
71Top-258
72MilBra-121
72Top-780
73OPC-456
73Top-456
74OPC-392
74Top-392
75OPC-91
75Top-91
86A'sGreT-2
Green, Don (Donald)
89HamRedS-18
90SavCarP-2066
Green, Fred
60KeyChal-21
60Top-272
61Top-181
Green, G. Dallas
60Lea-52
60Top-366
61Top-359
62SalPlaC-219
62ShiPlaC-219
62Top-111
62TopVen-111
63Top-91
64PhiJayP-6
64Top-464
65OPC-203
65PhiJayP-6
65Top-203
78TCM60I-187
80PhiBurK-1
80Top-526
81Don-415
81Top-682
83PhiPosGPaM-11
84CubUno-12
87CubCan-12
89Top-104
89TopTif-104
89YanScoNW-31
91MetWIZ-150
93MetColP-110
93TopTra-36T
94MetColP-3
94MetShuST-5
96MetKah-10
96MetKah-11
Green, Gary
85BeaGolGT-18
85Top-396
85TopTif-396
86LasVegSP-6
87LasVegSP-22
88LasVegSC-17
88LasVegSP-232
89UppDec-722
90CMC-163
90OklCit8C-13
90OklCit8P-439
90ProAAAF-685
91OPC-184
91StaClu-323
91Top-184
91TopDesS-184
91TopMic-184
91TopTif-184
92NasSouF-1837
93IndIndF-1494
93RanKee-164
95OmaRoyTI-11
Green, Gene
55DonWin-21
58Top-366
59Top-37
59TopVen-37
60Lea-82
60Top-269
61Top-206
62Jel-72
62Pos-72
62PosCan-72
62SalPlaC-70
62ShiPlaC-70
62Top-78
62TopVen-78
63Top-506
91OriCro-163
Green, Harvey
90DodTar-962
Green, Jason
94Bow-545
94DanBraC-15
94DanBraF-3527
95AubAstTI-20
95DurBulTI-10
96AubDouB-2
Green, Jeff
83BufBisT-8
Green, Joe
87NegLeaPD-8
Green, Joey
90OklSoo-5
Green, John
86GenCubP-7
86PeoChiP-9
87PeoChiP-3
87PeoChiPW-3
89Ft.LauYS-7
Green, Larry
76DubPacT-13
Green, Lenny
58Top-471
59Top-209
60Top-99
60TopVen-99
61Top-4
61TwiCloD-8
61TwiJayP-3
61TwiPetM-15
61TwiUniMC-5
62Jel-87
62Pos-87
62PosCan-87
62SalPlaC-69A
62SalPlaC-69B
62ShiPlaC-69
62Top-84
62TopBuc-32
62TopStal-75
62TopVen-84
63Jel-6
63Pos-6
63Top-198
63TwiVol-4
64Top-386
65Top-588
66Top-502
81RedSoxBG2S-83
91OriCro-164
Green, Marcie
91FreStaLBS-3
Green, Nat
85BenPhiC-8
Green, Otis
86SyrChiP-11
87SyrChiP-1942
87SyrChiT-14
88SyrChiC-19
88SyrChiP-831
89SyrChiC-12
89SyrChiMB-11
89SyrChiP-793
90CMC-68
90IndIndC-18
90IndIndP-293
90ProAAAF-576
91StoPorC-2
91StoPorP-3028
92DenZepF-2633
92DenZepS-129
92ProFS7-88
92SkyAAAF-63
93VanCanF-2589
Green, Pumpsie (Elijah)
60KeyChal-22
60RedSoxJP-5
60Top-317
61Top-454
62SalPlaC-187
62ShiPlaC-187
62Top-153
62TopVen-153
63Top-292
64Top-442
76Met63 S-7
81TCM60I-297
91MetWIZ-151
Green, Randy
77ModA'sC-10
79WatA'sT-12
80OgdA'sT-5
Green, Rick
77VisOakT-6
92SalSpuF-3749
Green, Scarborough
96StPetCB-10
Green, Shawn
92ClaFS7-348
92DunBluJC-8
92DunBluJF-2011
92OPC-276
92StaCluD-67
92Top-276
92TopGol-276
92TopGolW-276
92TopMic-276
92UppDec-55
92UppDecML-225
93Bow-27
93ClaFS7-72
93KnoSmoF-1262
94Bow-253
94BowBes-B46
94BowBes-X110
94BowBesR-B46
94BowBesR-X110
94Cla-190
94ClaCreotC-C25
94ColC-9
94ColChoGS-9
94ColChoSS-9
94Don-607
94FleUpd-98
94LeaLimR-52
94ScoRoo-RT91
94ScoRooGR-RT91
94SpoRoo-48
94SpoRooAP-48
94SpoRooRS-TR16
94StaClu-66
94StaCluFDI-66
94StaCluGR-66
94StaCluMOP-66
94StaCluT-159
94StaCluTFDI-159
94SyrChiF-984
94SyrChiTI-15
94Top-237
94TopGol-237
94TopSpa-237
94UppDec-15
94UppDec-297
94UppDec-493
94UppDecED-15
94UppDecED-297
94UppDecED-493
95Bow-261
95BowBes-R75
95BowBes-X4
95BowBesR-R75
95BowBesR-X4
95BowGolF-261
95ColCho-144
95ColChoGS-144
95ColChoSE-58
95ColChoSEGS-58
95ColChoSESS-58
95ColChoSS-144
95Don-464
95DonPreP-464
95Emo-94
95EmoRoo-6
95Fin-327
95FinRef-327
95Fla-316
95FlaWavotF-7
95Fle-94
95FleUpdRU-3
95Lea-285
95LeaGolR-3
95LeaLim-82
95LinVen-167
95Pin-135
95Pin-279
95PinArtP-135
95PinArtP-279
95PinMusC-135
95PinMusC-279
95PinNewB-NB2
95PinPer-PP15
95PinUps-US16
95Sco-304
95ScoGolR-304
95ScoPlaTS-304
95ScoRooDT-RDT6
95Sel-202
95Sel-240
95SelArtP-202
95SelArtP-240
95SelCanM-CM12
95SelCer-105
95SelCerF-4
95SelCerMG-105
95SelCerPU-14
95SelCerPU9-14
95SP-204
95SPCha-199
95SPChaDC-199
95Spo-143
95SpoArtP-143
95SPSil-204
95StaClu-233
95StaCluCB-CB6
95StaCluFDI-233
95StaCluMOP-233
95StaCluMOP-CB6
95StaCluSTWS-233
95StaCluVR-118
95Stu-28
95StuGolS-28
95SumNewA-NA14
95Top-514
95TopCyb-302
95TopTra-13T
95UC3-106
95UC3ArtP-106
95UC3CleS-CS2
95Ult-338
95UltGolM-338
95UppDec-289
95UppDecED-289
95UppDecEDG-289
95UppDecPAW-H13
95UppDecPAWE-H13
95UppDecSE-68
95UppDecSEG-68
95Zen-150
95ZenRooRC-4
96Baz-105
96BluJayOH-11
96Bow-10
96ColCho-751
96ColChoGS-751
96ColChoSS-751
96Don-229
96DonPreP-229
96EmoXL-132
96Fin-S41
96FinRef-S41
96Fla-184
96Fle-274
96FleRooS-6
96FleTif-274
96Lea-66
96LeaPre-6
96LeaPreP-6
96LeaPrePB-66
96LeaPrePG-66
96LeaPrePS-66
96LeaPreSG-62
96LeaPreSte-62
96MetUni-120
96MetUniMFG-3
96MetUniP-120
96Pac-443
96PanSti-161
96Pin-125
96PinAfi-104
96PinAfiAP-104
96PinArtP-33
96PinFirR-16
96PinSta-33
96Sco-24
96ScoDugC-A23
96ScoDugCAP-A23
96Sel-2
96SelArtP-2
96SelCer-44
96SelCerAP-44
96SelCerCB-44
96SelCerCR-44
96SelCerMB-44
96SelCerMG-44
96SelCerMR-44
96SelTeaN-7
96SP-183
96StaClu-34
96StaClu-231

96StaCluEPB-34
96StaCluEPG-34
96StaCluEPS-34
96StaCluMOP-34
96StaCluMOP-231
95StaCluVRMC-118
96Stu-108
96StuPrePB-108
96StuPrePG-108
96StuPrePS-108
96Sum-16
96SumAbo&B-16
96SumArtP-16
96SumFoi-16
96Top-417
96TopChr-163
96TopChrR-163
96TopGal-120
96TopGalPPI-120
96TopLas-65
96Ult-146
96UltGolM-146
96UppDec-216
96Zen-11
96ZenArtP-11
97BluJayS-13
97Cir-301
97CirRav-301
97ColCho-503
97Don-315
97DonEli-75
97DonEliGS-75
97DonLim-51
97DonLimLE-51
97DonPre-90
97DonPreCttC-90
97DonPreP-315
97DonPrePGold-315
97FlaSho-A131
97FlaSho-B131
97FlaSho-C131
97FlaShoLC-131
97FlaShoLC-B131
97FlaShoLC-C131
97FlaShoLCM-A131
97FlaShoLCM-B131
97FlaShoLCM-C131
97Fle-240
97FleTif-240
97Lea-140
97LeaFraM-140
97LeaFraMDC-140
97MetUni-184
97NewPin-135
97NewPinAP-135
97NewPinMC-135
97NewPinPP-135
97Pac-220
97PacLigB-220
97PacSil-220
97PinIns-54
97PinInsCE-54
97PinInsDE-54
97Sco-281
97ScoPreS-281
97ScoShoS-281
97ScoShoSAP-281
97Sel-74
97SelArtP-74
97SelRegG-74
97StaClu-147
97StaCluMOP-147
97Stu-106
97StuPrePG-106
97StuPrePS-106
97Top-214
97Ult-396
97UltGolME-396
97UltPlaME-396
97UppDec-514

Green, Stephen W.
89VerBeaDS-9

Green, Steve R.
78HolMilT-9
80OrlTwiT-4
82OrlTwi8SCT-15
88BakDodCLC-248
90LonTigP-1279
93VerBeaDC-6
93VerBeaDF-2230

Green, Terry
86OscAstP-9
87OscAstP-25
88ColAstB-22

Green, Tom (Tom)
86SumBraP-7
90WelPirP-13
91AugPirC-20
91AugPirP-819
92BufBisBS-10
92CarMudF-1193
92ClaFS7-241
92SalBucC-17
93CarMudF-2068
93CarMudTI-14

Green, Trent
92DavLipB-12

Green, Tyler
90WicStaSGD-13
91BatCliC-20
91BatCliP-3479
91Cla/Bes-416
91ClaDraP-7
91ClaDraPP-1
91ClaGolB-BC19
91FroRowDP-34
92ClaFS7-230
92DonRooP-BC5
92FroRowTG-1
92FroRowTG-2
92FroRowTG-3
92FroRowTG-4
92FroRowTG-5
92FroRowTG-6
92FroRowTG-7
92OPC-764
92Pin-303
92ProFS7-303
92ReaPhiF-569
92ReaPhiS-531
92Sco-810
92SkyAA F-229
92StaCluD-68
92Top-764
92TopGol-764
92TopGolW-764
92TopMic-764
92UppDec-68
92UppDecML-40
92UppDecML-68
92UppDecML-167
93Bow-400
93ClaGolF-36
93ExcFS7-85
93PhiMed-15
93Pin-581
93ScrRedBF-2542
93ScrRedBTI-10
93TopTra-37T
93UppDec-505
93UppDecGold-505
94Bow-362
94Bow-422
94Don-433
94Fin-256
94FinRef-256
94PhiMed-11
94PhiUSPC-12S
94Pin-503
94PinArtP-503
94PinMusC-503
94ScrRedBF-920
94StaCluT-239
94StaCluTFDI-239
94Top-294
94TopGol-294
94TopSpa-294
94UppDec-72
94UppDecED-72
95BowBes-R73
95BowBesR-R73
95DonTopotO-304
95Fla-389
95FleUpd-119
95Phi-13
95PhiMel-10
95SPCha-76
95SPChaDC-76
95TopTra-131T
95TopTra-152T
95UltGolMR-M14
95UppDec-476T
96ColCho-253
96ColChoGS-253
96ColChoSS-253
96Don-188
96DonPreP-188
96Fle-498

96FleTif-498
96Pac-163
96PacPri-P53
96PacPriG-P53
96PhiTeal-15
96Sco-42
96ScoDugC-A37
96ScoDugCAP-A37
96StaClu-175
96StaCluMOP-175
96Top-418
96Ult-252
96UltGolM-252
96UppDec-167
97Sco-398
97ScoHobR-398
97ScoResC-398
97ScoShoS-398
97ScoShoSAP-398

Greenberg, Hank
34DiaStaR-54A
34DiaStaR-54B
34Gou-62
35GouPreR-12
35GouPuzR-8F
35GouPuzR-9F
35TigFreP-9
36GouBWR-15
36GouWidPPR-A42
36GouWidPPR-B11
36GouWidPPR-C14
36NatChiFPR-35
36NatChiFPR-109
36OveCanR-20
36R31PasP-12
36R31Pre-G9
36WheBB3-5
36WorWidGV-41
37OPCBatUV-107
38BasTabP-13
38ExhFou-12
38GouHeaU-253
38GouHeaU-277
38OurNatGPP-13
38WheBB11-5
38WheBB15-4
39ExhSal-22A
39ExhSal-22B
39GouPreR303A-20
39GouPreR303B-12
39PlaBal-56
39WheBB12-7
39WorWidGTP-20
40PlaBal-40
40WheM4-2A
40WheM4-7B
41DouPlaR-51
41DouPlaR-85
41PlaBal-18
41WheM5-16
43MPR302-1-12
46SpaExcW-4-1B
48BluTin-35
48IndTeal-11
48IndTeal-12
49IndTeal-12
50IndTeal-12
51R42SmaS-38
55IndGolS-27
60NuHi-42
61GolPre-4
61NuSco-442
63BasMagM-31
63BazA-19
68LauWorS-42
70FleWorS-42
71FleWorS-43
76BooProC-6
76GalBasGHoF-13
76RowExh-7
76ShaPiz-81
76TayBow4-36
76TigOldTS-11
77GalGloG-82
80MarExhH-14
80PacLeg-30
80PerHaloFP-81
80SSPHOF-81
80TigGreT-4
81ConTSN-79
81TigDetN-54
81TigDetN-133
81TigSecNP-17
82DiaCla-49

83DonHOFH-16
83TigAlKS-39
83YanYealT-11
84OCoandSI-120
84TCMPla1-4
85TCMPla1-42
85TopGloA-22
86SpoDecG-4
86TigSpoD-6
87HygAllG-22
87SpoRea-39
88WilMulP-5
89PacLegI-195
90PerGreM-88
91ConTSN-14
92ConTSN-430
92ConTSN-590
93ActPacA-107
93ActPacA2-41G
93ConTSN-733
94ConTSN-1005
94ConTSNB-1005
94TedWil-32
94UppDecTAE-54
94UppDecTAEGM-4
95ConTSN-1335

Greenberg, Steve
74SpoIndC-40

Greene, Al (Altar)
80EvaTriT-8
80Top-666

Greene, Bart
92BriTigC-23
92BriTigF-1424

Greene, Carl
57SeaPop-17

Greene, Charlie
92ChaRaiC-12
92ChaRaiF-122
93SpoIndC-30
93WatDiaC-16
93WatDiaF-1771
94St.LucMF-1199
95BinMetTI-21
96BinBeeB-9

Greene, Ed
86BelBreP-8

Greene, Grant
76LauIndC-8

Greene, Henry
77DayBealT-7

Greene, Jeff
86SumBraP-6
87DurBulP-22
87PenWhiSP-20
88BurBraP-14
88TamTarS-8

Greene, Joe (James)
78LauLonABS-13

Greene, Keith
86BenPhiC-137
87SpaPhiP-8

Greene, Nelson
90DodTar-963

Greene, Rick
92Bow-563
92ClaDraP-12
92LSUTigM-5
92TopTra-44T
92TopTraG-44T
92UppDecML-9
93Bow-263
93ClaFS7-193
93LakTigC-9
93LakTigF-1302
93StaCluM-188
93Top-233
93TopGol-233
93TopInaM-233
93TopMic-233
93UppDec-446
93UppDecGold-446
94Bow-425
94Cla-146
94ClaGolF-110
94ExcFS7-55
94SigRoo-27
94SigRooS-27
94TreThuF-2116
94Ult-356
94UppDecML-49
95JacSunTI-13
96JacSunB-15

Greene, Steve
77BurBeeT-11

Greene, Todd
91TopTra-50T
91TopTraT-50T
92StaCluD-69
92TopDaiQTU-20
93BoiHawC-1
93BoiHawF-3928
94ExcFirYPF-7
94ExcFS7-27
94LakElsSC-1
94LakElsSF-1666
95ARuFalLS-8
95Bes-9
95Bes-AU1
95Bow-227
95BowBes-B18
95BowBes-X12
95BowBesR-B18
95BowBesR-X12
95BowGolF-227
95ColCho-34
95ColChoGS-34
95ColChoSS-34
95Exc-20
95ExcAll-9
95MidAngOHP-13
95MidAngTI-11
95SPMLA-26
95Top-633
95UppDec-6
95UppDecED-6
95UppDecEDG-6
95UppDecML-25
95UppDecMLOP-OP4
95UppDecSE-127
95UppDecSEG-127
96BesAutSA-22
96Bow-178
96BowBes-128
96BowBesAR-128
96BowBesP-BBP18
96BowBesPAR-BBP18
96BowBesPR-BBP18
96BowBesR-128
96ColCho-440
96ColCho-664
96ColChoGS-440
96ColChoGS-664
96ColChoSS-440
96ColChoSS-664
96EmoXL-27
96Fla-38
96FlaWavotF-12
96Fle-48
96FlePro-6
96FleTif-48
96FleUpdNH-8
96LeaSig-138
96LeaSigPPG-138
96LeaSigPPP-138
96MetUni-28
96MetUniMFG-4
96MetUniP-28
96MetUniProS-28
96SP-14
96Top-213
96TopChr-75
96TopChrR-75
96TopGal-130
96TopGalPPI-130
96Ult-325
96UltGolM-325
96UppDec-240
96UppDecFSP-FS12
96UppDecPHE-H24
96UppDecPreH-H24
96VanCanB-15
97Bow-208
97BowBes-137
97BowBesAR-137
97BowBesR-137
97BowCerBIA-CA31
97BowCerGIA-CA31
97BowChr-191
97BowChrI-191
97BowChrIR-191
97BowChrR-191
97BowInt-208
97Cir-63
97CirRav-63
97ColCho-259
97Don-374
97DonEli-84

97DonEliGS-84
97DonEliTotC-10
97DonEliTotCDC-10
97DonLim-41
97DonLim-82
97DonLimLE-41
97DonLimLE-82
97DonPre-151
97DonPreCttC-151
97DonPreP-374
97DonPrePGold-374
97DonRatR-26
97FlaSho-A11
97FlaSho-B11
97FlaSho-C11
97FlaShoLC-11
97FlaShoLC-B11
97FlaShoLC-C11
97FlaShoLCM-A11
97FlaShoLCM-B11
97FlaShoLCM-C11
97FlaShoWotF-1
97Fle-44
97FleTif-44
97Lea-331
97LeaFraM-331
97LeaFraMDC-331
97PacPriGotD-GD5
97Pin-179
97PinArtP-179
97PinCer-120
97PinCerMBlu-120
97PinCerMG-120
97PinCerMR-120
97PinCerR-120
97PinIns-136
97PinInsCE-136
97PinInsDE-136
97PinMusC-179
97PinTotCPB-120
97PinTotCPG-120
97PinTotCPR-120
97Sco-277
97ScoPreS-277
97ScoShoS-277
97ScoShoSAP-277
97Sel-109
97SelArtP-109
97SelRegG-109
97SelRooR-17
97SpoIll-7
97SpoIllEE-7
97StaClu-112
97StaCluM-M19
97StaCluMOP-112
97StaCluMOP-M19
97Stu-156
97StuPrePG-156
97StuPrePS-156
97Top-288
97TopSta-107
97TopStaAM-107
97Ult-28
97UltGolME-28
97UltPlaME-28
97UppDec-296
95UppDecMLFS-25
97UppDecU-47
97UppDecUGN-GN13
Greene, Tommy (Ira Thomas)
88RicBraC-1
88RicBraP-2
89RicBraBC-7
89RicBraC-3
89RicBraP-831
89RicBraTI-8
89TriAAP-AAA54
90Bow-1
90BowTif-1
90ClaUpd-T22
90CMC-296
90Don-576
90Fle-584
90FleCan-584
90ProAAAF-398
90RicBraBC-9
90RicBraC-20
90RicBraP-253
90RicBraTI-10
90Sco-640
90ScoYouS2-24
90Spo-224
90TopDeb89-45
90UppDec-49
91ClaGam-66
91Don-635
91FleUpd-108
91Lea-524
91OPC-486
91PhiMed-15
91Sco-808
91StaClu-549
91StaCluMO-3
91Top-486
91TopDesS-486
91TopMic-486
91TopTif-486
91UltUpd-99
91UppDecFE-62F
92Bow-227
92ClaGam-64
92Don-94
92Don-109
92Fle-531
92Lea-292
92OPC-83
92PhiMed-14
92Pin-155
92PinTea2-53
92Sco-336
92Sco-426
92StaClu-27
92Top-83
92TopGol-83
92TopGolW-83
92TopMic-83
92Ult-242
92UppDec-567
93Don-568
93Fin-149
93FinRef-149
93Fla-101
93Fle-489
93Lea-132
93OPC-144
93PhiMed-16
93Pin-313
93Sco-464
93SP-174
93StaClu-559
93StaCluFDI-559
93StaCluMOP-559
93StaCluP-27
93Top-291
93TopGol-291
93TopInaM-291
93TopMic-291
93Ult-441
93UppDec-549
93UppDecGold-549
94Bow-580
94ColC-115
94ColChoGS-115
94ColChoSS-115
94Don-482
94ExtBas-333
94Fin-152
94FinRef-152
94Fla-412
94Fle-589
94Lea-133
94OPC-137
94Pac-475
94PhiMed-12
94PhiMel-8
94PhiUSPC-7S
94PhiUSPC-13D
94Pin-78
94PinArtP-78
94PinMusC-78
94RedFolMI-13
94Sco-380
94ScoGolR-380
94Sel-155
94StaClu-705
94StaCluFDI-705
94StaCluGR-705
94StaCluMOP-705
94StaCluT-222
94StaCluTFDI-222
94Top-570
94TopGol-570
94TopSpa-570
94TriPla-174
94Ult-244
94UppDec-203
94UppDecED-203
95Don-518
95DonPreP-518
95Emb-55
95EmbGolI-55
95Fin-41
95FinRef-41
95Fla-180
95Fle-392
95Sco-36
95ScoGolR-36
95ScoPlaTS-36
95StaClu-356
95StaCluMOP-356
95StaCluSTWS-356
95StaCluVR-186
95Top-144
95TopCyb-88
95Ult-419
95UltGolM-419
95UppDec-379
95UppDecED-379
95UppDecEDG-379
96StaClu-399
96StaCluMOP-399
95StaCluVRMC-186
97BobCamRB-15
Greene, Willie
90AugPirP-2470
90Bow-173
90BowTif-173
90CMC-849
90ProAaA-96
90Sco-682
91Bow-448
91Cla/Bes-350
91WesPalBEC-20
91WesPalBEP-1236
92Bow-429
92CedRapRC-20
92ChaLooF-3826
92ClaFS7-48
92FleUpd-81
92ProFS7-263
93Bow-349
93Bow-638
93ClaFS7-194
93Don-143
93Fin-148
93FinRef-148
93Fle-34
93IndIndF-1495
93Lea-456
93Pin-285
93Sco-250
93ScoBoyoS-12
93ScoProaG-8
93Sel-348
93StaClu-704
93StaCluFDI-704
93StaCluMOP-704
93Top-764
93TopGol-764
93TopInaM-764
93TopMic-764
93Toy-46
93ToyMasP-4
93UppDec-4
93UppDecGold-4
94Bow-430
94BowBes-B69
94BowBesR-B69
94ColC-116
94ColChoGS-116
94ColChoSS-116
94Don-539
94Fle-410
94FUnPac-169
94Lea-326
94Pin-522
94PinArtP-522
94PinMusC-522
94ScoBoyoS-34
94Sel-102
94Top-428
94TopGol-428
94TopSpa-428
94TriPla-212
94Ult-170
94UppDec-230
94UppDecED-230
95ActPac2GF-12G
95ActPacF-17
95ActPacF-73
95ColCho-428
95ColChoGS-428
95ColChoSS-428
95Don-210
95DonPreP-210
95IndIndF-101
95Lea-72
95Pac-105
95Pin-331
95PinArtP-331
95PinMusC-331
95PinUps-US28
95RedKah-8
95Sel-190
95SelArtP-190
95SigRoo-22
95SigRooSig-22
95Spo-110
95SpoArtP-110
95StaClu-308
95StaCluMOP-308
95StaCluSTWS-308
95Stu-83
95Sum-39
95SumNthD-39
95Top-467
95UppDec-160
95UppDecED-168
95UppDecEDG-168
96FleUpd-U121
96FleUpdTC-U121
96Pin-295
96PinAfi-144
96PinAfiAP-144
96PinFoil-295
97Cir-177
97CirRav-177
97ColCho-303
97Fle-294
97FleTif-294
97Lea-122
97LeaFraM-122
97LeaFraMDC-122
97NewPin-137
97NewPinAP-137
97NewPinMC-137
97NewPinPP-137
97Pac-268
97PacLigB-268
97PacSil-268
97Sco-425
97ScoHobR-425
97ScoResC-425
97ScoShoS-425
97ScoShoSAP-425
97Top-371
97Ult-328
97UltGolME-328
97UltPlaME-328
97UppDec-335
Greenfield, Kent
90DodTar-295
92ConTSN-617
Greenfield, Monroe
77PhoGiaVNB-6
Greengrass, Jim
47Exh-83
53Top-209
54Bow-28
54Top-22
55Bow-49
56Top-275
56YelBasP-12
58UniOil-3
79DiaGre-321
91TopArc1-209
94TopArc1-22
94TopArc1G-22
Greenhalgh, Dan
77ReaPhiT-11
Greenhalgh, Ted
46SunBre-7
Greenlee, Darren
93PocPosSP-18
Greenlee, Gus
88NegLeaD-5
Greenlee, Robert
87SanBerSP-19
Greenstein, Stu
77LynMetT-16A
77LynMetT-16B
Greenwell, Mike
85IntLeaAT-44
85PawRedST-4
86PawRedSP-10
86Spo-178
87Don-585
87DonRoo-4
87FleUpd-37
87FleUpdG-37
87SpoRool-8
87SpoTeaP-9
87Top-259
87TopTif-259
88ClaBlu-227
88Don-339
88DonBasB-177
88DonTeaBRS-339
88Fle-354
88Fle-630
88FleExcS-16
88FleGlo-354
88FleGlo-630
88FleHotS-14
88FleMin-7
88FleStiC-9
88Lea-153
88OPC-274
88PanSti-32
88Sco-175
88ScoGlo-175
88ScoYouSI-24
88Spo-118
88StaGre-1
88StaGre-2
88StaGre-3
88StaGre-4
88StaGre-5
88StaGre-6
88StaGre-7
88StaGre-8
88StaGre-9
88StaGre-10
88StaGre-11
88StaGreP-1
88StaGreP-2
88StaGreP-3
88StaGreP-4
88StaGreP-5
88StaGreP-6
88StaGreP-7
88StaGreP-8
88StaGreP-9
88StaGreP-10
88StaGreP-11
88StaLinRS-10
88Top-493
88TopBig-233
88TopCoi-14
88TopGloS-20
88TopRoo-3
88TopSti-249
88TopSti-312
88TopTif-493
88ToyRoo-12
89Bow-34
89BowTif-34
89CadEllD-24
89ClaTraO-149
89ColPosG-1
89ColPosG-2
89ColPosG-3
89ColPosG-4
89ColPosG-5
89ColPosG-6
89ColPosG-7
89ColPosG-8
89Don-1
89Don-186
89DonAll-15
89DonBasB-28
89DonBonM-BC13
89DonGraS-5
89DonSupD-1
89Fle-90
89FleAll-6
89FleBasA-16
89FleBasM-16
89FleExcS-18
89FleGlo-90
89FleHeroB-19
89FleLeaL-18
89FleSup-20
89FleWaxBC-C11
89KayB-15
89Nis-6
89OPC-374
89PanSti-280
89Sco-66

89Sco-659
89ScoHot1S-70
89ScoSco-36
89Spo-143
89Spo-221
89SpoIllFKI-31
89Top-402
89Top-630
89TopBasT-119
89TopBig-211
89TopCoi-41
89TopDouA-6
89TopGloS-31
89TopHeaUT-22
89TopHilTM-15
89TopMinL-48
89TopSti-255
89TopStiB-16
89TopTif-402
89TopTif-630
89TopUKM-32
89TVSpoM-61
89TVSpoM-128
89UppDec-432
90Bow-274
90BowTif-274
90ClaBlu-47
90Don-66
90DonBesA-115
90DOnBonM-BC17
90DonLeaS-32
90Fle-277
90Fle-632
90FleBasA-13
90FleBasM-13
90FleCan-277
00FloCan 632
90FleLeaL-13
90FleWaxBC-C8
90Lea-143
90MLBBasB-71
90MSAIceTD-18
90OPC-70
90PanSti-16
90PubSti-287
90PubSti-457
90RedFolSB-39
90RedSoxP-11
90Sco-345
90Sco100S-67
90Spo-50
90Top-70
90TopBig-61
90TopDou-28
90TopSti-254
90TopTif-70
90TopTVA-22
90TopTVRS-30
90UppDec-354
90VenSti-213
90VenSti-214
91Bow-116
91Cla3-T29
91ClaGam-18
91Don-553
91DonGraS-14
91Fle-96
91FlePro-8
91Lea-19
91OPC-792
91PanCanT1-32
91PanFreS-268
91RedSoxP-8
91Sco-130
91Sco100S-82
91StaClu-253
91Stu-15
91Top-792
91TopCraJ2-34
91TopDesS-792
91TopMic-792
91TopTif-792
91TopTriH-A2
91Ult-32
91UppDec-43
91UppDec-165
92Bow-615
92ClaGam-72
92Don-523
92Fle-39
92Lea-89
92OPC-113
92PanSti-91
92Pin-131
92RedSoxDD-14
92Sco-545
92Sco100S-10
92SpoStaCC-19
92StaClu-446
92Top-113
92TopGol-113
92TopGolW-113
92TopKid-69
92TopMic-113
92TriPla-252
92Ult-16
92UppDec-275
93Bow-607
93DiaMar-43
93Don-223
93Fin-197
93FinRef-197
93Fla-164
93Fle-559
93FunPac-164
93Lea-197
93OPC-285
93PacSpa-33
93PanSti-96
93Pin-102
93RedSoxWHP-12
93Sco-385
93Sel-228
93SP-202
93StaClu-86
93StaCluFDI-86
93StaCluMOP-86
93Stu-161
93Top-323
93TopGol-323
03TopInaM 323
93TopMic-323
93TriPla-46
93Ult-152
93UppDec-154
93UppDecGold-154
94Bow-259
94ColC-440
94ColChoGS-440
94ColChoSS-440
94Don-163
94ExtBas-20
94Fin-322
94FinRef-322
94Fla-263
94Fle-33
94FUnPac-39
94FUnPac-228
94Lea-182
94LeaL-10
94OPC-49
94Pac-56
94PanSti-30
94Pin-285
94PinArtP-285
94PinMusC-285
94ProMag-13
94Sco-83
94ScoGolR-83
94Sel-10
94SP-155
94SPDieC-155
94Spo-110
94StaClu-386
94StaCluFDI-386
94StaCluGR-386
94StaCluMOP-386
94Stu-162
94TomPiz-20
94Top-502
94TopGol-502
94TopSpa-502
94TriPla-204
94Ult-314
94UppDec-187
94UppDecED-187
95Bow-388
95ColCho-411
95ColChoGS-411
95ColChoSE-193
95ColChoSEGS-193
95ColChoSESS-193
95ColChoSS-411
95D3-34
95Don-547
95DonPreP-547
95DonTopotO-20
95Emb-64
95EmbGolI-64
95Emo-12
95Fin-152
95FinRef-152
95Fla-12
95Fle-31
95Lea-298
95Lea300C-5
95LeaLim-74
95Pac-38
95PacPri-14
95Pin-40
95PinArtP-40
95PinMusC-40
95Sco-33
95ScoGolR-33
95ScoPlaTS-33
95Sel-110
95SelArtP-110
95Spo-106
95SpoArtP-106
95StaClu-121
95StaClu-311
95StaCluFDI-121
95StaCluMOP-121
95StaCluMOP-311
95StaCluSTDW-RS121
95StaCluSTWS-121
95StaCluSTWS-311
95Stu-121
95Top-215
95Ult-263
95UltGolM-263
95UppDec-400
95UppDecED-400
95UppDecEDG-400
06UppDooSE 80
95UppDecSEG-80
96Cir-11
96CirRav-11
96ColCho-472
96ColChoGS-472
96ColChoSS-472
96Don-307
96DonPreP-307
96EmoXL-14
96Fin-B178
96FinRef-B178
96Fla-19
96Fle-27
96FleRedS-7
96FleTif-27
96Lea-170
96LeaPrePB-170
96LeaPrePG-170
96LeaPrePS-170
96LeaSigA-84
96LeaSigAG-84
96LeaSigAS-84
96MetUni-16
96MetUniP-16
96Pac-251
96PanSti-138
96Pin-28
96Pin-303
96PinArtP-187
96PinFoil-303
96PinSta-187
96ProSta-108
96Sco-335
96ScoDugC-B60
96ScoDugCAP-B60
96StaClu-162
96StaCluEPB-162
96StaCluEPG-162
96StaCluEPS-162
96StaCluMOP-162
96Top-143
96TopGal-54
96TopGalPPI-54
96Ult-17
96UltGolM-17
96UppDec-23
97Fle-24
97FleTif-24
97Pac-41
97PacLigB-41
97PacSil-41
97Sco-226
97ScoPreS-226
97ScoRedS-12
97ScoRedSPl-12
97ScoRedSPr-12
97ScoShoS-226
97ScoShoSAP-226
97StaClu-63
97StaCluMOP-63
97Top-123

Greenwell, Richard
89HigSchPLS-12

Greenwood, Bob
55Bow-42

Greenwood, John
88PulBraP-1753

Greenwood, Mike
87PocGiaTB-9

Greenwood, William
87OldJudN-215

Greer, Brian K.
80Top-685
82AmaGolST-2

Greer, Edward C.
88AugBecN-13

Greer, Ken
88OneYanP-2047
89PriWilCS-8
90Ft.LauYS-9
91Ft.LauYC-4
91Ft.LauYP-2418
92AlbYanF-2219
93ColCliF-1105
93ColCliP-4
94NorTidF-2914
95PhoFirTI-44

Greer, Michael
87OldJudN-216

Greer, Randy
80PenPilBT-14
80PenPilCT-20

Greer, Rusty
00ButCopKSP 4
91ChaRanC-21
91ChaRanP-1325
91Cla/Bes-172
91FloStaLAP-FSL4
92ProFS7-156
92SkyAA F-267
92TulDriF-2701
92TulDriS-607
93TulDriF-2741
94BowBes-B90
94BowBesR-B90
94LeaLimR-66
94OklCit8F-1504
94TopTra-29T
95ColCho-405
95ColChoGS-405
95ColChoSE-182
95ColChoSEGS-182
95ColChoSESS-182
95ColChoSS-405
95Don-513
95DonPreP-513
95DonTopotO-161
95Emo-86
95Fin-15
95FinRef-15
95Fla-89
95Lea-61
95LeaLim-73
95Pac-427
95PanSti-107
95Pin-253
95PinArtP-253
95PinMusC-253
95RanCra-12
95Sco-540
95ScoAi-AM18
95ScoGolR-540
95ScoPlaTS-540
95Sel-215
95SelArtP-215
95Spo-109
95SpoArtP-109
95StaClu-486
95StaCluMOP-486
95StaCluSTWS-486
95StaCluVR-266
95Stu-89
95Top-279
95TopCyb-151
95Ult-110
95UltAllR-3
95UltAllRGM-3
95UltGolM-110
95UltSecYS-3
95UltSecYSGM-3
95UppDec-156
95UppDecED-156
95UppDecEDG-156
95UppDecSE-173
95UppDecSEG-173
95Zen-96
96Cir-87
96CirRav-87
96ColCho-741
96ColChoGS-741
96ColChoSS-741
96Don-183
96DonPreP-183
96EmoXL-122
96Fla-170
96Fle-251
96FleRan-7
96FleTif-251
96Lea-71
96LeaLim-46
96LeaLimG-46
96LeaPrePB-71
96LeaPrePG-71
96LeaPrePS-71
96LeaSig-104
96LeaSigA-85
96LeaSigAG-85
96LeaSigAS-85
96LeaSigPPG-104
96LeaSigPPP-104
96MetUni-114
96MetUniP-114
96Pac-431
96RanMot-9
96Sco-30
96ScoDugC-A29
96ScoDugCAP-A29
06StaClu 315
96StaCluMOP-315
95StaCluVRMC-266
96Stu-97
96StuPrePB-97
96StuPrePG-97
96StuPrePS-97
96Top-87
96Ult-136
96UltGolM-136
96UppDec-211
97Bow-284
97BowChr-95
97BowChrI-95
97BowChrIR-95
97BowChrR-95
97BowInt-284
97Cir-43
97CirRav-43
97ColCho-239
97Don-226
97Don-422
97DonEli-127
97DonEliGS-127
97DonLim-44
97DonLim-133
97DonLimFotG-48
97DonLimLE-44
97DonLimLE-133
97DonPre-76
97DonPreCttC-76
97DonPreP-226
97DonPreP-422
97DonPrePGold-226
97DonPrePGold-422
97Fin-193
97FinRef-193
97FlaSho-A156
97FlaSho-B156
97FlaSho-C156
97FlaShoLC-156
97FlaShoLC-B156
97FlaShoLC-C156
97FlaShoLCM-A156
97FlaShoLCM-B156
97FlaShoLCM-C156
97Fle-222
97FleTif-222
97Lea-28
97Lea-387
97LeaFraM-28
97LeaFraM-387
97LeaFraMDC-28
97LeaFraMDC-387
97LeaKnoG-7
97LeaWarT-8
97MetUni-163
97NewPin-63

97NewPinAP-63
97NewPinMC-63
97NewPinPP-63
97Pac-201
97PacLigB-201
97PacPri-69
97PacPriLB-69
97PacPriP-69
97PacSil-201
97PinCer-56
97PinCerMBlu-56
97PinCerMG-56
97PinCerMR-56
97PinCerR-56
97PinIns-95
97PinInsCE-95
97PinInsDE-95
97PinTotCPB-56
97PinTotCPG-56
97PinTotCPR-56
97PinX-P-22
97PinX-PMoS-22
97Sco-43
97Sco-534
97ScoHobR-534
97ScoPreS-43
97ScoRan-4
97ScoRanPl-4
97ScoRanPr-4
97ScoResC-534
97ScoShoS-43
97ScoShoS-534
97ScoShoSAP-43
97ScoShoSAP-534
97Sel-30
97SelArtP-30
97SelRegG-30
97SelTooотT-21
97SelToootTMB-21
97SP-174
97SpoIll-43
97SpoIllEE-43
97StaClu-52
97StaCluMat-52
97StaCluMOP-52
97Stu-48
97StuPrePG-48
97StuPrePS-48
97Top-12
97TopChr-6
97TopChrR-6
97TopGal-94
97TopGalPPI-94
93TulDriTI-11
97Ult-133
97UltGolME-133
97UltPlaME-133
97UppDec-180
97UppDec-387

Gregg, Eric
88T/MUmp-34
89T/MUmp-32
90T/MUmp-31

Gregg, Hal
47TipTop-95
49EurSta-161
52Top-318
76TayBow4-73
83TopRep5-318
90DodTar-296

Gregg, Sylvanus
16FleBreD-34

Gregg, Tommy
86NasPirP-9
87HarSenP-19
88BufBisC-12
88BufBisP-1474
88Don-203
88FleUpd-113
88FleUpdG-113
88ScoRoo-69T
88ScoRooG-69T
89BraDub-13
89ClaTraP-192
89Don-121
89DonBasB-170
89Fle-592
89FleGlo-592
89PanSti-32
89TopTra-39T
89TopTraT-39T
89UppDec-751
90BraDubP-9
90BraDubS-11
90Don-239
90Fle-585
90FleCan-585
90Lea-86
90OPC-223
90PanSti-224
90PubSti-114
90Sco-78
90ScoYouSI-39
90Top-223
90TopTif-223
90UppDec-121
90VenSti-215
91BraDubP-13
91BraSubS-17
91Don-244
91Fle-691
91Lea-144
91OPC-742
91PanFreS-19
91Sco-606
91StaClu-571
91Top-742
91TopDesS-742
91TopMic-742
91TopTif-742
91Ult-6
92BraLykP-14
92BraLykS-15
92Don-485
92OPC-53
92Sco-623
92StaClu-244
92Top-53
92TopGol-53
92TopGolW-53
92TopMic-53
93IndIndF-1496
96ChaKniB-12
97RicBraBC-22

Gregg, Vean
09SpoNewSM-71
11PloCanE-30
12T207-71
13NatGamW-17
13TomBarW-16
14CraJacE-29
14TexTomE-21
14TexTomE-53
15CraJacE-29
15SpoNewP-4
19W514-33

Gregory, B.
09PC7HHB-17

Gregory, Brad
90MiaMirIS-10

Gregory, Bull
72Dia-121

Gregory, Howie
09PC7HHB-17

Gregory, Jim
72CedRapCT-7

Gregory, John
83VerBeaDT-17

Gregory, Lee (Grover)
62KahAtl-9
77FriOneYW-74

Gregory, Paul
47SigOil-7

Gregory, Scott
78DunBluJT-10

Gregson, Goose (Glenn)
77ReaPhiT-12
83MidCubT-3
84MidCubT-14
87WinSpiP-12
88GreFalDTI-27
89GreFalDSP-33
90BakDodCLC-246
91BakDodCLC-29
91CalLeLA-24
93AlbDukF-1480
94AlbDukF-859

Greif, Bill
72OPC-101
72PadTeal-11
72Top-101
73OPC-583
73Top-583
74OPC-102
74PadDea-10
74PadMcDD-4
74Top-102A
74Top-102B
74TopSta-92
75OPC-168
75Top-168
76OPC-184
76Top-184
77OPC-243
77Top-112

Greiner, Dan
19W514-80

Greisinger, Seth
97Bow-99
97BowBes-108
97BowBesAR-108
97BowBesR-108
97BowChr-121
97BowChrI-121
97BowChrIR-121
97BowChrR-121
97BowInt-99

Grejtak, Bryan
90OklSoo-1
91BluOriC-13
91BluOriP-4130

Greminger, Edward
09T206-486
10CouT21-25
11SpoLifCW-147

Grenert, Geoff
93BoiHawC-12
93BoiHawF-3909
94CedRapKC-11
94CedRapKF-1105
95CedRapKTI-21
96CedRapKTI-10

Grennan, Steve
91PocPioP-3777
91PocPioSP-19
92KinMetC-7
92KinMetF-1525
93PitMetC-7
93PitMetF-3701
94CapCitBC-9
94CapCitBF-1746
95StLucMTI-14

Grensky, Herb
80PenPilCT-15

Gresham, Kris
91BluOriC-1
91BluOriP-4131
92KanCouCC-9
92KanCouCF-93
92KanCouCTI-12
93FreKeyC-9
93FreKeyF-1029
94BowBayF-2416
94OriPro-42
95RocRedWTI-17
96BowBayB-15

Gress, Loren
90IdaFalBP-3270
91IdaFalBP-4336
91MacBraP-871

Gretzky, Wayne
91StaCluCM-46
91StaCluCM-47
91StaCluMO-44

Grewal, Ranbir
90JamExpP-17
91MidLeaAP-MWL45
91RocExpC-5
91RocExpP-2040
92ClaFS7-304
92WesPalBEC-12
92WesPalBEF-2084

Grich, Bob
71OPC-193
71Top-193
72OPC-338
72Top-338
73Kel2D-39
73LinPor-10
73OPC-418
73OriJohP-3A
73OriJohP-3B
73Top-418
74OPC-109
74Top-109
74TopDecE-8
74TopSta-125
75Hos-72
75Kel-4A
75Kel-4B
75OPC-225
75Top-225
76Hos-13
76HosTwi-13
76OPC-335
76SSP-388
76Top-335
77BurCheD-126
77Hos-131
77Kel-39
77OPC-28
77PepGloD-25
77RCColC-26
77Spo-3502
77Top-521
78AngFamF-13
78Hos-62
78OPC-133
78RCColC-57
78SSP270-194
78Top-18
79Hos-112
79OPC-248
79Top-477
80OPC-326
80Top-621
81AllGamPI-13
81Don-289
81Fle-269
81FleStiC-50
81LonBeaPT-2
81OPC-182
81Top-182
81TopSti-53
81TopSupHT-58
82Don-90
82Fle-461
82FleSta-218
82Kel-38
82OPC-284
82PerAll-5
82PerAllG-5
82Top-162
82Top-284
82TopSti-4
82TopSti-162
83AllGamPI-13
83Don-468
83Fle-91
83Kel-60
83OPC-381
83OPC-387
83SevCoi-11
83Top-387
83Top-790
83TopSti-43
84AllGamPI-104
84AngSmo-10
84Don-179
84Fle-518
84Nes792-315
84OPC-315
84Top-315
84TopRubD-20
84TopSti-228
84TopTif-315
85AllGamPI-14
85AngSmo-12
85AngStrH-7
85Don-280
85Fle-302
85Lea-88
85OPC-155
85Top-465
85TopRubD-20
85TopSti-230
85TopTif-465
86AngSmo-12
86Don-207
86Fle-157
86OPC-155
86Top-155
86Top-486
86TopSti-181
86TopTat-23
86TopTif-155
86TopTif-486
86Woo-12
87AngGriS-1
87AngGriS-2
87AngGriS-3
87AngGriS-4
87AngGriS-5
87AngGriS-6
87AngGriS-7
87AngGriS-8
87AngGriS-9
87AngGriS-10
87AngGriS-11
87AngGriS-12
87AngGriS-13
87AngGriS-14
87AngGriS-15
87AngGriS-16
87AngGriS-17
87Don-456
87Fle-81
87FleGlo-81
87OPC-4
87RedFolSB-30
87Spo-184
87Top-677
87TopTif-677
89AngSmo-11
90PacLeg-31
90SweBasG-58
91OriCro-165
91UppDecS-12
92ActPacA-71
93OriCroASU-5
93TedWil-19
93UppDecAH-59
94UppDecAH-132
94UppDecAH1-132

Grier, Antron
87EriCarP-12
88HamRedP-1723
88SavCarP-355
89SprCarB-3
90St.PetCS-10

Grier, Dave
80BurBeeT-5
82ElPasDT-17

Grier, Mark
79NewCoPT-14

Griesser, Grant
90AppFoxBS-10
90AppFoxP-2097

Grieve, Ben
94Cla#1DPMF-DD2
94ClaUpdCotC-CC2
94SigRooDP-3
94SigRooDPS-3
94SouOreAC-7
94SouOreAF-3636
94StaCluDP-84
94StaCluDPFDI-84
94TopTra-44T
94UppDecAHNIL-18
95ActPac2GF-18G
95ActPacF-53
95ActPacF-79
95Bes-37
95BesFra-F5
95Bow-258
95BowBes-B25
95BowBesR-B25
95BowGolF-258
95ColCho-40
95ColChoGS-40
95ColChoSS-40
95Exc-108
95ExcFirYP-7
95ModA'sTI-8
95Pin-175
95PinArtP-175
95PinETA-1
95PinMusC-175
95ScoDraP-DP12
95SelSurS-SS1
95SigRooFD-FD2
95SigRooFDS-FD2
95SPML-8
95SPML-125
95SPMLA-10
95SPMLDtS-DS5
95StaClu-103
95StaCluFDI-103
95StaCluMOP-103
95StaCluSTWS-103
95Top-212
95UppDec-3
95UppDecED-3
95UppDecEDG-3
95UppDecML-150
95UppDecML-216
95UppDecSE-107
95UppDecSEG-107
95WesMicWTI-22
96BesAutSA-23

96Bow-187
96BowBes-118
96BowBesAR-118
96BowBesMI-7
96BowBesMIR-7
96BowBesR-118
96Exc-98
96HunStaTI-8
96ModA'sB-4
96SigRooOJRS-R2
96Top-436
97Bow-386
97BowBes-169
97BowBesAR-169
97BowBesR-169
97BowCerBIA-CA32
97BowCerGIA-CA32
97BowChr-255
97BowChrI-255
97BowChrIR-255
97BowChrR-255
97BowChrSHR-SHR7
97BowChrSHRR-SHR7
97BowInt-386
97BowScoHR-7
97Top-488
95UppDecMLFS-150
95UppDecMLFS-216

Grieve, Tim

94EugEmeC-11
94EugEmeF-3705
94StaCluDP-90
94StaCluDPFDI-90
94TopTra-66T
95Exc-60

Grieve, Tom

71MLBOffS-540
71OPC-167
71Top-167
72Top-609
73OPC-579
73Top-579
74OPC-268
74Top-268
75Hos-38
75OPC-234
75Top-234
76Hos-130
76OPC-106
76SSP-270
76Top-106
77BurCheD-25
77Hos-93
77Top-403
78MetDaiPA-8
78Top-337
79OPC-138
79Top-277
79TucTorT-14
91MetWIZ-152
93RanKee-13
96BowBesMIAR-7

Grieve, William

55Bow-275

Griffen, Leonard

91CedRapRC-5
91CedRapRP-2713
92CedRapRC-3
92CedRapRF-1067

Griffey, Craig

92BelMarC-25
92BelMarF-1459
92LimRocGH-3
92UppDec-85
93AppFoxC-10
93AppFoxF-2471
93RivPilCLC-27
94JacSunF-1424
94SigRooFCD-1
94SigRooFCD-2
94SigRooFCS-AU1
94SigRooFCS-AU2
94SigRooFCS-AU3
94SigRooFCS-AU5
95PorCitRTI-12
95UppDecML-59
96PorCitRB-13
95UppDecMLFS-59

Griffey, Ken Jr.

83KelCerB-14
84OCoandSI-237
87BelMarTI-15
88CalLeaACLC-26
88SanBerSB-1
88SanBerSCLC-34
88VerMarP-NNO
89Bow-220
89Bow-259
89BowTif-220
89BowTif-259
89ClaTraO-131
89ClaTraP-193
89Don-33
89DonBasB-192
89DonRoo-3
89Fle-548
89FleGlo-548
89MarMot-3
89MotGriJ-1
89MotGriJ-2
89MotGriJ-3
89MotGriJ-4
89ScoRoo-100T
89ScoSco-30
89ScoYouS2-18
89SpoIllFKI-158
89TopHeaUT-5
89TopTra-41T
89TopTraT-41T
89UppDec-1
89UppDecS-2
89UppDecS-3
90AllBasT-17
90Baz-18
90Bow-481
90BowTif-481
90ClaBlu-20
90ClaYel-T1
90Col-3
90Don-4
90Don-365
90DonBesA-1
90DonLeaS-8
90DonSupD-4
90Fle-513
90FleAwaW-16
90FleBasA-14
90FleBasM-14
90FleCan-513
90FleLeaL-14
90FleSoaS-6
90FleWaxBC-C10
90GooHumICBLS-11
90Hot50RS-19
90KinDis-16
90Lea-245
90LeaPre-4
90MarMot-3
90MLBBasB-117
90MSAIceTD-8
90OPC-336
90PanSti-155
90PlaPri-2
90Pos-23
90PubSti-30
90PubSti-433
90PubSti-595
90RedFolSB-40
90Sco-560
90Sco100RS-3
90Spo-7
90StaGriJ-1
90StaGriJ-2
90StaGriJ-3
90StaGriJ-4
90StaGriJ-5
90StaGriJ-6
90StaGriJ-7
90StaGriJ-8
90StaGriJ-9
90StaGriJ-10
90StaGriJ-11
90SunSee-2
90SupActM-3
90Top-336
90TopBig-250
90TopCoi-16
90TopDeb89-46
90TopDou-29
90TopGloS-20
90TopHeaU-5
90TopMag-3
90TopMag-27
90TopRoo-11
90TopSti-225
90TopSti-323
90TopStiB-49
90TopTif-336
90ToyRoo-13
90UppDec-24
90UppDec-156
90UppDecS-3
90USPlaCA-11S
90VenSti-216
90WinDis-7
90WonBreS-18
91AlrGriG-1
91AlrGriG-2
91AlrGriG-3
91AlrGriG-4
91AlrGriP-1
91AreHol-2
91AreHol-5
91BasBesHM-7
91Ble23KGJ-1
91Ble23KGJ-2
91Ble23KGJ-3
91BlePro-1
91Bow-246
91CadEIlD-26
91CarGuaPG-1
91Cla1-T3
91Cla2-T1
91Cla3-T30
91ClaGam-120
91Col-4
91ColGriJ-1
91ColGriJ-2
91ColGriJ-3
91ColGriJ-4
91ColGriJ-5
91ColGriJ-6
91ColGriJ-7
91ColGriJ-8
91ColGriJ-9
91ColGriJ-10
91ColGriJ-11
91ColGriJ-12
91Don-49
91Don-77
91Don-392
91DonPre-4
91Fle-450
91Fle-450A
91Fle-710
91FleAll-7
91FroRowKGJ-1
91FroRowKGJ-1P
91FroRowKGJ-2
91FroRowKGJ-2P
91FroRowKGJ-3
91FroRowKGJ-3P
91FroRowKGJ-4
91FroRowKGJ-4P
91FroRowKGJ-5
91FroRowKGJ-5P
91FroRowKGJ-6
91FroRowKGJ-7
91FroRowKGJ-8
91FroRowKGJ-9
91FroRowKGJ-10
91JimDea-2
91KinDis-6
91Lea-372
91MajLeaCP-4
91MarCouH-15
91MarCouH-28
91MooSna-4
91MotGri-1
91MotGri-3
91MotGri-4
91MSAHolD-9
91OPC-392
91OPC-790
91OPCPre-56
91PanCanT1-116
91PanFreS-172
91PanFreS-233
91PanSti-189
91PepGri-1
91PepGri-2
91PepGri-3
91PepGri-4
91PepGri-5
91PepGri-6
91PetSta-23
91PlaGriJ-1
91PlaGriJ-32
91PlaGriJ-33
91PlaGriJ-34
91PlaGriJ-35
91PlaGriJ-36
91PlaGriJ-37
91PlaGriJ-38
91PlaGriJ-49
91PlaGriJ-50
91PlaGriJ-61
91PlaGriJ-62
91PlaGriJ-63
91PlaGriJ-64
91PlaGriJ-65
91PlaGriJ-66
91PlaGriJ-xx
91Pos-11
91PosCan-26
91RedFolS-41
91RedFolS-120
91Sco-2
91Sco-396
91Sco-697
91Sco-841
91Sco-858
91Sco-892
91Sco100S-5
91ScoCoo-B3
91Sev3DCN-6
91SevCoi-A4
91SevCoi-F7
91SevCoi-M7
91SevCoi-NW4
91SevCoi-T8
91SevCoi-NC6
91SevCoi-NE6
91SevCoi-NW5
91SevCoi-SC3
91SimandSMLBL-18
91StaClu-270
91StaCluCM-10
91StaGri-1
91StaGri-2
91StaGri-4
91StaGri-6
91StaGri-8
91StaGri-10
91StaPinB-21
91Stu-112
91SunSee-11
91Top-392
91Top-790
91TopCraJI-36
91TopDesS-392
91TopDesS-790
91TopGloA-7
91TopMic-392
91TopMic-790
91TopSta-17
91TopTif-392
91TopTif-790
91TopTriH-A12
91Ult-336
91UltGol-4
91UppDec-555
91UppDec-572
91UppDecFE-79F
91UppDecFE-87F
91USPlaCA-1D
92AlrGriAAS-1
92AlrGriAAS-2
92AlrGriAAS-3
92AlrGriAAS-4
92AlrGriAAS-5
92AlrGriAAS-6
92AlrGriAAS-7
92AlrGriAAS-8
92AlrGriAAS-9
92AlrGriAAS-10
92AlrGriGM-1
92AlrGriGM-2
92AlrGriGM-3
92AlrGriGM-4
92AlrGriGM-5
92AlrGriGM-6
92AlrGriGM-7
92AlrGriGM-8
92AlrGriGM-9
92AlrGriGM-10
92AlrGriGMS-1
92AlrGriM-1
92AlrGriM-2
92AlrGriM-3
92AreKidGCH-1
92AreKidGCH-2
92AreKidGCH-3
92AreKidGCH-4
92AreKidGCH-5
92Bow-100
92Cla1-T40
92Cla2-T44
92ClaBluBF-BC12
92ClaFS7-200
92ClaGam-186
92ClaRedB-BC12
92ColAllG-11
92ColAllP-11
92ColPro-8
92DEL-AU1
92Don-24
92Don-165
92DonCraJ1-12
92DonEli-13
92DonMcD-22
92DonPre-7
92Fle-279
92Fle-709
92FleAll-23
92FleCitTP-4
92FleTeaL-15
92FleUpdH-1
92Fre-15
92FroRowGCH-1
92FroRowGCH-2
92FroRowGCH-3
92FroRowGCH-4
92FroRowGCH-5
92FroRowGCH-6
92FroRowGCH-7
92FroRowGCH-8
92FroRowGCH-9
92FroRowGCH-10
92FroRowGG-1
92FroRowGG-2
92FroRowGG-3
92FroRowGH-1
92FroRowGH-2
92FroRowGH-3
92FroRowGJOC-NNO
92Hig5-107
92Hig5S-17
92Hig5S-32
92JimDea-11
92KinDis-8
92Lea-392
92LeaBlaG-392
92LeaGolP-24
92LeaPre-24
92LimRocGH-2
92MarMot-2
92MooSna-7
92Mr.TurS-12
92MSABenSHD-10
92MTVRocnJ-3
92New-9
92OPC-50
92OPCPre-167
92PanSti-60
92PanSti-277
92PepDieM-26
92PerGamGJ-1
92PerGamGJ-2
92PerGamGJ-3
92PerGamGJ-4
92PerGamGJ-5
92PerGamGJ-6
92PerGamGJ-7
92PerGamGJ-8
92PerGamGJ-9
92Pin-283
92Pin-549
92PinSlu-7
92PinTea2-47
92PinTeaP-9
92PlaGriJ-1
92PlaGriJ-2
92PlaGriJ-3
92PlaGriJ-4
92Pos-20
92Sco-1
92Sco-436
92Sco100
92ScoIm
92ScoPr
92ScoS
92Sev
92Sp
92S
92S
92
9
9

92StaCluMP-7
92StaGriJ-1
92StaGriJ-2
92StaGriJ-3
92StaGriJ-4
92StaGriJ-5
92StaGriJ-6
92StaGriJ-7
92StaGriJ-8
92StaGriJ-9
92StaGriJ-10
92StaGriJ-11
92Stu-232
92SunSee-14
92Top-50
92TopGol-50
92TopGolW-50
92TopKid-122
92TopMcD-8
92TopMic-50
92TopMic-G50
92TriPla-152
92TriPlaG-GS8
92TriPlaP-1
92Ult-123
92UltAllS-6
92UltAwaW-22
92UppDec-85
92UppDec-424
92UppDec-650
92UppDecF-24
92UppDecFG-24
92UppDecTMH-22
92UppDecWB-T15
93AlrGri2TT-1
93AlrGri2TT-2
93AlrGri2TT-3
93AlrGri2TT-4
93AlrGri2TT-5
93AlrGri2TT-6
93AlrGrifMVO-1
93AlrGrifMVO-2
93AlrGrifMVO-3
93AlrGriT-1
93AlrGriTP-1
93Ble23KGJ-1
93Ble23KGJ-2
93Bow-375
93Bow-703
93CadDis-28
93ClaGam-38
93ColAllG-3
93DiaMar-44
93DiaMarA-3
93DiaMarP-5
93Don-553
93DonDiaK-DK1
93DonEliD-12
93DonLonBL-LL9
93DonMasotG-8
93DonMVP-20
93DonPre-20
93DurPowP2-15
93Fin-110
93FinJum-110
93FinRef-110
93Fla-270
93Fle-307
93FleAll-AL7
93FleAtl-11
93FleFruotL-25
93FleTeaL-AL10
93FroRowGJGC-1
93FroRowGJGC-2
93FroRowGJGC-3
93FroRowGJGC-4
93FroRowGJGC-5
93FroRowGJGC-6
93FroRowGJGC-7
93FroRowGJGC-8
93FroRowGJGC-9
93FroRowGJGC-10
93FunPac-16
93FunPac-24
93FunPac-30
93FunPac-111
3FunPac-114
FunPac-224
unPacA-AS8
s-25
nDumC-15
ea-11
-2

93Lea-319
93LeaGolA-R7
93LeaGolA-U8
93MarDaiQ-4
93MarMot-4
93MetBak-9
93OPC-91
93OPCPreSP-9
93OPCPreSPF-9
93PacJugC-7
93PacSpa-286
93PanSti-63
93Pin-110
93PinCoo-22
93PinCooD-22
93PinHomRC-13
93PinSlu-28
93Pos-7
93PosCan-9
93Sco-1
93Sco-504
93Sco-536
93ScoFra-12
93ScoGolDT-5
93Sel-2
93SelChaS-19
93SelDufIP-7
93SelStaL-15
93SP-4
93SpeGolSGJ-1
93SPPlaP-PP9
93StaClu-591
93StaClu-707
93StaCluFDI-591
93StaCluFDI-707
93StaClul-B4
93StaCluM-56
93StaCluMari-1
93StaCluMMP-3
93StaCluMO-11
93StaCluMOP-591
93StaCluMOP-707
93StaCluMOP-MB4
93StaCluMP-26
93Stu-96
93StuSupoC-1
93Top-179
93Top-405
93TOPBLAG-33
93TopFulS-2
93TopGol-179
93TopGol-405
93TopInaM-179
93TopInaM-405
93TopMic-179
93TopMic-405
93TopMic-P179
93TopPre-179
93TopPreS-6
93Toy-1
93ToyMasP-5
93TriPla-1
93TriPlaA-24
93TriPlaN-5
93TriPlaP-1
93Ult-619
93UltAllS-17
93UltAwaW-16
93UltPer-3
93UppDec-55
93UppDec-355
93UppDec-525
93UppDecCP-R11
93UppDecDG-13
93UppDecFA-A1
93UppDecFAJ-A1
93UppDecFH-59
93UppDecGold-55
93UppDecGold-355
93UppDecGold-525
93UppDecHRH-HR9
93UppDecIC-WI13
93UppDecICJ-WI13
93UppDecOD-D13
93UppDecS-19
93UppDecSH-HI9
93UppDecTriCro-TC4
93USPlaCA-4C
94AlrTacGJ-1
94AlrTacGJ-2
94AlrTacGJ-3
94AlrTacGJ-4
94AlrTacGJ-5
94AlrTacGJ-6

94AlrTacGJ-SP1
94AlrTacGJ-SP2
94AlrTacGJ-SP3
94AlrTacGJ-SP4
94AlrTacGJ-SP5
94Bow-5
94BowBes-R40
94BowBes-X96
94BowBesR-R40
94BowBesR-X96
94ChuShoS-3
94ColC-117
94ColC-317
94ColC-324
94ColC-340
94ColC-634
94ColChoGS-117
94ColChoGS-317
94ColChoGS-324
94ColChoGS-340
94ColChoGS-634
94ColChoHRA-HA2
94ColChoSS-117
94ColChoSS-317
94ColChoSS-324
94ColChoSS-340
94ColChoSS-634
94ColChoT-2
94ColChoT-7
94DaiQueKGJ-1
94DaiQueKGJ-2
94DaiQueKGJ-3
94DaiQueKGJ-4
94DaiQueKGJ-5
94DaiQueKGJ-6
94DaiQueKGJ-7
94DaiQueKGJ-8
94DaiQueKGJ-9
94DaiQueKGJ-10
94DenHol-12
94Don-4
94DonDiaK-DK14
94DonDom-A9
94DonDom-B6
94DonEli-45
94DonLonBL-5
94DonMVP-26
94DonPro-7
94DonSpeE-4
94DonSpiotG-3
94ExtBas-166
94ExtBasGB-14
94Fin-232
94FinJum-232
94FinRef-232
94Fla-103
94FlaHotG-3
94FlaOutP-6
94Fle-286
94FleAllS-10
94FleGolM-4
94FleLumC-5
94FleSun-13
94FleTeaL-12
94FUnPac-24
94FUnPac-182
94FUnPac-193
94FUnPac-200
94FUnPac-216
94FUnPac-224
94FUnPac-229
94FUnPac-235
94KinDis-6
94Kra-5
94Lea-368
94LeaGam-1
94LeaGolS-4
94LeaL-66
94LeaLimGA-11
94LeaMVPC-A8
94LeaMVPCG-A8
94LeaPowB-5
94LeaPro-3
94LeaSli-9
94LeaStaS-6
94MarMot-4
94NinGriJ-1
94OPC-22
94OPCAllR-8
94OPCJumA-8
94OscMayR-6
94Pac-570
94PacGolP-2
94PacPro-P4

94PacSilP-8
94PanSti-118
94Pin-100
94PinArtP-100
94PinMusC-100
94PinPowS-PS23
94PinRunC-RC3
94PinTeaP-6
94PinTheN-3
94PinTri-TR17
94Pos-15
94PosCan-10
94PosCanG-10
94ProMag-127
94ProMagP-1
94RedFolMI-33
94Sco-3
94Sco-628
94ScoCyc-TC17
94ScoGolR-3
94ScoGolR-628
94ScoGolS-32
94ScoSam-3
94ScoSam-3GR
94Sel-1
94SelCroC-CC10
94SigBatP-1
94SigRooFCD-3
94SigRooFCS-AU2
94SigRooFCS-AU4
94SigRooFCS-AU5
94SigRooFCS-AU6
94SP-105
94SPDieC-105
94SPHol-12
94SPHolDC-12
94Spo-143
94Spo-181
94SpoFanA-AS7
94SpoRooGGG-GG4
94SPPre-WR3
94StaClu-85
94StaClu-262
94StaClu-529
94StaCluDD-DD7
94StaCluF-F5
94StaCluFDI-85
94StaCluFDI-262
94StaCluFDI-529
94StaCluGR-85
94StaCluGR-262
94StaCluGR-529
94StaCluMO-17
94StaCluMOF-2
94StaCluMOP-85
94StaCluMOP-262
94StaCluMOP-529
94StaCluMOP-F5
94StaCluMOP-DD7
94Stu-101
94StuEdiC-3
94StuSerS-4
94TomPiz-21
94Top-388
94Top-400
94Top-606
94TopBlaG-8
94TopGol-388
94TopGol-400
94TopGol-606
94TopSpa-388
94TopSpa-400
94TopSpa-606
94TopSupS-19
94TopTraFI-5
94TriPla-127
94TriPlaBS-8
94TriPlaM-11
94TriPlaP-4
94Ult-120
94UltAllS-8
94UltAwaW-6
94UltHomRK-2
94UltOnBL-6
94UppDec-53
94UppDec-224
94UppDec-292
94UppDec-GM1
94UppDec-KG1
94UppDecAJ-1
94UppDecAJ-48
94UppDecAJG-1
94UppDecAJG-48
94UppDecDC-W4

94UppDecED-53
94UppDecED-224
94UppDecED-292
94UppDecGJ-CL1
94UppDecGJ-CL2
94UppDecGJ-CL3
94UppDecGJ-CL4
94UppDecGP-172
94UppDecGP-50
94UppDecGP-24
94UppDecGP-224
94UppDecGP-48
94UppDecGP-24
94UppDecGP-6
94UppDecGP-125
94UppDecGP-100
94UppDecMLS-MM10
94UppDecMLSED-MM10
94UppDecNG-6
94UppDecNGED-6
94USPlaCA-12C
95Baz-31
95BazRedH-RH7
95Bow-321
95BowBes-R49
95BowBes-X12
95BowBesJR-2
95BowBesR-R49
95BowBesR-X12
95ClaFanFPCP-4
95ClaPhoC-50
95ColCho-62
95ColCho-70
95ColCho-88
95ColChoCtG-CG8
95ColChoCtG-CG8B
95ColChoCtG-CG8C
95ColChoCtGE-8
95ColChoCtGG-CG8
95ColChoCtGG-CG8B
95ColChoCtGG-CG8C
95ColChoCtGGE-8
95ColChoGS-62
95ColChoGS-70
95ColChoGS-88
95ColChoSE-26
95ColChoSE-125
95ColChoSE-261
95ColChoSEGS-26
95ColChoSEGS-125
95ColChoSEGS-261
95ColChoSESS-26
95ColChoSESS-125
95ColChoSESS-261
95ColChoSS-62
95ColChoSS-70
95ColChoSS-88
95ConTSNGJ-1
95ConTSNGJ-2
95ConTSNGJ-3
95ConTSNGJ-4
95ConTSNGJ-5
95ConTSNGJ-6
95ConTSNGJ-7
95ConTSNGJ-8
95D3-43
95DenHol-11
95Don-340
95DonAll-AL8
95DonBomS-1
95DonDiaK-DK27
95DonDom-8
95DonEli-54
95DonLonBL-3
95DonPreP-340
95DonTopotO-150
95Emb-51
95EmbGolI-51
95Emo-77
95EmoMas-3
95EmoN-6
95Fin-118
95FinPowK-PK10
95FinRef-118
95Fla-81
95FlaHotG-3
95FlaHotN-4
95FlaOutP-7
95Fle-269
95FleAllF-7
95FleAllS-7
95FleLeaL-2
95FleLumC-6
95FleTeaL-12

95FleUpdDT-6
95FleUpdH-11
95FleUpdSL-3
95KinDis-11
95Kra-5
95Lea-211
95Lea300C-10
95LeaGolS-4
95LeaGreG-6
95LeaHeaftH-2
95LeaLim-118
95LeaLimG-6
95LeaLimIBP-5
95LeaLimL-4
95LeaOpeD-4
95LeaSli-8A
95LeaSli-8B
95LeaStaS-2
95MarMot-4
95MarPac-1
95MarPac-6
95MarPac-9
95MarPac-32
95MegGriJWL-2
95MegGriJWL-3
95MegGriJWL-4
95MegGriJWL-5
95MegGriJWL-6
95MegGriJWL-7
95MegGriJWL-8
95MegGriJWL-9
95MegGriJWL-10
95MegGriJWL-11
95MegGriJWL-12
95MegGriJWL-13
95MegGriJWL-14
95MegGriJWL-15
95MegGriJWL-16
95MegGriJWL-17
95MegGriJWL-18
95MegGriJWL-19
95MegGriJWL-20
95MegGriJWL-21
95MegGriJWL-22
95MegGriJWL-23
95MegGriJWL-24
95MegGriJWL-25
95MegGriJWL-XX
95MegRut-14
95MegRut-21
95NatPac-6
95Pac-398
95PacGolCDC-16
95PacGolP-21
95PacPri-126
95PanSti-86
95PanSti-123
95Pin-128
95Pin-304
95Pin-447
95Pin-450
95PinArtP-128
95PinArtP-304
95PinArtP-447
95PinArtP-450
95PinFan-11
95PinGatA-GA1
95PinMusC-128
95PinMusC-304
95PinMusC-447
95PinMusC-450
95PinPin-14
95PinPinR-14
95PinRedH-RH2
95PinTeaP-TP7
95PinWhiH-WH2
95Pos-4
95PosCan-1
95RedFol-5
95Sco-437
95Sco-551
95ScoDouGC-GC2
95ScoDreT-DG7
95ScoGolR-1
95ScoGolR-437
95ScoGolR-551
95ScoHaloG-HG1
95ScoPlaTS-1
95ScoPlaTS-437
95ScoPlaTS-551
95ScoRul-SR1
95ScoRulJ-SR1
95Sel-89
95Sel-243
95Sel-250
95SelArtP-89
95SelArtP-243
95SelArtP-250
95SelBigS-BS2
95SelCer-70
95SelCerC-1
95SelCerGT-1
95SelCerMG-70
95SP-190
95SP-AU190
95SPCha-183
95SPCha-185
95SPChaDC-183
95SPChaDC-185
95SPChaDFC-1
95SPChaFCDC-1
95Spo-1
95Spo-168
95SpoArtP-1
95SpoArtP-168
95SpoDet-DE3
95SpoDouT-9
95SpoHamT-HT1
95SpoPro-PM1
95SPPlaP-PP12
95SPSil-190
95SPSpeF-18
95StaClu-241
95StaClu-521
95StaCluCC-CC18
95StaCluCT-9
95StaCluFDI-241
95StaCluMO-19
95StaCluMOP-241
95StaCluMOP-521
95StaCluMOP-CC18
95StaCluMOP-PZ7
95StaCluMOP-RL14
95StaCluMOP-SS11
95StaCluMOP-VRE2
95StaCluPZ-PZ7
95StaCluRL-RL14
95StaCluSS-SS11
95StaCluSTDW-M241
95StaCluSTWS-241
95StaCluSTWS-521
95StaCluVE-VRE2
95StaCluVR-120
95Stu-5
95StuGolS-5
95StuPlaS-5
95Sum-1
95Sum-174
95Sum-195
95SumBigB-BB1
95SumNthD-1
95SumNthD-174
95SumNthD-195
95TomPiz-9
95Top-388
95Top-397
95TopCyb-199
95TopFin-3
95TopLeaL-LL31
95TopPre-PP6
95TopTra-2T
95TopTra-160T
95TopTraPB-2
95UC3-73
95UC3-124
95UC3ArtP-73
95UC3ArtP-124
95UC3CycS-CS2
95UC3InM-IM2
95UllHomRK-6
95Ult-101
95UltAllS-7
95UltAllSGM-7
95UltAwaW-6
95UltAwaWGM-6
95UltGolM-101
95UltHitM-6
95UltHitMGM-6
95UltHomRK-1
95UltHomRKGM-1
95UltPowP-2
95UltPowPGM-2
95UppDec-100
95UppDec-110
95UppDecED-100
95UppDecED-110
95UppDecEDG-100
95UppDecEDG-110
95UppDecPAW-H3
95UppDecPAWE-H3
95UppDecPC-MLB4
95UppDecPLL-R4
95UppDecPLL-R45
95UppDecPLL-R52
95UppDecPLLE-R4
95UppDecPLLE-R45
95UppDecPLLE-R52
95UppDecSE-255
95UppDecSEG-255
95USPlaCMLA-13C
95Zen-61
95ZenAllS-15
95ZenZ-2
96Baz-1
96Bow-79
96BowBes-71
96BowBesAR-71
96BowBesC-1
96BowBesCAR-1
96BowBesCR-1
96BowBesMI-7
96BowBesMIAR-7
96BowBesMIR-7
96BowBesP-BBP30
96BowBesPAR-BBP30
96BowBesPR-BBP30
96BowBesR-71
96Cir-78
96Cir-198
96CirAcc-12
96CirBos-20
96CirRav-78
96CirRav-198
96Cla7/1PC-5
96ColCho-310
96ColCho-370T
96ColCho-415
96ColChoCtG-CG26
96ColChoCtG-CG26B
96ColChoCtG-CG26C
96ColChoCtGE-CR26
96ColChoCtGG-CG26
96ColChoCtGG-CG26B
96ColChoCtGG-CG26C
96ColChoCtGGE-CR26
96ColChoGACA-CA1
96ColChoGACA-CA2
96ColChoGACA-CA3
96ColChoGACA-CA4
96ColChoGACA-CA5
96ColChoGACA-CA6
96ColChoGACA-CA7
96ColChoGACA-CA8
96ColChoGACA-CA9
96ColChoGACA-CA10
96ColChoGS-310
96ColChoGS-415
96ColChoSS-310
96ColChoSS-415
96ColChoYMtP-16
96ColChoYMtP-16A
96ColChoYMtPGS-16
96ColChoYMtPGS-16A
96CUIMCG-1
96CUIMCG-2
96CUIMCG-3
96CUIMCG-4
96CUIMCG-NNO
96Don-338
96Don-490
96DonEli-70
96DonFreF-2
96DonHitL-2
96DonLonBL-6
96DonPowA-10
96DonPowADC-10
96DonPreP-338
96DonPreP-490
96DonRouT-6
96DonSam-4
96DonSho-3
96EmoLegoB-4
96EmoN-4
96EmoXL-113
96EmoXLD-4
96Fin-B24
96Fin-G135
96Fin-S305
96FinBro-4
96FinRef-B24
96FinRef-G135
96FinRef-S305
96Fla-160
96FlaDiaC-5
96FlaHotG-4
96FlaPow-4
96Fle-238
96FleChe-2
96FleLumC-4
96FlePosG-2
96FleTeaL-12
96FleTif-238
96FleUpd-U223
96FleUpd-U247
96FleUpd-3
96FleUpdH-7
96FleUpdSL-4
96FleUpdSS-4
96FleUpdTC-U223
96FleUpdTC-U247
96FleZon-3
96GriNik-1
96Kin-6
96Lea-41
96LeaAllGMC-18
96LeaAllGMCG-18
96LeaGolS-4
96LeaHatO-5
96LeaLim-11
96LeaLimG-11
96LeaLimL-1
96LeaLimLB-1
96LeaLimPC-4
96LeaPicP-7
96LeaPre-1
96LeaPre-149
96LeaPreP-1
96LeaPreP-149
96LeaPrePB-41
96LeaPrePG-41
96LeaPrePS-41
96LeaPreSG-52
96LeaPreSP-3
96LeaPreSta-6
96LeaPreSte-52
96LeaSig-10
96LeaSigPPG-10
96LeaSigPPP-10
96LeaStaS-4
96LeaTotB-9
96MarMot-4
96MetImpG-1
96MetImpG-2
96MetImpG-3
96MetImpG-4
96MetImpG-5
96MetImpG-6
96MetImpG-7
96MetImpG-8
96MetImpG-9
96MetImpG-10
96MetUni-107
96MetUniHM-4
96MetUniML-3
96MetUniP-107
96MetUniT-3
96Pac-410
96PacCraC-CC8
96PacGolCD-DC13
96PacHom-HP11
96PacMil-M9
96PacOctM-OM6
96PacPri-P131
96PacPriFB-FB6
96PacPriG-P131
96PacPriRHS-RH7
96PanSti-223
96Pin-122
96Pin-134
96Pin-195
96Pin-255
96Pin-301
96Pin-394
96Pin-399
96PinAfi-75
96PinAfi-196
96PinAfiAP-75
96PinAfiAP-196
96PinAfiFPP-75
96PinAfiMN-1
96PinAfiR-1
96PinAfiR-4
96PinAfiR-5
96PinAfiR-7
96PinAfiR-9
96PinAfiR-10
96PinAfiSP-3
96PinArtP-41
96PinArtP-61
96PinArtP-155
96PinArtP-185
96PinEssotG-7
96PinFan-3
96PinFirR-1
96PinFoil-255
96PinFoil-301
96PinFoil-394
96PinFoil-399
96PinPow-3
96PinSky-1
96PinSlu-2
96PinSta-41
96PinSta-61
96PinSta-155
96PinSta-185
96PinTeaP-6
96PinTeaS-2
96Pro-6
96ProMagA-3
96ProMagDM-21
96ProSta-61
96SchDis-16
96Sco-273
96Sco-282
96ScoAll-3
96ScoBigB-2
96ScoDiaA-14
96ScoDreT-7
96ScoDugC-B7
96ScoDugCAP-B7
96ScoGolS-1
96ScoNumG-3
96ScoPowP-12
96ScoRef-2
96ScoTitT-4
96Sel-6
96Sel-151
96Sel-197
96SelArtP-6
96SelArtP-151
96SelArtP-197
96SelCer-47
96SelCer-136
96SelCerAP-47
96SelCerAP-136
96SelCerCB-47
96SelCerCB-136
96SelCerCR-47
96SelCerCR-136
96SelCerIP-1
96SelCerMB-47
96SelCerMB-136
96SelCerMG-47
96SelCerMG-136
96SelCerMR-47
96SelCerMR-136
96SelCerSF-3
96SelClaTF-3
96SelEnF-1
96SelTeaN-9
96SigRooOHKG-J1
96SigRooOHKG-J2
96SigRooOHKG-J3
96SigRooOHKG-J4
96SigRooOHKG-J5
96SP-170
96SP-188
96SPBasH-90
96SPBasH-NNO
96SPMarM-MM1
96SPMarMDC-1
96Spo-18
96Spo-98
96Spo-142
96SpoArtP-18
96SpoArtP-98
96SpoArtP-142
96SpoDouT-4
96SpoHitP-1
96SpoPowS-2
96SpoPro-6
96SPPreF-1
96SPSpeFX-10
96SPSpeFXDC-10
96SPx-55
96SPx-KG1
96SPx-KGAU
96SPxBoufG-1
96SPxGol-55
96StaClu-105

96StaCluEPB-105
96StaCluEPG-105
96StaCluEPS-105
96StaCluEWB-EW8
96StaCluEWG-EW8
96StaCluEWS-EW8
96StaCluMeg-MH2
96StaCluMOP-105
96StaCluMOP-MH2
96StaCluMOP-PC3
96StaCluMOP-PP6
96StaCluMOP-TSCA5
96StaCluPC-PC3
96StaCluPP-PP6
96StaCluTA-5
95StaCluVRMC-120
96Stu-116
96StuHitP-2
96StuMas-7
96StuPrePB-116
96StuPrePG-116
96StuPrePS-116
96StuStaGS-2
96Sum-86
96Sum-158
96Sum-197
96SumAbo&B-86
96SumAbo&B-158
96SumAbo&B-197
96SumArtP-86
96SumArtP-158
96SumArtP-197
96SumBal-5
96SumBigB-2
96SumBigBM-2
96SumFoi-86
96SumFoi-158
96SumFoi-197
96SumHitI-4
96SumPos-8
96TeaOut-32
96TeaOut-C95
96Top-205
96Top-230
96TopBigC-3
96TopChr-70
96TopChr-90
96TopChrR-70
96TopChrR-90
96TopChrWC-WC9
96TopChrWCR-WC9
96TopClaC-CC1
96TopGal-146
96TopGalE-3
96TopGalPG-PG10
96TopGalPPI-146
96TopLas-42
96TopLasPC-14
96TopLasSS-4
96TopMysF-M16
96TopMysF-M25
96TopMysFR-M16
96TopMysFR-M25
96TopPro-AL5
96TopWreC-WC9
96Ult-126
96Ult-579
96UltCalttH-2
96UltCalttHGM-2
96UltChe-A4
96UltChe-B3
96UltCheGM-A4
96UltCheGM-B3
96UltDiaP-3
96UltDiaPGM-3
96UltGolM-126
96UltGolM-579
96UltHitM-4
96UltHitMGM-4
96UltHomRKGM-6
96UltHomRKR-6
96UltPowP-3
96UltPowPGM-3
96UltPriL-6
96UltPriLGM-6
96UltPro-2
96UltRaw-4
96UltRawGM-4
96UltRes-2
96UltResGM-2
96UltThu-11
96UltThuGM-11
96UppDec-200
96UppDec-376
96UppDecA-9
96UppDecDD-DD35
96UppDecDDG-DD35
96UppDecDDS-DD35
96UppDecG-GF1
96UppDecHC-HC1
96UppDecMtSGR-1
96UppDecPD-PD7
96UppDecPHE-H4
96UppDecPRE-R4
96UppDecPRE-R15
96UppDecPRE-R24
96UppDecPreH-H4
96UppDecPreR-R4
96UppDecPreR-R15
96UppDecPreR-R24
96UppDecRunP-RP7
96UppDecVJLS-VJ10
96Zen-1
96Zen-135
96ZenArtP-1
96ZenArtP-135
96ZenDiaC-3
96ZenDiaCP-3
96ZenMoz-5
96ZenZ-1
97Bow-16
97BowBes-1
97BowBesAR-1
97BowBesBC-BC6
97BowBesBCAR-BC6
97BowBesBCR-BC6
97BowBesMI-MI5
97BowBesMIAR-MI5
97BowBesMIARI-MI5
97BowBesMII-MI5
97BowBesMIR-MI5
97BowBesMIRI-MI5
97BowBesP-2
97BowBesPAR-2
97BowBesPR-2
97BowBesR-1
97BowChr-12
97BowChrI-12
97BowChrIR-12
97BowChrR-12
97BowInt-16
97BowIntB-BBI2
97BowIntBAR-BBI2
97BowIntBR-BBI2
97Cir-24
97Cir-395
97CirBos-6
97CirIco-2
97CirLimA-5
97CirRav-24
97CirRav-395
97CirRavR-4
97CirSupB-6
97ColCho-230
97ColCho-244
97ColCho-245
97ColCho-246
97ColCho-247
97ColCho-248
97ColCho-249
97ColCho-334
97ColChoAC-5
97ColChoBS-1
97ColChoBSGS-1
97ColChoCtG-28A
97ColChoCtG-28B
97ColChoCtG-28C
97ColChoCtGIW-CG28
97ColChoGriCD-CD1
97ColChoGriCD-CD2
97ColChoGriCD-CD3
97ColChoGriCD-CD4
97ColChoGriCD-CD5
97ColChoNF-NF11
97ColChoPP-PP3
97ColChoPPG-PP3
97ColChoS-24
97ColChoTBS-43
97ColChoTBSWH-43
97ColChoTotT-T27
97Don-21
97Don-399
97Don-439
97Don-450
97DonArmaD-1
97DonDiaK-1
97DonDiaKC-1
97DonDom-2
97DonEli-5
97DonEli-7
97DonEliGS-5
97DonEliLaL-1
97DonFraFea-1
97DonLim-1
97DonLim-18
97DonLim-19
97DonLimFotG-5
97DonLimFotG-45
97DonLimLE-1
97DonLimLE-18
97DonLimLE-19
97DonLonL-6
97DonPowA-2
97DonPowADC-2
97DonPre-2
97DonPre-175
97DonPreCttC-2
97DonPreCttC-175
97DonPreP-21
97DonPreP-399
97DonPreP-439
97DonPreP-450
97DonPrePGold-21
97DonPrePGold-399
97DonPrePGold-439
97DonPrePGold-450
97DonPrePM-2
97DonPreS-9
97DonPreTB-6
97DonPreTBG-6
97DonPreTF-6
97DonPreTP-6
97DonPreTPG-6
97DonPreXP-7A
97DonTea-136
97DonTeaSMVP-13
97DonTeaSPE-136
97Fin-139
97Fin-238
97Fin-342
97FinEmb-139
97FinEmb-342
97FinEmbR-139
97FinEmbR-342
97FinRef-139
97FinRef-238
97FinRef-342
97FlaSho-A24
97FlaSho-B24
97FlaSho-C24
97FlaShoDC-5
97FlaShoHG-4
97FlaShoLC-24
97FlaShoLC-B24
97FlaShoLC-C24
97FlaShoLCM-A24
97FlaShoLCM-B24
97FlaShoLCM-C24
97Fle-206
97Fle-492
97Fle-701
97Fle-745
97FleBleB-4
97FleDiaT-4
97FleGouG-2
97FleGouGF-2
97FleHea-6
97FleLumC-9
97FleNig&D-4
97FleSoaS-4
97FleTeaL-12
97FleTif-206
97FleTif-492
97FleTif-701
97FleTif-745
97FleZon-7
97Lea-193
97Lea-204
97Lea-371
97LeaBanS-2
97LeaDrefS-12
97LeaFraM-193
97LeaFraM-204
97LeaFraM-371
97LeaFraMDC-193
97LeaFraMDC-204
97LeaFraMDC-371
97LeaGet-1
97LeaGolS-3
97LeaKnoG-2
97LeaLeaotN-6
97LeaStaS-3
97LeaWarT-1
97MetUni-145
97MetUniBF-6
97MetUniMF-4
97MetUniML-4
97MetUniT-3
97NewPin-1
97NewPinAP-1
97NewPinIE-3
97NewPinKtP-4
97NewPinMC-1
97NewPinPP-1
97NewPinPP-I3A
97NewPinPP-K4
97NewPinPP-KG1
97NewPinPP-KG2
97NewPinPP-KG3
97NewPinPP-KG4
97NewPinPP-KG5
97NewPinPP-KG6
97NewPinS-KG1
97NewPinS-KG2
97NewPinS-KG3
97NewPinS-KG4
97NewPinS-KG5
97NewPinS-KG6
97Pac-186
97PacCar-17
97PacCarM-17
97PacCerCGT-13
97PacCraC-5
97PacFirD-11
97PacGolCD-16
97PacLigB-186
97PacPri-63
97PacPriGA-GA14
97PacPriGotD-GD86
97PacPriLB-63
97PacPriP-63
97PacPriSH-SH6A
97PacPriSL-SL6A
97PacSil-186
97PacTriCD-9
97Pin-193
97PinArtP-193
97PinCar-14
97PinCer-53
97PinCer-136
97PinCerCMGT-13
97PinCerCT-13
97PinCerLI-2
97PinCerMBlu-53
97PinCerMBlu-136
97PinCerMG-53
97PinCerMG-136
97PinCerMR-53
97PinCerMR-136
97PinCerR-53
97PinCerR-136
97PinHom-3
97PinHom-4
97PinIns-19
97PinInsC-8
97PinInsCE-19
97PinInsDD-6
97PinInsDE-19
97PinInsFS-12
97PinMin-1
97PinMinB-1
97PinMinCB-1
97PinMinCG-1
97PinMinCGR-1
97PinMinCN-1
97PinMinCS-1
97PinMinG-1
97PinMinS-1
97PinMusC-193
97PinPasttM-2
97PinSha-1
97PinTeaP-7
97PinTeaP-10
97PinTotCPB-53
97PinTotCPB-136
97PinTotCPG-53
97PinTotCPG-136
97PinTotCPR-53
97PinTotCPR-136
97PinX-P-7
97PinX-P-139
97PinX-PF&A-14
97PinX-PMoS-7
97PinX-PMoS-139
97PinX-PMP-6
97PinX-PMW-1
97PinX-PMWG-1
97PinX-PMWS-1
97PinX-PSfF-1
97PinX-PSfFU-1
97ProMag-71
97ProMagIM-1
97ProMagML-71
97Sco-156
97Sco-499
97Sco-548
97ScoAllF-11
97ScoBla-6
97ScoFra-1
97ScoFraG-1
97ScoHeaotO-9
97ScoHigZ-2
97ScoHobR-499
97ScoHobR-548
97ScoMar-6
97ScoMarPl-6
97ScoMarPr-6
97ScoPitP-14
97ScoPreS-156
97ScoResC-499
97ScoResC-548
97ScoShoS-156
97ScoShoS-499
97ScoShoS-548
97ScoShoSAP-156
97ScoShoSAP-499
97ScoShoSAP-548
97ScoStaaD-5
97ScoSteS-6
97ScoTitT-3
97Sel-47
97Sel-145
97Sel-150
97SelArtP-47
97SelArtP-145
97SelArtP-150
97SelRegG-47
97SelRegG-145
97SelRegG-150
97SelToootT-1
97SelToootTMB-1
97SkyE-X-40
97SkyE-XACA-2
97SkyE-XC-40
97SkyE-XEC-40
97SkyE-XHoN-2
97SP-165
97SP-183
97SPGamF-GF10
97SPGriH-91
97SPGriH-92
97SPGriH-93
97SPGriH-94
97SPGriH-95
97SPGriH-96
97SPGriH-97
97SPGriH-98
97SPGriH-99
97SPGriH-100
97SPInsI-1
97SPMarM-MM1
97SpoIll-28
97SpoIll-157
97SpoIll-172
97SpoIll-178
97SpoIllEE-28
97SpoIllEE-157
97SpoIllEE-172
97SpoIllEE-178
97SpoIllGS-25
97SPSpeF-1
97SPSpxF-1
97SPSPxFA-1
97SPVinAu-8
97SPVinAu-9
97SPVinAu-10
97SPVinAu-11
97SPVinAu-12
97SPx-45
97SPx-S45
97SPxBoufG-19
97SPxBoufGSS-2
97SPxBro-45
97SPxCorotG-1
97SPxGraF-45
97SPxSil-45
97SPxSte-45
97StaClu-50
97StaClu-385
97StaCluFR-F5

97StaCluMat-50
97StaCluMOP-50
97StaCluMOP-385
97StaCluMOP-FB5
97StaCluMOP-PG15
97StaCluMOP-PL4
97StaCluPG-PG15
97StaCluPL-PL4
97Stu-16
97Stu-163
97StuHarH-3
97StuMasS-3
97StuMasS8-3
97StuPor8-1
97StuPrePG-16
97StuPrePG-163
97StuPrePS-16
97StuPrePS-163
97Top-300
97TopAll-AS13
97TopChr-101
97TopChrAS-AS13
97TopChrDD-DD3
97TopChrDDR-DD3
97TopChrR-101
97TopChrSAR-AS13
97TopChrSB-8
97TopChrSBR-8
97TopGal-79
97TopGalGoH-GH4
97TopGalPG-PG4
97TopGalPMS-5
97TopGalPMSSS-1
97TopGalPPI-79
97TopHobM-HM1
97TopIntF-ILM3
97TopIntFR-ILM3
97TopScr-7
97TopScrSI-1
97TopSeaB-SB8
97TopSta-4
97TopSta1AS-AS16
97TopStaAM-4
97TopStaASGM-ASM5
97TopSweS-SS6
97TopTeaT-TT1
97Ult-121
97UltBasR-2
97UltChe-A3
97UltChe-B2
97UltDiaP-3
97UltDouT-9
97UltFamGam-1
97UltFieC-6
97UltGolME-121
97UltHitM-2
97UltHRK-4
97UltLeaS-1
97UltPlaME-121
97UltPowP-A4
97UltPowP-B1
97UltRBIK-7
97UltStaR-2
97UltThu-8
97UltTop3-2
97UltTop3GM-2
97UppDec-150
97UppDec-175
97UppDec-385
97UppDec-424
97UppDecAG-AG1
97UppDecGJ-GJ1
97UppDecHC-HC5
97UppDecKGJHR-1
97UppDecKGJHR-2
97UppDecKGJHR-3
97UppDecKGJHR-4
97UppDecKGJHR-5
97UppDecLDC-LD3
97UppDecMM-9
97UppDecP-26
97UppDecPP-PP1
97UppDecPPJ-PP1
97UppDecRP-RP1
97UppDecU-3
97UppDecUMA-MA1
97UppDecUSS-2
97Zen-20
97Zen Z-Z-1
97Zen8x1-4
97Zen8x1D-4
97ZenV-2-1
Griffey, Ken Sr.
74OPC-598
74Top-598
75OPC-284
75Top-284
76CraDis-17
76Kel-44
76LinSup-94
76OPC-128
76RedIceL-6
76RedKro-10
76RedPos-9
76SSP-40
76Top-128
77BurCheD-206
77Hos-59
77Kel-49
77MSADis-25
77OPC-11
77PepGloD-50
77RCColC-27
77Top-320
78Kel-4
78OPC-140
78Pep-12
78RCColC-11
78SSP270-118
78Top-80
79Hos-45
79Kel-39
79OPC-216
79Top-420
80OPC-285
80RedEnq-30
80Top-550
81AllGamPI-145
81CokTeaS-42
81Don-184
81Fle-199
81FleStiC-60
81OPC-280
81Top-280
81TopScr-91
81TopSti-163
81TopSupHT-36
82Don-634
82Fle-67
82FleSta-16
82OPC-171
82OPC-330
82Top-620
82Top-621
82Top-756
82TopTra-40T
83Don-486
83Fle-382
83FleSta-71
83FleSti-46
83OPC-110
83Top-110
83TopFol-3
83TopSti-98
83YanRoyRD-3
84AllGamPI-94
84Don-613
84DonActAS-21
84DonCha-25
84Fle-126
84Nes792-770
84OPC-306
84Top-770
84TopSti-317
84TopTif-770
85Don-347
85Fle-128
85Lea-193
85OPC-380
85Top-380
85TopTif-380
86Don-126
86Fle-105
86Lea-48
86OPC-40
86Top-40
86TopTif-40
86TopTra-41T
86TopTraT-41T
86YanTCM-32
87BraSmo-19
87Don-513
87DonOpeD-42
87Fle-516
87FleGlo-516
87FleMin-46
87FleStiC-49
87OPC-114
87SpoTeaP-24
87StuPan-2
87Top-711
87TopTif-711
88Don-202
88DonBasB-141
88Fle-540
88FleGlo-540
88Lea-165
88OPC-255
88PanSti-248
88RedFolSB-28
88Sco-390
88ScoGlo-390
88Spo-178
88StaLinBra-7
88Top-443
88Top-549
88TopBig-110
88TopSti-38
88TopTif-443
88TopTif-549
89Bow-259
89BowTif-259
89FleUpd-84
89RedKah-30
89Sco-609
89TopTra-40T
89TopTraT-40T
90Bow-60
90BowTif-60
90Don-469
90Fle-420
90FleCan-420
90KayB-13
90OPC-581
90RodKah-10
90Sco-338A
90Sco-338B
90StaGriJ-9
90Top-581
90TopBig-100
90TopMag-27
90TopTif-581
90UppDec-682
91AlrGriG-4
91Bow-255
91Cla2-T21
91ClaGam-141
91Don-452
91Lea-503
91MajLeaCP-5
91MarCouH-19
91MarCouH-28
91MotGri-2
91MotGri-3
91MotGri-4
91MSAHolD-11
91OPC-465
91PepGri-5
91PepGri-6
91PepGri-7
91PepGri-8
91Sco-835
91Sco-841
91SevCoi-NW4
91StaClu-342
91StaCluCM-10
91StaGri-1
91StaGri-3
91StaGri-5
91StaGri-7
91StaGri-9
91StaGri-11
91Stu-113
91Top-465
91TopDesS-465
91TopMic-465
91TopTif-465
91TopTriH-A12
91Ult-335
91UppDec-572
92AlrGriAAS-5
92AlrGriAAS-10
92AlrGriGM-5
92AlrGriGM-10
92LimRocGH-1
92OPC-250
92PerGamGJ-8
92Top-250
92TopGol-250
92TopGolW-250
92TopMic-250
92UppDec-85
92UppDec-335
92YanWIZ8-69
93Bow-703
93MarMot-28
94SigRooFCD-3
94SigRooFCS-AU3
94SigRooFCS-AU4
94SigRooFCS-AU6
96Red76K-7
Griffin, Alan
75TucTorC-18
75TucTorTI-5
76TucTorCa-13
76TusTorCr-34
78SanJosMMC-9
Griffin, Alfredo
79BluJayBY-10
79Top-705
80OPC-290
80Top-558
81AllGamPI-22
81Don-149
81Fle-430
81OPC-277
81OPCPos-15
81Top-277
81TopSti-140
82Don-101
82Fle-615
82FleSta-236
82OPC-148
82Top-677
82TopSti-252
83AllGamPI-21
83Don-180
83Fle-429
83OPC-294
83Top-488
83TopSti-129
84AllGamPI-111
84BluJayFS-15
84Don-605
84Fle-156
84Nes792-76
84OPC-76
84Top-76
84TopSti-369
84TopTif-76
85A'sMot-5
85AllGamPI-22
85Don-73
85Fle-106
85FleUpd-47
85Lea-230
85OPC-361
85Top-361
85TopSti-366
85TopTif-361
85TopTifT-42T
85TopTra-42T
86A'sMot-5
86Don-101
86Fle-417
86Lea-34
86OPC-121
86Spo-136
86Top-566
86TopSti-168
86TopTat-16
86TopTif-566
87A'sSmoC-4
87Don-256
87DonOpeD-28
87Fle-392
87FleGlo-392
87Lea-198
87OPC-111
87Spo-164A
87Spo-164B
87SpoTeaP-23
87StuPan-24
87Top-111
87TopSti-166
87TopTif-111
88DodMot-7
88DodPol-7
88Don-226
88DonBasB-92
88Fle-280
88FleGlo-280
88FleUpd-94
88FleUpdG-94
88OPC-42
88PanSti-172
88Sco-88
88ScoGlo-88
88ScoRoo-37T
88ScoRooG-37T
88Spo-156
88StaLinAs-6
88StaLinD-5
88Top-726
88TopBig-247
88TopSti-169
88TopTif-726
88TopTra-43T
88TopTraT-43T
89Bow-345
89BowTif-345
89DodMot-7
89DodPol-5
89DodStaSV-1
89Don-79
89DonBasB-178
89Fle-58
89FleGlo-58
89OPC-62
89Sco-167
89Top-62
89TopSti-59
89TopTif-62
89UppDec-631
90Bow-95
90BowTif-95
90DodMot-8
90DodPol-7
90DodTar-297
90Don-195
90DonBesN-103
90Fle-395
90FleCan-395
90Lea-95
90OPC-643
90PanSti-270
90PubSti-6
90Sco-156
90Top-643
90TopBig-18
90TopSti-58
90TopTif-643
90UppDec-338
91BluJayFS-10
91Bow-592
91DodMot-8
91DodPol-7
91Don-488
91Fle-201
91Lea-344
91OPC-226
91OPCBoxB-G
91PanFreS-58
91Sco-442
91StaClu-524
91Top-226
91TopDesS-226
91TopMic-226
91TopTif-226
91TopWaxBC-G
91Ult-161
91UppDec-119
92Don-692
92Fle-455
92OPC-418
92PanSti-195
92Sco-254
92Top-418
92TopGol-418
92TopGolW-418
92TopMic-418
92UppDec-282
93BluJayD-12
93BluJayD4-6
93BluJayFS-11
93Fle-692
93StaClu-561
93StaCluFDI-561
93StaCluMOP-561
94Fle-332
94Pac-641
96BluJayOH-12
97BluJayS-25
Griffin, Barry
88BoiHawP-1614
Griffin, Bob
88MisStaB-8
Griffin, Chad
95EveAqaTI-8
Griffin, Dave

83AndBraT-20
84DurBulT-8
85DurBulT-24
86GreBraTI-11
87IntLeaAT-35
87RicBraBC-9
87RicBraC-24
87RicBraT-13
88RicBraC-19
88RicBraP-20
88TriAAC-17
89ColCliC-27
89TolMudHC-12
89TolMudHP-785
97BobCamRB-14
Griffin, Doug
71OPC-176
71RedSoxA-5
71Top-176
72Top-703
72Top-704
73LinPor-21
73OPC-96
73Top-96
74OPC-219
74Top-219
75OPC-454
75Top-454
76OPC-654
76SSP-412
76Top-654
77Top-191
89PacSenL-53
Griffin, Frankie
83ReaPhiT-6
Griffin, Greg
83KnoBluJT-17
Griffin, Ivy M.
23WilChoV-53
Griffin, Mark
89Sta-29
89VerBeaDS-10
90VerBeaDS-16
91Cla/Bes-236
91FloStaLAP-FSL38
91VerBeaDC-27
91VerBeaDP-787
93WesPalBEC-6
93WesPalBEF-1353
94HarSenF-2104
Griffin, Mike Leroy
77AshTouT-7
79WesHavYT-17
81ColCliP-36
81ColCliT-10
81Fle-107
81Top-483
82Don-533
82Top-146
83OklCit8T-8
84OklCit8T-7
85OmaRoyT-13
86OmaRoyP-8
86OmaRoyT-15
87OldJudN-217
87OriFreB-42
87RocRedWP-9
87RocRedWT-3
88Don-494
88Fle-561
88FleGlo-561
88RocRedWC-7
88RocRedWGCP-8
88RocRedWP-210
88RocRedWTI-9
89EdgR.WG-12
89NasSouC-4
89NasSouP-1274
89NasSouTI-6
90ChaWheB-27
90ChaWheP-2258
90DodTar-298
91ChaLooLD-175
91ChaLooP-1975
91LinDriAA-175
92ChaLooF-3834
92YanWIZ7-59
92YanWIZ8-68
93IndIndF-1504
94IndIndF-1825
95IndIndF-112
95May-12
98CamPepP-30
Griffin, Nuje
91OriCro-166
Griffin, Rick
88MarMot-28
89MarMot-28
90MarMot-28
Griffin, Ryan
94AlbPolC-13
94AlbPolF-2231
94BluOriC-10
94BluOriF-3557
Griffin, Steve
91FreStaBS-5
92SouOreAC-15
92SouOreAF-3410
Griffin, Terry
87LitFalMP-2384
88LitFalMP-16
89St.LucMS-8
Griffin, Tim
90GreFalDSP-25
91VerBeaDC-20
91VerBeaDP-781
91YakBeaC-11
91YakBeaP-4253
92VerBeaDC-6
Griffin, Tom
69Top-614
70AstTeal-5
70Top-578
71MLBOffS-81
71OPC-471
71Top-471
72MilBra-122
73OPC-468
73Top-468
74AstFouTIP-3
74OPC-256
74Top-256
75OPC-188
75Top-188
76OPC-454
76Top-454
77PadSchC-24
77Top-39
78AngFamF-14
78Top-318
79GiaPol-43
79Top-291
80GiaPol-43
80Top-649
81Don-75
81Fle-456
81Top-538
82Don-474
82Fle-389
82Top-777
87AstShoSO-10
87AstShowSTh-26
87AstShowSTh-28
Griffin, Ty
87PanAmTURB-2
88TopTra-44T
88TopTraT-44T
89Bow-289
89BowTif-289
89ChaKniTI-14
89PeoChiTI-1
89PeoChiTI-21
89Top-713
89TopBig-170
89TopTif-713
90Bow-37
90BowTif-37
90ChaKniTI-14
90TopTVCu-45
91ChaKniLD-134
91ChaKniP-1700
91LinDriAA-134
92ChaLooF-3827
92ChaLooS-183
92SkyAA F-81
95ArkTraTI-13
87PanAmTUBI-14
Griffith, Calvin
78TwiFri-6
Griffith, Clark C.
04FanCraAL-22
05RotCP-6
05RotCP-7
09RamT20-52
09SpoNewSM-88
09T206-147
09T206-148
10CouT21-140
10CouT21-285
10DomDisP-50
10RedCroT-27
10RedCroT-114
10RedCroT-195
10StaCarE-15
10SweCapPP-101A
10SweCapPP-101B
10W555-32
11S74Sil-76
11SpoLifCW-148
11SpoLifM-195
11T205-69
11TurRedT-17
12HasTriFT-59
13NatGamW-18
13TomBarW-17
14PieStaT-25
15CraJacE-167
15VicT21-13
16SpoNewM-72
19W514-41
31SenTealPW-11
36PC7AlbHoF-43
48ExhHoF-13
50CalHOFW-35
60ExhWriH-12
60Fle-15
60SenUniMC-6
61Fle-36
63BazA-37
76ShaPiz-43
77GalGloG-150
80PacLeg-37
80PerHaloFP-43
80SSPHOF-43
87OldJudN-218
92ConTSN-464
92YanWIZH-13
93ConTSN-840
94OriofB-77
95ConTSN-1374
Griffith, Derrell (Robert D.)
65DodTeal-6
65OPC-112
65Top-112
66Top-573
67Top-502
90DodTar-299
Griffith, Jeff
87WatPirP-22
88AugPirP-363
Griffith, Kerry
86EriCarP-10
Griffith, Lynn
93DavLipB-23
94DavLipB-12
Griffith, Tommy
89BoiHawP-1984
91SalSpuC-6
91SalSpuP-2255
Griffith, Tommy (Thomas H.)
14B18B-49A
14B18B-49B
14B18B-49C
15SpoNewM-72
16ColE13-64
16FleBreD-35
16SpoNewM-73
20NatCarE-36
21E121So1-35
21E121So8-31
21Nei-58
22AmeCarE-25
22E120-139
22W572-34
22W575-47
23W501-107
23W515-35
23WilChoV-54
90DodTar-300
Griffiths, Brian
89AshTouP-955
90OscAstS-8
91OscAstC-3
91OscAstP-675
92ClaFS7-324
92JacGenF-3994
92JacGenS-332
92SkyAA F-141
93ShrCapF-2752
93Top-483
93TopGol-483
93TopInaM-483
93TopMic-483
Griffiths, Everard
96ButCopKB-13
Grifol, Pedro
91EliTwiP-4303
92ClaFS7-12
92Ft.MyeMCB-6
92Ft.MyeMF-2749
92ProFS7-101
93Bow-185
93NasXprF-406
94NasXprF-389
95HarCitRCTI-7
96BinBeeB-10
Griggs, Art
09PC7HHB-18
Griggs, Hal
58Top-455
59SenTealW-8
59Top-434
60Lea-34
60Top-244
Griggs, Rod
96BilMusTI-10
Griggs, Skeet (Acie)
93NegLeaRL2-12
Griggs, Wiley
92NegLeaRLI-26
Grigsby, Benji
92ClaDraP-15
92ClaDraPFB-BC14
92UppDecML-11
93ClaFS7-195
93ModA'sC-1
93ModA'sF-794
93Pin-463
93Sco-495
93Sel-354
93StaCluM-151
93Top-518
93TopGol-518
93TopInaM-518
93TopMic-518
94ModA'sC-12
94ModA'sF-3060
95HunStaTI-10
95UppDecML-153
95UppDecMLFS-153
Grijak, Kevin
91IdaFalBP-4337
91IdaFalBSP-17
92ProFS7-197
92PulBraC-17
92PulBraF-3191
93MacBraC-11
93MacBraF-1406
94DurBulC-9
94DurBulF-339
94DurBulTI-8
94GreBraTI-12
95Exc-151
95RicBraRC-4
95RicBraTI-5
95SigRooOJ-15
95SigRooOJP-15
95SigRooOJPS-15
95SigRooOJS-15
96BesAutS-33
96RicBraUB-10
Grilione, Dave
86SalAngC-94
87QuaCitAP-29
Grilk, Jim
40SolHug-8
Grilli, Guido
66Top-558
Grilli, Steve
76OPC-591
76Top-591
77Top-506
78SyrChiT-11
79SyrChiT-17
79SyrChiTI-21
80SyrChiTI-9
81SyrChiT-4
Grilone, Dave
88BurBraP-18
Grim, Bob
55Bow-167
55RedMan-AL5
55Top-80
55TopDouH-57
56Top-52
57Top-36
58Top-224
59Top-423
60Lea-10
60Top-78
60TopVen-78
62Top-564
83YanASFY-17
84FifNatCT-7
92YanWIZA-26
94TopArc1-252
94TopArc1G-252
Grim, John
90DodTar-964
Grimes, Bob
88ChaWheB-27
89PeoChiTI-32
90ChaKniTI-24
96IowCubB-5
Grimes, Burleigh A.
21Exh-61
21Nei-89
21OxfConE-7
22E120-140
22W572-35
22W573-52
22WilPatV-31
23W515-16
23WilChoV-55
25Exh-12
26Exh-11
27Exh-7
27YorCarE-1
28PorandAR-A12
28PorandAR-B12
28W502-1
28W513-72
28Yue-1
29PorandAR-32
30W554-5
32CubTeal-8
32OrbPinNP-26
32OrbPinUP-21
33Gou-64
33GouCanV-64
33TatOrb-21
33TatOrbSDR-191
35GouPuzR-1F
35GouPuzR-3D
35GouPuzR-14D
35GouPuzR-15D
60Fle-59
61Fle-37
75SheGrePG-6
75TCMAllG-12
76GrePlaG-6
76RowExh-11
76ShaPiz-97
77BobParHoF-24
77GalGloG-97
79DiaGre-76
80PacLeg-51
80PerHaloFP-97
80SSPHOF-97
82DiaCla-36
83DonHOFH-21
89DodSmoG-8
90DodTar-301
91ConTSN-25
92CarMcD-20
92ConTSN-433
92YanWIZH-14
93ConTSN-706
94ConTSN-997
94ConTSNB-997
95ConTSN-1382
Grimes, Dave (David)
89SprCarB-2
90St.PetCS-11
91ArkTraLD-35
91ArkTraP-1278
91LinDriAA-35
Grimes, John
84EveGiaC-25
85FreGiaP-14
86ShrCapP-9
87ShrCapP-22
Grimes, Lee
87WinSpiP-14
88ChaWheB-6
Grimes, Mike (Michael)
88CapCodPPaLP-122
89MedAthB-6
91MadMusC-4

92ClaFS7-36
92ModA'sC-20
92ModA'sF-3894
93CenValRC-12
93CenValRF-2888
Grimes, Oscar Ray
21Exh-62
21Nei-105
22E120-157
22W572-36
43YanSta-13
79DiaGre-282
95ConTSN-1419
Grimes, Steve
76CedRapGT-11A
76CedRapGT-11B
78HolMilT-10
Grimm, Charlie
20NatCarE-37
21E121So1-36
21Exh-63
22E120-218
22W575-48
22WilPatV-43
23W501-82
23WilChoV-56
25Exh-21
26Exh-21
26SpoComoA-17
27AmeCarE-19
27Exh-10
28StaPlaCE-30
29ExhFou-6
30ChiEveAP-4
30SchR33-15
31CubTeal-8
31Exh-6
32CubTeal-6
32OrbPinNP-37
32OrbPinUP-22
32R33So2-423
33CraJacP-11
33ExhFou-3
33GeoCMil-16
33Gou-51
33GouCanV-51
33TatOrb-22
34DiaMatCSB-73
34DiaMatCSB-74
34ExhFou-3
34Gou-3
34GouCanV-61
34WarBakSP-6
35DiaMatCS2-7
35DiaMatCS3T1-62
35ExhFou-3
36DiaMatCS4-5
36SandSW-25
36WorWidGV-89
40PlaBal-228
41CubTeal-25
46SpoExcW-2-5
48BabRutS-23
53BowC-69
53BraJohC-1
54BraJohC-40
55Bow-298
55BraGolS-2
55BraJohC-40
56BraBilaBP-10
60Top-217
76ChiGre-8
77GalGloG-115
79DiaGre-101
80CubGreT-7
80PacLeg-75
83DiaClaS2-100
84CubUno-8
87ConSer2-40
88ConSer4-12
91ConTSN-95
91TopArc1-321
92CubOldS-9
93ConTSN-821
Grimm, John
92BriTigC-12
92BriTigF-1402
94LakTigC-10
94LakTigF-3031
95Exc-49
Grimshaw, Moose (Myron)
09ColChiE-120A
09ColChiE-120B
09T206-425
11SpoLifCW-149
12ColRedB-120A
12ColRedB-120B
12ColTinT-120A
12ColTinT-120B
Grimsley, Jason
85BenPhiC-9
88ClePhiS-12
89BasAmeAPB-AA4
89EasLeaAP-16
89ReaPhiB-10
89ReaPhiP-670
89ReaPhiS-12
90Bow-151
90BowTif-151
90CMC-229
90Fle-653
90FleCan-653
90OPC-493
90PhiTas-10
90ProAAAF-297
90Sco-649
90ScrRedBC-3
90ScrRedBP-595
90Top-493
90TopDeb89-47
90TopTif-493
90UppDec-27
91Don-653
91Fle-396
91Lea-288
91OPC-173
91PhiMed-16
91Sco-818
91StaClu-294
91Top-173
91TopDesS-173
91TopMic-173
91TopTif-173
92Don-599
92Fle-532
92Sco-711
92StaClu-418
92TucTorF-482
92TucTorS-608
92UppDec-406
93ChaKniF-537
93LinVenB-220
94ChaKniF-887
94FleUpd-31
94VenLinU-25
95Don-164
95DonPreP-164
95Fla-31
95Fle-135
95Ult-279
95UltGolM-279
96AngMot-20
Grimsley, Ross
72OPC-99
72Top-99
73OPC-357
73Top-357
74OPC-59
74Top-59
74TopTra-59T
75Kel-2
75OPC-458
75Top-458
76OPC-257
76SSP-377
76Top-257
77BurCheD-40
77FriOneYW-4
77OPC-47
77Top-572
78ExpPos-5
78Top-691
79Hos-5
79Kel-3
79OPC-4
79Top-15
79TopCom-26
80ExpPos-10
80Kel-1
80OPC-195
80Top-375
81Fle-406
81Top-170
84ChaLooT-7
86CalCanP-10
87CalCanP-2313
89BurBraP-1614
89BurBraS-28
89PacSenL-117
89T/MSenL-40
90EliSenL-81
90PenPilS-26
91CalCanLD-75
91CalCanP-531
91LinDriAAA-75
91OriCro-167
92CalCanF-3746
92CalCanS-75
93CalCanF-1183
96RocRedWB-3
Griner, Craig
90GeoColC-6
Griner, Dan
90DodTar-965
Grinstead, Carl
94ButCopKSP-11
Grisham, Wes
90LSUTigA-2
90LSUTigP-2
90WelPirP-15
Grissom, Antonio
90MarPhiP-3195
91BatCliC-13
91BatCliP-3496
91SpaPhiC-24
91SpaPhiP-909
92AlbPolC-26
92AlbPolF-2316
93BurBeeC-9
93BurBeeF-170
93ExcFS7-59
94WesPalBEC-11
94WesPalBEF-55
95HarSenTI-38
Grissom, Lee
38CinOraW-13
39OrcPhoAP-12
39PlaBal-2
79DiaGre-262
90DodTar-302
Grissom, Marquis
88JamExpP-1910
89BasAmeAPB-AA14
89JacExpB-1
89JacExpP-175
90Bow-115
90BowTif-115
90ClaBlu-65
90Don-36
90DonBesN-128
90DonRoo-45
90ExpPos-13
90Fle-347
90FleCan-347
90Hot50RS-20
90Lea-107
90OPC-714
90Sco-591
90Sco100RS-99
90ScoRooDT-B9
90ScoYouS2-6
90Spo-134
90Top-714
90TopBig-138
90TopDeb89-48
90TopTif-714
90UppDec-9
90UppDec-702
90UppDecS-2
91Bow-435
91Cla2-T38
91ClaGam-119
91Don-307
91Fle-234
91Lea-22
91OPC-283
91PanFreS-151
91Sco-234
91Sco100RS-38
91StaClu-8
91Stu-198
91Top-283
91TopDesS-283
91TopMic-283
91TopRoo-10
91TopTif-283
91ToyRoo-9
91Ult-204
91UppDec-477
92Bow-14
92ClaGam-39
92DenHol-1
92Don-137
92DonCraJ1-21
92ExpDonD-10
92ExpPos-15
92Fle-482
92Hig5-58
92Lea-273
92OPC-647
92OPCPre-176
92PanSti-207
92Pin-129
92PinTea2-11
92Sco-66
92ScoImpP-63
92SpoIllFK1-144
92StaClu-120
92Stu-55
92Top-647
92TopGol-647
92TopGolW-647
92TopKid-8
92TopMic-647
92TriPla-47
92Ult-518
92UppDec-455
92UppDec-719
93Bow-268
93ClaGam-39
93DenHol-10
93DiaMar-45
93Don-300
93ExpDonM-5
93Fin-40
93FinRef-40
93Fla-83
93Fle-461
93Fle-706
93FleFruotL-26
93FleTeaL-NL7
93FunPac-93
93FunPac-95
93FunPac-216
93FunPacA-AS8
93HumDumC-37
93Lea-129
93LeaFas-20
93LeaGolA-R17
93LeaGolA-U8
93OPC-209
93PacSpa-185
93PanSti-230
93Pin-346
93PinTea2-17
93Sco-28
93Sel-99
93SelStaL-18
93SelStaL-58
93SP-12
93StaClu-529
93StaClu-598
93StaCluFDI-529
93StaCluFDI-598
93StaCluMOP-529
93StaCluMOP-598
93Stu-178
93Top-15
93TOPBLAG-7
93TopGol-15
93TopInaM-15
93TopMic-15
93Toy-30
93ToyMasP-6
93TriPla-159
93Ult-415
93UppDec-356
93UppDec-481
93UppDecDG-10
93UppDecGold-356
93UppDecGold-481
93USPlaCA-1H
94Bow-284
94BowBes-R69
94BowBesR-R69
94ChuHomS-24
94ChuHomSG-24
94ColC-465
94ColChoGS-465
94ColChoSS-465
94Don-37
94DonSpeE-37
94ExtBas-306
94Fin-229
94FinJum-229
94FinRef-229
94Fla-190
94Fle-540
94FleAllS-38
94FleTeaL-22
94FUnPac-159
94Lea-174
94LeaL-125
94OPC-18
94OPCAllR-11
94OPCJumA-11
94OscMayR-22
94Pac-382
94PanSti-210
94Pin-358
94PinArtP-358
94PinMusC-358
94PinRunC-RC38
94ProMag-83
94Sco-352
94ScoGolR-352
94ScoGolS-25
94Sel-242
94SelSki-SK7
94SP-84
94SPDieC-84
94Spo-48
94StaClu-706
94StaCluF-F6
94StaCluFDI-706
94StaCluGR-706
94StaCluMO-35
94StaCluMOP-706
94StaCluMOP-F6
94StaCluMOP-ST8
94StaCluST-ST8
94Stu-78
94TomPiz-7
94Top-590
94TopBlaG-34
94TopGol-590
94TopSpa-590
94TopSupS-20
94TriPla-95
94Ult-228
94UltAwaW-16
94UltRisS-6
94UppDec-39
94UppDec-390
94UppDecAJ-28
94UppDecAJG-28
94UppDecED-39
94UppDecED-390
94USPlaCA-10H
95Baz-37
95Bow-320
95BowBes-R68
95BowBesR-R68
95ColCho-237
95ColCho-537T
95ColCho-TC3
95ColChoGS-237
95ColChoSE-98
95ColChoSEGS-98
95ColChoSESS-98
95ColChoSS-237
95Don-251
95DonDom-8
95DonPreP-251
95DonTopotO-184
95Emo-101
95Fin-95
95Fin-237
95FinRef-95
95FinRef-237
95Fla-324
95FlaHotG-4
95Fle-351
95FleAllS-17
95FleUpd-90
95FleUpdSL-4
95Lea-335
95LeaGreG-7
95LeaLim-60
95Pac-268
95PacPri-87
95Pin-34
95PinArtP-34
95PinMusC-34
95Sco-246
95ScoGolR-246
95ScoHaloG-HG35
95ScoPlaTS-246
95Sel-39
95SelArtP-39

95SP-29
95SPCha-22
95SPChaDC-22
95Spo-28
95SpoArtP-28
95SPSil-29
95StaClu-440
95StaClu-617
95StaCluMO-20
95StaCluMOP-440
95StaCluMOP-617
95StaCluMOP-SS12
95StaCluSS-SS12
95StaCluSTWS-440
95StaCluSTWS-617
95StaCluVR-231
95Stu-34
95StuGolS-34
95Top-315
95TopCyb-171
95TopLeaL-LL43
95TopTra-65T
95UC3-49
95UC3ArtP-49
95Ult 403
95UltAwaW-16
95UltAwaWGM-16
95UltGolM-403
95UppDec-81
95UppDec-290
95UppDecED-81
95UppDecED-290
95UppDecEDG-81
95UppDecEDG-290
95UppDecSE-148
95UppDecSEG-148
95USPlaCMLA-9H
95Zen-72
96Baz-57
96Bow-102
96BowBes-50
96BowBesAR-50
96BowBesR-50
96Cir-100
96CirRav-100
96ColCho-41
96ColChoGS-41
96ColChoSS-41
96Don-19
96DonPreP-19
96EmoXL-141
96Fin-B190
96FinRef-B190
96Fla-199
96Fle-292
96FleBra-5
96FleTif-292
96Lea-47
96LeaPrePB-47
96LeaPrePG-47
96LeaPrePS-47
96LeaSig-148
96LeaSigPPG-148
96LeaSigPPP-148
96MetUni-128
96MetUniP-128
96MLBPin-14
96Pac-17
96PanSti-5
96Pin-96
96PinAfi-63
96PinAfiAP-63
96PinAfiFPP-63
96PinChrBC-8
96Sco-334
96ScoDugC-B59
96ScoDugCAP-B59
96Sel-113
96SelArtP-113
96SelCerIP-25
96StaClu-422
96StaCluEPB-422
96StaCluEPG-422
96StaCluEPS-422
96StaCluMOP-422
95StaCluVRMC-231
96Stu-20
96StuPrePB-20
96StuPrePG-20
96StuPrePS-20
96Sum-83
96SumAbo&B-83
96SumArtP-83
96SumFoi-83
96TeaOut-33
96Top-297
96TopChr-117
96TopChrR-117
96TopGal-7
96TopGalPPI-7
96TopLas-66
96Ult-155
96UltGolM-155
96UppDec-8
97Bow-230
97BowBes-25
97BowBesAR-25
97BowBesR-25
97BowChr-57
97BowChrI-57
97BowChrIR-57
97BowChrR-57
97BowInt-230
97Cir-146
97CirRav-146
97ColCho-31
97Don-64
97Don-278
97DonEli-143
97DonEliGS-143
97DonLim-8
97DonLimLE-8
97DonPre-8
97DonPreCttC-8
97DonPreP-64
97DonPreP-278
97DonPrePGold-64
97DonPrePGold-278
97DonTea-85
97DonTeaSPE-85
97Fin-219
97FinRef-219
97FlaSho-A154
97FlaSho-B154
97FlaSho-C154
97FlaShoHG-5
97FlaShoLC-154
97FlaShoLC-B154
97FlaShoLC-C154
97FlaShoLCM-A154
97FlaShoLCM-B154
97FlaShoLCM-C154
97Fle-256
97Fle-640
97FleTif-256
97FleTif-640
97Lea-292
97LeaFraM-292
97LeaFraMDC-292
97MetUni-29
97Pac-233
97PacLigB-233
97PacSil-233
97Pin-8
97PinArtP-8
97PinCer-89
97PinCerMBlu-89
97PinCerMG-89
97PinCerMR-89
97PinCerR-89
97PinMusC-8
97PinTotCPB-89
97PinTotCPG-89
97PinTotCPR-89
97PinX-P-33
97PinX-PMoS-33
97Sco-246
97Sco-334
97ScoBra-14
97ScoBraPl-14
97ScoBraPr-14
97ScoHobR-334
97ScoPreS-246
97ScoResC-334
97ScoShoS-246
97ScoShoS-334
97ScoShoSAP-246
97ScoShoSAP-334
97SP-57
97SpoIll-44
97SpoIllEE-44
97StaClu-201
97StaCluMat-201
97StaCluMOP-201
97Stu-69
97StuPrePG-69
97StuPrePS-69
97Top-184
97TopChr-71
97TopChrR-71
97TopGal-87
97TopGalPPI-87
97TopSta-48
97TopStaAM-48
97Ult-386
97UltFieC-7
97UltGolME-386
97UltPlaME-386
97UppDec-11
97UppDec-531

Grissom, Marv
53RedSoxTI-11
54NewYorJA-22
55Bow-123
55GiaGolS-7
55RedMan-NL25
56Top-301
57Top-216
58GiaSFCB-10
58Hir-64
58Top-399
59Top-243
78AngFamF-15
79DiaGre-46

Grissom, Scott
94DavLipB-13

Groat, Dick
47Exh-84
52Top-369
53Top-154
54Top-43
55Top-26
55TopDouH-99
56Top-24
56TopHocF-A1
56TopHocF-B3
56TopPin-42
57Kah-10
57Kah-11
57Top-12
58HarSta-17
58Hir-21
58Kah-11
58Top-45
59Kah-12
59Top-160
59TopVen-160
60Kah-11
60PirJayP-6
60PirTag-24
60Top-258
60TopTat-20
61Baz-8
61ChePat-4
61Kah-16
61NuSco-413
61PirJayP-5
61PirRigF-3
61Pos-129A
61Pos-129B
61Top-1
61Top-41
61Top-486
61TopDicG-5
61TopStaI-64
62ExhStaB-15
62Jel-172
62Kah-15
62Pos-172
62PosCan-172
62SalPlaC-138
62ShiPlaC-138
62Top-270
62TopBuc-33
62TopStaI-177
63BasMagM-32
63CarJayP-9
63ExhStaB-27
63Jel-139
63Kah-13
63Pos-139
63SalMetC-16
63Top-130
64Baz-2
64CarTeal-3
64ChatheY-30
64Raw-3
64Top-7
64Top-40
64TopCoi-5
64TopCoi-147
64TopGia-19
64TopSta-81
64TopStaU-30
64TopTatI-40
64TopVen-7
64TopVen-40
64WheSta-20
65CarJayP-4
65ChaTheY-29
65OldLonC-11
65OPC-275
65Top-275
65TopTraI-15
66OPC-103
66PhiTeal-8
66Top-103A
66Top-103B
66TopVen-103
67CokCapPh-6
67DexPre-83
67PhiPol-8
67Top-205
67TopVen-338
75OPC-198
75Top-198
78TCM60I-150
79DiaGre-372
81TCM60I-414
83TopRep5-369
87Pir196T-3
88PacLegI-108
89SweBasG-91
90PacLeg-26
90SweBasG-49
91SweBasG-35
91TopArc1-154
92ActPacA-28
92BazQua5A-15
92CarMcD-28
92MDAMVP-2
94TopArc1-43
94TopArc1G-43
94UppDecS-2

Grob, Connie
59DarFar-8

Groch, Dick
89EasLeaDDP-DD47

Grodzicki, Johnny
81TCM60I-362

Groennert, John
87SalLakTTT-8
88BilMusP-1815

Groeschner, David
96BelGiaTI-36

Groh, Don
83PeoSunF-5
85EdmTraC-4

Groh, Heinie
15CraJacE-159
15SpoNewM-73
16ColE13-65
16FleBreD-36
16SpoNewM-74
19W514-46
20NatCarE-38
20RedWorCP-8
20WalMaiW-19
21E121So1-37
21E121So8-32
21Exh-64
21Exh-65
21Nei-88
22E120-186
22W572-37
22W573-53
22W575-49
22W575-50
22WilPatV-23
23W501-67
23W503-34
23W515-52
25Exh-34
68LauWorS-19
69SCFOldT-32
77GalGloG-139
81ConTSN-90
83DiaClaS2-80
86RedGreT-8
88PacEigMO-81
91ConTSN-163
94ConTSN-1270
94ConTSNB-1270
20W516-2

Grohs, Michael
91SpoIndC-4
91SpoIndP-3943
92ChaRaiF-117

Gromek, Steve
46SpoExcW-3-12
47Exh-85
47IndTeal-12
47IndVanPP-11
48IndTeal-13
49Bow-198
49IndTeal-13
50Bow-131
50IndNumN-12
50IndTeal-13
51Bow-115
52Bow-203
52IndNumN-8
52Top-258
53BowBW-63
53IndPenCBP-14
54Bow-199
55Bow-203
56Top-310
56YelBasP-13
57Top-258
79DiaGre-293
79TCM50-133
83TopRep5-258

Groninger, Gerry
88BilMusP-1803
89CedRapRB-23
89CedRapRP-930
89CedRapRS-23
90BilMusP-3238
91FayGenC-14
91FayGenP-1186
92FayGenC-24
92FayGenF-2184
93LakTigC-26
93LakTigF-1326

Groom, Bob
08AmeCarE-77
09AmeCarE-47
09ColChiE-121
09SenBarP-5
09T206-149
10CouT21-141
10DomDisP-51
10RedCroT-115
10RedCroT-196
10SweCapPP-59
11T205-70
11TurRedT-96
12ColRedB-121
12ColTinT-121
12HasTriFT-44
14CraJacE-46
14PieStaT-26
15CraJacE-46
15VicT21-14
16ColE13-66
92ConTSN-350

Groom, Buddy
88TamTarS-9
89BirBarB-24
89BirBarP-109
89SouLeaAJ-17
90BirBarB-16
90BirBarP-1104
91LinDriAA-386
91LonTigLD-386
91LonTigP-1872
92DonRoo-44
92FleUpd-22
92TolMudHF-1037
92TolMudHS-585
93Don-569
93TigGat-11
93TolMudHF-1649
93Top-353
93TopGol-353
93TopInaM-353
93TopMic-353
94Don-637
94FleUpd-45
94TolMudHF-1023
95Fle-55
95Pac-155
96A'sMot-22
96LeaSigEA-63

Groot, Franz
92GreFalDSP-14
93YakBeaC-10
93YakBeaF-3880
95VerBeaDTI-9

Groover, Larry
79WatA'sT-17
Groppuso, Mike
91ClaDraP-39
91FroRowDP-39
92OscAstC-13
92OscAstF-2537
92Pin-543
93ClaFS7-196
93JacGenF-2112
94JacGenF-224
95JacGenTI-22
Groseclose, David
96AshTouB-20
Groski, Gary
87ModA'sC-27
Gross, Bob
87GasRanP-5
Gross, Deryk
89KenTwiP-1064
89KenTwiS-8
90KenTwiB-4
90KenTwiP-2306
90KenTwiS-5
Gross, Don
57Kah-12
57RedSoh-7
57Top-341
58Top-172
59Top-228
60Top-284
Gross, George
78DayBeaAT-8
80TucTorT-10
81TucTorT-22
Gross, Greg
73LinPor-81
74AstFouTIP-1
75Hos-101
75Kel-5
75OPC-334
75Top-334
76Hos-90
76Kel-56A
76Kel-56B
76OPC-171
76SSP-64
76Top-171
77Top-614
78SSP270-257
78Top-397
79OPC-302
79PhiBurK-22
79Top-579
80OPC-364
80PhiBurK-12
80Top-718
81Don-508
81Fle-18
81Top-459
82Don-371
82Fle-246
82Top-53
83Don-441
83Fle-162
83PhiTas-12
83Top-279
84Don-285
84Fle-31
84Nes792-613
84OCoandSI-236
84PhiTas-35
84Top-613
84TopTif-613
85Don-407
85Fle-251
85FleStaS-53
85OPC-117
85PhiCIG-5
85PhiTas-12
85PhiTas-35
85Top-117
85TopMin-117
85TopTif-117
86Don-163
86Fle-441
86OPC-302
86PhiCIG-5
86PhiTas-21
86Top-302
86TopTif-302
87AstShoSTw-9
87Don-385
87Fle-173
87FleGlo-173
87OPC-338
87PhiTas-21
87RedFolSB-20
87Top-702
87TopTif-702
88Don-412
88Fle-302
88FleGlo-302
88PhiTas-11
88Sco-386
88ScoGlo-386
88StaLinPh-8
88Top-518
88TopTif-518
89AstLenH-2
89AstMot-12
89AstSmo-17
89Fle-568
89FleGlo-568
89OPCBoxB-E
89Sco-125
89Top-438
89TopTif-438
89TopWaxBC-E
89UppDec-534
91PadMag-12
95NewHavRTI-6
96NewHavRB-2
Gross, John
90AppFoxBS-11
91BasCitRC-4
91BasCitRP-1391
91Cla/Bes-35
92BasCitRC-9
92BasCitRF-3839
93WilBluRC-12
93WilBluRF-1992
Gross, Kevin
83PorBeaT-5
84Don-381
84Fle-32
84Nes792-332
84PhiTas-20
84Top-332
84TopTif-332
85Don-477
85Fle-252
85PhiCIG-14
85PhiTas-9
85PhiTas-18
85Top-584
85TopTif-584
86BasStaB-49
86Don-529
86Fle-442
86PhiCIG-8
86PhiTas-46
86Top-764
86TopSti-119
86TopTif-764
87Don-236
87Fle-174
87FleGlo-174
87OPC-163
87PhiTas-46
87SpoTeaP-6
87Top-163
87TopTif-163
88Don-113
88DonBasB-103
88Fle-303
88FleGlo-303
88OPC-20
88PhiTas-12
88Sco-468
88ScoGlo-468
88Top-20
88TopSti-118
88TopTif-20
89Bow-355
89BowTif-355
89Don-194
89DonAll-48
89DonBasB-202
89DonBonM-BC12
89DonTra-3
89ExpPos-11
89Fle-569
89FleGlo-569
89FleUpd-96
89OPC-215
89PanSti-147
89Sco-227
89ScoRoo-39T
89Spo-213
89Top-215
89TopSti-116
89TopTif-215
89TopTra-42T
89TopTraT-42T
89UppDec-31
89UppDec-719
90Bow-109
90BowTif-109
90Don-248
90DonBesN-18
90ExpPos-14
90Fle-348
90FleCan-348
90Lea-61
90OPC-465
90PubSti-174
90Sco-251
90Top-465
90TopBig-3
90TopSti-76
90TopTif-465
90UppDec-468
91Bow-611
91DodMot-17
91DodPol-45
91Don-569
91Fle-235
91FleUpd-94
91Lea-279
91OPC-674
91Sco-22
91ScoRoo-51T
91SimandSMLBL-19
91Top-674A
91Top-674B
91TopDesS-674
91TopMic-674
91TopTif-674
91UppDec-380
91UppDec-713
92DodMot-16
92DodPol-46
92DodSmo-5892
92Don-279
92Fle-456
92Lea-33
92OPC-334
92Pin-344
92Sco-34
92ScoProP-10
92StaClu-72
92StaCluMO-16
92Top-334
92TopGol-334
92TopGolW-334
92TopMic-334
92UppDec-515
93DodMot-19
93DodPol-7
93Don-458
93DonSpiotG-SG19
93Fle-448
93Lea-181
93OPC-111
93PacSpa-145
93Pin-177
93Sco-519
93StaClu-473
93StaCluD-5
93StaCluFDI-473
93StaCluMOP-473
93Top-714
93TopGol-714
93TopInaM-714
93TopMic-714
93Ult-399
93UppDec-198
93UppDecGold-198
94ColC-394
94ColChoGS-394
94ColChoSS-394
94DodMot-21
94DodPol-9
94Don-587
94ExtBas-287
94Fla-396
94Fle-510
94Lea-153
94Pac-308
94Sco-530
94ScoGolR-530
94Sel-157
94StaClu-281
94StaCluFDI-281
94StaCluGR-281
94StaCluMOP-281
94Top-516
94TopGol-516
94TopSpa-516
94Ult-516
94UppDec-166
94UppDecED-166
95ColCho-402
95ColChoGS-402
95ColChoSS-402
95Don-424
95DonPreP-424
95Fle-540
95FleUpd-82
95Lea-371
95RanCra-13
95StaClu-187
95StaCluFDI-187
95StaCluMOP-187
95StaCluSTWS-187
95StaCluVR-97
95Top-123
95TopCyb-78
95TopTra-14T
95Ult-335
95UltGolM-335
95UppDec-389
95UppDecED-389
95UppDecEDG-389
96ColCho-733
96ColChoGS-733
96ColChoSS-733
96Don-93
96DonPreP-93
96EmoXL-123
96Fla-171
96Fle-252
96FleRan-8
96FleTif-252
96LeaSigEA-64
96Pac-425
96RanMot-10
95StaCluVRMC-97
96Ult-419
96UltGolM-419
96UppDec-208
97Fle-223
97FleTif-223
97PacPriGotD-GD96
97Top-328
Gross, Kip
86AncGlaPTI-13
87LynMetP-5
88FloStaLAS-6
88St.LucMS-10
89JacMetGS-22
91LinDriAAA-259
91NasSouLD-259
91NasSouP-2150
91TopDeb90-60
92DodPol-57
92DodSmo-5992
92Fle-407
92OPC-372
92Sco-740
92Sco100RS-92
92StaClu-247
92Top-372
92TopGol-372
92TopGolW-372
92TopMic-372
93DodPol-8
93Don-194
93StaClu-7
93StaCluFDI-7
93StaCluMOP-7
94VenLinU-36
Gross, Rafael
94GreFalDSP-15
95YakBeaTI-12
96SanBerSB-11
Gross, Wayne
76TucTorCa-10
76TusTorCr-25
77Top-479
78Hos-141
78OPC-106
78Top-139
79Top-528
80OPC-189
80Top-363
81A'sGraG-10
81AllGamPI-32
81Don-237
81Fle-587
81OPC-86
81Top-86
81TopSti-118
82A'sGraG-2
82Don-139
82Fle-90
82FleSta-124
82OPC-303
82Top-692
83A'sGraG-10
83Don-591
83Fle-517
83Top-233
84Don-375
84Fle-444
84FleUpd-45
84Nes792-741
84OPC-263
84Top-741
84TopSti-333
84TopTif-741
84TopTra-44T
84TopTraT-44T
85Don-228
85Fle-179
85OPC-233
85Top-416
85TopTif-416
86Don-535
86Fle-276
86OPC-173
86Top-173
86TopTif-173
87A'sMot-17
91OriCro-168
Grossman, Bob
75OklCit8TI-1
75SanAntBT-7
76WilTomT-6
Grossman, Dave
82EdmTraT-24
86IowCubP-12
88IowCubP-531
89IowCubP-1703
Grossman, Jim
87KinIndP-8
Grote, Bob
79JacMetT-8
Grote, Jason
95ButCopKtI-9
96BurBeeTI-4
Grote, Jerry (Gerald)
64Top-226
64TopVen-226
65AstBigLBPP-7
65Top-504
66Top-328
66TopVen-328
67CokCapYM-V34
67DexPre-84
67MetTeaI-6
67Top-413
68Top-582
69MetCit-4
69MetNewYDN-7
69MilBra-98
69MLBOffS-165
69OPC-55
69Top-55
69TopSta-63
69TopTeaP-24
70MetTra-22C
70MLBOffS-76
70OPC-183
70Top-183
71MLBOffS-154
71OPC-278
71Top-278
71TopGreM-54
72MilBra-123
72Top-655
73NewYorN-13
73OPC-113
73Top-113
74MetDaiPA-18
74OPC-311
74Top-311
74TopSta-62
75OPC-158

75Top-158
76Hos-78
76MetMSAP-1
76OPC-143
76Spo-9
76Top-143
77MetDaiPA-6
78SSP270-60
78Top-464
79Top-279
81TCM60I-438
84OCoandSI-186
86MetGreT-8
87Met196T-8
89Met196C-4
89PacSenL-120
89PacSenL-125
89RinPosM1-11
89T/MSenL-41
89TopSenL-34
90DodTar-303
91LinDri-17
91MetWIZ-153
91SweBasG-36
93UppDecAH-60
93UppDecS-10
94Met69CCPP-17
94Met69CS-16
94Met69T-8
94UppDecAH-181
94UppDecAH1-181
96Met69Y-3

Grotewold, Jeff
87SpaPhiP-21
88ClePhiS-13
89ClePhiS-10
90ReaPhiB-17
90ReaPhiP-1227
90ReaPhiS-10
91LinDriAAA-484
91ScrRedBLD-484
91ScrRedBP-2544
92DonRoo-45
92FleUpd-110
92PhiMed-40
92Ult-545
93Fle-490
93LinVenB-155
93Sco-305
93StaClu-63
93StaCluFDI-63
93StaCluMOP-63
93Top-72
93TopGol-72
93TopInaM-72
93TopMic-72
94SanBerSC-4
96OmaRoyB-13

Groth, Ernest
50RemBre-9

Groth, Johnny (John)
47Exh-86
50Bow-243
51Bow-249
51TopBluB-11
52Bow-67
52NatTeaL-12
52RedMan-AL10
52StaCalL-72F
52StaCalS-86C
52TipTop-12
52Top-25
53Top-36
54Bow-165
54Wil-7
55Bow-117
56Top-279
56YelBasP-14
57Top-360
58Top-262
59Top-164
59TopVen-164
60Lea-133
60Top-171
60TopVen-171
79DiaGre-392
79TCM50-38
81TigDetN-33
83TopRep5-25
91TopArc1-36

Grott, Matt
90MidLeaASGS-54
90ModA'sC-11
90ProAaA-115
91HunStaC-11
91HunStaLD-285
91HunStaP-1789
91HunStaTI-11
91LinDriAA-285
92ChaLooF-3812
92ChaLooS-184
93IndIndF-1482
94IndIndF-1804
96ScrRedBB-15

Grott, Matthew
90MadMusP-2261

Grout, Ron
79WisRapTT-7

Grove, George M.
20WalMaiW-20

Grove, Lefty (Robert M.)
28PorandAR-A13
28PorandAR-B13
28StaPlaCE-31
28W56PlaC-C13
29ExhFou-27
29PorandAR-33
30SchR33-49
30W554-6
31Exh-28
31W517-39
32OrbPinUP-23
32R33So2-408
32USCar-27
33ButCanV-21
33ButCre-11
33CraJacP-12
33DelR33-23
33ExhFou-14
33GeoCMil-17
33Gou-220
33RitCE-8D
33TatOrb-23
33TatOrbSDR-182
34BatR31-31
34BatR31-153
34ButPreR-28
34DiaStaR-1
34ExhFou-9
34ExhFou-14
34Gou-19
34GouCanV-54
35ExhFou-9
35WheBB1-15
36ExhFou-9
36NatChiFPR-36
36OveCanR-21
36PC7AlbHoF-52
36R31PasP-36
36WheBB4-4
36WheBB5-10
36WorWidGV-88
37ExhFou-9
37OPCBatUV-137
37WheBB6-9
37WheBB8-6
37WheBB9-7
38BasTabP-14
38ExhFou-9
38WheBB10-9
38WheBB11-4
38WheBB15-5
39ExhSal-23
41DouPlaR-105
46SpoExcW-4-4
48ExhHoF-14
50CalHOFW-36
51R42SmaS-39
60Fle-60
60Fle-80B
61Fle-38
61GolPre-17
63BasMagM-33
67TopVen-168
68SpoMemAG-6
69EquSpoHoF-BB6
72KelATG-7
72LauGreF-16
75TCMAllG-13
76OPC-350
76RowExh-13
76ShaPiz-52
76Top-350
77GalGloG-55
77GalGloG-195
77ShaPiz-7
79RedSoxEF-4
79RedSoxEF-12
79RedSoxEF-13
80Lau300-19
80LauFamF-8
80PacLeg-27
80PerHaloFP-52
80SSPHOF-52
81ConTSN-38
82DiaCla-43
82OhiHaloF-25
83ConMar-20
84OCoandSI-83
85FegMurCG-9
86ConSer1-47
86RedSoxGT-2
86SpoDecG-3
87HygAllG-23
87SpoRea-26
88ConAmeA-13
88ConSer4-13
88GreBasS-69
89HOFStiB-74
89PacLegI-185
89SweBasG-15
90BasWit-94
90HOFStiB-31
90SweBasG-70
91ConTSN-23
91ConTSN-255
91SweBasG-139
92ConTSN-431
92ConTSN-533
92ConTSNCI-2
93ActPacA-99
93ActPacA2-33G
93ConTSN-669
93ConTSN-930
93ConTSNP-1140
94ConTSN-999
94ConTSN-1140
94ConTSNB-999
94ConTSNB-1140
94TedWil-67
94UppDecTAE-41

Grove, LeRoy Orval
47Exh-87
48KelPep*-BB2
48WhiSoxTI-8
49Lea-66
79DiaGre-131
83TCMPla1943-11

Grove, Scott
88PulBraP-1752
89SumBraP-1114
90BurBraB-18
90BurBraP-2344
90BurBraS-13
92DunBluJC-13
92DunBluJF-1994
93DunBluJC-8
93DunBluJF-1789
93DunBluJFFN-8
93KnoSmoF-1248

Grove, Wayne
85DalNatCC-12

Groves, Jeff
86GreBraTI-12

Groves, Larry
86IndIndTI-27

Grovom, Carl
86AubAstP-11
87ChaWheP-15
88OscAstS-11
91JacGenP-920

Grow, Lorin
76IndIndTI-14

Grubb, Cary
87SalAngP-26
88RenSilSCLC-281

Grubb, Christopher
93JamExpC-7
93JamExpF-3333

Grubb, Dennis
95AusFut-45

Grubb, Johnny (John)
73LinPor-155
74OPC-32
74PadDea-11
74PadMcDD-5
74Top-32A
74Top-32B
74TopSta-93
75Hos-109
75Kel-43
75OPC-298
75PadDea-2
75SSPPuzB-11
75Top-298
76OPC-422
76SSP-130
76Top-422
77OPC-165
77PadSchC-25
77PepGloD-10
77Top-286
78Top-608
79OPC-99
79Top-198
80OPC-165
80Top-313
81Don-148
81Fle-631
81Top-545
82Don-467
82Fle-317
82OPC-193
82Top-496
83Don-341
83Fle-567
83FleSta-72
83FleSti-167
83Tig-13
83Top-724
83TopSti-123
83TopTra-38T
84Don-90
84Fle-81
84Nes792-42
84TigFarJ-5
84TigWavP-18
84Top-42
84TopTif-42
85Don-578
85Fle-9
85TigCaiD-9
85TigWen-10
85Top-643
85TopTif-643
86Don-615
86Fle-227
86TigCaiD-7
86Top-243
86TopTif-243
87Don-476
87Fle-152
87FleGlo-152
87TigCaiD-12
87TigCok-18
87Top-384
87TopSti-265
87TopTif-384
88Sco-199
88ScoGlo-199
88Top-128
88TopTif-128
89PacSenL-191
89RicBraBC-8
89RicBraC-24
89RicBraP-821
89RicBraTI-25
89T/MSenL-42
90EliSenL-57
90ProAAAF-420
90RicBraC-2
90RicBraP-275
90RicBraTI-11
91RicBraBC-41
91RicBraP-2586
93RanKee-165
95ColSilB-10
96ColSilB-12
97BobCamRB-23

Grubb, Sean
89HamRedS-17

Grube, Frank
32OrbPinNP-5
32OrbPinUP-24
33TatOrb-24
34DiaMatCSB-75
34Gou-64
35DiaMatCS3T1-63
35GouPuzR-8C
35GouPuzR-9C
41BroW75-13
92ConTSN-399
94ConTSN-1162
94ConTSNB-1162

Gruber, Henry
87OldJudN-219

Gruber, Kelly
80BatTroT-21
81WatIndT-22
82ChaLooT-16
83BufBisT-16
84BluJayFS-16
84SyrChiT-27
85BluJayFS-13
85Fle-645
85IntLeaAT-37
85SyrChiT-22
86BluJayAF-12
86BluJayFS-15
86DonRoo-16
87BluJayFS-11
87Don-444
87Fle-227
87FleGlo-227
87GenMilB-1D
87OPC-191
87Top-458
87TopTif-458
88BluJayFS-14
88Don-244
88DonBasB-255
88Fle-111
88FleGlo-111
88OPC-113
88PanSti-221
88Sco-422
88ScoGlo-422
88Top-113
88TopBig-134
88TopTif-113
89BluJayFS-12
89Bow-251
89BowTif-251
89Don-113
89DonBasB-31
89Fle-234
89FleGlo-234
89OPC-29
89PanSti-469
89Sco-194
89ScoYouS2-12
89Spo-163
89SpoIllFKI-189
89Top-29
89Top-201
89TopBig-95
89TopSti-187
89TopTif-29
89TopTif-201
89UppDec-575
90BluJayFS-10
90BluJayHS-1
90BluJayHS-5
90Bow-519
90BowTif-519
90ClaYel-T70
90Don-12
90Don-113A
90Don-113B
90DonBesA-84
90DonLeaS-30
90DonSupD-12
90Fle-83
90FleCan-83
90Lea-106
90OPC-505
90PanSti-171
90PubSti-515
90RedFolSB-41
90Sco-425
90ScoMcD-9
90Spo-57
90Top-505
90TopBig-17
90TopSti-193
90TopTif-505
90UppDec-111
90USPlaCA-5S
90WinDis-5
91BasBesHRK-8
91BluJayFS-11
91BluJayS-15
91Bow-18
91Bow-369
91CadEllD-27
91ClaGam-19
91DenHol-6
91Don-149
91Fle-175
91Lea-9

91MSAHoID-15
91OPC-370
91OPC-388
91OPCPre-57
91PanCanT1-22
91PanCanT1-112
91PanFreS-338
91PanSti-161
91PetSta-26
91PosCan-15
91RedFolS-42
91Sco-595
91Sco100S-64
91SimandSMLBL-20
91StaClu-331
91StaPinB-22
91Stu-135
91SunSee-12
91Top-370
91Top-388
91TopCraJ2-4
91TopDesS-370
91TopDesS-388
91TopMic-370
91TopMic-388
91TopTif-370
91TopTif-388
91TopTriH-A14
91Ult-361
91UppDec-44
91UppDec-374
91UppDecSS-SS7
92Bow-510
92Cla2-T20
92ClaGam-122
92Don-65
92DonCraJ1-5
92DonMcD-G3
92DonPre-8
92Fle-329
92Hig5-118
92Lea-27
92MSABenSHD-5
92OPC-298
92OPCPre-116
92PanSti-27
92PepDieM-20
92Pin-134
92PosCan-14
92Sco-495
92Sco100S-64
92ScoCokD-11
92StaClu-570
92StaCluD-71
92Stu-255
92Top-298
92TopGol-298
92TopGolW-298
92TopKid-92
92TopMic-298
92TriPla-242
92Ult-146
92UppDec-324
93AngMot-13
93AngPol-5
93BluJayD4-7
93BluJayDM-5
93BluJayDM-17
93BluJayDM-18A
93BluJayDM-18B
93BluJayDM-19
93Don-453
93Fle-334
93Lea-532
93OPC-156
93OPCWorC-5
93PacSpa-323
93PanSti-5
93Pin-198
93Sco-156
93Sel-200
93StaCluM-31
93Top-628
93TopGol-628
93TopInaM-628
93TopMic-628
93UppDec-406
93UppDec-807
93UppDecGold-406
93UppDecGold-807
96BluJayOH-13
97BluJayS-50
Grudzielanek, Mark
91JamExpC-4
91JamExpP-3553
92RocExpC-20
92RocExpF-2123
93WesPalBEC-7
93WesPalBEF-1346
94AriFalLS-6
94HarSenF-2097
95Bow-224
95BowBes-R86
95BowBesR-R86
95BowGolF-224
95ColCho-549T
95Exc-222
95Fin-250
95FinRef-250
95Fla-376
95FleUpd-106
95SelCer-115
95SelCerMG-115
95SP-7
95SPSil-7
95StaClu-571
95StaCluCB-CB11
95StaCluMOP-571
95StaCluMOP-CB11
95StaCluSTWS-571
95Sum-124
95SumNthD-124
95TopTra-73T
95UC3-112
95UC3ArtP-112
95UppDec-234
95UppDecED-234
95UppDecEDG-234
95UppDecML-131
95UppDecPAW-H32
95UppDecPAWE-H32
95UppDecSE-136
95UppDecSEG-136
95Zen-122
96Bow-47
96BowBes-84
96BowBesAR-84
96BowBesR-84
96Cir-149
96CirRav-149
96ColCho-213
96ColChoGS-213
96ColChoSS-213
96Don-13
96DonPreP-13
96ExpBoo-3
96ExpDis-9
96ExpDis-10
96Fin-B348
96FinRef-B348
96Fla-307
96Fle-458
96FleTif-458
96Lea-50
96LeaPre-73
96LeaPreP-73
96LeaPrePB-50
96LeaPrePG-50
96LeaPrePS-50
96LeaSig-76
96LeaSigA-86
96LeaSigAG-86
96LeaSigAS-86
96LeaSigPPG-76
96LeaSigPPP-76
96Sco-253
96SP-122
96StaClu-449
96StaCluMOP-449
96Stu-106
96StuPrePB-106
96StuPrePG-106
96StuPrePS-106
96TeaOut-34
96Ult-504
96UltGolM-504
96UppDec-132
97Bow-267
97BowInt-267
97Cir-6
97CirRav-6
97ColCho-163
97ColChoAC-31
97Don-112
97DonEli-82
97DonEliGS-82
97DonLim-40
97DonLimLE-40
97DonPre-21
97DonPreCttC-21
97DonPreP-112
97DonPrePGold-112
97Fin-70
97FinRef-70
97FlaSho-A147
97FlaSho-B147
97FlaSho-C147
97FlaShoLC-147
97FlaShoLC-B147
97FlaShoLC-C147
97FlaShoLCM-A147
97FlaShoLCM-B147
97FlaShoLCM-C147
97Fle-380
97FleTif-380
97Lea-94
97LeaFraM-94
97LeaFraMDC-94
97MetUni-155
97NewPin-104
97NewPinAP-104
97NewPinMC-104
97NewPinPP-104
97Pac-345
97PacLigB-345
97PacPri-118
97PacPriLB-118
97PacPriP-118
97PacSil-345
97Pin-16
97PinArtP-16
97PinCer-93
97PinCerMBlu-93
97PinCerMG-93
97PinCerMR-93
97PinCerR-93
97PinIns-80
97PinInsCE-80
97PinInsDE-80
97PinMusC-16
97PinTotCPB-93
97PinTotCPG-93
97PinTotCPR-93
97PinX-P-83
97PinX-PMoS-83
97Sco-133
97ScoPreS-133
97ScoShoS-133
97ScoShoSAP-133
97Sel-13
97SelArtP-13
97SelRegG-13
97SP-111
97SpoIll-86
97SpoIllEE-86
97StaClu-44
97StaCluM-M2
97StaCluMat-44
97StaCluMOP-44
97StaCluMOP-M2
97Stu-38
97StuPrePG-38
97StuPrePS-38
97Top-260
97TopChr-91
97TopChrR-91
97TopGal-173
97TopGalPPI-173
97Ult-230
97UltGolME-230
97UltPlaME-230
97UppDec-110
95UppDecMLFS-131
Grudzinski, Gary
85PriWilPT-19
Gruesbeck, Mark
94BriTigC-30
96WesOahCHWB-NNO
Grump, Mascot
96ScrRedBB-30
Grundler, Frank
75ShrCapT-4
76ShrCapT-17
Grundt, Ken
91EveGiaC-18
91EveGiaP-3906
92CliGiaC-23
92CliGiaF-3591
92MidLeaATI-13
92ProFS7-358
93ExcFS7-117
95AshTouTI-26
95NewHavRTI-25
96PawRedSDD-10
96TreThuB-11
Grundy, Phil
93EugEmeC-1
93EugEmeF-3851
94MidLeaAF-MDW23
94RocRoyC-11
94RocRoyF-559
95WilBluRTI-32
96WilBluRB-6
Grunewald, Keith
94AshTouC-10
94AshTouF-1791
95SalAvaTI-16
96NewHavRB-12
Grunhard, Danny (Dan)
85AncGlaPTI-12
86QuaCitAP-13
87PalSprP-8
88MidAngGS-16
89MidAngGS-17
90CMC-493
90EdmTraC-16
90EdmTraP-528
90ProAAAF-104
91EdmTraLD-165
91EdmTraP-1528
91LinDriAAA-165
92TacTigF-2514
92TacTigS-534
Grunsky, Gary
76BatRouCT-11
Grunwald, Al
57JetPos-7
60Top-427
Gryboski, Kevin
95EveAqaTI-9
96WisTimRB-10
Grygiel, Joe
91SpoIndC-16
91SpoIndP-3944
Gryskevich, Larry
89HamRedS-14
90SavCarP-2073
Grzanich, Mike
93AubAstC-12
93AubAstF-3436
94QuaCitRBC-11
94QuaCitRBF-529
95JacGenTI-3
96JacGenB-9
96TexLeaAB-7
Grzelaczyk, Kenneth
92SpoIndC-2
92SpoIndF-1286
93RanCucQC-13
93RanCucQF-825
94RanCucQC-13
94RanCucQF-1630
Grzenda, Joe
69OPC-121
69Top-121
69TopFou-20
70Top-691
71CarTeal-19
71MLBOffS-541
71OPC-518
71SenTealW-11
71Top-518
72OPC-13
72Top-13
91MetWIZ-154
Grzybeck, Ben
77DayBealT-8
Gsellman, Bob
87ChaWheP-8
Guanchez, Harry
90EugEmeGS-9
91AppFoxC-18
91AppFoxP-1724
93LinVenB-143
94VenLinU-85
95LinVen-233
Guante, Cecilio
81PorBeaT-10
82PorBeaT-3
83Don-423
84Don-78
84Fle-250
84Nes792-122
84Top-122
84TopTif-122
85Don-357
85Fle-465
85Top-457
85TopTif-457
86Don-142
86Fle-609
86Top-668
86TopTat-8
86TopTif-668
87Don-238
87Fle-610
87FleGlo-610
87FleUpd-38
87FleUpdG-38
87OPC-219
87Top-219
87TopSti-127
87TopTif-219
87TopTra-40T
87TopTraT-40T
88DonBasB-276
88DonReaBY-NEW
88Top-84
88TopTif-84
89Don-260
89Fle-519
89FleGlo-519
89RanMot-23
89RanSmo-10
89Sco-439
89Top-766
89TopTif-766
89UppDec-576
90Don-403
90Fle-298
90FleCan-298
90IndTeal-14
90Lea-365
90OPC-532
90PubSti-410
90Sco-438
90Top-532
90TopTif-532
92YanWIZ8-70
93LimRocDWB-117
93RanKee-166
Guarache, Jose
88St.CatBJP-2011
93LinVenB-108
Guardado, Eddie
91EliTwiP-4296
92KenTwiC-3
92KenTwiF-598
92ProFS7-102
93FleFinE-235
93NasXprF-395
94Don-139
94Fle-203
94SalLakBF-812
94Top-677
94TopGol-677
94TopSpa-677
94Ult-86
95FleUpd-59
96LeaSigEA-65
96Pac-355
97Pac-136
97PacLigB-136
97PacSil-136
Guarnaccia, John
77ReaPhiT-13
Guarnera, Rick
75SpoIndC-5
Gubanich, Creighton
91SouOreAP-3850
92ClaFS7-177
92MadMusC-1
92MadMusF-1238
93MadMusC-12
93MadMusF-1824
94ModA'sC-13
94ModA'sF-3065
95HunStaTI-11
Gubicza, Mark
84FleUpd-46
84TopTra-45T
84TopTraT-45T
85Don-344
85Fle-201
85OPC-127
85Top-127
85TopTif-127
86Don-583
86Fle-8
86Lea-226

86RoyKitCD-19
86RoyNatP-23
86Top-644
86TopTif-644
87Don-466
87Fle-368
87FleExcS-20
87FleGlo-368
87FleMin-47
87Lea-238
87OPC-326
87SpoTeaP-13
87Top-326
87TopTif-326
88Don-54
88DonBasB-95
88Fle-259
88FleGlo-259
88FleRecS-15
88OPC-378
88RoySmo-12
88Sco-516
88ScoGlo-516
88StaLinRo-6
88Top-507
88TopBig-199
88TopSti-262
88TopTif-507
89Bow-117
89BowTif-117
89CadEllD-25
89ClaTraO-138
89Don-179
89DonAll-18
89DonBasB-119
89Fle-283
89FleBasA-17
89FleExcS-19
89FleGlo-283
89OPC-379
89PanSti-350
89RoyTasD-9
89Sco-291
89ScoHot1S-69
89ScoYouS2-14
89Spo-102
89Top-430
89TopBig-26
89TopMinL-55
89TopSti-271
89TopStiB-26
89TopTif-430
89TopUKM-33
89UppDec-202
90Bow-363
90BowTif-363
90Don-204
90DonBesA-77
90Fle-109
90Fle-633
90FleBasA-15
90FleCan-109
90FleCan-633
90FleLeaL-15
90Lea-145
90MLBBasB-105
90OPC-20
90PanSti-82
90PubSti-349
90Sco-121
90Top-20
90TopBig-201
90TopSti-272
90TopTif-20
90UppDec-676
91ClaGam-20
91Don-145
91Fle-560
91OPC-265
91PanSti-228
91RoyPol-11
91Sco-212
91StaClu-240
91Stu-67
91Top-265
91TopDesS-265
91TopMic-265
91TopTif-265
91Ult-148
91UppDec-541
92Bow-215
92ClaGam-83
92Don-282
92Fle-159
92Lea-332
92OPC-741
92Pin-102
92RoyPol-9
92Sco-459
92StaClu-542
92Stu-183
92Top-741
92TopGol-741
92TopGolW-741
92TopMic-741
92TriPla-233
92Ult-70
92UppDec-459
93Don-703
93Fle-618
93OPC-99
93PacSpa-135
93Pin-81
93RoyPol-10
93Sco-581
93Sel-227
93StaClu-555
93StaCluFDI-555
93StaCluMOP-555
93StaCluRoy-11
93Top-674
93TopGol-674
93TopInaM-674
93TopMic-674
93TriPla-168
93Ult-208
93UppDec-85
93UppDecGold-85
94Fle-156
94StaClu-197
94StaCluFDI-197
94StaCluGR-197
94StaCluMOP-197
94Top-357
94TopGol-357
94TopSpa-357
95ColCho-464
95ColChoGS-464
95ColChoSS-464
95Don-80
95DonPreP-80
95DonTopotO-89
95Fla-45
95Fle-159
95Lea-157
95Pac-202
95Pin-427
95PinArtP-427
95PinMusC-427
95Sco-20
95ScoGolR-20
95ScoPlaTS-20
95TopTra-94T
95Ult-290
95UltGolM-290
96ColCho-572
96ColChoGS-572
96ColChoSS-572
96Don-56
96DonPreP-56
96EmoXL-67
96Fla-89
96Fle-128
96FleTif-128
96LeaSigA-87
96LeaSigAG-87
96LeaSigAS-87
96MetUni-65
96MetUniP-65
96Pac-330
96Pin-115
96ProSta-118
96RoyPol-9
96Sco-82
96StaClu-72
96StaCluMOP-72
96Top-157
96Ult-354
96UltGolM-354
96UppDec-352
97Cir-262
97CirRav-262
97Fle-579
97FleTif-579
97Ult-350
97UltGolME-350
97UltPlaME-350

Gudat, Marv

32CubTeal-7

Guenther, Bob

87MyrBeaBJP-1460

Guercio, Maurice

86FloStaLAP-19
86Ft.LauYP-10
87AlbYanP-6

Guerra, Esmili

92PeoChiC-16
93LinVenB-68
93PeoChiTI-6
94VenLinU-210
95LinVen-65

Guerra, Fernando

80VenLeaS-145

Guerra, Mark

94PitMetC-9
94PitMetF-3517
95StLucMTI-15
96BinBeeB-11

Guerra, Mike (Fermin)

49Bow-155
49PhiBul-21
50Bow-157
51Bow-202

Guerra, Pete

91BurIndP-3303

Guerra, Rich

75SanAntBT-8
76WilTomT-7

Guerra, Robert

94VenLinU-97
95LinVen-237

Guerrero, Alex

75QuaCitAT-11

Guerrero, Ino (Inocencio)

83DurBulT-4
85DomLeaS-85
85GreBraTI-6
86GreBraTI-13
87GreBraB-17
87RicBraBC-10
88GreBraB-4
89DurBullS-28
89DurBulTI-26

Guerrero, Juan

87PocGiaTB-27
88CliGiaP-701
89SanJosGB-21
89SanJosGCLC-219
89SanJosGP-451
89SanJosGS-11
89Sta-86
90ShrCapP-1450
90ShrCapS-8
91LinDriAA-305
91ShrCapLD-305
91ShrCapP-1828
92AstMot-15
92DonRoo-46
92FleUpd-85
92Lea-428
92Pin-552
92ProFS7-348
92StaClu-775
92StaCluECN-775
92Ult-490
93Don-240
93Fle-435
93LimRocDWB-72
93Sco-259
93StaClu-16
93StaCluFDI-16
93StaCluMOP-16
93Top-414
93TopGol-414
93TopInaM-414
93TopMic-414
93Ult-41
94TucTorF-766
95TusTorTI-7

Guerrero, Mario

73LinPor-22
73OPC-607
73Top-607
74OPC-192
74Top-192
75OPC-152
75Top-152
75TulOil7-23
76OPC-499
76SSP-285
76Top-499
77Top-628
78Top-339
79Hos-78
79Kel-43
79OPC-131
79Top-261
80Top-49
81Fle-591
81Top-547
85DomLeaS-151
89PacSenL-36
89T/MSenL-43

Guerrero, Mike

88BelBreGS-15
89BelBreIS-8
90StoPorB-8
90StoPorP-2193
91ElPasDP-2754
92ClaFS7-97
92ElPasDF-3930
92ElPasDS-211
93LimRocDWB-20
93MemChiF-381

Guerrero, Patrick

88St.CatBJP-2038

Guerrero, Pedro

79AlbDukT-16
79Top-719
80DodPol-28
81Dod-5
81DodPol-28
81LonBeaPT-7
81Top-651
82DodPol-28
82DodPos-3
82DodUniOV-6
82DogBuiE-4
82Don-136
82Fle-7
82FleSta-6
82LouSlu-2
82OPC-247
82Top-247
82TopSti-55
82TopSti-260
83AllGamPI-121
83DodPol-28
83DodPos-3
83Don-110
83Dra-9
83Fle-207
83FleSti-117
83Kel-20
83OPC-116
83PerCreC-5
83PerCreCG-5
83SevCoi-4
83Top-425
83Top-681
83TopFol-3
83TopSti-248
84AllGamPI-30
84DodPol-28
84Don-24
84Don-24A
84Don-174
84DonActAS-17
84Dra-11
84Fle-100
84FleSti-19
84FleSti-34
84FunFooP-26
84MilBra-11
84Nes792-90
84Nes792-306
84OPC-90
84RalPur-30
84SevCoi-W14
84Top-90
84Top-306
84TopCer-30
84TopGloS-25
84TopRubD-7
84TopSti-75
84TopSup-24
84TopTif-90
84TopTif-306
85AllGamPI-142
85DodCokP-11
85Don-174
85DonActA-34
85DonHig-19
85Dra-13
85Fle-370
85Lea-211
85OPC-34
85SevCoi-W10
85ThoMcAD-31
85Top-575
85TopMin-575
85TopRubD-8
85TopSti-70
85TopSup-44
85TopTif-575
86BasStaB-50
86DodCokP-10
86DodPol-28
86DodUniOP-6
86Don-174
86Dra-6
86Fle-130
86FleAll-8
86FleLimE-21
86FleMin-28
86FleSlu-13
86FleStiC-47
86GenMilB-5B
86Lea-105
86MeaGolBB-6
86MeaGolSB-18
86OPC-145
86OPCBoxB-G
86SevCoi-C4
86SevCoi-E4
86SevCoi-S4
86SevCoi-W4
86Spo-14
86Spo-148
86Spo-181
86SpoDecG-74
86Top-145
86Top-706
86Top3-D-8
86TopGloS-25
86TopMinL-44
86TopSti-65
86TopSup-27
86TopTat-23
86TopTif-145
86TopTif-706
86TopWaxBC-G
86TruVal-1
87BoaandB-27
87BurKinA-7
87ClaGam-39
87DodMot-2
87DodPol-14
87DodSmoA-10
87Don-53
87Fle-440
87FleGlo-440
87FleSlu-16
87GenMilB-6D
87KayB-14
87Lea-237
87MSAJifPD-10
87OPC-360
87RedFolSB-83
87SevCoi-W4
87Spo-27
87SpoTeaP-14
87StuPan-6
87Top-360
87TopSti-69
87TopTif-360
88DodMot-2
88DodPol-28
88DodSmo-28
88Don-278
88DonAll-48
88DonBasB-122
88DonBonM-BC16
88Dra-26
88Fle-514
88Fle-623
88FleAwaW-15
88FleGlo-514
88FleGlo-623
88FleMin-83
88FleSlu-16
88FleStiC-91
88K-M-11
88KayB-12
88Lea-101
88MSAFanSD-20
88Nes-24
88OPC-111
88PanSti-314
88RedFolSB-29

88Sco-9
88ScoGlo-9
88Spo-97
88StaLinD-6
88Top-489
88Top-550
88TopBig-171
88TopCoi-43
88TopGloS-24
88TopMinL-52
88TopRitTM-5
88TopSti-75
88TopStiB-15
88TopTif-489
88TopTif-550
88TopUKM-28
88TopUKMT-28
89Bow-440
89BowTif-440
89CadEllD-26
89CarSmo-7
89ClaLigB-60
89DodSmoG-94
89Don-418
89DonBasB-75
89Fle-451
89FleGlo-451
89K-M-33
89KayB-16
89KinDis-20
89OPC-68
89PanSti-183
89RedFolSB-52
89Sco-564
89ScoHot1S-44
89Top-780
89TopAme2C-15
89TopBasT-74
89TopBatL-6
89TopBig-285
89TopCoi-16
89TopSti-40
89TopTif-780
89TopUKM-34
89TVSpoM-27
89UppDec-306
90Bow-201
90BowTif-201
90CarSmo-7
90ClaBlu-146
90DodTar-304
90Don-63
90Don-674A
90Don-674B
90DonBesN-95
90DOnBonM-BC6
90Fle-250
90FleBasA-16
90FleBasM-15
90FleCan-250
90FleLeaL-16
90FleWaxBC-C11
90HOFStiB-85
90Hot50PS-18
90K-M-15
90Lea-44
90MLBBasB-32
90OPC-610
90PanSti-211
90PanSti-335
90Pos-22
90PubSti-219
90RedFolSB-42
90Sco-13
90Sco100S-61
90Spo-66
90SunSee-10
90Top-610
90TopBatL-6
90TopBig-13
90TopCoi-47
90TopDou-30
90TopGloS-32
90TopHilHM-6
90TopMinL-75
90TopSti-35
90TopSti-151
90TopStiB-3
90TopTif-610
90TopTVA-50
90TopTVCa-25
90UppDec-244
90UppDecS-5
91BasBesHM-8
91Bow-403
91CarPol-28
91ClaGam-21
91DenHol-22
91Don-25
91Don-558
91DonSupD-25
91Fle-634A
91Fle-634B
91Lea-204
91LouRedTI-16
91OPC-20
91OPCPre-58
91PanFreS-31
91PanSti-37
91RedFolS-43
91Sco-140
91StaClu-314
91Stu-232
91Top-20
91TopCraJI-8
91TopDesS-20
91TopMic-20
91TopTif-20
91TopTriH-N12
91Ult-289
91UppDec-98
91UppDec-327
92Bow-377
92CarPol-7
92ClaGam-80
92DodStaTA-26
92Don-158
92Fle-579
92Lea-18
92OPC-470
92PanSti-172
92Pin-392
92Sco-376
92StaClu-320
92Stu-91
92Top-470
92TopGol-470
92TopGolW-470
92TopKid-26
92TopMic-470
92TriPla-9
92Ult-263
92UppDec-357
93Don-600
93Fle-509
95MidAngOHP-14
95MidAngTI-12
Guerrero, Rafael
92GulCoaMF-3493
93KinMetC-13
93KinMetF-3809
94CapCitBC-9
94CapCitBF-1763
96StLucMTI-7
Guerrero, Ramces
88IdaFalBP-1844
89IdaFalBP-2010
Guerrero, Sandy
86VenGulP-8
87StoPorP-4
88CalLeaACLC-15
88StoPorCLC-196
88StoPorP-727
89ElPasDGS-22
90ElPasDGS-15
91LinDriAAA-139
91DenZepLD-139
91DenZepP-130
92DenZepF-2646
92ElPasDS-212
93LimRocDWB-119
Guerrero, Sergio
95HelBreTI-7
96HelBreTI-6
Guerrero, Tony
81WisRapTT-4
83OrlTwiT-22
85VisOakT-21
Guerrero, Vladimir
95Bes-80
95Bow-90
95BowBes-B2
95BowBesR-B2
95SPML-7
95SPML-90
95SPMLA-11
95SPMLDtS-DS7
95UppDecML-127
96Bow-374
96BowBes-97
96BowBesAR-97
96BowBesMI-7
96BowBesMIAR-7
96BowBesMIR-7
96BowBesR-97
96BowMinLP-14
96Exc-187
96ExcAll-6
96ExcSeaC-5
96HarSenB-14
96LeaSig-110
96LeaSigPPG-110
96LeaSigPPP-110
96SigRooOJ-12
96Top-435
96WesPalBEB-1
96WesPalBEB-31
97Bow-416
97BowBes-101
97BowBesAR-101
97BowBesBC-BC18
97BowBesBCAR-BC18
97BowBesBCR-BC18
97BowBesMI-MI10
97BowBesMIAR-MI10
97BowBesMIARI-MI10
97BowBesMII-MI10
97BowBesMIR-MI10
97BowBesMIRI-MI10
97BowBesP-17
97BowBesPAR-17
97BowBesPR-17
97BowBesR-101
97BowCerBIA-CA33
97BowCerGIA-CA33
97BowChr-276
97BowChrI-276
97BowChrIR-276
97BowChrR-276
97BowChrSHR-SHR3
97BowChrSHRR-SHR3
97BowInt-416
97BowIntB-BBI14
97BowIntBAR-BBI14
97BowIntBR-BBI14
97BowScoHR-3
97Cir-313
97CirFasT-1
97CirRav-313
97ColCho-10
97ColChoCtG-21A
97ColChoCtG-21B
97ColChoCtG-21C
97ColChoCtGIW-CG21
97ColChoNF-NF33
97ColChoNF-NF34
97ColChoS-28
97ColChoTotT-T17
97Don-355
97DonEli-11
97DonEliGS-11
97DonFraFea-7
97DonLim-6
97DonLim-138
97DonLimFotG-23
97DonLimLE-6
97DonLimLE-138
97DonPowA-19
97DonPowADC-19
97DonPre-155
97DonPre-197
97DonPreCttC-155
97DonPreCttC-197
97DonPreP-355
97DonPrePGold-355
97DonPrePM-24
97DonRatR-27
97DonRooDK-2
97DonRooDKC-2
97Fin-167
97Fin-315
97FinEmb-167
97FinEmb-315
97FinEmbR-167
97FinEmbR-315
97FinRef-167
97FinRef-315
97FlaSho-A27
97FlaSho-B27
97FlaSho-C27
97FlaShoLC-27
97FlaShoLC-B27
97FlaShoLC-C27
97FlaShoLCM-A27
97FlaShoLCM-B27
97FlaShoLCM-C27
97FlaShoWotF-14
97FleNewH-5
97Lea-184
97Lea-398
97LeaFraM-184
97LeaFraM-398
97LeaFraMDC-184
97LeaFraMDC-398
97LeaGolS-27
97LeaLeaotN-15
97MetUni-156
97MetUniMfG-4
97NewPin-169
97NewPin-198
97NewPinAP-169
97NewPinAP-198
97NewPinIE-6
97NewPinMC-169
97NewPinMC-198
97NewPinPP-169
97NewPinPP-198
97NewPinPP-I6B
97PinCer-111
97PinCer-137
97PinCerMBlu-111
97PinCerMBlu-137
97PinCerMG-111
97PinCerMG-137
97PinCerMR-111
97PinCerMR-137
97PinCerR-111
97PinCerR-137
97PinIns-120
97PinInsCE-129
97PinInsDD-20
97PinInsDE-129
97PinTotCPB-111
97PinTotCPB-137
97PinTotCPG-111
97PinTotCPG-137
97PinTotCPR-111
97PinTotCPR-137
97PinX-P-123
97PinX-PMoS-123
97PinX-PMP-2
97PinX-PSfF-53
97PinX-PSfFU-53
97Sco-489
97ScoBla-16
97ScoHobR-489
97ScoResC-489
97ScoShoS-489
97ScoShoSAP-489
97Sel-105
97SelArtP-105
97SelRegG-105
97SelRooR-10
97SelToootT-7
97SelToootTMB-7
97SkyE-X-83
97SkyE-XC-83
97SkyE-XEC-83
97SkyE-XSD2-15
97SP-10
97SPInsI-14
97SpollI-8
97SpollIEE-8
97SPSpeF-47
97SPSpxF-10
97SPSPxFA-10
97SPx-33
97SPxBro-33
97SPxCorotG-5
97SPxGraF-33
97SPxSil-33
97SPxSte-33
97StaClu-185
97StaClu-210
97StaCluM-M36
97StaCluMat-210
97StaCluMOP-185
97StaCluMOP-210
97StaCluMOP-M36
97Stu-151
97StuAut-1
97StuMasS-15
97StuMasS8-15
97StuPor8-21
97StuPrePG-151
97StuPrePS-151
97Top-433
97TopAweI-AI5
97TopChr-153
97TopChrR-153
97TopGal-144
97TopGalPPI-144
97TopStaFAS-FAS3
97Ult-509
97UltGolME-509
97UltGolP-2
97UltPlaME-509
97UppDec-271
97UppDecBCP-BC10
97UppDecHC-HC17
95UppDecMLFS-127
97UppDecU-42
97UppDecUGN-GN2
97UppDecUSS-3
97Zen-48
97Zen8x1-23
97Zen8x1D-23
97ZenV-2-8
Guerrero, Wilton
93GreFalDSP-19
94VerBeaDC-8
94VerBeaDF-79
95Bes-77
95SanAntMTI-4
95SigRooOJ-16
95SigRooOJP-16
95SigRooOJPS-16
95SigRooOJS-16
95SPML-76
95UppDecML-152
96Bow-361
96BowBes-108
96BowBesAR-108
96BowBesR-108
96ColCho-443
96ColChoGS-443
96ColChoSS-443
96Exc-175
96ExcAll-5
96ExcSeaTL-3
96FleUpd-U145
96FleUpdNH-9
96FleUpdTC-U145
96Pin-383
96PinAfi-180
96PinAfiAP-180
96PinFoil-383
96Sel-182
96SelArtP-182
96SelCer-113
96SelCerAP-113
96SelCerCB-113
96SelCerCR-113
96SelCerMB-113
96SelCerMG-113
96SelCerMR-113
96Sum-180
96SumAbo&B-180
96SumArtP-180
96SumFoi-180
96Ult-498
96UltGolM-498
96UltGolP-7
96UltGolPHGM-7
96UppDec-254
96Zen-120
96ZenArtP-120
97Bow-109
97BowBes-183
97BowBesA-183
97BowBesAAR-183
97BowBesAR-183
97BowBesBC-BC12
97BowBesBCAR-BC12
97BowBesBCR-BC12
97BowBesMI-MI8
97BowBesMIAR-MI8
97BowBesMIARI-MI8
97BowBesMII-MI8
97BowBesMIR-MI8
97BowBesMIRI-MI8
97BowBesP-11
97BowBesPAR-11
97BowBesPR-11
97BowBesR-183
97BowChr-129
97BowChrI-129
97BowChrIR-129
97BowChrR-129
97BowChrSHR-SHR14

97BowChrSHRR-SHR14
97BowInt-109
97BowScoHR-14
97Cir-113
97CirRav-113
97ColCho-368
97Don-246
97DonFraFea-4
97DonLim-57
97DonLim-62
97DonLimFotG-53
97DonLimLE-57
97DonLimLE-62
97DonPre-152
97DonPreCttC-152
97DonPreP-246
97DonPrePGold-246
97DonRooDK-10
97DonRooDKC-10
97DonTea-116
97DonTeaSPE-116
97Fin-339
97FinEmb-339
97FinEmbR-339
97FinRef-339
97FlaSho-A91
97FlaSho-B91
97FlaSho-C91
97FlaShoLC-91
97FlaShoLC-B91
97FlaShoLC-C91
97FlaShoLCM-A91
97FlaShoLCM-B91
97FlaShoLCM-C91
97Fle-363
97FleNewH-6
97FleRooS-14
97FleTif-363
97Lea-318
97LeaFraM-318
97LeaFraMDC-318
97LeaLeaotN-14
97MetUni-99
97MetUniMfG-5
97NewPin-168
97NewPinAP-168
97NewPinMC-168
97NewPinPP-168
97PacPriGotD-GD159
97Pin-181
97PinArtP-181
97PinCer-116
97PinCerMBlu-116
97PinCerMG-116
97PinCerMR-116
97PinCerR-116
97PinMusC-181
97PinTotCPB-116
97PinTotCPG-116
97PinTotCPR-116
97PinX-P-121
97PinX-PMoS-121
97PinX-PMP-15
97Sco-480
97ScoHeaotO-23
97ScoHobR-480
97ScoResC-480
97ScoShoS-480
97ScoShoSAP-480
97Sel-140
97SelArtP-140
97SelRegG-140
97SelRooA-2
97SP-11
97SpoIll-9
97SpoIllEE-9
97Ult-217
97UltGolME-217
97UltPlaME-217
97UppDec-399
95UppDecMLFS-152
97Zen-46
Guerry, Kyle
93OscAstC-12
93OscAstF-621
Guess, Tom
77ForLauYS-16
Guetterman, Lee
84ChaLooT-15
85DomLeaS-171
86FleUpd-45
87Don-322
87Fle-585
87FleGlo-585
87Top-307
87TopTif-307
88Don-270
88DonReaBY-NEW
88Fle-374
88FleGlo-374
88OPC-382
88Sco-323
88ScoGlo-323
88Spo-45
88Top-656
88TopTif-656
89DonBasB-108
89TopTra-43T
89TopTraT-43T
89YanScoNW-24
90Don-127
90Fle-443
90FleCan-443
90Lea-333
90OPC-286
90PanSti-118
90PubSti-534
90Sco-294
90Top-286
90TopTif-286
90TopTVY-9
90UppDec-318
90YanScoNW-17
91Don-124
91Fle-664
91Lea-52
91OPC-62
91Sco-34
91SimandSMLBL-21
91StaClu-361
91Top-62
91TopDesS-62
91TopMic-62
91TopTif-62
91Ult-232
91UppDec-481
92Don-507
92Fle-227
92Lea-320
92OPC-578
92Sco-244
92ScoRoo-74T
92StaClu-346
92Top-578
92TopGol-578
92TopGolW-578
92TopMic-578
92UppDec-610
92YanWIZ8-71
93Don-542
93Fle-475
93StaClu-214
93StaCluFDI-214
93StaCluMOP-214
93Top-134
93TopGol-134
93TopInaM-134
93TopMic-134
94Fle-632
94Pac-590
94StaClu-216
94StaCluFDI-216
94StaCluGR-216
94StaCluMOP-216
95MarPac-33
96TacRaiB-12
Guevara, Giomar
93BelMarC-14
93BelMarF-3216
94AppFoxC-5
94AppFoxF-1061
94MidLeaAF-MDW1
95Exc-116
95LinVen-17
95UppDecML-81
96PorCitRB-14
95UppDecMLFS-81
Guggiana, Todd
90ButCopKSP-30
91Bow-697
91ChaRanC-18
91ChaRanP-1322
91Cla/Bes-204
93ChaRanC-13
93ChaRanF-1949
93FloStaLAF-2
94TulDriF-251
94TulDriTI-9
Gugino, Mark
94ElmPioF-3486
94ElmPioC-6
Guides, Maine
87IntLeaAT-45
Guidi, Jim
91SalLakTP-3205
91SalLakTSP-24
92SalLakTSP-26
Guidry, Ron
76OPC-599
76Top-599
77Spo-6102
77Top-656
77YanBurK-11
78Hos-25
78PapGinD-28
78SSP270-17
78Top-135
78YanBurK-4
78YanSSPD-17
79Hos-89
79Kel-11
79OPC-264
79Top-5
79Top-7
79Top-202
79Top-500
79TopCom-13
79YanBurK-4
79YanPicA-15
80BurKinPHR-4
80Kel-4
80OPC-157
80Top-207
80Top-300
80TopSup-7
81AllGamPI-82
81Don-227
81Fle-88
81FleStiC-76
81Kel-45
81OPC-250
81Top-250
81TopSti-112
81TopSupHT-64
82Don-548
82Don-558
82Fle-38
82FleSta-120
82Kel-26
82OPC-9
82OPC-10
82Squ-9
82Top-9
82Top-10
82WilSpoG-3
83Don-17
83Don-31
83DonActA-15
83Fle-383
83FleSta-73
83FleSti-47
83OPC-104
83Top-440
83TopSti-102
83YanRoyRD-4
84Don-173
84DonActAS-51
84Fle-127
84FunFooP-96
84MilBra-12
84Nes792-110
84Nes792-406
84Nes792-486
84Nes792-717
84NesDreT-10
84OCoandSI-45
84OPC-110
84OPC-204
84RalPur-31
84SevCoi-E16
84Top-110
84Top-406
84Top-486
84Top-717
84TopCer-31
84TopGloS-14
84TopRubD-11
84TopSti-194
84TopSti-318
84TopSup-17
84TopTif-110
84TopTif-406
84TopTif-486
84TopTif-717
85AllGamPI-77
85Don-214
85Fle-129
85Lea-237
85OPC-388
85PolMet-Y3
85ThoMcAD-11
85Top-790
85TopRubD-11
85TopSti-313
85TopTif-790
86BasStaB-51
86Don-103
86Dra-32
86Fle-106
86FleMin-22
86FleSlu-14
86FleStiC-48
86Lea-36
86OPC-109
86OPCBoxB-H
86SevCoi-C6
86SevCoi-E6
86SevCoi-S6
86SevCoi-W6
86Spo-18
86Spo-59
86Spo-149
86Spo-179
86Spo-185
86SpoDecG-71
86Top-610
86Top-721
86Top3-D-9
86TopGloS-12
86TopMinL-26
86TopSti-302
86TopSup-28
86TopTat-14
86TopTif-610
86TopTif-721
86TopWaxBC-H
86YanTCM-9
87ClaGam-68
87Don-93
87Fle-100
87FleAwaW-16
87FleGlo-100
87Lea-101
87OPC-375
87RedFolSB-54
87Spo-83
87Top-375
87TopSti-301
87TopTif-375
88Don-175
88DonReaBY-175
88Fle-207
88FleGlo-207
88FleStiWBC-S3
88Lea-180
88OPC-127
88Sco-310
88ScoGlo-310
88StaLinY-5
88Top-535
88TopBig-50
88TopSti-296
88TopStiB-61
88TopTif-535
89Sco-342
89Top-255
89TopBasT-110
89TopTif-255
89UppDec-307
89YanScoNW-28
90HOFStiB-97
91UppDecS-16
92YanWIZ7-60
92YanWIZ8-72
92YanWIZA-27
Guiel, Aaron
94CedRapKC-12
94CedRapKF-1115
95LakElsSTI-15
96Exc-27
96MidAngB-17
96MidAngOHP-13
96TexLeaAB-24
Guilfoyle, Mike
90BriTigP-3166
90BriTigS-7
91FayGenC-2
91FayGenP-1163
92LakTigC-13
92LakTigF-2272
93LakTigC-10
93LakTigF-1303
94TreThuF-2117
95JacSunTI-14
96TolMudHB-12
Guiliano, Matt
94MarPhiC-7
94MarPhiF-3301
95PiePhiF-191
96ReaPhiB-18
Guillen, Carlos
96Bow-353
96BowBes-162
96BowBesAR-162
96BowBesR-162
97Bow-138
97BowBes-135
97BowBesAR-135
97BowBesR-135
97BowChr-146
97BowChrI-146
97BowChrIR-146
97BowChrR-146
97BowInt-138
Guillen, Jose
93MadMusC-13
93MadMusF-1828
94WesMicWC-10
94WesMicWF-2305
95ModA'sTI-9
96BesAutS-34
96Bow-116
96BowBes-109
96BowBesAR-109
96BowBesR-109
96CarLeaA1B-20
96CarLeaA2B-20
96CarLeaAIB-B9
96LynHilB-11
97Bow-106
97BowBes-189
97BowBesAR-189
97BowBesBC-BC16
97BowBesBCAR-BC16
97BowBesBCR-BC16
97BowBesMI-MI6
97BowBesMIAR-MI6
97BowBesMIARI-MI6
97BowBesMII-MI6
97BowBesMIR-MI6
97BowBesMIRI-MI6
97BowBesR-189
97BowCerBIA-CA34
97BowCerGIA-CA34
97BowChr-126
97BowChrI-126
97BowChrIR-126
97BowChrR-126
97BowInt-106
97ColCho-465
97Don-367
97DonFraFea-11
97DonLim-136
97DonLim-146
97DonLimFotG-55
97DonLimLE-136
97DonLimLE-146
97DonPre-164
97DonPreCttC-164
97DonPreP-367
97DonPrePGold-367
97DonPrePM-25
97DonRooDK-6
97DonRooDKC-6
97Fin-182
97FinRef-182
97FlaSho-A120
97FlaSho-B120
97FlaSho-C120
97FlaShoLC-120
97FlaShoLC-B120
97FlaShoLC-C120
97FlaShoLCM-A120
97FlaShoLCM-B120
97FlaShoLCM-C120
97FlaShoWotF-21
97Fle-554
97FleNewH-7
97FleTif-554
97Lea-319

97LeaFraM-319
97LeaFraMDC-319
97LeaGolS-36
97NewPin-161
97NewPinAP-161
97NewPinMC-161
97NewPinPP-161
97PinCer-107
97PinCerMBlu-107
97PinCerMG-107
97PinCerMR-107
97PinCerR-107
97PinTotCPB-107
97PinTotCPG-107
97PinTotCPR-107
97PinX-P-119
97PinX-PMoS-119
97PinX-PMP-1
97Sco-484
97ScoHobR-484
97ScoResC-484
97ScoShoS-484
97ScoShoSAP-484
97Sel-134
97SelArtP-134
97SelRegG-134
97SelRooA-1
97SP-4
97SpolII-10
97SpolIIEE-10
97TopStaFAS-FAS5
97Ult-495
97UltGolME-495
97UltGolP-8
97UltPlaME-495
97UppDec-542
97Zen-50

Guillen, Ozzie
83BeaGolGT-2
84LasVegSC-236
85DonHig-55
85FleUpd-48
85TopTifT-43T
85TopTra-43T
85WhiSoxC-13
86Don-208
86Fle-206
86FleLeaL-17
86FleMin-44
86FleStiC-49
86FleWaxBC-C3
86GenMilB-2E
86KayB-16
86Lea-140
86MSAJayPCD-9
86OPC-254
86QuaGra-20
86SevCoi-C13
86Spo-22
86Spo-176
86Top-254
86TopGaloC-5
86TopGloS-58
86TopSti-294
86TopSti-309
86TopSup-7
86TopTat-5
86TopTif-254
86WhiSoxC-13
87Don-87
87DonOpeD-235
87Fle-497
87FleAwaW-17
87FleGlo-497
87FleMin-48
87FleRecS-13
87FleStiC-50
87KraFoo-11
87Lea-117
87OPC-89
87RedFolSB-67
87SevCoi-C9
87Spo-186
87SpoTeaP-26
87StuPan-17
87Top-89
87TopSti-287
87TopTif-89
87WhiSoxC-12
88Don-137
88DonBasB-81
88Fle-398
88FleGlo-398
88FleMin-15
88FleRecS-16
88FleStiC-16
88Lea-59
88Nes-7
88OPC-296
88PanSti-61
88Sco-603
88ScoGlo-603
88ScoYouSI-21
88Spo-14
88StaLinWS-8
88Top-585
88TopBig-27
88TopSti-284
88TopTif-585
88WhiSoxC-9
88WhiSoxK-1
89Bow-64
89BowTif-64
89ClaTraP-175
89Don-176
89DonBasB-137
89DonBonM-BC23
89Fle-497
89FleBasA-18
89FleGlo-497
89KinDis-6
89OPC-195
89PanSti-309
89RedFolSB-53
89Sco-433
89ScoHot1S-51
89Spo-85
89Top-195
89TopBasT-149
89TopBig-148
89TopSti-303
89TopTif-195
89TopUKM-35
89TVSpoM-114
89UppDec-175
89UppDec-628A
89WhiSoxC-10
89WhiSoxK-6
90Bow-315
90BowTif-315
90ClaBlu-92
90Don-15
90Don-135
90DonBesA-74
90DonLeaS-13
90DonSupD-15
90Fle-533
90FleCan-533
90Lea-128
90OPC-365
90PanSti-41
90PubSti-388
90Sco-6
90ScoMcD-21
90Spo-48
90Top-365
90TopBig-215
90TopSti-298
90TopTif-365
90TopTVA-3
90UppDec-79
90UppDec-267
90USPlaCA-6C
90WhiSoxC-7
90WhiSoxC-29
90WhiSoxK-3
90WinDis-9
91BasBesHM-9
91Bow-356
91ClaGam-53
91Don-577
91Fle-121
91Lea-331
91MooSna-12
91OPC-620
91PanCanT1-113
91PanFreS-315
91PanSti-261
91RedFolS-44
91Sco-11
91Sco-394
91Sco100S-15
91SevCoi-M8
91StaClu-70
91Top-620
91TopDesS-620
91TopMic-620
91TopTif-620
91Ult-74
91UppDec-325
91USPlaCA-2H
91WhiSoxK-13
91WhiSoxK-NNO0
92Bow-565
92ClaGam-98
92Don-229
92Fle-82
92Fle-706
92HitTheBB-15
92Lea-149
92OPC-210
92PacSea-57
92PanSti-128
92Pin-79
92Sco-92
92Sco100S-13
92ScoCokD-12
92ScoImpP-84
92ScoProP-22
92StaClu-20
92StaCluD-72
92Top-210
92TopGol-210
92TopGolW-210
92TopKid-100
92TopMic-210
92Ult-35
92UppDec-436
92WhiSoxK-13
93Bow-287
93Don-255
93Fin-128
93FinRef-128
93Fla-184
93Fle-203
93Lea-85
93LinVenB-270
93OPC-102
93PacBeiA-4
93PacSpa-72
93PacSpaPl-15
93PanSti-138
93Pin-166
93Sco-94
93Sel-128
93SP-254
93StaClu-517
93StaCluFDI-517
93StaCluMOP-517
93StaCluWS-12
93Stu-167
93Top-474
93TopGol-474
93TopInaM-474
93TopMic-474
93TriPla-115
93Ult-532
93UppDec-139
93UppDecGold-139
93WhiSoxK-10
94Bow-511
94ColC-435
94ColChoGS-435
94ColChoSS-435
94Don-359
94DonSpeE-359
94ExtBas-47
94Fin-393
94FinRef-393
94Fla-31
94Fle-82
94FUnPac-113
94Lea-107
94OPC-115
94Pac-125
94PanSti-47
94Pin-428
94PinArtP-428
94PinMusC-428
94Sco-93
94ScoGolR-93
94Sel-25
94Spo-33
94StaClu-389
94StaCluFDI-389
94StaCluGR-389
94StaCluMOP-389
94StaCluT-141
94StaCluTFDI-141
94Stu-206
94Top-5
94TopGol-5
94TopSpa-5
94TriPla-264
94Ult-337
94UppDec-156
94UppDecED-156
94VenLinU-90
94WhiSoxK-10
95Baz-8
95ColCho-494
95ColChoGS-494
95ColChoSE-236
95ColChoSEGS-236
95ColChoSESS-236
95ColChoSS-494
95Don-294
95DonPreP-294
95DonTopotO-49
95Emb-116
95EmbGolI-116
95Emo-27
95Fla-25
95Fle-118
95Lea-117
95LeaLim-191
95LinVen-250
95Pac-88
95PacPri-29
95PanSti-67
95Pin-107
95PinArtP-107
95PinMusC-107
95Sco-428
95ScoGolR-428
95ScoPlaTS-428
95Sel-185
95SelArtP-185
95StaClu-206
95StaCluFDI-206
95StaCluMOP-206
95StaCluSTWS-206
95Stu-157
95Top-598
95TopCyb-370
95Ult-274
95UltGolM-274
95UppDec-196
95UppDecED-196
95UppDecEDG-196
95UppDecSE-21
95UppDecSEG-21
95WhiSoxK-12
96ColCho-94
96ColCho-340
96ColChoGS-94
96ColChoGS-340
96ColChoSS-94
96ColChoSS-340
96Don-509
96DonPreP-509
96EmoXL-37
96Fin-B80
96FinRef-B80
96Fla-51
96Fle-66
96FleTif-66
96FleWhiS-6
96Lea-193
96LeaPrePB-193
96LeaPrePG-193
96LeaPrePS-193
96MetUni-37
96MetUniP-37
96Pac-286
96PacEstL-EL13
96PacPri-P89
96PacPriG-P89
96PanSti-170
96Pin-310
96PinFoil-310
96ProSta-132
96Sco-404
96StaClu-117
96StaCluMOP-117
96TeaOut-35
96Top-129
96Ult-38
96UltGolM-38
96UppDec-41
97Cir-182
97CirRav-182
97ColCho-296
97DonTea-75
97DonTeaSPE-75
97Fin-224
97FinRef-224
97Fle-61
97FleTif-61
97Pac-53
97PacLigB-53
97PacSil-53
97Sco-160
97ScoPreS-160
97ScoShoS-160
97ScoShoSAP-160
97StaClu-67
97StaCluMOP-67
97Top-147
97Ult-39
97UltGolME-39
97UltPlaME-39
97UppDec-206
97UppDec-331

Guillot, Don
87PanAmTURB-9
87PanAmTUBI-10

Guin, Greg
82ArkTraT-14
83ArkTraT-17
84ArkTraT-10

Guindon, Bob
65Top-509

Guinn, Brian
84ModA'sC-15
85ModA'sC-7
86SouLeaAJ-8
87PitCubP-11
88IowCubC-15
88IowCubP-526
89IowCubC-16
89IowCubP-1709
90CMC-87
90IowCubC-12
90IowCubP-324
90ProAAAF-631
90TopTVCu-46
91IowCubLD-206
91IowCubP-1066
91LinDriAAA-206
92VanCanS-629
86HumStaDS-20

Guinn, Skip (Drannon E.)
69Top-614
70OPC-316
70Top-316
71MLBOffS-82
71OPC-741
71Top-741

Guinn, Wayne
80CedRapRT-26

Guintini, Ben
48SomandK-14

Guise, Witt
41HarHarW-9

Guisto, Lou
16ColE13-67
23W503-58

Gulan, Mike
92ClaDraP-38
92ClaFS7-426
92FroRowDP-11
92HamRedC-26
92HamRedF-1597
93Bow-656
93ExcFS7-98
93SprCarC-11
93SprCarF-1858
93StaCluM-90
94ExcFS7-266
94St.PetCC-10
94St.PetCF-2592
94UppDecML-136
94UppDecMLPotYF-PY7
95ArkTraTI-14
95Bes-95
96BesAutSA-24
96Bow-304
96Exc-227
96LouRedB-19

Gulbit, German
89EasLeaDDP-DD3

Guldahl, Ralph
40WheM4-6A
40WheM4-6C

Gulden, Brad
77LodDodT-4
79ColCliT-1
80ColCliP-20
80ColCliT-6

80NasSouTI-10
80Top-670
81SpolndT-30
83ColCliT-4
84RedEnq-15
85Don-365
85Fle-537
85OPC-251
85RedYea-7
85Top-251
85TopMin-251
85TopTif-251
86GiaMot-25
90DodTar-305
92YanWIZ7-61
92YanWIZ8-73
Gull, Sterling
80SalLakCGT-20
Gulledge, Derek
94BluOriF-3558
Gulledge, Hugh
90MadMusB-16
91MadMusC-8
91MadMusP-2125
92RenSilSCLC-41
Gullett, Don
70DayDaiNM-78
71MLBOffS-60
71OPC-124
71Top-124
72OPC-157
72Top-157
73LinPor-56
73OPC-595
73Top-595
74OPC-385
74Top-385
74TopSta-27
75Hos-107
75OPC-65
75Top-65
76CraDis-18
76Hos-45
76HosTwi-45
76Kel-3
76LinSup-90
76OPC-390
76RedIceL-7
76RedKro-11
76RedPos-10
76SSP-27
76Top-390
77BurCheD-172
77Hos-143
77MSADis-26
77OPC-250
77PepGloD-35
77RCColC-28
77Top-15
77YanBurK-6
78OPC-30
78RCColC-28
78SSP270-18
78Top-225
78WifBalD-28
78YanBurK-8
78YanSSPD-18
79OPC-64
79Top-140
79YanPicA-16
80Top-435
90ChaLooGS-2
91LinDriAAA-275
91NasSouLD-275
91NasSouP-2173
92YanWIZ7-62
92YanWIZ8-74
93RedKah-8
94RedKah-33
95RedKah-34
96Red76K-8
Gulley, Napolean
93NegLeaRL2-13
95NegLeaL2-26
Gullickson, Bill
80ExpPos-11
81Don-91
81Fle-150
81OPC-41
81Top-203
81Top-578
82Don-162
82ExpHygM-9
82ExpPos-15
82ExpZel-15
82FBIDis-9
82Fle-190
82OPC-94
82OPC-172
82OPCPos-21
82Top-172
82Top-526
83Don-288
83ExpPos-8
83ExpStu-15
83Fle-284
83FleSti-263
83OPC-31
83Top-31
84Don-401
84ExpPos-11
84ExpStu-16
84Fle-276
84Nes792-318
84OPC-318
84Top-318
84TopSti-96
84TopTif-318
85Don-97
85Fle-399
85Lea-236
85OPC-143
85Top-687
85TopSti-91
85TopTif-687
86Don-331
86DonHig-40
86Fle-249
86FleUpd-46
86OPC-229
86RedTexG-34
86Top-229
86TopSti-78
86TopTif-229
86TopTra-42T
86TopTraT-42T
87Don-369
87Fle-203
87FleAwaW-18
87FleGlo-203
87FleMin-49
87FleRecS-14
87FleStiC-51
87RedKah-34
87SmoNatL-4
87SpoTeaP-4
87Top-281
87Top-489
87TopSti-140
87TopTif-489
88Don-586
88Fle-208
88FleGlo-208
88OPC-329
88Sco-585
88ScoGlo-585
88Top-711
88TopTif-711
90AstLenH-14
90AstMot-13
90Bow-65
90BowTif-65
90TopTra-34T
90TopTraT-34T
90UppDec-799
91Bow-133
91Fle-508
91Lea-402
91Sco-177
91ScoRoo-56T
91Stu-55
91TigCok-36
91UppDec-590
92Bow-558
92Don-131
92Fle-137
92Lea-61
92OPC-508
92PanSti-112
92Pin-87
92Sco-242
92ScoProP-21
92StaClu-119
92SunSee-2
92Top-508
92TopGol-508
92TopGolW-508
92TopMic-508
92TriPla-161
92Ult-362
92UppDec-317
92UppDecTMH-23
92YanWIZ8-75
93Don-523
93Fle-606
93Lea-103
93OPC-124
93PacSpa-110
93PanSti-112
93Pin-352
93Sco-643
93Sel-85
93StaClu-574
93StaCluFDI-574
93StaCluMOP-574
93TigGat-12
93Top-325
93TopComotH-7
93TopGol-325
93ToplnaM-325
93TopMic-325
93UppDec-398
93UppDecGold-398
94ColC-118
94ColChoGS-118
94ColChoSS-118
94Don-195
94Fin-398
94FinRef-398
94Fle-134
94Lea-147
94PanSti-65
94Sco-198
94ScoGolR-198
94StaClu-370
94StaCluFDI-370
94StaCluGR-370
94StaCluMOP-370
94Top-654
94TopGol-654
94TopSpa-654
94TriPla-245
94UppDec-458
94UppDecED-458
95ColCho-479
95ColChoGS-479
95ColChoSS-479
95Don-434
95DonPreP-434
95StaClu-250
95StaCluFDI-250
95StaCluMOP-250
95StaCluSTWS-250
95Top-249
95TopCyb-136
Gulliver, Glenn
77EvaTriT-13
80EvaTriT-21
81EvaTriT-15
82RocRedWT-12
83Don-131
83Fle-62
83RocRedWT-15
83Top-293
84RocRedWT-11
85RicBraT-13
86HagSunP-7
86RocRedWP-4
87HagSunP-11
91OriCro-169
91PacSenL-155
Gully, Scott
91OneYanP-4149
92GreHorC-13
92GreHorF-774
93PriWilCC-13
93PriWilCF-652
Gulseth, Mark
93EveGiaC-12
93EveGiaF-3773
95BurBeeTI-4
96BurBeeTI-17
Gumbert, Addison
87OldJudN-220
90DodTar-306
Gumbert, Harry
39PlaBal-54
40PlaBal-86
41CarW75-9
41DouPlaR-27
41DouPlaR-91
41PlaBal-26
49Bow-192
50Bow-171
79DiaGre-48
Gumbert, Rich
83GreHorT-9
Gumbs, Lincoln
90AubAstB-17
90AubAstP-3409
Gump, Chris
92AriWilP-5
93EveGiaC-13
93EveGiaF-3774
Gumpert, Dave
82BirBarT-5
83EvaTriT-3
84EvaTriT-8
84Nes792-371
84Top-371
84TopTif-371
85IowCubT-14
86IowCubP-13
87Fle-565
87FleGlo-565
87Top-487
87TopTif-487
90BirBarDGB-16
86STaoftFT-9
Gumpert, Randy
48BluTin-23
48YanTeal-10
49Bow-87
50Bow-184
51Bow-59
52Bow-106
52Top-247
78ReaRem-7
83TopRep5-247
Gumpf, John
90EliTwiS-11
91KenTwiC-9
91KenTwiP-2089
92Ft.MyeMCB-22
92Ft.MyeMF-2756
Gundelfinger, Matt
81RedPioT-14
83SprCarF-18
Gunderson, Eric
87EveGiaC-13
88CalLeaACLC-5
88SanJosGCLC-131
88SanJosGP-114
89ShrCapP-1833
90Bow-225
90BowTif-225
90CMC-534
90PhoFirC-7
90ScoRoo-99T
90UppDec-752
91Bow-628
91Don-416
91Sco-744
91Sco100RS-57
91TopDeb90-61
91UppDec-315
92ClaGam-41
92Fle-637
92JacSunS-357
92StaClu-397
93CalCanF-1160
96MetKah-11
Gunderson, Greg
89BatCliP-1938
90SpaPhiB-6
90SpaPhiP-2487
90SpaPhiS-11
Gunderson, Mike
94AubAstC-4
94AubAstF-3751
96QuaCitRB-15
Gunderson, Shane
96Exc-77
96FtMyeMB-22
Gunn, Clay
86BelMarC-126
87WauTimP-10
88SanBerSB-18
88SanBerSCLC-32
Gunn, Jeffrey
90PriPatD-9
Gunnarson, Bob
86ChaLooP-10
87ChaLooB-13
Gunner, Chie
97Top-471
Gunnett, Chris
94LetMouF-3874
94LetMouSP-12
Gunning, Thomas
87OldJudN-221
90KalBatN-24
Gunson, Joseph
87OldJudN-222
Gunter, Chet
76ShrCapT-19
77ShrCapT-6
Gunter, Reid
87PocGiaTB-8
Gunther, Kevin
96WesMicWB-10
Gura, Larry
71OPC-203
71Top-203
73OPC-501
73Top-501
74OPC-616
74Top-616
74TopTra-616T
75OPC-557
75Top-557
75YanSSP-7
76OPC-319
76Top-319
76VenLeaS-135
77Top-193
78Roy-6
78SSP270-237
78Top-441
79RoyTeal-3
79Top-19
80OPC-154
80Top-295
81AllGamPI-83
81CokTeaS-75
81Don-461
81Fle-38
81FleStiC-102
81Kel-59
81OPC-130
81Top-130
81TopScr-51
81TopSti-88
82Don-338
82Fle-410
82FleSta-205
82OPC-147
82Roy-9
82Top-96
82Top-790
82TopSti-195
83AllGamPI-79
83Don-160
83Fle-113
83FleSti-103
83Kel-42
83OPC-340
83OPC-395
83Roy-10
83Top-340
83Top-395
83TopSti-77
84AllGamPI-171
84Don-100
84Fle-347
84Nes792-96
84Nes792-625
84OPC-264
84Top-96
84Top-625
84TopSti-285
84TopTif-96
84TopTif-625
85Don-217
85Fle-202
85Top-595
85TopSti-278
85TopTif-595
92UppDecS-20
92YanWIZ7-63
Gurchiek, Chris
88AppFoxP-156
88BoiHawP-1609
Gurtcheff, Jeff
86WatPirP-8
Gust, Chris
88MadMusP-12
Gustafson, Cliff
92TexLon-19
93Tex-1

Gustafson, Ed (Edward)
89EveGiaS-9
90Bes-85
90CliGiaB-6
90CliGiaP-2550
90ProAaA-118
91VisOakC-2
91VisOakP-1736
92OrlSunRF-2841
92OrlSunRS-506
Gustafson, Marc
94AshTouC-29
95NewHavRTI-NNO
96NewHavRB-4
Gustave, Michael
78WisRapTT-6
Gustavson, Dan
92HunCubC-13
92HunCubF-3141
Gustavson, Duane
82ForMyeRT-10
83ChaRoyT-25
85Ft.MyeRT-26
86Ft.MyeRP-13
87MemChiB-2
87MemChiP-21
88OrlTwiB-3
Gustine, Frank
47Exh-88A
47Exh-88B
47TipTop-140
49Bow-99
49EurSta-57
49Lea-88
79DiaGre-369
83TCMPla1943-33
Guth, Bucky
73TacTwiC-10
Guthrie, David
96BilMusTI-11
Guthrie, Mark
87LSUTigP-3
88VisOakCLC-167
89OrlTwiB-14
89OrlTwiP-1335
89SouLeaAJ-19
90Don-622
90LSUTigGM-9
90OPC-317
90PorBeaP-174
90ProAAAF-244
90Top-317
90TopDeb89-49
90TopTif-317
90UppDec-436
91Don-64
91Fle-612
91Lea-171
91OPC-698
91Sco-778
91StaClu-219
91Top-698
91TopDesS-698
91TopMic-698
91TopTif-698
91UppDec-505
92Don-691
92Lea-263
92OPC-548
92Pin-511
92Sco-164
92StaClu-456
92Top-548
92TopGol-548
92TopGolW-548
92TopMic-548
92Ult-396
92UppDec-604
93Don-714
93Fle-265
93Lea-251
93PacSpa-170
93Pin-361
93StaClu-550
93StaCluFDI-550
93StaCluMOP-550
93Top-777
93TopGol-777
93TopInaM-777
93TopMic-777
93Ult-581
93UppDec-399
93UppDecGold-399
94Don-530
94Fle-204
94Pac-352
95Fle-202
95Top-553
95TopCyb-332
96DodMot-26
96DodPol-15
96LeaSigEA-66
Gutierrez, Alfredo
96OgdRapTI-34
Gutierrez, Anthony
90AshTouP-2742
90CMC-677
91BurAstC-4
91BurAstP-2795
92OscAstC-18
92OscAstF-2524
93QuaCitRBC-10
93QuaCitRBF-93
Gutierrez, Bob (Robert)
84NewOriT-21
85NewOriT-15
Gutierrez, Cesar
69OPC-16
69Top-16
70OPC-269
70Top-269
71MLBOffS-392
71OPC-154
71Top-154
72Top-743
87SpoRea-4
93LinVenB-172
95LinVen-70
Gutierrez, Dimas
85PriWilPT-8
86NasPirP-10
87HarSenP-22
88EasLeaAP-15
88HarSenP-841
89MiaMirIS-8
Gutierrez, Felipe
85VerBeaDT-7
Gutierrez, Israel
78AshTouT-8
79WauTimT-7
Gutierrez, Jackie (Joaquin)
79ElmPioRST-7
84FleUpd-47
84TopTra-46T
84TopTraT-46T
85AllGamPI-23
85Don-335
85Fle-160
85Top-89
85TopSti-216
85TopSti-373
85TopTif-89
86Don-335
86Fle-350
86FleUpd-47
86OPC-73
86Top-633
86TopTif-633
87Don-601
87Fle-471
87FleGlo-471
87Top-276
87TopTif-276
88PhiTas-33
89PawRedSC-19
89PawRedSP-694
89PawRedSTI-10
89UppDec-430
90MiaMirIS-11
90MiaMirIS-9
91OriCro-170
Gutierrez, Javier
96EveAquB-10
Gutierrez, Jim
89BelMarL-6
90PenPilS-10
91SanBerSC-5
91SanBerSP-1981
93RivPilCLC-8
94JacSunF-1407
95JacSunTI-15
96JacSunB-16
Gutierrez, Julian
78St.PetCT-11
80ArkTraT-16
82ArkTraT-15
Gutierrez, Rafael
90EugEmeGS-10
92VerBeaDC-23
92YakBeaC-21
92YakBeaF-3442
Gutierrez, Ricky
89FreKeyS-8
90CarLeaA-4
90FreKeyTI-18
91Cla/Bes-55
91HagSunLD-231
91HagSunP-2462
91LinDriAA-231
92Bow-103
92RocRedWF-1945
92RocRedWS-453
92SkyAAAF-206
93Bow-462
93FleFinE-140
93Lea-493
93PacSpa-596
93PadMot-10
93Pin-577
93SelRoo-63T
93SP-166
93StaClu-676
93StaCluFDI-676
93StaCluMOP-676
93TopTra-21T
93UppDec-660
93UppDecGold-660
94Bow-560
94ColC-119
94ColChoGS-119
94ColChoSS-119
94Don-159
94Fin-53
94FinRef-53
94Fla-233
94Fle-664
94FUnPac-37
94Lea-196
94OPC-47
94Pac-524
94PadMot-9
94Pin-138
94PinArtP-138
94PinMusC-138
94Sco-271
94ScoBoyoS-13
94ScoGolR-271
94Sel-175
94StaClu-75
94StaCluFDI-75
94StaCluGR-75
94StaCluMOP-75
94StaCluMOP-ST13
94StaCluST-ST13
94Top-42
94TopGol-42
94TopSpa-42
94TriPla-166
94Ult-279
94UppDec-104
94UppDecED-104
94WatIndC-14
94WatIndF-3943
95Don-416
95DonPreP-416
95Fle-559
95FleUpd-140
95KinIndTI-12
95Pac-361
95Sco-65
95ScoGolR-65
95ScoPlaTS-65
95StaClu-119
95StaCluFDI-119
95StaCluMOP-119
95StaCluSTWS-119
95TusTorTI-8
95Top-524
95TopCyb-309
96AstMot-26
96CanIndB-13
96ColCho-358
96ColChoGS-358
96ColChoSS-358
96Exc-44
96Fle-407
96FleTif-407
96Pac-99
97Fle-345
97FleTif-345
97Pac-317
97PacLigB-317
97PacSil-317
Gutierrez, Willie
79KnoKnoST-13
Gutteridge, Don
60Top-458
70OPC-123
70Top-123
70WhiSoxTI-4
79DiaGre-156
83TCMPla1944-1
92ConTSN-636
96Bro194F-2
Guy, Mark
91MelBusF-9
Guyton, Duffy
92JohCitCC-23
92JohCitCF-3109
Guzik, Brian
93CedRapKC-7
93CedRapKF-1746
Guzik, Robbi (Rob)
89KinMetS-11
90PitMetP-5
91ColMetPI-22
91ColMetPPI-2
92ColMetC-13
92ColMetF-289
92ColMetPI-15
93St.LucMC-12
94St.LucMC-11
94St.LucMF-1188
93StLucMF-2917
Guzman, Correa (Juan)
86VerBeaDP-8
87BakDodP-5
88KnoBluJB-18
89SyrChiC-9
89SyrChiMB-12
89SyrChiP-797
90Bes-79
90CMC-814
90KnoBluJB-8
90KnoBluJP-1242
91BluJayFS-12
91BluJayS-25
91LinDriAAA-504
91SyrChiLD-504
91SyrChiMB-6
91SyrChiP-2476
91UltUpd-60
92Bow-294
92Cla2-T18
92ClaGam-12
92ColAllP-NNO
92Don-534
92Fle-330
92FleRooS-13
92Lea-35
92OPC-662
92OPCPre-168
92Pin-183
92PinTea2-27A
92PinTea2-27B
92ProFS7-161
92Sco-424
92Sco100RS-27
92ScoImpP-3
92StaClu-402
92Stu-256
92SyrChiTT-3
92Top-662
92TopDeb91-68
92TopGol-662
92TopGolW-662
92TopMic-662
92Ult-449
92UppDec-625
92UppDecTMH-24
93BluJayCP1-7
93BluJayCP1-12
93BluJayD-1
93BluJayD4-17
93BluJayFS-12
93Bow-55
93ClaGam-40
93DiaMar-46
93Don-189
93Fin-56
93FinRef-56
93Fla-290
93Fle-693
93FleFruotL-27
93FunPac-57
93HumDumC-25
93Lea-3
93LeaFas-9
93MSABenSPD-14
93OPC-187
93OPCPre-36
93OPCWorC-6
93PacSpa-324
93PacSpaGE-15
93PanSti-33
93Pin-364
93PosCan-2
93Sco-372
93Sel-180
93SelAce-11
93SP-48
93StaClu-244
93StaCluFDI-244
93StaCluM-2
93StaCluM-63
93StaCluMOP-244
93Stu-144
93Top-75
93TopComotH-15
93TopGol-75
93TopInaM-75
93TopMic-75
93Toy-73
93TriPla-28
93TriPlaA-28
93Ult-640
93UltStrK-2
93UppDec-266
93UppDecGold-266
93USPlaCA-5S
94BluJayP-5
94BluJayUSPC-6S
94BluJayUSPC-13D
94Bow-553
94ColC-120
94ColChoGS-120
94ColChoSS-120
94Don-404
94ExtBas-190
94Fin-132
94FinRef-132
94Fla-349
94Fle-333
94FleSmo'nH-3
94FUnPac-66
94Lea-262
94OPC-177
94Pac-642
94PanSti-138
94Pin-172
94PinArtP-172
94PinMusC-172
94PosCan-6
94PosCanG-6
94ProMag-138
94Sco-375
94ScoGolR-375
94Sel-253
94SP-43
94SPDieC-43
94Spo-116
94StaClu-149
94StaCluFDI-149
94StaCluGR-149
94StaCluMOP-149
94StaCluT-170
94StaCluTFDI-170
94Top-181
94TopGol-181
94TopSpa-181
94TriPla-33
94Ult-438
94UppDec-430
94UppDecED-430
95BluJayP-3
95BluJayUSPC-3C
95BluJayUSPC-11D
95ColCho-148
95ColChoGS-148
95ColChoSE-56
95ColChoSEGS-56
95ColChoSESS-56
95ColChoSS-148
95Don-174
95DonPreP-174
95Fin-151
95FinFlaT-FT3
95FinRef-151
95Fla-97
95Fle-95

95Lea-85
95Pac-445
95PacPri-142
95Pin-261
95PinArtP-261
95PinMusC-261
95Sco-474
95ScoGolR-474
95ScoPlaTS-474
95StaClu-162
95StaCluFDI-162
95StaCluMOP-162
95StaCluSTWS-162
95StaCluVR-86
95Top-290
95TopCyb-157
95Ult-339
95UltGolM-339
95UppDec-287
95UppDecED-287
95UppDecEDG-287
95UppDecSE-66
95UppDecSEG-66
96BluJayOH-14
96Cir-95
96CirRav-95
96ColCho-745
96ColChoGS-745
96ColChoSS-745
96Don-374
96DonPreP-374
96Fla-185
96Fle-275
96FleTif-275
96LeaSigA-88
96LeaSigAG-88
96LeaSigAS-88
96Pac-438
96StaClu-324
96StaCluMOP-324
95StaCluVRMC-86
96Ult-430
96UltGolM-430
96UppDec-474
97BluJayS-8
97Cir-167
97CirRav-167
97ColCho-62
97ColCho-499
97Don-94
97DonLim-119
97DonLimLE-119
97DonPre-77
97DonPreCttC-77
97DonPreP-94
97DonPrePGold-94
97Fin-72
97FinRef-72
97FlaSho-A103
97FlaSho-B103
97FlaSho-C103
97FlaShoLC-103
97FlaShoLC-B103
97FlaShoLC-C103
97FlaShoLCM-A103
97FlaShoLCM-B103
97FlaShoLCM-C103
97Fle-241
97FleTif-241
97Lea-237
97LeaFraM-237
97LeaFraMDC-237
97MetUni-185
97NewPin-64
97NewPinAP-64
97NewPinMC-64
97NewPinPP-64
97Pac-221
97PacLigB-221
97PacPri-74
97PacPriLB-74
97PacPriP-74
97PacSil-221
97Sco-83
97ScoPreS-83
97ScoShoS-83
97ScoShoSAP-83
97SkyE-X-50
97SkyE-XC-50
97SkyE-XEC-50
97SP-181
97SpollI-135
97SpollIEE-135
97StaClu-207
97StaCluMat-207
97StaCluMOP-207
97Top-458
97TopGal-124
97TopGalPPI-124
97Ult-144
97UltGolME-144
97UltPlaME-144
97UppDec-516
97UppDecAWJ-13

Guzman, Doinini
89MedAthB-10

Guzman, Domingo
95IdaFalBTI-32
96IdaFalB-9

Guzman, Edwards
96SanJosGB-5

Guzman, Hector
83VerBeaDT-18

Guzman, Ismael
93BriTigC-10
93BriTigF-3661
94JamJamC-11
94JamJamF-3978

Guzman, Johnny
90CMC-665
90ModA'sC-12
90ModA'sP-2207
90ProAaA-144
91LinDriAAA-536
91TacTigLD-536
91TacTigP-2299
92ClaFS7-136
92DonRoo-47
92HunStaF-3943
92HunStaS-310
92SkyAA F-131
92StaClu-498
92TopDeb91-67
93ClaFS7-197
93LimRocDWB-100
93Pin-261
93Sco-270
93StaClu-284
93StaCluAt-23
93StaCluFDI-284
93StaCluMOP-284
93TacTigF-3026

Guzman, Jonathan
96HelBreTI-7

Guzman, Jose Alberto
83BurRanF-7
83BurRanT-4
84TulDriTI-29
85OklCit8T-11
86Don-30
86DonRoo-24
86Fle-559
86RanLit-2
86RanPer-23
86TopTra-43T
86TopTraT-43T
87Don-101
87Fle-124
87FleGlo-124
87Lea-50
87RanMot-23
87RanSmo-3
87Top-363
87TopTif-363
88Don-136
88DonBasB-88
88Fle-467
88FleGlo-467
88Lea-55
88OPC-98
88RanMot-23
88RanSmo-20
88Sco-322
88ScoGlo-322
88StaLinRa-5
88Top-563
88TopTif-563
89BimBreD-11
89Don-284
89Fle-520
89FleGlo-520
89OPC-209
89PanSti-445
89RanMot-25
89RanSmo-11
89Sco-143
89ScoYouS2-11
89Top-462
89TopSti-241
89TopTif-462
89UppDec-73
90OPC-308
90PubSti-411
90Top-308
90TopTif-308
90UppDec-617
91FleUpd-60
92Bow-668
92Don-271
92Fle-306
92Lea-222
92OPC-188
92Pin-98
92RanMot-19
92RanTeal-9
92Sco-502
92ScoProP-21
92StaClu-153
92Stu-243
92Top-188
92TopGol-188
92TopGolW-188
92TopMic-188
92TriPla-215
92Ult-442
92UppDec-204
93Bow-412
93CubMar-8
93Don-687
93Fin-145
93FinRef-145
93Fle-323
93FleFinE-7
93Lea-266
93OPC-121
93OPCPre-23
93PacBeiA-17
93PacSpa-377
93Pin-505
93RanKee-167
93Sco-256
93SelRoo-107T
93SP-84
93StaClu-648
93StaCluCu-19
93StaCluFDI-648
93StaCluMOP-648
93Stu-91
93Top-253
93TopGol-253
93TopInaM-253
93TopMic-253
93TriPla-142
93Ult-313
93UppDec-323
93UppDec-515
93UppDecGold-323
93UppDecGold-515
94Bow-578
94ColC-463
94ColChoGS-463
94ColChoSS-463
94Don-507
94Fin-93
94FinPre-93P
94FinRef-93
94Fla-137
94Fle-384
94Lea-186
94OPC-180
94Pac-99
94Pin-55
94PinArtP-55
94PinMusC-55
94Sco-178
94ScoGolR-178
94Sel-90
94StaClu-615
94StaCluFDI-615
94StaCluGR-615
94StaCluMOP-615
94StaCluT-342
94StaCluTFDI-342
94Top-35
94TopGol-35
94TopSpa-35
94TriPla-73
94Ult-456
94UppDec-196
94UppDecED-196
95Pac-71
95PacPri-23

Guzman, Jose Antonio
89BriTigS-10
90FayGenP-2400

Guzman, Luis
79KnoKnoST-3
80UtiBluJT-17

Guzman, Pete (Pedro)
85DomLeaS-58
90ChaRaiB-10
90ChaRaiP-2037

Guzman, Ramon
92SouBenWSC-19

Guzman, Ruben
83WatRedT-18
86GleFalTP-8
87GleFalTP-1

Guzman, Santiago
70Top-716
72OPC-316
72Top-316

Guzman, Toribio
96JohCitCTI-14

Gwaltney, Gary
85RedWinA-16

Gwaltney, Scott
85RedWinA-18

Gwinn, Tony
87PriWilYP-27

Gwosdz, Doug
81HawIslT-5
82Top-731
84Don-383
84Nes792-753
84PadMot-16
84PadSmo-11
84Top-753
84TopTif-753
85GiaMot-22
85GiaPos-13
86JacMetT-11
87CalCanP-2331
88NasSouC-16
88NasSouP-480
88NasSouTI-11
89NasSouC-11
89NasSouP-1277
89NasSouTI-7

Gwynn, Chris
87AlbDukP-27
88AlbDukC-12
88AlbDukP-259
88Fle-647
88FleGlo-647
88SanDieSAAG-7
88SanDieSAAG-8
88Sco-640
88ScoGlo-640
88TriAAAP-2
89AlbDukC-15
89AlbDukP-64
89Fle-59
89FleGlo-59
89SanDieSAG-6
89SanDieSAG-7
89ScoHot1R-21
89UppDec-607
90ClaBlu-111
90DodMot-14
90DodPol-15
90DodTar-307
90Lea-411
90OPC-456
90ScoYouS2-39
90Top-456
90TopTif-456
90UppDec-526
91DodMot-14
91DodPol-15
91Don-598
91Fle-202
91OPC-99
91Sco-178
91StaClu-480
91Top-99
91TopDesS-99
91TopMic-99
91TopTif-99
91UppDec-560
92Don-648
92Fle-457
92Lea-518
92OPC-604
92OPCPre-9
92RoyPol-10
92Sco-449
92ScoRoo-56T
92StaClu-815
92Top-604
92TopGol-604
92TopGolW-604
92TopMic-604
92Ult-371
92UppDec-83
92UppDec-689
93Don-657
93Lea-453
93RoyPol-11
93StaCluRoy-9
93Top-472
93TopGol-472
93TopInaM-472
93TopMic-472
93UppDec-632
93UppDecGold-632
94ColC-121
94ColChoGS-121
94ColChoSS-121
94DodMot-17
94DodPol-10
94Don-223
94Fle-157
94Lea-209
94Pac-284
94Pin-297
94PinArtP-297
94PinMusC-297
94Sco-381
94ScoGolR-381
94Top-731
94TopGol-731
94TopSpa-731
94Ult-63
95DodMot-15
95Sco-205
95ScoGolR-205
95ScoPlaTS-205
95Top-357
96PadMot-22
97PacPriGotD-GD206

Gwynn, Tony (Anthony)
82HawIslT-10
83Don-598
83Fle-360
83OPC-143
83Top-482
84AllGamPI-52
84Don-324
84Fle-301
84FunFooP-28
84Nes792-251
84OCoandSI-233
84PadMot-9
84PadSmo-12
84Top-251
84TopSti-160
84TopTif-251
85AllGamPI-143
85Don-25
85Don-63
85DonActA-19
85DonSupD-25
85Dra-14
85Fle-34
85FleLimE-11
85FleStaS-8
85KASDis-4
85KitCloD-4
85Lea-25
85OPC-383
85PadMot-2
85SevCoi-W11
85ThoMcAD-32
85Top-660
85Top-717
85Top3-D-13
85TopGaloC-4
85TopGloA-6
85TopGloS-29
85TopRubD-3
85TopSti-146
85TopSti-170
85TopSti-174
85TopSup-5
85TopTif-660
85TopTif-717
86BasStaB-52
86Don-112
86DonAll-1

86DonPop-1
86Fle-323
86FleLimE-22
86FleMin-69
86FleSlu-15
86FleStiC-50
86KayB-17
86Lea-41
86OPC-10
86QuaGra-7
86SevCoi-W10
86Spo-13
86Spo-140
86Spo-181
86Top-10
86TopGloA-17
86TopGloS-57
86TopMinL-65
86TopSti-105
86TopSti-146
86TopSup-29
86TopTat-24
86TopTif-10
86Woo-13
87ClaGam-26
87Don-64
87DonAll-16
87DonHig-12
87DonOpeD-146
87DonP-16
87Dra-11
87Fle-416
87FleAwaW-19
87FleBasA-20
87FleGlo-416
87FleLimE-19
87FleMin-50
87FleSlu-17
87FleStiC-52
87GenMilB-6E
87HosSti-16
87KayB-15
87KraFoo-44
87Lea-235
87MandMSL-23
87MSAIceTD-16
87OPC-198
87PadBohHB-19
87RedFolSB-113
87Spo-31
87Spo-117
87Spo-197
87SpoDeaP-3
87SpoSupD-7
87SpoTeaP-16
87StuPan-12
87Top-530
87Top-599
87TopCoi-34
87TopGaloC-6
87TopGloA-6
87TopGloS-2
87TopMinL-35
87TopSti-106
87TopSti-155
87TopTif-530
87TopTif-599
87Woo-16
88Baz-9
88CheBoy-6
88ClaBlu-220
88Don-164
88DonAll-51
88DonBasB-154
88DonBonM-BC6
88Dra-14
88Fle-585
88Fle-631
88Fle-634
88FleAwaW-16
88FleBasA-13
88FleBasM-17
88FleExcS-17
88FleGlo-585
88FleGlo-631
88FleGlo-634
88FleHotS-15
88FleLeaL-16
88FleMin-112
88FleRecS-17
88FleSlu-17
88FleStiC-123
88FleTeaL-11
88GreBasS-26
88K-M-12
88KayB-13
88KinDis-5
88Lea-90
88MSAFanSD-18
88Nes-40
88OPC-360
88OPCBoxB-F
88PadCok-19
88PadSmo-10
88PanSti-410
88PanSti-437
88SanDieSAAG-9
88Sco-385
88ScoGlo-385
88Spo-16
88StaBog/G-1
88StaBog/G-3
88StaBog/G-5
88StaBog/G-7
88StaBog/G-9
88StaBog/G-11
88StaGwy-1
88StaGwy-2
88StaGwy-3
88StaGwy-4
88StaGwy-5
88StaGwy-6
88StaGwy-7
88StaGwy-8
88StaGwy-9
88StaGwy-10
88StaGwy-11
88StaLinAl-13
88StaLinPa-5
88Top-360
88Top-402
88Top-699
88TopBig-161
88TopCoi-36
88TopGaloC-7
88TopGloS-38
88TopMinL-74
88TopRevLL-1
88TopRitTM-11
88TopSti-115
88TopStiB-16
88TopTif-360
88TopTif-402
88TopTif-699
88TopUKM-29
88TopUKMT-29
88TopWaxBC-F
88Woo-12
89Baz-13
89Bow-461
89BowTif-461
89CadEllD-27
89ClaLigB-30
89DodStaSV-7
89Don-6
89Don-128
89DonBasB-42
89DonBonM-BC20
89DonSupD-6
89Fle-305
89FleBasA-19
89FleBasM-17
89FleExcS-20
89FleGlo-305
89FleHeroB-20
89FleLeaL-19
89FleSup-21
89FleWaxBC-C12
89K-M-29
89KayB-17
89KinDis-21
89MSAHolD-6
89OPC-51
89PadCok-6
89PadMag-3
89PanSti-203
89PanSti-222
89RedFolSB-54
89SanDieSAG-8
89Sco-90
89ScoHot1S-40
89ScoSco-37
89Spo-160
89SpollIFKI-33
89Top-570
89Top-699
89TopBasT-62
89TopBatL-2
89TopBig-58
89TopCapC-5
89TopCoi-4
89TopGaloC-7
89TopGloS-58
89TopHeaUT-1
89TopHilTM-16
89TopMinL-39
89TopSti-109
89TopStiB-50
89TopTif-570
89TopUKM-36
89TVSpoM-45
89TVSpoM-130
89UppDec-384
89UppDec-683
90AllBasT-14
90BasWit-2
90Baz-6
90Bow-217
90BowTif-217
90ClaBlu-17
90ClaBlu-87A
90ClaBlu-87B
90Col-17
90Don-86
90Don-705
90Don-705A
90DonBesN-11
90DOnBonM-BC4
90DonLeaS-48
90DonPre-9
90Fle-157
90FleBasM-16
90FleCan-157
90FleLeaL-17
90FleWaxBC-C12
90Hot50PS-19
90K-M-5
90KayB-14
90KinDis-3
90Lea-154
90MLBBasB-55
90MSAHolD-18
90OPC-403
90OPC-730
90PacGwyCB-1
90PadCok-6
90PadMag-1
90PadMag-15
90PanSti-207
90PanSti-351
90Pos-5
90PubSti-50
90PubSti-261
90RedFolSB-43
90Sco-255
90Sco-685
90Sco100S-3
90Spo-98
90StaLonJS-4
90StaLonJS-29
90SunSee-11
90Top-403
90Top-730
90TopBatL-2
90TopBig-93
90TopCoi-36
90TopDou-31
90TopGaloC-3
90TopGloA-8
90TopGloS-56
90TopHeaU-1
90TopMag-60
90TopMinL-80
90TopSti-101
90TopSti-146
90TopStiB-15
90TopTif-403
90TopTif-730
90TopTVA-39
90UppDec-344
90USPlaCA-11D
90WonBreS-12
91BasBesHM-10
91Bow-647
91CadEllD-28
91Cla2-T93
91Cla3-T33
91ClaGam-156
91Col-19
91Don-243
91Fle-529
91Lea-290
91LeaPre-11
91MajLeaCP-54
91MooSna-6
91MSAHolD-5
91OPC-180
91OPCPre-59
91PadMag-22
91PadSmo-11
91PanCanT1-104
91PanFreS-97
91PanSti-99
91PetSta-24
91Pos-10
91Sco-500
91Sco100S-94
91SevCoi-SC4
91StaClu-308
91StaPinB-23
91Stu-245
91Top-180
91TopCraJl-26
91TopDesS-180
91TopMic-180
91TopSta-18
91TopTif-180
91TopTriH-N10
91Ult-303
91UppDec-255
91UppDecFE-97F
91USPlaCA-1C
92Bow-50
92Cla2-T52
92ClaGam-61
92ColAllG-18
92ColAllP-18
92ColGwy-1
92ColGwy-2
92ColGwy-3
92ColGwy-4
92ColGwy-5
92ColGwy-6
92ColGwy-7
92ColGwy-8
92ColGwy-9
92ColGwy-10
92ColGwy-11
92ColGwy-12
92Don-425
92Don-441
92DonCraJ1-16
92DonEli-14
92Fle-605
92FleAll-2
92FleCitTP-10
92FleTeaL-7
92Fre-16
92Hig5-122
92Hig5S-18
92HitTheBB-16
92JimDea-13
92KinDis-10
92Lea-206
92Mr.TurS-13
92MSABenSHD-15
92OPC-270
92OPCPre-106
92PadCarJ-7
92PadMot-7
92PadPolD-8
92PadSmo-9
92PanSti-236
92PanSti-286
92Pin-400
92Pin-591
92Pos-26
92Sco-625
92Sco-779
92Sco-887
92Sco100S-81
92ScoProaG-16
92SevCoi-23
92SpollIFK1-288
92SpoStaCC-21
92StaClu-825
92StaCluD-73
92StaCluNC-825
92Stu-104
92StuPre-22
92Top-270
92TopGol-270
92TopGolW-270
92TopKid-53
92TopMic-270
92TopMic-G270
92TriPla-219
92Ult-277
92UltAwaW-12
92UltGwy-1
92UltGwy-2
92UltGwy-3
92UltGwy-4
92UltGwy-5
92UltGwy-6
92UltGwy-7
92UltGwy-8
92UltGwy-9
92UltGwy-10
92UltGwy-S1
92UltGwy-S2
92UltGwy-AU0
92UppDec-83
92UppDec-274
92UppDec-717
92UppDecF-25
92UppDecFG-25
92UppDecWB-T6
93Bow-630
93CadDis-29
93ClaGam-41
93ColAllG-18
93DiaMar-47
93Don-126
93DurPowP1-14
93Fin-77
93FinRef-77
93Fla-133
93Fle-138
93FleFruotL-28
93FunPac-138
93FunPac-211
93FunPacA-AS9
93HumDumC-47
93Kra-23
93Lea-28
93LeaGolA-R9
93LeaHeaftH-2
93MetBak-10
93OPC-94
93PacJugC-28
93PacSpa-257
93PadMot-3
93PanSti-262
93Pin-98
93Pin-289
93PinCoo-20
93PinCooD-20
93Pos-8
93Sco-24
93Sco-525
93Sel-5
93SelChaS-8
93SelDufIP-8
93SP-167
93StaClu-538
93StaCluFDI-538
93StaCluM-3
93StaCluMMP-4
93StaCluMOP-538
93Stu-100
93Top-5
93TOPBLAG-8
93TopFulS-7
93TopGol-5
93TopInaM-5
93TopMic-5
93TriPla-51
93Ult-472
93UppDec-165
93UppDec-474
93UppDecDG-17
93UppDecGold-165
93UppDecGold-474
93UppDecOD-D14
93UppDecTAN-TN11
93USPlaCA-6D
94Bow-120
94BowBes-R78
94BowBesR-R78
94ColC-122
94ColC-344
94ColChoGS-122
94ColChoGS-344
94ColChoSS-122
94ColChoSS-344
94ColChoT-5
94DenHol-14
94Don-10
94Don-440

94DonAnn8-10
94DonDiaK-DK11
94DonDom-B1
94DonEli-38
94DonMVP-13
94DonSpeE-10
94ExtBas-372
94Fin-201
94FinJum-201
94FinRef-201
94Fla-436
94Fle-665
94Fle-711
94FleAllS-39
94FlePro-9
94FleTeaL-27
94FleUpdDT-5
94FUnPac-119
94FUnPac-206
94Kra-24
94Lea-254
94LeaL-152
94LeaLimGA-12
94LeaStaS-9
94OPC-109
94OscMayR-23
94Pac-525
94PacSilP-35
94PadMot-2
94PanSti-256
94Pin-4
94PinArtP-4
94PinMusC-4
94PinRunC-RC35
94PinTheN-12
94Pos-13
94ProMag-119
94RedFolMI-5
94Sco-12
94ScoGolR-12
94ScoGolS-23
94Sel-77
94SP-130
94SPDieC-130
94SPHol-13
94SPHolDC-13
94Spo-25
94SpoMov-MM5
94StaClu-151
94StaClu-537
94StaCluFDI-151
94StaCluFDI-537
94StaCluGR-151
94StaCluGR-537
94StaCluMO-43
94StaCluMOP-151
94StaCluMOP-537
94Stu-132
94StuSerS-1
94SucSav-10
94TomPiz-8
94Top-620
94TopGol-620
94TopSpa-620
94TopSupS-21
94TriPla-167
94Ult-280
94UltHitM-6
94UppDec-219
94UppDec-279
94UppDecAJ-17
94UppDecAJG-17
94UppDecDC-W5
94UppDecED-219
94UppDecED-279
95Baz-30
95BazRedH-RH6
95Bow-304
95BowBes-R21
95BowBes-X11
95BowBesJR-3
95BowBesR-R21
95BowBesR-X11
95ClaPhoC-46
95ColCho-61
95ColCho-73
95ColChoGS-61
95ColChoGS-73
95ColChoSE-27
95ColChoSE-140
95ColChoSE-160
95ColChoSEGS-27
95ColChoSEGS-140
95ColChoSEGS-160
95ColChoSESS-27
95ColChoSESS-140
95ColChoSESS-160
95ColChoSS-61
95ColChoSS-73
95D3-42
95DenHol-12
95Don-224
95DonAll-NL8
95DonDiaK-DK24
95DonDom-9
95DonPreP-224
95DonTopotO-341
95Emb-6
95EmbGolI-6
95Emo-187
95EmoMas-4
95Fin-196
95FinRef-196
95Fla-201
95Fle-560
95FleAllF-8
95FleAllS-7
95FleLeaL-6
95FleTeaL-27
95Kra-22
95Lea-299
95Lea300C-13
95LeaChe-7
95LeaGolS-3
95LeaHeaftH-7
95LeaLim-87
95LeaLimG-20
95LeaLimIBP-2
95NatPac-15
95Pac-362
95PacGolP-36
95PacPri-116
95PadCHP-1
95PadMot-2
95PanSti-79
95PanSti-115
95Pin-93
95Pin-291
95PinArtP-93
95PinArtP-291
95PinFan-20
95PinGatA-GA9
95PinMusC-93
95PinMusC-291
95PinPin-17
95PinPinR-17
95PinRedH-RH8
95PinTeaP-TP9
95PinWhiH-WH8
95Pos-7
95PosCan-13
95RedFol-32
95Sco-28
95Sco-561
95ScoDouGC-GC4
95ScoDreT-DG8
95ScoGolR-28
95ScoGolR-561
95ScoHaloG-HG14
95ScoPlaTS-28
95ScoPlaTS-561
95ScoRul-SR23
95ScoRulJ-SR23
95Sel-94
95SelArtP-94
95SelBigS-BS7
95SelCer-66
95SelCerGT-10
95SelCerMG-66
95SP-105
95SPCha-88
95SPCha-90
95SPChaDC-88
95SPChaDC-90
95Spo-16
95SpoArtP-16
95SpoDouT-11
95SpoHamT-HT10
95SPSil-105
95SPSpeF-46
95StaClu-475
95StaClu-508
95StaCluCC-CC3
95StaCluMO-21
95StaCluMOP-475
95StaCluMOP-508
95StaCluMOP-CC3
95StaCluMOP-RL7
95StaCluMOP-VRE6
95StaCluRL-RL7
95StaCluSTWS-475
95StaCluSTWS-508
95StaCluVE-VRE6
95StaCluVR-261
95Stu-25
95StuGolS-25
95StuPlaS-25
95Sum-6
95Sum-183
95SumBigB-BB10
95SumNthD-6
95SumNthD-183
95TomPiz-24
95Top-389
95Top-431
95TopCyb-228
95TopFin-12
95TopLeaL-LL4
95TopTra-7T
95TopTra-160T
95TopTraPB-7
95UC3-69
95UC3-133
95UC3ArtP-69
95UC3ArtP-133
95UC3CycS-CS13
95Ult-233
95UltAllS-8
95UltAllSGM-8
95UltGolM-233
95UltHitM-7
95UltHitMGM-7
95UltLeaL-6
95UltLeaLGM-6
95UltOnBL-7
95UltOnBLGM-7
95UppDec-135
95UppDecC-2B
95UppDecED-135
95UppDecEDG-135
95UppDecPC-MLB1
95UppDecPLL-R27
95UppDecPLLE-R27
95UppDecSE-270
95UppDecSEG-270
95USPlaCMLA-1D
95Zen-104
95ZenAllS-6
95ZenZ-12
96Baz-124
96Bow-71
96BowBes-38
96BowBesAR-38
96BowBesMI-7
96BowBesMIAR-7
96BowBesMIR-7
96BowBesP-BBP10
96BowBesPAR-BBP10
96BowBesPR-BBP10
96BowBesR-38
96Cir-186
96CirAcc-27
96CirBos-47
96CirRav-186
96ColCho-2
96ColCho-290
96ColCho-408
96ColCho-760
96ColChoGS-2
96ColChoGS-290
96ColChoGS-408
96ColChoGS-760
96ColChoSS-2
96ColChoSS-290
96ColChoSS-408
96ColChoSS-760
96ColChoYMtP-17
96ColChoYMtP-17A
96ColChoYMtPGS-17
96ColChoYMtPGS-17A
96DenHol-15
96DenHolGS-4
96DenHolGSAP-4
96Don-525
96Don-550
96DonDiaK-9
96DonEli-72
96DonHitL-1
96DonPreP-525
96DonPreP-550
96DonSho-4
96EmoN-5
96EmoXL-277
96Fin-B61
96Fin-B320
96Fin-G6
96FinBro-2
96FinRef-B61
96FinRef-B320
96FinRef-G6
96Fla-374
96Fle-567
96FleRoaW-2
96FleTeaL-27
96FleTif-567
96FleUpd-U224
96FleUpd-4
96FleUpdH-8
96FleUpdTC-U224
96FleZon-4
96Kin-10
96Lea-99
96LeaAllGMC-8
96LeaAllGMCG-8
96LeaGolS-11
96LeaLim-53
96LeaLimG-53
96LeaPicP-6
96LeaPre-79
96LeaPreP-79
96LeaPrePB-99
96LeaPrePG-99
96LeaPrePS-99
96LeaPreSG-48
96LeaPreSta-4
96LeaPreSte-48
96LeaSig-98
96LeaSigEA-67
96LeaSigEACM-10
96LeaSigPPG-98
96LeaSigPPP-98
96LeaStaS-2
96MetUni-235
96MetUniP-235
96MetUniT-4
96Pac-184
96Pac-198
96PacCraC-CC6
96PacGolCD-DC35
96PacHom-HP3
96PacMil-M3
96PacPri-P61
96PacPriG-P61
96PacPriRHS-RH12
96PadMot-2
96PanSti-97
96PanSti-113
96Pin-205
96Pin-267
96Pin-336
96PinAfi-30
96PinAfiAP-30
96PinAfiFPP-30
96PinAfiR-16
96PinAfiR-18
96PinAfiR-20
96PinAfiR-21
96PinAfiR-23
96PinAfiR-24
96PinAfiSP-15
96PinArtP-105
96PinArtP-167
96PinArtP-200
96PinFan-7
96PinFoil-205
96PinFoil-267
96PinFoil-336
96PinSky-13
96PinSta-105
96PinSta-167
96PinSta-200
96Pro-7
96ProMagA-20
96ProMagDM-19
96ProSta-81
96Sco-16
96Sco-378
96ScoAll-9
96ScoBigB-9
96ScoDiaA-23
96ScoDugC-A15
96ScoDugC-B103
96ScoDugCAP-A15
96ScoDugCAP-B103
96ScoGolS-6
96ScoNumG-9
96ScoRef-7
96Sel-59
96SelArtP-59
96SelCer-21
96SelCerAP-21
96SelCerCB-21
96SelCerCR-21
96SelCerIP-13
96SelCerMB-21
96SelCerMG-21
96SelCerMR-21
96SelClaTF-14
96SelEnF-13
96SelTeaN-22
96SP-160
96Spo-9
96SpoArtP-9
96SpoDouT-10
96SpoHitP-13
96SpoPro-11
96SPSpeFX-40
96SPSpeFXDC-40
96SPx-49
96SPxBoufG-9
96SPxGol-49
96StaClu-301
96StaCluEPB-301
96StaCluEPG-301
96StaCluEPS-301
96StaCluMM-MM9
96StaCluMO-15
96StaCluMOP-301
96StaCluMOP-MM9
96StaCluMOP-PC4
96StaCluPC-PC4
95StaCluVRMC-261
96Stu-145
96StuHitP-1
96StuMas-1
96StuPrePB-145
96StuPrePG-145
96StuPrePS-145
96Sum-134
96SumAbo&B-134
96SumArtP-134
96SumBal-18
96SumFoi-134
96SumHitI-1
96TeaOut-36
96Top-1
96Top-250
96TopChr-1
96TopChr-97
96TopChrMotG-12
96TopChrMotGR-12
96TopChrR-1
96TopChrR-97
96TopClaC-CC9
96TopGal-147
96TopGalE-15
96TopGalPPI-147
96TopLas-43
96TopLasSS-11
96TopMasotG-12
96TopMysF-M9
96TopMysFR-M9
96TopPowB-1
96Ult-284
96Ult-580
96UltCalttH-3
96UltCalttHGM-3
96UltChe-B4
96UltCheGM-B4
96UltDiaP-4
96UltDiaPGM-4
96UltGolM-284
96UltGolM-580
96UltOn-L-3
96UltOn-LGM-3
96UltPriL-16
96UltPriLGM-16
96UltRes-3
96UltResGM-3
96UltSeaC-2
96UltSeaCGM-2
96UppDec-116
96UppDec-377
96UppDec-450
96UppDecA-10
96UppDecDD-DD32
96UppDecDDG-DD32
96UppDecDDS-DD32
96UppDecHC-HC19
96UppDecPHE-H34

96UppDecPRE-R57
96UppDecPreH-H34
96UppDecPreR-R57
96UppDecRunP-RP8
96UppDecVJLS-VJ19
96Zen-91
96Zen-150
96ZenArtP-91
96ZenArtP-150
96ZenMoz-20
97Bow-274
97BowBes-29
97BowBesA-29
97BowBesAAR-29
97BowBesAR-29
97BowBesR-29
97BowChr-91
97BowChrI-91
97BowChrIR-91
97BowChrR-91
97BowInt-274
97Cir-150
97CirBos-7
97CirIco-3
97CirLimA-6
97CirRav-150
97CirRavR-5
97CirSupB-7
97ColCho-56
97ColCho-210
97ColChoAC-23
97ColChoBS-19
97ColChoBSGS-19
97ColChoNF-NF1
97ColChoNF-NF2
97ColChoS-19
97ColChoTBS-39
97ColChoTBSWH-39
97ColChoTotT-T25
97Don-3
97Don-407
97DonEli-15
97DonEliGS-15
97DonFraFea-15
97DonLim-91
97DonLim-107
97DonLim-136
97DonLimFotG-2
97DonLimFotG-25
97DonLimLE-91
97DonLimLE-107
97DonLimLE-136
97DonPowA-18
97DonPowADC-18
97DonPre-46
97DonPre-172
97DonPreCttC-46
97DonPreCttC-172
97DonPreP-3
97DonPreP-407
97DonPrePGold-3
97DonPrePGold-407
97DonPrePM-7
97DonPreS-10
97DonPreTB-7
97DonPreTBG-7
97DonPreTF-7
97DonPreTP-7
97DonPreTPG-7
97DonPreXP-10A
97Fin-169
97Fin-298
97FinEmb-169
97FinEmb-298
97FinEmbR-169
97FinEmbR-298
97FinRef-169
97FinRef-298
97FlaSho-A37
97FlaSho-B37
97FlaSho-C37
97FlaShoDC-6
97FlaShoLC-37
97FlaShoLC-B37
97FlaShoLC-C37
97FlaShoLCM-A37
97FlaShoLCM-B37
97FlaShoLCM-C37
97Fle-462
97Fle-702
97Fle-743
97FleDecoE-4
97FleDecoERT-4
97FleDiaT-5
97FleGouG-3
97FleGouGF-3
97FleHea-7
97FleMilDM-46
97FleTeaL-27
97FleTif-462
97FleTif-702
97FleTif-743
97FleZon-8
97Lea-17
97Lea-356
97LeaFraM-17
97LeaFraM-356
97LeaFraMDC-17
97LeaFraMDC-356
97LeaGolS-15
97LeaKnoG-4
97LeaLeaotN-12
97LeaWarT-6
97MetUni-219
97NewPin-71
97NewPinAP-71
97NewPinIE-3
97NewPinKtP-12
97NewPinMC-71
97NewPinPP-71
97NewPinPP-I3B
97NewPinPP-K12
97Pac-424
97PacCar-35
97PacCarM-35
97PacCraC-10
97PacFirD-19
97PacGolCD-35
97PacLigB-424
97PacPri-144
97PacPriGA-GA31
97PacPriGotD-GD207
97PacPriLB-144
97PacPriP-144
97PacPriSH-SH12A
97PacPriSL-SL12A
97PacSil-424
97Pin-42
97PinArtP-42
97PinCer-45
97PinCer-147
97PinCerLI-10
97PinCerMBlu-45
97PinCerMBlu-147
97PinCerMG-45
97PinCerMG-147
97PinCerMR-45
97PinCerMR-147
97PinCerR-45
97PinCerR-147
97PinIns-56
97PinInsC-24
97PinInsCE-56
97PinInsDD-10
97PinInsDE-56
97PinMin-21
97PinMinB-21
97PinMinCB-21
97PinMinCG-21
97PinMinCGR-21
97PinMinCN-21
97PinMinCS-21
97PinMinG-21
97PinMinS-21
97PinMusC-42
97PinTotCPB-45
97PinTotCPB-147
97PinTotCPG-45
97PinTotCPG-147
97PinTotCPR-45
97PinTotCPR-147
97PinX-P-13
97PinX-PMoS-13
97PinX-PMW-11
97PinX-PMWG-11
97PinX-PMWS-11
97ProMag-38
97ProMagML-38
97Sco-249
97Sco-535
97ScoAllF-10
97ScoHeaotO-25
97ScoHobR-535
97ScoPreS-249
97ScoResC-535
97ScoShoS-249
97ScoShoS-535
97ScoShoSAP-249
97ScoShoSAP-535
97Sel-3
97SelArtP-3
97SelRegG-3
97SelTooотT-8
97SelToootTMB-8
97SkyE-X-93
97SkyE-XC-93
97SkyE-XEC-93
97SkyE-XHoN-8
97SP-155
97SPInsI-19
97SPMarM-MM7
97SpoIll-119
97SpoIllEE-119
97SPSpeF-17
97SPSpxF-9
97SPSPxFA-9
97SPVinAu-13
97SPVinAu-14
97SPVinAu-15
97SPVinAu-16
97SPVinAu-17
97SPx-42
97SPxBoufG-15
97SPxBro-42
97SPxCorotG-4
97SPxGraF-42
97SPxSil-42
97SPxSte-42
97StaClu-219
97StaCluC-CO10
97StaCluMat-219
97StaCluMOP-219
97StaCluMOP-PG6
97StaCluPG-PG6
97Stu-121
97StuMasS-20
97StuMasS8-20
97StuPor8-20
97StuPrePG-124
97StuPrePS-124
97Top-410
97TopChr-145
97TopChrR-145
97TopChrSB-1
97TopChrSBR-1
97TopGal-5
97TopGalGoH-GH9
97TopGalPPI-5
97TopHobM-HM5
97TopIntF-ILM4
97TopIntFR-ILM4
97TopScr-8
97TopSeaB-SB1
97TopSta-11
97TopSta1AS-AS9
97TopStaAM-11
97TopSweS-SS7
97Ult-283
97UltDouT-19
97UltFamGam-11
97UltGolME-283
97UltHitM-9
97UltLeaS-6
97UltPlaME-283
97UltStaR-12
97UltTop3-12
97UltTop3GM-12
97UppDec-378
97UppDec-492
97UppDecAG-AG6
97UppDecAWJ-2
97UppDecGJ-GJ2
97UppDecHC-HC16
97UppDecP-23
97UppDecU-35
97Zen-2
97Zen8x1-2
97Zen8x1D-2

Gyarmati, Jeff
83BelBreF-4
89BoiHawP-1985

Gyselman, Dick
34DiaMatCSB-76
43CenFlo-11
44CenFlo-10

Gyselman, Jeff
93BatCliC-10
93BatCliF-3147
94BatCliC-5
94BatCliF-3448
95ClePhiF-219
96ReaPhiB-14

Haag, Charlie
55JetPos-5

Haag, Jeff
93WatIndC-11
93WatIndF-3564
94WatIndC-15
94WatIndF-3940

Haag, Mike
93JamExpC-28

Haaland, Bill
85RedWinA-9
86RedWinA-20

Haar, Rich
93JamExpC-8
93JamExpF-3334
94WesPalBEC-12
94WesPalBEF-49

Haas, Bert (Berthold)
46SpoExcW-5-9
47Exh-89
49EurSta-105
84TCMPla1-38
90DodTar-308

Haas, Bill
63Top-544
64Top-398

Haas, Bruno
78HalHalR-3

Haas, Chris
96Exc-228
96HilStaHWB-20
96PeoChiB-13
96Top-434

Haas, Dave
87AncGlaP-16
89LakTigS-7
90LonTigP-1260
91Bow-151
91LinDriAAA-585
91TolMudHLD-585
91TolMudHP-1926
92OPC-665
92Sco-825
92SkyAAAF-262
92StaClu-362
92TolMudHF-1038
92TolMudHS-586
92Top-665
92TopDeb91-69
92TopGol-665
92TopGolW-665
92TopMic-665
93Don-335
93Sco-215
93TigGat-13
93Top-536
93TopGol-536
93TopInaM-536
93TopMic-536
93Ult-551
93USPlaCR-8S
94Pac-221

Haas, Eddie (G. Edwin)
59Top-126
59TopVen-126
79SavBraT-16
79SavBraT-18
81RicBraT-21
82RicBraT-27
83RicBraT-23
84RicBraT-27
85BraHos-1
85BraPol-22
85TopTifT-44T
85TopTra-44T

Haas, Jeff
92EugEmeC-3
92EugEmeF-3025
93RocRoyC-14
93RocRoyF-713
93StaCluM-119

Haas, Matt
94VerExpC-12
94VerExpF-3912
96WesPalBEB-18

Haas, Moose (Bryan)
75BurBeeT-10
76SpoIndC-10
78Top-649
79Top-448
80Top-181
81Don-85
81Fle-516
81OPC-327
81Top-327
81TopSti-98
82BrePol-30
82Don-206
82Fle-143
82FleSta-139
82OPC-12
82Top-12
83BreGar-9
83BrePol-30
83Don-204
83Fle-35
83OPC-317
83Top-503
84BreGar-8
84BrePol-30
84Don-368
84Fle-202
84FleSti-61
84Nes792-271
84Nes792-726
84OPC-271
84Top-271
84Top-726
84TopRubD-22
84TopSti-292
84TopTif-271
84TopTif-726
85BreGar-8
85BrePol-30
85Don-473
85Fle-583
85OPC-151
85Top-151
85TopMin-151
85TopRubD-23
85TopSti-293
85TopTif-151
86A'sMot-16
86Don-237
86Fle-489
86FleUpd-48
86OPC-9
86Top-759
86TopSti-201
86TopTat-2
86TopTif-759
86TopTra-44T
86TopTraT-44T
87A'sSmoC-5
87Don-528
87Fle-393
87FleGlo-393
87Lea-54
87OPC-369
87Top-413
87TopTif-413
88Sco-177
88ScoGlo-177
88Top-606
88TopTif-606
92BreCarT-9
94BreMilB-33

Haas, Mule (George W.)
28PorandAR-A14
28PorandAR-B14
31Exh-28
31W517-32
32OrbPinNP-19
32OrbPinUP-25
33ButCanV-22
33Gou-219
33RitCE-1H
33TatOrb-25
34BatR31-170
34ButPreR-29
35AlDemDCR3-11
35GouPuzR-8B
35GouPuzR-9B
36GouWidPPR-A43
36OveCanR-22
36R31PasP-38
36SandSW-26
36WorWidGV-68
38BasTabP-15
39WhiSoxTI-5
40PlaBal-184
40WhiSoxL-6
61Fle-109
81ConTSN-60
84OCoandSI-176
91ConTSN-323
94ConTSN-1138
94ConTSNB-1138

Haas, Randy
75CliPilT-8
Haase, Dean
91UtiBluSC-11
91UtiBluSP-3242
92SarWhiSCB-10
92SouBenWSF-179
Haber, Dave
90EugEmeGS-11
91EugEmeC-2
91EugEmeP-3732
Haberle, Dave
83CedRapRF-11
83CedRapRT-18
84CedRapRT-28
Habetz, Alyson
95ColSilB-11
96ColSilB-13
Habyan, John
85ChaO'sT-21
86Don-45
86RocRedWP-5
87ClaGam-95
87Don-494
87OriFreB-54
87RocRedWP-24
87RocRedWT-4
88Don-354
88Fle-562
88FleGlo-562
88RocRedWC-6
88RocRedWGCP-9
88RocRedWP-215
88RocRedWTI-10
88Sco-353
88ScoGlo-353
88Top-153
88TopTif-153
90CMC-203
90ColCliC-3
90ColCliP-16
90ColCliP-671
90ProAAAF-321
90TopTVY-44
91Bow-167
91FleUpd-42
91Lea-480
91OriCro-171
91StaClu-590
91UltUpd-40
92Don-32
92Fle-228
92Lea-189
92OPC-698
92Pin-433
92Sco-451
92StaClu-576
92Top-698
92TopGol-698
92TopGolW-698
92TopMic-698
92TriPla-228
93Don-107
93Fle-277
93Lea-162
93PacSpa-205
93Pin-409
93Sco-459
93StaClu-383
93StaCluFDI-383
93StaCluMOP-383
93StaCluY-20
93Top-86
93TopGol-86
93TopInaM-86
93TopMic-86
93Ult-241
93UppDec-719
93UppDecGold-719
94Don-562
94Fle-158
94FleUpd-179
94Pac-285
94Sco-294
94ScoGolR-294
94StaClu-618
94StaCluFDI-618
94StaCluGR-618
94StaCluMOP-618
94StaCluT-325
94StaCluTFDI-325
94Top-614
94TopGol-614
94TopSpa-614
95Fle-498
95FleUpd-158
Hacen, Abraham
96BluOriB-14
Hack, Stan
32CubTeal-9
34DiaMatCSB-77
34BatR31-137
34DiaStaR-34
34DiaStaR-107
35DiaMatCS3T1-64
36DiaMatCS3T2-12
36NatChiFPR-37
36R31PasP-29
36R31PasP-31
36SandSW-27
36WorWidGV-105
39CubTeal-9
40WheM4-12
41CubTeal-8
41DouPlaR-3
41DouPlaR-97
41WheM5-21
43CubTeal-9
43MPR302-1-13
47TipTop-107
52MotCoo-60
53MotCoo-49
54Wil-8
55Top-6
55TopDouH-23
55TopTesS-3
61Fle-110
75ShaPiz-18
76TayBow4-90
77GalGloG-78
80PacLeg-83
83TCMPla1942-40
83TCMPla1945-24
91ConTSN-126
92CubOldS-10
Hacker, Rich
86CarTeal-14
90TopTVCa-3
91BluJayFS-12
91BluJayFS-13
93BluJayFS-13
Hacker, Steve
96EugEmeB-10
Hacker, Warren
51Bow-318
52StaCalL-80G
52Top-324
53BowC-144
53DixLid-7
53DixPre-7
53NorBreL-10
53RedMan-NL23
54Bow-125
55Bow-8
56Top-282
57Kah-13
57RedSoh-8
57Top-370
58Top-251
83TopRep5-324
Hackett, Jason
96BluOriB-15
Hackett, John
86EriCarP-11
Hackett, Tom
52LaPat-6
52LavPro-108
Hackman, Luther
95AshTouTI-22
96MauStiHWB-25
96SalAvaB-12
Hacopian, Derek
92ClaDraP-96
92WatIndC-24
92WatIndF-3252
93ColRedC-1
93ColRedF-611
93SouAtlLAGF-13
94ClaGolF-44
94ExcFS7-44
94KinIndC-6
94KinIndF-2656
95BelBreTI-12
95Bes-22
95MidLeaA-20
96BesAutSA-25
Haddan, Russell
91SydWavF-17
Haddix, Harvey
53CarHunW-8
53Top-273
54CarHunW-7
54Top-9
55ArmCoi-8
55CarHunW-7
55Top-43
55TopDouH-41
55TopTesS-4
56Top-77
56TopHocF-A6
56TopHocF-B8
56TopPin-47
57Top-265
58Kah-12
58RedEnq-15
58RedJayP-6
58Top-118
59Kah-13
59Top-184
59TopVen-184
60Kah-12
60KeyChal-23
60NuHi-9
60PirJayP-7
60Top-340
61Kah-17
61NuSco-478
61Pos-134
61Top-100
61Top-410
61TopMagR-33
62Jel-180
62Kah-16
62Pos-180
62PosCan-180
62Top-67
62TopVen-67
63Kah-14
63PirIDL-11
63PirJayP-7
63Top-239
64Top-439
65OPC-67
65Top-67
76LauDiaJ-31
76SSP-623
77GalGloG-241
79DiaGre-171
79TCM50-39
82Don-651
82OhiHaloF-46
87SpoRea-33
88PacLegI-11
89SweBasG-13
90HOFStiB-57
90SweBasG-73
91OriCro-172
91TopArc1-273
92ActPacA-63
92BazQua5A-19
93TedWil-75
93UppDecAH-61
94TopArc1-9
94TopArc1G-9
94UppDecAH-12
94UppDecAH-81
94UppDecAH1-12
94UppDecAH1-81
Haddock, Darren
91BenBucC-7
91BenBucP-3692
Haddock, George
87OldJudN-223
95May-13A
95May-13B
Haden, Paris
90HagSunB-11
Hadley, Bump (Irving)
29PorandAR-34
31SenTealPW-12
32OrbPinNP-24
32OrbPinUP-26
33Gou-140
33TatOrb-26
34DiaMatCSB-78
34ExhFou-15
34GouCanV-15
35DiaMatCS3T1-65
35GouPuzR-1C
35GouPuzR-2C
35GouPuzR-16C
35GouPuzR-17C
38GouHeaU-251
38GouHeaU-275
38OurNatGPP-14
61Fle-111
75YanDyn1T-20
92ConTSN-508
93DiaStaES-131
Hadley, Kent
59Top-127
59TopVen-127
60Lea-135
60Top-102
60TopVen-102
61UniOil-SD3
92YanWIZ6-50
Haeberle, Kevin
89IdaFalBP-2037
90SumBraB-27
90SumBraP-2427
Haefner, Mickey
47SenGunBP-4
49Bow-144
50Bow-183
83TCMPla1944-22
Haeger, Greg
90BriTigP-3159
90BriTigS-8
91FayGenC-3
91FayGenP-1164
92FayGenC-9
92FayGenF-2163
Haeussinger, Jason
96CliLumKTI-13
Hafey, Bud (Daniel A.)
34BatR31-163
79DiaGre-366
Hafey, Chick (Charles J.)
28StaPlaCE-32
29ExhFou-16
29PorandAR-35
30SchR33-5
31Exh-16
31W517-29
32OrbPinUP-27
32USCar-8
33ButCanV-23
33DelR33-19
33ExhFou-4
33GeoCMil-18
33NatLeaAC-10
33RitCE-2D
33TatOrb-27
33TatOrbSDR-207
34DiaMatCSB-79
34BatR31-16
34ButPreR-30
34DiaStaR-18
34ExhFou-4
34Gou-34
34GouCanV-78
35DiaMatCS2-8
35ExhFou-4
36WorWidGV-94
61Fle-39
66CarCoi-6
76RowExh-8
76ShaPiz-121
77BobParHoF-25
77GalGloG-217
80PacLeg-116
80PerHaloFP-121
80SSPHOF-121
83CarGreT-6
83ConMar-42
87ConSer2-14
88ConNatA-10
89HOFStiB-34
91ConTSN-33
91ConTSN-259
92CarMcD-11
92ConTSN-657
93ConTSN-677
93ConTSN-889
Hafey, Tom
46RemBre-12
47RemBre-11
47SigOil-46
47SmiClo-18
48SmiClo-12
96Bro194F-27
Hafey, Will
47RemBre-16
47SmiClo-19
48SigOil-9
48SmiClo-3
Haffley, Jay
90WicStaSGD-15
Haffner, Les
90QuaCitAGS-11
Hafner, Frank
87OldJudN-224
Hagan, Danny
93PriRedC-13
93PriRedF-4173
94ChaWheC-12
94ChaWheF-2696
Hageman, Kurt
12T207-72
Hagemann, Tim
80CliGiaT-9
Hagen, Kevin
81ArkTraT-16
82ArkTraT-2
83LouRedR-6
84LouRedR-11
84Nes792-337
84Top-337
84TopTif-337
85LouRedR-7
86MaiGuiP-10
87PorBeaP-13
87TucTorP-17
88TucTorJP-12
88TucTorP-180
88TucTorC-5
Hagen, Walter
28W512-39
Hagermann, Ken
79ElmPioRST-3
Haggas, Josh
92GulCoaMF-3490
93PitMetC-8
93PitMetF-3715
Hagge, Kirk
94BriTigF-3511
Haggerty, Roger
86ElmPioRSP-7
87WinHavRSP-26
88WinHavRSS-9
89LynRedSS-26
Haggins, Ray
93NegLeaRL2-14
Hagman, Keith
81DurBulT-9
82DurBulT-2
Hague, Joe
69Top-559
70CarTeal-6
70OPC-362
70Top-362
71CarTeal-20
71MLBOffS-274
71OPC-96
71Top-96
71TopCoi-139
72Top-546
73OPC-447
73Top-447
81TCM60I-427
Hagy, Gary
91BoiHawC-19
91BoiHawP-3886
92MidLeaATI-14
92QuaCitRBC-22
92QuaCitRBF-818
93PalSprAC-9
93PalSprAF-77
95KinIndTI-13
96KenIndB-10
Hahn, Brent
90SalSpuCLC-134
90SalSpuP-2725
Hahn, Don
71ExpPS-9
71MLBOffS-129
71OPC-94
71Top-94
72OPC-269
72Top-269
74OPC-291
74Top-291
75OPC-182
75Top-182
76PhoGiaVNB-8
77PhoGiaCC-7
77PhoGiaCP-6
77PhoGiaVNB-7
91MetWIZ-155

Hahn, Ed
09T206-150
10ChiE-15
11SpoLifCW-151
11SpoLifM-24
12ColTinT-122
Hahn, Eric
87SavCarP-5
Hahn, Noodles (Frank)
03BreE10-62
09ColChiE-122
11SpoLifCW-152
12ColRedB-122
82OhiHaloF-47
Hahn, Willie
87OldJudN-225
Haid, Harold
34DiaMatCSB-80
Hailey, Freddie (Fred)
87OneYanP-15
88Ft.LauYS-11
89Ft.LauYS-8
90AlbYanB-20
90AlbYanP-1044
90AlbYanS-6
Hailey, Roger
88PulBraP-1766
89PulBraP-1907
90Bes-160
90CMC-728
90ProAaA-93
90SouAtlLAS-31
90SumBraB-4
90SumBraP-2428
91DurBulP-1539
92DurBulF-1093
92DurBulTI-32
Hain, Bill
60HenHouW-6
60UniOil-7
61TacBan-9
Haines, Abner (Allan)
80GleFalWSBT-27
80GleFalWSCT-22
Haines, Dennis
77SanJosMC-11
79OgdA'sT-8
Haines, Jesse
21E121So1-38
21Exh-66
21Nei-103
22E120-230
22W573-54
22W575-51
23W501-76
23WilChoV-57
27YorCarE-30
28StaPlaCE-33
28W513-78
28W56PlaC-S10
29PorandAR-36
32OrbPinUP-767
33Gou-73
33TatOrb-28
34DiaMatCSB-81
34GouCanV-44
36WorWidGV-93
40PlaBal-227
61Fle-40
66CarCoi-8
74Car193T-13
76RowExh-3
76ShaPiz-118
77GalGloG-125
80PerHaloFP-118
80SSPHOF-118
82OhiHaloF-6
89PacLegI-208
91ConTSN-43
92CarMcD-17
92ConTSN-358
92ConTSN-647
93ConTSN-768
93DiaStaES-132
Haines, Michael
86JamExpP-11
Hainline, Jeff
88ButCopKSP-25
Hairston, Jerry
74OPC-96
74Top-96
75OPC-327
75Top-327
76OPC-391
76SSP-153
76Top-391
83Don-616
83Fle-236
83Top-487
83WhiSoxTV-17
84Don-86
84Fle-60
84Nes792-177
84Top-177
84TopTif-177
84WhiSoxTV-15
85Don-135
85Fle-515
85Top-596
85TopTif-596
85WhiSoxC-17
86Don-424
86Fle-207
86Top-778
86TopTif-778
86WhiSoxC-17
87Don-285
87Fle-498
87FleGlo-498
87OPC-299
87Top-685
87TopTif-685
87WhiSoxC-13
88Don-285
88StaLinWS-9
88Top-281
88TopTif-281
Hairston, John
90SouBenWSB-3
90SouBenWSGS-5
91SouBenWSC-8
91SouBenWSP-2863
Hairston, Rodd
91BurlndP-3308
Hairston, Sam Sr.
86BirBarTI-26
87BirBarB-2
87NegLeaPD-1
89BirBarB-29
89BirBarP-112
90BirBarB-26
90BirBarP-1398
91BirBarP-1470
91LinDriAA-75
94BirBarC-29
94BirBarF-640
Hajeck, David
90AshTouP-2754
90CMC-675
90ProAaA-102
90SouAtlLAS-10
91OscAstC-18
91OscAstP-692
92JacGenF-4003
93JacGenF-2113
94TucTorF-767
95TusTorTI-9
96TusTorB-10
Haku, Jinten
79TCMJapPB-2
Halama, John
94AubAstC-5
94AubAstF-3752
95QuaCitRBTI-8
96JacGenB-10
Halama, Scott
87EriCarP-22
88HamRedP-1720
89JohCitCS-14
Halberg, Eric
83CliGiaF-2
Halcovich, Frank
87AriWilP-4
88AriWilP-4
Halderman, Gerlach
90IBAWorA-25
Hale, Bob
56Top-231
57Top-406
59Top-507
60Top-309
61Top-532
61Yan61RL-28
79TCM50-129
91OriCro-173
91RinPos1Y3-3
92YanWIZ6-51
Hale, Chad
95MicBatCTI-14
96SarRedSB-18
Hale, Chip
84AriWilP-7
86AriWilP-3
87AriWilP-5
88OrlTwiB-18
88PorBeaC-24
89PorBeaP-208
90CMC-571
90Don-690
90OPC-704
90PorBeaC-19
90PorBeaP-183
90ProAAAF-253
90Sco-588
90Sco100RS-98
90Spo-223
90Top-704
90TopDeb89-50
90TopTif-704
90UppDec-475
91LinDriAAA-409
91PorBeaLD-409
91PorBeaP-1570
91Sco100RS-39
92PorBeaF-2673
92PorBeaS-408
93FleFinE-236
93PorBeaF-2387
93SelRoo-74T
94ColC-573
94ColChoGS-573
94ColChoSS-573
94Don-168
94Fle-205
94Lea-115
94Pac-353
94Sco-609
94ScoGolR-609
94Sel-162
94StaClu-501
94StaCluFDI-501
94StaCluGR-501
94StaCluMOP-501
94Top-583
94TopGol-583
94TopSpa-583
95Don-467
95DonPreP-467
95Fle-203
95LinVen-103
95Sco-490
95ScoGolR-490
95ScoPlaTS-490
96FleUpd-U52
96FleUpdTC-U52
96LeaSigEA-68
Hale, Dad (Ray Luther)
08RosComP-2
Hale, Dan
86GreHorP-10
87GreHorP-20
Hale, DeMarlo
86NewBriRSP-12
88HunStaTI-5
88MadMusP-13
92NewBriRSS-500
93ForLauRSC-27
93ForLauRSFP-1613
94SarRedSC-29
94SarRedSF-1968
96HilStaHWB-34
96SarRedSB-1
Hale, John
75AlbDukC-5
76OPC-228
76Top-228
77Top-253
78Top-584
79OPC-23
79Top-56
80IndIndTI-6
80VenLeaS-178
81RocRedWT-6
81RocRedWW-18
90DodTar-309
Hale, Mark
72CedRapCT-2
96ButCopKB-14
Hale, Odell (A. Odell)
34DiaMatCSB-82
34BatR31-112
35DiaMatCS3T1-66
36GouWidPPR-A44
36NatChiFPR-38
36WheBB5-8
37OPCBatUV-128
38ExhFou-11
40PlaBal-203
81ConTSN-55
92ConTSN-415
93DiaStaES-133
Hale, Sammy (Samuel)
25Exh-108
29ExhFou-28
31W517-44
81ConTSN-56
91ConTSN-293
94ConTSN-1155
94ConTSNB-1155
Hale, Shane
91FreKeyC-3
91FreKeyP-2357
94AlbPolC-14
94AlbPolF-2232
94OriPro-43
96BowBayB-16
Halemanu, Josh
94AubAstC-6
94AubAstF-3765
95AubAstTI-7
Haley, Bart
86ElmPioRSP-8
87WinHavRSP-6
88LynRedSS-8
89LynRedSS-10
Haley, Bill
78GreBraT-11
Haley, Bo
91PitMotC 10
94PitMetF-3527
Haley, Mark
85AncGlaPTI-13
91SouBenWSC-23
91SouBenWSP-2875
92SouBenWSC-25
92SouBenWSF-195
93NasSouF-584
94HicCraC-28
94HicCraF-2194
96PriWilCB-3
Haley, Rich
93YakBeaC-11
93YakBeaF-3895
Haley, Ryan
91NiaFalRC-5
91NiaFalRP-3635
Haley, Sam
83WauTimF-23
86WesPalBEP-19
Halicki, Ed
75OPC-467
75Top-467
76OPC-423
76Top-423
77Gia-8
77Top-343
78Hos-12
78Top-107
79GiaPol-28
79OPC-354
79Top-672
80GiaPol-28
80OPC-115
80Top-217
81Don-53
81Top-69
89PacSenL-74
Halicki, Kevin
82RedPioT-4
Hall, Albert
82RicBraT-19
82RicBraT-31
83RicBraT-18
85BraHos-10
85BraPol-2
85Fle-326
85Top-676
85TopTif-676
86RicBraP-8
87BraSmo-25
87FleUpd-39
87FleUpdG-39
87TopTra-41T
87TopTraT-41T
88Don-290
88DonBasB-253
88Fle-541
88FleGlo-541
88OPC-213
88PanSti-249
88Sco-148
88ScoGlo-148
88StaLinBra-8
88Top-213
88Top-549
88TopSti-39
88TopTif-213
88TopTif-549
89BlaYNPRWL-156
89BlaYNPRWLU-60
89BlaYNPRWLU-63
89Fle-593
89FleGlo-593
89OPC-153
89Sco-74
89Top-433
89TopBig-104
89TopSti-30
89TopTif-433
89UppDec-93
Hall, Andy
86MacPirP-11
86TriTriC-198
88CarLeaAS-8
88SalBucS-7
89BufBisC-10
89BufBisP-1672
89HarSenS-8
90MidAngGS-21
95NewJerCTI-11
96MidLeaAB-19
96PeoChiB-14
Hall, Bill (William B.)
90DodTar-967
Hall, Bill (William Lemuel)
59Top-49
59TopVen-49
Hall, Billy
90WicStaSGD-16
92CalLeaACL-39
92HigDesMC-7
92UppDecML-285
93Bow-306
93ClaFS7-276
93ClaGolF-57
93WicWraF-2984
94ExcFS7-281
94UppDec-175
94UppDecED-175
94UppDecML-35
94WicWraF-197
95MidLeaA-21
95QuaCitRBTI-9
96ChaLooB-14
96KisCobB-10
Hall, Bob
49EurSta-10
55Bow-113
90DodTar-1103
Hall, Carl
90WicStaSGD-17
94VerExpC-13
94VerExpF-3921
Hall, Charles Louis
09AmeCarE-48
11SpoLifCW-153
11SpoLifM-9
12T207-73
Hall, Chris
89BriTigS-11
90BriTigP-3155
90BriTigS-9
Hall, Darren
87MyrBeaBJP-1438
88DunBluJS-8
89DunBluJS-6
90KnoBluJB-21
90KnoBluJP-1244
90KnoBluJS-4
91KnoBluJLD-358
91KnoBluJP-1762
91LinDriAA-358
92ProFS7-165
92SyrChiF-1961
92SyrChiMB-7
92SyrChiS-507
93PriRedC-14
93PriRedF-4194
93SyrChiF-995
94Bow-85

94FleUpd-99
94LeaLimR-58
94PriRedC-11
94PriRedF-3276
94TopTra-26T
95ColCho-141
95ColChoGS-141
95ColChoSS-141
95Don-81
95DonPreP-81
95Fle-96
95FleRooS-6
95Lea-131
95Pac-446
95StaClu-466
95StaCluMOP-466
95StaCluSTWS-466
95Top-174
95Ult-120
95UltGolM-120
95UltSecYS-4
95UltSecYSGM-4
96ColCho-354
96ColChoGS-354
96ColChoSS-354
96DodMot-24
96DodPol-16
96LeaSigEA-69
Hall, Dave
63MilSau-1
81CedRapRT-26
82CedRapRT-19
83TamTarT-14
Hall, Dean
78NewWayCT-18
Hall, Drew
86PitCubP-8
87Don-594
87IowCubTI-2
88DonTeaBC-NEW
88Top-262
88TopTif-262
89Bow-221
89BowTif-221
89Don-522
89Fle-643
89FleGlo-643
89OklCit8P-1517
89RanSmo-12
89Top-593
89TopTif-593
89UppDec-324
90ExpPos-15
90Fle-299
90FleCan-299
90Lea-423
90OPC-463
90Sco-516
90Top-463
90TopTif-463
90UppDec-631
91Fle-236
91OPC-77
91Sco-581
91Top-77
91TopDesS-77
91TopMic-77
91TopTif-77
93RanKee-168
93ScrRedBTI-11
Hall, Gardner C. (Grady)
87BirBarB-14
88VanCanC-8
88VanCanP-761
89BirBarB-11
89BirBarP-108
89Fle-650
89FleGlo-650
90CMC-633
90ProAAAF-162
90VanCanC-6
90VanCanP-484
91LinDriAAA-632
91VanCanLD-632
91VanCanP-1589
92AlbDukF-713
Hall, Greg
85SpolndC-6
87ChaRaiP-5
88RivRedWCLC-219
88RivRedWP-1415
89RivRedWB-26
89RivRedWCLC-6
89RivRedWP-1397
89SpolndSP-8
Hall, Halsey
78HalHalR-1
Hall, Irv
83TCMPla1944-15
Hall, Jeff
80ElmPioRST-11
Hall, Jimmie
64Top-73
64TopCoi-16
64TopSta-3
64TopVen-73
64TwiJayP-4
65Top-580
66OPC-190
66Top-190
66TopRubI-37
66TopVen-190
66TwiFaiG-5
67CokCapDA-23
67Top-432
68OPC-121
68Top-121
68TopVen-121
69MilBra-99
69OPC-61
69Top-61
70Top-649
78TwiFri-7
92YanWIZ6-52
Hall, Joe
88HamRedP-1747
89St.PetCS-15
90ArkTraGS-16
90TexLeaAGS-30
91LinDriAAA-633
91VanCanLD-633
91VanCanP-1600
92VanCanF-2730
92VanCanS-636
93LinVenB-178
93NasSouF-579
94Bow-651
94Fla-32
94FleUpd-26
94ScoRoo-RT143
94ScoRooGR-RT143
94Sel-404
94SpoRoo-114
94SpoRooAP-114
94TopTra-61T
94Ult-338
94VenLinU-257
94WhiSoxK-11
95LinVen-143
95Pac-89
95Sco-290
95ScoGolR-290
95ScoPlaTS-290
95TolMudHTI-15
96RocRedWB-15
Hall, Johnny
90DodTar-968
Hall, Kevin
88PocGiaP-2093
89EveGiaS-10
Hall, Lamar
88IdaFalBP-1840
89SumBraP-1106
Hall, Larry
80AppFoxT-27
Hall, Marty
86MadMusP-10
87AshTouP-10
Hall, Matthew
86ChaLooP-11
87ChaLooB-21
Hall, Mel
82IowCubT-4
83CubThoAV-27
83Don-126
83TopTra-39T
84Don-411
84Fle-493
84FleSti-106
84IndWhe-34
84Nes792-508
84OPC-4
84Top-508
84TopSti-380
84TopTif-508
84TopTra-47T
84TopTraT-47T
85Don-338
85Fle-449
85Ind-16
85IndPol-27
85OPC-263
85Top-263
85TopMin-263
85TopSti-254
85TopTif-263
86Don-276
86Fle-587
86IndOhH-27
86IndTeal-23
86OPC-138
86Top-647
86TopTif-647
87Don-473
87Fle-252
87FleExcS-21
87FleGlo-252
87FleStiC-53
87IndGat-27
87OPC-51
87Spo-180
87SpoTeaP-3
87Top-51
87TopSti-208
87TopTif-51
88Don-342
88DonBasB-173
88Fle-610
88FleGlo-610
88IndGat-27
88Lea-109
88OPC-318
88PanSti-79
88Sco-441
88ScoGlo-441
88Spo-189
88StaLinI-12
88Top-318
88TopBig-114
88TopSti-205
88TopTif-318
89Don-73
89DonTra-36
89Fle-406
89FleGlo-406
89FleUpd-49
89OPC-173
89PanSti-328
89RedFolSB-55
89Sco-17
89ScoRoo-54T
89Spo-144
89Top-173
89TopBig-13
89TopTif-173
89TopTra-44T
89TopTraT-44T
89TVSpoM-86
89UppDec-538
89UppDec-729
89YanScoNW-20
90Bow-437
90BowTif-437
90Don-598
90DonBesA-66
90Fle-444
90FleCan-444
90Lea-227
90MLBBasB-92
90OPC-436
90PanSti-122
90PubSti-535
90Sco-383
90Top-436
90TopBig-123
90TopSti-313
90TopTif-436
90TopTVY-30
90UppDec-458
90YanScoNW-7
91Bow-179
91Cla3-T34
91Don-442
91Fle-665
91Lea-283
91OPC-738
91Sco-166
91StaClu-333
91Top-738
91TopDesS-738
91TopMic-738
91TopTif-738
91Ult-233
91UppDec-392
92Bow-425
92Cla2-T83
92Don-248
92Fle-229
92Hig5-86
92Lea-88
92OPC-223
92PanSti-141
92Pin-144
92Sco-154
92StaClu-9
92Top-223
92TopGol-223
92TopGolW-223
92TopKid-87
92TopMic-223
92Ult-101
92UppDec-291
92UppDecS-1
92YanWIZ8-76
93Fle-278
93Sel-89
93Top-114
93TopGol-114
93TopInaM-114
93TopMic-114
93UppDec-291
93UppDecGold-291
96GiaMot-16
Hall, Richard W.
55Top-126
55TopDouH-57
56Top-331
57Top-308
60Top-308
61Top-197
61TopStal-160
62Top-189
62TopVen-189
63Top-526
67Top-508
68OPC-17
68Top-17
68TopVen-17
70OPC-182
70Top-182
71MLBOffS-297
71OPC-417
71Ori-5
71Top-417
78TCM60I-170
81Ori6F-15
91OriCro-174
Hall, Robert P.
09T206-426
Hall, Rocky
78NewWayCT-19
79BurBeeT-6
79HolMilT-24
Hall, Ronnie
94BenRocF-3608
95AshTouTI-25
96SalAvaB-13
Hall, Roy
85GreHorT-15
Hall, Ryan
94JohCitCC-12
94JohCitCF-3705
95PeoChiTI-16
96StPetCB-11
Hall, Tim
91SpolndC-26
91SpolndP-3950
92ChaRaiF-123
Hall, Todd
87PenWhiSP-24
88TamTarS-10A
89SarWhiSS-9
90BirBarB-17
90BirBarP-1105
90CMC-747
Hall, Tom E.
69Top-658
70OPC-169
70Top-169
71MLBOffS-462
71OPC-313
71Top-313
72MilBra-124
72OPC-417
72Top-417
73OPC-8
73Top-8
74OPC-248
74Top-248
75MetSSP-3
75OPC-108
75Top-108
76OPC-621
76SSP-556
76Top-621
77TacTwiDQ-13
78TwiFri-31
91MetWIZ-156
Hall, Yates
94NewJerCC-14
94NewJerCF-3412
94SigRooBS-2
94StaCluDP-55
94StaCluDPFDI-55
95Exc-267
96StPetCB-12
Halla, John
09ColChiE-123
12ColRedB-123
12ColTinT-123
Halladay, Roy
06Boc-126
96DunBluJB-12
96DunBluJTI-14
96DunBluJUTI-3
97BluJayS-59
97Bow-308
97BowBes-134
97BowBesAR-134
97BowBesR-134
97BowCerBIA-CA35
97BowCerGIA-CA35
97BowChr-212
97BowChrl-212
97BowChrIR-212
97BowChrR-212
97BowInt-308
Hallahan, Bill
31Exh-16
32OrbPinNP-72
32OrbPinUP-29
33ExhFou-8
33Gou-200
33NatLeaAC-13
33TatOrb-29
34DiaMatCSB-83
34BatR31-40
34BatR31-121
34DiaStaR-23
34ExhFou-8
34Gou-82
34TarThoBD-8
35DiaMatCS3T1-67
35GolMedFR-7
36GouWidPPR-A45
36NatChiFPR-39
36SandSW-28
36WorWidGV-70
46SpoExcW-5-4
74Car193T-14
77GalGloG-211
87ConSer2-15
91ConTSN-214
92CarMcD-18
92ConTSN-639
93ConTSN-685
Halland, Jon
91BelMarC-4
91BelMarP-3674
91PenPilP-385
Hallas, Bob
83MadMusF-16
84AlbA'sT-13
Hallberg, Lance
78WisRapTT-7
80OrlTwiT-8
82OrlTwi8SCT-11
Halle, Andrew
88BurIndP-1797
Hallead, John
96AshTouB-21
96PorRocB-14
Haller, Jim
75AlbDukC-19
90GreHorB-7
90GreHorP-2653
90GreHorS-4
90ProAaA-87
91Cla/Bes-144
91PriWilC-29

91PriWilCP-1418
92ForLauYTI-15
92Ft.LauYF-2606
93AlbYanF-2157
Haller, Tom
60TacBan-7
62GiaJayP-5
62Top-356
63GiaJayP-5
63Jel-108
63Pos-108
63Top-85
64GiaJayP-5
64Top-485
65GiaTeal-3
65Top-465
65TopTral-16
66Top-308
66TopVen-308
67CokCapG-9
67DexPre-85
67OPC-65
67Top-65
68OPC-185
68Top-185
68TopVen-185
69MilBra-100
69MLBOffS-148
69OPCDec-10
69Top-310
69TopDec-23
69TopDecl-14
69TopSta-45
69TopSup-47
69TopTeaP-22
69TraSta-43
70DayDaiNM-27
70Kel-25
70MilBra-9
70MLBOffS-51
70Top-685
71MLBOffS-105
71OPC-639
71Top-639
72MilBra-125
72OPC-175
72OPC-176
72Top-175
72Top-176
73OPC-454
73TigJew-8
73Top-454
77Gia-9
78TCM60I-188
79GiaPol-5
84GiaMot-5
86BirBarTI-25
87DodSmoA-11
89DodSmoG-74
90DodTar-310
92DodStaTA-7
93UppDecS-7
Halley, Allen
96PriWilCB-13
Hallgren, Robert
76DubPacT-14
77CocAstT-7
78AshTouT-9
Hallgren, Tim
80SanJosMJitB-11
86SalRedBP-11
Halliday, Doc
90IdaFalBP-3264
Halliday, Troy
91ParPatF-6
Hallinan, Ed
12T207-74
Hallion, Tom
88T/MUmp-57
89T/MUmp-55
90T/MUmp-53
Hallman, Bill (William W.)
03BreE10-63
09T206-427
11SpoLifCW-154
87OldJudN-226
90DodTar-311
95May-34
Hallmark, Patrick
95SpoIndTI-6
96LanLugB-13
Halloran, Matt
96BesAutS1RP-FR5
97Bow-203
97BowChr-189
97BowChrI-189
97BowChrIR-189
97BowChrR-189
97BowInt-203
97Top-271
Halls, Gary
77BurBeeT-12
Hallstrom, Bill
79WatIndT-3A
Hallstrom, Charles
87OldJudN-227
Halperin, Mike
94St.CatBJC-11
94St.CatBJF-3637
94StaCluDP-76
94StaCluDPFDI-76
95DunBluJTI-8
96KnoSmoB-14
Halter, Shane
91EugEmeC-4
91EugEmeP-3733
92AppFoxC-8
92AppFoxF-991
92MidLeaATI-15
92StaCluD-74
93ExcFS7-173
93WilBluRC-13
93WilBluRF-2004
94Bow-31
94MemChiF-366
95OmaRoyTI-12
96ChaKniB-13
Haltiwanger, Garrick
96PitMetB-11
Ham, Kevin
94BoiHawC-12
94BoiHawF-3368
95BoiHawTI-19
96CedRapKTI-11
Ham, Mike (Michael)
87EveGiaC-17
88CliGiaP-709
89PhoFirP-1478
89SanJosGB-26
89SanJosGCLC-220
89SanJosGP-461
89SanJosGS-12
90ShrCapP-1447
90ShrCapS-9
Hambright, Roger
72OPC-124
72Top-124
74SyrChiTI-9
92YanWIZ7-64
Hamburg, Leon
94SouOreAC-8
94SouOreAF-3637
95WesMicWTI-23
Hamel, Todd
85CloHSS-20
Hamelin, Bob
88EugEmeB-1
89BasAmeAPB-AA17
89MemChiB-1
89MemChiP-1201
89MemChiS-12
89SouLeaAJ-9
89Sta-42
90Bow-379
90BowTif-379
90CMC-199
90OmaRoyC-24
90OmaRoyP-71
90ProAAAF-606
90UppDec-45
91Bow-310
91LinDriAAA-336
91OmaRoyLD-336
91OmaRoyP-1042
92Fle-672
93Bow-617
93ClaFS7-198
93OmaRoyF-1684
94Bow-143
94ColC-393
94ColChoGS-393
94ColChoSS-393
94Don-435
94ExtBas-90
94ExtBasRS-7
94Fin-110
94FinRef-110
94Fla-58
94FleAllR-M5
94FleUpd-48
94Lea-363
94LeaGolR-11
94LeaL-39
94LeaLimRP-2
94Pin-404
94PinArtP-404
94PinMusC-404
94PinRooTP-2
94Sco-622
94ScoBoyoS-44
94ScoGolR-622
94ScoRoo-RT73
94ScoRooGR-RT73
94ScoRooSR-SU5
94Sel-191
94SelRooS-RS2
94Spo-152
94SpoRooRS-TR8
94StaClu-294
94StaClu-626
94StaCluFDI-294
94StaCluFDI-626
94StaCluGR-294
94StaCluGR-626
94StaCluMOP-294
94StaCluMOP-626
94Top-769
94TopGol-769
94TopSpa-769
94Ult-64
94UppDec-249
94UppDecED-249
95Baz-46
95Bow-381
95ColCho-78
95ColChoCtG-CG9
95ColChoCtG-CG9B
95ColChoCtG-CG9C
95ColChoCtGE-9
95ColChoCtGG-CG9
95ColChoCtGG-CG9B
95ColChoCtGG-CG9C
95ColChoCtGGE-9
95ColChoGS-78
95ColChoSE-215
95ColChoSEGS-215
95ColChoSESS-215
95ColChoSS-78
95D3-40
95Don-520
95DonPreP-520
95DonTopotO-90
95Emb-117
95EmbGolI-117
95Fin-11
95FinPowK-PK1
95FinRef-11
95Fla-46
95Fle-160
95FleAwaW-5
95FleRooS-7
95FleTeaL-7
95Lea-198
95LeaChe-1
95LeaLim-51
95NatPac-4
95Pac-203
95PacGolP-8
95PacPri-64
95PanSti-97
95PanSti-106
95PanSti-114
95Pin-22
95PinArtP-22
95PinMusC-22
95Sco-433
95ScoAi-AM1
95ScoGolR-433
95ScoHaloG-HG107
95ScoPlaTS-433
95Sel-50
95SelArtP-50
95Spo-75
95SpoArtP-75
95StaClu-79
95StaCluCC-CC14
95StaCluFDI-79A
95StaCluFDI-79B
95StaCluMO-49
95StaCluMOP-79
95StaCluMOP-CC14
95StaCluSTWS-79
95StaCluVR-49
95Stu-30
95StuGolS-30
95Sum-72
95SumNthD-72
95TomPiz-3
95Top-143
95TopCyb-87
95UC3-93
95UC3ArtP-93
95Ult-57
95UltAllR-4
95UltAllRGM-4
95UltAwaW-23
95UltAwaWGM-23
95UltGolM-57
95UltSecYS-5
95UltSecYSGM-5
95UppDec-180
95UppDecED-180
95UppDecEDG-180
95UppDecSE-187
95UppDecSEG-187
96ColCho-571
96ColChoGS-571
96ColChoSS-571
96Don-190
96DonPreP-190
96Fla-90
96Fle-129
96FleTif-129
96Lea-53
96LeaPrePB-53
96LeaPrePG-53
96LeaPrePS-53
96Pac-324
96Pin-289
96PinFoil-289
96RoyPol-10
96StaCluMOF-1
95StaCluVRMC-49
96Ult-355
96UltGolM-355
97Pac-101
97PacLigB-101
97PacSil-101
Hamilton, Bill
52LavPro-55
Hamilton, Billy
61Fle-112
76ShaPiz-86
80PerHaloFP-86
80SSPHOF-86
87OldJudN-228
89HOFStiB-43
94OriofB-79
95May-35
98CamPepP-31
Hamilton, Bo (Paul)
93MarPhiF-3466
94MarPhiC-8
94MarPhiF-3284
95BatCliTI-16
95PiePhiF-182
Hamilton, Bob
79NaSouTI-10
80WatRedT-13
85VerBeaDT-1
87SanAntDTI-18
Hamilton, Carl
86PitCubP-9
87IowCubTI-1
88PeoChiTI-13
90MidAngGS-17
91CarMudLD-108
91CarMudP-1081
91LinDriAA-108
Hamilton, Charlie
91KisDodP-4205
Hamilton, Darryl
85AncGlaPTI-14
87StoPorP-8
88DenZepC-24
88DenZepP-1274
88FleUpd-38
88FleUpdG-38
88ScoRoo-72T
88ScoRooG-72T
89DenZepC-13
89DenZepP-39
89Fle-187
89FleGlo-187
89ScoHot1R-44
89Top-88
89TopTif-88
89UppDec-301
90Bow-397
90BowTif-397
90BreMilB-10
90BrePol-24
90Fle-325
90FleCan-325
90TopTra-35T
90TopTraT-35T
91BreMilB-9
91BrePol-9
91Don-517
91Fle-585
91OPC-781
91Sco-107
91StaClu-234
91Top-781
91TopDesS-781
91TopMic-781
91TopTif-781
91UltUpd-30
91UppDec-42
92Bow-74
92BrePol-10
92Don-593
92Fle-177
92Lea-12
92OPC-278
92Pin-151
92Sco-497
92StaClu-253
92Top-278
92TopGol-278
92TopGolW-278
92TopMic-278
92TriPla-260
92Ult-383
92UppDec-460
93Bow-239
93BrePol-9
93BreSen5-5
93DiaMar-48
93Don-527
93Fin-45
93FinRef-45
93Fla-224
93Fle-250
93Lea-199
93OPC-158
93PacSpa-157
93PanSti-41
93Pin-144
93Sco-118
93Sel-168
93SP-65
93StaClu-303
93StaCluFDI-303
93StaCluMOP-303
93Stu-40
93Top-556
93TopGol-556
93TopInaM-556
93TopMic-556
93Ult-219
93UppDec-192
93UppDecGold-192
94Bow-289
94BreMilB-34
94BrePol-9
94ColC-386
94ColChoGS-386
94ColChoSS-386
94Don-398
94ExtBas-102
94Fin-142
94FinRef-142
94Fla-67
94Fle-177
94FUnPac-98
94Lea-281
94OPC-58
94Pac-329
94PanSti-80
94Pin-94
94PinArtP-94
94PinMusC-94
94ProMag-71
94Sco-395
94ScoGolR-395
94Sel-307
94Spo-57
94StaClu-188
94StaCluFDI-188

94StaCluGR-188
94StaCluMOP-188
94Stu-43
94Top-435
94TopGol-435
94TopSpa-435
94TriPla-53
94Ult-74
94UppDec-326
94UppDecED-326
95ColCho-178
95ColChoGS-178
95ColChoSS-178
95Don-443
95DonPreP-443
95DonTopotO-97
95Fla-270
95Fle-179
95Lea-247
95LeaLim-6
95Pin-207
95PinArtP-207
95PinMusC-207
95Sco-84
95ScoGolR-84
95ScoPlaTS-84
95StaClu-176
95StaCluFDI-176
95StaCluMOP-176
95StaCluSTWS-176
95Sum-49
95SumNthD-49
95Top-245
95Ult-64
95UltGolM-64
96ColCho-788
96Don-527
96DonPreP-527
96Fla-172
96Fle-145
96FleRan-9
96FleTif-145
96FleUpd-U89
96FleUpdTC-U89
96LeaPre-60
96LeaPreP-60
96LeaSigA-89
96LeaSigAG-89
96LeaSigAS-89
96Pac-348
96Pin-353
96PinFoil-353
96RanMot-5
96Sco-85
96Top-365
96Ult-80
96Ult-420
96UltGolM-80
96UltGolM-420
96UppDec-467
97Cir-249
97CirRav-249
97ColCho-455
97Don-251
97Don-294
97DonLim-85
97DonLimLE-85
97DonPreP-251
97DonPreP-294
97DonPrePGold-251
97DonPrePGold-294
97Fin-210
97FinRef-210
97Fle-224
97Fle-631
97FleTif-224
97FleTif-631
97Lea-210
97LeaFraM-210
97LeaFraMDC-210
97NewPin-157
97NewPinAP-157
97NewPinMC-157
97NewPinPP-157
97Pac-202
97PacLigB-202
97PacSil-202
97Pin-4
97PinArtP-4
97PinMusC-4
97Sco-231
97Sco-363
97ScoHobR-363
97ScoPreS-231
97ScoRan-13
97ScoRanPl-13
97ScoRanPr-13
97ScoResC-363
97ScoShoS-231
97ScoShoS-363
97ScoShoSAP-231
97ScoShoSAP-363
97StaClu-126
97StaCluMOP-126
97Top-194
97Ult-134
97Ult-447
97UltGolME-134
97UltGolME-447
97UltPlaME-134
97UltPlaME-447

Hamilton, Dave
74OPC-633
74Top-633
75OPC-428
75Top-428
76OPC-237
76Top-237
77OPC-224
77Top-367
78Top-288
79Top-147
80Top-86
81TacTigT-8

Hamilton, Earl
12T207-75
14B18B-31A
14B18B-31B
14FatPlaT-15
15CraJacE-171
15SpoNewM-74
16BF2FP-41
16ColE13-68
16SpoNewM-75
21Nei-68
22E120-219
22W573-57
92ConTSN-339

Hamilton, George W.
88KimN18-16

Hamilton, Jack
62Top-593
63Top-132
65Top-288
66Top-262
66TopVen-262
67CokCapYM-V35
67DexPre-86
67OPC-2
67Top-2
68OPC-193
68Top-193
68TopVen-193
69Top-629
91MetWIZ-157

Hamilton, Jamie
80ElPasDT-23

Hamilton, Jason
93BriTigC-11
93BriTigF-3653

Hamilton, Jeff
86AlbDukP-10
87AlbDukP-19
87DodPol-16
87Don-464
87Top-266
87TopTif-266
88DodMot-19
88DodPol-33
88Don-525
88Fle-515
88FleGlo-515
88PanSti-312
88Top-62
88TopTif-62
89DodMot-19
89DodPol-3
89DodStaSV-6
89Don-550
89DonBasB-290
89Fle-60
89FleGlo-60
89Sco-570
89Top-736
89TopTif-736
89UppDec-615
90Bow-94
90BowTif-94
90DodMot-23
90DodPol-3
90DodTar-312
90Don-321
90Fle-396
90FleCan-396
90Lea-306
90OPC-426
90PubSti-7
90Sco-132
90ScoYouS2-17
90Top-426
90TopBig-98
90TopSti-67
90TopTif-426
90UppDec-296
91DodMot-23
91DodPol-3
91Lea-509
91OPC-552
91StaClu-550
91Top-552
91TopDesS-552
91TopMic-552
91TopTif-552
91UppDec-779
92AlbDukF-726
92AlbDukS-10
92DodPol-3
92OPC-151
92Sco-684
92SkyAAAF-4
92StaClu-339
92Top-151
92TopGol-151
92TopGolW-151
92TopMic-151
86STaoftFT-18

Hamilton, Jimmy
96AppLeaAB-8
96BurIndB-5

Hamilton, Joe
94UtiBluSC-13
94UtiBluSF-3833
95MicBatCTI-15
96MicBatCB-12

Hamilton, Joey
88MisStaB-9
89MisStaB-16
90MisStaB-15
91MisStaB-20
92CalLeaACL-42
92ChaRaiC-21
92ClaDraP-90
92ClaFS7-54
92FroRowDP-35
92UppDec-67
92UppDecML-39
92UppDecML-76
93ClaFS7-199
93RanCucQC-14
93RanCucQF-826
93StaCluM-49
94Bow-525
94BowBes-B8
94BowBesR-B8
94Cla-122
94Fla-437
94FlaWavotF-B3
94FleUpd-185
94LasVegSF-869
94LeaLimR-42
94ScoRoo-RT124
94ScoRooGR-RT124
94Sel-403
94SigRoo-26
94SigRooS-26
94SPDieC-5
94SP-5
94SpoRoo-139
94SpoRooAP-139
94TopTra-48T
94Ult-575
94UppDec-513
94UppDecED-513
94UppDecML-229
95Bow-283
95ColCho-346
95ColChoGS-346
95ColChoSE-161
95ColChoSEGS-161
95ColChoSESS-161
95ColChoSS-346
95Don-267
95DonPreP-267
95DonTopotO-342
95Emb-87
95EmbGoll-87
95Emo-188
95Fin-10
95FinRef-10
95Fla-419
95Fle-561
95FleRooS-8
95Lea-114
95PadCHP-15
95PadMot-24
95PanSti-103
95Pin-344
95PinArtP-344
95PinMusC-344
95PinUps-US20
95Sco-482
95ScoGolR-482
95ScoPlaTS-482
95Sel-27
95SelArtP-27
95SelCer-83
95SelCerMG-83
95SP-109
95SPCha-91
95SPChaDC-91
95Spo-54
95SpoArtP-54
95SPSil-109
95StaClu-339
95StaCluMO-47
95StaCluMOP-339
95StaCluSTWS-339
95StaCluVR-178
95Stu-69
95Sum-68
95SumNthD-68
95Top-54
95TopCyb-39
95Ult-234
95UltAllR-5
95UltAllRGM-5
95UltGolM-234
95UltSecYS-6
95UltSecYSGM-6
95UppDec-137
95UppDecED-137
95UppDecEDG-137
95UppDecSE-266
95UppDecSEG-266
96ColCho-701
96ColChoGS-701
96ColChoSS-701
96Don-204
96DonPreP-204
96EmoXL-278
96Fla-375
96Fle-568
96FleTif-568
96Lea-73
96LeaPre-41
96LeaPreP-41
96LeaPrePB-73
96LeaPrePG-73
96LeaPrePS-73
96LeaSig-44
96LeaSigA-90
96LeaSigAG-90
96LeaSigAS-90
96LeaSigPPG-44
96LeaSigPPP-44
96MetUni-236
96MetUniP-236
96Pac-197
96PadMot-20
96PanSti-104
96Pin-23
96Sco-412
96StaClu-29
96StaClu-251
96StaCluMOP-29
96StaCluMOP-251
95StaCluVRMC-178
96Stu-136
96StuPrePB-136
96StuPrePG-136
96StuPrePS-136
96Top-403
96TopGal-112
96TopGalPPI-112
96TopLas-119
96Ult-285
96UltGolM-285
96UppDec-451
97Cir-20
97CirRav-20
97ColCho-444
97Don-45
97DonLim-74
97DonLimLE-74
97DonPre-118
97DonPreCttC-118
97DonPreP-45
97DonPrePGold-45
97Fin-27
97FinRef-27
97FlaSho-A150
97FlaSho-B150
97FlaSho-C150
97FlaShoLC-150
97FlaShoLC-B150
97FlaShoLC-C150
97FlaShoLCM-A150
97FlaShoLCM-B150
97FlaShoLCM-C150
97Fle-463
97FleTif-463
97Lea-125
97LeaFraM-125
97LeaFraMDC-125
97MetUni-220
97Pac-425
97PacLigB-425
97PacSil-425
97PinX-P-97
97PinX-PMoS-97
97Sco-261
97ScoPreS-261
97ScoShoS-261
97ScoShoSAP-261
97SP-153
97Spolll-45
97SpollIEE-45
97StaClu-155
97StaCluMOP-155
97Stu-46
97StuPrePG-46
97StuPrePS-46
97Top-117
97TopChr-45
97TopChrR-45
97TopGal-95
97TopGalPPI-95
97Ult-284
97UltGolME-284
97UltPlaME-284
97UppDec-493

Hamilton, Kenny
90GreFalDSP-19
91YakBeaC-17
91YakBeaP-4243
92VerBeaDC-5
92VerBeaDF-2869
93VerBeaDC-7
93VerBeaDF-2211

Hamilton, Mike
88ButCopKSP-1

Hamilton, Scott W.
86EriCarP-12
87SprCarB-17
88St.PetCS-8
90StoPorB-19
90StoPorCLC-180
90StoPorP-2180

Hamilton, Steve
55DonWin-22
63Top-171
64ChatheY-11
64Top-206
64TopVen-206
65ChaTheY-9
65Top-309
66Top-503
67CokCapYM-V15
67DexPre-87
67Top-567
68Top-496
69MilBra-101
69MLBOffS-75
69OPC-69
69Top-69
70MLBOffS-246
70OPC-349
70Top-349
71OPC-627
71Top-627

72MilBra-126
72Top-766
73OPC-214
73Top-214
92YanWIZ6-53
92YanWIZ7-65
Hamilton, Z.B.
89PriPirS-8
Hamlet, Macot
95LakElsSTI-28
96LakElsSB-30
Hamlin, Jonas
91St.PetCC-21
91St.PetCP-2284
92SavCarC-12
92SavCarF-670
93SprCarC-12
93SprCarF-1859
94BelBreC-11
94BelBreF-108
95Bes-27
96El PasDB-11
96Exc-70
96TexLeaAB-25
Hamlin, Ken
55DonWin-23
60A'sTeal-6
60Top-542
61Pos-89A
61Pos-89B
61Top-263
62SalPlaC-34A
62SalPlaC-34B
62ShiPlaC-34
62Top-296
66OPC-69
66Top-69
66TopVen-69
Hamlin, Luke
34DiaMatCSB-84
35TigFreP-10
39PlaBal-13
40DodTeal-11
40PlaBal-70
41DodTeal-3
41PlaBal-53
76TigOldTS-12
90DodTar-313
Hamlin, Mark
96PorRocB-15
Hamm, Albert
87AllandGN-24
Hamm, Pete
71OPC-74
71Top-74
72OPC-501
72Top-501
Hamm, Stacy
91PocPioP-3796
91PocPioSP-26
92ChaRaiC-4
92ChaRaiF-132
92SpoIndC-23
92SpoIndF-1306
Hamm, Tim
82HawIslT-18
Hammack, Brandon
96MidLeaAB-48
96RocCubTI-9
Hammagren, Roy (Tucker)
88CapCodPPaLP-166
90BilMusP-3225
91ChaWheC-12
91ChaWheP-2889
92ChaWheF-10
92ChaWVWC-7
93ClaGolF-186
93SouAtlLAPI-14
Hammaker, Atlee
81OmaRoyT-6
82Top-471
83AllGamPI-166
83Don-298
83Fle-261
83FleSta-74
83FleSti-50
83GiaMot-13
83Top-342
83TopSti-324
84Don-236
84Fle-373
84FleSti-65
84GiaMot-9
84GiaPos-7
84Nes792-85
84Nes792-137
84Nes792-576
84OPC-85
84SevCoi-W15
84Top-85
84Top-137
84Top-576
84TopGloS-7
84TopRubD-4
84TopSti-165
84TopSti-175
84TopTif-85
84TopTif-137
84TopTif-576
85Don-509
85Fle-608
85GiaMot-6
85GiaPos-14
85OPC-351
85Top-674
85TopMin-674
85TopRubD-4
85TopSti-165
85TopTif-674
86BasStaB-53
86Don-445
86Fle-544
86GiaMot-6
86Lea-220
86Top-223
86TopTif-223
87FleUpd-40
87FleUpdG-40
87OPC-358
87PhoFirP-24
87Top-781
87TopTif-781
88Don-450
88Fle-83
88FleGlo-83
88GiaMot-19
88Sco-528
88ScoGlo-528
88StaLinG-8
88Top-157
88TopBig-259
88TopTif-157
89Don-414
89Fle-329
89FleGlo-329
89GiaMot-19
89OPC-2
89Sco-422
89Top-572
89TopBig-21
89TopTif-572
89UppDec-544
90Don-532
90Fle-57
90FleCan-57
90GiaMot-13
90GiaSmo-9
90OPC-447
90PubSti-69
90Sco-231
90Top-447
90TopTif-447
90UppDec-620
91Don-707
91Fle-530
91OPC-34
91PadSmo-12
91StaClu-347
91Stu-246
91Top-34
91TopDesS-34
91TopMic-34
91TopTif-34
92Sco-233
94BirBarC-11
Hamman, Ed
76LauIndC-1
76LauIndC-12
76LauIndC-23
76LauIndC-32
76LauIndC-40
Hammell, Al
92GulCoaMF-3484
94CapCitBC-10
94CapCitBF-1754
94St.LucMC-12
95StLucMTI-16
Hammer, Ben
95AusFutGP-4
Hammer, M.C.
92MTVRocnJ-1
Hammer, Pete (James)
77WauMetT-9
79JacMetT-12
Hammerschmidt, Andy
96RanCucQB-17
Hammon, Randy
77PhoGiaVNB-8
78PhoGiaC-9
79PhoGiaVNB-13
Hammond, Allan
92SavCarC-19
92SavCarF-657
Hammond, Arthur S.
81VerBeaDT-6
Hammond, Chris
87TamTarP-15
88BasAmeAAB-17
88ChaLooB-2
88SouLeaAJ-36
89NasSouP-1279
89NasSouTI-8
90CMC-130
90Fle-421
90FleCan-421
90NasSouC-5
90NasSouP-225
90ProAAAF-537
90Sco-629
90TriAllGP-AAA51
90UppDec-52
91Bow-680
91Don-759
91DonRoo-19
91Fle-65
91Lea-373
91OPC-258
91OPCPre-60
91RedKah-45
91StaClu-575
91Stu-165
91Top-258
91TopDeb90-62
91TopDesS-258
91TopMic-258
91TopTif-258
91UltUpd-76
91UppDec-748
92Bow-328
92Don-172
92Fle-408
92Lea-178
92OPC-744
92Pin-335
92RedKah-45
92Sco-513
92Sco100RS-89
92StaClu-751
92StaCluNC-751
92Top-744
92TopGol-744
92TopGolW-744
92TopMic-744
92Ult-189
92UppDec-105
93Don-346
93Fla-51
93Fle-35
93FleFinE-61
93Lea-475
93MarPub-11
93MarUSPC-4H
93MarUSPC-12C
93Pin-449
93Sco-195
93SelRoo-104T
93SP-140
93StaClu-209
93StaCluFDI-209
93StaCluMOP-209
93Top-437
93TopGol-437
93TopInaM-437
93TopMic-437
93TopTra-86T
93Ult-29
93Ult-376
93UppDec-216
93UppDec-661
93UppDecGold-216
93UppDecGold-661
94Bow-150
94ColC-362
94ColChoGS-362
94ColChoSS-362
94Don-315
94ExtBas-260
94Fin-200
94FinRef-200
94Fla-163
94Fle-467
94Lea-284
94Pac-242
94Pin-59
94PinArtP-59
94PinMusC-59
94Sco-124
94ScoGolR-124
94SP-111
94SPDieC-111
94StaClu-367
94StaCluFDI-367
94StaCluGR-367
94StaCluMOP-367
94StaCluT-64
94StaCluTFDI-64
94Stu-109
94Top-189
94TopGol-189
94TopSpa-189
94TriPla-136
94Ult-492
94UppDec-209
94UppDecED-209
95ColCho-309
95ColChoGS-309
95ColChoSS-309
95Don-428
95DonPreP-428
95DonTopotO-243
95Emo-130
95Fin-315
95FinRef-315
95Fla-353
95Fle-333
95Lea-378
95Pin-96
95PinArtP-96
95PinMusC-96
95StaClu-360
95StaCluMOP-360
95StaCluSTWS-360
95Top-18
95Ult-162
95UltGolM-162
95UppDec-354
95UppDecED-354
95UppDecEDG-354
95UppDecSE-112
95UppDecSEG-112
96ColCho-153
96ColChoGS-153
96ColChoSS-153
96Don-98
96DonPreP-98
96EmoXL-186
96Fla-262
96Fle-387
96FleTif-387
96LeaSigA-91
96LeaSigAG-91
96LeaSigAS-91
96MetUni-165
96MetUniP-165
96PanSti-10
96ProSta-69
96Sco-107
96StaClu-314
96StaCluMOP-314
96Top-374
96Ult-200
96UltGolM-200
96UppDec-336
97Ult-479
97UltGolME-479
97UltPlaME-479
Hammond, Chuck
75LynRanT-11
Hammond, David
90PriPatD-10
Hammond, Greg
91ChaWheC-13
91ChaWheP-2890
92ChaWheF-11
92ChaWVWC-17
93WinSpiC-7
93WinSpiF-1573
Hammond, Steve
78GreBraT-12
80RicBraT-6
81RicBraT-16
83Fle-114
83OmaRoyT-18
84OmaRoyT-10
86IowCubP-14
87JapPlaB-38
86STaoftFT-8
Hammonds, Jeffrey
91TopTra-51T
91TopTraT-51T
92Bow-617
92ClaDraP-4
92ClaDraPFB-BC4
92ClaDraPP-BB4
92ClaDraPP-1
92DEL-BB4
92StaCluD-75
92TopDaiQTU-21
92TopTra-45T
92TopTraG-45T
92UppDecML-3
93BowBayF-2200
93ClaFS7-AU3
93ClaGolF-166
93ClaYouG-YG4
93FlaWavotF-6
93FleFinE-159
93LeaGolR-U2
93RocRedWF-252
93SelRoo-82T
93SelRooAR-6
93SP-156
93StaCluM-73
94ColC-123
94ColChoGS-123
94ColChoSS-123
94Don-629
94ExtBas-5
94ExtBasRS-8
94Fla-2
94Fle-5
94FleRooS-8
94FUnPac-11
94Lea-403
94LeaL-1
94LeaLimRP-6
94OriPro-44
94OriUSPC-4D
94OriUSPC-12C
94Pac-32
94Pin-417
94PinArtP-417
94PinMusC-417
94PinNewG-NG4
94PinRooTP-7
94ProMag-10
94Sco-560
94ScoBoyoS-8
94ScoGolR-560
94ScoRoo-RT77
94ScoRooGR-RT77
94ScoRooSR-SU7
94Sel-180
94SelRooS-RS5
94SP-121
94SPDieC-121
94SPHol-14
94SPHolDC-14
94Spo-150
94SpoRooRS-TR3
94Stu-123
94TriPla-284
94Ult-1
94UltAllR-4
94UltAllRJ-4
94UltSecYS-3
94UppDec-210
94UppDecED-210
94UppDecNG-7
94UppDecNGED-7
95ColCho-335
95ColChoGS-335
95ColChoSE-156
95ColChoSEGS-156
95ColChoSESS-156
95ColChoSS-335
95Don-231
95DonPreP-231
95DonTopotO-9
95Emo-4

95Fle-8
95Lea-385
95LeaLim-43
95Pac-22
95PacPri-7
95Pin-10
95PinArtP-10
95PinMusC-10
95Sco-450
95ScoGolR-450
95ScoHaloG-HG101
95ScoPlaTS-450
95Sel-18
95SelArtP-18
95SP-123
95Spo-2
95SpoArtP-2
95SPSil-123
95Stu-40
95StuGolS-40
95Sum-62
95SumNthD-62
95Ult-3
95UltGolM-3
95UltSecYS-7
95UltSecYSGM-7
95UppDec-129
95UppDecED-129
95UppDecEDG-129
95UppDecSE-184
95UppDecSEG-184
96Bow-87
96BowBes-76
96BowBesAR-76
96BowBesR-76
96ColCho-467
96ColChoGS-467
96ColChoSS-467
96Don-372
96DonPreP-372
96EmoXL-4
96Fla-5
96Fle-9
96FleOri-6
96FleTif-9
96Lea-208
96LeaPrePB-208
96LeaPrePG-208
96LeaPrePS-208
96Pac-235
96Sco-86
96SP-31
96Stu-117
96StuPrePB-117
96StuPrePG-117
96StuPrePS-117
96Ult-304
96UltGolM-304
96UppDec-277
97ColCho-277
97Don-303
97DonLim-108
97DonLim-160
97DonLimLE-108
97DonLimLE-160
97DonPreP-303
97DonPrePGold-303
97DonTea-41
97DonTeaSPE-41
97Fle-7
97FleTif-7
97Pac-23
97PacLigB-23
97PacSil-23
97Sco-205
97ScoOri-12
97ScoOriPl-12
97ScoOriPr-12
97ScoPreS-205
97ScoShoS-205
97ScoShoSAP-205
97Top-438
97Ult-4
97UltGolME-4
97UltPlaME-4

Hammonds, Reggie
86NasPirP-11

Hammons, Matthew
96RocCubTI-10

Hamner, Granny
47PM1StaP1-76
49EurSta-135
49PhiBul-22
49PhiLumPB-4
50Bow-204
51BerRos-B7
51Bow-148
51TopBluB-29
52Bow-35
52NatTeaL-13
52RedMan-NL7
52TipTop-13
52Top-221
53BowC-60
53RedMan-NL18
53Top-146
54Bow-47
54Top-24
55Bow-112
55RedMan-NL15
55RobGouS-18
55RobGouW-18
56Top-197
57Top-335
58Hir-20
58PhiJayP-6
58Top-268
59Top-436
60RawGloT-9
79TCM50-30
83PhiPosGPaM-4
83TopRep5-221
87Phi195T-5
91TopArc1-146
94TopArc1-24
94TopArc1G-24

Hamner, Ralph
49Bow-212

Hampton, Anthony
86OscAstP-10

Hampton, Ike (Isaac)
75SalLakCC-11
76SalLakCGC-12
76SSP-601
78AngFamF-16
78SSP270-196
78Top-503
91MetWIZ-158

Hampton, Lionel
95NegLeaL2-9

Hampton, Mark
90AubAstB-14
90AubAstP-3401
92GasRanC-5
92GasRanF-2247
93StoPorC-13
93StoPorF-740

Hampton, Mike
90HigSchPLS-20
91SanBerSC-6
91SanBerSP-1982
92Bow-638
92CalLeaACL-40
92ProFS7-145
92SanBerC-17
92SanBerSF-947
92UppDecML-252
93Bow-459
93ExcFS7-225
93FleFinE-270
93MarMot-24
93OPCPre-80
93StaClu-731
93StaCluFDI-731
93StaCluMari-22
93StaCluMOP-731
93TopTra-58T
93Ult-620
93UppDec-783
93UppDecGold-783
94AstMot-25
94BilMusF-3678
94BilMusSP-7
94Fin-407
94FinRef-407
94Pin-415
94PinArtP-415
94PinMusC-415
94StaClu-237
94StaClu-614
94StaCluDP-50
94StaCluDPFDI-50
94StaCluFDI-237
94StaCluFDI-614
94StaCluGR-237
94StaCluGR-614
94StaCluMOP-237
94StaCluMOP-614
95AstMot-22
95Bow-50
95Fle-461
95Top-133
96AstMot-10
96ColCho-158
96ColChoGS-158
96ColChoSS-158
96Don-202
96DonPreP-202
96EmoXL-199
96Fle-408
96FleTif-408
96Lea-83
96LeaPrePB-83
96LeaPrePG-83
96LeaPrePS-83
96LeaSigA-92
96LeaSigAG-92
96LeaSigAS-92
96StaClu-91
96StaClu-239
96StaCluMOP-91
96StaCluMOP-239
96Ult-209
96UltGolP-209
96UppDec-82
97Cir-387
97CirRav-387
97ColCho-121
97Don-244
97DonPreP-244
97DonPrePGold-244
97Fin-64
97FinRef-64
97Fle-346
97FleTif-346
97PacPriGotD-GD151
97StaClu-352
97StaCluMOP-352
97Top-366
97UppDec-362

Hampton, Ray
82EvaTriT-21

Hampton, Robbie
96StCatSB-11

Hampton, Scott
89TenTecGE-10

Hampton, Tony
85OscAstTI-23

Hamric, Bert (Odbert)
55Top-199
58Top-336
91OriCro-175
95TopArcBD-107

Hamric, Rusty
80PenPilBT-18
80PenPilCT-24
81ReaPhiT-14
82OklCit8T-10
84PorBeaC-216

Hamrick, Ray
47RemBre-17
47SmiClo-5
48SigOil-10
48SmiClo-7
49RemBre-9
50RemBre-10

Hamrick, Stephen
78SanJosMMC-15

Hamza, Tony
86GenCubP-8
86PeoChiP-10

Hance, Bill
83TriTriT-13
84TulDriTI-28

Hancken, Buddy (Morris)
67Ast-13

Hancock, Andy
80AshTouT-5

Hancock, Brian
92UppDecML-188
93El PasDF-2944
94StoPorC-9
94StoPorF-1687

Hancock, Chris
89CliGiaP-890
89EveGiaS-11
90Bes-113
90CliGiaB-8
90CliGiaP-2543
90CliGiaUTI-U11
90MidLeaASGS-34
90ProAaA-119
92SanJosGC-19
93ShrCapF-2753
93StaCluG-16
94ShrCapF-1599

Hancock, Garry
79RedSoxTI-3
79Top-702
81Fle-229
82Don-608
82Fle-295
82RedSoxC-8
82Top-322
84A'sMot-16
84Fle-445
84Nes792-197
84Top-197
84TopTif-197

Hancock, Jeff
89WatIndS-9

Hancock, Lee
87BelMarL-14
89SanBerSB-16
89SanBerSCLC-71
90Bes-32
90WilBilB-1
90WilBilP-1054
90WilBilS-9
91CarMudLD-109
91CarMudP-1082
91LinDriAA-109
92CarMudF-1176
92CarMudS-135
93CarMudF-2047
93CarMudTI-19
93ClaFS7-137
94BufBisF-1830
96LeaSigEA-70

Hancock, Michael
92StoPorC-14
92StoPorF-31

Hancock, Ryan
94Bow-619
94LakElsSC-8
94LakElsSF-1657
94MidAngOHP-7
94Top-760
94TopGol-760
94TopSpa-760
94UppDec-523
94UppDecED-523
95Bow-82
95MidAngOHP-15
95MidAngTI-13
96VanCanB-16
97DonPreP-158
97DonPrePGold-158
97Lea-186
97LeaFraM-186
97LeaFraMDC-186
97Pin-158
97PinArtP-158
97PinMusC-158

Hand, James
82TucTorT-23

Hand, Rich
71MLBOffS-369
71OPC-24
71Top-24
72OPC-317
72Top-317
73OPC-398
73Top-398
74OPC-571
74Top-571
93RanKee-14

Handford, Charles
12ImpTobC-21

Handler, Marve
80ElmPioRST-34

Handley, Gene
40SolHug-9
49BowPCL-34
49W72HolS-6
50W720HolS-11
52MotCoo-7
53MotCoo-21

Handley, Jim
76AppFoxT-7

Handley, Lee E.
40PlaBal-221
41DouPlaR-33
49BowPCL-28
49W725AngTI-11
84TCMPla1-42
93ConTSN-744

Hands, Bill (William Alfred)
66Top-392
67CubProPS-5
67OPC-16
67Top-16
68Top-279
68TopVen-279
69CubJewT-5
69MLBOffS-120
69OPC-115
69Top-115
69TopFou-10
69TopSta-13
69TopTeaP-4
70DayDaiNM-24
70MLBOffS-16
70OPC-405
70Top-405
71MLBOffS-31
71OPC-670
71Top-670
71TopTat-63
72CubTeal-3
72MilBra-127
72OPC-335
72Top-335
73OPC-555
73Top-555
74OPC-271
74Top-271
75OPC-412
75Top-412
76OPC-509
76SSP-253
76Top-509
78TwiFri-32
93RanKee-169

Handy, Russell
94BurBeeF-1076
94VerExpC-14
94VerExpF-3907

Hanebrink, Harry
58Top-454
59Top-322A
59Top-322B

Hanel, Marcus
90WelPirP-17
91AugPirC-13
91AugPirP-807
92ClaFS7-242
92SalBucC-14
92SalBucF-67
93SalBucC-12
93SalBucF-435
94SalBucC-11
94SalBucF-2326
95CarMudF-160
96CarMudB-14

Haney, Chris
90JamExpP-18
91Bow-443
91Cla/Bes-23
91DonRoo-44
91ExpPos-9
91HarSenLD-255
91HarSenP-618
91LinDriAA-255
91UppDecFE-23F
92Cla1-T41
92ClaGam-133
92Don-291
92ExpDonD-2A
92ExpPos-16
92Fle-483
92OPC-626
92OPCPre-186
92Pin-521
92ProFS7-258
92Sco-873
92Sco100RS-15
92StaClu-449
92Top-626
92TopDeb91-70
92TopGol-626
92TopGolW-626
92TopMic-626
92Ult-519
92UppDec-662
93ClaFS7-200
93Don-279
93FleFinE-219
93Lea-538

93OmaRoyF-1676
93Pin-194
93RoyPol-12
93Top-581
93TopGol-581
93TopInaM-581
93TopMic-581
94ColC-398
94ColChoGS-398
94ColChoSS-398
94Don-251
94Fle-159
94Pac-286
94Sco-279
94ScoGolR-279
94StaClu-154
94StaCluFDI-154
94StaCluGR-154
94StaCluMOP-154
94Top-9
94TopGol-9
94TopSpa-9
94Ult-65
95Top-382
96ColCho-573
96ColChoGS-573
96ColChoSS-573
96Don-212
96DonPreP-212
96FleUpd-U40
96FleUpdTC-U40
96LeaSigA-93
96LeaSigAG-93
96LeaSigAS-93
96RoyPol-11
96Ult-356
96UltGolM-356
96UppDec-349
97ColCho-357
97Fle-114
97FleTif-114
97RoyPol-9
Haney, Fred G.
26Exh-66
27Exh-34
29ExhFou-16
47SigOil-8
49W72HolS-7
52MotCoo-13
54Top-75
56BraBilaBP-11
57BraSpiaS4-10
58JayPubA-8
58Top-475
59Top-551
78AtlCon-9
83ASASpa-6
86BraGreT-12
87ConSer2-16
91TopArc1-316
93ConTSN-856
94TopArc1-75
94TopArc1G-75
Haney, Joe
86BelBreP-9
Haney, Larry (Wallace Larry)
67CokCapO-17
67Top-507
68CokCapO-17
68OPC-42
68Top-42
68TopVen-42
69OPC-209
69PilPos-28
69Top-209
69TopFou-7
70Top-648
73OPC-563
73Top-563
75OPC-626
75Top-626
76OPC-446
76SSP-502
76Top-446
77Top-12
78TCM60I-228
78Top-391
81Ori6F-16
82BrePol-NNO
83BrePol-NNO
83Pil69G-39
85BrePol-NNO
86BrePol-12
87BrePol-NNO
88BrePol-NNO
89BrePol-NNO
90BreMilB-32
90BrePol-NNO
91BreMilB-32
91BrePol-NNO
91OriCro-176
92BreCarT-xx
94BreMilB-35
Haney, Todd
87BelMarTI-11
88WauTimGS-14
89SanBerSB-25
89SanBerSCLC-81
89WilBilS-8
90CalCanC-18
90CalCanP-657
90CMC-445
90ProAAAF-122
90TriAllGP-AAA43
91IndIndLD-185
91IndIndP-468
91LinDriAAA-185
92ProFS7-257
93Don-342
93OttLynF-2442
93TriAAAGF-17
94ClaGolF-138
94IowCubF-1282
95IowCubTI-15
96LeaSigA-94
96LeaSigAG-94
96LeaSigAS-94
Hanford, Charles
09ColChiE-125
11T205-190
12ColRedB-125
12ColTinT-125
Hanger, Charlie
96OklCit8B-27
Hanggie, Dan
81NasSouTI-5
84ChaLooT-3
85OrlTwiT-6
Hanifin, Pat
90DodTar-970
Hanisch, Ron
89BelBreIS-12
90AshTouC-29
90StoPorB-23
90StoPorCLC-202
93AshTouC-28
Hanker, Fred
88MadMusP-14
Hankins, Jay
77FriOneYW-25
Hankins, Mike
90OneYanP-3385
91CarLeaAP-CAR31
91Cla/Bes-143
91PriWilCC-5
91PriWilCP-1434
92Ft.LauYF-2620
92PriWilCC-4
93AlbYanF-2171
Hankinson, Frank
87BucN28-60
87FouBasHN-5
87OldJudN-230A
87OldJudN-230B
88GandBCGCE-19
Hanks, Chris
89ElmPioP-4
89WinHavRSS-9
90LynRedSTI-12
Hanlan, Ed
87AllandGN-25
88KimN18-17
Hanlan, Oarsman
88GooN16-23
Hanley, John
78AppFoxT-11
79KnoKnoST-15
81AppFoxT-17
Hanlin, Rich
89BelMarL-26
Hanlon, Larry (Lawrence)
92ChaRanC-12
92ChaRanF-2232
92StaCluD-76
93OklCit8F-1632
94ChaRivC-9
94ChaRivF-2683
Hanlon, Ned (Edward J.)
03BreE10-64
06FanCraNL-20
11SpoLifCW-155
75FlePio-9
76SSP188WS-11
80PerHaloFP-227
87BucN28-31
87OldJudN-231
87ScrDC-14
88WG1CarG-22
90DodTar-314
Hanna, Dave
83IdaFalAT-5
Hanna, Preston
76VenLeaS-7
79Top-296
80Top-489
81BraPol-49
81Don-523
81Fle-264
81Top-594
82BraBurKL-9
82BraPol-49
82Fle-435
83Top-127
Hannah, Joe
61MapLeaBH-7
Hannah, Mike
75OklCit8TI-18
75SanAntBT-9
76WilTomT-8
Hannah, Neal
96YakBeaTI-27
Hannahs, Gerry (Gerald)
77ExpPos-17
79AlbDukT-9
80AlbDukT-25
81TolMudHT-5
90DodTar-315
Hannahs, Mitch
88CapCodPPaLP-45
89BelBreIS-13
90ElPasDGS-16
91ElPasDLD-184
91ElPasDP-2755
91LinDriAA-184
Hannan, Jim
63Top-121
64Top-261
64TopVen-261
65Top-394
66Top-479
67CokCapS-14
67Top-291
69OPC-106
69SenTeal-8
69Top-106
69TopSta-236
69TopTeaP-23
70Top-697
71OPC-229
71Top-229
72MilBra-128
94BreMilB-36
Hanneman, Blair
92EveGiaC-5
93EveGiaC-14
93EveGiaF-3765
Hannifan, John J.
09T206-428
Hannon, John
76BurBeeT-17
77HolMilT-12
Hannon, Phil
87GenCubP-22
87WinSpiP-6
88PeoChiTI-12
89WinSpiS-9
90ChaKniTI-2
90TopTVCu-47
91GenCubC-29
91GenCubP-4235
92HunCubC-28
93HunCubC-29
93HunCubF-3255
94HigDesMC-27
94HigDesMF-2804
Hanrahan, William
87OldJudN-232
Hansel, Damon
87MacPirP-18
Hansell, Greg
90WinHavRSS-10
91BakDodCLC-17
91CalLeLA-14
92AlbDukF-714
92Bow-314
92ClaFS7-344
92SanAntMS-566
92SkyAA F-246
92UppDecML-150
93AlbDukF-1454
93Bow-478
94AlbDukF-838
95Bow-72
95DodMot-26
95DodPol-8
95FleUpd-172
95SigRoo-23
95SigRooSig-23
95Top-429
95UppDec-317
95UppDecED-317
95UppDecEDG-317
Hanselman, Carl
88PocGiaP-2099
89CliGiaP-903
89EveGiaS-12
90CliGiaB-14
90CliGiaP-2540
91CalLeLA-45
91SanJosGC-16
91SanJosGP-4
92SanJosGC-18
93Bow-84
93ShrCapF-2754
95ReaPhiTI-23
Hansen, Andy
49EurSta-106
52Top-74
53BowBW-64
83TopRep5-74
Hansen, Bob
75IntLeaASB-7
75PacCoaLAB-7
75OPC-508
75SacSolC-1
75Top-508
76SpoIndC-17
82BrePol-NNO
94BreMilB-37
Hansen, Brent
93ForLauRSC-1
93ForLauRSFP-1590
94SarRedSC-11
94SarRedSF-1944
95TreThuTI-9
Hansen, Darel
83IdaFalAT-6
84MadMusP-15
85MadMusP-12
85MadMusT-15
86ModA'sC-8
86ModA'sP-10
Hansen, Dave
87BakDodP-21
88FloStaLAS-7
88VerBeaDS-9
89SanAntMB-17
90AlbDukC-17
90AlbDukP-350
90AlbDukT-9
90Bow-93
90BowTif-93
90CMC-419
90Fle-642
90FleCan-642
90FleUpd-21
90ProAAAF-71
90TriAllGP-AAA45
91AlbDukLD-7
91AlbDukP-1145
91Cla2-T35
91ClaGam-155
91Don-45
91Fle-203
91LinDriAAA-7
91TopDeb90-63
91UppDec-4
92Cla2-T23
92ClaGam-103
92DodMot-17
92DodPol-15
92DodSmo-9692
92Don-506
92Lea-389
92ProFS7-238
92Sco-754
92StaClu-36
92Ult-505
93DodMot-24
93DodPol-9
93Don-244
93Fle-449
93PacSpa-146
93Pin-209
93RemUltK-5
93StaClu-263
93StaCluFDI-263
93StaCluMOP-263
93Top-469
93TopGol-469
93TopInaM-469
93TopMic-469
93UppDec-537
93UppDecGold-537
94ColC-416
94ColChoGS-416
94ColChoSS-416
94DodMot-22
94DodPol-11
94Don-616
94Fle-511
94Pac-309
94PanSti-199
94Sco-259
94ScoGolR-259
94Sel-219
94StaClu-587
94StaCluFDI-587
94StaCluGR-587
94StaCluMOP-587
94Top-697
94TopGol-697
94TopSpa-697
95DodMot-10
95DodPol-9
95FleUpd-173
95Sco-169
95ScoGolR-169
95ScoPlaTS-169
95Top-218
96DodMot-15
96DodPol-17
96Fle-435
96FleTif-435
96LeaSigEA-71
Hansen, Elston
92Bow-548
92ClaFS7-148
92ForLauYC-13
92ForLauYTI-16
92GreHorF-787
93GreHorC-9
93GreHorF-891
93OneYanC-8
93OneYanF-3509
94SanBerSC-5
94SanBerSF-2767
95TamYanYI-9
Hansen, Guy
83ButCopKT-31
89MemChiB-26
89MemChiP-1192
89MemChiS-24
90MemChiB-25
90MemChiP-1026
90MemChiS-26
91LinDriAAA-350
91OmaRoyP-1050
92RoyPol-27
93RoyPol-27
Hansen, Jed
94SigRooBS-3
95MidLeaA-22
95SprSulTI-11
96Bow-300
96Exc-60
96TexLeaAB-26
96WicWraB-18
97Top-203
Hansen, Jon
82ElPasDT-11
Hansen, Mike
87LakTigP-16
88FloStaLAS-39
88LakTigS-13
89LonTigP-1376
Hansen, Ray
86GreHorP-11
87GreHorP-17

Hansen, Roger
81ChaRoyT-6
82ChaRoyT-2
84MemChiT-18
86OmaRoyP-9
86OmaRoyT-5
87ChaLooB-14
88CalCanC-21
88CalCanP-790
89CalCanC-15
89CalCanP-530
92MarMot-27
96EveAquB-28
Hansen, Ron
83TriTriT-17
Hansen, Ron Lavern
47PM1StaP1-77
59Top-444
60OriJayP-4
60Top-127
60TopVen-127
61Pos-72A
61Pos-72B
61SevElev-10
61Top-240
61TopStal-102
62Jel-30
62Pos-30A
62Pos-30B
62PosCan-30
62SalPlaC-89
62ShiPlaC-89
62Top-245
62TopStal-6
63BasMagM-34
63Fle-2
63Jel-60
63Pos-60
63Top-88
63WhiSoxJP-3
63WhiSoxTS-8
64Top-384
64TopCoi-41
64WhiSoxTS-10
65MacSta-4
65OPC-146
65Top-146
65WhiSoxJP-1
66Top-261
66TopVen-261
66WhiSoxTI-5
67CokCapWS-10
67DexPre-88
67OPC-9
67Top-9
67TopVen-233
68SenTeal-5
68Top-411
69MilBra-102
69Top-566
70MLBOffS-184
70OPC-217
70Top-217
71MLBOffS-489
71OPC-419
71Top-419
72MilBra-129
72Top-763
78TCM60I-142
83BrePol-NNO
83FraBroR-7
85ExpPos-9
86ExpProPa-28
87ExpPos-9
87SpoRea-11
89ExpPos-12
91OriCro-177
92BreCarT-xx
92YanWIZ7-66
Hansen, Snipe (Roy)
34DiaMatCSB-85
93ConTSN-953
Hansen, Terrel
87JamExpP-2547
89RocExpLC-11
90Bes-169
90CMC-690
90JacExpB-9
90JacExpP-1384
90ProAaA-54
91LinDriAAA-556
91TidTidLD-556
91TidTidP-2522
92SkyAAAF-251
92StaClu-878
92StaCluECN-878
92TidTidF-905
92TidTidS-557
93ClaFS7-277
93OttLynF-2445
94JacSunF-1425
95JacSunTI-16
96JacSunB-17
Hansen, Todd
86MacPirP-12
88ChaRaiP-1206
89RivRedWB-6
89RivRedWCLC-22
89RivRedWP-1413
90WicWraRD-7
Hanson, Craig
91SpoIndC-15
91SpoIndP-3945
92ChaRaiF-118
93WatDiaC-17
93WatDiaF-1762
94RanCucQC-14
94RanCucQF-1631
95MemChiTI-19
96PorCitRB-15
Hanson, Erik
87ChaLooB-10
88CalCanP-786
89BlaYNPRWL-191
89Bow-206
89BowTif-206
89ChaLooLITI-11
89ClaTraO-145
89Don-32
89DonBasB-320
89DonRoo-49
89Fle-549
89FleGlo-549
89MarMot-16
89TopTra-45T
89TopTraT-45T
89UppDec-766
90Bow-469
90BowTif-469
90ClaYel-T78
90Don-345
90DonBesA-68
90Fle-514
90FleCan-514
90Lea-430
90MarMot-8
90OPC-118
90PubSti-434
90Sco-530
90Sco100RS-85
90ScoYouS2-18
90Top-118
90TopBig-289
90TopTif-118
90UppDec-235
91Bow-260
91Cla2-T22
91ClaGam-147
91Don-550
91Fle-451
91Lea-142
91MarCouH-24
91OPC-655
91PanCanT1-79
91PanFreS-235
91PanSti-186
91Sco-486
91Sco-688
91SevCoi-NW6
91StaClu-9
91Stu-114
91Top-655
91TopDesS-655
91TopMic-655
91TopTif-655
91Ult-337
91UppDec-551
92Bow-583
92Don-138
92Fle-280
92Lea-23
92MarMot-7
92OPC-71
92Pin-188
92Sco-8
92StaClu-37
92Stu-233
92Top-71
92TopGol-71
92TopGolW-71
92TopKid-124
92TopMic-71
92TriPla-20
92Ult-124
92UppDec-572
93Don-317
93Fin-150
93FinRef-150
93Fla-271
93Fle-308
93Lea-354
93MarMot-12
93OPC-115
93PacSpa-287
93Pin-152
93Sco-136
93SP-131
93StaClu-423
93StaCluFDI-423
93StaCluMari-17
93StaCluMOP-423
93Top-342
93TopGol-342
93TopInaM-342
93TopMic-342
93Ult-621
93UppDec-338
93UppDecGold-338
94ColC-124
94ColC-597
94ColChoGS-124
94ColChoGS-597
94ColChoSS-124
94ColChoSS-597
94Don-211
94ExtBas-232
94Fin-395
94FinRef-395
94Fle-287
94FleUpd-119
94Lea-426
94OPC-243
94Pin-472
94PinArtP-472
94PinMusC-472
94RedKah-13
94RedKah-30
94Sco-387
94ScoGolR-387
94ScoRoo-RT7
94ScoRooGR-RT7
94Sel-290
94StaClu-623
94StaCluFDI-623
94StaCluGR-623
94StaCluMOP-623
94Top-529
94TopGol-529
94TopSpa-529
94TopTra-73T
94Ult-472
94UppDec-508
94UppDecED-508
95DonTopotO-21
95Emo-13
95Fle-436
95Pac-106
95StaClu-95
95StaCluFDI-95
95StaCluMOP-95
95StaCluSTWS-95
95Top-322
95TopTra-78T
95UppDec-483T
96BluJayOH-15
96ColCho-65
96ColCho-790
96ColChoGS-65
96ColChoSS-65
96Don-175
96DonPreP-175
96EmoXL-133
96Fla-186
96Fle-28
96FleTif-28
96FleUpd-U96
96FleUpdTC-U96
96LeaSigA-95
96LeaSigAG-95
96LeaSigAS-95
96MetUni-121
96MetUniP-121
96Pac-247
96Pin-311
96PinFoil-311
96Sco-318
96ScoDugC-B43
96ScoDugCAP-B43
96SP-184
96StaClu-394
96StaCluEPB-394
96StaCluEPG-394
96StaCluEPS-394
96StaCluMOP-394
96Top-383
96Ult-431
96UltGolM-431
96UppDec-510U
97BluJayS-14
97ColCho-501
97Sco-467
97ScoHobR-467
97ScoResC-467
97ScoShoS-467
97ScoShoSAP-467
97Top-38
Hanson, Kris
93WatIndC-12
93WatIndF-3557
94ColRedF-438
95KinIndTI-14
96KenIndB-11
Hanson, R.C.
40WheM4-9
41WheM5-14
Hanson, Roy
35DiaMatCS3T1-68
Hanyuda, Tad
88SanJosGCLC-119
88SanJosGP-128
Hanyzewski, Ed
43CubTeal-10
44CubTeal-11
Hara, Hidefumi
92SalSpuC-18
92SalSpuF-3768
Hara, Shunsuke
96HonShaHWB-2
Haraguchi, Ted
87SanJosBP-10
Hard, Shelby
90EveGiaB-23
Hardamon, Derrick
86GenCubP-9
Hardaway, Anfernee
93StaCluMO-32
Harden, Curry
88CapCodPPaLP-67
Harden, Jon
88MisStaB-10
89MisStaB-17
90MisStaB-16
91MisStaB-21
92MisStaB-16
92SalLakTSP-20
Harden, Nat
92MisStaB-17
93MisStaB-17
Harden, Ty
85BurRanT-21
86DayBealP-10
Harder, Mel
32OrbPinNP-29
32OrbPinUP-30
33TatOrb-30
34DiaMatCSB-86
34BatR31-134
34Gou-66
35DiaMatCS3T1-69
35ExhFou-11
35GouPuzR-8I
35GouPuzR-9I
36ExhFou-11
36GouWidPPR-A46
36GouWidPPR-C15
36NatChiFPR-40
36R31PasP-13
36R31Pre-G10
36R31Pre-L5
36SandSW-29
41DouPlaR-133
47IndTeal-13
47IndVanPP-12
48IndTeal-14
49IndTeal-29
55IndGolS-28
59Ind-6
60Top-460
76GrePlaG-27
77GalGloG-81
79DiaGre-287
81DiaStaCD-113
82OhiHaloF-37
83ConMar-23
83DiaClaS2-91
88ConAmeA-14
89PacLegI-205
89SweBasG-41
93UppDecS-30
94ConTSN-1079
94ConTSNB-1079
Hardge, Michael
92RocExpC-6
92RocExpF-2124
93WesPalBEC-8
93WesPalBEF-1347
94HarSenF-2098
95PawRedSDD-11
95PawRedTI-10
95TreThuTI-29
Hardgrave, Eric
86BeaGolGP-13
87ElPasDP-7
88GleFalTP-915
Hardgrove, Tom
88CapCodPPaLP-132
89MarPhiS-14
89Sta-144
90Bes-38
90SpaPhiB-1
90SpaPhiP-2498
90SpaPhiS-12
Hardin, Jim
68Top-222
68TopVen-222
69MilBra-103
69Top-532
69Top-610
69TopSta-124
70Top-656
71MLBOffS-298
71OPC-491
71Top-491
72MilBra-130
72OPC-287
72Top-287
73OPC-124
73Top-124
91OriCro-178
92YanWIZ7-67
Harding, Greg
88St.CatBJP-2029
89MyrBeaBJP-1469
Harding, Warren G.
94UppDecTAE-36
Hardtke, Jason
91Cla/Bes-7
91ColIndC-25
91ColIndP-1492
92MidLeaATI-16
92ProFS7-59
92UppDecML-98
92WatDiaC-21
92WatDiaF-2150
93RanCucQC-15
93RanCucQF-840
94ClaGolF-141
94ExcFS7-282
94Top-527
94TopGol-527
94TopSpa-527
94WicWraF-198
95BinMetTI-20
96BinBeeB-12
96NorTidB-17
Hardwick, Anthony
86BakDodP-12
Hardwick, Bill
94ClaGolF-175
Hardwick, Bubba
93StoPorC-14
93StoPorF-741
Hardwick, Joe
92BoiHawC-3
92BoiHawF-3643
93CedRapKC-8
93CedRapKF-1751
Hardwick, Willie
82AmaGolST-19
83BeaGolGT-18

84ArkTraT-15
Hardy, Alex
12ImpTobC-78
Hardy, Bryan
96BurIndB-20
Hardy, Carlton
91MarPhiC-10
91MarPhiP-3461
Hardy, Carroll
58Top-446
59Ind-7
59Top-168
59TopVen-168
60Top-341
61Top-257
62SalPlaC-220
62ShiPlaC-220
62Top-101
62TopVen-101
63Col45"P-7
63Top-468
Hardy, Hayland
93HelBreF-4109
93HelBreSP-16
Hardy, Jack
82GleFalWST-18
86BirBarTI-16
87BirBarB-18
87HawIsIP-3
88VanCanC-10
88VanCanP-755
89VanCanC-5
89VanCanP-586
90CMC-151
90OklCit8C-1
90OklCit8P-425
90ProAAAF-671
90TopDeb89-51
Hardy, Larry (Howard L.)
74PadDea-12
75HawIsIC-15
75OPC-112
75Top-112
76SSP-120
78ChaChaT-8
79ChaChaT-15
80KnoBluJT-18
80UtiBluJT-1
82KnoBluJT-21
84SyrChiT-2
86KnoBluJP-9
87PhoFirP-11
90CMC-688
90PhoFirC-26
90PhoFirP-29
90ProAAAF-55
91LinDriAAA-400
91PhoFirP-85
92TexLon-20
95RanCra-14
96RanMot-28
Hardy, Mark
86JamExpP-12
Hare, Shawn
89LakTigS-8
89Sta-156
90CMC-391
90ProAAAF-392
90TolMudHC-14
90TolMudHP-162
91LinDriAAA-586
91TolMudHLD-586
91TolMudHP-1944
92DonRoo-48
92FleUpd-23
92Pin-598
92Sco-828
92SkyAAAF-263
92StaClu-465
92TolMudHS-587
92TopDeb91-71
92Ult-363
93Don-305
93TolMudHF-1663
93Top-491
93TopGol-491
93TopInaM-491
93TopMic-491
94SpoRoo-47
94SpoRooAP-47
94TolMudHF-1037
95RanCra-15
96LouRedB-20
Harer, Wayne
80ColCliT-4
81ColCliP-22
81ColCliT-19
82ColCliP-22
82ColCliT-3
Harford, Bill
90PeoChiTI-34
Hargan, Steve
66Top-508
67Kah-14
67Top-233
67Top-440
67TopVen-262
68Kah-B13
68OPC-35
68Top-35
68TopActS-7A
68TopGamI-15
68TopVen-35
69Top-348
70Ind-5
70OPC-136
70Top-136
71Ind-5
71MLBOffS-370
71OPC-375
71Top-375
71TopCoi-110
72MilBra-131
72Top-615
75OPC-362
75Top-362
76Kel-1
76OPC-463
76SSP-254
76Top-463
77OPC-247
77Top-37
93RanKee-170
Hargesheimer, Al
81Fle-457
81PhoGiaVNB-13
81Top-502
83IowCubT-4
84OmaRoyT-4
85OmaRoyT-26
86OmaRoyT-21
87OmaRoyP-13
88OmaRoyC-6
88OmaRoyP-1517
82PhoGiaVNB-27
Hargis, Dan
89RocExpLC-12
90JamExpP-34
91RocExpP-2050
Hargis, Gary
76ShrCapT-1
77ColCliT-6
78ColCliT-9
79PorBeaT-13
80PorBeaT-15
81BufBisT-15
Hargis, Steve
91RocExpC-29
Hargrave, Bubbles (Eugene F.)
20WalMaiW-21
21Nei-60
22E120-173
22W573-55
28Exh-14
28W502-33
28Yue-33
76ISCHooHA-21
81ConTSN-96
91ConTSN-245
94ConTSN-1179
94ConTSNB-1179
Hargrave, Pinky (William M.)
26Exh-113
27Exh-57
31SenTealPW-13
33Gou-172
76ISCHooHA-21
81ConTSN-97
94ConTSN-1179
94ConTSNB-1179
94ConTSNB-1180
Hargraves, Charles R.
27YorCarE-33
28Exh-7
29ExhFou-14
Hargreaves, Charlie
79DiaGre-77
90DodTar-316
Hargrove, Mike (Dudley M.)
75Hos-106
75OPC-106
75Top-106
76Hos-88
76Kel-51A
76Kel-51B
76OPC-485
76SSP-263
76Top-485
77BurCheD-24
77Hos-18
77Kel-30
77MSADis-27
77OPC-35
77PepGloD-5
77RCColC-29
77Top-275
77TopCloS-20
78Hos-41
78Kel-56
78OPC-176
78RanBurK-11
78RCColC-32
78SSP270-82
78Top-172
79Hos-148
79OPC-311
79Top-591
80OPC-162
80Top-308
81AllGamPI-5
81Don-78
81Fle-387
81Kel-66
81MSAMinD-15
81OPC-74
81Top-74
81TopScr-32
81TopSti-68
82Don-389
82Dra-16
82Fle-368
82FleSta-198
82Ind-17
82IndTeal-16
82IndWhe-24
82OPC-310
82Top-310
82Top-559
82TopSti-180
83Don-450
83Fle-409
83FleSta-75
83FleSti-242
83IndPos-17
83IndWhe-16
83OPC-37
83Top-660
83TopSti-56
84Don-495
84Fle-543
84FunFooP-101
84Ind-16
84IndWhe-21
84Nes792-546
84Nes792-764
84OPC-79
84SevCoi-C10
84Top-546
84Top-764
84TopSti-260
84TopTif-546
84TopTif-764
85Don-398
85Fle-450
85GenMilS-18
85Ind-17
85IndPol-21
85OPC-252
85ThoMcAD-12
85Top-425
85TopSti-248
85TopTif-425
86Don-590
86Fle-588
86Lea-228
86RanGreT-5
86Top-136
86TopTif-136
88EasLeaAP-52
88WilBilP-1306
89ColSprSSC-10
89ColSprSSP-246
90IndTeal-15
91IndFanC-30
91TopTra-52T
91TopTraT-52T
92IndFanC-10
92OPC-609
92Top-609
92TopGol-609
92TopGolW-609
92TopMic-609
93IndWUA-10
93RanKee-171
93Top-505
93TopGol-505
93TopInaM-505
93TopMic-505
94RanAllP-3
Harigen, Charlie
81TacTigT-29
Harikkala, Tim
92BelMarC-9
92BelMarF-1437
93BelMarF-3203
94AppFoxC-10
94AppFoxF-1048
94MidLeaAF-MDW2
95Exc-117
95TacRaiTI-8
96TacRaiB-13
Harimoto, Isao
79TCMJapPB-61
Harker, Paul
92PenPilC-30
95PorCitRTI-13
96PorCitRB-4
Harkey, Mike
88BasAmeAAB-2
88EasLeaAP-26
88PeoChiTI-35
88PitCubP-1377
88TriAAC-15
89Bow-286
89BowTif-286
89Don-43
89Fle-427
89FleGlo-427
89IowCubC-5
89IowCubP-1704
89PanSti-48
89Sco-624
89ScoHot1R-48
89ScoYouS2-31
89Spo-132
89Top-742
89TopTif-742
89UppDec-14
90Bow-28
90BowTif-28
90ClaYel-T47
90CubMar-10
90Don-522
90DonRoo-22
90Fle-33
90FleCan-33
90Lea-309
90PeoChiTI-20
90TopTra-36T
90TopTraT-36T
90TopTVCu-9
90UppDec-107
91Bow-417
91ClaGam-22
91CubMar-22
91CubVinL-13
91Don-447
91Fle-423
91Lea-90
91OPC-376
91PanFreS-51
91PanSti-46
91Sco-322
91Sco100RS-63
91StaClu-197
91Top-376
91TopDesS-376
91TopMic-376
91TopRoo-11
91TopTif-376
91ToyRoo-10
91Ult-62
91UppDec-475
92Don-241
92Fle-382
92OPC-98
92Pin-197
92Sco-67
92StaClu-501
92Top-98
92TopGol-98
92TopGolW-98
92TopMic-98
92UppDec-218
93CubMar-9
93Don-450
93Fle-378
93Lea-533
93OPC-110
93Pin-395
93Sco-111
93Sel-397
93StaClu-656
93StaCluCu-14
93StaCluFDI-656
93StaCluMOP-656
93Top-657
93TopGol-657
93TopInaM-657
93TopMic-657
93Ult-314
93UppDec-610
93UppDecGold-610
94ColC-417
94ColChoGS-417
94ColChoSS-417
94Don-121
94Fin-259
94FinRef-259
94Fla-154
94Fle-385
94FleUpd-124
94Lea-276
94Pac-100
94Pin-171
94PinArtP-171
94PinMusC-171
94RocPol-11
94Sco-96
94ScoGolR-96
94ScoRoo-RT68
94ScoRooGR-RT68
94SpoRoo-13
94SpoRooAP-13
94StaClu-41
94StaCluFDI-41
94StaCluGR-41
94StaCluMOP-41
94StaCluT-95
94StaCluTFDI-95
94Top-272
94TopGol-272
94TopSpa-272
94Ult-161
94UppDec-372
94UppDecED-372
95AthMot-23
95FleUpd-71
95Pin-343
95PinArtP-343
95PinMusC-343
96Fle-49
96FleTif-49
96Sco-434
Harkins, John
87OldJudN-234
Harkness, Don
77CocAstT-8
78DayBeaAT-9
Harkness, Tim (Thomas W.)
61UniOil-SP7
62Top-404
63Top-436
64MetJayP-5
64Top-57
64TopVen-57
90DodTar-317
91MetWIZ-159
Harkrider, Tim
93Tex-2
94Bow-201
94MidAngF-2445
94MidAngOHP-8
95MidAngOHP-16
95MidAngTI-14
96BesAutS-35

96Top-427
Harlan, Dan
88BasCitRS-13
Harley, Al
91AshTouP-575
91Cla/Bes-101
92BurAstC-23
92BurAstF-555
93OscAstC-13
93OscAstF-637
Harley, Quentin
95MemChiTI-3
Harley, Richard
03BreE10-65
Harlow, Larry
76SSP-397
77RocRedWM-13
78Top-543
79Top-314
80Top-68
81Fle-289
81LonBeaPT-25
81Top-121
82Fle-462
82Top-257
83LasVegSBHN-9
89TopSenL-103
91OriCro-179
91PacSenL-20
Harmes, Kris
90MedHatBJB-20
91DunBluJC-29
91DunBluJP-210
91St.CatBJC-4
91St.CatBJP-3397
92DunBluJC-9
92St.CatBJC-16
92St.CatBJF-3388
93HagSunC-12
93HagSunF-1881
93SouAtlLAGF-26
94ClaGolF-89
94DunBluJC-11
94DunBluJF-2559
95AusFut-32
95KnoSmoF-43
96KnoSmoB-15
Harmon, Brian
94GreFalDSP-9
95YakBeaTI-13
96SavSanB-5
Harmon, Chuck (Charles)
54Top-182
55Top-82
55TopDouH-55
56Top-308
57Top-299
58Top-48
94TopArc1-182
94TopArc1G-182
Harmon, Glen
43ParSpo-35
Harmon, Kevin
86SumBraP-8
87SumBraP-12
95RocRedWTI-48
Harmon, Larry
76BatTroTI-11
Harmon, Mark
92ColMetPI-38
Harmon, Merle
75BreBro-4
Harmon, Robert
09PC7HHB-19
09SpoNewSM-78
10DomDisP-52
10JuJuDE-20
10SweCapPP-147
11PloCanE-31
11SpoLifCW-156
11SpoLifM-269
11T205-71A
11T205-71B
12HasTriFT-12
12T207-76
14TexTomE-22
15SpoNewM-75
16FleBreD-37
16SpoNewM-76
Harmon, Terry
69Top-624
70OPC-486
70Top-486
71MLBOffS-179
71OPC-682
71PhiArcO-4
71Top-682
72OPC-377
72Top-377
72TopCloT-16
73OPC-166
73Top-166
74OPC-642
74Top-642
75OPC-399
75Top-399
76OPC-247
76Top-247
77Top-388
78PhiSSP-37
78SSP270-37
78Top-118
Harmon, Tommy
75TulOil7-22
76TulOilGP-3
82CubRedL-NNO
83MidCubT-2
92TexLon-21
Harmon, Wayne
83CedRapRF-6
83CedRapRT-28
Harms, Tom
87NewOriP-28
88HagSunS-8
89FreKeyS-9
Harnisch, Pete
88BasAmeAAB-11
88ChaKniTI-18
88RocRedWGCP-10
88SouLeaAJ-32
89Bow-4
89BowTif-4
89Don-44
89OriFreB-42
89RocRedWP-1649
89ScoRoo-110T
89UppDec-744
90Bow-247
90BowTif-247
90ClaBlu-44
90Don-596
90DonBesA-101
90Fle-177
90FleCan-177
90Lea-39
90OPC-324
90Sco-355
90Sco100RS-76
90ScoYouS2-19
90Top-324
90TopRoo-12
90TopTif-324
90ToyRoo-14
90UppDec-623
91AstMot-3
91Bow-555
91Don-181
91Fle-474
91FleUpd-89
91Lea-245
91OPC-179
91OriCro-180
91RedFolS-45
91Sco-492
91ScoRoo-36T
91StaClu-343
91StaCluMO-17
91Stu-177
91Top-179
91TopDesS-179
91TopMic-179
91TopTif-179
91TopTra-53T
91TopTraT-53T
91UltUpd-83
91UppDec-302
91UppDec-772
91USPlaCA-3S
92AstMot-3
92Bow-514
92Cla2-T9
92ClaGam-4
92Don-235
92Fle-435
92Hig5-40
92Lea-77
92OPC-765
92PanSti-159
92Pin-196
92PinTea2-67
92Sco-224
92Sco100S-12
92StaClu-391
92StaCluD-77
92Stu-36
92Top-765
92TopGol-765
92TopGolW-765
92TopMic-765
92TriPla-175
92Ult-204
92UppDec-635
92UppDecTMH-25
93AstMot-3
93Bow-448
93Don-272
93Fin-62
93FinRef-62
93Fla-64
93Fle-52
93Lea-51
93OPC-185
93PacSpa-124
93PanSti-168
93Pin-113
93Sco-395
93Sel-219
93SP-35
93StaClu-110
93StaCluAs-19
93StaCluFDI-110
93StaCluMOP-110
93Top-195
93TopComotH-21
93TopGol-195
93TopInaM-195
93TopMic-195
93TriPla-241
93Ult-42
93UppDec-97
93UppDecGold-97
94AstMot-9
94Bow-286
94ColC-534
94ColChoGS-534
94ColChoSS-534
94Don-113
94ExtBas-275
94Fin-120
94FinRef-120
94Fla-171
94Fle-492
94FleSmo'nH-4
94Lea-398
94OPC-73
94Pac-267
94Pin-45
94PinArtP-45
94PinMusC-45
94Sco-78
94ScoGolR-78
94Sel-284
94Spo-113
94StaClu-190
94StaCluFDI-190
94StaCluGR-190
94StaCluMOP-190
94Top-456
94TopGol-456
94TopSpa-456
94TriPla-28
94Ult-504
94UppDec-379
94UppDecED-379
94USPlaCA-7S
95Bow-379
95ColCho-322
95ColChoGS-322
95ColChoSS-322
95Don-119
95DonPreP-119
95DonTopotO-292
95Fin-317
95FinRef-317
95Fla-384
95Fle-462
95FleUpd-112
95Lea-302
95Pac-188
95Pin-121
95PinArtP-121
95PinMusC-121
95Sco-509
95ScoGolR-509
95ScoPlaTS-509
95Sel-151
95SelArtP-151
95StaClu-535
95StaCluMOP-535
95StaCluSTWS-535
95Top-48
95TopCyb-36
95TopTra-141T
95UppDec-361
95UppDecED-361
95UppDecEDG-361
96ColCho-624
96ColChoGS-624
96ColChoSS-624
96Don-346
96DonPreP-346
96FleUpd-U157
96FleUpdTC-U157
96LeaSigA-96
96LeaSigAG-96
96LeaSigAS-96
96MetKah-12
96Sco-456
96StaClu-320
96StaCluMOP-320
96Top-333
96UppDec-403
97ColCho-172
97Fle-396
97FleTif-396
97StaClu-68
97StaCluMOP-68
97Top-125
97Ult-397
97UltGolME-397
97UltPlaME-397
97UppDec-432
Harnisch, Ron
92AshTouC-30
Haro, Sam
84PriWilPT-22
85NasPirT-11
86HawIslP-11
87VanCanP-1607
Harp, Scott
96SpoIndB-13
Harper, Brian
78QuaCitAT-8
80ElPasDT-9
80VenLeaS-217
81SalLakCGT-15
84Don-142
84Nes792-144
84Top-144
84TopTif-144
85CarTeal-11
85Don-566
85Fle-466
85Top-332
85TopTif-332
86CarKASD-8
86CarTeal-15
86Don-547
86Fle-36
86NasSouTI-10
86Top-656
86TopTif-656
88FleUpd-42
88FleUpdG-42
88MarPhiS-16
88PorBeaC-11
88PorBeaP-651
89Bow-155
89BowTif-155
89Don-641
89Fle-114
89FleGlo-114
89Sco-408
89Top-472
89TopTif-472
89UppDec-379
90Don-355
90DonBesA-37
90El PasDAGTI-35
90Fle-377
90FleCan-377
90Lea-479
90OPC-47
90PanSti-116
90PubSti-329
90Sco-189
90Spo-121
90Top-47
90TopSti-290
90TopTif-47
90UppDec-391
91Bow-333
91Cla3-T35
91Don-22
91Don-398
91Don-582
91DonSupD-22
91Fle-613
91Lea-54
91OPC-554
91PanFreS-299
91PanSti-242
91Sco-312
91Sco100S-46
91StaClu-589
91Stu-86
91Top-554
91TopDesS-554
91TopMic-554
91TopTif-554
91Ult-188
91UppDec-212
92Bow-149
92Don-83
92Fle-204
92Lea-131
92OPC-217
92PanSti-114
92Pin-73
92Sco-215
92ScoFacI-B4
92StaClu-296
92Stu-204
92Top-217
92TopGol-217
92TopGolW-217
92TopMic-217
92TriPla-76
92Ult-91
92UppDec-527
93Bow-537
93ColAllG-21
93Don-547
93Fin-51
93FinRef-51
93Fla-235
93Fle-266
93FleAll-AL10
93Lea-186
93OPC-125
93PacSpa-520
93PanSti-124
93Pin-54
93Sco-72
93Sel-154
93SP-246
93StaClu-95
93StaCluFDI-95
93StaCluMOP-95
93Stu-27
93Top-389
93Top-408
93TOPBLAG-34
93TopGol-389
93TopGol-408
93TopInaM-389
93TopInaM-408
93TopMic-389
93TopMic-408
93TriPla-68
93TriPla-250
93Ult-582
93UppDec-110
93UppDecGold-110
94Bow-645
94BreMilB-315
94BrePol-10
94ColC-492
94ColChoGS-492
94ColChoSS-492
94Don-196
94DonDiaK-DK6
94ExtBas-103
94Fin-247
94FinRef-247
94Fla-304
94Fle-206
94FleUpd-54
94Lea-290
94LeaL-43

94OPC-102
94Pac-354
94PanSti-90
94Pin-494
94PinArtP-494
94PinMusC-494
94Sco-37
94ScoGolR-37
94ScoGolS-55
94ScoRoo-RT32
94ScoRooGR-RT32
94Sel-225
94SP-58
94SPDieC-58
94SpoRoo-7
94SpoRooAP-7
94StaClu-707
94StaCluFDI-707
94StaCluGR-707
94StaCluMOP-707
94Stu-44
94Top-706
94TopGol-706
94TopSpa-706
94TopTra-21T
94TriPlaM-1
94Ult-371
94UppDec-441
94UppDecED-441
95ColCho-181
95ColChoGS-181
95ColChoSS-181
95Don-448
95DonPreP-448
95Fle-180
95Pac-232
95Sco-25
95ScoGolR-25
95ScoPlaTS-25
95UppDecSE-99
95UppDecSEG-99

Harper, David
77RocRedWM-21
77RocRedWM-22
77TucTorC-59
78TucTorC-59A

Harper, Devallon
83KinBluJTI-7

Harper, George W.
21Exh-68
23W501-108
25Exh-41
26Exh-43
27Exh-18
28W513-85
29ExhFou-2
91ConTSN-246

Harper, Greg
88IdaFalBP-1847
88SumBraP-401
89SumBraP-1117
90BurBraB-22
90BurBraS-14

Harper, Harry C.
16ColE13-69
20GasAmeMBD-9
21E121So1-39
21E121So8-33
21KoBreWSI-33
22W575-52
90DodTar-318

Harper, Jack (Charles W.)
03BreE10-66
11SpoLifCW-157

Harper, Jon
77CedRapGT-18

Harper, Marshal
76AppFoxT-8
77AppFoxT-7

Harper, Milt
86WatIndP-12
87KinIndP-22
88WilBilP-1327
90RenSilSCLC-275

Harper, Terry
82RedPioT-22
83RedPioT-12

Harper, Terry (Terry Joe)
79RicBraT-14
80RicBraT-17
81BraPol-19
81Top-192
82BraBurKL-10
82RicBraT-24
82Top-507
83BraPol-19
83Don-607
83Fle-137
83Top-339
84BraPol-19
84Fle-180
84Nes792-624
84Top-624
84TopTif-624
85BraPol-19
85Fle-327
85TopTifT-45T
85TopTra-45T
86BraPol-19
86Don-627
86Fle-516
86Lea-246
86OPC-247
86Top-247
86TopSti-41
86TopTif-247
87DonOpeD-217
87Fle-517
87FleExcS-22
87FleGlo-517
87Top-49
87TopTif-49
87TopTra-42T
87TopTraT-42T
88Fle-331
88FleGlo-331
90GreBraP-1145
91GreBraC-27
91GreBraLD-225
91GreBraP-3019
91LinDriAA-225

Harper, Tommy
62RedEnq-11
63RedEnq-11
63RedFreBC-7
63Top-158
64Kah-11
64RedJayP-3
64Top-330
64TopCoi-40
64TopSta-43
64TopVen-330
65Kah-15
65OPC-47
65RedEnq-10
65Top-47
66Kah-14
66Top-214
66TopVen-214
67CokCapR-4
67DexPre-89
67Kah-15
67Top-392
67TopVen-294
68Top-590
69MilBra-104
69MLBOffS-95
69OPC-42
69PilPos-2
69Top-42
69TopSta-225
69TopTeaP-9
70BreMcD-9
70BreMil-6
70BreTeal-3
70DayDaiNM-100
70Kel-74
70MLBOffS-270
70OPC-370
70SunPin-10
70Top-370
70TopBoo-11
70TopSup-9
71BazNumT-30
71BazUnn-9
71BreTeal-3
71Kel-47
71MilDud-8
71MLBOffS-437
71OPC-260
71Top-260
71TopCoi-140
71TopGreM-42
71TopSup-63
71TopTat-11
72MilBra-132
72OPC-455
72Top-455
73LinPor-23
73OPC-620
73Top-620
74GreHeroBP-5
74OPC-204
74OPC-325
74Top-204
74Top-325
74TopSta-134
75OPC-537
75Top-537
76OPC-274
76Top-274
77Top-414
81TCM60I-399
83Pil69G-37
90ExpPos-16
91OriCro-181
92ExpPos-17
94BreMilB-128

Harradon, Willie
88AllandGN-20

Harrah, Doug
92SalBucC-6
92SalBucF-57
93CarMudF-2048
93CarMudTI-10
94OrlCubF-1380
95OrlCubF-3

Harrah, Toby
71SenPolP-5
71SenTealW-12
72OPC-104
72Top-104
73LinPor-176
73OPC-216
73Top-216
74OPC-511
74Top-511
74TopSta-235
75Hos-14
75HosTwi-14
75OPC-131
75Top-131
76Hos-48
76HosTwi-48
76OPC-412
76SSP-264
76Top-412
77BurCheD-26
77Hos-37
77OPC-208
77Top-301
78Hos-123
78OPC-74
78RanBurK-13
78SSP270-89
78Top-44
79Hos-150
79OPC-119
79Top-234
80OPC-333
80Top-636
81AllGamPI-33
81Don-318
81Fle-389
81OPC-67
81Top-721
81TopScr-46
81TopSti-65
82Don-72
82Fle-369
82FleSta-193
82Ind-18
82IndTeal-17
82IndWhe-5
82OPC-16
82Top-532
82TopSti-177
83AllGamPI-33
83Don-13
83Don-337
83DonActA-39
83Fle-410
83Fle-635
83FleSta-76
83FleSti-247
83IndPos-18
83IndWhe-17
83Kel-44
83OPC-356
83PerCreC-25
83PerCreCG-25
83Top-141
83Top-480
83TopGloS-13
83TopSti-58
84AllGamPI-123
84Don-251
84Fle-544
84FleUpd-48
84Nes792-348
84OPC-348
84Top-348
84TopRubD-23
84TopSti-251
84TopTif-348
84TopTra-48T
84TopTraT-48T
85Fle-130
85FleUpd-49
85RanPer-11
85Top-94
85TopTif-94
85TopTifT-46T
85TopTra-46T
86Don-159
86Fle-560
86Lea-86
86OPC-72
86RanGreT-7
86RanPer-11
86Top-535
86TopMinL-32
86TopSti-238
86TopTat-19
86TopTif-535
87Don-408
87Fle-125
87FleGlo-125
87OklCit8P-12
87Top-152
87TopTif-152
88OklCit8C-25
88OklCit8P-46
88TriAAAP-51
89PacSenL-162
89RanMot-27
89RanSmo-13
89T/MSenL-44
89TopSenL-58
90EliSenL-22
90RanMot-27
91LinDri-10
91RanMot-28
91SweBasG-37
92RanMot-28
92UppDecS-12
92YanWIZ8-77
93RanKee-15
93RanKee-172
93UppDecAH-62
94RanAllP-3
94RanAllP-4
94UppDecAH-143
94UppDecAH1-143
95NorTidTI-1

Harrel, Donny
90EugEmeGS-12
91AppFoxC-12
91AppFoxP-1718

Harrel, Greg
96OklCit8B-3

Harrell, Bill
58Top-443
59Top-433
61Top-354
63MilSau-2

Harrell, Greg
87PorChaRP-13
88TulDriTI-27
89TulDriGS-4
89TulDriTI-9
90TexLeaAGS-38
90TulDriTI-9
91TulDriTI-10

Harrell, John
70OPC-401
70Top-401

Harrell, Matt
93JamExpC-9
93JamExpF-3329

Harrell, Ray
93ConTSN-960

Harrelson, Bill
69Top-224

Harrelson, Bud (Derrel M.)
67Top-306
68OPC-132
68Top-132
68TopVen-132
69MetBoyS-2
69MetNewYDN-8
69MilBra-105
69MLBOffS-166
69MLBPin-45
69Top-456
69TopSta-64
69TopTeaP-24
70DayDaiNM-105
70MetTra-25B
70MLBOffS-77
70Top-634
71Kel-66A
71Kel-66B
71Kel-66C
71MilDud-45
71MLBOffS-155
71OPC-355
71Top-355
71TopCoi-67
71TopGreM-55
71TopTat-104
72Kel-32A
72Kel-32B
72MilBra-133
72OPC-53
72OPC-54
72OPC-496
72Top-53
72Top-54
72Top-496
72TopPos-22
73LinPor-112
73MetAllEB-2
73NewYorN-9
73OPC-223
73Top-223
73TopCanL-20
74MetDaiPA-10
74OPC-380
74Top-380
74TopSta-63
75Hos-45
75OPC-395
75SSP42-16
75Top-395
76Hos-52
76HosTwi-52
76MetMSAP-1
76OPC-337
76SSP-545
76Top-337
77BurCheD-144
77MetDaiPA-7
77OPC-172
77Top-44
78Top-403
79Top-118
80OPC-294
80Top-566
81TCM60I-425
81Top-694
82MetPhoA-28
84FifNatC-2
84LitFalMT-13
84OCoandSI-79
86MetColP-17
86MetGreT-3
86MetTCM-38
86TopRos-70
87Met196T-2
87MetColP-34
88MetColP-25
88MetKah-3
89Met196C-5
89MetColP-32
89MetKah-10
89RinPosM1-14
90MetColP-8
90MetHalof-2
90MetKah-3
90SweBasG-111
90TopTra-37T
90TopTraT-37T
90TopTVM-4
91MetColP-9
91MetKah-3
91MetWIZ-160
91OPC-261
91SweBasG-38
91Top-261

91TopDesS-261
91TopMic-261
91TopTif-261
92ActPacA-58
92UppDecS-10
93RanKee-173
93TedWil-56
93UppDecAH-63
94Met69CCPP-18
94Met69CS-17
94Met69T-6
94MetColP-10
94MetComR-1
94UppDecAH-69
94UppDecAH1-69
96Met69Y-4
96MetTeal-8
Harrelson, Ken
64A's-8
64AthJayP-6
64Top-419
65AthJayP-7
65Top-479
66OPC-55
66Top-55
66TopRubl-38
66TopVen-55
67CokCapS-17
67DexPre-90
67OPC-188
67SenTeal-4
67Top-188
68Top-566
68TopActS-10C
69MilBra-106
69MLBOffS-13
69MLBPin-8
69OPC-3
69OPC-5
69OPCDec-8
69Top-3
69Top-5
69Top-240
69Top-417
69TopDec-3
69TopDecl-15
69TopSta-134
69TopSup-4
69TopTeaP-3
69TraSta-23
70Ind-6
70Kel-68
70MLBOffS-198
70OPC-545
70Top-545
70TopPos-6
71BazNumT-15
71Ind-6
71MLBOffS-371
71OPC-510
71Top-510
71TopCoi-134
72MilBra-134
78TCM60I-247
81RedSoxBG2S-84
86WhiSoxC-NNO
88PacLegI-14
Harridge, Will
56Top-1
57Top-100
58Top-300
76ShaPiz-130
80PerHaloFP-130
80SSPHOF-130
Harriger, Dennis
89PitMetS-6
90St.LucMS-9
91St.LucMC-21
92St.LucMCB-8
92St.LucMF-1741
93BinMetF-2329
94LasVegSF-870
96LasVegSB-13
Harriger, Mark
96BoiHawB-14
Harring, Ken
89IdaFalBP-2014
90DurBulTI-5
Harrington, Jody
89EliTwiS-10
90KenTwiB-19
90KenTwiP-2288
90KenTwiS-6
Harrington, John
86MiaMarP-8
87MiaMarP-20
Harrington, Mark
94AubAstC-28
95AubAstTI-29
96AubDouB-30
Harris, Adoldo
90TamYanD-10
Harris, B. Gail
56Top-91
57Top-281
58Top-309
59Top-378
60Top-152
60TopVen-152
79TCM50-275
Harris, Bill (William)
23WilChoV-58
60Top-128
60TopVen-128
77OrlTwiT-13
90DodTar-971
Harris, Billy (James William)
58MonRoyF-11
60DarFar-18
69Top-569
70OPC-512
70Top-512
Harris, Bryan
93BoiHawC-13
93BoiHawF-3910
94LakElsSC-9
94LakElsSF-1658
95MidAngOHP-17
95MidAngTI-15
Harris, Bubba (Charlie)
49PhiBul-23
Harris, Bucky (Stanley)
22E120-109
22W572-39
23MapCriV-21
23WilChoV-59
25Exh-124
26Exh-124
26SpoComoA-18
27YorCarE-41
28Exh-62
28W502-41
28Yue-41
31W517-9
33ButCanV-24
34ButPreR-31
34DiaStaR-91
36GouBWR-16
36GouWidPPR-A47
36NatChiFPR-41
36R31PasP-32
36WorWidGV-130
40PlaBal-129
48BabRutS-24
48YanTeal-11
51Bow-275
52Bow-158
53BowBW-46
59FleWil-68
60SenUniMC-7
75TCMAllG-14
76RowExh-10
76ShaPiz-148
77GalGloG-132
80PerHaloFP-148
80SSPHOF-148
81ConTSN-68
81TigDetN-105
86ConSer1-25
91ConTSN-61
91TopArc1-313
92ConTSN-593
92YanWIZH-15
93ConTSN-845
Harris, Buddy (Walter)
71OPC-404
71Top-404
Harris, Candy (Alonzo)
67Top-564
68OPC-128
68Top-128
68TopVen-128
Harris, Carry
83KnoBluJT-10
Harris, Craig
80WesHavWCT-11
Harris, D.J.
93PocPosF-4216
93PocPosSP-19
95DunBluJTI-9
96DunBluJB-13
96DunBluJTI-15
Harris, Dannie
90Bes-126
90HunStaB-7
Harris, David Stanley
25Exh-7
31SenTeaIPW-14
33Gou-9
33GouCanV-9
Harris, Donald
89ButCopKSP-4
90Bow-499
90BowTif-499
90CMC-793
90OPC-314
90Sco-661
90Top-314
90TopTif-314
90TulDriP-1167
90TulDriTI-10
91Bow-269
91Cla/Bes-12
91LinDriAA-583
91TulDriLD-583
91TulDriP-2785
91TulDriTI-11
92Bow-332
92ClaFS7-287
92Don-652
92Fle-660
92OPC-554
92Pin-597
92PinRool-16
92ProFS7-155
92SkyAA F-268
92StaClu-691
92StaCluNC-691
92Top-554
92TopDeb91-72
92TopGol-554
92TopGolW-554
92TopMic-554
92TulDriS-608
92Ult-443
92UppDec-11
93ClaFS7-201
93Don-291
93LinVenB-186
93OklCit8F-1637
93RanKee-174
93Sco-254
93ScoBoyoS-21
93Sel-341
93StaClu-318
93StaCluFDI-318
93StaCluMOP-318
93StaCluR-7
93Top-731
93TopGol-731
93TopInaM-731
93TopMic-731
94Don-133
94OklCit8F-1505
94StaCluT-249
94StaCluTFDI-249
Harris, Doug
90EugEmeGS-13
91AppFoxC-4
91AppFoxP-1710
92BasCitRF-3840
94MemChiF-353
96RocRedWB-16
Harris, Doyle
83LouRedR-29
84LouRedR-7
86LouRedTI-30
Harris, Eric
92KinMetC-8
92KinMetF-1534
93PitMetC-9
93PitMetF-3716
93SouOreAC-10
93SouOreAF-4077
94SouOreAC-9
94SouOreAF-3638
Harris, Frank
77EvaTriT-14
80OgdA'sT-12
82MadMusF-18
89ColMetB-26
89MedAthB-3
Harris, G.G.
93AugPirC-9
93AugPirF-1552
93WelPirC-6
93WelPirF-3364
94AugGreF-3015
Harris, Gary
90ArkRaz-14
Harris, Gene
86JamExpP-13
87WesPalBEP-677
88JacExpB-5
88JacExpP-980
89BlaYNPRWL-192
89DonBasB-325
89ExpPos-13
89FleUpd-58
89TopTra-46T
89TopTraT-46T
90Don-247
90Fle-515
90FleCan-515
90Lea-378
90MarMot-15
90OPC-738
90Sco-548
90Sco100RS-54
90Top-738
90TopDeb89-52
90TopTif-738
90UppDec-565
91Don-651
91Fle-452
91OPC-203
91Sco-627
91Top-203
91TopDesS-203
91TopMic-203
91TopTif-203
92OPC-390
92PadSmo-10
92StaClu-425
93Don-494
93Fla-134
93FleFinE-141
93Lea-517
93PacSpa-597
93PadMot-18
93SP-168
93TopTra-64T
93UppDec-657
93UppDecGold-657
94ColC-125
94ColChoGS-125
94ColChoSS-125
94Don-468
94ExtBas-76
94Fin-340
94FinRef-340
94Fle-666
94Lea-407
94Pac-526
94PadMot-16
94Pin-363
94PinArtP-363
94PinMusC-363
94Sco-138
94ScoGolR-138
94ScoRoo-RT33
94ScoRooGR-RT33
94Sel-125
94StaClu-325
94StaCluFDI-325
94StaCluGR-325
94StaCluMOP-325
94Top-514
94TopGol-514
94TopSpa-514
94TriPla-168
94Ult-576
95FleUpd-120
95Phi-14
95PhiMel-11
Harris, Glenn
84SavCarT-18
Harris, Greg A.
79JacMetT-21
80TidTidT-11
81TidTidT-23
82IndIndTI-13
82RedCok-7
82Top-783
82TopTra-41T
83Don-295
83Fle-590
83IndIndTI-6
83Top-296
84ExpPos-12
84ExpStu-22
85Fle-35
85RanPer-27
85Top-242
85TopTif-242
85TopTifT-47T
85TopTra-47T
86Don-465
86Fle-561
86OPC-128
86RanPer-27
86Top-586
86TopSti-245
86TopTif-586
87Don-382
87Fle-126
87FleGlo-126
87FleStiC-54
87Lea-82
87OPC-44
87RanMot-11
87RanSmo-2
87Spo-126
87SpoTeaP-1
87Top-44
87TopSti-238
87TopTif-44
88AlaGolAA'TI-15
88Don-427
88Fle-468
88FleGlo-468
88FleUpd-109
88FleUpdG-109
88PhiTas-34
88Sco-179
88ScoGlo-179
88Top-369
88TopTif-369
89Don-548
89Fle-570
89FleGlo-570
89PhiTas-8
89Sco-476
89Top-627
89TopTif-627
90Don-582
90FleUpd-71
90Lea-499
90OPC-529
90PubSti-237
90Top-529
90TopTif-529
90TopTVRS-11
91Don-306
91Fle-97
91Lea-83
91MetWIZ-161
91OPC-123
91RedSoxP-9
91Sco-109
91StaClu-324
91Top-123
91TopDesS-123
91TopMic-123
91TopTif-123
91Ult-33
91UppDec-509
92Don-113
92Lea-154
92OPC-468
92RedSoxDD-15
92Sco-156
92StaClu-49
92Stu-133
92Top-468
92TopGol-468
92TopGolW-468
92TopMic-468
92UppDec-658
93Don-663
93Fla-165
93Fle-560
93Lea-131
93PacSpa-359
93RanKee-175
93RedSoxWHP-13
93Sco-640
93StaClu-315
93StaCluFDI-315

93StaCluMOP-315
93Ult-511
93UppDec-414
93UppDecGold-414
94ColC-506
94ColChoGS-506
94ColChoSS-506
94Don-512
94Fin-303
94Fin-372
94FinRef-303
94Fle-34
94Pin-476
94PinArtP-476
94PinMusC-476
94Sco-272
94ScoGolR-272
94StaClu-407
94StaCluFDI-407
94StaCluGR-407
94StaCluMOP-407
94Top-738
94TopGol-738
94TopSpa-738
94Ult-15
96HudValRB-25
Harris, Greg W.
85SpoIndC-7
86ChaRaiP-10
86SpoIndC-161
87ChaRaiP-3
87TexLeaAF-23
87WicPilRD-11
88BlaYNPRWLU-32
88LasVegSC-3
88LasVegSP-227
88TriAAAP-23
89BlaYNPRWLU-21
89Don-34
89DonRoo-46
89Fle-306
89FleGlo-306
89PadMag-18
89ScoRoo-87T
89Top-194
89TopTif-194
89UppDec-724
89WicWraR-19
90ClaYel-T13
90Don-65
90Fle-158
90FleCan-158
90Lea-452
90OPC-572
90PadCok-7
90PadMag-24
90PanSti-353
90Sco-257
90Sco100RS-24
90ScoYouSI-18
90Top-572
90TopRoo-13
90TopTif-572
90UppDec-622
91Bow-657
91Don-131
91Fle-531
91Lea-422
91OPC-749
91PadMag-13
91PadSmo-13
91Sco-251
91StaClu-205
91Top-749
91TopMic-749
91TopDesS-749
91TopTif-749
91Ult-304
91UppDec-489
92Bow-269
92Don-49
92Fle-606
92Lea-10
92OPC-636
92PadCarJ-8
92PadMot-2
92PadPolD-9
92PadSmo-11
92Pin-169
92Sco-378
92StaClu-275
92Stu-105
92Top-636
92TopGol-636
92TopGolW-636
92TopMic-636
92TriPla-157
92Ult-278
92UppDec-306
93Don-154
93Fle-139
93Lea-82
93PacSpa-258
93PadMot-5
93Sco-599
93StaClu-312
93StaCluFDI-312
93StaCluMOP-312
93Top-78
93Top-436
93TopGol-78
93TopGol-436
93TopInaM-78
93TopInaM-436
93TopMic-78
93TopMic-436
93Ult-117
93UppDec-724
93UppDecGold-724
94ColC-126
94ColChoGS-126
94ColChoSS-126
94Don-193
94ExtBas-246
94FinRef-372
94Fle-442
94Lea-416
94Pin-470
94PinArtP-470
94PinMusC-470
94ProMag-44
94RocPol-12
94Sco-374
94ScoGolR-374
94StaClu-560
94StaCluFDI-560
94StaCluGR-560
94StaCluMOP-560
94StaCluT-99
94StaCluTFDI-99
94Top-18
94TopGol-18
94TopSpa-18
94Ult-481
94UppDec-194
94UppDecED-194
95Don-400
95DonPreP-400
95Fle-520
95Top-268
Harris, Gregg S.
88WicPilRD-19
Harris, James
89KinMetS-12
89Sta-172
90ColMetGS-7
90ColMetPPI-5
90SouAtlLAS-32
90StaFS7-99
91St.LucMC-8
91St.LucMP-717
92St.LucMCB-6
92St.LucMF-1751
Harris, Jeff
96ForWayWB-10
Harris, Joe
22E120-4
22W572-38
22W573-56
28W502-51
28W513-81
28Yue-51
90DodTar-319
94ConTSN-1241
94ConTSNB-1241
Harris, John
92GulCoaMF-3472
93YakBeaF-3896
Harris, John Thomas
77QuaCitAT-14
79SalLakCGT-16A
80SalLakCGT-12
81Top-214
82Don-444
82Fle-463
82SpoIndT-16
82Top-313
83IndIndTI-29
84EvaTriT-15
Harris, Josh
96BilMusTI-12
Harris, Keith
89UtiBluSP-10
Harris, Kyle
86AncGlaPTI-39
Harris, Larry
81WisRapTT-5
Harris, Lenny
84CedRapRT-25
86VerRedP-9
87NasSouTI-9
88NasSouC-12
88NasSouP-489
88NasSouTI-12
89BlaYNPRWLU-2
89DodStaSV-7
89Fle-645
89FleGlo-645
89RedKah-7
89UppDec-781
90CedRapRDGB-3
90DodMot-18
90DodPol-29
90DodTar-320
90Don-434
90Fle-397
90FleCan-397
90Lea-437
90OPC-277
90PubSti-31
90Sco-23
90Sco100RS-83
90ScoYouSI-37
90Top-277
90TopTif-277
90UppDec-423
91Bow-607
91DodMot-18
91DodPol-29
91Don-224
91Fle-204
91OPC-453
91PanFreS-57
91PanSti-51
91Sco-144
91StaClu-65
91Top-453
91TopDesS-453
91TopMic-453
91TopTif-453
91Ult-162
91UppDec-239
92DodMot-5
92DodPol-29
92DodSmo-9792
92Don-226
92Fle-458
92Hig5-52
92Lea-213
92OPC-92
92PanSti-194
92Pin-57
92Sco-291
92ScoProP-12
92StaClu-121
92Top-92
92TopGol-92
92TopGolW-92
92TopMic-92
92Ult-211
92UppDec-191
93DodMot-13
93DodPol-10
93Don-590
93Fle-61
93Lea-127
93PacSpa-147
93PanSti-220
93Pin-119
93Sco-546
93Sel-384
93StaClu-98
93StaCluD-13
93StaCluFDI-98
93StaCluMOP-98
93Top-177
93TopGol-177
93TopInaM-177
93TopMic-177
93Ult-54
93UppDec-184
93UppDecGold-184
94RedKah-14
94Sco-152
94ScoGolR-152
95Don-500
95DonPreP-500
95DonTopotO-213
95RedKah-9
95Sco-359
95ScoGolR-359
95ScoPlaTS-359
95Top-401
95TopCyb-202
96Fle-341
96FleTif-341
97Pac-269
97PacLigB-269
97PacSil-269
Harris, Luman
60Top-455
65AstBigLBPP-12
65OPC-274
65Top-274
66OPC-147
66Top-147
66TopVen-147
67AstTeal2-13
68Top-439
69OPC-196
69Top-196
69TopFou-6
70OPC-86
70Top-86
71OPC-346
71Top-346
72OPC-484
72Top-484
83TCMPla1943-21
87AstSer1-30
Harris, Mark
79WesHavYT-26
90LitSunW-19
93HicCraC-10
93HicCraF-1291
Harris, Matt
96BelSnaTI-16
Harris, Michael
92StoPorF-48
93StoPorC-15
93StoPorF-757
Harris, Mickey (Maurice)
46RedSoxTI-11
47TipTop-6
48RedSoxTI-9
49Bow-151
49Lea-27
50Bow-160
51Bow-311
52Bow-135
52Top-207
83TopRep5-207
87RedSox1T-9
Harris, Mike
82SprCarF-19
83ArkTraT-13
84ArkTraT-26
86BirBarTI-10
94ElPasDF-3158
96El PasDB-12
Harris, Moon
81ConTSN-66
Harris, Pep
91BurIndP-3296
91HigSchPLS-26
92ColRedC-15
92ColRedF-2384
93ColRedC-11
93ColRedF-592
94KinIndC-7
94KinIndF-2636
96MidAngB-18
96VanCanB-17
Harris, Rafael
80UtiBluJT-6
Harris, Ray
86AncGlaPTI-14
88SouOreAP-1713
89MadMusS-28
Harris, Reggie
87ElmPio(C-30
88ElmPio1C-1
88LynRedSS-9
89WinHavRSS-10
90Bow-446
90BowTif-446
91Cla1-T71
91Don-704
91OPC-177
91Sco-643
91Sco100RS-49
91TacTigP-2300
91Top-177
91TopDeb90-64
91TopDesS-177
91TopMic-177
91TopTif-177
91UppDec-672
92Don-781
92Sco100RS-48
92SkyAAAF-239
92StaClu-158
92TacTigF-2497
92TacTigS-535
93JacSunF-2707
Harris, Robbie
85CloHSS-21
Harris, Robert
87WatPirP-3
88AugPirP-386
89SalBucS-NNO
90HarSenP-1205
90HarSenS-9
92BirBarF-2594
92BirBarS-83
Harris, Robert A.
41BroW75-14
79DiaGre-182
Harris, Rodger
96JohCitCTI-15
Harris, Rusty
87AubAstP-2
88OscAstS-12
89OscAstS-7
90ColMudB-7
90ColMudP-1353
90ColMudS-12
91JacGenLD-559
91JacGenP-931
91LinDriAA-559
92JacGenF-4004
92JacGenS-333
94AubAstF-3777
96JacGenB-2
Harris, Sam
20NatCarE-40
21Exh-69
Harris, Sheriff
81ConTSN-67
Harris, Steve
85BenPhiC-10
Harris, Tony
91AdeGiaF-3
95AusFut-108
95VerBeaDTI-10
96VerBeaDB-2
Harris, Tracy
80SanJosMJitB-10
81LynSaiT-5
82SalLakCGT-10
83ChaLooT-17
Harris, Twayne
83IdaFalAT-21
85ModA'sC-4
86ModA'sC-9
86ModA'sP-11
Harris, Vic (Elander Victor)
87NegLeaPD-2
94TedWil-107
Harris, Vic Lanier
73LinPor-177
73OPC-594
73Top-594
74OPC-157
74Top-157
74TopSta-13
75OPC-658
75Top-658
76SSP-321
77PhoGiaCC-8
77PhoGiaCP-7
78Top-436
79Top-338
79VanCanT-2
80VanCanT-21
84LouRedR-18
93RanKee-16
94BreMilB-129
Harris, Vince
88UtiBluSP-6

89ChaRaiP-976
90Bes-315
90CalLeaACLC-5
90CMC-718
90RivRedWB-9
90RivRedWCLC-12
90RivRedWP-2619
91LinDriAA-607
91WicWraLD-607
91WicWraP-2610
91WicWraRD-20
92SkyAA F-281
92WicWraF-3666
92WicWraS-633
93WicWraF-2989
Harris, Walt
88HagSunS-9
89RocRedWC-19
89RocRedWP-1651
90HagSunS-10
Harris, William
34DiaMatCSB-88
Harris, Wilmer
93NegLeaRL2-15
95NegLeaL2-25
Harrison, Bob (Robert Lee)
79TCM50-76
91OriCro-182
Harrison, Brett
87St.PetCP-7
88ArkTraGS-13
88TexLeaAGS-13
Harrison, Brian Lee
86SpoIndC-164
87ChaRaiP-8
88RivRedWCLC-210
88RivRedWP-1428
89RivRedWB-7
89RivRedWCLC-17
89RivRedWP-1410
90Bes-27
90ProAaA-133
90RivRedWB-10
90RivRedWCLC-17
90RivRedWP-2601
92AppFoxF-979
93CarLeaAGF-12
93WilBluRC-14
93WilBluRF-1993
94MemChiF-354
94SanBerSC-6
95MemChiTI-13
96WicWraB-7
Harrison, Chuck (Charles)
66Top-244
66TopVen-244
67CokCapAs-6
67DexPre-91
67OPC-8
67Top-8
69OPC-116
69RoySol-7
69Top-116
69TopFou-10
87AstShoSO-11
87AstShoSTw-23
Harrison, Craig
89SanDieSAS-11
Harrison, Doug
78CliDodT-12
80AlbDukT-9
Harrison, Keith
86ElmPioRSP-9
86SpoIndC-173
87ChaRaiP-22
88ChaRaiP-1207
Harrison, Mack
77ModA'sC-12
79OgdA'sT-7
Harrison, Matt (Mathew)
86FloStaLAP-20
86Ft.LauYP-11
87AlbYanP-13
88ColCliC-5
88ColCliP-3
88ColCliP-317
90AlbDecGB-8
Harrison, Mike
91BilMusP-3756
91BilMusSP-21
92ChaWheF-12
92ChaWVWC-8
92StaCluD-78
93WinSpiC-8
93WinSpiF-1574
94WinSpiC-10
94WinSpiF-275
Harrison, Pat
89AlaGol-7
Harrison, Phil
86GenCubP-10
87PeoChiP-23
88CarLeaAS-28
88WinSpiS-5
89ChaKniTI-21
90TopTVCu-48
Harrison, R.J.
78ArkTraT-12
80LynSaiT-19
81LynSaiT-6
82WauTimF-17
83WauTimF-30
86ChaLooP-12
Harrison, Robert
77St.PetCT-20
89JohCitCS-26
90HamRedS-28
Harrison, Ron
82MadMusF-21
83AlbA'sT-18
85TacTigC-137
87BelBreP-16
87DenZepP-8
Harrison, Roric E.
72OPC-474
72Top-474
73OPC-229
73Top-229
74OPC-298
74Top-298
74TopSta-5
75OPC-287
75Top-287
76OPC-547
76SSP-507
76Top-547
77EvaTriT-15
78Top-536
91OriCro-183
Harrison, Scott
92JamExpC-20
92JamExpF-1496
93JamExpC-10
93JamExpF-3320
96BurIndB-6
Harrison, Tommy
95DurBulTI-11
96GreBraB-13
96GreBraTI-36
96RicBraB-15
Harrison, Wayne
85DurBulT-25
86DurBulP-13
Harriss, Robin
94WatIndC-16
94WatIndF-3941
96KenIndB-12
Harriss, Slim (Bryan)
20NatCarE-39
21Nei-38
22E120-80
27AmeCarE-46
28Exh-34
Harriss, Slim (William)
21Exh-70
Harrist, Earl
48WhiSoxTI-9
50RemBre-11
52Top-402
53Top-65
83TopRep5-402
91TopArc1-65
Harry, Whitney
82BurRanF-24
82BurRanT-22
83BurRanF-15
83BurRanT-18
84TulDriTI-20
Harryman, Jeff
77NewCoPT-16
78BurBeeT-15
Harsh, Nick
82ForMyeRT-7
Harshman, Jack
54Top-173
55RedMan-AL6
55Top-104
55TopDouH-65
56Top-29
56TopPin-33
57Top-152
58Top-217
59Top-475
60Top-112
60TopVen-112
79DiaGre-146
79TCM50-33
91OriCro-184
94TopArc1-173
94TopArc1G-173
Hart, Bob
94ConTSN-1195
94ConTSNB-1195
Hart, Brian
89BurIndS-12
Hart, Chris
85MiaHur-6
90SouOreAB-18
90SouOreAP-3431
91ModA'sP-3103
91SouOreAP-3861
92ModA'sC-5
93HunStaF-2094
94HunStaF-1343
95HunStaTI-12
Hart, Darrin
89WatDiaS-10
89WatDiaS-30
Hart, Hub (James Henry)
09T206-489
10CouT21-26
10CouT21-27
11SpoLifCW-158
Hart, James Aristotle
89N526N7C-6
Hart, James M.
81RocRedWW-17
83ColCliT-24
Hart, Jason
94PeoChiC-11
94PeoChiF-2260
96OrlCubB-10
Hart, Jeff
89ChaRaiP-987
89WatDiaP-1781
90CMC-703
90WatDiaB-6
90WatDiaP-2373
Hart, Jim Ray
47PM1StaP1-78
64Top-452
65GiaTeal-4
65OPC-4
65Top-4
65Top-395
65TopEmbl-4
66Top-295
66TopRubl-39
66TopVen-295
67CokCapG-6
67DexPre-92
67Top-220
67TopVen-335
68AtlOilPBCC-21
68OPC-73
68Top-73
68TopVen-73
69MilBra-107
69MLBOffS-199
69MLBPin-46
69Top-555
69TopSta-104
69TopTeaP-14
70OPC-176
70Top-176
71OPC-461
71Top-461
72Top-733
73OPC-538
73Top-538
74OPC-159
74Top-159
78TCM60I-269
84GiaMot-20
92YanWIZ7-68
93UppDecS-7
Hart, John
75WatRoyT-15
85ChaO'sT-14
86RocRedWP-6
87RocRedWP-3
87RocRedWT-24
88OriFreB-47
90OPC-141
90Top-141
90TopTif-141
Hart, Kim
82IowCubT-31
83IowCubT-28
Hart, Leon
51BerRos-A14
Hart, Mike (Michael Lawrence)
79TucTorT-17
80ChaChaT-10
80LynSaiT-7
81RocRedWT-7
81SpoIndT-7
82SalLakCGT-11
83TolMudHT-20
85IntLeaAT-30
85TolMudHT-21
86RocRedWP-7
87NewOriP-3
87RocRedWP-10
87RocRedWT-18
88CarLeaAS-2
88Top-69
88TopTif-69
89ReaPhiB-26
89ReaPhiP-658
89ReaPhiS-26a
90Ft.LauYS-23
91CarLeaAP-CAR32
91OriCro-185
91PriWilCC-24
91PriWilCP-1442
92PriWilCC-26
92PriWilCF-164
93AlbYanF-2177
93LinVenB-265
93RanKee-176
95BurBeeTI-32
Hart, Shelby
90EveGiaP-3139
91CliGiaC-17
91CliGiaP-846
92EveGiaC-11
92EveGiaF-1696
Hart, Tommy
80CarMudF-9
81ReaPhiT-3
Hart, William F.
09T206-488
87BucN28-53
87OldJudN-235
90DodTar-321
98CamPepP-32
Hart, William W.
46RemBre-6
47SmiClo-15
90DodTar-972
Hartas, Peter
91DaiDolF-13
Hartenstein, Chuck
68OPC-13
68Top-13
68TopVen-13
69Top-596
70OPC-216
70Top-216
75IntLeaASB-8
75PacCoaLAB-8
76HawIslC-1
77OPC-157
77Top-416
80HawIslT-11
81HawIslT-22
82HawIslT-24
84HawIslC-134
86PenWhiSP-11
87BrePol-NNO
88BrePol-NNO
89BrePol-NNO
92TexLon-22
Harter, Andy
88AshTouP-1052
Hartgraves, Dean
87AubAstP-24
88AshTouP-1072
89AshTouP-960
90ColMudB-6
90ColMudP-1343
90ColMudS-13
91JacGenLD-560
91JacGenP-921
91LinDriAA-560
92JacGenF-3995
92TucTorS-609
93LinVenB-48
93TucTorF-3054
94TucTorF-755
96Don-115
96DonPreP-115
96Fle-409
96FleTif-409
96RicBraUB-11
96TusTorB-11
Hartgrove, Lyle
94UtiBluSF-3812
96SarRedSB-19
Hartje, Chris
90DodTar-973
Hartley, Grover
12T207-77
16ColE13-70
92ConTSN-520
Hartley, Mike (Michael)
83St.PetCT-7
85SprCarT-13
87BakDodP-1
88AlbDukC-9
88AlbDukP-263
88BlaYNPRWL-182
89AlbDukC-4
89AlbDukP-67
89BlaYNPRWL-24
90Bow-87
90BowTif-87
90ClaYel-T63
90DodPol-46
90DodTar-974
90DonRoo-34
90Fle-651
90FleCan-651
90FleUpd-22
90Sco-641
90SprCarDGB-15
90TopDeb89-53
91DodMot-19
91DodPol-46
91Don-545
91Fle-205
91OPC-199
91Sco-252
91Sco100RS-67
91Top-199
91TopDesS-199
91TopMic-199
91TopTif-199
91UppDec-686
92Don-726
92OPC-484
92PhiMed-41
92Sco-670
92ScrRedBS-485
92Top-484
92TopGol-484
92TopGolW-484
92TopMic-484
92UppDec-613
93Don-596
93Fle-102
93OPCPre-67
93StaClu-124
93StaCluFDI-124
93StaCluMOP-124
93Top-208
93TopGol-208
93TopInaM-208
93TopMic-208
94Don-225
94Fle-207
95PawRedSDD-12
95PawRedTI-27
Hartley, Todd
86MedA'sC-63
Hartley, Tom
86AppFoxP-10
Hartline, Danny
87NewOriP-18
Hartman, Albert
82BurRanF-5
82BurRanT-23
Hartman, Doc (Ralph)
81RedPioT-26
82RedPioT-27
Hartman, Ed
87WatPirP-16
88AugPirP-366

89SalBucS-10
89Sta-94
Hartman, Harry
41HarHarW-34
Hartman, J.C.
61TopStal-161
62Col.45B-9
63Col45"P-8
63Top-442
Hartman, Jeff
86VerBeaDP-9
88VerBeaDS-10
Hartman, Kelly
92BelMarC-10
92BelMarF-1438
Hartman, Red
77ColCliT-7
Hartman, Robert
59Top-128
59TopVen-128
60Top-129
60TopVen-129
Hartman, Ron
96AriBlaDB-20
97Top-251
Hartman, Trey
86DavLipB-14
Hartmann, Brian
92Min-7
Hartmann, Pete
93EriSaiC-10
93EriSaiF-3108
94ChaRanF-2492
Hartmann, Reid
89KinMetS-13
90ColMetGS-8
90ColMetPPI-4
Hartmann, Rich
94NewJerCC-15
94NewJerCF-3413
Hartnett, Bill
93AubAstC-13
93AubAstF-3437
94OscAstC-11
94OscAstF-1132
Hartnett, Dave
86BelMarC-101
87WauTimP-22
Hartnett, Gabby (Charles)
21Exh-67
22E120-158
25Exh-22
26Exh-22
26SpoComoA-19
27Exh-11
27YorCarE-5
28Exh-10
28StaPlaCE-34
28W502-5
28Yue-5
29ExhFou-5
30ChiEveAP-5
30SchR33-38
31CubTeal-9
31Exh-5
32CubTeal-10
32OrbPinUP-31
33ButCre-12
33CraJacP-13
33Gou-202
33NatLeaAC-7
33RitCE-13H
33TatOrb-31
33TatOrbSDR-200
34DiaMatCSB-87
34BatR31-136
35DiaMatCS3T1-70
35ExhFou-3
36DiaMatCS3T2-13
36ExhFou-3
36GouWidPPR-A48
36GouWidPPR-C16
36NatChiFPR-91
36NatChiFPR-93
36NatChiFPR-102
36NatChiFPR-119
36R31PasP-31
36R31PasP-33
36R31PasP-48
36R31Pre-L6
36SandSW-30
36WheBB3-6
36WorWidGV-57
37DixLid-3
37DixPre-3
37ExhFou-3
37KelPepS-BB7
38BasTabP-16
38ExhFou-3
38OurNatGPP-15
39CubTeal-10
39ExhSal-24
40WheM4-6C
47PM1StaP1-79
50CalHOFW-37
60Fle-29
61Fle-41
61GolPre-11
76GalBasGHoF-14
76RowExh-9
76ShaPiz-75
77GalGloG-62
77GalGloG-206
80CubGreT-5
80PacLeg-72
80PerHaloFP-76
80SSPHOF-76
81ConTSN-89
84CubUno-3
84CubUno-6
85FegMurCG-10
86SpoDecG-13
87ConSer2-17
87HygAllG-24
88ScoBoxC-T4
91ConTSN-59
91ConTSN-313
92ConTSN-586
92ConTSNGI-880
92CubOldS-11
93ConTSN-675
93ConTSN-880
93DiaStaES-134
94ConTSN-1052
94ConTSN-1103
94ConTSNB-1052
94ConTSNB-1103
94TedWil-16
95ConTSN-1404
95ConTSNP-1404
Harts, Greg
91MetWIZ-162
Hartsel, Topsy (Tully)
03BreE10-67
08AmeCarE-11
08RosComP-60
09BriE97-12
09ColChiE-126A
09ColChiE-126B
09T206-151
10CouT21-28
10DomDisP-53
10E101-22
10E12AmeCDC-18
10MelMinE-22
10NadCarE-23
10NadE1-20
10PeoT21-26A
10PeoT21-26B
10RedCroT-28
10RedCroT-116
10RedCroT-197
10SweCapPP-45
10W555-33
11A'sFirT20-7
11S74Sil-31
11SpoLifCW-159
11SpoLifM-93
11T205-72
12ColRedB-126A
12ColRedB-126B
12ColTinT-126A
12ColTinT-126B
12ColTinT-127A
12ColTinT-127B
Hartsfield, Bob
75CedRapGT-18
75CedRapGT-19
76CliPilT-19
82AubAstT-2
92JacSunF-3724
92JacSunS-374
Hartsfield, Roy
51Bow-277
52Bow-28
52Top-264
73OPC-237
73Top-237A
73Top-237B
74HawIslC-108
75IntLeaASB-9
75PacCoaLAB-9
76HawIslC-4
77OPC-238
77Top-113
78BluJayP-8
78OPC-218
78Top-444
79BluJayBY-11
79OPC-262
79TCM50-123
79Top-282
83IndIndTI-3
83TopRep5-264
Hartshorn, Kyle
85LynMetT-12
86JacMetT-5
87JacMetF-19
88JacMetGS-6
Hartshorn, Tyson
95HagSunF-62
95StCatSTI-3
96HagSunB-7
Hartsock, Brian
82DanSunF-24
83PeoSunF-24
86MidAngP-9
87SanBerSP-13
89RenSilSCLC-249
Hartsock, Jeff
88GreFalDTI-21
89BakDodCLC-183
89CalLeaA-15
90SanAntMGS-14
91AlbDukLD-8
91AlbDukP-1135
91LinDriAAA-8
92IowCubF-4048
92IowCubS-209
92SkyAAAF-102
93Bow-648
93Don-160
94LouRedF-2978
Hartung, Andrew
90GenCubP-3044
90GenCubS-13
90ProAaA-180
91Cla/Bes-433
91PeoChiC-28
91PeoChiP-1349
91PeoChiTI-17
92ClaFS7-430
92WinSpiC-13
92WinSpiF-1214
93ClaFS7-202
93DayCubC-1
93DayCubF-864
93ExcFS7-9
94DayCubC-8
94DayCubF-2358
Hartung, Clinton
47TipTop-124
48BluTin-47
48Bow-37
49Bow-154
49EurSta-107
50Bow-118
50Dra-2
51Bow-234
52BerRos-22
52Top-141
75Gia195T-6
83TopRep5-141
Hartvigson, Chad
94EveGiaC-11
94EveGiaF-3646
96SanJosGB-19
96WesOahCHWB-42
Hartwell, Ed
94CliLumF-1994
94CliLumC-11
Hartwig, Dan
77CedRapGT-21
Hartwig, Rob
90BatCliP-3079
91SpaPhiC-25
91SpaPhiP-910
Hartzell, Paul
75QuaCitAT-25
77BurCheD-118
77Top-179
78AngFamF-17
78SSP270-191
78Top-529
79OPC-212
79Top-402
79TwiFriP-9
80OPC-366
80Top-721
80VenLeaS-187
84ElPasDT-20
91OriCro-186
94BreMilB-130
Hartzell, Roy A.
08AmeCarE-48
09AmeCarE-49
09AmeCarE-50
09ColChiE-127A
09ColChiE-127B
09PC7HHB-20
09RamT20-53
10NadCarE-24A
10NadCarE-24B
10PeoT21-27A
10PeoT21-27B
11MecDFT-4
11SpoLifCW-160
11SpoLifM-109
12ColRedB-127A
12ColRedB-127B
12HasTriFT-43
12HasTriFT-44
14B18B-23
15AmeCarE-20
15SpoNewM-76
16FleBreD-38
16SpoNewM-77
92ConTSN-544
Hartzog, Cullen
90PriWilCTI-11
90TopTVY-45
91AlbYanLD-7
91AlbYanP-1003
91LinDriAA-7
95LynHilTI-9
Harvell, Pete
93BilMusF-3938
93BilMusSP-9
94ChaWheC-13
94ChaWheF-2697
Harvell, Rod
89GreFalDSP-26
Harvey, Aaron
95KanCouCTI-9
96BreCouMB-18
Harvey, Bob
91NegLeaRL-3
93NegLeaRL2-16
95NegLeaLI-3
Harvey, Bryan
86PalSprAP-12
86PalSprAP-16
87MidAngP-25
88AngSmo-21
88DonRoo-53
88EdmTraC-5
88FleUpd-14
88FleUpdG-14
88ScoRoo-87T
88ScoRooG-87T
88TopTra-45T
88TopTraT-45T
89Bow-40
89BowTif-40
89Don-525
89DonBasB-317
89Fle-479
89FleBasM-18
89FleGlo-479
89FleHeroB-21
89OPC-287
89PanSti-284
89Sco-185
89ScoHot1R-92
89ScoYouSI-30
89Spo-130
89Top-632
89TopSti-180
89TopTif-632
89ToyRoo-13
89UppDec-594
90AngSmo-7
90Don-372
90Fle-134
90FleCan-134
90Lea-116
90OPC-272
90RedFolSB-44
90Sco-8
90Spo-31
90Top-272
90TopSti-175
90TopTif-272
90UppDec-686
91AngSmo-17
91Bow-211
91Don-206
91Fle-315
91Lea-213
91OPC-153
91Sco-108
91StaClu-98
91Top-153
91TopDesS-153
91TopMic-153
91TopTif-153
91Ult-45
91UppDec-592
91USPlaCA-7D
92Bow-172
92Cla1-T42
92ClaGam-57
92Don-211
92Fle-61
92Fle-696
92Fre-6
92Hig5-13
92Lea-309
92OPC-568
92PepDieM-9
92Pin-145
92Sco-322
92StaClu-410
92StaCluD-79
92Stu-146
92Top-407
92Top-568
92TopGol-407
92TopGol-568
92TopGolW-407
92TopGolW-568
92TopMic-407
92TopMic-568
92TriPla-37
92Ult-27
92UppDec-434
92UppDecF-26
92UppDecFG-26
93Bow-234
93Don-728
93Fin-3
93FinRef-3
93Fla-52
93FlaPro-4
93Fle-193
93FleFinE-62
93FunPac-120
93Lea-361
93MarPub-12
93MarUSPC-3D
93MarUSPC-10C
93OPC-14
93OPCPre-90
93PacSpa-463
93Pin-235
93Sco-558
93ScoFra-27
93Sel-126
93SP-141
93StaClu-604
93StaCluFDI-604
93StaCluMarI-2
93StaCluMOP-604
93Top-439
93TopGol-439
93TopInaM-439
93TopMic-439
93TriPla-225
93Ult-377
93UppDec-684
93UppDecGold-684
94Bow-10
94ColC-127
94ColChoGS-127
94ColChoSS-127
94Don-374
94DonMVP-5
94DonSpeE-374
94ExtBas-261
94Fin-164

94FinRef-164
94Fla-164
94Fle-468
94FleAllS-40
94FUnPac-134
94Lea-140
94LeaL-107
94OPC-239
94Pac-243
94PanSti-183
94Pin-344
94PinArtP-344
94PinMusC-344
94RedFolMI-24
94Sco-66
94ScoGolR-66
94Sel-103
94SP-112
94SPDieC-112
94Spo-47
94StaClu-452
94StaCluFDI-452
94StaCluGR-452
94StaCluMO-31
94StaCluMOP-452
94StaCluT-61
94StaCluTFDI-61
94Stu-110
94TomPiz-9
94Top-20
94TopGol-20
94TopSpa-20
94TriPla-137
94Ult-493
94UltFir-8
94UppDec-405
94UppDecAJ-3
94UppDecAJG-3
94UppDecED-405
95ColCho-310
95ColChoGS-310
95ColChoSS-310
95Don-345
95DonPreP-345
95Emb-32
95EmbGolI-32
95Fin-97
95FinRef-97
95Fle-334
95Pin-239
95PinArtP-239
95PinMusC-239
95Sco-548
95ScoGolR-548
95ScoPlaTS-548
95Sel-139
95SelArtP-139
95StaClu-3
95StaCluFDI-3
95StaCluMOP-3
95StaCluSTWS-3
95Stu-103
95Top-311
95Ult-163
95UltGolM-163
96LeaSigEA-72
96Sco-450
96Ult-326
96UltGolM-326

Harvey, Craig
76BatTroTI-12
77WatIndT-11

Harvey, Don
88PacEigMO-16

Harvey, Doug (Harold)
43ParSpo-36
84PadSmo-13
88T/MUmp-1
89T/MUmp-1
90T/MUmp-1

Harvey, Greg
88EugEmeB-3
89AppFoxP-853
90BasCitRS-10
90FloStaLAS-31
91BasCitRC-5
91BasCitRP-1392
92MemChiF-2413

Harvey, Ken
87SanAntDTI-23

Harvey, Randy
82BirBarT-12
85ModA'sC-11
86QuaCitAP-14

Harvey, Raymond
91ColIndC-1
91ColIndP-1498
92KinIndC-12
92KinIndF-2484
93KinIndC-11
93KinIndF-2260
93KinIndTI-10
94CanIndF-3130

Harvey, Robert
90SanBerSCLC-xxx

Harvey, Steve
82ReaPhiT-20

Harvey, Terry
93BazTeaU-1
93TopTra-41T
95WatIndTI-14
96KenIndB-13
96WesOahCHWB-20

Harvey, Wayne
91ParPatF-17

Harvick, Brad
87EriCarP-19
88SavCarP-345
89SavCarP-365

Harwell, David
88KinIndS-10

Harwell, Ernie
81TigDetN-62
83TigAlKS-26
88TigDom-6
89PacLegI-172

Harwell, Jim
61UniOil-SP8

Haryd, Mark
87BurExpP-1086

Hasbach, Dave
76OmaRoyTT-7

Hasegawa, Shigetoshi
97ColCho-258
97Don-379
97DonPreP-379
97DonPrePGold-379
97DonTea-13
97DonTeaSPE-13
97FlaSho-A180
97FlaSho-B180
97FlaSho-C180
97FlaShoLC-180
97FlaShoLC-B180
97FlaShoLC-C180
97FlaShoLCM-A180
97FlaShoLCM-B180
97FlaShoLCM-C180
97Fle-690
97FleTif-690
97Ult-516
97UltGolME-516
97UltPlaME-516

Haselman, Bill
88ChaRanS-9
89TexLeaAGS-33
89TulDriGS-11
89TulDriTI-10
90CMC-745
90ProAaA-68
90TexLeaAGS-25
90TulDriP-1158
90TulDriTI-11
91Don-679
91Fle-287
91LinDriAAA-310
91OklCit8LD-310
91OklCit8P-182
91Sco-377
91TopDeb90-65
92CalCanF-3734
92StaClu-574
93Bow-79
93FleFinE-271
93PacSpa-623
93RanKee-177
93StaCluMari-7
93Ult-622
94ColC-552
94ColChoGS-552
94ColChoSS-552
94Don-654
94Fle-288
94Lea-58
94MarMot-20
94Pac-571
94Sco-189
94ScoGolR-189
94StaClu-114
94StaCluFDI-114
94StaCluGR-114
94StaCluMOP-114
94Top-138
94TopGol-138
94TopSpa-138
95Sco-42
95ScoGolR-42
95ScoPlaTS-42
96LeaSigEA-73
97Cir-82
97CirRav-82
97Fle-681
97FleTif-681
97PacPriGotD-GD21
97Ult-473
97UltGolME-473
97UltPlaME-473

Haskins, Dean
89AncBucTI-18

Hasler, Curt
88SouBenWSGS-21
89SarWhiSS-10
91LinDriAAA-634
91VanCanLD-634
91VanCanP-1590
93HicCraC-28
93HicCraF-1296
94HicCraC-27
94HicCraF-2195
96SouBenSHS-2

Haslerig, Bill
78GreBraT-13
79SavBraT-4

Hasley, Mike
75DubPacT-30
76DubPacT-15

Haslin, Mickey
34BatR31-104

Haslock, Chris
88SpoIndP-1945
89ChaRaiP-981
90RivRedWB-11
90RivRedWCLC-18
90RivRedWP-2602
91HigDesMC-5
91HigDesMP-2388

Hassan, Theodore
92PulBraC-1
92PulBraF-3172

Hassel, Bob
84IdaFalATI-11

Hassel, Jay
92HunCubC-25
92HunCubF-3142
93ExcFS7-10
93PeoChiC-7
93PeoChiF-1079
93PeoChiTI-8

Hasselhoff, Derek
96MidLeaAB-51
96SouBenSHS-15

Hassett, Buddy (John)
36NatChiFPR-110
39ExhSal-25
39GouPreR303A-21
39PlaBal-57
39WorWidGTP-21
40PlaBal-62
41DouPlaR-121
90DodTar-322
93ConTSN-752
94ConTSN-1067
94ConTSNB-1067
95ConTSN-1333

Hassey, Ron
79TacTugT-1
80Top-222
81AllGamPI-41
81Don-80
81Fle-405
81OPC-187
81Top-564
81TopSti-71
82Don-463
82Fle-370
82Ind-19
82IndTeaI-20
82IndWhe-6
82OPC-54
82Top-54
83Don-159
83Fle-411
83Fle-642
83IndPos-19
83IndWhe-18
83Top-689
83TopSti-62
84CubChiT-14
84CubSev-15
84Don-460
84Fle-545
84FleUpd-49
84Ind-17
84Nes792-308
84OPC-308
84Top-308
84TopSti-262
84TopTif-308
84TopTra-49T
84TopTraT-49T
85FleUpd-50
85Top-742
85TopTif-742
85TopTifT-48T
85TopTra-48T
86Don-370
86Fle-107
86OPC-157
86Top-157
86TopTat-13
86TopTif-157
86YanTCM-20
87Don-532
87Fle-499
87FleGlo-499
87OPC-61
87SpoTeaP-26
87Top-667
87TopSti-285
87TopTif-667
87WhiSoxC-14
88A'sMot-16
88Don-580
88DonBasB-302
88DonTeaBA-NEW
88Fle-399
88FleGlo-399
88ScoRoo-33T
88ScoRooG-33T
88Top-458
88TopTif-458
88TopTra-46T
88TopTraT-46T
89A'sMot-15
89Bow-194
89BowTif-194
89Don-361
89Fle-9
89FleGlo-9
89OPC-272
89Sco-334
89Top-272
89TopBig-171
89TopSti-173
89TopTif-272
89UppDec-564
90A'sMot-12
90Bow-464
90BowTif-464
90Don-450
90Fle-8
90FleCan-8
90Lea-326
90OPC-527
90PubSti-305
90Sco-168A
90Sco-168B
90Top-527
90TopBig-4
90TopTif-527
90UppDec-195
91Don-476
91ExpPos-10
91Fle-8
91FleUpd-98
91Lea-359
91OPC-327
91OPCPre-61
91Sco-806
91ScoRoo-43T
91StaClu-490
91Top-327
91TopDesS-327
91TopMic-327
91TopTif-327
91UppDec-401
92Sco-273
92YanWIZ8-78
94RocPol-27

Hassinger, Brad
90PriPatD-11
91Cla/Bes-140
91SpaPhiC-5
91SpaPhiP-890
92SpaPhiF-1259
94GreBraF-408
94GreBraTI-13

Hassler, Andy
75OPC-261
75Top-261
76OPC-207
76SSP-186
76Top-207
77Top-602
78SSP270-225
78Top-73
79Top-696
80Top-353
81Don-581
81Fle-290
81LonBeaPT-14
81Top-454
81TopSti-55
82Don-519
82Fle-464
82Top-94
83Don-290
83Fle-92
83Top-573
84ArkTraT-25
84Don-255
84Fle-519
84Nes792-719
84Top-719
84TopTif-719
85LouRedR-6
91MetWIZ-163

Hasson, Gene
39WorWidGV-14

Hastings, Lionel
94ElmPioF-3483
95BreCouMF-254
96PorSeaDB-14
94ElmPioC-7

Hasty, Robert
22E120-81
23WilChoV-60

Hatcher, Billy
83MidCubT-13
84IowCubT-24
85CubSev-22
85Don-41
85Fle-649
85IowCubT-10
86AstMilL-10
86AstPol-23
86AstTeaI-7
86Don-433
86Fle-371
86FleUpd-49
86Top-46
86TopTif-46
86TopTra-45T
86TopTraT-45T
87AstMot-26
87AstPol-6
87Don-481
87DonOpeD-18
87Fle-59
87FleGlo-59
87FleRecS-15
87Top-578
87TopTif-578
88AstMot-6
88AstPol-11
88Don-23
88Don-261
88DonBasB-150
88DonSupD-23
88Fle-449
88FleGlo-449
88Lea-23
88Lea-110
88OPC-306
88PanSti-300
88RedFolSB-30
88Sco-505
88ScoGlo-505
88Spo-63
88StaLinAst-10

88Top-291
88Top-306
88TopBig-3
88TopMinL-49
88TopSti-28
88TopTif-291
88TopTif-306
88TopUKM-30
88TopUKMT-30
89AstLenH-1
89AstMot-5
89AstSmo-18
89Don-187
89DonBasB-150
89Fle-359
89FleGlo-359
89OPC-252
89PanSti-92
89Sco-61
89Spo-174
89Top-252
89TopBig-118
89TopSti-19
89TopTif-252
89TVSpoM-55
89UppDec-344
90Don-616
90DonBesN-125
90Fle-467
90FleCan-467
90FleUpd-13
90Lea-241
90OPC-119
90PirHomC-11
90PubSti-96
90RedKah-11
90Sco-562
90ScoRoo-42T
90Top-119
90TopBig-222
90TopTif-119
90TopTra-38T
90TopTraT-38T
90UppDec-598
90UppDec-778
91Bow-670
91Don-196
91Don-763
91Fle-66
91FleWorS-2
91Lea-205
91OPC-604
91PanFreS-132
91RedFolS-46
91RedKah-22
91RedPep-10
91Sco-469
91StaClu-371
91StaCluCM-11
91Stu-166
91Top-604
91TopDesS-604
91TopMic-604
91TopTif-604
91Ult-94
91Ult-95
91UppDec-114
91Woo-27
92Don-537
92Fle-409
92OPC-432
92Pin-460
92Sco-447
92ScoRoo-72T
92StaClu-363
92Top-432
92TopGol-432
92TopGolW-432
92TopMic-432
92TriPla-222
92Ult-190
92UppDec-699
93Don-754
93Fla-166
93Fle-561
93Lea-109
93PacSpa-83
93RedSoxWHP-6
93Sco-657
93Sel-225
93Stu-186
93Top-725
93TopGol-725
93TopInaM-725
93TopMic-725
93TriPla-157
93Ult-512
93UppDec-618
93UppDecGold-618
94ColC-128
94ColChoGS-128
94ColChoSS-128
94Don-434
94ExtBas-334
94Fla-14
94Fla-413
94Fle-35
94FleUpd-164
94Lea-34
94Pac-57
94PanSti-31
94PhiMel-19
94Pin-362
94PinArtP-362
94PinMusC-362
94Sco-443
94ScoGolR-443
94Sel-96
94Top-26
94TopGol-26
94TopSpa-26
94TriPla-205
94Ult-16
94UppDec-461
94UppDecED-461
95Don-470
95DonPreP-470
95Sco-515
95ScoGolR-515
95ScoPlaTS-515
95Top-383

Hatcher, Chris
90AubAstP-3395
91BurAstC-20
91BurAstP-2814
91Cla/Bes-312
91MidLeaAP-MWL16
92OscAstC-6
92OscAstF-2542
92ProFS7-230
93ClaFS7-203
93ClaGolF-167
93ExcFS7-43
93JacGenF-2119
94TucTorF-773
94VenLinU-3
95TusTorTI-10
96JacGenB-11
96TusTorB-12

Hatcher, Hal
81ChaRoyT-5
82ForMyeRT-2
84MemChiT-20

Hatcher, Johnny
83DurBulT-5
84DurBulT-5
85DurBulT-26
87GreBraB-25

Hatcher, Ken
52LavPro-39

Hatcher, Mickey
79AlbDukT-11
80DodPol-44
80Top-679
81DodPol-44A
81Don-526
81Fle-135
81Top-289
81TopTra-768
82Don-480
82OPC-291
82Top-467
82TopSti-212
82TwiPos-14
83Don-615
83Fle-614
83Top-121
83TwiTeal-6
84Don-147
84Fle-566
84MinTwiP-15
84Nes792-746
84Top-746
84TopTif-746
84TwiTeal-6
85Don-194
85Fle-279
85Lea-224
85Top-18
85TopSti-304
85TopTif-18
85Twi7-3
85TwiTeal-6
86Don-269
86Fle-396
86Lea-143
86OPC-356
86Top-356
86Top-786
86TopTif-356
86TopTif-786
86TwiTeal-6
87DodMot-25
87Don-491
87Fle-542
87FleGlo-542
87FleUpd-41
87FleUpdG-41
87OPC-341
87Top-504
87TopSti-276
87TopTif-504
87TopTra-43T
87TopTraT-43T
88DodMot-25
88DodPol-9
88Don-299
88Fle-516
88FleGlo-516
88Lea-122
88OPC-339
88Sco-298
88ScoGlo-298
88StaLinD-7
88Top-607
88TopSti-71
88TopTif-607
89Bow-347
89BowTif-347
89DodMot-25
89DodPol-6
89DodStaSV-14
89Don-346
89FleGlo-WS1
89FleWorS-1
89OPC-254
89OPC-390
89PanSti-23
89PanSti-105
89Sco-332
89Top-483
89TopBig-63
89TopTif-483
89UppDec-709
89Woo-31
90DodMot-6
90DodPol-8
90DodTar-323
90Don-439
90Fle-398
90FleCan-398
90Lea-332
90OPC-226
90PubSti-8
90Sco-359
90Top-226
90TopTif-226
90UppDec-283
91Fle-206
91OPC-152
91Sco-153
91Top-152
91TopDesS-152
91TopMic-152
91TopTif-152
91UppDec-666
92AlbDukF-738
93RanKee-436
94RanMagM-6
95GreFalDTI-32
96GreFalDB-1
96GreFalDTI-33

Hatcher, Rick
82DurBulT-18

Hatfield, Fred
52Bow-153
52Top-354
53BowC-125
53TigGle-12
53Top-163
54Bow-119
55Bow-187
56Top-318
57Top-278
58Top-339
59DarFar-9
80RicBraT-5
83TopRep5-354
86MiaMarP-9
91TopArc1-163

Hatfield, Gil (Gilbert)
87OldJudN-237
89SFHaCN-10
90DodTar-975

Hatfield, Rick
94AshTouC-11
94AshTouF-1784

Hatfield, Rob
86MacPirP-13
87SalBucP-4

Hathaway, Hilly
90BoiHawP-3311
90ProAaA-157
92MidAngOHP-7
92PalSprAF-831
93Bow-61
93ClaFS7-6
93Don-329
93FleFinE-183
93SelRoo-55T
93TopTra-87T
93VanCanF-2590
94ColC-129
94ColChoGS-129
94ColChoSS-129
94Don-170
94Fle-59
94LasVegSF-871
94Pin-127
94PinArtP-127
94PinMusC-127
94Sco-612
94ScoBoyoS-10
94ScoGolR-612
94StaClu-385
94StaCluFDI-385
94StaCluGR-385
94StaCluMOP-385
94Top-596
94TopGol-596
94TopSpa-596

Hathaway, Ray
43ParSpo-79

Hathaway, Shawn
88SprCarB-6
89St.PetCS-16
89Sta-50

Hattabaugh, Matt
91UtiBluSC-10
91UtiBluSP-3243

Hattaway, Wayne
85OrlTwiT-23
88OrlTwiB-26
89OrlTwiB-27
89OrlTwiP-1336
90OrlSunRB-26
90OrlSunRS-28

Hatteberg, Scott
91Cla/Bes-442
91ClaDraP-38
91FroRowDP-15
92Bow-83
92ClaFS7-196
92NewBriRSF-437
92NewBriRSS-487
92OPC-734
92Pin-569
92SkyAA F-207
92StaCluD-80
92Top-734
92TopGol-734
92TopGolW-734
92TopMic-734
92UppDecML-238
93Bow-87
93ClaFS7-7
93ClaGolF-28
93NewBriRSF-1225
94NewBriRSF-653
94PawRedSDD-8
94SigRoo-8
94SigRooS-8
94Top-764
94TopGol-764
94TopSpa-764
94UppDecML-246
95PawRedSDD-13
95PawRedTI-12
95Top-632
96PawRedSDD-11
96Sco-508
97DonLim-175
97DonLimLE-175

Hatten, Joe
47HomBon-19
47TipTop-96
49Bow-116
49EurSta-36
50Bow-166
51Bow-190
52Bow-144
52Top-194
79DiaGre-91
83TopRep5-194
90DodTar-324
91RinPosBD4-7

Hatter, Clyde
35DiaMatCS3T1-71

Hattig, Keith
94BoiHawC-13
94BoiHawF-3362

Hatton, Grady
47Exh-90
47PM1StaP1-80
49Bow-62
49EurSta-85
50Bow-26
51Bow-47
51TopRedB-34
52Top-6
53Top-45
54Top-208
55Top-131
55TopDouH-71
56Top-26
56TopPin-23
66Top-504
67Ast-14
67AstTeal1-6
67Top-347
68Top-392
73OPC-624
73Top-624
74OPC-31
74Top-31
79DiaGre-268
83TopRep5-6
84TCMPla1-39
91OriCro-187
91TopArc1-45
92TexLon-23
94TopArc1-208
94TopArc1G-208

Haugen, Troy
89HelBreSP-7
90BelBreB-24
90BelBreS-10
91StoPorC-12
91StoPorP-3039

Haughey, Chris
90DodTar-976

Haughney, Trevor
91GulCoaRSP-14

Haught, Gary
92SouOreAC-17
92SouOreAF-3411
93MadMusC-14
93MadMusF-1818
93MidLeaAGF-13
94ModA'sC-14
94ModA'sF-3061
95ModA'sTI-10
96HunStaTI-9

Haugstad, Phil
52Top-198
83TopRep5-198
90DodTar-325
95TopArcBD-11

Haurado, Yanko
87PriWilYP-2

Hause, Brendan
92HigSchPLS-8
94SouOreAC-10
94SouOreAF-3614
95MidLeaA-23
95WesMicWTI-16
96ModA'sB-15

Hauser, Arnold
09SpoNewSM-89
10DomDisP-54

10SweCapPP-148
11MecDFT-25
11PloCanE-32
11S74Sil-119
11T205-73
12HasTriFT-70C
14PieStaT-27
Hauser, Jeff
88RocExpLC-16
Hauser, Joe
21Nei-53
22E120-82
22W572-40
26Exh-108
28Exh-55
61Fle-113
78HalHalR-16
79DiaGre-328
88LitSunMLL-10
92ConTSN-548
94ConTSN-1071
94ConTSNB-1071
95ConTSN-1386
Hausladen, Bob
83BurRanF-1
83BurRanT-19
Hausman, Tom (Thomas)
74SacSolC-52
76OPC-452
76Top-452
77SpoIndC-18
77Top-99
78TidTidT-10
79OPC-339
79Top-643
80Top-151
81Don-396
81Fle-333
81Top-359
82Don-301
82Fle-526
82MetPhoA-9
82Top-524
83Top-417
91MetWIZ-164
94BreMilB-131
Hausmann, Clem
50WorWidGV-13
Hausmann, George
49EurSta-109
83TCMPla1944-36
Hausmann, Jeff
88NebCor-4
Hausterman, David
86DayBealP-11
Hauswirth, Trentor
93RocRoyC-15
93RocRoyF-720
Havens, Brad
78QuaCitAT-9
82Don-382
82OrlTwi8SCT-16
82Top-92
82TwiPos-15
83Don-480
83Fle-615
83Top-751
83TwiTeal-19
84Nes792-509
84TolMudHT-8
84Top-509
84TopTif-509
85IntLeaAT-40
85RocRedWT-16
86Don-599
87Fle-472
87FleGlo-472
87RocRedWP-17
87RocRedWT-5
87Top-398
87TopTif-398
87TopTra-44T
87TopTraT-44T
88DodMot-22
88DodPol-41
88Fle-517
88FleGlo-517
88Top-698
88TopTif-698
89Fle-407
89FleGlo-407
89IndTeal-13
89Top-204
89TopTif-204
90DodTar-326
91OriCro-188
Havens, Jeff
94WilCubF-3758
96AugGreB-13
Havens, Tom
92MadMusC-8
92MadMusF-1242
Havens, Will
92PulBraC-15
92PulBraF-3173
93DanBraC-13
93DanBraF-3614
Havlin, Jack
88AllandGN-9
Hawarny, Dave
82BirBarT-16
83BirBarT-6
Hawblitzel, Ryan
90HunCubP-3276
91CarLeaAP-CAR42
91WinSpiC-4
91WinSpiP-2823
92Bow-138
92ChaKniF-2765
92ChaKniS-158
92ClaFS7-61
92DonRoo-49
92ProFS7-205
92SkyAA F-73
92UppDec-59
92UppDecML-31
92UppDecML-298
93Bow-64
93ClaFS7-8
93ClaGolF-91
93ColSprSSF-3081
93ExcFS7-11
93FleFinE-32
93Top-648
93TopGol-648
93TopInaM-648
93TopMic-648
93Ult-349
94ColSprSSF-727
96ColSprSSTI-17
Hawes, Roy Lee
55Bow-268
88ChaLooLTI-14
Hawkins, Al
96OgdRapTI-50
Hawkins, Andy
82HawIsIT-14
84Fle-302
84Nes792-778
84PadMot-18
84Top-778
84TopTif-778
85Don-528
85DonHig-14
85DonHig-15
85Fle-36
85PadMot-13
85Top-299
85TopTif-299
86Don-284
86Fle-324
86FleMin-70
86FleStiC-51
86Lea-158
86OPC-5
86SevCoi-W12
86Spo-191
86Top-478
86TopSti-108
86TopTat-12
86TopTif-478
87Don-264
87Fle-417
87FleGlo-417
87PadBohHB-40
87SpoTeaP-16
87Top-81
87Top-183
87TopTif-81
87TopTif-183
88Fle-586
88FleGlo-586
88PadSmo-11
88Sco-347
88ScoGlo-347
88Top-9
88TopBig-257
88TopTif-9
89Bow-166
89BowTif-166
89Don-583
89DonBasB-52
89DonTra-52
89Fle-307
89FleGlo-307
89FleUpd-50
89PanSti-194
89Sco-118
89ScoRoo-14T
89Spo-84
89Top-533
89TopSti-111
89TopTif-533
89TopTra-47T
89TopTraT-47T
89UppDec-495
89UppDec-708
89YanScoNW-19
90ClaBlu-135
90Don-159
90Fle-445
90FleCan-445
90Lea-281
90OPC-335
90PanSti-130
90PubSti-536
90Top-335
90TopBig-36
90TopSti-317
90TopTif-335
90TopTVY-10
90UppDec-339
90YanScoNW-18
91Don-611
91DonBonC-BC12A
91DonBonC-BC12B
91Fle-666
91FleWaxBC-6
91OPC-635
91PanFreS-357
91PanSti-6
91Sco-47
91Sco-704
91StaClu-487
91StaCluCM-12
91Top-635
91TopDesS-635
91TopMic-635
91TopTif-635
91Ult-234
91UppDec-333
92CalCanS-59
92YanWIZ8-79
Hawkins, Cedric
86LitFalMP-13
Hawkins, Chris
87AubAstP-11
Hawkins, Craig
91EliTwiP-4306
92EliTwiC-14
92EliTwiF-3694
Hawkins, Hersey
88PeoChiTI-14
Hawkins, J.R.
93YakBeaC-12
93YakBeaF-3897
Hawkins, Joe
90PitMetP-28
91St.LucMC-30
95NorTidTI-4
96NorTidB-4
Hawkins, John
84NasSouTI-9
85AlbYanT-32
86FloStaLAP-21
86Ft.LauYP-12
91SouBenWSC-28
Hawkins, Kraig
92OneYanC-25
93GreHorC-10
93GreHorF-898
94ExcFS7-104
94TamYanC-12
94TamYanF-2396
95AusFut-72
95NorNavTI-11
95TamYanYI-10
96TamYanY-12
Hawkins, LaTroy
93ForWayWC-10
93ForWayWF-1963
94BowBes-B65
94BowBesR-B65
94Cla-54
94ClaTriF-T46
94ExcFS7-95
94ExcLeaLF-9
94ForMyeMC-1
94ForMyeMF-1163
94SigRooTPD-T4
94SigRooTPS-T4
94SPDieC-8
94Ult-389
94UppDec-548
94UppDecAHNIL-6
94UppDecED-548
94UppDecML-248
94UppDecMLPotYF-PY26
95ActPac2GF-15G
95ActPacF-28
95ActPacF-76
95ARuFalLS-9
95Bow-256
95BowBes-B53
95BowBesR-B53
95BowGolF-256
95ColChoSE-7
95ColChoSEGS-7
95ColChoSESS-7
95Exc-86
95ExcLeaL-8
95Fla-280
95Fle-204
95SelCer-103
95SelCerMG-103
95SigRooOP-OP4
95SigRooOPS-OP4
95StaCluCB-CB15
95StaCluMOP-CB15
95Sum-172
95SumNthD-172
95Top-179
95UltGolP-5
95UltGolPGM-5
95UppDec-223
95UppDecED-223
95UppDecEDG-223
95UppDecML-7
95UppDecML-163
95UppDecMLMLA-5
95UppDecSE-81
95UppDecSEG-81
95Zen-136
95ZenRooRC-15
96ColCho-198
96ColCho-659
96ColChoGS-198
96ColChoGS-659
96ColChoSS-198
96ColChoSS-659
96Don-514
96DonPreP-514
96Fla-113
96FleUpd-U53
96FleUpdTC-U53
96Lea-56
96LeaPre-140
96LeaPreP-140
96LeaPrePB-56
96LeaPrePG-56
96LeaPrePS-56
96LeaSigA-97
96LeaSigAG-97
96LeaSigAS-97
96Pin-185
96PinAfi-170
96PinAfiAP-170
96Sco-224
96ScoDugC-A104
96ScoDugCAP-A104
96Sel-185
96SelArtP-185
96SelCer-125
96SelCerAP-125
96SelCerCB-125
96SelCerCR-125
96SelCerMB-125
96SelCerMG-125
96SelCerMR-125
96Stu-131
96StuPrePB-131
96StuPrePG-131
96StuPrePS-131
96Sum-183
96SumAbo&B-183
96SumArtP-183
96SumFoi-183
96Top-407
96Ult-373
96UltGolM-373
96UppDec-367
97DonEli-138
97DonEliGS-138
97DonRatR-2
97Sco-260
97ScoPreS-260
97ScoShoS-260
97ScoShoSAP-260
95UppDecMLFS-7
95UppDecMLFS-163
Hawkins, Todd
87EveGiaC-18
88FreSunCLC-9
88FreSunP-1242
Hawkins, Ty
91SouBenWSP-2869
Hawkins, Walter
87IdaFalBP-11
Hawkins, Wes
93BluOriF-4139
94AlbPolF-2250
Hawkins, Wynn
60Top-536
61Top-34
63Top-334
Hawks, Boise
95BoiHawTI-35
Hawks, Larry
90SpoIndSP-5
91BenBucC-24
91BenBucP-3696
91WatDiaC-28
91WatDiaP-1258
Hawks, Nelson
21KoBreWSI-34
22W575-53
25Exh-42
Hawley, Billy
83CedRapRF-10
86VerRedP-10
87TamTarP-26
Hawley, Pink (Emerson P.)
98CamPepP-33
Haws, Scott
92MarPhiC-16
92MarPhiF-3060
93SpaPhiC-14
93SpaPhiF-1059
94ClePhiC-16
94ClePhiF-2331
Haydel, Hal
71OPC-692
71Top-692
72OPC-28
72Top-28
Hayden, Alan
86ColMetP-12
87JacMetF-22
87LynMetP-11
88JacMetGS-25
89ChaLooB-25
89ChaLooGS-23
89JacMetGS-30
89NasSouTI-9
90ChaLooGS-15
Hayden, David
91BatCliC-10
91BatCliP-3492
92SpaPhiC-18
92SpaPhiF-1269
93ClePhiC-13
93ClePhiF-2691
94ReaPhiF-2070
95ReaPhiTI-16
Hayden, John F.
09T206-429
Hayden, Paris
89FreKeyS-10
90FreKeyTI-13
90HagSunP-1427
90HagSunS-11
91FloStaLAP-FSL22
91MiaMirC-28
91MiaMirP-421
Hayden, Richard
84ButCopKT-12
Hayes, Ben
82IndIndTI-21
83Fle-591
84Fle-470

84Nes792-448
84Top-448
84TopTif-448
85LouRedR-25
Hayes, Bill
80WicAerT-5
82IowCubT-5
83IowCubT-12
84IowCubT-15
85IowCubT-2
86OmaRoyP-10
86OmaRoyT-1
87IowCubTI-14
88GenCubP-1654
90GenCubP-3053
90GenCubS-26
91PeoChiC-22
91PeoChiP-1359
91PeoChiTI-1
92WinSpiC-26
92WinSpiF-1223
93DayCubC-24
93DayCubF-873
94CenValRC-26
94CenValRF-3218
95SalAvaTI-29
96NewHavRB-1
Hayes, Blimp (Frank)
39PlaBal-108
40PlaBal-24
41DouPlaR-47
41Gou-13
41PlaBal-41
47TipTop-7
92ConTSN-380
93ConTSN-864
Hayes, Brian
78LodDodT-7
79LodDodT-19
Hayes, Charlie
85FreGiaP-11
86ShrCapP-11
87ShrCapP-17
87TexLeaAF-27
88BlaYNPRWL-151
88PhoFirC-15
88PhoFirP-57
89BlaYNPRWL-157
89Fle-330
89FleGlo-330
89FleUpd-106
89PhiTas-41
89PhoFirC-13
89PhoFirP-1487
89Sco-628
89ScoHot1R-39
89UppDec-707
90ClaBlu-98
90Don-548
90DonBesN-106
90Fle-558
90FleCan-558
90Hot50RS-21
90Lea-131
90OPC-577
90PhiTas-11
90Sco-507
90Sco100RS-12
90ScoYouSI-38
90Spo-36
90Top-577
90TopTif-577
90UppDec-437
91Bow-508
91Don-278
91Fle-397
91Lea-214
91OPC-312
91PanFreS-105
91PanSti-102
91PhiMed-17
91Sco-238
91Sco100S-19
91StaClu-163
91Stu-214
91Top-312
91TopDesS-312
91TopMic-312
91TopTif-312
91Ult-263
91UppDec-269
92Bow-147
92Don-547
92Fle-533
92FleUpd-42
92Lea-220
92OPC-754
92OPCPre-6
92PanSti-244
92Pin-497
92Sco-301
92ScoRoo-16T
92StaClu-711
92StaCluNC-711
92Stu-212
92Top-754
92TopGol-754
92TopGolW-754
92TopMic-754
92TopTra-46T
92TopTraG-46T
92Ult-243
92Ult-407
92UppDec-208
92UppDec-768
93Bow-500
93CadDis-30
93DiaMar-49
93Don-181
93Don-776
93DurPowP2-4
93Fin-60
93FinRef-60
93Fla-41
93Fle-279
93FleFinE-33
93FunPac-177
93JimDea-26
93Lea-360
93OPC-54
93OPCPre-66
93PacSpa-429
93Pin-447
93PinExpOD-5
93PinHomRC-19
93RocUSPC-1H
93RocUSPC-2C
93Sco-411
93Sel-194
93SP-222
93StaClu-743
93StaCluFDI-743
93StaCluMOP-743
93StaCluRoc-3
93Stu-136
93Top-142
93Top-759
93TopGol-142
93TopGol-759
93TopInaM-142
93TopInaM-759
93TopMic-142
93TopMic-759
93TriPla-257
93Ult-350
93UppDec-647
93UppDecGold-647
94Bow-254
94ColC-130
94ColChoGS-130
94ColChoSS-130
94Don-46
94DonSpeE-46
94ExtBas-247
94Fin-32
94FinRef-32
94Fla-374
94Fle-443
94FUnPac-89
94Lea-134
94LeaL-104
94OPC-171
94Pac-197
94PacSilP-21
94PanSti-175
94Pin-14
94PinArtP-14
94PinMusC-14
94PinRunC-RC40
94RedFolMI-12
94RocPol-13
94Sco-50
94ScoCyc-TC7
94ScoGolR-50
94Sel-42
94SP-167
94SPDieC-167
94Spo-82
94StaClu-249
94StaCluFDI-249
94StaCluGR-249
94StaCluMOP-249
94StaCluT-114
94StaCluTFDI-114
94Stu-179
94Top-655
94TopGol-655
94TopSpa-655
94TriPla-225
94Ult-482
94UppDec-167
94UppDecAJ-39
94UppDecAJG-39
94UppDecED-167
95ColCho-445
95ColCho-567T
95ColChoGS-445
95ColChoSE-207
95ColChoSEGS-207
95ColChoSESS-207
95ColChoSS-445
95Don-252
95DonPreP-252
95DonTopotO-305
95Emo-166
95Fin-261
95FinRef-261
95Fla-390
95Fle-521
95FleUpd-121
95Lea-325
95LeaLim-18
95Pac-138
95Phi-15
95PhiMel-12
95Pin-79
95PinArtP-79
95PinMusC-79
95Sco-58
95ScoGolR-58
95ScoPlaTS-58
95SP-89
95Spo-9
95SpoArtP-9
95SPSil-89
95StaClu-123
95StaClu-559
95StaCluFDI-123
95StaCluMOP-123
95StaCluMOP-559
95StaCluSTWS-123
95StaCluSTWS-559
95StaCluVR-62
95Top-81
95TopCyb-57
95TopTra-140T
95Ult-154
95UltGolM-154
95UppDec-172
95UppDec-378
95UppDecED-172
95UppDecED-378
95UppDecEDG-172
95UppDecEDG-378
95UppDecSE-209
95UppDecSEG-209
96Cir-171
96CirRav-171
96ColCho-255
96ColCho-680
96ColChoGS-255
96ColChoGS-680
96ColChoSS-255
96ColChoSS-680
96Don-140
96DonPreP-140
96EmoXL-254
96Fin-B226
96FinRef-B226
96Fla-346
96Fle-499
96FleTif-499
96FleUpd-U176
96FleUpdTC-U176
96LeaSigA-98
96LeaSigAG-98
96LeaSigAS-98
96Pac-149
96PanSti-34
96Pin-124
96Pin-343
96PinAfi-44
96PinAfiAP-44
96PinAfiFPP-44
96PinFoil-343
96Sco-307
96ScoDugC-B32
96ScoDugCAP-B32
96Sel-131
96SelArtP-131
96SP-148
96StaClu-441
96StaCluEPB-441
96StaCluEPG-441
96StaCluEPS-441
96StaCluMOP-441
95StaCluVRMC-62
96Top-255
96Ult-253
96Ult-532
96UltGolM-253
96UltGolM-532
96UppDec-436
97ColCho-403
97Don-99
97DonPreP-99
97DonPrePGold-99
97DonTea-127
97DonTeaSPE-127
97Fle-167
97FleTif-167
97PacPriGotD-GD73
97Sco-64
97ScoPreS-64
97ScoShoS-64
97ScoShoSAP-64
97Ult-323
97UltGolME-323
97UltPlaME-323
97UppDec-442
Hayes, Chris
87ModA'sC-19
87ModA'sP-13
95StCatSTI-19
96DunBluJUTI-4
96HagSunB-8
Hayes, Damon
47RemBre-21
47SmiClo-21
48SmiClo-13
Hayes, Dan
84NewOriT-13
Hayes, Darren
96PriWilCB-14
Hayes, Emanuel
92MedHatBJF-3213
92MedHatBJSP-5
93St.CatBJC-9
93St.CatBJF-3980
Hayes, Jackie (Minter)
29ExhFou-32
31SenTeaIPW-15
34Gou-63
35AlDemDCR3-15
35GouPuzR-8B
35GouPuzR-9B
37OPCBatUV-102
39WhiSoxTI-6
40WhiSoxL-7
81ConTSN-36
91ConTSN-71
95ConTSN-1429
Hayes, Jimmy (Jim)
88BriTigP-1874
90TamYanD-11
Hayes, Randy
84AriWilP-8
Hayes, Robbie
91MisStaB-22
92MisStaB-18
93MisStaB-18
Hayes, Terry
82WauTimF-29
Hayes, Todd
87SanBerSP-22
88SanBerSB-25
88SanBerSCLC-51
Hayes, Tom
81DurBulT-7
84RicBraT-6
85GreBraTI-7
Hayes, Von
80WatIndT-35
81ChaChaT-15
82Don-237
82Fle-371
82Ind-20
82IndTeal-18
82IndWhe-25
82Top-141
82TopTra-42T
83AllGamPI-146
83Don-324
83Fle-412
83OPC-325
83PhiTas-13
83Top-325
83TopSti-311
83TopTra-40T
84Don-477
84Fle-33
84Nes792-587
84OPC-259
84PhiTas-36
84Top-587
84TopSti-124
84TopTif-587
85AllGamPI-144
85Don-326
85DonHig-16
85Fle-253
85Lea-93
85OPC-68
85PhiCIG-2
85PhiTas-12
85PhiTas-36
85Top-68
85TopMin-68
85TopSti-115
85TopTif-68
86BasStaB-54
86Don-305
86Fle-443
86FleMin-92
86FleStiC-52
86Lea-176
86OPC-146
86PhiCIG-3
86PhiKel-2
86PhiTas-9
86Top-420
86TopSti-120
86TopTat-10
86TopTif-420
87BurKinA-8
87ClaGam-63
87Don-12
87Don-113
87DonOpeD-152
87DonSupD-12
87Dra-3
87Fle-175
87FleExcS-23
87FleGamW-19
87FleGlo-175
87FleMin-51
87FleStiC-55
87KraFoo-24
87Lea-12
87Lea-130
87OPC-389
87PhiCha-1
87PhiTas-9
87RedFolSB-72
87Spo-193
87SpoTeaP-6
87Top-481
87Top-666
87TopCoi-35
87TopMinL-28
87TopSti-121
87TopTif-481
87TopTif-666
88Don-207
88DonBasB-128
88Dra-17
88Fle-304
88FleExcS-18
88FleGlo-304
88FleMin-99
88FleStiC-108
88Lea-197
88OPC-215
88PanSti-356
88PhiTas-13
88Sco-515
88ScoGlo-515
88Spo-62
88StaLinPh-9
88Top-215

88TopBig-139
88TopSti-117
88TopTif-215
89Bow-406
89BowTif-406
89Don-160
89DonBasB-47
89Fle-571
89FleGlo-571
89KinDis-18
89OPC-385
89PanSti-151
89PhiTas-9
89RedFolSB-56
89Sco-38
89Spo-181
89Top-385
89TopBig-302
89TopSti-115
89TopTif-385
89TVSpoM-30
89UppDec-246
90Bow-160
90BowTif-160
90ClaBlu-113
90Don-278
90DonBesN-140
90DOnBonM-BC25
90DonLeaS-18
90Fle-559
90FleAwaW-17
90FleBasA-17
90FleCan-559
90GooHumICBLS-12
90KinDis-7
90Lea-52
90MLBBasB-2
90OPC-710
90PanSti-319
90PhiTas-12
90Pos-27
90PubSti-238
90RedFolSB-45
90Sco-36
90Sco100S-62
90Spo-147
90SunSee-12
90Top-710
90TopBig-69
90TopCoi-48
90TopDou-32
90TopMinL-69
90TopSti-114
90TopStiB-16
90TopTif-710
90TopTVA-54
90UppDec-7
90UppDec-453
91BasBesHRK-9
91Bow-487
91ClaGam-25
91Don-222
91Fle-398
91Lea-280
91OPC-15
91PanFreS-107
91PanSti-105
91PhiMed-18
91RedFolS-47
91Sco-426
91StaClu-127
91Top-15
91TopCraJ2-5
91TopDesS-15
91TopMic-15
91TopTif-15
91Ult-264
91Ult-398
91UppDec-368
92AngPol-12
92Bow-197
92Don-580
92Fle-534
92Lea-177
92OPC-135
92OPCPre-127
92PanSti-248
92Pin-326
92Sco-207
92SpoStaCC-22
92StaClu-880
92Stu-147
92Top-135
92TopGol-135
92TopGolW-135
92TopKid-19
92TopMic-135
92TopTra-47T
92TopTraG-47T
92Ult-326
92UppDec-427
92UppDec-707

Hayford, Don
79ElmPioRST-10

Hayman, David
93MisStaB-19
96AriBlaDB-21
97Top-251

Haynes, Heath
91JamExpC-25
91JamExpP-3538
92MidLeaATI-17
92ProFS7-272
92RocExpC-21
92RocExpF-2109
93ClaGolF-37
93HarSenF-266
94ExcFS7-225
94OttLynF-2897
94VenLinU-212
94WatIndC-17
94WatIndF-3944
95EdmTraTI-9
95LinVen-59
96LakElsSB-5

Haynes, Jimmy
91HigSchPLS-6
92KanCouCC-18
92KanCouCF-85
92KanCouCTI-13
92UppDecML-168
93Bow-493
93ClaFS7-73
93FreKeyC-10
93FreKeyF-1021
94Bow-543
94BowBayF-2410
94BowBes-B15
94BowBesR-B15
94Cla-35
94ExcFS7-7
94OriPro-45
94UppDecML-194
95ActPacF-39
95Bow-130
95BowBes-B69
95BowBesR-B69
95Exc-6
95ExcLeaL-9
95RocRedWTI-18
95Sel-196
95SelArtP-196
95SigRooOJA-AS3
95SigRooOJAS-AS3
95UppDecML-61
96Bow-184
96BowBes-159
96BowBesAR-159
96BowBesR-159
96ColCho-22
96ColChoGS-22
96ColChoSS-22
96Don-475
96DonPreP-475
96Fin-B220
96FinRef-B220
96Fla-6
96Fle-10
96FleOri-7
96FleTif-10
96Lea-189
96LeaPrePB-189
96LeaPrePG-189
96LeaPrePS-189
96LeaSigA-99
96LeaSigAG-99
96LeaSigAS-99
96Pin-179
96PinAfi-186
96PinAfiAP-186
96Sco-509
96Sel-165
96SelArtP-165
96SelCer-132
96SelCerAP-132
96SelCerCB-132
96SelCerCR-132
96SelCerMB-132
96SelCerMG-132
96SelCerMR-132
96SP-8
96Spo-132
96SpoArtP-132
96Sum-195
96SumAbo&B-195
96SumArtP-195
96SumFoi-195
96Top-354
96TopChr-143
96TopChrR-143
96TopGal-132
96TopGalPPI-132
96TopLasBS-11
96Ult-305
96UltGolM-305
96UppDec-229
96UppDecFSP-FS13
97Sco-234
97ScoOri-14
97ScoOriPl-14
97ScoOriPr-14
97ScoPreS-234
97ScoShoS-234
97ScoShoSAP-234
95UppDecMLFS-61

Haynes, Joe
48WhiSoxTI-10
49Bow-191
51Bow-240
52Bow-103
52Top-145
54Top-223
83TopRep5-145
94TopArc1-223
94TopArc1G-223

Haynes, Marvin
87VerRedP-26

Haynes, Nathan
97Bow-428
97BowChr-288
97BowChrI-288
97BowChrIR-288
97BowChrR-288
97BowInt-428

Haynes, Rick
75DubPacT-14

Haynie, Jason
96EriSeaB-12

Hays, Darrin
89ButCopKSP-23
90ChaRanS-9

Hays, David
89EasLeaDDP-DD50

Hays, Rob
90SpoIndSP-9
91WatDiaC-5
91WatDiaP-1252

Haysbert, Dennis
89MajLeaM-4
89MajLeaM-10

Hayward, Brent
92GulCoaMF-3473

Hayward, Jeff
86TamTarP-6

Hayward, Joe
94HigDesMC-13
94HigDesMF-2800

Hayward, Ray
83BeaGolGT-19
84LasVegSC-219
85LasVegSC-104
86LasVegSP-7
87Don-632
87LasVegSP-12
88FleUpd-63
88FleUpdG-63
88OklCit8C-7
88OklCit8P-49
88RanMot-16
88ScoRoo-67T
88ScoRooG-67T
88TopTra-47T
88TopTraT-47T
89Don-521
89Fle-521
89FleGlo-521
89Sco-514
90OklCit8P-426
90ProAAAF-672
93RanKee-178

Hayward, Steve
94LynRedSC-12
94LynRedSF-1889

Haywood, Buster (Albert)
78LauLonABS-20
86NegLeaF-42
87NegLeaPD-36
89RinPosNL1-4
92NegLeaK-8
92NegLeaRLI-27

Hayworth, Ray
33GeoCMil-19
34BatR31-165
34DiaStaR-90
35DiaMatCS3T1-72
35TigFreP-11
36GouWidPPR-A49
36SandSW-31
36WorWidGV-50
39PlaBal-140
40PlaBal-155
76TigOldTS-13
79DiaGre-385
90DodTar-327
95MegRut-5

Hayworth, Red
96Bro194F-22

Hazelette, Moe
83KinBluJTI-8

Hazewood, Drungo L.
80ChaO'sP-10
80ChaO'sW-10
81RocRedWT-8
81RocRedWW-16
83RocRedWT-20
91OriCro-189

Hazle, Hurricane (Robert S.)
58BraJayP-6
58Top-83
87Bra195T-3

Hazlett, Steve
91EliTwiP-4307
92KenTwiC-11
92KenTwiF-617
92MidLeaATI-18
93FloStaLAF-15
93ForMyeMC-10
93ForMyeMF-2668
94ClaGolF-66
94NasXprF-399

Head, Ed
42DodTeal-9
43DodTeal-12
90DodTar-328
91RinPosBD2-5

Headley, Kent
88VirGenS-9

Heakins, Craig
86WatPirP-9
87MacPirP-19

Healey, John
87OldJudN-238

Healy, Bob
77LynMetT-17
77QuaCitAT-15

Healy, Fran
72Top-663
73OPC-361
73Top-361
74Car193T-15
74OPC-238
74Top-238
74TopSta-182
75OPC-120
75OPC-251
75Top-120
75Top-251
76OPC-394
76SSP-184
76Top-394
77Top-148
77YanBurK-3
78SSP270-19
78Top-582
78YanSSPD-19
92YanWIZ7-69

Healy, J.C.
87OldJudN-239

Healy, John
87BucN28-42

Heams, Shane
95EveAqaTI-10

Heap, James
52LavPro-79

Heaps, Chris
92GulCoaYF-3796

Heard, Jehosie
54OriEss-14
54Top-226
91NegLeaRL-15
91OriCro-190
93NegLeaRL2-17
94TopArc1-226
94TopArc1G-226
95NegLeaLI-15

Hearn, Ed
83LynMetT-22
84JacMetT-NNO
85IntLeaAT-10
85TidTidT-21
86DonRoo-54
86MetTCM-32
86MetWorSC-8
86TidTidP-13
87Don-446
87DonOpeD-201
87Fle-10
87FleGlo-10
87Top-433
87TopTif-433
87ToyRoo-11
88Sco-569
88ScoGlo-569
88Top-56
88TopTif-56
89Don-297
89OmaRoyC-12
89OmaRoyP-1732
89Top-348
89TopTif-348
89TriAAP-AAA4
89UppDec-42
91MetWIZ-165

Hearn, Jim
49Bow-190
49EurSta-184
50Bow-208
50JJKCopP-5
51Bow-61
51R42SmaS-44
52BerRos-23
52Bow-49
52RedMan-NL8
52TipTop-14
52Top-337
53BowC-76
53NorBreL-11
53Top-38
54NewYorJA-24
55Bow-220
55GiaGolS-8
56Top-202
57Top-348
58Top-298
59Top-63
59TopVen-63
75Gia195T-7
79TCM50-97
83TopRep5-337
91TopArc1-38

Hearn, Sean
92MedHatBJF-3219
92MedHatBJSP-3
93St.CatBJC-10
93St.CatBJF-3986
94DunBluJC-12
94DunBluJF-2569

Hearn, Tommy
86MiaMarP-10

Hearne, Hugh
90DodTar-977

Hearne, John
91PerHeaF-14

Hearron, Jeff
86BluJayFS-16
87BluJayFS-13
87Don-490
87KnoBluJP-1514
87OPC-274
87SyrChiT-3
87Top-274
87TopTif-274
89LasVegSC-17
89LasVegSP-11
90CMC-98
90IowCubC-23
90IowCubP-320
90ProAAAF-627
90TopTVCu-49

86STaoftFT-30
Heath, Al
82AppFoxF-28
83AppFoxF-29
84MadMusP-8
85ModA'sC-8
86KinEagP-9
87PalSprP-2
Heath, Bill (William)
66Top-539
67AstTeal1-7
67CokCapAs-7
67OPC-172
67Top-172
70OPC-541
70Top-541
87AstShowSTh-27
Heath, Dave
83PeoSunF-6
85MidAngT-6
86MidAngP-10
87EdmTraP-2063
Heath, Jason
92OklStaC-11
94BelMarC-15
94BelMarF-3240
Heath, Jeff (John Jeffrey)
39ExhSal-26A
39ExhSal-26B
39GouPreR303A-22
39GouPreR303B-13
39WorWidGTP-22
46SeaSLP-21
46SpoExcW-4-2
47TipTop-64
49Bow-169
49EurSta-11
83TCMPla1945-15
93ConTSN-939
Heath, Kelly
80OmaRoyP-14
81OmaRoyT-17
83OmaRoyT-16
84ColCliP-11
84ColCliT-2
85ColCliP-12
85ColCliT-16
85IntLeaAT-31
86RicBraP-9
87RicBraBC-11
87RicBraC-1
87RicBraT-18
88SyrChiC-20
88SyrChiP-811
89SyrChiC-17
89SyrChiMB-13
89SyrChiP-800
90CMC-239
90ProAAAF-307
90ScrRedBC-13
90ScrRedBP-605
92ReaPhiF-593
93ReaPhiF-312
96ReaPhiB-28
Heath, Lee
89PulBraP-1911
90SumBraB-5
90SumBraP-2445
91MacBraC-23
91MacBraP-876
92DurBulC-7
92DurBulF-1112
92DurBulTI-33
92UppDecML-88
93Bow-114
93GreBraF-360
94HigDesMC-14
94HigDesMF-2801
Heath, Mike
75ForLauYS-19
76ForLauYS-14
77WesHavYT-11
79Top-710
80Top-687
81A'sGraG-2
81Don-120
81Fle-583
81Top-437
82A'sGraG-3
82Don-413
82Fle-91
82OPC-318
82Top-318
83A'sGraG-2
83AllGamPI-41
83Don-517
83Fle-518
83Top-23
83TopSti-104
84A'sMot-9
84AllGamPI-130
84Don-223
84Fle-446
84Nes792-567
84Top-567
84TopSti-337
84TopTif-567
85A'sMot-4
85AllGamPI-41
85Don-298
85Fle-424
85OPC-396
85Top-662
85TopSti-326
85TopTif-662
86CarIGAS-5
86CarSchM-7
86Don-253
86Fle-418
86FleUpd-50
86OPC-148
86Top-148
86TopSti-174
86TopTif-148
86TopTra-46T
86TopTraT-46T
87Don-496
87DonOpeD-214
87FleUpd-42
87FleUpdG-42
87TigCaiD-3
87TigCok-8
87Top-492
87TopTif-492
88Don-338
88DonBasB-69
88Fle-56
88FleGlo-56
88RedFolSB-31
88Sco-156
88ScoGlo-156
88StaLinTi-6
88TigPep-8
88Top-237
88TopTif-237
89Don-271
89DonBasB-147
89Fle-132A
89Fle-132B
89FleGlo-132
89Sco-131
89TigMar-8
89Top-609
89Top-743
89TopTif-609
89TopTif-743
89UppDec-654
90Bow-352
90BowTif-352
90ClaYel-T40
90Don-209
90DonBesA-90
90Fle-603
90FleCan-603
90Lea-60
90MLBBasB-91
90OPC-366
90PanSti-66
90PubSti-471
90Sco-172
90TigCok-7
90Top-366
90TopBig-166
90TopSti-280
90TopTif-366
90UppDec-306
91Bow-589
91BraDubP-14
91BraSubS-18
91Don-230
91Fle-339
91Lea-320
91OPC-16
91PanFreS-287
91PanSti-237
91Sco-112
91ScoPro-112
91ScoRoo-69T
91StaClu-393
91Top-16
91TopDesS-16
91TopMic-16
91TopTif-16
91UppDec-318
91UppDec-701
92OPC-512
92Sco-344
92StaClu-128
92TacTigF-2506
92Top-512
92TopGol-512
92TopGolPS-512
92TopGolW-512
92TopMic-512
92TopPreS-16
92UppDec-304
92YanWIZ7-70
96BirBarB-22
Heath, Thomas
36GouWidPPR-D11
52MotCoo-46
53MotCoo-43
Heathcock, Jeff
83ColAstT-14
84TucTorC-65
86Don-182
86Fle-302
86TucTorP-6
87TucTorP-18
88AstMot-18
88AstPol-12
88Fle-450
88FleGlo-450
89TucTorC-7
89TucTorJP-7
89TucTorP-196
90CMC-486
90EdmTraC-9
90EdmTraP-515
90ProAAAF-91
Heathcote, Clifton E.
21Exh-71
22E120-231
22W573-58
26Exh-23
27Exh-12
27YorCarE-35A
27YorCarE-35B
28StaPlaCE-35
33Gou-115
34GouCanV-9
94ConTSN-1058
94ConTSNB-1058
95ConTSN-1409
Heathcott, Mike
91UtiBluSC-8
91UtiBluSP-3235
93SarWhiSC-12
93SarWhiSF-1365
94BirBarC-12
94BirBarF-617
95PriWilCTI-19
Heaton, Mike
78QuaCitAT-10
Heaton, Neal
82ChaChaT-5
82Ind-21
82IndTeal-19
83IndPos-20
83IndWhe-19
84Don-373
84Don-608
84Fle-546
84FleSti-113
84Ind-18
84IndWhe-44
85Don-373
85Fle-451
85Ind-18
85IndPol-44
86Don-338
86Fle-589
86IndOhH-44
86IndTeal-24
86Lea-203
87Don-615
87ExpPos-10
87Fle-543
87FleGlo-543
87FleUpd-43
87FleUpdG-43
87TopTra-45T
87TopTraT-45T
88Don-134
88DonBasB-124
88Fle-185
88FleGlo-185
88FleMin-89
88MSAHosD-10
88OPC-354
88PanSti-319
88RedFolSB-32
88Sco-430
88ScoGlo-430
88Spo-81
88StaLinE-7
88Top-765
88TopBig-33
88TopSti-80
88TopStiB-29
88TopTif-765
89Don-224
89Fle-377
89FleGlo-377
89FleUpd-113
89OPC-197
89PirVerFJ-26
89Sco-253
89Top-197
89TopTif-197
89UppDec-99
90Don-658
90Fle-468
90FleCan-468
90Lea-460
90OPC-539
90PirHomC-12
90PubSti-156
90Top-539
90TopBig-255
90TopTif-539
90UppDec-86
90USPlaCA-7D
91BasBesAotM-9
91Don-475
91Fle-38
91OPC-451
91PanFreS-123
91PanSti-115
91Sco-233
91StaClu-53
91Top-451
91TopDesS-451
91TopMic-451
91TopTif-451
91Ult-279
91UppDec-36
92Don-522
92Fle-554
92OPC-89
92Sco-723
92StaClu-357
92StaClu-877
92StaCluNC-877
92Top-89
92TopGol-89
92TopGolW-89
92TopMic-89
92UppDec-417
93PacSpa-554
94BreMilB-132
Heaverlo, Dave
76OPC-213
76SSP-95
76Top-213
77PhoGiaCC-9
77PhoGiaCP-8
77Top-97
78Top-338
79Top-432
80Top-177
81Don-407
81Fle-594
81TacTigT-26
82TacTigT-3
83TacTigT-21
Hebb, Michael
91KanCouCC-6
91KanCouCP-2654
91KanCouCTI-9
Hebbert, Allan
94ElmPioF-3466
95KanCouCTI-32
94ElmPioC-8
Hebel, Jon
93BilMusF-3939
93BilMusSP-22
94ChaWheC-14
94ChaWheF-2698
Heberling, Keith
93OneYanF-3497
94BowBes-B89
94BowBesR-B89
94Cla-72
94ExcFS7-105
94FloStaLAF-FSL20
94TamYanC-13
94TamYanF-2377
95Exc-95
Hebert, Roger
52LavPro-65
Heble, Kurt
91St.CatBJC-11
91St.CatBJP-3403
92MyrBeaHC-26
92MyrBeaHF-2191
93DunBluJC-9
93DunBluJF-1790
93DunBluJFFN-9
94ExcFS7-144
94KnoSmoF-1299
95KnoSmoF-37
Hebner, Rich
69OPC-82
69Top-82
69TopTeaP-16
70DayDaiNM-66
70DayDaiNM-95
70MLBOffS-101
70OPC-264
70PirTeal-4
70Top-264
71MLBOffS-203
71OPC-212
71Pir-4
71PirActP-17
71PirArc-5
71Top-212
72MilBra-136
72Top-630
73OPC-2
73Top-2
74OPC-450
74Top-450
74TopDecE-35
74TopSta-84
75Hos-57
75Kel-57
75OPC-492
75Pir-3
75Top-492
76OPC-376
76SSP-579
76Top-376
77OPC-168
77Top-167
78OPC-194
78PhiSSP-35
78RCColC-62
78SSP270-35
78Top-26
79OPC-293
79Top-567
80OPC-175
80Top-331
81CokTeaS-51
81Don-125
81Fle-474
81OPC-217
81Top-217
82Don-328
82Fle-268
82OPC-96
82Top-603
83Fle-307
83Top-778
84CubChiT-15
84CubSev-18
84Fle-251
84FleUpd-50
84Nes792-433
84Top-433
84TopTif-433
84TopTra-50T
84TopTraT-50T
85CubSev-18
85Don-564
85Fle-59
85Top-124
85TopTif-124

86Top-19
86TopTif-19
88MyrBeaBJP-1188
88SouAtlLAGS-1
90TopTVRS-5
91MetWIZ-166
91MetWIZ-172
91UppDecS-13
95SyrChiTI-14
96SyrChiTI-13
Hebrard, Mike
82AmaGolST-24
Hechinger, Mike
09MaxPubP-20
90DodTar-978
Hecht, Steve
87PanAmTURB-7
89CalLeaA-35
89SanJosGB-24
89SanJosGCLC-221
89SanJosGP-457
89SanJosGS-13
90ShrCapP-1451
90ShrCapS-10
91IndIndLD-186
91IndIndP-474
91LinDriAAA-186
92HarSenF-470
92HarSenS-282
93ShrCapF-2768
94ShrCapF-1614
87PanAmTUBI-15
Heckel, Wally
90St.CatBJP-3477
Hecker, Doug
92ClaDraP-64
92FroRowDP-24
93Bow-411
93CarLeaAGF-7
93ClaGolF-151
93LynRedSC-11
93LynRedSF-2523
93StaCluM-64
94SarRedSC-12
94SarRedSF-1957
96SarRedSB-20
Hecker, Guy
87OldJudN-240
90HOFStiB-3
Heckman, Andy
92EveGiaC-29
92EveGiaF-1680
93CliGiaC-12
93CliGiaF-2485
94SanJosGC-9
94SanJosGF-2811
Heckman, Tom
82MadMusF-8
Hedfelt, Pancho
85UtiBluST-10
Hedge, Pat
89EriOriS-5
91FreKeyC-25
91FreKeyP-2380
Hedgearner, Pat
90FreKeyTI-28
Hedley, Brian
96HelBreTI-8
Hedley, Darren
90MarPhiP-3183
Hedlund, Mike
65Top-546
69RoySol-8
69Top-591
70OPC-187
70Top-187
71OPC-662
71Top-662
72MilBra-137
72OPC-81
72Top-81
73OPC-591
73Top-591
Hedrick, Craig
79CedRapGT-23
Hedspeth, Dennis
94GreFalDSP-14
Hee, Dong
96WesOahCHWB-31
Heeney, Tom
28W513-89
Heep, Danny
80TucTorT-1
81Fle-72
81Top-82
82AstAstI-5
82Fle-217
82Top-441
83Don-443
83Fle-449
83Top-538
83TopTra-41T
84Don-434
84Fle-586
84Nes792-29
84Top-29
84TopTif-29
85Don-556
85Fle-84
85MetColP-13
85MetTCM-34
85OPC-339
85Top-339
85TopTif-339
86Don-556
86Fle-403
86MetColP-18
86MetTCM-26
86MetWorSC-14
86Top-619
86TopTif-619
87Don-649
87Fle-11
87FleGlo-11
87Top-241
87TopTif-241
88DodMot-20
88DodPol-12
88Sco-417
88ScoGlo-417
88Top-753
88TopTif-753
89Don-368
89Fle-61A
89Fle-61B
89FleGlo-61
89Sco-343
89ScoRoo-57T
89Top-198
89TopTif-198
90Bow-276
90BowTif-276
90DodTar-329
90Don-358
90Fle-278
90FleCan-278
90OPC-573
90Sco-113
90Top-573
90TopBig-90
90TopTif-573
90TopTVRS-24
91BraDubP-15
91LinDriAAA-635
91MetWIZ-167
91Sco-827
91VanCanLD-635
91VanCanP-1601
Heffernan, Bert
87PanAmTURB-18
89BelBreIS-9
89BelBreIS-14
89Sta-109
90ElPasDGS-17
90TexLeaAGS-5
91AlbDukLD-9
91AlbDukP-1143
91LinDriAAA-9
92CalCanS-60
92DonRoo-50
93CalCanF-1169
93ShrCapF-2762
87PanAmTUBI-22
Heffernan, Greg
96NewJerCB-13
Heffernan, Jerry
43ParSpo-37
Heffner, Don
39PlaBal-44
40PlaBal-51
41BroW75-15
41DouPlaR-147
41Gou-11
60Top-462
66Top-269
66TopVen-269
75YanDyn1T-21
92ConTSN-521
Heffner, Robert
64Top-79
64TopVen-79
65OPC-199
65Top-199
66Top-432
Heflin, Bailey
92DavLipB-13
93DavLipB-11
Heflin, Bronson
94BatCliC-6
94BatCliF-3438
95ClePhiF-212
95ReaPhiELC-17
95TenVolW-3
96Exc-203
96ReaPhiB-6
Heflin, Randy
46RedSoxTI-12
Hegan, J. Mike
67Top-553
68Top-402
69PilPos-38
69Top-577
70BreMcD-10
70BreMil-7
70BreTeal-4
70DayDaiNM-43
70MLBOffS-271
70OPC-111
70SunPin-11
70Top-111
70TopScr-8
71BreTeal-4
71MLBOffS-438
71OPC-415
71Top-415
71TopCoi-116
72Top-632
73OPC-382
73Top-382
74OPC-517
74SyrChiTI-10
74Top-517
75OPC-99
75Top-99
76BreA&P-4
76LauDiaJ-21
76OPC-69
76OPC-377
76SSP-235
76Top-69
76Top-377
77Top-507
83Pil69G-8
92YanWIZ6-54
92YanWIZ7-71
94BreMilB-133
Hegan, Jim
46SpoExcW-4-12
47Exh-91
47IndTeal-14
47IndVanPP-13
47PM1StaP1-81
48IndTeal-15
49IndTeal-14
49IndVisEI-10
49Lea-28
50Bow-7
50IndNumN-13
50IndTeal-14
51Bow-79
51TopRedB-12
52Bow-187
52IndNumN-2
52RedMan-AL11
52StaCalL-74D
52StaCalS-88A
52Top-17
53BowC-102
53IndPenCBP-15
53Top-80
54DanDee-10
54RedHeaF-11
54Top-29
55Ind-3
55IndCarBL-3
55IndGolS-10
55RedMan-AL7
55RobGouS-5
55RobGouW-5
55Top-7
55TopDouH-67
56Top-48
56TopPin-8
57IndSoh-6
57Top-136
58Top-345
59TigGraASP-7
59Top-372
61Yan61RL-31
73OPC-116
73Top-116A
73Top-116B
76OPC-69
76TayBow4-105
76Top-69
79DiaGre-286
79TCM50-139
79YanPicA-17
81TCM60I-481
83TigAlKS-15
83TopRep5-17
84TCMPla1-16
86IndGreT-8
91TopArc1-80
93UppDecAH-64
94TopArc1-29
94TopArc1G-29
Hegan, Steve
90MisStaB-17
91MisStaB-23
92MisStaB-19
93MisStaB-20
Hegman, Bob
81ChaRoyT-10
84MemChiT-13
85OmaRoyT-30
86OmaRoyP-11
86OmaRoyT-8
Hehl, Jake
90DodTar-979
Heib, Earl
92ButCopKSP-22
Heidelberg, Khary
91HigSchPLS-15
Heidemann, Jack
71MLBOffS-372
71OPC-87
71Top-87
72OPC-374
72Top-374
73OPC-644
73Top-644
75OPC-649
75Top-649
76SSP-544
77Top-553
78SpoIndC-9
79SpoIndT-15
91MetWIZ-168
94BreMilB-134
Heiden, Shawn
89BluOriS-11
90Bes-110
90WauTimB-13
90WauTimP-2126
90WauTimS-9
Heidenreich, Curt
82CedRapRT-3
83WatRedT-3
84WicAerRD-9
Heiderscheit, Pat
89JamExpP-2143
93JamExpC-27
93JamExpF-3343
94VerExpC-22
94VerExpF-3924
Heidrick, Emmet
03BreE10-68
Heifferon, Mike
86AlbYanT-11
87PriWilYP-14
88AlbYanP-1354
89ColCliP-24
89ColCliP-755
89TriAAP-AAA3
92ColCliF-368
Height, Ron
87LitFalMP-2398
88LitFalMP-5
Heilgeist, Jim
90GatCitPP-3346
90GatCitPSP-11
Heilmann, Harry E.
16ColE13-71
17HolBreD-41
20NatCarE-41
21E121So1-40A
21E121So1-40B
21E121So8-34
21Exh-72
21Nei-27
22AmeCarE-26
22E120-54
22W572-41
22W573-59
22W575-54
22WilPatV-22
23W501-6
23W515-18
23WilChoV-61
25Exh-92
26Exh-93
27Exh-48
27YorCarE-22
28StaPlaCE-36
28W502-22
28Yue-22
29ExhFou-24
31Exh-7
31W517-14
36PC7AlbHoF-61
40PlaBal-171
50CalHOFW-38
51R42SmaS-46
60Fle-65
61Fle-42
63BazA-2
76ShaPiz-61
77GalGloG-95
80Lau300-28
80PerHaloFP-61
80SSPHOF-61
80TigGreT-7
81ConTSN-76
81TigDetN-4
81TigSecNP-8
86ConSer1-42
86TigSpoD-3
90PerGreM-47
91ConTSN-52
93ConTSN-915
Heimach, Fred
90DodTar-330
92ConTSN-480
Heimer, Todd
79TacTugT-8
80TacTigT-18
81ChaLooT-10
Heimueller, Gorman
81WesHavAT-20
82TacTigT-5
83TacTigT-4
84Don-131
84TacTigC-95
85OrlTwiT-25
86TolMudHP-12
87VisOakP-24
88VisOakCLC-174
88VisOakP-105
89VisOakCLC-119
89VisOakP-1420
90OrlSunRB-24
90OrlSunRP-1100
90OrlSunRS-26
91LinDriAAA-425
91PorBeaP-1583
92PorBeaF-2683
93PorBeaF-2397
94SalLakBF-832
95HarCitRCTI-8
96HarCitRCB-4
Heineman, Rick
96BriWhiSB-16
Heinen, Joe
75CedRapGT-4
Heinkel, Don
83BirBarT-9
84EvaTriT-19
86NasSouTI-11
87TolMudHP-7
87TolMudHT-2
88BlaYNPRWL-85
88FleUpd-27
88FleUpdG-27
88ScoRoo-79T
88ScoRooG-79T
89Bow-427
89BowTif-427
89Fle-133
89FleGlo-133

89LouRedBTI-21
89Sco-168
89Top-499
89TopTif-499
90BirBarDGB-17
90WicStaSGD-14
93WicWraF-2974
Heinle, Dana
87KenTwiP-15
88VisOakCLC-168
88VisOakP-82
89VerBeaDS-11
Heins, C.H.
88KimN18-18
Heins, Jim
89NiaFalRP-10
Heintz, Chris
96BriWhiSB-17
Heintzelman, Ken
49Bow-108
49EurSta-136
49PhiBul-24
50Bow-85
51BerRos-C10
51Bow-147
51R42SmaS-42
52Bow-148
52Top-362
53Top-136
79DiaGre-367
79TCM50-78
83TopRep5-362
91TopArc1-136
Heintzelman, Tom
74OPC-607
74Top-607
75PhoGiaC-13
75PhoGiaCK-17
76PheGiaCr-23
76PhoGiaCa-16
76PhoGiaCC-10
76PhoGiaVNB-9
77PhoGiaVNB-9
79PhoGiaVNB-12
Heise, Benjamin
75OklCit8TI-12
Heise, Larry Wayne
84NewOriT-19
87GreBraB-22
Heise, Robert
70OPC-478
70Top-478
71MLBOffS-250
71OPC-691
71Top-691
72OPC-402
72Top-402
73OPC-547
73Top-547
74OPC-51
74Top-51
74TopTra-51T
75OPC-441
75Top-441
91MetWIZ-169
94BreMilB-224
Heiser, Roy
77FriOneYW-57
Heiserman, Rick
94WatIndF-3931
95KinIndTI-15
95Top-398
96Exc-45
96StPetCB-13
Heisler, Laurence
92BatCliC-16
92BatCliF-3257
94ClePhiC-17
94ClePhiF-2523
94SpaPhiF-1718
Heisler, Toni
95ColSilB-12
Heist, Al
58UniOil-4
61Top-302
62Col45'HC-8
62SalPlaC-195
62ShiPlaC-195
62Top-373
62TopStal-126
89AstCol4S-24
Heitmuller, Heinie (William)
09AmeCarE-51
10LuxCigPP-11
11SpoLifM-94
Held, Dan
93BatCliC-11
93BatCliF-3148
94SouAtlLAF-SAL54
94SpaPhiF-1727
94SparPhiC-13
95ClePhiF-224
95ReaPhiELC-18
96BesAutS-36
96Exc-204
96ExcSeaTL-4
96ReaPhiB-19
Held, Matt
83IdaFalAT-16
Held, Mel
64TopVen-105
91OriCro-191
Held, Woodie
58A'sJayP-4
58Top-202
59Ind-8
59Kah-14
59Top-266
60IndJayP-3
60Kah-13
60Lea-2
60Top-178
60TopVen-178
61Baz-33
61Kah-18
61NuSco-405
61Top-60
61TopStal-136
62Baz-8
62IndJayP-5
62Jel-44
62Kah-17
62Pos-44
62PosCan-44
62SalPlaC-5
62ShiPlaC-5
62Top-215
62TopBuc-34
62TopStal-35
63BasMagM-35
63IndJayP-8
63Jel-69
63Pos-69
63Top-435
64IndJayP-7
64Kah-12
64Top-105
64TopCoi-29
64TopSta-29
64TopStaU-31
64TopTatl-41
65Top-336
66OPC-136
66SenTeal-6
66Top-136
66TopVen-136
67Top-251
68Top-289
68TopVen-289
69MilBra-108
69Top-636
78TCM60I-284
79TCM50-174
81Ori6F-17
91OriCro-192
Helf, Henry
46SeaSLP-22
Helfand, Eric
88NebCor-5
89AlaGol-3
90ProAaA-167
90SouOreAB-2
90SouOreAP-3426
91Cla/Bes-128
91ModA'sC-21
92CalLeaACL-3
92ClaFS7-188
92ModA'sC-3
92ModA'sF-3903
93ExcFS7-217
93HunStaF-2085
94A'sMot-23
94TacTigF-3178
94Top-363
94TopGol-363
94TopSpa-363
95AthMot-15
96BufBisB-10
Helfrich, Chris
94SouOreAC-11
94SouOreAF-3615
Heller, Brad
95ChaRivTI-16
Heller, John
83LynMetT-17
Heller, Mark
86AlbDukP-11
Helling, Rick
91TopTra-54T
91TopTraT-54T
92Bow-641
92ClaDraP-17
92FroRowDP-81
92FroRowDPPS-81
92StaCluD-81
92TopTra-48T
92TopTraG-48T
92UppDecML-13
93Bow-165
93ClaFS7-204
93ClaPro-3
93Pin-459
93Sco-491
93Sel-358
93StaCluM-96
94Bow-297
94ClaGolF-181
94ExcFS7-134
94ExtBas-179
94ExtBasRS-9
94Fin-434
94FinJum-434
94FinRef-434
94Fla-110
94FleUpd-92
94LeaLimR-47
94Pin-525
94PinArtP-525
94PinMusC-525
94SigRooBS-P1
94SP-149
94SPDieC-149
94StaClu-632
94StaClu-697
94StaCluFDI-632
94StaCluFDI-697
94StaCluGR-632
94StaCluGR-697
94StaCluMOP-632
94StaCluMOP-697
94TopTra-58T
94Ult-431
94UppDecML-147
94UppDecML-240
94UppDecMLPotYF-PY20
95ColCho-397
95ColChoGS-397
95ColChoSE-181
95ColChoSEGS-181
95ColChoSESS-181
95ColChoSS-397
95Don-314
95DonPreP-314
95Fle-286
95Lea-123
95StaClu-387
95StaCluMOP-387
95StaCluSTWS-387
95UppDec-157
95UppDecED-157
95UppDecEDG-157
95UppDecSE-174
95UppDecSEG-174
96ColCho-323
96ColChoGS-323
96ColChoSS-323
96OklCit8B-11
96RanMot-11
97Fle-521
97FleTif-521
97Sco-380
97ScoHobR-380
97ScoResC-380
97ScoShoS-380
97ScoShoSAP-380
97Ult-472
97UltGolME-472
97UltPlaME-472
Hellman, Anthony
87OldJudN-241
Hellman, Jeff
87Ft.LauYP-25
Helm, J. Ross
09T206-490
Helm, Wayne
89BenBucL-4
90BoiHawP-3315
Helmick, Tony
89GreFalDSP-6
90BakDodCLC-238
Helmquist, Doug
84BufBisT-25
Helms, Mike
90EveGiaB-18
90EveGiaP-3134
Helms, Ryan
94SigRooBS-4
96SigRooOJRS-R3
Helms, Tommy
65OPC-243
65RedEnq-11
65Top-243
66Top-311
66TopVen-311
67CokCapR-5
67DexPre-93
67Kah-16A
67Kah-16B
67Top-505
67TopVen-315
68Top-405
69MilBra-109
69MLBOffS-129
69MLBPin-47
69OPC-70
69OPCDec-9
69Top-70
69Top-418
69TopDec-20
69TopDecl-16
69TopSta-24
69TopSup-40
69TopTeaP-20
70DayDaiNM-33
70MLBOffS-28
70OPC-159
70Top-159
71MLBOffS-61
71OPC-272
71Top-272
72MilBra-138
72OPC-204
72Top-204
73OPC-495
73Top-495
74AstFouTIP-3
74OPC-67
74Top-67
74TopSta-32
75OPC-119
75Top-119
76OPC-583
76SSP-56
76Top-583
76TopTra-583T
77Top-402
78Top-618
82AstAstl-2
84RedEnq-27
86RedTexG-NNO
87AstShoSO-12
87AstShowSTh-25
87RedKah-NNO
88RedKah-NNO
89RedKah-xx
90ChaKniTI-19
90OPC-110
90Top-110
90TopTif-110
91UtiBluSC-17
91UtiBluSP-3248
92SalSpuC-12
93RanKee-179
93UppDecS-8
Helms, Wes
94StaCluDP-77
94StaCluDPFDI-77
95MacBraTI-10
96BesAutS-37
96BesAutSA-26
96BowBes-152
96BowBesAR-152
96BowBesR-152
96BowMinLP-6
96CarLeaA1B-15
96CarLeaA2B-15
96CarLeaAIB-B1
96CarLeaAIB-B4
96DurBulBIB-30
96DurBulBrB-18
96Exc-126
96GreBraB-14
96GreBraTI-33
97Bow-295
97BowBes-151
97BowBesAR-151
97BowBesR-151
97BowCerBIA-CA36
97BowCerGIA-CA36
97BowChr-203
97BowChrl-203
97BowChrIR-203
97BowChrR-203
97BowInt-295
97StaClu-183
97StaCluMOP-183
97Top-490
Helsel, Ronald
93DunBluJF-1808
Helsom, Bob
83St.PetCT-21
84ArkTraT-7
Helton, Keith
87BelMarTI-6
88CalLeaACLC-29
88SanBerSB-19
88SanBerSCLC-44
89Sta-123
89WilBilP-645
89WilBilS-9
90CalCanC-21
90CalCanP-040
90CMC-448
90ProAAAF-111
91CalCanLD-58
91CalCanP-510
91LinDriAAA-58
92JacGenF-3996
Helton, Todd
93BazTeaU-11
93TopTra-19T
95AshTouUTI-9
95Bes-126
95SPML-112
95TenVolW-4
95TenVolW-5
96Bow-378
96BowBes-171
96BowBesAR-171
96BowBesMI-1
96BowBesMIAR-1
96BowBesMIR-1
96BowBesR-171
96Exc-154
96ExcFirYP-5
96NewHavRB-13
96NewHavRUSTI-22
96SigRooOJPP-P4
96Top-13
96TopChr-13
96TopChrR-13
96TopPowB-13
97Bow-331
97Bow98ROY-ROY3
97BowBes-109
97BowBesAR-109
97BowBesMI-MI7
97BowBesMIAR-MI7
97BowBesMIARI-MI7
97BowBesMII-MI7
97BowBesMIR-MI7
97BowBesMIRI-MI7
97BowBesR-109
97BowChr-227
97BowChr1RC-ROY3
97BowChr1RCR-ROY3
97BowChrl-227
97BowChrIR-227
97BowChrR-227
97BowInt-331
97Fin-286
97FinEmb-286
97FinEmbR-286
97FinRef-286
97StaClu-187
97StaCluMOP-187
97TopSta-104
97TopStaAM-104
Helvey, Rob

94JohCitCC-13
94JohCitCF-3694
95NewJerCTI-12
Heman, Russell
59Top-283
60MapLeaSF-8
Hembree, Kirk
89CarNewE-24
Heming, Tom
92EugEmeC-15
92EugEmeF-3026
Hemm, Warren
78MemChiBC-5
79MemChiT-23
Hemmerich, Mike
89PitMetS-7
Hemmerly, John
89EriOriS-6
89SanDieSAS-12
Hemond, Scott
87HunStaTI-12
87MadMusP-9
87MadMusP-3
88HunStaTI-6
89HunStaB-1
90Bow-453
90BowTif-453
90CMC-593
90Fle-646
90FleCan-646
90ProAAAF-146
90Sco-598
90TacTigC-16
90TacTigP-99
90TopDeb89-54
90UppDec-727
91Bow-232
91Sco100RS-22
91TacTigP-2314
92AthMot-26
92Don-637
92Sco-617
92StaClu-62
92Ult-422
93AthMot-19
93Don-623
93StaCluAt-21
93Ult-607
94A'sMot-17
94ColC-408
94ColChoGS-408
94ColChoSS-408
94Don-141
94Fle-263
94Pac-451
94StaClu-12
94StaCluFDI-12
94StaCluGR-12
94StaCluMOP-12
94Top-226
94TopGol-226
94TopSpa-226
95StaClu-167
95StaCluFDI-167
95StaCluMOP-167
95StaCluSTWS-167
96LouRedB-21
Hempen, Hal
88SavCarP-342
Hempfield, Keith
83ChaRoyT-7
Hemphill, Bret
94BoiHawC-1
94BoiHawF-3358
95CedRapKTI-31
95Exc-21
95Top-480
96LakElsSB-12
Hemphill, Charles
03BreE10-69
08RosComP-48
09BriE97-13
09RamT20-54
09T206-152
10W555-35
11S74Sil-22
11SpoLifCW-161
11T205-74
Hemphill, James
96HelBreTI-9
Hemsley, Rollie (Ralston)
31CubTeal-10
32CubTeal-11
34BatR31-71
34ExhFou-15
35ExhFou-15
35GouPuzR-8C
35GouPuzR-9C
36ExhFou-15
36GouBWR-17
36GouWidPPR-A50
36OveCanR-23
36R31PasP-26
36SandSW-32
36WheBB4-5
37ExhFou-15
38BasTabP-17
40PlaBal-205
41DouPlaR-133
41PlaBal-34
43YanSta-14
47CenFlo-8
54Top-143
91ConTSN-299
92YanWIZA-28
94TopArc1-143
94TopArc1G-143
95ConTSN-1420
Hemus, Solly
52Bow-212
52Top-196
53BowC-85
53CarHunW-9
53Top-231
54Bow-94
54CarHunW-8
54Top-117
55Bow-107
55CarHunW-8
57Top-231
58Top-207
59Top-527
60Top-218
61CarJayP-5
61Top-139
79DiaGre-172
79TCM50-93
81TCM60I-362
82MetGal62-28
91TopArc1-231
94TopArc1-117
94TopArc1G-117
Hence, Sam
90BurIndP-3020
91BurIndP-3315
92ColRedC-7
92ColRedF-2405
92WatIndF-3247
93ColRedC-12
93ColRedF-612
94KinIndC-8
94KinIndF-2657
Henderson, Bill
88FayGenP-1102
89LakTigS-9
Henderson, Brad
86FloStaLAP-22
86St.PetCP-10
87ArkTraP-24
88ArkTraGS-2
Henderson, Bruce
72CedRapCT-12
Henderson, Carl
90MisStaB-18
91MisStaB-24
92MisStaB-20
93MisStaB-21
Henderson, Chris
92BenRocC-12
92BenRocF-1469
93BenRocC-10
93BenRocF-3261
94CenValRC-9
94CenValRF-3196
95AshTouUTI-13
Henderson, Craig
82WisRapTF-26
83VisOakF-20
85OrlTwiT-26
Henderson, Daryl
91GulCoaRSP-22
92GasRanC-10
92GasRanF-2248
92UppDecML-243
93Bow-25
93ChaRanC-14
93ChaRanF-1936
93FloStaLAF-3
94ClaGolF-34
Henderson, Dave
80SpoIndT-16
82Top-711
83Fle-481
83Top-732
84Don-557
84Fle-611
84MarMot-3
84Nes792-154
84OPC-154
84Top-154
84TopSti-343
84TopTif-154
85Fle-489
85MarMot-4
85OPC-344
85Top-344
85TopSti-338
85TopTif-344
86Don-318
86Fle-465
86Lea-187
86MarMot-4
86OPC-221
86Top-221
86Top-546
86TopSti-222
86TopTif-221
86TopTif-546
87Don-622
87DonOpeD-189
87Fle-36
87FleGlo-36
87FleGlo-WS10
87FleHotS-19
87FleWorS-10
87Lea-103
87SpoTeaP-9
87Top-452
87TopSti-23
87TopTif-452
87Woo-22
88A'sMot-14
88DonTeaBA-NEW
88Fle-84
88FleGlo-84
88FleUpd-53
88FleUpdG-53
88Sco-228
88ScoGlo-228
88ScoRoo-49T
88ScoRooG-49T
88StaLinAs-7
88Top-628
88TopBig-131
88TopTif-628
88TopTra-48T
88TopTraT-48T
89A'sMot-13
89Bow-200
89BowTif-200
89Don-20
89Don-450
89DonBasB-190
89DonSupD-20
89Fle-10
89FleGlo-10
89OPC-327
89PanSti-423
89Sco-533
89Spo-127
89SpoIllFKI-289
89Top-527
89TopBig-326
89TopSti-164
89TopStiB-17
89TopTif-527
89TVSpoM-100
89UppDec-174
90A'sMot-18
90Bow-458
90BowTif-458
90Don-243
90DonBesA-39
90Fle-9
90FleCan-9
90OPC-68
90PanSti-133
90PubSti-306
90Sco-325
90Sco-702
90Top-68
90TopBig-309
90TopMag-59
90TopSti-184
90TopTif-68
90UppDec-206
90Woo-29
91A'sMot-18
91A'sSFE-5
91Bow-226
91Cla3-T36
91Don-326
91Fle-9
91Lea-232
91OPC-144
91PanFreS-197
91PanSti-150
91Sco-644
91StaClu-284
91Stu-103
91Top-144
91TopDesS-144
91TopMic-144
91TopTif-144
91TopTriH-A11
91Ult-247
91UppDec-108
91UppDecFE-88F
91USPlaCA-13H
92A'sUno7P-5
92AthMot-18
92Bow-488
92ClaGam-9
92Don-21
92Don-311
92Fle-257
92Hig5-104
92Lea-232
92OPC-335
92PanSti-20
92PanSti-276
92Pin-16
92PinRool-8
92Sco-5
92Sco100S-92
92ScoCokD-13
92ScoProP-3
92ScoProP-4
92StaClu-218
92StaCluD-82
92Stu-224
92Top-335
92TopGol-335
92TopGolW-335
92TopKid-116
92TopMic-335
92TriPla-130
92TriPla-166
92Ult-113
92UppDec-172
93AthMot-9
93Don-373
93Fle-664
93Lea-139
93OPC-155
93PacSpa-568
93PanSti-20
93Pin-170
93Sco-134
93StaClu-349
93StaCluAt-11
93StaCluFDI-349
93StaCluMOP-349
93Stu-30
93Top-473
93TopGol-473
93TopInaM-473
93TopMic-473
93TriPla-119
93Ult-608
93UppDec-607
93UppDecGold-607
94ColC-431
94ColChoGS-431
94ColChoSS-431
94Don-513
94ExtBas-91
94Fin-260
94FinRef-260
94Fla-59
94Fle-264
94FleUpd-49
94Pac-452
94PanSti-109
94Pin-508
94PinArtP-508
94PinMusC-508
94Sco-463
94ScoGolR-463
94ScoRoo-RT18
94ScoRooGR-RT18
94Sel-298
94SpoRoo-15
94SpoRooAP-15
94StaClu-253
94StaClu-689
94StaCluFDI-253
94StaCluFDI-689
94StaCluGR-253
94StaCluGR-689
94StaCluMOP-253
94StaCluMOP-689
94Top-708
94TopGol-708
94TopSpa-708
94TopTra-23T
94Ult-365
94UppDec-507
94UppDecED-507
95Fle-161
95Pac-204
95StaClu-251
95StaCluFDI-251
95StaCluMOP-251
95StaCluSTWS-251
95Top-276
95TopCyb-149
Henderson, David
89AubAstP-2185
90OscAstS-9
91BurAstC-15
91BurAstP-2809
92SanBerSF-966
Henderson, Derek
89PitMetS-8
91St.LucMC-7
91St.LucMP-718
92KnoBluJF-2996
92KnoBluJS-381
93KnoSmoF-1258
94KnoSmoF-1310
Henderson, Frank
88AppFoxP-154
88EugEmeB-23
89AppFoxP-857
Henderson, Hardie (James H.)
87OldJudN-242
87OldJudN-243
87OldJudN-398
88KimN18-19
Henderson, Harry IV
89BilMusP-2059
Henderson, Jeff
91KinMetC-1
91KinMetP-3808
Henderson, Jim
92JamExpC-2
Henderson, Joe
76IndIndTI-5
77IndIndTI-3
77Top-487
81CliGiaT-22
82BelBreF-2
83ElPasDT-3
84MidCubT-1
96BatCliTI-31
Henderson, John
77QuaCitAT-16
Henderson, Juan
94CedRapKC-13
94CedRapKF-1116
95CedRapKTI-11
96LakElsSB-17
Henderson, Kenneth J.
91EveGiaC-19
91EveGiaP-3929
92EveGiaC-6
92EveGiaF-1681
Henderson, Kenneth Jos.
65Top-497
66OPC-39
66Top-39
66TopVen-39
67Top-383
68Top-309
68TopVen-309
70DayDaiNM-89
70Gia-4
70OPC-298

70Top-298
71GiaTic-5
71MLBOffS-251
71OPC-155
71Top-155
71TopCoi-97
71TopTat-12
72OPC-443
72OPC-444
72Top-443
72Top-444
72WhiSox-4
73OPC-101
73Top-101
74OPC-394
74Top-394
74TopSta-154
75Hos-136
75HosTwi-136
75OPC-59
75Top-59
76OPC-464
76SSP-147
76Top-464
76TopTra-464T
77Top-242
78MetDaiPA-9
78Pep-13
78Top-612
79Top-73
80Top-523
91MetWIZ-170
93RanKee-180

Henderson, Kenny
96CliLumKTI-14

Henderson, Lee
89GeoColC-10
90ChaRaiB-11
90ChaRaiP-2041
90GeoColC-7
91WatDiaC-12
91WatDiaP-1259
92HigDesMC-26
93RanCucQC-16
93RanCucQF-835
93WicWraF-2980
94SprSulC-12
94SprSulF-2039

Henderson, Lester
94MedHatBJF-3676
94MedHatBJSP-16

Henderson, Matt
79WisRapTT-8
80WisRapTT-22

Henderson, Mike
78HolMilT-11
79HolMilT-17
80VanCanT-17

Henderson, Pedro
90BurIndP-3021
91CollndP-1499
91WatIndC-26
91WatIndP-3381

Henderson, Ramon
86ReaPhiP-9
87ReaPhiP-15
88MaiPhiC-19
88MaiPhiP-295
89ReaPhiB-13
89ReaPhiP-653
89ReaPhiS-13
90PriPatD-29
91ClePhiC-5
91ClePhiP-1639
92ClePhiC-24
92ClePhiF-2074

Henderson, Rats
86NegLeaF-34

Henderson, Rickey
77ModA'sC-5
79OgdA'sT-9
80Top-482
81A'sGraG-35
81AllGamPI-52
81Don-119
81Fle-351
81Fle-574
81FleStiC-54
81Kel-33
81OPC-261
81PerCreC-19
81Squ-28
81Top-4
81Top-261
81TopScr-39
81TopSti-15
81TopSti-115
82A'sGraG-4
82Don-113
82Fle-92
82Fle-643
82FleSta-123
82Kel-4
82OPC-268
82PerAll-6
82PerAllG-6
82PerCreC-23
82PerCreCG-23
82Top-156
82Top-164
82Top-610
82TopSti-8
82TopSti-221
82TopStiV-221
83A'sGraG-35
83AllGamPI-54
83Don-11
83Don-35
83DonActA-22
83Fle-519
83Fle-639
83Fle-646
83FleSta-77
83FleSti-144
83FleSti-192
83Kel-8
83OPC-180
83OPC-391
83PerCreC-26
83PerCreCG-26
83Top-2
83Top-180
83Top-391
83Top-531
83Top-704
83TopFol-5
83TopGloS-33
83TopSti-21
83TopSti-103
83TopSti-159
83TopSti-197
83TopSti-198
83TopSti-199
83TopSti-200
83TopSti-201
83TopSti-202
83TopStiB-8
84A'sMot-2
84AllGamPI-143
84Don-54
84DonActAS-9
84Fle-447
84FleSti-53
84FleSti-92
84FunFooP-17
84MilBra-13
84Nes792-2
84Nes792-134
84Nes792-156
84Nes792-230
84OCoandSI-27
84OPC-230
84RalPur-15
84SevCoi-W21
84Top-2
84Top-134
84Top-156
84Top-230
84TopCer-15
84TopGloS-6
84TopPewB-8
84TopRubD-24
84TopSti-3
84TopSti-4
84TopSti-202
84TopSti-327
84TopSup-19
84TopTif-2
84TopTif-134
84TopTif-156
84TopTif-230
85AllGamPI-58
85Don-176
85DonHig-17
85DonHig-42
85Fle-425
85Fle-629
85FleStaS-54
85FleUpd-51
85Lea-208
85OPC-115
85SevCoi-W12
85Top-115
85Top-706
85Top3-D-10
85TopRubD-24
85TopSti-283
85TopSti-321
85TopSup-14
85TopTif-115
85TopTif-706
85TopTifT-49T
85TopTra-49T
85Woo-17
86BasStaB-55
86Don-51
86DonAll-10
86DonPop-10
86DorChe-7
86Dra-5
86Fle-108
86FleAll-7
86FleLimE-23
86FleMin-23
86FleStiC-53
86GenMilB-1C
86Lea-37
86OPC-243
86QuaGra-25
86SevCoi-E12
86Spo-6
86Spo-184
86SpoDecG-69
86Top-500
86Top-716
86Top3-D-11
86TopGloA-7
86TopGloS-5
86TopMinL-27
86TopSti-155
86TopSti-297
86TopSup-30
86TopTat-24
86TopTif-500
86TopTif-716
86YanTCM-33
87A'sMot-20
87BoaandB-8
87BurKinA-9
87ClaGam-12
87Don-228
87DonAll-6
87DonOpeD-248
87DonP-6
87Dra-12
87Fle-101
87FleExcS-24
87FleGlo-101
87FleHea-4
87FleHotS-20
87FleMin-52
87FleSlu-18
87FleStiC-56
87GenMilB-2D
87K-M-27
87KayB-16
87KraFoo-31
87Lea-191
87MSAIceTD-18
87MSAJifPD-14
87OPC-7
87OPCBoxB-E
87RedFolSB-80
87SevCoi-E3
87Spo-4
87Spo-157
87Spo-159
87Spo-198
87SpoDeaP-4
87SpoSupD-14
87SpoTeaP-7
87StuPan-23
87Top-311
87Top-406
87Top-735
87TopCoi-12
87TopGloA-18
87TopGloS-21
87TopMinL-64
87TopSti-147
87TopSti-296
87TopTif-311
87TopTif-406
87TopTif-735
87TopWaxBC-E
87Woo-3
88CheBoy-20
88ClaBlu-234
88Don-277
88DonAll-4
88DonBasB-76
88DonPop-4
88DonReaBY-277
88Dra-7
88Fle-209
88FleGlo-209
88FleHotS-16
88FleMin-40
88FleSluBC-C2
88FleStiWBC-S4
88FleSupBC-C2
88K-M-13
88Lea-145
88OPC-60
88OPCBoxB-M
88PanSti-158
88PanSti-231
88PanSti-434
88Sco-13
88ScoBoxC-7
88ScoGlo-13
88Spo-11
88SpoGam-8
88StaLinAl-14
88StaLinY-6
88Top-60
88TopBig-165
88TopGloA-7
88TopGloS-25
88TopMinL-26
88TopSti-155
88TopSti-297
88TopStiB-51
88TopTif-60
88TopUKM-31
88TopUKMT-31
88TopWaxBC-M
89Baz-14
89Bow-181
89BowTif-181
89CadEllD-28
89ClaLigB-50
89Don-245
89DonAll-4
89DonBasB-78
89DonPop-4
89Fle-254
89FleBasA-20
89FleExcS-21
89FleGlo-254
89FleSup-22
89FleUpd-54
89KayB-18
89ModA'sC-33
89OPC-282
89OPCBoxB-F
89PanSti-239
89PanSti-408
89Sco-70
89Sco-657
89ScoHot1S-45
89ScoRoo-50T
89Spo-145
89SpollIFKI-46
89Top-380
89TopAme2C-16
89TopBasT-55
89TopBatL-15
89TopBig-271
89TopDouM-16
89TopGloA-7
89TopGloS-35
89TopMinL-66
89TopSti-145
89TopSti-312
89TopStiB-18
89TopTif-380
89TopTra-48T
89TopTraT-48T
89TopUKM-37
89TopWaxBC-F
89TVSpoM-83
89TVSpoM-127
89UppDec-210
90A'sMot-4
90AllBasT-5
90BasWit-37
90Baz-9
90Bow-457
90BowTif-457
90ClaBlu-37
90ClaYel-T27
90Col-8
90Don-304
90DonBesA-124
90DonLeaS-7
90Fle-10
90FleAwaW-18
90FleBasM-17
90FleCan-10
90FleLeaL-18
90FleWorS-11
90HOFStiB-87
90Hot50PS-20
90K-M-23
90KayB-15
90KinDis-19
90Lea-84
90Lea-160
90MSAHolD-8
90OPC-7
90OPC-450
90OPCBoxB-F
90PanSti-138
90Pos-25
90PubSti-288
90PubSti-537
90Sco-360
90Sco-686
90Sco-698
90Sco-702
90Sco100S-90
90SooMoD 5
90Spo-208
90StaHen-1
90StaHen-2
90StaHen-3
90StaHen-4
90StaHen-5
90StaHen-6
90StaHen-7
90StaHen-8
90StaHen-9
90StaHen-10
90StaHen-11
90SunSee-13
90Top-7
90Top-450
90TopAmeA-13
90TopBatL-21
90TopBig-292
90TopCoi-17
90TopDou-33
90TopGloS-37
90TopMag-30
90TopMinL-28
90TopSti-7
90TopSti-181
90TopStiB-50
90TopTif-7
90TopTif-450
90TopTVA-10
90TopWaxBC-F
90UppDec-334
90USPlaCA-13C
90WinDis-8
90Woo-14
90Woo-23
90Woo-31
91A'sMot-4
91A'sSFE-6
91BasBesRB-7
91Baz-2
91Bow-213
91Bow-371
91Bow-692
91CadEllD-29
91Cla1-T72
91Cla2-T75
91ClaGam-189
91Col-25
91Don-53
91Don-387
91Don-648
91Don-761
91DonEli-7
91Fle-10
91FleAll-6
91FlePro-F2
91FleWorS-4

91JimDea-17
91KinDis-5
91Lea-101
91LeaGolR-BC26
91LeaPre-23
91MajLeaCP-40
91MSAHolD-12
91OPC-391
91OPC-670
91OPCBoxB-H
91OPCPre-62
91PanCanT1-6
91PanCanT1-38
91PanCanT1-45
91PanCanT1-53
91PanFreS-171
91PanFreS-196
91PanSti-146
91PepRicH-1
91PepRicH-2
91PepRicH-3
91PepRicH-4
91PepRicH-5
91PepRicH-6
91PepRicH-7
91PepRicH-8
91PepRicH-9
91PepRicH-10
91PepRicHD-1
91PepRicHD-2
91PepRicHD-3
91PepRicHD-4
91PetSta-21
91Pos-27
91PosCan-24
91RedFolS-48
91RedFolS-121
91Sco-10
91Sco-397
91Sco-857
91Sco-875
91Sco-890
91Sco100S-10
91ScoCoo-B4
91Sev3DCN-7
91SevCoi-A5
91SevCoi-NC7
91SevCoi-NE7
91SevCoi-NW7
91SilHol-1
91StaClu-120
91StaCluCM-13
91StaCluCM-14
91StaCluMO-4
91StaCluMO-18
91StaHen-1
91StaHen-2
91StaHen-3
91StaHen-4
91StaHen-5
91StaHen-6
91StaHen-7
91StaHen-8
91StaHen-9
91StaHen-10
91StaHen-11
91StaPinB-24
91Stu-104
91Top-391
91Top-670
91TopCraJI-18
91TopDesS-391
91TopDesS-670
91TopGaloC-7
91TopGloA-6
91TopMic-391
91TopMic-670
91TopSta-19
91TopTif-391
91TopTif-670
91TopTriH-A11
91TopWaxBC-H
91Ult-248
91Ult-393
91UltGol-5
91UppDec-444
91UppDec-636
91UppDec-636A
91UppDec-SP2
91UppDecFE-86F
91UppDecSS-SS3
91USPlaCA-11H
91Woo-2
91Woo-26
92A'sUno7P-2
92AthMot-4
92Bow-166
92Cla1-T43
92ClaGam-118
92Don-30
92Don-193
92Don-215
92DonCraJ2-19
92DonEli-L2
92Fle-258
92Fle-681
92FleCitTP-17
92Fre-17
92Hig5-105
92Hig5S-19
92Lea-116
92MooSna-19
92Mr.TurS-14
92New-10
92OPC-2
92OPC-560
92OPCPre-147
92PanSti-21
92PanSti-278
92PepDieM-28
92Pin-283
92Pin-401
92Pin-614
92PinRool-7
92PosCan-18
92Sco-430
92Sco-441
92Sco-480
92Sco100S-100
92SpoStaCC-23
92StaClu-750
92StaCluD-83
92StaCluMP-8
92StaPro-4
92Top-2
92Top-560
92TopGol-2
92TopGol-560
92TopGolW-2
92TopGolW-560
92TopKid-118
92TopMcD-3
92TopMic-2
92TopMic-560
92TopMic-G2
92TriPla-63
92Ult-114
92UppDec-90
92UppDec-155
92UppDec-640
92UppDec-648
92UppDec-782
92UppDecF-27
92UppDecFG-27
92UppDecWB-T7
92YanWIZ8-80
92YanWIZA-29
93AthMot-6
93Bow-625
93CadDis-31
93ClaGam-42
93DenHol-3
93DiaMar-50
93Don-315
93Fin-86
93FinJum-86
93FinRef-86
93Fla-260
93Fle-294
93FleFruotL-29
93FunPac-50
93FunPac-212
93Hos-23
93HumDumC-14
93Lea-291
93MetBak-30
93OPC-130
93PacSpa-222
93PanSti-19
93Pin-29
93Pin-308
93PinCoo-7
93PinCooD-7
93PinHomRC-21
93Sco-71
93Sel-106
93SelRoo-1T
93SP-40
93StaClu-558
93StaCluAt-8
93StaCluFDI-558
93StaCluMOP-558
93StaCluMP-19
93Stu-84
93Top-750
93TopGol-750
93TopInaM-750
93TopMic-750
93TriPla-219
93Ult-258
93UppDec-136
93UppDecCP-R12
93UppDecDG-29
93UppDecGold-136
93UppDecSH-HI10
93UppDecTAN-TN3
93USPlaCA-8H
94A'sMot-6
94Bow-80
94BowBes-R4
94BowBesR-R4
94ColC-131
94ColC-510
94ColChoGS-131
94ColChoGS-510
94ColChoSS-131
94ColChoSS-510
94DenHol-15
94Don-19
94Don-290
94DonAnn8-4
94DonSpeE-19
94ExtBas-150
94Fin-223
94FinJum-223
94FinRef-223
94Fla-331
94Fle-334
94FleUpd-74
94FUnPac-124
94FUnPac-213
94Lea-259
94LeaL-60
94OPC-37
94OPCWorC-1
94Pac-643
94PanSti-139
94Pin-450
94PinArtP-450
94PinMusC-450
94PinRunC-RC10
94ProMag-100
94Sco-35
94ScoGolR-35
94ScoGolS-34
94ScoRoo-RT13
94ScoRooCP-CP6
94ScoRooGR-RT13
94Sel-254
94SP-34
94SPDieC-34
94SpoMov-MM8
94StaClu-107
94StaClu-654
94StaCluFDI-107
94StaCluFDI-654
94StaCluGR-107
94StaCluGR-654
94StaCluMO-38
94StaCluMOP-107
94StaCluMOP-654
94Stu-3
94SucSav-1
94Top-248
94TopGol-248
94TopSpa-248
94TopTra-65T
94TriPla-4
94Ult-408
94UppDec-60
94UppDecDC-W6
94UppDecED-60
94USPlaCA-9H
95AthMot-5
95Baz-62
95BluJayUSPC-3S
95BluJayUSPC-11H
95Bow-316
95ClaPhoC-42
95ColCho-53
95ColCho-125
95ColChoGS-53
95ColChoGS-125
95ColChoSE-48
95ColChoSEGS-48
95ColChoSESS-48
95ColChoSS-53
95ColChoSS-125
95Don-305
95DonPreP-305
95DonTopotO-137
95Emb-103
95EmbGolI-103
95Emo-71
95Fin-47
95FinRef-47
95Fla-74
95Fle-246
95FleUpdDT-7
95Lea-22
95LeaLim-29
95Pac-312
95PacPri-102
95Pin-201
95PinArtP-201
95PinFan-15
95PinMusC-201
95Sco-441
95ScoGolR-441
95ScoHaloG-HG102
95ScoPlaTS-441
95Sel-134
95SelArtP-134
95SelCer-41
95SelCerMG-41
95SP-182
95SPCha-178
95SPChaDC-178
95Spo-4
95SpoArtP-4
95SPSil-182
95StaClu-415
95StaCluMOP-415
95StaCluMOP-RL35
95StaCluRL-RL35
95StaCluSTWS-415
95StaCluVR-213
95Stu-123
95Sum-54
95SumNthD-54
95Top-559
95TopCyb-335
95UC3-41
95UC3ArtP-41
95Ult-318
95UltGolM-318
95UppDec-30
95UppDecED-30
95UppDecEDG-30
95UppDecSE-245
95UppDecSEG-245
95Zen-87
96Baz-129
96Bow-38
96Cir-187
96CirAcc-28
96CirBos-48
96CirRav-187
96ColCho-240
96ColCho-783
96ColChoGS-240
96ColChoSS-240
96Don-61
96DonPreP-61
96EmoXL-279
96Fin-S229
96FinRef-S229
96Fla-376
96Fle-209
96FleTif-209
96FleUpd-U197
96FleUpd-5
96FleUpdTC-U197
96LeaLim-78
96LeaLimG-78
96LeaPre-88
96LeaPreP-88
96LeaPreSG-57
96LeaPreSte-57
96LeaSig-142
96LeaSigPPG-142
96LeaSigPPP-142
96MetUni-237
96MetUniP-237
96Pac-396
96PacGolCD-DC9
96PacPri-P125
96PacPriG-P125
96PadMot-4
96PanSti-222
96Pin-338
96PinAfi-36
96PinAfiAP-36
96PinAfiFPP-36
96PinFoil-338
96Sco-10
96ScoDugC-A10
96ScoDugCAP-A10
96Sel-108
96SelArtP-108
96SelCer-70
96SelCerAP-70
96SelCerCB-70
96SelCerCR-70
96SelCerMB-70
96SelCerMG-70
96SelCerMR-70
96SP-159
95StaCluVRMC-213
96Stu-149
96StuPrePB-149
96StuPrePG-149
96StuPrePS-149
96Sum-66
96SumAbo&B-66
96SumArtP-66
96SumFoi-66
96Top-397
96TopChr-159
96TopChrMotG-6
96TopChrMotGR-6
96TopChrR-159
96TopGal-79
96TopGalPPI-79
96TopLas-44
96TopMasotG-6
96Ult-114
96Ult-558
96UltCalttH-4
96UltCalttHGM-4
96UltGolM-114
96UltGolM-558
96UltOn-L-4
96UltOn-LGM-4
96UppDec-110
96UppDec-378
96UppDec-445
96Zen-42
96ZenArtP-42
96ZenMoz-20
97Cir-341
97CirRav-341
97ColCho-211
97Don-73
97DonEli-104
97DonEliGS-104
97DonLim-85
97DonLimFotG-4
97DonLimLE-85
97DonPreP-73
97DonPrePGold-73
97Fin-63
97FinRef-63
97Fle-464
97FleDecoE-5
97FleDecoERT-5
97FleMilDM-24
97FleTif-464
97Lea-261
97LeaFraM-261
97LeaFraMDC-261
97MetUni-221
97Pac-426
97PacLigB-426
97PacPriGotD-GD208
97PacSil-426
97Pin-104
97PinArtP-104
97PinCer-76
97PinCerMBlu-76
97PinCerMG-76
97PinCerMR-76
97PinCerR-76
97PinIns-51
97PinInsCE-51
97PinInsDE-51
97PinMusC-104
97PinPreP-3
97PinTotCPB-76
97PinTotCPG-76

97PinTotCPR-76
97Sco-51
97ScoPreS-51
97ScoShoS-51
97ScoShoSAP-51
97Sel-50
97SelArtP-50
97SelRegG-50
97SkyE-X-94
97SkyE-XC-94
97SkyE-XEC-94
97SP-152
97StaClu-66
97StaCluMOP-66
97Stu-42
97StuPrePG-42
97StuPrePS-42
97Top-96
97TopChr-39
97TopChrR-39
97TopGal-11
97TopGalPPI-11
97TopSta-74
97TopStaAM-74
97Ult-285
97UltDouT-19
97UltGolME-285
97UltPlaME-285
97UppDec-494
Henderson, Robbie
78CedRapGT-9
79CedRapGT-6
Henderson, Rod (Rodney)
92ClaDraP-76
92JamExpC-1
92JamExpF-1497
93ClaFS7-278
93FloStaLAF-49
93OPCPreTDP-3
93StaCluM-178
93WesPalBEC-9
93WesPalBEF-1333
94Bow-584
94BowBes-B37
94BowBesR-B37
94Cla-39
94ClaGolF-189
94ExcFS7-226
94Fla-191
94HarSenF-2085
94SigRoo-6
94SigRooS-6
94Ult-523
94UppDecML-81
94UppDecML-92
94UppDecML-267
94UppDecMLPotYF-PY10
95Bow-269
95BowGolF-269
95ColCho-12
95ColChoGS-12
95ColChoSE-10
95ColChoSEGS-10
95ColChoSESS-10
95ColChoSS-12
95Pin-418
95PinArtP-418
95PinMusC-418
95PinMusC-437
Henderson, Ryan
92GreFalDSP-17
93VerBeaDC-8
93VerBeaDF-2212
94ExcFS7-214
95VerBeaDTI-11
96SanAntMB-6
Henderson, Steve
77IndIndTI-14
78Hos-126
78MetDaiPA-10
78OPC-53
78Top-134
79OPC-232
79Top-445
80OPC-156
80Top-299
81AllGamPI-146
81CokTeaS-17
81Don-157
81Fle-321
81Kel-25
81OPC-44
81Top-619
81TopScr-79
81TopSti-193
81TopTra-769
82CubRedL-28
82Don-183
82FBIDis-10
82Fle-597
82FleSta-98
82OPC-89
82Top-89
82TopSti-30
83Don-252
83Fle-496
83Top-335
83TopTra-42T
84Don-389
84Fle-612
84MarMot-21
84Nes792-501
84OPC-274
84Top-501
84TopRubD-25
84TopSti-341
84TopTif-501
85A'sMot-26
85Don-145
85Fle-490
85FleUpd-52
85OPC-38
85Top-640
85TopRubD-25
85TopTif-640
85TopTifT-50T
85TopTra-50T
86A'sMot-20
86Don-375
86Fle-419
86Top-748
86TopTif-748
87TacTigP-13
88AstMot-12
88AstPol-13
88Sco-547
88ScoGlo-547
88Top-527
88TopTif-527
89BufBisC-14
89BufBisP-1676
89PacSenL-5
89T/MSenL-45
89TopSenL-9
89TriA AAC-9
89TriAAP-AAA22
90BufBisP-391
90BufBisTI-8
90EliSenL-17
90ProAAAF-506
90TriAAAC-9
91MetWIZ-171
91PacSenL-144
94AstMot-27
95AstMot-28
96AstMot-28
Henderson, Tim
89MisStaB-18
90MisStaB-19
Henderson, Todd
92HamRedC-27
92HamRedF-1606
Henderson, Valentine
89WelPirP-13
Henderson, Wendell
82QuaCitCT-15
Hendley, Brett
90ModA'sC-13
91MadMusC-15
91MadMusP-2134
91MidLeaAP-MWL41
92ModA'sC-16
92ModA'sF-3906
Hendley, C. Bob
61Top-372
62Top-361
63BraJayP-5
63Top-62
64Top-189
64TopCoi-94
64TopVen-189
65Top-444
66OPC-82
66Top-82
66TopVen-82
67CokCapC-4
67Top-256
68Top-345
68TopVen-345
69OPC-144
69Top-144
Hendrick, George
71A'sPos-10
72OPC-406
72Top-406
73LinPor-63
73OPC-13
73OPC-201
73Top-13
73Top-201
74OPC-303
74Top-303
74TopSta-167
75Hos-140
75Kel-46
75OPC-109
75Top-109
76OPC-570
76SSP-527
76Top-570
77BurCheD-129
77Hos-123
77OPC-218
77PadSchC-26A
77PadSchC-26B
77PepGloD-40
77Top-330
78Hos-82
78OPC-178
78Top-30
79Car5-8
79Hos-66
79OPC-82
79Top-175
80OPC-184
80Top-350
81AllGamPI-147
81Car5x7-6
81CokTeaS-122
81Don-430
81Dra-22
81Fle-542
81Kel-35
81OPC-230
81Top-230
81TopScr-85
81TopSti-22
81TopSti-220
81TopSti-256
82Don-9
82Don-40
82Dra-17
82Fle-113
82FleSta-25
82OPC-295
82Squ-16
82Top-420
82TopSti-91
83AllGamPI-147
83Car-7
83Don-404
83Dra-10
83Fle-7
83FleSti-269
83Kel-25
83OPC-148
83PerCreC-6
83PerCreCG-6
83Top-650
83TopSti-153
83TopSti-285
84AllGamPI-53
84Car-9
84Car5x7-9
84Don-475
84DonActAS-32
84Dra-12
84Fle-324
84FleSti-9
84FunFooP-52
84Nes792-386
84Nes792-540
84OPC-163
84OPC-386
84Top-386
84Top-540
84TopGloS-23
84TopRubD-2
84TopSti-139
84TopSti-185
84TopStiB-11
84TopTif-386
84TopTif-540
85AllGamPI-145
85Don-181
85Fle-225
85FleStaS-27
85FleUpd-53
85Lea-259
85OPC-60
85Pir-7
85Top-60
85TopRubD-2
85TopSti-134
85TopTif-60
85TopTifT-51T
85TopTra-51T
86AngSmo-14
86Fle-158
86OPC-190
86Top-190
86TopTif-190
87AngSmo-22
87DonOpeD-3
87Fle-82
87FleGlo-82
87OPC-248
87Top-725
87TopTif-725
88AngSmo-24
88Don-479
88Sco-308
88ScoGlo-308
88StaLinAn-8
88Top-304
88TopTif-304
89PacSenL-61
89T/MSenL-46
89TopSenL-12
90EliSenL-82
92CarMcD-45
Hendrick, Harvey
28PorandAR-C2
29ExhFou-3
29PorandAR-37
34DiaMatCSB-89
34DiaStaR-41
90DodTar-331
92ConTSN-522
Hendrick, Pete
86ElPasDP-14
Hendricks, Ellie (Elrod)
69MilBra-110
69Top-277
70DayDaiNM-160
70OPC-528
70Top-528
71MLBOffS-299
71OPC-219
71Ori-6
71Top-219
72MilBra-139
72OPC-508
72Top-508
73OriJohP-10
75OPC-609
75Top-609
76OPC-371
76SSP-384
76Top-371
83OriPos-11
84OriTeal-12
87OriFreB-44
88OriFreB-44
89OriFreB-44
89SweBasG-64
91OriCro-193
92YanWIZ7-72
Hendricks, Kacy
92GulCoaDF-3561
93ButCopKSP-10
Hendricks, Ryan
94BluOriC-11
94BluOriF-3567
96HigDesMB-12
Hendricks, Steve
87SpoIndP-22
88RivRedWCLC-221
88RivRedWP-1409
89WatDiaP-1772
89WatDiaS-11
89WicStaR-7
90CalLeaACLC-7
90RivRedWB-12
90RivRedWCLC-11
90RivRedWP-2615
91LinDriAA-462
91NewBriRSLD-462
91NewBriRSP-357
Hendrickson, Craig
77QuaCitAT-17
78CedRapGT-10
Hendrickson, Dan
89EveGiaS-13
Hendriksen, Claude
16FleBreD-39
16FleBreD-40
Hendrix, Claude
13PolGroW-9
14CraJacE-76
15CraJacE-76
15SpoNewM-77
16BF2FP-66
16ColE13-72
16SpoNewM-78
19W514-9
20NatCarE-42
92ConTSN-343
Hendrix, James
87ChaWheP-2
88VirGenS-10
Hendry, Keith
79WatIndT-4B
Hendry, Ted
88T/MUmp-35
89T/MUmp-33
90T/MUmp-32
Hendy, Jim
94ElmPioF-3489
94ElmPioC-24
Hengel, Dave
86CalCanP-11
87CalCanP-2317
88CalCanC-18
88CalCanP-1550
88Don-629
88Fle-375
88FleGlo-375
89ChaLooLITI-12
89ColSprSSC-18
89ColSprSSP-243
89Top-531
89TopTif-531
92PhoFirS-382
Hengle, Emory
87OldJudN-244
Henika, Ron
84CedRapRT-27
86VerRedP-11
87NasSouTI-10
90CedRapRDGB-17
Henion, Scott
87ColMetP-17
88SalBucS-8
89WesPalBES-12
Henke, Rick
83WatIndF-26
86WatIndP-13
87WilBilP-15
Henke, Tom
82TulDriT-1
83OklCit8T-9
84Don-134
84OklCit8T-10
85BluJayFS-14
85Don-403
85IntLeaAT-41
85SyrChiT-8
86BluJayAF-13
86BluJayFS-17
86Don-437
86Fle-60
86FleStiC-54
86Lea-206
86OPC-333
86Top-333
86TopSti-189
86TopTif-333
87BluJayFS-12
87Don-197
87Fle-228
87FleExcS-25
87FleGlo-228
87FleSlu-19
87FleStiC-57
87GenMilB-1E
87Lea-73
87OPC-277
87SmoAmeL-14
87SpoTeaP-5

87SyrChi1A-6
87Top-510
87TopMinL-76
87TopSti-185
87TopTif-510
88BluJay5-6
88BluJayFS-15
88Don-490
88DonAll-28
88DonBasB-104
88Fle-112
88FleAll-2
88FleAwaW-18
88FleExcS-19
88FleGlo-112
88FleLeaL-17
88FleMin-62
88FleStiC-73
88FleTeaL-12
88MSAHosD-23
88OPC-220
88PanSti-213
88RedFolSB-33
88Sco-57
88ScoGlo-57
88Spo-65
88StaLinBJ-8
88Top-220
88Top-396
88TopBig-41
88TopGloS-35
88TopMinL-38
88TopRevLL-31
88TopSti-186
88TopStiB-64
88TopTif-220
88TopTif-396
88TopUKM-32
88TopUKMT-32
89BluJayFS-13
89Bow-246
89BowTif-246
89Don-385
89DonBasB-301
89Fle-235
89FleExcS-22
89FleGlo-235
89OPC-75
89PanSti-461
89Sco-318
89ScoHot1S-63
89Spo-126
89Top-75
89TopBasT-118
89TopSti-195
89TopTif-75
89UppDec-264
90BluJayFS-11
90BluJayHS-3
90BluJayHS-4
90Bow-506
90BowTif-506
90Don-349
90DonBesA-14
90Fle-84
90FleCan-84
90Lea-158
90MSAHolD-3
90OPC-695
90PubSti-516
90Sco-157
90Spo-42
90Top-695
90TopBig-101
90TopSti-196
90TopTif-695
90TulDriDGB-19
90TulDriTI-28
90UppDec-282
91BluJayFS-13
91BluJayFS-14
91BluJayS-2
91Bow-16
91Don-205
91Fle-176
91Lea-517
91OPC-110
91OPCPre-63
91PanFreS-345
91Sco-579
91StaClu-24
91Top-110
91TopDesS-110
91TopMic-110
91TopTif-110
91Ult-362
91UppDec-149
92Don-141
92DonMcD-G5
92Fle-331
92Lea-159
92OPC-451
92PepDieM-3
92Pin-417
92Sco-385
92Sco-439
92Sco100S-31
92StaClu-819
92StaCluECN-819
92SyrChiTT-4
92Top-451
92TopGol-451
92TopGolW-451
92TopKid-93
92TopMic-451
92Ult-450
92UppDec-395
93BluJayD4-18
93BluJayDM-7
93Bow-461
93Don-723
93Fin-164
93FinRef-164
93Fla-281
93Fle-335
93FleFinE-279
93KinDis-15
93Lea-278
93MSABenSPD-16
93OPC-202
93OPCPre-77
93OPCWorC-7
93PacSpa-640
93Pin-546
93RanKee-409
93Sco-602
93Sel-211
93SelRoo-15T
93SP-195
93StaClu-637
93StaCluFDI-637
93StaCluMOP-637
93StaCluR-17
93Top-376
93TopGol-376
93TopInaM-376
93TopMic-376
93TopTra-14T
93Ult-629
93UppDec-557
93UppDecGold-557
94Bow-269
94ColC-628
94ColChoGS-628
94ColChoSS-628
94Don-162
94ExtBas-180
94Fin-64
94FinRef-64
94Fla-111
94Fle-308
94Lea-434
94OPC-242
94Pac-618
94PanSti-128
94Pin-42
94PinArtP-42
94PinMusC-42
94RanMagM-7
94Sco-542
94ScoGolR-542
94Sel-237
94Spo-104
94StaClu-19
94StaCluFDI-19
94StaCluGR-19
94StaCluMO-2
94StaCluMOP-19
94StaCluT-270
94StaCluTFDI-270
94Top-644
94TopGol-644
94TopSpa-644
94TriPla-195
94Ult-128
94UltFir-3
94UppDec-367
94UppDecED-367
95BluJayUSPC-4S
95BluJayUSPC-12H
95ColCho-196
95ColChoGS-196
95ColChoSS-196
95Don-473
95DonPreP-473
95DonTopotO-327
95Fin-238
95FinRef-238
95Fla-407
95Fle-287
95FleUpd-159
95Lea-351
95Pin-363
95PinArtP-363
95PinMusC-363
95Sco-150
95ScoGolR-150
95ScoPlaTS-150
95SP-101
95SPSil-101
95StaClu-261
95StaClu-545
95StaCluFDI-261
95StaCluMOP-261
95StaCluMOP-545
95StaCluSTWS-261
95StaCluSTWS-545
95StaCluVR-129
95TopTra-98T
95Ult-429
95UltGolM-429
95UppDec-455T
96ColCho-285
96ColChoGS-285
96ColChoSS-285
96Don-320
96DonPreP-320
96Fle-544
96FleTif-544
96Pac-227
96PacPri-P70
96PacPriG-P70
96Sco-160
96StaClu-13
96StaClu-263
96StaCluEPB-13
96StaCluEPG-13
96StaCluEPS-13
96StaCluMOP-13
96StaCluMOP-263
95StaCluVRMC-129
96Top-90
96Ult-274
96UltGolM-274
96UppDec-185
97BluJayS-38

Henkel, Rob
91ElmPioC-20
91ElmPioP-3267
92ProFS7-26
92WinHavRSF-1770
93CarLeaAGF-8
93ClaFS7-9
93LynRedSC-12
93LynRedSF-2513
94SarRedSC-13
94UppDecML-176

Henkemeyer, Dick
82WisRapTF-17

Henley, Bobby
93JamExpC-11
93JamExpF-3330
94BurBeeC-9
94BurBeeF-1083
94MidLeaAF-MDW32
95AusFut-74
96HarSenB-15
97Sel-121
97SelArtP-121
97SelRegG-121

Henley, Dan
85AncGlaPTI-15
88BakDodCLC-235
89SanAntMB-12
90AlbDukC-18
90AlbDukP-351
90AlbDukT-10
90CMC-420
90ProAAAF-72
91LinDriAAA-636
91VanCanLD-636
91VanCanP-1602

Henley, Gail
57JetPos-8

Henley, Mike
83AppFoxF-11

Henley, Weldon
03BreE10-70
09ColChiE-128
11SpoLifCW-162
12ColRedB-128
12ColTinT-128
90DodTar-332

Henline, Butch (Walter)
20NatCarE-43
21Nei-59
22E120-198
22W572-42
23WilChoV-62
25Exh-43
26Exh-44
27AmeCarE-31
27Exh-8
87ConSer2-18
90DodTar-333
92ConTSN-581

Henline, Noah
12ImpTobC-64

Henneman, Blair
92EveGiaF-1679

Henneman, Mike
86NasSouTI-12
87DonRoo-32
87FleUpd-44
87FleUpdG-44
87IntLeaAT-15
87SpoRoo2-29
87TolMudHP-16
87TolMudHT-13
87TopTra-46T
87TopTraT-46T
88ClaBlu-241
88Don-420
88DonBasB-91
88Fle-57
88FleGlo-57
88FleStiC-25
88OPC-3
88Sco-520
88ScoGlo-520
88ScoYouSI-15
88Spo-129
88StaLinTi-7
88TigPep-39
88Top-582
88TopBig-256
88TopGloS-10
88TopRoo-7
88TopTif-582
88ToyRoo-13
89Bow-98
89BowTif-98
89ClaLigB-94
89Don-327
89DonBasB-237
89Fle-134
89FleExcS-23
89FleGlo-134
89OPC-365
89PanSti-333
89Sco-293
89ScoHot1S-59
89Spo-56
89TigMar-39
89TigPol-39
89Top-365
89TopBig-252
89TopSti-273
89TopTif-365
89UppDec-373
90BirBarDGB-18
90Bow-345
90BowTif-345
90Don-296
90DonBesA-105
90Fle-604
90FleCan-604
90Lea-2
90OPC-177
90PanSti-69
90PubSti-472
90Sco-184
90Spo-144
90TigCok-8
90TigMilH-1
90TigMilH-2
90TigMilH-3
90TigMilH-4
90TigMilH-6
90Top-177
90TopBig-41
90TopSti-282
90TopTif-177
90UppDec-537
91Don-76
91Fle-340
91Lea-18
91OPC-641
91PanSti-236
91RedFolS-49
91Sco-142
91Sco100S-51
91StaClu-287
91TigCok-39
91Top-641
91TopDesS-641
91TopMic-641
91TopTif-641
91Ult-123
91UppDec-386
92Bow-441
92Don-253
92Fle-138
92Lea-325
92OPC-293
92Pin-164
92Sco-217
92StaClu-34
92Stu-175
92Top-293
92TopGol-293
92TopGolW-293
92TopMic-293
92Ult-364
92UppDec-339
93Bow-559
93Don-259
93Fla-204
93Fle-229
93Lea-81
93OPC-149
93Pin-385
93Sco-166
93Sel-138
93SP-238
93StaClu-480
93StaCluFDI-480
93StaCluMOP-480
93TigGat-14
93Top-756
93TopGol-756
93TopInaM-756
93TopMic-756
93Ult-199
93UppDec-403
93UppDecGold-403
94Bow-181
94ColC-132
94ColChoGS-132
94ColChoSS-132
94Don-496
94ExtBas-77
94Fin-34
94FinRef-34
94Fle-135
94Lea-183
94OPC-52
94Pin-154
94PinArtP-154
94PinMusC-154
94RedFolMI-10
94Sco-117
94ScoGolR-117
94Sel-368
94SP-178
94SPDieC-178
94StaClu-401
94StaCluFDI-401
94StaCluGR-401
94StaCluMOP-401
94Top-438
94TopGol-438
94TopSpa-438
94TriPla-246
94Ult-55
94UppDec-321
94UppDecED-321
95ColCho-468
95ColChoGS-468
95ColChoSS-468

95DonTopotO-78
95Fin-153
95FinRef-153
95Fla-257
95Fle-56
95Sco-148
95ScoGolR-148
95ScoPlaTS-148
95StaClu-329
95StaCluMOP-329
95StaCluSTWS-329
95StaCluVR-170
95Top-307
95TopCyb-165
96ColCho-162
96ColChoGS-162
96ColChoSS-162
96Don-532
96DonPreP-532
96Fla-173
96LeaSigEA-74
96RanMot-16
96StaClu-390
96StaCluMOP-390
95StaCluVRMC-170
96Top-390
96Ult-421
96UltGolM-421
97Fle-225
97FleTif-225
97Pac-203
97PacLigB-203
97PacSil-203
97Top-76
97Ult-135
97UltGolME-135
97UltPlaME-135

Hennessey, Scott
91BasCitRC-25
91BasCitRP-1411

Hennessey, Sean
93HunCubC-10
93HunCubF-3231

Hennessy, Brendan
83BurRanF-18
83BurRanT-20
83TriTriT-24

Hennessy, Mike
82CedRapRT-9
86SumBraP-9

Hennigan, Phil
71MLBOffS-373
71OPC-211
71Top-211
72Top-748
73OPC-107
73Top-107
91MetWIZ-173

Henning, Rich
85FreGiaP-24
90BriTigP-3176
90BriTigS-28

Henninger, Rai
88IdaFalBP-1852

Henninger, Rich
74SpoIndC-30
74OPC-602
74Top-602
75OklCit8TI-4
93RanKee-181

Hennis, Randy (Randall)
87AubAstP-10
88FloStaLAS-8
88OscAstS-13
89ColMudB-9
89ColMudP-137
89ColMudS-12
90CMC-608
90TucTorC-6
90TucTorP-200
91Cla1-T45
91LinDriAAA-611
91Sco-752
91TopDeb90-66
91TucTorLD-611
91TucTorP-2209
96BreCouMB-3

Hennisaire, Randy
90ProAAAF-190

Henrich, Bobby
58RedEnq-16
58Top-131
59RedEnq-10

Henrich, Tommy (Tom)
39GouPreR303A-23
39PlaBal-52
39WorWidGTP-23
39WorWidGV-15
40PlaBal-4
41DouPlaR-111
41PlaBal-39
43MPR302-1-14
46SpoExcW-5-7
47Exh-92
47PM1StaP1-82
47PM1StaP1-83
47TipTop-51
48BluTin-42
48Bow-19
48YanTeal-12
49Bow-69
49Lea-55
49MPR302-2-xx
50Bow-10
50Dra-23
50RoyDes-12
51BerRos-B3
51Bow-291
51R42SmaS-47
53ExhCan-27
59TigGraASP-8
69EquSpoHoF-BB7
74NewYorNTDiS-23
75YanDyn1T-22
76SSPYanOD-3
79TCM50-35
82OhiHaloF-38
83YanASFY-18
84TCMPla1-9
92ConTSNGI-770
92UppDecS-16
92YanWIZA-30
93ConTSN-770
94ConTSN-1061
94ConTSNB-1061

Henrichs, Shawn
91EveGiaC-16
91EveGiaP-3907

Henrickson, John
94LetMouF-3875
94LetMouSP-13

Henriksen, Olaf
12T207-78
15SpoNewM-78
16ColE13-73
16SpoNewM-79

Henrikson, Dan
90BenBucL-12
91CliGiaC-3
91CliGiaP-828
94CliLumF-1975
94CliLumC-12

Henriquez, Oscar
93AshTouC-8
93AshTouF-2270
93LinVenB-259
94Bow-418
96Bow-385
96KisCobB-11

Henry Allen, Colt (Newton)
87NegLeaPD-41

Henry, Antoine
92JohCitCC-12
92JohCitCF-3130
93GleFalRC-15
93GleFalRF-4019
94SavCarC-14
94SavCarF-520

Henry, Bill F.
68Top-384

Henry, Bill R.
55Bow-264
59Top-46
59TopVen-46
60Kah-14
60Top-524
61Top-66
62Kah-18
62RedEnq-12
62Top-562
63RedEnq-12
63RedFreBC-8
63Top-378
64Top-49
64TopVen-49
65RedEnq-12
65Top-456
66OPC-115
66Top-115
66TopVen-115
67Top-579
68Top-239
68TopVen-239
82Bow195E-259
92YanWIZ6-55

Henry, Butch
88CedRapRP-1159
88MidLeaAGS-12
89ChaLooB-9
89ChaLooGS-11
90CedRapRDGB-23
90ChaLooGS-16
91LinDriAAA-612
91TucTorLD-612
91TucTorP-2210
92AstMot-18
92Bow-502
92DonRoo-51
92FleUpd-86
92Lea-435
92Pin-567
92StaClu-742
92StaCluECN-742
92Stu-37
92TopTra-49T
92TopTraG-49T
92UppDec-796
92UppDecSR-SR9
93Don-348
93Don-767
93Fle-411
93OPC-200
93OPCPre-30
93PacSpa-430
93Pin-511
93RocUSPC-5S
93RocUSPC-11C
93Sco-569
93StaClu-311
93StaCluFDI-311
93StaCluMOP-311
93StaCluRoc-24
93Top-281
93Top-719
93TopGol-281
93TopGol-719
93TopInaM-281
93TopInaM-719
93TopMic-281
93TopMic-719
93Ult-351
93UppDec-770
93UppDecGold-770
93USPlaCR-2S
94Fle-541
94TopTra-88T
95ColCho-247
95ColChoGS-247
95ColChoSS-247
95Don-455
95DonPreP-455
95Fle-352
95Sco-518
95ScoGolR-518
95ScoPlaTS-518
95StaClu-283
95StaCluMOP-283
95StaCluSTWS-283
95StaCluVR-146
95Top-498
95TopCyb-288
95Ult-191
95UltGolM-191
96ColCho-214
96ColChoGS-214
96ColChoSS-214
96Don-125
96DonPreP-125
95StaCluVRMC-146

Henry, Carlos
88AshTouP-1074
89AshTouP-965

Henry, Chris
80WauTimT-17

Henry, Dan
77CliDodT-10
77LodDodT-5

Henry, Doug
86BelBreP-10
87BelBreP-12
88StoPorCLC-177
88StoPorP-747
89ElPasDGS-8
90StoPorCLC-184
91DenZepLD-140
91DenZepP-120
91LinDriAAA-140
91TriA AAGP-AAA9
92BrePol-11
92ClaGam-78
92Don-663
92Lea-80
92OPC-776
92ProFS7-82
92Sco-421
92ScoImpP-17
92StaClu-615
92Top-776
92TopDeb91-73
92TopGol-776
92TopGolW-776
92TopMic-776
92Ult-384
92UppDec-43
93BrePol-10
93Don-471
93Fle-251
93Lea-530
93OPC-181
93PacSpa-158
93Pin-415
93Sco-177
93Sel-399
93StaClu-521
93StaCluFDI-521
93StaCluMOP-521
93Top-343
93TopGol-343
93TopInaM-343
93TopMic-343
93Ult-220
93UppDec-395
93UppDecGold-395
94BreMilB-225
94BrePol-11
94ColC-413
94ColChoGS-413
94ColChoSS-413
94Don-119
94Fin-404
94FinRef-404
94Fle-178
94Lea-393
94Pac-330
94Pin-283
94PinArtP-283
94PinMusC-283
94Sco-119
94ScoGolR-119
94Top-16
94TopGol-16
94TopSpa-16
94Ult-75
95FleUpd-113
95Top-131
96ColCho-627
96ColChoGS-627
96ColChoSS-627
96LeaSigEA-75
96MetKah-13

Henry, Dutch
90DodTar-334
93ConTSN-783

Henry, Dwayne
82BurRanF-4
82BurRanT-24
83TulDriT-11
84TulDriTI-36
85TulDriTI-29
86Don-603
86Fle-562
87Don-637
87OklCit8P-18
88BlaYNPRWL-183
88OklCit8C-2
88OklCit8P-33
88Top-178
88TopTif-178
89RicBraBC-9
89RicBraC-4
89RicBraP-844
89RicBraTI-9
89Top-496
89TopTif-496
89UppDec-51
90BraDubP-10
90BraDubS-12
91AstMot-24
91Fle-692
91Lea-329
91OPC-567
91Top-567
91TopDesS-567
91TopMic-567
91TopTif-567
92Don-114
92Fle-436
92Lea-433
92OPC-668
92RedKah-48
92Sco-204
92StaClu-892
92StaCluECN-892
92Top-668
92TopGol-668
92TopGolW-668
92TopMic-668
92Ult-483
92UppDec-430
93Don-478
93Fle-391
93FleFinE-272
93MarMot-8
93RanKee-182
93Sco-474
93StaClu-577
93StaCluFDI-577
93StaCluMOP-577
93Top-29
93TopGol-29
93TopInaM-29
93TopMic-29
94Pac-572
95TolMudHTI-16

Henry, Harold
91UtiBluSC-18
91UtiBluSP-3253
92SouBenWSC-16
92SouBenWSF-189
93SarWhiSC-13

Henry, Jim (James Francis)
79RedSoxEF-6

Henry, Jimmy
90BriTigP-3171
90BriTigS-10
91NiaFalRP-3627
92LakTigC-17
92LonTigF-629

Henry, John M.
87OldJudN-245

Henry, John Park
12T207-79
14FatPlaT-16
15SpoNewM-79
16ColE13-74
16SpoNewM-80
17HolBreD-42

Henry, Jon
90EliTwiS-12
91VisOakC-3
91VisOakP-1737
92OrlSunRF-2842
92OrlSunRS-507
93PorBeaF-2380
94NasXprF-380

Henry, Kevin
88IdaFalBP-1846

Henry, Mark
86PenWhiSP-12
87DayBeaAP-10

Henry, Michael
87SavCarP-10
88SprCarB-4

Henry, Paul
88NebCor-6

Henry, Prince Jo
76LauIndC-22

Henry, Ron
64TwiJayP-5
77FriOneYW-48

Henry, Ryan
89CarNewE-11

Henry, Santiago
92St.CatBJC-10
92St.CatBJF-3396
93HagSunC-13
93HagSunF-1889
94DunBluJC-13
94DunBluJF-2564

95KnoSmoF-48
96KnoSmoB-16
Henry, Scott
90MadMusB-7
90SouOreAB-29
91MadMusC-17
91MadMusP-2135
92RenSilSCLC-42
Henry, Sugar (Jim)
43ParSpo-38
91NiaFalRC-25
93LonTigF-2302
Henry, Tim
82BurRanF-14
82BurRanT-1
82TulDriT-6
83TulDriT-10
Henshaw, Roy
90DodTar-335
Hensich, Phil
36GouWidPPR-D12
36WorWidGV-123
Hensley, Chuck
82WesHavAT-6
83TacTigT-5
84TacTigC-86
86PhoFirP-9
87RicBraBC-12
87RicBraC-37
87RicBraT-6
88AlbDukC-10
88AlbDukP-273
89CalCanC-2
89CalCanP-531
90WilBilB-9
90WilBilP-1055
90WilBilS-10
Hensley, Mike
88OklSoo-2
89SavCarP-364
90Bes-235
90SprCarB-19
91St.PetCP-2272
Henson, Hunter
94DavLipB-14
95DavLipB-14
Henson, Joey
92DavLipB-14
93DavLipB-12
93GleFalRC-16
93GleFalRF-4010
Henson, Mickey
91Cla/Bes-22
91GasRanC-7
91GasRanP-2684
Hentgen, Pat
87MyrBeaBJP-1444
88DunBluJS-9
89DunBluJS-7
90Bes-295
90KnoBluJB-4
90KnoBluJP-1240
90KnoBluJS-5
90ProAaA-45
91Bow-23
91LinDriAAA-505
91SyrChiK-2
91SyrChiLD-505
91SyrChiMB-7
91SyrChiP-2477
92Bow-696
92Cla2-T16
92Don-704
92FleUpd-64
92Pin-563
92ScoRoo-96T
92SyrChiF-1962
92SyrChiMB-8
92TopDeb91-74
93BluJayD-19
93BluJayD4-33
93BluJayFS-14
93Don-247
93Fla-291
93Fle-694
93Lea-540
93LinVenB-29
93OPC-245
93Sco-343
93Sel-309
93SP-49
93StaClu-26
93StaCluFDI-26
93StaCluMOP-26
93Top-752
93TopGol-752
93TopInaM-752
93TopMic-752
93Ult-641
93UppDec-693
93UppDecGold-693
94BluJayUSPC-4S
94BluJayUSPC-9H
94BluJayUSPC-11D
94Bow-323
94ColC-133
94ColChoGS-133
94ColChoSS-133
94Don-200
94ExtBas-191
94Fin-400
94FinRef-400
94Fla-118
94Fle-335
94FleAllS-11
94Lea-185
94Pac-644
94Pin-316
94PinArtP-316
94PinMusC-316
94Sco-509
94ScoGolR-509
94Sel-48
94Spo-133
94StaClu-242
94StaCluFDI-242
94StaCluGR-242
94StaCluMOP-242
94StaCluT-158
94StaCluTFDI-158
94Stu-28
94Top-304
94TopGol-304
94TopSpa-304
94TriPla-34
94Ult-138
94UppDec-126
94UppDecED-126
95BluJayUSPC-2C
95BluJayUSPC-9D
95Bow-339
95ColCho-149
95ColChoGS-149
95ColChoSS-149
95Don-127
95DonPreP-127
95Emb-5
95EmbGolI-5
95Emo-95
95Fin-78
95FinRef-78
95Fla-98
95Fle-97
95FleAllS-22
95FleTeaL-14
95FleUpdSS-5
95Lea-156
95PanSti-15
95Pin-27
95PinArtP-27
95PinMusC-27
95Sco-110
95ScoGolR-110
95ScoPlaTS-110
95Sel-26
95SelArtP-26
95SP-207
95Spo-102
95SpoArtP-102
95SPSil-207
95StaClu-454
95StaCluMOP-454
95StaCluSTWS-454
95StaCluVR-244
95Top-213
95TopCyb-121
95TopLeaL-LL21
95Ult-121
95UltGolM-121
95UppDec-37
95UppDecED-37
95UppDecEDG-37
95UppDecSE-196
95UppDecSEG-196
96BluJayB-2
96BluJayOH-16
96ColCho-743
96ColChoGS-743
96ColChoSS-743
96Don-433
96DonPreP-433
96EmoXL-134
96Fin-B87
96FinRef-B87
96Fla-187
96Fle-276
96FleTif-276
96MetUni-122
96MetUniP-122
96Pac-440
96ProSta-17
96Sco-451
96StaClu-149
96StaCluMOP-149
95StaCluVRMC-244
96Top-148
96Ult-147
96UltGolM-147
96UppDec-473
97BluJayS-2
97BluJayS-30
97Bow-245
97BowBes-14
97BowBesAR-14
97BowBesR-14
97BowChr-70
97BowChrI-70
97BowChrIR-70
97BowChrR-70
97BowInt-245
97Cir-355
97CirRav-355
97ColCho-495
97ColChoAC-9
97Don-177
97Don-430
97DonEli-128
97DonEliGS-128
97DonLim-183
97DonLimLE-183
97DonPre-85
97DonPreCttC-85
97DonPreP-177
97DonPreP-430
97DonPrePGold-177
97DonPrePGold-430
97Fin-43
97FinRef-43
97FlaSho-A87
97FlaSho-B87
97FlaSho-C87
97FlaShoLC-87
97FlaShoLC-B87
97FlaShoLC-C87
97FlaShoLCM-A87
97FlaShoLCM-B87
97FlaShoLCM-C87
97Fle-242
97FleTeaL-14
97FleTif-242
97Lea-59
97LeaBanS-13
97LeaFraM-59
97LeaFraMDC-59
97LeaGet-6
97MetUni-186
97NewPin-32
97NewPinAP-32
97NewPinMC-32
97NewPinPP-32
97Pac-222
97PacLigB-222
97PacPri-75
97PacPriLB-75
97PacPriP-75
97PacSil-222
97Pin-88
97PinArtP-88
97PinCar-6
97PinCer-55
97PinCerMBlu-55
97PinCerMG-55
97PinCerMR-55
97PinCerR-55
97PinIns-97
97PinIns-149
97PinInsCE-97
97PinInsCE-149
97PinInsDE-97
97PinInsDE-149
97PinMusC-88
97PinTotCPB-55
97PinTotCPG-55
97PinTotCPR-55
97PinX-P-79
97PinX-PMoS-79
97ProMag-79
97ProMagML-79
97Sco-264
97ScoPreS-264
97ScoShoS-264
97ScoShoSAP-264
97Sel-46
97SelArtP-46
97SelRegG-46
97SkyE-X-51
97SkyE-XC-51
97SkyE-XEC-51
97SP-182
97SpoIll-134
97SpoIllEE-134
97StaClu-39
97StaCluMat-39
97StaCluMOP-39
97Stu-87
97StuPrePG-87
97StuPrePS-87
97Top-330
97TopAll-AS19
97TopChr-111
97TopChrAS-AS19
97TopChrR-111
97TopChrSAR-AS19
97TopChrSB-18
97TopChrSBR-18
97TopGal-123
97TopGalPPI-123
97TopSeaB-SB18
97TopSta-68
97TopStaAM-68
97Ult-145
97UltGolME-145
97UltPlaME-145
97UltTop3-26
97UltTop3GM-26
97UppDec-213
97UppDecAWJ-22
Henthorne, Kevin
96TamYanY-13
Hepler, William
66Top-574
67OPC-144
67Top-144
91MetWIZ-174
Herbel, Ron
61TacBan-10
61UniOil-T28
63Top-208
64Top-47
64TopVen-47
65OPC-84
65Top-84
66Top-331
66TopVen-331
67OPC-156
67Top-156
68Top-333
68TopVen-333
69Top-251
70OPC-526
70Top-526
71MLBOffS-11
71OPC-387
71Top-387
72MilBra-140
72OPC-469
72Top-469
91MetWIZ-175
Herberholz, Craig
81BurBeeT-7
Herbert, Ray
47Exh-93
53TigGle-13
54Top-190
55A'sRodM-18
55Top-138
55TopDouH-105
58Top-379
59Top-154
59TopVen-154
60A'sJayP-5
60A'sTeal-7
60Top-252
60TopTat-21
61A'sTeal-7
61AthJayP-9
61Pos-87A
61Pos-87B
61Top-498
61TopStal-162
62SalPlaC-6
62ShiPlaC-6
62Top-8
62TopStal-25
62TopVen-8
63Baz-29
63ExhStaB-28
63Fle-9
63Jel-45
63Pos-45
63SalMetC-42
63Top-8
63Top-560
63TopStil-17
63WhiSoxJP-4
63WhiSoxTS-9
64Top-215
64TopVen-215
64WhiSoxTS-11
65Top-399
66OPC-121
66Top-121
66TopVen-121
67TopVen-183
76A'sRodMC-12
79DiaGre-396
94TopArc1-190
94TopArc1G-190
Herbert, Russ
96CarLeaA1B-8
96CarLeaA2B-8
96PriWilCB-15
Herbison, Brett
96AppLeaAB-22
96BesAutSA-27
97Bow-408
97BowInt-408
Herbst, Michael
93CapCitBC-27
96BinBeeB-13
Herde, Kevin
93JohCitCF-3681
Heredia, Felix
94KanCouCC-11
94KanCouCF-156
94KanCouCTI-11
95BreCouMF-240
96PorSeaDB-15
97Bow-72
97BowBes-124
97BowBesAR-124
97BowBesR-124
97BowInt-72
97Cir-55
97CirRav-55
97Fle-622
97FleTif-622
97Ult-514
97UltGolME-514
97UltPlaME-514
97UppDec-278
Heredia, Geysi
86OscAstP-11
Heredia, Gil (Gilbert)
86AriWilP-4
87AriWilP-6
87EveGiaC-2
88CalLeaACLC-2
88SanJosGCLC-132
88SanJosGP-130
90CMC-530
90PhoFirC-3
90PhoFirP-6
90ProAAAF-32
91LinDriAAA-383
91PhoFirLD-383
91PhoFirP-61
92Don-737
92Fle-665
92GiaPacGaE-18
92Sco-771
92SkyAAAF-294
92StaClu-895
92StaCluECN-895
92TopDeb91-75
93OttLynF-2430
94Pac-383
94StaClu-664
94StaCluFDI-664
94StaCluGR-664

94StaCluMOP-664
95Fla-162
95Fle-353
95Pac-269
95Top-509
95TopCyb-298
96Fle-459
96FleTif-459
96LeaSigEA-76
96RanMot-18
97PacPriGotD-GD97
Heredia, Hector
87AlbDukP-10
88AlbDukC-11
88AlbDukP-274
89AlbDukC-5
89AlbDukP-66
Heredia, Julian
91BoiHawC-29
91BoiHawP-3871
91Cla/Bes-444
92ClaFS7-227
92ProFS7-40
92QuaCitRBC-1
92QuaCitRBF-803
93LimRocDWB-41
93MidAngF-319
94MidAngOHP-9
96PhoFirB-17
97MidAngOHP-15
Heredia, Ubaldo
76VenLeaS-85
77LodDodT-6
78LodDodT-8
80VenLeaS-101
87IndIndTI-11
Heredia, Wilson
91GulCoaRSP-6
92GasRanC-7
92GasRanF-2249
93ChaRanC-15
93ChaRanF-1937
93FloStaLAF-4
93LimRocDWB-124
94TulDriF-239
94TulDriTI-10
95Fla-306
95FleUpd-83
95Sum-129
95SumNthD-129
Herges, Matt
92YakBeaC-15
92YakBeaF-3443
93BakDodCLC-10
94VerBeaDC-9
94VerBeaDF-65
95SanAntMTI-53
96SanAntMB-7
Herling, Keith
94SigRoo-7
94SigRooS-7
Herman, Babe (Floyd C.)
28PorandAR-A15
28PorandAR-B15
28W513-84
28W513-92
28W56PlaC-H7
29ExhFou-4
29PorandAR-38
31Exh-4
32OrbPinUP-32
32R33So2-418
33ButCre-13
33Gou-5
33GouCanV-5
33RitCE-1D
33TatOrb-32
33TatOrbSDR-195
34DiaMatCSB-90
35DiaMatCS3T1-73
36ExhFou-4
36GouWidPPR-A51
61Fle-114
79DiaGre-78
88ConSer5-16
90DodTar-336
91ConTSN-169
93DiaStaES-135
Herman, Billy
32CubTeal-12
32OrbPinNP-67
32OrbPinUP-33
33Gou-227
33RitCE-2S
33TatOrb-33
34DiaMatCSB-91
34BatR31-138
35GouPuzR-8K
35GouPuzR-9K
36DiaMatCS3T2-14
36ExhFou-3
36R31PasP-29
36R31PasP-31
36SandSW-33
36WheBB4-6
36WheBB5-2
36WorWidGV-16
37ExhFou-3
37KelPepS-BB8
37WheBB14-6
37WheBB6-10
37WheBB9-8
38ExhFou-3
39CubTeal-11
39GouPreR303A-24
39GouPreR303B-14
39WorWidGTP-24
40WheM4-10
41DouPlaR-3
42DodTeal-10
43DodTeal-13
46SpoExcW-3-5
50RemBre-12
52Top-394
54Top-86
55DodGolS-27
55Top-19
55TopDouH-53
56Dod-12
60Top-456
65OPC-251
65Top-251
66OPC-37
66Top-37
66TopVen-37
75TCMAllG-15
76ChiGre-9
76RowExh-9
76ShaPiz-149
76SSPYanOD-4
76TayBow4-98
77GalGloG-84
78PadFamF-15
79DiaGre-105
79TCM50-187
80CubGreT-9
80PacLeg-23
80PerHaloFP-149
80SSPHOF-149
83DiaClaS2-72
83TopRep5-394
89DodSmoG-9
89KahCoo-6
89PerCelP-17
90DodTar-337
90PacLeg-30
90PerGreM-41
90SweBasG-59
91RinPosBD4-1
91SweBasG-39
92ActPacA-9
92ActPacA2-9G
92ConTSN-421
92ConTSN-473
92CubOldS-12
93ConTSN-787
93DiaStaES-136
93SpeGolSH-1
93TedWil-21
94ConTSN-1092
94ConTSNB-1092
94TopArc1-86
94TopArc1G-86
95TopArcBD-31
95TopArcBD-70
95TopArcBD-92
Herman, Greg
77AppFoxT-8
Herman, Ty
80ElmPioRST-8
Hermann, Jeff
86GleFalTP-9
87GleFalTP-18
88WicPilRD-27
Hermann, LeRoy
36GouWidPPR-D13
Hermansen, Chad
95Bes-112
95SPML-106
96AugGreB-14
96BesAutSA-28
96Exc-217
96ExcFirYP-6
96HonShaHWB-17
96LynHilUB-1
97Bow-87
97BowBes-129
97BowBesAR-129
97BowBesR-129
97BowCerBIA-CA37
97BowCerGIA-CA37
97BowChr-111
97BowChrI-111
97BowChrIR-111
97BowChrR-111
97BowInt-87
Hermanski, Gene
47Exh-94
47TipTop-97
49Bow-20
49EurSta-37
49Lea-102A
49Lea-102B
50Bow-113
51Bow-55
51TopRedB-11
52Bow-136
52TipTop-15
52Top-16
53Top-179
54Top-228
79DiaGre-92
79TCM50-165
83TopRep5-16
84FifNatC-3
88RinPosD1-12C
90DodTar-338
91TopArc1-179
94TopArc1-228
94TopArc1G-228
Hermanson, Dustin
93BazTeaU-7
93TopTra-22T
94Cla#1DPMF-DD3
94ClaUpdCotC-CC3
94SigRooDP-4
94SigRooDPS-4
94StaCluDP-87
94StaCluDPFDI-87
94TopTra-95T
94UppDecAHNIL-19
95ActPacF-54
95ARuFalLS-10
95Bow-274
95BowBes-B48
95BowBesR-B48
95BowGolF-274
95ColCho-25
95ColChoGS-25
95ColChoSE-3
95ColChoSEGS-3
95ColChoSESS-3
95ColChoSS-25
95Exc-284
95ExcFirYP-10
95Fin-302
95FinRef-302
95Fla-420
95FlaWavotF-8
95FleUpd-185
95ScoDraP-DP15
95SelSurS-SS5
95SP-5
95SPCha-7
95SPChaDC-7
95SPSil-5
95StaClu-107
95StaClu-572
95StaCluCB-CB2
95StaCluFDI-107
95StaCluMOP-107
95StaCluMOP-572
95StaCluMOP-CB2
95StaCluSTWS-107
95StaCluSTWS-572
95Sum-127
95SumNthD-127
95Top-231
95UppDec-219
95UppDecED-219
95UppDecEDG-219
95UppDecML-130
95UppDecML-164
95UppDecML-217
95UppDecSE-134
95UppDecSEG-134
95Zen-117
96Bow-303
96BowBes-114
96BowBesAR-114
96BowBesR-114
96ColCho-651
96ColCho-702
96ColChoGS-651
96ColChoGS-702
96ColChoSS-651
96ColChoSS-702
96Don-393
96DonPreP-393
96Fle-569
96FleTif-569
96LasVegSB-14
96Pin-187
96PinArtP-100
96PinSta-100
96Sco-266
96Spo-133
96SpoArtP-133
96Top-218
97Fle-635
97FleTif-635
97Top-434
97Ult-511
97UltGolME-511
97UltPlaME-511
95UppDecMLFS-130
95UppDecMLFS-164
95UppDecMLFS-217
Hermanson, Mike
92SpoIndC-9
92SpoIndF-1287
93WatDiaC-18
93WatDiaF-1763
94RanCucQC-15
94RanCucQF-1632
95RanCucQT-20
96LakElsSB-6
Hermoso, Angel
70OPC-147
70Top-147
76VenLeaS-225
Hermoso, Remigio
76VenLeaS-149
80VenLeaS-137
93LinVenB-32
Hernaiz, Jesus R.
76OklCit8TI-11
77ReaPhiT-14
80CarMudF-23
83ColCliT-12
84IdaFalATI-12
88SouOreAP-1718
89BlaYNPRWL-31
91KinMetC-26
91KinMetP-3830
92KinMetC-24
92KinMetF-1549
93KinMetC-26
93KinMetF-3812
94KinMetC-26
94KinMetF-3840
Hernaiz, Juan
92GulCoaDF-3580
93GreFalDSP-2
95VerBeaDTI-12
95YakBeaTI-14
96SavSanB-19
Hernandez, Alex
95TopTra-69T
96EriSeaB-13
Hernandez, Angel
76VenLeaS-15
80VenLeaS-11
Hernandez, Arned
90AppFoxBS-12
90AppFoxP-2110
Hernandez, Bobby (Roberto)
87ColMetP-15
Hernandez, Carlos
80VenLeaS-143
85BurRanT-19
87BakDodP-25
88BakDodCLC-243
89SanAntMB-13
89TexLeaAGS-17
90AlbDukC-16
90AlbDukP-349
90AlbDukT-11
90CMC-418
90DonRoo-37
90ProAAAF-70
91AlbDukLD-10
91AlbDukP-1144
91Don-711
91Fle-207
91LinDriAAA-10
91MadMusC-24
91MadMusP-2138
91TopDeb90-67
91TriA AAGP-AAA2
92Bow-5
92Cla1-T44
92DodMot-18
92DodPol-41
92DodSmo-9892
92Don-778
92FleUpd-91
92Lea-54
92Pin-456
92PinRoo-30
92ProFS7-239
92ScoRoo-91T
92TopTra-50T
92TopTraG-50T
92Ult-506
92UppDec-797
93DodMot-18
93DodPol-11
93Don-406
93Fle-62
93Lea-442
93LinVenB-250
93PacSpa-148
93Pin-146
93Sco-348
93Sel-317
93StaClu-149
93StaCluD-4
93StaCluFDI-149
93StaCluMOP-149
93Top-589
93TopGol-589
93TopInaM-589
93TopMic-589
93Ult-400
93UppDec-148
93UppDecGold-148
94DodMot-26
94DodPol-12
94Don-122
94Fle-512
94Pac-310
94Sco-174
94ScoGolR-174
94StaClu-145
94StaCluFDI-145
94StaCluGR-145
94StaCluMOP-145
94Top-353
94TopGol-353
94TopSpa-353
94VenLinU-54
95DodMot-20
95DodPol-10
95FleUpd-174
95LinVen-26
95Pac-217
95QuaCitRBTI-10
95Top-94
96DodMot-20
96DodPol-18
96Fle-436
96FleTif-436
96LeaSigEA-77
96QuaCitRB-16
Hernandez, Cesar
86BurExpP-8
87WesPalBEP-665
88RocExpLC-17
90JacExpB-10
90JacExpP-1385
91HarSenLD-256
91HarSenP-639
91LinDriAA-256
92ChaLooS-185
92DonRoo-52
92OPC-618
92SkyAA F-82
92Top-618

92TopGol-618
92TopGolW-618
92TopMic-618
93Don-558
93Fle-392
93LimRocDWB-54
93PacSpa-400
93Pin-591
93Sco-302
93Top-301
93TopGol-301
93TopInaM-301
93TopMic-301
94Pac-148

Hernandez, Chico
43CubTeal-11

Hernandez, Chuck
86PalSprAP-3
86PalSprAP-17
87MidAngP-18
88EdmTraP-563
89EdmTraC-24
89EdmTraP-562
90CMC-485
90EdmTraC-8
90EdmTraP-532
90ProAAAF-108
93AngMot-28
94AngMot-28
95AngMot-28
96AngMot-28

Hernandez, Daniel
90HigSchPLS-8

Hernandez, Elvin
96AugGreB-15
97Bow-350
97BowInt-350

Hernandez, Enzo
71MLBOffS-229
71OPC-529
71Top-529
72OPC-7
72PadTeal-12
72Top-7
73OPC-438
73Top-438
74OPC-572
74PadDea-13
74PadMcDD-6
74Top-572
75OPC-84
75Top-84
76OPC-289
76SSP-125
76Top-289
76VenLeaS-113
77BurCheD-135
77PadSchC-27
77PadSchC-28
77Top-522
86PadGreT-3
90DodTar-339

Hernandez, Fernando
91BurIndP-3297
92ColRedC-16
92ColRedF-2385
93KinIndC-12
93KinIndF-2242
93KinIndTI-11
93LimRocDWB-103
96MemChiB-14
97Fle-633
97FleTif-633

Hernandez, Francis
96FreKeyB-26

Hernandez, Guillermo (Willie)
76OkICit8TI-18
77CubJewT-7
78SSP270-255
78Top-99
79Top-614
80Top-472
81Don-589
81Fle-310
81Top-238
82CubRedL-38
82Top-23
83Don-174
83Fle-497
83Top-568
83TopTra-45T
84Don-163
84Fle-34
84FleUpd-51
84FunFooP-79
84Nes792-199
84OPC-199
84TigFarJ-6
84TigWavP-19
84Top-199
84TopTif-199
84TopTra-51T
84TopTraT-51T
85AllGamPI-78
85Don-212
85Dra-37
85Fle-10
85FleStaS-101
85Lea-235
85OPC-333
85SevCoi-C7
85SevCoi-D10
85SevCoi-G1
85TigCaiD-10
85TigWen-11
85Top-333
85TopGaloC-5
85TopMin-333
85TopRubD-18
85TopSti-257
85TopSup-2
85TopTif-333
86Don-227
86DonAll-43
86DonWaxBC-PC5
86Fle-228
86FleLeaL-18
86FleStiC-56
86Lea-102
86OPC-341
86SevCoi-C9
86Spo-65
86Spo-85
86TigCaiD-8
86Top-670
86TopSti-275
86TopTat-8
86TopTif-670
87Don-522
87DonAll-43
87Fle-153
87FleExcS-26
87FleGamW-20
87FleGlo-153
87FleMin-54
87FleStiC-59
87OPC-339
87SevCoi-D4
87Spo-105
87SpoTeaP-15
87TigCaiD-13
87TigCok-15
87TolMudHP-27
87Top-515
87TopMinL-54
87TopSti-272
87TopTif-515
88Don-398
88DonBasB-125
88Fle-58
88FleGlo-58
88PanSti-84
88Sco-507
88ScoGlo-507
88StaLinTi-8
88TigPep-21
88Top-713
88TopBig-206
88TopTif-713
89BimBreD-9
89Don-62
89Fle-135
89FleGlo-135
89OPC-43
89Sco-275
89TigMar-21
89TigPol-21
89Top-43
89TopTif-43
89UppDec-279
90Don-610
90Fle-605
90FleCan-605
90PubSti-473
90RedFolSB-46
90Sco-267
90UppDec-518

Hernandez, Henry
90St.PetCS-12

Hernandez, Jackie
67CokCapDA-20
68Top-352
68TopVen-352
69RoySol-9
69Top-258
69TopSta-185
69TopTeaP-7
70MLBOffS-221
70RoyTeal-14
70Top-686
71MLBOffS-204
71OPC-144
71PirActP-18
71Top-144
72MilBra-141
72OPC-502
72Top-502
73OPC-363
73Top-363
74OPC-566
74Top-566
76VenLeaS-194

Hernandez, Javier
90AshTouC-5
91AshTouP-563
92OscAstF-2525

Hernandez, Jeremy
87EriCarP-26
88SprCarB-3
89St.PetCS-17
90TexLeaAGS-13
90WicWraRD-8
91LasVegSLD-283
91LasVegSP-230
91LinDriAAA-283
92Bow-73
92Don-756
92FleUpd-122
92LasVegSF-2792
92OPC-211
92PadMot-18
92PadSmo-12
92StaClu-734
92Top-211
92TopDeb91-76
92TopGol-211
92TopGolW-211
92TopMic-211
92Ult-576
92UppDec-42
93Don-180
93Fle-140
93Lea-502
93PacSpa-598
93StaClu-392
93StaCluFDI-392
93StaCluMOP-392
93Top-388
93TopGol-388
93TopInaM-388
93TopMic-388
93Ult-473
93Ult-649
93UppDec-811
93UppDecGold-811
94Don-95
94ExtBas-262
94Fle-105
94FleUpd-135
94Sco-204
94ScoGolR-204
94StaClu-420
94StaCluFDI-420
94StaCluGR-420
94StaCluMOP-420
94Top-537
94TopGol-537
94TopSpa-537
95Don-366
95DonPreP-366
95Fla-138

Hernandez, Jesus
93LinVenB-46
95LinVen-28
96BurIndB-27

Hernandez, Jose
89BlaYNPRWL-116
89GasRanP-1018
89GasRanS-8
90ChaRanS-10
91Cla/Bes-94
91LinDriAA-584
91TulDriLD-584
91TulDriP-2780
91TulDriTI-12
92CanIndF-698
92CanIndS-109
92Don-530
92Fle-307
92OPC-237
92Sco-866
92SkyAA F-51
92Top-237
92TopDeb91-77
92TopGol-237
92TopGolW-237
92TopMic-237
93OrlCubF-2793
93RanKee-183
94Ult-457
95Don-466
95DonPreP-466
95Fle-416
95Pac-72
96ColCho-498
96ColChoGS-498
96ColChoSS-498
96Don-136
96DonPreP-136
96Fle-320
96FleCub-8
96FleTif-320
96LeaSigEA-78
96Pac-23
97Pac-251
97PacLigB-251
97PacSil-251

Hernandez, Keith
75OPC-623
75Top-623
76OPC-542
76SSP-590
76Top-542
77BurCheD-11
77Car5-11
77CarTeal-10
77Hos-115
77OPC-150
77Top-95
78CarTeal-8
78Hos-22
78OPC-109
78Top-143
79Car5-10
79Hos-108
79OPC-371
79Top-695
80BurKinPHR-16
80Kel-43
80OPC-170
80Top-201
80Top-321
80TopSup-26
81AllGamPI-96
81Car5x7-7
81CokTeaS-123
81Don-67
81Fle-545
81Kel-31
81MSAMinD-16
81OPC-195
81PerCreC-8
81Top-420
81TopScr-67
81TopSti-18
81TopSti-219
82Don-278
82FBIDis-11
82Fle-114
82FleSta-23
82K-M-36
82Kel-23
82OPC-210
82PerCreC-8
82PerCreCG-8
82Top-186
82Top-210
82TopSti-92
83AllGamPI-95
83Car-8
83Don-20
83Don-152
83DonActA-20
83Fle-8
83FleSta-78
83FleSti-6
83Kel-49
83OPC-262
83PerCreC-7
83PerCreCG-7
83Top-700
83TopFol-3
83TopGloS-4
83TopSti-188
83TopSti-290
83TopTra-43T
84AllGamPI-6
84Don-238
84DonActAS-23
84DonCha-46
84Dra-13
84Fle-587
84FleSti-49
84FunFooP-104
84MetFanC-4
84Nes792-120
84OPC-120
84RalPur-32
84RawGloT-1
84SevCoi-E24
84Top-120
84TopCer-32
84TopRubD-5
84TopSti-107
84TopStiB-6
84TopSup-26
84TopTif-120
85AllGamPI-97
85Don-68
85DonActA-41
85DonHig-21
85DonHig-27
85Dra-15
85Fle-85
85FleLimE-12
85FleStaS-25
85KASDis-5
85KitCloD-5
85Lea-62
85MetColP-25
85MetFanC-6
85MetTCM-24
85OPC-80
85PolMet-M5
85SevCoi-E10
85ThoMcAD-33
85Top-80
85Top-712
85Top3-D-11
85TopGloS-13
85TopRubD-6
85TopSti-98
85TopSup-36
85TopTif-80
85TopTif-712
86BasStaB-56
86Don-190
86DorChe-9
86Dra-10
86Fle-84
86FleMin-20
86FleStiC-55
86Lea-124
86MetColP-6
86MetFanC-5
86MetTCM-18
86MetWorSC-1
86OPC-252
86SevCoi-C3
86SevCoi-E3
86SevCoi-S3
86SevCoi-W3
86Spo-15
86Spo-62
86Spo-127
86Spo-179
86Spo-181
86Top-203
86Top-520
86Top-701
86Top3-D-10
86TopGloS-7
86TopMinL-53
86TopSti-99
86TopSup-31
86TopTat-1
86TopTif-203
86TopTif-520
86TopTif-701

86Woo-14
87BoaandB-12
87BurKinA-10
87ClaGam-4
87Don-76
87DonAll-11
87DonOpeD-124
87DonP-11
87Dra-10
87Fle-12
87Fle-629
87Fle-637
87FleGlo-12
87FleGlo-629
87FleGlo-637
87FleGlo-WS2
87FleHea-5
87FleHotS-21
87FleLimE-20
87FleMin-53
87FleStiC-58
87FleWaxBC-C6
87FleWorS-2
87GenMilB-5C
87KayB-17
87Lea-233
87MetColP-13
87MSAIceTD-4
87MSAJifPD-4
87OPC-350
87RedFolSB-32
87SevCoi-E10
87SevCoi-M13
87Spo-133
87Spo-195
87SpoDeaP-3
87SpoSupD-13
87SpoTeaP-2
87StaHer-1
87StaHer-2
87StaHer-3
87StaHer-4
87StaHer-5
87StaHer-6
87StaHer-7
87StaHer-8
87StaHer-9
87StaHer-10
87StaHer-11
87StaHer-12
87StaHer-13
87StuPan-1
87Top-350
87Top-595
87TopCoi-36
87TopGloA-2
87TopGloS-26
87TopMinL-24
87TopSti-102
87TopSti-157
87TopTif-350
87TopTif-595
87Woo-31
88CheBoy-12
88Don-316
88DonAll-49
88DonBasB-152
88DonTeaBM-316
88Dra-5
88Fle-136
88Fle-639
88FleGlo-136
88FleGlo-639
88FleHotS-17
88FleLeaL-18
88FleMin-93
88FleStiC-103
88K-M-14
88Lea-117
88MetColP-5
88MetFanC-17
88MetKah-17
88MSAJifPD-9
88Nes-42
88OPC-68
88PanSti-339
88Sco-400
88ScoGlo-400
88Spo-31
88SpoGam-11
88StaLinAl-15
88StaLinMe-9
88Top-610
88TopBig-59
88TopGloS-32
88TopSti-97
88TopStiB-3
88TopTif-610
88TopUKM-33
88TopUKMT-33
89Bow-385
89BowTif-385
89ClaLigB-59
89Don-117
89DonBasB-208
89DonGraS-8
89Fle-37
89FleGlo-37
89MetCol8-57
89MetColP-9
89MetKah-11
89OPC-63
89OPCBoxB-G
89PanSti-137
89RedFolSB-57
89Sco-41
89ScoHot1S-23
89Spo-60
89Top-480
89TopBasT-48
89TopBatL-8
89TopBig-185
89TopDouM-8
89TopSti-93
89TopTif-291
89TopTif-480
89TopWaxBC-G
89TVSpoM-4
89UppDec-612
90BasWit-20
90Bow-342
90BowTif-342
90ClaYel-T36
90Don-388
90DonBesA-33
90Fle-205
90FleCan-205
90IndTeal-16
90KayB-16
90Lea-470
90MLBBasB-10
90OPC-230
90PubSti-135
90PubSti-262
90Sco-193
90Sco100S-29
90ScoRoo-57T
90Spo-106
90Top-230
90TopAmeA-8
90TopBatL-10
90TopBig-301
90TopTif-230
90TopTra-39T
90TopTraT-39T
90UppDec-222
90UppDec-777
91Fle-368
91MetWIZ-177
91Sco-89
92CarMcD-24
93ActPacA-148
94Yoo-7
Hernandez, Kiki (Enrique)
89OneYanP-2100
90PriWilCTI-12
91GreHorP-3062
91SouAtlLAGP-SAL26
92AlbYanF-2228
92AlbYanS-23
92Bow-637
92ClaFS7-102
92ForLauYTI-17
92ProFS7-125
92SkyAA F-3
92UppDecML-158
93ClaGolF-101
93ColCliF-1113
93ColCliP-11
94ColCliF-2954
94ColCliP-11
95ChaKniTI-11
Hernandez, Krandall
91HunCubC-12
91HunCubP-3337
Hernandez, Leo (Leonardo Jesus)
78CliDodT-13
79CliDodT-16
80VenLeaS-103
83TopTra-44T
84Nes792-71
84RocRedWT-15
84Top-71
84TopTif-71
85RocRedWT-5
86ColCliP-10
86ColCliP-11
91OriCro-194
92YanWIZ8-81
94VenLinU-182
Hernandez, Livan
96Bow-266
96ChaKniB-14
96ColCho-432
96ColChoGS-432
96ColChoSS-432
96Fin-G294
96FinRef-G294
96Pin-372
96PinFoil-372
96PinProS-13
96Sel-174
96SelCer-105
96SelCerAP-105
96SelCerCB-105
96SelCerCR-105
96SelCerMB-105
96SelCerMG-105
96SelCerMR-105
96Sum-172
96SumAbo&B-172
96SumArtP-172
96SumFoi-172
96UppDec-244
97Bow-153
97BowChr-153
97BowChrI-153
97BowChrIR-153
97BowChrR-153
97BowInt-153
97Top-382
Hernandez, Luis
90BriTigP-3153
90BriTigS-11
91BriTigC-5
91BriTigP-3614
92BriTigF-1418
Hernandez, Manny
82DayBeaAT-5
83DayBeaAT-6
84TucTorC-59
85DomLeaS-84
85TucTorC-56
86TucTorP-7
87TucTorP-7
88Don-481
88TucTorC-1
88TucTorJP-13
88TucTorP-169
89PorBeaC-2
89PorBeaP-221
90CMC-356
90ProAAAF-269
90TidTidC-5
90TidTidP-538
90TopTVM-45
91LinDriAAA-557
91MetWIZ-176
91TidTidLD-557
91TidTidP-2504
Hernandez, Marino
88PocGiaP-2085
89CliGiaP-884
90CliGiaB-16
Hernandez, Martin
86NasPirP-12
87SalBucP-11
Hernandez, Mike
94YakBeaF-3857
Hernandez, Nick
78NewWayCT-20
79BurBeeT-8
Hernandez, Pedro
80KnoBluJT-17
81SyrChiT-15
81SyrChiTI-9
82SyrChiT-21
82SyrChiTI-14
85DomLeaS-78
85TucTorC-71
Hernandez, Pete (Pedro Julio)
78DayBeaAT-10
Hernandez, Rafael
91KinMetC-11
91KinMetP-3822
92PitMetC-8
92PitMetF-3304
93PitMetC-10
93PitMetF-3717
Hernandez, Ramon
91BilMusP-3760
91BilMusSP-17
92PriRedC-22
92PriRedF-3094
93BatCliC-12
93BatCliF-3157
93SpaPhiC-15
93SpaPhiF-1061
96Bow-220
96WesMicWB-11
97Bow-418
97BowChr-278
97BowChrI-278
97BowChrIR-278
97BowChrR-278
97BowInt-418
Hernandez, Ramon Pitcher
67Top-576
68Top-382
73OPC-117
73Top-117
74OPC-222
74Top-222
75OPC-224
75Top-224
76OPC-647
76SSP-567
76Top-647
77Top-468
Hernandez, Rob
86LitFalMP-14
88St.LucMS-11
95ElmPioTI-11
95ElmPioUTI-11
Hernandez, Roberto M.
86SalAngC-100
87KenTwiP-2
87QuaCitAP-8
88BlaYNPRWL-70
88QuaCitAGS-20
89BlaYNPRWL-77
89MidAngGS-18
90Bes-216
90BirBarB-18
90BirBarP-1106
90CMC-820
91Bow-343
91LinDriAAA-637
91VanCanLD-637
91VanCanP-1591
92Bow-133
92Cla1-T45
92ClaGam-115
92Don-19
92Fle-677
92FleUpd-13
92OPC-667
92Pin-253
92PinRoo-9
92Sco-874
92SkyAAAF-284
92StaClu-356
92Top-667
92TopDeb91-78
92TopGol-667
92TopGolW-667
92TopMic-667
92Ult-336
92UppDec-7
92VanCanS-640
92WhiSoxK-39
93Don-403
93Fla-185
93Fle-583
93FleRooS-RSA4
93Lea-346
93OPC-126
93PacSpa-387
93Pin-129
93Sco-376
93Sel-311
93StaClu-21
93StaCluFDI-21
93StaCluMOP-21
93StaCluWS-8
93Top-70
93TopGol-70
93TopInaM-70
93TopMic-70
93Toy-88
93Ult-533
93UppDec-352
93UppDecGold-352
93USPlaCR-9D
93WhiSoxK-11
94Bow-138
94ColC-134
94ColChoGS-134
94ColChoSS-134
94Don-116
94Fin-376
94FinRef-376
94Fla-277
94Fle-83
94FUnPac-77
94Lea-167
94OPC-94
94Pac-127
94PanSti-48
94Pin-164
94PinArtP-164
94PinMusC-164
94Sco-457
94ScoGolR-457
94Sel-277
94StaClu-182
94StaCluFDI-182
94StaCluGR-182
94StaCluMOP-182
94StaCluT-129
94StaCluTFDI-129
94Top-572
94TopGol-572
94TopSpa-572
94TriPla-265
94Ult-34
94UltFir-4
94UppDec-468
94UppDecED-468
94WhiSoxK-12
95ColCho-507
95ColChoGS-507
95ColChoSS-507
95Don-279
95DonPreP-279
95DonTopotO-50
95Fin-161
95FinRef-161
95Fla-245
95Fle-119
95Lea-164
95Pac-90
95Sco-449
95ScoGolR-449
95ScoPlaTS-449
95StaClu-420
95StaCluMOP-420
95StaCluSTWS-420
95StaCluVR-218
95Top-191
95TopCyb-109
95TopPre-PP8
95Ult-29
95UltGolM-29
95UppDec-436
95UppDecED-436
95UppDecEDG-436
95UppDecSE-22
95UppDecSEG-22
95WhiSoxK-13
96Baz-87
96ColCho-96
96ColChoGS-96
96ColChoSS-96
96Don-205
96DonPreP-205
96Fin-B5
96FinRef-B5
96Fla-52
96Fle-67
96FleTif-67
96FleWhiS-7
96LeaSigA-100
96LeaSigAG-100
96LeaSigAS-100
96MetUni-38
96MetUniP-38
96Pac-288

96PacPri-P90
96PacPriG-P90
96Sco-192
96StaClu-22
96StaCluEPB-22
96StaCluEPG-22
96StaCluEPS-22
96StaCluMOP-22
95StaCluVRMC-218
96Top-405
96TopGal-86
96TopGalPPI-86
96Ult-39
96UltGolM-39
96UppDec-304
97Bow-285
97BowChr-96
97BowChrI-96
97BowChrIR-96
97BowChrR-96
97BowInt-285
97Cir-229
97CirRav-229
97ColCho-297
97Don-129
97DonPreP-129
97DonPrePGold-129
97DonTea-63
97DonTeaSPE-63
97Fin-19
97FinRef-19
97Fle-62
97FleTif-62
97Lea-10
97LeaFraM-10
97LeaFraMDC-10
97MetUni-59
97NewPin-46
97NewPinAP-46
97NewPinMC-46
97NewPinPP-46
97Pac-54
97PacLigB-54
97PacSil-54
97Sco-131
97ScoPreS-131
97ScoShoS-131
97ScoShoSAP-131
97ScoWhiS-6
97ScoWhiSPI-6
97ScoWhiSPr-6
97SP-47
97StaCluMat-38
97Top-232
97TopAll-AS21
97TopChr-82
97TopChrAS-AS21
97TopChrR-82
97TopChrSAR-AS21
97TopGal-104
97TopGalPPI-104
97Ult-40
97UltGolME-40
97UltPlaME-40
97UppDec-332

Hernandez, Rudy (Rudolph Albert)
55DonWin-24
61Top-229

Hernandez, Rudy J.
89St.LucMS-9
90JacMetGS-21
90TexLeaAGS-21
91LinDriAA-633
91WilBilLD-633
91WilBilP-301
93LinVenB-168
94VenLinU-45
95LinVen-113

Hernandez, Santos
95BurBeeTI-5
96BurBeeTI-5
96MidLeaAB-14

Hernandez, Toby
80UtiBluJT-18
80VenLeaS-56
83SyrChiT-14
84SyrChiT-15
85TolMudHT-13

Hernandez, Tom
91GasRanC-15
91GasRanP-2692

Hernandez, Wicho
94PitMetC-11
94PitMetF-3528

Hernandez, Xavier
88MyrBeaBJP-1178
88SouAtlLAGS-21
89KnoBluJB-9
89KnoBluJP-1144
89SyrChiMB-14
90AstLenH-15
90Don-682
90DonRoo-33
90Lea-517
90TopDeb89-55
90UppDec-26
91AstMot-26
91Bow-545
91Don-708
91Fle-509
91Lea-462
91OPC-194
91Sco-564
91StaClu-74
91Top-194
91TopDesS-194
91TopMic-194
91TopTif-194
92AstMot-26
92Don-782
92Fle-437
92OPC-640
92StaClu-736
92StaCluNC-736
92Top-640
92TopGol-640
92TopGolW-640
92TopMic-640
92Ult-205
93AstMot-23
93Don-636
93Fle-53
93Lea-543
93OPC-233
93PacSpa-477
93Pin-453
93Sco-417
93StaClu-271
93StaCluAs-24
93StaCluFDI-271
93StaCluMOP-271
93Top-252
93TopGol-252
93TopInaM-252
93TopMic-252
93Ult-43
93UppDec-319
93UppDecGold-319
94ColC-399
94ColChoGS-399
94ColChoSS-399
94Don-143
94ExtBas-130
94Fin-373
94FinRef-373
94Fla-81
94Fle-493
94FleUpd-67
94Lea-273
94Pac-268
94Pin-471
94PinArtP-471
94PinMusC-471
94ScoRoo-RT53
94ScoRooGR-RT53
94SpoRoo-18
94SpoRooAP-18
94StaClu-616
94StaCluFDI-616
94StaCluGR-616
94StaCluMOP-616
94StaCluT-201
94StaCluTFDI-201
94Top-512
94TopGol-512
94TopSpa-512
94TopTra-83T
94Ult-206
94Ult-399
94UppDec-342
94UppDecED-342
95Fle-69
95FleUpd-133
95Pac-296
95RedKah-10
96ColCho-518
96ColChoGS-518
96ColChoSS-518
96Don-170
96DonPreP-170
96Fle-342
96FleTif-342
96Pac-42
97Fle-641
97FleTif-641
97Pac-318
97PacLigB-318
97PacSil-318

Herndon, Larry
75PhoGiaC-9
75PhoGiaCK-20
75TulOil7-12
76PheGiaCr-11
76PhoGiaCC-11
77BurCheD-104
77Hos-47
77OPC-169
77Top-397
78Top-512
79GiaPol-31
79OPC-328
79Top-624
80GiaPol-31
80Top-257
81Don-196
81Fle-451
81OPC-108
81Top-409
81TopSti-236
82Don-172
82Fle-390
82OPC-182
82Top-182
82TopSti-109
82TopStiV-109
82TopTra-43T
83AllGamPI-55
83Don-585
83DonActA-5
83Fle-330
83FleSta-79
83FleSti-256
83OPC-13
83Tig-14
83Top-13
83Top-261
83TopSti-68
84AllGamPI-144
84Don-349
84Fle-82
84Nes792-333
84OPC-333
84TigFarJ-7
84TigWavP-20
84Top-333
84TopSti-264
84TopTif-333
85Don-150
85Fle-11
85Lea-249
85OPC-9
85SevCoi-D4
85TigCaiD-11
85TigWen-12
85Top-591
85TopSti-266
85TopTif-591
86Don-593
86Fle-229
86Lea-230
86OPC-61
86TigCaiD-9
86Top-688
86TopSti-271
86TopTif-688
87DonOpeD-211
87Fle-154
87FleGlo-154
87SevCoi-D5
87TigCaiD-11
87TigCok-2
87Top-298
87TopTif-298
88Don-353
88Fle-59
88FleGlo-59
88OPC-146
88RedFolSB-34
88Sco-138
88ScoGlo-138
88StaLinTi-9
88TigPep-31
88TigPol-6
88Top-743
88TopBig-56
88TopTif-743
89Sco-279
89UppDec-49
93TigGat-28

Herold, Bob
92OmaRoyF-2978
92OmaRoyS-350
96SpoIndB-1

Heron, Chico
57SeaPop-18

Herr, Edward
87OldJudN-246

Herr, Tommy (Thomas)
77St.PetCT-14
78ArkTraT-13
80Top-684
81Car5x7-8
81Car5x7-9
81CokTeaS-124
81Don-68
81Fle-550
81Top-266
82Don-530
82Fle-115
82FleSta-30
82Top-27
83AllGamPI-102
83Car-9
83Don-217
83Fle-9
83FleSta-80
83OPC-97
83Top-489
83TopSti-286
84AllGamPI-11
84Car-10
84Car5x7-10
84Don-596
84Fle-325
84Nes792-649
84OPC-117
84Top-649
84TopSti-142
84TopTif-649
85AllGamPI-101
85CarTeal-12
85Don-425
85DonActA-43
85Fle-226
85OPC-113
85Top-113
85TopMin-113
85TopSti-142
85TopTif-113
86BasStaB-57
86CarIGAS-6
86CarKASD-15
86CarSchM-8
86CarTeal-16
86Don-83
86DonAll-2
86DonPop-2
86Dra-21
86Fle-37
86FleAll-2
86FleMin-8
86FleStiC-57
86Lea-79
86OPC-94
86SevCoi-S14
86Spo-113
86Top-550
86Top-702
86TopGloA-14
86TopGloS-32
86TopMinL-62
86TopSti-49
86TopSti-147
86TopSup-32
86TopTat-22
86TopTif-550
86TopTif-702
87CarSmo-20
87Don-140
87DonOpeD-61
87Fle-296
87FleGlo-296
87FleLeaL-22
87Lea-121
87OPC-181
87RedFolSB-60
87SpoTeaP-12
87Top-721
87TopSti-49
87TopTif-721
88Don-208
88DonBasB-326
88Fle-35
88FleGlo-35
88FleGlo-WS7
88FleGlo-WS10
88FleHotS-18
88FleUpd-43
88FleUpdG-43
88FleWorS-7
88FleWorS-10
88Lea-201
88OPC-310
88PanSti-389
88PanSti-391
88Sco-84
88ScoGlo-84
88ScoRoo-8T
88ScoRooG-8T
88Spo-141
88StaLinCa-7
88Top-310
88TopBig-31
88TopSti-50
88TopStiB-4
88TopTif-310
88TopTra-49T
88TopTraT-49T
89Bow-403
89BowTif-403
89ClaTraP-166
89Don-301
89DonBasB-72
89DonTra-4
89Fle-115
89FleGlo-115
89FleUpd-107
89PhiTas-10
89Sco-191
89ScoRoo-9T
89Top-709
89TopBig-283
89TopTif-709
89TopTra-49T
89TopTraT-49T
89UppDec-558
89UppDec-720
90Bow-159
90BowTif-159
90Don-21
90Don-75
90DonBesN-32
90DonLeaS-16
90DonSupD-21
90Fle-560
90FleBasM-18
90FleCan-560
90Lea-184
90MLBBasB-1
90OPC-297
90PanSti-309
90PhiTas-13
90PubSti-239
90RedFolSB-47
90Sco-171
90Sco100S-77
90Spo-63
90Top-297
90TopBig-206
90TopCoi-49
90TopSti-122
90TopTif-297
90UppDec-488
91Bow-480
91Don-610
91Fle-149
91Lea-48
91MetColP-17
91MetKah-28
91MetWIZ-178
91OPC-64
91Sco-820
91StaClu-532
91Stu-205
91Top-64
91TopDesS-64
91TopMic-64
91TopTif-64
91Ult-219

91UppDec-416
92CarMcD-37
Herrera, Carl
93StaCluMO-33
Herrera, Desmond
96BilMusTI-13
Herrera, Edgar
89GeoColC-11
90GeoColC-8
93Bow-241
93ClaFS7-205
93EliTwiC-11
93EliTwiF-3428
93ForWayWC-11
93ForWayWF-1981
93LinVenB-51
94VenLinU-238
Herrera, Ezequiel
90Bes-41
90SprCarB-9
91St.PetCC-26
91St.PetCP-2289
92St.PetCC-22
92St.PetCF-2039
Herrera, Francisco
80VenLeaS-5
Herrera, Hector
87AubAstP-20
Herrera, Ivan
96BelGiaTI-27
Herrera, Jose C.
69Top-378
76VenLeaS-54
Herrera, Jose Ramon Catalina
91MedHatBJP-4115
91MedHatBJSP-9
92MedHatBJF-3220
92MedHatBJSP-9
93HagSunC-1
93HagSunF-1891
93SouAtlLAGF-27
94Bow-604
94Cla-8
94ClaTriF-T58
94ExcFS7-145
94ModA'sC-1
94ModA'sF-3075
94TedWil-122
94UppDecML-168
95Bow-177
95BowBes-B83
95BowBesR-B83
95Exc-109
95HunStaTI-13
95UppDecML-62
95UppDecML-108
96A'sMot-9
96ColChoGS-16
96ColChoSS-16
96Don-460
96DonPreP-460
96Fin-B352
96FinRef-B352
96Fle-210
96FleTif-210
96Lea-132
96LeaPre-144
96LeaPreP-144
96LeaPrePB-132
96LeaPrePG-132
96LeaPrePS-132
96Pin-190
96Sco-250
96Top-338
96UltGolP-7
96UltGolPGM-7
96UppDec-239
96UppDecPHE-H22
96UppDecPreH-H22
97Cir-22
97CirRav-22
97Fle-191
97FleTif-191
97Lea-283
97LeaFraM-283
97LeaFraMDC-283
97MetUni-130
97Pac-170
97PacLigB-170
97PacSil-170
97Sco-81
97ScoPreS-81
97ScoShoS-81
97ScoShoSAP-81
97StaClu-307
97StaCluMOP-307
97Top-48
95UppDecMLFS-62
95UppDecMLFS-108
Herrera, Pascuel
92MedHatBJSP-12
Herrera, Poncho (Juan)
58Top-433A
58Top-433B
59Top-129
59TopVen-129
60Lea-5
60PhiJayP-8
60Top-130
60TopVen-130
61Baz-27
61Pos-121A
61Pos-121B
61Top-569
61TopMagR-36
61TopStaI-56
62Jel-192
62Pos-192
62PosCan-192
62SalPlaC-122
62ShiPlaC-122
Herrera, Ramon
26Exh-67
86NegLeaF-84
Herrera, Raul
93ClaGolF-102
94VenLinU-254
Herrholtz, John
91UtiBluSC-3
91UtiBluSP-3236
92SouBenWSF-173
Herrick, Jason
94CedRapKC-14
94CedRapKF-1122
95CedRapKTI-14
96LakElsSB-24
Herrick, Neal
81MiaOriT-16
Herring, Art
90DodTar-340
Herring, Jonathan
96MedHatBJTI-12
Herring, Paul
80WatRedT-5
81IndIndTI-27
82WatRedT-16
Herring, Vince
90SanJosGB-20
90SanJosGCLC-48
90SanJosGP-2010
90SanJosGS-11
91SanJosGC-17
91SanJosGP-5
92SanJosGC-22
Herrmann, August
09SpoNewSM-93
95ConTSN-1396
Herrmann, Ed
69Top-439
70OPC-368
70Top-368
71OPC-169
71Top-169
72OPC-452
72Top-452
72WhiSox-5
72WhiSoxC-2
72WhiSoxDS-2
72WhiSoxTI1-5
73LinPor-48
73OPC-73
73Top-73
74OPC-438
74Top-438
74TopSta-155
75Hos-86
75OPC-219
75Top-219
75YanSSP-8
76OPC-406
76SSP-440
76Top-406
77Top-143
78AstBurK-3
78Top-677
79ExpPos-11
79OPC-194
79Top-374
92YanWIZ7-73
Herrmann, Gary
92BatCliC-13
92BatCliF-3258
94ClePhiC-18
94ClePhiF-2524
95ClePhiF-213
96ReaPhiB-7
Herrmann, Leroy
32CubTeal-13
93ConTSN-973
Herrmann, Tim
89NiaFalRP-11
90FayGenP-2401
Herrnstein, John
63Top-553
64PhiPhiB-14
64Top-243
64TopVen-243
65Top-534
66Top-304
66TopVen-304
78TCM60I-124
Herrolz, John
92UtiBluSC-26
Herron, Tony
84PawRedST-11A
84PawRedST-11B
85PawRedST-16
Herrscher, Rick
76DalCon-5
77FriOneYW-69
91MetWIZ-179
Herry, David
92LSUTigM-15
Hersh, Dave
77BurBeeT-13
78AppFoxT-12
Hersh, Earl
60MapLeaSF-9
61MapLeaBH-8
Hershberger, N. Mike
61UniOil-SD4
62Top-341
63Top-254
63WhiSoxJP-5
63WhiSoxTS-10
64A's-9
64Top-465
64WhiSoxTS-12
65AthJayP-8
65OPC-89
65Top-89
66Top-236
66TopVen-236
67CokCapAt-11
67DexPre-94
67Top-323
68OPC-18
68Top-18
68TopVen-18
69MilBra-111
69MLBOffS-86
69Top-655
69TopTeaP-21
70BreMcD-11
70BreMil-8
70BreTeal-5
70MLBOffS-272
70Top-596
71BreTeal-5
71OPC-149
71Top-149
72MilBra-142
78TCM60I-287
94BreMilB-226
Hershberger, Willard
38CinOraW-14
39OrcPhoAP-13
39OrcPhoAP-29
39PlaBal-119
40PlaBal-77
41HarHarW-10
Hershiser, Gordon
88VerBeaDS-11
89SanAntMB-7
Hershiser, Orel
76BooProC-19
82AlbDukT-4
83AlbDukT-3
84DodPol-55
84FunFooP-83
84OCoandSI-225
85DodCokP-12
85Don-581
85Fle-371
85FleStaS-96
85Lea-38
85OPC-273
85Top-493
85TopSti-74
85TopTif-493
86BasStaB-58
86DodCokP-11
86DodPol-55
86DodUniOP-7
86Don-18
86Don-226
86DonSupD-18
86Dra-31
86Fle-131
86FleLimE-24
86FleSlu-16
86FleStiC-58
86Lea-18
86OPC-159
86SevCoi-W12
86Spo-9
86Top-159
86Top3-D-12
86TopGloS-24
86TopMinL-45
86TopSti-73
86TopSup-33
86TopTat-20
86TopTif-159
87ClaGam-92
87DodMot-6
87DodPol-28
87DodSmoA-12
87Don-106
87DonHig-13
87DonOpeD-79
87Fle-441
87FleGlo-441
87FleRecS-16
87Lea-246
87OPC-385
87RedFolSB-5
87SevCoi-W6
87Spo-43
87SpoTeaP-14
87Top-385
87TopMinL-14
87TopTif-385
88DodMot-6
88DodPol-55
88Don-94
88DonAll-56
88DonBasB-148
88Fle-518
88Fle-632
88FleAwaW-17
88FleBasA-14
88FleExcS-20
88FleGlo-518
88FleGlo-632
88FleHotS-19
88FleLeaL-19
88FleMin-84
88FleRecS-18
88FleSlu-18
88FleStiC-92
88FleSup-15
88FleTeaL-13
88Lea-62
88OPC-40
88PanSti-303
88Sco-470
88ScoGlo-470
88Spo-160
88StaHer-1
88StaHer-2
88StaHer-3
88StaHer-4
88StaHer-5
88StaHer-6
88StaHer-7
88StaHer-8
88StaHer-9
88StaHer-10
88StaHer-11
88StaLinD-8
88Top-40
88TopBig-91
88TopMinL-53
88TopRevLL-12
88TopSti-68
88TopTif-40
88TopUKM-34
88TopUKMT-34
89Baz-15
89Bow-341
89BowTif-341
89CadEllD-29
89CerSup-5
89ClaLigB-1
89ClaTraO-105
89ClaTraP-173
89DodMot-6
89DodPol-29
89DodSmoG-100
89DodStaSV-8
89Don-197
89Don-648
89DonAll-50
89DonBasB-225
89DonBonM-BC4
89Fle-62
89FleAll-7
89FleBasA-21
89FleBasM-19
89FleExcS-24
89FleGlo-62
89FleGlo-WS6
89FleGlo-WS11
89FleHeroB-22
89FleLeaL-20
89FleSup-23
89FleWaxBC-C14
89FleWorS-6
89FleWorS-11
89KayB-19
89KinDis-12
89MSAHolD-18
89MSAIceTD-10
89Nis-18
89OPC-41
89OPC-380
89PanSti-9
89PanSti-13
89PanSti-18
89PanSti-19
89PanSti-25
89PanSti-97
89PanSti-225
89PanSti-474
89RedFolSB-58
89Sco-370
89Sco-582
89Sco-653
89ScoHot1S-35
89ScoSco-21
89SocHer-1
89SocHer-2
89SocHer-3
89SocHer-4
89SocHer-5
89SocHer-6
89SocHer-7
89Spo-36
89Spo-222
89SpoIllFKI-5
89Top-5
89Top-394
89Top-550
89Top-669
89TopBasT-82
89TopBig-1
89TopCapC-3
89TopCoi-2
89TopDouA-21
89TopGaloC-8
89TopGloS-48
89TopHilTM-17
89TopMinL-18
89TopSti-12
89TopSti-65
89TopStiB-60
89TopTif-5
89TopTif-394
89TopTif-550
89TopTif-669
89TopUKM-38
89TVSpoM-34
89TVSpoM-135
89UppDec-130
89UppDec-661
89UppDec-665
89UppDec-667
89Woo-4

89Woo-21
89Woo-25
89Woo-33
90AllBasT-9
90BasWit-1
90Bow-84
90BowTif-84
90ClaBlu-81
90Col-6
90DodMot-12
90DodPol-55
90DodTar-341
90Don-197
90DonBesN-54
90DOnBonM-BC5
90Fle-399
90FleBasA-18
90FleBasM-19
90FleCan-399
90FleWaxBC-C14
90HOFStiB-99
90Hot50PS-21
90Lea-280
90MLBBasB-8
90MSAHolD-12
90OPC-780
90PanSti-275
90Pos-8
90PubSti-9
90PubSti-263
90RedFolSB-48
90Sco-50
90Sco100S-94
90Spo-197
90Top-780
90TopBig-82
90TopDou-34
90TopMinL-58
90TopSti-63
90TopTif-780
90TopTVA-46
90UppDec-10
90UppDec-256
90VenSti-217
90VenSti-218
90WonBreS-4
91Bow-595
91CadEllD-30
91Cla3-T38
91ClaGam-23
91DodMot-12
91DodPol-55
91DodUno7P-3
91Don-280
91Fle-208
91Lea-243
91OPC-690
91OPCPre-64
91PetSta-22
91SanAntMP-2968
91Sco-550
91SevCoi-SC5
91StaClu-244
91StaPinB-25
91Stu-183
91Top-690
91TopCraJ2-17
91TopDesS-690
91TopMic-690
91TopTif-690
91UltUpd-88
91UppDec-524
92Bow-517
92ClaGam-33
92DodMot-6
92DodPol-55
92DodSmo-4492
92DodStaTA-27
92Don-247
92Fle-459
92Lea-81
92OPC-175
92OPCPre-162
92PanSti-199
92Pin-21
92Pin-592
92Sco-653
92ScoProP-8
92SpoStaCC-24
92StaClu-431
92Stu-44
92Top-175
92TopGol-175
92TopGolW-175
92TopKid-52
92TopMic-175
92TriPla-212
92Ult-507
92UppDec-261
93Bow-394
93CadDis-32
93DiaMar-51
93DodMot-10
93DodPol-12
93Don-274
93DonDiaK-DK14
93DurPowP1-4
93Fin-184
93FinRef-184
93Fla-70
93Fle-63
93FunPac-88
93Kra-24
93Lea-53
93OPC-136
93PacSpa-149
93Pin-319
93Sco-90
93Sel-49
93SP-93
93StaClu-544
93StaCluD-23
93StaCluFDI-544
93StaCluMOP-544
93Top-255
93TopGol-255
93TopInaM-255
93TopMic-255
93TriPla-121
93Ult-55
93UppDec-169
93UppDecGold-169
94Bow-566
94ColC-135
94ColChoGS-135
94ColChoSS-135
94DodMot-7
94DodPol-13
94Don-151
94ExtBas-288
94ExtBasPD-10
94Fin-98
94FinRef-98
94Fla-178
94Fle-513
94FUnPac-155
94Lea-16
94OPC-133
94Pac-311
94PanSti-200
94Pin-58
94PinArtP-58
94PinMusC-58
94ProMag-69
94RedFolMI-20
94Sco-102
94ScoGolR-102
94Sel-134
94SP-77
94SPDieC-77
94Spo-125
94StaClu-400
94StaCluFDI-400
94StaCluGR-400
94StaCluMOP-400
94Stu-68
94Top-460
94TopGol-460
94TopSpa-460
94TriPla-84
94Ult-517
94UppDec-355
94UppDecAJ-32
94UppDecAJG-32
94UppDecED-355
95ColCho-229
95ColCho-555T
95ColChoGS-229
95ColChoSE-89
95ColChoSEGS-89
95ColChoSESS-89
95ColChoSS-229
95Don-245
95DonPreP-245
95Emo-33
95Fin-304
95FinRef-304
95Fla-250
95Fle-541
95FleUpd-41
95Lea-370
95Pac-218
95Pin-378
95PinArtP-378
95PinMusC-378
95RedFol-22
95Sco-238
95ScoGolR-238
95ScoPlaTS-238
95SPCha-108
95SPChaDC-108
95StaClu-37
95StaClu-562
95StaCluFDI-37
95StaCluMOP-37
95StaCluMOP-562
95StaCluSTDW-I562
95StaCluSTMP-13
95StaCluSTWS-37
95StaCluSTWS-562
95StaCluVR-26
95Top-305
95TopCyb-164
95TopTra-61T
95Ult-396
95UltGolM-396
95UppDec-74
95UppDec-466T
95UppDec-TC1
95UppDecED-74
95UppDecEDG-74
96Baz-131
96ColCho-384T
96ColCho-393T
96ColCho-525
96ColChoGS-525
96ColChoSS-525
96Don-149
96DonPreP-149
96EmoXL-48
96Fin-B147
96FinRef-B147
96Fla-66
96Fle-87
96FleInd-5
96FlePosG-3
96FleTif-87
96Kin-8
96Lea-124
96LeaPrePB-124
96LeaPrePG-124
96LeaPrePS-124
96MetUni-45
96MetUniP-45
96Pac-296
96PanSti-178
96Pin-248
96PinArtP-148
96PinFoil-248
96PinSta-148
96SchDis-2
96Sco-96
96StaClu-350
96StaCluEPB-350
96StaCluEPG-350
96StaCluEPS-350
96StaCluMOP-350
95StaCluVRMC-26
96Stu-142
96StuPrePB-142
96StuPrePG-142
96StuPrePS-142
96Top-40
96TopGal-55
96TopGalPPI-55
96Ult-47
96UltGolM-47
96UppDec-59
96UppDec-220
97Cir-193
97CirRav-193
97ColCho-88
97Don-266
97DonPreP-266
97DonPrePGold-266
97DonTea-83
97DonTeaSPE-83
97Fin-261
97FinRef-261
97Fle-79
97FleMilDM-18
97FleTif-79
97Lea-76
97LeaFraM-76
97LeaFraMDC-76
97MetUni-81
97Pac-71
97PacLigB-71
97PacPriSH-SH4B
97PacSil-71
97Pin-121
97PinArtP-121
97PinMusC-121
97Sco-378
97ScoHobR-378
97ScoIndU-12
97ScoIndUTC-12
97ScoResC-378
97ScoShoS-378
97ScoShoSAP-378
97StaClu-357
97StaCluMOP-357
97Top-110
97TopGal-7
97TopGalPPI-7
97Ult-49
97UltGolME-49
97UltPlaME-49
97UppDec-53

Hershmann, William
86EriCarP-NNO
87St.PetCP-21
88SavCarP-340
89SavCarP-366

Hertel, Rick
78DunBluJT-11

Hertz, Steve
64Top-544

Hertzler, Paul
85IndIndTI-18
86JacMetT-15

Herz, Steve
80TolMudHT-13
81TolMudHT-12
82SpoIndT-11
82VanCanT-11
84HawIsIC-142
85HawIsIC-244

Herzig, Spike (Lynn)
77HolMilT-13
78HolMilT-12

Herzog, Buck (Charles)
09SpoNewSM-90
09T206-153
09T206-154
10CouT21-142
10CouT21-143
10CouT21-286
10DarChoE-19
10RedCroT-117
10RedCroT-198
10SweCapPP-67
10SweCapPP-114
11MecDFT-26
11S74Sil-44
11SpoLifM-141
11T205-75
11TurRedT-45
12PhiCarE-12
12T207-80
14CraJacE-85
15CraJacE-85
15SpoNewM-80
16BF2FP-73
16ColE13-75
16FleBreD-41
16SpoNewM-81
17HolBreD-43
19W514-104
40PlaBal-229
75FlePio-27
92ConTSN-489

Herzog, Hans
84SavCarT-8
86St.PetCP-11
87St.PetCP-16

Herzog, Whitey
47Exh-95
57Top-29
58Top-438
59Top-392
60A'sTeal-8
60Lea-71
60Top-92
60TopVen-92
61Pos-88A
61Pos-88B
61SevElev-14
61Top-106
61TopStal-163
62Top-513
63Top-302
73OPC-549
73Top-549
75SSP18-13
76OPC-236
76SSP-185
76Top-236
77Top-371
78Roy-7
78SSP270-224
78Top-299
79Top-451
81Car5x7-10
81Top-684
82Don-190
83Car-10
83Don-530A
83Don-530B
83Top-186
84Car-11
84Car5x7-11
84Fle-660
84Nes792-561
84Top-561
84TopGloA-12
84TopTif-561
85CarTeal-13
85Top-683
85TopTif-683
86CarTeal-17
86Top-441
86TopTif-441
87CarSmo-25
87DonAll-20
87DonP-20
87Top-243
87TopGloA-1
87TopTif-243
88CarSmo-1
88Top-744
88TopTif-744
89CarSmo-8
89DonAll-42
89DonPop-42
89Top-654
89TopGloA-12
89TopTif-654
90CarSmo-8
90OPC-261
90Top-261
90TopTif-261
90TopTVCa-1
91OriCro-195
92CarMcD-47
93RanKee-184

Hesketh, Joe
83MemChiT-19
84IndIndTI-6
85Don-157
85ExpPos-10
85Fle-652
85TopTifT-52T
85TopTra-52T
86Don-341
86ExpPos-5
86ExpProPa-21
86ExpProPo-6
86Fle-250
86Lea-150
86OPC-42
86SevCoi-S15
86Spo-177
86Top-472
86TopGloS-19
86TopTif-472
87Don-134
87ExpPos-11
87Fle-320
87FleGlo-320
87Lea-62
87OPC-189
87Top-189
87TopTif-189
88Don-504
88ExpPos-8
88IndIndP-512
88OPC-371
88Top-371
88TopTif-371

89Don-460
89ExpPos-14
89Fle-378
89FleGlo-378
89OPC-74
89Sco-498
89Top-614
89TopTif-614
89UppDec-60
90BraDubP-11
90Don-511
90Fle-349
90FleCan-349
90Lea-507
90OPC-24
90PubSti-175
90Sco-483
90Top-24
90TopTif-24
90TopTra-40T
90TopTraT-40T
90UppDec-512
90VenSti-219
91OPC-269
91Top-269
91TopDesS-269
91TopMic-269
91TopTif-269
92Don-611
92Fle-40
92Lea-22
92OPC-521
92Pin-415
92RedSoxDD-16
92Sco-359
92StaClu-636
92StaCluNC-636
92Top-521
92TopGol-521
92TopGolW-521
92TopMic-521
92Ult-17
92UppDec-570
93Fle-562
93PacSpa-360
93Pin-448
93RedSoxWHP-14
93Sco-467
93StaClu-107
93StaCluFDI-107
93StaCluMOP-107
93Top-162
93TopGol-162
93TopInaM-162
93TopMic-162
93UppDec-620
93UppDecGold-620
94StaClu-455
94StaCluFDI-455
94StaCluGR-455
94StaCluMOP-455
95ColCho-416
95ColChoGS-416
95ColChoSS-416
95Don-229
95DonPreP-229
95Fle-32
Heslet, Harry
50WorWidGV-27
Hess, Mark
91DaiDolF-3
Hess, Otto
05IndSouPSoCP-9
11SpoLifCW-163
Hessler, John
80ColAstT-13
Hester, Marshall
80ChaO'sW-11
Hester, Steve
88GreHorP-1570
89CedRapRB-29
89CedRapRP-919
89CedRapRS-8
89CedRapRS-27
90CedRapRB-26
90CedRapRP-2323
Hetki, John
53Top-235
54Top-161
55TopDouH-61
91TopArc1-235
94TopArc1-161
94TopArc1G-161
Hetrick, B.
84JacMetT-11
Hetrick, Kent
87SalLakTTT-3
88BelBreGS-13
89StoPorB-9
89StoPorCLC-161
89StoPorP-376
89StoPorS-10
Hetzel, Eric
85GreHorT-18
87WinHavRSP-22
88PawRedSC-8
88PawRedSP-449
89Don-660
89PawRedSC-3
89PawRedSP-703
89PawRedSTI-11
90Don-539
90Fle-279
90FleCan-279
90LSUTigGM-5
90OPC-629
90PawRedSDD-9
90Sco-543
90Sco100RS-23
90Top-629
90TopDeb89-56
90TopTif-629
90TopTVRS-45
90UppDec-673
91LinDriAAA-356
91PawRedSDD-7
91PawRedSLD-356
91PawRedSP-32
Heuer, Mark
87SanAntDTI-24
Heusser, Ed
93ConTSN-970
Heving, Joe (Joseph W.)
34BatR31-43
39PlaBal-20
40PlaBal-35
41DouPlaR-135
81ConTSN-47
94ConTSN-1176
94ConTSNB-1176
Heving, Johnnie (John A.)
28StaPlaCE-37
29ExhFou-17
81ConTSN-48
92ConTSN-455
94ConTSN-1176
94ConTSNB-1176
Hewatt, B.
88PocGiaP-2090
Hewes, Pat
87SavCarP-9
88St.PetCS-9
89PenPilS-7
Heydeman, Greg
74AlbDukTI-6
Heydler, John
94ConTSN-1112
94ConTSNB-1112
Heydler, Mrs. (John)
94ConTSN-1112
94ConTSNB-1112
Hiatt, Jack
65Top-497
66Top-373
67Top-368
68DexPre-38
68Top-419
69MilBra-112
69OPC-204
69Top-204
69TopFou-11
70OPC-13
70Top-13
71MLBOffS-83
71OPC-371
71Top-371
72MilBra-143
72Top-633
73OPC-402
73Top-402
74WicAerODF-117
80WicAerT-8
82HolMilT-23
83ColAstT-22
88PocGiaP-2101
Hiatt, Phil
90EugEmeGS-14
91BasCitRC-17
91BasCitRP-1403
91Cla/Bes-151
91FloStaLAP-FSL1
92Bow-529
92ClaFS7-181
92MemChiF-2426
92MemChiS-436
92ProFS7-76
92SkyAA F-183
92UppDecML-45
92UppDecML-176
92UppDecMLPotY-PY22
93Bow-69
93ClaGolF-25
93Don-393
93ExcAllF-9
93ExcFS7-174
93Fla-216
93FleFinE-220
93FunPac-4
93LeaGolR-R14
93PacSpa-488
93Pin-611
93SelRoo-66T
93SP-229
93StaClu-695
93StaCluFDI-695
93StaCluMOP-695
93StaCluRoy-6
93Stu-107
93TopTra-29T
93Ult-561
93UltAllR-3
93UppDec-457
93UppDec-645
93UppDecDG-33
93UppDecGold-457
93UppDecGold-645
94ColC-136
94ColChoGS-136
94ColChoSS-136
94Don-279
94Fin-56
94FinRef-56
94Fle-160
94FUnPac-172
94Lea-90
94Pac-287
94Pin-327
94PinArtP-327
94PinMusC-327
94Sco-515
94ScoGolR-515
94Top-94
94TopGol-94
94TopSpa-94
94Ult-66
94USPlaCR-4D
95DonTopotO-91
95SigRoo-24
95SigRooSig-24
96TolMudHB-13
Hibbard, Billy
95HagSunF-63
Hibbard, Greg
86EugEmeC-43
87AppFoxP-27
87Ft.MyeRP-6
88BlaYNPRWL-26
88VanCanC-11
88VanCanP-770
89VanCanC-3
89VanCanP-584
90Bow-303
90BowTif-303
90Don-384
90Fle-534
90FleCan-534
90Lea-523
90OPC-769
90Sco-369
90Sco100RS-77
90ScoYouS2-20
90Top-769
90TopDeb89-57
90TopRoo-14
90TopTif-769
90UppDec-543
90WhiSoxC-8
91Don-159
91Fle-122
91Lea-438
91OPC-256
91PanFreS-319
91PanSti-254
91Sco-128
91Stu-34
91Top-256
91TopDesS-256
91TopMic-256
91TopTif-256
91Ult-75
91UppDec-679
91WhiSoxK-27
92Bow-325
92Don-178
92Fle-83
92Lea-169
92OPC-477
92Pin-364
92Sco-266
92StaClu-586
92Stu-153
92Top-477
92TopGol-477
92TopGolW-477
92TopMic-477
92TriPla-261
92Ult-36
92UppDec-420
92WhiSoxK-27
93Bow-88
93CubMar-10
93Don-271
93Fla-15
93Fle-379
93FleFinE-8
93Lea-298
93PacSpa-378
93Pin-527
93Sco-622
93Sel-216
93SelRoo-103T
93StaClu-606
93StaCluCu-3
93StaCluFDI-606
93StaCluMOP-606
93Top-313
93TopGol-313
93TopInaM-313
93TopMic-313
93Ult-315
93UppDec-539
93UppDecGold-539
94ColC-462
94ColChoGS-462
94ColChoSS-462
94Don-542
94Fin-389
94FinRef-389
94Fla-104
94Fle-386
94Lea-402
94MarMot-9
94Pac-101
94Pin-480
94PinArtP-480
94PinMusC-480
94Sco-432
94ScoGolR-432
94ScoRoo-RT15
94ScoRooGR-RT15
94Sel-294
94StaClu-704
94StaCluFDI-704
94StaCluGR-704
94StaCluMOP-704
94Top-148
94TopGol-148
94TopSpa-148
94TopTra-124T
94Ult-162
94UppDec-472
94UppDecED-472
95ColCho-296
95ColChoGS-296
95ColChoSS-296
Hibbett, Wendell
78ChaPirT-9
Hibbs, Al
85UtiBluST-11
86BenPhiC-132
Hibbs, Jim
73WicAerKSB-4A
73WicAerKSB-4B
77FriOneYW-39
Hibbs, Loren
84EveGiaC-15
90WicStaSGD-40
Hibner, Dave
78AshTouT-10
79AshTouT-25
80AshTouT-8
Hice, Bob
84ChaO'sT-1
85ChaO'sT-27
86ChaOriW-13
87ChaO'sW-NNO
Hickerson, Bryan
87CliGiaP-28
89SanJosGB-15
89SanJosGCLC-212
89SanJosGP-443
89SanJosGS-14
90ShrCapP-1438
90ShrCapS-11
91LinDriAA-306
91ShrCapLD-306
91ShrCapP-1815
92ClaGam-135
92Don-783
92Fle-638
92GiaMot-16
92GiaPacGaE-19
92Lea-280
92OPC-8
92OPCPre-65
92ProFS7-349
92Sco-750
92StaClu-686
92StaCluECN-686
92Top-8
92TopDeb91-79
92TopGol-8
92TopGolW-8
92TopMic-8
92Ult-589
92UppDec-667
93Don-496
93Fle-530
93GiaMot-26
93GiaPos-17
93Lea-501
93OPC-162
93PacSpa-271
93StaClu-217
93StaCluFDI-217
93StaCluG-29
93StaCluMOP-217
93Top-147
93TopGol-147
93TopInaM-147
93TopMic-147
93Ult-485
93UppDec-778
93UppDecGold-778
94Don-181
94ExtBas-386
94Fla-242
94Fle-691
94GiaMot-26
94GiaUSPC-5H
94GiaUSPC-12S
94Pac-546
94StaClu-711
94StaCluFDI-711
94StaCluGR-711
94StaCluMOP-711
94StaCluT-11
94StaCluTFDI-11
94Top-429
94TopGol-429
94TopSpa-429
94Ult-588
95Fle-580
Hickey, Bob
75SanAntBT-10
Hickey, Jim
85BufBisT-20
86BirBarTI-18
87BirBarB-16
89ColMudB-19
91BurAstC-26
91BurAstP-2818
92AshTouC-28
95QuaCitRBTI-11
96JacGenB-3
Hickey, Kevin
79AppFoxT-6
80GleFalWSBT-10
80GleFalWSCT-7
82Don-631

82Fle-344
82OPC-362
82Top-778
83Don-445
83Fle-237
83Top-278
83WhiSoxTV-45
84Don-135
84Fle-61
84Nes792-459
84Top-459
84TopTif-459
86PorBeaP-8
87HawIsIP-18
88RocRedWGCP-11
89FleUpd-4
89OriFreB-23
90Don-583A
90Don-583B
90Fle-178
90FleCan-178
90OPC-546
90PubSti-577
90Sco-214
90Top-546
90TopTif-546
90UppDec-299
90VenSti-220
91Fle-475
91HagSunLD-237
91HagSunP-2450
91LinDriAA-237
91OriCro-196
Hickey, Michael
90OklSoo-6
92BelMarC-28
92BelMarF-1452
92ClaDraP-123
92FroRowDP-5
93AppFoxC-11
93AppFoxF-2469
94RivPilCLC-6
95PorCitRTI-14
96PorCitRB-16
Hickman, Braxton
93EugEmeC-16
93EugEmeF-3863
93Tex-3
94RocRoyC-12
94RocRoyF-574
Hickman, Dave J.
90DodTar-342
Hickman, Gordon J.
09T206-491
Hickman, Jess
77FriOneYW-36
Hickman, Jim
61UniOil-P8
62Top-598
63MetJayP-3
63Top-107
64MetJayP-6
64Top-514
64TopCoi-92
65MetJayP-6
65OPC-114
65Top-114
66Top-402
67Top-346
69CubJewT-6
69MilBra-113
69OPC-63
69Top-63
69TopTeaP-4
70DayDaiNM-72
70SunPin-3
70Top-612
71Kel-11
71MilDud-46
71MLBOffS-32
71OPC-175
71Top-175
71TopCoi-27
72CubTeal-4
72Top-534
73MetAllEB-3
73OPC-565
73Top-565
76Met63 S-8
82MetGal62-7
90DodTar-343
91MetWIZ-180
Hickman, Piano Legs (Charles)
03BreE10-71
04FanCraAL-23
08AmeLeaPC-8
10CouT21-29
11MecDFT-27
11SpoLifCW-164
Hickox, Tom
88CapCodPPaLP-86
91HelBreSP-21
Hicks, Aman
89EriOriS-7
90WauTimB-24
90WauTimP-2138
90WauTimS-10
91KanCouCC-23
91KanCouCP-2670
91KanCouCTI-10
Hicks, Charlie
92EveGiaC-27
92EveGiaF-1682
93SanJosGC-12
93SanJosGF-2
94SanJosGC-10
Hicks, Clarence Walter
50W720HolS-13
Hicks, Clay
77AppFoxT-9
78AppFoxT-13
Hicks, Ed
76WauMetT-13
89PacSenL-130
Hicks, Jamie
95DurBulTI-12
96MacBraB-14
Hicks, Jim
67Top-532
69Top-559
70OPC-173
70Top-173
Hicks, Joe (William J.)
60Lea-74
61Top-386
62Top-428
79QuaCitCT-11
83IowCubT-14
84IowCubT-9
86IowCubP-15
87PriWilYP-26
89PacSenL-69
89TopSenL-105
91MetWIZ-181
86STaoftFT-11
Hicks, Mike
77AshTouT-8
Hicks, Rob
86PorBeaP-9
87ReaPhiP-26
88ElPasDB-27
Hicks, Robert
82SprCarF-7
Hidalgo, Richard
93AshTouC-1
93AshTouF-2288
93SouAtlLAGF-30
94Bow-586
94MidLeaAF-MDW52
94QuaCitRBC-12
94QuaCitRBF-547
94UppDecML-23
94VenLinU-20
95ActPacF-49
95Bow-62
95Exc-203
95ExcLeaL-10
95JacGenTI-15
95LinVen-81
95SPML-65
95SPMLA-12
95SPMLDtS-DS2
95UppDecML-38
96Bow-131
96BowBes-99
96BowBesAR-99
96BowBesP-BBP20
96BowBesPAR-BBP20
96BowBesPR-BBP20
96BowBesR-99
96ColCho-439
96ColChoGS-439
96ColChoSS-439
96Exc-171
96Fla-278
96FlaWavotF-13
96FleUpd-U139
96FleUpdNH-10
96FleUpdTC-U139
96JacGenB-12
96PinAfi-174
96PinAfiAP-174
96PinProS-10
96Sel-191
96SelArtP-191
96SelCer-122
96SelCerAP-122
96SelCerCB-122
96SelCerCR-122
96SelCerMB-122
96SelCerMG-122
96SelCerMR-122
96SP-6
96Sum-193
96SumAbo&B-193
96SumArtP-193
96SumFoi-193
96TexLeaAB-8
96Top-438
96Ult-487
96UltGolM-487
96UltGolP-8
96UltGolPHGM-8
96UppDec-257
97Bow-84
97Bow98ROY-ROY4
97BowBes-102
97BowBesAR-102
97BowBesMI-MI6
97BowBesMIAR-MI6
97BowBesMIARI-MI6
97BowBesMII-MI6
97BowBesMIR-MI6
97BowBesMIRI-MI6
97BowBesR-102
97BowCerBIA-CA38
97BowCerGIA-CA38
97BowChr-110
97BowChr1RC-ROY4
97BowChr1RCR-ROY4
97BowChrI-110
97BowChrIR-110
97BowChrR-110
97BowInt-84
97Top-488
97Ult-207
97UltGolME-207
97UltPlaME-207
95UppDecMLFS-38
97UppDecTTS-TS12
Hierholzer, David
90EugEmeGS-15
91AppFoxC-5
91AppFoxP-1711
Higbe, Kirby
39ExhSal-27
41DouPlaR-23
41PlaBal-52
42DodTeal-18
43DodTeal-14
46SpoExcW-5-2
47Exh-96
47TipTop-141
49Bow-215
49EurSta-108
49Lea-129
50Bow-200
79DiaGre-83
89DodSmoG-50
90DodTar-344
91RinPosBD4-5
93ConTSN-764
94ConTSN-1213
94ConTSNB-1213
95ConTSN-1344
Higginbotham, Irv
09PC7HHB-21
Higginbotham, Robin
91NiaFalRC-15
91NiaFalRP-3647
92NiaFalRF-3338
Higgins, Bill
90MarPhiP-3184
Higgins, Bob
12T207-81
90DodTar-980
Higgins, Dennis
66Top-529
67OPC-52
67Top-52
68Top-509
69Top-441A
69Top-441B
69TopSta-237
70Ind-7
70OPC-257
70Top-257
71MLBOffS-374
71OPC-479
71Top-479
72MilBra-144
72OPC-278
72Top-278
Higgins, Frank
33ButCanV-25
34BatR31-171
36ExhFou-14
36GouWidPPR-A52
36NatChiFPR-42
36SandSW-34
39GouPreR303A-25
39GouPreR303B-15
39WorWidGTP-25
Higgins, Kevin
89SpoIndSP-19
90Bes-102
90RivRedWB-13
90RivRedWCLC-6
90RivRedWP-2610
91LasVegSLD-284
91LasVegSP-239
91LinDriAAA-284
92LasVegSF-2801
92LasVegSS-232
93Bow-574
93FleFinE-142
93LasVegSF-951
93Lea-441
93SelRoo-136T
94Don-387
94Fle-667
94LasVegSF-874
94Pac-527
94Pin-215
94PinArtP-215
94PinMusC-215
94Sco-642
94ScoGolR-642
94StaClu-83
94StaCluFDI-83
94StaCluGR-83
94StaCluMOP-83
94Top-279
94TopGol-279
94TopSpa-279
94TriAAF-AAA34
96VerExpB-1
Higgins, Mark
80BurBeeT-23
81BurBeeT-23
Higgins, Mark Douglas
86WatIndP-11
87WilBilP-9
88ColSprSSC-13
88ColSprSSP-1544
89ColSprSSC-15
89ColSprSSP-255
90CMC-471
90DenZepC-16
90DenZepP-631
90ProAAAF-656
90TopDeb89-58
Higgins, Mike
93BenRocC-11
93BenRocF-3271
94AshTouC-12
94AshTouF-1785
95SalAvaTI-15
96NewHavRB-14
96SalAvaB-14
Higgins, Pinky (Mike)
33RitCE-11H
34Gou-78
35GouPuzR-1B
35GouPuzR-2B
35GouPuzR-16B
35GouPuzR-17B
36GouBWR-18
36GouWidPPR-C17
36OveCanR-24
40PlaBal-199
41DouPlaR-55
41PlaBal-35
47PM1StaP1-84
55Top-150
58RedSoxJP-4
59RedSoxJP-3
61Top-221
62RedSoxJP-4
62Top-559
72FleFamF-30
72LauGreF-11
81TigDetN-89
83ConMar-10
83TCMPla1943-13
88ConAmeA-15
90HOFStiB-37
91ConTSN-271
94ConTSN-1115
94ConTSNB-1115
Higgins, Rudy
93FreKeyC-29
Higgins, Ted
86FloStaLAP-23
86Ft.LauYP-13
87AlbYanP-8
Higginson, Bobby (Robert Leigh)
92NiaFalRC-14
92NiaFalRF-3339
93LakTigC-11
93LakTigF-1322
94AriFalLS-7
94ExcFS7-56
94TolMudHF-1038
95Bow-127
95ColCho-581T
95DonTopotO-79
95Emo-45
95Exc-50
95Fin-257
95FinRef-257
95Fla-258
95FleUpd-20
95LeaLim-106
95SelCer-102
95SelCerMG-102
95SPCha-156
95SPChaDC-156
95StaClu-611
95StaCluMOP-611
95StaCluSTWS-611
95Sum-134
95SumNthD-134
95TopTra-35T
95UltGolMR-M15
95UppDec-233
95UppDecED-233
95UppDecEDG-233
95Zen-131
96Cir-40
96CirRav-40
96ColCho-146
96ColChoGS-146
96ColChoSS-146
96Don-104
96DonPreP-104
96Fla-82
96Fle-113
96FleTif-113
96Lea-72
96LeaPrePB-72
96LeaPrePG-72
96LeaPrePS-72
96LeaSig-113
96LeaSigA-101
96LeaSigAG-101
96LeaSigAS-101
96LeaSigPPG-113
96LeaSigPPP-113
96Pac-319
96Pin-102
96PinAfi-146
96PinAfiAP-146
96Sco-278
96ScoDugC-B3
96ScoDugCAP-B3
96Sel-150
96SelArtP-150
96StaClu-170
96StaClu-234
96StaCluMOP-170
96StaCluMOP-234
96Sum-46
96SumAbo&B-46
96SumArtP-46
96SumFoi-46
96TeaOut-37
96Top-98

96Ult-62
96UltGolM-62
96UppDec-68
97Bow-234
97BowChr-61
97BowChrI-61
97BowChrIR-61
97BowChrR-61
97BowInt-234
97Cir-52
97CirRav-52
97ColCho-108
97Don-61
97DonEli-81
97DonEliGS-81
97DonEliTotC-17
97DonEliTotCDC-17
97DonLim-200
97DonLimLE-200
97DonPre-56
97DonPreCttC-56
97DonPreP-61
97DonPrePGold-61
97Fin-76
97FinRef-76
97FlaSho-A146
97FlaSho-B146
97FlaSho-C146
97FlaShoLC-146
97FlaShoLC-B146
97FlaShoLC-C146
97FlaShoLCM-A146
97FlaShoLCM-B146
97FlaShoLCM-C146
97Fle-99
97FleTeaL-6
97FleTif-99
97Lea-127
97LeaFraM-127
97LeaFraMDC-127
97MetUni-110
97NewPin-51
97NewPinAP-51
97NewPinMC-51
97NewPinPP-51
97Pac-88
97PacLigB-88
97PacPri-32
97PacPriLB-32
97PacPriP-32
97PacSil-88
97PinIns-76
97PinInsCE-76
97PinInsDE-76
97PinX-P-85
97PinX-PMoS-85
97Sco-307
97ScoPreS-307
97ScoShoS-307
97ScoShoSAP-307
97Sel-67
97SelArtP-67
97SelRegG-67
97SkyE-X-22
97SkyE-XC-22
97SkyE-XEC-22
97SP-72
97SpoIll-136
97SpoIllEE-136
97StaClu-136
97StaCluMOP-136
97Stu-71
97StuPrePG-71
97StuPrePS-71
97Top-258
97TopChr-90
97TopChrR-90
97Ult-60
97UltGolME-60
97UltPlaME-60
97UppDec-355
Higgs, Darrel
87OrlTwiP-24
High, Andy (Andrew)
21Exh-73
26Exh-2
27Exh-3
29PorandAR-39
33Gou-182
88ConSer3-13
90DodTar-345
92ConTSN-648
94ConTSN-1174
94ConTSNB-1174
95ConTSN-1336
High, Brent
94DavLipB-15
High, Hugh
15SpoNewM-81
16ColE13-76A
16ColE13-76B
16ColE13-190A
16FleBreD-42
16SpoNewM-82
94ConTSN-1174
94ConTSNB-1174
Hightower, Barry
86ColMetP-13
87ColMetP-1
88SpoIndP-1942
Hightower, Mark
90GeoColC-9
Hightower, Vee
93PeoChiTI-9
96OrlCubB-11
Higson, Chuck
86EveGiaC-185
86EveGiaPC-8
88FreSunCLC-22
88FreSunP-1225
Higuchi, Alan
87HawRai-29
Higuchi, Roberta
96MedHatBJTI-13
Higuera, Teddy (Ted)
84ElPasDT-15
85BrePol-49
85FleUpd-54
85TopTifT-53T
85TopTra-53T
86BrePol-49
86Don-351
86Fle-490
86FleStiC-59
86Lea-157
86MSAJayPCD-10
86Spo-114
86Top-347
86TopTif-347
87BrePol-49
87BreTeaI-7
87ClaUpdY-147
87Don-16
87Don-49
87DonAll-57
87DonOpeD-56
87DonSupD-16
87Fle-346
87FleExcS-27
87FleGamW-21
87FleGlo-346
87FleHotS-22
87FleLeaL-23
87FleLimE-21
87FleMin-55
87FleSlu-20
87FleStiC-60
87Lea-16
87Lea-95
87OPC-250
87RedFolSB-74
87Spo-11
87Spo-111
87SpoTeaP-19
87Top-250
87Top-615
87TopGloA-22
87TopMinL-60
87TopSti-199
87TopTif-250
87TopTif-615
88BrePol-49
88Don-90
88DonBasB-127
88Fle-166
88FleAll-3
88FleAwaW-19
88FleBasA-15
88FleBasM-18
88FleExcS-21
88FleGlo-166
88FleHotS-20
88FleLeaL-20
88FleMin-30
88FleRecS-19
88FleSlu-19
88FleStiC-37
88FleSup-16
88FleTeaL-15
88GreBasS-60
88Lea-53
88OPC-110
88PanSti-116
88Sco-280
88ScoGlo-280
88Spo-20
88StaLinBre-9
88Top-110
88TopBig-87
88TopMinL-18
88TopSti-196
88TopTif-110
88TopUKM-35
88TopUKMT-35
89Bow-129
89BowTif-129
89BreGar-7
89BrePol-49
89BreYea-49
89ClaTraO-136
89Don-175
89DonBasB-183
89ElPasDGS-16
89Fle-188
89FleBasM-20
89FleGlo-188
89FleHeroB-23
89FleSup-24
89OPC-292
89PanSti-366
89RedFolSB-59
89Sco-132
89ScoHot1S-49
89Spo-47
89Top-595
89TopMinL-57
89TopSti-198
89TopStiB-28
89TopTif-595
89TopUKM-39
89TVSpoM-75
89UppDec-424
90Bow-384
90BowTif-384
90BreMilB-11
90BrePol-49
90ClaYel-T9
90Don-339
90DonBesA-92
90El PasDAGTI-6
90Fle-326
90FleCan-326
90Lea-506
90MLBBasB-83
90OPC-15
90PanSti-96
90PubSti-289
90PubSti-497
90Sco-305
90Spo-44
90Top-15
90TopBig-322
90TopSti-201
90TopTif-15
90UppDec-627
90VenSti-221
90VenSti-222
91BasBesAotM-10
91Bow-54
91BreMilB-10
91BrePol-10
91ClaGam-24
91Don-629
91Fle-586
91OPC-475
91Sco-260
91StaClu-46
91StuPre-6
91Top-475
91TopDesS-475
91TopMic-475
91TopTif-475
91Ult-175
91UppDec-341
92Bow-223
92BrePol-12
92Don-294
92Fle-178
92OPC-265
92Pin-439
92Sco-126
92StaClu-208
92Top-265
92TopGol-265
92TopGolW-265
92TopMic-265
92Ult-80
92UppDec-138
93BrePol-11
93PacSpa-511
93PacSpaPl-16
94BreMilB-227
94BrePol-12
94ColC-451
94ColChoGS-451
94ColChoSS-451
94PanSti-81
94Sco-348
94ScoGolR-348
94StaClu-273
94StaCluFDI-273
94StaCluGR-273
94StaCluMOP-273
95Pac-233
Hijus, Erik
93CapCitBF-454
Hilbert, Adam
88PocGiaP-2081
Hildebrand, George
21Exh-74
90DodTar-346
93ConTSN-708
94ConTSN-1208
94ConTSNB-1208
Hildebrand, Oral
33TatOrbSDR-163
34BatR31-123
34Gou-38
34GouCanV-95
35GouPuzR-1L
35GouPuzR-2E
35GouPuzR-16E
35GouPuzR-17E
36GouBWR-19
36GouWidPPR-A53
36GouWidPPR-B12
36NatChiFPR-43
36OveCanR-25
37ExhFou-15
40PlaBal-123
75YanDyn1T-23
77GalGloG-186
91ConTSN-278
Hildebrand, Tom
86PenWhiSP-13
Hildreth, Brad
88MisStaB-11
89EriOriS-8
89MisStaB-19
90FreKeyTI-30
90WauTimS-11
Hilgenberg, Scot
86CedRapRT-17
87TamTarP-24
Hilgendorf, Tom
70OPC-482
70Top-482
74OPC-13
74Top-13
75OPC-377
75Top-377
76OPC-168
76Top-168
Hiljus, Erik
92KinMetC-13
92KinMetF-1526
93CapCitBC-7
94St.LucMC-13
94St.LucMF-1189
95StLucMTI-17
96BesAutS-38
Hill, A.J.
77AppFoxT-10
80AppFoxT-17
80GleFalWSBT-21
80GleFalWSCT-30
81AppFoxT-18
83MidCubT-26
84ChaLooT-20
Hill, Belden
98CamPepP-34
Hill, Brad
85BurRanT-4
86SalRedBP-12
Hill, Carmen
93ConTSN-987
Hill, Chris
88LitFalMP-17
89ColMetB-13
89ColMetGS-9
89SouAtlLAGS-15
90St.LucMS-10
91LinDriAA-634
91WilBilLD-634
91WilBilP-286
92OscAstC-3
92OscAstF-2526
93ClaGolF-66
93ExcFS7-44
93JacGenF-2104
94JacGenF-212
Hill, Clay (Don)
83ChaLooT-15
84ChaLooT-27
85CalCanC-100
86CalCanP-12
88MiaMarS-9
93HelBreF-4110
Hill, Darryl
78DunBluJT-12
Hill, Donnie
82WesHavAT-14
83TacTigT-11
84A'sMot-13
84Don-96
84Fle-448
84Nes792-265
84Top-265
84TopTif-265
85A'sMot-12
85Don-375
85Fle-426
85TopTifT-54T
85TopTra-54T
86A'sMot-12
86Don-340
86Fle-420
86Lea-148
86OPC-310
86Top-484
86TopTif-484
87Don-405
87DonOpeD-237
87Fle-394
87FleGlo-394
87Top-339
87TopTif-339
87TopTra-47T
87TopTraT-47T
87WhiSoxC-15
88Don-87
88Fle-400
88FleGlo-400
88OPC-132
88Sco-572
88ScoGlo-572
88StaLinWS-10
88Top-132
88TopBig-137
88TopSti-286
88TopTif-132
88WhiSoxC-10
89Sco-583
89TacTigC-18
89TacTigP-1562
89Top-512
89TopTif-512
89UppDec-527
91AngSmo-12
91Don-376
91Fle-316
91Lea-177
91OPC-36
91Top-36
91TopDesS-36
91TopMic-36
91TopTif-36
91Ult-46
91UppDec-211
92Fle-60
92Lea-498
92OPC-731
92Sco-183
92StaClu-702
92Top-731
92TopGol-731
92TopGolW-731
92TopMic-731
92UppDec-413
93HelBreSP-7

Hill, Eric
90BatCliP-3058
91SpaPhiC-6
91SpaPhiP-891
92ClePhiC-2
92ReaPhiF-570
93ReaPhiF-294
94ReaPhiF-2056
95ReaPhiTI-30
95ScrRedBTI-12
Hill, Fred
89WytCubS-13
Hill, Garry
70OPC-172
70Top-172
Hill, Glenallen
85KinBluJT-19
86KnoBluJP-10
86SouLeaAJ-16
87Don-561
87SpoTeaP-5
87SyrChiP-1950
87SyrChiT-20
88SyrChiC-15
88SyrChiP-812
89SyrChiC-15
89SyrChiMB-15
89SyrChiP-804
89TriA AAC-22
89TriAAP-AAA31
90BluJayFS-12
90Bow-514
90BowTif-514
90ClaBlu-88
90Don-627
90DonRoo-24
90FleUpd-127
90Lea-317
90OPC-194
90Sco-601
90ScoYouS2-33
90Top-194
90TopDeb89-59
90TopTif-194
90TriAAAC-22
90UppDec-776
91BluJayFS-14
91Bow-24
91Don-380
91Fle-177
91FleUpd-17
91Lea-311
91OPC-509
91PanFreS-347
91Sco-514
91Sco100RS-60
91StaClu-425
91Stu-43
91Top-509
91TopDesS-509
91TopMic-509
91TopRoo-12
91TopTif-509
91TopTra-55T
91TopTraT-55T
91ToyRoo-11
91Ult-363
91UltUpd-19
91UppDec-276
91UppDecFE-52F
92Bow-659
92Don-643
92DonCraJ2-23
92Fle-110
92IndFanC-11
92Lea-70
92OPC-364
92Pin-420
92Sco-448
92StaClu-413
92Stu-166
92Top-364
92TopGol-364
92TopGolW-364
92TopMic-364
92TriPla-181
92Ult-347
92UppDec-558
93Bow-65
93Don-201
93Fle-592
93IndWUA-11
93Lea-128
93OPC-114
93PacSpa-411
93Pin-123
93Sco-398
93StaClu-576
93StaCluFDI-576
93StaCluMOP-576
93Top-666
93TopGol-666
93TopInaM-666
93TopMic-666
93TriPla-212
93Ult-540
93UppDec-584
93UppDecGold-584
94ColC-137
94ColChoGS-137
94ColChoSS-137
94Don-150
94Fla-138
94Fle-387
94Lea-18
94Sel-372
94StaCluT-351
94StaCluTFDI-351
94Top-63
94TopGol-63
94TopSpa-63
94Ult-458
94UppDec-149
94UppDecED-149
95ColCho-206
95ColCho-553T
95ColChoGS-206
95ColChoSS-206
95Don-90
95DonPreP-90
95DonTopotO-351
95Emo-194
95Fin-282
95FinRef-282
95Fla-424
95Fle-417
95FleUpd-193
95GiaMot-5
95Lea-375
95LeaLim-81
95Pin-249
95PinArtP-249
95PinMusC-249
95Sco-9
95ScoGolR-9
95ScoPlaTS-9
95SP-114
95SPCha-94
95SPChaDC-94
95SPSil-114
95StaClu-525
95StaCluMOP-525
95StaCluSTWS-525
95TopTra-84T
95Ult-137
95UltGolM-137
95UppDec-331
95UppDecED-331
95UppDecEDG-331
96ColCho-305
96ColChoGS-305
96ColChoSS-305
96Don-75
96DonPreP-75
96EmoXL-290
96Fin-B44
96FinRef-B44
96Fla-388
96Fle-588
96FleTif-588
96GiaMot-6
96Lea-183
96LeaPrePB-183
96LeaPrePG-183
96LeaPrePS-183
96LeaSigA-102
96LeaSigAG-102
96LeaSigAS-102
96MetUni-242
96MetUniP-242
96Pac-213
96PanSti-112
96Pin-63
96Pin-297
96PinFoil-297
96ProSta-55
96Sco-436
96SP-164
96StaClu-287
96StaCluB&B-BB8
96StaCluEPB-287
96StaCluEPG-287
96StaCluEPS-287
96StaCluMOP-287
96StaCluMOP-BB8
96Top-32
96TopChr-15
96TopChrR-15
96TopGal-76
96TopGalPPI-76
96Ult-294
96UltGolM-294
96UppDec-194
96UppDec-418
97Cir-194
97CirRav-194
97ColCho-215
97Don-332
97DonPreP-332
97DonPrePGold-332
97Fin-23
97FinRef-23
97Fle-482
97FleTif-482
97Lea-269
97LeaFraM-269
97LeaFraMDC-269
97MetUni-245
97PacPriGotD-GD217
97SP-161
97StaClu-146
97StaCluMOP-146
97Top-221
97TopGal-83
97TopGalPPI-83
97Ult-439
97UltGolME-439
97UltPlaME-439
97UppDec-495
Hill, Gus
88AllandGN-48
Hill, H.A.
79KnoKnoST-22
Hill, Herman
70OPC-267
70Top-267
Hill, Hunter
11SpoLifCW-165
Hill, Jason
94BoiHawC-14
94BoiHawF-3349
95CedRapKTI-19
96CedRapKTI-12
96LakElsSB-7
Hill, Jim
47CenFlo-9
92NegLeaRLI-28
Hill, Ken
87ArkTraP-19
89CarSmo-9
89Don-536
89DonBasB-304
89DonRoo-31
89Fle-652
89FleGlo-652
89FleUpd-119
89LouRedBP-1268
89LouRedBTI-22
89ScoRoo-98T
89TopTra-50T
89TopTraT-50T
90Don-397
90Fle-251
90FleCan-251
90LouRedBLBC-19
90OPC-233
90Sco-233
90Sco100RS-34
90ScoYouSI-32
90Top-233
90TopRoo-15
90TopTif-233
90TopTVCa-13
90ToyRoo-15
90TriAllGP-AAA53
90UppDec-336
91Bow-390
91CarPol-43
91Don-670
91Fle-635
91Lea-376
91LouRedTI-4
91OPC-591
91Sco-567
91StaClu-435
91Top-591
91TopDesS-591
91TopMic-591
91TopTif-591
91UltUpd-106
91UppDec-647
92Bow-507
92ClaGam-168
92Don-31
92ExpDonD-11
92ExpPos-18
92Fle-580
92FleUpd-98
92Lea-468
92OPC-664
92OPCPre-89
92Pin-486
92Sco-104
92ScoRoo-61T
92StaClu-138
92StaClu-735
92StaCluNC-735
92Stu-56
92Top-664
92TopGol-664
92TopGolW-664
92TopMic-664
92TopTra-51T
92TopTraG-51T
92Ult-520
92UppDec-628
92UppDec-790
93Bow-324
93Don-220
93ExpDonM-9
93Fin-35
93FinRef-35
93Fla-84
93Fle-76
93FunPac-96
93HumDumC-38
93Lea-201
93OPC-239
93PacSpa-186
93PanSti-223
93Pin-66
93Sco-48
93Sel-169
93SelAce-14
93SelStaL-89
93SP-104
93StaClu-227
93StaCluFDI-227
93StaCluMOP-227
93Top-495
93TopGol-495
93TopInaM-495
93TopMic-495
93TriPla-174
93Ult-68
93UppDec-138
93UppDecGold-138
94Bow-444
94ColC-138
94ColChoGS-138
94ColChoSS-138
94Don-180
94ExtBas-307
94Fin-25
94FinRef-25
94Fla-192
94Fle-542
94FUnPac-44
94Lea-282
94LeaL-126
94OPC-140
94PanSti-211
94Pin-355
94PinArtP-355
94PinMusC-355
94Sco-64
94ScoGolR-64
94Sel-371
94StaClu-445
94StaCluFDI-445
94StaCluGR-445
94StaCluMOP-445
94Stu-79
94Top-315
94TopGol-315
94TopSpa-315
94TriPla-96
94Ult-229
94UppDec-173
94UppDecED-173
95Bow-349
95ColCho-236
95ColCho-541T
95ColChoGS-236
95ColChoSE-99
95ColChoSEGS-99
95ColChoSESS-99
95ColChoSS-236
95Don-227
95DonPreP-227
95DonTopotO-328
95Emo-180
95Fin-276
95FinRef-276
95Fla-408
95Fle-354
95FleAllS-19
95FleLeaL-9
95FleTeaL-22
95FleUpd-160
95Lea-395
95Pac-270
95PanSti-8
95Pin-115
95PinArtP-115
95PinMusC-115
95PosCan-6
95RedFol-25
95Sco-50
95ScoGolR-50
95ScoHaloG-HG44
95ScoPlaTS-50
95SP-102
95SPCha-84
95SPChaDC-84
95SPSil-102
95StaClu-22
95StaClu-408
95StaClu-616
95StaCluFDI-22
95StaCluMO-22
95StaCluMOP-22
95StaCluMOP-408
95StaCluMOP-616
95StaCluMOP-VRE9
95StaCluSTWS-22
95StaCluSTWS-408
95StaCluSTWS-616
95StaCluVE-VRE9
95StaCluVR-16
95Stu-120
95Sum-8
95SumNthD-8
95Top-46
95TopCyb-35
95TopTra-64T
95Ult-192
95UltGolM-192
95UppDec-77
95UppDec-309
95UppDec-467T
95UppDecED-77
95UppDecED-309
95UppDecEDG-77
95UppDecEDG-309
95UppDecSE-227
95UppDecSEG-227
96Cir-88
96CirRav-88
96ColCho-789
96Don-454
96DonPreP-454
96EmoXL-124
96Fin-B310
96FinRef-B310
96Fla-174
96Fle-88
96FleRan-10
96FleTif-88
96FleUpd-U90
96FleUpdTC-U90
96LeaSigA-103
96LeaSigAG-103
96LeaSigAS-103
96Pin-348
96PinFoil-348
96RanMot-17
96SP-178
95StaCluVRMC-16
96Sum-44

96SumAbo&B-44
96SumArtP-44
96SumFoi-44
96Top-414
96Ult-422
96UltGolM-422
96UppDec-468
97Cir-239
97CirRav-239
97ColCho-491
97Don-181
97DonLim-155
97DonLimLE-155
97DonPre-122
97DonPreCttC-122
97DonPreP-181
97DonPrePGold-181
97Fin-11
97FinRef-11
97FlaSho-A144
97FlaSho-B144
97FlaSho-C144
97FlaShoLC-144
97FlaShoLC-B144
97FlaShoLC-C144
97FlaShoLCM-A144
97FlaShoLCM-B144
97FlaShoLCM-C144
97Fle-226
97FleTif-226
97Lea-148
97LeaFraM-148
97LeaFraMDC-148
97MetUni-164
97Pac-204
97PacLigB-204
97PacSil-204
97Pin-124
97PinArtP-124
97PinMusC-124
97PinX-P-17
97PinX-PMoS-17
97Sco-13
97ScoPreS-13
97ScoRan-3
97ScoRanPl-3
97ScoRanPr-3
97ScoShoS-13
97ScoShoSAP-13
97StaClu-250
97StaCluMat-250
97StaCluMOP-250
97Top-235
97Ult-136
97UltGolME-136
97UltPlaME-136
97UppDec-508

Hill, Lew
87OneYanP-1
89OneYanP-2111
90GreHorB-23
90GreHorP-2675
91GreHorP-3074
92ClaFS7-438
92GreHorC-20
92GreHorF-792
93ClaGolF-116
93ExcFS7-208
93PriWilCC-14
93PriWilCF-669
93SouAtlLAIPI-3
93SouAtlLAPI-15
94AbaYanF-1454
95ColCliP-12
95ColCliTI-12

Hill, Marc
75Gia-3
75OPC-620
75Top-620
76OPC-577
76SSP-100
76Top-577
77Gia-10
77Top-57
78Top-359
79GiaPol-2
79Top-11
80GiaPol-2
80OPC-125
80Top-236
81Top-486
81TopTra-770
82Top-748
83Don-230
83Top-124
83WhiSoxTV-7
84Don-330
84Fle-62
84Nes792-698
84Top-698
84TopTif-698
84WhiSoxTV-16
85Don-160
85Fle-516
85Top-312
85TopTif-312
85WhiSoxC-7
86Top-552
86TopTif-552
86WhiSoxC-7
88AstMot-27
92PenPilC-27
92PenPilF-2948
93ClaGolF-132
93ClaPla&MotYF-PM2
94JacSunF-1426
95LynHilTI-10
96CarMudB-26

Hill, Mike
93EriSaiC-11
93EriSaiF-3128
94HudValRF-3391
94HudValRC-6

Hill, Milt
90CMC-126
90NasSouC-1
95CarMudF-150

Hill, Milton
88CedRapRP-1163
89ChaLooB-6
89ChaLooGS-10
90NasSouP-226
90ProAAAF-538
91LinDriAAA-261
91NasSouLD-261
91NasSouP-2151
92Don-659
92NasSouF-1828
92NasSouS-282
92Sco-820
92StaClu-733
92StaCluECN-733
92TopDeb91-80
93Don-502
93Fle-36
93Top-642
93TopGol-642
93TopInaM-642
93TopMic-642
94BraLykP-10
94BraLykS-11
94BraUSPC-7H
94StaCluT-33
94StaCluTFDI-33

Hill, Moe (Elmore)
78WisRapTT-8

Hill, Nate
85SpoIndC-8

Hill, Orsino
83CedRapRF-23
83CedRapRT-23
88JacExpB-12
88JacExpP-965
89ChaKniTI-24
90CMC-644
90ProAAAF-177
90TriAllGP-AAA41
90VanCanC-17
90VanCanP-499
91LinDriAAA-638
91VanCanLD-638
91VanCanP-1606
92TacTigF-2515
92TacTigS-536

Hill, Perry W.
86DayBealP-12
90GasRanS-28
91GasRanP-2705
93RanKee-437

Hill, Pete
74LauOldTBS-10

Hill, Quency
76OklCit8TI-23
78KnoKnoST-8
82QuaCitCT-27

Hill, Roger
88WatIndP-685

Hill, Ron
80ElmPioRST-9

Hill, Sandy
78SalPirT-6

Hill, Shane
94ButCopKSP-13

Hill, Shawn
93GenCubC-13
93GenCubF-3168
94MidLeaAF-MDW48
94PeoChiC-12
94PeoChiF-2261
95Exc-163

Hill, Steve (Stephen F.)
85AncGlaPTI-16
86St.PetCP-12
87PeoChiP-7
87PeoChiPW-4
87SprCarB-12
88St.PetCS-10
88WinSpiS-6
89ArkTraGS-7
89SanBerSB-15
89SanBerSCLC-84

Hill, Still (William C.)
90DodTar-981

Hill, Tony
86ElmPioRSP-10
87GreHorP-14

Hill, Tripp
90MisStaB-20
91MisStaB-25
92MisStaB-21
93MisStaB-22

Hill, Tyrone
91ClaDraP-12
91HelBreSP-8
91HigSchPLC-3
92BelBreC-1
92BelBreF-401
92ClaFS7-364
92MidLeaATI-19
92OPC-444
92Pin-301
92Sco-807
92StaCluD-84
92Top-444
92TopGol-444
92TopGolW-444
92TopMic-444
92UppDecML-29
92UppDecML-135
93Bow-368
93Bow-619
93ClaYouG-YG5
93ExcFS7-186
93StoPorC-1
93StoPorF-742
93UppDec-427
93UppDecGold-427
94ActPac-27
94FleMajLP-13
94SigRoo-15
94SigRooS-15
94StoPorC-10
94StoPorF-1688
94Ult-372
94UppDecML-233
96StoPorB-8

Hilldales, Philadelphia
91PomBlaBPB-3
94PomNegLB-6

Hillebrand, Homer
11SpoLifCW-166

Hillegas, Shawn
87AlbDukP-11
87SpoRoo2-30
88AlbDukC-1
88AlbDukP-265
88DodPol-49
88Don-35
88Fle-519
88FleGlo-519
88Lea-35
88Sco-612
88ScoGlo-612
88Top-455
88TopTif-455
89Bow-58
89BowTif-58
89Don-503
89Fle-498
89FleGlo-498
89PanSti-301
89Sco-488
89ScoYouS2-29
89Top-247
89TopTif-247
89UppDec-72A
89UppDec-478
89WhiSoxC-11
90CMC-635
90DodTar-982
90Don-619
90Fle-535
90FleCan-535
90OPC-93
90ProAAAF-163
90PubSti-389
90Sco-329
90Top-93
90TopTif-93
90UppDec-541
90VanCanC-7
90VanCanP-485
90VenSti-223
91Don-589
91FleUpd-18
91IndFanC-13
91Lea-513
91ScoRoo-65T
92ColCliF-346
92Don-72
92Fle-111
92OPC-523
92Sco-93
92ScoProP-21
92StaClu-76
92Top-523
92TopGol-523
92TopGolW-523
92TopMic-523
93AthMot-26
93PacSpa-569
93StaCluAt-20
94Pac-453

Hillemann, Charlie (Charles)
87SpoIndP-9
88ChaRaiP-1197
89TexLeaAGS-9
89WicStaR-4
89WicUpdR-6
89WicWraR-18
90CMC-521
90LasVegSC-18
90LasVegSP-134
90ProAAAF-22
90WicWraRD-9
91Cla/Bes-50
91LinDriAA-608
91WicWraLD-608
91WicWraP-2611

Hillenbrand, Shea
96LowSpiB-9

Hiller, Chuck
61Top-538
62GiaJayP-6
62SalPlaC-106
62ShiPlaC-106
62Top-188
62TopVen-188
63GiaJayP-6
63Jel-102
63Pos-102
63Top-145
63Top-185
64Top-313
64TopVen-313
65Top-531
66OPC-154
66Top-154
66TopVen-154
67CokCapYM-V19
67MetTeal-7
67Top-198
68Top-461
73OPC-549
73Top-549
81Car5x7-11
83Car-11
85GiaMot-27
86GiaPos-15
91MetWIZ-182
93RanKee-185

Hiller, Dutch
43ParSpo-39

Hiller, Frank
48BluTin-37
48YanTeal-13
52Bow-114
52Top-156
83TopRep5-156

Hiller, John
66Top-209
66TopVen-209
68TigDetFPB-6
68Top-307
68TopVen-307
69MilBra-114
69TigTealC-4
69Top-642
70OPC-12
70Top-12
71MLBOffS-393
71OPC-629
71Top-629
72MilBra-146
73LinPor-70
73OPC-448
73Top-448
74OPC-24
74OPC-208
74Tig-5
74Top-24
74Top-208
74TopDecE-17
74TopSta-175
75Kel-19
75OPC-415
75Top-415
76OPC-37
76SSP-353
76Top-37
77BurCheD-95
77Hos-28
77OPC-257
77Top-595
78TigBurK-9
78Top-258
79OPC-71
79Top-151
80OPC-229
80TigGreT-12
80Top-614
81TigDetN-12
83TigAlKS-52
86GleFalTP-10
86TigSpoD-22
87TolMudHP-25
88TigDom-7

Hillerman, Charlie
91WicWraRD-21

Hillis, Jon
94HelBreF-3610
94HelBreSP-19

Hillman, Dave
57Top-351
58Top-41
59Top-319
60Top-68
60TopVen-68
61Top-326
62RedEnq-13
62Top-282
91MetWIZ-183

Hillman, Eric
87LitFalMP-2385
88ColMetGS-5
89ColMetB-11
89ColMetGS-10
91LinDriAAA-558
91MetColP-33
91TidTidLD-558
91TidTidP-2505
92Bow-326
92FleUpd-102
92SkyAAAF-252
92StaClu-847
92StaCluECN-847
92TidTidF-891
92TidTidS-558
93Fle-87
93MetColP-35
93NorTidF-2565
93Sco-280
93Sel-350
93Top-751
93TopGol-751
93TopInaM-751
93TopMic-751
94ColC-139
94ColChoGS-139

94ColChoSS-139
94Don-514
94Fle-564
94MetColP-11
94Pac-403
94StaClu-480
94StaCluFDI-480
94StaCluGR-480
94StaCluMOP-480
94Top-453
94TopGol-453
94TopSpa-453
95Pac-281
Hillman, Greg
93GenCubC-14
93GenCubF-3169
94PeoChiC-13
94PeoChiF-2262
Hillman, Joe
88SouOreAP-1716
89ModA'sC-29
89ModA'sCLC-275
Hillman, Stewart
90CliGiaB-18
90CliGiaP-2542
Hillman, Trey
86WatIndP-12
87KinIndP-19
89PriWilCS-29
90OneYanP-3389
91GreHorP-3075
91SouAtlLAGP-SAL27
92GreHorC-26
92GreHorF-796
93PriWilCC-26
93PriWilCF-672
94GreBatF-491
95GreBatTI-29
96TamYanY-1
97GreBatC-27
Hills, Rich
95IdaFalBTI-17
96CliLumKTI-15
Hilo, Johnny
94GreFalDSP-10
95SanBerSTI-7
95YakBeaTI-15
Hilpert, Adam
86AncGlaPTI-15
89CliGiaP-883
Hilt, Scott
96HarCitRCB-14
Hilton, Howard
86St.PetCP-13
87SprCarB-13
88ArkTraGS-12
89LouRedBC-6
89LouRedBP-1251
89LouRedBTI-23
90Bow-189
90BowTif-189
90CMC-106
90LouRedBC-6
90LouRedBLBC-20
90LouRedBP-398
90ProAAAF-512
90TopTVCa-14
91TopDeb90-68
Hilton, John David
73OPC-615
73Top-615
74OPC-148
74PadDea-14
74Top-148A
74Top-148B
75OPC-509
75Top-509
76HawIsIC-9
77OPC-139
77Top-163
79TCMJapPB-18
81PorBeaT-11
84VisOakT-10
85BrePol-NNO
88BrePol-NNO
89PacSenL-216
89SanJosGCLC-30
90EliSenL-113
91PacSenL-124
91PacSenL-133
92IdaFalGF-3531
93GreBraF-365
94IdaFalBSP-28
94MacBraC-30
94MacBraF-2223
95MacBraTI-11
Hilton, Stan
84ModA'sC-16
85ModA'sC-22
88WilBilP-1316
89BurIndS-28
89ColSprSSP-244
90BurIndP-3027
91BurIndP-3321
86HumStaDS-22
Hilton, Willy
96SouOreTI-27
Hina, Fred
88ColMetGS-18
89St.LucMS-27
90JacMetGS-6
Hinch, A.J.
93BazTeaU-14
93TopTra-12T
Hinchliffe, Brett
94AppFoxC-11
94AppFoxF-1049
95Exc-118
96LanJetB-15
Hinchman, Bill (William)
08AmeLeaPC-9
08RosComP-25
09BriE97-14
09T206-155
10W555-34
11SpoLifCW-168
91ConTSN-155
94ConTSN-1113
94ConTSNB-1113
Hinchman, Harry
09ColChiE-129
09T206-430
11MecDFT-27
11SpoLifCW-167
12ColRedB-129
12ColTinT-129
Hinde, Michael
88CapCodPPaLP-62
89EliTwiS-11
Hindman, Randy
86CedRapRT-18
Hinds, Kevin
81CedRapRT-11
Hinds, Robert
92OneYanC-14
93GreHorC-11
93GreHorF-892
94FloStaLAF-FSL21
94TamYanC-14
94TamYanF-2392
95NorNagUTI-21
95NorNavTI-21
Hinds, Sam
77SpoIndC-17
78SpoIndC-19
78Top-303
79HolMilT-29
79VanCanT-19
94BreMilB-228
Hindy, Mark
95OdgRapTI-8
Hine, Frank
85CloHSS-22
Hine, Steve
96LowSpiB-10
Hines, Ben
84MarMot-27
86DodCokP-12
86DodPol-NNO
87AlbDukP-2
88DodMot-28
89DodMot-27
89DodPol-1
90DodMot-28
90DodPol-NNO
91DodMot-28
91DodPol-NNO
92DodMot-28
92DodPol-NNO
93DodMot-28
93DodPol-30
94AstMot-27
Hines, Bruce
94LakElsSC-28
94LakElsSF-1682
Hines, Hunkey (Henry)
87OldJudN-247
90DodTar-347
Hines, Keith
90MedHatBJB-14
91St.CatBJC-12
91St.CatBJP-3408
92St.CatBJC-2
93HagSunC-14
93HagSunF-1892
Hines, Maurice
90MarPhiP-3187
Hines, Paul
87BucN28-114A
87BucN28-114B
87OldJudN-248
88WG1CarG-33
94OriofB-37
Hines, Pooh
95EugEmeTI-16
96EugEmeB-11
Hines, Rich
91GreHorP-3053
91SouAtlLAGP-SAL28
94ColCliP-12
95ColCliMCTI-5
95NorNavTI-39
96ColCliB-15
Hines, Richard
90TamYanD-12
92PriWilCC-6
92PriWilCF-141
93AlbYanF-2158
Hines, Tim
89PitMetS-9
89St.LucMS-10
89Sta-158
90SalBucS-7
91CarMudLD-110
91CarMudP-1089
91LinDriAA-110
93WesPalBEF-1344
Hingle, Larry
92BoiHawC-30
92BoiHawF-3620
92FroRowDP-73
93CedRapKC-9
93CedRapKF-1732
93MidLeaAGF-35
94LakElsSC-10
94LakElsSF-1659
Hinkel, John
78WauMetT-11
Hinkle, Gordon
35DiaMatCS3T1-74
Hinkle, Mike
87EriCarP-28
88SavCarP-331
89ArkTraGS-8
90CMC-105
90LouRedBC-5
90LouRedBLBC-21
90LouRedBP-399
90ProAAAF-513
90TopTVCa-52
91LouRedTI-10
92LouRedF-1883
92LouRedS-264
Hinnrichs, Dave
84EveGiaC-16
86FreGiaP-13
Hinrichs, Phil
81PhoGiaVNB-17
83PhoGiaBHN-11
Hinshaw, George
82AmaGolST-1
83LasVegSBHN-10
84LasVegSC-234
85LasVegSC-113
87AlbDukP-28
88AlbDukC-13
88AlbDukP-268
88TriAAC-40
90CMC-542
90PhoFirC-15
90PhoFirP-22
90ProAAAF-48
Hinsley, Jerry
64Top-576
65Top-449
91MetWIZ-184
Hinson, Bo
82AubAstT-10
Hinson, Dean
91WelPirC-9
91WelPirP-3576
94HigDesMC-15
94HigDesMF-2783
Hinson, Gary
79WatIndT-8
80WatIndT-23
82BirBarT-14
Hinton, Chuck
47Exh-97
62Top-347
62TopStal-96
63Baz-25
63ExhStaB-29
63Jel-93
63Pos-93
63Top-2
63Top-330
63TopStil-18
64Baz-25
64Top-52
64TopCoi-38
64TopCoi-162A
64TopCoi-162B
64TopGia-20
64TopSta-47
64TopStaU-32
64TopVen-52
65Baz-3
65Kah-16
65OldLonC-26
65OPC-235
65Top-235
65TopEmbl-60
65TopTral-48
66IndTeal-5
66Top-391
67CokCapl-18
67DexPre-95
67OPC-189
67Top-189
68Top-531
69MilBra-115
69MLBOffS-22
69Top-644
70MLBOffS-199
70OPC-27
70Top-27
71Ind-7
71MLBOffS-375
71OPC-429
71Top-429
72MilBra-147
78TCM60I-252
78TCM60I-265
89SweBasG-93
Hinton, Rich
72Top-724
73OPC-321
73Top-321
76IndIndTI-20
76OPC-607
76SSP-158
76Top-607
92YanWIZ7-74
93RanKee-17
Hinton, Steve
91EugEmeC-9
91EugEmeP-3734
92AppFoxC-23
92AppFoxF-992
92MidLeaATI-20
93WilBluRC-15
93WilBluRF-2005
95AusFut-3
95AusFut-87
Hinzo, Thomas
86AriWilP-5
87KinIndP-21
88ColSprSSC-14
88ColSprSSP-1527
88Don-526
88Fle-611
88FleGlo-611
88OPC-294
88PanSti-73
88Sco-567
88ScoGlo-567
88StaLinI-13
88Top-576
88TopTif-576
89ColSprSSC-16
89ColSprSSP-256
89UppDec-34
93RocRedWF-249
93TriAAAGF-28
94CalCanF-795
Hipp, Mike
93Sou-10
Hippauf, Herb A.
66Top-518
87IdaFalBP-18
88IdaFalBP-1860
Hiraldo, Jerry
92GulCoaMF-3494
94KinMetC-4
94KinMetF-3834
Hird, Jeff
86AriWilP-6
Hirooka, Tatsuro
79TCMJapPB-25
Hirose, Sam
87SanJosBP-1
88SanJosGCLC-142
88SanJosGP-123
Hirsch, Chris
91SumFlyC-13
91SumFlyP-2336
93CedRapKF-1741
Hirsch, Elroy
53SpoMagP-3
Hirsch, Jeff
86PeoChiP-11
87WinSpiP-23
88IowCubC-6
88IowCubP-532
89ChaKniTI-18
90PeoChiTI-20
Hirschbeck, John
88T/MUmp-50
89T/MUmp-48
90T/MUmp-46
Hirschbeck, Mark
89T/MUmp-59
90T/MUmp-57
Hirtensteiner, Rick
87PanAmTURB-17
88CapCodPPaLP-25
89BenBucL-20
90QuaCitAGS-27
91SalLakTP-3225
91SalLakTSP-6
92Bow-658
92HarSenF-471
92HarSenS-283
93OttLynF-2445
94PorSeaDF-690
94PorSeaDTI-15
87PanAmTUBI-9
Hiser, Gene
72OPC-61
72Top-61
74OPC-452
74Top-452
74WicAerODF-120
76SSP-314
Hisey, Jason
88AlaGolTI-9
90AriWilP-7
91HamRedC-11
91HamRedP-4034
92SavCarC-16
92SavCarF-658
93ClaFS7-243
93FloStaLAF-45
93St.PetCC-14
93St.PetCF-2623
94ClaGolF-171
Hisey, Steve
88SanBerSB-20
88SanBerSCLC-39
Hisle, Larry
68Top-579
69OPC-206
69PhiTeal-4
69Top-206
69TopFou-22
69TopTeaP-8
70DayDaiNM-49
70Kel-45
70MLBOffS-89
70OPC-288
70PhiTeal-4
70Top-288
71MLBOffS-180
71OPC-616
71PhiArcO-5
71Top-616
72MilBra-148
72OPC-398
72Top-398

73OPC-622
73Top-622
74OPC-366
74Top-366
75Hos-128
75OPC-526
75Top-526
76Hos-73
76OPC-59
76SSP-220
76Top-59
77BurCheD-49
77OPC-33
77Top-375
78Hos-13
78OPC-3
78PapGinD-38
78RCColC-79
78TasDis-24
78Top-203
78Top-520
78WifBalD-29
79Hos-95
79OPC-87
79Top-180
79TopCom-10
80Kel-22
80OPC-222
80Top-430
81Don-87A
81Don-87B
81Fle-509
81FleStiC-94
81OPC-215
81Top-215
82BrePol-9
82Don-358
82Fle-144
82Top-93
83Top-773
86TwiGreT-6
91BluJayFS-15
93BluJayFS-15
94BreMilB-316
Hiss, William
75SanAntBT-11
77WatIndT-12
Hitchcock, Billy
48RedSoxTI-10
51Bow-191
52Bow-89
52Top-182
53TigGle-14
53Top-17
60Top-461
62Top-121
62TopVen-121
63Top-213
67Top-199
79DiaGre-183
83TopRep5-182
91TopArc1-17
Hitchcock, Sterling
90CMC-822
90GreHorB-2
90GreHorP-2654
90GreHorS-5
90ProAaA-88
90TopTVY-46
91Cla/Bes-385
91PriWilCC-2
91PriWilCP-1419
92AlbYanF-2220
92AlbYanS-8
92SkyAA F-4
93Bow-606
93ClaFS7-74
93ColCliF-1106
93ColCliP-5
93Don-345
93FleMajLP-A2
93Pin-579
93PinRooTP-2
93PinTea2-30
93Sco-311
93ScoBoyoS-22
93SelRoo-53T
93StaCluY-17
93Top-530
93TopGol-530
93TopInaM-530
93TopMic-530
93UppDec-16
93UppDecGold-16
94Bow-333
94ColC-539
94ColChoGS-539
94ColChoSS-539
94ColCliF-2948
94ColCliP-13
94Don-638
94Fla-320
94FleUpd-68
94Pin-213
94PinArtP-213
94PinMusC-213
94Sco-565
94ScoGolR-565
94ScoRoo-RT83
94ScoRooGR-RT83
94Sel-397
94Spo-157
94StaClu-658
94StaCluFDI-658
94StaCluGR-658
94StaCluMOP-658
94StaCluT-203
94StaCluTFDI-203
94Top-103
94TopGol-103
94TopSpa-103
94UppDec-138
94UppDecED-138
95Don-51
95DonPreP-51
95Fla-284
95Fle-70
95Lea-59
95Pin-74
95PinArtP-74
95PinMusC-74
95Sco-546
95ScoGolR-546
95ScoPlaTS-546
95Sel-54
95SelArtP-54
95Top-266
95TopCyb-145
95Ult-309
95UltGolM-309
96ColCho-229
96ColChoGS-229
96ColChoSS-229
96Don-179
96DonPreP-179
96EmoXL-114
96Fin-S230
96FinRef-S230
96Fla-161
96Fle-239
96FleTif-239
96FleUpd-U79
96FleUpdTC-U79
96LeaLim-73
96LeaLimG-73
96LeaSigA-104
96LeaSigAG-104
96LeaSigAS-104
96MarMot-10
96Pac-373
96Pin-345
96PinAfi-108
96PinAfiAP-108
96PinFoil-345
96Sco-71
96Sel-105
96SelArtP-105
96SelCer-38
96SelCerAP-38
96SelCerCB-38
96SelCerCR-38
96SelCerMB-38
96SelCerMG-38
96SelCerMR-38
96StaClu-177
96StaCluMOP-177
96Sum-41
96SumAbo&B-41
96SumArtP-41
96SumFoi-41
96Ult-411
96UltGolM-411
96UppDec-463
96Zen-15
96ZenArtP-15
97Cir-227
97CirRav-227
97ColCho-231
97ColCho-448
97Don-168
97Don-290
97DonEli-101
97DonEliGS-101
97DonPreP-168
97DonPreP-290
97DonPrePGold-168
97DonPrePGold-290
97Fin-239
97FinRef-239
97Fle-207
97Fle-671
97FleTif-207
97FleTif-671
97MetUni-146
97Pac-187
97PacLigB-187
97PacSil-187
97Sco-66
97Sco-335
97ScoHobR-335
97ScoPreS-66
97ScoResC-335
97ScoShoS-66
97ScoShoS-335
97ScoShoSAP-66
97ScoShoSAP-335
97StaClu-106
97StaCluMOP-106
97Top-149
97Ult-122
97Ult-310
97UltGolME-122
97UltGolME-310
97UltPlaME-122
97UltPlaME-310
97UppDec-178
Hitchcox, Wally
93DavLipB-24
Hithe, Victor
87AshTouP-19
88OscAstS-14
89EasLeaAP-21
89HagSunB-5
89HagSunP-272
89HagSunS-11
90Bes-135
90CMC-323
90HagSunB-14
90HagSunP-1426
90ProAAAF-471
90RocRedWC-22
90RocRedWGC-24
90RocRedWP-714
Hitt, Danny (Daniel)
89SavCarP-369
90St.PetCS-13
Hitta, Chief Powa
78RicBraT-20
79RicBraT-8
Hitting, Scott
90BatCliP-3084
Hittle, Red (Floyd)
48SmiClo-21
53MotCoo-42
Hivizda, Jim
88ButCopKSP-2
Hixon, Alan
86MiaMarP-11
Hiyama, Yasuhiro
87SalLakTTT-20
Hmielewski, Chris
92AlbPolC-8
92AlbPolF-2317
93BurBeeC-10
93BurBeeF-166
93MidLeaAGF-30
94WesPalBEC-13
94WesPalBEF-34
Hoag, Myril
34Gou-95
34TarThoBD-9
36GouWidPPR-A54
36NatChiFPR-44
36R31PasP-34
39PlaBal-109
40PlaBal-52
75YanDyn1T-24
91ConTSN-233
93ConTSN-894
Hoak, Don
47Exh-98
52LaPat-7
52Par-57
53ExhCan-33
53Top-176
54Top-211
55Bow-21
55DodGolS-25
55Top-40
55TopDouH-25
56Top-335
57Kah-14
57RedSoh-9
57Top-274
58Kah-13
58RedEnq-17
58RedJayP-7
58Top-160
59Kah-15
59Top-25
59TopVen-25
60Kah-15
60KeyChal-24
60PirJayP-8
60PirTag-12
60Top-373
61Kah-19
61PirJayP-6
61PirRigF-4
61Pos-130A
61Pos-130B
61Top-230
61TopStal-65
61WilSpoGH828-1
61WilSpoGH828-1-2
62ExhStaB-16
62Jel-171
62Kah-19
62Pos-171
62PosCan-171
62SalPlaC-107
62ShiPlaC-107
62Top-95
62TopBuc-35
62TopStal-178
62TopVen-95
63ExhStaB-30
63Jel-140
63Pos-140
63Top-305
64Top-254
64TopVen-254
79TCM50-273
81TCM60I-388
90DodTar-348
91TopArc1-176
94TopArc1-211
94TopArc1G-211
95TopArcBD-50
95TopArcBD-81
95TopArcBD-94
95TopArcBD-121
Hoalton, Brandon
94IdaFalBF-3579
94IdaFalBSP-12
Hoban, John
80WatIndT-1
81WatIndT-9
82BelBreF-7
Hobaugh, Brian
83WisRapTF-17
84VisOakT-12
Hobaugh, Ed
55DonWin-25
60Top-131
60TopVen-131
61Top-129
62Top-79
62TopVen-79
63Top-423
Hobbie, Glen
58Top-467
59Top-334
60Baz-32
60CubJayP-7
60Lea-20
60Top-182
60TopTat-22
60TopVen-182
61CubJayP-8
61Pos-197A
61Pos-197B
61Top-264
61Top-273A
61Top-393
62CubJayP-7
62SalPlaC-145
62ShiPlaC-145
62Top-585
62TopStal-108
63Fle-31
63Top-212
64CubJayP-6
64Top-578
Hobbie, Matt
93BurIndC-1
93BurIndF-3311
94BurIndC-7
94BurIndF-3807
96BoiHawB-15
Hobbs, Jack
82OrlTwi8SCT-17
82OrlTwiT-5
83OrlTwiT-16
Hobbs, John
80VenLeaS-106
Hobbs, Jon
88FreSunCLC-4
88FreSunP-1237
Hobbs, Rodney
80LynSaiT-3
81LynSaiT-22
82WesHavAT-22
84AlbA'sT-4
86NasSouTI-13
Hobbs, Shane
93MarPhiC-13
93MarPhiF-3478
Hobbs, Tyler
89KinMetS-29
Hoblitzell, Doc (Richard C.)
09ColChiE-130
09RamT20-55
09T206-156
10CouT21-144
10CouT21-145
10CouT21-146
10CouT21-287
10DomDisP-55
10JHDABE-8
10OrnOvaPP-6
10RedCroT-29
10RedCroT-118
10RedCroT-199
10SweCapPP-102
11PloCanE-33
11S74Sil-77
11SpoLifCW-169
11SpoLifM-196
11T205-76
11TurRedT-97
12ColRedB-130
12ColTinT-130
12HasTriFT-40
12HasTriFT-71
13NatGamW-19
13TomBarW-18
14CraJacE-55
15CraJacE-55
15SpoNewM-82
16ColE13-77
16FleBreD-43
16SpoNewM-83
91ConTSN-148
Hobson, Butch
77Top-89
78Hos-1
78OPC-187
78PapGinD-4
78RCColC-59
78SSP270-172
78Top-155
79Hos-129
79OPC-136
79Top-270
80OPC-216
80Top-420
81AllGamPI-34
81Don-542
81Fle-227
81LonBeaPT-4
81OPC-7
81Top-595
81TopSti-54
81TopSupHT-59
81TopTra-771
82Don-577
82Fle-465
82FleSta-213

82OPC-357
82Top-357
82TopSti-164
83ColCliT-21
83Top-652
84ColCliP-12
84ColCliT-16
85ColCliP-13
85ColCliT-17
87ColMetP-10
88ColMetGS-1
89NewBriRSP-617
89NewBriRSS-23
89PacSenL-32
89T/MSenL-47
89TopSenL-49
90EasLeaAP-EL11
90NewBriRSB-23
90NewBriRSP-1334
90NewBriRSS-25
91LinDriAAA-374
91PawRedSDD-8
91PawRedSLD-374
91PawRedSP-54
92RedSoxDD-17
92TopTra-52T
92TopTraG-52T
92YanWIZ8-82
93Top-502
93TopGol-502
93TopInaM-502
93TopMic-502
96ScrRedBB-1

Hobson, Daren
94SarRedSC-14
94SarRedSF-1945

Hobson, Todd
90ArkRaz-15
91AubAstC-18
91AubAstP-4286
92AshTouC-6
93AshTouC-9
93AshTouF-2289

Hockenberry, Charlie
75SalLakCC-13
76SalLakCGC-13

Hockenbury, Bill
52Par-81

Hockett, Oris
83TCMPla1944-12
90DodTar-349

Hockette, George
35DiaMatCS3T1-75

Hockey, Gavin
95AusFut-47

Hocking, David
89EveGiaS-14

Hocking, Denny
91KenTwiC-4
91KenTwiP-2081
91MidLeaAP-MWL37
92ClaFS7-295
92VisOakC-20
92VisOakF-1020
93Bow-73
93ExcFS7-201
93ExcLeaLF-8
94Fla-313
94FleMajLP-14
94FleUpd-61
94LeaLimR-26
94Pin-421
94PinArtP-421
94PinMusC-421
94SalLakBF-823
94ScoRoo-RT106
94ScoRooGR-RT106
94Sel-379
94SpoRoo-34
94SpoRooAP-34
94StaClu-9
94StaCluFDI-9
94StaCluGR-9
94StaCluMOP-9
94Top-771
94TopGol-771
94TopSpa-771
94UppDec-114
94UppDecED-114
95ColCho-22
95Don-272
95DonPreP-272
95Fle-205
95Lea-52
95PacPri-79
95Sco-585
95ScoGolR-585
95ScoPlaTS-585
95StaClu-52
95StaCluFDI-52
95StaCluMOP-52
95StaCluSTWS-52
95Top-122
95Ult-302
95UltGolM-302
95UppDec-192
95UppDecED-192
95UppDecEDG-192
96StaClu-448
96StaCluMOP-448
97Pac-137
97PacLigB-137
97PacSil-137

Hocutt, Mike
86IndIndTI-22
87JacMetF-10
88LouRedBTI-22

Hodapp, Johnny (Urban J.)
29PorandAR-40
33DouDisP-22
79DiaGre-132
83ConMar-13
88ConAmeA-16
92ConTSN-538
93ConTSN-810

Hodde, Rodney
82BurRanF-11
82BurRanT-2

Hoderlein, Mel
53Bri-7
54Bow-120

Hodge, Clarence
21E121So1-41
22E120-20
22W573-60
23W501-42

Hodge, Eddie
80OrlTwiT-5
82OrlTwiT-24
83TolMudHT-4
84FleUpd-52
85TolMudHT-8
85Top-639
85TopTif-639

Hodge, Gomer
81WatIndT-1
82WatIndF-2
82WatIndT-26
83WatIndF-28
86BelBreP-11
87BelBreP-18
88BelBreGS-1
89JacExpB-20
90IndIndP-308
90ProAAAF-591
91IndIndLD-200
91IndIndP-479
91LinDriAAA-200
92IndIndF-1877
92IndIndS-200
93HarSenF-285
96TreThuB-2

Hodge, Hal
95SpoIndTI-7

Hodge, Jim
94BelBreC-12
94BelBreF-115
94HelBreF-3624
94HelBreSP-15

Hodge, Kevin
88BufBisP-1482

Hodge, Nick
92IndIndF-NNO

Hodge, Pat
83DurBulT-6
84DurBulT-4

Hodge, Roy
92BluOriC-12
92BluOriF-2371
92KanCouCC-3
92KanCouCF-105
93AlbPolF-2038
94FreKeyF-2628
96HigDesMB-13
94FreKeyC-11

Hodge, Tim
88St.CatBJP-2016
89MyrBeaBJP-1457
90DunBluJS-10
91DunBluJC-20
91DunBluJP-218
92DunBluJC-15
92DunBluJF-2012
93KnoSmoF-1263

Hodges, Darren
90OneYanP-3377
90ProAaA-177
91CarLeaAP-CAR33
91PriWilCC-3
91PriWilCP-1420
92AlbYanF-2221
92AlbYanS-9
92SkyAA F-5
93AlbYanF-2159
94AbaYanF-1436

Hodges, Gil
47Exh-99A
47Exh-99B
47HomBon-20
47PM1StaP1-85
47PM1StaP1-86
47PM1StaP1-87
47PM1StaP1-88
49Bow-100
49EurSta-38
50Bow-112
50Dra-11
51Bow-7
51FisBakL-9
51TopRedB-31
52BerRos-24
52Bow-80
52CokTip-3
52StaCalL-79A
52StaCalS-91A
52TipTop-16
52Top-36
53BowC-92
53Bri-31
53Dor-129
53ExhCan-13
53StaMey-3
54Bow-138
54DanDee-11
54NewYorJA-7
54RedMan-NL22
54StaMey-3
54Top-102
54Wil-9
55BigLeaIS-8
55Bow-158
55DaiQueS-8
55DodGolS-13
55RedMan-NL3
55StaMey-3
55Top-187
56Dod-13
56Top-145
56TopPin-50
56YelBasP-15
57Top-80
57Top-400
58DodBelB-5
58DodJayP-6
58PacBel-4
58Top-162
59DodMor-4
59DodTeal-9
59DodVol-7
59HomRunD-7
59Top-270
60Baz-23
60DodJayP-6
60DodMor-5
60DodPos-4
60DodTeal-8
60DodUniO-8
60NuHi-41
60Top-295
60Top-388
61DodBelB-14
61DodUniO-9
61NuSco-441
61Pos-168A
61Pos-168B
61SevElev-21
61Top-460
62Baz-27
62Jel-101
62MetJayP-4
62Pos-101
62PosCan-101
62SalPlaC-146A
62SalPlaC-146B
62ShiPlaC-146
62Top-85
62TopBuc-36
62TopStal-155
62TopVen-85
63BasMagM-36
63Jel-193
63MetJayP-4
63Pos-193
63Top-68
63Top-245
64Top-547
65OPC-99
65Top-99
66SenTeal-7
66Top-386
67SenTeal-5
67Top-228
68OPC-27
68Top-27
68TopVen-27
69MetNewYDN-9
69Top-564
70OPC-394
70Top-394
71OPC-183
71Top-183
72OPC-465
72Top-465
74MetJapEB-3
74NewYorNTDiS-7
76BooProC-20
76TayBow4-7
77GalGloG-15
77GalGloG-233
77Spo-6318
79TCM50-43
79TCM50-71
80DodGreT-1
80MarExh-10
80PacLeg-63
81TCM60I-315
81TCM60I-407
81TCM60I-423
81TCM60I-482
82MetGal62-10
83TopRep5-36
84FifNatCT-8
84OCoandSI-113
84OCoandSI-151
85CirK-29
86MetGreT-12
86SpoDecG-38
86SpoDesJM-19
86TCMSupS-5
87Dod195T-5
88PacLegI-87
88RinPosD1-7C
89BowInsT-4
89BowRepI-4
89BowTif-R4
89DodSmoG-54
89Met196C-6
89RinPosM1-15
89SweBasG-33
89Top-664
89TopTif-664
90DodTar-350
90MetHaloF-1
90SweBasG-132
91MetWIZ-185
91PacRyaTEI-11
91SweBasG-131
91TopArc1-296
92BazQua5A-16
93ActPacA-137
93TedWilM-3
93UppDecAH-65
94Met69CCPP-2
94Met69CS-1
94Met69T-29
94TedWil-11
94TedWil-148
94TopArc1-102
94TopArc1G-102
95TopArcBD-4
95TopArcBD-59
95TopArcBD-72
95TopArcBD-105
95TopArcBD-118
95TopArcBD-131
95TopArcBD-150
95UppDecSHoB-12

Hodges, Kevin
94RocRoyC-13
94RocRoyF-560
95WilBluRTI-31

Hodges, Randy
95EugEmeTI-20
96MacBraB-18

Hodges, Reid
96BriWhiSB-18

Hodges, Ron (Ronald W.)
74MetDaiPA-3
74MetOriEB-4
74OPC-448
74Top-448
75CedRapGT-27
75OPC-134
75TidTidTI-13
75Top-134
76CedRapGT-12
77MetDaiPA-8
77Top-329
78MetDaiPA-11
78Top-653
79Top-46
80Top-172
81Top-537
82Fle-527
82MetPhoA-10
82Top-234
83Don-476
83Fle-545
83Top-713
84Don-603
84Fle-588
84Nes792-418
84Top-418
84TopTif-418
85Top-363
85TopTif-363
91MetWIZ-186

Hodges, Scott
97Bow-426
97BowChr-286
97BowChrI-286
97BowChrIR-286
97BowChrR-286
97BowInt-426
97TopSta-113
97TopStaAM-113

Hodges, Steve
90IdaFalBP-3242

Hodgin, Elmer Ralph
47TipTop-20
48WhiSoxTI-11
49BowPCL-3
49SolSunP-6
79DiaGre-137

Hodgkins, Ellis
63GadFunC-71

Hodgson, Gordon
79QuaCitCT-18
80QuaCitCT-23

Hodgson, Paul
80KnoBluJT-5
82KnoBluJT-13
83KnoBluJT-18

Hodkinson, Chris
91ParPatF-7

Hodo, Doug
86BenPhiC-134

Hodson, Blair
94ColRedC-11
94ColRedF-449

Hodson, Steven
93WatIndC-13
93WatIndF-3568

Hoeft, Billy
52Top-370
53BowBW-18
53TigGle-15
53Top-165
54Bow-167
54DixLid-4
56Top-152
57Top-60
58Top-13A
58Top-13B
59TigGraASP-9
59Top-343
60Lea-90
60Top-369
61Top-256
62Top-134A

62Top-134B
62TopVen-134
63Top-346
64Top-551
65Top-471
66Top-409
79TCM50-37
81TigDetN-32
83TopRep5-370
91OriCro-197
91TopArc1-165
Hoeksema, Dave
83MemChiT-9
85IndIndTI-23
Hoelskoetter, Art
08RosComP-164
11SpoLifCW-173
Hoeme, Steve
88EugEmeB-2
89AppFoxP-852
90BasCitRS-11
92WatDiaC-9
92WicWraF-3654
93RanCucQF-827
93WicWraF-2975
94HarSenF-2086
95PawRedSDD-14
95PawRedTI-39
95TreThuTI-5
Hoenstine, Dave
80CedRapRT-3
81CedRapRT-12
Hoerner, Joe
64Top-544
66Top-544
67OPC-41
67Top-41
68Top-227
68TopVen-227
69Top-522
70MLBOffS-90
70OPC-511
70Top-511
71MLBOffS-181
71OPC-166
71PhiArcO-6
71Top-166
72OPC-482
72Top-482
73OPC-653
73Top-653
74OPC-493
74Top-493
75OPC-629
75Top-629
76SSP-456
77Top-256
93RanKee-186
Hoerner, Troy
90KenTwiB-5
90KenTwiP-2307
90KenTwiS-7
Hofer, John
89AppFoxP-878
Hofer, Ray
94IdaFalBF-3592
94IdaFalBSP-17
Hoff, Jim
83TamTarT-28
88BilMusP-1827
Hoff, Red (Chester)
12T207-82
Hoffer, Bill
98CamPepP-27
Hoffert, Troy
93ClePhiC-29
94SparPhiC-28
96PieBolWB-3
Hoffinger, Glenn
86MedA'sC-61
Hoffman, Artie
07CubA.CDPP-4
07CubGFGCP-4
08AmeCarE-49
08CubPos-2
09PhiCarE-11
10ChiE-6
10SepAnoP-15
11PloCanE-34
14CraJacE-9
15CraJacE-9
Hoffman, Daniel
96BatCliTI-33
Hoffman, Danny
08RosComP-68
09PC7HHB-22
09T206-157
10CouT21-30
10CouT21-148
10DomDisP-56
10RedCroT-30
10SweCapPP-52
11SpoLifCW-170
11SpoLifM-110
11T205-77
Hoffman, Dennis
88MarPhiS-17
Hoffman, Edson
94OgdRapF-3732
94OgdRapSP-8
Hoffman, Frank J.
87OldJudN-249
Hoffman, Fred
22W575-55
28Exh-35
46SeaSLP-23
92ConTSN-575
Hoffman, Glenn
81CokTeaS-5
81Don-95
81Fle-237
81OPC-349
81Top-349
81TopSupHT-5
82Don-460
82Fle-296
82FleSta-168
82RedSoxC-9
82Top-189
83AllGamPI-22
83Don-282
83Fle-185
83OPC-108
83Top-108
84AllGamPI-112
84Don-606
84Fle-399
84Nes792-523
84OPC-141
84Top-523
84TopSti-223
84TopTif-523
85Top-633
85TopTif-633
86Don-457
86Fle-351
86OPC-38
86Top-38
86TopTif-38
87PawRedSP-63
87Top-374
87TopTif-374
88PawRedSC-13
88PawRedSP-465
88StaLinD-9
88Top-202
88TopTif-202
90AlbDukC-26
90AlbDukP-352
90AlbDukT-12
90CMC-653
90DodTar-351
90Don-407
90ProAAAF-73
91BakDodCLC-30
92VerBeaDC-29
92VerBeaDF-2893
93SanAntMF-3020
Hoffman, Guy
79IowOakP-8
80IowOakP-7
80Top-664
81EdmTraRR-6
82EdmTraT-6
86CubGat-50
86FleUpd-51
86IowCubP-16
87Fle-566
87FleGlo-566
87FleUpd-45
87FleUpdG-45
87RedKah-30
87TopTra-48T
87TopTraT-48T
88Don-452
88Fle-235
88FleGlo-235
88Sco-609
88ScoGlo-609
88Top-496
88TopTif-496
93RanKee-187
Hoffman, Harry C.
09T206-431
Hoffman, Hunter
89WauTimGS-18
90FayGenP-2410
Hoffman, Jeff
88OneYanP-2057
90Bes-230
90CMC-704
90GreHorB-3
90GreHorP-2655
90GreHorS-6
90SouAtlLAS-11
91PriWilCC-4
91PriWilCP-1421
92AlbYanF-2222
92AlbYanS-10
92SkyAA F-6
Hoffman, John
87BelMarTI-7
88WauTimGS-9
89SanBerSCLC-77
Hoffman, John Edward
77FriOneYW-33
Hoffman, Rich
89St.PetCS-18
90ArkTraGS-17
Hoffman, Rob
90KisDodD-14
Hoffman, Trevor
88AriWilP-5
89BilMusP-2068
90ChaWheB-16
90ChaWheP-2247
91CedRapRC-6
91CedRapRP-2714
92Bow-11
92ChaLooS-186
92NasSouF-1829
92ProFS7-219
92SkyAA F-83
92UppDecML-105
93Bow-390
93Fla-135
93FlaWavotF-7
93FleFinE-143
93Lea-531
93MarUSPC-7D
93MarUSPC-12H
93OPCPre-113
93PacSpa-464
93Pin-602
93SP-169
93StaClu-451
93StaCluFDI-451
93StaCluMarl-20
93StaCluMOP-451
93Top-572
93TopGol-572
93TopInaM-572
93TopMic-572
93Ult-378
93UppDec-773
93UppDecGold-773
94ColC-494
94ColChoGS-494
94ColChoSS-494
94Don-187
94ExtBas-373
94ExtBasSYS-9
94Fin-417
94FinRef-417
94Fla-234
94Fle-668
94Lea-421
94Pac-528
94PadMot-23
94PanSti-257
94Pin-272
94PinArtP-272
94PinMusC-272
94SP-131
94SPDieC-131
94StaClu-312
94StaCluFDI-312
94StaCluGR-312
94StaCluMOP-312
94Stu-133
94Top-222
94TopGol-222
94TopSpa-222
94Ult-577
94UppDec-153
94UppDecED-153
94USPlaCR-4S
95ColCho-355
95ColChoGS-355
95ColChoSE-163
95ColChoSEGS-163
95ColChoSESS-163
95ColChoSS-355
95Don-318
95DonPreP-318
95DonTopotO-343
95Fin-269
95FinRef-269
95Fla-202
95Fle-562
95Lea-17
95Pac-363
95PadCHP-5
95PadMot-21
95Pin-85
95PinArtP-85
95PinMusC-85
95Sco-46
95ScoGolR-46
95ScoPlaTS-46
95StaClu-382
95StaCluMOP-382
95StaCluSTWS-382
95StaCluVR-201
95Stu-101
95Top-7
95TopCyb-5
95Ult-439
95UltGolM-439
95UppDec-374
95UppDecED-374
95UppDecEDG-374
95UppDecSE-135
95UppDecSEG-135
96ColCho-296
96ColChoGS-296
96ColChoSS-296
96Don-198
96DonPreP-198
96EmoXL-280
96Fin-B134
96FinRef-B134
96Fla-377
96Fle-570
96FleTif-570
96Lea-190
96LeaPrePB-190
96LeaPrePG-190
96LeaPrePS-190
96LeaSigA-105
96LeaSigAG-105
96LeaSigAS-105
96MetUni-238
96MetUniP-238
96Pac-193
96PadMot-17
96PanSti-99
96Pin-321
96PinAfi-117
96PinAfiAP-117
96PinFoil-321
96Sco-175
96Sel-80
96SelArtP-80
96StaClu-171
96StaCluMOP-171
95StaCluVRMC-201
96Sum-56
96SumAbo&B-56
96SumArtP-56
96SumFoi-56
96Top-313
96TopGal-90
96TopGalPPI-90
96Ult-286
96UltGolM-286
96UppDec-447
97Bow-39
97BowInt-39
97Cir-287
97CirRav-287
97ColCho-212
97Don-93
97DonPreP-93
97DonPrePGold-93
97Fin-149
97FinEmb-149
97FinEmbR-149
97FinRef-149
97FlaSho-A151
97FlaSho-B151
97FlaSho-C151
97FlaShoLC-151
97FlaShoLC-B151
97FlaShoLC-C151
97FlaShoLCM-A151
97FlaShoLCM-B151
97FlaShoLCM-C151
97Fle-465
97FleTif-465
97Lea-75
97LeaFraM-75
97LeaFraMDC-75
97MetUni-222
97Pac-427
97PacLigB-427
97PacSil-427
97Pin-21
97PinArtP-21
97PinMusC-21
97Sco-36
97ScoPreS-36
97ScoShoS-36
97ScoShoSAP-36
97SP-157
97StaClu-202
97StaCluMat-202
97StaCluMOP-202
97Top-70
97TopChr-25
97TopChrR-25
97TopGal-130
97TopGalPPI-130
97Ult-286
97UltGolME-286
97UltPlaME-286
97UppDec-488
Hoffmann, Greg
85IowCubT-24
Hoffner, Jamie
89PitMetS-27
91St.LucMC-6
91St.LucMP-719
92BinMetF-524
92BinMetS-58
Hofheinz, Roy
84WilMay-31
Hofman, Bobby (Robert G.)
49Bow-223
50RemBre-13
52Top-371
53Top-182
54NewYorJA-25
54Top-99
55GiaGolS-28
55Top-17
55TopDouH-95
55TopTesS-5
56Top-28
56TopPin-40
79TCM50-59
83TopRep5-371
91TopArc1-182
94TopArc1-99
94TopArc1G-99
Hofman, Rich
92HigSchPLS-29
Hofman, Solly (Arthur)
08RosComP-103
09ColChiE-131
09SpoNewSM-55
09T206-158
10CouT21-147
10RedCroT-119
10RedCroT-200
11BasBatEU-24
11MecDFT-28
11SpoLifCW-171
11SpoLifM-170
11TurRedT-98
12ColRedB-131
12ColTinT-131
Hofmann, Fred
21KoBreWSI-35
26SpoComoA-20
41BroW75-16
Hogan, Ben
51BerRos-A16
52Whe-14A
52Whe-14B

74NewYorNTDiS-2
Hogan, David
91BriBanF-16
Hogan, Happy (William)
09ColChiE-132
12ColRedB-132
12ColTinT-132
12T207-83
Hogan, Mike
82AubAstT-8
83DayBeaAT-8
86ModA'sP-12
88PhoFirC-6
88PhoFirP-73
Hogan, Rob
91WavRedF-6
Hogan, Robert
87OldJudN-250
Hogan, Sean
93GenCubC-15
93GenCubF-3170
94WilCubC-10
94WilCubF-3759
Hogan, Shanty (J. Francis)
28Exh-18
29ExhFou-10
29PorandAR-41
31Exh-9
33DouDisP-23
33Gou-30
33GouCanV-30
34DiaMatCSB-92
34ButPreR-32
34DiaStaR-20
34ExhFou-1
34Gou-20
34GouCanV-66
35DiaMatCS2-9
35ExhFou-1
35GouPuzR-4E
35GouPuzR-7E
35GouPuzR-12E
87ConSer2-42
91ConTSN-294
Hogan, Shorty
33ButCanV-26
Hogan, Todd
96JohCitCTI-16
Hoganson, Dale
72Dia-75
Hogdin, Ralph
83TCMPla1944-17
Hogestyn, Don
77ForLauYS-21
Hogg, Bill
11SpoLifCW-172
Hogg, David
82EdmTraT-16
Hogge, Shawn
96JohCitCTI-17
Hogsett, Chief (Elon)
34DiaMatCSB-93
34TarThoBD-10
35TigFreP-12
76TigOldTS-14
79DiaGre-177
93ConTSN-969
Hogue, Bobby
49EurSta-12
52Top-9
83TopRep5-9
Hogue, Cal
53Top-238
54Top-134
91TopArc1-238
94TopArc1-134
94TopArc1G-134
Hohlmeyer, Lefty (Alice)
93TedWil-116
Hohn, Bill
90T/MUmp-60
Hohn, Eric
86EriCarP-13
Hohno, Takayuki
92SalSpuC-26
Hoiles, Chris
87GleFalTP-2
88BlaYNPRWL-86
88TolMudHC-19
88TolMudHP-597
89RocRedWP-1640
90Bow-259
90BowTif-259
90CMC-313
90FleUpd-65
90Lea-513
90ProAAAF-461
90RocRedWC-14
90RocRedWGC-4
90RocRedWP-704
90ScoRoo-96T
90TopDeb89-60
91Bow-99
91Cla1-T13
91Don-358
91Fle-476
91Lea-131
91OPC-42
91OPCPre-65
91OriCro-198
91Sco-334
91Sco100RS-34
91StaClu-489
91StaCluMO-10
91Stu-4
91Top-42
91TopDesS-42
91TopMic-42
91TopTif-42
91Ult-17
91UppDec-306
92Bow-472
92Don-156
92Fle-9
92Lea-211
92LeaGolP-31
92OPC-125
92PanSti-64
92Pin-83
92Sco-641
92StaClu-161
92Stu-124
92Top-125
92TopGol-125
92TopGolW-125
92TopMic-125
92TriPla-256
92Ult-5
92UppDec-183
92UppDecWB-T16
93Bow-549
93Don-323
93Fla-151
93Fle-168
93Lea-133
93OPC-142
93PacSpa-18
93PanSti-70
93Pin-186
93Sco-54
93Sel-144
93SP-157
93StaClu-345
93StaCluFDI-345
93StaCluMOP-345
93Stu-156
93Top-524
93TopGol-524
93TopInaM-524
93TopMic-524
93TriPla-205
93Ult-495
93UppDec-402
93UppDecGold-402
94Bow-131
94ColC-140
94ColChoGS-140
94ColChoSS-140
94Don-99
94ExtBas-6
94Fin-141
94FinPre-141P
94FinRef-141
94Fla-3
94Fle-6
94FUnPac-63
94KinDis-11
94Lea-195
94OPC-167
94OriPro-46
94OriUSPC-1C
94OriUSPC-8D
94Pac-33
94PanSti-20
94Pin-112
94PinArtP-112
94PinMusC-112
94PinPowS-PS2
94PinRunC-RC18
94Sco-357
94ScoGolR-357
94Sel-15
94SP-122
94SPDieC-122
94Spo-114
94Spo-180
94StaClu-451
94StaCluFDI-451
94StaCluGR-451
94StaCluMOP-451
94StaCluT-288
94StaCluTFDI-288
94Top-295
94TopBlaG-9
94TopGol-295
94TopSpa-295
94TriPla-154
94TriPlaM-1
94Ult-2
94UltAllS-1
94UppDec-77
94UppDecAJ-19
94UppDecAJG-19
94UppDecED-77
95Baz-98
95Bow-288
95ColCho-331
95ColChoGS-331
95ColChoSE-158
95ColChoSEGS-158
95ColChoSESS-158
95ColChoSS-331
95Don-295
95DonPreP-295
95DonTopotO-10
95Emb-34
95EmbGolI-34
95Fin-60
95FinRef-60
95Fla-221
95Fle-9
95Lea-54
95Pac-23
95PanSti-27
95Pin-38
95PinArtP-38
95PinMusC-38
95SP-121
95SPCha-119
95SPChaDC-119
95SPSil-121
95StaClu-135
95StaCluFDI-135
95StaCluMOP-135
95StaCluSTWS-135
95StaCluVR-70
95Top-546
95TopCyb-327
95Ult-4
95UltGolM-4
95UppDec-131
95UppDecED-131
95UppDecEDG-131
95UppDecSE-185
95UppDecSEG-185
96ColCho-54
96ColChoGS-54
96ColChoSS-54
96Don-412
96DonPreP-412
96EmoXL-5
96Fin-B108
96FinRef-B108
96Fla-7
96Fle-11
96FleOri-8
96FleTif-11
96MetUni-4
96MetUniP-4
96MLBPin-15
96Pac-238
96PanSti-132
96Sco-136
96StaClu-219
96StaClu-279
96StaCluEPB-279
96StaCluEPG-279
96StaCluEPS-279
96StaCluMOP-219
96StaCluMOP-279
95StaCluVRMC-70
96Top-191
96TopGal-53
96TopGalPPI-53
96Ult-6
96UltGolM-6
96UppDec-14
97Cir-46
97CirRav-46
97ColCho-38
97Don-342
97DonPreP-342
97DonPrePGold-342
97DonTea-43
97DonTeaSPE-43
97Fin-195
97FinRef-195
97Fle-8
97FleTif-8
97MetUni-4
97Pac-24
97PacLigB-24
97PacSil-24
97Sco-223
97ScoOri-13
97ScoOriPl-13
97ScoOriPr-13
97ScoPreS-223
97ScoShoS-223
97ScoShoSAP-223
97StaClu-330
97StaCluMOP-330
97Top-174
97Ult-5
97UltGolME-5
97UltPlaME-5
97UppDec-305
Hokanson, Mark
91KinMetC-21
91KinMetP-3809
92PitMetF-3289
93CapCitBC-8
93CapCitBF-455
Hoke, Leon
81MiaOriT-17
83SanJosBC-23
Hokuf, Ken
91ModA'sC-6
91ModA'sP-3081
92ModA'sC-22
92ModA'sF-3895
Holbert, Aaron
90ClaDraP-18
90HigSchPLS-4
90JohCitCS-14
91Bow-399
91Sco-676
92SavCarC-21
92SavCarF-671
92UppDecML-172
93Bow-304
93ClaFS7-206
93SouAtlLAIPI-2
93SouAtlLAPI-16
93St.PetCC-15
93St.PetCF-2634
93StaCluCa-30
94ArkTraF-3096
94Bow-68
94ExcFS7-267
94UppDecML-221
95Bow-57
95LouRedF-282
95SPML-156
96BesAutS-39
96BesAutSA-29
96Bow-365
96FleUpd-U190
96FleUpdTC-U190
96LouRedB-22
96Ult-548
96UltGolM-548
97Fle-444
97FleTif-444
97Ult-271
97UltGolME-271
97UltPlaME-271
Holbert, Ray
89WatDiaP-1791
89WatDiaS-12
90Bes-9
90WatDiaB-1
90WatDiaP-2384
91HigDesMC-22
91HigDesMP-2405
92SkyAA F-282
92UppDecML-103
92WicWraF-3664
92WicWraS-634
93Bow-194
93ClaFS7-207
93WicWraF-2985
94Bow-532
94ColC-665
94ColChoGS-665
94ColChoSS-665
94ExcFS7-283
94LeaLimR-73
94SpoRoo-55
94SpoRooAP-55
94UppDecML-102
95FleUpd-186
95PadMot-16
95Pin-415
95PinArtP-415
95PinMusC-415
95Sel-179
95SelArtP-179
95StaClu-606
95StaCluMOP-606
95StaCluSTWS-606
95Sum-142
95SumNthD-142
95Top-571
Holbert, William
87OldJudN-251A
87OldJudN-251B
Holbrook, Sammy (James)
35DiaMatCS3T1-76
Holcomb, Scott
87ModA'sC-6
87ModA'sP-24
88HunStaTI-7
89HunStaB-16
92AlbYanS-11
93ChaLooF-2358
Holcomb, Shawn
92FroRowDP-65
Holcomb, Ted
86BakDodP-13
87BakDodP-18
88DurBulS-7
Holcombe, Ken
49BowPCL-19
51Bow-267
52Top-95
53RedSoxTI-12
83TopRep5-95
Holden, Bill
84IowCubT-10
Holden, Gary
81BatTroT-21
Holder, Brooks
46RemBre-23
47RemBre-3
47SigOil-47
47SmiClo-4
48SigOil-11
48SmiClo-2
49SomandK-16
Holding, Brook
95ButCopKtl-10
Holdren, Nate
93BenRocC-12
93BenRocF-3277
94AshTouC-13
94AshTouF-1792
95SalAvaTI-14
95UppDecML-142
96SalAvaB-15
95UppDecMLFS-142
Holdridge, Dave
88QuaCitAGS-11
89ClePhiS-11
90Bes-17
90CMC-802
90ReaPhiB-1
90ReaPhiP-1216
90ReaPhiS-13
91Cla/Bes-155
91LinDriAA-510
91ReaPhiLD-510
91ReaPhiP-1368
92PalSprAC-9
92PalSprAF-832
93MidAngF-320
94MidAngF-2431
94MidAngOHP-10
94VanCanF-1860
95MidAngOHP-18

95MidAngTI-16
97MidAngOHP-16
Holdsworth, Fred
74OPC-596
74Top-596
75OPC-323
75Top-323
77Top-466
78ExpPos-6
80VanCanT-18
81TacTigT-21
91OriCro-199
94BreMilB-229
Holiday, Billie
96NoiSatP-10
Holifield, Rickey (Rick)
89St.CatBJP-2096
90MyrBeaBJP-2787
91MyrBeaHC-24
91MyrBeaHP-2958
92MyrBeaHC-13
92MyrBeaHF-2211
93DunBluJC-10
93DunBluJF-1809
93DunBluJFFN-10
94KnoSmoF-1316
95Bow-200
95ReaPhiELC-19
95ScrRedBTI-13
96TreThuB-26
Holin, Andrew
94HunCubF-3556
94HunCubC-13
Holke, Walter
16ColE13-78
17HolBreD-44
20GasAmeMBD-21
21E121So1-42A
21E121So1-42B
21E121So8-35A
21E121So8-35B
21Exh-75
21Exh-76
21OxfConE-8
22AmeCarE-27
22E120-127
22W575-56
23W501-92
23WilChoV-63
25Exh-44
91ConTSN-207
92ConTSN-491
Hollacher, Charlie
20GasAmeMBD-25
21E121So8-36
22AmeCarE-28
Holladay, Kolin
92DavLipB-15
94DavLipB-16
95DavLipB-15
Holland, Al
77ShrCapT-7
78ColCliT-10
79PorBeaT-1
80GiaEurFS-1
80GiaPol-19
81Fle-445
81Top-213
82Don-377
82Fle-391
82Top-406
83Don-146
83Fle-262
83FleSta-81
83FleSti-56
83PhiTas-14
83Top-58
83TopSti-306
83TopTra-46T
84AllGamPI-79
84Don-204
84Fle-35
84FleSti-68
84FunFooP-87
84Nes792-138
84Nes792-564
84NesDreT-22
84OPC-206
84PhiTas-21
84Top-138
84Top-564
84TopSti-125
84TopSti-289
84TopSup-10
84TopTif-138
84TopTif-564
85Don-427
85Fle-254
85Fle-637
85FleStaS-107
85FleUpd-55
85Lea-151
85OPC-185
85PhiTas-9
85PhiTas-19
85Top-185
85TopMin-185
85TopSti-113
85TopTif-185
85TopTifT-55T
85TopTra-55T
86ColCliP-11
86ColCliP-12
86Don-573
86Fle-159
86OPC-369
86Top-369
86TopTif-369
86YanTCM-3
87ColCliP-12
87ColCliP-22
87ColCliT-6
89PacSenL-26
89PacSenL-113
90EliSenL-114
91PacSenL-139
92YanWIZ8-83
93UppDecS-12
Holland, Bill
78LauLonABS-21
Holland, Donny
82WauTimF-20
Holland, Jay
92BenRocC-13
92BenRocF-1470
Holland, Jim
94PriRedC-27
Holland, John
81BufBisT-2
82BufBisT-12
Holland, Mike
74CedRapAT-26
90EriSaiS-9
Holland, Monty
80BatTroT-9
Holland, Randy
86KnoBluJP-11
87KnoBluJP-1515
88SyrChiC-2
88SyrChiP-829
88TriAAAP-53
89SyrChiC-13
89SyrChiP-795
90SyrChiMB-12
91SyrChiMB-8
Holland, Rod
93ButCopKSP-15
Holland, Sid
91GasRanC-23
91GasRanP-2700
92ChaRanC-16
92ChaRanF-2237
Holland, Tim
89WatDiaP-1779
89WatDiaS-13
90CarLeaA-5
90FreKeyTI-15
91HagSunLD-232
91HagSunP-2463
91LinDriAA-232
91PerHeaF-8
92HagSunF-2562
92HagSunS-259
93BowBayF-2195
95AusFut-2
Hollandsworth, Todd
91FroRowDP-46
92BakDodCLC-1
92StaCluD-85
92UppDecML-160
92UppDecMLPotY-PY9
93Bow-98
93ClaFS7-138
93SanAntMF-3017
93StaCluD-28
94ActPac-50
94ActPac-66
94ActPac2G-12G
94AlbDukF-856
94Bow-359
94Bow-426
94BowBes-B45
94BowBesR-B45
94Cla-101
94ClaCreotC-C8
94ColC-658
94ColChoGS-658
94ColChoSS-658
94ExcFS7-215
94SigRoo-14
94SigRooHP-S3
94SigRooS-14
94SP-6
94SPDieC-6
94UppDec-531
94UppDecED-531
94UppDecML-60
94UppDecML-266
95ActPacF-13
95Bow-268
95BowBes-B44
95BowBesR-B44
95BowGolF-268
95ColCho-231
95ColChoGS-231
95ColChoSE-91
95ColChoSEGS-91
95ColChoSESS-91
95ColChoSS-231
95DodMot-16
95DodPol-11
95Exc-213
95Fla-365
95FleAllR-M7
95Pin-420
95PinArtP-420
95PinMusC-420
95SelCer-120
95SelCerF-6
95SelCerMG-120
95SelCerPU-16
95SelCerPU9-16
95SigRoo-25
95SigRooOJSS-4
95SigRooOJSSS-4
95SigRooSig-25
95StaClu-590
95StaCluMOP-590
95StaCluSTWS-590
95Sum-159
95SumNewA-NA12
95SumNthD-159
95Top-247
95UC3-111
95UC3ArtP-111
95UppDec-224
95UppDecED-224
95UppDecEDG-224
95UppDecML-10
95UppDecMLMLA-6
95UppDecMLT1PF-10
95UppDecSE-34
95UppDecSEG-34
95Zen-147
95ZenRooRC-5
96Bow-40
96Bow-42
96Bow-40
96BowBes-149
96BowBesAR-149
96BowBesR-149
96ColCho-182
96ColChoGS-182
96ColChoSS-182
96DodMot-9
96DodPol-19
96Don-339
96DonPreP-339
96EmoXL-209
96Fin-B246
96FinRef-B246
96Fla-293
96Fle-437
96FleDod-9
96FleTif-437
96Lea-143
96LeaPre-133
96LeaPreP-133
96LeaPrePB-143
96LeaPrePG-143
96LeaPrePS-143
96LeaPreSG-13
96LeaPreSte-13
96LeaSig-93
96LeaSigPPG-93
96LeaSigPPP-93
96Pin-252
96PinAfi-165
96PinAfiAP-165
96PinArtP-152
96PinFoil-252
96PinProS-16
96PinSta-152
96Sco-112
96ScoDiaA-28
96ScoDugC-A76
96ScoDugCAP-A76
96Sel-181
96SelArtP-181
96SelCer-117
96SelCerAP-117
96SelCerCB-117
96SelCerCR-117
96SelCerMB-117
96SelCerMG-117
96SelCerMR-117
96Spo-122
96SpoArtP-122
96Stu-4
96StuPrePB-4
96StuPrePG-4
96StuPrePS-4
96Sum-189
96SumAbo&B-189
96SumArtP-189
96SumFoi-189
96Top-48
96TopLasBS-12
96Ult-210
96UltGolM-219
96UppDec-118
96UppDecPHE-H55
96UppDecPreH-H55
97Bow-282
97BowBes-20
97BowBesAR-20
97BowBesR-20
97BowCerBIA-CA39
97BowCerGIA-CA39
97BowInt-282
97Cir-251
97CirEmeA-251
97CirEmeAR-AU2
97CirFasT-2
97CirRav-251
97ColCho-139
97ColChoTBS-25
97ColChoTBSWH-25
97Don-125
97DonEli-67
97DonEliGS-67
97DonLim-15
97DonLimLE-15
97DonPre-119
97DonPreCttC-119
97DonPreP-125
97DonPrePGold-125
97DonTea-110
97DonTeaSPE-110
97Fin-121
97FinEmb-121
97FinEmbR-121
97FinRef-121
97FlaSho-A82
97FlaSho-B82
97FlaSho-C82
97FlaShoLC-82
97FlaShoLC-B82
97FlaShoLC-C82
97FlaShoLCM-A82
97FlaShoLCM-B82
97FlaShoLCM-C82
97Fle-364
97FleRooS-6
97FleTif-364
97Lea-58
97LeaBanS-15
97LeaFraM-58
97LeaFraMDC-58
97MetUni-100
97MetUniEAR-AU2
97MetUniPP-3
97NewPin-121
97NewPinAP-121
97NewPinMC-121
97NewPinPP-121
97Pac-331
97PacCar-29
97PacCarM-29
97PacGolCD-29
97PacLigB-331
97PacPri-111
97PacPriGA-GA24
97PacPriLB-111
97PacPriP-111
97PacSil-331
97Pin-118
97PinArtP-118
97PinCer-52
97PinCerMBlu-52
97PinCerMG-52
97PinCerMR-52
97PinCerR-52
97PinIns-25
97PinIns-148
97PinInsCE-25
97PinInsCE-148
97PinInsDD-19
97PinInsDE-25
97PinInsDE-148
97PinMusC-118
97PinTotCPB-52
97PinTotCPG-52
97PinTotCPR-52
97PinX-P-105
97PinX-PMoS-105
97Sco-113
97ScoDod-3
97ScoDodPl-3
97ScoDodPr-3
97ScoPreS-113
97ScoShoS-113
97ScoShoSAP-113
97ScoStaaD-16
97Sel-9
97SelArtP-9
97SelRegG-9
97SelRooR-3
97SelToootT-13
97SelToootTMB-13
97SkyE-X-78
97SkyE-XC-78
97SkyE-XEAR-AU2
97SkyE-XEC-78
97SkyE-XSD2-12
97SP-93
97SpoIll-114
97SpoIllEE-114
97SPSpxF-7
97SPSPxFA-7
97SPVinAu-18
97StaClu-87
97StaCluC-CO5
97StaCluMOP-87
97Stu-6
97StuPrePG-6
97StuPrePS-6
97Top-177
97TopAwel-AI6
97TopChr-69
97TopChrR-69
97TopGal-175
97TopGalPPI-175
97Ult-218
97UltAutE-6
97UltGolME-218
97UltPlaME-218
97UltRooR-4
97UltTop3-27
97UltTop3GM-27
97UppDec-92
97UppDecAWJ-19
97UppDecBCP-BC16
95UppDecMLFS-10
97UppDecU-56
97UppDecUGN-GN14
Holle, Gary
77HolMilT-14
78HolMilT-13
81EdmTraRR-1
93RanKee-188
Holleday, Juan
92AubAstC-25
92AubAstF-1349
Hollenback, Dave
88ModA'sCLC-83
88ModA'sTI-3
89ModA'sC-3
89ModA'sCLC-290
90ModA'sC-14

90ModA'sCLC-173
91ModA'sC-19
92CalLeaACL-23
92ModA'sC-27
95HunStaTI-14
96HunStaTI-10
Holley, Battle
94St.CatBJC-12
94St.CatBJF-3652
95HagSunF-74
95StCatSTI-18
Holley, Bobby
88EugEmeB-22
90BasCitRS-12
91CarLeaAP-CAR28
91PenPilC-21
91PenPilP-386
92JacSunF-3715
92JacSunS-359
92SkyAA F-151
93ClaFS7-279
Holley, Ed
33ButCanV-27
34ButPreR-33
34Gou-55
Holley, Kenny
88WytCubP-1994
Holliday, Brian
92BurAstC-15
92BurAstF-538
92StaCluD-86
93OscAstC-14
93OscAstF-622
Holliday, Bug (James)
87OldJudN-252
98CamPepP-35
Holliday, Tom
91OklStaC-11
92OklStaC-5
Hollifield, David
76QuaCitAT-16
77QuaCitAT-18
Hollimon, Ulysses
96NegLeaBMKC-1
Hollinger, Adrian
92SpoIndC-19
92SpoIndF-1288
93WatDiaC-19
93WatDiaF-1764
94RanCucQC-16
94RanCucQF-1633
95BreCouMF-241
Hollingsworth, Al
79DiaGre-140
90DodTar-352
96Bro194F-4
Hollingsworth, Scot
91MisStaB-26
Hollins, Damon
92HigSchPLS-25
93Bow-170
93ClaGolF-149
93DanBraC-14
93DanBraF-3631
93StaCluM-185
94Bow-161
94CarLeaAF-CAR28
94Cla-75
94DurBulC-1
94DurBulF-340
94DurBulTI-9
94ExcFS7-154
95Bes-51
95Bow-10
95BreBtaTI-7
95Exc-152
95SigRoo-26
95SigRooSig-26
95SPML-12
95Top-645
95UppDec-5
95UppDecED-5
95UppDecEDG-5
95UppDecML-50
95UppDecSE-13
95UppDecSEG-13
96BesAutSA-30
96Bow-332
96Exc-127
96RicBraB-16
96RicBraRC-13
96RicBraUB-12
95UppDecMLFS-50
Hollins, Dave
87SpoIndP-8
88CalLeaACLC-44
88RivRedWCLC-222
88RivRedWP-1418
89WicChaR-11
89WicStaR-12
89WicWraR-7
90Bow-161
90BowTif-161
90ClaYel-T14
90DonRoo-47
90FleUpd-43
90PhiTas-14
90ScoRoo-75T
90ScoYouS2-35
90TopTra-41T
90TopTraT-41T
90UppDec-785
91Fle-399
91OPC-264
91PhiMed-19
91Sco-61
91Sco100RS-96
91ScrRedBP-2545
91Top-264
91TopDeb90-69
91TopDesS-264
91TopMic-264
91TopTif-264
91UppDec-518
92Bow-6
92Don-685
92Fle-535
92Lea-278
92OPC-383
92PhiMed-15
92Pin-67
92PinTea2-16
92ProFS7-296
92Sco-553
92ScoProP-16
92StaClu-246
92Top-383
92TopGol-383
92TopGolW-383
92TopMic-383
92Ult-244
92UppDec-586
93Bow-216
93DenHol-18
93DiaMar-52
93Don-68
93Fin-23
93FinRef-23
93Fla-102
93Fle-353
93Fle-491
93FunPac-145
93Lea-239
93OPC-169
93PacSpa-236
93PanSti-273
93PhiMed-17
93Pin-127
93PinHomRC-11
93PinSlu-8
93Sco-99
93Sel-187
93SelStaL-41
93SP-175
93SPPlaP-PP10
93StaClu-339
93StaCluFDI-339
93StaCluMOP-339
93StaCluP-11
93Stu-158
93Top-17
93TopGol-17
93TopInaM-17
93TopMic-17
93Toy-18
93TriPla-38
93Ult-88
93UltHomRK-10
93UppDec-153
93UppDec-458
93UppDec-485
93UppDecDG-18
93UppDecGold-153
93UppDecGold-458
93UppDecGold-485
93UppDecHRH-HR10
93USPlaCA-2C
94Bow-524
94ColC-141
94ColChoGS-141
94ColChoSS-141
94Don-29
94DonSpeE-29
94ExtBas-335
94Fin-47
94FinPre-47P
94FinRef-47
94Fla-207
94Fle-590
94FleAllS-41
94FUnPac-115
94Lea-54
94LeaCleC-3
94OPC-186
94Pac-476
94PanSti-228
94PhiMed-13
94PhiMel-9
94PhiUSPC-1S
94PhiUSPC-7H
94Pin-121
94PinArtP-121
94PinMusC-121
94ProMag-103
94Sco-354
94ScoGolR-354
94Sel-28
94SP-136
94SPDieC-136
94Spo-145
94StaClu-96
94StaCluFDI-96
94StaCluGR-96
94StaCluMOP-96
94StaCluT-225
94StaCluTFDI-225
94Stu-139
94Top-476
94TopGol-476
94TopSpa-476
94TriPla-175
94TriPlaM-10
94Ult-245
94UppDec-432
94UppDecED-432
95Bow-281
95BowBes-R47
95BowBesR-R47
95ColCho-362
95ColChoGS-362
95ColChoSS-362
95Don-453
95DonPreP-453
95DonTopotO-306
95Emb-47
95EmbGolI-47
95Emo-167
95Fin-159
95FinRef-159
95Fla-391
95Fle-393
95Lea-229
95LeaLim-45
95Phi-16
95PhiMel-13
95Pin-104
95PinArtP-104
95PinMusC-104
95Sco-77
95ScoGolR-77
95ScoHaloG-HG91
95ScoPlaTS-77
95SP-88
95Spo-71
95SpoArtP-71
95SPSil-88
95StaClu-144
95StaCluFDI-144
95StaCluMOP-144
95StaCluSTWS-144
95Stu-124
95Top-586
95TopCyb-359
95UC3-80
95UC3ArtP-80
95Ult-205
95UltGolM-205
95UppDec-377
95UppDecED-377
95UppDecEDG-377
95UppDecSE-207
95UppDecSEG-207
96ColCho-601
96ColChoGS-601
96ColChoSS-601
96Fin-B255
96FinRef-B255
96Fla-114
96FleUpd-U54
96FleUpdTC-U54
96LeaSigA-106
96LeaSigAG-106
96LeaSigAS-106
96TopLas-67
96Ult-374
96UltGolM-374
97Cir-141
97CirRav-141
97ColCho-262
97DonLim-58
97DonLimLE-58
97DonTea-14
97DonTeaSPE-14
97Fle-506
97FleTif-506
97Pac-188
97PacLigB-188
97PacSil-188
97Pin-123
97PinArtP-123
97PinMusC-123
97Ult-311
97UltGolME-311
97UltPlaME-311
Hollins, Jessie
89WytCubS-16
90GenCubP-3041
90GenCubS-14
90ProAaA-175
91Bow-423
91Cla/Bes-36
91WinSpiC-5
91WinSpiP-2824
92ChaKniF-2766
92ChaKniS-159
92SkyAA F-74
93Bow-348
93Bow-580
93Don-368
93StaCluCu-27
93Top-487
93TopGol-487
93TopInaM-487
93TopMic-487
93UppDec-18
93UppDecGold-18
94Bow-278
Hollins, Paul
86ChaLooP-13
Hollins, Stacy
93MadMusC-15
93MadMusF-1819
94AriFalLS-8
94ModA'sC-15
94ModA'sF-3062
95Bow-99
95HunStaTI-15
95SigRooOJ-17
95SigRooOJP-17
95SigRooOJPS-17
95SigRooOJS-17
96HunStaTI-11
Hollins, Steve
90PriPatD-12
Hollinshed, Joe
86EriCarP-14
Hollis, Jack
52MotCoo-62
78DunBluJT-13
90ChaWheB-21
90ChaWheP-2252
Hollis, Ron
94YakBeaC-6
94YakBeaF-3841
95VerBeaDTI-13
96SanAntMB-8
96VerBeaDB-14
Hollmig, Stan
49EurSta-137
49PhiBul-25
Hollocher, Charles J.
19W514-53
20NatCarE-44
21E121So1-43
21Exh-77
21Nei-110
22E120-159
22W572-43
22W573-61
22W575-57
23W501-57
23W515-59
23WilChoV-64
93ConTSN-799
Holloman, Bobo
63GadFunC-38
77FriOneYW-11
90BasWit-69
90HOFStiB-47
91TopArc1-306
Holloway, Crush
78LauLonABS-24
86NegLeaF-22
Holloway, Ken
29ExhFou-22
93ConTSN-700
Holloway, Rick
81WesHavAT-13
Hollowell, Chuck
80BatTroT-12
Hollrah, Scot
93HicCraC-11
93HicCraF-1284
Holly, Chuck**
88MisStaB-12
89MisStaB-20
90MisStaB-21
91MisStaB-27
Holly, Jeff
77TacTwiDQ-24B
78OrlTwiT-8
79Top-371
79TwiFriP-10
Holm, Dave
75CliPilT-15
Holm, Jerry
86RedWinA-11
Holm, Mike
85NewOriT-8
Holm, Roscoe
33Gou-173
Holm, Vivian
94ColSilBC-3
95ColSilB9-9
Holm, Wattie
93ConTSN-691
Holm, William
44CubTeal-12
Holman, Brad
90EugEmeGS-16
91PenPilC-5
91PenPilP-371
92JacSunF-3704
92PenPilC-24
93CalCanF-1161
93LinVenB-35
94CalCanF-784
94Don-462
94Fle-289
94Lea-35
94Pac-573
94StaClu-76
94StaCluFDI-76
94StaCluGR-76
94StaCluMOP-76
94Top-631
94TopGol-631
94TopSpa-631
94VenLinU-39
Holman, Brian
86JacExpT-23
86SouLeaAJ-21
87JacExpP-452
88ExpPos-9
88FleUpd-100
88FleUpdG-100
88IndIndC-9
88IndIndP-504
89Bow-357
89BowTif-357
89Don-511
89Fle-379
89FleGlo-379
89TopTra-51T
89TopTraT-51T
89UppDec-356
90ClaBlu-66
90Don-143
90Fle-516
90FleCan-516

90Lea-273
90MarMot-20
90OPC-616
90PanSti-146
90PubSti-176
90Sco-387
90ScoYouSI-7
90Top-616
90TopBig-282
90TopTif-616
90UppDec-362
90VenSti-224
91Bow-240
91Don-539
91Fle-453
91Lea-11
91MarCouH-21
91OPC-458
91Sco-285
91StaClu-106
91StaCluP-16
91Stu-115
91Top-458
91TopDesS-458
91TopMic-458
91TopTif-458
91Ult-338
91UppDec-252
92Don-43
92Fle-281
92MarMot-26
92OPC-239
92Pin-520
92Sco-228
92StaClu-295
92Top-239
92TopGol-239
92TopGolW-239
92TopMic-239
92UppDec-595
93Don-385
93StaCluMari-15
93UppDec-799
93UppDecGold-799

Holman, Craig
91BatCliC-28
91BatCliP-3480
92SpaPhiC-1
92SpaPhiF-1260
93ClePhiC-14
94ReaPhiF-2057
95ReaPhiELC-20
95ReaPhiTI-18
96ScrRedBB-16

Holman, Dale
82AlbDukT-20
84SyrChiT-28
85SyrChiT-5
86SyrChiP-12
87RicBraBC-13
87RicBraC-25
87RicBraT-23

Holman, Ed
75LynRanT-12
76SanAntBTI-12

Holman, Gary
69Top-361

Holman, Jeff
90StaFS7-92

Holman, R. Scott
77WauMetT-10
79TidTidT-17
82TidTidT-18
83Don-224
84Fle-589
84Nes792-13
84TidTidT-1
84Top-13
84TopTif-13
85IowCubT-15
91MetWIZ-187

Holman, Shawn
84PriWilPT-4
85PriWilPT-16
86NasPirP-13
87HarSenP-1
88BlaYNPRWL-87
88EasLeaAP-7
88GleFalTP-929
89BlaYNPRWLU-26
89TolMudHC-5
89TolMudHP-781
90CMC-381
90Fle-606
90FleCan-606
90ProAAAF-373
90Sco-620
90TolMudHC-4
90TolMudHP-143
90TopDeb89-61
93RicBraBB-14
93RicBraF-180
93RicBraP-23
93RicBraRC-9
93RicBraRC-10
94OttLynF-2898

Holman, Steve
78CedRapGT-11

Holmberg, Dennis
75BurBeeT-11
76BurBeeT-18
77NewCoPT-17
78DunBluJT-14
85SyrChiT-28
87DunBluJP-929
89DunBluJS-26
90DunBluJS-26
90FloStaLAS-48
91DunBluJC-25
91DunBluJP-223
92DunBluJC-26
92DunBluJF-2013
93DunBluJC-26
93DunBluJF-1811
93DunBluJFFN-11
96DunBluJB-27
96DunBluJTI-16

Holmberg, Kenny
92DunBluJC-30
93DunBluJC-29

Holmes, Bill
89PriPirS-9
90AugPirP-2471

Holmes, Bob
12ImpTobC-79

Holmes, Carl
86SpoIndC-158

Holmes, Chris
88RenSilSCLC-282

Holmes, Craig
94OgdRapSP-27
95OdgRapTI-9

Holmes, Darren
86VerBeaDP-10
87VerBeaDP-5
89SanAntMB-4
90AlbDukC-6
90AlbDukP-339
90AlbDukT-13
90CMC-408
90ProAAAF-60
91BreMilB-11
91DenZepLD-141
91Don-669
91Lea-387
91LinDriAAA-141
91TopDeb90-70
92DenZepS-130
92Don-504
92Fle-179
92OPC-454
92Sco-753
92Sco100RS-39
92StaClu-155
92Top-454
92TopGol-454
92TopGolW-454
92TopMic-454
93Don-149
93Don-779
93Fle-412
93FleFinE-34
93Lea-383
93OPCPre-104
93PacSpa-431
93Pin-521
93RocUSPC-6D
93RocUSPC-9S
93Sco-600
93StaClu-506
93StaCluFDI-506
93StaCluMOP-506
93StaCluRoc-17
93Top-681
93TopGol-681
93TopInaM-681
93TopMic-681
93TriPla-22
93Ult-352
93UppDec-668
93UppDecGold-668
94Bow-310
94BreMilB-230
94ColC-422
94ColChoGS-422
94ColChoSS-422
94Don-222
94Fin-307
94FinRef-307
94Fle-444
94Lea-119
94Pac-198
94Pin-375
94PinArtP-375
94PinMusC-375
94RocPol-14
94Sco-207
94ScoGolR-207
94StaClu-672
94StaCluFDI-672
94StaCluGR-672
94StaCluMOP-672
94StaCluT-117
94StaCluTFDI-117
94Top-562
94TopGol-562
94TopSpa-562
94TriPla-226
94Ult-483
94UppDec-128
94UppDecED-128
95FleUpd-167
95Top-26
96ColCho-533
96ColChoGS-533
96ColChoSS-533
96Don-476
96DonPreP-476
96Fla-247
96Fle-364
96FleRoc-6
96FleTif-364
96LeaSigEA-79
96Pac-54
96RocPol-9
96Top-51
96Ult-190
96UltGolM-190
97Cir-164
97CirRav-164
97PacPriGotD-GD134

Holmes, Ducky
11SpoLifCW-174
12ImpTobC-60

Holmes, Michael
95RocCubTI-NNO
96RocCubTI-11

Holmes, Stan
83VisOakF-10
85TolMudHT-22
86OrlTwiP-8
87MidAngP-17
88EdmTraC-14
88EdmTraP-571
89EdmTraC-11
89EdmTraP-555

Holmes, Tammy
96ColSilB-14

Holmes, Tim
88WatPirP-6

Holmes, Tommy
39ExhSal-28A
39ExhSal-28B
46SpoExcW-5-10
47HomBon-21
49Bow-72
49EurSta-13
49Lea-133
50AmeNut&CCP-8
50Bow-110
50JJKCopP-6
51TopRedB-52A
51TopRedB-52B
52Top-289
53ExhCan-18
76TayBow4-8
79DiaGre-215
83TCMPla1942-43
83TCMPla1945-39
86BraGreT-7
90DodTar-353

Holmes, William
04FanCraAL-24

Holmquist, Doug
83NasSouTI-8
85ColCliT-25

Holsman, Rich (Richard)
87SpoIndP-6
88RivRedWCLC-211
88RivRedWP-1427
89TexLeaAGS-12
89WicChaR-4
89WicChaR-14
89WicStaR-20
89WicUpdR-20
89WicWraR-17
90WicWraRD-10
91HarSenLD-257
91HarSenP-619
91LinDriAA-257

Holt, Chris
92AubAstC-1
92AubAstF-1350
92ClaDraP-50
92FroRowDP-33
93Bow-264
93MidLeaAGF-47
93QuaCitRBC-1
93QuaCitRBF-94
93StaCluM-75
94ExcFS7-201
94JacGenF-213
95Exc-204
95JacGenTI-4
95TusTorTI-11
96Bow-315
96TusTorB-13
97Bow-120
97BowInt-120
97Cir-263
97CirRav-263
97ColCho-351
97DonLim-104
97DonLimLE-104
97Fle-628
97FleTif-628
97PinCer-132
97PinCerMBlu-132
97PinCerMG-132
97PinCerMR-132
97PinCerR-132
97PinTotCPB-132
97PinTotCPG-132
97PinTotCPR-132
97Sco-487
97ScoHobR-487
97ScoResC-487
97ScoShoS-487
97ScoShoSAP-487
97Ult-457
97UltGolME-457
97UltPlaME-457

Holt, Darren
90VisOakCLC-86

Holt, Dave
79ElmPioRST-14
86FloStaLAP-24
86WinHavRSP-10
87NewBriRSP-18
89WinHavRSS-29
90WinHavRSS-26
91ElmPioC-27
91ElmPioP-3287
92ElmPioC-24
93UtiBluSC-25
93UtiBluSF-3548
94UtiBluSC-28
94UtiBluSF-3836

Holt, Gene
44CenFlo-11

Holt, Goldie
49EurSta-162

Holt, Jim
71MLBOffS-463
71OPC-7
71Top-7
72Top-588
73A'sPos-39
73OPC-259
73Top-259
74OPC-122
74Top-122
74TopSta-207
75OPC-607
75Top-607
76OPC-603
76SSP-498
76Top-603
76TucTorCa-11
76TusTorCr-37
77Top-349
78TwiFri-33

Holt, Kevin
94LetMouF-3886
94LetMouSP-25

Holt, Mike
78CliDodT-14

Holt, Norman
87HawRai-20

Holt, Roger
77ForLauYS-13
79ColCliT-18
80ColCliP-11
80ColCliT-7
92YanWIZ8-84

Holter, Brian
92BurIndC-27
92BurIndF-1650

Holtgrave, Vern
77FriOneYW-30

Holton, Brian
81AlbDukT-10
82AlbDukT-5
83AlbDukT-4
84AlbDukC-168
85AlbDukC-164
86AlbDukP-12
87DodMot-26
87DodPol-27
87Don-598
87DonRoo-54
87TopTra-49T
87TopTraT-49T
88DodMot-26
88DodPol-51
88Don-402
88RedFolSB-35
88Sco-208
88ScoGlo-208
88StaLinD-10
88Top-338
88TopTif-338
89Bow-2
89BowTif-2
89Don-439
89DonTra-20
89Fle-63
89FleGlo-63
89FleUpd-5
89OriFreB-37
89Sco-507A
89Sco-507B
89ScoRoo-59T
89Top-368
89TopTif-368
89TopTra-52T
89TopTraT-52T
89UppDec-72A
89UppDec-72B
90DodTar-354
90Don-635
90Fle-179
90FleCan-179
90Lea-487
90OPC-179
90PubSti-578
90RocRedWGC-32
90Sco-177
90Top-179
90TopTif-179
90UppDec-175
90VenSti-225
91OriCro-200
92AlbDukF-715

Holton, Mark
80UtiBluJT-19

Holtz, Ed
76AppFoxT-28
80KnoBluJT-28
84ChaLooT-5
88SumBraP-420
89SumBraP-1088

Holtz, Gerald
86ChaOriW-14
87ChaO'sW-17
88ChaKniTI-19
88RocRedWGCP-12
89ReaPhiS-14

Holtz, Mike
94BoiHawC-15

94BoiHawF-3350
95Exc-22
95LakElsSTI-16
96Exc-28
96MidAngB-19
96MidAngOHP-14
97Cir-335
97CirRav-335
97Fle-45
97FleTif-45
Holtzclaw, Shawn
90MyrBeaBJP-2788
90ProAaA-100
90SouAtlLAS-33
91DunBluJC-21
91DunBluJP-219
Holtzman, Ken
67CokCapC-14
67CubProPS-6
67DexPre-96
67OPC-185
67Top-185
68Baz-4
68OPC-60
68Top-60
68Top-356A
68Top-356B
68Top-380
68TopVen-60
68TopVen-356
69CubJewT-7
69CubPho-5
69CubTealC-3
69MilBra-116
69Top-288
69TopTeaP-4
70MLBOffS-18
70OPC-505
70Top-505
71MilDud-47
71MLBOffS-33
71OPC-410
71Top-410
72MilBra-149
72Top-670
73OPC-60
73Top-60
74Kel-31
74OPC-180
74Top-180
74TopSta-224
75Hos-16
75HosTwi-16
75OPC-145
75Top-145
76OPC-115
76OriEngCL-2
76SSP-482
76Top-115
77Top-625
77YanBurK-8
78SSP270-6
78Top-387
78YanSSPD-6
79Top-522
80Top-298
86A'sGreT-10
87A'sMot-11
89PacLegI-138
89SweBasG-129
91LinDri-21
91OriCro-201
91SweBasG-40
92ActPacA-57
92YanWIZ7-75
93TedWil-45
93UppDecAH-66
93UppDecS-3
Holub, Edward
88BoiHawP-1612
Holub, Sean
92HelBreF-1720
92HelBreSP-12
Holum, Brett
90AshTouP-2755
Holway, John
90LitSunW-20
Holyfield, Vince
85BenPhiC-11
87SpaPhiP-20
88ReaPhiP-883
89ReaPhiB-14
89ReaPhiP-661
89ReaPhiS-15
90EasLeaAP-EL23
90ReaPhiB-21
90ReaPhiP-1231
90ReaPhiS-14
Holzemer, Mark
88BenBucL-22
89QuaCitAB-9
89QuaCitAGS-21
90MidAngGS-16
92MidAngF-4021
92PalSprAC-27
93Bow-117
93VanCanF-2591
94Don-583
94Top-765
94TopGol-765
94TopSpa-765
94VanCanF-1861
96AngMot-26
96LeaSigEA-80
Homan, John
94OgdRapF-3733
94OgdRapSP-9
Hommel, Brian
95HelBreTI-27
Hommel, Ken
58RedEnq-18
Homstedt, Vic
78WatIndT-12
Honeycutt, Rick
77ShrCapT-8
79Top-612
80Top-307
81Don-46
81OPC-33
81Top-33
81TopTra-772
82Don-494
82Fle-318
82Top-751
83AllGamPI-80
83Don-415
83Fle-568
83RanAffF-40
83Top-557
84AllGamPI-80
84DodPol-40
84Don-494
84Fle-101
84FleSti-66
84Nes792-37
84Nes792-137
84Nes792-222
84OPC-222
84Top-37
84Top-137
84Top-222
84TopSti-84
84TopSti-176
84TopTif-37
84TopTif-137
84TopTif-222
85DodCokP-13
85Don-215
85Fle-372
85Lea-156
85OPC-174
85Top-174
85TopSti-78
85TopTif-174
86DodCokP-13
86DodPol-40
86DodUniOP-8
86Don-372
86Fle-132
86Top-439
86TopTif-439
87ClaGam-93
87DodMot-16
87DodPol-20
87Don-402
87Fle-442
87FleExcS-28
87FleGlo-442
87OPC-167
87Top-753
87TopSti-71
87TopTif-753
88A'sMot-23
88Don-590
88DonBasB-211
88DonTeaBA-590
88Fle-281
88FleGlo-281
88Sco-87
88ScoGlo-87
88Top-641
88TopTif-641
89A'sMot-25
89Bow-187
89BowTif-187
89Don-328
89DonBasB-313
89Fle-11
89FleGlo-11
89Sco-416
89Top-328
89TopTif-328
89UppDec-278
89Woo-28
90A'sMot-13
90Bow-450
90BowTif-450
90DodTar-355
90Don-386
90Fle-11
90FleCan-11
90Lea-372
90OPC-582
90PubSti-307
90Sco-317
90Top-582
90TopBig-42
90TopTif-582
90UppDec-151
91A'sMot-13
91A'sSFE-7
91Don-373
91Fle-11
91Lea-210
91OPC-67
91Sco-539
91StaClu-415
91Stu-105
91Top-67
91TopDesS-67
91TopMic-67
91TopTif-67
91Ult-249
91UppDec-379
92AthMot-13
92Don-269
92Fle-259
92OPC-202
92Sco-456
92StaClu-581
92Top-202
92TopGol-202
92TopGolW-202
92TopMic-202
92UppDec-684
93AthMot-8
93Fle-665
93PacSpa-223
93RanKee-189
93StaCluAt-13
94Don-169
94Fle-265
94Pac-454
94RanAllP-11
94RanMagM-8
94Sco-208
94ScoGolR-208
94StaCluT-242
94StaCluTFDI-242
95AthMot-17
95Pac-428
96CarPol-11
96LeaSigEA-81
97PacPriGotD-GD199
Honeywell, Brent
90AugPirP-2457
Honig, Donald
92MegRut-155
Honma, Mitsuru
96MauStiHWB-3
Honochick, Jim
55Bow-267
Hood, Dennis
86SumBraP-10
87DurBulP-27
88GreBraB-5
89GreBraB-1
89GreBraP-1169
89GreBraS-8
90CMC-291
90ProAAAF-415
90RicBraBC-18
90RicBraC-15
90RicBraP-270
90RicBraTI-12
91CalCanLD-59
91CalCanP-527
91LinDriAAA-59
Hood, Don
74OPC-436
74Top-436
75OPC-516
75Top-516
76OPC-132
76SSP-508
76Top-132
77Top-296
78Top-398
79Top-667
79YanPicA-18
80Top-89
81Fle-547A
81Fle-547B
81OmaRoyT-8
82OmaRoyT-5
83Don-390
83Fle-115
83Roy-11
83Top-443
84Fle-348
84Nes792-743
84Top-743
84TopTif-743
89PacSenL-108
91OriCro-202
92YanWIZ7-76
Hood, Mike
80WauTimT-16
Hood, Randall
91HelBreSP-23
91StoPorC-16
91StoPorP-3045
92SarWhiSCB-16
92SarWhiSF-220
93SarWhiSC-14
93SarWhiSF-1383
94BirBarC-13
94BirBarF-632
Hood, Scott
82DurBulT-3
83DurBulT-7
84DurBulT-17
Hood, Wally
90DodTar-983
Hoog, James
88CapCodPPaLP-178
Hoog, Michael
90IdaFalBP-3244
Hook, Chris
90ChaWheB-2
90ChaWheP-2234
91ChaWheC-4
91ChaWheP-2881
92CedRapRC-10
92CedRapRF-1068
93ChaLooF-2359
94ExcFS7-175
94PhoFirF-1516
95FleUpd-194
95GiaMot-18
95SigRoo-27
95SigRooSig-27
96Don-462
96DonPreP-462
96LeaSigEA-82
Hook, Ed
90HagSunDGB-13
Hook, Jay
58RedEnq-19
59RedShiBS-7
60Kah-16
60RedJayP-3
60Top-187
60TopVen-187
61Kah-20
61Top-162
62MetJayP-5
62Top-94
62TopStaI-156
62TopVen-94
63MetJayP-5
63Top-469
64Top-361
64TopVen-361
82MetGal62-23
91MetWIZ-188
Hook, Mike
88AshTouP-1073
89Ft.LauYS-9
90MidLeaASGS-35
90QuaCitAGS-6
91FreKeyC-4
91FreKeyP-2358
92HagSunS-260
Hooker, Buck (W.E.)
09T206-492
Hooker, Kevin
95MarPhiTI-9
96Exc-205
Hooker, Len
91PomBlaBPB-22
Hooks, Alex
35DiaMatCS3T1-77
36GouWidPPR-B13
Hooper, Bob (Robert)
49OlmStu-4
51Bow-33
52Bow-10
52Top-340
53Top-84
54Bow-4
55Bow-271
79DiaGre-344
83TopRep5-340
91TopArc1-84
Hooper, Ed
20W516-27
Hooper, Harry
08AmeCarE-78
09ColChiE-133A
09ColChiE-133B
10E12AmeCDC-19
10SweCapPP-4
11SpoLifM-10
12ColRedB-133A
12ColRedB-133B
12ColTinT-133A
12ColTinT-133B
12T207-84
14CraJacE-35
14TexTomE-54
15CraJacE-35
15SpoNewM-83
16BF2FP-4
16ColE13-79
16SpoNewM-84
19W514-64
20GasAmeMBD-2
20NatCarE-45
21E121So1-44
21E121So8-37
21Nei-13
22AmeCarE-29
22E120-21
22W572-44
22W573-62
22W575-58
23W501-47
23WilChoV-65
25Exh-75
40PlaBal-226
76ShaPiz-122
76WhiSoxTAG-3
77GalGloG-172
80PerHaloFP-122
80SSPHOF-122
80WhiSoxGT-11
81ConTSN-15
87ConSer2-35
89HOFStiB-52
91ConTSN-135
92ConTSN-470
93ConTSN-802
93CraJac-14
Hooper, Jeff
87BelMarTI-1
88WauTimGS-16
89WilBilP-639
89WilBilS-10
90WilBilB-10
90WilBilP-1060
90WilBilS-11
Hooper, Mike
90HelBreSP-2
91BelBreC-25
91BelBreP-2097
92SalSpuF-3750
92SarWhiSCB-26
Hooper, Troy
92SalSpuF-3751

Hoosiers, Indianapolis
76ISCHooHA-25
Hooten, Leon
75IntLeaASB-10
75PacCoaLAB-10
75TucTorC-17
75TucTorTI-6
76TucTorCa-12
76TusTorCr-16
77OPC-67
77Top-478
Hooton, Burt
72OPC-61
72Top-61
73OPC-367
73Top-367
74OPC-378
74Top-378
74TopDecE-18
74TopSta-14
75Hos-11A
75Hos-11B
75HosTwi-11
75OPC-176
75Top-176
76OPC-280
76SSP-67
76Top-280
77Top-484
78Kel-42
78SSP270-55
78Top-41
79DodBlu-5
79Hos-49
79OPC-370
79Top-694
80DodPol-46
80OPC-96
80Top-170
81AllGamPI-169
81Dod-6
81DodPol-46
81Don-541
81Fle-113
81FleStiC-61
81LonBeaPT-11
81LonBeaPT-22
81OPC-53
81Top-565
81TopSti-180
81TopSupHT-46
82DodPol-46
82DodUniOV-7
82Don-32
82Fle-8
82FleSta-5
82Kel-15
82OPC-315
82Top-311
82Top-315
82TopSti-53
82TopStiV-53
83DodPol-46
83DodPos-4
83Don-32
83Fle-208
83FleSta-82
83FleSti-115
83OPC-82
83Top-775
84DodPol-46
84Don-459
84Fle-102
84Nes792-15
84OPC-15
84Top-15
84TopTif-15
85Don-104
85Fle-373
85FleUpd-56
85OPC-201
85RanPer-46
85Top-201
85TopMin-201
85TopTif-201
85TopTifT-56T
85TopTra-56T
86Don-300
86Fle-563
86OPC-36
86Top-454
86TopSti-242
86TopTat-18
86TopTif-454
87DodSmoA-13
88DodSmo-19
89DodSmoG-95
89PacLegI-219
89SalDodTI-2
90DodTar-356
90SanAntMGS-2
91SanAntMP-2992
92DodStaTA-20
92TexLon-24
93RanKee-190
93SanAntMF-3021
Hoover, Charles
87OldJudN-253
Hoover, John
85ChaO'sT-22
85Top-397
85TopTif-397
86ChaOriW-15
87ChaO'sW-20
88JacExpB-4
88JacExpP-989
89TulDriTI-11
90CMC-153
90OklCit8C-3
90OklCit8P-427
90ProAAAF-673
91TopDeb90-71
93RanKee-191
Hoover, Sgt. (Dick)
81ColCliP-NNO
Hoover, William
87OldJudN-9
87OldJudN-254
Hope, John
89HigSchPLS-18
91WelPirC-26
91WelPirP-3667
92SalBucC-15
92SalBucF-58
93CarMudF-2049
93CarMudTI-11
94BufBisF-1831
94FleMajLP-15
94Top-491
94TopGol-491
94TopSpa-491
Hopke, Fred
60Lea-91
Hopkins, Dave
83BurRanF-23
83BurRanT-5
Hopkins, Don
75SSP18-12
76TucTorCa-2
76TusTorCr-11
77SanJosMC-13
Hopkins, Gail
70OPC-483
70Top-483
70WhiSoxTI-5
71MLBOffS-416
71OPC-269
71Top-269
72Top-728
73OPC-441
73Top-441
74OPC-652
74Top-652
90DodTar-357
Hopkins, Hoppy (Gordon)
93NegLeaRL2-18
Hopkins, Randy
75ShrCapT-5
76ShrCapT-22
77ColCliT-8
78ColCliT-11
Hopkins, Rick
86WinSpiP-9
87PitCubP-20
Hopp, Dean
91MarPhiC-17
91MarPhiP-3455
92BatCliC-24
92BatCliF-3269
93ClePhiC-15
93ClePhiF-2685
Hopp, Johnny (John)
41CarW75-10
46SpoExcW-6-9
47Exh-100
49Bow-207
49EurSta-163
49Lea-139
50Bow-122
50PirTeal-8
51Bow-146
52Top-214
54Top-193
76GrePlaG-26
79DiaGre-160
82Bow195E-265
83TCMPla1944-24
83TopRep5-214
84TCMPla1-33
89PacLegI-139
90DodTar-358
94TopArc1-193
94TopArc1G-193
Hoppe, Denny
91Cla/Bes-341
91KenTwiC-10
91KenTwiP-2068
92Ft.MyeMCB-21
92Ft.MyeMF-2740
Hoppe, Jim
73TacTwiC-11
Hoppel, Monty
90MidAngGS-NNO
Hopper, Brad
88EugEmeB-9
90BasCitRS-13
91BasCitRC-6
91BasCitRP-1393
Hopper, Clay
52MotCoo-55
53MotCoo-51
Hopper, Jim
47CenFlo-10
Hopper, Lefty
90DodTar-984
Horan, Dave
89SalSpuCLC-128
89SalSpuP-1800
Horgan, Joe
96BurIndB-7
Horincewich, Thomas
92EliTwiC-6
92EliTwiF-3685
93ForMyeMC-11
93ForMyeMF-2663
Horlen, Joel
62Top-479
63Top-332
63WhiSoxJP-6
64Top-584
64WhiSoxTS-13
65OPC-7
65Top-7
65Top-480
66Top-560
66TopRubI-40
66WhiSoxTI-6
67CokCapWS-14
67DexPre-97
67OPC-107
67ProPizC-8
67Top-107
67Top-233
67TopVen-228
68AtlOilPBCC-22
68Baz-11
68Kah-B14
68OPC-8
68OPC-125
68Top-8
68Top-125
68Top-377
68TopActS-1A
68TopActS-8B
68TopActS-14A
68TopVen-8
68TopVen-125
69Kah-B9
69KelPin-7
69MilBra-117
69MLBOffS-30
69MLBPin-9
69Top-328
69TopSta-154
69TopSup-12
69TopTeaP-11
69WhiSoxTI-5
70Kel-23
70MLBOffS-185
70OPC-35
70Top-35
70TopPos-1
70TopSup-20
70WhiSoxTI-6
71OPC-345
71Top-345
71TopCoi-120
72MilBra-150
72Top-685
81TCM60I-318
88ColMetGS-28
89PacLegI-217
89St.LucMS-26
90St.LucMS-29
91LinDriAA-638
91WilBilLD-638
91WilBilP-311
92OmaRoyF-2979
93PhoFirF-1534
94PhoFirF-1537
96PhoFirB-3
Horn, Doc (Herman)
93NegLeaRL2-19
96NegLeaBMKC-2
Horn, Jeff
92EliTwiC-10
92EliTwiF-3682
93ForWayWC-12
93ForWayWF-1971
94ForMyeMC-9
94ForMyeMF-1170
95ForMyeMTI-10
Horn, Keith
95WatIndTI-15
Horn, Larry
75WesPalBES-25
Horn, Sam
86NewBriRSP-13
87IntLeaAT-7
87PawRedSP-52
87PawRedST-14
87SpoRoo2-38
88BlaYNPRWL-58
88ClaBlu-204
88Don-498
88DonTeaBRS-498
88Fle-355
88FleGlo-355
88FleMin-8
88Lea-237
88OPC-377
88Sco-201
88ScoGlo-201
88ScoYouSI-3
88Spo-114
88StaHor-1
88StaHor-2
88StaHor-3
88StaHor-4
88StaHor-5
88StaHor-6
88StaHor-7
88StaHor-8
88StaHor-9
88StaHor-10
88StaHor-11
88StaLinRS-11
88Top-377
88TopBig-252
88TopSti-246
88TopTif-377
88ToyRoo-14
90ClaYel-T28
90PubSti-458
90RocRedWGC-11
90TopBig-307
90TopTra-42T
90TopTraT-42T
90UppDec-796
90VenSti-226
91Don-733
91Fle-477
91Lea-332
91OPC-598
91OriCro-203
91Sco-605
91StaClu-316
91Stu-5
91Top-598
91TopDesS-598
91TopMic-598
91TopTif-598
91UppDec-530
92Bow-177
92Don-278
92Fle-10
92Lea-219
92OPC-422
92Pin-221
92Sco-290
92StaClu-269
92Stu-125
92Top-422
92TopGol-422
92TopGolW-422
92TopMic-422
92Ult-6
92UppDec-338
93ChaKniF-549
93Don-617
93Fle-542
93Pin-128
93Top-109
93TopGol-109
93TopInaM-109
93TopMic-109
94ColCliF-2959
94ColCliP-14
94Pin-170
94PinArtP-170
94PinMusC-170
94Sco-543
94ScoGolR-543
94StaCluT-187
94StaCluTFDI-187
Horn, Terry
91ClaDraP-46
91FroRowDP-24
91HigSchPLS-24
92StaCluD-87
Horn, Tim
89TenTecGE-11
Horn, Walt
79WatA'sT-3
82WesHavAT-29
86TacTigP-8
89TacTigP-1543
93TriAAAGF-51
95EdmTraTI-10
Hornacek, Jay
86BakDodP-14
87VerBeaDP-20
88BakDodCLC-245
89SouBenWSGS-29
90SarWhiSS-12
Hornbeck, Ryan
94EveGiaC-12
94EveGiaF-3647
Horne, Geoff
91MedHatBJSP-25
Horne, Jeffrey
82AleDukT-5
84GreHorT-5
Horne, Lena
91PomBlaBPB-17
Horne, Tyrone
90GatCitPP-3348
90GatCitPSP-12
91SumFlyC-23
91SumFlyP-2348
92MidLeaATI-21
92RocExpC-24
92RocExpF-2127
93ExcFS7-60
93FloStaLAF-50
93WesPalBEC-10
93WesPalBEF-1354
94ClaGolF-190
94HarSenF-2105
95Bes-32
95HarSenTI-19
Horner, Bob
78BraCok-6
79Hos-98
79Top-586
79TopCom-18
80OPC-59
80Top-108
80TopSup-27
81AllGamPI-120
81BraPol-5
81Don-99
81Dra-17
81Fle-244
81FleStiC-99
81Kel-61
81MSAMinD-17
81OPC-355
81PerCreC-6
81Top-355

81TopScr-61
81TopSti-20
81TopSti-145
82BraBurKL-11
82BraPol-5
82Don-173
82Dra-18
82Fle-436
82FleSta-69
82Kel-13
82OPC-145
82Top-145
82TopSti-18
83AllGamPI-122
83BraPol-5
83Don-58
83DonActA-46
83Dra-11
83Fle-138
83FleSta-83
83FleSti-84
83Kel-54
83OPC-50
83Top-50
83TopGloS-12
83TopSti-214
84AllGamPI-31
84BraPol-5
84Don-14
84Don-14A
84Don-535
84DonActAS-10
84Dra-14
84Fle-181
84FunFooP-122
84Nes792-760
84OCoandSI-44
84OPC-239
84SevCoi-W10
84Top-760
84TopGloS-13
84TopRubD-10
84TopSti-30
84TopTif-760
85AllGamPI-120
85BraHos-11
85BraPol-11
85Don-77
85Fle-328
85KASDis-6
85KitCloD-6
85Lea-240
85OPC-262
85ThoMcAD-34
85Top-276
85Top-410
85TopRubD-10
85TopSti-24
85TopTif-276
85TopTif-410
86BraPol-11
86Don-188
86DonHig-22
86Fle-517
86Fle-635
86FleLeaL-19
86FleMin-104
86FleStiC-60
86Lea-121
86OPC-220
86SevCoi-S13
86Spo-66
86Spo-115
86Top-220
86TopGloS-44
86TopSti-34
86TopTat-3
86TopTif-220
87BoaandB-23
87ClaGam-38
87Don-389
87Fle-518
87Fle-632
87FleGlo-518
87FleGlo-632
87FleHotS-23
87FleLeaL-24
87FleStiC-61
87FleStiWBC-S7
87JapPlaB-1
87Lea-136
87OPC-116
87RedFolSB-21
87Spo-73
87Spo-196
87Top-660
87TopMinL-1
87TopSti-41
87TopTif-660
88CarSmo-14
88FleMin-107
88FleUpd-120
88FleUpdG-120
88StaLinCa-8
88TopBig-245
88TopTra-50T
88TopTraT-50T
89Fle-452
89FleGlo-452
89OPC-255
89Sco-68
89Top-510
89TopSti-35
89TopTif-510
89UppDec-125
90HOFStiB-89
90PacLeg-54
92ActPacA-30
93TedWil-47
93UppDecAH-67
94TedWil-149
94UppDecAH-194
94UppDecAH1-194

Horner, William F.
87OldJudN-255

Hornsby, Dave
84EveGiaC-11
85EveGialC-4
86CliGiaP-10

Hornsby, Mascot
96TulDriTI-12

Hornsby, Rogers
16ColE13-80
17HolBreD-47
19W514-56
20NatCarE-46
21E121So1-45
21E121So8-38
21Exh-78
21Nei-81
21OxfConE-9
22AmeCarE-30
22E120-232
22W572-45
22W573-63
22W575-59
22WilPatV-21
23W501-115
23W503-42
23W515-55
23WilChoV-66
24MrsShePP-3
25Exh-61
26Exh-60
26SpoComoA-21
26SpoNewSM-3
27Exh-19
27YorCarE-13
28Exh-2
28PorandAR-A16
28PorandAR-B16
28W502-13
28W512-9
28W56PlaC-H4
28Yue-13
29ExhFou-5
29PorandAR-42
30ChiEveAP-6
30SchR33-7
31CubTeal-11
31Exh-5
31W517-38
32OrbPinUP-34
32USCar-11
33Gou-119
33Gou-188
33RitCE-6H
33TatOrb-34
34BatR31-35
34ButPreR-34
34DiaStaR-44
34GouCanV-1
36NatChiFPR-45
36PC7AlbHoF-27
36R31PasP-14
36R31PasP-35
36R31Pre-L7
37OPCBatUV-140
46SpoExcW-6-4
47PM1StaP1-89
48ExhHoF-15
50CalHOFW-39
51R42SmaS-48
61Fle-43
61GolPre-7
61Top-404
63BasMagM-37
63BazA-32
63GadFunC-22
63HalofFB-11
67TopVen-142
68SpoMemAG-13
69Baz-2
69Baz-12
71FleWorS-24
72FleFamF-2
72KelATG-2
72LauGreF-15
73HalofFPP-9
74MetOriEB-5
76JerJonPC-5
76OPC-342
76RowExh-2
76ShaPiz-27
76Top-342
77BobParHoF-26
77GalGloG-92
77ShaPiz-14
79Top-414
80CubGreT-11
80Lau300-17
80LauFamF-39
80PacLeg-20
80PerHaloFP-27
80SSPHOF-27
81ConTSN-19
81DiaStaCD-119
82DiaCla-7
82MetGal62-29
83CarGreT-2
84CubUno-3
84DonCha-20
84GalHaloFRL-27
85Woo-18
86ConSer1-44
87HygAllG-25
87NesDreT-2
88ConSer3-14
89PacLegI-148
89SweBasG-20
90BasWit-97
90HOFStiB-27
90SweBasG-51
91ConTSN-1
91ConTSN-251
91SweBasG-137
91TopArc1-289
91USGamSBL-7C
91USGamSBL-7D
91USGamSBL-7H
91USGamSBL-7S
92BazQua5A-7
92CarMcD-4
92ConTSN-527
92ConTSN-622
92ConTSNCI-20
92CubOldS-13
92St.VinHHS-6
93ActPacA-95
93ActPacA2-29G
93ConMasB-8
93ConTSN-766
93ConTSN-842
93LegFoi-4
93SpeHOFI-4
93TedWil-91
93TedWil-124
93UppDecAH-68
93UppDecAH-132
93UppDecAH-139
93UppDecAH-160
93UppDecAH-162
94ConTSN-1253
94ConTSNB-1253
94UppDecAH-108
94UppDecAH-140
94UppDecAH-162
94UppDecAH1-108
94UppDecAH1-140
94UppDecAH1-162
94UppDecTAE-35
20W516-7

Hornung, Michael
87BucN28-7
87OldJudN-257
88WG1CarG-3

Horowitz, Ed
88CapCodPPaLP-140
89EriOriS-9
90FreKeyTI-21
91CarLeaAP-CAR8
91FreKeyC-13
91FreKeyP-2367
92HagSunS-261

Horowitz, Robert
90QuaCitAGS-4

Horsley, Clinton
88SavCarP-343

Horsman, Vince
87MyrBeaBJP-1440
88DunBluJS-10
89DunBluJS-8
90DunBluJS-11
91KnoBluJP-1763
92AthMot-23
92DonRoo-53
92FleUpd-49
92Lea-487
92Pin-524
92ProFS7-164
92ScoRoo-106T
92StaClu-637
92StaCluECN-637
92TopDeb91-81
92TopTra-53T
92TopTraG-53T
93Don-347
93Fle-295
93Sco-406
93Sel-316
93StaClu-256
93StaCluFDI-256
93StaCluMOP-256
93Top-263
93TopGol-263
93TopInaM-263
93TopMic-263
93Ult-259
94A'sMot-24
94Fle-266
94Top-436
94TopGol-436
94TopSpa-436
96SyrChiTI-14

Horstmann, Gary
75WesPalBES-22

Horta, Nedar
86AshTouP-13
87AshTouP-15
88AshTouP-1057
88AubAstP-1965

Horton, Aaron
96HudValRB-20

Horton, David
86EriCarP-15
87St.PetCP-12

Horton, Eric
94MedHatBJF-3677
94MedHatBJSP-17
95StCatSTI-9
96HagSunB-9

Horton, Ricky
82ArkTraT-3
82LouRedE-11
83LouRedR-23
84Car-12
84Car5x7-12
84FleUpd-53
84TopTra-52T
84TopTraT-52T
85CarTeal-14
85Don-83
85Fle-227
85Lea-253
85OPC-321
85Top-321
85TopTif-321
86CarSchM-9
86CarTeal-18
86Don-138
86Fle-38
86Top-783
86TopTif-783
87CarSmo-5
87Don-234
87Fle-297
87FleGlo-297
87OPC-238
87Top-542
87TopTif-542
88Don-430
88Fle-36
88FleGlo-36
88FleUpd-17
88FleUpdG-17
88OPC-34
88Sco-412
88ScoGlo-412
88ScoRoo-24T
88ScoRooG-24T
88StaLinCa-9
88Top-34
88TopSti-48
88TopTif-34
88TopTra-51T
88TopTraT-51T
88WhiSoxC-11
88WhiSoxK-3
89Bow-338
89BowTif-338
89DodMot-20
89DodPol-18
89Don-582
89Sco-145
89Top-232
89TopTif-232
89UppDec-629
90CarSmo-9
90DodTar-985
90Don-666
90OPC-133
90PubSti-10
90Top-133
90TopTif-133
90TopTVCa-15
90VenSti-227
91ColSprSSLD-83
91LinDriAAA-83
92KinIndC-27
92KinIndF-2492

Horton, Tony
68Kah-B15
69Kah-B10
69MilBra-118
69MLBOffS-41
69MLBPin-10
69NabTeaF-10
70DayDaiNM-21
70MLBOffS-200
71Kel-69
71MLBOffS-376
72MilBra-151
78TCM60I-128
81RedSoxBG2S-85

Horton, Willie
64Top-512
65OPC-206
65Top-206
66Baz-2
66OPC-20
66Top-20
66Top-218
66Top-220
66TopRubI-41
66TopVen-20
66TopVen-218
66TopVen-220
67CokCapA-32
67CokCapAAm-23
67CokCapTi-18
67DexPre-98
67TigDexP-3
67Top-465
67TopVen-195
68Baz-8
68CokCapT-18
68Kah-B16
68TigDetFPB-7
68Top-360
68TopActS-5C
68TopVen-360
69CitMetC-6
69MilBra-119
69MLBOffS-48
69MLBPin-11
69OPC-5
69OPC-163
69OPC-169
69OPC-180
69OPCDec-11

69TigTeal-3
69TigTealC-5
69Top-5
69Top-163
69Top-169
69Top-180
69Top-429
69TopDec-9
69TopDecI-17
69TopFou-15
69TopFou-16
69TopFou-23
69TopSta-173
69TopSup-16
69TopTeaP-1
69TraSta-2
70DayDaiNM-92
70Kel-69
70MLBOffS-207
70OPC-520
70Top-520
71AllBasA-8
71MLBOffS-394
71MLBOffS-560
71OPC-120
71Top-120
71TopCoi-130
72MilBra-152
72OPC-494
72Top-494
72Top-750
73LinPor-71
73OPC-433
73TigJew-9
73Top-433
74Kel-23
74OPC-115
74Top-115
74TopDecE-72
74TopSta-176
75Hos-36
75HosTwi-36
75OPC-66
75Top-66
76CraDis-19
76Hos-26
76HosTwi-26
76OPC-320
76SSP-360
76Top-320
77BurCheD-97
77PepGloD-31
77Top-660
78Top-290
79OPC-252
79Top-239
80OPC-277
80Top-532
81PorBeaT-12
81TigDetN-78
82PorBeaT-14
86TigSpoD-19
88TigDom-8
90PacLeg-83
91LinDri-29
91SweBasG-41
91UppDecS-22
92ActPacA-73
93RanKee-192
93UppDecS-15
93UppDecS-26
Hoscheidt, John
77DayBeaIT-9
Hoscheit, Vern
73OPC-179
73Top-179A
73Top-179B
85MetTCM-2
86MetTCM-39
87MetColP-35
88MetColP-26
89MetColP-33
90MetColP-33
Hosey, Dwayne
88SouBenWSGS-7
89MadMusS-11
90CalLeaACLC-42
90ModA'sC-15
90ModA'sCLC-169
90ModA'sP-2225
91HunStaC-12
91HunStaLD-286
91HunStaP-1809
91LinDriAA-286
92SkyAA F-283
92WicWraF-3667
92WicWraS-635
93WicWraF-2990
94OmaRoyF-1235
94SigRooDP-93
94SigRooDPS-93
94TriAAF-AAA10
95Bow-221
95BowGolF-221
95OmaRoyTI-13
95Sel-209
95SelArtP-209
95StaClu-493
95StaCluMOP-493
95StaCluSTWS-493
96ColCho-473
96ColChoGS-473
96ColChoSS-473
96Don-344
96DonPreP-344
96EmoXL-15
96Fla-20
96Fle-29
96FleRedS-8
96FleTif-29
96Lea-32
96LeaPrePB-32
96LeaPrePG-32
96LeaPrePS-32
96LeaSigA-107
96LeaSigAG-107
96LeaSigAS-107
96Pac-254
96PawRedSDD-12
96Pin-290
96PinFoil-290
96Ult-315
96UltGolM-315
97PacPriGotD-GD22
Hosey, Steve
89EveGiaS-15
89FreStaBS-11
89Sta-193
90Bes-15
90Bow-242
90BowTif-242
90CMC-856
90SanJosGB-1
90SanJosGCLC-28
90SanJosGP-2025
90SanJosGS-12
90SanJosGS-26
90Sco-666
91Bow-629
91Cla/Bes-233
91LinDriAA-307
91ShrCapLD-307
91ShrCapP-1835
92Bow-544
92DonRoo-54
92FleUpd-127
92LeaGolR-BC23
92OPC-618
92PhoFirF-2832
92PhoFirS-383
92ProFS7-346
92SkyAAAF-176
92Top-618
92TopGol-618
92TopGolW-618
92TopMic-618
92UppDec-62
93Bow-360
93Bow-492
93ClaFS7-52
93Don-704
93FleMajLP-A11
93Lea-48
93PhoFirF-1527
93Pin-253
93PinRooTP-8
93PinTea2-21
93Sco-303
93Sel-346
93StaClu-333
93StaCluFDI-333
93StaCluG-15
93StaCluMOP-333
93Top-653
93TopGol-653
93TopInaM-653
93TopMic-653
93TriPla-54
93Ult-132
93UppDec-15
93UppDecGold-15
94ColC-613
94ColChoGS-613
94Don-655
94GiaUSPC-3C
94Spo-155
94StaCluT-7
94StaCluTFDI-7
94Top-547
94TopGol-547
94TopSpa-547
94VanCanF-1874
95MidAngOHP-19
95MidAngTI-17
Hoshino, Senichi
79TCMJapPB-72
Hoskins, Dave
54Top-81
55Top-133
55TopDouH-77
86NegLeaF-81
94TopArc1-81
94TopArc1G-81
Hoskinson, Keith
86LakTigP-7
Hosley, Tim
72OPC-257
72Top-257
76OPC-482
76SSP-313
76Top-482
77SanJosMC-10
78Top-261
79OgdA'sT-2
80OgdA'sT-1
82TacTigT-12
89PacSenL-93
Hosmer, George
87AllandGN-26
Hostetler, Brian
92HelBreF-1718
92HelBreSP-15
93BelBreF-1713
93ExcFS7-187
93StoPorC-16
93StoPorF-747
94StoPorC-11
94StoPorF-1697
Hostetler, Dave
79MemChiT-9
83Don-89
83Fle-569
83OPC-339
83RanAffF-12
83Top-584
83TopSti-312
84Don-159
84Fle-418
84Nes792-62
84OPC-62
84Top-62
84TopTif-62
85IndIndTI-17
85IowCubT-23
87JapPlaB-39
93RanKee-193
Hostetler, Jeff
91FroRowDP-37
91JamExpC-20
91JamExpP-3539
92StaCluD-88
93BurBeeC-11
93BurBeeF-152
94HigDesMC-16
94HigDesMF-2784
Hostetler, Marcus
94MacBraC-8
94MacBraF-2197
95BreBtaTI-51
95Exc-153
96BowBayB-17
Hostetler, Mike
90IBAWorA-44
92DurBulC-17
92DurBulF-1094
92DurBulTI-24
92UppDecML-206
93Bow-30
93ClaGolF-89
93RicBraBB-7
93RicBraF-181
93RicBraRC-13
93RicBraRC-11
94ExcFS7-155
94RicBraF-2842
95BreBtaTI-33
96RicBraB-17
96RicBraRC-11
96RicBraUB-13
Hostetler, Tom
87EveGiaC-16
88CliGiaP-697
88MidLeaAGS-7
89SanJosGB-19
89SanJosGCLC-213
89SanJosGP-444
89SanJosGS-15
90ProAaA-66
90ShrCapP-1439
90ShrCapS-12
91LinDriAA-308
91ShrCapLD-308
91ShrCapP-1816
Hotaling, Pete
87OldJudN-258
88GandBCGCE-20
Hotchkiss, John
83TacTigT-12
84TacTigC-93
86MidAngP-11
87MidAngP-11
Hotchkiss, Thomas
90MedHatBJB-23
92DunBluJC-23
92DunBluJF-1995
93DunBluJC-11
93DunBluJF-1791
93DunBluJFFN-12
Hotz, Todd
90UtiBluSP-19
Houck, Byron Simon
14FatPlaT-17
Houck, Jeff
90ArkRaz-16
Hough, Charlie
72OPC-198
72Top-198
73OPC-610
73Top-610
74OPC-408
74Top-408
75OPC-71
75Top-71
76OPC-174
76SSP-68
76Top-174
77Kel-47
77Top-298
78SSP270-81
78Top-22
79DodBlu-6
79OPC-266
79Top-508
80DodPol-49
80Top-644
81Top-371
82Don-447
82Fle-319
82Top-718
83Don-69
83Fle-570
83FleSti-163
83OPC-343
83RanAffF-49
83Top-412
83Top-479
83TopSti-125
84Don-638
84Fle-419
84FunFooP-114
84Nes792-118
84OPC-118
84RanJarP-49
84Top-118
84TopSti-356
84TopTif-118
85Don-422
85Fle-558
85Lea-108
85OPC-276
85RanPer-49
85SpoIndGC-8
85Top-571
85TopSti-345
85TopTif-571
86Don-342
86Fle-564
86FleStiC-61
86Lea-152
86OPC-275
86RanPer-49
86Top-275
86Top-666
86TopMinL-33
86TopSti-241
86TopTat-9
86TopTif-275
86TopTif-666
87Don-7
87Don-470
87DonAll-49
87DonOpeD-178
87DonSupD-7
87Fle-127
87Fle-641
87FleBasA-21
87FleGlo-127
87FleGlo-641
87FleMin-56
87FleStiC-62
87Lea-7
87OPC-70
87RanMot-3
87RanSmo-1
87RedFolSB-26
87SmoAmeL-12
87SpoTeaP-1
87Top-70
87TopSti-240
87TopTif-70
88Don-99
88DonBasB-256
88Fle-160
88FleAwaW-20
88FleBasA-16
88FleBasM-19
88FleGlo-469
88FleMin-55
88FleStiC-64
88GreBasS-42
88Lea-89
88OPC-121
88PanSti-197
88RanMot-3
88RanSmo-13
88Sco-140
88ScoGlo-140
88Spo-87
88StaLinRa-6
88Top-680
88TopBig-47
88TopCoi-15
88TopMinL-36
88TopRevLL-32
88TopSti-236
88TopTif-680
88TopUKM-36
88TopUKMT-36
89Bow-224
89BowTif-224
89Don-165
89Fle-522
89FleGlo-522
89OPC-345
89PanSti-446
89RanMot-4
89RanSmo-14
89RedFolSB-60
89Sco-295
89Spo-92
89Top-345
89TopBasT-160
89TopSti-245
89TopTif-345
89TopUKM-40
89TVSpoM-119
89UppDec-437
90DodTar-359
90Don-411
90Fle-300
90FleCan-300
90KayB-17
90Lea-390
90OPC-735
90PubSti-412
90RanMot-5
90Sco-202
90Top-735
90TopBig-242
90TopTif-735

90UppDec-314
90VenSti-228
91Bow-355
91Don-146
91Fle-288
91FleUpd-12
91Lea-472
91OPC-495
91Sco-141
91StaClu-579
91Stu-35
91Top-495
91TopDesS-495
91TopMic-495
91TopTif-495
91TopTra-56T
91TopTraT-56T
91UppDec-313
91UppDec-792
91WhiSoxK-49
92Bow-153
92Don-69
92Fle-84
92Lea-39
92OPC-191
92Pin-422
92Sco-302
92StaClu-894
92StaCluNC-894
92Top-191
92TopGol-191
92TopGolW-191
92TopMic-191
92Ult-37
92UppDec-418
92WhiSoxK-49
93Bow-530
93Fin-169
93FinRef-169
93Fle-584
93FleFinE-63
93Lea-384
93MarPub-13
93MarUSPC-8H
93MarUSPC-9S
93OPC-41
93PacSpa-465
93Pin-523
93PinExpOD-1
93RanKee-194
93Sco-223
93SelRoo-117T
93StaClu-610
93StaCluFDI-610
93StaCluI-C2
93StaCluMarI-6
93StaCluMOP-610
93StaCluMOP-MC2
93Stu-205
93Top-520
93TopGol-520
93TopInaM-520
93TopMic-520
93Ult-379
93UppDec-207
93UppDec-518
93UppDecGold-207
93UppDecGold-518
94Bow-618
94ColC-359
94ColChoGS-359
94ColChoSS-359
94Don-269
94ExtBas-263
94Fin-180
94FinRef-180
94Fla-382
94Fle-469
94Lea-188
94OPC-62
94Pac-244
94Pin-288
94PinArtP-288
94PinMusC-288
94ProMag-52
94RanAllP-14
94Sco-452
94ScoGolR-452
94StaClu-245
94StaCluFDI-245
94StaCluGR-245
94StaCluMOP-245
94StaCluT-69
94StaCluTFDI-69
94Top-625
94TopGol-625
94TopSpa-625
94Ult-494
94UppDec-449
94UppDecED-449
95ColCho-311
95ColChoGS-311
95ColChoSS-311
95UppDec-117
95UppDecED-117
95UppDecEDG-117
96SanBerSB-2

Hough, Stan
79JacMetT-22A
79TidTidT-16
83DayBeaAT-2
85TucTorC-62
86OscAstP-12
88TulDriTI-11
89OklCit8C-24
89OklCit8P-1521
90CMC-173
90OklCit8C-23
90OklCit8P-450
91LinDriAAA-325
91OklCit8LD-325
91OklCit8P-195

Houk, Ralph
52Top-200
53Dor-106
60Top-465
61Top-133
61Yan61RL-26
61YanJayP-5
62Top-88
62TopVen-88
62YanJayP-7
63Top-382
63YanJayP-4
67Top-468
68OPC-47
68Top-47
68TopVen-47
69Top-447A
69Top-447B
70OPC-273
70Top-273
71OPC-146
71Top-146
71YanCliDP-7
72Top-533
73NewYorN-2
73OPC-116
73SyrChiTI-10
73Top-116A
73Top-116B
74OPC-578
74Top-578
75OPC-18
75Top-18
76OPC-361
76SSP-352
76Top-361
77Top-621
78TigBurK-1
78Top-684
81TCM60I-455
81TCM60I-481
81Top-662
82Don-282
83Top-786
83TopRep5-200
84Nes792-381
84Top-381
84TopTif-381
85Top-11
85TopTif-11
87Yan196T-9
89SweBasG-42
90SweBasG-131
91LinDri-25
91RinPos1Y1-10
91SweBasG-42
91TopArc1-282

Houk, Tom
91Cla/Bes-351
91KenTwiC-26
91KenTwiP-2082
92VisOakC-12
92VisOakF-1021
93NasXprF-408
96OgdRapTI-5

Houle, Rejean
72Dia-76
82MonNew-7

Houp, Scott
85OscAstTI-24

House, Brian
86WinSpiP-10
87PitCubP-7
88EasLeaAP-27
88PitCubP-1361
89IowCubC-17
89IowCubP-1700
90CMC-164
90OklCit8C-14
90OklCit8P-440
90ProAAAF-686

House, Gary
77NewCoPT-18

House, H. Frank
52Top-146
54Top-163
55Top-87
55TopDouH-13
56Top-32
56TopPin-37
57Top-223
58A'sJayP-5
58Top-318
59TigGraASP-10
59Top-313
60Top-372
79TCM50-214
83TopRep5-146
94TopArc1-163
94TopArc1G-163

House, Howard
92Bow-581

House, Mike
89EliTwiS-12
89Sta-149
90VisOakCLC-73
90VisOakP-2167

House, Mitch
91WelPirC-7
91WelPirP-3578
92LetMouSP-16
93WelPirC-1
93WelPirF-3365
94AugGreC-5
94AugGreF-3016
94Cla-181
94ClaTriF-T64

House, Pat
77FriOneYW-22

House, Thomas R.
69Top-331
72OPC-351
72Top-351
74OPC-164
74Top-164
75OPC-525
75Top-525
76OPC-231
76RedSoxSM-7
76SSP-2
76Top-231
76TopTra-231T
77Top-358
78Top-643
79Top-31
82AmaGolST-25
83LasVegSBHN-11
84LasVegSC-232
86RanPer-NNO
87RanMot-28
87RanSmo-20
88AlaGolAA'TI-8
88RanMot-27
89RanMot-27
89RanSmo-15
90RanMot-27
90RicBra2ATI-10
91RanMot-28
92PacRyaTEI-208
92RanMot-28
93RanKee-195

House, Trini
92BelBreC-14
92BelBreF-420

Householder, Brian
87ChaO'sW-21
88ChaKniTI-1
88SouLeaAJ-33

Householder, Ed
90DodTar-986

Householder, Paul
79NaSouTI-11
80IndIndTI-15
81Don-303
81Fle-217
81IndIndTI-4
81Top-606
82Don-314
82Fle-68
82RedCok-8
82Top-351
83Don-566
83Fle-592
83RedYea-21
83Top-34
84Fle-471
84Nes792-214
84Top-214
84TopSti-61
84TopTif-214
85BrePol-7
86BrePol-7
86Don-414
86Fle-491
86Top-554
86TopTif-554
94BreMilB-231

Houser, Ben
12T207-85

Houser, Brett
78St.PetCT-12

Houser, Chris
87EriCarP-24
88HamRedP-1719

Houser, Kyle
94BenRocF-3601
95AshTouTI-14
96CarLeaA1B-14
96CarLeaA2B-14
96SalAvaB-16
97BenRocC-9

Housey, Joe
81QuaCitCT-20
84MidCubT-7
86GenCubP-12
87PeoChiP-11
89WinSpiS-20
90GenCubP-3054
91GenCubC-28

Housie, Wayne
87LakTigP-1
88GleFalTP-913
89LonTigP-1382
90SalSpuP-2731
91LinDriAA-463
91NewBriRSLD-463
91NewBriRSP-365
92OPC-639
92PawRedSF-935
92PawRedSS-357
92Sco-836
92SkyAAAF-161
92StaClu-352
92Top-639
92TopDeb91-82
92TopGol-639
92TopGolW-639
92TopMic-639
92Ult-314
92UppDec-664
94NewBriRSF-662
97DunDonPPS-10

Housley, Adam
96BelSnaTI-17

Houston, Barry
82WisRapTF-16

Houston, Erv
87EugEmeP-2651

Houston, Ken (K.R.)
81EvaTriT-21
82EvaTriT-24
83WauTimF-1
86OscAstP-13
87OscAstP-24

Houston, Kevin
78DayBeaAT-11
82BufBisT-10

Houston, Maceo
91HigSchPLS-29
91HunCubC-13
91HunCubP-3347
92HunCubC-9
92HunCubF-3162

Houston, Mel
86WesPalBEP-20
87WesPalBEP-670
88IndIndC-23
88IndIndP-507
89JacExpB-3
89JacExpP-170
90CMC-70
90IndIndC-20
90IndIndP-295
90ProAAAF-578
91IndIndLD-196
91IndIndP-469
91LinDriAAA-196

Houston, Pete
88RenSilSCLC-289

Houston, Tyler
89HigSchPLS-5
89IdaFalBP-2021
90Bes-16
90Bes-324
90Bow-14
90BowTif-14
90CMC-827
90OPC-564
90ProAaA-104
90Sco-677
90SumBraB-1
90SumBraP-2436
90Top-564
90TopTif-564
91Bow-581
91Cla/Bes-267
91MacBraC-16
91MacBraP-869
91SouAtlLAGP-SAL32
92ClaFS7-91
92DurBulC-16
92DurBulF-1104
92DurBulTI-19
92UppDecML-151
93ClaFS7-208
93GreBraF-352
94ClaGolF-87
94RicBraF-2948
94StaCluT-45
94StaCluTFDI-45
94UppDecML-88
95RicBraRC-5
95RicBraTI-6
96PinAfi-192
96PinAfiAP-192
96Sum-194
96SumAbo&B-194
96SumArtP-194
96SumFoi-194
97DonRatR-12
97Fle-277
97FleTif-277
97Lea-312
97LeaFraM-312
97LeaFraMDC-312
97PacPriGotD-GD119
97Sco-259
97ScoPreS-259
97ScoShoS-259
97ScoShoSAP-259
97Ult-165
97UltGolME-165
97UltPlaME-165

Houtteman, Art
50Bow-42
51Bow-45
52Top-238
53BowC-4
53TigGle-16
54Bow-20
54DanDee-12
55Bow-144
55IndCarBL-4
55IndGolS-6
56Top-281
57Top-385
79TCM50-242
81TigDetN-46
83TopRep5-238
91OriCro-204

Hovey, James
92BenRocC-14
92BenRocF-1471
93CenValRC-13
93CenValRF-2889

Hovley, Steve
69PilPos-20
70BreMcD-12

70BreMil-9
70MLBOffS-273
70OPC-514
70Top-514
71MLBOffS-515
71OPC-109
71Top-109
72Top-683
73OPC-282
73Top-282
83Pil69G-9
94BreMilB-317
Howard, Bob
63BasMagM-38
Howard, Brent
89CalLeaA-52
90CalLeaACLC-35
Howard, Bruce
64Top-107
64TopVen-107
65OPC-41
65Top-41
66Top-281
66TopVen-281
67OPC-159
67Top-159
68Top-293
68TopVen-293
69Top-226
91OriCro-205
Howard, Chris
94BenRocF-3587
Howard, Chris (Christian)
87PriWilYP-11
88CarLeaAS-9
88PriWilYS-12
89Ft.LauYS-10
80Sta 78
89WauTimGS-27
90AlbYanP-1033
90Bes-239
90WilBilB-11
90WilBilP-1061
90WilBilS-12
91BirBarLD-62
91BirBarP-1450
91CalCanLD-60
91CalCanP-519
91LinDriAA-62
91LinDriAAA-60
92Bow-309
92CalCanF-3735
92CalCanS-61
92SkyAAAF-283
92TopDeb91-83
92VanCanF-2717
92VanCanS-638
93CalCanF-1170
93NasSouF-568
94CalCanF-793
94FleUpd-12
94PawRedSDD-9
94PawRedSF-944
94Top-686
94TopGol-686
94TopSpa-686
94TopTra-68T
94TriAAF-AAA1
95Don-261
95DonPreP-261
95Fle-33
95Pac-39
95TacRaiTI-9
95Top-177
95Ult-11
95UltGolM-11
96LeaSigEA-83
96NorTidB-18
97BenRocC-10
Howard, Dave (David)
87Ft.MyeRP-32
88AppFoxP-145
89BasCitRS-9
89PriPirS-10
90MemChiB-5
90MemChiP-1015
90MemChiS-11
91Bow-295
91FleUpd-27
91Lea-325
91ScoRoo-83T
92Bow-307
92Don-567
92Fle-160
92Lea-4
92OPC-641
92Pin-86
92RoyPol-11
92Sco-704
92Sco100RS-2
92ScoProP-25
92StaClu-245
92Top-641
92TopDeb91-84
92TopGol-641
92TopGolW-641
92TopMic-641
92TriPla-201
92Ult-71
92UppDec-216
93Fle-619
93PacSpa-136
93Sco-645
93Top-519
93TopGol-519
93TopInaM-519
93TopMic-519
94Pac-288
94Sco-206
94ScoGolR-206
95Sco-206
95ScoGolR-206
95ScoPlaTS-206
95TamYanYI-30
96Fle-130
96FleTif-130
96RoyPol-12
96StaClu-353
96StaCluMOP-353
97Pac-102
97PacLigB-102
97PacSil-102
97RoyPol-10
Howard, Del (George Elmer)
06FanCraNL-21
09ColChiE-134
09RamT20-56
09T206-159
10RedCroT-31
10RedCroT-201
11SpoLifCW-175
12ColRedB-134
12ColTinT-134
Howard, Dennis
80UtiBluJT-20
82KnoBluJT-4
83SyrChiT-8
84SyrChiT-4
85SyrChiT-9
86SyrChiP-13
Howard, Doug
74TacTwiC-18
75TulOil7-13
77OPC-112
88SalLakCTTI-19
Howard, Elston
47Exh-101
47PM1StaP1-90
47StaPinP2-17
53Dor-139
55Bow-68
55DonWin-26
56Top-208
57Top-82
57YanJayP-4
58Top-275
59Top-395
60Top-65
60TopVen-65
60YanJayP-4
61Pos-2A
61Pos-2B
61Top-495
61TopStaI-194
61Yan61RL-4
61YanJayP-6
62Jel-8
62Pos-8
62PosCan-8
62SalPlaC-95
62ShiPlaC-95
62Top-51
62Top-400
62Top-473
62TopBuc-37
62TopStaI-86
62TopVen-51
62YanJayP-8
63Jel-18
63Kah-15
63Pos-18
63SalMetC-45
63Top-60
63Top-306
63YanJayP-5
64Baz-29
64ChatheY-12
64Top-100
64TopCoi-23
64TopCoi-135
64TopGia-21
64TopSta-72
64TopStaU-33
64TopVen-100
64WheSta-21
64YanJayP-5
64YanReqKP-8
65Baz-29
65ChaTheY-10
65OPC-1
65Top-1
65Top-450
66Top-405
66YanTeal-4
67AshOil-2
67CokCapA-25
67CokCapAAm-29
67CokCapYM-V9
67DexPre-99
67OPC-25
67Top-25
67TopVen-255
68CokCapRS-18
68OPC-167
68Top-167
68TopVen-167
73OPC-116
73Top-116A
73Top-116B
74SyrChiTI-11
75OPC-201
75SyrChiTI-6
75Top-201
76SSP-619
78TCM60I-236
79DiaGre-24
79TCM50-271
81RedSoxBG2S-86
81TCM60I-474
82K-M-3
84OCoandSI-109
85GeoSteM-4
86SpoDecG-49
87SpoCubG-3
87Yan196T-5
88PacLegI-19A
88PacLegI-19B
90RinPosYMP-4
91RinPos1Y2-12
92YanWIZ6-56
92YanWIZA-31
94TedWil-59
94TedWilM-M26
94TopArc1-253
94TopArc1G-253
Howard, Ernest E.
09T206-493
Howard, Frank
47Exh-102
60DarFar-17
60DodJayP-7
60DodTeal-9
60DodUniO-9
60Top-132
60TopVen-132
61DodJayP-4
61DodMor-3
61DodUniO-10
61Top-280
61TopMagR-34
61TopStaI-27
62Baz-15
62DodBelB-25
62DodJayP-5
62Top-175
62TopBuc-38
62TopStaI-135
62TopVen-175
63DodJayP-7
63ExhStaB-31
63Top-123
64DodHea-5
64Top-139
64Top-371
64TopCoi-61
64TopGia-24
64TopSta-83
64TopStaU-34
64TopTatI-42
64TopVen-139
65OPC-40
65Top-40
65TopTraI-49
66Baz-3
66SenTeal-8
66Top-515
66TopRubI-42
67Baz-3
67CokCapAAm-20
67CokCapS-6
67DexPre-100
67OPCPapI-7
67SenTeal-6
67Top-255
67TopGiaSU-15
67TopPos-7
67TopTesF-7
67TopVen-201
68Baz-7
68OPC-6
68SenTeal-6
68Top-6
68Top-320
68TopActS-11C
68TopGamI-21
68TopPla-4
68TopPos-3
68TopVen-320
69CitMetC-10
69MilBra-120
69MLBOffS-105
69MLBPin-12
69OPC-3
69OPC-5
69OPC-170
69OPCDec-12
69SenTeal-9
69SenTeal8-12
69Top-3
69Top-5
69Top-170
69TopDec-16
69TopDecI-18
69TopFou-20
69TopSta-238
69TopSup-30
69TopTeaP-23
69TraSta-29
70DayDaiNM-36
70Kel-6
70MilBra-10
70MLBOffS-283
70OPC-66
70SenPolY-5
70Top-66
70Top-550
70TopPos-22
70TopSup-16
70TraSta-12B
71AllBasA-9
71BazNumT-20
71BazUnn-20
71Kel-14
71MilDud-9
71MLBOffS-542
71MLBOffS-561
71OPC-65
71OPC-620
71SenPolP-6
71SenTealW-13
71Top-63
71Top-65
71Top-620
71TopCoi-22
71TopGreM-48
71TopSup-17
71TopTat-64
71TopTat-65
72MilBra-153
72OPC-350
72Top-350
72TopCloT-17
73OPC-560
73Top-560
76SpoIndC-13
78TCM60I-220
78TigDeaCS-7
81Top-685
82MetPhoA-28
83MLBPin-9
83TopTra-47T
84Nes792-621
84OCoandSI-195
84Top-621
84TopTif-621
85BrePol-NNO
85CirK-23
85Woo-19
86BrePol-33
87MarMot-28
88DodSmo-3
88PacLegI-17
90DodTar-360
90HOFStiB-75
93RanKee-18
94TedWil-88
95DodROY-5
96MetKah-14
Howard, Fred
77AppFoxT-11
78KnoKnoST-9
80Top-72
Howard, Ivan Chester
15SpoNewM-84
16ColE13-81
16SpoNewM-85
Howard, Jamie
94ClaGolF-47
Howard, Jim
86KnoBluJP-12
87AlbYanP-3
Howard, Larry
71OPC-102
71Top-102
87AstShowSTh-29
Howard, Matt (Mathew)
88CapCodPPaLP-120
89GreFalDSP-23
90BakDodCLC-253
90CalLeaACLC-14
91FloStaLAP-FSL39
91VerBeaDC-21
91VerBeaDP-782
92ClaFS7-244
92ProFS7-246
92SanAntMF-3983
92SanAntMS-567
92SkyAA F-247
93AlbDukF-1468
94AlbDukF-850
95BowBayTI-22
96ColCliB-16
Howard, Mike
75QuaCitAT-14
Howard, Mike (Michael Frederick)
78CliDodT-15
79JacMetT-14
80VenLeaS-160
81TidTidT-12
82MetPhoA-11
82TidTidT-5
83TidTidT-18
84HawIsIC-135
91MetWIZ-189
Howard, Mike (Michael Stephen)
81PawRedST-2
Howard, Rich
94ButCopKSP-6
Howard, Rob
89AncBucTI-5
Howard, Ron
88BriTigP-1870
89FayGenP-1592
90FayGenP-2413
91LakTigC-19
91LakTigP-272
92LakTigC-6
92LakTigF-2286
Howard, Steve
83IdaFalAT-27
85ModA'sC-16
86ModA'sC-10
86ModA'sP-13
87HunStaTI-13
88HunStaTI-8
88SouLeaAJ-3
89TacTigC-21

89TacTigP-1552
90CMC-594
90ProAAAF-155
90TacTigC-17
90TacTigP-108
90TopTra-43T
90TopTraT-43T
91Sco-364
91TopDeb90-72
91UppDec-277
92RicBraS-426

Howard, Thomas
86SpoIndC-171
87TexLeaAF-18
87WicPilRD-13
88BlaYNPRWL-88
88LasVegSC-11
88LasVegSP-239
89BlaYNPRWL-126
89LasVegSC-15
89LasVegSP-8
89UppDec-726
90Bow-212
90BowTif-212
90FleUpd-56
90LasVegSP-135
90ProAAAF-23
91Bow-644
91Don-746
91Fle-532
91LasVegSP-248
91PadMag-3
91PadSmo-14
91Sco-335
91Sco100RS-9
91StaClu-403
91TopDeb90-73
91Ult-305
91UppDecFE-39F
92Don-266
92Fle-607
92FleUpd-15
92IndFanC-12
92Lea-84
92Lea-456
92OPC-539
92Sco-293
92StaClu-401
92Top-539
92TopGol-539
92TopGolW-539
92TopMic-539
92Ult-279
92Ult-348
92UppDec-416
93Don-257
93Fle-215
93IndWUA-12
93OPC-139
93Pin-399
93Sco-426
93StaClu-515
93StaCluFDI-515
93StaCluMOP-515
93Top-113
93TopGol-113
93TopInaM-113
93TopMic-113
93Ult-185
93UppDec-299
93UppDecGold-299
94Don-164
94Fle-411
94RedKah-15
94Sco-501
94ScoGolR-501
94StaClu-496
94StaCluFDI-496
94StaCluGR-496
94StaCluMOP-496
94Top-246
94TopGol-246
94TopSpa-246
94Ult-473
95Don-100
95DonPreP-100
95ElmPioTI-12
95ElmPioUTI-12
95Fle-437
95RedKah-11
95Sco-391
95ScoGolR-391
95ScoPlaTS-391
95StaClu-280
95StaCluMOP-280
95StaCluSTDW-RE280
95StaCluSTWS-280
95Top-381
96ColCho-109
96ColChoGS-109
96ColChoSS-109
96Don-245
96DonPreP-245
96Fle-343
96FleTif-343
96LeaSigA-108
96LeaSigAG-108
96LeaSigAS-108
96Pac-36
96StaClu-330
96StaCluMOP-330
96Top-283
96Ult-461
96UltGolM-461
96UppDec-49
97Cir-157
97CirRav-157
97ColCho-84
97Fle-295
97Fle-596
97FleTif-295
97FleTif-596
97Pac-270
97PacLigB-270
97PacSil-270
97Top-231

Howard, Tim
89PitMetS-10
90ColMetGS-11
90ColMetPPI-6
90SouAtlLAS-34
91Bow-538
91Cla/Bes-232
91St.LucMC-23
91St.LucMP-720
92BinMetF-527
92BinMetS-59
92SkyAA F-25
92UppDecML-218
93NorTidF-2582
95NasSouTI-6
95PawRedSDD-15
95PawRedTI-11

Howard, Wilbur
74OPC-606
74Top-606
75OPC-563
75Top-563
76OPC-97
76SSP-65
76Top-97
77Top-248
78AstBurK-20
78Top-534
79ChaChaT-17
79Top-642
94BreMilB-318

Howarth, Jim
73OPC-459
73Top-459
74OPC-404
74Top-404

Howatt, Jeff
95PitMetTI-46

Howe, Art
76SSP-585
78AstBurK-16
78Top-13
79AstTeal-7
79OPC-165
79Top-327
80OPC-287
80Top-554
81CokTeaS-64
81Don-258
81Fle-51
81OPC-129
81Top-129
81TopScr-99
81TopSti-170
81TopSupHT-99
82AstAstI-4
82Don-92
82Fle-218
82FleSta-48
82Kel-34
82OPC-248
82Top-66
82Top-453
82TopSti-43
83Don-396
83Fle-450
83FleSta-84
83FleSti-211
83OPC-372
83Top-639
83TopSti-236
84Car-13
84Car5x7-13
84Fle-227
84FleUpd-54
84Nes792-679
84Top-679
84TopTif-679
84TopTra-53T
84TopTraT-53T
85Fle-228
85RanPer-NNO
85Top-204
85TopTif-204
86RanLit-3
86RanPer-NNO
87RanMot-28
87RanSmo-25
88RanMot-27
89AstLenH-25
89AstMot-1
89AstSmo-19
89TopTra-53T
89TopTraT-53T
90AstLenH-16
90AstMot-1
90OPC-579
90Top-579
90TopTif-579
91AstMot-1
91OPC-51
91Top-51
91TopDesS-51
91TopMic-51
91TopTif-51
92AstMot-1
92OPC-729
92Top-729
92TopGol-729
92TopGolW-729
92TopMic-729
93AstMot-1
93RanKee-196
93Top-506
93TopGol-506
93TopInaM-506
93TopMic-506
96A'sMot-1

Howe, Gordie
83TigAlKS-13

Howe, Greg
83VisOakF-21
85TolMudHT-23

Howe, Steve
81DodPol-57
81Don-511
81Fle-136
81LonBeaPT-15
81OPC-159
81Top-693
81TopSupHT-47
82DodPol-57
82DodPos-4
82DodUniOV-8
82Don-158
82Fle-9
82OPC-14
82Top-14
83DodPol-57
83DodPos-5
83Don-630
83Fle-209
83FleSta-85
83FleSti-119
83OPC-170
83Top-170
84Fle-103
84Nes792-425
84OPC-196
84Top-425
84TopTif-425
85DodCokP-14
85DomLeaS-27
86SanJosBP-10
87DodSmoA-14
88Don-593
88Sco-543
88ScoGlo-543
89DodSmoG-98
89LonTigP-1357
90DodTar-361
90SalSpuCLC-117
91ColCliLD-105
91ColCliP-5
91ColCliP-592
91FleUpd-43
91Lea-440
91LinDriAAA-105
91StaClu-401
91Stu-93
91UppDecFE-31F
92DodStaTA-21
92Don-106
92Fle-230
92OPC-318
92Pin-507
92Sco-275
92StaClu-827
92StaCluNC-827
92Top-318
92TopGol-318
92TopGolW-318
92TopMic-318
92Ult-408
92UppDec-630
93Don-763
93PacSpa-555
93Pin-559
93RanKee-197
93StaClu-738
93StaCluFDI-738
93StaCluMOP-738
93Ult-594
93UppDec-707
93UppDecGold-707
94ColChoSS-613
94Fle-231
94StaClu-595
94StaCluFDI-595
94StaCluGR-595
94StaCluMOP-595
94StaCluT-193
94StaCluTFDI-193
94Top-637
94TopGol-637
94TopSpa-637
95Baz-91
95ColCho-522
95ColChoGS-522
95ColChoSS-522
95DodROY-9
95Don-381
95DonPreP-381
95Fle-71
95Pac-297
95Pin-435
95PinArtP-435
95PinMusC-435
95Sco-23
95ScoGolR-23
95ScoPlaTS-23
95StaClu-372
95StaCluMOP-372
95StaCluSTWS-372
95StaCluVR-195
95Top-294
95TopCyb-175
96LeaSigA-109
96LeaSigAG-109
96LeaSigAS-109
95StaCluVRMC-195

Howe, Tom
91MisStaB-28
92MisStaB-22

Howell, Dave (David)
89OneYanP-2113
90PriWilCTI-13
91Ft.LauYC-20
91Ft.LauYP-2433
92ArkTraF-1137
92St.PetCC-11

Howell, Dixie (Homer)
48SomandK-19
49EurSta-86
51Bow-252
52Bow-222
52Top-135
53Top-255
83TopRep5-135
90DodTar-362
91TopArc1-255
95TopArcBD-54
95TopArcBD-113

Howell, Dixie (Millard)
56Top-149
57Top-221
58Top-421

Howell, Harry
03BreE10-72
04FanCraAL-25
08RosComP-69
09AmeCarE-52
09AmeCarE-53
09PC7HHB-23
09RamT20-57
09T206-160
09T206-161
10CouT21-31
10NadCarE-25A
10NadCarE-25B
11SpoLifCW-176
11SpoLifM-111
90DodTar-363

Howell, Jack
85EdmTraC-24
86Don-524
86EdmTraP-15
86OPC-127
86Top-127
86TopTif-127
87AngSmo-16
87Don-305
87Fle-83
87FleGlo-83
87OPC-2
87Top-422
87TopTif-422
88AngSmo-3
88Don-333
88DonBasB-59
88Fle-491
88FleGlo-491
88OPC-114
88PanSti-44
88PanSti-187
88Sco-124
88ScoGlo-124
88StaLinAn-9
88Top-381
88Top-631
88TopBig-121
88TopSti-175
88TopTif-381
88TopTif-631
89Bow-48
89BowTif-48
89Don-288
89DonBasB-307
89Fle-480
89FleGlo-480
89OPC-216
89PanSti-293
89RedFolSB-61
89Sco-261
89Top-216
89TopBig-228
89TopSti-181
89TopTif-216
89UppDec-138
90AngSmo-8
90Bow-296
90BowTif-296
90Don-254
90DonBesA-45
90Fle-135
90FleCan-135
90Lea-327
90OPC-547
90PubSti-371
90Sco-206
90Top-547
90TopBig-34
90TopTif-547
90UppDec-19
90VenSti-229
91AngSmo-11
91Don-247
91OPC-57
91PanFreS-182
91Sco-842
91StaClu-198
91Top-57
91TopDesS-57
91TopMic-57

91TopTif-57
91Ult-47
91UppDec-213
92Don-646
92OPC-769
92PanSti-234
92Sco-706
92Top-769
92TopGol-769
92TopGolW-769
92TopMic-769
92UppDec-419
93GolCar-1
96AngMot-19
96LeaSigEA-84
97PacPriGotD-GD6

Howell, Jay
79IndIndTI-24
80IndIndTI-11
82IowCubT-16
82Top-51
83Don-587
84Fle-128
84Nes792-239
84Top-239
84TopTif-239
85A'sMot-18
85Don-103
85DonHig-18
85Fle-131
85FleUpd-57
85Lea-244
85Top-559
85TopTif-559
85TopTifT-57T
85TopTra-57T
86A'sMot-18
86Don-223
86DonAll-57
86Fle-421
86FleMin-89
86FleStiC-62
86Lea-100
86OPC-115
86SevCoi-W15
86Spo-192
86Top-115
86TopSti-175
86TopSup-34
86TopTat-11
86TopTif-115
87A'sMot-25
87A'sSmoC-6
87Don-503
87Fle-395
87FleGlo-395
87FleStiC-63
87OPC-391
87RedFolSB-89
87Top-391
87TopTif-391
88DodMot-16
88DodPol-50
88Don-55
88DonAll-11
88Fle-282
88FleGlo-282
88FleUpd-95
88FleUpdG-95
88OPC-91
88Sco-522
88ScoGlo-522
88ScoRoo-35T
88ScoRooG-35T
88Spo-86
88Top-690
88TopSti-166
88TopTif-690
88TopTra-52T
88TopTraT-52T
89Bow-335
89BowTif-335
89CarNewE-8
89DodMot-16
89DodPol-26
89DodSmoG-89
89DodStaSV-9
89Don-610
89DonBasB-36
89Fle-64
89FleGlo-64
89OPC-212
89PanSti-22
89PanSti-98
89Sco-378
89Top-425
89TopBig-79
89TopSti-61
89TopTif-425
89UppDec-610
89Woo-30
90Bow-83
90BowTif-83
90DodMot-15
90DodPol-50
90DodTar-364
90Don-203
90DonBesN-66
90Fle-400
90FleCan-400
90K-M-13
90Lea-42
90OPC-40
90PanSti-274
90PubSti-11
90RedFolSB-49
90Sco-227
90Spo-78
90Top-40
90TopMinL-59
90TopSti-65
90TopStiB-32
90TopTif-40
90TopTVA-47
90UppDec-508
90VenSti-230
91Bow-603
91DodMot-15
91DodPol-50
91Don-486
91Fle-209
91Lea-98
91OPC-770
91Sco-29
91StaClu-278
91StaCluP-17
91Top-770
91TopDesS-770
91TopMic-770
91TopTif-770
91Ult-163
91UppDec-558
92Bow-408
92DodMot-19
92DodPol-50
92DodSmo-9992
92DodStaTA-28
92Don-395
92Fle-460
92OPC-205
92Pin-444
92Sco-119
92StaClu-457
92Top-205
92TopGol-205
92TopGolW-205
92TopMic-205
92UppDec-511
92YanWIZ8-85
93BraLykP-12
93BraLykS-15
93Don-538
93Fle-450
93FleFinE-2
93OPC-160
93PacSpa-150
93StaCluB-19
93Top-311
93TopGol-311
93TopInaM-311
93TopMic-311
93UppDec-731
93UppDecGold-731
94Fle-360
94Lea-322
94StaCluT-262
94StaCluTFDI-262
94Top-592
94TopGol-592
94TopSpa-592

Howell, Ken
84AlbDukC-165
85DodCokP-15
85DomLeaS-17
85Don-592
85Fle-374
85TopTifT-58T
85TopTra-58T
86DodCokP-14
86DodPol-43
86DodUniOP-9
86Don-275
86Fle-133
86OPC-349
86Top-654
86TopSti-69
86TopTif-654
87DodMot-19
87DodPol-22
87Don-229
87Fle-443
87FleGlo-443
87OPC-187
87PhiTas-37
87Top-477
87TopTif-477
88DodMot-24
88DodPol-43
88Don-130
88Fle-520
88FleGlo-520
88OPC-149
88Sco-406
88ScoGlo-406
88Top-149
88TopTif-149
89Bow-394
89BowTif-394
89DonBasB-184
89FleUpd-108
89PhiTas-11
89Top-93
89TopTif-93
89TopTra-54T
89TopTraT-54T
90Bow-147
90BowTif-147
90DodTar-365
90Don-430
90DonBesN-44
90Fle-561
90FleCan-561
90Lea-316
90OPC-756
90PanSti-314
90PhiTas-15
90PubSti-240
90Top-756
90TopBig-269
90TopSti-116
90TopTif-756
90UppDec-559
90VenSti-231
91Don-204
91Fle-400
91OPC-209
91PanFreS-110
91PanSti-108
91PhiMed-20
91Sco-458
91StaClu-71
91Top-209
91TopDesS-209
91TopMic-209
91TopTif-209
91Ult-265
91UppDec-488
94SanBerSC-7

Howell, Pat
89PitMetS-11
89Sta-159
90ColMetGS-9
90ColMetPPI-3
90SouAtlLAS-35
91Cla/Bes-217
91FloStaLAP-FSL32
91St.LucMC-25
91St.LucMP-724
92DonRoo-55
92FleUpd-103
92ProFS7-284
92SkyAAAF-253
92TidTidF-910
92TidTidS-559
93Don-116
93PorBeaF-2393
93Top-215
93TopGol-215
93TopInaM-215
93TopMic-215
93UppDec-161
93UppDecGold-161
94BinMetF-717
94NorTidF-2932

Howell, Peter
92KanCouCC-28
92KanCouCTI-14
93AlbPolC-25
94AlbPolC-29

Howell, Roy Lee
74SpoIndC-41
76OPC-279
76SSP-265
76Top-279
77Top-608
78BluJayP-9
78Hos-84
78OPC-31
78Top-394
79BluJayBY-12
79Hos-137
79Kel-54
79OPC-45
79Top-101
80OPC-254
80Top-488
81Don-392
81Fle-417
81OPC-40
81Top-581
81TopTra-773
82BrePol-13
82Don-204
82Fle-145
82Top-68
83BrePol-13
83Don-358
83Fle-36
83Top-218
84BreGar-9
84BrePol-13
84Fle-203
84Nes792-687
84Top-687
84TopTif-687
85Don-577
85Top-372
85TopTif-372
86BluJayGT-4
89PacSenL-12
89T/MSenL-48
89TopSenL-88
90EliSenL-6
92BreCarT-10
93RanKee-198
94BreMilB-319

Hower, Dan
94HudValRF-3377
94StaCluDP-57
94StaCluDPFDI-57
95ChaRivTI-20
94HudValRC-7

Howerton, Bill
50Bow-239
51Bow-229
52Bow-119
52Top-167
53MotCoo-16
83TopRep5-167

Howerton, R.J.
96ButCopKB-15

Howerton, Rick
77WatIndT-13

Howerton, Troy
84NewOriT-3

Howes, Jeff
84LitFalMT-12
87HawRai-25

Howes, John
87BurExpP-1088
88WesPalBES-12

Howes, William
87OldJudN-259

Howey, Todd
87ClePhiP-26
88ClePhiS-14

Howie, Mark
85MadMusP-13
85MadMusT-16
86MadMusP-11
87HunStaTI-14
88EasLeaAP-39
88WilBilP-1322
89MidAngGS-19
90LSUTigGM-2
90MidAngGS-7
91LinDriAA-436
91MidAngLD-436
91MidAngOHP-13
91MidAngP-442
92NasSouF-1838
92NasSouS-285
92ProFS7-31
92SkyAA F-292
92SkyAAAF-132

Howitt, Dann
86MedA'sC-67
87ModA'sC-7
87ModA'sP-20
88ModA'sCLC-67
88ModA'sTI-27
89HunStaB-7
90CMC-597
90Fle-644
90FleCan-644
90ProAAAF-147
90TacTigC-20
90TacTigP-100
90TopDeb89-62
90UppDec-747
91Bow-229
91LinDriAAA-538
91TacTigLD-538
91TacTigP-2315
91UppDec-442
92Bow-521
92Don-751
92Sco-861
92Sco100RS-68
92SkyAAAF-240
92TacTigS-537
93CalCanF-1177
93Don-349
94NasSouF-1261
94WhiSoxK-13

Howley, Dan
33Gou-175

Howry, Bob
94EveGiaC-13
94EveGiaF-3648
94SigRooDP-89
94SigRooDPS-89

Howser, Dick
61A'sTeal-8
61AthJayP-10
61Top-416
62Baz-10
62Jel-94
62Pos-94
62PosCan-94
62SalPlaC-31
62ShiPlaC-31
62Top-13
62TopBuc-39
62TopStal-53
62TopVen-13
63AthJayP-5
63BasMagM-39
63Fle-15
63Top-124
64Top-478
65Kah-17
65OPC-92
65Top-92
66IndTeal-6
66Top-567
67Top-411
68Top-467
69MilBra-121
73OPC-116
73Top-116A
73Top-116B
78TCM60I-233
80Top-424
81Fle-84
82Roy-10
83Don-590
83Roy-12
83Top-96
84Nes792-471
84Top-471
84TopTif-471
85Top-334
85TopTif-334
86RoyNatP-10
86Top-199
86TopTif-199
87DonAll-10
87DonP-10
87Top-18

87TopGloA-12
87TopTif-18
90OPC-661
90Top-661
90TopTif-661
92YanWIZ6-57
93RoySta2-4
Howze, Ben
89RocExpLC-13
90RocExpLC-10
91RocExpC-6
91RocExpP-2041
94DayCubC-9
94DayCubF-2346
Hoy, Dummy (William)
73FleWilD-8
87OldJudN-260
88WG1CarG-65
89EdgR.WG-13
94OriofB-44
98CamPepP-36
Hoy, Pete
89ElmPioP-5
90WinHavRSS-11
91LinDriAA-464
91NewBriRSLD-464
91NewBriRSP-349
92Bow-292
92Cla2-T92
92DonRoo-56
92Lea-515
92PawRedSF-917
92Pin-526
92Ult-315
93ForLauRSC-13
93ForLauRSFP-1591
93NewBriRSF-1214
93RedSoxWHP-15
93Sco-230
97DunDonPPS-11
Hoy, Wayne
94St.CatBJC-13
94St.CatBJF-3638
95StCatSTI-7
Hoyer, Brad
88SpoIndP-1937
89WatDiaP-1794
89WatDiaS-14
90WatDiaB-8
90WatDiaP-2374
91LynRedSC-4
91LynRedSP-1193
Hoyt, Dave
82WisRapTF-5
83SprCarF-16
Hoyt, Dewey (LaMarr)
78AppFoxT-14
79IowOakP-9
80IowOakP-8
81Don-160
81Top-164
82Don-117
82Fle-345
82FleSta-190
82Top-428
83Don-632
83Fle-238
83FleSta-86
83FleSti-159
83OPC-226
83Top-591
83Top-618
83Top-705
83TopLeaS-4
83TopSti-16
83TopSti-53
83WhiSoxTV-31
84Don-488
84Fle-63
84FunFooP-91
84Nes792-97
84Nes792-135
84Nes792-405
84NesDreT-9
84OPC-97
84OPC-177
84SevCoi-C23
84Top-97
84Top-135
84Top-405
84TopGloS-32
84TopRubD-26
84TopSti-11
84TopSti-178
84TopSti-192
84TopSti-240
84TopSup-3
84TopTif-97
84TopTif-135
84TopTif-405
84WhiSoxTV-17
85Don-86
85DonHig-23
85Fle-517
85FleUpd-58
85Lea-37
85OPC-312
85PadMot-17
85Top-520
85TopMin-520
85TopRubD-26
85TopTif-520
85TopTifT-59T
85TopTra-59T
86Don-139
86DonAll-9
86DonPop-9
86Fle-325
86FleLimE-25
86FleStiC-63
86Lea-61
86OPC-380
86Spo-59
86Spo-193
86Top-380
86TopGloA-21
86TopSti-113
86TopSti-154
86TopTat-14
86TopTif-380
87Don-434
87Fle-418
87FleGlo-418
87Top-275
87TopTif-275
92PacSea-59
Hoyt, Todd
94AugGreC-30
Hoyt, Waite
20GasAmeMBD-10
20NatCarE-47
21E121So1-46
21E121So8-39
21KoBreWSI-36
21Nei-44
22E120-64
22W572-46
22W573-64
22W575-60
22WilPatV-32
23MapCriV-7
23W501-32
23W503-11
23W515-8
23WilChoV-67
26SpoComoA-22
28StaPlaCE-38
28W502-30
28W513-62
28W56PlaC-H11
28Yue-30
29ExhFou-25
29PorandAR-43
30W554-7
31Exh-24
33ButCanV-28
33Gou-60
33GouCanV-60
34DiaMatCSB-94
34ButPreR-35
35DiaMatCS3T1-78
35GouPuzR-1E
35GouPuzR-3C
35GouPuzR-5C
35GouPuzR-14C
36GouWidPPR-A55
36NatChiFPR-46
36WorWidGV-39
40PlaBal-118
56RedBurB-7
59RedBurBP-5
60Fle-69
61Fle-44
68LauWorS-18
71FleWorS-19
76ShaPiz-114
77GalGloG-117
79DiaGre-32
80PerHaloFP-113
80SSPHOF-113
82DiaCla-28
82OhiHaloF-7
84OCoandSI-111
85FegMurCG-11
86ConSer1-26
87Yan192T-4
89DodSmoG-10
89HOFStiB-71
90DodTar-366
91ConTSN-115
92ConTSN-468
92MegRut-157
92YanWIZH-16
93ConTSN-757
93DiaStaES-137
Hrabar, Shaun
91KanCouCC-1
91KanCouCP-2671
91KanCouCTI-11
91PerHeaF-3
Hrabcsak, Edward
52Par-87
Hrabosky, Al
71OPC-594
71Top-594
73OPC-153
73Top-153
74OPC-108
74Top-108
75OPC-122
75Top-122
76CraDis-20
76Hos-50
76HosTwi-50
76Kel-23
76OPC-205
76OPC-315
76SSP-291
76Top-205
76Top-315
77BurCheD-10
77Car5-12
77CarTeal-11
77MSADis-28
77PepGloD-37
77Top-495
78RCColC-80
78Roy-8
78SSP270-228
78Top-230
78WifBalD-30
79Hos-25
79OPC-19
79Top-45
80OPC-306
80Top-585
81BraPol-39
81Don-550
81Fle-262
81OPC-354
81Top-636
82BraBurKL-12
82BraPol-39
82Don-97
82Fle-438A
82Fle-438B
82Fle-438C
82OPC-393
82Top-393
83Don-475
89PacLegI-115
89PacSenL-179
89T/MSenL-49
89TopSenL-15
91SweBasG-43
91UppDecS-14
92CarMcD-55
Hrbek, Kent
80WisRapTT-18
82Don-557
82Top-766
82TopTra-44T
82TwiPos-16
83AllGamPI-4
83Don-19
83Don-179
83DonActA-49
83Fle-616
83Fle-633
83FleSta-87
83FleSti-135
83Kel-53
83OPC-251
83Top-690
83Top-771
83TopGloS-35
83TopSti-88
83TopSti-313
83TwiTeal-9
83TwiTeal-31
83TwiTeal-33
84AllGamPI-95
84Don-70
84DonActAS-37
84Fle-567
84FunFooP-111
84MinTwiP-16
84Nes792-11
84Nes792-345
84OCoandSI-38
84OPC-345
84SevCoi-C11
84Top-11
84Top-345
84TopRubD-17
84TopSti-305
84TopTif-11
84TopTif-345
84TwiTeal-10
85AllGamPI-5
85Don-70
85DonActA-40
85Dra-16
85Fle-281
85FleLimE-13
85KASDis-7
85KitCloD-7
85Lea-200
85OPC-308
85SevCoi-C11
85ThoMcAD-13
85Top-510
85TopRubD-16
85TopSti-296
85TopSup-41
85TopTif-510
85Twi7-4
85TwiTeal-10
86Don-70
86DonHig-19
86DorChe-6
86Fle-397
86FleLeaL-20
86FleMin-84
86FleSlu-17
86FleStiC-64
86GenMilB-2F
86Lea-67
86OPC-63
86Spo-36
86Top-430
86TopSti-277
86TopTat-17
86TopTif-430
86TruVal-24
86TwiTeal-9
87BoaandB-28
87ClaGam-53
87Don-73
87DonOpeD-228
87Fle-544
87FleExcS-29
87FleGlo-544
87FleLimE-22
87FleMin-57
87FleStiC-64
87KraFoo-25
87Lea-99
87OPC-161
87RedFolSB-49
87Spo-15
87SpoTeaP-17
87StuPan-22
87Top-679
87TopCoi-13
87TopGloS-25
87TopSti-281
87TopTif-679
88ClaRed-192
88Don-320
88DonBasB-102
88Fle-13
88FleBasA-17
88FleGlo-13
88FleGlo-WS9
88FleLeaL-21
88FleMin-35
88FleStiC-44
88FleSup-17
88FleTeaL-14
88FleWorS-9
88Lea-139
88MSAJifPD-10
88OPC-45
88PanSti-136
88Sco-43
88ScoGlo-43
88Spo-95
88StaLinTw-10
88Top-45
88Top-609
88TopBig-84
88TopGloS-8
88TopMinL-22
88TopSti-24
88TopSti-274
88TopTif-45
88TopTif-609
88TopUKM-37
88TopUKMT-37
88TwiMasBD-10
88TwiSmoC-3
88TwiTeal-8
88Woo-30
89Bow-157
89BowTif-157
89CadEllD-30
89ClaLigB-55
89Don-199
89DonBasB-18
89Fle-116
89FleGlo-116
89OPC-265
89PanSti-387
89RedFolSB-62
89Sco-382
89ScoHot1S-14
89Spo-188
89Top-265
89TopBasT-157
89TopBatL-16
89TopBig-209
89TopCoi-42
89TopGloS-7
89TopSti-287
89TopTif-265
89TopUKM-41
89TVSpoM-101
89UppDec-213
90AllBasT-20
90Bow-418
90BowTif-418
90ClaUpd-T23
90Don-81
90DonBesA-65
90DonLeaS-36
90Fle-378
90FleBasM-20
90FleCan-378
90Lea-228
90MLBBasB-97
90OPC-125
90PanSti-112
90PubSti-290
90PubSti-330
90RedFolSB-50
90Sco-381
90Spo-203
90Top-125
90TopAmeA-19
90TopBatL-22
90TopBig-27
90TopCoi-18
90TopHilHM-11
90TopSti-287
90TopTif-125
90UppDec-452
90VenSti-232
90VenSti-233
91BasBesHRK-10
91Bow-321
91Cla2-T15
91ClaGam-118
91DenHol-7
91Don-95
91Fle-614
91Lea-313
91OPC-710
91PanFreS-300
91PanSti-251

91RedFolS-50
91Sco-292
91Sco100S-78
91StaClu-248
91Stu-87
91SunSee-13
91Top-710
91TopCraJ2-24
91TopDesS-710
91TopMic-710
91TopTif-710
91TopTriH-A9
91Ult-189
91UppDec-167
92Bow-445
92ClaGam-94
92DenHol-19
92Don-326
92DonCraJ1-29
92Fle-205
92Hig5-83
92Lea-362
92New-11
92OPC-347
92OPCPre-46
92PanSti-115
92Pin-68
92Sco-530
92Sco100S-98
92ScoProP-17
92StaClu-235
92StaCluD-89
92Stu-205
92Top-347
92TopGol-347
92TopGolW-347
92TopKid-111
92TopMic-347
92TriPla-135
92Ult-92
92UppDec-334
93Bow-677
93DiaMar-53
93Don-283
93DonLonBL-LL7
93Fin-117
93FinRef-117
93Fla-236
93Fle-267
93Lea-76
93MetBak-31
93OPC-150
93PacSpa-171
93PanSti-125
93Pin-27
93Pin-307
93PinHomRC-45
93Sco-98
93Sel-80
93SP-247
93StaClu-525
93StaCluFDI-525
93StaCluMOP-525
93Stu-35
93Top-9
93TopGol-9
93TopInaM-9
93TopMic-9
93TriPla-128
93Ult-231
93UppDec-50
93UppDec-74
93UppDecGold-50
93UppDecGold-74
94ColC-486
94ColChoGS-486
94ColChoSS-486
94DenHol-16
94Don-443
94ExtBas-117
94Fin-261
94FinRef-261
94Fla-75
94Fle-208
94Lea-269
94LeaL-48
94OPC-261
94Pac-355
94PanSti-91
94Pin-206
94PinArtP-206
94PinMusC-206
94ProMag-76
94Sco-65
94ScoGolR-65
94Sel-261
94Spo-100
94StaClu-224
94StaCluFDI-224
94StaCluGR-224
94StaCluMOP-224
94StaCluMOP-ST23
94StaCluST-ST23
94Stu-196
94Top-490
94TopGol-490
94TopSpa-490
94TriPla-253
94Ult-87
94UppDec-98
94UppDecAJ-14
94UppDecAJG-14
94UppDecED-98
95ColChoSE-227
95ColChoSEGS-227
95ColChoSESS-227
95Pac-249
95UppDec-195
95UppDecED-195
95UppDecEDG-195

Hreha, Dan
90ArkRaz-17

Hriniak, Walt
69Top-611
70OPC-392
70Top-392
90WhiSoxC-30
91WhiSoxK-NNO
92WhiSoxK-NNO
93WhiSoxK-30
94WhiSoxK-30
95WhiSoxK-27
95WhiSoxK-31

Hritz, Derrick
93BurIndC-12
93BurIndF-3291
95WatIndTI-16

Hrovat, Dale
75WatRoyT-16
76WatRoyT-11
77HolMilT-15
78SpoIndC-4

Hrusovsky, John
91PriRedC-8
91PriRedP-3507
92ChaWheF-3
92ChaWVWC-3
92ProFS7-221
93CarLeaAGF-41
93ClaGolF-187
93SouAtlLAPI-17
93WinSpiC-9
93WinSpiF-1564
94CanIndF-3116
94ChaLooF-1357
94ExcFS7-176

Hrynko, Larry
80WatIndT-11
81WatIndT-4
82ChaChaT-6
83ChaChaT-3

Hubacek, Doug
57SeaPop-19

Hubbard, Cal
55Bow-315
76ShaPiz-154
80PerHaloFP-154
80SSPHOF-154
89HOFStiB-99
90BasWit-75

Hubbard, Don
78WatIndT-13

Hubbard, Glenn
78BraCok-7
78RicBraT-5
79Top-715
80RicBraT-15
81AllGamPI-102
81BraPol-17
81Don-459
81Fle-260
81OPC-247
81Top-247
81TopSti-149
82BraBurKL-13
82BraPol-17
82Don-436
82Fle-437
82Top-482
82TopSti-23
83AllGamPI-103
83BraPol-17
83Don-184
83Fle-139
83OPC-322
83Top-624
83TopSti-215
84AllGamPI-12
84BraPol-17
84Don-432
84Fle-182
84Nes792-25
84OPC-25
84Top-25
84TopSti-29
84TopTif-25
85AllGamPI-102
85BraHos-12
85BraPol-17
85Don-199
85Fle-329
85Lea-242
85OPC-195
85Top-195
85TopSti-33
85TopTif-195
86BraPol-17
86Don-141
86Fle-518
86Lea-71
86OPC-112
86Top-539
86TopSti-36
86TopTat-4
86TopTif-539
87BraSmo-21
87Don-634
87DonOpeD-48
87Fle-519
87FleGlo-519
87OPC-68
87SpoTeaP-24
87Top-31
87Top-745
87TopTif-31
87TopTif-745
88A'sMot-18
88Don-22
88Don-314
88DonSupD-22
88DonTeaBA-NEW
88Fle-542
88FleGlo-542
88Lea-22
88OPC-325
88PanSti-243
88RedFolSB-36
88Sco-111
88ScoGlo-111
88ScoRoo-58T
88ScoRooG-58T
88StaLinBra-9
88Top-325
88TopBig-200
88TopTif-325
88TopTra-53T
88TopTraT-53T
89A'sMot-19
89Bow-199
89BowTif-199
89Don-568
89Fle-12
89FleGlo-12
89Sco-34
89Top-237
89TopBig-232
89TopTif-237
89UppDec-395
90RicBra2ATI-11
90VenSti-234
91MacBraC-10
91MacBraP-882
92MacBraC-27
92MacBraF-285
92UppDecS-4
93RicBraF-203
93RicBraRC-3
94MacBraC-29
94MacBraF-2224
95RicBraTI-28
96RicBraB-3

Hubbard, Jack
89Ft.LauYS-28

Hubbard, Jeff
89ChaRanS-28
90ChaRanS-30
91LinDriAA-600
91TulDriP-2790
91TulDriTI-13

Hubbard, Joe
90EliTwiS-26

Hubbard, Mark
91OneYanP-4165
92ClaFS7-306
92GreHorC-24
92GreHorF-793
92StaCluD-90
93PriWilCC-15
93PriWilCF-670
94GreBatF-467
95NorNagUTI-38
95TamYanYI-11
96SigRooOJTP-T3
97GreBatC-9

Hubbard, Mike
92GenCubC-15
92GenCubF-1563
93DayCubC-10
93DayCubF-862
93FloStaLAF-31
94Bow-606
94ClaGolF-50
94OrlCubF-1389
95Bow-34
95Exc-164
95IowCubTI-16
96Fle-321
96FleTif-321
06IowCubB 15

Hubbard, Trenidad
86AubAstP-12
87AshTouP-2
88OscAstS-15
89ColMudP-132
89ColMudS-13
91JacGenLD-561
91JacGenP-932
91LinDriAA-561
92TucTorF-496
92TucTorS-610
93ColSprSSF-3094
93ExcFS7-45
93LinVenB-89
94ColSprSSF-744
94TopTra-56T
94TriAAF-AAA28
96ColSprSSTI-18
96Don-64
96DonPreP-64
96FleUpd-U128
96FleUpdTC-U128
96RocPol-10
96StaClu-447
96StaCluMOP-447
96Top-103
96Ult-468
96UltGolM-468

Hubbard, Ty III
83TamTarT-15

Hubbell, Carl
28PorandAR-A17
28PorandAR-B17
30SchR33-22
32GiaSch-1
33Gou-230
33Gou-234
33NatLeaAC-12
33SpoKin-42
34DiaMatCSB-95
34BatR31-5
34DiaStaR-39
34ExhFou-5
34Gou-12
34GouCanV-71
35DiaMatCS2-10
35DiaMatCS3T1-79
35ExhFou-5
35WheBB1-16
36DiaMatCS4-6
36ExhFou-5
36GouWidPPR-C18
36PC7AlbHoF-53
36SandSW-35
36WheBB3-7
36WheBB5-11
37DixLid-4
37DixPre-4
37ExhFou-5
37WheBB14-7
37WheBB6-6
37WheBB8-7
37WheBB9-9
38DixLid-4
38DixLidP-4
38ExhFou-5
38OurNatGPP-16
38WheBB10-5
38WheBB15-6
39ExhSal-29
39PlaBal-53
40PlaBal-87
41DouPlaR-139
41Gou-20
41PlaBal-6
43MPR302-1-15
46SpoExcW-7-4
47PM1StaP1-91
47PM1StaP1-92
48ExhHoF-16
48SweSpoT-8
50CalHOFW-40
51R42SmaS-49
59OklTodML-13
60Fle-4
60NuHi-11
61Fle-45
61GolPre-6
61NuSco-479
67TopVen-172
68LauWorS-34
69EquSpoHoF-BB8
70FleWorS-34
71FleWorS-31
72LauGreF-36
74LauAllG-34
74NewYorNTDiS-10
75SheGrePG-2
76GalBasGHoF-15
76GrePlaG-2
76RowExh-12
76ShaPiz-53
77BobParHoF-27
77GalGloG-88
77GalGloG-208
77GalGloG-240
79DiaGre-35
80GiaGreT-3
80PacLeg-89
80PerHaloFP-53
80SSPHOF-53
82DiaCla-6
83ConMar-43
83DonHOFH-33
83TCMPla1942-34
84DonCha-55
84OCoandSI-130
85FegMurCG-12
86ConSer1-15
86SpoDecG-6
86TCM-4
87HygAllG-26
87NesDreT-10
87SpoRea-31
88ConNatA-11
88ConSer3-15
89HOFStiB-75
90BasWit-95
90HOFStiB-32
90PerGreM-35
91ConTSN-10
91ConTSN-253
92ConTSN-360
92ConTSN-552
92ConTSNCI-12
92ConTSNGI-665
93ActPacA-103
93ActPacA2-37G
93ConTSN-665
93ConTSNP-1105
93LegFoi-5
93UppDecAH-69
93UppDecAH-136
94ConTSN-1105
94ConTSNB-1105
94UppDecTAE-46

Hubbell, Wilbert
20NatCarE-48
21Exh-79
21Nei-96
22E120-199

22W572-47
25Exh-45
90DodTar-987
Hubbs, Dan
93GreFalDSP-21
94SanAntMF-2462
95SanAntMTI-34
Hubbs, Ken
47Exh-103
62CubJayP-8
62Top-461
63Baz-27
63CubJayP-6
63ExhStaB-32
63Jel-174
63Pos-174
63Top-15
63TopStil-19
64Top-550
66Top-447
84CubUno-2
92CubOldS-14
Huber, Aaron
94SouOreAC-12
94SouOreAF-3616
Huber, Clarence
26Exh-45
Huber, Jeff
91ChaRaiC-7
91ChaRaiP-93
92ChaRaiC-10
92ChaRaiF-119
93RanCucQC-17
93RanCucQF-828
94WicWraF-185
Huble, Ian
91WavRedF-5
Huckaby, Ken
91GreFalDSP-17
92ClaFS7-353
92VerBeaDC-27
92VerBeaDF-2878
93FloStaLAF-47
93VerBeaDC-9
93VerBeaDF-2223
94BakDodC-10
94ExcFS7-216
94SanAntMF-2472
Hudak, Joe
88MisStaB-37
90MisStaB-41
91MisStaB-29
Hudek, John
88SouBenWSGS-22
89SarWhiSS-11
89Sta-59
90Bes-296
90BirBarB-19
90BirBarP-1107
90CMC-771
91BirBarLD-63
91BirBarP-1451
91LinDriAA-63
92BirBarS-84
92SkyAA F-40
92VanCanF-2718
92VanCanS-641
93TolMudHF-1650
94AstMot-17
94Bow-34
94ExtBas-276
94Fla-390
94FlaWavotF-B4
94FleAllR-M6
94FleUpd-143
94LeaLimR-57
94ScoRoo-RT104
94ScoRooGR-RT104
94Sel-405
94SP-31
94SPDieC-31
94SpoRooRS-TR1
94TopTra-45T
94UppDec-517
94UppDecED-517
94VenLinU-13
95AstMot-18
95Bow-400
95ColCho-108
95ColChoGS-108
95ColChoSE-42
95ColChoSEGS-42
95ColChoSESS-42
95ColChoSS-108
95Don-170
95DonPreP-170
95DonTopotO-254
95Emo-138
95Fin-9
95FinFlaT-FT4
95FinRef-9
95Fla-147
95Fle-463
95FleAllS-21
95FleRooS-9
95Lea-187
95Pac-189
95PanSti-104
95Pin-149
95PinArtP-149
95PinMusC-149
95Sco-543
95ScoGolR-543
95ScoPlaTS-543
95StaClu-279
95StaCluMOP-279
95StaCluSTWS-279
95StaCluVR-143
95Top-500
95TopCyb-290
95Ult-173
95UltAllR-6
95UltAllRGM-6
95UltGolM-173
95UltSecYS-8
95UltSecYSGM-8
95UppDec-277
95UppDecED-277
95UppDecEDG-277
95UppDecSE-43
95UppDecSEG-43
96AstMot-19
96Fle-410
96FleTif-410
96LeaSigA-110
96LeaSigAG-110
96LeaSigAS-110
96StaClu-406
96StaCluMOP-406
95StaCluVRMC-143
96UppDec-419
97Fle-694
97FleTif-694
97Ult-317
97UltGolME-317
97UltPlaME-317
Hudgens, Dave
79WatIndT-29
83TacTigT-16
84TacTigC-74
93JacGenF-2124
Hudik, Matt
90St.CatBJP-3452
Hudler, Rex
82NasSouTI-14
84ColCliP-13
84ColCliT-8
85ColCliP-14
85ColCliT-18
85Don-469
86RocRedWP-8
87RocRedWT-28
88BlaYNPRWL-152
88ExpPos-10
88FleUpd-101
88FleUpdG-101
88IndIndC-10
88IndIndP-513
89Bow-364
89BowTif-364
89Don-452
89Fle-380
89FleGlo-380
89OPC-346
89Sco-470
89Top-346
89TopBig-248
89TopTif-346
89UppDec-405
90CarSmo-10
90Don-366
90ExpPos-17
90Lea-439
90OPC-647
90PubSti-177
90Sco-287
90Top-647
90TopTif-647
90UppDec-411
90VenSti-235
91Bow-409
91CarPol-10
91Don-599
91FleUpd-116
91Lea-212
91OPC-228
91OriCro-206
91PanFreS-37
91Sco-589
91StaClu-280
91Stu-233
91Top-228
91TopDesS-228
91TopMic-228
91TopTif-228
91UppDec-482
92CarPol-8
92Don-438
92Fle-581
92Lea-25
92OPC-47
92Pin-315
92Pin-589
92Sco-184
92StaClu-851
92StaCluNC-851
92Stu-92
92Top-47
92TopGol-47
92TopGolW-47
92TopMic-47
92TriPla-41
92TriPla-207
92Ult-568
92UppDec-670
92YanWIZ8-86
93Don-96
93Fle-510
93StaClu-113
93StaCluFDI-113
93StaCluMOP-113
94AngLAT-16
94AngMot-20
94FleUpd-17
94ScoRoo-RT56
94ScoRooGR-RT56
94Sel-367
94SpoRoo-141
94SpoRooAP-141
94StaClu-685
94StaCluFDI-685
94StaCluGR-685
94StaCluMOP-685
95AngCHP-10
95AngMot-26
95Fle-226
95Sco-66
95ScoGolR-66
95ScoPlaTS-66
95StaClu-51
95StaCluFDI-51
95StaCluMOP-51
95StaCluSTWS-51
95Ult-269
95UltGolM-269
96AngMot-21
96ColCho-484
96ColChoGS-484
96ColChoSS-484
96LeaSigA-111
96LeaSigAG-111
96LeaSigAS-111
97ColCho-422
97Fle-46
97Fle-557
97FleTif-46
97FleTif-557
97Pac-9
97PacLigB-9
97PacSil-9
97Sco-415
97ScoHobR-415
97ScoResC-415
97ScoShoS-415
97ScoShoSAP-415
97StaClu-358
97StaCluMOP-358
97Top-254
97Ult-344
97UltGolME-344
97UltPlaME-344
97UppDec-454
Hudlin, Willis
29PorandAR-44
33Gou-96
33GouCanV-72
34BatR31-48
34BatR31-103
34DiaStaR-79
35GouPuzR-5B
35GouPuzR-6B
35GouPuzR-11K
35GouPuzR-13B
36GouWidPPR-B14
36NatChiFPR-47
96Bro194F-5
Hudson, Charles
84Don-448
84Fle-36
84Nes792-432
84PhiTas-22
84Top-432
84TopTif-432
85Don-355
85Fle-255
85OPC-379
85PhiTas-9
85PhiTas-20
85Top-379
85TopMin-379
85TopSti-120
85TopTif-379
86Don-622
86Fle-444
86PhiClG-13
86PhiTas-49
86Top-792
86TopTat-13
86TopTif-792
87Don-630
87Fle-176
87FleGlo-176
87FleUpd-46
87FleUpdG-46
87Top-191
87TopTif-191
87TopTra-50T
87TopTraT-50T
88Don-374
88DonReaBY-374
88Fle-210
88FleGlo-210
88Top-639
88TopBig-212
88TopTif-636
89Don-514
89DonTra-50
89OPC-236
89Sco-415
89TigMar-27
89Top-236
89TopBig-88
89TopTif-236
89UppDec-586
90PubSti-474
90UppDec-520
90VenSti-236
92YanWIZ8-87
93RanKee-199
Hudson, Charlie
75SalLakCC-18
76SalLakCGC-21
76TucTorCa-18
83PorBeaT-19
84TopSti-17
85PhiClG-16
86Lea-239
Hudson, Deryk
90RocExpLC-11
90RocExpP-2701
Hudson, Hap (David)
86LouRedTI-3
87LouRedTI-29
88LouRedBP-434
88LouRedBTI-51
89LouRedBC-5
89LouRedBP-1253
89LouRedBTI-38
89TriAAP-AAA12
Hudson, Jack
76WatRoyT-12
Hudson, Jesse James
70OPC-348
70Top-348
91MetWIZ-190
Hudson, Jim
87EugEmeP-2671
89BasCitRS-10
Hudson, Joe
92ElmPioC-18
92ElmPioF-1378
93ClaFS7-102
93LynRedSC-13
93LynRedSF-2514
94SarRedSC-15
94SarRedSF-1946
95TreThuTI-10
96PawRedSDD-13
Hudson, John
39PlaBal-154
40DodTeal-12
40PlaBal-147
41CubTeal-9
90DodTar-367
Hudson, Kevin
89BilMusP-2039
91BilMusSP-26
Hudson, Lance
86MiaMarP-12
88LakTigS-14
90MiaMirIS-10
Hudson, Maryann
87SalSpuP-4
Hudson, Nathaniel
87LonJacN-6
87OldJudN-261A
87OldJudN-261B
Hudson, Rex
74AlbDukTI-7
75AlbDukC-13
Hudson, Robert
79WatIndT-31
81WauTimT-3
83ChaLooT-14
Hudson, Sid
41PlaBal-46
47SenGunBP-5
49Lea-84
50Bow-17
51Bow-169
51TopRedB-44
52Bow-123
52Top-60
53BowBW-29
53RedSoxTI-13
53Top-251
54Bow-194
54Top-93
55Bow-318
68SenTeal81/2-2
76TayBow4-87
79DiaGre-66
83TopRep5-60
91TopArc1-251
93RanKee-42
94TopArc1-93
94TopArc1G-93
Hudson, Stan
75AlbDukC-14
Hudson, Todd
92LetMouSP-1
Hudson, Tony
80TulDriT-3
81TulDriT-21
82BurRanF-21
82BurRanT-3
85TulDriTI-20
86KnoBluJP-13
87SyrChiP-1939
Huebner, John
88GreFalDTI-18
89BakDodCLC-196
Hueda, Alejandro
96StCatSB-12
Huelsmann, Mike
96WatIndTI-10
Huenneke, Derek
86AriWilP-7
Hueston, Steve
96SpoIndB-14
Huey, John
83MadMusF-26
84MidCubT-5
Huff, B.J.
96PitMetB-12
Huff, Brad
88WytCubP-1979
89WytCubS-14
90GenCubP-3032
90GenCubS-15

91WinSpiC-14
Huff, Larry
94MarPhiC-1
94MarPhiF-3302
95PiePhiF-192
Huff, Matt
87SalLakTTT-23
88MiaMarS-10
93ButCopKSP-8
Huff, Michael
86VerBeaDP-11
87SanAntDTI-16
88SanAntMB-19
88TexLeaAGS-33
89AlbDukC-24
89AlbDukP-79
89TriA AAC-38
89TriAAP-AAA48
90AlbDukC-24
90AlbDukP-358
90AlbDukT-14
90ClaUpd-T24
90CMC-426
90Fle-649
90FleCan-649
90ProAAAF-79
90Sco-597
90TopDeb89-63
90TriAAAC-38
90TriAllGP-AAA46
91Bow-73
91Fle-210
91IndFanC-14
91LeaGolR-BC22
91ScoRoo-52T
92Don-579
92Fle-85
92Lea-342
92OPC-532
92OPCPre-21
92Pin-485
92Sco-664
92StaClu-329
92Top-532
92TopGol-532
92TopGolW-532
92TopMic-532
92Ult-337
92WhiSoxK-12
93Don-788
93PacSpa-388
93StaCluWS-24
93WhiSoxK-12
94FleUpd-100
94StaCluT-140
94StaCluTFDI-140
95Don-140
95DonPreP-140
95Fla-99
95Fle-98
95Pin-324
95PinArtP-324
95PinMusC-324
95Sco-549
95ScoGolR-549
95ScoPlaTS-549
95Ult-340
95UltGolM-340
96SyrChiTI-15
Huffman, Jason
94EugEmeC-27
94EugEmeF-3706
94RocRoyC-14
94RocRoyF-561
Huffman, Jeff
94UtiBluSC-14
94UtiBluSF-3813
Huffman, Kris
88SavCarP-351
89SprCarB-9
Huffman, Phil
79BluJayBY-13
80OPC-79
80SyrChiT-9
80SyrChiTI-10
80Top-142
81OPC-2
81SyrChiT-5
81SyrChiTI-10
81Top-506
82OmaRoyT-6
85RocRedWT-17
86RocRedWP-9
87RocRedWP-1
87RocRedWT-6
91OriCro-207
Huffman, Rod
91CliGiaC-5
91CliGiaP-829
91MidLeaAP-MWL4
92ProFS7-355
92SanJosGC-20
Huffman, Ryan
94LSUTig-10
Hufford, Scott
87SpaPhiP-26
88LakTigS-15
Huffstickler, Danny
79ElmPioRST-4
Huggins, Miller
06FanCraNL-22
08RosComP-116
09ColChiE-135
09PC7HHB-24
09RamT20-58
09T206-162
09T206-163
10CouT21-32
10CouT21-33
10CouT21-149
10CouT21-150
10CouT21-288
10CouT21-289
10DomDisP-57
10RedCroT-32
10RedCroT-120
10RedCroT-121
10RedCroT-202
10RedCroT-203
10SweCapPP-149A
10SweCapPP-149B
11DiaGumP-15
11MecDFT-5
11PloCanE-35
11S74Sil-120
11SpoLifCW-178
11SpoLifM-270
11T205-78
12ColRedB-135
12ColTinT-135
12HasTriFT-67A
13NatGamW-20
13TomBarW-19
14B18B-85A
14B18B-85B
14CraJacE-75
14FatPlaT-18
14PieStaT-28
15CraJacE-75
15SpoNewM-85
16BF2FP-95
16SpoNewM-86
19W514-34
20GasAmeMBD-11
21E121So1-47
21E121So8-40
21KoBreWSI-37
22W575-61
22WilPatV-10
23W501-26
23W515-36
23WilChoV-68
61Fle-46
62Top-137
62TopVen-137
75TCMAllG-16
76ShaPiz-98
77BobParHoF-28
77GalGloG-128
80PerHaloFP-98
80SSPHOF-98
81ConTSN-3
81SpoHaloF-2
82OhiHaloF-39
86ConSer1-16
87SpoCubG-3
87Yan192T-1
89CMCRut-17
91ConTSN-101
92CarMcD-5
92ConTSN-649
92MegRut-124
92YanWIZH-17
93ConTSN-830
93CraJac-22
94MegRutS-5
95MegRut-18
Hughes, Bobby
92ClaDraP-35
93BelBreC-10
93BelBreF-1714
93Bow-507
93ClaFS7-280
94BowBes-X104
94BowBesR-X104
94ExcFS7-81
94StoPorC-1
94StoPorF-1698
94VerExpC-15
95SigRooOJ-18
95SigRooOJP-18
95SigRooOJPS-18
95SigRooOJS-18
96FleUpd-U46
96FleUpdTC-U46
96Ult-363
96UltGolM-363
Hughes, Butch
82ReaPhiT-3
83PhoGiaBHN-18
86ModA'sC-24
86ModA'sP-14
87ModA'sC-24
87ModA'sP-9
94WilCubC-27
Hughes, Danan
92HelBreF-1727
92HelBreSP-17
93ExcFS7-188
Hughes, Dick (Richard)
62KahAtl-10
67Top-384
68Top-253
68TopVen-253
69OPC-39
69Top-39
Hughes, Doc (Leo)
48SomandK-29
49SomandK-23
Hughes, Gregory
79NaSouTI-12
80WatRedT-22
81TulDriT-23
Hughes, Jim (James Jay)
11SpoLifCW-179
90DodTar-368
Hughes, Jim (James Michael)
74TacTwiC-7
76Hos-53
76HosTwi-53
76OPC-11
76SSP-211
76Top-11
76VenLeaS-96
77TacTwiDQ-21
77Top-304
78Top-395
78TucTorC-59B
Hughes, Jim (James Robert)
49W72HolS-8
52Par-56
53Top-216
54NewYorJA-8
54Top-169
55Bow-156
55DodGolS-7
55Top-51
55TopDouH-19
79TCM50-268
90DodTar-369
91TopArc1-216
94TopArc1-169
94TopArc1G-169
95TopArcBD-51
95TopArcBD-78
95TopArcBD-96
95TopArcBD-130
Hughes, John
83CliGiaF-16
Hughes, Keith
85AlbYanT-35
86AlbYanT-7
87ColCliP-13
87ColCliP-17
87ColCliT-21
88BlaYNPRWLU-26
88Don-643
88Fle-305
88FleGlo-305
88RocRedWC-15
88RocRedWGCP-13
88RocRedWP-213
88RocRedWTI-11
88Sco-635
88ScoGlo-635
88Top-781
88TopTif-781
89RocRedWC-13
89RocRedWP-1659
89TriAAP-AAA23
90AlbDecGB-32
90CMC-375
90MetColP-34
90ProAAAF-287
90TidTidC-24
90TidTidP-556
90TopTVM-46
90TriAllGP-AAA6
91ColCliLD-106
91ColCliP-6
91ColCliP-601
91LinDriAAA-106
91MetWIZ-191
91OriCro-208
92PorBeaF-2674
92PorBeaS-409
92YanWIZ8-88
93IndIndF-1501
95OmaRoyTI-14
96HonShaHWB-30
96WilBluRB-30
Hughes, Kiley
93Sou-11
Hughes, Mickey (Michael)
90DodTar-370
96BoiHawB-16
Hughes, Mickey J.
87OldJudN-82
87OldJudN-262
Hughes, Roy
47RoyMon-2
84TCMPla1-37
92ConTSN-566
94ConTSN-1069
94ConTSNB-1069
Hughes, Sammy T.
78LauLonABS-15
86NegLeaF-111
90NegLeaS-35
Hughes, Steve
80CedRapRT-8
Hughes, Terry W.
73OPC-603
73Top-603
74OPC-604
74Top-604
75OPC-612
75Top-612
Hughes, Tom (Thomas)
08AmeCarE-79
09ColChiE-136A
09ColChiE-136B
09ColChiE-136C
09ColChiE-137
11SpoLifCW-180
11SpoLifM-283
12ColRedB-136A
12ColRedB-136B
12ColRedB-136C
12ColRedB-137
12ColTinT-136A
12ColTinT-136B
12ColTinT-136C
12ColTinT-137
12ImpTobC-66
75CedRapGT-1
77FriOneYW-110
91ConTSN-161
Hughes, Troy
90PulBraB-20
90PulBraP-3088
91MacBraC-24
91MacBraP-877
92ClaFS7-92
92DurBulC-15
92DurBulF-1113
92DurBulTI-27
92ProFS7-191
93GreBraF-361
94RicBraF-2859
94UppDecML-18
95BreBtaTI-10
96OrlCubB-12
Hughey, Jim
98CamPepP-37
Hughs, Eric
89AlaGol-18
Hughson, Tex (Cecil)
42RedSoxTI-14
43RedSoxTI-9
46RedSoxTI-13
46SpoExcW-6-2
47Exh-104
47TipTop-8
49Bow-199
76TayBow4-63
83TCMPla1942-5
87RedSox1T-8
92TexLon-25
Hugo, Sean
92OklStaC-12
95BowBayTI-24
Huisman, Rick
90CliGiaUTI-U6
91CalLeLA-31
91Cla/Bes-32
91SanJosGC-27
91SanJosGP-6
92Bow-217
92ClaFS7-255
92ProFS7-350
92ShrCapF-3865
92ShrCapS-585
92SkyAA F-258
92UppDecML-186
93ClaFS7-281
93ExcFS7-118
94JacGenF-214
95Bow-118
95BowBes-B43
95BowBesR-B43
95Exc-205
95TusTorTI-12
95Top-650
96OmaRoyB-14
96RoyPol-13
97RoyPol-11
Huismann, Mark
81ChaRoyT-18
82ForMyeRT-16
84Don-339
85DomLeaS-204
85Don-583
85Fle-203
85OmaRoyT-15
85Top-644
85TopTif-644
86RoyNatP-38
87Fle-586
87FleGlo-586
87MarMot-16
87Top-187
87TopTif-187
88TolMudHC-11
88TolMudHP-588
88TriAAAP-42
88TriAAC-26
89RocRedWC-10
89RocRedWP-1650
90BufBisC-4
90BufBisP-367
90BufBisTI-9
90CMC-4
90ProAAAF-482
91BufBisLD-30
91BufBisP-535
91LinDriAAA-30
91OriCro-209
92OmaRoyF-2956
92OmaRoyS-331
Huizenga, Ken
77BriRedST-8
Hulbert, William
80PerHaloFP-222
94OriofB-24
Hulett, Tim
81GleFalWST-12
82GleFalWST-6
84WhiSoxTV-18
85Don-645
85FleUpd-59
85TopTifT-60T
85TopTra-60T
85WhiSoxC-32
86Don-404
86Fle-208
86OPC-87
86Top-724

86TopSti-295
86TopTif-724
86WhiSoxC-32
87Don-260
87DonOpeD-231
87Fle-500
87FleGlo-500
87OPC-286
87Top-566
87TopSti-289
87TopTif-566
87WhiSoxC-16
88IndIndC-17
88IndIndP-522
88Top-158
88TopTif-158
89RocRedWC-16
89RocRedWP-1653
90FleUpd-66
91Don-706
91Fle-478
91OPC-468
91OriCro-210
91Sco-632
91StaClu-517
91Top-468
91TopDesS-468
91TopMic-468
91TopTif-468
92Fle-11
92OPC-396
92Sco-391
92StaClu-104
93Don-661
93Fle-543
93OPC-167
93PacSpa-343
93StaClu-14
93StaCluFDI-14
93StaCluMOP-14
93Top-327
93TopGol-327
93TopInaM-327
93TopMic-327
94Don-129
94Fle-7
94OriPro-47
94OriUSPC-6S
94OriUSPC-11D
94Pac-34
94Sco-165
94ScoGolR-165
94StaClu-430
94StaCluFDI-430
94StaCluGR-430
94StaCluMOP-430
94StaCluT-298
94StaCluTFDI-298
94Top-32
94TopGol-32
94TopSpa-32

Hull, Brett
91StaCluCM-48
91StaCluCM-49
91StaCluMO-45

Hull, Jeff
85Ft.MyeRT-8
86Ft.MyeRP-14
87SalSpuP-25
88BlaYNPRWLU-4
88EasLeaAP-35
88VerMarP-961
89CalCanC-8
89CalCanP-526
90OrlSunRB-8
90OrlSunRP-1085

Hulme, Pat
90UtiBluSP-20

Hulse, David
90ButCopKSP-8
91ChaRanC-22
91ChaRanP-1326
91Cla/Bes-197
92SkyAA F-269
92TulDriF-2707
92TulDriS-609
93Bow-601
93Don-706
93Fla-282
93Fle-683
93Lea-355
93OPC-146
93OPCPre-40
93PacSpa-641
93Pin-269
93PinRooTP-10
93RanKee-410
93Sco-293
93ScoBoyoS-26
93SelRoo-35T
93SelRooAR-7
93StaClu-705
93StaCluFDI-705
93StaCluMOP-705
93StaCluR-4
93Top-118
93TopGol-118
93TopInaM-118
93TopMic-118
93Toy-75
93Ult-630
93UppDec-374
93UppDecGold-374
94ColC-142
94ColChoGS-142
94ColChoSS-142
94Don-560
94Fin-148
94FinRef-148
94Fla-112
94Fle-309
94Lea-278
94Pac-620
94Pin-162
94PinArtP-162
94PinMusC-162
94RanMagM-9
94Sco-523
94ScoBoyoS-22
94ScoCyc-TC14
94ScoGolR-523
94Sel-302
94StaClu-449
94StaCluFDI-449
94StaCluGR-449
94StaCluMOP-449
94StaCluT-251
94StaCluTFDI-251
94Stu-155
94Top-498
94TopGol-498
94TopSpa-498
94TriPla-196
94Ult-129
94UppDec-377
94UppDecED-377
94USPlaCR-10H
94USPlaCR-13D
95ColCho-392
95ColChoGS-392
95ColChoSS-392
95Don-228
95DonPreP-228
95Fin-323
95FinRef-323
95Fla-271
95Fle-288
95FleUpd-51
95Pac-429
95Sco-130
95ScoGolR-130
95ScoPlaTS-130
95StaClu-293
95StaCluMOP-293
95StaCluSTWS-293
95Ult-111
95UltGolM-111
96Don-410
96DonPreP-410
96Fle-146
96FleTif-146
96LeaSigEA-85
96Pac-346
96Ult-81
96UltGolM-81
97Pac-118
97PacLigB-118
97PacSil-118

Hulse, Jeff
88EugEmeB-14
89AppFoxP-866
90ClePhiS-8

Hulstrom, Bruce
87PenWhiSP-14

Hulswitt, Rudy
08RosComP-117
09ColChiE-138A
09ColChiE-138B
09ColChiE-138C
09PC7HHB-25
09T206-164
11SpoLifCW-181
11SpoLifM-271
12ColRedB-138A
12ColRedB-138B
12ColRedB-138C
12ColTinT-138A
12ColTinT-138B
12ColTinT-138C

Humber, Frank
89GreFalDSP-21
90BakDodCLC-239

Hume, Thomas H.
88KimN18-20

Hume, Tom (Thomas Hubert)
76IndIndTI-9
77IndIndTI-5
78Pep-14
78SSP270-120
78Top-701
79Top-301
80RedEnq-47
80Top-149
81CokTeaS-43
81Fle-211
81OPC-292
81Top-8
81Top-419
81TopSti-31
81TopSti-166
81TopSupHT-37
82Don-229
82Fle-69
82OPC-79
82RedCok-9
82Top-763
82TopSti-38
83Don-229
83Fle-593
83FleSta-88
83FleSti-146
83FleSti-213
83OPC-86
83RedYea-47
83Top-86
84Don-550
84Fle-472
84Nes792-607
84OPC-186
84RedEnq-19
84Top-607
84TopSti-59
84TopTif-607
85Don-408
85Fle-538
85OPC-223
85Top-223
85TopMin-223
85TopTif-223
86Don-365
86Fle-179
86FleUpd-52
86PhiTas-41
86Top-573
86TopTif-573
86TopTra-47T
86TopTraT-47T
87Fle-177
87FleGlo-177
87OPC-251
87PhiTas-41
87Top-719
87TopTif-719
88Fle-236
88FleGlo-236
88Sco-494
88ScoGlo-494

Hummel, Dean
86ShrCapP-10

Hummel, John E.
08RosComP-94
09ColChiE-139
09RamT20-59
09T206-165
10CouT21-151
10CouT21-152
10CouT21-290
10DomDisP-58
10RedCroT-33
10RedCroT-122
10RedCroT-204
10SweCapPP-74
11PloCanE-36
11S74Sil-53
11SpoLifCW-182
11SpoLifM-156
11T205-79
12ColRedB-139
12ColTinT-139
12HasTriFT-27
14B18B-58
14CraJacE-50
14PieStaT-29
15CraJacE-50
90DodTar-371

Humphrey, Al
90DodTar-988

Humphrey, Daryl
83GreHorT-10

Humphrey, Rich
93AubAstC-14
93AubAstF-3438
96JacGenB-13

Humphrey, Sly
83IdaFalAT-28

Humphrey, Terry
72Dia-20
72OPC-489
72Top-489
73OPC-106
73Top-106
76OPC-552
76SSP-373
76Top-552
77Top-369
78AngFamF-18
78SSP270-210
78Top-71
79Top-503

Humphreys, Bob (Robert W.)
65OPC-154
65Top-154
66Top-342
66TopVen-342
67CokCapS-1
67Top-478
68Top-268
68TopVen-268
69OPC-84
69Top-84
70OPC-538
70Top-538
71MLBOffS-439
71OPC-236
71Top-236
72MilBra-154
80KnoBluJT-25
81SyrChiT-23
81SyrChiTI-11
83SyrChiT-26
94BreMilB-320

Humphreys, Kevin
96BoiHawB-17

Humphreys, Mike
87SalLakTTT-16
88SpoIndP-1926
89CalLeaA-10
89RivRedWB-8
89RivRedWCLC-5
89RivRedWP-1400
90TexLeaAGS-7
90WicWraRD-11
91Bow-162
91ColCliLD-107
91ColCliP-7
91ColCliP-608
91LinDriAAA-107
91UppDecFE-35F
92ColCliF-363
92ColCliP-21
92ColCliS-105
92Don-769
92Fle-231
92Pin-277
92Sco-815
92ScoRoo-26
92SkyAAAF-47
92StaClu-319
92TopDeb91-85
92UppDec-432
93ColCliF-1121
93ColCliP-21
93FleFinE-246
93StaCluY-10
93Ult-595
94ColCliF-2963
94ColCliP-15

Humphries, Joe
87MyrBeaBJP-1459
88SanAntMB-20

Humphries, John
93ConTSN-951

Humphry, Brandt
80ElPasDT-1
81HolMilT-22

Humphry, Trevor
92ClaDraP-59
92MarPhiF-3051
93MarPhiC-14
93MarPhiF-3467
93SpaPhiC-16
93SpaPhiF-1051
93StaCluM-87
93StaCluP-16
95PiePhiF-183

Hund, John
75QuaCitAT-18

Hundhammer, Paul
84PawRedST-10A
84PawRedST-10B
85PawRedST-5

Hundley, Randy
66Top-392
67CokCapC-10
67CubProPS-7
67DexPre-101
67OPC-106
67ProPizC-9
67Top-106
68OPC-136
68Top-136
68TopVen-136
69CubJewT-8
69CubPho-6
69CubTeaIC-4
69MilBra-122
69MLBOffS-121
69Top-347
69TopSta-14
69TopTeaP-4
70CubDunD-3
70DayDaiNM-146
70Kel-31
70MLBOffS-17
70OPC-265
70SunPin-4
70Top-265
71BazNumT-46
71BazUnn-16
71MilDud-48
71MLBOffS-34
71OPC-592
71Top-592
71TopCoi-51
71TopTat-20
72CubTeal-5
72MilBra-155
72OPC-258
72Top-258
73OPC-21
73Top-21
74OPC-319
74Top-319
74TopSta-15
74TopTra-319T
75PadDea-3
76OPC-351
76SSP-121
76Top-351
77Top-502
78TwiFri-34
84CubUno-2
84CubUno-6
89PacLegI-207
92CubOldS-15
92UppDecS-28

Hundley, Todd
87LitFalMP-2396
88LitFalMP-6
89ColMetB-1
89ColMetGS-11
89SouAtlLAGS-17
90Bow-142
90BowTif-142
90ClaYel-T100
90FleUpd-36
90JacMetGS-1
90MetColP-35

90ScoRoo-76T
90TopTra-44T
90TopTraT-44T
90TopTVM-47
90UppDec-726
91Bow-467
91Don-641
91Fle-150
91LinDriAAA-559
91MajLeaCP-75
91MetColP-34
91MetWIZ-192
91OPC-457
91OPCPre-66
91RedFolS-108
91Sco-340
91Sco100RS-79
91ScoRoo-23
91StaClu-349
91TidTidLD-559
91TidTidP-2513
91Top-457
91TopDeb90-74
91TopDesS-457
91TopMic-457
91TopTif-457
91TriA AAGP-AAA49
91Ult-220
91UppDec-440
92Bow-101
92ClaGam-54
92Don-568
92Fle-506
92LeaGolR-BC7
92MetColP-16
92MetKah-9
92OPC-673
92Pin-571
92PinRoo-17
92PinRool-10
92PinTea2-78
92ProFS7-277
92Sco-602
92Sco100RS-80
92ScoHotR-6
92ScoImpP-31
92ScoRoo-6
92StaClu-290
92Stu-66
92Top-673
92TopGol-673
92TopGolW-673
92TopMcD-42
92TopMic-673
92TriPla-104
92Ult-233
92UppDec-260
92UppDecSR-SR10
93Bow-398
93Don-66
93Fla-92
93Fle-88
93Lea-75
93MetColP-36
93MetKah-9
93OPC-116
93PacSpa-542
93PanSti-246
93Pin-126
93Sco-167
93Sel-293
93SelChaR-19
93SP-150
93StaClu-72
93StaCluFDI-72
93StaCluMOP-72
93Stu-206
93Top-380
93TopGol-380
93TopInaM-380
93TopMic-380
93Toy-12
93TriPla-218
93Ult-75
93UppDec-293
93UppDecGold-293
94Bow-456
94ColC-143
94ColChoGS-143
94ColChoSS-143
94Don-128
94ExtBas-318
94Fin-319
94FinRef-319
94Fla-198
94Fle-565
94Lea-323
94MetColP-12
94MetShuST-8
94Pac-404
94PanSti-218
94Pin-155
94PinArtP-155
94PinMusC-155
94ProMag-92
94Sco-458
94ScoGolR-458
94Sel-73
94SP-117
94SPDieC-117
94StaClu-82
94StaCluFDI-82
94StaCluGR-82
94StaCluMOP-82
94Stu-115
94Top-8
94TopGol-8
94TopSpa-8
94TriPla-144
94Ult-237
94UppDec-242
94UppDecED-242
95ColCho-324
95ColChoGS-324
95ColChoSS-324
95Don-65
95DonPreP-65
95DonTopotO-293
95Fin-138
95FinRef-138
95Fla-171
95Fle-370
95Lea-3
95LeaLim-124
95Pac-282
95Pin-32
95PinArtP-32
95PinMusC-32
95Sco-416
95ScoGolR-416
95ScoPlaTS-416
95Sel-154
95SelArtP-154
95StaClu-205
95StaCluFDI-205
95StaCluMOP-205
95StaCluSTWS-205
95StaCluVR-107
95Top-223
95TopCyb-125
95Ult-412
95UltGolM-412
95UppDec-123
95UppDecED-123
95UppDecEDG-123
95UppDecSE-194
95UppDecSEG-194
96Baz-86
96Bow-62
96Cir-157
96CirRav-157
96ColCho-221
96ColChoGS-221
96ColChoSS-221
96Don-249
96DonPreP-249
96EmoXL-232
96Fin-B85
96FinRef-B85
96Fla-320
96Fle-479
96FleTif-479
96Lea-100
96LeaPrePB-100
96LeaPrePG-100
96LeaPrePS-100
96LeaSig-45
96LeaSigPPG-45
96LeaSigPPP-45
96MetKah-15
96MetMod-5
96MetUni-200
96MetUniP-200
96Pac-147
96PanSti-28
96ProSta-71
96Sco-73
96SP-128
96StaClu-70
96StaCluEPB-70
96StaCluEPG-70
96StaCluEPS-70
96StaCluMOP-70
95StaCluVRMC-107
96Stu-100
96StuPrePB-100
96StuPrePG-100
96StuPrePS-100
96Sum-28
96SumAbo&B-28
96SumArtP-28
96SumFoi-28
96TeaOut-38
96Top-409
96TopGal-10
96TopGalPPI-10
96TopLas-68
96Ult-242
96UltGolM-242
96UppDec-399
97Bow-288
97BowBes-4
97BowBesAR-4
97BowBesR-4
97BowChr-98
97BowChrI-98
97BowChrIR-98
97BowChrR-98
97BowInt-288
97Cir-366
97CirRav-366
97ColCho-395
97ColChoAC-35
97ColChoNF-NF37
97ColChoNF-NF38
97ColChoPP-PP11
97ColChoPPG-PP11
97ColChoTotT-T18
97Don-26
97Don-443
97DonEli-141
97DonEliGS-141
97DonLim-179
97DonLim-188
97DonLimLE-179
97DonLimLE-188
97DonPre-62
97DonPreCttC-62
97DonPreP-26
97DonPreP-443
97DonPrePGold-26
97DonPrePGold-443
97Fin-171
97Fin-324
97FinEmb-171
97FinEmb-324
97FinEmbR-171
97FinEmbR-324
97FinRef-171
97FinRef-324
97FlaSho-A90
97FlaSho-B90
97FlaSho-C90
97FlaShoDC-7
97FlaShoLC-90
97FlaShoLC-B90
97FlaShoLC-C90
97FlaShoLCM-A90
97FlaShoLCM-B90
97FlaShoLCM-C90
97Fle-397
97Fle-738
97FleGolM-3
97FleLumC-10
97FleMilDM-6
97FleTeaL-23
97FleTif-397
97FleTif-738
97Lea-248
97LeaFraM-248
97LeaFraMDC-248
97MetUni-194
97MetUniBF-7
97NewPin-132
97NewPinAP-132
97NewPinMC-132
97NewPinPP-132
97Pac-365
97PacCar-32
97PacCarM-32
97PacGolCD-32
97PacLigB-365
97PacPri-124
97PacPriGA-GA27
97PacPriLB-124
97PacPriP-124
97PacSil-365
97Pin-73
97PinArtP-73
97PinCer-87
97PinCerMBlu-87
97PinCerMG-87
97PinCerMR-87
97PinCerR-87
97PinIns-117
97PinInsCE-117
97PinInsDE-117
97PinInsFS-5
97PinMusC-73
97PinTotCPB-87
97PinTotCPG-87
97PinTotCPR-87
97PinX-P-29
97PinX-PMoS-29
97PinX-PSfF-50
97PinX-PSfFU-50
97ProMag-27
97ProMagML-27
97Sco-219
97Sco-330
97Sco-493
97ScoHobR-493
97ScoPreS-219
97ScoPreS-330
97ScoResC-493
97ScoShoS-219
97ScoShoS-330
97ScoShoS-493
97ScoShoSAP-210
97ScoShoSAP-330
97ScoShoSAP-493
97ScoTitT-9
97Sel-83
97SelArtP-83
97SelRegG-83
97SkyE-X-85
97SkyE-XC-85
97SkyE-XEC-85
97SP-120
97SpoIll-88
97SpoIllEE-88
97SPSpeF-29
97SPx-34
97SPxBro-34
97SPxGraF-34
97SPxSil-34
97SPxSte-34
97StaClu-41
97StaCluC-CO2
97StaCluI-I3
97StaCluMat-41
97StaCluMOP-41
97StaCluMOP-I3
97Stu-141
97StuPrePG-141
97StuPrePS-141
97Top-145
97Top-466
97TopAll-AS2
97TopChr-55
97TopChrAS-AS2
97TopChrR-55
97TopChrSAR-AS2
97TopGal-64
97TopGalPPI-64
97TopIntF-ILM10
97TopIntFR-ILM10
97TopSta-61
97TopStaAM-61
97Ult-239
97UltGolME-239
97UltHRK-5
97UltPlaME-239
97UppDec-322
97UppDec-430
97UppDecLDC-LD11
97UppDecU-11

Hundrick, Gink

28W513-63

Hunger, Chris

81WauTimT-9
83ChaLooT-3

Hungling, Bernie (Bernard)

22E120-141
90DodTar-989

Hunnefield, William

26Exh-76
27Exh-38
30ChiEveAP-15
31Exh-21
93ConTSN-696

Hunsacker, Frank

77St.PetCT-8
80ArkTraT-15
81BirBarT-9

Hunsinger, Alan

82SprCarF-17
83ArkTraT-18
90SprCarDGB-7

Hunt, Ben

75CliPilT-19

Hunt, Chris

92BoiHawF-3630
93PocPosSP-9

Hunt, John

96HicCraB-9

Hunt, Ken L.

60Lea-33
60Top-522
61Top-156
62AngJayP-5
62Jel-79
62Pos-79
62PosCan-79
62Top-68
62TopBuc-40
62TopVen-68
63AngJayP-6
63Top-207
64Top-294
64TopCoi-89
64TopVen-294
92YanWIZ0-58

Hunt, Ken R.

61Top-556
62Jel-129
62Kah-20
62Pos-129
62PosCan-129
62RedEnq-14
62SalPlaC-76A
62SalPlaC-76B
62ShiPlaC-76
62Top-364
62TopStaI-65
63RedEnq-13

Hunt, Kenya

94SpoIndC-11
94SpoIndF-3329
95IdaFalBTI-16

Hunt, Randy

82SprCarF-20
83ArkTraT-11
85LouRedR-11
86IndIndTI-6
86Top-218
86TopTif-218
87Don-625
88MemChiB-15
90SprCarDGB-33

Hunt, Riegal

92WelPirC-10
92WelPirF-1337
93WelPirC-7
93WelPirF-3372

Hunt, Ron (Ronald K.)

61TopStaI-172
63Top-558
64Baz-26
64MetJayP-7
64Top-235
64TopCoi-164
64TopGia-6
64TopSta-93
64TopStaU-35
64TopVen-235
65Baz-26
65MetJayP-7
65OldLonC-12
65Top-285
65TopEmbI-35
65TopTraI-50
66Top-360
66TopVen-360
67CokCapD-6
67CokCapDA-6
67DexPre-102
67OPCPapI-31
67Top-525
67TopPos-31

68DexPre-39
68OPC-15
68Top-15
68TopVen-15
69MilBra-123
69MLBOffS-200
69Top-664
69TopSta-105
69TopTeaP-14
70ExpPin-7
70Gia-5
70MLBOffS-125
70OPC-276
70Top-276
71ExpPS-10
71MLBOffS-130
71OPC-161
71Top-578
72Dia-21
72MilBra-156
72OPC-110
72ProStaP-6
72Top-110
73OPC-149
73Top-149
74ExpWes-5
74Kel-25
74OPC-275
74Top-275
74TopSta-55
75OPC-610
75Top-610
78TCM60I-212
81RedPioT-15
81TCM60I-357
82HolMilT-15
86MetGreT-2
90DodTar-372
90PacLeg-84
91MetWIZ-193
92Nab-5
93UppDecAH-70
94UppDecAH-33
94UppDecAH1-33

Hunt, Ronald
82RedPioT-21

Hunt, Shannon
90BenBucL-28

Hunt, Tom
80LynSaiT-16
81WauTimT-28
82WauTimF-30
83ChaLooT-23
84ChaLooT-9
86ChaLooP-14
87ChaLooB-26

Hunt, Will
93BriTigF-3644
93LSUTigM-6
94FayGenC-14
94FayGenF-2140

Hunter, Andy
96IdaFalB-10

Hunter, Bert
86AshTouP-14
86AubAstP-13
87AshTouP-16
88OscAstS-16
89ColMudP-148
89ColMudS-14
90ColMudB-8
90ColMudP-1358
90ColMudS-14
91JacGenLD-562
91JacGenP-937
91LinDriAA-562
92BinMetF-528
92BinMetS-60
93NorTidF-2583

Hunter, Billy (Gordon)
53Top-166
54Bow-5
54Top-48
55Bow-69
57Top-207
58Top-98A
58Top-98B
59Top-11
59TopVen-11
73OPC-136
73Top-136A
73Top-136B
74OPC-306
74Top-306
78RanBurK-1
78SSP270-104
78Top-548
79TCM50-118
81Ori6F-18
86RanGreT-4
91OriCro-211
91TopArc1-166
93RanKee-200
94TopArc1-48
94TopArc1G-48

Hunter, Bobby (Bob)
88OneYanP-2056
91AugPirC-8
92CarMudF-1177
92SalBucC-13
92SalBucF-59
93CarMudF-2050
93CarMudTI-20

Hunter, Brian L.
90AshTouP-2761
91OscAstC-24
91OscAstP-698
92ClaFS7-206
92OscAstC-9
92OscAstF-2543
92UppDecML-324
93Bow-12
93ClaFS7-209
93JacGenF-2120
93StaCluAs-21
94ActPac-52
94AriFalLS-9
94Bow-670
94BowBes-B31
94BowBesR-B31
94Cla-147
94ColC-659
94ColChoGS-659
94ColChoSS-659
94ExcAllF-8
94ExcFS7-202
94FleUpd-144
94LeaLimR-63
94ScoRoo-RT142
94ScoRooGR-RT142
94SP-7
94SPDieC-7
94SpoRoo-31
94SpoRooAP-31
94StaClu-651
94StaCluFDI-651
94StaCluGR-651
94StaCluMOP-651
94TedWilDGC-DG7
94TucTorF-774
94Ult-505
94UppDec-16
94UppDecED-16
94UppDecML-100
94UppDecML-135
94UppDecML-159
94VenLinU-7
95ActPac2GF-9G
95ActPacF-7
95ActPacF-70
95AstMot-26
95Bow-267
95BowBes-B82
95BowBes-X11
95BowBesR-B82
95BowBesR-X11
95BowGolF-267
95ColCho-111
95ColChoGS-111
95ColChoSE-43
95ColChoSEGS-43
95ColChoSESS-43
95ColChoSS-111
95Don-184
95DonPreP-184
95DonTopotO-255
95Fin-300
95FinRef-300
95FleMajLP-6
95LeaGolR-10
95LeaLim-104
95Pin-164
95PinArtP-164
95PinMusC-164
95PinNewB-NB3
95Sco-297
95ScoGolR-297
95ScoPlaTS-297
95ScoPlaTS-403
95ScoRooDT-RDT7
95Sel-162
95Sel-238
95SelArtP-162
95SelArtP-238
95SelCer-116
95SelCerF-7
95SelCerMG-116
95SelCerPU-17
95SelCerPU9-17
95SP-59
95SPCha-53
95SPChaDC-53
95Spo-153
95SpoArtP-153
95SPSil-59
95StaClu-437
95StaCluMOP-322
95StaCluMOP-437
95StaCluSTWS-322
95StaCluSTWS-437
95Stu-172
95TusTorTI-13
95Top-237
95TopTra-39T
95Ult-387
95UltGolM-387
95UltGolP-6
95UltGolPGM-6
95UppDec-27
95UppDecED-27
95UppDecEDG-27
95UppDecPAW-H17
95UppDecPAWE-H17
95Zen-137
95ZenRooRC-10
96AstMot-12
96Baz-9
96Bow-15
96BowBes-60
96BowBesAR-60
96BowBesR-60
96Cir-137
96CirRav-137
96ColCho-161
96ColChoGS-161
96ColChoSS-161
96Don-68
96DonPreP-68
96EmoRarB-3
96EmoXL-200
96Fin-B75
96FinRef-B75
96Fla-279
96Fle-411
96FleRooS-7
96FleTif-411
96FleTomL-3
96Lea-179
96LeaLim-33
96LeaLimG-33
96LeaPre-48
96LeaPreP-48
96LeaPrePB-179
96LeaPrePG-179
96LeaPrePS-179
96LeaSig-115
96LeaSigA-112
96LeaSigAG-112
96LeaSigAS-112
96LeaSigPPG-115
96LeaSigPPP-115
96MetUni-178
96MetUniMFG-5
96MetUniP-178
96Pac-84
96PanSti-58
96Pin-54
96PinAfi-105
96PinAfiAP-105
96PinArtP-21
96PinSta-21
96ScoDiaA-2
96ScoDugC-A28
96ScoDugCAP-A28
96ScoRef-4
96Sel-55
96SelArtP-55
96SelCer-83
96SelCerAP-83
96SelCerCB-83
96SelCerCR-83
96SelCerIP-20
96SelCerMB-83
96SelCerMG-83
96SelCerMR-83
96SP-92
96Spo-59
96SpoArtP-59
96StaClu-230
96StaCluMOP-230
96Stu-81
96StuPrePB-81
96StuPrePG-81
96StuPrePS-81
96Sum-50
96SumAbo&B-50
96SumArtP-50
96SumFoi-50
96TacRaiB-14
96Top-268
96TopChr-108
96TopChrR-108
96TopGal-107
96TopGalPPI-107
96TopLas-107
96TopLasBS-1
96Ult-210
96UltFreF-4
96UltFreFGM-4
96UltGolM-210
96UltRisS-5
96UltRisSGM-5
96UppDec-84
96UppDecBCP-BC18
96Zen-64
96ZenArtP-64
97Bow-62
97BowInt-62
97Cir-369
97CirRav-369
97ColCho-126
97ColCho-335
97Don-116
97Don-293
97DonEli-107
97DonEliGS-107
97DonPre-87
97DonPreCttC-87
97DonPreP-116
97DonPreP-293
97DonPrePGold-116
97DonPrePGold-293
97Fin-194
97FinRef-194
97Fle-208
97Fle-347
97Fle-526
97FleTif-347
97FleTif-526
97Lea-280
97LeaFraM-280
97LeaFraMDC-280
97MetUni-137
97NewPin-75
97NewPinAP-75
97NewPinMC-75
97NewPinPP-75
97Pac-319
97PacLigB-319
97PacSil-319
97PinCer-11
97PinCerMBlu-11
97PinCerMG-11
97PinCerMR-11
97PinCerR-11
97PinTotCPB-11
97PinTotCPG-11
97PinTotCPR-11
97PinX-P-95
97PinX-PMoS-95
97Sco-140
97Sco-424
97ScoHobR-424
97ScoPreS-140
97ScoResC-424
97ScoShoS-140
97ScoShoS-424
97ScoShoSAP-140
97ScoShoSAP-424
97SP-69
97StaClu-73
97StaCluM-M15
97StaCluMOP-73
97StaCluMOP-M15
97Stu-111
97StuPrePG-111
97StuPrePS-111
97Top-208
97Ult-404
97UltGolME-404
97UltPlaME-404

Hunter, Brian R.
88BurBraP-25
88MidLeaAGS-18
89GreBraB-2
89GreBraP-1158
89GreBraS-9
89Sta-35
90CMC-295
90CMC-848
90ProAAAF-416
90RicBraC-19
90RicBraP-271
90RicBraTI-13
91BraSubS-19
91Cla3-T39
91DonRoo-9
91LinDriAAA-431
91RicBraBC-25
91RicBraLD-431
91RicBraP-2581
91RicBraTI-18
91UltUpd-67
91UppDecFE-54F
92Bow-662
92BraLykP-15
92BraLykS-17
92ClaGam-16
92Don-163
92Fle-359
92Lea-374
92OPC-611
92OPCPre-78
92Pin-412
92PinTea2-29
92ProFS7-177
92Sco-417
92Sco100RS-3
92ScoImpP-9
92StaClu-432
92Top-611
92TopDeb91-86
92TopGol-611
92TopGolW-611
92TopMic-611
92Ult-163
92UppDec-366
93BraLykP-13
93BraLykS-16
93Don-290
93Fle-5
93OPC-157
93PacSpa-7
93Pin-414
93Sco-549
93Sel-189
93StaClu-491
93StaCluB-23
93StaCluFDI-491
93StaCluMOP-491
93Top-102
93TopGol-102
93TopInaM-102
93TopMic-102
93Ult-305
93UppDec-582
93UppDecGold-582
94ColC-586
94ColChoGS-586
94ColChoSS-586
94ExtBas-346
94Fin-336
94FinRef-336
94Fla-421
94FleUpd-173
94Lea-275
94Pin-502
94PinArtP-502
94PinMusC-502
94PirQui-8
94ScoRoo-RT42
94ScoRooGR-RT42
94Sel-91
94TopTra-39T
95ColCho-426
95ColChoGS-426
95ColChoSS-426
95FleUpd-134
95RedKah-12
95Sco-403

95ScoGolR-403
95StaClu-322
95Ult-366
95UltGolM-366
95UppDec-164
95UppDecED-164
95UppDecEDG-164
97FleTif-208
Hunter, Catfish (Jim)
65Top-526
66OPC-36
66Top-36
66TopVen-36
67CokCapAt-15
67Top-369
67TopGiaSU-23
68Baz-2
68Top-385
68TopActS-10A
68TopPla-5
68TopPos-5
69A'sJacitB-8
69MilBra-124
69MLBOffS-87
69Top-235
69TopSta-216
69TopTeaP-21
70DayDaiNM-75
70MLBOffS-259
70Top-565
71BazNumT-48
71BazUnn-18
71MilDud-10
71MLBOffS-516
71OPC-45
71Top-45
71TopCoi-80
71TopTat-74
72Kel-22
72MilBra-157
72OPC-330
72Top-330
73A'sPos-29
73Kel2D-20
73LinPor-140
73OPC-235
73OPC-344
73Top-235
73Top-344
73TopCanL-21
74Kel-44
74OPC-196
74OPC-339
74Top-7
74Top-339
74TopDecE-6
74TopSta-225
75BlaBacD-3
75Hos-148
75Kel-44A
75Kel-44B
75OPC-230
75OPC-310
75OPC-311
75SSPSam-2
75Top-230
75Top-310
75Top-311
75YanSSP-1
76CraDis-21
76Hos-141
76Kel-5
76LauDiaJ-7
76OPC-100
76OPC-200
76OPC-202
76SafSupLB-3
76SafSupLB-7
76SafSupLB-10
76SafSupLB-11
76SafSupLB-12
76SSP-425
76SSP-593A
76SSP-593B
76Top-100
76Top-200
76Top-202
77BurCheD-178
77Hos-79
77MSADis-29
77OPC-10
77RCColC-30
77Spo-1409
77Spo-1410
77Top-280
77TopCloS-21
77YanBurK-4
78OPC-69
78RCColC-58
78SSP270-23
78Top-460
78WifBalD-31
78YanBurK-7
78YanSSPD-23
79OPC-352
79Top-670
79YanBurK-6
79YanPicA-19
80PerHaloFP-198
80SSPHOF-198
83MLBPin-10
83YanASFY-20
86A'sGreT-9
86SpoDecG-63
87A'sMot-6
87DonHig-19
88PacLegI-16
88TopGloA-11
89HOFStiB-82
89PacLegI-193
89PerCelP-18
89SweBasG-10
90PacLeg-68
90PerGreM-62
91UppDecS-7
91UppDecS-16
92A'sUno7P-3
92A'sUno7P-4
92Pin-587
92UppDecS-27
92YanWIZ7-77
92YanWIZA-32
92YanWIZH-18
93ActPacA-126
93ActPacA2-60G
93MCIAmb-8
93NabAllA-3
94TedWil-68
95JimDeaAG-2
Hunter, George
09ColChiE-140
09T206-166
10CouT21-34
11SpoLifM-157
12ColRedB-140
12ColTinT-140
90DodTar-990
Hunter, Greg
91Cla/Bes-178
91SanBerSC-15
91SanBerSP-1992
92PenPilC-19
92PenPilF-2938
Hunter, Herb H.
16FleBreD-44
Hunter, Jeff
80ElmPioRST-21
Hunter, Jim (James McGregor)
86BurExpP-9
87StoPorP-19
88ElPasDB-28
89ElPasDGS-9
91BreMilB-12
92DenZepF-2634
92DenZepS-148
92ElPasDS-214
92Sco-741
92SkyAA F-94
92TopDeb91-87
93NewOrlZF-965
94BreMilB-321
Hunter, Marion
81RedPioT-16
Hunter, Mark
82MonNew-8
Hunter, Marty
90BenBucL-5
Hunter, Rich
93MarPhiC-15
93MarPhiF-3468
94MarPhiC-9
94MarPhiF-3285
95Bes-90
95PiePhiF-184
95ReaPhiELC-21
96Bow-283
96Exc-206
96ExcCli-4
96Fin-B207
96FinRef-B207
96FleUpd-U165
96FleUpdTC-U165
96Top-430
96Ult-522
96UltGolM-522
96UppDec-262
97PacPriGotD-GD182
Hunter, Scott
94GreFalDSP-16
95SanBerSTI-8
96HilStaHWB-6
96StLucMTI-18
Hunter, Torii
94Bow-104
94Cla-182
94ClaGolF-80
94ClaGolN1PLF-LP5
94ClaGolREF-RE5
94Pin-267
94PinArtP-267
94PinMusC-267
94Sco-640
94ScoGolR-640
95Bow-143
95ForMyeMTI-11
95UppDecML-128
96Bow-111
96HarCitRCB-15
97Bow-176
97BowChr-168
97BowChrI-168
97BowChrIR-168
97BowChrR-168
97BowInt-176
97Sel-116
97SelArtP-116
97SelRegG-116
95UppDecMLFS-128
Hunter, Traver
92OklStaC-13
Hunter, Willard
82MetGal62-21
90DodTar-373
91MetWIZ-194
Huntley, James
94HunCubF-3560
94HunCubC-14
Hunts, Chris
93PocPosF-4210
Huntsman, Brandon
96BluOriB-16
96HigDesMB-14
Huntsman, Scott
95BelBreTI-23
96StoPorB-6
Huntz, Steve
69OPC-136
69Top-136
69TopFou-25
70OPC-282
70Top-282
71MLBOffS-252
71OPC-486
71Top-486
72OPC-73
72Top-73
75HawIsIC-2
75IntLeaASB-11
75PacCoaLAB-11
76HawIsIC-20
76SSP-126
Hunziker, Kent
76CliPilT-20
77AppFoxT-12
Hupke, Doug
87EugEmeP-2650
Huppert, Dave (David B.)
80ChaO'sP-11
80ChaO'sW-12
81RocRedWT-9
81RocRedWW-15
83RocRedWT-11
84VanCanC-37
86ElPasDP-13
88CalLeaACLC-19
88StoPorCLC-202
88StoPorP-740
89StoPorB-29
89StoPorCLC-176
89StoPorP-386
89StoPorS-22
90ElPasDGS-1
90TexLeaAGS-18
91ElPasDLD-199
91ElPasDP-2762
91LinDriAA-199
91OriCro-212
92WhiSoxK-NNO
93SarWhiSC-28
93SarWhiSF-1386
94BreMilB-322
94PriWilCC-25
94PriWilCF-1936
95PriWilCTI-28
96PriWilCB-1
Hurd, Thomas
55Top-116
55TopDouH-119
56Top-256
Hurdle, Clint (Clinton)
76WatRoyT-13
78Roy-9
78SSP270-229
78Top-705
79Top-547
80OPC-273
80Top-525
81Don-224
81Fle-45
81OPC-98
81RoyPol-4
81Top-98
81TopSti-85
82Don-516
82Fle-411
82RedCok-10
82Top-297
83TidTidT 4
84TidTidT-28
85MetColP-14
85MetTCM-38
86CarSchM-10
86CarTeal-19
86Don-434
86Top-438
86TopTif-438
87Fle-298
87FleGlo-298
87MetColP-36
87OPC-317
87TidTidP-1
87TidTidT-22
87Top-317
87TopTif-317
89MetColP-34
89PacSenL-111
89St.LucMS-6
89T/MSenL-50
89TidTidC-12
89TopSenL-98
90EliSenL-115
90JacMetGS-5
90MetColP-15
91LinDriAA-649
91MetColP-35
91MetWIZ-195
91WilBilLD-649
91WilBilP-309
92MetColP-35
92TidTidF-912
92TidTidS-574
93NorTidF-2585
Hurdle, Mike
80UtiBluJT-29
Hurlbert, Gordon
90EasLeaAP-EL47
90NewBriRSB-15
90NewBriRSS-27
Hurlbutt, Robert
90AshTouC-18
90AubAstB-7
90AubAstP-3416
91AshTouP-570
Hurley, Battling
11TurRedT-71
Hurley, Edwin
55Bow-260
Hurley, Mike
89OklSoo-15
Hurley, Pat
90DodTar-991
Hurni, Rick
88SalLakCTTI-12
Hursey, Darren
87FayGenP-13
88LakTigS-16
89LonTigP-1370
90LakTigS-13
91LinDriAA-387
91LonTigLD-387
91LonTigP-1873
Hurst, Bill
91JohCitCP-3973
95BreCouMF-242
96PorSeaDB-16
Hurst, Bruce
81PawRedST-3
81Top-689
82Fle-297
82Top-381
83Don-134
83Fle-186
83Top-82
84AllGamPI-172
84Don-213
84Fle-400
84Nes792-213
84OPC-213
84Top-213
84TopSti-226
84TopTif-213
85Don-493
85Fle-161
85Lea-73
85OPC-134
85Top-451
85TopSti-211
85TopTif-451
86Don-517
86DonHig-47
86Fle-352
86OPC-193
86Top-581
86TopMinL-6
86TopTif-581
87ClaGam-83
87Don-174
87Fle-37
87FleBasA-22
87FleGlo-37
87FleGlo-WS1
87FleStiC-65
87FleWorS-1
87Lea-253
87OPC-31
87RedSoxSAP-8
87Spo-38
87SpoTeaP-9
87Top-705
87TopMinL-43
87TopSti-19
87TopTif-705
87Woo-19
87Woo-28
88Don-252
88DonAll-14
88DonBasB-233
88DonTeaBRS-252
88Fle-356
88FleBasA-18
88FleGlo-356
88FleStiC-10
88Lea-179
88OPC-125
88PanSti-22
88RedFolSB-37
88Sco-380
88ScoGlo-380
88Spo-197
88StaLinRS-12
88Top-125
88TopSti-253
88TopStiB-62
88TopTif-125
89Bow-451
89BowTif-451
89ClaTraP-194
89Don-423
89DonBasB-77
89DonTra-45
89Fle-91
89FleGlo-91
89FleUpd-124
89PadCok-7
89PadMag-21
89PanSti-271
89Sco-325
89ScoHot1S-79
89ScoRoo-19T

89Spo-175
89Top-675
89TopBasT-111
89TopGloS-28
89TopMinL-49
89TopStiB-29
89TopTif-675
89TopTra-55T
89TopTraT-55T
89TopUKM-42
89UppDec-387
89UppDec-792
90Bow-208
90BowTif-208
90ClaBlu-102
90Don-183
90DonBesN-84
90Fle-159
90FleBasA-19
90FleCan-159
90Lea-23
90MLBBasB-57
90OPC-315
90PadCok-8
90PadMag-23
90PanSti-357
90PubSti-51
90Sco-270
90Sco100S-18
90Spo-47
90Top-315
90TopBig-324
90TopMinL-81
90TopSti-108
90TopTif-315
90TopTVA-48
90UppDec-433
90VenSti-237
91Bow-661
91ClaGam-84
91Don-83
91Fle-533
91Lea-469
91MajLeaCP-56
91OPC-65
91PadMag-5
91PadMag-19B
91PadSmo-15
91PanCanT1-90
91Sco-145
91StaClu-475
91Top-65
91TopDesS-65
91TopMic-65
91TopTif-65
91Ult-306
91UppDec-602
92Bow-187
92Don-123
92Fle-608
92Hig5-123
92Lea-216
92OPC-595
92PadCarJ-9
92PadMot-20
92PadPolD-10
92PadSmo-13
92PanSti-238
92Pin-40
92Sco-111
92ScoProP-4
92ScoProP-9
92StaClu-312
92Top-595
92TopGol-595
92TopGolW-595
92TopMic-595
92TriPla-57
92Ult-280
92UppDec-437
93Don-576
93Fle-521
93Lea-341
93OPC-118
93PadMot-9
93PanSti-256
93Pin-327
93Sco-133
93Sel-141
93SelAce-19
93StaClu-347
93StaCluFDI-347
93StaCluMOP-347
93Top-111
93TopGol-111
93TopInaM-111
93TopMic-111
93Ult-474
93UppDec-304
93UppDecGold-304
94Pin-504
94PinArtP-504
94PinMusC-504
94StaCluT-243
94StaCluTFDI-243

Hurst, Charlie (Charles)
89MarPhiS-15
90BatCliP-3059
91SpaPhiC-7
91SpaPhiP-892
92SpaPhiC-13
92SpaPhiF-1261

Hurst, Don (Frank O.)
29ExhFou-11
29PorandAR-45
31Exh-12
33ExhFou-6
33RitCE-6S
33RitCE-11D
34ExhFou-6
34Gou-33
34GouCanV-80
86PhiGreT-11
92ConTSN-519

Hurst, Harry
43ParSpo-85

Hurst, James Lavon
92ChaRanC-7
92ChaRanF-2223
93TulDriF-2730
94Bow-625
94OklCit8F-1493
94RanMagM-10
94Sel-199
94SpoRoo-75
94SpoRooAP-75
94VenLinU-98
95LinVen-244
93TulDriTI-13

Hurst, Jimmy
93SouBenWSC-11
93SouBenWSF-1444
94Bow-483
94BowBes-B58
94BowBes-X98
94BowBesR-B58
94BowBesR-X98
94CarLeaAF-CAR8
94PriWilCC-1
94PriWilCF-1934
95Bow-44
95BowBes-B70
95BowBesR-B70
95Exc-29
95SigRooOJ-19
95SigRooOJP-19
95SigRooOJPS-19
95SigRooOJS-19
95SP-12
95SPSil-12
95UppDec-254
95UppDecED-254
95UppDecEDG-254
95UppDecML-36
95UppDecSE-156
95UppDecSEG-156
96BirBarB-4
96Bow-142
95UppDecMLFS-36
92UtiBluSC-4

Hurst, Jody
88CapCodPPaLP-110
88MisStaB-13
88MisStaB-21
89NiaFalRP-12
90LakTigS-14
90StaFS7-35
92TolMudHF-1054
92TolMudHS-588
93TolMudHF-1664

Hurst, Jonathan
88ChaRanS-10
89ChaRanS-10
90Bes-105
90GasRanB-9
90GasRanP-2518
90GasRanS-11
90SouAtlLAS-12
91Cla/Bes-199
91FloStaLAP-FSL23
91MiaMirC-8
91MiaMirP-402
92Bow-388
92DonRoo-57
92IndIndS-184
92SkyAAAF-90
93OttLynF-2431
93Pin-242
93Sco-299
93StaClu-306
93StaCluFDI-306
93StaCluMOP-306
93Top-727
93TopGol-727
93TopInaM-727
93TopMic-727
94MetColP-13
94Ult-529
95Sco-307
95ScoGolR-307
95ScoPlaTS-307

Hurst, Roy
94WilCubC-11
94WilCubF-3768

Hurta, Bob (Robert)
87UtiBluSP-28
88SpaPhiP-1026
88SpaPhiS-24
90AubAstB-2
90AubAstP-3399
91BurAstC-5
91BurAstP-2796
92JacGenF-3997
92JacGenS-334
92TucTorF-483
93JacGenF-2105
93TucTorF-3055

Hurtado, Edwin
93LinVenB-38
93St.CatBJC-11
93St.CatBJF-3969
94HagSunC-8
94HagSunF-2722
94VenLinU-121
95Bow-134
95LinVen-184
96ColCho-16
96Don-327
96DonPreP-327
96FleUpd-U80
96FleUpdTC-U80
96LeaSigEA-86
96MarMot-26
96Ult-412
96UltGolM-412
96UppDec-217

Hurtado, Jose
85BenPhiC-12

Hurtado, Victor
96KanCouCTI-13
96KanCouCUTI-7
96MidLeaAB-33

Husband, Perry
85VisOakT-3

Huseby, Ken
87TamTarP-4
88GreHorP-1564
89AugPirP-503

Huskey, Butch
90KinMetS-11
91ColMetPI-29
91ColMetPI-30
91ColMetPPI-5
91SouAtlLAGP-SAL16
92Bow-539
92ClaFS7-273
92ColMetPI-42
92ColMetPIISPI-2
92ColMetPIISPI-4
92St.LucMCB-1
92St.LucMF-1752
92UppDecML-37
92UppDecML-269
93BinMetF-2340
93Bow-46
93ClaGolF-70
93ClaYouG-YG6
93Don-506
93ExcFS7-74
93UppDec-436
93UppDecGold-436
94ActPac-37
94Bow-100
94Cla-40
94ColC-10
94ColChoGS-10
94ColChoSS-10
94Don-426
94FleMajLP-16
94LeaGolR-3
94NorTidF-2926
94Pac-405
94Pin-235
94PinArtP-235
94PinMusC-235
94PinNewG-NG12
94PinRooTP-4
94Sco-605
94ScoBoyoS-52
94ScoGolR-605
94Spo-149
94Top-179
94TopGol-179
94TopSpa-179
94TriPla-297
94UppDec-17
94UppDecED-17
95NorTidTI-14
95Sel-174
95SelArtP-174
96Bow-123
96ColCho-227
96ColChoGS-227
96ColChoSS-227
96Don-351
96DonPreP-351
96Fin-B264
96FinRef-B264
96Fle-480
96FleTif-480
96LeaPre-83
96LeaPreP-83
96LeaSigA-113
96LeaSigAG-113
96LeaSigAS-113
96MetKah-16
96Pin-309
96PinAfi-118
96PinAfiAP-118
96PinFoil-309
96Sel-72
96SelArtP-72
96SelCer-78
96SelCerAP-78
96SelCerCB-78
96SelCerCR-78
96SelCerMB-78
96SelCerMG-78
96SelCerMR-78
96SigRooOJ-13
96SigRooOJS-13
96StaClu-86
96StaClu-257
96StaCluMOP-86
96StaCluMOP-257
96Stu-17
96StuPrePB-17
96StuPrePG-17
96StuPrePS-17
96Sum-93
96SumAbo&B-93
96SumArtP-93
96SumFoi-93
96Top-103
96Top-104
96Ult-243
96UltGolM-243
97ColCho-173
97Don-222
97DonEli-147
97DonEliGS-147
97DonLim-178
97DonLimLE-178
97DonPreP-222
97DonPrePGold-222
97Fle-398
97FleTif-398
97Lea-266
97LeaFraM-266
97LeaFraMDC-266
97Pac-366
97PacLigB-366
97PacSil-366
97Sco-278
97ScoPreS-278
97ScoShoS-278
97ScoShoSAP-278
97StaClu-308
97StaCluMOP-308
97Top-73
97Ult-240
97UltGolME-240
97UltPlaME-240
97UppDec-116

Huslig, James
88OklSoo-1
89OklSoo-16
90CliGiaUTI-U7
90EveGiaB-6
90EveGiaP-3122
90OklSoo-14

Huson, Jeff
86BurExpP-10
87WesPalBEP-674
88JacExpB-18
88JacExpP-966
88SouLeaAJ-18
89IndIndC-18
89IndIndP-1233
89ScoHot1R-69
89TriA AAC-4
89TriAAP-AAA11
90Don-693
90DonBesA-83
90DonRoo-11
90ExpPos-18
90Fle-350
90FleCan-350
90FleUpd-123
90Lea-285
90OPC-72
90RanMot-23
90Sco-615
90Sco100RS-14
90ScoRoo-41T
90ScoRooDT-B7
90ScoYouSI-41
90Spo-176
90Top-72
90TopTif-72
90TopTra-45T
90TopTraT-45T
90TriAAAC-4
90UppDec-434
90UppDec-788
91Baz-16
91Bow-273
91Don-305
91Fle-289
91Lea-134
91OPC-756
91PanFreS-255
91PanSti-206
91RanMot-23
91Sco-263
91Sco100RS-18
91StaClu-160
91Top-756
91TopDesS-756
91TopMic-756
91TopRoo-13
91TopTif-756
91ToyRoo-12
91Ult-349
91UppDec-195
92Don-456
92Fle-308
92Lea-251
92OPC-314
92PanSti-78
92RanMot-23
92RanTeal-11
92Sco-466
92StaClu-341
92Top-314
92TopGol-314
92TopGolW-314
92TopMic-314
92Ult-133
92UppDec-196
93Don-583
93Fle-324
93Lea-137
93PacSpa-312
93PanSti-83
93RanKee-411
93StaClu-281
93StaCluFDI-281
93StaCluMOP-281
93StaCluR-12

93Top-143
93TopGol-143
93TopInaM-143
93TopMic-143
93Ult-280
93UppDec-289
93UppDecGold-289
94Don-432
94Pac-619
94StaCluT-253
94StaCluTFDI-253
95RocRedWTI-19
96LeaSigEA-87
Hust, Gary
90HigSchPLS-15
91SouOreAC-16
91SouOreAP-3862
92MadMusC-9
92MadMusF-1249
92ProFS7-134
93MadMusC-16
93MadMusF-1836
94ModA'sC-16
94ModA'sF-3076
95ModA'sTI-11
96HunStaTI-12
Huston, Pat
91GenCubC-9
91GenCubP-4224
Hutcheon, Mike
88MisStaB-37
89MisStaB-44
Hutcheson, Dave
93PeoChiTI-10
94DayCubC-10
94DayCubF-2347
95Exc-165
96OrlCubB-13
95OrlCubF-4
Hutcheson, Joe
90DodTar-992
Hutcheson, Todd
83MiaMarT-28
84BeaGolGT-23
85BeaGolGT-23
86LasVegSP-8
87LasVegSP-13
88LasVegSP-226
89LasVegSP-28
90CMC-683
90LasVegSC-25
Hutchings, John R.
41HarHarW-11
Hutchingson, Chris
86OscAstP-14
Hutchins, Jason
92BenRocC-15
92BenRocF-1472
93Bow-584
93CenValRC-14
93CenValRF-2890
93ClaFS7-103
93ExcFS7-34
93Top-537
93TopGol-537
93TopInaM-537
93TopMic-537
94CenValRC-10
94CenValRF-3197
Hutchins, Lance
88SanJosGCLC-144
88SanJosGP-124
Hutchins, Norm
96Bow-314
96CedRapKTI-13
97Bow-340
97BowInt-340
Hutchinson, Don
88CapCodPPaLP-68
Hutchinson, Fred
39GouPreR303A-26
39WorWidGTP-26
39WorWidGV-16
47Exh-105
47TipTop-33
49Bow-196
49Lea-163
50Bow-151
51Bow-141
52Bow-3
52StaCalL-72E
52StaCalS-86C
52Top-126
53BowC-132
53NorBreL-12
53Top-72
56RedBurB-8
59RedBurBP-6
60RedJayP-4
60Top-219
61RedJayP-5
61Top-135
62RedEnq-15
62RedJayP-5
62Top-172
62TopVen-172
63RedEnq-14
63RedFreBC-9
63RedJayP-3
63Top-422
64RedJayP-4
64Top-207
64TopVen-207
75ShaPiz-11
76TayBow4-65
79TCM50-138
80PacLeg-25
81TigDetN-48
82OhiHaloF-40
83TopRep5-126
85TCMPla1-4
91TopArc1-72
95HutPop-1
95HutPop-2
95HutPop-3
95HutPop-4
96HutPop-1
96HutPop-2
96HutPop-3
96HutPop-4
Hutchinson, Harpo (Ray)
76DubPac1-16
Hutchinson, Ira
39PlaBal-142
41CarW75-11
90DodTar-374
Hutchinson, Sean
89PulBraP-1909
Hutchinson, Tom
94ButCopKSP-8
Hutchinson, William
87OldJudN-264
Hutchison, Bernard
96PorRocB-16
Huth, Ken
84SavCarT-7
Hutson, Jason
90MyrBeaBJP-2771
Hutson, Roy
90DodTar-993
Hutson, Scott
89St.CatBJP-2074
Hutto, Jim
75IntLeaAT-11
75IntLeaAT-17
76SSP-385
84NewOriT-23
84RocRedWT-4
91OriCro-213
Hutto, Paul
90GatCitPP-3351
90GatCitPSP-13
Hutton, Mark
89OneYanP-2118
90GreHorB-4
90GreHorP-2656
90GreHorS-7
91FloStaLAP-FSL13
91Ft.LauYC-5
91Ft.LauYP-2419
92AlbYanF-2223
92AlbYanS-12
92Bow-598
92ClaBluBF-BC2
92ClaFS7-5
92ClaRedB-BC2
92DonRoo-58
92LeaGolR-BC6
92SkyAA F-7
92UppDecML-147
93Bow-651
93ClaFS7-75
93ClaGolF-2
93ColCliF-1107
93ColCliP-8
93Don-671
93ExcFS7-209
93StaCluY-24
93Top-806
93TopGol-806
93TopInaM-806
93TopMic-806
94Bow-437
94Cla-117
94ColC-11
94ColChoGS-11
94ColChoSS-11
94ColCliF-2949
94ColCliP-16
94Don-87
94Pac-423
94Pin-412
94PinArtP-412
94PinMusC-412
94PinRooTP-9
94Sco-608
94ScoBoyoS-32
94ScoGolR-608
94ScoRoo-RT133
94ScoRooGR-RT133
94Spo-166
94StaClu-279
94StaCluFDI-279
94StaCluGR-279
94StaCluMOP-279
94StaCluT-182
94StaCluTFDI-182
94Top-269
94TopGol-269
94TopSpa-269
94UppDec-18
94UppDecED-18
95ColCliMCTI-14
95ColCliP-13
95ColCliTI-13
95Sco-600
95ScoGolR-600
95ScoPlaTS-600
96LeaSigA-114
96LeaSigAG-114
96LeaSigAS-114
97ColCho-343
97Fle-661
97FleTif-661
Hutton, Tom
67Top-428
69Top-266
72Dia-22
72Top-741
73OPC-271
73Top-271
74OPC-443
74Top-443
75OPC-477
75Top-477
76OPC-91
76SSP-472
76Top-91
77Top-264
78Hos-103
78Top-568
79ExpPos-12
79OPC-355
79Top-673
80ExpPos-12
80OPC-219
80Top-427
81Don-93
81Fle-164
81OPC-374
81Top-374
85SpoIndGC-9
90DodTar-375
90SweBasG-87
Hutzler, Jeff
96BurBeeTI-6
Huyke, Woody
78ChaPirT-10
Huyler, Mike
88WatPirP-19
89AugPirP-509
90CarLeaA-22
90SalBucS-8
91CarMudLD-111
91CarMudP-1093
91Cla/Bes-300
91LinDriAA-111
92BelBreC-26
92BelBreF-411
93StoPorC-17
93StoPorF-752
Hvizda, Jim (James)
89BlaYNPRWLU-27
89GasRanP-1019
89GasRanS-9
89SouAtlLAGS-25
89Sta-140
90ChaRanS-11
90TulDriTI-12
91BelBreC-28
91BelBreP-2098
Hyatt, Robert Ham
10JuJuDE-21
10NadE1-21
10PirAmeCE-4
10PirTipTD-20
11SpoLifCW-183
11SpoLifM-251
12T207-86
14B18B-77A
14B18B-77B
Hyde, Bubba
91NegLeaRL-29
91PomBlaBPB-5
Hyde, Cowan
92NegLeaRLI-29
93TedWil-106
95NegLeaLI-29
Hyde, Dick
57Top-403
58SenJayP-4
58Top-156
59Top-498
60Top-193
60TopVen-193
91OriCro-214
Hyde, Matt
91QuaCitAC-5
91QuaCitAP-2647
91QuaCitAP-2648
92QuaCitRBC-28
92QuaCitRBF-828
93CedRapKC-27
93CedRapKF-1756
Hyde, Mickey
89BatCliP-1931
90BenBucL-4
91ClePhiC-21
91ClePhiP-1632
92ClePhiC-6
92ReaPhiF-587
93ReaPhiF-307
Hyde, Rich
91EveGiaP-3908
92CliGiaC-2
93SanJosGC-13
93SanJosGF-3
Hyde, Scott
75TopPho-123
Hydes, Kyle
75PhoGiaC-20
Hyers, Matt
96AubDouB-14
Hyers, Tim
90MedHatBJB-3
91MyrBeaHC-20
91MyrBeaHP-2954
92DunBluJC-10
92DunBluJF-2007
93KnoSmoF-1259
94Bow-148
94ClaGolF-109
94ColC-612
94ColChoGS-612
94ColChoSS-612
94ExtBas-374
94Fla-438
94FleAllR-M7
94FleUpd-186
94PadMot-15
94Pin-530
94PinArtP-530
94PinMusC-530
94ScoRoo-RT100
94ScoRooGR-RT100
94Sel-416
94SpoRoo-90
94SpoRooAP-90
94Ult-578
94UppDec-516
94UppDecED-516
95Don-393
95DonPreP-393
95Pac-364
96TolMudHB-14
Hyman, Don
81QuaCitCT-2
83MidCubT-17
84MidCubT-3
Hyman, Pat
89ColMetB-24
Hymel, Gary
90LSUTigP-7
91LSUTigP-7
91LSUTigP-12
92AlbPolC-24
92AlbPolF-2309
92ClaFS7-9
93BurBeeC-12
93BurBeeF-160
93OttLynF-2438
94HarSenF-1096
95HarSenTI-6
Hypes, Kyle
75LafDriT-17
76PheGiaCr-36
76PhoGiaCa-3
76PhoGiaCC-12
76PhoGiaVNB-10
77PhoGiaCC-10
77PhoGiaCP-9
77PhoGiaVNB-10
78PhoGiaC-10
79PhoGiaVNB-2
Hyson, Cole
89AubAstP-2170
90OscAstS-10
91OscAstC-4
91OscAstP-676
92WatDiaC-25
93RanCucQC-18
93RanCucQF-829
Hyuk Lim, Soo
96HilStaHWB-31
Hyun Kim, Sang
96HilStaHWB-28
Hyzdu, Adam
90ClaDraP-15
90ClaYel-T90
90EveGiaB-1
90EveGiaP-3140
90ProAaA-169
91Bow-617
91Cla/Bes-321
91CliGiaC-20
91CliGiaP-847
91Sco-388
92CalLeaACL-5
92SanJosGC-8
92UppDecML-244
93SanJosGC-1
93SanJosGF-25
94ChaLooF-1363
95ChaLooTI-7
96TreThuB-27
Iannini, Steve
87ModA'sC-8
87ModA'sP-15
Iapoce, Anthony
96BelSnaTI-18
Iasparro, Donnie
86VisOakP-11
Iatarola, Aaron
93BoiHawC-14
93BoiHawF-3929
94CedRapKF-1123
95CedRapKTI-16
95MidLeaA-24
Iavarone, Greg
87PeoChiP-9
90TulDriP-1159
90TulDriTI-13
91LinDriAA-585
91TulDriLD-585
91TulDriP-2775
91TulDriTI-14
Ibanez, Raul
93AppFoxC-12
93AppFoxF-2462
93BelMarC-15
93BelMarF-3213
94AppFoxC-12
94AppFoxF-1057
94MidLeaAF-MDW3
95SPML-150
96BesAutS-40
96Bow-267
96BowBes-172
96BowBesAR-172
96BowBesR-172

96ColCho-431
96ColChoGS-431
96ColChoSS-431
96Exc-105
96ExcAll-9
96FleUpd-U81
96FleUpdNH-11
96FleUpdTC-U81
96TacRaiB-15
96Top-432
96Ult-413
96UltGolM-413
96UltGolP-9
96UltGolPHGM-9
97Fle-209
97FleTif-209
97PacPriGotD-GD87
97Sco-258
97ScoMar-13
97ScoMarPl-13
97ScoMarPr-13
97ScoPreS-258
97ScoShoS-258
97ScoShoSAP-258
97Sel-120
97SelArtP-120
97SelRegG-120
97Top-201
97Ult-123
97UltGolME-123
97UltPlaME-123
97UppDec-233
Ibarguen, Ricky
89BriTigS-12
Ibarguen, Steve
82JacMetT-5
Ibarra, Carlos
82EdmTraT-1
Ibarra, Jesse
94EveGiaC-14
94EveGiaF-3659
94StaCluDP-71
94StaCluDPFDI-71
95BurBeeTI-6
95SPML-145
96BesAutS-41
96Bow-246
96Exc-245
96Top-424
Ibarra, Jesus
96SanJosGB-1
Ibarra, Luis
85MexCitTT-28
Ibarra, Miguel
80CarMudF-6
81ReaPhiT-12
Ickes, Mike
87WinHavRSP-25
Iddon, Brent
95EveAqaTI-11
96MidLeaAB-4
96WisTimRB-11
Iglesias, Luis
87SpaPhiP-18
88ClePhiS-15
Iglesias, Marlo
96BriWhiSB-19
96HicCraB-10
Iglesias, Michael
91KisDodP-4178
94VerBeaDC-10
Iglesias, Mike
93BakDodCLC-11
94VerBeaDF-66
95BakBlaTI-14
96MauStiHWB-35
96VerBeaDB-15
Ignash, Reggie
93ButCopKSP-19
94BurIndC-8
94BurIndF-3808
Ignasiak, Mike
89CalLeaA-39
89StoPorB-3
89StoPorCLC-157
89StoPorP-400
89StoPorS-5
90ElPasDGS-18
90StoPorB-16
90StoPorCLC-177
90StoPorP-2176
91DenZepLD-142
91DenZepP-121
91LinDriAAA-142
92Bow-15
92DenZepF-2635
92DenZepS-131
92Sco-837
92SkyAAAF-64
92TopDeb91-88
93FleFinE-224
93NewOrlZF-966
94BreMilB-38
94BrePol-13
94Fle-179
94NewOrlZF-1462
94StaClu-489
94StaCluFDI-489
94StaCluGR-489
94StaCluMOP-489
94Top-564
94TopGol-564
94TopSpa-564
94Ult-76
95StaClu-575
95StaCluMOP-575
95StaCluSTWS-575
Ihde, Alan Dale
49W725AngTI-12
Ikebe, Iwao
79TCMJapPB-49
Ikegaya, Kojiro
79TCMJapPB-26
Ikesue, Kazutaka
91SalSpuC-21
91SalSpuP-2236
Ikeue, Kouichi
87SalLakTTT-15
Illig, Brett
95GreFalDTI-24
96GreFalDB-15
Ilsley, Blaise
86AshTouP-15
87ColAstP-8
88ColAstB-17
89OscAstS-8
91LinDriAAA-613
91TucTorLD-613
91TucTorP-2211
92LouRedF-1884
92LouRedS-265
93IowCubF-2131
94Bow-188
94SpoRoo-95
94SpoRooAP-95
94Ult-459
95Pac-73
95Sco-289
95ScoGolR-289
95ScoPlaTS-289
95ScrRedBTI-14
Imes, Rod (Rodney)
87OneYanP-25
88Ft.LauYS-12
89AlbYanB-21
89AlbYanP-314
89AlbYanS-8
89BasAmeAPB-AA8
89EasLeaAP-10
90AlbDecGB-16
90CMC-132
90NasSouC-7
90NasSouP-227
90ProAAAF-539
91LinDriAAA-262
91NasSouLD-262
91NasSouP-2152
92ChaLooF-3813
92ChaLooS-187
Impagliazzo, Joe
86AlbYanT-27
Imperial, Jason
92BelBreF-412
93BelBreC-11
93BelBreF-1717
Imrisek, Jason
96TamYanY-15
Inaba, Atsunori
96WesOahCHWB-27
Inabata, Nelson
87HawRai-2
Inagaki, Shuji
87MiaMarP-13
88MiaMarS-12
Incaviglia, Pete
86DonRoo-23
86FleUpd-53
86RanPer-29
86SpoRoo-3
86TopTra-48T
86TopTraT-48T
87ClaGam-16
87ClaUpdY-131
87Don-224
87DonOpeD-175
87Fle-128
87Fle-625
87FleGlo-128
87FleGlo-625
87FleHotS-24
87FleLeaL-25
87FleMin-58
87FleSlu-21
87FleStiC-66
87KraFoo-39
87Lea-185
87OPC-384
87RanMot-2
87RanSmo-15
87RedFolSB-130
87Spo-37
87SpoTeaP-1
87StuPan-26
87Top-550
87TopCoi-14
87TopGloS-29
87TopRoo-6
87TopSti-236
87TopSti-308
87TopTif-550
87ToyRoo-12
88ClaRed-177
88Don-304
88DonBasB-55
88Fle-470
88FleGlo-470
88FleMin-56
88FleSlu-20
88FleStiC-65
88FleSupBC-C1
88GreBasS-33
88HouSho-20
88Lea-147
88Nes-20
88OPC-280
88PanSti-207
88RanMot-2
88RanSmo-4
88Sco-485
88ScoGlo-485
88ScoYouSI-32
88Spo-169
88StaLinRa-7
88Top-201
88Top-280
88TopBig-73
88TopSti-239
88TopTif-201
88TopTif-280
89Bow-238
89BowTif-238
89Don-3
89Don-56
89DonBasB-144
89DonSupD-3
89Fle-523
89FleGlo-523
89FleLeaL-21
89KinDis-24
89OPC-42
89PanSti-455
89RanMot-10
89RanSmo-16
89RedFolSB-63
89Sco-201
89Spo-112
89Top-706
89TopBasT-127
89TopBig-127
89TopSti-249
89TopTif-706
89TVSpoM-118
89UppDec-484
90Bow-491
90BowTif-491
90Don-48
90Fle-301
90FleCan-301
90Lea-231
90OPC-430
90PanSti-157
90PubSti-413
90RanMot-4
90Sco-93
90Top-430
90TopBig-81
90TopSti-247
90TopTif-430
90UppDec-333
90VenSti-238
91Bow-131
91Don-464
91Fle-290
91Lea-366
91OPC-172
91OPCPre-67
91PanFreS-258
91RedFolS-51
91Sco-278
91ScoRoo-3T
91StaClu-78
91TigCok-29
91Top-172
91TopDesS-172
91TopMic-172
91TopTif-172
91TopTra-57T
91TopTraT-57T
91UppDec-453
91UppDec-747
92AstMot-4
92Bow-43
92Fle-139
92Lea-458
92OPC-679
92OPCPre-126
92Pin-325
92Sco-306
92ScoRoo-17T
92StaClu-874
92StaCluNC-874
92Top-679
92TopGol-679
92TopGolW-679
92TopMic-679
92TopTra-54T
92TopTraG-54T
92Ult-491
92UppDec-271
92UppDec-759
93Don-480
93Fla-103
93Fle-436
93FleFinE-110
93Lea-276
93OPC-242
93OPCPre-95
93PacSpa-577
93PhiMed-18
93Pin-492
93RanKee-201
93Sco-568
93SelRoo-114T
93SP-176
93StaClu-47
93StaClu-636
93StaCluFDI-47
93StaCluFDI-636
93StaCluMOP-47
93StaCluMOP-636
93StaCluP-22
93Top-7
93TopGol-7
93TopInaM-7
93TopMic-7
93TopPreS-7
93TopTra-73T
93Ult-442
93UppDec-522
93UppDecGold-522
94Bow-84
94ColC-144
94ColChoGS-144
94ColChoSS-144
94Don-594
94ExtBas-336
94Fin-140
94FinRef-140
94Fle-591
94Lea-265
94Pac-477
94PhiMed-14
94PhiMel-10
94PhiUSPC-1C
94PhiUSPC-4H
94Pin-468
94PinArtP-468
94PinMusC-468
94Sco-416
94ScoGolR-416
94Sel-280
94StaClu-559
94StaCluFDI-559
94StaCluGR-559
94StaCluMOP-559
94StaCluT-215
94StaCluTFDI-215
94Stu-140
94Top-323
94TopGol-323
94TopSpa-323
94Ult-246
94UppDec-491
94UppDecED-491
95Don-98
95DonPreP-98
95Fle-394
95Sco-131
95ScoGolR-131
95ScoPlaTS-131
96Cir-166
96CirRav-166
96FleUpd-U166
96FleUpdTC-U166
96PhiTeaI-16
97DonTea-45
97DonTeaSPE-45
97Sco-44
97ScoPreS-44
97ScoShoS-44
97ScoShoSAP-44
Incaviglia, Tony
81BufBisT-20
Indians, Burlington
92BurIndF-1674
Indians, Cleveland
13FatT20-3
35GouPreR-2
48ExhTea-2
48ExhTea-12
56Top-85A
56Top-85B
56Top-85C
57Top-275
58Top-158
59Top-476
60Top-174
60TopTat-67
60TopVen-174
61Top-467
61TopMagR-10
62GuyPotCP-6
62Top-537
63GadFunC-65
63Top-451
64Top-172
64TopTatI-7
64TopVen-172
65Top-481
66Top-303
66TopRubI-107
66TopVen-303
67Top-544
69FleCloS-8
69FleCloS-33
69TopStaA-8
70FleWorS-45
70Top-637
71FleWorS-18
71FleWorS-46
71FleWorS-52
71OPC-584
71Top-584
71TopTat-60
72Top-547
73OPC-629
73OPCBTC-8
73Top-629
73TopBluTC-8
74OPC-541
74OPCTC-8
74Top-541
74TopStaA-8
74TopTeaC-8
78Top-689
80MarExh-31
83FleSta-232
83FleSti-NNO
87IndGat-NNO
87SpoTeaL-3

87Top-11
87TopTif-11
88IndGat-NNO
88PanSti-459
88RedFolSB-114
90PubSti-647
90RedFolSB-105
90VenSti-522
93TedWilPC-9
94ImpProP-5
94Sco-321
94ScoGolR-321
95PanSti-143
95StaCluSTWS-R19L
96FleInd-19
96PanSti-179
Indians, Indianapolis
38BasTabP-38
77IndIndTI-1
78IndIndTI-1
79IndIndTI-1
80IndIndTI-1
81IndIndTI-1
82IndIndTI-1
83IndIndTI-1
84IndIndTI-1
85IndIndTI-1
86IndIndTI-14
87IndIndTI-1
96IndIndB-1
Indians, Kinston
95KinIndTI-30
Indriago, Juan
92AppFoxC-24
92AppFoxF-993
Infante, Alexis
85SyrChiT-14
86SyrChiP-14
87SyrChiP-1935
87SyrChiT-15
88SyrChiC-21
88SyrChiP-813
89DonRoo-30
90Bow-17
90BowTif-17
90BraDubP-12
90BraDubS-14
90PubSti-517
90VenSti-239
93LinVenB-153
94VenLinU-109
94VenLinU-169
95LinVen-165
86STaoftFT-27
Infante, Ken (Kennedy)
86St.PetCP-14
87ArkTraP-5
88ArkTraGS-11
89CedRapRB-15
89CedRapRS-28
90ClePhiS-9
Infante, Tom
89HamRedS-19
90SprCarB-17
Ingalls, Rick
88BenBucL-29
89BenBucL-28
Inge, Adele
40WheM4-10
Ingle, Mike
86KinEagP-10
Ingle, Randy
83AndBraT-4
84DurBulT-29
85GreBraTI-8
86GreBraTI-14
87GreBraB-4
89GreBraB-21
89GreBraP-1177
90GreBraP-1146
90GreBraS-24
90PulBraB-26
90PulBraP-3114
91GreBraC-28
91LinDriAA-225
91PulBraC-14
91PulBraP-4022
92GreBraS-250
92PulBraC-27
92PulBraF-3195
93MacBraC-27
93MacBraF-1417
93SouAtlLAGF-37
94GreBraF-430
94GreBraTI-4
95BreBtaTI-12
96DurBulBIB-13
Inglin, Jeff
96BriWhiSB-20
Ingram, Darron
94PriRedC-12
94PriRedF-3277
96BilMusTI-14
Ingram, Garey (Gerald)
88EugEmeB-26
90GreFalDSP-18
91BakDodCLC-14
91CalLeLA-12
92SanAntMF-3986
93SanAntMF-3011
94BowBes-B82
94BowBesR-B82
94FleUpd-150
94LeaLimR-65
94SanAntMF-2477
94SpoRoo-32
94SpoRooAP-32
95ColChoGS-22
95ColChoSS-22
95Don-258
95DonPreP-258
95Fle-542
95Pac-219
95PacPri-69
95Pin-154
95PinArtP-154
95PinMusC-154
95Sco-287
95ScoGolR-287
95ScoPlaTS-287
95Ult-397
95UltGolM-397
96DodPol-20
Ingram, Jeff
89UtiBluSP-11
90SouBenWSB-5
90SouBenWSGS-6
Ingram, John
90BatCliP-3061
91MarPhiC-22
91MarPhiP-3449
Ingram, Linty
89FayGenP-1572
90FayGenP-2402
92HigDesMC-10
92LasVegSS-242
Ingram, Riccardo
89LakTigS-10
90LonTigP-1280
91LinDriAA-388
91LonTigLD-388
91LonTigP-1890
92Bow-164
92SkyAAAF-264
92TolMudHF-1055
92TolMudHS-589
92UppDecML-213
93TolMudHF-1665
94TolMudHF-1039
94TopTra-30T
96LasVegSB-15
Ingram, Todd
91SouOreAC-9
91SouOreAP-3835
92RenSilSCLC-43
93ModA'sC-12
93ModA'sF-795
94HunStaF-1325
95KnoSmoF-38
95TreThuTI-11
Inks, Bert
90DodTar-994
Inman, Bert
90OklSoo-16
91OneYanP-4150
92GreHorC-17
92GreHorF-775
92OneYanC-11
93GreHorC-12
93GreHorF-881
94SanBerSC-8
94SanBerSF-2751
Inman, Wade
88OklSoo-21
89OklSoo-17
Innis, Brian
83VerBeaDT-5
Innis, Jeff
84JacMetT-6
85LynMetT-4
86JacMetT-6
87TidTidP-8
87TidTidT-5
88DonTeaBM-NEW
88FleUpd-105
88FleUpdG-105
88TidTidCa-21
88TidTidCM-3
88TidTidP-1582
88TopTra-54T
88TopTraT-54T
89MetColP-35
89MetKah-U1
89TidTidC-3
89TidTidP-1950
90CMC-357
90Don-408
90Fle-206
90FleCan-206
90MetColP-36
90MetKah-40
90OPC-557
90ProAAAF-270
90TidTidC-6
90TidTidP-539
90Top-557
90TopTif-557
90TopTVM-13
90UppDec-562A
90UppDec-562B
91FleUpd-103
91MetColP-36
91MetKah-40
91MetWIZ-196
91OPC-443
91StaClu-547
91Top-443
91TopDesS-443
91TopMic-443
91TopTif-443
91UltUpd-97
92Don-587
92Fle-507
92MetColP-40
92MetKah-40
92OPC-139
92Sco-327
92StaClu-863
92Top-139
92TopGol-139
92TopGolW-139
92TopMic-139
92TriPla-64
92TriPlaP-8
92Ult-234
92UppDec-298
93Don-330
93Fle-476
93MetColP-37
93MetKah-40
93OPC-141
93PacSpa-543
93Pin-557
93Sco-409
93StaClu-433
93StaCluFDI-433
93StaCluMOP-433
93Top-297
93TopGol-297
93TopInaM-297
93TopMic-297
93Ult-428
93UppDec-119
93UppDecGold-119
94Fle-566
94Pac-406
94Sco-291
94ScoGolR-291
94Top-37
94TopGol-37
94TopSpa-37
Inouye, Kelly
94ColSilBC-4
95ColSilB9-7
Intorcia, Trent
87WauTimP-21
88MiaMarS-13
Inzunza, Miguel
95NewJerCTI-13
96PeoChiB-15
Iopoce, Anthony
95HelBreTI-2
Iorg, Dane
76OklCit8TI-8
79Car5-11
80Top-139
81Car5x7-12
81Don-311
81Fle-543
81Top-334
82Don-166
82Fle-116
82FleSta-24
82Top-86
83Car-17
83Don-469
83Fle-10
83FleSti-5
83Top-788
83TopFol-3
83TopSti-189
83TopSti-190
84Don-571
84Fle-326
84FleUpd-55
84Nes792-416
84Top-416
84TopTif-416
84TopTra-54T
84TopTraT-54T
85Don-252
85Fle-204
85Top-671
85TopTif-671
86Fle-9
86FleUpd-54
86RoyKitCD-9
86Spo-186
86Top-269
86TopSti-18
86TopTif-269
86TopTra-49T
86TopTraT-49T
87OPC-151
87Top-690
87TopTif-690
Iorg, Garth
75ForLauYS-26
76VenLeaS-72
78Top-704
79SyrChiT-12
79SyrChiTI-9
80SyrChiT-1
80SyrChiTI-11
80VenLeaS-72
81Fle-423
81OPC-78
81OPCPos-16
81Top-444
82Don-353
82Fle-616
82OPC-83
82Top-518
83Don-306
83Fle-430
83FleSta-89
83FleSti-110
83OPC-326
83Top-326
84BluJayFS-17
84Don-561
84Fle-157
84Nes792-39
84OPC-39
84Top-39
84TopTif-39
85BluJayFS-15
85Don-363
85Fle-107
85OPC-168
85Top-168
85TopTif-168
86BasStaB-59
86BluJayAF-14
86BluJayFS-18
86Don-640
86Fle-61
86Lea-252
86OPC-277
86Top-694
86TopTif-694
87BluJayFS-14
87Don-394
87Fle-229
87FleGlo-229
87OPC-59
87SyrChi1A-4
87Top-751
87TopTif-751
88Don-444
88Fle-113A
88Fle-113B
88FleGlo-113
88OPC-273
88PanSti-220
88Sco-204
88ScoGlo-204
88StaLinBJ-9
88Top-273
88TopTif-273
89PacSenL-152
89T/MSenL-51
89TopSenL-86
90EliSenL-36
91MyrBeaHC-27
91MyrBeaHP-2961
91PacSenL-41
92KnoBluJF-3006
92KnoBluJS-399
92Nab-28
92UppDecS-3
93KnoSmoF-1265
93LinVenB-255
94KnoSmoF-1319
95KnoSmoF-55
Ippolito, Rob
92AriWilP-6
94BelMarC-16
94BelMarF-3229
Irabu, Hideki
97Bow-221
97BowBes-149
97BowBesAR-149
97BowBesR-149
97BowChr-198
97BowChrI-198
97BowChrIR-198
97BowChrR-198
97BowInt-221
97Don-361
97DonLim-121
97DonLim-135
97DonLimLE-121
97DonLimLE-135
97DonPreP-361
97DonPrePGold-361
97DonTea-135
97DonTeaSPE-135
97Fin-320
97FinEmb-320
97FinEmbR-320
97FinRef-320
97FlaShoWotF-WF1
97Fle-751
97FleNewH-8
97FleTif-751
97Lea-324
97LeaFraM-324
97LeaFraMDC-324
97PinCer-129
97PinCerMBlu-129
97PinCerMG-129
97PinCerMR-129
97PinCerR-129
97PinTotCPB-129
97PinTotCPG-129
97PinTotCPR-129
97PinX-P-137
97PinX-PMoS-137
97Sco-551
97ScoShoSAP-551
97SP-184
97SpoIll-11
97SpoIll-31
97SpoIllEE-11
97SpoIllEE-31
97TopStaFAS-FAS15
97Ult-553
97UltGolME-553
97UltPlaME-553
97UppDec-550
97Zen-45
97Zen8x1-20
97Zen8x1D-20
Ireland, Billy
83MiaMarT-13
Ireland, Rich
92ClaDraP-72
92FroRowDP-61
93ClaGolF-190

93StaCluM-192
93Top-767
93TopGol-767
93TopInaM-767
93TopMic-767
Ireland, Tim
77JacSunT-10
80OmaRoyP-15
80VenLeaS-216
81OmaRoyT-18
81Top-66
89PacSenL-104
89SalSpuCLC-146
89SalSpuP-1822
89T/MSenL-52
89TopSenL-67
90CMC-552
90EliSenL-69
90PhoFirC-25
90PhoFirP-28
90ProAAAF-54
92StoPorC-23
92StoPorF-51
93ElPasDF-2966
94ElPasDF-3161
95ElPasDTI-10
Irisawa, Jun
89VerBeaDS-29
Irish, Jeffrey
90DunBluJS-12
90St.CatBJP-3475
Irons, Alex
93DavLipB-13
Irvin, Kyle
88EugEmeB-7
Irvin, Monte
47Exh-106
47PM1StaP1-93
47PM1StaP1-94
47PM1StaP1-95
51Bow-198
51TopRedB-50
52BerRos-25
52Bow-162
52DixLid-10
52DixPre-10
52RedMan-NL9
52StaCalL-78F
52StaCalS-90A
52Top-26
53BowC-51
53Bri-32
53DixLid-8
53DixPre-8
53ExhCan-6
53NorBreL-13
53StaMey-4
53Top-62
54DanDee-13
54DixLid-5
54NewYorJA-26
54RedMan-NL5
54StaMey-4
54Top-3
55GiaGolS-20
55StaMey-4
55Top-100
55TopDouH-3
56Top-194
75Gia195T-8
75TCMAllG-17
76ShaPiz-137
76SSPYanOD-5
77GalGloG-26
79BasGre-65
79DiaGre-45
79TCM50-168
80PerHaloFP-137
80SSPHOF-137
83DonHOFH-15
83TopRep5-26
84WilMay-4
86NegLeaF-6
86NegLeaF-89
86NegLeaFS-89
88NegLeaD-20
88PacLegI-79
89HOFStiB-32
89PerCelP-19
89RinPosNL1-1
90NegLeaS-9
90PacLeg-32
90PerGreM-27
90SweBasG-85
91LinDri-42
91NegLeaRL-20
91SweBasG-44
91TopArc1-62
92ActPacA-10
92ActPacA2-10G
92BazQua5A-10
92FroRowI-1
92FroRowI-2
92FroRowI-3
92FroRowI-4
92FroRowI-5
92NegLeaK-4
92NegLeaPL-1
92NegLeaRLI-30
93ActPacAC-10
93TedWil-54
93TedWil-136
93TedWil-146
93UppDecAH-71
93UppDecAH-154
93UppDecAH-163
94TedWilM-M21
94TopArc1-3
94TopArc1G-3
94UppDecAH-53
94UppDecAH1-53
95NegLeaL2-4
95NegLeaLI-20
95UppDecSHoB-13
97St.VinHHS-8
97TopStaHRR-5
97TopStaHRRA-5
Irvine, Daryl
85GreHorT-17
86WinHavRSP-11
87NewBriRSP-14
88NewBriRSP-890
89EasLeaAP-12
89NewBriRSP-611
89NewBriRSS-7
89Sta-127
90CMC-256
90PawRedSC-5
90PawRedSDD-10
90PawRedSP-457
90ProAAAF-429
90TopTVRS-46
91Fle-98
91OPC-189
91PawRedSDD-9
91PawRedSP-33
91Sco-333
91StaClu-122
91Top-189
91TopDeb90-75
91TopDesS-189
91TopMic-189
91TopTif-189
91TriA AAGP-AAA30
91Ult-34
92Fle-41
92PawRedSF-918
92PawRedSS-358
92Sco-726
92SkyAAAF-162
93BufBisF-511
93RedSoxWHP-16
97DunDonPPS-12
Irvine, Ed
81ElPasDT-1
82VanCanT-8
84VanCanC-44
Irvine, Michael
95IdaFalBTI-11
Irvis, Damon
96AppLeaAB-16
Irwin, Arthur
87BucN28-81
88WG1CarG-52
89EdgR.WG-14
90KalBatN-25
90KalBatN-26
Irwin, Charles
90DodTar-376
98CamPepP-39
Irwin, Dennis
78TacYanC-14
Irwin, Jim
75BreBro-1
Irwin, John
87OldJudN-265
87OldJudN-266
87OldJudN-383
88WG1CarG-66
Irwin, Michael
90AubAstB-13
90AubAstP-3412
Irwin, Tom
92BatCliC-27
92BatCliF-3259
93BatCliC-13
93BatCliF-3141
93SpaPhiF-1052
Isa, Kelsey
87PenWhiSP-21
Isaac, Joe Keith
78WisRapTT-9
Isaac, Luis
76WilTomT-12
81BatTroT-28
88IndGat-7
89BlaYNPRWL-32
89IndTeal-28
90IndTeal-17
91IndFanC-30
92ColSprSSF-767
92ColSprSSS-100
93ChaKniF-560
Isaacson, Christopher
88KinIndS-11
Isales, Orlando
81OklCit8T-8
82IndIndTI-10
83IndIndTI-18
Isbell, Cecil
40WheM4-7A
40WheM4-7C
Isbell, Frank
03BreE10-73
04FanCraAL-26
07WhiSoxGWH-5
08RosComP-14
09AmeCarE-55
09T206-167
11SpoLifCW-184
Ishee, Gabe
96OgdRapTI-3
Ishibashi, Keith
87HawRai-9
Ishige, Hiromichi
87JapPlaB-36
Ishimaru, Taisuke
96GreFalDB-16
Ishimine, Kazuhiko
87JapPlaB-28
Ishimoto, Yoshiaki
87JapPlaB-17
Ishiwata, Shigeru
79TCMJapPB-47
Ishmael, Mike (Michael)
87BurExpP-1085
87JamExpP-2540
Isom, Jeff
93WelPirC-8
93WelPirF-3350
94AugGreC-6
Isom, Johnny
96CarLeaA1B-19
96CarLeaA2B-19
96FreKeyB-20
Isringhausen, Jason
92GulCoaMF-3474
93PitMetC-11
93PitMetF-3702
94Bow-326
94Cla-68
94ExcFS7-235
94FloStaLAF-FSL39
94St.LucMC-14
94St.LucMF-1190
95BinMetTI-44
95Bow-180
95BowBes-B38
95BowBesR-B38
95ColChoSE-19
95ColChoSEGS-19
95ColChoSESS-19
95Exc-231
95NorTidTI-15
95SigRooOJ-20
95SigRooOJP-20
95SigRooOJPS-20
95SigRooOJS-20
95SPCha-19
95SPChaDC-19
95Top-653
95UltGolMR-M16
95UppDec-14
95UppDecED-14
95UppDecEDG-14
95UppDecML-65
95UppDecSE-63
95UppDecSEG-63
96Baz-69
96Bow-83
96BowBes-70
96BowBesAR-70
96BowBesC-2
96BowBesCAR-2
96BowBesCR-2
96BowBesR-70
96Cir-158
96CirRav-158
96ColCho-30
96ColChoGS-30
96ColChoSS-30
96DenHol-17
96Don-101
96DonDiaK-19
96DonPreP-101
96EmoRarB-4
96EmoXL-233
96Fin-G51
96FinRef-G51
96Fla-321
96Fle-481
96FleRooS-8
96FleTif-481
96FleTomL-4
96FleUpd-U225
96FleUpdTC-U225
96Lea-26
96LeaPre-37
96LeaPreP-37
96LeaPrePB-26
96LeaPrePG-26
96LeaPrePS-26
96LeaPreSG-42
96LeaPreSte-42
96LeaSig-33
96LeaSigPPG-33
96LeaSigPPP-33
96MetKah-16
96MetKah-17
96MetUni-201
96MetUniP-201
96MetUniPP-4
96Pac-146
96PacPri-P48
96PacPriG-P48
96PanSti-25
96PanSti-241
96Pin-223
96PinAfi-101
96PinAfiAP-101
96PinArtP-123
96PinFan-28
96PinFoil-223
96PinSta-123
96Sco-131
96Sco-380
96ScoDugC-A82
96ScoDugC-B105
96ScoDugCAP-A82
96ScoDugCAP-B105
96ScoFutF-1
96ScoGolS-10
96Sel-61
96SelArtP-61
96SelCer-16
96SelCerAP-16
96SelCerCB-16
96SelCerCR-16
96SelCerIP-10
96SelCerMB-16
96SelCerMG-16
96SelCerMR-16
96SelTeaN-21
96SP-125
96Spo-42
96SpoArtP-42
96SPSpeFX-7
96SPSpeFXDC-7
96SPx-40
96SPxGol-40
96StaClu-286
96StaCluEPB-286
96StaCluEPG-286
96StaCluEPS-286
96StaCluMOP-286
96Stu-38
96StuPrePB-38
96StuPrePG-38
96StuPrePS-38
96Sum-99
96SumAbo&B-99
96SumArtP-99
96SumFoi-99
96Top-369
96TopChr-151
96TopChrR-151
96TopGal-106
96TopGalPPI-106
96TopLas-120
96Ult-244
96UltGolM-244
96UppDec-140
96UppDec-147
96UppDecBCP-BC3
96UppDecPHE-H43
96UppDecPreH-H43
96Zen-41
96ZenArtP-41
96ZenMoz-24
97Cir-38
97CirRav-38
97ColCho-394
97Don-33
97DonEli-63
97DonEliGS-63
97DonPre-9
97DonPreCttC-9
97DonPreP-33
97DonPrePGold-33
97Fle-399
97FleTif-399
97Lea-156
97LeaFraM-156
97LeaFraMDC-156
97NewPin-5
97NewPinAP-5
97NewPinMC-5
97NewPinPP-5
97Pac-367
97PacLigB-367
97PacSil-367
97PinCer-105
97PinCerMBlu-105
97PinCerMG-105
97PinCerMR-105
97PinCerR-105
97PinIns-11
97PinInsCE-11
97PinInsDE-11
97PinTotCPB-105
97PinTotCPG-105
97PinTotCPR-105
97Sco-306
97Sco-530
97ScoHobR-530
97ScoPreS-306
97ScoResC-530
97ScoShoS-306
97ScoShoS-530
97ScoShoSAP-306
97ScoShoSAP-530
97Sel-77
97SelArtP-77
97SelRegG-77
97StaClu-257
97StaCluMOP-257
97Stu-3
97StuPrePG-3
97StuPrePS-3
97Top-317
97TopGal-172
97TopGalPPI-172
97Ult-241
97UltGolME-241
97UltPlaME-241
97UppDec-433
95UppDecMLFS-65
Issac, Richard
86AppFoxP-11
Ithier, Pete
76WilTomT-13
78SanJosMMC-10
Iverson, Tom
89GreHorP-430
90ChaWheB-28
91PriRedC-30
92CedRapRC-30
93WesVirWC-27
94ChaWheC-27
Ives, F.F.

88AllandGN-21
Ivie, Lonnie
81MiaOriT-15
Ivie, Mike
72OPC-457
72Top-457
73OPC-613
73Top-613
76Hos-103
76OPC-134
76SSP-127
76Top-134
77BurCheD-134
77OPC-241
77PadSchC-29A
77PadSchC-29B
77PadSchC-29C
77Top-325
78Top-445
79GiaPol-15
79Top-538
80GiaPol-15
80OPC-34
80Top-62
81Don-312
81Fle-435
81OPC-236
81Top-236
81TopTra-774
82Don-396
82Top-734
82TopTra-45T
83Don-485
83Fle-331
83OPC-117
83Top-613
Ivie, Ryan
92WatDiaC-7
92WatDiaF-2139
Ivie, Tamara
95ColSilB-13
96ColSilB-15
Ivie, Tom
91ChaRaiC-27
Ivory, Sap (James)
93NegLeaRL2-20
Iwema, Todd
91HelBreSP-17
Izquierdo, Hank
77FriOneYW-58
Jabalera, Francisco
83ColAstT-12
85DomLeaS-205
Jablonowski, Pete
33Gou-83
34GouCanV-34
Jablonski, Ray
53CarHunW-10
53Top-189
54CarHunW-9
54Top-26
54Wil-10
55RedMan-NL21
55Top-56
55TopDouH-51
56Kah-7
56Top-86
57Top-218
58GiaSFCB-11
58Hir-35
58Top-362
59Top-342
61UniOil-H1
79DiaGre-173
91TopArc1-189
94CarLeaA-DJ9
94TopArc1-26
94TopArc1G-26
Jacas, Andre
86MadMusP-12
88St.LucMS-12
Jacas, Dave (David)
87KenTwiP-12
88KenTwiP-1389
89CalLeaA-8
89VisOakCLC-109
89VisOakP-1447
90CMC-572
90PorBeaC-20
90PorBeaP-192
90ProAAAF-262
91ElPasDLD-186
91ElPasDP-2760
91LinDriAA-186
92HunStaF-3962
92HunStaS-311
92SkyAA F-132
Jaccar, Mike
77AshTouT-9
Jacinto, Larry
91GreFalDSP-8
Jacklitsch, Fred
03BreE10-74
09T206-168
10E101-23
10MelMinE-23
10NadCarE-26
10NadE1-22
10PeoT21-28A
10PeoT21-28B
11SpoLifCW-185
11SpoLifM-231
11T205-80
12ImpTobC-62
15AmeCarE-21
16TanBraE-13
90DodTar-377
Jackman, Bill
86NegLeaF-68
Jackowski, Bill
55Bow-284
Jackson, Alvin
62MetJayP-6
62Top-464
63Baz-19
63Fle-48
63MetJayP-6
63Top-111
63TopStil-20
64MetJayP-8
64Top-494
64TopCoi-17
64TopSta-85
64TopStaU-36
64TopTatI-43
65MetJayP-8
65Top-381
65TopTraI-17
66Top-206
66TopVen-206
67OPC-195
67Top-195
68Top-503
69MilBra-125
69Top-590
70OPC-443
70Top-443
73MetAllEB-4
78TCM60I-193
82MetGal62-11
83TidTidT-24
84TidTidT-22
87LitFalMP-2410
88LitFalMP-27
89OriFreB-31
91MetWIZ-197
Jackson, Andrew
92SalLakTSP-3
Jackson, Bo
84OCoandSI-204
86DonHig-43
86DonRoo-38
86MemChiSTOS-10
86MemChiTOS-10
86SouLeaAJ-13
86SpoRoo-40
86TopTra-50T
86TopTraT-50T
87ClaGam-15
87ClaUpdY-109
87Don-35
87DonOpeD-205
87DonRoo-14
87Fle-369
87FleGlo-369
87FleSluBC-M4
87FleStiC-132
87Lea-35
87Spo-190
87SpoSupD-16
87SpoTeaP-13
87Top-170
87TopTif-170
87ToyRoo-13
88ClaBlu-208
88Don-220
88DonBasB-119
88Fle-260
88FleGlo-260
88Lea-187
88OPC-8
88PanSti-110
88RedFolSB-38
88RoySmo-5
88Sco-180
88ScoGlo-180
88Spo-148
88StaLinRo-7
88Top-750
88TopBig-49
88TopSti-258
88TopTif-750
89Bow-126
89BowTif-126
89ClaTraO-122
89ClaTraP-157
89Don-208
89DonBasB-169
89Fle-285
89FleGlo-285
89KinDis-11
89OPC-84
89PanSti-358
89RedFolSB-64
89RoyTasD-6
89Sco-330
89ScoSco-1
89ScoYouSI-5
89Spo-70
89SpoIllFKI-75
89Top-540
89Top-789
89TopAme2C-17
89TopBig-238
89TopHeaUT-8
89TopSti-265
89TopTif-540
89TopTif-789
89TopUKM-43
89TVSpoM-108
89UppDec-221
90AllBasT-7
90Bow-378
90BowIns-4
90BowInsT-4
90BowTif-378
90BowTif-A4
90ClaBlu-2
90ClaBlu-59A
90ClaBlu-59B
90ClaUpd-T25
90ClaUpd-T26
90Col-1
90ColtheSBM-85
90Don-1
90Don-61
90Don-650A
90Don-650B
90DonBesA-63
90DOnBonM-BC1
90DonGraS-12
90DonLeaS-38
90DonPre-3
90DonSupD-1
90Fle-110
90Fle-635
90FleAwaW-19
90FleBasA-20
90FleBasM-21
90FleCan-110
90FleCan-635
90FleLeaL-19
90FleWaxBC-C15
90FraGloT-1
90Hot50PS-22
90KinDis-17
90Lea-125
90MLBBasB-104
90MSAIceTD-5
90OPC-300
90PanSti-84
90PanSti-198
90PanSti-384
90Pos-14
90PubSti-350
90PubSti-596
90RedFolSB-51
90Sco-280A
90Sco-280B
90Sco-566
90Sco-687
90Sco-697
90Sco100S-40
90ScoYouSI-1
90Spo-200
90SunSee-4
90Top-300
90TopBig-6
90TopCoi-19
90TopDou-35
90TopGloA-17
90TopGloS-44
90TopHeaU-8
90TopMag-9
90TopMag-52
90TopMinL-16
90TopSti-155
90TopSti-264
90TopStiB-51
90TopTif-300
90TopTVA-5
90UppDec-32
90UppDec-75
90UppDec-105
90UppDec-555
90VenSti-240
90VenSti-241
90WonBreS-1
91BasBesHRK-11
91CadElID-32
91Cla1-T48
91ClaGam-186
91Don-632
91DonBonC-BC10
91Fle-561
91FlePro-5
91LeaPre-19
91MajLeaCP-20
91OPC-600
91PanFreS-281
91PanSti-226
91RoyPol-12
91Sco-5
91Sco-412
91Sco-420
91Sco-692
91Sco-773
91Sco100S-2
91ScoRoo-1T
91StaClu-224
91Top-600
91TopCraJI-25
91TopDesS-600
91TopMic-600
91TopSta-20
91TopTif-600
91TopTra-58T
91TopTraT-58T
91Ult-149
91UltGol-6
91UppDec-545
91UppDec-744
91WhiSoxK-8
92ClaGam-108
92Don-470
92Fle-86
92Fle-701
92New-12
92OPC-290
92Sco-361
92ScoImpP-53
92SpoStaCC-25
92StaBoJ-1
92StaBoJ-2
92StaBoJ-3
92StaBoJ-4
92StaBoJ-5
92StaBoJ-6
92StaBoJ-7
92StaBoJ-8
92StaBoJ-9
92StaBoJ-10
92StaBoJ-11
92StaClu-654
92StaCluMO-17
92Top-290
92TopGol-290
92TopGolW-290
92TopKid-103
92TopMcD-33
92TopMic-290
92TriPla-164
92UppDec-555
93Bow-415
93CadDis-33
93DiaMar-54
93Fin-91
93FinJum-91
93FinRef-91
93Fla-186
93FleFinE-195
93FunPac-31
93FunPac-199
93Lea-316
93OPC-151
93PacJugC-8
93PacSpa-389
93Pin-524
93PinHomRC-43
93SP-255
93StaClu-495
93StaCluFDI-495
93StaCluMOP-495
93StaCluWS-2
93Stu-110
93Top-400
93TopGol-400
93TopInaM-400
93TopMic-400
93Ult-534
93UppDec-775
93UppDecGold-775
93UppDecOD-D15
93WhiSoxK-13
94AngLAT-7
94AngMot-7
94Bow-535
94ColC-356
94ColChoGS-356
94ColChoSS-356
94Don-173
94DonLonBL-4
94ExtBas-36
94Fin-241
94FinRef-241
94Fla-23
94Fle-84
94FleGolM-5
94FleUpd-18
94FUnPac-151
94Lea-307
94OPC-116
94Pac-128
94PanSti-49
94Pin-509
94PinArtP-509
94PinMusC-509
94PinTri-TR4
94Sco-513
94ScoGolR-513
94ScoGolS-35
94ScoRoo-RT3
94ScoRooCP-CP4
94ScoRooGR-RT3
94ScoRooS-RT3
94Sel-356
94SP-24
94SPDieC-24
94SPHol-15
94SPHolDC-15
94SpoRoo-150
94SpoRooAP-150
94StaClu-167
94StaClu-547
94StaCluFDI-167
94StaCluFDI-547
94StaCluGR-167
94StaCluGR-547
94StaCluMOP-167
94StaCluMOP-547
94Stu-12
94Top-500
94TopGol-500
94TopSpa-500
94TopTra-90T
94Ult-330
94UppDec-117
94UppDecDC-W7
94UppDecED-117
95ColCho-95
95ColChoGS-95
95ColChoSE-36
95ColChoSEGS-36
95ColChoSESS-36
95ColChoSS-95
95Don-507
95DonPreP-507
95Fle-227
95Pac-61
95PacPri-20

95Pin-208
95PinArtP-208
95PinMusC-208
95PinSam-208
95Sco-342
95ScoGolR-342
95ScoPlaTS-342
95Spo-140
95SpoArtP-140
95StaClu-2
95StaCluFDI-2
95StaCluMOP-2
95StaCluSTWS-2
95Top-592
95TopCyb-364
95UppDec-20
95UppDecED-20
95UppDecEDG-20

Jackson, Bubba
88TulDriTI-17

Jackson, Chief
92ColCliP-25

Jackson, Chuck
85TucTorC-67
86TucTorP-8
87DonRoo-55
87FleUpd-47
87FleUpdG-47
88AstMot-25
88AstPol-14
88Sco-222
88ScoGlo-222
88Top-94
88TopTif-94
89AstSmo-20
89Sco-584
89TucTorC-20
89TucTorJP-8
89TucTorP-205
89UppDec-323
91CalCanLD-61
91CalCanP-521
91LinDriAAA-61
92OklCit8F-1921
92OklCit8S-311
92SkyAAAF-143
93EdmTraF-1143
94OklCit8F-1499

Jackson, Damian
92BurIndC-3
92BurIndF-1664
93ColRedC-13
93ColRedF-604
94CanIndF-3122
95Bes-14
95Bow-132
95Exc-40
95UppDecML-179
96Bow-163
96BufBisB-11
97Bow-78
97BowCerBIA-CA40
97BowCerGIA-CA40
97BowInt-78
97ColCho-7
97Fle-626
97FleTif-626
97StaClu-337
97StaCluMOP-337
97UppDec-471
95UppDecMLFS-179

Jackson, Danny
82ChaRoyT-6
83OmaRoyT-6
84Don-461
85Don-374
85Fle-205
86Don-95
86Fle-10
86Lea-30
86RoyKitCD-16
86RoyNatP-25
86Spo-186
87Don-157
87DonOpeD-203
87Fle-370
87FleGlo-370
87TopTra-51T
87TopTraT-51T
88Don-132
88DonBasB-166
88Fle-261
88FleGlo-261
88FleSlu-21
88FleUpd-84
88FleUpdG-84
88OPC-324
88RedKah-20
88Sco-398
88ScoGlo-398
88ScoRoo-2T
88ScoRooG-2T
88Top-324
88TopTif-324
88TopTra-55T
88TopTraT-55T
89Bow-304
89BowTif-304
89CadEllD-31
89ClaLigB-100
89ClaTraO-123
89Don-124
89DonAll-52
89DonBasB-54
89Fle-163
89Fle-636
89FleBasA-22
89FleBasM-21
89FleExcS-25
89FleGlo-163
89FleGlo-636
89FleHeroB-24
89FleLeaL-22
89FleWaxBC-C15
89KinDis-23
89OPC-319
89PanSti-67
89PanSti-225
89RedKah-20
89Sco-555
89ScoHot1S-75
89ScoYouS2-41
89Spo-80
89Top-395
89Top-730
89TopBasT-107
89TopDouA-22
89TopGloS-57
89TopHilTM-18
89TopMinL-10
89TopSti-143
89TopStiB-62
89TopTif-395
89TopTif-730
89TVSpoM-40
89UppDec-640
90Bow-44
90BowTif-44
90Don-80
90Fle-422
90FleCan-422
90Lea-279
90OPC-445
90PanSti-255
90PubSti-32
90PubSti-264
90RedKah-13
90Sco-289
90Spo-89
90Top-445
90TopSti-142
90TopTif-445
90UppDec-120
90VenSti-242
90VenSti-243
91Bow-412
91ClaGam-69
91CubMar-32
91CubVinL-14
91Don-96
91Don-678
91Fle-67
91FleUpd-78
91Lea-268
91OPC-92
91OPCPre-68
91Sco-601
91ScoRoo-17T
91StaClu-433
91Top-92
91TopDesS-92
91TopMic-92
91TopTif-92
91TopTra-59T
91TopTraT-59T
91UltUpd-70
91UppDec-414
91UppDec-723
92Bow-142
92ClaGam-86
92CubMar-32
92Don-91
92Fle-383
92Lea-381
92OPC-619
92Pin-457
92Sco-120
92StaClu-406
92Top-619
92TopGol-619
92TopGolW-619
92TopMic-619
92Ult-176
92UppDec-104
93Don-202
93Fla-104
93Fle-492
93FleFinE-111
93Lea-308
93PacSpa-578
93PhiMed-19
93Pin-514
93Sco-421
93Sel-371
93SelRoo-94T
93StaCluP-5
93Ult-443
93UppDec-753
93UppDecGold-753
94ColC-145
94ColChoGS-145
94ColChoSS-145
94Don-131
94ExtBas-337
94Fin-320
94FinRef-320
94Fla-208
94Fle-592
94Lea-83
94LeaL-137
94OPC-240
94Pac-478
94PhiMed-15
94PhiMel-11
94PhiUSPC-2S
94PhiUSPC-5D
94Pin-144
94PinArtP-144
94PinMusC-144
94Sco-209
94ScoGolR-209
94SP-137
94SPDieC-137
94StaClu-296
94StaCluFDI-296
94StaCluGR-296
94StaCluMOP-296
94StaCluT-235
94StaCluTFDI-235
94Stu-141
94Top-199
94TopGol-199
94TopSpa-199
94TriPla-176
94Ult-247
94UppDec-453
94UppDecED-453
95ColCho-189
95ColChoGS-189
95ColChoSE-172
95ColChoSEGS-172
95ColChoSESS-172
95ColChoSS-189
95Don-105
95DonPreP-105
95DonTopotO-329
95Fla-409
95Fle-395
95FleAllS-22
95FleTeaL-24
95FleUpd-161
95Lea-301
95Pac-330
95PanSti-5
95Pin-369
95PinArtP-369
95PinMusC-369
95Sco-107
95ScoGolR-107
95ScoPlaTS-107
95Spo-123
95SpoArtP-123
95Top-393
95Top-420
95TopCyb-220
95Ult-430
95UltGolM-430
95UppDec-308
95UppDecED-308
95UppDecEDG-308
95UppDecSE-224
95UppDecSEG-224
96CarPol-12
96ColCho-284
96ColChoGS-284
96ColChoSS-284
96Top-167

Jackson, Darrell
78OrlTwiT-9
79TolMudHT-18
79Top-246
80Top-386
81Don-547
81Fle-567
81OPC-89
81Top-89
82Don-179
82Fle-555A
82Fle-555B
82Fle-555C
82Top-193
82TwiPos-17

Jackson, Darrin
82QuaCitCT-22
84MidCubT-16
86PitCubP-10
87IowCubTI-25
88CubDavB-30
88DonRoo-45
88DonTeaBC-NEW
88Fle-641
88FleGlo-641
88FleUpd-78
88FleUpdG-78
88ScoRoo-109T
88ScoRooG-109T
88TopTra-56T
88TopTraT-56T
89Fle-428
89FleGlo-428
89Sco-360
89Top-286
89TopRoo-12
89TopTif-286
89ToyRoo-14
89UppDec-214
90Don-641
90Fle-160
90FleCan-160
90OPC-624
90PadMag-6
90PubSti-195
90Sco-541
90Top-624
90TopTif-624
90UppDec-414
90VenSti-244
91FleUpd-124
91Lea-346
91OPC-373
91PadMag-6
91PadSmo-16
91Sco-169
91Top-373
91TopDesS-373
91TopMic-373
91TopTif-373
91UltUpd-112
92Bow-456
92Don-292
92Fle-609
92Lea-129
92OPC-88
92PadCarJ-10
92PadMot-15
92PadPolD-11
92PadSmo-14
92PanSti-237
92Pin-207
92Sco-521
92StaClu-226
92Top-88
92TopGol-88
92TopGolW-88
92TopMic-88
92TriPla-189
92UppDec-328
93BluJayD-22
93BluJayDM-33
93BluJayFS-16
93Don-230
93Fle-141
93FleFinE-102
93Lea-140
93OPC-143
93PacSpa-259
93PanSti-264
93Pin-125
93Sco-155
93Sel-199
93SelRoo-133T
93StaClu-19
93StaCluFDI-19
93StaCluMOP-19
93Top-761
93TopGol-761
93TopInaM-761
93TopMic-761
93TriPla-138
93Ult-118
93Ult-642
93UppDec-258
93UppDec-673
93UppDecGold-258
93UppDecGold-673
94ColC-370
94ColChoGS-370
94ColChoSS-370
94ExtBas-48
94Fin-262
94FinRef-262
94Fla-33
94Fle-567
94FleUpd-27
94Lea-300
94Pin-531
94PinArtP-531
94PinMusC-531
94ScoRoo-RT38
94ScoRooGR-RT38
94Sel-352
94SpoRoo-8
94SpoRooAP-8
94StaClu-157
94StaClu-659
94StaCluFDI-157
94StaCluFDI-659
94StaCluGR-157
94StaCluGR-659
94StaCluMOP-157
94StaCluMOP-659
94StaCluT-150
94StaCluTFDI-150
94Top-576
94TopGol-576
94TopSpa-576
94TopTra-108T
94Ult-339
94UppDec-411
94UppDecED-411
94WhiSoxK-14
95Don-384
95DonPreP-384
95Fle-120
95Pac-91
95Pin-66
95PinArtP-66
95PinMusC-66
95Sco-16
95ScoGolR-16
95ScoPlaTS-16
95StaClu-71
95StaCluFDI-71
95StaCluMOP-71
95StaCluSTWS-71
95StaCluVR-44
95Top-106
95TopCyb-69
95UppDec-203
95UppDecED-203
95UppDecEDG-203
95StaCluVRMC-44

Jackson, Doug
78DayBeaAT-12

Jackson, Evan
95DurBulTI-14
96DurBulBIB-18

Jackson, Gavin
94SarRedSC-16
94SarRedSF-1958

96HilStaHWB-9
96PawRedSDD-14
96SarRedSB-21
Jackson, Gayron
86AubAstP-14
Jackson, Grant
66Top-591
67Top-402A
67Top-402B
68Top-512
69OPC-174
69Top-174
69TopFou-21
70MLBOffS-91
70OPC-6
70PhiTeal-5
70Top-6
71MLBOffS-300
71OPC-392
71Top-392
72MilBra-158
72OPC-212
72Top-212
73OPC-396
73OriJohP-23
73Top-396
74OPC-68
74Top-68
74TopSta-126
75OPC-303
75Top-303
76OPC-233
76SSP-378
76Top-233
77PirPosP-10
77Top-49
78Top-661
79Top-117
80OPC-218
80Top-426
81Don-15
81Fle-378
81OPC-232
81Top-518
82Don-518
82Fle-191
82OPC-104
82Top-779
82TopTra-46T
88EasLeaAP-48
89ChaKniTI-3
89ChaLooLITI-13
89PacSenL-66
89T/MSenL-53
91IowCubLD-225
91IowCubP-1077
91LinDriAAA-225
91OriCro-215
92YanWIZ7-78
93ChaLooF-2376
94RedKah-33
95RedKah-34
96IndIndB-4
Jackson, Greg
86SalAngC-85
87QuaCitAP-30
87SalAngP-9
87WytCubP-12
Jackson, Harold
74NewYorNTDiS-31
80WisRapTT-8
Jackson, James
84IdaFalATI-13
Jackson, James B.
05IndSouPSoCP-10
09T206-432
Jackson, Jason
87BriYouC-8
88NewBriRSP-912
90CanIndS-7
Jackson, Jeff
89MarPhiS-16
90BatCliP-3080
90Bow-157
90BowTif-157
90OPC-74
90Sco-678
90Top-74
90TopTif-74
91Bow-491
91Cla/Bes-125
91SpaPhiC-26
91SpaPhiP-911
92Bow-72
92ClePhiC-1
92ClePhiF-2070
92UppDecML-301
93ClaGolF-99
93ReaPhiF-308
93StaCluP-24
94ReaPhiF-2075
Jackson, Jelly
86NegLeaF-96
Jackson, Joe
09AmeCarE-56
09ColChiE-141
09SpoNewSM-69
11SpoLifCW-186
12ColRedB-141
13NatGamW-21
13PolGroW-10
13TomBarW-20
14B18B-4A
14B18B-4B
14CraJacE-103
14E&SP-3
14TexTomE-23
15CraJacE-103
15SpoNewM-86
16BF2FP-13
16ColE13-82
16SpoNewM-87
19W514-15
40PlaBal-225
75WhiSox1T-10
76CliPilT-21
77GalGloG-154
77GalGloG-259
77SerSta-11
77ShaPiz-21
80Lau300-13
80LauFamF-24
82OhiHaloF-48
84OCoandSI-199
86IndGreT-5
88FriBasCM-4
91ConTSNP-14
91ConTSNP-400
92Man191BSR-11
92Man191BSR-12
93ConTSNP-1030
94ConTSNB-1030
95UppDecSHoB-17
Jackson, John
90EveGiaB-25
90EveGiaP-3141
91Cla/Bes-255
91SanJosGC-26
91SanJosGP-23
91SanJosGP-26
92ClaFS7-186
92MidAngOHP-8
92MidAngS-459
92UppDecML-205
93MidAngF-332
94VanCanF-1875
97MidAngOHP-17
Jackson, Karun
93GenCubC-16
93GenCubF-3183
Jackson, Ken (Kenneth)
85PhiTas-44
86ReaPhiP-10
87MaiGuiP-7
87MaiGuiT-11
87PhiTas-51
88MaiPhiP-287
89ScrRedBC-17
89ScrRedBP-729
90StoPorB-12
90StoPorCLC-197
92DenZepS-132
Jackson, Kenny
86EugEmeC-37
87AppFoxP-28
88BasCitRS-14
88MaiPhiC-17
89BelBreIS-15
90StoPorP-2197
91ElPasDLD-187
91ElPasDP-2761
91LinDriAA-187
92DenZepF-2653
92LSUTigM-13
93LSUTigM-7
94LSUTigMP-2
Jackson, Larry
81CedRapRT-1
Jackson, Larry (Lawrence C.)
55CarHunW-9
56Top-119
57Top-196
58CarJayP-5
58Top-97A
58Top-97B
59Top-399
60CarJayP-4
60Lea-15
60Top-492
61CarJayP-6
61Pos-174A
61Pos-174B
61Top-535
61TopStal-88
62CarJayP-5
62Jel-165
62Pos-165
62PosCan-165
62Top-83
62Top-306
62TopBuc-41
62TopStal-184
62TopVen-83
63CubJayP-7
63Top-95
64CubJayP-7
64Top-444
64TopCoi-114
64TopSta-13
64TopTatl-44
64WheSta-22
65Baz-2
65CubJayP-8
65OPC-10
65Top-10
65Top-420
66CubTeal-8
66Top-595
67CokCapPh-14
67DexPre-103
67PhiPol-9
67Top-229
68OPC-81
68Top-81
68TopVen-81
69MilBra-126
78TCM60I-222
78TCM60I-286
84CubUno-2
Jackson, LaVerne
85GreHorT-26
86WinHavRSP-12
87WinHavRSP-8
89EasLeaDDP-DD31
89NewBriRSP-615
89NewBriRSS-2
90CanIndP-1303
Jackson, Lee
90CanIndB-13
Jackson, Lloyd
85EveGialC-5
86CliGiaP-11
Jackson, Lonnie
91KisDodP-4201
Jackson, Lou
59Top-130
59TopVen-130
61MapLeaBH-9
64Top-511
78TCM60I-115
91OriCro-216
Jackson, Mark
86CedRapRT-20
87TamTarP-18
Jackson, Martinez
92NegLeaK-18
Jackson, Miccal
91SavCarC-17
91SavCarP-1658
Jackson, Mike (Michael)
86ReaPhiP-11
87DonRoo-36
87FleUpd-48
87FleUpdG-48
87PhiTas-33
87SpoRoo2-33
88Don-139
88Fle-306
88FleGlo-306
88FleUpd-60
88FleUpdG-60
88MarMot-19
88RedFolSB-39
88Sco-144
88ScoGlo-144
88ScoRoo-62T
88ScoRooG-62T
88Top-651
88TopTif-651
89Bow-207
89BowTif-207
89Don-652
89Fle-550
89FleBasM-22
89FleGlo-550
89MarMot-19
89OPC-169
89Sco-398
89ScoYouSI-14
89Top-169
89TopTif-169
89UppDec-142
90Fle-517
90FleCan-517
90Lea-351
90MarMot-19
90OPC-761
90PubSti-435
90Sco-546
90Top-761
90TopTif-761
90UppDec-494
90VenSti-245
91Don-676
91Fle-454
91Lea-452
91MarCouH-23
91OPC-534
91Sco-91
91Top-534
91TopDesS-534
91TopMic-534
91TopTif-534
91UltUpd-51
91UppDec-496
92Bow-513
92Don-584
92Fle-282
92FleUpd-128
92GiaMot-12
92GiaPacGaE-20
92Lea-481
92OPC-411
92Pin-437
92Sco-194
92ScoRoo-40T
92StaClu-653
92StaCluECN-653
92Stu-116
92Top-411
92TopGol-411
92TopGolW-411
92TopMic-411
92Ult-590
92UppDec-593
92UppDec-738
93Don-314
93Fla-142
93Fle-156
93GiaMot-20
93GiaPos-19
93Lea-84
93PacSpa-611
93StaClu-373
93StaCluFDI-373
93StaCluG-18
93StaCluMOP-373
93Top-283
93TopGol-283
93TopInaM-283
93TopMic-283
93Ult-133
93UppDec-170
93UppDecGold-170
94ColC-622
94ColChoGS-622
94ColChoSS-622
94Don-525
94ExtBas-387
94Fin-311
94FinRef-311
94Fla-243
94Fle-692
94GiaAMC-10
94GiaMot-23
94GiaUSPC-5C
94GiaUSPC-11H
94Lea-301
94Pac-547
94Sco-243
94ScoGolR-243
94StaClu-565
94StaCluFDI-565
94StaCluGR-565
94StaCluMOP-565
94StaCluT-25
94StaCluTFDI-25
94Top-58
94TopGol-58
94TopSpa-58
94Ult-290
94UppDec-311
94UppDecED-311
95ColCho-261
95ColChoGS-261
95ColChoSS-261
95Don-459
95DonPreP-459
95Fle-581
95RedKah-13
95Sco-524
95ScoGolR-524
95ScoPlaTS-524
95Top-333
95TopCyb-181
95Ult-444
95UltGolM-444
96Don-523
96DonPreP-523
96Fle-344
96FleTif-344
96FleUpd-U82
96FleUpdTC-U82
96MarMot-18
96Ult-414
96UltGolM-414
97PacPriGotD-GD88
97Ult-524
97UltGolME-524
97UltPlaME-524
Jackson, Mikki
83MadMusF-20
Jackson, Paige
88OklSoo-19
Jackson, Randy (Ransom)
52Bow-175
52StaCalL-80C
52StaCalS-92B
52Top-322
53BowBW-12
54Bow-189
55Bow-87
56Dod-14
56Top-223
57Top-190
58Top-301
59Top-394
79DiaGre-117
83TopRep5-322
90DodTar-378
92TexLon-26
95TopArcBD-156
Jackson, Ray
91EveGiaC-7
91EveGiaP-3930
92ClaFS7-78
92CliGiaC-9
92CliGiaF-3609
Jackson, Reggie
83LynMetT-1
84JacMetT-5
Jackson, Reggie (Reginald M.)
69A'sJacitB-9
69MilBra-127
69Raw-1
69Top-260
69TopDecl-19
69TopSup-28
69TopTeaP-21
70DayDaiNM-31
70Kel-32
70MilBra-11
70MLBOffS-260
70OPC-64
70OPC-66
70OPC-140
70OPC-459
70Top-64

70Top-66
70Top-140
70Top-459
70TopBoo-10
70TopSup-28
70TraSta-11B
71AllBasA-10
71BazNumT-18
71BazUnn-3
71MLBOffS-517
71MLBOffS-562
71OPC-20
71Top-20
71TopCoi-108
71TopGreM-47
71TopSup-38
71TopTat-21
72'sA'sPos-14
72Kel-20
72MilBra-159
72OPC-90
72OPC-435
72OPC-436
72ProStaP-26
72Top-90
72Top-435
72Top-436
73Kel2D-22
73LinPor-141
73OPC-255
73Top-255
73TopCanL-22
73TopCom-8
73TopPin-8
74A'sPos-52
74Kel-20
74LauAllG-71
74OPC-130
74OPC-202
74OPC-203
74OPC-338
74OPC-470
74OPC-477
74Top-130
74Top-202
74Top-203
74Top-338
74Top-470
74Top-477
74TopDecE-61
74TopPuz-6
74TopSta-226
75Hos-88
75Kel-54
75OPC-211
75OPC-300
75OPC-461
75SSP42-11
75SSPPuzB-12
75Top-211
75Top-300
75Top-461
76CraDis-22A
76CraDis-22B
76Hos-146
76Kel-8
76OPC-194
76OPC-500
76SSP-494
76Top-194
76Top-500
77BurCheD-176
77Hos-3
77MSADis-30
77OPC-200
77PepGloD-34
77Spo-1409
77Top-10
77TopCloS-22
77YanBurK-17
78Hos-47
78Kel-40
78OPC-110
78OPC-242
78PapGinD-26
78Pep-32
78RCColC-81
78SSP270-26
78Top-7
78Top-200
78Top-413
78WifBalD-32
78YanBurK-21
78YanSSPD-26
79Hos-120
79Kel-46
79OPC-374
79Top-700
79TopCom-12
79YanBurK-21
79YanPicA-20
80BurKinPHR-17
80Kel-26
80OPC-314
80PerHaloFP-216
80Top-600
80TopSup-6
81AccRegJ-1
81AccRegJ-2
81AccRegJ-3
81AllGamPI-53
81Don-228
81Don-348
81Don-468
81Dra-10
81Fle-79
81Fle-650
81Fle-650B
81FleStiC-115
81FleStiC-126
81Kel-3
81MSAMinD-18
81OPC-370
81PerAll-14
81PerCreC-7
81Squ-5
81TigDetN-120
81Top-2
81Top-400
81TopScr-3
81TopSti-11
81TopSti-107
81TopSti-245
81TopSupHT-65
81TopSupN-8
82Don-535
82Don-575
82Dra-19
82Fle-39
82Fle-646
82Fle-646B
82FleSta-110
82FleSta-112
82K-M-23
82Kel-14
82OPC-300
82OPC-301
82OPC-377
82PerAll-7
82PerAllG-7
82PerCreC-20
82PerCreCG-20
82Squ-5
82Top-300
82Top-301
82Top-551
82TopSti-216
82TopStiV-216
82TopTra-47T
83AllGamPI-56
83Don-3
83Don-115
83DonActA-3A
83DonActA-3B
83Dra-12
83Fle-93
83Fle-640
83Fle-645
83FleSta-90
83FleSti-32
83Kel-3
83KelCerB-15
83OPC-56
83OPC-219
83OPC-390
83PerCreC-27
83PerCreCG-27
83SevCoi-5
83Top-390
83Top-500
83Top-501
83Top-702
83TopFol-2
83TopGloS-39
83TopLeaS-2
83TopSti-5
83TopSti-17
83TopSti-41
83TopSti-163
83TopStiB-4
84AllGamPI-145
84AngSmo-11
84DodUniOP-10
84Don-57
84DonActAS-36
84DonCha-9
84Dra-15
84Fle-520
84FunFooP-16
84GalRegJ-1
84GalRegJ-2
84GalRegJ-3
84GalRegJ-4
84GalRegJ-5
84GalRegJ-6
84GalRegJ-7
84GalRegJ-8
84GalRegJ-9
84GalRegJ-10
84GalRegJ-11
84GalRegJ-12
84GalRegJ-13
84GalRegJ-14
84GalRegJ-15
84GalRegJ-16
84GalRegJ-17
84GalRegJ-18
84GalRegJ-19
84GalRegJ-20
84GalRegJ-21
84GalRegJ-22
84GalRegJ-23
84GalRegJ-24
84GalRegJ-25
84GalRegJ-26
84GalRegJ-27
84GalRegJ-28
84GalRegJ-29
84GalRegJ-30
84MilBra-14
84Nes792-100
84Nes792-711
84Nes792-712
84Nes792-713
84OCoandSI-21
84OCoandSI-95
84OPC-100
84RalPur-19
84SevCoi-W12
84Top-100
84Top-711
84Top-712
84Top-713
84TopCer-19
84TopGaloC-6
84TopRubD-27
84TopSti-102B
84TopSti-231
84TopSup-21
84TopTif-100
84TopTif-711
84TopTif-712
84TopTif-713
85AllGamPI-59
85AngSmo-2
85AngStrH-8
85CirK-13
85Don-57
85DonActA-39
85Dra-17
85Fle-303
85Fle-639
85FleLimE-14
85GenMilS-19
85Lea-170
85OPC-200
85SevCoi-C12
85SevCoi-W13
85Top-200
85Top3-D-14
85TopGloA-19
85TopGloS-15
85TopRubD-27
85TopSti-187
85TopSti-220
85TopSup-29
85TopTif-200
86AngSmo-2
86BurKinA-12
86Don-377
86DonHig-10
86DorChe-11
86Dra-3
86Fle-160
86FleFutHoF-6
86FleLimE-26
86FleMin-32
86FleSlu-18
86FleStiC-65
86GenMilB-2G
86Lea-173
86MeaGolBB-7
86MeaGolSB-6
86MSAJifPD-8
86OPC-394
86OPCBoxB-I
86QuaGra-26
86SevCoi-W9
86Spo-37
86Spo-57
86Spo-61
86Spo-71
86Spo-147
86Spo-150
86SpoDecG-53
86Top-700
86Top3-D-13
86TopGloS-2
86TopSti-177
86TopSup-35
86TopTat-17
86TopTif-700
86TopWaxBC-I
86TruVal-13
86Woo-15
87A'sMot-5
87A'sMot-27
87A'sSmoC-7
87ClaGam-24
87Don-210
87DonOpeD-22
87Fle-84
87FleGlo-84
87FleUpd-49
87FleUpdG-49
87GenMilB-3E
87K-M-16
87Lea-201
87OPC-300
87RedFolSB-108
87Spo-44
87SpoTeaP-23
87Top-300
87Top-312
87TopCoi-15
87TopGloS-54
87TopTif-300
87TopTif-312
87TopTra-52T
87TopTraT-52T
87Woo-4
88Fle-283
88FleGlo-283
88GreBasS-3
88PanSti-175
88Sco-500
88Sco-501
88Sco-502
88Sco-503
88Sco-504
88ScoGlo-500
88ScoGlo-501
88ScoGlo-502
88ScoGlo-503
88ScoGlo-504
88Spo-120
88StaLinAs-8
89AngSmo-15
89PacLegI-111
89TopBasT-9
90BasWit-42
90HOFStiB-88
90UppDecJH-1
90UppDecJH-2
90UppDecJH-3
90UppDecJH-4
90UppDecJH-5
90UppDecJH-6
90UppDecJH-7
90UppDecJH-8
90UppDecJH-9
90UppDecJH-AU1
90UppDecJH-NNO0
90UppDecS-2
91A'sMot-28
91BasBesRB-8
91FouBal-32
91OriCro-217
91UppDecCBP-4
91UppDecHoB5-1
91UppDecS-1
91UppDecS-5
91UppDecS-11
91UppDecS-12
92A'sUno7P-2
92A'sUno7P-5
92TVSpoMF5HRC-4
92UppDecF-46
92UppDecFG-46
92UppDecHH-HI5
92UppDecS-4
92UppDecS-17
92UppDecS-27
92UppDecS-34
92YanWIZ7-79
92YanWIZ8-89
92YanWIZA-33
93FunPac-28
93UppDecAH-72
93UppDecAH-135
93UppDecAH-165
93UppDecAHP-2
93UppDecAHP-3
93UppDecAHP-4
93UppDecCRJ-C1
93UppDecCRJ-C2
93UppDecCRJ-C3
93UppDecFA-A9
93UppDecFAJ-A9
93UppDecJHJ-1
93UppDecJHJ-2
93UppDecJHJ-3
93UppDecJHJ-4
93UppDecJHJ-5
93UppDecJHJ-6
93UppDecJHJ-7
93UppDecJHJ-8
93UppDecJHJ-9
93UppDecS-1
93UppDecS-3
93UppDecS-18
93UppDecS-20
93UppDecS-23
93UppDecTAN-TN16
94TedWil5C-2
94UppDecAH-9
94UppDecAH-44
94UppDecAH-107
94UppDecAH-122
94UppDecAH-167
94UppDecAH-210
94UppDecAH-P44
94UppDecAH1-9
94UppDecAH1-44
94UppDecAH1-107
94UppDecAH1-122
94UppDecAH1-167
94UppDecAH1-210
94UppDecS-5
94UppDecS-8
94UppDecTAE-75
94UppDecTAELD-LD15
95EagBalL-2
95SPCha-109
95SPChaCP-CP1
95SPChaCPDC-CP1
95SPChaDC-109
95UppDecA-2
95UppDecSDRJ-1
95UppDecSDRJ-2
95UppDecSDRJ-3
95UppDecSHoB-10
97St.VinHHS-9

Jackson, Robert

85EveGialC-6

Jackson, Roderick

93NiaFalRF-3380
96IdaFalB-11

Jackson, Ron

85LouRedR-30
86BakDodP-15
87GasRanP-20

Jackson, Ron H.

55ArmCoi-9
55Top-66
55TopDouH-49
56Top-186
58Top-26
59Top-73
59TopVen-73

60Lea-29
60Top-426
Jackson, Ronnie D.
75IntLeaASB-12
75PacCoaLAB-12
75SalLakCC-4
77BurCheD-120
77Top-153
78AngFamF-19
78SSP270-213
78Top-718
79Kel-59
79OPC-173
79Top-339
79TwiFriP-11
80OPC-5
80Top-18
81Don-489
81Fle-557
81OPC-271
81Top-631
81TopSti-103
82Don-602
82Fle-269
82OPC-359
82SpoIndT-21
82Top-488
82TopTra-48T
83Don-639A
83Don-639B
83Don-639C
83Fle-94
83Top-262
84AngSmo-12
84Don-133
84Fle-521
84Nes792-548
84Top-548
84TopTif-548
88VanCanP-768
89BirBarB-26
89BirBarP-113
89PacSenL-92
89T/MSenL-54
89TopSenL-117
90EliSenL-70
90SarWhiSS-28
91OriCro-218
91PacSenL-5
93NewOrlZF-988
94NewOrlZF-1485
95WhiSoxK-31
Jackson, Roy Lee
78TidTidT-11
79TidTidT-1
80TidTidT-19
81Don-36
81Top-223
81TopTra-775
82Don-541
82OPC-71
82OPCPos-7
82Top-71
83Don-479
83Fle-431
83OPC-194
83Top-427
84BluJayFS-18
84Don-195
84Fle-158
84Nes792-339
84OPC-339
84Top-339
84TopTif-339
85Don-606
85Fle-108
85Lea-106
85OPC-37
85Top-516
85TopSti-364
85TopTif-516
86Fle-326
86Top-634
86TopTif-634
87Fle-545
87FleGlo-545
87Top-138
87TopTif-138
91MetWIZ-198
Jackson, Ryan
94ElmPioF-3487
95KanCouCLTI-6
95KanCouCTI-17
95MidLeaA-25
96Exc-162
94ElmPioC-9
Jackson, Shoeless (Joe)
12ColTinT-141
17HolBreD-48
46SpoExcW-4-11
80PacLeg-107
88PacEigMO-13
88PacEigMO-31
88PacEigMO-32
88PacEigMO-36
88PacEigMO-37
88PacEigMO-55
88PacEigMO-62
88PacEigMO-69
88PacEigMO-77
88PacEigMO-110
89PacLegI-220
92ConTSN-444
92ConTSN1N-400
92ConTSNCI-21
93ActPacA-131
93CraJac-2
94ConTSN-1030
94ConTSN-1042
94ConTSNB-1042
94UppDecTAE-29
95ConTSNGJ-6
Jackson, Sonny (Roland)
65AstBigLBPP-8
65OPC-16
65Top-16
66Top-244
66TopVen-244
67AstTeal1-8
67CokCapAs-8
67DexPre-104
67Top 415
68CokCapB-14
68DexPre-40
68OPC-187
68Top-187
68TopVen-187
69MilBra-128
69OPC-53
69Top-53
69TopSta-5
69TopTeaP-2
70OPC-413
70Top-413
71MLBOffS-12
71OPC-587
71Top-587
72MilBra-160
72OPC-318
72Top-318
73OPC-403
73Top-403
74GreHeroBP-6
74OPC-591
74Top-591
75HawIsIC-10
76LauIndC-37
79SavBraT-8
80AndBraT-8
83BraPol-36
84DurBulT-30
85RicBraT-25
87AstSer1-12
87AstShoSO-13
87GreBraB-3
89RicBraBC-10
89RicBraC-24
89RicBraP-832
90ProAAAF-422
90RicBraC-2
90RicBraP-277
90RicBraTI-14
91LinDriAAA-450
91RicBraBC-39
91RicBraP-2587
92RicBraBB-23
92RicBraF-393
92RicBraRC-7
96SanJosGB-28
Jackson, Stonewall (Travis C.)
22WilPatV-36
25Exh-35
28PorandAR-A18
28PorandAR-B18
29ExhFou-10
31Exh-9
31W517-12
33CraJacP-14
33Gou-102
34BatR31-180
34DiaStaR-63
34GouCanV-24
35GouPuzR-1K
35GouPuzR-3B
35GouPuzR-14B
35GouPuzR-15B
35WheBB1-17
40PlaBal-158
46SpoExcW-4-8
61Fle-115
79DiaGre-33
80PacLeg-87
80PerHaloFP-179
80SSPHOF-180
83DiaClaS2-102
91ConTSN-42
94ConTSN-1101
94ConTSNB-1101
Jackson, Vince
91HigSchPLS-9
91KisDodP-4202
92GreFalDSP-2
93YakBeaC-13
93YakBeaF-3898
Jackson, Wade
96BoiHawB-18
Jackson, William
52LavPro-34
96BurIndB-28
Jacob, Mark
83SanJosBC-12
Jacobo, Ed
85VerBeaDT-10
86VerBeaDP-12
Jacobs, Anthony R.
55CarHunW-10
55Top-183
Jacobs, Dwayne
96MacBraB-8
Jacobs, Elmer
20WalMaiW-22
Jacobs, Frank
91Cla/Bes-398
91PitMetC-4
91PitMetP-3429
92ClaFS7-274
92St.LucMCB-24
92St.LucMF-1753
93BinMetF-2341
93ClaFS7-139
94BinMetF-711
95BinMetTI-47
Jacobs, Jake
89EugEmeB-4
90AppFoxBS-13
90AppFoxP-2090
91BasCitRC-7
91BasCitRP-1394
Jacobs, Lamar
77FriOneYW-68
Jacobs, Ron
76SpoIndC-5
77HolMilT-16
78HolMilT-14
79VanCanT-3
Jacobs, Russell
96HonShaHWB-31
96WisTimRB-12
Jacobs, Ryan
93DanBraC-16
93DanBraF-3615
94MacBraC-9
94MacBraF-2198
95DurBulTI-13
96Exc-128
96GreBraB-15
96GreBraTI-48
Jacobs, Spook (Forrest)
47PM1StaP1-96
52Par-54
53ExhCan-46
54Top-129
55A'sRodM-19
55JetPos-6
55Top-61
55TopDouH-47
56Top-151
56TopHocF-A17
58JetPos-9
88ChaLooLTI-15
94TopArc1-129
94TopArc1G-129
Jacobs, Terrell
40WheM4-9
Jacobsen, Joe
93YakBeaC-14
93YakBeaF-3881
94SanAntMF-2463
96Exc-176
96SanAntMB-9
Jacobsen, Nels
87BurExpP-1069
88FloStaLAS-9
88WesPalBES-13
Jacobsen, Robert
85VerBeaDT-16
86VerBeaDP-13
Jacobson, Albert
04FanCraAL-27
Jacobson, Baby Doll (William)
17HolBreD-49
19W514-61
20GasAmeMBD-19
20NatCarE-49
21E121So8-41
21Exh-80
22AmeCarE-31
22E120-97
22W572-48
23MapCriV-18
23WilChoV-69
25Exh-114
26Exh-114
27AmeCarE-45
87ConSer2-43
88ConSer4-14
93ConTSN-740
Jacobson, Brian
96GreFalDB-17
96GreFalDTI-11
Jacobson, Jeff
82AubAstT-3
85ChaO'sT-3
Jacobson, Kelton
95FayGenTI-13
96LakTigB-14
Jacobson, Kevin
82RedPioT-23
Jacobson, Merwin
22W575-62
90DodTar-379
Jacobucci, Steve
89PitMetS-26
90St.LucMS-30
91ElmPioC-30
Jacoby, Brook
80AndBraT-27
82RicBraT-13
83RicBraT-13
84Don-542
84FleUpd-56
84Ind-19
84IndWhe-26
84TopTra-55T
84TopTraT-55T
85Don-154
85Fle-452
85Ind-19
85IndPol-26
85OPC-327
85Top-327
85TopSti-251
85TopSti-370
85TopTif-327
86Don-154
86Fle-590
86FleMin-116
86IndOhH-26
86IndTeal-25
86Lea-82
86OPC-116
86Top-116
86TopSti-207
86TopTat-5
86TopTif-116
87ClaGam-40
87Don-8
87Don-104
87DonAll-37
87DonOpeD-112
87DonSupD-8
87Fle-253
87FleGlo-253
87HosSti-22
87IndGat-26
87Lea-8
87Lea-134
87OPC-98
87RedFolSB-53
87Spo-109
87SpoTeaP-3
87Top-405
87TopSti-212
87TopTif-405
88Don-131
88DonBasB-229
88Fle-612
88FleExcS-22
88FleGlo-612
88FleStiC-20
88IndGat-26
88Lea-51
88OPC-248
88PanSti-76
88Sco-39
88ScoGlo-39
88Spo-72
88StaLinI-14
88Top-555
88TopBig-17
88TopSti-211
88TopTif-555
88TopUKM-38
88TopUKMT-38
89Bow-86
89BowTif-86
89Don-114
89DonBasB-61
89Fle-408
89FleGlo-408
89IndTeal-14
89OPC-1
89PanSti-326
89RedFolSB-65
89Sco-19
89Spo-192
89Top-141
89Top-739
89TopBig-195
89TopSti-212
89TopTif-141
89TopTif-739
89UppDec-198
90Bow-341
90BowTif-341
90Don-83
90DonBesA-75
90Fle-493
90FleCan-493
90IndTeal-18
90Lea-74
90OPC-208
90PanSti-58
90PubSti-561
90RicBra2ATI-12
90Sco-56
90Spo-155
90Top-208
90TopBig-276
90TopSti-219
90TopTif-208
90UppDec-459
90USPlaCA-5C
90VenSti-246
91Bow-59
91DenHol-9
91Don-176
91Fle-369
91IndFanC-11
91Lea-421
91OPC-47
91PanFreS-216
91PanSti-178
91Sco-162
91Sco100S-92
91StaClu-286
91Stu-44
91Top-47
91TopDesS-47
91TopMic-47
91TopTif-47
91Ult-113
91UltUpd-46
91UppDec-137
91UppDecFE-78F
92Cla1-T46
92Don-670
92Fle-260

92IndFanC-13
92OPC-606
92Pin-376
92Sco-577
92StaClu-828
92StaCluNC-828
92Top-606
92TopGol-606
92TopGolW-606
92TopMic-606
92Ult-349
92UppDec-528
93Don-493
93Fle-593
93Sco-567
93Top-303
93TopGol-303
93TopInaM-303
93TopMic-303
93UppDec-200
93UppDecGold-200
Jacoby, Don
91BurIndP-3322
Jacome, Jason
91KinMetC-23
91KinMetP-3810
92ColMetC-10
92ColMetPI-28
92ColMetPIISPI-9
92ProFS7-292
92St.LucMF-1742
93St.LucMC-13
94Bow-210
94Cla-76
94LeaLimR-24
94NorTidF-2915
94SigRooDP-94
94SigRooDPS-94
95ColCho-327
95ColChoGS-327
95ColChoSE-146
95ColChoSEGS-146
95ColChoSESS-146
95ColChoSS-327
95Don-136
95DonPreP-136
95Fle-371
95Lea-307
95NorTidTI-16
95Pin-383
95PinArtP-383
95PinMusC-383
95Sel-147
95SelArtP-147
95StaClu-321
95StaCluMOP-321
95StaCluSTWS-321
95StaCluVR-167
95Top-337
95TopCyb-183
95UC3-120
95UC3ArtP-120
95Ult-413
95UltGolM-413
95UppDec-124
95UppDecED-124
95UppDecEDG-124
96Fle-131
96FleTif-131
96LeaSigA-115
96LeaSigAG-115
96LeaSigAS-115
96RoyPol-14
96StaClu-282
96StaCluMOP-282
95StaCluVRMC-167
96Ult-71
96UltGolM-71
96UppDec-92
93St.LucMF-2918
97Pac-103
97PacLigB-103
97PacSil-103
97RoyPol-12
Jacques, Eric
89WytCubS-17
91WinSpiP-2825
Jaeckel, Paul
65Top-386
Jagnow, Jim
85BurRanT-17
Jaha, John
86TriTriC-195
87BelBreP-3
88StoPorCLC-193
88StoPorP-743
89CalLeaA-45
89StoPorB-16
89StoPorCLC-165
89StoPorP-380
89StoPorS-3
91Cla/Bes-291
91DaiDolF-18
91ElPasDLD-188
91ElPasDP-2756
91LinDriAA-188
92Bow-399
92Bow-542
92DenZepF-2647
92DenZepS-133
92Don-398
92FleUpd-35
92OPC-126
92ProFS7-84
92SkyAA F-290
92SkyAAAF-65
92Top-126
92TopGol-126
92TopGolW-126
92TopMic 126
93Bow-183
93BrePol-12
93Don-207
93Fin-152
93FinRef-152
93Fla-225
93Fle-252
93Lea-350
93OPC-190
93PacSpa-159
93Pin-228
93Sco-236
93Sel-308
93SP-66
93StaClu-701
93StaCluFDI-701
93StaCluMOP-701
93Stu-89
93Top-181
93TopGol-181
93TopInaM-181
93TopMic-181
93Toy-91
93Ult-221
93UppDec-177
93UppDecGold-177
94Bow-65
94BreMilB-39
94BrePol-14
94ColC-146
94ColChoGS-146
94ColChoSS-146
94Don-569
94ExtBas-104
94Fin-106
94FinRef-106
94Fla-68
94Fle-180
94Lea-317
94LeaL-44
94OPC-131
94Pac-331
94PanSti-82
94Pin-312
94PinArtP-312
94PinMusC-312
94ProMag-74
94Sco-173
94ScoGolR-173
94Sel-216
94Spo-40
94StaClu-105
94StaCluFDI-105
94StaCluGR-105
94StaCluMOP-105
94StaCluMOP-ST22
94StaCluST-ST22
94Stu-45
94Top-283
94TopGol-283
94TopSpa-283
94TriPla-54
94Ult-77
94UppDec-476
94UppDecED-476
95ColCho-184
95ColChoGS-184
95ColChoSS-184
95Don-232
95DonPreP-232
95Fin-195
95FinRef-195
95Fle-181
95Lea-275
95LeaLim-117
95Pac-234
95Pin-356
95PinArtP-356
95PinMusC-356
95Sco-235
95ScoGolR-235
95ScoPlaTS-235
95StaClu-371
95StaCluMOP-371
95StaCluSTWS-371
95Stu-131
95Top-505
95TopCyb-295
95Ult-65
95UltGolM-65
95UppDec-299
95UppDecED-299
95UppDecEDG-299
96ColCho-595
96ColChoGS-595
96ColChoSS-595
96Don-84
96DonPreP-84
96EmoXL-73
96Fla-101
96Fle-147
96FleTif-147
96Lea-104
96LeaPrePB-104
96LeaPrePG-104
96LeaPrePS-104
96LeaSig-119
96LeaSigA-116
96LeaSigAG-116
96LeaSigAS-116
96LeaSigPPG-119
96LeaSigPPP-119
96MetUni-70
96MetUniP-70
96Pac-340
96PacPri-P109
96PacPriG-P109
96PanSti-193
96Pin-98
96ProSta-28
96Sco-315
96ScoDugC-B40
96ScoDugCAP-B40
96SelTeaN-28
96StaClu-102
96StaCluMOP-102
96Sum-74
96SumAbo&B-74
96SumArtP-74
96SumFoi-74
96Top-317
96Ult-364
96UltGolM-364
96UppDec-123
97Bow-250
97BowBes-39
97BowBesAR-39
97BowBesR-39
97BowInt-250
97Cir-379
97CirRav-379
97ColCho-370
97Don-252
97DonEli-116
97DonEliGS-116
97DonLim-176
97DonLimLE-176
97DonPre-57
97DonPreCttC-57
97DonPreP-252
97DonPrePGold-252
97Fin-114
97FinEmb-114
97FinEmbR-114
97FinRef-114
97FlaSho-A169
97FlaSho-B169
97FlaSho-C169
97FlaShoLC-169
97FlaShoLC-B169
97FlaShoLC-C169
97FlaShoLCM-A169
97FlaShoLCM-B169
97FlaShoLCM-C169
97Fle-129
97FleTeaL-8
97FleTif-129
97Lea-27
97LeaFraM-27
97LeaFraMDC-27
97MetUni-65
97NewPin-23
97NewPinAP-23
97NewPinMC-23
97NewPinPP-23
97Pac-119
97PacLigB-119
97PacPri-39
97PacPriLB-39
97PacPriP-39
97PacSil-119
97PinCer-57
97PinCerMBlu-57
97PinCerMG-57
97PinCerMR-57
97PinCerR-57
97PinIns-98
97PinInsCE-98
97PinInsDE-98
97PinTotCPB-57
97PinTotCPG-57
97PinTotCPR-57
97PinX-P-93
97PinX-PMoS-93
97PinX-PSfF-24
97PinX-PSfFU-24
97ProMag-59
97ProMagML-59
97Sco-68
97ScoPreS-68
97ScoShoS-68
97ScoShoSAP-68
97Sel-54
97SelArtP-54
97SelRegG-54
97SP-100
97SpoIll-151
97SpoIllEE-151
97StaClu-35
97StaCluMat-35
97StaCluMOP-35
97Stu-63
97StuPrePG-63
97StuPrePS-63
97Top-446
97TopChr-158
97TopChrR-158
97TopGal-98
97TopGalPPI-98
97TopIntF-ILM9
97TopIntFR-ILM9
97Ult-76
97UltGolME-76
97UltPlaME-76
97UppDec-100
Jaime, Angel
92GreFalDSP-23
93BakDodCLC-12
93YakBeaC-15
94VerBeaDC-11
94VerBeaDF-87
95SanAntMTI-23
96StLucMTI-24
Jaime, Ismael
85MexCitTT-16
Jaime, Jorge
89HigSchPLS-17
Jaime, Juan
90MyrBeaBJP-2780
91MyrBeaHC-13
91MyrBeaHP-2947
Jakubowski, John
81BatTroT-30
Jakubowski, Stan
77AshTouT-10
79TucTorT-6
Jakucki, Jack (Sigmund)
47CenFlo-11
47SigOil-77
96Bro194F-6
James, Artie (Arthur)
77EvaTriT-16
79RocRedWT-6
James, Author (Bill)
92MegRut-143
92MegRut-144
92MegRut-145
95MegGriJWL-15
James, Bevan
91SydWavF-5
James, Bill (William)
14B18B-50A
14B18B-50B
15CraJacE-153
15SpoNewM-87
16BF2FP-53
16ColE13-84
16SpoNewM-88
75WhiSox1T-11
88ConSer5-17
88PacEigMO-61
94ConTSN-1035
94ConTSN-1041
94ConTSNB-1035
94ConTSNB-1041
James, Bob
82ExpHygM-10
82ExpPos-16
83ExpPos-9
83WicAerDS-11
84Don-87
84ExpPos-13
84ExpStu-10
84Fle-277
84Nes792-579
84OPC-336
84Top-579
84TopTif-579
85Don-279
85Fle-400
85FleUpd-60
85OPC-114
85Top-114
85TopMin-114
85TopTif-114
85TopTifT-61T
85TopTra-61T
85WhiSoxC-43
86BasStaB-60
86Don-379
86Fle-209
86FleStiC-66
86OPC-284
86SevCoi-C11
86Spo-158
86Top-467
86TopSti-290
86TopSup-36
86TopTat-3
86TopTif-467
86WhiSoxC-43
87Don-493
87Fle-501
87FleGlo-501
87FleStiC-67
87OPC-342
87RedFolSB-15
87SpoTeaP-26
87Top-342
87TopTif-342
87WhiSoxC-17
88Don-507
88Fle-401
88FleGlo-401
88OPC-232
88PanSti-54
88Top-232
88TopSti-289
88TopTif-232
James, Calvin
85MiaHur-7
86OscAstP-15
87OscAstP-7
88ColAstB-26
James, Charlie (Charles)
60Top-517
61Top-561
62Top-412
63Jel-163
63Pos-163
63Top-83
64CarTeal-4
64Top-357
64TopVen-357
65OPC-141
65RedEnq-13
65Top-141
78TCM60I-292
James, Chris
85PhiTas-43

85PorBeaC-29
86FleUpd-55
86PhiTas-26
86PorBeaP-10
87Don-42
87FleUpd-50
87FleUpdG-50
87Lea-42
87PhiTas-18
87TopTra-53T
87TopTraT-53T
88Don-453
88DonBasB-159
88Fle-307
88FleGlo-307
88OPC-1
88PanSti-362
88PhiTas-14
88Sco-409
88ScoGlo-409
88ScoYouSI-14
88StaLinPh-10
88Top-572
88TopSti-122
88TopTif-572
89Bow-404
89BowTif-404
89Don-312
89DonBasB-266
89Fle-572
89FleGlo-572
89OPC-298
89PadCok-8
89PadMag-23
89PanSti-156
89PhiTas-12
89RedFolSB-66
89Sco-202
89ScoRoo-46T
89Top-298
89TopSti-119
89TopTif-298
89TopTra-56T
89TopTraT-56T
89UppDec-513
90Bow-340
90BowTif-340
90Don-323
90DonGraS-3
90Fle-161
90FleCan-161
90FleUpd-92
90IndTeal-20
90Lea-319
90OPC-178
90PanSti-350
90PubSti-241
90Sco-498
90ScoRoo-60T
90Top-178
90TopSti-105
90TopTif-178
90TopTra-46T
90TopTraT-46T
90UppDec-435
90UppDec-798
90VenSti-247
91Bow-67
91Don-227
91Fle-370
91IndFanC-15
91Lea-175
91OPC-494
91PanSti-181
91Sco-491
91StaClu-422
91Stu-45
91Top-494
91TopDesS-494
91TopMic-494
91TopTif-494
91Ult-114
91UppDec-140
92Don-82
92Fle-112
92GiaMot-27
92GiaPacGaE-21
92Lea-497
92OPC-709
92OPCPre-20
92Sco-262
92StaClu-23
92StaClu-747
92StaCluECN-747
92Top-709
92TopGol-709
92TopGolW-709
92TopMic-709
92UppDec-560
93AstMot-21
93Don-604
93Fle-531
93FleFinE-79
93PacSpa-272
93Pin-120
93RanKee-412
93StaCluAs-5
93Top-38
93TopGol-38
93TopInaM-38
93TopMic-38
94ColC-507
94ColChoGS-507
94ColChoSS-507
94ExtBas-181
94Fin-385
94FinRef-385
94FleUpd-93
94Lea-358
94StaClu-621
94StaCluFDI-621
94StaCluGR-621
94StaCluMOP-621
94Ult-432
94UppDec-398
94UppDecED-398
95Fle-289
95Sco-108
95ScoGolR-108
95ScoPlaTS-108
95Top-150
James, Cleo
72OPC-117
72Top-117A
72Top-117B
74WicAerODF-113
90DodTar-380
James, Darin
84EveGiaC-6B
85EveGialC-7
James, Dewey
82BelBreF-11
83BelBreF-3
James, Dion
82ElPasDT-2
84BrePol-14
84Don-31
84FleUpd-57
85BreGar-9
85BrePol-14
85Don-211
85Fle-584
85Lea-162
85Top-228
85TopTif-228
86Don-89
86Top-76
86TopTif-76
86VanCanP-13
87BraSmo-24
87ClaUpdY-144
87DonOpeD-44
87FleUpd-51
87FleUpdG-51
87SpoTeaP-24
87TopTra-54T
87TopTraT-54T
88Don-190
88DonBasB-29
88Fle-543
88FleGlo-543
88FleMin-64
88FleStiC-76
88OPC-82
88PanSti-250
88Sco-395
88ScoGlo-395
88ScoYouSI-7
88Spo-36
88StaLinBra-10
88Top-408
88Top-549
88TopBig-220
88TopCoi-44
88TopMinL-40
88TopSti-42
88TopTif-408
88TopTif-549
88TopUKM-39
88TopUKMT-39
89Bow-277
89BowTif-277
89Don-340
89DonBasB-253
89Fle-594
89FleGlo-594
89PanSti-44
89Sco-163
89ScoRoo-51T
89Top-678
89TopBig-223
89TopSti-24
89TopTif-678
89UppDec-587
90Bow-331
90BowTif-331
90Don-428
90El PasDAGTI-14
90Fle-494
90FleCan-494
90IndTeal-19
90OPC-319
90PanSti-64
90PubSti-115
90Sco-514
90Top-319
90TopBig-132
90TopTif-319
90UppDec-591
90VenSti-248
91Don-348
91Fle-371
91OPC-117
91Sco-131
91Top-117
91TopDesS-117
91TopMic-117
91TopTif-117
91UppDec-399
92Bow-494
92Lea-365
92StaClu-884
92StaCluNC-884
92Ult-409
93Don-735
93Fle-649
93PacSpa-556
93StaClu-266
93StaCluFDI-266
93StaCluMOP-266
94BreMilB-40
94Don-446
94Fle-232
94Pac-424
94Sco-175
94ScoGolR-175
James, Duane
85TulDriTI-29
86SalRedBP-13
James, Howard
90CedRapRB-27
James, Jeff
69Top-477
70OPC-302
70Top-302
James, Joey
89WatIndS-10
90Bes-127
90CliGiaB-20
90CliGiaP-2554
90MidLeaASGS-36
90ProAaA-127
91CalLeLA-33
91Cla/Bes-378
91SanJosGC-29
91SanJosGP-18
James, John
60Top-499
61Top-457
61Yan61RL-27
91RinPos1Y2-11
92YanWIZ6-59
James, Keith
87PocGiaTB-22
James, Kenny
95TopTra-129T
James, Mike
88GreFalDTI-23
89BakDodCLC-186
90SanAntMGS-15
90TexLeaAGS-14
91LinDriAA-536
91SanAntMLD-536
91SanAntMP-2969
92AlbDukS-11
92SanAntMF-3970
93AlbDukF-1455
93Bow-674
93StaCluD-26
94VanCanF-1862
95AngMot-27
95FleUpd-66
96AngMot-23
96Don-257
96DonPreP-257
96Fle-50
96FleTif-50
96LeaSigEA-88
97Fle-47
97FleTif-47
97Sco-369
97ScoHobR-369
97ScoResC-369
97ScoShoS-369
97ScoShoSAP-369
97Top-431
James, Paul
86DayBealP-13
James, Richard
83St.PetCT-22
James, Robert Byrne
33Gou-208
James, Skip
74PhoGiaC-80
75PhoGiaC-5
75PhoGiaCK-14
76PhoGiaCr-15
76PhoGiaCa-5
76PhoGiaCC-13
76PhoGiaVNB-11
77Gia-11
77PhoGiaCC-11
77PhoGiaCP-10
77PhoGiaCP-11
77PhoGiaVNB-11
79VanCanT-1
James, Sonny
84SavCarT-1
James, Todd
88BenBucL-23
89PalSprACLC-56
91LinDriAA-437
91MidAngLD-437
91MidAngP-431
92EdmTraS-161
92MidAngF-4022
92MidAngOHP-9
92SkyAAAF-80
James, Troy
86ColMetP-14
87LynMetP-23
88VisOakCLC-164
88VisOakP-88
Jameyson, Rick
92WatIndC-29
94ColRedC-29
Jamieson, Charles
16ColE13-85
21Exh-81
22E120-35
22W572-49
23WilChoV-70
25Exh-82
27AmeCarE-21
28Exh-41
28StaPlaCE-39
29PorandAR-46
33Gou-171
77Ind192T-9
93ConTSN-692
95ConTSN-1360
Jamison, Bob
81NasSouTI-14
87NasSouTI-25
89NasSouTI-26
Jamison, David
85CloHSS-23
Jamzy, Mascot
93FayGenC-29
Janeski, Gerry
71MLBOffS-543
71OPC-673
71Top-673
93RanKee-19
Janiak, Joseph
52LavPro-8
Janicki, Pete
92ClaDraP-119
93Bow-641
93PalSprAC-10
93Pin-468
93Sco-500
93UppDec-422
93UppDecGold-422
94MidAngF-2432
94MidAngOHP-11
95LakElsSTI-17
96Bow-363
96VanCanB-18
Janikowski, Randy
88BoiHawP-1619
Janke, Jared
95MarPhiTI-10
96PieBolWB-13
Janney, Barry
77SpaPhiT-22
Janowicz, Vic
53Top-222
54Bow-203
54Top-16
55Bow-114
72TopTes5-6
91TopArc1-222
94TopArc1-16
94TopArc1G-16
Jansen, Larry
46SpoExcW-5-11
47HomBon-22
48BluTin-6
48Bow-23
49Bow-202
49EurSta-110
49Lea-56
50Bow-66
50JJKCopP-7
51Bow-162
51FisBakL-10
51TopRedB-21
52BerRos-26
52Bow-90
52RedMan-NL10
52StaCalL-78D
52StaCalS-90B
52TipTop-17
52Top-5
53BowBW-40
54Bow-169
54NewYorJA-27
54Top-200
57HygMea-6
57SeaPop-20
73OPC-81
73Top-81A
73Top-81B
75Gia195T-9
76TayBow4-95
79TCM50-255
83TopRep5-5
93UppDecAH-73
94TopArc1-200
94TopArc1G-200
Jantzen, A.C.
87OldJudN-267
Janus, Ed
82MadMusF-33
83MadMusF-1
Janvrin, Harold
15CraJacE-149
15SpoNewM-88
16ColE13-83
16FleBreD-45
16SpoNewM-89
17HolBreD-50
90DodTar-381
91ConTSN-144
Janzen, Marty
92GulCoaYF-3786
95TamYanYI-12
96BesAutS-42
96BluJayOH-17
96Bow-265
96BowBes-170
96BowBesAR-170
96BowBesR-170
96Exc-90
96Fin-G300
96FinRef-G300
96FleUpd-U97
96FleUpdTC-U97
96SyrChiTI-16

96Top-429
96Ult-432
96UltGolM-432
96UltGolP-10
96UltGolPHGM-10
97BluJayS-53
97ColCho-11
97Fle-243
97FleTif-243
97PacPriGotD-GD101
97StaClu-356
97StaCluMOP-356
97Top-225
97Ult-146
97UltGolME-146
97UltPlaME-146
97UppDec-231

Jaques, Eric
89Sta-164
90PeoChiTI-24
91WinSpiC-6
92ChaKniF-2767
92ChaKniS-160

Jaquette, Bryan
92BelBreC-30
93BelBreC-29
95ElPasDTI-11
96El PasDB-5
92BelBreC-30

Jaramillo, Rudy
76SanAntBTI-13
90AstMot-27
91AstMot-28
92AstMot-27
93AstMot-28
95RanCra-16
96RanMot-28
97BenRocC-28

Jarlett, Al
46SunBre-8

Jarolimek, Jonathan
92GenCubC-14
92GenCubF-1556

Jaroncyk, Ryan
95Bes-115
95BowBes-X4
95BowBesR-X4
95SPML-114
95TopTra-30T
96AppLeaAB-23
96BesAutSA-31
96Top-19
96TopPowB-19

Jarquin, Skeeter (Gersan)
77RocRedWM-21
78RocRedWT-9
79HolMilT-13

Jarrell, Joe
86MemChiSTOS-11
86MemChiTOS-11
87ChaO'sW-13
88ChaKniTI-9

Jarrett, Link
94BenRocF-3602
95AshTouTI-5
96NewHavRB-15
97BenRocC-11

Jarrett, Mark
82MadMusF-12

Jarvis, Jason
94OneYanC-10
94OneYanF-3786
95Exc-96
95GreBatTI-13
96DunBluJB-14
96DunBluJTI-17

Jarvis, John
90GreHorB-14
90GreHorP-2666
90GreHorS-8
91PriWilCC-15
91PriWilCP-1431

Jarvis, Kevin
91PriRedC-23
91PriRedP-3508
92ChaWheF-4
92ChaWVWC-12
93WinSpiC-10
93WinSpiF-1565
94Bow-48
94IndIndF-1805
94SpoRoo-116
94SpoRooAP-116
95Bow-202
95Fle-438
95Pac-107
95RedKah-14
95TopTra-93T
95Ult-144
95UltGolM-144
96ColCho-517
96ColChoGS-517
96ColChoSS-517
96IndIndB-11
96UppDec-51
97ColCho-81
97UppDec-337

Jarvis, LeRoy
47TipTop-142
49SomandK-9
90DodTar-382

Jarvis, Matt
92KanCouCC-6
92KanCouCF-86
92KanCouCTI-15
93AlbPolC-15
93AlbPolF-2023
93SouAtlLAGF-3
94Bow-599
94ClaGolF-6
94FreKeyF-2608
94OriPro-48
95BowBayTI-37
96BowBayB-18
94FreKeyC-12

Jarvis, Pat (Robert Pat)
67OPC-57
67Top-57
68CokCapB-4
68DexPre-41
68OPC-134
68Top-134
68TopVen-134
69MilBra-129
69MLBOffS-114
69Top-282
69TopSta-6
69TopTeaP-2
70MLBOffS-7
70OPC-438
70Top-438
71MLBOffS-13
71OPC-623
71Top-623
71TopCoi-85
72MilBra-161
72Top-675
73OPC-192
73Top-192
78AtlCon-10
78TCM60I-264

Jarvis, Ray
70OPC-361
70Top-361
71OPC-526
71Top-526

Jasco, Elinton
94HunCubF-3561
96RocCubTI-12
94HunCubC-15

Jaster, Larry
65CarTeal-12
67Top-356
68OPC-117
68Top-117
68TopVen-117
69Top-496
69TopSta-56
69TopTeaP-10
70ExpPos-13
70OPC-124
70Top-124
71MLBOffS-14
71RicBraTI-8
72MilBra-162
86DurBulP-14
87SumBraP-21
88SumBraP-415
89DurBullS-27
89DurBulTI-27
90DurBulTI-28
91DurBulC-16
91DurBulP-1678
92MacBraC-28
92MacBraF-286
93MacBraC-29
93MacBraF-1418
94MacBraC-28
94MacBraF-2225
95MacBraTI-12

Jaster, Scott
86ColMetP-15
87LynMetP-21
88ColMetGS-25
88St.LucMS-13
89St.LucMS-11
90SalSpuP-2732
91BirBarLD-64
91BirBarP-1465
91LinDriAA-64
92BirBarF-2595
92BirBarS-85
92SkyAA F-41
93MemChiF-387

Jaszczak, Steve
93MisStaB-23

Jata, Paul
72OPC-257
72Top-257

Jauss, Dave
89WesPalBES-29
90WesPalBES-30
91WesPalBEC-27
91WesPalBEP-1246
92WesPalBEC-26
92WesPalBEF-2103
94HarSenF-2107
95LinVen-35

Javery, Al
77TCMTheWY-62
83TCMPla1943-39

Javier, Ignacio Alfredo
73CedRapAT-21
75IowOakT-9
80WicAerT-10
85DomLeaS-170

Javier, M. Julian
60Top-133
60TopVen-133
61CarJayP-7
61Top-148
61TopStal-89
62CarJayP-6
62Top-118
62TopStal-185
62TopVen-118
63CarJayP-10
63Jel-159
63Pos-159
63Top-226
64CarTeal-5
64Top-446
64WheSta-23
65CarJayP-5
65CarTeal-13
65Top-447
66CarTeal-6
66Top-436
67Top-226
67TopVen-320
68Baz-5
68OPC-25
68Top-25
68TopVen-25
69MilBra-130
69MLBOffS-212
69Top-497
69TopSta-116
69TopTeaP-18
70CarTeal-7
70MLBOffS-140
70OPC-415
70Top-415
71CarTeal-21
71MLBOffS-275
71OPC-185
71Top-185
71TopCoi-39
72MilBra-163
72Top-745
78TCM60I-288
81TCM60I-414
92CarMcD-27

Javier, Stan
83GreHorT-24
84NasSouTI-10
85DomLeaS-45
85HunStaJ-20
86Don-584
86FleUpd-56
86TacTigP-9
87Don-590
87FleUpd-52
87FleUpdG-52
87Top-263
87TopTif-263
88A'sMot-15
88DonBasB-155
88DonTeaBA-NEW
88Sco-367
88ScoGlo-367
89A'sMot-21
89Don-185
89Fle-13
89FleGlo-13
89OPC-248
89Sco-322
89Top-622
89TopBig-277
89TopTif-622
89UppDec-581
90A'sMot-23
90Don-568
90Fle-12
90FleCan-12
90FleUpd-23
90Lea-445
90OPC-102
90PubSti-308
90Sco-394
90ScoRoo-52T
90ScoYouS2-21
90Top-102
90TopTif-102
90TopTra-47T
90TopTraT-47T
90UppDec-209
90VenSti-249
91Bow-599
91DodMot-27
91DodPol-5
91Don-239
91Fle-211
91Lea-155
91OPC-61
91PanFreS-61
91Sco-281
91StaClu-39
91StaCluP-18
91Top-61
91TopDesS-61
91TopMic-61
91TopTif-61
91UppDec-688
92DodMot-20
92DodPol-5
92DodSmo-10092
92Don-322
92Fle-461
92OPC-581
92Sco-583
92StaClu-187
92Top-581
92TopGol-581
92TopGolW-581
92TopMic-581
92Ult-212
92YanWIZ8-90
93AngMot-23
93Don-280
93Fle-493
93PacBeiA-2
93PacSpa-237
93PanSti-276
93Top-712
93TopGol-712
93TopInaM-712
93TopMic-712
93UppDec-249
93UppDec-730
93UppDecGold-249
93UppDecGold-730
94A'sMot-8
94ColC-598
94ColChoGS-598
94ColChoSS-598
94ExtBas-151
94Fin-403
94FinRef-403
94Fla-92
94Fle-60
94FleUpd-75
94Lea-325
94Pac-80
94Pin-313
94PinArtP-313
94PinMusC-313
94Sco-252
94ScoGolR-252
94ScoRoo-RT36
94ScoRooGR-RT36
94Sel-115
94SpoRoo-143
94SpoRooAP-143
94StaClu-613
94StaCluFDI-613
94StaCluGR-613
94StaCluMOP-613
94Top-446
94TopGol-446
94TopSpa-446
94TopTra-107T
94Ult-409
94UppDec-384
94UppDecED-384
95AthMot-9
95ColCho-129
95ColChoGS-129
95ColChoSS-129
95Don-485
95DonPreP-485
95DonTopotO-138
95Fla-75
95Fle-247
95Lea-323
95Pac-313
95Pin-109
95PinArtP-109
95PinMusC-109
95Sco-39
95ScoGolR-39
95ScoPlaTS-39
95StaClu-50
95StaCluFDI-50
95StaCluMOP-50
95StaCluSTWS-50
95StaCluVR-32
95Top-338
95TopCyb-184
95Ult-93
95UltGolM-93
96Don-155
96DonPreP-155
96EmoXL-291
96Fla-389
96Fle-211
96FleTif-211
96FleUpd-U207
96FleUpdTC-U207
96GiaMot-14
96MetUni-243
96MetUniP-243
96Pac-400
96Sco-420
96StaClu-207
96StaCluMOP-207
95StaCluVRMC-32
96Top-57
96Ult-568
96UltGolM-568
97Fle-483
97FleTif-483
97Pac-444
97PacLigB-444
97PacSil-444
97Top-308

Javier, Vicente
88BilMusP-1824
89GreHorP-422
90CedRapRB-4
90CedRapRP-2327
91CedRapRC-18
91CedRapRP-2727

Jay, Joe
47Exh-107
54BraJohC-47
54Top-141
55BraGolS-11
55BraJohC-47
55Top-134
56RedBurB-9
58Top-472
59RedBurBP-7
59Top-273
60BraJayP-6
60BraLaktL-12
60BraSpiaS-9
60Lea-23
60Top-266
61Kah-21

61RedJayP-6
61SevElev-3
61Top-233
61TopStaI-43
62Baz-13
62Jel-124
62Kah-21
62Pos-124A
62Pos-124B
62PosCan-124
62RedEnq-16
62RedJayP-6
62SalPlaC-126
62ShiPlaC-126
62Top-58
62Top-233
62Top-263
62Top-440
62TopBuc-42
62TopStaI-116
62TopVen-58
63BasMagM-40
63ExhStaB-33
63Jel-133
63Kah-16
63Pos-133
63RedEnq-15
63RedFreBC-10
63RedJayP-4
63Top-7
63Top-225
64Kah-13
64RedJayP-5
64Top-346
64TopVen-346
65Kah-18
65OPC-174
65RedEnq-14
65Top-174
66Top-406
78TCM60I-216
90BasWit-81
94TopArc1-141
94TopArc1G-141

Jaye, Jamie
95BakBlaTI-25

Jean, Domingo
91MidLeaAP-MWL10
91SouBenWSC-16
91SouBenWSP-2852
92Bow-130
92ForLauYTI-18
92Ft.LauYF-2607
92UppDecML-307
93AlbYanF-2160
93Bow-159
93ClaFS7-76
93FlaWavotF-8
93StaCluY-30
94Bow-90
94Cla-136
94ColC-147
94ColChoGS-147
94ColChoSS-147
94Don-117
94Fle-233
94Pac-425
94Pin-238
94PinArtP-238
94PinMusC-238
94Sco-256
94ScoBoyoS-14
94ScoGolR-256
94Top-212
94TopGol-212
94TopSpa-212
94TucTorF-756
94Ult-506
96ChaLooB-15

Jeannette, Joe
11TurRedT-68

Jeansonne, Kevin
76BatTroTI-13
77WatIndT-14

Jeffcoat, George
90DodTar-383

Jeffcoat, Hal
49EurSta-58
51Bow-211
52Bow-104
52Top-341
53BowBW-37
53Top-29
54Bow-205
55Bow-223
56RedBurB-10
56Top-289
57Kah-15
57RedSoh-10
57Top-93
58Kah-14
58RedEnq-20
58RedJayP-8
58Top-294
59RedEnq-11
59RedShiBS-8
59Top-81
59TopVen-81
83TopRep5-341
91TopArc1-29

Jeffcoat, Mike
81WatIndT-10
82WatIndT-4
83ChaChaT-2
84Don-43
84FleUpd-58
84Ind-20
84IndWhe-46
84TopTra-56T
84TopTraT-56T
85Don-251
85Fle-453
85Ind-20
85Top-303
85TopTif-303
86Fle-545
86PhoFirP-10
86Top-571
86TopTif-571
87OklCit8P-10
88BlaYNPRWLU-17
89Fle-524
89FleGlo-524
89OklCit8C-4
89OklCit8P-1520
90Don-521
90Fle-302
90FleCan-302
90Lea-416
90OPC-778
90RanMot-19
90Sco-158
90Top-778
90TopTif-778
91Bow-278
91Fle-291
91Lea-386
91OPC-244
91RanMot-19
91Sco-174
91StaClu-216
91Top-244
91TopDesS-244
91TopMic-244
91TopTif-244
92Don-351
92Fle-309
92OklCit8S-312
92OPC-464
92RanTeal-10
92Sco-174
92StaClu-265
92Top-464
92TopGol-464
92TopGolW-464
92TopMic-464
92Ult-134
92UppDec-597
93RanKee-202
94EdmTraF-2870

Jefferies, Gregg
86ColMetP-16
87JacMetF-24
87TexLeaAF-11
88ClaBlu-243
88Don-657
88DonTeaBM-657
88Fle-137
88FleGlo-137
88FleMin-94
88Lea-259
88MetColP-27
88Sco-645
88ScoGlo-645
88StaJef-1
88StaJef-2
88StaJef-3
88StaJef-4
88StaJef-5
88StaJef-6
88StaJef-7
88StaJef-8
88StaJef-9
88StaJef-10
88StaJef-11
88TidTidCa-9
88TidTidCM-15A
88TidTidCM-15B
88TidTidP-1600
88TriAAAP-40
88TriAAC-27
89Baz-16
89Bow-381
89BowTif-381
89ClaLigB-6
89ClaTraP-154
89Don-35
89DonBasB-152
89DonRoo-2
89Fle-38
89FleExcS-26
89FleGlo-38
89FleLeaL-23
89FleSup-25
89JefCarCC-1
89JefCarCC-2
89JefCarCC-3
89JefCarCC-4
89JefCarCC-5
89JefCarCC-6
89JefCarCC-7
89JefCarCC-8
89JefCarCC-9
89JefCarCC-10
89JefCarCC-11
89JefCarCC-12
89JefCarCC-13
89JefCarCC-14
89JefCarCC-15
89JefCarCC-16
89K-M-11
89MetCol8-9
89MetCol8-32
89MetColP-10
89MetFanC-9
89MetKah-12
89MSAHolD-11
89Nis-11
89OPC-233
89PanSti-128
89Sco-600
89ScoHot1R-1
89ScoSco-39
89ScoYouSI-1
89Spo-90
89Spo-223
89Top-233
89TopBasT-87
89TopBig-253
89TopDouM-2
89TopHeaUT-10
89TopRoo-13
89TopTif-233
89TopUKM-44
89ToyRoo-15
89TVSpoM-8
89UppDec-9
89Woo-22
90Baz-14
90Bow-140
90BowTif-140
90ClaUpd-T1
90Don-270
90DonBesN-117
90Fle-207
90FleCan-207
90Hot50RS-22
90Lea-171
90MetCol8-17
90MetColP-5
90MetFanC-9
90MetKah-9
90MLBBasB-18
90OPC-457
90PanSti-298
90PubSti-136
90PubSti-614
90Sco-468
90Sco100RS-10
90Spo-14
90StaLonJS-12
90StaLonJS-32
90Top-457
90TopBig-57
90TopDou-36
90TopGloS-60
90TopRoo-16
90TopSti-324
90TopStiB-5
90TopTif-457
90TopTVM-24
90ToyRoo-16
90UppDec-166
90UppDecS-4
90VenSti-250
90VenSti-251
91BasBesHM-11
91Bow-481
91Cla2-T40
91ClaGam-117
91Don-79
91Fle-151
91Lea-465
91MajLeaCP-77
91MetColP-5
91MetKah-9
91MetTro-4
91MetWIZ-199
91OPC-30
91PanFreS-80
91PanSti-83
91Pos-9
91Sco-660
91Sco100S-80
91Sev3DCN-8
91SevCoi-NE8
91StaClu-257
91Stu-206
91Top-30
91TopDesS-30
91TopMic-30
91TopTif-30
91Ult-221
91Ult-397
91UppDec-95
91UppDec-156
92Bow-13
92ClaGam-171
92Don-372
92Fle-508
92FleUpd-26
92Hig5-73
92Lea-215
92OPC-707
92OPCPre-95
92PanSti-223
92Pin-330
92PinTea2-45
92RoyPol-12
92Sco-192
92ScoRoo-39T
92SpoIllFK1-292
92StaClu-737
92StaCluNC-737
92Stu-184
92Top-707
92TopGol-707
92TopGolW-707
92TopKid-14
92TopMic-707
92TopTra-55T
92TopTraG-55T
92Ult-372
92UppDec-133
92UppDec-725
93Bow-544
93CarPol-7
93DiaMar-55
93Don-307
93Fin-83
93FinRef-83
93Fla-121
93Fle-238
93FleFinE-124
93FunPac-75
93Lea-265
93OPC-123
93OPCPre-98
93PacSpa-137
93PanSti-106
93Pin-24
93Pin-480
93Sco-17
93ScoFra-7
93Sel-152
93SelRoo-12T
93SP-75
93StaClu-628
93StaCluCa-12
93StaCluFDI-628
93StaCluMOP-628
93Stu-90
93Top-105
93TopGol-105
93TopInaM-105
93TopMic-105
93TopTra-122T
93TriPla-130
93Ult-209
93Ult-463
93UppDec-54
93UppDec-176
93UppDec-545
93UppDec-818
93UppDecGold-54
93UppDecGold-176
93UppDecGold-545
93UppDecGold-818
94Bow-536
94BowBes-R27
94BowBesR-R27
94CarLeaA-DJ32
94CarPol-6
94ColC-148
94ColChoGS-148
94ColChoSS-148
94Don-9
94DonDiaK-DK21
94DonMVP-12
94DonSpeE-9
94ExtBas-359
94Fin-92
94FinPro-92P
94FinRef-92
94Fla-429
94Fle-633
94FleTeaL-26
94FUnPac-153
94Lea-56
94LeaL-145
94LeaLimGA-2
94LeaMVPC-N6
94LeaMVPCG-N6
94OPC-77
94OscMayR-24
94Pac-591
94PacSilP-27
94PanSti-243
94Pin-204
94PinArtP-204
94PinMusC-204
94PinRunC-RC27
94Pos-28
94ProMag-115
94Sco-29
94ScoCyc-TC5
94ScoGolR-29
94ScoGolS-9
94Sel-232
94SP-63
94SPDieC-63
94Spo-74
94SpoMov-MM1
94StaClu-109
94StaClu-531
94StaCluFDI-109
94StaCluFDI-531
94StaCluGR-109
94StaCluGR-531
94StaCluMO-19
94StaCluMOP-109
94StaCluMOP-531
94StaCluMOP-ST12
94StaCluST-ST12
94StaCluT-317
94StaCluTFDI-317
94Stu-51
94StuHer-7
94TomPiz-10
94Top-660
94TopBlaG-35
94TopGol-660
94TopSpa-660
94TopSupS-22
94TriPla-62
94TriPlaN-8
94Ult-266
94UltOnBL-7
94UppDec-265
94UppDecAJ-4

94UppDecAJG-4
94UppDecED-265
94USPlaCA-6H
94USPlaCA-12D
95Baz-25
95Bow-315
95ColCho-360
95ColChoGS-360
95ColChoSE-80
95ColChoSEGS-80
95ColChoSESS-80
95ColChoSS-360
95Don-417
95DonAll-NL3
95DonDiaK-DK28
95DonPreP-417
95DonTopotO-307
95Emo-168
95Fin-219
95FinRef-219
95Fla-392
95Fle-499
95FleAllS-2
95FleTeaL-26
95FleUpd-122
95KinDis-12
95Kra-23
95Lea-398
95LeaLim-72
95Pac-407
95PacGolP-2
95PacPri-131
95PanSti-33
95Phi-17
95PhiMel-14
95Pin-364
95PinArtP-364
95PinMusC-364
95PinPer-PP10
95RedFol-31
95Sco-354
95ScoGolR-354
95ScoPlaTS-354
95Sel-220
95SelArtP-220
95SP-86
95SPCha-75
95SPChaDC-75
95Spo-133
95SpoArtP-133
95SPSil-86
95StaClu-361
95StaClu-625
95StaCluMOP-361
95StaCluMOP-625
95StaCluSTWS-361
95StaCluSTWS-625
95Stu-47
95StuGolS-47
95Sum-56
95SumNthD-56
95Top-526
95TopCyb-311
95TopTra-77T
95UC3-44
95UC3ArtP-44
95Ult-420
95UltGolM-420
95UppDec-59
95UppDec-475T
95UppDec-TC5
95UppDecED-59
95UppDecEDG-59
95UppDecPLL-R28
95UppDecPLLE-R28
95UppDecSE-76
95UppDecSEG-76
95USPlaCMLA-2D
95Zen-38
96Baz-82
96Bow-44
96ColCho-670
96ColChoGS-670
96ColChoSS-670
96Don-341
96DonDiaK-17
96DonPreP-341
96EmoXL-246
96Fin-S37
96FinRef-S37
96Fla-335
96Fle-500
96FleTif-500
96Lea-93
96LeaLim-25
96LeaLimG-25
96LeaPre-3
96LeaPreP-3
96LeaPrePB-93
96LeaPrePG-93
96LeaPrePS-93
96LeaPreSG-7
96LeaPreSte-7
96LeaSig-13
96LeaSigPPG-13
96LeaSigPPP-13
96MetUni-211
96MetUniP-211
96Pac-159
96PacPri-P54
96PacPriG-P54
96PanSti-39
96PhiTeal-17
96Pin-47
96PinAfi-89
96PinAfiAP-89
96PinAfiFPP-89
96PinArtP-19
96PinSta-19
96ProSta-87
96Sco-321
96ScoDugC-B46
96ScoDugCAP-B46
96Sel-23
96SelArtP-23
96SelCer-23
96SelCerAP-23
96SelCerCB-23
96SelCerCR-23
96SelCerMB-23
96SelCerMG-23
96SelCerMR-23
96SelTeaN-10
96SP-145
96Spo-78
96SpoArtP-78
96StaClu-425
96StaCluEPB-425
96StaCluEPG-425
96StaCluEPS-425
96StaCluMOP-425
96Stu-5
96StuPrePB-5
96StuPrePG-5
96StuPrePS-5
96Sum-17
96SumAbo&B-17
96SumArtP-17
96SumFoi-17
96Top-180
96TopChr-53
96TopChrR-53
96TopGal-63
96TopGalPPI-63
96TopLas-24
96Ult-254
96UltGolM-254
96UppDec-170
96Zen-23
96ZenArtP-23
97Bow-262
97BowBes-68
97BowBesAR-68
97BowBesR-68
97BowInt-262
97Cir-311
97CirRav-311
97ColCho-195
97Don-87
97DonPre-128
97DonPreCttC-128
97DonPreP-87
97DonPrePGold-87
97Fin-38
97FinRef-38
97Fle-413
97FleTif-413
97Lea-12
97LeaFraM-12
97LeaFraMDC-12
97MetUni-201
97NewPin-6
97NewPinAP-6
97NewPinMC-6
97NewPinPP-6
97Pac-379
97PacLigB-379
97PacPri-129
97PacPriLB-129
97PacPriP-129
97PacSil-379
97ProMag-30
97ProMagML-30
97Sco-10
97ScoPreS-10
97ScoShoS-10
97ScoShoSAP-10
97SkyE-X-88
97SkyE-XC-88
97SkyE-XEC-88
97SP-138
97StaClu-76
97StaCluC-CO4
97StaCluMOP-76
97Top-229
97TopChr-81
97TopChrR-81
97TopGal-23
97TopGalPPI-23
97TopIntF-ILM12
97TopIntFR-ILM12
97Ult-336
97UltGolME-336
97UltPlaME-336
97UppDec-155

Jeffers, Steve
87EriCarP-6
88SprCarB-20

Jefferson, David
96RocCubTI-13

Jefferson, George
86NegLeaF-105
91PomBlaBP-2

Jefferson, Jesse
73OPC-604
73Top-604
74OPC-509
74Top-509
75OPC-539
75Top-539
76OPC-47
76Top-47
76VenLeaS-30
77OPC-184
77Top-326
78BluJayP-10
78OPC-22
78Top-144
79BluJayBY-14
79OPC-112
79Top-221
80OPC-244
80Top-467
81Fle-419A
81Fle-419B
81Fle-419C
81LonBeaPT-10
82Fle-466
82Top-682
91OriCro-219
92Nab-32

Jefferson, Jim
86FloStaLAP-25
86TamTarP-7
87VerRedP-2
88ChaLooB-19
88NasSouTI-13

Jefferson, Reggie
87CedRapP-14
88CedRapRP-1146
89ChaLooB-1
89ChaLooGS-12
90Bow-51
90BowTif-51
90CedRapRDGB-9
90CMC-147
90NasSouC-22
90NasSouP-238
90ProAAAF-550
91Bow-678
91Cla1-T35
91DonRoo-55
91Lea-514
91LinDriAAA-263
91NasSouLD-263
91NasSouP-2164
91TopTra-60T
91TopTraT-60T
91Ult-379
91UppDec-746
91UppDecFE-73F
92Bow-25
92ClaGam-47
92Don-12
92Fle-113
92IndFanC-14
92Lea-86
92OPC-93
92Pin-476
92PinTea2-79
92ProFS7-213
92Sco-409
92ScoHotR-10
92StaClu-335
92Top-93
92TopDeb91-89
92TopGol-93
92TopGolW-93
92TopMic-93
92TriPla-24
92Ult-50
92UppDec-656
93Bow-557
93Don-303
93Fin-139
93FinRef-139
93Fle-594
93IndWUA-13
93Lea-302
93OPC-163
93PacSpa-412
93PanSti-48
93Pin-550
93Sco-433
93Sel-330
93SP-121
93StaClu-425
93StaCluFDI-425
93StaCluMOP-425
93Stu-152
93Top-496
93TopGol-496
93TopInaM-496
93TopMic-496
93Toy-83
93Ult-541
93UppDec-544
93UppDecGold-544
93USPlaCR-2D
94ColC-149
94ColC-428
94ColChoGS-149
94ColChoGS-428
94ColChoSS-149
94ColChoSS-428
94Don-653
94ExtBas-167
94Fin-333
94FinRef-333
94Fla-105
94Fle-106
94FleUpd-83
94Lea-298
94MarMot-8
94Pac-170
94Pin-161
94PinArtP-161
94PinMusC-161
94Sco-391
94ScoGolR-391
94ScoRoo-RT43
94ScoRooGR-RT43
94Sel-292
94SpoRoo-11
94SpoRooAP-11
94Top-121
94TopGol-121
94TopSpa-121
94UppDec-478
94UppDecED-478
95ColCho-295
95ColChoGS-295
95ColChoSE-128
95ColChoSEGS-128
95ColChoSESS-128
95ColChoSS-295
95Don-338
95DonPreP-338
95Fle-270
95Pin-48
95PinArtP-48
95PinMusC-48
95Sco-353
95ScoGolR-353
95ScoPlaTS-353
95Sel-106
95SelArtP-106
95Spo-44
95SpoArtP-44
95StaClu-284
95StaCluMOP-284
95StaCluSTWS-284
95Top-614
95TopCyb-382
95Ult-102
95UltGolM-102
95UppDec-111
95UppDecED-111
95UppDecEDG-111
96Don-359
96DonPreP-359
96FleUpd-U13
96FleUpdTC-U13
96LeaSigA-117
96LeaSigAG-117
96LeaSigAS-117
96Sco-425
97Cir-267
97CirRav-267
97ColCho-278
97Don-103
97DonLim-7
97DonLimLE-7
97DonPreP-103
97DonPrePGold-103
97DonTea-47
97DonTeaSPE-47
97Fle-25
97FleTif-25
97Lea-91
97LeaFraM-91
97LeaFraMDC-91
97Pac-42
97PacLigB-42
97PacPri-16
97PacPriLB-16
97PacPriP-16
97PacSil-42
97Pin-72
97PinArtP-72
97PinMusC-72
97Sco-110
97ScoPreS-110
97ScoRedS-4
97ScoRedSPI-4
97ScoRedSPr-4
97ScoShoS-110
97ScoShoSAP-110
97StaClu-173
97StaCluMOP-173
97Top-29
97Ult-304
97UltGolME-304
97UltPlaME-304
97UppDec-313

Jefferson, Stan
86MetColP-23
86MetTCM-33
86TidTidP-14
87Don-642
87DonRoo-43
87FleUpd-53
87FleUpdG-53
87PadBohHB-22
87SpoRool-9
87TopTra-55T
87TopTraT-55T
88BlaYNPRWL-119
88Don-187
88Fle-587
88FleGlo-587
88OPC-223
88PadCok-22
88PadSmo-12
88PanSti-411
88Sco-114
88ScoGlo-114
88ScoYouSI-11
88StaLinPa-6
88Top-223
88TopBig-86
88TopSti-109
88TopTif-223
89Bow-180
89BowTif-180
89ColCliC-28
89Sco-519
89Top-689A
89Top-689B
89TopBig-165

89TopTif-689
91ColSprSSLD-84
91LinDriAAA-84
91MetWIZ-200
91OriCro-220
92YanWIZ8-91
94ButCopKSP-29
95PitMetTI-11
86STaoftFT-31
Jeffery, Scott
88GreHorP-1553
89CedRapRB-3
89CedRapRP-913
89CedRapRS-9
90CedRapRB-25
91ChaLooP-1955
93MedHatBJF-3734
93MedHatBJSP-17
Jeffries, James
11TurRedT-55
82BurRanF-25
82BurRanT-4
Jefts, Chris
86PenWhiSP-14
87DayBeaAP-16
Jelic, Chris
86Ft.MyeRP-15
87LynMetP-4
88JacMetGS-8
88MetColP-28
89JacMetGS-5
89MetColP-36
90CMC-369
90ProAAAF-284
90TidTidC-18
90TidTidP-553
90TopTVM-48
91Cla1-T66
91LasVegSLD-285
91LasVegSP-249
91LinDriAAA-285
91MetWIZ-201
91TopDeb90-76
92LasVegSF-2802
92WicWraS-636
93LasVegSF-957
Jelinek, Joey
91MarPhiC-9
91MarPhiP-3462
92MarPhiC-8
92MarPhiF-3065
Jelks, Greg
86PorBeaP-11
87MaiGuiP-9
87MaiGuiT-12
87PhiTas-45
88Fle-648
88FleGlo-648
88MaiPhiC-18
88MaiPhiP-298
89LouRedBC-19
89LouRedBP-1258
89LouRedBTI-24
95AusFut-101
Jelks, Pat
85GreHorT-22
86NewBriRSP-14
88RivRedWCLC-228
88RivRedWP-1411
88WicPilRD-28
Jeltz, Steve
82ReaPhiT-15
83PorBeaT-6
84PorBeaC-205
85Don-44
85Fle-653
85PhiCIG-10
85PhiTas-11
85PhiTas-30
85TopTifT-62T
85TopTra-62T
86PhiCIG-9
86PhiTas-30
86Top-453
86TopTif-453
87Don-359
87DonOpeD-157
87Fle-178
87FleGlo-178
87PhiCha-2
87PhiTas-30
87Top-294
87TopTif-294
88Don-576
88Fle-308
88FleGlo-308
88OPC-126
88PanSti-361
88PhiTas-15
88Sco-435
88ScoGlo-435
88StaLinPh-11
88Top-126
88TopTif-126
89Don-431
89DonBasB-271
89Fle-573
89FleGlo-573
89PhiTas-13
89Sco-355
89Top-707
89TopBig-52
89TopSti-114
89TopTif-707
89UppDec-219
90Don-133
90Fle-562
90FleCan-562
90OPC-607
90PubSti-242
90RedFolSB-52
90Sco-421
90ScoRoo-59T
90Top-607
90TopSti-113
90TopTif-607
90UppDec-495
90VenSti-252
91LinDriAAA-457
91OPC-507
91RocRedWLD-457
91RocRedWP-1908
91Sco-272
91Top-507
91TopDesS-507
91TopMic-507
91TopTif-507
Jemison, Greg
77AshTouT-11
79WesHavYT-15
80NasSouTI-11
83BurRanF-26
83BurRanT-27
84TulDriTI-14
Jendra, Rick
80CedRapRT-11
Jenkins, Ab
40WheM4-5
Jenkins, Anthony
91SavCarC-25
91SavCarP-1666
Jenkins, Arthur
94SpoIndC-12
94SpoIndF-3318
Jenkins, Ben
96MarPhiB-10
Jenkins, Bernie
88AubAstP-1959
89OscAstS-9
90Bes-66
90ColMudB-10
90ColMudP-1359
90ColMudS-15
91JacGenLD-563
91JacGenP-938
91LinDriAA-563
92CedRapRF-1085
93ChaLooF-2373
Jenkins, Bob
57SeaPop-21
Jenkins, Brett
92WesPalBEC-21
92WesPalBEF-2094
93SanJosGC-14
93SanJosGF-18
Jenkins, Buddy
91JamExpC-21
91JamExpP-3540
Jenkins, Corey
95Bes-113
95BowBes-X8
95BowBesR-X8
95TopTra-106T
96LowSpiB-11
96Top-20
96TopPowB-20
Jenkins, Daniel
96BilMusTI-15
Jenkins, Dee
91PriRedC-14
91PriRedP-3522
92BenMusSP-12
92BilMusF-3363
93ExcFS7-22
93WesVirWC-9
93WesVirWF-2871
94UppDecML-109
94WinSpiC-11
94WinSpiF-278
Jenkins, Fats
74LauOldTBS-28
86NegLeaF-113
Jenkins, Fergie
66Top-254
66TopVen-254
67CokCapC-1
67CubProPS-8
67ProPizC-10
67Top-333
67TopVen-306
68Baz-10
68Kah-B17
68OPC-9
68OPC-11
68Top-9
68Top-11
68Top-410
68TopActS-11C
68TopVen-9
68TopVen-11
69CubJewT-9
69CubPho-7
69CubTealC-5
69MilBra-131
69MLBOffS-122
69OPC-10
69OPC-12
69Top-10
69Top-12
69Top-640
69TopDecl-20
69TopSta-15
69TopSup-37
69TopTeaP-4
70MLBOffS-19
70OPC-69
70OPC-71
70OPC-240
70SunPin-5
70Top-69
70Top-71
70Top-240
71AllBasA-11
71BazNumT-13
71MilDud-49
71MLBOffS-35
71MLBOffS-563
71OPC-70
71OPC-72
71OPC-280
71Top-70
71Top-72
71Top-280
71TopCoi-7
71TopSup-42
71TopTat-81
71TopTat-82
72CubChi-3
72CubTeal-6
72Dia-60
72Kel-8
72MilBra-164
72OPC-93
72OPC-95
72OPC-410
72ProStaP-16
72Top-93
72Top-95
72Top-410
72TopPos-10
73Kel2D-28
73LinPor-178
73OPC-180
73Top-180
73TopCanL-23
74LauAllG-67
74OPC-87
74Top-87
74TopDecE-59
74TopSta-236
75Hos-116
75Kel-22
75OPC-60
75OPC-310
75Top-60
75Top-310
76Hos-138
76LinSup-105
76OPC-250
76RedSoxSM-8
76SSP-255
76Top-250
76TopTra-250T
77BurCheD-31
77Kel-3
77OPC-187
77Spo-4702
77Top-430
78RanBurK-8
78SSP270-84
78Top-720
79Top-544
80Kel-47
80OPC-203
80PerHaloFP-208
80Top-390
81Don-146
81Fle-622
81FleStiC-84
81Top-158
82CubRedL-31
82Don-643
82Fle-320
82FleSta-173
82OPC-137
82Top-624
82TopTra-49T
83AllGamPI-167
83CubThoAV-31
83Don-300
83Fle-498
83FleSta-91
83FleSti-130
83OPC-230
83OPC-231
83Top-51
83Top-230
83Top-231
83TopFol-1
83TopSti-224
84CubUno-5
84Don-189
84DonCha-33
84Fle-494
84Nes792-456
84Nes792-483
84Nes792-706
84OPC-343
84SevCoi-C20
84Top-456
84Top-483
84Top-706
84TopSti-48
84TopTif-456
84TopTif-483
84TopTif-706
88HouSho-19
88OklCit8C-6
88OklCit8P-50
88PacLegI-43
89ChaLooLITI-14
89OklCit8C-25
89OklCit8P-1513
89PacSenL-29
89T/MSenL-55
89TopSenL-119
90EliSenL-97
90EliSenL-125
90PerGreM-93
91CubVinL-15
91PacSenL-108
91SweBasG-45
91UppDecHoB-H3
91UppDecHoB-AU3
91UppDecS-11
91UppDecS-18
91UppDecS-21
92ActPacA-4
92ActPacA2-4G
92CubOldS-16
92KodCelD-2
92MCIAmb-13
92MCIAmb-15
93RanKee-203
93TedWil-22
93UppDecAH-74
93UppDecAH-159
93UppDecS-1
93UppDecS-21
94MCIAmb-5
94UppDecAH-97
94UppDecAH-212
94UppDecAH1-97
94UppDecAH1-212
95SonGre-4
97St.VinHHS-10
Jenkins, Garrett
89ElmPioP-6
90FloStaLAS-32
90WinHavRSS-12
91Cla/Bes-72
91WinHavRSC-22
91WinHavRSP-501
Jenkins, Geoff
95Bes-114
95SPML-107
96BesAutSA-32
96Bow-362
96BowBes-136
96BowBesAR-136
96BowBesR-136
96El PasDB-1
96Exc-71
96ExcFirYP-7
96Top-24
96TopPowB-24
97Bow-188
97Bow98ROY-ROY5
97BowBes-133
97BowBesAR-133
97BowBesR-133
97BowChr-176
97BowChr1RC-ROY5
97BowChr1RCR-ROY5
97BowChrl-176
97BowChrIR-176
97BowChrR-176
97BowInt-188
97Top-201
Jenkins, Jack
70OPC-286
70Top-286
90DodTar-384
Jenkins, Jerry
77NewCoPT-19
78BurBeeT-16
82ElPasDT-13
Jenkins, Joe
75WhiSox1T-24
92Man191BSR-13
Jenkins, Jon (Jonathan)
90UtiBluSP-21
91Cla/Bes-219
91SouBenWSC-17
91SouBenWSP-2853
92SouBenWSC-12
93SouBenWSC-12
93SouBenWSF-1425
Jenkins, Mack
88GreHorP-1566
90BilMusP-3239
91BilMusP-3771
91BilMusSP-27
91CedRapRC-28
91CedRapRP-2737
92CedRapRC-29
93WesVirWC-26
93WesVirWF-2881
94ChaWheC-26
94ChaWheF-2719
96ChaLooB-2
Jenkins, Pete
96OgdRapTI-48
Jennette, Les
92SalLakTSP-27
Jennings, Doug
86PalSprAP-26
86PalSprAP-18
87MidAngP-16
87TexLeaAF-4
88A'sMot-24
88DonRoo-13
88DonTeaBA-NEW
88FleSlu-22
88FleUpd-54
88FleUpdG-54
89Don-505
89Fle-14
89FleGlo-14
89Sco-459

89TacTigC-19
89TacTigP-1541
89Top-166
89TopTif-166
89UppDec-585
90CMC-595
90ProAAAF-148
90TacTigC-18
90TacTigP-101
91Fle-12
91LinDriAAA-539
91Sco-819
91TacTigLD-539
92RocRedWF-1950
92RocRedWS-454
93CubMar-11
93IowCubF-2139
93LinVenB-128
94IndIndF-1821
94Pac-102
94SigRooDP-95
94SigRooDPS-95
94TriAAF-AAA31

Jennings, Hugh
03WilCarE-16
07TigACDPP-6
07TigACDPP-21
09AmeCarE-57
09BusBroBPP-7
09ColChiE-142
09SpoNewSM-12
09T206-169
09T206-170
09T206-171
09TigHMTP-7
09TigHMTP-8
09TigHMTP-9
09TigMorPenWBPP-5
09TigTaCP-7
09WolNewDTPP-8
10CouT21-153
10CouT21-154
10CouT21-291
10CouT21-292
10DomDisP-59
10E101-24
10E98-16
10MelMinE-24
10NadCarE-27
10NadE1-23
10PeoT21-29A
10PeoT21-29B
10RedCroT-34
10RedCroT-35
10RedCroT-123
10RedCroT-205
10RedCroT-206
10StaCarE-16
10SweCapPP-25A
10SweCapPP-25B
10W555-36
11DiaGumP-16
11E94-16
11L1L-128
11MecDFT-29
11S81LarS-103
11SpoLifCW-188
11SpoLifM-59
11T205-81
11TurRedT-18
12ColRedB-142
12ColTinT-142
12HasTriFT-48G
12HasTriFT-75A
12PhiCarE-13
13NatGamW-22
13PolGroW-11
13TomBarW-21
14CraJacE-77
14FatPlaT-19
15AmeCarE-22
15CraJacE-77
15SpoNewM-89
16ColE13-86
16FleBreD-46
16SpoNewM-90
16TanBraE-11
17HolBreD-51
19W514-106
20GasAmeMBD-29
21E121So8-42
21KoBreWSI-13
22W575-63
23W515-34
36PC7AlbHoF-35
40PlaBal-223
48ExhHoF-17
50CalHOFW-41
60Fle-67
61Fle-47
72LauGreF-23
76ShaPiz-35
80PerHaloFP-35
80SSPHOF-35
81ConTSN-2
81TigDetN-34
81TigSecNP-2
84GalHaloFRL-35
86TigSpoD-2
89DodSmoG-11
89HOFStiB-16
90DodTar-385
91ConTSN-16
91ConTSNP-450
92ConTSN-556
93ConMasC-9
93ConTSN-847
94ConTSNCI-25
93UppDecTR-2
93UppDecTR-5

Jennings, Lance
77GalGloG-176
91AppFoxC-13
91AppFoxP-1719
92BasCitRC-5
92Bow-633
92ClaFS7-21
92MemChiF-2423
92UppDecML-107
93ExcFS7-175
93MemChiF-379
94CarLeaAF-CAR17
94WilBluRC-11
94WilBluRF-303

Jennings, Robin
92GenCubC-13
92GenCubF-1572
93LinVenB-277
93PeoChiC-8
93PeoChiF-1095
93PeoChiTI-11
94DayCubC-11
94DayCubF-2365
96BesAutS-43
96BowBes-175
96BowBesAR-175
96BowBesR-175
96Exc-137
96Fla-217
96FlaWavotF-14
96FleCub-9
96FleUpd-U110
96FleUpdNH-12
96FleUpdTC-U110
96IowCubB-16
96LeaPre-119
96LeaPreP-119
96SelCer-103
96SelCerAP-103
96SelCerCB-103
96SelCerCR-103
96SelCerMB-103
96SelCerMG-103
96SelCerMR-103
96Ult-449
96UltGolM-449
96UltGolP-11
96UltGolPHGM-11
96Zen-104
96ZenArtP-104
97Cir-74
97CirRav-74
97ColCho-22
97DonRatR-10
97Fle-278
97FleTif-278
97Lea-180
97LeaFraM-180
97LeaFraMDC-180
95OrlCubF-21
97PacPriGotD-GD120
97Pin-165
97PinArtP-165
97PinIns-137
97PinInsCE-137
97PinInsDE-137
97PinMusC-165
97Sco-319
97ScoPreS-319
97ScoShoS-319
97ScoShoSAP-319
97Ult-166
97UltGolME-166
97UltPlaME-166
97UppDec-242

Jennings, William
52Par-5

Jenny, Shane
88KenTwiP-1401

Jensen, Blair
94BurIndC-9

Jensen, Dave
85LynMetT-8

Jensen, Jackie
47Exh-108
47PM1StaP1-97
47PM1StaP1-98
47PM1StaP1-99
47PM1StaP1-100
49RemBre-10
51Bow-254
52Bow-161
52Top-122
53BowC-24
53Bri-8
53DixLid-9
53DixPre-9
53NorBreL-14
53RedMan-AL6
53Top-265
54Bow-2
54DixLid-6
54Top-80
55ArmCoi-10
55RedMan-AL19
55Top-200
56Top-115
56TopPin-24
57SwiFra-15
57Top-220
58Hir-56
58JayPubA-9
58RedSoxJP-5
58Top-130
58Top-489
59ArmCoi-10
59Baz-12
59HomRunD-8
59RedSoxJP-4
59Top-400
60Baz-21
60KeyChal-25
60TopTat-23
60TopTat-90
61Top-173
61Top-476
61Top-540
61TopStal-112
62Jel-50
62Pos-62
62PosCan-62
62SalPlaC-73
62ShiPlaC-73
63BasMagM-41
75OPC-196
75Top-196
77GalGloG-18
79TCM50-229
80MarExh-11
83DiaClaS2-65
83TopRep5-122
91TopArc1-265
92BazQua5A-11
94TopArc1-80
94TopArc1G-80

Jensen, Jeff
94BatCliC-7
94BatCliF-3453

Jensen, John
49BowPCL-13
89WinSpiS-10
90WinSpiTI-15
91CarLeaAP-CAR43
91WinSpiC-25
91WinSpiP-2842
92ChaKniF-2784
92ChaKniS-161
92ProFS7-206
93OrlCubF-2798

Jensen, Marcus
90EveGiaB-14
90EveGiaP-3130
90ProAaA-171
92CliGiaC-24
92CliGiaF-3602
93CliGiaC-13
93CliGiaF-2492
93MidLeaAGF-40
94Cla-5
94ExcFS7-292
94SanJosGC-11
94SanJosGF-2820
95Bow-30
95UppDecML-158
96Bow-242
96FleUpd-U208
96FleUpdNH-13
96FleUpdTC-U208
96PhoFirB-18
96Ult-569
96UltGolM-569
96UppDec-252
97Don-238
97DonPreP-238
97DonPrePGold-238
97Fle-484
97FleTif-484
97Sco-327
97ScoPreS-327
97ScoShoS-327
97ScoShoSAP-327
97StaClu-324
97StaCluMOP-324
97Ult-296
97UltGolME-296
97UltPlaME-296
95UppDecMLFS-158

Jensen, Ryan
96BelGiaTI-26

Jensen, Woody (Forrest)
36GouWidPPR-A56
36NatChiFPR-48
79DiaGre-362

Jenson, Jeff
91SouOreAP-3836

Jericho, Mascot
90MiaMirIS-30
90MiaMirIS-31

Jernigan, Pete
63MilSau-3
63Top-253

Jersild, Aaron
92St.CatBJC-26
92St.CatBJF-3383
93HagSunC-15
93HagSunF-1875
94DunBluJC-14
94DunBluJF-2552
94FloStaLAF-FSL6
95Exc-137
95KnoSmoF-39

Jerzembeck, Mike
93OneYanC-9
94TamYanC-15
94TamYanF-2378
96NorNavB-12

Jesperson, Bob
91BilMusP-3767
91BilMusSP-24
92ChaWheF-20
93WesVirWC-10
93WesVirWF-2877
94CarLeaAF-CAR48
94ChaWheC-15

Jessop, Kim
91BriBanF-15
95AusFutSFP-SFFP2

Jessup, Steve
88UtiBluSP-28

Jestadt, Garry
70OPC-109
70Top-109
71OPC-576
71Top-576
72OPC-143
72PadTeal-13
72Top-143
74HawIslC-102
77PhoGiaCC-12
77PhoGiaCP-12
77PhoGiaVNB-12

Jester, Billy
86ClePhiP-10

Jester, Virgil
83Bra53F-22

Jeter, Derek
92ClaBluBF-BC22
92ClaDraP-6
92ClaDraPFB-BC6
92ClaFS7-402
92FroRowDP-55
92FroRowDPPS-55
92GulCoaYF-3797
92HigSchPLS-2
92UppDecML-5
93Bow-511
93ClaFS7-91
93ClaFS7-AU4
93ClaGolF-115
93ClaPro-1
93ExcFS7-210
93GreHorC-1
93GreHorF-893
93Pin-457
93Sco-489
93Sel-360
93SouAtlLAGF-21
93SP-279
93StaCluM-117
93Top-98
93TopGol-98
93TopInaM-98
93TopMic-98
93UppDec-449
93UppDecGold-449
94ActPac-43
94AlbYanTI-2
94Bow-376
94Bow-633
94BowBes-B2
94BowBes-X95
94BowBesR-B2
94BowBesR-X95
94Cla-60
94ClaCreotC-C17
94ClaGolA-SH3
94ClaGolF-83
94ClaTriF-T55
94ColC-644
94ColChoGS-644
94ColChoSS-644
94ExcFS7-106
94ExcLeaLF-10
94FloStaLAF-FSL22
94SigRoo-35
94SigRooHP-S4
94SigRooS-35
94TamYanC-1
94TamYanF-2393
94TedWil-124
94TedWilDGC-DG3
94Top-158
94TopGol-158
94TopSpa-158
94UppDec-550
94UppDecAHNIL-7
94UppDecED-550
94UppDecML-185
95ActPac2GF-6G
95ActPac2GF-AU1
95ActPac2GF-AU2
95ActPacF-1
95ActPacF-10
95ActPacF-67
95Bow-229
95BowBes-B1
95BowBesR-B1
95BowGolF-229
95ColCho-15
95ColChoGS-15
95ColChoSE-2
95ColChoSEGS-2
95ColChoSESS-2
95ColChoSS-15
95ColCliMCTI-13
95ColCliP-14
95ColCliTI-14
95Emo-60
95Exc-97
95ExcAll-5
95Fin-279
95FinRef-279
95FleMajLP-7
95SelCer-122
95SelCerMG-122
95SigRooFD-FD3
95SigRooFDS-FD3
95SigRooOJSS-3
95SigRooOJSSS-3
95SP-181

95SPCha-20
95SPChaDC-20
95SPSil-181
95StaCluCB-CB14
95StaCluMOP-CB14
95Top-199
95UltGolP-7
95UltGolPGM-7
95UppDec-225
95UppDecED-225
95UppDecEDG-225
95UppDecML-1
95UppDecML-165
95UppDecMLMLA-7
95UppDecMLT1PF-1
95UppDecPAW-H14
95UppDecPAWE-H14
95UppDecSE-5
95UppDecSEG-5
95Zen-134
95ZenRooRC-2
96Baz-80
96Bow-112
96BowBes-79
96BowBesAR-79
96BowBesC-3
96BowBesCAR-3
96BowBesCR-3
96BowBesP-BBP15
96BowBesPAR-BBP15
96BowBesPR-BBP15
96BowBesR-79
96Cir-65
96CirRav-65
96ColCho-231
96ColChoGS-231
96ColChoSS-231
96Don-491
96DonPreP-491
96EmoXL-90
96Fin-B92
96Fin-S350
96FinRef-B92
96FinRef-S350
96Fla-129
96Fle-184
96FleTif-184
96FleUpd-U226
96FleUpdTC-U226
96Lea-211
96LeaLimR-4
96LeaLimRG-4
96LeaPre-116
96LeaPreP-116
96LeaPrePB-211
96LeaPrePG-211
96LeaPrePS-211
96LeaPreSG-40
96LeaPreSta-3
96LeaPreSte-40
96LeaSig-67
96LeaSigA-118
96LeaSigAG-118
96LeaSigAS-118
96LeaSigEA-89
96LeaSigEACM-11
96LeaSigPPG-67
96LeaSigPPP-67
96MetUni-87
96MetUniMFG-6
96MetUniP-87
96MLBPin-16
96Pac-383
96Pin-171
96Pin-279
96PinAfi-163
96PinAfiAP-163
96PinAfiSP-18
96PinArtP-97
96PinArtP-179
96PinFirR-13
96PinFoil-279
96PinProS-2
96PinSta-97
96PinSta-179
96PinTeaS-3
96PinTeaT-9
96Sco-240
96Sco-384
96ScoDiaA-11
96ScoDugC-A106
96ScoDugC-B109
96ScoDugCAP-A106
96ScoDugCAP-B109
96ScoFutF-3
96ScoNumG-26
96ScoRef-10
96ScoSam-240
96Sel-161
96SelArtP-161
96SelCer-100
96SelCerAP-100
96SelCerCB-100
96SelCerCR-100
96SelCerIP-6
96SelCerMB-100
96SelCerMG-100
96SelCerMR-100
96SelCerSF-2
96SP-135
96SPMarM-MM3
96SPMarMDC-4
96Spo-139
96SpoArtP-139
96SpoDouT-9
96SPSpeFX-48
96SPSpeFXDC-48
96SPx-43
96SPxGol-43
96StaClu-123
96StaClu-260
96StaCluEPB-123
96StaCluEPG-123
96StaCluEPS-123
96StaCluMOP-123
96StaCluMOP-260
96Stu-33
96StuPrePB-33
96StuPrePG-33
96StuPrePS-33
96Sum-154
96Sum-171
96SumAbo&B-154
96SumAbo&B-171
96SumArtP-154
96SumArtP-171
96SumBal-6
96SumFoi-154
96SumFoi-171
96TeaOut-39
96Top-219
96TopBigC-4
96TopChr-80
96TopChrR-80
96TopGal-143
96TopGalPPI-143
96TopLas-82
96TopLasBS-2
96TopLasBS-13
96Ult-386
96UltChe-B5
96UltCheGM-B5
96UltGolM-386
96UltGolP-8
96UltGolPGM-8
96UppDec-156
96UppDecBCP-BC17
96UppDecDD-DD28
96UppDecDDG-DD28
96UppDecDDS-DD28
96UppDecPHE-H25
96UppDecPreH-H25
96UppDecVJLS-VJ3
96Zen-93
96Zen-147
96ZenArtP-93
96ZenArtP-147
97Bow-1
97BowBes-82
97BowBesA-82
97BowBesAAR-82
97BowBesAR-82
97BowBesBC-BC1
97BowBesBCAR-BC1
97BowBesBCR-BC1
97BowBesMI-MI1
97BowBesMIAR-MI1
97BowBesMIARI-MI1
97BowBesMII-MI1
97BowBesMIR-MI1
97BowBesMIRI-MI1
97BowBesP-4
97BowBesPAR-4
97BowBesPR-4
97BowBesR-82
97BowCerBIA-CA41
97BowCerGIA-CA41
97BowCerGIJA-CA41
97BowChr-1
97BowChrI-1
97BowChrIR-1
97BowChrR-1
97BowInt-1
97Cir-200
97CirBos-8
97CirFasT-3
97CirIco-4
97CirLimA-7
97CirRav-200
97CirSupB-8
97ColCho-180
97ColCho-331
97ColChoAC-40
97ColChoBS-13
97ColChoBSGS-13
97ColChoNF-NF29
97ColChoTBS-34
97ColChoTBSWH-34
97ColChoTotT-T19
97Don-49
97Don-415
97DonArmaD-11
97DonEli-24
97DonEliGS-24
97DonEliPtT-11
97DonEliPtT-12
97DonEliPtTA-11
97DonEliPtTA-12
97DonEliTotC-7
97DonEliTotC-P7
97DonEliTotCDC-7
97DonFraFea-14
97DonLim-22
97DonLim-83
07DonLim 116
97DonLimFotG-61
97DonLimLE-22
97DonLimLE-83
97DonLimLE-116
97DonPowA-24
97DonPowADC-24
97DonPre-125
97DonPre-184
97DonPreCttC-125
97DonPreCttC-184
97DonPreP-49
97DonPreP-415
97DonPrePGold-49
97DonPrePGold-415
97DonPrePM-21
97DonPreS-7
97DonPreTB-8
97DonPreTBG-8
97DonPreTF-8
97DonPreTP-8
97DonPreTPG-8
97DonTea-123
97DonTeaSPE-123
97Fin-15
97Fin-166
97Fin-310
97FinEmb-166
97FinEmb-310
97FinEmbR-166
97FinEmbR-310
97FinPro-15
97FinRef-15
97FinRef-166
97FinRef-310
97FlaSho-A2
97FlaSho-B2
97FlaSho-C2
97FlaShoDC-13
97FlaShoHG-6
97FlaShoLC-2
97FlaShoLC-B2
97FlaShoLC-C2
97FlaShoLCM-A2
97FlaShoLCM-B2
97FlaShoLCM-C2
97Fle-168
97Fle-703
97Fle-739
97FleGouG-4
97FleGouGF-4
97FleHea-8
97FleMilDM-2
97FleRooS-7
97FleSoaS-5
97FleTif-168
97FleTif-703
97FleTif-739
97Lea-165
97Lea-200
97Lea-358
97LeaBanS-14
97LeaFraM-165
97LeaFraM-200
97LeaFraM-358
97LeaFraMDC-165
97LeaFraMDC-200
97LeaFraMDC-358
97LeaGet-14
97LeaGolS-7
97LeaLeaotN-4
97LeaStaS-12
97MetUni-118
97MetUniMF-5
97MetUniPP-5
97NewPin-53
97NewPinAP-53
97NewPinIE-6
97NewPinKtP-9
97NewPinMC-53
97NewPinPP-53
97NewPinPP-I6A
97NewPinPP-K9
97Pac-152
97PacCar-13
97PacCarM-13
97PacCerCGT-3
97PacFirD-7
97PacGolCD-11
97PacLigB-152
97PacPri-51
97PacPriGA-GA9
97PacPriLB-51
97PacPriP-51
97PacPriSH-SH5A
97PacPriSL-SL4A
97PacSil-152
97Pin-139
97PinArtP-139
97PinCer-51
97PinCer-141
97PinCerCMGT-3
97PinCerCT-3
97PinCerMBlu-51
97PinCerMBlu-141
97PinCerMG-51
97PinCerMG-141
97PinCerMR-51
97PinCerMR-141
97PinCerR-51
97PinCerR-141
97PinHom-17
97PinHom-18
97PinIns-87
97PinIns-148
97PinInsC-16
97PinInsCE-87
97PinInsCE-148
97PinInsDD-11
97PinInsDE-87
97PinInsDE-148
97PinMin-16
97PinMinB-16
97PinMinCB-16
97PinMinCG-16
97PinMinCGR-16
97PinMinCN-16
97PinMinCS-16
97PinMinG-16
97PinMinS-16
97PinMusC-139
97PinTotCPB-51
97PinTotCPB-141
97PinTotCPG-51
97PinTotCPG-141
97PinTotCPR-51
97PinTotCPR-141
97PinX-P-32
97PinX-PMoS-32
97PinX-PMP-19
97PinX-PMW-5
97PinX-PMWG-5
97PinX-PMWS-5
97ProMag-64
97ProMagIM-6
97ProMagML-64
97Sco-35
97Sco-545
97ScoHeaotO-16
97ScoHobR-545
97ScoPreS-35
97ScoResC-545
97ScoShoS-35
97ScoShoS-545
97ScoShoSAP-35
97ScoShoSAP-545
97ScoStaaD-9
97ScoYan-3
97ScoYanPI-3
97ScoYanPr-3
97Sel-60
97Sel-148
97SelArtP-60
97SelArtP-148
97SelRegG-60
97SelRegG-148
97SelRooR-2
97SelToootT-25
97SelToootTMB-25
97SkyE-X-33
97SkyE-XC-33
97SkyE-XEC-33
97SkyE-XSD2-7
97SP-125
97SPGamF-GF6
97SPInsI-17
97SPMarM-MM10
97SpoIll-62
97SpoIll-128
97SpoIll-179
97SpoIllEE-62
97SpoIllEE-128
97SpoIllEE-179
97SpoIllGS-16
97SPSpeF-16
97SPSpxF-6
97SPSPxFA-6
97SPx-36
97SPxBoufG-13
97SPxBro-36
97SPxCorotG-10
97SPxGraF-36
97SPxSil-36
97SPxSte-36
97StaClu-55
97StaCluC-CO1
97StaCluI-I17
97StaCluM-M1
97StaCluMat-55
97StaCluMOP-55
97StaCluMOP-I17
97StaCluMOP-M1
97StaCluMOP-PG19
97StaCluMOP-PL13
97StaCluPG-PG19
97StaCluPL-PL13
97Stu-91
97StuHarH-13
97StuMasS-1
97StuMasS8-1
97StuPor8-10
97StuPrePG-91
97StuPrePS-91
97Top-13
97Top-NNO
97TopAweI-AI7
97TopChr-7
97TopChrDD-DD2
97TopChrDDR-DD2
97TopChrR-7
97TopGal-161
97TopGalGoH-GH1
97TopGalP-PP2
97TopGalPG-PG6
97TopGalPMS-1
97TopGalPMSSS-5
97TopGalPPI-161
97TopHobM-HM18
97TopScr-9
97TopStaFAS-FAS1
97Ult-99
97UltBasR-3
97UltChe-B9
97UltDouT-7
97UltFamGam-7
97UltGolME-99
97UltHitM-7
97UltLeaS-4
97UltPlaME-99
97UltRooR-5
97UltStaR-9
97UltTop3-9
97UltTop3GM-9
97UppDec-421
97UppDec-440
97UppDecAWJ-18

97UppDecBCP-BC2
97UppDecHC-HC3
95UppDecMLFS-1
95UppDecMLFS-165
97UppDecP-19
97UppDecRSF-RS3
97UppDecTTS-TS5
97UppDecU-55
97UppDecUGN-GN15
97UppDecUSS-4
97Zen-17
97Zen Z-Z-7
97Zen8x1-17
97Zen8x1D-17
97ZenV-2-7

Jeter, John
70OPC-141
70Top-141
71MLBOffS-205
71OPC-47
71Top-47
72OPC-288
72PadTeal-14
72Top-288
73OPC-423
73Top-423
74OPC-615
74Top-615

Jeter, Shawn
87DunBluJP-943
88DunBluJS-12
89KnoBluJB-10
89KnoBluJP-1130
89KnoBluJS-8
90KnoBluJB-6
90KnoBluJP-1257
90KnoBluJS-6
91LinDriAAA-506
91SyrChiLD-506
91SyrChiMB-9
91SyrChiP-2493
92DonRoo-59
92FleUpd-14
92VanCanS-639
93LinVenB-196
93NasSouF-580
93Pin-265
93StaClu-453
93StaCluFDI-453
93StaCluMOP-453
93Top-800
93TopGol-800
93TopInaM-800
93TopMic-800

Jethroe, Sam
47Exh-109
50Bow-248
51BerRos-D10
51Bow-242
51TopBluB-12
52Bow-84
52Top-27
53BowC-3
53ExhCan-10
79TCM50-44
83TopRep5-27
84OCoandSI-133
86NegLeaF-38
89PacLegI-206
89SweBasG-62
91PomBlaBPB-2
92NegLeaK-10
92NegLeaRLI-31
93TedWil-137
95NegLeaL2-19

Jevne, Frederick
87OldJudN-268

Jevyak, Brian
89CarNewE-13

Jewell, Jim
43CenFlo-12

Jewell, Mike
91WatIndC-7
91WatIndP-3362
92WatIndC-6
92WatIndF-3228

Jewett, Earl
89PulBraP-1897
90SumBraB-7
90SumBraP-2429
91MacBraC-2
91MacBraP-856

Jewett, Trent
89SalBucS-11
90HarSenP-1197
90HarSenS-10
91CarMudLD-125
91LinDriAA-125
92WelPirC-28
92WelPirF-1340
94SalBucC-26
94SalBucF-2339
95CarMudF-173

Jim, Diamond
90ColMudS-27

Jimaki, Jim
88CapCodPPaLP-84

Jimenez, Alex
87LitFalMP-2399
88ColMetGS-15
89ColMetB-29
89ColMetGS-12
90JacMetGS-3
91LinDriAAA-560
91TidTidLD-560
91TidTidP-2518

Jimenez, Cesar
86DurBulP-15
87DurBulP-1
88DurBulS-8
88FleUpd-72
88FleUpdG-72

Jimenez, D'Angelo
96Bow-124
96GreBatB-12

Jimenez, Elvio (Felix)
65OPC-226
65Top-226
69Top-567
85DomLeaS-42
92YanWIZ6-62

Jimenez, German
88FleUpd-72
88FleUpdb-72
89GreBraB-23
89GreBraP-1153
89GreBraS-10
89Top-569
89TopTif-569
89UppDec-113

Jimenez, Houston (Alfonso)
83TolMudHT-15
84MinTwiP-17
84Nes792-411
84Top-411
84TopTif-411
84TwiTeal-3
85Don-269
85Fle-282
85TolMudHT-16
85Top-562
85TopTif-562
87VanCanP-1609

Jimenez, Jhonny
96EveAquB-11

Jimenez, Jose
96PeoChiB-16

Jimenez, Juan
85DomLeaS-74
86BurExpP-11

Jimenez, Luis
78ChaPirT-11
80VenLeaS-141

Jimenez, Manny
92MacBraF-274
93DurBulC-9
93DurBulF-491
93DurBulTI-10
94GreBraTI-14
95DurBulTI-15
96GreBraB-16
96GreBraTI-12

Jimenez, Manuel
75QuaCitAT-12
91PulBraC-7
91PulBraP-4013
92MacBraC-8
92ProFS7-194
94GreBraF-421

Jimenez, Manuel Emilio
61AthJayP-11
62Top-598
63AthJayP-6
63Jel-87
63Pos-87
63Top-195
64A's-10
64AthJayP-7
64Top-574
66Top-458
67Top-586
68Top-538
69MilBra-132

Jimenez, Miguel
91SouOreAC-14
91SouOreAP-3837
92MadMusC-7
92MadMusF-1228
93Bow-133
93ClaFS7-210
93HunStaF-2078
93LimRocDWB-86
94A'sMot-11
94Bow-108
94ColC-12
94ColChoGS-12
94ColChoSS-12
94FleMajLP-17
94LeaGolR-13
94LeaLimR-50
94ScoRoo-RT152
94ScoRooGR-RT152
94SpoRoo-86
94SpoRooAP-86
94StaClu-356
94StaCluFDI-356
94StaCluGR-356
94StaCluMOP-356
94Top-773
94TopGol-773
94TopSpa-773
94Ult-108
95Don-262
95DonPreP-262
95EdmTraTI-11
95Lea-46
95Pac-314
95StaClu-201
95StaCluFDI-201
95StaCluMOP-201
95StaCluSTWS-201

Jimenez, Oscar
93EugEmeC-17
93EugEmeF-3869
94Bow-583
94RocRoyC-15
94RocRoyF-576
95WilBluRTI-17

Jimenez, Ramon
90Bes-40
90CMC-697
90GreHorB-17
90GreHorP-2669
90GreHorS-9
90SouAtlLAS-13
90StaFS7-93
91PriWilCC-18
91PriWilCP-1435
92PriWilCC-11
92PriWilCF-156

Jimenez, Ray
83PeoSunF-1

Jimenez, Roberto
90BurIndP-3011

Jimenez, Ruben
94JohCitCC-14
94JohCitCF-3709
96NewJerCB-14

Jimenez, Steve
93Sou-12

Jimenez, Vincent
91IdaFalBSP-21

Jiminez, Alex
86LitFalMP-15
87ColMetP-28

Jiminez, Vincent
90PulBraB-14
90PulBraP-3092

Jirschele, Mike
78AshTouT-11
79WauTimT-21
80AshTouT-28
80TulDriT-15
81TulDriT-29
82TulDriT-19
83OklCit8T-10
84OklCit8T-9
85OklCit8T-4
89OmaRoyC-17
90AppFoxBS-14
90AppFoxP-2112
90TulDriDGB-20
91AppFoxC-27
91AppFoxP-1732
93RocRoyC-28
93RocRoyF-731
94CarLeaAF-CAR18
94WilBluRC-24
94WilBluRF-315
95OmaRoyTI-15
96OmaRoyB-1

Joanette, Rosario
43ParSpo-40

Job, Ryan
85OscAstTI-18
86ColAstP-15

Jobes, Tracy
88MisStaB-14
89MisStaB-22
90MisStaB-22

Jockish, Mike
88St.CatBJP-2031
89St.CatBJP-2078
90EriSaiS-10

Jodo, Daijiro
88SanJosGCLC-120

Joe, Tokio
72Dia-130

Johdo, Joe
88SanJosGP-136

Johjima, Kenji
96MauStiHWB-8

John, Tommy
64Top-146
64TopVen-146
65OPC-208
65Top-208
66Top-486
66WhiSoxTI-7
67CokCapWS-15
67DexPre-105
67Top-609
68OPC-72
68Top-72
68TopVen-72
69MilBra-133
69MLBOffS-31
69NabTeaF-11
69Top-465
69TopSta-155
69TopTeaP-11
69TraSta-22
69WhiSoxTI-6
70MLBOffS-186
70OPC-180
70Top-180
70WhiSoxTI-7
71Kel-74
71MilDud-11
71OPC-520
71Top-520
71TopCoi-56
72MilBra-165
72OPC-264
72Top-264
73OPC-258
73Top-258
74OPC-451
74Top-451
75OPC-47
75Top-47
76OPC-416
76SSP-69
76Top-416
77Spo-3204
77Top-128
78Hos-7
78Kel-36
78RCColC-82
78SSP270-75
78Top-375
79OPC-129
79Top-255
79YanBurK-9
79YanPicA-21
80OPC-348
80Top-690
80TopSup-23
80WilGloT-3
81AllGamPI-84
81Don-107
81Fle-81
81FleStiC-121
81Kel-52
81OPC-96
81Top-550
81TopScr-52
81TopSti-2
81TopSti-114
81TopSti-250
81TopSupHT-66
82Don-409
82Don-558
82Fle-40
82FleSta-115
82OPC-75
82Top-75
82Top-486
82TopSti-214
82WilSpoG-4
83Don-570
83Fle-95
83FleSta-92
83FleSti-25
83OPC-144
83OPC-196
83SevCoi-9
83Top-735
83Top-736
83TopFol-1
84AngSmo-13
84Don-301
84DonCha-36
84Fle-522
84FunFooP-92
84Nes792-415
84Nes792-715
84OPC-284
84Top-415
84Top-715
84TopRubD-28
84TopSti-232
84TopTif-415
84TopTif-715
85AngSmo-23
85Don-423
85Fle-304
85OPC-179
85Top-179
85TopSti-229
85TopTif-179
86Fle-422
86FleUpd-57
86Top-240
86TopTif-240
86WilGloT-1
86YanTCM-1
87DodSmoA-15
87Fle-102
87FleGlo-102
87OPC-236
87Top-236
87TopTif-236
88Don-17
88Don-401
88DonBasB-220
88DonReaBY-401
88DonSupD-17
88Fle-211
88FleGlo-211
88Lea-17
88Lea-230
88PanSti-148
88Sco-240
88ScoGlo-240
88Spo-122
88StaLinY-7
88Top-611
88TopTif-611
89ClaLigB-40
89DodSmoG-91
89Fle-255
89FleGlo-255
89Sco-477
89Top-359
89TopBasT-139
89TopSti-310
89TopTif-359
89UppDec-230
90DodTar-386
92DodStaTA-17
92YanWIZ7-80
92YanWIZ8-92
92YanWIZA-34
93ActPacA-157
93UppDecAH-75
94TedWil-12
94UppDecAH-78
94UppDecAH1-78

95SonGre-5
Johnigan, Steve
87WatIndP-4
92MisStaB-23
93MisStaB-24
Johns, Clarence
94JohCitCC-15
94JohCitCF-3695
Johns, Douglas
90SouOreAB-5
91MadMusC-9
91MadMusP-2126
92RenSilSCLC-44
93HunStaF-2079
94HunStaF-1326
94TacTigF-3168
95EdmTraTI-12
96A'sMot-8
96ColCho-31
96ColChoGS-31
96ColChoSS-31
96Don-377
96DonPreP-377
96EmoXL-103
96Fla-149
96Fle-212
96FleTif-212
96StaClu-154
96StaCluMOP-154
96Ult-401
96UltGolM-401
96UppDec-163
97UppDec-129
Johns, Jeffrey
80VenLeaS-34
Johns, Keith
92FroRowDP-52
92HamRedC-12
92HamRedF-1600
93ClaGolF-118
93ExcFS7-99
93MidLeaAGF-51
93SprCarC-13
93SprCarF-1860
94St.PetCC-11
94St.PetCF-2593
95ArkTraTI-15
96ArkTraB-15
Johns, Ronald M.
86FloStaLAP-26
86St.PetCP-15
87SprCarB-6
88HarSenP-849
Johnson, A.J.
92KenTwiC-9
Johnson, Abner
78WisRapTT-10
81ChaRoyT-19
Johnson, Adam
96EugEmeB-12
97Bow-369
97BowChr-247
97BowChrI-247
97BowChrIR-247
97BowChrR-247
97BowInt-369
Johnson, Alex
64PhiPhiB-15
65Top-352
66CarTeal-7
66OPC-104
66Top-104A
66Top-104B
66TopVen-104
67OPC-108
67Top-108
68Top-441
69Kah-B11
69Top-280
69TopSta-25
69TopTeaP-20
70DayDaiNM-13
70MLBOffS-173
70OPC-115
70Top-115
71AllBasA-12
71AngJacitB-5
71Kel-54A
71Kel-54B
71Kel-54C
71MilDud-12
71MLBOffS-346
71MLBOffS-564
71OPC-61
71OPC-590
71Top-61
71Top-590
71TopCoi-84
71TopGreM-17
71TopSup-8
71TopTat-122
72MilBra-166
72OPC-215
72Top-215
73OPC-425
73Top-425
74OPC-107
74Top-107
74TopSta-237
75OPC-534
75Top-534
75YanSSP-17
77Top-637
85AngStrH-9
92YanWIZ7-81
93RanKee-204
Johnson, Andre
91PulBraC-12
91PulBraP-4018
92IdaFalGF-3527
92IdaFalGSP-7
Johnson, Andrew
94OriofB-14
Johnson, Angela
89GeoColC-12
Johnson, Anthony
89SanDieSAS-13
90PulBraB-21
90PulBraP-3086
Johnson, Anthony Clair
79MemChiT-10
80MemChiT-3
83Don-629
83SyrChiT-22
84SyrChiT-7
Johnson, Arthur
77TCMTheWY-77
91NiaFalRC-3
92BriTigF-1419
Johnson, Artis
93HunCubC-11
93HunCubF-3250
94HunCubF-3567
94HunCubC-16
Johnson, Avery
89BurIndS-13
Johnson, B.J. (Brian Lloyd)
88BurIndP-1798
89KinIndS-10
90KinIndTI-6
Johnson, Ban
04FanCraAL-28
09SpoNewSM-14
36PC7AlbHoF-7
50CalHOFW-42
61Fle-48
63BazA-16
69Baz-2
76ShaPiz-10
77GalGloG-170
80PerHaloFP-7
80SSPHOF-7
84GalHaloFRL-10
88PacEigMO-78
89HOFStiB-96
94OriofB-80
95ConTSN-1396
Johnson, Barry
90AriWilP-8
93SarWhiSC-15
94BirBarC-14
94BirBarF-618
96BirBarB-16
Johnson, Bart (C. Barth)
70Top-669
71OPC-156
71Top-156
72OPC-126
72Top-126
72WhiSoxDS-3
73OPC-506
73Top-506
74OPC-147
74Top-147
75OPC-446
75Top-446
76OPC-513
76Top-513
77BurCheD-77
77Top-177
Johnson, Ben
88AlaGolTI-10
90WelPirP-6
Johnson, Ben (Benjamin F.)
54BraJohC-12
60Top-528
Johnson, Bert
82ChaRoyT-9
Johnson, Bill
43YanSta-15
46SpoExcW-6-10
47Exh-110
48BluTin-1
48Bow-33
48YanTeal-14
49Bow-129
75JohMiz-13
83ReaPhiT-7
84IowCubT-29
85IowCubT-16
89SpoIndSP-12
90ChaRaiB-12
90ChaRaiP-2040
91ChaRaiC-8
91ChaRaiP-94
Johnson, Billy
49Lea-14
50Bow-102
51BerRos-A5
51Bow-74
51TopBluB-21
52Bow-122
52Top-83
53Top-21
79TCM50-230
83TopRep5-83
83YanASFY-21
85TCMPla1-9
87LouRedTI-30
91TopArc1-21
92WatDiaC-5
92YanWIZA-35
Johnson, Bo
94JohCitCC-16
94JohCitCF-3696
95PeoChiTI-26
Johnson, Bob
79WauTimT-12
Johnson, Bob (Robert Dale)
70Top-702
71OPC-71
71OPC-365
71PirActP-7
71Top-71
71Top-365
72MilBra-167
72OPC-27
72Top-27
73OPC-657
73Top-657
74SpoIndC-29
74OPC-269
74Top-269
76OmaRoyTT-8
91MetWIZ-202
Johnson, Bob (Robert Wallace)
55DonWin-27
60A'sTeal-9
61SenJayP-4
62Top-519
62TopStal-97
63Jel-96
63Pos-96
63Top-504
64Top-304
64TopVen-304
65Top-363
66OPC-148
66Top-148
66TopVen-148
67OPC-38
67Top-38
68Top-338
68TopVen-338
69MilBra-134
69Top-261
70Top-693
91MetWIZ-204
Johnson, Bobby E.
76VenLeaS-125
78AshTouT-12
80TulDriT-21
82Top-418
83Don-494
83RanAffF-8
83TopTra-48T
84Don-500
84Fle-420
84Nes792-608
84Top-608
84TopTif-608
87OPC-234
88OPC-228
93RanKee-205
Johnson, Boo (Curley)
90PeoChiTI-10
Johnson, Brian David
90Bes-214
90CarLeaA-40
90GreHorB-13
90GreHorP-2665
90GreHorS-10
90SouAtlLAS-14
90TopTVY-47
91Cla/Bes-9
91ColSprSSLD-85
91ColSprSSP-2186
91FloStaLAP-FSL14
91Ft.LauYC-16
91Ft.LauYP-2429
91LinDriAAA-85
92ColSprSSF-754
92WicWraF-3659
92WicWraS-637
93LasVegSF-948
94ExcFS7-284
94PadMot-12
94SpoRoo-115
94SpoRooAP-115
94StaClu-601
94StaCluFDI-601
94StaCluGR-601
94StaCluMOP-601
94Top-789
94TopGol-789
94TopSpa-789
94Ult-579
95Fin-321
95FinRef-321
95Fla-203
95HelBreTI-10
95PadCHP-4
95PadMot-10
95Sco-149
95ScoGolR-149
95ScoPlaTS-149
96ColCho-713
96ColChoGS-713
96ColChoSS-713
96Don-416
96DonPreP-416
96Fle-571
96FleTif-571
96LeaSigEA-90
96PadMot-9
97ColCho-336
97Fle-466
97Fle-688
97FleTif-466
97FleTif-688
97Pac-428
97PacLigB-428
97PacSil-428
97Ult-318
97UltGolME-318
97UltPlaME-318
97UppDec-357
Johnson, Carl
88VerBeaDS-12
89KenTwiP-1065
89KenTwiS-9
90BurIndP-3006
91KinIndC-3
91KinIndP-315
92KinIndC-13
94KinIndC-9
94KinIndF-2637
Johnson, Charles
81GleFalWST-4
82GleFalWST-19
Johnson, Charles Edward
91MiaHurBB-7
91TopTra-61T
91TopTraT-61T
92Bow-661
92StaCluD-91
92TopDaiQTU-27
92TopTra-56T
92TopTraG-56T
93ClaExp#PF-EP2
93ClaFS7-211
93KanCouCC-1
93KanCouCF-918
93MidLeaAGF-8
93StaCluM-76
93UppDec-435
93UppDecGold-435
93WorUniG-1
94ActPac-7
94ActPac-58
94ActPac2G-4G
94AriFalLS-10
94Cla-180
94ClaCreotC-C18
94ClaGolF-105
94ColC-660
94ColChoGS-660
94ColChoSS-660
94ExcAllF-1
94ExcFS7-191
94LeaLimR-1
94PorSeaDF-681
94PorSeaDTI-16
94ScoRoo-RT120
94ScoRooGR-RT120
94Sel-407
94SigRooBS-P2
94SP-113
94SPDieC-113
94SpoRoo-35
94SpoRooAP-35
94SpoRooRS-TR18
94TedWil-125
94TedWilDGC-DG4
94UppDec-536
94UppDecED-536
94UppDecML-93
94UppDecML-110
94UppDecML-269
94UppDecMLPotYF-PY14
94UppDecMLT1PJF-TP4
94UppDecMLT1PMF-4
95ActPac2GF-1G
95ActPacF-3
95ActPacF-62
95ColCho-1
95ColChoGS-1
95ColChoSE-135
95ColChoSEGS-135
95ColChoSESS-135
95ColChoSS-1
95Don-27
95DonPreP-27
95DonTopotO-244
95Emo-131
95EmoRoo-7
95Fla-139
95Fla-354
95FleMajLP-8
95FleUpd-97
95FleUpdRU-4
95KanCouCLTI-7
95Lea-345
95LeaGolR-9
95LeaLim-67
95PacPri-56
95Pin-158
95PinArtP-158
95PinMusC-158
95PinNewB-NB5
95Sco-575
95ScoAi-AM5
95ScoGolR-575
95ScoPlaTS-575
95ScoRooDT-RDT5
95Sel-102
95Sel-236
95SelArtP-102
95SelArtP-236
95SelCanM-CM3
95SelCer-117
95SelCerMG-117
95SelCerPU-8
95SelCerPU9-8
95SigRooMR-MR3
95SigRooMRS-MR3

95SigRooOJSS-2
95SigRooOJSSS-2
95SP-58
95SPCha-46
95SPChaDC-46
95Spo-150
95SpoArtP-150
95SPSil-58
95SPSpeF-36
95Stu-140
95Sum-130
95SumNewA-NA8
95SumNthD-130
95SumSam-130
95UC3-122
95UC3ArtP-122
95UC3CleS-CS4
95Ult-380
95UltGolM-380
95UltGolP-8
95UltGolPGM-8
95UppDec-220
95UppDecED-220
95UppDecEDG-220
95UppDecPAW-H18
95UppDecPAWE-H18
95UppDecSE-113
95UppDecSEG-113
95Zen-133
95ZenRooRC-17
96Cir-129
96CirBos-35
96CirRav-129
96ColCho-155
96ColChoGS-155
96ColChoSS-155
96Don-313
96DonPreP-313
96EmoRarB-5
96EmoXL-187
96Fla-263
96Fle-388
96FleRooS-9
96FleTif-388
96FleTomL-5
96Lea-22
96LeaLim-60
96LeaLimG-60
96LeaPre-42
96LeaPreP-42
96LeaPrePB-22
96LeaPrePG-22
96LeaPrePS-22
96LeaPreSG-50
96LeaPreSte-50
96LeaSig-60
96LeaSigPPG-60
96LeaSigPPP-60
96MetUni-166
96MetUniMFG-7
96MetUniP-166
96Pac-80
96PacPri-P26
96PacPriG-P26
96PanSti-11
96PanSti-245
96Pin-52
96PinAfi-150
96PinAfiAP-150
96PinArtP-20
96PinProS-7
96PinSta-20
96Sco-289
96ScoDugC-B14
96ScoDugCAP-B14
96ScoFutF-15
96Sel-44
96SelArtP-44
96SelCer-39
96SelCerAP-39
96SelCerCB-39
96SelCerCR-39
96SelCerMB-39
96SelCerMG-39
96SelCerMR-39
96SelTeaN-16
96SP-87
96Spo-61
96SpoArtP-61
96Stu-51
96StuPrePB-51
96StuPrePG-51
96StuPrePS-51
96Sum-51
96SumAbo&B-51
96SumArtP-51
96SumFoi-51
96SumPos-5
96Ult-201
96UltGolM-201
96UppDec-73
96Zen-60
96ZenArtP-60
96ZenMoz-16
97Cir-176
97CirRav-176
97ColCho-114
97Don-18
97DonArmaD-12
97DonEli-129
97DonEliGS-129
97DonLim-167
97DonLimLE-167
97DonPre-37
97DonPreCttC-37
97DonPreP-18
97DonPrePGold-18
97FlaSho-A78
97FlaSho-B78
97FlaSho-C78
97FlaShoLC-78
97FlaShoLC-B78
97FlaShoLC-C78
97FlaShoLCM-A78
97FlaShoLCM-B78
97FlaShoLCM-C78
97Fle-330
97FleTif-330
93KanCouCTI-9
97Lea-131
97LeaFraM-131
97LeaFraMDC-131
97MetUni-175
97NewPin-38
97NewPinAP-38
97NewPinMC-38
97NewPinPP-38
97Pac-301
97PacLigB-301
97PacPri-102
97PacPriLB-102
97PacPriP-102
97PacSil-301
97PinCer-99
97PinCerMBlu-99
97PinCerMG-99
97PinCerMR-99
97PinCerR-99
97PinIns-99
97PinInsCE-99
97PinInsDE-99
97PinTotCPB-99
97PinTotCPG-99
97PinTotCPR-99
97Sco-294
97ScoPreS-294
97ScoShoS-294
97ScoShoSAP-294
97Sel-61
97SelArtP-61
97SelRegG-61
97SelToootT-20
97SelToootTMB-20
97SP-79
97Stu-62
97StuPrePG-62
97StuPrePS-62
97Ult-197
97UltFieC-8
97UltGolME-197
97UltPlaME-197
97UppDec-79
97UppDec-139
97UppDecRSF-RS8

Johnson, Chet
45CenFlo-12

Johnson, Chip
91OklStaC-12

Johnson, Chris
88BelBreGS-25
89BelBreIS-10
89BelBreIS-16
90CalLeaACLC-56
90CMC-712
90ProAaA-137
90StoPorB-15
90StoPorCLC-176
90StoPorP-2174
91Bow-45
91Cla/Bes-282
91ElPasDLD-189
91ElPasDP-2743
91LinDriAA-189
91UppDec-56
92HarSenF-456
92HarSenS-284
92SkyAA F-120
93HarSenF-267
93OrlCubF-2779
94OrlCubF-1381
95OrlCubF-5

Johnson, Chuck
86AriWilP-8

Johnson, Chuck (Charles)
87SavCarP-2
88SprCarB-12
89St.PetCS-19

Johnson, Cliff
75OPC-143
75Top-143
76OPC-249
76SSP-51
76Top-249
77Top-514
78SSP270-2
78Top-309
78YanBurK-3
78YanSSPD-2
79OPC-50
79Top-114
79YanBurK-3
80OPC-321
80Top-612
81Don-484
81Fle-303
81OPC-17
81Top-17
81TopTra-776
82A'sGraG-5
82Don-339
82Fle-93
82OPC-333
82Top-422
82TopSti-226
82TopStiV-226
83Don-601
83Fle-520
83Top-762
83TopTra-49T
84BluJayFS-19
84Don-512
84Fle-159
84Nes792-221
84OPC-221
84Top-221
84TopSti-366
84TopTif-221
85Don-512
85Fle-109
85FleUpd-61
85Lea-115
85OPC-7
85RanPer-44
85Top-4
85Top-568
85TopMin-568
85TopSti-367
85TopTif-4
85TopTif-568
85TopTifT-63T
85TopTra-63T
85Woo-20
86BluJayAF-15
86BluJayFS-19
86Don-639
86Fle-62
86Lea-250
86OPC-348
86Top-348
86TopTif-348
87AstShoSTw-10
87Don-645
87Fle-231
87FleGlo-231
87OPC-118
87Top-663
87TopTif-663
90EliSenL-83
92Nab-2
92YanWIZ7-82
93RanKee-206
93UppDecAH-76

Johnson, Clinton
81BriRedST-20

Johnson, Connie (Clifford)
56Top-326
57Top-43
58OriJayP-4
58Top-266
59Top-21
59TopVen-21
87NegLeaPD-43
91OriCro-222
92NegLeaRLI-32
96NegLeaBMKC-3

Johnson, Curtis
88St.CatBJP-2022
89MyrBeaBJP-1471

Johnson, Damon
94MedHatBJF-3693
94MedHatBJSP-6
95StCatSTI-22
96StCatSB-13

Johnson, Dana
87DunBluJP-930

Johnson, Dane
93ElPasDF-2945
94FleUpd-28
94NasSouF-1246
94WhiSoxK-15
95NasSouTI-7
96SyrChiTI-17

Johnson, Dante
88BilMusP-1812
89GreHorP-417

Johnson, Darrell
54OriEss-15
57Top-306
58Top-61A
58Top-61B
59Top-533
60Top-263
62RedEnq-17
62Top-16
62TopVen-16
63RocRedWSP-7
74OPC-403
74Top-403
75OPC-172
75Top-172
76OPC-118
76SSP-417
76Top-118
77Top-597
78Top-79
79Top-659
80Top-282
83Top-37
91OriCro-223
93RanKee-207

Johnson, Darron
90EugEmeGS-17

Johnson, Dave (David Wayne)
67CokCapO-8
67DexPre-106
67Top-363
67TopVen-256
68CokCapO-8
68DexPre-42
68Top-273
68TopVen-273
69MilBra-135
69MLBOffS-4
69OPC-203
69Top-203
69TopSta-125
70DayDaiNM-107
70MLBOffS-150
70OPC-45
70Ori-6
70Top-45
71MilDud-13
71MLBOffS-301
71OPC-595
71Ori-7
71Top-595
71TopCoi-2
71TopTat-28
72Kel-43A
72Kel-43B
72MilBra-168
72OPC-224
72OriPol-5
72Top-224
72Top-680
73LinPor-4
73OPC-550
73Top-550
74Kel-50
74OPC-45
74Top-45
74TopDecE-50
74TopSta-6
75OPC-57
75Top-57
77SanJosMC-24
77Top-478
78St.PetCT-13
78Top-317
78TwiFriP-9
79Top-513
81Ori6F-20
83FraBroR-22
83FraBroR-26
84JacMetF-6
84MetFanC-1
84PriWilPT-30
84TopTra-57T
84TopTraT-57T
85MetColP-1
85NasPirT-12
85Top-492
85TopTif-492
86HawIsIP-12
86MetColP-5
86OriGreT-12
86QuaCitAP-15
86Top-501
86TopTif-501
87MetColP-15
87Top-543
87TopTif-543
87VanCanP-1606
88BufBisC-4
88BufBisP-1476
88BufBisTI-2
88MetColP-29
88Top-164
88TopGloA-12
88TopTif-164
89MetColP-37
89RocRedWC-11
89RocRedWP-1656
89Top-684
89TopTif-684
90Don-702
90FleUpd-67
90Lea-434
90MetCol8-8
90MetColP-9
90OPC-291
90OPC-416
90PacLeg-33
90Sco-528
90Sco100RS-43
90Top-291
90Top-416
90TopTif-291
90TopTif-416
90TopTVM-1
90UppDec-425
91Don-126
91Fle-479
91Lea-248
91LinDri-34
91OriCro-224
91PanSti-199
91Sco-506
91StaClu-117
91StaCluP-19
91Top-163
91TopDesS-163
91TopMic-163
91TopTif-163
91Ult-18
91UppDec-299
92EdmTraS-162
92Fle-12
92MVP-5
92MVP2H-20
92OPC-657
92Sco-604
92Top-657
92TopGol-657
92TopGolW-657
92TopMic-657
92UppDecS-4
93TolMudHF-1651

Johnson, Davey (David

Allen)
65Top-473
66Top-579
69TopFou-11
69TopTeaP-5
83TidTidT-23
85MetTCM-1
85PolMet-M2
86MetTCM-37
86MetWorSC-23
88DonAll-42
88DonPop-20
88MetKah-5
89MetKah-13
90MetKah-5
90SweBasG-61
91MDAA-13
91OriCro-225
91SweBasG-46
92ActPacA-75
93RedKah-10
93TedWil-83
93TopTra-36T
93UppDecAH-77
94RedKah-16
95RedKah-15
Johnson, David
83AleDukT-20
87PalSprP-3
91OPC-163
Johnson, David C.
78Top-627
91OriCro-226
Johnson, David M.
79ArkTraT-21
80ArkTraT-14
Johnson, Dean
85LitFalMT-25
Johnson, Deron
86BelMarC-105
87WauTimP-18
Johnson, Deron Andre
88WatPirP-20
89WelPirP-14
90AugPirP-2472
Johnson, Deron Roger
59Top-131
59TopVen-131
60Top-134
60TopVen-134
61Top-68
61Yan61RL-41
62Top-82
62TopVen-82
64Top-449
65Kah-19
65MacSta-5
65OPC-75
65RedEnq-15
65Top-75
66Kah-15
66Top-219
66Top-440
66TopRubI-43
66TopVen-219
67CokCapR-6
67DexPre-107
67Kah-17
67OPC-135
67Top-135
67TopVen-331
68CokCapB-15
68Kah-B18
68Top-323
68TopVen-323
69MilBra-136
69PhiTeal-5
69Top-297
70OPC-125
70PhiTeal-6
70Top-125
70TopBoo-20
71MLBOffS-182
71OPC-490
71PhiArcO-7
71Top-490
71TopCoi-79
71TopSup-58
72MilBra-169
72OPC-167
72OPC-168
72Top-167
72Top-168
73OPC-590
73Top-590
74OPC-312
74Top-312
74TopSta-227
75SSP18-18
76OPC-529
76Top-529
78TCM60I-213
84PhiTas-11
85MarMot-27
86MarMot-28
88AlbYanP-1351
90SweBasG-34
91RinPos1Y3-2
92YanWIZ6-60
94BreMilB-41
97CraSalLCG-7
Johnson, Dodd
86SumBraP-11
87DurBulP-28
88DurBulS-9A
89PenPilS-8
91RenSilSCLC-22
91SydWavF-14
Johnson, Dominick
87PocGiaTB-15
89CliGiaP-904
90SanJosGB-25
90SanJosGCLC-47
90SanJosGP-2011
90SanJosGS-13
91RenSilSCLC-6
92PalSprAF-833
93PalSprAC-11
93PalSprAF-63
94MidAngF-2433
94MidAngOHP-12
Johnson, Don
44CubTeal-13
47TipTop-108
52Top-190
53BowBW-55
53Top-219
54Top-146
55Bow-101A
55Bow-101B
55Bow-157A
55OriEss-10
55Top-165
83TopRep5-190
91OriCro-227
91TopArc1-219
94TopArc1-146
94TopArc1G-146
Johnson, Drew
92KanCouCC-2
92KanCouCF-98
92KanCouCTI-16
Johnson, Duan
96EveAquB-12
Johnson, Earl
93SpoIndC-9
93SpoIndF-3603
94SprSulC-13
94SprSulF-2050
95AusFut-20
95RanCucQT-3
96MemChiB-15
Johnson, Earl Douglas
46RedSoxTI-14
47TipTop-9
48RedSoxTI-11
49Bow-231
50Bow-188
51Bow-321
52MotCoo-14
77TCMTheWY-88
95Exc-285
95ExcLeaL-11
96BesAutSA-33
Johnson, Earnie
90SouBenWSGS-7
91OriCro-228
91SarWhiSC-5
91SarWhiSP-1108
92BirBarF-2576
93OrlCubF-2780
Johnson, Erik
87PocGiaTB-29
88CliGiaP-708
88MidLeaAGS-3
89ShrCapP-1845
90PhoFirP-19
90ProAAAF-45
90ShrCapS-13
91LinDriAA-309
91ShrCapLD-309
91ShrCapP-1829
92PhoFirF-2827
92PhoFirS-384
93PhoFirF-1523
94PhoFirF-1526
95Pac-378
Johnson, Ernest R.
21Exh-82
22E120-22
22W573-65
23WilChoV-71
Johnson, Ernest T.
53BraJohC-7
53BraSpiaS3-13
54Bow-144
54BraJohC-32
54BraSpiaSP-10
55Bow-157A
55Bow-157B
55BraGolS-10
55BraJohC-32
55BraSpiaSD-9
56Top-294
57BraSpiaS4-11
57Top-333
58Top-78A
58Top-78B
59Top-279
60Top-228
78AtlCon-11
83Bra53F-32
Johnson, Frank
69Top-227
71MLBOffS-253
71OPC-128
71Top-128
74PhoGiaC-88
75PhoGiaCK-23
Johnson, Gary
92DavLipB-16
93DavLipB-14
94DavLipB-17
94DavLipB-18
Johnson, George
78LauLonABS-25
Johnson, Greg
77QuaCitAT-19
79SavBraT-10
79WatIndT-30
81ChaRoyT-1
82ForMyeRT-6
87AubAstP-18
88AshTouP-1051
89AshTouP-959
90OrlSunRB-15
90OrlSunRP-1078
90OrlSunRS-7
90ProAaA-42
91Cla/Bes-105
91LinDriAA-482
91OrlSunRLD-482
91OrlSunRP-1844
92KenTwiC-10
92KenTwiF-613
92PorBeaF-2662
92PorBeaS-410
92SkyAAAF-187
Johnson, Hank
32R33So2-409
33Gou-14
33GouCanV-14
36GouWidPPR-D14
92ConTSN-382
Johnson, Herman
92SouOreAC-23
92SouOreAF-3418
Johnson, Home Run (Grant)
74LauOldTBS-22
86NegLeaF-109
Johnson, Howard
81BirBarT-12
83Don-328
83Fle-332
83Tig-15
84TigFarJ-8
84TigWavP-21
85Don-247
85Fle-12
85FleUpd-62
85MetColP-4
85MetTCM-25
85OPC-192
85Top-192
85TopSti-262
85TopTif-192
85TopTifT-64T
85TopTra-64T
86Don-312
86Fle-85
86MetColP-11
86MetFanC-6
86MetTCM-19
86MetWorSC-15
86OPC-304
86Top-751
86TopSti-101
86TopTif-751
87Don-646
87DonHig-43
87DonOpeD-132
87Fle-13
87FleGlo-13
87MetColP-5
87OPC-267
87Top-267
87TopTif-267
88Don-569
88DonBasB-97
88DonTeaBM-569
88Fle-138
88FleGlo-138
88FleMin-95
88FleRecS-20
88FleStiC-104
88KayB-14
88Lea-238
88MetColP-6
88MetFanC-20
88MetKah-20
88OPC-85
88OPCBoxB-K
88PanSti-343
88PanSti-439
88RedFolSB-40
88Sco-69
88ScoGlo-69
88Spo-138
88SpoGam-17
88StaLinMe-10
88Top-85
88TopBig-129
88TopGloS-52
88TopMinL-61
88TopSti-99
88TopTif-85
88TopWaxBC-K
89Don-235
89DonBasB-126
89Fle-39
89FleGlo-39
89MetColP-11
89MetKah-14
89OPC-383
89Sco-136
89Top-383
89TopAme2C-18
89TopBig-208
89TopDouM-10
89TopGloS-22
89TopSti-91
89TopStiB-41
89TopTif-383
89UppDec-582
90BirBarDGB-2
90Bow-133
90BowTif-133
90ClaBlu-144
90Don-18
90Don-99
90Don-654A
90Don-654B
90DonBesN-19
90DOnBonM-BC2
90DonPre-8
90DonSupD-18
90Fle-208
90Fle-639
90FleAll-4
90FleAwaW-20
90FleBasA-21
90FleBasM-22
90FleCan-208
90FleCan-639
90FleWaxBC-C16
90K-M-3
90Lea-272
90MetColP-4
90MetFanC-20
90MetKah-20
90MLBBasB-16
90MSAHolD-10
90MSAIceTD-2
90OPC-399
90OPC-680
90PanSti-210
90PanSti-306
90PanSti-385
90PubSti-137
90PubSti-265
90Sco-124
90Sco100S-83
90Spo-109
90SunSee-3
90Top-399
90Top-680
90TopBig-216
90TopCoi-50
90TopDou-37
90TopGloA-4
90TopGloS-43
90TopHilHM-33
90TopMag-80
90TopMinL-67
90TopSti-90
90TopSti-150
90TopStiB-8
90TopTif-399
90TopTif-680
90TopTVA-53
90TopTVM-25
90UppDec-263
90UppDecS-1
90VenSti-253
90VenSti-254
90WonBreS-17
91BasBesHRK-12
91BasBesRB-9
91Bow-464
91CadEllD-33
91Cla3-T40
91ClaGam-76
91DenHol-11
91Don-454
91Fle-152
91Lea-34
91MetColP-18
91MetKah-20
91MetTro-5
91MetWIZ-203
91OPC-470
91PanFreS-81
91PanSti-86
91RedFolS-52
91Sco-185
91Sco100S-86
91SpoNSP-1
91StaClu-86
91StaCluMO-19
91StaCluP-20
91Stu-207
91Top-470
91TopCraJ2-33
91TopDesS-470
91TopMic-470
91TopTif-470
91TopTriH-N7
91Ult-222
91UppDec-124
91USPlaCA-4C
92Bow-10
92Cla1-T47
92Cla2-T41
92ClaGam-145
92DenHol-16
92Don-341
92DonCraJ2-17
92DonEli-15
92DonMcD-25
92Fle-509
92Fle-689
92FleTeaL-2
92Fre-4
92Hig5-74
92Hig5S-20
92HitTheBB-17
92KinDis-6
92Lea-132

92LeaGolP-7
92LeaPre-7
92MetColP-4
92MetKah-20
92MSABenSHD-16
92New-13
92OPC-590
92OPCPre-42
92PanSti-147
92PanSti-224
92PepDieM-23
92Pin-15
92Pos-28
92Sco-550
92Sco-776
92Sco100S-68
92SpoStaCC-26
92StaClu-430
92StaClu-610
92StaCluD-92
92StaCluECN-610
92Stu-67
92SunSee-6
92Top-388
92Top-590
92TopGol-388
92TopGol-590
92TopGolW-388
92TopGolW-590
92TopKid-12
92TopMcD-23
92TopMic-388
92TopMic-590
92TriPla-236
92Ult-235
92UppDec-37
92UppDec-256
92UppDec-720
92UppDecF-28
92UppDecFG-28
92UppDecHRH-HR3
92UppDecTMH-26
93Bow-130
93CadDis-34
93DiaMar-56
93Don-434
93Fin-143
93FinRef-143
93Fla-93
93Fle-89
93FunPac-127
93Lea-39
93MetBak-11
93MetColP-24
93MetKah-20
93OPC-166
93PacSpa-199
93PanSti-251
93Pin-389
93PinHomRC-44
93PinSlu-18
93Sco-62
93Sel-101
93SP-151
93StaClu-404
93StaCluFDI-404
93StaCluMOP-404
93Stu-128
93Top-106
93TopGol-106
93TopInaM-106
93TopMic-106
93TriPla-86
93Ult-76
93UppDec-484
93UppDec-676
93UppDecGold-484
93UppDecGold-676
93UppDecIC-WI14
93UppDecICJ-WI14
93UppDecTAN-TN12
94Bow-142
94ColC-530
94ColChoGS-530
94ColChoSS-530
94Don-487
94ExtBas-248
94Fin-374
94FinRef-374
94Fle-568
94FleUpd-125
94FUnPac-86
94Lea-432
94OPC-31
94Pac-407
94PanSti-219
94Pin-518
94PinArtP-518
94PinMusC-518
94RocPol-15
94Sco-414
94ScoGolR-414
94ScoRoo-RT63
94ScoRooGR-RT63
94Sel-315
94SpoRoo-23
94SpoRooAP-23
94StaClu-640
94StaCluFDI-640
94StaCluGR-640
94StaCluMOP-640
94StaCluT-109
94StaCluTFDI-109
94Top-302
94TopGol-302
94TopSpa-302
94TopTra-82T
94TriPla-227
94Ult-484
94UppDec-462
94UppDecED-462
95ColCho-542T
95Sco-505
95ScoGolR-505
95ScoPlaTS-505
95StaCluMOP-RL9
95StaCluRL-RL9
95Top-206
95UppDec-316
95UppDecED-316
95UppDecEDG-316
95UppDecSE-260
95UppDecSEG-260
96ButCopKB-4
96ColCho-83
96ColChoGS-83
96ColChoSS-83
96MetMod-6

Johnson, Indian Bob (Robert Lee)
34BatR31-20
34Gou-68
35ExhFou-14
35GouPuzR-8J
35GouPuzR-9J
36ExhFou-14
36GouWidPPR-A57
36OveCanR-26
37ExhFou-14
37OPCBatUV-123
38ExhFou-14
38WheBB10-6
39ExhSal-30
39GouPreR303A-27
39PlaBal-97
39WorWidGTP-27
40PlaBal-25
41DouPlaR-49
41PlaBal-22
47CenFlo-12
47SigOil-78
75SheGrePG-17
76GrePlaG-17
77ShaPiz-C
79DiaGre-326
81ConTSN-33
82DiaCla-53
83TCMPla1942-22
83TCMPla1944-10
91ConTSN-96
92ConTSN-547
93ConTSN-776
93DiaStaES-138
94ConTSN-1173
94ConTSNB-1173

Johnson, J.J.
91ClaDraP-33
91FroRowDP-48
91YakBeaC-6
92Pin-577
93UtiBluSC-10
93UtiBluSF-3546
94Bow-7
94CenValRF-3198
94Cla-66
94LynRedSC-13
94LynRedSF-1905
96BowBes-141
96BowBesAR-141
96BowBesR-141
96HarCitRCB-16
97Bow-89
97BowCerBIA-CA69
97BowCerGIA-CA69
97BowChr-113
97BowChrI-113
97BowChrIR-113
97BowChrR-113
97BowInt-89
97Sel-124
97SelArtP-124
97SelRegG-124

Johnson, Jace
96SouOreTI-25

Johnson, Jack
11TurRedT-76
87SpoCubG-1
89AncGlaP-16
90AriWilP-9
92BakDodCLC-13
93ClaFS7-282
93OrlCubF-2788
93PeoChiC-9
93PeoChiF-1088
94PriWilCC-10
94PriWilCF-1923
95RocCubTI-29

Johnson, James
81CliGiaT-19
96CliLumKTI-16

Johnson, James H.
21Exh-83

Johnson, Jason
93BenRocC-13
93BenRocF-3262
94AugGreC-7
94AugGreF-3001
94Bow-498
94CenValRC-11
95HudValRTI-20
95NewHavRTI-32
96ChaRivTI-9615
96LynHilB-12
96MarPhiB-11

Johnson, Jay
87SumBraP-30
94SpoIndC-13
94SpoIndF-3336

Johnson, Jeff
88OneYanP-2069
89PriWilCS-9
90Ft.LauYS-10
91Bow-159
91ColCliLD-108
91ColCliP-8
91ColCliP-593
91DonRoo-47
91FleUpd-44
91LinDriAAA-108
91ScoRoo-110T
91TopTra-62T
91TopTraT-62T
92Bow-362
92ColCliP-11
92Don-275
92OPC-449
92Pin-464
92PinTea2-23
92ProFS7-109
92Sco-523
92Sco100RS-40
92StaClu-471
92Top-449
92TopDeb91-90
92TopGol-449
92TopGolW-449
92TopMic-449
92TriPla-93
92Ult-410
92UppDec-626
93ColCliF-1108
93Fle-650
93ForLauRSC-14
93ForLauRSFP-1592
93UtiBluSC-10
94ChaKniF-888

Johnson, Jeffrey
96SouBenSHS-16

Johnson, Jerome
75LynRanT-14

Johnson, Jerry
81ArkTraT-11
83ArkTraT-9
84BeaGolGT-19
84LouRedR-26
85RocRedWT-18

Johnson, Jerry Michael
69Top-253
70OPC-162
70Top-162
71MLBOffS-254
71OPC-412
71Top-412
72OPC-35
72OPC-36
72Top-35
72Top-36
73OPC-248
73Top-248
75HawIslC-18
75IntLeaASB-13
75PacCoaLAB-13
75OPC-218
75Top-218
76HawIslC-19
76OPC-658
76Top-658
78OPC-184
78Top-169
81TCM60I-440
82HawIslT-5
83LasVegSBHN-12

Johnson, Jim
82TucTorT-24

Johnson, Jimmy (Jim)
80TucTorT-9
81TucTorT-12
85TucTorC-53
95NorNagUTI-NNO
95NorNavTI-14
96GreBatB-1

Johnson, Jody
89GeoColC-13

Johnson, Joe
84RicBraT-21
85GreBraTI-9
85IntLeaAT-17
86BraPol-38
86Don-624
86Fle-519
87BluJayFS-15
87Don-650
87Fle-230
87FleGlo-230
87Lea-91
87TopTra-56T
87TopTraT-56T
88EdmTraC-7
88EdmTraP-560
88OPC-347
88Top-347
88TopTif-347
90CMC-258
90PawRedSC-7
90PawRedSDD-11
90PawRedSP-458
90ProAAAF-430
90TopTVRS-47

Johnson, Joel
91EugEmeC-26
91EugEmeP-3720
92ColRedF-2386
92Ult-72

Johnson, John
86BirBarTI-9
86VanCanP-14
87Ft.LauYP-23

Johnson, John Henry
75CedRapGT-14
75TulOil7-19
76CedRapGT-13
79Hos-39
79Kel-6
79OPC-361
79Top-681
80OPC-97
80Top-173
81Top-216
82Don-550
82Fle-321
82Top-527
84Don-91
84Fle-401
84Nes792-419
84Top-419
84TopTif-419
85Fle-162
85HawIslC-246
85Top-734
85TopTif-734
87BrePol-38
87Fle-347
87FleGlo-347
87Top-377
87TopTif-377
93RanKee-208
94BreMilB-42

Johnson, John Ralph
87OldJudN-269

Johnson, Jonathan
95Bes-121
95SPML-102
96Bow-270
96Exc-111
96SigRooOJPP-P3
96TexLeaAB-9
96TulDriTI-13
97Bow-103
97BowInt-103
97Top-242

Johnson, Josh
86NegLeaF-13
86NegLeaF-63
91NegLeaRL-26
92NegLeaRLI-33
95NegLeaL2-8
95NegLeaLI-26

Johnson, Judd
89SumBraP-1102
90Bes-193
90GreBraB-13
90GreBraS-8
91GreBraC-2
91GreBraLD-208
91GreBraP-2996
91LinDriAA-208
92GreBraF-1151
92GreBraS-234
93RicBraBB-22
93RicBraF-182
93RicBraP-24
93RicBraRC-22
93RicBraRC-12
94RicBraF-2843

Johnson, Judy (William Julius)
74LauOldTBS-36
76ShaPiz-150
80PerHaloFP-150
80SSPHOF-150
83ConMar-59
86NegLeaF-4
86NegLeaF-5
88ConNegA-6
88NegLeaD-9
89PerCelP-20
90NegLeaS-18
90PerGreM-46
90PomBlaBNLP-2547
91PomBlaBPB-11
93TedWil-107
94PomNegLB-4

Johnson, Karl
89EliTwiS-13

Johnson, Keith
92FroRowDP-21
92YakBeaC-6
92YakBeaF-3458
93StaCluM-110
93VerBeaDC-10
93VerBeaDF-2227
94BakDodC-11
95SanBerSTI-9
96MauStiHWB-15
96SanAntMB-10

Johnson, Ken (Kenneth Travis)
49EurSta-185
51Bow-293
60A'sTeal-10
60Top-135
60TopVen-135
61A'sTeal-9
61MapLeaBH-10
61Top-24
62Col.45B-10
62Col45'HC-9
62Col45'JP-7
62Top-278
63Col45"P-9

63Top-352
64Col.45JP-5
64Top-158
64TopGia-2
64TopSta-70
64TopStaU-37
64TopTatl-45
64TopVen-158
65OldLonC-13
65Top-359
66Top-466
67CokCapB-10
67DexPre-108
67Kah-18
67OPC-101
67Top-101
68CokCapB-10
68DexPre-43
68Top-342
68TopVen-342
69Top-238
78AtlCon-12
78TCM60I-232
87AstSer1-13
89AstCol4S-5
92YanWIZ6-61

Johnson, Kent
79CliDodT-14

Johnson, Kevin
80CliGiaT-12
91SpoIndC-20
91SpoIndP-3951

Johnson, Lamar
76OPC-596
76Top-596
76VenLeaS-204
77BurCheD-76
77Top-443
77WhiSoxJT-6
78SSP270-137
78Top-693
79Hos-43
79OPC-192
79Top-372
80Top-242
81CokTeaS-30
81Don-38
81Fle-350
81OPC-366
81Top-589
81TopScr-26
81TopSti-58
81TopSupHT-16
82Don-269
82Fle-346
82Top-13
82TopTra-50T
83Don-142
83Fle-571
83FleSti-162
83Top-453
90EliSenL-7
91DenZepLD-150
91DenZepP-138
91LinDriAAA-150
92DenZepF-2657
92DenZepS-150
93RanKee-209
93StoPorC-27
93StoPorF-760
94StoPorC-27
94StoPorF-1708

Johnson, Lance
86ArkTraP-8
87LouRedTI-16
88Don-31
88Fle-37
88FleGlo-37
88Lea-31
88StaLinCa-10
88TopBig-251
88WhiSoxC-12
89Don-606
89Fle-499
89FleGlo-499
89PanSti-312
89RedFolSB-67
89ScoHot1R-33
89Top-122
89TopTif-122
89TriAAP-AAA30
89VanCanC-18
89VanCanP-576
90Don-573
90Fle-536
90FleCan-536
90Lea-259
90OPC-587
90Sco-570
90ScoYouS2-38
90Top-587
90TopBig-274
90TopTif-587
90UppDec-90
90WhiSoxC-9
91Bow-349
91Don-259
91Fle-123
91Lea-403
91OPC-243
91PanFreS-317
91PanSti-253
91Sco-157
91StaClu-199
91Top-243
91TopDesS-243
91TopMic-243
91TopTif-243
91Ult-76
91UppDec-248
91WhiSoxK-1
92Bow-208
92Don-267
92Fle-87
92Lea-237
92OPC-736
92PanSti-130
92Pin-373
92Sco-146
92StaClu-444
92StaCluMP-9
92Stu-154
92Top-736
92TopGol-736
92TopGolW-736
92TopMic-736
92TriPla-239
92Ult-38
92UppDec-188
92WhiSoxK-1
93Don-301
93Fin-64
93FinRef-64
93Fla-187
93Fle-204
93Lea-373
93OPC-176
93PacSpa-390
93PanSti-141
93Pin-137
93Sco-109
93Sel-266
93SelStaL-19
93SP-256
93StaClu-359
93StaCluFDI-359
93StaCluMOP-359
93StaCluWS-15
93Stu-192
93Top-94
93TopGol-94
93TopInaM-94
93TopMic-94
93Ult-174
93UppDec-280
93UppDecGold-280
93WhiSoxK-14
94Bow-623
94BowBes-R10
94BowBesR-R10
94ColC-150
94ColChoGS-150
94ColChoSS-150
94Don-552
94ExtBas-49
94Fin-54
94FinRef-54
94Fla-278
94Fle-85
94Lea-13
94OPC-262
94Pac-129
94Pin-86
94PinArtP-86
94PinMusC-86
94Sco-69
94ScoCyc-TC11
94ScoGolR-69
94Sel-13
94Spo-123
94StaClu-194
94StaCluFDI-194
94StaCluGR-194
94StaCluMOP-194
94StaCluT-134
94StaCluTFDI-134
94Top-452
94TopGol-452
94TopSpa-452
94TriPla-266
94Ult-35
94UppDec-118
94UppDecED-118
94WhiSoxK-16
95ColCho-499
95ColChoGS-499
95ColChoSS-499
95Don-298
95DonPreP-298
95DonTopotO-51
95Emb-78
95EmbGolI-78
95Fin-168
95FinRef-168
95Fla-246
95Fle-121
95Lea-200
95Pac-92
95Pin-41
95PinArtP-41
95PinMusC-41
95Sco-360
95ScoGolR-360
95ScoPlaTS-360
95StaClu-173
95StaCluFDI-173
95StaCluMO-24
95StaCluMOP-173
95StaCluSTWS-173
95StaCluVR-90
95Stu-97
95Top-314
95TopCyb-170
95Ult-30
95UltGolM-30
95UppDec-437
95UppDecED-437
95UppDecEDG-437
95WhiSoxK-14
96Baz-107
96Cir-159
96CirRav-159
96ColCho-97
96ColCho-625
96ColChoGS-97
96ColChoGS-625
96ColChoSS-97
96ColChoSS-625
96Don-48
96DonPreP-48
96EmoXL-234
96Fin-B200
96FinRef-B200
96Fla-322
96Fle-68
96FleTif-68
96FleUpd-U158
96FleUpdTC-U158
96MetKah-18
96MetUni-202
96MetUniP-202
96Pac-277
96PanSti-169
96Pin-352
96PinAfi-29
96PinAfiAP-29
96PinAfiFPP-29
96PinFoil-352
96Sco-148
96Sel-115
96SelArtP-115
96StaClu-152
96StaCluEPB-152
96StaCluEPG-152
96StaCluEPS-152
96StaCluMO-16
96StaCluMOP-152
95StaCluVRMC-90
96Sum-9
96SumAbo&B-9
96SumArtP-9
96SumFoi-9
96TeaOut-40
96Top-375
96TopGal-60
96TopGalPPI-60
96Ult-40
96Ult-513
96UltGolM-40
96UltGolM-513
96UppDec-502U
97Bow-258
97BowBes-69
97BowBesAR-69
97BowBesR-69
97BowChr-80
97BowChrI-80
97BowChrIR-80
97BowChrR-80
97BowInt-258
97Cir-207
97CirRav-207
97ColCho-396
97ColChoAC-41
97Don-249
97DonLim-73
97DonLimLE-73
97DonPre-97
97DonPreCttC-97
97DonPreP-249
97DonPrePGold-249
97Fin-119
97FinEmb-119
97FinEmbR-119
97FinRef-119
97FlaSho-A139
97FlaSho-B139
97FlaSho-C139
97FlaShoLC-139
97FlaShoLC-B139
97FlaShoLC-C139
97FlaShoLCM-A139
97FlaShoLCM-B139
97FlaShoLCM-C139
97Fle-400
97FleTif-400
97Lea-32
97LeaFraM-32
97LeaFraMDC-32
97MetUni-195
97Pac-369
97PacLigB-369
97PacPri-125
97PacPriGA-GA28
97PacPriLB-125
97PacPriP-125
97PacSil-369
97Pin-20
97PinArtP-20
97PinMusC-20
97PinX-P-51
97PinX-PMoS-51
97Sco-237
97ScoPreS-237
97ScoShoS-237
97ScoShoSAP-237
97SP-118
97StaClu-222
97StaCluMat-222
97StaCluMOP-222
97Top-261
97TopChr-92
97TopChrR-92
97TopChrSB-25
97TopChrSBR-25
97TopGal-22
97TopGalPPI-22
97TopSeaB-SB25
97TopSta-24
97TopStaAM-24
97Ult-242
97UltGolME-242
97UltPlaME-242
97UppDec-435

Johnson, Larry D.
80RocRedWT-20
81EvaTriT-12

Johnson, Ledowick
95HelBreTI-13
96HelBreTI-1

Johnson, Lee
90DurBulUTI-1
90GreBraP-1124
90GreBraS-9
91OscAstC-5
91OscAstP-677

Johnson, Lefty (Arthur Henry)
77TCMTheWY-63

Johnson, Lindsey
86KinEagP-11
89MiaMirIS-9
89MiaMirIS-7

Johnson, Lloyd
34Gou-86

Johnson, Lou
60Top-476
61MapLeaBH-11
63Top-238
65DodJayP-6
65DodTeal-7
66OPC-13
66Top-13
66TopVen-13
67CokCapD-8
67CokCapDA-8
67DexPre-109
67Top-410
67TopVen-290
68OPC-184
68Top-184
68TopVen-184
69AngJacitB-4
69MilBra-137
69Top-367
69TopTeaP-13
90DodTar-387

Johnson, Luther
88MarPhiS-18
89AubAstP-2176
90AshTouP-2762
91OscAstC-25
91OscAstP-699

Johnson, Marcel
88NebCor-22
90KinMetB-23
90KinMetS-12
92PulBraC-9
92PulBraF-3184
93IdaFalBF-4045
93IdaFalBSP-13

Johnson, Mark
86DavLipB-15
88T/MUmp-51
89T/MUmp-49
90T/MUmp-47

Johnson, Mark L.
94SigRooDP-25
94SigRooDPS-25
94StaCluDP-12
94StaCluDPFDI-12
95Exc-254
95Pin-174
95PinArtP-174
95PinMusC-174
95ScoDraP-DP11
95SigRooOJA-AS4
95SigRooOJAS-AS4
95StaClu-104
95StaCluFDI-104
95Top-605
95UppDecML-193
96FleTif-522
96MidLeaAB-52
96SouBenSHS-17
97Fin-9
97FinRef-9
97Lea-119
97LeaFraM-119
97LeaFraMDC-119
97ScoShoSAP-265
97Top-99
97UltGolME-261
97UltPlaME-261
95UppDecMLFS-193

Johnson, Mark Patrick
88CapCodPB-2
88CapCodPPaLP-1
90ArkRaz-18
91AugPirC-15
91AugPirP-811
91EugEmeC-11
91EugEmeP-3738
92AppFoxC-10
92AppFoxF-994
92CarMudF-1187
92CarMudS-136
92MidLeaATI-22
92ProFS7-79
93CarMudF-2061

93CarMudTI-17
93ClaFS7-140
93ClaGolF-104
93MemChiF-388
94CarMudF-1585
95Bow-225
95BowGolF-225
95DonTopotO-316
95Emo-174
95Fin-236
95FinRef-236
95Fla-400
95FleUpd-149
95PirFil-13
95StaCluMOP-104
95StaCluSTWS-104
95UppDec-252
95UppDecED-252
95UppDecEDG-252
95UppDecML-209
96ColCho-260
96ColChoGS-260
96ColChoSS-260
96Don-286
96DonPreP-286
96Fle-522
96LeaSigEA-92
96Sco-40
96Ult-264
96UltGolM-264
96UppDec-176
97Cir-169
97CirRav-169
97ColCho-423
97Don-215
97DonPreP-215
97DonPrePGold-215
97Fle-428
97FleTif-428
97Pac-393
97PacLigB-393
97PacSil-393
97Pin-90
97PinArtP-90
97PinMusC-90
97Sco-265
97ScoPreS-265
97ScoShoS-265
97Ult-261
97UppDec-459
95UppDecMLFS-209

Johnson, Mark U of Hawaii
97Bow-323
97BowChr-222
97BowChrI-222
97BowChrIR-222
97BowChrR-222
97BowInt-323
97Top-483

Johnson, Matt
92MedHatBJF-3214
92MedHatBJSP-1
93DunBluJC-12
93DunBluJF-1804
93DunBluJFFN-13
94DunBluJC-15
94DunBluJF-2565
95KnoSmoF-49

Johnson, Mike
79AppFoxT-10
82WauTimF-18
84ChaLooT-13
93KinMetC-14
93KinMetF-3802
94MedHatBJF-3678
94MedHatBJSP-18
96HagSunB-10
97Bow-314
97BowInt-314
97Fle-532
97FleTif-532

Johnson, Mitch
80ElmPioRST-18
85PawRedST-19
86PawRedSP-11
87PawRedSP-58
87PawRedST-7
88PawRedSC-3
88PawRedSP-455
89TucTorC-2
89TucTorJP-9
89TucTorP-187

Johnson, North
91KinIndC-30

Johnson, Otis
11MecDFT-30

Johnson, Owen
66Top-356
66TopVen-356

Johnson, Paul
22W573-68
89PitMetS-12
89Sta-160
90St.LucMS-11

Johnson, Perry
83IdaFalAT-7

Johnson, Randy (Randall David)
86WesPalBEP-21
87JacExpP-451
87SouLeaAJ-16
88IndIndC-1
88IndIndP-510
88TriAAC-13
89ClaLigB-95
89Don-42
89DonBasB-80
89DonRoo-43
89ExpPos-15
89Fle-381
89FleGlo-381
89FleUpd-59
89OPC-186
89PanSti-111
89Sco-645
89ScoHot1R-63
89ScoRoo-77T
89ScoYouS2-32
89Spo-224
89Top-647
89TopBig-287
89TopTif-647
89TopTra-57T
89TopTraT-57T
89UppDec-25
89Woo-13
90Bow-468
90BowTif-468
90ClaYel-T22
90Don-379
90DonBesA-111
90Fle-518
90FleCan-518
90Hot50RS-23
90Lea-483
90MarMot-13
90OPC-431
90PanSti-154
90Sco-415
90Sco100RS-52
90Spo-64
90Top-431
90TopSti-230
90TopTif-431
90UppDec-563
90USPlaCA-3S
91Bow-253
91ClaGam-35
91Don-134
91DonBonC-BC2
91Fle-455
91FleWaxBC-2
91Lea-319
91MajLeaCP-6
91MarCouH-26
91OPC-225
91PanFreS-353
91PanSti-2
91PanSti-188
91RedFolS-53
91Sco-290
91Sco-700
91SevCoi-NW9
91StaClu-409
91StaCluCM-15
91Stu-116
91Top-225
91TopDesS-225
91TopMic-225
91TopTif-225
91Ult-339
91UppDec-376
92Bow-178
92Don-207
92DonDiaK-DK22
92Fle-283
92FleSmo'nH-S11
92Hig5-108
92Lea-302
92MarMot-13
92OPC-525
92OPCPre-173
92PanSti-62
92Pin-379
92Pin-595
92Sco-584
92SpoIllFK1-199
92StaClu-720
92Stu-234
92SunSee-15
92Top-525
92TopGol-525
92TopGolW-525
92TopKid-126
92TopMic-525
92TriPla-71
92Ult-125
92UppDec-164
92UppDecTMH-27
93Bow-431
93CadDis-35
93Don-581
93Fin-154
93FinRef-154
93Fla-272
93Fle-676
93FunPac-115
93Lea-380
93MarDaiQ-1
93MarMot-15
93OPC-140
93PacSpa-288
93PanSti-60
93Pin-41
93Sco-384
93Sel-118
93SelStaL-73
93SP-132
93StaClu-501
93StaCluFDI-501
93StaCluMari-16
93StaCluMOP-501
93Stu-153
93Top-460
93TopComotH-16
93TopGol-460
93TopInaM-460
93TopMic-460
93TriPla-167
93Ult-269
93UltStrK-3
93UppDec-336
93UppDec-824
93UppDecGold-336
93UppDecGold-824
94Bow-285
94ColC-307
94ColC-357
94ColChoGS-307
94ColChoGS-357
94ColChoSS-307
94ColChoSS-357
94Don-352
94DonSpeE-352
94ExtBas-168
94ExtBasPD-2
94Fin-213
94FinJum-213
94FinRef-213
94Fla-337
94Fle-290
94FleAllS-12
94FleSmo'nH-5
94FUnPac-51
94FUnPac-175
94FUnPac-197
94Lea-164
94LeaL-67
94MarMot-2
94OPC-81
94Pac-574
94PacSilP-7
94PanSti-9
94PanSti-119
94Pin-278
94PinArtP-278
94PinMusC-278
94PinTheN-10
94PinTri-TR9
94ProMag-128
94RedFolMI-7
94Sco-33
94ScoGolR-33
94ScoGolS-43
94Sel-19
94SelCroC-CC4
94SelSam-19
94SelSki-SK1
94SP-106
94SPDieC-106
94Spo-30
94StaClu-438
94StaCluDD-DD11
94StaCluFDI-438
94StaCluGR-438
94StaCluMO-22
94StaCluMOP-438
94StaCluMOP-DD11
94Stu-102
94Top-290
94TopBlaG-10
94TopGol-290
94TopSpa-290
94TopSupS-23
94TriPla-128
94TriPlaM-13
94Ult-419
94UltLeaL-5
94UltStrK-1
94UppDec-31
94UppDec-330
94UppDecAJ-20
94UppDecAJG-20
94UppDecED-31
94UppDecED-330
95Baz-54
95BazRedH-RH11
95Bow-395
95BowBes-R1
95BowBes-X14
95BowBesR-R1
95BowBesR-X14
95ClaPhoC-51
95ColCho-74
95ColChoGS-74
95ColChoSE-123
95ColChoSE-143
95ColChoSE-250
95ColChoSEGS-123
95ColChoSEGS-143
95ColChoSEGS-250
95ColChoSESS-123
95ColChoSESS-143
95ColChoSESS-250
95ColChoSS-74
95Don-18
95DonMouM-7
95DonPreP-18
95DonTopotO-151
95Emb-69
95EmbGolI-69
95Emo-78
95Fin-76
95FinFlaT-FT5
95FinRef-76
95Fla-82
95Fle-271
95FleAllS-21
95FleLeaL-5
95FleTeaL-12
95Lea-244
95LeaLim-40
95MarMot-2
95MarPac-5
95MarPac-14
95MarPac-34
95NatPac2-3
95Pac-399
95PacPri-127
95PanSti-16
95PanSti-126
95Pin-330
95PinArtP-330
95PinArtP-351
95PinMusC-330
95RedFol-34
95Sco-222
95ScoGolR-222
95ScoHaloG-HG7
95ScoPlaTS-222
95Sel-135
95SelArtP-135
95SelCer-61
95SelCerMG-61
95SP-189
95SPCha-186
95SPChaDC-186
95Spo-29
95SpoArtP-29
95SPSil-189
95SPSpeF-19
95StaClu-340
95StaCluMO-23
95StaCluMOP-340
95StaCluMOP-SS20
95StaCluSS-SS20
95StaCluSTDW-M340
95StaCluSTWS-340
95StaCluVR-179
95Stu-48
95StuGolS-48
95Sum-97
95Sum-193
95SumNthD-97
95SumNthD-193
95Top-203
95TopCyb-116
95TopLeaL-LL46
95TopTra-164T
95UC3-64
95UC3-130
95UC3ArtP-64
95UC3ArtP-130
95Ult-103
95UltGolM-103
95UltLeaL-4
95UltLeaLGM-4
95UltStrK-3
95UltStrKGM-3
95UppDec-102
95UppDec-112
95UppDecC-4B
95UppDecED-102
95UppDecED-112
95UppDecEDG-102
95UppDecEDG-112
95UppDecSE-118
95UppDecSEG-118
95USPlaCMLA-3S
95Zen-83
95ZenAllS-9
96Baz-95
96Bow-48
96BowBes-21
96BowBesAR-21
96BowBesMI-10
96BowBesMIAR-10
96BowBesMIR-10
96BowBesR-21
96Cir-79
96CirAcc-13
96CirBos-21
96CirRav-79
96ColCho-7
96ColCho-8
96ColCho-269
96ColCho-315
96ColCho-365
96ColCho-708
96ColChoGS-7
96ColChoGS-8
96ColChoGS-269
96ColChoGS-315
96ColChoGS-365
96ColChoGS-708
96ColChoSS-7
96ColChoSS-8
96ColChoSS-269
96ColChoSS-315
96ColChoSS-365
96ColChoSS-708
96ColChoYMtP-18
96ColChoYMtP-18A
96ColChoYMtPGS-18
96ColChoYMtPGS-18A
96Don-478
96DonPreP-478
96DonSho-2
96EmoN-6
96EmoXL-115
96Fin-G270
96Fin-S77
96FinRef-G270
96FinRef-S77
96Fla-162
96Fle-240
96FlePosG-4
96FleSmo'H-5
96FleTif-240
96FleUpd-U227

96FleUpdH-9
96FleUpdTC-U227
96FleZon-5
96Kin-5
96Lea-165
96LeaLim-38
96LeaLimG-38
96LeaPre-52
96LeaPreP-52
96LeaPrePB-165
96LeaPrePG-165
96LeaPrePS-165
96LeaPreSG-60
96LeaPreSte-60
96LeaSig-37
96LeaSigEA-91
96LeaSigEACM-12
96LeaSigPPG-37
96LeaSigPPP-37
96MarMot-2
96MetUni-108
96MetUniP-108
96Pac-401
96Pac-418
96PacGolCD-DC33
96PacOctM-OM7
96PacPri-P132
96PacPriFT-FT1
96PacPriG-P132
96PacPriRHS-RH17
96PanSti-124
96PanSti-226
96Pin-236
96Pin-273
96PinAfi-10
96PinAfiAP-10
96PinAfiFPP-10
96PinAfiSP-25
96PinArtP-136
96PinArtP-173
96PinFan-25
96PinFoil-236
96PinFoil-273
96PinSta-136
96PinSta-173
96PinTeaP-9
96ProMagDM-22
96ProSta-62
96SchDis-15
96Sco-34
96Sco-193
96Sco-367
96Sco-512
96ScoAll-11
96ScoDugC-A33
96ScoDugC-B92
96ScoDugCAP-A33
96ScoDugCAP-B92
96ScoGolS-29
96ScoNumG-25
96ScoRef-18
96Sel-63
96SelArtP-63
96SelCer-17
96SelCerAP-17
96SelCerCB-17
96SelCerCR-17
96SelCerIP-13
96SelCerMB-17
96SelCerMG-17
96SelCerMR-17
96SelClaTF-19
96SelEnF-19
96SelTeaN-9
96SP-169
96Spo-51
96SpoArtP-51
96SPSpeFX-31
96SPSpeFXDC-31
96SPx-56
96SPxGol-56
96StaClu-16
96StaClu-235
96StaCluEPB-16
96StaCluEPG-16
96StaCluEPS-16
96StaCluMM-MM1
96StaCluMO-17
96StaCluMOP-16
96StaCluMOP-235
96StaCluMOP-MM1
96StaCluMOP-PS1
96StaCluMOP-TSCA9
96StaCluPS-PS1
96StaCluTA-9
95StaCluVRMC-179
96Stu-73
96StuPrePB-73
96StuPrePG-73
96StuPrePS-73
96Sum-110
96SumAbo&B-110
96SumArtP-110
96SumFoi-110
96SumPos-6
96TeaOut-41
96Top-150
96Top-224
96TopBroLL-5
96TopChr-43
96TopChr-84
96TopChrR-43
96TopChrR-84
96TopClaC-CC11
96TopGal-162
96TopGalE-10
96TopGalPG-PG2
96TopGalPPI-162
96TopLas-56
96TopLasSS-12
96TopMysF-M3
96TopMysFR-M3
96TopPro-AL6
96Ult-127
96Ult-581
96UltGolM-127
96UltGolM-581
96UltSeaC-3
96UltSeaCGM-3
96UppDec-460
96UppDooDD DD37
96UppDecDDG-DD37
96UppDecDDS-DD37
96UppDecHC-HC9
96UppDecPHE-H14
96UppDecPreH-H14
96UppDecVJLS-VJ12
96Zen-75
96ZenArtP-75
96ZenDiaC-17
96ZenDiaCP-17
96ZenMoz-5
97Bow-225
97BowBes-93
97BowBesAR-93
97BowBesR-93
97BowChr-55
97BowChrI-55
97BowChrIR-55
97BowChrR-55
97BowInt-225
97Cir-276
97CirRav-276
97ColCho-485
97ColChoTBS-44
97ColChoTBSWH-44
97Don-89
97Don-426
97DonArmaD-5
97DonEli-30
97DonEliGS-30
97DonLim-52
97DonLim-120
97DonLim-187
97DonLimLE-52
97DonLimLE-120
97DonLimLE-187
97DonPre-104
97DonPreCltC-104
97DonPreP-89
97DonPreP-426
97DonPrePGold-89
97DonPrePGold-426
97DonTea-139
97DonTeaSPE-139
97Fin-110
97Fin-348
97FinEmb-110
97FinEmb-348
97FinEmbR-110
97FinEmbR-348
97FinRef-110
97FinRef-348
97FlaSho-A20
97FlaSho-B20
97FlaSho-C20
97FlaShoLC-20
97FlaShoLC-B20
97FlaShoLC-C20
97FlaShoLCM-A20
97FlaShoLCM-B20
97FlaShoLCM-C20
97Fle-210
97FleTif-210
97Lea-132
97Lea-379
97LeaFraM-132
97LeaFraM-379
97LeaFraMDC-132
97LeaFraMDC-379
97LeaGet-4
97MetUni-147
97NewPin-100
97NewPinAP-100
97NewPinKtP-17
97NewPinMC-100
97NewPinPP-100
97NewPinPP-K17
97Pac-189
97PacLigB-189
97PacPriSH-SH6B
97PacSil-189
97PinCar-3
97PinCer-54
97PinCerLI-17
97PinCerMBlu-54
97PinCerMG-54
97PinCerMR-54
97PinCerR-54
97PinIns-127
97PinInsCE-127
97PinInsDE-127
97PinTotCPB-54
97PinTotCPG-54
97PinTotCPR-54
97PinX-P-96
97PinX-P-142
97PinX-PMoS-96
97PinX-PMoS-142
97ProMag-72
97ProMagML-72
97Sco-192
97Sco-529
97ScoHigZ-17
97ScoHobR-529
97ScoMar-9
97ScoMarPl-9
97ScoMarPr-9
97ScoPitP-15
97ScoPreS-192
97ScoResC-529
97ScoShoS-192
97ScoShoS-529
97ScoShoSAP-192
97ScoShoSAP-529
97ScoStaaD-8
97Sel-78
97SelArtP-78
97SelRegG-78
97SkyE-X-41
97SkyE-XC-41
97SkyE-XEC-41
97SP-167
97SpoIll-36
97SpoIll-159
97SpoIllEE-36
97SpoIllEE-159
97SpoIllGS-22
97SPSPxFA-5
97StaClu-247
97StaCluMat-247
97StaCluMOP-247
97Stu-113
97StuPrePG-113
97StuPrePS-113
97Top-325
97TopChr-110
97TopChrR-110
97TopGal-52
97TopGalPPI-52
97TopHobM-HM7
97TopScr-10
97TopSta-43
97TopSta1AS-AS2
97TopStaAM-43
97TopStaASGM-ASM4
97Ult-124
97UltGolME-124
97UltPlaME-124
97UppDec-72
97UppDec-501
97Zen-31

Johnson, Randy (Randall Glenn)
81RicBraT-22
82BraBurKL-14
82BraPol-6
83BraPol-6
83Top-596
84BraPol-6
84Don-321
84Fle-183
84Nes792-289
84Top-289
84TopTif-289
85Don-531
85Fle-330
85RicBraT-14
85Top-458
85TopTif-458
86PhoFirP-11
89EveGiaS-16
90CliGiaB-15
90CliGiaP-2561

Johnson, Randy (Randall Stuart)
80GleFalWSBT-18
80GleFalWSCT-4
81GleFalWST-18
82TopTra-51T
82TwiPos-18
83Don-305
83Fle-617
83TolMudHT-21
83Top-354
85BufBisT-14
87JapPlaB-12
89PacSenL-181
90EliSenL-23
91BriBanF-17

Johnson, Reginald
92GreFalDSP-11
93VerBeaDC-11
93VerBeaDF-2228

Johnson, Ric
96QuaCitRB-17

Johnson, Rich
86AshTouP-16
87ColAstP-23
88ColAstB-14

Johnson, Rocky
88NebCor-12

Johnson, Roger
86KinEagP-12

Johnson, Ron (Rondin)
81OmaRoyT-19
82OmaRoyT-17A
82OmaRoyT-17B
83Roy-13
84IndIndTI-24
84OmaRoyT-25
85OmaRoyT-21
86OmaRoyP-12
86OmaRoyT-2
87Ft.MyeRP-34
87OmaRoyP-11
88OmaRoyC-10
88OmaRoyP-1515
89BasCitRS-27
90BasCitRS-30
91BasCitRC-29
91BasCitRP-1415
91DaiDolF-5
92BasCitRC-24
92BasCitRF-3860
93CarLeaAGF-13
93WilBluRC-27
93WilBluRF-2013
94MemChiF-373
95AusFut-6
95WicWraTI-21
96WicWraB-27

Johnson, Roy Cleveland
29PorandAR-47
32OrbPinUP-35
32R33So2-xx
33Gou-8
33GouCanV-8
33TatOrb-35
34BatR31-63
34ExhFou-9
38ExhFou-1
39CubTeal-12
44CenFlo-12
75YanDyn1T-25
81ConTSN-32
83ConMar-11
88ConAmeA-17
91ConTSN-199
93ConTSN-777
94ConTSN-1173
94ConTSNB-1173

Johnson, Roy Edward
82ExpPos-17
82WicAerTI-6
82WicAerTI-7
83Don-492
83WicAerDS-12
83WicAerDS-24
84ExpPos-14
84IndIndTI-7
84IndIndTI-15
85IndIndTI-5
87TacTigP-15
88TacTigC-15
88TacTigP-621
86HumStaDS-45

Johnson, Russ
92LSUTigM-14
93BazTeaU-12
93LSUTigM-13
93TopTra-115T
94LSUTig-3
94LSUTigMP-3
94SigRooBS-5
94StaCluDP-15
94StaCluDPFDI-15
95JacGenTI-23
95SigRooDDS-DD3
95SigRooDDSS-DD3
95Top-423
96Bow-294
96JacGenB-14
96TexLeaAB-10
97Bow-148
97Bow98ROY-ROY6
97BowBes-152
97BowBesAR-152
97BowBesR-152
97BowChr-152
97BowChr1RC-ROY6
97BowChr1RCR-ROY6
97BowChrI-152
97BowChrIR-152
97BowChrR-152
97BowInt-148
97Fle-516
97FleTif-516
97SpoIll-12
97SpoIllEE-12
97Top-487
97Ult-480
97UltGolME-480
97UltPlaME-480

Johnson, Scott
81MiaOriT-21
87WatIndP-9
88KinIndS-12
89SouBenWSGS-6
90SouBenWSB-25
90SouBenWSGS-8
92SarWhiSCB-30
94ElmPioF-3467
95ButCopKtl-6
94ElmPioC-10

Johnson, Sean
88SalLakCTTI-30

Johnson, Silas
30SchR33-34
33DouDisP-24
34DiaMatCSB-96
43PhiTeal-11
47TipTop-80
77TCMTheWY-57

Johnson, Stan
61UniOil-SD5
77FriOneYW-63

Johnson, Steve
83BeaGolGT-3
84BeaGolGT-20
86WatIndP-13
92SavCarC-9
92SavCarF-659
93SprCarC-14
93SprCarF-1845
94St.PetCC-12
94St.PetCF-2579

Johnson, Swede (John Clifford)
77TCMTheWY-85

Johnson, Sylvester
21Nei-24
22E120-55
22W572-50
22W573-66
23MapCriV-13
34DiaMatCSB-97
34BatR31-54
39PlaBal-28
40PlaBal-99
43CenFlo-13
44CenFlo-13
45CenFlo-13
92ConTSN-654
93ConTSN-901
Johnson, T.J. (Terence)
84LitFalMT-14
85LitFalMT-19
Johnson, Terry
83BurRanF-10
83BurRanT-6
83TulDriT-24
84TulDriTI-34
85TulDriTI-30
Johnson, Tim
74OPC-554
74Top-554
75OPC-556
75Top-556
76BreA&P-6
76OPC-613
76Top-613
76VenLeaS-205
77Top-406
78BluJayP-11
78Top-542
79OPC-89
79Top-182
80OPC-155
80Top-297
86BreGreT-3
88GreFalDTI-26
89BakDodCLC-206
89CalLeaA-23
90CMC-75
90IndIndC-25
90IndIndP-307
90ProAAAF-590
93ExpPosN-13
94BreMilB-43
Johnson, Todd
91FreStaBS-6
91TopTra-63T
91TopTraT-63T
92StaCluD-93
92TopDaiQTU-24
93BurIndC-13
93BurIndF-3301
94KinIndC-10
94KinIndF-2646
95KinIndTI-16
Johnson, Tom
81QuaCitCT-13
83MidCubT-23
86BurExpP-12
87Ft.MyeRP-19
88VirGenS-11
89BasCitRS-11
Johnson, Tom R.
75OPC-618
75TacTwiK-11
75Top-618
76OPC-448
76TacTwiDQ-9
76Top-448
77BurCheD-46
77Top-202
78Hos-59
78Kel-9
78Top-54
78TwiFriP-10
79OPC-77
79Top-162
80GleFalWSBT-3
80GleFalWSCT-28
Johnson, Tony
84IdaFalATI-14
Johnson, Tookie
90LSUTigA-5
90LSUTigP-16
91LSUTigP-5
Johnson, Travis
96ForWayWB-11
Johnson, Wade
85RedWinA-10
86RedWinA-19
Johnson, Wally (Wallace)
82ExpPos-18
82Fle-192
82WicAerTI-8
83Fle-285
85IndIndTI-21
86IndIndTI-19
87ExpPos-12
87Fle-321
87FleGlo-321
87Top-588
87TopTif-588
88Fle-186
88FleGlo-186
88Sco-433
88ScoGlo-433
88StaLinE-8
88Top-228
88TopTif-228
89Don-484
89Fle-382
89FleGlo-382
89OPC-138
89PanSti-120
89Sco-196
89Top-138
89TopTif-138
89UppDec-124
90Don-570
90ExpPos-19
90Fle-351
90FleCan-351
90Lea-344
90OPC-318
90PubSti-178
90Sco-479
90Top-318
90TopBig-46
90TopTif-318
90VenSti-255
95EugEmeTI-31
96MacBraB-27
Johnson, Walter P.
08AmeCarE-80
08RosComP-80
09RamT20-60
09SenBarP-6
09SpoNewSM-40
09T206-172
09T206-173
10CouT21-155
10CouT21-293
10DarChoE-20
10DomDisP-60
10OrnOvaPP-7
10RedCroT-36
10RedCroT-124
10RedCroT-207
10SenWasT-2
10SepAnoP-16
10SweCapPP-60A
10SweCapPP-60B
11BasBatEU-25
11L1L-135
11MecDFT-44
11PloCanE-37
11S74Sil-39
11S81LarS-110
11SpoLifM-125
11T205-82
11TurRedT-99
12HasTriFT-7
12HasTriFT-49
12SenNatPC-1
12SenVasS-3
12T207-87
13NatGamW-23
13TomBarW-22
14B18B-41
14CraJacE-57
14FatPlaT-20
14TexTomE-24
14TexTomE-55
14TexTomE-59
15CraJacE-57
15SpoNewM-90
15SpoNewP-5
15VicT21-15
16BF2FP-46
16ColE13-87
16SpoNewM-91
19W514-94
20NatCarE-50
20WalMaiW-23
21E121So1-48
21E121So8-43A
21E121So8-43B
21Exh-84
21Nei-47
21OxfConE-10
22AmeCarE-32
22E120-110
22W572-51
22W573-67
22W575-64
22WilPatV-47
23MapCriV-30
23W501-17
23W503-23
23W515-38
23W551-5
23WilChoV-72
24MrsShePP-4
25Exh-125
25SenOakT-1
26Exh-125
26SpoComoA-23
27AmeCarE-28
27Exh-62
27YorCarE-45
28W56PlaC-S2
31SenTeaPW-16
34ButPreR-36
36PC7AlbHoF-2
37KelPepS-BB9
40PlaBal-120
47PM1StaP1-101
48ExhHoF-18
48SweSpoT-4
49LeaPre-4
50CalHOFW-43
51R42SmaS-54
51TopConMA-6
60ExhWriH-13
60Fle-6
60NuHi-40
60SenUniMC-8
61Fle-49
61GolPre-29
61NuSco-440
61Top-409
63BasMagM-42
63BazA-12
63GadFunC-39
63HalofFB-12
67TopVen-139
68LauWorS-22
68SpoMemAG-3
69Baz-2
69Baz-6
70FleWorS-22
71FleWorS-22
71FleWorS-23
72FleFamF-8
72KelATG-1
72LauGreF-2
73OPC-476
73OPC-478
73Top-476
73Top-478
74NewYorNTDiS-30
75McCCob-6
75SheGrePG-15
76BooProC-7
76GrePlaG-15
76OPC-349
76RowExh-10
76ShaPiz-3
76Top-349
77GalGloG-105
77GalGloG-144
77GalGloG-234
77ShaPiz-4
79Pew-3
79Top-417
79Top-418
80Lau300-3
80LauFamF-25
80PacLeg-45
80PerHaloFP-2
80SSPHOF-3
81ConTSN-37
81SpoHaloF-23
82DiaCla-37
83DonHOFH-2
84DonCha-37
84GalHaloFRL-3
84OCoandSI-81
85UltBasC-13
85Woo-21
86ConSer1-4
86TCM-14
86TCMSupS-8
87ConSer2-6
87HygAllG-27
87NesDreT-9
87SpoRea-36
89PacLegI-192
89SweBasG-3
90BasWit-62
90HOFStiB-28
90PerGreM-8
90SweBasG-75
91ConTSN-9
91ConTSN-258
91LinDri-45
91SweBasG-130
91USGamSBL-9C
91USGamSBL-9D
91USGamSBL-9H
91USGamSBL-9S
92ConTSN-353
92ConTSN-564
92ConTSNCI-7
92ConTSNGI-934G
92MegRut-9
92MegRut-73
92MegRut-95
92MegRut-126
93ActPacA-90
93ActPacA2-24G
93ConMasB-3
93ConMasC-3
93ConTSN-758
93ConTSN-804
93ConTSN-934
93ConTSNP-934
93CraJac-5
93Hoy-4
93LegFoi-6
93PacRyaFM-12
93UppDecAH-78
93UppDecAH-138
93UppDecAH-142
93UppDecAH-143
94ConTSN-1255
94ConTSNB-1255
94ConTSNCI-30
94TedWil-89
94TedWilLC-LC15
94UppDecAH-80
94UppDecAH-109
94UppDecAH-152
94UppDecAH1-80
94UppDecAH1-109
94UppDecAH1-152
94UppDecTAE-15
94UppDecTAELD-LD6
95UppDecSHoB-18
93UppDecTR-4
96ColCho-502
96ColChoGS-502
96ColChoSS-502
20W516-8
Johnson, Wayne
82WatIndF-25
82WatIndT-5
83BufBisT-2
85WatIndT-10
91MarPhiC-4
91MarPhiP-3467
92BatCliC-9
92BatCliF-3277
Johnson, Wes
88MisStaB-15
Johnson, William Russell
53CarHunW-11
75LynRanT-13
77TCMTheWY-55
78LauLonABS-29
Johnson, Willy
88SumBraP-417
89SumBraP-1092
90SumBraB-26
93MacBraC-30
93SouAtlLAGF-38
94SouAtlLAF-SAL44
95MacBraTI-13
96DurBulBIB-9
Johnston, Chris
83KnoBluJT-11
86STaoftFT-29
Johnston, Craig
88MarPhiS-19
89KinMetS-14
91SydWavF-11
Johnston, Dan
88GenCubP-1644
90GreHorB-5
90GreHorP-2657
90GreHorS-11
91PriWilCC-6
91PriWilCP-1422
92ForLauYC-8
92ForLauYTI-19
92Ft.LauYF-2608
93UtiBluSF-3528
Johnston, Doc (Wheeler)
15CraJacE-150
22E120-83
77Ind192T-10
Johnston, Fred Ivy
90DodTar-388
Johnston, Greg
78PhoGiaC-11
79PhoGiaVNB-10
79Top-726
80Top-686
80VenLeaS-18
81Top-328
91ParPatF-12
Johnston, James H.
16ColE13-88
17HolBreD-54
20NatCarE-51
21E121So8-44
22AmeCarE-33
22E120-142
22W572-52
22W575-65
23W515-41
23WilChoV-73
25Exh-13
90DodTar-389
Johnston, Jody
82JacMetT-6
82LynMetT-22
Johnston, Joel
86SyrChiP-15
88EugEmeB-11
89BasCitRS-12
90MemChiB-17
90MemChiP-1010
91Bow-297
91LinDriAAA-337
91OmaRoyLD-337
91OmaRoyP-1031
92Bow-199
92DonRoo-60
92Fle-673
92OPC-328
92Pin-259
92PinRoo-10
92ProFS7-73
92RoyPol-13
92Sco-764
92ScoRoo-15
92StaClu-345
92Top-328
92TopDeb91-91
92TopGol-328
92TopGolW-328
92TopMic-328
93BufBisF-512
93Don-791
93SelRoo-137T
94Don-246
94Fle-610
94Sco-308
94ScoGolR-308
94Top-557
94TopGol-557
94TopSpa-557
94TriPla-184
Johnston, John
16FleBreD-47
Johnston, Len
77SerSta-12
92BluOriC-24
93BluOriC-25
94BluOriC-25
94BluOriF-3579
Johnston, Mark
79WesHavYT-1

82ElPasDT-10
83BelBreF-10
94IowCubF-1292
Johnston, Rex
64PirKDK-14
77FriOneYW-59
Johnston, Richard
87BucN28-8
87OldJudN-270
88GandBCGCE-21
88WG1CarG-4
89N526N7C-7
Johnston, Rusty
77ShrCapT-9
Johnston, Ryan
88SavCarP-352
Johnston, Sean
93MidLeaAGF-23
93SouBenWSC-13
93SouBenWSF-1426
94CarLeaAF-CAR9
94ClaGolF-156
94PriWilCC-11
94PriWilCF-1915
94SigRooDP-33
94SigRooDPS-33
95SPML-115
96BesAutS-44
96StLucMTI-8
92UtiBluSC-21
Johnston, Stan
86BakDodP-16
87BakDodP-14
88BakDodCLC-264
89AlbDukP-74
93TriAAAGF-14
Johnston, Tom
93WelPirC-9
93WelPirF-3366
94OgdRapF-3741
94OgdRapSP-3
Johnstone, Jay
67CokCapDA-34
67Top-213
68Top-389
69AngJacitB-5
69MilBra-138
69OPC-59
69Top-59
70DayDaiNM-115
70MLBOffS-174
70OPC-485
70Top-485
70TopBoo-3
71OPC-292
71Top-292
72MilBra-170
72OPC-233
72Top-233
75OPC-242
75Top-242
76OPC-114
76SSP-463
76Top-114
77BurCheD-166
77Kel-33
77OPC-226
77PepGloD-71
77Top-415
78PhiSSP-43
78SSP270-43
78Top-675
79OPC-287
79Top-558
79YanBurK-5
80DodPol-21
80OPC-15
80Top-31
81DodPol-21
81Don-300
81Fle-128
81OPC-372
81Top-372
82CubRedL-21
82DodPol-21
82Don-262
82Fle-10
82Top-774
82TopTra-52T
83CubThoAV-21
83Don-561
83Fle-499
83OPC-152
83Top-152
83TopSti-220
84CubSev-21
84Don-540
84Fle-495
84Nes792-249
84Top-249
84TopSti-50
84TopTif-249
85DodCokP-16
86Top-496
86TopTif-496
90DodTar-390
92YanWIZ7-83
Johnstone, John
89PitMetS-13
89Sta-169
90FloStaLAS-7
90St.LucMS-12
91Cla/Bes-64
91LinDriAA-635
91MetColP-37
91WilBilLD-635
91WilBilP-287
92BinMetF-510
92BinMetS-61
92SkyAA F-26
92UppDecML-310
93Don-784
93EdmTraF-1131
93StaClu-734
93StaCluFDI-734
93StaCluMOP-734
93Top-454
93TopGol-454
93TopInaM-454
93TopMic-454
94EdmTraF-2871
95Sco-311
95ScoGolR-311
95ScoPlaTS-311
Joiner, Dave
87LitFalMP-2400
88ColMetGS-16
89ColMetB-8
89ColMetGS-13
Joiner, Pop (Roy)
34DiaMatCSB-98
35DiaMatCS3T1-80
40PlaBal-211
Jok, Stan
52Par-93
54Top-196
55Bow-251
94TopArc1-196
94TopArc1G-196
Jolley, Mike
91SavCarC-6
91SavCarP-1647
92SavCarC-2
92SavCarF-660
Jolley, Smead
28PorandAR-C3
28PorandAR-D3
30ChiEveAP-16
31Exh-20
32OrbPinNP-25
32OrbPinUP-36
33TatOrb-36
36WorWidGV-98
79DiaGre-136
79RedSoxEF-19
87ConSer2-23
88LitSunMLL-8
93ConTSN-858
Jolly, Dave
53BraJohC-8
53BraSpiaS3-14
54BraJohC-17
54BraSpiaSP-11
54Top-188
55Bow-71
55BraGolS-9
55BraJohC-16
55BraSpiaSD-10
55Top-35
55TopDouH-95
55TopTesS-6
57Top-389
58Top-183
83Bra53F-16
94TopArc1-188
94TopArc1G-188
Jonas, John
90SalSpuCLC-144
Jonas, Pete
43CenFlo-14
47CenFlo-13
47SigOil-79
Jonathan, Don Leo
72Dia-122
Jones, Al
82AppFoxF-7
83AppFoxF-20
85Don-404
85Top-437
85TopTif-437
86BufBisP-13
86Top-227
86TopTif-227
87DenZepP-26
Jones, Alan
72Dia-141
Jones, Allen
60MapLeaSF-10
Jones, Andruw
92SpoIllFK1-582
95Bes-50
95Bes-106
95Bes-AU2
95BesFra-F9
95Bow-23
95BowBes-B7
95BowBesR-B7
95MacBraTI-14
95MacBraUTI-3
95SPML-1
95SPML-15
95SPMLA-13
95SPMLDtS-DS1
96BesAutSA-34
96BesPlaotYAJ-1
96BesPlaotYAJ-2
96BesPlaotYAJ-3
96BesPlaotYAJ-4
96BesPlaotYAJ-5
96BesPlaotYAJA-2
96BesPlaotYAJA-3
96BesPlaotYAJA-4
96BesPlaotYAJA-5
96Bow-192
96BowBes-91
96BowBesAR-91
96BowBesC-4
96BowBesCAR-4
96BowBesCR-4
96BowBesMI-6
96BowBesMIAR-6
96BowBesMIR-6
96BowBesP-BBP9
96BowBesPAR-BBP9
96BowBesPR-BBP9
96BowBesR-91
96BowMinLP-1
96CarLeaA1B-18
96CarLeaA2B-18
96CarLeaAIB-B5
96CarLeaAIB-B6
96CarLeaAIB-B7
96Cir-101
96CirRav-101
96DurBulBIB-1
96DurBulBrB-2
96Exc-129
96ExcAll-7
96ExcSeaC-6
96GreBraB-17
96GreBraTI-6
96LeaLimR-8
96LeaSig-101
96LeaSigEA-93
96LeaSigEACM-13
96LeaSigPPG-101
96LeaSigPPP-101
96RicBraRC-23
96RicBraUB-1
96RicBraUB-14
96RicBraUB-15
96Top-435
97Bow-107
97BowBes-186
97BowBesAR-186
97BowBesBC-BC14
97BowBesBCAR-BC14
97BowBesBCR-BC14
97BowBesMI-MI5
97BowBesMIAR-MI5
97BowBesMIARI-MI5
97BowBesMII-MI5
97BowBesMIR-MI5
97BowBesMIRI-MI5
97BowBesP-15
97BowBesPAR-15
97BowBesPR-15
97BowBesR-186
97BowCerBIA-CA42
97BowCerGIA-CA42
97BowChr-127
97BowChrI-127
97BowChrIR-127
97BowChrR-127
97BowChrSHR-SHR13
97BowChrSHRR-SHR13
97BowInt-107
97BowIntB-BBI13
97BowIntBAR-BBI13
97BowIntBR-BBI13
97BowScoHR-13
97Cir-329
97Cir-394
97CirBos-9
97CirFasT-4
97CirRav-329
97CirRav-394
97CirSupB-9
97ColCho-1
97ColCho-320
97ColChoCtG-3A
97ColChoCtG-3B
97ColChoCtG-3C
97ColChoCtGIW-CG3
97ColChoNF-NF17
97ColChoNF-NF18
97ColChoS-2
97ColChoTBS-3
97ColChoTBSWH-3
97ColChoTotT-T1
97Don-358
97DonEli-10
97DonEliGS-10
97DonEliPtT-5
97DonEliPtT-6
97DonEliPtTA-5
97DonEliPtTA-6
97DonEliTotC-2
97DonEliTotCDC-2
97DonFraFea-1
97DonLim-94
97DonLim-128
97DonLimFotG-51
97DonLimLE-94
97DonLimLE-128
97DonPowA-6
97DonPowADC-6
97DonPre-143
97DonPre-179
97DonPreCttC-143
97DonPreCttC-179
97DonPreP-358
97DonPrePGold-358
97DonPrePM-23
97DonPreS-18
97DonPreTB-9
97DonPreTBG-9
97DonPreTF-9
97DonPreTP-9
97DonPreTPG-9
97DonPreXP-8B
97DonRatR-20
97DonRooDK-1
97DonRooDKC-1
97DonTea-28
97DonTeaSPE-28
97Fin-100
97Fin-162
97Fin-306
97FinEmb-162
97FinEmb-306
97FinEmbR-162
97FinEmbR-306
97FinRef-100
97FinRef-162
97FinRef-306
97FlaSho-A1
97FlaSho-B1
97FlaSho-C1
97FlaShoDC-8
97FlaShoLC-1
97FlaShoLC-B1
97FlaShoLC-C1
97FlaShoLCM-A1
97FlaShoLCM-B1
97FlaShoLCM-C1
97FlaShoWotF-2
97Fle-257
97Fle-493
97Fle-704
97Fle-NNO
97FleAndJA-1
97FleHea-9
97FleMilDM-26
97FleNewH-9
97FleRooS-15
97FleSoaS-6
97FleTif-257
97FleTif-493
97FleTif-704
97Lea-168
97Lea-199
97Lea-349
97LeaDrefS-17
97LeaFraM-168
97LeaFraM-199
97LeaFraM-349
97LeaFraMDC-168
97LeaFraMDC-199
97LeaFraMDC-349
97LeaGet-10
97LeaGolS-4
97LeaWarT-4
97MetUni-30
97MetUniMfG-6
97MetUniML-5
97NewPin-175
97NewPinAP-175
97NewPinIE-2
97NewPinMC-175
97NewPinPP-175
97NewPinPP-I2A
97NewPinPP-AJ1
97NewPinPP-AJ2
97NewPinPP-AJ3
97NewPinPP-AJ4
97NewPinPP-AJ5
97NewPinPP-AJ6
97NewPinS-AJ1
97NewPinS-AJ2
97NewPinS-AJ3
97NewPinS-AJ4
97NewPinS-AJ5
97NewPinS-AJ6
97Pac-234
97PacCar-21
97PacCarM-21
97PacCerCGT-14
97PacFirD-14
97PacGolCD-21
97PacLatotML-23
97PacLigB-234
97PacPri-78
97PacPriGA-GA17
97PacPriLB-78
97PacPriP-78
97PacPriSH-SH8A
97PacPriSL-SL8C
97PacSil-234
97PacTriCD-12
97Pin-163
97Pin-198
97PinArtP-163
97PinArtP-198
97PinCer-106
97PinCer-150
97PinCerCMGT-14
97PinCerCT-14
97PinCerMBlu-106
97PinCerMBlu-150
97PinCerMG-106
97PinCerMG-150
97PinCerMR-106
97PinCerMR-150
97PinCerR-106
97PinCerR-150
97PinIns-128
97PinInsC-18
97PinInsCE-128
97PinInsDD-6
97PinInsDE-128
97PinMin-10
97PinMinB-10
97PinMinCB-10
97PinMinCG-10
97PinMinCGR-10
97PinMinCN-10
97PinMinCS-10
97PinMinG-10
97PinMinS-10

97PinMusC-163
97PinMusC-198
97PinTotCPB-106
97PinTotCPB-150
97PinTotCPG-106
97PinTotCPG-150
97PinTotCPR-106
97PinTotCPR-150
97PinX-P-116
97PinX-P-NNO
97PinX-PF&A-8
97PinX-PMoS-116
97PinX-PMP-3
97PinX-PMW-3
97PinX-PMWG-3
97PinX-PMWS-3
97ProMag-1
97ProMagML-1
97Sco-310
97Sco-500
97ScoAllF-12
97ScoBla-7
97ScoBra-15
97ScoBraPl-15
97ScoBraPr-15
97ScoHeaotO-20
97ScoHobR-500
97ScoPreS-310
97ScoResC-500
97ScoShoS-310
97ScoShoS-500
97ScoShoSAP-310
97ScoShoSAP-500
97ScoStaaD-1
97Sel-101
97SelArtP-101
97SelRegG-101
97SelRooA-3
97SelRooR-1
97SelToootT-1
97SelToootTMB-1
97SkyE-X-53
97SkyE-XC-53
97SkyE-XEC-53
97SkyE-XSD2-2
97SP-1
97SPGamF-GF3
97SPInsI-25
97Spolll-13
97SpollIEE-13
97SPSpeF-45
97SPSpxF-10
97SPSPxFA-10
97SPx-4
97SPxBoufG-1
97SPxBoufGSS-3
97SPxBro-4
97SPxCorotG-5
97SPxGraF-4
97SPxSil-4
97SPxSte-4
97StaClu-181
97StaClu-255
97StaClul-I21
97StaCluM-M21
97StaCluMat-255
97StaCluMOP-181
97StaCluMOP-255
97StaCluMOP-I21
97StaCluMOP-M21
97Stu-149
97StuMasS-9
97StuMasS8-9
97StuPor8-4
97StuPrePG-149
97StuPrePS-149
97Top-455
97TopAwel-AI8
97TopChr-160
97TopChrDD-DD1
97TopChrDDR-DD1
97TopChrR-160
97TopGal-146
97TopGalP-PP1
97TopGalPPI-146
97TopScr-11
97TopStaFAS-FAS2
97Ult-153
97Ult-NNO
97UltChe-B1
97UltGolME-153
97UltGolP-1
97UltHitM-1
97UltPlaME-153
97UltStaR-1
97UltTop3-1
97UltTop3GM-1
97UppDec-196
97UppDec-240
97UppDec-262
97UppDec-324
97UppDec-415
97UppDecBCP-BC1
97UppDecHC-HC2
97UppDecLDC-LD20
97UppDecMM-1
97UppDecP-1
97UppDecTTS-TS14
97UppDecU-41
97UppDecUGN-GN5
97Zen-43
97Zen Z-Z-8
97Zen8x1-21
97Zen8x1D-21
97ZenV-2-2

Jones, Available (Sheldon)
47HomBon-23
48Bow-34
49Bow-68
49EurSta-111
50Bow-83
50Dra-7
51Bow-199
52BerRos-27
52Bow-215
52Top-130
75Gia195T-10
83TopRep5-130

Jones, B.J. (Bobby)
94BriTigC-15
94BriTigF-3518

Jones, Barry
85PriWilPT-3
86HawIsIP-13
86SumBraP-12
87Don-602
87DurBulP-2
87Fle-611
87FleGlo-611
87Top-494
87TopTif-494
88FleUpd-114
88FleUpdG-114
88GreBraB-8
88SouLeaAJ-14
88Top-168
88TopTif-168
89BlaYNPRWL-25
89Don-647
89Fle-500
89FleGlo-500
89RicBraBC-11
89RicBraC-20
89RicBraP-846
89RicBraTI-10
89Sco-333
89Top-539
89TopTif-539
89UppDec-457
89WhiSoxC-12
90CMC-288
90Lea-431
90OPC-243
90ProAAAF-417
90PubSti-390
90RicBraBC-11
90RicBraC-12
90RicBraP-272
90RicBraTI-15
90Sco-152
90Top-243
90TopTif-243
90VenSti-256
90WhiSoxC-10
91Bow-439
91ColSprSSLD-86
91ColSprSSP-2196
91Don-534
91ExpPos-11
91Fle-124
91Lea-406
91LinDriAAA-86
91OPC-33
91OPCPre-69
91PanSti-259
91Sco-115
91ScoPro-115
91ScoRoo-75T
91StaClu-551
91Top-33
91TopDesS-33
91TopMic-33
91TopTif-33
91TopTra-64T
91TopTraT-64T
91UltUpd-91
91UppDec-39
91UppDec-789
92Don-155
92Fle-484
92Lea-484
92OPC-361
92PhiMed-16
92Sco-297
92StaClu-671
92StaCluECN-671
92Top-361
92TopGol-361
92TopGolW-361
92TopMic-361
92Ult-546
92UppDec-681
93NasSouF-569
93RicBraBB-17
93RicBraF-195
93RicBraRC-13
94NewOrlZF-1463
88RicBraBC-24

Jones, Ben
92ClaDraP-102
92FroRowDP-66
93EliTwiC-12
93EliTwiF-3429
94ForWayWC-10
94ForWayWF-2022
95FtMyeMTI-12
96FtMyeMB-23

Jones, Bill
86St.PetCP-16

Jones, Bobby
88StoPorCLC-190
88StoPorP-732
89BenBucL-21
89CalLeaA-32
89StoPorB-24
89StoPorCLC-166
89StoPorP-383
89StoPorS-15
90FloStaLAS-50
90QuaCitAGS-30
91MidAngLD-438
91MidAngOHP-14
91MidAngP-445
92HelBreF-1710
92HelBreSP-7
92MidAngOHP-10
92MidAngS-460
93BelBreC-12
93BelBreF-1705
93BriTigC-12
93BriTigF-3662
94StoPorF-1689
95NewHavRTI-33
96ColSprSSTI-19

Jones, Bobby (Robert Joseph)
91ClaDraP-32
91FreStaBS-7
91FroRowDP-11
91LinDriAA-438
92BinMetF-511
92BinMetS-62
92Bow-389
92ClaFS7-341
92ColMetPI-40
92ColMetPIISPI-5
92Pin-548
92SkyAA F-27
92StaCluD-94
92UppDecML-294
92UppDecMLPotY-PY14
93Bow-355
93Bow-650
93ClaFS7-104
93ClaGolF-61
93ExcAllF-5
93ExcFS7-75
93NorTidF-2566
93Top-817
93TopGol-817
93TopInaM-817
93TopMic-817
93Ult-429
93UppDec-19
93UppDecGold-19
94Bow-652
94ColC-151
94ColChoGS-151
94ColChoSS-151
94Don-501
94ExtBas-319
94Fin-109
94FinRef-109
94Fla-199
94Fle-569
94FUnPac-46
94Lea-304
94MetColP-14
94MetShuST-7
94OPC-108
94OPCDiaD-6
94Pin-380
94PinArtP-380
94PinMusC-380
94PinNewG-NG14
94Sel-167
94SP-118
94SPDieC-118
94Spo-148
94StaClu-620
94StaCluFDI-620
94StaCluGR-620
94StaCluMOP-620
94StoPorC-12
94Stu-116
94Top-539
94TopGol-539
94TopSpa-539
94TriPla-145
94Ult-530
94UppDec-119
94UppDecED-119
95Bow-401
95ColCho-328
95ColChoGS-328
95ColChoSE-149
95ColChoSEGS-149
95ColChoSESS-149
95ColChoSS-328
95Don-6
95DonPreP-6
95DonTopotO-294
95Emb-27
95EmbGolI-27
95Emo-160
95Fin-73
95FinRef-73
95Fla-385
95Fle-372
95LeaLim-69
95Pin-71
95PinArtP-71
95PinMusC-71
95Sco-232
95ScoGolR-232
95ScoPlaTS-232
95SP-83
95SPCha-69
95SPCha-71
95SPChaDC-69
95SPChaDC-71
95SPSil-83
95StaClu-342
95StaCluMOP-342
95StaCluSTWS-342
95StaCluVR-181
95Stu-188
95Top-252
95TopCyb-139
95Ult-197
95UltGolM-197
95UppDec-125
95UppDecED-125
95UppDecEDG-125
95UppDecSE-193
95UppDecSEG-193
95USPlaCMLA-4S
96ColCho-222
96ColChoGS-222
96ColChoSS-222
96Don-430
96DonPreP-430
96EmoXL-235
96Fla-323
96Fle-482
96FleTif-482
96LeaSigA-119
96LeaSigAG-119
96LeaSigAS-119
96MetKah-17
96MetKah-19
96MetUni-203
96MetUniP-203
96Pac-141
96ProSta-75
96Sco-433
96StaClu-273
96StaCluMOP-273
95StaCluVRMC-181
96Top-133
96TopGal-40
96TopGalPPI-40
96Ult-245
96UltGolM-245
96UppDec-398
97Cir-344
97CirRav-344
97ColCho-391
97DonLim-25
97DonLimLE-25
97Fin-137
97FinEmb-137
97FinEmbR-137
97FinRef-137
97Fle-401
97FleTif-401
97Lea-304
97LeaFraM-304
97LeaFraMDC-304
97MetUni-196
97Pac-368
97PacLigB-368
97PacSil-368
97Sco-401
97ScoHobR-401
97ScoResC-401
97ScoShoS-401
97ScoShoSAP-401
97SpolII-90
97SpolIIEE-90
97StaClu-95
97StaCluMOP-95
97Top-361
97TopSta-54
97TopStaAM-54
97Ult-243
97UltGolME-243
97UltPlaME-243
97UppDec-434

Jones, Bobby (Robert O.)
74SpoIndC-36
75IntLeaASB-14
75PacCoaLAB-14
75SpoIndC-9
76SacSolC-5
77Top-16
77Top-431
79TCMJapPB-78
83RanAffF-6
84Nes792-451
84RanJarP-6
84Top-451
84TopTif-451
85Don-134
85Fle-559
85RanPer-6
85Top-648
85TopTif-648
86OklCit8P-8
86Top-142
86TopTif-142
88ChaRanS-14
89ChaRanS-26
89PacSenL-98
89TopSenL-3
90ChaRanS-29
90EliSenL-71
91LinDriAA-599
91PacSenL-59
91TulDriLD-599
91TulDriP-2788
91TulDriTI-15
92TulDriF-2709
92TulDriS-624
93OklCit8F-1639
93RanKee-210
94OklCit8F-1508
95TulDriTI-28
96TulDriTI-14
97CraSalLCG-15

Jones, Brian
85PriWilPT-31
86PriWilPP-13
87HarSenP-17
95Lea-16
Jones, Bryan
76WatRoyT-14
Jones, Butter
92EveGiaC-13
92EveGiaF-1703
Jones, Calvin
87ChaLooB-6
88VerMarP-962
89SanBerSCLC-64
89WilBilS-11
90SanBerSB-3
90SanBerSCLC-96
90SanBerSP-2629
91CalCanLD-62
91CalCanP-511
91LinDriAAA-62
92Don-690
92Lea-71
92MarMot-21
92ProFS7-139
92Sco-868
92StaClu-127
92TopDeb91-92
92Ult-433
92UppDec-731
93Don-749
93Fle-413
93StaClu-578
93StaCluFDI-578
93StaCluMOP-578
93Top-664
93TopGol-664
93TopInaM-664
93TopMic-664
94ChaKniF-889
95LinVen-25
95PawRedSDD-16
95PawRedTI-36
Jones, Carl
87SumBraP-14
Jones, Casey (Clinton)
92NegLeaK-2
92NegLeaRLI-34
Jones, Charlie
03BreE10-75
11SpoLifCW-189
83VerBeaDT-6
Jones, Chipper
90ClaDraP-1
90ClaDraP-NNO
90ClaYel-T92
90ClaYel-NNO0
91Bow-569
91Cla/Bes-268
91MacBraC-19
91MacBraP-872
91OPC-333
91Sco-671
91SouAtlLAGP-SAL33
91Top-333
91TopDesS-333
91TopMic-333
91TopTif-333
91UppDec-55
92Bow-28
92ClaBluBF-BC7
92ClaFS7-93
92ClaRedB-BC7
92DurBulC-1
92DurBulF-1108
92DurBulTI-10
92OPC-551
92ProFS7-190
92SpoIllFK1-447
92StaCluFDP-1
92Top-551
92TopGol-551
92TopGolW-551
92TopMic-551
92UppDecML-66
92UppDecML-165
92UppDecMLPotY-PY5
92UppDecMLTPHF-TP3
93Bow-86
93Bow-347
93ClaFisN-5
93ClaGolF-172
93ClaYouG-YG7
93Don-721
93EliTwiC-27
93ExcAllF-2
93ExcFS7-2
93LeaGolR-R19
93RicBraBB-13
93RicBraF-190
93RicBraP-6
93RicBraRC-15
93RicBraRC-14
93SanBerSC-27
93SP-280
93StaClu-638
93StaCluB-9
93StaCluFDI-638
93StaCluMOP-638
93Top-529
93TopGol-529
93TopInaM-529
93TopMic-529
93TriAAAGF-1
93UppDec-24
93UppDec-459
93UppDecFA-A11
93UppDecFAJ-A11
93UppDecGold-24
93UppDecGold-459
93UppDecOD-D16
93UtiBluSC-27
94Bow-353
94Bow-489
94BowBes-B1
94BowBes-X108
94BowBesR-B1
94BowBesR-X108
94BraLykP-11
94BraLykS-12
94BraUSPC-2C
94ColC-152
94ColChoGS-152
94ColChoSS-152
94Don-453
94FleMajLP-18
94FUnPac-5
94Lea-46
94OPC-57
94Pac-10
94Pin-236
94PinArtP-236
94PinMusC-236
94PinNewG-NG20
94PinRooTP-5
94Sco-572
94ScoBoyoS-58
94ScoGolR-572
94Spo-160
94StaClu-638
94StaCluFDI-638
94StaCluGR-638
94StaCluMOP-638
94StaCluT-50
94StaCluTFDI-50
94Top-777
94TopGol-777
94TopSpa-777
94TriPla-281
94Ult-152
94UppDec-185
94UppDecED-185
95Bow-262
95BowGolF-262
95ClaPhoC-1
95ColCho-154
95ColChoGS-154
95ColChoSS-154
95DonTopotO-185
95Emo-102
95EmoRoo-8
95Fin-221
95FinRef-221
95Fla-325
95FlaWavotF-9
95FleUpd-91
95FleUpdRU-5
95Lea-369
95LeaLim-78
95LeaLimG-22
95Pin-111
95Pin-303
95PinArtP-111
95PinArtP-303
95PinMusC-111
95PinMusC-303
95PinNewB-NB6
95Sel-173
95Sel-235
95SelArtP-173
95SelArtP-235
95SelCanM-CM11
95SelCer-107
95SelCerF-1
95SelCerMG-107
95SelCerPU-11
95SelCerPU9-11
95SP-34
95SPCha-26
95SPChaDC-26
95Spo-162
95SpoArtP-162
95SpoSam-162
95SPSil-34
95StaClu-543
95StaCluCB-CB1
95StaCluMOP-543
95StaCluMOP-CB1
95StaCluSTDW-B543
95StaCluSTMP-3
95StaCluSTWS-543
95Stu-160
95Sum-115
95SumNewA-NA11
95SumNthD-115
95Top-535
95TopTra-128T
95UC3-101
95UC3ArtP-101
95UC3CleS-CS9
95Ult-347
95UltGolM-347
95UppDec-293
95UppDecED-293
95UppDecEDG-293
95UppDecPAW-H39
95UppDecPAWE-H39
95UppDecSE-14
95UppDecSEG-14
95Zen-111
95ZenRooRC-3
96Baz-96
96Bow-76
96BowBes-7
96BowBesAR-7
96BowBesC-5
96BowBesCAR-5
96BowBesCR-5
96BowBesMI-3
96BowBesMIAR-3
96BowBesMIR-3
96BowBesP-BBP1
96BowBesPAR-BBP1
96BowBesPR-BBP1
96BowBesR-7
96Cir-102
96CirRav-102
96ColCho-42
96ColCho-374T
96ColChoCtG-CG1
96ColChoCtG-CG1B
96ColChoCtG-CG1C
96ColChoCtGE-CR1
96ColChoCtGG-CG1
96ColChoCtGG-CG1B
96ColChoCtGG-CG1C
96ColChoCtGGE-CR1
96ColChoGS-42
96ColChoSS-42
96ColChoYMtP-19
96ColChoYMtP-19A
96ColChoYMtPGS-19
96ColChoYMtPGS-19A
96Don-437
96DonEli-66
96DonFreF-7
96DonPreP-437
96EmoRarB-6
96EmoXL-142
96Fin-B16
96Fin-G141
96Fin-G192
96FinRef-B16
96FinRef-G141
96FinRef-G192
96Fla-200
96Fle-293
96FleBra-6
96FleChe-3
96FleRooS-10
96FleTif-293
96FleTomL-6
96FleUpd-U228
96FleUpdH-10
96FleUpdSS-5
96FleUpdTC-U228
96Lea-28
96LeaAllGMC-11
96LeaAllGMCG-11
96LeaGolS-9
96LeaLim-27
96LeaLimG-27
96LeaLimL-7
96LeaLimLB-7
96LeaLimPC-10
96LeaPicP-5
96LeaPre-40
96LeaPreP-40
96LeaPrePB-28
96LeaPrePG-28
96LeaPrePS-28
96LeaPreSG-33
96LeaPreSta-1
96LeaPreSte-33
96LeaSig-26
96LeaSigPPG-26
96LeaSigPPP-26
96LeaStaS-8
96MetUni-129
96MetUniMFG-8
96MetUniP-129
96MetUniPP-5
96MetUniProS-129
96Pac-4
96PacGolCD-DC31
96PacHom-HP7
96PacOctM-OM8
96PacPri-P2
96PacPriFR-FR7
96PacPriG-P2
96PacPriRHS-RH3
96PanSti-8
96PanSti-243
96Pin-114
96Pin-200
96Pin-266
96Pin-396
96Pin-399
96PinAfi-127
96PinAfiAP-127
96PinAfiMN-6
96PinAfiSP-30
96PinArtP-45
96PinArtP-166
96PinChrBC-5
96PinEssotG-5
96PinFan-21
96PinFirR-4
96PinFoil-266
96PinFoil-396
96PinFoil-399
96PinProS-6
96PinSky-15
96PinSta-45
96PinSta-166
96PinTeaS-10
96PinTeaT-6
96Sco-322
96ScoAll-18
96ScoBigB-20
96ScoDiaA-8
96ScoDugC-B47
96ScoDugCAP-B47
96ScoFutF-2
96ScoGolS-12
96ScoNumG-19
96ScoRef-1
96Sel-41
96SelArtP-41
96SelCer-7
96SelCer-142
96SelCerAP-7
96SelCerAP-142
96SelCerCB-7
96SelCerCB-142
96SelCerCR-7
96SelCerCR-142
96SelCerIP-11
96SelCerMB-7
96SelCerMB-142
96SelCerMG-7
96SelCerMG-142
96SelCerMR-7
96SelCerMR-142
96SelCerSF-9
96SelClaTF-11
96SelEnF-12
96SelTeaN-12
96SP-26
96SPBasH-85
96SPMarM-MM18
96SPMarMDC-18
96Spo-19
96Spo-97
96SpoArtP-19
96SpoArtP-97
96SpoDouT-3
96SpoHitP-15
96SpoPowS-1
96SpoPro-10
96SPSpeFX-15
96SPSpeFXDC-15
96SPx-2
96SPxBoufG-6
96SPxGol-2
96StaClu-10
96StaClu-226
96StaCluEPB-10
96StaCluEPG-10
96StaCluEPS-10
96StaCluMO-48
96StaCluMOP-10
96StaCluMOP-226
96StaCluMOP-TSCA8
96StaCluTA-8
96Stu-72
96StuPrePB-72
96StuPrePG-72
96StuPrePS-72
96StuStaGS-5
96Sum-126
96Sum-161
96SumAbo&B-126
96SumAbo&B-161
96SumArtP-126
96SumArtP-161
96SumBigB-15
96SumBigBM-15
96SumFoi-126
96SumFoi-161
96SumHitI-14
96SumPos-3
96TeaOut-42
96Top-177
96TopChr-52
96TopChrR-52
96TopGal-100
96TopGalE-6
96TopGalPPI-100
96TopLas-45
96TopLasBS-14
96TopMysF-M4
96TopMysFR-M4
96TopPro-NL15
96Ult-156
96Ult-582
96Ult-596
96UltChe-A5
96UltCheGM-A5
96UltFreF-5
96UltFreFGM-5
96UltGolM-156
96UltGolM-582
96UltGolM-596
96UltRisS-6
96UltRisSGM-6
96UppDec-5
96UppDec-149
96UppDec-219
96UppDecBCP-BC10
96UppDecDD-DD1
96UppDecDDG-DD1
96UppDecDDS-DD1
96UppDecG-GF7
96UppDecHC-HC11
96UppDecPHE-H35
96UppDecPRE-R34
96UppDecPreH-H35
96UppDecPreR-R34
96Zen-55
96Zen-137
96ZenArtP-55
96ZenArtP-137
96ZenDiaC-20
96ZenDiaCP-20
96ZenMoz-1
96ZenZ-7
97Bow-3
97BowBes-9
97BowBesAR-9

97BowBesBC-BC2
97BowBesBCAR-BC2
97BowBesBCR-BC2
97BowBesMI-MI9
97BowBesMIAR-MI9
97BowBesMIARI-MI9
97BowBesMII-MI9
97BowBesMIR-MI9
97BowBesMIRI-MI9
97BowBesP-5
97BowBesPAR-5
97BowBesPR-5
97BowBesR-9
97BowChr-2
97BowChrI-2
97BowChrIR-2
97BowChrR-2
97BowInt-3
97Cir-381
97CirBos-10
97CirFasT-5
97CirIco-5
97CirLimA-8
97CirRav-381
97CirSupB-10
97ColCho-270
97ColCho-326
97ColChoAC-30
97ColChoBS-15
97ColChoBSGS-15
97ColChoCtG-2A
97ColChoCtG-2B
97ColChoCtG-2C
97ColChoCtGIW-CG2
97ColChoNF-NF29
97ColChoNF-NF30
97ColChoS-10
97ColChoTBS-2
97ColChoTBSWH-2
97ColChoTotT-T2
97Don-34
97Don-401
97DonArmaD-3
97DonDiaK-10
97DonDiaKC-10
97DonDom-9
97DonEli-8
97DonEli-5
97DonEliGS-8
97DonEliLaL-4
97DonEliTotC-3
97DonEliTotCDC-3
97DonFraFea-6
97DonLim-23
97DonLim-45
97DonLim-55
97DonLimFotG-6
97DonLimLE-23
97DonLimLE-45
97DonLimLE-55
97DonPowA-10
97DonPowADC-10
97DonPre-93
97DonPre-170
97DonPreCttC-93
97DonPreCttC-170
97DonPreP-34
97DonPreP-401
97DonPrePGold-34
97DonPrePGold-401
97DonPrePM-16
97DonPreS-3
97DonPreTB-10
97DonPreTBG-10
97DonPreTF-10
97DonPreTP-10
97DonPreTPG-10
97DonPreXP-8A
97DonRocL-3
97DonTea-18
97DonTeaSMVP-10
97DonTeaSPE-18
97Fin-108
97Fin-273
97Fin-330
97FinEmb-108
97FinEmb-330
97FinEmbR-108
97FinEmbR-330
97FinRef-108
97FinRef-273
97FinRef-330
97FlaSho-A10
97FlaSho-B10
97FlaSho-C10
97FlaShoDC-9
97FlaShoHG-7
97FlaShoLC-10
97FlaShoLC-B10
97FlaShoLC-C10
97FlaShoLCM-A10
97FlaShoLCM-B10
97FlaShoLCM-C10
97Fle-258
97Fle-494
97Fle-705
97FleGouG-5
97FleGouGF-5
97FleHea-10
97FleMilDM-10
97FleSoaS-7
97FleTeaL-15
97FleTif-258
97FleTif-494
97FleTif-705
97FleZon-9
97Lea-189
97Lea-201
97Lea-374
97LeaBanS-9
97LeaDrefS-18
97LeaFraM-189
97LeaFraM-201
97LeaFraM-374
97LeaFraMDC-189
97LeaFraMDC-201
97LeaFraMDC-374
97LeaGet-4
97LeaGolS-5
97LeaKnoG-9
97LeaLeaotN-2
97LeaStaS-6
97MetUni-31
97MetUniML-6
97MetUniPP-5
97MetUniT-4
97NewPin-123
97NewPin-194
97NewPinAP-123
97NewPinAP-194
97NewPinIE-4
97NewPinMC-123
97NewPinMC-194
97NewPinPP-123
97NewPinPP-194
97NewPinPP-I4B
97NewPinPP-CJ1
97NewPinPP-CJ2
97NewPinPP-CJ3
97NewPinPP-CJ4
97NewPinPP-CJ5
97NewPinPP-CJ6
97NewPinPP-CJ7
97NewPinS-CJ1
97NewPinS-CJ2
97NewPinS-CJ3
97NewPinS-CJ4
97NewPinS-CJ5
97NewPinS-CJ6
97NewPinS-CJ7
97Pac-235
97PacCar-22
97PacCarM-22
97PacCerCGT-4
97PacCraC-7
97PacFirD-15
97PacGolCD-22
97PacLigB-235
97PacPri-79
97PacPriGA-GA18
97PacPriGotD-GD112
97PacPriLB-79
97PacPriP-79
97PacPriSH-SH9A
97PacPriSL-SL8B
97PacSil-235
97PacTriCD-13
97Pin-96
97PinArtP-96
97PinCar-7
97PinCer-59
97PinCerCMGT-4
97PinCerCT-4
97PinCerMBlu-59
97PinCerMG-59
97PinCerMR-59
97PinCerR-59
97PinHom-1
97PinHom-2
97PinIns-31
97PinInsC-15
97PinInsCE-31
97PinInsDD-7
97PinInsDE-31
97PinMin-9
97PinMinB-9
97PinMinCB-9
97PinMinCG-9
97PinMinCGR-9
97PinMinCN-9
97PinMinCS-9
97PinMinG-9
97PinMinS-9
97PinMusC-96
97PinPasttM-8
97PinTeaP-4
97PinTeaP-10
97PinTotCPB-59
97PinTotCPG-59
97PinTotCPR-59
97PinX-P-23
97PinX-PF&A-9
97PinX-PMoS-23
97PinX-PMW-8
97PinX-PMWG-8
97PinX-PMWS-8
97PinX-PSfF-44
97PinX-PSfFU-44
97ProMag-2
97ProMagIM-5
97Sco-193
97Sco-509
97ScoAllF-6
97ScoBla-8
97ScoBra-10
97ScoBraPI-10
97ScoBraPr-10
97ScoFra-4
97ScoFraG-4
97ScoHeaotO-19
97ScoHigZ-11
97ScoHobR-509
97ScoPreS-193
97ScoResC-509
97ScoShoS-193
97ScoShoS-509
97ScoShoSAP-193
97ScoShoSAP-509
97ScoStaaD-3
97ScoTitT-14
97Sel-63
97SelArtP-63
97SelRegG-63
97SelToootT-3
97SelToootTMB-3
97SkyE-X-54
97SkyE-XC-54
97SkyE-XEC-54
97SkyE-XSD2-5
97SP-25
97SPGamF-GF8
97SPInsI-22
97SPMarM-MM9
97SpollI-33
97SpollI-76
97SpollIEE-33
97SpollIEE-76
97SpollIGS-1
97SPSpeF-7
97SPSpxF-6
97SPSPxFA-6
97SPVinAu-19
97SPVinAu-20
97SPVinAu-21
97SPx-5
97SPxBoufG-2
97SPxBro-5
97SPxCorotG-3
97SPxGraF-5
97SPxSil-5
97SPxSte-5
97StaClu-1
97StaClu-376
97StaCluFR-F8
97StaCluM-M6
97StaCluMat-1
97StaCluMOP-1
97StaCluMOP-376
97StaCluMOP-M6
97StaCluMOP-FB8
97StaCluMOP-PG7
97StaCluPG-PG7
97StaCluPP-PP1
97Stu-79
97StuHarH-12
97StuMasS-17
97StuMasS8-17
97StuPor8-8
97StuPrePG-79
97StuPrePS-79
97Top-277
97TopAll-AS8
97TopAwel-AI9
97TopChr-97
97TopChrAS-AS8
97TopChrDD-DD1
97TopChrDDR-DD1
97TopChrR-97
97TopChrSAR-AS8
97TopGal-137
97TopGalGoH-GH2
97TopGalPG-PG5
97TopGalPMS-4
97TopGalPMSSS-10
97TopGalPPI-137
97TopHobM-HM13
97TopIntF-ILM13
97TopIntFR-ILM13
97TopScr-12
97TopScrSI-2
97TopSta-5
97TopStaAM-5
97TopSweS-SS8
97TopTeaT-TT15
97Ult-154
97UltBasR-4
97UltChe-B8
97UltDiaP-4
97UltDouT-11
97UltGolME-154
97UltPlaME-154
97UltPowP-A5
97UltPowP-B6
97UltStaR-8
97UltThu-7
97UltTop3-8
97UltTop3GM-8
97UppDec-10
97UppDec-246
97UppDec-416
97UppDecAG-AG5
97UppDecBCP-BC15
97UppDecHC-HC6
97UppDecLDC-LD18
97UppDecMM-2
97UppDecP-2
97UppDecRP-RP20
97UppDecRSF-RS5
97UppDecTTS-TS1
97UppDecU-60
97UppDecUGN-GN10
97Zen-12
97Zen8x1-14
97Zen8x1D-14

Jones, Chris
78WauMetT-12
82TucTorT-2
83TucTorT-19
84TucTorC-52
85TucTorC-51

Jones, Chris C.
86CedRapRT-21
86PhoFirP-12
87DunBluJP-939
87PhoFirP-1
87VerRedP-22
88ChaLooB-6
88IdaFalBP-1843
88KnoBluJB-16
88SanDieSAAG-10
89KnoBluJB-11
89KnoBluJP-1134
89KnoBluJS-9
89NasSouC-20
89NasSouP-1290
89SanDieSAG-9
90CMC-141
90NasSouC-16
90NasSouP-246
90ProAAAF-558
91AlbDukLD-11
91AlbDukP-1136
91Bow-676
91DonRoo-50
91ScoRoo-92T
91TopTra-65T
91TopTraT-65T
92AstMot-22
92Don-464
92Fle-410
92Lea-444
92OPC-332
92Sco-811
92Sco100RS-69
92StaClu-698
92Top-332
92TopDeb91-93
92TopGol-332
92TopGolW-332
92TopMic-332
93Fla-42
93FleFinE-35
93StaCluRoc-19
93TopTra-102T
94Don-510
94Fle-445
94Pac-199
94PanSti-176
94Sco-148
94ScoGolR-148
94Top-496
94TopGol-496
94TopSpa-496
96ColCho-226
96ColChoGS-226
96ColChoSS-226
96Fle-483
96FleTif-483
96LeaSigEA-94
96MetKah-18
96MetKah-20

Jones, Chris L.
88CapCodPPaLP-164
90KnoBluJB-20
90KnoBluJP-1243
90KnoBluJS-7
91LinDriAAA-11

Jones, Clarence W.
68Top-506
86SumBraP-13
87SumBraP-6
88RicBraC-25
88RicBraP-17
89BraDub-14
90BraDubS-15
91BraSubS-20
92BraLykS-18
93BraLykS-17
94BraLykP-12
94BraLykS-13

Jones, Cleon Joseph
65Top-308
66OPC-67
66Top-67
66TopVen-67
67CokCapA-31
67CokCapNLA-35
67CokCapYM-V24
67DexPre-110
67Kah-19
67MetTeal-8
67OPC-165
67OPCPapI-13
67Top-165
67TopPos-13
67TopTesF-8
68Top-254
68TopVen-254
69MetBoyS-6
69MetCit-7
69MetNewYDN-10
69MilBra-139
69MLBOffS-167
69Top-512
69TopSta-65
69TopSup-50
70Kel-3
70MetTra-24C
70MLBOffS-78
70OPC-61
70Top-61
70Top-575
70TopBoo-19
70TraSta-1C
71MLBOffS-156
71OPC-527
71Top-527
71TopCoi-103
71TopTat-4
72MilBra-171

72OPC-31
72OPC-32
72Top-31
72Top-32
73LinPor-113
73MetAllEB-5
73NewYorN-15
73OPC-540
73Top-540
74MetDaiPA-17
74OPC-245
74OPC-476
74Top-245
74Top-476
74TopSta-64
75Hos-123
75Kel-21
75MetSSP-11
75OPC-43
75Top-43
81TCM60I-322
86MetGreT-5
87Met196T-3
89Met196C-7
89RinPosM1-16
91MetWIZ-207
92UppDecS-10
94Met69CCPP-19
94Met69CS-18
94Met69T-14
96Met69Y-5
Jones, Cliff
92PitMetC-17
92PitMetF-3290
Jones, Craig
84RicBraT-13
Jones, D.J.
87DurBulP-23
Jones, Dan
83MiaMarT-15
91Cla/Bes-423
91WelPirC-29
91WelPirP-3568
92SalBucC-21
92SalBucF-60
92StaCluD-95
93CarMudF-2051
93CarMudTI-9
Jones, Darryl
78TacYanC-15
79ColCliT-28
80Top-670
92YanWIZ7-84
Jones, David
85DurBulT-7
86SumBraP-14
Jones, Davy (David Jefferson)
03WilCarE-17
07TigACDPP-7
09ColChiE-144
09TigMorPenWBPP-6
09TigTaCP-8
09WolNewDTPP-9
10NadE1-24
10StaCarE-17
10W555-37
11S74Sil-15
11SpoLifCW-190
11SpoLifM-60
11T205-83
11TurRedT-100
12ColRedB-144
12ColTinT-144
12HasTriFT-47
81TigDetN-19
93ConTSN-753
Jones, Dax
91Cla/Bes-421
91EveGiaC-8
91EveGiaP-3931
92ClaFS7-79
92CliGiaC-1
92CliGiaF-3610
93ShrCapF-2771
94PhoFirF-1532
95PhoFirTI-24
96PhoFirB-19
97Sco-323
97ScoPreS-323
97ScoShoS-323
97ScoShoSAP-323
Jones, Deacon (Grover)
63Top-253
63WhiSoxTS-11
84PadMot-27
85PadMot-27
Jones, Dennis
87MyrBeaBJP-1447
88BasAmeAAB-19
88KnoBluJB-19
89KnoBluJB-12
89KnoBluJP-1136
89KnoBluJS-10
90KnoBluJB-24
90KnoBluJS-8
Jones, DeWayne
88SouOreAP-1698
Jones, Donny
77QuaCitAT-20
78QuaCitAT-11
80ElPasDT-18
93UtiBluSC-12
94HigDesMC-17
94HigDesMF-2803
Jones, Doug
78NewWayCT-21
79BurBeeT-12
81ElPasDT-11
82BrePol-45
82VanCanT-13
84ElPasDT-7
84VanCanC-39
85WatIndT-12
86MaiGuiP-11
87IndGat-46
88Don-588
88DonBasB-325
88Fle-613
88FleGlo-613
88IndGat-11
88Sco-594
88ScoGlo-594
88StaLinI-15
88Top-293
88TopTif-293
89Bow-78
89BowTif-78
89ClaLigB-89
89Don-438
89DonAll-20
89DonBasB-173
89Fle-409
89FleBasA-23
89FleBasM-23
89FleGlo-409
89IndTeal-15
89OPC-312
89PanSti-5
89PanSti-319
89Sco-387
89Sco-656
89ScoHot1S-41
89Spo-38
89Top-6
89Top-690
89TopBasT-161
89TopMinL-51
89TopSti-3
89TopSti-215
89TopStiB-32
89TopTif-6
89TopTif-690
89UppDec-540
89Woo-14
90Bow-328
90BowTif-328
90ClaBlu-114
90Don-320
90DonBesA-61
90El PasDAGTI-15
90Fle-495
90FleBasA-22
90FleCan-495
90FleLeaL-20
90GeoColC-10
90IndTeal-21
90Lea-153
90OPC-75
90PanSti-63
90PubSti-562
90Sco-130
90Spo-96
90Top-75
90TopBig-316
90TopSti-215
90TopTif-75
90UppDec-632
90USPlaCA-7S
90VenSti-257
91Bow-77
91ClaGam-55
91Don-232
91Fle-372
91IndFanC-16
91Lea-57
91OPC-745
91PanCanT1-87
91PanFreS-224
91PanSti-173
91RedFolS-54
91Sco-45
91Sco-884
91Sco100S-54
91StaClu-145
91Stu-46
91Top-745
91TopDesS-745
91TopMic-745
91TopTif-745
91Ult-115
91UppDec-216
92AstMot-16
92Don-674
92Fle-114
92FleUpd-87
92Lea-253
92OPC-461
92OPCPre-51
92Pin-499
92Sco-53
92ScoProP-11
92ScoRoo-38T
92StaClu-616
92StaCluNC-616
92Stu-38
92Top-461
92TopGol-461
92TopGolW-461
92TopMic-461
92TopTra-57T
92TopTraG-57T
92UppDec-798
93AstMot-14
93Bow-532
93Don-296
93Fin-69
93FinRef-69
93Fla-65
93Fle-54
93Lea-161
93OPC-267
93PacSpa-478
93Pin-443
93Sco-197
93Sel-67
93StaClu-411
93StaCluAs-15
93StaCluFDI-411
93StaCluM-53
93StaCluMOP-411
93Stu-115
93Top-171
93TopGol-171
93TopInaM-171
93TopMic-171
93TriPla-175
93Ult-44
93UppDec-171
93UppDecGold-171
94BreMilB-135
94ColC-513
94ColChoGS-513
94ColChoSS-513
94Don-533
94ExtBas-338
94Fin-380
94FinRef-380
94Fla-209
94Fle-494
94FleUpd-165
94Lea-377
94PanSti-195
94PhiMed-16
94PhiMel-12
94Pin-222
94PinArtP-222
94PinMusC-222
94Sco-544
94ScoGolR-544
94ScoRoo-RT69
94ScoRooGR-RT69
94StaClu-580
94StaCluFDI-580
94StaCluGR-580
94StaCluMOP-580
94StaCluT-216
94StaCluTFDI-216
94Top-334
94TopGol-334
94TopSpa-334
94TopTra-126T
94Ult-207
94Ult-548
94UppDec-374
94UppDecED-374
95ColCho-368
95ColCho-563T
95ColChoGS-368
95ColChoSE-174
95ColChoSEGS-174
95ColChoSESS-174
95ColChoSS-368
95DonTopotO-11
95Fin-268
95FinRef-268
95Fla-222
95Fle-396
95FleAllS-25
95FleUpd-5
95Lea-394
95Sco-467
95ScoGolR-467
95ScoPlaTS-467
95StaClu-89
95StaClu-564
95StaCluFDI-89
95StaCluMOP-89
95StaCluMOP-564
95StaCluSTWS-89
95StaCluSTWS-564
95StaCluVR-55
95Top-495
95TopCyb-285
95TopTra-113T
95UppDecSE-74
95UppDecSEG-74
96ColCho-767
96Don-237
96DonPreP-237
96Fla-218
96Fle-12
96FleCub-10
96FleTif-12
96FleUpd-U111
96FleUpdTC-U111
96StaClu-38
96StaCluMOP-38
95StaCluVRMC-55
96Top-183
96Ult-7
96Ult-450
96UltGolM-7
96UltGolM-450
96UppDec-487U
Jones, Elijah
12ImpTobC-52
Jones, Eric
81BatTroT-22
Jones, Eugene
89GreHorP-416
90Bes-207
90ChaWheB-22
90ChaWheP-2253
90CMC-695
91CedRapRC-22
91CedRapRP-2732
92ChaWheF-21
93WinSpiF-1580
Jones, Fielder
03BreE10-76
04FanCraAL-29
07WhiSoxGWH-6
08RosComP-15
09T206-176
09T206-177
15SpoNewM-91
16BF2FP-42
16ColE13-89
16SpoNewM-92
19W514-50
87ConSer2-44
90DodTar-391
90HOFStiB-20
Jones, Gary
83QuaCitCT-21
86FreGiaP-4
87TacTigP-5
88SanJosGCLC-121
88SanJosGP-112
88TacTigC-23
88TacTigP-612
89HunStaB-17
91MadMusC-22
91MadMusP-2146
92RenSilSCLC-59
93MadMusC-27
93MadMusF-1838
94BenRocF-3603
94HunStaF-1347
95EdmTraTI-13
97BenRocC-12
86HumStaDS-11
Jones, Gary (Gareth Howell)
71OPC-559
71Top-559
92YanWIZ7-85
Jones, Geary
86ColMetP-17
87LynMetP-17
88JacMetGS-3
88St.LucMS-14
92KinMetC-26
92KinMetF-1548
Jones, George
85EveGiaC-6A
85EveGiaC-6B
Jones, Glenn
82CliGiaF-21
91AdeGiaF-1
Jones, Golfer (Bobby)
32USCar-3
87SpoCubG-1
Jones, Gordon
82RedPioT-5
Jones, Gordon Bassett
55CarHunW-11
55Top-78
55TopDouH-5
57SeaPop-22
59Top-458
60Lea-73
60Top-98
60TopVen-98
61Top-442
91OriCro-229
Jones, Greg
95ArkTraTI-16
Jones, Grier
94ForWayWC-11
94ForWayWF-2012
Jones, Gus
86EugEmeC-47
87Ft.MyeRP-14
Jones, Guy
78QuaCitAT-12
Jones, Hank
77LodDodT-7
78LodDodT-9
79LodDodT-20
Jones, Harold
62Top-49
62TopVen-49
Jones, Ivory
96FtMyeMB-24
Jones, J. Dalton
64Top-459
65OPC-178
65Top-178
66Top-317
66TopVen-317
67CokCapRS-8
67DexPre-111
67OPC-139
67Top-139
67TopRedSS-8
67TopVen-237
68CokCapRS-8
68DexPre-44
68OPC-106
68Top-106
68TopVen-106
69MilBra-140
69RedSoxAO-5
69RedSoxTI-4
69Top-457
70Top-682
71MLBOffS-395
71OPC-367

71Top-367
72MilBra-172
72OPC-83
72Top-83
73OPC-512
73Top-512
81RedSoxBG2S-87
89PacSenL-55
93RanKee-20
Jones, Jacque
97Bow-329
97BowChr-225
97BowChrI-225
97BowChrIR-225
97BowChrR-225
97BowInt-329
Jones, Jaime
95Bes-122
95ElmPioUTI-NNO
95SPML-105
96KanCouCTI-15
96KanCouCUTI-8
96MauStiHWB-27
Jones, Jake
48RedSoxTI-12
85TCMPla1-2
Jones, James
86EveGiaC-25
86EveGiaPC-9
86ModA'sC-11
88CapCodPB-3
88CapCodPPaLP-70
89BenBucL-5
Jones, Jeffrey A.
79OgdA'sT-23
81Top-687
82Don-213
82Fle-94
82FleSta-130
82TacTigT-24
82Top-139
83Don-651
83TacTigT-28
83Top-259
84Nes792-464
84Top-464
84TopTif-464
85Top-319
85TopTif-319
91PacSenL-32
Jones, Jeffrey R.
80CedRapRT-19
81CedRapRT-16
82CedRapRT-24
84Don-262
84MidCubT-20
84TacTigC-82
87GleFalTP-4
88GleFalTP-936
89FayGenP-1570
90CedRapRDGB-19
90CMC-399
90ProAAAF-395
90TolMudHC-26
90TolMudHP-165
91LinDriAA-400
91LonTigLD-400
91LonTigP-1893
92LonTigF-650
93TolMudHF-1669
94SpoIndC-14
94SpoIndF-3319
94TolMudHF-1042
96JacSunB-3
Jones, Jim
84MadMusP-14
85ModA'sC-15
86ModA'sP-15
87PocGiaTB-7
87SpoTeaP-16
88TacTigP-618
89CalLeaA-30
89DenZepP-40
89SanJosGB-23
89SanJosGCLC-222
89SanJosGP-460
89SanJosGS-16
90SanJosGB-11
90SanJosGCLC-38
90SanJosGP-2016
90SanJosGS-14
91RenSilSCLC-5
Jones, Jimmy (James C.)
84BeaGolGT-1
85BeaGolGT-8
86LasVegSP-9
87Don-557
87Fle-650
87FleGlo-650
87FleUpd-54
87FleUpdG-54
87HunStaTI-15
87LasVegSP-17
87SouLeaAJ-12
87SpoRoo2-35
88Don-141
88DonBasB-189
88Fle-588
88FleGlo-588
88HunStaTI-9
88PadCok-45
88PadSmo-13
88Sco-246
88ScoGlo-246
88TacTigC-21
88Top-63
88TopTif-63
89Bow-169
89BowTif-169
89ColCliC-9
89ColCliP-6
89ColCliP-752
89DenZepC-17
89Don-247
89DonBasB-217
89Fle-308
89FleGlo-308
89Sco-294
89Top-748
89TopTif-748
89TopTra-58T
89TopTraT-58T
89UppDec-286
89YanScoNW-26
90CMC-223
90ColCliC-23
90ColCliP-19
90ColCliP-672
90OPC-359
90ProAAAF-322
90Top-359
90TopTif-359
90TopTVY-48
90YanScoNW-21
91AstMot-12
91Bow-553
91Fle-667
91Lea-371
91Sco-583
92AstMot-12
92Don-272
92Fle-438
92OPC-184
92Sco-33
92ScoProP-6
92StaClu-53
92Top-184
92TopGol-184
92TopGolW-184
92TopMic-184
92UppDec-392
92YanWIZ8-93
93Don-324
93ExpPosN-14
93Fle-437
93OPC-293
93PacSpa-125
93Sco-463
93Top-477
93TopGol-477
93TopInaM-477
93TopMic-477
93UppDec-698
93UppDecGold-698
Jones, Joe
77SpaPhiT-9
80CarMudF-7
Jones, John
94SouOreAC-13
94SouOreAF-3629
Jones, Keith
82BurRanF-10
82BurRanT-5
84TulDriTI-6
91JohCitCC-16
91JohCitCP-3989
92SprCarC-10
92SprCarF-882
93St.PetCC-16
93St.PetCF-2641
94MadHatC-12
94MadHatF-146
Jones, Ken
78WauMetT-13
81WatRedT-4
82WatRedT-4
83WatRedT-4
87MadMusP-14
Jones, Kenneth
93GenCubC-17
93GenCubF-3191
Jones, Kevin
85OscAstTI-28
89EveGiaS-17
90BilMusP-3229
90ChaWheB-17
Jones, Kiki (Keith Tyrone)
89GreFalDSP-18
90BakDodCLC-230
90Bow-86
90BowTif-86
90CalLeaACLC-20
90Sco-676
91Cla/Bes-212
91UppDec-59
91VerBeaDC-8
91VerBeaDP-769
92ClaFS7-292
92VerBeaDC-1
93VerBeaDC-12
93VerBeaDF-2213
Jones, Kirk
80BatTroT-6
80WatIndT-12
85OscAstTI-29
Jones, Lance
88CapCodPPaLP-133
89AncBucTI-20
Jones, Larry K.
80RocRedWT-7
81RocRedWT-19
81RocRedWW-10
82IowCubT-17
83IowCubT-5
Jones, Lee
83RedPioT-13
Jones, Lefty (Earl)
48SigOil-12
49RemBre-11
Jones, Lynn
78IndIndTI-20
80Top-123
81Top-337
82Don-542
82Fle-270
82Top-64
83Fle-333
83Tig-16
83Top-483
84Nes792-731
84Top-731
84TopTif-731
84TopTra-58T
84TopTraT-58T
85Top-513
85TopTif-513
86Don-466
86Fle-11
86RoyNatP-35
86Top-671
86TopTif-671
91RoyPol-26
92RoyPol-27
93ElmPioC-27
93ElmPioF-3839
94KanCouCC-27
94KanCouCF-178
94KanCouCTI-12
95KanCouCTI-10
96KanCouCTI-16
Jones, Mack
62Top-186
62TopVen-186
63Top-137
65OPC-241
65Top-241
66Kah-16
66Top-446
67BraIrvD-2
67CokCapB-18
67Top-435
67TopVen-277
68CokCapB-18
68Kah-B19
68Top-353
68TopVen-353
69ExpFudP-5
69MLBOffS-159
69Top-625
69TopSta-57
69TopTeaP-10
70DayDaiNM-22
70ExpPin-8
70ExpPos-10
70MLBOffS-66
70OPC-38
70Top-38
70TopScr-9
71ExpPS-11
71MLBOffS-131
71OPC-142
71Top-142
71TopCoi-135
72MilBra-173
76LauDiaJ-20
78TCM60I-277
92Nab-27
93ExpDonM-15
Jones, Mark
88VisOakCLC-173
Jones, Marty
90AubAstB-15
90AubAstP-3403
Jones, Matt
92WelPirC-11
92WelPirF-1331
93LetMouF-4156
93LetMouSP-13
95ButCopKtI-11
Jones, Mike
74CedRapAT-8
88BriTigP-1889
88KnoBluJB-4
88NasSouC-6
88NasSouP-485
88NasSouTI-14
89LakTigS-11
89RocRedWC-1
89RocRedWP-1657
89Sta-31
90CMC-305
90RocRedWC-4
91BilMusP-3761
91BilMusSP-18
92CedRapRC-16
92CedRapRF-1077
96EugEmeB-13
Jones, Mike (Michael C.)
81OmaRoyT-9
81Top-66
82CliGiaF-7
82Fle-412
82Top-471
84OmaRoyT-20
84ShrCapFB-9
85Don-640A
85Don-640B
85FreGiaP-6
85Top-244
85TopTif-244
86Don-419
86Fle-12
86RicBraP-10
86ShrCapP-12
86Top-514
86TopTif-514
86VenGulP-9
87DunBluJP-926
88BlaYNPRWL-184
90WicStaSGD-18
Jones, Motorboat
92ChaWVWC-10
93CarLeaAGF-42
93WinSpiC-11
94UppDecML-29
Jones, Neil
91MelBusF-2
Jones, Nippy (Vernal)
49EurSta-186
49MPR302-2-111
50Bow-238
51R42SmaS-51
52Top-213
58UniOil-5
79DiaGre-169
83TopRep5-213
85TCMPla1-25
Jones, Norm
89DenZepP-56
Jones, Odell
77PirPosP-11
78ColCliT-12
78Top-407
80PorBeaT-17
80Top-342
80VenLeaS-191
81PorBeaT-13
82PorBeaT-4
83RanAffF-21
83TopTra-50T
84Don-256
84Fle-421
84Nes792-734
84OPC-382
84RanJarP-21
84Top-734
84TopTif-734
85Don-525
85Fle-560
85RocRedWT-19
85Top-29
85TopTif-29
86RocRedWP-10
87Don-582
87SyrChiT-5
88BrePol-28
89Fle-189
89FleGlo-189
89PacSenL-171
89Sco-579
89T/MSenL-56
89UppDec-608
91OriCro-231
91PacSenL-27
93RanKee-211
94BreMilB-232
Jones, Oscar
11SpoLifCW-191
90DodTar-392
Jones, P.J.
93BluOriC-14
Jones, Parnelli
68AtlOil-6
Jones, Paul
92BluOriC-18
92BluOriF-2365
Jones, Percy
22E120-160
27AmeCarE-18
29PorandAR-48
92ConTSN-456
Jones, Pookie
94BenRocF-3609
95Exc-187
96SalAvaB-17
97BenRocC-13
Jones, Randy
74OPC-173
74PadDea-15
74PadMcDD-7
74Top-173A
74Top-173B
74TopSta-94
75OPC-248
75Top-248
76CraDis-23
76Hos-143
76Kel-4
76OPC-199
76OPC-201
76OPC-310
76Spo-6
76SSP-118
76Top-199
76Top-201
76Top-310
77BurCheD-132
77Hos-26
77Kel-17
77MSADis-31
77OPC-5
77OPC-113
77PadSchC-30A
77PadSchC-30B
77PadSchC-31
77RCColC-31
77Spo-1704
77Top-5
77Top-550
77TopCloS-23

78OPC-101
78PadFamF-16
78RCColC-61
78Top-56
78WifBalD-33
79OPC-95
79Top-194
80OPC-160
80Top-305
80TopSup-48
81CokTeaS-88
81Don-122
81Fle-487
81OPC-148
81Top-458
81TopTra-777
82Fle-528
82MetPhoA-12
82OPC-274
82Top-626
83Fle-546
83FleSti-222
83OPC-29
83Top-29
86PadGreT-10
88GreBasS-36
89PadMag-16
91MetWIZ-205
93UppDecS-13
93UppDecS-22
94TedWil-84

Jones, Rex
80ColAstT-22
83ColAstT-24
84TucTorC-56
85TucTorC-74
86TucTorP-9
88TucTorP-192
94AstMot-28

Jones, Rick
89SpaPhiP-1032
89SpaPhiS-26
90SpaPhiB-27
90SpaPhiP-2509

Jones, Rick (Thomas F.)
77Top-118
79PorBeaT-23
80VenLeaS-164
82RocRedWT-13
83RocRedWT-16
86RocRedWP-11

Jones, Ricky
85ChaO'sT-23
85RocRedWT-6
87ChaO'sW-7
88PorBeaC-14
88PorBeaP-656
91OriCro-230

Jones, Robert Walter
22E120-56
23WilChoV-74
83OklCit8T-11
87BelBreP-8
87UtiBluSP-8
88CalLeaACLC-13

Jones, Ron
85BenPhiC-13
86ClePhiP-11
86FloStaLAP-27
87MaiGuiP-23
87MaiGuiT-17
88BlaYNPRWL-89
88MaiPhiC-14
88MaiPhiP-280
88PhiTas-27
89Bow-407
89BowTif-407
89ClaLigB-96
89Don-40
89DonRoo-42
89Fle-574
89FleGlo-574
89PanSti-143
89PhiTas-14
89Sco-639
89ScoHot1R-25
89ScoYouS2-3
89Spo-178
89Spo-225
89Top-349
89TopTif-349
89ToyRoo-16
89UppDec-11
90CMC-245
90Don-487
90Fle-563
90FleCan-563
90OPC-129
90PhiTas-16
90ProAAAF-312
90PubSti-243
90Sco-364
90Sco100RS-31
90ScrRedBC-19
90ScrRedBP-610
90Top-129
90TopTif-129
90UppDec-94
90VenSti-258
91Sco-653
92Don-738
92Sco-342
93RicBraBB-9
93RicBraF-196
93RicBraP-14
93RicBraRC-23
93RicBraRC-15

Jones, Ronnie
81BurBeeT-25

Jones, Ross
82AlbDukT-17
83AlbDukT-16
84TidTidT-18
85BurRanT-26
85TidTidT-22
85UtiBluST-2
86ChaLooP-15
86DayBealP-14
87GasRanP-17
88Fle-262
88FleGlo-262
88Sco-598
88ScoGlo-598
88Top-169
88TopTif-169
88WesPalBES-14
89WesPalBES-13
91MetWIZ-208
95AusFut-100
95AusFutSFP-SFFP6

Jones, Ruppert
75OmaRoyTI-7
76OmaRoyTT-9
76VenLeaS-118
77Top-488
78Hos-121
78OPC-20
78Top-141
79Hos-99
79OPC-218
79Top-422
80OPC-43
80Top-78
81Don-349
81Fle-101
81OPC-225
81Top-225
81TopSupHT-67
81TopTra-778
82Don-346
82Fle-573
82FleSta-102
82OPC-217
82Top-511
82TopSti-99
83AllGamPI-148
83Don-373
83Fle-361
83FleSta-93
83OPC-287
83Top-695
83TopGloS-38
83TopSti-295
84Don-261
84Fle-303
84FleUpd-59
84Nes792-327
84OPC-327
84TigWavP-22
84Top-327
84TopSti-158
84TopTif-327
84TopTra-59T
84TopTraT-59T
85AngSmo-19
85Don-612
85Fle-13
85FleUpd-63
85Top-126
85TopTif-126
85TopTifT-65T
85TopTra-65T
86AngSmo-19
86Don-423
86Fle-161
86OPC-186
86Top-464
86TopSti-184
86TopTif-464
87AngSmo-21
87Don-428
87Fle-85
87FleGlo-85
87SpoTeaP-11
87Top-53
87TopTif-53
88Fle-492
88FleGlo-492
88PanSti-47
88Sco-333
88ScoGlo-333
88StaLinAn-10
92YanWIZ8-94

Jones, Ryan
93MedHatBJF-3745
94ExcFS7-146
94HagSunC-9
94HagSunF-2739
95DunBluJTI-10
96Bow-355
96BowBes-134
96BowBesAR-134
96BowBesR-134
96Exc-115
96KnoSmoB-17
97ColCho-472
97FlaShoWotF-25
97Fle-513
97FleTif-513
97Sel-132
97SelArtP-132
97SelRegG-132
97Ult-462
97UltGolME-462
97UltPlaME-462

Jones, Sad Sam (Samuel)
52IndNumN-19
52NatTeaL-14
52Top-382
53Top-6
56Top-259
57Top-287
58CarJayP-6
58Top-287
59Top-75
59TopVen-75
60GiaJayP-6
60KeyChal-26
60Lea-14
60Top-410
60TopTat-24
61GiaJayP-6
61Pos-143A
61Pos-143B
61Top-49
61Top-555
61TopMagR-31
62Jel-138
62Pos-138
62PosCan-138
62SalPlaC-162
62ShiPlaC-162
62Top-92
62TopStal-127
62TopVen-92
83TopRep5-382
84GiaMot-15
86NegLeaF-80
91OriCro-232
91TopArc1-6

Jones, Sam
75BurBeeT-12
76BurBeeT-19
77DayBealT-10

Jones, Sam P.
19W514-8
21Exh-85
21Nei-43
22E120-65
22W573-69
22WilPatV-17
23W515-43
23WilChoV-75
28Exh-63
28W502-38
28Yue-38
29ExhFou-32
29PorandAR-49
31SenTeaIPW-17
33Gou-81
34GouCanV-31
35DiaMatCS3T1-81
77GalGloG-129
91ConTSN-140
91ConTSN-174
92ConTSN-356
93ConTSN-801
94ConTSN-1003
94ConTSNB-1003

Jones, Scott
83CedRapRF-18
83CedRapRT-2
93PitMetC-12
93PitMetF-3703
96MicBatCB-13
96MidLeaAB-44

Jones, Sean
91PerHeaF-9
95AusFut-31

Jones, Shane
94OgdRapF-3742
94OgdRapSP-4
95OdgRapTI-10

Jones, Shannon
89GenCubP-1881
90CarLeaA-46
90WinSpiTI-12
91ChaKniLD-135
91ChaKniP-1685
91LinDriAA-135
92SalLakTSP-10

Jones, Sherman
60TacBan-8
61Top-161
74MetOriEB-6
91MetWIZ-206

Jones, Slim
86NegLeaF-79

Jones, Stacy
89FreKeyS-11
90FreKeyTI-12
91HagSunLD-233
91HagSunP-2451
91LinDriAA-233
92Fle-701
92FreKeyC-25
92FreKeyF-1801
92ProFS7-7
92Sco-832
92TopDeb91-94
93FreKeyC-11
93FreKeyF-1022
94ShrCapF-1600

Jones, Steve
91JohCitCC-25
91JohCitCP-3974
92HamRedC-10
92HamRedF-1587
92ProFS7-328

Jones, Steve H.
69OPC-49
69Top-49A
69Top-49B

Jones, Terry
87Ft.MyeRP-21

Jones, Terry Lee
93BenRocC-14
93BenRocF-3281
94CenValRC-12
94CenValRF-3215
95Exc-188
95NewHavRTI-10
96ColSprSSTI-20
96Exc-155

Jones, Terry R.
76OklCit8TI-1

Jones, Thomas
07TigACDPP-22
08RosComP-70
09BusBroBPP-8
09ColChiE-145
09PC7HHB-27
09RamT20-61
09T206-174
09T206-175
09TigTaCP-9
10NadE1-25
10SweCapPP-26
11SpoLifCW-192
11SpoLifM-61
11T205-84
12ColRedB-145
12ColTinT-145
12HasTriFT-28
12HasTriFT-73A
12HasTriFT-73B

Jones, Tim
92BriTigC-13
92BriTigF-1403
94ChaKniF-903
96SouOreTI-2

Jones, Tim (William Timothy)
87ArkTraP-14
87LouRedTI-17
88LouRedBC-13
88LouRedBP-433
88LouRedBTI-23
89Bow-439
89BowTif-439
89CarSmo-10
89Don-555
89DonRoo-28
89Fle-453
89FleGlo-453
89Sco-649
89ScoHot1R-28
89UppDec-348
90CarSmo-11
90Don-686
90OPC-533
90Sco-579
90Sco100RS-62
90Top-533
90TopTif-533
90TopTVCa-26
90UppDec-501
91Don-66
91FleUpd-117
91LouRedTI-19
91OPC-262
91StaClu-121
91Top-262
91TopDesS-262
91TopMic-262
91TopTif-262
92StaClu-206
92Ult-569
93Don-624
93LouRedF-222
93StaClu-280
93StaCluFDI-280
93StaCluMOP-280
94Pac-592

Jones, Timothy Byron
75ShrCapT-6
77CliDodT-11
77ColCliT-9
78CliDodT-16
78Top-703

Jones, Todd
90OscAstS-12
91Cla/Bes-333
91OscAstC-6
91OscAstP-678
92Bow-202
92JacGenF-3998
92JacGenS-335
92SkyAA F-142
92UppDecML-219
93Bow-352
93Bow-392
93ExcFS7-46
93LinVenB-58
93StaCluAs-25
93TucTorF-3056
93UppDec-423
93UppDecGold-423
94AstMot-20
94Bow-22
94ColC-153
94ColChoGS-153
94ColChoSS-153
94Don-171
94Fin-265
94FinRef-265
94Fla-172
94Fle-495
94Lea-415
94Pac-269

94Sco-246
94ScoGolR-246
94StaClu-226
94StaCluFDI-226
94StaCluGR-226
94StaCluMOP-226
94Top-97
94TopGol-97
94TopSpa-97
94Ult-507
95AstMot-23
95ColCho-121
95ColChoGS-121
95ColChoSS-121
95Don-60
95DonPreP-60
95DonTopotO-256
95Fla-360
95Fle-464
95Lea-161
95Sco-516
95ScoGolR-516
95ScoPlaTS-516
95StaClu-129
95StaCluFDI-129
95StaCluMOP-129
95StaCluSTWS-129
95StaCluVR-65
95Top-560
95TopCyb-336
95Ult-174
95UltGolM-174
96AstMot-25
96ColCho-562
96ColChoGS-562
96ColChoSS-562
96Don-228
96DonPreP-228
96Fla-280
96Fle-412
96FleTif-412
96LeaSigA-120
96LeaSigAG-120
96LeaSigAS-120
96Pac-90
95StaCluVRMC-65
96Ult-211
96UltGolM-211
96UppDec-341
97Cir-274
97CirRav-274
97ColCho-122
97ColCho-324
97Fle-348
97Fle-576
97FleTif-348
97FleTif-576
97PacPriGotD-GD152
97Top-68
97Ult-208
97Ult-402
97UltGolME-208
97UltGolME-402
97UltPlaME-208
97UltPlaME-402

Jones, Tommy

80CliGiaT-27
81PhoGiaVNB-16
83ButCopKT-30
86MemChiSTOS-12
86MemChiTOS-12
87AlbYanP-19
88AlbYanP-1352
89WauTimGS-2
90BatCliP-3060
90CalCanC-23
90CalCanP-664
90CMC-450
90ProAAAF-129
91SanBerSC-27
91SanBerSP-2003
93OrlCubF-2801

Jones, Tracy

83TamTarT-26
86BasStaB-61
86DonRoo-2
86FleUpd-58
86RedTexG-29
87Don-413
87Fle-651
87FleGlo-651
87FleUpd-55
87FleUpdG-55
87RedKah-29
87SpoTeaP-4
87Top-146
87TopTif-146
88ClaRed-185
88Don-310
88DonBasB-174
88ExpPos-11
88Fle-237
88FleGlo-237
88Lea-107
88OPC-101
88PanSti-283
88RedKah-29
88Sco-326
88ScoGlo-326
88ScoYouSI-38
88Spo-38
88StaLinRe-11
88Top-553
88TopTif-553
89Bow-479
89BowTif-479
89Don-574
89Fle-383
89FleGlo-383
89FleUpd-31
89GiaMot-14
89OPC-373
89PanSti-124
89Sco-510
89ScoRoo-43T
89Top-373
89TopTif-373
89UppDec-96
89UppDec-798
90Don-636
90Fle-607
90FleCan-607
90OPC-767
90PubSti-70
90Sco-291
90TigCok-9
90Top-767
90TopTif-767
90UppDec-309
90VenSti-259
91Don-594
91FleUpd-53
91MarCouH-16
91OPC-87
91Sco-87
91StaClu-446
91Top-87
91TopDesS-87
91TopMic-87
91TopTif-87
92Don-519
92Fle-284
92OPC-271
92Sco-206
92Top-271
92TopGol-271
92TopGolW-271
92TopMic-271

Jones, Victor

91CollndC-2
91CollndP-1500

Jones, Willie

47PM1StaP1-102
49Bow-92
49EurSta-138
49PhiBul-26
49PhiLumPB-5
50Bow-67
51BerRos-B8
51Bow-112
51FisBakL-11
51TopBluB-43
52Bow-20
52RedMan-NL11
52Top-47
53BowC-133
53Top-88
54Bow-143
54Top-41
55Bow-172
56Top-127
57Top-174
58Hir-60
58Top-181
59Top-208
60Lea-98
60Top-289
61RedJayP-7
61Top-497
79TCM50-29
83PhiPosGPaM-10
83TopRep5-47
87SpoCubG-2
91TopArc1-88
94TopArc1-41
94TopArc1G-41

Jongewaard, Steve

87EriCarP-8

Jonnard, Clarence

23W503-24
35GouPuzR-6C
35GouPuzR-11E
35GouPuzR-13C
35GouPuzR-15C

Joost, Eddie (Edwin)

38CinOraW-15
39OrcPhoAP-14
39PlaBal-67
40PlaBal-151
41DouPlaR-117
41HarHarW-12
46SpoExcW-3-11
47HomBon-24
48Bow-15
49Bow-55
49Lea-62
49MPR302-2-115
49PhiBul-27
50Bow-103
51Bow-119
51FisBakL-12
51R42SmaS-50
51TopBluB-15
52Bow-26
52RedMan-AL12
52TipTop-18
52Top-45
53BowC-105
53RedMan-AL7
54Bow-35
55Bow-263
61Fle-116
76TayBow4-13
79DiaGre-264
83TopRep5-45
85TCMPla1-21

Joppie, Dave

95HunStaTI-16
96HunStaTI-13

Jordan, Adrian

90BriTigP-3152
90BriTigS-12
93LinVenB-237
94VenLinU-261
95LinVen-208

Jordan, Brian

90ArkTraGS-18
91LinDriAAA-238
91LouRedLD-238
91LouRedP-2927
91LouRedTI-24
91LouRedTI-32
92Bow-464
92DonRooP-BC14
92DonUpd-U3
92JimDeaRS-3
92Lea-337
92Pin-555
92PinTea2-39
92ScoRoo-83T
92Stu-93
92TopTra-58T
92TopTraG-58T
92UppDec-3
92UppDec-702
92UppDecSR-SR11
93CarPol-8
93Don-442
93Fle-511
93Lea-229
93OPC-134
93PacSpa-632
93Pin-540
93Sco-217
93Sel-280
93StaClu-435
93StaCluCa-25
93StaCluFDI-435
93StaCluMOP-435
93Top-754
93TopGol-754
93TopInaM-754
93TopMic-754
93Toy-97
93TriPla-62
93Ult-107
93UppDec-596
93UppDecGold-596
93USPlaCR-6D
94Bow-676
94CarPol-7
94ColC-154
94ColChoGS-154
94ColChoSS-154
94Don-586
94Fin-360
94FinRef-360
94Fla-225
94Fle-634
94Lea-272
94PanSti-244
94Pin-124
94PinArtP-124
94PinMusC-124
94Sco-201
94ScoGolR-201
94Sel-62
94Spo-105
94StaClu-63
94StaCluFDI-63
94StaCluGR-63
94StaCluMOP-63
94StaCluT-308
94StaCluTFDI-308
94Top-632
94TopGol-632
94TopSpa-632
94TriPla-63
94Ult-267
94UppDec-223
94UppDecAJ-4
94UppDecAJG-4
94UppDecED-223
95BowBes-R54
95BowBesR-R54
95ColCho-192
95ColChoGS-192
95ColChoSS-192
95Don-221
95DonPreP-221
95DonTopotO-330
95Emo-181
95Fin-326
95FinRef-326
95Fla-410
95Fle-500
95Lea-64
95LeaLim-34
95Pin-271
95PinArtP-271
95PinMusC-271
95Sco-143
95ScoGolR-143
95ScoPlaTS-143
95Sel-90
95SelArtP-90
95SP-103
95Spo-55
95SpoArtP-55
95SPSil-103
95StaClu-355
95StaCluMOP-355
95StaCluSTWS-355
95Top-62
95TopCyb-44
95Ult-223
95UltGolM-223
95UppDec-58
95UppDecED-58
95UppDecEDG-58
95UppDecSE-226
95UppDecSEG-226
95Zen-11
96Baz-115
96Bow-33
96CarPol-13
96Cir-177
96CirRav-177
96ColCho-289
96ColChoGS-289
96ColChoSS-289
96Don-87
96DonDiaK-25
96DonPreP-87
96EmoXL-267
96Fin-B28
96FinRef-B28
96Fla-360
96Fle-545
96FleTif-545
96Lea-142
96LeaLim-79
96LeaLimG-79
96LeaPre-81
96LeaPreP-81
96LeaPrePB-142
96LeaPrePG-142
96LeaPrePS-142
96LeaPreSG-61
96LeaPreSte-61
96LeaSig-126
96LeaSigA-121
96LeaSigAG-121
96LeaSigAS-121
96LeaSigPPG-126
96LeaSigPPP-126
96MetUni-226
96MetUniP-226
96MLBPin-17
96Pac-229
96PacPri-P71
96PacPriG-P71
96PanSti-78
96Pin-233
96PinAfi-103
96PinAfiAP-103
96PinArtP-133
96PinFoil-233
96PinSta-133
96ProSta-31
96Sco-22
96ScoDugC-A21
96ScoDugCAP-A21
96Sel-90
96SelArtP-90
96SelCer-90
96SelCerAP-90
96SelCerCB-90
96SelCerCR-90
96SelCerMB-90
96SelCerMG-90
96SelCerMR-90
96SelTeaN-2
96SP-157
96StaClu-118
96StaCluEPB-118
96StaCluEPG-118
96StaCluEPS-118
96StaCluMOP-118
96Stu-147
96StuPrePB-147
96StuPrePG-147
96StuPrePS-147
96Sum-122
96SumAbo&B-122
96SumArtP-122
96SumFoi-122
96TeaOut-43
96Top-126
96TopChr-35
96TopChrR-35
96TopGal-75
96TopGalPPI-75
96TopLas-9
96Ult-275
96UltGolM-275
96UppDec-180
96Zen-56
96ZenArtP-56
96ZenMoz-11
97Bow-272
97BowBes-46
97BowBesAR-46
97BowBesR-46
97BowChr-89
97BowChrI-89
97BowChrIR-89
97BowChrR-89
97BowInt-272
97Cir-196
97CirRav-196
97ColCho-220
97ColCho-440
97ColChoBS-3
97ColChoBSGS-3
97ColChoNF-NF27
97ColChoNF-NF28
97Don-9
97Don-444
97DonEli-65

97DonEliGS-65
97DonLim-146
97DonLim-148
97DonLimLE-146
97DonLimLE-148
97DonPre-45
97DonPre-190
97DonPreCttC-45
97DonPreCttC-190
97DonPreP-9
97DonPreP-444
97DonPrePGold-9
97DonPrePGold-444
97DonTea-151
97DonTeaSPE-151
97Fin-3
97Fin-293
97FinEmb-293
97FinEmbR-293
97FinRef-3
97FinRef-293
97FlaSho-A56
97FlaSho-B56
97FlaSho-C56
97FlaShoLC-56
97FlaShoLC-B56
97FlaShoLC-C56
97FlaShoLCM-A56
97FlaShoLCM-B56
97FlaShoLCM-C56
97Fle-445
97Fle-746
97FleTeaL-26
97FleTif-445
97FleTif-746
97Lea-116
97Lea-394
97LeaDrefS-14
97LeaFraM-116
97LeaFraM-394
97LeaFraMDC-116
97LeaFraMDC-394
97LeaGet-11
97MetUni-231
97NewPin-44
97NewPinAP-44
97NewPinIE-1
97NewPinMC-44
97NewPinPP-44
97NewPinPP-I1B
97Pac-411
97PacGolCD-33
97PacLigB-411
97PacPri-139
97PacPriLB-139
97PacPriP-139
97PacSil-411
97Pin-41
97PinArtP-41
97PinCar-17
97PinCer-80
97PinCerLI-4
97PinCerMBlu-80
97PinCerMG-80
97PinCerMR-80
97PinCerR-80
97PinIns-18
97PinInsCE-18
97PinInsDD-10
97PinInsDE-18
97PinMin-29
97PinMinB-29
97PinMinCB-29
97PinMinCG-29
97PinMinCGR-29
97PinMinCN-29
97PinMinCS-29
97PinMinG-29
97PinMinS-29
97PinMusC-41
97PinSha-7
97PinTotCPB-80
97PinTotCPG-80
97PinTotCPR-80
97PinX-P-108
97PinX-PMoS-108
97PinX-PSfF-60
97PinX-PSfFU-60
97ProMag-34
97ProMagML-34
97Sco-55
97ScoAllF-14
97ScoBla-17
97ScoHeaotO-28
97ScoPreS-55
97ScoShoS-55
97ScoShoSAP-55
97Sel-38
97SelArtP-38
97SelRegG-38
97SelToootT-21
97SelToootTMB-21
97SkyE-X-99
97SkyE-XC-99
97SkyE-XEC-99
97SP-146
97Spolll-103
97SpolllEE-103
97StaClu-4
97StaClul-I16
97StaCluMat-4
97StaCluMOP-4
97StaCluMOP-I16
97Stu-140
97StuHarH-24
97StuPrePG-140
97StuPrePS-140
97Top-415
97TopChr-147
97TopChrR-147
97TopGal-134
97TopGalPPI-134
97TopIntF-ILM7
97Ult-272
97UltGolME-272
97UltPlaME-272
97UppDec-162
97UppDec-245
97UppDec-258
Jordan, Buck (Baxter)
31SenTealPW-18
34DiaMatCSB-99
34DiaStaR-49
34Gou-31
34GouCanV-75
35DiaMatCS3T1-82
36DiaMatCS4-7
36GouWidPPR-A58
36OveCanR-27
37WheBB9-10
79DiaGre-203
Jordan, Dutch (Adolph)
09T206-494
10CouT21-35
11SpoLifCW-193
90DodTar-995
Jordan, Harry K.
75PhoGiaCK-24
76PheGiaCr-NNO
76PhoGiaCC-24
76PhoGiaVNB-12
77PhoGiaCC-13
77PhoGiaCP-13
77PhoGiaVNB-13
78PhoGiaC-12
79PhoGiaVNB-24
80PhoGiaVNB-26
81PhoGiaVNB-2
82PhoGiaVNB-9
Jordan, Jason
94JamJamC-12
94JamJamF-3959
95FayGenTI-14
Jordan, Jim
78BurBeeT-17
Jordan, Jim William
33ButCanV-29
34ButPreR-37
Jordan, Joe
85EveGialC-8
89OklSoo-4
Jordan, Kevin
90NebCor-13
90OneYanP-3386
90ProAaA-181
91Cla/Bes-96
91FloStaLAP-FSL15
91Ft.LauYC-21
91Ft.LauYP-2434
92ClaFS7-223
92PriWilCC-22
92PriWilCF-157
93AlbYanF-2172
93ClaFS7-77
93ClaGolF-35
93ExcFS7-211
94Bow-224
94ExcFS7-107
94ScrRedBF-925
94UppDecML-113
94VenLinU-181
95Bow-108
95ScrRedBTI-15
95Top-654
96ColCho-33
96ColChoGS-33
96ColChoSS-33
96Don-497
96DonPreP-497
96Fle-501
96FleTif-501
96LeaSigA-122
96LeaSigAG-122
96LeaSigAS-122
96PhiTeal-18
96Sco-230
96Top-426
96UltGolP-9
96UltGolPGM-9
97Pac-380
97PacLigB-380
97PacSil-380
Jordan, Michael
91UppDec-SP1
92SpollIFK1-270
93StaCluMO-34
94ActPac-23
94BirBarC-23
94BirBarF-633
94Cla-1
94ColC-635
94ColC-661
94ColChoGS-635
94ColChoGS-661
94ColChoSS-635
94ColChoSS-661
94FUnPac-170
94SP-8
94SPHol-16
94SPHolDC-16
94SPPre-CR2
94TedWilDGC-DG1
94UppDec-19
94UppDecDC-C2
94UppDecED-19
94UppDecML-MJ23
94UppDecNG-8
94UppDecNGED-8
94UppDecTAE-BC2
95ColCho-500
95ColChoGS-500
95ColChoSE-238
95ColChoSEGS-238
95ColChoSESS-238
95ColChoSS-500
95SPMLA-14
95SPMLMJC-TC1
95SPMLMJC-TC2
95SPMLMJC-TC3
95SPMLMJC-TC4
95UppDec-200
95UppDecED-200
95UppDecEDG-200
95UppDecML-45
95UppDecMLMJS-MJ1
95UppDecMLMJS-MJ2
95UppDecMLMJS-MJ3
95UppDecMLMJS-MJ4
95UppDecMLMJS-MJ5
95UppDecMLMJS-MJ6
95UppDecMLMJS-MJ7
95UppDecMLMJS-MJ8
95UppDecMLMJS-MJ9
95UppDecMLMJS-MJ10
95UppDecMLOP-OP6
95UppDecSoaD-SD15
95UppDecMLFS-45
95UppDecMLMJJ-MJ1
95UppDecMLMJJ-MJ2
95UppDecMLMJJ-MJ3
95UppDecMLMJJ-MJ4
95UppDecMLMJJ-MJ5
95UppDecMLMJOoO-1
95UppDecMLMJOoO-2
95UppDecMLMJOoO-3
95UppDecMLMJOoO-4
95UppDecMLMJOoO-5
95UppDecMLMJOoO-6
95UppDecMLMJOoO-7
95UppDecMLMJOoO-8
95UppDecMLMJOoO-9
95UppDecMLMJOoO-10
Jordan, Milton
53TigGle-17
Jordan, Ricardo
91MyrBeaHC-7
91MyrBeaHP-2941
92DunBluJC-11
92DunBluJF-1996
94KnoSmoF-1300
95Exc-138
96ScrRedBB-17
97Pac-381
97PacLigB-381
97PacSil-381
Jordan, Ricky
86PhiTas-xx
86ReaPhiP-12
87ReaPhiP-16
88BlaYNPRWL-90
88FleUpd-110
88FleUpdG-110
88MaiPhiC-11
88MaiPhiP-286
88PhiTas-35
88ScoRoo-68T
88ScoRooG-68T
88StaJor-1
88StaJor-2
88StaJor-3
88StaJor-4
88StaJor-5
88StaJor-6
88StaJor-7
88StaJor-8
88StaJor-9
88StaJor-10
88StaJor-11
88TriAAC-28
89Baz-17
89Bow-401
89BowTif-401
89ClaTraO-129
89Don-624
89DonBasB-103
89Fle-575
89FleBasA-24
89FleExcS-27
89FleGlo-575
89FleHeroB-25
89PanSti-144
89PhiTas-15
89Sco-548
89ScoHot1R-88
89ScoYouSI-15
89Spo-44
89Top-358
89TopBig-246
89TopCoi-17
89TopHeaUT-4
89TopRoo-14
89TopTif-358
89TopUKM-45
89ToyRoo-17
89TVSpoM-31
89UppDec-35
90Bow-156
90BowTif-156
90ClaBlu-32A
90ClaBlu-32B
90Don-76
90DonBesN-8
90Fle-564
90FleCan-564
90FleLeaL-21
90FleSoaS-11
90Hot50PS-23
90Lea-236
90MLBBasB-3
90OPC-216
90PanSti-315
90PhiTas-17
90PubSti-244
90PubSti-615
90Sco-16
90Spo-153
90Top-216
90TopBig-172
90TopDou-38
90TopSti-112
90TopTif-216
90UppDec-576
90VenSti-260
90VenSti-261
91Bow-494
91DenHol-13
91Don-466
91Fle-401
91OPC-712
91PanFreS-103
91PhiMed-21
91RedFolS-55
91Sco-15
91StaClu-192
91Stu-215
91Top-712
91TopDesS-712
91TopMic-712
91TopTif-712
91UltUpd-100
91UppDec-160
92Don-458
92Fle-536
92OPC-103
92PhiMed-42
92Pin-530
92Sco-476
92StaClu-188
92Top-103
92TopGol-103
92TopGolW-103
92TopMic-103
92Ult-245
92UppDec-106
93CadDis-36
93Don-514
93Fle-103
93Lea-169
93PacSpa-579
93PhiMed-20
93Pin-187
93Sco-141
93StaClu-229
93StaCluFDI-229
93StaCluMOP-229
93Top-585
93TopGol-585
93TopInaM-585
93TopMic-585
93Ult-89
93UppDec-561
93UppDecGold-561
94ColC-447
94ColChoGS-447
94ColChoSS-447
94Don-394
94ExtBas-339
94Fin-297
94FinRef-297
94Fla-414
94Fle-593
94PhiMed-17
94PhiMel-13
94PhiUSPC-6H
94PhiUSPC-10S
94Sco-116
94ScoGolR-116
94Sel-95
94StaClu-657
94StaCluFDI-657
94StaCluGR-657
94StaCluMOP-657
94StaCluT-228
94StaCluTFDI-228
94Top-86
94TopGol-86
94TopSpa-86
94Ult-248
95ColCho-369
95ColChoGS-369
95ColChoSS-369
95Don-395
95DonPreP-395
95Fle-397
95Sco-234
95ScoGolR-234
95ScoPlaTS-234
95Top-269
96FleUpd-U83
96FleUpdTC-U83
96LeaSigEA-95
96MarMot-5
Jordan, Rocky
75SalLakCC-10
Jordan, Scott
86WatIndP-14
87KinIndP-12
88EasLeaAP-40
88WilBilP-1326
89Don-609

Jordan, Steve
81BurBeeT-16
Jordan, Tim
77NewCoPT-20
78NewWayCT-22
90JohCitCS-15
91SavCarC-26
91SavCarP-1667
92HamRedC-20
92HamRedF-1607
93SprCarC-15
93SprCarF-1863
Jordan, Tim Joseph
03WilCarE-18
09AmeCarE-58
09T206-178
09T206-179
10CouT21-156
10CouT21-157
10CouT21-294
11SpoLifM-158
11TurRedT-20
11TurRedT-45
12ImpTobC-87
90DodTar-393
Jordan, Tom (Thomas Jefferson)
77TCMTheWY-70
Jordan, Tony
80WauTimT-4
Jordon, J.H.
88KimN18-21
Jorgens, Arndt
34DiaMatCSB-100
34Gou-72
35DiaMatCS3T1-83
39PlaBal-42
40PlaBal-2
75YanDyn1T-26
91ConTSN-78
Jorgensen, Mike
70OPC-348
70Top-348
71OPC-596
71Top-596
72Dia-23
72Dia-65
72OPC-16
72ProStaP-7
72Top-16
73ExpPos-5
73OPC-281
73Top-281
74ExpWes-6
74OPC-549
74Top-549
74TopSta-56
75Hos-105
75OPC-286
75Top-286
76ExpRed-14
76Hos-144
76OPC-117
76SSP-327
76Top-117
77ExpPos-18
77OPC-9
77Top-368
78SSP270-107
78Top-406
79Top-22
80Top-213
81Don-274
81Fle-324
81Top-698
82Don-224
82Fle-529
82MetPhoA-13
82Top-566
83Fle-547
83Top-107
83TopTra-51T
84BraPol-11
84Car-14
84Nes792-313
84Top-313
84TopTif-313
84TopTra-60T
84TopTraT-60T
85CarTeal-15
85Fle-229
85Top-783
85TopTif-783
86CarTeal-20
86Top-422
86TopTif-422
87LouRedTI-1
88LouRedBC-25
88LouRedBP-441
88LouRedBTI-1
89LouRedBC-25
89LouRedBP-1256
89LouRedBTI-6
91MetWIZ-209
93RanKee-212
Jorgensen, Randy
93BelMarC-16
93BelMarF-3217
94RivPilCLC-11
96BesAutS-45
96PorCitRB-17
Jorgensen, Spider (John)
43ParSpo-80
47TipTop-98
49EurSta-39
53MotCoo-55
75Gia195T-11
85TCMPla1-28
90DodTar-394
Jorgensen, Terry
86AncGlaPTI-16
88OrlTwiB-15
89OrlTwiB-15
89OrlTwiP-1352
89SouLeaAJ-12
90CMC-569
90PorBeaC-17
90PorBeaP-184
90ProAAAF-254
90Sco-655
90TopDeb89-64
91LinDriAAA-410
91PorBeaLD-410
91PorBeaP-1571
92PorBeaF-2675
92PorBeaS-411
92SkyAAAF-188
93Don-151
93Fle-268
93OPCPre-106
93PacSpa-521
93Pin-594
93Sco-458
93SelRoo-144T
93Top-805
93TopGol-805
93TopInaM-805
93TopMic-805
93Ult-232
93UppDec-697
93UppDecGold-697
94Don-563
94Fle-209
94Pac-356
94PorSeaDF-685
94PorSeaDTI-17
94Ult-88
95ChaKniTI-12
Jorgensen, Tim
95WatIndTI-17
96KenIndB-14
Jorn, David A.
78St.PetCT-14
80ArkTraT-25
81ArkTraT-12
89PriWilCS-28
90GreHorB-30
90GreHorP-2680
90GreHorS-26
91AlbYanLD-25
91AlbYanP-1024
91LinDriAA-25
92AlbYanF-2349
92AlbYanS-25
93CapCitBC-26
94CapCitBC-27
94CapCitBF-1769
Jose, Elio
88ChaWheB-23
Jose, Felix (Domingo Felix)
84IdaFalATI-15
85MadMusP-14
85MadMusT-17
86ModA'sC-12
86ModA'sP-16
87HunStaTI-16
88TacTigC-24
88TacTigP-614
89A'sMot-22
89Don-38
89Fle-15
89FleGlo-15
89Sco-629
89ScoHot1R-22
89TacTigC-14
89TacTigP-1542
89UppDec-22
90A'sMot-17
90Bow-455
90BowTif-455
90ClaYel-T33
90Don-564
90DonRoo-5
90Fle-13
90FleCan-13
90Hot50RS-24
90Lea-385
90OPC-238
90Sco-321
90Top-238
90TopTif-238
90UppDec-228
91Baz-17
91Bow-401
91CarPol-34
91Cla3-T41
91ClaGam-64
91Don-656
91Fle-636
91Lea-392
91OPC-368
91Sco-784
91Sco100RS-90
91StaClu-366
91Top-368
91TopDesS-368
91TopMic-368
91TopRoo-14
91TopTif-368
91ToyRoo-13
91UltUpd-107
91UppDec-387
91USPlaCA-9S
92Bow-176
92CarPol-9
92Cla2-T53
92DenHol-4
92Don-233
92DonDiaK-DK13
92Fle-582
92FleAll-1
92Hig5-96
92Lea-63
92LeaGolP-10
92LeaPre-10
92MooSna-9
92OPC-105
92PanSti-176
92Pin-159
92Sco-40
92Sco100S-99
92StaClu-407
92StaCluD-96
92Stu-94
92Top-105
92TopGol-105
92TopGolW-105
92TopKid-29
92TopMic-105
92TriPla-75
92Ult-264
92UppDec-264
93Bow-393
93ClaGam-43
93Don-574
93DonLonBL-LL12
93Fin-81
93FinRef-81
93Fla-217
93Fle-126
93FleAll-NL5
93FunPac-183
93Lea-349
93LeaFas-12
93LimRocDWB-82
93OPC-182
93OPCPre-128
93PacBeiA-8
93PacSpa-295
93PacSpaGE-4
93PanSti-198
93Pin-36
93RoyPol-13
93Sco-110
93Sel-131
93SelRoo-110T
93SP-230
93StaClu-653
93StaCluFDI-653
93StaCluMOP-653
93StaCluRoy-21
93Top-67
93TopGol-67
93TopInaM-67
93TopMic-67
93TopTra-66T
93TriPla-114
93Ult-562
93UppDec-156
93UppDec-542
93UppDec-835
93UppDecGold-156
93UppDecGold-542
93UppDecGold-835
94Bow-667
94ColC-493
94ColChoGS-493
94ColChoSS-493
94Don-529
94ExtBas-92
94Fin-306
94FinRef-306
94Fla-300
94Fle-161
94Lea-168
94OPC-191
94Pac-289
94PanSti-74
94Pin-77
94PinArtP-77
94PinMusC-77
94Sco-433
94ScoGolR-433
94Sel-37
94SP-173
94SPDieC-173
94StaClu-298
94StaCluFDI-298
94StaCluGR-298
94StaCluMOP-298
94Stu-185
94Top-672
94TopGol-672
94TopSpa-672
94TriPla-235
94Ult-67
94UppDec-226
94UppDecED-226
95ColChoSE-212
95ColChoSEGS-212
95ColChoSESS-212
95Don-95
95DonPreP-95
95Fle-162
95Pac-205
95PacLatD-19
95PacPri-65
95Pin-43
95PinArtP-43
95PinMusC-43
95Sco-82
95ScoGolR-82
95ScoPlaTS-82
95Top-607
95TopCyb-377
96SyrChiTI-18
Jose, Manny
85GreHorT-4
86WinHavRSP-13
87WinHavRSP-17
88NewBriRSP-897
89LonTigP-1385
91LinDriAAA-265
91NasSouLD-265
91NasSouP-2170
93LimRocDWB-123
Joseph, Newt (Walter Lee)
87NegLeaPD-31
Joseph, Ricardo
68Top-434
69Top-329
70OPC-186
70PhiTeal-7
70Top-186
72MilBra-174
Joseph, Sam
86QuaCitAP-16
Joseph, Terry
96RocCubTI-14
Josepher, Rich
93OneYanC-10
93OneYanF-3510
Josephina, Michael
92MacBraC-16
92MacBraF-279
Josephson, Duane
66WhiSoxTI-8
67Top-373
68Top-329
68TopVen-329
69MilBra-141
69MLBOffS-32
69Top-222
69TopSta-156
69TopTeaP-11
69WhiSoxTI-7
70MLBOffS-187
70OPC-263
70Top-263
70WhiSoxTI-8
71OPC-56
71RedSoxTI-4
71Top-56
71TopCoi-92
72MilBra-175
72Top-543
Josephson, Paul
81BirBarT-24
83AlbA'sT-5
84DurBulT-21
Joshua, Von
71OPC-57
71Top-57
73OPC-544
73Top-544
74OPC-551
74Top-551
75OPC-547
75Top-547
76BreA&P-5
76Kel-39
76OPC-82
76SSP-109
76Top-82
77BurCheD-85
77Top-651
78Top-108
80Top-209
85SpoIndGC-10
88AlbDukP-254
89AlbDukP-73
90AlbDukC-28
90AlbDukP-362
90AlbDukT-15
90DodTar-395
90ProAAAF-84
91AlbDukLD-25
91AlbDukP-1158
91LinDriAAA-25
92AlbDukF-739
92AlbDukS-25
93SouBenWSC-29
93SouBenWSF-1448
94BreMilB-323
94PriWilCC-27
94PriWilCF-1937
Joslin, Chris
83BurRanF-16
83BurRanT-7
Joslyn, John
88VirGenS-12
Joss, Addie (Adrian)
03BreE10-77
04FanCraAL-30
05IndSouPSoCP-11
08AmeLeaPC-10
08RosComP-26
09AmeCarE-59
09AmeCarE-60
09ColChiE-147
09SpoNewSM-29
09T206-180
09T206-181
10StaCarE-18
10W555-38
11SpoLifM-44
11T205-85
11TurRedT-19
12ColRedB-147

12ColTinT-147
61Fle-117
77GalGloG-168
80PacLeg-114
80PerHaloFP-164
80SSPHOF-164
91ConTSN-272
94ConTSN-1016
94ConTSNB-1016
94OriofB-97
94UppDecTAE-23

Jourdan, Ted
92Man191BSR-14

Joyce, Bill (William)
90DodTar-396
95May-14

Joyce, Dick
77FriOneYW-27

Joyce, James
91PocPioP-3784

Joyce, Jim
90T/MUmp-59

Joyce, Kevin
78CliDodT-17
79CliDodT-24

Joyce, Michael
63Top-66
63WhiSoxTS-12
64Top-477

Joyce, Richard
91PocPioSP-4

Joyce, Robert Emmett
48SomandK-6

Joyce, Tom
76AppFoxT-9

Joyner, Wally
85EdmTraC-2
86AngSmo-22
86BasStaB-62
86DonHig-23
86DonRoo-1
86FleSlu-19
86FleUpd-59
86SpoRoo-7
86StaJoyR-1
86StaJoyR-2
86StaJoyR-3
86StaJoyR-4
86StaJoyR-5
86StaJoyR-6
86StaJoyR-7
86StaJoyR-8
86StaJoyR-9
86StaJoyR-10
86StaJoyR-11
86StaJoyR-12
86StaJoyR-13
86StaJoyR-14
86StaJoyR-15
86StaStiJ-1
86StaStiJ-2
86StaStiJ-3
86StaStiJ-4
86StaStiJ-5
86StaStiJ-6
86StaStiJ-7
86StaStiJ-8
86StaStiJ-9
86StaStiJ-10
86StaStiJ-11
86StaStiJ-12
86StaStiJ-13
86StaStiJ-14
86StaStiJ-15
86TopTra-51T
86TopTraT-51T
87AngSmo-12
87BurKinA-11
87ClaGam-6
87ClaUpdY-108
87Don-1
87Don-135
87DonAll-1
87DonHig-35
87DonOpeD-7
87DonP-1
87DonSupD-1
87Dra-2
87Fle-86
87Fle-628
87FleBasA-23
87FleExcS-30
87FleGamW-22
87FleGlo-86
87FleGlo-628
87FleHotS-25
87FleLeaL-26
87FleLimE-23
87FleMin-59
87FleRecS-17
87FleSlu-22
87FleStiC-68
87FleWaxBC-C7
87GenMilB-3F
87HosSti-20
87KayB-18
87KraFoo-9
87Lea-1
87Lea-252
87MandMSL-1
87MSAIceTD-10
87OPC-80
87RedFolSB-82
87SevCoi-W3
87Spo-26
87Spo-75
87SpoDeaP-2
87SpoTeaP-11
87StuPan-16
87Top-80
87TopCoi-16
87TopGloA-13
87TopGloS-39
87TopMinL-45
87TopRoo-7
87TopSti-150
87TopSti-174
87TopSti-313
87TopTif-80
87ToyRoo-14
88AngSmo-17
88Baz-10
88ClaBlu-206
88Don-110
88DonBasB-115
88DonBonM-BC13
88Fle-493
88Fle-622
88FleAwaW-21
88FleBasA-19
88FleBasM-20
88FleExcS-23
88FleGlo-493
88FleGlo-622
88FleHotS-21
88FleLeaL-22
88FleMin-11
88FleRecS-21
88FleStiC-12
88FleSup-18
88FleTeaL-16
88FleWaxBC-C4
88GreBasS-8
88KayB-15
88KinDis-9
88Lea-50
88MSAFanSD-4
88MSAJifPD-11
88Nes-44
88OPC-168
88PanSti-38
88RedFolSB-41
88Sco-7
88ScoGlo-7
88ScoYouSI-27
88Spo-75
88StaLinAn-11
88Top-381
88Top-420
88TopBig-52
88TopCoi-16
88TopGloS-48
88TopMinL-6
88TopRitTM-15
88TopSti-179
88TopStiB-34
88TopTif-381
88TopTif-420
88TopUKM-40
88TopUKMT-40
88UppDecP-A700
88UppDecP-B700
88UppDecP-C700
89AngSmo-18
89Bow-47
89BowTif-47
89ClaLigB-29
89Don-52
89DonBasB-139
89DonBonM-BC21
89Fle-481
89FleExcS-28
89FleGlo-481
89FleSup-26
89FleWaxBC-C16
89MasBreD-7
89MSAHolD-1
89Nis-1
89OPC-270
89PanSti-291
89RedFolSB-68
89Sco-65
89ScoHot1S-73
89Spo-2
89Top-270
89TopBasT-49
89TopBig-201
89TopSti-183
89TopTif-270
89TopUKM-46
89TVSpoM-109
89UppDec-573
89UppDec-668
90AngSmo-9
90Bow-299
90BowTif-299
90ClaUpd-T42
90Don-94
90DonBesA-31
90Fle-136
90FleCan-136
90Hot50PS-24
90Lea-24
90MLBBasB-93
90OPC-525
90PanSti-31
90PubSti-372
90Sco-120
90Sco100S-81
90Spo-49
90SunSee-19
90Top-525
90TopAmeA-30
90TopBig-168
90TopSti-166
90TopTif-525
90UppDec-693
90VenSti-262
91AngSmo-6
91Bow-195
91Cla3-T42
91DenHol-23
91Don-677
91Fle-317
91Lea-31
91OPC-195
91PanFreS-180
91PanSti-141
91RedFolS-56
91Sco-470
91Sco-873
91Sco100S-57
91SevCoi-SC7
91StaClu-2
91StaPinB-26
91Stu-26
91Top-195
91TopDesS-195
91TopMic-195
91TopTif-195
91TopTriH-A3
91Ult-48
91UppDec-575
92Bow-435
92ClaGam-164
92Don-333
92DonUpd-U14
92Fle-62
92FleUpd-27
92Lea-438
92OPC-629
92OPCPre-61
92PanSti-5
92Pin-284
92Pin-537
92Pos-4
92RoyPol-14
92Sco-535
92Sco100S-29
92ScoRoo-13T
92SpoStaCC-27
92StaClu-122
92StaClu-710
92StaCluNC-710
92Stu-185
92StuPre-10
92Top-629
92TopGol-629
92TopGolW-629
92TopKid-95
92TopMic-629
92TopTra-59T
92TopTraG-59T
92TriPlaG-GS2
92Ult-373
92UppDec-343
92UppDec-744
92UppDecF-29
92UppDecFG-29
93Bow-645
93ClaGam-44
93DenHol-24
93DiaMar-57
93Don-129
93DonDiaK-DK8
93Fin-59
93FinRef-59
93Fla-218
93Fle-239
93FunPac-184
93Hos-24
93Lea-376
93MetBak-12
93MilBonSS-11
93OPC-148
93PacSpa-138
93PanSti-103
93Pin-51
93RoyPol-11
93Sco-43
93Sel-34
93SP-231
93StaClu-537
93StaCluFDI-537
93StaCluMOP-537
93StaCluRoy-4
93Stu-164
93Top-375
93TopGol-375
93TopInaM-375
93TopMic-375
93TriPla-153
93TriPlaA-25
93Ult-210
93UppDec-54
93UppDec-252
93UppDecGold-54
93UppDecGold-252
94Bow-443
94ColC-155
94ColChoGS-155
94ColChoSS-155
94Don-345
94DonMVP-21
94DonSpeE-345
94ExtBas-93
94Fin-176
94FinRef-176
94Fla-60
94Fle-162
94FUnPac-48
94Lea-141
94LeaL-40
94OPC-91
94Pac-290
94PanSti-75
94Pin-291
94PinArtP-291
94PinMusC-291
94ProMag-64
94Sco-67
94ScoGolR-67
94Sel-35
94SP-174
94SPDieC-174
94Spo-23
94StaClu-431
94StaCluFDI-431
94StaCluGR-431
94StaCluMOP-431
94Stu-186
94Top-275
94TopGol-275
94TopSpa-275
94TriPla-236
94Ult-366
94UppDec-169
94UppDec-287
94UppDecED-169
94UppDecED-287
95Bow-364
95BowBes-R43
95BowBesR-R43
95ColCho-453
95ColChoGS-453
95ColChoSE-214
95ColChoSEGS-214
95ColChoSESS-214
95ColChoSS-453
95Don-447
95DonPreP-447
95DonTopotO-92
95Emb-63
95EmbGolI-63
95Fin-39
95FinRef-39
95Fla-47
95Fle-163
95Lea-194
95LeaLim-102
95Pac-206
95PacPri-66
95Pin-77
95PinArtP-77
95PinMusC-77
95Sco-256
95ScoGolR-256
95ScoPlaTS-256
95Sel-74
95SelArtP-74
95SelCer-29
95SelCerMG-29
95SP-150
95SPCha-158
95SPChaDC-158
95Spo-74
95SpoArtP-74
95SPSil-159
95StaClu-419
95StaCluMOP-419
95StaCluSTWS-419
95StaCluVR-217
95Stu-192
95Sum-61
95SumNthD-61
95Top-115
95TopCyb-74
95UC3-29
95UC3ArtP-29
95Ult-291
95UltGolM-291
95UppDec-181
95UppDecED-181
95UppDecEDG-181
95Zen-108
96Cir-188
96CirRav-188
96ColCho-700
96ColChoGS-700
96ColChoSS-700
96Don-520
96DonDiaK-24
96DonPreP-520
96EmoXL-281
96Fin-S263
96FinRef-S263
96Fla-378
96Fle-132
96FleTif-132
96FleUpd-U198
96FleUpdTC-U198
96LeaLim-36
96LeaLimG-36
96MetUni-239
96MetUniP-239
96Pac-336
96PacPri-P107
96PacPriG-P107
96PadMot-3
96PanSti-188
96Pin-367
96PinAfi-4
96PinAfiAP-4
96PinAfiFPP-4
96PinFoil-367
96Sco-53
96ScoDugC-A46
96ScoDugCAP-A46
96Sel-124
96SelArtP-124

96SP-161
96StaClu-93
96StaCluMOP-93
95StaCluVRMC-217
96Stu-61
96StuPrePB-61
96StuPrePG-61
96StuPrePS-61
96Sum-21
96SumAbo&B-21
96SumArtP-21
96SumFoi-21
96TeaOut-44
96Top-386
96TopChr-155
96TopChrR-155
96Ult-72
96Ult-559
96UltGolM-72
96UltGolM-559
96UppDec-88
96UppDec-509U
96Zen-53
96ZenArtP-53
96ZenMoz-20
97Cir-30
97CirRav-30
97ColCho-445
97Don-152
97DonLim-185
97DonLimLE-185
97DonPreP-152
97DonPrePGold-152
97Fin-201
97FinRef-201
97Fle-467
97FleTif-467
97Lea-279
97LeaFraM-279
97LeaFraMDC-279
97MetUni-223
97NewPin-105
97NewPinAP-105
97NewPinMC-105
97NewPinPP-105
97Pac-429
97PacLigB-429
97PacPri-145
97PacPriLB-145
97PacPriP-145
97PacSil-429
97PinCer-33
97PinCerMBlu-33
97PinCerMG-33
97PinCerMR-33
97PinCerR-33
97PinTotCPB-33
97PinTotCPG-33
97PinTotCPR-33
97Sco-152
97ScoPreS-152
97ScoShoS-152
97ScoShoSAP-152
97StaClu-342
97StaCluMOP-342
97Stu-53
97StuPrePG-53
97StuPrePS-53
97Top-132
97TopChr-50
97TopChrR-50
97TopGal-30
97TopGalPPI-30
97Ult-337
97UltGolME-337
97UltPlaME-337
97UppDec-168

Ju Cha, Myung
96HilStaHWB-7

Juarbe, Ken
88BlaYNPRWL-106
89BlaYNPRWL-117
89OneYanP-2114
90GreHorB-6
90GreHorP-2658
90GreHorS-12

Juarez, Raul
96ForWayWB-12

Jubyna, Chad
90GeoColC-11

Juday, Bob
92ClaDraP-105
92ElmPioC-23
92ElmPioF-1389
93CarLeaAGF-9
93LynRedSC-14
93LynRedSF-2524
94LynRedSC-14
94LynRedSF-1899

Juday, Richard
91EriSaiC-6
91EriSaiP-4076
92WinSpiC-5
92WinSpiF-1215
93SalBucF-441
95WesMicWTI-9

Judd, Mike
96GreBatB-13
96SavSanB-26

Judd, Oscar
40SolHug-10
42RedSoxTI-15
43RedSoxTI-10
83TCMPla1943-19
85TCMPla1-36

Juden, Jeff
90Bes-243
90Bow-64
90BowTif-64
90FloStaLAS-8
90OPC-164
90OscAstS-11
90StaFS7-2
90Top-164
90TopTif-164
91Bow-547
91Cla/Bes-302
91Cla3-T43
91JacGenLD-564
91JacGenP-922
91UppDec-52
92Bow-188
92ClaGam-5
92Don-405
92OPC-34
92ProFS7-226
92SkyAAAF-272
92StaClu-479
92Top-34
92TopDeb91-95
92TopGol-34
92TopGolW-34
92TopMic-34
92TucTorF-484
92TucTorS-611
92Ult-492
92UppDec-6
93Bow-180
93ExcFS7-47
93OPC-309
93StaClu-698
93StaCluAs-6
93StaCluFDI-698
93StaCluMOP-698
93Top-709
93TopGol-709
93TopInaM-709
93TopMic-709
93Toy-94
93TucTorF-3057
94ColC-662
94ColChoGS-662
94ColChoSS-662
94Fla-210
94PhiMed-18
94ScoRoo-RT153
94ScoRooGR-RT153
94Sel-409
94SpoRoo-120
94SpoRooAP-120
94StaClu-609
94StaCluFDI-609
94StaCluGR-609
94StaCluMOP-609
94StaCluT-218
94StaCluTFDI-218
94Top-541
94TopGol-541
94TopSpa-541
94Ult-549
94UppDec-504
94UppDecED-504
95ScrRedBTI-16
96GiaMot-23
96LeaSigA-123
96LeaSigAG-123
96LeaSigAS-123

Judge, Joe
16BF2FP-47
16ColE13-90A
16ColE13-90B
16SpoNewM-93
17HolBreD-55
20NatCarE-52
21E121So1-49
21E121So8-45
21Exh-86
22AmeCarE-34
22E120-111
22W572-53
22W575-66
22WilPatV-44
23W501-13
23WilChoV-76
25Exh-126
26Exh-126
26SpoComoA-24
27AmeCarE-26
28StaPlaCE-40
28W502-35
28Yue-35
29ExhFou-31
29PorandAR-50
30W554-8
31Exh-32
31SenTeaIPW-19
31W517-53
33DouDisP-25
33ExhFou-16
33Gou-155
33GouCanV-88
60SenUniMC-9
61Fle-118
77GalGloG-130
77GalGloG-171
88ConSer3-16
90DodTar-397
91ConTSN-68

Judice, Bryan
95SpoIndTI-8

Judnich, Walt
41BroW75-17
41PlaBal-67
46SeaSLP-24
47Exh-111
47TipTop-65
48IndTeal-16
49SomandK-28
52MotCoo-8
53IndPenCBP-16
76TayBow4-84
77TCMTheWY-60
83TCMPla1942-7
93ConTSN-816

Judson, Erik
90BatCliP-3072
91SpaPhiC-16
91SpaPhiP-900

Judson, Howie (Howard)
48WhiSoxTI-12
50Bow-185
51Bow-123
52Bow-149
52NatTeaL-15
52Top-169
53BowBW-42
53Top-12
55Bow-193
83TopRep5-169
91TopArc1-12

Juelsgaard, Jarod
91EveGiaC-14
91EveGiaP-3909
92CliGiaC-15
92CliGiaF-3592
93KanCouCC-9
93KanCouCF-911
94PorSeaDF-673
94PorSeaDTI-18
95PorSeaDTI-7
96ChaKniB-15
93KanCouCTI-10

Juenke, Dan
86FloStaLAP-28
86MiaMarP-13

Juhl, Mike
92SpaPhiC-6
92SpaPhiF-1262
93ClePhiC-16
93ClePhiF-2680
93FloStaLAF-27
94ClaGolF-38
95ReaPhiELC-22
95ReaPhiTI-15

Jumonville, Joe
93GleFalRC-1
93GleFalRF-4011
94SavCarC-15
94SavCarF-515
95PeoChiTI-22
96StPetCB-14

Jundy, Lorin
85LitFalMT-6
86LitFalMP-16
87LitFalMP-2386
89BasCitRS-13

Junker, Lance
81CliGiaT-27
83RedPioT-14

Jurado, Pat
91RocExpC-7
91RocExpP-2042

Jurak, Ed
77BriRedST-9
81BriRedST-12
84Don-127
84Fle-402
84Nes792-628
84Top-628
84TopTif-628
85Don-579
85Top-233
85TopTif-233
86Top-749
86TopTif-749
87TexLeaAF-9
88DonTeaBA-NEW
88TacTigC-13
88TacTigP-615
88TriAAAP-6
89GiaMot-20
90CalCanC-10
90CalCanP-658
90CMC-437
90ProAAAF-123
90TulDriDGB-21

Jurewicz, Mike
77FriOneYW-49
92YanWIZ6-63

Jurgens, Scott
89BoiHawP-1980

Jurges, Bill
31CubTeal-12
32CubTeal-14
32OrbPinNP-33A
32OrbPinNP-33B
32OrbPinUP-37
33Gou-225
33TatOrb-37
34DiaMatCSB-101
34BatR31-139
35DiaMatCS3T1-84
36DiaMatCS3T2-15
36NatChiFPR-101
36R31PasP-31
36SandSW-36
36WorWidGV-97
39PlaBal-35
40PlaBal-89
41PlaBal-59
60RedSoxJP-6
60Top-220
84TCMPla1-30
95ConTSN-1376

Jury, Frank
88BoiHawP-1630

Justice, Choo Choo (Charlie)
51BerRos-D15

Justice, Dave (David)
86SumBraP-15
87GreBraB-9
88RicBraC-17
88RicBraP-24
89RicBraBC-12
89RicBraC-15
89RicBraP-838
89RicBraTI-11
89ScoHot1R-26
89SpoIllFKI-259
90BraDubP-13
90BraDubS-16
90CarColJB-1
90CarColJB-2
90CarColJB-3
90CarColJB-4
90CarColJB-5
90CarColJB-6
90CarColJB-7
90CarColJB-8
90CarColJB-9
90CarColJB-10
90CarColJB-11
90CarColJB-12
90CarColJB-13
90CarColJB-14
90CarColJB-15
90CarColJB-16
90ClaYel-T97
90CMC-285
90Don-704
90DonRoo-14
90Fle-586
90FleCan-586
90Lea-297
90ProAAAF-418
90RicBraC-9
90RicBraP-273
90RicBraTI-16
90Sco-650
90StaJus-1
90StaJus-2
90StaJus-3
90StaJus-4
90StaJus-5
90StaJus-6
90StaJus-7
90StaJus-8
90StaJus-9
90StaJus-10
90StaJus-11
90TopDeb89-65
90TopMag-36
90TopTra-48T
90TopTraT-48T
90UppDec-711
91Baz-18
91BlePro-2
91Bow-574
91BraDubP-16
91BraSubS-21
91CadEllD-31
91Cla1-T11
91Cla1-NNO
91Cla2-T63
91Cla3-T24
91ClaGam-193
91Col-33
91ColJus-1
91ColJus-2
91ColJus-3
91ColJus-4
91ColJus-5
91ColJus-6
91ColJus-7
91ColJus-8
91ColJus-9
91ColJus-10
91ColJus-11
91ColJus-12
91ColJus-xx
91DenHol-25
91Don-402
91Don-548
91Don-683
91DonPre-1
91Fle-693
91JimDea-14
91KinDis-18
91Lea-77
91Lea-84
91LeaPre-1
91MajLeaCP-46
91MooSna-9
91OPC-329
91OPCPre-70
91PanFreS-25
91PanSti-29
91PepSup-9
91Pos-1
91PosCan-12
91Sco-55
91Sco-861
91Sco-880
91Sco100RS-45
91ScoHotR-1
91SevCoi-A7
91SevCoi-F9
91SevCoi-NW10
91SilHol-3

91StaClu-26
91StaCluCM-16
91StaPinB-27
91Stu-146
91StuPre-10
91SunSee-15
91Top-329
91TopCraJI-14
91TopDesS-329
91TopGaloC-8
91TopMic-329
91TopRoo-15
91TopSta-21
91TopTif-329
91TopTriH-N1
91ToyRoo-14
91Ult-7
91Ult-394
91UppDec-363
91Woo-5
92Ble23KJ-1
92Ble23KJ-2
92Ble23KJ-3
92Bow-312
92BraLykP-16
92BraLykS-19
92Cla2-T15
92ClaGam-17
92ColPro-9
92Don-327
92DonCraJ2-3
92DonDiaK-DK6
92DonMcD-23
92Fle-360
92Fle-713
92FleCitTP-8
92Fre-15
92Hig5-24
92Hig5S-21
92Hig5S-33
92HitTheBB-18
92Lea-404
92LeaBlaG-404
92Mr.TurS-15
92OPC-80
92OPCPre-117
92PanSti-166
92Pin-100
92Pin-588
92Pin-604
92Pin-620
92PinSlu-5
92PinTea2-9
92PinTeaP-10
92Pos-29
92Sco-4
92Sco100S-42
92ScoFacl-B3
92ScoFacl-B5
92ScoImpP-44
92ScoProP-3
92ScoProP-24
92ScoSam-2
92SevCoi-10
92SpoStaCC-28
92StaClu-182
92StaClu-592
92StaCluD-97
92StaJus-1
92StaJus-2
92StaJus-3
92StaJus-4
92StaJus-5
92StaJus-6
92StaJus-7
92StaJus-8
92StaJus-9
92StaJus-10
92StaJus-11
92Stu-5
92StuPre-8
92Top-80
92TopGol-80
92TopGolW-80
92TopKid-31
92TopMcD-28
92TopMic-80
92TriPla-217
92TriPlaG-GS9
92Ult-164
92UppDec-29
92UppDec-546
92UppDecWB-T17
93Bow-578
93BraLykP-14
93BraLykS-18
93CadDis-37
93ClaGam-45
93ColAllG-16
93DiaMar-58
93DiaMarA-4
93Don-580
93DonEliD-5
93DonLonBL-LL5
93DonMasotG-12
93DonSpiotG-SG2
93Fin-1
93FinRef-1
93Fla-5
93FlaPro-5
93Fle-367
93FleFruotL-30
93FunPac-64
93Lea-50
93LeaFas-18
93LeaGolA-R8
93LeaGolA-U9
93MetBak-13
93OPC-180
93PacSpa-8
93PanSti-187
93Pin-344
93PinHomRC-31
93PinSlu-15
93Sco-107
93Sel-39
93SP-13
93SPPlaP-PP11
93StaClu-660
93StaCluB-3
93StaCluFDI-660
93StaCluMOP-660
93Stu-173
93Top-170
93TopGol-170
93TopInaM-170
93TopMic-170
93Toy-14
93TriPla-249
93TriPlaA-29
93Ult-306
93UppDec-366
93UppDec-460
93UppDecFA-A7
93UppDecFAJ-A7
93UppDecGold-366
93UppDecGold-460
93UppDecHRH-HR17
93UppDecS-19
94Bow-133
94BowBes-R63
94BowBesR-R63
94BraLykP-13
94BraLykS-14
94BraUSPC-1H
94BraUSPC-8C
94ChuShoS-4
94ClaGolF-AU1
94ColC-156
94ColC-325
94ColC-332
94ColC-636
94ColChoGS-156
94ColChoGS-325
94ColChoGS-332
94ColChoGS-636
94ColChoHRA-HA7
94ColChoSS-156
94ColChoSS-325
94ColChoSS-332
94ColChoSS-636
94ColChoT-4
94ColEdgDJ-1
94DenHol-17
94Don-25
94DonLonBL-6
94DonMVP-1
94DonSpeE-25
94DonSpiotG-8
94ExtBas-202
94ExtBasGB-15
94Fin-233
94FinJum-233
94FinRef-233
94Fla-126
94FlaOutP-7
94Fle-361
94Fle-706
94FleAllS-42
94FleLumC-6
94FleSun-14
94FleTeaL-15
94FUnPac-23
94FUnPac-192
94Kra-25
94Lea-263
94LeaGam-5
94LeaGolS-3
94LeaL-83
94LeaLimGA-14
94LeaMVPC-N7
94LeaMVPCG-N7
94LeaPowB-2
94LeaPro-4
94LeaSli-10
94OPC-233
94OPCAllR-24
94OPCJumA-24
94Pac-11
94PacGolP-12
94PanSti-146
94Pin-40
94PinArtP-40
94PinMusC-40
94PinPowS-PS1
94PinRunC-RC32
94PinTeaP-8
94PinTheN-5
94PinTri-TR5
94Pos-6
94PosCan-17
94PosCanG-17
94ProMag-4
94Sco-422
94ScoCyc-TC19
94ScoGolR-422
94ScoGolS-24
94Sel-236
94SP-50
94SPDieC-50
94SPHol-17
94SPHolDC-17
94Spo-6
94Spo-192
94StaClu-94
94StaClu-111
94StaClu-263
94StaClu-530
94StaCluF-F7
94StaCluFDI-94
94StaCluFDI-111
94StaCluFDI-263
94StaCluFDI-530
94StaCluGR-94
94StaCluGR-111
94StaCluGR-263
94StaCluGR-530
94StaCluMO-5
94StaCluMOP-94
94StaCluMOP-111
94StaCluMOP-263
94StaCluMOP-530
94StaCluMOP-F7
94StaCluT-49
94StaCluTF-6
94StaCluTFDI-49
94Stu-35
94SucSav-13
94TomPiz-11
94Top-389
94Top-630
94TopBlaG-36
94TopGol-389
94TopGol-630
94TopSpa-389
94TopSpa-630
94TopSupS-24
94TriPla-45
94TriPlaBS-5
94Ult-442
94UltAllS-18
94UltHomRK-8
94UltRBIK-8
94UppDec-267
94UppDec-375
94UppDecAJ-33
94UppDecAJG-33
94UppDecDC-E7
94UppDecED-267
94UppDecED-375
94UppDecMLS-MM11
94UppDecMLSED-MM11
94UppDecNG-9
94UppDecNGED-9
94USPlaCA-10C
95Baz-6
95Bow-386
95BowBes-R34
95BowBesR-R34
95ClaPhoC-2
95ColCho-156
95ColChoCtG-CG10
95ColChoCtG-CG10B
95ColChoCtG-CG10C
95ColChoCtGE-10
95ColChoCtGG-CG10
95ColChoCtGG-CG10B
95ColChoCtGG-CG10C
95ColChoCtGGE-10
95ColChoGS-156
95ColChoSE-67
95ColChoSEGS-67
95ColChoSESS-67
95ColChoSS-156
95D3-1
95Don-1
95DonAll-NL9
95DonPreP-1
95DonTopotO-186
95Emb-101
95EmbGolI-101
95Emo-103
95Fin-98
95FinRef-98
95Fla-326
95Fle-305
95FleAllS-8
95FleTeaL-15
95KinDis-15
95Lea-62
95LeaLim-95
95Pac-5
95PacGolP-27
95PacPri-1
95PanSti-77
95Pin-50
95Pin-285
95PinArtP-50
95PinArtP-285
95PinMusC-50
95PinMusC-285
95PinPin-15
95PinPinR-15
95PinRedH-RH20
95PinTeaP-TP8
95PinWhiH-WH20
95Pos-10
95RedFol-9
95Sco-271
95Sco-555
95ScoGolR-271
95ScoGolR-555
95ScoHaloG-HG5
95ScoPlaTS-271
95ScoPlaTS-555
95ScoRul-SR26
95ScoRulJ-SR26
95Sel-67
95SelArtP-67
95SelCer-64
95SelCerMG-64
95SP-28
95Spo-32
95SpoArtP-32
95SpoDouT-8
95SPSil-28
95StaClu-446
95StaCluMOP-446
95StaCluSTDW-B446
95StaCluSTMP-4
95StaCluSTWS-446
95StaCluVR-237
95Stu-31
95StuGolS-31
95Sum-111
95SumBigB-BB18
95SumNthD-111
95Top-620
95TopCyb-388
95UC3-67
95UC3ArtP-67
95Ult-126
95UltGolM-126
95UltOnBL-8
95UltOnBLGM-8
95UppDec-295
95UppDecED-295
95UppDecEDG-295
95UppDecPC-MLB10
95UppDecPLL-R39
95UppDecPLLE-R39
95UppDecSE-15
95UppDecSEG-15
95Zen-22
96Baz-116
96Bow-72
96BowBes-41
96BowBesAR-41
96BowBesR-41
96Cir-103
96CirRav-103
96ColCho-43
96ColCho-394T
96ColChoGS-43
96ColChoSS-43
96Don-197
96DonPreP-197
96EmoXL-143
96Fin-B56
96Fin-B248
96FinRef-B56
96FinRef-B248
96Fla-201
96Fle-294
96FleBra-7
96FleTif-294
96Lea-60
96LeaPrePB-60
96LeaPrePG-60
96LeaPrePS-60
96LeaPreSG-10
96LeaPreSte-10
96LeaSig-120
96LeaSigPPG-120
96LeaSigPPP-120
96MetUni-130
96MetUniP-130
96Pac-16
96PacOctM-OM9
96PacPri-P3
96PacPriFB-FB8
96PacPriG-P3
96PanSti-1
96Pin-286
96PinAfi-91
96PinAfiAP-91
96PinAfiFPP-91
96PinChrBC-3
96PinFoil-286
96ProMagA-17
96ProMagDM-1
96ProSta-23
96Sco-58
96Sco-385
96ScoDugC-A51
96ScoDugC-B110
96ScoDugCAP-A51
96ScoDugCAP-B110
96ScoPowP-17
96Sel-53
96SelArtP-53
96SP-28
96Spo-62
96SpoArtP-62
96StaClu-159
96StaCluEPB-159
96StaCluEPG-159
96StaCluEPS-159
96StaCluMOP-159
95StaCluVRMC-237
96Stu-109
96StuPrePB-109
96StuPrePG-109
96StuPrePS-109
96Sum-96
96SumAbo&B-96
96SumArtP-96
96SumFoi-96
96Top-60
96TopChr-22
96TopChrR-22
96TopGal-59
96TopGalPG-PG12
96TopGalPPI-59
96TopLas-69
96TopPro-NL16
96Ult-157
96UltGolM-157
96UppDec-4
88RicBraBC-13

97Bow-273
97BowBes-79
97BowBesAR-79
97BowBesR-79
97BowChr-90
97BowChrI-90
97BowChrIR-90
97BowChrR-90
97BowInt-273
97Cir-137
97CirRav-137
97ColChoNF-NF21
97Don-175
97Don-291
97DonLim-99
97DonLim-154
97DonLimFotG-20
97DonLimLE-99
97DonLimLE-154
97DonPre-34
97DonPreCttC-34
97DonPreP-175
97DonPreP-291
97DonPrePGold-175
97DonPrePGold-291
97DonTea-86
97DonTeaSPE-86
97Fin-271
97FinRef-271
97FlaSho-A73
97FlaSho-B73
97FlaSho-C73
97FlaShoLC-73
97FlaShoLC-B73
97FlaShoLC-C73
97FlaShoLCM-A73
97FlaShoLCM-B73
97FlaShoLCM-C73
97Fle-259
97Fle-514
97FleTif-259
97FleTif-514
97Lea-299
97Lea-378
97LeaFraM-299
97LeaFraM-378
97LeaFraMDC-299
97LeaFraMDC-378
97LeaWarT-17
97NewPin-33
97NewPinAP-33
97NewPinMC-33
97NewPinPP-33
97Pac-236
97PacLigB-236
97PacSil-236
97PinX-P-34
97PinX-PMoS-34
97PinX-PSfF-27
97PinX-PSfFU-27
97Sco-33
97Sco-442
97ScoBra-2
97ScoBraPl-2
97ScoBraPr-2
97ScoHobR-442
97ScoPreS-33
97ScoResC-442
97ScoShoS-33
97ScoShoS-442
97ScoShoSAP-33
97ScoShoSAP-442
97ScoStaaD-19
97SP-58
97SpoIll-143
97SpoIllEE-143
97StaClu-223
97StaCluMat-223
97StaCluMOP-223
97Stu-19
97StuPrePG-19
97StuPrePS-19
97Top-244
97TopChr-86
97TopChrR-86
97TopGal-86
97TopGalPPI-86
97TopSta-6
97TopStaAM-6
97Ult-373
97UltGolME-373
97UltPlaME-373
97UppDec-298
97UppDec-532
97Zen-30
Justiniano, Rene
95ButCopKtl-12
Justis, Walter
12ImpTobC-42
Jutze, Skip (Alfred Henry)
73OPC-613
73Top-613
74OPC-328
74Top-328
76OPC-489
76SSP-52
76Top-489
78Top-532
87AstShowSTh-29
Ka'akimaka, Lehua
91HawWomS-4
Kaage, George
77CliDodT-12
78LodDodT-10
Kaaihue, Kala
76HawIslC-17
87HawIslP-20
Kaat, Jim
60Top-136
60TopVen-136
61Top-63
61TopStal-180
61TwiCloD-9
61TwiJayP-4
61TwiPetM-7
61TwiUniMC-6
62Top-21
62TopVen-21
63Fle-22
63Jel-10
63Pos-10
63SalMetC-40
63Top-10
63Top-165
63TwiJayP-5
64Top-567
64TwiJayP-6
65OPC-62
65Top-62
66Top-224
66Top-445
66TopVen-224
66TwiFaiG-6
67Baz-18
67CokCapTw-16
67Top-235
67Top-237
67Top-278
67Top-300
67TopVen-236
68DexPre-45
68OPC-67
68Top-67
68Top-450
68TopVen-67
69MilBra-142
69MLBOffS-67
69Top-290
69TopSta-194
69TopTeaP-15
69TwiTeaIC-5
70DayDaiNM-145
70MLBOffS-233
70OPC-75
70Top-75
71MLBOffS-464
71OPC-245
71Top-245
71TopGreM-7
72MilBra-176
72Top-709
72Top-710
73OPC-530
73Top-530
74OPC-440
74Top-440
75Hos-110
75HosTwi-110
75OPC-243
75SSPPuzB-13
75Top-243
76CraDis-24
76Kel-25A
76Kel-25B
76OPC-80
76SSP-136
76Top-80
76TopTra-80T
77BurCheD-169
77Top-638
78Top-715
79Top-136
79YanPicA-22
80Top-250
81Car5x7-13
81Don-536
81Fle-536
81Top-563
82Don-217
82Fle-117
82FleSta-240
82Top-367
83Car-12
83Don-343
83Fle-11
83OPC-211
83OPC-383
83Top-672
83Top-673
83TopSti-135
83TopSti-136
86TwiGreT-10
87HygAllG-28
88ChaLooLTI-16
88PacLegI-88
89SweBasG-88
92YanWIZ7-86
92YanWIZ8-95
93ActPacA-149
94TedWil-48
94Yoo-8
Kable, David
81ArkTraT-9
82LouRedE-12
83LouRedR-28
84LouRedR-29
85LouRedR-9
86ArkTraP-9
Kaczmarski, Randy
82AmaGolST-21
83BeaGolGT-4
Kadota, Hiromitsu
87JapPlaB-41
Kaelin, Kris
91PocPioP-3789
91PocPioSP-20
Kagawa, Nobuyuki
87JapPlaB-37
Kagawa, Ross
87HawRai-11
Kahl, Nick
05IndSouPSoCP-12
Kahler, George
12T207-88
Kahlon, Bobby
95HudValRTI-11
Kahmann, Jim
86WesPalBEP-22
87JacExpP-456
88JacExpP-974
89OrlTwiB-6
89OrlTwiP-1349
Kahn, Roger
79HawIslT-20
90LitSunW-13
Kahoe, Michael
03BreE10-78
09RamT20-62
11SpoLifCW-194
Kail, Joe
94HudValRF-3392
94HudValRC-8
Kain, Marty
82AmaGolST-20
84EdmTraC-100
85EdmTraC-11
Kainer, Don W.
79TucTorT-11
93RanKee-213
Kainer, Ronald
76WatRoyT-15
Kairis, Bob
88BurIndP-1794
Kaiser, Bart
86ClePhiP-12
87ClePhiP-25
Kaiser, C. Don
56Top-124
57Top-134
Kaiser, Jeff
85A'sMot-25
86TacTigP-10
87BufBisP-16
88ColSprSSC-4
88ColSprSSP-1531
88IndGat-47
89ColSprSSC-3
89Fle-410
89FleGlo-410
89SalSpuCLC-142
89SalSpuP-1805
90CMC-462
90ColSprSSC-10
90TopTra-49T
90TopTraT-49T
91DenZepLD-143
91DenZepP-122
91LinDriAAA-143
91OPC-576
91Top-576
91TopDesS-576
91TopMic-576
91TopTif-576
92StaClu-526
92TolMudHF-1039
92TolMudHS-590
92TriA AAS-590
Kaiser, Keith
88GreHorP-1573
89ChaLooB-2
89ChaLooGS-13
90ChaLooGS-17
91JacGenLD-565
91JacGenP-923
91LinDriAA-565
Kaiser, Ken
88T/MUmp-31
89T/MUmp-29
90T/MUmp-28
Kaiser, Nick
91EugEmeC-6
91EugEmeP-3735
Kaiserling, George
15CraJacE-157
Kajima, Ken
89SalSpuCLC-148
Kakefu, Masayuki
79TCMJapPB-83
87JapPlaB-22
Kalas, Harry
84PhiTas-7
88PhiTas-39
90PhiTas-35
Kalin, Frank
53MotCoo-44
Kaline, Al
47Exh-112A
47Exh-112B
54Top-201
55Bow-23
55Top-4
55TopDouH-45
56Top-20
56TopPin-38
56YelBasP-16
57Top-125
58Top-70A
58Top-70B
58Top-304
59HomRunD-9
59Top-34
59Top-360
59Top-463
59Top-562
59TopVen-34
60ArmCoi-12
60Baz-18
60KeyChal-27
60NuHi-65
60Pos-4
60RawGloT-10
60TigJayP-7
60Top-50
60Top-561
60TopTat-25
60TopVen-50
61Baz-20
61ChePat-5
61NuSco-465
61Pos-35A
61Pos-35B
61TigJayP-9
61Top-429
61Top-580
61TopDicG-6
61TopStal-152A
61TopStal-152B
62AurRec-8
62Baz-12
62ExhStaB-17
62Jel-20
62Pos-20
62PosCan-20
62SalPlaC-67
62ShiPlaC-67
62TigJayP-7
62Top-51
62Top-150
62Top-470
62TopBuc-43
62TopStal-47
62TopVen-51
62TopVen-150
63BasMagM-43
63Baz-34
63ExhStaB-34
63Jel-51
63Pos-51
63SalMetC-63
63TigJayP-8
63Top-25
63TopStil-21
64Baz-34
64ChatheY-31
64TigJayP-6
64TigLid-7
64Top-8
64Top-12
64Top-250
64Top-331
64TopCoi-100
64TopCoi-129
64TopGia-12
64TopSta-95
64TopStaU-38
64TopTatl-46
64TopVen-8
64TopVen-12
64TopVen-250
64TopVen-331
64WheSta-24
65Baz-34
65ChaTheY-30
65OldLonC-27
65OPC-130
65Top-130
65TopEmbl-13
65TopTral-51
66Baz-46
66Top-410
66TopRubl-44
67AshOil-3
67Baz-46
67CokCapA-22
67CokCapAAm-19
67CokCapTi-17
67DexPre-112
67DexPre-113
67OPC-30
67OPCPapl-21
67TigDexP-4
67Top-30
67Top-216
67Top-239
67TopGiaSU-10
67TopPos-21
67TopVen-210
68AtlOilPBCC-23
68Baz-1
68CokCapT-17
68OPC-2
68TigDetFPB-8
68Top-2
68Top-240
68TopActS-1C
68TopActS-6B
68TopActS-16C
68TopGamI-27
68TopPla-6
68TopPos-9
68TopVen-2
68TopVen-240
69EquSpoHoF-BB9
69KelPin-8
69MilBra-143
69MLBOffS-49
69MLBPin-13
69NabTeaF-12
69OPC-166
69TigTeal-4

69Top-166
69Top-410
69TopFou-24
69TopSta-174
69TopTeaP-1
69TraSta-6
70DayDaiNM-15
70Kel-52
70MLBOffS-208
70Top-640
70TopScr-10
70TraSta-14A
71AllBasA-13
71BazNumT-14
71Kel-44
71MatMin-5
71MatMin-6
71MLBOffS-396
71MLBOffS-565
71OPC-180
71Top-180
71TopCoi-62
71TopGreM-19
71TopSup-54
71TopTat-36
71TopTat-37
72MilBra-177
72ProStaP-27
72Top-600
73Kel2D-52
73LinPor-72
73OPC-280
73TigJew-10
73Top-280
73TopCanL-24
74LauAllG-57
74OPC-215
74SunPopK-1
74SupBlaB-5
74Tig-6
74Top-215
74TopSta-177
75OPC-4
75SSP42-34
75Top-4
76GalBasGHoF-16
77Spo-8720
78TCM60I-40
78TigDeaCS-12
79TCM50-184
80PacLeg-65
80PerHaloFP-170
80SSPHOF-171
80TigGreT-5
81SanDieSC-4
81TigDetN-100
81TigDetN-132
82CraJac-4
83DonHOFH-18
83FraBroR-13
83MLBPin-11
83Oco& SSBG-9
83TigAlKS-1A
83TigAlKS-1B
83TigAlKS-2
83TigAlKS-3
83TigAlKS-4
83TigAlKS-5
83TigAlKS-6
83TigAlKS-7
83TigAlKS-8
83TigAlKS-9
83TigAlKS-10
83TigAlKS-11
83TigAlKS-12
83TigAlKS-13
83TigAlKS-14
83TigAlKS-15
83TigAlKS-16
83TigAlKS-17
83TigAlKS-18
83TigAlKS-19
83TigAlKS-20
83TigAlKS-21
83TigAlKS-22
83TigAlKS-23
83TigAlKS-24
83TigAlKS-25
83TigAlKS-26
83TigAlKS-27
83TigAlKS-28
83TigAlKS-29
83TigAlKS-30
83TigAlKS-31
83TigAlKS-32
83TigAlKS-33
83TigAlKS-34
83TigAlKS-35
83TigAlKS-36
83TigAlKS-37
83TigAlKS-38
83TigAlKS-39
83TigAlKS-40
83TigAlKS-41
83TigAlKS-42
83TigAlKS-43
83TigAlKS-44
83TigAlKS-45
83TigAlKS-46
83TigAlKS-47
83TigAlKS-48
83TigAlKS-49
83TigAlKS-50
83TigAlKS-51
83TigAlKS-52
83TigAlKS-53
83TigAlKS-54
83TigAlKS-55
83TigAlKS-56
83TigAlKS-57
83TigAlKS-58
83TigAlKS-59
83TigAlKS-60
83TigAlKS-61
83TigAlKS-62
83TigAlKS-63
83TigAlKS-64
83TigAlKS-65
83TigAlKS-66
83TigAlKS-67
83TigAlKS-68
83TigAlKS-69
83TigAlKS-70
83TigAlKS-71
83TigAlKS-72
84OCoandSI-4
84OCoandSI-115
84SpoDesPW-12
85CirK-21
86SpoDecG-51
86TigSpoD-12
87LeaSpeO*-H10
88GreBasS-12
88PacLegI-104
88TigDom-9
89PerCelP-21
89SweBasG-40
89TopBasT-24
90AGFA-5
90HOFStiB-52
90PerGreM-2
91MDAA-18
91SweBasG-53
91UppDecS-22
92ActPacA-6
92ActPacA2-6G
93ActPacAC-6
93TedWil-38
93UppDecS-18
93Yoo-8
94TedWilM-M30
94TopArc1-201
94TopArc1G-201
94UppDecAH-98
94UppDecAH-173
94UppDecAH1-98
94UppDecAH1-173
95EagBalL-7
95JimDeaAG-3
95MrTurBG-2
95UppDecSHoB-16
97FleMilDM-21
97SpollICC-6
97TopMan-36
97TopManF-36
97TopManFR-36
97TopStaHRR-6
97TopStaHRRA-6
Kaline, Louise
83TigAlKS-7
83TigAlKS-32
Kaline, Mark
83TigAlKS-28
83TigAlKS-32
Kaline, Michael
83TigAlKS-28
83TigAlKS-32
Kaline, Naomi
83TigAlKS-54
83TigAlKS-65
Kaline, Nicholas
83TigAlKS-54
83TigAlKS-65
Kallevig, Dane
90WatIndS-11
Kallevig, Greg
86PeoChiP-12
87WinSpiP-2
88MidLeaAGS-28
88PeoChiTI-18
89ChaKniTI-16
90CMC-79
90IowCubC-4
90IowCubP-314
90ProAAAF-621
90TopTVCu-50
Kamanaka, Masaaki
89VerBeaDS-12
Kamei, Kat
87SanJosBP-8
Kamenshek, Dotty
93TedWil-117
Kamerschen, Robbie
90MarPhiP-3199
Kamieniecki, Scott
87PriWilYP-6
88Ft.LauYS-13
89AlbYanB-25
89AlbYanP-316
89EasLeaAP-15
90AlbYanB-5
90AlbYanP-1034
90AlbYanS-7
90Bes-63
90TopTVY-49
91ColCliLD-109
91ColCliP-9
91ColCliP-594
91DonRoo-51
91FleUpd-45
91LinDriAAA-109
91StaClu-568
91TopTra-66T
91TopTraT-66T
91UppDecFE-33F
92Don-195
92Fle-232
92ForLauYC-14
92OPC-102
92OPCPre-110
92ProFS7-110
92Sco-415
92Sco100RS-23
92StaClu-649
92Top-102
92TopDeb91-96
92TopGol-102
92TopGolW-102
92TopMic-102
92UppDec-46
93Don-681
93Fle-651
93Lea-520
93PacSpa-557
93Pin-570
93Sco-377
93StaClu-410
93StaCluFDI-410
93StaCluMOP-410
93StaCluY-19
93Top-749
93TopGol-749
93TopInaM-749
93TopMic-749
94ColC-487
94ColChoGS-487
94ColChoSS-487
94Don-553
94Fin-60
94FinRef-60
94Fle-234
94Pin-309
94PinArtP-309
94PinMusC-309
94Sco-350
94ScoGolR-350
94StaClu-101
94StaCluFDI-101
94StaCluGR-101
94StaCluMOP-101
94StaCluT-186
94StaCluTFDI-186
94Top-489
94TopGol-489
94TopSpa-489
94Ult-94
95ColCho-523
95ColChoGS-523
95ColChoSS-523
95Don-59
95DonPreP-59
95Fle-72
95Pin-438
95PinArtP-438
95PinMusC-438
95Sco-92
95ScoGolR-92
95ScoPlaTS-92
95StaClu-310
95StaCluMOP-310
95StaCluSTWS-310
95StaCluVR-165
95TamYanYI-13
95Top-352
95TopCyb-195
95Ult-81
95UltGolM-81
96ColCho-628
96ColChoGS-628
96ColChoSS-628
96Fle-185
96FleTif-185
96Sco-191
95StaCluVRMC-165
96UppDec-408
97Ult-498
97UltGolME-498
97UltPlaME-498
Kamm, Willie
21Exh-87
22WilPatV-7
23W503-29
23W515-42
25Exh-76
26Exh-77
26SpoComoA-25
27Exh-39
28StaPlaCE-41
28W502-40
28W56PlaC-H3A
28Yue-40
29ExhFou-19
29PorandAR-51
30ChiEveAP-17
31Exh-19
31W517-13
32OrbPinNP-10
32OrbPinUP-38
33Gou-75
33GouCanV-68
33TatOrb-38
33TatOrbSDR-164
34BatR31-39
34ExhFou-11
34Gou-14
34GouCanV-60
34TarThoBD-11
35DiaMatCS3T1-85
35ExhFou-11
35GouPuzR-1L
35GouPuzR-2E
35GouPuzR-5A
35GouPuzR-6A
35GouPuzR-11J
35GouPuzR-13A
35GouPuzR-16E
35GouPuzR-17E
76WhiSoxTAG-4
79DiaGre-134
80WhiSoxGT-6
91ConTSN-166
93ConTSN-899
Kammerer, James
96AshTouB-22
Kammeyer, Bob
78TacYanC-21
79ColCliT-23
80ColCliP-29
80ColCliT-10
92YanWIZ7-87
Kammeyer, Tim
82RedPioT-6
83RedPioT-15
Kampouris, Alex
35GouPuzR-8D
35GouPuzR-9D
36ExhFou-4
36GouWidPPR-A59
41DouPlaR-13
42DodTeal-12
90DodTar-398
Kampsen, Doug
85CedRapRT-9
Kane, Frank
90DodTar-997
Kane, Jim (James Joseph)
08RosComP-151
Kane, Joey
88AlaGolTI-11
89AlaGol-13
Kane, John Francis
11SpoLifM-171
Kane, Johnny
88KimN18-22
Kane, Kevin
81BriRedST-3
85PawRedST-18
Kane, Mike
93BoiHawC-15
93BoiHawF-3911
Kane, Ryan
95BoiHawTI-20
96CedRapKTI-14
96Exc-29
Kane, Thomas
91LinDriAA-465
91NewBriRSLD-465
Kane, Tom
86GreHorP-12
87GreHorP-1
91NewBriRSP-350
Kaneda, Tomehiro
79TCMJapPB-28
Kanehl, Rod
62Top-597
63Fle-49
63Jel-199
63MetJayP-7
63Pos-199
63Top-371
64MetJayP-9
64Top-582
74MetOriEB-7
76Met63 S-9
82MetGal62-8
90SweBasG-44
91MetWIZ-210
Kaney, Joe
47CenFlo-14
Kanikeberg, Ken
76SeaRaiC-7
Kannenberg, Scott
86QuaCitAP-17
87QuaCitAP-9
88PalSprACLC-88
88PalSprAP-1444
Kanter, John
85MadMusP-15
85MadMusT-18
86ModA'sP-17
Kantlehner, Erving
16FleBreD-48
Kantor, Brad
91WatIndC-18
91WatIndP-3373
92WatIndC-20
92WatIndF-3243
Kanwisher, Billy
91OklStaC-13
92OklStaC-14
Kanwisher, Gary
85BelBreT-20
86StoPorP-11
87StoPorP-25
Kapano, Corey
89BenBucL-17
90QuaCitAGS-19
91CalLeLA-16
91PalSprAP-2023
92MidAngOHP-11
92MidAngS-461
92SkyAA F-195
92WinSpiF-1220
93ClaFS7-212
93OrlCubF-2799
Kaplan, Kid (Louis)
28W513-98
Kapler, Gabe
96FayGenB-19
96WesOahCHWB-19

Kappell, Henry
87OldJudN-272
Kappesser, Bob
89HelBreSP-19
90CalLeaACLC-48
90StoPorB-4
90StoPorCLC-189
90StoPorP-2188
91VisOakC-25
91VisOakP-1745
92ElPasDF-3925
92ElPasDS-215
93ElPasDF-2952
94ElPasDF-3149
95ElPasDTI-12
Karakas, Michael
43ParSpo-41
Karasinski, Dave
88BurBraP-16
89BurBraP-1611
89BurBraS-11
90DurBulTI-26
91SalSpuC-20
91SalSpuP-2237
Karcher, Carl
92AngPol-13
93AngPol-2
Karcher, Kevin
86EugEmeC-41
Karcher, Rick
90IdaFalBP-3255
91MacBraC-20
91MacBraP-873
92DurBulC-3
92DurBulF-1109
92DurBulTI-22
Karchner, Matt
89EugEmeB-6
90AppFoxBS-15
90AppFoxP-2091
91BasCitRC-8
91BasCitRP-1395
92MemChiF-2414
92MemChiS-437
93ClaGolF-126
93MemChiF-370
94BirBarC-15
94BirBarF-619
96ColCho-509
96ColChoGS-509
96ColChoSS-509
96Fle-69
96FleTif-69
96FleWhiS-8
96LeaSigEA-96
96StaClu-85
96StaCluMOP-85
Karcl, Darin
90ProAaA-114
Karczewski, Ray
88SalLakCTTI-7
89SalLakTTI-7
Kardamis, Mike
93AlbPolC-28
Karger, Edwin
08RosComP-165
09AmeCarE-61
09RamT20-63
09T206-182
10DomDisP-61
10SweCapPP-5
11SpoLifCW-195
11SpoLifM-11
11T205-86
12PhiCarE-14
Karkovice, Ron
83AppFoxF-22
86BirBarTI-8
86SouLeaAJ-5
87Don-334
87DonOpeD-234
87Fle-645
87FleGlo-645
87SevCoi-C11
87SpoTeaP-26
87Top-491
87TopTif-491
87WhiSoxC-18
88BlaYNPRWLU-33
88Sco-374
88ScoGlo-374
88Top-86
88TopTif-86
88VanCanC-15
88VanCanP-773
89Top-308
89TopTif-308
89UppDec-183
89WhiSoxC-13
90BirBarDGB-19
90Don-413
90Lea-307
90OPC-717
90PubSti-391
90Sco-22
90Top-717
90TopTif-717
90UppDec-69
90VenSti-263
90WhiSoxC-11
91Don-220
91DonGraS-12
91Fle-125
91Lea-515
91OPC-568
91Sco-833
91StaClu-102
91Top-568
91TopDesS-568
91TopMic-568
91TopTif-568
91UltUpd-16
91UppDec-209
91WhiSoxK-20
92Don-374
92Fle-88
92Lea-105
92OPC-153
92Pin-413
92Sco-532
92StaClu-257
92Top-153
92TopGol-153
92TopGolW-153
92TopMic-153
92Ult-39
92UppDec-169
92WhiSoxK-20
93Don-331
93Fle-205
93Lea-63
93OPC-198
93PacSpa-391
93PanSti-142
93Pin-195
93Sco-152
93Sel-381
93SP-257
93StaClu-427
93StaCluFDI-427
93StaCluMOP-427
93StaCluWS-17
93Top-286
93TopGol-286
93TopInaM-286
93TopMic-286
93TriPla-216
93Ult-175
93UppDec-199
93UppDecGold-199
93WhiSoxK-15
94Bow-71
94ColC-157
94ColChoGS-157
94ColChoSS-157
94Don-416
94ExtBas-50
94Fin-71
94FinRef-71
94Fla-279
94Fle-86
94Lea-184
94OPC-71
94Pac-130
94Pin-116
94PinArtP-116
94PinMusC-116
94Sco-403
94ScoGolR-403
94Sel-33
94StaClu-57
94StaCluFDI-57
94StaCluGR-57
94StaCluMOP-57
94StaCluT-123
94StaCluTFDI-123
94Top-684
94TopGol-684
94TopSpa-684
94Ult-36
94UppDec-121
94UppDecED-121
94WhiSoxK-17
95ColCho-502
95ColChoGS-502
95ColChoSS-502
95Don-198
95DonPreP-198
95DonTopotO-52
95Fla-247
95Fle-122
95Lea-44
95Pin-68
95PinArtP-68
95PinMusC-68
95Sco-481
95ScoGolR-481
95ScoPlaTS-481
95StaClu-88
95StaCluFDI-88
95StaCluMOP-88
95StaCluSTWS-88
95StaCluVR-54
95Top-372
95TopCyb-197
95Ult-31
95UltGolM-31
95WhiSoxK-15
96ColCho-508
96ColChoGS-508
96ColChoSS-508
96Don-88
96DonPreP-88
96Fla-53
96Fle-70
96FleTif-70
96FleWhiS-9
96LeaSigA-124
96LeaSigAG-124
96LeaSigAS-124
96Pac-291
96ProSta-134
96Sco-182
96StaClu-220
96StaClu-432
96StaCluMOP-220
96StaCluMOP-432
95StaCluVRMC-54
96Top-52
96Ult-41
96UltGolM-41
97Cir-261
97CirRav-261
97ColCho-298
97Fle-63
97FleTif-63
97Pac-55
97PacLigB-55
97PacSil-55
97Sco-233
97ScoPreS-233
97ScoShoS-233
97ScoShoSAP-233
97ScoWhiS-12
97ScoWhiSPl-12
97ScoWhiSPr-12
97StaClu-346
97StaCluMOP-346
97Top-81
Karl, Andy
43RedSoxTI-11
83TCMPla1945-44
Karl, Scott
92HelBreF-1711
92HelBreSP-16
93ElPasDF-2946
93ExcFS7-189
94AriFalLS-11
94Bow-477
94ExcFS7-82
94NewOrlZF-1464
95FleUpd-52
95TopTra-43T
96ColCho-596
96ColChoGS-596
96ColChoSS-596
96Don-414
96DonPreP-414
96Fle-148
96FleTif-148
96LeaSigEA-97
96Pac-347
96UppDec-124
97Cir-154
97CirRav-154
97ColCho-144
97Fle-130
97FleTif-130
97Lea-74
97LeaFraM-74
97LeaFraMDC-74
97MetUni-66
97Pac-120
97PacLigB-120
97PacSil-120
97Top-58
97Ult-77
97UltGolME-77
97UltPlaME-77
97UppDec-406
Karli, Todd
90RenSilSCLC-291
Karmeris, Joe
85VerBeaDT-14
Karp, Ryan
92OneYanC-7
93GreHorC-13
93GreHorF-882
93SouAtlLAGF-22
94Bow-552
94ClaGolF-84
94ExcFS7-108
94ExcLeaLF-11
94ReaPhiF-2058
94UppDecML-64
94UppDecMLPotYF-PY28
95ReaPhiELC-23
95ReaPhiTI-11
95ScrRedBTI-17
95SigRooOJ-21
95SigRooOJP-21
95SigRooOJPS-21
95SigRooOJS-21
96ScrRedBB-18
Karpoel, Herb
50W720HolS-14
Karpuk, Greg
86WatIndP-15
87WilBilP-26
Karr, Benjamin
22E120-5
22W573-70
27AmeCarE-20
Karr, Jeff
84LitFalMT-7
Karrmann, Jason
92Min-8
Karros, Eric
88GreFalDTI-2
89BakDodCLC-201
89CalLeaA-2
90SanAntMGS-16
90TexLeaAGS-1
90TopMag-100
91AlbDukLD-12
91AlbDukP-1146
91Bow-604
91Cla2-T36
91ClaGam-171
91LinDriAAA-12
91Ult-380
91UppDec-24
92Bow-288
92Cla2-T21
92ClaGam-34
92DodMot-21
92DodPol-23
92DodSmo-4992
92Don-16
92DonRooP-BC6
92Fle-462
92JimDeaRS-4
92Lea-293
92OPC-194
92OPCPre-63
92Pin-256
92PinRoo-24
92PinTea2-76
92ProFS7-240
92Sco-827
92ScoRoo-31
92SpollIFK1-390
92StaClu-236
92StaCluMO-18
92StaPro-5
92Stu-45
92Top-194
92TopDeb91-97
92TopGol-194
92TopGolW-194
92TopMcD-43
92TopMic-194
92Ult-508
92UltAllR-1
92UppDec-534
92UppDecSR-SR12
93Bow-14
93ClaGam-46
93DiaMar-59
93DodMot-2
93DodPol-13
93Don-430
93DonDiaK-DK30
93DonMVP-8
93DonPre-5
93Fin-32
93FinRef-32
93Fla-71
93Fle-64
93FleFruotL-31
93FleRooS-RSA6
93FleTeaL-NL4
93FunPac-86
93FunPac-89
93HumDumC-34
93JimDea-24
93Lea-234
93LeaFas-7
93OPC-208
93OPCPreSP-8
93OPCPreSPF-8
93PacSpa-151
93PanSti-166
93PanSti-214
93Pin-14
93PinTea2-26
93Pos-6
93RemUltK-1
93RemUltK-2
93RemUltK-3
93RemUltK-4
93RemUltK-5
93Sco-63
93Sco-486
93Sel-278
93SelChaR-5
93SP-94
93StaClu-292
93StaClu-528
93StaCluD-8
93StaCluFDI-292
93StaCluFDI-528
93StaCluMOP-292
93StaCluMOP-528
93Stu-92
93StuHer-10
93Top-11
93TOPBLAG-9
93TopGol-11
93TopInaM-11
93TopMic-11
93TopPre-11
93Toy-63
93TriPla-4
93TriPlaA-7
93TriPlaLL-L3
93TriPlaP-4
93Ult-56
93UltAwaW-20
93UltPer-4
93UppDec-385
93UppDec-490
93UppDecFA-A10
93UppDecFAJ-A10
93UppDecGold-385
93UppDecGold-490
93UppDecHRH-HR19
93UppDecIC-WI9
93UppDecICJ-WI9
93UppDecOD-D17
93USPlaCR-1S
94Bow-14
94ColC-158
94ColChoGS-158
94ColChoSS-158
94DodMot-4
94DodPol-16
94Don-338
94DonSpeE-338
94ExtBas-289

94Fin-356
94FinRef-356
94Fla-397
94Fle-514
94Fle-713
94FUnPac-146
94Lea-171
94LeaL-118
94OPC-163
94Pac-312
94PanSti-201
94Pin-87
94PinArtP-87
94PinMusC-87
94PinPowS-PS18
94ProMag-66
94Sco-26
94ScoGolR-26
94Sel-44
94SP-78
94SPDieC-78
94Spo-5
94StaClu-240
94StaCluFDI-240
94StaCluGR-240
94StaCluMOP-240
94Stu-69
94Top-115
94TopGol-115
94TopSpa-115
94TriPla-85
94Ult-518
94UppDec-208
94UppDecED-208
95Baz-66
95Bow-402
95BowBes-R14
95BowBesR-R14
95ColCho-220
95ColChoGS-220
95ColChoSE-92
95ColChoSEGS-92
95ColChoSESS-92
95ColChoSS-220
95DodMot-5
95DodPol-12
95DodROY-12
95Don-488
95DonPreP-488
95DonTopotO-265
95Emb-119
95EmbGolI-119
95Emo-141
95Fin-58
95FinRef-58
95Fla-366
95Fle-543
95Lea-252
95LeaLim-36
95Pac-220
95Pin-7
95PinArtP-7
95PinMusC-7
95Sco-399
95ScoGolR-399
95ScoPlaTS-399
95SelCer-80
95SelCerMG-80
95SP-66
95SPCha-59
95SPChaDC-59
95Spo-50
95SpoArtP-50
95SPSil-66
95SPSpeF-40
95StaClu-278
95StaCluMOP-278
95StaCluSTDW-D278
95StaCluSTWS-278
95StaCluVR-142
95Stu-147
95Top-487
95TopCyb-279
95Ult-181
95UltGolM-181
95UppDec-70
95UppDecED-70
95UppDecEDG-70
95UppDecSE-172
95UppDecSEG-172
95Zen-31
96Baz-36
96Bow-66
96BowBes-81
96BowBesAR-81
96BowBesR-81
96Cir-141
96CirRav-141
96ColCho-183
96ColChoCtG-CG20
96ColChoCtG-CG20B
96ColChoCtG-CG20C
96ColChoCtGE-CR20
96ColChoCtGG-CG20
96ColChoCtGG-CG20B
96ColChoCtGG-CG20C
96ColChoCtGGE-CR20
96ColChoGS-183
96ColChoSS-183
96DodMot-5
96DodPol-21
96Don-158
96DonPreP-158
96EmoXL-210
96Fin-B163
96FinRef-B163
96Fla-294
96Fle-438
96FleDod-10
96FleTif-438
96Lea-23
96LeaPre-69
96LeaPreP-69
96LeaPrePB-23
96LeaPrePG-23
96LeaPrePS-23
96LeaSig-114
96LeaSigPPG-114
96LeaSigPPP-114
96MetUni-183
96MetUniP-183
96MetUniProS-183
96Pac-111
96PacPri-P34
96PacPriFB-FB9
96PacPriG-P34
96PanSti-96
96Pin-62
96Pin-132
96PinAfi-70
96PinAfiAP-70
96PinAfiFPP-70
96PinArtP-25
96PinSta-25
96ProSta-42
96Sco-355
96ScoDugC-B80
96ScoDugCAP-B80
96ScoPowP-18
96Sel-83
96SelArtP-83
96SP-101
96Spo-41
96SpoArtP-41
96SPSpeFX-2
96SPSpeFXDC-2
96SPx-32
96SPxGol-32
96StaClu-63
96StaCluEPB-63
96StaCluEPG-63
96StaCluEPS-63
96StaCluMO-18
96StaCluMOP-63
95StaCluVRMC-142
96Stu-7
96StuPrePB-7
96StuPrePG-7
96StuPrePS-7
96Sum-127
96SumAbo&B-127
96SumArtP-127
96SumFoi-127
96Top-196
96TopChr-64
96TopChrR-64
96TopGal-69
96TopGalPPI-69
96TopLas-70
96Ult-220
96UltGolM-220
96UppDec-355
96UppDecPD-PD8
96UppDecPHE-H36
96UppDecPreH-H36
97Bow-25
97BowBes-75
97BowBesAR-75
97BowBesR-75
97BowChr-21
97BowChrI-21
97BowChrIR-21
97BowChrR-21
97BowInt-25
97Cir-186
97CirRav-186
97ColCho-140
97ColChoCtG-19A
97ColChoCtG-19B
97ColChoCtG-19C
97ColChoCtGIW-CG19
97Don-216
97DonEli-108
97DonEliGS-108
97DonLim-11
97DonLimLE-11
97DonPre-124
97DonPreCttC-124
97DonPreP-216
97DonPrePGold-216
97DonTea-115
97DonTeaSPE-115
97Fin-255
97FinRef-255
97FlaSho-A69
97FlaSho-B69
97FlaSho-C69
97FlaShoLC-69
97FlaShoLC-B69
97FlaShoLC-C69
97FlaShoLCM-A69
97FlaShoLCM-B69
97FlaShoLCM-C69
97Fle-365
97FleTif-365
97Lea-72
97LeaFraM-72
97LeaFraMDC-72
97MetUni-101
97Pac-332
97PacLigB-332
97PacSil-332
97Pin-116
97PinArtP-116
97PinCer-37
97PinCerMBlu-37
97PinCerMG-37
97PinCerMR-37
97PinCerR-37
97PinIns-66
97PinInsCE-66
97PinInsDE-66
97PinMusC-116
97PinTotCPB-37
97PinTotCPG-37
97PinTotCPR-37
97ProMag-20
97ProMagML-20
97Sco-103
97ScoDod-14
97ScoDodPl-14
97ScoDodPr-14
97ScoPreS-103
97ScoShoS-103
97ScoShoSAP-103
97SkyE-X-79
97SkyE-XC-79
97SkyE-XEC-79
97SP-94
97SpoIll-113
97SpoIllEE-113
97SpoIllGS-14
97SPSpeF-31
97StaClu-23
97StaCluC-CO7
97StaCluMat-23
97StaCluMOP-23
97Stu-83
97StuPrePG-83
97StuPrePS-83
97Top-321
97TopChr-108
97TopChrR-108
97TopGal-119
97TopGalPPI-119
97Ult-355
97UltGolME-355
97UltPlaME-355
97UppDec-400
Karsay, Steve
90ProAaA-179
90St.CatBJP-3472
91BluJayS-31
91Bow-12
91Cla/Bes-119
91Cla2-T60
91ClaGam-88
91MyrBeaHC-8
91MyrBeaHP-2942
91Sco-675
91UppDec-54
92Bow-158
92ClaFS7-193
92DunBluJC-1
92DunBluJF-1997
92ProFS7-171
92UppDecML-154
93Bow-83
93ClaFS7-78
93ExcFS7-244
93KnoSmoF-1249
94A'sMot-12
94Bow-220
94Bow-377
94ColC-13
94ColChoGS-13
94ColChoSS-13
94Don-197
94ExtBas-152
94ExtBasRS-10
94Fin-438
94FinJum-438
94FinRef-438
94Fla-93
94FlaWavotF-A3
94FleMajLP-19
94FleUpd-76
94FUnPac-8
94LeaGolR-9
94LeaLimR-32
94OPC-11
94Pin-247
94PinArtP-247
94PinMusC-247
94Sco-558
94ScoBoyoS-50
94ScoGolR-558
94ScoRoo-RT74
94ScoRooGR-RT74
94ScoRooSR-SU6
94Sel-179
94SelRooS-RS8
94SP-35
94SPDieC-35
94SPHol-18
94SPHolDC-18
94Spo-163
94SpoRooRS-TR14
94StaClu-631
94StaClu-708
94StaCluFDI-631
94StaCluFDI-708
94StaCluGR-631
94StaCluGR-708
94StaCluMOP-631
94StaCluMOP-708
94Top-131
94TopGol-131
94TopSpa-131
94TriPla-291
94Ult-109
94UppDec-20
94UppDecED-20
95ColCho-133
95ColChoGS-133
95ColChoSE-47
95ColChoSEGS-47
95ColChoSESS-47
95ColChoSS-133
95Don-203
95DonPreP-203
95Fin-21
95FinRef-21
95Fle-248
95Pin-358
95PinArtP-358
95PinMusC-358
95PinUps-US26
95Sco-194
95ScoGolR-194
95ScoPlaTS-194
95Sel-49
95SelArtP-49
95StaClu-345
95StaCluMOP-345
95StaCluSTWS-345
95Stu-184
95SumNthD-110
95Top-569
95Ult-319
95UltGolM-319
95UppDec-31
95UppDecED-31
95UppDecEDG-31
95UppDecSoaD-SD7
96ModA'sB-12
97ColCho-412
97Don-351
97DonPreP-351
97DonPrePGold-351
97Fle-592
97FleTif-592
97Lea-281
97LeaFraM-281
97LeaFraMDC-281
97Sco-375
97ScoHobR-375
97ScoResC-375
97ScoShoS-375
97ScoShoSAP-375
Karvala, Kyle
94MarPhiC-10
94MarPhiF-3286
95BatCliTI-17
Kaseda, Yuki
89SalSpuCLC-130
89SalSpuP-1808
Kashiwabara, Junichi
79TCMJapPB-39
Kasko, Eddie
56RedBurB-11
57Top-363
58CarJayP-7
58Top-8A
58Top-8B
59RedBurBP-8
59RedShiBS-9
59Top-232
60Kah-17
60Lea-9
60Top-61
60TopVen-61
61Kah-22
61Pos-185A
61Pos-185B
61RedJayP-8
61Top-534
61TopStaI-18
62Jel-119
62Kah-22
62Pos-119
62PosCan-119
62RedEnq-18
62RedJayP-7
62SalPlaC-147
62ShiPlaC-147
62Top-193
62TopStaI-117
62TopVen-193
63Jel-128
63Kah-17
63Pos-128
63RedEnq-16
63RedFreBC-11
63RedJayP-5
63Top-498
65AstBigLBPP-9
67AstTeal2-14
70OPC-489
70Top-489
71OPC-578
71Top-31
72OPC-218
72Top-218
73OPC-131
73Top-131A
73Top-131B
78TCM60I-249
81RedSoxBG2S-88
87AstSer1-14
87AstSer1-29
Kasper, Kevin
89EveGiaS-18
90CliGiaB-17
90CliGiaP-2556
91SanJosGC-7
91SanJosGP-19
92ShrCapF-3882
92ShrCapS-586
93ShrCapF-2769

Kaspryzak, Dennis
77JacSunT-11
Kast, Nick
95NewJerCTI-14
96PeoChiB-17
Kastelic, Bruce
82LynMetT-5
Kastelic, Matt
96ButCopKB-16
Kasunick, Joe
83ButCopKT-29
Katalinas, Ed
81TigDetN-127
Katcher, Sy
95BurBeeTI-35
Kath, Merlin
93LetMouF-4147
93LetMouSP-11
Kating, Jim
87BakDodP-11
88SanAntMB-9
89HunStaB-6
90HunStaB-17
Kato, Hideki
92SalSpuC-10
92SalSpuF-3764
Kato, Toshio
79TCMJapPB-38
Kats, Bill
43CenFlo-15
45CenFlo-14
Katt, Ray
54Bow-121
54NewYorJA-28
55Bow-183
55GiaGolS-24
57Top-331
58Hir-57
58Top-284
60Top-468
61UniOil-P9
79TCM50-235
Katz, Bob
78ReaRem-8
Katz, Jason
96DanBraB-12
Katzaroff, Rob (Robert)
90JamExpP-8
91Cla/Bes-20
91HarSenLD-258
91HarSenP-640
91LinDriAA-258
92BinMetF-529
92BinMetS-63
92ClaFS7-26
92ProFS7-262
92SkyAA F-28
93PhoFirF-1528
93ShrCapF-2772
94MidAngOHP-13
95PorSeaDTI-8
Kaub, Keith
88JamExpP-1911
89MiaMirIS-21
89RocExpLC-14
90RocExpP-2704
Kauff, Bennie (Benjamin)
10OrnOvaPP-9
15CraJacE-160
15SpoNewM-92
16BF2FP-78
16ColE13-92
16FleBreD-49
16SpoNewM-94
17HolBreD-56
19W514-100
77SerSta-13
92ConTSN-484
94ConTSN-1269
94ConTSNB-1269
20W516-16
Kauffman, Ewing M.
93UppDecS-5
Kauflin, Dave
94BriTigF-3498
94StaCluDP-63
94StaCluDPFDI-63
Kaufman, Al
11TurRedT-73
Kaufman, Brad
93SpoIndC-10
93SpoIndF-3586
94SprSulC-14
94SprSulF-2032
95MemChiTI-14
96MemChiB-16
Kaufman, Curt
81NasSouTI-6
82ColCliP-24
82ColCliT-5
83ColCliT-11
84AngSmo-14
85Don-524
85EdmTraC-20
85Fle-305
85Top-61
85TopTif-61
92YanWIZ8-96
Kaufman, John
96ButCopKB-17
Kaufman, Ron
82QuaCitCT-9
Kaufmann, Tony (Anthony)
21Exh-88
47TipTop-157
93ConTSN-927
Kaull, Kurt
83EriCarT-25
84SavCarT-5
Kausnicka, Jay
90VisOakCLC-72
Kautz, Scott
88HarSenP-862
Kautzer, Bill
75AppFoxT-8
76AppFoxT-10
Kavanagh, Mike
75ShrCapT-7
77ShrCapT-10
Kavanaugh, Marty
14B18B-18
Kavanaugh, Tim
83EriCarT-19
Kawabata, Kyle
95BatCliTI-18
96BatCliTI-4
Kawabata, Yasuhiro
89VerBeaDS-13
Kawahara, Orin
96MauStiHWB-11
Kawakami, Mark
87HawRai-13
Kawano, Rye
91SalSpuC-11
91SalSpuP-2256
Kay, Belinda
90ColMudS-29
Kaye, Jeff
86ClePhiP-13
87ClePhiP-8
87PhiTas-xx
88ReaPhiP-872
Kayser, Tom
77HolMilT-17
79HolMilT-30
80HolMilT-10
81HolMilT-3
Kaysner, Brent
95SpoIndTI-9
96LanLugB-14
Kazak, Eddie (Edward)
49EurSta-187
50Bow-36
51Bow-85
52Top-165
53Top-194
79DiaGre-164
79TCM50-250
83TopRep5-165
91TopArc1-194
Kazama, Yuhito
95OdgRapTI-11
Kazanski, Ted
54Top-78
55Top-46
55TopDouH-5
57Top-27
58Top-36
59Top-99
59TopVen-99
94TopArc1-78
94TopArc1G-78
Kazmierczak, Bill (William)
87PeoChiP-28
88WinSpiS-7
90ChaKniTI-13
Kazmirski, Bob
96WesMicWB-12
Kea, Rusty
89GeoColC-14
90GeoColC-12
Keagle, Greg
93SpoIndC-11
93SpoIndF-3587
94RanCucQC-17
94RanCucQF-1634
94Top-753
94TopGol-753
94TopSpa-753
95MemChiTI-15
95UppDecML-63
96Bow-276
96SigRooOJ-14
96SigRooOJS-14
96Ult-346
96UltGolM-346
95UppDecMLFS-63
Kealey, Steve
69Top-224
71OPC-43
71Top-43
72OPC-146
72Top-146
73OPC-581
73Top-581
Keane, Johnny
60Top-468
62CarJayP-7
62Top-198
63CarJayP-11
63CarJayP-12
63Top-166
64Top-413
65OPC-131
65Top-131
66Top-296
66TopVen-296
66YanTeal-5
81TCM60I-371
Kearney, Bob (Robert)
78CedRapGT-12
80PhoGiaVNB-15
81TacTigT-5
82TacTigT-27
83Don-539
83TopTra-52T
84Don-462
84Fle-449
84FleUpd-60
84MarMot-4
84Nes792-326
84Top-326
84TopSti-381
84TopTif-326
84TopTra-61T
84TopTraT-61T
85Don-362
85Fle-491
85MarMot-13
85OPC-386
85Top-679
85TopSti-335
85TopTif-679
86Don-74
86Fle-466
86MarMot-23
86OPC-13
86Top-13
86TopTif-13
87Don-445
87Fle-587
87FleGlo-587
87MarMot-12
87OPC-73
87Top-498
87TopTif-498
92TexLon-27
Kearney, Chad
94MarPhiF-3308
95MarPhiTI-11
Kearns, John
83WisRapTF-10
Kearse, Edward
46RemBre-14
47RemBre-7
47SmiClo-14
Keas, Ed
87OldJudN-273
Keathley, Davan
96MedHatBJTI-14
Keathley, Don
91ModA'sP-3090
Keathley, Robin
83TriTriT-8
85BurRanT-22
Keating, Dave
89NiaFalRP-5a
90BriTigS-13
93SarWhiSC-16
93SarWhiSF-1366
94PriWilCC-12
94PriWilCF-1916
Keating, Dennis
79AppFoxT-2
80AppFoxT-24
Keating, Mike
90SavCarP-2074
Keating, Ray H.
14B18B-24
14CraJacE-95
14FatPlaT-21
15CraJacE-95
16FleBreD-50
Keatley, Greg
81OmaRoyT-14
82OmaRoyT-11
Keaveney, Jeff
96LowSpiB-12
Kebedgy, Nik
43ParSpo-86
Keck, Brian
96PorRocB-17
Keckler, Mike
85Ft.MyeRT-23
Keedy, Pat
81HolMilT-16
82HolMilT-16
84EdmTraC-118
85EdmTraC-1
86EdmTraP-16
87HawIslP-27
88Top-486
88TopTif-486
88TucTorC-22
88TucTorJP-14
88TucTorP-175
89IndTeal-16
Keefe, Bob
11SpoLifCW-196
Keefe, Dave
93ConTSN-885
Keefe, George
87OldJudN-276
Keefe, Jamie (Jim)
92ClaDraP-69
92FroRowDP-42
93ClaGolF-199
94AugGreC-8
96MemChiB-17
Keefe, Kevin
79AlbDukT-8
80AlbDukT-17
81AlbDukT-11
Keefe, Tim (Timothy)
76ShaPiz-99
77BobParHoF-29
80PerHaloFP-99
80SSPHOF-99
86OldJudN-9
87AllandGN-7
87BucN28-70A
87BucN28-70B
87OldJudN-274
87OldJudN-275
88AugBecN-14
88GandBCGCE-22
88GooN16-7
88SpoTimM-14
88WG1CarG-41
89EdgR.WG-7
90HOFStiB-4
90KalBatN-27
94OriofB-57
Keefer, Paul
89WelPirP-15
Keegan, Bob (Robert)
53Top-196
54Top-100
55Top-10
55TopDouH-51
56Top-54
57Top-99
58Top-200
59Top-86
59TopVen-86
60Top-291
77Top-436
91TopArc1-196
94TopArc1-100
94TopArc1G-100
Keegan, Ed
61Top-248
62Top-249
Keehn, Mike
83TriTriT-18
Keel, David
93SouOreAC-11
93SouOreAF-4078
94WesMicWC-11
94WesMicWF-2310
Keeler, Devo (Jay)
83WatIndF-9
Keeler, Willie
03BreE10-79
04FanCraAL-31
08RosComP-49
09AmeCarE-62
09AmeCarE-63
09AmeCarE-64
09BriE97-15
09ColChiE-150
09RamT20-64
09T206-183
09T206-184
10W555-39
11SpoLifCW-197
11TurRedT-101
12ColRedB-150
12ColTinT-150
36PC7AlbHoF-23
40PlaBal-237
48ExhHoF-19
50CalHOFW-44
63BazA-31
63HalofFB-25
72FleFamF-40
72LauGreF-31
76ShaPiz-19
80PacLeg-99
80PerHaloFP-23
80SSPHOF-23
84GalHaloFRL-19
89DodSmoG-12
89HOFStiB-51
90BasWit-74
90DodTar-399
90PerGreM-25
92YanWIZH-19
94ConTSN-1018
94ConTSNB-1018
94OriofB-81
96PitPosH-7
Keeline, Jason
91PulBraC-8
91PulBraP-4014
92MacBraC-19
92MacBraF-275
93MacBraC-12
93MacBraF-1407
94DurBulC-10
94DurBulF-333
94DurBulTI-10
Keely, Bob (Robert William)
54BraJohC-35
54Top-176
55BraJohC-35
56BraBilaBP-12
94TopArc1-176
94TopArc1G-176
Keen, Vic
93ConTSN-976
Keenan, Brad
92BenMusSP-3
92BilMusF-3364
93PriRedC-15
93PriRedF-4174
93WesVirWC-11
93WesVirWF-2872
94ChaWheC-16
94ChaWheF-2699
Keenan, Chris
93BriTigC-13
93BriTigF-3663
Keenan, James
23WilChoV-77
87OldJudN-277
Keenan, Kerry
77AshTouT-12

79WauTimT-4
Keenan, Kevin
80ElmPioRST-10
Keene, Andre
92CliGiaC-10
92CliGiaF-3604
92MidLeaATI-23
92UppDecML-123
93ExcFS7-119
94SanJosGC-12
94SanJosGF-2824
Keener, Jeff
82ArkTraT-4
83LouRedR-10
84LouRedR-22
85LouRedR-8
Keenum, Larry
76BatRouCT-12
Keeter, Lonnie
90WicWraRD-26
91HigDesMP-2413
Keeton, Buster (Rickey)
79VanCanT-10
82Don-618
82Fle-146
82Top-268
82TucTorT-13
83TucTorT-3
84OmaRoyT-6
85DomLeaS-203
85OmaRoyT-28
91AugPirC-27
91AugPirP-824
92SalBucC-27
92SalBucF-80
94BreMilB-44
96SpoIndB-2
Keeton, Garry
83AppFoxF-26
Kehn, Chet
90DodTar-998
Kehoe, John
96HagSunB-11
Kehrli, Ed
93GleFalRC-17
93GleFalRF-3998
Keifer, Greg
94EveGiaC-15
94EveGiaF-3667
Keighley, Chris
95OdgRapTI-12
Keighley, Steve
91RocExpC-15
91RocExpP-2051
92WesPalBEC-6
92WesPalBEF-2092
Keim, Chris
89BilMusP-2062
90BilMusP-3216
Keister, Bill
11SpoLifCW-198
Keister, Tripp
92PitMetC-3
92PitMetF-3306
93St.LucMC-14
94St.LucMC-15
94St.LucMF-1207
95StLucMTI-18
Keitges, Jeff
89WauTimGS-24
90SanBerSB-6
90SanBerSCLC-110
90SanBerSP-2639
91SanBerSC-16
91SanBerSP-1993
Keith, James
92ClaDraP-69
Keith, Jeff
94EveGiaC-16
94EveGiaF-3649
95BurBeeTI-7
96BurBeeTI-7
Kekich, Mike
65Top-561
69Top-262
70OPC-536
70Top-536
71MLBOffS-490
71OPC-703
71Top-703
72OPC-138
72Top-138
73OPC-371
73SyrChiTI-11
73Top-371
74OPC-199
74Top-199
76OPC-582
76Top-582
76VenLeaS-131
78SanJosMMC-24
89PacSenL-73
89T/MSenL-57
90DodTar-400
90EliSenL-84
92YanWIZ6-64
92YanWIZ7-88
93RanKee-214
Kelbe, Frank
89WatIndS-27
Keliher, Paul
91PulBraC-2
Keliipuleole, Carl
88KinIndS-13
89CanIndB-18
89CanIndP-1300
89CanIndS-9
90Bes-137
90CanIndB-21
90CanIndP-1290
90CanIndS-8
90CMC-835
90IndTeal-22
91HarSenP-620
Keling, Korey
88OklSoo-14
89OklSoo-18
90OklSoo-23
91BoiHawC-25
91BoiHawP-3872
92CalLeaACL-31
92PalSprAC-10
92PalSprAF-834
92ProFS7-37
93PalSprAC-12
93PalSprAF-64
94MidAngF-2434
94MidAngOHP-14
95AusFut-15
95MidAngOHP-20
95MidAngTI-18
96LakElsSB-8
96MidAngB-20
96MidAngOHP-15
Kelipuleole, Carl
87BriYouC-4
Kell, George
47Exh-113
47TipTop-34
49Bow-26
49Lea-120
50Bow-8
50RoyDes-3
51Bow-46
51FisBakL-13
51R42SmaS-57
51TopCurA-5
52BerRos-28
52Bow-75
52RedMan-AL13
52RoyPre-6
52StaCalL-72A
52StaCalS-86A
52TipTop-19
52Top-246
52Whe-15A
52Whe-15B
53BowC-61
53RedMan-AL8
53RedSoxTI-14
53Top-138
54Bow-50
54RedHeaF-12
54RedMan-AL4A
54RedMan-AL4B
55Bow-213
56Top-195
57Top-230
58Top-40
76TayBow4-31
77GalGloG-9
79TCM50-86
80MarExh-13
80PacLeg-118
80PerHaloFP-182
80SSPHOF-183
80TigGreT-1
81TigDetN-10
82DiaCla-15
82GSGalAG-14
83TigAlKS-26
83TigAlKS-30
83TigAlKS-39
83TigAlKS-57
83TigAlKS-58
83TopRep5-246
84TCMPla1-5
86SpoDecG-24
86TigSpoD-10
88PacLegI-69
89HOFStiB-24
89PerCelP-22
90PacLeg-86
90PerGreM-59
91OriCro-233
91SweBasG-47
91TopArc1-138
92ActPacA-11
92ActPacA2-11G
92BazQua5A-11
93ActPacAC-11
93TedWil-39
93UppDecAH-79
93UppDecS-2
94UppDecAH-96
94UppDecAH1-96
Kell, Rob
93EriSaiC-12
93EriSaiF-3109
94ChaRivC-10
94ChaRivF-2667
95ChaRivUTIS-33
Kell, Skeeter (Everett)
52Bow-242
Kollohor, Frank
47SigOil-9
49BowPCL-27
49W72HolS-9
50W720HolS-15
53MotCoo-37
Kelleher, Hal
93ConTSN-968
Kelleher, John
21Nei-87
22E120-161
90DodTar-401
Kelleher, Mick
75TulOil7-7
76SSP-605
76VenLeaS-88
77Top-657
78SSP270-269
78Top-564
79Top-53
80Top-323
81Don-513
81Top-429
81TopTra-779
82Don-601
82Top-184
82TopTra-53T
83Top-79
93StoPorC-28
93StoPorF-761
Kellelmark, Joe
87VerBeaDP-19
Keller, Buzz (Carlton)
77ArkTraT-2A
77ArkTraT-2B
Keller, Charlie
39ExhSal-31A
39ExhSal-31B
39PlaBal-88
40PlaBal-9
41DouPlaR-83
41PlaBal-21
43YanSta-16
47Exh-114
47HomBon-25
47TipTop-52
48BluTin-48
48YanTeal-15
49Bow-209
50AmeNut&CCP-9
50Bow-211
51Bow-177
75YanDyn1T-27
76TayBow4-34
77TCMTheWY-55
80MarExh-12
80RicBraT-12
83YanASFY-22
84OCoandSI-171
84TCMPla1-8
89PacLegI-194
90SweBasG-22
91SweBasG-48
92YanWIZA-36
93TedWil-64
Keller, Clyde
87PanAmTURB-21
90Bes-82
90MidLeaASGS-37
90SprCarB-18
91MidLeaAP-MWL14
91SprCarC-18
91SprCarP-739
92ProFS7-318
92St.LucMCB-11
87PanAmTUBI-4
Keller, Dave (David)
86TamTarP-8
88BilMusP-1802
89BilMusP-2048
90BurIndP-3026
91BurIndP-3320
91CanIndLD-100
91CanIndP-997
91LinDriAA-100
92KinIndC-26
92KinIndF-2491
93CarLeaAGF-31
93KinIndC-27
93KinIndF-2263
93KinIndTI-12
94KinIndC-23
94KinIndF-2660
96SouBenSHS-1
Keller, Edward
94ConTSN-1113
Keller, Harold
47SenGunBP-3
Keller, Jeremy
96BilMusTI-16
Keller, Jerry
79RicBraT-19
81RicBraT-3
82RicBraT-10
83PorBeaT-7
84SyrChiT-10
85SyrChiT-18
90RicBra2ATI-13
Keller, Phil
74AlbDukTI-70
74AlbDukTI-8
Keller, Ron
77FriOneYW-51
Keller, Steve
89SpaPhiP-1055
89SpaPhiS-10
Kellert, Frank
55DodGolS-20
56Top-291
90DodTar-402
91OriCro-234
95TopArcBD-114
Kelley, Anthony
86ColAstP-16
86SouLeaAJ-22
87TucTorP-21
88TucTorC-2
88TucTorJP-15
88TucTorP-186
89TucTorC-3
89TucTorJP-10
89TucTorP-186
90FloStaLAS-9
90MiaMirIS-13
90MiaMirIS-11
90RocRedWGC-30
90StaFS7-73
Kelley, Brad
94PriRedC-28
94PriRedF-3280
87PanAmTUBI-NNO
Kelley, Chris
92ButCopKSP-23
93ButCopKSP-12
Kelley, Dean Alan
87OneYanP-29
88CarLeaAS-10
88PriWilYS-13
89Ft.LauYS-11
90WicWraRD-12
91LasVegSLD-286
91LasVegSP-242
91LinDriAAA-286
Kelley, Erskine
92WelPirC-12
92WelPirF-1338
93WelPirC-10
93WelPirF-3373
94AugGreC-9
94AugGreF-3020
96LynHilB-13
Kelley, Harry
37ExhFou-14
37OPCBatUV-121
38ExhFou-14
93ConTSN-721
Kelley, Jack
12ImpTobC-15
Kelley, Jason
94HunCubF-3547
94SigRooDP-76
94SigRooDPS-76
94StaCluDP-70
94StaCluDPFDI-70
95Bow-7
94HunCubC-17
Kelley, Joe
03BreE10-80
06FanCraNL-23
09BriE97-16
09T206-433
10CouT21-158
10CouT21-159
10CouT21-295
10RedCroT-125
10RedCroT-208
11SpoLifCW-199
12ImpTobC-27
14B18B-78A
14B18B-78B
76ShaPiz-123
80PerHaloFP-123
80SSPHOF-123
89DodSmoG-13
89HOFStiB-35
90DodTar-403
94OriofB-96
Kelley, M.
20W516-26
Kelley, Mike
80QuaCitCT-21
Kelley, Rich
91NiaFalRC-18
91NiaFalRP-3628
92FayGenF-2164
93FloStaLAF-18
93LakTigF-1304
94LakTigC-11
94LakTigF-3032
Kelley, Richard
64Top-476
66OPC-84
66Top-84
66TopVen-84
67CokCapB-16
67OPC-138
67Top-138
67Top-214
68CokCapB-16
68Top-203
68TopVen-203
69MLBOffS-193
69Top-359
69TopTeaP-12
70MLBOffS-114
70OPC-474
70Top-474
72MilBra-178
72OPC-412
72Top-412
Kelley, Rodd
94BoiHawC-16
94BoiHawF-3363
Kelley, Steve
75QuaCitAT-26
Kelley, Thomas
64Top-552
66OPC-44
66Top-44
66TopVen-44
71OPC-463
71Top-463
72OPC-97
72Top-97
Kelliher, Paul
91IdaFalBP-4332

91PulBraP-4008
Kellman, Howard
85IndIndTI-27
88IndIndP-525
89IndIndP-1216
Kellner, Alex
47Exh-115
49Bow-222
49PhiBul-28
50Bow-14
51Bow-57
51FisBakL-14
52Bow-226
52Top-201
53BowC-107
53ExhCan-64
54Bow-51
55A'sRodM-20
55Bow-53
56Top-176
57Top-280
58Top-3
59Top-101
59TopVen-101
76A'sRodMC-13
79TCM50-55
80MarExh-14
83TopRep5-201
Kellner, Frank
90OscAstS-13
91OscAstC-19
91OscAstP-693
92JacGenF-4005
92JacGenS-336
93JacGenF-2114
94TucTorF-768
96TusTorB-14
Kellogg, Geoff
90HelBreSP-17
91BelBreC-4
91BelBreP-2099
92HigDesMC-18
93WicWraF-2976
Kelly, Bill
47SigOil-27
49W725AngTI-13
79NaSouTI-13
80IndIndTI-23
81IndIndTI-22
82OmaRoyT-7
Kelly, Brian
75CliPilT-4
Kelly, Bryan
83EvaTriT-4
85NasSouTI-7
86NasSouTI-14
87TolMudHP-29
Kelly, Charles H.
87OldJudN-281
Kelly, Christopher
92IndIndF-NNO
Kelly, Eliqio
78NewWayCT-23
Kelly, Gene
59RedBurBP-9
Kelly, George L.
20NatCarE-53
21E121So1-50
21E121So8-46
21Exh-89
21KoBreWSI-14
21Nei-119
22AmeCarE-35
22E120-187
22W572-54
22W575-67
22WilPatV-15
23W501-72
23W503-6
23W515-32
23WilChoV-78
27AmeCarE-60
27YorCarE-20
28StaPlaCE-42
28W502-20
28Yue-20
29ExhFou-7
31W517-11
40PlaBal-142
49RemBre-12
50RemBre-14
69SCFOldT-23
76RowExh-8
76ShaPiz-138
77GalGloG-119
80PacLeg-62
80PerHaloFP-138
80SSPHOF-138
83DiaClaS2-88
87ConSer2-45
89DodSmoG-14
89HOFStiB-8
90DodTar-404
91ConTSN-60
92ConTSN-561
93ConTSN-908
Kelly, Hal
79TulDriT-22
Kelly, Jeff
96AugGreB-16
Kelly, Jim
85RedWinA-17
86RedWinA-18
88KnoBluJB-5
89DunBluJS-9
90St.LucMS-13
93StaCluMO-48
Kelly, Joe (Joseph)
88CapCodPPaLP-173
90YakBeaTI-17
Kelly, John
90JohCitCS-16
91Cla/Bes-166
91SavCarC-7
91SavCarP-1648
91SouAtlLAGP-SAL42
92ClaFS7-279
92ProFS7-319
92St.PetCC-20
92St.PetCF-2024
93ArkTraF-2810
93ExcFS7-100
93ExcLeaLF-11
94ArkTraF-3085
94ExcFS7-268
94PitMetC-12
94PitMetF-3518
95JacSunTI-17
96HonShaHWB-22
96StLucMTI-13
Kelly, John O.
87OldJudN-279
Kelly, Kevin
89BurBraP-1623
89BurBraS-12
90BurBraB-21
90BurBraP-2345
90BurBraS-15
Kelly, King (Michael Joseph)
36PC7AlbHoF-36
50CalHOFW-45
75FlePio-8
76ShaPiz-36
77BobParHoF-30
80PerHaloFP-36
80SSPHOF-36
84GalHaloFRL-36
87AllandGN-8
87BucN28-9A
87BucN28-9B
87FouBasHN-6
87OldJudN-278
88AugBecN-15
88GandBCGCE-23
88GooN16-8
88SpoTimM-15
88WG1CarG-5
89EdgR.WG-9
89N526N7C-8
90PerGreM-61
94OriofB-48
94UppDecAH-23
94UppDecAH-102
94UppDecAH1-23
94UppDecAH1-102
94UppDecTAE-9
94UppDecTAELD-LD3
Kelly, Leonard
87BurExpP-1067
Kelly, Mike
87ElmPio(C-15
88WinHavRSS-10
89LynRedSS-11
90Bes-191
90EasLeaAP-EL39
90NewBriRSB-11
90NewBriRSP-1330
90NewBriRSS-6
Kelly, Mike (Michael Raymond)
88CapCodPPaLP-10
89AlaGol-6
91Cla/Bes-399
91ClaDraP-2
91ClaDraPP-2
91ClaGolB-BC16
91DurBulC-6
91DurBulUP-1
91TopGolS-2
92ClaBluBF-BC9
92ClaDraP-87
92ClaDraPFB-BC19
92ClaFS7-116
92ClaRedB-BC9
92GreBraF-1164
92GreBraS-235
92ProFS7-185
92SkyAA F-100
92UppDec-794
92UppDecCPH-CP2
92UppDecML-28
92UppDecML-275
92UppDecMLTPHF-TP4
93ClaFisN-6
93ClaFS7-10
93ClaFS7-AU5
93ClaGolF-18
93ClaGolLF-4
93ClaGolP-1
93ExcFS7-3
93RicBraBB-8
93RicBraF-197
93RicBraP-16
93RicBraRC-14
93RicBraRC-16
93UppDec-756
93UppDecGold-756
94Bow-261
94BowBes-B54
94BowBesR-B54
94BraLykP-14
94BraLykS-15
94BraUSPC-9D
94ClaGolF-144
94ColC-663
94ColChoGS-663
94ColChoSS-663
94ExcFS7-156
94ExtBas-203
94Fin-329
94FinRef-329
94Fla-127
94FleMajLP-20
94FleUpd-101
94LeaLimR-60
94Pin-534
94PinArtP-534
94PinMusC-534
94RicBraF-2860
94ScoRoo-RT159
94ScoRooGR-RT159
94Sel-386
94SigRoo-34
94SigRooHP-S5
94SigRooS-34
94SpoRoo-101
94SpoRooAP-101
94TopTra-35T
94Ult-443
94UppDec-338
94UppDecED-338
94UppDecML-15
95ColCho-157
95ColChoGS-157
95ColChoSS-157
95Don-299
95DonPreP-299
95Fle-306
95LeaGolR-13
95Pac-6
95Pin-440
95PinArtP-440
95PinMusC-440
95PinUps-US21
95RicBraRC-6
95Sco-283
95ScoAi-AM16
95ScoGolR-283
95ScoPlaTS-283
95Sel-118
95SelArtP-118
95Spo-163
95SpoArtP-163
95StaClu-439
95StaCluMOP-439
95StaCluSTWS-439
95Top-61
95TopCyb-43
95Ult-348
95UltGolM-348
95UppDec-47
95UppDecED-47
95UppDecEDG-47
96Don-298
96DonPreP-298
96Fla-233
96Fle-295
96FleTif-295
96FleUpd-U122
96FleUpdTC-U122
96IndIndB-12
96Pin-363
96PinAfi-115
96PinAfiAP-115
96PinFoil-363
96Sco-180
96Sel-139
96SelArtP-139
96SelCer-60
96SelCerAP-60
96SelCerCB-60
96SelCerCR-60
96SelCerMB-60
96SelCerMG-60
96SelCerMR-60
96Sum-68
96SumAbo&B-68
96SumArtP-68
96SumFoi-68
96Ult-462
96UltGolM-462
97PacPriGotD-GD126
Kelly, Pat
95RicBraRC-7
Kelly, Pat (Dale Patrick)
75QuaCitAT-17
78SyrChiT-12
79SyrChiTI-6
79Top-714
80OPC-329
80SyrChiT-15
80SyrChiTI-12
80Top-674
83GleFalWST-11
86ChaRaiP-11
88WicPilRD-40
89WicChaR-15
89WicStaR-15
89WicUpdR-2
89WicWraR-6
90CMC-525
90CMC-787
90LasVegSC-22
90LasVegSP-136
90ProAAAF-25
90SumBraB-8
90SumBraP-2440
91DurBulP-1555
91RocExpC-27
91RocExpP-2062
92GreBraF-1160
92GreBraS-236
92IndIndF-1875
92IndIndS-199
93ChaLooF-2375
93DurBulC-10
93DurBulF-492
93DurBulTI-11
94ChaLooF-1373
94RicBraF-2852
95HarSenTI-30
96HarSenB-1
Kelly, Pat (Harold Patrick)
69RoySol-10
69RoyTeal-7
69Top-619
69TopTeaP-7
70MLBOffS-222
70OPC-57
70RoyTeal-16
70Top-57
71OPC-413
71Top-413
72MilBra-179
72OPC-326
72Top-326
72WhiSox-6
72WhiSoxC-3
72WhiSoxTI1-6
73OPC-261
73Top-261
74Kel-47
74OPC-46
74Top-46
74TopSta-156
75OPC-82
75Top-82
76OPC-212
76SSP-152
76Top-212
77Top-469
78Top-616
79Top-188
80Top-543
81Don-600
82Fle-372
82Top-417
89PacSenL-134
91OriCro-235
91PacSenL-56
Kelly, Pat F.
88OneYanP-2043
89PriWilCS-10
89Sta-89
89TexLeaAGS-1
90AlbYanB-16
90AlbYanP-1041
90AlbYanS-8
90EasLeaAP-EL21
90ProAaA-32
90TopMag-63
91AlbYanCB-1
91Bow-155
91Cla3-T44
91ColCliLD-110
91ColCliP-10
91ColCliP-602
91DonRoo-1
91FleUpd-46
91LeaGolR-BC17
91LinDriAAA-110
91ScoRoo-107T
91StaClu-381
91TopTra-67T
91TopTraT-67T
91Ult-381
91UltUpd-41
91UppDec-76
92Bow-535
92Cla1-T48
92Don-370
92Fle-233
92Lea-104
92OPC-612
92OPCPre-71
92PanSti-137
92Pin-54
92PinTea2-7
92ProFS7-108
92Sco-185
92Sco100RS-5
92StaClu-89
92Stu-213
92Top-612
92TopDeb91-98
92TopGol-612
92TopGolW-612
92TopMic-612
92TriPla-46
92TriPla-193
92Ult-102
92UppDec-435
92UppDecS-1
93Bow-187
93Don-503
93Fla-246
93Fle-280
93Lea-447
93OPC-24
93PacSpa-206
93PanSti-150
93Pin-134
93Sco-370
93Sel-255
93StaClu-155
93StaCluFDI-155
93StaCluMOP-155
93StaCluY-16
93Stu-111

93Top-196
93TopGol-196
93TopInaM-196
93TopMic-196
93Ult-242
93UppDec-215
93UppDecGold-215
94Bow-549
94ColC-483
94ColChoGS-483
94ColChoSS-483
94Don-483
94ExtBas-131
94Fin-63
94FinRef-63
94Fla-321
94Fle-235
94Lea-51
94OPC-156
94Pac-426
94PanSti-101
94Pin-197
94PinArtP-197
94PinMusC-197
94Sco-397
94ScoGolR-397
94Sel-142
94StaClu-52
94StaCluFDI-52
94StaCluGR-52
94StaCluMOP-52
94StaCluT-196
94StaCluTFDI-196
94Stu-213
94Top-88
94TopGol-88
94TopSpa-88
94TriPla-274
94Ult-95
94UppDec-264
94UppDecED-264
95ColCho-512
95ColChoGS-512
95ColChoSS-512
95Don-93
95DonPreP-93
95Fla-285
95Fle-73
95Lea-242
95Pin-9
95PinArtP-9
95PinMusC-9
95Sco-369
95ScoGolR-369
95ScoPlaTS-369
95StaClu-394
95StaCluMOP-394
95StaCluSTWS-394
95StaCluVR-207
95TamYanYI-14
95Top-468
95TopCyb-262
95Ult-82
95UltGolM-82
95UppDec-442
95UppDecED-442
95UppDecEDG-442
96ColCho-631
96ColChoGS-631
96ColChoSS-631
96DonPreP-71
96Fle-186
96FleTif-186
96MLBPin-18
96Sco-93
96StaClu-363
96StaCluMOP-363
95StaCluVRMC-207
96Ult-387
96UltGolM-387
96UppDec-404
97PacPriGotD-GD74
97Sco-440
97ScoHobR-440
97ScoResC-440
97ScoShoS-440
97ScoShoSAP-440

Kelly, Rafael
75QuaCitAT-13
76QuaCitAT-17

Kelly, Rich
92FayGenC-14
93ClaGolF-52
93SouAtlLAPI-18

Kelly, Robert Edward
49W725AngTI-14
52Top-348
58RedEnq-21
83TopRep5-348
97Sco-454
97ScoHobR-454
97ScoResC-454
97ScoShoS-454
97ScoShoSAP-454

Kelly, Roberto
83GreHorT-19
84GreHorT-4
86AlbYanT-2
87ColCliP-14
87ColCliT-22
87IntLeaAT-4
88Don-635
88DonReaBY-635
88DonRoo-16
88Fle-212
88FleGlo-212
88Sco-634
88ScoGlo-634
88TopTra-57T
88TopTraT-57T
89Bow-183
89BowTif-183
89ClaTraP-167
89Don-433
89DonBasB-273
89Fle-256
89FleGlo-256
89PanSti-395
89Sco-487
89ScoHot1R-90
89ScoYouS2-25
89Top-691
89TopBig-152
89TopTif-691
89ToyRoo-18
89UppDec-590
89YanScoNW-18
90AlbDecGB-3
90Bow-444
90BowTif-444
90ClaUpd-T27
90Don-192
90DonBesA-94
90Fle-446
90FleCan-446
90Lea-17
90OPC-109
90PanSti-119
90PubSti-538
90PubSti-597
90Sco-100
90Sco100S-57
90Spo-184
90Top-109
90TopBig-247
90TopSti-312
90TopTif-109
90TopTVY-31
90UppDec-193
90VenSti-264
90VenSti-265
90YanScoNW-6
91Bow-166
91ClaGam-28
91Don-400
91Don-538
91Fle-668
91Lea-38
91OPC-11
91PanCanT1-31
91PanCanT1-47
91PanFreS-328
91PanSti-268
91RedFolS-57
91Sco-119
91Sco100S-96
91ScoPro-119
91Sev3DCN-9
91SevCoi-NE9
91StaClu-319
91Stu-94
91Top-11
91TopCraJ2-16
91TopDesS-11
91TopMic-11
91TopTif-11
91Ult-235
91UppDec-49
91UppDec-372
92Bow-12
92Cla2-T81
92ClaGam-51
92Don-73
92DonMcD-4
92Fle-234
92Hig5-87
92Lea-156
92OPC-266
92OPCPre-83
92PanSti-140
92Pin-114
92Sco-324
92Sco100S-96
92ScoImpP-80
92StaClu-393
92Stu-214
92Top-266
92TopGol-266
92TopGolW-266
92TopKid-88
92TopMic-266
92TriPla-72
92Ult-103
92UltAllS-7
92UppDec-577
92YanWIZ8-97
93Bow-610
93ClaGam-47
93DiaMar-60
93Don-313
93DonDiaK-DK12
93Fin-120
93FinRef-120
93Fla-26
93Fle-393
93FleFinE-15
93FunPac-169
93Lea-289
93OPC-79
93OPCPre-109
93PacJugC-29
93PacSpa-401
93PanSti-295
93Pin-520
93RedKah-11
93Sco-438
93Sel-64
93SelRoo-20T
93SP-209
93StaClu-632
93StaCluFDI-632
93StaCluM-162
93StaCluMOP-632
93Stu-23
93Top-60
93TopGol-60
93TopInaM-60
93TopMic-60
93TopTra-105T
93Ult-329
93UppDec-47
93UppDec-473
93UppDec-655
93UppDecGold-47
93UppDecGold-473
93UppDecGold-655
94Bow-626
94BraLykP-15
94ColC-484
94ColChoGS-484
94ColChoSS-484
94Don-344
94DonSpeE-344
94ExtBas-204
94Fin-163
94FinPre-163P
94FinRef-163
94Fla-353
94Fle-412
94FleUpd-102
94Lea-40
94LeaL-84
94OPC-139
94Pac-149
94PanSti-162
94Pin-286
94PinArtP-286
94PinMusC-286
94Sco-334
94ScoGolR-334
94ScoRoo-RT65
94ScoRooCP-CP3
94ScoRooGR-RT65
94Sel-312
94SP-51
94SPDieC-51
94SpoRoo-5
94SpoRooAP-5
94StaClu-372
94StaCluFDI-372
94StaCluGR-372
94StaCluMOP-372
94Stu-36
94Top-457
94TopGol-457
94TopSpa-457
94TopTra-103T
94TriPla-213
94Ult-171
94UppDec-387
94UppDecED-387
95Baz-52
95Bow-300
95ColCho-158
95ColCho-546T
95ColChoGS-158
95ColChoSE-61
95ColChoSEGS-61
95ColChoSESS-61
95ColChoSS-158
95DodMot-6
95Don-301
95DonPreP-301
95DonTopotO-266
95Emb-46
95EmbGolI-46
95Fin-33
95Fin-297
95FinRef-33
95FinRef-297
95Fla-102
95Fle-307
95FleUpd-107
95Lea-377
95LeaLim-149
95Pac-7
95Pin-254
95PinArtP-254
95PinMusC-254
95PinUps-US24
95Sco-59
95ScoGolR-59
95ScoHaloG-HG45
95ScoPlaTS-59
95Sel-230
95SelArtP-230
95Spo-113
95SpoArtP-113
95StaClu-219
95StaClu-414
95StaCluFDI-219
95StaCluMOP-219
95StaCluMOP-414
95StaCluSTWS-219
95StaCluSTWS-414
95StaCluVR-212
95Stu-57
95Top-532
95TopCyb-317
95TopTra-139T
95Ult-127
95UltGolM-127
95UppDec-43
95UppDec-326
95UppDec-461T
95UppDecED-43
95UppDecED-326
95UppDecEDG-43
95UppDecEDG-326
95UppDecSE-139
95UppDecSEG-139
96Cir-56
96CirRav-56
96ColCho-184
96ColCho-336
96ColCho-604
96ColChoGS-184
96ColChoGS-336
96ColChoGS-604
96ColChoSS-184
96ColChoSS-336
96ColChoSS-604
96Don-543
96DonPreP-543
96EmoXL-81
96Fla-115
96Fle-439
96FleTif-439
96FleUpd-U55
96FleUpdTC-U55
96LeaSigA-125
96LeaSigAG-125
96LeaSigAS-125
96Pac-114
96PacHom-HP15
96Sco-457
95StaCluVRMC-212
96Ult-375
96UltGolM-375
96UppDec-501U
97Cir-99
97CirRav-99
97ColCho-377
97Fle-146
97FleTif-146
97Lea-298
97LeaFraM-298
97LeaFraMDC-298
97Pac-138
97PacLatotML-12
97PacLigB-138
97PacPri-45
97PacPriLB-45
97PacPriP-45
97PacSil-138

Kelly, Tim
86BakDodP-17
87PalSprP-18
88MidAngGS-3

Kelly, Tom
73TacTwiC-12
74TacTwiC-25
75TacTwiK-19
77TacTwiDQ-10
82OrlTwi8SCT-12
82OrlTwiT-13
83TwiTeal-26
83TwiTeal-34
84MinTwiP-19
84TwiTeal-27
85TwiTeal-30
86TwiTeal-28
87Top-618
87TopTif-618
88Top-194
88TopTif-194
88TwiTeal-7
89DonAll-10
89DonPop-10
89Top-14
89TopGloA-1
89TopTif-14
90OPC-429
90Top-429
90TopTif-429
91OPC-201
91Top-201
91TopDesS-201
91TopMic-201
91TopTif-201
92OPC-459
92Top-459
92TopGol-459
92TopGolW-459
92TopMic-459
93Top-509
93TopGol-509
93TopInaM-509
93TopMic-509

Kelly, Van
71RicBraTI-9

Kelly, William J.
09SpoNewSM-70
12ColRedB-151A
12ColRedB-151B
12T207-89

Kelso, Bill
65OPC-194
65Top-194
67Top-367
68Top-511
92AubAstC-29
92AubAstF-1371

Kelso, Jeff
88BenBucL-9
89BenBucL-22
90PalSprACLC-214
90PalSprAP-2590

Keltner, Ken
36OveCanR-28

36R31Pre-G11
39ExhSal-32
39GouPreR303A-28
39GouPreR303B-16
39WorWidGTP-28
41DouPlaR-79
46SpoExcW-1-11
47Exh-116
47HomBon-26
47IndTeal-15
47IndVanPP-14
48IndTeal-17
49Bow-125
49IndTeal-15
49IndVisEl-8
49Lea-45
50AmeNut&CCP-10
50Bow-186
53IndPenCBP-17
75SheGrePG-19
76GrePlaG-19
76TayBow4-35
79DiaGre-288
83TCMPla1942-11
89PacLegl-143
89SweBasG-87
91UppDecS-4
94ConTSN-1043
94ConTSNB-1043
Kemmerer, Russ
55Bow-222
55DonWin-28
55Top-18
55TopDouH-3
58Top-137
59SenTealW-9
59Top-191
59TopVen-191
60Top-362
61Top-56
61TopStal-121
62Top-576
62WhiSoxJP-4
63Top-338
Kemmler, Rudolph
87OldJudN-283A
87OldJudN-283B
Kemnitz, Brent
85AncGlaPTI-17
86AncGlaPTI-17
87AncGlaP-17
90WicStaSGD-41
Kemp, Bill
90GeoColC-13
Kemp, Hugh
84CedRapRT-7
87NasSouTI-11
88NasSouC-7
88NasSouP-479
88NasSouTI-15
88TriAAAP-27
89NasSouC-5
89NasSouP-1294
89NasSouTI-10
90BufBisC-5
90BufBisP-368
90BufBisTI-10
90CMC-5
90ProAAAF-483
Kemp, Joe
88SanBerSB-21
88SanBerSCLC-35
89ModA'sCLC-280
Kemp, Rick
75SpoIndC-15
Kemp, Rod
79LodDodT-1
Kemp, Steve
77Top-492
78Hos-55
78OPC-167
78TigBurK-18
78Top-21
79Hos-15
79OPC-97
79Top-196
80Kel-33
80OPC-166
80Top-315
80TopSup-29
81AllGamPI-54
81CokTeaS-52
81Don-249
81Dra-27
81Fle-459
81FleStiC-7
81MSAMinD-19
81OPC-152
81Squ-27
81TigDetN-86
81Top-593
81TopScr-11
81TopSti-74
82Don-594
82Fle-271
82FleSta-160
82Kel-39
82OPC-296
82Top-666
82Top-670
82TopSti-185
82TopTra-54T
83AllGamPI-57
83Don-269
83Dra-13
83Fle-239
83FleSta-94
83FleSti-149
83OPC-260
83Top-260
83TopSti-50
83TopTra-53T
83YanRoyRD-5
84AllGamPI-146
84Don-469
84Dra-16
84Fle-129
84FunFooP-58
84Nes792-440
84OPC-301
84Top-440
84TopRubD-12
84TopTif-440
85AllGamPI-146
85Don-225
85Fle-132
85FleUpd-64
85Lea-100
85OPC-120
85Pir-8
85Top-120
85TopMin-120
85TopRubD-15
85TopTif-120
85TopTifT-66T
85TopTra-66T
86Don-200
86Fle-610
86LasVegSP-10
86Top-387
86TopTif-387
87OklCit8P-11
88AlaGolAA'TI-19
88RanMot-8
89PacSenL-10
89T/MSenL-58
89TopSenL-52
90EliSenL-8
90SouCalS-6
92YanWIZ8-98
93RanKee-215
Kemper, Robbie
89CliGiaP-896
90EriSaiS-11
Kempfer, Jason
91IdaFalBSP-24
92PulBraC-16
92PulBraF-3174
Kenady, Jake
93BakDodCLC-13
93GreFalDSP-25
94YakBeaC-7
94YakBeaF-3842
95BakBlaTI-16
96SanBerSB-12
Kenaga, Jeff
81BirBarT-13
82EvaTriT-22
83EvaTriT-20
84ChaO'sT-8
Kenan, Kerry
80AshTouT-15
Kendall, Fred
72PadTeal-15
72Top-532
73OPC-221
73Top-221
74OPC-53
74PadDea-16
74PadMcDD-8
74Top-53A
74Top-53B
74TopSta-95
75OPC-332
75Top-332
76OPC-639
76SSP-122
76Top-639
77OPC-213
77PadSchC-32A
77PadSchC-32B
77Top-576
78PapGinD-13
78SSP270-182
78Top-426
79Top-83
80Top-598
86PadGreT-8
93HicCraC-26
93HicCraF-1295
94HicCraC-26
94HicCraF-2192
94SouAtlLAF-SAL24
94VenLinU-166
Kendall, Jason
92ClaBluBF-BC26
92ClaDraP-18
92ClaFS7-408
92FroRowDP-89
92HigSchPLS-11
92UppDecML-14
93AugPirC-1
93AugPirF-1547
93Bow-162
93ClaFS7-105
93ClaGolF-195
93Pin-458
93Sco-490
93Sel-359
93SouAtlLAGF-33
93StaCluM-148
93Top-334
93TopGol-334
93TopInaM-334
93TopMic-334
94Bow-246
94CarLeaAF-CAR40
94ClaGolF-19
94ExcFS7-252
94SalBucC-12
94SalBucF-2327
94SigRoo-33
94SigRooS-33
94Top-686
94TopGol-686
94TopSpa-686
94UppDecML-124
95ARuFalLS-12
95Bes-91
95Bes-101
95BesFra-F11
95Bow-41
95CarMudF-161
95Exc-255
95SPML-137
95SPMLA-15
95SPMLDtS-DS16
95Top-480
95UppDecML-27
96BesAutSA-35
96Bow-293
96BowBes-15
96BowBesAR-15
96BowBesR-15
96Cir-172
96CirRav-172
96ColCho-445
96ColChoGS-445
96ColChoSS-445
96EmoXL-255
96Exc-218
96ExcAll-1
96Fin-S241
96FinRef-S241
96Fla-347
96FlaWavotF-15
96FleUpd-U177
96FleUpdNH-14
96FleUpdTC-U177
96LeaLimR-6
96LeaLimRG-6
96LeaPre-124
96LeaPreP-124
96LeaSig-68
96LeaSigEA-98
96LeaSigEACM-14
96LeaSigPPG-68
96LeaSigPPP-68
96Pin-376
96PinAfi-190
96PinAfiAP-190
96PinFoil-376
96Sel-169
96SelArtP-169
96SelCer-108
96SelCerAP-108
96SelCerCB-108
96SelCerCR-108
96SelCerMB-108
96SelCerMG-108
96SelCerMR-108
96SP-17
96SPSpeFX-21
96SPSpeFXDC-21
96SPx-46
96SPxGol-46
96Stu-79
96StuPrePB-79
96StuPrePG-79
96StuPrePS-79
96Sum-156
96Sum-188
96SumAbo&B-156
96SumAbo&B-188
96SumArtP-156
96SumArtP-188
96SumFoi-156
96SumFoi-188
96TeaOut-45
96Top-342
96TopChr-135
96TopChrR-135
96TopLasBS-3
96Ult-533
96UltChe-B6
96UltCheGM-B6
96UltGolM-533
96UppDec-241
96UppDecPHE-H57
96UppDecPreH-H57
96Zen-113
96ZenArtP-113
96ZenMoz-23
97Bow-57
97BowInt-57
97Cir-226
97CirRav-226
97ColCho-430
97ColChoTBS-37
97ColChoTBSWH-37
97Don-43
97DonEli-77
97DonEliGS-77
97DonEliTotC-14
97DonEliTotCDC-14
97DonLim-167
97DonLim-192
97DonLimLE-167
97DonLimLE-192
97DonPre-91
97DonPreCttC-91
97DonPreP-43
97DonPrePGold-43
97Fin-124
97FinEmb-124
97FinEmbR-124
97FinRef-124
97FlaSho-A81
97FlaSho-B81
97FlaSho-C81
97FlaShoLC-81
97FlaShoLC-B81
97FlaShoLC-C81
97FlaShoLCM-A81
97FlaShoLCM-B81
97FlaShoLCM-C81
97Fle-429
97Fle-742
97FleRooS-8
97FleTif-429
97FleTif-742
97Lea-31
97LeaFraM-31
97LeaFraMDC-31
97MetUni-238
97MetUniPP-6
97NewPin-120
97NewPinAP-120
97NewPinMC-120
97NewPinPP-120
97Pac-394
97PacLigB-394
97PacPri-135
97PacPriLB-135
97PacPriP-135
97PacSil-394
97Pin-91
97PinArtP-91
97PinCer-46
97PinCerMBlu-46
97PinCerMG-46
97PinCerMR-46
97PinCerR-46
97PinIns-62
97PinInsCE-62
97PinInsDE-62
97PinMusC-91
97PinTotCPB-46
97PinTotCPG-46
97PinTotCPR-46
97PinX-P-111
97PinX-PMoS-111
97PirPosG-1
97ProMag-32
97ProMagML-32
97Sco-31
97ScoPreS-31
97ScoShoS-31
97ScoShoSAP-31
97Sel-42
97SelArtP-42
97SelRegG-42
97SelRooR-5
97SelToootT-4
97SelToootTMB-4
97SkyE-X-91
97SkyE-XC-91
97SkyE-XEC-91
97SkyE-XSD2-8
97SP-140
97SpoIll-63
97SpoIllEE-63
97StaClu-77
97StaCluC-CO5
97StaCluM-M10
97StaCluMOP-77
97StaCluMOP-M10
97Stu-60
97StuPrePG-60
97StuPrePS-60
97Top-195
97TopAwel-AI10
97TopChr-75
97TopChrR-75
97TopGal-152
97TopGalPPI-152
97Ult-262
97UltGolME-262
97UltPlaME-262
97UltRooR-6
97UppDec-157
97UppDecBCP-BC19
95UppDecMLFS-27
97UppDecRSF-RS12
97UppDecTTS-TS8
97UppDecU-48
97UppDecUGN-GN8
Kendall, Jeremey
92MarPhiC-15
92MarPhiF-3071
93BatCliC-14
93BatCliF-3158
94SouAtlLAF-SAL55
94SpaPhiF-1735
94SparPhiC-14
95Bow-116
95Exc-243
96ReaPhiB-22
Kendall, Phil
91BilMusP-3748
91BilMusSP-25
96HelBreTI-10
Kenders, Al
77FriOneYW-80
Kendrena, Ken
92EriSaiC-15
92EriSaiF-1614
93HigDesMC-6
93HigDesMF-33
93Top-726

93TopGol-726
93TopInaM-726
93TopMic-726
94BreCouMC-6
94BreCouMF-4
95HarSenTI-32
Kendrick, Patrick
92HunCubC-22
92HunCubF-3143
Kendrick, Pete
83MadMusF-23
84AlbA'sT-14
85ModA'sC-14
87ElPasDP-4
88DenZepP-1269
Kenna, David
96BelGiaTI-13
Kennedy, Adam
97Bow-430
97BowChr-290
97BowChrI-290
97BowChrIR-290
97BowChrR-290
97BowInt-430
97TopSta-118
97TopStaAM-118
Kennedy, Bill (William G.)
49Bow-105
52Top-102
53RedSoxTI-15
53Top-94
57HygMea-7
60HenHouW-25
83TopRep5-102
91TopArc1-94
Kennedy, Bo
87PenWhiSP-23
88SouBenWSGS-23
89SarWhiSS-12
90BirBarB-20
90BirBarP-1108
90CMC-770
91BirBarLD-65
91BirBarP-1452
91LinDriAA-65
92BirBarF-2577
92BirBarS-86
92SkyAA F-42
92VanCanF-2719
93IndIndF-1483
Kennedy, Brad
96NewJerCB-15
Kennedy, Brickyard (William V.)
03BreE10-81
11SpoLifCW-200
90DodTar-406
95May-15
Kennedy, Dan
89WinSpiS-11
89WytCubS-18
Kennedy, Darryl
92GasRanC-11
93ChaRanC-16
93ChaRanF-1944
93FloStaLAF-5
94ChaRanF-2500
94FloStaLAF-FSL2
95TulDriTI-9
Kennedy, Dave
89ElmPioP-23
Kennedy, David
93BoiHawC-16
93BoiHawF-3923
95NewHavRTI-31
96ColSprSSTI-21
96Exc-156
Kennedy, Gregg
94LynRedSC-15
94LynRedSF-1890
Kennedy, Gus
94DanBraC-16
95MacBraTI-15
95MacBraUTI-4
96DurBulBIB-17
96DurBulBrB-17
96Exc-130
Kennedy, James
91GulCoaRSP-12
Kennedy, Jesse
94DanBraF-3545
Kennedy, John E.
64Top-203
64TopVen-203
65DodTeal-8
65OPC-119
65Top-119
66Top-407
67CokCapD-11
67CokCapDA-11
67DexPre-114
67OPC-111
67Top-111
69PilPos-14
69Top-631
70BreMcD-13
70BreMil-10
70OPC-53
70Top-53
71MLBOffS-319
71OPC-498
71Top-498
72Top-674
73LinPor-24
73OPC-437
73Top-437
86AlbYanT-24
90DodTar-407
92YanWIZ6-65
94BreMilB-45
Kennedy, John Fitzgerald
94UppDecTAE-65
Kennedy, Junior
76IndIndTI-13
77PhoGiaCC-14
77PhoGiaCP-14
77PhoGiaVNB-14
78Pep-15
78SSP270-134
79Top-501
80RedEnq-20
80Top-377
81Don-424
81Fle-203
81Top-447
82CubRedL-15
82Don-188
82Fle-70
82Top-723
82TopTra-55T
83Don-529
83Fle-500
83Top-204
Kennedy, Justin
95MarPhiTI-12
Kennedy, Kevin
77RocRedWM-24
78RocRedWT-10
79RocRedWT-3
80RocRedWT-11
81RocRedWT-10
87BakDodP-15
88BlaYNPRWL-161
88SanAntMB-23
88TexLeaAGS-22
89AlbDukP-72
90AlbDukC-27
90AlbDukP-361
90AlbDukT-16
90CMC-667
90ProAAAF-82
90TriAllGP-AAA32
91AlbDukLD-24
91AlbDukP-1157
91LinDriAAA-24
93RanKee-393
93Top-513
93TopGol-513
93TopInaM-513
93TopMic-513
Kennedy, Kyle
92MisStaB-24
93MisStaB-25
Kennedy, Mike
90ModA'sC-16
91SouOreAC-21
91SouOreAP-3849
Kennedy, Monte
47TipTop-125
49Bow-237
49EurSta-112
50Bow-175
51Bow-163
52BerRos-29
52Bow-213
52Top-124
75Gia195T-12
83TopRep5-124
Kennedy, Robert D.
39WhiSoxTI-7
40WhiSoxL-8
47TipTop-21
48IndTeal-18
48WhiSoxTI-13
49IndTeal-16
50IndNumN-14
50IndTeal-15
51Bow-296
51TopRedB-29
52IndNumN-16
52Top-77
53IndPenCBP-18
53Top-33
54OriEss-16
54Top-155
55OriEss-11
55Top-48
55TopDouH-87
56Top-38
56TopPin-34
57Top-149
64CubJayP-8
64Top-486
65CubJayP-9
65Top-457
68OPC-183
68Top-183
68TopVen-183
76TayBow4-85
82Bow195E-253
83TopRep5-77
85Top-135
85TopTif-135
90DodTar-405
91OriCro-236
91TopArc1-33
94TopArc1-155
94TopArc1G-155
Kennedy, Scott
93MedHatBJF-3731
93MedHatBJSP-6
Kennedy, Shawn
91ButCopKSP-12
Kennedy, Terry
78ArkTraT-14
79Car5-12
79Top-724
80Top-569
81AllGamPI-131
81Don-428
81Fle-541
81OPC-353
81Top-353
81TopTra-780
82Don-121
82Dra-20
82Fle-574
82FleSta-105
82OPC-65
82Top-65
82TopSti-100
83AllGamPI-132
83Don-26
83Don-220
83DonActA-11
83Fle-364
83FleSti-223
83OPC-274
83Top-274
83Top-742
83TopGloS-6
83TopSti-293
84AllGamPI-42
84Don-112
84DonActAS-8
84Fle-304
84FunFooP-47
84Nes792-366
84Nes792-455
84OPC-166
84PadMot-5
84PadSmo-14
84SevCoi-W17
84Top-366
84Top-455
84TopRubD-28
84TopSti-154
84TopTif-366
84TopTif-455
85AllGamPI-131
85Don-429
85Fle-37
85Lea-33
85OPC-194
85PadMot-10
85Top-135
85Top-635
85TopRubD-28
85TopSti-148
85TopTif-135
85TopTif-635
86Don-356
86DonAll-7
86DonPop-7
86Fle-327
86GenMilB-5C
86OPC-230
86Top-230
86Top-306
86TopGloA-20
86TopSti-111
86TopSti-152
86TopTif-230
86TopTif-306
87Don-205
87DonOpeD-142
87Fle-419
87FleGlo-419
87FleUpd-56
87FleUpdG-56
87OPC-303
87OriFreB-15
87SpoTeaP-21
87Top-81
87Top-540
87TopSti-108
87TopTif-81
87TopTif-540
87TopTra-57T
87TopTraT-57T
88Don-150
88DonAll-9
88DonBasB-30
88DonPop-9
88Fle-563
88FleGlo-563
88Lea-99
88OPC-180
88OriFreB-15
88PanSti-7
88PanSti-227
88Sco-123
88ScoBoxC-1
88ScoGlo-123
88Spo-94
88StaLinAl-16
88StaLinO-6
88Top-180
88TopGloA-9
88TopSti-161
88TopSti-225
88TopStiB-55
88TopTif-180
89Bow-470
89BowTif-470
89Don-141
89Fle-610
89FleGlo-610
89FleUpd-128
89GiaMot-8
89OPC-309
89PanSti-256
89Sco-123
89ScoRoo-30T
89Top-705
89TopBig-180
89TopSti-235
89TopTif-705
89TopTra-59T
89TopTraT-59T
89UppDec-469
90Bow-241
90BowTif-241
90Don-602
90DonBesN-132
90Fle-58
90FleCan-58
90GiaMot-12
90GiaSmo-10
90Lea-67
90OPC-372
90PubSti-71
90Sco-7
90Top-372
90TopBig-16
90TopTif-372
90UppDec-397
90VenSti-266
91Bow-631
91Don-94
91Fle-263
91GiaMot-12
91GiaPacGaE-5
91GiaPos-1
91Lea-216
91OPC-66
91OriCro-237
91PanFreS-66
91Sco-548
91SimandSMLBL-22
91StaClu-91
91Top-66
91TopDesS-66
91TopMic-66
91TopTif-66
91Ult-321
91Ult-399
91UppDec-404
92OPC-253
92Sco-503
92Top-253
92TopGol-253
92TopGolW-253
92TopMic-253
92UppDec-192
93St.PetCC-29
93St.PetCF-2644
94VerExpC-21
94VerExpF-3923
95TacRaiTI-3
96TacRaiB-2
Kennedy, Theodore A.
87OldJudN-284
Kennedy, Vern
34DiaMatCSB-102
35DiaMatCS3T1-86
36SandSW-37
37ExhFou-10
37OPCBatUV-135
38GouHeaU-256
38GouHeaU-280
79DiaGre-188
92ConTSN-365
94ConTSN-1123
94ConTSNB-1123
95ConTSN-1392
Kennedy, William
87BucN28-50
Kennelley, Steve
87ColMetP-11
Kennemur, Paul
76BatRouCT-13
Kenner, Jeff
86ArkTraP-10
Kenney, Jerry
69Top-519
70OPC-219
70Top-219
70YanCliDP-11
71MLBOffS-491
71OPC-572
71Top-572
71YanCliDP-8
72MilBra-180
72OPC-158
72Top-158
73OPC-514
73Top-514
75SyrChiTI-7
92YanWIZ6-66
92YanWIZ7-89
Kennison, Kyle
96EveAquB-13
Kenny, Brian
91GenCubC-10
91GenCubP-4210
92MidLeaATI-24
92PeoChiC-7
92PeoChiTI-9
92PeoChiTI-31
Kenny, Sean
93PitMetF-3704
94CapCitBC-11
94CapCitBF-1747
95StLucMTI-19
Kenny, Terry
75CedRapGT-31
Kent, Bernard
85BelBreT-12
Kent, Bo (John)

86MedA'sC-73
86ModA'sC-4
87ModA'sC-9
87ModA'sP-1
88HunStaTI-10
Kent, Dave
89OneYanP-2119
Kent, Jeff
88CapCodPPaLP-169
89St.CatBJP-2091
90DunBluJS-13
90FloStaLAS-33
90StaFS7-65
91Cla/Bes-108
91KnoBluJLD-360
91KnoBluJP-1775
91LinDriAA-360
92DonRoo-61
92FleUpd-104
92Lea-445
92Pin-522
92ScoRoo-84T
93BluJayD4-41
93Bow-426
93Don-302
93Fle-90
93Lea-185
93LinVenB-160
93MetColP-38
93MetKah-12
93OPC-213
93Pin-155
93Sco-189
93Sel-318
93StaClu-269
93StaCluFDI-269
93StaCluMOP-269
93Top-703
93TopGol-703
93TopInaM-703
93TopMic-703
93Toy-84
93Ult-77
93UppDec-401
93UppDecGold-401
93USPlaCR-7S
94Bow-296
94Bow-385
94ColC-159
94ColChoGS-159
94ColChoSS-159
94Don-185
94ExtBas-320
94Fin-33
94FinRef-33
94Fla-200
94Fle-570
94FUnPac-157
94Lea-112
94LeaL-131
94MetColP-4
94MetShuST-1
94OPC-166
94Pac-408
94PanSti-220
94Pin-122
94PinArtP-122
94PinMusC-122
94Sco-516
94ScoGolR-516
94Sel-85
94SP-119
94SPDieC-119
94SPHol-19
94SPHolDC-19
94StaClu-362
94StaCluDD-DD10
94StaCluFDI-362
94StaCluGR-362
94StaCluMOP-362
94StaCluMOP-DD10
94Stu-117
94Top-424
94TopGol-424
94TopSpa-424
94TriPla-146
94Ult-238
94UppDec-178
94UppDecAJ-38
94UppDecAJG-38
94UppDecED-178
95Baz-82
95Bow-342
95ClaPhoC-37
95ColCho-315
95ColChoGS-315
95ColChoSE-147
95ColChoSEGS-147
95ColChoSESS-147
95ColChoSS-315
95Don-97
95DonPreP-97
95DonTopotO-295
95Emb-9
95EmbGolI-9
95Fin-121
95FinRef-121
95Fla-172
95Fle-373
95Lea-220
95LeaLim-107
95Pac-283
95PacPri-93
95Pin-242
95PinArtP-242
95PinMusC-242
95PinUps-US13
95Sco-46
95ScoGolR-48
95ScoPlaTS-48
95Sel-77
95SelArtP-77
95SP-81
95Spo-30
95SpoArtP-30
95SpoDouT-3
95SPSil-81
95StaClu-61
95StaCluFDI-61
95StaCluMOP-61
95StaCluSTWS-61
95StaCluVR-37
95Stu-64
95Sum-107
95SumNthD-107
95Top-185
95TopCyb-105
95Ult-198
95UltGolM-198
95UppDec-359
95UppDecED-359
95UppDecEDG-359
95UppDecSE-61
95UppDecSEG-61
95Zen-49
96ColCho-225
96ColChoGS-225
96ColChoSS-225
96Don-285
96DonPreP-285
96EmoXL-236
96Fla-324
96Fle-484
96FleTif-484
96Lea-20
96LeaPrePB-20
96LeaPrePG-20
96LeaPrePS-20
96MetKah-19
96MetTeal-4
96MetUni-204
96MetUniP-204
96Pac-144
96Pin-41
96ProSta-73
96Sco-316
96ScoDugC-B41
96ScoDugCAP-B41
96SP-126
96StaClu-99
96StaCluEPB-99
96StaCluEPG-99
96StaCluEPS-99
96StaCluMOP-99
95StaCluVRMC-37
96Top-207
96Ult-246
96UltGolM-246
96UppDec-143
97Bow-65
97BowInt-65
97Cir-36
97CirRav-36
97Don-338
97DonPreP-338
97DonPrePGold-338
97Fin-254
97FinRef-254
97Fle-509
97FleTif-509
97Lea-273
97LeaFraM-273
97LeaFraMDC-273
97Pac-72
97PacLigB-72
97PacSil-72
97PinX-PSfF-37
97PinX-PSfFU-37
97Sco-230
97Sco-352
97ScoHobR-352
97ScoInd-13
97ScoIndPl-13
97ScoIndPr-13
97ScoPreS-230
97ScoResC-352
97ScoShoS-230
97ScoShoS-352
97ScoShoSAP-230
97ScoShoSAP-352
97SP-163
97Top-346
97Ult-388
97UltGolME-388
97UltPlaME-388
97UppDec-546
Kent, Lewis
87KinIndP-7
88KinIndS-14
Kent, Matt
86StoPorP-12
Kent, Maury
90DodTar-999
Kent, Robert
96IdaFalB-12
Kent, Troy
88MarPhiS-20
89SpaPhiP-1033
89SpaPhiS-11
91SanBerSC-7
91SanBerSP-1983
92JacSunF-3705
92JacSunS-360
92SkyAA F-152
93CalCanF-1162
96WatIndTI-11
Kent, Wes
81AppFoxT-26
82AppFoxF-13
83GleFalWST-3
Kenworthy, Dick
68OPC-63
68Top-63
68TopVen-63
77SerSta-14
81TCM60I-332
Kenworthy, Duke (William)
20WalMaiW-24
Kenyon, J.J.
87OldJudN-285
Kenyon, Robert
81VerBeaDT-7
82VerBeaDT-7
Keon, Kevin
90NiaFalRP-19
Keough, Joseph
69RoyTeal-8
69Top-603
70RoyTeal-17
70Top-589
71MLBOffS-417
71OPC-451
71Top-451
72OPC-133
72Top-133
93UppDecS-4
Keough, Matt
78Top-709
79Hos-59
79OPC-284
79Top-554
80OPC-74
80Top-134
81A'sGraG-27
81AllGamPI-85
81Don-358
81Fle-588
81OPC-301
81Top-301
82A'sGraG-6
82Don-71
82Fle-95
82FleSta-129
82OPC-87
82Top-87
82TopSti-225
83A'sGraG-27
83Don-239
83Fle-521
83Top-413
83TopSti-109
83TopTra-54T
84Don-627
84Fle-130
84Nes792-203
84OPC-203
84Top-203
84TopTif-203
85LouRedR-16
87A'sMot-18
87JapPlaB-15
88ChaLooLTI-17
90SweBasG-127
92YanWIZ8-99
Keough, R. Marty
58Top-371
59Top-303
60Top-71
60TopVen-71
61Top-146
62Jel-69
62Pos-69
62PosCan-69
62RedEnq-19
62SalPlaC-79
62ShiPlaC-79
62Top-258
63Jel-135
63Pos-135
63RedEnq-17
63RedFreBC-12
63RedJayP-6
63Top-21
64Top-166
64TopVen-166
65OPC-263
65RedEnq-16
65Top-263
66Top-334
66TopVen-334
Keppen, Jeff
95YakBeaTI-16
96SanBerSB-13
96SavSanB-20
Kepshire, Kurt
81CedRapRT-2
82CedRapRT-5
83ArkTraT-4
84LouRedR-17
85CarTeal-16
85Don-382
85Fle-230
85Top-474
85TopTif-474
86CarKASD-13
86CarSchM-11
86CarTeal-21
86Don-504
86Fle-39
86LouRedTI-14
86Top-256
86TopTif-256
88IndIndC-2
88IndIndP-506
89PorBeaC-3
89PorBeaP-215
Kerfeld, Charlie
85TucTorC-73
86AstMilL-11
86AstPol-10
86AstTeal-8
86BasStaB-63
86DonRoo-6
86Fle-303
86SpoRoo-23
86TopTra-52T
86TopTraT-52T
87AstMot-12
87Don-209
87Fle-60
87FleExcS-31
87FleGlo-60
87Lea-195
87OPC-145
87Spo-146
87SpoTeaP-8
87Top-145
87TopSti-28
87TopTif-145
87ToyRoo-15
88ColAstB-1
88OPC-392
88Sco-479
88ScoGlo-479
88Top-608
88TopTif-608
89AstSmo-21
89TucTorC-8
89TucTorJP-11
89TucTorP-188
90BraDubP-14
Kerfut, George
90FloStaLAS-10
90MiaMirIS-14
90MiaMirIS-12
90StaFS7-74
91MiaMirC-15
91MiaMirP-403
92SalLakTSP-17
93HigDesMC-7
93HigDesMF-34
Keriazakos, Gus (Const.)
55Bow-14
Kerins, John
87OldJudN-286
Kerkes, Kevin
89WauTimGS-22
Kerley, Collin
92GenCubC-12
92GenCubF-1557
93PeoChiC-10
93PeoChiF-1080
93PeoChiTI-12
94DayCubC-12
94DayCubF-2348
95HarSenTI-45
Kermode, Al
92JamExpC-11
92JamExpF-1498
94BurBeeC-10
94BurBeeF-1077
Kern, Bill
77FriOneYW-65
Kern, Jim (James)
75OklCit8TI-8
75OPC-621
75Top-621
76SSP-509
77PepGloD-7
77Top-41
78OPC-165
78Top-253
79OPC-297
79Top-573
80OPC-192
80Top-369
81Don-27
81Fle-618
81FleStiC-18
81OPC-197
81Top-197
82Don-89
82Fle-322
82OPC-59
82RedCok-11
82Top-463
82TopTra-56T
83Don-355
83Fle-240
83Top-772
83TopFol-4
83WhiSoxTV-67
86IndOhH-46
86IndTeal-26
86RanGreT-3
92UppDecS-12
93RanKee-216
94BreMilB-46
94RanAllP-7
Kern, Lloyd D.
77WesHavYT-12
79WesHavYT-28
80LynSaiT-22
81LynSaiT-26
Kernan, Phil
95ButCopKtI-13
Kernek, George B.
65CarTeal-14
66Top-544
Kernels, Cedar Rapids

96CedRapKTI-31
Kernick, Craig
91WavRedF-7
Kerns, Mickey
92BoiHawC-13
92BoiHawF-3637
93CedRapKC-10
93CedRapKF-1752
Kerns, Russ
50WorWidGV-38
Kerr, Buddy (John J.)
46SpoExcW-7-9
47HomBon-27
48Bow-20
49Bow-186
49EurSta-113
49MPR302-2-102
50Bow-55
50Dra-15
51Bow-171
79DiaGre-127
79TCM50-113
83TCMPla1945-37
Kerr, Dickie (Richard)
19W514-23
20GasAmeMBD-3
20NatCarE-54
21E121So1-51
21E121So8-47
21Exh-90
22AmeCarE-36
22W575-68
23W501-37
69SCFOldT-18
75WhiSox1T-12
75WhiSox1T-24
88PacEigMO-47
88PacEigMO-56
88PacEigMO-97
94ConTSN-1037
94ConTSN-1041
94ConTSNB-1037
94ConTSNB-1041
Kerr, Frank
49RemBre-13
Kerr, Jason
91YakBeaC-16
91YakBeaP-4244
92ProFS7-250
92VerBeaDC-9
92VerBeaDF-2870
93RanCucQC-19
93RanCucQF-830
Kerr, Jim
96ButCopKB-18
Kerr, John Francis
33Gou-214
34DiaMatCSB-103
35DiaMatCS3T1-87
Kerr, John L.
29ExhFou-19
Kerr, Paul S.
80PerHaloFP-C
Kerr, Zach (Zackary)
89EriOriS-10
90CarLeaA-1
90FreKeyTI-10
91FreKeyC-5
Kerrigan, Joe
75WesPalBES-9
76ExpRed-15
77ExpPos-19
77OPC-171
77Top-341
78OPC-108
78Top-549
79RocRedWT-2
79Top-37
81IndIndTI-24
82OklCit8T-13
83ExpPos-10
84ExpPos-15
84ExpStu-33
84ExpStu-38
86ExpProPa-14
87JacExpP-454
88IndIndC-25
88IndIndP-499
89IndIndC-24
89IndIndP-1227
90IndIndP-309
90ProAAAF-592
91HarSenLD-275
91HarSenP-644
91LinDriAA-275
91OriCro-238
92ExpPos-19
Kerrigan, Patsey
88AllandGN-10
Kerrigan, Rob
87JamExpP-2558
88JamExpP-1898
88RocExpLC-18
89RocExpLC-15
90WesPalBES-11
Kersgeiter, Greg
93ChaRanC-30
Kershaw, Scott
86AppFoxP-12
Kershner, Jason
95MarPhiTI-13
96PieBolWB-14
Keshock, Christopher
87ChaWheP-22
Kesler, Mike
87QuaCitAP-13
Kessel, Kyle
96PitMetB-13
Kesselmark, Joe
88SanAntMB-11
89SanAntMB-9
90CanIndB-10
90CanIndP-1304
Kessels, Steve
76WauMetT-14
77LynMetT-18
Kessinger, Don
66OPC-24
66Top-24
66TopVen-24
67CubProPS-9
67ProPizC-11
67Top-419
68OPC-159
68Top-159
68TopVen-159
69CubJewT-10
69CubPho-8
69CubTealC-6
69KelPin-9
69MilBra-144
69MLBOffS-123
69MLBPin-48
69Top-225
69Top-422
69TopDec-18
69TopSta-16
69TopTeaP-4
70CubDunD-4
70DayDaiNM-108
70MLBOffS-20
70OPC-80
70OPC-456
70SunPin-6
70Top-80
70Top-456
71Kel-9A
71Kel-9B
71Kel-9C
71MilDud-50
71MLBOffS-36
71OPC-455
71Top-455
71TopCoi-119
71TopTat-123
72CubChi-4
72CubTeal-7
72MilBra-181
72OPC-145
72Top-145
73LinPor-41
73OPC-285
73Top-285
74OPC-38
74Top-38
74TopDecE-52
74TopSta-16
75Hos-77
75HosTwi-77
75OPC-315
75Top-315
76CraDis-25
76Hos-134
76OPC-574
76SSP-315
76Top-574
77CarTeal-12
77Top-229
78SSP270-154
78Top-672
79Top-404
79Top-467
84CubUno-2
84CubUno-7
89SweBasG-112
90PacLeg-34
90SweBasG-69
91SweBasG-115
91UppDecS-21
92ActPacA-76
92UppDecS-28
93UppDecAH-80
94TedWil-17
Kessinger, Keith
89BluOriS-12
90WauTimB-18
90WauTimP-2131
90WauTimS-12
91FreKeyC-29
92CedRapRC-8
92CedRapRF-1078
93ChaLooF-2366
94IndIndF-1817
94Pin-251
94PinArtP-251
94PinMusC-251
94PinRooTP-3
94Sco-621
94ScoBoyoS-42
94ScoGolR-621
95IowCubTI-17
96IowCubB-17
Kessler, Dave
92BoiHawC-5
92BoiHawF-3631
93CedRapKC-11
93CedRapKF-1742
94CedRapKC-16
94CedRapKF-1112
Kessler, Greg
89WytCubS-19
90GenCubP-3037
90GenCubS-16
Kester, Rick
70Top-621
71OPC-494
71RicBraTI-10
71Top-494
72OPC-351
72Top-351
Kester, Tim
93AubAstC-15
93AubAstF-3439
94OscAstC-12
94OscAstF-1133
95MidLeaA-26
95QuaCitRBTI-12
96JacGenB-15
Ketcham, Lee Anne
95ColSilB-14
96ColSilB-16
Ketchel, Stanley
11TurRedT-67
Ketchen, Douglas
90AshTouC-6
90AubAstB-8
91AshTouP-564
92OscAstC-10
92OscAstF-2527
93JacGenF-2106
94JacGenF-215
Ketchen, J.B.
90AubAstP-3415
Ketleers, Cotuit
88CapCodPB-24
Keusch, Joe
94HudValRF-3378
94HudValRC-9
Keuter, Greg
89WytCubS-30
92HunCubC-30
95RocCubTI-NNO
96RocCubTI-15
Key, Denny
91BurIndP-3298
92WatIndC-5
92WatIndF-3229
Key, Greg
83RedPioT-16
85MidAngT-3
Key, Jeffrey
93MarPhiC-16
93MarPhiF-3489
95PiePhiF-197
Key, Jimmy
84BluJayFS-20
84FleUpd-61
84TopTra-62T
84TopTraT-62T
85BluJayFS-16
85Don-559
85Fle-110
85OPC-193
85Top-193
85TopTif-193
86BluJayAF-16
86BluJayFS-20
86Don-561
86DonAll-53
86Fle-63
86Fle-642
86KayB-18
86Lea-219
86OPC-291
86Top-545
86TopMinL-35
86TopSti-191
86TopTif-545
87BluJayFS-16
87Don-244
87DonOpeD-37
87Fle-232
87FleGlo-232
87GenMilB-1F
87Lea-187
87OPC-29
87SpoTeaP-5
87SyrChi1A-8
87Top-29
87TopSti-192
87TopTif-29
88BluJay5-7
88BluJayFS-16
88ClaBlu-249
88Don-72
88DonBasB-143
88Fle-114
88FleAwaW-22
88FleExcS-24
88FleGlo-114
88FleHotS-22
88FleLeaL-23
88FleMin-63
88FleRecS-22
88FleStiC-74
88FleSup-19
88FleTeaL-17
88Lea-67
88MSAHosD-24
88OPC-47
88PanSti-214
88RedFolSB-42
88Sco-216
88ScoGlo-216
88Spo-116
88StaLinBJ-10
88Top-395
88Top-682
88TopCoi-17
88TopMinL-39
88TopRevLL-27
88TopSti-190
88TopTif-395
88TopTif-682
89BluJayFS-14
89Bow-243
89BowTif-243
89Don-188
89DonBasB-87
89Fle-236
89FleGlo-236
89OPC-229
89PanSti-462
89Sco-480
89Spo-167
89Top-229
89TopBasT-129
89TopSti-186
89TopTif-229
89UppDec-291
90BluJayFS-13
90BluJayHS-3
90Bow-509
90BowTif-509
90Don-231
90DonBesA-42
90Fle-85
90FleCan-85
90Lea-211
90OPC-371
90PanSti-181
90PubSti-518
90RedFolSB-53
90Sco-407
90Top-371
90TopSti-191
90TopTif-371
90UppDec-462
90VenSti-267
90VicPos-2
91BluJayFS-15
91BluJayFS-16
91BluJayS-3
91BluJayS-38
91Bow-19
91Cla3-T45
91ClaGam-63
91Don-98
91Fle-178
91Lea-103
91OPC-741
91OPCPre-71
91PanFreS-351
91Sco-422
91StaClu-221
91Top-741
91TopDesS-741
91TopMic-741
91TopTif-741
91Ult-364
91UppDec-667
91USPlaCA-8D
92Bow-500
92Don-219
92DonMcD-14
92Fle-332
92Lea-111
92OPC-482
92Pin-193
92Sco-96
92SpoIllFK1-305
92StaClu-259
92StaCluD-98
92Top-482
92TopGol-482
92TopGolW-482
92TopMic-482
92Ult-147
92UppDec-302
93BluJayD4-19
93BluJayDM-20
93BluJayDWS-5
93Bow-427
93Don-710
93Fin-174
93FinRef-174
93Fla-247
93Fle-336
93FleFinE-247
93FunPac-207
93Lea-317
93MSABenSPD-19
93OPC-269
93OPCPre-15
93OPCWorC-8
93OPCWorSH-2
93PacSpa-558
93Pin-9
93Sco-639
93Sel-376
93SelRoo-13T
93SP-264
93StaClu-639
93StaCluFDI-639
93StaCluM-24
93StaCluMOP-639
93StaCluY-13
93Stu-168
93Top-596
93TopGol-596
93TopInaM-596
93TopMic-596
93TopTra-68T
93Ult-596
93UppDec-358
93UppDec-543
93UppDecGold-358
93UppDecGold-543
94Bow-465
94BowBes-R60

94BowBesR-R60
94ColC-160
94ColChoGS-160
94ColChoSS-160
94Don-30
94DonSpeE-30
94ExtBas-132
94ExtBasPD-3
94Fin-299
94FinRef-299
94Fla-82
94Fle-236
94FleAllS-13
94FUnPac-165
94Lea-412
94LeaL-55
94LeaLimGA-17
94OPC-174
94Pac-427
94Pin-52
94PinArtP-52
94PinMusC-52
94Sco-75
94ScoGolR-75
94Sel-43
94SP-197
94SPDieC-197
94Spo-34
94StaClu-469
94StaCluFDI-469
94StaCluGR-469
94StaCluMOP-469
94StaCluT-205
94StaCluTFDI-205
94Stu-214
94Top-120
94Top-393
94TopGol-120
94TopGol-393
94TopSpa-120
94TopSpa-393
94TriPla-275
94Ult-96
94UppDec-259
94UppDecED-259
94USPlaCA-3S
95Baz-85
95BazRedH-RH17
95BluJayUSPC-6H
95BluJayUSPC-13S
95Bow-383
95ColCho-68
95ColChoGS-68
95ColChoSE-141
95ColChoSE-248
95ColChoSEGS-141
95ColChoSEGS-248
95ColChoSESS-141
95ColChoSESS-248
95ColChoSS-68
95Don-78
95DonAll-AL1
95DonMouM-5
95DonPreP-78
95Emb-128
95EmbGolI-128
95Emo-61
95Fin-160
95FinRef-160
95Fla-64
95Fle-74
95FleAllS-9
95FleLeaL-4
95FleTeaL-10
95KinDis-24
95Kra-6
95Lea-75
95LeaLim-28
95Pac-298
95PacGolP-34
95PacPri-96
95PanSti-12
95PanSti-127
95Pin-268
95PinArtP-268
95PinMusC-268
95PosCan-10
95RedFol-27
95Sco-76
95ScoDreT-DG10
95ScoGolR-76
95ScoHaloG-HG47
95ScoPlaTS-76
95Sel-73
95SelArtP-73
95SelCer-13
95SelCerMG-13
95SP-177
95Spo-66
95SpoArtP-66
95SpoDouT-12
95SPSil-177
95StaClu-418
95StaCluMO-25
95StaCluMOP-418
95StaCluMOP-VRE10
95StaCluSTWS-418
95StaCluVE-VRE10
95StaCluVR-216
95Stu-155
95Sum-98
95SumNthD-98
95TomPiz-10
95Top-393
95Top-549
95TopCyb-330
95UC3-9
95UC3ArtP-9
95Ult-83
95UltGolM-83
95UltLeaL-3
95UltLeaLGM-3
95UppDec-205
95UppDecED-205
95UppDecEDG-205
95UppDecSE-142
95UppDecSEG-142
95Zen-52
96Don-381
96DonPreP-381
96Fla-130
96FleUpd-U62
96FleUpdTC-U62
96ProSta-137
96Sco-444
95StaCluVRMC-216
96Top-273
96Ult-388
96UltGolM-388
97Cir-333
97CirRav-333
97ColCho-273
97Don-309
97DonLim-60
97DonLimLE-60
97DonPreP-309
97DonPrePGold-309
97DonTea-42
97DonTeaSPE-42
97Fin-211
97FinRef-211
97FlaSho-A122
97FlaSho-B122
97FlaSho-C122
97FlaShoLC-122
97FlaShoLC-B122
97FlaShoLC-C122
97FlaShoLCM-A122
97FlaShoLCM-B122
97FlaShoLCM-C122
97Fle-169
97Fle-585
97FleTif-169
97FleTif-585
97Lea-249
97LeaFraM-249
97LeaFraMDC-249
97NewPin-89
97NewPinAP-89
97NewPinMC-89
97NewPinPP-89
97Sco-410
97ScoHobR-410
97ScoResC-410
97ScoShoS-410
97ScoShoSAP-410
97SpoIll-46
97SpoIllEE-46
97StaClu-343
97StaCluMOP-343
97Top-121
97Ult-356
97UltGolME-356
97UltPlaME-356
97UppDec-526
Key, Scott
96LanLugB-15
Keyes, Stewart
88CapCodPPaLP-148
Keyote, Mascot
93FreKeyC-30
96FreKeyB-29
Keys, Woody
77ForLauYS-2
Keyser, Brian
89UtiBluSP-12
90SarWhiSS-13
91SarWhiSC-6
91SarWhiSP-1109
92BirBarF-2578
93LinVenB-252
93NasSouF-570
94NasSouF-1247
94VenLinU-152
95LinVen-134
95NasSouTI-8
95WhiSoxK-16
96Don-187
96DonPreP-187
96LeaSigEA-99
96Pac-281
96UppDec-43
Khalifa, Sammy
83AleDukT-2
85HawIslC-227
86Don-308
86Fle-611
86Lea-178
86Top-316
86TopSti-127
86TopTat-6
86TopTif-316
87Top-164
87TopTif-164
87VanCanP-1608
89BufBisC-15
89BufBisP-1667
Khoury, Mike
86WatPirP-10
Khoury, Scott
86HagSunP-8
87HagSunP-26
88WatIndP-672
89CanIndB-19
89CanIndP-1310
89CanIndS-10
Khoury, Tony
93HunCubC-12
93HunCubF-3238
95RocCubTI-25
Kibbe, Jay
81RedPioT-4
84EdmTraC-119
Kibbee, Jim
77ForLauYS-15
Kibler, John
88T/MUmp-4
89T/MUmp-2
90T/MUmp-2
Kibler, Russell
85MadMusP-16
85MadMusT-19
86MadMusP-13
87HunStaTI-17
Kibota, Richie
87HawRai-5
Kida, Masao
88MiaMarS-14
Kidd, Dennis
90MiaMirIS-12
90MiaMirIS-13
91MiaMirC-29
91MiaMirP-422
Kidd, Pete
92SkyAA F-270
Kidder, Jim
77ShrCapT-11
Kiecker, Dana
86NewBriRSP-15
87NewBriRSP-17
88PawRedSC-10
88PawRedSP-461
89PawRedSC-4
89PawRedSP-701
89PawRedSTI-12
90DonRoo-28
90FleUpd-72
90Lea-525
90ScoRoo-102T
90TopTra-50T
90TopTraT-50T
90TopTVRS-12
91Bow-108
91Don-347
91Fle-99
91Lea-341
91OPC-763
91RedSoxP-10
91Sco-77
91Sco100RS-92
91StaClu-140
91Top-763
91TopDeb90-77
91TopDesS-763
91TopMic-763
91TopTif-763
91ToyRoo-15
91UltUpd-6
91UppDec-507
92OPC-163
92Sco-732
92Top-163
92TopGol-163
92TopGolW-163
92TopMic-163
Kiefer, Mark
89BelBrelS-11
89BelBrelS-17
91ElPasDLD-190
91ElPasDP-2744
91LinDriAA-190
92Bow-674
92DenZepF-2636
92DenZepS-134
92SkyAAAF-66
93Bow-155
93BrePol-13
93Don-263
93ElPasDF-2947
93LeaGolR-R3
93StaClu-417
93StaCluFDI-417
93StaCluMOP-417
94BreMilB-136
94BrePol-15
94ColC-161
94ColChoGS-161
94ColChoSS-161
94Fla-69
94Pin-526
94PinArtP-526
94PinMusC-526
94ScoRoo-RT139
94ScoRooGR-RT139
94Sel-380
94SpoRoo-107
94SpoRooAP-107
94Top-770
94TopGol-770
94TopSpa-770
94Ult-373
95Fla-272
95FleUpd-53
95Lea-143
95Sco-294
95ScoGolR-294
95ScoPlaTS-294
95StaClu-581
95StaCluMOP-581
95StaCluSTWS-581
95TopTra-17T
96Don-448
96DonPreP-448
96Fle-149
96FleTif-149
96LeaSigA-126
96LeaSigAG-126
96LeaSigAS-126
Kiefer, Steve
82MadMusF-3
83AlbA'sT-12
84TacTigC-78
85Don-35
85Fle-647
85Lea-27
85TacTigC-139
86Don-420
86VanCanP-15
87DenZepP-18
88BrePol-30
88Don-542
88Fle-167
88FleGlo-167
88Sco-630
88ScoGlo-630
88StaLinBre-10
88Top-187
88TopTif-187
89ColCliC-15
89ColCliP-15
89ColCliP-740
90BufBisC-17
90BufBisP-379
90BufBisTI-11
90CMC-17
90ProAAAF-494
92YanWIZ8-100
94BreMilB-137
Kiely, John
89LakTigS-12
90CMC-768
90LonTigP-1264
90ProAaA-18
91LinDriAAA-587
91TolMudHLD-587
91TolMudHP-1927
92FleUpd-24
92SkyAAAF-265
92StaClu-384
92TolMudHF-1040
92TolMudHS-591
92TopDeb91-99
93Don-203
93Fle-230
93StaClu-212
93StaCluFDI-212
93StaCluMOP-212
93Top-107
93TopGol-107
93TopInaM-107
93TopMic-107
93Ult-200
93UppDec-378
93UppDecGold-378
94TolMudHF-1024
Kiely, Leo
52Top-54
54Top-171
55Top-36
55TopDouH-43
58Top-204
59Top-199
60Top-94
60TopVen-94
83TopRep5-54
94TopArc1-171
94TopArc1G-171
Kieran, Jack
95ConTSN-1400
Kiernan, J.F.
09T206-495
Kierst, Kevin
87KnoBluJP-1517
Kies, Norman
36WorWidGV-120
Kieschnick, Brooks
93Tex-4
94ActPac-4
94ActPac-57
94ActPac2G-3G
94AriFalLS-12
94Bow-354
94Bow-438
94BowBes-B5
94BowBes-X92
94BowBesR-B5
94BowBesR-X92
94Cla-200
94Cla-AU3
94ClaBonB-BB4
94ClaCreotC-C4
94ClaGolF-130
94ClaGolN1PLF-LP6
94ClaGolREF-RE6
94ClaGolREF-RE20
94ClaTriF-T13
94ColC-28
94ColChoGS-28
94ColChoSS-28
94ExcFS7-165
94ExtBas-219
94ExtBasMLH-5
94OrlCubF-1398
94Pin-262
94PinArtP-262
94PinMusC-262
94Sco-517
94ScoGolR-517
94SigRoo-32
94SigRooS-32

94SP-9
94SPDieC-9
94SPHol-20
94SPHolDC-20
94Top-205
94TopGol-205
94TopSpa-205
94Ult-460
94UppDec-530
94UppDecED-530
94UppDecML-2
95Bes-57
95Bow-263
95BowBes-B12
95BowBesR-B12
95BowGolF-263
95Exc-166
95Fle-418
95IowCubTI-18
95PinETA-6
95Sel-164
95SelArtP-164
95SPML-2
95SPML-30
95SPMLA-16
95SPMLDtS-DS4
95Top-246
95UppDecML-15
95UppDecMLOP-OP5
96BesAutSA-36
96Bow-196
96BowBes-113
96BowBesAR-113
96BowBesP-BBP3
96BowBesPAR-BBP3
96BowBesPR-BBP3
96BowBesR-113
96ColCho-430
96ColChoGS-430
96ColChoSS-430
96Exc-138
96ExcSeaTL-5
96Fin-B316
96FinRef-B316
96FleCub-11
96FleUpd-U112
96FleUpdNH-15
96FleUpdTC-U112
96IowCubB-1
96LeaPre-130
96LeaPreP-130
96LeaSig-95
96LeaSigA-127
96LeaSigAG-127
96LeaSigAS-127
96LeaSigPPG-95
96LeaSigPPP-95
96Pin-377
96PinAfi-181
96PinAfiAP-181
96PinFoil-377
96PinProS-11
96Sel-121
96SelArtP-121
96SelCer-114
96SelCerAP-114
96SelCerCB-114
96SelCerCR-114
96SelCerMB-114
96SelCerMG-114
96SelCerMR-114
96Stu-115
96StuPrePB-115
96StuPrePG-115
96StuPrePS-115
96Sum-164
96SumAbo&B-164
96SumArtP-164
96SumFoi-164
96Top-344
96TopChr-136
96TopChrR-136
96TopGal-135
96TopGalPPI-135
96TopLasBS-4
96Ult-451
96UltGolM-451
96UppDec-242
96UppDecBCP-BC12
96UppDecPHE-H58
96UppDecPreH-H58
96Zen-121
96ZenArtP-121
97Bow-141
97BowCerBIA-CA43
97BowCerGIA-CA43
97BowChr-149
97BowChrI-149
97BowChrIR-149
97BowChrR-149
97BowInt-141
97ColCho-286
97Don-368
97DonEliTotC-16
97DonEliTotCDC-16
97DonLim-33
97DonLim-156
97DonLimLE-33
97DonLimLE-156
97DonPre-154
97DonPreCttC-154
97DonPreP-368
97DonPrePGold-368
97DonRatR-17
97Fin-218
97FinRef-218
97Fle-279
97FleTif-279
97Lea-133
97Lea-344
97LeaFraM-133
97LeaFraM-344
97LeaFraMDC-133
97LeaFraMDC-344
97Pac-252
97PacLigB-252
97PacPri-86
97PacPriLB-86
97PacPriP-86
97PacSil-252
97PinCer-118
97PinCerMBlu-118
97PinCerMG-118
97PinCerMR-118
97PinCerR-118
97PinTotCPB-118
97PinTotCPG-118
97PinTotCPR-118
97PinX-P-127
97PinX-PMoS-127
97Sco-71
97ScoPreS-71
97ScoShoS-71
97ScoShoSAP-71
97SkyE-XSD2-4
97StaClu-94
97StaCluM-M29
97StaCluMOP-94
97StaCluMOP-M29
97Stu-153
97StuPrePG-153
97StuPrePS-153
97Top-389
97TopAwel-AI11
95UppDecMLFS-15

Kiess, Paul
80PenPilBT-17
80PenPilCT-23

Kiker, Ed
89GeoColC-15

Kildoo, Don
57JetPos-9

Kilduff, Pete
17HolBreD-57
20GasAmeMBD-22
20NatCarE-55A
20NatCarE-55B
21E121So1-52
21E121So8-48
22AmeCarE-37
22W575-69
23W501-94
23WilChoV-79

Kile, Darryl
89BasAmeAPB-AA12
89ColMudB-4
89ColMudP-133
89ColMudS-15
89TucTorJP-12
90Bow-61
90BowTif-61
90CMC-606
90ProAAAF-191
90TucTorC-4
90TucTorP-201
91AstMot-27
91Bow-548
91DonRoo-5
91FleUpd-90
91ScoRoo-86T
91Stu-178
91TopTra-68T
91TopTraT-68T
91UltUpd-84
91UppDec-774
92AstMot-24
92Bow-601
92Cla1-T49
92ClaGam-116
92Don-309
92Fle-439
92Lea-198
92OPC-134
92OPCPre-196
92Pin-225
92Sco-494
92Sco100RS-4
92StaClu-837
92StaCluNC-837
92Stu-39
92Top-134
92TopDeb91-100
92TopGol-134
92TopGolW-134
92TopMic-134
92Ult-206
92UppDec-374
93AstMot-19
93Don-668
93Fla-66
93Fle-438
93Lea-143
93PacSpa-479
93Pin-430
93Sco-430
93SP-36
93StaClu-518
93StaCluAs-17
93StaCluFDI-518
93StaCluMO-12
93StaCluMOP-518
93Top-308
93TopGol-308
93TopInaM-308
93TopMic-308
93Ult-393
93UppDec-314
93UppDecGold-314
94AstMot-6
94Bow-614
94ColC-162
94ColChoGS-162
94ColChoSS-162
94Don-32
94DonSpeE-32
94ExtBas-277
94Fin-244
94FinRef-244
94Fla-173
94Fle-496
94FleAllS-43
94FleGolM-10
94FUnPac-52
94Lea-314
94OPC-176
94Pac-270
94PanSti-196
94Pin-321
94PinArtP-321
94PinMusC-321
94Sco-231
94Sco-630
94ScoGolR-231
94ScoGolR-630
94Sel-326
94Spo-72
94StaClu-327
94StaCluFDI-327
94StaCluGR-327
94StaCluMOP-327
94Stu-23
94Top-703
94TopGol-703
94TopSpa-703
94TriPla-29
94Ult-208
94UppDec-435
94UppDecED-435
95AstMot-4
95ColCho-118
95ColChoGS-118
95ColChoSE-41
95ColChoSEGS-41
95ColChoSESS-41
95ColChoSS-118
95Don-398
95DonPreP-398
95Fla-148
95Fle-465
95Lea-110
95Pin-238
95PinArtP-238
95PinMusC-238
95Sco-177
95ScoGolR-177
95ScoPlaTS-177
95Sel-20
95SelArtP-20
95StaClu-447
95StaCluMOP-447
95StaCluSTWS-447
95StaCluVR-238
95Top-228
95TopCyb-128
95Ult-388
95UltGolM-388
95UppDec-22
95UppDecED-22
95UppDecEDG-22
95UppDecSE-178
95UppDecSEG-178
96AstMot-5
96Cir-138
96CirRav-138
96ColCho-564
96ColChoGS-564
96ColChoSS-564
96Don-519
96DonPreP-519
96Fle-413
96FleTif-413
95StaCluVRMC-238
96Ult-488
96UltGolM-488
96UppDec-346
97Cir-199
97CirRav-199
97ColCho-349
97Don-337
97DonLim-114
97DonLimLE-114
97DonPreP-337
97DonPrePGold-337
97FlaSho-A157
97FlaSho-B157
97FlaSho-C157
97FlaShoLC-157
97FlaShoLC-B157
97FlaShoLC-C157
97FlaShoLCM-A157
97FlaShoLCM-B157
97FlaShoLCM-C157
97Fle-349
97FleTif-349
97Lea-293
97LeaFraM-293
97LeaFraMDC-293
97MetUni-138
97Pac-320
97PacLigB-320
97PacSil-320
97Pin-49
97PinArtP-49
97PinMusC-49
97Sco-371
97ScoShoS-371
97ScoShoSAP-371
97ScoHobR-371
97ScoResC-371
97SP-81
97StaClu-295
97StaCluMOP-295
97Top-315
97TopSta-99
97TopStaAM-99
97Ult-209
97UltGolME-209
97UltPlaME-209
97UppDec-368

Kiley, Craig
84LitFalMT-15

Kilgo, Dub
94HelBreF-3628
94HelBreSP-25
95BelBreTI-29

Kilgo, Rusty
89JamExpP-2156
90MidLeaASGS-11
90ProAaA-110
90RocExpLC-12
90RocExpP-2685
91FloStaLAP-FSL43
91WesPalBEC-6
91WesPalBEP-1222
92CedRapRC-15
92CedRapRF-1069
92ChaLooF-3814
92RocExpC-4
93ChaLooF-2360
94IndIndF-1806
95ChaLooTI-8
96MemChiB-18

Kilgus, Paul
86TulDriTI-20
87OklCit8P-1
88Don-469
88DonBasB-111
88Fle-471
88FleGlo-471
88RanMot-19
88Sco-536
88ScoGlo-536
88Top-427
88TopTif-427
89Bow-285
89BowTif-285
89CubMar-39
89Don-283
89DonBasB-149
89DonTra-42
89Fle-525
89FleGlo-525
89FleUpd-76
89OPC-276
89Sco-271
89Top-276
89TopTif-276
89TopTra-60T
89TopTraT-60T
89UppDec-335
89UppDec-797
90BluJayFS-14
90Bow-508
90BowTif-508
90CMC-335
90Don-276
90Fle-34
90FleCan-34
90OPC-86
90ProAAAF-346
90PubSti-196
90Sco-196
90SyrChiC-9
90SyrChiMB-13
90SyrChiP-566
90Top-86
90TopTif-86
90UppDec-155
90VenSti-268
91OriCro-499
92LouRedF-1885
92LouRedS-266
92Sco-268
92StaClu-722
93FleFinE-125
93LouRedF-209
93RanKee-217
94CarPol-8
94Pac-593
94StaCluT-324
94StaCluTFDI-324
94Top-737
94TopGol-737
94TopSpa-737

Kilkenny, Mike
69TigTeal-5
69Top-544
70MLBOffS-209
70OPC-424
70Top-424
71MLBOffS-397
71OPC-86
71Top-86
72OPC-337
72Top-337
73OPC-551
73Top-551
77PadSchC-33

Killebrew, Cameron
79WauTimT-22

Killebrew, Harmon
47Exh-117A
47Exh-117B
47Exh-117C
47PM1StaP1-103
55DonWin-29
55DonWin-43
55Top-124
55TopDouH-111
56Top-164
58HarSta-16
58Top-288
59HomRunD-10
59Top-515
59WilSpoG-4
60Baz-20
60KeyChal-28
60NuHi-49
60Pos-5
60RawGloT-11
60SenJayP-7
60SenUniMC-10
60Top-210
60TopTat-26
60TopTat-91
61ChePat-6
61NuSco-449
61Pos-92A
61Pos-92B
61Top-80
61TopStal-181
61TwiCloD-10
61TwiJayP-5
61TwiPetM-18
61TwiUniMC-7
62Baz-44
62ExhStaB-18
62Jel-85
62Pos-85
62PosCan-85
62SalPlaC-36
62ShiPlaC-36
62Top-53
62Top-70
62Top-316
62TopBuc-44
62TopStal-76
62TopVen-53
62TopVen-70
63BasMagM-44
63Baz-7
63ExhStaB-35
63Jel-5
63Pos-5
63Top-4
63Top-500
63TopStil-22
63TwiJayP-6
64Baz-7
64Top-10
64Top-12
64Top-81
64Top-177
64TopCoi-112
64TopCoi-133
64TopGia-38
64TopSta-34
64TopStaU-39
64TopTatl-47
64TopVen-10
64TopVen-12
64TopVen-81
64TopVen-177
64TwiJayP-7
64WheSta-25
65Baz-7
65OldLonC-28
65OPC-3
65OPC-5
65Top-3
65Top-5
65Top-400
65TopEmbl-56
65TopTral-52
66Baz-11
66OPC-120
66Top-120
66TopRubl-45
66TopVen-120
66TwiFaiG-7
67AshOil-4
67Baz-11
67CokCapA-18
67CokCapAAm-26
67CokCapTw-6
67DexPre-115
67DexPre-116
67OPCPapl-23
67Top-241
67Top-243
67Top-334
67Top-460
67TopGiaSU-6
67TopPos-23
67TopVen-206
68Baz-8
68DexPre-46
68OPC-4
68OPC-6
68Top-4
68Top-6
68Top-220
68Top-361
68Top-490
68TopActS-2B
68TopActS-9A
68TopActS-14B
68TopGaml-5
68TopPla-7
68TopPos-10
68TopVen-4
68TopVen-6
68TopVen-220
68TopVen-361
69CitMetC-4
69MilBra-145
69MLBOffS-68
69MLBPin-14
69Top-375
69TopDecl-21
69TopSta-195
69TopSup-19
69TopTeaP-15
69TraSta-11
69TwiTealC-6
70DayDaiNM-4
70Kel-61
70MilBra-12
70MLBOffS-234
70OPC-64
70OPC-66
70OPC-150
70Top-64
70Top-66
70Top-150
70TopScr-11
70TopSup-4
70TraSta-15B
71AllBasA-14
71BazNumT-17
71BazUnn-2
71Kel-55
71MilDud-14
71MLBOffS-465
71MLBOffS-566
71OPC-65
71OPC-550
71Top-65
71Top-550
71TopCoi-100
71TopGreM-8
71TopSup-60
71TopTat-49
71TopTat-50
72MilBra-182
72OPC-51
72OPC-52
72OPC-88
72ProStaP-28
72Top-51
72Top-52
72Top-88
72TopPos-20
73OPC-170
73Top-170
73TopCanL-25
73TopCom-9
73TopPin-9
74OPC-400
74Top-400
74TopSta-208
75OPC-207
75OPC-640
75Top-207
75Top-640
76LauDiaJ-13
76SSP-168
77SerSta-15
78TCM60I-90
78TwiFri-8
80Lau300-14
80MarExh-15
80PacLeg-69
80PerHaloFP-188
80SSPHOF-185
82CraJac-5
82K-M-15
83DiaClaS2-89
83FraBroR-28
83FraBroR-40
83YanYealT-7
84OCoandSI-19
84SpoDesPW-23
84TwiTeal-33
85CirK-5
86BigLeaC-5
86SpoDecG-48
86TCMSupS-12
86TwiGreT-1
87K-M-4
87NesDreT-22
88ChaLooLTI-18
88GreBasS-18
88PacLegI-86
89KahCoo-7
89PacLegI-163
89PerCelP-23
89SweBasG-70
89TopBasT-13
90AGFA-3
90PacLeg-35
90PerGreM-48
91Col-34
91Kel3D-6
91LinDri-41
91MDAA-16
91SweBasG-49
91UppDecHoB-H1
91UppDecHoB-AU1
91UppDecHoB5-1
92MDAMVP-6
92MDAMVP-20
92MVP-6
92MVP2H-8
92TVSpoMF5HRC-5
93ActPacA-118
93ActPacA2-52G
93MCIAmb-10
93Pin-481
93UppDecS-15
94TedWil-49
94TedWil5C-3
94TopArc1-254
94TopArc1G-254
95EagBalL-4
95MCIAmb-6
95SonGre-6
95TopLegot6M-11

Killeen, Evans
77FriOneYW-104

Killeen, Tim
92SouOreAC-12
92SouOreAF-3419
93MadMusC-17
93MadMusF-1825
94ModA'sC-17
94ModA'sF-3066
95MemChiTI-23
96MemChiB-19

Killefer, Bill
09ColChiE-152A
09ColChiE-152B
10JuJuDE-22
12ColRedB-152A
12ColRedB-152B
12ColTinT-152A
12ColTinT-152B
14CraJacE-135
15CraJacE-135
15SpoNewM-93
16BF2FP-88
17HolBreD-58
21E121So8-49A
21Exh-91
22AmeCarE-38
23WilChoV-80
94ConTSN-1178
94ConTSN-1274
94ConTSNB-1178
94ConTSNB-1274

Killefer, Red (Wade H.)
09BusBroBPP-9
11SpoLifM-126
16FleBreD-51
94ConTSN-1178
94ConTSNB-1178

Killen, Brent
92NiaFalRC-23
92NiaFalRF-3332
93LakTigC-12
94LakTigC-12
94LakTigF-3044

Killen, Frank
98CamPepP-41

Killian, Ed
07TigACDPP-8
08RosComP-35
09ColChiE-153A
09ColChiE-153B
09T206-185
09T206-186
09TigTaCP-10
09WolNewDTPP-10
10CouT21-36
10SweCapPP-27
11MecDFT-21
11SpoLifCW-201
11T205-87
12ColRedB-153A
12ColRedB-153B
12ColTinT-153A
12ColTinT-153B
81TigDetN-87

Killifer, William
14PieStaT-30
16ColE13-93
16SpoNewM-95
19W514-87
21E121So1-53A
21E121So1-53B
21E121So8-49B
23W501-56

Killingsworth, Kirk
83TulDriT-12
85TulDriTI-32
86TulDriTI-3
87OklCit8P-9

Killingsworth, Sam
75BurBeeT-13

Kilner, John Steven
86DurBulP-16
87GreBraB-14
88GreBraB-20
89GreBraS-11
89RicBraTI-12
90Bes-289
90GreBraB-21
90GreBraB-22
90GreBraP-1125
90GreBraS-10

Kilrain, Jake
87AllandGN-14
88GooN16-24

Kilroy, Mathew
87BucN28-3
87OldJudN-287
88SpoTimM-16

Kim, Bobby
93BoiHawC-17
93BoiHawF-3930

Kim, Kwang Ung
87AncGlaP-18

Kim, Wendell
75LafDriT-2
77PhoGiaCC-15
77PhoGiaCP-15
77PhoGiaVNB-15
78PhoGiaC-13
81CliGiaT-2
82CliGiaF-2
85FreGiaP-1
86ShrCapP-13
86ShrCapP-14
87PhoFirP-23
88PhoFirC-24
88PhoFirP-65
89GiaMot-28
90GiaMot-21
90GiaSmo-11
91GiaMot-27
92GiaMot-28
92GiaPacGaE-22
93GiaMot-28
93GiaPos-20
94GiaMot-28
95GiaMot-28
96GiaMot-28

Kimata, Tatsuhiko
79TCMJapPB-73

Kimball, Doug
92GreFalDSP-18

Kimball, Newt
40DodTeal-13
41DodTeal-4
42DodTeal-13
43PhiTeal-12
90DodTar-409

Kimball, Ricky
88CapCodPPaLP-142
91SouOreAC-6
91SouOreAP-3838
92ProFS7-137

Kimball, Scott
90BelBreB-8
90BelBreS-11
90Bes-124
90MidLeaASGS-12

Kimber, Doug
95RocCubTI-30

Kimberlin, Keith
89NiaFalRP-13
90FloStaLA3-34
90LakTigS-15
90StaFS7-36
91Cla/Bes-170
91LinDriAA-389
91LonTigLD-389
91LonTigP-1885
93ReaPhiF-301
94ReaPhiF-2071
94ScrRedBF-926

Kimberling, Shannon
94ColSilBC-5
95ColSilB-15
95ColSilB9-5

Kimbler, Doug
90NiaFalRP-2
91FayGenC-19
91FayGenP-1178

Kimbrell, Mike
96ButCopKB-19

Kimbro, Henry
93NegLeaRL2-21
93UppDecS-17
95NegLeaL2-16

Kimbrough, Larry
86NegLeaF-37
86NegLeaF-61
92NegLeaRLI-35

Kimel, Jack
92ButCopKSP-11
93ChaRaiC-8
93ChaRaiF-1903
93SouAtlLAGF-7
94ClaGolF-30
94TulDriF-240
94TulDriTI-11
95TulDriTI-10

Kimler, Mike
92LetMouSP-17

Kimm, Bruce
77Top-554
81Fle-355
81Top-272
83CedRapRF-22
83CedRapRT-1
84RedEnq-28
86RedTexG-NNO
87RedKah-NNO
88RedKah-NNO
89PirVerFJ-36
90CedRapRDGB-27
91PadSmo-17
92PadMot-27
92PadPolD-28
92PadSmo-16
93GreBraF-364
94RicBraF-2864
96OrlCubB-1
95OrlCubF-25

Kimm, Tyson
95BatCliTI-19
96PieBolWB-15

Kimsey, Chad
92ConTSN-511

Kimsey, Keith
91BriTigC-12
91BriTigP-3618
92NiaFalRC-22
92NiaFalRF-3340

93FayGenC-12
93FayGenF-141
94Bow-561
94LakTigC-13
Kinard, Rudy
75SpoIndC-3
Kindall, Jerry
58Top-221
59Top-274
60Top-444
61CubJayP-9
61Pos-199A
61Pos-199B
61Top-27
62AmeTraS-51A
62AmeTraS-51B
62Jel-191
62Pos-191
62PosCan-191
62Top-292
63Fle-13
63Jel-68
63Pos-68
63Top-36
78TCM60I-218
78TCM60I-271
78TwiFri-35
84AriWilP-9
86AriWilP-9
87AriWilP-7
88AriWilP-6
90AriWilP-10
92AriWilP-7
Kindelan, Orestes
90IBAWorA-41
Kindell, Scott
94KinMetC-5
94KinMetF-3815
95PitMetTI-45
Kinder, Ellis
46SeaSLP-25
47Exh-118
48RedSoxTI-13
50Bow-152
51Bow-128
51R42SmaS-55
52Top-78
53RedSoxFNSMS-2
53RedSoxTI-16
53Top-44
54Bow-98
54Top-47
55Top-115
55TopDouH-129
56Top-336
57Top-352
79TCM50-115
83TopRep5-78
91TopArc1-44
94TopArc1-47
94TopArc1G-47
Kindler, Tom
92SpoIndC-8
92SpoIndF-1289
93WatDiaC-20
93WatDiaF-1765
94SprSulC-15
94SprSulF-2033
Kindred, Curt
83VisOakF-22
84VisOakT-2
86CedRapRT-6
87CedRapRP-4
Kindred, Vincent L.
87SprCarB-23
89SavCarP-355
90Bes-302
90SprCarB-10
Kiner, Ralph
46SpoExcW-6-7
47Exh-119
47HomBon-28
47PM1StaP1-104
47TipTop-143
48BluTin-7
48Bow-3
49Bow-29
49EurSta-164
49IndVisEI-9
49Lea-91
49MPR302-2-110
50AmeNut&CCP-12
50Bow-33
50PirTeal-9
51BerRos-C1
51R42SmaS-58
51TopCurA-6
51TopRedB-15
52BerRos-30
52Bow-11
52DixLid-11
52DixPre-11
52RedMan-NL12
52StaCalL-77B
52StaCalS-89D
52Whe-16A
52Whe-16B
53BowC-80
53DixLid-10
53DixPre-10
53ExhCan-22
53MacSta-1
53RedMan-NL15
53Top-191
54Bow-45
54DixLid-7
54RedHeaF-13
55Bow-197
55IndCarBL-5
55IndGolS-16
60Fle-79
61Fle-50
74LauAllG-51
74NewYorNTDiS-7
75TCMAllG-18
76ShaPiz-151
76TayBow4-9
77GalGloG-2
77Top-437
79BasGre-80
79TCM50-13
80PacLeg-81
80PerHaloFP-151
80SSPHOF-151
82CraJac-11
82GSGalAG-15
83DiaClaS2-110
83DonHOFH-38
85CirK-30
86PirGreT-5
86SpoDecG-35
86TCMSupS-14
87HygAllG-29
87MetColP-51
88PacLegI-9
89PerCelP-24
89RinPosM1-32
89TopBasT-36
90PacLeg-36
90PerGreM-75
90SweBasG-80
91Col-12
91Kel3D-15
91SweBasG-50
91TopArc1-191
92ActPacA-5
92ActPacA2-5G
92BazQua5A-17
93ActPacAC-5
93TedWil-76
93TedWil-127
94UppDecAH-49
94UppDecAH1-49
97TopStaHRR-7
97TopStaHRRA-7
King, Andre
93DanBraC-1
93DanBraF-3632
94Bow-217
94ClaGolF-48
94ExcFS7-157
94MacBraC-1
94MacBraF-2218
94SigRoo-13
94SigRooS-13
94Top-752
94TopGol-752
94TopSpa-752
94UppDecML-126
95DurBulTI-16
95UppDecML-109
95UppDecML-118
96BesAutSA-37
95UppDecMLFS-109
95UppDecMLFS-118
King, Anthony
93HunCubC-13
93HunCubF-3251
King, Bill
94SigRooDP-55
94SigRooDPS-55
94SouOreAC-14
94SouOreAF-3617
95MidLeaA-27
95WesMicWTI-34
96ModA'sB-22
King, Billie Jean
74NewYorNTDiS-10
King, Brett
93EveGiaC-15
93EveGiaF-3775
94Bow-603
94ClaGolF-62
94SanJosGC-13
94SanJosGF-2825
King, Brion
96DunBluJUTI-5
King, Bryan
88SanBerSB-22
88SanBerSCLC-28
89SanBerSB-20
89SanBerSCLC-80
90WilBilB-12
90WilBilP-1063
90WilBilS-13
91SanBerSC-17
91SanBerSP-1994
King, Cesar
96ChaRivTI-9616
King, Chick (Charles G.)
55Bow-133
59Top-538
King, Clarence
92NegLeaRLI-36
King, Clay
92EveGiaC-14
92EveGiaF-1697
93CliGiaC-14
94SanJosGC-14
94SanJosGF-2826
King, Clyde
50WorWidGV-26
51Bow-299
52Bow-56
52Top-205
58JetPos-10
69Top-274
70Top-624
71RicBraTI-11
75OPC-589
75Top-589
83Top-486
83TopRep5-205
88RinPosD1-12A
90DodTar-410
90SweBasG-117
91SweBasG-51
95TopArcBD-12
King, Curtis
94NewJerCC-16
94NewJerCF-3414
King, David
90AppFoxBS-16
90AppFoxP-2101
91BasCitRC-18
91BasCitRP-1404
King, Douglas
90CedRapRB-21
90ChaWheP-2235
91ChaWheC-5
91ChaWheP-2882
King, Eric
86DonRoo-27
86SpoRoo-42
86TopTra-53T
86TopTraT-53T
87Don-250
87Fle-155
87FleGlo-155
87SpoTeaP-15
87TigCaiD-19
87Top-36
87TopRoo-8
87TopTif-36
87ToyRoo-16
88Don-50
88Fle-60
88FleGlo-60
88OPC-108
88Sco-471
88ScoGlo-471
88StaLinTi-10
88TigPep-25
88TolMudHC-5
88TolMudHP-592
88Top-499
88TopSti-271
88TopTif-499
89Don-535
89DonBasB-235
89DonTra-37
89Fle-136
89FleGlo-136
89FleUpd-19
89Sco-471
89ScoRoo-26T
89ScoYouS2-7
89Top-238
89TopTif-238
89TopTra-61T
89TopTraT-61T
89UppDec-493
89WhiSoxC-14
90Bow-304
90BowTif-304
90Don-337
90DonBesA-46
90Fle-537
90FleCan-537
90Lea-43
90OPC-786
90PubSti-392
90Sco-28
90Top-786
90TopTif-786
90UppDec-651
90VenSti-269
90WhiSoxC-12
91Bow-63
91ClaGam-56
91Don-271
91Fle-126
91IndFanC-17
91Lea-382
91OPC-121
91Sco-124
91ScoRoo-60T
91StaClu-328
91Stu-47
91Top-121
91TopDesS-121
91TopMic-121
91TopTif-121
91UppDec-281
91UppDec-782
92Bow-317
92Fle-115
92OPC-326
92OPCPre-80
92Pin-503
92Sco-144
92ScoRoo-42T
92StaClu-125
92StaClu-638
92StaCluECN-638
92Top-326
92TopGol-326
92TopGolW-326
92TopMic-326
92UppDec-679
King, Frank J.
09T206-496
King, Hal (Harold)
36GouWidPPR-D15
36WorWidGV-121
67Ast-15
69MilBra-146
70OPC-327
70Top-327
71MLBOffS-15
71OPC-88
71Top-88
72Top-598
74OPC-362
74Top-362
76LauIndC-32
93RanKee-21
King, Hank
85PhiTas-8
93BoiHawC-18
93BoiHawF-3924
94LakElsSC-11
94LakElsSF-1671
King, Jake
91ColMetPI-18
King, Jason
90PitMetP-8
92St.LucMCB-23
92St.LucMF-1754
93St.LucMC-15
King, Jeff
87SalBucP-24
88EasLeaAP-16
88Fle-653
88FleGlo-653
88HarSenP-859
89BufBisC-16
89BufBisP-1671
89FleUpd-114
90Don-480
90Fle-469
90FleCan-469
90Hot50RS-25
90Lea-163
90OPC-454
90PirHomC-13
90Sco-549
90Sco100RS-71
90ScoYouS2-16
90Top-454
90TopBig-117
90TopDeb89-66
90TopRoo-17
90TopTif-454
90UppDec-557
91Bow-520
91Don-233
91Fle-39
91Lea-71
91OPC-272
91PanFreS-117
91Sco-244
91StaClu-528
91Top-272
91TopDesS-272
91TopMic-272
91TopTif-272
91Ult-280
91UppDec-687
92Don-468
92Fle-555
92Lea-420
92OPC-693
92Pin-317
92PirNatI-9
92Sco-511
92StaClu-24
92Top-693
92TopGol-693
92TopGolW-693
92TopMic-693
92Ult-553
92UppDec-111
93Bow-654
93Don-252
93Fla-113
93Fle-113
93Lea-207
93OPC-96
93PacSpa-245
93PanSti-284
93Pin-355
93PirHil-4
93PirNatI-13
93Sco-159
93SP-185
93StaClu-93
93StaCluFDI-93
93StaCluMOP-93
93Stu-102
93Top-136
93TopGol-136
93TopInaM-136
93TopMic-136
93TriPla-182
93Ult-97
93UppDec-240
93UppDecGold-240
94Bow-490
94ColC-163
94ColChoGS-163
94ColChoSS-163
94Don-538
94DonMVP-11
94ExtBas-347
94Fin-65
94FinRef-65
94Fla-422
94Fle-611
94FUnPac-128

94Lea-145
94LeaL-140
94OPC-151
94Pac-499
94PanSti-236
94Pin-208
94PinArtP-208
94PinMusC-208
94PirQui-9
94Sco-382
94ScoGolR-382
94Sel-56
94SP-142
94SPDieC-142
94StaClu-338
94StaCluFDI-338
94StaCluGR-338
94StaCluMOP-338
94Stu-146
94Top-44
94TopGol-44
94TopSpa-44
94TriPla-185
94Ult-256
94UppDec-238
94UppDecAJ-27
94UppDecAJG-27
94UppDecED-238
95ColCho-379
95ColChoGS-379
95ColChoSS-379
95Don-108
95DonPreP-108
95DonTopotO-317
95Emo-175
95Fin-133
95FinRef-133
95Fla-401
95Fle-480
95Lea-270
95LeaLim-46
95Pac-344
95Pin-35
95PinArtP-35
95PinMusC-35
95PirFil-14
95Sco-109
95ScoGolR-109
95ScoPlaTS-109
95StaClu-433
95StaClu-506
95StaCluMOP-433
95StaCluMOP-506
95StaCluSTWS-433
95StaCluSTWS-506
95StaCluVR-228
95Stu-180
95Top-501
95TopCyb-291
95Ult-216
95UltGolM-216
95UppDec-384
95UppDecED-384
95UppDecEDG-384
95UppDecSE-87
95UppDecSEG-87
95Zen-50
96Baz-75
96Cir-173
96CirRav-173
96ColCho-258
96ColChoGS-258
96ColChoSS-258
96Don-498
96DonDiaK-13
96DonPreP-498
96EmoXL-256
96Fin-S78
96FinRef-S78
96Fla-348
96Fle-523
96FleTeaL-25
96FleTif-523
96Lea-55
96LeaPrePB-55
96LeaPrePG-55
96LeaPrePS-55
96LeaSigA-128
96LeaSigAG-128
96LeaSigAS-128
96MetUni-216
96MetUniP-216
96MetUniProS-216
96Pac-172
96PanSti-68
96Pin-49
96PinAfi-34
96PinAfiAP-34
96PinAfiFPP-34
96Sco-462
96Sel-54
96SelArtP-54
96SelTeaN-3
96Spo-38
96SpoArtP-38
96StaClu-194
96StaClu-335
96StaCluEPB-335
96StaCluEPG-335
96StaCluEPS-335
96StaCluMOP-194
96StaCluMOP-335
95StaCluVRMC-228
96Stu-31
96StuPrePB-31
96StuPrePG-31
96StuPrePS-31
96Sum-27
96SumAbo&B-27
96SumArtP-27
96SumFoi-27
96Top-116
96TopChr-32
96TopChrR-32
96TopGal-20
96TopGalPPI-20
96TopLas-25
96Ult-534
96UltGolM-534
96UppDec-175
97Bow-68
97BowChr-49
97BowChrI-49
97BowChrIR-49
97BowChrR-49
97BowInt-68
97Cir-386
97CirRav-386
97Don-323
97DonPreP-323
97DonPrePGold-323
97Fin-244
97FinRef-244
97Fle-430
97Fle-656
97FleTeaL-25
97FleTif-430
97FleTif-656
97Lea-253
97LeaFraM-253
97LeaFraMDC-253
97MetUni-239
97NewPin-152
97NewPinAP-152
97NewPinMC-152
97NewPinPP-152
97Pac-395
97PacLigB-395
97PacSil-395
97Pin-74
97PinArtP-74
97PinMusC-74
97RoyPol-13
97Sco-17
97Sco-362
97ScoHobR-362
97ScoPreS-17
97ScoResC-362
97ScoShoS-17
97ScoShoS-362
97ScoShoSAP-17
97ScoShoSAP-362
97SP-91
97SpolII-155
97SpolIIEE-155
97StaClu-326
97StaCluMOP-326
97Top-28
97TopChr-11
97TopChrR-11
97TopGal-74
97TopGalPPI-74
97TopIntF-ILM8
97TopIntFR-ILM8
97Ult-263
97Ult-412
97UltGolME-263
97UltGolME-412
97UltPlaME-263
97UltPlaME-412
97UppDec-539

King, Jerome
83TacTigT-6

King, Jerry
81BriRedST-13

King, Jim (James H.)
56Top-74
57Top-186
58Top-332
60MapLeaSF-11
61Top-351
62Top-42
62TopVen-42
63Top-176
64Top-217
64TopVen-217
65OPC-38
65Top-38
65TopEmbl-54
65TopTral-53
66Top-369
66TopVen-369
67CokCapS-8
67DexPre-117
67Top-509
78TCM60I-207

King, Joe
82DanSunF-22
83PeoSunF-2

King, John
90GeoColC-14

King, Kenny
87MiaMarP-1
88BakDodCLC-254

King, Kevin
80WauTimT-20
81WauTimT-27
83ChaLooT-18
84ChaLooT-1B
86MidAngP-12
87EdmTraP-2068
88EdmTraC-25
88EdmTraP-573
89TenTecGE-33

King, Kevin Ray
88CapCodPPaLP-99
88OklSoo-20
89OklSoo-19
90OklSoo-13
91PenPilC-6
91PenPilP-372
92SanBerC-22
92SanBerSF-948
93RivPilCLC-9
94MarMot-26
94Top-774
94TopGol-774
94TopSpa-774
94Ult-420
95Sco-590
95ScoGolR-590
95ScoPlaTS-590

King, Lee
21Nei-92
22E120-200
22W572-55
23WilChoV-81

King, Lynn
40SolHug-11
43CenFlo-16

King, Mike
81QuaCitCT-17
84NasSouTI-11
87ChaRaiP-4
88ChaRaiP-1202
89WatDiaP-1787
89WatDiaS-15
96ButCopKB-20

King, Nelson
55Top-112
57Top-349
79TCM50-247

King, Randy
85NewOriT-2

King, Raymond
95BilRedTI-21
96DurBulBrB-3
96MacBraB-9

King, Richard
76LauIndC-5
76LauIndC-31
91WavRedF-10
92SouOreAF-3412
93SouOreAC-12
93SouOreAF-4057

King, Ron
86SalRedBP-14

King, Silver (Charles F.)
87OldJudN-288
89EdgR.WG-15

King, Steve
86JamExpP-14
89BoiHawP-2002
90QuaCitAGS-10
91LinDriAA-439
91MidAngLD-439
91MidAngOHP-15
91MidAngP-432

King, Thomas
93HunCubC-14
93HunCubF-3252

King, Tiger
93ButCopKSP-3

King, Tom
74SacSolC-54
75AppFoxT-9
76CliPilT-22
87WytCubP-28
94WilCubC-12
94WilCubF-3779

King, Willie
96YakBeaTI-55

Kingery, Mike
82ChaRoyT-12
84MemChiT-7
85OmaRoyT-23
86OmaRoyP-13
86OmaRoyT-4
86SpoRoo-37
87Don-424
87DonOpeD-119
87Fle-371
87FleGlo-371
87FleUpd-57
87FleUpdG-57
87MarMot-17
87Top-203
87TopTif-203
87TopTra-58T
87TopTraT-58T
88Don-322
88Fle-376
88FleGlo-376
88Lea-104
88MarMot-17
88OPC-119
88PanSti-193
88Sco-178
88ScoGlo-178
88StaLinMa-7
88Top-532
88TopBig-160
88TopTif-532
89CalCanC-20
89CalCanP-545
89Top-413
89TopTif-413
90CMC-538
90Don-601
90PhoFirC-11
90PhoFirP-23
90ProAAAF-49
91Don-573
91GiaMot-21
91GiaPacGaE-16
91Lea-224
91OPC-657
91Sco-547
91Top-657
91TopDesS-657
91TopMic-657
91TopTif-657
92StaClu-862
92TacTigF-2516
93OmaRoyF-1690
94FleUpd-126
95ColCho-441
95ColChoGS-441
95ColChoSS-441
95Don-96
95DonPreP-96
95DonTopotO-229
95Fle-522
95Pac-139
95PacPri-46
95Pin-29
95PinArtP-29
95PinMusC-29
95RocPol-8
95Sco-156
95ScoGolR-156
95ScoPlaTS-156
95StaClu-307
95StaCluMOP-307
95StaCluSTWS-307
95StaCluVR-163
95Top-615
95TopCyb-383
95Ult-155
95UltGolM-155
95UppDec-411
95UppDecED-411
95UppDecEDG-411
96ColCho-684
96ColChoGS-684
96ColChoSS-684
96Don-400
96DonPreP-400
96Fla-349
96Fle-365
96FleTif-365
96FleUpd-U178
96FleUpdTC-U178
96LeaSigEA-100
96Pac-60
95StaCluVRMC-163
96Ult-535
96UltGolM-535
96UppDec-437
97PacPriGotD-GD193

Kingman, Brendan
94KanCouCC-12
94KanCouCF-164
94KanCouCTI-13
95AusFut-26
95AusFut-99
95AusFutGP-5
95AusFutSFP-SFFP8
95BreCouMF-248

Kingman, Brian
77SanJosMC-19
79OgdA'sT-13
80Top-671
80VenLeaS-224
81Don-360
81Fle-579
81Top-284
82Don-87
82Fle-96
82OPC-231
82TacTigT-25
82Top-476
83Fle-522
83Top-312
84PhoGiaC-15

Kingman, Dave
72OPC-147
72Top-147
73Kel2D-44
73LinPor-159
73OPC-23
73Top-23
74OPC-610
74Top-610
74TopSta-106
75Hos-85
75MetSSP-9
75OPC-156
75SSPSam-3
75Top-156
76CraDis-26
76Hos-15
76HosTwi-15
76MetMSAP-2
76OPC-40
76OPC-193
76Spo-1
76SSP-542
76Top-40
76Top-193
77BurCheD-141
77Hos-60
77Kel-35
77MetDaiPA-9
77MSADis-32
77OPC-98
77PepGloD-69
77RCColC-32
77Spo-2721
77Spo-4208

77Top-500
77TopCloS-24
78Hos-26
78Pep-33
78RCColC-5
78SSP270-252
78TasDis-19
78Top-570
78WifBalD-34
79Hos-146
79OPC-191
79Top-370
79TopCom-20
80Kel-6
80OPC-127
80Top-202
80Top-240
80TopSup-16
81AllGamPI-148
81CokTeaS-87
81Don-553
81Dra-19
81Fle-291
81FleStiC-111
81Kel-47
81OPC-361
81PerCreC-18
81Squ-14
81Top-450
81TopScr-69
81TopSti-151
81TopSupHT-26
81TopTra-781
82Don-17
82Don-182
82Dra-21
82Fle-530
82FleSta-85
82Kel-19
82MetPhoA-14
82OPC-276
82Top-690
82TopSti-72
83Don-301
83Dra-14
83Fle-548
83FleSti-232
83OPC-160
83OPC-161
83Top-160
83Top-161
83Top-702
83TopFol-2
83TopLeaS-7
83TopSti-11
83TopSti-207
83TopSti-259
84A'sMot-15
84Don-360
84DonCha-3
84Fle-590
84FleUpd-62
84FunFooP-36
84Nes792-573
84Nes792-703
84OPC-172
84Top-573
84Top-703
84TopTif-573
84TopTif-703
84TopTra-63T
84TopTraT-63T
85A'sMot-2
85CirK-26
85Don-54
85DonActA-32
85Fle-427
85FleLimE-15
85FleStaS-14
85FleStaS-29
85FleStaS-48
85Lea-182
85OPC-123
85Top-730
85Top3-D-12
85TopGloS-5
85TopSti-320
85TopSup-59
85TopTif-730
86A'sMot-2
86BasStaB-64
86Don-54
86Fle-423
86FleStiC-67
86OPC-322
86SevCoi-W9
86Spo-68
86Spo-116
86Spo-150
86Top-410
86TopSti-167
86TopTif-410
86Woo-16
87Don-425
87Fle-396
87FleGlo-396
87FleLeaL-27
87OPC-266
87RedFolSB-115
87Spo-178
87Top-709
87TopMinL-69
87TopSti-173
87TopTif-709
88AlaGolAA'TI-7
89PacLegI-175
89PacSenL-164
89PacSenL-186
89T/MSenL-59
89TopSenL-101
90EliSenL-24
90EliSenL-126
90PacLeg-87
90SouCalS-7
91MetWIZ-211
91SweBasG-52
91UppDecS-21
92ActPacA-56
92MCIAmb-7
92UppDecS-7
92YanWIZ7-90
93TedWil-57
94UppDecAH-86
94UppDecAH-208
94UppDecAH1-86
94UppDecAH1-208

Kingman, Eamon
88CapCodPPaLP-17

Kingsale, Eugene
96Bow-157
96FreKeyB-12
97Bow-129
97BowBes-156
97BowBesAR-156
97BowBesR-156
97BowCerBIA-CA44
97BowCerGIA-CA44
97BowChr-141
97BowChrI-141
97BowChrIR-141
97BowChrR-141
97BowInt-129
97Cir-223
97CirRav-223
97Sel-118
97SelArtP-118
97SelRegG-118
97UppDec-470

Kingsolver, Kurt
80BurBeeT-19
82ElPasDT-4

Kingston, Mark
92HelBreF-1721
92HelBreSP-3
93PeoChiTI-13
94DayCubC-13
94DayCubF-2359
96OrlCubB-14

Kingwood, Tyrone
88WesPalBES-15
90SanBerSCLC-102
90SanBerSP-2644
91Cla/Bes-304
91HagSunLD-234
91HagSunP-2467
91LinDriAA-234
92LonTigF-646
92LonTigS-411
92SkyAA F-175
92UppDecML-220

Kinkade, Mike
95HelBreTI-6
96BelSnaTI-19
96MidLeaAB-11

Kinlaw, Jeff
92AlbPolC-28

Kinnard, Ken (Kenneth Joe)
83KinBluJTI-9
86VenGulP-10
87GreBraB-27

Kinney, Brad
84ButCopKT-13

Kinney, Dennis
75SanAntBT-12
76WilTomT-14
79HawIsIC-17
79HawIsIT-18
81Don-363
81EvaTriT-22
81Fle-505
81Top-599
82TacTigT-6

Kinney, Matt
96LowSpiB-13

Kinney, Michael
93GreFalDSP-11
94BakDodC-12

Kinney, Tom
91Cla/Bes-139
91SavCarC-8
91SavCarP-1649

Kinnon, Duane
93NiaFalRF-3397

Kinnunen, Mike
81TolMudHT-6
83MemChiT-24
85OmaRoyT-18
86RocRedWP-12
88BlaYNPRWL-60
88ColCliC-9
88ColCliP-4
88ColCliP-316
88TriAAAP-10
89BlaYNPRWLU-6
89DenZepC-4
89DenZepP-33
91OriCro-239

Kinsel, David
83AppFoxF-23

Kinsella, W.P.
90LitSunW-15

Kinslow, Thomas
90DodTar-1000
95May-16A
95May-16B

Kinugasa, Sachio
79TCMJapPB-9
87JapPlaB-9
93UppDecS-22

Kinyoun, Tavis
89BriTigS-13
91BasCitRC-14
91BasCitRP-1400

Kinzer, Matt
85SprCarT-14
86St.PetCP-17
88ArkTraGS-14
88LouRedBTI-24
88BlaYNPRWL-92
89LouRedBC-7
89LouRedBP-1255
89LouRedBTI-25
90CMC-382
90Fle-652
90FleCan-652
90ProAAAF-374
90Sco-628
90SprCarDGB-13
90TolMudHC-5
90TolMudHP-144
90TopDeb89-67

Kiper, Kory
92GulCoaYF-3787

Kipfer, Greg
82WisRapTF-2

Kipila, Jeff
88BenBucL-2
89BenBucL-18
90PalSprACLC-205
90PalSprAP-2584
91QuaCitAC-18
91QuaCitAP-2637
92MidAngF-4038
92MidAngOHP-12
92MidAngS-462
92SkyAA F-196
93ExcFS7-144
93VanCanF-2610
94HarSenF-2099
97MidAngOHP-18

Kipp, Fred
59DodTeal-10
59Top-258
60Top-202
90DodTar-1001
92YanWIZ6-67

Kipper, Bob
83PeoSunF-25
83TriTriT-3
86Don-44
86DonRoo-46
86Fle-648
86TopTra-54T
86TopTraT-54T
87Don-572
87Fle-612
87FleGlo-612
87Top-289
87TopTif-289
88Don-115
88Fle-332
88FleGlo-332
88Top-723
88TopBig-141
88TopTif-723
89Bow-414
89BowTif-414
89Don-409
89Fle-211
89FleGlo-211
89PirVerFJ-16
89Sco-354
89Top-114
89TopTif-114
89UppDec-520
90Don-362
90Fle-470
90FleCan-470
90OPC-441
90PirHomC-14
90Top-441
90TopTif-441
90UppDec-560
91Don-720
91Fle-40
91OPC-551
91Sco-646
91StaClu-334
91Top-551
91TopDesS-551
91TopMic-551
91TopTif-551
91UppDec-407
92Don-622
92Fle-556
92Lea-506
92OPC-64
92Pin-495
92Sco-340
92StaClu-752
92Top-64
92TopGol-64
92TopGolW-64
92TopMic-64

Kipper, Thornton
54Top-108
55Top-62
55TopDouH-9
94TopArc1-108
94TopArc1G-108

Kiraly, Jeff
92KinMetC-6
92KinMetF-1539
93CapCitBC-9
93CapCitBF-466
94CapCitBC-12
94CapCitBF-1756

Kirby, Butch
81BurBeeT-18
82BelBreF-15
83BelBreF-1

Kirby, Chris
78WauMetT-14

Kirby, Clay
69Top-637
70MLBOffS-115
70OPC-79
70Top-79
71MLBOffS-230
71OPC-333
71Top-333
72OPC-173
72OPC-174
72PadTeal-16
72Top-173
72Top-174
73OPC-655
73Top-655
73TopCanL-26
74OPC-287
74Top-287
74TopSta-96
75OPC-423
75Top-423
76ExpRed-16
76OPC-579
76SSP-28
76Top-579
76TopTra-579T
77PadSchC-34A
77PadSchC-34B

Kirby, Doug
96BilMusTI-17

Kirby, Scott
96HelBreTI-11

Kirby, Wayne
76TusTorCr-15

Kirby, Wayne Edward
85VerBeaDT-8
86VerBeaDP-14
87BakDodP-23
88BakDodCLC-249
88SanAntMB-8
89SanAntMB-8
90AlbDukC-23
90AlbDukP-359
90AlbDukT-17
90CMC-425
90ProAAAF-80
91ColSprSSLD-87
91ColSprSSP-2197
91LinDriAAA-87
92ColSprSSF-764
92ColSprSSS-87
92Fle-670
92TopDeb91-101
92TriA AAS-87
93ChaKniF-557
93Don-380
93Fla-193
93FleFinE-201
93IndWUA-14
93JimDeaR-5
93Lea-528
93Sco-328
93SelRoo-56T
93SP-122
93SP-123
93StaClu-35
93StaCluFDI-35
93StaCluMOP-35
94ColC-164
94ColChoGS-164
94ColChoSS-164
94Don-125
94ExtBas-59
94ExtBasSYS-10
94Fin-36
94FinRef-36
94Fla-40
94Fle-107
94FleRooS-9
94Lea-283
94OPC-219
94OPCDiaD-3
94Pac-171
94PanSti-57
94Pin-132
94PinArtP-132
94PinMusC-132
94Sco-230
94ScoBoyoS-16
94ScoGolR-230
94Sel-342
94StaClu-43
94StaCluFDI-43
94StaCluGR-43
94StaCluMOP-43
94Top-508
94TopGol-508
94TopSpa-508
94TriPla-114
94Ult-43
94USPlaCR-8D
95ColCho-276
95ColChoGS-276
95ColChoSS-276
95Don-237
95DonPreP-237

95Fle-136
95Lea-176
95Pac-121
95Sco-517
95ScoGolR-517
95ScoPlaTS-517
95StaClu-377
95StaCluMOP-377
95StaCluSTWS-377
95Top-227
95UppDec-342
95UppDec-347
95UppDecED-342
95UppDecEDG-342
96LeaSigEA-101
97Ult-521
97UltGolME-521
97UltPlaME-521
Kirchenwitz, Arno
78St.PetCT-15
79ArkTraT-1
Kirgan, Chris
94BluOriC-12
94BluOriF-3568
96HigDesMB-15
Kirk, Chuck
90HunCubP-3277
91PeoChiC-6
91PeoChiP-1338
91PeoChiTI-9
92WinSpiC-17
92WinSpiF-1205
93DayCubC-11
93DayCubF-855
Kirk, Thomas
52Par-79
Kirk, Tim
86WatPirP-11
87SalBucP-8
88CarLeaAS-11
88SalBucS-9
89PenPilS-9
Kirke, Judson
12T207-90
Kirkland, Kris
93BatCliC-15
93BatCliF-3142
94BatCliC-8
94BatCliF-3439
Kirkland, Willie
58GiaJayP-5
58GiaSFCB-12
58Top-128
59Top-484
60GiaJayP-7
60Top-172
60TopVen-172
61Kah-23
61Pos-146A
61Pos-146B
61Top-15
62IndJayP-6
62Jel-41
62Kah-23
62Pos-41
62PosCan-41
62SalPlaC-61
62ShiPlaC-61
62Top-447
63BasMagM-45
63IndJayP-9
63Jel-72
63Pos-72
63Top-187
64OriJayP-6
64Top-17
64TopVen-17
65OPC-148
65Top-148
66Top-434
91OriCro-240
Kirkpatrick, Bill
75IntLeaAT-14
Kirkpatrick, Ed
63Top-386
64Top-296
64TopVen-296
65Top-393
66OPC-102
66Top-102
66TopVen-102
67CokCapDA-35
67Top-293
68Top-552
69MilBra-147
69MLBOffS-59
69Top-529
70MLBOffS-223
70OPC-165
70RoyTeal-18
70Top-165
70TopPos-19
71MLBOffS-418
71OPC-299
71Top-299
72MilBra-183
72Top-569
72Top-570
73LinPor-150
73OPC-233
73Top-233
74OPC-262
74Top-262
74TopSta-183
74TopTra-262T
75OPC-171
75Top-171
76OPC-294
76SSP-580
76Top-294
77Top-582
78Top-77
86RoyGreT-8
93RanKee-218
94BreMilB-138
Kirkpatrick, Enos
90DodTar-411
Kirkpatrick, Jay
91GreFalDSP-18
92VerBeaDC-7
92VerBeaDF-2882
93BakDodCLC-14
93ClaGolF-98
93ExcFS7-52
94SanAntMF-2478
95AusFut-103
95SanBerSTI-10
96SanAntMB-11
96SigRooOJ-15
96SigRooOJS-15
Kirkpatrick, Stephen
87UtiBluSP-18
88ClePhiS-16
88SpaPhiS-9
89ClePhiS-12
90ReaPhiB-22
90ReaPhiP-1232
90ReaPhiS-15
Kirkreit, Daron
92TopTra-60T
92TopTraG-60T
93StaCluM-21
94ActPac-9
94Bow-495
94CarLeaAF-CAR34
94Cla-163
94ClaGolF-186
94ClaGolN1PLF-LP7
94ClaGolREF-RE7
94ClaTriF-T22
94ExcFS7-45
94KinIndF-2638
94Pin-263
94PinArtP-263
94PinMusC-263
94Sco-527
94ScoGolR-527
94TedWil-126
94UppDec-534
94UppDecAHNIL-8
94UppDecED-534
94UppDecML-122
95ActPacF-38
95Bow-144
95Exc-41
95UppDecML-75
95UppDecMLOP-OP8
95UppDecMLFS-75
Kirkwood, Don
76OPC-108
76Top-108
77Top-519
78BluJayP-12
78Top-251
79OPC-334
79Top-632
Kirsch, Paul
82CedRapRT-14
84CedRapRT-5
85CedRapRT-26
86CedRapRT-24
87CedRapRP-24
91LinDriAAA-425
91RoyPlaP-1584
92PorBeaF-2682
92PorBeaS-425
95ElmPioTI-13
95ElmPioUTI-13
Kirt, Tim
90NiaFalRP-3
Kirtlan, Josh
94OgdRapF-3734
94OgdRapSP-20
Kirwin, Steve
88BenBucL-8
Kiser, Bob
88CapCodPB-10
88CapCodPPaLP-74
Kiser, Dan
84ModA'sC-26
89ModA'sC-4
Kiser, Garland
86BenPhiC-154
89WatIndS-12
90CarLeaA-37
90KinIndTI-12
91CanIndLD-84
91CanIndP-976
91CarLeaAP-CAR17
91LinDriAA-84
92CanIndF-687
92TopDeb91-102
93NewOrlZF-967
Kiser, Larry G.
76OklCit8TI-28
Kish, Bobby
82SprCarF-14
83St.PetCT-8
84SavCarT-12
Kisinger, Rube (Charles S.)
09T206-434
Kison, Bruce
72OPC-72
72Top-72
73OPC-141
73Top-141
75OPC-598
75Top-598
76OPC-161
76SSP-568
76Top-161
77PirPosP-12
77Top-563
78Top-223
79Top-661
80Top-28
81Fle-284
81Top-340
82Don-66
82Fle-467
82Top-442
83Don-267
83Fle-96
83FleSta-95
83FleSti-27
83Top-712
84AngSmo-15
84Don-499
84Fle-523
84Nes792-201
84OPC-201
84Top-201
84TopSti-235
84TopTif-201
85Don-377
85Fle-306
85FleUpd-65
85Top-544
85TopTif-544
85TopTifT-67T
85TopTra-67T
86Don-616
86Fle-353
86Top-117
86TopTif-117
89PacSenL-136
89T/MSenL-60
89TopSenL-11
90EliSenL-37
91UppDecS-13
92RoyPol-27
93RoyPol-27
Kissell, George
71CarTeal-22
71CarTeal-23
73OPC-497
73Top-497A
73Top-497B
74OPC-236
74Top-236
90JohCitCS-28
Kissick, David
91BriBanF-7
Kissinger, John
11SpoLifCW-202
12ImpTobC-72
Kistaitis, Dale
88NebCor-7
90MedHatBJB-18
Kisten, Dale
88HamRedP-1728
89SprCarB-20
90ArkTraGS-19
90LouRedBLBC-22
90SprCarDGB-19
91ArkTraLD-36
91ArkTraP-1279
91LinDriAA-36
Kitabeppu, Manabu
87JapPlaB-8
Kitagawa, Hirotoshi
96HilStaHWB-10
Kitchen, Ron
93BluOriF-4120
Kite, Dan
87LSUTigP-4
88ElmPioC-6
90LSUTigGM-3
90WinHavRSS-13
91WinHavRSC-3
91WinHavRSP-483
Kitson, Frank R.
03BreE10-82
90DodTar-412
Kittle, Hub
73OPC-624
73Top-624
74OPC-31
74Top-31
77St.PetCT-13
81Car5x7-14
83Car-13
95NewJerCTI-15
Kittle, Ron
77CliDodT-13
79KnoKnoST-12
80AppFoxT-9
81GleFalWST-19
82EdmTraT-13
83Fle-241
83TopTra-55T
83WhiSoxTV-42
84AllGamPI-147
84Don-18
84Don-18A
84Don-244
84Dra-17
84Fle-64
84FleSti-22
84FleSti-109
84FunFooP-53
84MilBra-15
84Nes792-480
84OCoandSI-56
84OPC-373
84SevCoi-C17
84Top-480
84TopRubD-2
84TopSti-382
84TopSup-11
84TopTif-480
84WhiSoxTV-19
85AllGamPI-60
85Don-180
85DonActA-13
85DonWaxBC-PC3
85Fle-518
85FleLimE-16
85Lea-210
85OPC-105
85Top-105
85TopRubD-2
85TopSti-232
85TopTif-105
85WhiSoxC-42
86Don-526
86Fle-210
86FleMin-45
86FleStiC-68
86Lea-257
86MSAJayPCD-11
86OPC-288
86Spo-67
86Spo-86
86Top-574
86TopSti-289
86TopTat-6
86TopTif-574
86WhiSoxC-42
87Don-351
87Fle-103
87FleGlo-103
87Top-584
87TopTif-584
88Don-422
88Fle-213
88FleGlo-213
88IndGat-33
88Lea-251
88Sco-449
88ScoGlo-449
88ScoRoo-44T
88ScoRooG-44T
88Top-259
88TopTif-259
88TopTra-58T
88TopTraT-58T
89Bow-69
89BowTif-69
89Don-428
89DonBasB-249
89DonTra-51
89FleUpd-20
89OPC-268
89Sco-96
89Top-771
89TopTif-771
89TopTra-62T
89TopTraT-62T
89UppDec-228
89UppDec-711
89WhiSoxC-15
90Don-148
90Fle-538
90FleCan-538
90Lea-405
90OPC-79
90PanSti-51
90PubSti-393
90RedFolSB-54
90Sco-529
90Top-79
90TopSti-302
90TopTif-79
90UppDec-790
90VenSti-270
90WhiSoxC-13
90WhiSoxK-4
91Don-613
91Fle-480
91OPC-324
91OriCro-241
91Top-324A
91Top-324B
91TopDesS-324
91TopMic-324
91TopTif-324
92YanWIZ8-101
Kittredge, Malachi
03BreE10-83
03BreE10-84
11SpoLifCW-203
98CamPepP-42
Kiyohara, Kazuhiro
87JapPlaB-35
Kizer, Bubba (Hal)
79QuaCitCT-15
Kizer, Craig
82AubAstT-14
Kizziah, Daren
89St.CatBJP-2076
90MyrBeaBJP-2772
91DunBluJC-4
91DunBluJP-200
92KnoBluJF-2985
92KnoBluJS-382
93KnoSmoF-1250
Kjos, Ryan
96SouOreTI-15

Klages, Fred
67Top-373
68Top-229
68TopVen-229
69MilBra-148
Klamm, Ted
92WelPirC-14
92WelPirF-1317
93AugPirC-10
93AugPirF-1537
94SalBucC-13
94SalBucF-2319
Klancnik, Joe
86AncGlaPTI-18
88JamExpP-1919
89JamExpP-2155
91QuaCitAP-2622
Klass, Klinton
93AubAstC-16
93AubAstF-3455
Klassen, Danny
94BelBreC-13
94BelBreF-109
95BelBreTI-20
95Exc-70
95UppDecML-171
96Bow-328
96StoPorB-1
97Bow-395
97BowChr-261
97BowChrI-261
97BowChrIR-261
97BowChrR-261
97BowInt-395
95UppDecMLFS-171
Klaus, Billy (William)
47Exh-120
55Bow-150
56Top-217
57Top-292
58Top-89
59Top-299
60Top-406
61Pos-79
61Top-187
62Jel-67
62Pos-67
62PosCan-67
62SalPlaC-10
62ShiPlaC-10
62Top-571
63Top-551
79TCM50-251
83Bra53F-2
91OriCro-242
Klaus, Robert
61TopStal-203
64Top-524
65OPC-227
65Top-227
66OPC-108
66Top-108
66TopVen-108
69Top-387
78TCM60I-19
91MetWIZ-212
Klavitter, Clay
91BelMarC-2
91BelMarP-3668
91SanBerSC-13
91SanBerSP-1989
Klawitter, Tom
84TolMudHT-14
85TwiTeal-25
Klebba, Rob
79WatA'sT-13
80WesHavWCT-6
Klee, Chuck
96BriWhiSB-21
Kleean, Tom
86BelBreP-12
Klein, Bob
75AppFoxT-10
Klein, Bruce
89AugPirP-513
Klein, Chuck
28PorandAR-A19
28PorandAR-B19
29PorandAR-52
30SchR33-17
30W554-9
31Exh-11
31W517-10
32USCar-21
33ButCre-14
33DelR33-22
33DouDisP-26
33ExhFou-6
33GeoCMil-20
33Gou-128
33NatLeaAC-4
33RitCE-3D
33TatOrbSDR-157
34DiaMatCSB-104
34BatR31-185
34ExhFou-3
34Gou-10
34GouCanV-56
35DiaMatCS2-11
35DiaMatCS3T1-88
35ExhFou-3
35GouPuzR-1F
35GouPuzR-3D
35GouPuzR-14D
35GouPuzR-15D
35WheBB1-18
36DiaMatCS4-8
36GouBWR-20
36GouWidPPR-A60
36R31PasP-31
36SandSW-38
36WorWidGV-13
38BasTabP-18
38ExhFou-6
39ExhSal-33
39PlaBal-82
40PlaBal-102
41PlaBal-60
43PhiTeal-13
60Fle-30
61Fle-51
72FleFamF-36
76ISCHooHA-3
77GalGloG-48
77GalGloG-218
80LauFamF-6
80PacLeg-112
80PerHaloFP-171
80SSPHOF-172
81ConTSN-88
81SpoHaloF-8
82DiaCla-22
83ConMar-25
83PhiPosGPaM-1
84OCoandSI-201
86PhiGreT-1
88ConNatA-12
88GreBasS-13
89HOFStiB-48
90PerGreM-60
91ConTSN-30
91ConTSN-300
92ConTSN-438
92ConTSN-531
93ConTSN-671
93DiaStaES-139
94ConTSN-1095
94ConTSNB-1095
94TedWil-74
Klein, Gary
83ButCopKT-6
Klein, Jeff
79WatIndT-4A
Klein, Larry
85BurRanT-3
86TulDriTI-24
88OklCit8C-17
88OklCit8P-32
Klein, Lou
46SeaSLP-26
49EurSta-188
60Top-457
Klein, Mark
77ReaPhiT-15
Klein, Mike
96ButCopKB-6
Kleiner, Stacy
96NewJerCB-16
Kleinhans, Ted
34DiaMatCSB-105
35DiaMatCS3T1-89
75YanDyn1T-28
Kleinke, Norbert
40SolHug-12
Kleinow, Red (John)
08RosComP-50
09BriE97-17
09RamT20-66
09T206-187
09T206-188
09T206-189
10E101-25
10E102-12
10MelMinE-25
10NadCarE-28
10PeoT21-30
10W555-40
11E94-17
11SpoLifCW-204
11T205-88
11TurRedT-21
Klem, Bill
09SpoNewSM-38
21Exh-92
30SchR33-6
34DiaMatCSB-106
50CalHOFW-46
72FleFamF-31
76ShaPiz-68
77GalGloG-173
80PerHaloFP-67
80SSPHOF-67
84OCoandSI-106
86ConSer1-5
87SpoCubG-3
88ConSer4-15
89T/MUmp-63
92ConTSN-460
93ConTSNP-1190
94ConTSN-1190
94ConTSNB-1190
95ConTSN-1378
Klenoshek, Bill
88CapCodPPaLP-50
Klesko, Ryan
89HigSchPLS-20
90Bes-236
90CMC-826
90DurBulUTI-7
90ProAaA-106
90SumBraB-9
90SumBraP-2441
91Bow-590
91Cla/Bes-388
91Cla2-T53
91ClaGolB-BC15
91GreBraC-17
91GreBraLD-209
91GreBraP-3011
91LeaGolR-BC21
91LinDriAA-209
91UppDecFE-1F
91UppDecFE-8F
92Bow-549
92Bow-623
92Don-13
92DonPre-9
92DonRooP-BC15
92OPC-126
92ProFS7-181
92RicBraBB-4
92RicBraF-383
92RicBraRC-8
92RicBraS-430
92SkyAAAF-197
92Top-126
92TopGol-126
92TopGolW-126
92TopMcD-39
92TopMic-126
92TriPlaG-GS10
92UppDec-1
92UppDec-24
93Bow-634
93BraLykP-15
93ClaGam-48
93ClaGam-NNO
93Don-422
93Fle-6
93Lea-469
93OPC-189
93PacSpa-9
93Pin-251
93PinRooTP-4
93PinTea2-27
93RicBraBB-1
93RicBraF-191
93RicBraP-1
93RicBraRC-17
93Sco-294
93ScoBoyoS-8
93ScoProaG-5
93Sel-405
93StaClu-541
93StaCluB-26
93StaCluFDI-541
93StaCluMOP-541
93Top-423
93TopGol-423
93TopInaM-423
93TopMic-423
93Toy-4
93TriAAAGF-2
93Ult-7
93UppDec-376
93UppDecGold-376
94Bow-105
94BowBes-R84
94BowBesR-R84
94BraLykP-16
94BraLykS-16
94BraUSPC-3S
94BraUSPC-9H
94ColC-165
94ColChoGS-165
94ColChoSS-165
94Don-617
94ExtBas-205
94ExtBasRS-11
94Fin-437
94FinJum-437
94FinRef-437
94Fla-128
94FlaWavotF-A4
94Fle-362
94FUnPac-7
94Lea-286
94LeaL-85
94LeaLimRR-7
94OPC-75
94OPCHotP-9
94Pac-12
94Pin-157
94PinArtP-157
94PinMusC-157
94ProMag-2
94Sco-464
94ScoBoyoS-41
94ScoGolR-464
94ScoRoo-RT75
94ScoRooGR-RT75
94ScoRooSR-SU3
94Sel-197
94SelRooS-RS3
94SelSam-197
94SP-52
94SPDieC-52
94SPHol-21
94SPHolDC-21
94Spo-20
94SpoRoo-R01
94SpoRooRS-TR9
94StaClu-148
94StaClu-628
94StaCluFDI-148
94StaCluFDI-628
94StaCluGR-148
94StaCluGR-628
94StaCluMOP-148
94StaCluMOP-628
94StaCluT-38
94StaCluTFDI-38
94Stu-37
94Top-777
94TopGol-777
94TopSpa-777
94TriPla-282
94Ult-444
94UltAllR-5
94UltAllRJ-5
94UppDec-64
94UppDecED-64
94UppDecNG-10
94UppDecNGED-10
95Baz-18
95Bow-309
95ColCho-155
95ColChoCtG-CG11
95ColChoCtG-CG11B
95ColChoCtG-CG11C
95ColChoCtGE-11
95ColChoCtGG-CG11
95ColChoCtGG-CG11B
95ColChoCtGG-CG11C
95ColChoCtGGE-11
95ColChoGS-155
95ColChoSE-62
95ColChoSEGS-62
95ColChoSESS-62
95ColChoSS-155
95Don-253
95DonPreP-253
95DonTopotO-187
95Emb-21
95EmbGolI-21
95Emo-104
95Fin-8
95FinPowK-PK3
95FinRef-8
95Fla-103
95Fle-308
95FleRooS-10
95Lea-214
95LeaLim-145
95Pac-8
95PacPri-2
95PanSti-100
95Pin-224
95PinArtP-224
95PinMusC-224
95PinSam-224
95Sco-332
95Sco-RG1
95Sco-SG1
95ScoAi-AM9
95ScoGolR-332
95ScoHaloG-HG75
95ScoPlaTS-332
95ScoRul-SR28
95ScoRulJ-SR28
95Sel-41
95SelArtP-41
95SelCanM-CM2
95SelCer-53
95SelCerMG-53
95Spo-65
95SpoArtP-65
95SPSpeF-27
95StaClu-19
95StaCluFDI-19
95StaCluMO-50
95StaCluMOP-19
95StaCluSTDW-B19
95StaCluSTMP-5
95StaCluSTWS-19
95StaCluVR-13
95Stu-109
95Sum-89
95SumNthD-89
95Top-324
95TopCyb-177
95TopCybSiR-6
95UC3-54
95UC3ArtP-54
95Ult-349
95UltAllR-7
95UltAllRGM-7
95UltGolM-349
95UltSecYS-9
95UltSecYSGM-9
95UppDec-296
95UppDecED-296
95UppDecEDG-296
95UppDecSE-11
95UppDecSEG-11
95Zen-97
96Baz-17
96Bow-11
96BowBes-19
96BowBesAR-19
96BowBesC-6
96BowBesCAR-6
96BowBesCR-6
96BowBesR-19
96Cir-104
96CirBos-26
96CirRav-104
96ColCho-460
96ColChoGS-460
96ColChoSS-460
96Don-138
96DonLonBL-2
96DonPreP-138
96EmoXL-144
96Fin-B333
96Fin-G321
96Fin-S88
96FinRef-B333
96FinRef-G321
96FinRef-S88

96Fla-202
96Fle-296
96FleBra-8
96FleTif-296
96FleTomL-7
96FleUpd-U229
96FleUpdH-11
96FleUpdTC-U229
96Lea-176
96LeaLim-49
96LeaLimG-49
96LeaPre-66
96LeaPreP-66
96LeaPrePB-176
96LeaPrePG-176
96LeaPrePS-176
96LeaPreSG-55
96LeaPreSte-55
96LeaSig-43
96LeaSigEA-102
96LeaSigEACM-15
96LeaSigPPG-43
96LeaSigPPP-43
96MetUni-131
96MetUniP-131
96MetUniPP-6
96Pac-2
96PacOctM-OM10
96PacPri-P4
96PacPriG-P4
96PanSti-7
96Pin-253
96PinAfi-107
96PinAfiAP-107
96PinAfiP-107
96PinAfiSP-21
96PinArtP-153
96PinChrBC-2
96PinFoil-253
96PinProS-18
96PinSta-153
96ProMagA-15
96ProMagDM-2
96ProSta-22
96Sco-3
96Sco-368
96ScoDugC-A3
96ScoDugC-B93
96ScoDugCAP-A3
96ScoDugCAP-B93
96ScoGolS-19
96ScoSam-3
96Sel-77
96SelArtP-77
96SelCer-82
96SelCer-144
96SelCerAP-82
96SelCerAP-144
96SelCerCB-82
96SelCerCB-144
96SelCerCR-82
96SelCerCR-144
96SelCerIP-5
96SelCerMB-82
96SelCerMB-144
96SelCerMG-82
96SelCerMG-144
96SelCerMR-82
96SelCerMR-144
96SelCerSF-11
96SelTeaN-12
96SP-22
96Spo-28
96SpoArtP-28
96StaClu-178
96StaCluEPB-178
96StaCluEPG-178
96StaCluEPS-178
96StaCluMOP-178
95StaCluVRMC-13
96Stu-150
96StuPrePB-150
96StuPrePG-150
96StuPrePS-150
96Sum-136
96Sum-157
96SumAbo&B-136
96SumAbo&B-157
96SumArtP-136
96SumArtP-157
96SumBigB-9
96SumBigBM-9
96SumFoi-136
96SumFoi-157
96SumHitI-11
96SumPos-7
96Top-193
96TopChr-61
96TopChrR-61
96TopGal-110
96TopGalPPI-110
96TopLas-10
96Ult-158
96Ult-597
96UltChe-B7
96UltCheGM-B7
96UltFreF-6
96UltFreFGM-6
96UltGolM-158
96UltGolM-597
96UltRisS-7
96UltRisSGM-7
96UppDec-272
96UppDecDD-DD4
96UppDecDDG-DD4
96UppDecDDS-DD4
96Zen-37
96Zen-139
96ZenArtP-37
96ZenArtP-139
96ZenDiaC-10
96ZenDiaCP-10
96ZenMoz-1
96ZenZ-9
97Bow-14
97BowBes-61
97BowBesAR-61
97BowBesR-61
97BowChr-10
97BowChrI-10
97BowChrIR-10
97BowChrR-10
97BowInt-14
97Cir-365
97CirRav-365
97ColCho-32
97ColChoCtG-1A
97ColChoCtG-1B
97ColChoCtG-1C
97ColChoCtGIW-CG1
97Don-144
97DonEli-22
97DonEliGS-22
97DonLim-105
97DonLim-182
97DonLimLE-105
97DonLimLE-182
97DonLonL-14
97DonPre-43
97DonPreCttC-43
97DonPreP-144
97DonPrePGold-144
97DonTea-21
97DonTeaSPE-21
97Fin-116
97Fin-343
97FinEmb-116
97FinEmb-343
97FinEmbR-116
97FinEmbR-343
97FinRef-116
97FinRef-343
97FlaSho-A118
97FlaSho-B118
97FlaSho-C118
97FlaShoLC-118
97FlaShoLC-B118
97FlaShoLC-C118
97FlaShoLCM-A118
97FlaShoLCM-B118
97FlaShoLCM-C118
97Fle-260
97FleLumC-11
97FleTif-260
97Lea-233
97LeaFraM-233
97LeaFraMDC-233
97LeaKnoG-10
97LeaKnoG-P10
97MetUni-32
97NewPin-127
97NewPinAP-127
97NewPinMC-127
97NewPinPP-127
97Pac-237
97PacCar-23
97PacCarM-23
97PacGolCD-23
97PacLigB-237
97PacPri-80
97PacPriLB-80
97PacPriP-80
97PacPriSL-SL8A
97PacSil-237
97Pin-38
97PinArtP-38
97PinCer-14
97PinCerMBlu-14
97PinCerMG-14
97PinCerMR-14
97PinCerR-14
97PinIns-81
97PinInsC-14
97PinInsCE-81
97PinInsDE-81
97PinMin-28
97PinMin-P28
97PinMinB-28
97PinMinB-P28
97PinMinCB-28
97PinMinCG-28
97PinMinCGR-28
97PinMinCN-28
97PinMinCS-28
97PinMinG-28
97PinMinS-28
97PinMusC-38
97PinTotCPB-14
97PinTotCPG-14
97PinTotCPR-14
97PinX-P-92
97PinX-PMoS-92
97PinX-PSfF-58
97PinX-PSfFU-58
97RicBraBC-3
97RicBraBC-25
97Sco-7
97Sco-536
97ScoBra-1
97ScoBraPl-1
97ScoBraPr-1
97ScoHeaotO-21
97ScoHigZ-16
97ScoHobR-536
97ScoPreS-7
97ScoResC-536
97ScoShoS-7
97ScoShoS-536
97ScoShoSAP-7
97ScoShoSAP-536
97ScoSteS-18
97ScoTitT-10
97Sel-20
97SelArtP-20
97SelRegG-20
97SkyE-X-55
97SkyE-XC-55
97SkyE-XEC-55
97SP-26
97SpoIll-47
97SpoIllEE-47
97SpoIllGS-2
97SPSpeF-38
97StaClu-16
97StaCluMat-16
97StaCluMOP-16
97Stu-125
97StuPrePG-125
97StuPrePS-125
97Top-390
97TopChr-135
97TopChrR-135
97TopGal-101
97TopGalPPI-101
97Ult-155
97UltGolME-155
97UltHRK-6
97UltPlaME-155
97UppDec-299
97UppDecPP-PP13
97UppDecPPJ-PP13
97UppDecRSF-RS7

Kleven, Jay
75TidTidTI-14
91MetWIZ-213

Kleven, Mark
88ChaRaiP-1205

Kliafas, Steve
92BakDodCLC-14
92SanAntMF-3984
92VerBeaDF-2883
94SanAntMF-2479

Klieman, Ed
47IndTeal-16
47IndVanPP-15
48IndTeal-19
79DiaGre-292
83TCMPla1944-13

Klimas, Phil
77CocAstT-9
80TulDriT-13
81TulDriT-3
82GleFalWST-7
90TulDriDGB-22

Klimchock, Lou
60Lea-116
60Top-137
60TopVen-137
61A'sTeal-10
61Top-462
62Top-259
63Top-542
65Top-542
66Top-589
70OPC-247
70Top-247
91MetWIZ-214

Klimek, Josh
96HelBreTI-12

Klimkowski, Ron
70Top-702
71MLBOffS-492
71OPC-28
71Top-28
72OPC-363
72Top-363
72TopCloT-18
73SyrChiTI-12
92YanWIZ6-73
92YanWIZ7-91

Kline, Bob
55Top-173
84NewOriT-24

Kline, Bob (Robert George)
34DiaMatCSB-107

Kline, Doug
88VisOakCLC-169
88VisOakP-107
89WesPalBES-14
90JacMetGS-2
91LinDriAA-636
91WilBilLD-636
91WilBilP-288

Kline, Greg
75CliPilT-5
76CliPilT-23

Kline, Jason
95OdgRapTI-13

Kline, Kris
83PeoSunF-7

Kline, Peter
94OgdRapSP-28

Kline, Ron
53Top-175
56Top-94
57Kah-16
57Top-256
58Hir-31
58Kah-15
58Top-82
59Kah-16
59Top-265
59Top-428
60CarJayP-5
60Kah-18A
60Kah-18B
60Lea-105
60Top-197
61Top-127
61TopStal-90
62TigPosCF-10
62Top-216
63Top-84
64Top-358
64TopVen-358
65OPC-56
65Top-56
65TopTral-54
66Top-453
67CokCapTw-1
67OPC-133
67Top-133
68PirKDK-27
68PirTeal-8
68Top-446
69MilBra-149
69Top-243
69TopSta-86
78TCM60I-251
91TopArc1-175

Kline, Steve (Steven Jack)
71MLBOffS-493
71OPC-51
71Top-51
72OPC-467
72Top-467
73Kel2D-50
73LinPor-64
73OPC-172
73SyrChiTI-13
73Top-172
74OPC-324
74SyrChiTI-12
74Top-324
75OPC-639
75Top-639
76SSP-532
92YanWIZ7-92

Kline, Steve James
93BurIndC-14
93BurIndF-3292
94ColRedC-12
94ColRedF-439
94SouAtlLAF-SAL9
95Exc-42
95Top-635
95UppDecML-178
96CanIndB-14
97ColCho-315
97Fle-692
97FleTif-692
95UppDecMLFS-178

Klinefelter, David
88AubAstP-1972

Kling, Johnny (John)
06FanCraNL-24
07CubA.CDPP-5
07CubGFGCP-5
08AmeCarE-12
08CubPos-3
08RosComP-104
09ColChiE-154
09SpoNewSM-41
09T206-190
10E98-17
10JHDABE-9
11BasBatEU-26
11MecDFT-12
11PloCanE-38
11S74Sil-63
11SpoLifCW-205
11SpoLifM-172
11T205-89
11TurRedT-102
12ColRedB-154
12ColTinT-154A
12ColTinT-154B
12HasTriFT-20
12HasTriFT-50A
12HasTriFT-50B
12HasTriFT-50C
12HasTriFT-50D
12PhiCarE-15
12T207-91
61Fle-52
87Cub190T-4
93ConTSN-867
93UppDecTR-3

Klingbell, Scott
85VisOakT-23

Klingenbeck, Scott
92FroRowDP-45
92KanCouCTI-17
93FreKeyC-12
93FreKeyF-1023
93StaCluM-80
94Bow-86
94BowBayF-2411
94ExcFS7-8
94OriPro-49
95RocRedWTI-20
95Top-631
96ColCho-203
96ColChoGS-203
96ColChoSS-203
96Don-137
96DonPreP-137

Klinger, Robert
39PlaBal-90
40PlaBal-165

41DouPlaR-35
41DouPlaR-97
48SmiClo-25
Klink, Joe
85LynMetT-13
86OrlTwiP-9
87SpoTeaP-17
89HunStaB-27
90A'sMot-26
90ClaYel-T26
90Lea-503
90TopTra-51T
90TopTraT-51T
91A'sMot-26
91Don-591
91Fle-13
91Lea-461
91OPC-553
91Sco-588
91Top-553
91TopDesS-553
91TopMic-553
91TopTif-553
91UppDec-468
92Don-183
92OPC-678
92Sco-151
92StaClu-326
92Top-678
92TopGol-678
92TopGolW-678
92TopMic-678
92UppDec-530
93FleFinE-64
93MarPub-14
93MarUSPC-5H
93TopTra-95T
93Ult-380
93UppDec-715
93UppDecGold-715
94Fle-470
94Sco-283
94ScoGolR-283
94StaClu-68
94StaCluFDI-68
94StaCluGR-68
94StaCluMOP-68
94StaCluT-87
94StaCluTFDI-87
94Top-409
94TopGol-409
94TopSpa-409
Klippstein, John
51Bow-248
52Top-148
53Top-46
54Bow-29
54Top-31
55Bow-152
56Kah-8
56Top-249
57Kah-17
57RedSoh-11
57Top-296
58RedEnq-22
58Top-242
59Top-152
59TopVen-152
60DodBelB-12
60Top-191
60TopVen-191
61Top-539
61TopStal-204
62RedEnq-20
62Top-151
62TopVen-151
63RedEnq 18
63Top-571
64Top-533
65Top-384
66Top-493
67Top-588
78TwiFri-36
79DiaGre-120
79TCM50-62
83TopRep5-148
90DodTar-413
91TopArc1-46
94TopArc1-31
94TopArc1G-31
Klipstein, Dave
84ElPasDT-18
86VanCanP-16
87DenZepP-12
88NasSouC-20
88NasSouP-474
Kloek, Kevin
92FroRowDP-30
93ElPasDF-2948
95ElPasDTI-13
96El PasDB-13
Kloff, August
87OldJudN-289
Klonoski, Jason
87AriWilP-8
88AriWilP-7
88CapCodPPaLP-127
90BenBucL-10
91Cla/Bes-370
91KenTwiC-27
91KenTwiP-2069
92OrlSunRF-2843
92OrlSunRS-508
93NasXprF-396
Klopp, Betz
78ReaRem-9
Klopp, Frank
85PriWilPT-26
Klopper, Rod
88AlaGolTI-12
Kluge, Matt
92SanBerC-5
92SanBerSF-957
Klugman, Joe
90DodTar-1002
Klump, Ken
83WisRapTF-21
85OrlTwiT-17
Klumpp, Elmer
90DodTar-414
Klusener, Matt
90WicStaSGD-19
Klusman, William F.
87OldJudN-290
Kluss, Dennis
90WatIndS-12
Kluszewski, Ted
47Exh-121A
47Exh-121B
47Exh-121C
47PM1StaP1-105
47PM1StaP1-106
49EurSta-87
49Lea-38
50Bow-62
51Bow-143
51FisBakL-15
51TopRedB-39
52BasPho-3
52Top-29
53BowC-62
53DixLid-11
53DixPre-11
53MacSta-2
53NorBreL-15
53RedMan-NL6
53Top-162
54DixLid-8
54RedHeaF-14
54RedMan-NL6
54Top-7
55ArmCoi-11
55Kah-2
55RedMan-NL16
55RobGouS-10
55RobGouW-10
55Top-120
55TopDouH-121
56Kah-9
56Top-25
56TopHocF-A12
56TopHocF-B14
56TopPin-56
56YelBasP-17
57Kah-18
57RedSoh-12
57Top-165
58Hir-67
58Kah-16
58Top-178
58Top-321
59Kah-17
59Top-17
59Top-35
59TopVen-17
59TopVen-35
60Kah-19
60MacSta-10
60NuHi-57
60Top-505
60WhiSoxJP-4
60WhiSoxTS-8
61AngJayP-7
61Baz-18
61NuSco-457
61Pos-31
61Top-65
61TopStal-173
62AngJayP-6
62Pos-82
62PosCan-82
63BasMagM-47
67TopVen-183
73OPC-296
73Top-296
74OPC-326
74Top-326
76SSP-618
79DiaGre-269
79TCM50-13
81TCM60I-439
82GSGalAG-17
82OhiHaloF-18
83DiaClaS2-62
83TopRep5-29
84OCoandSI-213
85AngStrH-10
86RedGreT-9
86SpoDecG-38
88PacLegI-72
89WhiSoxK-1
91TopArc1-162
92BazQua5A-17
93ActPacA-138
94TodWil-22
94TopArc1-7
94TopArc1G-7
Klutts, Mickey (Gene)
77Top-490
78SSP270-21
78Top-707
78YanSSPD-21
80Top-717
81Don-110
81Fle-584
81Top-232
82Fle-97
82Top-148
83Don-465
83Top-571
83TopTra-56T
92YanWIZ7-93
Kluttz, Clyde
46SeaSLP-27
50WorWidGV-41
52Top-132
83TCMPla1944-39
83TopRep5-132
Klvac, David
92LynRedSC-15
92LynRedSF-2902
93ForLauRSC-15
93ForLauRSFP-1593
Kmak, Joe
85EveGiaC-7
86FreGiaP-6
88ShrCapP-1280
89CalLeaA-46
89FleUpd-127
89RenSilSCLC-252
90ElPasDGS-19
91DenZepLD-144
91DenZepP-125
91LinDriAAA-144
92Bow-545
92DenZepF-2643
92DenZepS-135
93Bow-15
93BrePol-14
93ExcFS7-190
93FleFinE-225
93Pin-575
93Ult-570
93UppDec-782
93UppDecGold-782
94BreMilB-139
94NorTidF-2924
94USPlaCR-3D
95IowCubTI-19
96IndIndB-13
Knabe, Otto (Franz Otto)
08RosComP-141
09ColChiE-156
09T206-191
10CouT21-37
10CouT21-160
10E101-26
10E102-13
10LuxCigPP-12
10MelMinE-26
10NadCarE-29
10NadE1-26
10PeoT21-31A
10PeoT21-31B
11SpoLifM-232
12ColRedB-156
12ColTinT-156
12T207-92
14CraJacE-1
14TexTomE-25
15AmeCarE-23
15CraJacE-1
Knabenshue, Chris
85SpoIndC-9
86ChaRaiP-12
87WicPilRD-7
88TexLeaAGS-34
88WicPilRD-14
89LasVegSC-23
89LasVegSP-19
90CMC-246
90ProAAAF-313
90ScrRedBC-20
90ScrRedBP-611
91LinDriAAA-485
91ScrRedBLD-485
91ScrRedBP-2551
92HunStaS-312
Knackert, Brent
88FloStaLAS-40
88TamTarS-11
89SarWhiSS-13
90DonRoo-52
90MarMot-18
90MetColP-37
90TopTra-52T
90TopTraT-52T
91Don-662
91MarCouH-17
91OPC-563
91Sco-774
91Top-563
91TopDeb90-78
91TopDesS-563
91TopMic-563
91TopTif-563
91UppDec-378
92Don-608
92JacSunS-372
92SkyAA F-153
93JacSunF-2708
95BinMetTI-34
96PawRedSDD-15
Knapland, Greg
91WatIndC-8
91WatIndP-3363
Knapp, Chris (Robert C.)
77Top-247
77WhiSoxJT-7
78AngFamF-20
78SSP270-212
78Top-361
79Top-453
80Top-658
81Don-173
81SalLakCGT-7
81Top-557
82IowCubT-18
83KinBluJTI-10
Knapp, John
87ChaWheP-12
88BakDodCLC-236
89VerBeaDS-14
90VerBeaDS-17
91AdeGiaF-10
92GulCoaDF-3584
Knapp, Michael
86SalAngC-87
87QuaCitAP-27
88MidAngGS-13
88TexLeaAGS-36
89MidAngGS-20
90MidAngGS-13
90TexLeaAGS-6
91ChaKniP-1691
91ChaKniLD-136
91LinDriAA-136
92IowCubF-4053
92IowCubS-210
93OmaRoyF-1681
94OmaRoyF-1225
96TacRaiB-16
Knapp, Rick
86TulDriTI-9B
88GasRanP-1000
92GulCoaRSP-29
93OklCit8F-1641
94OklCit8F-1510
Knauss, Tom
92ClaDraP-49
92FroRowDP-19
93ClaFS7-213
93EliTwiC-13
93EliTwiF-3420
93ForWayWC-13
93ForWayWF-1974
93StaCluM-38
94ForWayWC-12
94ForWayWF-2023
95ForMyeMTI-13
96FtMyeMB-25
Knecht, Bobby
88AppFoxP-161
88MidLeaAGS-41
Knell, Phillip
87OldJudN-291
Knepper, Bob
75PhoGiaC-16
75PhoGiaCK-10
76PheGiaCr-34
76PhoGiaCa-15
76PhoGiaCC-14
76PhoGiaVNB-13
77Gia-12
77PhoGiaCC-16
77PhoGiaCP-16
77PhoGiaVNB-16
78Top-589
79GiaPol-39
79Hos-52
79Kel-35
79OPC-255
79Top-486
80GiaPol-39
80OPC-61
80Top-111
81AllGamPI-170
81Don-194
81Fle-447
81OPC-279
81Top-279
81TopTra-782
82AstAstI-5
82Don-41
82Fle-219
82FleSta-49
82Kel-31
82OPC-389
82Top-672
82TopSti-45
82TopStiV-45
83AllGamPI-168
83Don-92
83Fle-451
83Top-382
84AstMot-16
84Don-572
84Fle-228
84Nes792-93
84OPC-93
84Top-93
84TopTif-93
85AstHouP-18
85AstMot-20
85Don-476
85Fle-352
85Lea-61
85OPC-289
85Top-455
85Top-721
85TopSti-62
85TopTif-455
85TopTif-721
86AstMilL-12
86AstMot-22
86AstPol-15
86AstTeal-9
86Don-161
86Fle-304
86Lea-90

86OPC-231
86Top-590
86TopTif-590
87AstMot-5
87AstPol-20
87Don-112
87Fle-61
87FleAwaW-20
87FleGamW-23
87FleGlo-61
87FleMin-60
87Lea-249
87OPC-129
87RedFolSB-17
87Spo-29
87SpoTeaP-8
87Top-722
87TopGloS-13
87TopMinL-10
87TopSti-32
87TopTif-722
88AstMot-5
88AstPol-15
88Don-138
88DonBasB-176
88Fle-451
88FleGlo-451
88Sco-344
88ScoGlo-344
88Top-151
88TopTif-151
89AstLenH-10
89AstMot-7
89AstSmo-22
89Don-123
89DonAll-54
89Fle-360
89FleBasA-25
89FleGlo-360
89OPC-280
89PanSti-82
89Sco-273
89ScoHot1S-38
89Top-280
89TopSti-22
89TopStiB-63
89TopTif-280
89UppDec-422
90Don-485
90OPC-104
90PhoFirP-7
90ProAAAF-33
90PubSti-97
90Top-104
90TopTif-104
90UppDec-599
90VenSti-271

Knetzer, Elmer
12T207-93
14CraJacE-84
15CraJacE-84
16FleBreD-52
90DodTar-1003

Kneuer, Frank
83NasSouTI-9

Knicely, Alan
75DubPacT-18
76DubPacT-17
80Top-678
80TucTorT-14
81Top-82
81TucTorT-4
82AstAstI-7
83Don-620
83Fle-452
83Top-117
83TopTra-57T
84Fle-473
84Nes792-323
84Top-323
84TopTif-323
84WicAerRD-18
85TopTifT-68T
85TopTra-68T
86LouRedTI-15
86OPC-316
86Top-418
86TopTif-418
87OklCit8P-22

Knickerbocker, Bill (Wm.)
34DiaMatCSB-108
34BatR31-58
35DiaMatCS3T1-90
35GouPuzR-8I
35GouPuzR-9I
36GouWidPPR-B15
36NatChiFPR-49
40PlaBal-182
75YanDyn1T-29
91ConTSN-79

Knieper, Aaron
93JamExpC-12
93JamExpF-3321
94BurBeeC-11
94BurBeeF-1078

Kniffen, Chuck
88WauTimGS-2
89SanBerSB-10
89SanBerSCLC-89
90SanBerSB-8
90SanBerSCLC-115
90SanBerSP-2650
91SanBerSC-26
91SanBerSP-2004
92WesPalBEC-30
92WesPalBEF-2104
93HarSenF-286
94WesPalBEC-29
94WesPalBEF-59

Knight, Brandon
95ChaRivUTIS-37
96HudValRB-5

Knight, Brock
85ElmPioT-9

Knight, Brooke
95HelBreTI-1

Knight, Dennis
83TriTriT-5

Knight, Jack
09AmeCarE-65
09ColChiE-157A
09ColChiE-157B
09RamT20-67
09T206-192
09T206-193
10DomDisP-62A
10DomDisP-62B
10E101-27
10MelMinE-27
10NadCarE-30
10PeoT21-32
10SweCapPP-36A
10SweCapPP-36B
11S74Sil-23
11SpoLifM-80
11T205-90
12ColRedB-157A
12ColRedB-157B
12ColTinT-157A
12ColTinT-157B
12HasTriFT-49
14PieStaT-31
93UppDecTR-4

Knight, Randy
89TenTecGE-12

Knight, Ray (C. Ray)
76IndIndTI-3
78Pep-16
78SSP270-110
78Top-674
79OPC-211
79Top-401
80OPC-98
80RedEnq-25
80Top-174
81AllGamPI-121
81CokTeaS-44
81Don-61
81Fle-198
81OPC-325
81Top-325
81TopSupHT-38
82AstAstI-6
82Don-374
82Fle-71
82FleSta-18
82OPC-319
82Top-525
82TopSti-39
82TopTra-57T
83AllGamPI-96
83Don-522
83Fle-453
83FleSta-96
83FleSti-145
83FleSti-147
83FleSti-208
83OPC-275
83Top-275
83Top-441
83TopGloS-18
83TopSti-238
84AllGamPI-7
84AstMot-6
84Don-12
84Don-12A
84Don-232
84Fle-229
84FleSti-10
84Nes792-660
84OPC-321
84Top-660
84TopRubD-3
84TopSti-68
84TopStiB-9
84TopTif-660
85AllGamPI-121
85Don-617
85Fle-86
85IndIndTI-28
85MetColP-11
85MetTCM-26
85OPC-274
85Top-590
85TopTif-590
86AstMot-24
86Don-597
86Fle-86
86MetColP-10
86MetTCM-20
86MetWorSC-29
86OPC-27
86Top-27
86TopTif-27
87Don-586
87DonOpeD-137
87Fle-14
87FleAwaW-21
87FleGlo-14
87FleGlo-WS11
87FleGlo-WS12
87FleRecS-18
87FleUpd-58
87FleUpdG-58
87FleWorS-11
87FleWorS-12
87Lea-166
87OPC-275
87OriFreB-25
87Spo-89
87SpoTeaP-21
87Top-488
87TopSti-24
87TopTif-488
87TopTra-59T
87TopTraT-59T
87Woo-30
87Woo-33
88Don-108
88Fle-564
88FleGlo-564
88FleUpd-28
88FleUpdG-28
88OPC-124
88PanSti-12
88RedFolSB-43
88Sco-96
88ScoGlo-96
88ScoRoo-17T
88ScoRooG-17T
88Spo-115
88StaLinO-7
88StaLinTi-11
88TigPep-22
88Top-124
88TopSti-229
88TopTif-124
88TopTra-59T
88TopTraT-59T
89Sco-135A
89Sco-135B
89UppDec-259
91MetWIZ-215
91OriCro-243
91UppDecS-8
92MDAMVP-16
93RedKah-8
94RedKah-33
95RedKah-34

Knight, Shawn
94SpoIndC-15
94SpoIndF-3330

Knight, Steve
80SanJosMJitB-12

Knight, Tim
82NasSouTI-15
83NasSouTI-10
84NasSouTI-12
85AlbYanT-33
85ColCliP-15
85ColCliT-20
86PorBeaP-12

Knighton, Toure'
94ChaRivC-11
94ChaRivF-2668
95ChaRivTI-11

Knoblauch, Chuck
88CapCodPB-15
88CapCodPPaLP-94
90Bes-146
90Bes-322
90Bow-415
90BowTif-415
90CMC-807
90OrlSunRB-3
90OrlSunRP-1090
90OrlSunRS-8
90ProAaA-56
90Sco-672
91Bow-330
91Cla3-T46
91Don-421
91DonRoo-39
91FleUpd-37
91Lea-396
91ScoAllF-10
91ScoRoo-93T
91StaClu-548
91StaCluMO-20
91TopTra-69T
91TopTraT-69T
91Ult-382
91UltUpd-37
91UppDec-40
92Bow-24
92Cla1-T50
92Cla2-T71
92ClaGam-181
92ColAllG-10
92ColAllP-10
92Don-390
92DonBonC-BC5
92DonCraJ1-24
92Fle-206
92FleRooS-10
92Fre-1
92JimDea-12
92Lea-230
92MJBHolK-R1
92MJBHolK-R2
92MJBHolK-R3
92MJBHolK-R4
92MJBHolP-R1
92MotKno-1
92MotKno-2
92MotKno-3
92MotKno-4
92OPC-23
92OPCPre-35
92PanSti-116
92Pin-119
92Pin-285
92Pin-307
92PinTea2-6
92Pos-6
92Sco-572
92Sco-792
92Sco-X672
92Sco100RS-11
92ScoCokD-14
92ScoImpP-1
92SpoIllFK1-433
92StaClu-601
92StaClu-830
92StaCluECN-601
92StaCluNC-830
92StaKno-1
92StaKno-2
92StaKno-3
92StaKno-4
92StaKno-5
92StaKno-6
92StaKno-7
92StaKno-8
92StaKno-9
92StaKno-10
92StaKno-11
92Top-23
92TopDeb91-103
92TopGol-23
92TopGolW-23
92TopKid-112
92TopMcD-35
92TopMic-23
92TriPla-171
92Ult-93
92UltAwaW-2
92UppDec-446
93Bow-481
93ClaGam-49
93DiaMar-61
93Don-415
93Fin-76
93FinRef-76
93Fla-237
93Fle-357
93Fle-639
93FleFruotL-32
93FunPac-193
93KinDis-24
93Lea-98
93LeaFas-6
93LeaGolA-R5
93OPC-175
93PacSpa-172
93PanSti-126
93Pin-107
93PinTea2-4
93Sco-148
93Sel-36
93SP-248
93StaClu-314
93StaCluFDI-314
93StaCluM-8
93StaCluMMP-5
93StaCluMOP-314
93Stu-109
93Top-250
93TopGol-250
93TopInaM-250
93TopMic-250
93TopPre-250
93Toy-39
93ToyMasP-7
93TriPla-48
93Ult-583
93UppDec-254
93UppDecGold-254
94Bow-229
94ColC-166
94ColChoGS-166
94ColChoSS-166
94Don-28
94DonSpeE-28
94ExtBas-118
94Fin-324
94FinRef-324
94Fla-314
94Fle-210
94Fle-712
94FUnPac-147
94Lea-64
94LeaL-49
94OPC-155
94Pac-357
94PanSti-92
94Pin-83
94PinArtP-83
94PinMusC-83
94ProMag-80
94Sco-89
94ScoGolR-89
94Sel-29
94SP-185
94SPDieC-185
94Spo-83
94StaClu-416
94StaCluFDI-416
94StaCluGR-416
94StaCluMOP-416
94Stu-197
94Top-555
94TopGol-555
94TopSpa-555
94TriPla-254
94Ult-89
94UppDec-152
94UppDecED-152
95Baz-112
95Bow-365

95BowBes-R44
95BowBesR-R44
95ColCho-490
95ColChoGS-490
95ColChoSE-28
95ColChoSE-226
95ColChoSEGS-28
95ColChoSEGS-226
95ColChoSESS-28
95ColChoSESS-226
95ColChoSS-490
95D3-8
95Don-286
95DonPreP-286
95DonTopotO-109
95Emb-99
95EmbGolI-99
95Emo-57
95Fin-88
95FinRef-88
95Fla-57
95FlaTodS-4
95Fle-206
95FleAllS-10
95Kra-7
95Lea-238
95LeaLim-53
95Pac-250
95PanSti-47
95Pin-91
95PinArtP-91
95PinMusC-91
95Sco-431
95ScoGolR-431
95ScoHaloG-HG80
95ScoPlaTS-431
95Sel-122
95SelArtP-122
95SelCer-38
95SelCerMG-38
95SP-173
95SPCha-169
95SPChaDC-169
95Spo-91
95SpoArtP-91
95SPSil-173
95StaClu-249
95StaCluFDI-249
95StaCluMO-26
95StaCluMOP-249
95StaCluSTWS-249
95StaCluVR-123
95Stu-104
95Sum-71
95SumNthD-71
95Top-250
95TopCyb-138
95TopLeaL-LL44
95UC3-38
95UC3ArtP-38
95Ult-303
95UltAllS-9
95UltAllSGM-9
95UltGolM-303
95UltRisS-5
95UltRisSGM-5
95UppDec-193
95UppDecED-193
95UppDecEDG-193
95UppDecSE-218
95UppDecSEG-218
95USPlaCMLA-8H
95Zen-17
96Baz-65
96Bow-84
96BowBes-34
96BowBesAR-34
96BowBesR-34
96Cir-57
96CirBos-12
96CirRav-57
96ColCho-205
96ColChoGS-205
96ColChoSS-205
96Don-536
96DonPreP-536
96EmoXL-82
96Fin-B49
96Fin-S261
96FinRef-B49
96FinRef-S261
96Fla-116
96Fle-166
96FleTif-166
96Lea-43
96LeaLim-19
96LeaLimG-19
96LeaPre-16
96LeaPreP-16
96LeaPrePB-43
96LeaPrePG-43
96LeaPrePS-43
96LeaPreSG-75
96LeaPreSte-75
96LeaSig-20
96LeaSigEA-103
96LeaSigEACM-16
96LeaSigPPG-20
96LeaSigPPP-20
96MetUni-76
96MetUniP-76
96Pac-367
96PacPri-P114
96PacPriG-P114
96PanSti-199
96Pin-8
96PinAfi-78
96PinAfiAP-78
96PinAfiFPP-78
96PinArtP-6
96PinSta-6
96PinTeaP-2
96ProSta-126
96Sco-285
96ScoDugC-B10
96ScoDugCAP-B10
96ScoRef-20
96Sel-5
96SelArtP-5
96SelCer-18
96SelCerAP-18
96SelCerCB-18
96SelCerCR-18
96SelCerMB-18
96SelCerMG-18
96SelCerMR-18
96SelTeaN-19
96SP-116
96StaClu-187
96StaClu-414
96StaCluEPB-414
96StaCluEPG-414
96StaCluEPS-414
96StaCluEWB-EW4
96StaCluEWG-EW4
96StaCluEWS-EW4
96StaCluMO-19
96StaCluMOP-187
96StaCluMOP-414
95StaCluVRMC-123
96Stu-21
96StuPrePB-21
96StuPrePG-21
96StuPrePS-21
96Sum-141
96SumAbo&B-141
96SumArtP-141
96SumFoi-141
96SumPos-2
96TeaOut-46
96Top-248
96TopChr-95
96TopChrR-95
96TopGal-170
96TopGalPPI-170
96TopLas-83
96Ult-89
96UltGolM-89
96UltOn-L-5
96UltOn-LGM-5
96UppDec-125
96UppDecDD-DD26
96UppDecDDG-DD26
96UppDecDDS-DD26
96UppDecPRE-R25
96UppDecPreR-R25
96Zen-72
96ZenArtP-72
96ZenMoz-19
97Bow-37
97BowBes-51
97BowBesAR-51
97BowBesMI-MI8
97BowBesMIAR-MI8
97BowBesMIARI-MI8
97BowBesMII-MI8
97BowBesMIR-MI8
97BowBesMIRI-MI8
97BowBesR-51
97BowChr-32
97BowChrI-32
97BowChrIR-32
97BowChrR-32
97BowInt-37
97Cir-350
97CirRav-350
97ColCho-153
97ColChoAC-2
97Don-25
97Don-444
97DonDiaK-4
97DonDiaKC-4
97DonEli-33
97DonEliGS-33
97DonEliLaL-8
97DonFraFea-4
97DonLim-12
97DonLim-54
97DonLim-149
97DonLimFotG-24
97DonLimLE-12
97DonLimLE-54
97DonLimLE-149
97DonPre-4
97DonPre-189
97DonPreCttC-4
97DonPreCttC-189
97DonPreP-25
97DonPreP-444
97DonPrePGold-25
97DonPrePGold-444
97DonPreXP-2B
97DonTeaSMVP-5
97Fin-140
97Fin-211
97FinEmb-140
97FinEmbR-140
97FinRef-140
97FinRef-214
97FlaSho-A45
97FlaSho-B45
97FlaSho-C45
97FlaShoLC-45
97FlaShoLC-B45
97FlaShoLC-C45
97FlaShoLCM-A45
97FlaShoLCM-B45
97FlaShoLCM-C45
97Fle-147
97FleTif-147
97Lea-192
97Lea-220
97Lea-376
97LeaBanS-7
97LeaFraM-192
97LeaFraM-220
97LeaFraM-376
97LeaFraMDC-192
97LeaFraMDC-220
97LeaFraMDC-376
97LeaGolS-26
97LeaKnoG-1
97MetUni-210
97NewPin-108
97NewPin-179
97NewPinAP-108
97NewPinAP-179
97NewPinKtP-8
97NewPinMC-108
97NewPinMC-179
97NewPinPP-108
97NewPinPP-179
97NewPinPP-K8
97Pac-139
97PacCar-10
97PacCarM-10
97PacLigB-139
97PacPri-46
97PacPriGotD-GD62
97PacPriLB-46
97PacPriP-46
97PacSil-139
97Pin-188
97PinArtP-188
97PinCer-73
97PinCerLI-6
97PinCerMBlu-73
97PinCerMG-73
97PinCerMR-73
97PinCerR-73
97PinIns-10
97PinInsCE-10
97PinInsDD-5
97PinInsDE-10
97PinMin-19
97PinMinB-19
97PinMinCB-19
97PinMinCG-19
97PinMinCGR-19
97PinMinCN-19
97PinMinCS-19
97PinMinG-19
97PinMinS-19
97PinMusC-188
97PinTeaP-2
97PinTeaP-10
97PinTotCPB-73
97PinTotCPG-73
97PinTotCPR-73
97PinX-P-18
97PinX-PMoS-18
97ProMag-62
97ProMagML-62
97Sco-165
97Sco-533
97ScoAllF-3
97ScoHeaotO-34
97ScoHobR-533
97ScoPreS-165
97ScoResC-533
97ScoShoS-165
97ScoShoS-533
97ScoShoSAP-165
97ScoShoSAP-533
97ScoSteS-2
97Sel-69
97SelArtP-69
97SelRegG-69
97SelToootT-18
97SelToootTMB-18
97SkyE-X-28
97SkyE-XC-28
97SkyE-XEC-28
97SP-110
97SpollI-145
97SpollIEE-145
97StaClu-206
97StaCluMat-206
97StaCluMOP-206
97Stu-127
97StuHarH-4
97StuPrePG-127
97StuPrePS-127
97Top-65
97TopAll-AS5
97TopChr-22
97TopChrAS-AS5
97TopChrR-22
97TopChrSAR-AS5
97TopChrSB-5
97TopChrSBR-5
97TopGal-105
97TopGalPPI-105
97TopSeaB-SB5
97TopSta-38
97TopStaAM-38
97Ult-87
97UltDouT-6
97UltFieC-9
97UltGolME-87
97UltPlaME-87
97UppDec-411
97Zen-32

Knoblauh, Jay
88OneYanP-2067
89PenPilS-10
90FloStaLAS-35
90Ft.LauYS-11
90StaFS7-40
91AlbYanLD-8
91AlbYanP-1019
91LinDriAA-8
92AlbYanF-2238
92ColCliS-106
93ColCliF-1122
93ColCliP-22
95LynHilTI-11

Knoll, Brian
95BelGiaTI-29
96BurBeeTI-8

Knoll, Randy
96PieBolWB-16

Knoop, Bobby
64Top-502
65OPC-26
65Top-26
65TopTral-18
66AngDexP-2
66Top-280
66TopRubI-46
66TopVen-280
67CokCapDA-28
67OPC-175
67OPCPapI-17
67Top-175
67TopPos-17
67TopTesF-9
67TopVen-260
68Baz-3
68Top-271
68TopVen-271
69MilBra-150
69MLBOffS-23
69Top-445
69TopSta-145
69TopTeaP-17
69TraSta-17
70MLBOffS-188
70Top-695
70WhiSoxTI-9
71OPC-506
71Top-506
72MilBra-184
72Top-664
75QuaCitAT-6
78TCM60I-234
85AngStrH-7
89AngSmo-4
90El PasDAGTI-44
93AngMot-28
94AngMot-28
95AngMot-28
96AngMot-20

Knorr, Randy
87MyrBeaBJP-1446
88MyrBeaBJP-1182
89DunBluJS-10
90Bes-273
90CMC-813
90KnoBluJB-26
90KnoBluJP-1248
90KnoBluJS-9
91Cla/Bes-21
91KnoBluJLD-361
91KnoBluJP-1770
91LinDriAA-361
91SyrChiMB-10
92FleUpd-65
92SkyAAAF-226
92SyrChiF-1981
92SyrChiMB-9
92SyrChiS-508
92TopDeb91-104
93BluJayD-17
93BluJayD4-25
93BluJayFS-17
93Don-717
93Fle-695
93OPCPre-25
93StaClu-321
93StaCluFDI-321
93StaCluMOP-321
93Top-534
93TopGol-534
93TopInaM-534
93TopMic-534
93Ult-643
93UppDec-682
93UppDecGold-682
94BluJayUSPC-3S
94BluJayUSPC-10D
94Fle-336
94Pac-645
94StaClu-174
94StaCluFDI-174
94StaCluGR-174
94StaCluMOP-174
94StaCluT-176
94StaCluTFDI-176
94Top-96
94TopGol-96
94TopSpa-96
95BluJayUSPC-10D
95Don-183
95DonPreP-183
95Fle-99
95Top-327
96ColCho-357
96ColChoGS-357
96ColChoSS-357

Knose, Mark
75WesPalBES-26
Knott, Jack
34DiaMatCSB-109
35DiaMatCS3T1-91
39WhiSoxTI-8
40PlaBal-13
40WhiSoxL-9
79DiaGre-181
91ConTSN-178
95ConTSN-1339
Knott, James
92GulCoaMF-3475
Knott, John
39PlaBal-91
41PlaBal-68
93MacBraC-13
93MacBraF-1408
94MacBraC-10
94MacBraF-2214
95AusFut-25
95DurBulTI-17
Knott, Shawn
93BluOriC-15
Knout, Fred (Edward)
87OldJudN-292
Knowland, Sam
95DanBraTI-14
Knowles, Brian
94HigDesMC-18
94HigDesMF-2802
Knowles, Darold
64Top-418
65Top-577
66OPC-27
66Top-27
66TopVen-27
67CokCapS-15
67Top-362
68Top-483
69SenTeal8-13
70OPC-106
70SenPolY-6
70Top-106
71MLBOffS-544
71OPC-261
71Top-261
72Top-583
73OPC-274
73Top-274
74OPC-57
74OPC-472
74Top-57
74Top-472
75OPC-352
75Top-352
76OPC-617
76SSP-307
76Top-617
77Top-169
78ExpPos-7
78Top-414
79Car5-13
79OPC-303
79Top-581
80Top-286
88LouRedBTI-3
89PhiTas-16
90PhiTas-34
91ClePhiC-10
91ClePhiP-1640
91OriCro-244
92ClePhiC-25
92ClePhiF-2075
93ClePhiC-28
93ClePhiF-2700
93RanKee-219
94ClePhiC-28
94ClePhiF-2543
95ClePhiF-232
Knowles, Eric
92OneYanC-24
93PriWilCC-16
93PriWilCF-665
94GreBatF-483
94SouAtlLAF-SAL14
95Bow-27
95TamYanYI-15
96NorNavB-13
97GreBatC-10
Knowles, Greg
91MiaHurBB-8
92SavCarF-661
93SprCarC-16
93SprCarF-1846
94St.PetCC-13
94St.PetCF-2580
95BowBayTI-35
Knox, Jeff
86ClePhiP-14
87AlbYanP-17
94BoiHawC-17
94BoiHawF-3351
94Bow-591
94CedRapKC-17
95CedRapKTI-35
Knox, John
74OPC-604
74Tig-7
74Top-604
75OPC-546
75Top-546
76IndIndTI-21
76OPC-218
76SSP-361
76SSP-592
76Top-218
Knox, Kerry
89SpoIndSP-14
90Bes-221
90RivRedWB-14
90RivRedWP-2603
91LinDriAA-609
91WicWraLD-609
91WicWraP-2594
91WicWraRD-4
92BelBreC-27
92BelBreF-402
93ArkTraF-2811
94LouRedF-2979
Knox, Mike
83CedRapRF-9
83CedRapRT-4
83DurBulT-8
84DurBulT-15
85GreBraTI-10
Knox, Scott
85PriWilPT-29
Knudsen, Kurt
89LakTigS-13
90LakTigS-16
91LonTigP-1874
92DonRoo-62
92FleUpd-25
92SkyAAAF-266
92TolMudHS-592
93Don-145
93Fle-231
93Sco-264
93Sel-306
93StaClu-65
93StaCluFDI-65
93StaCluMOP-65
93TigGat-15
93TolMudHF-1652
93Top-272
93TopGol-272
93TopInaM-272
93TopMic-272
94Fle-136
94TolMudHF-1025
95PhoFirTI-7
Knudson, Mark
83DayBeaAT-7
85TucTorC-60
86TucTorP-10
87DenZepP-20
88DenZepC-1
88DenZepP-1275
88Don-495
88Top-61
88TopTif-61
89BrePol-41
90BreMilB-12
90BrePol-41
90Don-575
90Fle-327
90FleCan-327
90Lea-348
90OPC-566
90Sco-539
90Top-566
90TopTif-566
91BreMilB-13
91BrePol-12
91Don-328
91Fle-587
91Lea-159
91OPC-267
91PanFreS-211
91PanSti-165
91Sco-239
91Top-267
91TopDesS-267
91TopMic-267
91TopTif-267
91Ult-176
91UppDec-393
92LasVegSF-2793
92LasVegSS-233
92Sco-373
94BreMilB-140
Knudtson, Jim
87CedRapRP-27
95ChaLooTI-27
96ChaLooB-4
Knupfer, Jason
96BatCliTI-1
Koba, Takeshi
79TCMJapPB-33
Kobayashi, Shigeru
79TCMJapPB-85
Kobbe, Eric
89GeoColC-16
90GeoColC-15
Kobel, Kevin
74OPC-605
74Top-605
75OPC-337
75Top-337
76OPC-588
76SpoIndC-8
76Top-588
77SpoIndC-22
79OPC-6
79Top-21
80OPC-106
80Top-189
91MetWIZ-216
94BreMilB-141
Kobernus, Jeff
82MadMusF-25
84ModA'sC-24
Kobetitsch, Kevin
91EugEmeC-16
91EugEmeP-3721
92AppFoxC-22
92BasCitRF-3841
Kobza, Greg
89UtiBluSP-13
90SouBenWSB-15
90SouBenWSGS-24
91Cla/Bes-73
91SarWhiSC-14
91SarWhiSP-1116
92StoPorC-10
92StoPorF-36
Koch, Alan
77FriOneYW-99
Koch, Barney
90DodTar-1004
Koch, Billy
97BluJayS-58
97Bow-73
97BowInt-73
97Top-481
Koch, Donn
82AppFoxF-17
Koch, Ken
86BirBarTI-24
87OrlTwiP-8
Kochanski, Mark
82IdaFalAT-9
Kocher, Bradley W.
12ImpTobC-82
16FleBreD-53
Koegel, Pete
71OPC-633
71Top-633
72OPC-14
72Top-14
77JacSunT-12
94BreMilB-142
Koehler, Ben
11SpoLifCW-206
Koehler, James
91ButCopKSP-1
93RivPilCLC-26
94RivPilCLC-26
Koehler, Jason
96StCatSB-14
Koehler, P.K.
95DanBraTI-15
96EugEmeB-14
Koehnke, Odie
75AppFoxT-11
Koelling, Brian
91BilMusP-3762
91BilMusSP-20
92Bow-65
92CedRapRC-26
92CedRapRF-1079
92ClaFS7-49
92MidLeaATI-25
92UppDecML-330
93Bow-554
93ChaLooF-2367
93ClaFS7-214
94Bow-542
94IndIndF-1818
94StaClu-503
94StaCluFDI-503
94StaCluGR-503
94StaCluMOP-503
94UppDec-217
94UppDecED-217
95ChaLooTI-9
Koeman, Matt
96BurIndB-9
Koenecke, Len (Leonard)
34ExhFou-2
90DodTar-415
Koenig, Fred
83CubThoAV-NNO
88PulBraP-1749
89PulBraP-1900
91PulBraC-23
91PulBraP-4024
91PulBraP-4025
92PulBraF-3198
93RanKee-220
Koenig, Gary
90BasCitRS-14
Koenig, Mark
28PorandAR-A20
28PorandAR-B20
28W513-83
29ExhFou-26
29PorandAR-53
31Exh-24
32CubTeal-15
32OrbPinNP-30
32OrbPinUP-39
33Gou-39
33GouCanV-39
33TatOrb-39
34DiaMatCSB-110
34Gou-56
35DiaMatCS3T1-92
35GouPuzR-8A
35GouPuzR-8M
79DiaGre-252
87ConSer2-41
88ConSer4-16
91ConTSN-125
92MegRut-154
93ConTSN-751
93ConTSNP-1230
94ConTSN-1121
94ConTSN-1230
94ConTSNB-1121
94ConTSNB-1230
Koenig, Matt
94KinMetC-6
94KinMetF-3816
95PitMetTI-44
Koenigsfeld, Ron
82ElPasDT-3
84VanCanC-25
Koeyers, Ramsey
93JamExpC-1
93JamExpF-3331
94WesPalBEC-14
94WesPalBEF-43
96HarSenB-16
Koga, Hide
90SalSpuCLC-142
90SalSpuP-2735
91SalSpuC-24
91SalSpuP-2260
92SalSpuC-25
92SalSpuF-3773
Koh, Joe
87IdaFalBP-20
Kohl, Jim
92Ft.MyeMCB-25
92Ft.MyeMF-2741
93ForMyeMC-12
93ForMyeMF-2650
Kohli, John
87BelMarL-15
88NebCor-23
Kohlogi, Asst. (Acey)
89VisOakCLC-121
Kohno, Takayuki
90SalSpuCLC-143
90SalSpuP-2736
91SalSpuC-26
91SalSpuP-2262
92SalSpuF-3775
Koike, Takuichi
96HonShaHWB-12
Koklys, Wayne
91IdaFalBP-4322
Kokora, Pat
89AncGlaP-17
Kokos, Dick
49Bow-31
50Bow-50
51Bow-68
51TopRedB-19
53Top-232
54Bow-37
54OriEss-17
54Top-106
79DiaGre-196
91OriCro-245
91TopArc1-232
94TopArc1-106
94TopArc1G-106
Kolarek, Frank
79OgdA'sT-19
79WatA'sT-8
Kolb, Brandon
96CliLumKTI-17
Kolb, Dan
96ChaRivTI-9617
Kolb, Gary
64Top-119
64TopVen-119
65Top-287
68PirKDK-10
68PirTeal-9
68Top-407
69MilBra-151
69Top-307
78TCM60I-268
78TCM60I-283
91MetWIZ-217
Kolb, Pete
86ElPasDP-15
87ElPasDP-9
88DenZepP-1252
89DenZepP-50
Kolbe, Brian
82JacMetT-7
Kolinsky, Steve
93HunCubC-28
93HunCubF-3254
94HunCubF-3569
94HunCubC-28
Koller, Jerry
91IdaFalBP-4323
92MacBraF-263
93DurBulC-11
93DurBulF-481
93DurBulTI-27
94GreBraF-409
94GreBraTI-15
95BreBtaTI-30
Koller, Mark
87WatPirP-25
88WatPirP-7
Koller, Mike
88BriTigP-1880
89FayGenP-1576
90FayGenP-2403
Koller, Rodney
91BurIndP-3299
92BurIndC-7
92BurIndF-1651
93ColRedC-14
93ColRedF-593
Kolloway, Don
47Exh-122
48WhiSoxTI-14
49Bow-28
50Bow-133
51Bow-105
52Bow-91

52Top-104
53Top-97
77TCMTheWY-58
83TCMPla1943-10
83TopRep5-104
91TopArc1-97
Kolodny, Mike
80BatTroT-5
Kolotka, Chuck
82MadMusF-6
83MiaMarT-8
84BeaGolGT-22
Kolovitz, Mike
87SalSpuP-28
Kolp, Ray
23WilChoV-82
33Gou-150
33GouCanV-82
94ConTSN-1160
94ConTSNB-1160
Kolstad, Hal (Harold)
62Top-276
63Top-574
Komadina, Tony
75AppFoxT-12
Komazaki, Yukiichi
83SanJosBC-9
Kominek, Tobias
95BelBreTI-21
95HelBreTI-29
96StoPorB-3
Komminsk, Brad
80AndBraT-28
81DurBulT-10
83RicBraT-19
84Don-36
84FleUpd-63
84RicBraT-10
84RicBraT-11
85BraHos-13
85BraPol-36
85BraTBSAT-1
85Don-321
85Fle-331
85Top-292
85TopTif-292
86Fle-520
86OPC-210
86RicBraP-11
86Top-698
86TopTif-698
87DenZepP-6
88DenZepC-21
88DenZepP-1263
88Don-583
89FleUpd-28
89IndTeal-17
90Don-350
90Fle-496
90FleCan-496
90Lea-303
90OPC-476
90RicBra2ATI-14
90RocRedWGC-27
90Sco-496
90ScoRoo-53T
90Top-476
90TopTif-476
90TopTra-53T
90TopTraT-53T
90UppDec-428
91LinDriAAA-540
91OriCro-246
91Sco-259
91TacTigLD-540
92Sco-735
93NasSouF-581
94BreMilB-233
Konderla, Mike
83CedRapRF-14
83CedRapRT-7
84CedRapRT-9
87NasSouTI-12
88DenZepC-2
88DenZepP-1276
Kondo, Akihiko
79TCMJapPB-23
Konemann, Troy
92SprCarC-12
92SprCarF-862
Konerko, Paul
94ClaUpdCotC-CC12
94SigRooDP-13
94SigRooDPS-13
94StaCluDP-80
94StaCluDPFDI-80
94TopTra-112T
94YakBeaC-8
94YakBeaF-3854
95Bes-79
95Bow-241
95BowBes-B28
95BowBesR-B28
95BowGolF-241
95Exc-214
95ExcFirYP-1
95Pin-170
95PinArtP-170
95PinMusC-170
95SanBerSTI-11
95ScoDraP-DP7
95SelSurS-SS4
95SPML-77
95SPMLDtS-DS8
95StaClu-102
95StaCluFDI-102
95StaCluMOP-102
95StaCluSTWS-102
95Top-139
95UppDecML-194
95UppDecML-222
95UppDecMLOP-OP14
96BesAutSA-38
96Bow-338
96BowBes-156
96BowBesAR-156
96BowBesR-156
96Exc-177
96SanAntMB-12
96TexLeaAB-27
96Top-432
97Bow-130
97Bow98ROY-ROY7
97BowBes-103
97BowBesAR-103
97BowBesMI-MI7
97BowBesMIAR-MI7
97BowBesMIARI-MI7
97BowBesMII-MI7
97BowBesMIR-MI7
97BowBesMIRI-MI7
97BowBesR-103
97BowCerBIA-CA45
97BowCerGIA-CA45
97BowChr-142
97BowChr1RC-ROY7
97BowChr1RCR-ROY7
97BowChrI-142
97BowChrIR-142
97BowChrR-142
97BowChrSHR-SHR4
97BowChrSHRR-SHR4
97BowInt-130
97BowScoHR-4
97Top-489
97TopSta-105
97TopStaAM-105
95UppDecMLFS-194
95UppDecMLFS-222
Konetchy, Ed
08RosComP-166
09ColChiE-158
09PC7HHB-28
09RamT20-65
09SpoNewSM-34
09T206-194
09T206-195
10CouT21-161
10CouT21-162
10CouT21-163
10CouT21-296
10DarChoE-21
10DomDisP-63
10OrnOvaPP-8
10RedCroT-37
10RedCroT-126
10RedCroT-209
10SweCapPP-150
11S74Sil-121
11SpoLifCW-207
11SpoLifM-272
11T205-91
11TurRedT-103
12ColRedB-158
12ColTinT-158
12HasTriFT-70C
12PhiCarE-16
12T207-94
13NatGamW-24
13TomBarW-23
14B18B-79A
14B18B-79B
14CraJacE-118
15CraJacE-118
15SpoNewM-94
15VicT21-16
16ColE13-94
16FleBreD-54
16SpoNewM-96
19W514-93
21Exh-93
90DodTar-416
91ConTSN-263
92ConTSN-638
Konieczki, Dom
91EriSaiC-17
91EriSaiP-4062
92KenTwiF-599
93NasXprF-397
94ForMyeMC-10
92KenTwiC-23
94ForMyeMF-1164
95HarCitRCTI-9
96FtMyeMB-16
96HarCitRCB-17
Konieczny, Doug
75OPC-624
75Top-624
76OPC-602
76SSP-49
76Top-602
Konikowski, Alex
75Gia195T-13
Konopa, Bob
80WisRapTT-7
82OrlTwi8SCT-18
82OrlTwiT-6
84ChaO'sT-15
90HagSunDGB-14
Konopki, Mark
91ElmPioC-22
91ElmPioP-3268
92LynRedSC-21
92LynRedSF-2903
Konrady, Dennis
96WatIndTI-12
Konstanty, Jim
47Exh-123
47PM1StaP1-107
49EurSta-139
49PhiBul-29
50Bow-226
51BerRos-D6
51Bow-27
51FisBakL-16
51R42SmaS-56
51TopCurA-7
52Top-108
53BowBW-58
53Dor-138
55Bow-231
56Top-321
60RawGloT-12
61Top-479
63GadFunC-27
76SSPYanOD-6
79TCM50-53
83TCMPla1944-30
83TopRep5-108
86PhiGreT-7
87Phi195T-3
90HOFStiB-44
Kontorinis, Andrew
92KenTwiF-614
93ForMyeMC-13
93ForMyeMF-2664
94FloStaLAF-FSL9
94ForMyeMC-11
94ForMyeMF-1173
Kontos, Chris
92StaCluMO-45
Konuszewski, Dennis
92WelPirC-13
93ClaGolF-178
93SalBucC-13
93SalBucF-426
94CarMudF-1572
95CarMudF-151
96CarMudB-3
Koob, Ernie
92ConTSN-349
Kooiman, Bill
90IdaFalBP-3267
Kooman, Chris
87EveGiaC-14
Koonce, Cal
63Top-31
65OPC-34
65Top-34
66Top-278
66TopVen-278
67CokCapC-15
67DexPre-118
67OPC-171
67Top-171
68Top-486
69Top-303
70OPC-521
70Top-521
71MLBOffS-320
71OPC-254
71Top-254
72MilBra-185
89RinPosM1-18
91MetWIZ-218
94Met69CCPP-20
94Met69CS-19
94Met69T-28
Koonce, Graham
94BriTigC-16
96FayGenB-20
Koontz, Jim
81ElPasDT-10
82ElPasDT-20
84VanCanC-45
Koopman, Bob
86PriWilPP-14
87SalBucP-20
Koosman, Jerry
68OPC-177
68Top-177
68TopVen-177
69CitMetC-12
69MetCit-6
69MetNewYDN-11
69MLBOffS-168
69MLBPin-49
69OPC-90
69Top-90
69Top-434
69TopDec-25
69TopDecI-22
69TopSta-66
69TopSup-51
69TopTeaP-24
69TraSta-46
70DayDaiNM-44
70MetTra-22B
70MLBOffS-79
70OPC-309
70OPC-468
70Top-309
70Top-468
70Top-610
70TraSta-5C
71MLBOffS-157
71OPC-335
71Top-335
71TopCoi-23
71TopTat-22
72MilBra-186
72Top-697
72Top-698
73LinPor-114
73MetAllEB-6
73OPC-184
73Top-184
74MetDaiPA-19
74MetJapEB-4
74OPC-356
74Top-356
74TopSta-65
75MetSSP-14
75OPC-19
75SSP42-17
75Top-19
76CraDis-27
76LauDiaJ-22
76MetMSAP-4
76OPC-64
76SSP-591
76SSP-609
76Top-64
77BurCheD-143
77Hos-77
77Kel-29
77MetDaiPA-10
77MSADis-33
77OPC-26
77Top-300
78Hos-80
78MetDaiPA-12
78Pep-34
78TasDis-12
78Top-565
78WifBalD-35
79Hos-149
79OPC-345
79Top-655
79TwiFriP-12
80BurKinPHR-5
80OPC-144
80Top-275
80TopSup-38
81Don-531
81Fle-552
81FleStiC-19
81OPC-298
81Top-476
81TopSti-104
82Don-603
82Fle-347
82OPC-63
82Top-714
83Don-39
83Fle-242
83FleSta-97
83FleSti-152
83OPC-153
83Top-153
83TopFol-1
83WhiSoxTV-36
84Don-501
84Fle-65
84FleUpd-64
84Nes792-311
84Nes792-716
84OPC-311
84PhiTas-23
84Top-311
84Top-716
84TopTif-311
84TopTif-716
84TopTra-64T
84TopTraT-64T
85Don-233
85Fle-256
85Lea-178
85OPC-15
85PhiCIG-7
85PhiTas-9
85PhiTas-21
85Top-15
85TopMin-15
85TopSti-117
85TopTif-15
86Don-23
86DonSupD-23
86Lea-23
86MetGreT-10
86OPC-343
86Spo-64
86Top-505
86TopTif-505
87Met196T-4
88PacLegI-66
89Met196C-8
89RinPosM1-19
89SweBasG-109
90MetHaloF-5
90PacLeg-88
91MetWIZ-219
91PitMetC-26
91PitMetP-3440
91UppDecRH-10
92ColMetC-27
92ColMetPI-2
92UppDecS-10
93ActPacA-160
94Met69CCPP-21
94Met69CS-20
94Met69SP-P2
94Met69T-4
94Met69T-37
94Met69T-39
94Met69T-48
94Met69T-54
96Met69Y-6
Kopacz, Derek
96FayGenB-21

Kopacz, George
71OPC-204
71Top-204
Koperda, Mike
80AndBraT-21
Kopetsky, Brian
86BakDodP-18
Kopf, Dave
86PitCubP-11
87IowCubTI-10
88PitCubP-1373
Kopf, Larry (William)
19W514-118
20NatCarE-56
20RedWorCP-9
22E120-128
22W572-56
88PacEigMO-91
Kopitzke, Chad
93HelBreF-4088
93HelBreSP-21
94BelBreC-14
94BelBreF-95
95BelBreTI-13
Koplitz, Howard
62Top-114
62TopVen-114
63Top-406
64Top-372
66OPC-46
66Top-46
66TopVen-46
78TCM60I-221
Koppe, Clint
94BilMusF-3664
94BilMusSP-17
Koppe, Joe
59Top-517
60Top-319
61Top-179
62SalPlaC-209
62ShiPlaC-209
62Top-39
62TopVen-39
63Jel-26
63Pos-26A
63Pos-26B
63Top-396
64Top-279
64TopVen-279
Kopriva, Dan
92PriRedC-25
92PriRedF-3095
93SouAtlLAGF-55
93WesVirWC-12
93WesVirWF-2873
94WinSpiC-12
94WinSpiF-279
95ChaLooTI-10
96PriWilCB-16
Kopyta, Jeff
86MedA'sC-66
86ModA'sC-27
87MadMusP-10
87MadMusP-18
88ModA'sCLC-63
88ModA'sTI-12
89ModA'sCLC-272
Koranda, Jim
58MonRoyF-12
Korcheck, Steve
58Top-403
59Top-284
60Lea-79
60SenJayP-8
60Top-56
60TopVen-56
Korczyk, Steve
82TolMudHT-3
83TolMudHT-5
Kordish, Steve
83TriTriT-2
84TulDriTI-30
86SalRedBP-15
Korince, George
67OPC-72
67Top-72
67Top-526
68Top-447
Korn, Ray
91EriSaiC-27
91EriSaiP-4085
94HunCubF-3570
94HunCubC-29
Korneev, Leonid
89EasLeaDDP-DD15
Kornfeld, Craig
79QuaCitCT-16
80QuaCitCT-17
Korolev, Sergey
89EasLeaDDP-DD4
Kortmeyer, Scott
95SpoIndTI-10
Kortright, Jim
88IdaFalBP-1858
89IdaFalBP-2031
Korwan, Jim
90DodTar-1005
Kosc, Greg
88T/MUmp-25
89T/MUmp-23
90T/MUmp-22
Kosco, Andy
66Top-264
66TopVen-264
67CokCapTw-18
67Top-366
68Top-524
69MilBra-152
69OPC-139
69Top-139
69TopFou-8
69TopSta-204
69TopTeaP-22
70OPC-535
70Top-535
71MLBOffS-440
71OPC-746
71Top-746
72MilBra-187
72OPC-376
72Top-376
74OPC-34
74Top-34
90DodTar-417
92YanWIZ6-69
94BreMilB-234
Kosco, Bryn
88JamExpP-1896
89RocExpLC-16
90JacExpB-6
90JacExpP-1382
91HarSenLD-259
91HarSenP-633
91LinDriAA-259
92HarSenF-465
92HarSenS-285
93HigDesMC-8
93HigDesMF-47
94ExcFS7-192
94NewHavRF-1557
94SigRoo-31
94SigRooS-31
95IowCubTI-20
96IowCubB-18
Kosco, Dru (Andrew)
87WauTimP-14
88WauTimGS-26
89WilBilP-626
90WilBilB-13
90WilBilP-1068
90WilBilS-14
Kosek, Kory
95MarPhiTI-14
Kosenski, John
88CapCodPPaLP-108
88OklSoo-13
89OklSoo-20
90OklSoo-15
91FayGenC-4
91FayGenP-1165
92LakTigC-14
92LakTigF-2273
93LakTigC-13
93LakTigF-1305
Koshevoy, Alexei
89EasLeaDDP-DD7
Koshorek, Clem
52Top-380
53BowC-147
53Top-8
83TopRep5-380
91TopArc1-8
Koskie, Corey
95ForWayWTI-17
95MidLeaA-28
96Exc-78
96FtMyeMB-17
Koslo, Dave (George B.)
47TipTop-126
48Bow-48
49Bow-34
49EurSta-114
50Bow-65
51Bow-90
52BerRos-31
52Bow-182
52Top-336
54OriEss-18
55BraGolS-12
55BraJohC-20
75Gia195T-14
79TCM50-231
83TopRep5-336
85TCMPla1-45
91OriCro-247
Koslofski, Kevin
86Ft.MyeRP-16
87Ft.MyeRP-24
88BasCitRS-15
89BasCitRS-14
90MemChiB-10
90MemChiP-1021
90MemChiS-12
91LinDriAA-408
91MemChiLD-408
91MemChiP-666
92DonRoo-63
92FleUpd-28
92OmaRoyF-2975
92OmaRoyS-332
92ProFS7-74
92SkyAAAF-152
93Don-205
93Fle-240
93OmaRoyF-1691
93RoyPol-15
93Sco-226
93Sel-394
93StaClu-505
93StaCluFDI-505
93StaCluMOP-505
93Top-158
93TopGol-158
93TopInaM-158
93TopMic-158
93Ult-211
93UppDec-351
93UppDecGold-351
93USPlaCR-4D
94Pac-291
Kosman, Cody
93EugEmeC-18
93EugEmeF-3852
Kosnik, Jim
87BelMarL-16
Kostich, Billy
89HigSchPLS-15
91PenPilC-7
91PenPilP-373
92PenPilC-21
92PenPilF-2928
93AppFoxC-13
93AppFoxF-2457
Kostickhka, Steve
87BelBreP-6
Kostro, Frank
63Top-407
65Top-459
68OPC-44
68Top-44
68TopVen-44
69Top-242
Kotarski, Mike
92BenRocC-16
92BenRocF-1473
93CenValRC-15
93CenValRF-2891
93Top-621
93TopGol-621
93TopInaM-621
93TopMic-621
94NewHavRF-1545
96NorNavB-14
Kotch, Darrin
90JamExpP-19
91SumFlyC-6
91SumFlyP-2329
92RocExpC-5
92RocExpF-2110
Kotchman, Randy
89MiaMirIS-8
90BoiHawP-3325
Kotchman, Tom
86PalSprAP-2
86PalSprAP-19
87EdmTraP-2072
88EdmTraC-22
88EdmTraP-580
89EdmTraC-25
89EdmTraP-549
89TriAAP-AAA28
90BoiHawP-3331
91BoiHawP-3899
92BoiHawF-3646
93BoiHawC-27
94BoiHawC-30
94BoiHawF-3372
95BoiHawTI-21
96BoiHawB-1
Kotes, Chris
91St.CatBJC-17
91St.CatBJP-3389
92MyrBeaHC-14
92MyrBeaHF-2192
93DunBluJC-13
93DunBluJF-1792
93DunBluJFFN-14
93SouAtlLAPI-19
94DunBluJC-16
94DunBluJF-2553
95KnoSmoF-40
Kotkas, Jim
90IBAWorA-27
Kotrany, Joe
76DalCon-6
Kotsay, Mark
96BesAutS1RP-FR2
96KanCouCUTI-9
96MauStiHWB-9
97Bow-108
97Bow98ROY-ROY8
97BowBes-197
97BowBesAR-197
97BowBesR-197
97BowChr-128
97BowChr1RC-ROY8
97BowChr1RCR-ROY8
97BowChrI-128
97BowChrIR-128
97BowChrR-128
97BowInt-108
97DonLim-88
97DonLimLE-88
97Top-483
97TopSta-108
97TopStaAM-108
Kouba, Curtis
82WauTimF-5
Koufax, Sandy
47Exh-124
55DodGolS-8
55Top-123
56Dod-15
56Top-79
57Top-302
58DodBelB-6
58Top-187
59DodMor-5
59DodTeal-11
59Top-163
59TopVen-163
60DodBelB-9
60DodMor-6
60DodPos-5
60DodTeal-10
60DodUniO-10
60Top-343
61DodBelB-32
61DodMor-4
61DodUniO-11
61Top-49
61Top-207
61Top-344
62AurRec-9
62Baz-16
62DodBelB-32
62DodJayP-6
62ExhStaB-19
62Jel-109
62Pos-109A
62Pos-109B
62PosCan-109
62SalPlaC-109
62ShiPlaC-109
62Top-5
62Top-60
62TopBuc-45
62TopStal-136
62TopVen-5
62TopVen-60
63DodJayP-8
63ExhStaB-36
63Fle-42
63Jel-121
63Pos-121
63SalMetC-4
63Top-5
63Top-9
63Top-210
63Top-412
63TopStil-23
64Baz-32
64DodHea-6
64Top-1
64Top-3
64Top-5
64Top-136
64Top-200
64TopCoi-106
64TopCoi-159
64TopGia-3
64TopSta-91
64TopStaU-40
64TopTatI-48
64TopVen-1
64TopVen-3
64TopVen-5
64TopVen-136
64TopVen-200
65Baz-32
65DodJayP-7
65DodTeal-9
65OPC-8
65Top-8
65Top-300
65TopEmbl-8
65TopTral-55
66Baz-1
66OPC-100
66Top-100
66Top-221
66Top-223
66Top-225
66TopRubl-47
66TopVen-100
66TopVen-221
66TopVen-223
66TopVen-225
67Top-234
67Top-236
67Top-238
67TopTesF-10
67TopVen-162
68LauWorS-60
68LauWorS-62
72LauGreF-4
73HalofFPP-10
74NewYorNTDiS-5
74SupBlaB-6
75OPC-201
75TCMAllG-19
75Top-201
76JerJonPC-1
76LauDiaJ-4
76ShaPiz-131
77GalGloG-244
77Spo-2902
77Spo-6023
78TCM60I-130
79TCM50-49
80DodGreT-5
80PacLeg-10
80PerHaloFP-131
80SSPHOF-131
81AlbDukT-23B
82BasCarN-17
82K-M-4
83DiaClaS2-60
83MLBPin-24
84OCoandSI-3
84OCoandSI-101
86SpoDesJM-17
86TCM-3
86TCMSupS-20
87DodSmoA-16
88DodSmo-4
88DodSmo-6
89DodSmoG-15
89HOFStiB-79

90DodTar-418
90HOFStiB-69
90OPC-665
90PerGreM-16
90Top-665
90TopTif-665
91DodUno7P-4
91DodUno7P-6
92DodStaTA-4
95TopArcBD-102
95TopArcBD-146
95TopArcBD-AU
Koukalik, Joe
90DodTar-1006
Kounas, Tony
88CapCodPPaLP-144
91PenPilC-14
91PenPilP-380
92SanBerC-8
92SanBerSF-958
93JacSunF-2715
94JacSunF-1414
95HarSenTI-20
Koupal, Lou
90DodTar-1007
93ConTSN-713
Kovach, Ty
89WatIndS-13
90CarLeaA-34
90KinIndTI-4
91CanIndLD-85
91CanIndP-977
91Cla/Bes-309
91LinDriAA-85
92KinIndC-6
92KinIndF-2470
Kowalik, Fabian
35DiaMatC33T1-93
36OveCanR-28
Kowalski, Killer (Wladek)
72Dia-123
Kowar, Frank
90St.CatBJP-3462
Kowitz, Brian
90ProAaA-192
90PulBraB-22
90PulBraP-3087
91Cla/Bes-66
91DurBulC-25
91DurBulP-1559
92DurBulF-1114
92GreBraS-237
93ClaGolF-90
93ExcFS7-4
93GreBraF-362
94RicBraF-2861
95RicBraRC-8
95RicBraTI-7
96SyrChiTI-19
96TolMudHB-15
Koy, Ernest
41DouPlaR-117
79DiaGre-161
90DodTar-419
92TexLon-28
Koza, Dave
77BriRedST-10
81PawRedST-16
83PawRedST-17
Kozar, Al
47SenGunBP-5
49Bow-16
49MPR302-2-xx
50Bow-15
Kozeniewski, Blaise
92OneYanC-21
93GreHorC-14
93GreHorF-894
93OneYanC-11
93OneYanF-3498
94GreBatF-468
95NorNagUTI-39
97GreBatC-11
Kozyrez, Alexander
89EasLeaDDP-DD18
Krablin, Justin
92GulCoaMF-3476
94KinMetC-7
94KinMetF-3817
Kracl, Darin
87BriYouC-10
89MedAthB-13
90CMC-867
90MadMusP-2262
90MidLeaASGS-55
Kraeger, Don
79AppFoxT-23
Kraemer, Joe
85MadMusP-17
85MadMusT-20
86ModA'sP-18
86PeoChiP-13
87HunStaTI-18
87IowCubTI-9
88IowCubC-7
88IowCubP-549
89IowCubC-3
89IowCubP-1715
90DonRoo-10
90FleUpd-8
90TopDeb89-68
90TopTVCu-10
90UppDec-740
91IowCubLD-207
91IowCubP-1054
91LinDriAAA-207
91Sco-755
92MidAngF-4023
92MidAngOHP-13
92MidAngS-463
92SkyAA F-197
Kraft, Bob
76SeaRaiC-8
Kraft, Ken
86ClePhiP-15
Kraft, Mike
89JohCitCS-15
90SprCarB-11
Krafve, Keith
86EveGiaC-24
86EveGiaPC-10
Krahenbuhl, Ken
90HunCubP-3278
91PeoChiC-26
91PeoChiTI-10
92PeoChiTI-10
92WinSpiC-15
Krajewski, Chris
80SanJosMJitB-13
Krakauskas, Joe
40PlaBal-188
41DouPlaR-77
47SigOil-10
91ConTSN-228
Kralick, Jack
61Top-36
61TwiCloD-11
61TwiJayP-6
61TwiPetM-6
61TwiUniMC-8
62Top-346
62TopStal-77
63Jel-11
63Pos-11
63Top-448
64IndJayP-8
64Kah-14
64Top-338
64TopVen-338
65Kah-20
65Top-535
65TopEmbl-72
66IndTeal-7
66OPC-129
66Top-129
66TopVen-129
67CokCapl-14
67Top-316
78TCM60I-134
78TwiFri-37
Kraly, Steve
54NewYorJA-47
55Top-139
Kramer, Jack (John)
41BroW75-18
41Gou-14
43ParSpo-87
46SeaSLP-28
47TipTop-66
48RedSoxTI-14
49Bow-53
50Bow-199
51Bow-200
52Whe-17A
52Whe-17B
75Gia195T-15
76TayBow4-32
79DiaGre-180
79TCM50-107
84TCMPla1-19
96Bro194F-14
Kramer, Jeff
94HelBreF-3611
94HelBreSP-24
95Exc-71
96El PasDB-14
Kramer, Mark
85BurRanTI-18
86DayBealP-15
87PorChaRP-19
88ChaRanS-11
89MiaMirIS-9
Kramer, Matt
96YakBeaTI-24
Kramer, Randy
83BurRanF-5
83BurRanT-8
86KinEagP-13
86TulDriTI-23
87VanCanP-1613
88BlaYNPRWLU-39
88BufBisC-5
88BufBisP-1464
89BlaYNPRWL-158
89Don-480
89DonBasB-213
89DonRoo-48
89Fle-647
89FleGlo-647
89FleUpd-115
89PanSti-159
89ScoHot1R-57
89Top-522
89TopTif-522
90BufBisTI-12
90Don-409
90Fle-471
90FleCan-471
90Hot50RS-26
90OPC-126
90PanSti-327
90PirHomC-15
90Sco100RS-41
90Top-126
90TopTif-126
90UppDec-519
91LinDriAAA-432
91RicBraBC-8
91RicBraLD-432
91RicBraP-2561
91RicBraTI-17
92Bow-398
92CalCanS-62
92SkyAAAF-27
93EdmTraF-1132
Kramer, Scott
94WatIndC-18
94WatIndF-3932
Kramer, Tommy (Tom)
88MidLeaAGS-22
88WatIndP-689
89KinIndS-11
89Sta-76
90CarLeaA-38
91CanIndLD-86
91CanIndP-978
91LinDriAA-86
92ColSprSSF-748
92ColSprSSS-88
92SkyAAAF-38
92TopDeb91-105
93Bow-37
93FleFinE-202
93IndWUA-15
93Pin-585
93SelRoo-73T
94ChaKniF-890
94Don-384
94Fle-108
94Pac-172
94Sco-314
94ScoGolR-314
94Top-642
94TopGol-642
94TopSpa-642
94Ult-44
95ChaLooTI-11
96ColSprSSTI-22
Kranepool, Ed
47Exh-125
47PM1StaP1-108
63Top-228
64Top-393
64Top-566
65MetJayP-9
65OPC-144
65Top-144
65TopEmbl-6
65TopTral-56
66Baz-9
66Top-212
66TopRubl-48
66TopVen-212
67AshOil-5
67CokCapYM-V21
67DexPre-119
67Kah-20A
67Kah-20B
67MetTeal-9
67OPC-186
67Top-186
67Top-452
67TopVen-282
68OPC-92
68Top-92
68TopActS-5C
68TopVen-92
69MetCit-5
69MetNewYDN-12
69MilBra-153
69MLBOffS-169
69Top-381
69TopSta-67
69TopTeaP-24
70Kel-1
70MetTra-21A
70MLBOffS-80
70OPC-310
70Top-557
71MLBOffS-158
71OPC-573
71Top-573
72MilBra-188
72OPC-181
72OPC-182
72Top-181
72Top-182
73MetAllEB-7
73OPC-329
73Top-329
74MetDaiPA-11
74MetJapEB-5
74OPC-561
74Top-561
75MetSSP-10
75OPC-324
75Top-324
76MetMSAP-2
76OPC-314
76SSP-533
76Top-314
77BurCheD-136
77MetDaiPA-11
77OPC-60
77Top-201
78MetDaiPA-13
78OPC-205
78Top-49
78WifBalD-36
79OPC-265
79Top-505
80OPC-336
80Top-641
86MetGreT-1
87Met196T-1
89Met196C-9
89PacLegl-114
89RinPosM1-17
89SweBasG-28
90MetHaloF-6
91MetWIZ-220
92UppDecS-10
94Met69CCPP-22
94Met69CS-21
94Met69T-13
94Met69T-36
Kranitz, Rick
80HolMilT-1
81ElPasDT-17
82VanCanT-19
86WinSpiP-11
87WytCubP-29
88PeoChiTI-19
89PeoChiTI-31
90ChaKniTI-25
91ChaKniLD-150
91ChaKniP-1705
91LinDriAA-150
92IowCubF-4066
92IowCubS-225
93OrlCubF-2802
Kratochvil, Tim
96LowSpiB-14
Krattli, Tom
77DayBealT-11
Kratz, Ron
92BatCliC-15
92BatCliF-3273
Kraus, Jack
43PhiTeal-14
Kraus, Jeff
77SpaPhiT-18
80CarMudF-8
Kraus, Ralph
87PriWilYP-5
88Ft.LauYS-14
89Ft.LauYS-12
Kraus, Tim
96SouBenSHS-18
Krause, Andrew
85MadMusP-18
85MadMusT-21
Krause, Guy
75WesPalBES-28
75WesPalBES-29B
Krause, Harry
08AmeCarE-50
09AmeCarE-66
09PhiCarE-12
09SpoNewSM-27
09T206-196
09T206-197
10CouT21-164
10DomDisP-64
10E12AmeCDC-20
10LuxCigPP-13
10NadE1-27
10RedCroT-38
10RedCroT-127
10RedCroT-210
10SweCapPP-46
11A'sFirT20-8
11S74Sil-32
11SpoLifCW-208
11SpoLifM-95
11T205-92
11TurRedT-22
12HasTriFT-70D
12T207-95
20WalMaiW-25
Krause, Kevin
94WilCubC-13
94WilCubF-3760
95RocCubTI-8
Krause, Ron
90RocExpLC-13
90RocExpP-2700
91WesPalBEC-21
92WesPalBEC-2
92WesPalBEF-2095
93HarSenF-275
Krause, Scott
95BelBreTI-17
96El PasDB-15
96StoPorB-9
Krause, Tom
87SalSpuP-21
Krauss, Ron
82ChaRoyT-15
Krauss, Timothy
81RedPioT-17
82HolMilT-17
84EdmTraC-98
85DomLeaS-92
85EdmTraC-17
86BufBisP-14
87HawIslP-23
Krausse, Lew
63Top-104
64Top-334
64TopVen-334
65Top-462
66Top-256
66TopVen-256
67CokCapAt-16
67DexPre-120
67Top-565
67TopVen-205
68Top-458
69MilBra-154

69OPC-23
69Top-23
69TopSta-217
70BreMcD-14
70BreMil-11
70BreTeal-6
70OPC-233
70SunPin-12
70Top-233
71BreTeal-6
71MLBOffS-441
71OPC-372
71Top-372
71TopCoi-20
72Top-592
73OPC-566
73Top-566
75OPC-603
75Top-603
75TucTorC-13
75TucTorTI-7
94BreMilB-235
Krauza, Ron
89BufBisC-19
Kravec, Ken
77Top-389
77WhiSoxJT-8
78Top-439
79OPC-141
79Top-283
80OPC-299
80Top-575
81Top-67
81TopTra-783
82CubRedL-37
82Don-378
82IowCubT-19
82Top-639
87Ft.MyeRP-28
88MemChiB-14
89PacSenL-151
91PacSenL-10
Kravitz, Dan
57JetPos-10
57Top-267
58Top-444
59Top-536
60Top-238
61Top-166
Krawczyk, Ray
82AleDukT-4
84HawIslC-129
85DomLeaS-60
85HawIslC-245
86HawIslP-14
87HawIslP-17
88BlaYNPRWL-120
89BlaYNPRWL-127
89DenZepC-7
89DenZepP-32
94BreMilB-236
Krebs, Dave
87SavCarP-3
88SavCarP-338
Kreevich, Mike
36R31PasP-38
36SandSW-39
38ExhFou-10
39ExhSal-34
39GouPreR303A-29
39GouPreR303B-17
39WhiSoxTI-9
39WorWidGTP-29
40WhiSoxL-10
83TCMPla1944-3
93DiaStaES-140
96Bro194F-30
Kremblas, Frank
90CedRapRP-2324
91ChaLooLD-160
91ChaLooP-1966
91LinDriAA-160
92ChaLooF-3828
92ChaLooS-188
93IndIndF-1497
94ChaLooF-1364
Kremblas, Kris
95IndIndF-110
Kremer, Ken
89BelBreIS-12
89BelBreIS-18
Kremer, Ray (Remy)
20WalMaiW-26
25Exh-53
26Exh-53
27Exh-26
28Exh-25
28W56PlaC-C9
29ExhFou-14
31Exh-14
33ButCre-15
33Gou-54
34GouCanV-38
91ConTSN-279
Kremers, Jimmy
89BlaYNPRWLU-35
89GreBraB-24
89GreBraP-1163
89GreBraS-12
89SouLeaAJ-8
90BraDubS-17
90CMC-286
90FleUpd-4
90ProAAAF-406
90RicBraBC-12
90RicBraC-10
90RicBraP-261
90RicBraTI-17
91Don-739
91Fle-694
91IndIndLD-187
91IndIndP-464
91LinDriAAA-187
91Sco-736
91TopDeb90-79
91UppDec-262
92IndIndF-1862
92IndIndS-185
92SkyAAAF-91
94NewOrlZF-1472
94VenLinU-268
95PorSeaDTI-9
Kremmel, Jim
93RanKee-221
Kremmeyer, Charles
87OldJudN-293
Krenchicki, Wayne
78RocRedWT-11
80RocRedWT-16
80Top-661
82Fle-168
82RedCok-12
82Top-107
82TopTra-58T
83Don-314
83Fle-594
83FleSti-220
83Top-374
84Don-334
84Fle-83
84FleUpd-65
84Nes792-223
84RedEnq-8
84Top-223
84TopTif-223
84TopTra-65T
84TopTraT-65T
84WicAerRD-7
85Don-140
85Fle-539
85RedYea-8
85Top-468
85TopTif-468
86Don-140
86ExpPos-6
86ExpProPa-20
86Fle-180
86FleUpd-60
86OPC-81
86Top-777
86TopTif-777
86TopTra-55T
86TopTraT-55T
87Don-406
87Fle-322
87FleGlo-322
87OPC-81
87TacTigP-6
87Top-774
87TopTif-774
88LouRedBTI-25
88TacTigC-14
88TacTigP-635
89PacSenL-157
89TopSenL-75
90EliSenL-38
91OriCro-248
91PacSenL-42
92BelBreC-28
92BelBreF-422
93BelBreC-26
93BelBreF-1726
94BelBreC-27
94BelBreF-118
Krenke, Keith
92BenRocC-17
92BenRocF-1487
92Min-9
93CenValRC-16
93CenValRF-2905
Kress, Chuck (Charlie)
54Top-219
90DodTar-420
94TopArc1-219
94TopArc1G-219
Kress, Red (Ralph)
29ExhFou-29
29ProandAR-54
31Exh-30
33Gou-33
33GouCanV-33
34BatR31-169
35AlDemDCR3-20
35DiaMatCS3T1-94
35GouPuzR-4C
35GouPuzR-7C
35GouPuzR-12C
38BasTabP-19
39PlaBal-115
40PlaBal-45
54Top-160
55IndGolS-29
55Top-151
60Top-460
82MetGal62-30
92ConTSN-383
94TopArc1-160
94TopArc1G-160
Kretlow, Lou
52Bow-221
52Top-42
53BowC-50
54Bow-197
54OriEss-19
55Bow-108
55OriEss-12
57Top-139
83TopRep5-42
91OriCro-249
Kreuter, Chad
86SalRedBP-16
87PorChaRP-25
88TexLeaAGS-3
88TulDriTI-19
89ClaLigB-27
89Don-579
89Fle-526
89FleGlo-526
89PanSti-444
89RanSmo-17
89Sco-638
89ScoHot1R-51
89ScoYouS2-40
89Spo-43
89Top-432
89TopTif-432
89UppDec-312
90Don-520
90Fle-303
90FleCan-303
90OPC-562
90PubSti-414
90Sco-406
90Sco100RS-51
90Top-562
90TopTif-562
90TulDriDGB-23
90UppDec-609
90VenSti-272
92Bow-515
92Lea-496
92Ult-365
93Don-673
93Fla-205
93Fle-607
93Lea-463
93PacSpa-444
93RanKee-222
93TigGat-16
93Top-692
93TopGol-692
93TopInaM-692
93TopMic-692
93Ult-201
94Bow-13
94ColC-167
94ColChoGS-167
94ColChoSS-167
94Don-224
94Fin-388
94FinRef-388
94Fle-137
94Lea-5
94Pac-223
94Pin-125
94PinArtP-125
94PinMusC-125
94Sco-503
94ScoGolR-503
94Sel-327
94StaClu-411
94StaCluFDI-411
94StaCluGR-411
94StaCluMOP-411
94Top-257
94TopGol-257
94TopSpa-257
94Ult-56
94UppDec-392
94UppDecED-392
95Don-219
95DonPreP-219
95Fle-57
95FleUpd-75
95MarMot-18
95Pac-156
95Sco-504
95ScoGolR-504
95ScoPlaTS-504
95Top-362
95Ult-48
95UltGolM-48
96LeaSigEA-104
Kreutzer, Frank
63WhiSoxTS-13
64Top-107
64TopVen-107
65Top-371
66Top-211
66TopVen-211
78TCM60I-116
Krevokuch, Jim
91WelPirC-8
91WelPirP-3579
92AugPirC-3
92AugPirF-246
93CarMudF-2062
93CarMudTI-18
94CarMudF-1586
95CarMudF-166
Krichell, Paul
09ColChiE-159
12ColRedB-159
12ColTinT-159
Krieg, William
87OldJudN-294
87OldJudN-295
Kries, John
89SalDodTI-14
Kripner, Mike
80CedRapRT-23
82WatRedT-12
Krippner, Curt
88BelBreGS-16
89BelBreIS-19
90StoPorCLC-185
90StoPorP-2184
91Cla/Bes-403
91EriSaiP-4063
Krislock, Zak
92AubAstC-24
92AubAstF-1351
93AshTouC-10
93AshTouF-2271
Krist, Howie
41CarW75-12
46SeaSLP-29
79DiaGre-165
Kristan, Kevin
85LasVegSC-124
87WesPalBEP-673
Kritscher, Ryan
96JohCitCTI-18
Krivda, Rick
91BluOriC-18
91BluOriP-4123
92KanCouCC-14
92KanCouCF-87
92KanCouCTI-18
92MidLeaATI-26
92ProFS7-27
93ClaFS7-53
93ExcFS7-124
94ActPac-44
94Bow-159
94ExcFS7-9
94ExcLeaLF-12
94OriPro-50
94RocRedWF-993
94RocRedWTI-9
94TriAAF-AAA13
94Ult-306
94UppDecML-226
95Fle-10
95RocRedWTI-21
96ColCho-11
96ColChoGS-11
96ColChoSS-11
96Don-262
96DonPreP-262
96Fle-13
96FleOri-9
96FleTif-13
96StaClu-294
96StaCluMOP-294
96Top-352
96TopChr-142
96TopChrR-142
96UppDec-16
97ColCho-44
97Top-323
Krizmanich, Mike
75IntLeaAT-3
75IntLeaAT-23
Kroc, Ray
77PadSchC-35
78PadFamF-17
91FouBal-23
Krock, August
87OldJudN-296
88AugBecN-16
88GandBCGCE-24
Kroener, Chris
86VisOakP-12
Kroh, Rube (Floyd)
09BriE97-18
09ColChiE-160
09T206-198
10SweCapPP-83
11SpoLifM-173
11T205-93
12ColRedB-160
12ColTinT-160
Krokroskia, Sean
90BenBucL-3
Krol, David
88CapCodPPaLP-180
Krol, Jack
76ArkTraT-4
77Car5-13
77CarTeal-13
78CarTeal-9
79Car5-14
84PadMot-27
84PadSmo-15
85PadMot-27
87LasVegSP-3
88ChaRaiP-1219
89ChaRaiP-991
90ChaRaiB-26
90ChaRaiP-2054
92LouRedF-1902
92LouRedS-274
Kroll, Gary
65Top-449
66Top-548
66TopRubI-49
78TCM60I-127
91MetWIZ-221
Kroll, Todd
87BakDodP-8
88BakDodCLC-255
Kromy, Ted
79WisRapTT-19
82OrlTwi8SCT-19
82OrlTwiT-17
83OrlTwiT-17
Kroon, Marc
92KinMetC-18
92KinMetF-1527

92StaCluD-99
93CapCitBC-10
93CapCitBF-456
94RanCucQC-18
94RanCucQF-1635
95Bow-207
95BowBes-B17
95BowBesR-B17
95MemChiTI-16
96BesAutS-46
96ColCho-699
96ColChoGS-29
96ColChoGS-699
96ColChoSS-29
96ColChoSS-699
96Fle-572
96FleTif-572
96MemChiB-20
96Sco-238
96Sco-498
96Top-433
97Bow-402
97BowCerBIA-CA46
97BowCerGIA-CA46
97BowInt-402
Kropke, Keri
95ColSilB-16
Krsnich, Joe
77BriRedST-11
Krsnich, Mike
62Top-289
Krsnich, Rocky (Rocco)
53Top-229
91TopArc1-229
Krueger, Arthur T.
09T206-435
10JuJuDE-23
11SpoLifCW-209
11SpoLifM-284
Krueger, Bill
82WesHavAT-7
84Fle-450
84Nes792-178
84OPC-178
84TacTigC-84
84Top-178
84TopTif-178
85A'sMot-21
85Don-467
85Fle-428
85Top-528
85TopTif-528
86A'sMot-21
86Don-298
86Fle-424
86Top-58
86TopTif-58
87Top-238
87TopTif-238
88AlbDukC-3
88AlbDukP-271
88TriAAC-42
90BreMilB-13
90BrePol-47
90DodTar-421
90Fle-328
90FleCan-328
90Lea-421
90OPC-518
90Sco-366
90Top-518
90TopTif-518
91Bow-248
91Don-647
91Fle-588
91FleUpd-54
91OPC-417
91Sco-598
91Top-417
91TopDesS-417
91TopMic-417
91TopTif-417
91TopTra-70T
91TopTraT-70T
91UltUpd-52
91UppDecFE-60F
92Don-672
92DonUpd-U16
92Fle-285
92Lea-477
92OPC-368
92Pin-501
92Sco-253
92StaClu-861
92Top-368
92TopGol-368
92TopGolW-368
92TopMic-368
92TopTra-61T
92TopTraG-61T
92Ult-397
92UppDec-403
92UppDec-781
93Don-352
93FleFinE-211
93Lea-348
93OPCPre-38
93PacSpa-445
93Pin-547
93TigGat-17
93Ult-552
93UppDec-530
93UppDecGold-530
94BreMilB-237
94Don-252
94Fle-138
94Pac-222
94Top-552
94TopGol-552
94TopSpa-552
Krueger, Ernie
90DodTar-422
Krueger, Kirby
81WisRapTT-6
83OrlTwiT-18
Krueger, Rick
79TCMJapPB-58
Krueger, Robert
94AppFoxC-13
94AppFoxF-1050
Krueger, Steve
81LynSaiT-7
82LynSaiT-5
Krug, Chris (Everett B.)
66CubTeal-9
66OPC-166
66Top-166
66TopVen-166
Krug, Martin
22E120-162
Kruger, Andy
94BriTigC-17
94BriTigF-3519
Kruk, John
83BeaGolGT-11
84LasVegSC-228
84LasVegSC-250
85LasVegSC-103
86DonRoo-42
86FleUpd-61
86SpoRoo-1
86TopTra-56T
86TopTraT-56T
87Don-328
87Fle-420
87FleGlo-420
87Lea-217
87PadBohHB-8
87Spo-61
87SpoTeaP-16
87StuPan-12
87Top-123
87TopSti-113
87TopTif-123
87ToyRoo-17
88ClaBlu-203
88ClaRed-162
88Don-205
88DonBasB-245
88Fle-589
88FleGlo-589
88FleMin-113
88FleStiC-124
88FleSup-20
88Lea-176
88OPC-32
88OPCBoxB-G
88PadCok-8
88PadSmo-14
88PanSti-326
88PanSti-403
88RedFolSB-44
88Sco-36
88ScoGlo-36
88ScoYouSI-17
88Spo-64
88StaLinPa-7
88Top-596
88TopBig-60
88TopCoi-45
88TopMinL-75
88TopSti-110
88TopTif-596
88TopUKM-41
88TopUKMT-41
88TopWaxBC-G
89Bow-460
89BowTif-460
89Don-86
89DonBasB-240
89Fle-309
89FleGlo-309
89FleUpd-109
89OPC-235
89PadMag-5
89PanSti-200
89PhiTas-42
89RedFolSB-69
89Sco-148
89ScoRoo-70T
89Spo-184
89Top-235
89TopBasT-145
89TopBig-216
89TopSti-102
89TopTif-235
89TopTra-63T
89TopTraT-63T
89TVSpoM-48
89UppDec-280
90Bow-154
90BowTif-154
90ClaYel-T3
90Don-160
90DonBesN-69
90Fle-565
90FleCan-565
90Lea-284
90OPC-469
90PanSti-310
90PhiTas-18
90PubSti-52
90Sco-467
90Spo-124
90Top-469
90TopBig-214
90TopMag-96
90TopSti-117
90TopTif-469
90UppDec-668
90VenSti-273
91Bow-503
91Cla3-T47
91Don-260
91Fle-402
91Lea-278
91OPC-689
91PanSti-107
91PhiMed-22
91Sco-94
91SimandSMLBL-23
91StaClu-227
91Top-689
91TopDesS-689
91TopMic-689
91TopTif-689
91TopTriH-N8
91Ult-266
91UppDec-199
91USPlaCA-4S
92Bow-541
92Don-230
92DonDiaK-DK12
92Fle-537
92Hig5-78
92Lea-313
92LeaGolP-8
92LeaPre-8
92OPC-30
92OPCPre-134
92PanSti-242
92PhiMed-17
92Pin-147
92Sco-235
92SpoIllFK1-196
92StaClu-209
92StaCluD-100
92Stu-76
92StuPre-4
92Top-30
92TopGol-30
92TopGolW-30
92TopKid-18
92TopMic-30
92TriPla-38
92Ult-246
92UppDec-38
92UppDec-326
92UppDecHRH-HR23
92UppDecTMH-28
93Bow-540
93ClaGam-50
93ColAllG-4
93DiaMar-62
93Don-436
93DurPowP2-3
93Fin-38
93FinRef-38
93Fla-105
93Fle-104
93FleAtl-12
93FleFruotL-33
93FleTeaL-NL8
93FunPac-146
93Hos-4
93Lea-366
93LeaGolA-U3
93OPC-216
93OPCPre-76
93PacJugC-30
93PacSpa-238
93PanSti-270
93PhiMed-21
93Pin-8
93PinSlu-17
93Pos-29
93Sco-79
93Sel-33
93SelStaL-6
93SelStaL-53
93SP-14
93StaClu-83
93StaCluFDI-83
93StaCluM-84
93StaCluMOP-83
93StaCluP-30
93Stu-183
93StuHer-12
93StuSil-7
93Top-340
93TopFulS-16
93TopGol-340
93TopInaM-340
93TopMic-340
93TriPla-139
93Ult-90
93UppDec-247
93UppDec-485
93UppDecGold-247
93UppDecGold-485
93USPlaCA-10D
94Bow-412
94ColC-168
94ColC-326
94ColChoGS-168
94ColChoGS-326
94ColChoSS-168
94ColChoSS-326
94Don-7
94DonDiaK-DK9
94DonDom-B10
94DonEli-41
94DonSpeE-7
94ExtBas-340
94Fin-416
94FinRef-416
94Fla-415
94Fle-594
94FleAllS-44
94FleSun-15
94FUnPac-120
94FUnPac-214
94FUnPac-230
94Lea-347
94LeaGam-11
94LeaL-138
94OPC-257
94OscMayR-25
94Pac-479
94PacSilP-32
94PanSti-229
94PhiMed-19
94PhiMel-14
94PhiUSPC-7D
94PhiUSPC-13C
94Pin-63
94PinArtP-63
94PinMusC-63
94PinRunC-RC25
94ProMag-104
94RedFolMI-13
94Sco-28
94ScoGolR-28
94ScoGolS-7
94Sel-24
94SelSam-24
94SP-138
94SPDieC-138
94SPHol-22
94SPHolDC-22
94Spo-101
94StaClu-361
94StaClu-533
94StaCluDD-DD3
94StaCluFDI-361
94StaCluFDI-533
94StaCluGR-361
94StaCluGR-533
94StaCluMO-3
94StaCluMOP-361
94StaCluMOP-533
94StaCluMOP-DD3
94StaCluT-226
94StaCluTFDI-226
94Stu-142
94TomPiz-12
94Top-401
94TopBlaG-37
94TopGol-401
94TopSpa-401
94TriPla-177
94Ult-249
94Ult-P249
94UltPhiF-6
94UltPhiF-7
94UltPhiF-8
94UltPhiF-9
94UltPhiF-10
94UltPhiF-16
94UltPhiF-17
94UltPhiF-18
94UltPhiF-19
94UltPhiF-20
94UltPhiF-M2
94UltPhiF-M4
94UltPhiF-AU2
94UppDec-276
94UppDec-410
94UppDecAJ-7
94UppDecAJG-7
94UppDecED-276
94UppDecED-410
94USPlaCA-2D
95ColCho-373
95ColCho-584T
95ColChoGS-373
95ColChoSS-373
95Don-61
95DonPreP-61
95Fin-132
95Fin-319
95FinRef-132
95FinRef-319
95Fle-398
95Lea300C-14
95Pac-331
95Pin-395
95PinArtP-395
95PinMusC-395
95RedFol-29
95ScoHaloG-HG76
95ScoHaloGYTE-HG76T
95StaClu-331
95StaCluMOP-331
95StaCluSTWS-331
95StaCluVR-171
95Top-572
95TopCyb-346
95TopTra-116T
95Ult-421
95UltGolM-421
95UppDec-145
95UppDecED-145
95UppDecEDG-145
95WhiSoxK-17
96ColCho-98
96ColChoGS-98
96ColChoSS-98
95StaCluVRMC-171
Krukow, Mike

77CubJewT-8
77Top-493
78SSP270-267
78Top-17
79Top-592
80OPC-223
80Top-431
81CokTeaS-18
81Fle-312
81OPC-176
81Top-176
81TopSupHT-27
82Don-351
82Fle-598
82FleSta-92
82OPC-215
82Top-215
82TopSti-31
82TopTra-59T
83Don-119
83Fle-163
83GiaMot-12
83OPC-331
83Top-331
83TopTra-58T
84Don-509
84Fle-374
84GiaPos-8
84Nes792-633
84OPC-37
84Top-633
84TopTif-633
85AllGamPl-171
85Don-630
85Fle-609
85GiaMot-11
85GiaPos-16
85OPC-74
85Top-74
85TopSti-163
85TopTif-74
86Don-143
86DonHig-49
86Fle-546
86GiaMot-11
86OPC-126
86Top-752
86TopSti-93
86TopTat-8
86TopTif-752
87BurKinA-12
87ClaGam-67
87Don-609
87DonAll-58
87DonAllB-PC15
87DonOpeD-98
87Fle-275
87Fle-630
87FleGamW-24
87FleGlo-275
87FleGlo-630
87FleLimE-24
87FleMin-61
87FleStiC-69
87GiaMot-6
87HosSti-17
87Lea-86
87OPC-241
87SmoNatL-12
87Spo-62
87SpoTeaP-10
87Top-580
87TopMinL-36
87TopSti-92
87TopTif-580
88Don-116
88DonBasB-50
88Fle-85
88FleGlo-85
88GiaMot-6
88OPC-393
88PanSti-417
88RedFolSB-45
88Sco-185
88ScoGlo-185
88Top-445
88TopTif-445
89ClaTraO-114
89Don-258
89DonBasB-135
89Fle-331
89FleGlo-331
89GiaMot-6
89OPC-125
89Sco-190
89Top-125
89TopSti-83
89TopTif-125
89UppDec-46
90OPC-241
90PubSti-72
90Sco-215
90Top-241
90TopTif-241
90UppDec-639
90VenSti-274
Krum, Sandy
88CedRapRP-1140
89ChaLooB-24
89ChaLooGS-3
90SalBucS-27
91SalBucC-24
95CarMudF-176
Krumback, Mark
88BoiHawP-1625
89GreHorP-425
90CedRapRB-12
90CedRapRP-2335
91CalLeLA-34
91RenSilSCLC-2
Krumm, Todd
90LakTigS-17
91LinDriAA-390
91LonTigLD-390
91LonTigP-1875
Krupenchemkov, Alex.
89EasLeaDDP-DD14
Kruppa, Ken
75ForLauYS-15
76ForLauYS-10
Krusch, Lawrence
80VenLeaS-155
Kruse, Kelly
96SouBenSHS-19
Krusinski, Clar
89PeoChiTI-33
Krusinski, Mark
91PeoChiTI-30
Krusinski, Scott
93PeoChiC-25
Kryhoski, Dick
49Bow-218
49RemBre-14
50Bow-242
52Bow-133
52Top-149
53BowC-127
54Bow-117
54OriEss-20
54Top-150
55JetPos-7
79TCM50-241
83TopRep5-149
91OriCro-250
94TopArc1-150
94TopArc1G-150
Kryka, Mark
77CliDodT-14
78CliDodT-18
Kryzanowski, Rusty
86AubAstP-15
87KenTwiP-9
88KenTwiP-1383
89KenTwiP-1077
89KenTwiS-10
Ksenich, Michael
91ElmPioC-29
Kubala, Brian
86SanJosBP-11
87SanJosBP-30
Kubek, Tony
47Exh-126A
47Exh-126B
57Top-312
58Top-393
58YanJayP-4
59Top-505
59Yoo-3
60Top-83
60TopVen-83
60YanJayP-5
61Pos-9A
61Pos-9B
61Top-265
61TopDicG-7
61TopStal-195
61Yan61RL-42
61YanJayP-7
62Jel-4
62Pos-4
62PosCan-4
62SalPlaC-18
62ShiPlaC-18
62Top-311
62Top-430
62TopStal-87
63Kah-18
63Top-20
63YanJayP-6
64ChatheY-13
64Top-415
64YanJayP-6
64YanReqKP-9
65ChaTheY-11
65OPC-65
65Top-65
65TopEmbl-71
79DiaGre-19
79TCM50-244
81TCM60I-477
83FraBroR-16
87Yan196T-4
88PacLegI-29
89SweBasG-68
91RinPos1Y1-9
92YanWIZ6-70
92YanWIZA-37
Kubenka, Jeff
96YakBeaTI-37
Kubiak, Ted
68OPC-79
68Top-79
68TopVen-79
69Top-281
70BreMcD-15
70BreMil-12
70BreTeal-7
70SunPin-13
70Top-688
71BreTeal-7
71MLBOffS-442
71OPC-516
71Top-516
72MilBra-189
72OPC-23
72Top-23
73OPC-652
73Top-652
74A'sPos-53
74OPC-228
74Top-228
75OPC-329
75Top-329
76OPC-578
76SSP-129
76Top-578
77Top-158
89ModA'sC-1
90ModA'sC-33
90ModA'sCLC-171
90ModA'sP-2229
91ModA'sC-17
91ModA'sP-3106
92CalLeaACL-21
92ModA'sC-25
92ModA'sF-3910
93ModA'sC-26
93ModA'sF-815
93RanKee-22
94BreMilB-238
94CanIndF-3133
96WatIndTI-13
Kubicki, Marc
91UtiBluSC-1
91UtiBluSP-3237
92ProFS7-48
92SalSpuC-6
Kubinski, Tim
94WesMicWC-12
94WesMicWF-2290
95ModA'sTI-12
96HunStaTI-14
Kubiszyn, Jack
60MapLeaSF-12
77FriOneYW-42
Kubit, Joe
80WisRapTT-23
83VisOakF-17
Kuboto, Masahiro
90SalSpuCLC-148
Kubski, Gil
79SalLakCGT-16B
80SalLakCGT-21
81SyrChiT-18
81VanCanT-9
82IndIndTI-28
91HunCubP-3354
92HunCubC-29
97CraSalLCG-16
Kucab, John
52Top-358
83TopRep5-358
Kucek, Jack
75OPC-614
75Top-614
76OPC-597
76Top-597
77Top-623
80SyrChiT-11
80SyrChiTI-13
81SyrChiT-6
81SyrChiTI-12
Kucharski, Joe
84RocRedWT-18
85RocRedWT-20
86ChaOriW-16
87ChaO'sW-37
87RocRedWT-27
Kucks, John
56Top-88
57Top-185
57YanJayP-5
58Top-87
59Top-289
60A's-7
60A'sTeal-11
60Lea-96
60Top-177
60TopVen-177
61Top-94
62KahAtl-11
62Top-241
79DiaGre-23
83YanASFY-23
92YanWIZA-38
Kuder, Jeff
89AugPirP-491
89WelPirP-16
Kuecker, Mark
77CedRapGT-20
79PhoGiaVNB-20
Kuehl, John
88SpoIndP-1934
89ChaRaiP-986
89SouAtlLAGS-12
91Cla/Bes-354
91MidLeaAP-MWL30
91WatDiaC-17
91WatDiaP-1264
92ClaFS7-130
92HigDesMC-15
93HunStaF-2089
Kuehl, Karl
75IntLeaAT-25
76ExpRed-17
76OPC-216
76SSP-611
76Top-216
79TwiFriP-13
82TwiPos-19
Kuehne, William
87OldJudN-297
88WG1CarG-60
89WelPirP-33
Kuen Kim, Bong
96HilStaHWB-14
Kuenn, Harvey
47Exh-127A
47Exh-127B
47Exh-127C
53TigGle-18
54Bow-23
54RedHeaF-15
54Top-25
54Wil-11
55ArmCoi-12A
55ArmCoi-12B
55BigLeaIS-9
55Bow-132A
55Bow-132B
55DaiQueS-9
56Top-155
57Top-88
58Top-304
58Top-434
59ArmCoi-11
59Baz-13
59TigGraASP-11
59Top-70
59TopVen-70
60Baz-34
60IndJayP-4
60Kah-20
60NuHi-59
60Top-330
60Top-429
60TopTat-27
61Baz-15
61GiaJayP-7
61NuSco-459
61Pos-57A
61Pos-57B
61Top-500
61TopStal-77
61WilSpoGH828-2
61WilSpoGH828-1-3
62GiaJayP-7
62Jel-135
62Pos-135
62PosCan-135
62SalPlaC-121
62ShiPlaC-121
62Top-480
62TopBuc-46
62TopStal-197
63ExhStaB-37
63Jel-105
63Pos-105
63Top-30
64Top-242
64TopVen-242
65OPC-103
65Top-103
66CubTeal-10
66Top-372
73OPC-646
73Top-646
74Top-99
75SSP42-41
76GrePlaG-34
78NewWayCT-24
78TigDeaCS-6
79DiaGre-399
79TCM50-104
80PacLeg-66
81TigDetN-96
82Don-578
83BreGar-1
83BrePol-32
83Don-608
83TigAlKS-15
83TigAlKS-16
83Top-726
84Nes792-321
84Top-321
84TopGloA-1
84TopTif-321
86BreGreT-12
86TigSpoD-11
88PacLegI-56
89SweBasG-9
91SweBasG-114
91TopArc1-301
92BazQua5A-20
92BreCarT-11
92UppDecS-9
94TopArc1-25
94TopArc1G-25
Kuenzi, Kevin
89BoiHawP-1978
Kuhaulua, Fred
77SalLakCGC-12
79HawIslC-23
80HawIslT-25
81HawIslT-17
82HawIslT-17
82Top-731
Kuhel, Joe
31SenTealPW-20
33Gou-108
34BatR31-80
34BatR31-128
34ButPreR-38
34DiaStaR-78
34ExhFou-16
34Gou-16
34GouCanV-52
35GouPuzR-8H
35GouPuzR-9H
36GouWidPPR-A61

36NatChiFPR-50
36WorWidGV-63
37ExhFou-16
37OPCBatUV-127
38GouHeaU-243
38GouHeaU-267
39ExhSal-35
39WhiSoxTI-10
40PlaBal-185
40WhiSoxL-11
41PlaBal-31
47SenGunBP-1
47TipTop-22
60SenUniMC-11
61Fle-119
83ConMar-8
83DiaClaS2-95
83TCMPla1945-4
88ConAmeA-18
88ConSer5-18
91ConTSN-188
Kuhlman, Eric
88IdaFalBP-1851
89IdaFalBP-2028
Kuhn, Bowie
69TopBowK-1
77PadSchC-31
83TigAlKS-64
Kuhn, Chad
88SpoIndP-1935
89WatDiaP-1797
89WatDiaS-16
90MadMusB-17
90MadMusP-2263
91HunStaC-13
91HunStaLD-287
91HunStaP-1790
91HunStaTI-12
91LinDriAA-287
92HunStaF-3944
Kuhn, Ken
57Top-266
60Lea-115
Kuhn, Red (Walter)
12T207-96
Kuhn, Todd
85FreGiaP-21
Kuilan, Hector
96KanCouCTI-17
96KanCouCUTI-10
Kuilan, Jorge
88WinHavRSS-11
Kuiper, Duane
76OPC-508
76SSP-522
76SSP-529
76Top-508
77BurCheD-55
77OPC-233
77PepGloD-19
77Top-85
78Hos-34
78OPC-39
78Top-332
79Hos-13
79OPC-67
79Top-146
80OPC-221
80Top-429
81AllGamPI-14
81Don-319A
81Don-319B
81OPC-226
81Top-612
82Don-198
82Fle-373
82OPC-233
82Top-233
82TopTra-60T
83Fle-263
83FleSta-98
83FleSti-58
83GiaMot-11
83Top-767
84Don-553
84Fle-375
84GiaPos-9
84Nes792-542
84OPC-338
84Top-542
84TopSti-169
84TopTif-542
85Fle-610
85Top-22
85TopTif-22
Kuiper, Glen
85SpoIndC-10
86EriCarP-16
Kulakov, Vadim
89EasLeaDDP-DD5
Kuld, Pete
88WatIndP-682
89MiaMirIS-22
90HunStaB-14
91LinDriAA-610
91WicWraLD-610
91WicWraP-2602
91WicWraRD-12
92TulDriS-610
Kulle, Chuck
93WatIndC-14
93WatIndF-3576
Kulpa, Stephen
93GenCubC-18
93GenCubF-3184
Kume, Mike
52Par-100
57SeaPop-23
Kummerfeldt, Jason
92BenMusSP-11
92BilMusF-3348
93ExcFS7-23
93WesVirWC-13
93WesVirWF-2861
94WinSpiC-13
94WinSpiF-266
Kunkel, Bill (William)
61Top-322
62Top-147A
62Top-147B
62TopVen-147
63Top-523
85Top-136
85TopTif-136
92YanWIZ6-71
Kunkel, Jeff
84RanJarP-20
85Don-587
85Fle-561
85OklCit8T-3
85OPC-288
85Top-136
85Top-288
85TopSti-350
85TopTif-136
85TopTif-288
86OklCit8P-9
87RanMot-24
88OklCit8C-18
88OklCit8P-30
88Sco-407
88ScoGlo-407
89Bow-231
89BowTif-231
89Don-496
89Fle-527
89FleGlo-527
89RanMot-19
89RanSmo-18
89Sco-484
89Top-92
89TopTif-92
89UppDec-463
90Don-496
90Fle-304
90FleCan-304
90OPC-174
90PubSti-415
90RanMot-18
90Sco-431
90Top-174
90TopSti-246
90TopTif-174
90UppDec-394
90VenSti-275
91Fle-292
91OPC-562
91Sco-783
91StaClu-580
91Stu-126
91Top-562
91TopDesS-562
91TopMic-562
91TopTif-562
92DenZepF-2648
92DenZepS-136
93ChaKniF-550
93RanKee-223
94TolMudHF-1032
Kunkel, Kevin
86MedA'sC-70
87MadMusP-11
87MadMusP-19
Kuntz, Lee
86WatIndP-16
88WilBilP-1303
90CanIndB-3
90CanIndS-21
Kuntz, Rusty
78KnoKnoST-10
81Don-282
81Top-112
82EdmTraT-20
82Fle-348
82Top-237
84Fle-568
84FleUpd-66
84Nes792-598
84TigWavP-24
84Top-598
84TopTif-598
84TopTra-66T
84TopTraT-66T
85Don-516
85Fle-14
85NasSouTI-8
85TigWen-13
85Top-73
85TopTif-73
89MarMot-27
90MarMot-27
92MarMot-27
Kunz, Devin
93EriSaiC-13
93EriSaiF-3110
Kuoda, Masa
89SalSpuCLC-134
89SalSpuP-1804
Kupsey, John
89PulBraP-1913
90SumBraB-10
90SumBraP-2442
92SpaPhiC-11
92SpaPhiF-1270
94ReaPhiF-2072
Kurczewski, Tommy
88WatIndP-665
89BurBraP-1603
Kurek, Chris
94UtiBluSC-15
95MicBatCTI-16
Kurosaki, Ryan
76ArkTraT-5
77ArkTraT-3A
77ArkTraT-3B
78ArkTraT-15
80ArkTraT-13
Kurowski, Whitey (George)
46SpoExcW-4-1A
47Exh-128
47TipTop-158
49Lea-81
50AmeNut&CCP-11
76TayBow4-96
78ReaRem-10
83TCMPla1943-26
92CarMcD-8
Kurpiel, Ed
76SalLakCGC-8
78TidTidT-12
Kurri, Jari
92StaCluMO-46
Kurtz, Dan
96WisTimRB-13
Kurtz, John
89GeoColC-17
90GeoColC-16
Kurtz, Rodd
93HunCubC-15
93HunCubF-3232
94PeoChiC-14
94PeoChiF-2263
Kurys, Sophie
94TedWil-97
Kush, Emil
47TipTop-109
49EurSta-59
80CubGreT-6
Kusick, Craig
73TacTwiC-13
74TacTwiC-3
75OPC-297
75Top-297
76VenLeaS-14
77Top-38
78Top-137
78TwiFriP-11
79Top-472
79TwiFriP-14
80HawIslT-7
80OPC-374
80Top-693
81EvaTriT-16
Kusiewicz, Mike
95AshTouTI-10
96BesAutS-47
96Bow-113
96Exc-157
96NewHavRB-16
Kusnyer, Art
72OPC-213
72Top-213
74SacSolC-47
75IntLeaASB-15
75PacCoaLAB-15
75SacSolC-10
76SpoIndC-12
77SpoIndC-10
79IowOakP-10
84WhiSoxTV-8
89A'sMot-27
90A'sMot-27
91A'sMot-28
92AthMot-28
93AthMot-27
93Don-396
94A'sMot-28
94BreMilB-324
95AthMot-28
Kustus, Joe
90DodTar-1008
Kutcher, Randy
80CliGiaT-14
83PhoGiaBHN-15
84PhoGiaC-18
85DomLeaS-94
85PhoGiaC-177
86PhoFirP-13
87Don-547
87Fle-276
87FleGlo-276
87PhoFirP-12
88PawRedSC-11
88PawRedSP-464
89Fle-98A
89TopTra-64T
89TopTraT-64T
90OPC-676
90PubSti-459
90Sco-551
90Top-676
90TopTif-676
90TopTVRS-31
90VenSti-276
91Fle-100
91Sco-837
Kutina, Joe
12T207-97
Kutner, Mike
82MiaMarT-20
Kutsukos, Pete
84BeaGolGT-2
85BeaGolGT-7
Kutyna, Marty
58RedEnq-23
60A'sTeal-12
60Top-516
61SenJayP-5
61Top-546
62Top-566
Kutzler, Jerry
88TamTarS-12
89BirBarB-15
89BirBarP-117
89SouLeaAJ-15
90Don-503
90DonRoo-25
90ScoRoo-80T
90WhiSoxC-14
90WhiSoxC-28
91LinDriAAA-639
91Sco-749
91TopDeb90-80
91VanCanLD-639
91VanCanP-1592
93AlbDukF-1456
93LinVenB-203
94OmaRoyF-1219
95OmaRoyTI-16
Kuykendall, Kevin
87WatIndP-12
Kuzava, Bob (Robert)
50Bow-5
51Bow-97
51TopBluB-22
52BerRos-32
52Bow-233
52Top-85
53BowBW-33
54NewYorJA-48
54OriEss-21
54Top-230
55Bow-215
55OriEss-13
57JetPos-11
83TopRep5-85
91OriCro-251
94TopArc1-230
94TopArc1G-230
Kuzma, Greg
88ButCopKSP-3
Kuzniar, Kooz (Paul)
87WatIndP-19
88WilBilP-1321
89CanIndB-20
89CanIndP-1305
89CanIndS-11
90NewBriRSS-7
Kvansnicka, Jay
89KenTwiP-1063
89KenTwiS-11
90VisOakP-2168
91LinDriAA-483
91OrlSunRLD-483
91OrlSunRP-1862
92OrlSunRF-2859
92PorBeaF-2679
92PorBeaS-412
Kwasny, Joe
75ForLauYS-18
Kwolek, Chuck
79AshTouT-24
Kwolek, Joe
86OscAstP-16
Kyles, Stan
81QuaCitCT-19
83MidCubT-19
84AlbA'sT-15
85TacTigC-138
87TacTigP-3
88AlbDukC-2
88AlbDukP-275
91BenBucC-3
91BenBucP-3712
92GenCubC-27
92GenCubF-1577
93IowCubF-2150
93IowCubF-2151
96AshTouB-4
86HumStaDS-30
Kynerd, Jay
89CarNewE-25
Kyslinger, Dan
92FroRowDP-95
92HelBreF-1712
92HelBreSP-1
93BelBreC-13
93BelBreF-1706
94StoPorC-13
94StoPorF-1690
Kyte, Frank
92BasCitRC-27
La Babra, Fidel
28W513-96
Laabs, Chet (Chester)
40PlaBal-206
41BroW75-19
46SeaSLP-30
50WorWidGV-31
77TCMTheWY-60
79DiaGre-187
83TCMPla1943-16
94ConTSN-1278
94ConTSNB-1278
96Bro194F-33
Laake, Pete
91GasRanP-2694
Labarca, Argenis
93PriRedC-16
93PriRedF-4186

94PriRedC-13
94PriRedF-3269
LaBare, Jay
80ElmPioRST-40
Labastidas, Mario
93LinVenB-139
94VenLinU-258
Labay, Steve
86ReaPhiP-13
Labine, Clem
52Top-342
53Top-14
54Bow-106
54NewYorJA-9
54Top-121
55DodGolS-11
55Top-180
56Dod-16
56Dod-17
56Top-295
57Top-53
58DodJayP-7
58Hir-34
58Top-305
59DodMor-6
59DodTeal-12
59DodVol-8
59Top-262
59Top-403
60DodBelB-6
60Lea-60
60Top-29
60TopVen-29
61Top-22
74MetOriEB-8
79TCM50-31
81TCM60I-482
83TopRep5-342
87Dod195T-8
88RinPosD1-7B
89DodSmoG-61
90DodTar-423
90PacLeg-89
91MetWIZ-222
91SweBasG-54
91TopArc1-14
92ActPacA-59
94TopArc1-121
94TopArc1G-121
95TopArcBD-25
95TopArcBD-39
95TopArcBD-73
95TopArcBD-104
95TopArcBD-162
LaBlanche, George
88AllandGN-11
Labossiere, Dave
77BriRedST-12
80TucTorT-12
81TucTorT-14
82TucTorT-27
83TucTorT-25
88AstMot-28
89AstMot-28
90AstMot-28
92AstMot-28
94AstMot-28
Laboy, Carlos
87AubAstP-14
88AshTouP-1056
88BlaYNPRWL-166
89BlaYNPRWL-141
89OscAstS-10
91PalSprAP-2029
92SalSpuC-22
92SalSpuF-3769
Laboy, Coco (Jose A.)
69ExpPin-4
69ExpFudP-6
69Top-524
70ExpPin-9
70ExpPos-8
70Kel-66
70MLBOffS-67
70OPC-238
70Top-238
71ExpLaPR-5
71ExpPS-12
71MLBOffS-132
71OPC-132
71Top-132
72Dia-24
72MilBra-190
72Top-727
73OPC-642
73Top-642
87Ft.LauYP-20
88PriWilYS-14
89BlaYNPRWL-198
92Nab-9
Labozzetta, Al
86GleFalTP-11
LaCasse, Michael
79NewCoPT-10
Lacer, Mike
86PitCubP-12
LaCerra, Tony
88RenSilSCLC-270
Lacey, Kerry
91ButCopKSP-14
Lacey, Robert
76TucTorCa-7
76TusTorCr-19
77SanJosMC-14
78Top-29
79Top-647
80OPC-167
80Top-316
81Don-240A
81Don-240B
81Fle-578
81Top-481
81TopTra-784
82Top-103
85Fle-611
85PhoGiaC-191
93RanKee-224
Lach, Elmer
43ParSpo-42
LaChance, Candy (George)
03BreE10-85
04RedSoxUP-9
11SpoLifCW-210
90DodTar-424
98CamPepP-43
LaChance, Vince (Vincent)
93JamExpC-13
93JamExpF-3338
94BurBeeC-12
94BurBeeF-1095
LaChapelle, Yan
96StCatSB-15
LaChappa, Matt
94SprSulC-16
94SprSulF-2034
95RanCucQT-15
Lachemann, Bill
83CliGiaF-29
86QuaCitAP-18
87PalSprP-17
88CalLeaACLC-35
88PalSprACLC-112
88PalSprAP-1436
89PalSprACLC-63
89PalSprAP-489
95AngMot-28
96AngMot-28
Lachemann, Bret
91QuaCitAC-6
91QuaCitAP-2623
Lachemann, Marcel
71MLBOffS-518
71OPC-84
71Top-84
75WesPalBES-11
82DanSunF-14
93MarPub-28
94AngLAT-26
94AngMot-1
95AngCHP-16
95AngMot-1
96AngMot-1
Lachemann, Rene
65Top-526
66OPC-157
66Top-157
66TopVen-157
67CokCapAt-10
67Top-471
68Top-422
76VenLeaS-242
77SanJosMC-2
78SanJosMMC-2
79SpoIndT-16
80SpoIndT-18
80VenLeaS-181
81SpoIndT-13
82Don-600
83Top-336
84BreGar-1
84BrePol-9
84Fle-655
84TopTra-67T
84TopTraT-67T
85Top-628
85TopTif-628
86MarGreT-12
87Top-556
87TopTif-556
88ChaLooLTI-19
89A'sMot-27
90A'sMot-27
91A'sMot-28
92AthMot-28
93MarPub-15
93Top-505
93TopGol-505
93TopInaM-505
93TopMic-505
Lachmann, Tom
88OklSoo-22
89BurIndS-14
Lachowetz, Anthony J.
81VerBeaDT-8
82VerBeaDT-23
Lachowicz, Al
82TulDriT-7
84OklCit8T-1
85TulDriTI-36
93RanKee-225
Lackey, John
81BirBarT-1
82GleFalWST-20
83LynPirT-4
Lackey, Stephen
92GulCoaMF-3491
92HigSchPLS-23
93KinMetC-15
93KinMetF-3803
94KinMetF-3830
95PitMetTI-26
96FayGenB-22
Lacko, Rich
87LakTigP-14
88GleFalTP-920
Lacks, Charles K.
54BraJohC-49
55BraGolS-31
55BraJohC-49
LaCock, R. Pete
73WicAerKSB-5
74WicAerODF-124
75OPC-494
75Top-494
76OPC-101
76SSP-317
76Top-101
77Top-561
78Roy-10
78SSP270-223
78Top-157
79Top-248
80OPC-202
80Top-389
81Don-344
81Fle-47
81Top-9
89PacSenL-33
89TopSenL-99
90EliSenL-98
91PacSenL-53
91PacSenL-120
LaCorte, Frank
76OPC-597
76SSP-612
76Top-597
78RicBraT-6
80Top-411
81Don-143
81Fle-55
81OPC-348
81Top-513
82AstAstI-7
82Don-270
82Fle-220
82Top-248
83Don-218
83Fle-454
83Top-14
84AngSmo-16
84Don-283
84Fle-230
84FleUpd-67
84Nes792-301
84Top-301
84TopTif-301
84TopTra-68T
84TopTraT-68T
85OPC-153
85Top-153
85TopTif-153
LaCoss, Mike
77IndIndTI-11
78IndIndTI-4
79Top-717
80OPC-111
80RedEnq-51
80Top-199
81Don-183
81OPC-134
81Top-474
82AstAstI-8
82Don-440
82Fle-72
82Top-294
82TopTra-61T
83Don-344
83Fle-455
83Top-92
84AstMot-24
84Don-206
84Fle-231
84Nes792-507
84Top-507
84TopTif-507
85Don-405
85Fle-353
85FleUpd-66
85Top-666
85TopTif-666
85TopTifT-69T
85TopTra-69T
86FleUpd-62
86GiaMot-17
86Top-359
86TopTif-359
86TopTra-57T
86TopTraT-57T
87Don-636
87Fle-277
87FleGlo-277
87GiaMot-21
87Top-151
87TopTif-151
88Don-436
88Fle-86
88FleGlo-86
88GiaMot-21
88PanSti-418
88Sco-465
88ScoGlo-465
88Top-754
88TopTif-754
89Don-602
89FleUpd-129
89GiaMot-21
89RedFolSB-70
89Sco-500
89Top-417
89TopTif-417
89UppDec-48
90Don-652
90Fle-59
90FleCan-59
90GiaMot-11
90GiaSmo-12
90Lea-463
90OPC-53
90PubSti-73
90Sco-253
90Top-53
90TopTif-53
90UppDec-140
90VenSti-277
91Fle-264
91GiaMot-11
91GiaPacGaE-17
91GiaSFE-9
91Lea-309
91OPC-242
91Sco-652
91StaClu-479
91Top-242
91TopDesS-242
91TopMic-242
91TopTif-242
91UppDec-691
Lacy, Kerry
92GasRanC-15
92GasRanF-2250
93ChaRaiC-9
93ChaRaiF-1904
93SouAtlLAGF-8
94Bow-241
94ClaGolF-31
94ExcFS7-135
94TulDriF-241
94TulDriTI-12
95SigRoo-28
95TulDriTI-11
96OklCit8B-12
Lacy, Lee
73OPC-391
73Top-391
74OPC-658
74Top-658
75OPC-631
75Top-631
76OPC-99
76SSP-78
76Top-99
76TopTra-99T
77Top-272
78SSP270-69
78Top-104
79OPC-229
79Top-441
80Top-536
81Don-376
81Fle-374
81Top-332
82Don-276
82Fle-483
82FleSta-80
82Top-752
83Don-276
83Fle-308
83FleSti-78
83FleSti-142
83OPC-69
83Top-69
84Don-479
84Fle-252
84Nes792-462
84OPC-229
84Top-462
84TopSti-138
84TopTif-462
85AllGamPI-61
85Don-508
85Fle-467
85FleStaS-9
85FleUpd-67
85Lea-40
85OriHea-8
85Top-669
85TopSti-126
85TopTif-669
85TopTifT-70T
85TopTra-70T
86Don-228
86Fle-277
86Lea-104
86OPC-226
86Spo-87
86Top-226
86TopSti-229
86TopTif-226
87Don-336
87Fle-473
87FleGlo-473
87OPC-182
87OriFreB-27
87Spo-86
87SpoTeaP-21
87Top-182
87TopSti-231
87TopTif-182
88Fle-565
88FleGlo-565
88Sco-173
88ScoGlo-173
88StaLinO-8
88Top-598
88TopTif-598
89PacSenL-184
89T/MSenL-61
89TopSenL-72
90DodTar-425
90EliSenL-25

90SweBasG-94
91DodUno7P-2
91OriCro-252
Lacy, Steve
75WatRoyT-17
76WatRoyT-16
77DayBealT-12
Ladd, Jeff
92St.CatBJC-18
92St.CatBJF-3389
93HagSunC-16
93HagSunF-1882
94HagSunC-10
94HagSunF-2734
94St.CatBJC-14
94St.CatBJF-3646
95HagSunF-71
Ladd, Pete
80Top-678
80VenLeaS-83
81TucTorT-19
82VanCanT-17
83BrePol-27
83Fle-37
84BreGar-10
84BrePol-27
84Don-124
84Fle-204
84FleSti-77
84Nes792-243
84Top-243
84TopTif-243
85BreGar-10
85BrePol-27
85Don-271
85Fle-585
85Top-471
85TopTif-471
86Fle-492
86FleUpd-63
86MarMot-17
86Top-163
86TopTif-163
86TopTra-58T
86TopTraT-58T
87AlbDukP-12
87Don-660
87Fle-588
87FleGlo-588
87Top-572
87TopTif-572
92BreCarT-12
94BreMilB-47
Lade, Doyle
49Bow-168
49EurSta-60
50Bow-196
51Bow-139
76TayBow4-76
85TCMPla1-31
Ladell, Cleveland
92PriRedC-4
92PriRedF-3098
93CarLeaAGF-43
93WinSpiC-12
93WinSpiF-1581
94Bow-46
94ChaLooF-1370
94Cla-191
94ExcFS7-177
95ChaLooTI-12
96ChaLooB-16
Ladjevich, Rick
94BelMarC-17
94BelMarF-3243
96PorCitRB-18
Ladnier, Deric
86Ft.MyeRP-17
87AppFoxP-8
89MemChiB-11
89MemChiP-1189
89MemChiS-13
89Sta-43
91LinDriAA-409
91MemChiLD-409
91MemChiP-662
Lafata, Joe
49EurSta-115
LaFever, Greg
86WatIndP-17
87WilBilP-17
88SanAntMB-4
Lafitte, Doc (Edward)
09ColChiE-161A
09ColChiE-161B
12ColRedB-161A
12ColRedB-161B
12ColTinT-161A
12ColTinT-161B
Lafitte, James A.
09T206-497
Lafleur, Guy
72Dia-77
72Dia-78
Laforce, Ernest
43ParSpo-43
LaFountain, James
77VisOakT-7
LaFrancois, Roger
81PawRedST-23
83Don-534
83PawRedST-12
83Top-344
84RicBraT-14
85DurBulT-27
88JamExpP-1894
89SouBenWSGS-4
90CMC-671
90ProAAAF-185
90VanCanC-27
90VanCanP-507
91LinDriAAA-650
91VanCanLD-650
91VanCanP-1611
92VanCanF-2735
92VanCanS-650
93NasSouF-585
94NasSouF-1266
95NasSouTI-9
96NasSouB-3
Laga, Mike
81BirBarT-8
82EvaTriT-16
83EvaTriT-15
84Don-491
84EvaTriT-16
85NasSouTI-9
86Don-578
86TopTra-59T
86TopTraT-59T
87CarSmo-15
87Don-293
87LouRedTI-23
87Top-321
87TopTif-321
88LouRedBTI-26
89PhoFirC-17
89PhoFirP-1493
89Sco-536
90BirBarDGB-20
90CMC-548
90PhoFirC-21
Lagarde, Joe
93YakBeaC-16
95SanBerSTI-12
96VerBeaDB-16
97Bow-149
97BowInt-149
Lagattuta, Rico
96SouOreTI-7
Lagimas, Tracie
91HawWomS-5
Lago, Pete
89CarNewE-15
Lagrandeur, Yan
96DanBraB-13
LaGrow, Lerrin
71OPC-39
71Top-39
73OPC-369
73Top-369
74OPC-433
74Top-433
75OPC-116
75Top-116
76OPC-138
76SSP-356
76Top-138
76TulOilGP-13
77WhiSoxJT-9
78OPC-152
78SSP270-161
78Top-14
79Top-527
80Top-624
90DodTar-426
Lague, Raymond
52LavPro-14
Lahey, Kevin
75WatRoyT-18
LaHonta, Ken
76DubPacT-18
Lahoud, Joe
69OPC-189
69Top-189
69TopFou-14
70OPC-78
70Top-78
71MLBOffS-321
71OPC-622
71Top-622
72MilBra-191
72OPC-321
72Top-321
72TopCloT-19
73OPC-212
73Top-212
74OPC-512
74Top-512
75Hos-10
75HosTwi-10
75OPC-317
75Top-317
76OPC-612
76SSP-201
76Top-612
78SSP270-226
78Top-382
81RedSoxBG2S-89
93RanKee-226
94BreMilB-48
Lahrman, Tom
86PenWhiSP-15
87PenWhiSP-22
88TamTarS-13
Lahti, Jeffrey Allen
80WatRedT-2
81IndIndTI-16
82LouRedE-13
83Car-14
83Fle-12
83Top-284
84Car-15
84Don-327
84Fle-327
84Nes792-593
84Top-593
84TopTif-593
85CarTeal-18
85Fle-231
85Top-447
85TopTif-447
86CarIGAS-8
86CarKASD-18
86CarSchM-12
86CarTeal-22
86Don-475
86Fle-40
86Lea-233
86SevCoi-S12
86Top-33
86TopTif-33
87Don-577
87Fle-299
87FleGlo-299
87Top-367
87TopTif-367
Lain, Marty
83BeaGolGT-9
Lair, Scott
94JohCitCC-17
94JohCitCF-3697
Laird, Tony
85NasPirT-13
86NasPirP-14
Lairsey, Eric
91PulBraC-24
91PulBraP-4001
92IdaFalGF-3507
92IdaFalGSP-26
Lajeskie, Dick
48SomandK-22
49BowPCL-16
49SomandK-12
Lajoie, Nap (Napoleon)
03BreE10-86
03WilCarE-19
04FanCraAL-32
05IndSouPSoCP-13
08AmeLeaPC-11
08RosComP-27
09AmeCarE-67
09ColChiE-162
09SpoNewSM-4
09SpoNewSM-6
09T206-199
09T206-200
09T206-201
10CouT21-165
10CouT21-166
10CouT21-167
10CouT21-297
10DomDisP-65
10E-UOraBSC-13
10E101-28
10E102-14
10E98-18
10MelMinE-28
10NadCarE-31
10OrnOvaPP-10
10PeoT21-33A
10PeoT21-33B
10PeoT21-33C
10RedCroT-39
10RedCroT-128
10RedCroT-211
10SepAnoP-17
10StaCarE-19
10SweCapPP-18
10W555-41
11BasBatEU-27
11DiaGumP-17
11E94-18
11L1L-121
11MecDFT-20
11PloCanE-39
11S81LarS-96
11SpoLifCW-211
11SpoLifM-45
11TurRedT-23
12ColRedB-162
12ColTinT-162
12PhiCarE-17
12SenVasS-4
13NatGamW-25
13PolGroW-12
13TomBarW-24
14CraJacE-66
14TexTomE-26
15AmeCarE-24
15CraJacE-66
15SpoNewM-95
15VicT21-17
16BF2FP-36
16SpoNewM-97
19W514-62
33Gou-106
36PC7AlbHoF-8
40PlaBal-173
48ExhHoF-20
50CalHOFW-47
60Fle-1
61Fle-120
61GolPre-31
63BazA-8
63HalofFB-26
67TopVen-159
69Baz-10
69Baz-11
72FleFamF-28
73FleWilD-35
75FlePio-18
76MotOldT-2
76ShaPiz-6
77BobParHoF-31
77GalGloG-137
77GalGloG-260
77ShaPiz-15
80Lau300-9
80PacLeg-74
80PerHaloFP-8
80SSPHOF-8
81SpoHaloF-12
82OhiHaloF-26
84GalHaloFRL-6
86IndGreT-2
89HOFStiB-10
92ConTSN-528
93ConMasC-2
93ConTSN-837
93CraJac-8
94ConTSN-1218
94ConTSNB-1218
94OriofB-83
94UppDecAH-25
94UppDecAH-103
94UppDecAH-175
94UppDecAH1-25
94UppDecAH1-103
94UppDecAH1-175
94UppDecTAE-22
96PitPosH-8
Lajszky, Werner
80WauTimT-21
Lak, Carlos
91CliGiaP-842
Lake, Dan
85AncGlaPTI-18
Lake, Edward
41CarW75-13
43RedSoxTI-12
47Exh-129
47TipTop-35
49Bow-107
50Bow-240
51Bow-140
83TCMPla1945-19
Lake, Fred
11SpoLifM-142
Lake, Joe
09T206-202
09T206-203
09T206-204
10RedCroT-129
10RedCroT-212
10W555-42
11E94-19
11MecDFT-48
11SpoLifCW-212
11SpoLifM-112
Lake, Ken
89JamExpP-2148
89MiaMirIS-10
90WesPalBeS-12
91HarSenLD-260
91HarSenP-641
91LinDriAA-260
Lake, Kevin
94EveGiaC-17
94EveGiaF-3650
95BurBeeTI-8
96BurBeeTI-9
Lake, Mike
77LodDodT-8
78LodDodT-11
Lake, Steve
80HolMilT-17
81VanCanT-25
82TucTorT-5
83CubThoAV-16
84CubChiT-16
84Don-198
84Nes792-691
84Top-691
84TopTif-691
85CubLioP-14
85CubSev-16
85Top-98
85TopTif-98
86CubGat-29
86Top-588
86TopTif-588
87CarSmo-10
87Don-604
87Fle-300
87FleGlo-300
87Top-84
87TopTif-84
88CarSmo-11
88Don-510
88Fle-38
88FleGlo-38
88Sco-596
88ScoGlo-596
88StaLinCa-11
88Top-208
88TopTif-208
89Bow-399
89BowTif-399
89Fle-454
89FleGlo-454
89PhiTas-17
89Sco-363
89ScoRoo-12T
89Top-463
89TopTif-463
89TopTra-65T
89TopTraT-65T
90Don-431
90Fle-566

90FleCan-566
90Lea-395
90OPC-183
90PhiTas-19
90PubSti-245
90Sco-435
90Top-183
90TopBig-191
90TopTif-183
90UppDec-491
90VenSti-278
91Don-334
91Fle-403
91Lea-385
91OPC-661
91PhiMed-23
91Sco-572
91StaClu-395
91Stu-216
91Top-661
91TopDesS-661
91TopMic-661
91TopTif-661
92OPC-331
92PhiMed-18
92Sco-467
92StaClu-54
92Top-331
92TopGol-331
92TopGolW-331
92TopMic-331
93CubMar-12
93Sco-443
93StaCluCu-10
94Fle-388

Lakeman, Al
49EurSta-14
55JetPos-9

Laker, Tim
88JamExpP-1904
89JamExpP-2137
90MidLeaASGS-13
90RocExpLC-14
90RocExpP-2696
91Cla/Bes-205
91WesPalBEC-16
91WesPalBEP-1232
92ClaFS7-125
92HarSenF-463
92HarSenS-286
92SkyAA F-121
93Bow-156
93Don-440
93Fle-77
93Lea-367
93OPC-276
93OPCPre-120
93PacSpa-534
93Pin-583
93StaClu-18
93StaCluFDI-18
93StaCluMOP-18
93Top-816
93TopGol-816
93TopInaM-816
93TopMic-816
93Toy-7
93Ult-416
94Pin-465
94PinArtP-465
94PinMusC-465
94Top-524
94TopGol-524
94TopSpa-524
94TriAAF-AAA39
96Don-211
96DonPreP-211
96Fle-460
96FleTif-460
96Sco-452

Lakman, Jason
96AppLeaAB-5
96BriWhiSB-22

Lakovic, Greg
96ForWayWB-13

Lamabe, Jack
62Top-593
63Top-251
64Top-305
64TopVen-305
65OPC-88
65Top-88
66Top-577
67Top-208
68Top-311
68TopVen-311
81RedSoxBG2S-90
85BeaGolGT-24
91MetWIZ-223
92ChaRaiC-23
92ChaRaiF-136
93CenValRC-27
93CenValRF-2910
94AshTouC-27
94AshTouF-1798
95AshTouTI-36
96NewHavRB-3

LaManna, Frank
77TCMTheWY-63

Lamanno, Ray
46SpoExcW-8-9
49Bow-113

Lamanske, Frank
90DodTar-1009

Lamar, Bill
90DodTar-427
93ConTSN-852

LaMar, Danny
82CedRapRT-12
83TamTarT-16
84CedRapRT-18

Lamar, Johnny
92BriTigC-24
92BriTigF-1425
93LakTigC-14
93LakTigF-1323
94ChaWheC-17
94ChaWheF-2712

LaMarche, Michel
87SpaPhiP-10

LaMarque, Jim
92NegLeaRLI-37
96NegLeaBMKC-4

LaMaster, Wayne
90DodTar-428

Lamb, David
94AlbPolF-2243
94Bow-36
94OriPro-51
96HigDesMB-16

Lamb, Randy
77CocAstT-10
78WauMetT-15

Lamb, Ray
70OPC-131
70Top-131
71Ind-8
71MLBOffS-377
71OPC-727
71Top-727
72OPC-422
72Top-422
73OPC-496
73Top-496
85SpoIndGC-11
90DodTar-429

Lamb, Todd
84DurBulT-19
85GreBraTI-11
86DurBulP-17

Lambert, Gene
82CliGiaF-17
83CliGiaF-10

Lambert, Ken
87VerBeaDP-10

Lambert, Layne
90AubAstP-3396
91BurAstC-16
91BurAstP-2810
92OscAstC-15

Lambert, Mark
90HigSchPLS-17

Lambert, Reese
87HunStaTI-19
87MadMusP-23
88TacTigC-4
88TacTigP-631
89TacTigC-3
89TacTigP-1548
90CMC-585
90ProAAAF-134
90TacTigC-8
90TacTigP-87
92OmaRoyF-2957
92OmaRoyS-333

Lambert, Reggie
86PalSprAP-27
86PalSprAP-20
87PalSprP-5
88PalSprACLC-113
88PalSprAP-1461

Lambert, Rob
87PriWilYP-25
88ColCliC-14
88ColCliP-319

Lambert, Tim
82IdaFalAT-10
84AlbA'sT-17
85TacTigC-140
86TacTigP-11
87MemChiB-16
87MemChiP-13
90AlbDecGB-24

Lambert, Yvon
72Dia-79

Lamkey, William
80WisRapTT-6

Lamle, Adam
88ChaRanS-12
88FloStaLAS-41
89MiaMirIS-10
89TulDriGS-12

Lammon, John
90ElmPioP-14
91ElmPioC-7
91ElmPioP-3272

Lamonde, Larry
82AleDukT-3
84HawIslC-124
85NasPirT-14

Lamont, Gene
71OPC-39
71Top-39
75OPC-593
75Top-593
84OmaRoyT-2
85OmaRoyT-22
89PirVerFJ-36
90PirHomC-16
92TopTra-62T
92TopTraG-62T
92WhiSoxK-33
92WhiSoxK-NNO
93Top-504
93TopGol-504
93TopInaM-504
93TopMic-504
93WhiSoxK-16
93WhiSoxK-30
94WhiSoxK-18
94WhiSoxK-30

LaMotta, Jake
47HomBon-29
51BerRos-C12

Lamoureux, Leo
43ParSpo-44

Lamp, Dennis
78SSP270-260
78Top-711
79Top-153
80OPC-129
80Top-54
81Don-573
81Fle-305
81Top-331
81TopTra-785
82Don-619
82Fle-349
82Top-216
82Top-622
83AllGamPI-81
83Don-165
83Fle-243
83OPC-26
83Top-434
83WhiSoxTV-53
84BluJayFS-21
84Don-526
84Fle-66
84FleUpd-68
84Nes792-541
84Top-541
84TopSti-239
84TopTif-541
84TopTra-69T
84TopTraT-69T
85BluJayFS-17
85Don-119
85Fle-111
85OPC-83
85Top-774
85TopTif-774
86BluJayAF-17
86BluJayFS-21
86Don-626
86Fle-64
86Lea-244
86OPC-219
86Top-219
86TopSti-193
86TopTat-12
86TopTif-219
87Fle-233
87FleGlo-233
87OPC-336
87Top-768
87TopTif-768
88DonTeaBRS-NEW
88Fle-284
88FleGlo-284
88Sco-616
88ScoGlo-616
88ScoRoo-6T
88ScoRooG-6T
89Don-633
89Fle-92
89FleGlo-92
89Sco-508
89Top-188
89TopBig-169
89TopTif-188
89UppDec-503
90Don-423
90Fle-280
90FleCan-280
90Lea-315
90OPC-338
90PubSti-460
90RedSoxP-12
90Sco-471
90Top-338
90TopTif-338
90TopTVRS-13
90VenSti-279
91Don-138
91Fle-101
91OPC-14
91RedSoxP-11
91Sco-612
91Top-14
91TopDesS-14
91TopMic-14
91TopTif-14
92Fle-42
92OPC-653
92Sco-335
92Top-653
92TopGol-653
92TopGolW-653
92TopMic-653

Lampard, Keith (C. Keith)
70OPC-492
70Top-492
71OPC-728
71Top-728
72OPC-489
72Top-489

Lampe, Ed
88HamRedP-1742

Lampert, Ken
86VerBeaDP-15

Lamphere, Larry (Lawrence)
87PanAmTURB-11
88AubAstP-1947
89AshTouP-967
89SouAtlLAGS-4
90OscAstS-14
87PanAmTUBI-2

Lampkin, Steve
92LetMouSP-22

Lampkin, Tom
87WatIndP-23
88BasAmeAAB-7
88EasLeaAP-41
88WilBilP-1304
89ColSprSSP-254
89Don-639
89TriAAP-AAA35
90CMC-464
90ColSprSSC-12
90ColSprSSP-39
90IndTeal-23
90OPC-172
90ProAAAF-220
90Top-172
90TopTif-172
91Lea-512
91PadMag-4
91PadSmo-18
91Sco-720
91Sco100RS-70
91StaClu-530
92Fle-610
92LasVegSS-234
92PadPolD-12
92PadSmo-15
92Sco-338
92StaClu-453
93Don-654
93FleFinE-226
93NewOrlZF-976
93Top-492
93TopGol-492
93TopInaM-492
93TopMic-492
94BreMilB-49
94PhoFirF-1523
94StaClu-147
94StaCluFDI-147
94StaCluGR-147
94StaCluMOP-147
94Top-558
94TopGol-558
94TopSpa-558
95GiaMot-15
96GiaMot-22
96LeaSigEA-105
97PacPriGotD-GD218

Lamplugh, Ian
92CalLeaACL-26

Lamson, Chuck
78AshTouT-14
80TulDriT-20

Lancaster, Brian
96EriSeaB-3

Lancaster, Les (Lester)
86WinSpiP-12
87CubCan-13
87DonRoo-10
88CubDavB-50
88Don-561
88DonBasB-172
88DonTeaBC-561
88Fle-421
88FleGlo-421
88Sco-602
88ScoGlo-602
88Top-112
88TopTif-112
89CubMar-50
89Don-341
89Fle-429
89FleGlo-429
89IowCubC-8
89IowCubP-1689
89Sco-60
89Top-694
89TopTif-694
89UppDec-84
90CubMar-11
90Don-628
90DonBesN-38
90Fle-35
90FleCan-35
90Lea-361
90OPC-437
90Sco-413
90Top-437
90TopTif-437
90TopTVCu-11
90UppDec-584
91CubMar-50
91CubVinL-16
91Don-256
91Fle-424
91OPC-86
91Sco-293A
91Sco-293B
91Top-86
91TopDesS-86
91TopMic-86
91TopTif-86
91Ult-63
92Don-296
92Fle-384
92Lea-402
92OPC-213
92Sco-348
92StaClu-88

92Top-213
92TopGol-213
92TopGolW-213
92TopMic-213
92Ult-177
92UppDec-481
93FleFinE-126
93PacSpa-111
93StaCluCa-26
94Fle-635
94Pac-594
94Sco-269
94ScoGolR-269
94StaCluT-330
94StaCluTFDI-330
94SyrChiF-969
94SyrChiTI-16
Lance, Gary
75OmaRoyTI-8
76OmaRoyTT-10
76VenLeaS-36
79SpoIndT-11
83IdaFalAT-32
84MadMusP-2
85HunStaJ-24
87ChaRaiP-9
88ChaRaiP-1212
89BlaYNPRWL-130
89WicStaR-28
89WicWraR-38
90CMC-526
90LasVegSC-23
90LasVegSP-138
90MarPhiP-3191
90ProAAAF-26
91PacSenL-62
91SumFlyC-27
91SumFlyP-2352
92AlbPolC-29
92AlbPolF-2322
92AlbPolF-2323
93CarLeaAGF-14
93WilBluRC-28
93WilBluRF-2014
94CarLeaAF-CAR19
94WilBluRC-25
94WilBluRF-316
95WicWraTI-11
96WicWraB-29
Lance, Mark
83DurBulT-19
84DurBulT-2
Lancellotti, Rick
78SalPirT-7
79BufBisT-3
80PorBeaT-20
81HawIslT-9
82HawIslT-11
84LasVegSC-230
85TidTidT-1
86PhoFirP-14
87JapPlaB-3
89PawRedSTI-13
90CMC-270
90PawRedSC-19
90PawRedSDD-12
90PawRedSP-472
90ProAAAF-444
90TopTVRS-48
91LinDriAAA-358
91PacSenL-122
91PawRedSDD-10
91PawRedSLD-358
91PawRedSP-47
Landaker, Dave
92ClaDraP-26
92FroRowDP-94
92HigSchPLS-19
93Top-743
93TopGol-743
93TopInaM-743
93TopMic-743
94QuaCitRBF-542
96KisCobB-12
Landers, Hank
83BelBreF-7
Landers, Lee
76TulOilGP-26
78SprRedWK-12
Landers, Mark
94MedHatBJF-3688
94MedHatBJSP-1
95StCatSTI-20
Landestoy, Rafael
75WatDodT-9
78SSP270-74
79AstTeal-8
79Top-14
80Top-268
81AllGamPI-103
81CokTeaS-65
81Don-19
81Fle-70
81OPC-326
81Top-597
81TopSti-168
81TopTra-786
82Fle-73
82RedCok-13
82Top-361
83Fle-595
83Top-684
83TopTra-59T
84DodPol-17
84Nes792-477
84Top-477
84TopTif-477
85AlbYanT-17
85DomLeaS-11
85TucTorC-61
87PocGiaTB-2
89ExpPos-16
89PacSenL-60
89T/MSenL-62
89TopSenL-5
90DodTar-430
90EliSenL-85
90ExpPos-20
91PacSenL-24
94St.LucMC-27
94St.LucMF-1211
95StLucMTI-1
Landinez, Carlos
90SprCarB-12
91SavCarC-18
91SavCarP-1659
92St.PetCF-2035
93LinVenB-53
93SprCarC-17
93SprCarF-1861
Landis, Craig
78CedRapGT-13
80PhoGiaVNB-14
81RicBraT-5
Landis, Jim
47Exh-130
57Top-375
58Top-108A
58Top-108B
59Top-493
60MacSta-11
60Top-550
60WhiSoxJP-5
60WhiSoxTS-9
61Pos-27A
61Pos-27B
61Top-271
61TopStal-122
61WhiSoxTS-6
62Baz-19
62ExhStaB-20
62Jel-50
62Pos-50
62PosCan-50
62SalPlaC-49
62ShiPlaC-49
62Top-540
62TopBuc-47
62TopStal-26
62WhiSoxJP-5
62WhiSoxTS-9
63BasMagM-48
63ExhStaB-38
63Fle-10
63Jel-40
63Pos-40
63SalMetC-60
63Top-485
63WhiSoxJP-7
63WhiSoxTS-14
64A's-11
64Top-264
64TopVen-264
64WhiSoxTS-14
65AthJayP-9
65Top-376
66OPC-128
66Top-128
66TopVen-128
67CokCapAs-17
67DexPre-121
67Top-483
79DiaGre-148
85WhiSoxC-8
87AstShowSTh-10
89WhiSoxK-4
Landis, Judge (Kenesaw M.)
36PC7AlbHoF-28
50CalHOFW-48
60Fle-64
61Fle-53
63BazA-30
69SCFOldT-35
70FleWorS-18
75TCMAllG-20
76ShaPiz-28
77GalGloG-123
80PerHaloFP-28
80SSPHOF-28
82OhiHaloF-49
84GalHaloFRL-28
88PacEigMO-67
88PacEigMO-79
89HOFStiB-95
91FouBal-9
93DiaStaES-153
94UppDecTAE-33
Landis, William
68OPC-189
68Top-189
68TopVen-189
69RedSoxTI-5
69Top-264
72MilBra-192
Landmark, Neil
85VisOakT-20
Landphere, Ed
90SalSpuCLC-130
90SalSpuP-2728
Landreaux, Ken
78AngFamF-21
78SSP270-190
79Top-619
79TwiFriP-15
80OPC-49
80Top-88
81AllGamPI-149
81DodPol-44B
81Don-565
81Fle-553
81FleStiC-46
81Kel-30
81LonBeaPT-6
81OPC-219
81Top-219
81TopScr-41
81TopSti-101
81TopTra-787
82DodPol-44
82DodUniOV-9
82Don-388
82Fle-11
82OPC-114
82Top-114
82TopSti-49
82TopStiV-49
83AllGamPI-149
83DodPol-44
83DodPos-6
83Don-236
83Fle-210
83FleSta-99
83FleSti-120
83Top-376
83TopSti-246
84AllGamPI-54
84DodPol-44
84DodSmo-1
84Don-470
84Fle-104
84FleSti-2
84Nes792-533
84OPC-216
84Top-533
84TopSti-76
84TopTif-533
85DodCokP-17
85Don-494
85Fle-375
85Top-418
85TopSti-75
85TopTif-418
86DodCokP-15
86DodPol-44
86DodUniOP-11
86Don-470
86Fle-134
86OPC-2
86Top-782
86TopTif-782
87DodMot-24
87DodPol-23
87Don-352
87DonOpeD-81
87Fle-444
87FleGlo-444
87OPC-123
87Top-699
87TopTif-699
88RocRedWGCP-14
88Sco-247
88ScoGlo-247
88Top-23
88TopTif-23
89T/MSenL-63
89TopSenL-109
90DodTar-431
90El PasDAGTI-41
90EliSenL-9
91PacSenL-134
Landress, Roger
91EugEmeC-24
91EugEmeP-3722
92AppFoxC-5
92AppFoxF-980
92BasCitRF-3842
93WilBluRC-16
93WilBluRF-1994
Landreth, Harry
83ChaLooT-25
84ChaLooT-14
Landreth, Larry
78Top-701
Landrith, Dave
83ButCopKT-13
Landrith, Hobie
54Bow-220
55Bow-50
56Top-314
57Top-182
58Top-24A
58Top-24B
59Top-422
60Top-42
60TopVen-42
61Pos-150A
61Pos-150B
61Top-114
61TopStal-78
62MetJayP-7
62SalPlaC-181
62ShiPlaC-181
62Top-279
62TopStal-157
63Top-209
74MetOriEB-9
81TCM60I-344
91MetWIZ-224
91OriCro-253
Landrum, Bill
82WatRedT-1
83WatRedT-5
84WicAerRD-17
87RedKah-43
88BlaYNPRWL-59
88Fle-238
88FleGlo-238
88IowCubC-8
88IowCubP-541
88Top-42
88TopTif-42
89BufBisC-2
89BufBisP-1674
89FleUpd-116
89PirVerFJ-43
90Bow-166
90BowTif-166
90Don-668
90DonBesN-58
90Fle-472
90FleCan-472
90Lea-222
90OPC-425
90PanSti-326
90PirHomC-17
90PubSti-157
90Sco-456
90Top-425
90TopBig-164
90TopSti-128
90TopTif-425
90UppDec-442
90VenSti-280
91Bow-523
91Don-350
91Fle-41
91OPC-595
91Sco-98
91SimandSMLBL-24
91StaClu-431
91Stu-225
91Top-595
91TopDesS-595
91TopMic-595
91TopTif-595
91Ult-281
91UppDec-614
92Don-221
92ExpDonD-17A
92ExpPos-20
92Fle-557
92Lea-333
92OPC-661
92OPCPre-68
92Pin-116
92Sco-196
92StaClu-672
92StaCluECN-672
92Top-661
92TopGol-661
92TopGolW-661
92TopMic-661
92TriPla-248
92UppDec-636
93RedKah-12
94Fle-413
Landrum, Ced (Cedric)
86GenCubP-13
87WinSpiP-4
88PitCubP-1370
89ChaKniTI-4
90CMC-94
90IowCubC-19
90IowCubP-330
90ProAAAF-637
90TopTVCu-51
91Cla3-T49
91DonRoo-11
91IowCubLD-208
91IowCubP-1075
91LinDriAAA-208
92Don-662
92Fle-385
92IowCubS-211
92OPC-81
92Sco-418
92Sco100RS-30
92StaClu-334
92Top-81
92TopDeb91-106
92TopGol-81
92TopGolW-81
92TopMic-81
92UppDec-50
94Pac-409
Landrum, Darryl
86VenGulP-11
87DunBluJP-933
88WilBilP-1319
Landrum, Don
58Top-291
61Top-338
62Top-323
63CubJayP-8
63Jel-175
63Pos-175
63Top-113
64Top-286
64TopVen-286
65Top-596
66OPC-43
66Top-43A
66Top-43B
66Top-43C
66TopRubI-50
66TopVen-43
Landrum, Tito (Terry)
76ArkTraT-6
77ArkTraT-4A

77ArkTraT-4B
78St.PetCT-16
79ArkTraT-4
81Fle-539
81Top-244
82Don-292
82Fle-118
82Top-658
83Don-498
83Fle-13
83LouRedR-12
83Top-337
84Car-16
84FleUpd-69
84TopSti-14
85CarTeal-19
85Don-168
85Fle-232
85OPC-33
85Top-33
85TopTif-33
86CarIGAS-7
86CarKASD-3
86CarSchM-13
86CarTeal-23
86Don-425
86Fle-41
86OPC-171
86Top-498
86TopSti-19
86TopTat-15
86TopTif-498
87CarSmo-23
87Don-386
87DonOpeD-66
87Fle-301
87FleGlo-301
87OPC-288
87Top-288
87TopTif-288
88DodPol-21
88RocRedWC-22
88Top-581
88TopTif-581
89NasSouTI-11
89PacSenL-168
89T/MSenL-64
89TopSenL-94
90DodTar-432
90EliSenL-26
90MiaMirIS-15
91GreFalDSP-28
91OriCro-254
91PacSenL-149
92YakBeaC-11
92YakBeaF-3462
93VerBeaDC-13
93VerBeaDF-2231
94BakDodC-13
95SanAntMTI-32
96SanBerSB-14
Landry, Greg
89BelBreIS-13
89HelBreSP-10
90BelBreB-9
Landry, Howard
89WinHavRSS-11
90LynRedSTI-19
Landry, Lonny
93BriTigC-14
93BriTigF-3664
94JamJamC-13
94JamJamF-3979
96LakTigB-15
Landry, Todd
93HelBreF-4101
93HelBreSP-9
94StoPorC-14
94StoPorF-1700
95ElPasDTI-14
96BesAutSA-39
Landstad, Rob
96BurIndB-18
Landuyt, Doug
78CedRapGT-14
81ShrCapT-14
83PhoGiaBHN-25
Landy, Brian
88BilMusP-1820
89GreHorP-412
Landy, Ron
89GeoColC-18
Lane, Aaron
93AlbPolF-2024
94AlbPolC-15
94AlbPolF-2233
95AusFut-51
95BowBayTI-19
96RocRedWB-17
Lane, Brian
88GreHorP-1555
88SouAtlLAGS-7
89BasAmeAPB-AA16
89ChaLooB-4
89ChaLooGS-14
90Bow-48
90BowTif-48
90CMC-145
90NasSouC-20
90NasSouP-239
90ProAAAF-551
92ChaLooS-189
92ClaFS7-87
92NasSouF-1839
92SkyAA F-84
93ChaLooF-2368
93ClaFS7-215
Lane, Dan
94WesPalBEC-15
94WesPalBEF-50
95HarSenTI-7
Lane, Danny
92JamExpC-14
92JamExpF-1507
Lane, Frank
59Ind-9
61A'sTeal-11
83FraBroR-29
Lane, Gene
82DurBulT-24
90BurBraB-29
90BurBraS-31
Lane, Heath
87AriWilP-9
88AriWilP-8
89BelBreIS-14
90RivRedWB-26
90RivRedWCLC-19
90RivRedWP-2604
Lane, Ira
82DayBeaAT-14
Lane, Jerry
81ElPasDT-7
Lane, Jerry (Jerald H.)
54Top-97
94TopArc1-97
94TopArc1G-97
Lane, Kevin
91BurAstC-6
91BurAstP-2797
92OscAstC-25
92OscAstF-2528
93FloStaLAF-35
93OscAstC-15
93OscAstF-623
94ClaGolF-134
Lane, Marvin
77EvaTriT-17
Lane, Mike
94BluOriF-3559
Lane, Nolan
88CapCodPPaLP-46
89BurIndS-15
89Sta-179
90CarLeaA-42
90KinIndTI-10
91CanIndLD-87
91CanIndP-990
91LinDriAA-87
92CanIndS-111
92Ft.MyeMCB-20
92SkyAA F-52
Lane, Ryan
94EliTwiC-10
94EliTwiF-3739
95ForWayWTI-18
96FtMyeMB-18
Lane, Scott
88RocExpLC-19
Lane, William C.
52Par-50
Lanfair, Dave
75WatDodT-10
Lanfranco, Luis
90SouOreAB-6
90SouOreAP-3432
91MadMusC-23
91MadMusP-2139
Lanfranco, Raphael
90AshTouC-19
91AshTouP-571
92BurAstC-8
92BurAstF-550
Lanfranconi, Walt
49W725AngTI-15
85TCMPla1-34
Lang, Chip (Robert)
76ExpRed-18
77OPC-216
77Top-132
Lang, Perry
88PacEigMO-15
Lang, Stephen
91TopRut-2
Langaigne, Selwyn
96DunBluJUTI-6
96MedHatBJTI-15
Langbehn, Gregg
89PitMetS-14
90ColMetGS-16
90ColMetPPI-7
91St.LucMC-20
91St.LucMP-705
92BinMetF-512
92BinMetS-64
92SkyAA F-29
93NorTidF-2567
94BinMetF-700
94NorTidF-2916
Langdon, Ted
83TamTarT-17
84CedRapRT-2
86TamTarP-9
87VerRedP-3
Langdon, Tim
91KinIndC-4
91KinIndP-316
Lange, Clark
85OscAstTI-19
87VisOakP-26
Lange, E.D.
88AllandGN-36
Lange, Frank H.
09ColChiE-164
11T205-94
12ColRedB-164
12ColTinT-164
12T207-98
Lange, Fred
87OldJudN-298
Lange, Richard
74OPC-429
74Top-429
75OPC-114
75Top-114
76OPC-176
76SalLakCGC-15
76Top-176
77SalLakCGC-20
Langfield, Paul
80UtiBluJT-28
Langford, Rick
75ShrCapT-8
78Hos-120
78OPC-33
78Top-327
79Top-29
80OPC-284
80Top-546
81A'sGraG-22
81Don-238
81Fle-572
81FleStiC-27
81Kel-55
81OPC-154
81Top-154
81TopSti-121
82A'sGraG-7
82Don-161
82Fle-98
82FleSta-126
82OPC-43
82Top-454
83A'sGraG-22
83Don-365
83Fle-523
83FleSti-190
83Top-286
83Top-531
83TopSti-106
84Fle-451
84Nes792-629
84OPC-304
84Top-629
84TopTif-629
85ThoMcAD-14
85Top-347
85TopTif-347
86A'sMot-14
86Fle-425
86Top-766
86TopTif-766
88ColCliC-10
88ColCliP-5
88ColCliP-308
91BilMusP-3749
91BilMusSP-19
91CedRapRC-7
91CedRapRP-2715
91Cla/Bes-347
92BenMusSP-9
92BilMusF-3349
92ChaWheF-5
92ChaWVWC-9
93WesVirWC-14
93WesVirWF-2862
96KnoSmoB-2
Langford, Sam
11TurRedT-65
Langiotti, Fred
89SprCarB-24
90SprCarB-13
91St.PetCC-16
91St.PetCP-2279
Langley, Lee
87VerBeaDP-28
88BakDodCLC-256
89ClePhiS-13
90ClePhiS-10
91MiaMirC-14
91MiaMirP-404
92ClePhiC-11
92ClePhiF-2054
Langowski, Ted
91MedHatBJP-4107
Langston, Keith
88CapCodPPaLP-109
89NiaFalRP-14
Langston, Mark
83ChaLooT-11
84FleUpd-70
84FunFooP-18
84MarMot-13
84TopTra-70T
84TopTraT-70T
85AllGamPI-79
85Don-557
85Dra-38
85Fle-492
85FleLimE-17
85FleStaS-109
85Lea-56
85MarMot-3
85OPC-259
85Top-625
85Top3-D-22
85TopMin-625
85TopRubD-29
85TopSti-281
85TopSti-337
85TopSti-371
85TopSup-20
85TopTif-625
86Don-118
86Fle-467
86MarMot-3
86OPC-198
86Top-495
86TopSti-225
86TopTif-495
87ClaGam-89
87Don-568
87DonHig-34
87DonOpeD-116
87Fle-589
87FleAwaW-22
87FleGlo-589
87FleHotS-26
87FleMin-62
87FleStiC-70
87Lea-55
87MarMot-5
87OPC-215
87RedFolSB-45
87Spo-102
87SpoTeaP-25
87StuPan-25
87Top-215
87TopMinL-71
87TopSti-219
87TopTif-215
87ClaBlu-250
88Don-20
88Don-317
88DonAll-26
88DonBasB-136
88DonSupD-20
88Fle-377
88FleBasA-20
88FleBasM-21
88FleGlo-377
88FleHotS-23
88FleLeaL-24
88FleMin-52
88FleSlu-23
88FleStiC-60
88FleTeaL-18
88GreBasS-16
88Lea-20
88Lea-123
88MarMot-5
88OPC-80
88PanSti-181
88RedFolSB-46
88Sco-30
88ScoGlo-30
88ScoSam-30
88Spo-46
88StaLinMa-8
88Top-80
88TopBig-176
88TopCoi-18
88TopGaloC-8
88TopMinL-34
88TopRevLL-33
88TopSti-214
88TopStiB-63
88TopTif-80
88TopUKM-42
88TopUKMT-42
89Bow-205
89BowTif-205
89Don-227
89DonBasB-68
89ExpPos-17
89Fle-551
89FleExcS-29
89FleGlo-551
89FleSup-27
89FleUpd-97
89K-M-21
89MarMot-5
89OPC-355
89PanSti-430
89RedFolSB-71
89Sco-161
89ScoHot1S-67
89ScoRoo-25T
89ScoSco-13
89Spo-159
89Top-355
89TopBasT-85
89TopHilTM-19
89TopMinL-73
89TopSti-221
89TopTif-355
89TopTra-66T
89TopTraT-66T
89TopUKM-47
89TVSpoM-121
89UppDec-526
90AngSmo-10
90Bow-284
90BowTif-284
90ClaBlu-72
90ClaUpd-T28
90Don-338
90DonBesA-17
90Fle-352
90FleCan-352
90FleUpd-78
90Lea-155
90LeaPre-6
90OPC-530
90PanSti-287
90PubSti-179
90RedFolSB-55
90Sco-401
90Sco-688
90Sco100S-96

90ScoRoo-11T
90Spo-110
90Top-530
90TopBig-232
90TopMinL-62
90TopSti-70
90TopStiB-29
90TopTif-530
90TopTra-54T
90TopTraT-54T
90UppDec-647
90UppDec-783
90VenSti-281
91AngSmo-8
91Bow-202
91Don-190
91DonBonC-BC1
91Fle-318
91FleWaxBC-1
91Lea-67
91MajLeaCP-25
91OPC-755
91PanFreS-352
91PanSti-1
91Sco-21
91Sco-411
91Sco-699
91SimandSMLBL-25
91StaClu-27
91StaCluCM-17
91Stu-27
91Top-755
91TopCraJI-17
91TopDesS-755
91TopMic-755
91TopTif-755
91Ult-49
91UppDec-234
91USPlaCA-5H
92AngPol-14
92Bow-520
92Cla2-T6
92ClaGam-113
92Don-531
92DonCraJ2-20
92DonDiaK-DK20
92DonMcD-19
92Fle-63
92Hig5-14
92Hig5S-22
92HitTheBB-19
92Lea-229
92OPC-165
92PanSti-11
92Pin-132
92Sco-12
92Sco100S-32
92ScoProP-2
92SpoStaCC-29
92StaClu-670
92StaCluD-101
92Stu-148
92Top-165
92TopGol-165
92TopGolW-165
92TopKid-98
92TopMic-165
92TriPla-36
92Ult-327
92UltAwaW-16
92UppDec-305
93AngMot-8
93AngPol-8
93Bow-469
93Don-593
93Fin-82
93FinRef-82
93Fla-175
93Fle-194
93FunPac-40
93JimDea-9
93Lea-324
93LeaGolA-U1
93OPC-232
93PacSpa-48
93PanSti-2
93Pin-56
93Sco-66
93ScoFra-3
93Sel-52
93SP-5
93StaClu-355
93StaCluAn-4
93StaCluFDI-355
93StaCluM-107
93StaCluMOP-355
93Top-210
93TopGol-210
93TopInaM-210
93TopMic-210
93TriPla-235
93Ult-166
93UltAwaW-10
93UppDec-53
93UppDec-128
93UppDecGold-53
93UppDecGold-128
94AngLAT-14
94AngMot-2
94Bow-235
94ColC-169
94ColChoGS-169
94ColChoSS-169
94Don-31
94Don-660
94DonSpeE-31
94ExtBas-37
94Fin-24
94FinRef-24
94Fla-271
94Fle-61
94FleAllS-14
94FleSmo'nH-6
94FUnPac-112
94Kra-6
94Lea-162
94LeaL-17
94OPC-175
94Pac-81
94PanSti-38
94Pin-311
94PinArtP-311
94PinMusC-311
94ProMag-17
94RedFolMI-23
94Sco-71
94ScoGolR-71
94Sel-351
94SP-25
94SPDieC-25
94Spo-38
94StaClu-442
94StaCluFDI-442
94StaCluGR-442
94StaCluMO-16
94StaCluMOP-442
94Stu-13
94SucSav-11
94Top-665
94TopGol-665
94TopSpa-665
94TriPla-17
94Ult-331
94UltAwaW-9
94UltStrK-2
94UppDec-485
94UppDecED-485
95AngCHP-3
95AngMot-2
95Baz-108
95Bow-404
95ColCho-103
95ColChoGS-103
95ColChoSS-103
95Don-155
95DonPreP-155
95DonTopotO-37
95Emb-122
95EmbGolI-122
95Fin-142
95FinRef-142
95Fla-236
95Fle-228
95Lea-236
95LeaLim-169
95Pac-62
95Pin-225
95PinArtP-225
95PinMusC-225
95Sco-126
95ScoGolR-126
95ScoPlaTS-126
95Sel-136
95SelArtP-136
95SP-132
95Spo-87
95SpoArtP-87
95SPSil-132
95StaClu-246
95StaCluFDI-246
95StaCluMOP-246
95StaCluSTWS-246
95Stu-87
95Top-95
95TopCyb-62
95UC3-79
95UC3ArtP-79
95Ult-22
95UltAwaW-9
95UltAwaWGM-9
95UltGolM-22
95UppDec-271
95UppDecED-271
95UppDecEDG-271
95UppDecSE-129
95UppDecSEG-129
96AngMot-3
96Baz-119
96ColCho-73
96ColChoGS-73
96ColChoSS-73
96Don-426
96DonPreP-426
96EmoXL-28
96Fin-B114
96FinRef-B114
96Fla-39
96Fle-51
96FleTif-51
96Lea-97
96LeaPrePB-97
96LeaPrePG-97
96LeaPrePS-97
96MetUni-29
96MetUniP-29
96Pac-261
96PanSti-214
96Pin-127
96Sco-291
96ScoDugC-B16
96ScoDugCAP-B16
96SP-47
96StaClu-385
96StaCluEPB-385
96StaCluEPG-385
96StaCluEPS-385
96StaCluMOP-385
96Top-423
96TopGal-4
96TopGalPPI-4
96TopLas-57
96Ult-31
96UltGolM-31
96UppDec-28
97Cir-166
97CirRav-166
97ColCho-261
97Don-228
97DonPreP-228
97DonPrePGold-228
97DonTea-6
97DonTeaSPE-6
97Fin-185
97FinRef-185
97Fle-48
97FleTif-48
97Lea-73
97LeaFraM-73
97LeaFraMDC-73
97Pac-10
97PacLigB-10
97PacSil-10
97Sco-287
97ScoPreS-287
97ScoShoS-287
97ScoShoSAP-287
97StaClu-334
97StaCluMOP-334
97Top-128
97UppDec-136
97UppDec-289

Laniauskas, Vitas

89AshTouP-941

Lanier, H. Max

41CarW75-14
50Bow-207
51Bow-230
52Bow-110
52Top-101
79DiaGre-155
83TopRep5-101
92ConTSN-620

Lanier, Hal

47PM1StaP1-109
65OPC-118
65Top-118
66OPC-156
66Top-156
66Top-271
66TopVen-156
66TopVen-271
67CokCapG-8
67DexPre-122
67OPC-4
67Top-4
67TopVen-287
68Top-436
69MilBra-155
69MLBOffS-201
69Top-316
69TopSta-106
69TopTeaP-14
70Gia-6
70MLBOffS-126
70Top-583
71MLBOffS-255
71OPC-181
71Top-181
72MilBra-193
72Top-589
73OPC-479
73Top-479
74OPC-588
74Top-588
75TulOil7-8
78St.PetCT-29
81Car5x7-15
83Car-15
84Car-17
84Car5x7-14
85CarTeal-17
86AstMilL-13
86AstPol-6
86CarTeal-24
86TopTra-60T
86TopTraT-60T
87AstMot-1
87AstPol-7
87Top-343
87TopTif-343
88AstMot-1
88AstPol-25
88Top-684
88TopTif-684
89Top-164
89TopTif-164
90PhiTas-34
91PhiMed-24
92YanWIZ7-94

Lanier, Tom

94LSUTigMP-4

Lankard, Steve

86SalRedBP-17
87PorChaRP-3
88TulDriTI-20
89TexLeaAGS-35
89TulDriGS-13
90CMC-152
90OklCit8C-2
90OklCit8P-428
90ProAAAF-674

Lankford, Frank

93OneYanC-12
93OneYanF-3499
94GreBatF-469
95TamYanYI-16
96NorNavB-15
97GreBatC-12

Lankford, Ray

88MidLeaAGS-26
88SprCarB-14
89ArkTraGS-9
89BasAmeAPB-AA23
89BlaYNPRWL-93
89BlaYNPRWLU-62
89TexLeaAGS-22
90Bow-192
90BowTif-192
90ClaUpd-T29
90CMC-114
90Lea-308
90LouRedBC-14
90LouRedBLBC-23
90LouRedBP-416
90ProAAAF-530
90ScoRoo-84T
90SprCarDGB-24
90TopMag-56
90TopTVCa-53
90UppDec-755
91Bow-388
91CarPol-16
91Cla3-T48
91ClaGam-83
91Don-43
91DonRoo-8
91Fle-637
91Lea-523
91LeaPre-10
91MajLeaCP-50
91OPC-682
91OPCPre-72
91Sco-731
91ScoAllF-1
91ScoHotR-7
91ScoRoo-2
91SevCoi-M10
91StaClu-537
91StaCluMO-21
91Stu-234
91Top-682
91TopDeb90-81
91TopDesS-682
91TopMic-682
91TopTif-682
91Ult-290
91UppDec-346
92Bow-643
92CarPol-10
92Cla1-T51
92ClaGam-130
92Don-350
92Fle-583
92FleRooS-17
92Hig5-97
92Lea-195
92OPC-292
92OPCPre-148
92PanSti-177
92Pin-126
92PinTea2-51
92Sco-223
92Sco100RS-43
92ScoImpP-8
92StaClu-8
92Top-292
92TopGol-292
92TopGolW-292
92TopMic-292
92TriPla-194
92Ult-265
92UppDec-262
92UppDecF-8
92UppDecFG-8
93Bow-404
93CadDis-38
93CarPol-9
93ClaGam-51
93DenHol-7
93Don-366
93DonMVP-12
93Fin-187
93FinRef-187
93Fla-122
93Fle-127
93FleFruotL-34
93FleTeaL-NL3
93FunPac-76
93Hos-5
93JimDea-20
93Lea-297
93LeaFas-8
93OPC-191
93OPCPre-44
93PacSpa-296
93PanSti-196
93Pin-116
93PinTea2-19
93Sco-56
93ScoFra-24
93Sel-155
93SelStaL-17
93SP-76
93StaClu-49
93StaCluCa-17
93StaCluFDI-49
93StaCluMOP-49
93Stu-175
93Top-386
93TOPBLAG-10

93TopGol-386
93TopInaM-386
93TopMic-386
93Toy-100
93TriPla-254
93Ult-108
93Ult-298
93UltAllS-7
93UppDec-244
93UppDec-461
93UppDec-482
93UppDecDG-7
93UppDecGold-244
93UppDecGold-461
93UppDecGold-482
93UppDecHRH-HR20
94Bow-96
94BowBes-R64
94BowBesR-R64
94CarPol-9
94ColC-365
94ColChoGS-365
94ColChoSS-365
94Don-367
94DonSpeE-367
94ExtBas-360
94Fin-347
94FinRef-347
94Fla-226
94Fle-636
94Lea-384
94LeaL-146
94LeaMVPC-N8
94LeaMVPCG-N8
94OPC-251
94PanSti-245
94Pin-36
94PinArtP-36
94PinMusC-36
94ProMag-111
94RedFolMI-14
94Sco-16
94ScoGolR-16
94Sel-152
94SP-64
94SPDieC-64
94Spo-65
94StaClu-353
94StaCluFDI-353
94StaCluGR-353
94StaCluMOP-353
94StaCluT-310
94StaCluTFDI-310
94Stu-52
94Top-530
94TopGol-530
94TopSpa-530
94TriPla-64
94Ult-566
94UppDec-446
94UppDecED-446
95Baz-74
95Bow-299
95BowBes-R18
95BowBesR-R18
95ColCho-190
95ColChoGS-190
95ColChoSE-77
95ColChoSEGS-77
95ColChoSESS-77
95ColChoSS-190
95Don-324
95DonPreP-324
95DonTopotO-331
95Emb-25
95EmbGolI-25
95Emo-182
95Fin-136
95FinRef-136
95Fla-411
95Fle-501
95Lea-79
95LeaLim-181
95Pac-408
95Pin-195
95PinArtP-195
95PinMusC-195
95Sco-264
95ScoGolR-264
95ScoPlaTS-264
95Sel-76
95SelArtP-76
95SelCer-63
95SelCerMG-63
95SP-104
95SPCha-87
95SPChaDC-87
95Spo-130
95SpoArtP-130
95SPSil-104
95StaClu-424
95StaClu-507
95StaCluMO-27
95StaCluMOP-424
95StaCluMOP-507
95StaCluSTWS-424
95StaCluSTWS-507
95StaCluVR-221
95Stu-190
95Sum-38
95SumNthD-38
95Top-82
95TopCyb-58
95UC3-66
95UC3ArtP-66
95Ult-431
95UltGolM-431
95UppDec-305
95UppDecED-305
95UppDecEDG-305
95UppDecSE-90
95UppDecSEG-90
95Zen-85
96ArkTraB-29
96Baz-11
96Bow-28
96BowBes-90
96BowBesAR-90
96BowBesR-90
96CarPol-14
96Cir-178
96CirRav-178
96ColCho-690
96ColChoGS-690
96ColChoSS-690
96Don-379
96DonPreP-379
96EmoXL-268
96Fin-B334
96Fin-S10
96FinRef-B334
96FinRef-S10
96Fla-361
96Fle-546
96FleTeaL-26
96FleTif-546
96Lea-37
96LeaLim-7
96LeaLimG-7
96LeaPre-10
96LeaPreP-10
96LeaPrePB-37
96LeaPrePG-37
96LeaPrePS-37
96LeaPreSG-29
96LeaPreSte-29
96LeaSig-6
96LeaSigPPG-6
96LeaSigPPP-6
96MetUni-227
96MetUniP-227
96MLBPin-19
96Pac-219
96PanSti-73
96Pin-57
96PinAfi-57
96PinAfiAP-57
96PinAfiFPP-57
96PinArtP-22
96PinSta-22
96ProSta-32
96Sco-279
96ScoDugC-B4
96ScoDugCAP-B4
96Sel-18
96SelArtP-18
96SelCer-26
96SelCerAP-26
96SelCerCB-26
96SelCerCR-26
96SelCerIP-7
96SelCerMB-26
96SelCerMG-26
96SelCerMR-26
96SelTeaN-2
96SP-151
96Spo-77
96SpoArtP-77
96StaClu-209
96StaClu-283
96StaCluB&B-BB7
96StaCluEPB-283
96StaCluEPG-283
96StaCluEPS-283
96StaCluMOP-209
96StaCluMOP-283
96StaCluMOP-BB7
95StaCluVRMC-221
96Stu-112
96StuPrePB-112
96StuPrePG-112
96StuPrePS-112
96Sum-33
96SumAbo&B-33
96SumArtP-33
96SumFoi-33
96TeaOut-47
96Top-327
96TopChr-130
96TopChrR-130
96TopGal-5
96TopGalE-11
96TopGalPPI-5
96TopLas-71
96Ult-549
96UltGolM-549
96UppDec-441
96Zen-38
96ZenArtP-38
96ZenMoz-11
97Bow-33
97BowBes-24
97BowBesAR-24
97BowBesR-24
97BowChr-28
97BowChrI-28
97BowChrIR-28
97BowChrR-28
97BowInt-33
97Cir-28
97CirRav-28
97ColCho-202
97Don-67
97DonLim-148
97DonLim-150
97DonLimLE-148
97DonLimLE-150
97DonPre-80
97DonPreCttC-80
97DonPreP-67
97DonPrePGold-67
97DonTea-153
97DonTeaSPE-153
97Fin-256
97FinRef-256
97FlaSho-A116
97FlaSho-B116
97FlaSho-C116
97FlaShoLC-116
97FlaShoLC-B116
97FlaShoLC-C116
97FlaShoLCM-A116
97FlaShoLCM-B116
97FlaShoLCM-C116
97Fle-446
97FleTif-446
97Lea-6
97LeaFraM-6
97LeaFraMDC-6
97MetUni-232
97NewPin-67
97NewPinAP-67
97NewPinMC-67
97NewPinPP-67
97Pac-412
97PacLigB-412
97PacSil-412
97PinCer-13
97PinCerMBlu-13
97PinCerMG-13
97PinCerMR-13
97PinCerR-13
97PinTotCPB-13
97PinTotCPG-13
97PinTotCPR-13
97ProMag-35
97ProMagML-35
97Sco-236
97ScoPreS-236
97ScoShoS-236
97ScoShoSAP-236
97SkyE-X-100
97SkyE-XC-100
97SkyE-XEC-100
97SP-145
97SpoIll-104
97SpoIllEE-104
97StaClu-236
97StaCluMat-236
97StaCluMOP-236
97Stu-28
97StuPrePG-28
97StuPrePS-28
97Top-87
97TopChr-33
97TopChrR-33
97TopGal-70
97TopGalPPI-70
97TopSta-89
97TopSta1AS-AS17
97TopStaAM-89
97Ult-273
97UltDouT-18
97UltGolME-273
97UltPlaME-273
97UppDec-485

Lanning, David P.
81VerBeaDT-9

Lanning, Johnny
79DiaGre-202
94ConTSN-1301
94ConTSNB-1301

Lannon, Joe
87AllandGN-15

Lanok, Dale
85BurRanT-7

Lanoux, Marty
86KenTwiP-11
87VisOakP-23
88CalLeaACLC-39
88VisOakCLC-153
88VisOakP-104
89OrlTwiB-26
89OrlTwiP-1328
90PorBeaP-186
90ProAAAF-256

Lansford, Carney
76QuaCitAT-18
78AngFamF-22
78SSP270-207
79Top-212
80OPC-177
80Top-337
81AllGamPI-35
81CokTeaS-6
81Don-409
81Fle-270
81FleStiC-12
81OPC-245
81Top-639
81TopScr-25
81TopSti-43
81TopSupHT-6
81TopTra-788
82Don-82
82Fle-298
82FleSta-164
82Kel-41
82OPC-91
82PerCreC-15
82PerCreCG-15
82RedSoxC-10
82Top-91
82Top-161
82Top-786
82TopSti-2
82TopSti-156
82TopStiV-156
83A'sGraG-4
83AllGamPI-34
83Don-408
83Fle-187
83FleSta-100
83FleSti-67
83OPC-318
83Top-523
83TopSti-32
83TopTra-60T
84A'sMot-7
84AllGamPI-124
84Don-176
84DonActAS-39
84Fle-452
84FunFooP-55
84Nes792-767
84OPC-59
84Top-767
84TopRubD-18
84TopSti-328
84TopTif-767
85A'sMot-8
85AllGamPI-34
85Don-8
85Don-345
85DonSupD-8
85Fle-429
85Lea-8
85OPC-347
85Top-422
85TopRubD-17
85TopSti-330
85TopTif-422
86A'sMot-8
86Don-131
86Fle-426
86Lea-55
86OPC-134
86SevCoi-W10
86Spo-75
86Top-134
86TopSti-169
86TopTat-7
86TopTif-134
86Woo-17
87A'sSmoC-8
87Don-158
87DonOpeD-20
87Fle-397
87FleBasA-24
87FleGlo-397
87FleMin-63
87FleStiC-71
87OPC-69
87RedFolSB-37
87Spo-138
87SpoTeaP-23
87StuPan-24
87Top-678
87TopSti-171
87TopTif-678
88A'sMot-6
88ActPacT-4
88Don-178
88DonBasB-246
88DonTeaBA-178
88Fle-285
88FleGlo-285
88FleSluBC-C3
88FleStiC-55
88Lea-195
88OPC-292
88PanSti-169
88Sco-253
88ScoGlo-253
88Spo-202
88StaLinAs-9
88Top-292
88TopBig-221
88TopSti-167
88TopTif-292
89A'sMot-5
89Bow-198
89BowTif-198
89Don-243
89DonAll-17
89DonBasB-22
89Fle-16
89Fle-633
89FleGlo-16
89FleGlo-633
89OPC-47
89PanSti-421
89RedFolSB-72
89Sco-179
89ScoHot1S-12
89Spo-53
89Top-47
89TopBasT-103
89TopBatL-20
89TopBig-57
89TopSti-170
89TopTif-47
89TVSpoM-99
89UppDec-562
90A'sMot-8
90Bow-452
90BowTif-452
90ClaBlu-12
90Don-95
90DonBesA-117

90El PasDAGTI-40
90Fle-14
90FleCan-14
90Lea-213
90MLBBasB-73
90OPC-316
90PanSti-134
90PanSti-184
90PubSti-309
90RedFolSB-56
90Sco-296
90Sco-702
90Sco100S-20
90Spo-84
90Top-316
90TopBatL-12
90TopBig-83
90TopDou-39
90TopGloS-6
90TopMinL-29
90TopSti-183
90TopStiB-42
90TopTif-316
90TopTVA-4
90UppDec-253
90VenSti-282
91A'sMot-8
91BasBesHM-12
91Don-273
91Fle-14
91OPC-502
91PanFreS-194
91Sco-630
91StaClu-231
91Top-502
91TopDesS-502
91TopMic-502
91TopTif-502
91Ult-250
91UppDec-194
92AthMot-8
92Bow-78
92Don-775
92Fle-261
92Lea-148
92OPC-495
92PanSti-17
92Pin-455
92Sco-648
92StaClu-45
92Stu-225
92Top-495
92TopGol-495
92TopGolW-495
92TopMic-495
92Ult-423
92UppDec-682
93PanSti-17
93Sel-156
93Top-127
93TopGol-127
93TopInaM-127
93TopMic-127
94A'sMot-28
95AthMot-28

Lansford, Joe
82HawIslT-6
83LasVegSBHN-13
84LasVegSC-220
85TacTigC-146
87LasVegSP-4

Lansing, Mike
90MiaMirIS-16
90WicStaSGD-20
91Cla/Bes-45
91FloStaLAP-FSL24
91MiaMirC-21
91MiaMirP-415
92HarSenF-466
92HarSenS-287
92UppDecML-131
93Bow-184
93ExcFS7-61
93ExpPosN-15
93Fin-186
93FinRef-186
93Fla-85
93FleFinE-95
93JimDeaR-6
93Lea-464
93OPCPre-82
93PacSpa-535
93Pin-620
93SelRoo-60T
93SelRooAR-3
93SP-105
93StaClu-691
93StaCluFDI-691
93StaCluMOP-691
93Stu-46
93TopTra-99T
93Ult-417
93UltAllR-4
93UppDec-677
93UppDecGold-677
94Bow-228
94ColC-170
94ColChoGS-170
94ColChoSS-170
94Don-208
94ExtBas-308
94Fin-10
94FinJum-10
94FinRef-10
94Fla-402
94Fle-543
94FleRooS-10
94Lea-89
94OPC-218
94Pac-384
94PanSti-212
94Pin-455
94PinArtP-455
94PinMusC-455
94Sco-488
94ScoBoyoS-17
94ScoGolR-488
94Sel-88
94StaClu-577
94StaCluFDI-577
94StaCluGR-577
94StaCluMO-48
94StaCluMOP-577
94Top-287
94TopGol-287
94TopSpa-287
94TriPla-97
94Ult-230
94UppDec-244
94UppDecED-244
94USPlaCR-7H
94USPlaCR-12D
95ColCho-233
95ColChoGS-233
95ColChoSS-233
95Don-15
95DonPreP-15
95DonTopotO-281
95Fla-163
95Fle-355
95Lea-11
95Pin-408
95PinArtP-408
95PinMusC-408
95Sco-127
95ScoGolR-127
95ScoPlaTS-127
95StaClu-431
95StaCluMOP-431
95StaCluSTWS-431
95Top-548
95TopCyb-329
95Ult-404
95UltGolM-404
95UppDec-328
95UppDecED-328
95UppDecEDG-328
96ColCho-615
96ColChoGS-615
96ColChoSS-615
96Don-252
96DonPreP-252
96ExpDis-11
96Fla-308
96Fle-461
96FleTif-461
96Lea-206
96LeaPrePB-206
96LeaPrePG-206
96LeaPrePS-206
96LeaSigA-129
96LeaSigAG-129
96LeaSigAS-129
96Pac-118
96SP-119
96StaClu-369
96StaCluMOP-369
96TeaOut-48
96Top-86
96Ult-232
96UltGolM-232
96UppDec-133
97Bow-21
97BowChr-17
97BowChrI-17
97BowChrIR-17
97BowChrR-17
97BowInt-21
97Cir-118
97CirRav-118
97ColCho-164
97Fin-69
97FinRef-69
97Fle-381
97FleTif-381
97Lea-37
97LeaFraM-37
97LeaFraMDC-37
97MetUni-157
97Pac-346
97PacLigB-346
97PacSil-346
97Sco-289
97ScoPreS-289
97ScoShoS-289
97ScoShoSAP-289
97SP-112
97StaClu-145
97StaCluMOP-145
97Stu-123
97StuPrePG-123
97StuPrePS-123
97Top-83
97TopChr-31
97TopChrR-31
97TopGal-106
97TopGalPPI-106
97Ult-384
97UltGolME-384
97UltPlaME-384
97UppDec-428

Lantigua, Eduardo
92GulCoaDF-3573
93VerBeaDC-14
93VerBeaDF-2229
94Bow-266

Lantigua, Manny
75SanAntBT-13
79PorBeaT-16

Lantrip, Joe
92BluOriC-16
92BluOriF-2357

Lantrip, Rick
88AriWilP-9
90OneYanP-3387
91GreHorP-3066
92GreHorC-15
92GreHorF-788

Lantz, Tom
75CliPilT-14

Lanza, Mike
94BelMarC-18
94BelMarF-3244
96LanJetB-16

LaPalme, Paul
52Top-166
53BowBW-19
53Top-201
54Bow-107
54DanDee-14
55Bow-61
55CarHunW-12
57Top-344
58MonRoyF-15
83TopRep5-166
91TopArc1-201

Lapenta, Jerry
86GenCubP-14
87PeoChiP-6
88PeoChiTI-20
88PitCubP-1366

Laperriere, Jacques
72Dia-80
72Dia-81

Lapka, Rick
94PriRedC-14
94PriRedF-3258
95BilRedTI-5

LaPlante, Michel
92WelPirC-15
92WelPirF-1318
93AugPirC-11
93AugPirF-1538
94CarMudF-1573

LaPoint, Dave
77NewCoPT-21
78BurBeeT-18
79CliDodT-19
80VanCanT-7
81Car5x7-16
83Car-16
83Don-544
83Fle-14
83Top-438
84AllGamPI-81
84Car-18
84Car5x7-15
84Don-290
84Fle-328
84Nes792-627
84Top-627
84TopSti-146
84TopTif-627
85Don-138
85Fle-233
85FleUpd-68
85GiaMot-16
85GiaPos-17
85OPC-229
85Top-229
85TopMin-229
85TopSti-143
85TopTif-229
85TopTifT-71T
85TopTra-71T
86Don-387
86Fle-547
86FleUpd-64
86OPC-162
86TigCaiD-10
86Top-551
86TopTif-551
86TopTra-61T
86TopTraT-61T
87Don-607
87Fle-421
87FleGlo-421
87OPC-319
87Top-754
87TopTif-754
88Don-552
88DonBasB-123
88Fle-402
88FleBasA-21
88FleGlo-402
88FleSlu-24
88Sco-589
88ScoGlo-589
88StaLinWS-11
88Top-334
88TopTif-334
88WhiSoxC-13
89Bow-165
89BowTif-165
89Don-488
89DonBasB-244
89DonTra-27
89Fle-212
89FleGlo-212
89OPC-89
89Sco-384
89ScoRoo-4T
89Top-89
89TopTif-89
89TopTra-67T
89TopTraT-67T
89UppDec-600
89UppDec-706
89YanScoNW-15
90Don-72
90OPC-186
90PubSti-539
90Sco-357
90Top-186
90TopTif-186
90TopTVY-11
90UppDec-507
90VenSti-283
90YanScoNW-12
91Don-481
91Fle-669
91OPC-484
91Sco-218
91Top-484
91TopDesS-484
91TopMic-484
91TopTif-484
91UppDec-483
92YanWIZ8-102
93PorBeaF-2381
94BreMilB-50

LaPoint, Tony (J. Anthony)
86GenCubP-15
87ChaWheP-19

Lapointe, Guy
72Dia-82
72Dia-83

LaPorte, Frank
08RosComP-3
09ColChiE-165A
09ColChiE-165B
09T206-205
10CouT21-38
10DomDisP-66
10E-UOraBSC-12
10JHDABE-10
10SweCapPP-53A
10SweCapPP-53B
11MecDFT-42
11SpoLifCW-213
11SpoLifM-81
11T205-95
12ColRedB-165A
12ColRedB-165B
12ColTinT-165A
12ColTinT-165B
12HasTriFT-1A
14CraJacE-98
14PieStaT-32
15CraJacE-98

Lapp, John
10NadE1-28
11A'sFirT20-9
11MecDFT-2
11PloCanE-40
11SpoLifM-96
12T207-99
14FatPlaT-22
15SpoNewM-96
16BF2FP-14
16SpoNewM-98

Lapple, Bob
80CedRapRT-10

Laprade, Edgar
43ParSpo-45

Lara, Carlos
91PulBraC-3
91PulBraP-4009

Lara, Crucito
87St.PetCP-20
88St.PetCS-11
89St.LucMS-12
90JacMetGS-25

Lara, Eddie
96WesMicWB-13

Lara, Giovanni
96VerExpB-15

Lara, Luis
85DomLeaS-61

Larcom, Mark
82WisRapTF-22
83WisRapTF-12

Lardizabal, Ruben
90ModA'sC-17
91ModA'sC-7
91ModA'sP-3082

Lardner, Ring
88PacEigMO-30
88PacEigMO-35
88PacEigMO-42

Largusa, Levon
92ClaDraP-70
92St.CatBJC-25
92St.CatBJF-3384
93HagSunC-17
93HagSunF-1876
93StaCluM-23
94DunBluJF-2554
95DunBluJTI-11

Laribee, Russ
81PawRedST-20

Larios, John
86EugEmeC-35
87AppFoxP-3

Lariviere, Chris
88RocExpLC-20

Lariviere, Jason
95NewJerCTI-16
96PeoChiB-18

Larker, Norm

53ExhCan-37
59DodMor-7
59DodTeal-13
59Top-107
59TopVen-107
60DodBelB-1
60DodJayP-8
60DodTeal-11
60DodUniO-11
60KeyChal-29
60Top-394
61Baz-34
61DodBelB-5
61DodJayP-5
61DodMor-5
61DodUniO-12
61Pos-156A
61Pos-156B
61Top-41
61Top-130
61TopStal-28
62Baz-39
62Col.45B-11
62Col45'HC-10
62Col45'JP-8
62Jel-113
62Pos-113
62PosCan-113
62SalPlaC-194
62ShiPlaC-194
62Top-23
62TopBuc-48
62TopVen-23
63BraJayP-6
63Jel-188
63Pos-188
63Top-536
89AstCol4S-14
89DodSmoG-67
90DodTar-433

Larkin, Andy

93ElmPioC-9
93ElmPioF-3818
94Bow-262
94Cla-62
94KanCouCC-13
94KanCouCF-157
94KanCouCTI-14
94MidLeaAF-MDW16
95Bow-166
95BowBes-B9
95BowBesR-B9
95Exc-195
95KanCouCLTI-8
95PorSeaDTI-10
95UppDecML-64
96SigRooOJTP-T8
97Bow-132
97BowInt-132
97UppDec-478
95UppDecMLFS-64

Larkin, Barry

86SpoRoo-34
87ClaGam-18
87ClaUpdY-133
87Don-492
87DonOpeD-191
87Fle-204
87FleGlo-204
87RedKah-15
87SpoTeaP-4
87Top-648
87TopTif-648
87ToyRoo-18
88Don-492
88DonBasB-222
88Fle-239
88FleGlo-239
88Lea-226
88OPC-102
88PanSti-280
88RedKah-11
88Sco-72
88ScoGlo-72
88ScoSam-72
88ScoYouS2-34
88StaLinRe-12
88Top-102
88TopBig-74
88TopSti-140
88TopTif-102
89Bow-311
89BowTif-311
89CadEllD-32
89ClaLigB-70
89ClaTraP-165
89Don-257
89DonAll-47
89DonBasB-110
89Fle-164
89FleBasA-26
89FleGlo-164
89OPC-363
89PanSti-74
89RedFolSB-73
89RedKah-11
89Sco-31
89ScoHot1S-52
89ScoSco-24
89Spo-136
89Top-515
89TopBasT-90
89TopBig-199
89TopMinL-11
89TopSti-137
89TopStiB-44
89TopTif-515
89TVSpoM-39
89UppDec-270
89UppDecS-2
90Bow-50
90BowTif-50
90ClaBlu-48
90Don-71
90DonBesN-52
90DonLeaS-51
90Fle-423
90FleBasA-23
90FleCan-423
90FleLeaL-22
90FleLeaS-1
90Lea-18
90LeaPre-5
90MLBBasB-21
90OPC-10
90PanSti-253
90PubSti-33
90PubSti-266
90RedFolSB-57
90RedKah-12
90Sco-155
90Sco-689
90Spo-160
90StaLar-1
90StaLar-2
90StaLar-3
90StaLar-4
90StaLar-5
90StaLar-6
90StaLar-7
90StaLar-8
90StaLar-9
90StaLar-10
90StaLar-11
90Top-10
90TopBig-189
90TopCoi-51
90TopDou-40
90TopGloS-5
90TopMag-18
90TopMag-81
90TopSti-136
90TopStiB-11
90TopTif-10
90TopTVA-36
90UppDec-99
90UppDec-167
90USPlaCA-6D
90VenSti-284
90VenSti-285
91BasBesHM-13
91Bow-379
91Bow-673
91CadEllD-34
91Cla2-T33
91ClaGam-142
91Col-31
91Don-5
91Don-471
91DonSupD-5
91Fle-68
91Fle-711
91FleAll-2
91JimDea-10
91Lea-168
91LeaPre-3
91OPC-400
91OPC-730
91PanCanT1-28
91PanFreS-130
91PanSti-129
91Pos-18
91RedFolS-58
91RedKah-11
91RedPep-11
91Sco-505
91Sco-666
91Sco-795
91Sco-888
91Sco100S-20
91ScoCoo-B2
91SevCoi-F10
91SimandSMLBL-26
91StaClu-92
91StaPinB-28
91Stu-167
91SunSee-16
91Top-400
91Top-730
91TopCraJ2-11
91TopDesS-400
91TopDesS-730
91TopMic-400
91TopMic-730
91TopTif-400
91TopTif-730
91TopTriH-N3
91Ult-96
91UppDec-353
91UppDecSS-SS18
91USPlaCA-6C
91Woo-30
92Bow-353
92Bow-694
92Cla2-T74
92ClaGam-76
92Don-185
92DonCraJ1-19
92DonMcD-15
92Fle-411
92Fle-704
92FleAll-16
92FleCitTP-14
92Hig5-32
92HitTheBB-20
92Lea-73
92New-14
92OPC-465
92OPCPre-96
92PanSti-265
92PepDieM-18
92Pin-5
92PinRool-9
92PinTeaP-7
92Pos-23
92RedKah-11
92Sco-100
92Sco-775
92Sco100S-77
92ScoImpP-50
92SevCoi-13
92SpoIllFK1-402
92StaClu-100
92StaClu-596
92StaCluD-102
92Stu-23
92Top-389
92Top-465
92TopDaiQTU-4
92TopGol-389
92TopGol-465
92TopGolW-389
92TopGolW-465A
92TopGolW-465B
92TopKid-37
92TopMcD-21
92TopMic-389
92TopMic-465
92TriPla-31
92Ult-191
92UltAllS-13
92UppDec-144
92UppDecF-30
92UppDecFG-30
92UppDecTMH-29
93Bow-470
93ClaGam-52
93ColAllG-20
93DiaMar-63
93Don-426
93DonEli-23
93DonEliS-5
93DonPre-3
93DonSpiotG-SG13
93DurPowP2-17
93Fin-114
93FinJum-114
93FinRef-114
93Fla-27
93Fle-394
93FleAll-NL4
93FleFruotL-35
93FunPac-167
93FunPac-170
93Hos-8
93JimDea-2
93Kra-25
93Lea-311
93LeaGolA-R14
93LeaGolA-U6
93MetBak-32
93MilBonSS-3
93OPC-147
93OPCPre-103
93PacSpa-84
93PanSti-293
93Pin-22
93Pin-300
93Pin-306
93PinCoo-26
93PinCooD-26
93Pos-28
93PosCan-15
93RedKah-13
93Sco-16
93ScoFra-17
93Sel-23
93SP-15
93StaClu-415
93StaCluFDI-415
93StaCluMOP-415
93Stu-43
93StuHer-7
93Top-110
93Top-404
93TOPBLAG-11
93TopFulS-17
93TopGol-110
93TopGol-404
93TopInaM-110
93TopInaM-404
93TopMic-110
93TopMic-404
93TriPla-31
93TriPlaA-8
93Ult-30
93UltAllS-4
93UppDec-245
93UppDec-473
93UppDecCP-R13
93UppDecDG-22
93UppDecGold-245
93UppDecGold-473
93UppDecIC-WI21
93UppDecICJ-WI21
94Bow-471
94BowBes-X95
94BowBesR-X95
94ChuHomS-12
94ChuHomSG-12
94ColC-171
94ColC-349
94ColChoGS-171
94ColChoGS-349
94ColChoSS-171
94ColChoSS-349
94ColChoT-8
94Don-45
94DonDiaK-DK17
94DonSpeE-45
94ExtBas-233
94Fin-240
94FinJum-240
94FinRef-240
94Fla-146
94Fle-414
94FleAllS-45
94FleTeaL-17
94FUnPac-111
94KinDis-17
94Kra-26
94Lea-126
94LeaL-95
94LeaMVPC-N9
94LeaMVPCG-N9
94OPC-125
94Pac-150
94PanSti-163
94Pin-12
94PinArtP-12
94PinMusC-12
94Pos-12
94ProMag-32
94RedFolMI-15
94RedKah-17
94Sco-74
94ScoDreT-5
94ScoGolR-74
94ScoGolS-15
94ScoSam-DT5
94Sel-7
94SelSki-SK2
94SP-159
94SPDieC-159
94SPHol-23
94SPHolDC-23
94Spo-109
94StaClu-414
94StaCluFDI-414
94StaCluGR-414
94StaCluMOP-414
94StaCluMOP-ST3
94StaCluST-ST3
94Stu-168
94TomPiz-13
94Top-250
94TopGol-250
94TopSpa-250
94TopSupS-25
94TriPla-214
94TriPlaM-8
94Ult-474
94UppDec-269
94UppDec-385
94UppDecAJ-26
94UppDecAJG-26
94UppDecDC-C3
94UppDecED-269
94UppDecED-385
95Baz-40
95BazRedH-RH8
95Bow-415
95BowBes-R25
95BowBesR-R25
95ClaPhoC-15
95ColCho-430
95ColChoGS-430
95ColChoSE-200
95ColChoSEGS-200
95ColChoSESS-200
95ColChoSS-430
95D3-48
95DenHol-13
95Don-241
95DonDom-6
95DonPreP-241
95DonTopotO-214
95Emb-129
95EmbGolI-129
95Emo-117
95Fin-96
95FinRef-96
95Fla-339
95FlaHotG-5
95Fle-439
95Kra-24
95Lea-283
95LeaGreG-9
95LeaLim-49
95LeaLimIBP-18
95Pac-108
95PacPri-33
95PanSti-62
95Pin-382
95PinArtP-382
95PinMusC-382
95RedFol-15
95RedKah-16
95Sco-254
95ScoGolR-254
95ScoHaloG-HG8
95ScoPlaTS-254
95Sel-52
95SelArtP-52
95SelCer-27
95SelCerMG-27
95SP-45
95SPCha-36
95SPChaDC-36
95Spo-94

95SpoArtP-94
95SPSil-45
95SPSpeF-32
95StaClu-35
95StaClu-211
95StaClu-407
95StaClu-498
95StaCluFDI-35
95StaCluFDI-211
95StaCluMOP-35
95StaCluMOP-211
95StaCluMOP-407
95StaCluMOP-498
95StaCluMOP-SS17
95StaCluSS-SS17
95StaCluSTDW-RE3T
95StaCluSTDW-RE35
95StaCluSTWS-35
95StaCluSTWS-211
95StaCluSTWS-407
95StaCluSTWS-498
95StaCluVR-24
95Stu-37
95StuGolS-37
95Sum-10
95SumNthD-10
95SumSam-10
95TomPiz-25
95Top-350
95TopCyb-189
95UC3-26
95UC3ArtP-26
95Ult-145
95UltAllS-10
95UltAllSGM-10
95UltAwaW-14
95UltAwaWGM-14
95UltGolM-145
95UppDec-405
95UppDecED-405
95UppDecEDG-405
95UppDecSE-163
95UppDecSEG-163
95Zen-4
96Baz-97
96Bow-18
96BowBes-66
96BowBesAR-66
96BowBesMI-4
96BowBesMIAR-4
96BowBesMIR-4
96BowBesP-BBP17
96BowBesPAR-BBP17
96BowBesPR-BBP17
96BowBesR-66
96Cir-117
96CirAcc-17
96CirBos-31
96CirRav-117
96ColCho-276
96ColCho-401
96ColCho-520
96ColCho-707
96ColChoGS-276
96ColChoGS-401
96ColChoGS-520
96ColChoGS-707
96ColChoSS-276
96ColChoSS-401
96ColChoSS-520
96ColChoSS-707
96ColChoYMtP-20
96ColChoYMtP-20A
96ColChoYMtPGS-20
96ColChoYMtPGS-20A
96DenHol-13
96Don-442
96DonPreP-442
96EmoXL-165
96Fin-B167
96Fin-B319
96Fin-S7
96FinRef-B167
96FinRef-B319
96FinRef-S7
96Fla-234
96Fle-345
96FleTeaL-17
96FleTif-345
96FleUpd-U230
96FleUpdTC-U230
96Kin-15
96Lea-122
96LeaGolS-13
96LeaHatO-2
96LeaLim-43
96LeaLimG-43
96LeaPre-38
96LeaPreP-38
96LeaPrePB-122
96LeaPrePG-122
96LeaPrePS-122
96LeaPreSG-69
96LeaPreSte-69
96LeaSig-42
96LeaSigPPG-42
96LeaSigPPP-42
96MetUni-149
96MetUniP-149
96Pac-40
96Pac-50
96PacPri-P16
96PacPriG-P16
96PanSti-49
96Pin-90
96PinAfi-38
96PinAfiAP-38
96PinAfiFPP-38
96PinArtP-51
96PinFan-18
96PinFirR-15
96PinSta-51
96PinTeaP-4
96ProMagA-19
96ProMagDM-9
96ProSta-101
96Sco-5
96Sco-362
96Sco-516
96ScoDugC-A5
96ScoDugC-B87
96ScoDugCAP-A5
96ScoDugCAP-B87
96ScoGolS-14
96ScoRef-10
96ScoSam-5
96Sel-32
96SelArtP-32
96SelCer-41
96SelCerAP-41
96SelCerCB-41
96SelCerCR-41
96SelCerIP-24
96SelCerMB-41
96SelCerMG-41
96SelCerMR-41
96SelTeaN-25
96SP-63
96SPMarM-MM11
96SPMarMDC-11
96Spo-60
96SpoArtP-60
96SpoDouT-1
96SPSpeFX-9
96SPSpeFXDC-9
96SPx-17
96SPxGol-17
96StaClu-197
96StaClu-271
96StaCluEPB-271
96StaCluEPG-271
96StaCluEPS-271
96StaCluEWB-EW6
96StaCluEWG-EW6
96StaCluEWS-EW6
96StaCluMM-MM6
96StaCluMO-20
96StaCluMOP-197
96StaCluMOP-271
96StaCluMOP-MM6
95StaCluVRMC-24
96Stu-26
96StuPrePB-26
96StuPrePG-26
96StuPrePS-26
96Sum-108
96SumAbo&B-108
96SumArtP-108
96SumFoi-108
96SumPos-4
96TeaOut-49
96Top-6
96Top-293
96TopBroLL-1
96TopChr-6
96TopChr-116
96TopChrR-6
96TopChrR-116
96TopGal-169
96TopGalE-20
96TopGalPPI-169
96TopLas-84
96TopLasSS-5
96TopPowB-6
96TopPro-NL17
96Ult-179
96Ult-583
96UltGolM-179
96UltGolM-583
96UltPriL-13
96UltPriLGM-13
96UppDec-219
96UppDec-310
96UppDecA-11
96UppDecDD-DD15
96UppDecDDG-DD15
96UppDecDDS-DD15
96UppDecPHE-H37
96UppDecPRE-R58
96UppDecPreH-H37
96UppDecPreR-R58
96Zen-19
96ZenArtP-19
96ZenMoz-10
97Bow-9
97BowBes-30
97BowBesAR-30
97BowBesMI-MI1
97BowBesMIAR-MI1
97BowBesMIARI-MI1
97BowBesMII-MI1
97BowBesMIR-MI1
97BowBesMIRI-MI1
97BowBesR-30
97BowChr-7
97BowChrI-7
97BowChrIR-7
97BowChrR-7
97BowInt-9
97Cir-332
97CirRav-332
97ColCho-80
97ColChoAC-22
97ColChoS-11
97ColChoTBS-17
97ColChoTBSWH-17
97ColChoTotT-T12
97Don-23
97Don-441
97DonArmaD-15
97DonDom-17
97DonEli-88
97DonEliGS-88
97DonLim-10
97DonLim-61
97DonLim-131
97DonLim-153
97DonLimFotG-41
97DonLimLE-10
97DonLimLE-61
97DonLimLE-131
97DonLimLE-153
97DonPre-109
97DonPre-185
97DonPreCttC-109
97DonPreCttC-185
97DonPreP-23
97DonPreP-441
97DonPrePGold-23
97DonPrePGold-441
97DonTeaSMVP-8
97Fin-66
97Fin-157
97Fin-323
97FinEmb-157
97FinEmb-323
97FinEmbR-157
97FinEmbR-323
97FinRef-66
97FinRef-157
97FinRef-323
97FlaSho-A32
97FlaSho-B32
97FlaSho-C32
97FlaShoHG-8
97FlaShoLC-32
97FlaShoLC-B32
97FlaShoLC-C32
97FlaShoLCM-A32
97FlaShoLCM-B32
97FlaShoLCM-C32
97Fle-296
97Fle-706
97Fle-727
97FleTeaL-17
97FleTif-296
97FleTif-706
97FleTif-727
97Lea-55
97Lea-365
97LeaFraM-55
97LeaFraM-365
97LeaFraMDC-55
97LeaFraMDC-365
97LeaGolS-23
97LeaKnoG-11
97LeaLeaotN-8
97MetUni-47
97NewPin-116
97NewPinAP-116
97NewPinMC-116
97NewPinPP-116
97Pac-271
97PacLigB-271
97PacPri-93
97PacPriLB-93
97PacPriP-93
97PacSil-271
97Pin-109
97PinArtP-109
97PinCer-25
97PinCerMBlu-25
97PinCerMG-25
97PinCerMR-25
97PinCerR-25
97PinIns-112
97PinInsCE-112
97PinInsDD-11
97PinInsDE-112
97PinMin-27
97PinMinB-27
97PinMinCB-27
97PinMinCG-27
97PinMinCGR-27
97PinMinCN-27
97PinMinCS-27
97PinMinG-27
97PinMinS-27
97PinMusC-109
97PinTotCPB-25
97PinTotCPG-25
97PinTotCPR-25
97PinX-P-31
97PinX-PMoS-31
97PinX-PSfF-46
97PinX-PSfFU-46
97ProMag-8
97ProMagML-8
97Sco-242
97Sco-538
97ScoHobR-538
97ScoPreS-242
97ScoResC-538
97ScoShoS-242
97ScoShoS-538
97ScoShoSAP-242
97ScoShoSAP-538
97Sel-92
97SelArtP-92
97SelRegG-92
97SkyE-X-64
97SkyE-XC-64
97SkyE-XEC-64
97SP-55
97SPMarM-MM18
97SpoIll-99
97SpoIllEE-99
97SPSpeF-19
97SPx-19
97SPxBro-19
97SPxGraF-19
97SPxSil-19
97SPxSte-19
97StaClu-17
97StaClul-I8
97StaCluMat-17
97StaCluMOP-17
97StaCluMOP-I8
97StaCluMOP-PL9
97StaCluPL-PL9
97Stu-9
97StuHarH-11
97StuPrePG-9
97StuPrePS-9
97Top-420
97TopAll-AS10
97TopChr-149
97TopChrAS-AS10
97TopChrR-149
97TopChrSAR-AS10
97TopGal-34
97TopGalPG-PG16
97TopGalPPI-34
97TopIntF-ILM6
97TopIntFR-ILM6
97TopSta-15
97TopStaAM-15
97Ult-177
97UltFieC-10
97UltGolME-177
97UltPlaME-177
97UppDec-45
97UppDecU-34
97Zen-9

Larkin, Gene

85VisOakT-14
86OrlTwiP-10
87DonRoo-23
87FleUpd-59
87FleUpdG-59
87PorBeaP-19
87SpoRoo2-34
87TopTra-60T
87TopTraT-60T
88Don-564
88DonBasB-158
88Fle-14
88FleGlo-14
88OPC-384
88PanSti-145
88RedFolSB-47
88Sco-276
88ScoGlo-276
88Spo-107
88StaLinTw-11
88Top-746
88TopBig-264
88TopSti-279
88TopTif-746
88TwiSmoC-5
88TwiTeal-6
89Bow-160
89BowTif-160
89Don-355
89Fle-117
89FleGlo-117
89PanSti-388
89Sco-280
89ScoYouS2-6
89Top-318
89TopBig-226
89TopSti-294
89TopTif-318
89UppDec-580
90ClaYel-T53
90Don-436
90Fle-379
90FleCan-379
90Lea-215
90OPC-556
90PubSti-331
90Sco-276
90Top-556
90TopBig-302
90TopSti-291
90TopTif-556
90UppDec-471
90VenSti-286
91Don-152
91Fle-615
91Lea-157
91OPC-102
91PanFreS-306
91PanSti-246
91Sco-471
91StaClu-132
91Top-102
91TopDesS-102
91TopMic-102
91TopTif-102
91Ult-190
91UppDec-501
92Bow-479
92Don-496
92Fle-207
92Lea-415
92OPC-284
92Pin-435
92Sco-272
92ScoFacI-B7

92StaClu-66
92Top-284
92TopGol-284
92TopGolW-284
92TopMic-284
92UppDec-187
93Don-575
93Fle-269
93PacSpa-173
93Sco-444
93StaClu-42
93StaCluFDI-42
93StaCluMOP-42
93Top-61
93TopGol-61
93TopInaM-61
93TopMic-61
93Ult-584
93UppDec-540
93UppDecGold-540
94Fle-211
94Pac-358
94Sco-288
94ScoGolR-288
Larkin, Jim
94UtiBluSF-3828
Larkin, Pat
84EvaTriT-5
Larkin, Stephen
34Gou-92
Larkin, Steve
94TopTra-56T
95ChaRivTI-6
94HudValRF-3399
94HudValRC-10
Larkin, Ted (Henry)
87OldJudN-299
90KalBatN-28
90KalBatN-40
LaRocca, Greg
94SpoIndC-16
94SpoIndF-3331
95Bes-98
95RanCucQT-18
95SPML-142
96Exc-237
96MemChiB-21
LaRocca, Todd
95SigRoo-29
95SigRooSig-29
LaRoche, Dave
71OPC-174
71Top-174
72OPC-352
72Top-352
73OPC-426
73Top-426
74OPC-502
74Top-502
74WicAerODF-107
75OPC-258
75Top-258
76OPC-21
76SSP-510
76Top-21
77BurCheD-60
77MSADis-34
77OPC-61
77PepGloD-15
77RCColC-33
77Top-385
78AngFamF-23
78RCColC-22
78SSP270-197
78Top-454
79OPC-317
79Top-601
80Top-263
81Fle-285
81Top-529
81TopTra-789
82Don-569
82Top-142
83Fle-384
83OPC-333
83OPC-334
83Top-333
83Top-334
85AlbYanT-24
86ColCliP-25
86ColCliP-13
87SyrChiP-1946
87SyrChiT-24
89PacSenL-97
89T/MSenL-65
89TopSenL-89
90SweBasG-108
90WhiSoxC-30
91WhiSoxK-NNO
92MetColP-36
92MetKah-28
94PitMetC-26
94PitMetF-3539
LaRock, Scott
94BenRocF-3588
95SalAvaTI-20
96SalAvaB-18
97BenRocC-14
LaRocque, Gary
76BurBeeT-20
77HolMilT-18
88BakDodCLC-262
Larocque, Michel
72Dia-84
LaRosa, Bill
78AshTouT-13
Larosa, John
87UtiBluSP-23
88SpaPhiP-1031
88SpaPhiS-10
89PacSenL-43
89SpaPhiP-1054
89SpaPhiS-12
LaRosa, Mark
88CapCodPPaLP-77
91JamExpC-15
91JamExpP-3541
91LSUTigP-9
92AlbPolC-9
92AlbPolF-2300
93WesPalBEC-11
93WesPalBEF-1334
94ExcFS7-227
Larose, Claude
72Dia-85
72Dia-86
Larose, Steve
87LitFalMP-2387
88ColMetGS-6
89St.LucMS-13
90JacMetGS-8
91JacGenLD-566
91JacGenP-924
91LinDriAA-566
92JacGenS-337
LaRose, Vic
69Top-404
Larreal, Guillermo
96BelGiaTI-25
Larregui, Ed
90HunCubP-3300
91GenCubC-11
91GenCubP-4231
92ClaFS7-221
92MidLeaATI-27
92PeoChiC-13
92PeoChiTI-11
93DayCubC-12
93DayCubF-869
94DayCubC-14
94DayCubF-2366
96Exc-139
96OrlCubB-15
96SigRooOJ-16
96SigRooOJS-16
95OrlCubF-22
Larsen, Bill
88RocExpLC-21
Larsen, Don
47Exh-131
54Bow-101
54OriEss-22
55Bow-67
56Top-251
56Top-332
57Top-175
57YanJayP-6
58Top-161
58YanJayP-5
59Top-205
59Top-383
60A's-5
60A'sJayP-6
60NuHi-18
60Top-353
61A'sTeal-12
61NuSco-418
61Top-177
61Top-402
62Top-33
62TopVen-33
63Top-163
64Top-513
65Top-389
68LauWorS-53
72LauGreF-45
76ISCHooHA-13
76LauDiaJ-17
77GalGloG-3
77Spo-6204
78TCM60I-211
78TCM60I-266
79DiaGre-21
79TCM50-272
86TCMSupS-45
87AstSer1-15
87AstSer1-24
87AstShoSTw-28
87HygAllG-30
88PacLegI-42A
88PacLegI-42B
90BasWit-7
90HOFStiB-54
91OriCro-255
93ActPacA-144
94UppDecTAE-64
95SkiBra-1
97FleMilDM-23
Larsen, Jim
86EugEmeC-36
Larson, Dan
77Top-641
81OklCit8T-7
83IowCubT-6
84ButCopKT-14
84OklCit8T-6
86KinEagP-14
86WauTimP-12
87BurExpP-1092
87SalSpuP-15
91MarPhiC-3
91MarPhiP-3468
93SpaPhiC-17
93SpaPhiF-1068
Larson, Duane
80KnoBluJT-27
82SyrChiT-27A
Larson, Jamie
85AncGlaPTI-36
86AncGlaPTI-40
Larson, Joe
92JohCitCC-16
92JohCitCF-3110
93GleFalRC-18
93GleFalRF-3999
Larson, Kirk
92AubAstC-13
92AubAstF-1360
Larson, Lance
89AncBucTI-6
Larson, Mike (Michael)
88BoiHawP-1620
89BoiHawP-2003
90EriSaiS-12
Larson, Toby
94PitMetC-13
94PitMetF-3519
95StLucMTI-20
LaRue, Jason
95BilRedTI-3
LaRussa, Tony
64Top-244
64TopVen-244
68Top-571
72OPC-451
72Top-451
73WicAerKSB-6
78KnoKnoST-11
78TCM60I-229
79IowOakP-1
80Top-112
81Don-402
81Fle-344
81Top-664
82Don-319
83Don-571
83Top-216
83WhiSoxTV-10
84Fle-649
84FleSti-126
84Nes792-591
84Top-591
84TopTif-591
84WhiSoxTV-8
84WhiSoxTV-20
85Top-466
85TopTif-466
85WhiSoxC-10
86Top-531
86TopTif-531
86WhiSoxC-NNO
87ModA'sC-A1
87Top-68
87TopTif-68
88A'sMot-1
88Top-344
88TopTif-344
89A'sMot-1
89PacLegI-140
89Top-224
89TopBasT-132
89TopTif-224
90A'sMot-1
90K-M-33
90OPC-639
90PacLeg-90
90Top-639
90TopGloA-12
90TopTif-639
90TopTVA-33
91A'sMot-1
91OPC-171
91Stu-263
91Top-171
91TopDesS-171
91TopGloA-1
91TopMic-171
91TopTif-171
92AthMot-1
92OPC-429
92Top-429
92TopGol-429
92TopGolW-429
92TopMic-429
93AthMot-1
93Top-511
93TopGol-511
93TopInaM-511
93TopMic-511
94A'sMot-1
95AthMot-1
96CarPol-15
Lary, Al
77FriOneYW-118
Lary, Frank
55Bow-154
56Top-191
57Top-168
58Top-245
59Top-393
60Lea-3
60TigJayP-8
60Top-85
60TopTat-28
60TopVen-85
61Pos-38A
61Pos-38B
61TigJayP-10
61Top-48
61Top-50
61Top-243
61TopStal-153
62Jel-22
62Pos-22
62PosCan-22
62SalPlaC-58
62ShiPlaC-58
62TigJayP-8
62Top-57
62Top-474
62TopBuc-49
62TopStal-48
62TopVen-57
63Fle-14
63Jel-55
63Pos-55
63TigJayP-9
63Top-140
63Top-218
64TigJayP-7
64TigLid-8
64Top-197
64TopVen-197
65OPC-127
65Top-127
78TCM60I-253
79DiaGre-398
79TCM50-183
81TigDetN-125
91MetWIZ-225
Lary, Lyn (Lynford H.)
31Exh-26
33Gou-193
35GouPuzR-1C
35GouPuzR-2C
35GouPuzR-16C
35GouPuzR-17C
36GouWidPPR-A62
90DodTar-434
91ConTSN-318
Lasbury, Robert
93BenRocC-15
93BenRocF-3263
94AshTouC-14
94AshTouF-1774
Lasek, Jim
77SpaPhiT-8
Laseke, Eric
85ElmPioT-10
86WinHavRSP-14
87WinHavRSP-7
89WinHavRSS-12
Laseter, Tom
75WatRoyT-19
76WatRoyT-17
Lash, Herbie
52LaPat-8
Lasher, Fred
68TigDetFPB-9
68Top-447
69Top-373
70OPC-356
70Top-356
71MLBOffS-347
71OPC-707
71Top-707
72MilBra-194
88TigDom-10
Lashley, Mickey
77CliDodT-15
78LodDodT-12
Laskey, Bill
80OmaRoyP-16
81OmaRoyT-10
83Don-424
83Fle-264
83FleSta-101
83FleSti-57
83GiaMot-15
83OPC-218
83Top-171
83Top-518
83TopSti-325
84Don-358
84Fle-376
84GiaPos-10
84Nes792-129
84OPC-129
84Top-129
84TopSti-172
84TopTif-129
85Don-387
85Fle-612
85GiaMot-9
85GiaPos-18
85OPC-331
85Top-331
85TopTif-331
86Don-585
86Fle-251
86GiaMot-24
86OPC-281
86Top-603
86TopTif-603
87TolMudHP-21
87TolMudHT-4
88IndGat-17
90CMC-300
90ProAAAF-399
90RicBraBC-3
90RicBraC-24
90RicBraP-254
90RicBraTI-18
Lasky, Larry
85OscAstTI-27
86AshTouP-17
87ColAstP-21
88ColAstB-15
89TucTorP-182
Lasorda, Tom

50WorWidGV-45
52Par-58
53ExhCan-50
54Top-132
55DodGolS-23
58MonRoyF-13
73OPC-569
73Top-569
74OPC-144
74Top-144
77Spo-7509
77Top-504
78SSP270-63
78Top-189
79DodBlu-7
79Top-526
80Top-302
81DodPol-2
81DodPol-NNO
81Don-420
81Fle-116
81LonBeaPT-26
81Top-679
82DodPol-2
82DodPos-5
82DodUniOV-10
82DogBuiE-5
82Don-110
82FleSta-111
83DodPol-2
83DodPos-7
83Don-136
83Top-306
84DodPol-2
84Fle-651
84FleSti-124
84Nes792-681
84Top-681
84TopTif-681
85DodCokP-18
85SpoIndGC-12
85Top-601
85TopTif-601
86DodCokP-16
86DodPol-2
86DodUniOP-10
86Top-291
86TopTif-291
87DodMot-1
87DodPol-1
87DodPol-29
87DodSmoA-17
87Top-493
87TopTif-493
88DodMot-1
88DodPol-2
88DodPol-NNO
88DodSmo-23
88RinPosD1-1B
88Top-74
88TopTif-74
89DodMot-1
89DodPol-1
89DodPol-2
89DodStaSV-10
89OPCBoxB-H
89Top-254
89TopBasT-54
89TopTif-254
89TopWaxBC-H
90DodMot-1
90DodPol-1
90DodPol-NNO
90DodTar-435
90OPC-669
90OPCBoxB-G
90Top-669
90TopGloA-1
90TopTif-669
90TopWaxBC-G
91DodMot-1
91DodPol-NNO
91OPC-789
91Stu-262
91Top-789
91TopDesS-789
91TopMic-789
91TopTif-789
92DodMot-1
92DodPol-2
92DodPol-NNO
92DodSmo-5092
92DodStaTA-18
92DodStaTA-22
92DodUno7P-5
92OPC-261
92Top-261
92TopGol-261
92TopGolPS-261
92TopGolW-261
92TopMic-261
92TopPreS-798
93DodMot-1
93DodPol-14
93DodPol-30
93Top-507
93TopGol-507
93TopInaM-507
93TopMic-507
94DodMot-1
94DodPol-15
94DodPol-30
94TopArc1-132
94TopArc1G-132
95DodMot-1
95DodPol-13
95DodPol-30
95TopArcBD-75
95TopArcBD-115
96DodMot-1
96DodPol-8
96DodPol-22
96UppDec-478
97UppDec-221

Lassard, Paul
87Ft.LauYP-14

Lassiter, David
94BurIndC-30

Lata, Tim
88CapCodPPaLP-129
80HamRedS-20
90Bes-267
90SprCarB-16
91St.PetCC-29
91St.PetCP-2273

Latarola, Aaron
94CedRapKC-15

Latham, Bill
83LynMetT-3
84TidTidT-6
85MetColP-16
85TidTidT-10
86TwiTeal-25
87PorBeaP-18
87TidTidP-22
87TidTidT-28
91ColMetPI-2
91MetWIZ-226
92St.LucMCB-28
92St.LucMF-1765
93St.LucMC-27
94St.LucMC-28
94St.LucMF-1213
95BinMetTI-39
96BinBeeB-14
93St.LucMF-2938

Latham, Chris
91KisDodP-4194
92GreFalDSP-7
93YakBeaC-17
93YakBeaF-3899
94YakBeaC-9
94YakBeaF-3862
95Bes-76
95SPML-74
95VerBeaDTI-14
96Exc-178
96ExcCli-5

Latham, John
89WelPirP-17
90SalBucS-9
91AugPirC-9
91AugPirP-801

Latham, W. Arlie
09T206-206
10RedCroT-40
10SweCapPP-115
11T205-96
12HasTriFT-69
12T207-100
76SSP188WS-3
87BucN28-99
87LonJacN-8
87OldJudN-300A
87OldJudN-300B
87ScrDC-6
88SpoTimM-17
89EdgR.WG-2
89SFHaCN-11
94OriofB-55
95ConTSN-1383
95May-17

Lathers, Charles
11SpoLifM-62

Latimer, Tacks
90DodTar-1010

Latimer, William
92HunCubC-20
92HunCubF-3144

Latman, Barry
59Top-477
60IndJayP-5
60Top-41
60TopVen-41
60WhiSoxTS-10
61Top-560
61TopStal-137
62IndJayP-7
62Kah-24
62Top-37
62Top-145
62TopStal-36
62TopVen-37
62TopVen-145
63IndJayP-10
63Top-426
64Top-227
64TopVen-227
65Top-307
66Top-451
67CokCapAs-5
67OPC-28
67Top-28
87AstShowSTh-11

Latmore, Dob
86MiaMarP-14
87MiaMarP-10
88HagSunS-10
89HagSunB-4
89HagSunP-271
89HagSunS-12
90EasLeaAP-EL34
90HagSunB-7
90HagSunP-1422
90HagSunS-12

Latta, Greg
85BufBisT-3
86BufBisP-15
87HawIsIP-25
89VanCanP-574
95NasSouTI-10
96NasSouB-4

Latter, Dave
89MedAthB-12
90MadMusB-18
90MadMusP-2264
91HunStaC-14
91HunStaLD-288
91HunStaP-1791
91HunStaTI-13
91LinDriAA-288
92HunStaF-3945
92HunStaS-313
93HunStaF-2080

Lattimore, William
09T206-436

Lau, Charley
58Top-448
60Top-312
61Top-261
62Top-533
63Top-41
64AthJayP-8
64Top-229
64TopVen-229
65OPC-94
65Top-94
66Top-368
66TopVen-368
67Top-329
73OPC-593
73Top-593
74Top-166
79YanPicA-23
91OriCro-256
94FUnPac-189

Lau, David
87ColMetP-5
88ColMetGS-13
89St.LucMS-14

Laubhan, John
77CedRapGT-NNO

Lauck, Jeff
84SavCarT-2

Laudenslager, Kevin
90GeoColC-17

Laudner, Tim
80OrlTwiT-12
82Don-549
82OrlTwi8SCT-8
82Top-766
83Don-177
83Fle-618
83Top-529
83TopSti-93
83TopSti-314
83TwiTeal-10
83TwiTeal-31
83TwiTeal-32
84Fle-569
84MinTwiP-18
84Nes792-363
84Top-363
84TopTif-363
84TwiTeal-11
85Don-652
85Fle-283
85Top-71
85TopTif-71
85Twi7-12
85TwiTeal-11
86Don-391
86Fle-398
86Top-184
86TopTif-184
86TwiTeal-10
87Don-320
87Fle-546
87FleGlo-546
87OPC-392
87Top-206
87Top-478
87TopTif-206
87TopTif-478
88Don-631
88Fle-15
88FleGlo-15
88OPC-78
88PanSti-135
88Sco-153
88ScoGlo-153
88StaLinTw-12
88Top-671
88TopBig-243
88TopSti-278
88TopTif-671
88TwiMasBD-5
88TwiSmoC-7
88TwiTeal-9
89Bow-154
89BowTif-154
89Don-615
89DonAll-19
89Fle-118
89FleGlo-118
89OPC-239
89PanSti-384
89Sco-134
89Spo-152
89Top-239
89TopSti-290
89TopTif-239
89UppDec-62
90Don-419
90Fle-380
90FleCan-380
90OPC-777
90PubSti-332
90Sco-318
90Top-777
90TopBig-218
90TopTif-777
90UppDec-419
90VenSti-287

Lauer, John Charles
87OldJudN-301

Laureano, Frank (Francisco)
86BurExpP-13
87AppFoxP-7
88VirGenS-13
89BasCitRS-15
90MemChiB-7
90MemChiP-1018
90MemChiS-13
91LinDriAAA-338
91OmaRoyLD-338
91OmaRoyP-1043

Laurent, Rick (Milfred)
93NegLeaRL2-22

Lauterhahn, Michael
94HunCubF-3568
94HunCubC-18

Lauzerique, George
69Top-358
70BreMcD-16
70OPC-41
70Top-41
75DubPacT-27
76DubPacT-19
76DubPacT-40
94BreMilB-51

Lavagetto, Cookie (Harry)
34BatR31-51
36GouWidPPR-A63
36NatChiFPR-51
36OveCanR-29
39PlaBal-74
40DodTeal-14
40PlaBal-69
41DouPlaR-17
46SpoExcW-7-7
47TipTop-99
48SigOil-13
49RemBre-15
50RemBre-15
52Top-365
58SenJayP-5
59Top-74
59TopVen-74
60SenJayP-9
60Top-221
61Top-226
61TwiPetM-10
61TwiUniMC-9
81TCM60I-482
82Bow195E-266
82MetGal62-27
83TopRep5-365
88RinPosD1-10A
88RinPosD1-11C
89DodSmoG-40
90DodTar-436
90HOFStiB-43
95ConTSN-1411
95TopArcBD-27

LaValley, Todd
92YakBeaC-17
92YakBeaF-3444

LaValliere, Mike
83ReaPhiT-12
85LouRedR-22
86CarSchM-14
86DonRoo-35
86FleUpd-65
87Don-331
87Fle-302
87FleGlo-302
87FleUpd-60
87FleUpdG-60
87Top-162
87TopTif-162
87TopTra-61T
87TopTraT-61T
87ToyRoo-19
88Don-312
88DonBasB-129
88Fle-333
88FleGlo-333
88FleSlu-25
88Lea-112
88OPC-57
88PanSti-369
88Sco-421
88ScoGlo-421
88Spo-193
88StaLinPi-13
88Top-539
88TopBig-61
88TopSti-131
88TopTif-539
89Bow-417
89BowTif-417
89Don-244
89DonBasB-201
89Fle-213
89FleGlo-213
89OPC-218
89PanSti-168
89PirVerFJ-12

89RedFolSB-74
89Sco-33
89Spo-98
89Top-218
89TopBasT-126
89TopBig-306
89TopSti-128
89TopStiB-56
89TopTif-218
89UppDec-417
90Bow-172
90BowTif-172
90ClaBlu-42
90Don-211
90DonBesN-107
90DonLeaS-43
90Fle-473
90FleCan-473
90Lea-32
90OPC-478
90PanSti-333
90PirHomC-18
90PubSti-158
90Sco-116
90Spo-157
90Top-478
90TopBig-104
90TopSti-133
90TopTif-478
90TopTVA-57
90UppDec-578
90VenSti-288
91Bow-514
91Don-121
91Fle-42
91Lea-15
91OPC-665
91PanFreS-114
91Sco-222
91StaClu-279
91Stu-226
91Top-665
91TopDesS-665
91TopMic-665
91TopTif-665
91Ult-282
91UppDec-129
92Bow-245
92Don-121
92Fle-558
92FleAll-5
92Lea-228
92OPC-312
92PanSti-251
92Pin-146
92PirNatI-10
92Sco-38
92StaClu-216
92StaCluD-103
92Stu-85
92Top-312
92TopGol-312
92TopGolW-312
92TopMic-312
92TriPla-232
92Ult-254
92UppDec-113
93Don-306
93Fle-114
93FleFinE-196
93Lea-510
93OPC-145
93PacSpa-246
93PanSti-280
93Pin-219
93Sco-83
93Sel-203
93StaClu-496
93StaCluFDI-496
93StaCluMOP-496
93Top-54
93TopGol-54
93TopInaM-54
93TopMic-54
93TriPla-110
93Ult-98
93UppDec-120
93UppDecGold-120
93WhiSoxK-17
94Don-201
94Fle-87
94Pac-131
94Sco-181
94ScoGolR-181
94StaClu-118
94StaCluFDI-118
94StaCluGR-118
94StaCluMOP-118
94StaCluT-124
94StaCluTFDI-124
94Top-147
94TopGol-147
94TopSpa-147
94WhiSoxK-19
95Don-517
95DonPreP-517
95Fla-26
95Fle-123
95Sco-168
95ScoGolR-168
95ScoPlaTS-168
95WhiSoxK-18

Lavan, Doc (John)
15SpoNewM-97
16BF2FP-43
16ColE13-95
16SpoNewM-99
19W514-4
21E121So1-54
21E121So8-50
21Exh-94
21Nei-102
22AmeCarE-39
22E120-233
22W573-71
22W575-70
23W501-109
23WilChoV-83

Lavelle, Gary
75OPC-624
75Top-624
76OPC-105
76SSP-96
76Top-105
77Gia-13
77Top-423
78Hos-32
78Top-671
79GiaPol-46
79Top-311
80GiaEurFS-2
80GiaPol-46
80Top-84
81Don-314
81Fle-448
81OPC-62
81Top-588
82Don-60
82Fle-392
82OPC-209
82Top-209
83Don-60
83Fle-265
83FleSta-102
83FleSti-52
83GiaMot-14
83OPC-376
83Top-791
83TopFol-4
84AllGamPI-82
84Don-573
84DonActAS-1
84Fle-377
84GiaMot-10
84GiaPos-11
84Nes792-145
84OPC-145
84Top-145
84TopSti-164
84TopTif-145
85BluJayFS-18
85Don-265
85Fle-613
85FleUpd-69
85Lea-114
85OPC-2
85OPCPos-24
85Top-462
85TopSti-159
85TopTif-462
85TopTifT-72T
85TopTra-72T
86BluJayAF-18
86BluJayFS-22
86Don-621
86Fle-65
86OPC-22
86Top-622
86TopTif-622
87BluJayFS-17

Lavenda, John
91CalLeLA-27

Lavender, Jeff
89TenTecGE-13

Lavender, Jimmy (James)
09SpoNewSM-91
09T206-437
13PolGroW-13
14CraJacE-105
15CraJacE-105
15SpoNewM-98
16BF2FP-67
16ColE13-96
16SpoNewM-100
92ConTSN-344

Lavender, Robert
88GasRanP-996
89ChaRanS-11

Lavenia, Mark
93HunCubC-16
93HunCubF-3233
94HunCubF-3548
95MacBraTI-16
94HunCubC-19

Laverty, Pat
93LetMouSP-23
95KanCouCTI-NNO

Laviano, Frank
90TamYanD-13
91OneYanP-4151
92GreHorC-6

Lavigne, Ben
92IdaFalGF-3515

Lavigne, Martin
91KisDodP-4179
93VerBeaDC-15
93VerBeaDF-2214

LaVigne, Randy
82lowCubT-6
83MidCubT-24

Lavoie, Marc
90AriWilP-11

Lavrusky, Chuck
87IdaFalBP-7
88BoiHawP-1621

Law, Joe
83IdaFalAT-14
84ModA'sC-17
85HunStaJ-40
87ModA'sC-10
87ModA'sP-19
89TacTigC-6
89TacTigP-1550
90CMC-587
90ProAAAF-135
90TacTigC-10
90TacTigP-88

Law, Rudy
77LodDodT-9
79AlbDukT-19
79Top-719
81AlbDukT-20
81DodPol-3
81Don-180
81Fle-139
81Top-127
83Don-521
83Fle-244
83FleSti-150
83Top-514
83WhiSoxTV-11
84Don-257
84Fle-67
84FleSti-93
84Nes792-47
84OPC-47
84Top-47
84TopSti-245
84TopTif-47
84WhiSoxTV-21
85Don-244
85Fle-519
85Lea-117
85OPC-286
85Top-286
85TopSti-241
85TopTif-286
85WhiSoxC-23
86Don-632
86Fle-211
86FleUpd-66
86OPC-6
86Top-637
86TopSti-291
86TopTif-637
86TopTra-62T
86TopTraT-62T
87Don-343
87Fle-372
87FleGlo-372
87Top-382
87TopTif-382
90DodTar-437

Law, Travis
88ButCopKSP-23
89ChaRanS-12

Law, Vance
79PorBeaT-5
80PorBeaT-9
81PorBeaT-14
81Top-551
82Don-582
82Fle-484
82Top-291
83Don-117
83Fle-245
83OPC-98
83Top-98
83WhiSoxTV-5
84AllGamPI-125
84Don-546
84Fle-68
84Nes792-667
84Top-667
84TopSti-249
84TopTif-667
84WhiSoxTV-22
85Don-122
85ExpPos-11
85Fle-520
85FleUpd-70
85Lea-183
85OPC-81
85Top-137
85Top-413
85TopSti-242
85TopTif-137
85TopTif-413
85TopTifT-73T
85TopTra-73T
86Don-132
86ExpProPa-23
86ExpProPo-12
86Fle-252
86GenMilB-6D
86Lea-57
86OPC-99
86Top-787
86TopSti-81
86TopTif-787
87Don-212
87DonOpeD-94
87ExpPos-13
87Fle-323
87FleGlo-323
87GenMilB-4D
87OPC-127
87Top-127
87TopTif-127
88CubDavB-2
88CubVanLS-1
88CubVanLS-2
88CubVanLS-3
88Don-212
88DonBasB-60
88DonTeaBC-NEW
88Fle-187
88FleGlo-187
88FleUpd-79
88FleUpdG-79
88OPC-346
88PanSti-324
88Sco-85
88ScoGlo-85
88ScoRoo-16T
88ScoRooG-16T
88Spo-41
88StaLinE-9
88Top-111
88Top-346
88TopTif-111
88TopTif-346
88TopTra-60T
88TopTraT-60T
89Bow-293
89BowTif-293
89CubMar-2
89Don-276
89DonAll-49
89Fle-430
89FleBasA-27
89FleGlo-430
89MSAHoID-12
89Nis-12A
89OPC-338
89PanSti-57
89Sco-102
89Spo-162
89Top-501
89TopBig-143
89TopSti-46
89TopStiB-42
89TopTif-501
89TVSpoM-24
89UppDec-473
90Don-629
90Fle-36
90FleCan-36
90OPC-287
90PubSti-197
90Sco-73
90Top-287
90TopTif-287
90UppDec-380
90VenSti-289
91A'sMot-12
91Bow-222
91Lea-355
91UppDec-760

Law, Vern (Vernon)
50PirTeal-10
51Bow-203
52Bow-71
52Top-81
54Bow-187
54Top-235
55Bow-199
56Top-252
57Top-199
58HirTes-5
58Kah-17
58Top-132
59Kah-18
59Top-12
59Top-428
59TopVen-12
60Kah-21
60KeyChal-30
60Top-453
60TopTat-29
61Kah-24
61NuSco-406
61PirJayP-7
61PirRigF-5
61Pos-126A
61Pos-126B
61Top-47
61Top-250
61Top-400
61TopStal-66
62Jel-179
62Pos-179
62PosCan-179
62Top-295
63Fle-58
63PirJayP-8
63Top-184
64PirKDK-15
64Top-472
65Top-515
66Baz-18
66OPC-15
66PirEasH-32
66Top-15
66Top-221
66TopRubI-51
66TopVen-15
66TopVen-221
67CokCapPi-16
67DexPre-123
67PirTeal-9
67Top-351
67TopPirS-11
78TCM60I-239
79DiaGre-371
79TCM50-42
79TCMJapPB-17
82PorBeaT-24
83TopRep5-81
85Top-137

85TopTif-137
87Pir196T-9
90PacLeg-37
91SweBasG-55
91TopArc1-324
92ActPacA-19
92BazQua5A-18
93UppDecAH-81
94TopArc1-235
94TopArc1G-235
Lawler, Brian
93SpaPhiF-1062
Lawler, Chris
92Min-10
Lawless, Thomas
80WatRedT-18
81WatRedT-14
82IndIndTI-15
83Don-400
83IndIndTI-12
83Top-423
84RedEnq-4
85CarTeal-20
86CarSchM-15
86CarTeal-25
86Top-228
86TopTif-228
87CarSmo-19
87Top-647
87TopTif-647
88CarSmo-15
88Top-183
88TopSti-22
88TopTif-183
88Woo-25
89BluJayFS-15
89Bow-255
89BowTif-255
89Top-312
89TopTif-312
90BluJayFS-15
90Don-681
90OPC-49
90PubSti-519
90Top-49
90TopTif-49
90VenSti-290
94CedRapKC-23
94CedRapKF-1124
96CedRapKTI-27
Lawn, Mike
91HelBreSP-4
92SalSpuC-8
92SalSpuF-3770
92StoPorF-49
Lawrence, Andy
85LynMetT-22
86JacMetT-16
87JacExpP-435
88JacExpB-19
88JacExpP-972
Lawrence, Bill
34DiaMatCSB-111
43CenFlo-17
Lawrence, Brooks
55Bow-75
55CarHunW-13
55RedMan-NL4
56Kah-10
56Top-305
57Kah-19
57RedSoh-13
57Top-66
58Kah-18
58RedEnq-24
58Top-374
59RedEnq-12
59RedShiBS-10
59Top-67
59TopVen-67
60Kah-22
60Lea-25A
60Lea-36
60Top-434
79TCM50-217
93UppDecS-8
Lawrence, Chip
96BluOriB-17
Lawrence, Clint
96StCatSB-16
Lawrence, Joe
96BesAutS1RP-FR6
97Bow-368
97BowChr-246
97BowChrI-246
97BowChrIR-246
97BowChrR-246
97BowInt-368
97Top-480
Lawrence, Matt
92HunCubC-14
92HunCubF-3145
Lawrence, Randy
92ElmPioC-7
92ElmPioF-1379
93ForLauRSC-16
93ForLauRSFP-1594
93UtiBluSC-13
93UtiBluSF-3529
Lawrence, Richard
95BilRedTI-26
Lawrence, Scott
86EriCarP-17
87SavCarP-25
88St.PetCS-12
89SprCarB-13
Lawrence, Sean
92WelPirC-16
92WelPirF-1319
93AugPirC-12
94CarLeaAF-CAR41
94SalBucC-14
94SalBucF-2320
95LynHilTI-12
95SigRoo-30
95SigRooSig-30
96CarMudB-4
Lawrenson, Scott
87LynMetP-27
90CMC-687
90TidTidC-30
Lawson, Cale
91BurIndP-3304
Lawson, David
92BelMarC-24
92BelMarF-1457
93AppFoxC-14
93AppFoxF-2472
94AppFoxF-1067
Lawson, Jim (James)
88SouOreAP-1712
89MadMusS-12
90MadMusB-19
90ModA'sCLC-152
90ModA'sP-2209
Lawson, Roxie (Alfred V.)
36WorWidGV-104
92ConTSN-513
Lawson, Steve
73OPC-612
73Top-612
93RanKee-23
Lawton, Alycia
91FreStaLBS-13
Lawton, Marcus
86LynMetP-14
87JacMetF-16
87MetColP-37
87TexLeaAF-24
88MetColP-30
88TidTidP-1591
89TidTidC-23
89TidTidP-1967
90CMC-643
90OPC-302
90ProAAAF-178
90Top-302
90TopDeb89-69
90TopTif-302
90VanCanC-16
90VanCanP-500
91LinDriAA-440
91MidAngLD-440
91MidAngOHP-16
91MidAngP-446
92MemChiS-438
92MidAngOHP-14
92SkyAA F-184
92YanWIZ8-103
96ColCho-34
Lawton, Matt
93ForWayWC-14
93ForWayWF-1982
94FloStaLAF-FSL10
94ForMyeMC-12
94ForMyeMF-1180
95HarCitRCTI-10
96Bow-261
96ColChoGS-34
96ColChoSS-34
96Don-432
96DonPreP-432
96Fin-B312
96FinRef-B312
96Fla-117
96Fle-167
96FleTif-167
96Lea-10
96LeaPre-145
96LeaPreP-145
96LeaPrePB-10
96LeaPrePG-10
96LeaPrePS-10
96LeaSigA-130
96LeaSigAG-130
96LeaSigAS-130
96Pac-354
96Pin-168
96PinAfi-184
96PinAfiAP-184
96Sco-495
96SelCer-131
96SelCerAP-131
96SelCerCB-131
96SelCerCR-131
96SelCerMB-131
96SelCerMG-131
96SelCerMR-131
96Spo-136
96SpoArtP-136
96StaClu-437
96StaCluMOP-437
96Ult-376
96UltGolM-376
96UppDooPHE H27
96UppDecPreH-H27
97ColCho-381
97Don-344
97DonLim-35
97DonLimLE-35
97DonPre-53
97DonPreCttC-53
97DonPreP-344
97DonPrePGold-344
97Fle-148
97FleTif-148
97Lea-217
97LeaFraM-217
97LeaFraMDC-217
97NewPin-126
97NewPinAP-126
97NewPinMC-126
97NewPinPP-126
97Pac-140
97PacLigB-140
97PacSil-140
97Sco-394
97ScoHobR-394
97ScoResC-394
97ScoShoS-394
97ScoShoSAP-394
97Top-428
97Ult-88
97UltGolME-88
97UltPlaME-88
Laxamana, Brian
90CalLeaACLC-34
91CalLeLA-50
Laxton, Brett
93LSUTigM-15
94LSUTig-8
94LSUTigMP-5
96SouOreTI-20
Laxton, William
75TidTidTI-15
76SSP-615
77Top-394
Lay, Shane
92HelBreF-1728
92HelBreSP-6
Laya, Jesus
87PocGiaTB-28
88PocGiaP-2096
89EveGiaS-19
93LinVenB-113
Layana, Tim
87AlbYanP-11
88AlbYanP-1333
89AlbYanB-5
89AlbYanP-329
89AlbYanS-9
89EasLeaAP-14
90AlbDecGB-11
90Bow-41
90BowTif-41
90ClaYel-T46
90DonRoo-23
90FleUpd-14
90Lea-410
90RedKah-14
90ScoRoo-107T
90TopTra-55T
90TopTraT-55T
90UppDec-717
91Bow-689
91Don-516
91Fle-69
91OPC-627
91Sco-64
91Sco100RS-54
91StaClu-396
91Top-627
91TopDeb90-82
91TopDesS-627
91TopMic-627
91TopTif-627
91UppDec-396
92RocRedWF-1933
92RocRedWS-460
92Sco-628
92StaClu-419
93PhoFirF-1512
94SanBerSF-2752
Laycoe, Hal
43ParSpo-46
Layne, Hillis
47CenFlo-15
47SigOil-80
00ChaLooLTI-21
Layne, Jason
96SpoIndB-15
Layne, Jerry
90T/MUmp-58
Layton, Tom
83KinBluJTI-11
87IowCubTI-8
Lazar, John Dan
69Top-439
70Top-669
72MilBra-195
Lazor, Joe
87CedRapRP-5
88ChaLooB-4
88SouLeaAJ-35
89ChaLooB-5
89ChaLooGS-15
90ChaLooGS-18
Lazor, John Paul
43RedSoxTI-13
49BowPCL-30
83TCMPla1945-20
Lazorko, Jack
80TulDriT-6
81TulDriT-19
83ElPasDT-23
84VanCanC-48
85PhoGiaC-176
85Top-317
85TopTif-317
86Don-628
86NasSouTI-15
87EdmTraP-2062
87FleUpd-61
87FleUpdG-61
87TopTra-62T
87TopTraT-62T
88Don-160
88EdmTraC-3
88EdmTraP-556
88Fle-494
88FleGlo-494
88Sco-437
88ScoGlo-437
88Top-601
88TopTif-601
89EdmTraC-1
89Fle-482
89FleGlo-482
89Top-362
89TopTif-362
90TulDriDGB-13
91PacSenL-113
94BreMilB-143
Lazzaro, Sam
93SalBucC-29
94SalBucC-28
95SalAvaTI-30
Lazzeri, Tony (Anthony)
26Exh-100
26SpoComoA-26
26SpoNewSM-4
27Exh-50
28PorandAR-A21
28PorandAR-B21
28StaPlaCE-43
28W502-29
28W513-79
28Yue-29
29ExhFou-25
31Exh-25
31W517-27
32OrbPinNP-107
32USCar-18
33CraJacP-15
33ExhFou-13
33Gou-31
33GouCanV-31
34BatR31-45
34DiaStaR-74
35ExhFou-13
35GouPuzR-4D
35GouPuzR-7D
35GouPuzR-12D
36ExhFou-13
36OveCanR-30
36R31Pre-L12
37ExhFou-13
37OPCBatUV-117
38BasTabP-20
40PlaBal-238
51R42SmaS-62
60ExhWriH-14
60Fle-31
61Fle-54
68LauWorS-23
69Baz-3
70FleWorS-23
71FleWorS-35
75ShaPiz-16
75YanDyn1T-30
75YanDyn1T-51
75YanDyn1T-52
77GalGloG-116
77GalGloG-191
80LauFamF-26
80PerHaloFP-209
80YanGreT-2
81ConTSN-11
83ConMar-18
87Yan192T-3
88ConAmeA-19
88ConSer3-17
90DodTar-438
91ConTSN-113
92YanWIZA-39
92YanWIZH-20
93ActPacA-101
93ActPacA2-35G
93ConTSN-761
93ConTSN-762
93ConTSN-911
93LegFoi-7
94ConTSN-1053
94ConTSNB-1053
95ConTSN-1412
Le Grand, Todd
95AusFut-19
Lea, Charles
79MemChiT-8
80ExpPos-13
80MemChiT-2
81ExpPos-3
81Fle-165
81OPC-293
81Top-293
82Don-320
82ExpHygM-11
82ExpPos-19
82Fle-193
82OPC-38
82Top-38
83AllGamPI-169
83Don-414
83ExpPos-11
83ExpStu-23
83Fle-286
83FleSta-103
83FleSti-266
83OPC-253
83Top-629

84AllGamPl-83
84Don-376
84ExpPos-16
84ExpStu-8
84Fle-278
84Nes792-421
84Nes792-516
84OPC-142
84OPC-332
84Top-421
84Top-516
84TopSti-98
84TopTif-421
84TopTif-516
85Don-21
85Don-177
85DonSupD-21
85Fle-401
85Fle-632
85Lea-21
85OPC-345
85OPCPos-10
85Top-345
85TopGloA-10
85TopGloS-30
85TopMin-345
85TopSti-84
85TopSti-182
85TopTif-345
86Don-376
86Fle-253
86Lea-172
86OPC-376
86Top-526
86TopTat-21
86TopTif-526
87WesPalBEP-668
88FleUpd-44
88FleUpdG-44
89Don-473
89Fle-119
89FleGlo-119
89Sco-501
89UppDec-81
91UppDecS-23
93ExpDonM-23

Lea, Corey
93LetMouF-4162
93LetMouSP-18

Leach, Chris
89WinHavRSS-13
90LynRedSTI-2
91LynRedSC-21
91LynRedSP-1211

Leach, Don
80ElmPioRST-19

Leach, Fred
09T206-207
09T206-208
10W555-43
11SpoLifM-252
11TurRedT-3
28Exh-21
28PorandAR-A22
28PorandAR-B22
29PorandAR-55
33Gou-179
79DiaGre-28
94ConTSN-1130
94ConTSNB-1130

Leach, Jay (Jalal)
90OneYanP-3420
90ProAaA-183
91Cla/Bes-270
91Ft.LauYC-27
91Ft.LauYP-2441
92PriWilCC-5
92PriWilCF-161
94ColCliF-2964
94ColCliP-17
94VenLinU-179
95ColCliMCTI-21
95ColCliP-15
95ColCliTI-15
96HarSenB-17

Leach, Jumaane
94SpoIndC-17
94SpoIndF-3320

Leach, Martin
82TulDriT-3
85WatIndT-13

Leach, Matthew
94EliTwiC-11
94EliTwiF-3725

Leach, Nick
96GreFalDB-18
96GreFalDTI-23

Leach, Rick
80EvaTriT-24
82Don-583
82Fle-272
82Top-266
83Don-81
83Fle-334
83Tig-17
83Top-147
84BluJayFS-22
84Fle-84
84FleUpd-71
84Nes792-427
84SyrChiT-6
84Top-427
84TopTif-427
84TopTra-71T
84TopTraT-71T
85Fle-112
85IntLeaAT-29
85OPC-52
85SyrChiT-11
85Top-593
85TopTif-593
86BluJayFS-23
86TopTra-63T
86TopTraT-63T
87BluJayFS-18
87Don-567
87Fle-234
87FleGlo-234
87FleUpd-63
87FleUpdG-63
87OPC-5
87SyrChi1A-7
87Top-716
87TopTif-716
88BluJayFS-17
88Don-518
88Fle-115
88FleGlo-115
88Lea-247
88OPC-323
88Sco-257
88ScoGlo-257
88StaLinBJ-11
88Top-323
88TopTif-323
89Bow-234
89BowTif-234
89Don-638
89Fle-237
89FleGlo-237
89OPC-284
89RanMot-16
89RanSmo-19
89Sco-540
89Top-682
89TopTif-682
89TopTra-68T
89TopTraT-68T
89UppDec-554
90Don-613
90Fle-305
90FleCan-305
90GiaMot-14
90Lea-436
90OPC-27
90PubSti-416
90Sco-426
90Top-27
90TopTif-27
90TopTra-56T
90TopTraT-56T
90UppDec-640
90VenSti-291
91Lea-136
93RanKee-227

Leach, Ron
80WatIndT-3

Leach, Terry
76BatRouCT-14
79SavBraT-19
81TidTidT-29
82TidTidT-14
82Top-623
83Don-634
83TidTidT-5
83Top-187
84RicBraT-19
84TidTidT-26
85TidTidT-2
86Fle-87
86TidTidP-15
86Top-774
86TopTif-774
87FleUpd-62
87FleUpdG-62
87MetColP-38
87TopTra-63T
87TopTraT-63T
88Don-603
88DonTeaBM-603
88Fle-139
88FleGlo-139
88MetColP-31
88MetKah-26
88OPC-391
88Sco-203
88ScoGlo-203
88Spo-139
88Top-457
88TopTif-457
89Don-502
89Fle-40
89FleGlo-40
89MetColP-38
89Sco-431
89ScoRoo-24T
89Top-207
89TopBig-96
89TopTif-207
89TopTra-69T
89TopTraT-69T
89UppDec-288
90Don-534
90Fle-111
90FleCan-111
90Lea-360
90OPC-508
90Sco-502
90ScoRoo-43T
90Top-508
90TopTif-508
90TopTra-57T
90TopTraT-57T
90UppDec-642
91Bow-340
91Don-715
91Fle-616
91MetWIZ-227
91Sco-556
91StaClu-397
92Don-484
92Fle-208
92Lea-486
92OPC-644
92Sco-296
92StaClu-778
92StaCluECN-778
92Top-644
92TopGol-644
92TopGolW-644
92TopMic-644
92UppDec-311
92WhiSoxK-34
93Don-720
93Fle-585
93Sco-479
93StaCluWS-29
93Top-443
93TopGol-443
93TopInaM-443
93TopMic-443
93UppDec-418
93UppDecGold-418
93WhiSoxK-18
94Don-441

Leach, Thomas
03BreE10-87
03WilCarE-20
06FanCraNL-25
08AmeCarE-81
08RosComP-152
09AmeCarE-68
09AmeCarE-69
09ColChiE-166
09PhiCarE-13
09SpoNewSM-24
10CouT21-168
10CouT21-169
10CouT21-170
10DarChoE-22
10DomDisP-67
10E12AmeCDC-21
10JuJuDE-24
10NadE1-29
10PirAmeCE-5
10PirHerP-7
10PirTipTD-5
10RedCroT-41
10RedCroT-130
10StaCarE-20
10SweCapPP-138
11E94-20
11MecDFT-23
11S74Sil-111
11SpoLifCW-215
11T205-97
12ColRedB-166
12ColTinT-166
12HasTriFT-30C
12T207-101
14CraJacE-41
14FatPlaT-23
15CraJacE-41
95ConTSN-1368

Leader, Ramon
77CocAstT-11
78DayBeaAT-13

Leahy, Pat
92ClaDraP-114
92EriSaiC-14
92EriSaiF-1615
93KanCouCC-10
93KanCouCF-912
93Top-641
93TopGol-641
93TopInaM-641
93TopMic-641
94BreCouMC-7
94BreCouMF-5
94FloStaLAF-FSL27
95PorSeaDTI-11
93KanCouCTI-11

Leahy, Tom (Thomas)
91MacBraC-3
91MacBraP-857
92DurBulC-18
92DurBulF-1095
92DurBulTI-25
93DurBulC-12
93DurBulF-482
93DurBulTI-20

Leake, Jon
85MiaHur-8
87SalLakTTT-24

Leal, Carlos
80UtiBluJT-27
80VenLeaS-54

Leal, Luis
80SyrChiTI-14
80VenLeaS-64
81OPC-238
81Top-577
82Don-255
82Fle-617
82OPC-368
82OPCPos-9
82Top-412
83Don-129
83Fle-432
83OPC-109
83Top-109
84AllGamPI-173
84BluJayFS-23
84Don-485
84Fle-160
84Nes792-783
84OPC-207
84Top-783
84TopSti-371
84TopTif-783
85BluJayFS-19
85Don-317
85Fle-113
85Lea-29
85OPC-31
85Top-622
85TopSti-361
85TopTif-622
86Don-315
86OPC-365
86SyrChiP-16
86Top-459
86TopTif-459
88SyrChiP-806
93LinVenB-112

Leaman, Jeff
95BatCliTI-20

Leandro, Francisco
80VenLeaS-195

Leard, Bill
90DodTar-1011

Leary, Rob
87WesPalBEP-652
88RocExpLC-22
89WesPalBES-15
90LSUTigGM-8
90RocExpLC-15
90RocExpP-2697
92MadMusC-6
92MadMusF-1243
92RocExpC-28
92RocExpF-2131
93MadMusC-18
93MadMusF-1829
93WesPalBEC-26
93WesPalBEF-1357
94WesPalBEC-28
94WesPalBEF-58
95LynHilTI-13

Leary, Timothy
82Top-623
83TidTidT-9
84JacMetF-7
85VanCanC-203
86BrePol-39
86Don-577
86TopTra-64T
86TopTraT-64T
87DodMot-21
87DodPol-11
87Don-232
87Fle-348
87FleGlo-348
87Top-32
87TopTif-32
87TopTra-64T
87TopTraT-64T
88AlaGolAA'TI-20
88DodMot-21
88DodPol-54
88Fle-521
88FleGlo-521
88Sco-224
88ScoGlo-224
88Top-367
88TopTif-367
89Bow-339
89BowTif-339
89DodMot-21
89DodPol-28
89Don-552
89DonBasB-309
89Fle-65
89FleExcS-30
89FleGlo-65
89OPC-249
89PanSti-99
89Sco-429
89ScoHot1S-9
89ScoRoo-52T
89Spo-81
89Top-249
89TopBig-17
89TopSti-62
89TopTif-249
89UppDec-94
90Bow-429
90BowTif-429
90DodTar-439
90Don-670
90DonBesA-53
90Fle-424
90FleCan-424
90Lea-148
90OPC-516
90PubSti-12
90Sco-504
90ScoRoo-27T
90Top-516
90TopTif-516
90TopTra-58T
90TopTraT-58T
90TopTVY-12
90UppDec-662
90UppDec-705
90VenSti-292
90YanScoNW-13
91Don-67
91Fle-670
91Lea-206

91MetWIZ-228
91OPC-161
91Sco-631
91StaClu-423
91Stu-95
91Top-161
91TopDesS-161
91TopMic-161
91TopTif-161
91Ult-236
91UppDec-693
92Don-433
92Fle-235
92OPC-778
92Pin-349
92Sco-286
92StaClu-291
92Top-778
92TopGol-778
92TopGolW-778
92TopMic-778
92Ult-411
93Don-289
93Fle-677
93MarMot-21
93PacSpa-624
94BreMilB-144
94Don-240
94Fle-291
94Sco-240
94ScoGolR-240

Leatherman, Jeff
91WelPirC-17
91WelPirP-3580
92AugPirC-22

Leatherwood, Anthony
90GeoColC-18

Leatherwood, Del
78DayBeaAT-14
80ColAstT-5
81TucTorT-2

Leavell, Gregg
91WelPirC-12
91WelPirP-3586

Lebak, David
91SpoIndC-7
91SpoIndP-3960
92ChaRaiC-14
92ChaRaiF-133

LeBlanc, Michael
88CapCodPPaLP-61
89BelMarL-7

LeBlanc, Richie
88BasCitRS-16
88FloStaLAS-42
90MemChiB-16
90MemChiP-1024
90MemChiS-14

Lebo, Mike
78DunBluJT-15

LeBoeuf, Alan
85PorBeaC-32
86PorBeaP-13
87MaiGuiP-22
87MaiGuiT-13
88ReaPhiP-864
89MarPhiS-35
90ClePhiS-27
91LinDriAA-525
91ReaPhiLD-525
91ReaPhiP-1386
92ScrRedBF-2463
92ScrRedBS-500
93BatCliC-29
93BatCliF-3163
94BatCliC-27
94BatCliF-3464

Lebron, David
78NewWayCT-25

LeBron, Jose
89BlaYNPRWL-142
89WatDiaP-1775
89WatDiaS-17
90Bes-37
90WatDiaB-27
90WatDiaP-2375
91HigDesMC-6
91HigDesMP-2389
92HigDesMC-22

LeBron, Juan
95Bes-127
95BowBes-X5
95BowBesR-X5
95SPML-108
95TopTra-12T
96Exc-61
96Top-17
96TopPowB-17

Lebron, Ruben
96LowSpiB-15
96MicBatCB-14

Leclair, Jean-Claude
72Dia-138

Leclair, Keith
88IdaFalBP-1850

LeClair, Morgan
90WicStaSGD-22

LeClair, Paul
94KinMetC-8
94KinMetF-3835
95PitMetTI-35

LeClaire, Frenchy (George)
12ImpTobC-3

LeCoste, Rene
28W513-100

LeCronier, Jason
96HigDesMB-17

Ledbetter, Gary
77CedRapGT-9

Ledbetter, Jeff
86ArkTraP-11

Leddon, Charles
95PitMetTI-NNO

Ledduke, Dan
79WesHavYT-9
80NasSouTI-12
81NasSouTI-7

Ledee, Ricky
90TamYanD-14
92GulCoaYF-3702
93OneYanC-13
93OneYanF-3516
94GreBatF-488
94SouAtlLAF-SAL15
95GreBatTI-14
96NorNavB-16
97Bow98ROY-ROY9
97BowBes-191
97BowBesAR-191
97BowBesR-191
97BowChr-103
97BowChr1RC-ROY9
97BowChr1RCR-ROY9
97BowChrI-103
97BowChrIR-103
97BowChrR-103
97Fle-560
97FleTif-560
97GreBatC-13

Ledeit, Richard
96OgdRapTI-49

Ledesma, Aaron
90KinMetB-1
90KinMetS-13
91ColMetPI-13
91ColMetPPI-6
92ClaFS7-275
92St.LucMCB-17
92St.LucMF-1755
93BinMetF-2342
93Bow-102
94NorTidF-2927
95NorTidTI-17
95SigRoo-31
95SigRooSig-31
96MetKah-20
96Sco-507
96VanCanB-19

Ledezma, Carlos
75WesPalBES-8
81BufBisT-8
82PorBeaT-26
84HawIslC-143
86HawIslP-15
87VanCanP-1601
88BufBisP-1481
88TriAAAP-48
89BufBisC-3
89BufBisP-1678
90BufBisTI-13

Ledinsky, Ray
91MiaMirC-22
91MiaMirP-416

Ledoux, Charley
28W512-50

Leduc, Jean
78ChaPirT-12

Ledwick, Shannon
91IdaFalBP-4324
91IdaFalBSP-16

Lee, Annabel
94UppDecTAE-53
94UppDecTAELD-LD8

Lee, Anthony
92AppFoxC-7
92AppFoxF-981
93PeoChiC-11
93PeoChiF-1081
93PeoChiTI-14
94DayCubC-15

Lee, Ben
87AppFoxP-13

Lee, Bob
64Top-502
65OPC-46
65Top-46
66Top-481
67Top-313
68Kah-B20
68Top-543
85VisOakT-15
86AngGreT-11
86KenTwiP-12
87VisOakP-6
88KenTwiP-1403
89KenTwiP-1058
90DodTar-440

Lee, Calvin
95OdgRapTI-14

Lee, Carlos
96BesAutS-48
96Exc-33
96HicCraB-11
96HicCraB-30

Lee, Charles
92JamExpC-12
92JamExpF-1513
94BurBeeC-13
94WesPalBEC-16
94WesPalBEF-56

Lee, Chong Bum
90IBAWorA-18

Lee, Chris
88AshTouP-1059

Lee, Corey
97Bow-376
97BowChr-250
97BowChrI-250
97BowChrIR-250
97BowChrR-250
97BowInt-376
97Top-270

Lee, David
87RocRedWT-14
88RocRedWC-17
96PorRocB-18

Lee, Derek
88UtiBluSP-7
89SouBenWSGS-27
90Bes-144
90BirBarB-10
90BirBarP-1118
90CMC-769
91BirBarLD-66
91BirBarP-1466
91Cla/Bes-272
91LinDriAA-66
92Bow-210
92SkyAAAF-285
92UppDecML-148
92VanCanF-2733
92VanCanS-642
93Bow-335
93PorBeaF-2394
94OttLynF-2908
95NorTidTI-18
96OklCit8B-13

Lee, Derrek
94ActPac-35
94Bow-232
94Cla-130
94ClaGolF-142
94ClaGolN1PLF-LP8
94ClaGolREF-RE8
94ClaTriF-T67
94ColC-645
94ColChoGS-645
94ColChoSS-645
94Pin-438
94PinArtP-438
94PinMusC-438
94RanCucQC-1
94RanCucQF-1645
94Sco-585
94ScoGolR-585
94SP-10
94SPDieC-10
94UppDec-539
94UppDecED-539
94UppDecML-116
95ARuFalLS-13
95Bes-100
95Bes-102
95BesFra-F10
95Bow-25
95BowBes-B22
95BowBesR-B22
95Exc-286
95RanCucQT-34
95SPML-140
95SPMLA-17
95SPMLDtS-DS12
95UppDecML-66
96Bow-278
96BowBes-160
96BowBesAR-160
96BowBesR-160
96Exc-238
96MemChiB-22
96Top-424
97Bow-292
97Bow98ROY-ROY11
97BowBes-178
97BowBesAR-178
97BowBesMI-MI2
97BowBesMIAR-MI2
97BowBesMIARI-MI2
97BowBesMII-MI2
97BowBesMIR-MI2
97BowBesMIRI-MI2
97BowBesR-178
97BowCerBIA-CA47
97BowCerGIA-CA47
97BowChr-200
97BowChr1RC-ROY11
97BowChr1RCR-ROY11
97BowChrI-200
97BowChrIR-200
97BowChrR-200
97BowChrSHR-SHR9
97BowChrSHRR-SHR9
97BowInt-292
97BowScoHR-9
97ColCho-476
97Don-383
97DonLim-96
97DonLim-100
97DonLimLE-96
97DonLimLE-100
97DonPreP-383
97DonPrePGold-383
97FlaSho-A80
97FlaSho-B80
97FlaSho-C80
97FlaShoLC-80
97FlaShoLC-B80
97FlaShoLC-C80
97FlaShoLCM-A80
97FlaShoLCM-B80
97FlaShoLCM-C80
97Fle-620
97FleTif-620
97Lea-321
97LeaFraM-321
97LeaFraMDC-321
97Sel-128
97SelArtP-128
97SelRegG-128
97SP-9
97Top-489
97Ult-541
97UltGolME-541
97UltGolP-10
97UltPlaME-541
97UppDec-543
95UppDecMLFS-66

Lee, Don
57Top-379
59Top-132
59TopVen-132
60Top-503
61Top-153
61TwiCloD-12
61TwiJayP-7
61TwiPetM-9
62Top-166
62TopVen-166
63AngJayP-7
63Fle-18
63Top-372
64Top-493
65Top-595

Lee, Dudley
21Exh-95

Lee, Eddie
79ElmPioRST-11

Lee, Greg
88PocGiaP-2086
89SalSpuCLC-141
89SalSpuP-1806

Lee, Hal
33ButCanV-30
34ButPreR-39
90DodTar-441

Lee, Harvey
86Ft.LauYP-14
87SanJosBP-5

Lee, Jason
96JohCitCTI-19

Lee, Jeremy
94ClaGolF-69
94St.CatBJC-15
94St.CatBJF-3639
94Top-206
94TopGol-206
94TopSpa-206
95HagSunF-64
96DunBluJUTI-7

Lee, John
76DubPacT-20
89CarNewE-17

Lee, Leon
72CedRapCT-24
75TulOil7-2
76TulOilGP-12
79TCMJapPB-70
87JapPlaB-4

Lee, Leron
70CarTeal-8
70DayDaiNM-140
70OPC-96
70Top-96
71MLBOffS-276
71OPC-521
71Top-521
72OPC-238
72PadTeal-17
72Top-238
73OPC-83
73Top-83
74OPC-651
74Top-651
75OPC-506
75Top-506
76OPC-487
76Top-487
79TCMJapPB-67
86SyrChiP-17
87JapPlaB-21
90DodTar-442

Lee, Manny
85BluJayFS-20
85FleUpd-71
86KnoBluJP-14
86OPC-23
86Top-23
86TopTif-23
87Don-518
87OPC-289
87SyrChiP-1941
87SyrChiT-16
87Top-574
87TopTif-574
88BluJayFS-18
88Don-650
88Fle-116
88FleGlo-116
88OPC-303
88Sco-561
88ScoGlo-561
88StaLinBJ-12
88Top-722
88TopTif-722
89BluJayFS-16
89Don-504
89Fle-238
89FleGlo-238
89OPC-371
89PanSti-468
89Sco-326

89Top-371
89TopBig-70
89TopTif-371
89UppDec-271
90BluJayFS-16
90Bow-512
90BowTif-512
90Don-620
90Fle-86
90FleCan-86
90Lea-370
90OPC-113
90PubSti-520
90Sco-482
90Top-113
90TopBig-219
90TopTif-113
90UppDec-285
90VenSti-293
91BluJayFS-16
91BluJayFS-17
91BluJayS-16
91Bow-21
91Don-211
91Fle-179
91Lea-399
91OPC-297
91PanFreS-337
91Sco-534
91StaClu-168
91Top-297
91TopDesS-297
91TopMic-297
91TopTif-297
91Ult-365
91UppDec-142
92Bow-421
92Don-499
92Fle-333
92Lea-382
92OPC-634
92PanSti-28
92Pin-245
92Sco-518
92StaClu-283
92Top-634
92TopGol-634
92TopGolW-634
92TopMic-634
92Ult-148
92UppDec-118
93BluJayD4-8
93Don-688
93Fle-337
93Lea-381
93OPC-320
93OPCWorC-9
93PacSpa-325
93Pin-493
93RanKee-413
93Sco-205
93Sel-380
93SelRoo-119T
93StaClu-713
93StaCluFDI-713
93StaCluM-118
93StaCluMOP-713
93StaCluR-18
93Top-488
93TopGol-488
93TopInaM-488
93TopMic-488
93Ult-631
93UppDec-205
93UppDec-637
93UppDecGold-205
93UppDecGold-637
94ColC-172
94ColChoGS-172
94ColChoSS-172
94ExtBas-182
94Fin-188
94FinRef-188
94Fla-113
94Fle-310
94Lea-372
94PanSti-129
94Sel-364
94StaClu-423
94StaCluFDI-423
94StaCluGR-423
94StaCluMOP-423
94StaCluT-248
94StaCluTFDI-248
94Top-51
94TopGol-51
94TopSpa-51
94UppDec-216
94UppDecED-216
95BluJayUSPC-8D
95ColCho-404
95ColChoGS-404
95ColChoSS-404
95Don-215
95DonPreP-215
95Fle-290
95Pac-430

Lee, Mark L.
78PadFamF-18
79Top-138
80HawIsIT-17
80Top-557
81PorBeaT-15

Lee, Mark Owen
82EvaTriT-4
86LakTigP-8
87GleFalTP-15
87LakTigP-17
88LakTigS-17
89MemChiB-4
89MemChiP-1190
89MemChiS-14
91BreMilB-14
91BrePol-11
91FleUpd-30
91Lea-343
91OPC-721
91Sco-372
91Top-721
91TopDesS-721
91TopMic-721
91TopTif-721
92DenZepF-2637
92DenZepS-137
92Don-313
92Fle-180
92OPC-384
92Sco-277
92StaClu-32
92Top-384
92TopGol-384
92TopGolW-384
92TopMic-384
92UppDec-507
93OklCit8F-1622
94BreMilB-145
94IowCubF-1272
94TriAAF-AAA33
95RocRedWTI-22
96NorTidB-19
96RicBraUB-16

Lee, Michael
60Top-521

Lee, Ronnie
50WorWidGV-25
53ExhCan-51

Lee, Terry
75CedRapGT-9
80HolMilT-21
81VanCanT-14
83CedRapRF-13
83CedRapRT-19

Lee, Terry James
89ChaLooB-10
89ChaLooGS-16
90ChaLooGS-19
91Bow-683
91Don-752
91Fle-70
91LinDriAAA-266
91NasSouLD-266
91NasSouP-2165
91TopDeb90-83
91TriA AAGP-AAA23
91UppDec-37
92ColSprSSS-89
92OPC-262
92Top-262
92TopGol-262
92TopGolW-262
92TopMic-262

Lee, Thomas
91EugEmeC-23
91EugEmeP-3723
92LetMouSP-18

Lee, Thornton
34DiaMatCSB-112
34BatR31-109
36NatChiFPR-52
39WhiSoxTI-11
40WhiSoxL-12
47TipTop-23
85WhiSoxC-37
89PacLegI-158

Lee, Tony
94DayCubF-2349

Lee, Travis
97Bow-389
97Bow98ROY-ROY10
97BowBes-187
97BowBesAR-187
97BowBesMI-MI2
97BowBesMIAR-MI2
97BowBesMIARI-MI2
97BowBesMII-MI2
97BowBesMIR-MI2
97BowBesMIRI-MI2
97BowBesR-187
97BowCerBIA-CA48
97BowCerGIA-CA48
97BowChr-257
97BowChr1RC-ROY10
97BowChr1RCR-ROY10
97BowChrI-257
97BowChrIR-257
97BowChrR-257
97BowChrSHR-SHR12
97BowChrSHRR-SHR12
97BowInt-389
97BowScoHR-12
97TopSta-106
97TopStaAM-106

Lee, Watty (Wyatt)
03BreE10-88
03BreE10-89
11SpoLifCW-216
11T205-193
12ColRedB-167
12ColTinT-167
12ImpTobC-71

Lee, Wiley
87SalAngP-19
88MidLeaAGS-24
88QuaCitAGS-4
89CalLeaA-11
89PalSprACLC-39
89PalSprAP-485
90MidAngGS-11

Lee, William C.
34DiaMatCSB-113
34BatR31-140
35DiaMatCS3T1-95
36DiaMatCS3T2-16
36SandSW-40
36WorWidGV-109
37ExhFou-3
39CubTeal-13
39ExhSal-36
39WheBB12-4
41CubTeal-10
41DouPlaR-103
43CubTeal-12
47PM1StaP1-110
47TipTop-110
89ChaLooLITI-15
91ConTSN-128
92CubOldS-17
93ConTSN-724

Lee, William F.
70OPC-279
70Top-279
71MLBOffS-322
71OPC-58
71Top-58
72Dia-25
72Top-636
73LinPor-25
73OPC-224
73Top-224
74OPC-118
74Top-118
74TopSta-135
75Hos-66
75OPC-128
75Top-128
76Kel-29
76LinSup-111
76OPC-396
76RedSoxSM-9
76SSP-421
76Top-396
77BurCheD-32
77Top-503
78PapGinD-9
78SSP270-167
78Top-295
79ExpPos-13
79ExpPos-14
79OPC-237
79Top-455
80ExpPos-14
80OPC-53
80Top-97
81Don-211
81ExpPos-4
81Fle-157
81OPC-371
81Top-633
82Don-194
82ExpPos-20
82Fle-194
82OPC-323
82Top-323
88AlaGolAA'TI-6
89PacSenL-28
89T/MSenL-66
89TopSenL-33
90EliSenL-99
90SouCalS-8
91PacSenL-146
92Nab-1
93ExpDonM-24
95MCIAmb-11

Leech, Skip
77ChaPatT-7

Leek, Eugene
61Top-527
62SalPlaC-82A
62SalPlaC-82B
62ShiPlaC-82

Leeper, Dave
83OmaRoyT-22
84OmaRoyT-22
85OmaRoyT-24
86Don-461
86HawIsIP-16
87VanCanP-1611

Leese, Brandon
96BelGiaTI-24

Leetch, Brian
91StaCluMO-46

Leever, Sam
03BreE10-90
08AmeCarE-82
09AmeCarE-70
10DomDisP-68
10NadE1-30
10PirAmeCE-6
10PirHerP-8
10PirTipTD-18
10SweCapPP-139
11SpoLifCW-217
11SpoLifM-253
11T205-98

Lefebvre, Jim
65DodJayP-8
65Top-561
66OPC-57
66Top-57
66TopVen-57
67CokCapD-12
67CokCapDA-12
67DexPre-124
67Top-260
67TopVen-286
68Baz-2
68Top-457
68TopActS-4A
68TopActS-13A
69MilBra-156
69MLBOffS-149
69OPC-140
69Top-140
69TopFou-9
69TopSta-46
69TopTeaP-22
69TraSta-47
70MLBOffS-52
70Top-553
71DodTic-8
71MLBOffS-106
71OPC-459
71Top-459
72MilBra-196
72OPC-369
72Top-369
72TopCloT-20
78TCM60I-263
80GiaPol-5
85PhoGiaC-187
86PhoFirP-15
87DodSmoA-18
88A'sMot-27
89DodSmoG-71
89MarMot-1
89TopTra-70T
89TopTraT-70T
90DodTar-443
90MarMot-1
90OPC-459
90Top-459
90TopTif-459
91MarCouH-1
91OPC-699
91Top-699
91TopDesS-699
91TopMic-699
91TopTif-699
92CubMar-5
92DodStaTA-5
92TopTra-63T
92TopTraG-63T
93CubMar-13
93Top-502
93TopGol-502
93TopInaM-502
93TopMic-502
94A'sMot-28
95AthMot-28
95DodROY-6
86STaoftFT-37

Lefebvre, Joe
77ForLauYS-6
79WesHavYT-25
80ColCliP-14
80ColCliT-26
81Don-571
81Fle-103
81OPC-88
81Top-88
81TopTra-790
82Don-373
82Fle-575
82Top-434
83Don-523
83Fle-363
83Top-644
83TopTra-61T
84AllGamPI-55
84Don-82
84Fle-37
84Nes792-148
84PhiTas-37
84Top-148
84TopTif-148
85Don-285
85Fle-257
85PhiTas-12
85PhiTas-37
85Top-531
85TopTif-531
86PhiTas-23
87ReaPhiP-3
88MaiPhiC-25
88MaiPhiP-301
89ScrRedBC-18
89ScrRedBP-722
90AlbYanB-25
90AlbYanP-1181
90AlbYanS-25
92YanWIZ8-104
96PhoFirB-4

Lefebvre, Ryan
92Min-11

Lefebvre, Tip
84PhoGiaC-14

Lefferts, Craig
82IowCubT-20
83CubThoAV-32
84Don-388
84Fle-496
84FleUpd-72
84Nes792-99
84PadMot-19
84Top-99
84TopTif-99
84TopTra-72T
84TopTraT-72T
85Don-261
85Fle-38

85OPC-76
85PadMot-15
85Top-608
85TopMin-608
85TopTif-608
86Don-307
86Fle-328
86OPC-244
86Top-244
86TopTif-244
87Don-387
87Fle-422
87FleGlo-422
87FleRecS-19
87FleUpd-64
87FleUpdG-64
87OPC-287
87PadBohHB-37
87SpoTeaP-16
87Top-501
87TopTif-501
88Don-515
88DonBasB-330
88Fle-87
88FleGlo-87
88GiaMot-24
88Sco-553
88ScoGlo-553
88StaLinG-9
88Top-734
88TopTif-734
89Bow-464
89BowTif-464
89Don-59
89Fle-332
89FleGlo-332
89GiaMot-24
89Sco-178
89Top-372
89TopTif-372
89UppDec-541
90Bow-206
90BowTif-206
90ClaBlu-109
90Don-376
90DonBesN-23
90Fle-60
90FleCan-60
90FleUpd-57
90Lea-339
90OPC-158
90PadCok-9
90PadMag-11
90PanSti-362
90PubSti-74
90Sco-209
90ScoRoo-22T
90Spo-130
90Top-158
90TopSti-80
90TopTif-158
90TopTra-59T
90TopTraT-59T
90UppDec-399
90UppDec-792
90VenSti-294
91Bow-650
91Don-515
91Fle-534
91Lea-390
91OPC-448
91PadCok-4
91PadMag-21
91PadSmo-19
91PanCanT1-84
91RedFolS-59
91Sco-184
91StaClu-533
91Top-448
91TopDesS-448
91TopMic-448
91TopTif-448
91Ult-307
91UppDec-228
92Bow-105
92Don-162
92Fle-611
92Lea-408
92OPC-41
92PadCarJ-11
92PadMot-24
92PadPolD-13
92PadSmo-17
92PanSti-239
92Pin-478
92Sco-175
92StaClu-618
92StaCluNC-618
92Top-41
92TopGol-41
92TopGolW-41
92TopMic-41
92Ult-577
92UppDec-589
93Bow-249
93Don-1
93Fle-544
93Lea-309
93Pin-522
93RanKee-414
93Sco-435
93Sel-373
93SelRoo-112T
93Top-617
93TopGol-617
93TopInaM-617
93TopMic-617
93Ult-632
93UppDec-718
93UppDecGold-718
94AngLAT-17
94AngMot-18
94Don-472
94Fle-311
94Pac-621
94Top-288
94TopGol-288
94TopSpa-288
Lefley, Chuck
72Dia-87
72Dia-88
LeFlore, Ron
75OPC-628
75Top-628
76GreHeroBP-3
76Hos-69
76Kel-17
76OPC-61
76SSP-363
76Top-61
77BurCheD-98
77Hos-50
77Kel-25
77OPC-167
77PepGloD-28
77RCColC-34
77Spo-3601
77TigBurK-2
77Top-240
78Hos-95
78OPC-88
78RCColC-12
78TigBurK-19
78Top-480
78WifBalD-37
79Hos-34
79OPC-348
79Top-4
79Top-660
79TopCom-8
80BurKinPHR-27
80ExpPos-15
80OPC-45
80Top-80
81AllGamPI-55
81CokTeaS-31
81Don-576
81Fle-154
81FleStiC-2
81MSAMinD-20
81OPC-104
81Squ-26
81Top-4
81Top-204
81Top-710
81TopSti-23
81TopSupHT-17
81TopTra-791
82Don-165
82Fle-350
82FleSta-182
82OPC-140
82Top-140
82TopSti-172
83Don-543
83Fle-246
83FleSta-104
83FleSti-151
83OPC-297
83Top-560
83TopFol-5
89PacSenL-4
89T/MSenL-67
89TopSenL-111
90EliSenL-39
91PacSenL-63
94MCIAmb-8
Leftwich, Phil
90BoiHawP-3306
90ProAaA-158
91Cla/Bes-247
91MidLeaAP-MWL27
91QuaCitAC-7
91QuaCitAP-2624
92MidAngF-4024
93VanCanF-2592
94AngAdoF-2
94AngLAT-9
94ColC-173
94ColChoGS-173
94ColChoSS-173
94Don-403
94Fin-391
94FinRef-391
94Fla-272
94Fle-62
94Lea-132
94Pac-82
94Pin-441
94PinArtP-441
94PinMusC-441
94Top-471
94TopGol-471
94TopSpa-471
94Ult-23
94UppDec-139
94UppDecED-139
95ColCho-106
95ColChoGS-106
95ColChoSS-106
95Don-199
95DonPreP-199
95Fle-229
95Top-619
95TopCyb-387
Legault, Kevin
92EliTwiC-8
92EliTwiF-3675
93ClaFS7-216
93ForWayWC-15
93ForWayWF-1964
94ForMyeMC-13
94ForMyeMF-1165
95HarCitRCTI-11
Legendre, Rob
91YakBeaC-25
91YakBeaP-4245
92YakBeaC-10
92YakBeaF-3445
Leger, Frank
83LynPirT-24
Leger, Roger
43ParSpo-47
Leger, Tim
92FroRowDP-23
93StaCluM-67
94WelPirC-12
94WelPirF-3508
Legett, Lou
35DiaMatCS3T1-96
Legg, Greg
83ReaPhiT-14
85PorBeaC-48
87MaiGuiP-4
87MaiGuiT-14
87PhiTas-11
88ReaPhiP-882
89ScrRedBC-19
89ScrRedBP-708
90ProAAAF-311
90ScrRedBP-609
91LinDriAAA-486
91ScrRedBLD-486
91ScrRedBP-2546
92ScrRedBF-2452
92ScrRedBS-486
93ScrRedBF-2547
93ScrRedBTI-12
94ClePhiC-29
94ClePhiF-2544
95ClePhiF-233
96ScrRedBB-3
Leggatt, Rich
82BufBisT-1
83DurBulT-20
84DurBulT-18
85GreBraTI-12
86TolMudHP-13
Legree, Keith
92EliTwiF-3686
95HarCitRCTI-12
Legrow, Brett
94BatCliC-9
94BatCliF-3440
Legumina, Gary
83SanJosBC-15
85VerBeaDT-9
Lehew, Jim
91OriCro-257
Lehman, Bill
76AppFoxT-11
Lehman, Ken
50W720HolS-16
55Bow-310
57Top-366
58Hir-52
58Top-141
59Top-31
59TopVen-31
79TCM50-258
90DodTar-444
91OriCro-258
95TopArcBD-140
Lehman, Mike
87NewOriP-2
89FreKeyS-12
90FreKeyTI-16
91HagSunLD-235
91HagSunP-2159
91LinDriAA-235
92RocRedWS-455
92SkyAAAF-207
Lehman, Toby
93HicCraC-12
93HicCraF-1274
94SouBenSHC-7
94SouBenSHF-588
96HigDesMB-18
Lehmann, Arthur
63GadFunC-70
Lehner, Ken
95BreCouMF-265
Lehner, Paul
47TipTop-67
49Bow-131
50Bow-158
51Bow-8
85TCMPla1-18
Lehnerz, Daniel
88IdaFalBP-1857
Lehnerz, Mike
89KinMetS-15
91PitMetC-20
91PitMetP-3417
Lehoisky, Russ
93EliTwiC-14
93EliTwiF-3413
94ForWayWC-13
94ForWayWF-2005
95ForMyeMTI-14
Leibee, Skye
94SouOreAC-15
94SouOreAF-3618
95WesMicWTI-21
Leiber, Hank
38ExhFou-5
39CubTeal-14
41CubTeal-11
79DiaGre-37
95ConTSN-1426
Leibert, Allen
90CanIndS-10
Leibold, Nemo (Harry)
14B18B-5A
14B18B-5B
14FatPlaT-24
15SpoNewM-99
16ColE13-97
16SpoNewM-101
17HolBreD-60
17HolBreD-61
21E121So8-51
22E120-6
22W575-71
23WilChoV-84
75WhiSox1T-13
88PacEigMO-101
94ConTSN-1036
94ConTSN-1042
94ConTSNB-1036
94ConTSNB-1042
Leibrandt, Charles
79IndIndTI-7
80RedEnq-44
81Don-421
81Fle-208
81IndIndTI-5
81OPC-126
81Top-126
82Fle-74
82RedCok-14
82Top-169
83Don-421
83Fle-596
83IndIndTI-4
83Top-607
84OmaRoyT-1
85AllGamPI-80
85Don-399
85DonHig-4
85DonHig-46
85Fle-206
85IndIndTI-33
85Top-459
85TopTif-459
86BasStaB-67
86Don-297
86Fle-13
86FleLeaL-21
86FleSlu-20
86FleStiC-69
86Lea-171
86OPC 77
86RoyKitCD-10
86RoyNatP-37
86Spo-159
86Spo-186
86Top-77
86TopMinL-19
86TopSti-262
86TopSup-37
86TopTat-1
86TopTif-77
87Don-220
87Fle-373
87FleGlo-373
87OPC-223
87SpoTeaP-13
87Top-223
87TopSti-258
87TopTif-223
88Don-157
88DonBasB-151
88Fle-263
88FleGlo-263
88FleStiC-31
88Lea-76
88OPC-218
88PanSti-100
88RoySmo-13
88Sco-61
88ScoGlo-61
88Spo-21
88StaLinRo-8
88Top-569
88TopSti-260
88TopTif-569
89Bow-116
89BowTif-116
89ClaLigB-82
89Don-89
89DonBasB-231
89Fle-286
89FleGlo-286
89OPC-301
89PanSti-351
89RoyTasD-10
89Sco-133
89Top-301
89TopTif-301
89UppDec-637
90Bow-8
90BowTif-8
90BraDubP-15
90BraDubS-18
90Don-208
90Fle-112
90FleCan-112
90Lea-428
90MLBBasB-103

90OPC-776
90PubSti-351
90Sco-82
90Top-776
90TopTif-776
90TopTra-60T
90TopTraT-60T
90UppDec-658
90VenSti-295
91Bow-573
91BraDubP-17
91BraSubS-22
91Don-562
91Fle-695
91Lea-209
91OPC-456
91PanFreS-27
91PanSti-23
91Sco-536
91StaClu-527
91Top-456
91TopDesS-456
91TopMic-456
91TopTif-456
91UppDec-460
92BraLykP-17
92BraLykS-20
92Don-84
92Fle-361
92Lea-113
92OPC-152
92Pin-423
92Sco-105
92StaClu-366
92Top-152
92TopGol-152
92TopGolW-152
92TopMic-152
92Ult-459
92UppDec-170
93Bow-433
93Don-630
93Fle-7
93FleFinE-280
93Lea-407
93OPC-204
93OPCPre-116
93PacSpa-642
93Pin-115
93RanKee-415
93Sco-393
93Sel-209
93SelRoo-91T
93StaClu-723
93StaCluFDI-723
93StaCluMOP-723
93StaCluR-16
93Top-677
93TopGol-677
93TopInaM-677
93TopMic-677
93UppDec-678
93UppDecGold-678
94Don-190
94Fle-312
94Sco-467
94ScoGolR-467

Leiby, Brent
90PriPatD-30
91SpaPhiC-30
95ReaPhiELC-24
96ReaPhiB-29

Leifield, Lefty (Albert)
09T206-209
09T206-210
10DomDisP-69
10PirTipTD-10
10RedCroT-42
10RedCroT-131
10RedCroT-213
10SweCapPP-140
11MecDFT-40
11S74Sil-112
11SpoLifM-254
11T205-99
12HasTriFT-16C
12T207-102

Leighton, John
87OldJudN-303

Leimeister, Eric
90NiaFalRP-20
91LakTigC-7
91LakTigP-263

Lein, Chris
82NasSouTI-16
83AleDukT-14
85PriWilPT-13
87SalBucP-28
89HarSenP-301
90SalBucS-26
91BluOriC-25
91BluOriP-4142
95BowBayTI-25
96BowBayB-2

Leinen, Michael
90WauTimS-13

Leinen, Pat
88NebCor-13
89EriOriS-11
90Bes-96
90WauTimB-3
90WauTimP-2116
91FreKeyP-2359
91HagSunP-2452
91PerHeaF-7
92RocRedWF-1934
92RocRedWS-456

Leinhard, Steve
90ShrCapS-14
94CliLumF-1998

Leiper, Dave
82IdaFalAT-11
83MadMusF-27
84ModA'sC-18
86TacTigP-12
87Don-472
87Fle-398
87FleGlo-398
87ModA'sC-A4
87Top-441
87TopTif-441
88Don-557
88FleUpd-123
88FleUpdG-123
88PadSmo-15
88Sco-348
88ScoGlo-348
89Don-465
89DonBasB-133
89Fle-310
89FleGlo-310
89Sco-515
89Top-82
89TopTif-82
89UppDec-363
90OPC-773
90PubSti-53
90Sco-212
90Top-773
90TopTif-773
90VenSti-296
91EdmTraLD-166
91EdmTraP-1514
91LinDriAAA-166
94TacTigF-3169
95AthMot-16
96PhiTeal-19

Leiper, Tim (Timothy)
86FloStaLAP-29
86LakTigP-9
87GleFalTP-9
88GleFalTP-938
88TolMudHC-21
88TolMudHP-603
89LonTigP-1373
90CMC-838
90EasLeaAP-EL5
90LonTigP-1281
91LinDriAAA-561
91TidTidLD-561
91TidTidP-2523
92MemChiF-2431
92MemChiS-441
93CarMudF-2063
93CarMudTI-23
94BufBisF-1849
95JacSunTI-18
96BinBeeB-15

Leister, John
86PawRedSP-12
87PawRedSP-55
87PawRedST-26
88PawRedSC-4
88PawRedSP-470
89PawRedSC-5
89PawRedSP-681
89PawRedSTI-14
90CMC-257
90PawRedSC-6
90PawRedSDD-13
90PawRedSP-459
90ProAAAF-431
90TopTVRS-49

Leiter, Al
82RegGloT-2
87ColCliP-15
87ColCliP-26
87IntLeaAT-38
88ClaBlu-238
88Don-43
88DonBasB-132
88DonReaBY-43
88DonRoo-27
88FleUpd-49
88FleUpdG-49
88Lea-43
88ScoRoo-97T
88ScoRooG-97T
88Top-18A
88Top-18B
88TopTif-18
89Bow-170
89BowTif-170
89ClaTraO-112
89Don-315
89Fle-257
89FleGlo-257
89FleUpd-70
89PanSti-396
89Sco-580
89ScoHot1R-80
89ScoYouSI-17
89Top-659
89TopBig-125
89TopRoo-15
89TopTif-659
89TopTra-71T
89TopTraT-71T
89ToyRoo-19
89UppDec-588
89UppDec-705
90BluJayFS-17
90Don-543
90OPC-138
90PubSti-521
90Top-138
90TopTif-138
90VenSti-297
91BluJayFS-17
91BluJayS-4
91Don-697
91OPC-233
91Top-233
91TopDesS-233
91TopMic-233
91TopTif-233
92Fle-334
92OPC-394
92SkyAAAF-227
92StaClu-231
92SyrChiF-1963
92SyrChiMB-10
92SyrChiS-509
92YanWIZ8-105
93BluJayD-18
93BluJayD4-34
93BluJayFS-18
93FleFinE-294
93PacSpa-652
93Pin-568
93StaClu-670
93StaCluFDI-670
93StaCluMOP-670
93UppDec-638
93UppDecGold-638
94BluJayUSPC-2C
94BluJayUSPC-10H
94ColC-512
94ColChoGS-512
94ColChoSS-512
94Don-229
94Fle-337
94Lea-95
94Pac-646
94Pin-334
94PinArtP-334
94PinMusC-334
94StaClu-667
94StaCluFDI-667
94StaCluGR-667
94StaCluMOP-667
94StaCluT-171
94StaCluTFDI-171
94Top-732
94TopGol-732
94TopSpa-732
94Ult-139
95Don-419
95DonPreP-419
95Fle-100
95StaClu-256
95StaCluFDI-256
95StaCluMOP-256
95StaCluSTWS-256
95TopTra-135T
95Ult-341
95UltGolM-341
96Cir-130
96CirRav-130
96ColCho-356
96ColCho-772
96ColChoGS-356
96ColChoSS-356
96Don-89
96DonPreP-89
96Fin-B208
96FinRef-B208
96Fla-264
96Fle-277
96FleTif-277
96FleUpd-U132
96FleUpdTC-U132
96LeaSigA-131
96LeaSigAG-131
96LeaSigAS-131
96MetUni-167
96MetUniP-167
96Pac-444
96PanSti-165
96Pin-24
96Sco-464
96StaClu-236
96StaCluMOP-236
96Ult-479
96UltGolM-479
96UppDec-339
97Cir-319
97CirRav-319
97ColCho-111
97Don-213
97DonEli-149
97DonEliGS-149
97DonPreP-213
97DonPrePGold-213
97Fin-183
97FinRef-183
97Fle-331
97FleTif-331
97Lea-118
97LeaFraM-118
97LeaFraMDC-118
97LeaGet-14
97MetUni-176
97NewPin-35
97NewPinAP-35
97NewPinMC-35
97NewPinPP-35
97Pac-302
97PacLigB-302
97PacSil-302
97PinCer-81
97PinCerMBlu-81
97PinCerMG-81
97PinCerMR-81
97PinCerR-81
97PinTotCPB-81
97PinTotCPG-81
97PinTotCPR-81
97Sco-124
97ScoPreS-124
97ScoShoS-124
97ScoShoSAP-124
97SpoIll-81
97SpoIllEE-81
97StaClu-110
97StaCluMOP-110
97Top-101
97Top-280
97Ult-198
97UltGolME-198
97UltPlaME-198
97UppDec-78

Leiter, Kurt
83SanJosBC-24
84ChaO'sT-23
86MiaMarP-15

Leiter, Mark
89ColCliC-29
89Ft.LauYS-13
90CMC-204
90ColCliC-4
90ColCliP-11
90ColCliP-673
90ProAAAF-323
90TopTVY-51
91Bow-138
91DonRoo-29
91LinDriAAA-588
91Sco-727
91TigCok-23
91TolMudHLD-588
91TopDeb90-84
92Bow-476
92Cla1-T52
92Don-633
92Fle-140
92Lea-207
92OPC-537
92OPCPre-48
92Sco-626
92StaClu-889
92Top-537
92TopGol-537
92TopGolW-537
92TopMic-537
92Ult-366
92UppDec-319
93Don-495
93Fle-608
93OPC-174
93PacSpa-112
93StaClu-116
93StaCluFDI-116
93StaCluMOP-116
93TigGat-18
93Top-216
93TopGol-216
93TopInaM-216
93TopMic-216
93UppDec-95
93UppDecGold-95
94AngLAT-13
94AngMot-24
94Fla-24
94FleUpd-19
94Pac-224
94StaClu-663
94StaCluFDI-663
94StaCluGR-663
94StaCluMOP-663
94Top-133
94TopGol-133
94TopSpa-133
94TopTra-117T
95Fle-230
95GiaMot-11
95Sco-225
95ScoGolR-225
95ScoPlaTS-225
95Top-41
96ColCho-301
96ColChoGS-301
96ColChoSS-301
96Don-296
96DonPreP-296
96EmoXL-292
96Fin-B34
96FinRef-B34
96Fla-390
96Fle-589
96FleTif-589
96GiaMot-12
96LeaSigA-132
96LeaSigAG-132
96LeaSigAS-132
96MetUni-244
96MetUniP-244
96Pac-205
96ProSta-54
96Sco-459
96StaClu-165
96StaCluMOP-165
96Top-107
96Ult-295
96UltGolM-295
96UppDec-452
97Cir-170
97CirRav-170
97ColCho-417
97Fle-627

97FleTif-627
97PacPriGotD-GD169
97Sco-453
97ScoHobR-453
97ScoResC-453
97ScoShoS-453
97ScoShoSAP-453
97Top-327
97Ult-453
97UltGolME-453
97UltPlaME-453
Leitner, Ted
90PadMag-16
91PadCok-5
Leius, Scott
87KenTwiP-21
88VisOakCLC-154
88VisOakP-102
89BasAmeAPB-AA18
89OrlTwiB-16
89OrlTwiP-1332
89SouLeaAJ-6
90Bow-423
90BowTif-423
90CMC-568
90Fle-647
90FleCan-647
90PorBeaC-16
90PorBeaP-185
90ProAAAF-255
91Bow-337
91DonRoo-4
91FleUpd-38
91LeaGolR-BC1
91Sco-370
91StaClu-338
91TopDeb90-85
91TopTra-71T
91TopTraT-71T
91UltUpd-38
91UppDec-35
92Bow-209
92Don-359
92Fle-209
92FleRooS-20
92Lea-214
92OPC-74
92OPCPre-118
92Pin-365
92Sco-320
92ScoFacI-B2
92StaClu-350
92StaCluD-104
92Stu-206
92Top-74
92TopGol-74
92TopGolW-74
92TopMic-74
92Ult-94
92UppDec-313
93Don-369
93Fle-270
93Lea-208
93PacSpa-522
93PanSti-128
93Pin-192
93Sco-178
93Sel-251
93StaClu-254
93StaCluFDI-254
93StaCluMOP-254
93Top-146
93TopGol-146
93TopInaM-146
93TopMic-146
93TriPla-165
93Ult-233
93UppDec-212
93UppDecGold-212
94ColC-382
94ColChoGS-382
94ColChoSS-382
94ExtBas-119
94Fin-377
94FinRef-377
94Fla-76
94FleUpd-62
94Lea-337
94Pac-359
94Sco-545
94ScoGolR-545
94StaClu-670
94StaCluFDI-670
94StaCluGR-670
94StaCluMOP-670
94Top-517
94TopGol-517
94TopSpa-517
94UppDec-322
94UppDecED-322
95ColCho-486
95ColChoGS-486
95ColChoSS-486
95D3-18
95Don-247
95DonPreP-247
95DonTopotO-110
95Fin-57
95FinRef-57
95Fla-58
95Fle-207
95Lea-49
95LeaLim-175
95Pac-251
95Pin-44
95PinArtP-44
95PinMusC-44
95Sco-142
95ScoGolR-142
95ScoPlaTS-142
95StaClu-292
95StaCluMOP-292
95StaCluSTWS-292
95StaCluVR-151
95Top-573
95TopCyb-347
95Ult-74
95UltGolM-74
96Don-240
96DonPreP-240
96LeaSigEA-106
96Pac-362
96PacPri-P115
96PacPriG-P115
96Sco-392
96StaClu-338
96StaCluMOP-338
95StaCluVRMC-151
96Top-78
Leiva, Jose
86ReaPhiP-14
87ReaPhiP-22
88ReaPhiP-884
89CanIndB-22
89CanIndP-1312
89CanIndS-24
93LinVenB-165
Leix, Tom
81WisRapTT-2
Leja, Frank
54NewYorJA-49
54Top-175
55Top-99
60Lea-121
94TopArc1-175
94TopArc1G-175
LeJeune, Larry
90DodTar-1105
LeJohn, Ducky (Don)
66OPC-41
66Top-41
66TopVen-41
75WatDodT-11
77CliDodT-16
78CliDodT-19
86BakDodP-19
90DodTar-445
Lekew, Jim
77FriOneYW-88
Leland, Stan
78DayBeaAT-15
80ColAstT-4
81TucTorT-15
Lelivelt, John Frank
14FatPlaT-25
Lelivelt, William
09ColChiE-168
12ColRedB-168
12ColTinT-168
Lemaire, Jacques
72Dia-89
72Dia-90
Lemanczyk, Dave
75OPC-571
75Top-571
76OPC-409
76SSP-355
76Top-409
77OPC-229
77Top-611
78BluJayP-13
78OPC-85
78Top-33
79BluJayBY-15
79OPC-102
79Top-207
80OPC-68
80Top-124
81Don-292
81Top-391
86BluJayGT-9
LeMaster, Denny
63Top-74
64BraJayP-5
64Top-152
64TopVen-152
65Kah-21
65Top-441
66Kah-17
66Top-252
66TopVen-252
67Ast-16
67CokCapB-7
67Top-288
68CokCapA-16
68DexPre-47
68Top-491
69MilBra-157
69OPC-96
69Top-96
69TopSta-34
69TopTeaP-6
70AstTeal-6
70MLBOffS-42
70OPC-178
70Top-178
71MLBOffS-84
71OPC-636
71Top-636
72MilBra-197
72OPC-371
72Top-371
78AtlCon-13
78TCM60I-17
87AstShoSO-14
87AstShowSTh-28
LeMaster, Johnnie
75IntLeaASB-16
75PacCoaLAB-16
75PhoGiaC-12
75PhoGiaCK-12
76OPC-596
76PheGiaCr-2
76PhoGiaCa-1
76PhoGiaCC-15
76PhoGiaVNB-14
76Top-596
77Top-151
78Top-538
79GiaPol-10
79Top-284
80GiaEurFS-3
80GiaPol-10
80OPC-224
80Top-434
81Don-432
81Fle-450
81OPC-84
81Top-84
82Don-524
82Fle-393
82Top-304
82TopSti-108
83Don-125
83Fle-266
83GiaMot-4
83OPC-154
83Top-154
83TopSti-304
84AllGamPI-22
84Don-649
84Fle-378
84GiaPos-12
84Nes792-663
84OPC-107
84Top-663
84TopRubD-2
84TopSti-168
84TopTif-663
85Don-114
85Fle-614
85GiaMot-14
85GiaPos-19
85OPC-302
85Top-772
85TopRubD-2
85TopSti-164
85TopTif-772
85TopTifT-74T
85TopTra-74T
86OPC-289
86Top-289
86TopTif-289
90SweBasG-68
LeMasters, Jim
87SumBraP-20
88BurBraP-13
88MidLeaAGS-20
89GreBraB-10
89GreBraP-1176
89GreBraS-13
89Sta-36
90CMC-180
90OmaRoyC-5
90OmaRoyP-63
90ProAAAF-598
91LinDriAAA-339
91OmaRoyLD-339
91OmaRoyP-1032
Lemay, Bob
91NiaFalRC-27
91NiaFalRP-3629
92FayGenC-8
92FayGenF-2165
Lemay, Richard
62Top-71
62TopVen-71
63Top-459
Lembo, Steve
50WorWidGV-7
53ExhCan-36
90DodTar-446
Lemieux, Mario
91StaCluCM-50
91StaCluMO-47
91StaCluMO-48
93StaCluMO-56
Lemke, Mark
86SumBraP-16
87DurBulP-26
88BasAmeAAB-16
88GreBraB-10
88SouLeaAJ-15
89ClaLigB-52
89Don-523
89RicBraBC-13
89RicBraC-19
89RicBraP-830
89RicBraTI-13
89Top-327
89TopTif-327
89TriA AAC-18
89TriAAP-AAA55
89UppDec-19
90Bow-11
90BowTif-11
90BraDubP-16
90BraDubS-19
90Don-624
90DonRoo-43
90Fle-587
90FleCan-587
90OPC-451
90Sco-593
90ScoRooDT-B5
90ScoYouS2-22
90Top-451
90TopBig-120
90TopTif-451
90TriAAAC-18
90UppDec-665
91BraDubP-18
91BraSubS-23
91Don-604
91Fle-696
91OPC-251
91Sco-779
91Sco100RS-89
91StaClu-203
91Top-251
91TopDesS-251
91TopMic-251
91TopTif-251
91UppDec-419
92Bow-663
92BraLykP-18
92BraLykS-21
92Don-606
92Fle-362
92Lea-94
92OPC-689
92PanSti-163
92Pin-426
92Sco-386
92ScoFacI-B3
92StaClu-316
92StaCluD-105
92Stu-6
92Top-689
92TopGol-689
92TopGolW-689
92TopMic-689
92Ult-165
92UppDec-47
93BraFloA-6
93BraLykP-16
93BraLykS-19
93Don-316
93Fla-6
93Fle-368
93Lea-68
93OPC-236
93PacSpa-334
93PanSti-182
93Pin-368
93Sco-147
93Sel-161
93StaClu-172
93StaCluB-4
93StaCluFDI-172
93StaCluM-37
93StaCluMOP-172
93Top-116
93TopGol-116
93TopInaM-116
93TopMic-116
93TriPla-215
93Ult-8
93UppDec-109
93UppDecGold-109
94BraLykP-17
94BraLykS-17
94BraUSPC-2H
94BraUSPC-12D
94ColC-501
94ColChoGS-501
94ColChoSS-501
94Don-147
94ExtBas-206
94Fin-95
94FinRef-95
94Fla-354
94Fle-363
94Lea-392
94Pac-13
94Pin-447
94PinArtP-447
94PinMusC-447
94Sco-392
94ScoGolR-392
94Sel-60
94StaClu-402
94StaCluFDI-402
94StaCluGR-402
94StaCluMOP-402
94StaCluT-46
94StaCluTFDI-46
94Top-23
94TopGol-23
94TopSpa-23
94Ult-153
94UppDec-489
94UppDecED-489
95ColCho-164
95ColChoGS-164
95ColChoSS-164
95Don-146
95DonPreP-146
95DonTopotO-188
95Fla-327
95Fle-309
95Lea-174
95Pac-9
95Pin-126
95PinArtP-126
95PinMusC-126
95Sco-87
95ScoGolR-87
95ScoPlaTS-87
95StaClu-285

95StaCluMOP-285
95StaCluSTWS-285
95StaCluVR-147
95Top-486
95TopCyb-278
95Ult-128
95UltGolM-128
96ColCho-44
96ColChoGS-44
96ColChoSS-44
96Don-279
96DonPreP-279
96Fla-203
96Fle-297
96FleBra-9
96FleTif-297
96MetUni-132
96MetUniP-132
96Pac-12
96Sco-124
96ScoDugC-A78
96ScoDugCAP-A78
96StaClu-382
96StaCluEPB-382
96StaCluEPG-382
96StaCluEPS-382
96StaCluMOP-382
95StaCluVRMC-147
96Top-83
96Ult-439
96UltGolM-439
96UppDec-7
97Cir-48
97CirRav-48
97ColCho-269
97Fle-261
97FleTif-261
97Pac-238
97PacLigB-238
97PacSil-238
97Sco-163
97ScoBra-8
97ScoBraPl-8
97ScoBraPr-8
97ScoPreS-163
97ScoShoS-163
97ScoShoSAP-163
97StaClu-322
97StaCluMOP-322
97Top-94
97Ult-419
97UltGolME-419
97UltPlaME-419
97UppDec-13

Lemke, Steve
92SouOreAC-4
92SouOreAF-3413
93SouOreAC-13
93SouOreAF-4058
94MidLeaAF-MDW31
94WesMicWC-13
94WesMicWF-2291
95Exc-110
95HunStaTI-17

Lemle, Rob
87LitFalMP-2403
88ColMetGS-21
89ColMetB-4
89ColMetGS-14

Lemon, Bob (Robert)
46SpoExcW-5-12
47Exh-132A
47Exh-132B
47IndTeal-17
47IndVanPP-16
47PM1StaP1-111
47PM1StaP1-112
48IndTeal-20
49Bow-238
49IndTeal-17
49IndVisEl-11
49MPR302-2-119
50Bow-40
50IndNumN-15
50IndTeal-16
51BerRos-A2
51Bow-53
51FisBakL-17
51R42SmaS-59
51TopCurA-8
52BerRos-33
52Bow-23
52IndNumN-4
52StaCalL-74C
52StaCalS-88A
52Top-268
52Whe-18A
52Whe-18B
53BowBW-27
53DixLid-12
53DixPre-12
53ExhCan-31
53IndPenCBP-19
53NorBreL-16
53RedMan-AL17
54Bow-196
54DanDee-15
54RedHeaF-16
54RedMan-AL21
55BigLealS-10
55Bow-191
55DaiQueS-10
55Ind-4
55IndCarBL-6
55IndGolS-2
55RedMan-AL8
56Top-255
57IndSoh-7
57Top-120
58Top-2A
58Top-2B
60RawGloT-13
60Top-460
70RoyTeal-19
71OPC-91
71Top-91
72OPC-449
72Top-449
74SacSolC-62
76RowExh-5
76ShaPiz-155
76TayBow4-104
77Top-418
78SSP270-139
78Top-574
79TCM50-19
79Top-626
79YanBurK-1
80PacLeg-120
80PerHaloFP-155
80SSPHOF-155
82Don-635
82OhiHaloF-32
83DiaClaS2-79
83DonHOFH-30
83TopRep5-268
85TCMPla1-16
86SpoDecG-39
88PacLegI-32
89HOFStiB-68
89PerCelP-25
90PerGreM-67
91TopArc1-284
92BazQuaSA-1
93ActPacA-113
93ActPacA2-47G

Lemon, Chet
75TucTorTI-8
76OPC-590
76Top-590
77BurCheD-73
77OPC-195
77Top-58
77WhiSoxJT-10
78Hos-124
78OPC-224
78SSP270-146
78Top-127
79Hos-40
79OPC-169
79Top-333
79TopCom-5
80Kel-46
80OPC-309
80Top-589
80TopSup-57
81AllGamPI-56
81CokTeaS-32
81Don-281
81Fle-354
81Kel-19
81OPC-242
81Squ-33
81Top-242
81TopScr-34
81TopSti-57
81TopSupHT-18
82Don-291
82Fle-351
82FleSta-191
82Kel-54
82OPC-13
82Top-216
82Top-493
82TopSti-168
82TopTra-62T
83AllGamPI-58
83Don-511
83Fle-335
83FleSti-251
83OPC-53
83Tig-18
83Top-727
84AllGamPI-148
84Don-171
84Fle-85
84FunFooP-97
84Nes792-611
84OPC-86
84TigFarJ-9
84TigWavP-23
84Top-611
84TopSti-271
84TopTif-611
85AllGamPI-62
85Don-90
85Fle-15
85Lea-77
85OPC-20
85SevCoi-D11
85SevCoi-G9
85TigCaiD-12
85TigWen-14
85Top-20
85TopGloA-18
85TopSti-21
85TopSti-190
85TopSti-260
85TopTif-20
86BasStaB-65
86Don-90
86Fle-230
86Lea-85
86OPC-160
86SevCoi-C14
86TigCaiD-11
86Top-160
86TopSti-274
86TopTat-10
86TopTif-160
87Don-353
87DonOpeD-213
87Fle-156
87FleGlo-156
87Lea-227
87OPC-206
87SevCoi-D6
87SpoTeaP-15
87TigCaiD-10
87TigCok-10
87Top-739
87TopSti-268
87TopTif-739
88Don-215
88DonBasB-147
88Fle-61
88FleGlo-61
88Lea-166
88OPC-366
88PanSti-96
88Sco-119
88ScoGlo-119
88StaLinTi-12
88TigPep-34
88TigPol-7
88Top-366
88TopBig-147
88TopTif-366
89Bow-108
89BowTif-108
89Don-209
89DonBasB-69
89Fle-137
89FleGlo-137
89OPC-328
89PanSti-344
89Sco-44
89Spo-171
89TigMar-34
89TigPol-34
89Top-514
89TopBig-202
89TopSti-283
89TopTif-514
89UppDec-128
90Bow-354
90BowTif-354
90Don-60
90DonBesA-76
90Fle-608
90FleCan-608
90Lea-133
90MLBBasB-87
90OPC-271
90PanSti-77
90PubSti-475
90Sco-106
90TigCok-10
90Top-271
90TopBig-86
90TopSti-278
90TopTif-271
90UppDec-348
90VenSti-298
91Don-301
91Fle-341
91OPC-469
91PanFreS-292
91Sco-557
91StaClu-23
91Top-469
91TopDesS-469
91TopMic-469
91TopTif-469
91UppDec-389

Lemon, Don
89IdaFalBP-2033

Lemon, Don (Donald)
92EriSaiC-5
92EriSaiF-1616
93HigDesMC-9
93HigDesMF-35
93TopGol-441
93TopInaM-441
93TopMic-441
94PorSeaDF-674
94PorSeaDTI-19

Lemon, Jim
47PM1StaP1-113
54Top-103
55Bow-262
57Top-57
58SenJayP-6
58Top-15
59HomRunD-11
59Top-74
59Top-215
59TopVen-74
60SenJayP-10
60Top-440
61Baz-12
61Pos-93A
61Pos-93B
61Top-44
61Top-450
61TopStal-182
61TwiCloD-13
61TwiJayP-8
61TwiPetM-17
61TwiUniMC-10
62Jel-89
62Pos-89
62PosCan-89
62SalPlaC-9B
62ShiPlaC-9
62Top-510
63Top-369
67SenTeal-7
68SenTeal-7
68Top-341
68TopVen-341
69Top-294
78TwiFri-9
79TCM50-180
82TwiPos-20
83TwiTeal-29
83TwiTeal-34
84MinTwiP-20
84TwiTeal-30
89EliTwiS-30
90EliTwiS-25
91EliTwiP-4316
94TopArc1-103
94TopArc1G-103

Lemon, Leo
81RedPioT-19

Lemonds, Dave
71OPC-458
71Top-458
72OPC-413
72Top-413
73OPC-534
73Top-534

Lemongello, Mark
77Top-478
78AstBurK-9
78Top-358
79Top-187
80WicAerT-22

Lemons, Richard
92AriWilP-8
93BurIndC-15
93BurIndF-3312
94ColRedC-13
94ColRedF-455

Lemons, Tim
86BurExpP-14
87SprCarB-7

Lemp, Chris
91BluOriC-21
91BluOriP-4124
92KanCouCC-11
92KanCouCF-88
92KanCouCTI-19
92ProFS7-12
93FreKeyC-13
93FreKeyF-1024
94FreKeyF-2609
94OriPro-52
95Exc-7
96BowBayB-19
94FreKeyC-13

Lemperle, John
85AlbYanT-30
86AlbYanT-19

Lemuth, Steve
89MedAthB-19

Lenderman, Dave
86PitCubP-13

Lenhardt, Don
51TopBluB-33
52Top-4
53BowC-20
54Bow-53
54OriEss-23
54Top-157
73OPC-131
73Top-131A
73Top-131B
79DiaGre-144
83TopRep5-4
91OriCro-259
94TopArc1-157
94TopArc1G-157

Lennon, Patrick
86BelMarC-128
87WauTimP-7
88VerMarP-947
89WilBilP-632
89WilBilS-12
90Bes-153
90SanBerSB-9
90SanBerSCLC-101
90SanBerSP-2645
91Bow-250
91CalCanLD-63
91CalCanP-528
91LinDriAAA-63
91UppDecFE-43F
92Bow-192
92CalCanS-64
92ClaGam-172
92Don-17
92Pin-542
92SkyAAAF-28
92StaClu-679
92StaCluECN-679
92TopDeb91-107
92UppDec-13
94NewBriRSF-657
95PawRedSDD-17
95PawRedTI-22
95TreThuTI-26

Lennon, Robert
55Top-119
56Top-104
57Top-371
58MonRoyF-14

Lennox, Ed (James E.)
09T206-211

10CouT21-39
10CouT21-171
11SpoLifM-159
11T205-100
11TurRedT-104
12HasTriFT-42
12T207-103
15VicT21-18
90DodTar-447
Lenti, Mike
81CliGiaT-23
Lentine, James
78ArkTraT-16
81ChaChaT-17
81Don-250
81Fle-476
Lentz, Harry
09T206-498
10CouT21-40
Leon, Angel
93LinVenB-242
Leon, Danny (Danilo)
87JamExpP-2560
88JamExpP-1913
88WesPalBES-16
89JacExpB-21
89JacExpP-169
92DonRoo-64
92FleUpd-61
92TopTra-64T
92TopTraG-64T
92TulDriF-2691
93Don-387
93LinVenB-247
93OklCit8F-1623
93RanKee-228
94VenLinU-247
95LinVen-64
Leon, Donny
97Bow-360
97BowChr-241
97BowChrI-241
97BowChrIR-241
97BowChrR-241
97BowInt-360
Leon, Eddie (Eduardo)
70OPC-292
70Top-292
71MLBOffS-378
71OPC-252
71Top-252
72Top-721
72WhiSox-7
73LinPor-49
73OPC-287
73Top-287
74OPC-501
74Top-501
75OPC-528
75Top-528
92YanWIZ7-95
Leon, Felix
93LinVenB-4
Leon, Johnny
90TamYanD-15
Leon, Jose
89EliTwiS-14
93LinVenB-171
94VenLinU-176
96JohCitCTI-20
Leon, Maximino
75OPC-442
75Top-442
76OPC-576
76SSP-3
76Top-576
77Top-213
Leon, Mike
87AppFoxP-22
88AppFoxP-163
89MemChiB-27
89MemChiP-1191
90MemChiB-27
90MemChiS-27
95ChaKniTI-4
96ChaKniB-4
Leon, Mike (Michael)
93JamExpC-14
93JamExpF-3322
Leon, Richard
75TulOil7-5
Leon, Ron
85SprCarT-15
87EriCarP-5
Leon, Scott
96HudValRB-12
Leonard, Andy
86BurExpP-15
Leonard, Benny
28W512-48
Leonard, Bernardo
78HolMilT-15
Leonard, Buck (Walter)
74LauOldTBS-11
76ShaPiz-132
80PerHaloFP-132
80SSPHOF-132
83ConMar-56
86NegLeaF-1
87NegLeaPD-30
88ConNegA-7
88NegLeaD-16
89PerCelP-26
89RinPosNL1-11
90NegLeaS-26
90PerGreM-58
90PomBlaBNLP-2542
91NegLeaRL-22
91PomBlaBPB-2
91PomBlaBPB-12
91PomBlaBPB-15
91PomBlaBPB-19
91PomBlaBPB-29
92FroRowBL-1
92FroRowBL-2
92FroRowBL-3
92FroRowBL-4
92FroRowBL-5
92NegLeaK-16
92NegLeaPL-2
92NegLeaRLI-38
93NegLeaRL2-41
93TedWil-108
93UppDecS-17
94PomNegLB-2
95NegLeaL2-3
95NegLeaLI-22
Leonard, Dennis
75OPC-615
75Top-615
76OPC-334
76SSP-164
76Top-334
77BurCheD-70
77Hos-72
77OPC-91
77Top-75
78Hos-88
78OPC-5
78OPC-41
78Roy-11
78SSP270-220
78Top-205
78Top-665
79Hos-109
79OPC-109
79RoyTeal-4
79Top-218
80OPC-293
80Top-565
81AllGamPI-86
81CokTeaS-76
81Don-102
81Fle-42
81OPC-185
81RoyPol-5
81Top-185
81TopSti-87
82Don-264
82Fle-413
82FleSta-208
82OPC-369
82Roy-11
82Squ-10
82Top-495
82TopSti-191
82TopStiV-191
83Don-412
83Fle-116
83FleSta-105
83FleSti-95
83OPC-87
83Roy-14
83RoyPol-3
83Top-785
84Fle-349
84Nes792-375
84OPC-375
84Top-375
84TopTif-375
86FleUpd-67
86RoyNatP-22
86TopTra-65T
86TopTraT-65T
87Fle-374
87FleGlo-374
87OPC-38
87RedFolSB-33
87Top-38
87TopTif-38
89PacSenL-84
89T/MSenL-68
89TopSenL-125
90EliSenL-72
90PacLeg-91
93RoySta2-5
93UppDecAH-82
93UppDecS-20
Leonard, Dutch (Emil)
34DiaMatCSB-114
35DiaMatCS3T1-97
39PlaBal-21
40PlaBal-23
41PlaBal-24
48Bow-24
49Bow-115
49EurSta-61
49Lea-113
50Bow-170
51Bow-102
52Bow-159
52StaCalL-80B
52StaCalS-92A
52TipTop-20
52Top-110
53BowBW-50
55Bow-247
61Fle-121
76GrePlaG-28
79DiaGre-55
83TCMPla1943-4
83TopRep5-110
90DodTar-448
91TopArc1-155
94ConTSNB-1276
Leonard, Dutch (Hubert)
15SpoNewM-100
16BF2FP-5
16ColE13-98
16FleBreD-56
16SpoNewM-102
17HolBreD-62
20NatCarE-57
34TarThoBD-12
53Top-155
72FleFamF-17
72LauGreF-34
79Top-418
85Woo-22
91ConTSN-142
91ConTSN-276
92ConTSN-346
93ConTSN-712
94ConTSN-1276
Leonard, Jeff (Jeffrey)
80Top-106
81Don-264
81Fle-67
81Top-469
82Don-438
82RegGloT-3
82RegGloT-4
82RegGloT-5
82Top-47
83Don-474
83GiaMot-8
83Top-309
84AllGamPI-56
84Don-567
84Fle-379
84GiaPos-13
84Nes792-576
84Nes792-748
84Top-576
84Top-748
84TopRubD-29
84TopSti-166
84TopTif-576
84TopTif-748
85AllGamPI-147
85Don-358
85Fle-615
85FleLimE-18
85GenMilS-4
85GiaMot-4
85GiaPos-20
85Lea-92
85OPC-132
85SevCoi-W14
85ThoMcAD-35
85Top-619
85Top-718
85TopMin-619
85TopRubD-30
85TopSti-161
85TopTif-619
85TopTif-718
86BasStaB-66
86Don-79
86Fle-548
86GiaMot-4
86Lea-74
86OPC-381
86Top-490
86TopSti-84
86TopTat-15
86TopTif-490
87ClaGam-64
87Don-391
87DonOpeD-103
87Fle-278
87FleGamW-25
87FleGlo-278
87FleSlu-23
87GiaMot-8
87OPC-280
87RedFolSB-102
87SpoTeaP-10
87StuPan-13
87Top-280
87TopSti-90
87TopTif-280
88ClaRed-175
88Don-327
88DonAll-54
88Fle-88
88FleGlo-88
88FleMin-117
88FleRecS-23
88FleStiC-128
88FleSup-21
88FleUpd-39
88FleUpdG-39
88GiaMot-8
88GreBasS-31
88Lea-118
88OPC-152
88PanSti-246
88PanSti-427
88PanSti-446
88RedFolSB-48
88Sco-580
88ScoGlo-580
88Spo-82
88StaLinG-10
88Top-570
88TopCoi-46
88TopRitTM-32
88TopSti-16
88TopSti-86
88TopStiB-17
88TopTif-570
88TopTra-61T
88TopTraT-61T
88TopUKM-43
88TopUKMT-43
88Woo-17
89Bow-218
89BowTif-218
89Don-457
89DonBasB-107
89DonTra-1
89Fle-190
89FleGlo-190
89FleUpd-60
89MarMot-8
89OPC-160
89Sco-557
89ScoRoo-7T
89Top-160
89TopAme2C-19
89TopSti-199
89TopTif-160
89TopTra-72T
89TopTraT-72T
89UppDec-263
89UppDec-789
90Bow-472
90BowTif-472
90ClaBlu-93
90DodTar-449
90Don-93
90DonBesA-125
90DonGraS-2
90Fle-519
90FleCan-519
90Lea-219
90MarMot-4
90OPC-455
90PanSti-150
90PubSti-436
90RedFolSB-58
90Sco-98
90Sco100S-91
90Spo-20
90Top-455
90TopBig-303
90TopSti-223
90TopTif-455
90UppDec-331
90VenSti-299
91Fle-456
91OPC-55
91Sco-44
91Top-55
91TopDesS-55
91TopMic-55
91TopTif-55
91UppDec-107
94BreMilB-146
96ModA'sB-28
Leonard, Kathy
81RedPioT-24
Leonard, Mark
86EveGiaC-182
86EveGiaPC-11
87CliGiaP-14
88CalLeaACLC-3
88SanJosGCLC-122
88SanJosGP-134
89PhoFirC-5
89PhoFirP-1498
90CMC-546
90PhoFirC-19
90PhoFirP-24
90ProAAAF-50
90TriAllGP-AAA52
91Bow-624
91Don-526
91Fle-265
91GiaMot-13
91GiaPacGaE-22
91Lea-369
91Sco-719
91ScoRoo-18
91TopDeb90-86
91Ult-322
91UppDec-557
92Don-761
92GiaMot-13
92GiaPacGaE-23
92GiaPacGaE-24
92PhoFirF-2833
92Pin-233
92Sco-499
92Sco100RS-62
92StaClu-538
92Ult-591
93Don-288
93Fle-532
93PanSti-241
93RocRedWF-253
93Sco-381
93StaClu-497
93StaCluFDI-497
93StaCluMOP-497
93Top-729
93TopGol-729
93TopInaM-729
93TopMic-729
94PhoFirF-1533
95PhoFirTI-27
Leonard, Mathew
88GenCubP-1645
88WytCubP-1996
89ChaWheB-9
89ChaWheP-1758
Leonard, Tom
81RedPioT-23
Leonard, Wilfred

48SomandK-20
Leonardo, Juan
75AppFoxT-13
Leones, Escogidio
93LimRocDWB-152
Leonette, Mark
83IdaFalAT-8
84IdaFalATI-16
85MadMusP-19
85MadMusT-22
87PitCubP-16
88PitCubP-1371
86HumStaDS-26
Leonhard, Dave
68OPC-56
68Top-56
68TopVen-56
69MilBra-158
69Top-228
70Top-674
71MLBOffS-302
71OPC-716
71Ori-8
71Top-716
72MilBra-198
72Top-527
91OriCro-260
Leonhardt, Dave
92FayGenC-21
92FayGenF-2175
94PitMetC-14
94PitMetF-3520
Leopold, Jim
83BeaGolGT-6
84BeaGolGT-14
85LasVegSC-119
86NasPirP-15
88LouRedBC-10
88LouRedBP-437
88LouRedBTI-27
Lepcio, Ted
52Top-335
53RedSoxTI-17
53Top-18
54Bow-162
54Top-66
55Top-128
55TopDouH-125
57Top-288
58Top-29
59Top-348
60Top-97
60TopVen-97
61Top-234
83TopRep5-335
91TopArc1-18
94TopArc1-66
94TopArc1G-66
Lepel, Joel
91KenTwiC-19
91KenTwiP-2091
Lepley, John
88HamRedP-1737
88NebCor-8
89ArkTraGS-10
90ArkTraGS-20
91ArkTraLD-37
91ArkTraP-1280
91LinDriAA-37
Leppert, Don
62Top-36
62TopVen-36
63Top-243
64Top-463
64WheSta-26
73OPC-517
73Top-517A
73Top-517B
74OPC-489
74Top-489
76VenLeaS-145
77OPC-58
77Top-113
78BluJayP-14
78TCM60I-101
78TCM60I-110
84AstMot-27
85AstMot-27
86KenTwiP-13
87KenTwiP-27
88KenTwiP-1399
89KenTwiP-1070
91OriCro-261
Lepson, Mark
79BurBeeT-11
80BurBeeT-4
81BurBeeT-9
Lerch, Randy
76OklCit8TI-15
76OPC-595
76Top-595
77Top-489
78PhiSSP-44
78SSP270-44
78Top-271
79PhiBurK-8
79Top-52
80OPC-181
80PhiBurK-18
80Top-344
81Don-574
81Fle-25
81Top-584
81TopTra-792
82BrePol-35
82Don-595A
82Don-595B
82Fle-147
82Top-466
83ExpPos-12
83ExpStu-28
83Fle-287
83OPC-22
83Top-686
84Fle-380
84GiaPos-14
85Don-309
85Fle-616
85Top-103
85TopTif-103
86PhiTas-35
86PorBeaP-14
89PacSenL-23
89TopSenL-23
90EliSenL-10
94BreMilB-147
LeRoy, John
95DurBulTI-18
96CarLeaA1B-7
96CarLeaA2B-7
96DurBulBIB-8
96DurBulBrB-9
97Bow-337
97BowInt-337
LeRoy, Louis
11SpoLifCW-214
Lersch, Barry
69OPC-206
69Top-206
69TopFou-22
71MLBOffS-183
71OPC-739
71Top-739
72OPC-453
72Top-453
73OPC-559
73Top-559
74OPC-313
74Top-313
74TopTra-313T
75OklCit8TI-2
Lesch, J.R.
93EriSaiC-14
Lesch, Paul
92ButCopKSP-29
93EriSaiF-3111
Leshay, Maney
96HelBreTI-13
Lesher, Brian
92SouOreAC-6
92SouOreAF-3434
93MadMusC-19
93MadMusF-1837
94ModA'sC-18
94ModA'sF-3077
95HunStaTI-18
96BesAutS-49
97ColCho-24
97Pac-171
97PacLigB-171
97PacSil-171
Leshnock, Don
75ShrCapT-9
Leshnock, Donnie
91TopTra-72T
91TopTraT-72T
92ClaDraP-81
92OneYanC-8
92StaCluD-106
93StaCluM-137
93Top-701
93TopGol-701
93TopInaM-701
93TopMic-701
94GreBatF-470
95TamYanYI-17
97GreBatC-14
Leskanic, Curt (Curtis)
90KinIndTI-5
91Cla/Bes-297
91KinIndC-5
91KinIndP-317
92OrlSunRF-2844
92OrlSunRS-509
92ProFS7-57
92SkyAA F-218
93ColSprSSF-3082
93Lea-527
93Top-774
93TopGol-774
93TopInaM-774
93TopMic-774
94ColSprSSF-728
94Don-580
94Pac-200
94StaClu-507
94StaCluFDI-507
94StaCluGR-507
94StaCluMOP-507
94StaCluT-118
94StaCluTFDI-118
94Top-191
94TopGol-191
94TopSpa-191
95ColCho-442
95ColChoGS-442
95ColChoSS-442
95Don-533
95DonPreP-533
96ColCho-537
96ColChoGS-537
96ColChoSS-537
96Don-268
96DonPreP-268
96Fla-248
96Fle-366
96FleRoc-7
96FleTif-366
96LeaSigA-133
96LeaSigAG-133
96LeaSigAS-133
96Pac-62
96RocPol-11
96Sco-485
96StaClu-290
96StaCluMOP-290
96Ult-469
96UltGolM-469
97Fle-311
97FleTif-311
97PacPriGotD-GD135
97Ult-186
97UltGolME-186
97UltPlaME-186
97UppDec-56
Lesley, Brad
81CedRapRT-3
82IndIndTI-5
83Don-547
83IndIndTI-26
85Top-597
85TopTif-597
85VanCanC-202
87JapPlaB-16
90CedRapRDGB-21
94BreMilB-148
Leslie, Reggie
91ChaWheC-6
91ChaWheP-2883
92CedRapRC-9
92CedRapRF-1070
92ChaLooS-190
Leslie, Roy Reid
22E120-201
Leslie, Sam
34BatR31-46
34DiaStaR-68
34ExhFou-2
34Gou-49
35GouPuzR-1G
35GouPuzR-3E
35GouPuzR-5E
35GouPuzR-14E
36GouWidPPR-A64
36OveCanR-31
36WorWidGV-4
37ExhFou-5
79DiaGre-27
92ConTSN-504
Leslie, Sean
96DelShoB-19
96VerExpB-16
Lesperance, Frank
94ButCopKSP-12
Lesslie, Bob
75WatDodT-12
Lester, Jimmy
88WicPilRD-22
89ChaRaiP-989
90ChaRaiB-27
90ChaRaiP-2056
91WatDiaC-11
91WatDiaP-1273
Letchas, Charlie
89ChaLooLITI-16
Letendre, Mark
79ColCliT-11
80ColCliP-NNO
80ColCliT-18
81ColCliP-NNO
81ColCliT-25
91GiaMot-28
Letourneau, Jeff
91EriSaiC-18
91EriSaiP-4064
Lett, Jim
80CedRapRT-22
82WatRedT-23
83WatRedT-19
84CedRapRT-12
86RedTexG-NNO
87RedKah-NNO
88RedKah-NNO
89RedKah-xx
90ChaWheB-26
90ChaWheP-2257
91LinDriAAA-275
91NasSouP-2174
92NasSouF-1850
97BluJayS-23
Letterio, Shane
88GreHorP-1556
89MiaMirIS-11
90CMC-758
90WilBilB-14
90WilBilP-1064
90WilBilS-15
91CalCanLD-64
91CalCanP-522
91LinDriAAA-64
92JacSunF-3716
92JacSunS-361
Levan, Jesse
78ReaRem-12
88ChaLooLTI-20
LeVander, Scott
84IdaFalATI-17
Levangie, Dana
91ElmPioC-8
91ElmPioP-3273
92WinHavRSC-20
92WinHavRSF-1781
93ForLauRSC-17
93ForLauRSFP-1600
94LynRedSC-16
94LynRedSF-1894
95TreThuTI-17
96TreThuB-17
LeVasseur, Tom
86SpoIndC-169
88RivRedWCLC-223
88RivRedWP-1417
89WicChaR-9
89WicStaR-26
89WicWraR-21
90CMC-520
90LasVegSC-17
90LasVegSP-129
90ProAAAF-17
94CalCanF-796
Levenda, John
90CalLeaACLC-31
Leverette, Dixie (Gorham)
22W572-57
22W573-72
Leverette, Horace
22E120-23
Levey, James
32OrbPinNP-52
32OrbPinUP-40
33TatOrb-40
92ConTSN-395
Levi, Stan
80BurBeeT-27
83ElPasDT-11
Levias, Andres
94HicCraC-13
94HicCraF-2188
95ButCopKtI-14
96PriWilCB-17
Levine, Al
91UtiBluSC-21
91UtiBluSP-3238
92SouBenWSC-18
92SouBenWSF-174
93SarWhiSC-17
93SarWhiSF-1367
94BirBarC-16
94BirBarF-620
94VenLinU-139
95LinVen-138
96NasSouB-15
Levinson, Davis
81RedPioT-25
Levinson, Steve
81RedPioT-30
Levis, Jesse
88CapCodPB-13
88CapCodPPaLP-116
89BurIndS-16
90CarLeaA-39
90KinIndTI-8
91CanIndLD-88
91CanIndP-981
91LinDriAA-88
92ColSprSSF-755
92ColSprSSS-90
92DonRoo-65
92FleUpd-16
93ChaKniF-546
93Don-669
93FleFinE-203
93FleMajLP-A14
93Pin-288
93PinRooTP-3
93Sco-330
93StaClu-468
93StaCluFDI-468
93StaCluMOP-468
93Top-801
93TopGol-801
93TopInaM-801
93TopMic-801
94ChaKniF-898
94Pac-174
94VenLinU-222
97Fle-131
97FleTif-131
97Pac-121
97PacLigB-121
97PacSil-121
Levrault, Allen
96HelBreTI-14
Levsen, Dutch
94ConTSN-1304
94ConTSNB-1304
Lewallyn, Dennis
75AlbDukC-20
76VenLeaS-200
79AlbDukT-7
80AlbDukT-8
82Ind-22
82IndTeal-21
82IndWhe-7
82Top-356
83VerBeaDT-29
85VerBeaDT-25
89VerBeaDS-28
90DodTar-451
90VerBeaDS-30
91VerBeaDP-793
92VerBeaDC-30
92VerBeaDF-2896
93RanKee-229
93VerBeaDC-30
94VerBeaDC-28
95SanBerSTI-30
96AriBlaDB-2
96HonShaHWB-26
Lewandowski, John

92BurIndC-1
92BurIndF-1659
Lewis, A.D.
94ChaRivF-2684
Lewis, Alan
88BakDodCLC-237
89VerBeaDS-15
90VerBeaDS-18
91BakDodCLC-9
92ElPasDF-3931
92ElPasDS-216
93ElPasDF-2957
96SanBerSB-3
Lewis, Amos
79AshTouT-17
Lewis, Andreaus
94BurIndC-10
94BurIndF-3809
94ChaRivC-12
Lewis, Anthony
90SavCarP-2083
91Cla/Bes-137
91St.PetCC-27
91St.PetCP-2290
92St.PetCC-17
92St.PetCF-2040
93ArkTraF-2823
93ExcFS7-101
94ArkTraF-3102
95ArkTraTI-17
96HarCitRCB-18
Lewis, Bill
81TCM60I-362
Lewis, Bob
31CubTeal-13
93WatIndC-15
93WatIndF-3565
94ColRedC-14
94ColRedF-446
Lewis, Brett
87PocGiaTB-3
Lewis, Brian
92GulCoaYF-3703
93OneYanC-14
93OneYanF-3517
Lewis, Buddy (John K.)
38OurNatGPP-17
38WheBB15-7
39PlaBal-47
40PlaBal-20
41PlaBal-47
47Exh-133
60SenUniMC-12
79DiaGre-60
84TCMPla1-12
89PacLegI-119
95ConTSN-1348
Lewis, Chris
92DavLipB-4
93DavLipB-15
Lewis, Craig
88WatPirP-8
Lewis, Curt
78OrlTwiT-10
Lewis, Dan
87AubAstP-8
88AshTouP-1061
89OscAstS-11
90CalLeaACLC-40
91LinDriAA-310
91ShrCapLD-310
91ShrCapP-1830
92PhoFirF-2828
92PhoFirS-385
93IowCubF-2140
94JacSunF-1417
Lewis, Darren
89CalLeaA-33
89ModA'sC-30
89ModA'sCLC-278
90Bes-22
90Bow-463
90BowTif-463
90HunStaB-1
91Cla2-T54
91DonRoo-35
91Fle-15
91LinDriAAA-384
91OPC-239
91OPCPre-73
91PhoFirLD-384
91PhoFirP-80
91Sco-350
91ScoRoo-28
91StaClu-362
91Top-239
91TopDeb90-87
91TopDesS-239
91TopMic-239
91TopTif-239
91TriA AAGP-AAA33
91Ult-323
91UppDec-564
91UppDecFE-38F
92Bow-683
92Cla1-T53
92Don-615
92Fle-639
92FleRooS-6
92GiaMot-11
92GiaPacGaE-25
92Lea-441
92OPC-743
92OPCPre-151
92Pin-409
92PinTea2-63
92ProFS7-340
92Sco-562
92Sco100RS-10
92StaClu-31
92Stu-117
92Top-743
92TopGol-743
92TopGolW-743
92TopMic-743
92TriPla-111
92Ult-292
92UppDec-565
93Don-392
93Fla-143
93Fle-157
93GiaMot-13
93GiaPos-21
93Lea-369
93OPC-193
93PacSpa-273
93Pin-94
93Sco-203
93SP-113
93StaClu-143
93StaCluFDI-143
93StaCluG-25
93StaCluMO-13
93StaCluMOP-143
93Top-176
93TopGol-176
93TopInaM-176
93TopMic-176
93Ult-134
93UppDec-173
93UppDecGold-173
94Bow-659
94ColC-174
94ColChoGS-174
94ColChoSS-174
94Don-424
94ExtBas-388
94Fin-85
94FinRef-85
94Fla-244
94Fle-693
94GiaAMC-11
94GiaMot-12
94GiaTeal-8
94GiaUSPC-6S
94GiaUSPC-12D
94Lea-399
94OPC-132
94Pac-548
94Pin-169
94PinArtP-169
94PinMusC-169
94ProMag-124
94Sco-480
94ScoGolR-480
94Sel-304
94Spo-8
94StaClu-453
94StaCluFDI-453
94StaCluGR-453
94StaCluMOP-453
94StaCluT-19
94StaCluTFDI-19
94Stu-85
94Top-354
94TopGol-354
94TopSpa-354
94TriPla-105
94Ult-291
94UppDec-207
94UppDecED-207
94USPlaCA-5H
95Bow-341
95ColCho-256
95ColChoGS-256
95ColChoSE-106
95ColChoSEGS-106
95ColChoSESS-106
95ColChoSS-256
95D3-36
95Don-311
95DonPreP-311
95DonTopotO-215
95Emb-140
95EmbGolI-140
95Emo-195
95Fin-157
95FinRef-157
95Fla-209
95FlaHotG-6
95Fle-582
95FleUpdSL-5
95GiaMot-14
95Lea-76
95Pac-379
95Pin-199
95PinArtP-199
95PinMusC-199
95Sco-274
95ScoGolR-274
95ScoPlaTS-274
95Sel-191
95SelArtP-191
95Spo-95
95SpoArtP-95
95StaClu-74
95StaCluFDI-74
95StaCluMO-28
95StaCluMOP-74
95StaCluSTWS-74
95Top-39
95TopCyb-31
95TopLeaL-LL45
95Ult-241
95UltAwaW-17
95UltAwaWGM-17
95UltGolM-241
95UppDec-87
95UppDec-487T
95UppDecED-87
95UppDecEDG-87
95UppDecSE-204
95UppDecSEG-204
95USPlaCMLA-5H
96Don-287
96DonPreP-287
96EmoXL-38
96Fla-54
96Fle-346
96FleTif-346
96FleUpd-U25
96FleUpdTC-U25
96FleWhiS-10
96LeaSigA-134
96LeaSigAG-134
96LeaSigAS-134
96Sco-41
96Ult-180
96Ult-332
96UltGolM-180
96UltGolM-332
96UppDec-303
97Fle-64
97FleTif-64
97Pac-56
97PacLigB-56
97PacSil-56
97Sco-374
97ScoHobR-374
97ScoResC-374
97ScoShoS-374
97ScoShoSAP-374
97Top-292
97Ult-41
97UltGolME-41
97UltPlaME-41
Lewis, Duffy (George)
12T207-104
15SpoNewM-101
16BF2FP-6
16ColE13-99
16FleBreD-57
16SpoNewM-103
17HolBreD-63
21E121So8-52
22AmeCarE-40
22W575-72
55BraJohC-50
79DiaGre-10
81ConTSN-16
87ConSer2-36
88ConSer4-17
91ConTSN-146
Lewis, Dwayne
95SpoIndTI-11
Lewis, Dwight
94IdaFalBF-3599
94IdaFalBSP-3
Lewis, Ed
94QuaCitRBC-13
94QuaCitRBF-530
95TenVolW-6
Lewis, Harry
11TurRedT-63
Lewis, Herman
80UtiBluJT-26
Lewis, Irving
12T207-105A
12T207-105B
Lewis, Jay
83PeoSunF-18
Lewis, Jeremy
96RocCubTI-16
Lewis, Jerry
78NewWayCT-26
Lewis, Jim
94OscAstC-13
96BufBisB-12
Lewis, Jim L.
80ColCliP-21
80ColCliT-16
81ColCliP-21
81ColCliT-6
82ColCliP-21
82ColCliT-22
83TolMudHT-6
85CalCanC-77
Lewis, Jim M.
79SpoIndT-13
84SalLakCGC-180
92YanWIZ8-106
Lewis, Jim S.
86ChaRaiP-13
88RivRedWCLC-212
88RivRedWP-1423
89WicStaR-14
89WicWraR-20
90CMC-509
90LasVegSC-6
90LasVegSP-114
90ProAAAF-2
91AubAstC-3
91AubAstP-4269
91Cla/Bes-411
91LinDriAA-611
91WicWraLD-611
91WicWraRD-5
92Fle-612
92JacGenF-3999
92OscAstC-20
92OscAstF-2529
92RocRedWF-1935
92RocRedWS-457
92TopDeb91-108
Lewis, Jimmy
91ClaDraP-44
-44
91FroRowDP-28
92Sco-852
92StaCluD-107
94OscAstF-1134
Lewis, Joe
89GasRanP-1007
89GasRanS-10
90GasRanB-20
90GasRanP-2523
90GasRanS-12
Lewis, John
37OPCBatUV-101
37WheBB6-7
86PeoChiP-14
87WinSpiP-16
88WinSpiS-8
91MetWIZ-229
Lewis, Johnny
62KahAtl-12
64Top-479
65OPC-277
65Top-277
66Top-282
66TopRubI-52
66TopVen-282
67CokCapYM-V20
67DexPre-125
67OPC-91
67Top-91
74OPC-236
74Top-236
85CarTeal-21
86CarTeal-26
Lewis, Ken
89BriTigS-14
89Sta-188
Lewis, Kevin
93PitMetC-13
93PitMetF-3713
94CapCitBC-13
94CapCitBF-1755
Lewis, Marc
96CarLeaAIB-B8
96DurBulBrB-19
96MacBraB-23
97Bow-393
97BowInt-393
Lewis, Mark
88BurIndP-1800
89Bow-87
89BowTif-87
89KinIndS-12
89Sta-168
89Top-222
89TopTif-222
90Boo 4
90Bes-320
90Bow-338
90BowTif-338
90CanIndB-1
90CanIndP-1299
90CanIndS-9
90CMC-831
90EasLeaAP-EL36
90ProAaA-27
90StaFS7-13
91Bow-70
91Cla1-T37
91Cla2-T11
91ClaGam-185
91ColSprSSLD-88
91ColSprSSP-2190
91Don-29
91DonRoo-42
91FleUpd-19
91Lea-289
91LinDriAAA-88
91ScoRoo-106T
91StaClu-492
91StaLewRG-1
91StaLewRG-2
91StaLewRG-3
91StaLewRG-4
91StaLewRG-5
91StaLewRG-6
91StaLewRG-7
91StaLewRG-8
91StaLewRG-9
91StaLewRG-10
91StaLewRG-11
91Stu-48
91TopTra-73T
91TopTraT-73T
91TopTriH-A5
91UppDec-17
92Bow-439
92ClaGam-48
92Don-273
92Fle-116
92IndFanC-15
92Lea-49
92OPC-446
92PanSti-46
92Pin-91
92PinTea2-57
92ProFS7-49
92Sco-528
92Sco100RS-50
92ScoImpP-82
92ScoProP-25
92StaClu-193
92Stu-167
92Top-446

92TopDeb91-109
92TopGol-446
92TopGolW-446
92TopMic-446
92TriPla-205
92Ult-51
92UppDec-235
93ChaKniF-551
93ClaFS7-217
93Don-125
93Fle-216
93IndWUA-16
93OPC-194
93PacSpa-96
93PanSti-49
93Pin-374
93Sco-164
93Sel-150
93StaClu-337
93StaCluFDI-337
93StaCluMOP-337
93Top-762
93TopGol-762
93TopInaM-762
93TopMic-762
93TriPla-155
93Ult-186
93UppDec-88
93UppDecGold-88
94ColC-533
94ColChoGS-533
94ColChoSS-533
94Don-464
94Fin-91
94FinRef-91
94Fle-109
94Lea-423
94Sco-483
94ScoGolR-483
94Top-678
94TopGol-678
94TopSpa-678
94UppDec-381
94UppDecED-381
94VerExpC-16
94VerExpF-3917
95RedKah-17
96ColCho-373T
96ColCho-551
96ColChoGS-551
96ColChoSS-551
96Fla-83
96Fle-114
96FleTif-114
96FleUpd-U34
96FleUpdTC-U34
96LeaSigA-135
96LeaSigAG-135
96LeaSigAS-135
96Pin-328
96PinFoil-328
96Sco-144
96Sum-150
96SumAbo&B-150
96SumArtP-150
96SumFoi-150
96Ult-347
96UltGolM-347
97Cir-348
97CirRav-348
97ColCho-109
97ColCho-456
97Don-236
97DonPreP-236
97DonPrePGold-236
97Fle-100
97Fle-570
97FleTif-100
97FleTif-570
97MetUni-111
97Pac-89
97PacLigB-89
97PacSil-89
97Sco-48
97Sco-339
97ScoHobR-339
97ScoPreS-48
97ScoResC-339
97ScoShoS-48
97ScoShoS-339
97ScoShoSAP-48
97ScoShoSAP-339
97Top-442
97Ult-523
97UltGolME-523
97UltPlaME-523
97UppDec-61

Lewis, Matt
94FayGenC-30
95FayGenTI-15
96FayGenB-4

Lewis, Mica
88AubAstP-1974
89AshTouP-966
89AubAstP-2186
90OscAstS-15
91VisOakC-16
91VisOakP-1748
92ClaFS7-71
92OrlSunRF-2858
92OrlSunRS-510
92SkyAA F-219
93ReaPhiF-302

Lewis, Mike
92ClaFS7-296
92VisOakC-15
92VisOakF-1009
95BreCouMF-243

Lewis, Phil
11SpoLifCW-218
90DodTar-1012

Lewis, Richie
88JacExpB-10
88JacExpP-992
90JacExpB-20
90WesPalBES-13
91HarSenP-621
92RocRedWF-1936
92RocRedWS-458
92SkyAAAF-208
93Bow-502
93Don-265
93FleFinE-65
93MarFloA-5
93MarPub-16
93MarUSPC-4D
93MarUSPC-13S
93Pin-608
93SelRoo-139T
93StaClu-619
93StaCluFDI-619
93StaCluMOP-619
93TopTra-90T
93Ult-381
94Don-297
94Fle-471
94Lea-14
94Pac-245
94Sco-280
94ScoGolR-280
94StaClu-427
94StaCluFDI-427
94StaCluGR-427
94StaCluMOP-427
94StaCluT-74
94StaCluTFDI-74
94Top-47
94TopGol-47
94TopSpa-47
94Ult-196
95Fle-335
95Top-373

Lewis, Rufus
91NegLeaRL-30
95NegLeaLI-30

Lewis, Scott
89MidAngGS-21
89TexLeaAGS-5
90CMC-487
90EdmTraC-10
90EdmTraP-516
90ProAAAF-92
91AngSmo-19
91Bow-192
91Sco-759
91ScoRoo-9
91TopDeb90-88
91UppDec-594
92EdmTraF-3537
92Sco-165
92StaClu-43
92Ult-328
93AngMot-19
93Don-167
93Fle-575
93PacSpa-49
93StaCluAn-14
93Top-668
93TopGol-668
93TopInaM-668
93TopMic-668
94AngMot-19
96LasVegSB-16

Lewis, Steve
83AleDukT-25
84PriWilPT-19
85PriWilPT-9

Lewis, T.R.
89BluOriS-13
90Bes-10
90CMC-869
90StaFS7-32
90WauTimB-1
90WauTimP-2133
90WauTimS-14
91Cla/Bes-238
91FreKeyC-18
91FreKeyP-2372
91PerHeaF-10
92FreKeyF-1811
92KanCouCC-8
92KanCouCF-99
92UppDecML-183
93Bow-85
93BowBayF-2196
93ClaFS7-54
94ExcFS7-10
94OriPro-53
94RocRedWF-1004
94RocRedWTI-10
94UppDecML-11
95BowBayTI-44
95RocRedWTI-23
96PawRedSDD-16

Lewis, Tim
94DavLipB-19
95DavLipB-16

Lewis, Timothy
76ForLauYS-25
77WesHavYT-13
79WesHavYT-18

Lewis, Tony
87SpoIndP-3
88ChaRaiP-1214
89RivRedWB-9
89RivRedWCLC-24
89RivRedWP-1395
90WatDiaB-9
90WatDiaP-2376

Lewis, Tyrone
92GulCoaDF-3574
93BakDodCLC-15
96SanBerSB-15

Lewis, Willie
11TurRedT-74

Lewright, Cleo
52LavPro-23

Lexa, Michael
87KenTwiP-10
88KenTwiP-1395

Ley, Terry
72OPC-506
72Top-506
92YanWIZ7-96

Leyland, Jim
75CliPilT-1
80EvaTriT-17
81EvaTriT-1
84WhiSoxTV-8
86TopTra-66T
86TopTraT-66T
87Top-93
87TopTif-93
88Top-624
88TopTif-624
89PirVerFJ-10
89Top-284
89TopTif-284
90OPC-699
90PirHomC-19
90Top-699
90TopTif-699
91OPC-381
91Top-381
91TopDesS-381
91TopMic-381
91TopTif-381
92OPC-141
92PirNatl-11
92Top-141
92TopGol-141
92TopGolW-141
92TopMic-141
93PirHil-5
93PirNatl-14
93Top-511
93TopGol-511
93TopInaM-511
93TopMic-511
94PirQui-10
95PirFil-15
96UppDec-479

Leyritz, Jim
87Ft.LauYP-24
88AlbYanP-1344
89AlbYanB-2
89AlbYanP-325
89AlbYanS-10
89EasLeaAP-9
90AlbDecGB-6
90ClaYel-T60
90CMC-211
90ColCliC-11
90ColCliP-5
90ColCliP-681
90FleUpd-112
90Lea-465
90ProAAAF-331
90ScoRoo-83T
90TopTra-61T
90TopTraT-61T
90TopTVY-50
90UppDec-723
90YanScoNW-10
91Bow-171
91Don-219
91Fle-671
91OPC-202
91PanFreS-326
91Sco-65
91Sco100RS-29
91Top-202
91TopDeb90-89
91TopDesS-202
91TopMic-202
91TopRoo-16
91TopTif-202
91Ult-237
91UppDec-243
92Don-649
92StaClu-198
92Ult-412
92UppDec-117
93Don-477
93Fla-248
93FleFinE-248
93Lea-468
93PacSpa-559
93StaClu-234
93StaCluFDI-234
93StaCluMOP-234
93Top-385
93TopGol-385
93TopInaM-385
93TopMic-385
93Ult-597
94ColC-453
94ColChoGS-453
94ColChoSS-453
94Don-146
94Fla-83
94Fle-237
94Lea-158
94Pac-428
94Pin-517
94PinArtP-517
94PinMusC-517
94Sco-213
94ScoGolR-213
94Sel-350
94StaClu-283
94StaCluFDI-283
94StaCluGR-283
94StaCluMOP-283
94StaCluT-192
94StaCluTFDI-192
94Top-728
94TopGol-728
94TopSpa-728
94Ult-97
95ColCho-521
95ColChoGS-521
95ColChoSE-242
95ColChoSEGS-242
95ColChoSESS-242
95ColChoSS-521
95Don-401
95DonPreP-401
95Fla-65
95Fle-75
95Lea-168
95Sco-102
95ScoGolR-102
95ScoPlaTS-102
95StaClu-341
95StaCluMOP-341
95StaCluSTWS-341
95StaCluVR-180
95Top-450
95TopCyb-246
95Ult-310
95UltGolM-310
95UppDecSE-8
95UppDecSEG-8
96ColCho-369T
96ColCho-629
96ColChoGS-629
96ColChoSS-629
96Fla-131
96Fle-187
96FleTif-187
96MetUni-88
96MetUniP-88
96Sco-181
95StaCluVRMC-180
96Ult-100
96UltGolM-100
97Cir-353
97CirRav-353
97ColCho-179
97ColCho-224
97Don-339
97DonPreP-339
97DonPrePGold-339
97DonTea-9
97DonTeaSPE-9
97Fin-209
97FinRef-209
97Fle-170
97Fle-610
97FleTif-170
97FleTif-610
97Lea-264
97LeaFraM-264
97LeaFraMDC-264
97Pac-153
97PacLigB-153
97PacSil-153
97Sco-466
97ScoHobR-466
97ScoResC-466
97ScoShoS-466
97ScoShoSAP-466
97SpoIll-165
97SpoIllEE-165
97StaClu-288
97StaCluI-I22
97StaCluMOP-288
97StaCluMOP-I22
97Top-98
97Ult-338
97UltGolME-338
97UltPlaME-338
97UppDec-265
97UppDec-523

Leystra, Jeff
93MedHatBJF-3732
93MedHatBJSP-18
94St.CatBJC-16
94St.CatBJF-3640

Leyva, Damian
92BurIndC-19
92BurIndF-1652
93BurIndC-16
93BurIndF-3293

Leyva, Nick
77ArkTraT-5A
77ArkTraT-5B
83ArkTraT-23
84Car-19
84Car5x7-16
85CarTeal-22
86CarTeal-27
89PhiTas-18
89Top-74
89TopTif-74
90OPC-489
90PhiTas-20
90Top-489
90TopTif-489

91OPC-141
91Top-141
91TopDesS-141
91TopMic-141
91TopTif-141
92SyrChiF-1986
92SyrChiMB-11
92SyrChiS-524
93SyrChiF-1013
96BluJayOH-18
97BluJayS-26

Lezcano, Carlos
81Don-521
81Fle-307
81Top-381
82Top-51
83IowCubT-23
84TacTigC-79
88BlaYNPRWLU-5
89BlaYNPRWL-199
91PenPilP-395
93AppFoxC-26
93AppFoxF-2476
94AppFoxC-22
94AppFoxF-1069
96SanJosGB-27

Lezcano, Sixto
74SacSolC-57
76BreA&P-7
76OPC-353
76SSP-241
76Top-353
77BurCheD-89
77Hos-12
77Kel-27
77OPC-71
77Top-185
78Hos-35
78OPC-102
78Top-595
78WifBalD-38
79Hos-136
79OPC-364
79Top-685
80OPC-114
80Top-215
80TopSup-31
81AllGamPI-150
81CokTeaS-125
81Don-207
81Fle-513
81OPC-25
81Top-25
81TopScr-45
81TopSti-218
81TopTra-793
82Don-64
82Fle-119
82OPC-271
82Top-727
82TopSti-95
82TopTra-63T
83AllGamPI-150
83Don-499
83Fle-364
83FleSta-106
83FleSti-229
83OPC-244
83Top-455
83TopSti-298
84Fle-38
84Nes792-185
84OPC-185
84PhiTas-38
84Top-185
84TopTif-185
85Don-529
85Fle-258
85FleUpd-72
85OPC-89
85Pir-9
85Top-556
85TopMin-556
85TopTif-556
85TopTifT-75T
85TopTra-75T
86BreGreT-5
86Top-278
86TopTif-278
88BlaYNPRWL-167
88BlaYNPRWLU-18
94BreMilB-149
94CarLeaAF-CAR20
94WilBluRC-26
94WilBluRF-317
95WilBluRTI-16
96OmaRoyB-2

Lezeau, Jim
94BenRocF-3610
97BenRocC-15

Libke, Al
44CenFlo-14
47SigOil-11
83TCMPla1945-40

Liborio, Dennis
88AstMot-28
89AstMot-28
90AstMot-28
92AstMot-28
94AstMot-28

Liburdi, John
84AlbA'sT-10
85AlbYanT-34
86AlbYanT-13

Lich, Rod
84CedRapRT-23
85CedRapRT-29
86TamTarP-10
87VerRedP-27
92AugPirC-27
93AugPirC-28
95LynHilTI-14

Lichtenberger, Tom
96SarRedSB-4

Lickert, John
83PawRedST-13
85RicBraT-11

Licursi, Richard
92SalLakTSP-1
93VerBeaDC-16
94HigDesMC-19
94HigDesMF-2785

Liddell, Dave
86PeoChiP-15
87ColMetP-13
88RenSilSCLC-287
89JacMetGS-25
89MetColP-39
89TidTidC-18
90CMC-371
90ProAAAF-278
90TidTidC-20
90TidTidP-547
90TopTVM-49
91MetWIZ-230
91TopDeb90-90
92DenZepF-2644
92DenZepS-138

Liddle, Don
53BraJohC-9
53BraSpiaS3-15
54NewYorJA-29
54Top-225
55Bow-146
55GiaGolS-12
56Top-325
83Bra53F-43
94TopArc1-225
94TopArc1G-225

Liddle, Steve
82RedPioT-7
83NasAngT-10
84EdmTraC-107
85EdmTraC-13
86EdmTraP-17
87PorBeaP-10
88PorBeaC-12
88PorBeaP-655
89KenTwiP-1084
89KenTwiS-25
90KenTwiB-27
90KenTwiP-2310
90KenTwiS-25
91VisOakC-24
91VisOakP-1757
92VisOakC-24
92VisOakF-1029
93ForMyeMC-26
93ForMyeMF-2672
94ForMyeMC-26
94ForMyeMF-1183

Lidle, Cory
92EliTwiC-15
92EliTwiF-3676
93PocPosF-4205
93PocPosSP-10
94StoPorC-15
94StoPorF-1691
95ElPasDTI-15
96BinBeeB-16

Lidle, Kevin
92BriTigF-1414
93FayGenC-13
93FayGenF-132
94LakTigC-14
94LakTigF-3038
95JacSunTI-19
96LakTigB-16
96WesOahCHWB-40

Lieber, Jon
92ClaDraP-29
92ClaFS7-421
92EugEmeC-16
92EugEmeF-3027
92FroRowDP-76
93CarLeaAGF-15
93ClaFS7-110
93StaCluM-57
93WilBluRC-17
93WilBluRF-1995
94BowBes-B18
94BowBesR-B18
94CarMudF-1574
94ExcFS7-68
94Fla-423
94FlaWavotF-B5
94FleUpd-174
94LeaLimR-34
94PirQui-11
94TopTra-67T
94UppDecML-132
95Bow-301
95ColCho-385
95ColChoGS-385
95ColChoSE-177
95ColChoSEGS-177
95ColChoSESS-177
95ColChoSS-385
95Don-163
95DonPreP-163
95Fin-7
95FinRef-7
95Fla-402
95Fle-481
95Lea-38
95Pac-345
95Pin-153
95PinArtP-153
95PinMusC-153
95PirFil-16
95Sco-461
95ScoGolR-461
95ScoPlaTS-461
95StaClu-386
95StaCluMOP-386
95StaCluSTWS-386
95Stu-136
95Top-537
95TopCyb-320
95Ult-217
95UltGolM-217
95UppDec-146
95UppDecED-146
95UppDecEDG-146
95UppDecSE-223
95UppDecSEG-223
96ColCho-262
96ColChoGS-262
96ColChoSS-262
96FleUpd-U179
96FleUpdTC-U179
96LeaSigEA-107
97Cir-4
97CirRav-4
97ColCho-431
97Fle-431
97FleTif-431
97Pac-396
97PacLigB-396
97PacSil-396
97UppDec-462

Liebert, Allen
86LakTigP-10
87FayGenP-15
88CarLeaAS-29
88KinIndS-15
89CanIndB-21
89CanIndP-1314
89CanIndS-12
90Bes-188
90CanIndB-6
90CanIndP-1294
90EasLeaAP-EL35
92BirBarF-2586
92BirBarS-88

Lieberthal, Mike
90ClaDraP-3
90ClaYel-T62
90HigSchPLS-2
90MarPhiP-3197
90ProAaA-193
91Bow-506
91Cla/Bes-290
91OPC-471
91Sco-683
91SouAtlLAGP-SAL44
91SpaPhiC-14
91SpaPhiP-899
91Top-471
91TopDesS-471
91TopMic-471
91TopTif-471
91UppDec-67
92ClaDraP-93
92ClaFS7-231
92ProFS7-302
92ReaPhiF-578
92ReaPhiS-532
92SkyAA F-230
92UppDecML-184
92UppDecMLPotY-PY17
93Bow-20
93ClaFisN-11
93ClaYouG-YG8
93ExcAllF-4
93ExcFS7-86
93ScrRedBF-2546
93ScrRedBTI-13
93StaCluP-19
94Bow-112
94Cla-74
94ExcFS7-246
94FleMajLP-21
94FleUpd-166
94LeaLimR-27
94ScrRedBF-922
94StaCluT-233
94StaCluTFDI-233
94Ult-550
94UppDecML-54
95Bow-419
95ColCho-371
95ColChoGS-371
95ColChoSE-24
95ColChoSEGS-24
95ColChoSESS-24
95ColChoSS-371
95Don-240
95DonPreP-240
95Fin-13
95FinRef-13
95Fle-399
95Lea-65
95PacPri-108
95Pin-156
95PinArtP-156
95PinMusC-156
95Sco-309
95ScoGolR-309
95ScoPlaTS-309
95ScrRedBTI-18
95StaClu-203
95StaCluFDI-203
95StaCluMOP-203
95StaCluSTWS-203
95Top-554
95TopCyb-333
95Ult-206
95UltGolM-206
96FleUpd-U167
96FleUpdTC-U167
96PhiTeal-20
97Cir-258
97CirRav-258
97ColCho-419
97Don-343
97DonPreP-343
97DonPrePGold-343
97Fin-82
97FinRef-82
97Fle-414
97FleTif-414
97PinX-PSfF-32
97PinX-PSfFU-32
97SpoIll-93
97SpoIllEE-93
97StaClu-364
97StaCluMOP-364
97Top-56
97Ult-251
97UltGolME-251
97UltPlaME-251
97UppDec-452

Liebhardt, Glenn
08AmeLeaPC-12
08RosComP-28
09T206-212

Liebold, Harry
20NatCarE-58
21Exh-96
21Exh-97
92Man191BSR-15

Liebovitz, Neil
75ForLauYS-4

Liefer, Jeff
96MidLeaAB-53
96SouBenSHS-20
96Top-243
97Bow-82
97BowBes-168
97BowBesAR-168
97BowBesR-168
97BowChr-109
97BowChrI-109
97BowChrIR-109
97BowChrR-109
97BowInt-82

Lien, Al
48SomandK-7
49SomandK-5
52MotCoo-47

Liendo, Temis
93LinVenB-201
94VenLinU-191
95LinVen-114

Lienhard, Steve
87PocGiaTB-5
88CliGiaP-694
89CalLeaA-47
89SanJosGB-20
89SanJosGCLC-214
89SanJosGP-456
89SanJosGS-17
90ShrCapP-1440
91ElPasDLD-185
91ElPasDP-2745
91LinDriAA-185
92ElPasDS-217
93CliGiaC-28
93CliGiaF-2506
95ButCopKtI-24
94CliLumC-27

Liepa, John
94LetMouF-3882
94LetMouSP-20

Lieppman, Keith
75TucTorC-10
76TucTorCa-3
76TusTorCr-6
79OgdA'sT-26
82IdaFalAT-30
82WesHavAT-27
84AlbA'sT-7
85TacTigC-126
86TacTigP-13
87TacTigP-14

Lifgren, Kelly
88SpoIndP-1925
89RivRedWB-10
89RivRedWCLC-16
89RivRedWP-1392
90Bes-190
90RivRedWB-15
90RivRedWCLC-22
90RivRedWP-2605
91Cla/Bes-120
91HigDesMC-7
91HigDesMP-2390
92HigDesMC-8
93WicWraF-2977

Liggett, Troy
89TenTecGE-14

Light, Tal
95AshTouUTI-26
96AshTouB-23

Lightner, Ed
91BenBucC-23
91BenBucP-3701

Lightner, Fred
48BabRutS-11

Ligtenberg, Kerry
96DurBulBlB-16
96DurBulBrB-16
Liles, Greyson
90ArkRaz-19
Lillard, Robert E.
37WheBB7-29P
39CubTeal-15
46SunBre-10
47RemBre-22
47SigOil-48
47SmiClo-6
48SigOil-14
48SmiClo-8
Lilliquist, Derek
88RicBraC-2
88RicBraP-21
89Bow-264
89BowTif-264
89BraDub-15
89ClaTraP-172
89Don-653
89DonBasB-226
89DonRoo-54
89FleUpd-73
89Sco-631
89ScoHot1R-23
89TopTra-73T
89TopTraT-73T
89UppDec-753
90Bow-7
90BowTif-7
90BraDubP-17
90Don-286
90Fle-588
90FleCan-588
90Hot50RS-27
90OPC-282
90PanSti-223
90PubSti-116
90Sco-243
90Sco100RS-19
90ScoYouSI-30
90Spo-24
90Top-282
90TopBig-192
90TopDeb89-70
90TopRoo-18
90TopTif-282
90ToyRoo-17
90UppDec-234
90VenSti-300
91Don-570
91Fle-535
91LasVegSLD-287
91LasVegSP-231
91LinDriAAA-287
91OPC-683
91Sco-571
91StaClu-268
91Top-683
91TopDesS-683
91TopMic-683
91TopTif-683
91UppDec-251
92IndFanC-16
92Lea-451
92ScoRoo-44T
92StaClu-864
92StaCluECN-864
93Don-9
93Fla-194
93Fle-217
93IndWUA-17
93Lea-444
93OPC-211
93PacSpa-413
93Sco-548
93StaClu-441
93StaCluFDI-441
93StaCluMOP-441
93Top-31
93TopGol-31
93TopInaM-31
93TopMic-31
93Ult-187
93UppDec-70
93UppDecGold-70
94ColC-175
94ColChoGS-175
94ColChoSS-175
94Don-154
94Fle-110
94Pin-219
94PinArtP-219
94PinMusC-219
94Sco-194
94ScoGolR-194
94StaClu-508
94StaCluFDI-508
94StaCluGR-508
94StaCluMOP-508
94Top-301
94TopGol-301
94TopSpa-301
94Ult-344
95Top-189
88RicBraBC-7
Lillis, Bob
59DarFar-10
59DodTeal-14
59Top-133
59TopVen-133
60Top-354
61DodBelB-11
61Top-38
62Col.45B-12
62SalPlaC-108A
62SalPlaC-108B
62ShiPlaC-108
62Top-74
62TopVen-74
63Col45"P-10
63Col45'JP-5
63Jel-191
63Pos-191
63Top-119
64Top-321
64TopVen-321
65AstBigLBPP-10
67AstTeal2-15
74OPC-31
74Top-31
78TCM60I-42
83Top-66
84AstMot-15
84Don-84
84Fle-656
84Nes792-441
84Top-441
84TopTif-441
85AstMot-1
85Top-186
85TopTif-186
86GiaMot-28
86Top-561
86TopTif-561
87AstSer1-16
87GiaMot-27
88GiaMot-27
89AstCol4S-17
89GiaMot-28
90DodTar-452
90GiaMot-21
90GiaSmo-13
91GiaMot-27
92GiaMot-28
92GiaPacGaE-26
93GiaMot-28
93GiaPos-22
94GiaMot-28
95GiaMot-28
96GiaMot-28
Lilly, Ted
96YakBeaTI-10
Lim, Ron
90LSUTigP-12
Lima, Jose
90BriTigP-3156
90BriTigS-14
92LakTigC-9
92LakTigF-2274
93LimRocDWB-87
93LimRocDWB-143
93LonTigF-2303
94Bow-481
94ScoRoo-RT158
94ScoRooGR-RT158
94TolMudHF-1026
94UppDecML-101
95Bow-427
95Don-137
95DonPreP-137
95Lea-113
95Pin-148
95PinArtP-148
95PinMusC-148
95Sco-292
95ScoGolR-292
95ScoPlaTS-292
95ScoRooDT-RDT10
95Sel-205
95SelArtP-205
95TolMudHTI-17
96ColCho-547
96ColChoGS-547
96ColChoSS-547
96Don-502
96DonPreP-502
96Fle-115
96FleTif-115
96Pac-310
96Sco-466
96TolMudHB-16
96Top-366
96Ult-348
96UltGolM-348
96UppDec-332
97Pac-90
97PacLigB-90
97PacSil-90
Limbach, Chris
86BenPhiC-147
88ClePhiS-17
88FloStaLAS-10
90SouAtlLAS-15
90SpaPhiB-7
90SpaPhiP-2488
90SpaPhiS-13
91ClePhiC-6
91ClePhiP-1617
92ReaPhiF-571
92ReaPhiS-533
92SkyAA F-231
93MemChiF-371
Limmer, Lou
52Par-86
54Top-232
55Bow-80
55Top-54
55TopDouH-15
79DiaGre-342
94TopArc1-232
94TopArc1G-232
Limon, Vinny
88NebCor-24
Limoncelli, Bill
79ElmPioRST-23
80ElmPioRST-35
87ElmPio(C-2
88ElmPioC-27
Limoncelli, Jeff
90ElmPioP-7
Linares, Antonio
88MarPhiS-22
89SpaPhiP-1046
89SpaPhiS-13
89Sta-55
90SpaPhiB-20
90SpaPhiP-2503
90SpaPhiS-14
Linares, Ifrain
93LinVenB-39
94VenLinU-24
95LinVen-92
Linares, Julio
94AstMot-27
95AstMot-28
96AstMot-28
Linares, Mario
91AubAstC-15
91AubAstP-4277
92AshTouC-22
93QuaCitRBC-11
93QuaCitRBF-103
93QuaCitRBF-130
Linares, Omar
90IBAWorA-4
90IBAWorA-43
Linares, Ramon
85DomLeaS-109
Linares, Rich
93FloStaLAF-48
93VerBeaDC-17
93VerBeaDF-2215
94BakDodC-14
94ClaGolF-185
94ExcFS7-217
95BakBlaTI-17
96SanBerSB-16
Linares, Rufino
79SavBraT-3
81BraPol-25
82BraBurKL-15
82BraPol-25
82Don-310
82Fle-439
82Top-244
83Don-275
83Fle-140
83Top-467
84RicBraT-2
85DomLeaS-180
85Top-167
85TopTif-167
86EdmTraP-18
Linares, Yfrain
95BelBreTI-4
Linarez, Jose
87PocGiaTB-32
Lincoln, Abraham
39WheBB13-2
88WilMulP-10
94OriofB-13
Lincoln, Lance
84AriWilP-10
86BelBreP-13
87BelBreP-14
Lind, Carl
29ExhFou-21
94ConTSN-1262
94ConTSNB-1262
Lind, Jack
74SacSolC-60
75SacSolC-4
83RedPioT-30
87NasSouTI-13
88NasSouC-23
88NasSouP-486
94BreMilB-239
Lind, Jose
85PriWilPT-17
86NasPirP-16
87VanCanP-1616
88BlaYNPRWL-168
88ClaRed-195
88Don-38
88DonBasB-145
88Fle-334
88FleGlo-334
88Lea-38
88PanSti-371
88Sco-597
88ScoGlo-597
88ScoYouS2-4
88StaLinPi-14
88Top-767
88TopBig-106
88TopSti-127
88TopTif-767
89BimBreD-7
89BlaYNPRWL-143
89Bow-421
89BowTif-421
89ClaLigB-20
89Don-290
89DonBasB-101
89Fle-214
89FleGlo-214
89OPC-273
89PanSti-170
89PirVerFJ-13
89RedFolSB-75
89Sco-87
89Spo-62
89Top-273
89TopBig-25
89TopSti-126
89TopTif-273
89UppDec-334
90Bow-170
90BowTif-170
90Don-172
90DonBesN-82
90Fle-474
90FleCan-474
90Lea-77
90OPC-168
90PanSti-328
90PirHomC-20
90PubSti-159
90PubSti-616
90Sco-83
90Spo-58
90Top-168
90TopBig-196
90TopSti-131
90TopTif-168
90UppDec-424
90VenSti-301
90VenSti-302
91Bow-530
91Don-58
91Fle-43
91Lea-146
91OPC-537
91PanFreS-116
91PanSti-117
91Sco-461
91Sco100S-33
91StaClu-233
91Stu-227
91Top-537
91TopDesS-537
91TopMic-537
91TopTif-537
91Ult-283
91UppDec-258
92Bow-351
92ClaGam-178
92Don-189
92Fle-559
92Lea-175
92OPC-43
92PanSti-253
92Pin-49
92Pin-603
92PirNatl-12
92Sco-265
92StaClu-859
92Stu-86
92Top-43
92TopGol-43
92TopGolW-43
92TopMic-43
92Ult-255
92UppDec-205
93Bow-153
93Don-675
93Fla-219
93Fle-115
93FleFinE-221
93Lea-402
93OPC-120
93OPCPre-42
93PacBeiA-8
93PacSpa-489
93PacSpaPl-2
93Pin-103
93RoyPol-16
93Sco-660
93Sel-105
93SelRoo-22T
93StaClu-729
93StaCluFDI-729
93StaCluMOP-729
93StaCluRoy-10
93Stu-189
93Top-108
93TopGol-108
93TopInaM-108
93TopMic-108
93Ult-563
93UltAwaW-4
93UppDec-309
93UppDec-513
93UppDecGold-309
93UppDecGold-513
94Bow-611
94ColC-176
94ColChoGS-176
94ColChoSS-176
94Don-306
94ExtBas-94
94Fin-46
94FinRef-46
94Fla-301
94Fle-163
94Lea-65
94OPC-68
94Pac-292
94PanSti-76
94Pin-199
94PinArtP-199
94PinMusC-199
94Sco-39
94ScoGolR-39
94Sel-51
94SelSam-51
94StaClu-135

94StaCluFDI-135
94StaCluGR-135
94StaCluMOP-135
94StaCluMOP-ST21
94StaCluP-135
94StaCluST-ST21
94Top-332
94TopGol-332
94TopSpa-332
94TriPla-237
94Ult-68
94UppDec-161
94UppDecED-161
95ColCho-454
95ColChoGS-454
95ColChoSS-454
95Don-225
95DonPreP-225
95Fla-265
95Fle-164
95Lea-32
95Pac-207
95PanSti-48
95Pin-108
95PinArtP-108
95PinMusC-108
95Sco-172
95ScoGolR-172
95ScoPlaTS-172
95StaClu-232
95StaCluFDI-232
95StaCluMOP-232
95StaCluSTWS-232
95Top-578
95TopCyb-352
95Ult-58
95UltGolM-58
95UppDec-183
95UppDecED-183
95UppDecEDG-183

Lind, Orlando
85PriWilPT-1
86NasPirP-17
87HarSenP-14
88BlaYNPRWL-135
88HarSenP-847
89BlaYNPRWL-7
89HarSenP-300
89HarSenS-9
90OrlSunRS-9
90PorBeaP-175
90ProAAAF-245
91LinDriAA-484
91OrlSunRLD-484
91OrlSunRP-1845
92PorBeaF-2663
92PorBeaS-413

Lind, Randy
87EveGiaC-11

Lindaman, Vivian
08RosComP-91
09ColChiE-170A
09ColChiE-170B
09ColChiE-170C
09RamT20-68
09T206-213
11SpoLifCW-219
12ColRedB-170A
12ColRedB-170B
12ColRedB-170C
12ColTinT-170A
12ColTinT-170B
12ColTinT-170C

Lindbeck, Em
77FriOneYW-111

Lindblad, Paul
66Top-568
67Top-227
68OPC-127
68Top-127
68TopVen-127
69Top-449
70OPC-408
70Top-408
71MLBOffS-519
71OPC-658
71SenTeaIW-14
71Top-658
72OPC-396
72Top-396
73OPC-406
73Top-406
74OPC-369
74Top-369
75OPC-278
75Top-278
76Kel-52A
76Kel-52B
76OPC-9
76SSP-479
76Top-9
77BurCheD-117
77Top-583
78SSP270-85
78Top-314
79Top-634
87ElPasDP-20
88ElPasDB-10
89ElPasDGS-2
90ElPasDGS-2
91ElPasDLD-200
91ElPasDP-2763
91LinDriAA-200
92PenPilC-29
92PenPilF-2950
92YanWIZ7-97
93AppFoxC-28
93RanKee-24

Lindell, Johnny (John)
43YanSta-17
46SpoExcW-5-3
47Exh-134
47HomBon-30
47TipTop-53
48BluTin-5
48Bow-11
48SweSpoT-17
48YanTeal-17
49Bow-197
49Lea-82
50Bow-209
50W720HolS-17
52MotCoo-1
53Top-230
54Bow-159
54Top-51
76TayBow4-106
77TCMTheWY-55
79DiaGre-17
83TCMPla1943-3
91TopArc1-230
92YanWIZA-40
93ConTSN-715
94TopArc1-51
94TopArc1G-51

Lindell, Rick
91PacSenL-72

Lindeman, Jim
86LouRedTI-16
87CarSmo-14
87ClaUpdY-111
87Don-37
87DonOpeD-59
87DonRoo-41
87FleMin-66
87FleUpd-65
87FleUpdG-65
87Lea-37
87SpoRoo2-43
87TopTra-65T
87TopTraT-65T
88Don-540
88Fle-39
88FleGlo-39
88LouRedBTI-28
88OPC-16
88Sco-302
88ScoGlo-302
88StaLinCa-12
88Top-562
88TopTif-562
89BlaYNPRWL-94
89CarSmo-11
89LouRedBTI-26
89Top-791
89TopTif-791
90CMC-392
90ProAAAF-386
90SprCarDGB-29
90TolMudHC-15
90TolMudHP-156
91LinDriAAA-487
91ScrRedBLD-487
92Don-701
92Fle-538
92OPC-258
92PhiMed-19
92Sco-321
92StaClu-893
92StaCluECN-893
92Top-258
92TopGol-258
92TopGolW-258
92TopMic-258
93TucTorF-3066
94NorTidF-2933
95ColCho-317
95ColChoGS-317
95ColChoSS-317
95Fla-173
95Fle-374
95Sco-216
95ScoGolR-216
95ScoPlaTS-216
95StaClu-380
95StaCluMOP-380
95StaCluSTWS-380

Lindemann, Skip
89GeoColC-19
89GeoColC-28

Lindemann, Wayne
93HicCraC-13
93HicCraF-1275
94SouBenSHC-8
94SouBenSHF-589
95PriWilCTI-20

Lindemuth, John
90BasWit-87

Linden, Mark
89GenCubP-1878

Lindner, Brian
96EveAquB-14

Lindquist, Dan
83TriTriT-11
84VisOakT-25

Lindquist, John
95OdgRapTI-15

Lindros, Eric
90ScoRoo-100T
92StaCluMO-47

Lindsay, Chuck
80LynSaiT-5

Lindsay, Darian
90KinMetB-2
90KinMetS-14
91ParPatF-4
91PitMetC-19
91PitMetP-3418
92ColMetC-8
92ColMetF-290
92ColMetPI-12

Lindsay, John
84WilMay-38

Lindsay, Jon
91GulCoaRSP-16

Lindsay, Tim
91St.CatBJC-21
91St.CatBJP-3390
92MyrBeaHC-18
92MyrBeaHF-2193
93DunBluJC-14
93DunBluJFFN-15

Lindsey, Bill (William D.)
85AlbYanT-12
86AlbYanT-22
87BirBarB-26
88Fle-403
88FleGlo-403
88VanCanC-16
88VanCanP-758

Lindsey, Darrell
88MarPhiS-21
89SpaPhiP-1040
89SpaPhiS-14
90ClePhiS-11
91LinDriAA-511
91ReaPhiLD-511
91ReaPhiP-1369
92ClePhiF-2055

Lindsey, Dave
75SacSolC-2

Lindsey, Don
89EugEmeB-5

Lindsey, Doug (Douglas)
82DanSunF-12

Lindsey, Doug (Michael Douglas)
87UtiBluSP-10
88SpaPhiP-1042
88SpaPhiS-11
90CMC-776
90ReaPhiB-12
90ReaPhiP-1223
90ReaPhiS-16
91Cla/Bes-100
91LinDriAA-512
91ReaPhiLD-512
91ReaPhiP-1372
92ScrRedBF-2449
92ScrRedBS-487
92TopDeb91-110
93ScrRedBTI-14
93StaCluP-10
94NasSouF-1254

Lindsey, Jim
74Car193T-16
90DodTar-453

Lindsey, John
85CloHSS-24
96PorRocB-19

Lindsey, Jon
82ReaPhiT-16

Lindsey, Joseph
75TulOil7-18

Lindsey, Rodney L.
95IdaFalBTI-7
96IdaFalB-13

Lindstrom, Fred
26Exh-36
27Exh-20
28Exh-19
28PorandAR-A23
28PorandAR-B23
28W56PlaC-D8
29ExhFou-10
29PorandAR-56
31Exh-9
31W517-24
32USCar-16
33ButCre-16
33DelR33-11
33ExhFou-5
33Gou-133
34BatR31-122
34GouCanV-17
35DiaMatCS3T1-98
36ExhFou-2
36GouWidPPR-A64
36R31PasP-31
36WorWidGV-65
75SheGrePG-23
76GrePlaG-23
76RowExh-9
76ShaPiz-156
77BobParHoF-32
77GalGloG-127
79DiaGre-351
80GiaGreT-11
80PacLeg-100
80PerHaloFP-156
80SSPHOF-156
83ConMar-35
88ConNatA-13
89DodSmoG-103
90DodTar-454
91ConTSN-58
92ConTSN-596
93DiaStaES-141

Linduyt, Doug
79CedRapGT-31

Linebarger, Keith
92EliTwiC-2
92EliTwiF-3677
93ForWayWC-16
93ForWayWF-1965
94ForWayWC-14
94ForWayWF-2006
95ForMyeMTI-15
96HarCitRCB-19

Linehan, Andrew
94ElmPioF-3468
94ElmPioC-11

Linemann, Wayne
92UtiBluSC-20

Lines, Richard
61UniOil-SD6
67CokCapS-10
67Top-273
68Top-291
68TopVen-291

Lineweaver, Aaron
96SpoIndB-16

Linfante, Rob
91OklStaC-14
92OklStaC-15
94ButCopKSP-5

Linfonte, Ron
79WatIndT-3B

Ling, Holly
91HawWomS-6

Lingerman, Nemo
78WisRapTT-11

Liniak, Cole
96MicBatCB-15
97Bow-417
97BowChr-277
97BowChrI-277
97BowChrIR-277
97BowChrR-277
97BowInt-417

Link, Bryan
93BluOriC-16
93BluOriF-4132
94Bow-349
94ExcFirYPF-2
94ExcFS7-11
94FreKeyF-2629
94OriPro-54
95HudValRTI-12
94FreKeyC-14

Link, Dave
83St.PetCT-30

Link, Robert
86WatIndP-14
87WilBilP-7
88GleFalTP-937
89TolMudHC-6
89TolMudHP-778

Linke, Ed
35DiaMatCS3T1-99
93ConTSN-961

Linke, Fred
11SpoLifM-46

Linnert, Tom
75SanAntBT-14
76WilTomT-9

Lino, Rivera Ortiz
87GasRanP-9

Linskey, Mike
89FreKeyS-13
90Bes-21
90HagSunB-20
90HagSunDGB-15
90HagSunP-1407
90ProAaA-1
90ProAAAF-475
90RocRedWGC-20
90RocRedWP-718
91Bow-105
91LinDriAAA-468
91RocRedWLD-468
91RocRedWP-1897
92Fle-663
92WicWraF-3655
92WicWraS-638
93LasVegSF-940

Lint, Royce
54CarHunW-10
55Bow-62

Lintern, Cory
94EveGiaC-18
94EveGiaF-3651
95BurBeeTI-9

Linton, Dave
85UtiBluST-3
86DayBealP-16

Linton, Doug
87MyrBeaBJP-1439
88KnoBluJB-15
90CMC-331
90ProAAAF-347
90SyrChiC-5
90SyrChiMB-14
90SyrChiP-567
91LinDriAAA-507
91SyrChiLD-507
91SyrChiMB-11
91SyrChiP-2478
92Bow-277
92SkyAAAF-228
92SyrChiF-1964
92SyrChiMB-12
92SyrChiS-510
93BluJayD4-35
93Don-321
93LinVenB-261
93Sco-295
93SyrChiF-996
93Top-159
93TopGol-159

93TopInaM-159
93TopMic-159
94MetColP-15
94VenLinU-126
95ColCho-323
95ColChoGS-323
95ColChoSS-323
95LinVen-187
95OmaRoyTI-17
96OmaRoyB-15
Lintz, Larry
72Dia-26
74OPC-121
74Top-121
75OPC-416
75Top-416
76OPC-109
76SSP-286
76Top-109
77Top-323
Lintz, Ricky
81WatIndT-11
82WatIndF-5
82WatIndT-6
Linz, Phil
47Exh-135
62Top-596
63Top-264
64ChatheY-14
64Top-344
64TopVen-344
64YanReqKP-10
65ChaTheY-12
65Top-369
66PhiTeaI-9
66Top-522
67CokCapPh-8
67OPC-14
67Top-14
68Top-594
78TCM60I-97
91MetWIZ-231
92YanWIZ6-72
Linzy, Frank
65Top-589
66OPC-78
66Top-78
66TopVen-78
67CokCapG-13
67Top-279
68DexPre-48
68OPC-147
68Top-147
68TopVen-147
69MLBOffS-202
69Top-345
70Gia-7
70MLBOffS-127
70OPC-77
70Top-77
71CarTeaI-24
71MLBOffS-277
71OPC-551
71Top-551
72MilBra-199
72OPC-243
72Top-243
73OPC-286
73Top-286
75HawIsIC-13
94BreMilB-240
Lipe, Perry H.
09T206-499
Lipon, John
51Bow-285
52Bow-163
52Top-89
53BowC-123
53RedSoxTI-18
53Top-40
54Top-19
57JetPos-12
58JetPos-11
61MapLeaBH-12
76ShrCapT-13
77ShrCapT-12
78ColCliT-13
79DiaGre-382
79PorBeaT-9
81BufBisT-1
81TigDetN-26
82AleDukT-21
83AleDukT-11
83TopRep5-89
84PriWilPT-29
85NasPirT-27
87FayGenP-17
88FloStaLAS-28
89LakTigS-26
90FloStaLAS-49
90LakTigS-26
91LakTigC-29
91LakTigP-282
91TopArc1-40
92LakTigC-27
92LakTigF-2293
94TopArc1-19
94TopArc1G-19
Lipscomb, Bruce
89ChaRanS-13
Lipski, Robert
63Top-558
Lipson, Marc
90Bes-101
90KenTwiB-20
90KenTwiP-2289
90KenTwiS-9
90MidLeaASGS-14
90ProAaA-113
91Cla/Bes-229
91VisOakC-4
91VisOakP-1738
92OrlSunRF-2845
Lipson, Stefan
83ButCopKT-7
Lira, Felipe
90BriTigP-3165
90BriTigS-15
92LakTigC-16
92LakTigF-2275
93Bow-643
93LinVenB-177
93LonTigF-2304
94Cla-2
94ExcFS7-57
94TolMudHF-1027
94VenLinU-78
95Fin-329
95FinRef-329
95Fla-259
95FleUpd-21
95LinVen-242
95StaClu-585
95StaCluMOP-585
95StaCluSTWS-585
95TopTra-68T
95UppDec-422
95UppDecED-422
95UppDecEDG-422
96ColCho-138
96ColChoGS-138
96ColChoSS-138
96Don-207
96DonPreP-207
96EmoXL-62
96Fla-84
96Fle-116
96FleTif-116
96LeaSigA-136
96LeaSigAG-136
96LeaSigAS-136
96MetUni-61
96MetUniP-61
96Pac-322
96PacPri-P102
96PacPriG-P102
96PanSti-145
96Sco-47
96StaClu-302
96StaCluMOP-302
96Top-71
96Ult-63
96UltGolM-63
96UppDec-71
97Cir-86
97CirRav-86
97ColCho-106
97Fle-101
97FleTif-101
97Pac-91
97PacLigB-91
97PacSil-91
97Top-31
97UppDec-73
Liranzo, Rafael
77RocRedWM-3
78RocRedWT-12
Liriano, Felix
88FayGenP-1093
Liriano, Julio
88WatIndP-675
Liriano, Nelson
85KinBluJT-13
86KnoBluJP-15
87IntLeaAT-8
87SyrChiP-1929
87SyrChiT-17
88BluJay5-8
88BluJayFS-19
88Don-32
88Fle-117
88FleGlo-117
88Lea-32
88OPC-205
88Sco-621
88ScoGlo-621
88ScoYouSI-13
88StaLinBJ-13
88Top-205
88TopBig-155
88TopTif-205
89BluJayFS-17
89ClaTraP-196
89Don-627
89DonBasB-160
89Fle-239
89FleGlo-239
89OPC-76
89Sco-577
89Top-776
89TopBig-207
89TopTif-776
89UppDec-109
90BluJayFS-18
90Bow-518
90BowTif-518
90Don-267
90Fle-87
90FleCan-87
90OPC-543
90PanSti-182
90PubSti-522
90Sco-77
90Top-543
90TopBig-142
90TopSti-197
90TopTif-543
90UppDec-134
90VenSti-303
91Don-603
91Fle-617
91OPC-18
91Sco-288
91Top-18
91TopDesS-18
91TopMic-18
91TopTif-18
91UppDec-360
92ColSprSSF-758
92ColSprSSS-91
93ColSprSSF-3095
93LimRocDWB-21
93TopTra-53T
94Fla-375
94FleUpd-127
94RocPol-16
94StaCluT-110
94StaCluTFDI-110
95DonTopotO-318
95Fle-523
95Pac-140
95PirFil-17
96ColCho-678
96ColChoGS-678
96ColChoSS-678
96Don-91
96DonPreP-91
96Fle-524
96FleTif-524
96LeaSigEA-108
96Pac-175
96Ult-536
96UltGolM-536
97Pac-397
97PacLigB-397
97PacSil-397
Lis, Joe
91St.CatBJC-9
91St.CatBJP-3404
92MyrBeaHC-15
92MyrBeaHF-2204
93ClaGolF-129
93KnoSmoF-1260
93SouAtlLAPI-20
94SyrChiF-979
94SyrChiTI-17
95SyrChiTI-15
96BufBisB-13
Lis, Joe (Joseph)
70OPC-56
70Top-56
71OPC-138
71Top-138
74OPC-659
74Top-659
75OklCit8TI-20
75OPC-86
75Top-86
76SSP-523
77Hos-125
77Top-269
Liscio, Joe
60DarFar-5
Lisenbee, Hod (Horace)
33Gou-68
34GouCanV-45
92ConTSN-540
Lisi, Rick
75AndRanT-2
76AshTouT-7
79TulDriT-14
80ChaChaT-9
80VenLeaS-214
82RocRedWT-14
83RocRedWT-21
84RicBraT-7
93RanKee-230
Lisiecki, David
91BelMarC-22
91BelMarP-3658
92ProFS7-147
Lisio, Joe
94KinMetC-9
94KinMetF-3818
95PitMetTI-42
Liska, Ad
29PorandAR-57
Liss, Tom
87BelMarL-17
89BelMarL-8
List, Joe
95NewHavRTI-7
List, Lew
94NewHavRF-1561
List, Paul
87SalAngP-20
88BenBucL-32
91AugPirC-21
91AugPirP-820
92GasRanF-2264
93TulDriF-2747
93TulDriTI-14
Listach, Pat
89StoPorB-22
89StoPorCLC-173
89StoPorP-379
89StoPorS-4
90CalLeaACLC-36
90StoPorB-5
90StoPorCLC-191
90StoPorP-2190
90TopMag-98
91ElPasDLD-191
91ElPasDP-2753
91LinDriAA-191
92Bow-526
92BrePol-13
92DonRooP-BC7
92DonUpd-U1
92FleUpd-36
92JimDeaRS-2
92Lea-370
92Pin-562
92PinRoo-5
92ScoRoo-80T
92StaClu-757
92StaCluECN-757
92StaCluMO-19
92TopTra-65T
92TopTraG-65T
92Ult-385
92UppDec-775
92UppDecSR-SR13
93Bow-395
93BrePol-15
93BreSen5-1
93ClaGam-53
93DiaMar-64
93Don-309
93DonDiaK-DK29
93Fin-109
93FinJum-109
93FinRef-109
93Fla-226
93Fle-253
93FleAll-AL4
93FleFruotL-36
93FleRooS-RSA3
93FleTeaL-AL3
93FunPac-71
93Hos-32
93JimDea-28
93Lea-264
93LeaFas-10
93OPC-205
93OPCPreSP-15
93OPCPreSPF-15
93PacSpa-160
93PanSti-39
93PanSti-163
93Pin-33
93PinTeaP-7
93Sco-357
93Sco-485
93Sel-273
93SelChaR-1
93SelStaL-56
93SP-67
93StaClu-293
93StaClu-432
93StaCluFDI-293
93StaCluFDI-432
93StaCluMOP-293
93StaCluMOP-432
93Stu-146
93Top-480
93TOPBLAG-35
93TopGol-480
93TopInaM-480
93TopMic-480
93Toy-5
93TriPla-116
93TriPlaLL-L3
93Ult-571
93UltAwaW-19
93UltPer-5
93UppDec-43
93UppDec-253
93UppDec-491
93UppDec-817
93UppDecFA-A13
93UppDecFAJ-A13
93UppDecGold-43
93UppDecGold-253
93UppDecGold-491
93UppDecGold-817
93USPlaCA-12H
93USPlaCR-1H
93USPlaCR-JK
94Bow-617
94BreMilB-241
94BrePol-16
94BreSen-3
94ColC-333
94ColC-520
94ColChoGS-333
94ColChoGS-520
94ColChoSS-333
94ColChoSS-520
94ColChoT-9
94Don-148
94ExtBas-105
94Fin-79
94FinPre-79P
94FinRef-79
94Fla-305
94Fle-181
94FUnPac-92
94Lea-420
94LeaL-45
94OPC-216
94Pac-332
94PanSti-83
94Pin-449
94PinArtP-449
94PinMusC-449
94Sco-371
94ScoGolR-371
94Sel-220
94SP-59

94SPDieC-59
94SPHol-24
94SPHolDC-24
94StaClu-354
94StaCluFDI-354
94StaCluGR-354
94StaCluMOP-354
94Top-130
94TopGol-130
94TopSpa-130
94TriPla-55
94Ult-374
94UppDec-305
94UppDecAJ-9
94UppDecAJG-9
94UppDecED-305
95ColCho-179
95ColChoGS-179
95ColChoSS-179
95Don-410
95DonPreP-410
95DonTopotO-98
95Fla-52
95Fle-182
95Lea-120
95LeaLim-33
95PacPri-75
95Pin-433
95PinArtP-433
95PinMusC-433
95Sco-417
95ScoGolR-417
95ScoPlaTS-417
95StaClu-244
95StaCluFDI-244
95StaCluMOP-244
95StaCluSTWS-244
95Stu-185
95TopTra-144T
95Ult-296
95UltGolM-296
95UppDec-54
95UppDecED-54
95UppDecEDG-54
96ColCho-597
96ColChoGS-597
96ColChoSS-597
96Don-80
96DonPreP-80
96Fle-150
96FleTif-150
96Lea-194
96LeaPrePB-194
96LeaPrePG-194
96LeaPrePS-194
96LeaSigA-137
96LeaSigAG-137
96LeaSigAS-137
96Pac-342
96ProSta-29
96Sco-81
97ColCho-353
97Fle-648
97FleTif-648
97ProMag-60
97ProMagML-60
97Sco-52
97Sco-405
97ScoHobR-405
97ScoPreS-52
97ScoResC-405
97ScoShoS-52
97ScoShoS-405
97ScoShoSAP-52
97ScoShoSAP-405
97Ult-405
97UltGolME-405
97UltPlaME-405
Lister, Martin
92BenMusSP-18
92BilMusF-3350
93WesVirWC-15
93WesVirWF-2863
94ExcFS7-178
94WinSpiC-14
94WinSpiF-267
95JacGenTI-5
Littell, Mark
74OPC-596
74Top-596
75OmaRoyTI-9
76OPC-593
76SSP-181
76Top-593
77Top-141
78CarTeal-10
78Top-331
79Car5-15
79Top-466
80Top-631
81Don-580
81Fle-544
81Top-255
82Don-442
82Fle-120
82Top-56
86RoyGreT-11
89WatDiaP-1784
89WatDiaS-27
90ChaRaiB-25
90ChaRaiP-2055
90SweBasG-112
91HigDesMC-30
91HigDesMP-2414
92StoPorC-24
92StoPorF-52
93StoPorC-29
93StoPorF-762
94StoPorC-28
94StoPorF-1709
Littimer, Dave
91CalLeLA-54
Little, Bryan
82ExpPos-21
83ExpPos-13
83ExpStu-24
83TopTra-62T
84Don-157
84ExpPos-17
84ExpStu-30
84Fle-279
84Nes792-188
84OPC-188
84Top-188
84TopTif-188
85BufBisT-9
85Fle-402
85OPC-257
85Top-257
85TopTif-257
86Don-452
86Fle-212
86Top-346
86TopTif-346
87ColCliP-16
87ColCliP-10
87ColCliT-14
88BufBisC-16
88BufBisP-1491
88BufBisTI-3
89WicStaR-27
89WicWraR-4
90WatDiaB-19
90WatDiaP-2393
91WatDiaC-25
91WatDiaP-1272
92HigDesMC-29
92YanWIZ8-107
Little, Dick
91SalSpuC-25
91SalSpuP-2263
92SalSpuC-27
92SalSpuF-3776
Little, Dick (Richard)
82WicAerTI-9
Little, Doug
87DayBeaAP-8
88BirBarB-26
89BirBarB-22
89BirBarP-93
Little, Grady
84ChaO'sT-10
85KinBluJT-24
88BurBraP-11
89DurBullS-26
89DurBulTI-28
90DurBulTI-29
90HagSunDGB-16
91DurBulC-15
91DurBulP-1676
92GreBraF-1168
92GreBraS-249
93RicBraBB-25
93RicBraF-201
93RicBraP-25
93RicBraRC-25
93RicBraRC-1
94RicBraF-2862
95RicBraRC-9
95RicBraTI-1
96PadMot-28
Little, Jeff
75LafDriT-19
78PhoGiaC-14
79PhoGiaVNB-4
82TolMudHT-4
83Fle-619
83TolMudHT-7
83Top-499
Little, Marc
92WinSpiC-10
Little, Mark
94HudValRF-3400
94StaCluDP-73
94StaCluDPFDI-73
96TexLeaAB-11
96TulDriTI-15
94HudValRC-11
Little, Martin
80WauTimT-5
Little, Mike
89WytCubS-20
90HunCubP-3301
91PeoChiC-21
91PeoChiP-1358
91PeoChiTI-27
92WinSpiF-1221
Little, Randy
86BelMarC-119
Little, Ronald
82WatRedT-21
83IndIndTI-20
Little, Scott
84LitFalMT-4
85LynMetT-27
86JacMetT-21
88HarSenP-838
89BufBisC-20
89BufBisP-1681
90BufBisC-25
90BufBisP-388
90BufBisTI-14
90CMC-25
90ProAAAF-503
90TopDeb89-71
91BufBisLD-31
91BufBisP-552
91LinDriAAA-31
92AugPirC-25
92AugPirF-255
93SalBucC-26
93SalBucF-448
93SouAtlLAPI-21
94AugGreC-28
94AugGreF-3024
Little, Thomas
86BelMarC-109
Littlefield, Dick (Richard)
52Bow-209
54Bow-213
54OriEss-24
55Bow-200
57Top-346
58Top-241
79DiaGre-123
79TCM50-14
91OriCro-262
Littlefield, John
77St.PetCT-4
78ArkTraT-17
79ArkTraT-6
81Don-309
81Fle-535
81Top-489
81TopTra-794
82Don-145
82Fle-576A
82Fle-576B
82SyrChiT-5
82SyrChiTI-15
82Top-278
Littlejohn, Dennis
78PhoGiaC-15
79PhoGiaVNB-19
80PhoGiaVNB-16
80Top-686
81Don-313
81Fle-455
81PhoGiaVNB-18
81Top-561
Littleton, Larry
77ShrCapT-13
79PorBeaT-19
80TacTigT-3
82ChaChaT-20
Littlewood, Mike
87BriYouC-9
Litton, Greg
84EveGiaC-1
85FreGiaP-12
86ShrCapP-15
87ShrCapP-8
89FleUpd-130
89ScoRoo-86T
90Don-453
90Fle-61
90FleCan-61
90GiaMot-18
90GiaSmo-14
90Hot50RS-28
90Lea-331
90OPC-66
90PhoFirP-20
90ProAAAF-46
90Sco-497
90Sco100RS-91
90ScoYouSI-33
90Top-66
90TopBig-308
90TopDeb89-72
90TopTif-66
90UppDec-677
91Bow-621
91Don-198
91Fle-266
91GiaMot-18
91GiaPacGaE-8
91OPC-628
91Sco-533
91StaClu-45
91Top-628
91TopDesS-628
91TopMic-628
91TopTif-628
91Ult-324
92Fle-640
92GiaMot-18
92OPC-238
92PhoFirS-386
92Sco-603
92StaClu-439
92Top-238
92TopGol-238
92TopGolW-238
92TopMic-238
93CalCanF-1171
93Don-340
93Fle-533
93FleFinE-273
93StaCluMari-10
94Fle-292
94Pac-575
94PawRedSDD-10
94PawRedSF-950
94Top-111
94TopGol-111
94TopSpa-111
95TacRaiTI-10
Littrell, Jack
78CliDodT-20
79WauTimT-15
Littrell, Jack Sr.
49PorBeaP-2
55A'sRodM-22
76A'sRodMC-14
Litwhiler, Dan
36OveCanR-32
41DouPlaR-45
41DouPlaR-99
47TipTop-81
49Bow-97
49EurSta-88
50Bow-198
51Bow-179
79DiaGre-313
Litzinger, Jeff
88CapCodPB-8
88CapCodPPaLP-185
Livchak, Robert
87St.PetCP-27
88St.PetCS-13
Lively, Everett
49EurSta-89
Lively, Henry
12T207-106
Livengood, Wes
38CinOraW-16
Livernois, Derek
85ElmPioT-11
86GreHorP-13
87WinHavRSP-23
89LynRedSS-12
90Bes-307
90CMC-805
90NewBriRSB-24
90NewBriRSP-1314
90NewBriRSS-8
90TopTVRS-50
91Bow-123
91LinDriAAA-359
91PawRedSDD-11
91PawRedSLD-359
91PawRedSP-34
92ClaFS7-197
92NewBriRSF-428
92NewBriRSS-488
92SkyAA F-208
93PawRedSDD-13
93PawRedSF-2405
93PawRedSTI-13
Livesey, Jeff
87AncGlaP-19
88OneYanP-2052
89PriWilCS-11
90Ft.LauYS-12
91AlbYanLD-10
91AlbYanP-1011
91LinDriAA-10
92AlbYanF-2229
92ColCliS-107
93AlbYanF-2165
94AbaYanF-1444
95ColCliP-16
95ColCliTI-16
96HarSenB-2
Livesey, Steve
91OneYanP-4162
92PriWilCC-19
92PriWilCF-158
93SanBerSC-22
93SanBerSF-788
94SanBerSC-27
94SanBerSF-2776
96HudValRB-26
96WesOahCHWB-30
Livesy, Shawn
95RocCubTI-12
Livin, Jeff
86OscAstP-17
87ColAstP-20
Livingston, Bob
89SanDieSAS-14
Livingston, Clyde
95MarPhiTI-15
Livingston, Dennis
86AlbDukP-13
87AlbDukP-13
86STaoftFT-14
Livingston, Doug
96PorRocB-20
Livingston, Mickey (T.)
43PhiTeal-15
47TipTop-111
83TCMPla1943-42
90DodTar-1013
Livingston, Paddy
09T206-214
10DomDisP-70
10LuxCigPP-14
10NadE1-31
10SweCapPP-47
11A'sFirT20-10
11SpoLifCW-220
11SpoLifM-97
11T205-101
12T207-107
12T207-108
12T207-109
Livingstone, Scott
87PanAmTURB-4
89LonTigP-1381
90CMC-393
90ProAAAF-387
90TolMudHC-16
90TolMudHP-157
91Cla3-T50
91LinDriAAA-589
91TolMudHLD-589
91TolMudHP-1940
91TriA AAGP-AAA46

91UppDecFE-53F
92Bow-3
92Cla1-T54
92Don-675
92Fle-141
92Lea-127
92OPC-685
92OPCPre-56
92Pin-490
92ProFS7-64
92Sco-414
92Sco100RS-57
92StaClu-317
92Top-685
92TopDeb91-111
92TopGol-685
92TopGolW-685
92TopMic-685
92Ult-61
92UppDec-538
92UppDecSR-SR14
93Bow-235
93Don-409
93Fla-206
93Fle-232
93FleRooS-RSB6
93Lea-375
93OPC-219
93PacSpa-446
93PanSti-116
93Pin-106
93Sco-196
93Sel-320
93StaClu-328
93StaCluFDI-328
93StaCluMOP-328
93TigGat-19
93Top-298
93TopGol-298
93TopInaM-298
93TopMic-298
93Toy-71
93ToyMasP-8
93Ult-202
93UppDec-63
93UppDecGold-63
93USPlaCR-12H
94ColC-421
94ColChoGS-421
94ColChoSS-421
94Don-597
94Fle-139
94Lea-202
94Sco-171
94ScoGolR-171
94StaClu-351
94StaCluFDI-351
94StaCluGR-351
94StaCluMOP-351
94Stu-134
94Top-19
94TopGol-19
94TopSpa-19
95Don-218
95DonPreP-218
95Lea-99
95PadMot-11
95Sco-211
95ScoGolR-211
95ScoPlaTS-211
95StaClu-196
95StaCluFDI-196
95StaCluMOP-196
95StaCluSTWS-196
95Top-483
95TopCyb-275
96Fle-573
96FleTif-573
96LeaSigEA-109
96PadMot-16
96Ult-560
96UltGolM-560
97Pac-430
97PacLigB-430
97PacSil-430
87PanAmTUBI-30

Livsey, Shawn
91Cla/Bes-434
91ClaDraP-25
91FroRowDP-38
92OPC-124
92Pin-545
92StaCluD-108
92Top-124
92TopGol-124
92TopGolW-124
92TopMic-124
93AshTouC-11
93AshTouF-2290
94OscAstC-14
94OscAstF-1150
96DayCubB-15

Liz, Jesus
95SpoIndTI-12

Llanes, Pedro
86MiaMarP-16
87SavCarP-13

Llano, Jorge
82MiaMarT-11

Llanos, Aurelio
88MarPhiS-23
89MarPhiS-17
90PriPatD-13
95HagSunF-80

Llanos, Bobby
92BelMarC-29
92BelMarF-1453
93AppFoxC-15
93AppFoxF-2473

Llanos, Victor
93GleFalRC-19
93GleFalRF-4012
94SavCarC-16
94SavCarF-516
95PeoChiTI-24

Llenas, Chilote
85DomLeaS-77

Llenas, Winston
71OPC-152
71Top-152
74OPC-467
74Top-467
75OPC-597
75Top-597
76SSP-195
83NasAngT-20
85EdmTraC-14
86EdmTraP-19
88BluJayFS-20

Llewellyn, Paul
83AndBraT-28

Llig, Brett
96GreFalDTI-22

Llodrat, Fernando
76WatRoyT-18

Lloyd, Graeme
88MyrBeaBJP-1167
91DunBluJC-5
91DunBluJP-201
92KnoBluJF-2986
92KnoBluJS-383
92SkyAA F-161
93Bow-423
93BrePol-16
93Fla-227
93FleFinE-227
93Lea-459
93OPCPre-71
93PacSpa-512
93Pin-616
93SelRoo-76T
93Ult-572
93UppDec-725
93UppDecGold-725
94BreMilB-242
94BrePol-17
94ColC-518
94ColChoGS-518
94ColChoSS-518
94Don-176
94Fin-48
94FinRef-48
94Fle-182
94Lea-351
94Pac-333
94Sco-284
94ScoGolR-284
94Sel-262
94Top-187
94TopGol-187
94TopSpa-187
94Ult-78
94UppDec-332
94UppDecED-332
95Fla-273
95Fle-183
95Pac-235
95Sco-275
95ScoGolR-275
95ScoPlaTS-275
95Ult-66
95UltGolM-66
96FleUpd-U47
96FleUpdTC-U47
96LeaSigEA-110
97Fle-663
97FleTif-663
97Sco-443
97ScoHobR-443
97ScoResC-443
97ScoShoS-443
97ScoShoSAP-443

Lloyd, John
93BoiHawC-19
93BoiHawF-3912
94CedRapKF-1106
96CedRapKTI-15

Lloyd, Mike
89EliTwiS-15
90KenTwiB-6
90KenTwiP-2301
90KenTwiS-10

Lloyd, Pop (John Henry)
74LauOldTBS-33
80PerHaloFP-160
80SSPHOF-160
83ConMar-54
86NegLeaF-16
88ConNegA-8
88NegLeaD-6
90NegLeaS-5
91PomBlaBPB-21
93TedWil-109
94PomNegLB-9
94UppDecTAE-19

Loaiza, Esteban
93SalBucC-14
93SalBucF-427
94Bow-134
95Bow-162
95BowBes-R82
95BowBesR-R82
95Exc-256
95Fin-253
95FinRef-253
95Fla-403
95FleUpd-150
95FleUpdRU-6
95PirFil-18
95SigRoo-32
95SigRooSig-32
95StaClu-531
95StaCluMOP-531
95StaCluSTWS-531
95Sum-147
95SumNthD-147
95Top-655
95UppDec-260
95UppDecED-260
95UppDecEDG-260
96ColCho-263
96ColChoGS-263
96ColChoSS-263
96Don-273
96DonPreP-273
96Fle-525
96FleTif-525
96Pac-166
96PacEstL-EL14
96PacPri-P58
96PacPriG-P58
96Sco-439
96StaClu-288
96StaCluMOP-288
96Top-172
96TopGal-101
96TopGalPPI-101
96Ult-265
96UltGolM-265
96UppDec-174
97ColCho-424
97Don-312
97DonLim-98
97DonLimLE-98
97DonPreP-312
97DonPrePGold-312
97Pac-398
97PacLigB-398
97PacSil-398
97Sco-459
97ScoHobR-459
97ScoResC-459
97ScoShoS-459
97ScoShoSAP-459

Loaiza, Steve
92AugPirC-4
92AugPirF-233
94CarMudF-1575

Lobaton, Jose
94OneYanC-11
94OneYanF-3800
95GreBatTI-15
96TamYanY-16

Lobaton, Pedro
76VenLeaS-44

Lobb, Dave
71RicBraTI-12

Lobe, Bill
55IndGolS-31

Loberg, Tim
77TacTwiDQ-8A

Lobert, Hans (John)
08RosComP-118
09AmeCarE-71
09RamT20-69
09SpoNewSM-97
09T206-215
10DomDisP-71
10E101-29
10E102-15
10MelMinE-29
10NadCarE-32
10PeoT21-34A
10PeoT21-34B
10SweCapPP-127
11E94-21
11MecDFT-36
11S74Sil-101
11SpoLifCW-221
11SpoLifM-197
11T205-102
11TurRedT-105
12HasTriFT-31B
12HasTriFT-50A
12HasTriFT-50B
12HasTriFT-50C
12HasTriFT-50D
12HasTriFT-51
14FatPlaT-26
14PieStaT-33
15AmeCarE-25
15CraJacE-170
15SpoNewM-102
16BF2FP-79
16ColE13-91
16SpoNewM-104
40PlaBal-160
91ConTSN-172
92ConTSN-392

Lobozzetta, Al
87CedRapRP-1

Locanto, Pat
70RoyTeal-20

Locas, Jacques
43ParSpo-48

Locey, Tony
93GenCubC-19
93GenCubF-3171
94PeoChiC-15
94PeoChiF-2264

Lochner, Dave
83CedRapRF-8
83CedRapRT-3

Lock, Dan
94SigRooDP-44
94SigRooDPS-44
94StaCluDP-8
94StaCluDPFDI-8
95QuaCitRBTI-13
96KisCobB-13

Lock, Don
47Exh-136
63Top-47
64Top-114
64TopCoi-53
64TopSta-24
64TopStaU-41
64TopTatl-49
64TopVen-114
65ChaTheY-31
65OldLonC-29
65Top-445
66OPC-165
66SenTeal-9
66Top-165
66TopRubl-53
66TopVen-165
67CokCapPh-18
67DexPre-126
67Top-376
68OPC-59
68Top-59
68TopVen-59
69MilBra-159
69Top-229
69TopSta-76
78TCM60I-34

Locke, Bobby
60Top-44
60TopVen-44
61Top-537
62Top-359
65Top-324
68OPC-24
68Top-24
68TopVen-24

Locke, Charlie
91OriCro-263

Locke, Roger Dale
88AshTouP-1064

Locke, Ron
64Top-556
65Top-511
91MetWIZ-232

Locke, William H.
10PirTipTD-2

Lockenmeyer, Mark
84JacMetT-3

Locker, John
89ElmPioP-29
90ElmPioP-18

Locker, Robert
65Top-541
66Top-374
67CokCapWS-16
67DexPre-127
67Top-338
68OPC-51
68Top-51
68TopVen-51
69Top-548
70BreMcD-17
70BreMil-13
70MLBOffS-274
70OPC-249
70Top-249
71MLBOffS-520
71OPC-356
71Top-356
72Top-537
73LinPor-42
73OPC-645
73Top-645
74OPC-62
74Top-62
74TopTra-62T
75OPC-434
75Top-434
83Pil69G-19
94BreMilB-243

Lockett, Lester
91NegLeaRL-28
92NegLeaK-3
93TedWil-110
95NegLeaL2-2
95NegLeaLI-28

Lockett, Ron
90PriPatD-14
91Cla/Bes-348
91ClePhiC-17
91ClePhiP-1628
91FloStaLAP-FSL7
92Bow-303
92ClaFS7-232
92ReaPhiF-588
92ReaPhiS-534
92SkyAA F-232
92UppDecML-231
93ReaPhiF-303
93StaCluP-26
94ScrRedBF-933

Lockhart, Bruce
85GreHorT-6
86WinHavRSP-15
87WinHavRSP-13

Lockhart, Keith
87CedRapRP-13
88ChaLooB-9
88SouLeaAJ-5
89NasSouC-16

89NasSouP-1278
89NasSouTI-12
90CedRapRDGB-12
90CMC-144
90NasSouC-19
90NasSouP-247
90ProAAAF-559
91LinDriAAA-264
91NasSouLD-264
91NasSouP-2166
92TacTigF-2510
92TacTigS-538
93LouRedF-223
93TriAAAGF-23
94Bow-111
94PadMot-19
94ScoRoo-RT146
94ScoRooGR-RT146
94Sel-395
94SpoRoo-56
94SpoRooAP-56
94Ult-580
94VenLinU-82
95Sco-306
95ScoGolR-306
95ScoPlaTS-306
96Cir-45
96CirRav-45
96ColCho-574
96ColChoGS-574
96ColChoSS-574
96Don-386
96DonPreP-386
96Fla-91
96Fle-133
96FleTif-133
96LeaSigA-138
96LeaSigAG-138
96LeaSigAS-138
96Pin-56
96ProSta-117
96RoyPol-15
96Sco-114
96StaClu-305
96StaCluMOP-305
96Ult-357
96UltGolM-357
96UppDec-498U
97Fle-115
97FleTif-115
97Lea-45
97LeaFraM-45
97LeaFraMDC-45
97MetUni-94
97Pac-104
97PacLigB-104
97PacSil-104
97Sco-59
97Sco-472
97ScoHobR-472
97ScoPreS-59
97ScoResC-472
97ScoShoS-59
97ScoShoS-472
97ScoShoSAP-59
97ScoShoSAP-472
97StaClu-159
97StaCluMOP-159
97Top-312
97Ult-67
97UltGolME-67
97UltPlaME-67
97UppDec-84

Lockhart, Mike
92WatIndC-19
92WatIndF-3238

Lockhart, Tim
89FreStaBS-12

Lockie, Randy
83QuaCitCT-13

Locklear, Dean
91Cla/Bes-206
91SouBenWSC-18
91SouBenWSP-2854
92SarWhiSCB-7
92SarWhiSF-201
93SarWhiSC-18
94MidAngOHP-15
94PriWilCC-13
94PriWilCF-1917

Locklear, Gene
74HawIslC-101
74PadDea-17
75OPC-13
75Top-13
76OPC-447
76Top-447
92YanWIZ7-98

Locklear, Jeff
92CliGiaF-3593
93CliGiaC-15
93CliGiaF-2486
94CliLumF-1976
94SanJosGC-15
94SanJosGF-2812
94CliLumC-13

Lockley, Blain
86WatPirP-12
87MacPirP-12

Lockman, Whitey (Carroll)
47Exh-137
47HomBon-31
47PM1StaP1-114
47TipTop-127
48Bow-30
49Bow-2
49EurSta-116
50Bow-82
50Dra-8
50JJKCopP-8
51Bow-37
51R42SmaS-60
51TopRedB-41
52BerRos-34
52Bow-38
52RedMan-NL13
52StaCalL-78G
52TipTop-21
53BowC-128
53Bri-33
53RedMan-NL7
53StaMey-5
54Bow-153
54NewYorJA-30
54StaMey-5
55Bow-219
55GiaGolS-16
55StaMey-5
56Top-205
57Top-232
58GiaJayP-6
58GiaSFCB-13
58Hir-62
58Top-195
59Top-411
60Top-535
73OPC-81
73Top-81A
73Top-81B
74OPC-354
74Top-354
75Gia195T-16
79TCM50-26
84FifNatCT-9
91OriCro-264
91TopArc1-292

Lockwood, Rick
85ChaO'sT-4
86JacMetT-18
88LouRedBTI-29

Lockwood, Skip (Claude)
65Top-526
70OPC-499
70Top-499
71MLBOffS-443
71OPC-433
71Top-433
72OPC-118
72Top-118
73OPC-308
73Top-308
74OPC-532
74Top-532
75OPC-417
75Top-417
75TucTorC-16
75TucTorTI-9
76OPC-166
76SSP-549
76Top-166
77BurCheD-139
77MetDaiPA-12
77Top-65
78MetDaiPA-14
78Top-379
79OPC-250
79Top-481
80OPC-295
80Top-567
81Don-217
81Top-233
91MetWIZ-233
94BreMilB-244

Lodbell, Dick
87AncGlaP-38

Lodding, Richard
89BelMarL-9
91PenPilC-8
91PenPilP-374
92SanBerC-6
92SanBerSF-949

Lodes, Lance
90ArkRaz-32

Lodgek, Scott
89BelMarL-10
90PenPilS-11

Lodigiani, Dario
41Gou-15
47RemBre-19
47SigOil-49
48SigOil-15
48SmiClo-15
49RemBre-16
79DiaGre-339
84TCMPla1-14

LoDuca, Paul
94BakDodC-15
94Bow-594
95AusFut-52
95SanAntMTI-17
96VerBeaDB-17

Loe, Darin
89BelMarL-11
90PenPilS-12
91SanBerSC-8
91SanBerSP-1984

Loeb, Marc
90MedHatBJB-24
91MyrBeaHC-14
91MyrBeaHP-2948
93DunBluJC-15
93DunBluJF-1799
93DunBluJFFN-16
94DunBluJC-17
94DunBluJF-2560
95DunBluJTI-12

Loehr, Ted
75AppFoxT-14

Loera, Javier
89GreFalDSP-7

Loes, Billy
47StaPinP2-18
52Bow-240
52Top-20
53BowC-14
53Top-174
54Bow-42
54NewYorJA-10
55Bow-240
55DodGolS-5
56Top-270
57Top-244
58Hir-48
58OriJayP-5
58Top-359
59Top-336A
59Top-336B
60Top-181
60TopVen-181
61Top-237
76BooProC-8
79TCM50-50
90DodTar-455
91OriCro-265
91RinPosBD2-10
91TopArc1-174
95TopArcBD-3
95TopArcBD-49
95TopArcBD-136
95TopArcBD-160

Loewer, Carlton
92MisStaB-25
93BazTeaU-21
93MisStaB-26
93TopTra-4T
94SigRooBS-6
95Bes-88
95ClePhiF-214
95ReaPhiELC-25
95SPML-131
95UppDecML-202
96Exc-207
96ExcFirYP-8
96ReaPhiB-8
97Bow-218
97BowInt-218
95UppDecMLFS-202

Loewer, Stan
87LSUTigP-5

Lofthus, Kevin
90ModA'sCLC-170
90ModA'sP-2219

Loftin, Bo
90LSUTigA-10
91BilMusP-3757
91BilMusSP-5
92BenMusSP-1
92BilMusF-3351
93ExcFS7-24
93WinSpiC-13
93WinSpiF-1566

Lofton, James
93PriRedC-17
93PriRedF-4187
94BilMusF-3679
94BilMusSP-8
95Exc-177

Lofton, Kenny (Kenneth)
88AubAstP-1953
89AubAstP-2166
90FloStaLAS-11
90OscAstS-16
90StaFS7-3
91Bow-565
91LinDriAAA-614
91TriA AAGP-AAA52
91TucTorLD-614
91TucTorP-2225
91UppDecFF-24F
92Bow-110
92Cla2-T46
92ClaGam-177
92Don-5
92DonRooP-BC8
92DonUpd-U6
92Fle-655
92FleUpd-17
92IndFanC-17
92JimDeaRS-8
92LeaGolR-BC4
92OPC-69
92OPCPre-72
92Pin-290
92Pin-582
92PinRoo-3
92PinRooI-7
92PinTea2-35
92ProFS7-223
92Sco-845
92ScoHotR-3
92ScoImpP-32
92ScoRoo-14T
92ScoRoo-10
92SpoIllFK1-359
92StaClu-695
92StaCluNC-695
92Stu-168
92Top-69
92TopDeb91-112
92TopGol-69
92TopGolW-69
92TopMic-69
92TopTra-66T
92TopTraG-66T
92Ult-350
92UltAllR-7
92UppDec-25
92UppDec-766
92UppDecSR-SR15
93Bow-417
93ClaGam-54
93DiaMar-65
93Don-537
93DonSpiotG-SG11
93Fin-43
93FinRef-43
93Fla-195
93Fle-218
93Fle-346
93FleFruotL-37
93FleRooS-RSA1
93FunPac-109
93IndWUA-18
93JimDea-23
93Lea-40
93LeaFas-3
93OPC-251
93OPCPreSP-17
93OPCPreSPF-17
93PacJugC-9
93PacSpa-97
93PanSti-53
93Pin-40
93PinTea2-18
93Sco-58
93Sel-275
93SelChaR-4
93SelStaL-55
93StaClu-277
93StaCluFDI-277
93StaCluMOP-277
93Stu-180
93Top-331
93TOPBLAG-36
93TopGol-331
93TopInaM-331
93TopMic-331
93Toy-69
93TriPla-144
93TriPla-181
93Ult-542
93UppDec-45
93UppDec-262
93UppDecGold-45
93UppDecGold-262
93UppDecSH-HI11
93USPlaCA-13H
93USPlaCR-1C
94Bow-195
94BowBes-R68
94BowBesR-R68
94ColC-315
94ColC-565
94ColChoGS-315
94ColChoGS-565
94ColChoSS-315
94ColChoSS-565
94Don-39
94DonSpeE-39
94ExtBas-60
94Fin-218
94FinJum-218
94FinRef-218
94Fla-283
94FlaHotG-4
94Fle-111
94FleLeaL-4
94FUnPac-107
94Lea-350
94LeaL-28
94OPC-237
94OPCAllR-25
94OPCJumA-25
94OscMayR-7
94Pac-173
94PacSilP-17
94PanSti-58
94Pin-179
94PinArtP-179
94PinMusC-179
94PinRunC-RC14
94PinTheN-7
94Sco-81
94ScoCyc-TC2
94ScoGolR-81
94ScoGolS-41
94Sel-231
94SelSki-SK4
94SP-98
94SPDieC-98
94Spo-43
94SpoSha-SH1
94StaClu-301
94StaCluFDI-301
94StaCluGR-301
94StaCluMO-27
94StaCluMOP-301
94StaCluMOP-ST19
94StaCluST-ST19
94Stu-93
94Top-149
94TopBlaG-11
94TopGol-149
94TopPre-331
94TopSpa-149
94TopTraFI-6
94TriPla-115
94Ult-45
94UltAwaW-7
94UltLeaL-3

94UltRisS-7
94UppDec-215
94UppDecAJ-29
94UppDecAJG-29
94UppDecED-215
94USPlaCA-1H
94USPlaCA-8D
95Baz-22
95BazRedH-RH4
95Bow-305
95BowBes-R20
95BowBes-X10
95BowBesR-R20
95BowBesR-X10
95ClaPhoC-22
95ColCho-81
95ColChoGS-81
95ColChoSE-119
95ColChoSE-139
95ColChoSE-258
95ColChoSEGS-119
95ColChoSEGS-139
95ColChoSEGS-258
95ColChoSESS-119
95ColChoSESS-139
95ColChoSESS-258
95ColChoSS-81
95D3Zon-6
95Don-371
95DonDiaK-DK11
95DonDom-8
95DonPreP-371
95DonTopotO-59
95Emb-1
95EmbGolI-1
95Emo-34
95EmoMas-5
95Fin-56
95FinRef-56
95FlaHotG-7
95FlaHotN-5
95FlaTodS-5
95Fle-137
95FleAllS-16
95FleUpdH-12
95FleUpdSL-6
95FleUpdSS-6
95Kra-8
95Lea-8
95Lea300C-18
95LeaGreG-8
95LeaLim-12
95LeaLimG-18
95LeaLimIBP-9
95NatPac-16
95Pac-122
95PacGolP-24
95PacPri-39
95PanSti-81
95PanSti-125
95Pin-189
95Pin-284
95PinArtP-189
95PinArtP-284
95PinGatA-GA17
95PinMusC-189
95PinMusC-284
95PinRedH-RH21
95PinWhiH-WH21
95Sco-422
95ScoDouGC-GC8
95ScoGolR-422
95ScoHaloG-HG57
95ScoPlaTS-422
95ScoRul-SR14
95ScoRulJ-SR14
95Sel-120
95SelArtP-120
95SelCer-91
95SelCerMG-91
95SP-150
95SPCha-149
95SPChaDC-149
95Spo-81
95SpoArtP-81
95SpoDouT-8
95SpoHamT-HT16
95SPSil-150
95SPSpeF-10
95StaClu-470
95StaCluMO-29
95StaCluMOP-470
95StaCluMOP-SS14
95StaCluMOP-VRE7
95StaCluSS-SS14
95StaCluSTDW-I19T
95StaCluSTDW-I470
95StaCluSTMP-14
95StaCluSTWS-470
95StaCluVE-VRE7
95StaCluVR-257
95Stu-11
95StuGolS-11
95StuPlaS-11
95Sum-48
95SumNthD-48
95TomPiz-11
95Top-104
95TopCyb-67
95TopCybSiR-7
95TopFin-10
95TopLeaL-LL16
95TopLeaL-LL30
95UC3-85
95UC3-143
95UC3ArtP-85
95UC3ArtP-143
95UC3CycS-CS19
95Ult-38
95UltAllS-11
95UltAllSGM-11
95UltAwaW-7
95UltAwaWGM-7
95UltGolM-38
95UltLeaL-2
95UltLeaLGM-2
95UltRisS-6
95UltRisSGM-6
95UppDec-90
95UppDecED-90
95UppDecEDG-90
95UppDecPAW-H24
95UppDecPAWE-H24
95UppDecPLL-R22
95UppDecPLLE-R22
95UppDecSE-159
95UppDecSEG-159
95UppDecSoaD-SD3
95USPlaCMLA-1H
95USPlaCMLA-9D
95Zen-62
95ZenZ-15
96Baz-12
96Bow-55
96BowBes-23
96BowBesAR-23
96BowBesMI-6
96BowBesMIAR-6
96BowBesMIR-6
96BowBesR-23
96Cir-33
96CirAcc-6
96CirBos-9
96CirRav-33
96ColCho-5
96ColCho-127
96ColCho-385T
96ColCho-388T
96ColCho-410
96ColChoGS-5
96ColChoGS-127
96ColChoGS-410
96ColChoSS-5
96ColChoSS-127
96ColChoSS-410
96ColChoYMtP-21
96ColChoYMtP-21A
96ColChoYMtPGS-21
96ColChoYMtPGS-21A
96Don-396
96DonPreP-396
96EmoXL-49
96EmoXLD-5
96Fin-B233
96Fin-G81
96Fin-S327
96FinRef-B233
96FinRef-G81
96FinRef-S327
96Fla-67
96FlaHotG-5
96Fle-89
96FleInd-6
96FleTeaL-5
96FleTif-89
96FleUpd-U231
96FleUpdH-12
96FleUpdSL-5
96FleUpdTC-U231
96FleZon-6
96Lea-127
96LeaAllGMC-12
96LeaAllGMCG-12
96LeaLim-29
96LeaLimG-29
96LeaPre-24
96LeaPreP-24
96LeaPrePB-127
96LeaPrePG-127
96LeaPrePS-127
96LeaPreSG-3
96LeaPreSte-3
96LeaSig-55
96LeaSigA-139
96LeaSigAG-139
96LeaSigAS-139
96LeaSigEA-111
96LeaSigEACM-17
96LeaSigPPG-55
96LeaSigPPP-55
96MetUni-46
96MetUniML-4
96MetUniP-46
96Pac-303
96PacBaeS-7
96PacOctM-OM11
96PacPri-P95
96PacPriG-P95
96PanSti-123
96PanSti-180
96Pin-105
96Pin-312
96PinAfi-114
96PinAfiAP-114
96PinAfiSP-23
96PinArtP-40
96PinArtP-194
96PinChrBC-R15
96PinFoil-312
96PinSta-40
96PinSta-194
96ProMagA-4
96ProSta-56
96SchDis-12
96Sco-325
96ScoBigB-16
96ScoDugC-B50
96ScoDugCAP-B50
96ScoNumG-22
96ScoRef-4
96Sel-14
96SelArtP-14
96SelCer-4
96SelCerAP-4
96SelCerCB-4
96SelCerCR-4
96SelCerIP-20
96SelCerMB-4
96SelCerMG-4
96SelCerMR-4
96SP-73
96Spo-39
96SpoArtP-39
96SPSpeFX-23
96SPSpeFXDC-23
96SPx-18
96SPxGol-18
96StaClu-208
96StaClu-325
96StaCluEPB-325
96StaCluEPG-325
96StaCluEPS-325
96StaCluMM-MM8
96StaCluMO-21
96StaCluMOP-208
96StaCluMOP-325
96StaCluMOP-MM8
95StaCluVRMC-257
96Stu-45
96StuPrePB-45
96StuPrePG-45
96StuPrePS-45
96StuStaGS-12
96Sum-39
96SumAbo&B-39
96SumArtP-39
96SumFoi-39
96TeaOut-50
96Top-420
96TopChr-164
96TopChrR-164
96TopGal-161
96TopGalPPI-161
96TopLas-108
96TopLasSS-13
96TopPro-AL15
96Ult-48
96Ult-584
96UltGolM-48
96UltGolM-584
96UltPriL-7
96UltPriLGM-7
96UltRaw-5
96UltRawGM-5
96UltSeaC-4
96UltSeaCGM-4
96UppDec-319
96UppDecA-12
96UppDecDD-DD18
96UppDecDDG-DD18
96UppDecDDS-DD18
96UppDecHC-HC18
96UppDecPHE-H2
96UppDecPRE-R26
96UppDecPreH-H2
96UppDecPreR-R26
96UppDecRunP-RP9
96Zen-66
96ZenArtP-66
97Bow-224
97BowBes-11
97BowBesAR-11
97BowBesMI-MI10
97BowBesMIAR-MI10
97BowBesMIARI-MI10
97BowBesMII-MI10
97BowBesMIR-MI10
97BowBesMIRI-MI10
97BowBesP-8
97BowBesPAR-8
97BowBesPR-8
97BowBesR-11
97BowChr-54
97BowChrI-54
97BowChrIR-54
97BowChrR-54
97BowInt-224
97Cir-1
97CirRav-1
97ColCho-59
97ColCho-264
97ColChoAC-25
97ColChoS-7
97ColChoTBS-18
97ColChoTBSWH-18
97ColChoTotT-T5
97Don-50
97Don-276
97Don-411
97DonArmaD-9
97DonDom-16
97DonEli-19
97DonEliGS-19
97DonFraFea-12
97DonLim-73
97DonLim-94
97DonLim-141
97DonLimFotG-31
97DonLimLE-73
97DonLimLE-94
97DonLimLE-141
97DonPowA-15
97DonPowADC-15
97DonPre-24
97DonPre-174
97DonPreCttC-24
97DonPreCttC-174
97DonPreP-50
97DonPreP-276
97DonPreP-411
97DonPrePGold-50
97DonPrePGold-276
97DonPrePGold-411
97DonPrePM-6
97DonPreTB-11
97DonPreTBG-11
97DonPreTP-11
97DonPreTPG-11
97DonTea-24
97DonTeaSMVP-14
97DonTeaSPE-24
97Fin-174
97Fin-283
97FinEmb-174
97FinEmb-283
97FinEmbR-174
97FinEmbR-283
97FinRef-174
97FinRef-283
97FlaSho-A7
97FlaSho-B7
97FlaSho-C7
97FlaShoHG-9
97FlaShoLC-7
97FlaShoLC-B7
97FlaShoLC-C7
97FlaShoLCM-A7
97FlaShoLCM-B7
97FlaShoLCM-C7
97Fle-80
97Fle-501
97FleGouG-6
97FleGouGF-6
97FleTif-80
97FleTif-501
97Lea-110
97Lea-363
97LeaBanS-6
97LeaFraM-110
97LeaFraM-363
97LeaFraMDC-110
97LeaFraMDC-363
97LeaGolS-17
97LeaLeaotN-4
97LeaWarT-5
97MetUni-82
97MetUniMF-6
97MetUniML-7
97NewPin-25
97NewPinAP-25
97NewPinKtP-11
97NewPinMC-25
97NewPinPP-25
97NewPinPP-K11
97Pac-73
97PacLigB-73
97PacPri-26
97PacPriGA-GA5
97PacPriLB-26
97PacPriP-26
97PacPriSH-SH4A
97PacPriSL-SL3C
97PacSil-73
97Pin-186
97PinArtP-186
97PinCer-58
97PinCerLI-14
97PinCerMBlu-58
97PinCerMG-58
97PinCerMR-58
97PinCerR-58
97PinIns-71
97PinInsC-1
97PinInsCE-71
97PinInsDD-12
97PinInsDE-71
97PinMusC-186
97PinTotCPB-58
97PinTotCPG-58
97PinTotCPR-58
97PinX-P-6
97PinX-PMoS-6
97PinX-PMW-19
97PinX-PMWG-19
97PinX-PMWS-19
97ProMag-53
97ProMagML-53
97Sco-157
97Sco-340
97Sco-540
97ScoHobR-340
97ScoHobR-540
97ScoInd-7
97ScoIndPl-7
97ScoIndPr-7
97ScoIndU-7
97ScoIndUTC-7
97ScoPreS-157
97ScoResC-340
97ScoResC-540
97ScoShoS-157
97ScoShoS-340
97ScoShoS-540
97ScoShoSAP-157
97ScoShoSAP-340
97ScoShoSAP-540
97Sel-27
97SelArtP-27
97SelRegG-27

97SelToootT-11
97SelToootTMB-11
97SkyE-X-56
97SkyE-XC-56
97SkyE-XEC-56
97SkyE-XHoN-20
97SP-24
97SPInsI-3
97SpoIll-77
97SpoIllEE-77
97SpoIllGS-3
97SPSpeF-12
97SPx-8
97SPxBoufG-4
97SPxBro-8
97SPxGraF-8
97SPxSil-8
97SPxSte-8
97StaClu-3
97StaCluMat-3
97StaCluMOP-3
97StaCluMOP-PG13
97StaCluMOP-PL8
97StaCluPG-PG13
97StaCluPL-PL8
97StaCluPP-PP2
97Stu-85
97StuMasS-10
97StuMasS8-10
97StuPor8-17
97StuPrePG-85
97StuPrePS-85
97Top-350
97TopChr-117
97TopChrDD-DD4
97TopChrDDR-DD4
97TopChrR-117
97TopChrSB-21
97TopChrSBR-21
97TopGal-117
97TopGalPG-PG9
97TopGalPPI-117
97TopHobM-HM10
97TopScr-13
97TopSeaB-SB21
97TopSta-64
97TopStaAM-64
97Ult-50
97Ult-406
97UltDiaP-5
97UltDouT-5
97UltFamGam-14
97UltFieC-11
97UltGolME-50
97UltGolME-406
97UltHitM-12
97UltLeaS-11
97UltPlaME-50
97UltPlaME-406
97UltSeaC-4
97UltTop3-17
97UltTop3GM-17
97UppDec-52
97UppDec-153
97UppDec-525
97UppDecAG-AG7
97UppDecAWJ-7
97UppDecP-12
97UppDecRP-RP17
97UppDecU-37
97Zen-37
Lofton, Rodney
89FreKeyS-14
90CMC-765
90HagSunB-9
90HagSunP-1423
90HagSunS-13
91HagSunLD-236
91HagSunP-2464
91LinDriAA-236
92HagSunS-262
92RocRedWF-1946
92SkyAA F-107
92UppDecML-327
93Bow-258
93ElPasDF-2958
94ElPasDF-3152
Loftus, Dick
90DodTar-1014
Loftus, Thomas
87OldJudN-305
Logan, Chris
94SpoIndC-18
94SpoIndF-3321
96RanCucQB-18
Logan, H. Dan
80RocRedWT-4
81RocRedWT-11
81RocRedWW-11
82RocRedWT-15
83RocRedWT-17
Logan, Joe
88CapCodPPaLP-19
89JamExpP-2158
90RocExpLC-16
90RocExpP-2689
91FloStaLAP-FSL44
91WesPalBEC-7
91WesPalBEP-1223
Logan, Johnny
47Exh-138
53BraJohC-20
53BraSpiaS3-16
53BraSpiaS7-7
53Top-158
54Bow-80
54BraJohC-23
54BraMer-2
54BraSpiaSP-12
54RedMan-NL20
54Top-122
55Bow-180
55BraGolS-19
55BraJohC-23
55BraSpiaSD-11
55RedMan-NL5
56Top-136
56YelBasP-18
57BraSpiaS4-12
57SwiFra-12
57Top-4
58BraJayP-7
58Top-110
59Top-225
60BraLaktL-13
60BraSpiaS-10
60Top-205
61Pos-105A
61Pos-105B
61Top-524
62Top-573
63PirIDL-12
63Top-259
78BraTCC-8
79TCM50-158
83Bra53F-23
87Bra195T-4
91TopArc1-158
92BazQua5A-3
93UppDecAH-83
94TopArc1-122
94TopArc1G-122
94UppDecAH-83
94UppDecAH1-83
Logan, Lefty (Robert Dean)
77SerSta-16
86IndIndTI-18
90DodTar-456
Logan, Marcus
94NewJerCC-17
94NewJerCF-3415
96StPetCB-15
Logan, Todd
90VisOakCLC-76
90VisOakP-2157
92VisOakC-13
Loggins, Mike
86Ft.MyeRP-18
87MemChiB-18
87MemChiP-4
88OmaRoyC-13
88OmaRoyP-1504
89OmaRoyC-20
89OmaRoyP-1738
90CMC-187
90OmaRoyC-12
90OmaRoyP-76
90ProAAAF-611
91LinDriAAA-433
91RicBraBC-26
91RicBraLD-433
91RicBraTI-2
LoGrande, Angelo
78WatIndT-14
81ChaChaT-14
82ChaChaT-15
83ChaChaT-10
Logsdon, Kevin
91WatIndC-9
91WatIndP-3364
92ColRedC-11
92ColRedF-2387
93KinIndC-13
93KinIndF-2243
93KinIndTI-13
94CanIndF-3117
Logue, Matt
89NiaFalRP-15
Lohrke, Jack
47TipTop-128
48Bow-16
49Bow-59
49EurSta-117
51Bow-235
52Bow-251
53BowBW-47
57HygMea-8
57SeaPop-24
75Gia195T-17
76TayBow4-61
85TCMPla1-44
Lohrman, Bill
40PlaBal-210
79DiaGre-40
90DodTar-457
Lohry, Adin
90OneYanP-3367
92PriWilCC-8
92PriWilCF-151
93SanBerSC-11
93SanBerSF-775
94SanBerSC-9
94SanBerSF-2762
Lohuis, Mark
81ShrCapT-21
Lois, Alberto
77ColCliT-10A
77ColCliT-10B
78ColCliT-14
79PorBeaT-14
80Top-683
Loiselle, Richard
92ChaRaiC-13
92ChaRaiF-116
93WatDiaC-21
93WatDiaF-1766
94RanCucQC-19
94RanCucQF-1636
95MemChiTI-17
96JacGenB-16
Loiz, Niuman
96QuaCitRB-18
Lolich, Mickey
64Top-128
64TopVen-128
65TigJayP-7
65Top-335
65TopEmbl-55
66Top-226
66Top-455
66TopRubl-54
66TopVen-226
67CokCapTi-14
67DexPre-128
67OPC-88
67Top-88
67TopVen-239
68CokCapT-14
68TigDetFPB-10
68Top-414
69KelPin-10
69MilBra-160
69MLBOffS-50
69MLBPin-15
69OPC-168
69TigTeal-6
69TigTealC-6
69Top-168
69Top-270
69TopFou-14
69TopSta-175
69TopTeaP-1
70DayDaiNM-35
70Kel-65
70MilBra-13
70MLBOffS-210
70OPC-72
70Top-72
70Top-715
71MLBOffS-398
71OPC-71
71OPC-133
71Top-71
71Top-133
71TopCoi-106
71TopGreM-23
71TopTat-105
72Kel-38
72MilBra-200
72OPC-94
72OPC-96
72OPC-450
72ProStaP-29
72Top-94
72Top-96
72Top-450
72TopPos-5
73Kel2D-3
73LinPor-73
73OPC-390
73TigJew-11
73Top-390
73TopCanL-27
73TopCom-10
73TopPin-10
74OPC-166
74Top-9
74TopSta-178
75Hos-6
75HosTwi-6
75OPC-245
75SSP42-21
75Top-245
76CraDis-28
76LauDiaJ-3
76MetMSAP-4
76OPC-3
76OPC-385
76SSP-354
76Top-3
76Top-385
76TopTra-385T
77Spo-5209
77Top-565
78PadFamF-19
79Top-164
80Top-459
81TCM60I-347
81TigDetN-55
83TigAIKS-62
84OCoandSI-156
86TigSpoD-20
88PacLegI-39
88TigDom-11
89SweBasG-97
90SweBasG-81
91MetWIZ-234
91SweBasG-56
91UppDecS-22
92ActPacA-36
93MetIma-11
93TedWil-40
93TigLitC-7
93UppDecAH-84
93UppDecS-26
94TedWilM-M31
94UppDecAH-91
94UppDecAH1-91
97FleMilDM-33
Lolich, Ron
71OPC-458
71Top-458
Lollar, Sherm
50Bow-142
51Bow-100
51TopBluB-24
52Bow-237
52NatTeaL-16
52Top-117
52WhiSoxH-5
53BowC-157
53Top-53
54Bow-182
54RedHeaF-17
54RedMan-AL5
54Top-39
55Bow-174
55Top-201
56Top-243
57Top-23
58Top-267
58Top-491
58WhiSoxJP-6
59Top-385
60Top-495
60Top-567
60WhiSoxJP-6
60WhiSoxTS-11
61Pos-28A
61Pos-28B
61Top-285
61TopStal-123
61WhiSoxTS-7
62Jel-53
62Pos-53
62PosCan-53
62SalPlaC-55
62ShiPlaC-55
62Top-514
62WhiSoxJP-6
62WhiSoxTS-10
63Jel-42
63Pos-42
63Top-118
76ChiGre-10
79TCM50-73
81Ori6F-21
83TopRep5-117
85WhiSoxC-7
89WhiSoxK-3
91TopArc1-53
94TopArc1-39
94TopArc1G-39
Lollar, Tim
79WesHavYT-20
80ColCliP-23
80ColCliT-1
81Fle-108
81Top-424
82Top-587
83Don-61
83DonActA-37
83Fle-365
83FleSti-228
83OPC-185
83Top-185
83Top-742
83TopSti-296
84Don-284
84Fle-305
84Nes792-644
84OPC-267
84PadMot-3
84PadSmo-16
84Top-644
84TopTif-644
85Don-324
85Fle-39
85FleUpd-73
85Lea-111
85OPC-13
85Top-13
85TopSti-153
85TopTif-13
85TopTifT-76T
85TopTra-76T
85WhiSoxC-46
86Don-620
86Fle-354
86Top-297
86TopTif-297
87Fle-38
87FleGlo-38
87Top-396
87TopTif-396
92YanWIZ8-108
Loman, Doug
78BurBeeT-19
80HolMilT-15
81ElPasDT-8
82VanCanT-10
84VanCanC-28
85BrePol-5
85Don-46
94BreMilB-325
Loman, Kevin
95RicBraRC-10
96RicBraUB-17
Lomasney, Steve
96LowSpiB-16
Lomastro, Jerry
83OrlTwiT-12
85TolMudHT-24
86TolMudHP-14
87HagSunP-7
87RocRedWT-26
86STaoftFT-25
Lombard, George
94StaCluDP-14
94StaCluDPFDI-14

95EugEmeTI-1
96BesAutS-50
96Bow-204
96Exc-131
96MacBraB-24
97Bow-168
97BowChr-164
97BowChrI-164
97BowChrIR-164
97BowChrR-164
97BowInt-168

Lombardi, Al
89PenPilS-11

Lombardi, Ernie
32OrbPinNP-58
32OrbPinUP-41
33TatOrb-41
34DiaMatCSB-115
34BatR31-129
34DiaStaR-36A
34DiaStaR-36B
34DiaStaR-105
34ExhFou-4
34Gou-35
34GouCanV-82
35DiaMatCS2-12
35DiaMatCS3T1-100
35ExhFou-4
36ExhFou-4
36GouWidPPR-A66
36NatChiFPR-111
36R31PasP-15
37ExhFou-4
37WheBB14-8
37WheBB7-29E
38CinOraW-17
38ExhFou-4
38GouHeaU-246
38GouHeaU-270
38WheBB10-8
38WheBB11-6
39ExhSal-37A
39ExhSal-38B
39GouPreR303A-30
39GouPreR303B-18
39OrcPhoAP-30
39OrcPhoAP-32
39WheBB12-1
39WorWidGTP-30
40WheM4-8A
40WheM4-8B
41DouPlaR-11
41HarHarW-13
47TipTop-129
48SigOil-16
60Fle-17
61Fle-55
75JohMiz-1
75ShaPiz-5
77GalGloG-64
80PacLeg-11
80PerHaloFP-195
80SSPHOF-191
81ConTSN-28
82DiaCla-32
82OhiHaloF-8
86DonHig-33
86SpoDecG-23
89DodSmoG-102
89HOFStiB-58
91ConTSN-27
92ConTSN-427
93ConTSN-877
94ConTSN-1064
94ConTSNB-1064

Lombardi, John
91MedHatBJP-4102
94AlbPolC-16
94AlbPolF-2234
94OriPro-55

Lombardi, Phil
83GreHorT-15
85AlbYanT-13
86ColCliP-12
86ColCliP-14
87ColCliP-17
87ColCliP-12
87ColCliT-15
87Don-401
87Fle-648
87FleGlo-648
87Spo-118
87SpoTeaP-7
88MetColP-32
88TidTidCa-10
88TidTidCM-12
88TidTidP-1578
88Top-283
88TopTif-283
89MetColP-40
89TidTidC-12
89TidTidP-1975
90MetColP-38
91MetWIZ-235
92YanWIZ8-109
86STaoftFT-4

Lombardi, Vic
46SpoExcW-8-7
47TipTop-100
49EurSta-165
50PirTeal-11
51Bow-204
52Par-7
79DiaGre-88
84TCMPla1-27
90DodTar-459

Lombardi, Vince
87SpoCubG-1

Lombardo, Chris
78St.PetCT-17

Lombardozzi, Chris
87PriWilYP-13
89CedRapRB-28
89CedRapRP-935
89ChaLooB-17
89ChaLooGS-25
90NasSouP-240
90ProAAAF-552

Lombardozzi, Steve
83OrlTwiT-6
84TolMudHT-1
85TolMudHT-17
86Don-598
86DonRoo-18
86FleUpd-68
86Spo-178
86SpoRoo-17
86TwiTeal-2
87Don-318
87DonOpeD-227
87Fle-547
87FleGlo-547
87SpoTeaP-17
87TopTra-66T
87TopTraT-66T
88Don-196
88Fle-16
88FleGlo-16
88PanSti-137
88Sco-174
88ScoGlo-174
88StaLinTw-13
88Top-697
88TopTif-697
88TwiMasBD-6
88TwiTeal-1
89AstSmo-23
89Don-554
89Fle-120
89FleGlo-120
89OPC-376
89Sco-421
89Top-376
89TopTif-376
89TucTorC-23
89TucTorJP-13
89TucTorP-181
89UppDec-179
90Don-688

Lombarski, Tom
80CarMudF-12
81ReaPhiT-16
82OklCit8T-14
83MidCubT-14
84IowCubT-17
85IowCubT-4
86PeoChiP-16
87TidTidP-17
87TidTidT-14

Lomeli, Michael
87IdaFalBP-14
88BoiHawP-1622
89BoiHawP-2004
90EriSaiS-13

Lomon, Kevin
92DurBulC-8
92DurBulTI-14
93DurBulF-483
93DurBulTI-21
94Bow-401
94RicBraF-2844
95FleUpd-114
95RicBraTI-8
96RicBraB-18
96RicBraRC-1

Lonborg, Jim
65Top-573
66OPC-93
66Top-93
66TopVen-93
67CokCapRS-16
67DexPre-129
67Top-371
67TopGiaSU-4
67TopRedSS-9
67TopVen-213
68AtlOilPBCC-24
68Baz-11
68CokCapRS-16
68DexPre-49
68OPC-10
68OPC-12
68OPC-155
68Top-10A
68Top-10B
68Top-12
68Top-155
68Top-460
68Top3-D-5
68TopActS-4C
68TopActS-15C
68TopGamI-14
68TopPla-8
68TopPos-11
68TopVen-10
68TopVen-12
68TopVen-155
69CitMetC-3
69MilBra-161
69MLBOffS-14
69MLBPin-16
69NabTeaF-13
69OPC-109
69RedSoxAO-6
69RedSoxTI-6
69Top-109
69TopSta-135
69TopTeaP-3
70Kel-49
70MLBOffS-159
70RedSoxCPPC-17
70Top-665
71MLBOffS-323
71OPC-577
71RedSoxTI-5
71Top-577
72MilBra-201
72OPC-255
72Top-255
73OPC-3
73Top-3
74OPC-342
74PhiJohP-41
74Top-342
74TopSta-75
75OPC-94
75Top-94
76OPC-271
76SSP-462
76Top-271
77Kel-41
77Top-569
78PhiSSP-52
78SSP270-52
78Top-52
79OPC-233
79Top-446
81RedSoxBG2S-66
81RedSoxBG2S-91
83PhiPosGM-12
88PacLegI-80A
88PacLegI-80B
89SweBasG-48
90SweBasG-124
91LinDri-16
91SweBasG-57
92ActPacA-50
92UppDecS-6
93TedWil-3
93UppDecAH-85
94BreMilB-326
94UppDecAH-128
94UppDecAH1-128
94UppDecS-8

Lonchar, John
77TacTwiDQ-9

Lond, Joel
86FloStaLAP-30

London, Darren
90PriWilCTI-3

Long, Bill (William)
82AmaGolST-18
83LasVegSBHN-14
84BeaGolGT-11
85BufBisT-21
86BufBisP-16
87DonRoo-48
87FleUpd-66
87FleUpdG-66
87HawIsIP-16
87TopTra-67T
87TopTraT-67T
88Don-306
88Fle-404
88FleGlo-404
88OPC-309
88RedFolSB-49
88Sco-539
88ScoGlo-539
88Top-309
88TopTif-309
88WhiSoxC-14
89Bow-56
89BowTif-56
89Don-573
89Fle-501
89FleGlo-501
89OPC-133
89Sco-351
89Top-133
89TopTif-133
89UppDec-499
89WhiSoxC-16
90CubMar-12
90OPC-499
90PubSti-394
90Sco-526
90ScoRoo-62T
90Top-499
90TopTif-499
90TopTVCu-52
90VenSti-304
91Fle-425
91OPC-668
91Sco-559
91Top-668
91TopDesS-668
91TopMic-668
91TopTif-668
91UppDec-495
94ElmPioF-3490
94ElmPioC-25

Long, Bob
52LavPro-22

Long, Bob (Robert E.)
75LynRanT-15
78SalPirT-8
79BufBisT-20
80PorBeaT-21
81PorBeaT-16
82PorBeaT-5
82Top-291
84SalLakCGC-179
85CalCanC-95
86Fle-468
86RicBraP-12
87ChaO'sW-14
89ChaLooLITI-17

Long, Bruce
86ReaPhiP-15
87ReaPhiP-10

Long, Dale
47Exh-139A
47Exh-139B
55DonWin-30
55Top-127
55TopDouH-115
56Top-56
56TopPin-43
56YelBasP-19
57Kah-20
57SwiFra-3
57Top-3
58Top-7
59Top-147
59Top-414
59TopVen-147
60CubJayP-8
60Top-375
61Top-117
61TopStaI-205
62Jel-65
62Pos-65
62PosCan-65
62SalPlaC-35
62ShiPlaC-35
62Top-228
63BasMagM-49
63Top-484
72LauGreF-48
78TCM60I-223
79TCM50-41
80MarExh-16
87SpoRea-15
90HOFStiB-53
90PacLeg-92
92YanWIZ6-73

Long, Danny
87OldJudN-308

Long, Dennis
81TulDriT-14
82TulDriT-4
83TulDriT-8

Long, Don
87QuaCitAP-19
88BenBucL-27
88BenBucL-26
89PalSprACLC-60
89PalSprAP-476
90QuaCitAGS-1
91LinDriAA-449
91MidAngLD-449
91MidAngOHP-17
91MidAngP-449
92MidAngF-4040
92MidAngS-474
93MidAngF-337
94VanCanF-1878
96VanCanB-1

Long, Garrett
96EriSeaB-14
96Exc-219
96Top-241

Long, Germany (Herman)
03BreE10-91
11SpoLifCW-222
87OldJudN-307
95May-18
98CamPepP-44

Long, James V.
88PalSprACLC-89
88PalSprAP-1460

Long, Jeoff
64Top-497

Long, Joe
91SpoIndP-3946
92GulCoaYF-3788
93GreHorC-15
93GreHorF-883
94TamYanC-16
94TamYanF-2379
95NorNavTI-43
96Bow-295
97Bow-152
97BowInt-152

Long, Joey
91SpoIndC-2
93WatDiaC-22
93WatDiaF-1767
94RanCucQC-20
94RanCucQF-1637
96LasVegSB-17

Long, Justin
95ElmPioTI-14
95ElmPioUTI-14

Long, Kevin
88AriWilP-10
88CapCodPPaLP-98
89EugEmeB-14
90BasCitRS-15
92OmaRoyF-2976
92OmaRoyS-334
92SkyAAAF-153
93OmaRoyF-1692
94MemChiF-369
96WicWraB-3

Long, R.D.
92OneYanC-15
93GreHorC-16
93GreHorF-895

94TamYanC-17
94TamYanF-2394
95NorNavTI-24
95TamYanYI-18
Long, Rich (Richard)
89UtiBluSP-14
90SouBenWSB-10
90SouBenWSGS-9
Long, Ryan
91ClaDraP-40
91FroRowDP-18
91HigSchPLS-30
92Bow-79
92EugEmeC-2
92EugEmeF-3035
92StaCluD-109
93RocRoyC-16
93RocRoyF-722
94WilBluRC-12
94WilBluRF-305
95WicWraTI-9
96WicWraB-13
Long, Steve
90JamExpP-20
91SumFlyC-7
91SumFlyP-2330
92WesPalBEC-11
92WesPalBEF-2085
93BinMetF-2330
94EdmTraF-2872
95ChaKniTI-13
Long, Terrence
94ClaUpdCotC-CC17
94KinMetC-10
94KinMetF-3836
94SigRooDP-20
94SigRooDPS-20
94StaCluDP-83
94StaCluDPFDI-83
94TopTra-33T
95Exc-232
95Pin-173
95PinArtP-173
95PinMusC-173
95PitMetTI-23
95ScoDraP-DP10
95SelSurS-SS10
95SPML-99
95StaClu-98
95StaCluFDI-98
95StaCluMOP-98
95StaCluSTWS-98
95Top-112
95UppDecML-175
96Bow-368
96HilStaHWB-12
97Bow-187
97BowBes-157
97BowBesAR-157
97BowBesR-157
97BowCerBIA-CA49
97BowCerGIA-CA49
97BowInt-187
95UppDecMLFS-175
Long, The Kid (Ernest)
93NegLeaRL2-23
Long, Thomas
15SpoNewM-103
16ColE13-100
16SpoNewM-105
Long, Tony
86LakTigP-11
90EugEmeGS-18
91BasCitRC-9
91BasCitRP-1396
91FloStaLAP-FSL2
92BasCitRF-3843
95ArkTraTI-18
Longaker, Scott
91HamRedC-9
91HamRedP-4035
Longenecker, Jere
83ButCopKT-18
86MemChiSTOS-13
86MemChiTOS-13
87MemChiB-19
87MemChiP-9
Longmire, Tony
87MacPirP-8
88SalBucS-10
91Bow-489
91Cla/Bes-98
91LinDriAA-513
91ReaPhiLD-513
91ReaPhiP-1382
92ProFS7-297
93Bow-596
93ClaFS7-67
93ScrRedBF-2555
93ScrRedBTI-15
93TriAAAGF-20
94Bow-168
94FleUpd-167
94LeaLimR-37
94Pac-480
94PhiMed-20
94PhiMel-15
94PhiUSPC-2H
94PhiUSPC-8S
94Pin-528
94PinArtP-528
94PinMusC-528
94ScoRoo-RT148
94ScoRooGR-RT148
94Sel-382
94SpoRoo-57
94SpoRooAP-57
94StaClu-394
94StaCluFDI-394
94StaCluGR-394
94StaCluMOP-394
94StaCluT-213
94StaCluTFDI-213
94Top-28
94TopGol-28
94TopSpa-28
94Ult-551
95Don-420
95DonPreP-420
95Fla-181
95Fle-400
95Pac-332
95PacPri-109
95Phi-18
95PhiMel-15
95Sco-242
95ScoGolR-242
95ScoPlaTS-242
95Top-608
95TopCyb-362
96ColCho-252
96ColChoGS-252
96ColChoSS-252
96Don-90
96DonPreP-90
96Fle-502
96FleTif-502
96Ult-255
96UltGolM-255
97PacPriGotD-GD183
Longuil, Rich
87SumBraP-15
88DurBulS-10
89BurBraP-1624
89BurBraS-14
90DurBulTI-21
Lonigro, Greg
87CedRapRP-15
88CedRapRP-1152
88MidLeaAGS-9
89ChaLooB-16
89ChaLooGS-17
90ChaLooGS-20
91ChaLooLD-161
91ChaLooP-1967
91LinDriAA-161
93IowCubF-2141
93OrlCubF-2794
Lonnett, Joe
57Top-241
58Top-64
73OPC-356
73Top-356
74OPC-221
74Top-221
77PirPosP-13
93CarMudF-2071
Lono, Joel
86TamTarP-11
87CedRapRP-6
Look, Bruce
69Top-317
Lookout, Chief
83ChaLooT-24
Lookouts, Chattanooga
83ChaLooT-28
Loomis, Geoff
92SouOreAC-10
92SouOreAF-3425
93SouOreAC-14
93SouOreAF-4072
Looney, Brian
91JamExpC-17
91JamExpP-3542
92ProFS7-269
92RocExpC-18
92RocExpF-2111
93WesPalBEC-12
93WesPalBEF-1335
94Bow-472
94Fle-544
94UppDec-125
94UppDecED-125
95PawRedSDD-18
95PawRedTI-17
96PawRedSDD-17
Looney, Steve
91FayGenC-24
91FayGenP-1183
Looper, Braden
97Bow-77
97BowBes-172
97BowBesAR-172
97BowBesR-172
97BowChr-105
97BowChrI-105
97BowChrIR-105
97BowChrR-105
97BowInt-77
97Top-477
Looper, Eddie
87SavCarP-18
88SavCarP-350
89SprCarB-23
Lootens, Brian
93EveGiaC-16
93EveGiaF-3783
Lopat, Ed
47Exh-140
47StaPinP2-19
47TipTop-24
48BluTin-40
48YanTeal-16
49Bow-229
50Bow-215
51BerRos-C6
51Bow-218
51R42SmaS-61
51TopBluB-39
52BerRos-35
52Bow-17
52CokTip-4
52StaCalL-70B
52StaCalS-84B
52TipTop-22
52Top-57
53Dor-103
53ExhCan-15
53Top-87
54NewYorJA-50
54Top-5
55Top-109
55TopDouH-41
56TopHocF-A2
60RawGloT-14
60Top-465
61TwiPetM-2
63AthJayP-7
63Top-23
64AthJayP-9
64Top-348
64TopVen-348
71FleWorS-49
79DiaGre-135
81TCM60I-345
83ASAJohM-11
83TCMPla1945-17
83TopRep5-57
83YanASFY-24
84FifNatC-4
90PacLeg-38
90SweBasG-24
91OriCro-266
91SweBasG-58
91TopArc1-87
92ActPacA-67
92BazQua5A-12
92YanWIZA-41
93TedWil-65
94TopArc1-5
94TopArc1G-5
94UppDecAH-68
94UppDecAH1-68
Lopata, Stan
47PM1StaP1-115
49Bow-177
49EurSta-140
49PhiBul-30
50Bow-206
51BerRos-B9
51Bow-76
54Bow-207
55Bow-18
56Top-183
57Top-119
58Hir-29
58HirTes-6
58PhiJayP-7
58Top-353
59Top-412
60BraJayP-7
60RawGloT-15
60Top-515
79TCM50-151
83PhiPosGPaM-3
Lopes, Dave
73LinPor-95
73OPC-609
73Top-609
74GreHeroBP-4
74GreHeroBP-6
74OPC-112
74Top-112
74TopSta-46
75GreHeroBP-2
75GreHeroBP-6
75Hos-67
75HosTwi-67
75OPC-93
75Top-93
76GreHeroBP-2
76GreHeroBP-6
76Hos-105
76LinSup-114
76OPC-4
76OPC-197
76OPC-660
76Spo-10
76SSP-79
76Top-4
76Top-197
76Top-660
77BurCheD-145
77Hos-14
77OPC-4
77OPC-96
77Spo-5102
77Spo-7401
77Top-4
77Top-180
78Hos-112
78OPC-222
78SSP270-67
78Top-412
78Top-440
78WifBalD-39
79DodBlu-8
79Hos-114
79Kel-52
79OPC-144
79Top-290
80BurKinPHR-28
80DodPol-15
80Kel-29
80OPC-291
80Top-560
80TopSup-60
81AllGamPI-104
81Dod-7
81DodPol-15
81Don-416
81Fle-114A
81Fle-114B
81FleStiC-67
81Kel-29
81LonBeaPT-2
81OPC-50
81PerAll-5
81Top-50
81TopScr-92
81TopSti-175
81TopSupHT-48
82A'sGraG-8
82Don-327
82Fle-12
82FleSta-10
82OPC-85
82OPC-218
82OPC-338
82Top-338
82Top-740
82Top-741
82TopTra-64T
83A'sGraG-15
83Don-339
83Fle-524
83FleSta-107
83FleSti-188
83OPC-365
83Top-365
83TopFol-5
83TopSti-105
84A'sMot-21
84CubChiT-17
84Don-400
84Fle-453
84Nes792-669
84Nes792-714
84OPC-17
84Top-669
84Top-714
84TopRubD-19
84TopSti-331
84TopTif-669
84TopTif-714
85CubLioP-15
85CubSev-15
85Don-604
85Fle-60
85OPC-12
85SpoIndGC-13
85Top-12
85TopMin-12
85TopTif-12
86CubGat-15
86CubUno-11
86Don-9
86Don-388
86DonSupD-9
86Fle-372
86Lea-9
86OPC-125
86Spo-144
86Spo-194
86Top-125
86TopTif-125
87AstMot-16
87AstPol-8
87DodSmoA-19
87Don-455
87Fle-62
87FleGlo-62
87OPC-311
87Top-4
87Top-445
87TopSti-7
87TopTif-4
87TopTif-445
88DodSmo-15
88DodSmo-18
88RanMot-27
88Sco-489
88ScoGlo-489
88Top-226
88TopTif-226
89DodSmoG-96
89RanMot-27
89RanSmo-20
90DodTar-460
90RanMot-27
91DodUno7P-1
91RanMot-28
92DodStaTA-20
92UppDecS-15
93RanKee-231
95PadMot-28
96PadMot-28
Lopez, Al
33DouDisP-27
33ExhFou-2
34DiaMatCSB-116
34BatR31-3
34DiaStaR-28
34DiaStaR-97
34ExhFou-2
35DiaMatCS2-13
35DiaMatCS3T1-101
35ExhFou-2
36DiaMatCS4-9
36GouWidPPR-A67

36R31PasP-44
36WorWidGV-131
37ExhFou-1
38GouHeaU-257
38GouHeaU-281
47IndTeal-18
47IndVanPP-17
51Bow-295
52IndNumN-20
53BowC-143
53IndPenCBP-20
54DanDee-16
55Bow-308
55Ind-5
55IndGolS-1
60MacSta-12
60Top-222
60WhiSoxJP-7
60WhiSoxTS-12
61Top-132
61Top-337
61WhiSoxTS-8
62Top-286
62WhiSoxJP-7
62WhiSoxTS-11
63Top-458
63WhiSoxJP-8
63WhiSoxTS-15
64Top-232
64TopVen-232
64WhiSoxTS-15
65Top-414
65WhiSoxJP-2
69Top-527
69WhiSoxTI-8
76ChiGre-11
76RowExh-14
76WhiSoxTAG-5
77GalGloG-32
77TCMTheWY-10
79DiaGre-80
80PacLeg-98
80PerHaloFP-161
80SSPHOF-161
80WhiSoxGT-3
81TCM60I-348
82OhiHaloF-27
83TCMPla1942-39
84OCoandSI-116
85WhiSoxC-10
86IndGreT-12
86IndIndTI-21
89DodSmoG-38
89PacLegI-197
89PerCelP-27
89SweBasG-90
90DodTar-461
90PerGreM-64
91TopArc1-329
91TopGloA-11
93ActPacA-104
93ActPacA2-38G
93ConTSN-844
93ConTSN-873
94ConTSN-1010
94ConTSN-1104
94ConTSNB-1010
94ConTSNB-1104

Lopez, Albie
91BurIndP-3300
92ColRedC-19
92ColRedF-2388
92ProFS7-60
93Bow-613
93CanIndF-2835
93ClaFS7-141
93ClaGolF-12
93SouAtlLAPI-22
94Bow-635
94ChaKniF-891
94ColC-177
94ColChoGS-177
94ColChoSS-177
94Don-648
94FleMajLP-22
94Pin-426
94PinArtP-426
94PinMusC-426
94Top-178
94TopGol-178
94TopSpa-178
95ColCho-278
95ColChoGS-278
95ColChoSS-278
95Fle-138
95Pin-442
95PinArtP-442
95PinMusC-442
95Sco-512
95ScoGolR-512
95ScoPlaTS-512
95Sel-183
95SelArtP-183
95SigRoo-33
95SigRooSig-33
95Spo-70
95SpoArtP-70
95StaClu-353
95StaCluMOP-353
95StaCluSTWS-353
95Top-478
95TopCyb-271
95UppDecSE-23
95UppDecSEG-23
96BufBisB-14
96Sco-447
97PacPriGotD-GD36
97Sco-377
97ScoHobR-377
97ScoResC-377
97ScoShoS-377
97ScoShoSAP-377
97StaClu-260
97StaCluMOP-260
97Ult-474
97UltGolME-474
97UltPlaME-474

Lopez, Andres
93EugEmeC-19
93EugEmeF-3853
93LimRocDWB-115
94EugEmeC-12
94EugEmeF-3707

Lopez, Antonio
79WisRapTT-1
80VenLeaS-23
93LinVenB-61

Lopez, Art
65Top-566
92YanWIZ6-74

Lopez, Aurelio
78SprRedWK-22
79Top-444
80Top-101
81CokTeaS-53
81OPC-291
81TigDetN-75
81Top-291
82Don-359
82Fle-273
82Top-728
83Tig-19
83TopTra-63T
84Don-516
84Fle-86
84FunFooP-98
84Nes792-95
84OPC-95
84TigWavP-25
84Top-95
84TopSti-268
84TopTif-95
85Don-349
85Fle-16
85Lea-160
85SevCoi-D9
85TigCaiD-13
85TigWen-15
85Top-539
85TopSti-265
85TopTif-539
86AstTeal-10
86Don-293
86Fle-231
86FleUpd-69
86Top-367
86TopTif-367
87AstMot-18
87AstPol-13
87Don-629
87Fle-63
87FleGlo-63
87Top-659
87TopTif-659

Lopez, Carlos
76SalLakCGC-5
77Top-492
78OPC-219
78Top-166
79RocRedWT-8
79Top-568
89GeoColC-20
90GeoColC-19
90GeoColC-34
91OriCro-267
93LinVenB-134
94VenLinU-151
95LinVen-146

Lopez, Craig
87NewOriP-10

Lopez, Dina
91FreStaLBS-4

Lopez, Francisco
74WicAerODF-101

Lopez, Fred
89IdaFalBP-2016
90SumBraB-19
90SumBraP-2437
91GreBraC-13
91GreBraP-3007
91MedHatBJP-4095
91MedHatBJSP-13

Lopez, Gil
96WesMicWB-3

Lopez, Hector
47StaPinP2-20
52LavPro-56
55A'sRodM-23
56A'sRodM-6
56Top-16
56TopPin-13
57Top-6
58A'sJayP-6
58Top-155
59Top-402
60Top-163
60TopVen-163
60YanJayP-6
61Pos-12A
61Pos-12B
61Top-28
61Yan61RL-10
62Top-502
63Top-92
64ChatheY-15
64Top-325
64TopVen-325
65Top-532
66OPC-177
66Top-177
66TopVen-177
66YanTeal-6
76A'sRodMC-15
78TCM60I-272
79TCM50-195
91RinPos1Y1-8
92YanWIZ6-75

Lopez, Javier
78CedRapGT-15
88BlaYNPRWL-136
89BlaYNPRWL-8
89PulBraP-1892
90BurBraP-2352
92GreBraS-238
93RicBraRC-10
93StaCluMOP-630
93TopInaM-811
93TopMic-811
93TriAAAGF-3
94BraUSPC-3H
94BraUSPC-7S
94ColChoSS-178
94FinJum-425
94ScoGolR-620
94ScoRooGR-RT78
94StaCluMOP-630
94StaCluMOP-703
94StaCluTFDI-52
94TopGol-194
94TopSpa-194
94UppDecED-255
94UppDecNGED-11
95ScoRulJ-SR27
95StaCluMOP-200
95StaCluSTWS-200
96ColChoGS-46
96ColChoSS-46
96FleBra-10
96FleTif-298
96LeaSig-128
96LeaSigPPG-128
96LeaSigPPP-128
96PacPriG-P5
96PanSti-3
96PinFoil-326
96ScoDugCAP-A89
96StaCluMOP-103
96TeaOut-51
97ColCho-33
97Don-301
97DonPre-14
97DonPreCttC-14
97DonPreP-301
97DonPrePGold-301
97DonTea-25
97DonTeaSPE-25
97Fle-262
97FleTif-262
97Lea-93
97LeaFraM-93
97LeaFraMDC-93
97NewPin-13
97NewPinAP-13
97NewPinMC-13
97NewPinPP-13
97Pac-239
97PacLatotML-24
97PacLigB-239
97PacPri-81
97PacPriLB-81
97PacPriP-81
97PacSil-239
97PinCer-42
97PinPasttM-11
97PinTotCPB-42
97PinTotCPG-42
97PinTotCPR-42
97PinX-P-53
97PinX-PMoS-53
97PinX-PSfF-56
97PinX-PSfFU-56
97Sco-105
97ScoBra-5
97ScoBraPl-5
97ScoBraPr-5
97ScoPreS-105
97ScoShoS-105
97ScoShoSAP-105
97SP-27
97Stu-110
97StuPrePG-110
97StuPrePS-110
97Ult-156
97UltGolME-156
97UltPlaME-156
97UppDec-255
97UppDec-301
97Zen-27

Lopez, Javy (Javier Torres)
90Bes-107
90BurBraB-20
90BurBraS-16
90MidLeaASGS-38
90ProAaA-132
91Bow-587
91CarLeaAP-CAR2
91Cla/Bes-62
91DurBulC-19
91DurBulP-1547
92Bow-452
92ClaBluBF-BC10
92ClaFS7-117
92ClaRedB-BC10
92GreBraF-1156
92ProFS7-186
92SkyAA F-101
93Bow-343
93Bow-466
93BraLykS-20
93ClaMVPF-2
93Don-782
93FleMajLP-B15
93RicBraBB-15
93RicBraF-187
93RicBraP-2
93RicBraRC-18
93SP-281
93StaClu-630
93StaCluB-27
93StaCluFDI-630
93Top-811
93TopGolI-811
93Toy-92
93Ult-9
93UppDec-29
93UppDecGold-29
94Bow-273
94BowBes-R85
94BowBes-X106
94BowBesR-R85
94BowBesR-X106
94BowPre-4
94BraLykP-18
94BraLykS-18
94ColC-178
94ColChoGS-178
94Don-613
94ExtBas-207
94ExtBasRS-12
94Fin-425
94FinRef-425
94Fla-129
94FlaWavotF-A5
94Fle-364
94FUnPac-6
94LeaGolR-1
94LeaL-86
94LeaLimRP-8
94OPC-162
94OPCHotP-7
94Pac-14
94Pin-239
94PinArtP-239
94PinMusC-239
94PinNewG-NG15
94PinRooTP-1
94Sco-620
94ScoBoyoS-20
94ScoRoo-RT78
94ScoRooSR-SU11
94Sel-188
94SelRooS-RS9
94SP-53
94SPDieC-53
94Spo-172
94SpoRooRS-TR5
94SpoSam-7
94SpoSha-SH7
94SPPre-ER3
94StaClu-630
94StaClu-703
94StaCluFDI-630
94StaCluFDI-703
94StaCluGR-630
94StaCluGR-703
94StaCluT-52
94Stu-38
94StuHer-6
94Top-194
94TriPla-283
94Ult-445
94UltAllR-6
94UltAllRJ-6
94UppDec-255
94UppDecNG-11
95Baz-123
95ColCho-160
95ColChoGS-160
95ColChoSE-63
95ColChoSEGS-63
95ColChoSESS-63
95ColChoSS-160
95Don-166
95DonPreP-166
95DonTopotO-189
95Emb-36
95EmbGolI-36
95Emo-105
95Fin-25
95FinRef-25
95Fla-104
95FlaTodS-6
95Fle-310
95FleRooS-11
95Lea-140
95LeaLim-172
95Pac-10
95PacGolP-33
95PacLatD-20
95PacPri-3
95Pin-229
95PinArtP-229
95PinMusC-229
95PinUps-US4
95Sco-119
95ScoGolR-119
95ScoPlaTS-119
95ScoRul-SR27
95Sel-51
95SelArtP-51

95SelCer-37
95SelCerMG-37
95Spo-78
95SpoArtP-78
95StaClu-200
95StaCluFDI-200
95StaCluSTDW-B200
95StaCluSTMP-6
95Stu-61
95Sum-78
95SumNthD-78
95Top-567
95TopCyb-343
95Ult-350
95UltGolM-350
95UppDec-48
95UppDecED-48
95UppDecEDG-48
95UppDecSE-149
95UppDecSEG-149
95Zen-44
96Bow-32
96ColCho-46
96ColCho-376T
96ColCho-387T
96Don-230
96DonPreP-230
96EmoXL-145
96Fin-B158
96FinRef-B158
96Fla-204
96Fle-298
96Lea-119
96LeaPrePB-119
96LeaPrePG-119
96LeaPrePS-119
96MetUni-133
96MetUniP-133
96Pac-14
96PacEstL-EL15
96PacOctM-OM12
96PacPri-P5
96Pin-326
96PinChrBC-7
96Sco-154
96ScoDugC-A89
96SP-21
96StaClu-103
96StaCluEPB-103
96StaCluEPG-103
96StaCluEPS-103
96Stu-47
96StuPrePB-47
96StuPrePG-47
96StuPrePS-47
96Top-367
96TopChr-149
96TopChrR-149
96TopGal-125
96TopGalPPI-125
96TopLas-26
96Ult-159
96UltGolM-159
96UppDec-6
97Cir-266
97CirRav-266
97ColCho-222
97ColChoAC-44
97DonEli-53
97DonEliGS-53
97DonLim-81
97DonLim-175
97DonLimLE-81
97DonLimLE-175
97Fin-52
97FinRef-52
97PinCerMBlu-42
97PinCerMG-42
97PinCerMR-42
97PinCerR-42
97PinIns-82
97PinInsCE-82
97PinInsDE-82
97Sel-28
97SelArtP-28
97SelRegG-28
97StaClu-215
97StaCluMat-215
97StaCluMOP-215
97Top-395
97TopChr-137
97TopChrR-137
97TopGal-100
97TopGal-129
97TopGalPPI-100
97TopGalPPI-129
97TopSta-95
97TopStaAM-95
97UppDecRSF-RS15

Lopez, Johan
94AubAstF-3753
95LinVen-31
96KisCobB-14

Lopez, Jose
90JohCitCS-17
91SavCarC-9
91SavCarP-1650
92JohCitCC-15
92JohCitCF-3111
96StLucMTI-19

Lopez, Jose Muisi
76VenLeaS-41

Lopez, Juan
74SacSolC-59
75SacSolC-22
76SpoIndC-7
77SpoIndC-14
78SpoIndC-13
79VanCanT-12
80EvaTriT-23
81EvaTriT-17
82EvaTriT-17
83EvaTriT-16
83WatIndF-6
84EvaTriT-1
87FayGenP-18
87OscAstP-2
88ColAstB-10
89BlaYNPRWL-65
89BlaYNPRWL-78
89NiaFalRP-26
90EveGiaP-3147
90NiaFalRP-28
91BriTigC-20
91BriTigP-3622
94EveGiaC-30
95BelGiaTI-13
96GiaMot-28
96PitMetB-3

Lopez, Louis
95OdgRapTI-17

Lopez, Luis (Luis Santos)
88SpoIndP-1930
89BlaYNPRWL-79
89BlaYNPRWLU-28
89ChaRaiP-984
89SanAntMB-15
90AlbDukC-21
90RivRedWCLC-5
91ColSprSSLD-90
91ColSprSSP-2191
91LinDriAA-612
91WicWraLD-612
91WicWraP-2604
91WicWraRD-14
92LasVegSF-2803
92LasVegSS-235
93Bow-250
93ClaFS7-218
93LasVegSF-952
93LinVenB-319
94ColC-669
94ColChoGS-669
94ColChoSS-669
94Don-393
94Fla-439
94FleAllR-M8
94FleUpd-187
94LeaLimR-38
94Pac-529
94PadMot-24
94Pin-259
94PinArtP-259
94PinMusC-259
94RicBraF-2853
94SigRooDP-96
94SigRooDPS-96
94Spo-159
94SpoRoo-147
94SpoRooAP-147
94Top-336
94TopGol-336
94TopSpa-336
94TriAAF-AAA42
95ColCho-348
95ColChoGS-348
95ColChoSS-348
95Don-4
95DonPreP-4
95Fle-563
95Pac-365
95PacLatD-21
95PacPri-117
95Sco-117
95ScoGolR-117
95ScoPlaTS-117
95SigRoo-34
95SigRooSig-34
95StaClu-306
95StaCluMOP-306
95StaCluSTWS-306
95StaCluVR-162
95Top-118
95Ult-235
95UltGolM-235
95UppDec-138
95UppDecED-138
95UppDecEDG-138
96LeaSigEA-112
96PadMot-23
95StaCluVRMC-162

Lopez, Luis Antonio
85VerBeaDT-21
86FloStaLAP-31
86VerBeaDP-16
87BakDodP-10
88BlaYNPRWL-71
88BlaYNPRWL-169
88SanAntMB-26
88TexLeaAGS-37
89BlaYNPRWL-144
90AlbDukP-360
90AlbDukT-18
90CMC-423
90CMC-852
90ProAAAF-81
90RivRedWP-2616
91LinDriAAA-90
91ScoRoo-109T
91TopDeb90-91
92Sco-716
92Sco100RS-84
92StaClu-556
93CanIndF-2846
96StCatSB-17

Lopez, Marcelino
63Top-549
65Top-537
66AngDexP-3
66OPC-155
66Top-155
66TopVen-155
67CokCapA-4
67CokCapAAm-31
67CokCapDA-32
67Top-513
70OPC-344
70Top-344
71MLBOffS-303
71OPC-137
71Top-137
72Top-652
91OriCro-268
94BreMilB-327
95TopCyb-75

Lopez, Marcos
87UtiBluSP-16
88ChaWheB-16
89PeoChiTI-4

Lopez, Mendy
95Bow-173
95SPML-69
95WilBluRTI-27
96BesAutSA-40
96ColCho-427
96ColChoGS-427
96ColChoSS-427
96TexLeaAB-28
96UppDec-253
96WicWraB-19
97Bow-134
97BowInt-134
97Sel-130
97SelArtP-130
97SelRegG-130

Lopez, Mickey
95HelBreTI-17
96BelSnaTI-20

Lopez, Mike
92NiaFalRC-11
92NiaFalRF-3318

Lopez, Omar
96BriWhiSB-23

Lopez, Orangel
92GulCoaYF-3798
93LinVenB-238

Lopez, Orlando
93HunCubC-17
93HunCubF-3234
94PeoChiC-16
94PeoChiF-2265
96RocCubTI-17

Lopez, Pancho
73CedRapAT-27

Lopez, Pedro
88BlaYNPRWL-107
89BlaYNPRWL-118
89WatDiaP-1790
89WatDiaS-18
90ChaRaiB-13
90ChaRaiP-2043
92WicWraS-639
94WicWraF-192
95ElPasDTI-16
96El PasDB-16

Lopez, Pee Wee
96AppLeaAB-24
97Bow-169
97BowInt-169

Lopez, Rene
93ForWayWC-17
93ForWayWF-1972
94ForMyeMC-14
94ForMyeMF-1171
95HarCitRCTI-13
96HarCitRCB-20

Lopez, Rich
94JohCitCC-18
94JohCitCF-3617

Lopez, Rob
86FloStaLAP-32
86TamTarP-12
87VerRedP-9
88NasSouC-8
88NasSouP-487
89NasSouC-6
89NasSouP-1295
89NasSouTI-13
90CMC-133
90NasSouC-8
90NasSouP-228
90ProAAAF-540
91LinDriAAA-267
91NasSouLD-267

Lopez, Robert
92OklStaC-16

Lopez, Roberto
95ElPasDTI-17
96BesAutS-51
96BesAutSA-41
96Exc-72

Lopez, Rodrigo
96IdaFalB-14

Lopez, Steve
88IdaFalBP-1859
89SumBraP-1096

Lopiccolo, Gina
91FreStaLBS-5

Lopiccolo, Jamie
95OdgRapTI-16
96BelSnaTI-21
96Bow-250

Lora, Jose
90ElmPioP-10
91ElmPioC-9
91ElmPioP-3284
91WinHavRSC-28

Lora, Luis
85DomLeaS-113

Lora, Ramon Antonio
81SyrChiT-10
81SyrChiTI-13
82SyrChiT-12
85DomLeaS-18

Loranger, Bob
52LavPro-53

Lord, Bristol
08RosComP-4
09ColChiE-171
10NadE1-32
11A'sFirT20-11
11SpoLifCW-223
11SpoLifM-47
11T205-103
11TurRedT-106
12ColRedB-171
12ColTinT-171
12ColTinT-172A
12T207-110
14PieStaT-34
14TexTomE-27

Lord, Harry
03WilCarE-21
08AmeCarE-83
09ColChiE-172A
09ColChiE-172B
09PhiCarE-14
09RamT20-70
09SpoNewSM-51
09T206-216
10DomDisP-72
10E-UOraBSC-14
10E12AmeCDC-22
10RedCroT-43
10RedCroT-132
10RedCroT-214
10SepAnoP-18
10SweCapPP-11A
10SweCapPP-11B
11DiaGumP-18
11E94-22
11MecDFT-15
11SpoLifCW-224
11SpoLifM-12
11T205-104
12ColRedB-172A
12ColRedB-172B
12ColTinT-172B
12HasTriFT-42
12HasTriFT-45
12HasTriFT-52
12HasTriFT-57
12HasTriFT-60
12T207-111
14CraJacE-48

Lorenz, Joe
82DurBulT-4

Lorenzana, Jose
90IBAWorA-40

Lorenzo, Martin
96HelBreTI-15

Loretta, Mark
94Bow-149
94ElPasDF-3153
95Bow-150
95Exc-72
96Bow-372
96ColCho-591
96ColChoGS-591
96ColChoSS-591
96Fle-151
96FleTif-151
96Lea-219
96LeaPre-136
96LeaPreP-136
96LeaPrePB-219
96LeaPrePG-219
96LeaPrePS-219
96Sco-493
96SelCer-121
96SelCerAP-121
96SelCerCB-121
96SelCerCR-121
96SelCerMB-121
96SelCerMG-121
96SelCerMR-121
96StaClu-440
96StaCluMOP-440
96Top-340
96TopChr-134
96TopChrR-134
96TopGal-139
96TopGalPPI-139
96Ult-365
96UltGolM-365
96UppDec-499U
97ColCho-147
97Don-256
97DonPreP-256
97DonPrePGold-256
97Fle-132
97FleTif-132
97Pac-122
97PacLigB-122
97PacSil-122
97Pin-129
97PinArtP-129
97PinMusC-129
97StaClu-369
97StaCluMOP-369

97Top-112
97UppDec-101
Lorms, John
90WatIndS-13
91ColIndC-20
91ColIndP-1487
92KinIndC-10
92KinIndF-2478
Lorraine, Andrew
94Bow-675
94Cla-186
94SigRooTPD-T3
94SigRooTPS-T3
94TriAAF-AAA23
94VanCanF-1863
94VenLinU-67
95ActPacF-40
95Bow-420
95BowBes-B57
95BowBesR-B57
95ColCho-13
95ColChoGS-13
95ColChoSS-13
95Don-524
95DonPreP-524
95Fla-19
95LeaGolR-16
95NasSouTI-11
95Pin-406
95PinArtP-406
95PinMusC-406
95Sel-194
95SelArtP-194
95SigRooOJHP-HP3
95SigRooOJHPS-HP3
95StaClu-492
95StaCluMOP-492
95StaCluSTWS-492
95Top-221
95Ult-270
95UltGolM-270
96ColCho-647
96ColCho-665
96ColChoGS-647
96ColChoGS-665
96ColChoSS-647
96ColChoSS-665
Losa, Bill
88ButCopKSP-13
88GasRanP-1013
89ChaRanS-14
90ChaRanS-23
91KinIndC-14
91KinIndP-325
Losauro, Carmelo
86DayBeaIP-17
88VirGenS-14
Loscalzo, Bob
82IdaFalAT-24
83MadMusF-15
84MadMusP-13
85ModA'sC-24
Loscrey, Mike
89ChaLooGS-18
Loseke, Scott
84CedRapRT-22
Lotshaw, Andy
31CubTeal-14
Lott, Billy (Bill)
89HigSchPLS-4
90BakDodCLC-259
90YakBeaTI-18
91BakDodCLC-15
92ClaFS7-357
92VerBeaDC-13
92VerBeaDF-2891
93SanAntMF-3018
94SanAntMF-2481
Lott, Brian
94PriRedC-15
94PriRedF-3259
Lotzar, Greg
85ElmPioT-12
86FloStaLAP-33
86WinHavRSP-16
87NewBriRSP-6
Loubier, Stephen
88RivRedWCLC-213
88RivRedWP-1432
89RivRedWB-11
89RivRedWCLC-20
89RivRedWP-1389
89WicStaR-24
89WicUpdR-14
90WicWraRD-13
91PalSprAP-2008
Loucks, Scott
78DayBeaAT-16
80ColAstT-17
81TucTorT-11
82AstAstI-3
82AstAstI-10
83TucTorT-22
85HawIsIC-228
Louden, William
16ColE13-101
Loudenslager, Charlie
90DodTar-1015
Loudermilk, Darren
96BurIndB-10
Loughlin, Larry
77FriOneYW-96
Loughlin, Mark
91AubAstC-1
91AubAstP-4270
92AshTouC-25
92ProFS7-236
93QuaCitRBC-12
93QuaCitRBF-95
Louis, Albert
76ShrCapT-14
Louis, Joe
47HomBon-32
87SpoCubG-3
Loun, Don
65OPC-181
65Top-181
Lovdal, Stewart
89MarPhiS-18
90BatCliP-3062
Love, James
92ElmPioC-26
93ForLauRSC-30
Love, Jeff
96NewJerCB-17
Love, John
87MacPirP-6
88SalBucS-11
Love, Slim (Edward H.)
16FleBreD-58
Love, Steve
76WauMetT-15
Love, Sylvester
90StoPorB-9
90StoPorCLC-194
90StoPorP-2194
Love, Will (William)
89MadMusS-13
89Sta-66
90ModA'sC-18
90ModA'sCLC-157
90ModA'sP-2210
91ModA'sP-3083
92RenSilSCLC-45
Lovelace, Dan
94WilCubC-30
Lovelace, Vance
82QuaCitCT-10
83VerBeaDT-7
86MidAngP-13
87MidAngP-24
88EdmTraC-4
88EdmTraP-557
89EdmTraP-559
89Fle-651
89FleGlo-651
90CalCanC-7
90CalCanP-647
90CMC-434
90ProAAAF-112
91CalCanLD-65
91CalCanP-512
91LinDriAAA-65
92TolMudHF-1041
92TolMudHS-593
93GreBraF-343
Lovell, Don
86WatIndP-15
87BufBisP-1
88ColSprSSC-15
88ColSprSSP-1523
Lovell, Jim
88GreBraB-11
89GreBraB-22
89GreBraP-1167
91GreBraC-29
93RicBraRC-19
95RicBraTI-30
96RicBraB-4
Lovenguth, Lynn
61TacBan-11
Lovett, Tom (Thomas)
87OldJudN-309
90DodTar-1016
95May-19
Loviglio, Jay (John)
81EdmTraRR-23
81Top-526
82EdmTraT-8
82Top-599
83IowCubT-15
86GenCubP-16
87WinSpiP-13
89WinSpiS-19
90ChaKniTI-16
91ChaKniLD-149
91ChaKniP-1704
91LinDriAA-149
96AugGreB-1
Lovinger, Allan
90PenPilS-27
Lovinger, Kevin
94NewJerCC-18
94NewJerCF-3416
94StaCluDP-5
94StaCluDPFDI-5
95Exc-268
96ArkTraB-16
Lovins, Sarge (Steve)
79MemChiT-1
80MemChiT-1
Lovitto, Joe
73OPC-276
73Top-276
74OPC-639
74Top-639
75OPC-36
75Top-36
76OPC-604
76SSP-271
76Top-604
93RanKee-25
Lovrich, Pete
63Top-549
64Top-212
64TopVen-212
65Top-462
Lovullo, Torey
88EasLeaAP-8
88GleFalTP-923
89DonRoo-17
89Fle-648
89FleGlo-648
89PanSti-332
89ScoHot1R-17
89TigMar-23
89UppDec-782
90CMC-401
90ProAAAF-388
90TolMudHC-24
90TolMudHP-158
90UppDec-332
91Bow-175
91ColCliP-603
92ColCliF-359
92ColCliP-17
92ColCliS-108
92SkyAAAF-48
92StaClu-809
92StaCluNC-809
93AngMot-18
93FleFinE-184
93Lea-476
93StaCluAn-29
93Ult-521
94ColC-179
94ColChoGS-179
94ColChoSS-179
94Don-612
94Fle-63
94Lea-204
94MarMot-27
94Pac-83
94PanSti-39
94Sco-179
94ScoGolR-179
94StaClu-506
94StaCluFDI-506
94StaCluGR-506
94StaCluMOP-506
94Top-634
94TopGol-634
94TopSpa-634
94Ult-24
96A'sMot-20
96LeaSigEA-113
Lowdermilk, Grover
75WhiSox1T-24
Lowdermilk, Louis
12T207-112
Lowe, Benny
95StCatSTI-4
96HagSunB-13
Lowe, Chris
88MarPhiS-24
89MarPhiS-19
90HamRedS-14
Lowe, Derek
92BelMarC-11
92BelMarF-1439
92Bow-98
92UppDecML-192
93Bow-107
93ClaGolF-213
93ExcFS7-226
93RivPilCLC-2
94Bow-585
94Cla-138
94JacSunF-1408
94UppDecML-89
95SigRooOJ-22
95SigRooOJP-22
95SigRooOJPS-22
95SigRooOJS-22
96Bow-228
96PorCitRB-19
Lowe, Doc (Steve)
78WauMetT-16
Lowe, Donald
79WauTimT-17
Lowe, Jamie
89OrlTwiB-29
Lowe, Jason
92HigSchPLS-15
93SouOreAC-15
93SouOreAF-4059
94SouOreAC-16
94SouOreAF-3619
Lowe, Kevin
95DanBraTI-16
Lowe, Q.V.
82OneYanT-6
83GreHorT-29
85ColCliP-25
86JacExpT-10
87JamExpP-2678
88JamExpP-2039
89JamExpP-2152
90JamExpP-28
91JamExpC-28
91JamExpP-3561
92JamExpC-26
92JamExpF-1516
Lowe, Robert
87OldJudN-310
95May-20
98CamPepP-45
Lowe, Sean
92ClaDraP-11
92ClaDraPFB-BC11
92ClaFS7-404
92UppDecML-119
93Bow-572
93ClaFS7-244
93ClaGolF-119
93Pin-461
93Sco-493
93Sel-356
93St.PetCC-17
93St.PetCF-2624
93StaCluCa-27
93StaCluM-121
93Top-191
93TopGol-191
93TopInaM-191
93TopMic-191
94SigRoo-40
94SigRooS-40
94St.PetCC-14
94St.PetCF-2581
95ArkTraTI-19
Lowell, Mike
96GreBatB-14
Lowenstein, John
71OPC-231
71Top-231
72OPC-486
72Top-486
73OPC-327
73Top-327
74OPC-176
74Top-176
75OPC-424
75Top-424
76OPC-646
76SSP-528
76Top-646
77OPC-175
77Top-393
78RanBurK-21
78SSP270-87
78Top-87
79Top-173
80Top-287
81Don-235
81Fle-186
81OPC-199
81Top-591
82Don-599
82Fle-169
82Top-747
83Don-153
83Fle-63
83FleSta-108
83FleSti-197
83OPC-337
83OriPos-12
83Top-473
83TopSti-24
84AllGamPI-149
84Don-228
84DonActAS-26
84Fle-10
84FleSti-116
84Nes792-604
84OriEng-6
84OriTeal-13
84Top-604
84TopSti-20
84TopSti-209
84TopTif-604
85Don-245
85Fle-180
85OPC-316
85Top-316
85TopSti-206
85TopTif-316
91OriCro-269
93RanKee-232
Lowery, David
91GasRanC-18
91GasRanP-2695
91SouAtlLAGP-SAL23
92ChaRanC-1
92ChaRanF-2233
93BinMetF-2343
Lowery, John
92CliGiaF-3594
92Min-12
Lowery, Josh
89BatCliP-1942
Lowery, Terrell
91ButCopKSP-17
92UppDecML-81
93Bow-373
93ChaRanC-1
93ChaRanF-1952
93FloStaLAF-6
94Bow-17
94Cla-18
94ClaTriF-T79
94TulDriF-255
94TulDriTI-13
94UppDecML-216
95Bow-260
95BowGolF-260
95Exc-129
95Top-643
95UppDecML-67
96BinBeeB-17
95UppDecMLFS-67
Lowman, Mel
77DayBeaIT-13
Lown, Turk (Omar)
50WorWidGV-14
52Bow-16
52Top-330
53BowC-154
53Top-130
54Bow-157

57Top-247
58Top-261
59Top-277
60Top-57
60Top-313
60TopVen-57
60WhiSoxTS-13
61Pos-32
61Top-424
61TopMagR-35
62Top-528
62WhiSoxTS-12
79DiaGre-147
83TopRep5-330
91TopArc1-130
Lowrey, Peanuts (Harry)
43CubTeal-13
46SpoExcW-6-11
47Exh-141A
47Exh-141B
47TipTop-112
49Bow-22
49EurSta-62
49Lea-33
50Bow-172
51Bow-194
52Bow-102
52Top-111
53CarHunW-12
53ExhCan-29
53Top-16
54CarHunW-11
54Top-158
60RawGloT-16
72TopTes5-7
83TCMPla1943-37
83TopRep5-111
91TopArc1-16
94TopArc1-158
94TopArc1G-158
Lowrey, Steve
82CedRapRT-4
Lowry, Curt
96CliLumKTI-18
Lowry, Dwight
81BirBarT-3
83BirBarT-4
85DomLeaS-133
85NasSouTI-10
87Don-338
87Fle-157
87FleGlo-157
87SevCoi-D7
87SpoTeaP-15
87TigCaiD-5
87TigCok-11
87TolMudHT-25
87Top-483
87TopTif-483
89PacSenL-21
89TopSenL-2
90CMC-64
90IndIndC-14
90IndIndP-297
90ProAAAF-580
91FayGenC-11
91FayGenP-1188
92FayGenC-25
92FayGenF-2185
93FayGenC-26
93FayGenF-146
94FayGenC-27
94FayGenF-2164
95FayGenTI-16
96FayGenB-1
Lowry, Elliot
94BurIndC-11
Lowry, Mike
78WauMetT-17
Loy, Darren
86ReaPhiP-16
87MaiGuiP-21
87MaiGuiT-9
87PhiTas-xx
88ChaRanS-13
89OklCit8C-20
89OklCit8P-1526
89TulDriTI-12
Loynd, Mike
86RanPer-46
86TulDriTI-8
87Don-506
87FleUpd-67
87FleUpdG-67
87RanMot-21
87RanSmo-27
87SpoTeaP-1
87Top-126
87TopTif-126
88Don-550
88Fle-472
88FleGlo-472
88Sco-491
88ScoGlo-491
88Top-319
88TopTif-319
88TucTorC-3
88TucTorP-185
89ColMudP-147
89ColMudS-16
90CMC-332
90ProAAAF-348
90SyrChiC-6
90SyrChiMB-15
90SyrChiP-568
91LouRedTI-11
92LouRedF-1886
92LouRedS-259
93RanKee-233
93RicBraP-13
93RicBraRC-21
Loyola, Juan
91PriRedC-2
91PriRedP-3526
Lozado, Willie
79BurBeeT-7
81ElPasDT-2
82VanCanT-5
83IndIndTI-10
85Don-595
85Fle-644
85LouRedR-19
86OklCit8P-10
88BlaYNPRWL-7
94BreMilB-328
Lozano, Steve
89FreStaBS-13
Lozinski, Tony
89BatCliP-1916
90ClePhiS-12
Lubert, Dennis
83DurBulT-21
Lubratich, Steve
80SalLakCGT-14
81SalLakCGT-19
82SpoIndT-17
84Don-377
84EdmTraC-112
84EdmTraC-249
84Fle-524
84Nes792-266
84Top-266
84TopTif-266
85LasVegSC-106
86BeaGolGP-14
86LasVegSP-11
87SpoIndP-10
88LasVegSP-243
88SpoIndP-1928
89RivRedWB-22
89RivRedWCLC-25
89RivRedWP-1411
90WicWraRD-25
91LinDriAA-624
91WicWraLD-624
91WicWraP-2614
91WicWraRD-24
Luby, Hugh
48SomandK-23
Lucadello, John
41BroW75-20
46SeaSLP-31
84TCMPla1-20
Lucarelli, Vito
79AppFoxT-3
80AppFoxT-8
Lucas, Arbrey
85OscAstTI-8
Lucas, Brian
78ChaPirT-13
Lucas, Charles S.
36GouWidPPR-D16
Lucas, Dave
86AncGlaPTI-19
Lucas, Gary
79HawIslC-26
79HawIslT-9
81Don-243
81Fle-502
81OPC-259
81Top-436
82Don-296
82Don-422A
82Fle-577
82OPC-120
82Top-120
82TopSti-102
83Don-187
83Fle-366
83OPC-364
83Top-761
84Don-307
84ExpPos-18
84ExpStu-12
84Fle-306
84FleUpd-73
84Nes792-7
84OPC-7
84Top-7
84TopSti-161
84TopTif-7
84TopTra-73T
84TopTraT-73T
85Don-498
85Fle-403
85OPC-297
85Top-297
85TopTif-297
86Don-453
86Fle-254
86OPC-351
86Top-601
86TopTif-601
87AngSmo-4
87Don-618
87Fle-87
87FleGlo-87
87OPC-382
87Top-696
87TopTif-696
88Don-579
88Fle-495
88FleGlo-495
88Top-524
88TopTif-524
91CalLeLA-48
91SanJosGC-24
91SanJosGP-29
92CliGiaC-28
92CliGiaF-3614
93QuaCitRBC-27
93QuaCitRBF-117
94QuaCitRBC-26
94QuaCitRBF-552
Lucas, Pepe
85DomLeaS-142
Lucas, Ray
33DouDisP-28
90DodTar-462
Lucas, Red (Charles Fred.)
29ExhFou-8
29PorandAR-58
30SchR33-43
31Exh-8
32OrbPinNP-40
32OrbPinUP-42
33DouDisP-29
33ExhFou-4
33Gou-137
33TatOrb-42
34DiaMatCSB-117
34DiaStaR-46
34DiaStaR-106
34GouCanV-7
35GouPuzR-4B
35GouPuzR-7B
35GouPuzR-12B
36NatChiFPR-53
79DiaGre-352
83DiaClaS2-98
91ConTSN-190
Lucas, Scott
91HelBreSP-6
Lucca, Lou
91OklStaC-15
92EriSaiC-16
92EriSaiF-1631
92OklStaC-17
93ExcFS7-37
93KanCouCC-11
93KanCouCF-923
93Top-494
93TopGol-494
93TopInaM-494
93TopMic-494
94BreCouMC-8
94BreCouMF-19
95PorSeaDTI-12
96ChaKniB-16
93KanCouCTI-12
Lucchesi, Frank
70Top-662
71OPC-119
71Top-119
72OPC-188
72Top-188
74OPC-379
74Top-379
76OPC-172
76SSP-272
76Top-172
77Top-428
87CubCan-14
88ChaLooLTI-22
88NasSouTI-25
88Top-564
88TopTif-564
89NasSouC-25
89NasSouP-1284
89NasSouTI-30
91FouBal-13
93RanKee-234
Lucchetti, Larry
92SavCarC-4
92SavCarF-663
93SavCarC-16
93SavCarF-684
94St.PetCC-15
94St.PetCF-2582
Luce, Robert
96EveAquB-15
Luce, Roger
92ChaRanC-4
92ChaRanF-2227
92ClaFS7-111
93TulDriF-2735
94TulDriF-246
94TulDriTI-14
96JacGenB-17
96TusTorB-15
93TulDriTI-15
Lucero, Kevin
91HamRedC-4
91HamRedP-4036
92SavCarC-3
92SavCarF-662
Lucero, Nathan
95QuaCitRBTI-14
96QuaCitRB-4
Lucero, Robert
88CliGiaP-714
Lucia, Danny
78GreBraT-14
81DurBulT-20
Luciani, Randy
88FayGenP-1098
Luciano, Medina
89PitMetS-15
Luciano, Ron
77Spo-8021
Luciano, Suliban
91KinMetC-5
91KinMetP-3825
Luciano, Virgilio
95ChaRivTI-26
Lucier, Lou
43RedSoxTI-14
Luckham, Ken
89SalDodTI-15
90OscAstS-17
91OscAstC-7
91OscAstP-679
92JacGenS-338
Luderus, Fred
10DarChoE-23
11PloCanE-41
14CraJacE-45
15CraJacE-45
15SpoNewM-104
16BF2FP-89
16ColE13-102
16FleBreD-55
16SpoNewM-106
Ludwick, Bob
53ExhCan-38
Ludwick, Eric
93PitMetC-1
93PitMetF-3705
94ExcFS7-236
94St.LucMC-16
94St.LucMF-1191
95AusFut-41
95Bes-74
95BinMetTI-38
96BesAutSA-42
96Bow-222
96Exc-188
Ludwig, Jeff
89GenCubP-1869
Ludwig, William
09ColChiE-173A
09ColChiE-173B
12ColRedB-173A
12ColRedB-173B
12ColTinT-173A
12ColTinT-173B
Ludy, John
85BelBreT-19
86StoPorP-13
87StoPorP-16
Luebber, Steve
72Top-678
76VenLeaS-123
77TacTwiDQ-18
77Top-457
79SyrChiT-20
79SyrChiTI-31
80RocRedWT-15
81RocRedWT-12
81RocRedWW-12
83EvaTriT-5
86BeaGolGP-15
87WicPilRD-23
88WicPilRD-42
89LasVegSC-25
89LasVegSP-26
89PacSenL-94
90RivRedWB-20
90RivRedWCLC-25
90RivRedWP-2623
91HagSunLD-240
91HagSunP-2473
91LinDriAA-240
91OriCro-270
91PacSenL-7
92RocRedWF-1956
92RocRedWS-475
93RocRedWF-258
94RocRedWF-1014
94RocRedWTI-11
Luebbers, Larry
90BilMusP-3217
91CedRapRC-8
91CedRapRP-2716
91Cla/Bes-373
91MidLeaAP-MWL22
92CedRapRC-11
92CedRapRF-1071
92ChaLooF-3815
92ClaFS7-50
93IndIndF-1484
94Don-192
94Fle-415
94IowCubF-1273
94Pac-151
94Sco-603
94ScoGolR-603
94StaCluT-335
94StaCluTFDI-335
94Top-221
94TopGol-221
94TopSpa-221
94Ult-172
95ChaLooTI-13
96ChaLooB-17
Luebke, Dick
77FriOneYW-66
91OriCro-271
Luecken, Rick
84ChaLooT-18
85CalCanC-98
86ChaLooP-16
87MemChiB-22
87MemChiP-18
88MemChiB-20
89OmaRoyC-7
89OmaRoyP-1734
89TriAAP-AAA38
90Bow-5
90BowTif-5

90BraDubP-18
90CMC-656
90Don-562
90Fle-113
90FleCan-113
90OPC-87
90RicBraC-26
90RicBraTI-19
90Top-87
90TopDeb89-73
90TopTif-87
90UppDec-621
Luedtke, John
90ArkRaz-27
Lugo, Angel
89EliTwiS-16
90MiaMirIS-14
91St.CatBJC-23
91St.CatBJP-3391
Lugo, Arquimedes
93AubAstC-17
93AubAstF-3440
Lugo, Elias
76VenLeaS-87
93LinVenB-232
Lugo, Jesus
95LinVen-144
95PeoChiTI-32
96JohCitCTI-21
96StPetCB-16
Lugo, Julio
95AubAstTI-8
96QuaCitRB-19
Lugo, Urbano (Rafael)
82DanSunF-26
83PeoSunF-20
85EdmTraC-9
85FleUpd-74
86Don-329
86Fle-162
86Top-373
86TopTif-373
87AngSmo-9
87Top-92A
87Top-92B
87TopTif-92A
87TopTif-92B
88EdmTraC-6
88EdmTraP-581
88TriAAAP-15
89IndIndP-1232
90TigCok-11
93LinVenB-8
93LinVenB-322
94VenLinU-40
95LinVen-8
95LinVen-299
Luis, Bevan
76ForLauYS-26
77ForLauYS-7
Luis, Joe
91LynRedSC-12
91LynRedSP-1202
92WinHavRSC-12
Lujack, Johnny
51Whe-2
52Whe-19A
52Whe-19B
Lukachyk, Rob
88UtiBluSP-1
89SouBenWSGS-22
90SarWhiSS-14
91FloStaLAP-FSL29
91SarWhiSC-23
91SarWhiSP-1124
92StoPorC-13
92StoPorF-50
93ElPasDF-2964
93ExcFS7-191
94BowBayF-2424
94ClaGolF-61
94OriPro-56
95TolMudHTI-18
96HarSenB-18
Lukasiewicz, Mark
92OklStaC-18
94HagSunC-11
94HagSunF-2723
95DunBluJTI-13
96DunBluJB-15
96DunBluJTI-18
Luke, Matt
92ClaDraP-115
92FroRowDP-69
92OneYanC-1
93GreHorC-17
93GreHorF-899
94ClaGolF-85
94ExcFS7-109
94FloStaLAF-FSL23
94TamYanC-18
94TamYanF-2397
95Exc-99
95NorNagUTI-48
95NorNavTI-48
95SigRooOJ-23
95SigRooOJP-23
95SigRooOJPS-23
95SigRooOJS-23
95UppDecML-184
96Bow-217
96ColCliB-17
96FleUpd-U63
96FleUpdTC-U63
96Sel-190
96SelArtP-190
96Ult-389
96UltGolM-389
95UppDecMLFS-184
Luketich, Stan
91NiaFalRC-30
91NiaFalRP-3651
92NiaFalRC-29
92NiaFalRF-3343
Lukevics, Mitch
76AppFoxT-12
78KnoKnoST-12
79KnoKnoST-11
Lukish, Tom
80UtiBluJT-25
82KnoBluJT-5
83SyrChiT-9
84SyrChiT-20
Lukon, Eddie
79DiaGre-260
85TCMPla1-38
Lum, Mike
68Top-579
69MilBra-162
69Top-514
70OPC-367
70Top-367
71MLBOffS-16
71OPC-194
71Top-194
72Top-641
73LinPor-5
73OPC-266
73Top-266
74OPC-227
74Top-227
74TopSta-7
75Hos-33
75HosTwi-33
75OPC-154
75Top-154
76LinSup-93
76OPC-208
76SSP-11
76Top-208
76TopTra-208T
77Top-601
78Pep-17
78SSP270-119
78Top-326
79OPC-286
79Top-556
80Top-7
81Fle-258
81Top-457
81TopTra-795
82Don-300
82Fle-599
82Top-732
88RoySmo-2
Luman, Charley
83ButCopKT-8
Lumenti, Ralph
58Top-369
59SenTealW-10
59Top-316A
59Top-316B
60Lea-130
61Top-469
Lumley, Harry G.
06FanCraNL-26
08RosComP-95
09AmeCarE-72
09RamT20-71
09T206-217
11SpoLifCW-225
43ParSpo-49
90DodTar-464
Lumley, Mike
89LakTigS-14
90CMC-837
90LonTigP-1265
91LakTigC-9
91LakTigP-264
92ClaFS7-173
92LonTigF-630
92LonTigS-412
93ClaGolF-63
93TolMudHF-1653
Lumpe, Jerry
58Top-193
58YanJayP-6
59Top-272
60A'sJayP-7
60A'sTeal-13
60Lea-47
60Top-290
61A'sTeal-13
61AthJayP-12
61AthJayP-13
61Pos-81A
61Pos-81B
61Top-119
61Top-365
61TopStal-164
62Jel-93
62Pos-93
62PosCan-93
62SalPlaC-25
62ShiPlaC-25
62Top-127
62Top-305
62TopBuc-50
62TopStal-54
62TopVen-127
63AthJayP-8
63BasMagM-50
63Fle-16
63Jel-86
63Pos-86
63Top-256
63TopStil-24
64A's-12
64TigJayP-8
64TigLid-9
64Top-165
64TopCoi-28
64TopCoi-124
64TopSta-86
64TopStaU-42
64TopVen-165
65TigJayP-8
65Top-353
66OPC-161
66Top-161
66TopVen-161
67CokCapTi-3
67DexPre-130
67TigDexP-5
67Top-247
78TCM60I-55
Luna, Alexis
92MedHatBJF-3215
92MedHatBJSP-17
Luna, Memo (Guillermo)
52MotCoo-26
54Bow-222
54CarHunW-12
Luna, Rich
93WelPirC-11
93WelPirF-3367
94AugGreF-3017
Lunar, Fernando
95Bow-201
95EugEmeTI-2
95MacBraTI-17
96BesAutS-52
96MacBraB-15
Lunar, Luis
76VenLeaS-111
76WauMetT-16
77WauMetT-11
79JacMetT-13
80VenLeaS-204
93LinVenB-42
95LinVen-211
Lunar, Manuel
80VenLeaS-243
80WisRapTT-5
Lunar, Victor
95LinVen-239
Lund, Don
53TigGle-19
53Top-277
54Bow-87
54Top-167
90DodTar-465
91TopArc1-277
94TopArc1-167
94TopArc1G-167
Lund, Ed
90GreFalDSP-4
91BakDodCLC-13
92VerBeaDF-2879
93BakDodCLC-16
Lund, Gordy (Gordon)
70Top-642
75AppFoxT-15
79KnoKnoST-4
80AppFoxT-29
81EdmTraRR-8
82EdmTraT-22
Lund, Greg
89EveGiaS-27
Lundahl, Rich
86LitFalMP-17
87ColMetP-7
Lundberg, Bryan
93MarPhiC-17
93MarPhiF-3469
94BatCliC-10
94BatCliF-3441
Lundblade, Rick
87PhiTas-xx
87ReaPhiP-13
88MaiPhiC-15
88MaiPhiP-291
89TidTidC-19
89TidTidP-1968
90HagSunP-1424
Lundeen, Larry
88BoiHawP-1615
Lundgren, Carl
06FanCraNL-27
07CubA.CDPP-6
07CubGFGCP-6
09T206-218
09T206-438
11SpoLifCW-226
Lundgren, Jason
89BenBucL-25
Lundgren, Kurt
86JacMetT-7
87JacMetF-8
Lundquist, David
94HicCraC-14
94HicCraF-2173
Lundstedt, Thomas
73WicAerKSB-7
74OPC-603
74Top-603
75TacTwiK-4
Lundy, Dick
78LauLonABS-6
86NegLeaF-75
90NegLeaS-25
91PomBlaBPB-23
Lunetta, Dan
90RocRedWGC-33
Lung, Rod
88QuaCitAGS-16
Lunte, Harry
77Ind192T-11
Lupien, Tony (Ulysses)
42RedSoxTI-16
43RedSoxTI-15
47SigOil-12
48WhiSoxTI-15
49Bow-141
77TCMTheWY-11
79DiaGre-230
83TCMPla1943-18
Luplow, Al
62Top-598
63Jel-73
63Pos-73
63Top-351
64Top-184
64TopVen-184
66OPC-188
66Top-188
66TopVen-188
67CokCapYM-V22
67Top-433
91MetWIZ-236
Luque, Dolph (Adolpho)
19W514-17
20RedWorCP-10
21Exh-98
21Nei-72
22E120-174
22WilPatV-9
23W503-43
27YorCarE-18
28Exh-15
28StaPlaCE-44
28W502-18
28W513-71
28Yue-18
33Gou-209
40PlaBal-231
61Fle-56
87ConSer2-46
88ConSer5-19
88PacEigMO-90
90DodTar-466
92ConTSN-413
94ConTSN-1021
94ConTSNB-1021
Lusader, Scott
86GleFalTP-12
87IntLeaAT-16
87TolMudHP-3
87TolMudHT-8
88Don-615
88Fle-62
88FleGlo-62
88TolMudHC-13
88TolMudHP-594
89ScoHot1R-15
89Top-487
89TopTif-487
90CMC-396
90Don-696
90OPC-632
90ProAAAF-393
90Sco-575
90Sco100RS-42
90TolMudHC-19
90TolMudHP-163
90Top-632
90TopTif-632
91Bow-174
91UppDec-241
Luse, Kelly
92SalSpuC-28
Lush, Ernie
09RamT20-72
Lush, John Charles
08RosComP-167
09PC7HHB-29
11MecDFT-25
11SpoLifCW-227
11SpoLifM-273
11T205-105
12ColRedB-174
12ColTinT-174
12ImpTobC-33
Lush, William L.
03BreE10-92
03BreE10-93
Lussier, Pat
92WelPirC-17
92WelPirF-1339
93LetMouF-4163
93LetMouSP-22
Lusted, Chuck
84ShrCapFB-10
Lutes, Brian
89SanDieSAS-15
Luther, Brad
83St.PetCT-18
85SprCarT-16
Luther, Tim
91EveGiaC-15
91EveGiaP-3910
92EveGiaC-3
92EveGiaF-1683
Lutt, Jeff
93WelPirC-12
93WelPirF-3351
94AugGreC-10
94AugGreF-3002
Lutticken, Bob
86SpoIndC-156

87SpoIndP-18
88ChaRaiP-1217
89RivRedWB-1
89RivRedWCLC-11
89RivRedWP-1403
90WicWraRD-14
91HigDesMC-16
91HigDesMP-2399
Luttrell, Lyle
57Top-386
Luttrull, Bruce
85BenPhiC-14
Lutz, Brent
91MedHatBJP-4103
92MyrBeaHC-21
92MyrBeaHF-2200
93DunBluJC-16
93DunBluJF-1800
93DunBluJFFN-17
94KnoSmoF-1306
Lutz, Chris
88GenCubP-1653
89ChaWheP-1760
90MidLeaASGS-39
90PeoChiTI-25
91WinSpiC-9
Lutz, Manuel
96BriWhiSB-24
Lutz, Rollin Joseph
52Par-74
73OPC-449
73Top-449A
73Top-449B
Lutzke, Rube (Walter)
25Exh-83
26Exh-82
27Exh-42
94ConTSN-1045
94ConTSNB-1045
Luuloa, Keith
95LakElsSTI-18
96MidAngB-21
96MidAngOHP-16
96TexLeaAB-29
Luzinski, Bill
80AppFoxT-25
Luzinski, Greg
71OPC-439
71Top-439
72OPC-112
72Top-112
73LinPor-146
73OPC-189
73Top-189
73TopCanL-28
74Kel-9
74OPC-360
74PhiJohP-19
74Top-360
74TopDecE-24
74TopSta-76
75Hos-27
75HosTwi-27
75OPC-630
75SSPPuzB-14
75Top-630
76CraDis-29
76Hos-125
76Kel-18
76OPC-193
76OPC-195
76OPC-610
76SSP-467
76Top-193
76Top-195
76Top-610
77BurCheD-163
77Hos-25
77Kel-12
77MSADis-35
77OPC-118
77PepGloD-72
77RCColC-35
77Spo-3424
77Top-30
78Hos-8
78Kel-33
78OPC-42
78PhiSSP-31
78RCColC-42
78SSP270-31
78TasDis-5
78Top-420
78WifBalD-40
79Hos-30
79OPC-278
79PhiBurK-19
79PhiTeal-4
79Top-540
80OPC-66
80PhiBurK-11
80Top-120
81AllGamPI-57
81CokTeaS-100
81Don-175
81Fle-10
81FleStiC-75
81OPC-270
81Top-270
81TopScr-74
81TopSupHT-82
81TopTra-796
82Don-193
82Dra-22
82Fle-352
82FleSta-187
82OPC-69
82OPC-152
82Top-720
82Top-721
82TopSti-165
83AllGamPI-59
83Don-395
83DonActA-4
83Fle-247
83FleSta-109
83FleSti-158
83Kel-50
83OPC-310
83PhiPosGM-12
83PhiPosGPaM-6
83Top-310
83Top-591
83TopFol-2
83TopSti-51
83WhiSoxTV-19
84AllGamPI-150
84Don-122
84DonActAS-41
84DonCha-13
84Dra-18
84Fle-69
84FleSti-47
84FunFooP-34
84Nes792-20
84Nes792-712
84OCoandSI-8
84OPC-20
84RalPur-5
84Top-20
84Top-712
84TopCer-5
84TopRubD-12
84TopSti-7
84TopSti-8
84TopSti-244
84TopTif-20
84TopTif-712
84WhiSoxTV-23
85Don-546
85Fle-521
85Lea-75
85OPC-328
85Top-650
85TopRubD-15
85TopSti-238
85TopTif-650
89SweBasG-24
92UppDecS-24
93AthMot-27
Luzinski, Ryan
92ClaDraP-23
92ClaDraPFB-BC16
92GreFalDSP-1
92UppDecML-144
93BakDodCLC-2
93StaCluM-140
93Top-481
93TopGol-481
93TopInaM-481
93TopMic-481
93YakBeaC-1
93YakBeaF-3885
94ActPac-53
94ClaGolF-197
94ExcFS7-218
94FloStaLAF-FSL47
94VerBeaDC-1
94VerBeaDF-75
95SanAntMTI-42
95UppDecML-68
95UppDecMLFS-68
Luzon, Bob
82DurBulT-5
83DurBulT-9
85GreBraTI-13
Lychak, Perry
83KinBluJTI-12
85KinBluJT-6
86KinEagP-15
Lyden, Mitch
87ColCliP-18
87ColCliP-5
87ColCliT-11
89AlbYanB-14
89AlbYanP-320
89AlbYanS-11
89Sta-98
90AlbDecGB-34
90AlbYanB-11
90AlbYanP-1037
90AlbYanS-9
90Bes-179
90EasLeaAP-EL15
90ProAaA-33
90StaFS7-52
91LinDriAAA-590
91TolMudHLD-590
91TolMudHP-1935
92TidTidF-901
92TidTidS-561
93EdmTraF-1139
93FleFinE-66
93TopTra-61T
94EdmTraF-2877
94Pac-246
95OmaRoyTI-18
96SigRooOJ-17
96SigRooOJS-17
Lydy, Scott
89MedAthB-8
91Cla/Bes-436
91MadMusC-20
91MadMusP-2142
92HunStaF-3963
92RenSilSCLC-34
92UppDecML-171
92UppDecMLPotY-PY3
93Bow-49
93ClaFS7-144
93FleFinE-256
93StaCluAt-24
93TacTigF-3047
94Cla-47
94ColC-180
94ColChoGS-180
94ColChoSS-180
94Don-226
94Fle-267
94Lea-27
94Pac-455
94Pin-232
94PinArtP-232
94PinMusC-232
94Spo-175
94StaClu-391
94StaCluFDI-391
94StaCluGR-391
94StaCluMOP-391
94TacTigF-3187
94Top-160
94TopGol-160
94TopSpa-160
94Ult-110
94UppDec-218
94UppDecED-218
95EdmTraTI-14
Lyle, Don
79IndIndTI-15
80IndIndTI-24
80VenLeaS-177
Lyle, Jeff
90WelPirP-22
91AugPirP-802
Lyle, Sparky (Albert)
69MilBra-163
69RedSoxAO-7
69RedSoxTI-7
69Top-311
70MLBOffS-160
70OPC-116
70RedSoxCPPC-7
70Top-116
71MLBOffS-324
71OPC-649
71RedSoxTI-6
71Top-649
72MilBra-202
72OPC-259
72Top-259
73Kel2D-15
73LinPor-130
73NewYorN-21
73OPC-68
73OPC-394
73SyrChiTI-14
73Top-68
73Top-394
73Yan-2
74Kel-41
74OPC-66
74SyrChiTI-13
74Top-66
74TopSta-212
75Hos-134
75Kel-47
75OPC-485
75SSP42-28
75SyrChiTI-8
75Top-485
75YanSSP-22
76OPC-545
76SSP-429
76Top-545
77OPC-89
77Top-598
77YanBurK-10
78Hos-68
78Kel-43
78OPC-214
78OPC-237
78RCColC-84
78SSP270-11
78Top-2
78Top-35
78YanBurK-9
78YanSSPD-11
79Hos-143
79OPC-188
79Top-365
80OPC-62
80Top-115
81Don-284
81Fle-17
81FleStiC-91
81OPC-337
81RedSoxBG2S-92
81Top-719
82Don-189
82Fle-247
82OPC-285
82Top-285
83OPC-92
83OPC-208
83Top-693
83Top-694
83YanASFY-25
90PacLeg-93
92YanWIZ7-99
92YanWIZA-42
93MCIAmb-13
93RanKee-235
94MCIAmb-1
94TedWil-60
94TedWil-138
95MCIAmb-7
95SonGre-7
Lyman, Billy
44CenFlo-15
45CenFlo-15
Lyman, Jason
93WatIndC-16
93WatIndF-3569
94ColRedC-15
94ColRedF-450
Lymberpoulos, Nick
93PocPosF-4206
93PocPosSP-11
Lynch, Charlie
80ElmPioRST-41
Lynch, David
89TulDriGS-14
90CMC-154
90OklCit8C-4
90OklCit8P-429
90ProAAAF-675
90TulDriDGB-16
90TulDriTI-14
91AlbDukLD-13
91AlbDukP-1137
91LinDriAAA-13
92ChaLooF-3816
92ChaLooS-191
93IndIndF-1485
94ChaKniF-892
Lynch, Ed
78AshTouT-15
78ChaPirT-14
79TucTorT-20
80TidTidT-21
81TidTidT-16
82Don-641
82Fle-531
82MetPhoA-15
82Top-121
83Don-308
83Fle-549
83Top-601
84Don-75
84Fle-591
84Nes792-293
84Top-293
84TopTif-293
85Don-623
85Fle-87
85MetColP-3
85MetTCM-14
85Top-467
85TopTif-467
86Don-631
86Fle-88
86MetTCM-7
86OPC-68
86Top-68
86TopTif-68
87CubCan-15
87CubDavB-37
87Don-516
87Fle-567
87FleGlo-567
87OPC-16
87Top-697
87TopTif-697
88Don-77
88Fle-422
88FleGlo-422
88Sco-506
88ScoGlo-506
88Top-336
88TopTif-336
91MetWIZ-237
94MetColP-16
Lynch, Jerry
54Top-234
55Top-142
55TopDouH-73
56RedBurB-12
56Top-97
57Top-358
58RedEnq-25
58Top-103
59Kah-19
59RedShiBS-11
59Top-97
59TopVen-97
60Kah-23
60Lea-45
60Top-198
60Top-352
61Kah-25
61Pos-187A
61Pos-187B
61RedJayP-9
61Top-97
61TopStal-19
62Jel-127
62Kah-25
62Pos-127
62PosCan-127
62RedEnq-21
62RedJayP-8
62SalPlaC-198
62ShiPlaC-198
62Top-487
63Jel-129
63Kah-19
63Pos-129
63RedEnq-19
63RedJayP-7
63Top-37

64Kah-15
64PirKDK-16
64Top-193
64TopVen-193
65Kah-22
65Top-291
66OPC-182
66PirEasH-24
66Top-182
66TopVen-182
72LauGreF-22
79DiaGre-275
94TopArc1-234
94TopArc1G-234
Lynch, Jim
96QuaCitRB-20
Lynch, Joe
85SpoIndC-11
87TexLeaAF-3
87WicPilRD-10
88LasVegSC-9
88LasVegSP-223
89LasVegSC-3
89LasVegSP-22
90CMC-513
90LasVegSC-10
90LasVegSP-115
90ProAAAF-3
Lynch, John
92ClaDraP-122
92ClaFS7-434
92EriSaiC-17
92EriSaiF-1617
92UppDecML-21
93ExcFS7-38
93KanCouCC-12
Lynch, John H.
87OldJudN-311A
87OldJudN-311B
90KalBatN-29
Lynch, Mike
91EriSaiC-19
91EriSaiP-4065
92WinHavRSF-1771
94LetMouF-3890
94LetMouSP-2
Lynch, Rich
80WesHavWCT-21B
81WesHavAT-22
Lynch, Ty
92UtiBluSC-24
Lynes, Mike
83AlbA'sT-6
Lynn, Byrd
75WhiSox1T-14
92Man191BSR-16
Lynn, Chuck
86LynMetP-15
Lynn, Fred
75BlaBacD-4
75OPC-622
75SSPPuzB-15
75Top-622
76CraDis-30
76Hos-1
76HosTwi-1
76Kel-31
76LinSup-103
76OPC-50
76OPC-192
76OPC-196
76RedSox-5
76RedSoxSM-10
76SafSupLB-2
76SafSupLB-8
76SafSupLB-11
76SafSupLB-13
76SafSupLB-14
76SSP-402
76Top-50
76Top-192
76Top-196
77BurCheD-35
77Hos-51
77MSADis-36
77OPC-163
77PepGloD-21
77RCColC-36
77Top-210
78OPC-62
78PapGinD-19
78SSP270-174
78Top-320
78WifBalD-41
79Kel-30
79OPC-249
79Top-480
80BurKinPHR-18
80Kel-40
80OPC-60
80Top-110
80Top-201
80TopSup-10
80WilGloT-4
81AllGamPI-58
81Don-218
81Dra-9
81Fle-223
81FleStiC-98
81Kel-40
81LonBeaPT-6
81MSAMinD-21
81OPC-313
81PerCreC-20
81Squ-25
81Top-720
81TopScr-5
81TopSti-42
81TopSupHT-60
81TopTra-797
82Don-367
82Fle-468
82Fle-642
82FleSta-214
82K-M-27
82LouSlu-3
82OPC-251
82OPC-252
82PerAll-8
82PerAllG-8
82Top-251
82Top-252
82TopSti-161
82TopStiV-161
82WilSpoG-5A
82WilSpoG-5B
83AllGamPI-60
83Don-241
83DonActA-59
83Fle-97
83FleSta-110
83FleSti-31
83Kel-51
83OPC-182
83OPC-392
83PerAll-3
83PerAllG-3
83SevCoi-3
83Top-392
83Top-520
83TopFol-3
83TopSti-44
83TopSti-158
84AllGamPI-151
84AngSmo-18
84Don-17
84Don-17A
84Don-108
84DonActAS-27
84DonCha-59
84Dra-19
84Fle-525
84Fle-626
84FunFooP-54
84Nes792-680
84OCoandSI-61
84OPC-247
84RalPur-29
84SevCoi-W16
84Top-680
84TopCer-29
84TopGloA-7
84TopRubD-15
84TopSti-5
84TopSti-6
84TopSti-230
84TopSup-23
84TopTif-680
85AllGamPI-63
85Don-133
85Fle-307
85FleUpd-75
85Lea-198
85OPC-220
85OriHea-9
85SevCoi-S9
85Top-220
85TopRubD-13
85TopSti-225
85TopTif-220
85TopTifT-77T
85TopTra-77T
86BasStaB-68
86Don-245
86Fle-278
86FleStiC-70
86Lea-120
86OPC-55
86SevCoi-E16
86Spo-38
86Spo-63
86Spo-71
86Spo-73
86Spo-137
86Spo-150
86SpoRoo-46
86Top-55
86TopSti-228
86TopTat-8
86TopTif-55
86Woo-18
87ClaGam-23
87Don-9
87Don-108
87DonOpeD-135
87DonSupD-9
87Fle-474
87FleBasA-25
87FleExcS-32
87FleGlo-474
87FleStiC-72
87Lea-9
87Lea-83
87OPC-370
87OriFreB-19
87Spo-49
87Spo-198
87SpoTeaP-21
87StuPan-14
87Top-370
87TopSti-226
87TopTif-370
88Don-248
88DonBasB-297
88Fle-566
88FleGlo-566
88Lea-163
88OriFreB-19
88PanSti-15
88RedFolSB-50
88Sco-42
88ScoBoxC-T2
88ScoGlo-42
88Spo-23
88StaLinO-9
88Top-707
88TopBig-169
88TopTif-707
89AngSmo-14
89Don-563
89Fle-138
89FleGlo-138
89OPC-27
89RedFolSB-76
89Sco-126
89Spo-68
89TigMar-9
89TigPol-9
89Top-416
89TopBasT-163
89TopTif-416
89UppDec-761
90BasWit-28
90Bow-216
90BowTif-216
90ClaYel-T59
90Fle-609
90FleCan-609
90HOFStiB-83
90Lea-188
90MLBBasB-90
90OPC-107
90OPC-663
90OPCBoxB-H
90PadCok-10
90PadMag-17
90PanSti-73
90PubSti-476
90Sco-131
90ScoRoo-20T
90SouCalS-9
90Top-107
90Top-663
90TopAmeA-10
90TopBig-277
90TopHilHM-14
90TopSti-279
90TopTif-107
90TopTif-663
90TopTra-62T
90TopTraT-62T
90TopWaxBC-H
90UppDec-247
90UppDec-771
90VenSti-305
91Don-673
91Fle-536
91OPC-586
91OriCro-272
91Sco-554
91Top-586
91TopDesS-586
91TopMic-586
91TopTif-586
91UppDec-273
94TedWil-4
94TedWilM-M34
95SonGre-8
Lynn, Greg
83CliGiaF-6
91GiaMot-28
Lynn, Ken
83AndBraT-11
Lynn, Red (Japhet)
47SigOil-28
49W725AngTI-16
53MotCoo-58
Lynn, Thomas
83LynPirT-26
Lyons, Albert
52MotCoo-42
Lyons, Barry
86MetColP-24
86MetTCM-15
86TidTidP-16
87MetColP-55
87TopTra-68T
87TopTraT-68T
88Don-619
88DonTeaBM-619
88Fle-140
88FleGlo-140
88MetColP-33
88MetKah-33
88Sco-387
88ScoGlo-387
88StaLinMe-11
88Top-633
88TopTif-633
89Don-572
89FleUpd-101
89MetColP-41
89MetKah-15
89Sco-456
89Top-412
89TopTif-412
89UppDec-176
90Bow-139
90BowTif-139
90Don-526
90Fle-209
90FleCan-209
90Lea-119
90MetColP-16
90MetKah-33
90OPC-258
90Sco-29
90Top-258
90TopBig-97
90TopTif-258
90TopTVM-20
90UppDec-473
91DodMot-25
91DodPol-40
91MetWIZ-238
92TucTorF-490
92TucTorS-612
93LouRedF-218
94IndIndF-1814
94TriAAF-AAA32
95NasSouTI-12
Lyons, Bill (William Allen)
82LouRedE-14
82SprCarF-4
83LouRedR-27
84Car-20
84Car5x7-17
84LouRedR-14
85LouRedR-17
86LouRedTI-17
87LouRedTI-24
88LouRedBC-12
88LouRedBP-432
88LouRedBTI-30
90SprCarDGB-32
Lyons, Bobby
83AleDukT-1
Lyons, Curt
92PriRedC-11
92PriRedF-3083
93BilMusF-3940
93BilMusSP-6
96ChaLooB-18
97BowCerBIA-CA50
97BowCerGIA-CA50
97Cir-41
97CirRav-41
97MetUniMfG-7
97UppDec-469
Lyons, Dennis
87OldJudN-312
90KalBatN-2
90KalBatN-30
90KalBatN-31
98CamPepP-46
Lyons, Eddie
90MisStaB-23
91MisStaB-30
92MisStaB-26
93MisStaB-27
Lyons, Edward Hoyte
47SenGunBP-9
Lyons, Harry P.
87OldJudN-313
Lyons, Jimmie
74LauOldTBS-14
86NegLeaF-114
Lyons, Mario
90BenBucL-23
Lyons, Steve
89TopBig-105
92ClaDraP-78
93CapCitBC-11
93CapCitBF-457
93StaCluM-45
94St.LucMC-17
94St.LucMF-1192
Lyons, Steve (Stephen John)
84PawRedST-18
85Don-29
85FleUpd-76
86Don-579
86Fle-355
86SevCoi-E9
86Top-233
86TopTif-233
86TopTra-67T
86TopTraT-67T
87Don-409
87Fle-502
87FleGlo-502
87Top-511
87TopTif-511
87WhiSoxC-19
88Don-532
88DonBasB-291
88Fle-405
88FleGlo-405
88PanSti-60
88StaLinWS-12
88Top-108
88TopTif-108
88WhiSoxC-15
89Bow-63
89BowTif-63
89Don-253
89Fle-502
89FleGlo-502
89OPC-334
89PanSti-308
89Sco-388
89Top-334
89TopSti-298
89TopTif-334
89UppDec-224
89WhiSoxC-17
89WhiSoxK-2
90Bow-321
90BowTif-321

90Don-651
90Fle-539
90FleCan-539
90OPC-751
90PanSti-40
90PubSti-395
90Sco-88
90Top-751
90TopBig-32
90TopSti-301
90TopTif-751
90UppDec-390
90VenSti-306
90WhiSoxC-15
91Fle-127
91FleUpd-6
91OPC-612
91Sco-269
91Top-612
91TopDesS-612
91TopMic-612
91TopTif-612
91Ult-77
91UltUpd-7
91UppDec-601
92ClaDraP-78
92Don-758
92OPC-349
92Sco-294
92Top-349
92TopGol-349
92TopGolW-349
92TopMic-349
93PawRedSDD-14
93PawRedSF-2420

Lyons, Ted
28Exh-39
28StaPlaCE-45
30SchR33-33
31Exh-19
31W517-45
32OrbPinUP-43
33ButCre-17
33CraJacP-16
33DouDisP-30
33ExhFou-10
33Gou-7
33GouCanV-7
33TatOrb-43
33TatOrbSDR-172
34DiaMatCSB-118
34BatR31-36
34BatR31-111
34BatR31-119
34DiaStaR-43
35AlDemDCR3-19
35ExhFou-10
35GouPuzR-8B
35GouPuzR-9B
36ExhFou-10
36OveCanR-33
38BasTabP-21
38ExhFou-10
39WhiSoxTI-12
40WhiSoxL-13
46SpoExcW-4-5
48BabRutS-22
48WhiSoxTI-16
50CalHOFW-49
61Fle-122
63BazA-38
67TopVen-174
76ChiGre-12
76RowExh-1
76ShaPiz-76
76TayBow4-92
76WhiSoxTAG-6
77GalGloG-110
80PacLeg-77
80PerHaloFP-77
80SSPHOF-77
80WhiSoxGT-1
81ConTSN-92
82DiaCla-41
83TCMPla1942-18
85WhiSoxC-41
91ConTSN-19
92ConTSN-359
93ConTSN-822
93ConTSN-935
94ConTSN-1248
94ConTSNB-1248

Lysander, Rick (Richard)
76TucTorCa-17
76TusTorCr-28
79OgdA'sT-11
80OgdA'sT-6
80VenLeaS-8
81TacTigT-23
82TucTorT-16
83TwiTeal-13
84Don-560
84Fle-570
84Nes792-639
84TolMudHT-23
84Top-639
84TopTif-639
85Don-560
85Fle-284
85Top-383
85TopTif-383
85TwiTeal-14
86Fle-399
86Top-482
86TopTif-482
89PacSenL-143
89TopSenL-68
90CMC-338
90ProAAAF-349
90SyrChiC-12
90SyrChiMB-16
90SyrChiP-569
91PacSenL-39
91PacSenL-52

Lysgaard, Jim
76ForLauYS-8
77WesHavYT-14
78TacYanC-18

Lytle, Wade
89PriPirS-11

Lyttle, Jim
70OPC-516
70Top-516
71OPC-234
71Top-234
71YanCliDP-9
72Top-648
74OPC-437
74Top-437
76ExpRed-19
76SSP-337
79TCMJapPB-32
90DodTar-467
92YanWIZ6-76
92YanWIZ7-100

Maack, Mike
83WisRapTF-18

Maas, Duke (Duane)
56Top-57
57Top-405
58Top-228
59Top-167
59TopVen-167
60Top-421
61Top-387
61TopMagR-28
61Yan61RL-30
79TCM50-117
91RinPos1Y3-5
92YanWIZ6-77

Maas, Jason
86Ft.LauYP-15
87PriWilYP-24
88AlbYanP-1346
89AlbYanB-24
89AlbYanP-334
89AlbYanS-12
90CMC-215
90ColCliC-15
90ColCliP-8
90ColCliP-690
90ProAAAF-340
90TopTVY-52
91ColCliLD-111
91ColCliP-11
91ColCliP-609
91LinDriAAA-111

Maas, Kevin
87Ft.LauYP-19
88EasLeaAP-2
88PriWilYS-15
89ColCliC-17
89ColCliP-22
89ColCliP-737
89TriA AAC-24
89TriAAP-AAA18
90AlbDecGB-12
90StaMaa-1
90StaMaa-2
90StaMaa-3
90StaMaa-4
90StaMaa-5
90StaMaa-6
90StaMaa-7
90StaMaa-8
90StaMaa-9
90StaMaa-10
90StaMaa-11
90Bow-440
90BowTif-440
90ClaUpd-T30
90CMC-217
90ColCliC-17
90ColCliP-4
90ColCliP-691
90ColMaa-1
90ColMaa-2
90ColMaa-3
90ColMaa-4
90ColMaa-5
90ColMaa-6
90ColMaa-7
90ColMaa-8
90ColMaa-9
90ColMaa-10
90ColMaa-11
90ColMaa-12
90Fle-641
90FleCan-641
90FleUpd-113
90Lea-446
90ProAAAF-341
90Sco-606
90Sco100RS-27
90StaFS7-19
90TopMag-31
90TopTra-63T
90TopTraT-63T
90TopTVY-53
90TriAAAC-24
90UppDec-70
90UppDecS-2
91Bow-158
91Cla1-T63
91Cla1-NNO
91Cla3-T51
91ClaGam-130
91Col-21
91Don-554
91Fle-672
91JimDea-23
91KinDis-3
91Lea-393
91MajLeaCP-2
91MLBKeyC-2
91OPC-4
91OPC-435
91OPCPre-74
91PanSti-264
91Pos-30
91PosCan-20
91Sco-600
91Sco100RS-40
91ScoHotR-2
91Sev3DCN-10
91SevCoi-NE10
91StaClu-282
91StaCluCM-18
91StaCluP-21
91Stu-96
91Top-4
91Top-435
91TopCraJI-20
91TopDeb90-92
91TopDesS-4
91TopDesS-435
91TopMic-4
91TopMic-435
91TopRoo-17
91TopSta-22
91TopTif-4
91TopTif-435
91ToyRoo-16
91Ult-238
91UppDec-375
91Woo-13
92Bow-205
92ClaGam-55
92ColPro-10
92Don-153
92Fle-236
92Hig5-88
92Lea-284
92MooSna-5
92OPC-710
92Pin-90
92Sco-613
92Sco100S-46
92ScoProP-24
92SpoStaCC-30
92StaClu-35
92StaPro-6
92Stu-215
92Top-710
92TopGol-710
92TopGolW-710
92TopKid-86
92TopMic-710
92TriPla-225
92Ult-104
92UppDec-98
92UppDec-377
93Don-635
93Fle-652
93Lea-206
93PacSpa-207
93PanSti-147
93Pin-165
93Sco-634
93Sel-142
93StaClu-395
93StaCluFDI-395
93StaCluMOP-395
93StaCluY-8
93Top-168
93TopGol-168
93TopInaM-168
93TopMic-168
93TriPla-57
93Ult-243
93UppDec-594
93UppDecGold-594
94Fle-238
94Pac-429
94Sco-425
94ScoGolR-425
94WicWraF-199
95ColCliP-17
95ColCliTI-17
95FleUpd-60

Maasberg, Gary
88SpaPhiP-1041

Mabe, Bobby (Robert)
59RedEnq-13
59Top-356
60Top-288
91OriCro-273

Mabe, Todd
85Ft.MyeRT-2

Mabee, Vic
77AshTouT-13
79WauTimT-6

Maberry, Louis
92PriRedC-17
92PriRedF-3084
93WesVirWC-16
93WesVirWF-2864
94ClaGolF-192

Mabry, John
91HamRedC-17
91HamRedP-4053
92ProFS7-331
92SprCarC-19
92SprCarF-883
92UppDecML-234
93ArkTraF-2824
94Bow-124
94ExcFS7-269
94LeaLimR-29
94LouRedF-2993
94ScoRoo-RT130
94ScoRooGR-RT130
94SigRooDP-97
94SigRooDPS-97
94SpoRoo-100
94SpoRooAP-100
95Bow-185
95BowBes-R77
95BowBesR-R77
95ColCho-21
95ColChoGS-21
95ColChoSS-21
95Don-260
95DonPreP-260
95DonTopotO-332
95Fin-303
95FinRef-303
95Fla-412
95Fle-502
95Lea-6
95Pin-151
95PinArtP-151
95PinMusC-151
95Sco-301
95ScoAi-AM2
95ScoGolR-301
95ScoPlaTS-301
95SelCer-126
95SelCerMG-126
95TopTra-83T
95UC3-119
95UC3ArtP-119
95Ult-432
95UltGolM-432
95UppDec-56
95UppDecED-56
95UppDecEDG-56
96CarPol-16
96Cir-179
96CirRav-179
96ColCho-693
96ColChoGS-693
96ColChoSS-693
96Don-253
96DonPreP-253
96EmoXL-269
96Fla-362
96Fle-547
96FleRooS-11
96FleTif-547
96Lea-197
96LeaPre-98
96LeaPreP-98
96LeaPrePB-197
96LeaPrePG-197
96LeaPrePS-197
96LeaSig-56
96LeaSigA-140
96LeaSigAG-140
96LeaSigAS-140
96LeaSigPPG-56
96LeaSigPPP-56
96MetUni-228
96MetUniP-228
96Pac-222
96PanSti-76
96Pin-12
96PinAfi-126
96PinAfiAP-126
96PinArtP-60
96PinSta-60
96Sco-293
96ScoDugC-B18
96ScoDugCAP-B18
96Sel-40
96SelArtP-40
96Spo-88
96SpoArtP-88
96StaClu-46
96StaCluMOP-46
96Sum-112
96SumAbo&B-112
96SumArtP-112
96SumFoi-112
96Top-73
96TopGal-102
96TopGalPPI-102
96Ult-276
96UltGolM-276
96UppDec-184
97Cir-346
97CirRav-346
97ColCho-203
97Don-90
97DonEli-94
97DonEliGS-94
97DonLim-97
97DonLimLE-97
97DonPre-127
97DonPreCttC-127
97DonPreP-90
97DonPrePGold-90
97DonTea-154
97DonTeaSPE-154
97Fin-97
97FinRef-97
97Fle-447
97FleTif-447
97Lea-35
97LeaFraM-35

97LeaFraMDC-35
97MetUni-233
97Pac-413
97PacLigB-413
97PacPri-140
97PacPriLB-140
97PacPriP-140
97PacSil-413
97PinIns-15
97PinInsCE-15
97PinInsDE-15
97Sco-118
97ScoPreS-118
97ScoShoS-118
97ScoShoSAP-118
97StaClu-167
97StaCluMOP-167
97Stu-86
97StuPrePG-86
97StuPrePS-86
97Top-102
97Top-171
97Ult-274
97UltGolME-274
97UltPlaME-274
97UppDec-163
97UppDec-316
Macaluso, Nick
88MarPhiS-25
Macalutas, Jon
96OgdRapTI-39
MacArthur, John
84AriWilP-11
MacArthur, Mark
90HamRedB-21
90HamRedS-15
91SavCarC-19
91SavCarP-1660
92VisOakC-11
92VisOakF-1022
Macauley, Drew
80BufBisT-6
81BufBisT-7
Macavage, Joe
87WatPirP-26
88AugPirP-372
Macca, Chris
96AshTouB-24
96MauStiHWB-14
MacCauley, John
92SouOreAC-21
92SouOreAF-3414
93SouOreAC-16
93SouOreAF-4060
MacCormack, Franc
78SanJosMMC-4
MacDonald, Bill
50PirTeal-12
51Bow-239
52Top-138
83TopRep5-138
MacDonald, Jim
78DayBeaAT-17
80ColAstT-20
81TucTorT-23
MacDonald, Ken
91BriBanF-10
95AusFut-73
MacDonald, Kevin
79NewCoPT-11
MacDonald, Mike
95MidLeaA-29
95SprSulTI-12
MacDonald, Robert
88MyrBeaBJP-1191
89KnoBluJB-13
89KnoBluJP-1139
89KnoBluJS-11
90KnoBluJP-1247
90KnoBluJS-10
90ProAaA-44
91BluJayFS-18
91BluJayS-32
91Don-636
91LinDriAAA-508
91StaClu-585
91SyrChiLD-508
91SyrChiMB-15
91TopDeb90-93
91UltUpd-61
92Don-588
92Fle-335
92OPC-87
92OPCPre-152
92Sco-405
92Sco100RS-46
92StaClu-372
92Top-87
92TopGol-87
92TopGolW-87
92TopMic-87
93BluJayD4-36
93Don-689
93Fle-696
93FleFinE-212
93OPC-131
93PacSpa-447
93StaClu-434
93StaCluFDI-434
93StaCluMOP-434
93TigGat-20
93Top-427
93TopGol-427
93TopInaM-427
93TopMic-427
93Ult-289
94CalCanF-785
94Don-415
94Fle-140
94Pac-225
94Sco-286
94ScoGolR-286
94Top-162
94TopGol-162
94TopSpa-162
94Ult-57
MacDonald, Ronald
79JacMetT-23
80TidTidT-9
82TidTidT-10
Mace, Jeff
83BurRanF-24
83BurRanT-21
85TulDriTI-24
88BoiHawP-1616
89BoiHawP-1977
Macey, Fausto
95Bow-218
Macfarlane, Mike
86MemChiSTOS-16
86MemChiTOS-16
87OmaRoyP-24
88DonRoo-55
88FleUpd-31
88FleUpdG-31
88RoySmo-17
88ScoRoo-76T
88ScoRooG-76T
88StaLinRo-9
88TopTra-62T
88TopTraT-62T
89Bow-118
89BowTif-118
89Don-416
89Fle-287
89FleGlo-287
89Sco-319
89ScoHot1R-97
89ScoYouSI-13
89Top-479
89TopBig-86
89TopTif-479
89UppDec-546
90Don-498
90Fle-114
90FleCan-114
90Lea-389
90OPC-202
90PubSti-352
90Top-202
90TopTif-202
90UppDec-307
90VenSti-307
91Bow-301
91Don-313
91Fle-562
91Lea-30
91OPC-638
91PanFreS-275
91RoyPol-13
91Sco-839
91StaClu-15
91Top-638
91TopDesS-638
91TopMic-638
91TopTif-638
91Ult-151
91UppDec-570
92Bow-589
92Don-161
92Fle-161
92Lea-83
92OPC-42
92Pin-517
92RoyPol-15
92Sco-27
92StaClu-74
92Top-42
92TopGol-42
92TopGolW-42
92TopMic-42
92TriPla-144
92Ult-73
92UppDec-497
93Bow-505
93DiaMar-66
93Don-525
93Fla-220
93Fle-241
93Lea-422
93OPC-265
93PanSti-102
93Pin-332
93RoyPol-17
93Sco-323
93SP-232
93StaClu-470
93StaCluFDI-470
93StaCluMOP-470
93StaCluRoy-2
93Top-768
93TopGol-768
93TopInaM-768
93TopMic-768
93Ult-564
93UppDec-327
93UppDecGold-327
93UppDecHRH-HR25
94Bow-227
94ColC-181
94ColChoGS-181
94ColChoSS-181
94Don-324
94ExtBas-95
94Fin-300
94FinRef-300
94Fla-61
94Fle-164
94Lea-159
94OPC-154
94Pac-294
94PanSti-77
94Pin-488
94PinArtP-488
94PinMusC-488
94Sco-459
94ScoGolR-459
94Sel-27
94StaClu-250
94StaCluFDI-250
94StaCluGR-250
94StaCluMOP-250
94Stu-187
94Top-578
94TopGol-578
94TopSpa-578
94TriPla-239
94Ult-69
94UppDec-107
94UppDecED-107
95ColCho-459
95ColCho-574T
95ColChoGS-459
95ColChoSE-213
95ColChoSEGS-213
95ColChoSESS-213
95ColChoSS-459
95Don-439
95DonPreP-439
95DonTopotO-22
95Fin-165
95Fin-227
95FinRef-165
95FinRef-227
95Fla-228
95Fle-165
95FleUpd-11
95Lea-379
95Pac-208
95Pin-113
95PinArtP-113
95PinMusC-113
95Sco-96
95ScoGolR-96
95ScoPlaTS-96
95SP-126
95SPSil-126
95StaClu-175
95StaClu-530
95StaCluFDI-175
95StaCluMOP-175
95StaCluMOP-530
95StaCluSTDW-RS530
95StaCluSTWS-175
95StaCluSTWS-530
95Top-296
95TopCyb-159
95TopTra-37T
95Ult-292
95UltGolM-292
95UppDec-396
95UppDecED-396
95UppDecEDG-396
95UppDecSE-54
95UppDecSEG-54
96ColCho-64
96ColCho-575
96ColChoGS-64
96ColChoGS-575
96ColChoSS-64
96ColChoSS-575
96Don-119
96DonPreP-119
96Fle-30
96FleTif-30
96FleUpd-U41
96FleUpdTC-U41
96LeaSigA-141
96LeaSigAG-141
96LeaSigAS-141
96Pac-257
96RoyPol-16
96Sco-108
96StaClu-108
96StaCluEPB-108
96StaCluEPG-108
96StaCluEPS-108
96StaCluMOP-108
96TeaOut-52
96Top-33
96Ult-18
96Ult-358
96UltGolM-18
96UltGolM-358
96UppDec-347
97Cir-35
97CirRav-35
97ColCho-355
97Fin-227
97FinRef-227
97Fle-116
97FleTif-116
97Pac-105
97PacLigB-105
97PacSil-105
97RoyPol-14
97StaClu-281
97StaCluMOP-281
97Top-198
97Ult-482
97UltGolME-482
97UltPlaME-482
97UppDec-88
MacFayden, Dan
31Exh-18
33ExhFou-9
33Gou-156
33GouCanV-87
34DiaMatCSB-119
35GouPuzR-4F
35GouPuzR-7F
35GouPuzR-12F
36ExhFou-1
36GouWidPPR-A68
37ExhFou-1
38ExhFou-1
79RedSoxEF-7
91ConTSN-215
Macha, Ken
72Dia-27
76VenLeaS-168
77ColCliT-11
78ColCliT-15
78Top-483
79ExpPos-16
80ExpPos-16
81Don-540
81Fle-167
82Fle-618
82OPC-282
82Top-282
86ExpPos-7
86ExpProPa-28
87ExpPos-16
89ExpPos-18
90ExpPos-21
93AngMot-28
94AngMot-28
95TreThuTI-1
96TreThuB-1
Macha, Mike
78RicBraT-7
80VenLeaS-127
Machado, Gregorio
76VenLeaS-146
80VenLeaS-138
93LinVenB-142
Machado, Julio
87ClePhiP-21
89JacMetGS-11
89PenPilS-12
89TriA AAC-28
90ClaUpd-T31
90Don-47
90DonRoo-41
90FleUpd-37
90MetColP-39
90MetKah-48
90OPC-684
90ScoRoo-92T
90Top-684
90TopDeb89-74
90TopTif-684
90TopTVM-14
90TriAAAC-28
90UppDec-93
91Bow-50
91BreMilB-15
91BrePol-13
91Don-764
91FleUpd-31
91Lea-247
91MetWIZ-240
91OPC-434
91Sco100RS-87
91Top-434
91TopDesS-434
91TopMic-434
91TopTif-434
91UppDec-716
92Don-262
92Fle-181
92OPC-208
92Sco-353
92Top-208
92TopGol-208
92TopGolW-208
92TopMic-208
92UppDec-479
93LinVenB-59
94BreMilB-52
94VenLinU-211
Machado, Robert
93LinVenB-156
93MidLeaAGF-24
93SouBenWSC-14
93SouBenWSF-1433
94PriWilCC-14
94PriWilCF-1924
94VenLinU-251
95LinVen-197
95PriWilCTI-14
96BirBarB-10
92UtiBluSC-14
Machalec, Mark
84ButCopKT-15
Machemer, Dave
77SalLakCGC-11
80EvaTriT-16
81TolMudHT-13
82TolMudHT-14
85BelBreT-26
86StoPorP-14
87StoPorP-3
88ElPasDB-6
89DenZepC-25
89DenZepP-37
90CMC-50
90DenZepC-25
90DenZepP-641

90ProAAAF-666
90TriAllGP-AAA26
96El PasDB-4
78STLakCGC-3
Machuca, Freddy
82DanSunF-19
Macias, Angel
91EugEmeC-19
91EugEmeP-3724
Macias, Bob
82AmaGolST-6
Macias, Henry
77CedRapGT-8
78CedRapGT-16
Macias, Jamie
96CedRapKTI-30
Macias, Jose
96DelShoB-20
Mack, Connie III
76TayBow4-81
Mack, Cornelius McGillicuddy (Connie)
04FanCraAL-33
09SpoNewSM-37
10E98-19
10JHDABE-11
10NadE1-33
11A'sFirT20-12
11SpoLifCW-228
11SpoLifM-98
12PhiCarE-18
13NatGamW-26
13TomBarW-25
14CraJacE-12
14TexTomE-28
14TexTomE-56
15CraJacE-12
16SpoNewM-105
16BF2FP-37
16SpoNewM-107
23WilChoV-85
32OrbPinUP-44
33TatOrb-44
33TatOrbSDR-188
36NatChiFPR-94
36PC7AlbHoF-9
36R31PasP-36
36R31Pre-L8
36WorWidGV-110
40PlaBal-132
48ExhHoF-21
49PhiBul-31
50CalHOFW-50
50H80FouMH-1
51R42SmaS-67
51TopConMA-7
60Fle-14
61Fle-123
63BasMagM-51
63BazA-18
68SpoMemAG-2
69Baz-10
69SCFOldT-19
76ShaPiz-12
76TayBow4-47
76TayBow4-81
77BobParHoF-33
77GalGloG-145
77GalGloG-194
77ShaPiz-1
80LauFamF-37
80PerHaloFP-9
80SSPHOF-9
81ConTSN-58
81SpoHaloF-4
82BHCRSpoL-9
84GalHaloFRL-12
86ConSer1-18
87OldJudN-314
88ConHar-4
88GandBCGCE-25
88WG1CarG-67
89HOFStiB-85
90BasWit-99
90HOFStiB-45
91ConTSN-45
91ConTSN-46
91ConTSN-47
92ConTSN-439
92ConTSN-599
92ConTSNCI-14
93ConTSN-824
93CraJac-10
93DiaStaES-142
94ConTSN-1159
94ConTSN-1217
94ConTSNB-1159
94ConTSNB-1217
94OriofB-84
94TedWil-69
94UppDecTAE-43
Mack, Earle
49PhiBul-32
76TayBow4-82
81ConTSN-57
92ConTSN-453
Mack, Henry
77SpaPhiT-7
Mack, Jerry
86KenTwiP-14
Mack, Joseph
87OldJudN-315
Mack, Quinn
88WesPalBES-17
89JacExpB-14
89JacExpP-153
90CMC-66
90IndIndC-16
90IndIndP-299
90ProAAAF-582
91IndIndLD-188
91IndIndP-475
91LinDriAAA-188
92IndIndF-1874
92IndIndS-186
93LinVenB-41
94CalCanF-801
95LinVen-207
95TacRaiTI-11
Mack, Ray
77TCMTheWY-2
83TCMPla1943-6
Mack, Raymond
89WytCubS-21
90PulBraP-3090
91MacBraC-4
91MacBraP-858
Mack, Roy
76TayBow4-81
Mack, Shane
85BeaGolGT-4
85Top-398
85TopTif-398
86BeaGolGP-16
87DonRoo-42
87LasVegSP-18
87SpoRoo2-31
87SpoTeaP-16
87TopTra-69T
87TopTraT-69T
88Don-411
88Fle-590
88FleGlo-590
88LasVegSC-10
88LasVegSP-233
88OPC-283
88PadSmo-16
88Sco-414
88ScoGlo-414
88ScoYouS2-36
88Top-548
88TopTif-548
89Don-538
89Sco-270
89UppDec-182
90ClaYel-T17
90DonBesA-122
90Lea-136
90TopTra-64T
90TopTraT-64T
91Bow-326
91Don-320
91Fle-618
91Lea-40
91OPC-672
91Sco-284
91StaClu-259
91StaCluP-22
91Stu-88
91Top-672
91TopDesS-672
91TopMic-672
91TopTif-672
91Ult-191
91UppDec-188
92Bow-592
92Cla1-T55
92Don-345
92Fle-210
92Lea-82
92OPC-164
92PanSti-119
92Pin-230
92Sco-284
92ScoSam-6
92StaClu-47
92Stu-207
92Top-164
92TopDaiQTU-8
92TopGol-164
92TopGolW-164
92TopMic-164
92TriPla-197
92Ult-95
92UppDec-428
93Bow-101
93ClaGam-55
93Don-395
93Fin-61
93FinRef-61
93Fla-238
93Fle-640
93FleFruotL-38
93FunPac-194
93Lea-315
93OPC-263
93PacSpa-174
93PanSti-129
93Pin-78
93Sco-19
93Sel-104
93SP-249
93StaClu-420
93StaCluFDI-420
93StaCluMOP-420
93Top-282
93TopGol-282
93TopInaM-282
93TopMic-282
93TriPla-180
93Ult-585
93UppDec-236
93UppDec-837
93UppDecGold-236
93UppDecGold-837
93USPlaCA-5D
94ColC-182
94ColChoGS-182
94ColChoSS-182
94Don-253
94ExtBas-120
94Fin-105
94FinRef-105
94Fla-315
94Fle-212
94Lea-435
94LeaL-50
94Pac-360
94PanSti-93
94Pin-148
94PinArtP-148
94PinMusC-148
94Sco-383
94ScoGolR-383
94Sel-274
94StaClu-429
94StaCluFDI-429
94StaCluGR-429
94StaCluMOP-429
94Stu-198
94Top-337
94TopGol-337
94TopSpa-337
94TriPla-255
94Ult-390
94UppDec-197
94UppDecED-197
95ColChoSE-228
95ColChoSEGS-228
95ColChoSESS-228
95Don-526
95DonPreP-526
95Fle-208
95PacPri-80
95Sco-43
95ScoGolR-43
95ScoHaloG-HG54
95ScoPlaTS-43
95StaClu-362
95StaCluMOP-362
95StaCluSTWS-362
95StaCluVR-189
95Top-8
95TopCyb-6
95UppDec-190
95UppDecED-190
95UppDecEDG-190
95StaCluVRMC-189
97ColCho-282
97DonTea-56
97DonTeaSPE-56
97Fle-603
97FleTif-603
97Ult-463
97UltGolME-463
97UltPlaME-463
Mack, Toby (Tony Lynn)
83RedPioT-17
85EdmTraC-6
86EdmTraP-20
87MidAngP-19
88SanAntMB-5
89MiaMirIS-12
MacKanin, Pete
74SpoIndC-42
74OPC-597
74Top-597
76ExpRed-20
76OPC-287
76SSP-324
76Top-287
76VenLeaS-55
77ExpPos-20
77OPC-260
77Top-156
78Top-399
79PhiBurK-17
81Fle-565
81Top-509
82Don-354
82Fle-556
82Top-438
83OklCit8T-12
84IowCubT-12
86PeoChiP-17
88IowCubC-24
88IowCubP-543
89IowCubC-25
89IowCubP-1707
89TriAAP-AAA43
90CMC-149
90NasSouC-24
90NasSouP-249
90ProAAAF-561
91LinDriAAA-274
91NasSouLD-274
91NasSouP-2172
91PacSenL-66
91TriA AAGP-AAA24
92NasSouF-1848
92NasSouS-299
93FreKeyC-26
93FreKeyF-1042
93RanKee-236
94BowBayF-2427
MacKay, Bill
83AndBraT-1
MacKay, Joey
83GreHorT-25
84GreHorT-8
MacKenzie, Chess
88GooN16-25
MacKenzie, Gordon
75WesPalBES-17
77JacSunT-13
82CubRedL-NNO
83EvaTriT-22
84EvaTriT-4
85NasSouTI-13
86GiaMot-28
87GiaMot-27
88GiaMot-27
89PhoFirC-25
89PhoFirP-1504
95KinIndTI-17
MacKenzie, Kenneth P.
60Top-534
61Top-496
62Top-421
63Top-393
64Top-297
64TopVen-297
67AstTeal2-16
81TCM60I-433
82MetGal62-14
91MetWIZ-239
MacKenzie, Shaun
86EveGiaC-20
86EveGiaPC-12
87EveGiaC-20
Mackey, Biz
74LauOldTBS-27
86NegLeaF-91
90NegLeaS-4
91PomBlaBPB-23
Mackey, Jason
93BurIndC-17
93BurIndF-3294
Mackie, Bart
81BatTroT-9
82WauTimF-6
Mackie, Ed
93HelBreF-4102
93HelBreSP-18
Mackie, Scott
89MiaMirIS-12
Mackiewicz, Felix
48SomandK-15
83TCMPla1945-14
Mackin, Jeff
90MisStaB-24
91MisStaB-31
92MisStaB-27
93MisStaB-28
MacKinnon, Tim
88BoiHawP-1629
Macko, Joe
76DalCon-7
90RanMot-28
Macko, Steve
80Top-676
80WicAerT-18
81Don-505
81Top-381
MacLeod, Kevin
88SouOreAP-1709
89ModA'sCLC-273
90HunStaB-8
Maclin, Lonnie
88St.PetCS-14
89SprCarB-25
90LouRedBLBC-24
90St.PetCS-14
91LinDriAAA-239
91LouRedLD-239
91LouRedP-2928
91LouRedTI-25
92LouRedF-1901
92LouRedS-267
92SkyAAAF-127
93LouRedF-227
94Pin-407
94PinArtP-407
94PinMusC-407
MacMillan, Darrell
89BoiHawP-1986
90EriSaiS-14
MacNeil, Doug
92ElmPioC-16
92ElmPioF-1380
92WinHavRSC-11
MacNeil, Tim
88ButCopKSP-4
89GasRanP-1024
89GasRanS-11
90MiaMirIS-15
Macon, Leland
94Bow-569
94ChaRivC-13
94ChaRivF-2685
Macon, Max
43DodTeal-15
77TCMTheWY-48
79DiaGre-218
90DodTar-468
MacPhail, Larry
80PerHaloFP-165
82OhiHaloF-62
88RinPosD1-8B
92YanWIZH-21
MacPherson, Bruce
77OrlTwiT-14
78OrlTwiT-11
80TolMudHT-4
81TolMudHT-7
82RocRedWT-3
MacQuarrie, Dave
75WesPalBES-24
MacRae, Scott
95BilRedTI-23

Macrina, Eric
91SalLakTP-3218
Macu, Andres
90KisDodD-15
Macullar, James
87OldJudN-316
MacWhorter, Keith
80VenLeaS-162
81Top-689
83PawRedST-8
84MaiGuiT-21
Macy, Frank
82IowCubT-30
84IowCubT-10
Madden, Billy
81TCM60I-391
Madden, Bob
76AppFoxT-13
77AppFoxT-13
79QuaCitCT-17
80QuaCitCT-11
Madden, Joey
93BatCliC-16
93BatCliF-3159
94BatCliC-11
94BatCliF-3458
Madden, Kid (Michael)
87OldJudN-317
88AugBecN-17
89N526N7C-9
Madden, Mike
81ElPasDT-14
82VanCanT-14
83TopTra-64T
84AstMot-25
84Don-161
84Fle-232
84Nes792-127
84Top-127
84TopTif-127
85Top-479
85TopTif-479
86AstMilL-14
86AstPol-18
86Top-691
86TopTif-691
Madden, Morris
83VerBeaDT-8
86GleFalTP-13
87TolMudHP-18
87TolMudHT-15
88BlaYNPRWL-153
88BufBisC-6
88BufBisP-1466
88BufBisTI-8
89BlaYNPRWLU-29
89ScoHot1R-32
89TriA AAC-11
90AlbDukC-5
90AlbDukP-340
90AlbDukT-19
90CMC-407
90ProAAAF-61
90TriAAAC-11
Madden, Scott
86ClePhiP-16
88RenSilSCLC-273
Madden, Thomas
09ColChiE-175
11SpoLifM-13
12ColRedB-175
12ColTinT-175
Maddern, Clarence
49Bow-152
49W725AngTI-17
52MotCoo-44
53MotCoo-34
Maddon, Joe
76QuaCitAT-19
85MidAngT-10
86MidAngP-14
94AngMot-28
95AngMot-28
96AngMot-28
Maddox, Elliott
71MLBOffS-545
71OPC-11
71SenPolP-7
71SenTeaIW-15
71Top-11
72OPC-277
72Top-277
72TopCloT-21
73OPC-658
73Top-658
74OPC-401
74Top-401
75Hos-90
75Kel-9
75OPC-113
75Top-113
75YanSSP-10
76OPC-503
76SSP-451
76Top-503
77Top-332
78Hos-40
78MetDaiPA-15
78Top-442
79OPC-28
79Top-69
80OPC-357
80Top-707
81Don-397
81Fle-326
81OPC-299
81Top-299
90SweBasG-109
91MetWIZ-241
91OriCro-274
92YanWIZ7-101
93RanKee-26
Maddox, Garry
73LinPor-160
73OPC-322
73Top-322
74OPC-178
74Top-178
74TopSta-107
75Hos-43
75HosTwi-43
75Kel-37
75OPC-240
75Top-240
76OPC-38
76Top-38
77BurCheD-167
77Kel-37
77OPC-42
77Top-520
78Hos-133
78Kel-28
78OPC-93
78PhiSSP-28
78RCColC-78
78SSP270-28
78Top-610
78WifBalD-42
79Kel-16
79OPC-245
79PhiBurK-20
79PhiTeal-5
79Top-470
80OPC-198
80PhiBurK-10
80Top-380
81AllGamPI-151
81CokTeaS-101
81Don-55
81Fle-19
81FleStiC-70
81OPC-160
81Top-160
81TopSti-204
81TopSupHT-83
82Don-315
82Fle-248
82FleSta-57
82OPC-20
82Top-20
82TopSti-73
82TopStiV-73
83AllGamPI-151
83Don-63
83Fle-164
83FleSta-111
83FleSti-173
83OPC-41
83PhiTas-15
83Top-615
83TopFol-5
84Don-305
84Fle-39
84FleSti-122
84Nes792-755
84OPC-187
84PhiTas-39
84Top-755
84TopSti-123
84TopTif-755
85Don-137
85Fle-259
85OPC-235
85PhiCIG-11
85PhiTas-38
85Top-235
85TopMin-235
85TopSti-121
85TopTif-235
86Don-407
86Fle-445
86OPC-362
86PhiTas-31
86Top-585
86TopSti-117
86TopTat-14
86TopTif-585
88PhiTas-39
90PhiTas-36
Maddox, Jerry
78RicBraT-8
79RicBraT-6
Maddox, Leland
87MadMusP-13
Maddox, Nicholas
08RosComP-153
09ColChiE-176A
09ColChiE-176B
09PhiCarE-15
09T206-219
10DomDisP-73
10NadE1-34
10PirAmeCE-7
10PirTipTD-11
10SweCapPP-141
11SpoLifCW-229
11SpoLifM-255
11T205-106
12ColRedB-176A
12ColRedB-176B
12ColTinT-176A
12ColTinT-176B
Maddux, Greg
86PitCubP-14
87CubCan-16
87CubDavB-31
87Don-36
87DonRoo-52
87FleUpd-68
87FleUpdG-68
87Lea-36
87SpoTeaP-22
87TopTra-70T
87TopTraT-70T
88CubDavB-31
88Don-539
88DonBasB-82
88DonTeaBC-539
88Fle-423
88FleGlo-423
88OPC-361
88PeoChiTI-21
88Top-361
88TopSti-59
88TopTif-361
89Bow-284
89BowTif-284
89CadEllD-33
89ClaTraO-121
89CubMar-31
89Don-373
89DonAll-56
89DonBasB-37
89Fle-431
89FleBasM-24
89FleForTR-5
89FleGlo-431
89FleSup-28
89OPC-240
89PanSti-49
89PeoChiTI-28
89RedFolSB-77
89Sco-119
89ScoHot1S-48
89ScoYouSI-39
89Spo-108
89Top-240
89TopMinL-4
89TopSti-48
89TopTif-240
89TVSpoM-23
89UppDec-241
90Bow-27
90BowTif-27
90ClaUpd-T32
90CubMar-13
90Don-158
90DonBesN-14
90Fle-37
90FleCan-37
90Lea-25
90MLBBasB-49
90OPC-715
90PanSti-237
90PeoChiTI-20
90PubSti-198
90Sco-403
90Spo-211
90Top-715
90TopBig-204
90TopDou-41
90TopMinL-50
90TopSti-51
90TopTif-715
90TopTVCu-12
90UppDec-213
90VenSti-308
91Bow-426
91Cla3-T52
91ClaGam-68
91CubMar-31
91CubVinL-17
91Don-374
91Fle-426
91Lea-127
91OPC-35
91PanCanT1-98
91PanFreS-50
91PanSti-43
91Sco-317
91StaClu-126
91Top-35
91TopDesS-35
91TopMic-35
91TopTif-35
91Ult-64
91UppDec-115
92Bow-148
92ClaGam-30
92CubMar-31
92Don-520
92Fle-386
92Hig5-29
92Lea-294
92OPC-580
92PanSti-189
92Pin-65
92Pin-608
92PinTea2-32
92Sco-269
92ScoImpP-77
92SpoIllFK1-162
92StaClu-665
92StaCluECN-665
92StaCluMO-20
92Stu-15
92Top-580
92TopGol-580
92TopGolW-580
92TopMic-580
92TriPla-19
92Ult-178
92UltAwaW-24
92UppDec-353
92UppDecTMH-30
93Bow-550
93BraLykP-17
93BraLykS-21
93ClaGam-56
93ClaGam-NNO
93Don-608
93DonEliD-3
93DurPowP2-12
93Fin-85
93FinJum-85
93FinRef-85
93Fla-7
93Fle-380
93Fle-707
93FleAll-NL10
93FleAtl-13
93FleFinE-3
93FleFruotL-39
93FunPac-65
93Lea-326
93LeaGolA-R19
93MSABenSPD-4
93OPC-135
93OPCPre-126
93OPCPreSP-19
93OPCPreSPF-19
93PacSpa-335
93PanSti-159
93PanSti-164
93Pin-517
93PinTeaP-1
93Sco-484
93Sco-527
93Sco-576
93Sel-31
93SelAce-4
93SelChaS-9
93SelDufIP-9
93SelRoo-123T
93SelStaL-66
93SelStaL-78
93SelStaL-84
93SelStaL-88
93SP-59
93StaClu-2
93StaClu-665
93StaClu-750
93StaCluB-18
93StaCluFDI-2
93StaCluFDI-665
93StaCluFDI-750
93StaCluM-126
93StaCluMO-14
93StaCluMOP-2
93StaCluMOP-665
93StaCluMOP-750
93StaCluMP-27
93Stu-196
93Top-183
93Top-409
93TOPBLAG-12
93TopComotH-17
93TopComotH-19
93TopGol-183
93TopGol-409
93TopInaM-183
93TopInaM-409
93TopMic-183
93TopMic-409
93TopTra-54T
93TriPlaG-GS4
93TriPlaLL-L2
93Ult-307
93UltAllS-9
93UltAwaW-1
93UltAwaW-22
93UltPer-6
93UppDec-472
93UppDec-488
93UppDec-535
93UppDecGold-472
93UppDecGold-488
93UppDecGold-535
93USPlaCA-13S
94Bow-245
94BowBes-R36
94BowBes-X101
94BowBesR-R36
94BowBesR-X101
94BraLykP-19
94BraLykS-19
94BraUSPC-1D
94BraUSPC-8S
94ChuHomS-4
94ChuHomSG-4
94ColC-183
94ColChoGS-183
94ColChoSS-183
94Don-380
94DonAwaWJ-2
94DonSpeE-380
94ExtBas-208
94ExtBasGB-16
94ExtBasPD-7
94Fin-209
94FinJum-209
94FinRef-209
94Fla-130
94FlaHotG-5
94Fle-365
94FleAwaW-4
94FleLeaL-12
94FleSmo'nH-7
94FleSun-16
94FUnPac-131

94FUnPac-184
94FUnPac-207
94KinDis-18
94Lea-94
94LeaGolS-8
94LeaL-87
94LeaLimGA-18
94LeaStaS-5
94OPC-101
94OPCAllR-22
94OPCJumA-22
94OscMayR-26
94Pac-15
94Pac-656
94PacPro-P5
94PacSilP-30
94PanSti-147
94Pin-11
94PinArtP-11
94PinMusC-11
94PinSam-11
94PinTeaP-9
94PinTheN-15
94PinTri-TR12
94ProMag-5
94ProMagP-2
94RedFolMI-16
94Sco-524
94Sco-634
94ScoGolR-524
94ScoGolR-634
94Sel-2
94SelCroC-CC2
94SP-54
94SPDieC-54
94Spo-53
94Spo-193
94SpoFanA-AS9
94SpoSam-193
94StaClu-544
94StaClu-716
94StaCluFDI-544
94StaCluFDI-716
94StaCluGR-544
94StaCluGR-716
94StaCluMO-42
94StaCluMOP-544
94StaCluMOP-716
94StaCluT-31
94StaCluTFDI-31
94Stu-39
94StuSerS-8
94TomPiz-14
94Top-392
94Top-499
94TopBlaG-38
94TopGol-392
94TopGol-499
94TopSpa-392
94TopSpa-499
94TopSupS-26
94TopTraFl-1
94TriPla-46
94TriPlaM-14
94TriPlaP-10
94Ult-446
94UltAllS-20
94UltAwaW-18
94UltAwaW-23
94UltStrK-3
94UppDec-320
94UppDecAJ-18
94UppDecAJG-18
94UppDecED-320
94USPlaCA-1S
95Baz-1
95BazRedH-RH1
95Bow-406
95BowBes-R15
95BowBesJR-4
95BowBesR-R15
95ClaPhoC-3
95ColCho-63
95ColCho-67
95ColChoGS-63
95ColChoGS-67
95ColChoSE-60
95ColChoSE-142
95ColChoSE-249
95ColChoSEGS-60
95ColChoSEGS-142
95ColChoSEGS-249
95ColChoSESS-60
95ColChoSESS-142
95ColChoSESS-249
95ColChoSS-63
95ColChoSS-67
95DenHol-14
95Don-331
95DonAll-NL1
95DonDiaK-DK22
95DonDom-1
95DonEli-51
95DonMouM-1
95DonPreP-331
95DonTopotO-190
95Emb-109
95EmbGolI-109
95Emo-106
95EmoMas-6
95Fin-213
95FinRef-213
95Fla-105
95FlaHotN-6
95Fle-311
95FleAllF-9
95FleAllS-9
95FleAwaW-4
95FleLeaL-9
95FlePro-4
95FleTeaL-15
95FleUpdDT-8
95FleUpdH-13
95KinDis-23
95Kra-25
95Lea-115
95LeaChe-6
95LeaGolS-9
95LeaGreG-11
95LeaLim-115
95LeaLimG-15
95NatPac2-4
95Pac-11
95PacGolCDC-1
95PacPri-4
95PanSti-6
95PanSti-109
95PanSti-120
95Pin-244
95PinArtP-244
95PinFan-21
95PinGatA-GA16
95PinMusC-244
95PinPer-PP12
95PinPin-1
95PinPinR-1
95PinRedH-RH12
95PinTeaP-TP1
95PinWhiH-WH12
95Pos-3
95PosCan-15
95RedFol-9
95Sco-32
95ScoDouGC-GC6
95ScoDreT-DG11
95ScoGolR-32
95ScoHaloG-HG18
95ScoPlaTS-32
95ScoRul-SR15
95ScoRulJ-SR15
95Sel-21
95SelArtP-21
95SelCer-59
95SelCerMG-59
95SP-31
95SPCha-25
95SPChaDC-25
95SPChaDFC-7
95SPChaFCDC-7
95Spo-45
95SpoArtP-45
95SpoDouT-12
95SPSil-31
95SPSpeF-29
95StaClu-46
95StaClu-425
95StaCluFDI-46
95StaCluMO-30
95StaCluMOP-46
95StaCluMOP-425
95StaCluSTDW-B425
95StaCluSTMP-7
95StaCluSTWS-46
95StaCluSTWS-425
95StaCluVR-222
95Stu-6
95StuGolS-6
95StuPlaS-6
95Sum-30
95Sum-189
95SumNthD-30
95SumNthD-189
95TomPiz-5
95Top-295
95Top-392
95TopCyb-158
95TopLeaL-LL24
95UC3-61
95UC3-129
95UC3ArtP-61
95UC3ArtP-129
95UC3InM-IM8
95Ult-129
95UltAllS-12
95UltAllSGM-12
95UltAwaW-18
95UltAwaW-22
95UltAwaWGM-18
95UltAwaWGM-22
95UltGolM-129
95UltLeaL-8
95UltLeaLGM-8
95UltStrK-4
95UltStrKGM-4
95UppDec-49
95UppDec-101
95UppDecC-5A
95UppDecC-3B
95UppDecED-49
95UppDecED-101
95UppDecEDG-49
95UppDecEDG-101
95UppDecPAW-H27
95UppDecPAWE-H27
95UppDecSF-151
95UppDecSEG-151
95USPlaCMLA-1S
95Zen-37
95ZenZ-8
96Baz-79
96Bow-67
96BowBes-85
96BowBesAR-85
96BowBesMI-9
96BowBesMIAR-9
96BowBesMIR-9
96BowBesP-BBP14
96BowBesPAR-BBP14
96BowBesPR-BBP14
96BowBesR-85
96Cir-105
96CirAcc-14
96CirBos-27
96CirRav-105
96Cla7/1PC-6
96ColCho-6
96ColCho-8
96ColCho-40
96ColCho-268
96ColCho-386T
96ColCho-396
96ColCho-709
96ColCho-754
96ColChoGS-6
96ColChoGS-8
96ColChoGS-40
96ColChoGS-268
96ColChoGS-396
96ColChoGS-709
96ColChoGS-754
96ColChoSS-6
96ColChoSS-8
96ColChoSS-40
96ColChoSS-268
96ColChoSS-396
96ColChoSS-709
96ColChoSS-754
96ColChoYMtP-22
96ColChoYMtP-22A
96ColChoYMtPGS-22
96ColChoYMtPGS-22A
96DenHol-1
96Don-394
96DonDiaK-15
96DonEli-68
96DonFreF-5
96DonPreP-394
96DonSam-8
96DonSho-3
96EmoN-7
96EmoXL-146
96EmoXLD-6
96Fin-G145
96Fin-S1
96Fin-S235
96FinLan-1
96FinRef-G145
96FinRef-S1
96FinRef-S235
96Fla-205
96FlaDiaC-6
96FlaHotG-6
96Fle-299
96FleBra-11
96FleChe-4
96FleGolM-3
96FleRoaW-3
96FleSmo'H-6
96FleTeaL-15
96FleTif-299
96FleUpd-U232
96FleUpd-6
96FleUpdH-13
96FleUpdSL-6
96FleUpdSS-6
96FleUpdTC-U232
96FleZon-7
96Kin-18
96Lea-192
96LeaAllGMC-19
96LeaAllGMCG-19
96LeaGolS-15
96LeaHatO-8
96LeaLim-10
96LeaLimG-10
96LeaLimPC-6
96LeaPicP-3
96LeaPre-12
96LeaPreP-12
96LeaPrePB-192
96LeaPrePG-192
96LeaPrePS-192
96LeaPreSG-53
96LeaPreSta-8
96LeaPreSte-53
96LeaSig-3
96LeaSigEA-114
96LeaSigEACM-18
96LeaSigPPG-3
96LeaSigPPP-3
96LeaStaS-6
96LeaTotB-12
96MetUni-134
96MetUniP-134
96MetUniT-5
96Pac-6
96Pac-18
96PacCraC-CC4
96PacGolCD-DC28
96PacHom-HP2
96PacMil-M7
96PacOctM-OM13
96PacPri-P6
96PacPriFT-FT7
96PacPriG-P6
96PacPriRHS-RH8
96PanSti-4
96PanSti-118
96Pin-1
96Pin-254
96Pin-397
96Pin-399
96PinAfi-22
96PinAfi-199
96PinAfiAP-22
96PinAfiAP-199
96PinAfiFPP-22
96PinAfiMN-2
96PinAfiSP-14
96PinArtP-1
96PinArtP-154
96PinChrBC-1
96PinEssotG-2
96PinFan-2
96PinFoil-254
96PinFoil-397
96PinFoil-399
96PinSam-1
96PinSky-3
96PinSta-1
96PinSta-154
96PinTeaP-9
96PinTeaS-1
96Pro-8
96ProMagA-12
96ProSta-24
96SchDis-3
96Sco-194
96Sco-275
96Sco-276
96Sco-515
96ScoAll-10
96ScoDiaA-7
96ScoDreT-9
96ScoDugC-B1
96ScoDugCAP-B1
96ScoGolS-17
96ScoNumG-6
96ScoRef-17
96Sel-7
96Sel-159
96Sel-198
96SelArtP-7
96SelArtP-159
96SelArtP-198
96SelCer-32
96SelCer-137
96SelCerAP-32
96SelCerAP-137
96SelCerCB-32
96SelCerCB-137
96SelCerCR-32
96SelCerCR-137
96SelCerIP-2
96SelCerMB-32
96SelCerMB-137
96SelCerMG-32
96SelCerMG-137
96SelCerMR-32
96SelCerMR-137
96SelCerSF-6
96SelClaTF-2
96SelEnF-4
96SelTeaN-12
96SP-25
96SPBasH-89
96SPMarM-MM10
96SPMarMDC-10
96Spo-8
96Spo-143
96SpoArtP-8
96SpoArtP-143
96SpoDouT-5
96SpoPro-2
96SPSpeFX-1
96SPSpeFXDC-1
96SPx-1
96SPxBoufG-5
96SPxGol-1
96StaClu-132
96StaClu-245
96StaCluEPB-132
96StaCluEPG-132
96StaCluEPS-132
96StaCluEWB-EW1
96StaCluEWG-EW1
96StaCluEWS-EW1
96StaCluMet-M6
96StaCluMO-22
96StaCluMOF-2
96StaCluMOP-132
96StaCluMOP-245
96StaCluMOP-M6
96StaCluMOP-TSCA7
96StaCluTA-7
95StaCluVRMC-222
96Stu-18
96StuMas-8
96StuPrePB-18
96StuPrePG-18
96StuPrePS-18
96StuStaGS-4
96Sum-91
96Sum-199
96SumAbo&B-91
96SumAbo&B-199
96SumArtP-91
96SumArtP-199
96SumBal-8
96SumFoi-91
96SumFoi-199
96SumPos-6
96TeaOut-53
96TeaOut-C96
96Top-3
96Top-318
96TopBigC-5
96TopBroLL-2
96TopChr-3
96TopChr-125

96TopChrMotG-19
96TopChrMotGR-19
96TopChrR-3
96TopChrR-125
96TopClaC-CC15
96TopGal-145
96TopGalPPI-145
96TopLas-121
96TopMasotG-19
96TopMysF-M2
96TopMysFR-M2
96TopPowB-3
96TopPro-NL4
96Ult-160
96Ult-585
96UltCalttH-5
96UltCalttHGM-5
96UltChe-B8
96UltCheGM-B8
96UltDiaP-5
96UltDiaPGM-5
96UltGolM-160
96UltGolM-585
96UltRaw-6
96UltRawGM-6
96UltRes-4
96UltResGM-4
96UltSeaC-5
96UltSeaCGM-5
96UppDec-10
96UppDec-379
96UppDec-422
96UppDecDD-DD5
96UppDecDDG-DD5
96UppDecDDS-DD5
96UppDecG-GF10
96UppDecHC-HC10
96UppDecPHE-H44
96UppDecPreH-H44
96UppDecVJLS-VJ5
96Zen-3
96Zen-134
96ZenArtP-3
96ZenArtP-134
96ZenDiaC-18
96ZenDiaCP-18
96ZenMoz-1
96ZenZ-5
97Bow-256
97BowBes-40
97BowBesAR-40
97BowBesMI-MI3
97BowBesMIAR-MI3
97BowBesMIARI-MI3
97BowBesMII-MI3
97BowBesMIR-MI3
97BowBesMIRI-MI3
97BowBesR-40
97BowChr-79
97BowChrI-79
97BowChrIR-79
97BowChrR-79
97BowInt-256
97Cir-337
97Cir-400
97CirBos-11
97CirIco-6
97CirLimA-9
97CirRav-337
97CirRav-400
97CirRavR-6
97CirSupB-11
97ColCho-266
97ColChoAC-36
97ColChoNF-NF35
97ColChoNF-NF36
97ColChoS-23
97ColChoTBS-1
97ColChoTBSWH-1
97ColChoTotT-T3
97Don-7
97Don-423
97Don-449
97DonArmaD-13
97DonDom-3
97DonEli-4
97DonEliGS-4
97DonLim-2
97DonLim-46
97DonLim-121
97DonLimLE-2
97DonLimLE-46
97DonLimLE-121
97DonPre-6
97DonPre-196
97DonPreCttC-6
97DonPreCttC-196
97DonPreP-7
97DonPreP-423
97DonPreP-449
97DonPrePGold-7
97DonPrePGold-423
97DonPrePGold-449
97DonPrePM-3
97DonPreS-13
97DonPreTB-12
97DonPreTBG-12
97DonPreTF-12
97DonPreTP-12
97DonPreTPG-12
97DonTea-16
97DonTeaSMVP-18
97DonTeaSPE-16
97Fin-158
97Fin-294
97FinEmb-158
97FinEmb-294
97FinEmbR-158
97FinEmbR-294
97FinRef-158
97FinRef-294
97FlaSho-A44
97FlaSho-B44
97FlaSho-C44
97FlaShoDC-10
97FlaShoHG-10
97FlaShoLC-44
97FlaShoLC-B44
97FlaShoLC-C44
97FlaShoLCM-A44
97FlaShoLCM-B44
97FlaShoLCM-C44
97Fle-263
97Fle-707
97Fle-722
97FleDecoE-6
97FleDecoERT-6
97FleDiaT-6
97FleGouG-7
97FleGouGF-7
97FleHea-11
97FleMilDM-44
97FleSoaS-8
97FleTif-263
97FleTif-707
97FleTif-722
97FleZon-10
97Lea-85
97Lea-351
97Lea-372
97LeaDrefS-1
97LeaFraM-85
97LeaFraM-351
97LeaFraM-372
97LeaFraMDC-85
97LeaFraMDC-351
97LeaFraMDC-372
97LeaGet-1
97LeaGolS-11
97LeaStaS-7
97MetUni-33
97MetUniT-5
97NewPin-3
97NewPinAP-3
97NewPinIE-7
97NewPinKtP-2
97NewPinMC-3
97NewPinPP-3
97NewPinPP-I7A
97NewPinPP-K2
97Pac-240
97PacCar-24
97PacCarM-24
97PacCerCGT-19
97PacCerCGT-S19
97PacLigB-240
97PacPri-82
97PacPriGA-GA19
97PacPriGotD-GD113
97PacPriLB-82
97PacPriP-82
97PacPriSH-SH8B
97PacSil-240
97Pin-189
97PinArtP-189
97PinCar-1
97PinCer-83
97PinCer-143
97PinCerCMGT-19
97PinCerCT-19
97PinCerMBlu-83
97PinCerMBlu-143
97PinCerMG-83
97PinCerMG-143
97PinCerMR-83
97PinCerMR-143
97PinCerR-83
97PinCerR-143
97PinIns-16
97PinInsC-10
97PinInsCE-16
97PinInsDD-15
97PinInsDE-16
97PinMin-11
97PinMinB-11
97PinMinCB-11
97PinMinCG-11
97PinMinCGR-11
97PinMinCN-11
97PinMinCS-11
97PinMinG-11
97PinMinS-11
97PinMusC-189
97PinPasttM-1
97PinTotCPB-83
97PinTotCPB-143
97PinTotCPG-83
97PinTotCPG-143
97PinTotCPR-83
97PinTotCPR-143
97PinX-P-9
97PinX-P-149
97PinX-PMoS-9
97PinX-PMoS-149
97PinX-PMW-10
97PinX-PMWG-10
97PinX-PMWS-10
97ProMag-3
97ProMagML-3
97Sco-215
97Sco-520
97ScoBra-12
97ScoBraPI-12
97ScoBraPr-12
97ScoHigZ-7
97ScoHobR-520
97ScoPreS-215
97ScoResC-520
97ScoShoS-215
97ScoShoS-520
97ScoShoSAP-215
97ScoShoSAP-520
97ScoStaaD-2
97Sel-23
97SelArtP-23
97SelRegG-23
97SelToootT-2
97SelToootTMB-2
97SkyE-X-57
97SkyE-XC-57
97SkyE-XEC-57
97SkyE-XHoN-12
97SP-23
97SPInsI-6
97SPMarM-MM13
97SpoIll-75
97SpoIll-173
97SpoIllEE-75
97SpoIllEE-173
97SpoIllGS-4
97SPSpeF-6
97SPSpxF-5
97SPSPxFA-5
97SPx-7
97SPxBoufG-3
97SPxBro-7
97SPxCorotG-3
97SPxGraF-7
97SPxSil-7
97SPxSte-7
97StaClu-196
97StaCluMat-196
97StaCluMOP-196
97StaCluMOP-PL5
97StaCluPL-PL5
97Stu-88
97StuMasS-12
97StuMasS8-12
97StuPor8-6
97StuPrePG-88
97StuPrePS-88
97Top-130
97TopChr-49
97TopChrR-49
97TopGal-26
97TopGalPPI-26
97TopHobM-HM3
97TopSta-17
97TopSta1AS-AS1
97TopStaAM-17
97Ult-157
97UltBasR-5
97UltChe-A4
97UltChe-B7
97UltDiaP-6
97UltDouT-11
97UltFamGam-6
97UltFieC-12
97UltGolME-157
97UltPlaME-157
97UltStaR-7
97UltTop3-7
97UltTop3GM-7
97UppDec-65
97UppDec-137
97UppDec-260
97UppDec-263
97UppDec-302
97UppDecAG-AG11
97UppDecHC-HC19
97UppDecP-3
97UppDecU-31
97Zen-8
97Zen8x1-6
97Zen8x1D-6

Maddux, Mike
85PhiTas-42
85PorBeaC-38
86PhiTas-xx
86PorBeaP-15
87Don-535
87Fle-179
87FleGlo-179
87MaiGuiT-5
87PhiTas-44
87Top-553
87TopTif-553
88Fle-309
88FleGlo-309
88PhiTas-16
88Top-756
88TopTif-756
89Bow-391
89BowTif-391
89Don-487
89Fle-576
89FleGlo-576
89OPC-39
89PhiTas-19
89Sco-393
89Top-39
89TopBig-74
89TopTif-39
89UppDec-338
90AlbDukC-8
90AlbDukP-341
90AlbDukT-20
90CMC-410
90Don-312
90OPC-154
90ProAAAF-62
90PubSti-246
90Top-154
90TopTif-154
90VenSti-309
91Lea-300
91PadSmo-20
91UltUpd-113
92Don-450
92Fle-613
92Lea-393
92OPC-438
92PadCarJ-12
92PadMot-26
92PadPolD-29
92PadSmo-18
92Pin-489
92Sco-313
92StaClu-26
92Top-438
92TopGol-438
92TopGolW-438
92TopMic-438
92TriPla-196
92Ult-281
92UppDec-330
93Don-286
93Fle-142
93FleFinE-103
93Lea-305
93MetColP-39
93MetKah-51
93OPC-168
93PacSpa-260
93Sco-451
93StaClu-103
93StaCluFDI-103
93StaCluMOP-103
93Top-329
93TopGol-329
93TopInaM-329
93TopMic-329
93Ult-430
93UppDec-58
93UppDec-650
93UppDecGold-58
93UppDecGold-650
94Don-213
94Fla-201
94Fle-571
94MetColP-17
94MetShuST-5
94Pac-410
94StaClu-33
94StaCluFDI-33
94StaCluGR-33
94StaCluMOP-33
94Top-217
94TopGol-217
94TopSpa-217
95Pac-284
96LeaSigEA-115
97PacPriGotD-GD23
97ProMag-47
97ProMagML-47

Mader, Chris
93HicCraC-14
93HicCraF-1285
93SouAtlLAGF-28
94ClaGolF-92
94HicCraC-15

Mader, Perry
83KinBluJTI-13

Maderfield, Steve
78NewWayCT-27

Madison, Dave
52Top-366
53TigGle-20
53Top-99
83TopRep5-366
91TopArc1-99

Madison, Jerry
90NebCor-14

Madison, Scott
96ButCopKB-21

Madison, Scotti
83AlbDukT-12
85NasSouTI-11
86NasSouTI-16
87OmaRoyP-17
88RoySmo-18
88TopTra-63T
88TopTraT-63T
89NasSouC-21
89NasSouP-1271
89NasSouTI-14
89TriAAP-AAA2

Madlock, Bill
74OPC-600
74Top-600
75Hos-125A
75Hos-125B
75HosTwi-125
75OPC-104
75SSPPuzB-16
75Top-104
76CraDis-31
76Hos-100
76Kel-20
76OPC-191
76OPC-640
76Spo-3
76SSP-309
76Top-191
76Top-640
77BurCheD-198
77Gia-14
77Hos-118
77Kel-43
77OPC-1

77OPC-56
77RCColC-37
77Top-1
77Top-250
77TopCloS-25
78Hos-117
78OPC-89
78Pep-35
78RCColC-54
78TasDis-15
78Top-410
79GiaPol-18
79Hos-138
79OPC-96
79Top-195
80OPC-30
80Top-55
81AllGamPI-122
81CokTeaS-114
81Don-252
81Fle-381
81OPC-137
81Top-715
81TopSti-213
82Don-653
82Dra-23
82Fle-485
82FleSta-77
82Kel-55
82OPC-365
82PerCreC-7
82PerCreCG-7
82Top-161
82Top-365
82Top-696
82TopSti-1
82TopSti-83
83AllGamPI-123
83Don-311
83DonActA-30
83Dra-15
83Fle-309
83FleSta-112
83FleSti-71
83Kel-18
83OPC-335
83PerCreC-8
83PerCreCG-8
83Top-291
83Top-645
83TopFol-3
83TopGloS-26
83TopSti-275
84AllGamPI-32
84Don-20
84Don-20A
84Don-113
84DonActAS-33
84DonCha-22
84Dra-20
84Fle-253
84FleSti-6
84FunFooP-31
84MilBra-16
84Nes792-131
84Nes792-250
84Nes792-696
84Nes792-701
84OCoandSI-71
84OPC-250
84RalPur-26
84SevCoi-E11
84Top-131
84Top-250
84Top-696
84Top-701
84TopCer-26
84TopGloS-19
84TopRubD-25
84TopSti-99
84TopSti-131
84TopStiB-12
84TopSup-8
84TopTif-131
84TopTif-250
84TopTif-696
84TopTif-701
85AllGamPI-122
85Don-200
85Fle-468
85FleLimE-19
85Lea-185
85OPC-157
85Pir-10
85SevCoi-E11
85Top-560
85TopMin-560
85TopRubD-25
85TopSti-122
85TopTif-560
86DodCokP-17
86DodPol-12
86DodUniOP-12
86Don-617
86Fle-135
86FleMin-29
86Lea-238
86OPC-47
86SevCoi-W14
86Spo-58
86Spo-88
86Spo-131
86Spo-181
86Top-470
86TopSti-12
86TopSti-70
86TopTat-19
86TopTif-470
86TruVal-23
86Woo-19
87DodMot-8
87DodPol-5
87Don-155
87DonOpeD-78
87Fle-445
87FleGlo-445
87FleMin-65
87FleStiC-73
87FleUpd-69
87FleUpdG-69
87Lea-120
87OPC-276
87RedFolSB-109
87Spo-130
87Top-734
87TopSti-67
87TopTif-734
87TopTra-71T
87TopTraT-71T
88Don-496
88Fle-63
88FleGlo-63
88Lea-232
88OPC-145
88Sco-445
88ScoGlo-445
88Spo-123
88StaLinTi-13
88Top-145
88TopSti-266
88TopTif-145
89PacSenL-214
89T/MSenL-69
89TopSenL-71
90DodTar-469
90EliSenL-116
92ActPacA-82
92KelAll-7
92MCIAmb-5
92MVP-15
92MVP2H-16
93RanKee-237
93TedWil-77
93UppDecAH-86
93UppDecS-9
93UppDecS-22
93UppDecS-24
94UppDecAH-74
94UppDecAH-216
94UppDecAH1-74
94UppDecAH1-216

Madrid, Alex
85BelBreT-18
87DenZepP-10
88BlaYNPRWL-91
88DenZepC-3
88DenZepP-1251
89Don-604
89PhiTas-20
89ScoHot1R-58
89ScrRedBC-5
89ScrRedBP-720
94BreMilB-53

Madrigal, Victor
91ButCopKSP-18
91Cla/Bes-266
91GasRanC-8
91GasRanP-2685
92ButCopKSP-21
93AshTouC-12
93AshTouF-2272

Madril, Bill
91ElmPioC-10
91ElmPioP-3274
91WinHavRSP-494
92WinHavRSC-5

Madril, Mike
83RedPioT-18
85EdmTraC-3
86MidAngP-15

Madsen, Dan
92GenCubC-11
92GenCubF-1573
93PeoChiC-12
93PeoChiF-1096
93PeoChiTI-15
94PeoChiC-17
94PeoChiF-2280

Madsen, Dave
94MadHatC-13
94MadHatF-141
96ModA'sB-20

Madsen, Erik
89GreFalDSP-24
90YakBeaTI-9

Madsen, Lance
89AubAstP-2164
90OscAstS-18
91JacGenLD-567
91JacGenP-933
91LinDriAA-567
92JacGenF-4006
92JacGenS-339
93JacGenF-2115
94TucTorF-769

Maduro, Calvin
93BluOriC-17
93BluOriF-4121
94FreKeyF-2610
94OriPro-57
95Bow-121
96BowBayB-20
97BowBes-158
97BowBesAR-158
97BowBesR-158
97ColCho-416
97Fle-575
97FleTif-575
94FreKeyC-15
97PinCer-133
97PinCerMBlu-133
97PinCerMG-133
97PinCerMR-133
97PinCerR-133
97PinTotCPB-133
97PinTotCPG-133
97PinTotCPR-133
97Ult-522
97UltGolME-522
97UltPlaME-522

Maduro, Noe
93LinVenB-162
95LinVen-70

Maebe, Art
80CliGiaT-11

Maeda, Katsuhiro
96Bow-121
97Bow-91
97BowBes-167
97BowBesAR-167
97BowBesP-20
97BowBesPAR-20
97BowBesPR-20
97BowBesR-167
97BowChr-115
97BowChrI-115
97BowChrIR-115
97BowChrR-115
97BowInt-91
97BowIntB-BBI18
97BowIntBAR-BBI18
97BowIntBR-BBI18
97StaClu-189
97StaCluM-M27
97StaCluMOP-189
97StaCluMOP-M27

Maeda, Koji
88SanJosGCLC-133
88SanJosGP-108

Maeda, Tomonori
93GolCar-5

Maema, Takashi
90GatCitPP-3358
90GatCitPSP-14

Maestas, Mickey
96YakBeaTI-35

Maffett, Chris
91BurIndP-3301
92BurIndC-12
92BurIndF-1653

Mag, Rick
88BriTigP-1862

Magadan, Dave
86MetWorSC-19
86TidTidP-17
87ClaGam-19
87Don-575
87DonRoo-34
87Fle-648
87FleGlo-648
87FleUpd-70
87FleUpdG-70
87MetColP-16
87SpoRool-10
87SpoRooP-3
87SpoTeaP-2
87Top-512
87TopRoo-9
87TopTif-512
88ClaBlu-230
88Don-323
88DonTeaBM-323
88Fle-141
88FleGlo-141
88Lea-108
88MetColP-34
88MetKah-29
88MSAIceTD-13
88OPC-58
88RedFolSB-51
88Sco-41
88ScoGlo-41
88ScoYouSI-23
88Spo-83
88StaLinMe-12
88Top-58
88TopSti-104
88TopTif-58
89Bow-384
89BowTif-384
89Don-408
89DonBasB-264
89Fle-41
89FleGlo-41
89MetColP-42
89MetKah-16
89OPC-81
89Sco-312
89Top-655
89TopBig-71
89TopTif-655
89UppDec-388
90Don-383
90DonBesN-56
90Fle-210
90FleCan-210
90Lea-330
90MetColP-18
90MetKah-10
90OPC-135
90PanSti-300
90PubSti-138
90Sco-46
90Spo-173
90Top-135
90TopBig-24
90TopSti-99
90TopTif-135
90TopTVM-26
90UppDec-243
90VenSti-310
91Bow-484
91Cla1-T67
91Cla2-T72
91ClaGam-100
91Don-17
91Don-362
91DonSupD-17
91Fle-153
91Lea-20
91MajLeaCP-76
91MetColP-6
91MetKah-10
91MetTro-6
91MetWIZ-242
91MooSna-13
91OPC-480
91PanCanT1-3
91PanFreS-79
91PanSti-81
91PosCan-4
91Sco-190
91Sco100S-34
91SimandSMLBL-27
91StaClu-210
91Stu-208
91Top-480
91TopDesS-480
91TopMic-480
91TopTif-480
91Ult-223
91UppDec-177
92Bow-263
92Don-45
92Fle-510
92Lea-306
92MetColP-7
92MetKah-29
92OPC-745
92PanSti-222
92Pin-201
92Sco-201
92StaClu-118
92Top-745
92TopGol-745
92TopGolW-745
92TopMic-745
92TriPla-82
92Ult-236
92UppDec-112
93Bow-614
93ClaGam-57
93Don-400
93Fle-477
93Lea-391
93MarUSPC-1D
93MarUSPC-2C
93MarUSPC-4C
93OPC-253
93OPCPre-61
93PacJugC-31
93PacSpa-466
93PanSti-250
93Pin-237
93PinExpOD-5
93Sco-631
93Sel-149
93SelRoo-116T
93StaClu-452
93StaCluFDI-452
93StaCluMarI-10
93StaCluMOP-452
93Stu-154
93Top-578
93TopGol-578
93TopInaM-578
93TopMic-578
93TopTra-106T
93Ult-382
93UppDec-479
93UppDec-528
93UppDecGold-479
93UppDecGold-528
94Bow-450
94ColC-184
94ColC-367
94ColChoGS-184
94ColChoGS-367
94ColChoSS-184
94ColChoSS-367
94Don-658
94ExtBas-264
94Fin-130
94FinPre-130P
94FinRef-130
94Fla-165
94Fle-293
94FleUpd-136
94Lea-386
94OPC-107
94Pac-247
94PacAll-2
94Pin-187
94PinArtP-187
94PinMusC-187
94ProMag-55
94Sco-14
94ScoGolR-14
94ScoRoo-RT23
94ScoRooGR-RT23

94Sel-143
94StaClu-365
94StaCluFDI-365
94StaCluGR-365
94StaCluMOP-365
94StaCluT-81
94StaCluTFDI-81
94Top-347
94TopGol-347
94TopSpa-347
94TopTra-80T
94TriPla-138
94Ult-197
94UppDec-73
94UppDecED-73
95AstMot-8
95ColCho-302
95ColCho-532T
95ColChoGS-302
95ColChoSS-302
95Don-489
95DonPreP-489
95DonTopotO-257
95Fle-336
95Pin-397
95PinArtP-397
95PinMusC-397
95Sco-475
95ScoGolR-475
95ScoPlaTS-475
95Top-283
95TopCyb-154
95TopTra-134T
96ColCho-163
96ColCho-766
96ColChoGS-163
96ColChoSS-163
96Don-280
96DonPreP-280
96Fla-219
96Fle-414
96FleTif-414
96FleUpd-U113
96FleUpdTC-U113
96LeaSigEA-116
96Pac-98
96Sco-116
96Ult-452
96UltGolM-452
86STaoftFT-32
97Ult-545
97UltGolME-545
97UltPlaME-545

Magallanes, Bobby (William)
86AppFoxP-13
90SanBerSB-12
90SanBerSCLC-107
90SanBerSP-2640
91Cla/Bes-263
91SanBerSC-18
91SanBerSP-1995
92PenPilF-2939
93LinVenB-209
94VenLinU-165
95LinVen-149

Magallanes, Ever
88KinIndS-16
89CanIndB-23
89CanIndP-1309
89CanIndS-13
90CMC-465
90ColSprSSC-13
90ColSprSSP-42
90ProAAAF-223
91Bow-61
91ColSprSSLD-91
91ColSprSSP-2192
91LinDriAAA-91
92SkyAAAF-286
92TopDeb91-113
92VanCanF-2731
92VanCanS-643
93TulDriF-2742
94TulDriF-252
94TulDriTI-15
93TulDriTI-16

Magallanes, Willie
88BirBarB-25
90Bes-125
90BirBarB-11
90BirBarP-1396

Magdaleno, Rick
92ClaDraP-36
93ClaFS7-106
93StaCluM-71
93WesVirWC-17
93WesVirWF-2874
94CarLeaAF-CAR49
94WinSpiC-15
94WinSpiF-280
96ChaLooB-19

Mageau, Fernand
43ParSpo-50

Magee, Bo
91ButCopKSP-22
92GasRanC-14
92GasRanF-2251
93ChaRanC-17
93ChaRanF-1938
94KinIndC-11
94KinIndF-2639

Magee, Danny
94MacBraC-11
94MacBraF-2215
95DurBulTI-19
96DurBulBIB-28
96DurBulBrB-28

Magee, Lee
09PC7HHB-30
14FatPlaT-27
15CraJacE-147
15SpoNewM-106
16ColE13-103
16SpoNewM-108
90DodTar-470
94ConTSN-1273
94ConTSNB-1273

Magee, Sherry
08RosComP-142
09SpoNewSM-7
09T206-220
09T206-221
09T206-222
10CouT21-172
10CouT21-173
10CouT21-174
10CouT21-298
10DomDisP-74
10E101-30
10E102-16
10MelMinE-30
10NadCarE-33
10PeoT21-35
10RedCroT-44
10RedCroT-215
10SweCapPP-128
10W555-44
11E94-23
11L1L-123
11PloCanE-42
11S81LarS-98
11SpoLifCW-230
11SpoLifM-233
11T205-107
11TurRedT-31
12HasTriFT-9
12HasTriFT-17
12HasTriFT-30D
14CraJacE-108
14FatPlaT-28
14PieStaT-35
15CraJacE-108
15VicT21-19
16BF2FP-54
16ColE13-104
16SpoNewM-109
20RedWorCP-11
83PhiPosGPaM-5
88FriBasCM-6
92ConTSN-449
93ConTSN-897
94ConTSN-1025
94ConTSN-1267
94ConTSNB-1025
94ConTSNB-1267

Magee, Warren
87ClePhiP-14
88EasLeaAP-33
88ReaPhiP-871
89ReaPhiB-2
89ReaPhiP-674
89ReaPhiS-16
90ReaPhiB-9
90ReaPhiP-1218
90ReaPhiS-17

Magee, Wendell
94BatCliC-12
94BatCliF-3459
95Bes-86
95ClePhiF-229
95ReaPhiELC-26
95SPML-132
96Bow-226
96Exc-208
96ExcCli-6
96ExcSeaTL-6
96ReaPhiB-23
97Bow-114
97BowInt-114
97ColCho-14
97Don-378
97DonPre-163
97DonPreCttC-163
97DonPreP-378
97DonPrePGold-378
97Fin-229
97FinRef-229
97FlaSho-A168
97FlaSho-B168
97FlaSho-C168
97FlaShoLC-168
97FlaShoLC-B168
97FlaShoLC-C168
97FlaShoLCM-A168
97FlaShoLCM-B168
97FlaShoLCM-C168
97Fle-415
97FleRooS-16
97FleTif-415
97Lea-183
97LeaFraM-183
97LeaFraMDC-183
97MetUni-202
97NewPin-163
97NewPinAP-163
97NewPinMC-163
97NewPinPP-163
97PacPriGotD-GD184
97PinCer-130
97PinCerMBlu-130
97PinCerMG-130
97PinCerMR-130
97PinCerR-130
97PinTotCPB-130
97PinTotCPG-130
97PinTotCPR-130
97PinX-P-132
97PinX-PMoS-132
97Sco-322
97ScoPreS-322
97ScoShoS-322
97ScoShoSAP-322
97StaClu-372
97StaCluM-M25
97StaCluMOP-372
97StaCluMOP-M25
97Top-302
97Ult-252
97UltGolME-252
97UltPlaME-252
97UppDec-472

Maggio, Aggie
80WesHavWCT-22A

Magill, Jim
93HigDesMC-10
93HigDesMF-36

Magistri, Greg
85ElmPioT-13

Maglie, Sal
47Exh-142
47PM1StaP1-116
51Bow-127
52BerRos-36
52Bow-66
52RedMan-NL14
52StaCalL-78C
52StaCalS-90B
52TipTop-23
53BowC-96
53RedMan-NL8
54Bow-105
54NewYorJA-31
55Bow-95
55GiaGolS-4
55RedMan-NL6
56Dod-18
57Top-5
58Top-43
59Top-309
60NuHi-70
60Top-456
61NuSco-470
67TopRedSS-17
69PilPos-32
74NewYorNTDiS-23
75Gia195T-18
77GalGloG-28
79TCM50-256
80MarExh-17
83Pil69G-21
84FifNatCT-10
88PacLegI-85
88RinPosD1-11A
89NiaFalRP-29
89SweBasG-99
90DodTar-471
90SweBasG-38
91SweBasG-59
91TopArc1-303
92BazQua5A-16
94TedWil-53
94TedWilM-M22

Magnante, Mike (Michael)
89MemChiB-21
89MemChiP-1198
89MemChiS-15
90CMC-181
90OmaRoyC-6
90OmaRoyP-64
90ProAAAF-599
91LinDriAAA-340
91OmaRoyLD-340
91OmaRoyP-1033
92Don-706
92OPC-597
92OPCPre-57
92RoyPol-16
92Sco-739
92StaClu-448
92Top-597
92TopDeb91-114
92TopGol-597
92TopGolW-597
92TopMic-597
93Fle-620
93OmaRoyF-1677
93StaClu-12
93StaCluFDI-12
93StaCluMOP-12
93StaCluRoy-13
93Top-186
93TopGol-186
93TopInaM-186
93TopMic-186
93UppDec-180
93UppDecGold-180
94Fle-165
94StaClu-607
94StaCluFDI-607
94StaCluGR-607
94StaCluMOP-607
95Fle-166
95OmaRoyTI-19
95Top-415
95TopCyb-215
96LeaSigEA-117

Magnante, Rick
89NiaFalRP-25

Magnelli, Tony
93GleFalRC-20
93GleFalRF-4000

Magner, Rich
75WatDodT-13
79AlbDukT-17

Magno, Chris
85MiaHur-9

Magnuson, Jim
72Top-597
92YanWIZ7-102

Magnusson, Brett
88GreFalDTI-3
89Sta-30
89VerBeaDS-16
90BakDodCLC-254
90CalLeaACLC-2
91AdeGiaF-9
91LinDriAA-537
91SanAntMLD-537
91SanAntMP-2988
92YakBeaC-25
93SanAntMF-3022
94SanAntMF-2487

Magoon, George
11SpoLifCW-231
90DodTar-472

Magrane, Joe
84AriWilP-12
86ArkTraP-12
87ClaUpdY-117
87DonRoo-40
87FleSlu-24
87FleUpd-71
87FleUpdG-71
87LouRedTI-25
87SpoRooI-11
87SpoTeaP-12
87TopTra-72T
87TopTraT-72T
88CarSmo-6
88ClaBlu-240
88Don-140
88DonBasB-100
88Fle-40
88FleGlo-40
88LouRedBTI-31
88OPC-380
88PanSti-385
88RedFolSB-52
88Sco-94
88ScoGlo-94
88ScoYouSI-9
88Spo-128
88Top-380
88TopGloS-40
88TopRoo-20
88TopSti-51
88TopTif-380
88ToyRoo-15
89Bow-432
89BowTif-432
89CarSmo-12
89ClaTraO-148
89Don-201
89DonBasB-131
89Fle-455
89FleGlo-455
89FleLeaL-24
89OPC-264
89PanSti-178
89Sco-460
89Top-657
89TopBasT-94
89TopBig-203
89TopMinL-36
89TopTif-657
89UppDec-103
90Bow-183
90BowTif-183
90CarSmo-12
90ClaBlu-145
90Don-13
90Don-163
90DonBesN-46
90DonLeaS-34
90DonSupD-13
90Fle-252
90FleAll-5
90FleCan-252
90K-M-12
90Lea-11
90OPC-406
90OPC-578
90PanSti-346
90PubSti-220
90PubSti-267
90Sco-17
90Spo-151
90Top-406
90Top-578
90TopBig-271
90TopCoi-52
90TopDou-42
90TopGloS-36
90TopMinL-76
90TopSti-41
90TopStiB-30
90TopTif-406
90TopTif-578
90TopTVA-64
90TopTVCa-16
90UppDec-242
90VenSti-311
90VenSti-312
91ClaGam-29
91Don-295
91Fle-638
91OPC-185
91PanFreS-38
91PanSti-31

91Sco-575
91StaClu-85
91StaCluP-23
91Stu-235
91Top-185
91TopDesS-185
91TopMic-185
91TopTif-185
91Ult-291
91UppDec-465
92CarPol-11
92Don-767
92OPC-783
92Pin-494
92StaClu-622
92StaCluECN-622
92Top-783
92TopGol-783
92TopGolW-783
92TopMic-783
93Don-492
93FleFinE-127
93PacSpa-633
93Pin-342
93StaClu-646
93StaCluCa-8
93StaCluFDI-646
93StaCluMOP-646
93Ult-464
93UppDec-703
93UppDecGold-703
94AngAdoF-3
94AngLAT-8
94AngMot-17
94ColC-185
94ColChoGS-185
94ColChoSS-185
94Fle-64
94Pac-84
94Pin-114
94PinArtP-114
94PinMusC-114
94SpoRoo-3
94SpoRooAP-3
94StaClu-509
94StaCluFDI-509
94StaCluGR-509
94StaCluMOP-509
94Top-27
94TopGol-27
94TopSpa-27
94UppDec-159
94UppDecED-159
96LeaSigEA-118
Magrann, Tom
86HagSunP-8
87MiaMarP-24
89CanIndB-10
89CanIndP-1313
89CanIndS-14
90CMC-466
90ColSprSSC-14
90ColSprSSP-40
90Don-374
90IndTeal-24
90ProAAAF-221
90TopDeb89-75
91BufBisLD-32
91BufBisP-545
91LinDriAAA-32
Magre, Pete
93BilMusF-3941
94ChaWheF-2700
Magria, Javier
89WelPirP-18
90MiaMirIS-16
Magrini, Paul
91BriTigC-27
91BriTigP-3598
92BriTigC-4
92BriTigF-1404
93NiaFalRF-3381
Magrini, Pete
66Top-558
Maguire, Chris
91DaiDolF-8
Maguire, Fred
29ExhFou-2
29PorandAR-59
31Exh-2
33ExhFou-1
93ConTSN-791
Maguire, Jack
75Gia195T-19
Maguire, Kevin
92AugPirC-20
92AugPirF-242
Maguire, Mike
91WelPirC-22
91WelPirP-3569
Mahaffey, Alan
96ForWayWB-14
Mahaffey, Art
47Exh-143
60Top-138
60TopVen-138
61Baz-1
61Top-433
61TopStal-57
62Baz-22
62ExhStaB-21
62Jel-199
62Pos-199
62PosCan-199
62SalPlaC-112
62ShiPlaC-112
62Top-550
62TopBuc-51
62TopStal-171
63BasMagM-52
63Baz-35
63ExhStaB-39
63Fle-54
63Jel-183
63Pos-183
63SalMetC-10
63Top-7
63Top-385
63TopStil-25
64ChatheY-32
64PhiJayP-7
64PhiPhiB-16
64Top-104
64TopVen-104
65ChaTheY-32
65PhiJayP-7
65Top-446
66Top-570
83PhiPosGM-3
94CarLeaA-DJ11
Mahaffey, Leroy
33Gou-196
33RitCE-4H
33TatOrbSDR-175
34DiaMatCSB-121
34BatR31-15
34DiaStaR-10A
34DiaStaR-10B
35ExhFou-14
35GouPuzR-1B
35GouPuzR-2B
35GouPuzR-16B
35GouPuzR-17B
92ConTSN-603
Mahalik, John
93ButCopKSP-7
94BurBeeF-1088
95BinMetTI-11
96BinBeeB-18
Mahambitov, Igor
89EasLeaDDP-DD20
Mahan, George
76WilTomT-15
Mahan, Russ
88MisStaB-16
89MisStaB-23
Mahar, Eddie
87SyrChiT-32
Maharg, Billy
88PacEigMO-17
Mahay, Ron
92WinHavRSC-14
93LynRedSC-15
93LynRedSF-2530
94SarRedSC-17
94SarRedSF-1966
95TreThuTI-25
Maher, Kim
91FreStaLBS-6
Mahlberg, Greg
76SacSolC-23
77TucTorC-8
78TucTorC-24
79TucTorT-15
80ChaChaT-6
80Top-673
81IndIndTI-12
87SalSpuP-32
88ChaWheB-3
89ChaWheB-25
89ChaWheP-1755
90PeoChiTI-31
91GenCubC-19
91GenCubP-4234
92GenCubC-26
93RanKee-238
93SanBerSC-21
93SanBerSF-786
94SanBerSC-25
94SanBerSF-2774
95BakBlaTI-31
96StoPorB-27
Mahlberg, John
96PorRocB-21
Mahler, Jim
81SpoIndT-22
Mahler, Mickey
78Top-703
79Top-331
80PorBeaT-10
81SalLakCGT-8
82SpoIndT-4
84LouRedR-28
85DomLeaS-130
85ExpPos-12
85FleUpd-77
85IndIndTI-16
86FleUpd-70
86TopTra-68T
86TopTraT-68T
87LouRedTI-18
89T/MSenL-70
89TopSenL-82
91PacSenL-37
93RanKoo-230
Mahler, Rick
78RicBraT-9
80RicBraT-11
80VenLeaS-189
81BraPol-42
82BraBurKL-16
82BraPol-42
82Don-349
82Fle-440
82Top-126
82Top-579
83Don-527
83Fle-141
83OPC-76
83Top-76
84BraPol-42
85AllGamPI-172
85BraHos-14
85BraPol-42
85Don-385
85Fle-332
85OPC-79
85Top-79
85TopSti-26
85TopTif-79
86BraPol-42
86Don-21
86Don-77
86DonSupD-21
86Fle-521
86Lea-21
86OPC-39
86Top-437
86TopSti-43
86TopTat-11
86TopTif-437
87BraSmo-5
87Don-190
87DonOpeD-41
87Fle-520
87FleGlo-520
87OPC-242
87SpoTeaP-24
87Top-242
87TopSti-43
87TopTif-242
88Don-389
88DonBasB-114
88OPC-171
88PanSti-239
88Sco-319
88ScoGlo-319
88StaLinBra-11
88Top-706
88TopTif-706
89Bow-302
89BowTif-302
89Don-222
89DonBasB-286
89DonTra-24
89Fle-595
89FleGlo-595
89FleUpd-85
89OPC-393
89PanSti-35
89RedKah-42
89Sco-229
89ScoRoo-79T
89Top-621
89TopSti-29
89TopTif-621
89TopTra-74T
89TopTraT-74T
89UppDec-74
89UppDec-760
90Don-375
90Fle-425
90FleCan-425
90OPC-151
90PubSti-34
90RedKah-15
90RicBra2ATI-15
90Sco-87
90Top-151
90TopSti-139
90TopTif-151
90UppDec-220
90VenSti-313
91ExpPos-12
91Fle-71
91Lea-284
91OPC-363
91Sco-464
91Top-363
91TopDesS-363
91TopMic-363
91TopTif-363
91UppDec-613
96ArkTraB-1
Mahnke, Jason
96YakBeaTI-NNO
Mahomes, Pat
89KenTwiP-1067
89KenTwiS-12
90CMC-861
90ProAaA-141
90VisOakCLC-60
90VisOakP-2149
91LinDriAA-485
91OrlSunRLD-485
91OrlSunRP-1846
92Bow-131
92Cla2-T97
92Don-403
92FleUpd-40
92LeaGolR-BC17
92OPC-676
92Pin-472
92PinRoo-11
92PinTea2-80
92PorBeaF-2664
92ProFS7-93
92ScoRoo-102T
92SkyAA F-295
92Stu-208
92Top-676
92TopGol-676
92TopGolW-676
92TopMic-676
92Ult-398
92UltAllR-9
92UppDec-776
92UppDecSR-SR16
93Bow-157
93Don-357
93Fle-271
93Lea-54
93PacSpa-523
93Pin-408
93Sco-337
93Sel-324
93StaClu-740
93StaCluFDI-740
93StaCluMOP-740
93Top-684
93TopGol-684
93TopInaM-684
93TopMic-684
93Toy-11
93Ult-234
93UppDec-337
93UppDecGold-337
93USPlaCR-2H
94Bow-160
94ColC-577
94ColChoGS-577
94ColChoSS-577
94ExtBas-121
94FleUpd-63
94Lea-413
94StaClu-688
94StaCluFDI-688
94StaCluGR-688
94StaCluMOP-688
94Top-43
94TopGol-43
94TopSpa-43
95ColCho-493
95ColChoGS-493
95ColChoSS-493
95Don-512
95DonPreP-512
95Fla-59
95Fle-209
95Lea-366
95Pin-252
95PinArtP-252
95PinMusC-252
95Sco-500
95ScoGolR-500
95ScoPlaTS-500
95Top-217
95Ult-304
95UltGolM-304
95UppDec-429
95UppDecED-429
95UppDecEDG-429
96ColCho-606
96ColChoGS-606
96ColChoSS-606
96Don-180
96DonPreP-180
96LeaSigEA-119
Mahon, Frank
96LowSpiB-3
Mahoney, Daniel
87OldJudN-318
Mahoney, Jim
73OPC-356
73Top-356
74OPC-221
74Top-221
77ChaPatT-8
78SalPirT-9
80PorBeaT-6
81GleFalWST-22
82GleFalWST-25
85MarMot-27
88PorBeaC-24
88PorBeaP-650
Mahoney, Mike
95EugEmeTI-14
96DurBulBIB-21
96DurBulBrB-22
Mahoney, Robert
52Top-58
83TopRep5-58
Mahony, Dan
91EriSaiC-7
91EriSaiP-4072
Mahovlich, Frank
72Dia-91
72Dia-92
Mahovlich, Pete
72Dia-93
72Dia-94
Maietta, Bub (Ron)
89BriTigS-15
89HigSchPLS-7
90BriTigP-3158
90BriTigS-16
Mails, Duster (Walter)
20NatCarE-59
20WalMaiW-27
21E121So1-55
21Exh-99
23WilChoV-88
90DodTar-473
95ConTSN-1365
Mails, John
22E120-36
23W501-23
77Ind192T-12
Main, Forrest
52Top-397

53Top-198
83TopRep5-397
91TopArc1-198
Main, Kevin
87ChaWheP-16
87GenCubP-21
Mainini, Marco
52LavPro-93
Mains, Willard
87OldJudN-319
98CamPepP-50
Mainville, Martin
94ClaGolF-72
Maisel, Fritz
13PolGroW-14
14B18B-25
14FatPlaT-29
15CraJacE-158
Maisel, George
21Exh-100
Maitland, Bill
92IdaFalGF-3508
92IdaFalGSP-6
Maitland, Mike
79AppFoxT-20
80AppFoxT-28
81GleFalWST-5
82GleFalWST-21
83GleFalWST-14
Maize, Dave
92WelPirC-18
92WelPirF-1326
93PitMetF-3714
Majcherek, Matt
96HudValRB-19
Majer, Steffen
90St.PetCS-15
91ArkTraP-1281
92ArkTraF-1125
92ArkTraS-36
Majeski, Brian
94GreFalDSP-11
95VerBeaDTI-16
96VerBeaDB-18
Majeski, Carl
91IdaFalBP-4325
91IdaFalBSP-22
Majeski, Henry (Hank)
41DouPlaR-119
47Exh-144
48BluTin-23
49Bow-127A
49Bow-127B
49Lea-149
49PhiBul-33
50Bow-92
51Bow-12
51TopBluB-2
52Bow-58
52Top-112
55Bow-127
55IndGolS-21
79DiaGre-206
83TopRep5-112
84TCMPla1-21
91OriCro-275
Majia, Roberto
96IndIndB-14
Majtyka, Roy
64TulOil-4
77IndIndTI-2
78IndIndTI-2
79IndIndTI-2
81BirBarT-2
82EvaTriT-25
83BirBarT-25
85IntLeaAT-22
85RicBraT-26
86RicBraP-13
87RicBraC-6
87RicBraT-21
89BraDub-16
90BirBarDGB-21
90BraDubS-20
91MacBraC-28
91MacBraP-881
91SouAtlLAGP-SAL34
92SpaPhiC-22
92SpaPhiF-1280
93SpaPhiC-25
93SpaPhiF-1071
94SpaPhiF-1738
94SparPhiC-25
95PiePhiF-202
96PieBolWB-1
Makarewicz, Scott
89AubAstP-2163
90FloStaLAS-12
90OscAstS-19
90StaFS7-4
91JacGenLD-568
91JacGenP-929
91LinDriAA-568
92JacGenF-4001
92JacGenS-340
93JacGenF-2111
94TucTorF-764
95TusTorTI-14
96JacSunB-18
Makemson, Jay
87OneYanP-18
88OneYanP-2063
89PenPilS-13
Maki, Timothy
82BurRanF-29
82BurRanT-6
83BurRanF-19
83BurRanT-9
Makosky, Frank
75YanDyn1T-31
Maksudian, Mike (Michael)
88MidLeaAGS-48
88SouBenWSGS-10
89MiaMirIS-15
89Sta-142
90Bes-111
90KnoBluJB-11
90KnoBluJP-1258
90KnoBluJS-11
90StaFS7-88
91LinDriAAA-509
91SyrChiLD-509
91SyrChiMB-12
91SyrChiP-2494
92SyrChiF-1982
92SyrChiMB-13
92SyrChiS-511
93BluJayD4-39
93Bow-297
93FleFinE-237
93LinVenB-103
94IowCubF-1279
95EdmTraTI-15
Malangone, John
52LavPro-96
Malarcher, Dave
74LauOldTBS-20
83ConMar-53
86NegLeaF-108
88ConNegA-9
Malarkey, John
11SpoLifCW-232
Malarkey, William
09T206-439
12ImpTobC-73
Malave, Benito
86WauTimP-13
87St.PetCP-22
88ArkTraGS-17
93LinVenB-67
94VenLinU-253
95LinVen-213
Malave, Jaime
95YakBeaTI-17
96YakBeaTI-30
Malave, Jose
90ElmPioP-11
92ElmPioC-13
92ElmPioF-1390
93Bow-696
93CarLeaAGF-10
93ClaFS7-11
93ExcFS7-133
93LinVenB-258
93LynRedSC-16
93LynRedSF-2531
94Bow-671
94BowBes-B22
94BowBes-X107
94BowBesR-B22
94BowBesR-X107
94Cla-137
94NewBriRSF-663
94UppDecML-204
95ActPac2GF-14G
95ActPacF-34
95ActPacF-75
95Bow-106
95Exc-11
95LinVen-84
95PawRedSDD-19
95PawRedTI-41
95Pin-429
95PinArtP-429
95PinMusC-429
95Sel-161
95SelArtP-161
95SelCer-101
95SelCerMG-101
95SP-13
95SPML-22
95SPSil-13
95Top-237
95UppDec-256
95UppDecED-256
95UppDecEDG-256
95UppDecML-18
95UppDecSE-211
95UppDecSEG-211
96Exc-13
96Fla-21
96FlaWavotF-16
96FleUpd-U14
96FleUpdTC-U14
96Ult-316
96UltGolM-316
97Fle-26
97FleTif-26
97PacPriGotD-GD24
97Ult-15
97UltGolME-15
97UltPlaME-15
95UppDecMLFS-18
Malave, Omar
80VenLeaS-69
85KinBluJT-17
86VenGulP-12
87KnoBluJP-1497
88MyrBeaBJP-1181
89KnoBluJB-14
89KnoBluJP-1127
89KnoBluJS-13
93LinVenB-122
93MedHatBJF-3752
93MedHatBJSP-23
94HagSunC-26
94HagSunF-2746
94SouAtlLAF-SAL17
95HagSunF-84
95LinVen-191
96KnoSmoB-1
Malaver, Johnny
93HicCraC-15
93HicCraF-1276
93LinVenB-36
Malay, Charlie
90DodTar-1017
Malchesky, Tom
88HamRedP-1741
89SprCarB-19
Malcolm, Trevor
91PerHeaF-12
Malden, Chris
79LodDodT-18
Maldonado, Al
90KisDodD-16
91GreFalDSP-2
92BakDodCLC-15
Maldonado, Candy
79CliDodT-26
81AlbDukT-21
82AlbDukT-21
82RegGloT-6
83AlbDukT-14
83DodPol-20
83Don-262
83Fle-212
84DodPol-20
84Don-93
84Nes792-244
84Top-244
84TopTif-244
85DodCokP-19
85Don-250
85Fle-376
85Top-523
85TopSti-81
85TopTif-523
86Fle-136
86FleUpd-71
86GiaMot-9
86Top-87
86TopTif-87
86TopTra-69T
86TopTraT-69T
87Don-327
87DonOpeD-102
87Fle-279
87FleAwaW-23
87FleGlo-279
87GiaMot-7
87Lea-216
87OPC-335
87Spo-78
87SpoTeaP-10
87Top-335
87TopMinL-37
87TopSti-94
87TopTif-335
88BlaYNPRWLU-6
88Don-391
88DonBasB-247
88Fle-89
88FleBasA-22
88FleGlo-89
88FleMin-118
88FleStiC-129
88GiaMot-7
88KinDis-16
88Lea-239
88OPC-190
88PanSti-428
88Sco-54
88ScoGlo-54
88Spo-126
88StaLinG-11
88Top-190
88TopBig-35
88TopSti-95
88TopTif-190
88TopUKM-44
88TopUKMT-44
89BimBreD-2
89Bow-478
89BowTif-478
89Don-177
89Fle-333
89FleGlo-333
89GiaMot-7
89OPC-269
89PanSti-221
89RedFolSB-78
89Sco-47
89Top-495
89TopBasT-137
89TopBig-197
89TopSti-89
89TopTif-495
89UppDec-502
90Bow-335
90BowTif-335
90ClaYel-T34
90DodTar-474
90Don-611
90DonBesA-132
90DonLeaS-42
90Fle-62
90FleCan-62
90FleUpd-93
90IndTeal-25
90Lea-338
90OPC-628
90PubSti-75
90Sco-138
90ScoRoo-8T
90Top-628
90TopBig-248
90TopTif-628
90TopTra-65T
90TopTraT-65T
90UppDec-136
90UppDec-780
90VenSti-314
91BluJayFS-19
91BluJayS-29
91BreMilB-16
91BrePol-14
91Don-391
91Don-480
91Fle-373
91Lea-434
91OPC-723
91PanFreS-220
91PanSti-179
91RedFolS-60
91Sco-93
91Sco100S-76
91ScoRoo-28T
91StaClu-350
91Stu-72
91Top-723
91TopDesS-723
91TopMic-723
91TopTif-723
91TopTra-74T
91TopTraT-74T
91UppDec-138
91UppDec-739
91UppDecFE-28F
92Don-664
92Fle-336
92OPC-507
92PanSti-31
92Sco-591
92StaClu-179
92Top-507
92TopGol-507
92TopGolW-507
92TopMic-507
92TriPla-15
92Ult-451
92UppDec-393
93BluJayD4-9
93BluJayDM-13
93BluJayDM-21
93BluJayDWS-4
93Bow-312
93CubMar-14
93Don-684
93Fle-338
93FleFinE-9
93Lea-329
93OPC-382
93OPCPre-83
93OPCWorC-10
93PacBeiA-20
93PacSpa-379
93Pin-422
93Sco-615
93Sel-110
93StaClu-669
93StaCluCu-4
93StaCluFDI-669
93StaCluMOP-669
93Top-213
93TopGol-213
93TopInaM-213
93TopMic-213
93Ult-316
93UppDec-741
93UppDecGold-741
94BreMilB-54
94Don-659
94Fle-112
94Pac-175
94Sco-154
94ScoGolR-154
94StaClu-464
94StaCluFDI-464
94StaCluGR-464
94StaCluMOP-464
94Top-667
94TopGol-667
94TopSpa-667
95BluJayUSPC-2H
95BluJayUSPC-8H
95DonTopotO-174
95Pac-123
Maldonado, Carlos
88BriTigP-1863
90Bes-117
90CMC-779
90MemChiB-21
90MemChiP-1007
90MemChiS-15
90ProAaA-35
91FayGenC-20
91FayGenP-1179
91LinDriAAA-341
91OmaRoyLD-341
91OmaRoyP-1034
91TopDeb90-94
92OmaRoyF-2958
92OmaRoyS-335
92SkyAAAF-154
92StaClu-569
93FleFinE-228
93PacSpa-513
93Ult-573

94BreMilB-55
94Pac-334
94TacTigF-3170
Maldonado, Efrain
89BlaYNPRWL-131
Maldonado, Esteban
96AubDouB-22
Maldonado, Felix
87ElmPio(C-30
92WinHavRSC-26
92WinHavRSF-1794
Maldonado, Jay
93St.CatBJC-12
93St.CatBJF-3970
94BowBes-B88
94BowBesR-B88
94HagSunC-12
94HagSunF-2724
Maldonado, Jerry
89RenSilSCLC-264
90RenSilSCLC-290
Maldonado, Johnny
89BlaYNPRWLU-3
89SumBraP-1105
Maldonado, Pete
87SpaPhiP-2
88ClePhiS-18
Maldonado, Phil
87IdaFalBP-3
88DurBulS-11
89DurBullS-13
89DurBulTI-13
90DurBulTI-22
Malejko, Matt
94LSUTig-6
Maler, Jim (James)
80SpoIndT-14
80VenLeaS-119
83SalLakCGT-17
83Top-54
84Nes792-461
84Top-461
84TopTif-461
85OklCit8T-20
86OklCit8P-11
Malespin, Gus
79ElmPioRST-19
82SprCarF-10
83SprCarF-25
Maley, Dennis
83MiaMarT-27
Malinak, Mike (Michael)
87SalLakTTT-2
88CedRapRP-1164
89CedRapRP-911
89CedRapRS-29
Malinoski, Chris
91RocExpC-20
91RocExpP-2055
92WesPalBEC-15
92WesPalBEF-2096
93ClaGolF-47
93HigDesMC-11
93HigDesMF-48
94ClaGolF-95
94PorSeaDF-686
94PorSeaDTI-20
Malinosky, Tony
90DodTar-475
Malkin, John
81WatIndT-19
82WatIndF-20
82WatIndT-12
83BufBisT-10
84HawIslC-145
85HawIslC-247
Malkmus, Robert
58Top-356
59Top-151
59TopVen-151
60Top-251
61Top-530
Mallard, Randi
96AppLeaAB-29
Mallea, Luis
87EugEmeP-2666
88AppFoxP-138
Mallee, Johnny
91MarPhiC-8
91MarPhiP-3463
92SpaPhiC-3
92SpaPhiF-1271
96BelSnaTI-22
Mallette, Mal (Malcolm)
52LaPat-9
52Par-60
90DodTar-1018
Malley, Mike
89GreHorP-424
90ChaWheB-3
90ChaWheP-2236
91KinIndC-6
91KinIndP-318
91WatIndC-10
91WatIndP-3365
Mallicoat, Rob
85OscAstTI-9
86ColAstP-17
86TucTorP-11
87ColAstP-22
87SouLeaAJ-15
88Fle-452
88FleGlo-452
89ColMudP-131
89ColMudS-17
91JacGenLD-569
91JacGenP-925
91LinDriAA-569
92AstMot-23
92Don-673
92Fle-440
92OPC-501
92Sco-819
92SkyAAAF-273
92Top-501
92TopGol-501
92TopGolW-501
92TopMic-501
92TucTorS-613
93Sco-253
93StaCluAs-10
94RanCucQF-1638
Mallinak, Mel
87HagSunP-24
Mallon, Jim
90WelPirP-32
Mallory, Sheldon
76OmaRoyTT-11
78SyrChiT-13
79TacTugT-21
Mallory, Steve
76VenLeaS-202
Mallory, Trevor
91ClaDraP-50
91FroRowDP-53
92MyrBeaHC-3
92St.CatBJC-6
92St.CatBJF-3385
92StaCluD-110
93HagSunC-18
93HagSunF-1877
94HagSunC-13
94HagSunF-2725
95DunBluJTI-14
Malloy, Bill
96BelGiaTI-23
Malloy, Bob
87GasRanP-11
88TulDriTI-22
89TexLeaAGS-37
89TulDriGS-15
89TulDriTI-13
90Bes-43
90JacExpB-19
90JacExpP-1370
93RanKee-240
Malloy, Charles
94UtiBluSC-16
94UtiBluSF-3814
Malloy, Marty
93MacBraC-14
93MacBraF-1409
93SouAtlLAGF-39
94ClaGolF-114
94DurBulC-11
94DurBulF-334
94DurBulTI-11
96Bow-224
96GreBraB-18
96GreBraTI-4
96RicBraB-19
96Ult-440
96UltGolM-440
Malmberg, Harry
60HenHouW-2
61UniOil-S4
Malone, Chuck (Charles)
86BenPhiC-136
87ClePhiP-4
88BasAmeAAB-6
88EasLeaAP-34
88ReaPhiP-869
89ReaPhiB-3
89ReaPhiP-656
89ReaPhiS-17
90Bow-144
90BowTif-144
90CMC-230
90ProAAAF-298
90ScrRedBC-4
90ScrRedBP-596
91Bow-497
91Fle-404
91LinDriAAA-488
91Sco-724
91ScoRoo-21
91ScrRedBLD-488
91ScrRedBP-2534
91TopDeb90-95
91UppDec-649
Malone, Earl
88BoiHawP-1617
Malone, Eddie
47SigOil-29
49W725AngTI-18
49BowPCL-31
50RemBre-16
53MotCoo-20
82IdaFalAT-25
Malone, J.L.
87AllandGN-50
Malone, Jack
89BoiHawP-1990
Malone, Kevin
80BatTroT 10
88JamExpP-1893
Malone, Lew
90DodTar-476
Malone, Pat (Perce)
29PorandAR-60
31CubTeal-15
32CubTeal-16
32OrbPinNP-13
32OrbPinUP-45
33Gou-55
33TatOrb-45
33TatOrbSDR-192
34DiaMatCSB-122
34GouCanV-30
35GouPuzR-4D
35GouPuzR-7D
35GouPuzR-12D
75YanDyn1T-32
91ConTSN-219
Malone, Rubio
79WisRapTT-18
Malone, Scott
92ButCopKSP-2
93ChaRaiC-25
93ChaRaiF-1920
94ChaRanF-2503
Malone, Todd
89OneYanP-2122
90Bes-18
90CMC-824
90GreHorB-1
90GreHorP-2659
90GreHorS-13
90OneYanP-3368
91GreHorP-3054
92PriWilCC-23
92PriWilCF-142
93SanBerSC-12
93SanBerSF-766
Maloney, Bill
96MicBatCB-3
Maloney, Chris
85LynMetT-17
88SprCarB-25
89ArkTraGS-2
90HamRedB-4
90HamRedS-27
91JohCitCC-29
91JohCitCP-3994
93SavCarC-26
93SavCarF-702
93SouAtlLAGF-48
94ArkTraF-3104
96StPetCB-1
Maloney, Jeffrey
96MedHatBJTI-16
Maloney, Jim
56RedBurB-13
59RedBurBP-10
61Kah-26
61Top-436
62Kah-26
62RedEnq-22
63Kah-20
63RedEnq-20
63RedFreBC-13
63Top-444
64Baz-19
64Kah-16
64RedJayP-6
64Top-3
64Top-5
64Top-420
64TopCoi-60
64TopCoi-158
64TopGia-34
64TopSta-32
64TopStaU-43
64TopVen-3
64TopVen-5
65Kah-23
65RedEnq-17
65Top-530
65TopEmbl-68
65TopTral-19
66Baz-45
66Kah-18
66OPC-140
66Top-140
66TopRubl-55
66TopVen-140
67AshOil-6
67Baz-45
67CokCapR-7
67DexPre-131
67Kah-21A
67Kah-21B
67OPC-80
67Top-80
67TopVen-325
68AtlOilPBCC-25
68Kah-A7
68Kah-B21
68Top-425
68Top3-D-6
68TopActS-3A
68TopActS-16A
69Kah-A2
69Kah-B12
69MilBra-164
69MLBOffS-130
69MLBPin-50
69Top-362
69TopSta-26
69TopTeaP-20
70DayDaiNM-150
70Kel-10
70MLBOffS-29
70OPC-320
70Top-320
71MLBOffS-348
71OPC-645
71Top-645
72MilBra-203
72Top-645
78TCM60I-10
Maloney, Kevin
89ColMetB-28
89ColMetGS-5
Maloney, Mark
88KinIndS-17
Maloney, Rich
71Top-13
87SumBraP-18
88DurBulS-12
89DurBullS-14
89DurBulTI-14
90GreBraB-14
90GreBraP-1139
90GreBraS-11
91GreBraC-18
91GreBraLD-210
91GreBraP-3012
91LinDriAA-210
Maloney, Ryan
92WinHavRSC-17
92WinHavRSF-1772
93LynRedSC-17
93LynRedSF-2515
Maloney, Sean
93HelBreF-4089
93HelBreSP-17
94BelBreC-15
94BelBreF-96
94MidLeaAF-MDW9
95ElPasDTI-18
96El PasDB-17
96TexLeaAB-30
97Bow-121
97BowInt-121
Maloney, William A.
06FanCraNL-28
08RosComP-96
09T206-440
11SpoLifCW-233
Maloof, Jack
76TacTwiDQ-10
77IndIndTI-24
79TCMJapPB-14
83BeaGolGT-21
85SpoIndC-12
91LinDriAA-625
91WicWraP-2616
91WicWraRD-26
Malpeso, Dave
84PawRedST-17
85PawRedST-7
Malpica, Omar
91PriRedC-3
91PriRedP-3527
Malseed, Jim (James)
87PocGiaTB-10
88FreSunCLC-12
88FreSunP-1232
89SanJosGB-22
89SanJosGCLC-223
89SanJosGP-437
89SanJosGS-18
Maltzberger, Gordon
49BowPCL-12
49W72HolS-10
50W720HolS-18
52LavPro-36
77TCMTheWY-38
Malzone, Frank
47Exh-145
47PM1StaP1-117
47PM1StaP1-118
55Bow-302
56Top-304
57Top-355
58JayPubA-10
58RedSoxJP-6
58Top-260
58Top-481
59ArmCoi-12
59RedSoxJP-5
59Top-220
59Top-519
59Top-558
60ArmCoi-13A
60ArmCoi-13B
60Baz-12
60RedSoxJP-7
60Top-310
60Top-557
60TopTat-30
61Baz-9
61ChePat-7
61Pos-48A
61Pos-48B
61Top-173
61Top-445
61TopStal-113
62ExhStaB-22
62Jel-58
62Pos-58
62PosCan-58
62RedSoxJP-5
62SalPlaC-14
62ShiPlaC-14
62Top-225
62TopBuc-52
62TopStal-14
63BasMagM-53
63ExhStaB-40
63Jel-79
63Pos-79
63Top-232
64ChatheY-33
64Top-60
64TopCoi-7
64TopCoi-126
64TopSta-6
64TopStaU-44

64TopTatI-50
64TopVen-60
64WheSta-27
65ChaTheY-33
65Top-315
65TopEmbI-37
66OPC-152
66Top-152
66TopVen-152
78TCM60I-177
80ElmPioRST-38
86RedSoxGT-7
87ElmPio(C-31
Malzone, John
91WinHavRSC-20
91WinHavRSP-499
92LynRedSC-22
92LynRedSF-2914
93PawRedSDD-15
93PawRedSF-2414
93PawRedSTI-14
94NewBriRSF-658
Mamaux, Al (Albert L.)
15SpoNewM-107
16BF2FP-93
16ColE13-105
16FleBreD-59
16SpoNewM-110
17HolBreD-64
19W514-19
21E121So8-53
22AmeCarE-41
22E120-143
22W572-58
22W575-73
23W515-2
90DodTar-477
Mammola, Mark
91BoiHawC-13
91BoiHawP-3873
92QuaCitRBC-19
Mamott, Joe
94UtiBluSC-17
94UtiBluSF-3815
96LowSpiB-17
Manabe, Bullet
88FreSunCLC-21
88FreSunP-1235
Manahan, Anthony
90Bes-83
91JacSunP-158
92ClaFS7-329
92JacSunF-3717
92JacSunS-362
92SkyAA F-154
93CalCanF-1172
93TriAAAGF-52
94CalCanF-797
94ClaGolF-23
94Ult-421
95ScrRedBTI-19
96ScrRedBB-19
Manahan, Austin
89Bow-420
89BowTif-420
90AugPirP-2473
90CMC-850
90ProAaA-97
90SouAtlLAS-36
91Bow-527
91Cla/Bes-218
91ParPatF-20
91SalBucC-6
91SalBucP-960
92CarMudF-1188
92CarMudS-137
92ClaFS7-44
92SkyAA F-64
92UppDecML-78
93WesPalBEC-13
93WesPalBEF-1348
94RanCucQF-1646
95OrlCubF-19
Manaure, Johanne
93LinVenB-47
94VenLinU-76
95LinVen-246
Mancini, Joe
88BoiHawP-1626
88FreSunCLC-3
88FreSunP-1247
89BoiHawP-1991
Mancini, Pete
85NewOriT-21
Mancuso, Frank
84OmaRoyT-28
85OmaRoyT-4
Mancuso, Frank Octavius
46SeaSLP-32
83TCMPla1945-8
96Bro194F-23
Mancuso, Gus (August)
30SchR33-24
33ButCanV-31
33Gou-41
33Gou-237
33GouCanV-41
33RitCE-2H
34BatR31-67
34ButPreR-40
35GouPuzR-1K
35GouPuzR-3B
35GouPuzR-4A
35GouPuzR-7A
35GouPuzR-12A
35GouPuzR-14B
35GouPuzR-15B
35WheBB1-19
36ExhFou-5
36WorWidGV-9
37ExhFou-5
38OurNatGPP-18
39CubTeal-16
39GouPreR303A-31
39GouPreR303B-19
39WorWidGTP-31
40DodTeal-15
40PlaBal-207
41CarW75-15
41DouPlaR-37
77TCMTheWY-31
79DiaGre-34
90DodTar-478
91ConTSN-129
Mancuso, Paul
83WisRapTF-22
84VisOakT-18
85OrlTwiT-18
86BeaGolGP-17
Mandel, Brett
94OgdRapF-3743
94OgdRapSP-12
Mandel, Mike
75TopPho-24
Mandell, Sammy
28W513-95
Manderbach, Gary
75TidTidTI-16
Manderfield, Steve
77NewCoPT-23
79BurBeeT-25
80BurBeeT-8
82ElPasDT-15
Manders, Jack
40WheM4-8A
Mandeville, Bob
86PeoChiP-18
Mandia, Sam
90St.CatBJP-3459
91MyrBeaHC-9
91MyrBeaHP-2943
Mandl, Steve
89JamExpP-2151
91HigSchPLS-33
Maneely, Bob
76TacTwiDQ-11
76VenLeaS-28
Manering, Mark
87Ft.LauYP-27
Maness, Don
89TenTecGE-15
Maness, Dwight
92ClaDraP-56
92GulCoaDF-3581
93ClaGolF-111
93VerBeaDC-18
93VerBeaDF-2232
94BakDodC-16
94SanAntMF-2482
95SanAntMTI-20
96BinBeeB-19
Manfre, Mike
83CedRapRF-20
83CedRapRT-20
84CedRapRT-21
86VerRedP-12
87NasSouTI-14
Manfred, Jim
91PitMetC-18
91PitMetP-3419
92ColMetC-6
92ColMetF-291
92ColMetPI-26
Manfredi, Joel
95GreFalDTI-12
Mangham, Eric
87BakDodP-19
88VerBeaDS-13
89SanAntMB-3
91LinDriAAA-591
91TolMudHLD-591
91TolMudHP-1945
Mangham, Mark
85OscAstTI-10
Mangiardi, Paul
83EriCarT-1
Mangrum, Lloyd
52Whe-20A
52Whe-20B
Mangual, Angel
70Top-654
71OPC-317
71Top-317
72OPC-62
72Top-62
73OPC-625
73Top-625
75OPC-452
75Top-452
76SSP-503
76TucTorCa-6
76TusTorCr-8
Mangual, Pepe (Jose)
75OPC-616
75Top-616
76ExpRed-21
76OPC-164
76SSP-335
76Top-164
77Top-552
78TidTidT-13
79SalLakCGT-22A
80SalLakCGT-22
81SalLakCGT-22
82SpoIndT-22
91MetWIZ-243
Mangual, Victor
87BelMarL-18
87BelMarTI-8
Mangum, Leo
33Gou-162
33GouCanV-92
34DiaMatCSB-123
Mangum, Mark
97Bow-435
97BowChr-295
97BowChrI-295
97BowChrIR-295
97BowChrR-295
97BowInt-435
Mangum, Wade
83IdaFalAT-9
Maniac, Miami
85AncGlaPTI-42
85MiaHur-10
91MiaHurBB-9
Manias, James
96ButCopKB-22
97Bow-345
97BowInt-345
Manicchia, Bryan
90PriPatD-15
91BatCliC-16
91BatCliP-3481
91SpaPhiC-8
91SpaPhiP-893
92SpaPhiC-7
92SpaPhiF-1263
Manion, Clyde
33Gou-80
34GouCanV-35
34TarThoBD-13
94ConTSN-1161
94ConTSNB-1161
Manion, George A.
09T206-500
Mankowski, Phil
77Top-477
78TigBurK-17
78Top-559
79Top-93
80Top-216
81TidTidT-6
82TidTidT-9
91MetWIZ-244
Manley, Greg
85Fle-280
90GeoColC-20
Mann, Bill
88JacExpB-15
Mann, Dave
61UniOil-S5
Mann, Fred
87OldJudN-320
90KalBatN-32
90KalBatN-48
Mann, Jim
96StCatSB-18
Mann, Kelly
86GenCubP-17
87PeoChiP-25
88CarLeaAS-30
88WinSpiS-9
89BlaYNPRWL-193
89ChaKniTI-9
89SouLeaAJ-4
90Bes-157
90Don-40
90Fle-642
90FleCan-642
90GreBraB-9
90GreBraP-1132
90GreBraS-12
90Hot50RS-29
90OPC-744
90ProAaA-63
90RicBraBC-21
90Sco-627
90Sco100RS-56
90Top-744
90TopDeb89-76
90TopTif-744
90UppDec-33
91Don-736
91LinDriAAA-434
91RicBraBC-3
91RicBraLD-434
91RicBraP-2571
91RicBraTI-24
91Stu-147
Mann, Les
14B18B-51A
14B18B-51B
14B18B-51C
15SpoNewM-108
16ColE13-106
16SpoNewM-111
19W514-49
94ConTSN-1134
94ConTSNB-1134
Mann, Mark
93BilMusSP-26
Mann, Red (Garth)
44CubTeal-14
46SunBre-11
47SigOil-63
47SigOil-81
47SunBre-9
Mann, Scott
86WesPalBEP-23
87JacExpP-436
88JacExpP-964
Mann, Skip
79LodDodT-5
81VerBeaDT-10
Mann, Tom
90HunCubP-3279
91PeoChiC-7
91PeoChiP-1339
91PeoChiTI-11
Manning, Al (Melvin)
77BurBeeT-14
78BurBeeT-20
81ElPasDT-3
Manning, Archie
74NewYorNTDiS-27
Manning, Brian
96BelGiaTI-12
Manning, Dave
92ClaDraP-68
93StaCluM-198
96TulDriTI-16
Manning, Derek
93SouOreAC-17
93SouOreAF-4061
94WesMicWC-14
94WesMicWF-2292
95ModA'sTI-13
96HunStaTI-15
Manning, Dick
83GleFalWST-24
Manning, Henry
88CapCodPPaLP-150
92SouBenWSC-22
92SouBenWSF-180
93SarWhiSC-19
94PriWilCC-15
94PriWilCF-1925
Manning, James
87BucN28-32
87OldJudN-321
Manning, Len
94MarPhiC-11
94MarPhiF-3287
95PiePhiF-185
96BesAutS-53
96Exc-209
Manning, Max
86NegLeaF-54
91NegLeaRL-13
92NegLeaRLI-39
93TodWil-111
95NegLeaL2-4
95NegLeaLI-13
Manning, Mike
94HudValRF-3379
94HudValRC-12
Manning, Rick
76Hos-12
76HosTwi-12
76OPC-275
76SSP-522
76SSP-529
76Top-275
77BurCheD-56
77Hos-53
77Kel-15
77MSADis-37
77OPC-190
77PepGloD-12
77Top-115
78Hos-91
78OPC-151
78Top-11
79Hos-76
79OPC-220
79Top-425
80OPC-292
80Top-564
80TopSup-44
81Don-202
81Fle-403
81OPC-308
81Top-308
81TopScr-19
81TopSti-69
82Don-85
82Fle-374
82FleSta-195
82Ind-23
82IndTeal-22
82IndWhe-8
82OPC-202
82Top-202
82TopSti-179
83AllGamPI-61
83Don-198
83Fle-413
83FleSta-113
83FleSti-246
83IndPos-21
83IndWhe-20
83OPC-147
83Top-757
83TopSti-60
83TopTra-65T
84BreGar-11
84BrePol-28
84Don-170
84Fle-205
84Nes792-128
84OPC-128
84Top-128
84TopSti-299
84TopTif-128
85BreGar-11
85BrePol-28
85Don-237
85Fle-586
85OPC-389

85Top-603
85TopMin-603
85TopSti-291
85TopTif-603
86BrePol-28
86Don-368
86Fle-493
86OPC-49
86Top-49
86TopTif-49
87BrePol-28
87Don-521
87Fle-349
87FleGlo-349
87OPC-196
87Top-706
87TopTif-706
88Don-486
88Fle-168
88FleGlo-168
88Sco-593
88ScoGlo-593
88Top-441
88TopTif-441
89PacSenL-86
89T/MSenL-71
89TopSenL-39
90EliSenL-73
94BreMilB-56

Manning, Rube
09RamT20-73
09T206-223
09T206-224
11TurRedT-107

Manning, Tony
75SanAntBT-15

Mannion, Greg
90SalSpuCLC-132

Manno, Don
77TCMTheWY-29

Manon, Julio
94JohCitCF-3698

Manon, Ramon
87PriWilYP-23
89Ft.LauYS-14
90AlbYanB-3
90AlbYanP-1175
90AlbYanS-10
90CedRapRB-17
90CedRapRP-2316
90FleUpd-124
91CedRapRC-9
91Ft.LauYC-6
91Ft.LauYP-2420
91TopDeb90-96
92PriWilCC-3
92PriWilCF-143
93BirBarF-1187
93LimRocDWB-12
93RanKee-241

Manos, Pete Charles
77ReaPhiT-16

Manrique, Fred
80VenLeaS-50
82SyrChiT-18
82SyrChiTI-12
83SyrChiT-17
84SyrChiT-12
85IndIndTI-12
86LouRedTI-18
87FleUpd-72
87FleUpdG-72
87WhiSoxC-20
88Don-493
88Fle-406
88FleGlo-406
88PanSti-57
88Sco-139
88ScoGlo-139
88StaLinWS-13
88Top-437
88TopRoo-6
88TopTif-437
88ToyRoo-16
88WhiSoxC-17
89Bow-66
89BowTif-66
89Don-489
89Fle-503
89FleGlo-503
89OPC-108
89Sco-457
89Top-108
89TopBig-84
89TopSti-300
89TopTif-108
89UppDec-628A
89UppDec-628B
90Don-165
90Fle-306
90FleCan-306
90Lea-518
90OPC-242
90PanSti-158
90PubSti-396
90Sco-166
90Top-242
90TopTif-242
90TopTra-66T
90TopTraT-66T
90UppDec-392
90VenSti-315
93RanKee-242
94VenLinU-155

Manrique, Marco
92BluOriC-19
92BluOriF-2363
93AlbPolC-16
93AlbPolF-2028
93LinVenB-54
94FreKeyF-2617
94VenLinU-137
95LinVen-154
94FreKeyC-16

Mansavage, Jay
96AubDouB-12

Manship, Jeff
92BenMusSP-19
92BilMusF-3368

Manship, Ray
78NewWayCT-28

Mansolino, Doug
85PhoGiaC-192
89VanCanP-575
92WhiSoxK-NNO
93WhiSoxK-30
94WhiSoxK-30
95WhiSoxK-31

Mansur, Jeff
92KenTwiC-2
92VisOakF-1010
93NasXprF-398
94NasXprF-381

Mantei, Matt
93BelMarC-17
93BelMarF-3204
94AppFoxF-1051
94MidLeaAF-MDW4
95Exc-119
96FleUpd-U133
96FleUpdTC-U133
96LeaSigEA-120
97PacPriGotD-GD142

Mantha, Georges
43ParSpo-51

Manti, Sam
89PenPilS-14

Mantick, Dennis
77OrlTwiT-15
78OrlTwiT-12
79TolMudHT-21

Mantilla, Felix
57BraSpiaS4-13
57Top-188
58Top-17
59Top-157
59TopVen-157
60BraJayP-8
60BraLaktL-14
60BraSpiaS-11
60Top-19
60TopVen-19
61Top-164
61TopStal-44
62SalPlaC-183
62ShiPlaC-183
62Top-436
62TopBuc-53
62TopStal-158
63Jel-198
63Pos-198
63Top-447
64Top-228
64TopVen-228
65OPC-29
65Top-29
66Top-557
66TopRubl-56
67Top-524
81RedSoxBG2S-93
81TCM60I-327
82MetGal62-13
91MetWIZ-245

Mantle, Mickey
47Exh-146A
47Exh-146B
47Exh-146C
47Exh-146D
47PM1StaP1-119
47PM1StaP1-120
47PM1StaP1-121
47PM1StaP1-122
47PM1StaP1-123
47PM1StaP1-124
47PM1StaP1-125
47StaPinP2-21
51Bow-253
52BerRos-37
52Bow-101
52StaCalL-70G
52TipTop-24
52Top-311
53BowC-44
53BowC-59
53Bri-34
53Dor-111
53Dor-111A
53Dor-111B
53Dor-111C
53StaMey-6
53Top-82
54Bow-65
54DanDee-17
54NewYorJA-51
54RedHeaF-18
54StaMey-6
55ArmCoi-13A
55ArmCoi-13B
55BigLealS-11
55Bow-202
55DaiQueS-11
55DonWin-31
55StaMey-6
56Top-135
56YelBasP-20
57Top-95
57Top-407
57YanJayP-7
58HarSta-1
58JayPubA-11
58Top-150
58Top-418
58Top-487
58YanJayP-7
59Baz-14
59HomRunD-12
59OklTodML-12
59Top-10
59Top-461
59Top-564
59TopVen-10
59Yoo-4
60ArmCoi-14
60Baz-31
60KeyChal-31
60NuHi-22
60NuHi-50
60Pos-7
60RawGloT-17
60Top-160
60Top-350
60Top-563
60TopTat-31
60TopTat-92
60TopVen-160
60YanJayP-7
61Baz-2
61NuSco-422
61NuSco-450
61Pos-4A
61Pos-4B
61Raw-5
61Top-44
61Top-300
61Top-307
61Top-406
61Top-475
61Top-578
61TopDicG-8
61TopStal-196
61Yan61RL-7
61YanJayP-8
62AurRec-10
62Baz-23
62ExhStaB-23
62Jel-5
62Pos-5A
62Pos-5B
62PosCan-5
62SalPlaC-41
62ShiPlaC-41
62Top-18
62Top-53
62Top-200
62Top-318
62Top-471
62TopBuc-54
62TopStal-88
62TopVen-18
62TopVen-53
62YanJayP-9
63BasMagM-54
63Baz-1
63ExhStaB-41
63Jel-15
63Pos-15
63SalMetC-56
63Top-2
63Top-173
63Top-200
63TopStil-26
63YanJayP-7
64Baz-1
64ChatheY-16
64Raw-4
64Top-50
64Top-331
64TopCoi-120
64TopCoi-131A
64TopCoi-131B
64TopGia-25
64TopSta-53
64TopStaU-45
64TopTatl-51
64TopVen-50
64TopVen-331
64YanJayP-7
65Baz-1
65ChaTheY-13
65OldLonC-30
65OPC-3
65OPC-5
65OPC-134
65Top-3
65Top-5
65Top-134
65Top-350
65TopEmbl-11
65TopTral-57
66Baz-7
66OPC-50
66Top-50
66TopRubl-57
66TopVen-50
66YanTeal-7
67Baz-7
67CokCapYM-V8
67DexPre-132
67OPC-103
67OPC-150
67OPCPapl-6
67Top-103
67Top-150
67TopGiaSU-8
67TopPos-6
67TopTesF-11
67TopVen-192
68AtlOil-7
68Baz-11
68LauWorS-61
68Top-280
68Top-490
68TopActS-7B
68TopActS-10A
68TopGamI-2
68TopPla-9
68TopPos-18
68TopVen-280
69Top-412
69Top-500A
69Top-500B
69TopDecl-23
69TopSta-205
69TopSup-24
69TopTeaP-19
69TraSta-30
70YanCliDP-13
71YanCliDP-10
72LauGreF-33
73SyrChiTI-15
74NewYorNTDiS-18
74SupBlaB-7
74SyrChiTI-14
75OPC-194
75OPC-195
75OPC-200
75SSP42-37
75SSPSam-4
75SyrChiTI-9
75TCMAllG-21
75Top-194
75Top-195
75Top-200
76BooProC-16
76GalBasGHoF-17
76GrePlaG-41
76ShaPiz-145
76Spo-D
76SSPYanOD-7
77BobParHoF-34
77GalGloG-7
77GalGloG-232
77Spo-716
78TCM60I-262
79BasGre-72
79TCM50-7
80Lau300-18
80PacLeg-6
80PerHaloFP-145
80SSPHOF-145
80YanGreT-6
81SanDieSC-10
81SanDieSC-11
81SanDieSC-12
81SanDieSC-13
81SpoHaloF-15
81TCM60I-303
81TCM60I-474
82BasCarN-1
82CraJac-6
82DiaCla-55
82K-M-1
83DonHOFH-7
83DonHOFH-43
83MLBPin-12
83Oco& SSBG-10
83TigAlKS-14
83TigAlKS-16
83TigAlKS-35
83TopRep5-311
83TopTraBP-4
83YanASFY-1
83YanASFY-26
83YanYealT-15
84DonCha-50
84FifNatCT-11
84OCoandSI-25
84OCoandSI-100
84OCoandSI-140
84OCoandSI-150
84OCoandSI-207
84SpoDesPW-4
84WilMay-29
85CirK-6
85DonHOFS-6
85GeoSteM-5
85Woo-23
86BigLeaC-6
86DonHig-10
86SpoDecG-26
86SpoDesJM-4
86TCM-20
86TCMSupS-4
86TCMSupS-7
86TCMSupS-9
86TCMSupS-11
86TCMSupS-18
86TCMSupS-23
86TCMSupS-24
87AstShoSO-26
87HygAllG-31
87K-M-5
87LeaSpeO*-H1
87NesDreT-17
87Yan196T-2
88GreBasS-46
88HouSho-9
88PacLegI-7
88WilMulP-23
89BowInsT-5

89BowInsT-6
89BowRepl-5
89BowRepl-6
89BowTif-R5
89BowTif-R6
89CMCMan-1
89CMCMan-2
89CMCMan-3
89CMCMan-4
89CMCMan-5
89CMCMan-6
89CMCMan-7
89CMCMan-8
89CMCMan-9
89CMCMan-10
89CMCMan-11
89CMCMan-12
89CMCMan-13
89CMCMan-14
89CMCMan-15
89CMCMan-16
89CMCMan-17
89CMCMan-18
89CMCMan-19
89CMCMan-20
89HOFStiB-40
89PerCelP-28
90BasWit-3
90HOFStiB-49
90PerGreM-19
90PerGreM-87
90PerMasW-6
90PerMasW-7
90PerMasW-8
90PerMasW-9
90PerMasW-10
90RinPosYMP-6
91RinPos1Y3-1
91ScoMan-1
91ScoMan-2
91ScoMan-3
91ScoMan-4
91ScoMan-5
91ScoMan-6
91ScoMan-7
91ScoMan-AU0
91TopArc1-82
91TopEasCN-2
92PinMan-1
92PinMan-2
92PinMan-3
92PinMan-4
92PinMan-5
92PinMan-6
92PinMan-7
92PinMan-8
92PinMan-9
92PinMan-10
92PinMan-11
92PinMan-12
92PinMan-13
92PinMan-14
92PinMan-15
92PinMan-16
92PinMan-17
92PinMan-18
92PinMan-19
92PinMan-20
92PinMan-21
92PinMan-22
92PinMan-23
92PinMan-24
92PinMan-25
92PinMan-26
92PinMan-27
92PinMan-28
92PinMan-29
92PinMan-30
92ScoFra-2
92ScoFra-4
92ScoFra-AU2
92ScoFra-AU4
92TVSpoMF5HRC-6
92YanWIZ6-78
92YanWIZA-43
92YanWIZH-22
93SelTriC-1
93UppDecAH-87
93UppDecAH-134
93UppDecAH-135
93UppDecAH-137
93UppDecAH-140
93UppDecAH-141
93UppDecAH-165
93UppDecAHP-1
93UppDecAHP-2
93UppDecAHP-4
93UppDecTAN-TN17
94MetImpM-1
94MetImpM-2
94MetImpM-3
94MetImpM-4
94MetImpM-5
94MetImpM-6
94MetImpM-7
94MetImpM-8
94MetImpM-9
94MetImpM-10
94TedWil5C-4
94UppDec-GM1
94UppDec-MM1
94UppDecAH-7
94UppDecAH-10
94UppDecAH-100
94UppDecAH-116
94UppDecAH-135
94UppDecAH-168
94UppDecAH-222
94UppDecAH-225
94UppDecAH1-7
94UppDecAH1-10
94UppDecAH1-100
94UppDecAH1-116
94UppDecAH1-135
94UppDecAH1-168
94UppDecAH1-222
94UppDecAH1-225
94UppDecAH1A-259
94UppDecAJ-46
94UppDecAJG-46
94UppDecMH-64
94UppDecMH-65
94UppDecMH-66
94UppDecMH-67
94UppDecMH-68
94UppDecMH-69
94UppDecMH-70
94UppDecMH-71
94UppDecMH-72
94UppDecMH-NNO0
94UppDecMLS-MM21
94UppDecMLS-NNO
94UppDecMLSED-MM21
94UppDecMPC-1
94UppDecMPC-2
94UppDecMPC-3
94UppDecMPC-4
94UppDecMPC-5
94UppDecMPC-6
94UppDecMPC-7
94UppDecMPC-8
94UppDecMPC-9
94UppDecMPC-10
94UppDecS-10
94UppDecTAE-63
94UppDecTAE-BC3
94UppDecTAEGM-5
94UppDecTAELD-LD12
96Baz-NNO
96Bow-M20
96BowBes-NNO
96BowBesAR-NNO
96BowBesR-NNO
96ManDonC-1
96StaCluMa-MM1
96StaCluMa-MM2
96StaCluMa-MM3
96StaCluMa-MM4
96StaCluMa-MM5
96StaCluMa-MM6
96StaCluMa-MM7
96StaCluMa-MM8
96StaCluMa-MM9
96StaCluMa-MM10
96StaCluMa-MM11
96StaCluMa-MM12
96StaCluMa-MM13
96StaCluMa-MM14
96StaCluMa-MM15
96StaCluMa-MM16
96StaCluMa-MM17
96StaCluMa-MM18
96StaCluMa-MM19
96Top-7
96Top-F7
96TopChr-7
96TopChrR-7
96TopGal-NNO
96TopMan-1
96TopMan-2
96TopMan-3
96TopMan-4
96TopMan-5
96TopMan-6
96TopMan-7
96TopMan-8
96TopMan-9
96TopMan-10
96TopMan-11
96TopMan-12
96TopMan-13
96TopMan-14
96TopMan-15
96TopMan-16
96TopMan-17
96TopMan-18
96TopMan-19
96TopManC-1
96TopManC-2
96TopManC-3
96TopManC-4
96TopManC-5
96TopManC-6
96TopManC-7
96TopManC-8
96TopManC-9
96TopManC-10
96TopManC-11
96TopManC-12
96TopManC-13
96TopManC-14
96TopManC-15
96TopManC-16
96TopManC-17
96TopManC-18
96TopManC-19
96TopManF-1
96TopManF-2
96TopManF-3
96TopManF-4
96TopManF-5
96TopManF-6
96TopManF-7
96TopManF-8
96TopManF-9
96TopManF-10
96TopManF-11
96TopManF-12
96TopManF-13
96TopManF-14
96TopManF-15
96TopManF-16
96TopManF-17
96TopManF-18
96TopManF-19
96TopManFR-1
96TopManFR-2
96TopManFR-3
96TopManFR-4
96TopManFR-5
96TopManFR-6
96TopManFR-7
96TopManFR-8
96TopManFR-9
96TopManFR-10
96TopManFR-11
96TopManFR-12
96TopManFR-13
96TopManFR-14
96TopManFR-15
96TopManFR-16
96TopManFR-17
96TopManFR-18
96TopManFR-19
96TopManR-1
96TopManR-2
96TopManR-3
96TopManR-4
96TopManR-5
96TopManR-6
96TopManR-7
96TopManR-8
96TopManR-9
96TopManR-10
96TopManR-11
96TopManR-12
96TopManR-13
96TopManR-14
96TopManR-15
96TopManR-16
96TopManR-17
96TopManR-18
96TopManR-19
97TopMan-21
97TopMan-22
97TopMan-23
97TopMan-24
97TopMan-25
97TopMan-26
97TopMan-27
97TopMan-28
97TopMan-29
97TopMan-30
97TopMan-31
97TopMan-32
97TopMan-33
97TopMan-34
97TopMan-35
97TopMan-36
97TopManF-21
97TopManF-22
97TopManF-23
97TopManF-24
97TopManF-25
97TopManF-26
97TopManF-27
97TopManF-28
97TopManF-29
97TopManF-30
97TopManF-31
97TopManF-32
97TopManF-33
97TopManF-34
97TopManF-35
97TopManF-36
97TopManFR-21
97TopManFR-22
97TopManFR-23
97TopManFR-24
97TopManFR-25
97TopManFR-26
97TopManFR-27
97TopManFR-28
97TopManFR-29
97TopManFR-30
97TopManFR-31
97TopManFR-32
97TopManFR-33
97TopManFR-34
97TopManFR-35
97TopManFR-36

Manto, Jeff

86QuaCitAP-19
87PalSprP-4
88BasAmeAAB-29
88BlaYNPRWL-185
88MidAngGS-21
88TexLeaAGS-39
89EdmTraC-20
89EdmTraP-570
89FleUpd-13
90CMC-467
90ColSprSSC-15
90ColSprSSP-43
90Fle-137
90FleCan-137
90FleUpd-94
90IndTeal-26
90ProAAAF-224
91Bow-75
91Don-602
91IndFanC-18
91OPC-488
91Sco-337
91StaClu-582
91Top-488
91TopDeb90-97
91TopDesS-488
91TopMic-488
91TopTif-488
91UppDec-238
92RicBraBB-1
92RicBraF-384
92RicBraRC-9
92RicBraS-431
92Sco-666
92StaClu-699
93ScrRedBF-2548
93ScrRedBTI-16
94NorTidF-2928
94Pac-481
94RocRedWTI-12
95Fin-299
95FinRef-299
95StaClu-597
95StaCluMOP-597
95StaCluSTWS-597
96ColCho-58
96ColChoGS-58
96ColChoSS-58
96Don-38
96DonPreP-38
96Fle-14
96FleTif-14
96Pac-233
96Ult-8
96UltGolM-8
96UppDec-17
97RicBraBC-12

Mantrana, Manny

87FayGenP-12
88ColMetGS-19
88St.LucMS-15

Manuare, Jose

91MedHatBJP-4096
91MedHatBJSP-3

Manuel, Barry

87LSUTigP-6
88ChaRanS-14
89TulDriGS-16
90ChaRanS-12
90FloStaLAS-36
90LSUTigGM-16
90StaFS7-24
91LinDriAA-586
91TulDriLD-586
91TulDriP-2768
91TulDriTI-16
92Don-401
92OklCit8F-1913
92ProFS7-154
92TopDeb91-115
93LinVenB-230
93Pin-257
93RanKee-243
93Sco-225
94OriPro-58
94RocRedWF-994
94RocRedWTI-13
97Fle-382
97FleTif-382
97Ult-231
97UltGolME-231
97UltPlaME-231

Manuel, Charlie (Charles)

70OPC-194
70Top-194
71MLBOffS-466
71OPC-744
71Top-744
74AlbDukTI-72
74AlbDukTI-9
76SSP-86
79TCMJapPB-44
83WisRapTF-27
85OrlTwiT-22
86TolMudHP-15
87PorBeaP-22
88IndGat-9
89IndTeal-28
90DodTar-479
91ColSprSSLD-99
91ColSprSSP-2200
91LinDriAAA-99
92ColSprSSF-766
92ColSprSSS-99
93ChaKniF-559
93TriAAAGF-37

Manuel, Jerry

76OPC-596
76Top-596
77EvaTriT-18
81ExpPos-5
82Fle-195
83IowCubT-17
86IndIndTI-36
87IndIndTI-5
89TopSenL-90
90JacExpB-25
90JacExpP-1391
91IndIndLD-199
91IndIndP-477
91LinDriAAA-199
92ExpPos-21

Manuel, Jose

88SanAntMB-18

Manush, Heinie

26SpoNewSM-5
29ExhFou-29

29PorandAR-61
31Exh-31
31SenTealPW-21
31W517-28
32R33So2-416
33ExhFou-16
33Gou-47
33Gou-107
33Gou-187
33GouCanV-47
33TatOrbSDR-178
34BatR31-77
34ButPreR-41
34DiaStaR-30A
34DiaStaR-30B
34ExhFou-16
34Gou-18
34GouCanV-68
35ExhFou-16
35GouPuzR-1C
35GouPuzR-2C
35GouPuzR-16C
35GouPuzR-17C
36GouWidPPR-B16
36WorWidGV-73
37WheBB6-8
38WheBB15-8
39PlaBal-94
40PlaBal-176
46SpoExcW-6-11
54Top-187
60Fle-18
61Fle-57
76RowExh-10
76ShaPiz-100
77BobParHoF-35
77GalGloG-56
79RedSoxEF-16
80PacLeg-2
80PerHaloFP-100
80SSPHOF-100
81ConTSN-77
81TigDetN-82A
81TigDetN-82B
81TigSecNP-3
83ConMar-2
86ConSer1-19
88ConAmeA-20
89DodSmoG-16
89HOFStiB-36
90DodTar-480
91ConTSN-63
91ConTSN-270
94ConTSN-1077
94ConTSNB-1077
94TopArc1-187
94TopArc1G-187

Manwaring, Kirt
87ShrCapP-10
87TexLeaAF-22
88BlaYNPRWL-92
88Don-39
88Fle-651
88FleGlo-651
88FleMin-119
88Lea-39
88PhoFirC-12
88PhoFirP-61
88Sco-627
88ScoGlo-627
88TopTra-64T
88TopTraT-64T
89Bow-469
89BowTif-469
89Don-494
89DonBasB-330
89Fle-334
89FleGlo-334
89GiaMot-23
89PanSti-208
89Sco-619
89ScoHot1R-46
89ScoYouSI-22
89Top-506
89TopTif-506
89UppDec-500
90CMC-537
90Don-59
90Fle-63
90FleCan-63
90OPC-678
90PhoFirC-10
90PhoFirP-14
90ProAAAF-40
90PubSti-76
90Sco-146
90Top-678
90TopTif-678
90UppDec-457
90VenSti-316
91GiaMot-23
91GiaPacGaE-25
91OPC-472
91Sco-101
91Top-472
91TopDesS-472
91TopMic-472
91TopTif-472
92Bow-361
92Don-494
92Fle-641
92GiaMot-23
92GiaPacGaE-27
92Lea-208
92OPC-726
92Pin-181
92Sco-636
92StaClu-271
92Top-726
92TopGol-726
92TopGolW-726
92TopMic-726
92TriPla-61
92Ult-293
92UppDec-740
93Bow-688
93Don-122
93Don-364
93Fla-144
93Fle-158
93GiaMot-9
93GiaPos-23
93Lea-66
93PacSpa-612
93PanSti-235
93Pin-122
93Sco-179
93Sel-247
93StaClu-690
93StaCluFDI-690
93StaCluG-6
93StaCluMOP-690
93Stu-151
93Top-337
93TopGol-337
93TopInaM-337
93TopMic-337
93Ult-135
93UppDec-179
93UppDecGold-179
94Bow-275
94ColC-186
94ColChoGS-186
94ColChoSS-186
94Don-209
94ExtBas-389
94Fin-415
94FinRef-415
94Fla-245
94Fle-694
94GiaAMC-12
94GiaMot-13
94GiaTeal-6
94GiaUSPC-6C
94GiaUSPC-12H
94Lea-55
94OPC-2
94Pac-549
94Pin-53
94PinArtP-53
94PinMusC-53
94Sco-344
94ScoGolR-344
94Sel-370
94StaClu-218
94StaCluFDI-218
94StaCluGR-218
94StaCluMOP-218
94StaCluMOP-ST14
94StaCluST-ST14
94StaCluT-3
94StaCluTFDI-3
94Top-30
94TopGol-30
94TopSpa-30
94TriPla-106
94TriPlaM-2
94Ult-292
94UltAwaW-10
94UppDec-100
94UppDecED-100
95ColCho-257
95ColChoGS-257
95ColChoSS-257
95Don-187
95DonPreP-187
95DonTopotO-352
95Fla-425
95Fle-583
95GiaMot-12
95Lea-190
95Pac-380
95Pin-203
95PinArtP-203
95PinMusC-203
95Sco-368
95ScoGolR-368
95ScoPlaTS-368
95StaClu-465
95StaCluMOP-465
95StaCluSTWS-465
95StaCluVR-254
95Top-211
95TopCyb-120
95Ult-242
95UltGolM-242
95UppDec-332
95UppDecED-332
95UppDecEDG-332
96ColCho-304
96ColChoGS-304
96ColChoSS-304
96Don-35
96DonPreP-35
96EmoXL-293
96Fla-391
96Fle-590
96FleTif-590
96GiaMot-7
96LeaSigA-142
96LeaSigAG-142
96LeaSigAS-142
96Pac-212
96Pin-69
96Sco-406
96StaClu-78
96StaCluMOP-78
95StaCluVRMC-254
96Top-260
96Ult-296
96UltGolM-296
96UppDec-454
97Cir-138
97CirRav-138
97ColCho-317
97DonTea-105
97DonTeaSPE-105
97PacPriGotD-GD153
97Sco-39
97ScoPreS-39
97ScoShoS-39
97ScoShoSAP-39
97Top-364
97Ult-413
97UltGolME-413
97UltPlaME-413
97UppDec-352

Manwarren, Marc
96KisCobB-15

Manz, George
74WicAerODF-105

Manzanillo, Josias
85ElmPioT-14
87NewBriRSP-21
89EasLeaAP-17
89NewBriRSP-606
89NewBriRSS-8
90Bes-70
90CMC-879
90NewBriRSB-4
90NewBriRSP-1315
90NewBriRSS-9
90TopTVRS-51
91PawRedSP-35
92MemChiS-429
92OmaRoyF-2959
92OmaRoyS-336
92Sco-838
92StaClu-504
92TopDeb91-116
93LimRocDWB-42
93PacSpa-514
93Ult-574
94BreMilB-150
94Fla-408
94FleUpd-157
94NorTidF-2917
94Pac-411
94TopTra-9T
94Ult-239
95Don-190
95DonPreP-190
95Fle-375
95StaClu-413
95StaCluMOP-413
95StaCluSTWS-413
95Top-308
95Ult-199
95UltGolM-199

Manzanillo, Ravelo
83AleDukT-27
85NasPirT-15
88FloStaLAS-43
88TamTarS-14
89BirBarB-13
90CMC-631
90ProAAAF-164
90VanCanC-4
90VanCanP-486
91LinDriAAA-510
91SyrChiLD-510
91SyrChiMB-13
94Bow-302
94Fla-424
94FleUpd-175
94PirQui-12
94SpoRoo-59
94SpoRooAP-59
94Ult-556
95Fla-186
95Fle-482
95Pac-346
95StaClu-490
95StaCluMOP-490
95StaCluSTWS-490

Manzon, Howard
86KenTwiP-15

Mapel, Steve
79WisRapTT-9
80OrlTwiT-6
80TolMudHT-1
82OrlTwi8SCT-20

Mapes, Cliff
48BluTin-33
48YanTeal-18
50Bow-218
51BerRos-D2
51Bow-289
51R42SmaS-64
52Bow-13
52Top-103
83TopRep5-103

Maples, Steve
79CliDodT-23

Maples, Tim
81MiaOriT-18

Mapp, Eric
96BilMusTI-18

Marabell, Scott
89BakDodCLC-195
90VerBeaDS-19
91SanAntMP-2989

Marabella, Tony
90GatCitPP-3347
90GatCitPSP-15
91SumFlyC-16
91SumFlyP-2341
94BurBeeC-14
94BurBeeF-1089

Marak, Paul
87SumBraP-9
88DurBulS-13
89GreBraB-17
89GreBraP-1174
89GreBraS-14
90CMC-284
90ProAAAF-400
90RicBraBC-10
90RicBraC-8
90RicBraP-255
90RicBraTI-20
91Cla2-T52
91Don-413
91Lea-260
91OPC-753
91RicBraP-2562
91Sco-712
91ScoRoo-13
91Top-753
91TopDeb90-98
91TopDesS-753
91TopMic-753
91TopTif-753
92ChaKniF-2768
93LinVenB-74

Maranda, Georges
52LaPat-10
52LavPro-5
60Top-479
61TacBan-12
61TwiCloD-15
61UniOil-T20

Maranville, Rabbit (Walter)
13PolGroW-15
14B18B-52A
14B18B-52B
14B18B-52C
14CraJacE-136
15CraJacE-136
15SpoNewM-109
16BF2FP-55
16ColE13-107
16FleBreD-60
16SpoNewM-112
17HolBreD-65
19W514-21
20NatCarE-60
20WalMaiW-28
21E121So1-56
21E121So8-54
21Exh-101
21Nei-90
22AmeCarE-42
22E120-220
22W572-59
22W573-73
22W575-74
22WilPatV-42
23W501-83
23W503-46
23W515-50
23WilChoV-87
24MrsShePP-5
25Exh-23
26Exh-15
26SpoComoA-27
29PorandAR-62
31Exh-1
32USCar-10
33CraJacP-17
33DelR33-13
33GeoCMil-21
33Gou-117
34DiaMatCSB-124
34BatR31-37
34DiaStaR-3
34GouCanV-4
35DiaMatCS2-14
35GouPuzR-1J
35GouPuzR-3A
35GouPuzR-14A
35GouPuzR-15A
36WorWidGV-129
50CalHOFW-51
60ExhWriH-15
60Fle-21
61Fle-124
63BazA-14
69Baz-10
69Baz-12
69SCFOldT-20
76RowExh-14
76ShaPiz-72
77GalGloG-114
80PacLeg-3
80PerHaloFP-72
80SSPHOF-72
83DiaClaS2-78
86BraGreT-3
87ConSer2-47
89DodSmoG-18
89HOFStiB-17
90DodTar-481
91ConTSN-4
93ConTSN-914
93CraJac-20
94ConTSN-1060
94ConTSNB-1060
95ConTSN-1329

95ConTSNCMP-1387
95ConTSNP-1500
Marberry, Firpo (Fred)
26SpoComoA-28
28PorandAR-A24
28PorandAR-B24
28W56PlaC-S7A
30SchR33-47
31Exh-31
31SenTeaIPW-22
33DouDisP-31
33ExhFou-16
33Gou-104
34BatR31-66
34ButPreR-42
34ExhFou-12
34GouCanV-8
35GolMedFR-8
35GouPuzR-5F
35GouPuzR-6F
35GouPuzR-11H
35GouPuzR-13F
35TigFreP-13
36WorWidGV-10
61Fle-125
76TigOldTS-15
78TigDeaCS-15
81TigSecNP-19
91ConTSN-326
Marcano, Gilberto
76VenLeaS-185
80VenLeaS-231
Marcano, Roberto
74CarSalLCA-92
76VenLeaS-142
79TCMJapPB-11
80VenLeaS-211
94VenLinU-10
Marcano, Tucupita
95LinVen-72
Marcell, Ziggy
86NegLeaF-56
Marcelle, Oliver
74LauOldTBS-3
90NegLeaS-17
Marcero, Doug
89NiaFalRP-16
90NiaFalRP-21
91LakTigP-265
Marchan, Jose
93LinVenB-24
94VenLinU-95
95LinVen-198
Marchese, Joe (Joseph)
86ElmPioRSP-11
87GreHorP-11
88CarLeaAS-12
88LynRedSS-10
89NewBriRSP-616
89NewBriRSS-9
91WinHavRSC-26
91WinHavRSP-506
92WinHavRSC-28
92WinHavRSF-1795
93LynRedSC-26
93LynRedSF-2535
94LynRedSC-28
94LynRedSF-1910
95AshTouTI-11
96SalAvaB-28
Marchese, John
88BenBucL-24
89QuaCitAB-18
89QuaCitAGS-10
90QuaCitAGS-15
Marchesi, Jim
92JohCitCC-21
92JohCitCF-3112
93JohCitCC-12
93JohCitCF-3672
Marcheskie, Lee
82AleDukT-2
83LynPirT-5
85NasPirT-16
Marchildon, Phil
39WorWidGV-17
49Bow-187
49PhiBul-34
60RawGloT-18
76TayBow4-100
Marchio, Frank
53ExhCan-53
Marchok, Chris
87JamExpP-2565
88RocExpLC-23
89JacExpB-4
89JacExpP-166
90CMC-55
90IndIndC-5
90IndIndP-300
90ProAAAF-583
91HarSenLD-262
91HarSenP-622
91LinDriAA-262
92HarSenF-457
92HarSenS-288
Marciano, Rocky
53SpoMagP-4
83FraBroR-20
Marcinczyk, T.R.
96SouOreTI-10
Marcon, Dave
90St.CatBJP-3463
91SalLakTP-3206
91SalLakTSP-23
93CedRapKC-12
93CedRapKF-1733
Marcucci, Lilo
46SunBre-12
Marcum, John
34Gou-69
35DiaMatCS3T1-102
35GouPuzR-8J
35GouPuzR-9J
36GouWidPPR-A69
36WorWidGV-58
79RedSoxEF-4
92ConTSN-574
Mardsen, Steve
84BufBisT-17
Marenghi, Matt
94BluOriC-13
94BluOriF-3560
96HigDesMB-19
Marett, John
89BluOriS-14
90WauTimP-2127
90WauTimS-15
Marge, Pete
93BilMusSP-15
Margenau, Eric
92ColMetPI-34
93ForWayWC-29
94ForWayWC-29
95ForWayWTI-31
96ForWayWB-30
Margheim, Greg
90BilMusP-3218
91CedRapRC-10
91CedRapRP-2717
Margoneri, Joe
57Top-191
Marguardt, Chuck
88GasRanP-1023
Maria, Esteban
75BurBeeT-14
Mariano, Bob
84ChaO'sT-12
85ChaO'sT-18
89AlbYanB-28
89AlbYanP-324
91AlbYanP-1025
91LinDriAA-25
92ForLauYTI-20
92Ft.LauYF-2630
93BelBreC-28
93BelBreF-1728
94ElPasDF-3163
94ElPasDF-3164
Marichal, Juan
47PM1StaP1-126
60TacBan-9
61GiaJayP-8
61Top-417
61TopStaI-79
62GiaJayP-8
62Jel-140
62Pos-140
62PosCan-140
62Top-505
62TopStaI-198
63Jel-109
63Pos-109
63SalMetC-5
63Top-440
64ChatheY-34
64GiaJayP-6
64Top-3
64Top-280
64TopCoi-36
64TopCoi-157
64TopGia-37
64TopSta-39
64TopStaU-46
64TopVen-3
64TopVen-280
64WheSta-28
65Baz-24
65ChaTheY-34
65GiaTeaI-5
65OPC-10
65OPC-50
65Top-10
65Top-50
65TopTraI-20
66Baz-10
66Top-221
66Top-420
66TopRubI-58
66TopVen-221
67Baz-10
67CokCapA-14
67CokCapG-7
67CokCapNLA-34
67OPCPapI-28
67Top-234
67Top-236
67Top-454A
67Top-454B
67Top-500
67TopPos-28
67TopTesF-12
67TopVen-300
68Baz-5
68DexPre-50
68OPC-107
68Top-107A
68Top-107B
68Top-205
68TopVen-107
68TopVen-205
69KelPin-11
69MilBra-165
69MLBOffS-203
69MLBPin-51
69NabTeaF-14
69OPC-10
69OPCDec-15
69Top-10
69Top-370
69Top-572
69TopDec-32
69TopSta-107
69TopSup-64
69TopTeaP-14
69TraSta-32
70Gia-8
70Kel-13
70MilBra-14
70MLBOffS-128
70OPC-67
70OPC-69
70OPC-210
70OPC-466
70Top-67
70Top-69
70Top-210
70Top-466
70TopScr-12
70TraSta-3A
71BazNumT-19
71BazUnn-19
71GiaTic-6
71MLBOffS-256
71OPC-325
71Top-325
71TopCoi-125
71TopTat-5
72EssCoi-7
72Kel-47
72MilBra-204
72ProStaP-17
72Top-567
72Top-568
73OPC-480
73Top-480
74OPC-330
74Top-330
74TopTra-330T
78TCM60I-2
80PerHaloFP-183
80SSPHOF-182
83DiaClaS2-70
83MLBPin-25
84GiaMot-3
85DomLeaS-1
85DomLeaS-2
85DomLeaS-3
85DomLeaS-4
85DomLeaS-5
85DomLeaS-6
85DomLeaS-7
85DomLeaS-8
85DomLeaS-9
86SpoDecG-46
86SpoDesJM-13
87K-M-6
88PacLegI-54
89DodSmoG-17
89PerCelP-29
90DodTar-482
90PerGreM-56
91FouBal-8
91TopGloA-22
92UppDecS-7
93ActPacA-124
93ActPacA2-58G
93UppDecS-7
93UppDecS-21
94TedWil-54
94TopSpa-L7
95TopLegot6M-9
97SpoIllCC-5
Marichal, Victor
75BurBeeT-15
Marie, Larry
90RicBra2ATI-16
Marietta, Lou
78CedRapGT-17
82WesHavAT-8
Marigny, Ron
87GleFalTP-11
87LakTigP-9
89LakTigS-15
90LakTigS-18
91LakTigC-20
91LakTigP-273
Marin, Jose
91ElmPioC-11
91ElmPioP-3278
92LynRedSC-4
92LynRedSF-2915
Marina, Juan
87ColMetP-18
88BlaYNPRWL-8
88ColMetGS-7
89St.LucMS-15
Marina, Vega
90St.LucMS-14
Marinaro, Bob
90PriWilCTI-4
Marine, Del
92BriTigC-16
92BriTigF-1415
93NiaFalRF-3393
94FayGenC-15
94FayGenF-2149
Marine, Justin
95BilRedTI-25
96BilMusTI-19
Mariners, Bellingham
87BelMarTI-33
Mariners, Harwich
88CapCodPB-29
Mariners, Seattle
78Top-499
83FleSta-248
83FleSti-NNO
87SpoTeaL-25
87Top-156
87TopTif-156
88PanSti-466
88RedFolSB-122
90PubSti-641
90RedFolSB-113
90VenSti-538
92UppDecS-22
94ImpProP-12
94Sco-328
94ScoGolR-328
95MarPac-4
95PanSti-148
96PanSti-227
Marini, Marc
92ColRedC-10
92ColRedF-2406
93ClaGolF-16
93ExcFS7-160
93KinIndC-14
93KinIndF-2261
93KinIndTI-14
93SouAtlLAIPI-11
93SouAtlLAPI-23
94CanIndF-3131
95SigRoo-35
95SigRooSig-35
96ColCliB-18
Marino, Bob
92ForLauYC-25
Marino, Dan
93StaCluMO-49
Marino, Mark
86QuaCitAP-20
87PalSprP-30
89StoPorP-402
89StoPorS-28
Marion, Mark
89StoPorB-31
Marion, Marty
39ExhSal-39
41CarW75-16
46SeaSLP-33
46SpoExcW-5-1A
47Exh-147
47PM1StaP1-127
47TipTop-159
48BluTin-3
48Bow-40
49Bow-54
49EurSta-189
49Lea-97
50Bow-88
51Bow-34
52Bow-85
53BowC-52
60Fle-19
61Fle-58
61NuSco-473
66CarCoi-5
77TCMTheWY-26
79TCM50-99
83CarGreT-4
83DiaClaS2-86
83TCMPla1942-27
90BasWit-47
91TopArc1-302
92CarMcD-6
92ConTSN-626
93ActPacA-134
Maris, Roger
47Exh-148
47PM1StaP1-128
47PM1StaP1-129
47PM1StaP1-130
47StaPinP2-22
47StaPinP2-23
55DonWin-32
57IndSoh-8
58HarSta-18
58Top-47
59Top-202
60KeyChal-32
60Top-377
60Top-565
60TopTat-32
60YanJayP-8
61Baz-5
61NuSco-416
61Pos-7A
61Pos-7B
61SevElev-25
61Top-2
61Top-44
61Top-478
61Top-576
61TopStaI-197
61Yan61RL-3
61YanJayP-9
62AurRec-11
62Baz-14
62ExhStaB-24
62Gol-1
62Jel-6
62Pos-6A
62Pos-6B
62PosCan-6
62SalPlaC-23
62ShiPlaC-23
62Top-1
62Top-53

62Top-234
62Top-313
62Top-401
62TopBuc-55
62TopStaI-89
62TopVen-1
62TopVen-53
62YanJayP-10
63BasMagM-55
63ExhStaB-42
63Jel-16
63Pos-16
63SalMetC-57
63Top-4
63Top-120
63Top-144
63YanJayP-8
64ChatheY-17
64Top-225
64Top-331
64TopVen-225
64TopVen-331
64YanJayP-8
65ChaTheY-14
65OldLonC-31
65OPC-155
65Top-155
66Top-365
66TopVen-365
66YanTeal-8
67OPC-45
67Top-45
67TopVen-328
68AtlOilPBCC-26
68Top-330
68TopVen-330
69OPC-164
69Top-164
72LauGreF-50
74SupBlaB-8
75OPC-198
75OPC-199
75SheGrePG-18
75Top-198
75Top-199
76GrePlaG-18
76LauDiaJ-30
77GalGloG-226
77Spo-716
78ReaRem-14
78TCM60I-11
79DiaGre-25
79TCM50-161
79Top-413
80MarExh-18
80PacLeg-101
81SanDieSC-15
81SanDieSC-16
81TCM60I-303
81TCM60I-382
81TCM60I-474
82BasCarN-5
82GSGalAG-16
83YanASFY-27
84OCoandSI-28
85GeoSteM-6
85Woo-24
86SpoDesJM-5
86TCMSupS-9
86TCMSupS-32
86Top-405
86TopTif-405
87K-M-7
87Yan196T-8
88PacLegI-89
89CMCMan-6
89CMCMan-10
90AGFA-10
90HOFStiB-63
90RinPosYMP-11
91RinPos1Y2-1
92YanWIZ6-79
92YanWIZA-44
94TedWil-139
94TedWilM-M27
94TedWilRM-ES1
94TedWilRM-ES2
94TedWilRM-ES3
94TedWilRM-ES4
94TedWilRM-ES5
94TedWilRM-ES6
94TedWilRM-ES7
94TedWilRM-ES8
94TedWilRM-ES9
94UppDecTAE-67
94Yoo-9
96StaCluMa-MM12
97TopMan-36
97TopManF-36
97TopManFR-36

Markert, Jim
86PenWhiSP-16
88BirBarB-5

Markert, Josh
95YakBeaTI-18

Markham, Andy
94BurBeeC-15
94BurBeeF-1079

Markham, Bobby
80WesHavWCT-12

Markham, Dan
92GulCoaDF-3562
93GreFalDSP-3

Markiewicz, Brandon
91BoiHawC-18
91BoiHawP-3887
92QuaCitRBC-5
92QuaCitRBF-819
93CedRapKC-13
93CedRapKF-1747
94BoiHawC-18
94BoiHawF-3364
94LakElsSC-12
94LakElsSF-1672

Markland, Gene
50WorWidGV-37

Markle, Cliff
22E120-175
22W573-74

Markley, Scot
86AshTouP-18
87OscAstP-23

Marks, John
82CliGiaF-28
83WisRapTF-26

Marks, Lance
91PulBraC-9
91PulBraP-4015
92MacBraC-3
92MacBraF-276
92ProFS7-193
93DurBulC-13
93DurBulF-493
93DurBulTI-23

Markulike, Joe
90IdaFalBP-3253

Marlin, Billy the
93MarFloA-2
93MarPub-29
94MasMan-2

Marlina, Mario
89PalSprACLC-37

Marlins, Florida
92DonBonC-BC8
92HitTheBB-14
93TedWilPC-11
94BreCouMC-29B
94ImpProP-19
94Sco-651
94ScoGolR-651
95PanSti-137
96PanSti-13
94ElmPioC-29A

Marlowe, Dick
53TigGle-21
55Bow-91

Marn, Kevin
96BilMusTI-20

Marnell, Dean
96PorRocB-22

Marois, Jean
43ParSpo-52

Marone, Lou
70Top-703
71MLBOffS-206

Maropis, Pete
76AppFoxT-14

Marotta, Chris
95StCatSTI-33

Marquard, Rube (Richard)
08AmeCarE-51
09AmeCarE-73
09ColChiE-178
09MaxPubP-5
09SpoNewSM-72
09T206-225
09T206-226
09T206-227
10CouT21-41
10CouT21-175
10CouT21-176
10CouT21-177
10CouT21-178
10CouT21-299
10CouT21-300
10DomDisP-75
10PeoT21-36
10RedCroT-45
10RedCroT-46
10RedCroT-133
10RedCroT-216
10RedCroT-217
10SweCapPP-116
11L1L-111
11PloCanE-43
11S74Sil-87
11S81LarS-86
11T205-108
12ColRedB-178
12ColTinT-178
12HasTriFT-48F
12HasTriFT-74E
12PhiCarE-19
12T207-113
12T22SeroC-4
13NatGamW-27
13PolGroW-16
13TomBarW-26
14CraJacE-43
14FatPlaT-30
14TexTomE-57
15AmeCarE-26
15CraJacE-43
15SpoNewM-110
15SpoNewP-6
16BF2FP-60
16ColE13-108
16FleBreD-61
16SpoNewM-113
22E120-129
22W572-60
22W575-75
23W503-37
23WilChoV-88
26SpoComoA-29
69SCFOldT-2
72LauGreF-14
76ShaPiz-124
77GalGloG-158
79DiaGre-26
80PerHaloFP-124
80SSPHOF-124
81ConTSN-45
82OhiHaloF-57
86ConSer1-27
89DodSmoG-19
89HOFStiB-66
90BasWit-91
90DodTar-483
90PerGreM-30
91ConTSN-252
92ConTSN-342
92ConTSNCI-6
93CraJac-9
94ConTSN-1015
94ConTSNB-1015
96PitPosH-9

Marquardt, Chuck
89GasRanP-1010
91ButCopKSP-28
93EriSaiC-30

Marquardt, John
84MadMusP-12
85HunStaJ-18
86OrlTwiP-11

Marquardt, Scott
93JohCitCC-13
93JohCitCF-3673
94SavCarC-17
94SavCarF-503

Marquess, Mark
88TopTra-65T
88TopTraT-65T

Marquez, Edgar
88MyrBeaBJP-1170
88St.CatBJP-2025
90St.CatBJP-3455
93LinVenB-117

Marquez, Edwin
86QuaCitAP-21
87MidAngP-12
88EdmTraC-19
88EdmTraP-575
89EdmTraC-13
89EdmTraP-552
90Bes-109
90CMC-62
90IndIndC-12
90IndIndP-301
90JacExpB-29
90ProAAAF-584
94VenLinU-96
95LinVen-235

Marquez, Gonzalo
73OPC-605
73Top-605
74OPC-422
74Top-422
76VenLeaS-91
80VenLeaS-98

Marquez, Ishovany
92BluOriC-6
92BluOriF-2358
92KanCouCC-23
92KanCouCF-89

Marquez, Isidrio
89SanAntMB-16
90SanAntMGS-17
91SanAntMP-2970
93SanAntMF-3000
94NasSouF-1248
95NasSouTI-13

Marquez, Jesus
93AppFoxC-16
93AppFoxF-2474
93LinVenB-197
94VenLinU-103
95LinVen-175
96LanJetB-17

Marquez, Luis
83Bra53F-29

Marquez, Robert
96DelShoB-21

Marquis, Jason
97Bow-401
97BowChr-265
97BowChrI-265
97BowChrIR-265
97BowChrR-265
97BowInt-401
97Top-274

Marquis, Roger
91OriCro-276

Marr, Alan
83CliGiaF-18
85EveGiaC-8

Marr, Charles
87OldJudN-322

Marrero, Conrado
51Bow-206
52Top-317
53Bri-9
53Top-13
54Bow-200
67TopVen-188
83TopRep5-317
91TopArc1-13

Marrero, Elieser
94SavCarC-18
94SavCarF-508
94SouAtlLAF-SAL50
95Bow-172
95Exc-269
96ArkTraB-17
96Bow-238
96TexLeaAB-12
97Bow-93
97Bow98ROY-ROY12
97BowBes-112
97BowBesAR-112
97BowBesMI-MI4
97BowBesMIAR-MI4
97BowBesMIARI-MI4
97BowBesMII-MI4
97BowBesMIR-MI4
97BowBesMIRI-MI4
97BowBesR-112
97BowCerBIA-CA51
97BowCerGIA-CA51
97BowChr-117
97BowChr1RC-ROY12
97BowChr1RCR-ROY12
97BowChrI-117
97BowChrIR-117
97BowChrR-117
97BowInt-93
97ColCho-477
97FlaShoWotF-23
97Fle-559
97FleTif-559
97Ult-549
97UltGolME-549
97UltPlaME-549

Marrero, Kenny
91EriSaiC-8
91EriSaiP-4073
92BriTigC-17
92BriTigF-1416
93NiaFalRF-3394
94JamJamC-14
94JamJamF-3960
96LakTigB-17

Marrero, Oreste
88BlaYNPRWL-41
89BelBreIS-15
89Sta-5
90BelBreB-18
90BelBreS-12
90Bes-292
91Cla/Bes-194
91StoPorC-6
91StoPorP-3040
92ElPasDS-218
92SkyAA F-95
92StoPorF-41
93HarSenF-276
94OttLynF-2904
94Pac-385
95SanAntMTI-28
97Pac-333
97PacLigB-333
97PacSil-333

Marrero, Roger
89AubAstP-2181

Marrero, Vilato
88BlaYNPRWL-42
89BelBreIS-16
89BelBreIS-20
90BelBreB-12
90BelBreS-13
90Bes-172
91StoPorC-21
91StoPorP-3041

Marrett, Scott
86PalSprAP-13
86PalSprAP-21
87SanBerSP-15

Marriott, Bill
90DodTar-484

Marris, Moose (Mark)
87OneYanP-26
88PriWilYS-16
89PriWilCS-12
91Ft.LauYC-7
91Ft.LauYP-2421

Marrow, Buck
34DiaMatCSB-125
90DodTar-485

Marrs, Terry
87ElmPio(C-10
88ElmPioC-22
89WinHavRSS-14

Marsans, Armando
12T207-114
14CraJacE-134
14TexTomE-29
15CraJacE-134
15SpoNewM-111
16ColE13-109
95ConTSN-1379

Marsh, Frank
93NegLeaRL2-24

Marsh, Freddie (Fred)
49SolSunP-7
52Top-8
53Top-240
54Top-218
55OriEss-14
55Top-13
55TopDouH-39
56Top-23
83TopRep5-8
91OriCro-277
91TopArc1-240
94TopArc1-218
94TopArc1G-218

Marsh, Quinn
88GreHorP-1552
89CedRapRB-4
89CedRapRP-929

89CedRapRS-10
90SalSpuCLC-124
90SalSpuP-2721
Marsh, Randy
88T/MUmp-43
89T/MUmp-41
89T/MUmp-60
90T/MUmp-39
Marsh, Roy
94AubAstC-7
94AubAstF-3770
94StaCluDP-66
94StaCluDPFDI-66
Marsh, Tom
88BatCliP-1676
89SpaPhiP-1047
89SpaPhiS-15
90ReaPhiB-23
90ReaPhiP-1233
90ReaPhiS-18
90SpaPhiB-28
90SpaPhiP-2495
90SpaPhiS-15
91LinDriAA-514
91ReaPhiLD-514
91ReaPhiP-1383
92DonRoo-66
92PhiMed-43
92ScrRedBS-488
93Fle-494
93Pin-256
93Sco-263
93ScrRedBF-2556
93ScrRedBTI-17
93StaClu-466
93StaCluFDI-466
93StaCluMOP-466
93Top-649
93TopGol-649
93TopInaM-649
93TopMic-649
94ScoRoo-RT147
94ScoRooGR-RT147
94Ult-552
95Pac-333
95PacPri-110
95ScrRedBTI-20
96BufBisB-15
96Fle-503
96FleTif-503
96Pac-156
Marsh, Trent
89StoPorS-26
Marshall, Bret
89SouBenWSGS-13
Marshall, Charlie
50WorWidGV-35
Marshall, Clarence
43CenFlo-18
52NatTeaL-17
52Top-174
83TopRep5-174
Marshall, Dave
69Top-464A
69Top-464B
70OPC-58
70Top-58
71MLBOffS-159
71OPC-259
71Top-259
72MilBra-205
72Top-673
73OPC-513
73Top-513
77PadSchC-36
91MetWIZ-247
Marshall, Doc (William R.)
09T206-228
10CouT21-42
11SpoLifCW-234
Marshall, Gary
96RocCubTI-18
Marshall, George
48BabRutS-12
Marshall, Jason
92EugEmeC-17
92EugEmeF-3036
93LetMouF-4152
93LetMouSP-12
93WilBluRC-18
93WilBluRF-2006
94WilBluRF-306
95WicWraTI-6
Marshall, Jim (R. James)
52MotCoo-9
58Top-441
59Top-153
59TopVen-153
60Top-267
61Top-188
62Top-337
73WicAerKSB-9
74OPC-354
74Top-354
75OPC-638
75Top-638
76OPC-277
76SSP-308
76Top-277
80Top-96
84NasSouTI-13
86BufBisP-17
91MetWIZ-248
91OriCro-278
91PacSenL-54
91PacSenL-127
91PacSenL-133
Marshall, John
88MarPhiS-26
89SanDieSAS-16
89SpaPhiP-1045
89SpaPhiS-16
89Sta-56
Marshall, Keith
75OmaRoyTI-10
76IndIndTI-19
Marshall, Max
40SolHug-13
47SmiClo-22
Marshall, Mike A.
79LodDodT-6
81AlbDukT-16
82AlbDukT-22
82DodUniOV-11
82Don-562
82Fle-13
82Top-681
83DodPol-5
83DodPos-8
83Don-362
83Fle-211
83OPC-324
83Top-324
84AllGamPI-58
84DodPol-5
84Don-348
84Fle-105
84FunFooP-64
84Nes792-634
84OPC-52
84Top-634
84TopSti-85
84TopTif-634
85AllGamPI-148
85DodCokP-20
85Don-12
85Don-296
85DonActA-22
85DonSupD-12
85Fle-377
85Lea-12
85OPC-85
85Top-85
85TopSti-72
85TopTif-85
86BasStaB-69
86DodCokP-18
86DodPol-5
86DodUniOP-13
86Don-52
86Dra-8
86Fle-137
86FleMin-30
86FleStiC-71
86Lea-40
86OPC-26
86SevCoi-W11
86Spo-89
86Top-728
86TopSti-71
86TopTat-17
86TopTif-728
87DodMot-5
87DodPol-3
87DodSmoA-21
87Don-176
87DonOpeD-77
87Fle-446
87FleGlo-446
87FleLimE-25
87OPC-186
87RedFolSB-31
87SevCoi-W8
87Spo-82
87SpoTeaP-14
87StuPan-6
87Top-664
87TopSti-66
87TopTif-664
88DodMot-5
88DodPol-5
88DodSmo-16
88DodSmo-29
88Don-229
88DonBasB-178
88Fle-522
88FleGlo-522
88OPC-249
88PanSti-315
88Sco-135
88ScoGlo-135
88Spo-220
88StaLinD-11
88Top-249
88TopBig-133
88TopSti-69
88TopTif-249
89Bow-350
89BowTif-350
89DodMot-5
89DodPol-4
89DodSmoG-101
89DodStaSV-4
89Don-110
89Don-552
89DonBasB-204
89DonGraS-2
89Fle-66
89FleBasM-25
89FleGlo-66
89FleGlo-WS7
89FleWorS-7
89OPC-323
89PanSti-108
89Sco-186
89Spo-54
89Top-582
89TopBasT-138
89TopBig-48
89TopCoi-18
89TopSti-67
89TopTif-582
89TopUKM-48
89TVSpoM-35
89UppDec-70
89Woo-26
90Bow-132
90BowTif-132
90ClaYel-T57
90DodTar-486
90Don-84
90Fle-401
90FleCan-401
90Lea-224
90MetColP-19
90MetKah-6
90OPC-198
90PanSti-272
90PubSti-13
90Sco-384
90Top-198
90TopSti-62
90TopTif-198
90TopTra-67T
90TopTraT-67T
90TopTVM-27
90UppDec-262
90UppDec-781
90VenSti-317
91Don-625
91Fle-102
91MetWIZ-249
91OPC-356
91Sco-617
91StaClu-226
91Top-356
91TopDesS-356
91TopMic-356
91TopTif-356
91Ult-35
91UppDec-681
92DodStaTA-23
Marshall, Mike G.
68CokCapT-3
68Top-201
68TopVen-201
69OPC-17
69PilPos-29
69Top-17
71ExpPS-13
71MLBOffS-133
71OPC-713
71Top-713
72Dia-28
72OPC-505
72Top-505
73OPC-355
73Top-355
73TopCanL-30
74OPC-73
74OPC-208
74Top-73
74Top-208
74TopSta-57
74TopTra-73T
75Kel-36
75OPC-6
75OPC-313
75OPC-330
75Top-6
75Top-313
75Top-330
76LinSup-122
76OPC-465
76Top-465
77Spo-4103
77Top-263
79TwiFriP-16
82Fle-532
83Pil69G-6
86ExpGreT-11
87AstShowSTh-12
87DodSmoA-20
89DodSmoG-84
90DodTar-487
90HOFStiB-79
91MetWIZ-246
92DodStaTA-13
93ExpDonM-25
93RanKee-244
Marshall, Monte
96GreFalDTI-24
Marshall, Randy
89ButCopKSP-20
89FayGenP-1581
90FayGenP-2404
90GasRanB-18
90GasRanP-2528
90GasRanS-13
90ProAaA-83
91GasRanC-19
91GasRanP-2696
91LinDriAA-391
91LonTigLD-391
91LonTigP-1876
92TidTidF-892
92TidTidS-562
92TriA AAS-562
94ColSprSSF-729
95TolMudHTI-19
96TolMudHB-17
Marshall, Steve
89CarNewE-2
Marshall, Todd
92SpoIndC-6
92SpoIndF-1290
Marshall, Willard
47Exh-149
47HomBon-33
47TipTop-130
48Bow-13
49Bow-48
49EurSta-118
50Bow-73
50Dra-17
50JJKCopP-9
50RoyDes-17
51Bow-98
51R42SmaS-65
52Bow-97
52Top-96
53BowC-58
53Top-95
54Bow-70
55Bow-131
75JohMiz-1
76TayBow4-107
79DiaGre-43
79TCM50-124
83TCMPla1942-33
83TopRep5-96
84FifNatC-8
91TopArc1-95
Marsland, David
93MisStaB-32
Marsonek, Sam
97Bow-305
97BowInt-305
Marsters, Brandon
96BatCliTI-6
Marte, Alexis
83KinBluJTI-14
84VisOakT-4
85DomLeaS-174
85OrlTwiT-7
86TolMudHP-16
87PorBeaP-17
89TulDriTI-14
Marte, Damaso
95EveAqaTI-12
96WisTimRB-14
Marte, Pedro
93WatIndC-17
93WatIndF-3577
94ColRedF-456
Marte, Roberto
86EriCarP-18
87EriCarP-10
88SavCarP-341
89SprCarB-21
91EriSaiC-26
91EriSaiP-4086
Marte, Vic
78ChaPirT-15
Martel, Ed
87OneYanP-30
88OneYanP-2040
89Ft.LauYS-15
90PriWilCTI-14
91AlbYanLD-11
91AlbYanP-1004
91LinDriAA-11
92Bow-607
92ColCliF-347
92ColCliP-6
92ColCliS-109
92DonRoo-67
92LeaGolR-BC14
92ProFS7-112
92SkyAAAF-49
Martel, Jay
87SavCarP-7
Marten, Greg
93Sou-2
Marten, Tom
88KenTwiP-1405
Marteniz, Ivan
88WytCubP-1995
Martes, Sixto
84EveGiaC-14
Martig, Rich
86ModA'sC-14
86ModA'sP-19
Martin, Al
86SumBraP-17
87SumBraP-24
88BurBraP-19
88MidLeaAGS-19
89DurBullS-15
89DurBulTI-15
90Bes-220
90GreBraB-17
90GreBraP-1141
90TopMag-102
91GreBraC-23
91GreBraLD-211
91GreBraP-3015
91LinDriAA-211
91RicBraBC-27
92BufBisBS-11
92BufBisF-333
92BufBisS-35
92DonRoo-68
92FleUpd-114
93Bow-246
93DiaMar-67
93Don-716
93Fin-155
93FinRef-155
93Fla-114

93FleFinE-113
93Lea-189
93OPCPre-57
93PacSpa-587
93Pin-614
93PirHil-6
93PirNatI-15
93Sco-322
93ScoBoyoS-27
93SelRoo-47T
93StaClu-579
93StaCluFDI-579
93StaCluMOP-579
93Stu-159
93Top-623
93TopGol-623
93TopInaM-623
93TopMic-623
93TriPla-242
93Ult-451
93UltAllR-5
93UppDec-340
93UppDecGold-340
94Bow-330
94ColC-187
94ColChoGS-187
94ColChoSS-187
94Don-494
94ExtBas-348
94ExtBasSYS-11
94Fin-11
94FinJum-11
94FinRef-11
94Fla-217
94Fle-612
94FleRooS-11
94FUnPac-76
94Lea-49
94LeaL-141
94OPC-241
94Pac-500
94Pin-211
94PinArtP-211
94PinMusC-211
94PirQui-13
94Sco-546
94ScoGolR-546
94Sel-50
94StaClu-6
94StaCluFDI-6
94StaCluGR-6
94StaCluMOP-6
94StaCluP-6
94Stu-147
94Top-366
94TopGol-366
94TopSpa-366
94TriPla-186
94Ult-257
94UppDec-243
94UppDecED-243
94USPlaCR-5H
94USPlaCR-7D
94USPlaCR-11C
95ColCho-381
95ColChoGS-381
95ColChoSS-381
95Don-147
95DonDiaK-DK26
95DonPreP-147
95DonTopotO-319
95Emo-176
95Fla-187
95Fle-483
95Lea-364
95LeaLim-135
95Pac-347
95Pin-275
95PinArtP-275
95PinMusC-275
95PirFil-19
95RedFol-30
95Sco-380
95ScoGolR-380
95ScoPlaTS-380
95Sel-3
95SelArtP-3
95StaClu-218
95StaClu-253
95StaCluFDI-218
95StaCluFDI-253
95StaCluMOP-218
95StaCluMOP-253
95StaCluSTWS-218
95StaCluSTWS-253
95Stu-163
95Top-51
95Ult-424
95UltGolM-424
95UppDec-383
95UppDecED-383
95UppDecEDG-383
95UppDecSE-219
95UppDecSEG-219
96Cir-174
96CirRav-174
96ColCho-682
96ColChoGS-682
96ColChoSS-682
96Don-127
96DonPreP-127
96EmoXL-257
96Fla-350
96Fle-526
96FleTif-526
96Lea-201
96LeaPrePB-201
96LeaPrePG-201
96LeaPrePS-201
96LeaSig-131
96LeaSigA-143
96LeaSigAG-143
96LeaSigAS-143
96LeaSigPPG-131
96LeaSigPPP-131
96MetUni-217
96MetUniP-217
96Pac-180
96PanSti-71
96ProSta-94
96Sco-123
96StaClu-26
96StaCluMOP-26
96Stu-94
96StuPrePB-94
96StuPrePG-94
96StuPrePS-94
96TeaOut-54
96Top-53
96Ult-266
96UltGolM-266
96UppDec-434
97Bow-30
97BowBes-36
97BowBesAR-36
97BowBesR-36
97BowChr-26
97BowChrI-26
97BowChrIR-26
97BowChrR-26
97BowInt-30
97Cir-354
97CirRav-354
97ColCho-435
97Don-211
97DonLim-166
97DonLim-192
97DonLimLE-166
97DonLimLE-192
97DonPre-70
97DonPreCttC-70
97DonPreP-211
97DonPrePGold-211
97Fin-6
97FinRef-6
97FlaSho-A93
97FlaSho-B93
97FlaSho-C93
97FlaShoLC-93
97FlaShoLC-B93
97FlaShoLC-C93
97FlaShoLCM-A93
97FlaShoLCM-B93
97FlaShoLCM-C93
97Fle-432
97FleTif-432
97Lea-134
97LeaFraM-134
97LeaFraMDC-134
97MetUni-240
97Pac-399
97PacLigB-399
97PacPri-136
97PacPriLB-136
97PacPriP-136
97PacSil-399
97PinX-P-86
97PinX-PMoS-86
97ProMag-33
97ProMagML-33
97Sco-282
97ScoPreS-282
97ScoShoS-282
97ScoShoSAP-282
97SP-142
97SpoIll-106
97SpoIllEE-106
97StaClu-316
97StaCluMOP-316
97Stu-90
97StuPrePG-90
97StuPrePS-90
97Top-356
97TopChr-121
97TopChrR-121
97TopGal-129
97TopGalPPI-129
97Ult-264
97UltGolME-264
97UltPlaME-264
97UppDec-460

Martin, Andy (Andrew)
92HamRedC-11
92HamRedF-1601
94MadHatC-14
94MadHatF-142

Martin, Ariel
93HunCubC-18
93HunCubF-3242

Martin, Babe (Boris)
49Bow-167
96Bro194F-21

Martin, Billy (Alfred)
47StaPinP2-24
48SigOil-17
48SmiClo-17
49RemBre-17
52BerRos-38
52Top-175
53BowC-93
53BowC-118
53Dor-130
53Top-86
54Bow-145
54RedHeaF-19
54Top-13
56Top-181
57Top-62
57YanJayP-8
58Top-271
59Ind-10
59Kah-20
59TigGraASP-12
59Top-295
60Kah-24
60Top-173
60TopVen-173
61Pos-190A
61Pos-190B
61Top-89
61TopMagR-26
62Jel-84
62Pos-84
62PosCan-84
62SalPlaC-43
62ShiPlaC-43
62Top-208
69Top-547
69TwiTealC-7
71OPC-208
71Top-208
72OPC-33
72OPC-34
72Top-33
72Top-34
73OPC-323
73TigJew-12
73Top-323
74OPC-379
74Top-379
75OPC-511
75Top-511
76BooProC-15
76SSP-453
76Top-17
77Spo-8309
77Top-387
77YanBurK-1
78SSP270-14
78Top-721
78TwiFri-10
78YanBurK-1
78YanSSPD-14
79TCM50-143
79YanPicA-24
81A'sGraG-1
81Don-479
81Fle-581
81TCM60I-364
81TigDetN-67
81TigDetN-107
81Top-671
82A'sGraG-9
82Don-491
82TopSti-115
83Don-575
83TigAlKS-15
83TigAlKS-16
83TigAlKS-43
83Top-156
83TopRep5-175
83TopTra-66T
83YanASFY-28
83YanYealT-5
84Fle-652
84Nes792-81
84OCoandSI-65
84Top-81
84TopTif-81
85PolMet-Y6
85TopTifT-78T
85TopTra-78T
86TCMSupS-17
86Top-651
86TopTif-651
87A'sMot-23
90YanScoNW-30
91ScoMan-1
91TopArc1-86
92BazQua5A-8
92PinMan-26
92RevLeg1-13
92RevLeg1-14
92RevLeg1-15
92YanWIZA-45
93ActPacA-140
93RanKee-245
93UppDecAH-88
93UppDecAH-141
93UppDecS-25
94TedWil-61
94TopArc1-13
94TopArc1G-13
94UppDecAH-99
94UppDecAH1-99

Martin, Chandler
96AshTouB-25

Martin, Chris
88KenTwiP-1397
91HarSenLD-263
91HarSenP-634
91LinDriAA-263
92Bow-493
92ClaFS7-126
92HarSenF-467
92HarSenS-289
92SkyAA F-122
92UppDecML-235
93HarSenF-277
94OttLynF-2905
94UppDecML-104

Martin, Darryl
87FayGenP-10
89FayGenP-1585
89SouAtlLAGS-39
90LakTigS-19
93CenValRC-17
93CenValRF-2906

Martin, Derrell
61UniOil-S6

Martin, Doug
91NiaFalRC-23
91NiaFalRP-3630
92NiaFalRF-3319

Martin, Eric
94EveGiaC-20
94EveGiaF-3668

Martin, Francine
91HawWomS-7

Martin, Fred
46SeaSLP-34
79TCM50-121

Martin, Gene
70Top-599
79TCMJapPB-51
90GreBraS-13
90SumBraB-11
90SumBraP-2446

Martin, Gregg
89St.CatBJP-2070
90MyrBeaBJP-2773
90ProAaA-91
91Cla/Bes-193
91DunBluJC-6
91DunBluJP-202
92MyrBeaHF-2194

Martin, Herschel
39PlaBal-12
40PlaBal-100
46RemBre-5
47RemBre-12
47SigOil-50
83TCMPla1944-9

Martin, J.C. (Joseph C.)
60Lea-92
60Top-346
60Top-407
61Top-124
61TopStal-124
61WhiSoxTS-10
62WhiSoxJP-8
62Top-91
62TopStal-27
62TopVen-91
62WhiSoxTS-13
63Top-499
63WhiSoxTS-16
64Top-148
64TopVen-148
64WhiSoxTS-16
65Top-382
65WhiSoxJP-3
66OPC-47
66Top-47
66TopVen-47
67Top-538
68Top-211
68TopVen-211
69MilBra-166
69OPC-112
69Top-112
69TopFou-17
70OPC-308
70OPC-488
70Top-308
70Top-488
71MLBOffS-37
71OPC-704
71Top-704
72MilBra-206
72Top-639
73OPC-552
73Top-552
73WicAerKSB-8
74OPC-354
74Top-354
81TCM60I-419
81TCM60I-438
85WhiSoxC-22
89RinPosM1-22
91MetWIZ-250
94Met69CCPP-23
94Met69CS-22
94Met69T-19

Martin, Jake
56Top-129

Martin, James
51BerRos-A15
92GreFalDSP-25
92OklStaC-19
95AusFut-69
95SanAntMTI-45

Martin, Jared
80WicAerT-16
82IowCubT-7

Martin, Jeff
93EveGiaC-17
93EveGiaF-3766
93LynRedSC-18
93LynRedSF-2519
94CliLumF-1977
94LynRedSC-17
94LynRedSF-1895
95Exc-291
95TreThuTI-18
96HonShaHWB-21
96SanJosGB-14
96WilBluRB-14
94CliLumC-14

Martin, Jerry

92GulCoaRSP-8
93ChaRaiC-11
93ChaRaiF-1906
94ChaRanF-2494
94FloStaLAF-FSL3
95Bow-122
95Exc-130
95TulDriTI-12
96TulDriTI-17
Martin, Jerry Lindsey
76SSP-475
77Top-596
78PhiSSP-51
78SSP270-51
78Top-222
79Top-382
80OPC-256
80Top-493
81AllGamPI-152
81Don-555A
81Don-555B
81Fle-295
81OPC-103
81Top-103
81TopScr-98
81TopTra-798
82Don-298
82Fle-394
82Roy-12
82Top-722
82TopTra-65T
83Don-138
83Fle-117
83OPC-309
83Roy-15
83Top-626
84FleUpd-74
84Nes792-74
84Top-74
84TopTif-74
84TopTra-74T
84TopTraT-74T
85Top-517
85TopTif-517
89PacSenL-6
89PacSenL-197
89TopSenL-14
91MetWIZ-251
91PacSenL-14
Martin, Jim
91SalLakTP-3226
91SalLakTSP-14
92AugPirF-234
93BakDodCLC-17
93SalBucC-15
93SalBucF-428
Martin, Joey
75LafDriT-3
76PhoGiaCa-17
76PhoGiaVNB-15
77PhoGiaCC-17
77PhoGiaCP-17
77PhoGiaVNB-17
Martin, John A.
87LouRedTI-19
88LouRedBTI-32
Martin, John Robert
77AppFoxT-14
80EvaTriT-14
81Car5x7-17
82Don-343
82Fle-121
82LouRedE-15
82Top-236
83Car-18
83Don-617
83St.PetCT-9
83Top-721
84ArkTraT-17
84Nes792-24
84Top-24
84TopTif-24
86ArkTraP-13
88LouRedBC-3
88LouRedBP-423
89ScrRedBC-3
89ScrRedBP-719
90ClePhiS-27
91LinDriAA-509
91ReaPhiLD-509
91ReaPhiP-1387
92BatCliF-3283
95PiePhiF-203
96PieBolWB-2
Martin, Jon
90WelPirP-4
Martin, Justin
88BenBucL-25
89QuaCitAB-11
90QuaCitAGS-9
91QuaCitAC-8
91QuaCitAP-2625
Martin, Lefty
49EurSta-40
Martin, Lincoln
93BluOriC-18
93BluOriF-4133
94FreKeyF-2621
94OriPro-59
96CarLeaA1B-16
96CarLeaA2B-16
96FreKeyB-13
94FreKeyC-17
Martin, Mark
87IdaFalBP-4
88OneYanP-2068
Martin, Matt
91BilMusP-3763
91BilMusSP-8
92BonMucSP-27
92BilMusF-3365
93WesVirWC-18
93WesVirWF-2875
94WinSpiC-16
94WinSpiF-281
95BilRedTI-29
96BilMusTI-21
Martin, Mike
81VerBeaDT-12
82AmaGolST-9
83BeaGolGT-1
84LasVegSC-227
85VanCanC-217
86PitCubP-15
93BazTeaU-20
93TopTra-128T
94JamJamC-15
94JamJamF-3973
94JohCitCC-19
94JohCitCF-3699
95AusFut-7
96CliLumKTI-19
Martin, Morrie (Morris)
52Top-131
53BowBW-53
53Top-227
54Bow-179
54Top-168
58Top-53A
58Top-53B
59Top-38
59TopVen-38
82Bow195E-256
83TopRep5-131
90DodTar-488
91OriCro-279
91TopArc1-227
94TopArc1-168
94TopArc1G-168
Martin, Norberto
87ChaWheP-25
88TamTarS-15
90CMC-648
90ProAAAF-173
90VanCanC-21
90VanCanP-495
91Bow-346
91LinDriAAA-640
91VanCanLD-640
91VanCanP-1603
92SkyAAAF-287
92VanCanF-2732
92VanCanS-644
93LimRocDWB-34
93NasSouF-578
94FleUpd-29
94LeaLimR-23
94NasSouF-1257
94Pac-132
94Pin-228
94PinArtP-228
94PinMusC-228
94ScoRoo-RT131
94ScoRooGR-RT131
94Spo-161
94StaCluT-139
94StaCluTFDI-139
94Top-527
94TopGol-527
94TopSpa-527
94WhiSoxK-20
95ColCho-508
95ColChoGS-508
95ColChoSS-508
95Don-165
95DonPreP-165
95Fle-124
95Pac-93
95Sco-503
95ScoGolR-503
95ScoPlaTS-503
95Top-258
95Ult-275
95UltGolM-275
95WhiSoxK-19
96Fle-71
96FleTif-71
96LeaSigA-144
96LeaSigAG-144
96LeaSigAS-144
96Ult-333
96UltGolM-333
97Pac-57
97PacLigB-57
97PacSil-57
Martin, Pepper (John Leonard)
30SchR33-36
32OrbPinNP-21
32OrbPinUP-46
33ButCre-18
33DelR33-17
33Gou-62
33GouCanV-62
33NatLeaAC-17
33TatOrb-46
33TatOrbSDR-159
34BatR31-7
34BatR31-125
34ButPreR-43
34DiaStaR-26
34ExhFou-8
35ExhFou-8
35GolMedFR-9
35GouPuzR-4F
35GouPuzR-7F
35GouPuzR-12F
35WheBB1-20A
35WheBB1-20B
36GouBWR-21
36GouWidPPR-A70
36NatChiFPR-54
36R31PasP-16
36R31Pre-G12
36WheBB3-8
37WheBB14-9
37WheBB7-29F
37WheBB9-11
59OklTodML-11
60Fle-80A
60Fle-80B
68LauWorS-28
70FleWorS-28
71FleWorS-29
74Car193T-17
74NewYorNTDiS-28
77GalGloG-66
77GalGloG-203
80PacLeg-106
81ConTSN-24
83ConMar-31
84OCoandSI-143
86ConSer1-22
87Car193T-3
88ConNatA-14
88ConSer3-18
91ConTSN-274
92CarMcD-12
92ConTSN-637
93ActPacA-132
93ConTSN-680
93ConTSNP-991
94ConTSN-991
94ConTSN-1108
94ConTSNB-991
94ConTSNB-1108
Martin, R. Hollis
81VerBeaDT-11
Martin, Renie
79RoyTeal-5
80Top-667
81Don-103
81Fle-39
81OPC-266
81Top-452
82Don-238
82Fle-414
82Top-594
82TopTra-66T
83Don-272
83Fle-267
83Top-263
84Don-445
84Fle-381
84GiaPos-15
84Nes792-603
84Top-603
84TopTif-603
85OmaRoyT-14
86OmaRoyP-14
91PacSenL-65
Martin, Rep. (Joe)
59FleWil-78
Martin, Russ
87JamExpP-2538
Martin, Ryan
94DanBraC-17
94DanBraF-3535
95DanBraTI-17
Martin, Sam
81BatTroT-17
82WatIndF-21
82WatIndT-17
83SprCarF-4
Martin, Speed (Elwood)
21E121So1-57
23W501-55
Martin, Steve
82VerBeaDT-8
85AlbDukC-172
Martin, Steve W.
89SpoIndSP-18
90Bes-209
90CMC-878
90WatDiaB-10
90WatDiaP-2385
91Bow-662
91Cla/Bes-85
91HigDesMC-25
91HigDesMP-2408
92HagSunS-263
92WicWraF-3668
Martin, Stuart
37ExhFou-8
38ExhFou-8
43CubTeal-14
79DiaGre-157
Martin, Todd
90UtiBluSP-2
Martin, Tom (Thomas)
89BluOriS-15
90Bes-178
90WauTimB-4
90WauTimP-2117
90WauTimS-16
91KanCouCC-7
91KanCouCP-2655
91KanCouCTI-12
92HigDesMC-24
92WatDiaF-2140
93RanCucQC-20
93RanCucQF-831
94GreBraF-410
94GreBraTI-16
96JacGenB-18
Martin, Tony
77LodDodT-10
Martin, Troy
91SydWavF-4
Martin, Vic
83ChaLooT-7
86CalCanP-13
Martindale, Denzel
77St.PetCT-5
Martindale, Ryan
88MisStaB-17
91WatIndC-13
91WatIndP-3368
92KinIndC-2
92KinIndF-2479
93CanIndF-2842
94CanIndF-3121
Martineau, Brian
95HudValRTI-19
Martineau, Paul Peter
86JamExpP-15
Martineau, Yves
92IdaFalGF-3509
92IdaFalGSP-27
93IdaFalBF-4026
93IdaFalBSP-3
Martinez, Abraham
89BlaYNPRWL-132
Martinez, Angel
88ModA'sTI-24
88VerBeaDS-14
89MadMusS-14
91MedHatBJP-4104
91MedHatBJSP-2
92MedHatBJF-3210
92MedHatBJSP-6
93HagSunC-19
93HagSunF-1883
94Bow-141
94Cla-7
94DunBluJC-18
94DunBluJF-2561
94FloStaLAF-FSL7
95Bow-216
95BowBes-B81
95BowBesR-B81
95Exc-139
95KnoSmoF-44
95Top-644
95UppDecML-69
96ColCho-13
96ColChoGS-13
96ColChoSS-13
96Sco-227
96UppDec-212
95UppDecMLFS-69
Martinez, Art
84MemChiT-4
86MemChiSTOS-14
86MemChiTOS-14
Martinez, Ben
92MarPhiC-7
92MarPhiF-3072
Martinez, Bert
83TriTriT-20
Martinez, Bill
92RocExpF-2112
Martinez, Buck (John Albert)
70Top-609
71OPC-163
71Top-163
72OPC-332
72Top-332
75OPC-314
75Top-314
76OPC-616
76SSP-165
76Top-616
77Top-46
78Top-571
79Top-243
80Top-477
81Don-444A
81Don-444B
81Fle-526
81Top-56
81TopTra-799
82Don-561
82OPC-314
82Top-314
83Don-178
83Fle-433
83OPC-308
83Top-733
84BluJayFS-24
84Don-612
84Fle-161
84Nes792-179
84OPC-179
84Top-179
84TopTif-179
85BluJayFS-21
85Fle-114
85OPC-119
85OPCPos-13
85Top-673
85TopMin-673
85TopTif-673
86BluJayAF-19
86BluJayFS-24
86Fle-66
86OPC-363
86Top-518
86TopTif-518

87Fle-235
87FleGlo-235
92Nab-24
94BreMilB-151
Martinez, Carlos
86AlbYanT-9
87HawIslP-21
88BirBarB-16
89DonRoo-14
89ScoRoo-103T
89VanCanC-17
89VanCanP-579
90Baz-13
90BirBarDGB-22
90Bow-322
90BowTif-322
90Don-531
90Fle-540
90FleCan-540
90Lea-438
90OPC-461
90PanSti-374
90Sco-314
90Sco100RS-70
90ScoYouSI-35
90Spo-213
90Top-461
90TopBig-116
90TopCoi-20
90TopGloS-9
90TopRoo-19
90TopSti-300
90TopSti-325
90TopTif-461
90ToyRoo-18
90UppDec-347
90WhiSoxC-16
91CanIndLD-89
91CanIndP-987
91Don-465
91Fle-128
91LinDriAA-89
91OPC-156
91PanFreS-312
91Sco-274
91Top-156
91TopDesS-156
91TopMic-156
91TopTif-156
91UppDec-625
92Don-521
92Fle-117
92OPC-280
92Sco-593
92Sco100RS-71
92StaClu-482
92Top-280
92TopGol-280
92TopGolW-280
92TopMic-280
92Ult-52
92UppDec-598
93Don-682
93Fla-196
93Fle-595
93IndWUA-19
93Lea-347
93LinVenB-251
93PacBeiA-6
93PacSpa-98
93SP-124
93StaClu-255
93StaCluFDI-255
93StaCluMOP-255
93Stu-125
93Top-59
93TopGol-59
93TopInaM-59
93TopMic-59
93Ult-188
93UppDec-520
93UppDecGold-520
94Pac-176
94VenLinU-61
95LinVen-222
95LinVen-268
95LinVen-288
95LinVen-289
Martinez, Carmelo
80QuaCitCT-29
83IowCubT-16
84Don-623
84Fle-497
84FleUpd-75
84Nes792-267
84PadMot-20
84Top-267
84TopSti-383
84TopTif-267
84TopTra-75T
84TopTraT-75T
85Don-478
85Fle-40
85OPC-365
85PadMot-24
85Top-558
85TopSti-157
85TopSti-375
85TopTif-558
86Don-324
86Fle-329
86OPC-67
86Top-67
86TopSti-109
86TopTif-67
87DonOpeD-151
87Fle-423
87FleGlo-423
87OPC-348
87PadBohHB-14
87Top-348
87TopTif-348
88Don-287
88Fle-591
88FleGlo-591
88Lea-142
88OPC-148
88PadCok-14
88PadSmo-17
88PanSti-412
88Sco-181
88ScoGlo-181
88StaLinPa-8
88Top-148
88TopBig-238
88TopCoi-47
88TopSti-106
88TopTif-148
89BimBreD-1
89Bow-459
89BowTif-459
89Don-601
89Fle-311
89FleGlo-311
89OPC-332
89PadCok-9
89PadMag-10
89PanSti-204
89Sco-517
89Top-449
89TopBig-11
89TopTif-449
89UppDec-365
90Bow-162
90BowTif-162
90ClaBlu-56
90Don-482
90Fle-162
90FleCan-162
90FleUpd-44
90Lea-448
90OPC-686
90PhiTas-21
90PubSti-54
90Sco-114
90ScoRoo-10T
90Top-686
90TopBig-287
90TopTif-686
90TopTra-68T
90TopTraT-68T
90UppDec-592
90VenSti-318
91Fle-44
91Lea-160
91Lea-467
91OPC-779
91Sco-792
91Top-779
91TopDesS-779
91TopMic-779
91TopTif-779
91UppDec-92
92Sco-686
92UppDec-696
93CalCanF-1178
Martinez, Cesar
92ElmPioC-12
92ElmPioF-1381
93ForLauRSC-18
93ForLauRSFP-1595
96SarRedSB-22
Martinez, Chito
85Ft.MyeRT-16
86MemChiSTOS-15
86MemChiTOS-15
87OmaRoyP-7
88MemChiB-21
89BlaYNPRWLU-36
89MemChiB-12
89MemChiP-1200
89MemChiS-16
90CMC-188
90OmaRoyC-13
90OmaRoyP-77
90ProAAAF-612
91DonRoo-54
91LinDriAAA-458
91RocRedWLD-458
91RocRedWP-1914
91TriA AAGP-AAA40
91UltUpd-2
91UppDecFE-30F
92Bow-19
92Cla1-T56
92Don-558
92Fle-13
92FleRooS-18
92Lea-300
92OPC-479
92OPCPre-77
92Pin-380
92ProFS7-4
92Sco-400
92Sco100RS-76
92StaClu-438
92Top-479
92TopDeb91-117
92TopGol-479
92TopGolW-479
92TopMcD-40
92TopMic-479
92TriPla-192
92Ult-7
92UppDec-672
93Don-221
93Fle-545
93Lea-274
93PacSpa-19
93Pin-214
93Sco-638
93StaClu-362
93StaCluFDI-362
93StaCluMOP-362
93Top-772
93TopGol-772
93TopInaM-772
93TopMic-772
93Ult-141
93UppDec-514
93UppDecGold-514
94ColCliF-2965
94ColCliP-18
Martinez, Christian
83St.PetCT-10
Martinez, Dalvis
93BriTigC-15
93BriTigF-3654
94JamJamC-16
94JamJamF-3974
Martinez, Dave
83QuaCitCT-26
86IowCubP-17
87CubCan-17
87CubDavB-1
87Don-488
87SpoTeaP-22
87TopTra-73T
87TopTraT-73T
88Don-438
88DonBasB-149
88DonTeaBC-438
88ExpPos-12
88Fle-424
88FleGlo-424
88PanSti-266
88Sco-223
88ScoGlo-223
88StaLinCu-5
88Top-439
88TopTif-439
89Bow-370
89BowTif-370
89Don-102
89ExpPos-19
89Fle-384
89FleGlo-384
89OPC-395
89Sco-77
89Top-763
89TopTif-763
89UppDec-444
90Bow-121
90BowTif-121
90Don-452
90DonBesN-79
90ExpPos-22
90Fle-353A
90Fle-353B
90FleCan-353
90Lea-318
90OPC-228
90PanSti-293
90PubSti-180
90Sco-27
90Top-228
90TopSti-71
90TopTif-228
90UppDec-470
90VenSti-319
91Bow-455
91Don-237
91ExpPos-13
91Fle-237
91Lea-8
91OPC-24
91PanFreS-144
91PanSti-66
91Sco-82
91StaClu-346
91Top-24
91TopDesS-24
91TopMic-24
91TopTif-24
91Ult-205
91UppDec-186
92Bow-220
92Don-732
92Fle-485
92Lea-457
92OPC-309
92OPCPre-75
92Pin-397
92RedKah-30
92Sco-501
92ScoRoo-33T
92StaClu-723
92StaCluNC-723
92Top-309
92TopGol-309
92TopGolW-309
92TopMic-309
92TopTra-67T
92TopTraG-67T
92Ult-484
92UppDec-382
92UppDec-784
93Don-534
93Fle-395
93FleFinE-153
93GiaMot-16
93GiaPos-24
93Lea-301
93OPC-172
93OPCPre-22
93PacSpa-613
93Pin-132
93Sco-601
93SelRoo-126T
93StaClu-640
93StaCluFDI-640
93StaCluG-19
93StaCluMOP-640
93Top-671
93TopGol-671
93TopInaM-671
93TopMic-671
93Ult-486
93UppDec-400
93UppDec-700
93UppDecGold-400
93UppDecGold-700
94Don-463
94Fle-695
94GiaAMC-13
94GiaMot-16
94GiaTarBCI-4
94GiaUSPC-5S
94GiaUSPC-11D
94Lea-15
94Pac-550
94StaCluT-15
94StaCluTFDI-15
94Top-174
94TopGol-174
94TopSpa-174
94Ult-293
95HudValRTI-16
95Pac-381
95WhiSoxK-20
96ColCho-499
96ColChoGS-499
96ColChoSS-499
96Don-95
96DonPreP-95
96Fle-72
96FleTif-72
96FleWhiS-11
96Pac-289
96StaClu-398
96StaCluMOP-398
86STaoftFt-8
97ColCho-293
97DonTea-74
97DonTeaSPE-74
97Fle-65
97FleTif-65
97Pac-58
97PacLatotML-7
97PacLigB-58
97PacSil-58
97Sco-447
97ScoHobR-447
97ScoResC-447
97ScoShoS-447
97ScoShoSAP-447
97Top-197
97UppDec-334
Martinez, David
86PalSprAP-22
87AriWilP-10
87MidAngP-2
88MidAngGS-20
89MidAngGS-22
90PalSprACLC-217
90PalSprAP-2573
91LinDriAAA-459
91RocRedWLD-459
91RocRedWP-1898
92ElPasDF-3916
92ElPasDS-219
96OgdRapTI-8
Martinez, Dennis Jr.
95SPML-104
96WatIndTI-15
Martinez, Denny (J. Dennis)
77Top-491
78Top-119
79Hos-32
79OPC-105
79Top-211
80OPC-2
80Top-10
81Don-533
81Fle-180
81OPC-367
81Top-367
82Don-79
82Fle-170
82OPC-135
82Top-165
82Top-712
82TopSti-10
83Don-231
83Fle-64
83FleSta-114
83FleSti-199
83OPC-167
83OriPos-13
83Top-553
84Don-633
84Fle-11
84Nes792-631
84OriTeal-14
84Top-631
84TopTif-631
85Don-514
85Fle-181
85OriHea-10

85Top-199
85TopTif-199
86Don-454
86Fle-280
86Top-416
86TopTif-416
87Fle-324
87FleGlo-324
87IndIndTI-31
87OPC-252
87Top-252
87TopTif-252
88Don-549
88DonBasB-146
88ExpPos-13
88Fle-188
88FleGlo-188
88Lea-262
88OPC-76
88Sco-601
88ScoGlo-601
88Top-76
88TopSti-84
88TopTif-76
89Bow-359
89BowTif-359
89ClaLigB-45
89Don-106
89DonBasB-90
89ExpPos-20
89Fle-385
89FleGlo-385
89OPC-313
89PanSti-114
89Sco-114
89ScoHot1S-13
89Spo-106
89Top-313
89TopSti-74
89TopTif-313
89UppDec-377
90Bow-111
90BowTif-111
90Don-156
90DonBesN-30
90ExpPos-23
90Fle-354
90FleCan-354
90Lea-54
90OPC-763
90PanSti-288
90PubSti-181
90Sco-47
90Spo-53
90Top-763
90TopBig-133
90TopSti-68
90TopTif-763
90UppDec-413
90USPlaCA-3D
90VenSti-320
91BasBesAotM-11
91Bow-434
91Cla3-T53
91ClaGam-30
91Don-139
91ExpPos-14
91Fle-238
91Lea-274
91OPC-528
91OPCPre-75
91OriCro-280
91PanFreS-150
91PanSti-68
91Sco-454
91StaClu-273
91StaCluMO-5
91StaCluP-24
91Top-528
91TopDesS-528
91TopMic-528
91TopTif-528
91TopTriH-N6
91Ult-206
91UppDec-385
91UppDecFE-50F
91USPlaCA-7S
92Bow-305
92Cla1-T57
92ClaGam-134
92Don-276
92Don-686
92DonDiaK-DK24
92DonMcD-16
92ExpDonD-12
92ExpPos-22
92Fle-486
92Fle-683
92Fle-695
92Hig5-59
92Lea-190
92OPC-15
92OPCPre-13
92PanSti-149
92PanSti-209
92PepDieM-4
92Pin-77
92PosCan-1
92Sco-470
92Sco-783
92Sco-784
92Sco100S-97
92ScoProP-17
92StaClu-860
92StaCluD-111
92StaCluNC-860
92Stu-57
92Top-15
92Top-394
92TopGol-15
92TopGol-394
92TopGolPS-15
92TopGolW-15
92TopGolW-394
92TopKid-10
92TopMic-15
92TopMic-394
92TopPreS-273
92TriPla-92
92Ult-223
92UppDec-365
92UppDecTMH-31
93Bow-480
93DiaMar-68
93Don-168
93DurPowP2-14
93ExpColP7-5
93ExpDonM-10
93Fla-86
93Fle-462
93FleFruotL-40
93FunPac-97
93HumDumC-41
93Lea-300
93MSABenSPD-5
93OPC-300
93PacBeiA-25
93PacSpa-187
93PacSpaGE-5
93PacSpaPI-3
93PanSti-228
93Pin-38
93Pin-291
93Sco-75
93Sel-147
93SelAce-6
93SelStaL-90
93SP-106
93StaClu-140
93StaCluFDI-140
93StaCluM-58
93StaCluMOP-140
93Top-610
93TopComotH-23
93TopGol-610
93TopInaM-610
93TopMic-610
93TriPla-74
93Ult-418
93UppDec-232
93UppDec-481
93UppDec-821
93UppDecGold-232
93UppDecGold-481
93UppDecGold-821
93USPlaCA-9S
94Bow-523
94ColC-546
94ColChoGS-546
94ColChoSS-546
94Don-422
94ExtBas-61
94Fin-412
94FinRef-412
94Fla-41
94Fle-545
94FleUpd-32
94FUnPac-132
94Lea-310
94OPC-21
94Pac-386
94PacAll-7
94Pin-516
94PinArtP-516
94PinMusC-516
94Sco-514
94ScoGolR-514
94ScoRoo-RT24
94ScoRooGR-RT24
94Sel-346
94SP-99
94SPDieC-99
94SpoRoo-92
94SpoRooAP-92
94StaClu-187
94StaClu-682
94StaCluFDI-187
94StaCluFDI-682
94StaCluGR-187
94StaCluGR-682
94StaCluMOP-187
94StaCluMOP-682
94Top-440
94TopGol-440
94TopSpa-440
94TopTra-7T
94Ult-345
94UppDec-358
94UppDecED-358
95Baz-13
95ColCho-65
95ColCho-274
95ColChoGS-65
95ColChoGS-274
95ColChoSE-122
95ColChoSEGS-122
95ColChoSESS-122
95ColChoSS-65
95ColChoSS-274
95D3-5
95Don-92
95DonPreP-92
95DonTopotO-60
95Emo-35
95Fin-188
95FinRef-188
95Fla-32
95Fle-139
95FleTeaL-5
95Lea-195
95LeaLim-190
95Pac-124
95PacLatD-22
95PacPri-40
95PanSti-20
95Pin-374
95PinArtP-374
95PinMusC-374
95ScoHaloG-HG88
95Sel-130
95SelArtP-130
95SelCer-86
95SelCerMG-86
95SP-147
95SPCha-147
95SPChaDC-147
95SPSil-147
95StaClu-484
95StaCluMOP-484
95StaCluSTDW-I484
95StaCluSTMP-15
95StaCluSTWS-484
95StaCluVR-264
95Stu-77
95Top-20
95TopCyb-16
95Ult-280
95UltGolM-280
95UppDec-94
95UppDecED-94
95UppDecEDG-94
95UppDecSE-158
95UppDecSEG-158
96Cir-34
96CirRav-34
96ColCho-122
96ColCho-335
96ColChoGS-122
96ColChoGS-335
96ColChoSS-122
96ColChoSS-335
96Don-284
96DonPreP-284
96EmoXL-50
96Fin-B131
96FinRef-B131
96Fla-68
96Fle-90
96FleInd-7
96FleTif-90
96Lea-139
96LeaPrePB-139
96LeaPrePG-139
96LeaPrePS-139
96LeaSigA-145
96LeaSigAG-145
96LeaSigAS-145
96MetUni-47
96MetUniP-47
96Pac-299
96PacEstL-EL16
96PacHom-HP16
96PacPri-P96
96PacPriG-P96
96Pin-112
96PinAfi-39
96PinAfi-157
96PinAfiAP-39
96PinAfiAP-157
96PinAfiFPP-39
96PinArtP-44
96PinSta-44
96SchDis-7
96Sco-306
96ScoDugC-B31
96ScoDugCAP-B31
96Sel-142
96SelArtP-142
96SP-71
96StaClu-100
96StaClu-253
96StaCluEPB-100
96StaCluEPG-100
96StaCluEPS-100
96StaCluMOP-100
96StaCluMOP-253
95StaCluVRMC-264
96Top-181
96TopChrMotG-2
96TopChrMotGR-2
96TopGalE-13
96TopLas-58
96TopMasotG-2
96Ult-49
96UltGolM-49
96UppDec-103
96UppDec-314
97ColCho-91
97Fle-81
97FleTif-81
97Lea-265
97LeaFraM-265
97LeaFraMDC-265
97Pac-74
97PacLigB-74
97PacSil-74
97Sco-115
97Sco-345
97ScoHobR-345
97ScoInd-4
97ScoIndPl-4
97ScoPreS-115
97ScoResC-345
97ScoShoS-115
97ScoShoS-345
97ScoShoSAP-115
97ScoShoSAP-345
97StaClu-62
97StaCluMOP-62
97Top-181
97UppDec-198

Martinez, Domingo

86VenGulP-13
87DunBluJP-945
88KnoBluJB-6
88SouLeaAJ-25
89KnoBluJB-15
89KnoBluJP-1148
89KnoBluJS-12
90KnoBluJB-15
90KnoBluJP-1254
90KnoBluJS-12
91LinDriAAA-511
91SyrChiLD-511
91SyrChiMB-14
91SyrChiP-2485
92ProFS7-160
92SkyAAAF-229
92SyrChiF-1975
92SyrChiMB-14
92SyrChiS-512
93BluJayD4-38
93BluJayFS-19
93Bow-203
93Don-363
93Lea-356
93LimRocDWB-24
93PacSpa-653
93Pin-596
93PinRooTP-6
93Sco-257
93StaClu-727
93StaCluFDI-727
93StaCluMOP-727
93SyrChiF-1004
93Top-810
93TopGol-810
93TopInaM-810
93TopMic-810
93Ult-644
93UppDec-651
93UppDecGold-651
94Don-584
94NasSouF-1258
94Pac-647
94StaCluT-157
94StaCluTFDI-157
95LouRedF-283

Martinez, Eddy

93BelMarC-18
96BesAutS-54
96Exc-5
96FreKeyB-14

Martinez, Edgar

86ChaLooP-17
87CalCanP-2309
88CalCanC-16
88CalCanP-782
88DonRoo-36
88Fle-378
88FleGlo-378
88TriAAC-34
89BlaYNPRWL-9
89BlaYNPRWLU-48
89BlaYNPRWLU-56
89Bow-216
89BowTif-216
89Don-645
89DonRoo-15
89Fle-552
89FleGlo-552
89MarMot-11
89PanSti-428
89Sco-637
89ScoHot1R-40
89SpoIllFKI-279
89UppDec-768
90ClaYel-T23
90CMC-439
90DonLeaS-45
90Fle-520
90FleCan-520
90Lea-299
90MarMot-10
90OPC-148
90PubSti-437
90Sco-324
90Top-148
90TopTif-148
90UppDec-532
90VenSti-321
91Bow-243
91Cla3-T54
91Don-16
91Don-606
91DonSupD-16
91Fle-457
91Lea-477
91MarCouH-7
91OPC-607
91PanFreS-230
91PanSti-187
91Sco-264
91Sco100S-17
91SevCoi-NW11
91StaClu-47
91Stu-117
91Top-607
91TopDesS-607
91TopMic-607

91TopTif-607
91Ult-340
91UppDec-574
92Bow-33
92Don-286
92DonCraJ2-24
92Fle-286
92Hig5-109
92Lea-197
92MarMot-20
92OPC-553
92PanSti-57
92Pin-13
92Sco-485
92Sco100S-17
92SpoIllFK1-407
92StaClu-267
92Stu-235
92Top-553
92TopGol-553
92TopGolW-553
92TopKid-125
92TopMic-553
92TriPla-127
92Ult-126
92UppDec-91
92UppDec-367
93Bow-515
93ClaGam-58
93DenHol-13
93DiaMar-69
93Don-421
93DonEli-27
93DonEliS-9
93DurPowP1-6
93Fin-190
93FinRef-190
93Fla-273
93Fle-309
93Fle-344
93Fle-716
93FleAll-AL3
93FleFruotL-41
93FunPac-116
93Lea-386
93LeaGolA-R15
93MarDaiQ-2
93MarMot-11
93OPC-164
93OPCPreSP-5
93OPCPreSPF-5
93PacBeiA-1
93PacBeiA-11
93PacSpa-290
93PacSpaGE-16
93PacSpaPI-17
93PanSti-62
93PanSti-155
93Pin-17
93PinTeaP-6
93Sco-49
93Sco-502
93Sel-82
93SelChaS-16
93SelStaL-1
93SelStaL-13
93SelStaL-44
93SP-133
93StaClu-331
93StaCluFDI-331
93StaCluM-159
93StaCluMari-24
93StaCluMOP-331
93Stu-126
93Top-315
93Top-403
93TOPBLAG-37
93TopGol-315
93TopGol-403
93TopInaM-315
93TopInaM-403
93TopMic-315
93TopMic-403
93TriPla-20
93TriPlaLL-L6
93Ult-270
93UltAllS-15
93UppDec-495
93UppDec-553
93UppDecGold-495
93UppDecGold-553
93USPlaCA-1D
94Bow-61
94ChuHomS-21
94ChuHomSG-21
94ColC-477
94ColC-480
94ColChoGS-477
94ColChoGS-480
94ColChoSS-480
94Don-268
94DonDom-B4
94ExtBas-169
94Fin-154
94FinPre-154P
94FinRef-154
94Fla-338
94Fle-294
94Lea-344
94LeaL-68
94MarMot-13
94OPC-44
94Pac-576
94PanSti-121
94Pin-302
94PinArtP-302
94PinMusC-302
94ProMag-130
94Sco-465
94ScoGolR-465
94Sel-72
94SP-107
94SPDieC-107
94Spo-151
94StaClu-364
94StaCluFDI-364
94StaCluGR-364
94StaCluMOP-364
94Stu-103
94Top-195
94TopGol-195
94TopSpa-195
94TriPla-129
94Ult-422
94UppDec-424
94UppDecED-424
95Bow-333
95ColCho-287
95ColChoGS-287
95ColChoSE-129
95ColChoSEGS-129
95ColChoSESS-129
95ColChoSS-287
95Don-151
95DonPreP-151
95DonTopotO-152
95Emo-79
95Fin-36
95FinRef-36
95Fla-301
95Fle-272
95Lea-271
95Lea300C-8
95LeaLim-150
95MarMot-5
95MarPac-7
95MarPac-8
95MarPac-35
95Pac-400
95PacPri-128
95Pin-97
95PinArtP-97
95PinMusC-97
95Sco-478
95ScoGolR-478
95ScoPlaTS-478
95SelCer-24
95SelCerMG-24
95SP-193
95SPCha-188
95SPChaDC-188
95SPSil-193
95StaClu-354
95StaCluMOP-354
95StaCluMOP-RL37
95StaCluRL-RL37
95StaCluSTDW-M354
95StaCluSTWS-354
95StaCluVR-185
95Stu-183
95Sum-17
95SumNthD-17
95Top-55
95TopCyb-40
95Ult-104
95UltGolM-104
95UppDec-349
95UppDecED-349
95UppDecEDG-349
95UppDecSE-119
95UppDecSEG-119
95Zen-30
96Baz-100
96Bow-20
96BowBes-2
96BowBesAR-2
96BowBesR-2
96Cir-80
96CirRav-80
96ColCho-2
96ColCho-275
96ColCho-371T
96ColCho-725
96ColChoGS-2
96ColChoGS-275
96ColChoGS-725
96ColChoSS-2
96ColChoSS-275
96ColChoSS-725
96Don-471
96DonDiaK-26
96DonHitL-12
96DonPreP-471
96EmoXL-116
96Fin-B323
96Fin-G335
96Fin-S35
96FinRef-B323
96FinRef-G335
96FinRef-S35
96Fla-163
96Fle-241
96FleGolM-4
96FleTif-241
96FleZon-8
96Lea-115
96LeaLim-42
96LeaLimG-42
96LeaPre-71
96LeaPreP-71
96LeaPrePB-115
96LeaPrePG-115
96LeaPrePS-115
96LeaSig-61
96LeaSigPPG-61
96LeaSigPPP-61
96MarMot-7
96MetUni-109
96MetUniP-109
96Pac-408
96Pac-419
96PacBaeS-6
96PacCraC-CC10
96PacEstL-EL17
96PacGolCD-DC5
96PacHom-HP20
96PacOctM-OM14
96PacPri-P133
96PacPriFB-FB10
96PacPriG-P133
96PacPriRHS-RH13
96PanSti-120
96PanSti-230
96Pin-67
96Pin-147
96Pin-313
96PinAfi-21
96PinAfiAP-21
96PinAfiFPP-21
96PinArtP-26
96PinArtP-74
96PinArtP-195
96PinFoil-313
96PinSta-26
96PinSta-74
96PinSta-195
96ProSta-64
96Sco-117
96Sco-376
96ScoAll-15
96ScoBigB-17
96ScoDugC-A77
96ScoDugC-B101
96ScoDugCAP-A77
96ScoDugCAP-B101
96ScoGolS-13
96ScoNumG-16
96ScoRef-13
96Sel-70
96SelArtP-70
96SelCer-61
96SelCerAP-61
96SelCerCB-61
96SelCerCR-61
96SelCerIP-22
96SelCerMB-61
96SelCerMG-61
96SelCerMR-61
96SelTeaN-9
96SP-172
96Spo-23
96Spo-111
96SpoArtP-23
96SpoArtP-111
96SpoPowS-15
96SPSpeFX-45
96SPSpeFXDC-45
96StaClu-221
96StaClu-300
96StaCluEPB-300
96StaCluEPG-300
96StaCluEPS-300
96StaCluMM-MM10
96StaCluMO-23
96StaCluMOP-221
96StaCluMOP-300
96StaCluMOP-MM10
96StaCluMOP-PC5
96StaCluPC-PC5
95StaCluVRMC-185
96Stu-34
96StuPrePB-34
96StuPrePG-34
96StuPrePS-34
96Sum-142
96SumAbo&B-142
96SumArtP-142
96SumFoi-142
96Top-247
96TopChr-94
96TopChrR-94
96TopClaC-CC3
96TopGal-158
96TopGalE-16
96TopGalPPI-158
96TopLas-27
96TopLasSS-14
96TopPro-AL16
96TopRoaW-RW9
96Ult-128
96UltGolM-128
96UltHitM-5
96UltHitMGM-5
96UltOn-L-6
96UltOn-LGM-6
96UltSeaC-6
96UltSeaCGM-6
96UppDec-205
96UppDec-218
96UppDecPRE-R16
96UppDecPRE-R27
96UppDecPreR-R16
96UppDecPreR-R27
96UppDecRunP-RP10
96Zen-35
96ZenArtP-35
97Bow-40
97BowBes-10
97BowBesAR-10
97BowBesR-10
97BowChr-34
97BowChrI-34
97BowChrIR-34
97BowChrR-34
97BowInt-40
97Cir-232
97CirRav-232
97ColCho-232
97Don-126
97Don-408
97DonEli-42
97DonEliGS-42
97DonLim-65
97DonLim-120
97DonLimFotG-15
97DonLimLE-65
97DonLimLE-120
97DonPre-32
97DonPreCttC-32
97DonPreP-126
97DonPreP-408
97DonPrePGold-126
97DonPrePGold-408
97DonTea-141
97DonTeaSPE-141
97Fin-99
97Fin-329
97FinEmb-329
97FinEmbR-329
97FinRef-99
97FinRef-329
97FlaSho-A137
97FlaSho-B137
97FlaSho-C137
97FlaShoLC-137
97FlaShoLC-B137
97FlaShoLC-C137
97FlaShoLCM-A137
97FlaShoLCM-B137
97FlaShoLCM-C137
97Fle-211
97FleTif-211
97Lea-246
97LeaFraM-246
97LeaFraMDC-246
97MetUni-148
97NewPin-155
97NewPinAP-155
97NewPinMC-155
97NewPinPP-155
97Pac-190
97PacGolCD-17
97PacLatotML-19
97PacLigB-190
97PacPri-64
97PacPriLB-64
97PacPriP-64
97PacSil-190
97Pin-29
97PinArtP-29
97PinCer-84
97PinCerMBlu-84
97PinCerMG-84
97PinCerMR-84
97PinCerR-84
97PinIns-42
97PinInsCE-42
97PinInsDE-42
97PinMusC-29
97PinPasttM-10
97PinTotCPB-84
97PinTotCPG-84
97PinTotCPR-84
97PinX-P-27
97PinX-PMoS-27
97PinX-PSfF-23
97PinX-PSfFU-23
97Sco-56
97ScoHigZ-14
97ScoMar-2
97ScoMarPl-2
97ScoMarPr-2
97ScoPitP-4
97ScoPreS-56
97ScoShoS-56
97ScoShoSAP-56
97Sel-64
97SelArtP-64
97SelRegG-64
97SkyE-X-42
97SkyE-XC-42
97SkyE-XEC-42
97SP-168
97StaClu-233
97StaCluMat-233
97StaCluMOP-233
97Stu-68
97StuPrePG-68
97StuPrePS-68
97Top-95
97TopChr-38
97TopChrR-38
97TopGal-21
97TopGalPPI-21
97TopSta-25
97TopSta1AS-AS10
97TopStaAM-25
97TopSweS-SS9
97Ult-125
97UltGolME-125
97UltPlaME-125
97UltSeaC-5
97UppDec-179
97UppDec-202
97UppDec-318
97UppDec-384
97Zen-40

Martinez, Eric

91AubAstC-13
91AubAstP-4280

91BoiHawC-24
91BoiHawP-3874
92AshTouC-9
92QuaCitRBC-9
92QuaCitRBF-804
Martinez, Erik
94SpoIndC-19
94SpoIndF-3332
95OdgRapTI-18
Martinez, Ernest
92AubAstC-12
92AubAstF-1361
Martinez, Felix Anthony
94Bow-162
94WilBluRC-13
94WilBluRF-307
95Bow-133
95WicWraTI-16
96Bow-383
96OmaRoyB-16
97Bow-88
97BowChr-112
97BowChrI-112
97BowChrIR-112
97BowChrR-112
97BowInt-88
Martinez, Fili
89BenBucL-7
90MidLeaASGS-40
90QuaCitAGS-25
91MidAngOHP-18
Martinez, Frank
92SprCarC-11
92SprCarF-863
93SavCarC-17
93SavCarF-685
94ArkTraF-3086
94ExcFS7-270
Martinez, Fred
85LouRedR-20
86LouRedTI-19
Martinez, Fred (Alfredo)
79JacMetT-24
81Don-172
81Fle-288
81SalLakCGT-9
81Top-227
82SpoIndT-5
82Top-659
Martinez, Gabby
92UppDecML-143
93BelBreC-14
93BelBreF-1718
93ClaFS7-283
94Bow-317
94Cla-24
94ClaTriF-T43
94StoPorC-16
94StoPorF-1701
96El PasDB-18
97Bow-341
97BowChr-233
97BowChrI-233
97BowChrIR-233
97BowChrR-233
97BowInt-341
Martinez, Gil
87GreHorP-15
88LynRedSS-11
89BlaYNPRWL-43
89LynRedSS-13
Martinez, Greg
93HelBreF-4111
94BelBreC-16
94BelBreF-116
96StoPorB-5
Martinez, Hector
93MedHatBJF-3739
93MedHatBJSP-4
Martinez, Jacen
93CapCitBC-12
93CapCitBF-467
Martinez, Jaime
93BelMarF-3218
Martinez, Javier
92BoiHawC-16
92BoiHawF-3638
94HunCubF-3549
95RocCubTI-32
94HunCubC-20
Martinez, Jesus
92ClaFS7-447
92GreFalDSP-10
92GulCoaDF-3563
93BakDodCLC-18
93ClaGolF-133
93LimRocDWB-118
94VerBeaDF-67
95AusFut-27
95SanAntMTI-47
96BesAutS-55
96SanAntMB-13
96TexLeaAB-31
Martinez, Joe
92ModA'sF-3896
Martinez, John
90BurIndP-3012
91PocPioP-3785
91PocPioSP-8
Martinez, Johnny
93BurIndC-18
93BurIndF-3295
94BurIndC-12
94BurIndF-3787
96CanIndB-15
Martinez, Jose
88St.CatBJP-2024
Martinez, Jose Luis
70OPC-8
70Top-8
71MLBOffS-207
71OPC-712
71Top-712
77DayBeaIT-14
83Roy-16
88CubDavB-NNO
89CubMar-NNO
90CubMar-28
90TopTVCu-4
91CubMar-NNO
92CubMar-NNO
93CubMar-15
Martinez, Jose Miguel
91ColMetPI-28
91ColMetPPI-6
91CubVinL-18
91SouAtlLAGP-SAL17
92ClaFS7-276
92ColMetPI-41
92ColMetPIISPI-1
92ColMetPIISPI-3
92ModA'sC-23
92ProFS7-287
92St.LucMCB-14
92St.LucMF-1743
92UppDecML-248
93Bow-331
93ClaFS7-219
93EdmTraF-1133
93ExcFS7-76
93LimRocDWB-104
93StaCluMarI-28
93UppDec-506
93UppDecGold-506
94WicWraF-186
95Pac-366
95Pin-160
95PinArtP-160
95PinMusC-160
96ChaRivTI-9618
96HudValRB-10
Martinez, Julian
87SavCarP-19
88St.PetCS-15
89ArkTraGS-11
89TexLeaAGS-20
90CMC-111
90LouRedBC-11
90LouRedBLBC-25
90LouRedBP-410
90ProAAAF-524
90TopTVCa-54
91LinDriAAA-240
91LouRedLD-240
91LouRedP-2929
91LouRedTI-26
92ArkTraF-1142
92ArkTraS-37
93LimRocDWB-33
Martinez, Julio
93MadMusC-20
93MadMusF-1820
Martinez, Leo
96ButCopKB-23
Martinez, Louie
91AubAstC-6
91AubAstP-4271
Martinez, Louie (Louis)
89SanAntMB-14
Martinez, Luis
80VenLeaS-21
86MedA'sC-57
87MadMusP-12
87MadMusP-8
88BlaYNPRWL-72
88BlaYNPRWLU-34
88FloStaLAS-11
88ModA'sCLC-74
89BlaYNPRWL-119
89SavCarP-350
90Bes-56
90SanAntMGS-18
90SprCarB-14
91AlbDukLD-14
91AlbDukP-1147
91ArkTraLD-38
91ArkTraP-1300
91LinDriAA-38
91LinDriAAA-14
92AlbDukF-727
92AlbDukS-12
93ClaGolF-138
Martinez, Manny (Manuel)
90SouOreAB-12
90SouOreAP-3433
91CalLeLA-44
91Cla/Bes-145
91ModA'sC-24
91ModA'sP-3104
92ClaFS7-35
92ModA'sC-17
93SanBerSC-13
93SanBerSF-785
94ClaGolF-149
94TacTigF-3188
95IowCubTI-21
96TacRaiB-17
Martinez, Martin
90RocExpLC-17
90RocExpP-2693
91Cla/Bes-252
91RocExpC-8
91RocExpP-2043
Martinez, Marty (Orlando)
61TwiCloD-16
67Top-504
68CokCapB-11
68Top-578
69MilBra-167
69Top-337
70OPC-126
70Top-126
71MLBOffS-85
71OPC-602
71Top-602
72MilBra-207
72OPC-336
72Top-336
72TopCloT-22
74SpoIndC-44
76SanAntBTI-14
80WauTimT-23
81SpoIndT-32
85MarMot-27
86MarMot-28
87AstShowSTh-13
92MarMot-27
93RanKee-27
Martinez, Matt
93ElmPioC-10
93ElmPioF-3830
Martinez, Nicio
88BatCliP-1667
90SavCarP-2076
Martinez, Obed R.
95IdaFalBTI-26
96IdaFalB-15
Martinez, Osvaldo
94BriTigC-18
94BriTigF-3499
Martinez, Pablo
90ChaRaiB-14
90ChaRaiP-2044
91ChaRaiC-19
91ChaRaiP-104
92HigDesMC-5
93WicWraF-2986
94NorTidF-2929
95BreBtaTI-5
96RicBraB-20
96RicBraRC-18
96RicBraUB-18
Martinez, Pedro A.
89ChaRaiP-992
89SouAtlLAGS-11
90WicWraRD-15
91WicWraLD-613
91WicWraP-2595
91WicWraRD-6
92WicWraF-3656
92WicWraS-640
93ExcFS7-110
93LasVegSF-941
94Bow-4
94ColC-188
94ColChoGS-188
94ColChoSS-188
94Don-526
94FinRef-101
94Fle-669
94OPC-26
94Pac-530
94PadMot-27
94StaClu-611
94StaClu-684
94StaCluFDI-684
94StaCluGR-684
94StaCluMOP-684
94Top-676
94TopGol-676
94TopSpa-676
94TriPla-169
94Ult-581
95Don-202
95DonPreP-202
95Fle-564
95FleUpd-141
95Pac-367
95Top-410
95TopCyb-210
95Ult-236
95UltGolM-236
96ColCho-358
96ColChoGS-358
96ColChoSS-358
96NorTidB-20
96Pac-92
Martinez, Pedro J.
90GreFalDSP-12
91BakDodCLC-32
91CalLeLA-2
91Cla/Bes-355
91Cla3-T55
91LinDriAA-613
91SanAntMP-2971
91UppDecFE-2F
92AlbDukF-716
92AlbDukS-13
92Bow-82
92DonRoo-69
92LeaGolR-BC3
92ProFS7-244
92SkyAAAF-5
92TriA AAS-13
92UppDec-18
92UppDec-79
93Bow-154
93DodMot-16
93DodPol-15
93Don-326
93Fla-72
93Fle-354
93FleMajLP-B4
93Lea-163
93LimRocDWB-126
93PacSpa-500
93Pin-259
93PinRooTP-1
93PinTea2-14
93Sco-321
93ScoBoyoS-3
93ScoProaG-2
93SelRoo-36T
93StaClu-365
93StaCluD-2
93StaCluFDI-365
93StaCluMOP-365
93Top-557
93TopGol-557
93TopInaM-557
93TopMic-557
93Ult-57
93UppDec-324
93UppDecGold-324
94ColC-189
94ColC-588
94ColChoGS-189
94ColChoGS-588
94ColChoSS-189
94ColChoSS-588
94Don-179
94ExtBas-309
94ExtBas-375
94ExtBasSYS-12
94Fin-101
94Fin-362
94FinRef-362
94Fla-193
94Fle-515
94FleUpd-153
94FUnPac-88
94Lea-367
94OPC-41
94Pac-313
94Pin-501
94PinArtP-501
94PinMusC-501
94ProMag-84
94Sco-554
94ScoBoyoS-49
94ScoGolR-554
94ScoRoo-RT62
94ScoRooGR-RT62
94Sel-332
94SP-85
94SPDieC-85
94SpoRoo-16
94SpoRooAP-16
94StaCluFDI-611
94StaCluGR-611
94StaCluMOP-611
94Top-268
94TopGol-268
94TopSpa-268
94TopTra-42T
94Ult-524
94UppDec-318
94UppDecAJ-32
94UppDecAJG-32
94UppDecED-318
94USPlaCR-11S
95AstMot-16
95Bow-350
95ColCho-244
95ColChoGS-244
95ColChoSE-101
95ColChoSEGS-101
95ColChoSESS-101
95ColChoSS-244
95Don-315
95DonPreP-315
95DonTopotO-282
95Emb-94
95EmbGolI-94
95Emo-153
95Fin-189
95FinFlaT-FT6
95FinRef-189
95Fla-164
95Fle-356
95Lea-88
95LeaLim-37
95Pac-271
95PacPri-88
95PanSti-4
95Pin-235
95PinArtP-235
95PinMusC-235
95Sco-170
95Sco-444
95ScoGolR-170
95ScoGolR-444
95ScoPlaTS-170
95ScoPlaTS-444
95Sel-87
95SelArtP-87
95SP-77
95SPCha-68
95SPChaDC-68
95Spo-99
95SpoArtP-99
95SPSil-77
95StaClu-485
95StaCluMOP-485
95StaCluSTWS-485
95StaCluVR-265
95Stu-73
95Top-622
95TopCyb-389
95TopLeaL-LL25

95Ult-405
95UltGolM-405
95UltStrK-5
95UltStrKGM-5
95UppDec-329
95UppDecED-329
95UppDecEDG-329
95UppDecSE-3
95UppDecSEG-3
96Baz-76
96Bow-37
96Cir-150
96CirRav-150
96ColCho-610
96ColChoGS-360
96ColChoGS-610
96ColChoSS-360
96ColChoSS-610
96Don-343
96DonDiaK-12
96DonPreP-343
96DonSho-6
96EmoXL-223
96ExpDis-12
96ExpDis-13
96Fin-B27
96FinRef-B27
96Fla-309
96Fle-462
96FleSmo'H-7
96FleTif-462
96Lea-92
96LeaLim-59
96LeaLimG-59
96LeaPre-53
96LeaPreP-53
96LeaPrePB-92
96LeaPrePG-92
96LeaPrePS-92
96LeaSigA-146
96LeaSigAG-146
96LeaSigAS-146
96MetUni-192
96MetUniP-192
96Pac-123
96PacEstL-EL9
96PacPri-P42
96PacPriG-P42
96PanSti-18
96Pin-79
96PinAfi-120
96PinAfiAP-120
96PinArtP-29
96PinSta-29
96ProSta-49
96Sco-277
96ScoDugC-B2
96ScoDugCAP-B2
96Sel-74
96SelArtP-74
96SelCer-93
96SelCerAP-93
96SelCerCB-93
96SelCerCR-93
96SelCerMB-93
96SelCerMG-93
96SelCerMR-93
96SP-118
96Spo-69
96SpoArtP-69
96StaClu-80
96StaCluEPB-80
96StaCluEPG-80
96StaCluEPS-80
96StaCluMOP-80
95StaCluVRMC-265
96Stu-92
96StuPrePB-92
96StuPrePG-92
96StuPrePS-92
96Top-303
96TopChr-121
96TopChrR-121
96TopGal-111
96TopGalPPI-111
96TopLas-122
96Ult-233
96UltGolM-233
96UppDec-136
96UppDecPHE-H45
96UppDecPreH-H45
96Zen-85
96ZenArtP-85
97Bow-223
97BowChr-53
97BowChrI-53
97BowChrIR-53
97BowChrR-53
97BowInt-223
97Cir-347
97CirRav-347
97ColCho-162
97Don-263
97DonLim-16
97DonLimLE-16
97DonPreP-263
97DonPrePGold-263
97Fin-40
97FinRef-40
97Fle-383
97FleTif-383
97Lea-44
97LeaFraM-44
97LeaFraMDC-44
97MetUni-158
97NewPin-40
97NewPin-182
97NewPinAP-40
97NewPinAP-182
97NewPinMC-40
97NewPinMC-182
97NewPinPP-40
97NewPinPP-182
97Pac-347
97PacLatotML-31
97PacLigB-347
97PacPri-119
97PacPriLB-119
97PacPriP-119
97PacSil-347
97Sco-72
97ScoPreS-72
97ScoShoS-72
97ScoShoSAP-72
97SP-113
97SpoIll-87
97SpoIllEE-87
97StaClu-12
97StaCluMat-12
97StaCluMOP-12
97Stu-139
97StuPrePG-139
97StuPrePS-139
97Top-158
97TopGal-132
97TopGalPPI-132
97TopSta-77
97TopStaAM-77
97Ult-232
97UltGolME-232
97UltPlaME-232
97UppDec-111
97UppDecRSF-RS16
Martinez, Porfi
86LakTigP-12
Martinez, Rafael
88St.CatBJP-2026
89MyrBeaBJP-1468
95GreFalDTI-30
96VerBeaDB-19
Martinez, Ramino
92GulCoaRSP-6
Martinez, Ramiro
93ChaRaiC-12
93ChaRaiF-1907
93StaCluM-173
94TulDriF-242
94TulDriTI-16
95TulDriTI-13
Martinez, Ramon
87SalAngP-12
88BenBucL-5
89PalSprACLC-38
89PalSprAP-467
89PriPirS-12
92SalBucC-2
Martinez, Ramon Dario
90AugPirP-2458
91AugPirC-16
91AugPirP-812
91PalSprAP-2024
92EdmTraF-3546
92SalBucF-11
93Bow-66
93ExcFS7-92
93HigDesMC-12
93HigDesMF-49
93StaClu-322
93StaCluFDI-322
93StaCluMarl-17
93StaCluMOP-322
93VanCanF-2604
94PorSeaDF-687
94PorSeaDTI-22
94UppDecML-223
94WilBluRC-14
94WilBluRF-308
95FinRef-200
95WicWraTI-15
96ColCho-360
96LynHilB-14
96OmaRoyB-17
96SanAntMB-14
Martinez, Ramon J.
86BakDodP-20
87VerBeaDP-7
88BasAmeAAB-21
88SanAntMB-1
88TexLeaAGS-28
88TriAAC-45
89AlbDukC-7
89AlbDukP-69
89ClaTraO-130
89DodPol-24
89DodStaSV-16
89Don-464
89DonRoo-45
89Fle-67
89FleGlo-67
89Sco-635
89ScoHot1R-55
89ScoYouSI-40
89Spo-224
89SpoIllFKI-303
89Top-225
89TopTif-225
89TriA AAC-40
89TriAAP-AAA47
89UppDec-18
90Bow-88
90BowTif-88
90ClaBlu-76
90DodMot-17
90DodTar-489
90Don-685
90DonBesN-141
90Fle-402
90FleCan-402
90Hot50RS-30
90Lea-147
90OPC-62
90PanSti-380
90Sco-461
90Sco100RS-59
90ScoMcD-13
90Spo-68
90Top-62
90TopRoo-20
90TopSti-61
90TopTif-62
90ToyRoo-19
90TriAAAC-40
90UppDec-675
90USPlaCA-1H
91BasBesRB-10
91Bow-610
91CadElID-35
91Cla1-T52
91ClaGam-99
91Col-18
91DodMot-10
91DodPol-48
91DodUno7P-6
91Don-15
91Don-557
91DonSupD-15
91Fle-212
91KinDis-12
91Lea-61
91LeaPre-5
91MajLeaCP-52
91OPC-340
91PanCanT1-58
91PanCanT1-75
91PanFreS-62
91PanSti-50
91Sco-300
91Sco-408
91Sco-419
91Sco100S-16
91SevCoi-F11
91SevCoi-SC8
91StaClu-516
91StaCluCM-19
91Stu-184
91Top-340
91TopCraJ2-25
91TopDesS-340
91TopMic-340
91TopSta-23
91TopTif-340
91TopTriH-N5
91Ult-164
91UltGol-7
91UppDec-78
91UppDec-136
92Bow-255
92Cla2-T40
92ClaGam-35
92DodMot-7
92DodPol-48
92DodSmo-4592
92DodStaTA-29
92Don-656
92DonCraJ1-30
92Fle-463
92Fle-706
92FleAll-7
92FleCitTP-21
92Hig5-53
92Hig5S-23
92Lea-297
92OPC-730
92Pin-429
92PinTea2-49
92PinTeaP-1
92Sco-610
92Sco-780
92Sco100S-75
92ScoImpP-75
92SpoStaCC-31
92StaClu-207
92Stu-46
92Top-730
92TopGol-730
92TopGolW-730
92TopKid-48
92TopMic-730
92TriPla-55
92Ult-213
92UppDec-79
92UppDec-346
92UppDecTMH-32
93Bow-590
93CadDis-39
93DiaMar-70
93DodMot-12
93DodPol-16
93Don-298
93Fin-29
93FinRef-29
93Fla-73
93Fle-65
93Fle-354
93FleFruotL-42
93FunPac-90
93FunPac-213
93Lea-335
93OPC-275
93PacSpa-152
93PacSpaPI-4
93PanSti-212
93Pin-377
93Sco-199
93Sel-213
93SP-95
93StaClu-71
93StaCluD-10
93StaCluFDI-71
93StaCluMOP-71
93Stu-149
93Top-120
93TopGol-120
93TopInaM-120
93TopMic-120
93TriPla-161
93Ult-401
93UppDec-133
93UppDecGold-133
94Bow-398
94ColC-190
94ColChoGS-190
94ColChoSS-190
94DodMot-11
94DodPol-17
94Don-368
94DonSpeE-368
94ExtBas-290
94Fin-405
94FinRef-405
94Fla-398
94Fle-516
94Lea-303
94OPC-76
94Pac-314
94Pin-353
94PinArtP-353
94PinMusC-353
94Sco-233
94ScoGolR-233
94Sel-107
94Spo-99
94StaClu-276
94StaCluFDI-276
94StaCluGR-276
94StaCluMOP-276
94Top-545
94TopGol-545
94TopSpa-545
94TriPla-86
94Ult-519
94UppDec-349
94UppDecAJ-32
94UppDecAJG-32
94UppDecED-349
95Bow-358
95ColCho-227
95ColChoGS-227
95ColChoSE-93
95ColChoSEGS-93
95ColChoSESS-93
95ColChoSS-227
95DodMot-4
95DodPol-14
95Don-481
95DonPreP-481
95DonTopotO-267
95Emo-142
95Fin-200
95Fla-367
95Fle-544
95FleTeaL-21
95Lea-104
95LeaLim-114
95Pac-221
95PacPri-70
95Pin-274
95PinArtP-274
95PinMusC-274
95Sco-155
95ScoGolR-155
95ScoPlaTS-155
95SP-69
95SPCha-61
95SPChaDC-61
95SPSil-69
95StaClu-434
95StaCluMOP-434
95StaCluSTDW-D434
95StaCluSTWS-434
95StaCluVR-229
95Stu-74
95Top-275
95TopCyb-148
95Ult-182
95UltGolM-182
95UppDec-321
95UppDecED-321
95UppDecEDG-321
95UppDecSE-37
95UppDecSEG-37
96Baz-68
96Cir-142
96CirRav-142
96ColCho-186
96ColCho-360
96ColChoGS-186
96ColChoGS-360
96ColChoSS-186
96ColChoSS-360
96DodMot-21
96DodPol-23
96Don-151
96DonPreP-151
96EmoXL-211
96Fin-B71
96FinRef-B71
96Fla-295
96Fle-440
96FleDod-11

96FleGolM-5
96FleTif-440
96Lea-198
96LeaPrePB-198
96LeaPrePG-198
96LeaPrePS-198
96MetUni-184
96MetUniP-184
96Pac-104
96PacPri-P35
96PacPriFT-FT9
96PacPriG-P35
96PanSti-94
96Pin-45
96PinAfi-93
96PinAfiAP-93
96PinAfiFPP-93
96Sco-294
96ScoDugC-B19
96ScoDugCAP-B19
96Sel-109
96SelArtP-109
96SP-103
96StaClu-140
96StaCluEPB-140
96StaCluEPG-140
96StaCluEPS-140
96StaCluMOP-140
95StaCluVRMC-229
96Stu-30
96StuPrePB-30
96StuPrePG-30
96StuPrePS-30
96Sum-103
96SumAbo&B-103
96SumArtP-103
96SumFoi-103
96Top-206
96TopChr-71
96TopChrR-71
96TopGal-8
96TopGalPPI-8
96Ult-221
96UltGolM-221
96UppDec-354
97Bow-238
97BowInt-238
97Cir-370
97CirRav-370
97ColCho-362
97Don-198
97DonLim-25
97DonLimLE-25
97DonPreP-198
97DonPrePGold-198
97DonTea-114
97DonTeaSPE-114
97Fin-31
97FinRef-31
97Fle-366
97FleTif-366
97Lea-109
97LeaFraM-109
97LeaFraMDC-109
97MetUni-102
97NewPin-79
97NewPinAP-79
97NewPinMC-79
97NewPinPP-79
97Pac-334
97PacLatotML-28
97PacLigB-334
97PacPri-112
97PacPriLB-112
97PacPriP-112
97PacSil-334
97Sco-248
97ScoDod-12
97ScoDodPI-12
97ScoDodPr-12
97ScoPreS-248
97ScoShoS-248
97ScoShoSAP-248
97SP-96
97SpoIll-117
97SpoIllEE-117
97StaClu-205
97StaCluMat-205
97StaCluMOP-205
97Top-182
97TopGal-53
97TopGalPPI-53
97Ult-219
97UltGolME-219
97UltPlaME-219
97UppDec-374
97UppDec-395
Martinez, Randy
83SprCarF-19
Martinez, Ray
81BatTroT-13
83WatIndF-19
Martinez, Rey
85LynMetT-23
90KinMetB-8
90KinMetS-15
90MadMusP-2265
90QuaCitAGS-23
92MidAngOHP-15
92MidAngS-464
92SkyAA F-198
Martinez, Rick
92NiaFalRC-6
92NiaFalRF-3333
Martinez, Roger
95PitMetTI-12
96PitMetB-14
Martinez, Sandy
91KisDodP-4195
92YakBeaF-3459
96BluJayOH-19
96Don-295
96DonPreP-295
96Fla-188
96Fle-278
96FleTif-278
96LeaSigA-147
96LeaSigAG-147
96LeaSigAS-147
96MetUni-123
96MetUniP-123
96StaClu-157
96StaCluMOP-157
96Top-321
96Ult-148
96UltGolM-148
97BluJayS-54
97Fle-244
97FleTif-244
97PacPriGotD-GD102
97StaClu-371
97StaCluMOP-371
97Top-418
Martinez, Silvio
76ShrCapT-15
76VenLeaS-198
78SprRedWK-18
79Car5-16
79Top-609
80OPC-258
80Top-496
81Don-429
81Fle-546
81Top-586
82ChaChaT-7
82Don-469
82Fle-122
82Top-181
Martinez, Ted
71OPC-648
71Top-648
72Top-544
73LinPor-115
73OPC-161
73Top-161
74OPC-487
74Top-487
75OPC-637
75Top-637
76OPC-356
76SSP-499
76Top-356
78SSP270-64
78Top-546
79OPC-59
79Top-128
80AlbDukT-14
80DodPol-23
80Top-191
85DomLeaS-38
90DodTar-490
91MetWIZ-252
Martinez, Thomas
83AleDukT-17
Martinez, Tino
87PanAmTURB-1
88TopTra-66T
88TopTraT-66T
89BasAmeAPB-AA6
89Bow-211
89BowTif-211
89EasLeaAP-18
89Sta-124
89TopBig-93
89WilBilP-635
89WilBilS-13
90Bow-484
90BowTif-484
90CalCanC-12
90CalCanP-659
90FleUpd-119
90ProAAAF-124
90Sco-596
90TopMag-46
90UppDec-37
91Bow-257
91CalCanLD-66
91CalCanP-523
91Cla1-T2
91ClaGam-150
91Don-28
91DonPre-6
91Fle-458
91LeaPre-24
91LinDriAAA-66
91MajLeaCP-7
91MarCouH-10
91OPC-482
91OPCPre-76
91Sco-798
91ScoRoo-38
91SevCoi-NW12
91StaClu-179
91Stu-118
91Top-482
91TopDeb90-99
91TopDesS-482
91TopMic-482
91TopTif-482
91TriA AAGP-AAA5
91Ult-341
91UppDec-553
92Bow-483
92Bow-626
92Cla2-T42
92ClaGam-50
92Don-410
92Don-525
92Fle-287
92Lea-329
92MarMot-11
92OPC-481
92OPCPre-64
92Pin-123
92PinTea2-62
92ProFS7-138
92Sco-596
92Sco100RS-51
92ScoHotR-7
92StaClu-573
92Stu-236
92Top-481
92TopGol-481
92TopGolW-481
92TopMic-481
92TriPla-259
92Ult-127
92UppDec-554
93Bow-303
93Don-217
93Fla-274
93Fle-310
93Lea-406
93MarMot-17
93OPC-212
93PacBeiA-11
93PacSpa-289
93PanSti-66
93Pin-213
93Sco-76
93Sel-246
93SP-134
93StaClu-273
93StaCluFDI-273
93StaCluMari-18
93StaCluMOP-273
93Stu-204
93Top-232
93TopGol-232
93TopInaM-232
93TopMic-232
93TriPla-35
93Ult-623
93UppDec-287
93UppDecGold-287
94Bow-669
94ColC-191
94ColChoGS-191
94ColChoSS-191
94Don-296
94ExtBas-170
94Fin-55
94FinRef-55
94Fla-106
94Fle-295
94Lea-92
94LeaL-69
94MarMot-16
94Pac-577
94PanSti-122
94Pin-129
94PinArtP-129
94PinMusC-129
94Sco-59
94ScoGolR-59
94Sel-163
94StaClu-60
94StaCluFDI-60
94StaCluGR-60
94StaCluMOP-60
94Stu-104
94Top-693
94TopGol-693
94TopSpa-693
94TriPla-130
94Ult-121
94UppDec-94
94UppDecED-94
95ColCho-283
95ColChoGS-283
95ColChoSE-127
95ColChoSEGS-127
95ColChoSESS-127
95ColChoSS-283
95Don-63
95DonPreP-63
95DonTopotO-153
95Emb-73
95EmbGolI-73
95Emo-80
95Fin-51
95FinRef-51
95Fla-83
95Fle-273
95Lea-90
95LeaLim-96
95MarMot-23
95MarPac-7
95MarPac-36
95Pac-401
95Pin-310
95PinArtP-310
95PinMusC-310
95Sco-128
95ScoGolR-128
95ScoPlaTS-128
95SP-191
95SPSil-191
95StaClu-227
95StaCluFDI-227
95StaCluMOP-227
95StaCluSTDW-M227
95StaCluSTWS-227
95StaCluVR-115
95Stu-82
95Top-377
95TopCyb-198
95Ult-328
95UltGolM-328
95UppDec-99
95UppDecED-99
95UppDecEDG-99
95UppDecSE-256
95UppDecSEG-256
95Zen-103
96Baz-113
96Bow-49
96BowBes-59
96BowBesAR-59
96BowBesR-59
96Cir-66
96CirRav-66
96ColCho-318
96ColCho-780
96ColChoGS-318
96ColChoSS-318
96Don-43
96DonPreP-43
96EmoXL-91
96Fin-B260
96Fin-S357
96FinRef-B260
96FinRef-S357
96Fla-132
96Fle-188
96FleTif-188
96FleUpd-U64
96FleUpdTC-U64
96LeaLim-4
96LeaLimG-4
96LeaPre-7
96LeaPreP-7
96LeaSig-123
96LeaSigPPG-123
96LeaSigPPP-123
96MetUni-89
96MetUniP-89
96MLBPin-20
96Pac-404
96PacEstL-EL18
96PacPri-P134
96PacPriG-P134
96PanSti-225
96Pin-27
96Pin-361
96PinAfi-64
96PinAfiAP-64
96PinAfiFPP-64
96PinAfiSP-24
96PinArtP-13
96PinFoil-361
96PinSta-13
96Sco-354
96ScoDugC-B79
96ScoDugCAP-B79
96Sel-104
96SelArtP-104
96SelCer-2
96SelCerAP-2
96SelCerCB-2
96SelCerCR-2
96SelCerMB-2
96SelCerMG-2
96SelCerMR-2
96Spo-84
96SpoArtP-84
96StaClu-185
96StaCluMO-24
96StaCluMOP-185
95StaCluVRMC-115
96Stu-144
96StuPrePB-144
96StuPrePG-144
96StuPrePS-144
96Sum-3
96SumAbo&B-3
96SumArtP-3
96SumFoi-3
96Top-168
96TopChr-48
96TopChrR-48
96TopLas-85
96TopRoaW-RW10
96Ult-129
96Ult-390
96UltGolM-129
96UltGolM-390
96UppDec-503U
96Zen-14
96ZenArtP-14
97Bow-48
97BowBes-66
97BowBesAR-66
97BowBesR-66
97BowChr-38
97BowChrI-38
97BowChrIR-38
97BowChrR-38
97BowInt-48
97Cir-104
97CirRav-104
97ColCho-181
97Don-55
97DonEli-105
97DonEliGS-105
97DonLim-56
97DonLim-93
97DonLimFotG-35
97DonLimLE-56
97DonLimLE-93

97DonPre-79
97DonPreCttC-79
97DonPreP-55
97DonPrePGold-55
97DonTea-124
97DonTeaSPE-124
97Fin-204
97FinRef-204
97Fle-171
97FleTif-171
97Lea-254
97LeaFraM-254
97LeaFraMDC-254
97LeaLeaotN-13
97MetUni-119
97NewPin-66
97NewPinAP-66
97NewPinMC-66
97NewPinPP-66
97Pac-154
97PacLatotML-13
97PacLigB-154
97PacPri-52
97PacPriLB-52
97PacPriP-52
97PacSil-154
87PanAmTUBI-19
97PinIns-55
97PinInsCE-55
97PinInsDE-55
97PinX-P-44
97PinX-P-144
97PinX-PMoS-44
97PinX-PMoS-144
97PinX-PSfF-3
97PinX-PSfFU-3
97Sco-208
97ScoPreS-208
97ScoShoS-208
97ScoShoSAP-208
97ScoYan-13
97ScoYanPl-13
97ScoYanPr-13
97SP-126
97SpoIll-29
97SpoIll-129
97SpoIllEE-29
97SpoIllEE-129
97StaClu-220
97StaCluMat-220
97StaCluMOP-220
97Stu-31
97StuPrePG-31
97StuPrePS-31
97Top-187
97TopChr-72
97TopChrR-72
97TopGal-89
97TopGalPPI-89
97TopSta-2
97TopSta1AS-AS3
97TopStaAM-2
97Ult-100
97UltGolME-100
97UltPlaME-100
97UppDec-123
97Zen-23

Martinez, Tippy (Felix)
75SyrChiTI-10
76OPC-41
76Top-41
77OPC-254
77Top-238
78Top-393
79Top-491
80Top-706
81Don-354
81Fle-179
81OPC-119
81Top-119
82Don-205
82Fle-171
82Top-583
83Don-357
83Fle-65
83FleSta-115
83FleSti-201
83OPC-263
83OriPos-14
83Top-631
84Don-472
84Fle-12
84Fle-635
84Nes792-215
84OPC-215
84OriEng-7
84OriTeal-15
84Top-215
84TopSti-208
84TopTif-215
85Don-210
85Fle-182
85OPC-247
85OriHea-11
85Top-445
85TopMin-445
85TopSti-200
85TopTif-445
86Don-514
86Fle-279
86OPC-82
86Top-82
86TopTif-82
87OPC-269
87RedFolSB-14
87Top-728
87TopTif-728
89PacSenL-144
89T/MSenL-72
90EliSenL-40
91OriCro-281
91PacSenL-28
92YanWIZ7-103
93OriCroASU-6

Martinez, Tommy
79WatIndT-26
80WatIndT-28

Martinez, Tony (Gabriel)
63Top-466
64Top-404
66Top-581

Martinez, Wilfredo
83EriCarT-5

Martinez, William
90GatCitPP-3344
91SouAtlLAGP-SAL46
91SumFlyC-8
91SumFlyP-2331
92RocExpC-19

Martinez, Willie
96WatIndTI-16
97Bow-172
97BowBes-131
97BowBesAR-131
97BowBesR-131
97BowInt-172

Marting, Tim
71OPC-423
71Top-423
90ColMetGS-28

Martino, R.J.
95AshTouTI-NNO

Martins, Eric
94SouOreAC-17
94SouOreAF-3630
95Exc-111
95ModA'sTI-14
96HunStaTI-16

Martinson, Evon
78CliDodT-21
79LodDodT-21

Martinson, Mike
75QuaCitAT-33
76QuaCitAT-20
76SalLakCGC-7

Marto, Johnny
11TurRedT-61

Martorana, Mutta (Dave)
91UtiBluSC-12
91UtiBluSP-3249
92SouBenWSF-186

Marty, Joe
36DiaMatCS3T2-17
40PlaBal-216
41PlaBal-28
46SunBre-13
47SigOil-64
47SunBre-10
49BowPCL-26
49SolSunP-8
52MotCoo-20
79DiaGre-308
93ConTSN-896

Martyn, Bob
58Top-39
59Top-41
59TopVen-41
79TCM50-254

Martz, Gary
75OmaRoyTI-11
76OmaRoyTT-12
76VenLeaS-203

Martz, Randy
80VenLeaS-166
80WicAerT-7
81Fle-300
81Top-381
82CubRedL-34
82Don-126
82Fle-600
82Top-188
82Top-456
83Don-151
83Fle-501
83FleSta-116
83FleSti-129
83Top-22
84RicBraT-18
85TucTorC-66

Marval, Raul
94CliLumF-1987
94EveGiaC-21
94EveGiaF-3660
95BurBeeTI-10
96BurBeeTI-21
94CliLumC-15

Marx, Bill
86ChaRaiP-14
88RivRedWCLC-214
88RivRedWP-1424
89RivRedWB-12
89RivRedWCLC-14
89RivRedWP-1416
90RivRedWCLC-20
90RivRedWP-2606

Marx, Tim
93SalBucC-16
93SalBucF-436

Marx, William
90ChaRaiB-16

Marzan, Jose
88BlaYNPRWLU-50
88VisOakCLC-155
88VisOakP-89
89BlaYNPRWL-145
89VisOakCLC-111
89VisOakP-1443
90OrlSunRB-6
90OrlSunRP-1091
90OrlSunRS-10
91LinDriAA-486
91OrlSunRLD-486
91OrlSunRP-1857
95ForMyeMTI-29

Marzano, John
85Top-399
85TopTif-399
86NewBriRSP-16
87IntLeaAT-19
87PawRedSP-51
87PawRedST-11
87SpoRoo2-49
88ClaRed-189
88Don-421
88DonTeaBRS-421
88Fle-357
88FleGlo-357
88Lea-245
88Sco-584
88ScoGlo-584
88StaLinRS-13
88Top-757
88TopTif-757
88ToyRoo-17
89PawRedSC-17
89PawRedSP-687
89PawRedSTI-15
90CMC-263
90PawRedSC-12
90PawRedSP-465
90ProAAAF-437
90TopTra-69T
90TopTraT-69T
90TopTVRS-19
91Bow-119
91Don-346
91Fle-103
91Lea-179
91OPC-574
91RedSoxP-12
91Sco-831
91StaClu-201
91Top-574
91TopDesS-574
91TopMic-574
91TopTif-574
92Don-448
92OPC-677
92RedSoxDD-18
92Sco-539
92StaClu-424
92Top-677
92TopDaiQTU-3
92TopGol-677
92TopGolW-677
92TopMic-677
92Ult-316
93Don-487
93RedSoxWHP-17
93StaClu-73
93StaCluFDI-73
93StaCluMOP-73
94ScrRedBF-923
96LeaSigEA-121
96MarMot-12
97PacPriGotD-GD89

Marze, Dickey
90BurBraB-15
90BurBraP-2357
90BurBraS-17

Marzetta, Angie
95ColSilB-17
96ColSilB-17

Masaoka, Onan
95YakBeaTI-19
96BesAutS-56
96Bow-119
96Exc-179
96SavSanB-18
97Bow-205
97BowInt-205

Mascia, Dan
92ButCopKSP-1

Mashore, Clyde
71ExpPS-14
71OPC-376
71Top-376
72Dia-29
73OPC-401
73Top-401

Mashore, Damon
90AriWilP-12
91SouOreAC-2
91SouOreAP-3863
92CalLeaACL-12
92ClaFS7-189
92ModA'sC-4
92ModA'sF-3909
92UppDecML-300
93HunStaF-2095
94HunStaF-1344
95EdmTraTI-16
96A'sMot-27
97Don-377
97DonLim-190
97DonLimLE-190
97DonPreP-377
97DonPrePGold-377
97DonRatR-30
97Fle-192
97FleTif-192
97Lea-327
97LeaFraM-327
97LeaFraMDC-327
97NewPin-167
97NewPinAP-167
97NewPinMC-167
97NewPinPP-167
97Pac-172
97PacLigB-172
97PacSil-172
97PinCer-113
97PinCerMBlu-113
97PinCerMG-113
97PinCerMR-113
97PinCerR-113
97PinTotCPB-113
97PinTotCPG-113
97PinTotCPR-113
97PinX-P-131
97PinX-PMoS-131
97Sco-321
97ScoPreS-321
97ScoShoS-321
97ScoShoSAP-321
97SpoIll-14
97SpoIllEE-14
97Ult-113
97UltGolME-113
97UltPlaME-113

Mashore, Justin
91BriTigC-3
91BriTigP-3619
92FayGenC-17
92FayGenF-2182
92StaCluD-112
92UppDecML-139
93Bow-447
93LakTigC-15
93LakTigF-1324
94Cla-104
94TreThuF-2131
94UppDecML-31
95TolMudHTI-20
96JacSunB-19

Masi, Phil
46SpoExcW-7-10
47TipTop-82
48BluTin-12
49Bow-153
49EurSta-15
50Bow-128
51Bow-160
51TopBluB-19
52Top-283
77TCMTheWY-14
79DiaGre-207
83TCMPla1943-38
83TopRep5-283

Masino, Ron
87BriYouC-7

Maskery, Sam
87OldJudN-324

Maskivish, Joe
94WelPirC-13
94WelPirF-3491
95Exc-257
96BesAutS-57
96Exc-220
96LynHilB-15

Maskovich, George
52Par-97

Mason, Andy
93EveGiaC-18
93EveGiaF-3784

Mason, Charlie
90KalBatN-33

Mason, Dan
95RocRedWTI-44

Mason, Don
66Top-524
69Top-584
71MLBOffS-231
71OPC-548
71Top-548
72Top-739

Mason, Henry
60Lea-80
60Top-331
96NegLeaBMKC-5

Mason, Jim
72Dia-30
72OPC-334
72Top-334
73OPC-458
73Top-458
74OPC-618
74Top-618
74TopTra-618T
75OPC-136
75Top-136
75YanSSP-18
76SSP-448
77OPC-211
77Top-212
78SSP270-94
78Top-588
79ExpPos-15
79Top-67
80OPC-259
80Top-497
92YanWIZ7-104
93RanKee-28

Mason, Kevin
89TenTecGE-16
89TenTecGE-35

Mason, Larry
81TCM60I-387

Mason, Marty (Martin)
82SprCarF-16

83SprCarF-7
84ArkTraT-19
86St.PetCP-18
87St.PetCP-19
88SavCarP-336
89St.PetCS-28
90ArkTraGS-2
91ArkTraP-1303
91LinDriAA-50
92ArkTraF-1145
92ArkTraS-50
93ArkTraF-2828
94ArkTraF-3105
95ArkTraTI-20
96ArkTraB-3
Mason, Mike
82TulDriT-5
83OklCit8T-20
84FleUpd-76
84RanJarP-16
84TopTra-76T
84TopTraT-76T
85Don-281
85Fle-562
85OPC-144
85RanPer-16
85Top-464
85TopMin-464
85TopSti-354
85TopTif-464
86Don-422
86Fle-565
86OPC-189
86RanPer-16
86Top-189
86TopTif-189
87Don-284
87Fle-129
87FleGlo-129
87FleUpd-73
87FleUpdG-73
87OPC-208
87RanSmo-4
87Top-646
87TopTif-646
88Top-87
88TopTif-87
91AppFoxC-28
91AppFoxP-1733
91AppFoxP-1734
92AppFoxC-28
92AppFoxF-1002
93MemChiF-392
93RanKee-246
94MemChiF-374
95SprSulTI-13
96LanLugB-3
Mason, Raymond
52LavPro-69
Mason, Rob
88WesPalBES-18
89RocExpLC-17
90WesPalBES-14
Mason, Roger
83BirBarT-24
84EvaTriT-21
85PhoGiaC-190
86Don-633
86FleUpd-72
86GiaMot-23
86TopTra-70T
86TopTraT-70T
87Don-204
87Fle-280
87FleGlo-280
87GiaMot-23
87Top-526
87TopTif-526
88BlaYNPRWLU-7
88PhoFirC-4
88PhoFirP-62
89AstSmo-24
89TucTorC-4
89TucTorJP-14
89TucTorP-195
90BufBisTI-15
91BufBisLD-33
91BufBisP-536
91LinDriAAA-33
91TriA AAGP-AAA3
92Don-715
92FleUpd-115
92Lea-454
92PirNatI-13
92Sco-727
92StaClu-266
92Ult-554
93Don-358
93Fle-116
93PadMot-25
93Sco-441
94Fle-595
94PhiMed-21
94PhiUSPC-3D
94PhiUSPC-10C
94Sco-123
94ScoGolR-123
94StaCluT-221
94StaCluTFDI-221
94Top-533
94TopGol-533
94TopSpa-533
95Don-430
95DonPreP-430
95Fle-376
Masone, Tony
80CedRapRT-9
Massarelli, John
87AubAstP-1
88AubAstP-1961
89AshTouP-945
90FloStaLAS-13
90OscAstS-20
91Cla/Bes-165
91OscAstC-15
91OscAstP-688
92JacGenS-341
92TucTorF-491
93TucTorF-3073
94EdmTraF-2887
95ChaKniTI-14
Massaro, Justo
80VenLeaS-240
93LinVenB-212
Masse, Billy (Bill)
88TopTra-67T
88TopTraT-67T
89PriWilCS-13
89Sta-90
89TopBig-179
90AlbYanB-21
90AlbYanP-1045
90AlbYanS-11
91AlbYanLD-9
91AlbYanP-1020
91LinDriAA-9
92ColCliF-364
92ColCliP-23
92ColCliS-110
92SkyAAAF-50
93ColCliF-1123
93ColCliP-23
93TriAAAGF-49
94ClaGolF-43
94ColCliF-2966
94ColCliP-19
94Top-79
94TopGol-79
94TopSpa-79
95ColCliMCTI-19
95ColCliP-18
95ColCliTI-18
Masse, Daniel
94BilMusF-3665
Massey, Jim
86EveGiaC-17
86EveGiaPC-13
87EveGiaC-21
Massey, Seth
95DavLipB-17
Massicotte, Jeff
87GenCubP-19
88PeoChiTI-15
89PeoChiTI-5
90WinSpiTI-20
Massie, Bret
88SpaPhiS-8
Masson, Todd
93Sou-13
Mast, Brian
92DavLipB-17
93DavLipB-16
93KinMetC-16
93KinMetF-3792
Masteller, Dan
90VisOakCLC-67
90VisOakP-2162
91Cla/Bes-330
91LinDriAA-487
91OrlSunRLD-487
91OrlSunRP-1858
92OrlSunRF-2854
92OrlSunRS-511
93NasXprF-409
94SalLakBF-830
94VenLinU-223
Masters, Burke
88CapCodPPaLP-101
88MisStaB-18
89MisStaB-24
90MisStaB-25
Masters, Dave (David)
86WinSpiP-13
87PitCubP-14
88IowCubC-9
88IowCubP-533
89IowCubC-6
89IowCubP-1698
90CMC-77
90IowCubC-2
90IowCubP-315
90ProAAAF-622
91IndIndLD-189
91IndIndP-458
91LinDriAAA-189
92PhoFirF-2816
92PhoFirS-387
93LinVenB-45
93ShrCapF-2755
Masters, Frank
86GleFalTP-14
87ModA'sC-20
88MadMusP-15
89MadMusS-15
Masters, Walt
31SenTeaIPW-24
79DiaGre-332
Masters, Wayne
90AugPirP-2459
Masterson, Walt
47SenGunBP-6
49Bow-157
50Bow-153
51Bow-307
52Bow-205
52Top-186
53BowBW-9
53Bri-11
60RawGloT-19
76TayBow4-108
79DiaGre-68
83TopRep5-186
Mastropietro, Dave
90NiaFalRP-5
Mastrullo, Michael
94BurIndC-13
94BurIndF-3810
Masuyama, Daryl
86ShrCapP-16
Masuzawa, Hideki
90GatCitPP-3342
Mata, Vic
83NasSouTI-11
84ColCliP-14
84ColCliT-10
85ColCliT-1
85DomLeaS-15
85Don-629
85Fle-644
86ColCliP-13
86ColCliP-15
86YanTCM-34
88RocRedWC-23
88RocRedWGCP-15
88RocRedWP-197
88RocRedWTI-12
92YanWIZ8-110
Matachun, Paul
90ButCopKSP-11
91GasRanC-20
91GasRanP-2697
92GasRanC-18
92GasRanF-2261
Matas, Jim
86GenCubP-18
87WinSpiP-26
88WinSpiS-10
Matchett, Steve
89BriTigS-16
Matchick, J. Tom
67OPC-72
67Top-72
68OPC-113
68TigDetFPB-14
68Top-113
68TopVen-113
69MilBra-168
69Top-344
70RoyTeal-21
70Top-647
71MLBOffS-419
71OPC-321
71Top-321
72MilBra-208
73OPC-631
73Top-631
81TCM60I-397
88TigDom-12
91OriCro-282
94BreMilB-152
Matcuk, Steven
96PorRocB-23
Mateo, Huascar
88BenBucL-13
Mateo, Jose
90ChaRaiB-15
90ChaRaiP-2047
95GreFalDTI-22
96SavSanB-25
Mateo, Luis
89MadMusS-16
Mateo, Ruben
96ChaRivTI-9619
Matheny, Mike (Michael)
91HelBreSP-11
92ClaFS7-393
92StoPorC-15
92StoPorF-37
93ElPasDF-2953
94Bow-673
94BreMilB-329
94ExcFS7-83
94Sel-204
94SpoRoo-127
94SpoRooAP-127
94Ult-375
95Pin-144
95PinArtP-144
95PinMusC-144
96Don-541
96DonPreP-541
96Fla-102
96Fle-152
96FleTif-152
96LeaSigA-148
96LeaSigAG-148
96LeaSigAS-148
96StaClu-446
96StaCluMOP-446
96Ult-366
96UltGolM-366
97ColCho-372
97Fle-133
97FleTif-133
97Pac-123
97PacLigB-123
97PacSil-123
97Top-485
97Ult-78
97UltGolME-78
97UltPlaME-78
Matheson, Bill
43CenFlo-19
44CenFlo-16
45CenFlo-16
Mathews, Byron
90OklSoo-11
92ClaDraP-120
93MidLeaAGF-25
93SouBenWSC-15
93SouBenWSF-1445
93StaCluM-186
93Top-612
93TopGol-612
93TopInaM-612
93TopMic-612
94SouBenSHC-9
94SouBenSHF-607
92UtiBluSC-7
Mathews, Chuck
85OscAstTI-11
86ColAstP-18
Mathews, Del
94MacBraC-12
94MacBraF-2199
95DurBulTI-20
96DurBulBIB-10
96DurBulBrB-11
Mathews, Eddie (Edwin Lee)
47Exh-150A
47Exh-150B
50JJKCopP-10
52Top-407
53BraJohC-21
53BraSpiaS3-17
53BowC-97
53BraSpiaS7-8
53Top-37
54Bow-64
54BraJohC-41
54BraSpiaSP-13
54RedMan-NL23
54Top-30
55Bow-103
55BraGolS-18
55BraJohC-41
55BraSpiaSD-12
55Top-155
55BigLeaIS-12
55DaiQueS-12
56BraBilaBP-13
56TopHocF-B21
56TopPin-18
56Top-107
56YelBasP-21
57BraSpiaS4-14
57Top-250
58BraJayP-8
58HarSta-4
58Top-351
58Top-440
58Top-480
59HomRunD-13
59Top-212
59Top-450
60BraSpiaS-12
60RawGloT-20
60ArmCoi-15
60BraDav-2
60KeyChal-33
60Pos-6
60Top-420
60Top-558
60TopTat-33
61Baz-11
61NuSco-412
61Pos-106
61Top-43
61Top-120
61TopStaI-45
62Baz-2
62Jel-147
62Pos-147
62TopStaI-148
62BraJayP-6
62ExhStaB-25
62PosCan-147
62SalPlaC-111
62ShiPlaC-111
62Top-30
62TopBuc-56
62TopVen-30
63BasMagM-56
63BraJayP-7
63ExhStaB-43
63Jel-151
63Pos-151
63SalMetC-28
63Top-275
64BraJayP-6
64ChatheY-35
64TopSta-97
64Top-35
64TopCoi-33
64TopStaU-47
64TopTatI-52
64TopVen-35
65ChaTheY-35
65Top-500
65TopEmbI-26
66Top-200
66TopRubI-59
66TopVen-200
67AstTeal1-9
67CokCapAs-18
67DexPre-133
67OPC-166
67Top-166
67TopVen-214

68CokCapT-16
68OPC-58
68Top-58
68TopVen-58
69EquSpoHoF-BB12
69MilBra-169
73OPC-237
73Top-237A
73Top-237B
74BraPhoC-4
74OPC-634
74Top-634
77GalGloG-34
78AtlCon-14
78BraTCC-9
79BasGre-78
79DiaGre-400
79TCM50-157
80Lau300-25
80PerHaloFP-166
80SSPHOF-166
82CraJac-12
83Bra53F-41
83MLBPin-26
83TopRep5-407
84OCoandSI-22
84OCoandSI-121
84SpoDesPW-17
85CirK-11
86SumBraP-18
86BigLeaC-10
86BraGreT-4
86SpoDecG-34
86SpoDesJM-16
86TCM-19
86TCMSupS-40
87AstShoSTw-23
87Bra195T-2
87DurBulP-16
87NesDreT-25
88GreBraB-22
88TigDom-13
89HOFStiB-25
89KahCoo-8
89PacLegI-116
89PerCelP-30
89RicBraBC-14
89RicBraC-10
89RicBraP-845
89RicBraTI-14
89TopBasT-32
90PacLeg-66
90PerGreM-28
90SumBraB-12
90SweBasG-65
91LinDri-40
91SweBasG-147
91TopArc1-37
91UppDecS-15
92BazQua5A-3
92TVSpoMF5HRC-7
93ActPacA-117
93ActPacA2-51G
94TedWil-43
94TopArc1-30
94TopArc1G-30
97TopStaHRR-8
97TopStaHRRA-8

Mathews, Gary Nathaniel
85AllGamPI-149

Mathews, Greg
86CarTeal-28
86DonRoo-26
86FleUpd-73
86SpoRoo-41
87CarSmo-8
87Don-208
87Fle-303
87FleGlo-303
87Top-567
87TopGloS-60
87TopTif-567
87ToyRoo-20
88CarSmo-7
88Don-84
88DonBasB-324
88Fle-41
88FleGlo-41
88LouRedBTI-33
88Sco-226
88ScoGlo-226
88ScoYouS2-35
88StaLinCa-13
88Top-133
88TopBig-177
88TopTif-133
89Don-281
89Fle-456
89FleGlo-456
89Sco-286
89Top-97
89TopTif-97
89UppDec-531
90CarSmo-13
90LouRedBLBC-26
90OPC-209
90PubSti-221
90Sco-537
90Top-209
90TopTif-209
90TopTVCa-17
90UppDec-678
90VenSti-322
92ScrRedBF-2443
92ScrRedBS-489
93Fle-495

Mathews, Jeremy
89BelMarL-22

Mathews, Jim
78AshTouT-16

Mathews, Jon
94BenRocF-3604
97BenRocC-16

Mathews, Michael
92ClaDraP-27
93WatIndF-3558

Mathews, Nelson
63Top-54A
63Top-54B
64Top-366
64TopVen-366
65OPC-87
65Top-87
81TCM60I-394

Mathews, Rick
81ChaRoyT-26
82ForMyeRT-22
84MemChiT-1

Mathews, Robert
87OldJudN-325
90KalBatN-34

Mathews, T.J.
92HamRedC-19
92HamRedF-1588
93ClaGolF-120
93ExcFS7-102
93MidLeaAGF-52
93SprCarC-18
93SprCarF-1847
94Bow-236
94ClaGolF-165
94ExcFS7-271
94FloStaLAF-FSL42
94St.PetCC-16
94St.PetCF-2583
95LouRedF-274
96Bow-255
96CarPol-17
96Fin-B297
96FinRef-B297
96Fla-363
96Fle-548
96FleTif-548
96LeaSigA-149
96LeaSigAG-149
96LeaSigAS-149
96SigRooOJ-18
96SigRooOJS-18
96Top-102
96Ult-550
96UltGolM-550
97Fle-448
97FleTif-448
97PacPriGotD-GD200
97Top-343
97Ult-275
97UltGolME-275
97UltPlaME-275

Mathews, Terry
88ChaRanS-15
89TulDriGS-17
89TulDriTI-15
90TulDriP-1171
90TulDriTI-15
91LinDriAAA-311
91OklCit8LD-311
91OklCit8P-173
92Don-694
92Fle-310
92ProFS7-151
92RanMot-20
92RanTeal-12
92Sco-737
92TopDeb91-118
92TopGol-131
92TopGolW-131
92Ult-135
93Fle-684
93JacGenF-2107
93RanKee-247
94EdmTraF-2873
95Fle-337
95Top-623
95TopCyb-390
95Ult-164
95UltGolM-164
96Fle-389
96FleTif-389
96LeaSigEA-122

Mathews, Tom
86FreGiaP-22

Mathewson, Christy
03BreE10-94
03WilCarE-22
06GiaUllAFS-6
08AmeCarE-13
08AmeCarE-52
08RosComP-128
09AmeCarE-74
09MaxPubP-6
09PhiCarE-16
09SpoNewSM-3
09T206-229
09T206-230
09T206-231
10CouT21-43
10CouT21-179
10CouT21-301
10DomDisP-76
10E-UOraBSC-15
10E101-31
10E102-17
10E12AmeCDC-23
10E98-20
10JHDABE-12
10JuJuDE-25
10MelMinE-31
10NadCarE-34
10OrnOvaPP-11
10PeoT21-37A
10PeoT21-37B
10RedCroT-47
10RedCroT-48
10RedCroT-134
10SepAnoP-19
10StaCarE-21
10SweCapPP-117A
10SweCapPP-117B
10W555-45
11DiaGumP-19
11L1L-133
11MecDFT-6
11PloCanE-44
11S74Sil-88
11S81LarS-108
11SpoLifCW-235
11SpoLifM-211
11T205-109
11TurRedT-27
12HasTriFT-29A
12HasTriFT-29B
12HasTriFT-29C
12HasTriFT-29D
12HasTriFT-48E
12HasTriFT-48H
12HasTriFT-74C
12HasTriFT-74D
13NatGamW-28
13PolGroW-17
13TomBarW-27
14CraJacE-88
14TexTomE-30
14TexTomE-58
15AmeCarE-27
15CraJacE-88
16FleBreD-62
19W514-72
30SchR33-10
36PC7AlbHoF-3
40PlaBal-175
48ExhHoF-22
49LeaPre-5
50CalHOFW-52
50H80FouMH-2
51R42SmaS-68
51TopConMA-8
60ExhWriH-16
60Fle-2
60NuHi-8
61Fle-59
61GolPre-24
61NuSco-477
61Top-408
63BasMagM-57
63BazA-4
63HalofFB-13
67TopVen-151
68LauWorS-2
68SpoMemAG-5
69Baz-3
69Baz-12
70FleWorS-2
71FleWorS-3
71FleWorS-11
72FleFamF-3
72LauGreF-25
73FleWilD-22
73HalofFPP-11
76ShaPiz-4
77GalGloG-152
77GalGloG-242
77ShaPiz-6
79Pew-4
80GiaGreT-10
80Lau300-5
80LauFamF-22
80PacLeg-34
80PerHaloFP-3
80SSPHOF-1
81ConTSN-9
82BHCRSpoL-6
83DonHOFH-3
84GalHaloFRL-4
84OCoandSI-119
84OCoandSI-172
85Woo-25
86ConSer1-23
86ConSer1-32
86ConSer1-46
87ConSer2-3
87HygAllG-32
89HOFStiB-65
90BasWit-104
90HOFStiB-10
90PerGreM-6
90SweBasG-134
91ConTSN-57
91ConTSNP-331
91SweBasG-141
91USGamSBL-12C
91USGamSBL-12D
91USGamSBL-12H
91USGamSBL-12S
92ConTSN-331
92ConTSNCI-9
93ActPacA-87
93ActPacA2-21G
93CokCasI-CM1
93ConMasC-8
93ConTSN-910
93CraJac-4
93UppDecAH-89
93UppDecAH-143
93UppDecAH-144
93UppDecAH-155
93UppDecAH-156
94ConTSN-1220
94ConTSNB-1220
94UppDecAH-35
94UppDecAH-104
94UppDecAH-153
94UppDecAH1-35
94UppDecAH1-104
94UppDecAH1-153
94UppDecTAE-14
94UppDecTAELD-LD5
95ConTSN-1322
93UppDecTR-1
96ColCho-503
96ColChoGS-503
96ColChoSS-503
20W516-24

Mathewson, Harry
06GiaUllAFS-7

Mathias, Bob
53SpoMagP-5

Mathias, Carl
60Top-139
60TopVen-139
61MapLeaBH-13
78ReaRem-13

Mathieu, Franz
82MonNew-9

Mathile, Michael
90JamExpP-21

Mathile, Mike
89AncBucTI-7
91RocExpC-9
91RocExpP-2044
92ClaFS7-127
92HarSenF-458
92HarSenS-290
92SkyAA F-123
93OttLynF-2432
94IndIndF-1807
95IndIndF-91

Mathiot, Mike
89KenTwiP-1059
89KenTwiS-13
90KenTwiB-7
90KenTwiP-2302
90KenTwiS-11

Mathis, Joe
94BelMarC-19
94BelMarF-3251
96WisTimRB-15

Mathis, Lefty (Verdell)
86NegLeaF-62
91NegLeaRL-7
91PomBlaBPB-2
92NegLeaRLI-40
93UppDecS-17
95NegLeaLI-7

Mathis, Monte
92SarWhiSCB-23

Mathis, Ron
81BirBarT-5
83TucTorT-4
84TucTorC-72
85AstMot-26
85FleUpd-78
85TopTifT-79T
85TopTra-79T
86Fle-305
86Top-476
86TopTif-476
86TucTorP-12
87TucTorP-14
88ColSprSSC-5
88ColSprSSP-1548

Mathis, Sammie
95WatIndTI-18

Mathis, Wayne
90KinMetB-4
90KinMetS-16

Mathison, Chuck
84GreHorT-15

Matias, John
70OPC-444
70Top-444
71OPC-546
71Top-546
73TacTwiC-14
87HawRai-8

Matilla, Pedro
88ElmPioC-14
89WinHavRSS-15
90WinHavRSS-14
91WinHavRSC-14

Matlack, Jon
71OPC-648
71Top-648
72OPC-141
72Top-141
73Kel2D-12
73LinPor-116
73OPC-55
73Top-55
74MetJapEB-6
74OPC-153
74OPC-471
74Top-153
74Top-471
74TopDecE-44
74TopSta-66
75Kel-10
75MetSSP-21
75OPC-290
75Top-290
76Hos-97

76Kel-49A
76Kel-49B
76MetMSAP-4
76OPC-190
76SSP-554
76Top-190
77BurCheD-137
77Hos-114
77MetDaiPA-14
77MSADis-38
77OPC-132
77PepGloD-68
77RCColC-38
77Top-440
78OPC-98
78RanBurK-5
78RCColC-38
78SSP270-99
78Top-25
78WifBalD-43
79Hos-122
79Kel-58
79OPC-159
79Top-315
80OPC-312
80Top-592
81Don-266
81Fle-621
81FleStiC-51
81OPC-339
81Top-656
81TopSti-135
81TopSupHT-92
82Don-215
82Fle-323
82FleSta-176
82OPC-239
82Top-239
83Don-195
83Fle-572
83FleSta-117
83FleSti-165
83RanAffF-32
83Top-749
84Don-378
84Fle-422
84Nes792-149
84Top-149
84TopTif-149
86RanGreT-2
89PacLegI-214
89PacSenL-9
89RivRedWB-23
89RivRedWCLC-26
89RivRedWP-1408
89T/MSenL-73
89TidTidC-3
89TopSenL-102
90EliSenL-11
90WicWraRD-27
91LasVegSLD-300
91LasVegSP-254
91LinDriAAA-300
91MetWIZ-253
92LasVegSF-2811
93RanKee-248
93SarWhiSC-29
93SarWhiSF-1387
94PriWilCC-26
94PriWilCF-1938

Matlock, Leroy
78LauLonABS-32

Matney, Ron
74WicAerODF-115

Matos, Alberto
93SpoIndC-12
93SpoIndF-3588

Matos, Carlos
82DanSunF-11

Matos, Domingo
90JamExpP-3
91JamExpC-14
91JamExpP-3554
92RocExpC-10
92RocExpF-2125
93WesPalBEC-14
93WesPalBEF-1349
94WesPalBEC-17
94WesPalBEF-51

Matos, Francisco
89ModA'sC-24
89ModA'sCLC-283
90ModA'sC-19
90ModA'sCLC-168
90ModA'sP-2220
91HunStaC-15
91HunStaLD-289
91HunStaP-1804
91LinDriAA-289
92HunStaS-314
92SkyAA F-133
93HunStaF-2090
94TacTigF-3183
95Pac-315

Matos, Jose
94AshTouC-15
94AshTouF-1775
94BenRocF-3589

Matos, Julius
94WatIndC-19
94WatIndF-3945

Matos, Luis
92HunCubF-3146

Matos, Malvin
90ButCopKSP-12
91GasRanC-24
91GasRanP-2701
92GasRanC-23
92GasRanF-2265
93ChaRaiC-13
93ChaRaiF-1924
93LinVenB-33
94ChaRanF-2508
94VenLinU-83
95LinVen-202

Matos, Pascual
94IdaFalBF-3588
94IdaFalBSP-15
94MacBraC-13
94MacBraF-2209
95MacBraTI-18
96DurBulBIB-24
96DurBulBrB-25

Matos, Rafael
84ButCopKT-16
85DomLeaS-96

Matouzas, Jeff
90TamYanD-16

Matranga, Dave
90NebCor-18

Matranga, Jeff
92JohCitCF-3113
94St.PetCC-17
94St.PetCF-2584
96ArkTraB-18

Matrisciano, Ron
80CliGiaT-7

Matsubara, Makoto
79TCMJapPB-5

Matsukubo, Shingo
89SalLakTTI-12

Matsumoto, Akira
96MauStiHWB-7

Matsunaga, Hiromi
87JapPlaB-29

Matsuo, Hideharu
87MiaMarP-22

Mattern, Al
09ColChiE-179
09T206-232
10DomDisP-77
10SweCapPP-68A
10SweCapPP-68B
11MecDFT-24
11S74Sil-45
11SpoLifM-274
11T205-110
12ColRedB-179
12ColTinT-179
12HasTriFT-50C

Mattes, Troy
96DelShoB-22

Matthews, Fran (Francis)
93NegLeaRL2-25

Matthews, Gary
73LinPor-161
73OPC-606
73Top-606
74OPC-386
74Top-386
75Gia-4
75Hos-31
75HosTwi-31
75OPC-79
75Top-79
76Hos-142
76OPC-133
76SSP-110
76Top-133
77BurCheD-210
77Hos-142
77RCColC-39
77Top-194
78BraCok-8
78Hos-19
78OPC-209
78RCColC-27
78Top-475
78WifBalD-44
79Hos-42
79OPC-35
79Top-85
80Kel-48
80OPC-186
80Top-355
81AllGamPI-153
81Don-306A
81Don-306B
81Fle-251A
81Fle-251B
81OPC-186
81Top-528
81TopScr-76
81TopSti-144
81TopTra-800
82Don-441
82Fle-249
82FleSta-58
82OPC-151
82Top-680
82TopSti-79
83AllGamPI-152
83Don-420
83Dra-16
83Fle-165
83FleSta-118
83FleSti-178
83OPC-64
83PhiPosGPaM-6
83PhiTas-16
83Top-780
83TopSti-269
84AllGamPI-59
84CubChiT-18
84CubSev-36
84Don-233
84Dra-21
84Fle-40
84FleSti-121
84FleUpd-77
84FunFooP-70
84Nes792-70
84Nes792-637
84OCoandSI-41
84OPC-70
84SevCoi-E23
84Top-70
84Top-637
84TopRubD-16
84TopSti-18
84TopSti-118
84TopTif-70
84TopTif-637
84TopTra-77T
84TopTraT-77T
85CubLioP-16
85CubSev-36
85Don-239
85Dra-18
85Fle-61
85FleStaS-24
85Lea-220
85OPC-210
85SevCoi-S10
85Top-210
85TopMin-210
85TopRubD-30
85TopSti-44
85TopSup-19
85TopTif-210
86BasStaB-70
86CubGat-36
86CubUno-12
86Don-76
86Fle-373
86GenMilB-4E
86OPC-292
86Spo-66
86Top-485
86TopSti-59
86TopTat-5
86TopTif-485
87CubCan-18
87CubDavB-36
87Fle-568
87FleGlo-568
87OPC-390
87SevCoi-C10
87Top-390
87TopSti-62
87TopTif-390
88OPC-156
88Sco-599
88ScoGlo-599
88Top-156
88TopSti-223
88TopTif-156
89SweBasG-118
93UppDecS-2
93UppDecS-12

Matthews, Gary Jr.
94SpoIndF-3337
96RanCucQB-19

Matthews, Jeff
78GreBraT-15

Matthews, Jeremy
89WauTimGS-15

Matthews, Joel
89MisStaB-25
90MisStaB-26
91MisStaB-32
92MisStaB-28
93MisStaB-29

Matthews, Michael
92ClaFS7-419
93Bow-261
93StaCluM-149
93Top-787
93TopGol-787
93TopInaM-787
93TopMic-787
93WatIndC-18
94ColRedF-440
96CanIndB-18

Matthews, Ron
92LetMouSP-24
93PocPosSP-14

Matthews, Tom
90KisDodD-17

Matthews, Wid (W.C.)
21Exh-102

Matthias, Brother
92MegRut-118

Mattick, Robert
39CubTeal-17
80Top-577
81Don-570
81Fle-431
81Top-674

Mattimore, Michael
87OldJudN-326

Mattingly, Dennis
89AncBucTI-25

Mattingly, Don
81NasSouTI-8
82ColCliP-19
82ColCliT-21
84Don-248
84Fle-131
84FunFooP-77
84Nes792-8
84OCoandSI-103
84OPC-8
84Top-8
84TopPewB-3
84TopSti-325
84TopTif-8
85AllGamPI-6
85Don-7
85Don-295
85Don-651A
85Don-651B
85DonActA-48
85DonHig-36
85DonHig-44
85DonHig-45
85DonSupD-7
85Dra-19
85Fle-133
85FleLimE-20
85FleStaS-4
85FleStaS-37
85Lea-7
85Lea-140
85OPC-324
85SevCoi-E12
85Top-665
85Top3-D-8
85TopGaloC-6
85TopGloS-27
85TopRubD-22
85TopSti-171
85TopSti-310
85TopSup-4
85TopTif-665
86BasStaB-71
86BurKinA-19
86Don-173
86DonAll-50
86DonHig-48
86DonHig-53
86DorChe-13
86Dra-7
86Fle-109
86Fle-627
86Fle-639
86FleAll-1
86FleLeaL-22
86FleLimE-27
86FleMin-24
86FleSlu-21
86FleStiC-72
86FraGloT-2
86FraGloT-3
86GenMilB-1D
86KayB-19
86Lea-103
86MeaGolBB-8
86MeaGolM-5
86MeaGolSB-5
86MSAJifPD-6
86OPC-180
86OPCBoxB-J
86QuaGra-18
86SevCoi-C3
86SevCoi-E3
86SevCoi-S3
86SevCoi-W3
86Spo-2
86Spo-54
86Spo-75
86Spo-176
86Spo-179
86Spo-180
86Spo-183
86Spo-184
86SpoDecG-65
86Top-180
86Top-712
86Top3-D-15
86TopGaloC-6
86TopGloS-31
86TopMinL-28
86TopSti-296
86TopSup-1
86TopTat-7
86TopTif-180
86TopTif-712
86TopWaxBC-J
86TruVal-5
86Woo-20
86YanTCM-24
87BoaandB-32
87BurKinA-13
87ClaGam-10
87ClaUpdY-104
87Don-52
87DonAll-33
87DonHig-17
87DonHig-23
87DonHig-48
87DonOpeD-241
87Dra-8
87Fle-104
87Fle-638
87FleAll-1
87FleAwaW-24
87FleBasA-26
87FleExcS-33
87FleGamW-26
87FleGlo-104
87FleGlo-638
87FleHotS-27
87FleLeaL-28
87FleLimE-26
87FleMin-66
87FleRecS-20
87FleSlu-25
87FleStiC-74
87FleStiC-131

87FleStiWBC-S8
87GenMilB-2E
87HosSti-27
87K-M-28
87KayB-19
87KraFoo-29
87Lea-150
87MandMSL-11
87MSAIceTD-6
87MSAJifPD-6
87OPC-229
87RalPur-5
87RedFolSB-106
87SevCoi-E12
87Spo-1
87Spo-75
87Spo-159
87SpoDeaP-1
87SpoRea-21
87SpoTeaP-7
87StaBlaM-1
87StaBlaM-2
87StaBlaM-3
87StaBlaM-4
87StaBlaM-5
87StaBlaM-6
87StaMat-1
87StaMat-2
87StaMat-3
87StaMat-4
87StaMat-5
87StaMat-6
87StaMat-7
87StaMat-8
87StaMat-9
87StaMat-10
87StaMat-11
87StaMat-12
87StaMat-13
87StaMat-14
87StaMat-15
87StaMat-16
87StaMat-17
87StaMat-18
87StaMat-19
87StaMat-20
87StaMat-21
87StaMat-22
87StaMat-23
87StaMat-24
87StuPan-23
87Top-406
87Top-500
87Top-606
87Top-606A
87TopCoi-17
87TopGaloC-7
87TopGloS-1
87TopMinL-65
87TopSti-294
87TopTif-406
87TopTif-500
87TopTif-606A
87TopTif-606B
87Woo-15
88ActPacT-5
88Baz-11
88CheBoy-16
88ClaBlu-211
88ClaBlu-247
88ClaRed-151
88ClaRed-152
88CMCMat-1
88CMCMat-2
88CMCMat-3
88CMCMat-4
88CMCMat-5
88CMCMat-6
88CMCMat-7
88CMCMat-8
88CMCMat-9
88CMCMat-10
88CMCMat-11
88CMCMat-12
88CMCMat-13
88CMCMat-14
88CMCMat-15
88CMCMat-16
88CMCMat-17
88CMCMat-18
88CMCMat-19
88CMCMat-20
88CMCMat-P1
88Don-217
88DonAll-1
88DonBasB-1
88DonBonM-BC21
88DonPop-1
88DonReaBY-217
88Dra-1
88Fle-214
88FleAwaW-23
88FleBasA-23
88FleBasM-22
88FleExcS-25
88FleGlo-214
88FleHea-1
88FleHotS-24
88FleLeaL-25
88FleMin-41
88FleRecS-24
88FleSlu-26
88FleStiC-48
88FleSup-22
88FleTeaL-19
88GreBasS-14
88K-M-15
88KayB-16
88KinDis-15
88Lea-177
88MSAFanSD-9
88MSAIceTD-3
88Nes-15
88OPC-300
88PanSti-152
88PanSti-155
88PanSti-227
88PanSti-430
88RedFolSB-53
88Sco-1
88Sco-650
88Sco-658
88ScoBoxC-2
88ScoGlo-1
88ScoGlo-650
88ScoGlo-658
88ScoYouS2-1
88Spo-1
88Spo-222
88SpoGam-1
88StaLinAl-17
88StaLinY-8
88StaMat-1
88StaMat-2
88StaMat-3
88StaMat-4
88StaMat-5
88StaMat-6
88StaMat-7
88StaMat-8
88StaMat-9
88StaMat-10
88StaMat-11
88StaMat/S-1
88StaMat/S-3
88StaMat/S-5
88StaMat/S-7
88StaMat/S-9
88StaMat/S-11
88Top-2
88Top-300
88Top-386
88TopBig-229
88TopCoi-19
88TopGloA-2
88TopGloS-11
88TopMinL-27
88TopRitTM-22
88TopSti-3
88TopSti-156
88TopSti-299
88TopStiB-35
88TopTif-2
88TopTif-300
88TopTif-386
88TopUKM-45
88TopUKMT-45
88Woo-4
89Bow-176
89BowTif-176
89CadEllD-34
89CerSup-11
89ClaLigB-5
89ClaTraO-106
89Don-26
89Don-74
89DonAll-21
89DonBasB-1
89DonSupD-26
89Fle-258
89FleBasA-28
89FleBasM-26
89FleExcS-31
89FleForTR-6
89FleGlo-258
89FleHeroB-26
89FleLeaL-25
89FleSup-29
89K-M-12
89KayB-20
89MasBreD-6
89MSAHolD-4
89MSAIceTD-1
89Nis-4
89OPC-26
89PanSti-404
89RedFolSB-79
89RinPosM-1
89RinPosM-2
89RinPosM-3
89RinPosM-4
89RinPosM-5
89RinPosM-6
89RinPosM-7
89RinPosM-8
89RinPosM-9
89RinPosM-10
89RinPosM-11
89RinPosM-12
89Sco-100
89ScoHot1S-10
89ScoSco-6
89Spo-50
89SpollIFKI-37
89Top-397
89Top-700
89TopBasT-123
89TopBatL-3
89TopBig-50
89TopCapC-8
89TopCoi-43
89TopDouA-1
89TopDouM-14
89TopGloS-51
89TopHeaUT-19
89TopRitM-1
89TopRitM-2
89TopRitM-3
89TopRitM-4
89TopRitM-5
89TopRitM-6
89TopRitM-7
89TopRitM-8
89TopRitM-9
89TopSti-314
89TopStiB-2
89TopTif-397
89TopTif-700
89TopUKM-49
89TVSpoM-82
89UppDec-200
89UppDec-693
89UppDecS-3
89YanScoNW-1
90AllBasT-11
90Bow-443
90BowIns-5
90BowInsT-5
90BowTif-443
90BowTif-A5
90ClaBlu-16
90ClaYel-T12
90ClaYel-NNO0
90Col-13
90ColMat-1
90ColMat-2
90ColMat-3
90ColMat-4
90ColMat-5
90ColMat-6
90ColMat-7
90ColMat-8
90ColMat-9
90ColMat-10
90ColMat-11
90ColMat-12
90ColtheSBM-97
90Don-190
90DonBesA-38
90DonLeaS-12
90Fle-447
90Fle-626
90Fle-638
90FleAwaW-21
90FleBasA-24
90FleBasM-23
90FleCan-447
90FleCan-626
90FleCan-638
90FleLeaL-23
90FleLeaS-2
90FleWaxBC-C19
90GooHumICBLS-13
90HOFStiB-90
90Hot50PS-25
90K-M-17
90KayB-18
90KinDis-14
90Lea-69
90MLBBasB-63
90MSAIceTD-14
90OPC-200
90PanSti-125
90Pos-1
90PubSti-291
90PubSti-540
90RedFolSB-59
90Sco-1
90Sco100S-10
90Spo-150
90StaLonJS-1
90StaLonJS-28
90StaLonJS-35
90SunSee-8
90Top-200
90TopAmeA-18
90TopBatL-4
90TopBig-85
90TopCoi-21
90TopDou-43
90TopGloS-11
90TopHeaU-19
90TopHilHM-3
90TopMag-17
90TopMinL-24
90TopSti-308
90TopStiB-34
90TopTif-200
90TopTVA-17
90TopTVY-25
90UppDec-191
90VenSti-323
90VenSti-324
90WonBreS-6
90YanScoNW-2
91BasBesHM-14
91BasBesRB-11
91Bow-178
91CadEllD-36
91Cla1-T33
91Cla3-T56
91ClaGam-98
91CokMat-1
91CokMat-2
91CokMat-3
91CokMat-4
91CokMat-5
91CokMat-6
91CokMat-7
91CokMat-8
91CokMat-9
91CokMat-10
91CokMat-11
91CokMat-12
91CokMat-13
91CokMat-14
91CokMat-15
91DenHol-8
91Don-107
91Fle-673
91FlePro-11
91Lea-425
91LeaPre-22
91MajLeaCP-1
91MooSna-15
91OPC-100
91OPCPre-77
91PanFreS-324
91PanSti-267
91PepSup-11
91PetSta-19
91PlaMat-26
91PlaMat-27
91PlaMat-28
91PlaMat-29
91PlaMat-30
91PlaMat-44
91PlaMat-45
91PlaMat-46
91PlaMat-47
91PlaMat-48
91PlaMatG-4
91PlaMatG-5
91Pos-29
91RedFolS-61
91RinPosM2-1
91RinPosM2-2
91RinPosM2-3
91RinPosM2-4
91RinPosM2-5
91RinPosM2-6
91RinPosM2-7
91RinPosM2-8
91RinPosM2-9
91RinPosM2-10
91RinPosM2-11
91RinPosM2-12
91Sco-23
91Sco-856
91Sco100S-23
91Sev3DCN-11
91SevCoi-NE11
91SimandSMLBL-28
91StaClu-21
91StaCluP-25
91StaPinB-29
91Stu-97
91Top-100
91Top-100A
91TopCraJl-7
91TopDesS-100
91TopMic-100
91TopSta-24
91TopTif-100
91TopTriH-A10
91Ult-239
91UppDec-354
92Bow-340
92Cla1-T58
92Cla2-T49
92ClaGam-105
92ColPro-11
92Don-596
92DonCraJ1-36
92DonMat#-1
92Fle-237
92FleCitTP-16
92FleTeaL-1
92Fre-11
92Hig5-89
92HitTheBB-21
92JimDea-8
92Lea-57
92LeaGolP-22
92LeaPre-22
92Mr.TurS-16
92New-15
92OPC-300
92OPCPre-92
92PanSti-135
92Pin-23
92Pin-584
92Pos-3
92Sco-23
92Sco100S-23
92ScoProP-7
92SevCoi-2
92SpoStaCC-32
92StaClu-420
92StaPro-7
92Stu-216
92StuHer-BC5
92StuPre-9
92Top-300
92TopGol-300
92TopGolW-300
92TopKid-84
92TopMic-300
92TopMic-G300
92TriPla-159
92TriPlaP-4
92Ult-105
92UltAwaW-19
92UppDec-356
92UppDecF-31
92UppDecFG-31
92UppDecS-1
92UppDecTMH-33
92YanWIZ8-111
92YanWIZA-46

93Bow-595
93CadDis-40
93ClaGam-59
93DiaMar-71
93Don-264
93Don-609
93DonEli-24
93DonEliD-6
93DonEliD-AU6
93DonEliS-6
93DonMVP-5
93DonPre-18
93DurPowP1-19
93Fin-98
93FinJum-98
93FinPro-98
93FinProR-98
93FinRef-98
93Fla-249
93Fle-281
93FleAtl-14
93FleFruotL-43
93FunPac-208
93Hos-28
93JimDea-6
93Kra-9
93Lea-237
93LeaGolA-R2
93MetBak-14
93OPC-103
93OPCPre-46
93PacSpa-208
93PanSti-154
93Pin-23
93Pin-470
93PinCoo-14
93PinCooD-14
93PinSlu-23
93Pos-12
93Sco-23
93ScoFra-10
93Sel-24
93SelSam-24
93SelStaL-14
93SP-265
93StaClu-557
93StaCluFDI-557
93StaClul-B2
93StaCluMOP-557
93StaCluMOP-MB2
93StaCluY-1
93Stu-193
93Top-32
93TopGol-32
93TopInaM-32
93TopMic-32
93TopMic-P32
93TopPre-32
93TriPla-120
93TriPlaA-19
93Ult-244
93UltAwaW-12
93UppDec-47
93UppDec-134
93UppDecCP-R14
93UppDecDG-28
93UppDecGold-47
93UppDecGold-134
93UppDecIC-WI26
93UppDecICJ-WI26
93UppDecTAN-TN13
94Bow-25
94Bow-386
94BowBes-R45
94BowBesR-R45
94ColC-192
94ColC-355
94ColChoGS-192
94ColChoGS-355
94ColChoSS-192
94ColChoSS-355
94ColChoT-3
94Don-340
94DonAnn8-8
94DonDiaK-DK16
94DonMVP-24
94DonPro-9
94DonSpeE-340
94DonSpiotG-9
94ExtBas-133
94ExtBasGB-17
94Fin-392
94FinRef-392
94Fla-84
94FlaHotG-6
94FlaInfP-4
94Fle-239
94FleSun-17
94FleTeaL-10
94FleUpdDT-6
94FUnPac-123
94FUnPac-200
94Lea-121
94LeaGam-4
94LeaGolS-6
94LeaL-56
94LeaPro-5
94OPC-54
94Pac-430
94PacSilP-10
94PanSti-102
94Pin-23
94PinArtP-23
94PinMusC-23
94Pos-2
94ProMag-88
94RedFolMI-17
94Sco-23
94ScoDreT-3
94ScoGolR-23
94ScoGolS-49
94Sel-23
94SP-198
94SPDieC-198
94SPHol-25
94SPHolDC-25
94Spo-127
94SpoMov-MM9
94SPPre-ER4
94StaClu-195
94StaCluFDI-195
94StaCluGR-195
94StaCluMOP-195
94StaCluMOP-ST24
94StaCluST-ST24
94StaCluT-181
94StaCluTF-7
94StaCluTFDI-181
94Stu-215
94StuHer-4
94StuSerS-10
94Top-600
94TopGol-600
94TopSpa-600
94TopSupS-27
94TriPla-276
94TriPlaP-9
94Ult-400
94UltAwaW-2
94UppDec-90
94UppDec-290
94UppDecAJ-8
94UppDecAJG-8
94UppDecDC-E8
94UppDecED-90
94UppDecED-290
94Yoo-10
95Baz-47
95Bow-282
95BowBes-R46
95BowBesR-R46
95ClaPhoC-38
95ColCho-510
95ColChoGS-510
95ColChoSE-240
95ColChoSEGS-240
95ColChoSESS-240
95ColChoSS-510
95D3-37
95DenHol-15
95Don-55
95Don-220
95Don-440
95DonPreP-55
95DonPreP-220
95DonPreP-440
95DonTopotO-120
95Emb-115
95EmbGolI-115
95Emo-62
95Fin-126
95FinRef-126
95Fla-66
95FlaHotG-8
95Fle-76
95FleTeaL-10
95FleUpdSL-7
95Lea-303
95Lea300C-15
95LeaCor-3
95LeaGolS-6
95LeaGreG-10
95LeaLim-55
95LeaLimG-12
95LeaLimIBP-21
95LeaStaS-3
95MegRut-13
95NatPac2-5
95Pac-299
95PacGolP-10
95PacPri-97
95PanSti-38
95Pin-21
95Pin-295
95PinArtP-21
95PinArtP-295
95PinFan-3
95PinGatA-GA12
95PinMusC-21
95PinMusC-295
95PinRedH-RH10
95PinWhiH-WH10
95RedFol-27
95Sco-239
95Sco-564
95ScoDouGC-GC5
95ScoGolR-239
95ScoGolR-564
95ScoHaloG-HG22
95ScoPlaTS-239
95ScoPlaTS-564
95ScoRul-SR25
95ScoRulJ-SR25
95Sel-101
95SelArtP-101
95SelBigS-BS5
95SelCer-21
95SelCerGT-8
95SelCerMG-21
95SP-175
95SPCha-171
95SPCha-175
95SPChaDC-171
95SPChaDC-175
95SPChaDFC-5
95SPChaFCDC-5
95Spo-13
95SpoArtP-13
95SpoHamT-HT8
95SpoPro-PM9
95SPSil-175
95SPSpeF-15
95StaClu-212
95StaClu-381
95StaCluFDI-212
95StaCluMOP-212
95StaCluMOP-381
95StaCluMOP-RL33
95StaCluMOP-SS5
95StaCluRL-RL33
95StaCluSS-SS5
95StaCluSTWS-212
95StaCluSTWS-381
95StaCluVR-200
95Stu-3
95StuGolS-3
95StuPlaS-3
95Sum-21
95Sum-181
95SumBigB-BB8
95SumNthD-21
95SumNthD-181
95Top-399
95TopCyb-200
95UC3-20
95UC3-139
95UC3ArtP-20
95UC3ArtP-139
95UC3CycS-CS11
95UC3InM-IM9
95Ult-311
95UltAwaW-2
95UltAwaWGM-2
95UltGolM-311
95UppDec-210
95UppDecED-210
95UppDecEDG-210
95UppDecPAW-H22
95UppDecPAWE-H22
95UppDecPC-MLB11
95UppDecPLL-R53
95UppDecPLLE-R53
95UppDecSE-145
95UppDecSEG-145
95UppDecSoaD-SD13
95Zen-29
95ZenZ-17
96Baz-23
96ColCho-100
96ColCho-237
96ColCho-368T
96ColChoGS-100
96ColChoGS-237
96ColChoSS-100
96ColChoSS-237
96ColChoYMtP-23
96ColChoYMtP-23A
96ColChoYMtPGS-23
96ColChoYMtPGS-23A
96Don-301
96DonDiaK-16
96DonHitL-15
96DonPreP-301
96Fle-189
96FleTeaL-10
96FleTif-189
96MetUni-90
96MetUniP-90
96MetUniProS-90
96Pac-376
96PacGolCD-DC4
96PacHom-HP5
96PacMil-M2
96PacOctM-OM15
96PacPri-P119
96PacPriG-P119
96PacPriRHS-RH18
96PanSti-151
96Pin-99
96Pin-157
96Pin-307
96PinArtP-37
96PinArtP-84
96PinArtP-192
96PinEssotG-15
96PinFoil-307
96PinSta-37
96PinSta-84
96PinSta-192
96Pro-9
96ProMagDM-18
96Sco-8
96Sco-377
96ScoDugC-A8
96ScoDugC-B102
96ScoDugCAP-A8
96ScoDugCAP-B102
96ScoNumG-23
96ScoRef-5
96SpoPro-12
96StaClu-73
96StaCluEPB-73
96StaCluEPG-73
96StaCluEPS-73
96StaCluMOP-73
95StaCluVRMC-200
96Top-185
96TopChr-56
96TopChrMotG-13
96TopChrMotGR-13
96TopChrR-56
96TopMasotG-13
96TopPro-AL17
96Ult-101
96UltGolM-101
96UppDec-154
Mattingly, Earl
90DodTar-491
Mattingly, Shane
89AncBucTI-21
Mattingly, Steve
89BoiHawP-1989
Mattocks, Rich
84GreHorT-24
Mattos, Tony
94EveGiaC-22
95BurBeeTI-11
Mattox, Frank
85BelBreT-11
86StoPorP-18
87ElPasDP-8
88ElPasDB-29
88TexLeaAGS-38
89ElPasDGS-23
90CMC-39
90DenZepC-14
90DenZepP-632
90ProAAAF-657
Mattson, Craig
94AugGreC-11
94AugGreF-3003
95Bow-101
96LynHilB-16
Mattson, Don
91MacBraC-5
Mattson, Kurt
83CliGiaF-22
84ShrCapFB-11
Mattson, Rob
91DurBulUP-3
91MacBraP-859
95MemChiTI-18
96MemChiB-23
Mattson, Ronnie
77SpaPhiT-13
Matula, Rick
80Top-596
81Don-317
81Fle-263
81Top-611
82EvaTriT-5
Matulevich, Jeff
92JohCitCC-20
92JohCitCF-3114
94MadHatC-15
94MadHatF-127
95Exc-270
96ArkTraB-19
96BesAutS-58
96Exc-229
Matusyavichus, Edmuntas
89EasLeaDDP-DD9
Matuszak, Mick
91AubAstC-23
Matuszek, Len
81OklCit8T-10
82OklCit8T-8
83PorBeaT-8
83Top-357
84Don-549
84Fle-41
84Nes792-275
84OPC-275
84PhiTas-31
84Top-275
84TopTif-275
85BluJayFS-22
85Don-259
85Fle-260
85FleUpd-79
85OPC-226
85Top-688
85TopTif-688
85TopTifT-80T
85TopTra-80T
86DodCokP-19
86DodPol-17
86Don-494
86Fle-138
86Top-109
86TopTif-109
87DodMot-20
87DodPol-8
87Don-423
87Fle-447
87FleGlo-447
87Top-457
87TopTif-457
88DodPol-21
88Sco-424
88ScoGlo-424
88Top-92
88TopTif-92
90DodTar-492
Matvey, Mike
93GleFalRC-21
93GleFalRF-4013
94SavCarC-19
94SavCarF-517
94SouAtlLAF-SAL51
96StPetCB-17
Matz, Brian
96VerExpB-17
Matzen, Mark
82CedRapRT-13
Matznick, Danny
90Bes-256
90MidLeaASGS-15
90SouBenWSB-20
90SouBenWSGS-10

91SarWhiSC-7
91SarWhiSP-1110
Mauch, Dennis
95GreFalDTI-20
Mauch, Gene
69ExpPin-5
49EurSta-63
51Bow-312
57Top-342
59RedSoxJP-6
61Top-219
62Top-374
63Top-318
64PhiJayP-8
64PhiPhiB-17
64Top-157
64TopVen-157
65PhiJayP-8
65Top-489
66Top-411
67PhiPol-10
67Top-248
68OPC-122
68Top-122
68TopVen-122
69Top-606
70OPC-442
70Top-442
71ExpLaPR-6
71ExpPS-15
71OPC-59
71Top-59
72Dia-31
72OPC-276
72Top-276
73OPC-377
73Top-377
74OPC-531
74Top-531
75OPC-101
75Top-101
76OPC-556
76SSP-597
76Top-556
77Top-228
78Top-601
78TwiFri-11
79Top-41
79TwiFriP-17
80Top-328
81TCM60I-359
82Don-141
83Top-276
85AngSmo-24
85TopTifT-81T
85TopTra-81T
86AngSmo-24
86Top-81
86TopTif-81
87Top-518
87TopTif-518
88Top-774
88TopTif-774
90DodTar-493
93ExpDonM-30
93UppDecS-27
Mauch, Thomas
87St.PetCP-17
88St.PetCS-16
Maugham, R.L
28W512-32
Maul, Al
87OldJudN-327
88WG1CarG-61
90DodTar-494
90KalBatN-26
90KalBatN-35
Mauldin, Eric
91MarPhiC-2
91MarPhiP-3469
Mauney, Terry
84ChaO'sT-2
85ChaO'sT-28
86ChaOriW-17
87ChaO'sW-NNO
Mauramatsu, Arihito
91SalSpuP-2257
Maurer, Mike
94SouOreAC-18
94SouOreAF-3620
95ModA'sTI-15
96BesAutSA-43
96HunStaTI-17
Maurer, Rob
88ButCopKSP-15
89ChaRanS-15
89Sta-7
90CMC-798
90ProAaA-69
90TexLeaAGS-20
90TulDriP-1163
90TulDriTI-16
91LinDriAAA-312
91OklCit8LD-312
91OklCit8P-186
91TriA AAGP-AAA26
92Bow-437
92ClaGam-184
92Don-703
92Fle-659A
92Fle-659B
92Fle-720A
92Fle-720B
92OklCit8F-1922
92OklCit8S-314
92Pin-273
92ProFS7-149
92Sco-767
92SkyAAAF-144
92StaClu-462
92TopDeb91-119
92UppDec-10
93Don-584
93PacSpa-313
93RanKee-249
93StaCluR-13
93Top-763
93TopGol-763
93TopInaM-763
93TopMic-763
94OklCit8F-1500
Maurer, Ron
90GreFalDSP-27
91BakDodCLC-2
91CalLeLA-21
92SanAntMF-3985
92SanAntMS-569
92SkyAA F-248
93AlbDukF-1469
93SanAntMF-3012
94AlbDukF-851
Mauriello, Ralph
90DodTar-1019
Mauro, Carmen
49W725AngTI-19
52LaPat-11
52Par-71
53Bri-10
53ExhCan-47
79TCM50-109
90DodTar-495
Mauro, Mike
90BriTigS-17
Mauser, Tim (Timothy)
88SpaPhiS-12
89ClePhiS-14
89EasLeaAP-24
89Sta-13
90Bes-115
90CMC-801
90ReaPhiB-8
90ReaPhiP-1217
90ReaPhiS-19
91LinDriAAA-489
91PhiMed-25
91ScrRedBLD-489
91ScrRedBP-2535
92Sco-744
92ScrRedBF-2444
92ScrRedBS-490
92SkyAAAF-221
92StaClu-558
92TopDeb91-120
93ScrRedBF-2543
93ScrRedBTI-18
94Don-215
94Fle-670
94PadMot-20
94StaClu-200
94StaCluFDI-200
94StaCluGR-200
94StaCluMOP-200
94Top-99
94TopGol-99
94TopSpa-99
94Ult-281
95Fla-204
95Fle-565
95Top-356
Mawhinney, Mindy
91FreStaLBS-13
Max, Bill
82BelBreF-21
83ElPasDT-13
84JacMetT-12
Maxcy, Brian
92BriTigC-5
92BriTigF-1405
93FayGenC-14
93FayGenF-125
95TopTra-16T
96ColCho-143
96ColChoGS-143
96ColChoSS-143
96Don-213
96DonPreP-213
96Fle-117
96FleTif-117
96SigRooOJ-19
96SigRooOJS-19
96TolMudHB-18
96Ult-64
96UltGolM-64
Maxey, Kevin
88St.PetCS-17
Maxie, Larry
64Top-94
64TopVen-94
71RicBraTI-13
78TCM60I-59
Maxim, Joey
51BerRos-B12
Maxson, Dan
78NewWayCT-29
Maxvill, Dal
63CarJayP-13
63Top-49
64Top-563
65CarTeal-15
65OPC-78
65Top-78
66Top-338
66TopVen-338
67Top-421
68OPC-141
68Top-141
68TopVen-141
69MilBra-174
69MLBOffS-213
69Top-320
69TopSta-117
69TopTeaP-18
70CarTeal-9
70MLBOffS-141
70OPC-503
70Top-503
71CarTeal-25
71CarTeal-26
71MLBOffS-278
71OPC-476
71Top-476
72MilBra-214
72OPC-206
72Top-206
73OPC-483
73Top-483
74OPC-358
74Top-358
78TCM60I-241
79Car5-17
82BraPol-53
83BraPol-53
84BraPol-53
Maxwell, Billy
92PriRedC-29
94BilMusSP-25
Maxwell, Charlie
52Top-180
55Bow-162
55OriEss-15
57Top-205
58Top-380
59Top-34
59Top-481
59TopVen-34
60Lea-48
60TigJayP-9
60Top-443
61Pos-37A
61Pos-37B
61TigJayP-11
61Top-37
61TopMagR-22
61TopStal-154
62Jel-25
62Pos-25
62PosCan-25
62TigJayP-9
62Top-506
63Jel-41
63Pos-41
63Top-86
63WhiSoxTS-17
64Top-401
79DiaGre-246
81TCM60I-320
81TigDetN-76
83TopRep5-180
91OriCro-283
Maxwell, Jason
93HunCubC-19
93HunCubF-3243
94DayCubC-16
94DayCubF-2360
96Exc-140
96FleUpd-U114
96FleUpdTC-U114
96OrlCubB-16
96Ult-453
96UltGolM-453
96UltGolP-12
96UltGolPHGM-12
97Ult-167
97UltGolME-167
97UltPlaME-167
Maxwell, Jim
80AshTouT-16
Maxwell, John
90ChaRaiB-24
91ChaRaiC-28
92WatDiaC-28
95IdaFalBTI-NNO
96IdaFalB-16
Maxwell, Marty
78OrlTwiT-13
Maxwell, Pat
91WatIndC-20
91WatIndP-3374
92ColRedC-5
92ColRedF-2397
93CarLeaAGF-32
93KinIndC-15
93KinIndF-2253
93KinIndTI-15
94CanIndF-3123
May, Carlos
69Top-654
69WHISoxTI-9
70DayDaiNM-85
70Kel-16
70OPC-18
70Top-18
70WhiSoxTI-10
71Kel-45
71OPC-243
71Top-243
71TopCoi-144
72MilBra-209
72OPC-525
72Top-525
72WhiSox-8
72WhiSoxC-4
72WhiSoxDS-4
72WhiSoxTI1-7
73Kel2D-45
73OPC-105
73Top-105
74OPC-195
74Top-195
74TopSta-157
75Hos-44
75OPC-480
75Top-480
76CraDis-32A
76CraDis-32B
76Hos-34
76HosTwi-34
76OPC-110
76SSP-148
76Top-110
77Top-568
77Top-633
77YanBurK-22
79TCMJapPB-68
85WhiSoxC-20
87SpoRea-1
92UppDecS-5
92YanWIZ7-105
94TedWil-21
May, Darrell
93MacBraC-15
93MacBraF-1396
93SouAtlLAGF-40
94CarLeaAF-CAR29
94ClaGolF-115
94DurBulTI-12
94ExcFS7-158
95BreBtaTI-25
95Exc-154
95RicBraRC-11
96RicBraRC-3
May, Dave
68CokCapO-7
68OPC-56
68Top-56
68TopVen-56
69OPC-113
69Top-113
69TopFou-17
70BreTeal-8
70OPC-81
70Top-81
71BreTeal-8
71MLBOffS-444
71OPC-493
71Ori-9
71Top-493
72Top-549
73LinPor-101
73OPC-152
73Top-152
74Kel-13
74OPC-12
74Top-12
74TopDecE-58
74TopSta-196
75OPC-650
75Top-650
76Hos-148
76OPC-281
76SSP-19
76Top-281
76VenLeaS-133
78SSP270-92
78Top-362
81TCM60I-385
83AndBraT-5
86BreGreT-7
91OriCro-284
93RanKee-250
94BreMilB-153
May, Davis
76TacTwiDQ-12
77TacTwiDQ-12
79SyrChiT-16
79SyrChiTI-22
80KnoBluJT-7
May, Derrick
87PeoChiP-12
88WinSpiS-11
89ChaKniTI-5
90CMC-89
90Fle-645
90FleCan-645
90IowCubC-14
90IowCubP-331
90ProAAAF-638
90TopTVCu-53
90UppDec-736
91Cla1-T28
91ClaGam-153
91Don-36
91Fle-427
91IowCubLD-209
91LinDriAAA-209
91MajLeaCP-69
91OPC-288
91Sco-379
91ScoRoo-36
91StaClu-73
91Top-288
91TopDeb90-100
91TopDesS-288
91TopMic-288
91TopTif-288
91Ult-65
91UppDec-334
92Cla2-T22
92CubMar-27
92DonRoo-70

92Fle-387
92IowCubS-212
92Pin-534
92SkyAAAF-108
92StaClu-148
92TopTra-68T
92TopTraG-68T
93CubMar-16
93Don-318
93Fla-16
93Fle-21
93FleRooS-RSA8
93Lea-200
93OPC-159
93PacBeiA-19
93PacJugC-32
93PacSpa-380
93PanSti-209
93Pin-371
93Sco-213
93Sel-402
93SP-85
93StaClu-109
93StaCluCu-12
93StaCluFDI-109
93StaCluMOP-109
93Stu-148
93Top-391
93TopGol-391
93TopInaM-391
93TopMic-391
93Toy-79
93Ult-19
93UppDec-248
93UppDecGold-248
93USPlaCR-10H
94ColC-193
94ColChoGS-193
94ColChoSS-193
94Don-178
94ExtBas-220
94Fin-162
94FinRef-162
94Fla-361
94Fle-389
94Lea-139
94LeaL-91
94OPC-40
94Pac-103
94PanSti-154
94Pin-196
94PinArtP-196
94PinMusC-196
94ProMag-24
94Sco-68
94ScoGolR-68
94Sel-38
94StaClu-287
94StaCluFDI-287
94StaCluGR-287
94StaCluMOP-287
94StaCluMOP-ST2
94StaCluST-ST2
94StaCluT-332
94StaCluTFDI-332
94Stu-61
94Top-6
94TopGol-6
94TopSpa-6
94TriPla-74
94Ult-461
94UppDec-328
94UppDecED-328
95AstMot-10
95ColCho-209
95ColCho-538T
95ColChoGS-209
95ColChoSE-84
95ColChoSEGS-84
95ColChoSESS-84
95ColChoSS-209
95Don-441
95DonPreP-441
95Fla-113
95Fle-419
95FleUpd-54
95Pac-74
95Pin-28
95PinArtP-28
95PinMusC-28
95Sco-334
95ScoGolR-334
95ScoPlaTS-334
95Spo-5
95SpoArtP-5
95StaClu-243
95StaCluFDI-243
95StaCluMOP-243
95StaCluSTWS-243
95Top-579
95TopCyb-353
95Ult-360
95UltGolM-360
95UppDec-68
95UppDecED-68
95UppDecEDG-68
96AstMot-8
96ColCho-567
96ColChoGS-567
96ColChoSS-567
96Don-489
96DonPreP-489
96EmoXL-201
96Fla-281
96Fle-415
96FleTif-415
96Pac-85
96Sco-476
96Ult-489
96UltGolM-489
97Fle-350
97Fle-505
97FleTif-350
97FleTif-505
97Pac-321
97PacLigB-321
97PacSil-321
97Ult-476
97UltGolME-476
97UltPlaME-476

May, Frank
31CubTeal-16

May, Freddy
96AugGreB-17

May, Jakie
27AmeCarE-56
32CubTeal-17
91ConTSN-319

May, Jerry
65OPC-143
65Top-143
66OPC-123
66PirEasH-12
66Top-123
66TopVen-123
67PirTeal-10
67Top-379
67TopPirS-13
68PirKDK-12
68PirTeal-10
68Top-598
69MilBra-170
69MLBOffS-186
69PirGre-5
69PirJacitB-5
69Top-263
69TopSta-87
69TopTeaP-16
70MLBOffS-102
70OPC-423
70Top-423
71MLBOffS-420
71OPC-719
71Top-719
72MilBra-210
72OPC-109
72Top-109
73OPC-558
73Top-558
91MetWIZ-254

May, Ken
76SeaRaiC-9

May, Kevin
81CliGiaT-9

May, Larry
80WisRapTT-4
82OrlTwiT-20

May, Lee
88LitFalMP-1
89ColMetB-10
89ColMetGS-15
89PitMetS-16
90St.LucMS-15
91LinDriAAA-562
91TidTidLD-562
91WilBilP-307
92SkyAAAF-254
92TidTidF-911
92TidTidS-563
93MemChiF-389

May, Lee Sr.
66Top-424
67Kah-22
67Top-222
68Kah-A8
68Kah-B22
68Top-487
69Kah-B13
69MilBra-171
69MLBOffS-131
69Top-405
69TopSta-27
69TopTeaP-20
69TraSta-52
70DayDaiNM-19
70MLBOffS-30
70OPC-65
70OPC-225
70Top-65
70Top-225
71MLBOffS-62
71OPC-40
71Top-40
71TopCoi-29
71TopTat-38
72Kel-37
72MilBra-211
72OPC-89
72OPC-480
72Top-89
72Top-480
73LinPor-11
73OPC-135
73Top-135
73TopCanL-31
74AstFouTIP-4
74OPC-500
74Top-500
74TopSta-33
75Hos-35
75Hos-142
75HosTwi-35
75OPC-25
75Top-25
76Hos-98
76OPC-210
76SSP-389
76Top-210
77BurCheD-45
77Hos-55
77OPC-3
77OPC-125
77Top-3
77Top-380
77Top-633
77TopCloS-26
78Hos-53
78OPC-47
78Top-640
78WifBalD-45
79OPC-1
79Top-10
80OPC-255
80Top-490
81Fle-183
82AstAstI-2
82Don-570
82Fle-415
82Top-132
83Don-538
83Fle-118
83FraBroR-36
83OPC-377
83OPC-378
83Top-377
83Top-378
83TopSti-9
85CirK-34
86AstMot-12
87AstShoSO-15
87AstShowSTh-25
88RedKah-NNO
89RedKah-xx
90PacLeg-55
90SweBasG-67
91OriCro-285
92RoyPol-27
93RoyPol-27
93UppDecAH-90
94UppDecAH-193
94UppDecAH1-193

May, Malcolm
91MelBusF-12

May, Milt
71OPC-343
71PirActP-8
71Top-343
72OPC-247
72Top-247
73OPC-529
73Top-529
74AstFouTIP-3
74OPC-293
74Top-293
75Hos-35
75HosTwi-35
75OPC-279
75Top-279
76OPC-532
76SSP-53
76Top-532
76TopTra-532T
77OPC-14
77Top-98
78Hos-115
78OPC-115
78TigBurK-2
78Top-176
79Top-316
80GiaEurFS-4
80GiaPol-7
80OPC-340
80Top-647
81AllGamPI-132
81Don-193
81Fle-442
81OPC-273
81Top-463
81TopSti-237
82Don-503
82Fle-395
82FleSta-62
82OPC-242
82Top-242
82Top-576
82TopSti-110
83Don-312
83Fle-268
83FleSta-119
83Top-84
83TopSti-301
84Don-386
84Fle-254
84Nes792-788
84Top-788
84TopTif-788
85Don-410
85Top-509
85TopTif-509
87AstShowSTh-14
89PirVerFJ-39
90PirHomC-21
92PirNatI-14
93PirNatI-16
94PirQui-14

May, Pinky (Merrill)
39ExhSal-40
39PlaBal-45
40PlaBal-98
41DouCubPlaR-45
41PlaBal-9
43PhiTeal-16
77TCMTheWY-32

May, Rudy
65Top-537
69AngJacitB-6
70MLBOffS-175
70OPC-203
70Top-203
71AngJacitB-6
71MLBOffS-349
71OPC-318
71Top-318
72Top-656
73OPC-102
73Top-102
74OPC-302
74Top-302
75OPC-321
75Top-321
76OPC-481
76SSP-427
76Top-481
77Top-56
78ExpPos-8
78Top-262
79OPC-318
79Top-603
80OPC-281
80Top-539
81Fle-90
81OPC-179
81Top-7
81Top-179
81TopSti-3
81TopSupHT-68
82Don-325
82Fle-41
82OPC-128
82Top-735
83Don-135
83Fle-385
83Top-408
84Don-626
84Nes792-652
84Top-652
84TopTif-652
91OriCro-286
92YanWIZ7-106
92YanWIZ8-112

May, Scott
86AlbDukP-14
87SanAntDTI-11
88OklCit8C-3
88OklCit8P-27
89Don-636
89OklCit8C-5
89OklCit8P-1523
90ElPasDGS-20
91IowCubLD-210
91IowCubP-1055
91LinDriAAA-210
92IowCubF-4049
92IowCubS-213
93RanKee-251
96EriSeaB-15

May, Steve
93PocPosF-4207
93PocPosSP-16

May, Ted
79QuaCitCT-7

Mayber, Chan
95AshTouTI-9
96SalAvaB-19

Mayberry, Germaine
92BurIndC-4
92BurIndF-1671

Mayberry, Greg
85VerBeaDT-20
88VerBeaDS-15
89SanAntMB-19
90AlbDukC-7
90AlbDukP-342
90AlbDukT-21
90CMC-409
90ProAAAF-63

Mayberry, John
70OPC-227
70Top-227
71MLBOffS-86
71OPC-148
71Top-148
72OPC-373
72Top-373
73LinPor-87
73OPC-118
73Top-118
73TopCanL-32
74Kel-29
74OPC-150
74Top-150
74TopDecE-51
74TopSta-184
75Hos-92
75OPC-95
75SSP42-31
75Top-95
76CraDis-33
76Hos-91
76Kel-46
76OPC-194
76OPC-196
76OPC-440
76SSP-169
76Top-194
76Top-196
76Top-440
77BurCheD-69
77Hos-56
77MSADis-39

77OPC-16
77Top-244
77TopCloS-27
78BluJayP-15
78OPC-168
78PapGinD-40
78Roy-12
78Top-550
78WifBalD-46
79BluJayBY-16
79Hos-82
79OPC-199
79Top-380
79TopCom-17
80OPC-338
80Top-643
81AllGamPI-7
81Don-29
81Dra-31
81Fle-416
81OPC-169
81OPCPos-13
81Top-169
81TopScr-15
81TopSti-139
82Don-25
82Don-306
82Dra-24
82FBIDis-12
82Fle-619
82FleSta-235
82OPC-53
82OPC-382
82OPCPos-1
82Top-470
82Top-606
82TopSti-248
82TopTra-67T
83Fle-386
83OPC-45
83Top-45
83TopFol-2
85SyrChiT-20
86BluJayGT-1
86RoyGreT-1
87AstShoSTw-22
87AstShowSTh-15
92UppDecS-3
92YanWIZ8-113
93RoySta2-6
Maye, Lee (A. Lee)
60BraLaktL-15
60BraSpiaS-13
60Top-246
61Top-84
62BraJayP-7
62Jel-156
62PC7HFGSS-3
62Pos-156
62PosCan-156
62SalPlaC-216
62ShiPlaC-216
62Top-518
63Top-109
64BraJayP-7
64Top-416
65Kah-24
65Top-407
65TopEmbl-62
65TopTral-21
66OPC-162
66Top-162
66TopVen-162
67CokCapl-10
67Top-258
68OPC-94
68Top-94
68TopVen-94
69MilBra-172
69SenTeal-10
69Top-595
69TopSta-165
70OPC-439
70SenPolY-7
70Top-439
71OPC-733
71Top-733
72MilBra-212
78AtlCon-15
78TCM60I-51
78TCM60I-107
Maye, Steve (Stephen)
86WinSpiP-14
88ModA'sCLC-66
88ModA'sTI-13
89HunStaB-10
90SalSpuCLC-128
91SalSpuC-17
91SalSpuP-2238
94SanBerSC-10
Mayer, Aaron
95BoiHawTI-22
96BoiHawB-19
Mayer, Bob
79NaSouTI-14
Mayer, Ed
58Top-461
Mayer, James Erskine
15CraJacE-172
15SpoNewM-112
16ColE13-110
16SpoNewM-114
75WhiSox1T-15
Mayers, Jerry
52LavPro-35
Mayes, Craig
92EveGiaC-26
92EveGiaF-1693
93CliGiaC-16
93CliGiaF-2493
94CliLumF-1983
96SanJosGB-11
96WesOahCHWB-29
94CliLumC-16
Mayhew, Keith
95EugEmeTI-24
Maynard, Tow (Ellerton)
87BelMarL-4
89WauTimGS-7
90Bes-84
90SanBerSB-13
90SanBerSCLC-111
90SanBerSP-2646
91SanBerSC-22
91SanBerSP-1999
92ClaFS7-141
92JacSunF-3719
92JacSunS-363
92SkyAA F-155
93CalCanF-1179
93ExcFS7-227
93RivPilCLC-10
94VenLinU-134
Mayne, Brent
90Bes-8
90Bow-372
90BowTif-372
90CMC-780
90MemChiB-1
90MemChiP-1012
90MemChiS-16
90ProAaA-52
90Sco-664
91Cla1-T50
91Don-617
91DonRoo-43
91FleUpd-28
91OPC-776
91Sco-765
91ScoRoo-8
91StaClu-418
91Top-776
91TopDeb90-101
91TopDesS-776
91TopMic-776
91TopTif-776
91Ult-150
91UppDec-72
92Don-265
92Fle-162
92Lea-200
92OPC-183
92OPCPre-40
92Pin-469
92RoyPol-17
92Sco-84
92Sco100RS-85
92ScoImpP-18
92ScoProP-23
92StaClu-229
92Stu-186
92Top-183
92TopGol-183
92TopGolW-183
92TopMic-183
92Ult-74
93Don-261
93Fle-621
93Lea-36
93PacSpa-490
93Pin-359
93RoyPol-18
93StaClu-25
93StaCluFDI-25
93StaCluMOP-25
93StaCluRoy-18
93Top-294
93TopGol-294
93TopInaM-294
93TopMic-294
93TriPla-36
93Ult-212
93UppDec-604
93UppDecGold-604
94Don-511
94Fle-166
94Pac-293
94Sco-183
94ScoGolR-183
94StaClu-333
94StaCluFDI-333
94StaCluGR-333
94StaCluMOP-333
94Top-38
94TopGol-38
94TopSpa-38
94Ult-367
95Don-238
95DonPreP-238
95DonTopotO-93
95Fle-167
95Lea-336
95Top-264
95Ult-59
95UltGolM-59
96ColCho-622
96ColChoGS-622
96ColChoSS-622
96Don-244
96DonPreP-244
96Fle-134
96FleTif-134
96FleUpd-U159
96FleUpdTC-U159
96MetKah-21
96Pac-333
96Sco-187
96Ult-73
96UltGolM-73
97Pac-370
97PacLigB-370
97PacSil-370
Maynor, Tonka
94WelPirC-14
94WelPirF-3509
Mayo, Blake
92MisStaB-29
96YakBeaTI-43
Mayo, Eddie (Edward)
47Exh-151
47TipTop-36
49Bow-75
54Top-247
83TCMPla1945-1
94TopArc1-247
94TopArc1G-247
95ConTSN-1427
Mayo, Jackie (John)
49Bow-228
49EurSta-141
49PhiBul-35
50WorWidGV-36
55JetPos-10
Mayo, Todd
88CapCodPPaLP-119
89JamExpP-2146
90WesPalBES-15
91WesPalBEC-26
91WesPalBEP-1241
92HarSenS-291
Mays, Al
87FouBasHN-7
87OldJudN-328A
87OldJudN-328B
90KalBatN-36
Mays, Carl W.
19W514-103
20NatCarE-61
21E121So1-58
21E121So8-55A
21E121So8-55B
21Exh-103
21KoBreWSI-38
21Nei-7
22AmeCarE-43
22E120-66
22W573-75
22W575-76
23W501-29
23W503-20
23W515-20
23WilChoV-89
27YorCarE-17
28W502-17
28Yue-17
30SchR33-8
77GalGloG-126
87ConSer2-48
88ConSer4-18
91ConTSN-150
Mays, David
89TenTecGE-17
Mays, Henry
77St.PetCT-16
Mays, Jarrod
96WatIndTI-14
Mays, Jeff
86SalRedBP-18
87PorChaRP-11
88ChaRanS-16
Mays, Mae
84WilMay-43
Mays, Marcus
94KanCouCC-14
94KanCouCF-158
94KanCouCTI-15
Mays, Mrs. (Willie)
84WilMay-46
Mays, Willie
47Exh-152A
47Exh-152B
47PM1StaP1-131
47PM1StaP1-132
47PM1StaP1-133
47PM1StaP1-134
47PM1StaP1-135
47PM1StaP1-136
47PM1StaP1-137
47StaPinP2-25
47StaPinP2-26
51Bow-305
52BerRos-39
52Bow-218
52RedMan-NL15
52StaCalL-78E
52StaCalS-90A
52Top-261
53Bri-35
53Top-244
54Bow-89
54NewYorJA-32
54RedMan-NL25
54StaMey-7
54Top-90
55Bow-184
55DonWin-33
55GiaGolS-21
55RedMan-NL7
55RobGouS-1
55RobGouW-1
55Top-194
56Top-31
56Top-130
56TopPin-41
57Top-10
58GiaJayP-7
58GiaSFCB-14
58HarSta-9
58Hir-25
58HirTes-7
58PacBel-5
58Top-5
58Top-436
58Top-486
59Baz-15
59HomRunD-14
59HowPhoSP-1
59Top-50
59Top-317
59Top-464
59Top-563
59TopVen-50
60ArmCoi-16
60Baz-13
60GiaJayP-8
60KeyChal-34
60MacSta-13
60NuHi-27
60RawGloT-21
60Top-7
60Top-200
60Top-564
60TopTat-34
60TopTat-93
60TopVen-7
61Baz-23
61ChePat-8
61GiaJayP-9
61NuSco-404
61NuSco-427
61Pos-145A
61Pos-145B
61SevElev-17
61Top-41
61Top-150
61Top-482
61Top-579
61TopDicG-9
62AurRec-12
62Baz-38
62ExhStaB-26
62GiaJayP-9
62Jel-142
62Pos-142
62PosCan-142
62SalPlaC-149
62ShiPlaC-149
62Top-18
62Top-54
62Top-300
62Top-395
62TopBuc-57
62TopStal-199
62TopVen-18
62TopVen-54
63BasMagM-58
63Baz-12
63ExhStaB-44
63Fle-5
63GiaJayP-7
63Jel-106
63Pos-106
63SalMetC-22
63Top-3
63Top-138
63Top-300
63TopStil-27
64Baz-12
64GiaJayP-7
64Top-9
64Top-150
64Top-306
64Top-423
64TopCoi-80
64TopCoi-151
64TopGia-51
64TopSta-20
64TopStaU-48
64TopTatl-53
64TopVen-9
64TopVen-150
64TopVen-306
64WheSta-29
65Baz-12
65GiaTeal-6
65MacSta-6
65OldLonC-14
65OPC-4
65OPC-6
65OPC-250
65Top-4
65Top-6
65Top-250
65TopEmbl-27
65TopTral-58
66AurSpoMK-3
66Baz-16
66OPC-1
66Top-1
66Top-215
66Top-217
66Top-219
66TopRubl-60
66TopVen-1
66TopVen-215
66TopVen-217
66TopVen-219
67Baz-16
67CokCapA-10
67CokCapG-17

67DexPre-134
67DexPre-135
67OPC-191
67OPCPapI-12
67Top-191A
67Top-191B
67Top-200
67Top-244
67Top-423
67TopGiaSU-19
67TopPos-12
67TopTesF-13
67TopVen-273
68AtlOil-8
68Baz-14
68DexPre-51
68OPC-50
68Top-50
68Top-490
68TopActS-5B
68TopActS-9C
68TopGamI-8
68TopPla-19
68TopPos-20
68TopVen-50
69KelPin-12
69MilBra-173
69MLBOffS-204
69MLBPin-52
69NabTeaF-15
69OPC-190
69OPCDec-16
69Top-190
69TopDec-33
69TopDecI-24
69TopFou-1
69TopSta-108
69TopSup-65
69TopTeaP-14
69TraSta-34
70Gia-9
70Kel-12
70MilBra-15
70MLBOffS-129
70Top-600
70TopBoo-24
70TopSup-18
70TraSta-1B
71AllBasA-15
71BazNumT-47
71BazUnn-17
71GiaTic-7
71Kel-10
71MatMin-7
71MatMin-8
71MilDud-51
71MLBOffS-257
71MLBOffS-567
71OPC-600
71Top-600
71TopCoi-153
71TopGreM-41
71TopSup-56
71TopTat-130
71TopTat-131
72Kel-54A
72Kel-54B
72MilBra-213
72OPC-49
72OPC-50
72ProStaP-18
72Top-49
72Top-50
72TopPos-17
73NewYorN-17
73OPC-1
73OPC-305
73Top-1
73Top-305
73TopCanL-33
74LauAllG-60
74OPC-473
74SupBlaB-9
74Top-473
75Gia195T-20
75Gia195T-34
75OPC-192
75OPC-203
75SSP42-35
75SSPSam-5
75Top-192
75Top-203
76GalBasGHoF-18
76JerJonPC-3
76LauDiaJ-18
76Spo-A
76SSP-595
76SSP-616
77GalGloG-8
77GalGloG-245
77SerSta-17
77Spo-1106
78HalHalR-20
78TCM60I-280
79BasGre-70
79DiaGre-50
79TCM50-6
80GiaGreT-1
80Lau300-10
80MarExh-19
80PacLeg-48
80PerHaloFP-168
80SSPHOF-168
81SanDieSC-12
82BasCarN-7
82CraJac-13
82DiaCla-18
82K-M-8
83KelCerB-5
83KelCerB-6
83MLBPin-27
83TopRep5-261
83TopSti-3
83TopTraBP-5
84FifNatCT-12
84GiaMot-1
84OCoandSI-20
84OCoandSI-131
84OCoandSI-165
84OCoandSI-216
84SpoDesPW-13
84WilMay-1A
84WilMay-1B
84WilMay-2
84WilMay-3
84WilMay-4
84WilMay-5
84WilMay-6
84WilMay-7
84WilMay-8
84WilMay-9
84WilMay-10
84WilMay-11
84WilMay-12
84WilMay-13
84WilMay-14
84WilMay-15
84WilMay-16
84WilMay-17
84WilMay-18
84WilMay-19
84WilMay-20
84WilMay-21
84WilMay-22
84WilMay-23
84WilMay-24
84WilMay-25
84WilMay-26
84WilMay-27
84WilMay-28
84WilMay-29
84WilMay-30
84WilMay-31
84WilMay-32
84WilMay-33
84WilMay-34
84WilMay-35
84WilMay-36
84WilMay-37
84WilMay-38
84WilMay-39
84WilMay-40
84WilMay-41
84WilMay-42
84WilMay-43
84WilMay-44
84WilMay-45
84WilMay-46
84WilMay-47
84WilMay-48
84WilMay-49
84WilMay-50
84WilMay-51
84WilMay-52
84WilMay-53
84WilMay-54
84WilMay-55
84WilMay-56
84WilMay-57
84WilMay-58
84WilMay-59
84WilMay-60
84WilMay-61
84WilMay-62
84WilMay-63
84WilMay-64
84WilMay-65
84WilMay-66
84WilMay-67
84WilMay-68
84WilMay-69
84WilMay-70
84WilMay-71
84WilMay-72
84WilMay-73
84WilMay-74
84WilMay-75
84WilMay-76
84WilMay-77
84WilMay-78
84WilMay-79
84WilMay-80
84WilMay-81
84WilMay-82
84WilMay-83
84WilMay-84
84WilMay-85
84WilMay-86
84WilMay-87
84WilMay-88
84WilMay-89
84WilMay-90
85CirK-3
85Woo-26
86BigLeaC-3
86SpoDecG-50
86SpoDesJM-22
86SpoRoo-46
86TCM-6
86TCMSupS-29
86Top-403
86TopTif-403
87AstShoSTw-21
87AstShoSTw-25
87HygAllG-33
87K-M-8
87NesDreT-28
88GreBasS-52
88HouSho-5
88PacLegI-24
88PhiTopAS-8
88WilMulP-22
89BowInsT-7
89BowRepI-7
89BowTif-R7
90AGFA-1
90BasWit-18
90El PasDAGTI-43
90HOFStiB-65
90PerGreM-65
90PerGreM-87
90PerMasW-11
90PerMasW-12
90PerMasW-13
90PerMasW-14
90PerMasW-15
91Kel3D-3
91MetWIZ-255
91NegLeaRL-21
91SweBasG-106
91TopArc1-244
92ActPacA-14
92ActPacA2-14G
92ActPacAP-3
92BazQua5A-1
92GiaCheHoFP-1
92GiaFanFFB-3
92MVP-16
92MVP2H-1
92RevLeg1-1
92RevLeg1-2
92RevLeg1-3
92TVSpoMF5HRC-8
92Zip-8
93ActPacAC-14
93MetIma-12
93MetIma-P1
93StaCluU-1
93StaCluU-2
93StaCluU-6
93StaCluU-8
93StaCluU-9
93TedWil-55
93TedWil-126
93TedWil-138
93TedWil-144
93TedWilLC-3
93UppDecAH-91
93UppDecAH-137
93UppDecAH-150
93UppDecAH-151
93UppDecAH-163
93UppDecAH-164
93UppDecMH-46
93UppDecMH-47
93UppDecMH-48
93UppDecMH-49
93UppDecMH-50
93UppDecMH-51
93UppDecMH-52
93UppDecMH-53
93UppDecMH-54
93UppDecTAN-TN18
94TedWil-150
94TopArc1-90
94TopArc1G-90
94UppDecAH-10
94UppDecAH-17
94UppDecAH-24
94UppDecAH-117
94UppDecAH-150
94UppDecAH-166
94UppDecAH1-10
94UppDecAH1-17
94UppDecAH1-24
94UppDecAH1-117
94UppDecAH1-150
94UppDecAH1-166
95NegLeaL2-1
95NegLeaLI-21
95TopLegot6M-1
95UppDecA-3
97SpoIllAM-4
97SpoIllCC-11
97TopMan-33
97TopManF-33
97TopManFR-33
97TopMay-1
97TopMay-2
97TopMay-3
97TopMay-4
97TopMay-5
97TopMay-6
97TopMay-7
97TopMay-8
97TopMay-9
97TopMay-10
97TopMay-11
97TopMay-12
97TopMay-13
97TopMay-14
97TopMay-15
97TopMay-16
97TopMay-17
97TopMay-18
97TopMay-19
97TopMay-20
97TopMay-21
97TopMay-22
97TopMay-23
97TopMay-24
97TopMay-25
97TopMay-26
97TopMay-27
97TopMay-J261
97TopMay-NNO
97TopMayF-1
97TopMayF-2
97TopMayF-3
97TopMayF-4
97TopMayF-5
97TopMayF-6
97TopMayF-7
97TopMayF-8
97TopMayF-9
97TopMayF-10
97TopMayF-11
97TopMayF-12
97TopMayF-13
97TopMayF-14
97TopMayF-15
97TopMayF-16
97TopMayF-17
97TopMayF-18
97TopMayF-19
97TopMayF-20
97TopMayF-21
97TopMayF-22
97TopMayF-23
97TopMayF-24
97TopMayF-25
97TopMayF-26
97TopMayF-27
97TopMayFR-1
97TopMayFR-2
97TopMayFR-3
97TopMayFR-4
97TopMayFR-5
97TopMayFR-6
97TopMayFR-7
97TopMayFR-8
97TopMayFR-9
97TopMayFR-10
97TopMayFR-11
97TopMayFR-12
97TopMayFR-13
97TopMayFR-14
97TopMayFR-15
97TopMayFR-16
97TopMayFR-17
97TopMayFR-18
97TopMayFR-19
97TopMayFR-20
97TopMayFR-21
97TopMayFR-22
97TopMayFR-23
97TopMayFR-24
97TopMayFR-25
97TopMayFR-26
97TopMayFR-27

Mayse, Gary
91CliGiaC-15

Maysey, Matt
85SpoIndC-13
86ChaRaiP-15
87ChaRaiP-14
88WicPilRD-43
89LasVegSC-6
89LasVegSP-5
90CMC-505
90LasVegSC-3
90LasVegSP-116
90ProAAAF-4
91HarSenLD-264
91HarSenP-623
91LinDriAA-264
92DonRoo-71
92IndIndF-1855
92IndIndS-187
92SkyAAAF-92
93LinVenB-183
93NewOrlZF-968
93Sco-316
94BreMilB-154
94Sco-610
94ScoGolR-610

Mayumi, Akinobu
87JapPlaB-23

Mazeroski, Bill
47Exh-153A
47Exh-153B
57Kah-21
57Top-24
58Hir-36
58JayPubA-12
58Kah-19
58Top-238
59Baz-16
59Kah-21
59Top-415
59Top-555
60Kah-25
60MacSta-14
60PirJayP-9
60PirTag-9
60Top-55
60TopVen-55
61Baz-24
61Kah-27
61NuSco-403
61PirJayP-8
61PirRigF-6
61Pos-128A
61Pos-128B
61Top-312
61Top-430
61Top-571
61TopDicG-10
61TopStaI-67
62AurRec-13

62Jel-170
62Kah-27
62Pos-170
62PosCan-170
62SalPlaC-131
62ShiPlaC-131
62Top-353
62Top-391
62TopStaI-179
63Baz-6
63ExhStaB-45
63Fle-59
63Jel-138
63Kah-21
63PirIDL-13
63PirJayP-9
63Pos-138
63SalMetC-14
63Top-323
63TopStil-28
64ChatheY-36
64Kah-17
64PirKDK-17
64Top-570
64TopCoi-27
64TopCoi-143
64TopSta-40
64TopStaU-49
64TopTatI-54
65ChaTheY-36
65Kah-25
65OldLonC-15
65OPC-95
65Top-95
65TopEmbl-23
65TopTraI-59
66Kah-19
66PirEasH-9
66Top-210
66TopRubI-61
66TopVen-210
67AshOil-7
67CokCapA-27
67CokCapNLA-28
67CokCapPi-6
67DexPre-136
67Kah-23A
67Kah-23B
67PirTeal-11
67Top-510
67TopPirS-14
67TopVen-313
68Baz-7
68DexPre-52
68Kah-A9
68Kah-B23
68PirKDK-9
68PirTeal-11
68Top-390
68TopActS-1A
68TopActS-14A
69Kah-B14
69MilBra-175
69MLBOffS-187
69PirGre-6
69PirJacitB-6
69Top-335
69TopSta-88
69TopTeaP-16
69TraSta-60
70DayDaiNM-138
70MLBOffS-103
70OPC-440
70Top-440
71BazNumT-3
71MLBOffS-208
71OPC-110
71PirActP-19
71PirArc-6
71Top-110
71TopCoi-15
71TopTat-90
72MilBra-215
72Top-760
73OPC-517
73Top-517A
73Top-517B
74OPC-489
74SupBlaB-10
74Top-489
76LauDiaJ-6
77GalGloG-261
78TCM60I-62
86PirGreT-2
87Pir196T-2
88PacLegI-60
89SweBasG-67
89TopBasT-19
90HOFStiB-62
90PacLeg-39
90SweBasG-93
91Col-24
91LinDri-13
91MDAA-4
91SweBasG-60
92ActPacA-69
92MVP-17
92MVP2H-14
93TedWil-78
93UppDecAH-92
94TedWil-79
94UppDecAH-8
94UppDecAH-76
94UppDecAH-118
94UppDecAH1-8
94UppDecAH1-76
94UppDecAH1-118
94UppDecS-5
94UppDecS-8
94UppDecTAE-66
95SkiBra-2
97FleMilDM-9
Mazey, Randy
88BurIndP-1776
89MiaMirIS-13
Mazion, Rodney
93PitMetC-14
93PitMetF-3724
Mazur, Bob
77SalPirT-14
Mazurek, Brian
96NewJerCB-18
Mazurek, Danny
52LavPro-18
Mazzella, Joe
72CedRapCT-22
Mazzilli, Lee
77MetDaiPA-15
77Spo-8712
77Top-488
78MetDaiPA-16
78OPC-26
78Top-147
79Hos-7
79Kel-42
79OPC-183
79Top-355
80Kel-38
80OPC-11
80Top-25
80TopSup-8
81AllGamPI-154
81CokTeaS-90
81Don-34
81Dra-33
81Fle-316
81FleStiC-42
81Kel-46
81MSAMinD-22
81OPC-167
81Squ-21
81Top-510
81TopScr-75
81TopSti-191
81TopSupHT-75
82Don-49
82Fle-533
82FleSta-90
82OPC-243
82Top-465
82TopSti-67
82TopTra-68T
83Don-638
83Fle-387
83FleSta-120
83FleSti-40
83OPC-306
83Top-685
83TopTra-67T
84Don-166
84Fle-255
84JacMetF-8
84Nes792-225
84OPC-225
84Top-225
84TopTif-225
85Don-386
85Fle-469
85OPC-323
85Pir-11
85Top-748
85TopMin-748
85TopTif-748
86Don-288
86Fle-612
86MetWorSC-13
86OPC-373
86Top-578
86TopTif-578
87Don-562
87Fle-15
87FleGlo-15
87MetColP-6
87Top-198
87TopTif-198
88Don-614
88DonBasB-209
88DonTeaBM-614
88Lea-223
88MetColP-35
88MetKah-13
88OPC-308
88Sco-158A
88Sco-158B
88ScoGlo-158A
88ScoGlo-158B
88StaLinMe-13
88Top-308
88TopTif-308
89MetColP-12
89MetKah-17
89Sco-217
89Top-58
89TopTif-58
89UppDec-657
90BasWit-8
90Don-584
90Fle-88
90FleCan-88
90OPC-721
90PubSti-139
90Sco-459
90Top-721
90TopTif-721
90VenSti-325
91MetWIZ-256
92YanWIZ8-114
93RanKee-252
Mazzone, Leo
75TucTorC-15
75TucTorTI-10
79SavBraT-17
83DurBulT-29
84DurBulT-9
85BraPol-52
86SumBraP-19
87GreBraB-2
87SouLeaAJ-25
88RicBraC-24
88RicBraP-16
89RicBraBC-15
89RicBraC-24
89RicBraP-833
89RicBraTI-25
90BraDubS-21
90CMC-278
90ProAAAF-421
90RicBraC-2
90RicBraP-276
90RicBraTI-21
91BraSubS-24
92BraLykS-22
93BraLykS-22
94BraLykP-20
94BraLykS-20
Mazzone, Tony
94IdaFalBF-3580
94IdaFalBSP-13
95EugEmeTI-25
Mazzotti, Mauro
89BelMarL-31
McAbee, Monte R.
82MadMusF-15
82WesHavAT-15
83GleFalWST-4
McAdams, Dennis
94AshTouC-16
94AshTouF-1776
McAfee, Bret
82WauTimF-13
McAleer, James
04FanCraAL-34
09PC7HHB-31
09RamT20-74
09SpoNewSM-17
11SpoLifCW-236
11SpoLifM-127
87OldJudN-329
98CamPepP-49
McAleese, John
09T206-233
McAllester, Bill
14B18B-32A
14B18B-32B
McAllister, Sport (Lewis)
03BreE10-95
11SpoLifCW-237
11T205-194
12ColRedB-181
12ColTinT-181
12ImpTobC-57
McAllister, Steve
83DayBeaAT-21
85NasPirT-17
86NasPirP-18
McAllister, Troy
92EugEmeC-18
92EugEmeF-3037
McAlpin, Mike
88St.CatBJP-2015
89St.CatBJP-2093
90St.CatBJP-3483
91KnoBluJLD-375
91KnoBluJP-1785
91LinDriAA-375
92KnoBluJF-3007
93KnoSmoF-1266
McAnally, Ernie
71OPC-376
71Top-376
72Dia-32
72OPC-58
72ProStaP-8
72Top-58
73OPC-484
73Top-484
74ExpWes-7
74OPC-322
74Top-322
75OPC-318
75Top-318
McAnany, Jim
88PalSprACLC-104
88PalSprAP-1452
McAnany, Michele
95ColSilB-18
96ColSilB-18
McAnarney, James
87LitFalMP-2388
88ColMetGS-8
McAndrew, Jamie
89GreFalDSP-5
90BakDodCLC-237
90CalLeaACLC-22
91AlbDukLD-15
91AlbDukP-1138
91Bow-601
91LinDriAAA-15
92AlbDukS-14
92Bow-591
92ProFS7-242
92SanAntMF-3971
92SkyAAAF-6
92UppDecML-197
93Don-774
93NewOrlZF-969
93Top-412
93TopGol-412
93TopInaM-412
93TopMic-412
94NewOrlZF-1465
McAndrew, Jim (James)
69MetNewYDN-13
69Top-321
69TopTeaP-24
70DayDaiNM-147
70OPC-246
70Top-246
71MLBOffS-160
71OPC-428
71Top-428
72Top-781
73LinPor-117
73OPC-436
73Top-436
89RinPosM1-20
91MetWIZ-257
94Met69CCPP-24
94Met69CS-23
94Met69T-24
McAninch, John
95BoiHawTI-23
96CedRapKTI-16
McArn, Brian
90NebCor-15
96VerExpB-3
McAulay, John
95HudValRTI-22
McAuliffe, David
89GreHorP-411
89SouAtlLAGS-32
90CedRapRB-22
90CedRapRP-2320
90MidLeaASGS-41
90ProAaA-123
91ChaLooLD-162
91ChaLooP-1956
91LinDriAA-162
91WavRedF-2
McAuliffe, Dick
62Top-527
63Jel-48
63Pos-48
63Top-64
64TigLid-10
64Top-363
64TopVen-363
65OPC-53
65TigJayP-9
65Top-53
66Top-495
66TopRubI-62
67CokCapTi-6
67DexPre-137
67OPC-170
67TigDexP-6
67Top-170
67TopVen-241
68CokCapT-6
68Kah-B24
68TigDetFPB-11
68Top-285
68TopVen-285
69MilBra-176
69MLBOffS-51
69OPC-169
69TigTeal-7
69Top-169
69Top-305
69TopFou-23
69TopSta-176
69TopTeaP-1
70MLBOffS-211
70OPC-475
70Top-475
71MLBOffS-399
71OPC-3
71Top-3
71TopCoi-10
71TopTat-75
72MilBra-216
72Top-725
73LinPor-74
73OPC-349
73TigJew-13
73Top-349
74OPC-495
74Top-495
78TCM60I-94
81TigDetN-134
88TigDom-14
89SweBasG-14
McAuliffe, Jack
87AllandGN-16
McAvoy, Thomas
60Lea-108
McBean, Al (Alvin)
62Top-424
63Jel-146
63PirIDL-14
63Pos-146
63Top-387
64Kah-18
64PirKDK-18
64Top-525
64TopCoi-66
64TopSta-17
65Kah-26
65OPC-25
65Top-25

65TopEmbl-14
66PirEasH-34
66Top-353
66TopVen-353
67CokCapPi-1
67PirTeal-12
67Top-203
67TopPirS-12
67TopVen-301
68PirKDK-34
68PirTeal-12
68Top-514
69MilBra-177
69OPC-14
69Top-14
69TopSta-96
69TopTeaP-12
70Top-641
72MilBra-217
81TCM60I-435
90DodTar-496
McBean, Douglas
52LavPro-71
McBride, Bake
74OPC-601
74Top-601
75Hos-41
75Kel-13
75OPC-174
75Top-174
76CraDis-34
76Hos-93
76OPC-135
76SSP-277
76Top-135
77BurCheD-17
77Hos-97
77Kel-34
77RCColC-40
77Top-516
78OPC-156
78PhiSSP-53
78RCColC-26
78SSP270-53
78Top-340
78WifBalD-47
79OPC-332
79PhiBurK-21
79PhiTeal-6
79Top-630
80OPC-257
80PhiBurK-9
80Top-495
81AllGamPI-155
81CokTeaS-102
81Don-404
81Fle-9
81FleStiC-31
81OPC-90
81Top-90
81TopScr-58
81TopSti-202
81TopSupHT-84
82Don-497
82Fle-250
82Ind-24
82IndTeal-23
82IndWhe-26
82OPC-92
82Top-745
82TopTra-69T
83Fle-414
83IndPos-22
83IndWhe-21
83OPC-248
83Top-248
83TopFol-3
84Fle-547
84Nes792-569
84OPC-81
84Top-569
84TopSti-256
84TopTif-569
89PacSenL-19
89PacSenL-201
89T/MSenL-74
90EliSenL-58
92CarMcD-44
McBride, Charles
93IdaFalBF-4040
93IdaFalBSP-4
McBride, Chris
94SigRooDP-71
94SigRooDPS-71
94St.CatBJC-1
94St.CatBJF-3641
94StaCluDP-42
94StaCluDPFDI-42
95HagSunF-65
96StCatSB-19
McBride, Gator
95DurBulTI-21
96DurBulBIB-7
96DurBulBrB-8
96GreBraB-19
96GreBraTI-2
McBride, George
08AmeCarE-84
08RosComP-81
09ColChiE-182
09SenBarP-7
09T206-234
10CouT21-44
10DomDisP-78
10SenWasT-3
10SweCapPP-61
11MecDFT-19
11SpoLifM-128
11T205-111
11TurRedT-110
12ColRedB-182
12ColTinT-182
12HasTriFT-58
12HasTriFT-59
12T207-115
14B18B-42
14FatPlaT-31
14PieStaT-36
14TexTomE-31
15SpoNewM-113
16BF2FP-48
16ColE13-111
16SpoNewM-115
17HolBreD-66
23WilChoV-90
McBride, Ivan
88WatIndP-677
McBride, Ken
47Exh-154
60Top-276
61Top-209
62Baz-25
62SalPlaC-91A
62SalPlaC-91B
62ShiPlaC-91
62Top-268
62TopBuc-58
62TopStal-66
63AngJayP-8
63ExhStaB-46
63Jel-33
63Pos-33
63SalMetC-41
63Top-510
64Baz-4
64ChatheY-37
64Top-405
64TopCoi-52
64TopSta-89
64TopStaU-50
64TopTatI-55
64WheSta-30
65ChaTheY-37
65OPC-268
65Top-268
65TopEmbl-30
McBride, Loy
89VisOakCLC-107
89VisOakP-1449
90St.LucMS-16
91LinDriAA-637
91WilBilLD-637
91WilBilP-308
McBride, Rodney
96ForWayWB-15
McBride, Thomas
47SenGunBP-7
49Bow-74
79DiaGre-237
McCabe, Bill
90DodTar-1020
McCabe, Brett
93GenCubC-20
93GenCubF-3185
McCabe, James
11MecDFT-41
McCabe, Joseph
64Top-564
65OPC-181
65Top-181
McCaffery, Dennis
92QuaCitRBC-16
92QuaCitRBF-822
93PalSprAC-13
93PalSprAF-82
McCahan, Bill
48Bow-31
49Bow-80
49PhiBul-36
McCain, Marcus
97Top-472
McCain, Mike
83OrlTwiT-7
83TolMudHT-27
McCall, Brian
77FriOneYW-79
McCall, Dutch (Robert)
47SigOil-30
49Lea-57
McCall, Larry
78TacYanC-29
79TucTorT-23
80TacTigT-8
91KanCouCC-27
91KanCouCP-2676
91KanCouCTI-26
92KanCouCC-27
92KanCouCF-109
92KanCouCTI-20
92YanWIZ7-107
93FreKeyC-28
93FreKeyF-1044
93RanKee-253
94FreKeyF-2632
96HigDesMB-2
94FreKeyC-26
McCall, Rod
91Cla/Bes-175
91ColIndC-26
91ColIndP-1493
91SouAtlLAGP-SAL18
92ColRedC-22
92ColRedF-2398
93ClaGolF-13
93KinIndC-16
93KinIndF-2254
93KinIndTI-16
93SouAtlLAPI-24
94KinIndC-12
94KinIndF-2651
95BakBlaTI-2
96CanIndB-16
McCall, Trey
85BenPhiC-15
87SpaPhiP-14
88ClePhiS-19
89ClePhiS-15
McCall, Windy (John)
55GiaGolS-13
55Top-42
55TopDouH-87
56Top-44
57Top-291
77RocRedWM-19
79TCM50-200
McCallum, John D.
75McCCob-14
McCallum, Thomas
87OldJudN-337
McCalmont, James
94EliTwiC-12
94EliTwiF-3740
95ForMyeMTI-19
96FtMyeMB-19
McCament, Randy
85EveGiaIC-9
86FreGiaP-11
87ShrCapP-16
88PhoFirC-9
88PhoFirP-71
89BlaYNPRWLU-15
89ShrCapP-1853
90CMC-529
90Fle-64
90FleCan-64
90OPC-361
90PhoFirC-2
90PhoFirP-8
90ProAAAF-34
90Sco-580
90Top-361
90TopDeb89-77
90TopTif-361
90UppDec-657
McCann, Brian
82AleDukT-19
83LynPirT-25
86WauTimP-14
87PitCubP-6
88EasLeaAP-49
88PitCubP-1364
89ChaKniTI-23
90CMC-100
90IowCubC-25
McCann, Frank
77JacSunT-14
82BirBarT-19
McCann, Gene
90DodTar-1021
McCann, Joe
79NewCoPT-12
89PitMetS-17
90ColMetGS-6
90ColMetPPI-5
91St.LucMC-19
91St.LucMP-706
92St.LucMCB-9
92St.LucMF-1744
93WinSpiC-14
93WinSpiF-1567
McCardell, Roger
52LavPro-7
McCarren, Bill
90DodTar-497
McCarter, Edward
86SanJosBP-12
McCarthy, Alex
09ColChiE-183
12ColRedB-183
12ColTinT-183
12T207-116
McCarthy, Dave
75AndRanT-20
76AshTouT-10
77AshTouT-14
McCarthy, Drew
96BatCliTI-28
McCarthy, Greg
87UtiBluSP-33
88SpaPhiP-1028
88SpaPhiS-13
89SpaPhiP-1034
89SpaPhiS-17
90ClePhiS-13
92KinIndC-21
92KinIndF-2471
93CanIndF-2836
93KinIndC-17
93KinIndF-2244
93KinIndTI-17
94CanIndF-3118
97PacPriGotD-GD90
McCarthy, J.D.
86SpoDesJM-1
McCarthy, Jack (John Arthur)
03BreE10-96
11SpoLifCW-238
90DodTar-498
McCarthy, Joe
30ChiEveAP-7
36GouWidPPR-A117
38OurNatGPP-19
43YanSta-18
48RedSoxTI-15
68LauWorS-40
75TCMAllG-22
75YanDyn1T-33
76ShaPiz-83
77GalGloG-70
80LauFamF-33
80PacLeg-58
80PerHaloFP-83
80SSPHOF-83
83TCMPla1942-4
84CubUno-8
86ConSer1-28
89HOFStiB-87
91ConTSN-28
92ConTSN-589
92YanWIZH-23
93ConTSN-823
93DiaStaES-143
93PinDiM-21
95ConTSN-1398
McCarthy, John A.
87OldJudN-331
McCarthy, John J.
36WorWidGV-53
40PlaBal-215
49Bow-220
93ConTSN-726
McCarthy, Shaun
76BurBeeT-21
80KnoBluJT-10
McCarthy, Steve
88BilMusP-1817
89CedRapRB-10
89CedRapRP-914
89CedRapRS-11
89Sta-192
90CedRapRP-2319
90ChaWheB-4
91ChaLooLD-163
91ChaLooP-1957
91LinDriAA-163
McCarthy, Thomas F.
36PC7AlbHoF-44
50CalHOFW-53
75FlePio-13
76ShaPiz-44
80PerHaloFP-44
80SSPHOF-44
87OldJudN-330
89DodSmoG-20
90DodTar-499
94OriofB-86
95May-21
McCarthy, Tom
79ElmPioRST-8
80ElmPioRST-17
85PawRedST-17
86TidTidP-19
87JacMetF-5
87MetColP-39
87TidTidP-13
87TidTidT-6
88BlaYNPRWL-93
88MetColP-36
88TidTidCa-22
88TidTidCM-7
88TidTidP-1599
89TopTra-75T
89TopTraT-75T
89VanCanC-4
89VanCanP-593
90Fle-541
90FleCan-541
90OPC-326
90Sco100RS-57
90Top-326
90TopTif-326
91LinDriAAA-435
91RicBraBC-10
91RicBraLD-435
91RicBraP-2563
91RicBraTI-14
92RicBraBB-24
92RicBraF-372
92RicBraRC-10
92RicBraS-432
93ChaKniF-538
97RicBraBC-15
McCartney, Sommer
94ElmPioF-3478
95ElmPioTI-15
95ElmPioUTI-15
96KanCouCTI-18
94ElmPioC-12
McCartney, Steve
74SacSolC-58
McCarty, David
91Cla/Bes-400
91ClaDraP-3
91ClaGolB-BC18
91VisOakUP-1
91VisOakUP-3
92ClaBluBF-BC17
92ClaDraP-88
92ClaFS7-350
92ClaRedB-BC17
92DEL-AU2
92OrlSunRF-2860
92OrlSunRS-512
92ProFS7-95
92SkyAA F-220
92UppDec-75
92UppDecCPH-CP1
92UppDecML-47
92UppDecML-255

93UppDecMLTPHF-TP5
93Bow-369
93Bow-649
93ClaFisN-15
93ClaGolF-93
93ClaGolLF-1
93ClaGolP-2
93ClaYouG-YG9
93ExcFS7-202
93Fla-239
93FlaWavotF-9
93FleFinE-238
93FunPac-5
93FunPac-221
93LeaGolR-U3
93PacSpa-524
93PorBeaF-2388
93SelRoo-45T
93SP-250
93StaClu-569
93StaCluFDI-569
93StaCluMOP-569
93TopFulS-12
93TopTra-17T
93Ult-586
93UppDec-450
93UppDec-462
93UppDecGold-450
93UppDecGold-462
94Bow-516
94ColC-194
94ColChoGS-194
94ColChoSS-194
94Don-281
94Fin-17
94FinJum-17
94FinRef-17
94Fle-213
94FUnPac-167
94Lea-78
94OPC-247
94OPCDiaD-7
94Pac-361
94Pin-333
94PinArtP-333
94PinMusC-333
94Sco-290
94ScoBoyoS-27
94ScoGolR-290
94Sel-154
94Spo-9
94StaClu-134
94StaCluFDI-134
94StaCluGR-134
94StaCluMOP-134
94Top-156
94TopGol-156
94TopSpa-156
94TriPla-256
94Ult-391
94UppDec-200
94UppDecED-200
95ColCho-485
95ColChoGS-485
95ColChoSS-485
95Don-217
95DonPreP-217
95FleUpd-61
95Lea-14
95Pac-252
95Pin-323
95PinArtP-323
95PinMusC-323
95Sel-12
95SelArtP-12
95StaClu-8
95StaCluFDI-8
95StaCluMOP-8
95StaCluSTWS-8
95Stu-65
95Top-98
95UppDec-427
95UppDecED-427
95UppDecEDG-427
96Fle-591
96FleTif-591
96GiaMot-21
96LeaSigA-150
96LeaSigAG-150
96LeaSigAS-150
96Sco-468
97Pac-445
97PacLigB-445
97PacSil-445

McCarty, G. Lewis
16ColE13-112
19W514-37
90DodTar-500
94ConTSN-1267
94ConTSNB-1267

McCarty, Matt
96GreFalDB-19
96GreFalDTI-29
96SanBerSB-17

McCarty, Scott
91MadMusC-10
91MadMusP-2127

McCarty, Tom
11MecDFT-31
12ImpTobC-89

McCarver, Tim
62KahAtl-13
62Top-167
62TopStal-186
62TopVen-167
63CarJayP-14
63Top-394
64CarTeal-6
64Top-429
64TopCoi-156
65CarJayP-6
65CarTeal-16
65ChaTheY-38
65OPC-136
65Top-136
65Top-294
65TopEmbl-7
66CarTeal-8
66Top-275
66TopRubl-63
66TopVen-275
67Top-485
67TopGiaSU-14
68Baz-3
68Top-275
68Top-376
68TopActS-6C
68TopGaml-18
68TopPla-20
68TopPos-19
68TopVen-275
69KelPin-13
69MilBra-178
69MLBOffS-214
69MLBPin-53
69OPC-164
69Top-164
69Top-475
69TopDecl-25
69TopFou-7
69TopSta-118
69TopSup-61
69TopTeaP-18
69TraSta-35
70Kel-34
70MLBOffS-92
70OPC-90
70PhiTeal-8
70Top-90
70TopScr-13
70TopSup-23
71BazNumT-1
71MLBOffS-184
71OPC-465
71PhiArcO-8
71Top-465
71TopCoi-107
71TopGreM-25
71TopSup-34
72Dia-33
72MilBra-218
72OPC-139
72Top-139
73OPC-269
73Top-269
74OPC-520
74Top-520
74TopSta-115
75OPC-586
75Top-586
76OPC-502
76Top-502
77Top-357
78PhiSSP-48
78SSP270-48
78Top-235
79PhiBurK-3
79Top-675
80Top-178
81Fle-27
81TCM60I-386
83CarGreT-10
92CarMcD-36
92SkyAA F-300

McCaskill, Kirk
83RedPioT-19
85EdmTraC-7
86AngSmo-5
86Don-474
86Fle-163
86Top-628
86TopTif-628
87AngSmo-5
87Don-381
87Fle-88
87FleGamW-27
87FleGlo-88
87FleHotS-29
87FleMin-67
87FleStiC-75
87GenMilB-3G
87Lea-223
87OPC-194
87SevCoi-W5
87Spo-127
87SpoTeaP-11
87Top-194
87TopSti-181
87TopTif-194
88AngSmo-12
88Don-381
88DonBasB-83
88Fle-496
88FleGlo-496
88PanSti-36
88Sco-552
88ScoGlo-552
88Spo-78
88StaLinAn-12
88Top-16
88TopBig-168
88TopTif-16
89Bow-38
89BowTif-38
89Don-136
89DonBasB-83
89Fle-483
89FleGlo-483
89OPC-348
89PanSti-285
89Sco-181
89Spo-214
89Top-421
89TopBig-149
89TopSti-184
89TopTif-421
89UppDec-223
90AngSmo-11
90Bow-283
90BowTif-283
90Don-170A
90Don-170B
90Fle-138
90FleCan-138
90Lea-264
90OPC-215
90PanSti-37
90PubSti-373
90PubSti-598
90Sco-217
90Sco100S-38
90Spo-169
90Top-215
90TopMinL-9
90TopSti-167
90TopTif-215
90UppDec-506
90VenSti-326
90VenSti-327
91AngSmo-10
91Don-637
91Fle-319
91Lea-199
91OPC-532
91Sco-590
91StaClu-313
91Stu-28
91Top-532
91TopDesS-532
91TopMic-532
91TopTif-532
91Ult-50
91UppDec-539
92Bow-2
92Don-340
92Fle-64
92Lea-517
92OPC-301
92OPCPre-60
92Pin-391
92Sco-79
92ScoProP-18
92ScoRoo-29T
92StaClu-688
92StaCluECN-688
92Stu-155
92Top-301
92TopGol-301
92TopGolW-301
92TopMic-301
92TopTra-69T
92TopTraG-69T
92Ult-338
92UppDec-128
92UppDec-722
92WhiSoxK-25
93Don-227
93Fle-206
93Lea-151
93OPC-230
93PacSpa-392
93Pin-560
93Sco-469
93Sel-387
93StaClu-166
93StaCluFDI-166
93StaCluMOP-166
93StaCluWS-28
93Top-175
93TopGol-175
93TopInaM-175
93TopMic-175
93TriPla-82
93Ult-535
93UppDec-608
93UppDecGold-608
93WhiSoxK-19
94Don-540
94Fla-34
94Fle-88
94Pac-133
94StaCluT-135
94StaCluTFDI-135
94Top-724
94TopGol-724
94TopSpa-724
94Ult-37
94WhiSoxK-21
95ColCho-496
95ColChoGS-496
95ColChoSS-496
95Don-425
95DonPreP-425
95Fle-125
95Sco-544
95ScoGolR-544
95ScoPlaTS-544
95Ult-32
95UltGolM-32
95WhiSoxK-21
96ColCho-511
96ColChoGS-511
96ColChoSS-511
96Fle-73
96FleTif-73

McCatty, Steve
78Top-701
80Top-231
81A'sGraG-54
81Don-478
81Fle-589
81OPC-59
81Top-503
82A'sGraG-10
82Don-35
82Fle-99
82FleSta-131
82OPC-113
82Top-113
82Top-156
82Top-165
82Top-167
82TopSti-10
82TopSti-14
82TopSti-228
83A'sGraG-54
83Don-491
83Fle-525
83Top-493
84A'sMot-8
84Don-420
84Fle-454
84Nes792-369
84OPC-369
84Top-369
84TopTif-369
85A'sMot-20
85Don-497
85Fle-430
85Top-63
85TopSti-324
85TopTif-63
86BufBisP-18
86Fle-427
86Top-624
86TopTif-624
87SanJosBP-26
89PacSenL-89
89T/MSenL-75
89TopSenL-110
91PacSenL-16

McCauley, Drew
82BufBisT-4

McCawley, Bill
52MotCoo-11
53MotCoo-22

McCawley, James
87OldJudN-332

McCerod, George
86PawRedSP-13

McClain, Charles
91BilMusP-3750
91BilMusSP-1
92ChaWheF-6
92ChaWVWC-2
93WinSpiC-15
93WinSpiF-1568

McClain, Joe
79QuaCitCT-8

McClain, Joe Sr.
61SenJayP-6
61Top-488
62SalPlaC-54
62ShiPlaC-54
62Top-324
62TopStal-98
63Top-311

McClain, Michael
82OrlTwiT-10
83MiaMarT-2
85BeaGolGT-12
86BeaGolGP-18

McClain, Ron
76IndIndTI-25
77IndIndTI-26
78IndIndTI-26
79IndIndTI-30
83ExpPos-14

McClain, Scott
92KanCouCC-10
92KanCouCF-100
92KanCouCTI-21
93CarLeaAGF-3
93FreKeyC-14
93FreKeyF-1032
94BowBayF-2419
94ExcFS7-12
94OriPro-60
95RocRedWTI-24
96Bow-245
96FleUpd-U3
96FleUpdTC-U3
96RocRedWB-18
96Ult-306
96UltGolM-306
96UltGolP-13
96UltGolPHGM-13

McClain, Terrence
95YakBeaTI-20

McClatchy, Kevin
96ModA'sB-30

McClear, Michael
86Ft.LauYP-16

McClellan, Bobby
75AppFoxT-16

McClellan, Dan
74LauOldTBS-32

McClellan, Garth
85CloHSS-25

McClellan, Harvey

22E120-24
22W573-76
23WilChoV-91
75WhiSox1T-16
McClellan, Paul
86EveGiaC-2
86EveGiaPC-14
87CliGiaP-21
88ShrCapP-1290
89BlaYNPRWL-26
89ShrCapP-1850
90CMC-528
90PhoFirC-1
90PhoFirP-9
90ProAAAF-35
91LinDriAA-311
91Sco-726
91ShrCapLD-311
91ShrCapP-1817
91TopDeb90-102
92Cla1-T59
92Don-700
92Fle-642
92OPC-424
92PhoFirF-2817
92PhoFirS-388
92ProFS7-344
92Sco-703
92SkyAAAF-177
92StaClu-566
92Top-424
92TopGol-424
92TopGolW-424
92TopMic-424
92UppDec-563
McClellan, Sean
96MedHatBJTI-17
McClellan, William
87BucN28-14
87OldJudN-333
McClelland, Tim
88T/MUmp-46
89T/MUmp-44
90T/MUmp-42
McClendon, Lloyd
82LynMetT-16
83WatRedT-9
87FleUpd-74
87FleUpdG-74
87RedKah-23
88RedKah-30
88Top-172
88TopTif-172
89Bow-287
89BowTif-287
89CubMar-10
89Don-595
89DonBasB-228
89FleUpd-77
89IowCubC-12
89IowCubP-1695
89Sco-521
89Top-644
89TopTif-644
89TopTra-76T
89TopTraT-76T
89UppDec-446
90Bow-36
90BowTif-36
90CubMar-14
90Don-341
90DonBesN-134
90Fle-38
90FleCan-38
90OPC-337
90Sco-176A
90Sco-176B
90Top-337
90TopBig-5
90TopTif-337
90TopTVCu-32
90UppDec-398
91FleUpd-111
91StaClu-385
92Don-338
92Fle-560
92OPC-209
92PirNatl-15
92Sco-566
92StaClu-302
92Top-209
92TopGol-209
92TopGolW-209
92TopMic-209
92Ult-256
93Don-384
93Fle-502
93PacSpa-247
93PirHil-7
93PirNatl-17
93Sco-380
93StaClu-66
93StaCluFDI-66
93StaCluM-69
93StaCluMOP-66
93Top-81
93TopGol-81
93TopInaM-81
93TopMic-81
93Ult-99
93UppDec-559
93UppDecGold-559
94Fle-613
94Pac-501
94PirQui-15
94StaClu-511
94StaCluFDI-511
94StaCluGR-511
94StaCluMOP-511
94Top-518
94TopGol-518
94TopSpa-518
McClendon, Travis
95NewJerCTI-17
96PeoChiB-19
McClinic, Nath
92NegLeaRLI-41
McClinton, Patrick
93BenRocC-16
93BenRocF-3264
94AshTouC-17
94AshTouF-1777
95AshTouUTI-21
96SalAvaB-20
McClinton, Tim
89KinMetS-16
90ColMetGS-3
90ColMetPPI-7
90PitMetP-10
91ColMetPI-21
91ColMetPPI-1
92St.LucMCB-21
92St.LucMF-1756
93St.LucMC-16
93StLucMF-2934
McClochlin, Mike
91ColIndP-1481
McCloskey, John
11SpoLifCW-239
McCloughan, Scot
90WicStaSGD-23
92St.CatBJC-20
92St.CatBJF-3398
93HagSunC-20
93HagSunF-1893
McClure, Bob (Robert)
76OmaRoyTT-13
76OPC-599
76SSP-182
76Top-599
77Top-472
78Top-243
79Top-623
80Top-357
81Don-510
81Fle-520
81OPC-156
81Top-156
82BrePol-10
82Top-487
83BreGar-10
83BrePol-10
83Don-582
83Fle-38
83FleSta-121
83FleSti-17
83Top-62
84BreGar-12
84BrePol-10
84Don-359
84Fle-206
84Nes792-582
84Top-582
84TopTif-582
85BreGar-12
85BrePol-10
85Don-536
85Fle-587
85Top-203
85TopTif-203
86BrePol-10
86Fle-494
86Top-684
86TopTif-684
86TopTra-71T
86TopTraT-71T
87ExpPos-14
87Fle-325
87FleGlo-325
87OPC-133
87Top-707
87TopTif-707
88Don-529
88Fle-189
88FleGlo-189
88OPC-313
88Sco-381
88ScoGlo-381
88StaLinE-10
88Top-313
88TopTif-313
89Bow-43
89BowTif-43
89Fle-42
89FleGlo-42
89FleUpd-14
89Sco-572
89ScoRoo-58T
89Top-182
89TopTif-182
90AngSmo-20
90Don-470
90Fle-139
90FleCan-139
90OPC-458
90PubSti-374
90Sco-117
90Top-458
90TopTif-458
90UppDec-81
90VenSti-328
91MetWIZ-258
91OPC-84
91Top-84
91TopDesS-84
91TopMic-84
91TopTif-84
92BreCarT-13
92Don-661
92Sco-717
92StaClu-484
93Fle-128
93MarUSPC-5C
93PacSpa-467
93Sco-434
93StaCluMarl-3
93Ult-383
94BreMilB-155
McClure, Brian
96IdaFalB-17
McClure, Craig
94Top-79
94TopGol-79
94TopSpa-79
96AppLeaAB-6
96BriWhiSB-25
McClure, Jack
44CenFlo-17
65Top-553
McClure, Rich
79QuaCitCT-9
McClure, Todd
87AshTouP-21
87AubAstP-3
88FloStaLAS-12
88OscAstS-17
89KenTwiS-14
89Sta-52
89VisOakP-1436
McClurg, Clint
94MarPhiC-12
94MarPhiF-3288
95BatCliTI-21
McCollom, Jim
87QuaCitAP-21
88MidAngGS-22
88TexLeaAGS-27
McCollough, Adam
96BluOriB-18
McCollough, Mike
91GulCoaRSP-1
92GasRanC-22
McCollum, Greg
87ElmPio(C-23
88LynRedSS-12
McCollum, Lou
47SunBre-11
McCommon, Jason
94VerExpC-17
94VerExpF-3908
96HarSenB-19
McConachie, Dale
89AlbYanB-26
McConathy, Doug
91BluOriC-15
91BluOriP-4135
92FreKeyC-21
92FreKeyF-1812
93FreKeyC-15
93FreKeyF-1033
McConnell, Ambrose
08AmeCarE-85
09BriE97-19
09ColChiE-184
09ColChiE-185
09RamT20-75
10E12AmeCDC-24
10W555-46
11S74Sil-6
11SpoLifCW-240
11SpoLifM-14A
11SpoLifM-14B
11T205-112
11TurRedT-29
12ColRedB-184
12ColRedB-185
12ColTinT-184
12ColTinT-185
12HasTriFT-4
12HasTriFT-41A
12HasTriFT-53
12HasTriFT-54
McConnell, Chad
92Bow-587
92ClaDraP-10
92ClaDraPFB-BC10
92TopTra-70T
92TopTraG-70T
92UppDecML-8
93Bow-132
93ClaFS7-245
93ClePhiF-2696
93StaCluM-35
93StaCluM-81
93StaCluP-4
93Top-161
93TopGol-161
93TopInaM-161
93TopMic-161
93UppDec-439
93UppDecGold-439
94Cla-21
94ClePhiC-19
94ClePhiF-2541
94SigRoo-39
94SigRooS-39
94UppDecML-39
95ReaPhiELC-27
95ReaPhiTI-14
96ReaPhiB-24
McConnell, Tim
92FayGenF-2171
93LakTigC-16
93LakTigF-1314
94LakTigC-15
94LakTigF-3039
94TreThuF-2122
McConnell, Walt
86FloStaLAP-34
86VerBeaDP-17
87SanAntDTI-14
88SanAntMB-16
89AlbDukC-21
89AlbDukP-83
90AlbDukC-28
90AlbDukP-353
90AlbDukT-22
90ProAAAF-74
91AlbDukP-1148
91MidAngOHP-19
92MidAngF-4033
92MidAngS-465
McCool, Bill
64Top-356
64TopVen-356
65Kah-27
65OPC-18
65RedEnq-18
65Top-18
66Kah-20
66Top-459
67CokCapR-14
67DexPre-138
67Kah-24
67Top-353
67TopVen-334
68Kah-B25
68Top-597
69MilBra-179
69MLBOffS-194
69OPC-129
69Top-129
69TopFou-15
70MLBOffS-116
70OPC-314
70Top-314
72MilBra-219
81TCM60I-351
McCord, Clinton
92NegLeaRLI-42
McCorkle, Dave
86WauTimP-15
87SalSpuP-12
88VerMarP-963
McCormack, Andy
94SouBenSHC-10
94SouBenSHF-590
96CanIndB-17
McCormack, Brian
87EugEmeP-2661
88AppFoxP-152
89BasCitRS-16
90MemChiB-19
90MemChiP-1009
90MemChiS-17
McCormack, Don R.
81OklCit8T-9
82EvaTriT-12
88BatCliP-1664
89BatCliP-1935
90ReaPhiB-24
90ReaPhiP-1234
90ReaPhiS-26
91LinDriAA-524
91ReaPhiLD-524
91ReaPhiP-1385
92ReaPhiF-591
92ReaPhiS-549
93ReaPhiF-310
94ClePhiC-27
95ClePhiF-231
McCormack, Hugh
88AllandGN-32
McCormack, John
87OldJudN-334
McCormack, Mark
83NasAngT-23
McCormack, Ron
83ChaRoyT-21
McCormack, Tim
86JacExpT-26
87IndIndTI-32
88IndIndP-498
89IndIndC-9
89IndIndP-1226
McCormick, Andrew
96DunBluJB-16
96DunBluJTI-19
96HagSunB-14
McCormick, Barry
03BreE10-97
McCormick, Buck (Frank A.)
38CinOraW-18
39ExhSal-41A
39ExhSal-41B
39OrcPhoAP-15
39PlaBal-36
40PlaBal-75
41DouPlaR-9
41HarHarW-14
41PlaBal-5
49Bow-239
79DiaGre-256
83TCMPla1942-35
91ConTSN-306
McCormick, Cody
96GreBatB-15
McCormick, Glenn
90BenBucL-17

90MadMusP-2277
McCormick, Jim
87BucN28-89
87OldJudN-335
McCormick, John
89AppFoxP-873
90BasCitRS-16
91BasCitRC-10
91BasCitRP-1397
McCormick, Kid (Michael J.)
90DodTar-501
McCormick, Mike
79ArkTraT-14
80ArkTraT-24
McCormick, Mike (Myron W.)
41DouPlaR-115
41HarHarW-15
49Bow-146
49EurSta-41
52MotCoo-57
76TayBow4-69
77TCMTheWY-65
90DodTar-1022
McCormick, Mike F.
58GiaSFCB-15
58Top-37
59Top-148
59TopVen-148
60GiaJayP-10
60MacSta-15
60Top-530
61GiaJayP-10
61Pos-141A
61Pos-141B
61Top-45
61Top-305
61Top-383
61TopStal-81
62GiaJayP-10
62Jel-139
62Pos-139
62PosCan-139
62SalPlaC-134
62ShiPlaC-134
62Top-56
62Top-107
62Top-319
62TopBuc-59
62TopStal-200
62TopVen-56
62TopVen-107
63Top-563
64Top-487
65Top-343
66OPC-118
66Top-118
66TopVen-118
67CokCapG-12
67DexPre-139
67OPC-86
67Top-86A
67Top-86B
67TopVen-289
68AtlOilPBCC-27
68Baz-12
68DexPre-53
68OPC-9
68Top-9
68Top-400A
68Top-400B
68TopActS-2A
68TopActS-15A
68TopGamI-17
68TopVen-9
69MilBra-180
69MLBOffS-205
69Top-517
70MLBOffS-130
70OPC-337
70Top-337
71MLBOffS-494
71OPC-438
71Top-438
72MilBra-220
72Top-682
73TacTwiC-15
79TCM50-245
84GiaMot-16
88PacLegI-67
91OriCro-287
92YanWIZ7-108
McCormick, Moose (Harry)
09ColChiE-186
09RamT20-76
09T206-235
11SpoLifCW-241
12ColRedB-186
12ColTinT-186
McCosky, W. Barney
40PlaBal-201
41DouPlaR-53
41PlaBal-36
41WheM5-20
47Exh-155A
47Exh-155B
48Bow-25
49Bow-203
49Lea-63
49PhiBul-37
51Bow-84
52Top-300
76TayBow4-93
79DiaGre-390
81TigDetN-114
81TigSecNP-25
82Bow195E-254
83TCMPla1942-14
83TopRep5-300
McCovey, Willie
47PM1StaP1-138
60GiaJayP-9
60NuHi-67
60Top-316
60Top-554
61Pos-147A
61Pos-147B
61Top-517
61TopStaI-82
62Jel-131
62Pos-131
62PosCan-131
62SalPlaC-142
62ShiPlaC-142
62Top-544
63GiaJayP-8
63Jel-112
63Pos-112
63Top-490
64Baz-21
64ChatheY-38
64GiaJayP-8
64Top-9
64Top-41
64Top-350
64TopCoi-22
64TopSta-94
64TopStaU-51
64TopVen-9
64TopVen-41
64TopVen-350
64WheSta-31
65ChaTheY-39
65GiaTeal-7
65OPC-176
65Top-176
66Baz-14
66Top-217
66Top-550
66TopRubI-64
66TopVen-217
67Baz-14
67CokCapG-11
67DexPre-140
67OPCPapI-32
67Top-423
67Top-480
67TopPos-32
67TopVen-303
68AtlOilPBCC-28
68Baz-13
68OPC-5
68Top-5
68Top-290
68TopActS-7A
68TopVen-5
68TopVen-290
69CitMetC-19
69MilBra-181
69MLBOffS-206
69MLBPin-54
69OPC-4
69OPC-6
69OPCDec-13
69Top-4
69Top-6
69Top-416
69Top-440A
69Top-440B
69Top-572
69TopDec-31
69TopDecI-26
69TopSta-109
69TopSup-66
69TopTeaP-14
69TraSta-36
70Gia-10
70Kel-4
70MilBra-16
70MLBOffS-131
70OPC-63
70OPC-65
70OPC-250
70OPC-450
70Top-63
70Top-65
70Top-250
70Top-450
70TopPos-7
70TopSup-13
70TraSta-2C
71BazNumT-4
71BazUnn-22
71GiaTic-8
71Kel-33
71MatMin-9
71MatMin-10
71MilDud-52
71MLBOffS-258
71OPC-50
71Top-50
71TopCoi-57
71TopGreM-52
71TopSup-46
71TopTat-106
71TopTat-107
72Dia-61
72Kel-7A
72Kel-7B
72MilBra-221
72OPC-280
72ProStaP-19
72Top-280
72TopCloT-23
72TopPos-24
73LinPor-162
73OPC-410
73Top-410
73TopCanL-29
73TopCom-11
73TopPin-11
74LauAllG-69
74OPC-250
74PadDea-18
74PadMcDD-9
74Top-250A
74Top-250B
74TopDecE-28
74TopSta-97
75Hos-19
75HosTwi-19
75OPC-207
75OPC-450
75Top-207
75Top-450
76Hos-124
76OPC-520
76Top-520
77GalGloG-263
77Gia-15
77PadSchC-37A
77PadSchC-37B
77Spo-7816
77Top-547
78Hos-73
78Kel-23
78OPC-185
78OPC-238
78RCColC-83
78Top-3
78Top-34
79GiaPol-44
79Kel-17
79OPC-107
79Top-215
80GiaEurFS-5
80GiaPol-44
80Lau300-30
80OPC-176
80PerHaloFP-196
80SSPHOF-190
80Top-2
80Top-335
81Fle-434
82K-M-16
83DiaClaS2-90
83MLBPin-28
84GiaMot-2
84OCoandSI-14
84SpoDesPW-14
85CirK-8
85TopGloA-11
86DonHig-34
86SpoDecG-48
87LeaSpeO*-H11
89HOFStiB-4
89PadMag-4
89PerCelP-31
89TopBasT-29
90AGFA-20
90PerGreM-22
92GiaCheHoFP-2
92TVSpoMF5HRC-9
92Zip-7
93ActPacA-123
93ActPacA2-57G
93Yoo-9
94CarLeaA-DJ4
95TopLegot6M-7
97St.VinHHS-11
McCoy, Benjamin
41DouPlaR-129
79DiaGre-334
McCoy, Brent
88PulBraP-1762
89PulBraP-1894
90Bes-59
90BurBraB-27
90BurBraP-2358
90BurBraS-18
90MidLeaASGS-42
90ProAaA-130
90StaFS7-57
91DurBulC-23
91DurBulP-1556
McCoy, Kevin
80BurBeeT-2
81BurBeeT-3
83ElPasDT-20
McCoy, Larry
88T/MUmp-10
89T/MUmp-8
90T/MUmp-8
McCoy, Tim (Timothy)
86EveGiaC-13
86EveGiaPC-15
88ShrCapP-1300
89PalSprACLC-57
89PalSprAP-468
90ModA'sC-20
90ModA'sCLC-156
90ModA'sP-2208
91LinDriAAA-541
91TacTigLD-541
McCoy, Tommy
93SavCarC-29
McCoy, Trey
88ButCopKSP-18
89GasRanP-1012
89GasRanS-12
89SouAtlLAGS-28
89Sta-138
90ChaRanS-13
91LinDriAA-587
91TulDriLD-587
91TulDriP-2781
91TulDriTI-17
92TulDriF-2702
92TulDriS-611
93TulDriF-2743
94ClaGolF-182
94ExcFS7-136
94ExcLeaLF-13
94OklCit8F-1506
93TulDriTI-17
McCrabb, Les
79DiaGre-333
McCracken, Quinton
92BenRocC-18
92BenRocF-1480
93Bow-260
93CenValRC-18
93CenValRF-2899
93StaCluRoc-2
93Top-451
93TopGol-451
93TopInaM-451
93TopMic-451
94ExcFS7-185
94NewHavRF-1562
94UppDecML-6
95ARuFalLS-14
95NewHavRTI-1
95UppDecML-119
96Bow-306
96ColCho-538
96ColCho-661
96ColChoGS-37
96ColChoGS-538
96ColChoGS-661
96ColChoSS-37
96ColChoSS-538
96ColChoSS-661
96Fle-367
96FleRoc-8
96FleTif-367
96Lea-44
96LeaPrePB-44
96LeaPrePG-44
96LeaPrePS-44
96Pin-391
96PinFoil-391
96RocPol-12
96Sco-504
96Sel-171
96SelArtP-171
96Sum-179
96SumAbo&B-179
96SumArtP-179
96SumFoi-179
96Ult-470
96UltGolM-470
96UppDec-234
96UppDecFSP-FS14
97Cir-327
97CirRav-327
97ColCho-101
97Don-385
97DonEli-130
97DonEliGS-130
97DonLim-123
97DonLimLE-123
97DonPre-75
97DonPreCttC-75
97DonPreP-385
97DonPrePGold-385
97DonRatR-8
97DonTea-99
97DonTeaSPE-99
97Fle-312
97FleTif-312
97Lea-21
97LeaFraM-21
97LeaFraMDC-21
97Pac-283
97PacLigB-283
97PacSil-283
97Pin-176
97PinArtP-176
97PinIns-101
97PinInsCE-101
97PinInsDE-101
97PinMusC-176
97Sco-189
97ScoPreS-189
97ScoRoc-10
97ScoRocPl-10
97ScoRocPr-10
97ScoShoS-189
97ScoShoSAP-189
97Top-443
97Ult-187
97UltGolME-187
97UltPlaME-187
97UppDec-57
95UppDecMLFS-119
McCrary, Arnold
77AshTouT-15
78AshTouT-17
79WauTimT-23
80WauTimT-22
McCrary, Sam
86JacMetT-23
87JacMetF-13
88TidTidCa-1
88TidTidP-1580
89TidTidC-28
89TidTidP-1947
McCraw, Tom

64Top-283
64TopVen-283
65Top-586
65WhiSoxJP-4
66OPC-141
66Top-141
66TopVen-141
66WhiSoxTI-9
67CokCapWS-11
67DexPre-141
67OPC-29
67Top-29
68Top-413
69MilBra-182
69MLBOffS-33
69Top-388
69TopTeaP-11
70MLBOffS-189
70Top-561
71OPC-373
71SenPolP-8
71Top-373
72MilBra-222
72Top-767
73Kel2D-21
73OPC-86
73Top-86
74OPC-449
74Top-449
75OPC-482
75Top-482
81TCM60I-353
82Ind-25
82IndBurK-5
82IndBurK-6
82IndBurK-7
82IndTeal-24
82IndWhe-9
84GiaPos-16
85GiaMot-27
85GiaPos-21
89OriFreB-40
92MetColP-37
92MetKah-27
96MetKah-21
96MetKah-22

McCray, Eric
89GasRanP-1008
89GasRanS-13
90CMC-766
90TulDriP-1151
90TulDriTI-17
91Bow-281
91TulDriTI-18

McCray, Justin
90AshTouP-2756
91SarWhiSC-17
91SarWhiSP-1119

McCray, Rod (Rodney)
86ChaRaiP-16
88SouBenWSGS-8
89SarWhiSS-14
90Bes-204
90BirBarB-12
90BirBarP-1119
91LinDriAAA-641
91OPC-523
91Sco-763
91Top-523
91TopDeb90-103
91TopDesS-523
91TopMic-523
91TopTif-523
91VanCanLD-641
91VanCanP-1607
92Sco-517
92StaClu-829
92StaCluNC-829
94LetMouF-3895
94LetMouSP-29

McCray, Todd
90BoiHawP-3307
91RenSilSCLC-18

McCreadie, Brant
89HigSchPLS-16
91SalSpuC-8
91SalSpuP-2239

McCready, Aaron
96BriWhiSB-6

McCready, Jim
92ColMetC-22
92ColMetF-292
92ColMetPI-16
93St.LucMC-17
94BinMetF-701
95BinMetTI-17
93StLucMF-2919

McCreary, Bob
88CapCodPPaLP-82
89EliTwiS-17
90VisOakCLC-69
90VisOakP-2163
91Cla/Bes-308
91LinDriAA-488
91OrlSunRLD-488
91OrlSunRP-1859
92CalLeaACL-33
92OrlSunRF-2846
92VisOakF-1011
93NasXprF-399

McCreedie, Judge
90DodTar-502

McCreery, Tom
90DodTar-503

McCreight, Kenneth
47SenGunBP-10

McCroskey, Jackie
93PriRedC-18
93PriRedF-4195
94PriRedC-16
94PriRedF-3278

McCubbin, Shane
93BurBeeC-13
93BurBeeF-161
93ButCopKSP-6
94BurBeeC-16
94BurBeeF-1084
94VerExpC-18
94VerExpF-3913

McCue, Deron
85FreGiaP-9
86ShrCapP-17
87ShrCapP-19
88PhoFirC-23
88PhoFirP-58
90EveGiaP-3145
91CliGiaC-28
91CliGiaP-852

McCulla, Harry
82SprCarF-22
83SprCarF-17
84SavCarT-16
85SprCarT-17
86ArkTraP-14
90SprCarDGB-3

McCullers, Lance
85LasVegSC-109
86Don-41
86Fle-330
86SpoRoo-8
86Top-44
86TopTif-44
87ClaGam-80
87Don-237
87Fle-424
87FleGlo-424
87FleMin-68
87FleStiC-76
87OPC-71
87PadBohHB-41
87PadFirPTB-3
87SpoTeaP-16
87Top-559
87TopSti-111
87TopTif-559
88Don-451
88DonBasB-210
88Fle-592
88FleGlo-592
88FleMin-114
88OPC-197
88PadCok-41
88PadSmo-18
88PanSti-399
88Sco-150
88ScoGlo-150
88Spo-85
88StaLinPa-9
88Top-197
88TopBig-38
88TopSti-114
88TopTif-197
89Bow-168
89BowTif-168
89Don-129
89DonBasB-220
89DonTra-13
89Fle-312
89FleGlo-312
89OPC-307
89Sco-158
89ScoRoo-63T
89ScoYouS2-19
89Spo-76
89Top-307
89TopSti-108
89TopTif-307
89TopTra-77T
89TopTraT-77T
89UppDec-382
89UppDec-710
89YanScoNW-14
90Don-433
90Fle-448
90FleCan-448
90Lea-456
90OPC-259
90PubSti-541
90Sco-186
90Top-259
90TopTif-259
90TopTVY-13
90UppDec-615
90VenSti-329
91Don-133
91Fle-342
91Sco-313
91UppDec-203
92OklCit8S-315
92YanWIZ8-115
93CalCanF-1163
93RanKee-254

McCullock, Alec
84BufBisT-10

McCullough, Carol
84IowCubT-19

McCullough, Clyde
41CubTeal-12
43CubTeal-15
47TipTop-113
49Bow-163
49EurSta-166
50Bow-124
50PirTeal-13
51Bow-94
52Bow-99
52Top-218
55Bow-280
61TwiPetM-21
72TopTes5-6
83TopRep5-218
84TCMPla1-32

McCune, Gary
83KnoBluJT-22
88KnoBluJB-21
89KnoBluJP-1121

McCurdy, Harry
28Exh-40
31Exh-12
33Gou-170
94ConTSN-1242
94ConTSNB-1242

McCurine, Jim
93NegLeaRL2-26

McCurry, Jeff
92AugPirC-17
92AugPirF-235
92UppDecML-207
93CarLeaAGF-50
93SalBucC-17
93SalBucF-429
94CarMudF-1576
94ExcFS7-253
95PirFil-20
95Sum-173
95SumNthD-173
96TolMudHB-19

McCutcheon, Greg
88St.CatBJP-2020
89St.CatBJP-2094
90EriSaiS-15

McCutcheon, James
87GasRanP-21
88GasRanP-1004
89GasRanP-1011
89GasRanS-14
93AshTouC-13
93AshTouF-2273
93QuaCitRBF-96

McCutcheon, Mike
96HonShaHWB-19

McDade, Neal
96EriSeaB-16

McDaniel, Cannonball (Booker T.)
49W725AngTI-20
87NegLeaPD-40

McDaniel, Donna
91FreStaLBS-7

McDaniel, Jim
59Top-134
59TopVen-134

McDaniel, Joey
93DavLipB-17

McDaniel, Lindy
47Exh-156
57Top-79
58CarJayP-8
58Top-180
59OklTodML-10
59Top-479
60CarJayP-6
60Top-195
60TopVen-195
61CarJayP-8
61Pos-175A
61Pos-175B
61Top-75
61Top-266
61TopStal-91
62CarJayP-8
62Jel-163
62Pos-163
62PosCan-163
62SalPlaC-144
62ShiPlaC-144
62Top-306
62Top-522
62TopStal-187
63CubJayP-9
63Jel-167
63Pos-167A
63Pos-167B
63Top-329
64CubJayP-9
64Top-510
65GiaTeal-8
65OPC-244
65Top-244
66Top-496
67CokCapG-16
67OPC-46
67Top-46
68Top-545
69MilBra-183
69OPC-191
69Top-191
69TopFou-10
70OPC-493
70Top-493
71MLBOffS-495
71OPC-303
71Top-303
71YanCliDP-11
72MilBra-223
72OPC-513
72Top-513
73OPC-46
73SyrChiTI-16
73Top-46
74OPC-182
74Top-182
74TopTra-182T
75OPC-652
75Top-652
79TCM50-280
84CubUno-9
92YanWIZ6-80
92YanWIZ7-109

McDaniel, M. Von
58Top-65A
58Top-65B
59OklTodML-9
89AstCol4S-21

McDaniel, Marty
89CarNewE-22

McDaniel, Terry
87LitFalMP-2404
88ColMetGS-22
89St.LucMS-16
90JacMetGS-27
90MetColP-40
90TexLeaAGS-28
90TopTVM-50
91MetColP-38
91TidTidP-2524
92Fle-511
92Sco-765
92TopDeb91-121
92TopGol-527
92TopGolW-527

McDarrah, Fred
75TopPho-52

McDavid, Ray
91ChaRaiC-21
91ChaRaiP-107
92CalLeaACL-29
92ClaFS7-131
92HigDesMC-9
92UppDecML-64
92UppDecML-256
92UppDecMLPotY-PY16
93Bow-26
93Bow-359
93ClaGolF-58
93ClaYouG-YG10
93SP-170
93UppDec-438
93UppDecGold-438
93WicWraF-2991
94Bow-260
94BowBes-B67
94BowBesR-B67
94Cla-92
94ExcFS7-285
94FleUpd-188
94LasVegSF-880
94LeaLimR-70
94SigRoo-12
94SigRooHP-S6
94SigRooS-12
94Top-152
94TopGol-152
94TopSpa-152
94Ult-582
94UppDecML-160
94UppDecML-165
94UppDecMLPotYF-PY17
95Bow-84
95ColCho-353
95ColChoGS-353
95ColChoSE-20
95ColChoSEGS-20
95ColChoSESS-20
95ColChoSS-353
95Don-117
95DonPreP-117
95LeaGolR-11
95Pin-409
95PinArtP-409
95PinMusC-409
95Sel-175
95SelArtP-175
95StaClu-43
95StaCluFDI-43
95StaCluMOP-43
95StaCluSTWS-43
95StaCluVR-31
95Top-147
95UppDec-139
95UppDecED-139
95UppDecEDG-139
96Don-482
96DonPreP-482
95StaCluVRMC-31

McDermont, Jim
93SouBenWSF-1427
92UtiBluSC-19

McDermott, Mickey (Maurice)
48RedSoxTI-16
50Bow-97
50Dra-31
51Bow-16
51TopRedB-43
52Bow-25
52Top-119
53BowC-35
53Bri-12
53NorBreL-17
53RedSoxTI-19
53Top-55
54Bow-56
55Bow-165
56Top-340
57Top-318
79TCM50-207
83TopRep5-119
91TopArc1-55

McDermott, Randall

92GulCoaYF-3789
McDermott, Ryan
96AppLeaAB-9
96BurIndB-11
McDermott, Terry
74AlbDukTI-67
74AlbDukTI-10
75AlbDukC-7
90DodTar-1023
McDevitt, Danny
58Top-357
59DodTeal-15
59Top-364
60DodBelB-3
60Lea-50
60Top-333
61Top-349
61Yan61RL-29
62Top-493
90DodTar-504
91RinPos1Y2-3
92YanWIZ6-81
McDevitt, Terry
86SpoIndC-170
87ChaRaiP-12
88RivRedWCLC-224
88RivRedWP-1430
89WatDiaS-31
90ClePhiS-14
McDill, Allen
92GulCoaMF-3477
92KinMetC-12
92KinMetF-1528
93PitMetF-3706
94CapCitBC-14
94CapCitBF-1748
95AusFut-30
95StLucMTI-21
96WicWraB-8
McDonald, Ashanti
96RocCubTI-19
McDonald, Ben
87AncGlaP-20
89Sta-200
90Baz-10
90Bes-7
90Bow-243
90BowTif-243
90ClaBlu-130
90CMC-302
90Don-32
90DonBesA-114
90DonPre-2
90DonRoo-30
90Fle-180
90FleCan-180
90HagSunB-1
90HagSunP-1408
90Lea-249
90LSUMcDM-1
90LSUMcDM-2
90LSUMcDM-3
90LSUMcDM-4
90LSUMcDM-5
90LSUMcDM-6
90LSUMcDM-7
90LSUMcDM-8
90LSUMcDM-9
90LSUMcDM-10
90LSUMcDM-11
90LSUMcDM-12
90LSUMcDM-13
90LSUMcDM-14
90LSUMcDM-15
90LSUMcDM-16
90LSUTigGM-7
90OPC-774
90PanSti-373
90ProAaA-2
90ProAAAF-456
90RocRedWC-1
90RocRedWGC-3
90RocRedWP-699
90Sco-680
90Sco100RS-93
90ScoYouS2-2
90StaFS7-28
90StaMcD-1
90StaMcD-2
90StaMcD-3
90StaMcD-4
90StaMcD-5
90StaMcD-6
90StaMcD-7
90StaMcD-8
90StaMcD-9
90StaMcD-10
90StaMcD-11
90Top-774
90TopBig-228
90TopDeb89-78
90TopMag-15
90TopTif-774
90TopTra-70T
90TopTraT-70T
90UppDec-54A
90UppDec-54B
91Bow-86
91Cla1-T14
91ClaGam-132
91Col-9
91Don-485
91Fle-481
91KinDis-4
91Lea-117
91MajLeaCP-31
91OPC-497
91OriCro-288
91PanFreS-247
91PanSti-197
91RedFolS-109
91Sco-645
91Sco100RS-50
91SevCoi-A8
91StaClu-264
91StaCluP-26
91Stu-6
91SunSee-17
91Top-497
91TopCraJ2-6
91TopDesS-497
91TopMic-497
91TopRoo-18
91TopSta-25
91TopTif-497
91TopTriH-A1
91ToyRoo-17
91Ult-19
91UppDec-446
92Bow-359
92ClaGam-59
92Don-436
92Fle-14
92Hig5-2
92HitTheBB-22
92Lea-145
92OPC-540
92Pin-44
92PinTea2-41
92Sco-658
92Sco100S-94
92ScoImpP-81
92StaClu-490
92Stu-126
92Top-540
92TopDaiQTU-10
92TopGol-540
92TopGolW-540
92TopKid-64
92TopMic-540
92TriPla-105
92Ult-303
92UppDec-93
92UppDec-163
92UppDecCPH-CP3
93Bow-437
93ClaGam-60
93Don-249
93Fin-65
93FinRef-65
93Fla-152
93Fle-169
93FunPac-133
93Lea-1
93MilBonSS-14
93OPC-254
93PacSpa-20
93PanSti-68
93Pin-72
93Sco-202
93Sel-224
93SP-158
93StaClu-259
93StaCluFDI-259
93StaCluMOP-259
93Top-218
93TopGol-218
93TopInaM-218
93TopMic-218
93TriPla-145
93Ult-142
93UppDec-276
93UppDecGold-276
94Bow-459
94BowBes-R22
94BowBesR-R22
94ColC-195
94ColChoGS-195
94ColChoSS-195
94Don-158
94ExtBas-7
94ExtBasGB-18
94ExtBasPD-2
94Fin-161
94FinRef-161
94Fla-4
94Fle-8
94Lea-127
94LeaL-2
94OPC-122
94OriPro-61
94OriUSPC-8C
94OriUSPC-13H
94Pac-35
94Pin-184
94PinArtP-184
94PinMusC-184
94ProMag-7
94Sco-111
94ScoGolR-111
94Sel-117
94SP-123
94SPDieC-123
94Spo-11
94StaClu-413
94StaCluFDI-413
94StaCluGR-413
94StaCluMOP-413
94StaCluT-284
94StaCluTFDI-284
94Stu-124
94Top-636
94TopGol-636
94TopSpa-636
94TriPla-155
94Ult-3
94UppDec-456
94UppDecED-456
95Baz-38
95Bow-311
95ColCho-339
95ColChoGS-339
95ColChoSE-159
95ColChoSEGS-159
95ColChoSESS-159
95ColChoSS-339
95Don-412
95DonPreP-412
95DonTopotO-12
95Emo-5
95Fin-83
95FinRef-83
95Fla-223
95Fle-11
95Lea-197
95Pac-24
95Pin-120
95PinArtP-120
95PinMusC-120
95Sco-273
95ScoGolR-273
95ScoHaloG-HG90
95ScoPlaTS-273
95Sel-144
95SelArtP-144
95Spo-49
95SpoArtP-49
95StaClu-84
95StaCluFDI-84
95StaCluMOP-84
95StaCluSTWS-84
95StaCluVR-51
95Stu-176
95Sum-4
95SumNthD-4
95Top-165
95TopCyb-99
95UC3-62
95UC3ArtP-62
95Ult-5
95UltGolM-5
95UppDec-127
95UppDecED-127
95UppDecEDG-127
95UppDecSE-49
95UppDecSEG-49
95Zen-6
96ColCho-56
96ColCho-776
96ColChoGS-56
96ColChoSS-56
96Don-82
96DonPreP-82
96EmoXL-74
96Fin-B210
96FinRef-B210
96Fla-103
96Fle-15
96FleTif-15
96FleUpd-U48
96FleUpdTC-U48
96LeaLim-22
96LeaLimG-22
96LeaPre-23
96LeaPreP-23
96LeaSigA-151
96LeaSigAG-151
96LeaSigAS-151
96MetUni-5
96MetUniP-5
96Pac-240
96PanSti-130
96Pin-120
96Pin-331
96PinAfi-56
96PinAfiAP-56
96PinAfiFPP-56
96PinFoil-331
96Sco-341
96ScoDugC-B66
96ScoDugCAP-B66
96Sel-102
96SelArtP-102
96SelCer-45
96SelCerAP-45
96SelCerCB-45
96SelCerCR-45
96SelCerMB-45
96SelCerMG-45
96SelCerMR-45
96SP-108
95StaCluVRMC-51
96Sum-80
96SumAbo&B-80
96SumArtP-80
96SumFoi-80
96Top-320
96Ult-367
96UltGolM-367
96UppDec-361
96Zen-28
96ZenArtP-28
96ZenMoz-14
97Cir-14
97CirRav-14
97ColCho-376
97Don-178
97DonLim-151
97DonLimLE-151
97DonPreP-178
97DonPrePGold-178
97Fin-96
97FinRef-96
97Fle-134
97FleTif-134
97Lea-139
97LeaFraM-139
97LeaFraMDC-139
97MetUni-67
97Pac-124
97PacLigB-124
97PacSil-124
97Pin-28
97PinArtP-28
97PinMusC-28
97Sco-27
97ScoPreS-27
97ScoShoS-27
97ScoShoSAP-27
97SkyE-X-27
97SkyE-XC-27
97SkyE-XEC-27
97SP-104
97StaClu-166
97StaCluMOP-166
97Top-25
97Ult-79
97UltGolME-79
97UltPlaME-79
97UppDec-99
McDonald, Chad
91WesPalBEC-22
91WesPalBEP-1237
92HarSenF-468
92HarSenS-292
McDonald, Clown (Ronald)
74PadMcDD-14
81TidTidT-3
McDonald, Dan
93BatCliC-17
93BatCliF-3160
McDonald, Dave
91SanBerSC-9
91SanBerSP-1985
McDonald, David B.
70OPC-189
70Top-189
92YanWIZ6-82
McDonald, Donzell
97Bow-347
97BowChr-235
97BowChrI-235
97BowChrIR-235
97BowChrR-235
97BowInt-347
McDonald, Ed
12T207-117
McDonald, George
45CenFlo-17
McDonald, James
86JamExpP-16
McDonald, Jason
91TopTra-75T
91TopTraT-75T
92StaCluD-113
94WesMicWC-15
94WesMicWF-2306
95ModA'sTI-16
95SPML-122
96Bow-288
96Exc-99
96ExcSeaTL-7
97DonLim-190
97DonLimLE-190
97Fle-758
97FleTif-758
97SpoIll-15
97SpoIllEE-15
McDonald, Jeff
84ChaLooT-28
86ChaLooP-18
McDonald, Jerry
77SalPirT-15A
77SalPirT-15B
79BufBisT-6
80PorBeaT-4
McDonald, Jim
76ForLauYS-5
77ForLauYS-14
79WesHavYT-10
80ColCliP-31
80ColCliT-11
82TucTorT-12
83ColAstT-15
86AriWilP-10
McDonald, Jimmie LeRoy
53Dor-117
55Bow-77
55OriEss-16
91OriCro-289
McDonald, John
96WatIndTI-17
McDonald, Keith
94JohCitCC-20
94JohCitCF-3706
95PeoChiTI-7
96StPetCB-18
McDonald, Kevin
90HelBreSP-5
91SalLakTP-3207
91SalLakTSP-5
92WesPalBEC-8
92WesPalBEF-2086
93WesPalBEC-15
93WesPalBEF-1336
McDonald, Kirk
86MadMusP-14
88HunStaTI-11
89ModA'sC-13
89ModA'sCLC-274

McDonald, Mac (Mark)
82MadMusF-29
McDonald, Manny
81OklCit8T-12
McDonald, Matt
96SavSanB-27
McDonald, Mike (Michael)
86BelMarC-103
87WauTimP-20
88MidLeaAGS-55
88WauTimGS-11
89EveGiaS-20
89SanBerSB-22
89SanBerSCLC-87
90Bes-226
90CMC-794
90WilBilB-15
90WilBilP-1069
90WilBilS-16
91JacSunLD-338
91JacSunP-162
91LinDriAA-338
92JacSunF-3720
92JacSunS-364
92SkyAA F-156
93NasXprF-416
86HumStaDS-42
McDonald, Rod
82WatIndF-8
82WatIndT-7
83BufBisT-5
McDonald, Russ
83TacTigT-7
McDonald, Rusty
78CliDodT-22
McDonald, Shelby
87UtiBluSP-6
88SpaPhiP-1030
88SpaPhiS-14
89ClePhiS-16
90ClePhiS-15
McDonald, T.J.
84EveGiaC-22B
86FreGiaP-24
87ShrCapP-18
88ShrCapP-1302
89SanJosGB-25
89SanJosGCLC-224
89SanJosGP-436
89SanJosGS-19
McDonald, Tony
80CarMudF-21
82OklCit8T-15
82ReaPhiT-21
McDonald, Webster
78LauLonABS-10
91PomBlaBPB-23
94TedWil-108
McDonnell, Mack (James William)
77TCMTheWY-69
McDonnell, Shawn
94PeoChiC-18
94PeoChiF-2269
McDonough, Brian
82MiaMarT-4
83SanJosBC-5
McDonough, Neil
91TopRut-6
McDougal, John
90DodTar-1024
McDougal, Julius
86WinSpiP-15
87PorBeaP-12
88EasLeaAP-9
88GleFalTP-919
89CanIndB-2
89CanIndP-1321
89CanIndS-15
90CMC-267
90NewBriRSB-3
90NewBriRSP-1326
90NewBriRSS-10
90PawRedSC-16
90PawRedSDD-14
90TopTVRS-53
91LinDriAAA-503
91SyrChiLD-503
91SyrChiMB-16
91SyrChiP-2486
McDougal, Mike
96NewJerCB-19
McDougald, Gil
47Exh-157
47PM1StaP1-139
47StaPinP2-27
52BerRos-40
52Bow-33
52CokTip-5
52RedMan-AL14
52TipTop-25
52Top-372
53BowC-63
53Bri-36
53Dor-110
53Dor-110A
53RedMan-AL23
53Top-43
54Bow-97
54DixLid-9
54NewYorJA-52
54RedHeaF-20
54RedMan-AL25
54StaMey-8
55Bow-9
55StaMey-7
56Top-225
57SwiFra-9
57Top-200
57YanJayP-9
58Top-20A
58Top-20B
58YanJayP-8
59Top-237
59Top-345
59Yoo-5
60MacSta-16
60Top-247
60YanJayP-9
61Pos-10
79TCM50-155
83TopRep5-372
90PacLeg-94
91TopArc1-43
92ActPacA-33
92YanWIZ6-83
92YanWIZA-47
93UppDecAH-93
94UppDecAH-26
94UppDecAH1-26
McDowell, Jack
88Don-47
88DonRoo-40
88Fle-407
88FleGlo-407
88FleHotS-25
88FleMin-16
88Lea-47
88ScoRoo-85T
88ScoRooG-85T
88TopTra-68T
88TopTraT-68T
88WhiSoxC-16
89Bow-61
89BowTif-61
89Don-531
89Fle-504
89FleGlo-504
89OPC-143
89PanSti-302
89Sco-289
89Top-486
89TopSti-302
89TopTif-486
89ToyRoo-20
89UppDec-530
89VanCanP-577
90Bow-305
90BowTif-305
90TopTra-71T
90TopTraT-71T
90UppDec-625
90WhiSoxC-17
91Bow-352
91Cla3-T66
91Don-57A
91Don-57B
91Fle-129
91Lea-340
91OPC-219
91Sco-27
91StaClu-87
91Stu-36
91Top-219
91TopDesS-219
91TopMic-219
91TopTif-219
91Ult-78
91UppDec-323
91USPlaCA-3H
91WhiSoxK-29
91WhiSoxK-NNO
92Bow-371
92Bow-605
92Cla2-T82
92Don-352
92DonCraJ2-36
92Fle-89
92FleSmo'nH-S2
92Hig5-17
92Lea-422
92OPC-11
92Pin-107
92Pin-291
92Pin-607
92Sco-62
92Sco100S-22
92ScoImpP-73
92ScoProP-16
92SpoIllFK1-136
92StaClu-52
92StaCluD-114
92Top-11
92TopGol 11
92TopGolW-11
92TopMic-11
92TriPla-129
92Ult-40
92UltAllS-10
92UppDec-553
92UppDecTMH-34
92WhiSoxK-29
93Bow-527
93ClaGam-61
93Don-433
93DurPowP2-20
93Fin-172
93FinRef-172
93Fla-188
93Fle-207
93FleAll-AL12
93FleFruotL-44
93FunPac-200
93Hos-31
93Lea-400
93MetBak-15
93MSABenSPD-10
93OPC-264
93PacSpa-73
93PanSti-134
93Pin-80
93Sco-70
93Sel-196
93SelAce-3
93SelStaL-61
93SelStaL-86
93SP-258
93StaClu-75
93StaCluFDI-75
93StaCluM-157
93StaCluMO-15
93StaCluMOP-75
93StaCluWS-18
93Stu-200
93Top-344
93TOPBLAG-38
93TopComotH-5
93TopGol-344
93TopInaM-344
93TopMic-344
93TriPla-158
93Ult-176
93UppDec-357
93UppDecGold-357
93WhiSoxK-20
94Bow-455
94BowBes-R23
94BowBesR-R23
94ColC-306
94ColC-309
94ColC-445
94ColChoGS-306
94ColChoGS-309
94ColChoGS-445
94ColChoSS-306
94ColChoSS-309
94ColChoSS-445
94Don-20
94DonAwaWJ-7
94DonEli-47
94DonSpeE-20
94ExtBas-51
94ExtBasPD-1
94Fin-226
94FinJum-226
94FinRef-226
94Fla-280
94Fle-89
94Fle-708
94FleAllS-15
94FleAwaW-3
94FleLeaL-5
94FlePro-7
94FleSun-18
94FUnPac-129
94KinDis-3
94Lea-125
94LeaGolS-15
94LeaL-22
94OPC-173
94OPCAllR-14
94OPCJumA-14
94OscMayR-8
94Pac-134
94Pac-657
94PanSti-8
94PanSti-50
94Pin-57
94PinArtP-57
94PinMusC-57
94PinTeaP-9
94Pos-7
94ProMag-26
94Sco-6
94Sco-633
94ScoGolR-6
94ScoGolR-633
94ScoGolS-39
94ScoSam-6
94ScoSam-6GR
94Sel-97
94SP-192
94SPDieC-192
94Spo-92
94Spo-184
94StaClu-24
94StaCluDD-DD5
94StaCluFDI-24
94StaCluGR-24
94StaCluMO-21
94StaCluMOP-24
94StaCluT-122
94StaCluTFDI-122
94Stu-207
94SupMcDP-1
94SupMcDP-2
94TomPiz-22
94Top-392
94Top-515
94TopBlaG-12
94TopGol-392
94TopGol-515
94TopSpa-392
94TopSpa-515
94TopSupS-28
94TriPla-267
94TriPlaM-13
94Ult-340
94UltAllS-10
94UltAwaW-22
94UltLeaL-4
94UppDec-395
94UppDecAJ-42
94UppDecAJG-42
94UppDecED-395
94USPlaCA-4S
94WhiSoxK-22
95Baz-106
95Bow-418
95ColCho-515
95ColChoGS-515
95ColChoSE-232
95ColChoSEGS-232
95ColChoSESS-232
95ColChoSS-515
95Don-418
95DonPreP-418
95DonTopotO-121
95Emo-63
95Fin-207
95Fin-258
95FinRef-207
95FinRef-258
95Fla-286
95Fle-126
95FleTeaL-4
95FleUpd-26
95Lea-399
95LeaLim-143
95Pac-94
95PacPri-30
95Pin-365
95PinArtP-365
95PinMusC-365
95Sco-255
95ScoGolR-255
95ScoPlaTS-255
95Sel-108
95SelArtP-108
95SP-176
95SPCha-176
95SPChaDC-176
95Spo-126
95SpoArtP-126
95SPSil-176
95StaClu-155
95StaClu-622
95StaCluFDI-155
95StaCluMOP-155
95StaCluMOP-622
95StaCluSTWS-155
95StaCluSTWS-622
95StaCluVR-81
95Stu-100
95Top-561
95TopCyb-337
95TopTra-36T
95UC3-42
95UC3ArtP-42
95Ult-312
95UltGolM-312
95UppDec-206
95UppDecED-206
95UppDecEDG-206
95UppDecSE-143
95UppDecSEG-143
96Baz-117
96Bow-24
96ColCho-233
96ColCho-771
96ColChoGS-233
96ColChoSS-233
96Don-418
96DonPreP-418
96EmoXL-51
96Fin-B203
96FinRef-B203
96Fla-69
96Fle-190
96FleTif-190
96FleUpd-U32
96FleUpdTC-U32
96LeaLim-90
96LeaLimG-90
96LeaPre-84
96LeaPreP-84
96MetUni-48
96MetUniP-48
96Pac-372
96PacPri-P120
96PacPriG-P120
96PanSti-157
96Pin-108
96Pin-359
96PinAfi-1
96PinAfiAP-1
96PinAfiFPP-1
96PinArtP-42
96PinFoil-359
96PinSta-42
96SchDis-11
96Sco-46
96ScoDugC-A40
96ScoDugCAP-A40
96Sel-117
96SelArtP-117
96SelCer-88
96SelCerAP-88
96SelCerCB-88
96SelCerCR-88
96SelCerMB-88
96SelCerMG-88
96SelCerMR-88
96SP-72
96Spo-87
96SpoArtP-87
96StaClu-8
96StaCluEPB-8
96StaCluEPG-8
96StaCluEPS-8

96StaCluMeg-MH6
96StaCluMOP-8
96StaCluMOP-MH6
95StaCluVRMC-81
96Stu-135
96StuPrePB-135
96StuPrePG-135
96StuPrePS-135
96Sum-62
96SumAbo&B-62
96SumArtP-62
96SumFoi-62
96Top-203
96TopChr-69
96TopChrR-69
96TopGal-28
96TopGalPPI-28
96TopLas-59
96Ult-102
96Ult-342
96UltGolM-102
96UltGolM-342
96UppDec-493U
96Zen-74
96ZenArtP-74
97Bow-12
97BowInt-12
97Cir-303
97CirRav-303
97ColCho-312
97Don-85
97DonPreP-85
97DonPrePGold-85
97DonTea-77
97DonTeaSPE-77
97Fin-55
97FinRef-55
97Fle-82
97FleTif-82
97MetUni-83
97NewPin-70
97NewPinAP-70
97NewPinMC-70
97NewPinPP-70
97Pac-75
97PacLigB-75
97PacSil-75
97PinCar-19
97Sco-85
97ScoInd-2
97ScoIndPl-2
97ScoIndPr-2
97ScoIndU-2
97ScoIndUTC-2
97ScoPreS-85
97ScoShoS-85
97ScoShoSAP-85
97SP-62
97StaClu-75
97StaCluMOP-75
97Top-307
97TopChr-103
97TopChrR-103
97TopGal-56
97TopGalPPI-56
97Ult-51
97UltGolME-51
97UltPlaME-51
97UppDec-342

McDowell, Mike (Michael)
89AubAstP-2173
90AshTouP-2743
91BurAstC-7
91BurAstP-2798

McDowell, Oddibe
85DonHig-24
85FleUpd-80
85OklCit8T-18
85RanPer-0
85Top-400
85TopTif-400
85TopTifT-82T
85TopTra-82T
86Don-56
86Fle-566
86FleLeaL-23
86FleLimE-28
86FleMin-111
86FleStiC-73
86KayB-20
86Lea-46
86OPC-192
86OPCBoxB-K
86RanPer-0
86SevCoi-S9
86Spo-160
86Top-480
86TopGloS-1
86TopSti-237
86TopSti-307
86TopTat-20
86TopTif-480
86TopWaxBC-K
87ClaUpdY-115
87Don-161
87DonOpeD-177
87Fle-130
87FleGlo-130
87FleLimE-27
87FleStiC-77
87Lea-51
87OPC-95
87RanMot-4
87RanSmo-16
87RedFolSB-78
87Spo-131
87SpoTeaP-1
87Top-95
87TopSti-243
87TopTif-95
88Don-382
88Fle-473
88FleGlo-473
88FleStiC-66
88Lea-154
88OPC-234
88PanSti-208
88RanMot-4
88RanSmo-5
88Sco-215
88ScoGlo-215
88ScoYouS2-27
88Spo-175
88StaLinRa-8
88Top-617
88TopBig-198
88TopSti-237
88TopTif-617
89Bow-90
89BowTif-90
89BraDub-17
89Don-378
89DonTra-49
89Fle-528
89FleGlo-528
89IndTeal-18
89OPC-183
89PanSti-456
89Sco-59
89ScoRoo-72T
89Top-183
89TopBasT-113
89TopBig-245
89TopTif-183
89TopTra-78T
89TopTraT-78T
89UppDec-333
89UppDec-796
90Bow-13
90BowTif-13
90BraDubP-19
90BraDubS-22
90Don-340
90DonBesN-100
90Fle-589
90FleCan-589
90Lea-112
90OPC-329
90PanSti-221
90PubSti-563
90Sco-476
90Spo-207
90Top-329
90TopBig-148
90TopSti-32
90TopTif-329
90UppDec-145
90VenSti-330
91Don-450
91Fle-697
91OPC-533
91RedFolS-62
91RocRedWP-1915
91Sco-121
91Top-533
91TopDesS-533
91TopMic-533
91TopTif-533
91Ult-8
91UppDec-497
92EdmTraS-163
93RanKee-255
94FleUpd-94
94RedFolMI-25
94TopTra-14T
95Fle-291

McDowell, Roger
85FleUpd-81
85MetColP-10
85MetTCM-40
85TopTifT-83T
85TopTra-83T
86BasStaB-72
86Don-629
86Fle-89
86KayB-21
86Lea-248
86MetColP-9
86MetFanC-7
86MetTCM-8
86MetWorSC-5
86OPC-139
86SevCoi-E15
86Spo-161
86Top-547
86TopGloS-39
86TopSti-103
86TopSti-312
86TopTat-20
86TopTif-547
87ClaGam-76
87Don-241
87Fle-16
87FleAwaW-25
87FloGlo 16
87Lea-49
87MetColP-7
87MetFanC-4
87OPC-185
87SmoNatL-6
87Spo-160
87Top-185
87TopGloS-8
87TopSti-104
87TopTif-185
88Don-651
88DonBasB-126
88DonTeaBM-651
88Fle-142
88FleBasA-24
88FleGlo-142
88FleMin-96
88FleStiC-105
88Lea-243
88MetColP-7
88MetFanC-42
88MetKah-42
88OPC-355
88Sco-188
88ScoGlo-188
88Spo-42
88StaLinMe-14
88Top-355
88TopBig-101
88TopMinL-62
88TopSti-100
88TopTif-355
89Don-265
89DonBasB-16
89Fle-43
89FleGlo-43
89FleUpd-110
89MetColP-43
89MetFanC-42
89OPC-296
89PanSti-132
89PhiTas-43
89Sco-281
89ScoRoo-53T
89Spo-79
89Top-735
89TopBasT-93
89TopSti-92
89TopTif-735
89TopTra-79T
89TopTraT-79T
89UppDec-296
90Bow-146
90BowTif-146
90ClaYel-T69
90Don-251
90DonBesN-57
90Fle-567
90FleCan-567
90Lea-20
90OPC-625
90PanSti-308
90PhiTas-22
90PubSti-140
90Sco-445
90Spo-75
90Top-625
90TopBig-230
90TopSti-121
90TopTif-625
90UppDec-416
90VenSti-331
91Bow-500
91ClaGam-80
91Don-166
91Fle-405
91Lea-410
91MetWIZ-259
91OPC-43
91PanFreS-111
91PhiMed-26
91RedFolS-63
91Sco-537
91StaClu-506
91Stu-217
91Top-43
91TopDesS-43
91TopMic-43
91TopTif-43
91Ult-267
91UppDec-406
91UppDecFE-57F
92Bow-657
92DodMot-22
92DodPol-31
92DodSmo-10192
92Don-750
92Fle-464
92Lea-58
92OPC-713
92Pin-445
92Sco-597
92StaClu-804
92StaCluNC-804
92Top-713
92TopGol-713
92TopGolW-713
92TopMic-713
92TriPla-80
92Ult-214
92UppDec-484
93DodMot-25
93DodPol-17
93Don-350
93Fla-74
93Fle-451
93Lea-537
93PacSpa-501
93Pin-528
93Sco-605
93Sel-375
93StaClu-251
93StaCluD-25
93StaCluFDI-251
93StaCluMOP-251
93Top-39
93TopGol-39
93TopInaM-39
93TopMic-39
93TriPla-263
93Ult-58
93UppDec-250
93UppDecGold-250
94ColC-196
94ColChoGS-196
94ColChoSS-196
94DodMot-25
94DodPol-18
94Don-207
94Fle-517
94Pac-315
94Pin-339
94PinArtP-339
94PinMusC-339
94StaClu-38
94StaCluFDI-38
94StaCluGR-38
94StaCluMOP-38
94Top-296
94TopGol-296
94TopSpa-296
95RanCra-17
96Fle-253
96FleTif-253
96FleUpd-U4
96FleUpdTC-U4

McDowell, Sam
62Top-591
63Top-317
64Top-391
65Kah-28
65OPC-76
65Top-76
66Baz-17
66IndTeal-8
66Kah-21
66Top-222
66Top-226
66Top-470
66TopRubl-65
66TopVen-222
66TopVen-226
67Baz-17
67CokCapl-15
67DexPre-142
67Kah-25
67OPCPapl-8
67Top-237
67Top-295
67Top-463
67TopPos-8
67TopTesF-14
67TopVen-259
68AtlOilPBCC-29
68Kah-B26
68OPC-12
68OPC-115
68Top-12
68Top-115
68TopActS-12C
68TopVen-12
68TopVen-115
69Kah-B15
69MilBra-184
69MLBOffS-42
69MLBPin-17
69OPC-7
69OPC-11
69Top-7
69Top-11
69Top-220
69Top-435
69TopDecl-27
69TopSta-166
69TopSup-14
69TopTeaP-13
70DayDaiNM-9
70Ind-8
70Kel-50
70MilBra-17
70MLBOffS-201
70OPC-72
70OPC-469
70Top-72
70Top-469
70Top-650
70TopScr-14
70TopSup-10
70TraSta-14C
71AllBasA-16
71BazNumT-11
71BazUnn-29
71Ind-9
71Kel-37
71MilDud-15
71MLBOffS-379
71MLBOffS-568
71OPC-71
71OPC-150
71Top-71
71Top-150
71TopCoi-86
71TopGreM-50
71TopSup-16
71TopTat-29
71TopTat-30
72Kel-33A
72Kel-33B
72MilBra-224
72Top-720
73LinPor-163
73OPC-342
73OPC-511
73Top-342
73Top-511

74OPC-550
74SyrChiTI-15
74Top-550
75SSP18-8
78TCM60I-103
86IndGreT-10
89PacLegI-155
89SweBasG-71
92ActPacA-48
92YanWIZ7-110
93UppDecAH-94
94TedWil-27
94UppDecAH-127
94UppDecAH1-127

McDowell, Tim
90SalBucS-10
91ParPatF-19
91SalBucC-16
91SalBucP-946

McElfish, Shawn
90BurIndP-3007

McElligott, Bob
94KinIndC-27
95KinIndTI-18

McElroy, Chuck (Charles)
87SpaPhiP-5
88ReaPhiP-875
89ReaPhiB-1
89ReaPhiP-669
89ReaPhiS-18
90Bow-150
90BowTif-150
90Fle-650
90FleCan-650
90PhiTas-23
90TopDeb89-79
90UppDec-706
91CubMar-33
91CubVinL-19
91Don-709
91DonRoo-49
91Fle-406
91FleUpd-79
91Sco-374
91ScoRoo-34
91StaClu-407
91UltUpd-71
91UppDecFE-29F
92Cla1-T60
92CubMar-35
92Don-650
92Fle-388
92Lea-158
92OPC-727
92OPCPre-85
92Pin-329
92Sco-366
92Sco100RS-63
92StaClu-474
92Stu-16
92Top-727
92TopGol-727
92TopGolW-727
92TopMic-727
92TriPla-245
92Ult-470
92UppDec-220
93Don-236
93Fla-17
93Fle-22
93Pin-341
93Sco-389
93StaClu-472
93StaCluCu-18
93StaCluFDI-472
93StaCluMOP-472
93Top-346
93TopGol-346
93TopInaM-346
93TopMic-346
93Ult-20
93UppDec-130
93UppDecGold-130
94ColC-503
94ColChoGS-503
94ColChoSS-503
94Don-639
94Fla-367
94Fle-390
94FleUpd-120
94RedKah-18
94Top-613
94TopGol-613
94TopSpa-613
94TopTra-19T
94Ult-163
95Don-290
95DonPreP-290
95Fle-440
95RedKah-18
95Top-141
95TopCyb-93
95Ult-146
95UltGolM-146
96LeaSigEA-123

McElroy, Glen
86PenWhiSP-17
87DayBeaAP-26
89BirBarP-116

McElveen, Pryor
09T206-236
10CouT21-45
11SpoLifM-160
11T205-113
90DodTar-1025

McElwain, Tim
85CloHSS-26

McEnaney, Will
75OPC-481
75Top-481
76OPC-362
76RedIceL-8
76Top-362
77ExpPos-21
77OPC-50
77Top-160
78OPC-81
78Top-603
80Top-563
91MiaMirC-2
91MiaMirP-424

McEntire, Ethan
94KinMetC-11
94KinMetF-3819
95PitMetTI-40

McEwing, Joe
93SavCarC-18
93SavCarF-701
94MadHatC-16
94MadHatF-147
94MidLeaAF-MDW44
95Exc-271
96ArkTraB-20

McFadden, Leon
69OPC-156
69Top-156
69TopFou-2
70Top-672
72MilBra-225

McFarland, Chappie (Charles A.)
11SpoLifCW-242
90DodTar-505

McFarland, Dustin
85AncGlaPTI-19
86AncGlaPTI-20
87AncGlaP-21

McFarland, Ed
03BreE10-98
07WhiSoxGWH-7

McFarland, Herm
03BreE10-99
11SpoLifCW-243

McFarland, Kelly
85AncGlaPTI-43
86AncGlaPTI-21

McFarland, Packey
11TurRedT-58

McFarland, Steve
85AncGlaPTI-20
86AncGlaPTI-22
87AncGlaP-22
95ElmPioTI-16
95ElmPioUTI-16

McFarland, Toby
92BriTigC-6
92BriTigF-1406
93NiaFalRF-3382
94FayGenC-16
94FayGenF-2141

McFarlane, Hemmy
85NewOriT-6

McFarlane, Orlando
62Top-229
64PirKDK-19
64Top-509
66Top-569
67Top-496
69MilBra-185

McFarlin, Jason
89EveGiaS-28
90CliGiaB-13
90CliGiaP-2563
90CMC-845
91CalLeLA-43
91Cla/Bes-70
91SanJosGC-10
91SanJosGP-24
91SanJosGP-26
92ClaFS7-249
92SanJosGC-15
94ShrCapF-1619
96GreBraB-20
96GreBraTI-50

McFarlin, Terry
91BakDodCLC-31
91CalLeLA-9
93SanAntMF-3001
94WicWraF-187

McFerrin, Chris
96AubDouB-13

McGaffigan, Andy
79WesHavYT-14
80NasSouTI-13
81ColCliT-8
82Top-83
83GiaMot-20
83TopTra-68T
84Don-309
84ExpPos-19
84ExpStu-34
84Fle-382
84FleUpd-78
84Nes792-31
84Top-31
84TopTif-31
84TopTra-78T
84TopTraT-78T
85Don-646
85Fle-540
85Top-323
85TopTif-323
86ExpPos-8
86ExpProPa-4
86ExpProPo-8
86Fle-181
86FleUpd-74
86Top-133
86TopTif-133
86TopTra-72T
86TopTraT-72T
87Don-380
87ExpPos-15
87Fle-326
87FleGlo-326
87GenMilB-4E
87Lea-220
87OPC-351
87Top-742
87TopTif-742
88Don-380
88Fle-190
88FleGlo-190
88OPC-56
88Sco-366
88ScoGlo-366
88StaLinE-11
88Top-488
88TopTif-488
89Bow-356
89BowTif-356
89Don-338
89ExpPos-21
89Fle-386
89FleGlo-386
89OPC-278
89Sco-138
89Top-278
89TopBig-315
89TopSti-75
89TopTif-278
89UppDec-359
90CMC-185
90Don-574
90Fle-355
90FleCan-355
90OmaRoyC-10
90OPC-559
90PubSti-182
90Sco-224
90Top-559
90TopTif-559
90UppDec-597A
90UppDec-597B
90VenSti-332
91LinDriAAA-342
91OmaRoyLD-342
91OPC-671
91RoyPol-14
91Sco-619
91Top-671
91TopDesS-671
91TopMic-671
91TopTif-671
92YanWIZ8-116
82PhoGiaVNB-19

McGah, Ed
46RedSoxTI-15

McGaha, Mel
60MapLeaSF-13
62IndJayP-8
62Top-242
64A's-13
65AthJayP-10
65Top-391
67Ast-17

McGann, Dan
06FanCraNL-29
06GiaUllAFS-8
11SpoLifCW-244
90DodTar-1026

McGann, Dennis
09ColChiE-187
09T206-441
12ColRedB-187
12ColTinT-187

McGann, Don
83GreHorT-30
84NasSouTI-14
85NasSouTI-12
86NasSouTI-17
87TolMudHP-23
88TolMudHP-606
89EdmTraP-560

McGannon, Paul
81OmaRoyT-3
82OmaRoyT-27
83OmaRoyT-26

McGarity, Jeremy
90JohCitCS-18
91SavCarC-10
91SavCarP-1651
92Bow-26
92ClaFS7-280
92St.PetCC-16
92St.PetCF-2025
93St.PetCC-18
93St.PetCF-2625
94MadHatC-17
94MadHatF-128

McGarr, Chippy (James)
87OldJudN-338
90KalBatN-37
98CamPepP-52

McGeachy, Jack (John)
87BucN28-44
87OldJudN-339

McGee, Brian
91BenBucC-22
91BenBucP-3697
92PeoChiC-26
92PeoChiTI-12

McGee, Jack
88AllandGN-12

McGee, Ron
80SpoIndT-6

McGee, Tim
86WinHavRSP-17
87GreHorP-16
88LynRedSS-13
88NewBriRSP-901

McGee, Tony
89SpoIndSP-5
90RivRedWB-16
90RivRedWCLC-4
90RivRedWP-2611

McGee, Willie D.
79WesHavYT-13
80NasSouTI-14
81NasSouTI-9
82LouRedE-16
83AllGamPI-153
83Car-19
83Don-190
83Fle-15
83FleSti-2
83OPC-49
83Top-49
83TopSti-147
83TopSti-326
84AllGamPI-57
84Car-21
84Car5x7-18
84Don-353
84Don-625
84DonActAS-2
84Fle-329
84FunFooP-33
84Nes792-310
84OPC-310
84SevCoi-C9
84Top-310
84TopSti-141
84TopStiB-8
84TopTif-310
85AllGamPI-150
85CarTeal-23
85Don-475
85DonHig-29
85DonHig-38
85DonHig-52
86Fle-231
85KASDis-8
85KitCloD-8
85Lea-125
85OPC-57
85ThoMcAD-36
85Top-757
85TopMin-757
85TopSti-141
85TopTif-757
86BasStaB-73
86BurKinA-16
86CarIGAS-9
86CarKASD-20
86CarSchM-16
86CarTeal-29
86Don-3
86Don-109
86Don-651
86DonAll-36
86DonSupD-3
86DorChe-15
86Dra-23
86Fle-42
86Fle-636
86FleLeaL-24
86FleLimE-29
86FleMin-9
86FleSlu-22
86FleStiC-74
86GenMilB-4F
86Lea-3
86Lea-225
86MeaGolBB-9
86MeaGolM-6
86MeaGolSB-10
86MSAJifPD-15
86OPC-117
86OPCBoxB-L
86QuaGra-1
86SevCoi-S16
86Spo-19
86Spo-176
86Spo-179
86Spo-183
86Spo-184
86Top-580
86Top-707
86Top3-D-14
86TopGaloC-7
86TopGloS-9
86TopMinL-63
86TopSti-45
86TopSti-144
86TopSup-2
86TopTat-23
86TopTif-580
86TopTif-707
86TopWaxBC-L
86Woo-21
87CarSmo-22
87ClaGam-31
87Don-84
87Dra-9
87Fle-304
87FleBasA-27
87FleGlo-304
87FleHotS-30
87FleLeaL-29

87GenMilB-5D
87Lea-113
87OPC-357
87RedFolSB-86
87Spo-74
87SpoTeaP-12
87Top-440
87TopSti-48
87TopTif-440
88Baz-12
88CarSmo-21
88ClaRed-173
88Don-307
88DonAll-44
88DonBasB-131
88Fle-42
88FleGlo-42
88FleMin-108
88FleStiC-118
88FleTeaL-20
88KayB-17
88Lea-103
88OPC-160
88PanSti-396
88Sco-40
88ScoGlo-40
88Spo-91
88StaLinCa-14
88Top-160
88TopBig-79
88TopGloS-36
88TopMinL-71
88TopSti-55
88TopTif-160
88TopUKM-46
88TopUKMT-46
88Woo-26
89Bow-442
89BowTif-442
89CarSmo-13
89ClaLigB-98
89Don-161
89DonAll-51
89Fle-457
89FleGlo-457
89LouRedBTI-27
89OPC-225
89PanSti-189
89Sco-88
89ScoHot1S-93
89Spo-206
89Top-640
89TopBasT-84
89TopBatL-12
89TopBig-183
89TopSti-36
89TopTif-640
89UppDec-621
90Bow-194
90BowTif-194
90CarSmo-14
90Don-632
90DonBesN-131
90Fle-253
90FleCan-253
90Lea-367
90MLBBasB-33
90OPC-285
90PanSti-339
90PubSti-222
90Sco-374
90Top-285
90TopBatL-14
90TopBig-158
90TopTif-285
90TopTVCa-34
90UppDec-505
90VenSti-333
91Baz-11
91Bow-640
91Cla1-T74
91Cla2-T76
91ClaGam-162
91Don-666
91DonBonC-BC22
91Fle-16
91FleUpd-130
91GiaMot-6
91GiaPacGaE-23
91GiaSFE-10
91KinDis-1
91Lea-360
91OPC-380
91OPCBoxB-I
91OPCPre-78
91PanCanT1-1
91RedFolS-64
91Sco-597
91Sco100S-37
91ScoRoo-19T
91StaClu-335
91StaCluCM-20
91Stu-256
91Top-380
91TopDesS-380
91TopGaloC-9
91TopMic-380
91TopTif-380
91TopTra-76T
91TopTraT-76T
91TopWaxBC-I
91Ult-325
91UltUpd-118
91UppDec-584
91UppDec-721
92Bow-604
92CarMcD-43
92ClaGam-42
92Don-60
92Fle-643
92GiaMot-6
92GiaPacGaE-28
92Hig5-127
92KinDis-15
92Lea-47
92OPC-65
92PanSti-217
92Pin-7
92Sco-112
92Sco100S-18
92ScoProP-1
92StaClu-239
92SunSee-24
92Top-65
92TopGol-65
92TopGolW-65
92TopKid-61
92TopMic-65
92TriPla-101
92Ult-294
92UppDec-34
92UppDec-194
93Bow-196
93Don-355
93Fla-145
93Fle-159
93GiaMot-8
93GiaPos-25
93Lea-396
93OPC-210
93PacSpa-274
93PanSti-240
93Pin-39
93Pin-490
93Sco-93
93Sel-119
93SP-114
93StaClu-91
93StaCluFDI-91
93StaCluG-11
93StaCluMOP-91
93Stu-179
93Top-435
93TopGol-435
93TopInaM-435
93TopMic-435
93TriPla-227
93Ult-487
93UppDec-281
93UppDecGold-281
94ColC-587
94ColChoGS-587
94ColChoSS-587
94Don-238
94DonDom-B8
94ExtBas-390
94Fin-184
94FinRef-184
94Fle-696
94GiaAMC-14
94GiaMot-15
94GiaTeal-9
94GiaUSPC-7S
94GiaUSPC-13D
94Lea-366
94Pac-551
94PanSti-265
94Pin-274
94PinArtP-274
94PinMusC-274
94ProMag-125
94Sco-70
94ScoGolR-70
94Sel-221
94StaClu-686
94StaCluFDI-686
94StaCluGR-686
94StaCluMOP-686
94StaCluT-6
94StaCluTFDI-6
94Stu-86
94Top-574
94TopGol-574
94TopSpa-574
94TriPla-107
94Ult-589
94UppDec-258
94UppDecED-258
95Sco-466
95ScoGolR-466
95ScoPlaTS-466
95StaCluMOP-RL39
95StaCluRL-RL39
95UppDec-484T
96CarPol-18
96Cir-180
96CirRav-180
96Don-521
96DonPreP-521
96FleUpd-U191
96FleUpdTC-U191
96Ult-551
96UltGolM-551
97ColCho-199
97Don-281
97DonPreP-281
97DonPrePGold-281
97DonTea-162
97DonTeaSPE-162
97Fle-449
97FleTif-449
97Pac-414
97PacLigB-414
97PacSil-414

McGeehee, Connor
82BufBisT-3
83LynPirT-21

McGehee, Kevin
90EveGiaP-3123
91CalLeLA-37
91SanJosGC-18
91SanJosGP-7
92Bow-616
92ClaFS7-256
92ProFS7-351
92ShrCapF-3866
92ShrCapS-587
92SkyAA F-259
92UppDecML-227
93ExcFS7-120
93PhoFirF-1513
94OriPro-62
94OriUSPC-3S
94RocRedWF-995
94RocRedWTI-14
94StaCluT-281
94StaCluTFDI-281
95RocRedWTI-25

McGehee, Mike
96ButCopKB-24

McGhee, Ed (Warren E.)
53Top-195
54Top-215
55Top-32
55TopDouH-77
91TopArc1-195
94TopArc1-215
94TopArc1G-215

McGilberry, Randy
77JacSunT-15
78SSP270-222
79Top-707
80OmaRoyP-17
80TidTidT-25

McGinley, James
09ColChiE-188
09T206-442
12ColRedB-188
12ColTinT-188
12ImpTobC-2

McGinn, Dan
69ExpFudP-7
69Top-646
70ExpPin-10
70ExpPos-3
70OPC-364
70Top-364
71ExpPS-16
71MLBOffS-134
71OPC-21
71Top-21
72MilBra-226
72OPC-473
72Top-473
73OPC-527
73Top-527

McGinn, Mark
92GulCoaMF-3478
94LetMouF-3876

McGinn, Shaun
90NebCor-16
93BatCliC-18
93BatCliF-3153
94BatCliC-13
94BatCliF-3454

McGinnis, Jumbo (George Washington)
87BucN28-100

McGinnis, Russ
86BelBreP-14
87BelBreP-13
89TacTigC-16
89TacTigP-1556
90CMC-598
90ProAAAF-143
90TacTigC-21
90TacTigP-96
91IowCubLD-211
91IowCubP-1063
91LinDriAAA-211
91TriA AAGP-AAA18
92DonRoo-72
92OklCit8S-316
92SkyAAAF-145
93OmaRoyF-1685
93RanKee-256
93TopGol-824
94OmaRoyF-1226

McGinnis, Shane
93GenCubC-21
93GenCubF-3186

McGinnity, Iron Man (Joe)
03BreE10-100
05RotCP-8
05RotMcG-1
05RotMcG-2
06FanCraNL-30
06GiaUllAFS-9
08AmeCarE-14
08RosComP-129
09ColChiE-189
09T206-443
10RedCroT-49
10RedCroT-218
11MecDFT-31
11SpoLifCW-245
12ColRedB-189
12ColTinT-189
12ImpTobC-77
36PC7AlbHoF-45
50CalHOFW-54
61Fle-126
72FleFamF-1
72LauGreF-6
76ShaPiz-45
77BobParHoF-36
80PerHaloFP-45
80SSPHOF-45
89DodSmoG-21
90DodTar-506
90HOFStiB-11
94ConTSN-1252
94ConTSNB-1252

McGivney, Tom
79AshTouT-3

McGlawn, Thomas
93MarPhiC-18
93MarPhiF-3483

McGlinchy, Kevin
96AppLeaAB-12
96DanBraB-14
97Bow-307
97BowBes-122
97BowBesAR-122
97BowBesR-122
97BowInt-307

McGlone, Brian
91AubAstC-20
91AubAstP-4281
92BurAstC-16
92BurAstF-556
93QuaCitRBC-13
93QuaCitRBF-108

McGlone, John
87OldJudN-340

McGlothen, Lynn
73LinPor-168
73OPC-114
73Top-114
75Kel-20
75OPC-272
75Top-272
76OPC-478
76SSP-297
76Top-478
77Top-47
78Top-581
79Top-323
80Top-716
81Don-562
81Fle-302
81Top-609
82Top-85
92YanWIZ8-117

McGlothin, Pat (Ezra)
50WorWidGV-10
52Par-53
90DodTar-1027

McGlothlin, Jim
66Top-417
67OPC-19
67Top-19
67TopVen-225
68Baz-8
68Top-493
68TopActS-12A
69AngJacitB-7
69MilBra-186
69MLBOffS-24
69Top-386
69TopSta-146
69TopTeaP-17
70DayDaiNM-37
70MLBOffS-31
70OPC-132
70Top-132
71MLBOffS-63
71OPC-556
71Top-556
71TopCoi-9
72MilBra-227
72OPC-236
72Top-236
73OPC-318
73Top-318
74OPC-557
74Top-557

McGlynn, Stoney (Ulysses)
08RosComP-168
09T206-444
11MecDFT-32

McGonigle, Bill
96StoPorB-22

McGonnigal, Brett
91CliGiaC-4
91EveGiaC-5
91EveGiaP-3932
92CliGiaF-3611
92SanJosGC-24

McGorkle, Robbie
82DayBeaAT-18

McGough, Greg
91SarWhiSC-13
91SarWhiSP-1117
92SalSpuC-14
92SalSpuF-3758

McGough, Keith
91ButCopKSP-24
91GasRanC-9
91GasRanP-2686

McGough, Tom
75OklCit8TI-3
76WilTomT-10

McGovern, Phil
11TurRedT-70

McGovern, Steve
90BatCliP-3063

McGowan, Bill
80PerHaloFP-213
93ConTSN-737

94ConTSN-1212
94ConTSNB-1212
McGowan, Donnie
85ElmPioT-15
86GreHorP-14
87WinHavRSP-5
88WinHavRSS-12
McGowan, Mike
93HigDesMC-29
93HigDesMF-NNO
94KanCouCC-30
94KanCouCTI-16
95PorSeaDTI-13
McGrath, Chuck (Charles)
83EriCarT-15
84SavCarT-6
85SprCarT-20
86St.PetCP-19
87ArkTraP-3
89ArkTraGS-12
89LouRedBTI-28
90CMC-48
90DenZepC-23
90DenZepP-622
90ElPasDGS-21
90ProAAAF-647
McGraw, Bob
90DodTar-507
McGraw, Doug
94OscAstF-1135
92UtiBluSC-18
McGraw, Gary
82IdaFalAT-26
McGraw, Hank
71RicBraTI-14
McGraw, John J.
03BreE10-101
05RotCP-5
06FanCraNL-31
06GiaUllAFS-10
08AmeCarE-15
08AmeCarE-53
09MaxPubP-7
09SpoNewSM-57
09T206-237
09T206-238
09T206-239
09T206-240
10CouT21-180
10CouT21-181
10CouT21-302
10CouT21-303
10DomDisP-79
10E-UOraBSC-16
10E101-32
10E98-21
10JuJuDE-26
10MelMinE-32
10NadCarE-35
10NadE1-35
10PeoT21-38A
10PeoT21-38B
10RedCroT-50
10RedCroT-51
10RedCroT-135
10RedCroT-136
10RedCroT-219
10RedCroT-220
10StaCarE-22
10SweCapPP-118A
10SweCapPP-118B
10W555-47
11E94-24
11L1L-116
11S74Sil-89
11S81LarS-91
11SpoLifCW-246
11SpoLifM-212
11T205-114
11TurRedT-26
12HasTriFT-48B
12HasTriFT-48G
12T207-118
13NatGamW-29
13PolGroW-18
13TomBarW-28
14CraJacE-69
14PieStaT-37
14TexTomE-32
14TexTomE-60
15AmeCarE-28
15CraJacE-69
15SpoNewM-114
16BF2FP-80
16ColE13-113
16SpoNewM-116
17HolBreD-67
19W514-52
21E121So1-59
21E121So8-56
21Exh-104
21KoBreWSI-15
22AmeCarE-44
22W575-77
22WilPatV-40
23W501-73
23W501-104
23W515-45
23WilChoV-92
27YorCarE-42
28W502-42
28Yue-42
30SchR33-41
35ClaBreD3-3
36NatChiFPR-94
36PC7AlbHoF-10
40PlaBal-235
48ExhHoF-23
49LeaPre-6
50CalHOFW-55
60ExhWriH-17
60Fle-66
61Fle-60
61GolPre-23
63BazA-20
68LauWorS-8
69Baz-5
69Baz-6
70FleWorS-8
70FleWorS-21
71FleWorS-2
72KelATG-3
75FlePio-15
75McCCob-13
75TCMAllG-23
76ShaPiz-11
77BobParHoF-37
77GalGloG-98
77GalGloG-215
77ShaPiz-2
80GiaGreT-12
80PacLeg-43
80PerHaloFP-10
80SSPHOF-10
81ConTSN-6
83DonHOFH-35
84GalHaloFRL-11
84OCoandSI-175
85FegMurCG-13
85UltBasC-10
86ConSer1-29
88ConSer5-20
89HOFStiB-89
90BasWit-59
91ConTSN-65
91FouBal-9
92ConTSN-584
92ConTSNGI-820
93ConMasC-7
93ConMasC-8
93ConTSN-820
93CraJac-21
94ConTSN-1001
94ConTSNB-1001
94OriofB-87
94UppDecTAE-12
94UppDecTAELD-LD4
93UppDecTR-5
McGraw, Tom
90BelBreS-14
91ElPasDLD-192
91ElPasDP-2746
91LinDriAA-192
92ElPasDF-3917
92StoPorF-32
93HigDesMF-37
93LinVenB-65
95PorSeaDTI-14
McGraw, Tug (Frank E.)
65Top-533
66OPC-124
66Top-124
66TopVen-124
67CokCapYM-V33
67Top-348
68AtlOilPBCC-30
68Top-236
68TopVen-236
69MetNewYDN-14
69Top-601
70MetTra-24B
70OPC-26
70OPC-310
70Top-26
71MLBOffS-161
71OPC-618
71Top-618
72MilBra-228
72OPC-163
72OPC-164
72Top-163
72Top-164
73LinPor-118
73MetAllEB-8
73NewYorN-22
73OPC-30
73Top-30
74OPC-265
74Top-265
74TopSta-67
75Hos-149
75OPC-67
75Top-67
76OPC-565
76SSP-457
76Top-565
77BurCheD-165
77OPC-142
77Top-164
78PhiSSP-42
78RCColC-85
78SSP270-42
78Top-446
78WifBalD-48
79OPC-176
79PhiBurK-10
79Top-345
80OPC-346
80PhiBurK-20
80Top-655
81CokTeaS-103
81Don-273
81Fle-7
81Fle-657A
81Fle-657B
81FleStiC-83
81Kel-37
81Top-40
81Top-404
81TopSti-205
81TopSti-262
81TopSupHT-85
82Don-420
82Fle-251
82FleSta-55
82OPC-250
82Top-250
83Don-371
83Fle-166
83FleSta-122
83FleSti-171
83OPC-166
83OPC-187
83PhiPosGM-10
83PhiTas-17
83Top-510
83Top-511
83TopFol-4
84Don-547
84DonCha-53
84Fle-42
84Nes792-709
84Nes792-728
84OPC-161
84PhiTas-24
84Top-709
84Top-728
84TopTif-709
84TopTif-728
85Fle-261
85Top-157
85TopTif-157
86MetGreT-11
87Met196T-6
88PacLegI-96
89Met196C-10
89RinPosM1-21
89SweBasG-96
91MetWIZ-260
91UppDecS-8
92MCIAmb-12
92UppDecS-24
94MCIAmb-6
94Met69CCPP-25
94Met69CS-24
94Met69T-12
94TedWil-58
95MCIAmb-3
95MrTurBG-3
McGregor, Scott
75OPC-618
75SyrChiTI-11
75Top-618
77Top-475
78Top-491
79OPC-206
79Top-393
80Top-237
81AllGamPI-87
81Don-114
81Fle-174
81FleStiC-10
81OPC-65
81Top-65
81TopSti-37
82Don-331
82Fle-172
82FleSta-149
82OPC-246
82OPC-316
82Top-555
82Top-617
82TopSti-143
82TopStiV-143
83Don-483
83Fle-66
83FleSta-123
83FleSti-194
83OPC-216
83OriPos-15
83Top-745
84Don-594
84Fle-13
84Fle-646
84FleSti-64
84FunFooP-102
84Nes792-260
84OPC-260
84OriEng-8
84OriTeal-16
84Top-260
84TopSti-207
84TopTif-260
85Don-413
85Fle-183
85Lea-72
85OPC-228
85OriHea-12
85Top-550
85TopSti-198
85TopTif-550
86Don-291
86Fle-281
86FleStiC-75
86Lea-165
86OPC-110
86Top-110
86TopSti-230
86TopTat-6
86TopTif-110
87Don-520
87Fle-475
87FleGlo-475
87Lea-243
87OPC-347
87OriFreB-16
87Top-708
87TopTif-708
88OPC-254
88Sco-315
88ScoGlo-315
88Top-419
88TopTif-419
89SweBasG-56
91OriCro-290
McGrew, Charley
86BelBreP-15
87StoPorP-12
88BelBreGS-7
89ModA'sCLC-284
McGriff, Fred
85DomLeaS-149
85SyrChiT-2
85SyrChiT-25
86Don-28
86Lea-28
86SyrChiP-18
87BluJayFS-20
87Don-621
87DonHig-39
87DonOpeD-38
87DonRoo-31
87FleUpd-75
87FleUpdG-75
87SpoRooI-12
87SpoTeaP-5
87TopTra-74T
87TopTraT-74T
88BluJayFS-21
88Don-195
88DonBasB-160
88Fle-118
88FleGlo-118
88MSAHosD-15
88OPC-395
88RedFolSB-54
88Sco-107
88ScoGlo-107
88ScoYouS2-28
88Spo-168
88StaLinBJ-14
88Top-463
88Top-729
88TopTif-463
88TopTif-729
88ToyRoo-18
89BluJayFS-18
89Bow-253
89BowTif-253
89CadEllD-35
89ClaTraO-116
89Don-16
89Don-70
89DonBasB-104
89DonBonM-BC19
89DonSupD-16
89Fle-240
89FleBasM-27
89FleGlo-240
89FleHeroB-27
89FleLeaL-26
89FleSup-30
89FleWaxBC-C19
89OPC-258
89PanSti-467
89Sco-6
89ScoHot1S-65
89Spo-14
89SpollIFKI-172
89Top-745
89TopBig-15
89TopCoi-44
89TopHilTM-20
89TopMinL-77
89TopSti-185
89TopTif-745
89TopUKM-50
89TVSpoM-77
89UppDec-572
89UppDec-671
90Baz-5
90BluJayFS-19
90BluJayHS-3
90BluJayHS-5
90Bow-513
90BowTif-513
90ClaBlu-19
90Don-188
90DonBesA-56
90DonGraS-9
90Fle-89
90FleAwaW-22
90FleBasM-24
90FleCan-89
90FleLeaL-24
90Hot50PS-26
90K-M-31
90KinDis-13
90Lea-132
90MSAHolD-13
90OPC-295
90OPC-385
90PanSti-170
90PubSti-523
90PubSti-599
90RedFolSB-60
90Sco-271
90Sco100S-45
90Spo-13
90SupActM-9

90Top-295
90Top-385
90TopBig-134
90TopCoi-22
90TopDou-44
90TopGaloC-4
90TopGloS-55
90TopMag-86
90TopMinL-43
90TopSti-187
90TopStiB-35
90TopTif-295
90TopTif-385
90TopTVA-26
90UppDec-108
90VenSti-334
90VenSti-335
90VicPos-3
91Bow-659
91CadElID-37
91Cla1-T88
91Cla2-T46
91ClaGam-163
91Don-261
91Don-389
91Fle-180
91FleUpd-125
91Lea-342
91OPC-140
91OPCPre-79
91PadMag-24
91PadSmo-21
91PanCanT1-16
91PanCanT1-40
91PanFreS-336
91PanSti-157
91RedFolS-65
91Sco-404
91Sco-480
91Sco100S-71
91ScoRoo-58T
91SevCoi-SC9
91StaClu-357
91Stu-247
91Top-140
91TopDesS-140
91TopMic-140
91TopTif-140
91TopTra-77T
91TopTraT-77T
91TopTriH-N10
91Ult-308
91UppDec-565
91UppDec-775
92Bow-650
92Cla1-T61
92ClaGam-149
92ColAllG-16
92ColAllP-16
92DenHol-3
92Don-283
92DonCraJ2-12
92DonDiaK-DK26
92DonMcD-9
92Fle-614
92Hig5-124
92Lea-274
92LeaGolP-11
92LeaPre-11
92MooSna-17
92New-16
92OPC-660
92OPCPre-166
92PadCarJ-13
92PadMot-4
92PadPolD-14
92PadPolD-30
92PadSmo-19
92PanSti-232
92Pin-112
92Sco-7
92Sco100S-65
92ScoImpP-56
92ScoProaG-11
92StaClu-580
92StaCluMO-29
92Stu-106
92SyrChiTT-5
92Top-660
92TopGol-660
92TopGolW-660
92TopKid-55
92TopMic-660
92TriPla-87
92Ult-282
92UppDec-33
92UppDec-344
92UppDecHRH-HR10
92UppDecTMH-35
92UppDecWB-T8
93BluJayDM-3
93Bow-686
93BraLykP-18
93BraLykS-23
93ClaGam-62
93DiaMar-72
93Don-390
93DonEli-19
93DonEliD-2
93DonEliS-1
93DonLonBL-LL2
93DonMasotG-4
93DonSpiotG-SG12
93DurPowP2-9
93Fin-106
93FinJum-106
93FinRef-106
93Fla-8
93Fle-143
93Fle-349
93FleAll-NL1
93FleAtl-15
93FleFruotL-45
93FunPac-136
93FunPac-139
93FunPacA-AS1
93HumDumC-48
93Lea-46
93LeaGolA-R2
93OPC-255
93OPCPreSP-2
93OPCPreSPF-2
93PacSpa-261
93PadMot-4
93PanSti-258
93Pin-71
93PinHomRC-2
93PinSlu-5
93PinTeaP-4
93Pos-5
93Sco-44
93Sco-528
93Sel-19
93SelChaS-1
93SelRoo-5T
93SelStaL-28
93SelStaL-36
93SelStaL-48
93SP-60
93SPPlaP-PP12
93StaClu-510
93StaClu-594
93StaCluFDI-510
93StaCluFDI-594
93StaCluM-78
93StaCluMOP-510
93StaCluMOP-594
93Stu-157
93Top-30
93Top-401
93TOPBLAG-13
93TopFulS-21
93TopGol-30
93TopGol-401
93TopInaM-30
93TopInaM-401
93TopMic-30
93TopMic-401
93TopTra-88T
93TriPla-95
93TriPlaLL-L4
93TriPlaN-10
93Ult-119
93UltHomRK-4
93UppDec-474
93UppDec-496
93UppDec-577
93UppDecCP-R15
93UppDecGold-474
93UppDecGold-496
93UppDecGold-577
93UppDecHRH-HR4
93UppDecIC-WI16
93UppDecICJ-WI16
93UppDecTriCro-TC5
93USPlaCA-11C
94Bow-405
94BowBes-R15
94BowBes-X92
94BowBesR-R15
94BowBesR-X92
94BraLykP-21
94BraLykS-21
94BraUSPC-7D
94BraUSPC-13C
94ChuShoS-6
94ColC-197
94ColChoGS-197
94ColChoSS-197
94Don-342
94DonDom-A3
94DonPro-8
94DonSpeE-342
94ExtBas-209
94ExtBasGB-19
94Fin-224
94FinJum-224
94FinRef-224
94Fla-131
94FlaHotN-4
94FlaInfP-5
94Fle-366
94Fle-706
94FleGolM-8
94FleLumC-7
94FleUpdDT-7
94FUnPac-27
94FUnPac-186
94KinDis-1
94Lea-345
94LeaCleC-9
94LeaGolS-14
94LeaL-88
94LeaMVPC-N10
94LeaMVPCG-N10
94LeaPowB-8
94OPC-13
94OPCAllR-13
94OPCJumA-13
94Pac-16
94PacGolP-14
94PanSti-148
94Pin-384
94PinArtP-384
94PinMusC-384
94PinRunC-RC26
94PinTheN-13
94ProMag-3
94RedFolMI-34
94Sco-82
94ScoGolR-82
94ScoGolS-18
94Sel-268
94SP-55
94SPDieC-55
94Spo-32
94Spo-185
94SpoFanA-AS1
94SpoRooGGG-GG9
94StaClu-111
94StaClu-180
94StaClu-264
94StaClu-665
94StaCluFDI-111
94StaCluFDI-180
94StaCluFDI-264
94StaCluFDI-665
94StaCluGR-111
94StaCluGR-180
94StaCluGR-264
94StaCluGR-665
94StaCluMO-30
94StaCluMOP-111
94StaCluMOP-180
94StaCluMOP-264
94StaCluMOP-665
94StaCluT-47
94StaCluTFDI-47
94Stu-40
94Top-384
94Top-565
94TopBlaG-39
94TopGol-384
94TopGol-565
94TopSpa-384
94TopSpa-565
94TopSupS-29
94TriPla-47
94TriPlaBS-6
94TriPlaM-4
94Ult-154
94UltAllS-12
94UltHomRK-10
94UppDec-225
94UppDecAJ-11
94UppDecAJG-11
94UppDecED-225
94UppDecMLS-MM12
94UppDecMLSED-MM12
94USPlaCA-7C
95Baz-63
95BluJayUSPC-5S
95BluJayUSPC-12D
95Bow-331
95BowBes-R56
95BowBesR-R56
95ClaPhoC-4
95ColCho-69
95ColCho-530
95ColChoCtA-3
95ColChoCtAG-3
95ColChoCtG-CG12
95ColChoCtG-CG12B
95ColChoCtG-CG12C
95ColChoCtGE-12
95ColChoCtGG-CG12
95ColChoCtGG-CG12B
95ColChoCtGG-CG12C
95ColChoCtGGE-12
95ColChoGS-69
95ColChoGS-530
95ColChoSE-65
95ColChoSEGS-65
95ColChoSESS-65
95ColChoSS-69
95ColChoSS-530
95D3Zon-4
95Don-349
95DonBomS-4
95DonDom-3
95DonEli-58
95DonLonBL-2
95DonPreP-349
95DonTopotO-191
95Emb-127
95EmbGolI-127
95Emo-107
95Fin-103
95FinPowK-PK16
95FinRef-103
95Fla-106
95FlaInfP-5
95Fle-312
95FleAllS-15
95FleLumC-7
95FleUpdH-14
95KinDis-13
95Lea-232
95LeaLim-184
95LeaLimIBP-22
95LeaLimL-5
95LeaSli-3A
95LeaSli-3B
95LeaStaS-4
95NatPac-14
95Pac-12
95PacGolCDC-2
95PacGolP-3
95PacPri-5
95PanSti-35
95Pin-12
95Pin-276
95PinArtP-12
95PinArtP-276
95PinMusC-12
95PinMusC-276
95RedFol-6
95Sco-316
95Sco-459
95ScoGolR-316
95ScoGolR-459
95ScoHaloG-HG67
95ScoPlaTS-316
95ScoPlaTS-459
95ScoRul-SR13
95ScoRulJ-SR13
95Sel-42
95SelArtP-42
95SelCer-62
95SelCerMG-62
95SP-30
95SPCha-21
95SPCha-23
95SPChaDC-21
95SPChaDC-23
95SPChaDFC-8
95SPChaFCDC-8
95Spo-3
95SpoArtP-3
95SpoDouT-2
95SpoHamT-HT14
95SpoSam-3
95SPPlaP-PP4
95SPSil-30
95SPSpeF-28
95StaClu-363
95StaClu-496
95StaCluCC-CC5
95StaCluCT-13
95StaCluMO-31
95StaCluMOP-363
95StaCluMOP-496
95StaCluMOP-CC5
95StaCluMOP-PZ9
95StaCluMOP-RL13
95StaCluPZ-PZ9
95StaCluRL-RL13
95StaCluSTDW-B393
95StaCluSTMP-8
95StaCluSTWS-363
95StaCluSTWS-496
95StaCluVR-190
95Stu-23
95StuGolS-23
95StuPlaS-23
95Sum-3
95SumBigB-BB17
95SumNthD-3
95SumSam-BB17
95TomPiz-26
95Top-355
95TopCyb-191
95TopCybSIR-4
95TopLeaL-LL15
95TopLeaL-LL34
95TopTra-156T
95UC3-65
95UC3-142
95UC3ArtP-65
95UC3ArtP-142
95UC3CycS-CS17
95Ult-351
95UltAllS-13
95UltAllSGM-13
95UltGolM-351
95UltHitM-8
95UltHitMGM-8
95UltHomRK-9
95UltHomRKGM-9
95UltRBIK-9
95UltRBIKGM-9
95UppDec-45
95UppDec-108
95UppDecC-2A
95UppDecED-45
95UppDecED-108
95UppDecEDG-45
95UppDecEDG-108
95UppDecPAW-H28
95UppDecPAWE-H28
95UppDecPC-MLB2
95UppDecPLL-R8
95UppDecPLL-R48
95UppDecPLLE-R8
95UppDecPLLE-R48
95UppDecSE-150
95UppDecSEG-150
95UppDecSoaD-SD2
95USPlaCMLA-8C
95Zen-34
96Baz-109
96Bow-4
96BowBes-61
96BowBesAR-61
96BowBesR-61
96Cir-106
96CirRav-106
96ColCho-45
96ColCho-107
96ColCho-375T
96ColCho-377T
96ColChoCtG-CG2
96ColChoCtG-CG2B
96ColChoCtG-CG2C
96ColChoCtGE-CR2
96ColChoCtGG-CG2
96ColChoCtGG-CG2B
96ColChoCtGG-CG2C
96ColChoCtGGE-CR2
96ColChoGS-45

96ColChoGS-107
96ColChoSS-45
96ColChoSS-107
96ColChoYMtP-24
96ColChoYMtP-24A
96ColChoYMtPGS-24
96ColChoYMtPGS-24A
96Don-349
96DonPreP-349
96EmoXL-147
96Fin-B40
96Fin-S218
96FinRef-B40
96FinRef-S218
96Fla-206
96Fle-300
96FleBra-12
96FleTif-300
96Lea-33
96LeaLim-37
96LeaLimG-37
96LeaPre-62
96LeaPreP-62
96LeaPrePB-33
96LeaPrePG-33
96LeaPrePS-33
96LeaPreSG-27
96LeaPreSte-27
96LeaSig-38
96LeaSigEA-124
96LeaSigEACM-19
96LeaSigPPG-38
96LeaSigPPP-38
96LeaTotB-8
96MetUni-135
96MetUniP-135
96Pac-9
96PacPri-P7
96PacPriG-P7
96Pin-161
96Pin-209
96PinAfi-8
96PinAfiAP-8
96PinAfiFPP-8
96PinArtP-88
96PinArtP-109
96PinChrBC-6
96PinFoil-209
96PinPow-12
96PinSta-88
96PinSta-109
96ProMagDM-3
96ProSta-21
96SchDis-10
96Sco-84
96ScoDugC-A67
96ScoDugCAP-A67
96Sel-68
96SelArtP-68
96SelCer-66
96SelCerAP-66
96SelCerCB-66
96SelCerCR-66
96SelCerMB-66
96SelCerMG-66
96SelCerMR-66
96SP-27
96SPMarM-MM20
96SPMarMDC-20
96Spo-36
96SpoArtP-36
96SPSpeFX-19
96SPSpeFXDC-19
96SPx-3
96SPxGol-3
96StaClu-407
96StaCluEPB-407
96StaCluEPG-407
96StaCluEPS-407
96StaCluMM-MM3
96StaCluMOP-407
96StaCluMOP-MM3
96StaCluMOP-PP13
96StaCluPP-PP13
95StaCluVRMC-190
96Stu-50
96StuPrePB-50
96StuPrePG-50
96StuPrePS-50
96Sum-69
96SumAbo&B-69
96SumArtP-69
96SumFoi-69
96Top-389
96TopChr-156
96TopChrR-156
96TopChrWC-WC10
96TopChrWCR-WC10
96TopGal-172
96TopGalPPI-172
96TopLas-72
96TopLasPC-3
96TopPro-NL5
96TopWreC-WC10
96Ult-441
96UltGolM-441
96UltThu-12
96UltThuGM-12
96UppDec-270
96UppDec-380
96UppDecDD-DD2
96UppDecDDG-DD2
96UppDecDDS-DD2
96UppDecPD-PD9
96UppDecPRE-R35
96UppDecPreR-R35
96UppDecRunP-RP11
96Zen-10
96ZenArtP-10
86STaoftFt-26
97BluJayS-49
97Bow-263
97BowBes-94
97BowBesAR-94
97BowBesR-94
97BowChr-84
97BowChrI-84
97BowChrIR-84
97BowChrR-84
97BowInt-263
97Cir-16
97CirRav-16
97ColCho-30
97Don-170
97Don-440
97DonEli-44
97DonEliGS-44
97DonLim-102
97DonLim-105
97DonLim-199
97DonLimFotG-54
97DonLimLE-102
97DonLimLE-105
97DonLimLE-199
97DonPre-78
97DonPreCttC-78
97DonPreP-170
97DonPreP-440
97DonPrePGold-170
97DonPrePGold-440
97DonRocL-7
97DonTea-22
97DonTeaSPE-22
97Fin-186
97Fin-325
97FinEmb-325
97FinEmbR-325
97FinRef-186
97FinRef-325
97FlaSho-A127
97FlaSho-B127
97FlaSho-C127
97FlaShoLC-127
97FlaShoLC-B127
97FlaShoLC-C127
97FlaShoLCM-A127
97FlaShoLCM-B127
97FlaShoLCM-C127
97Fle-264
97FleTif-264
97Lea-97
97Lea-391
97LeaFraM-97
97LeaFraM-391
97LeaFraMDC-97
97LeaFraMDC-391
97MetUni-34
97NewPin-65
97NewPinAP-65
97NewPinMC-65
97NewPinPP-65
97Pac-241
97PacLigB-241
97PacSil-241
97PinCer-8
97PinCerMBlu-8
97PinCerMG-8
97PinCerMR-8
97PinCerR-8
97PinIns-49
97PinInsCE-49
97PinInsDD-9
97PinInsDE-49
97PinTotCPB-8
97PinTotCPG-8
97PinTotCPR-8
97PinX-P-37
97PinX-PMoS-37
97PinX-PSfF-47
97PinX-PSfFU-47
97Sco-172
97Sco-512
97ScoBra-9
97ScoBraPl-9
97ScoBraPr-9
97ScoHobR-512
97ScoPreS-172
97ScoResC-512
97ScoShoS-172
97ScoShoS-512
97ScoShoSAP-172
97ScoShoSAP-512
97SkyE-X-58
97SkyE-XACA-10
97SkyE-XC-58
97SkyE-XEC-58
97SP-28
97SpoIll-78
97SpoIllEE-78
97StaClu-47
97StaCluMat-47
97StaCluMOP-47
97Stu-81
97StuPrePG-81
97StuPrePS-81
97Top-352
97TopChr-119
97TopChrR-119
97TopGal-33
97TopGalPPI-33
97TopSta-52
97TopStaAM-52
97TopStaASGM-ASM6
97Ult-158
97UltGolME-158
97UltPlaME-158
97UppDec-15
97UppDecP-4
97UppDecPP-PP6
97UppDecPPJ-PP6

McGriff, Terry (Terrence)
83TamTarT-18
87Don-512
88Don-556
88Fle-240
88FleGlo-240
88NasSouTI-16
88RedKah-8
88Sco-281
88ScoGlo-281
88Top-644
88TopTif-644
89BlaYNPRWL-159
89BlaYNPRWLU-61
89NasSouTI-15
89Top-151
89TopTif-151
90CMC-129
90NasSouC-4
90NasSouP-236
90ProAAAF-548
91LinDriAAA-615
91TucTorLD-615
91TucTorP-2215
93EdmTraF-1140
94FleUpd-180
95Fle-503
95Pac-409
95StaClu-202
95StaCluFDI-202
95StaCluMOP-202
95StaCluSTWS-202
95TolMudHTI-21
96SyrChiTI-20

McGuire, Bill
87ChaLooB-15
88BasAmeAAB-10
88VerMarP-943
89CalCanC-21
89CalCanP-533
89Fle-553
89FleGlo-553
90CalCanC-14
90CalCanP-653
90CMC-441
90ProAAAF-118
92PeoChiC-29
92PeoChiTI-13
93BenRocC-28
93BenRocF-3285
94AshTouC-28
94AshTouF-1799
94AshTouF-1800
95AshTouTI-32
96SalAvaB-26

McGuire, Deacon (James)
03BreE10-102
04FanCraAL-35
10JuJuDE-27
11SpoLifM-48
87OldJudN-341
90DodTar-508
90KalBatN-20
90KalBatN-38
90KalBatN-39

McGuire, Matt
96BelGiaTI-11

McGuire, Mickey
91OriCro-291

McGuire, Mike
87BelMarTI-22
88WauTimGS-20
89WauTimGS-1

McGuire, Ryan
94Bow-559
94Cla-185
94ExcFS7-20
94LynRedSC-18
94LynRedSF-1900
94Top-746
94TopGol-746
94TopSpa-746
94UppDecML-16
95Bes-4
95SPML-23
95TreThuTI-20
95UppDecML-71
96Bow-216
96ColCho-778
96Exc-14
96Fla-310
96FleUpd-U148
96FleUpdNH-16
96FleUpdTC-U148
96Ult-505
96UltGolM-505
96UppDec-266
97DonLim-56
97DonLimLE-56
97Fle-757
97FleTif-757
97SpoIll-16
97SpoIllEE-16
95UppDecMLFS-71

McGuire, Steve
86QuaCitAP-22
87MidAngP-26
88MidAngGS-12
89PalSprACLC-54
89QuaCitAB-14
89QuaCitAGS-17

McGunnigle, William
87OldJudN-342
90DodTar-509

McGwire, Mark
82AncGlaP-1
84TopPewB-5
85ModA'sC-17A
85ModA'sC-17B
85Top-401
85TopTif-401
86SouLeaAJ-3
87ClaUpdY-121
87ClaUpdY-150
87Don-46
87DonHig-27
87DonHig-40
87DonHig-46
87DonHig-54
87DonRoo-1
87FleSlu-26
87FleUpd-76
87FleUpdG-76
87Lea-46
87MotMcG-1
87MotMcG-2
87MotMcG-3
87MotMcG-4
87SpoRool-13
87SpoTeaP-23
87Top-366
87TopTif-366
88A'sMot-2
88A'sMot-28
88Baz-13
88CheBoy-1
88ClaBlu-212
88ClaBlu-247
88ClaRed-151
88ClaRed-153
88ClaRed-197
88Don-1
88Don-256
88DonAll-19
88DonBasB-169
88DonBonM-BC23
88DonSupD-1
88DonTeaBA-256
88Dra-6
88Fle-286
88Fle-624
88Fle-629
88Fle-633
88FleAwaW-24
88FleBasA-25
88FleBasM-23
88FleExcS-26
88FleGlo-286
88FleGlo-624
88FleGlo-629
88FleGlo-633
88FleHea-2
88FleHotS-26
88FleLeaL-26
88FleMin-46
88FleRecS-25
88FleSlu-27
88FleStiC-56
88FleStiWBC-S6
88FleSup-23
88FleTeaL-21
88GreBasS-77
88K-M-16
88KayB-18
88KinDis-6
88Lea-1
88Lea-194
88MotMcG-1
88MotMcG-2
88MotMcG-3
88MotMcG-4
88MSAFanSD-3
88MSAIceTD-4
88Nes-10
88OPC-394
88PanSti-167
88PanSti-438
88RedFolSB-55
88Sco-5
88Sco-648
88Sco-659
88ScoBoxC-T3
88ScoGlo-5
88ScoGlo-648
88ScoGlo-659
88ScoYouSI-1
88Spo-100
88Spo-221
88SpoGam-2
88StaDav-1
88StaDav-3
88StaDav-5
88StaDav-7
88StaDav-9
88StaDav-11
88StaLinAs-10
88StaMcG-1
88StaMcG-2
88StaMcG-3
88StaMcG-4
88StaMcG-5
88StaMcG-6
88StaMcG-7
88StaMcG-8
88StaMcG-9
88StaMcG-10
88StaMcG-11
88StaMcGG-1
88StaMcGG-2
88StaMcGG-3

88StaMcGG-4
88StaMcGG-5
88StaMcGG-6
88StaMcGG-7
88StaMcGG-8
88StaMcGG-9
88StaMcGG-10
88StaMcGG-11
88Top-3
88Top-3A
88Top-580
88Top-759
88TopBig-179
88TopCoi-3
88TopGaloC-9
88TopGloS-39
88TopMinL-31
88TopRevLL-17
88TopRitTM-23
88TopRoo-13
88TopSti-1
88TopSti-164
88TopSti-309
88TopStiB-36
88TopTif-3
88TopTif-580
88TopTif-759
88TopUKM-47
88TopUKMT-47
88ToyRoo-19
88Woo-15
89A'sMot-2
89A'sMot-28
89A'sMotR-2
89A'sMotR-4
89Bow-197
89BowTif-197
89CadEllD-36
89ClaLigB-4
89ClaTraO-104
89ClaTraP-190
89CMCCan-12
89ColPosMc-1
89ColPosMc-2
89ColPosMc-3
89ColPosMc-4
89ColPosMc-5
89ColPosMc-6
89ColPosMc-7
89ColPosMc-8
89Don-95
89DonAll-1
89DonBasB-43
89DonGraS-7
89DonPop-1
89Fle-17
89Fle-634
89FleBasA-29
89FleBasM-28
89FleExcS-32
89FleGlo-17
89FleGlo-634
89FleGlo-WS8
89FleHeroB-28
89FleLeaL-27
89FleSup-31
89FleWorS-8
89KayB-21
89KinDis-4
89ModA'sC-35
89MotMcG-1
89MotMcG-2
89MotMcG-3
89MotMcG-4
89MSAHolD-14
89MSAIceTD-3
89Nis-14
89OPC-70
89OPC-174
89PanSti-20
89PanSti-244
89PanSti-420
89PepMcG-1
89PepMcG-2
89PepMcG-3
89PepMcG-4
89PepMcG-5
89PepMcG-6
89PepMcG-7
89PepMcG-8
89PepMcG-9
89PepMcG-10
89PepMcG-11
89PepMcG-12
89RedFolSB-80
89Sco-3
89ScoHot1S-25
89ScoSco-32
89Spo-200
89SpoIllFKI-146
89TacTigP-1537
89Top-70
89TopBasT-64
89TopBig-34
89TopCapC-22
89TopCoi-45
89TopDouA-12
89TopGloA-2
89TopGloS-41
89TopHeaUT-14
89TopMinL-70
89TopSti-151
89TopSti-172
89TopStiB-3
89TopTif-70
89TopUKM-51
89TVSpoM-98
89TVSpoM-137
89UppDec-300
89UppDecS-2
89Woo-27
90A'sMot-2
90AllBasT-2
90Bow-454
90BowTif-454
90ClaBlu-59A
90ClaBlu-59B
90ClaUpd-T33
90Don-185
90Don-697A
90Don-697B
90DonBesA-54
90DonGraS-4
90Fle-15
90Fle-638
90FleBasA-25
90FleBasM-25
90FleCan-15
90FleCan-638
90FleLeaL-25
90FleWaxBC-C20
90HOFStiB-91
90K-M-32
90Lea-62
90MLBBasB-77
90MotMcG-1
90MotMcG-2
90MotMcG-3
90MotMcG-4
90MSAIceTD-15
90OPC-690
90OPCBoxB-I
90PanSti-132
90PanSti-204
90Pos-12
90PubSti-310
90PubSti-600
90RedFolSB-61
90Sco-385
90Sco100S-25
90SouCalS-10
90Spo-141
90StaLonJS-9
90StaLonJS-11
90StaLonJS-27
90Top-690
90TopBig-28
90TopDou-45
90TopGloA-13
90TopGloS-42
90TopHeaU-14
90TopMag-34
90TopMag-94
90TopMinL-30
90TopSti-162
90TopSti-176
90TopStiB-36
90TopTif-690
90TopTVA-1
90TopWaxBC-I
90UppDec-36
90UppDec-171
90UppDecS-1
90USPlaCA-WCO
90VenSti-336
90VenSti-337
91A'sMot-2
91A'sSFE-8
91BasBesHRK-13
91Bow-234
91CadEllD-38
91Cla1-T73
91ClaGam-131
91DenHol-10
91Don-56
91Don-105
91DonBonC-BC9
91DonGraS-11
91Fle-17
91FlePro-4
91Lea-487
91MajLeaCP-39
91MLBKeyC-3
91MSAHolD-16
91OPC-270
91PanCanT1-14
91PanCanT1-23
91PanCanT1-110
91PanFreS-167
91PanFreS-192
91PanSti-145
91Pos-2
91RedFolS-122
91Sco-324
91Sco100S-39
91SevCoi-NC9
91SimandSMLBL-29
91StaClu-399
91StaPinB-30
91Stu-106
91SunSee-18
91Top-270
91Top-270A
91TopCraJI-27
91TopDesS-270
91TopGloA-2
91TopMic-270
91TopSta-26
91TopTif-270
91Ult-251
91UppDec-174
91UppDec-656
92A'sUno7P-1
92AthMot-2
92Bow-384
92Bow-620
92Cla2-T10
92ClaGam-119
92ColAllG-1
92ColAllP-1
92ColMcG-1
92ColMcG-2
92ColMcG-3
92ColMcG-4
92ColMcG-5
92ColMcG-6
92ColMcG-7
92ColMcG-8
92ColMcG-9
92ColMcG-10
92ColMcG-11
92ColMcG-12
92Don-348
92DonUpd-U7
92Fle-262
92Lea-16
92LeaGolP-32
92New-17
92OPC-450
92OPCPre-99
92PanSti-15
92Pin-217
92PinSlu-2
92PolMcG-1
92PolMcG-2
92PolMcG-3
92PolMcG-4
92PolMcG-5
92PolMcG-6
92PolMcG-7
92PolMcG-8
92PolMcG-9
92PolMcG-10
92PolMcG-11
92PolMcG-12
92PolMcG-13
92PolMcG-14
92PolMcG-15
92PolMcG-16
92PolMcG-17
92PolMcG-18
92PolMcG-19
92PolMcG-20
92PolMcG-21
92PolMcG-22
92PolMcG-23
92PolMcG-24
92Sco-20
92Sco100S-63
92ScoProaG-2
92SpoIllFK1-412
92StaClu-475
92Stu-226
92StuPre-17
92Top-450
92TopDaiQTU-1
92TopGol-450
92TopGolW-450
92TopKid-121
92TopMic-450
92TriPla-231
92TriPla-262
92Ult-115
92UltAllS-1
92UppDec-153
92UppDecF-32
92UppDecFG-32
93AthMot-2
93Bow-161
93CadDis-41
93ClaGam-63
93ClaGam-NNO
93ColAllG-23
93DiaMar-73
93Don-479
93DonDiaK-DK18
93DonEli-33
93DonEliS-15
93DonLonBL-LL4
93DonMVP-19
93DurPowP1-9
93Fin-92
93FinJum-92
93FinRef-92
93Fla-261
93Fle-296
93Fle-710
93FleAtl-16
93FleFruotL-46
93FleTeaL-AL2
93FunPac-17
93FunPac-48
93FunPac-51
93FunPacA-AS3
93JimDea-22
93Kra-10
93Lea-323
93LeaGolA-R11
93MilBonSS-4
93OPC-201
93OPCPreSP-16
93OPCPreSPF-16
93PacJugC-10
93PacSpa-224
93PanSti-15
93Pin-58
93PinCoo-30
93PinCooD-30
93PinHomRC-8
93PinSlu-2
93Pos-19
93Sco-557
93Sel-16
93SelStaL-26
93SelStaL-43
93SP-41
93SPPlaP-PP13
93StaClu-478
93StaClu-595
93StaCluAt-7
93StaCluFDI-478
93StaCluFDI-595
93StaCluI-B1
93StaCluM-153
93StaCluMOP-478
93StaCluMOP-595
93StaCluMOP-MB1
93StaCluMP-20
93Stu-141
93StuHer-4
93StuSupoC-3
93Top-100
93TOPBLAG-39
93TopGol-100
93TopInaM-100
93TopMic-100
93TopPre-100
93TriPla-68
93TriPla-87
93TriPla-245
93TriPlaA-23
93Ult-609
93UltAllS-12
93UltHomRK-2
93UppDec-41
93UppDec-49
93UppDec-420
93UppDec-493
93UppDec-566
93UppDecDG-3
93UppDecFH-60
93UppDecGold-41
93UppDecGold-49
93UppDecGold-420
93UppDecGold-493
93UppDecGold-566
93UppDecHRH-HR2
93UppDecIC-WI3
93UppDecICJ-WI3
93UppDecOD-D18
93USPlaCA-13C
94A'sMot-2
94Bow-192
94ColC-330
94ColC-525
94ColChoGS-330
94ColChoGS-525
94ColChoSS-330
94ColChoSS-525
94ColChoT-10
94Don-335
94DonDom-A10
94DonSpeE-335
94ExtBas-153
94Fin-78
94FinPre-78P
94FinRef-78
94Fla-94
94Fle-268
94FleTeaL-11
94FUnPac-125
94Lea-391
94LeaL-61
94OPC-74
94Pac-456
94PanSti-110
94Pin-300
94PinArtP-300
94PinMusC-300
94ProMag-97
94RedFolMI-18
94Sco-550
94ScoGolR-550
94Sel-57
94SP-36
94SPDieC-36
94SPHol-26
94SPHolDC-26
94Spo-4
94StaClu-358
94StaCluFDI-358
94StaCluGR-358
94StaCluMOP-358
94Stu-4
94Top-340
94TopGol-340
94TopSpa-340
94TriPla-5
94TriPlaN-7
94Ult-111
94UppDec-67
94UppDecDC-W8
94UppDecED-67
94UppDecMLS-MM13
94UppDecMLSED-MM13
95A'sCHP-2
95AthMot-2
95Baz-27
95Bow-303
95BowBes-R69
95BowBesR-R69
95ClaPhoC-41
95ColCho-130
95ColChoCtA-4
95ColChoCtAG-4
95ColChoCtG-CG13
95ColChoCtG-CG13B
95ColChoCtG-CG13C
95ColChoCtGE-13
95ColChoCtGG-CG13

95ColChoCtGG-CG13B
95ColChoCtGG-CG13C
95ColChoCtGGE-13
95ColChoGS-130
95ColChoSE-45
95ColChoSEGS-45
95ColChoSESS-45
95ColChoSS-130
95DenHol-16
95Don-460
95DonPreP-460
95DonTopotO-139
95Emb-107
95EmbGolI-107
95Emo-72
95EmoN-7
95Fin-169
95FinRef-169
95Fla-76
95Fle-249
95Lea-240
95LeaLim-166
95Pac-316
95Pin-196
95PinArtP-196
95PinMusC-196
95RedFol-28
95Sco-377
95ScoGolR-377
95ScoPlaTS-377
95Sel-14
95SelArtP-14
95SelCer-50
95SelCerMG-50
95SelCerS-50
95SP-185
95SPCha-177
95SPCha-181
95SPChaDC-177
95SPChaDC-181
95Spo-121
95SpoArtP-121
95SPPlaP-PP13
95SPSil-185
95StaClu-289
95StaCluMOP-289
95StaCluMOP-RL2
95StaCluRL-RL2
95StaCluSTWS-289
95StaCluVR-176
95Stu-141
95Sum-27
95SumNthD-27
95Top-472
95TopCyb-266
95UC3-51
95UC3-137
95UC3ArtP-51
95UC3ArtP-137
95UllHomRK-7
95Ult-94
95UltGolM-94
95UppDec-35
95UppDecED-35
95UppDecEDG-35
95UppDecPAW-H26
95UppDecPAWE-H26
95UppDecSE-247
95UppDecSEG-247
95Zen-71
96A'sMot-2
96Baz-74
96Bow-22
96BowBes-75
96BowBesAR-75
96BowBesR-75
96Cir-73
96CirAcc-11
96CirBos-18
96CirRav-73
96ColCho-418
96ColCho-640
96ColCho-710
96ColChoGS-418
96ColChoGS-640
96ColChoGS-710
96ColChoSS-418
96ColChoSS-640
96ColChoSS-710
96ColChoYMtP-25
96ColChoYMtP-25A
96ColChoYMtPGS-25
96ColChoYMtPGS-25A
96DenHol-25
96Don-511
96DonDiaK-4
96DonLonBL-3
96DonPreP-511
96EmoLegoB-5
96EmoXL-104
96Fin-B162
96Fin-B236
96Fin-G74
96FinRef-B162
96FinRef-B236
96FinRef-G74
96Fla-150
96FlaPow-5
96Fle-213
96FleGolM-6
96FleLumC-5
96FleRoaW-4
96FleTeaL-11
96FleTif-213
96Kin-24
96Lea-15
96LeaLim-21
96LeaLimG-21
96LeaLimL-10
96LeaLimLB-10
96LeaPre-15
96LeaPreP-15
96LeaPrePB-15
96LeaPrePG-15
96LeaPrePS-15
96LeaPreSG-14
96LeaPreSte-14
96LeaSig-23
96LeaSigPPG-23
96LeaSigPPP-23
96MetUni-101
96MetUniHM-5
96MetUniP-101
96Pac-385
96PacGolCD-DC34
96PacPri-P126
96PacPriFB-FB11
96PacPriG-P126
96PanSti-218
96Pin-130
96Pin-158
96PinAfi-6
96PinAfiAP-6
96PinAfiFPP-6
96PinArtP-55
96PinArtP-85
96PinFan-27
96PinFirR-18
96PinSta-55
96PinSta-85
96ProSta-6
96Sco-310
96ScoDugC-B35
96ScoDugCAP-B35
96ScoPowP-1
96ScoRef-16
96ScoTitT-6
96Sel-31
96SelArtP-31
96SelCer-20
96SelCerAP-20
96SelCerCB-20
96SelCerCR-20
96SelCerIP-23
96SelCerMB-20
96SelCerMG-20
96SelCerMR-20
96SelTeaN-5
96SP-140
96SPMarM-MM7
96SPMarMDC-7
96Spo-16
96Spo-117
96SpoArtP-16
96SpoArtP-117
96SpoPowS-21
96SPSpeFX-27
96SPSpeFXDC-27
96SPx-45
96SPxGol-45
96StaClu-104
96StaCluEPB-104
96StaCluEPG-104
96StaCluEPS-104
96StaCluMO-25
96StaCluMOP-104
96StaCluMOP-PP2
96StaCluMOP-PS7
96StaCluPP-PP2
96StaCluPS-PS7
95StaCluVRMC-176
96Stu-118
96StuPrePB-118
96StuPrePG-118
96StuPrePS-118
96Sum-20
96SumAbo&B-20
96SumArtP-20
96SumFoi-20
96TeaOut-55
96TeaOut-C97
96Top-145
96TopChr-41
96TopChrR-41
96TopChrWC-WC11
96TopChrWCR-WC11
96TopGal-155
96TopGalE-8
96TopGalPPI-155
96TopLas-46
96TopPro-AL18
96TopRoaW-RW11
96TopWreC-WC11
96Ult-115
96UltGolM-115
96UltHomRKGM-7
96UltHomRKR-7
96UltThu-13
96UltThuGM-13
96UppDec-151
96UppDec-425
96UppDecDD-DD30
96UppDecDDG-DD30
96UppDecDDS-DD30
96UppDecPD-PD10
96UppDecPHE-H7
96UppDecPRE-R5
96UppDecPreH-H7
96UppDecPreR-R5
96UppDecRunP-RP12
96UppDecVJLS-VJ6
96Zen-5
96ZenArtP-5
96ZenMoz-21
97Bow-15
97BowBes-45
97BowBesAR-45
97BowBesBC-BC5
97BowBesBCAR-BC5
97BowBesBCR-BC5
97BowBesMI-MI7
97BowBesMIAR-MI7
97BowBesMIARI-MI7
97BowBesMII-MI7
97BowBesMIR-MI7
97BowBesMIRI-MI7
97BowBesP-6
97BowBesPAR-6
97BowBesPR-6
97BowBesR-45
97BowChr-11
97BowChrI-11
97BowChrIR-11
97BowChrR-11
97BowInt-15
97Cir-50
97CirBos-12
97CirIco-7
97CirLimA-10
97CirRav-50
97CirRavR-7
97CirSupB-12
97ColCho-57
97ColCho-190
97ColCho-330
97ColChoAC-1
97ColChoCtG-24A
97ColChoCtG-24B
97ColChoCtG-24C
97ColChoCtGIW-CG24
97ColChoNF-NF5
97ColChoPP-PP1
97ColChoPPG-PP1
97ColChoS-25
97ColChoTBS-36
97ColChoTBSWH-36
97ColChoTotT-T22
97Don-12
97Don-270
97Don-413
97DonDom-7
97DonEli-21
97DonEliGS-21
97DonEliLaL-10
97DonFraFea-8
86HumStaDS-33
97DonLim-64
97DonLim-101
97DonLim-106
97DonLimFotG-27
97DonLimLE-64
97DonLimLE-101
97DonLimLE-106
97DonLonL-12
97DonPowA-14
97DonPowADC-14
97DonPre-50
97DonPre-176
97DonPreCttC-50
97DonPreCttC-176
97DonPreP-12
97DonPreP-270
97DonPreP-413
97DonPrePGold-12
97DonPrePGold-270
97DonPrePGold-413
97DonPrePM-9
97DonPreS-14
97DonPreTB-13
97DonPreTBG-13
97DonPreTF-13
97DonPreTP-13
97DonPreTPG-13
97Fin-30
97Fin-155
97Fin-305
97FinEmb-155
97FinEmb-305
97FinEmbR-155
97FinEmbR-305
97FinPro-30
97FinRef-30
97FinRef-155
97FinRef-305
97FlaSho-A52
97FlaSho-B52
97FlaSho-C52
97FlaShoDC-11
97FlaShoLC-52
97FlaShoLC-B52
97FlaShoLC-C52
97FlaShoLCM-A52
97FlaShoLCM-B52
97FlaShoLCM-C52
97Fle-193
97Fle-495
97Fle-708
97Fle-740
97FleBleB-5
97FleDecoE-7
97FleDecoERT-7
97FleDiaT-7
97FleGolM-4
97FleGouG-8
97FleGouGF-8
97FleHea-12
97FleLumC-12
97FleNig&D-5
97FleSoaS-9
97FleTeaL-11
97FleTif-193
97FleTif-495
97FleTif-708
97FleTif-740
97FleZon-11
97Lea-38
97Lea-355
97LeaDrefS-9
97LeaFraM-38
97LeaFraM-355
97LeaFraMDC-38
97LeaFraMDC-355
97LeaGolS-22
97LeaLeaotN-3
97LeaStaS-10
97MetUni-131
97MetUniBF-8
97MetUniT-6
97NewPin-142
97NewPin-188
97NewPinAP-142
97NewPinAP-188
97NewPinMC-142
97NewPinMC-188
97NewPinPP-142
97NewPinPP-188
97Pac-173
97PacCar-15
97PacCarM-15
97PacFirD-10
97PacGolCD-15
97PacLigB-173
97PacPri-59
97PacPriGA-GA13
97PacPriGotD-GD80
97PacPriLB-59
97PacPriP-59
97PacPriSL-SL5A
97PacSil-173
97PacTriCD-8
97Pin-52
97PinArtP-52
97PinCar-4
97PinCer-49
97PinCer-139
97PinCerLI-5
97PinCerMBlu-49
97PinCerMBlu-139
97PinCerMG-49
97PinCerMG-139
97PinCerMR-49
97PinCerMR-139
97PinCerR-49
97PinCerR-139
97PinHom-19
97PinHom-20
97PinIns-78
97PinInsC-23
97PinInsCE-78
97PinInsDD-9
97PinInsDE-78
97PinInsFS-4
97PinMin-15
97PinMinB-15
97PinMinCB-15
97PinMinCG-15
97PinMinCGR-15
97PinMinCN-15
97PinMinCS-15
97PinMinG-15
97PinMinS-15
97PinMusC-52
97PinTotCPB-49
97PinTotCPB-139
97PinTotCPG-49
97PinTotCPG-139
97PinTotCPR-49
97PinTotCPR-139
97PinX-P-42
97PinX-P-143
97PinX-PF&A-2
97PinX-PMoS-42
97PinX-PMoS-143
97PinX-PMW-14
97PinX-PMWG-14
97PinX-PMWS-14
97PinX-PSfF-5
97PinX-PSfFU-5
97ProMag-69
97ProMagML-69
97Sco-187
97Sco-511
97ScoBla-2
97ScoHobR-511
97ScoPitP-6
97ScoPreS-187
97ScoResC-511
97ScoShoS-187
97ScoShoS-511
97ScoShoSAP-187
97ScoShoSAP-511
97ScoSteS-5
97ScoTitT-1
97Sel-75
97SelArtP-75
97SelRegG-75
97SelToootT-19
97SelToootTMB-19
97SkyE-X-38
97SkyE-XACA-6
97SkyE-XC-38
97SkyE-XEC-38
97SkyE-XHoN-10
97SP-130
97SPGamF-GF7
97SPInsI-2
97SPMarM-MM4
97SpoIll-168
97SpoIll-175
97SpoIllEE-168

97SpoIllEE-175
97SpoIllGS-17
97SPSpeF-11
97SPSpxF-2
97SPSPxFA-2
97SPx-38
97SPxBoufG-14
97SPxBro-38
97SPxCorotG-9
97SPxGraF-38
97SPxSil-38
97SPxSte-38
97StaClu-5
97StaClu-384
97StaCluFR-F7
97StaCluI-I6
97StaCluMat-5
97StaCluMOP-5
97StaCluMOP-384
97StaCluMOP-I6
97StaCluMOP-FB7
97StaCluMOP-PG8
97StaCluPG-PG8
97Stu-8
97StuMasS-22
97StuMasS8-22
97StuPor8-13
97StuPrePG-8
97StuPrePS-8
97Top-62
97TopChr-21
97TopChrR-21
97TopChrSB-6
97TopChrSBR-6
97TopGal-37
97TopGalGoH-GH6
97TopGalPG-PG8
97TopGalPM3-8
97TopGalPMSSS-9
97TopGalPPI-37
97TopIntF-ILM1
97TopIntFR-ILM1
97TopScr-14
97TopSeaB-SB6
97TopSta-51
97TopStaAM-51
97TopSweS-SS10
97TopTeaT-TT12
97Ult-114
97UltBasR-6
97UltChe-A5
97UltDiaP-7
97UltDouT-8
97UltFamGam-12
97UltGolME-114
97UltHitM-11
97UltHRK-7
97UltPlaME-114
97UltPowP-A6
97UltPowP-B10
97UltSeaC-6
97UltThu-3
97UltTop3-14
97UltTop3GM-14
97UppDec-320
97UppDec-386
97UppDec-420
97UppDec-450
97UppDecAWJ-3
97UppDecHC-HC10
97UppDecLDC-LD1
97UppDecMM-7
97UppDecP-21
97UppDecPP-PP10
97UppDecPPJ-PP10
97UppDecRP-RP4
97UppDecU-1
97UppDecUMA-MA2
97Zen-28
97Zen8x1-11
97Zen8x1D-11
McHenry, Austin
22E120-234
23WilChoV-93
McHenry, Vance
80SpoIndT-9
81SpoIndT-20
82SalLakCGT-12
85SyrChiT-23
McHugh, Chip
86LakTigP-13
87GleFalTP-25
McHugh, Mike
88GreFalDTI-6
95HudValRTI-21
96ChaRivTI-9620
McHugh, Scott
87JamExpP-2541
McHugh, Tom
82ChaRoyT-4
McIlvaine, Joe
91PadSmo-22
McIlwain, W. Stover
60Lea-114
McInerney, Steve
86GleFalTP-15
87GleFalTP-7
89TolMudHC-24
89TolMudHP-762
90CMC-476
90TolMudHC-27
95SyrChiTI-17
McInerny, Dan
83SanJosBC-7
McInnes, Chris
93HelBreF-4103
93HelBreSP-25
94BelBreC-17
94BelBreF-110
McInnis, Bill
86NewBriRSP-17
87NewBriRSP-8
88PawRedSC-12
88PawRedSP-456
McInnis, Stuffy (John)
09AmeCarE-75
09SpoNewSM-73
11PloCanE-45
11SpoLifM-99
13PolGroW-19
14CraJacE-10
14FatPlaT-32
14TexTomE-33
15CraJacE-10
15SpoNewM-115
16BF2FP-38
16ColE13-114
16SpoNewM-117
19W514-20
20WalMaiW-29
21E121So1-60
21E121So8-57
21Exh-105
21Exh-106
22AmeCarE-45
22E120-37
22W575-78
23W501-18
23WilChoV-94
25Exh-29
26SpoComoA-30
27AmeCarE-41
27Exh-22
27YorCarE-60
28W502-60
28Yue-60
69SCFOldT-33
77GalGloG-180
80LauFamF-29
88ConSer5-21
91ConTSN-191
McIntire, Harry
06FanCraNL-32
08RosComP-97
09AmeCarE-76
10DomDisP-81
10SweCapPP-84
11S74Sil-64
11SpoLifM-174
11SpoLifCW-247
11T205-115
11TurRedT-28
12T207-119
90DodTar-510
McIntosh, Joe
76OPC-497
76Top-497
76TopTra-497T
McIntosh, Tim
87BelBreP-26
88CalLeaACLC-12
88StoPorCLC-189
88StoPorP-733
89ElPasDGS-18
89TexLeaAGS-13
90Bow-394
90BowTif-394
90CMC-40
90DenZepC-15
90DenZepP-628
90El PasDAGTI-24
90Fle-329
90FleCan-329
90ProAAAF-653
90TriAllGP-AAA24
91Bow-36
91Cla1-T55
91DenZepLD-145
91DenZepP-126
91Don-414
91Fle-589
91LinDriAAA-145
91OPC-561
91Sco-347
91ScoRoo-35
91StaClu-321
91Stu-71
91Top-561
91TopDeb90-104
91TopDesS-561
91TopMic-561
91TopTif-561
91TriA AAGP-AAA10
91Ult-177
91UppDec-547
92Bow-402
92BrePol-14
92DonRoo-73
92Sco-469
92Sco100RS-93
92ScoRoo-20
92StaClu-477
92Ult-386
93BrePol-17
93Don-367
93ExpPosN-16
93Lea-78
93Sel-334
93StaClu-502
93StaCluFDI-502
93StaCluMOP-502
93Top-234
93TopGol-234
93TopInaM-234
93TopMic-234
94BreMilB-156
94SalLakBF-820
94TriAAF-AAA16
96ColCliB-19
McIntosh, Troy
94BatCliC-30
McIntyre, James J.
80ArkTraT-12
McIntyre, Joe (Joseph)
92BatCliC-19
92BatCliF-3260
McIntyre, Matthew
07TigACDPP-23
08RosComP-36
09BriE97-20
09BusBroBPP-10
09ColChiE-190A
09ColChiE-190B
09PhiCarE-17
09RamT20-77
09T206-241
09T206-242
09T206-243
09TigMorPenWBPP-7
09TigTaCP-11
10CouT21-46
10DomDisP-82
10JHDABE-13
10NadE1-36
10RedCroT-52
10RedCroT-221
10RedCroT-222
10SweCapPP-12A
10SweCapPP-12B
11BasBatEU-28
11SpoLifCW-248
11SpoLifM-63
11T205-116
11TurRedT-25
12ColRedB-190A
12ColRedB-190B
12ColTinT-190A
12ColTinT-190B
12HasTriFT-13B
12HasTriFT-41A
12HasTriFT-54
12T207-120
McIntyre, Rich
86AncGlaPTI-23
McIver, Jeryl
76WauMetT-18
77LynMetT-19
McIver, Larry
82AubAstT-9
McJames, Doc
90DodTar-1028
McKain, Archie
93ConTSN-945
McKamie, Sean
91VerBeaDC-22
91VerBeaDP-783
92VerBeaDC-10
92VerBeaDF-2884
93BakDodCLC-19
McKay, Alan
85KinBluJT-7
86PitCubP-16
McKay, Cody
96SouOreTI-5
McKay, Dave
75IntLeaASB-17
75PacCoaLAB-17
75TacTwiK-2
76OPC-592
76TacTwiDQ-13
76Top-592
77Hos-130
77OPC-40
77Top-377
79OPC-322
79Top-608
81A'sGraG-39
81Don-350
81Fle-592
81Top-461
82Don-391
82Fle-100
82Top-534
83Don-213
83Fle-526
83TacTigT-29B
83Top-47
85A'sMot-27
86A'sMot-27
88A'sMot-27
89A'sMot-27
90A'sMot-27
91A'sMot-28
92AthMot-28
92Nab-12
93AthMot-27
94A'sMot-28
95AthMot-28
McKay, John
87AllandGN-27
McKay, Karl
80BurBeeT-28
81BurBeeT-26
McKay, Tripp
96VerExpB-18
McKay, Troy
86JacExpT-16
McKean, Edward
87OldJudN-343
89EdgR.WG-12
98CamPepP-53
McKean, Jim
88T/MUmp-20
89T/MUmp-16
90T/MUmp-15
McKechnie, Bill (William B.)
12T207-121
16FleBreD-63
23MapCriV-25
34DiaMatCSB-126
35DiaMatCS3T1-103
36WorWidGV-108
38CinOraW-19
39OrcPhoAP-16
40PlaBal-153
41HarHarW-16
48IndTeal-21
49IndTeal-29
75TCMAllG-24
76RowExh-8
76ShaPiz-89
77GalGloG-213
80PacLeg-86
80PerHaloFP-88
80SSPHOF-88
82OhiHaloF-58
86RedGreT-2
89HOFStiB-88
91ConTSN-34
92ConTSN-592
93ConTSN-831
93DiaStaES-144
94ConTSN-1066
94ConTSNB-1066
McKee, Matt
89AshTouP-940
McKee, Ron
80AshTouT-9
88AshTouP-1077
89AshTouP-942
94AshTouC-30
95AshTouTI-NNO
96AshTouB-1
McKeel, Walt
92ClaFS7-389
92LynRedSC-9
92LynRedSF-2911
93LynRedSC-19
93LynRedSF-2520
94SarRedSC-18
94SarRedSF-1954
96TreThuB-18
McKelvey, Mitch
84PriWilPT-24
85NasPirT-18
86Ft.MyeRP-19
86MemChiSTOS-17
86MemChiTOS-17
McKelvie, Ron
83VisOakF-12
McKenna, Chris
96MedHatBJTI-18
McKenna, Kit
90DodTar-1029
McKenna, Sean
90NebCor-17
McKenzie, David
93BilMusF-3942
93BilMusSP-25
McKenzie, Don
81WauTimT-10
McKenzie, Doug
83PeoSunF-8
85MidAngT-7
McKenzie, Jason
96ForWayWB-16
McKenzie, Scott
96ChaLooB-20
McKeon, Brian
90Bes-264
90ProAaA-109
90WatDiaB-11
90WatDiaP-2377
91HigDesMC-8
91HigDesMP-2391
92HigDesMC-28
93StoPorC-18
93StoPorF-743
McKeon, Jack
73OPC-593
73Top-593
74Top-166
75OPC-72
75SSP18-7
75Top-72
77A'sPos-84
77Top-74
79Top-328
84PadSmo-17
88PadCok-15
88TopTra-69T
88TopTraT-69T
89PadCok-10
89PadMag-1
89Top-624
89TopTif-624
90OPC-231
90PadCok-11
90PadMag-25
90Top-231
90TopTif-231
94CarLeaA-DJ36
McKeon, Joel
83AppFoxF-5
85BufBisT-22
86DonRoo-55
86FleUpd-75
87Fle-503
87FleGlo-503

87WhiSoxC-21
88LasVegSC-4
88LasVegSP-225
88Top-409
88TopTif-409
89IndIndP-1212
89RicBraBC-16
90HagSunB-22
90HagSunP-1409
90HagSunS-14
90RocRedWGC-26
91HagSunLD-238
91HagSunP-2453
91LinDriAA-238
McKeon, Kasey
89BriTigS-17
89SanDieSAS-17
90FayGenP-2411
McKeown, Dan
85AncGlaPTI-37
McKercher, Tim
88SalLakCTTI-24
McKinion, Mickey
93HicCraC-16
93HicCraF-1277
94HicCraC-16
94HicCraF-2174
McKinley, Leif
92ElmPioC-14
92ElmPioF-1382
93UtiBluSC-14
93UtiBluSF-3530
McKinley, Michael
96LowSpiB-18
McKinley, Pat
88VirGenS-15
McKinley, Tim
88SalBucS-12
89HarSenP-312
89HarSenS-11
90MiaMirIS-17
McKinley, W.F.
55Bow-226
McKinley, William F.
82OhiHaloF-19
McKinney, Charlie
80CedRapRT-12
McKinney, Greg
81CedRapRT-25
McKinney, Jay
90MisStaB-44
McKinney, John
85BenPhiC-16
McKinney, Lynn
76OmaRoyTT-14
78SpolndC-24
79HawIslC-20
79HawIslT-2
McKinney, Rich (C. Rich)
71OPC-37
71Top-37
72Top-619
73OPC-587
73Top-587
75TucTorC-11
75TucTorTI-11
76SSP-587
76TucTorCa-8
76TusTorCr-22
92YanWIZ7-111
McKinnis, Bo
88MisStaB-39
89MisStaB-45
McKinnis, Leroy
93SpolndF-3595
94SprSulC-17
94SprSulF-2040
95RanCucQT-24
96RanCucQB-20
McKinnis, Roy
93SpolndC-13
McKinnis, Tim
88QuaCitAGS-26
McKinnon, Alex
87OldJudN-344
McKinnon, Sandy
94SouBenSHC-11
94SouBenSHF-608
95PriWilCTI-22
96PriWilCB-18
McKinnon, Tom
91Cla/Bes-426
91ClaDraP-24
91FroRowDP-41
91HigSchPLS-16
91JohCitCC-28
91JohCitCP-3975
92OPC-96
92ProFS7-326
92StaCluD-115
92Top-96
92TopGol-96
92TopGolW-96
92TopMic-96
93JohCitCC-14
93JohCitCF-3688
McKinzie, Phil
87AppFoxP-29
McKitrick, Greg
90OklSoo-21
McKnight, Chris
95EugEmeTI-10
McKnight, Jack
83KnoBluJT-5
86PhoFirP-16
87PhoFirP-14
McKnight, James
62SalPlaC-199
62ShiPlaC-199
62Top-597
81TCM60I-383
82DayBeaAT-21
McKnight, Jeff
86JacMetT-17
87JacMetF-2
87TidTidP-4
87TidTidT-15
88TidTidCa-16
88TidTidCM-19
88TidTidP-1587
89TidTidC-13
89TidTidP-1953
90CMC-320
90ProAAAF-467
90RocRedWC-12
90RocRedWGC-7
90RocRedWP-710
90TopDeb89-80
90UppDec-162
91LinDriAAA-460
91MetWIZ-261
91OPC-319
91OriCro-292
91RocRedWLD-460
91RocRedWP-1909
91Sco-369
91Top-319
91TopDesS-319
91TopMic-319
91TopTif-319
92StaClu-633
92StaCluECN-633
92TidTidF-906
92TidTidS-565
93MetColP-40
93MetKah-7
93PacSpa-544
94Don-634
94Fle-572
94MetColP-18
94Pac-412
94StaClu-324
94StaCluFDI-324
94StaCluGR-324
94StaCluMOP-324
94Top-331
94TopGol-331
94TopSpa-331
McKnight, Toby
95BowBes-X6
95BowBesR-X6
McKnight, Tony
95Bes-123
95TopTra-38T
96Exc-172
96SigRooOJPP-P6
96Top-18
96TopPowB-18
McKown, Steven
76CedRapGT-14
McKoy, Keith
90SpolndSP-1
91ChaRaiC-22
91ChaRaiP-108
92WatDiaC-20
92WatDiaF-2152
McKune, Jerry
81ArkTraT-22
82LouRedE-17
83LouRedR-3
84LouRedR-3
85LouRedR-4
McLain, Brian
93SpolndC-14
93SpolndF-3589
McLain, Dennis
65OPC-236
65Top-236
66Top-226
66Top-540
66TopVen-226
67Baz-13
67OPCPapI-20
67Top-235
67Top-420
67TopPos-20
67TopTesF-15
67TopVen-261
68CokCapT-15
68OPC-40
68TigDetFPB-12
68Top-40
68TopVen-40
69CitMetC-1
69KelPin-14
69MilBra-187
69MLBOffS-52
69MLBPin-18
69OPC-9
69OPC-11
69OPC-57
69OPC-150
69OPC-169
69OPCDec-14
69TigTeal-8
69TigTealC-7
69Top-9
69Top-11
69Top-57
69Top-150
69Top-169
69Top-433
69TopDec-8
69TopDecl-28
69TopFou-21
69TopFou-23
69TopSta-177
69TopSup-17
69TopTeaP-1
69TraSta-4
70DayDaiNM-87
70Kel-73
70MLBOffS-212
70OPC-70
70OPC-400
70OPC-467
70Top-70
70Top-400
70Top-467
70TopPos-24
70TopSup-17
70TraSta-11A
71AllBasA-17
71MLBOffS-546
71MLBOffS-569
71OPC-750
71SenPolP-9
71SenTealW-16
71Top-750
71TopGreM-20
72MilBra-229
72OPC-210
72Top-210
72Top-753
73OPC-630
73Top-630
75OPC-206
75Top-206
76GrePlaG-42
77GalGloG-239
78TCM60I-210
80TigGreT-10
81TigDetN-15
81TigDetN-79
81TigDetN-94
82K-M-13
83TigAlKS-39
86TigSpoD-21
88TigDom-15
90HOFStiB-72
91FouBal-6
93ActPacA-154
93TigLitC-5
94TedWil-33
94TedWilM-M32
McLain, Mike
92CliGiaF-3595
92EveGiaC-10
92EveGiaF-1684
94SanJosGC-16
94SanJosGF-2813
McLain, Ron
81ExpPos-7
McLain, Tim
86WauTimP-16
88SanBerSCLC-46
McLamb, Brian
93OneYanC-15
93OneYanF-3511
94GreBatF-484
94OneYanC-12
94OneYanF-3801
95GreBatTI-16
96TamYanY-17
97GreBatC-15
McLane, Larry
82BurRanF-20
82BurRanT-7
83TulDriT-6
McLaren, John
75DubPacT-9
83KnoBluJT-19
86BluJayFS-25
87BluJayFS-21
88BluJayFS-22
89BluJayFS-19
90BluJayFS-20
92RedKah-NNO
93MarMot-28
94MarMot-28
95MarMot-28
96MarMot-28
McLarnan, John
87ReaPhiP-23
88MaiPhiC-6
88MaiPhiP-281
90ReaPhiB-4
90ReaPhiP-1219
90ReaPhiS-20
McLauchlin, Dick
81AlbDukT-26
McLaughlin, Bo (Michael)
77Top-184
78ChaChaT-9
78Top-437
80RicBraT-23
80Top-326
82Top-217
McLaughlin, Burke
52Par-12
McLaughlin, Byron
78SanJosMMC-17
79Top-712
80Top-197
81Don-287
81Top-344
84Nes792-442
84Top-442
84TopTif-442
McLaughlin, Colin
82KnoBluJT-20
83SyrChiT-10
85SyrChiT-15
86KnoBluJP-16
87SyrChiT-6
88SyrChiC-3
88SyrChiP-823
89CalCanC-3
89CalCanP-532
McLaughlin, Dave
83AppFoxF-3
McLaughlin, Denis
94UtiBluSC-18
94UtiBluSF-3816
96MicBatCB-16
McLaughlin, J.F.
87AllandGN-34
McLaughlin, James
88KimN18-23
McLaughlin, Jockey
88GooN16-26
McLaughlin, Joey
78RicBraT-10
79RicBraT-1
80Top-384
81Don-271
81Fle-420
81OPC-248
81Top-248
82Don-507
82Fle-620
82OPC-376
82OPCPos-8
82Top-739
83Don-255
83Fle-434
83FleSti-107
83OPC-9
83Top-9
84Don-617
84Fle-162
84FleUpd-79
84Nes792-556
84OPC-11
84RanJarP-53
84Top-556
84TopTif-556
85Top-678
85TopTif-678
86BluJayGT-11
86TacTigP-14
87HawIslP-19
93RanKee-257
McLaughlin, Jud (Justin)
34DiaMatCSB-127
McLaughlin, Mac (Dick)
77CliDodT-17
78CliDodT-23
79CliDodT-17
82AlbDukT-26
83AlbDukT-25
84AlbDukC-169
85AlbDukC-160
86AlbDukP-15
McLaughlin, Mike
87BelMarL-5
McLaughlin, Steve
86AppFoxP-14
McLaughlin, Thomas
87OldJudN-345
McLaughlin, Tom
81CliGiaT-24
McLaughlin, Wm.
40SolHug-14
McLaurine, Bill (William)
77SpolndC-2
78SpolndC-2
McLean, Larry (John R.)
03WilCarE-23
08RosComP-119
09AmeCarE-77
09ColChiE-191A
09ColChiE-191B
09RamT20-78
09SpoNewSM-45
09T206-244
10CouT21-182
10DomDisP-80
10E101-33
10E98-22
10MelMinE-33
10NadCarE-36
10PeoT21-39
10RedCroT-137
10RedCroT-223
10SweCapPP-103A
10SweCapPP-103B
11MecDFT-33
11PloCanE-46
11SpoLifCW-249
11SpoLifM-198
11T205-117
12ColRedB-191A
12ColRedB-191B
12ColTinT-191A
12ColTinT-191B
12HasTriFT-10A
12HasTriFT-41B
12HasTriFT-73A
12HasTriFT-73B
12T207-122
13NatGamW-30
14FatPlaT-33
14PieStaT-38
McLemore, Mark
83PeoSunF-9
85MidAngT-17
86Don-35
86Fle-650
86MidAngP-16

87AngSmo-13
87ClaUpdY-119
87Don-479
87DonOpeD-8
87DonRoo-7
87FleUpd-77
87FleUpdG-77
87SpoRool-14
87TopTra-75T
87TopTraT-75T
88AngSmo-22
88Don-181
88DonBasB-251
88Fle-497
88FleGlo-497
88Lea-159
88OPC-162
88PanSti-41
88Sco-152
88ScoGlo-152
88ScoYouS2-29
88StaLinAn-13
88Top-162
88TopTif-162
89Don-94
89Fle-484
89FleGlo-484
89Sco-208
89Top-51
89Top-547
89TopBig-30
89TopTif-51
89TopTif-547
89UppDec-245
90AngSmo-12
90TopBig-310
91AstMot-17
91Lea-86
92Bow-446
92Lea-427
92Ult-304
93Don-485
93Fla-153
93Fle-546
93Lea-512
93PacSpa-344
93Pin-184
93SP-159
93Top-55
93TopGol-55
93TopInaM-55
93TopMic-55
93UppDec-801
93UppDecGold-801
94ColC-198
94ColChoGS-198
94ColChoSS-198
94Don-186
94ExtBas-8
94Fin-115
94FinRef-115
94Fla-5
94Fle-9
94Lea-36
94OriPro-63
94OriUSPC-1S
94OriUSPC-8H
94Pac-36
94Pin-379
94PinArtP-379
94PinMusC-379
94Sco-415
94ScoGolR-415
94Sel-80
94StaClu-342
94StaCluFDI-342
94StaCluGR-342
94StaCluMOP-342
94StaCluT-272
94StaCluTFDI-272
94Top-379
94TopGol-379
94TopSpa-379
94TriPla-156
94Ult-4
94UppDec-248
94UppDecED-248
95ColCho-569T
95Don-399
95DonPreP-399
95DonTopotO-162
95Fin-229
95FinRef-229
95Fla-307
95Fle-12
95FleUpd-84
95Lea-322
95Pac-25
95RanCra-18
95Sco-162
95ScoGolR-162
95ScoPlaTS-162
95StaClu-593
95StaCluMOP-593
95StaCluSTWS-593
95Top-602
95TopCyb-373
95TopTra-114T
96Cir-89
96CirRav-89
96ColCho-324
96ColChoGS-324
96ColChoSS-324
96Don-238
96DonPreP-238
96Fla-175
96Fle-254
96FleRan-11
96FleTif-254
96LeaSigEA-125
96Pac-421
96RanMot-14
96Top-166
96Ult-137
96UltGolM-137
96UppDec-466
97Cir-133
97CirRav-133
97ColCho-489
97Don-308
97DonPreP-308
97DonPrePGold-308
97Fin-243
97FinRef-243
97Fle-227
97FleTif-227
97Lea-271
97LeaFraM-271
97LeaFraMDC-271
97MetUni-165
97Pac-205
97PacLigB-205
97PacSil-205
97Sco-145
97ScoPreS-145
97ScoRan-7
97ScoRanPl-7
97ScoRanPr-7
97ScoShoS-145
97ScoShoSAP-145
97StaClu-99
97StaCluMOP-99
97Top-139
97Ult-137
97UltGolME-137
97UltPlaME-137
97UppDec-509

McLeod, Bill
63MilSau-4

McLeod, Brian
90EveGiaB-8
90EveGiaP-3124
91CliGiaP-830
92SanJosGC-6
93SanJosGC-15
93SanJosGF-4

McLeod, Jessie
41WheM5-15

McLeod, Kevin
90HamRedB-6
90HamRedS-16

McLin, Joe
91WelPirC-13
91WelPirP-3581

McLintock, Ron
87PocGiaTB-18

McLish, Cal
49EurSta-64
57Top-364
58Top-208
59Ind-11
59Kah-22
59OklTodML-8
59Top-445
60Kah-26
60Top-110
60TopTat-35
60TopVen-110
61Top-157
61WhiSoxTS-9
62Top-453
62WhiSoxTS-14
63Top-512
64Top-365
64TopVen-365
69ExpFudP-8
72Dia-34
73OPC-377
73Top-377
74OPC-531
74Top-531
79TCM50-221
81TCM60I-411
82BrePol-NNO
90DodTar-511
92BreCarT-xx

McLish, Tom
78NewWayCT-30

McLochlin, Mike
91CollndC-14

McLoughlin, Tim
86SalRedBP-19

McMahon, David
88MisStaB-19

McMahon, Don
58BraJayP-9
58Top-147
59Top-3
59TopVen-3
60BraLaktL-16
60BraSpiaS-14
60Top-189
60TopVen-189
61Top-278
62Col.45B-13
62Top-483
63Col45"P-11
63Col45'JP-6
63Top-395
64Top-122
64TopVen-122
65Kah-29
65Top-317
66IndTeal-9
66OPC-133
66Top-133
66TopVen-133
67CokCapRS-7
67OPC-7
67Top-7
67TopRedSS-10
68TigDetFPB-13
68Top-464
69Top-616
70OPC-519
70Top-519
71GiaTic-9
71MLBOffS-259
71OPC-354
71Top-354
72OPC-509
72Top-509
73OPC-252
73Top-252A
73Top-252B
74OPC-78
74Top-78
80GiaPol-47
81RedSoxBG2S-95
83IndPos-23
83IndWhe-22
84Ind-21
84IndWhe-NNO
85Ind-21
85IndPol-NNO
86DodPol-NNO
87DodMot-27
87DodPol-29
88TigDom-16

McMahon, Jack
83VisOakF-9

McMahon, John
87AllandGN-35

McMahon, Mike
43ParSpo-53

McMahon, Pat
88MisStaB-20
89MisStaB-42

McMahon, Sadie
90DodTar-1030
98CamPepP-54

McManaman, Steve
80OrlTwiT-17

McManus, Hugh
40WheM4-12

McManus, Jim (James M.)
61UniOil-H2
77FriOneYW-70
87RicBraT-24

McManus, Marty (Martin)
20WalMaiW-30
21Nei-41
22E120-98
22W572-61
22W573-77
25Exh-115
26Exh-115
27YorCarE-48
29ExhFou-23
31Exh-23
32OrbPinNP-7
32OrbPinUP-47
33DelR33-1
33Gou-48
33GouCanV-48
33TatOrb-47
34DiaMatCSB-128
34Gou-80
35GouPuzR-1J
35GouPuzR-3A
35GouPuzR-14A
35GouPuzR-15A
91ConTSN-189

McMath, Shelton
80AshTouT-27

McMichael, Chuck
81ChaRoyT-14

McMichael, Greg (Gregory)
88BurIndP-1796
89CanIndB-24
89CanIndP-1315
89CanIndS-16
90CanIndS-11
90CMC-459
90ColSprSSC-7
90ColSprSSP-31
90ProAAAF-212
91DurBulUP-7
92GreBraS-239
93Bow-317
93BraLykP-19
93BraLykS-24
93FleFinE-4
93Lea-489
93OPCPre-127
93SelRoo-59T
93SelRooAR-10
93TopTra-6T
93Ult-308
93UppDec-652
93UppDecGold-652
94BraLykP-22
94BraLykS-22
94BraUSPC-4D
94BraUSPC-11C
94ColC-199
94ColChoGS-199
94ColChoSS-199
94Don-175
94ExtBas-210
94ExtBasSYS-13
94Fin-3
94FinJum-3
94FinRef-3
94Fla-355
94Fle-367
94FleRooS-12
94Lea-207
94OPCDiaD-14
94Pac-17
94Pin-69
94PinArtP-69
94PinMusC-69
94Sco-551
94ScoBoyoS-21
94ScoGolR-551
94Sel-247
94StaClu-241
94StaCluFDI-241
94StaCluGR-241
94StaCluMOP-241
94StaCluT-55
94StaCluTFDI-55
94Top-81
94TopGol-81
94TopSpa-81
94Ult-155
94UltSecYS-8
94UppDec-407
94UppDecED-407
94USPlaCR-1S
95Baz-55
95ColCho-162
95ColChoGS-162
95ColChoSS-162
95Don-191
95DonPreP-191
95DonTopotO-192
95Fin-49
95FinRef-49
95Fle-313
95Pac-13
95Sco-250
95ScoGolR-250
95ScoPlaTS-250
95StaClu-449
95StaCluMOP-449
95StaCluSTWS-449
95StaCluVR-240
95Top-512
95TopCyb-300
95Ult-130
95UltGolM-130
96ColCho-458
96ColChoGS-458
96ColChoSS-458
96Don-281
96DonPreP-281
96Fla-207
96Fle-301
96FleBra-13
96FleTif-301
96LeaSigEA-126
96Pac-7
95StaCluVRMC-240
96Ult-442
96UltGolM-442
97Fle-265
97Fle-527
97FleTif-265
97FleTif-527
97Ult-329
97UltGolME-329
97UltPlaME-329

McMillan, Leonard
95BurBeeTI-12

McMillan, Norm
23W503-10

McMillan, Roy
52Bow-238
52Top-137
53BowC-26
53Top-259
54Bow-12
54RedHeaF-21
54Top-120
54Wil-12
55Kah-3
55Top-181
56Kah-11
56RedBurB-14
56Top-123
56TopPin-57
57Kah-22
57RedSoh-14
57Top-69
58JayPubA-13
58Kah-20
58RedEnq-26
58RedJayP-9
58Top-360
59Baz-17
59Kah-23
59RedEnq-14
59RedShiBS-12
59Top-405
60Baz-33
60Kah-27
60RedJayP-5
60Top-45
60TopVen-45
61Pos-183
61Top-465
61TopStal-46
61WilSpoGH828-1-4
62BraJayP-8
62Jel-148
62Pos-148
62PosCan-148

62SalPlaC-159
62ShiPlaC-159
62Top-211
62Top-393
62TopStaI-149
63BraJayP-8
63Jel-150
63Pos-150
63Top-156
64BraJayP-8
64Top-238
64TopCoi-148
64TopGia-8
64TopVen-238
65MetJayP-10
65OPC-45
65Top-45
65TopEmbI-44
66Baz-13
66Top-421
67CokCapYM-V31
70BreMcD-18
70BreMil-14
73OPC-257
73Top-257A
73Top-257B
74OPC-179
74Top-179
77VisOakT-8
79DiaGre-272
79TCM50-154
80OrlTwiT-22
83TopRep5-137
91MetWIZ-262
91TopArc1-259
94TopArc1-120
94TopArc1G-120
McMillan, Stu
90IdaFalBP-3261
McMillan, Thomas E.
75OklCit8TI-16
77Top-490
78SanJosMMC-18
79BufBisT-15
89PacSenL-40
90EliSenL-100
McMillan, Thomas Law
11SpoLifM-161
90DodTar-1032
McMillan, Tim
86PriWilPP-15
87ChaWheP-17
88SalBucS-13
McMillin, Darrell
90GeoColC-21
92EugEmeC-19
92EugEmeF-3043
McMillon, Billy
91TopTra-78T
91TopTraT-78T
92StaCluD-116
93ElmPioC-11
93ElmPioF-3836
94KanCouCC-15
94KanCouCF-175
94KanCouCTI-17
94MidLeaAF-MDW17
95Bes-71
95Exc-196
95KanCouCLTI-9
95PorSeaDTI-15
95SPML-60
95UppDecML-183
96Bow-209
96ChaKniB-17
96Exc-163
96Top-435
96UppDec-236
96UppDecFSP-FS15
97PacPriGotD-GD143
97Sco-311
97ScoShoS-311
97ScoShoSAP-311
97StaClu-104
97StaClu-186
97StaCluMOP-104
97StaCluMOP-186
97Top-206
95UppDecMLFS-183
McMorran, Pat
94HagSunC-29
95KnoSmoF-57
McMorris, Mark
86WinSpiP-16
87WinSpiP-1
McMullen, Dale
78MemChiBC-6
McMullen, Hugh
28StaPlaCE-46
McMullen, Jerry
95EugEmeTI-18
McMullen, Jon
92ClaDraP-116
93BatCliC-19
93BatCliF-3154
94SpaPhiF-1730
95ClePhiF-225
McMullen, Ken
63Top-537
64Top-214
64TopVen-214
65Top-319
66Top-401
66TopRubI-66
67CokCapS-12
67DexPre-143
67OPC-47
67SenTeal-8
67Top-47
68OPC-116
68SenTeal-8
68Top-116
68TopActS-8C
68TopVen-116
69MilBra-188
69MLBOffS-106
69SenTeal-11
69SenTeal8-14
69Top-319
69TopSta-239
69TopTeaP-23
70MLBOffS-284
70OPC-420
70Top-420
71MLBOffS-350
71OPC-485
71Top-485
72MilBra-230
72Top-765
73OPC-196
73Top-196
74OPC-434
74Top-434
75OPC-473
75Top-473
76OPC-566
76SSP-80
76Top-566
77Top-181
81TCM60I-338
90DodTar-512
94BreMilB-245
94BreMilB-330
McMullen, Kevin
91GreHorP-3063
McMullen, Mac
94SparPhiC-15
McMullen, Mike
95BurBeeTI-13
96BurBeeTI-11
McMullen, Rick
82JacMetT-15
McMullin, Fred
75WhiSox1T-17
88PacEigMO-15
88PacEigMO-105
92Man191BSR-17
94ConTSN-1039
94ConTSNB-1039
McMurray, Brock
88GreFalDTI-16
89SalDodTI-16
90BakDodCLC-250
91VerBeaDC-28
91VerBeaDP-788
92BakDodCLC-16
McMurray, Steve
79WatIndT-9
McMurtrie, Dan
86LitFalMP-18
87ColMetP-24
McMurtry, Craig
82RicBraT-6
83BraPol-29
83TopTra-69T
84BraPol-29
84Don-599
84Fle-184
84FleSti-105
84Nes792-126
84Nes792-543
84OPC-219
84Top-126
84Top-543
84TopRubD-30
84TopSti-384
84TopTif-126
84TopTif-543
85BraHos-15
85BraPol-29
85Don-188
85Fle-333
85Lea-45
85OPC-362
85Top-362
85TopMin-362
85TopRubD-31
85TopSti-28
85TopTif-362
86BraPol-29
86Top-194
86TopTif-194
87BluJayFS-22
87Top-461
87TopTif-461
88OklCit8C-4
88OklCit8P-44
89Don-520
89RanMot-20
89RanSmo-21
89Top-779
89TopTif-779
90OklCit8P-430
90OPC-294
90ProAAAF-676
90Top-294
90TopTif-294
91Sco-620
92PhoFirF-2818
92PhoFirS-389
93RanKee-258
94TriAAF-AAA46
94TucTorF-757
95TusTorTI-15
McNabb, Buck
91Cla/Bes-441
91ClaDraP-43
91FroRowDP-42
92BurAstC-25
92BurAstF-558
92MidLeaATI-28
92StaCluD-117
92UppDecML-328
93ClaFS7-107
93FloStaLAF-36
93OscAstC-1
93OscAstF-639
94ClaGolF-135
94JacGenF-229
95BakBlaTI-27
McNabb, Glenn
89AugPirP-508
89SouAtlLAGS-6
90SalBucS-11
McNair, Bob
80UtiBluJT-24
McNair, Donald Eric
33RitCE-12H
34DiaMatCSB-129
34BatR31-61
34TarThoBD-14
35DiaMatCS3T1-104
36GouWidPPR-A71
39GouPreR303A-32
39PlaBal-105
39WhiSoxTI-13
39WorWidGTP-32
40PlaBal-14
40WhiSoxL-14
92ConTSN-477
94ConTSN-1144
94ConTSNB-1144
McNair, Fred
92BelMarC-6
92BelMarF-1458
93ExcFS7-228
93RivPilCLC-11
94JacSunF-1418
95ReaPhiELC-28
95ReaPhiTI-19
96Exc-210
McNair, Hurley Allen
87NegLeaPD-17
McNally, Bob
86SumBraP-20
87SumBraP-5
McNally, Dave
63Top-562
64Top-161
64TopVen-161
65OPC-249
65Top-249
66OPC-193
66Top-193
66TopVen-193
67CokCapO-1
67DexPre-144
67OPC-154
67Top-154
67Top-382
67TopVen-248
68CokCapO-1
68DexPre-54
68Top-478
69CitMetC-2
69MilBra-189
69MLBOffS-5
69OPC-7
69OPC-9
69Top-7
69Top-9
69Top-340
69Top-532
69TopDecI-29
69TopSta-126
69TopSup-1
69TopTeaP-5
69TraSta-15
70DayDaiNM-51
70Kel-14
70MLBOffS-151
70OPC-20
70OPC-70
70Ori-7
70Top-20
70Top-70
71BazNumT-27
71BazUnn-15
71Kel-59
71MilDud-16
71MLBOffS-304
71OPC-69
71OPC-196
71OPC-320
71Ori-10
71Top-69
71Top-196
71Top-320
71TopCoi-26
71TopSup-18
71TopTat-96
72Kel-29A
72Kel-29B
72MilBra-231
72OPC-223
72OPC-344
72OPC-490
72OriPol-6
72ProStaP-30
72Top-223
72Top-344
72Top-490
72TopPos-1
73OPC-600
73OriJohP-19
73Top-600
74OPC-235
74Top-235
74TopSta-127
75Hos-150
75OPC-26
75Top-26
78TCM60I-270
81Ori6F-22
86OriGreT-4
88PacLegI-38
91OriCro-293
93ActPacA-153
McNally, Mike
20GasAmeMBD-12
21E121So1-61
21E121So8-58
21KoBreWSI-39
22E120-67
22W575-79
22WilPatV-39
23W501-33
McNally, Sean
94EugEmeC-13
94EugEmeF-3721
95MidLeaA-30
95NewJerCTI-18
95SprSulTI-14
96Exc-62
96PeoChiB-20
96WilBluRB-11
McNamara, Denny (Dennis)
90NiaFalRP-4
91LakTigC-25
91LakTigP-279
92ClaFS7-166
92LakTigC-8
92LakTigF-2291
93ClaGolF-163
McNamara, James
86EveGiaC-10
86EveGiaPC-16
87CliGiaP-9
88SanJosGCLC-123
88SanJosGP-133
89SalSpuCLC-145
89SalSpuP-1811
91LinDriAA-303
91LinDriAA-312
91ShrCapLD-312
91ShrCapP-1824
92DonRoo-74
92GiaMot-20
92GiaPacGaE-29
92Lea-514
92Ult-592
92UltAllR-5
93PacSpa-275
93PhoFirF-1518
93TopGol-395
94OklCit8F-1497
McNamara, John
70Top-706
73OPC-252
73Top-252A
73Top-252B
74OPC-78
74PadDea-19
74PadMcDD-10
74Top-78
75OPC-146
75Top-146
76OPC-331
76SSP-123
76Top-331
77PadSchC-38A
77PadSchC-38B
77PadSchC-38C
77Top-134
78AngFamF-24
80RedEnq-3
80Top-606
81Top-677
82Don-526
83TopTra-70T
84AngSmo-19
84Nes792-651
84Top-651
84TopTif-651
85Top-732
85TopTif-732
85TopTifT-84T
85TopTra-84T
86Top-771
86TopTif-771
87Top-306
87Top-368
87TopTif-306
87TopTif-368
88DonAll-10
88DonPop-10
88Top-414
88TopGloA-1
88TopTif-414
90IndTeal-27
90TopTra-72T
90TopTraT-72T
91IndFanC-19
91OPC-549
91Top-549
91TopDesS-549
91TopMic-549
91TopTif-549
McNamara, Mike

88CapCodPPaLP-85
McNamara, Tom
87BelMarL-6
McNamee, Graham
63GadFunC-31
McNaney, Scott
89WatDiaS-32
McNary, Mike
88CapCodPPaLP-32
McNeal, Clyde
91NegLeaRL-9
92NegLeaRLI-43
95NegLeaLI-9
McNeal, Paul
86HagSunP-10
87HagSunP-2
McNeal, Pepe
94BurIndC-14
94BurIndF-3798
94StaCluDP-59
94StaCluDPFDI-59
96JohCitCTI-22
McNealy, Derwin
83NasSouTI-12
85SyrChiT-29
86ColCliP-14
86ColCliP-16
McNealy, Rusty
82WesHavAT-23
83TacTigT-17
86ChaLooP-19
87SanJosBP-27
McNeely, Earl
25Exh-127
26Exh-127
91ConTSN-177
McNeely, Jeff
89ElmPioP-30
90ElmPioP-12
90WinHavRSS-15
91Bow-113
91CarLeaAP-CAR23
91Cla/Bes-169
91Cla3-T67
91LynRedSC-22
91LynRedSP-1212
91UppDecFE-20F
92Bow-193
92ClaFS7-198
92DonRoo-75
92NewBriRSF-447
92NewBriRSS-489
92OPC-618
92ProFS7-20
92SkyAA F-209
92StaClu-577
92Top-618
92TopGol-618
92TopGolW-618
92TopMic-618
92UppDecML-258
93ClaFS7-12
93ExcFS7-134
93PawRedSDD-16
93PawRedSF-2421
93PawRedSTI-15
93RedSoxWHP-18
94Bow-175
94Cla-98
94ColC-200
94ColChoGS-200
94ColChoSS-200
94Don-609
94FleMajLP-23
94Pac-58
94PawRedSDD-11
94PawRedSF-955
94Pin-231
94PinArtP-231
94PinMusC-231
94PinNewG-NG11
94Sco-646
94ScoBoyoS-33
94ScoGolR-646
94Spo-171
94StaClu-48
94StaCluFDI-48
94StaCluGR-48
94StaCluMOP-48
94TriPla-285
94UppDec-21
94UppDecED-21
94USPlaCR-2D
95LouRedF-289
96MidAngOHP-18
96SigRooOJ-20
96SigRooOJS-20
McNeely, Mitch
95YakBeaTI-21
McNeely, Rod
77ModA'sC-18
79WatA'sT-21
McNees, Kevin
87IdaFalBP-8
88HagSunS-11
McNeese, John
96DayCubB-16
McNeil, Gerry
43ParSpo-54
McNeill, Kevin
94JohCitCC-21
94JohCitCF-3700
96StPetCB-19
McNertney, Jerry (Gerald)
64Top-564
67CokCapWS-9
67DexPre-145
68OPC-14
68Top-14
68TopVen-14
69MilBra-190
69PilPos-4
69Top-534
69TopSta-226
69TopTeaP-9
70BreMcD-19
70BreMil-15
70BreTeal-9
70MLBOffS-275
70OPC-158
70Top-158
71BreTeal-9
71CarTeal-28
71MLBOffS-279
71OPC-286
71Top-286
71TopCoi-68
72MilBra-232
72Top-584
79ColCliT-9
80ColCliT-22
81ColCliT-28
82ColCliP-NNO
83Pil69G-15
85ColCliP-25
87AlbYanP-10
94BreMilB-246
McNichol, Brian
96DayCubB-17
96Top-239
McNulty, Bill
73OPC-603
73Top-603
74SacSolC-49
75SacSolC-6
McNulty, Pat
93ConTSN-978
McNutt, Brent
92DavLipB-18
92DavLipB-23
McNutt, Larry
83LynMetT-2
McPhail, Larry
80SSPHOF-165
McPhail, Lee
83TigAlKS-54
McPhail, Marlin
86TidTidP-18
87BirBarB-5
88VanCanC-25
88VanCanP-777
89VanCanC-15
89VanCanP-596
90CMC-645
90ProAAAF-179
90VanCanC-18
90VanCanP-501
91IndIndLD-190
91IndIndP-470
91LinDriAAA-190
92ColMetC-28
92ColMetF-313
92ColMetPI-3
93NorTidF-2587
94NorTidF-2938
McPhee, Bid (John)
87OldJudN-346
94OriofB-28
98CamPepP-55
McPheeters, Kourtney
87AncGlaP-35
McPherson, Barry
84SavCarT-3
McPherson, John
86DavLipB-16
88KimN18-24
McQuaid, Jack (John H.)
87OldJudN-347
87OldJudN-348
McQueen, David
93EliTwiC-26
McQueen, Mike
70Top-621
71OPC-8
71Top-8
72OPC-214
72Top-214
McQuillan, George
03WilCarE-24
08RosComP-143
09AmeCarE-78
09T206-245
09T206-246
10CouT21-183
10CouT21-184
10CouT21-185
10CouT21-304
10LuxCigPP-15
10PeoT21-40
11SpoLifM-234A
11SpoLifM-234B
12PhiCarE-20
15AmeCarE-29
15CraJacE-152
16TanBraE-12
McQuillan, Hugh
22E120-130
22WilPatV-14
23W515-33
26Exh-37
93ConTSN-807
McQuillen, Carl
52LavPro-59
McQuinn, George
36NatChiFPR-106
36NatChiFPR-112
36OveCanR-34
39ExhSal-42A
39ExhSal-42B
39PlaBal-122
40PlaBal-53
41BroW75-21
41Gou-5
41PlaBal-23
46SeaSLP-35
46SpoExcW-5-1B
48YanTeal-20
49Bow-232
52LavPro-1
76TayBow4-68
77TCMTheWY-60
83TCMPla1943-17
92ConTSN-391
92YanWIZA-48
96Bro194F-19
McRae, Brian
86EugEmeC-28
87Ft.MyeRP-26
88BasCitRS-17
89MemChiB-13
89MemChiP-1205
89MemChiS-17
89Sta-44
90Bes-276
90CMC-829
90MemChiB-13
90MemChiP-1022
90MemChiS-18
90ProAaA-50
90StaFS7-68
91Bow-292
91Cla1-T49
91Cla3-T68
91ClaGam-157
91Don-575
91DonRoo-31
91Fle-563
91Lea-235
91OPC-222
91RoyPol-15
91Sco-331
91StaClu-478
91Stu-68
91Top-222
91TopDeb90-105
91TopDesS-222
91TopMic-222
91TopTif-222
91ToyRoo-18
91Ult-152
91UppDec-543
92Bow-66
92Cla2-T77
92ClaGam-85
92DenHol-15
92Don-387
92DonCraJ1-20
92DonDiaK-DK16
92Fle-163
92FleRooS-9
92Hig5-63
92Lea-123
92OPC-659
92OPCPre-12
92PanSti-99
92Pin-117
92PinTea2-20
92RoyPol-18
92Sco-478
92StaClu-270
92Stu-187
92Top-659
92TopGol-659
92TopGolW-659
92TopKid-108
92TopMic-659
92TriPla-69
92Ult-75
92UppDec-157
93Bow-589
93Bow-704
93CadDis-42
93DiaMar-74
93Don-411
93Fla-221
93Fle-242
93Hos-12
93Lea-58
93OPC-287
93PacSpa-139
93PanSti-108
93Pin-367
93RoyPol-19
93Sco-128
93Sel-250
93SP-233
93StaClu-33
93StaCluFDI-33
93StaCluMOP-33
93StaCluMP-3
93StaCluRoy-25
93Stu-137
93Top-49
93TopGol-49
93TopInaM-49
93TopMic-49
93TriPla-21
93Ult-213
93UppDec-238
93UppDecGold-238
94Bow-115
94ChuHomS-1
94ChuHomSG-1
94ColC-201
94ColChoGS-201
94ColChoSS-201
94ColChoT-12
94Don-43
94DonDiaK-DK12
94DonSpeE-43
94ExtBas-96
94Fin-62
94FinPre-62P
94FinRef-62
94Fla-302
94Fle-167
94FleTeaL-7
94FUnPac-56
94Kra-7
94Lea-306
94LeaL-41
94OPC-245
94Pac-295
94PanSti-78
94Pin-18
94PinArtP-18
94PinMusC-18
94ProMag-62
94RedFolMI-19
94Sco-19
94ScoCyc-TC15
94ScoGolR-19
94ScoGolS-60
94Sel-47
94SP-175
94SPDieC-175
94StaClu-520
94StaCluFDI-520
94StaCluGR-520
94StaCluMOP-520
94Stu-188
94Top-425
94TopGol-425
94TopSpa-425
94TriPla-238
94Ult-368
94UppDec-253
94UppDecAJ-13
94UppDecAJG-13
94UppDecED-253
95Bow-328
95ColCho-460
95ColCho-543T
95ColChoGS-460
95ColChoSE-216
95ColChoSEGS-216
95ColChoSESS-216
95ColChoSS-460
95Don-167
95DonPreP-167
95DonTopotO-200
95Emo-111
95Fin-175
95Fin-256
95FinRef-175
95FinRef-256
95Fla-333
95Fle-168
95FleUpd-126
95Lea-347
95LeaLim-35
95Pac-209
95PacPri-67
95Pin-319
95PinArtP-319
95PinMusC-319
95RedFol-21
95Sco-493
95ScoGolR-493
95ScoHaloG-HG77
95ScoHaloGYTE-HG77T
95ScoPlaTS-493
95ScoYouTE-493T
95SP-40
95SPCha-32
95SPChaDC-32
95Spo-79
95SpoArtP-79
95SPSil-40
95StaClu-273
95StaClu-624
95StaCluMOP-273
95StaCluMOP-624
95StaCluSTWS-273
95StaCluSTWS-624
95StaCluVR-138
95Stu-154
95Top-624
95TopCyb-391
95TopTra-26T
95UC3-57
95UC3ArtP-57
95Ult-60
95UltGolM-60
95UppDec-457T
95UppDecSE-55
95UppDecSEG-55
95USPlaCMLA-2H
96Baz-90
96Bow-63
96Cir-110
96CirRav-110
96ColCho-84
96ColChoGS-84
96ColChoSS-84
96Don-55
96DonPreP-55
96EmoXL-156
96Fin-B26
96FinRef-B26

96Fla-220
96Fle-322
96FleCub-12
96FleTif-322
96Lea-109
96LeaPrePB-109
96LeaPrePG-109
96LeaPrePS-109
96MetUni-142
96MetUniP-142
96Pac-30
96PacPri-P11
96PacPriG-P11
96PanSti-41
96Pin-109
96ProSta-38
96Sco-68
96SP-52
96StaClu-180
96StaCluMO-26
96StaCluMOP-180
95StaCluVRMC-138
96Stu-148
96StuPrePB-148
96StuPrePG-148
96StuPrePS-148
96TeaOut-56
96Top-184
96TopChr-55
96TopChrR-55
96TopGal-56
96TopGalPPI-56
96TopLas-47
96Ult-454
96UltGolM-454
96UltPriL-17
96UltPriLGM-17
96UppDec-33
96UppDecRCJ-6
96UppDecRipC-6
97Bow-257
97BowBes-55
97BowBesAR-55
97BowBesR-55
97BowInt-257
97Cir-374
97CirRav-374
97ColCho-285
97Don-328
97DonPreP-328
97DonPrePGold-328
97Fin-26
97FinRef-26
97FlaSho-A95
97FlaSho-B95
97FlaSho-C95
97FlaShoLC-95
97FlaShoLC-B95
97FlaShoLC-C95
97FlaShoLCM-A95
97FlaShoLCM-B95
97FlaShoLCM-C95
97Fle-280
97FleTif-280
97Lea-2
97LeaFraM-2
97LeaFraMDC-2
97MetUni-12
97Pac-253
97PacLigB-253
97PacSil-253
97ProMag-5
97ProMagML-5
97Sco-99
97ScoPreS-99
97ScoShoS-99
97ScoShoSAP-99
97SP-41
97StaClu-175
97StaCluMOP-175
97Stu-78
97StuPrePG-78
97StuPrePS-78
97Top-74
97TopChr-27
97TopChrR-27
97TopGal-77
97TopGalPPI-77
97Ult-448
97UltGolME-448
97UltPlaME-448
97UppDec-326
McRae, Hal
68Top-384
70DayDaiNM-64
70Top-683
71MLBOffS-64
71OPC-177
71Top-177
72OPC-291
72OPC-292
72Top-291
72Top-292
72TopCloT-24
73OPC-28
73Top-28
74OPC-563
74Top-563
75Hos-104
75Kel-53
75OPC-268
75Top-268
76Hos-135
76OPC-72
76SSP-176
76Top-72
77BurCheD-72
77Hos-17
77Kel-10
77MSADis-40
77OPC-215
77RCColC-41
77Top-340
78Hos-6
78Kel-20
78RCColC-33
78Roy-13
78SSP270-219
78Top-465
78WifBalD-49
79Hos-90
79OPC-306
79RoyTeal-6
79Top-585
80OPC-104
80Top-185
81AllGamPI-59
81CokTeaS-77
81Don-463
81Fle-41A
81Fle-41B
81OPC-295
81RoyPol-6
81Top-295
81TopSti-86
82Don-196
82Fle-416
82FleSta-210
82OPC-384
82Roy-13
82Top-625
83AllGamPI-62
83Don-238
83DonActA-16
83Dra-17
83Fle-119
83FleSta-124
83FleSti-102
83FleSti-146
83Kel-5
83OPC-25
83PerCreC-28
83PerCreCG-28
83Roy-17
83RoyPol-4
83Top-25
83Top-703
83TopSti-19
83TopSti-75
84AllGamPI-152
84Don-11
84Don-11A
84Don-297
84DonActAS-25
84DonCha-17
84Fle-350
84FleSti-44
84FunFooP-63
84Nes792-96
84Nes792-340
84OPC-340
84Top-96
84Top-340
84TopRubD-14
84TopSti-278
84TopStiB-3
84TopTif-96
84TopTif-340
85Don-588
85Fle-207
85Lea-34
85OPC-284
85Top-773
85TopRubD-12
85TopSti-270
85TopTif-773
86Don-521
86Fle-14
86Lea-251
86OPC-278
86RoyKitCD-4
86RoyNatP-11
86Top-415
86Top-606
86TopTat-15
86TopTif-415
86TopTif-606
86Woo-22
87Don-471
87Fle-375
87FleGlo-375
87OPC-246
87RedFolSB-59
87SpoTeaP-13
87Top-573
87TopTif-573
88ClaBlu-235
89PacSenL-133
89T/MSenL-76
89TopSenL-122
90ExpPos-24
91TopTra-79T
91TopTraT-79T
92OPC-519
92RoyPol-19
92Top-519
92TopGol-519
92TopGolW-519
92TopMic-519
93Bow-704
93RoyPol-1
93RoySta2-7
93Top-507
93TopGol-507
93TopInaM-507
93TopMic-507
95RedKah-34
McRae, Norm
70OPC-207
70Top-207
71OPC-93
71Top-93
McReynolds, Kevin
83LasVegSBHN-15
84Don-34
84Fle-307
84PadMot-13
84PadSmo-18
85AllGamPI-151
85Don-139
85Fle-41
85Lea-43
85PadMot-3
86Don-80
86Fle-331
86Lea-76
87ClaUpdY-126
87Don-14A
87Don-14B
87Don-451
87DonOpeD-125
87DonSupD-14
87Fle-425
87FleGamW-28
87FleGlo-425
87FleUpd-78
87FleUpdG-78
87Lea-14
87Lea-214
87MetColP-17
87MetFanC-5
87RedFolSB-35
87Spo-135
87Spo-155
87SpoTeaP-2
87TopTra-76T
87TopTraT-76T
88Don-617
88DonBasB-153
88DonTeaBM-617
88Fle-143
88FleGlo-143
88FleSup-24
88Lea-228
88MetColP-37
88MetKah-22
88OPC-37
88PanSti-346
88RedFolSB-56
88Sco-21
88ScoGlo-21
88Spo-56
88SpoGam-22
88StaLinMe-15
88StaMcR-1
88StaMcR-2
88StaMcR-3
88StaMcR-4
88StaMcR-5
88StaMcR-6
88StaMcR-7
88StaMcR-8
88StaMcR-9
88StaMcR-10
88StaMcR-11
88Top-579
88Top-735
88TopBig-158
88TopSti-102
88TopTif-579
88TopTif-735
89Bow-388
89BowTif-388
89ClaLigB-24
89Don-99
89DonBasB-70
89DonGraS-4
89Fle-44
89FleBasM-29
89FleGlo-44
89FleHeroB-29
89MetColP-13
89MetFanC-22
89MetKah-18
89OPC-85
89PanSti-139
89Sco-93
89ScoHot1S-96
89Spo-97
89Top-7
89Top-85
89TopAme2C-20
89TopBig-116
89TopDouM-3
89TopGloS-26
89TopMinL-27
89TopSti-10
89TopSti-95
89TopStiB-51
89TopTif-7
89TopTif-85
89TopTif-291
89TopUKM-52
89TVSpoM-5
89UppDec-367
89Woo-15
90Bow-138
90BowTif-138
90ClaYel-T56
90Don-218
90DonBesN-129
90Fle-211
90FleBasA-26
90FleCan-211
90Lea-198
90MetColP-17
90MetKah-22
90MLBBasB-15
90OPC-545
90PanSti-305
90PubSti-141
90PubSti-268
90RedFolSB-62
90Sco-5
90Spo-127
90Top-545
90TopBig-194
90TopDou-46
90TopSti-94
90TopTif-545
90TopTVM-31
90UppDec-265
90VenSti-338
90VenSti-339
91Bow-479
91Cla3-T69
91ClaGam-31
91Don-191
91Fle-154
91Lea-151
91MetCol8-2
91MetColP-19
91MetKah-22
91MetTro-7
91MetWIZ-263
91OPC-105
91PanFreS-83
91Sco-327
91StaClu-35
91StaPinB-31
91Stu-209
91Top-105
91TopDesS-105
91TopMic-105
91TopTif-105
91Ult-224
91UppDec-105
92Bow-337
92ClaGam-170
92Don-288
92Fle-512
92FleUpd-29
92Hig5-75
92Lea-522
92OPC-625
92OPCPre-54
92PanSti-228
92Pin-427
92RoyPol-20
92Sco-168
92ScoRoo-31T
92StaClu-619
92StaCluECN-619
92Stu-188
92Top-625
92TopGol-625
92TopGolW-625
92TopKid-15
92TopMic-625
92TopTra-71T
92TopTraG-71T
92Ult-374
92UppDec-362
92UppDec-742
93Bow-321
93ClaGam-64
93Don-233
93Fle-622
93Lea-80
93OPC-359
93PacSpa-491
93PanSti-107
93Pin-164
93RoyPol-20
93Sco-69
93Sel-176
93StaClu-348
93StaCluFDI-348
93StaCluMOP-348
93StaCluRoy-15
93Stu-75
93Top-442
93TopGol-442
93TopInaM-442
93TopMic-442
93TriPla-104
93Ult-214
93UppDec-592
93UppDecGold-592
94Bow-568
94ColC-549
94ColChoGS-549
94ColChoSS-549
94Don-565
94ExtBas-321
94Fin-334
94FinRef-334
94Fle-168
94FleUpd-158
94Lea-280
94MetColP-19
94MetShuST-6
94Pac-296
94PanSti-79
94Sco-487
94ScoGolR-487
94ScoRoo-RT30
94ScoRooGR-RT30
94Sel-293
94StaClu-566

94StaCluFDI-566
94StaCluGR-566
94StaCluMOP-566
94Stu-118
94Top-218
94TopGol-218
94TopSpa-218
94Ult-531
94UppDec-319
94UppDecED-319
95Fle-377
95Sco-105
95ScoGolR-105
95ScoPlaTS-105
96MetTeal-5
McSherry, John
88T/MUmp-12
89T/MUmp-10
90T/MUmp-10
McSpadden, Gaylen
76HawIsIC-12
McSparin, Paul
96AugGreB-18
McSparron, Greg
81CliGiaT-25
McTammy, James
87OldJudN-349
McVey, George
87OldJudN-350
McWane, Rick
87LitFalMP-2411
88LitFalMP-28
89VisOakCLC-122
89VisOakP-1431
90OrlSunRB-25
90OrlSunRS-27
95HarCitRCTI-29
McWeeny, Douglas
23WilChoV-95
26Exh-13
29PorandAR-63
30W554-10
90DodTar-513
McWhirter, Kevin
78OrlTwiT-14
80OrlTwiT-20
81PawRedST-4
McWhite, Raymond
94DanBraC-18
94DanBraF-3541
95DanBraTI-18
McWilliam, Tim
89RivRedWB-13
89RivRedWCLC-2
89RivRedWP-1401
90WicWraRD-16
91LinDriAA-614
91WicWraLD-614
91WicWraP-2612
91WicWraRD-22
92WicWraS-641
94SpoIndC-26
94SpoIndF-3340
McWilliams, Jim
79AshTouT-13
McWilliams, Larry
78BraCok-9
79Top-504
80Top-309
81Fle-267
81RicBraT-14
81Top-44
82BraBurKL-17
82BraPol-27
82Don-527
82Top-733
83AllGamPI-170
83Don-45
83Fle-310
83Top-253
84Don-566
84Fle-256
84FleSti-58
84FleSti-80
84Nes792-668
84OPC-341
84Top-668
84TopSti-133
84TopTif-668
85Don-78
85Fle-470
85Lea-247
85OPC-183
85Pir-12
85Top-183
85TopSti-132
85TopTif-183
86Don-264
86Fle-613
86Lea-136
86OPC-204
86Top-425
86TopTif-425
87Fle-613
87FleGlo-613
87OPC-14
87Top-564
87TopTif-564
88CarSmo-22
88ScoRoo-23T
88ScoRooG-23T
88TopBig-261
88TopTra-70T
88TopTraT-70T
89Bow-397
89BowTif-397
89Don-516
89Fle-458
89FleGlo-458
89PhiTas-21
89Sco-259
89Top-259
89TopTif-259
89TopTra-80T
89TopTraT-80T
89UppDec-143
90Don-709
90PubSti-247
90VenSti-340
McWilliams, Matt
95EugEmeTI-6
McWilliams, Ryan
92BatCliC-20
92BatCliF-3261
Meacham, Bobby
83ColCliT-20
84Don-336
84Nes792-204
84Top-204
84TopTif-204
85Don-126
85Fle-134
85Lea-147
85OPC-16
85Top-16
85TopSti-315
85TopTif-16
86Don-638
86Fle-110
86OPC-379
86Top-379
86TopSti-304
86TopTif-379
86YanTCM-25
87ColCliP-19
87ColCliP-6
87ColCliT-16
87Fle-105
87FleGlo-105
87Top-62
87TopTif-62
88Don-616
88DonReaBY-616
88Fle-215
88FleGlo-215
88SanDieSAAG-11
88SanDieSAAG-12
88Sco-137
88ScoGlo-137
88StaLinY-9
88Top-659
88TopTif-659
89BufBisC-17
89BufBisP-1663
89SanDieSAG-10
89SanDieSAG-11
89Sco-509
89Top-436
89TopTif-436
89UppDec-77
90CMC-189
90OmaRoyC-14
90OmaRoyP-72
90ProAAAF-607
92YanWIZ8-118
93ColSprSSF-3103
94CarMudF-1594
Meacham, Buddy
87SalSpuP-18
Meacham, Rusty
88BriTigP-1868
89FayGenP-1575
90EasLeaAP-EL6
90LonTigP-1266
90ProAaA-17
91Bow-149
91DonRoo-53
91LinDriAAA-592
91TolMudHLD-592
91TolMudHP-1928
91UppDecFE-44F
92Bow-486
92Don-654
92DonRoo-76
92FleUpd-30
92Pin-600
92Sco-395
92Sco100RS-67
92StaClu-768
92TopDeb91-122
92TopTra-72T
92TopTraG-72T
92UppDec-453
93Don-439
93Fle-243
93Lea-14
93OPC-173
93Pin-149
93RoyPol-21
93Sco-378
93Sel-277
93StaClu-439
93StaCluFDI-439
93StaCluMOP-439
93StaCluRoy-29
93Top-321
93TopGol-321
93TopInaM-321
93TopMic-321
93Toy-76
93Ult-215
93UppDec-59
93UppDecGold-59
93USPlaCR-12S
94FleUpd-50
94OmaRoyF-1220
94StaClu-610
94StaCluFDI-610
94StaCluGR-610
94StaCluMOP-610
95Don-386
95DonPreP-386
95Fla-48
95Fle-169
95Sco-83
95ScoGolR-83
95ScoPlaTS-83
95Top-513
95TopCyb-301
96OmaRoyB-18
96RoyPol-17
Mead, Timber
85EveGiaIC-10
86CliGiaP-12
87TamTarP-16
88ChaLooB-1
89ChaLooB-13
89ChaLooGS-24
90CMC-550
90PhoFirC-23
90PhoFirP-10
90ProAAAF-36
91CalLeLA-56
Meade, Paul
92ColRedC-12
92ColRedF-2399
93KinIndC-18
93KinIndF-2255
93KinIndTI-18
94CanIndF-3124
95BakBlaTI-28
Meador, Paul
91OklStaC-16
92OklStaC-20
Meadows, Brian
94SigRooDP-60
94SigRooDPS-60
94StaCluDP-37
94StaCluDPFDI-37
95Bow-158
95KanCouCLTI-10
95KanCouCTI-44
95MidLeaA-31
95Top-570
96BesAutS-59
96BesAutSA-44
96BreCouMB-19
Meadows, Chuck
83AleDukT-3
Meadows, Henry
22E120-202
Meadows, Jeff
82AubAstT-7
Meadows, Jim
86DayBealP-18
86FloStaLAP-35
Meadows, Lee
16ColE13-115
20NatCarE-62
21Exh-107
21OxfConE-11
22W572-62
22W573-78
23W503-49
23W515-23
27AmeCarE-4
88ConSer3-19
93ConTSN-697
Meadows, Louie
83DayBeaAT-26
86TucTorP-13
87TucTorP-9
88FleUpd-92
88FleUpdG-92
88TucTorC-20
88TucTorP-177
89AstSmo-25
89Fle-361
89FleGlo-361
89Top-643
89TopTif-643
89TucTorC-14
89TucTorJP-15
89TucTorP-191
89UppDec-401
90CMC-614
90OPC-534
90ProAAAF-205
90Top-534
90TopTif-534
90TucTorC-12
90TucTorP-215
90UppDec-160
91LinDriAAA-490
91ScrRedBLD-490
91ScrRedBP-2552
91Top-603A
Meadows, Scott
89FreKeyS-15
89WatDiaP-1773
89WatDiaS-20
90Bes-294
90CMC-735
90EasLeaAP-EL9
90HagSunB-13
90HagSunP-1428
90HagSunS-15
90ProAaA-25
90StaFS7-75
91HagSunLD-239
91HagSunP-2468
91LinDriAA-239
92RocRedWF-1951
92RocRedWS-459
92SkyAAAF-209
Meads, Dave
86AshTouP-19
87AstMot-17
87AstPol-9
87DonRoo-46
87FleUpd-79
87FleUpdG-79
87TopTra-77T
87TopTraT-77T
88BlaYNPRWL-121
88Don-455
88Fle-453
88FleGlo-453
88RedFolSB-57
88Sco-243
88ScoGlo-243
88Top-199
88TopTif-199
88TucTorC-4
88TucTorJP-16
88TucTorP-183
89AstMot-26
89AstSmo-26
89Don-424
89Fle-362
89FleGlo-362
89Sco-593
89Top-589
89TopTif-589
89TucTorC-5
89TucTorJP-16
89TucTorP-180
Meagher, Adrian
86AlbDukP-16
88ElPasDB-24
91DaiDolF-15
95AusFut-29
95AusFut-94
95AusFutSFP-SFFP4
Meagher, Brad
77BurBeeT-15
Meagher, Tom
85SpoIndC-14
86ChaRaiP-17
88SanJosGCLC-134
88SanJosGP-120
Mealing, Allen
94HelBreF-3625
94HelBreSP-17
95HelBreTI-9
96BelSnaTI-23
Mealy, Tony
87MacPirP-5
88GreHorP-1563
89CedRapRB-21
89CedRapRP-926
89CedRapRS-12
Meamber, Tim
87EriCarP-14
88SavCarP-344
89SprCarB-22
90St.PetCS-16
Mean, Rick
79CedRapGT-19
Mear, Richard
96JohCitCTI-23
Meares, Pat
89AlaGol-8
90WicStaSGD-24
91VisOakC-17
91VisOakP-1749
92ClaFS7-201
92OrlSunRF-2855
92OrlSunRS-513
92SkyAA F-221
93Bow-45
93FleFinE-239
93Lea-451
93PorBeaF-2389
93SelRoo-67T
93TopTra-98T
94Bow-432
94ColC-202
94ColChoGS-202
94ColChoSS-202
94Don-392
94ExtBas-122
94Fin-119
94FinRef-119
94Fla-316
94Fle-214
94Lea-157
94Pac-362
94PanSti-94
94Pin-304
94PinArtP-304
94PinMusC-304
94Sco-238
94ScoBoyoS-4
94ScoGolR-238
94Sel-122
94StaClu-210
94StaClu-624
94StaCluFDI-210
94StaCluFDI-624
94StaCluGR-210
94StaCluGR-624
94StaCluMOP-210
94StaCluMOP-624
94Stu-199
94Top-223
94TopGol-223
94TopSpa-223
94TriPla-257
94Ult-90

94UppDec-501
94UppDecED-501
95ColCho-487
95ColChoGS-487
95ColChoSS-487
95Don-185
95DonPreP-185
95DonTopotO-111
95Fla-60
95Fle-210
95Lea-333
95Pac-253
95Sco-100
95ScoGolR-100
95ScoPlaTS-100
95StaClu-352
95StaCluMOP-352
95StaCluSTWS-352
95Top-432
95TopCyb-229
95Ult-75
95UltGolM-75
96ColCho-204
96ColChoGS-204
96ColChoSS-204
96Don-302
96DonPreP-302
96EmoXL-83
96Fla-118
96Fle-168
96FleTif-168
96LeaSigA-152
96LeaSigAG-152
96LeaSigAS-152
96MetUni-77
96MetUniP-77
96Pac-360
96PanSti-202
96Sco-135
96StaClu-111
96StaCluMOP-111
96Top-285
96Ult-90
96UltGolM-90
96UppDec-127
97ColCho-157
97Fle-149
97FleTif-149
97MetUni-211
97Pac-141
97PacLigB-141
97PacSil-141
97StaClu-116
97StaCluMOP-116
97Top-281
97Ult-89
97UltGolME-89
97UltPlaME-89
97UppDec-412
Mears, Ronnie
78WisRapTT-12
Mecerod, George
80ElmPioRST-16
Meche, Carl
75QuaCitAT-15
Meche, Gil
96BesAutS1RP-FR9
96EveAquB-30
97Top-271
Mecir, Jim
92SanBerC-11
92SanBerSF-950
92StaCluD-118
93RivPilCLC-12
94JacSunF-1409
95TacRaiTI-12
96ColCliB-20
Meckes, Tim
83ColAstT-16
84TulDriTI-24
Mecrina, Eric
91SalLakTSP-13
Meddaugh, Dean
89BurIndS-17
Medeiros, Jody
91HawWomS-8
Mediavilla, Rick
91HamRedC-26
91HamRedP-4054
92ClaFS7-365
92SavCarF-675
94SavCarC-20
94SavCarF-521
Medich, Doc (George)
73OPC-608
73SyrChiTI-17
73Top-608
74OPC-445
74SyrChiTI-16
74Top-445
74TopSta-213
75Hos-78
75OPC-426
75SSP42-25
75SyrChiTI-12
75Top-426
75YanSSP-15
76CraDis-35
76OPC-146
76SSP-430
76Top-146
76TopTra-146T
77OPC-222
77Top-294
78Hos-86
78RanBurK-7
78SSP270-102
78Top-583
79OPC-347
79Top-657
80Top-336
81Don-386
81Fle-627
81Top-702
82Don-142
82Fle-324
82Top-36
82Top-78
83Fle-39
89SweBasG-18
91MetWIZ-264
92BreCarT-14
92YanWIZ7-112
93RanKee-259
94BreMilB-247
Medina, Alger
95RocCubTI-22
Medina, Facanel
89MarPhiS-20
90MarPhiP-3180
91BatCliC-14
91BatCliP-3497
Medina, Julio
90IBAWorA-8
Medina, Luis
86WatIndP-18
87WilBilP-24
88ColSprSSC-21
88ColSprSSP-1543
88TriAAAP-8
88TriAAC-38
89ClaLigB-67
89Don-36
89DonRoo-20
89Fle-411
89FleGlo-411
89IndTeal-19
89PanSti-315
89Sco-633
89ScoHot1R-5
89ScoYouS2-26
89Top-528
89TopTif-528
89UppDec-2
90ClaBlu-103
90CMC-468
90ColSprSSC-16
90ColSprSSP-44
90Hot50RS-31
90ProAAAF-225
90PubSti-564
90VenSti-341
91ColSprSSLD-92
91ColSprSSP-2193
91LinDriAAA-92
91TriA AAGP-AAA6
92OmaRoyF-2969
92OmaRoyS-337
92SkyAAAF-157
Medina, Patrico
90MarPhiP-3186
Medina, Pedro
82OneYanT-17
83GreHorT-20
84GreHorT-23
Medina, Rafael
94OneYanC-13
94OneYanF-3787
95GreBatTI-17
96BowBes-179
96BowBesAR-179
96BowBesR-179
96NorNavB-17
97Bow-133
97BowCerBIA-CA52
97BowCerGIA-CA52
97BowInt-133
97Sel-119
97SelArtP-119
97SelRegG-119
Medina, Ricardo
89WytCubS-22
90GenCubP-3031
90GenCubS-17
91GenCubC-12
91GenCubP-4225
92MidLeaATI-29
92PeoChiC-12
92PeoChiTI-14
93ClaGolF-121
93PeoChiC-13
93PeoChiF-1091
93PeoChiTI-16
Medina, Robert
96MedHatBJTI-19
Medina, Val
82DayBeaAT-22
Medina, Victor
89BluOriS-16
Medlinger, Irving
50WorWidGV-33
52Par-11
Medrano, Anthony
94ClaGolF-70
95WilBluRTI-4
96Exc-63
96TexLeaAB-32
96WicWraB-9
Medrano, Theodoro
96WisTimRB-16
Medrick, John
91EugEmeC-18
91EugEmeP-3725
Medvin, Scott
86ShrCapP-18
87ShrCapP-7
88BufBisC-10
88BufBisP-1484
89Bow-412
89BowTif-412
89BufBisC-6
89BufBisP-1680
89Don-597
89PanSti-160
89ScoHot1R-38
89Top-756
89TopTif-756
90BufBisC-6
90BufBisP-369
90CMC-6
90ProAAAF-484
Medwick, Ducky (Joe)
34DiaMatCSB-130
34BatR31-145
34DiaStaR-66
35DiaMatCS3T1-105
35GolMedFR-10
35WheBB1-21
36DiaMatCS4-10
36ExhFou-8
36GouWidPPR-A72
36NatChiFPR-55
36SandSW-41
36WheBB4-7
36WheBB5-5
36WorWidGV-75
37DixLid-5
37DixPre-5
37ExhFou-8
37GouFliMR-11A
37GouFliMR-11B
37GouThuMR-11
37KelPepS-BB10
37WheBB6-12
37WheBB8-8
38BasTabP-22
38ExhFou-8
38GouHeaU-262
38GouHeaU-286
38OurNatGPP-20
38WheBB10-3
38WheBB11-7
38WheBB15-9
39ExhSal-43
39WheBB12-6
40DodTeal-16
40WheM4-5
41DouPlaR-21
42DodTeal-14
43DodTeal-16
43MPR302-1-16
51R42SmaS-69
60Fle-22
61Fle-61
66CarCoi-10
74Car193T-18
74Car193T-30
74LauAllG-37
75TCMAllG-25
76RowExh-11
76ShaPiz-108
77GalGloG-63
80LauFamF-19
80PerHaloFP-110
80SSPHOF-110
81ConTSN-84
83CarGreT-5
83ConMar-39
83TCMPla1943-44
86SpoDecG-15
87Car193T-7
88ConNatA-15
89DodSmoG-22
89PacLegI-160
90DodTar-514
91ConTSN-18
92CarMcD-9
92ConTSN-629
93ActPacA-108
93ActPacA2-42G
94ConTSN-1094
94ConTSNB-1094
Mee, Jimmy
88GreHorP-1571
Mee, Tommy
78GreBraT-16
Meegan, Pete
87OldJudN-351
Meek, Darryl
92JohCitCC-19
92JohCitCF-3115
93BelBreC-15
93BelBreF-1707
Meek, Rich
89EriOriS-12
Meek, Stan
88OklSoo-5
89OklSoo-2
90OklSoo-8
Meekin, Jouett
95NewN566-182
Meeks, Tim
85AlbDukC-169
86AlbDukP-17
87AlbDukP-14
88TacTigC-5
88TacTigP-633
89BlaYNPRWL-95
90PalSprACLC-227
91BufBisLD-34
91BufBisP-537
91LinDriAAA-34
Megabyte, Mascot
96HonShaHWB-NNO
Meggers, Mike
92BenMusSP-8
92BilMusF-3369
93WesVirWC-19
93WesVirWF-2878
94WinSpiC-17
94WinSpiF-284
96ChaLooB-21
Mehl, Steve
87ChaWheP-9
88UtiBluSP-8
89SouBenWSGS-18
Mehling, George
87AllandGN-33
Mehrtens, Pat
88TamTarS-16
88UtiBluSP-21
89UtiBluSP-15
Meier, Brad
86RedWinA-25
Meier, Brian
80BatTroT-14
80WatIndT-15
Meier, Dave
82OrlTwiT-9
83TolMudHT-22
84MinTwiP-21
84TwiTeal-4
85Don-147
85Fle-285
85Top-356
85TopTif-356
85TwiTeal-4
86Fle-400
87OklCit8P-6
88IowCubC-20
88IowCubP-536
93RanKee-260
Meier, Jeff
89SumBraP-1118
Meier, Kevin
87PocGiaTB-6
88SanJosGCLC-135
88SanJosGP-132
89CalLeaA-40
89SanJosGB-18
89SanJosGCLC-215
89SanJosGP-447
89SanJosGS-20
90ShrCapP-1441
90ShrCapS-15
91LinDriAA-313
91ShrCapLD-313
91ShrCapP-1818
92ArkTraF-1126
92ArkTraS-38
92ClaFS7-440
93ExcFS7-103
93LouRedF-210
94ColSprSSF-730
95OrlCubF-6
Meier, Pat
94PriRedC-17
94PriRedF-3260
Meier, Randy
81ChaRoyT-20
82WauTimF-8
83WauTimF-15
Meier, Scott
81AppFoxT-19
82AppFoxF-9
83GleFalWST-5
Meilan, Tony
94GreFalDSP-17
Meine, Heinie
30SchR33-50
33Gou-205
Meiners, Doug
93St.CatBJC-13
93St.CatBJF-3971
94HagSunC-14
94HagSunF-2726
96DunBluJUTI-8
Meinershagen, Adam
92St.CatBJC-5
92St.CatBJF-3386
93St.CatBJC-14
93St.CatBJF-3972
94Bow-29
94Cla-69
94DunBluJC-19
94DunBluJF-2555
95AusFut-43
Meischner, Otto
64TulOil-5
Meissner, Scooter
90BelBreB-22
90BelBreS-27
92HelBreSP-25
93StoPorC-30
Meister, Ralph
88SumBraP-418
Meizosa, Gus
87GasRanP-12
88BlaYNPRWL-43
88St.LucMS-16
89BlaYNPRWL-44
89JacMetGS-9
Mejia, Alfredo
79LodDodT-4
Mejia, Carlos
94UtiBluSC-19
94UtiBluSF-3817
Mejia, Cesar
88EasLeaAP-10
88GleFalTP-924

89RocRedWC-4
89RocRedWP-1635
90CMC-358
90ProAAAF-271
90TidTidC-7
90TidTidP-540
90TopTVM-51
Mejia, Delfino
91ModA'sC-12
92RenSilSCLC-47
Mejia, Diaz (Roberto)
91GreFalDSP-7
92ClaFS7-355
92UppDecML-209
92VerBeaDC-3
92VerBeaDF-2885
93Bow-692
93ClaFS7-13
93ColSprSSF-3096
93LeaGolR-U5
93SelRoo-87T
93SP-223
93StaClu-406
93StaCluFDI-406
93StaCluMOP-406
93StaCluRoc-8
94Bow-638
94ColC-203
94ColChoGS-203
94ColChoSS-203
94Don-250
94ExtBas-249
94Fin-153
94FinRef-153
94Fla-155
94Fle-446
94FUnPac-171
94Lea-63
94OPC-190
94OPCDiaD-2
94Pac-201
94PanSti-177
94Pin-181
94PinArtP-181
94PinMusC-181
94RocPol-17
94Sco-615
94ScoBoyoS-23
94ScoGolR-615
94Sel-75
94StaClu-21
94StaCluFDI-21
94StaCluGR-21
94StaCluMOP-21
94StaCluT-93
94StaCluTFDI-93
94Stu-180
94Top-258
94TopGol-258
94TopSpa-258
94TriPla-228
94Ult-186
94UppDec-105
94UppDecED-105
95ActPacF-27
95ColCho-439
95ColChoGS-439
95ColChoSS-439
95Don-383
95DonPreP-383
95FleUpd-168
95Lea-5
95Pac-141
95Pin-311
95PinArtP-311
95PinMusC-311
95Sco-521
95ScoGolR-521
95ScoPlaTS-521
95Top-169
95UppDec-412
95UppDecED-412
95UppDecEDG-412
95UppDecSE-104
95UppDecSEG-104
Mejia, Javier
96MarPhiB-13
Mejia, Juan
96MarPhiB-14
Mejia, Leandro
90MadMusB-13
90MadMusP-2266
91MadMusC-11
91MadMusP-2128
Mejia, Marlon
96AubDouB-8
Mejia, Miguel
94AlbPolC-17
94AlbPolF-2251
94BluOriC-14
94BluOriF-3576
94OriPro-64
96BowBes-110
96BowBesAR-110
96BowBesR-110
96FleUpd-U192
96FleUpdNH-17
96FleUpdTC-U192
96Ult-552
96UltGolM-552
97PacPriGotD-GD201
Mejia, Oscar
82TulDriT-16
84TulDriTI-7
85TulDriTI-7
86WatIndP-16
87WilBilP-4
Mejia, Secar
87MyrBeaBJP-1448
Mejias, Fernando
91MarPhiC-21
91MarPhiP-3450
92MarPhiC-27
92MarPhiF-3052
93MarPhiC-19
93MarPhiF-3470
95LinVen-125
95LinVen-285
Mejias, Marcos
75BurBeeT-16
Mejias, Roman
57Top-362
58Top-452
59Top-218
60Top-2
60TopVen-2
62Col.45B-14
62Col45'HC-11
62Col45'JP-9
62Top-354
63Jel-186
63Pos-186
63Top-432
64Top-186
64TopVen-186
81RedSoxBG2S-94
Mejias, Sam
77ExpPos-22
77Top-479
78OPC-99
78Top-576
79OPC-42
79Top-97
80RedEnq-28
81Fle-219
81Top-521
82Don-295
82Fle-75
82Top-228
91PriRedC-28
91PriRedP-3531
93MarMot-28
94MarMot-28
95MarMot-28
96MarMot-28
Mejias, Simeon
87GenCubP-20
87PeoChiP-21
Mejias, Stan
76TulOilGP-8
Mejias, Teodulo
91CliGiaC-19
91CliGiaP-838
94VenLinU-252
Mele, Dutch (Albert)
47Exh-158
50WorWidGV-48
Mele, Sam (Sabath)
47Exh-159
48RedSoxTI-17
49Bow-118
50Bow-52
51Bow-168
51TopBluB-25
52Bow-15
52StaCalL-73H
52Top-94
54Bow-22
54OriEss-25
54RedMan-AL6A
54RedMan-AL6B
54Top-240
55Bow-147
60Top-470
61TwiJayP-9
61TwiPetM-16
62Top-482
63Top-531
63TwiJayP-7
63TwiVol-5
64Top-54
64TopVen-54
65Top-506
66OPC-3
66Top-3
66TopVen-3
67Top-418
76TayBow4-64
78TwiFri-12
80ElmPioRST-37
81TCM60I-354
83TopRep5-94
86TwiGreT-12
91OriCro-294
94TopArc1-240
94TopArc1G-240
Melendez, Dan
91TopTra-80T
91TopTraT-80T
92ClaDraP-41
92FroRowDP-1
92StaCluD-119
92TopDaiQTU-22
93Bow-562
93ClaFS7-142
93SanAntMF-3013
95SanAntMTI-46
96SanAntMB-15
Melendez, David
96FayGenB-23
Melendez, Diego
77CocAstT-12
78DayBeaAT-18
80AppFoxT-3
Melendez, Esteban
94DayCubC-29
Melendez, Francisco
83ReaPhiT-15
84PorBeaC-199
85PhiTas-44
85PorBeaC-43
86PhiTas-xx
86PorBeaP-16
87PhoFirP-25
88BlaYNPRWL-9
88PhoFirP-64
88TriAAC-32
89BlaYNPRWL-178
89Don-611
89OriFreB-43
89RocRedWC-3
89RocRedWP-1654
90CanIndB-16
90CanIndP-1300
90CanIndS-12
91OriCro-295
Melendez, Jorge
92GulCoaRSP-18
93EriSaiC-15
93EriSaiF-3120
95LinVen-238
Melendez, Jose
85PriWilPT-4
86PriWilPP-16
87HarSenP-5
88BlaYNPRWL-44
88HarSenP-848
89BlaYNPRWL-45
89WilBilP-633
89WilBilS-14
90CalCanC-22
90CalCanP-648
90CMC-449
90ProAAAF-113
91DonRoo-23
91LasVegSLD-288
91LasVegSP-232
91LinDriAAA-288
91PadSmo-23
91TopDeb90-106
92Don-572
92Fle-615
92Lea-507
92OPC-518
92OPCPre-139
92PadCarJ-14
92PadMot-14
92PadPolD-29
92PadSmo-20
92Pin-536
92ProFS7-332
92Sco-397
92Sco100RS-19
92StaClu-342
92Top-518
92TopGol-518
92TopGolW-518
92TopMic-518
92Ult-578
92UppDec-566
93Don-626
93Fle-144
93FleFinE-175
93Lea-371
93PacSpa-361
93PawRedSDD-17
93PawRedSF-2406
93StaClu-87
93StaCluFDI-87
93StaCluMOP-87
93Top-58
93TopGol-58
93TopInaM-58
93TopMic-58
93UppDec-288
93UppDecGold-288
94Pac-59
94PawRedSDD-12
94PawRedSF-945
95OmaRoyTI-20
95Pac-40
Melendez, Luis A.
71CarTeal-27
71OPC-216
71Top-216
72Top-606
73CedRapAT-17
73OPC-47
73Top-47
74OPC-307
74Top-307
75OPC-353
75Top-353
76OPC-399
76SSP-282
76Top-399
77PadSchC-39
78SyrChiT-14
87FayGenP-22
88FayGenP-1083
88HamRedP-1733
89BlaYNPRWL-133
90HamRedB-27
90HamRedS-26
94SavCarC-29
94SavCarF-523
94SouAtlLAF-SAL52
95NewJerCTI-19
Melendez, Steve
86GenCubP-19
87GenCubP-5
88PeoChiTI-16
89WinSpiS-21
90WinSpiTI-27
91WinSpiC-28
92WinSpiC-28
93DayCubC-27
96OrlCubB-4
95OrlCubF-28
Melendez, William
76DubPacT-21
Meleski, Mark
86NewBriRSP-18
87PawRedSP-75
87PawRedST-28
88PawRedSC-25
88PawRedSP-454
89PawRedSC-24
89PawRedSP-696
89PawRedSTI-16
90CMC-259
90PawRedSC-8
90PawRedSDD-15
90PawRedSP-478
90ProAAAF-450
90TopTVRS-35
91LinDriAAA-360
91PawRedSDD-12
91PawRedSLD-360
91PawRedSP-56
92PawRedSF-940
93LynRedSC-25
93LynRedSF-2533
94LynRedSC-26
94LynRedSF-1908
95JacSunTI-20
96JacSunB-4
97DunDonPPS-13
Melhuse, Adam
93St.CatBJC-15
93St.CatBJF-3981
94HagSunC-15
94HagSunF-2735
95DunBluJTI-15
96DunBluJB-17
96DunBluJTI-20
96DunBluJUTI-9
Melhuse, Mike
94WilCubC-28
Melillo, Ski (Oscar)
26Exh-116
29ExhFou-30
29PorandAR-64
30SchR33-39
31Exh-29
33ButCanV-32
33DelR33-3
33DouDisP-32
33ExhFou-15
33GeoCMil-22
34BatR31-151
34ButPreR-44
34DiaStaR-53
34ExhFou-15
34Gou-45
34GouCanV-94
34TarThoBD-15
35DiaMatCS3T1-106
35ExhFou-15
35GouPreR-13
35GouPuzR-5D
35GouPuzR-6D
35GouPuzR-11F
35GouPuzR-13D
36NatChiFPR-56
55A'sRodM-24
61Fle-127
76A'sRodMC-16
91ConTSN-81
93ConTSN-890
Melito, Chuck
80BatTroT-17
Melito, Mark
95SpoIndTI-13
96LanLugB-16
96MidLeaAB-37
Mellix, Lefty (Ralph)
88NegLeaD-18
Mello, John
88MidLeaAGS-43
88RocExpLC-24
89WesPalBES-16
90FloStaLAS-14
90WesPalBES-16
Mellody, Honey
11TurRedT-72
Melo, Juan
95Bow-237
95BowGolF-237
96Bow-127
96RanCucQB-21
97Bow-182
97Bow98ROY-ROY13
97BowBes-121
97BowBesAR-121
97BowBesR-121
97BowCerBIA-CA53
97BowCerGIA-CA53
97BowChr-173
97BowChr1RC-ROY13
97BowChr1RCR-ROY13
97BowChrI-173
97BowChrIR-173
97BowChrR-173
97BowInt-182
97ColCho-462
Meloan, Paul
11SpoLifM-25
Melrose, Jeff
86DayBeaIP-19

86TulDriTI-21
88GasRanP-1012
Melson, Gary
79TacTugT-9
80RicBraT-8
Melton, Bill (William)
69Top-481
69TopTeaP-11
69WhiSoxTI-10
70MLBOffS-190
70OPC-518
70Top-518
70WhiSoxTI-11
71BazNumT-21
71BazUnn-21
71MilDud-17
71OPC-80
71Top-80
71TopCoi-76
71TopGreM-33
71TopSup-47
71TopTat-111
72Kel-12
72MilBra-233
72OPC-90
72OPC-183
72OPC-184
72OPC-495
72ProStaP-31
72Top-90
72Top-183
72Top-184
72Top-495
72TopPos-3
72WhiSox-9
72WhiSoxC-5
72WhiSoxDS-5
72WhiSoxTI1-8
73LinPor-50
73OPC-455
73Top-455
74OPC-170
74Top-170
74TopDecE-68
74TopSta-158
75Hos-8
75HosTwi-8
75OPC-11
75SSP42-3
75Top-11
76OPC-309
76SSP-155
76Top-309
76TopTra-309T
77Top-107
85WhiSoxC-3
92UppDecS-5
Melton, Cliff
39PlaBal-125
40PlaBal-83
41DouPlaR-25
41DouPlaR-93
47PM1StaP1-140
48SomandK-8
49SomandK-6
79DiaGre-42
92ConTSN-613
95ConTSN-1389
Melton, David
58Top-391
Melton, Larry
86PriWilPP-17
87SalBucP-3
88EasLeaAP-17
88HarSenP-857
89BufBisC-8
89BufBisP-1673
Melton, Rube (Reuben)
43DodTeal-17
47TipTop-101
83TCMPla1942-45
90DodTar-515
Melton, Sam
87ElmPio(C-11
Meltz, Rich
75ForLauYS-6
Meluskey, Mitch
92BurIndC-22
92BurIndF-1660
93ClaFS7-220
93ColRedC-15
93ColRedF-601
94KinIndC-13
94KinIndF-2647
96KisCobB-16
Melvin, Bill
87GenCubP-16
88PeoChiTI-17
89WinSpiS-NNO
90WinSpiTI-5
91WinSpiC-7
91WinSpiP-2826
92ChaKniF-2769
92ChaKniS-162
93OrlCubF-2781
Melvin, Bob
82BirBarT-7
83BirBarT-12
84EvaTriT-11
86Don-456
86GiaMot-12
86Top-479
86TopTif-479
87Don-239
87Fle-281
87FleGlo-281
87GiaMot-12
87Top-549
87TopTif-549
88Don-638
88Fle-91
88FleGlo-91
88GiaMot-12
88OPC-41
88Sco-477
88ScoGlo-477
88StaLinG-12
88Top-41
88TopTif-41
89Bow-8
89BowTif-8
89Fle-335
89FleGlo-335
89OPC-329
89OriFreB-36
89Sco-617
89ScoRoo-61T
89Top-329
89Top-351
89TopTif-329
89TopTif-351
89UppDec-227
90BirBarDGB-23
90Don-451
90Fle-181
90FleCan-181
90Lea-382
90OPC-626
90PubSti-579
90Sco-453
90Top-626
90TopTif-626
90UppDec-644
90VenSti-342
91Bow-89
91Don-335
91Fle-482
91Lea-240
91OPC-249
91OriCro-296
91StaClu-312
91Top-249
91TopDesS-249
91TopMic-249
91TopTif-249
91UltUpd-3
91UppDec-310
92Don-231
92Fle-15
92OPC-733
92RoyPol-21
92Sco-208
92ScoRoo-73T
92StaClu-642
92Top-733
92TopGol-733
92TopGolW-733
92TopMic-733
92UppDec-692
93RedSoxWHP-22
93Ult-513
94Fle-36
Melvin, Doug
75ForLauYS-17
76ForLauYS-27
77WesHavYT-15
Melvin, Ken
75ShrCapT-10
Melvin, Scott
86KinEagP-16
87SprCarB-24
88St.PetCS-18
89St.PetCS-20
90ArkTraGS-21
91ArkTraLD-50
91ArkTraP-1295
91LinDriAA-50
92HamRedC-30
92HamRedF-1609
93SprCarC-29
96NewJerCB-1
Melvin, William
87ChaWheP-1
Mena, Andres
87SanAntDTI-2
Menard, Dyrryl
86OscAstP-18
Mendazona, Mike
89GasRanP-1026
89GasRanS-15
Mendek, William
87ChaLooB-24
88VerMarP-958
Mendenhall, Casey
90OklSoo-22
92NiaFalRC-15
92NiaFalRF-3320
93ClaFS7-221
93LakTigC-17
93LakTigF-1306
Mendenhall, Kirk
90NiaFalRP-6
91FloStaLAP-FSL21
91LakTigC-21
91LakTigP-274
92LonTigF-640
92LonTigS-413
93LonTigF-2315
94TreThuF-2127
Mendenhall, Monte
78QuaCitAT-13
Mendenhall, Shannon
86ModA'sC-15
88LynRedSS-14
Mendes, Jaime
95BatCliTI-22
96PieBolWB-17
Mendez, Carlos
94RocRoyC-16
94RocRoyF-568
95LinVen-6
95WilBluRTI-28
96CarLeaA1B-11
96CarLeaA2B-11
96WilBluRB-2
Mendez, Eddie
89MyrBeaBJP-1453
Mendez, Emilio
93GenCubC-22
93GenCubF-3187
93PeoChiC-14
93PeoChiF-1092
94PeoChiC-19
94PeoChiF-2276
94WilCubC-14
94WilCubF-3771
Mendez, Jaime
90IBAWorA-29
Mendez, Jesus
86St.PetCP-20
87St.PetCP-3
88ArkTraGS-15
90CMC-118
90LouRedBC-18
90LouRedBLBC-27
90LouRedBP-411
90ProAAAF-525
90TopTVCa-55
91LouRedP-2930
92ArkTraF-1138
92ArkTraS-39
93LinVenB-70
94VenLinU-174
95LinVen-108
Mendez, John
96StPetCB-20
Mendez, Jose D.
74LauOldTBS-9
87NegLeaPD-7
90NegLeaS-32
Mendez, Julio
89SavCarP-361
Mendez, Mauro
93LinVenB-202
Mendez, Miguel
90SumBraB-13
90SumBraP-2443
Mendez, Raul
86BelMarC-124
Mendez, Ricardo
92MadMusC-10
92MadMusF-1244
92SouOreAF-3426
Mendez, Roberto
85MexCitTT-2
Mendez, Rodolfo
95MidLeaA-32
95SprSulTI-15
96Exc-64
Mendez, Sergio
93WelPirC-13
93WelPirF-3360
94AugGreC-12
94AugGreF-3012
94SouAtlLAF-SAL34
95LynHilTI-15
Mendon, Kevin
80MemChiT-14
Mendonca, Robert
89BatCliP-1918
Mendoza, Alonso
93PocPosF-4219
93PocPosSP-2
Mendoza, Carlos
96Exc-189
Mendoza, Dave
76CedRapGT-15
Mendoza, Francisco
92BelBreC-13
92BelBreF-413
93BelBreC-16
93BelBreF-1719
95SprSulTI-16
Mendoza, Jesus
88SumBraP-398
89BurBraP-1605
89BurBraS-13
95LinVen-159
Mendoza, Mario
75OPC-457
75Top-457
76SSP-606
77PirPosP-14
78Top-383
79Top-509
80OPC-344
80Top-652
81Don-45
81Fle-613
81OPC-76
81Top-76
81TopTra-801
82Don-394
82Fle-325
82OPC-212
82Top-212
91PalSprAP-2035
92CalLeaACL-49
92PalSprAC-28
92PalSprAF-855
93PalSprAC-26
93PalSprAF-86
93RanKee-261
94MidAngF-2453
94MidAngOHP-16
95MidAngOHP-21
95MidAngTI-19
96MidAngB-1
96MidAngOHP-17
Mendoza, Mike
75DubPacT-8
76DubPacT-22
79ChaChaT-19
80TucTorT-21
81TidTidT-19
Mendoza, Minnie
80ChaO'sP-12
80ChaO'sW-13
81MiaOriT-6
88OriFreB-40
96CanIndB-3
Mendoza, Ramiro
95NorNavTI-18
95SPML-119
96ColCliB-21
97Fle-172
97FleTif-172
97Ult-101
97UltGolME-101
97UltPlaME-101
97UppDec-475
Mendoza, Reynol
92EriSaiC-10
92EriSaiF-1618
93KanCouCC-13
93KanCouCF-913
93MidLeaAGF-9
93Top-782
93TopGol-782
93TopInaM-782
93TopMic-782
94BreCouMF-6
94ExcFS7-193
95PorSeaDTI-16
96PorSeaDB-17
93KanCouCTI-13
Menechino, Frank
94MidLeaAF-MDW27
94SouBenSHC-12
94SouBenSHF-599
95PriWilCTI-9
96BirBarB-6
96Exc-34
Menees, Gene
79NaSouTI-15
80IndIndTI-21
81IndIndTI-18
82WatRedT-5
Menefee, John
03BreE10-103
Menendez, Daniel
50W720HolS-19
Menendez, Tony (Antonio G.)
86BirBarTI-6
87BirBarB-10
88BirBarB-20
89BirBarB-3
89BirBarP-103
90BirBarDGB-24
92DonRoo-77
92NasSouF-1830
92NasSouS-286
92SkyAAAF-133
93Bow-106
93BufBisF-513
94GiaTarBCI-5
94PhoFirF-1517
94StaCluT-27
94StaCluTFDI-27
95PhoFirTI-36
Menendez, William
86WinSpiP-17
Mengel, Brad
90MyrBeaBJP-2782
91DunBluJC-17
91DunBluJP-214
92KnoBluJF-2997
Mengwasser, Brad
82TulDriT-2
Menhart, Paul
90St.CatBJP-3464
91DunBluJC-7
91DunBluJP-203
91FloStaLAP-FSL9
92KnoBluJF-2987
92KnoBluJS-384
92SkyAA F-162
93SyrChiF-997
95SyrChiTI-16
96Don-323
96DonPreP-323
96Fle-279
96FleTif-279
96MarMot-25
96StaClu-62
96StaCluMOP-62
Menke, Denis
62Top-597
63Top-433
64BraJayP-9
64Top-53
64TopCoi-90
64TopVen-53
65Kah-30
65Top-327
66Kah-22
66OPC-184
66Top-184
66TopRubI-67

66TopVen-184
67Ast-18
67BraIrvD-3
67CokCapB-6
67DexPre-146
67Kah-26
67Top-396
67Top-518
68CokCapA-8
68CokCapB-6
68DexPre-55
68Top-232
68TopVen-232
69MilBra-191
69MLBOffS-140
69Top-487
69TopSta-35
69TopTeaP-6
70AstTeal-7
70DayDaiNM-63
70MilBra-18
70MLBOffS-43
70OPC-155
70Top-155
70TopBoo-16
71AstCok-6
71Kel-8
71MilDud-53
71MLBOffS-87
71OPC-130
71Top-130
71TopCoi-89
72MilBra-234
72Top-586
73OPC-52
73Top-52
74OPC-134
74Top-134
77BurBeeT-16
78AtlCon-16
78DunBluJT-16
78TCM60I-58
82TucTorT-26
84AstMot-27
85AstMot-27
86AstMot-9
86AstPol-26
87AstMot-27
87AstPol-26
87AstShoSO-16
87AstShoSTw-24
87AstShoSTw-27
88AstMot-27
89PhiTas-22
90PhiTas-34
91PhiMed-27
92PhiMed-20
93PhiMed-22
94PhiMed-22
95Phi-19
96PhiTeal-21
Menosky, Mike
21Nei-46
22E120-7
22W572-63
22W573-79
23WilChoV-96
Mensik, Todd
96SouOreTI-3
Mensink, Brian
95BatCliTI-23
Mentzer, Troy
89EveGiaS-21
90SanJosGB-10
90SanJosGCLC-41
90SanJosGP-2013
90SanJosGS-15
Meola, Mike
39WorWidGV-18
Meoli, Rudy
74CarSalLCA-91
74OPC-188
74Top-188
75OPC-533
75Top-533
76IndIndTI-10
76OPC-254
76SSP-196
76Top-254
77IndIndTI-18
78SSP270-270
78Top-489
Mepri, Sal
94PriRedC-18
94PriRedF-3264
Mercado, Brian
90ButCopKSP-15
Mercado, Candy
75AppFoxT-17
76AppFoxT-15
77AppFoxT-15
77BurBeeT-17
Mercado, Gabby
95BelBreTI-7
96OgdRapTI-22
Mercado, Hector
94FloStaLAF-FSL35
94OscAstC-15
94OscAstF-1136
96KisCobB-17
Mercado, Manny
86WatIndP-19
87WatIndP-2
Mercado, Orlando
80LynSaiT-9
81SpoIndT-5
82SalLakCGT-13
83TopTra-71T
84Don-318
84Fle-613
84MarMot-14
84Nes792-314
84Top-314
84TopTif-314
85OklCit8T-1
85Top-58
85TopTif-58
86OklCit8P-12
87AlbDukP-16
87DonOpeD-209
87Top-514
87TopTif-514
88BlaYNPRWL-45
88TacTigC-22
88TacTigP-624
89BlaYNPRWL-46
89PorBeaC-12
89PorBeaP-209
89UppDec-624
90CMC-372
90DodTar-517
90MetColP-41
90MetKah-35
90ProAAAF-279
90TidTidC-21
90TidTidP-548
90TopTra-73T
90TopTraT-73T
90TopTVM-21
91LinDriAAA-563
91MetColP-39
91MetWIZ-265
91TidTidLD-563
91TidTidP-2514
92TidTidF-900
92TidTidS-566
93IowCubF-2136
93RanKee-262
Mercado, Rafael
90SouOreAP-3434
91MadMusC-27
91MadMusP-2140
91MidLeaAP-MWL42
92RenSilSCLC-48
93ColRedC-16
93ColRedF-605
Merced, Orlando
86MacPirP-15
88AugPirP-364
88BlaYNPRWLU-8
89BlaYNPRWL-179
89HarSenP-299
89HarSenS-10
89TriA AAC-15
90BufBisC-18
90BufBisP-380
90BufBisTI-16
90CMC-18
90ProAAAF-495
90TopMag-64
90TriAAAC-15
91Bow-512
91BufBisLD-35
91Cla3-T57
91DonRoo-22
91FleUpd-112
91Lea-489
91LinDriAAA-35
91MajLeaCP-58
91Sco-747
91TopDeb90-107
91TopTra-81T
91TopTraT-81T
91Ult-284
91UppDec-84
92Bow-291
92Cla1-T62
92ClaGam-154
92Don-310
92Fle-561
92FleRooS-3
92Lea-363
92OPC-637
92OPCPre-22
92PanSti-252
92Pin-62
92PirNatI-16
92Sco-153
92Sco100RS-75
92ScoImpP-7
92StaClu-134
92Top-637
92TopGol-637
92TopGolW-637
92TopMic-637
92TriPla-16
92Ult-257
92UppDec-517
93Bow-190
93DiaMar-75
93Don-282
93Fla-115
93Fle-117
93Lea-97
93PacJugC-33
93PacSpa-248
93PacSpaGE-6
93PanSti-281
93Pin-160
93PirHil-8
93PirNatI-18
93Sco-137
93Sel-183
93SP-186
93StaClu-372
93StaCluFDI-372
93StaCluMOP-372
93Stu-184
93Top-378
93TopGol-378
93TopInaM-378
93TopMic-378
93Ult-100
93UppDec-150
93UppDecGold-150
94Bow-546
94ColC-204
94ColChoGS-204
94ColChoSS-204
94Don-334
94DonDiaK-DK19
94DonSpeE-334
94ExtBas-349
94Fin-61
94FinPre-61P
94FinRef-61
94Fla-218
94Fle-614
94FUnPac-83
94Lea-388
94LeaL-142
94OPC-48
94Pac-502
94PacAll-9
94PacSilP-34
94PanSti-237
94Pin-76
94PinArtP-76
94PinMusC-76
94PirQui-16
94Pos-30
94ProMag-110
94Sco-58
94ScoGolR-58
94ScoGolS-2
94Sel-361
94SP-143
94SPDieC-143
94Spo-19
94StaClu-277
94StaCluFDI-277
94StaCluGR-277
94StaCluMOP-277
94Stu-148
94Top-281
94TopGol-281
94TopSpa-281
94TriPla-187
94Ult-557
94UltOnBL-8
94UppDec-182
94UppDecAJ-37
94UppDecAJG-37
94UppDecED-182
95Bow-335
95ColCho-375
95ColChoGS-375
95ColChoSE-179
95ColChoSEGS-179
95ColChoSESS-179
95ColChoSS-375
95D3-57
95DenHol-17
95Don-351
95DonPreP-351
95DonTopotO-320
95Emb-92
95EmbGolI-92
95Fin-204
95FinRef-204
95Fla-404
95Fle-484
95Lea-251
95LeaLim-165
95Pac-348
95PacPri-113
95Pin-60
95PinArtP-60
95PinMusC-60
95PirFil-21
95Sco-44
95ScoGolR-44
95ScoPlaTS-44
95SP-96
95SPCha-81
95SPChaDC-81
95Spo-31
95SpoArtP-31
95SPSil-96
95StaClu-198
95StaCluFDI-198
95StaCluMOP-198
95StaCluSTWS-198
95StaCluVR-104
95Stu-179
95TomPiz-27
95Top-21
95TopCyb-17
95Ult-218
95UltGolM-218
95UppDec-385
95UppDecED-385
95UppDecEDG-385
95UppDecSE-86
95UppDecSEG-86
96Baz-92
96ColCho-265
96ColChoGS-265
96ColChoSS-265
96Don-168
96DonPreP-168
96EmoXL-258
96Fin-B104
96FinRef-B104
96Fla-351
96Fle-527
96FleTif-527
96Lea-35
96LeaLim-62
96LeaLimG-62
96LeaPrePB-35
96LeaPrePG-35
96LeaPrePS-35
96LeaSigA-153
96LeaSigAG-153
96LeaSigAS-153
96MetUni-218
96MetUniP-218
96Pac-170
96PacEstL-EL19
96PacPri-P59
96PacPriG-P59
96PanSti-67
96Pin-71
96ProSta-91
96Sco-423
96SelCer-48
96SelCerAP-48
96SelCerCB-48
96SelCerCR-48
96SelCerMB-48
96SelCerMG-48
96SelCerMR-48
96SP-147
96StaClu-408
96StaCluEPB-408
96StaCluEPG-408
96StaCluEPS-408
96StaCluMOP-408
95StaCluVRMC-104
96Stu-90
96StuPrePB-90
96StuPrePG-90
96StuPrePS-90
96Sum-120
96SumAbo&B-120
96SumArtP-120
96SumFoi-120
96Top-265
96Ult-267
96UltGolM-267
96UppDec-178
96Zen-70
96ZenArtP-70
96ZenMoz-23
97BluJayS-11
97Cir-37
97CirRav-37
97ColCho-496
97Don-77
97Don-284
97DonPreP-77
97DonPreP-284
97DonPrePGold-77
97DonPrePGold-284
97Fin-196
97FinRef-196
97Fle-433
97Fle-577
97FleTif-433
97FleTif-577
97Lea-166
97LeaFraM-166
97LeaFraMDC-166
97MetUni-187
97Pac-400
97PacLigB-400
97PacSil-400
97StaClu-127
97StaCluMOP-127
97Top-278
97Ult-434
97UltGolME-434
97UltPlaME-434
97UppDec-549
Mercedes, Carlos
96BluOriB-19
Mercedes, Feliciano
92BluOriC-9
92BluOriF-2366
92KanCouCC-17
92KanCouCF-101
93FreKeyC-16
93FreKeyF-1034
94FreKeyF-2622
94OriPro-65
Mercedes, Fernando
92BurAstC-2
92BurAstF-539
Mercedes, Guillermo
86MacPirP-14
92GulCoaRSP-19
93ChaRaiC-14
93ChaRaiF-1921
94ChaRanF-2504
94Cla-43
95TulDriTI-14
96KenIndB-15
Mercedes, Hector
89St.CatBJP-2080
90MyrBeaBJP-2783
Mercedes, Henry
89MadMusS-26
89ModA'sC-20
90MadMusP-2272
90MidLeaASGS-16
91CalLeLA-38
91Cla/Bes-154
91ModA'sC-22
91ModA'sP-3091

92DonRoo-78
92ProFS7-131
92TacTigF-2507
92Ult-424
93Don-551
93FleFinE-257
93FleMajLP-B12
93LimRocDWB-131
93Pin-268
93Sco-290
93ScoBoyoS-24
93StaClu-733
93StaCluFDI-733
93StaCluMOP-733
93TacTigF-3035
93Top-602
93TopGol-602
93TopInaM-602
93TopMic-602
94Don-602
94Pac-457
94TacTigF-3179
95OmaRoyTI-21
96OmaRoyB-19
Mercedes, Jose
93Bow-309
93BowBayF-2185
93ClaFS7-55
93LimRocDWB-43
94BreMilB-331
94FleUpd-55
94Ult-376
95Don-250
95DonPreP-250
95Fle-184
95Pac-236
95Top-638
95Ult-297
95UltGolM-297
Mercedes, Juan
91BluOriC-6
91BluOriP-4125
92KanCouCC-16
92KanCouCF-90
92KanCouCTI-22
93HunCubC-20
93HunCubF-3244
Mercedes, Luis
89FreKeyS-16
89Sta-102
90Bes-313
90EasLeaAP-EL44
90HagSunB-12
90HagSunP-1429
90HagSunS-16
90ProAaA-24
90StaFS7-76
91Bow-94
91LinDriAAA-461
91RocRedWLD-461
91RocRedWP-1916
91UppDec-745
92Bow-163
92Cla1-T63
92ClaGam-173
92Don-6
92Fle-16
92Lea-130
92OPC-603
92Pin-248
92PinRoo-1
92PinRool-5
92PinTea2-71
92ProFS7-2
92RocRedWF-1952
92Sco-826
92StaClu-242
92Top-603
92TopDeb91-123
92TopGol-603
92TopGolW-603
92TopMic-603
92TriPla-145
92UppDec-652
93Don-645
93Fle-547
93GiaPos-26
93LimRocDWB-52
93OPC-43
93PacSpa-345
93Pin-376
93ScoBoyoS-4
93Sel-331
93StaClu-391
93StaCluFDI-391
93StaCluMOP-391
93Top-446
93TopGol-446
93TopInaM-446
93TopMic-446
93Ult-496
94GiaUSPC-2D
94GiaUSPC-9C
94StaCluT-24
94StaCluTFDI-24
Mercedes, Manuel
76QuaCitAT-21
Mercer, Mark
78AshTouT-18
79TulDriT-10
80ChaChaT-11
83OklCit8T-13
93RanKee-263
Mercerod, George
85PawRedST-21
Merchant, Andy (James A.)
76OPC-594
76Top-594
Merchant, John
81BatTroT-18
Merchant, Mark
88AugPirP-1576
89AugPirP-496
89CalLeaA-3
89SanBerSB-27
89SanBerSCLC-93
90Bes-277
90CMC-791
90WilBilB-16
90WilBilP-1070
90WilBilS-17
91PenPilC-24
91PenPilP-389
92JacSunF-3721
92JacSunS-366
93ChaLooF-2374
94ChaLooF-1371
95ChaLooTI-14
96NasSouB-16
Mercker, Kent
87DurBulP-12
88CarLeaAS-31
88DurBulS-14
89RicBraBC-17
89RicBraC-5
89RicBraP-835
89RicBraTI-16
89TriAAP-AAA5
90Bow-6
90BowTif-6
90ClaBlu-15
90CMC-657
90Don-31
90Fle-590
90FleCan-590
90RicBraBC-8
90RicBraC-27
90RicBraTI-22
90ScoRoo-72T
90TopDeb89-81
90UppDec-63
91Bow-568
91BraDubP-19
91BraSubS-25
91ClaGam-67
91Don-299
91FleUpd-74
91Lea-41
91OPC-772
91Sco-79
91Sco100RS-58
91StaClu-341
91StaCluMO-30
91Top-772
91TopDesS-772
91TopMic-772
91TopRoo-19
91TopTif-772
91ToyRoo-19
91UltUpd-68
91UppDec-642
92BraLykP-19
92BraLykS-23
92Cla1-T18
92Don-116
92Don-616
92Fle-363
92Fle-700
92OPC-596
92Sco-178
92Sco-787
92StaClu-147
92Top-596
92TopGol-596
92TopGolW-596
92TopMic-596
92Ult-460
92UppDec-472
93BraLykP-20
93BraLykS-25
93Don-2
93Fle-8
93Lea-521
93PacSpa-336
93Pin-418
93StaClu-111
93StaCluB-11
93StaCluFDI-111
93StaCluMOP-111
93Top-144
93TopGol-144
93TopInaM-144
93TopMic-144
93Ult-309
93UppDec-393
93UppDecGold-393
94BraLykP-23
94BraLykS-23
94BraUSPC-3D
94BraUSPC-11S
94ColC-446
94ColChoGS-446
94ColChoSS-446
94Don-203
94ExtBas-211
94Fla-132
94Fle-368
94Lea-410
94Pac-18
94Pin-440
94PinArtP-440
94PinMusC-440
94Sco-126
94ScoGolR-126
94SpoRoo-28
94SpoRooAP-28
94StaClu-360
94StaCluFDI-360
94StaCluGR-360
94StaCluMOP-360
94StaCluT-39
94StaCluTFDI-39
94Top-718
94TopGol-718
94TopSpa-718
94Ult-447
94UppDec-442
94UppDecED-442
95ColCho-163
95ColChoGS-163
95ColChoSS-163
95Don-54
95DonPreP-54
95Fla-328
95Fle-314
95Lea-98
95Pin-436
95PinArtP-436
95PinMusC-436
95Sco-313
95Sco-525
95ScoGolR-313
95ScoGolR-525
95ScoPlaTS-313
95ScoPlaTS-525
95StaClu-304
95StaCluMOP-304
95StaCluSTWS-304
95StaCluVR-160
95Top-202
95TopCyb-115
95Ult-131
95UltGolM-131
95UppDec-291
95UppDecED-291
95UppDecEDG-291
96ColCho-761
96Don-522
96DonPreP-522
96Fla-8
96Fle-302
96FleOri-10
96FleTif-302
96FleUpd-U5
96FleUpdTC-U5
96Pac-5
96Pin-340
96PinFoil-340
96Sco-219
95StaCluVRMC-160
96Top-266
96Ult-307
96UltGolM-307
96UppDec-482U
97Cir-210
97CirRav-210
97Fle-566
97FleTif-566
97Ult-435
97UltGolME-435
97UltPlaME-435
Mercurio, Tony
88TidTidCa-30
Meredith, Ryan
93BriTigF-3645
Meredith, Steve
90SalSpuCLC-136
Merejo, Domingo
87WatPirP-13
88WatPirP-21
89SalBucS-12
90SalBucS-12
Merejo, Jesus
88UtiBluSP-9
89UtiBluSP-16
Merejo, Luis
86SalAngC-92
87QuaCitAP-11
88PalSprACLC-90
88PalSprAP-1437
89MidAngGS-23
89TexLeaAGS-6
90MidAngGS-23
Meridith, Ron
80ColAstT-19
81TucTorT-16
82HawIslT-16
83TucTorT-5
84IowCubT-27
85IowCubT-17
86Don-533
86Fle-374
86IowCubP-18
87OklCit8P-13
87RanMot-16
88LouRedBTI-34
93RanKee-264
Merietta, Lou
79CedRapGT-22
Merigliano, Frank
88UtiBluSP-22
89SouBenWSGS-8
90SarWhiSS-15
91BirBarLD-67
91BirBarP-1453
91LinDriAA-67
92BirBarF-2579
92BirBarS-89
93BirBarF-1188
94VenLinU-146
Merila, Mark
92Min-13
93BazTeaU-15
93TopTra-70T
94SpoIndC-20
94SpoIndF-3333
95IdaFalBTI-22
Merkle, Fred
09ColChiE-192
09PhiCarE-18
09RamT20-79
09SpoNewSM-32
09T206-247
09T206-248
10CouT21-186
10CouT21-305
10DomDisP-83
10E12AmeCDC-25
10RedCroT-53
10RedCroT-224
10SweCapPP-119
11BasBatEU-29
11MecDFT-34
11PloCanE-47
11S74Sil-90
11SpoLifCW-250
11SpoLifM-213
11T205-118
11TurRedT-108
12ColRedB-192
12ColTinT-192
12HasTriFT-30B
12HasTriFT-32
14CraJacE-78
15CraJacE-78
15SpoNewM-116
16BF2FP-81
16ColE13-116
16SpoNewM-118
19W514-74
60NuHi-17
61NuSco-417
69SCFOldT-31
81ConTSN-27
86ConSer1-49
88ConSer4-19
90DodTar-516
94ConTSN-1260
94ConTSNB-1260
94UppDecTAE-17
95ConTSN-1406
Merloni, Lou
94SarRedSC-19
94SarRedSF-1959
95TreThuTI-21
96Bow-322
96TreThuB-22
Merrell, Philip
96BilMusTI-22
Merrick, Brett
95WatIndTI-19
Merrick, Jim
96HelBreTI-31
Merrifield, Bill
85MidAngT-19
86MidAngP-17
87EdmTraP-2074
88OklCit8C-15
88OklCit8P-36
Merrifield, Doug
81SpoIndT-12
82SalLakCGT-1
83SalLakCGT-26
86CalCanP-14
88CalCanC-22
88CalCanP-787
90KnoBluJB-7
Merrill, Durwood
88T/MUmp-30
89T/MUmp-28
90T/MUmp-27
Merrill, Ethan
94UtiBluSC-20
96SarRedSB-23
Merrill, Mike
86DurBulP-18
87DurBulP-17
Merrill, Stump (Carl)
77WesHavYT-16
79WesHavYT-8
80NasSouTI-15
84ColCliP-15
84ColCliT-23
85ColCliP-16
86YanTCM-8
89EasLeaDP-DD44
90CMC-225
90ColCliC-24
90ColCliC-25
90ColCliP-3
90ColCliP-693
90ProAAAF-343
90TopTra-74T
90TopTraT-74T
90YanScoNW-1
91OPC-429
91Top-429
91TopDesS-429
91TopMic-429
91TopTif-429
93ColCliF-1126
93ColCliP-14
93ColCliP-24
94ColCliF-2967
94ColCliP-20
96ColCliB-1
Merriman, Brett
88BurIndP-1795
89MiaMirIS-14

89Sta-182
89WatIndS-14
90PalSprAP-2574
91PalSprAP-2009
92MidAngF-4025
92MidAngOHP-16
92MidAngS-466
93Top-593
93TopGol-593
93TopInaM-593
93TopMic-593
94SalLakBF-813
95Sco-279
95ScoGolR-279
95ScoPlaTS-279

Merriman, Lloyd
49EurSta-90
50Bow-173
51Bow-72
52Bow-78
55Bow-135

Merritt, Bill
98CamPepP-56

Merritt, George
09ColChiE-193A
09ColChiE-193B
09T206-445
11T205-189
12ColRedB-193A
12ColRedB-193B
12ColTinT-193A
12ColTinT-193B

Merritt, Jim
66OPC-97
66Top-97
66TopVen-97
66TwiFaiG-8
67CokCapTw-4
67DexPre-147
67Top-523
68OPC-64
68Top-64
68TopVen-64
69MLBOffS-132
69Top-661
70MLBOffS-32
70Top-616
71BazNumT-7
71BazUnn-25
71Kel-25
71MilDud-54
71MLBOffS-65
71OPC-420
71Top-420
71TopCoi-129
71TopTat-124
72Top-738
74OPC-318
74Top-318
75OPC-83
75Top-83
78TwiFri-38
93RanKee-265

Merritt, Lloyd
58Top-231
59DarFar-11
84SavCarT-21
85SprCarT-10

Merriweather, James
92FayGenC-10
92FayGenF-2176

Mersh, Neil
78TacYanC-54
79WesHavYT-30

Merson, John
52Top-375
53RedSoxTI-20
82Bow195E-263
83TopRep5-375

Mertens, Warren
78OrlTwiT-15

Mertes, Sam
03BreE10-104
11SpoLifCW-251

Merullo, Lenny
43CubTeal-16
44CubTeal-15
77TCMTheWY-84
79DiaGre-107
83TCMPla1945-25

Merullo, Matt
87DayBeaAP-14
88BirBarB-22
88SouLeaAJ-7
89DonRoo-50
89FleUpd-21
90Bes-167
90BirBarB-3
90BirBarDGB-25
90BirBarP-1112
90CMC-819
90Fle-542
90FleCan-542
90Sco-605
90TopDeb89-82
90UppDec-67
91FleUpd-13
91StaClu-382
91WhiSoxK-5
92Don-264
92Fle-90
92OPC-615
92Sco-367
92StaClu-404
92Top-615
92TopGol-615
92TopGolW-615
92TopMic-615
92TriPla-121
92VanCanF-2725
92WhiSoxK-5
94StaCluT-148
94StaCluTFDI-148
96IowCubB-19

Mesa, Audy
90BenBucL-29
91PocPioP-3790
91PocPioSP-24

Mesa, Baltazar
90BakDodCLC-232

Mesa, Ivan
79AppFoxT-12
81GleFalWST-13
82TolMudHT-15

Mesa, Jose
85KinBluJT-8
86VenGulP-14
87KnoBluJP-1494
88Don-601
88RocRedWC-3
88RocRedWP-206
88RocRedWTI-13
89HagSunB-3
89RocRedWP-1636
90HagSunB-28
90HagSunP-1410
90HagSunS-17
90ProAaA-4
91Bow-91
91Don-765
91FleUpd-3
91Lea-166
91OPC-512
91OriCro-297
91StaClu-380
91Top-512
91TopDesS-512
91TopMic-512
91TopTif-512
91UppDec-703
92Don-773
92Fle-17
92Lea-351
92OPC-310
92Pin-496
92Sco-707
92SpolllFK1-485
92StaClu-888
92Top-310
92TopGol-310
92TopGolW-310
92TopMic-310
92Ult-305
93Don-465
93Fla-197
93Fle-596
93IndWUA-20
93Lea-374
93LimRocDWB-62
93PacBeiA-6
93PacSpa-414
93Pin-436
93Sco-424
93Top-696
93TopGol-696
93TopInaM-696
93TopMic-696
93UppDec-798
93UppDecGold-798
94ColC-205
94ColChoGS-205
94ColChoSS-205
94Don-182
94ExtBas-62
94Fin-138
94FinRef-138
94Fla-284
94Fle-113
94Lea-438
94Pac-177
94Pin-337
94PinArtP-337
94PinMusC-337
94Sco-419
94ScoGolR-419
94Top-7
94TopGol-7
94TopSpa-7
94TriPla-116
94Ult-46
95Don-58
95DonPreP-58
95DonTopotO-61
95Fin-267
95FinRef-267
95Fle-140
95Sco-196
95ScoGolR-196
95ScoPlaTS-196
95StaClu-550
95StaCluMOP-550
95StaCluSTDW-I550
95StaCluSTMP-16
95StaCluSTWS-550
95Top-161
95TopCyb-96
96Baz-55
96Cir-35
96CirRav-35
96ColCho-9
96ColCho-121
96ColCho-271
96ColChoGS-9
96ColChoGS-121
96ColChoGS-271
96ColChoSS-9
96ColChoSS-121
96ColChoSS-271
96Don-315
96DonPreP-315
96EmoXL-52
96Fin-B177
96FinRef-B177
96Fla-70
96Fle-91
96FleInd-8
96FleTif-91
96Lea-46
96LeaPrePB-46
96LeaPrePG-46
96LeaPrePS-46
96LeaSigA-154
96LeaSigAG-154
96LeaSigAS-154
96MetUni-49
96MetUniP-49
96Pac-297
96PacEstL-EL20
96PacPriFT-FT10
96PanSti-126
96PanSti-182
96SchDis-14
96Sco-186
96ScoDugC-A101
96ScoDugCAP-A101
96StaClu-4
96StaClu-262
96StaCluEPB-4
96StaCluEPG-4
96StaCluEPS-4
96StaCluMO-27
96StaCluMOP-4
96StaCluMOP-262
96StaCluMOP-TSCA10
96StaCluTA-10
96Stu-70
96StuPrePB-70
96StuPrePG-70
96StuPrePS-70
96Top-231
96Top-276
96TopChr-91
96TopChr-111
96TopChrR-91
96TopChrR-111
96TopGal-19
96TopGalPPI-19
96TopLas-123
96Ult-50
96UltGolM-50
96UppDec-57
96UppDecPHE-H13
96UppDecPreH-H13
97Cir-132
97CirRav-132
97ColCho-92
97Don-136
97DonPreP-136
97DonPrePGold-136
97DonTea-79
97DonTeaSPE-79
97Fin-93
97FinRef-93
97FlaSho-A136
97FlaSho-B136
97FlaSho-C136
97FlaShoLC-136
97FlaShoLC-B136
97FlaShoLC-C136
97FlaShoLCM-A136
97FlaShoLCM-B136
97FlaShoLCM-C136
97Fle-83
97FleTif-83
97Lea-153
97LeaFraM-153
97LeaFraMDC-153
97MetUni-84
97Pac-76
97PacLigB-76
97PacSil-76
97StaClu-230
97StaCluMat-230
97StaCluMOP-230
97Top-153
97TopChr-59
97TopChrR-59
97TopGal-81
97TopGalPPI-81
97Ult-52
97UltGolME-52
97UltPlaME-52

Mesa, Pablo
91PomBlaBPB-9

Mesa, Rafael
94BurIndC-15
94BurIndF-3788
95KinIndTI-19
96KenIndB-16

Mesewicz, Mark
92WelPirF-1320
93AugPirC-13
93AugPirF-1539
94CarMudF-1577
95LynHilTI-16

Mesh, Mike
85PawRedST-8
86PawRedSP-14
87PawRedSP-68
87PawRedST-15
88PawRedSC-18
88PawRedSP-463
89OmaRoyC-16
89OmaRoyP-1730

Meskauskas, John
94BenRocF-3597
95AshTouUTI-27
97BenRocC-17

Mesner, Steve
41CarW75-17
46SunBre-14
47SigOil-65
47SunBre-12

Messaros, Mike
80CedRapRT-20

Messer, Doug
87PocGiaTB-1
89SalSpuCLC-125
89SalSpuP-1817
91RenSilSCLC-11

Messerly, Mike (Michael)
88SouOreAP-1704
89MadMusS-7
90ModA'sC-21
90ModA'sCLC-160
90ModA'sP-2221
91Cla/Bes-44
91ModA'sC-20
91ModA'sP-3097

Messersmith, Andy (John)
69AngJacitB-8
69Top-296
70DayDaiNM-53
70MLBOffS-176
70OPC-72
70OPC-430
70Top-72
70Top-430
70TopPos-9
70TopSup-25
71AngJacitB-7
71MilDud-18
71MLBOffS-351
71OPC-15
71Top-15
71TopCoi-112
72Kel-42
72MilBra-235
72OPC-160
72Top-160
72TopPos-18
73OPC-515
73Top-515
74OPC-267
74Top-267
74TopSta-47
75Hos-79
75HosTwi-79
75Kel-30
75OPC-310
75OPC-440
75SSPPuzB-17
75Top-310
75Top-440
76CraDis-36A
76CraDis-36B
76OPC-199
76OPC-201
76OPC-203
76OPC-305
76SSP-70
76Top-199
76Top-201
76Top-203
76Top-305
77BurCheD-213
77Hos-150
77Kel-54
77MSADis-41
77OPC-155
77RCColC-42
77Top-80
77TopCloS-28
78OPC-79
78RCColC-17
78Top-156
78WifBalD-50
79OPC-139
79Top-278
87DodSmoA-22
88AlaGolAA'TI-5
89DodSmoG-85
90DodTar-518
92DodStaTA-14
92YanWIZ7-113

Messick, J.T.
95ButCopKtl-15

Messier, Mark
91StaCluMO-49

Messier, Tom
84EveGiaC-30A
86FreGiaP-10

Messitt, John
87OldJudN-352

Messner, Jake
96BurIndB-26

Mestek, Barney
75WatDodT-14

Metcalf, Clyde
90HigSchPLS-24

Metcalf, Scott
91PerHeaF-16
92BluOriC-10
92BluOriF-2367
93AlbPolC-17
93AlbPolF-2033

Metcalf, Thomas
64ChatheY-18
64Top-281
64TopVen-281

65ChaTheY-15
92YanWIZ6-84
Metcalfe, Mike
94BakDodC-17
94SigRooDP-63
94SigRooDPS-63
94StaCluDP-39
94StaCluDPFDI-39
95Top-571
95VerBeaDTI-15
96BesAutS-60
96Exc-180
Metheney, Michael
93BatCliC-20
Metheney, Nelson
93BatCliF-3143
94ClePhiC-20
94ClePhiF-2525
95ClePhiF-215
Metheny, Bud
43YanSta-19
77TCMTheWY-55
83TCMPla1944-7
Methven, Marlin
81WatIndT-23
82ChaLooI-12
82WatIndF-18
Metil, Bill
82CedRapRT-18
Metkovich, George
46RedSoxTI-16
47IndTeal-19
47IndVanPP-18
48SigOil-18
49BowPCL-2
49RemBre-18
50RemBre-17
51Bow-274
52Bow-108
52Top-310
53Top-58
54BraJohC-27
55BraGolS-27
79DiaGre-236
83TopRep5-310
91TopArc1-58
Metkovich, John
52Par-89
Metoyer, Tony
86AshTouP-20
87OscAstP-12
89MiaMirIS-13
Metro, Charles
46RemBre-11
70OPC-16
70RoyTeal-22
70Top-16
Metropolitans, New York
94OriofB-40
Mets, Columbia
90ColMetGS-30
90ColMetPPI-7
92ColMetPI-36
92ColMetPI-37
Mets, Hyannis
88CapCodPB-30
Mets, Kingsport
93KinMetC-28
Mets, New York
62GuyPotCP-14
63Top-473
64Top-27
64TopTatI-14
64TopVen-27
65Top-551
66OPC-172
66Top-172
66TopRubI-114
66TopVen-172
67OPC-42
67Top-42
68Top-401
69FleCloS-15
69FleCloS-34
69TopStaA-15
70FleWorS-66
70OPC-1
70Top-1
71FleWorS-67
71OPC-641
71Top-641
71TopTat-16
72OPC-362
72Top-362
73OPC-389
73OPCBTC-16
73Top-389
73TopBluTC-16
74OPC-56
74OPCTC-16
74Top-56
74TopTeaC-16
78Top-356
81MetMagM-1
81MetMagM-2
81MetMagM-3
81MetMagM-4
82MetGal62-24
83FleSta-240
83FleSti-NNO
85MetColP-29
86MetColP-1
87FleGlo-WS8
87FleWaxBC-C1
87FleWorS-8
87MetColP-1
87MetFanC-9
87SpoTeaL-2
88MetColP-12
88MetKah-NNO
88PanSti-475
88RedFolSB-126
89FleWaxBC-C1
89MetColP-1
89MetFanC-NNO
89MetKah-31
90FleWaxBC-C17
90MetColP-1
90MetKah-NNO
90PubSti-629
90RedFolSB-128
90VenSti-530
91MetColP-2
91MetKah-NNO
91PanCanT1-118
91PanCanT1-119
91PanCanT1-130
92MetColP-1
92MetKah-NNO
93MetColP-21
93MetKah-NNO
94ImpProP-23
94Met69T-2
94MetColP-1
94Sco-655
94ScoGolR-655
95PanSti-133
96Met69Y-9
96PanSti-29
Mettler, Bradley
85GreHorT-27
Metts, Carey
89EriOriS-13
Metzger, Butch (Clarence E.)
75HawIsIC-19
76OPC-593
76Top-593
77BurCheD-127
77Car5-14
77CarTeal-14
77Hos-99
77PadSchC-40
77Top-215
78MetDaiPA-17
78Top-431
80RicBraT-13
91MetWIZ-266
Metzger, Curt
86ArkTraP-15
Metzger, Erik
96LowSpiB-19
Metzger, Roger
71AstCok-7
71OPC-404
71Top-404
72OPC-217
72Top-217
73LinPor-82
73OPC-395
73Top-395
74AstFouTIP-4
74OPC-224
74Top-224
74TopSta-34
75Hos-115
75OPC-541
75Top-541
76Hos-67
76OPC-297
76SSP-57
76Top-297
77BurCheD-5
77Hos-20
77OPC-44
77Top-481
78AstBurK-15
78Hos-85
78Top-697
79GiaPol-16
79Top-167
80GiaPol-16
80OPC-164
80Top-311
82AstAstI-1
86AstGreT-3
87AstShoSTw-27
87AstShowSTh-25
Metzler, Alex
29ExhFou-20
94ConTSN-1265
94ConTSNB-1265
Meulens, Hensley
87PriWilYP-1
88AlbYanP-1349
88BasAmeAAB-1
88EasLeaAP-3
89AlbYanB-17
89AlbYanP-337
89AlbYanS-13
89ClaTraO-110
89Don-547
89FleUpd-51
89ScoHot1R-12
89Sta-99
89UppDec-746
90AlbDecGB-23
90ClaBlu-133A
90ClaBlu-133B
90CMC-209
90ColCliC-9
90ColCliP-23
90ColCliP-682
90Fle-449
90FleCan-449
90OPC-83
90ProAAAF-332
90Sco-636
90Sco100RS-53
90Top-83
90TopDeb89-83
90TopTif-83
90TopTVY-54
90TriAllGP-AAA13
90UppDec-546
91Bow-181
91Cla1-T69
91ClaGam-179
91Don-31
91FleUpd-47
91Lea-349
91MajLeaCP-3
91OPC-259
91OPCPre-80
91Sco-828
91Sco100RS-84
91ScoAllF-4
91ScoRoo-39
91StaClu-503
91Stu-98
91Top-259
91TopDesS-259
91TopMic-259
91TopTif-259
91Ult-240
91UppDec-675
92Bow-338
92ColCliF-360
92ColCliP-18
92ColCliS-111
92Don-711
92Fle-238
92OPC-154
92Pin-366
92Sco-89
92Sco100RS-72
92ScoProP-25
92SkyAAAF-51
92StaClu-64
92Top-154
92TopGol-154
92TopGolW-154
92TopMic-154
92TriA AAS-111
92Ult-106
92UppDec-606
92YanWIZ8-119
93ColCliF-1124
93ColCliP-19
93LimRocDWB-139
93Pin-124
93Sco-595
93Top-549
93TopGol-549
93TopInaM-549
93TopMic-549
93Ult-245
Meury, Bill
91Cla/Bes-339
91WatDiaC-18
91WatDiaP-1265
92HigDesMC-4
Meusel, Bob (Robert W.)
20GasAmeMBD-13
20NatCarE-63
20WalMaiW-31
21E121So1-63
21E121So8-60
21Exh-114
21KoBreWSI-40
22E120-68
22W572-64
22W575-80
22WilPatV-19
23W501-35
23W503-19
23W515-21
23WilChoV-98
25Exh-98
26Exh-101
27AmeCarE-39
27Exh-51
27YorCarE-7
28StaPlaCE-47
28W502-7
28Yue-7
31W517-49
77GalGloG-133
81ConTSN-43
86ConSer1-34
87ConSer2-21
87Yan192T-7
88ConSer5-22
91ConTSN-122
92MegRut-159
Meusel, Irish (Emil)
20NatCarE-64
21E121So1-62
21E121So8-59
21KoBreWSI-16
21Nei-55
22E120-188
22W572-65
22W573-80
22W575-81
22WilPatV-20
23MapCriV-17
23W501-36
23W501-114
23W503-18
23W515-21
23WilChoV-97
25Exh-36
26Exh-38
27AmeCarE-34
81ConTSN-42
87ConSer2-22
90DodTar-519
Meyer, Alfred
77St.PetCT-22
Meyer, Allen
86AncGlaPTI-24
Meyer, Basil
88KenTwiP-1404
89VisOakCLC-94
89VisOakP-1445
90CMC-755
90OrlSunRB-17
90OrlSunRP-1079
90OrlSunRS-11
Meyer, Benny
90DodTar-520
Meyer, Bob B.
64Top-488
65OPC-219
65Top-219
70BreMcD-20
70BreMil-16
70Top-667
71MLBOffS-445
71OPC-456
71Top-456
92YanWIZ6-85
94BreMilB-248
Meyer, Bobby
95GreFalDTI-14
96GreFalDB-20
96YakBeaTI-5
Meyer, Brad
88GasRanP-1015
Meyer, Brian
86AubAstP-16
87OscAstP-13
88ColAstB-5
88SouLeaAJ-31
89AstSmo-27
89Bow-319
89BowTif-319
89Don-640
89TucTorC-9
89TucTorJP-17
89TucTorP-189
90CMC-604
90Don-648
90Fle-232
90FleCan-232
90OPC-766
90ProAAAF-192
90Top-766
90TopTif-766
90TucTorC-2
90TucTorP-202
90UppDec-22
91Fle-510
Meyer, Dan
75OPC-620
75Top-620
76Hos-132
76OPC-242
76SSP-365
76Top-242
77Hos-135
77OPC-186
77Top-527
78Hos-97
78Kel-12
78OPC-55
78Top-57
79OPC-363
79Top-683
80OPC-207
80Top-396
81Don-43
81Fle-603
81MarPol-5
81OPC-143
81Top-143
81TopScr-40
81TopSti-125
82Don-176
82Fle-512
82Top-413
82TopTra-70T
83Don-413
83Fle-527
83Top-208
83TopSti-110
84Fle-455
84Nes792-609
84TacTigC-96
84Top-609
84TopTif-609
85A'sMot-23
85NasSouTI-14
86MarGreT-7
89PacSenL-155
89T/MSenL-77
89TopSenL-97
Meyer, David
94OneYanC-14
94OneYanF-3788
94StaCluDP-64
94StaCluDPFDI-64
96TamYanY-18
Meyer, Jack
56Top-269
57Top-162
58Top-186
59Top-269
60Lea-137

60Top-64
60TopVen-64
61Top-111
Meyer, Jay
91HunCubC-14
91HunCubP-3330
92PeoChiC-22
92PeoChiTI-15
Meyer, Joey
86VanCanP-17
87DenZepP-5
87Don-460
88BrePol-23
88Don-36
88DonBasB-239
88DonRoo-38
88Fle-645
88FleGlo-645
88FleUpd-40
88FleUpdG-40
88Lea-36
88ScoRoo-75T
88ScoRooG-75T
88Top-312
88TopTif-312
89Bow-138
89BowTif-138
89BreGar-13
89BrePol-23
89ClaLigB-10
89Don-339
89Fle-191
89FleGlo-191
89OPC-136
89PanSti-363
89Sco-374
89ScoHot1R-93
89ScoYouSI-33
89Spo-135
89Top-136
89TopBig-153
89TopTif-136
89UppDec-403
90OPC-673
90PubSti-498
90Sco-532
90Top-673
90TopTif-673
90VenSti-343
91BufBisLD-36
91BufBisP-547
91LinDriAAA-36
94BreMilB-249
Meyer, Lee
09ColChiE-194
12ColRedB-194
12ColTinT-194
Meyer, Matt
96YakBeaTI-18
Meyer, Paul
91KinMetC-9
91KinMetP-3823
Meyer, Rick
89MarPhiS-21
90MarPhiP-3178
92ClePhiC-21
92ClePhiF-2063
Meyer, Russ
49PhiBul-38
49PhiLumPB-6
51BerRos-D7
51Bow-75
52Bow-220
52Top-339
53BowC-129
54Bow-186
54NewYorJA-11
55Bow-196
55DodGolS-6
56Top-227
59Top-482
79TCM50-194
83TopRep5-339
88FloStaLAS-29
89AlbYanB-27
89AlbYanP-322
90AlbYanB-6
90AlbYanP-1182
90DodTar-521
91LinDriAAA-125
95TopArcBD-65
95TopArcBD-135
Meyer, Scott
79WatA'sT-23
80WesHavWCT-9
81WesHavAT-21
Meyer, Stephen W.
86EriCarP-19
87SprCarB-4
88SprCarB-18
Meyer, Travis
95YakBeaTI-22
Meyer, William
16TanBraE-13
46SpoExcW-6-12
47PM1StaP1-141
49EurSta-167
50PirTeal-14
51Bow-272
52Bow-155
52Top-387
83TopRep5-387
Meyers, Benny
12ImpTobC-28
Meyers, Brian
88AppFoxP-139
Meyers, Chief (John)
08AmeCarE-54
09BriE97-21
09ColChiE-195
09MaxPubP-8
09SpoNewSM-63
09T206-249
09T206-263
09T206-264
10CouT21-187
10CouT21-188
10CouT21-189
10CouT21-190
10DomDisP-84
10E98-23
10JuJuDE-28
10RedCroT-54
10RedCroT-225
10SweCapPP-120
10W555-48
11MecDFT-35
11PloCanE-51
11S74Sil-91
11SpoLifM-215
11T205-119
12ColRedB-195
12ColTinT-195
12HasTriFT-29D
12HasTriFT-48A
12HasTriFT-48C
12HasTriFT-48F
12HasTriFT-48H
12HasTriFT-48J
12HasTriFT-74A
12HasTriFT-74B
12HasTriFT-74E
12HasTriFT-74F
12PhiCarE-21
13NatGamW-31
13PolGroW-20
13TomBarW-29
14B18B-69
14CraJacE-71
14PieStaT-39
14TexTomE-34
14TexTomE-61
15CraJacE-71
15SpoNewM-117
15VicT21-20
16BF2FP-61
16ColE13-117
16FleBreD-64
16SpoNewM-119
23W501-95
90DodTar-522
91ConTSN-171
92ConTSN1N-775
93ConTSN-775
Meyers, Don
90GreFalDSP-17
91YakBeaC-12
91YakBeaP-4251
92BakDodCLC-17
Meyers, George
87BucN28-43
88WG1CarG-34
Meyers, Glenn
86QuaCitAP-23
Meyers, Henry W.
23WilChoV-99
Meyers, Jim
11TurRedT-50
Meyers, Paul
87ShrCapP-2
88ShrCapP-1288
89PhoFirC-22
89PhoFirP-1490
Meyers, Ryan
95TenVolW-7
96StCatSB-20
Meyett, Don
89BelBreIS-17
89BelBreIS-21
Meyhoff, Jason
94EliTwiC-13
94EliTwiF-3726
95ForWayWTI-7
Meyl, Brian
77ModA'sC-20
Meza, Lorenzo (Larry)
91HamRedC-28
91HamRedP-4046
92SprCarC-26
92SprCarF-874
93St.PetCC-19
93St.PetCF-2635
94St.PetCC-18
94St.PetCF-2594
Mezzanotte, Tom
91BriTigC-4
91BriTigP-3607
92ProFS7-70
Miceli, Dan
91EugEmeC-21
91EugEmeP-3726
92AppFoxC-6
92AppFoxF-982
92MemChiF-2415
92ProFS7-77
93Bow-293
93ClaFS7-222
93MemChiF-372
93StaCluRoy-30
94Bow-574
94BufBisF-1832
94FleMajLP-24
94FleUpd-176
94LeaLimR-44
94PirQui-17
94ScoRoo-RT126
94ScoRooGR-RT126
94Sel-378
94SpoRoo-64
94SpoRooAP-64
94Top-224
94TopGol-224
94TopSpa-224
94Ult-258
95Don-444
95DonPreP-444
95DonTopotO-321
95Emo-177
95Fle-485
95Lea-344
95PirFil-22
95Sco-534
95ScoGolR-534
95ScoPlaTS-534
95Top-109
96ColCho-264
96ColChoGS-264
96ColChoSS-264
96Don-114
96DonPreP-114
96EmoXL-259
96Fin-B15
96FinRef-B15
96Fla-352
96Fle-528
96FleTif-528
96MetUni-219
96MetUniP-219
96Pac-176
96PanSti-66
96StaClu-57
96StaCluMOP-57
96Top-322
96TopGal-117
96TopGalPPI-117
96Ult-268
96UltGolM-268
96UppDec-433
97Cir-349
97CirRav-349
97Ult-490
97UltGolME-490
97UltPlaME-490
Micelotta, Mickey (Robert Peter)
54Top-212
94TopArc1-212
94TopArc1G-212
Michael, Bill
75CliPilT-7
Michael, Gene
66PirEasH-45
67Top-428
68Top-299
68TopVen-299
69Top-626
70DayDaiNM-122
70OPC-114
70Top-114
70YanCliDP-7
71MLBOffS-496
71OPC-483
71Top-483
71YanArcO-7
71YanCliDP-4
72Top-713
72Top-714
73LinPor-131
73NewYorN-10
73OPC-265
73SyrChiTI-18
73Top-265
74OPC-299
74SyrChiTI-17
74Top-299
74TopSta-214
75OPC-608
75Top-608
76SSP-369
79ColCliT-7
81Don-500
81TCM60I-384
81Top-670
86CubGat-4
86TopTra-73T
86TopTraT-73T
86YanTCM-18
87CubCan-19
87CubDavB-4
87Top-43
87TopTif-43
90DodTar-523
92YanWIZ6-86
92YanWIZ7-114
94CarLeaA-DJ35
Michael, Jeff
94FreKeyF-2623
94FreKeyC-18
Michael, Matt
89PenPilS-15
Michael, Steve
79MemChiT-2
82ElPasDT-12
84ElPasDT-4
87ElmPio(C-19
88ElmPioC-3
89ElmPioP-7
90WinHavRSS-16
Michaels, Cass
47TipTop-25
48WhiSoxTI-17
49Bow-12
49Lea-13
50Bow-91
51Bow-132
51FisBakL-18
52Bow-36
52DixLid-12
52DixPre-12
52Top-178
53BowC-130
54Bow-150
55Bow-85
79DiaGre-142
83TopRep5-178
Michaels, John
35DiaMatCS3T1-107
Michalak, Chris
93SouOreAC-18
93SouOreAF-4062
94Top-316
94TopGol-316
94TopSpa-316
94WesMicWC-16
94WesMicWF-2293
95ModA'sTI-17
96HunStaTI-18
96ModA'sB-21
Michalak, Tony
87EveGiaC-15
88CliGiaP-710
Michel, Domingo
86VerBeaDP-18
87SanAntDTI-7
88SanAntMB-6
89AlbDukC-22
89AlbDukP-81
90CMC-389
90ProAAAF-389
90TolMudHC-12
90TolMudHP-159
91LinDriAA-392
91LonTigLD-392
91LonTigP-1886
93LimRocDWB-120
Michel, John
82IdaFalAT-19
83MadMusF-19
Micheu, Buddy
89ButCopKSP-25
90GasRanB-8
90GasRanP-2524
90GasRanS-14
Michlovitz, Doug
94HelBreSP-27
Michno, Tim
88WinSpiS-12
Michno, Tom
87NewOriP-8
89ChaKniTI-15
91FloStaLAP-FSL25
91MiaMirC-9
91MiaMirP-405
Mickan, Dan
84NewOriT-5
Mickens, Glenn
90DodTar-1033
Micknich, Steve
95ElmPioTI-17
95ElmPioUTI-17
MiCucci, Mike
94WilCubC-15
94WilCubF-3769
96DayCubB-18
Middaugh, Scott
90SarWhiSS-16
91BirBarLD-68
91BirBarP-1454
91LinDriAA-68
Middlekauff, Craig
89NiaFalRP-17
Middleton, Damon
77CliDodT-18
Miedreich, Kevin
95NewJerCTI-20
Mielke, Gary
88OklCit8C-5
88OklCit8P-35
89OklCit8C-6
89OklCit8P-1528
90Don-679
90FleUpd-125
90OPC-221
90RanMot-17
90Sco-574
90Top-221
90TopTif-221
90UppDec-612
91Fle-293
91OPC-54
91Sco-167
91Top-54
91TopDesS-54
91TopMic-54
91TopTif-54
92GasRanF-2270
93ChaRaiF-1928
93RanKee-266
Mientkiewicz, Doug
95ForMyeMTI-32
96FtMyeMB-20
Mieses, Melanio
91EliTwiP-4297
Mieske, Matt
90SpoIndSP-19
91Bow-694
91CalLeLA-4
91Cla/Bes-8
91ClaGolB-BC3
91HigDesMC-26

91HigDesMP-2409
92Bow-608
92DenZepF-2654
92DenZepS-139
92ProFS7-335
92SkyAAAF-67
92UppDecML-113
93Bow-99
93ExcFS7-192
93FleFinE-229
93NewOrlZF-984
93StaClu-687
93StaCluFDI-687
93StaCluMOP-687
93Top-616
93TopGol-616
93TopInaM-616
93TopMic-616
93TopTra-72T
93Ult-575
93UppDec-704
93UppDecGold-704
94Bow-589
94BreMilB-250
94BrePol-18
94Don-522
94Fin-399
94FinRef-399
94Fla-306
94FlaWavotF-B6
94Fle-183
94FUnPac-160
94LeaLimR-6
94Pin-258
94PinArtP-258
94PinMusC-258
94ScoRoo-RT156
94ScoRooGR-RT156
94Sel-206
94SpoRoo-89
94SpoRooAP-89
94StaClu-126
94StaCluFDI-126
94StaCluGR-126
94StaCluMOP-126
94Top-339
94TopGol-339
94TopSpa-339
95ColCho-180
95ColChoGS-180
95ColChoSE-73
95ColChoSEGS-73
95ColChoSESS-73
95ColChoSS-180
95Don-189
95DonPreP-189
95DonTopotO-99
95Fla-53
95Fle-185
95FleRooS-12
95Lea-89
95Pin-73
95PinArtP-73
95PinMusC-73
95Sco-402
95ScoGolR-402
95ScoPlaTS-402
95Sel-83
95SelArtP-83
95Spo-63
95SpoArtP-63
95StaClu-226
95StaCluFDI-226
95StaCluMOP-226
95StaCluSTWS-226
95StaCluVR-114
95Stu-170
95Top-64
95TopCyb-46
95Ult-67
95UltGolM-67
95UppDec-50
95UppDecED-50
95UppDecEDG-50
95UppDecSE-236
95UppDecSEG-236
96ColCho-193
96ColChoGS-193
96ColChoSS-193
96Don-243
96DonPreP-243
96EmoXL-75
96Fla-104
96Fle-153
96FleTif-153
96LeaSigA-155
96LeaSigAG-155
96LeaSigAS-155
96Pac-352
96Pin-35
96Sco-421
95StaCluVRMC-114
96Ult-368
96UltGolM-368
96UppDec-364
97Cir-211
97CirRav-211
97ColCho-145
97Don-52
97DonPreP-52
97DonPrePGold-52
97Fle-135
97FleTif-135
97Pac-125
97PacLigB-125
97PacSil-125
97Sco-285
97ScoPreS-285
97ScoShoS-285
97ScoShoSAP-285
97Top-168
97Ult-80
97UltGolME-80
97UltPlaME-80
97UppDec-402

Mifune, Hideyuki
91CalLeLA-32
91SalSpuC-4
91SalSpuP-2252

Miggins, Larry
53BowC-142
53CarHunW-13
79TCM50-285

Miggins, Mark
77CocAstT-13
79ChaChaT-10A
79ChaChaT-10B
79ChaChaT-11A
80ColAstT-21
81TucTorT-9
82TucTorT-17
83MiaMarT-26

Miglio, John
81QuaCitCT-21
82WatIndF-16
82WatIndT-8
83WatIndF-11
85WatIndT-8
87ElPasDP-12
87TexLeaAF-20
88DenZepC-4
88DenZepP-1260
89ElPasDGS-10

Mijares, Willie
85EveGiaC-9
86EveGiaPC-17
87CliGiaP-6
88SanJosGCLC-124
88SanJosGP-110

Mikan, George
51Whe-3
52Whe-21A
52Whe-21B

Mikesell, Larry James
82WisRapTF-12

Mikkelsen, Lincoln
90EriSaiS-16
91StoPorC-5
91StoPorP-3029
92StoPorC-9
92StoPorF-33
95HarSenTI-37

Mikkelsen, Pete
64Top-488
65ChaTheY-16
65OPC-177
65Top-177
66PirEasH-19
66Top-248
66TopVen-248
67CokCapPi-5
67PirTeal-13
67Top-425
67TopPirS-15
68Top-516
71DodTic-9
71MLBOffS-107
81TCM60I-431
90DodTar-524
92YanWIZ6-87

Miklos, John
44CubTeal-16
69PilPos-26

Miksis, Eddie
47TipTop-102
49EurSta-42
51Bow-117
52Bow-32
52StaCalL-80A
52StaCalS-92B
52Top-172
53Top-39
54Bow-61
55Bow-181
56Top-285
57Top-350
58Top-121
59RedShiBS-13
59Top-58
59TopVen-58
83TopRep5-172
88RinPosD1-12B
90DodTar-525
91OriCro-298
91TopArc1-39

Mikulik, Joe
86ColAstP-19
87ColAstP-15
88TucTorC-18
88TucTorJP-17
88TucTorP-176
90ColMudB-22
90ColMudP-1360
90ColMudS-16
91JacGenLD-570
91JacGenP-939
91LinDriAA-570
92JacGenF-4007
92TucTorF-499
92TucTorS-614
93TucTorF-3074

Milacki, Bob
86HagSunP-11
87ChaO'sW-30
88RocRedWGCP-16
88TriAAAP-35
89ClaLigB-92
89Don-651
89DonBasB-254
89DonRoo-22
89Fle-649
89FleGlo-649
89FleUpd-6
89OriFreB-18
89PanSti-251
89Sco-651
89Spo-224
89Top-324
89TopTif-324
89UppDec-735
90Don-333
90DonBesA-2
90Fle-182
90FleCan-182
90Lea-402
90OPC-73
90PanSti-6
90PubSti-580
90PubSti-601
90Sco-239
90Sco100RS-68
90ScoYouSI-20
90Top-73
90TopRoo-21
90TopSti-240
90TopTif-73
90ToyRoo-20
90UppDec-635
90VenSti-344
90VenSti-345
91Bow-101
91Don-69
91Fle-483
91HagSunP-2454
91OPC-788
91OriCro-299
91Sco-512
91StaCluMO-10
91Top-788
91TopDesS-788
91TopMic-788
91TopTif-788
91UppDec-328
92Bow-61
92Don-101
92Fle-18
92Lea-262
92OPC-408
92Pin-339
92Sco-314
92Sco-427
92StaClu-331
92Top-408
92TopGol-408
92TopGolW-408
92TopMic-408
92Ult-306
92UppDec-480
93ChaKniF-539
93Don-587
93Fle-548
93Top-192
93TopGol-192
93TopInaM-192
93TopMic-192
94OmaRoyF-1221
95OmaRoyTI-22
96TacRaiB-18

Milan, J. Clyde
08AmeCarE-86
08RosComP-83
09ColChiE-196
09RamT20-80
09SpoNewSM-62
09T206-250
10DomDisP-85
10SweCapPP-62
11SpoLifCW-252
11SpoLifM-129
11T205-120
12ColRedB-196
12ColTinT-196
12HasTriFT-33
12HasTriFT-34
12HasTriFT-58
12SenNatPC-2
12T207-123
13NatGamW-32
13TomBarW-30
14B18B-43
14CraJacE-56
15CraJacE-56
15SpoNewM-118
16BF2FP-49
16ColE13-118
16SpoNewM-120
17HolBreD-68
20GasAmeMBD-20
20NatCarE-65
21E121So1-64
21E121So8-61
21Exh-108
22AmeCarE-46
22E120-112
22W573-81
22W575-82
22WilPatV-34
23W501-15
23WilChoV-100
40PlaBal-130
60SenUniMC-13
77GalGloG-141
93ConTSN-806
20W516-25

Milbourne, Larry
75OPC-512
75Top-512
76SSP-58
78Top-366
79OPC-100
79Top-199
80Top-422
81Don-486
81Fle-611
81Top-583
81TopTra-802
82Don-614
82Fle-42
82Top-669
82TopTra-71T
83Don-411
83Fle-415
83PhiTas-18
83Top-91
83TopTra-72T
84MarMot-10
84Nes792-281
84Top-281
84TopTif-281
84TopTra-79T
84TopTraT-79T
85Fle-493
85Top-754
85TopTif-754
86MarGreT-2
87AstShowSTh-16
89PacSenL-112
89PacSenL-203
90EliSenL-86
91SavCarC-27
91SavCarP-1668
92YanWIZ8-120

Milburn, Adam
96EugEmeB-15

Milburn, Glyn
95D3-PF1

Milchin, Mike
89HamRedS-21
90SprCarDGB-26
90St.PetCS-17
90TopTVCa-56
91ArkTraLD-39
91ArkTraP-1282
91Bow-397
91Cla/Bes-107
91LinDriAA-39
91LouRedP-2910
91LouRedTI-9
92Bow-567
92LouRedS-273
92SkyAAAF-128
92UppDecML-79
93Bow-516
93ClaFS7-80
93LouRedF-211

Milene, Jeff
89EliTwiS-18
90KenTwiB-8
90KenTwiP-2296
90KenTwiS-12

Miles, Chad
94ElmPioF-3469
95ElmPioTI-18
95ElmPioUTI-18
95KanCouCTI-28
96BreCouMB-20
94ElmPioC-13

Miles, Dee (Wilson)
40PlaBal-195
43RedSoxTI-16
93ConTSN-743

Miles, Don
90DodTar-1034

Miles, Eddie
82AppFoxF-20
83GleFalWST-6

Miles, James
69Top-658
70OPC-154
70Top-154
76WauMetT-17

Miles, John
92NegLeaRLI-44

Mileur, Jerome
83NasAngT-25
85NasPirT-29

Miley, Dave
81CedRapRT-9
83WatRedT-10
84WicAerRD-2
87VerRedP-17
89CedRapRB-22
89CedRapRP-927
89CedRapRS-22
90CedRapRB-19
90CedRapRP-2337
91ChaWheP-2902
91SouAtlLAGP-SAL8
92ChaLooS-199
93RedKah-8
95ChaLooTI-28
96IndIndB-2

Miley, Mike (Michael)
75SalLakCC-8
76OPC-387
76SalLakCGC-6
76Top-387
77Top-257
90LSUTigGM-13

Milhaven, McGraw

88NebCor-25
Milholland, Eric
86AppFoxP-15
87DayBeaAP-3
88TamTarS-17
Militello, Sam
90OneYanP-3378
90ProAaA-176
91Bow-693
91CarLeaAP-CAR34
91Cla/Bes-150
91ClaGolB-BC8
91PriWilCC-7
91PriWilCP-1423
92Bow-21
92ColCliF-348
92ColCliP-7
92ColCliS-112
92Don-407
92DonRooP-BC16
92FleUpd-43
92OPC-676
92ProFS7-122
92ScoRoo-82T
92SkyAAAF-52
92Top-676
92TopGol-676
92TopGolW-676
92TopMic-676
92TriA AAS-112
93Bow-243
93ClaGam-65
93ClaGam-NNO
93ColCliF-1109
93ColCliP-9
93Don-371
93Fle-282
93FleRooS-RSB7
93Lea-52
93OPC-127
93Pin-225
93PinTea2-25
93Sco-351
93Sel-315
93SelChaR-8
93StaClu-11
93StaCluFDI-11
93StaCluMOP-11
93StaCluMP-4
93StaCluY-27
93Top-624
93TopGol-624
93TopInaM-624
93TopMic-624
93Toy-72
93ToyMasP-9
93TriPla-75
93Ult-246
93UppDec-383
93UppDecGold-383
94ColCliF-2950
Milius, Dennis
92HamRedC-13
92HamRedF-1589
Miljus, John
23WilChoV-101
28W513-65
90DodTar-526
Mill, Steve
91PocPioP-3778
91PocPioSP-3
Millan, Adan
94BatCliF-3449
95PiePhiF-190
Millan, Bernie
90KinMetB-5
90KinMetS-17
91ColMetPI-17
91ColMetPPI-3
91PitMetC-11
91PitMetP-3430
92St.LucMCB-2
92St.LucMF-1757
93FloStaLAF-40
93St.LucMC-18
94ClaGolF-168
94StoPorC-17
94StoPorF-1702
93StLucMF-2929
Millan, Felix
67OPC-89
67Top-89
68CokCapB-7
68Top-241
68TopVen-241
69MilBra-192
69MLBOffS-115
69OPC-210
69Top-210
69TopFou-10
69TopSta-7
69TopTeaP-2
70MLBOffS-8
70OPC-452
70Top-452
70Top-710
71MilDud-55
71MLBOffS-17
71OPC-81
71Top-81
71TopCoi-5
71TopSup-33
71TopTat-97
72EssCoi-8
72MilBra-236
72Top-540
73LinPor-119
73NewYorN-8
73OPC-407
73Top-407
74Kel-53
74MetJapEB-7
74OPC-132
74Top-132
74TopDecE-26
74TopSta-68
75Hos-111
75MetSSP-16
75OPC-445
75Top-445
76Hos-120
76Kel-9
76MetMSAP-3
76OPC-245
76SSP-536
76Top-245
77BurCheD-138
77Hos-96
77MetDaiPA-16
77OPC-249
77Top-605
78AtlCon-17
78TCM60I-31
78Top-505
79TCMJapPB-52
86BraGreT-2
89T/MSenL-78
89TopSenL-85
91MetWIZ-267
92GulCoaMF-3498
93UppDecS-10
Millan, Jorge
94JohCitCC-22
94JohCitCF-3710
Millar, Kevin
94ActPac-45
94KanCouCC-16
94KanCouCF-170
94KanCouCTI-18
94MidLeaAF-MDW18
95ActPacF-51
95BreCouMF-255
95Exc-197
96PorSeaDB-18
Millares, Jose
91KanCouCC-17
91KanCouCP-2664
91KanCouCTI-13
92FreKeyC-17
92FreKeyF-1813
93ClaFS7-284
93FreKeyC-17
93FreKeyF-1035
94BowBayF-2420
94OriPro-66
95BowBayTI-14
96BowBayB-21
Millay, Gar
84AriWilP-13
86AriWilP-11
87PorChaRP-23
88OklCit8C-13
88OklCit8P-40
88TulDriTI-21
89TulDriGS-18
89TulDriTI-16
90CMC-168
90OklCit8C-18
90OklCit8P-445
90ProAAAF-691
91LinDriAAA-313
91OklCit8LD-313
91OklCit8P-191
Millay, Keith
92MadMusF-1229
Miller, Barry
91CliGiaC-21
91CliGiaP-843
92CalLeaACL-10
92ClaFS7-248
92SanJosGC-9
93ShrCapF-2770
94ShrCapF-1615
95PhoFirTI-23
Miller, Bill
89GreFalDSP-31
89IdaFalBP-2020
89SalDodTI-17
89SanDieSAS-18
90MiaMirIS-18
92CalLeaACL-25
Miller, Bill (William Paul)
47StaPinP2-28
52Top-403
53BowBW-54
53Dor-107
53Top-100
54NewYorJA-53
55Bow-245
55OriEss-17
79TCM50-209
83TopRep5-403
91OriCro-300
91TopArc1-100
Miller, Bing (Edmund)
21Exh-109
21Nei-23
22E120-84
22W573-82
23WilChoV-102
25Exh-109
26Exh-109
28PorandAR-A25
28PorandAR-B25
29PorandAR-65
31Exh-27
31W517-31
33Gou-59
33GouCanV-59
33RitCE-2C
40PlaBal-137
48WhiSoxTI-18
60Fle-39
61Fle-62
75SheGrePG-14
76GrePlaG-14
91ConTSN-192
94ConTSN-1139
94ConTSNB-1139
Miller, Bob (Robert G.)
54Top-241
55Top-9
56Top-263
62RedEnq-23
62Top-572
91MetWIZ-268
94TopArc1-241
94TopArc1G-241
Miller, Bob (Robert J.)
50Bow-227
51Bow-220
52Top-187
55Bow-110
55Top-157
55TopDouH-59
56Top-334
57Top-46
58Top-326
59Top-379
79TCM50-289
83TopRep5-187
Miller, Bob (Robert L.)
60Top-101
60TopVen-101
61Top-314
62MetJayP-8
62SalPlaC-185
62ShiPlaC-185
62Top-293
62TopStal-159
63Top-261
64Top-394
65DodTeal-10
65OPC-98
65Top-98
66Top-208
66TopVen-208
67CokCapD-14
67CokCapDA-14
67Top-461
68Top-534
69Top-403
70OPC-47
70Top-47
71MLBOffS-38
71OPC-542
71Top-542
72OPC-414
72Top-414
73OPC-277
73Top-277
74MetOriEB-10
74OPC-624
74Top-624
75HawIslC-21
77OPC-58
77PadSchC-41
77Top-113
78BluJayP-16
81TCM60I-468
82MetGal62-18
85DomLeaS-111
85GiaMot-27
85GiaPos-22
90DodTar-527
91MetWIZ-269
Miller, Brent
91KanCouCC-18
91KanCouCP-2665
91KanCouCTI-14
92Bow-150
92HagSunF-2563
92HagSunS-264
92SkyAA F-108
93BowBayF-2197
94BowBayF-2421
94OriPro-67
Miller, Brian
95MarPhiTI-16
96BatCliTI-7
Miller, Damian
90EliTwiS-13
92KenTwiC-12
92KenTwiF-608
93FloStaLAF-16
93ForMyeMC-14
93ForMyeMF-2659
94NasXprF-390
Miller, Danny
75QuaCitAT-28
76SeaRaiC-10
94OgdRapF-3735
94OgdRapSP-22
Miller, Darrell
81HolMilT-17
82HolMilT-22
84EdmTraC-109
85Don-644
86AngSmo-18
86Top-524
86TopTif-524
87AngSmo-11
87SpoTeaP-11
87Top-337
87TopTif-337
88Don-551
88EdmTraC-12
88EdmTraP-579
88Fle-498
88FleGlo-498
88Sco-463
88ScoGlo-463
88StaLinAn-14
88Top-679
88TopTif-679
89ColCliC-19
89ColCliP-14
89ColCliP-733
89Sco-499
89Top-68
89TopTif-68
89UppDec-462
90CMC-324
90ProAAAF-462
90RocRedWC-23
90RocRedWP-705
Miller, Dave
79AshTouT-11
87DurBulP-11
88GreBraB-14
89FreKeyS-17
89OklCit8C-7
89OklCit8P-1522
89Sta-103
90HagSunB-24
90HagSunP-1411
90HagSunS-18
96WatIndTI-18
88RicBraBC-20
Miller, David
90CMC-156
90OklCit8C-6
90OklCit8P-431
90ProAAAF-677
92HagSunF-2551
92HagSunS-265
92SkyAA F-109
96Bow-329
96BreCouMB-21
96KenIndB-17
Miller, Doc (Roy)
09MaxPubP-21
10JuJuDE-29
12T207-127
93BelMarC-19
93BelMarF-3219
94RivPilCLC-7
Miller, Dots (John B.)
08AmeCarE-87
09AmeCarE-79
09ColChiE-197
09T206-251
10CouT21-191
10CouT21-306
10DomDisP-86
10E-UOraBSC-17
10E101-34A
10E101-34B
10E102-18A
10E102-18B
10E12AmeCDC-26
10MelMinE-34A
10MelMinE-34B
10NadCarE-37A
10NadCarE-37B
10NadE1-37
10PeoT21-41A
10PeoT21-41B
10PeoT21-41C
10PirAmeCE-8
10PirHerP-9
10PirTipTD-7
10RedCroT-55
10RedCroT-138
10SweCapPP-142
11DiaGumP-20
11MecDFT-26
11S74Sil-113
11SpoLifCW-253
11SpoLifM-256
11T205-121
12ColRedB-197
12ColRedB-198
12ColTinT-197
12ColTinT-198
12HasTriFT-62
12T207-124
14B18B-86A
14B18B-86B
14CraJacE-49
14PieStaT-40
15AmeCarE-30
15CraJacE-49
16SpoNewM-121
Miller, Dyar
75IntLeaAT-2
75OPC-614
75Top-614
76OPC-555
76SSP-379
76Top-555
77Top-77
78AngFamF-25
78SSP270-206
78Top-239
79Top-313
80TidTidT-10
81Top-472
82Fle-534
82LouRedE-18

82Top-178
83LouRedR-4
84LouRedR-4
86LouRedTI-2
89PacSenL-211
89TopSenL-129
90EliSenL-59
91ColIndP-1505
91MetWIZ-270
91OriCro-301
91PacSenL-12
92ColSprSSF-768
93ChaKniF-561
94ChaKniF-910
95LouRedF-293
96LouRedB-3
Miller, Edward Lee
76AshTouT-24
78RicBraT-11
79RicBraT-24
80RicBraT-22
80Top-675
80VenLeaS-120
81BraPol-45
81Top-192
82Don-425
82Fle-441
82Top-451
83PorBeaT-20
85BeaGolGT-13
93RanKee-267
Miller, Edward R.
40PlaBal-56
41PlaBal-1
49Lea-68
49PhiBul-39
83TCMPla1943-27
Miller, Edward S.
36GouWidPPR-D17
39PlaBal-49
Miller, Elmer
21E121So1-65
21E121So8-62
21KoBreWSI-41
22E120-69
22W573-83
22W575-83
23WilChoV-103
Miller, Eric
92JohCitCC-18
92JohCitCF-3116
93SprCarC-19
93SprCarF-1848
94FloStaLAF-FSL43
94St.PetCC-19
94St.PetCF-2585
95Exc-272
Miller, Frank
93RicBraRC-30
Miller, Gary
91St.CatBJC-15
91St.CatBJP-3392
92St.CatBJC-19
92St.CatBJF-3387
Miller, George
87BucN28-90
87OldJudN-353
88AllandGN-4
88AugBecN-18
88GandBCGCE-26
88SpoTimM-18
Miller, Gerry
81BurBeeT-24
82BelBreF-3
Miller, Gregg
90WicStaSGD-43
Miller, Hack (Lawrence H.)
20WalMaiW-32
21Exh-110
21Nei-86
22E120-163
22W573-85
90DodTar-1035
94ConTSN-1054
94ConTSNB-1054
Miller, Jeff
87BelMarL-9
89WauTimGS-23
92BurAstC-3
92BurAstF-540
Miller, Jerrod
94IdaFalBF-3581
94IdaFalBSP-19
Miller, Jerry
86MiaMarP-17
Miller, Jessica
93RicBraRC-30
Miller, Jim
55JetPos-11
77ChaPatT-9
91PriRedC-7
91PriRedP-3509
92PriRedC-8
92PriRedF-3085
Miller, Joey
92EliTwiC-22
92EliTwiF-3695
93ForWayWC-18
93ForWayWF-1983
Miller, John Allen
69Top-641
90DodTar-1036
92YanWIZ6-88
Miller, John E.
63Top-208
65Top-49
66Top-427
67OPC-141
67Top-141
81Ori6F-23
81TCM60I-392
91OriCro-302
Miller, Johnny
74NewYorNTDiS-4
Miller, Joseph
87OldJudN-354
Miller, Keith (Neal Keith)
86PorBeaP-17
86ReaPhiP-17
87MaiGuiP-8
87MaiGuiT-15
88MaiPhiC-20
88MaiPhiP-290
88PhiTas-27
88PhiTas-36
89ScrRedBC-13
89ScrRedBP-716
89Top-268
89TopTif-268
90ProAAAF-314
90ScrRedBC-21
90ScrRedBP-612
90TriAllGP-AAA7
91BufBisLD-37
91BufBisP-553
91LinDriAAA-37
91MetKah-25
92OklCit8F-1923
93OklCit8F-1633
Miller, Keith Alan
85LynMetT-18
86JacMetT-27
87IntLeaAT-18
87IntLeaAT-36
87MetColP-40
87SpoRoo2-50
87TidTidP-10
87TidTidT-16
88Don-562
88DonTeaBM-562
88Fle-144
88FleGlo-144
88MetColP-38
88Sco-639
88ScoGlo-639
88Spo-225
88TidTidCa-11
88TidTidCM-20
88TidTidP-1604
88Top-382
88TopTif-382
89Bow-380
89BowTif-380
89ClaLigB-16
89Don-623
89Fle-45
89FleGlo-45
89MetFanC-25
89MetKah-U2
89Sco-464
89ScoHot1R-62
89ScoYouSI-23
89TidTidC-14
89TidTidP-1948
89Top-557
89TopTif-557
89TriAAP-AAA24
89UppDec-739
90Bow-136
90BowTif-136
90CMC-247
90Don-507
90Lea-462
90MetColP-20
90MetColP-42
90MetFanC-25
90MetKah-25
90OPC-58
90Sco-559
90Top-58
90TopTif-58
90TopTVM-32
90UppDec-190
91Don-248
91Fle-155
91MetColP-40
91MetWIZ-272
91OPC-719
91Sco-318
91StaClu-239
91Top-719
91TopDesS-719
91TopMic-719
91TopTif-719
91Ult-225
91UppDec-196
92Bow-285
92Don-657
92Fle-513
92FleUpd-31
92Lea-459
92OPC-157
92OPCPre-94
92Pin-403
92RoyPol-22
92Sco-462
92ScoRoo-50T
92StaClu-786
92StaCluNC-786
92Stu-189
92Top-157
92TopGol-157
92TopGolW-157
92TopMic-157
92TopTra-73T
92TopTraG-73T
92Ult-375
92UppDec-383
92UppDec-704
93Bow-209
93Don-543
93Fle-244
93Lea-168
93PacSpa-492
93PanSti-109
93Pin-384
93RoyPol-22
93Sco-96
93Sel-54
93StaClu-401
93StaCluFDI-401
93StaCluMOP-401
93StaCluRoy-7
93Top-267
93TopGol-267
93TopInaM-267
93TopMic-267
93Ult-565
93UppDec-302
93UppDecGold-302
94ColC-409
94ColChoGS-409
94ColChoSS-409
94Fle-169
94Pac-297
94Top-454
94TopGol-454
94TopSpa-454
95Top-29
Miller, Ken
75LynRanT-16
Miller, Kenny
86BenPhiC-142
87SpaPhiP-9
Miller, Kevin
80WisRapTT-19
89MetColP-14
90BriTigP-3151
90BriTigS-18
91NiaFalRC-11
91NiaFalRP-3636
92FayGenC-7
92FayGenF-2172
Miller, Killer (Don)
88StoPorCLC-204
88StoPorP-750
89StoPorB-27
89StoPorCLC-175
89StoPorP-397
89StoPorS-24
Miller, Kumandae
95ElmPioTI-19
95ElmPioUTI-19
Miller, Kurt
90ClaDraP-5
90WelPirP-1
91AugPirC-28
91AugPirP-803
91Bow-521
91OPC-491
91Sco-682
91Top-491
91TopDesS-491
91TopMic-491
91TopTif-491
91UppDec-68
92ChaRanC-21
92ClaBluBF-BC5
92ClaFS7-67
92ClaRedB-BC5
92ProFS7-309
92UppDec-70
92UppDecML-42
92UppDecML-58
92UppDecML-166
92UppDecMLPotY-PY19
93Bow-53
93ClaYouG-YG11
93TulDriF-2731
93UppDec-9
93UppDec-20
93UppDecGold-9
93UppDecGold-20
94ActPac-54
94Bow-357
94Bow-478
94Cla-103
94EdmTraF-2874
94Fla-383
94FleUpd-137
94SigRoo-38
94SigRooHP-S7
94SigRooS-38
94TopTra-111T
94UppDec-307
94UppDecED-307
94UppDecML-51
95ChaKniTI-15
95ColCho-298
95ColChoGS-298
95ColChoSS-298
95Pin-161
95PinArtP-161
95PinMusC-161
95Sco-591
95ScoGolR-591
95ScoPlaTS-591
95Sel-193
95SelArtP-193
95Spo-164
95SpoArtP-164
95Top-251
95Ult-381
95UltGolM-381
96ChaKniB-18
97PacPriGotD-GD144
93TulDriTI-18
Miller, Larry Don
59DarFar-12
65Top-349
69Top-323
81TCM60I-373
90DodTar-528
91MetWIZ-271
Miller, Lemmie
83AlbDukT-22
84AlbDukC-150
85AlbDukC-165
90DodTar-1037
Miller, Mark
75AndRanT-3
76AshTouT-17
78QuaCitAT-14
79NaSouTI-16
80CedRapRT-16
80ElPasDT-8
80IndIndTI-18
Miller, Marvin
94UppDecTAE-74
Miller, Michael
87ReaPhiP-25
Miller, Mickey
76BatRouCT-15
Miller, Mike
79SavBraT-25
83ButCopKT-19
86ClePhiP-17
86MemChiSTOS-18
86MemChiTOS-18
86OmaRoyP-15
87LitFalMP-2389
87MemChiB-15
87PitCubP-9
87WinSpiP-20
88ColMetGS-9
88MemChiB-22
88SouAtlLAGS-14
89St.LucMS-17
90JacMetGS-18
Miller, Molly (Charles B.)
09T206-502
98CamPepP-56
Miller, Nancy
76LauIndC-9
Miller, Norm
67Ast-19
67Top-412
68OPC-161
68Top-161
68TopVen-161
69OPC-76
69Top-76
69TopTeaP-6
70Top-619
71MLBOffS-88
71OPC-18
71Top-18
72MilBra-237
72OPC-466
72Top-466
73OPC-637
73Top-637
74OPC-439
74Top-439
87AstSer1-26
87AstShoSO-17
87AstShoSTw-26
Miller, Orlando
89OneYanP-2124
90AshTouP-2757
90CMC-668
90ProAaA-101
90SouAtlLAS-16
91Cla/Bes-377
91JacGenLD-571
91JacGenP-934
91LinDriAA-571
92Bow-555
92ClaFS7-140
92JacGenS-342
92SkyAA F-143
92UppDecML-237
93Bow-588
93ExcFS7-203
93TucTorF-3067
94Bow-146
94Bow-358
94BowBes-B28
94BowBesR-B28
94Cla-109
94ExcFS7-203
94ExtBas-278
94ExtBasMLH-6
94Fla-391
94FlaWavotF-B7
94FleUpd-145
94LeaLimR-71
94SigRoo-11
94SigRooS-11
94Top-158
94TopGol-158
94TopSpa-158
94TucTorF-770
94Ult-508
94UppDecML-208
95AstMot-17
95Bow-436
95BowBes-R84
95BowBesR-R84
95ColCho-19

95ColChoGS-19
95ColChoSE-17
95ColChoSEGS-17
95ColChoSESS-17
95ColChoSS-19
95Don-94
95DonPreP-94
95DonTopotO-258
95Emo-139
95Fin-29
95FinRef-29
95Fla-361
95FleMajLP-9
95FleUpd-142
95Lea-221
95LeaGolR-6
95LinVen-77
95Pac-190
95PacLatD-23
95Pin-137
95PinArtP-137
95PinMusC-137
95Sco-291
95ScoGolR-291
95ScoPlaTS-291
95Sel-192
95SelArtP-192
95SelCer-129
95SelCerMG-129
95Spo-142
95SpoArtP-142
95StaClu-330
95StaCluMOP-330
95StaCluSTWS-330
95Sum-117
95SumNthD-117
95Top-371
95UC3-103
95UC3ArtP-103
95UC3CleS-CS5
95Ult-389
95UltGolM-389
95UppDec-211
95UppDecED-211
95UppDecEDG-211
95UppDecSE-42
95UppDecSEG-42
95Zen-135
96AstMot-9
96ColCho-166
96ColChoGS-166
96ColChoSS-166
96Don-328
96DonPreP-328
96EmoXL-202
96Fla-282
96Fle-416
96FleTif-416
96LeaSigA-156
96LeaSigAG-156
96LeaSigAS-156
96MetUni-179
96MetUniP-179
96Pac-91
96PanSti-64
96Sco-419
96StaClu-48
96StaCluMOP-48
96Top-64
96Ult-212
96UltGolM-212
96UppDec-81
97Cir-13
97CirRav-13
97Don-197
97DonPreP-197
97DonPrePGold-197
97Fle-351
97Fle-615
97FleTif-351
97FleTif-615
97Lea-108
97LeaFraM-108
97LeaFraMDC-108
97MetUni-139
97Pac-322
97PacLigB-322
97PacSil-322
97Pin-12
97PinArtP-12
97PinMusC-12
97Sco-80
97Sco-367
97ScoHobR-367
97ScoPreS-80
97ScoResC-367
97ScoShoS-80
97ScoShoS-367
97ScoShoSAP-80
97ScoShoSAP-367
97StaClu-335
97StaCluMOP-335
97Top-255
97Ult-210
97Ult-531
97UltGolME-210
97UltGolME-531
97UltPlaME-210
97UltPlaME-531
Miller, Otto (Lowell)
12T207-126
14B18B-59
14CraJacE-53
15CraJacE-53
15SpoNewM-119
16BF2FP-62
16ColE13-119
16FleBreD-65
16SpoNewM-122
17HolBreD-69
21E121So1-66
21E121So8-63
22AmeCarE-47
22W575-84
23W501-96
23WilChoV-104
90DodTar-529
Miller, Ox (John Anthony)
46SeaSLP-36
Miller, Pat
90HelBreSP-7
91BelBreC-5
91BelBreP-2100
92StoPorC-18
92StoPorF-34
93St.LucMC-19
Miller, Paul
89SalBucS-13
90CarLeaA-26
90SalBucS-13
91CarMudLD-112
91CarMudP-1083
91LinDriAA-112
92Bow-686
92BufBisBS-13
92BufBisF-319
92DonRoo-79
92Lea-492
92ProFS7-307
92TopDeb91-124
92Ult-555
93PacSpa-249
93Pin-258
93Sco-239
93ScoBoyoS-29
94BufBisF-1833
Miller, Pic (C. Bruce)
75OPC-606
75Top-606
76OPC-367
76PheGiaCr-14
76PhoGiaCa-20
76PhoGiaCC-17
76PhoGiaVNB-16
76SSP-102
76Top-367
82SprCarF-3
Miller, Ralph
77St.PetCT-25
78St.PetCT-18
83St.PetCT-27
Miller, Ralph Darwin
90DodTar-530
Miller, Ralph Joseph
22W573-84
Miller, Randall
77RocRedWM-15
80OPC-351
80Top-680
91OriCro-303
Miller, Ray
83OriPos-16
84OriTeal-17
86Top-381
86TopTif-381
86TwiTeal-31
89BlaYNPRWL-136
89PirVerFJ-31
90PirHomC-22
93PirNatI-19
94PirQui-18
Miller, Rich (Richard)
76DubPacT-23
78TidTidT-14
79JacMetT-18
86LitFalMP-19
87LitFalMP-2409
88TidTidCa-4
88TidTidCM-26
88TidTidP-1585
89TidTidC-25
90CMC-686
90ProAAAF-293
90TidTidC-29
90TidTidP-562
Miller, Rick (Richard A.)
72Top-741
73LinPor-26
74OPC-247
74Top-247
74TopSta-136
75OPC-103
75Top-103
76OPC-302
76RedSoxSM-11
76SSP-416
76Top-302
77Top-566
78AngFamF-26
78SSP270-199
78Top-482
79Top-654
80OPC-27
80Top-48
81Don-294
81Fle-279
81OPC-239
81Top-239
81TopTra-803
82Don-334
82Fle-299
82RedSoxC-11
82RegGloT-7
82Top-717
83Don-82
83Fle-188
83OPC-188
83Top-188
84Don-493
84Fle-403
84Nes792-344
84Top-344
84TopTif-344
85Don-517
85Fle-163
85Top-502
85TopTif-502
86Top-424
86TopTif-424
91ModA'sC-8
92SanJosGC-27
Miller, Roger
88CapCodPPaLP-184
90Bes-120
90CliGiaB-19
90CliGiaP-2553
90MidLeaASGS-43
91SanJosGC-2
91SanJosGP-13
94SanJosGC-17
94SanJosGF-2821
96NewHavRB-17
96NewHavRUSTI-13
Miller, Roger Wesley
74SacSolC-53
75SacSolC-19
77SpoIndC-25
94BreMilB-251
Miller, Roscoe
03BreE10-105
Miller, Russ
90BenBucL-15
Miller, Ryan
94PitMetC-15
94PitMetF-3529
95StLucMTI-22
96StLucMTI-25
Miller, Scott
82QuaCitCT-23
88CapCodPPaLP-87
90MedHatBJB-15
90MyrBeaBJP-2784
91MyrBeaHC-21
91MyrBeaHP-2955
92ClaDraP-66
92DunBluJC-25
92FroRowDP-47
92MedHatBJF-3223
92MedHatBJSP-27
93MedHatBJF-3754
93MedHatBJSP-25
94KnoSmoF-1321
95HagSunF-86
Miller, Shawn
92EliTwiC-1
92EliTwiF-3678
92StaCluD-120
93EliTwiC-15
93EliTwiF-3414
93ForWayWC-19
93ForWayWF-1966
94ForWayWC-15
94ForWayWF-2007
95ForMyeMTI-16
95HelBreTI-14
96OgdRapTI-35
Miller, Steve
86ShrCapP-19
87PhoFirP-26
Miller, Stu
53BowBW-16
53CarHunW-14
53Top-183
54Bow-158
54CarHunW-13
54Top-164
56Top-293
58GiaSFCB-16
58Top-111
59Top-183
59TopVen-183
60Top-378
61GiaJayP-11
61Top-72
62GiaJayP-11
62Jel-143
62Pos-143
62PosCan-143
62SalPlaC-205
62ShiPlaC-205
62Top-155
62TopBuc-60
62TopStal-201
62TopVen-155
63Top-286
64Top-565
65Top-499
66Top-265
66TopVen-265
67CokCapO-7
67Top-345
67TopVen-229
78TCM60I-254
81Ori6F-24
84GiaMot-18
91OriCro-304
91TopArc1-183
94TopArc1-164
94TopArc1G-164
Miller, Ted
86KenTwiP-16
Miller, Terry
92BurIndC-24
92BurIndF-1672
Miller, Todd
85EveGiaC-10
86CliGiaP-13
88CliGiaP-706
91ElmPioC-24
91ElmPioP-3269
92WinHavRSC-24
92WinHavRSF-1773
93LynRedSC-20
93LynRedSF-2516
Miller, Tom
82LynMetT-11
87OmaRoyP-26
Miller, Tony
91AubAstC-2
91AubAstP-4272
Miller, Travis
94SigRooDP-32
94SigRooDPS-32
94StaCluDP-16
94StaCluDPFDI-16
95Bow-48
95ColCho-44
95ColChoGS-44
95ColChoSS-44
95HarCitRCTI-14
95SPML-87
95Top-194
96Bow-143
97Cir-165
97CirRav-165
97Fle-150
97FleTif-150
97UppDec-285
Miller, Trever
91BriTigC-14
91BriTigP-3599
91Cla/Bes-406
91ClaDraP-37
91FroRowDP-7
92BriTigC-7
92BriTigF-1407
92OPC-684
92Pin-579
92ProFS7-72
92StaCluD-121
92Top-684
92TopGol-684
92TopGolW-684
92TopMic-684
93FayGenC-15
93FayGenF-126
94TreThuF-2118
95JacSunTI-21
96TolMudHB-20
Miller, Walt
90DodTar-531
Miller, Ward
12T207-125
14CraJacE-5
15CraJacE-5
Miller, Warren
11SpoLifM-130
Miller, Wayne
75AlbDukC-21
Miller-Jones, Gary
85PawRedST-9
86PawRedSP-15
87PawRedSP-69
87PawRedST-16
88PawRedSC-19
88PawRedSP-459
89PawRedSC-12
89PawRedSP-689
89PawRedSTI-17
Millerick, Edwin
91EriSaiC-20
91EriSaiP-4066
Millette, Joe
89BatCliP-1922
90ClePhiS-16
90FloStaLAS-15
90StaFS7-71
91ClePhiP-1629
91ReaPhiP-1374
92DonRoo-80
92ScrRedBF-2453
92ScrRedBS-491
93ScrRedBF-2549
93ScrRedBTI-19
93StaClu-360
93StaCluFDI-360
93StaCluMOP-360
93Top-531
93TopGol-531
93TopInaM-531
93TopMic-531
94EdmTraF-2879
95ChaKniTI-16
Millhauser, Glenn
80QuaCitCT-19
Milliard, Ralph
94KanCouCC-17
94KanCouCF-171
94KanCouCTI-19
94MidLeaAF-MDW19
95KanCouCLTI-11
95PorSeaDTI-17
96BesAutSA-45
96Bow-379
96ChaKniB-19
96LeaPre-146
96LeaPreP-146
96Zen-110
96ZenArtP-110
97Fle-332

97FleTif-332
97PacPriGotD-GD145
97Sco-288
97ScoPreS-288
97ScoShoS-288
97ScoShoSAP-288
97Ult-199
97UltGolME-199
97UltPlaME-199
97UppDec-279
Millican, Kevin
94HudValRF-3388
95ChaRivTI-14
94HudValRC-13
Millies, Walter
40PlaBal-218
79DiaGre-306
90DodTar-532
Milligan, John
87OldJudN-355
90KalBatN-40
90KalBatN-52
90KalBatN-54
Milligan, John Alexander
35DiaMatCS3T1-111
Milligan, Randy
82LynMetT-15
83LynMetT-7
84JacMetT-25
86JacMetT-26
86TidTidP-20
87IntLeaAT-5
87TidTidP-28
87TidTidT-17
88BlaYNPRWL-122
88DonRoo-32
88FleUpd-113
88FleUpd-115
88FleUpdG-113
88FleUpdG-115
88MetColP-39
88Sco-623
88ScoGlo-623
89Bow-10
89BowTif-10
89FleUpd-7
89OriFreB-15
89TidTidC-13
89TopTra-81T
89TopTraT-81T
89UppDec-559
89UppDec-740
90Bow-257
90BowTif-257
90Don-519
90DonBesA-85
90Fle-183
90FleCan-183
90Lea-92
90OPC-153
90PanSti-1
90Sco-252
90Top-153
90TopBig-263
90TopSti-233
90TopTif-153
90UppDec-663
91Don-542
91Fle-484
91Lea-109
91MetWIZ-273
91OPC-416
91OriCro-305
91PanFreS-240
91PanSti-201
91Sco-86
91Sco100S-43
91SevCoi-A9
91StaClu-80
91Stu-7
91Top-416
91TopDesS-416
91TopMic-416
91TopTif-416
91Ult-20
91UppDec-548
92Don-222
92Fle-19
92OPC-17
92PanSti-65
92Pin-179
92Sco-87
92StaClu-587
92Top-17
92TopGol-17
92TopGolW-17
92TopMic-17
92Ult-8
92UppDec-181
93Don-191
93Fle-170
93FleFinE-16
93Lea-513
93PacSpa-402
93PanSti-71
93Pin-157
93RedKah-14
93Sco-112
93Sel-212
93StaClu-158
93StaCluFDI-158
93StaCluMOP-158
93Stu-105
93Top-678
93TopGol-678
93TopInaM-678
93TopMic-678
93Ult-330
93UppDec-228
93UppDec-622
93UppDecGold-228
93UppDecGold-622
94Don-210
94FleUpd-154
94Lea-343
94Pin-485
94PinArtP-485
94PinMusC-485
94Sco-498
94ScoGolR-498
94ScoRoo-RT28
94ScoRooGR-RT28
95Sco-193
95ScoGolR-193
95ScoPlaTS-193
95Top-226
Milligan, Ricky
93UtiBluSC-15
93UtiBluSF-3547
Milligan, Sean
93RanCucQF-836
Milligan, William J.
09T206-446
11SpoLifCW-254
Milliken, Bob
53ExhCan-44
53Top-221
54Top-177
55Top-111
55TopDouH-117
62KahAtl-14
65CarTeal-17
79TCM50-234
90DodTar-533
91TopArc1-221
94TopArc1-177
94TopArc1G-177
95TopArcBD-52
95TopArcBD-79
95TopArcBD-101
Million, Doug
94BenRocF-3590
94ClaUpdCotC-CC6
94SigRooDP-7
94SigRooDPS-7
94StaCluDP-3
94StaCluDPFDI-3
94TopTra-85T
95ActPacF-57
95Bow-265
95BowBes-B88
95BowBesR-B88
95BowGolF-265
95ColCho-38
95ColChoGS-38
95ColChoSS-38
95Exc-189
95SalAvaTI-22
95ScoDraP-DP13
95SPML-48
95StaClu-109
95StaCluFDI-109
95StaCluMOP-109
95StaCluSTWS-109
95Top-286
95UppDecML-125
95UppDecML-223
96Bow-218
96BowBes-150
96BowBesAR-150
96BowBesR-150
96CarLeaA1B-9
96CarLeaA2B-9
96MauStiHWB-30
96SalAvaB-1
96Top-428
97BenRocC-18
97Top-200
95UppDecMLFS-125
95UppDecMLFS-223
Millner, Tim
80QuaCitCT-3
83MidCubT-9
Mills, Alan
86SalAngC-81
87PriWilYP-7
88PriWilYS-17
89Ft.LauYS-16
90Bow-428
90BowTif-428
90DonRoo-44
90FleUpd-114
90Lea-491
90ScoRoo-89T
90TopTra-75T
90TopTraT-75T
90TopTVY-14
90YanScoNW-29
91Cla1-T64
91ColCliLD-112
91ColCliP-12
91ColCliP-595
91Don-338
91LinDriAAA-112
91OPC-651
91Sco-73
91Sco100RS-62
91StaClu-473
91Top-651
91TopDeb90-108
91TopDesS-651
91TopMic-651
91TopTif-651
91UppDec-222
92Bow-342
92FleUpd-2
92StaClu-871
93Don-691
93Fle-171
93Lea-111
93OPC-195
93PacSpa-346
93Sco-440
93Sel-367
93StaClu-643
93StaCluFDI-643
93StaCluMOP-643
93Top-137
93TopGol-137
93TopInaM-137
93TopMic-137
93Ult-143
93UppDec-312
93UppDecGold-312
93USPlaCR-11C
94ColC-608
94ColChoGS-608
94ColChoSS-608
94Don-214
94Fle-10
94OriPro-68
94OriUSPC-5H
94OriUSPC-11S
94Pac-37
94StaClu-693
94StaCluFDI-693
94StaCluGR-693
94StaCluMOP-693
94StaCluT-277
94StaCluTFDI-277
94Top-324
94TopGol-324
94TopSpa-324
94Ult-5
95Fla-4
95Fle-13
97PacPriGotD-GD11
Mills, Art
47TipTop-37
Mills, Brad
80MemChiT-15
82ExpHygM-12
82ExpPos-22
82Fle-196
82OPC-118
82Top-118
83Don-366
83ExpPos-15
83ExpStu-30
83Fle-288
83OPC-199
83Top-744
83WicAerDS-13
84IndIndTI-9
85TucTorC-75
86IowCubP-19
87WytCubP-30
88ChaWheB-2
89PeoChiTI-30
90CarLeaA-51
90WinSpiTI-29
91CarLeaAP-CAR44
91WinSpiC-12
91WinSpiP-2845
92IowCubF-4065
92IowCubS-224
93ColSprSSF-3101
94ColSprSSF-748
96ColSprSSTI-23
Mills, Buster (Colonel)
48WhiSoxTI-19
54Top-227
79DiaGre-234
90DodTar-534
94TopArc1-227
94TopArc1G-227
Mills, Craig
86GleFalTP-16
87LakTigP-3
Mills, E.L.
87OldJudN-356
Mills, Gil
52Par-59
53ExhCan-55
Mills, Gotay
82LouRedE-19
83ArkTraT-21
84ArkTraT-21
Mills, Jethro
72CedRapCT-5
Mills, Ken
83CliGiaF-19
Mills, Lefty
93ConTSN-966
Mills, Michael
85BeaGolGT-17
86BeaGolGP-19
88WicPilRD-31
89DunBluJS-11
89KnoBluJB-16
89KnoBluJP-1141
89KnoBluJS-23
Mills, Rhadames
81ArkTraT-6
85DomLeaS-157
Mills, Richard Allen
71OPC-512
71Top-512
Mills, Tony
90WicStaSGD-25
Mills, William
80AppFoxT-4
Millwood, Kevin
94DanBraC-27
94DanBraF-3528
94MacBraC-14
94MacBraF-2200
95MacBraTI-19
96DurBulBIB-12
96DurBulBrB-13
Milnar, Al
40PlaBal-202
41PlaBal-33
79DiaGre-290
Milne, Blaine
92HamRedC-4
92HamRedF-1594
94MadHatF-135
Milne, Darren
92BriTigC-25
92BriTigF-1426
93LakTigC-18
94TreThuF-2132
Milne, Pete (William J.)
49EurSta-119
53MotCoo-28
Milner, Brian
78BluJayP-17
81OPC-238
81Top-577
82KnoBluJT-10
82OPC-203
82Top-203
90OneYanP-3392
91GreHorP-3076
92GreHorC-28
92GreHorF-797
93PriWilCC-28
93PriWilCF-674
94GreBatF-492
95GreBatTI-30
97GreBatC-29
Milner, Eddie
79IndIndTI-10
79NaSouTI-17
80IndIndTI-10
81IndIndTI-9
82TopTra-72T
83Don-169
83Fle-597
83FleSta-125
83OPC-363
83RedYea-20
83Top-449
84Don-365
84Fle-474
84Nes792-34
84OPC-34
84RedBor-20
84RedEnq-11
84Top-34
84TopSti-60
84TopTif-34
85Don-428
85Fle-541
85OPC-198
85RedYea-9
85Top-198
85TopMin-198
85TopSti-53
85TopTif-198
86Don-325
86Fle-182
86RedTexG-20
86Top-544
86TopTif-544
87Don-433
87Fle-205
87FleGlo-205
87GiaMot-15
87OPC-253
87Top-253
87TopSti-144
87TopTif-253
87TopTra-78T
87TopTraT-78T
88Fle-90
88FleGlo-90
88RedKah-9
88Sco-548
88ScoGlo-548
88Top-677
88TopTif-677
91PacSenL-25
Milner, John
72Top-741
73LinPor-120
73NewYorN-6
73OPC-4
73Top-4
74MetJapEB-5
74MetJapEB-8
74OPC-234
74Top-234
74TopSta-69
75Hos-15
75HosTwi-15
75MetSSP-1
75OPC-264
75Top-264
76OPC-517
76SSP-547
76Top-517
77MetDaiPA-17
77Top-172
78Top-304
79Top-523
80OPC-38
80Top-71
81Don-377

81Fle-386
81Top-618
82Don-266
82ExpHygM-13
82ExpPos-23
82Fle-197
82OPC-331
82Top-638
83Fle-311
91MetWIZ-274
Milner, Ted
84SavCarT-9
86SanJosBP-13
Miloszewski, Frank
78SalPirT-10
Milstien, David
86ElmPioRSP-12
87WinHavRSP-14
88WinHavRSS-13
89EasLeaDDP-DD23
89NewBriRSP-621
89NewBriRSS-10
90NewBriRSB-5
90NewBriRSP-1327
90NewBriRSS-11
91LinDriAA-466
91NewBriRSLD-466
91NewBriRSP-358
92PawRedSF-931
92PawRedSS-359
92SkyAAAF-163
93PawRedSDD-18
93PawRedSF-2415
93PawRedSTI-16
97DunDonPPS-14
Milton, Eric
97Bow-159
97BowBes-198
97BowBesAR-198
97BowBesR-198
97BowChr-157
97BowChrI-157
97BowChrIR-157
97BowChrR-157
97BowInt-159
97Top-272
Milton, Herb
90AppFoxBS-17
90AppFoxP-2092
91AppFoxC-6
91AppFoxP-1712
Mimbs, Mark
90GreFalDSP-9
91BakDodCLC-12
92AlbDukF-717
92AlbDukS-15
92SkyAAAF-7
92UppDecML-77
94AlbDukF-839
Mimbs, Mike (Michael)
90GreFalDSP-10
91FloStaLAP-FSL40
91VerBeaDC-9
91VerBeaDP-770
92ProFS7-247
92SanAntMF-3972
92SanAntMS-570
92SkyAA F-249
94HarSenF-2087
95Emo-169
95Fin-232
95FinRef-232
95Fla-393
95FleUpd-123
95Phi-20
95PhiMel-16
95StaClu-586
95StaCluMOP-586
95StaCluSTWS-586
95TopTra-19T
96ColCho-254
96ColChoGS-254
96ColChoSS-254
96Don-264
96DonPreP-264
96Fle-504
96FleTif-504
96LeaSigA-157
96LeaSigAG-157
96LeaSigAS-157
96Pac-150
96PhiTeal-22
96Sco-418
96Top-97
96Ult-256
96UltGolM-256
96UppDec-429
Mims, Fred
73CedRapAT-6
74CedRapAT-16
Mims, Gerry
80QuaCitCT-2
Mims, Larry
87MiaMarP-23
88HagSunS-12
89HagSunP-264
89WicStaR-6
89WicUpdR-13
Minarcin, John
78WisRapTT-13
79WisRapTT-10
Minarcin, Rudy
55Top-174
56Top-36
Minaya, Omar
81WauTimT-22
Minaya, Robert
88PulBraP-1767
89SumBraP-1111
Minch, John
87ModA'sC-11
87ModA'sP-7
88HunStaTI-12
Mincher, Don (Donald)
60Top-548
61Top-336
61TwiCloD-17
61TwiPetM-5
62Top-386
63Top-269
63TwiVol-6
64Top-542
65OPC-108
65Top-108
66Top-388
66TwiFaiG-9
67CokCapDA-25
67Top-312
67TopVen-223
68Baz-12
68OPC-75
68Top-75
68TopActS-8A
69MilBra-193
69MLBOffS-96
69PilPos-1
69Top-285
69TopDecl-30
69TopSta-227
69TopSup-33
69TopTeaP-9
70Kel-75
70MilBra-19
70MLBOffS-261
70OPC-185
70Top-185
70TopPos-17
71Kel-27
71MLBOffS-521
71OPC-680
71SenTealW-17
71Top-680
72MilBra-238
72OPC-242
72Top-242
78TCM60I-54
78TwiFri-14
83Pil69G-10
89AngSmo-5
93RanKee-29
Minchey, Nate
88OPC-6
88RocExpLC-25
89RocExpLC-18
90DurBulTI-27
91DurBulUP-5
91MiaMirC-10
91MiaMirP-406
92GreBraS-240
93Bow-331
93PawRedSDD-19
93PawRedSF-2407
93PawRedSTI-17
94Don-484
94FleMajLP-25
94PawRedSDD-13
94PawRedSF-946
94Pin-406
94PinArtP-406
94PinMusC-406
94ScoRoo-RT121
94ScoRooGR-RT121
94SpoRoo-136
94SpoRooAP-136
94Top-716
94TopGol-716
94TopSpa-716
95LouRedF-275
95Pac-41
95Sco-586
95ScoGolR-586
95ScoPlaTS-586
95SigRoo-36
95SigRooSig-36
96PawRedSDD-18
Minchk, Kevin
92SpoIndC-13
92SpoIndF-1303
93WatDiaC-23
93WatDiaF-1777
Mincho, Tom
90MiaMirIS-17
Minear, Clint
91KisDodP-4180
92YakBeaC-8
92YakBeaF-3446
93ButCopKSP-20
Miner, Gary
87BriYouC-17
Miner, J.R.
86BurExpP-16
87BurExpP-1090
87TucTorP-13
Miner, James
82ChaRoyT-1
84MemChiT-16
85TucTorC-72
86TucTorP-14
Miner, Richard
90IBAWorA-36
Minetto, Craig
77ModA'sC-3
80OgdA'sT-3
80Top-494
81Top-316
82RocRedWT-4
83RocRedWT-5
84TucTorC-69
Minford, Mitchell
96CarLeaA2B-23
Mingori, Steve
69Top-339
71OPC-612
71Top-612
72OPC-261
72Top-261
73OPC-532
73Top-532
74OPC-537
74Top-537
75OPC-544
75Top-544
76OPC-541
76SSP-161
76Top-541
77Top-314
78Roy-14
78SSP270-242
78Top-696
79Top-72
80Top-219
86SyrChiP-19
87DunBluJP-935
90MyrBeaBJP-2793
91KnoBluJP-1786
91KnoBluJP-1787
91LinDriAA-375
92KnoBluJF-3008
92KnoBluJS-400
93KnoSmoF-1267
Minici, Jason
95WatIndTI-20
Minick, Jeff
86LakTigP-14
Minier, Pablo
77SpaPhiT-1
Minik, Tim
91BenBucC-8
91BenBucP-3693
92MadMusF-1230
Minissale, Frank
88LitFalMP-29
Minium, Matt
80BatTroT-24
Minker, Al
79WatA'sT-16
80WesHavWCT-1
Minnehan, Dan
87OldJudN-357
Minnema, Dave
86LakTigP-15
Minner, Paul
49EurSta-43
52Bow-211
52Top-127
53BowC-71
53Top-92
54Bow-13
54Top-28
56Top-182
79TCM50-163
83TopRep5-127
90DodTar-535
91TopArc1-92
94TopArc1-28
94TopArc1G-28
Minnich, Bill
92AubAstC-5
92AubAstF-1366
Minnick, Don
80LynSaiT-8
Minnifield, Wallace
89KinMetS-17
90PitMetP-4
Minnis, Billy
91MidLeaAP-MWL28
91QuaCitAC-19
91QuaCitAP-2638
Minor, Blas
89SalBucS-14
90CMC-738
90HarSenP-1189
90HarSenS-11
90StaFS7-29
91BufBisLD-38
91BufBisP-538
91LinDriAAA-38
92BufBisBS-12
92BufBisF-320
92BufBisS-36
92DonRoo-81
92FleUpd-116
92SkyAAAF-15
93Bow-486
93FleFinE-114
93Lea-539
93PacSpa-588
93Pin-283
93PirHil-9
93PirNatl-20
93Sco-304
93SelRoo-71T
93TopTra-82T
93Ult-452
93UppDec-745
93UppDecGold-745
94ColC-206
94ColChoGS-206
94ColChoSS-206
94Don-189
94Fle-615
94Pac-503
94Pin-160
94PinArtP-160
94PinMusC-160
94Sco-211
94ScoGolR-211
94StaClu-465
94StaCluFDI-465
94StaCluGR-465
94StaCluMOP-465
94Top-253
94TopGol-253
94TopSpa-253
94Ult-259
95FleUpd-115
95Top-166
96LeaSigEA-127
96MetKah-23
Minor, Damon
96BelGiaTI-10
Minor, Tom
94NewJerCC-19
94NewJerCF-3417
95Exc-273
Minoso, Minnie (Orestes)
47Exh-160A
47Exh-160B
47PM1StaP1-142
52BerRos-41
52Bow-5
52RedMan-AL15
52StaCalL-73E
52StaCalS-87B
52Top-195
53BowC-36
53NorBreL-18
53Top-66
54Bow-38
54DixLid-10
54RedHeaF-22
54RedMan-AL7
55BigLealS-13
55Bow-25
55DaiQueS-13
55RedMan-AL24
56Top-125
56YelBasP-22
57Top-138
58Top-295
59Ind-12
59Kah-24
59Top-80
59Top-166
59TopVen-80
59TopVen-166
60Top-365
60WhiSoxJP-8
60WhiSoxTS-14
61Baz-7
61Pos-25A
61Pos-25B
61Top-42
61Top-380
61TopStal-125
61WhiSoxTS-11
62CarJayP-9
62Jel-51
62Pos-51
62PosCan-51
62SalPlaC-39A
62SalPlaC-39B
62ShiPlaC-39
62Top-28
62TopBuc-61
62TopStal-188
62TopVen-28
63BasMagM-59
63Top-190
64Top-538
67TopVen-187
76ChiGre-13
77OPC-262
77Top-232
78SSP270-160
79DiaGre-150
79TCM50-286
80MarExh-20
80PacLeg-96
83TopRep5-195
84OCoandSI-2
84WhiSoxTV-24
85WhiSoxC-42
86WhiSoxC-NNO
87SpoRea-23
87WhiSoxC-22
88PacLegI-51
88WhiSoxC-18
89SweBasG-59
89WhiSoxC-30
89WhiSoxK-4
91KelLey-9
91TopArc1-66
92ActPacA-37
92BazQua5A-8
93TedWil-27
93UppDecAH-95
93UppDecAH-153
93UppDecS-6
93UppDecS-22
93UppDecS-28
94TopSpa-L8
94UppDecAH-205
94UppDecAH1-205
95NegLeaL2-5
95UppDecSHoB-14
96IllLot-3
Minoso, Orestes
77AppFoxT-16A
77AppFoxT-16B

Minter, Larry
91PocPioP-3797
91PocPioSP-1
Minter, Matthew
96WatIndTI-19
Minton, Greg
75PhoGiaC-15
75PhoGiaCK-8
76PhoGiaVNB-17
77PhoGiaCC-18
77PhoGiaCP-18
77PhoGiaVNB-18
77Top-489
78PhoGiaC-16
78Top-312
79Top-84
80GiaPol-38
80Top-588
81Don-579
81Fle-449
81OPC-111
81Top-111
81TopSti-238
82Don-348
82Fle-396
82OPC-144
82Top-687
82TopSti-107
83Don-186
83DonActA-10
83Fle-269
83FleSta-126
83FleSti-54
83GiaMot-5
83Kel-46
83OPC-107
83Top-3
83Top-470
83TopFol-4
83TopSti-137
83TopSti-138
83TopSti-299
84Don-187
84Fle-383
84FleSti-69
84GiaMot-8
84GiaPos-17
84Nes792-205
84OPC-205
84Top-205
84TopTif-205
85Don-143
85Fle-617
85GiaMot-8
85GiaPos-23
85OPC-45
85Top-45
85TopSti-167
85TopTif-45
86Don-480
86Fle-549
86GiaMot-8
86Top-310
86Top-516
86TopTif-310
86TopTif-516
87Fle-282
87FleGlo-282
87FleUpd-80
87FleUpdG-80
87GiaMot-9
87OPC-333
87Top-724
87TopTif-724
87TopTra-79T
87TopTraT-79T
88AngSmo-11
88Don-505
88Fle-499
88FleGlo-499
88OPC-129
88Sco-176
88ScoGlo-176
88StaLinAn-15
88Top-129
88TopSti-176
88TopTif-129
89Don-490
89DonBasB-283
89Fle-485
89FleGlo-485
89OPC-306
89Sco-543
89Top-576
89TopTif-576
89UppDec-635
90Don-116
90Fle-140
90FleCan-140
90OPC-421
90PubSti-375
90Sco-48
90Top-421
90TopTif-421
90UppDec-83
90VenSti-346
91Sco-823
Minton, Jesse
87SumBraP-17
Mintz, Alan
80ElmPioRST-42
Mintz, Steve
90YakBeaTI-29
91BakDodCLC-11
92VerBeaDC-25
92VerBeaDF-2871
93NewBriRSF-1215
94ShrCapF-1601
96PhoFirB-20
Minutelli, Gino
86CedRapRT-7
87TamTarP-20
88ChaLooB-16
90ChaLooGS-21
91Bow-677
91LinDriAAA-268
91NasSouLD-268
91NasSouP-2153
91TopDeb90-109
92NasSouF-1831
92NasSouS-287
92Pin-261
92Sco-408
92SkyAAAF-134
92StaClu-452
93GiaMot-27
94TucTorF-758
Minyard, Sam
93ElmPioC-12
93ElmPioF-3819
Miquet, Felix
43ParSpo-88
Mirabella, Geno
91SalLakTP-3208
91SalLakTSP-17
Mirabella, Paul
76AshTouT-3
78TucTorC-10
79ColCliT-26
81Don-151
81OPC-11
81SyrChiTI-14
81Top-382
82Don-629
82OPC-163
82Top-499
83Don-541
83Fle-573
83Top-12
84MarMot-17
85CalCanC-89
85Fle-494
85Top-766
85TopTif-766
86MarMot-13
87DenZepP-9
88DenZepC-5
88DenZepP-1258
89BrePol-27
89Don-654
89Fle-192
89FleGlo-192
89PacSenL-165
89Sco-569
89T/MSenL-79
89Top-192
89TopSenL-51
89TopTif-192
89UppDec-322
90BreMilB-14
90BrePol-27
90EliSenL-27
90PubSti-499
90VenSti-347
91Fle-590
91OriCro-306
91Sco-558
92YanWIZ7-115
93RanKee-268
94BreMilB-252
Mirabelli, Doug
90WicStaSGD-26
93SanJosGC-16
93SanJosGF-14
93StaCluM-40
94ClaGolF-151
94ShrCapF-1610
Mirabito, Tim
86TamTarP-13
87VerRedP-8
Miracle, Miami
89MiaMirIS-22
90MiaMirIS-31
Miran, Tory
92YakBeaC-13
92YakBeaF-3463
93BakDodCLC-20
Miranda, Alex
94SouOreAC-19
94SouOreAF-3631
95WesMicWTI-33
96WesMicWB-14
Miranda, Angel
88BlaYNPRWL-10
88StoPorCLC-180
88StoPorP-749
89BelBreIS-22
89BlaYNPRWL-180
90CalLeaACLC-51
90ProAaA-139
90StoPorB-25
90StoPorCLC-175
90StoPorP-2175
91Bow-53
91ElPasDLD-193
91ElPasDP-2747
91LinDriAA-193
92Bow-63
92DenZepF-2638
92DenZepS-140
92SkyAAAF-68
93FleFinE-230
93SelRoo-72T
94BreMilB-253
94ColC-207
94ColChoGS-207
94ColChoSS-207
94Don-488
94Fle-184
94Pac-335
94Pin-341
94PinArtP-341
94PinMusC-341
94Top-709
94TopGol-709
94TopSpa-709
94Ult-79
94USPlaCR-6S
96Pac-350
96Ult-369
96UltGolM-369
97Pac-126
97PacLigB-126
97PacSil-126
Miranda, Giovanni
90AppFoxBS-18
90AppFoxP-2102
90CMC-723
90EugEmeGS-19
91AppFoxC-19
91AppFoxP-1725
92BasCitRC-18
92SarWhiSF-214
93BirBarF-1199
93SarWhiSF-1378
94PriWilCC-16
94PriWilCF-1929
Miranda, Tony
95SpoIndTI-14
96SpoIndB-17
Miranda, Walter
95KanCouCTI-43
96BreCouMB-22
Miranda, Willie
53Dor-123
53Top-278
54Top-56
55Bow-79
55OriEss-18
55Top-154
56Top-103
56TopPin-2
57Top-151
58Hir-32
58OriJayP-6
58Top-179
59Top-540
91OriCro-307
91TopArc1-278
94TopArc1-56
94TopArc1G-56
Misa, Joe
91SouOreAC-28
91SouOreAP-3839
92RenSilSCLC-57
Miscik, Bob
82BufBisT-2
84HawIslC-136
85HawIslC-239
86HawIslP-17
87EdmTraP-2064
88EdmTraC-15
88EdmTraP-577
90FreKeyTI-3
91KanCouCC-26
91KanCouCP-2674
91KanCouCTI-26
92FreKeyF-1822
93RocRedWF-257
94RocRedWF-1013
94RocRedWTI-15
95BowBayTI-10
Miscik, Dennis
77CocAstT-14
80TucTorT-13
81OklCit8T-11
Miskolczi, Levi
96BelGiaTI-9
Missions, San Jose
77SanJosMC-1
89SanAntMB-28
Misuraca, Mike
89EliTwiS-19
89KenTwiP-1071
89KenTwiS-15
89Sta-148
90Bes-272
90KenTwiB-21
90KenTwiP-2290
90KenTwiS-13
91VisOakC-5
91VisOakP-1739
92Ft.MyeMCB-18
92Ft.MyeMF-2742
93NasXprF-400
94NasXprF-382
Mitchell, Alvin
94UtiBluSC-21
94UtiBluSF-3818
95MicBatCTI-17
Mitchell, Bill
76BatTroTI-14
Mitchell, Bobby (Robert Van)
79AlbDukT-18
80AlbDukT-20
81AlbDukT-22
81PorBeaT-18
82Fle-14
82PorBeaT-15
82TolMudHT-28
82TwiPos-21
83Fle-620
83Top-647
83TopSti-91
83TwiTeal-7
84Fle-571
84Nes792-307
84PorBeaC-202
84TolMudHT-10
84Top-307
84TopTif-307
85NasSouTI-15
90DodTar-536
Mitchell, Bobby (Robert Vance)
71OPC-111
71Top-111
74OPC-497
74Top-497
75OPC-468
75Top-468
76OPC-479
76SSP-242
76Top-479
79HawIslC-12
79HawIslT-1
79TCMJapPB-41
80HawIslT-10
92YanWIZ7-116
94BreMilB-254
Mitchell, Charlie
84PawRedST-1
85Don-40
85IntLeaAT-18
85PawRedST-20
86TolMudHP-17
87AllandGN-17
88GooN16-27
88NasSouTI-17
89NasSouC-1
89NasSouP-1273
89NasSouTI-16
90CMC-131
90NasSouC-6
90NasSouP-229
90ProAAAF-541
91LinDriAAA-260
91NasSouLD-260
91NasSouP-2154
Mitchell, Chic
94MarPhiF-3289
Mitchell, Clarence
16ColE13-120
22E120-144
22W573-86
27YorCarE-15
28W502-15
28Yue-15
90DodTar-537
91ConTSN-202
Mitchell, Courtney
94MarPhiC-13
95BatCliTI-24
96BatCliTI-16
Mitchell, Craig
75TucTorC-14
75TucTorTI-12
76OPC-591
76Top-591
76TucTorCa-15
76TusTorCr-32
76VenLeaS-166
77SanJosMC-15
77Top-491
78Top-711
79OgdA'sT-5
79OgdA'sT-21
Mitchell, David
88MisStaB-21
89MisStaB-26
90MisStaB-27
Mitchell, Dean
96YakBeaTI-14
Mitchell, Donovan
92AubAstC-6
92AubAstF-1362
94ExcFS7-204
94OscAstC-16
94OscAstF-1145
95MidLeaA-33
95QuaCitRBTI-15
96JacGenB-19
Mitchell, Fred F.
03BreE10-106
09AmeCarE-81
09T206-447
11SpoLifCW-255
12ImpTobC-47
19W514-96
23WilChoV-105
90DodTar-539
Mitchell, Glenn
88IdaFalBP-1837
88SumBraP-408
89SumBraP-1116
92QuaCitRBC-11
92QuaCitRBF-805
Mitchell, Howie
78PhoGiaC-17
Mitchell, J.W.
79QuaCitCT-10
Mitchell, Jackie
88ChaLooTI-23
Mitchell, Joe
77NewCoPT-22
Mitchell, Joe (Joseph)
85BelBreT-3
86StoPorP-15
87ElPasDP-2

88ElPasDB-25
89DenZepC-20
89DenZepP-43
90CMC-37
90DenZepC-12
90DenZepP-633
90ProAAAF-658
Mitchell, John
93NegLeaRL2-27
Mitchell, John Kyle
83BelBreF-5
86TidTidP-21
87DonRoo-37
87FleUpd-81
87FleUpdG-81
87IdaFalBP-24
87TidTidP-20
87TidTidT-7
87TopTra-80T
87TopTraT-80T
88BurBraP-28
88Fle-145
88FleGlo-145
88MetColP-40
88Sco-249
88ScoGlo-249
88TidTidCa-23
88TidTidCM-8
88TidTidP-1577
88Top-207
88TopTif-207
89MetColP-44
89TidTidC-4
89TidTidP-1970
90CMC-322
90ProAAAF-457
90RocRedWC-21
90RocRedWP-700
91CalCanLD-67
91CalCanP-513
91Don-710
91Fle-485
91LinDriAAA-67
91MetWIZ-275
91OPC-708
91OriCro-308
91Sco-569
91Top-708
91TopDesS-708
91TopMic-708
91TopTif-708
86STaoftFt-34
Mitchell, Johnny
21KoBreWSI-42
22W575-85
90DodTar-540
93WelPirC-14
93WelPirF-3374
Mitchell, Jorge
87JamExpP-2548
88JamExpP-1916
93LinVenB-274
94VenLinU-156
Mitchell, Keith
88SumBraP-390
89BurBraP-1609
89BurBraS-15
90CarLeaA-29
90DurBulTI-2
91Bow-575
91BraSubS-26
91Cla/Bes-224
91Cla3-T58
91GreBraC-21
91GreBraLD-212
91GreBraP-3016
91LinDriAA-212
91RicBraBC-33
91UppDecFE-56F
92Bow-62
92Don-508
92Fle-364
92OPC-542
92Pin-258
92PinRool-8
92ProFS7-182
92RicBraBB-10
92RicBraF-387
92RicBraRC-11
92RicBraS-433
92Sco-748
92SkyAAAF-198
92StaClu-551
92Top-542
92TopDeb91-125
92TopGol-542
92TopGolW-542
92TopMic-542
92UppDec-80
92UppDec-454
92UppDecML-185
93RicBraBB-3
93RicBraF-198
93RicBraP-18
93RicBraRC-18
93RicBraRC-20
94FleUpd-84
94MarMot-19
94Pin-524
94PinArtP-524
94PinMusC-524
94ScoRoo-RT149
94ScoRooGR-RT149
94Sel-202
94SpoRoo-134
94SpoRooAP-134
94TopTra-51T
94Ult-423
95Pin-24
95PinArtP-24
95PinMusC-24
95Sco-410
95ScoGolR-410
95ScoPlaTS-410
96IndIndB-15
97RicBraBC-1
Mitchell, Kelvin
95EveAqaTI-13
Mitchell, Kendrick
95BakBlaTI-18
96VerBeaDB-20
Mitchell, Kevin
82LynMetT-6
84OCoandSI-205
84TidTidT-23
85IntLeaAT-4
85MetTCM-27
85TidTidT-18
86DonRoo-17
86FleUpd-76
86MetTCM-21
86MetWorSC-28
86SpoRoo-49
86TopTra-74T
86TopTraT-74T
87Don-599
87DonOpeD-145
87Fle-17
87FleGlo-17
87FleRecS-21
87FleUpd-82
87FleUpdG-82
87Lea-170
87MetColP-41
87OPC-307
87PadBohHB-7
87Spo-144
87SpoTeaP-16
87Top-653
87TopGloS-50
87TopTif-653
87TopTra-81T
87TopTraT-81T
87ToyRoo-21
88Don-66
88Fle-92
88FleGlo-92
88FleHotS-27
88FleStiWBC-S5
88GiaMot-3
88Lea-87
88OPC-387
88PanSti-424
88PanSti-448
88Sco-481
88ScoGlo-481
88StaLinG-13
88Top-497
88TopBig-57
88TopSti-88
88TopTif-497
88TopUKM-48
88TopUKMT-48
89Bow-474
89BowTif-474
89ClaLigB-31
89ClaTraP-198
89ColPosM-1
89ColPosM-2
89ColPosM-3
89ColPosM-4
89ColPosM-5
89ColPosM-6
89ColPosM-7
89ColPosM-8
89Don-485
89DonBasB-281
89Fle-336
89FleGlo-336
89GiaMot-3
89OPC-189
89PanSti-216
89Sco-39
89ScoSco-12
89ScoYouS2-38
89Spo-142
89SpoIllFKI-112
89StaMit-1
89StaMit-2
89StaMit-3
89StaMit-4
89StaMit-5
89StaMit-6
89StaMit-7
89StaMit-8
89StaMit-9
89StaMit-10
89StaMit-11
89StaMit/C-1
89StaMit/C-2
89StaMit/C-4
89StaMit/C-6
89StaMit/C-8
89StaMit/C-10
89Top-189
89TopAwaW-2
89TopBasT-159
89TopBig-129
89TopSti-84
89TopTif-189
89TVSpoM-51
89UppDec-163
89UppDecS-1
89UppDecS-3
90Baz-1
90Bow-232
90BowIns-6
90BowInsT-6
90BowTif-232
90BowTif-A6
90ClaBlu-64
90ClaBlu-150A
90ClaBlu-150B
90Col-16
90Don-11
90Don-98
90Don-715A
90Don-715B
90DonBesN-85
90DOnBonM-BC11
90DonLeaS-2
90DonPre-6
90DonSupD-11
90Fle-65
90Fle-637
90FleAll-6
90FleAwaW-23
90FleBasA-27
90FleBasM-26
90FleCan-65
90FleCan-637
90FleLeaL-26
90FleWaxBC-C21
90FleWorS-2
90GiaMot-5
90GiaSmo-15
90Hot50PS-27
90K-M-6
90KinDis-2
90Lea-120
90MLBBasB-24
90MSAHolD-9
90MSAIceTD-6
90OPC-401
90OPC-500
90PanSti-208
90PanSti-214
90PanSti-361
90Pos-15
90PubSti-77
90PubSti-617
90RedFolSB-64
90Sco-343
90Sco100S-50
90Spo-1
90StaMit-1
90StaMit-2
90StaMit-4
90StaMit-6
90StaMit-8
90StaMit-10
90SunSee-1
90Top-401
90Top-500
90TopBig-137
90TopCoi-33
90TopDou-47
90TopGaloC-5
90TopGloA-6
90TopGloS-21
90TopHeaU-15
90TopHilHM-5
90TopMag-7
90TopMinL-86
90TopSti-79
90TopSti-148
90TopStiB-17
90TopTif-401
90TopTif-500
90TopTVA-40
90UppDec-40
90UppDec-117
90USPlaCA-12H
90VenSti-348
90VenSti-349
90WonBreS-7
90Woo-2
90Woo-32
91BasBesHRK-14
91Bow-636
91CadEllD-39
91Cla1-T10
91Cla3-T59
91ClaGam-129
91Col-6
91Don-255
91Don-407
91Don-438
91Fle-267
91GiaActIS-2
91GiaMot-5
91GiaPacGaE-1
91GiaSFE-11
91JimDea-13
91Lea-85
91MajLeaCP-64
91MetWIZ-276
91MooSna-23
91MSAHolD-4
91OPC-40
91OPCPre-81
91PanCanT1-11
91PanCanT1-35
91PanFreS-71
91PanFreS-162
91PanSti-71
91Pos-24
91RedFolS-66
91RedFolS-123
91Sco-406
91Sco-451
91Sco100S-98
91SevCoi-NC10
91SimandSMLBL-30
91StaClu-250
91StaPinB-32
91Stu-257
91Top-40
91TopCraJI-30
91TopDesS-40
91TopGloA-17
91TopMic-40
91TopSta-27
91TopTif-40
91TopTriH-N11
91Ult-326
91UppDec-247
92Bow-276
92Cla1-T64
92Cla2-T91
92ClaGam-165
92Don-583
92Fle-644
92FleUpd-56
92Hig5-128
92Lea-185
92MarMot-4
92OPC-180
92OPCPre-97
92PanSti-218
92Pin-393
92Sco-640
92Sco100S-93
92ScoRoo-18T
92SpoStaCC-33
92StaClu-215
92StaClu-765
92StaCluECN-765
92Stu-237
92Top-180
92TopGol-180
92TopGolW-180
92TopKid-59
92TopMic-180
92TopTra-74T
92TopTraG-74T
92Ult-434
92UppDec-80
92UppDec-266
92UppDec-735
93Bow-386
93DiaMar-76
93Don-157
93Fin-136
93FinRef-136
93Fla-28
93Fle-396
93FleFinE-17
93FunPac-171
93Lea-321
93OPC-252
93PacSpa-403
93PanSti-296
93Pin-551
93PinHomRC-23
93PinSlu-21
93RedKah-15
93Sco-407
93Sel-108
93SelRoo-29T
93SP-210
93StaClu-694
93StaCluFDI-694
93StaCluMOP-694
93Stu-162
93Top-217
93TopGol-217
93TopInaM-217
93TopMic-217
93TopTra-112T
93Ult-331
93UppDec-55
93UppDec-213
93UppDec-646
93UppDecGold-55
93UppDecGold-213
93UppDecGold-646
94Bow-514
94BowBes-R33
94BowBesR-R33
94ColC-470
94ColChoGS-470
94ColChoSS-470
94Don-377
94DonSpeE-377
94ExtBas-234
94Fin-323
94FinRef-323
94Fla-368
94Fle-416
94Lea-370
94LeaL-96
94OPC-29
94Pac-152
94PanSti-164
94Pin-70
94PinArtP-70
94PinMusC-70
94ProMag-35
94RedKah-19
94Sco-24
94ScoGolR-24
94Sel-112
94SP-160
94SPDieC-160
94Spo-126
94StaClu-422
94StaCluFDI-422
94StaCluGR-422
94StaCluMOP-422

94Stu-169
94Top-335
94TopGol-335
94TopSpa-335
94TriPla-215
94Ult-173
94UppDec-58
94UppDecED-58
95Baz-7
95ColCho-435
95ColChoSE-203
95ColChoSEGS-203
95ColChoSESS-203
95Don-469
95DonBomS-6
95DonPreP-469
95Fin-146
95FinRef-146
95Fle-441
95FleLumC-8
95FleTeaL-17
95Pac-109
95Sco-336
95ScoGolR-336
95ScoHaloG-HG70
95ScoPlaTS-336
95StaClu-430
95StaCluMO-32
95StaCluMOP-430
95StaCluMOP-RL17
95StaCluRL-RL17
95StaCluSTWS-430
95StaCluVR-226
95Top-568
95TopCyb-344
95TopLeaL-LL2
95UppDec-169
95UppDecED-169
95UppDecEDG-169
95USPlaCMLA-3D
95USPlaCMLA-5C
96Fin-S293
96FinRef-S293
96FleRedS-9
96FleUpd-U15
96FleUpdTC-U15
96SP-42
95StaCluVRMC-226
96Sum-57
96SumAbo&B-57
96SumArtP-57
96SumFoi-57
96Ult-317
96UltGolM-317
96UppDec-484U
97ColCho-313
97Fle-297
97FleTif-297
97Lea-315
97LeaFraM-315
97LeaFraMDC-315
97Pin-33
97PinArtP-33
97PinMusC-33
97Sco-296
97Sco-366
97ScoHobR-366
97ScoPreS-296
97ScoResC-366
97ScoShoS-296
97ScoShoS-366
97ScoShoSAP-296
97ScoShoSAP-366
97Ult-378
97UltGolME-378
97UltPlaME-378

Mitchell, L. Dale
46SpoExcW-7-12
47Exh-161
47IndTeal-20
47IndVanPP-19
48IndTeal-22
49Bow-43
49IndTeal-18
49IndVisEI-12
49Lea-165
50Bow-130
50IndNumN-16
50IndTeal-17
51Bow-5
51TopRedB-13
52Bow-239
52IndNumN-15
52StaCalL-74F
52StaCalS-88C
52TipTop-26
52Top-92
53BowC-119
53IndPenCBP-21
53RedMan-AL9
53Top-26
54Bow-148
54DanDee-18
55Bow-314
55IndGolS-26
56Top-268
59OklTodML-7
79TCM50-140
83ASASpa-3
83TopRep5-92
85TCMPla1-15
90DodTar-538
91TopArc1-26

Mitchell, Larry
92FroRowDP-22
92MarPhiC-1
92MarPhiF-3053
93SpaPhiC-18
93SpaPhiF-1053
93StaCluM-39
94Bow-664
94ReaPhiF-2059
95ReaPhiELC-29
95ReaPhiTI-37
96ReaPhiB-9

Mitchell, Mark
87OneYanP-22
88Ft.LauYS-15

Mitchell, Michael F.
08RosComP-120
09AmeCarE-80
09ColChiE-199A
09ColChiE-199B
09RamT20-81
09T206-252
10CouT21-47
10CouT21-192
10DomDisP-87
10RedCroT-139
10RedCroT-226
10SweCapPP-104
11L1L-118
11S74Sil-78
11S81LarS-93
11SpoLifCW-256
11SpoLifM-199
11T205-122
11TurRedT-24
12ColRedB-199A
12ColRedB-199B
12ColTinT-199A
12ColTinT-199B
12HasTriFT-15A
12T207-128
14PieStaT-41

Mitchell, Mike
94OneYanF-3802
95TamYanYI-19

Mitchell, Parris
90IBAWorA-20
90IBAWorA-46
91PerHeaF-13

Mitchell, Paul
76OPC-393
76Top-393
77SanJosMC-25
77Top-53
78Top-558
79OPC-118
79Top-233
80Top-131
81Don-205
81Top-449
91OriCro-309
94BreMilB-255

Mitchell, Rivers
94BriTigC-19
94BriTigF-3520

Mitchell, Robert
91MarPhiC-20
91MarPhiP-3451
92MarPhiC-12
92MarPhiF-3054
93SpaPhiC-19
93SpaPhiF-1054

Mitchell, Ron
75ShrCapT-11
76ShrCapT-21
77ColCliT-12
78ColCliT-16
79PorBeaT-8
80BufBisT-2

Mitchell, Roy (Albert)
09ColChiE-201
12ColRedB-200
12ColRedB-201
12ColTinT-201
20RedWorCP-12

Mitchell, Scot
82MadMusF-11

Mitchell, Scott
88MisStaB-22
89MisStaB-27
90MisStaB-37
96DelShoB-23

Mitchell, Thomas
90EriSaiS-17
91RenSilSCLC-14

Mitchell, Tony (Antonio)
91WelPirC-5
91WelPirP-3587
92AugPirC-13
92AugPirF-252
92ClaFS7-18
93Bow-121
93ClaFS7-223
93ExcFS7-93
93KinIndC-19
93KinIndF-2262
93KinIndTI-19
93SouAtlLAPI-25
94CanIndF-3132
94Cla-195
95Exc-43
95JacGenTI-17
96JacSunB-20
96SigRooOJ-21
96SigRooOJS-21

Mitchell, Wes
80WatIndT-34

Mitchell, William
12T207-129
14B18B-6A
14B18B-6B
15CraJacE-62
15SpoNewM-120
16SpoNewM-123

Mitchelson, Mark
91Cla/Bes-168
91ElmPioC-25
91ElmPioP-3270
91WinHavRSC-4
91WinHavRSP-484
92WinHavRSC-25

Mitchem, Shannan
95ColSilB-19
96ColSilB-19

Mitchener, Mike
89SouBenWSGS-14
90Bes-131
90SouBenWSB-17
90SouBenWSGS-11

Mitta, Chris
88PulBraP-1763

Mittauer, Casey
94OneYanC-15
94OneYanF-3789
95GreBatTI-18
96TamYanY-19

Mitterwald, George
68Top-301
68TopVen-301
69Top-491A
69Top-491B
70OPC-118
70Top-118
71MLBOffS-467
71OPC-189
71Top-189
72OPC-301
72OPC-302
72Top-301
72Top-302
74OPC-249
74Top-249
74TopSta-209
74TopTra-249T
75OPC-411
75Top-411
76OPC-506
76SSP-318
76Top-506
77CubJewT-9
77Top-124
78SanJosMMC-20
78Top-688
84ModA'sC-23
85ModA'sC-26
86OrlTwiP-12
87OrlTwiP-9

Mix, Derek
93SpoIndC-15
93SpoIndF-3590
94SpoIndC-21
94SpoIndF-3322

Mix, Greg
93ElmPioC-13
93ElmPioF-3820
94BreCouMC-9
94BreCouMF-7
95PorSeaDTI-18
96PorSeaDB-19

Miyake, Chris
96AugGreB-19

Miyamoto, Shinya
96MauStiHWB-2

Miyauchi, Hector
88FreSunCLC-15
88FreSunP-1233

Mize, Johnny (John)
36OveCanR-35
36R31PasP-17
38ExhFou-8
39ExhSal-44A
39ExhSal-44B
40WheM4-6A
40WheM4-6B
41CarW75-18
41DouPlaR-39
41DouPlaR-99
42GilRazL-1
43MPR302-1-17
46SpoExcW-6-3
47HomBon-34
47TipTop-131
48BluTin-30
48Bow-4
49Bow-85A
49Bow-85B
49EurSta-120
49Lea-46
50Bow-139
51BerRos-A7
51Bow-50
51FisBakL-19
51R42SmaS-70
51TopBluB-50
52BerRos-42
52Bow-145
52Top-129
53BowBW-15
53Dor-112
53NorBreL-19
53RedMan-AL18
53Top-77
60Fle-38
61Fle-63
66CarCoi-3
67TopVen-182
68LauWorS-49
70FleWorS-49
71FleWorS-50
72LauGreF-17
72TopTes5-8
74LauAllG-47
75JohMiz-1
75JohMiz-2
75JohMiz-3
75JohMiz-4
75JohMiz-5
75JohMiz-6
75JohMiz-7
75JohMiz-8
75JohMiz-9
75JohMiz-10
75JohMiz-11
75JohMiz-12
75JohMiz-13
75JohMiz-14
75JohMiz-15
75JohMiz-16
75JohMiz-17
75JohMiz-18
75JohMiz-19
75JohMiz-20
76BooProC-9
76GalBasGHoF-19
76TayBow4-15
77ShaPiz-B
78AtlCon-18
79DiaGre-39
80PacLeg-49
80PerHaloFP-176
80SSPHOF-176
82DiaCla-24
83ASAJohM-1
83ASAJohM-2
83ASAJohM-3
83ASAJohM-4
83ASAJohM-5
83ASAJohM-6
83ASAJohM-7
83ASAJohM-8
83ASAJohM-9
83ASAJohM-10
83ASAJohM-11
83ASAJohM-12
83DonHOFH-10
83TCMPla1942-31
83TopRep5-129
83YanASFY-29
84OCoandSI-58
85CirK-32
85DonHOFS-4
85UltBasC-12
86SpoDecG-24
88PacLegI-63
89HOFStiB-3
89PacLegI-180
89PerCelP-32
89SweBasG-55
90PerGreM-23
90PerMasW-31
90PerMasW-32
90PerMasW-33
90PerMasW-34
90PerMasW-35
90SweBasG-90
91ConTSN-53
91SweBasG-62
91TopArc1-77
92ActPacA-13
92ActPacA2-13G
92BazQua5A-9
92CarMcD-3
92ConTSN-435
92ConTSN-628
92YanWIZA-49
92YanWIZH-24
93ActPacAC-13
93ConTSN-918
93DiaStaES-145
93MetIma-13
93TedWil-66
93TedWil-129
93TedWil-145
93TedWilLC-4
93UppDecAH-96
94ConTSN-1126
94ConTSNB-1126
94ConTSNCI-28
94UppDecAH-48
94UppDecAH-161
94UppDecAH1-48
94UppDecAH1-161

Mize, Paul
79WatA'sT-18
80WesHavWCT-8
81TacTigT-16
82TacTigT-15
82WesHavAT-16

Mizell, Wilmer
52Top-334
53BowBW-23
53CarHunW-15
53Top-128
54Top-249
56Top-193
57Top-113
58CarJayP-9
58Top-385
60CarJayP-7
61Kah-28
61Pos-140
74MetOriEB-11
82MetGal62-20
83TopRep5-334
91MetWIZ-277
91TopArc1-128
92BazQua5A-16

94TopArc1-249
94TopArc1G-249
Mizerock, John
84Don-380
85TucTorC-68
86Don-502
86TucTorP-15
87Don-653
87RicBraBC-14
87RicBraC-8
87RicBraT-10
87Top-408
87TopTif-408
88RicBraC-21
88RicBraP-19
89RicBraBC-18
89RicBraC-12
89RicBraP-827
89RicBraTI-15
90CMC-297
90ProAAAF-407
90RicBraBC-6
90RicBraC-21
90RicBraP-262
90RicBraTI-23
94RocRoyC-28
94RocRoyF-581
95WilBluRTI-7
96WilBluRB-28
88RicBraBC-10
Mizusawa, Hideki
90GatCitPSP-17
Mizutani, Jitsuo
79TCMJapPB-30
Mizutani, Shintaro
79TCMJapPB-24
Mlicki, Dave
91ColIndC-6
92Bow-413
92CanIndF-688
92CanIndS-112
92ClaFS7-39
92SkyAA F-53
93Bow-451
93ClaGolF-6
93Don-273
93FleMajLP-B9
93Pin-275
93Sco-285
93Top-571
93TopGol-571
93TopInaM-571
93TopMic-571
93UppDec-17
93UppDecGold-17
94ChaKniF-893
95Fin-248
95FinRef-248
95Fla-386
95FleUpd-116
95TopTra-46T
96ColCho-621
96ColChoGS-621
96ColChoSS-621
96Don-121
96DonPreP-121
96Fle-485
96FleTif-485
96LeaSigEA-128
96MetKah-22
96MetKah-23
96Pac-136
96UppDec-138
Mlicki, Doug
90ArkRaz-33
92AubAstC-18
92AubAstF-1352
93ClaFS7-108
93OscAstC-16
93OscAstF-624
94JacGenF-216
95Exc-206
95JacGenTI-6
95SigRoo-37
95SigRooSig-37
96BesAutS-61
96BesAutSA-46
96TusTorB-16
Mlodik, Kevin
96WesMicWB-15
Mmahat, Kevin
88FloStaLAS-44
88Ft.LauYS-16
89AlbYanB-23
89AlbYanP-341
89AlbYanS-14
90AlbDecGB-25
90CMC-205
90ColCliC-5
90ColCliP-20
90ColCliP-674
90Don-481
90ProAAAF-324
90Sco-643
90TopDeb89-84
90TopTVY-55
90TriAllGP-AAA15
91ColCliP-13
92YanWIZ8-121
Moates, Dave
74SpoIndC-37
75SpoIndC-2
76OPC-327
76Top-327
77Top-588
77TucTorC-2
93RanKee-269
Moberg, Mike
91Cla/Bes-317
91RocExpC-23
91RocExpP-2058
Mobilia, Bill
92Min-14
94BatCliC-14
94BatCliF-3455
95PiePhiF-193
Mobley, Anton
89St.CatBJP-2084
90MyrBeaBJP-2789
90St.CatBJP-3479
Moccia, Mario
89NiaFalRP-18
90NiaFalRP-7
Moeder, Tony
94CedRapKC-18
94CedRapKF-1117
94MidLeaAF-MDW39
95AusFut-71
96LakElsSB-18
96MidAngB-22
Moehler, Brian
93NiaFalRF-3383
94LakTigC-16
94LakTigF-3033
95JacSunTI-22
96JacSunB-21
97Don-384
97DonPreP-384
97DonPrePGold-384
97Fle-658
97FleTif-658
97Lea-332
97LeaFraM-332
97LeaFraMDC-332
Moeller, Chad
96AppLeaAB-17
Moeller, Daniel
09T206-448
12ImpTobC-76
14B18B-44
Moeller, Dennis
86EugEmeC-50
87AppFoxP-26
88AppFoxP-160
89BasCitRS-17
90MemChiS-19
92DonRoo-82
92OmaRoyF-2960
92OmaRoyS-338
92SkyAAAF-155
92TriA AAS-338
93Bow-50
93Don-648
93FleFinE-115
93FleMajLP-B14
93OPCPre-54
93PacSpa-589
93Pin-600
93PirNatI-21
93Ult-453
93UppDec-779
93UppDecGold-779
94OmaRoyF-1222
94VenLinU-79
Moeller, Joe
63Top-53
64DodHea-7
64Top-549
65OPC-238
65Top-238
66Top-449
67CokCapD-4
67CokCapDA-4
67OPC-149
67Top-149
68Top-359
68TopVen-359
69Top-444A
69Top-444B
70OPC-97
70Top-97
71DodTic-10
71MLBOffS-108
71OPC-288
71Top-288
81TCM60I-448
85SpoIndGC-14
90DodTar-541
Moeller, Ron
61Top-466
63Top-541
91OriCro-310
Moen, Eric
90YakBeaTI-21
91BenBucC-27
Moen, Robbie
90AriWilP-13
92AriWilP-9
93ElmPioC-14
93ElmPioF-3837
94KanCouCC-18
94KanCouCF-176
Moesche, Carl
84ButCopKT-7
Moffat, Donald
91TopRut-5
Moffet, Samuel
87OldJudN-358
Moffitt, G. Scott
76QuaCitAT-22
77QuaCitAT-21
80SalLakCGT-4
81SalLakCGT-23
Moffitt, Randy
73OPC-43
73Top-43
74OPC-156
74Top-156
75Gia-5
75OPC-132
75Top-132
76OPC-553
76Top-553
77BurCheD-101
77Gia-16
77Top-464
78Top-284
78WifBalD-51
79GiaPol-17
79Top-62
80GiaPol-17
80Top-359
81Don-195
81Fle-446
81Top-622
82AstAstI-9
83Don-545
83Fle-456
83Top-723
83TopFol-4
83TopTra-73T
84Don-390
84Fle-163
84Nes792-108
84OPC-108
84Top-108
84TopTif-108
Moford, Herb
59Top-91
59TopVen-91
91MetWIZ-278
Mogridge, George
12T207-130
22E120-113
22W572-66
22W573-87
23WilChoV-106
92ConTSN-376
Mohart, George
90DodTar-1038
Moharter, Dave
75SpoIndC-19
76SacSolC-3
77TucTorC-13
78TucTorC-13
79TucTorT-16
80ChaChaT-7
87MacPirP-25
88AugPirP-383
Mohler, Mike
90MadMusB-20
90MadMusP-2267
91CalLeLA-42
91ModA'sC-9
91ModA'sP-3084
92ClaFS7-137
92HunStaF-3946
92HunStaS-315
92SkyAA F-134
93AthMot-23
93Bow-105
93FleFinE-258
93PacSpa-570
93Pin-592
93StaCluAt-3
93Ult-610
94Don-505
94Fle-269
94Pac-458
94Top-282
94TopGol-282
94TopSpa-282
95EdmTraTI-17
96A'sMot-19
96LeaSigEA-129
97Fle-194
97FleTif-194
97Lea-161
97LeaFraM-161
97LeaFraMDC-161
97Top-19
Mohn, Solly
52LaPat-12
Mohorcic, Dale
81PorBeaT-17
85OklCit8T-26
86OklCit8P-13
86RanPer-34
87Don-531
87Fle-131
87FleGlo-131
87RanMot-15
87RanSmo-5
87Top-497
87TopTif-497
88Don-470
88DonBasB-144
88Fle-474
88FleGlo-474
88OPC-163
88RanMot-15
88RanSmo-6
88Sco-452
88ScoGlo-452
88StaLinRa-9
88Top-163
88TopSti-242
88TopTif-163
89Don-630
89Fle-259
89FleGlo-259
89Sco-420
89Top-26
89TopTif-26
89UppDec-727
89YanScoNW-16
90CMC-58
90Fle-450
90FleCan-450
90IndIndC-8
90IndIndP-298
90ProAAAF-581
90Sco-191
90UppDec-530
91Fle-239
91Sco-596
92YanWIZ8-122
93RanKee-270
Mohr, Ed
79QuaCitCT-2
Mohr, Tommy
83ButCopKT-25
85Ft.MyeRT-19
Moisan, William
52MotCoo-64
Mojica, Gonzalo
94BurIndF-3789
96BurIndB-12
Mokan, John
22E120-221
25Exh-46
26Exh-46
27Exh-23
Moldes, Orestes
80BatTroT-11
Moler, Dick
52LavPro-16
Moler, Jason
92FroRowDP-29
92TopTra-75T
92TopTraG-75T
93ClaFS7-285
93ClePhiC-1
93ClePhiF-2686
93FloStaLAF-28
93StaCluM-36
94Bow-636
94Cla-149
94ClaGolF-39
94ExcFS7-247
94ExcLeaLF-14
94ReaPhiF-2065
94TedWil-127
94UppDecML-111
94UppDecMLPotYF-PY18
95ReaPhiTI-22
95UppDecML-207
96ReaPhiB-20
95UppDecMLFS-207
Molero, Juan
87GreHorP-13
88LynRedSS-15
89LynRedSS-14
Molesworth, Carlton
09ColChiE-202
09T206-503
10CouT21-48
12ColRedB-202
12ColTinT-202
Molina, Albert
89SalBucS-15
Molina, Ben
95CedRapKTI-27
95MidLeaA-34
96MidAngB-23
96MidAngOHP-19
96TexLeaAB-33
Molina, Gabe
96BluOriB-20
Molina, Izzy (Islay)
91MadMusC-16
91MadMusP-2136
91MidLeaAP-MWL43
92CalLeaACL-16
92RenSilSCLC-49
93ModA'sC-13
93ModA'sF-802
93StaCluAt-17
94Bow-164
94ClaGolF-126
94ExcFS7-121
94HunStaF-1335
94UppDecML-79
95HunStaTI-19
Molina, Jose
94PeoChiC-20
94PeoChiF-2270
96RocCubTI-20
Molina, Luis
96LanJetB-18
Molina, Mario
87SalAngP-7
88QuaCitAGS-18
89PalSprAP-477
Molina, Norberto
80WisRapTT-20
Molinaro, Bob
77EvaTriT-19
78SSP270-158
79IowOakP-11
79Top-88
81CokTeaS-33
81Fle-340
81Top-466
81TopSti-61
81TopSupHT-19
82CubRedL-29
82Don-417
82Fle-353
82Top-363

83Don-596
83Fle-167
83PhiTas-19
83Top-664
85RocRedWT-12
86HagSunP-12
87RocRedWP-27
89CanIndB-17
89CanIndP-1319
89CanIndS-2
89PacSenL-80
89TopSenL-118
90CMC-477
90ColSprSSC-24
90ColSprSSP-54
90EliSenL-87
90HagSunDGB-17
90ProAAAF-235
91ChaRanC-27
91ChaRanP-1330
91OriCro-311
91PacSenL-13

Moline, Stan

76CedRapGT-16

Molitor, Paul

78Top-707
79Kel-20
79OPC-8
79Top-24
80OPC-211
80Top-406
81AllGamPI-60
81Don-203
81Fle-515
81FleStiC-82
81Kel-53
81OPC-300
81Top-300
81TopScr-35
81TopSti-91
82BrePol-4
82Don-78
82Fle-148
82FleSta-136
82OPC-195
82Top-195
82TopSti-200
83AllGamPI-35
83BreGar-11
83BrePol-4
83Don-484
83Fle-40
83FleSta-127
83FleSti-19
83OPC-371
83Top-630
83TopSti-83
83TopSti-139
83TopSti-140
83TopSti-156
84AllGamPI-126
84BreGar-13
84BrePol-4
84Don-107
84DonActAS-35
84DonCha-54
84Fle-207
84FunFooP-105
84Nes792-60
84OPC-60
84SevCoi-C18
84Top-60
84TopRubD-6
84TopSti-294
84TopTif-60
85AllGamPI-35
85BreGar-13
85BrePol-4
85Don-359
85Fle-588
85OPC-395
85Top-522
85TopRubD-7
85TopTif-522
86BrePol-4
86Don-124
86DonAll-39
86Fle-495
86FleLimE-30
86FleMin-101
86FleStiC-76
86Lea-70
86MSAJayPCD-12
86OPC-267
86SevCoi-C16
86Spo-39
86Spo-128
86Top-267
86TopSti-203
86TopTat-23
86TopTif-267
87BrePol-4
87BreTeal-8
87ClaGam-45
87Don-117
87DonHig-29
87DonOpeD-54
87Fle-350
87FleGlo-350
87FleStiC-78
87Lea-71
87OPC-184
87RedFolSB-22
87Spo-54
87SpoTeaP-19
87StuPan-21
87Top-741
87TopSti-200
87TopTif-741
88BrePol-4
88ClaBlu-232
88Don-7
88Don-249
88DonBasB-165
88DonBonM-BC3
88DonSupD-7
88Dra-11
88Fle-169
88FleAll-12
88FleAwaW-25
88FleGlo-169
88FleLeaL-27
88FleMin-31
88FleStiC-38
88FleTeaL-22
88GreBasS-29
88K-M-17
88KayB-19
88KinDis-23
88Lea-7
88Lea-168
88MSAFanSD-5
88MSAJifPD-12
88OPC-231
88PanSti-125
88PanSti-432
88Sco-340
88Sco-660
88ScoBoxC-T6
88ScoGlo-340
88ScoGlo-660
88Spo-79
88Spo-221
88StaLinBre-11
88Top-465
88TopBig-1
88TopCoi-20
88TopGloS-57
88TopMinL-19
88TopRevLL-20
88TopRitTM-20
88TopSti-194
88TopStiB-42
88TopTif-465
88TopUKM-49
88TopUKMT-49
89Bow-140
89BowTif-140
89BreGar-1
89BrePol-4
89BreYea-4
89CadEllD-37
89ClaLigB-12
89Don-291
89DonAll-3
89DonBasB-15
89DonBonM-BC9
89DonPop-3
89Fle-193
89FleAll-8
89FleBasA-30
89FleGlo-193
89MasBreD-8
89OPC-110
89PanSti-243
89PanSti-373
89RedFolSB-81
89Sco-565
89ScoHot1S-57
89Spo-209
89SpollIFKI-271
89Top-110
89TopBasT-153
89TopBatL-10
89TopBig-330
89TopCoi-46
89TopGloA-3
89TopGloS-43
89TopMinL-58
89TopSti-146
89TopSti-204
89TopStiB-9
89TopTif-110
89TopUKM-53
89TVSpoM-73
89UppDec-525
89UppDec-673
90AllBasT-22
90Bow-399
90BowTif-399
90BreMilB-15
90BrePol-4
90ClaUpd-T34
90Don-103
90DonBesA-64
90DOnBonM-BC15
90Fle-330
90FleBasM-27
90FleCan-330
90Hot50PS-28
90Lea-242
90MLBBasB-79
90OPC-360
90PanSti-98
90PubSti-500
90RedFolSB-65
90Sco-460
90Sco100S-98
90Spo-183
90Top-360
90TopAmeA-14
90TopBatL-8
90TopBig-103
90TopCoi-23
90TopMag-68
90TopMinL-20
90TopSti-199
90TopTif-360
90TopTVA-29
90UppDec-254
90VenSti-350
91Bow-32
91BreMilB-17
91BrePol-15
91Cla2-T14
91Cla3-T60
91ClaGam-79
91Don-85
91Fle-591
91Lea-302
91LeaPre-20
91MajLeaCP-42
91OPC-95
91OPCPre-82
91PanFreS-205
91PanSti-168
91PetSta-15
91Sco-49
91Sco100S-13
91StaClu-245
91StaCluMO-6
91StaPinB-33
91Stu-73
91Top-95
91TopCraJI-2
91TopDesS-95
91TopMic-95
91TopTif-95
91TopTriH-A8
91Ult-178
91UppDec-324
91USPlaCA-8H
92Bow-375
92Bow-645
92BreCarT-15
92BrePol-15
92BreUSO-2
92ClaGam-21
92Don-51
92DonCraJ2-22
92DonDiaK-DK1
92Fle-182
92Fle-702
92Hig5-67
92HitTheBB-23
92KinDis-14
92Lea-238
92LeaBlaG-238
92MooSna-14
92MSABenSHD-8
92OPC-600
92OPCPre-141
92Pin-8
92Pos-17
92Sco-61
92Sco100S-8
92ScoCokD-15
92ScoProP-2
92StaClu-230
92StaCluD-122
92Stu-194
92StuHer-BC11
92SunSee-13
92Top-600
92TopGol-600
92TopGolW-600
92TopKid-81
92TopMic-600
92TriPla-254
92Ult-81
92UppDec-423
92UppDecTMH-36
93BluJayCP1-13
93BluJayD-4
93BluJayDM-35
93BluJayFS-20
93Bow-167
93BreSen-1
93ClaGam-66
93DiaMar-77
93Don-75
93DonEli-22
93DonEliD-18
93DonEliD-AU18
93DonEliS-4
93DonMVP-4
93DurPowP2-24
93Fin-70
93FinRef-70
93Fla-292
93Fle-254
93FleFinE-295
93FleFinEDT-5
93FunPac-58
93HumDumC-18
93Lea-262
93LeaGolA-U10
93MetBak-33
93MilBonSS-1
93OPC-237
93OPCPre-124
93PacSpa-654
93Pin-428
93Pin-481
93PinCoo-23
93PinCooD-23
93Pos-16
93Sco-598
93Sel-42
93SelChaS-23
93SelRoo-16T
93SelStaL-9
93SP-50
93StaClu-627
93StaCluFDI-627
93StaCluM-131
93StaCluMO-16
93StaCluMOP-627
93Stu-172
93Top-207
93TopGol-207
93TopInaM-207
93TopMic-207
93TopTra-48T
93TriPla-97
93TriPlaG-GS6
93Ult-645
93UppDec-43
93UppDec-333
93UppDec-705
93UppDecGold-43
93UppDecGold-333
93UppDecGold-705
93UppDecIC-WI6
93UppDecICJ-WI6
93USPlaCA-7D
94BluJayP-6
94BluJayUSPC-1S
94BluJayUSPC-6D
94BluJayUSPC-7H
94Bow-281
94BowBes-R1
94BowBesR-R1
94BreMilB-256
94BreMilB-332
94BreSen-4
94BreSen-5
94BreUSO-1
94ColC-208
94ColChoGS-208
94ColChoSS-208
94Don-24
94DonAwaWJ-10
94DonDom-B3
94DonSpeE-24
94ExtBas-192
94ExtBas-P1
94ExtBasGB-20
94Fin-239
94FinJum-239
94FinRef-239
94Fla-119
94FlaI lotN-5
94Fle-338
94Fle-707
94FleAllS-16
94FleTeaL-14
94FUnPac-150
94KinDis-2
94Kra-8
94Lea-395
94LeaGolS-10
94LeaL-78
94LeaMVPC-A9
94LeaMVPCG-A9
94OPC-1
94OPCAllR-2
94OPCJumA-2
94OPCWorC-3
94OscMayR-9
94Pac-648
94PacSilP-4
94PanSti-140
94Pin-27
94PinArtP-27
94PinMusC-27
94PinRunC-RC4
94PinSam-TR1
94PinTri-TR1
94PosCan-2
94PosCanG-2
94ProMag-139
94Sco-427
94ScoCyc-TC3
94ScoGolR-427
94ScoGolS-57
94Sel-3
94Sel-MVP1
94SelSam-3
94SP-44
94SPDieC-44
94Spo-106
94Spo-NNO0
94StaClu-110
94StaClu-526
94StaClu-645
94StaCluFDI-110
94StaCluFDI-526
94StaCluFDI-645
94StaCluGR-110
94StaCluGR-526
94StaCluGR-645
94StaCluMO-4
94StaCluMOP-110
94StaCluMOP-526
94StaCluMOP-645
94StaCluT-161
94StaCluTFDI-161
94Stu-29
94Top-540
94Top-609
94TopBlaG-13
94TopGol-540
94TopGol-609
94TopSpa-540
94TopSpa-609
94TopSupS-30
94TriPla-35
94TriPlaM-15
94TriPlaP-5

94Ult-140
94UltAwaW-21
94UltCarA-2
94UltHitM-7
94UltOnBL-9
94UppDec-294
94UppDec-470
94UppDecAJ-16
94UppDecAJG-16
94UppDecED-294
94UppDecED-470
94USPlaCA-10D
95Baz-102
95BazRedH-RH19
95BluJayP-4
95BluJayUSPC-1S
95BluJayUSPC-7H
95Bow-324
95BowBes-R17
95BowBesR-R17
95BurBeeTI-21
95ColCho-145
95ColChoGS-145
95ColChoSE-55
95ColChoSEGS-55
95ColChoSESS-55
95ColChoSS-145
95Don-110
95Don-162
95DonPreP-110
95DonPreP-162
95DonTopotO-175
95Emb-19
95EmbGolI-19
95Emo-96
95Fin-115
95FinRef-115
95Fla-317
95Fle-101
95FleAllS-13
95KinDis-14
95Lea-181
95Lea300C-2
95LeaHeaftH-8
95LeaLim-100
95LeaStaS-5
95Pac-447
95PacGolP-25
95PacPri-143
95PanSti-98
95Pin-260
95Pin-297
95PinArtP-260
95PinArtP-297
95PinGatA-GA14
95PinMusC-260
95PinMusC-297
95PinPer-PP7
95PinRedH-RH14
95PinWhiH-WH14
95PosCan-3
95Sco-247
95Sco-566
95ScoDreT-DG9
95ScoGolR-247
95ScoGolR-566
95ScoHaloG-HG25
95ScoPlaTS-247
95ScoPlaTS-566
95Sel-35
95SelArtP-35
95SelBigS-BS10
95SelCer-23
95SelCerMG-23
95SP-203
95SPCha-110
95SPCha-195
95SPCha-198
95SPChaDC-110
95SPChaDC-195
95SPChaDC-198
95Spo-8
95SpoArtP-8
95SPSil-203
95SPSpeF-26
95StaClu-39
95StaCluCT-7
95StaCluFDI-39
95StaCluMO-33
95StaCluMOP-39
95StaCluMOP-PZ8
95StaCluMOP-RL4
95StaCluPZ-PZ8
95StaCluRL-RL4
95StaCluSTWS-39
95StaCluVR-28
95Stu-10
95StuGolS-10
95StuPlaS-10
95Sum-58
95Sum-186
95SumBigB-BB13
95SumNthD-58
95SumNthD-186
95TomPiz-12
95Top-30
95TopCyb-23
95UC3-22
95UC3ArtP-22
95Ult-122
95UltGolM-122
95UppDec-107
95UppDec-285
95UppDecED-107
95UppDecED-285
95UppDecEDG-107
95UppDecEDG-285
95UppDecPLL-R23
95UppDecPLLE-R23
95UppDecSE-65
95UppDecSEG-65
95USPlaCMLA-7D
95Zen-81
96Baz-64
96Bow-88
96BowBes-87
96BowBesAR-87
96BowBesR-87
96Cir-58
96CirAcc-8
96CirBos-13
96CirRav-58
96ColCho-355
96ColCho-414
96ColCho-600
96ColChoGS-355
96ColChoGS-414
96ColChoGS-600
96ColChoSS-355
96ColChoSS-414
96ColChoSS-600
96ColChoYMtP-26
96ColChoYMtP-26A
96ColChoYMtPGS-26
96ColChoYMtPGS-26A
96Don-325
96Don-419
96DonPreP-325
96DonPreP-419
96EmoXL-84
96Fin-B194
96Fin-G279
96FinRef-B194
96FinRef-G279
96Fla-119
96Fle-169
96FleTif-169
96FleUpd-U56
96FleUpdTC-U56
96Lea-80
96LeaLim-83
96LeaLimG-83
96LeaLimPC-7
96LeaPre-105
96LeaPreP-105
96LeaPrePB-80
96LeaPrePG-80
96LeaPrePS-80
96LeaPreSG-2
96LeaPreSte-2
96LeaSig-57
96LeaSigA-158
96LeaSigAG-158
96LeaSigAS-158
96LeaSigEA-130
96LeaSigEACM-20
96LeaSigPPG-57
96LeaSigPPP-57
96LeaTotB-7
96MetUni-78
96MetUniP-78
96Pac-435
96PacPri-P144
96PacPriG-P144
96PanSti-160
96Pin-61
96Pin-305A
96Pin-335
96PinAfi-48
96PinAfiAP-48
96PinAfiFPP-48
96PinArtP-24
96PinArtP-189
96PinFoil-305A
96PinFoil-335
96PinSta-24
96PinSta-189
96Sco-283
96ScoDugC-B8
96ScoDugCAP-B8
96Sel-110
96SelArtP-110
96SelCer-81
96SelCerAP-81
96SelCerCB-81
96SelCerCR-81
96SelCerMB-81
96SelCerMG-81
96SelCerMR-81
96SP-117
96Spo-27
96SpoArtP-27
96SPSpeFX-39
96SPSpeFXDC-39
96SPx-37
96SPxGol-37
96StaClu-2
96StaCluMOP-2
95StaCluVRMC-28
96Stu-138
96StuPrePB-138
96StuPrePG-138
96StuPrePS-138
96Sum-137
96SumAbo&B-137
96SumArtP-137
96SumFoi-137
96Top-30
96TopChr-14
96TopChrMotG-4
96TopChrMotGR-4
96TopChrR-14
96TopGal-51
96TopGalPPI-51
96TopLas-11
96TopMasotG-4
96Ult-149
96Ult-377
96UltGolM-149
96UltGolM-377
96UppDec-109
96UppDec-381
96UppDec-500U
96UppDecDD-DD25
96UppDecDDG-DD25
96UppDecDDS-DD25
96Zen-67
96ZenArtP-67
96ZenMoz-19
97BluJayS-37
97BluJayS-48
97Bow-10
97BowBes-33
97BowBesA-33
97BowBesAAR-33
97BowBesAR-33
97BowBesR-33
97BowChr-8
97BowChrI-8
97BowChrIR-8
97BowChrR-8
97BowInt-10
97Cir-300
97CirRav-300
97ColCho-155
97ColChoS-4
97ColChoTBS-29
97ColChoTBSWH-29
97ColChoTotT-T16
97Don-39
97Don-268
97Don-417
97DonEli-34
97DonEli-2
97DonEliGS-34
97DonLim-20
97DonLim-35
97DonLim-112
97DonLimFotG-22
97DonLimLE-20
97DonLimLE-35
97DonLimLE-112
97DonPowA-21
97DonPowADC-21
97DonPre-71
97DonPre-178
97DonPreCttC-71
97DonPreCttC-178
97DonPreP-39
97DonPreP-268
97DonPreP-417
97DonPrePGold-39
97DonPrePGold-268
97DonPrePGold-417
97DonPreXP-2A
97Fin-173
97Fin-181
97FinEmb-173
97FinEmbR-173
97FinRef-173
97FinRef-181
97FlaSho-A4
97FlaSho-B4
97FlaSho-C4
97FlaShoLC-4
97FlaShoLC-B4
97FlaShoLC-C4
97FlaShoLCM-A4
97FlaShoLCM-B4
97FlaShoLCM-C4
97Fle-151
97Fle-496
97Fle-709
97Fle-736
97FleDecoE-8
97FleDecoERT-8
97FleGolM-5
97FleHea-13
97FleTeaL-9
97FleTif-151
97FleTif-496
97FleTif-709
97FleTif-736
97Lea-24
97Lea-362
97LeaFraM-24
97LeaFraM-362
97LeaFraMDC-24
97LeaFraMDC-362
97LeaGolS-18
97LeaKnoG-12
97LeaLeaotN-8
97LeaStaS-15
97MetUni-212
97NewPin-129
97NewPinAP-129
97NewPinMC-129
97NewPinPP-129
97Pac-142
97PacCar-11
97PacCarM-11
97PacLigB-142
97PacPri-47
97PacPriGA-GA7
97PacPriGotD-GD63
97PacPriLB-47
97PacPriP-47
97PacSil-142
97Pin-78
97PinArtP-78
97PinCer-30
97PinCerLI-13
97PinCerMBlu-30
97PinCerMG-30
97PinCerMR-30
97PinCerR-30
97PinIns-14
97PinInsCE-14
97PinInsDE-14
97PinMusC-78
97PinTotCPB-30
97PinTotCPG-30
97PinTotCPR-30
97PinX-P-94
97PinX-PMoS-94
97ProMag-63
97ProMagML-63
97Sco-243
97Sco-329
97Sco-541
97ScoHeaotO-35
97ScoHobR-541
97ScoPreS-243
97ScoPreS-329
97ScoResC-541
97ScoShoS-243
97ScoShoS-329
97ScoShoS-541
97ScoShoSAP-243
97ScoShoSAP-329
97ScoShoSAP-541
97Sel-15
97SelArtP-15
97SelRegG-15
97SelToootT-15
97SelToootTMB-15
97SkyE-X-29
97SkyE-XC-29
97SkyE-XEC-29
97SP-105
97SPInsI-4
97SpoIll-146
97SpoIllEE-146
97SPSpeF-40
97SPSpxF-9
97SPSPxFA-9
97SPx-31
97SPxBro-31
97SPxCorotG-4
97SPxGraF-31
97SPxSil-31
97SPxSte-31
97StaClu-10
97StaCluI-I2
97StaCluMat-10
97StaCluMOP-10
97StaCluMOP-I2
97Stu-11
97StuMasS-24
97StuMasS8-24
97StuPrePG-11
97StuPrePS-11
97Top-138
97Top-463
97TopChr-53
97TopChr-164
97TopChrR-53
97TopChrR-164
97TopChrSB-4
97TopChrSBR-4
97TopGal-1
97TopGalPG-PG2
97TopGalPPI-1
97TopIntF-ILM8
97TopIntFR-ILM8
97TopScr-15
97TopSeaB-SB4
97TopSta-21
97TopStaAM-21
97Ult-90
97UltGolME-90
97UltPlaME-90
97UppDec-102
97UppDec-222
97UppDecAG-AG4
97UppDecRP-RP24
97UppDecU-30
97Zen-4
Mollwitz, Fred
15SpoNewM-121
16FleBreD-66
16SpoNewM-124
94ConTSN-1271
94ConTSNB-1271
Moloney, Bill
81BriRedST-2
83PawRedST-9
95MicBatCTI-20
Moloney, Richard
71OPC-13
Molta, Sal
96MarPhiB-15
Mompres, Danilo
91ColMetPI-20
91ColMetPPI-3
91PitMetC-10
91PitMetP-3431
92ColMetC-16
92ColMetF-304
92ColMetPI-5
93CapCitBC-13
93CapCitBF-468
Monahan, Shane
96BowBes-174
96BowBesAR-174
96BowBesR-174
96LanJetB-19
96Top-238
97Bow-180
97BowCerBIA-CA54

97BowCerGIA-CA54
97BowChr-172
97BowChrI-172
97BowChrIR-172
97BowChrR-172
97BowInt-180
97Top-491

Monarchs, Kansas City
90PomBlaBNLP-2541
91PomBlaBPB-13
92NegLeaRLI-85
92NegLeaRLI-86
93NegLeaRL2-47
93NegLeaRL2-69
93NegLeaRL2-70
93NegLeaRL2-71
93NegLeaRL2-72

Monasterio, Juan
76VenLeaS-144
76WauMetT-19
77LynMetT-20
80VenLeaS-201

Monastro, Frank
90BurIndP-3015

Monbouquette, Bill
47PM1StaP1-143
59Top-173
59TopVen-173
60Top-544
61Pos-54A
61Pos-54B
61Top-562
61TopStaI-114
62RedSoxJP-6
62SalPlaC-99
62ShiPlaC-99
62Top-580
62TopStaI-15
63Baz-21
63Fle-7
63Jel-84
63Pos-84
63SalMetC-35
63Top-480
63TopStil-29
64Top-25
64TopCoi-47
64TopSta-19
64TopTatI-56
64TopVen-25
65OPC-142
65Top-142
66Top-429
66TopRubI-68
67CokCapTi-16
67Top-482
68Top-234
68TopVen-234
69OPC-64
69Top-64
76WauMetT-20
78TCM60I-111
82MetPhoA-28
86AlbYanT-8
86AlbYanT-32
89MyrBeaBJP-1467
90DunBluJS-27
90SweBasG-106
91DunBluJC-26
91DunBluJP-224
92DunBluJC-29
92DunBluJF-2015
92YanWIZ6-89
93DunBluJC-27
93DunBluJF-1812
93DunBluJFFN-18
94DunBluJC-28
94DunBluJF-2573
95SyrChiTI-18
96SyrChiTI-21

Moncallo, Bernie
95HelBreTI-19
96OgdRapTI-24

Moncerratt, Pablo
84ButCopKT-17
86WauTimP-17
87SalSpuP-23

Monchak, Al
73OPC-356
73Top-356
74OPC-221
74Top-221
77PirPosP-15
86BraPol-52

Moncier, John
95BakBlaTI-30

Moncrief, Homer
82BirBarT-4
83GleFalWST-15

Moncrief, Tony
83IdaFalAT-29
84ModA'sC-19

Monda, Greg
85CedRapRT-17
86VerRedP-13
88NasSouC-13
88NasSouP-491

Monday, Rick
67Top-542
68Baz-10
68Top-282
68TopActS-7A
68TopGamI-26
68TopVen-282
69A'sJacitB-10
69MilBra-194
69MLBOffS-88
69MLBPin-19
69NabTeaF-16
69OPC-105
69Top-105
69TopDec-14
69TopDecI-31
69TopSta-218
69TopSup-27
69TopTeaP-21
69TraSta-10
70MLBOffS-262
70Top-547
71Kel-73A
71Kel-73B
71Kel-73C
71MLBOffS-522
71OPC-135
71Top-135
71TopCoi-40
71TopTat-125
72CubTeal-8
72MilBra-239
72Top-730
73LinPor-43
73OPC-44
73Top-44
74Kel-2
74OPC-295
74Top-295
74TopSta-17
75Hos-113
75HosTwi-113
75OPC-129
75Top-129
76CraDis-37
76Hos-80
76OPC-251
76SSP-311
76Top-251
77BurCheD-146
77Hos-30
77MSADis-42
77OPC-230
77RCColC-43
77Spo-4622
77Top-360
78RCColC-29
78SSP270-77
78Top-145
79Kel-57
79OPC-320
79Top-605
80DodPol-16
80OPC-243
80Top-465
81Dod-8
81DodPol-16
81Don-60
81Fle-122
81LonBeaPT-20
81OPC-177
81Top-726
81TopSupHT-49
82DodPol-16
82DodUniOV-12
82Don-514
82Fle-15
82FleSta-2
82OPC-6
82Top-577
83DodPol-16
83DodPos-9
83Don-643
83Fle-213
83FleSta-128
83FleSti-114
83OPC-63
83SevCoi-10
83Top-63
83TopFol-2
84DodPol-16
84Fle-106
84Nes792-274
84Top-274
84TopSti-83
84TopTif-274
86A'sGreT-6
87A'sMot-2
87DodSmoA-23
88AlaGolAA'TI-1
89DodSmoG-90
90DodTar-542
90PacLeg-40
90PadMag-8
91PadCok-6
91SweBasG-65
92DodStaTA-17
93UppDecAH-97
94TedWil-13

Mondesi, Raul
90GreFalDSP-6
91BakDodCLC-1
91Bow-593
91CalLeLA-3
92AlbDukS-16
92Bow-64
92DonRoo-83
92LeaGolR-BC16
92SanAntMF-3987
92SkyAAAF-8
92SpoIIIFK1-362
92UppDec-60
92UppDecML-32
92UppDecML-163
93AlbDukF-1475
93Bow-353
93Bow-618
93ClaYouG-YG12
93ExcFS7-53
93FleFinE-82
93Lea-473
93LimRocDWB-27
93LimRocDWB-142
93SP-96
93StaCluD-15
93Ult-402
94Bow-538
94BowBes-R86
94BowBes-X99
94BowBesR-R86
94BowBesR-X99
94ColC-209
94ColChoGS-209
94ColChoSS-209
94DodMot-9
94DodPol-19
94Don-313
94ExtBas-291
94ExtBasRS-13
94Fin-74
94FinRef-74
94Fla-179
94FlaWavotF-A6
94Fle-518
94FUnPac-143
94Lea-93
94LeaL-119
94LeaLimRP-1
94OPC-199
94OPCHotP-4
94Pac-316
94Pin-242
94PinArtP-242
94PinMusC-242
94Sco-618
94ScoBoyoS-47
94ScoGolR-618
94ScoRoo-RT82
94ScoRooGR-RT82
94ScoRooSR-SU4
94Sel-183
94SelRooS-RS17
94SP-79
94SPDieC-79
94SPHol-27
94SPHolDC-27
94Spo-162
94SpoRooRS-TR7
94StaClu-390
94StaCluFDI-390
94StaCluGR-390
94StaCluMOP-390
94Stu-70
94Top-783
94TopGol-783
94TopSpa-783
94TopSupS-31
94TopTraFI-4
94TriPla-288
94Ult-216
94UltAllR-7
94UltAllRJ-7
94UppDec-59
94UppDecED-59
94UppDecNG-12
94UppDecNGED-12
95Baz-58
95Bow-348
95BowBes-R53
95BowBesR-R53
95ClaPhoC-34
95ColCho-79
95ColChoCtA-5
95ColChoCtAG-5
95ColChoCtG-CG14
95ColChoCtG-CG14B
95ColChoCtG-CG14C
95ColChoCtGE-14
95ColChoCtGG-CG14
95ColChoCtGG-CG14B
95ColChoCtGG-CG14C
95ColChoCtGGE-14
95ColChoGS-79
95ColChoSE-95
95ColChoSEGS-95
95ColChoSESS-95
95ColChoSS-79
95D3Zon-5
95DodMot-3
95DodPol-15
95DodROY-14
95Don-543
95DonDiaK-DK16
95DonPreP-543
95DonTopotO-268
95Emb-102
95EmbGolI-102
95Emo-143
95EmoMas-7
95Fin-1
95FinPowK-PK2
95FinRef-1
95Fla-154
95FlaTodS-7
95Fle-545
95FleAwaW-6
95FlePro-2
95FleRooS-13
95FleUpdSS-7
95KinDis-10
95Lea-60
95LeaChe-5
95LeaGolS-7
95LeaLim-138
95LeaLimG-3
95LeaLimL-13
95LeaSli-1A
95LeaSli-1B
95NatPac-11
95Pac-222
95PacGolCDC-12
95PacGolP-15
95PacLatD-24
95PacPri-71
95PanSti-76
95PanSti-99
95PanSti-111
95Pin-292
95Pin-316
95PinArtP-292
95PinArtP-316
95PinFan-16
95PinGatA-GA10
95PinMusC-292
95PinMusC-316
95PinPer-PP6
95PinRedH-RH13
95PinUps-US9
95PinWhiH-WH13
95Sco-233
95Sco-567
95ScoAi-AM14
95ScoGolR-233
95ScoGolR-567
95ScoHaloG-HG33
95ScoPlaTS-233
95ScoPlaTS-567
95ScoRul-SR10
95ScoRulJ-SR10
95Sel-103
95Sel-247
95SelArtP-103
95SelArtP-247
95SelCanM-CM4
95SelCer-78
95SelCer-80
95SelCerC-7
95SelCerMG-78
95SelCerMG-80
95SelCerPU-3
95SelCerPU9-3
95SP-65
95SPCha-58
95SPChaDC-58
95Spo-21
95SpoArtP-21
95SpoDouT-10
95SpoHamT-HT17
95SPPlaP-PP5
95SPSil-65
95SPSpeF-42
95StaClu-57
95StaCluFDI-57
95StaCluMO-48
95StaCluMOP-57
95StaCluMOP-SS6
95StaCluSS-SS6
95StaCluSTDW-D57
95StaCluSTWS-57
95StaCluVR-35
95Stu-19
95StuGolS-19
95StuPlaS-19
95Sum-47
95SumNewA-NA3
95SumNthD-47
95TomPiz-6
95Top-180
95TopCyb-103
95UC3-84
95UC3-135
95UC3ArtP-84
95UC3ArtP-135
95UC3CycS-CS14
95Ult-183
95UltAllR-8
95UltAllRGM-8
95UltAwaW-24
95UltAwaWGM-24
95UltGolM-183
95UltRisS-7
95UltRisSGM-7
95UltSecYS-10
95UltSecYSGM-10
95UppDec-322
95UppDecA-4
95UppDecED-322
95UppDecEDG-322
95UppDecPLL-R56
95UppDecPLLE-R56
95UppDecSE-32
95UppDecSEG-32
95Zen-84
95ZenAllS-10
95ZenZ-7
96Baz-121
96Bow-104
96BowBes-46
96BowBesAR-46
96BowBesC-7
96BowBesCAR-7
96BowBesCR-7
96BowBesR-46
96Cir-143
96CirRav-143
96ColCho-102
96ColCho-328
96ColCho-580
96ColChoGS-102
96ColChoGS-328
96ColChoGS-580
96ColChoSS-102
96ColChoSS-328

96ColChoSS-580
96ColChoYMtP-27
96ColChoYMtP-27A
96ColChoYMtPGS-27
96ColChoYMtPGS-27A
96DodMot-4
96DodPol-24
96Don-160
96DonLonBL-4
96DonPreP-160
96DonPurP-1
96EmoRarB-7
96EmoXL-212
96EmoXLD-7
96Fin-B199
96Fin-S130
96FinRef-B199
96FinRef-S130
96Fla-296
96Fle-441
96FleDod-12
96FleTif-441
96FleUpd-U233
96FleUpdSL-7
96FleUpdTC-U233
96Lea-49
96LeaAllGMC-15
96LeaAllGMCG-15
96LeaLim-51
96LeaLimG-51
96LeaPre-33
96LeaPreP-33
96LeaPrePB-49
96LeaPrePG-49
96LeaPrePS-49
96LeaPreSG-38
96LeaPreSte-38
96LeaSig-41
96LeaSigA-159
96LeaSigAG-159
96LeaSigAS-159
96LeaSigPPG-41
96LeaSigPPP-41
96MetUni-185
96MetUniML-5
96MetUniP-185
96Pac-107
96PacEstL-EL21
96PacGolCD-DC16
96PacHom-HP18
96PacPri-P36
96PacPriG-P36
96PanSti-89
96Pin-132
96Pin-229
96Pin-283
96PinAfi-129
96PinAfiAP-129
96PinAfiSP-12
96PinArtP-129
96PinArtP-183
96PinFoil-229
96PinFoil-283
96PinProS-17
96PinSky-18
96PinSta-129
96PinSta-183
96PinTeaT-3
96ProSta-43
96Sco-7
96Sco-369
96ScoBigB-8
96ScoDiaA-9
96ScoDugC-A7
96ScoDugC-B94
96ScoDugCAP-A7
96ScoDugCAP-B94
96ScoFutF-16
96ScoNumG-11
96ScoRef-6
96ScoSam-7
96Sel-50
96SelArtP-50
96SelCer-57
96SelCerAP-57
96SelCerCB-57
96SelCerCR-57
96SelCerIP-17
96SelCerMB-57
96SelCerMG-57
96SelCerMR-57
96SelTeaN-11
96SP-102
96Spo-14
96SpoArtP-14
96SPSpeFX-4
96SPSpeFXDC-4
96SPx-34
96SPxGol-34
96StaClu-430
96StaCluB&B-BB5
96StaCluEPB-430
96StaCluEPG-430
96StaCluEPS-430
96StaCluMOF-4
96StaCluMOP-430
96StaCluMOP-BB5
95StaCluVRMC-35
96Stu-63
96Sum-32
96Sum-160
96SumAbo&B-32
96SumAbo&B-160
96SumArtP-32
96SumArtP-160
96SumBigB-14
96SumBigBM-14
96SumFoi-32
96SumFoi-160
96TeaOut-57
96TeaOut-C93
96Top-175
96TopChr-51
96TopChrR-51
96TopGal-115
96TopGalPPI-115
96TopLas-86
96TopLasSS-6
96TopMysF-M14
96TopMysFR-M14
96TopPro-NL6
96Ult-222
96Ult-586
96Ult-598
96UltFreF-7
96UltFreFGM-7
96UltGolM-222
96UltGolM-586
96UltGolM-598
96UltPowP-4
96UltPowPGM-4
96UltPriL-18
96UltPriLGM-18
96UltRaw-7
96UltRawGM-7
96UppDec-99
96UppDecVJLS-VJ9
96Zen-47
96ZenArtP-47
96ZenMoz-13
97Bow-51
97BowBes-97
97BowBesAR-97
97BowBesR-97
97BowChr-39
97BowChrI-39
97BowChrIR-39
97BowChrR-39
97BowInt-51
97Cir-296
97CirRav-296
97ColCho-135
97ColChoTBS-26
97ColChoTBSWH-26
97Don-6
97Don-447
97DonArmaD-2
97DonEli-71
97DonEliGS-71
97DonLim-26
97DonLim-128
97DonLimFotG-33
97DonLimLE-26
97DonLimLE-128
97DonPre-105
97DonPreCttC-105
97DonPreP-6
97DonPreP-447
97DonPrePGold-6
97DonPrePGold-447
97DonPreXP-9B
97DonTea-106
97DonTeaSPE-106
97Fin-13
97Fin-328
97FinEmb-328
97FinEmbR-328
97FinRef-13
97FinRef-328
97FlaSho-A43
97FlaSho-B43
97FlaSho-C43
97FlaShoLC-43
97FlaShoLC-B43
97FlaShoLC-C43
97FlaShoLCM-A43
97FlaShoLCM-B43
97FlaShoLCM-C43
97Fle-367
97FleTif-367
97Lea-78
97Lea-383
97LeaFraM-78
97LeaFraM-383
97LeaFraMDC-78
97LeaFraMDC-383
97LeaWarT-12
97MetUni-103
97NewPin-101
97NewPinAP-101
97NewPinMC-101
97NewPinPP-101
97Pac-335
97PacLatotML-29
97PacLigB-335
97PacPri-113
97PacPriLB-113
97PacPriP-113
97PacPriSL-SL11B
97PacSil-335
97PinCer-74
97PinCerMBlu-74
97PinCerMG-74
97PinCerMR-74
97PinCerR-74
97PinIns-40
97PinInsCE-40
97PinInsDE-40
97PinPasttM-17
97PinTotCPB-74
97PinTotCPG-74
97PinTotCPR-74
97PinX-P-104
97PinX-PMoS-104
97PinX-PSfF-33
97PinX-PSfFU-33
97ProMag-21
97ProMagML-21
97Sco-202
97ScoDod-7
97ScoDodPI-7
97ScoDodPr-7
97ScoHeaotO-24
97ScoPreS-202
97ScoShoS-202
97ScoShoSAP-202
97ScoStaaD-15
97Sel-57
97SelArtP-57
97SelRegG-57
97SkyE-X-80
97SkyE-XC-80
97SkyE-XEC-80
97SP-98
97SpoIll-115
97SpoIllEE-115
97SPSpxF-7
97SPSPxFA-7
97SPx-28
97SPxBro-28
97SPxGraF-28
97SPxSil-28
97SPxSte-28
97StaClu-216
97StaCluC-CO7
97StaCluMat-216
97StaCluMOP-216
97Stu-112
97StuPrePG-112
97StuPrePS-112
97Top-67
97TopChr-23
97TopChrR-23
97TopGal-91
97TopGalPPI-91
97TopHobM-HM8
97TopSta-23
97TopStaAM-23
97Ult-220
97UltFieC-13
97UltGolME-220
97UltPlaME-220
97UppDec-187
97UppDec-375
97UppDec-401
97UppDecRSF-RS20
97UppDecU-32

Mondile, Steve
89FreKeyS-18
90FreKeyTI-7

Mondroff, Perhsing
50W720HolS-20

Monds, Wonderful
94MacBraC-15
94MacBraF-2219
95DurBulTI-22
95Exc-155
95SPML-13
95SPMLA-18
95UppDecML-47
96Fla-208
96FlaWavotF-17
96FleUpd-U105
96FleUpdNH-18
96FleUpdTC-U105
96Ult-443
96UltGolM-443
96UltGolP-14
96UltGolPHGM-14
97Ult-159
97UltGolME-159
97UltPlaME-159
95UppDecMLFS-47

Monegro, David
88ElmPioC-15

Monegro, Miguel
87ElmPio(C-4
88WinHavRSS-14
90LynRedSTI-6

Monell, Johnny
85LitFalMT-26
86ColMetP-18
87ColMetP-9
88BlaYNPRWL-108
89JacMetGS-16
90TulDriTI-15

Monette, Jacques
52LaPat-13
52LavPro-114

Money, Don
69PhiTeal-6
69Top-454A
69Top-454B
69TopTeaP-8
70DayDaiNM-61
70PhiTeal-9
70Top-645
71MLBOffS-185
71OPC-49
71PhiArcO-9
71Top-49
71TopCoi-31
71TopTat-55
72MilBra-240
72Top-635
73LinPor-102
73OPC-386
73Top-386
74OPC-413
74Top-413
74TopSta-197
75Hos-112
75HosTwi-112
75OPC-175
75Top-175
76BreA&P-9
76Hos-136
76OPC-402
76SSP-236
76Top-402
77Top-79
78Top-24
79OPC-133
79Top-265
80OPC-313
80Top-595
81Don-443
81Fle-524
81OPC-106
81Top-106
82BrePol-7
82Don-384
82Fle-149
82OPC-294
82Top-709
83BreGar-12
83BrePol-7
83Don-132
83Fle-41
83OPC-259
83Top-608
84Fle-208
84Nes792-374
84Top-374
84TopTif-374
86BreGreT-4
91UppDecS-17
92BreCarT-16
94BreMilB-333
94BreMilB-334

Money, Kyle
82ReaPhiT-4
83PorBeaT-4
86PorBeaP-18

Moneypenny, Bubba
92DavLipB-19
93DavLipB-24

Monge, Christine
95ColSilB-20
96ColSilB-20

Monge, Sid (Isidro)
75IntLeaASB-18
75PacCoaLAB-18
75SalLakCC-17
76OPC-595
76Top-595
77Top-282
78Top-101
79Top-459
80OPC-39
80Top-74
81Don-81
81Fle-395
81OPC-333
81Top-333
82Don-620
82Fle-375
82Top-601
82TopTra-73T
83Don-245
83Fle-168
83PhiTas-20
83Top-564
83TopSti-274
83TopTra-74T
84Don-139
84Fle-308
84Nes792-224
84PadMot-21
84PadSmo-19
84TigWavP-26
84Top-224
84TopTif-224
84TopTra-80T
84TopTraT-80T
85Fle-17
85Top-408
85TopTif-408
89PacSenL-180
90EliSenL-88
90RocExpLC-18
90RocExpP-2711
92FayGenC-26
92FayGenF-2186
93LonTigF-2323
94JamJamC-28
95FayGenTI-17
96FayGenB-2

Mongiello, Michael
90Bes-282
90SouBenWSB-21
90SouBenWSGS-12
91SarWhiSC-8
91SarWhiSP-1111
92BirBarF-2580
92BirBarS-90
92ClaFS7-31
92SkyAA F-43
93BirBarF-1189
94NasSouF-1249
95NasSouTI-14

Monheimer, Len
88AugPirP-389

Monico, Mario
86StoPorP-16
87StoPorP-7
88ElPasDB-26
88TexLeaAGS-24
89ElPasDGS-30
90CMC-38

90DenZepC-13
90DenZepP-638
90ProAAAF-663
Monita, Greg
87VerRedP-21
Monk, Art
91StaCluMO-31
92StaCluMO-39
Monroe, Bill
74LauOldTBS-31
86NegLeaF-110
Monroe, Craig
96ChaRivTI-9621
Monroe, Darryl
94JamJamC-17
94JamJamF-3980
95FayGenTI-18
Monroe, Gary
81QuaCitCT-14
Monroe, Larry
75AppFoxT-18
78KnoKnoST-13
79KnoKnoST-14
Monroe, Zack
59Top-108
59TopVen-108
60Top-329
79TCM50-219
Mons, Jeffrey
88VerBeaDS-17
Monson, Mo (Steve)
87BelBreP-5
88StoPorCLC-175
88StoPorP-722
89ElPasDGS-11
89StoPorB-4
89StoPorCLC-160
89StoPorP-384
90ElPasDGS-22
91StoPorC-3
91StoPorP-3030
Montague, Ed
88T/MUmp-27
89T/MUmp-25
90T/MUmp-24
Montague, John
72Dia-35
75OPC-405
75Top-405
76OklCit8TI-25
78Top-117
79OPC-172
79Top-337
80Top-253
81Top-652
86MarGreT-10
Montalvo, Rafael
83VerBeaDT-9
85AlbDukC-173
86TucTorP-16
87TucTorP-5
88BlaYNPRWL-137
88TucTorC-6
88TucTorJP-18
88TucTorP-170
89BlaYNPRWL-10
90CMC-488
90EdmTraC-11
90EdmTraP-517
90ProAAAF-93
91Bow-189
91EdmTraLD-167
91EdmTraP-1515
91LinDriAAA-167
Montalvo, Robert
88St.CatBJP-2021
90MyrBeaBJP-2875
90St.CatBJP-3466
91DunBluJC-28
91DunBluJP-215
92KnoBluJF-2998
92KnoBluJS-385
92SyrChiF-1976
93SyrChiF-1005
94DunBluJC-20
94SyrChiTI-18
Montana, Joe
91AreHol-1
Montanari, Dave
86PalSprAP-21
86PalSprAP-23
Montane, Ivan
93BelMarC-20
93BelMarF-3205
94AppFoxC-14
94AppFoxF-1052
96LanJetB-20
Montanez, Willie
71OPC-138
71Top-138
72Dia-62
72EssCoi-9
72Top-690
73LinPor-147
73OPC-97
73Top-97
74OPC-515
74PhiJohP-27
74Top-515
74TopSta-77
75Gia-6
75Hos-137
75Kel-31
75OPC-162
75Top-162
76OPC-181
76SSP-103
76Top-181
77BurCheD-211
77Hos-19
77Kel-31
77OPC-79
77Top-410
77TopCloS-29
78Hos-143
78MetDaiPA-18
78OPC-43
78Top-38
78TopZes-4
79Hos-100
79OPC-153
79Top-305
80OPC-119
80Top-224
81AllGamPI-97
81ExpPos-6
81Fle-506
81OPC-63
81OPCPos-1
81Top-559
82Fle-486
82Top-458
89BlaYNPRWL-164
91MetWIZ-279
91UppDecS-17
93RanKee-271
Montano, Francisco
85MexCitTT-8
Montano, Martin
85BelBreT-22
86StoPorP-17
87StoPorP-13
88FreSunP-1245
Montaya, Ramon
93LinVenB-316
Montazvo, Rafael
91MidAngOHP-20
Monteagudo, Aurelio
64Top-466
65Top-286
66Top-532
67Top-453
70RoyTeal-23
71MLBOffS-421
71OPC-129
71Top-129
72OPC-458
72Top-458
74OPC-139
74Top-139
74TopTra-139T
76VenLeaS-114
80VenLeaS-203
81TCM60I-432
85MidAngT-20
86MidAngP-18
87KnoBluJP-1498
Monteau, Sam
75BurBeeT-17
76BurBeeT-22
Montefusco, John
76CraDis-38
76Hos-41
76HosTwi-41
76OPC-30
76OPC-203
76SSP-97
76Top-30
76Top-203
77BurCheD-106
77Gia-17
77Hos-31
77Kel-5
77MSADis-43
77OPC-232
77PepGloD-42
77RCColC-44
77Top-370
77TopCloS-30
78OPC-59
78Top-142
79GiaPol-26
79OPC-288
79Top-560
80GiaEurFS-6
80GiaPol-26
80OPC-109
80Top-195
81BraPol-24
81Don-434
81Fle-439
81Top-438
81TopTra-804
82Fle-442
82Top-697
82TopTra-74T
83Don-313
83Fle-367
83FleSta-129
83FleSti-270
83OPC-223
83Top-223
83TopSti-297
84Don-126
84Fle-132
84GiaMot-24
84Nes792-761
84OPC-265
84Top-761
84TopTif-761
85Don-580
85Fle-135
85OPC-301
85Top-301
85TopSti-319
85TopTif-301
86Fle-111
87Spo-71A
92UppDecS-7
92YanWIZ8-123
93UppDecS-9
Monteguedo, Rene
83TCMPla1945-45
Monteiro, Dave
87UtiBluSP-15
88IdaFalBP-1841
Montejo, Steve
88WatPirP-22
Monteleone, Rich
85NasSouTI-16
86CalCanP-15
87CalCanP-2332
87MarMot-24
88CalCanC-3
88CalCanP-797
89EdmTraC-2
89EdmTraP-564
89ScoRoo-92T
90CMC-208
90ColCliC-8
90ColCliP-675
90Don-462
90Fle-648
90FleCan-648
90OPC-99
90ProAAAF-325
90Sco-565
90Top-99
90TopTif-99
90TopTVY-56
91ColCliLD-113
91ColCliP-14
91ColCliP-596
91LinDriAAA-113
91TriA AAGP-AAA7
92Lea-352
92Sco-690
92StaClu-157
93Don-445
93Fle-653
93OPC-152
93StaClu-493
93StaCluFDI-493
93StaCluMOP-493
93StaCluY-23
93Top-779
93TopGol-779
93TopInaM-779
93TopMic-779
94Fle-240
94FleUpd-194
94GiaAMC-15
94GiaMot-19
94StaCluT-14
94StaCluTFDI-14
94Top-326
94TopGol-326
94TopSpa-326
95Fle-584
95Top-453
95TopCyb-249
96ColCliB-22
Montelongo, Joseph
94WilCubC-16
94WilCubF-3761
95RocCubTI-3
Montero, Alberto
90AshTouC-15
91AshTouP-576
92BurAstC-17
92BurAstF-557
Montero, Cesar
90HunCubP-3289
Montero, Danny
92HunCubC-4
92HunCubF-3151
93DayCubC-13
93DayCubF-863
93GenCubC-23
93GenCubF-3177
94DayCubC-17
94DayCubF-2356
Montero, Francisco
96MarPhiB-16
Montero, Jorge
87SalAngP-11
Montero, Sixto
89MarPhiS-22
Montes, Dan
89EveGiaS-22
Montgomery, Al
80UtiBluJT-23
Montgomery, Andre
95BilRedTI-4
Montgomery, Damin
91BilMusP-3768
91BilMusSP-12
92BenMusSP-28
Montgomery, Dan
87BakDodP-2
88BakDodCLC-238
89VerBeaDS-17
Montgomery, Don
91EveGiaC-6
91EveGiaP-3919
92SanJosGC-14
93SanJosGC-17
93SanJosGF-19
Montgomery, Jeff
87NasSouTI-15
88Fle-642
88FleGlo-642
88FleUpd-32
88FleUpdG-32
88OmaRoyC-7
88OmaRoyP-1501
88Sco-497
88ScoGlo-497
88ScoRoo-71T
88ScoRooG-71T
88Top-447
88TopTif-447
89Bow-113
89BowTif-113
89Don-440
89DonBasB-319
89Fle-288
89FleGlo-288
89Sco-367
89Top-116
89TopTif-116
89UppDec-618
90Bow-370
90BowTif-370
90Don-380
90Fle-115
90FleCan-115
90Lea-520
90OPC-638
90PanSti-85
90PubSti-353
90Sco-365
90Top-638
90TopSti-273
90TopTif-638
90UppDec-698
90VenSti-351
91Bow-308
91Don-505
91Fle-564
91OPC-371
91RoyPol-16
91Sco-143
91StaClu-369
91Top-371
91TopDesS-371
91TopMic-371
91TopTif-371
91Ult-153
91UppDec-637
92Bow-122
92Don-666
92Fle-164
92Hig5-64
92Lea-136
92OPC-16
92Pin-173
92RoyPol-23
92Sco-14
92ScoProP-5
92StaClu-12
92Stu-190
92Top-16
92TopGol-16
92TopGolW-16
92TopMic-16
92Ult-76
92UppDec-627
93Bow-533
93ClaGam-67
93Don-175
93Fin-42
93FinRef-42
93Fla-222
93Fle-245
93FleFruotL-47
93Lea-124
93OPC-261
93PacSpa-140
93Pin-336
93RoyPol-23
93Sco-212
93Sel-264
93SelStaL-69
93SP-234
93StaClu-125
93StaCluFDI-125
93StaCluM-184
93StaCluMOP-125
93StaCluRoy-19
93Top-130
93TopGol-130
93TopInaM-130
93TopMic-130
93TriPla-236
93Ult-566
93UppDec-62
93UppDecGold-62
94Bow-59
94BowBes-R73
94BowBesR-R73
94ColC-210
94ColChoGS-210
94ColChoSS-210
94Don-362
94DonSpeE-362
94ExtBas-97
94Fin-387
94FinRef-387
94Fla-62
94Fle-170
94FleAllS-17
94FUnPac-53
94Lea-25
94OPC-7
94Pac-298
94PanSti-10
94Pin-106
94PinArtP-106
94PinMusC-106

94ProMag-65
94Sco-155
94ScoGolR-155
94Sel-109
94StaClu-49
94StaCluFDI-49
94StaCluGR-49
94StaCluMO-41
94StaCluMOP-49
94TomPiz-23
94Top-394
94Top-535
94TopBlaG-14
94TopGol-394
94TopGol-535
94TopSpa-394
94TopSpa-535
94TriPla-240
94Ult-70
94UltFir-1
94UppDec-339
94UppDecED-339
95Baz-94
95Bow-345
95ColCho-455
95ColChoGS-455
95ColChoSE-211
95ColChoSEGS-211
95ColChoSESS-211
95ColChoSS-455
95D3-19
95DenHol-18
95Don-321
95DonPreP-321
95DonTopotO-94
95Emb-89
95EmbGolI-89
95Emo-50
95Fin-214
95FinRef-214
95Fla-49
95Fle-170
95Lea-29
95Pac-210
95Pin-90
95PinArtP-90
95PinMusC-90
95Sco-400
95ScoGolR-400
95ScoPlaTS-400
95SP-161
95SPCha-159
95SPChaDC-159
95SPSil-161
95SPSpeF-12
95StaClu-286
95StaCluMOP-286
95StaCluSTWS-286
95StaCluVR-148
95Stu-86
95Top-210
95TopCyb-119
95Ult-293
95UltGolM-293
95UppDec-182
95UppDecED-182
95UppDecEDG-182
95UppDecSE-188
95UppDecSEG-188
96Baz-5
96Cir-46
96CirRav-46
96ColCho-174
96ColChoGS-174
96ColChoSS-174
96Don-271
96DonPreP-271
96EmoXL-68
96Fin-B129
96FinRef-B129
96Fla-92
96Fle-135
96FleTif-135
96Lea-17
96LeaPrePB-17
96LeaPrePG-17
96LeaPrePS-17
96LeaSigA-160
96LeaSigAG-160
96LeaSigAS-160
96MetUni-66
96MetUniP-66
96PanSti-189
96RoyPol-18
96Sco-313
96ScoDugC-B38
96ScoDugCAP-B38
96SP-97
96StaClu-69
96StaCluEPB-69
96StaCluEPG-69
96StaCluEPS-69
96StaCluMOP-69
95StaCluVRMC-148
96Top-308
96TopGal-22
96TopGalPPI-22
96TopLas-124
96Ult-74
96UltGolM-74
96UppDec-348
97Cir-363
97CirRav-363
97ColCho-127
97Fin-300
97FinEmb-300
97FinEmbR-300
97FinRef-300
97Fle-117
97FleTif-117
97MetUni-95
97Pac-106
97PacLigB-106
97PacPri-37
97PacPriLB-37
97PacPriP-37
97PacSil-106
97RoyPol-15
97StaClu-135
97StaCluMOP-135
97Top-399
97Ult-68
97UltGolME-68
97UltPlaME-68
97UppDec-85

Montgomery, Josh
94ButCopKSP-21

Montgomery, Larry
77BurBeeT-18
78BurBeeT-21
80HolMilT-20
81ElPasDT-12
85TucTorC-58
91DaiDolF-2

Montgomery, Mike
90BatCliP-3064

Montgomery, Monty
72OPC-372
72Top-372
73OPC-164
73Top-164

Montgomery, Ray
90AubAstP-3394
91BurAstC-21
91BurAstP-2815
92JacGenF-4012
93JacGenF-2121
94TucTorF-775
95JacGenTI-18
95TusTorTI-16
96TusTorB-17
97Don-229
97DonPreP-229
97DonPrePGold-229
97Fle-611
97FleTif-611
97PinCer-134
97PinCerMBlu-134
97PinCerMG-134
97PinCerMR-134
97PinCerR-134
97PinTotCPB-134
97PinTotCPG-134
97PinTotCPR-134
97Sco-274
97Sco-491
97ScoHobR-491
97ScoResC-491
97ScoShoS-274
97ScoShoS-491
97ScoShoSAP-274
97ScoShoSAP-491

Montgomery, Reggie
85MidAngT-24
86EdmTraP-21
88RocRedWP-207

Montgomery, Robert
71OPC-176
71RedSoxA-6
71Top-176
72OPC-411
72Top-411
73LinPor-27
73OPC-491
73Top-491
74OPC-301
74Top-301
75OPC-559
75Top-559
76OPC-523
76SSP-414
76Top-523
77Top-288
78PapGinD-10
78Top-83
79OPC-219
79Top-423
80Top-618

Montgomery, Steve
92ClaDraP-61
92FroRowDP-87
93StaCluM-193
94ArkTraF-3087
95ArkTraTI-21
96BesAutS-62
96Exc-230
96HigDesMB-20
96LeaSigEA-131
96Top-431

Montiel, David
95BelBreTI-26
95LinVen-45

Montiel, Ivan
95LinVen-216

Montilla, Jose
94VenLinU-122
95LinVen-179

Montilla, Julio
93RocRoyC-17
93RocRoyF-723
96WilBluRB-24

Montoya, Albert
91MedHatBJP-4097
91MedHatBJSP-16
92MyrBeaHC-24
92MyrBeaHF-2195
93DunBluJC-17
93DunBluJF-1793
93DunBluJFFN-19
94KnoSmoF-1301

Montoya, Charlie
89StoPorCLC-172
90TexLeaAGS-4

Montoya, Norman
91QuaCitAC-9
91QuaCitAP-2626
92PalSprAC-3
92PalSprAF-835
95ElPasDTI-19
96El PasDB-19

Montoya, Wilmer
94VenLinU-157
94WatIndC-20
94WatIndF-3933
95LinVen-136

Montoyo, Charlie
88BlaYNPRWL-73
88CalLeaACLC-16
88StoPorCLC-199
88StoPorP-737
89BlaYNPRWL-80
89CalLeaA-29
89StoPorB-14
89StoPorP-381
89StoPorS-12
90ElPasDGS-23
91DenZepLD-146
91DenZepP-131
91LinDriAAA-146
92DenZepF-2649
92DenZepS-141
93OttLynF-2443
94ScrRedBF-927
95ScrRedBTI-21
96HarSenB-20

Montreuil, Al
73WicAerKSB-10
74WicAerODF-114

Monzant, Ray
56Top-264
58GiaSFCB-17
58Top-37
58Top-447
59Top-332
60TacBan-10
60Top-338
79TCM50-199

Monzon, Dan
73OPC-469
73Top-469
74OPC-613
74Top-613
78WauMetT-19
90UtiBluSP-3
91SouBenWSC-3

Monzon, Daniel F.
82LynMetT-1

Monzon, Jose
89MyrBeaBJP-1459
91KnoBluJLD-362
91KnoBluJP-1771
91LinDriAA-362
92KnoBluJF-2992
92KnoBluJS-386
92SyrChiF-1971
93LinVenB-99
93SyrChiF-1000
94MidAngF-2441
94MidAngOHP-17
94VenLinU-62
95LinVen-232
95MidAngOHP-22
95MidAngTI-20
96MidAngB-24
96MidAngOHP-20

Moock, Chris
92LSUTigM-3
92PeoChiTI-16

Moock, Joe
77FriOneYW-32
81TCM60I-340
91MetWIZ-280

Moock, Pat
76AshTouT-16

Moody, Eric
93EriSaiC-16
93EriSaiF-3112
94HudValRF-3380
96TulDriTI-18
94HudValRC-14

Moody, James
89OneYanP-2105
90PriWilCTI-15

Moody, Kyle
91SpoIndC-6
91SpoIndP-3957
92ChaRaiF-127

Moody, Lee
93NegLeaRL2-28

Moody, Ritchie
91OklStaC-17
92ClaDraP-43
92ClaFS7-429
92FroRowDP-79
92GasRanF-2252
92OklStaC-21
93Bow-377
93ClaFS7-224
93StaCluM-195
93StaCluR-2
93Top-438
93TopGol-438
93TopInaM-438
93TopMic-438
93TulDriF-2732
94Bow-457
94OklCit8F-1494
93TulDriTI-19

Moody, Willis
88NegLeaD-18

Moon Yang, Sang
96WesOahCHWB-37

Moon, Bradley
96MedHatBJTI-20

Moon, Glen
80CliGiaT-19

Moon, Ray
92PriRedC-5
92PriRedF-3099
93BilMusF-3958
93BilMusSP-3

Moon, Wally
47Exh-162
54Top-137
55CarHunW-14
55Top-67
55TopDouH-37
56Top-55
56TopPin-48
57Top-65
58CarJayP-10
58Top-210
59DodTeal-16
59DodVol-9
59Top-530
60Baz-3
60DodJayP-9
60DodMor-7
60DodPos-6
60DodTeal-12
60DodUniO-12
60Top-5
60TopTat-36
60TopVen-5
61DodBelB-9
61DodJayP-6
61DodUniO-13
61Pos-159A
61Pos-159B
61Raw-6
61Top-325
61TopStal-29
62DodBelB-9
62DodJayP-7
62ExhStaB-27
62SalPlaC-124
62ShiPlaC-124
62Top-52
62Top-190A
62Top-190B
62TopBuc-62
62TopStal-137
62TopVen-52
62TopVen-190
63BasMagM-60
63DodJayP-10
63ExhStaB-47
63Top-279
64Top-353
64TopVen-353
65OPC-247
65Top-247
79TCM50-137
81TCM60I-372
82GSGalAG-18
88PacLegI-81
89DodSmoG-65
89SweBasG-81
90CarLeaA-7
90DodTar-543
90FreKeyTI-1
91FreKeyC-26
91FreKeyP-2381
91SweBasG-64
92ActPacA-22
93UppDecAH-98
94TopArc1-137
94TopArc1G-137

Moon, Warren
91StaCluCM-36
91StaCluMO-32

Mooney, Eric
94EugEmeC-14
94EugEmeF-3708

Mooney, James
34DiaMatCSB-131
34Gou-83
74Car193T-19

Mooney, Troy
89PriPirS-13
90WelPirP-23
91AugPirC-10
91AugPirP-804
92SalBucC-22
92SalBucF-61

Mooneyham, Bill
81HolMilT-23
82HolMilT-6
83NasAngT-5
84EdmTraC-110
85HunStaJ-21
86DonRoo-50
86FleUpd-77
87Don-302
87Fle-399
87FleGlo-399
87TacTigP-18
87Top-548
87TopTif-548
88DenZepP-1254

88ElPasDB-9
Moore, Andy
92ElmPioC-22
92ElmPioF-1391
93UtiBluSC-16
93UtiBluSF-3541
Moore, Archie
64Top-581
81TCM60I-479
92YanWIZ6-90
Moore, Austin
33ButCanV-33
Moore, Balor
71OPC-747
71Top-747
72Dia-36
73OPC-211
73Top-211
74OPC-453
74Top-453
75OPC-592
75Top-592
78AngFamF-27
78BluJayP-18
78SSP270-202
78Top-368
79BluJayBY-17
79OPC-122
79Top-238
80OPC-6
80Top-19
80VenLeaS-29
81VanCanT-10
92UppDecS-3
Moore, Barry (R. Barry)
67OPC-11
67Top-11
68Top-462
69Top-639
70OPC-366
70Top-366
72MilBra-241
81TCM60I-360
Moore, Bart
89ElmPioP-9
90WinHavRSS-17
Moore, Billy
86IndIndTI-35
87IndIndTI-18
88BlaYNPRWLU-40
88IndIndC-13
88IndIndP-497
88TriAAC-6
89IndIndC-13
89IndIndP-1211
89RocRedWP-1647
90CMC-36
90DenZepC-11
90DenZepP-639
90ProAAAF-664
Moore, Bobby
95HudValRTI-27
Moore, Bobby (Robert Vincent)
88BasCitRS-18
89BasCitRS-18
90Bes-231
90MemChiB-9
90MemChiP-1019
90MemChiS-20
90ProAaA-51
90StaFS7-86
91LinDriAAA-343
91OmaRoyLD-343
91OmaRoyP-1047
92RicBraBB-9
92RicBraF-388
92RicBraRC-12
92RicBraS-434
92SkyAAAF-199
92TopDeb91-126
94MemChiF-370
95RicBraRC-12
95RicBraTI-9
96ChaRivTI-9622
96RicBraB-21
96RicBraRC-5
97RicBraBC-19
Moore, Bobby (Robert)
84ShrCapFB-12
86PhoFirP-17
87EugEmeP-2653
Moore, Boo
90WinHavRSS-18
91CarLeaAP-CAR24
91Cla/Bes-43
91LynRedSC-23
91LynRedSP-1213
92LynRedSC-19
92LynRedSF-2920
92UppDecML-200
93NewBriRSF-1233
94LynRedSC-19
94LynRedSF-1906
Moore, Brad
86BenPhiC-144
87ClePhiP-2
88PhiTas-27
88ReaPhiP-866
89BlaYNPRWL-61
89OPC-202
89ScrRedBC-8
89ScrRedBP-709
89Top-202
89TopTif-202
90FleUpd-45
90ProAAAF-299
90ScrRedBP-597
91LinDriAAA-564
91TidTidLD-564
91TidTidP-2506
92TidTidF-893
92TidTidS-567
Moore, Brandon
96PriWilCB-19
Moore, Brian
95MicBatCTI-21
96MicBatCB-4
Moore, Bud
96WatIndTI-20
Moore, Calvin
75CedRapGT-29
Moore, Cary
89EriOriS-14
Moore, Charlie
74OPC-603
74Top-603
75OPC-636
75Top-636
76BreA&P-8
76OPC-116
76SSP-231
76Top-116
76VenLeaS-201
77BurCheD-84
77Top-382
78Top-51
79Top-408
80OPC-302
80Top-579
81Don-324
81Fle-521
81OPC-237
81Top-237
82BrePol-22
82Don-280
82Fle-150
82OPC-308
82Top-308
83BreGar-13
83BrePol-22
83Don-206
83Fle-42
83Top-659
83TopSti-157
84BreGar-14
84BrePol-22
84Don-292
84Fle-209
84Nes792-751
84OPC-138
84Top-751
84TopSti-301
84TopTif-751
85BreGar-14
85BrePol-22
85Don-351
85Fle-589
85Top-83
85TopTif-83
86BrePol-22
86Don-246
86Fle-496
86OPC-137
86Top-137
86Top-426
86TopSti-204
86TopTif-137
86TopTif-426
87Don-372
87Fle-351
87FleGlo-351
87OPC-93
87SanJosBP-6
87Top-676
87TopTif-676
87TopTra-82T
87TopTraT-82T
88Sco-444
88ScoGlo-444
91UppDecS-10
92BreCarT-17
94BreMilB-335
Moore, Charlton
92MarPhiC-4
92MarPhiF-3073
93BatCliC-21
93BatCliF-3161
Moore, Cy (William Wilcey)
28StaPlaCE-48
28W513-77
79RedSoxEF-21
87Yan192T-5
90DodTar-544
91ConTSN-109
94ConTSN-1007
94ConTSNB-1007
Moore, Daryl
90Bes-121
90ProAaA-107
90WauTimB-5
90WauTimP-2118
91FreKeyP-2360
92HagSunS-266
92ProFS7-8
92RocRedWF-1937
92SkyAA F-110
Moore, Dave
78IndIndTI-11
79IndIndTI-4
80VenLeaS-25
81AlbDukT-1
82AlbDukT-6
Moore, Dee
43DodTeal-18
90DodTar-545
Moore, Don
81ArkTraT-3
82ArkTraT-17
87GenCubP-11
Moore, Donnie
96OgdRapTI-44
Moore, Donnie Ray
78SSP270-263
78Top-523
79Top-17
82RicBraT-7
84BraPol-31
84Fle-185
84Nes792-207
84Top-207
84TopTif-207
85AngSmo-21
85Don-650
85Fle-334
85FleUpd-82
85OPC-61
85Top-699
85TopTif-699
85TopTifT-85T
85TopTra-85T
86AngSmo-21
86Don-255
86DonAll-46
86Fle-164
86FleStiC-77
86Lea-130
86OPC-345
86SevCoi-W15
86Top-345
86TopSti-182
86TopTat-16
86TopTif-345
87AngSmo-8
87Don-110
87Fle-89
87FleGlo-89
87FleLeaL-30
87OPC-115
87RedFolSB-56
87SpoTeaP-11
87Top-115
87TopMinL-46
87TopSti-177
87TopTif-115
88AngSmo-20
88Don-621
88Fle-500
88FleGlo-500
88OPC-204
88Sco-195
88ScoGlo-195
88Top-471
88TopTif-471
89Sco-535
94BreMilB-336
Moore, Earl A.
03BreE10-107
04FanCraAL-36
05IndSouPSoCP-14
09BriE97-22
10LuxCigPP-16
10NadE1-38
10W555-49
11E94-25
11MecDFT-36
11SpoLifCW-257
11SpoLifM-235
12T207-131
14CraJacE-124
14TexTomE-35
15CraJacE-124
92ConTSN-373
Moore, Ed
79QuaCitCT-3
80QuaCitCT-4
Moore, Eddie (Graham E.)
33Gou-180
90DodTar-546
93ConTSN-850
Moore, Euel
93ConTSN-772
Moore, Gary D.
90DodTar-1039
Moore, Gene (Eugene)
36GouWidPPR-A73
39PlaBal-160
40PlaBal-143
41DouPlaR-121
41PlaBal-25
77TCMTheWY-27
81DiaStaCD-115
83TCMPla1945-7
90DodTar-547
91ConTSN-77
96Bro194F-32
Moore, Greg
86KnoBluJP-17
Moore, J.B.
85PriWilPT-27
Moore, Jackie S.
65Top-593
70BreMcD-21
73OPC-549
73Top-549
74OPC-379
74Top-379
77OPC-58
77Top-113
84A'sMot-27
84TopTra-81T
84TopTraT-81T
85A'sMot-1
85Top-38
85TopTif-38
86A'sMot-1
86Top-591
86TopTif-591
87ExpPos-17
89ExpPos-22
90RedKah-27
91RedKah-NNO
92RedKah-NNO
93RanKee-438
94RanMagM-11
Moore, Jason
96AriBlaDB-22
Moore, Jeramie
94LSUTig-16
Moore, Jim
30ChiEveAP-18
85Ft.MyeRT-25
Moore, Jo-Jo (Joe G.)
33Gou-126
33Gou-231
34DiaMatCSB-132
35DiaMatCS2-15
35DiaMatCS3T1-108
36WorWidGV-8
37WheBB14-10
37WheBB7-29D
38OurNatGPP-21
39PlaBal-79
40PlaBal-84
41DouPlaR-29
79DiaGre-31
94ConTSN-1182
94ConTSNB-1182
Moore, Joel
93BenRocC-17
93BenRocF-3265
94Bow-151
94CenValRC-1
94CenValRF-3199
95NewHavRTI-13
95SPML-49
96Exc-158
Moore, John
31CubTeal-17
34DiaMatCSB-133
35DiaMatCS3T1-109
37WheBB9-12
90WauTimS-17
91PerHeaF-5
Moore, Johnny (John F.)
32CubTeal-18
34ButPreR-45
36ExhFou-6
37ExhFou-6
37ExhFou-6
79DiaGre-103
93DiaStaES-146
94ConTSN-1184
94ConTSNB-1184
Moore, Junior (Alvin)
78GreBraT-17
78SSP270-159
78Top-421
79Top-275
80Top-186
81DurBulT-13
Moore, Kelvin
80OgdA'sT-20
81TacTigT-18
82Don-534
82TacTigT-31
82Top-531
83Don-87
83TacTigT-32
84ElPasDT-13
84VanCanC-31
85BufBisT-10
Moore, Kenderick
96SpoIndB-18
Moore, Kerwin
89EugEmeB-17
90AppFoxBS-19
90AppFoxP-2109
90CMC-873
91BasCitRC-26
91BasCitRP-1412
91Bow-312
91Cla/Bes-38
91UppDecFE-19F
92BasCitRC-14
92Bow-593
92ClaFS7-22
92UppDecML-278
93ClaGolF-82
93HigDesMC-13
93HigDesMF-55
94Bow-319
94Cla-61
94ExcFS7-194
94HunStaF-1345
94UppDecML-123
96SigRooOJ-22
96SigRooOJS-22
Moore, Lenny
78ReaRem-15
Moore, Marcus
89BenBucL-8
90QuaCitAGS-13
91DunBluJC-8
91DunBluJP-204
91MelBusF-6
92ClaFS7-160
92KnoBluJF-2988
92KnoBluJS-387

92SkyAA F-163
93Bow-288
93CenValRC-19
93CenValRF-2892
94Bow-2
94ColC-536
94ColChoGS-536
94ColChoSS-536
94ExtBas-250
94Fla-156
94FleUpd-128
94LeaGolR-12
94LeaLimR-61
94ScoRoo-RT157
94ScoRooGR-RT157
94SpoRoo-60
94SpoRooAP-60
94Top-186
94TopGol-186
94TopSpa-186
94Ult-485
94UppDec-234
94UppDecED-234
95Don-169
95DonPreP-169
95Lea-175
96FleUpd-U123
96FleUpdTC-U123
Moore, Mark
80CedRapRT-1
92SouOreAC-9
92SouOreAF-3420
93SouOreAC-19
93SouOreAF-4066
94WesMicWC-17
94WesMicWF-2299
95ModA'sTI-18
Moore, Meredith
89WinHavRSS-16
Moore, Michael
88BoiHawP-1608
92ClaBluBF-BC30
92ClaFS7-418
92YakBeaF-3464
93ClaGolF-183
93StaCluD-21
93StaCluM-26
93Top-576
93TopGol-576
93TopInaM-576
93TopMic-576
93UppDec-430
93UppDecGold-430
94BakDodC-18
94BowBesR-B60
94Cla-121
94UppDecML-250
94UppDecML-263
96SanAntMB-16
Moore, Mike (Michael W.)
80LynSaiT-1
83Don-428
83Fle-482
83SalLakCGT-7
83Top-209
84Don-634
84Fle-614
84MarMot-5
84Nes792-547
84Top-547
84TopTif-547
85Don-440
85Fle-495
85MarMot-8
85Top-279
85Top-373
85TopTif-279
85TopTif-373
86Don-240
86Fle-469
86Lea-114
86MarMot-21
86PenWhiSP-18
86Spo-162
86Top-646
86TopMinL-30
86TopSti-221
86TopTat-2
86TopTif-646
87Don-70
87Fle-590
87FleGlo-590
87MarMot-3
87OPC-102
87SmoAmeL-11
87SpoTeaP-25
87Top-727
87TopSti-215
87TopTif-727
88Don-75
88DonBasB-192
88Fle-379
88FleGlo-379
88MarMot-3
88Sco-464
88ScoGlo-464
88StaLinMa-9
88Top-432
88TopBig-241
88TopTif-432
89A'sMot-12
89Bow-189
89BowTif-189
89Don-448
89DonBasB-246
89DonTra-21
89Fle-554
89FleGlo-554
89FleUpd-55
89OPC-28
89PanSti-431
89PAORelT-3
89Sco-274
89ScoRoo-5T
89Spo-77
89Top-28
89TopSti-220
89TopTif-28
89TopTra-82T
89TopTraT-82T
89UppDec-123
89UppDec-758
90A'sMot-9
90Bow-445
90BowTif-445
90ClaBlu-104
90Don-214
90Fle-16
90FleCan-16
90FleWorS-1
90Lea-293
90OPC-175
90PanSti-136
90PubSti-311
90Sco-190
90Sco-700
90Sco100S-42
90Spo-185
90Top-175
90TopBig-200
90TopMinL-31
90TopSti-178
90TopTif-175
90UppDec-275
90VenSti-352
90Woo-27
91A'sMot-11
91A'sSFE-9
91Bow-212
91Don-161
91Fle-18
91Lea-218
91OPC-294
91Sco-516
91StaClu-464
91Top-294
91TopDesS-294
91TopMic-294
91TopTif-294
91Ult-252
91UppDec-423
91WatIndC-14
91WatIndP-3369
92AthMot-11
92Bow-216
92Don-337
92Fle-263
92Lea-164
92OPC-359
92Pin-109
92Sco-91
92StaClu-669
92Stu-227
92Top-359
92TopGol-359
92TopGolW-359
92TopMic-359
92Ult-425
92UppDec-661
92WatIndC-23
92WatIndF-3239
93BakDodCLC-1
93Bow-179
93Don-683
93Fle-666
93FleFinE-213
93Lea-401
93OPC-186
93OPCPre-110
93PacSpa-448
93Pin-202
93Sco-641
93Sel-270
93StaClu-693
93StaCluFDI-693
93StaCluMOP-693
93TigGat-21
93Top-73
93TopGol-73
93TopInaM-73
93TopMic-73
93Ult-553
93UppDec-182
93UppDec-512
93UppDecGold-182
93UppDecGold-512
94Bow-565
94BowBes-B60
94ColC-459
94ColChoGS-459
94ColChoSS-459
94Don-554
94ExtBas-78
94Fin-83
94FinRef-83
94Fla-51
94Fle-141
94Lea-197
94Pac-226
94PanSti-66
94Pin-212
94PinArtP-212
94PinMusC-212
94SanAntMF-2483
94Sco-143
94ScoGolR-143
94Sel-224
94StaClu-99
94StaCluFDI-99
94StaCluGR-99
94StaCluMOP-99
94Top-523
94TopGol-523
94TopSpa-523
94Ult-58
94UppDec-316
94UppDecED-316
95ColCho-469
95ColChoGS-469
95ColChoSS-469
95Don-154
95DonPreP-154
95Fle-58
95FleTeaL-6
95Lea-278
95Pac-157
95Sco-174
95ScoGolR-174
95ScoPlaTS-174
95Top-576
95TopCyb-350
95Ult-49
95UltGolM-49
95UppDec-187
95UppDecED-187
95UppDecEDG-187
Moore, Pat
87EriCarP-27
Moore, Randy
88BelBreGS-21
Moore, Randy (Randolph)
31Exh-1
33ButCanV-34
33Gou-69
33TatOrbSDR-171
34DiaMatCSB-134
34GouCanV-26
35GouPuzR-4E
35GouPuzR-7E
35GouPuzR-12E
36GouWidPPR-A74
36NatChiFPR-113
90DodTar-548
93ConTSN-924
Moore, Ray
55OriEss-19
55Top-208
56Top-43
57Top-106
58Top-249
58WhiSoxJP-7
59Top-293
60Top-447
61Top-289
61TopMagR-20
61TwiCloD-18
61TwiPetM-13
62Top-437
63Top-26
63TwiVol-7
78HalHalR-9
90DodTar-549
91OriCro-312
Moore, Red (James)
95NegLeaL2-30
Moore, Rick
86ChaLooP-20
87SalSpuP-10
Moore, Robert
79WatA'sT-25
80WesHavWCT-21C
83GleFalWST-16
90CMC-127
90NasSouC-2
90NasSouP-230
90ProAAAF-542
Moore, Rod
90ArkRaz-29
Moore, Ron
90ArkRaz-20
Moore, Ronald
86SpoIndC-159
Moore, Roy Daniel
22E120-85
Moore, Sam
86FreGiaP-8
87CliGiaP-23
95ElmPioTI-20
95ElmPioUTI-20
Moore, Steve
82TulDriT-13
Moore, Terry
36GouWidPPR-A75
36NatChiFPR-114
41CarW75-19
41DouPlaR-37
46SeaSLP-37
49Bow-174
51R42SmaS-71
66CarCoi-9
75JohMiz-11
76TayBow4-91
79DiaGre-154
82Bow195E-261
83TCMPla1942-25
92CarMcD-10
92ConTSN-641
Moore, Tim
90HunCubP-3290
90WinSpiTI-19
91EliTwiP-4312
91GenCubC-13
91GenCubP-4226
91PeoChiC-17
91PeoChiP-1350
91PeoChiTI-18
92FroRowDP-4
92KenTwiC-7
92KenTwiF-618
92PeoChiC-11
92PeoChiTI-17
93ForMyeMC-15
93ForMyeMF-2669
93SouBenWSC-16
93SouBenWSF-1428
93StaCluM-127
94NasXprF-400
94PriWilCC-17
94PriWilCF-1918
95HarCitRCTI-15
96BirBarB-15
92UtiBluSC-1
Moore, Tommy J.
89PacSenL-148
91MetWIZ-281
93RanKee-272
Moore, Tony
90KinMetB-9
90KinMetS-18
Moore, Trey
94SigRooDP-42
94SigRooDPS-42
94StaCluDP-32
94StaCluDPFDI-32
95SPML-151
95Top-538
96BesAutS-63
96PorCitRB-20
Moore, Vince
92Bow-443
92MacBraC-18
92MacBraF-280
92StaCluD-123
93CarLeaAGF-38
93DurBulC-1
93DurBulF-497
93DurBulTI-24
94Cla-14
94ExcFS7-159
94WicWraF-202
94Bow-476
94TedWil-128
94UppDecML-56
96MemChiB-24
Moore, Whitey
38CinOraW-20
39OrcPhoAP-18
39PlaBal-162
40PlaBal-150
41HarHarW-17
94ConTSN-1227
94ConTSNB-1227
Moorhead, Bob
62Top-593
82MetGal62-16
91MetWIZ-282
Moose, Bob
68OPC-36
68PirKDK-38
68PirTeal-13
68Top-36
68TopVen-36
69Top-409
70DayDaiNM-144
70MLBOffS-104
70OPC-110
70Top-110
70TopBoo-21
71MLBOffS-209
71OPC-690
71PirActP-20
71PirArc-7
71Top-690
71TopCoi-147
72MilBra-242
72Top-647
73OPC-499
73Top-499
74OPC-382
74Top-382
75OPC-536
75Top-536
76OPC-476
76SSP-570
76Top-476
81TCM60I-350
Moose, Juice
90MidAngGS-NNO
95MidAngTI-30
Moose, Mariner
91MarCouH-29
94MasMan-8
Mooty, Jake (J.T.)
36GouWidPPR-D18
41CubTeal-13
49BowPCL-23
Mora, Andres
77Top-646
78Top-517
79Top-287
91OriCro-313
Mora, Melvin
93AshTouC-14
93AshTouF-2284
93LinVenB-79
93SouAtlLAGF-31
94ClaGolF-15
94OscAstC-17
94OscAstF-1151
94VenLinU-18

95JacGenTI-16
95LinVen-75
96JacGenB-20
96TusTorB-18
Moraga, David
96WesPalBEB-11
Morales, Alex
95BelGiaTI-9
95HelBreTI-18
96BurBeeTI-22
96HelBreTI-30
Morales, Allen
94IdaFalBSP-30
Morales, Armando
91PriRedC-11
91PriRedP-3510
92ChaWheF-7
92ChaWVWC-13
93PriRedC-19
93PriRedF-4175
Morales, Edwin
87PorChaRP-8
Morales, Eric
94KinMetC-12
94KinMetF-3826
95PitMetTI-31
Morales, Francisco
92HunCubF-3152
96StPetCB-21
96WesPalBEB-19
Morales, Heriberto
92GulCoaMF-3485
Morales, Jerry (Julio)
70OPC-262
70Top-262
71OPC-696
71Top-696
72PadTeal-18
73OPC-268
73Top-268
74OPC-258
74Top-258
74TopSta-98
75OPC-282
75Top-282
76CraDis-39
76Hos-140
76OPC-79
76SSP-312
76Top-79
77BurCheD-196
77CubJewT-10
77Hos-49
77Top-639
78CarTeal-11
78OPC-23
78Top-175
79OPC-235
79Top-452
80Top-572
81Fle-338
81Top-377
81TopTra-805
82CubRedL-24
82Don-309
82Fle-601
82FleSta-93
82Top-33
83CubThoAV-24
83Fle-502
83Top-729
84Fle-498
89BlaYNPRWL-33
91MetWIZ-283
Morales, Joe Edwin
82BelBreF-16
84ElPasDT-21
Morales, Jorge
91PenPilC-15
91PenPilP-381
92PenPilC-6
92PenPilF-2936
93AppFoxC-17
93AppFoxF-2463
Morales, Jose
76ExpRed-22
76OPC-418
76SSP-323
76Top-418
77ExpPos-23
77OPC-90
77OPC-263
77Top-102
77Top-233
78OPC-63
78Top-374
78TwiFriP-12
79Top-552
79TwiFriP-18
80OPC-116
80Top-218
81Don-495
81Fle-571
81Top-43
81TopTra-806
82DodUniOV-13
82Don-203
82Fle-173
82Top-648
82TopTra-75T
83DodPol-43
83TopTra-75T
84DodPol-43
84Don-275
84Fle-107
84Nes792-143
84Top-143
84TopTif-143
86GiaMot-28
87GiaMot-27
88GiaMot-27
89SweBasG-38
90DodTar-550
90IndTeal-28
91IndFanC-30
91OriCro-314
92IndFanC-30
93IndWUA-33
Morales, Lester
76VenLeaS-112
Morales, Manuel
85MexCitTT-20
Morales, Rich
69Top-654
70OPC-91
70Top-91
71OPC-267
71Top-267
72Top-593
73OPC-494
73Top-494
74OPC-387
74PadDea-20
74Top-387A
74Top-387B
81QuaCitCT-30
88VerMarP-954
89CalCanC-24
89CalCanP-538
90SanBerSCLC-109
90WilBilB-25
90WilBilP-1072
90WilBilS-25
91PocPioP-3800
91PocPioSP-30
92SalSpuC-30
92SalSpuF-3777
94OgdRapF-3751
94OgdRapSP-25
95OdgRapTI-19
Morales, William
87PriWilYP-29
88PriWilYS-18
Morales, Willie
92AriWilP-10
93SouOreAC-20
93SouOreAF-4067
94WesMicWC-18
94WesMicWF-2300
95ModA'sTI-19
95SPML-127
96HunStaTI-19
Moralez, Paul
86KinEagP-17
87BakDodP-24
Moran, Al (Richard Alan)
63Top-558
64Top-288
64TopVen-288
76Met63 S-10
81TCM60I-430
91MetWIZ-284
Moran, Billy (William Nelson)
58Top-388
59Top-196
59TopVen-196
62Top-539
63AngJayP-9
63SalMetC-48
63Top-57
64Top-333
64TopSta-67
64TopVen-333
65Top-562
76VenLeaS-175
81TCM60I-429
Moran, Bugs (Bill)
60MapLeaSF-14
61MapLeaBH-14
63Jel-25
63Pos-25
78KnoKnoST-14
Moran, Charles
94ConTSN-1189
94ConTSNB-1189
Moran, Cyril
49W725AngTI-21
Moran, Dino
86WatPirP-13
Moran, Frank
88HamRedP-1746
Moran, Jim
53MotCoo-12
Moran, John Herbert
09ColChiE-203
09T206-449
12ColRedB-203
12ColTinT-203
15CraJacE-111
15SpoNewM-122
16FleBreD-67
90DodTar-1040
Moran, Opie
87EriCarP-2
89ArkTraGS-13
Moran, Owen
11TurRedT-60
Moran, Pat J.
07CubA.CDPP-7
07CubGFGCP-7
09ColChiE-204
09RamT20-82
09T206-253
10DomDisP-88A
10DomDisP-88B
10LuxCigPP-17
10SweCapPP-129
11S74Sil-102
11SpoLifCW-258
11SpoLifM-236
11T205-123
11TurRedT-109
12ColRedB-204
12ColTinT-204
12HasTriFT-9
12T207-132
14PieStaT-42
15SpoNewM-123
16BF2FP-90
16SpoNewM-125
19W514-12
20RedWorCP-13
20WalMaiW-33
23WilChoV-107
24MrsShePP-6
83PhiPosGPaM-11
88PacEigMO-89
Moran, Steve
86AppFoxP-16
Morandini, Mickey
88TopTra-71T
88TopTraT-71T
89SpaPhiP-1030
89SpaPhiS-18
89Sta-57
89Sta-120
89TopBig-162
90Bow-153
90BowTif-153
90CMC-240
90ProAAAF-308
90ScrRedBC-14
90ScrRedBP-606
91Bow-492
91Cla1-T79
91ClaGam-187
91Don-44
91Fle-407
91Lea-383
91LinDriAAA-491
91MajLeaCP-61
91OPC-342
91OPCPre-83
91PhiMed-28
91Sco-376
91ScoRoo-33
91ScrRedBLD-491
91Sev3DCN-12
91SevCoi-NE12
91StaClu-535
91Stu-218
91Top-342
91TopDeb90-110
91TopDesS-342
91TopMic-342
91TopTif-342
91Ult-268
91UppDec-18
92Bow-628
92Don-669
92Fle-539
92Lea-330
92OPC-587
92PanSti-243
92PhiMed-21
92Pin-103
92Sco-143
92StaClu-369
92StaCluMO-21
92Stu-77
92Top-587
92TopGol-587
92TopGolW-587
92TopMic-587
92Ult-247
92UppDec-449
93Bow-428
93Don-224
93Fle-105
93FleGolM-A2
93Lea-77
93OPC-256
93PacSpa-239
93PanSti-271
93PhiMed-23
93Pin-156
93Sco-415
93Sco-512
93Sel-245
93SP-177
93StaClu-449
93StaCluFDI-449
93StaCluMOP-449
93StaCluP-8
93Stu-208
93Top-262
93TopGol-262
93TopInaM-262
93TopMic-262
93TriPla-53
93Ult-91
93UppDec-285
93UppDecGold-285
93UppDecSH-HI12
94ColC-211
94ColChoGS-211
94ColChoSS-211
94Don-498
94Fin-273
94FinRef-273
94Fle-596
94Lea-424
94Pac-482
94PhiMed-23
94PhiMel-16
94PhiUSPC-4C
94PhiUSPC-12D
94Pin-159
94PinArtP-159
94PinMusC-159
94Sco-460
94ScoCyc-TC15
94ScoGolR-460
94StaClu-120
94StaCluFDI-120
94StaCluGR-120
94StaCluMOP-120
94StaCluMOP-ST10
94StaCluST-ST10
94StaCluT-234
94StaCluTFDI-234
94Top-692
94TopGol-692
94TopSpa-692
94Ult-250
94UppDec-463
94UppDecED-463
95Don-278
95DonPreP-278
95DonTopotO-308
95Fla-394
95Fle-401
95Lea-87
95Pac-334
95Phi-21
95PhiMel-17
95Pin-16
95PinArtP-16
95PinMusC-16
95PinSam-16
95Sco-494
95ScoGolR-494
95ScoPlaTS-494
95StaClu-291
95StaCluMOP-291
95StaCluSTWS-291
95Top-2
95TopCyb-2
95Ult-207
95UltGolM-207
96Cir-167
96CirRav-167
96ColCho-256
96ColChoGS-256
96ColChoSS-256
96Don-248
96DonPreP-248
96EmoXL-247
96Fla-336
96Fle-505
96FleTif-505
96Lea-42
96LeaPrePB-42
96LeaPrePG-42
96LeaPrePS-42
96LeaSigA-161
96LeaSigAG-161
96LeaSigAS-161
96MetUni-212
96MetUniP-212
96Pac-154
96PanSti-38
96PhiTeal-23
96ProSta-88
96SP-144
96StaClu-139
96StaCluMOP-139
96Top-370
96Ult-257
96UltGolM-257
96UppDec-168
97Cir-12
97CirRav-12
97ColCho-415
97FlaSho-A134
97FlaSho-B134
97FlaSho-C134
97FlaShoLC-134
97FlaShoLC-B134
97FlaShoLC-C134
97FlaShoLCM-A134
97FlaShoLCM-B134
97FlaShoLCM-C134
97Fle-416
97FleTif-416
97MetUni-203
97Pac-382
97PacLigB-382
97PacSil-382
97ProMag-31
97ProMagML-31
97SP-139
97StaClu-320
97StaCluMOP-320
97Top-64
97Ult-253
97UltGolME-253
97UltPlaME-253
97UppDec-154
Morando, Dean
78WisRapTT-14
Moraw, Carl
86BelBreP-16
87StoPorP-21
88StoPorCLC-184
88StoPorP-746
89ElPasDGS-12
89StoPorB-5
89StoPorCLC-156

89StoPorP-378
Mordecai, Mike
88CapCodPB-17
88CapCodPPaLP-42
90CarLeaA-28
90DurBulTI-7
91DurBulC-13
91DurBulP-1557
92GreBraF-1161
92GreBraS-241
93RicBraBB-6
93RicBraF-192
93RicBraP-4
93RicBraRC-1
93RicBraRC-21
94BraLykP-24
94RicBraF-2854
94TopTra-63T
95FleUpd-92
95LinVen-109
96ColCho-456
96ColChoGS-456
96ColChoSS-456
96Don-131
96DonPreP-131
96Fle-303
96FleTif-303
96LeaSigEA-132
96MLBPin-21
97PacPriGotD-GD114
More, Billy
87SpoTeaP-20
Moreau, Guy
36GouWidPPR-D19
Morehart, Ray
91ConTSN-102
Morehead, Dave
63Top-299
64Top-376
65Top-434
66OPC-135
66Top-135
66TopVen-135
67Top-297
67TopRedSS-11
68DexPre-57
68Top-212
68TopVen-212
69MLBOffS-60
69OPC-29
69Top-29
69TopTeaP-7
70MLBOffS-224
70OPC-495
70RoyTeal-24
70Top-495
71MLBOffS-422
71OPC-221
71Top-221
72MilBra-243
81RedSoxBG2S-96
Morehead, Seth
59Top-253
60Lea-87
60Top-504
61Top-107
Morehouse, Richard
86QuaCitAP-24
87PalSprP-28
88PalSprACLC-91
88PalSprAP-1449
89MidAngGS-24
Morehouse, Scott
88CapCodPPaLP-162
Morel, Plinio
94SavCarC-21
94SavCarF-509
Morel, Ramon
93WelPirC-15
93WelPirF-3352
94AugGreC-13
94AugGreF-3004
95Bow-151
95Exc-258
95LynHilTI-17
96Bow-135
96ColCho-679
96ColChoGS-679
96ColChoSS-679
96Fle-529
96FleTif-529
96Pac-169
97Fle-434
97FleTif-434
97Pac-401
97PacLigB-401
97PacSil-401
Moreland, Keith
80PhiBurK-3
81Don-382
81Fle-13
81Top-131
82CubRedL-6
82Don-119
82Fle-252
82Top-384
82TopTra-76T
83CubThoAV-6
83Don-309
83Fle-503
83FleSta-130
83FleSti-125
83OPC-58
83Top-619
83TopSti-222
84AllGamPI-60
84CubChiT-19
84CubSev-6
84Don-483
84Fle-499
84Nes792-23
84Nes792-456
84OPC-23
84Top-23
84Top-456
84TopSti-39
84TopTif-23
84TopTif-456
85AllGamPI-152
85CubLioP-17
85CubSev-6
85Don-117
85Fle-62
85Lea-197
85OPC-197
85Top-538
85TopMin-538
85TopSti-39
85TopTif-538
86BasStaB-74
86CubGat-6
86CubUno-13
86Don-167
86Dra-9
86Fle-375
86FleLeaL-25
86FleMin-79
86FleStiC-78
86Lea-94
86MSAJayPCD-13
86OPC-266
86Spo-90
86Top-266
86TopMinL-38
86TopSti-54
86TopTat-12
86TopTif-266
87CubCan-20
87CubDavB-6
87Don-24
87Don-169
87DonOpeD-71
87DonSupD-24
87Dra-7
87Fle-569
87FleGlo-569
87FleLeaL-31
87FleMin-69
87FleStiC-79
87Lea-24
87Lea-77
87OPC-177
87SevCoi-C12
87SevCoi-M7
87Spo-122
87SpoTeaP-22
87Top-177
87TopSti-65
87TopTif-177
88Don-201
88DonBasB-266
88Fle-425A
88Fle-425B
88FleGlo-425
88FleUpd-124
88FleUpdG-124
88Lea-160
88OPC-31
88PadCok-7
88PadSmo-19
88PanSti-263
88RedFolSB-58
88Sco-71
88ScoGlo-71
88ScoRoo-9T
88ScoRooG-9T
88ScoSam-71
88Spo-164
88StaLinCu-6
88Top-416
88TopBig-207
88TopSti-58
88TopTif-416
88TopTra-72T
88TopTraT-72T
89Bow-109
89BowTif-109
89Don-111
89DonBasB-203
89Fle-313
89FleGlo-313
89OPC-293
89Sco-42
89ScoRoo-29T
89Spo-141
89TigMar-10
89Top-773
89TopSti-105
89TopTif-773
89TopTra-83T
89TopTraT-83T
89UppDec-361
90PubSti-477
90Sco-444
90Spo-139
90UppDec-401
90VenSti-353
91OriCro-315
92TexLon-29
Moreland, Owen III
84LitFalMT-11
Morelli, Frank
89ElmPioP-10
Morelock, Charlie
83AndBraT-12
86DurBulP-19
87EdmTraP-2069
Moren, Lew
10NadE1-39
11SpoLifCW-259
11SpoLifM-237
Morena, Jamie
87ChaRaiP-18
Moreno, Angel
82Fle-469
84EdmTraC-99
93LinVenB-306
Moreno, Armando
86JacExpT-4
87JacExpP-440
88BlaYNPRWL-109
88JacExpB-27
88JacExpP-983
88SouLeaAJ-21
89BlaYNPRWL-120
89BlaYNPRWLU-16
89IndIndC-19
89IndIndP-1222
90BufBisC-19
90BufBisP-381
90BufBisTI-17
90CMC-19
90ProAAAF-496
91BufBisLD-39
91BufBisP-548
91LinDriAAA-39
92OPC-179
92Top-179
92TopGol-179
92TopGolW-179
92TopMic-179
Moreno, Carlos
76VenLeaS-116
80VenLeaS-184
82MiaMarT-5
Moreno, Chris
89StoPorB-26
Moreno, Claudio
96SanBerSB-18
Moreno, Douglas
86MacPirP-16
86WatPirP-14
93LinVenB-257
Moreno, Erik
93IdaFalBF-4036
93IdaFalBSP-6
Moreno, Jaime
86ChaRaiP-18
88ChaRaiP-1218
89BlaYNPRWL-66
89BlaYNPRWL-67
89WatDiaP-1785
89WatDiaS-26
91ChaRaiC-26
91ChaRaiP-111
92ChaRaiC-24
92ChaRaiF-137
Moreno, Jorge A.
73CedRapAT-28
74CedRapAT-15
75DubPacT-25
91BriTigC-13
91BriTigP-3615
92BriTigF-1427
93FayGenC-16
93FayGenF-142
93NiaFalRF-3404
94FayGenC-17
94FayGenF-2156
Moreno, Jose D.
91WatIndC-15
91WatIndP-3370
93LinVenB-111
94VenLinU-117
Moreno, Jose delos
77ReaPhiT-17
79TidTidT-3
80TidTidT-2
81HawIslT-2
91MetWIZ-285
Moreno, Juan
92ColMetC-17
92ColMetF-308
92ColMetPI-10
93CapCitBC-14
93CapCitBF-471
93KinMetC-17
93KinMetF-3793
96WesMicWB-16
Moreno, Julio
53Bri-13
96FreKeyB-15
Moreno, Michael
83WisRapTF-24
85OrlTwiT-8
Moreno, Omar
77PirPosP-16
77Top-104
78Top-283
79Hos-12
79OPC-321
79Top-4
79Top-607
80BurKinPHR-29
80OPC-372
80Top-165
80Top-204
81AllGamPI-156
81CokTeaS-115
81Don-17
81Fle-361
81FleStiC-100
81OPC-213
81Top-535
81TopScr-100
81TopSti-24
81TopSti-211
82Don-347
82Fle-487
82FleSta-79
82OPC-395
82Top-395
82TopSti-81
82TopStiV-81
83AllGamPI-154
83Don-347
83Fle-312
83FleSti-142
83OPC-332
83Top-485
83TopFol-5
83TopSti-278
83TopTra-76T
84Don-637
84Fle-133
84Nes792-16
84Nes792-714
84OPC-16
84Top-16
84Top-714
84TopSti-322
84TopTif-16
84TopTif-714
85Don-591
85Fle-136
85Top-738
85TopTif-738
86BraPol-18
86Fle-15
86FleUpd-78
86TopTra-75T
86TopTraT-75T
87Fle-521
87FleGlo-521
87Top-214
87TopSti-44
87TopTif-214
89PacSenL-138
89T/MSenL-80
90EliSenL-41
91PacSenL-46
92YanWIZ8-124
95MCIAmb-10
96MedHatBJTI-21
Moreno, Ric
87DunBluJP-936
93ModA'sC-28
94ModA'sC-28
96PawRedSDD-19
Morenz, Shea
95Bes-131
96Exc-91
96ExcFirYP-9
96GreBatB-16
96SigRooOJPP-P9
Moret, Roger (Rogelio)
71OPC-692
71Top-692
72OPC-113
72Top-113
73OPC-291
73Top-291
74OPC-590
74Top-590
74TopSta-137
75OPC-8
75Top-8
76OPC-632
76SSP-420
76Top-632
76TopTra-632T
77Top-292
78SSP270-106
78Top-462
93RanKee-273
Moreta, Manuel
75WatRoyT-20
76WatRoyT-19
Morfin, Arvid
84ButCopKT-18
86BelMarC-116
Morgan, Bill
79QuaCitCT-5
Morgan, Bob M.
50Bow-222
52Top-355
53BowC-135
53Top-85
55Bow-81
56Top-337
58Top-144
79DiaGre-323
79TCM50-193
83TopRep5-355
90DodTar-551
91TopArc1-85
95TopArcBD-26
95TopArcBD-45
Morgan, Chet
79DiaGre-381
Morgan, Chris
86FloStaLAP-36
86LakTigP-16
87GleFalTP-17
Morgan, Curt
86MiaMarP-18
Morgan, Cy (Harry)
09PhiCarE-19
09RamT20-83
10NadE1-40

11A'sFirT20-13
11PloCanE-48
11SpoLifCW-260
11SpoLifM-100
12T207-133
Morgan, David
93MedHatBJF-3740
93MedHatBJSP-19
95HagSunF-72
96DunBluJUTI-10
Morgan, Eddie
28StaPlaCE-49
31Exh-21
33ExhFou-11
33Gou-116
34BatR31-60
34GouCanV-2
90DodTar-552
93ConTSN-943
Morgan, Gary
90BatCliP-3081
Morgan, Gene
86MemChiSTOS-19
86MemChiTOS-19
87MemChiB-17
87MemChiP-16
Morgan, Jim
89ChaLooLITI-18
Morgan, Joe L.
65OPC-16
65Top-16
66OPC-195
66Top-195
66TopRubl-69
66TopVen-195
67Ast-20
67AstTeal1-10
67AstTeal2-17
67CokCapA-30
67CokCapAs-12
67CokCapNLA-24
67DexPre-148
67OPCPapl-25
67Top-337
67TopPos-25
67TopTesF-16
67TopVen-308
68CokCapA-12
68DexPre-56
68OPC-144
68Top-144
68Top-364
68TopVen-144
68TopVen-364
69MilBra-195
69MLBOffS-141
69OPC-35
69Top-35
69TopSta-36
69TopSup-42
69TopTeaP-6
70AstTeal-8
70DayDaiNM-112
70Kel-72
70MLBOffS-44
70OPC-537
70Top-537
71AstCok-8
71MLBOffS-89
71OPC-264
71Top-264
71TopCoi-117
71TopGreM-34
72MilBra-244
72OPC-132
72Top-132
72Top-752
73Kel2D-34
73LinPor-57
73OPC-230
73Top-230
74GreHeroBP-6
74Kel-36
74OPC-85
74OPC-333
74Top-85
74Top-333
74TopSta-28
75GreHeroBP-4
75Hos-5
75HosTwi-5
75Kel-27
75OPC-180
75Top-180
76BooProC-21
76CraDis-40
76GreHeroBP-4
76Hos-2
76HosTwi-2
76Kel-14
76LinSup-96
76OPC-197
76OPC-420
76RedIceL-9
76RedKro-12
76RedPos-11
76SSP-38
76Top-197
76Top-420
77BurCheD-207
77Hos-2
77MSADis-44
77OPC-220
77PepGloD-46
77RCColC-45
77Spo-1805
77Spo-3419
77Top-100
77Top-411
77TopCloS-31
78Hos-87
78OPC-160
78Pep-18
78RCColC-7
78SSP270-121
78Top-300
78WifBalD-52
79Hos-61
79OPC-5
79Top-20
80BurKinPHR-30
80OPC-342
80PerHaloFP-205
80Top-650
81Don-18
81Fle-78
81FleStiC-109
81Kel-22
81Top-560
81TopTra-807
82Don-312
82Fle-397
82FleSta-63
82K-M-28
82K-M-30
82OPC-146
82OPC-208
82Top-754
82Top-755
83AllGamPI-104
83Don-24
83Don-438
83Don-648
83Fle-270
83FleSta-131
83FleSti-55
83Oco& SSBG-11
83OPC-81
83OPC-264
83PhiTas-21
83Top-171
83Top-603
83Top-604
83TopFol-2
83TopFol-5
83TopSti-303
83TopTra-77T
84A'sMot-3
84Don-355
84DonCha-44
84Fle-43
84Fle-636
84FleSti-100
84FleSti-120
84FleUpd-80
84FunFooP-74
84Nes792-210
84Nes792-705
84OCoandSI-37
84OCoandSI-138
84OPC-210
84Top-210
84Top-705
84TopGaloC-7
84TopSti-116
84TopTif-210
84TopTif-705
84TopTra-82T
84TopTraT-82T
85Don-584
85Fle-431
85Lea-28
85OPC-352
85Top-5
85Top-352
85TopMin-352
85TopSti-5
85TopSti-6
85TopSti-325
85TopTif-5
85TopTif-352
86AstGreT-2
86AstMot-3
86RedGreT-10
86SpoDecG-56
87AstSer1-17
87AstSer1-25
87AstSer1-29
87AstShoSO-18
87AstShoSTw-22
87AstShoSTw-24
87AstShoSTw-27
89TopBasT-28
90AGFA-11
90PerGreM-89
90TopMag-13
92UppDecBH-40
92UppDecBH-41
92UppDecBH-43
92UppDecBH-44
92UppDecBH-AU5
93TedWil-30
93TedWilM-18
93UppDecS-12
93Yoo-10
94CarLeaA-DJ10
95SonGre-9
96Red76K-3
96Red76K-9
97SpolllCC-7
97St.VinHHS-12
Morgan, Joe M.
60Top-229
61Top-511
62KahAtl-15
81PawRedST-12
89Sco-660
89Top-714
89TopTif-714
90OPC-321
90Top-321
90TopTif-321
90TopTVRS-1
91OPC-21
91Top-21
91TopDesS-21
91TopMic-21
91TopTif-21
Morgan, Ken
87VisOakP-3
88VisOakCLC-146
88VisOakP-90
89OrlTwiB-17
89OrlTwiP-1341
90Bes-30
90CMC-751
90OrlSunRB-10
90OrlSunRP-1096
90OrlSunRS-12
91LinDriAAA-411
91PorBeaLD-411
91PorBeaP-1578
Morgan, Kevin
91NiaFalRC-1
91NiaFalRP-3642
92ClaFS7-104
92FayGenF-2177
93LakTigC-19
93LakTigF-1318
94St.LucMC-18
94St.LucMF-1202
95BinMetTI-15
96BinBeeB-20
Morgan, Mike (Michael)
79OgdA'sT-3
80Top-671
81NasSouTI-10
83Don-108
83Fle-388
83Top-203
83TopTra-78T
84Nes792-423
84OPC-6
84SyrChiT-22
84Top-423
84TopTif-423
85MarMot-25
86MarMot-25
86Top-152
86TopTif-152
87Don-366
87Fle-591
87FleGlo-591
87MarMot-8
87Top-546
87TopTif-546
88Don-120
88DonBasB-86
88Fle-380
88FleGlo-380
88OriFreB-12
88Sco-295
88ScoGlo-295
88Top-32
88TopBig-98
88TopTif-32
88TopTra-73T
88TopTraT-73T
89DodMot-13
89DodPol-23
89DodStaSV-8
89Don-164
89DonBasB-122
89FleUpd-91
89Top-788
89TopTif-788
89TopTra-84T
89TopTraT-84T
89UppDec-653
90DodMot-21
90DodPol-36
90DodTar-553
90Don-132
90Fle-403
90FleCan-403
90Lea-358
90OPC-367
90RedFolSB-66
90Sco-342
90Top-367
90TopTif-367
90UppDec-317
91DodMot-21
91DodPol-36
91Don-182
91Fle-213
91Lea-193
91OPC-631
91OriCro-316
91PanCanT1-89
91PanFreS-63
91PanSti-52
91RedFolS-67
91Sco-276
91StaClu-562
91Top-631
91TopDesS-631
91TopMic-631
91TopTif-631
91Ult-165
91UppDec-578
91USPlaCA-5C
92Bow-647
92CubMar-36
92DodStaTA-30
92Don-200
92Fle-465
92FleUpd-74
92Lea-204
92OPC-289
92OPCPre-180
92Pin-414
92Sco-171
92ScoRoo-66T
92StaClu-787
92StaCluD-124
92Stu-17
92Top-289
92TopGol-289
92TopGolW-289
92TopMic-289
92TopTra-76T
92TopTraG-76T
92Ult-471
92UppDec-513
92UppDec-703
92YanWIZ8-125
93Bow-144
93CubMar-17
93Don-394
93Fin-188
93FinRef-188
93Fla-18
93Fle-23
93FunPac-82
93Lea-123
93OPC-207
93PacSpa-59
93PanSti-201
93Pin-63
93Sco-73
93Sel-145
93SelAce-10
93SelStaL-90
93SP-86
93StaClu-285
93StaCluCu-17
93StaCluFDI-285
93StaCluMOP-285
93Top-373
93TopGol-373
93TopInaM-373
93TopMic-373
93TriPla-76
93Ult-21
93UppDec-106
93UppDecGold-106
93USPlaCA-7S
94Bow-26
94ColC-212
94ColChoGS-212
94ColChoSS-212
94Don-206
94Fin-96
94FinRef-96
94Fle-391
94Lea-192
94OPC-235
94Pac-104
94Pin-113
94PinArtP-113
94PinMusC-113
94Sco-214
94ScoGolR-214
94Sel-121
94StaClu-304
94StaCluFDI-304
94StaCluGR-304
94StaCluMOP-304
94StaCluT-359
94StaCluTFDI-359
94Top-479
94TopGol-479
94TopSpa-479
94TriPla-75
94Ult-164
94UppDec-451
94UppDecED-451
95ColCho-216
95ColChoGS-216
95ColChoSS-216
95Don-385
95DonPreP-385
95StaClu-336
95StaCluMOP-336
95StaCluSTWS-336
95Top-121
96CarPol-19
96ColCho-691
96ColChoGS-691
96ColChoSS-691
96Don-282
96DonPreP-282
96Fla-364
96Fle-549
96FleTif-549
96LeaSigEA-133
96Pac-225
96StaClu-87
96StaCluMOP-87
96UppDec-181
Morgan, Ray
12T207-134
14B18B-45
14FatPlaT-34
15SpoNewM-124
16BF2FP-50
16ColE13-90A
16ColE13-121A
16ColE13-121B

16SpoNewM-126
16TanBraE-14
17HolBreD-70
Morgan, Rick
80KnoBluJT-26
Morgan, Scott
91KinIndC-7
91KinIndP-319
92CanIndS-113
92KinIndF-2472
93KinIndC-20
93KinIndF-2245
93KinIndTI-20
95WatIndTI-21
96WesOahCHWB-44
97Top-488
Morgan, Steve
96LowSpiB-20
Morgan, Tom S.
47StaPinP2-29
52BerRos-43
52Bow-109
52Top-331
53Top-132
54NewYorJA-54
55Bow-100
57Top-239
58Top-365
59TigGraASP-13
59Top-545
60Lea-97
60Top-33
60TopVen-33
61AngJayP-8
61Top-272
62AngJayP-7
62Top-11
62TopVen-11
63AngJayP-10
63Top-421
73OPC-421
73Top-421A
73Top-421B
74OPC-276
74Top-276
83TopRep5-331
91TopArc1-132
Morgan, Vern
73OPC-49
73Top-49A
73Top-49B
74OPC-447
74Top-447
Morganna, Entertainer (Kissing Bandit)
90UtiBluSP-27
Morhardt, Greg
85OrlTwiT-9
86OrlTwiP-13
87PorBeaP-20
Morhardt, Moe
62Top-309
Mori, Dan
87SanJosBP-12
Moriarty, Edward
11SpoLifCW-261
36GouWidPPR-A76
Moriarty, George
07TigACDPP-24
09BusBroBPP-11
09ColChiE-205
09ColChiE-206A
09ColChiE-206B
09T206-254
09TigMorPenWBPP-8
09TigTaCP-12
10NadE1-41
11PloCanE-49
11S74Sil-16
11SpoLifM-64
11T205-124
12ColRedB-205
12ColRedB-206A
12ColRedB-206B
12ColTinT-205
12ColTinT-206A
12ColTinT-206B
12HasTriFT-39
12HasTriFT-55
12HasTriFT-75B
12T207-135
14B18B-19A
14B18B-19B
14B18B-19C
14CraJacE-114
15CraJacE-114
15SpoNewM-125
16SpoNewM-127
21Exh-111
94ConTSN-1209
94ConTSNB-1209
93UppDecTR-6
Moriarty, Mike
96FtMyeMB-11
Moriarty, Todd
84EveGiaC-26
Morillo, Cesar
91BasCitRC-19
91BasCitRP-1405
91Cla/Bes-60
92BasCitRC-12
92EugEmeC-20
92EugEmeF-3038
93RocRoyC-18
93RocRoyF-724
94VenLinU-6
94WilBluRC-15
94WilBluRF-309
95BakBlaTI-5
95LinVen-88
96WicWraB-21
Morillo, Donald
95ChaRivUTIS-31
95ChaRivUTIS-35
Morillo, Santiago
91SouOreAC-17
91SouOreAP-3840
Morimoto, Ken
95YakBeaTI-23
96GreFalDB-21
96GreFalDTI-25
Morin, Pete (Pierre)
43ParSpo-55
Moritz, Chris
85GreHorT-7
86WinHavRSP-18
87NewBriRSP-23
88NewBriRSP-907
89NewBriRSP-603
89NewBriRSS-11
Moritz, Tom
86BirBarTI-7
Mork, Dennis
80QuaCitCT-22
Morlan, John
75OPC-651
75Top-651
Morland, Mike
91St.CatBJC-1
91St.CatBJP-3398
92MyrBeaHC-8
92MyrBeaHF-2201
93KnoSmoF-1254
94KnoSmoF-1307
Morley, Mike
80OmaRoyP-18
Morlock, Allen
83SprCarF-24
84ArkTraT-8
86ArkTraP-16
Morman, Alvin
92AshTouC-20
93JacGenF-2108
94Bow-314
94Cla-115
94ExcFS7-205
94TucTorF-759
94UppDecML-70
95TusTorTI-17
96AstMot-17
96Fin-B201
96FinRef-B201
96FleUpd-U140
96FleUpdTC-U140
97PacPriGotD-GD154
Morman, Russ
86BufBisP-19
86SpoRoo-33
87Don-306
87Fle-645
87FleGlo-645
87HawIsIP-22
87SpoTeaP-26
87Top-233
87TopTif-233
87WhiSoxC-23
88VanCanC-17
88VanCanP-760
89VanCanC-16
89VanCanP-590
90CMC-190
90OmaRoyC-15
90OmaRoyP-73
90ProAAAF-608
90WicStaSGD-21
91Lea-263
92NasSouF-1840
93BufBisF-524
94EdmTraF-2880
95ChaKniTI-17
96ChaKniB-20
Morogiello, Dan
79RicBraT-18
80RicBraT-1
82LouRedE-20
83RocRedWT-6
84Nes792-682
84Top-682
84TopTif-682
85DomLeaS-50
85RicBraT-5
91OriCro-317
Morones, Geno
91HunCubC-15
91HunCubP-3331
92GenCubC-10
92GenCubF-1558
93PeoChiC-15
93PeoChiF-1082
95WicWraTI-32
96WilBluRB-16
Moronko, Jeff
80BatTroT-28
81ChaLooT-12
82ChaLooT-21
83BufBisT-17
84BufBisT-1
85MaiGuiT-19
85TulDriTI-22
86OklCit8P-14
87ColCliP-11
87ColCliT-17
87IntLeaAT-1
88ColCliC-18
88ColCliP-20
88ColCliP-328
89ChaLooLITI-19
92YanWIZ8-126
Morphy, Pat
90OneYanP-3379
91GreHorP-3055
92ForLauYC-17
92ForLauYTI-21
92Ft.LauYF-2609
Morreale, John
94BelBreC-18
94BelBreF-111
96StoPorB-19
Morrell, John
87BucN28-10A
87BucN28-10B
87OldJudN-359
88AllandGN-5
Morrelli, Anthony
85CloHSS-27
Morrill, Craig
93ButCopKSP-17
Morrill, John
88GandBCGCE-27
88WG1CarG-6
Morris, Aaron
91WatIndC-19
91WatIndP-3375
Morris, Angel
81BurBeeT-14
82BelBreF-26
85Ft.MyeRT-7
86MemChiSTOS-20
86MemChiTOS-20
87Ft.MyeRP-30
88BlaYNPRWL-170
88VirGenS-16
89BlaYNPRWL-146
89MemChiB-14
89MemChiP-1203
89MemChiS-18
90MiaMirIS-19
Morris, Bobby
93HunCubC-21
93HunCubF-3245
94MidLeaAF-MDW49
94PeoChiC-1
94PeoChiF-2277
95Bes-60
95Exc-167
95SPML-33
95UppDecML-172
96Bow-274
96Exc-141
96OrlCubB-17
96Top-426
95UppDecMLFS-172
Morris, Chad
96VerExpB-19
Morris, Danny W.
69OPC-99
69Top-99A
69Top-99B
Morris, Dave
81BurBeeT-1
83AndBraT-29
85DurBulT-8
85EveGiaIC-11
86CliGiaP-14
Morris, Don
80WesHavWCT-4
81WesHavAT-16
Morris, Edward
87OldJudN-360
Morris, Fred
78DayBeaAT-19
Morris, Frosty
57SeaPop-25
Morris, Greg
94BoiHawC-19
94BoiHawF-3365
94SigRooDP-83
94SigRooDPS-83
94StaCluDP-75
94StaCluDPFDI-75
95CedRapKTI-36
95MidLeaA-36
96LakElsSB-19
Morris, Hal
87AlbYanP-21
88ColCliC-20
88ColCliP-21
88ColCliP-327
89ClaLigB-28
89ColCliC-16
89ColCliP-16
89ColCliP-743
89Don-545
89Fle-260
89FleGlo-260
89ScoHot1R-8
89TriA AAC-17
89TriAAP-AAA20
89YanScoNW-29
90AlbDecGB-18
90Bow-57
90BowTif-57
90ClaUpd-T35
90Don-514
90FleUpd-15
90Hot50RS-32
90Lea-321
90OPC-236
90RedKah-16
90Sco-602
90Sco100RS-87
90ScoYouS2-37
90Top-236
90TopTif-236
90TopTra-76T
90TopTraT-76T
90TriAAAC-17
90UppDec-31
91Baz-13
91Bow-691
91Cla1-T98
91Cla3-T62
91ClaGam-178
91Don-141
91Fle-72
91Lea-51
91MajLeaCP-71
91OPC-642
91RedKah-23
91RedPep-12
91Sco-647
91Sco100RS-98
91ScoHotR-3
91StaClu-339
91Stu-168
91Top-642
91TopDesS-642
91TopMic-642
91TopRoo-20
91TopTif-642
91ToyRoo-20
91Ult-98
91UppDec-351
92Bow-468
92Cla1-T65
92ClaGam-137
92Don-258
92DonCraJ1-32
92DonDiaK-DK19
92Fle-412
92Hig5-33
92Lea-205
92OPC-773
92PanSti-262
92Pin-22
92RedKah-23
92RemUltP-P7
92RemUltP-P8
92RemUltP-P9
92Sco-125
92Sco100S-14
92ScoCokD-16
92ScoImpP-45
92SpoStaCC-34
92StaClu-63
92Stu-24
92Top-773
92TopGol-773
92TopGolW-773
92TopMic-773
92TriPla-30
92Ult-192
92UppDec-121
92YanWIZ8-127
93Don-294
93Fla-29
93Fle-37
93Lea-257
93OPC-197
93PacSpa-85
93PanSti-291
93Pin-222
93RedKah-16
93Sco-38
93Sel-45
93SP-211
93StaClu-534
93StaCluFDI-534
93StaCluMOP-534
93Top-546
93TopGol-546
93TopInaM-546
93TopMic-546
93TriPla-223
93Ult-31
93UppDec-121
93UppDec-833
93UppDecGold-121
93UppDecGold-833
94Bow-186
94ColC-482
94ColChoGS-482
94ColChoSS-482
94Don-221
94ExtBas-235
94Fin-70
94FinRef-70
94Fla-147
94Fle-417
94Lea-433
94LeaL-97
94OPC-153
94PanSti-165
94Pin-314
94PinArtP-314
94PinMusC-314
94RedKah-20
94Sco-526
94ScoGolR-526
94Sel-158
94StaClu-363
94StaCluFDI-363
94StaCluGR-363
94StaCluMOP-363
94Stu-170
94Top-126
94TopGol-126
94TopSpa-126
94TriPla-216
94Ult-475

94UppDec-494
94UppDecED-494
95Baz-92
95Bow-346
95ColCho-424
95ColChoGS-424
95ColChoSE-201
95ColChoSEGS-201
95ColChoSESS-201
95ColChoSS-424
95Don-234
95DonDiaK-DK20
95DonPreP-234
95DonTopotO-216
95Emb-3
95EmbGolI-3
95Fin-102
95FinRef-102
95Fla-121
95Fle-442
95Lea-210
95Lea300C-7
95LeaLim-75
95Pac-110
95PacPri-34
95Pin-332
95PinArtP-332
95PinMusC-332
95RedKah-19
95Sco-226
95ScoGolR-226
95ScoHaloG-HG46
95ScoPlaTS-226
95Sel-91
95SelArtP-91
95SelCer-35
95SelCerMG-35
95Spo-69
95SpoArtP-69
95StaClu-231
95StaCluCC-CC9
95StaCluFDI-231
95StaCluMO-34
95StaCluMOP-231
95StaCluMOP-CC9
95StaCluSTDW-RE231
95StaCluSTWS-231
95StaCluVR-117
95Stu-106
95Sum-51
95SumNthD-51
95Top-27
95TopCyb-22
95TopLeaL-LL29
95UC3-35
95UC3ArtP-35
95Ult-367
95UltGolM-367
95UppDec-406
95UppDecED-406
95UppDecEDG-406
95UppDecPLL-R29
95UppDecPLLE-R29
95UppDecSE-29
95UppDecSEG-29
95USPlaCMLA-5D
95Zen-42
96Baz-112
96ColCho-112
96ColChoGS-112
96ColChoSS-112
96Don-272
96DonPreP-272
96EmoXL-166
96Fin-B185
96FinRef-B185
96Fla-235
96Fle-347
96FleTif-347
96Lea-175
96LeaPre-106
96LeaPreP-106
96LeaPrePB-175
96LeaPrePG-175
96LeaPrePS-175
96MetUni-150
96MetUniP-150
96Pac-37
96PanSti-54
96Pin-119
96Pin-308
96PinAfi-49
96PinAfiAP-49
96PinAfiFPP-49
96PinArtP-193
96PinFoil-308
96PinSta-193
96Sco-330
96ScoDugC-B55
96ScoDugCAP-B55
96SelCer-89
96SelCerAP-89
96SelCerCB-89
96SelCerCR-89
96SelCerMB-89
96SelCerMG-89
96SelCerMR-89
96StaClu-97
96StaCluMOP-97
95StaCluVRMC-117
96Stu-36
96StuPrePB-36
96StuPrePG-36
96StuPrePS-36
96Sum-78
96SumAbo&B-78
96SumArtP-78
96SumFoi-78
96Top-158
96TopGal-83
96TopGalPPI-83
96TopLas-73
96Ult-463
96UltGolM-463
96UppDec-308
96Zen-51
96ZenArtP-51
96ZenMoz-10
97Bow-286
97BowChr-97
97BowChrI-97
97BowChrIR-97
97BowChrR-97
97BowInt-286
97Cir-372
97CirRav-372
97ColCho-307
97Don-117
97DonPreP-117
97DonPrePGold-117
97Fin-281
97FinEmb-281
97FinEmbR-281
97FinRef-281
97FlaSho-A123
97FlaSho-B123
97FlaSho-C123
97FlaShoLC-123
97FlaShoLC-B123
97FlaShoLC-C123
97FlaShoLCM-A123
97FlaShoLCM-B123
97FlaShoLCM-C123
97Fle-298
97FleTif-298
97Lea-276
97LeaFraM-276
97LeaFraMDC-276
97MetUni-48
97Pac-272
97PacLigB-272
97PacSil-272
97Sco-49
97ScoPreS-49
97ScoShoS-49
97ScoShoSAP-49
97SP-54
97StaClu-292
97StaCluMOP-292
97Top-44
97TopChr-16
97TopChrR-16
97Ult-407
97UltGolME-407
97UltPlaME-407
97UppDec-43
Morris, Jack
77EvaTriT-20
78TigBurK-8
78Top-703
79Top-251
80Top-371
81CokTeaS-54
81Don-127
81Fle-475
81OPC-284
81PerAll-15
81TigDetN-128
81Top-572
81TopSti-80
82Don-107
82Fle-274
82FleSta-159
82Kel-5
82OPC-47
82OPC-108
82Top-165
82Top-450
82Top-556
82TopSti-10
82TopSti-139
82TopSti-183
83Don-5
83Don-107
83Fle-336
83FleSti-252
83Kel-35
83OPC-65
83Tig-20
83Top-65
83TopSti-69
84AllGamPI-174
84Don-415
84Fle-87
84FleSti-83
84FunFooP-59
84Nes792-136
84Nes792-195
84Nes792-666
84OPC-195
84TigFarJ-10
84TigWavP-27
84Top-136
84Top-195
84Top-666
84TopGloS-10
84TopRubD-16
84TopSti-263
84TopTif-136
84TopTif-195
84TopTif-666
85AllGamPI-81
85Don-415
85Fle-18
85Fle-643
85FleLimE-21
85FleStaS-82
85Lea-142
85OPC-382
85SevCoi-D12
85ThoMcAD-15
85TigCaiD-14
85TigWen-16
85Top-610
85Top3-D-28
85TopGloS-26
85TopMin-610
85TopRubD-14
85TopSti-9
85TopSti-15
85TopSti-256
85TopSup-43
85TopTif-610
86BasStaB-75
86Don-105
86DonAll-18
86DonHig-27
86DonPop-18
86DorChe-2
86Fle-232
86FleMin-48
86FleSlu-23
86FleStiC-79
86GenMilB-1E
86Lea-38
86OPC-270
86SevCoi-C10
86Spo-117
86Spo-141
86TigCaiD-12
86Top-270
86Top3-D-17
86TopGloA-10
86TopMinL-14
86TopSti-163
86TopSti-268
86TopSup-38
86TopTat-11
86TopTif-270
87ClaGam-90
87Don-13
87Don-173
87DonOpeD-212
87DonSupD-13
87Dra-27
87Fle-158
87FleBasA-28
87FleGlo-158
87FleLimE-28
87FleMin-70
87FleSlu-27
87FleStiC-80
87GenMilB-2F
87KayB-20
87Lea-13
87Lea-135
87MandMSL-6
87MSAJifPD-3
87OPC-376
87RedFolSB-114
87SevCoi-D8
87SmoAmeL-6
87Spo-87
87Spo-111
87SpoTeaP-15
87StuPan-19
87TigCaiD-14
87TigCok-7
87Top-778
87TopCoi-18
87TopGloS-47
87TopMinL-55
87TopSti-266
87TopTif-778
88CheBoy-3
88ClaRed-174
88Don-127
88DonAll-24
88DonBasB-181
88Dra-32
88Fle-64
88Fle-626
88FleAwaW-26
88FleBasA-26
88FleBasM-24
88FleExcS-27
88FleGlo-64
88FleGlo-626
88FleHea-3
88FleHotS-28
88FleLeaL-28
88FleMin-22
88FleRecS-26
88FleStiC-26
88FleTeaL-23
88GreBasS-67
88Lea-85
88OPC-340
88PanSti-85
88Sco-545
88ScoGlo-545
88Spo-176
88StaLinAl-18
88StaLinTi-14
88TigPep-47
88TigPol-8
88Top-340
88TopBig-170
88TopCoi-21
88TopGloS-17
88TopMinL-11
88TopRitTM-27
88TopSti-268
88TopStiB-59
88TopTif-340
88TopUKM-50
88TopUKMT-50
89Bow-93
89BowTif-93
89Don-234
89Fle-139
89FleBasM-30
89FleGlo-139
89OPC-266
89PanSti-334
89RedFolSB-82
89Sco-250
89ScoSco-8
89Spo-5
89TigMar-47
89TigPol-47
89Top-645
89TopBasT-68
89TopBig-61
89TopSti-277
89TopTif-645
89TopUKM-54
89TVSpoM-71
89UppDec-352
90Don-639A
90Don-639B
90DonBesA-34
90Fle-610
90FleCan-610
90FleLeaL-27
90KayB-19
90Lea-482
90OPC-555
90PanSti-76
90PubSti-478
90Sco-203
90TigCok-12
90Top-555
90TopMag-78
90TopSti-276
90TopTif-555
90UppDec-573
90VenSti-354
91BluJayFS-20
91Bow-319
91Cla2-T49
91Cla3-T61
91Don-492
91Fle-343
91FleUpd-39
91Lea-294
91OPC-75
91OPCPre-84
91PanFreS-296
91Sco-114
91ScoPro-114
91ScoRoo-74T
91StaClu-447
91StaCluMO-22
91Stu-89
91Top-75
91TopDesS-75
91TopMic-75
91TopTif-75
91TopTra-82T
91TopTraT-82T
91UltUpd-39
91UppDec-45
91UppDec-336
91UppDec-736
91UppDecFE-80F
91USPlaCA-1H
92Bow-16
92Cla1-T66
92ClaGam-199
92Don-25
92Don-216
92DonMcD-G4
92Fle-211
92FleUpd-66
92Fre-18
92KinDis-18
92Lea-425
92New-18
92OPC-235
92OPCPre-79
92PanSti-122
92PanSti-279
92PepDieM-6
92Pin-483
92Pin-585
92Sco-652
92Sco-798
92ScoRoo-15T
92SpollFK1-81
92StaClu-640
92StaCluD-125
92StaCluD-126
92StaCluMO-7
92StaCluMO-22
92Stu-257
92Top-235
92TopGol-235
92TopGolW-235
92TopMic-235
92TopTra-77T
92TopTraG-77T
92TriPlaG-GS3
92Ult-452
92UltAwaW-1
92UppDec-315
92UppDec-732
93BluJayCP1-8
93BluJayD-7
93BluJayD4-20

93BluJayDM-9
93BluJayFS-21
93Bow-463
93ClaGam-68
93Don-351
93Fle-347
93Fle-697
93FunPac-59
93HumDumC-21
93Lea-113
93MSABenSPD-3
93OPC-179
93OPCWorC-11
93PacSpa-326
93PanSti-24
93Pin-57
93Pin-298
93Pin-472
93Sco-37
93Sco-508
93Sel-158
93SelAce-5
93SelStaL-85
93SP-51
93StaClu-356
93StaCluFDI-356
93StaCluMOP-356
93Top-185
93TopGol-185
93TopInaM-185
93TopMic-185
93TriPla-160
93Ult-290
93UppDec-164
93UppDecGold-164
94ColC-542
94ColChoGS-542
94ColChoSS-542
94ExtBas-63
94Fla-285
94Fle-339
94FleUpd-33
94Lea-401
94Pac-649
94Pin-532
94PinArtP-532
94PinMusC-532
94Sco-453
94ScoGolR-453
94ScoRoo-RT21
94ScoRooGR-RT21
94Sel-289
94SpoRoo-99
94SpoRooAP-99
94StaClu-556
94StaCluFDI-556
94StaCluGR-556
94StaCluMOP-556
94TopTra-36T
94Ult-346
94UppDec-331
94UppDecED-331
95BluJayUSPC-5D
95BluJayUSPC-12S
95ColCho-433
95ColChoGS-433
95ColChoSS-433
95Ult-368
95UltGolM-368
95UppDecSE-31
95UppDecSEG-31
97BluJayS-41

Morris, Jeff
83TucTorT-6
87EveGiaC-26
88CliGiaP-717
89CliGiaP-901
90SanJosGB-26
90SanJosGCLC-54
90SanJosGP-2028
90SanJosGS-29
92PitMetC-19
92PitMetF-3312
93BluOriC-26
94AlbPolC-28
94AlbPolF-2255
96FreKeyB-25
96MauStiHWB-33

Morris, Jim
87StoPorP-23
89SarWhiSS-15
87PanAmTUBI-NNO

Morris, Joe
90JamExpP-23

Morris, John Daniel
69PilPos-27
70BreMcD-22
70BreMil-17
71MLBOffS-446
71OPC-721
75OPC-577
83Pil69G-38
84OmaRoyT-8
85DomLeaS-136
85Don-32
85LouRedR-23
85OmaRoyT-19
86LouRedTI-20
87Don-480
87FleUpd-83
87FleUpdG-83
87LouRedTI-20
87SpoRoo2-42
87Top-211
87TopRoo-10
87TopTif-211
88Don-480
88Fle-43
88FleGlo-43
88LouRedBTI-35
88Sco-346
88ScoGlo-346
88Top-536
88TopTif-536
89CarSmo-14
89Top-578
89TopTif-578
90CarSmo-15
90Don-516
90Fle-254
90FleCan-254
90OPC-383
90Sco-134
90Top-383
90TopTif-383
90TopTVCa-35
91FleUpd-109
91Lea-496
91OriCro-318
91PhiMed-29
92Bow-474
92Don-92
92StaClu-796
93LouRedF-228
94BreMilB-337
94MidAngF-2456
94MidAngOHP-18
96VanCanB-3

Morris, Johnny (John W.)
69OPC-111
69Top-111
69TopFou-1
71Top-721
75Top-577

Morris, Ken
88AubAstP-1957

Morris, Marc
91PocPioP-3786
91PocPioSP-12
92VisOakC-5
92VisOakF-1012

Morris, Matt
95Bes-133
95NewJerCTI-22
96ArkTraB-21
96Bow-301
96BowBes-137
96BowBesAR-137
96BowBesR-137
96Exc-231
96ExcFirYP-10
96SigRooOJPP-P5
96StPetCB-3
96Top-232
96TopChr-92
96TopChrR-92
97Bow-113
97BowBes-150
97BowBesAR-150
97BowBesR-150
97BowChr-132
97BowChrI-132
97BowChrIR-132
97BowChrR-132
97BowInt-113
97ColCho-471
97Don-386
97DonLim-143
97DonLimLE-143
97DonPreP-386
97DonPrePGold-386
97DonTea-165
97DonTeaSPE-165
97Fin-316
97FinEmb-316
97FinEmbR-316
97FinRef-316
97Fle-683
97FleTif-683
97Lea-335
97LeaFraM-335
97LeaFraMDC-335
97PinX-P-133
97PinX-PMoS-133
97SpoIll-17
97SpoIllEE-17
97TopStaFAS-FAS13
97Ult-529
97UltGolME-529
97UltPlaME-529

Morris, Rick
87DurBulP-20
88CarLeaAS-32
88DurBulS-15
89GreBraB-5
89GreBraP-1172
89GreBraS-15
89Sta-37
90GreBraB-11
90GreBraP-1136
90GreBraS-14
91GreBraC-19
91GreBraLD-213
91GreBraP-3013
91LinDriAA-213

Morris, Rod
88ButCopKSP-19
89ChaRanS-16
89Sta-8
90ChaRanS-14
91LinDriAA-588
91TulDriLD-588
91TulDriP-2786
91TulDriTI-19
92TulDriF-2708

Morris, Rossi
91PriRedC-10
91PriRedP-3528
92PriRedC-20
92PriRedF-3100

Morris, Steve
87HawRai-12
89EliTwiS-20
89KenTwiP-1060
89KenTwiS-16
89Sta-53
90Bes-185
90KenTwiB-9
90KenTwiP-2308
90KenTwiS-14

Morris, Tom
63GadFunC-78
80QuaCitCT-5

Morrisette, James
89ColMetB-15
89ColMetGS-16
89SouAtlLAGS-20
90St.LucMS-17
91MiaMirC-25
91St.LucMC-3

Morrisey, Todd
85CloHSS-28

Morrison, Brian
87SanBerSP-17
88FloStaLAS-13
88MiaMarS-15
89KnoBluJB-17
89KnoBluJP-1146
90SalBucS-14

Morrison, Bruce
83LynMetT-9
91MelBusF-14

Morrison, Chris
96WesMicWB-17

Morrison, Dan
88T/MUmp-47
89T/MUmp-45
89T/MUmp-60
90T/MUmp-43

Morrison, Greg
95GreFalDTI-35
96SavSanB-8

Morrison, Jeff
87BelMarTI-13

Morrison, Jim
76OklCit8TI-6
79Top-722
80OPC-272
80Top-522
81CokTeaS-34
81Don-158
81Fle-357
81Top-323
81TopSti-60
81TopSupHT-20
82Don-395
82Fle-354
82OPC-154
82Top-654
82TopTra-77T
83Don-150
83Fle-313
83Top-173
84Don-322
84Fle-257
84Nes792-44
84Top-44
84TopTif-44
85Don-532
85Fle-471
85Pir-13
85Top-433
85TopTif-433
86Don-386
86ElmPioRSP-13
86Fle-614
86OPC-56
86Top-553
86TopSti-133
86TopTif-553
87Don-484
87DonOpeD-169
87Fle-614
87FleGamW-29
87FleGlo-614
87FleMin-71
87FleStiC-81
87GreHorP-22
87Lea-215
87OPC-237
87SpoTeaP-18
87StuPan-10
87Top-237
87TopSti-133
87TopTif-237
88Don-543A
88Don-543B
88Fle-65
88FleGlo-65
88OPC-288
88Sco-272
88ScoGlo-272
88StaLinTi-15
88Top-751
88TopBig-237
88TopSti-272
88TopTif-751
89ElmPioP-8
89PacSenL-137
89T/MSenL-81
89TopSenL-61
89UppDec-568
90EliSenL-42
91WinHavRSC-23
91WinHavRSP-502
92LynRedSC-25
92LynRedSF-2921
93NewBriRSF-1234

Morrison, John
21Exh-112
21Nei-115
22E120-222
22W572-67
22W573-88
23WilChoV-108
90DodTar-554
93ConTSN-794

Morrison, Keith
90PulBraB-6
90PulBraP-3104
91MacBraC-6
91MacBraP-860
92AlbPolC-20
92AlbPolF-2301
93PalSprAC-14
93PalSprAF-65
94MidAngF-2435
94MidAngOHP-19

Morrison, Perry
80ElPasDT-19
81HolMilT-24
82HolMilT-7

Morrison, Red
89Ft.LauYS-17
87OneYanP-2
88FloStaLAS-45
88Ft.LauYS-17

Morrison, Ryan
96PitMetB-15

Morrison, Scott
96YakBeaTI-21

Morrissey, Joe
33ButCanV-35
33Gou-97
34DiaMatCSB-135
34ButPreR-46

Morrissey, Tom
87BucN28-54
87OldJudN-361

Morrow, Ben
87SalBucP-9

Morrow, Brian
90WicStaSGD-27

Morrow, Chris
88GreFalDTI-5
89BakDodCLC-204
89SalDodTI-18
90BakDodCLC-247
90CalLeaACLC-12
91FloStaLAP-FSL41
91VerBeaDC-29
91VerBeaDP-789
92SanAntMS-571
92SkyAA F-250
93AlbDukF-1476
93VerBeaDC-19

Morrow, David
86JamExpP-17
87BurExpP-1083

Morrow, Nick
94BilMusF-3682
94BilMusSP-11
95Exc-178
96BesAutS-64

Morrow, Red
88CalLeaACLC-50

Morrow, Steve
82ForMyeRT-23
84MemChiT-22
86MemChiSTOS-21
86MemChiTOS-21
87MemChiB-27
87MemChiP-26
88MemChiB-4
89OmaRoyC-24
89OmaRoyP-1723

Morrow, Timmie
89ButCopKSP-26
90Bes-284
90CMC-847
90GasRanB-17
90GasRanP-2533
90GasRanS-15
91ChaRanC-23
91ChaRanP-1327
92ChaRanF-2238
92ClaFS7-68
93TulDriF-2748
94TulDriF-256
94TulDriTI-17
94TulDriTI-23
93TulDriTI-20

Morse, Jacob C.
90LitSunW-3

Morse, Matt
90EliTwiS-14
91KenTwiC-5
91KenTwiP-2083

Morse, Mike
81AppFoxT-20
82GleFalWST-8
83GleFalWST-7

Morse, Paul
94EliTwiC-14
94EliTwiF-3727
95ForMyeMTI-17
96FtMyeMB-12
96HarCitRCB-21

Morse, Randy
84ShrCapFB-13

Morse, Scott
87PorChaRP-4
89ChaRanS-17
Morseman, Robert
96FreKeyB-16
Morsler, Joseph
88KimN18-25
Mortensen, Tony
89FreStaBS-14
90SpoIndSP-4
91WatDiaC-6
91WatDiaP-1253
92HigDesMC-11
Mortillaro, John
83AndBraT-13
84DurBulT-24
Mortimer, Bob
86SalRedBP-20
Mortimer, Mike
94HudValRF-3381
94HudValRC-15
Morton, Bubba (Wycliffe)
62Top-554
63Top-164
67OPC-79
67Top-79
68Top-216
68TopVen-216
69MilBra-196
69Top-342
Morton, Carl
69ExpFudP-9
69Top-646
70ExpPin-11
70OPC-109
70Top-109
71ExpPS-17
71Kel-23
71MLBOffS-135
71OPC-515
71Top-515
71TopCoi-35
71TopGreM-4
71TopSup-28
71TopTat-132
72OPC-134
72ProStaP-9
72Top-134
73LinPor-6
73OPC-331
73Top-331
74OPC-244
74Top-244
74TopSta-8
75OPC-237
75Top-237
76Hos-43
76HosTwi-43
76OPC-328
76SSP-4
76Top-328
77Top-24
Morton, Guy
15SpoNewM-126
16BF2FP-24
16ColE13-122
16SpoNewM-128
20WalMaiW-34
21E121So8-64
22AmeCarE-48
22W575-86
23W503-33
77Ind192T-13
Morton, Kevin
88CapCodPB-12
88CapCodPPaLP-139
89ElmPioP-27
90Bes-211
90EasLeaAP-EL32
90NewBriRSB-14
90NewBriRSP-1316
90NewBriRSS-12
90ProAaA-5
90TopTVRS-52
91Bow-130
91Cla3-T63
91Don-37
91DonRoo-40
91LinDriAAA-361
91PawRedSDD-13
91PawRedSLD-361
91PawRedSP-36
91UppDecFE-66F
92Don-330
92OPC-724
92OPCPre-7
92PawRedSF-919
92PinTea2-14
92ProFS7-18
92RedSoxDD-19
92Sco-420
92Sco100RS-36
92StaClu-115
92Top-724
92TopDeb91-127
92TopGol-724
92TopGolW-724
92TopMic-724
92UppDec-676
94NorTidF-2918
95IowCubTI-22
97DunDonPPS-15
Morton, Lew
52Par-13
Morton, Maurice
85SpoIndC-15
Morton, Ron
88SpoIndP-1946
89Sta-190
89WatDiaP-1782
89WatDiaS-21
90WatDiaB-12
90WatDiaP-2378
Morton, Stan
80CliGiaT-22
Morton, Sydney
86NegLeaF-36
Morvay, Joe
93EriSaiC-17
93EriSaiF-3113
94ChaRivC-14
94ChaRivF-2669
95TulDriTI-16
96TulDriTI-19
Moryn, Walt
52Par-72
53ExhCan-39
55Bow-261
57Top-16
58Top-122
59Top-147
59Top-488
59TopVen-147
60CubJayP-9
60Lea-17
60Top-74
60TopTat-37
60TopVen-74
61CarJayP-9
61Top-91
61TopMagR-32
79DiaGre-122
79TCM50-141
90DodTar-555
95TopArcBD-137
Mosby, Linvel
78AshTouT-19
79AshTouT-4
80AshTouT-20
Moscaret, Jeff
84MidCubT-11
Moscat, Frank
85LynMetT-20
Moschetti, Mike
94SouOreAC-20
94SouOreAF-3632
Moschitto, Ross
65Top-566
81TCM60I-441
92YanWIZ6-91
Moscrey, Mike
88CedRapRP-1139
89ChaLooB-19
90ChaLooGS-22
Mosdell, Ken
43ParSpo-56
Moseby, Lloyd
80SyrChiT-16
80SyrChiTI-15
80VenLeaS-68
81Fle-421
81OPC-52
81OPCPos-24
81Top-643
82Don-129
82Fle-621
82OPC-223
82OPCPos-4
82Top-223
82TopSti-246
82TopStiV-246
83Don-556
83Fle-435
83OPC-124
83Top-452
83TopSti-130
84AllGamPI-153
84BluJayFS-25
84Don-363
84Fle-164
84FunFooP-132
84Nes792-92
84Nes792-403
84Nes792-606
84NesDreT-7
84OPC-3
84OPC-92
84OPC-289
84Top-92
84Top-403
84Top-606
84TopRubD-3
84TopSti-191
84TopSti-365
84TopStiB-4
84TopTif-92
84TopTif-403
84TopTif-606
85AllGamPI-64
85BluJayFS-23
85Don-437
85DonActA-5
85Fle-115
85Fle-636
85Lea-143
85OPC-77
85OPCPos-19
85Top-545
85TopMin-545
85TopRubD-3
85TopSti-359
85TopSup-39
85TopTif-545
86BluJayAF-20
86BluJayFS-26
86Don-73
86Fle-67
86FleLeaL-26
86GenMilB-3F
86Lea-72
86OPC-360
86Top-360
86TopSti-195
86TopTat-21
86TopTif-360
87BluJayFS-23
87Don-21
87Don-74
87DonAll-59
87DonOpeD-36
87DonSupD-21
87Fle-236
87FleGlo-236
87FleLimE-29
87FleMin-72
87FleRecS-22
87GenMilB-1G
87Lea-21
87Lea-105
87OPC-210
87RedFolSB-55
87Spo-96
87SpoTeaP-5
87StuPan-28
87SyrChi1A-1
87Top-210
87TopSti-190
87TopTif-210
88BluJay5-9
88BluJayFS-23
88Don-367
88DonBasB-199
88Fle-119
88FleGlo-119
88FleStiC-75
88GreBasS-61
88Lea-140
88MSAHosD-20
88OPC-272
88PanSti-225
88Sco-109
88ScoGlo-109
88Spo-74
88StaLinBJ-15
88Top-565
88TopBig-113
88TopSti-189
88TopTif-565
88TopUKM-51
88TopUKMT-51
89BluJayFS-20
89Don-231
89Fle-241
89FleGlo-241
89OPC-113
89PanSti-473
89RedFolSB-83
89Sco-12
89Top-113
89TopBig-262
89TopSti-188
89TopTif-113
89UppDec-381
90BluJayHS-2
90Bow-362
90BowTif-362
90Don-504
90DonBesA-62
90Fle-90
90FleCan-90
90FleUpd-97
90Lea-377
90OPC-779
90PubSti-524
90Sco-404
90ScoRoo-25T
90TigCok-13
90Top-779
90TopBig-305
90TopTif-779
90TopTra-77T
90TopTraT-77T
90UppDec-421
90UppDec-789
90VenSti-355
91Bow-135
91Don-188
91Fle-344
91Lea-223
91OPC-632
91PanFreS-293
91PanSti-239
91Sco-133
91StaClu-364
91Stu-56
91TigCok-15
91TigPol-7
91Top-632
91TopDesS-632
91TopMic-632
91TopTif-632
91Ult-124
91UppDec-559
92Don-443
92Fle-142
92New-19
92PanSti-111
92Sco-468
92UppDec-468
96BluJayOH-20
Moseley, Scott
90HelBreSP-8
Moser, Arnold
39WorWidGV-19
Moser, Larry
83AndBraT-30
Moser, Ricky
90EugEmeGS-20
Moser, Steve
86WatPirP-15
87SalBucP-13
Moses, Gerry (Gerald)
65Top-573
69Top-476A
69Top-476B
70DayDaiNM-104
70OPC-104
70RedSoxCPPC-8
70Top-104
71MLBOffS-352
71OPC-205
71Top-205
71TopCoi-6
72OPC-356
72Top-356
73OPC-431
73Top-431
74OPC-19
74Top-19
75OPC-271
75Top-271
81RedSoxBG2S-97
92YanWIZ7-117
Moses, John
81WauTimT-25
83AppFoxF-24
83SalLakCGT-19
84ChaLooT-24
84Don-74
84Nes792-517
84Top-517
84TopTif-517
85CalCanC-83
86CalCanP-16
87Don-393
87Fle-592
87FleGlo-592
87MarMot-18
87Top-284
87TopTif-284
88Don-440
88Fle-381
88FleGlo-381
88FleUpd-45
88FleUpdG-45
88PorBeaC-22
88PorBeaP-643
88Sco-309
88ScoGlo-309
88StaLinMa-10
88Top-712
88TopTif-712
89Don-626
89Fle-121A
89Fle-121B
89FleGlo-121
89Sco-432
89Top-72
89TopTif-72
89UppDec-242
90Don-590
90Fle-381
90FleCan-381
90Lea-433
90OPC-653
90PubSti-333
90Sco-391
90Top-653
90TopTif-653
90UppDec-240
90VenSti-356
91ColSprSSP-2198
91Fle-619
91OPC-341
91Sco-429
91Top-341
91TopDesS-341
91TopMic-341
91TopTif-341
92CalCanF-3743
92CalCanS-63
Moses, Mark
80AndBraT-13
Moses, Mike
93BilMusF-3943
93BilMusSP-20
Moses, Shane
94HelBreF-3612
94HelBreSP-9
Moses, Steve
85PorBeaC-30
86ReaPhiP-18
87WilBilP-6
Moses, Wally (Wallace)
34BatR31-98
35DiaMatCS3T1-110
36GouWidPPR-A77
36GouWidPPR-C19
36NatChiFPR-58
37ExhFou-14
37GouFliMR-5A
37GouFliMR-5B
37GouThuMR-5
37OPCBatUV-109
37WheBB9-13
38DixLid-5
38DixLidP-5
38ExhFou-14
39PlaBal-64
40PlaBal-26

41DouPlaR-125
41PlaBal-42
48RedSoxTI-18
49PhiBul-40
51Bow-261
53BowC-95
55Bow-294
60Top-459
61Yan61RL-32
68TigDetFPB-15
81TCM60I-481
91ConTSN-90
Mosher, Peyton
82VerBeaDT-9
Mosienko, Bill
43ParSpo-57
Moskau, Paul
77IndIndTI-9
78IndIndTI-3
78OPC-181
78Pep-19
78Top-126
79OPC-197
79Top-377
80RedEnq-31
80Top-258
81Fle-207
81OPC-358
81Top-546
82Don-355
82Fle-76
82Top-97
Mosley, Dave
87SalSpuP-8
Mosley, Reggie
83TriTriT-15
Mosley, Tim
96RocCubTI-21
Mosley, Tony
87ElmPio(C-17
88ElmPio1C-2
88WinHavRSS-15
89ElmPioP-11
90WinHavRSS-19
91LynRedSC-5
91LynRedSP-1194
92NewBriRSF-429
92NewBriRSS-490
92SkyAA F-210
Mosman, Marc
95BelGiaTI-23
Mosquea, Alberto
95MarPhiTI-17
96MarPhiB-17
Mosquera, David
94VenLinU-244
Mosquera, Julio
94MedHatBJF-3687
94MedHatBJSP-11
95HagSunF-73
96BesAutSA-47
96Exc-116
96KnoSmoB-18
96Top-432
97Bow-112
97BowCerBIA-CA55
97BowCerGIA-CA55
97BowInt-112
97PacPriGotD-GD103
Moss, Barry
77IndIndTI-23
87SalLakTTT-NNO
88SalLakCTTI-18
89SalLakTTI-15
91EriSaiC-28
91EriSaiP-4084
92SpoIndC-29
92SpoIndF-1312
93SpoIndC-29
96OrlCubB-3
Moss, Damian
94DanBraC-19
94DanBraF-3529
95AusFut-4
95Bes-55
95Bow-88
95MacBraTI-20
95MacBraUTI-5
95SPML-14
95UppDecML-72
96Bow-149
96BowBes-161
96BowBesAR-161
96BowBesR-161
96CarLeaA1B-3
96CarLeaA2B-3
96CarLeaAIB-B2
96DurBulBIB-14
96DurBulBrB-14
96Exc-132
96GreBraB-21
96GreBraTI-10
97Bow-412
97BowInt-412
97BowIntB-BBI20
97BowIntBAR-BBI20
97BowIntBR-BBI20
97Top-200
95UppDecMLFS-72
Moss, Darren
87AncGlaP-36
Moss, J. Lester
47TipTop-68
50Bow-251
51Bow-210
52Top-143
54Bow-181
54OriEss-26
55OriEss-20
57Top-213
58Top-153
59Top-453
77EvaTriT-21
79Top-66
83TopRep5-143
84AstMot-27
86AstPol-26
87AstMot-27
88AstMot-27
89AstLenH-14
89AstMot-27
89AstSmo-28
91OriCro-319
Moss, Ray
90DodTar-556
Mosser, Todd
90NebCor-19
Mossi, Don
55Bow-259
55Ind-6
55IndGolS-8
55Top-85
55TopDouH-83
55TopTesS-7
56Top-39
56TopPin-9
57IndSoh-9
57Top-8
58Top-35A
58Top-35B
59Top-302
60TigJayP-10
60Top-418
60TopTat-38
61Pos-42A
61Pos-42B
61SevElev-2
61Top-14
62Jel-23
62Pos-23
62PosCan-23
62TigJayP-10
62TigPosCF-11
62Top-55
62Top-105
62TopStal-49
62TopVen-55
62TopVen-105
63Jel-56
63Pos-56
63Top-218
63Top-530
64Top-335
64TopVen-335
66OPC-74
66Top-74
66TopVen-74
79DiaGre-297
79TCM50-215
81TCM60I-418
81TigDetN-49
84OCoandSI-152
90PacLeg-95
Mossor, Earl
90DodTar-1041
Mostil, Johnny A.
20WalMaiW-35
21E121So1-67
21Exh-113
21Nei-45
22E120-25
22W572-68
22W573-89
23W501-40
23WilChoV-109
26SpoNewSM-6
27YorCarE-24
28W502-24
28W56PlaC-S12A
28Yue-24
61Fle-64
76WhiSoxTAG-7
80WhiSoxGT-7
93ConTSN-912
Mota, Alfonso
95BoiHawTI-24
96CedRapKTI-17
Mota, Andy (Andres)
87AubAstP-7
88AubAstP-1966
89OscAstS-12
89Sta-16
90Bes-48
90CMC-752
90ColMudB-2
90ColMudP-1354
90ColMudS-17
90StaFS7-17
91LinDriAAA-616
91TucTorLD-616
91TucTorP-2220
91UppDecFE-22F
92Don-598
92Fle-441
92OPC-214
92Pin-257
92ProFS7-222
92Sco-872
92ScoImpP-33
92ScoRoo-16
92SkyAAAF-274
92StaClu-166
92Top-214
92TopDeb91-128
92TopGol-214
92TopGolW-214
92TopMic-214
92TucTorF-497
92TucTorS-615
92UppDec-564
93ColSprSSF-3097
93PhoFirF-1529
94ColSprSSF-745
Mota, Carlos
88BurIndP-1783
89Sta-183
89WatIndS-15
90RenSilSCLC-271
91Cla/Bes-118
91KinIndC-13
91KinIndP-326
92CanIndF-693
92CanIndS-114
93CanIndF-2843
93LimRocDWB-17
Mota, Christian
96BurIndB-21
Mota, Domingo
89AncBucTI-16
90KisDodD-18
91BakDodCLC-10
91Bow-696
92ClaFS7-182
92MemChiF-2427
92MemChiS-439
92SkyAA F-185
93ClaGolF-127
93MemChiF-382
Mota, Gary
92AshTouC-1
92ClaFS7-384
92UppDecML-25
92UppDecML-272
92UppDecMLPotY-PY2
93Bow-695
93ClaGolF-106
93ClaMVPF-6
93JacGenF-2122
93SouAtlLAIPI-16
93SouAtlLAPI-26
93StaCluAs-12
94JacGenF-230
94Top-782
94TopGol-782
94TopSpa-782
95ReaPhiTI-8
Mota, Gleydel
95PitMetTI-32
Mota, Guillermo
94KinMetC-13
94KinMetF-3831
96StLucMTI-31
Mota, Jose
77CocAstT-15
78DayBeaAT-20
80CedRapRT-13
Mota, Jose Manuel
86TulDriTI-27
89HunStaB-26
89WicChaR-7
89WicUpdR-11
90CMC-516
90LasVegSC-13
90LasVegSP-130
90ProAAAF-18
91FleUpd-126
91LasVegSLD-289
91LasVegSP-243
91LinDriAAA-289
91PadSmo-24
92Fle-616
92OmaRoyF-2970
92OmaRoyS-339
92Sco-742
92Sco100RS-47
92ScoRoo-19
92TopDeb91-129
93OmaRoyF-1686
94OmaRoyF-1230
96OmaRoyB-20
Mota, Manny
90AubAstB-1
90AubAstP-3398
93LimRocDWB-121
96MarPhiB-12
Mota, Manny Rafael
61TacBan-13
63Top-141
64PirKDK-20
64Top-246
64TopVen-246
65Top-463
66OPC-112
66PirEasH-15
66Top-112
66TopVen-112
67CokCapPi-8
67DexPre-149
67OPC-66
67PirTeal-14
67Top-66
67TopPirS-16
67TopVen-293
68PirKDK-15
68PirTeal-14
68Top-325
68TopVen-325
69ExpFudP-10
69MilBra-197
69MLBOffS-160
69Top-236
69TopSta-58
69TopTeaP-10
70DayDaiNM-117
70MLBOffS-53
70OPC-157
70Top-157
71DodTic-11
71MLBOffS-109
71OPC-112
71Top-112
72MilBra-245
72Top-596
73OPC-412
73Top-412
74Kel-49
74OPC-368
74Top-368
75OPC-414
75Top-414
76OPC-548
76SSP-87
76Top-548
77Top-386
78SSP270-79
78Top-228
78TopZes-5
79DodBlu-9
79Top-644
80Top-3
80Top-104
81DodPol-NNO
81Don-299
81Fle-141
83DodPol-NNO
83DodPos-10
84DodPol-NNO
84DodUniOP-5
85DodCokP-21
85DomLeaS-213
86DodCokP-20
87DodMot-27
87DodPol-29
87DodSmoA-24
88DodMot-28
88DodSmo-5
89DodMot-27
89DodPol-1
89DodSmoG-80
90BasWit-25
90DodMot-28
90DodPol-NNO
90DodTar-557
90PacLeg-41
90SweBasG-26
91DodMot-28
91DodPol-NNO
91DodUno7P-2
91LinDri-22
91SweBasG-63
92ActPacA-83
92DodMot-28
92DodPol-NNO
92DodStaTA-12
93DodMot-28
93DodPol-30
93UppDecAH-99
94CarLeaA-DJ29
94DodPol-30
94UppDecAH-139
94UppDecAH1-139
95DodMot-28
95DodPol-30
96DodMot-28
96DodPol-8
Mota, Miguel
87BakDodP-4
Mota, Santo
92JohCitCC-11
92JohCitCF-3124
94MadHatC-18
94MadHatF-143
Mota, Tony
96YakBeaTI-11
Mota, Willie
89EliTwiS-21
89Sta-151
90KenTwiB-10
90KenTwiP-2297
90KenTwiS-15
91KenTwiC-2
92ClaFS7-349
92Ft.MyeMCB-10
92Ft.MyeMF-2754
93ClaFS7-286
93ForMyeMC-16
93LinVenB-169
94VenLinU-228
95LinVen-55
Moten, Scott
92EliTwiC-4
92EliTwiF-3679
93ForWayWC-20
93ForWayWF-1967
94FloStaLAF-FSL11
94ForMyeMC-15
94ForMyeMF-1166
95HarCitRCTI-16
96IowCubB-20
Motes, Jeff
95PitMetTI-18
95StLucMTI-23
Mothell, Dink (Carroll Ray)
87NegLeaPD-19
Motley, Bob
96NegLeaBMKC-6
Motley, Darryl
81OmaRoyT-22
82Don-390
82Fle-417

82OmaRoyT-19
82Top-471
83EvaTriT-21
84Don-344
84FleUpd-81
85Don-461
85Fle-208
85Lea-69
85Top-561
85TopSti-276
85TopTif-561
86Don-217
86Fle-16
86Lea-95
86RoyKitCD-14
86RoyNatP-24
86Spo-186
86Top-332
86TopSti-22
86TopTif-332
87OPC-99
87RicBraBC-15
87RicBraC-30
87RicBraT-19
87Top-99
87TopTif-99
89IndIndC-22
89IndIndP-1238
90CMC-143
90NasSouC-18
90NasSouP-248
90ProAAAF-560
Motley, Mel
96WatIndTI-21
Motoi, Mitsuo
79TCMJapPB-53
Mott, Tom
94SigRooDP-74
94SigRooDPS-74
95ForWayWTI-8
95MidLeaA-37
96FtMyeMB-14
Motte, James
93EliTwiC-16
93EliTwiF-3421
94ForWayWC-16
94ForWayWF-2015
94MidLeaAF-MDW13
95ForMyeMTI-18
Mottola, Chad
92BenMusSP-2
92BilMusF-3370
92ClaDraP-5
92ClaDraPFB-BC5
92ClaDraPP-BB5
92DEL-BB5
92FroRowDP-82
92FroRowDPPC-1
92FroRowDPPS-82
92UppDecML-4
93Bow-90
93CarLeaAGF-44
93ClaYouG-YG13
93ExcFS7-25
93SP-282
93StaCluM-55
93StaCluMMP-6
93Top-56
93TopGol-56
93TopInaM-56
93TopMic-56
93UppDec-443
93UppDecGold-443
93WinSpiC-1
94ActPac-19
94Bow-214
94BowBes-B21
94BowBes-X102
94BowBesR-B21
94BowBesR-X102
94ChaLooF-1372
94Cla-152
94ClaGolF-196
94ExcFS7-179
94ExcLeaLF-15
94SigRooBS-P3
94TedWil-129
94Top-616
94TopGol-616
94TopSpa-616
94UppDecML-10
94UppDecML-265
94UppDecMLPotYF-PY22
94UppDecMLT1PJF-TP5
94UppDecMLT1PMF-5
95ChaLooTI-15
95Sel-167
95SelArtP-167
95SPML-41
95Sum-144
95SumNthD-144
95UppDecML-21
96Bow-244
96Fin-S284
96FinRef-S284
96FleUpd-U124
96FleUpdTC-U124
96IndIndB-16
96LeaPre-113
96LeaPreP-113
96LeaSig-70
96LeaSigPPG-70
96LeaSigPPP-70
96Zen-103
96ZenArtP-103
97DonEli-112
97DonEliGS-112
97DonEliTotC-20
97DonEliTotCDC-20
97DonRatR-21
97Fle-299
97FleTif-299
97Lea-83
97LeaFraM-83
97LeaFraMDC-83
97PacPriGotD-GD127
97Pin-144
97PinArtP-144
97PinIns-141
97PinInsCE-141
97PinInsDE-141
97PinMusC-144
97Sco-23
97ScoPreS-23
97ScoShoS-23
97ScoShoSAP-23
97StaClu-276
97StaCluM-M33
97StaCluMOP-276
97StaCluMOP-M33
97Top-358
97Ult-178
97UltGolME-178
97UltPlaME-178
97UppDec-477
95UppDecMLFS-21
Motton, Curt
68Top-549
69OPC-37
69Top-37
70OPC-261
70Ori-8
70Top-261
71MLBOffS-305
71OPC-684
71Top-684
72MilBra-246
72OPC-393
72Top-393
85EveGialC-12
86RocRedWP-13
87RocRedWP-13
87RocRedWT-23
88RocRedWC-25
88RocRedWGCP-29
88RocRedWP-218
88RocRedWTI-14
91OriCro-320
94BreMilB-338
Motuzas, Jeff
92ClaFS7-386
92PriWilCC-10
92PriWilCF-152
93PriWilCC-17
93PriWilCF-659
94SanBerSC-11
94SanBerSF-2763
95TamYanYI-20
Motz, Frank
98CamPepP-57
Motz, Willie
91KenTwiP-2079
Moulder, Glen
48WhiSoxTI-20
49Bow-159
49W72HolS-11
50W720HolS-21
90DodTar-1042
Moulton, Brian
77CedRapGT-6
Moultrie, Patrick
93St.CatBJC-16
93St.CatBJF-3987
94HagSunC-16
94HagSunF-2743
96HagSunB-15
Mounce, Tony
95Bes-75
95MidLeaA-35
95QuaCitRBTI-16
96BesAutSA-48
96Bow-125
96Exc-173
96KisCobB-18
Mount, Chuck
86EugEmeC-42
87AppFoxP-1
88BirBarB-27
89BirBarB-18
89BirBarP-92
90ChaKniTI-18
91IowCubLD-212
91IowCubP-1056
91LinDrIAAA-212
Mountain, Joe
92BelMarC-12
92BelMarF-1440
Moure, Brian
88CapCodPPaLP-12
Moushon, Dan
89SprCarB-28
Mouton, Brian
90ButCopKSP-21
Mouton, James
91AubAstC-17
91AubAstP-4282
92ClaFS7-207
92OscAstC-21
92OscAstF-2538
93Bow-236
93ClaFS7-225
93ExcFS7-48
93StaCluAs-3
93TriAAAGF-12
93TucTorF-3068
94AstMot-13
94Bow-258
94Bow-339
94BowBes-R82
94BowBesR-R82
94BowPre-10
94ClaGolF-136
94ColC-664
94ColChoGS-664
94ColChoSS-664
94ExcAllF-3
94ExcFS7-206
94ExtBas-279
94ExtBasRS-14
94Fin-421
94FinJum-421
94FinRef-421
94Fla-174
94FlaWavotF-A7
94FleAllR-M9
94FleUpd-146
94LeaGolR-15
94LeaLimR-76
94OPC-97
94OPCHotP-2
94Pin-535
94PinArtP-535
94PinMusC-535
94ScoRoo-RT99
94ScoRooGR-RT99
94ScoRooSR-SU15
94Sel-184
94SelRooS-RS15
94SpoRoo-109
94SpoRooAP-109
94StaClu-668
94StaCluFDI-668
94StaCluGR-668
94StaCluMOP-668
94Top-782
94TopGol-782
94TopSpa-782
94Ult-509
94UltAllR-8
94UltAllRJ-8
94UppDec-518
94UppDecED-518
94UppDecML-154
94UppDecML-215
95AstMot-14
95Baz-122
95ColCho-112
95ColChoGS-112
95ColChoSS-112
95Don-246
95DonPreP-246
95DonTopotO-259
95Fin-27
95FinRef-27
95Fla-362
95Fle-466
95Lea-101
95Pac-191
95Pin-58
95PinArtP-58
95PinMusC-58
95Sco-125
95ScoGolR-125
95ScoPlaTS-125
95Sel-109
95SelArtP-109
95Spo-67
95SpoArtP-67
95StaClu-305
95StaCluMOP-305
95StaCluSTWS-305
95StaCluVR-161
95Sum-63
95SumNthD-63
95Top-597
95TopCyb-369
95Ult-175
95UltGolM-175
95UppDec-28
95UppDecED-28
95UppDecEDG-28
95Zen-32
96AstMot-14
96ColCho-167
96ColChoGS-167
96ColChoSS-167
96Don-233
96DonPreP-233
96Fla-283
96Fle-417
96FleTif-417
96LeaSigA-163
96LeaSigAG-163
96LeaSigAS-163
96Pac-96
96Pin-95
96Sco-80
96StaClu-384
96StaCluMOP-384
95StaCluVRMC-161
96Ult-213
96UltGolM-213
96UppDec-83
97Don-209
97DonPreP-209
97DonPrePGold-209
97Fle-352
97FleTif-352
97Pac-323
97PacLigB-323
97PacSil-323
97Sco-293
97ScoPreS-293
97ScoShoS-293
97ScoShoSAP-293
97Ult-481
97UltGolME-481
97UltPlaME-481
Mouton, Lyle
91LSUTigP-12
91LSUTigP-13
91OneYanP-4166
92PriWilCC-16
92PriWilCF-162
92ProFS7-127
92UppDecML-194
93AlbYanF-2174
93ClaFS7-81
93ClaGolF-3
93ExcFS7-212
94AbaYanF-1455
94ExcFS7-110
94UppDecML-164
95ColCliMCTI-20
95SigRooOJ-24
95SigRooOJP-24
95SigRooOJPS-24
95SigRooOJS-24
95TopTra-130T
95UppDecML-208
96ColCho-17
96ColChoGS-17
96ColChoSS-17
96Don-54
96DonPreP-54
96EmoXL-39
96Fin-S168
96FinRef-S168
96Fla-55
96Fle-74
96FleTif-74
96FleWhiS-12
96Lea-103
96LeaPrePB-103
96LeaPrePG-103
96LeaPrePS-103
96LeaSigA-162
96LeaSigAG-162
96LeaSigAS-162
96MetUni-39
96MetUniP-39
96Pac-282
96Sco-257
96StaClu-54
96StaCluMOP-54
96Stu-60
96StuPrePB-60
96StuPrePG-60
96StuPrePS-60
96Top-119
96TopGal-105
96TopGalPPI-105
96Ult-42
96UltGolM-42
96UppDec-39
97Cir-109
97CirRav-109
97ColCho-73
97DonTea-73
97DonTeaSPE-73
97Fle-66
97FleTif-66
97Pac-59
97PacLigB-59
97PacSil-59
97Sco-218
97ScoPreS-218
97ScoShoS-218
97ScoShoSAP-218
97ScoWhiS-10
97ScoWhiSPI-10
97ScoWhiSPr-10
97Top-407
97UppDec-41
95UppDecMLFS-208
Mowrey, Mike (Harry)
08RosComP-121
09T206-255
10CouT21-49
10CouT21-193
10CouT21-194
10CouT21-195
10CouT21-307
10DarChoE-24
10RedCroT-140
10RedCroT-227
10W555-50
11PloCanE-50
11SpoLifCW-262
11SpoLifM-275
12PhiCarE-22
14B18B-80A
14B18B-80B
14TexTomE-36
16ColE13-123
16FleBreD-68
16SpoNewM-129
Mowry, Dave
90HigSchPLS-21
92ChaRaiF-128
92ClaFS7-55
92ChaRaiC-20
94SprSulC-18
94SprSulF-2045
95RanCucQT-33
Mowry, Joe
33ButCanV-36
34DiaMatCSB-136
34ButPreR-47
34Gou-59

Moya, Felix
90JamExpP-22
91WesPalBEC-8
91WesPalBEP-1224
92WesPalBEC-24
92WesPalBEF-2087
Moyer, Greg
81ShrCapT-22
Moyer, Jamie
86CubGat-49
86PitCubP-17
87CubCan-21
87CubDavB-49
87Don-315
87Fle-570
87FleGlo-570
87Top-227
87TopTif-227
88CubDavB-49
88Don-169
88DonBasB-228
88DonTeaBC-169
88Fle-426
88FleGlo-426
88OPC-36
88PanSti-255
88Sco-573
88ScoGlo-573
88StaLinCu-7
88Top-36
88TopSti-62
88TopTif-36
89Bow-223
89BowTif-223
89Don-157
89DonTra-39
89Fle-432
89FleGlo-432
89FleUpd-65
89OPC-171
89RanMot-17
89RanSmo-22
89Sco-263
89Top-549
89Top-717
89TopSti-53
89TopTif-549
89TopTif-717
89TopTra-85T
89TopTraT-85T
89UppDec-63
89UppDec-791
90Don-378
90Fle-307
90FleCan-307
90OPC-412
90PubSti-417
90RanMot-24
90Sco-107A
90Sco-107B
90Top-412
90TopTif-412
90UppDec-619
90VenSti-357
91Bow-391
91Fle-294
91LouRedTI-8
91OPC-138
91Sco-437
91StaClu-481
91Top-138
91TopDesS-138
91TopMic-138
91TopTif-138
91UppDec-610
92TolMudHF-1042
93FleFinE-160
93RanKee-274
93RocRedWF-234
94ColC-213
94ColChoGS-213
94ColChoSS-213
94Don-547
94Fla-6
94Fle-11
94Lea-215
94OriPro-69
94OriUSPC-6H
94OriUSPC-12S
94Pin-442
94PinArtP-442
94PinMusC-442
94Sco-270
94ScoGolR-270
94StaClu-284
94StaCluFDI-284
94StaCluGR-284
94StaCluMOP-284
94StaCluT-287
94StaCluTFDI-287
94Top-526
94TopGol-526
94TopSpa-526
94Ult-6
94UppDec-147
94UppDecED-147
95ColCho-342
95ColChoGS-342
95ColChoSS-342
95Don-66
95DonPreP-66
95Fla-5
95Fle-14
95Pac-26
95Sco-114
95ScoGolR-114
95ScoPlaTS-114
95Top-318
95TopCyb-172
95Ult-256
95UltGolM-256
96ColCho-479
96ColChoGS-479
96ColChoSS-479
96Don-69
96DonPreP-69
96Fle-16
96FleTif-16
96FleUpd-U16
96FleUpdTC-U16
96LeaSigA-164
96LeaSigAG-164
96LeaSigAS-164
96Sco-210
96StaClu-415
96StaCluMOP-415
96Ult-318
96UltGolM-318
97Cir-364
97CirRav-364
97ColCho-479
97Don-224
97DonPreP-224
97DonPrePGold-224
97DonTea-145
97DonTeaSPE-145
97Fle-212
97FleTif-212
97Pac-191
97PacLigB-191
97PacPriSH-SH7B
97PacSil-191
97Pin-30
97PinArtP-30
97PinMusC-30
97Sco-254
97ScoMar-14
97ScoMarPl-14
97ScoMarPr-14
97ScoPreS-254
97ScoShoS-254
97ScoShoSAP-254
97Top-283
97Ult-507
97UltGolME-507
97UltPlaME-507
97UppDec-504
Moyer, Jim
71MLBOffS-260
72OPC-506
72Top-506
Moyle, Michael
91PerHeaF-11
92BurIndC-20
92BurIndF-1661
93BurIndC-19
93BurIndF-3302
94ButCopKSP-17
95AusFut-18
95AusFutGP-3
96CarLeaA1B-10
96CarLeaA2B-10
96KenIndB-18
Mozzali, Mo
77Car5-15
77CarTeal-15
78CarTeal-12
Mraz, Don
76QuaCitAT-23
Mrowka, Jim
92KinMetF-1540
Mrozinski, Ron
55Bow-287
Mucerino, Greg
92ChaRaiC-6
92ChaRaiF-129
Mucker, Kelcey
94ClaGolF-81
94EliTwiC-15
94EliTwiF-3743
95ForWayWTI-23
96FtMyeMB-13
Mud Hens, Toledo
87IntLeaAT-43
Mudcat, Muddy the
96CarMudB-29
Mudcats, Columbus
89ColMudP-149
Mudd, Scott
95HudValRTI-4
96ChaRivTI-9623
Muddy, Mascot
95TolMudHTI-30
Mueller, Bill
93EveGiaC-19
93EveGiaF-3776
94SanJosGC-18
94SanJosGF-2827
96PhoFirB-21
97ColCho-8
97Don-380
97DonPreP-380
97DonPrePGold-380
97Fle-485
97FleTif-485
97MetUni-246
97Pac-446
97PacLigB-446
97PacSil-446
97Top-490
97Ult-297
97UltGolME-297
97UltPlaME-297
97UppDec-270
Mueller, Bret
95NewJerCTI-21
96PeoChiB-21
Mueller, Clarence F.
23WilChoV-110
25Exh-62
26Exh-61
Mueller, Don
47Exh-163
47PM1StaP1-144
49EurSta-121
50Bow-221
50JJKCopP-11
51Bow-268
52BerRos-44
52Bow-18
52CokTip-6
52DixLid-13
52DixPre-13
52NatTeaL-18
52TipTop-27
52Top-52
53BowC-74
53Bri-37
53DixLid-13
53DixPre-13
54Bow-73
54NewYorJA-33
54RedMan-NL7
54StaMey-9
54Top-42
55ArmCoi-14
55GiaGolS-22
55RedMan-NL8
55RobGouS-9
55RobGouW-9
55StaMey-8
56Top-241
57Top-148
58Top-253
59Top-368
75Gia195T-21
79TCM50-149
83TopRep5-52
94TopArc1-42
94TopArc1G-42
Mueller, Heinie (Emmett)
39PlaBal-63
40PlaBal-96
91ConTSN-179
92ConTSN-643
Mueller, Mark
72CedRapCT-26
Mueller, Pete
86OscAstP-19
Mueller, Ray
46SpoExcW-6-1B
49EurSta-122
50PirTeal-15
51Bow-313
61Fle-128
Mueller, Willard
75BurBeeT-18
76BurBeeT-23
76CliPilT-24
77BurBeeT-19
78HolMilT-16
79VanCanT-23B
80Top-668
80VanCanT-2
81VanCanT-15
82WicAerTI-10
94BreMilB-339
Muffett, Billy
58Top-143
59Top-241
61Top-16
62Top-336
71CarTeal-29
76SSP-614
88TigPep-NNO
89TigMar-NNO
90TigCok-28
91TigCok-NNO
93TigGat-28
Muh, Steve
89KenTwiP-1079
89KenTwiS-17
90OrlSunRB-20
90OrlSunRP-1080
91LinDriAA-489
91OrlSunRLD-489
91OrlSunRP-1847
Muhammad, Bob
87HawRai-23
89BelBrelS-18
Muhlethaler, Mike
90SouOreAB-26
90SouOreAP-3448
Muir, Harry
92MedHatBJF-3206
92MedHatBJSP-10
93St.CatBJC-17
93St.CatBJF-3973
94HagSunC-17
94HagSunF-2727
Muir, Joseph
52Top-154
83TopRep5-154
Mula, Jared
92LSUTigM-16
Mulcahy, Hugh
39ExhSal-45
39PlaBal-145
40PlaBal-95
41Gou-1
52LavPro-51
79DiaGre-309
93DiaStaES-147
95ConTSN-1346
Mulden, Chris
78CliDodT-24
Muldoon, William
87AllandGN-36
88GooN16-28
88KimN18-26
Mulholland, Terry
84EveGiaC-20
86PhoFirP-18
87Don-515
87PhoFirP-5
87SpoTeaP-10
87Top-536
87TopTif-536
88PhoFirC-10
88PhoFirP-77
89FleUpd-111
89PhiTas-44
89PhoFirC-4
89PhoFirP-1480
89Sco-474
89Top-41
89TopTif-41
90ClaBlu-127
90Don-515
90Fle-568
90FleCan-568
90Lea-474
90OPC-657
90PhiTas-24
90Sco-542
90Top-657
90TopTif-657
90UppDec-474
91Bow-504
91ClaGam-78
91Don-541
91DonBonC-BC14
91Fle-408
91FleWaxBC-8
91Lea-46
91OPC-413
91PanFreS-359
91PanSti-8
91PhiMed-30
91Sco-33
91Sco-706
91StaClu-58
91StaCluCM-21
91Stu-219
91Top-413
91TopDesS-413
91TopMic-413
91TopTif-413
91Ult-269
91UppDec-426
92Bow-39
92Don-268
92Fle-540
92Hig5-79
92Lea-464
92MooSna-16
92OPC-719
92PanSti-249
92PhiMed-22
92PhiMed-44
92Pin-199
92Sco-118
92StaClu-98
92Stu-78
92SunSee-4
92Top-719
92TopGol-719
92TopGolW-719
92TopMic-719
92TriPla-11
92Ult-248
92UppDec-129
93Bow-484
93Don-172
93Fla-106
93Fle-106
93Lea-22
93LeaGolA-U1
93OPC-283
93PacSpa-240
93PanSti-267
93PhiMed-24
93Pin-73
93Sco-117
93Sel-127
93SelStaL-64
93SP-16
93StaClu-716
93StaCluFDI-716
93StaCluMOP-716
93StaCluP-17
93Stu-10
93Top-555
93TopGol-555
93TopInaM-555
93TopMic-555
93TriPla-170
93Ult-92
93UppDec-279
93UppDecGold-279
94Bow-81
94ColC-508
94ColChoGS-508
94ColChoSS-508
94Don-160
94ExtBas-134
94Fin-305
94FinRef-305
94Fla-322
94Fle-597

94FleAllS-46
94FleUpd-69
94Lea-373
94OPC-34
94Pac-483
94PhiUSPC-1D
94PhiUSPC-6C
94PhiUSPC-9C
94Pin-47
94PinArtP-47
94PinMusC-47
94Sco-184
94ScoGolR-184
94ScoRoo-RT14
94ScoRooGR-RT14
94Sel-255
94Spo-134
94SpoRoo-22
94SpoRooAP-22
94StaClu-222
94StaClu-700
94StaCluFDI-222
94StaCluFDI-700
94StaCluGR-222
94StaCluGR-700
94StaCluMOP-222
94StaCluMOP-700
94StaCluT-207
94StaCluTFDI-207
94Top-170
94TopGol-170
94TopSpa-170
94TopTra-50T
94TriPla-178
94Ult-251
94Ult-401
94UppDec-399
94UppDecED-399
95ColCho-554T
95Don-404
95DonPreP-404
95DonTopotO-353
95Fla-426
95Fle-77
95FleUpd-195
95GiaMot-6
95Lea-350
95Pac-300
95Top-380
95TopTra-53T
95UppDec-337
95UppDecED-337
95UppDecEDG-337
96Fle-592
96FleTif-592
96FleUpd-U168
96FleUpdTC-U168
96Pac-208
96PhiTeal-24
86STaoftFt-39
97Cir-108
97CirRav-108
97Fle-634
97FleTif-634
97Ult-429
97UltGolME-429
97UltPlaME-429

Mull, Blaine
95SprSulTI-17
96LanLugB-17
96MidLeaAB-38

Mull, Jack
75PhoGiaC-6
75PhoGiaCK-2
76PheGiaCr-10
76PhoGiaCC-16
76PhoGiaVNB-18
77CedRapGT-11
78CedRapGT-18
81ShrCapT-1
83PhoGiaBHN-24
84PhoGiaC-24
85GiaMot-27
85GiaPos-24
86CliGiaP-15
87ShrCapP-25
87TexLeaAF-6
88ShrCapP-1279
88TexLeaAGS-1
89PhoFirC-21
89PhoFirP-1503
90CliGiaB-9
90CliGiaP-2565
91CliGiaC-26
91CliGiaP-851
93CliGiaC-26
93CliGiaF-2504
94CliLumF-1997
96KenIndB-28
94CliLumC-26

Mullan, Paul
92FleCle-NNO
93UltEck-P1

Mullane, Count (Anthony)
87OldJudN-362
94OriofB-66

Mullaney, Dominic
09T206-504

Mullaney, Jack
52LavPro-20

Mulleavy, Greg
59DodTeal-17
60DodUniO-23
60Top-463

Mullen, Adam
95DanBraTI-19

Mullen, Billy
90DodTar-1043

Mullen, Ford
43CenFlo-20

Mullen, Rebecca
96BatCliTI-29

Mullen, Scott
96SpoIndB-19

Mullen, Tom
81AppFoxT-5
81GleFalWST-6
82GleFalWST-22
83GleFalWST-17
85BufBisT-23
86OmaRoyP-16
86OmaRoyT-22
88OmaRoyC-8
88OmaRoyP-1507

Muller, Fred
37WheBB7-290

Muller, Mike
87MemChiP-22

Muller, S.
88KimN18-27

Mulligan, Bill
86Ft.MyeRP-20
87Ft.MyeRP-1

Mulligan, Bob
80WisRapTT-3
82OrlTwi8SCT-21
82OrlTwiT-21
83TolMudHT-8
84TolMudHT-9
85OrlTwiT-19

Mulligan, Edward
21E121So1-68
22W575-87
23W501-45

Mulligan, Sean
92ClaFS7-132
92HigDesMC-17
92StaCluD-127
92WatDiaF-2144
93RanCucQC-21
94AriFalLS-13
94RanCucQC-21
94RanCucQF-1642
96LasVegSB-18

Mullin, George
04FanCraAL-37
07TigACDPP-9
08RosComP-37
09AmeCarE-82
09BriE97-23
09BusBroBPP-12
09ColChiE-207
09SpoNewSM-33
09T206-256
09T206-257
09T206-258
09TigMorPenWBPP-9
09TigTaCP-13
09WolNewDTPP-11
10CouT21-196
10CouT21-197
10DomDisP-89
10E-UOraBSC-18
10E98-24
10JuJuDE-30
10NadE1-42
10RedCroT-56
10RedCroT-141
10RedCroT-228
10SweCapPP-28A
10SweCapPP-28B
10W555-51
11DiaGumP-21
11S74Sil-17
11SpoLifCW-263
11SpoLifM-65
11T205-125
11TurRedT-30
12ColRedB-207
12ColTinT-207
12HasTriFT-5
12PhiCarE-23
12T207-136
12T207-137
14CraJacE-24
15CraJacE-24
15VicT21-21
69SCFOldT-13
81TigDetN-119
81TigSecNP-4
92ConTSN-338

Mullin, Jay
89TenTecGE-18

Mullin, Pat
47TipTop-38
49Bow-56
50Bow-135
51Bow-106
52Bow-183
52Top-275
53BowBW-4
53TigGle-22
54Bow-151
79ExpPos-17
80ExpPos-17
81TigDetN-21
83TigAlKS-8
83TigAlKS-61
83TopRep5-275
85TCMPla1-6

Mullin, Williard
88WilMulP-1

Mulliniks, Rance (S. Rance)
75QuaCitAT-10
77SalLakCGC-4
78AngFamF-28
78SSP270-216
78Top-579
79SalLakCGT-11
81Don-504
81Fle-48
81Top-433
82Don-630
82Fle-418
82Top-104
82TopTra-78T
83Don-432
83Fle-436
83OPC-277
83Top-277
84BluJayFS-26
84Don-584
84Fle-165
84Nes792-762
84OPC-19
84Top-762
84TopSti-374
84TopTif-762
85AllGamPI-36
85BluJayFS-24
85Don-485
85Fle-116
85Lea-153
85OPC-336
85OPCPos-17
85Top-336
85TopTif-336
86BluJayAF-21
86BluJayFS-27
86Don-606
86Fle-68
86GenMilB-3G
86OPC-74
86Top-74
86TopTif-74
87BluJayFS-24
87Don-319
87DonOpeD-32
87Fle-237
87FleGlo-237
87OPC-91
87Top-537
87TopTif-537
88BluJayFS-24
88Don-197
88DonBasB-328
88Fle-120
88FleGlo-120
88Lea-204
88MSAHosD-14
88OPC-167
88Sco-235
88ScoGlo-235
88StaLinBJ-16
88Top-167
88TopTif-167
89BluJayFS-21
89Bow-250
89BowTif-250
89Don-87
89Fle-242
89FleGlo-242
89OPC-111
89Sco-385
89Top-618
89TopSti-192
89TopTif-618
89UppDec-43
90BluJayFS-21
90Don-607
90El PasDAGTI-42
90Fle-91
90FleCan-91
90OPC-466
90PubSti-525
90Sco-204
90Top-466
90TopTif-466
90UppDec-132
90VenSti-358
91BluJayFS-18
91BluJayFS-21
91BluJayS-17
91Don-663
91Fle-181
91OPC-229
91Sco-433
91Top-229
91TopDesS-229
91TopMic-229
91TopTif-229
91Ult-366
92Don-542
92Fle-337
92KnoBluJF-2999
92OPC-133
92Sco-132
92StaClu-202
92Top-133
92TopGol-133
92TopGolW-133
92TopMic-133
92Ult-149
93BluJayD4-26

Mullino, Ray
87GenCubP-9
87PeoChiP-1
88ChaWheB-25
89WinSpiS-12
90ChaKniTI-15
90PeoChiTI-26
90TopTVCu-54

Mullins, Fran
80GleFalWSBT-23
80GleFalWSCT-12
81EdmTraRR-20
81Top-112
82EdmTraT-9
84GiaPos-18
85PhoGiaC-180
85Top-283
85TopTif-283
86IndOhH-22

Mullins, Gregory
95BelBreTI-16
95HelBreTI-23
96El PasDB-20

Mullins, Ron
87CedRapRP-8
88GreHorP-1561
88SouAtlLAGS-9
89MiaMirIS-14
90PenPilS-13

Mullins, Sam
92PriRedC-7
92PriRedF-3086
93PriRedC-20
93PriRedF-4176

Mulvaney, Michael
88BilMusP-1808
89GreHorP-410
89SouAtlLAGS-33
90CedRapRB-7
90CedRapRP-2330
90MidLeaASGS-44

Mulvey, Joe (Joseph)
87AllandGN-9
87BucN28-82A
87BucN28-82B
87OldJudN-363
88WG1CarG-53
90DodTar-558
90KalBatN-41

Mulville, Duane
88BilMusP-1805
89CedRapRB-11
89CedRapRP-924
89CedRapRS-13
92ClePhiC-20
92ClePhiF-2059

Mumaw, Steve
86VenGulP-15
87DunBluJP-932
88DunBluJS-11
89ArkTraGS-14

Mummau, Rob
93St.CatBJC-18
93St.CatBJF-3982
94SouBenSHC-13
94SouBenSHF-600
95HagSunF-75
96DunBluJB-18
96DunBluJTI-21

Mumphrey, Jerry
75TulOil7-16
76SSP-289
77Car5-16
77CarTeal-16
77Top-136
78CarTeal-13
78Top-452
79Car5-18
79Top-32
80OPC-196
80Top-378
81Don-124
81Dra-26
81Fle-494
81OPC-196
81Squ-23
81Top-556
81TopScr-97
81TopSti-227
81TopTra-808
82Don-261
82Fle-43
82OPC-175
82Top-175
82Top-486
82TopSti-220
83AllGamPI-63
83Don-360
83Fle-389
83FleSta-132
83FleSti-41
83OPC-246
83Top-81
83Top-670
83TopSti-97
83YanRoyRD-6
84AllGamPI-61
84AstMot-9
84Don-426
84Fle-233
84Nes792-45
84OPC-45
84Top-45
84TopSti-70
84TopTif-45
85AllGamPI-153
85AstHouP-6
85AstMot-15
85Don-206
85Fle-354
85Lea-124
85OPC-186
85Top-736
85TopMin-736
85TopSti-60

85TopTif-736
86AstMot-27
86CubGat-22
86CubUno-14
86Don-84
86Fle-306
86FleUpd-79
86OPC-282
86SevCoi-S16
86Top-282
86TopTif-282
86TopTra-76T
86TopTraT-76T
87CubCan-22
87CubDavB-22
87Don-324
87Fle-571
87FleGlo-571
87FleMin-73
87FleStiC-82
87SpoTeaP-22
87Top-372
87TopSti-58
87TopTif-372
88CubDavB-22
88Don-447
88DonTeaBC-447
88Fle-427
88FleGlo-427
88FleMin-69
88OPC-63
88PanSti-267
88Sco-467
88ScoGlo-467
88StaLinCu-8
88Top-466
88TopBig-70
88TopTif-466
89Sco-288
92YanWIZ8-128
Muncrief, Bob
41BroW75-22
41Gou-8
46SeaSLP-38
46SpoExcW-5-8
47TipTop-69
48IndTeal-23
49Bow-221
79DiaGre-186
83TCMPla1945-9
96Bro194F-12
Munda, Steve
91OneYanP-4152
92GreHorC-22
92GreHorF-776
93PriWilCC-18
93PriWilCF-653
94SanBerSC-12
94TamYanF-2380
Mundroig, Jorge
79CedRapGT-4
Mundy, Rick
88GenCubP-1640
89GenCubP-1883
89PeoChiTI-12
90PeoChiTI-6
91PeoChiC-11
91PeoChiP-1345
91PeoChiTI-15
Munger, Red (George)
46SpoExcW-8-10
47TipTop-160
49Bow-40
49EurSta-190
50Bow-89
51Bow-11
51TopBluB-14
52Bow-243
52Top-115
83TopRep5-115
Mungin, Mike
88SouOreAP-1710
Mungo, Dave
89GenCubP-1859
Mungo, Van Lingle
34DiaMatCSB-138
34BatR31-26
34BatR31-131
34DiaStaR-19
34DiaStaR-102
35DiaMatCS2-16
35DiaMatCS3T1-112
35ExhFou-2
36DiaMatCS4-11
36ExhFou-2
36NatChiFPR-59
36R31PasP-18
36R31Pre-L9
36SandSW-42
36WheBB3-9
37ExhFou-2
37GouFliMR-6A
37GouFliMR-6B
37GouThuMR-6
37WheBB14-11
37WheBB7-29K
37WheBB9-14
38BasTabP-23
38ExhFou-2
38GouHeaU-254
38GouHeaU-278
39GouPreR303A-33
39PlaBal-111
39WorWidGTP-33
40DodTeal-17
40PlaBal-64
84OCoandSI-122
89DodSmoG-45
90DodTar-559
94ConTSN-1107
94ConTSNB-1107
Munley, John
83TriTriT-7
Munninghoff, Scott
81OklCit8T-13
82ChaLooT-2
Munns, Les
90DodTar-560
Munoz, Bobby (Bob)
91FloStaLAP-FSL16
91Ft.LauYC-9
91Ft.LauYP-2422
92AlbYanF-2224
92AlbYanS-13
92Bow-523
92ClaFS7-6
92SkyAA F-8
92UppDecML-222
93Bow-47
93ClaFS7-82
93ColCliF-1110
93ColCliP-10
93ExcFS7-213
93FlaWavotF-10
93FleFinE-249
93Lea-548
93SelRoo-32T
93TopTra-13T
93Ult-598
94Bow-56
94ColC-214
94ColC-553
94ColChoGS-214
94ColChoGS-553
94ColChoSS-214
94ColChoSS-553
94Don-174
94Fin-414
94FinRef-414
94Fla-416
94Fle-241
94FleUpd-168
94Pac-431
94PhiMed-24
94PhiMel-17
94Pin-188
94PinArtP-188
94PinMusC-188
94Sco-566
94ScoGolR-566
94SpoRoo-140
94SpoRooAP-140
94StaClu-246
94StaCluFDI-246
94StaCluGR-246
94StaCluMOP-246
94StaCluT-214
94StaCluTFDI-214
94Top-144
94TopGol-144
94TopSpa-144
94TopTra-102T
94Ult-98
94Ult-553
94UppDec-343
94UppDecED-343
95ColCho-372
95ColChoGS-372
95ColChoSE-173
95ColChoSEGS-173
95ColChoSESS-173
95ColChoSS-372
95Don-159
95DonPreP-159
95Emb-80
95EmbGolI-80
95Fin-84
95FinRef-84
95Fla-182
95Fle-402
95Lea-103
95Pac-335
95Phi-22
95Pin-243
95PinArtP-243
95PinMusC-243
95StaClu-385
95StaCluMOP-385
95StaCluSTWS-385
95StaCluVR-203
95Top-458
95TopCyb-253
95Ult-208
95UltGolM-208
95UppDec-143
95UppDecED-143
95UppDecEDG-143
95StaCluVRMC-203
97PacPriGotD-GD185
Munoz, Francisco
93LinVenB-96
94VenLinU-31
95LinVen-137
Munoz, J.J.
90MarPhiP-3196
90ProAaA-186
91SpaPhiC-9
91SpaPhiP-894
92ClePhiC-17
92ClePhiF-2056
93ClePhiC-17
93ClePhiF-2681
94ReaPhiF-2060
95OmaRoyTI-23
Munoz, Jose
88BakDodCLC-239
88BlaYNPRWL-46
89BlaYNPRWL-47
89VerBeaDS-18
90BakDodCLC-258
91LinDriAA-538
91SanAntMLD-538
91SanAntMP-2983
92AlbDukF-728
92AlbDukS-17
92SkyAAAF-9
93AlbDukF-1470
93LinVenB-299
94PawRedSDD-14
94PawRedSF-951
95RicBraRC-13
95RicBraTI-10
97Pac-60
97PacLigB-60
97PacSil-60
97Ult-42
97UltGolME-42
97UltPlaME-42
Munoz, Juan
96MidLeaAB-20
96PeoChiB-22
Munoz, Julio
90AshTouP-2744
Munoz, Lou
88ElmPioC-16
88WinHavRSS-16
89ElmPioP-12
90WinHavRSS-20
Munoz, Mario
93BenRocC-18
93BenRocF-3278
Munoz, Michael
87BakDodP-27
88BasAmeAAB-26
88BlaYNPRWL-186
88SanAntMB-7
88TexLeaAGS-30
89AlbDukC-8
89AlbDukP-62
90DodTar-561
90DonRoo-8
90Sco-653
90TopDeb89-85
91LinDriAAA-593
91Sco100RS-93
91TolMudHLD-593
91TolMudHP-1929
92StaClu-441
92Ult-367
93ColSprSSF-3083
93Don-627
93Fle-609
93Lea-191
93PacSpa-449
93Sco-228
93StaClu-248
93StaCluFDI-248
93StaCluMOP-248
93Top-379
93TopGol-379
93TopInaM-379
93TopMic-379
93UppDec-601
93UppDecGold-601
94FleUpd-129
94RocPol-18
94StaClu-492
94StaCluFDI-492
94StaCluGR-492
94StaCluMOP-492
94StaCluT-102
94StaCluTFDI-102
95Fla-131
95Fle-524
95Sco-228
95ScoGolR-228
95ScoPlaTS-228
95Ult-375
95UltGolM-375
96Fle-368
96FleRoc-9
96FleTif-368
96LeaSigEA-134
96RocPol-13
97PacPriGotD-GD136
Munoz, Noe
94SanAntMF-2473
Munoz, Omer
87WesPalBEP-669
88WesPalBES-19
90JacExpB-7
90JacExpP-1383
91HarSenLD-265
91HarSenP-635
91LinDriAA-265
92IndIndF-1868
92IndIndS-188
93BufBisF-525
94VenLinU-231
94VenLinU-245
95CarMudF-167
96LynHilB-29
Munoz, Orlando
92PalSprAC-14
92PalSprAF-848
93LinVenB-268
93PalSprAC-15
93PalSprAF-78
94VanCanF-1870
95LinVen-46
95MidAngOHP-23
95MidAngTI-21
97MidAngOHP-19
Munoz, Oscar
90WatIndS-14
91Cla/Bes-149
91KinIndC-8
91KinIndP-320
92OrlSunRF-2847
92OrlSunRS-522
92UppDecML-293
93NasXprF-401
94Bow-597
94ExcFS7-96
94SalLakBF-814
94Top-771
94TopGol-771
94TopSpa-771
94UppDecML-217
96Pac-366
96RocRedWB-19
96Sco-249
96SigRooOJ-23
96SigRooOJS-23
Munoz, Pedro
87DunBluJP-948
88BlaYNPRWL-110
88DunBluJS-13
89KnoBluJB-18
89KnoBluJP-1126
89KnoBluJS-14
89Sta-122
90ProAAAF-365
90SyrChiMB-17
90SyrChiP-585
91Bow-336
91Cla3-T64
91Don-758
91DonRoo-21
91Fle-620
91Lea-186
91LinDriAAA-412
91PorBeaLD-412
91PorBeaP-1579
91Sco-332
91StaClu-318
91TopDeb90-111
91Ult-192
91UppDec-432
92Don-305
92Fle-212
92Lea-53
92OPC-613
92Pin-139
92PinTea2-61
92ProFS7-91
92Sco-514
92Sco100RS-74
92StaClu-541
92Top-613
92TopGol-613
92TopGolW-613
92TopMic-613
92Ult-399
92UppDec-764
93Don-311
93Fla-240
93Fle-272
93Lea-219
93OPC-289
93PacSpa-175
93PanSti-132
93Pin-135
93Sco-130
93Sel-370
93SP-251
93StaClu-117
93StaCluFDI-117
93StaCluMOP-117
93Stu-166
93Top-119
93TopGol-119
93TopInaM-119
93TopMic-119
93Toy-26
93Ult-235
93UppDec-341
93UppDecGold-341
94ColC-543
94ColChoGS-543
94ColChoSS-543
94Don-55
94Fin-338
94FinRef-338
94Fle-215
94Lea-360
94Pac-363
94PanSti-95
94Pin-356
94PinArtP-356
94PinMusC-356
94Sco-435
94ScoGolR-435
94Sel-301
94StaClu-22
94StaCluFDI-22
94StaCluGR-22
94StaCluMOP-22
94Top-459
94TopGol-459
94TopSpa-459
94Ult-392
94UppDec-302
94UppDecED-302
95ColCho-489
95ColChoGS-489
95ColChoSS-489
95Don-436
95DonPreP-436
95DonTopotO-112

95Fla-61
95Fle-211
95Lea-125
95Pac-254
95PacPri-81
95Pin-125
95PinArtP-125
95PinMusC-125
95Sco-331
95ScoGolR-331
95ScoPlaTS-331
95SPCha-168
95SPChaDC-168
95StaClu-471
95StaCluMOP-471
95StaCluSTWS-471
95Top-274
95TopCyb-77
95Ult-305
95UltGolM-305
95UppDec-432
95UppDecED-432
95UppDecEDG-432
95UppDecSE-84
95UppDecSEG-84
96A'sMot-12
96ColCho-202
96ColCho-646
96ColChoGS-202
96ColChoGS-646
96ColChoSS-202
96ColChoSS-646
96Don-196
96DonPreP-196
96EmoXL-105
96Fla-151
96Fle-170
96FleTif-170
96FleUpd-U74
96FleUpdTC-U74
96MetUni-79
96MetUniP-79
96Pac-357
96PacPri-P116
96PacPriG-P116
96PanSti-206
96ProSta-129
96Sco-87
96Top-384
96Ult-91
96Ult-402
96UltGolM-91
96UltGolM-402
96UppDec-129
96UppDec-414
97PacPriGotD-GD81

Munoz, Ricky (Riccardo)
92BriTigC-8
92BriTigF-1408

Munoz, Roberto
76VenLeaS-16
89BlaYNPRWL-181
90Bes-192
90GreHorB-8
90GreHorP-2660
90GreHorS-14

Munro, Peter
91SydWavF-15
95Bow-208
96Bow-291
96SarRedSB-24

Munson, Jay
83CedRapRF-7
83CedRapRT-25

Munson, Joseph M.
26Exh-24

Munson, Thurman
70OPC-189
70Top-189
70YanCliDP-9
71MilDud-19
71MLBOffS-497
71OPC-5
71Top-5
71Top-275
71TopCoi-118
71TopGreM-1
71TopTat-83
71YanArcO-8
71YanCliDP-12
72OPC-441
72OPC-442
72Top-441
72Top-442
73LinPor-132
73NewYorN-14
73OPC-142
73SyrChiTI-19
73Top-142
73TopCanL-34
74OPC-340
74SyrChiTI-18
74Top-238
74Top-340
74TopDecE-7
74TopSta-215
75Hos-138
75OPC-20
75SSPPuzB-18
75SyrChiTI-13
75Top-20
75YanSSP-5
76CraDis-41
76Hos-16
76HosTwi-16
76Kel-53
76OPC-192
76OPC-650
76SSP-433
76Top-192
76Top-650
77BurCheD-177
77Hos-5
77Kel-23
77MSADis-45
77OPC-30
77PepGloD-36
77RCColC-46
77Spo-2005
77Top-170
77TopCloS-32
77YanBurK-2
78Hos-150
78Kel-30
78OPC-200
78PapGinD-27
78RCColC-15
78SSP270-1
78TasDis-7
78Top-60
78WifBalD-53
78YanBurK-2
78YanSSPD-1
79Hos-26
79OPC-157
79Top-310
79YanBurK-2
79YanPicA-25
80LauFamF-13
82K-M-29
82OhiHaloF-50
83FraBroR-39
84OCoandSI-32
84OCoandSI-158
84SpoDesPW-15
85GeoSteM-7
86SpoDecG-62
86TCMSupS-31
87SpoCubG-3
88PacLegI-34
89YanScoNW-32
90RinPosM-1
90RinPosM-2
90RinPosM-3
90RinPosM-4
90RinPosM-5
90RinPosM-6
90RinPosM-7
90RinPosM-8
90RinPosM-9
90RinPosM-10
90RinPosM-11
90RinPosM-12
90RinPosYMP-3
91Col-22
91LinDri-38
91SweBasG-149
92PinRool-10
92YanWIZ6-92
92YanWIZ7-118
92YanWIZA-50
93ActPacA-161
93UppDecS-20
94TedWil-62
94Yoo-11

Mura, Steve
79Top-725
80Top-491
81Don-362
81Fle-496
81Top-134
82Don-523
82Fle-578
82Top-641
82TopTra-79T
83Don-292
83Fle-16
83FleSta-133
83OPC-24
83Top-24
84PorBeaC-196
85TacTigC-147
86Top-281
86TopTif-281

Murakami, Les
87HawRai-1

Murakami, Masanori
65OPC-282
65Top-282
78TCM60I-182
79TCMJapPB-37

Murakami, Seiichi
90SalSpuCLC-119
90SalSpuP-2717

Muramatsu, Arihito
91SalSpuC-10

Murata, Katsuyoshi
96HonShaHWB-14

Muratti, Rafael
86MacPirP-17
87SalBucP-17
88BlaYNPRWL-138
88MiaMarS-16
89BlaYNPRWLU-7
91QuaCitAC-26
91QuaCitAP-2644

Murcer, Bobby
47PM1StaP1-145
66Top-469
67CokCapYM-V12
67OPC-93
67Top-93
69Top-657
70Kel-60
70MLBOffS-247
70OPC-333
70Top-333
70TopBoo-9
70YanCliDP-1
71BazNumT-9
71BazUnn-27
71MLBOffS-498
71OPC-635
71Top-635
71TopCoi-54
71TopGreM-46
71YanArcO-9
71YanCliDP-13
72Kel-16
72MilBra-247
72OPC-86
72ProStaP-32
72Top-86
72Top-699
72Top-700
73Kel2D-19
73LinPor-133
73NewYorN-18
73OPC-240
73OPC-343
73SyrChiTI-20
73Top-240
73Top-343
73TopCanL-35
73TopCom-12
73TopPin-12
73Yan-3
74Kel-22
74NewYorNTDiS-6
74OPC-90
74OPC-336
74SyrChiTI-19
74Top-90
74Top-336
74TopDecE-63
74TopPuz-7
74TopSta-216
75Hos-141
75OPC-350
75Top-350
76CraDis-42
76Hos-123
76Kel-38
76OPC-470
76SSP-111
76Top-470
77BurCheD-105
77CubJewT-11
77Hos-29
77MSADis-46
77OPC-83
77Top-40
77TopCloS-33
78Hos-90
78OPC-95
78RCColC-87
78SSP270-265
78Top-590
79Hos-6
79OPC-63
79Top-135
79YanPicA-26
80OPC-190
80Top-365
81Don-111
81Fle-94
81OPC-253
81Top-602
82Don-486
82Fle-44
82Top-208
83Don-261
83Fle-390
83OPC-122
83OPC-304
83Top-782
83Top-783
83TopFol-2
83YanASFY-30
84GiaMot-23
89PacLegI-196
91SweBasG-117
91UppDecS-16
92ActPacA-32
92PinRool-14
92YanWIZ6-93
92YanWIZ7-119
92YanWIZ8-129
92YanWIZA-51
93TedWil-67
93UppDecAH-100
94CarLeaA-DJ28

Murch, Simmy (Simeon)
09ColChiE-208A
09ColChiE-208B
12ColRedB-208A
12ColRedB-208B
12ColTinT-208A
12ColTinT-208B
90DodTar-562

Murdoch, Bob J.
72Dia-95

Murdock, Joe
89ChaRaiP-982
90ChaRaiB-17
90ChaRaiP-2036

Murdock, Kevin
88SouBenWSGS-4
88TamTarS-18

Murelli, Don
81MiaOriT-5

Murff, Red (John)
57Top-321

Murillo, Javier
89MiaMirIS-15

Murillo, Ray
79KnoKnoST-19
81EdmTraRR-15

Murnane, Tim
09RamT20-84

Murphy, Bob
87MetColP-52
88MetColP-53
89MetColP-45
89RinPosM1-33

Murphy, Brian
76OmaRoyTT-15
88BurBraP-7
91SydWavF-2
95AusFut-93
95AusFut-96

Murphy, Chris
92SpoIndC-10
92SpoIndF-1291
96Exc-148

Murphy, Dale
77Top-476
78BraCok-10
78Top-708
79Hos-121
79OPC-15
79Top-39
80OPC-143
80Top-274
81AllGamPI-157
81BraPol-3
81Don-437
81Fle-243
81FleStiC-119
81OPC-118
81Top-504
81TopScr-72
81TopSti-146
82BraBurKL-18
82BraPol-3
82Don-299
82Fle-443
82OPC-391
82PerAll-14
82PerAllG-14
82Top-668
82TopSti-19
83AllGamPI-155
83BraPol-3
83Don-12
83Don-47
83DonActA-45
83Dra-18
83Fle-142
83FleSta-134
83FleSti-90
83FleSti-140
83Kel-52
83OPC-21
83OPC-23
83PerAll-12
83PerAllG-12
83PerCreC-9
83PerCreCG-9
83Top-401
83Top-502
83Top-703
83Top-760
83TopGloS-16
83TopSti-160
83TopSti-206
83TopSti-211
84AllGamPI-62
84BraPol-3
84Don-66
84DonActAS-40
84DonCha-49
84Dra-22
84Fle-186
84FleSti-17
84FleSti-32
84FleSti-50
84FunFooP-103
84MilBra-17
84Nes792-126
84Nes792-133
84Nes792-150
84Nes792-391
84NesDreT-18
84OCoandSI-11
84OCoandSI-93
84OPC-150
84OPC-391
84RalPur-12
84SevCoi-C3
84SevCoi-E3
84SevCoi-W3
84Top-126
84Top-133
84Top-150
84Top-391
84TopCer-12
84TopGloA-19
84TopGloS-31
84TopRubD-29
84TopSti-27
84TopSti-180
84TopSti-199
84TopSup-2
84TopTif-126
84TopTif-133
84TopTif-150
84TopTif-391
85AllGamPI-154
85BraHos-16

85BraPol-3
85BraTBSAT-2
85Don-66
85DonActA-25
85DonHig-5
85Dra-20
85Fle-335
85FleLimE-22
85FleStaS-18
85FleStaS-33
85GenMilS-5
85Lea-222
85OPC-320
85SevCoi-S1
85SevCoi-W3
85SpoSam-1
85Top-320
85Top-716
85Top3-D-3
85TopGaloC-7
85TopGloA-7
85TopGloS-1
85TopRubD-30
85TopSti-22
85TopSti-96
85TopSti-177
85TopSup-11
85TopTif-320
85TopTif-716
86BasStaB-76
86BraPol-3
86BurKinA-11
86Don-66
86DonAll-4
86DonHig-41
86DonPop-4
86DorChe-10
86Dra-12
86Fle-522
86Fle-635
86Fle-640
86FleLeaL-27
86FleLimE-31
86FleMin-105
86FleSlu-24
86FleStiC-80
86FleStiC-132
86FleWaxBC-C4
86GenMilB-5D
86Lea-60
86MeaGolBB-10
86MeaGolM-7
86MeaGolSB-4
86MSAJifPD-16
86OPCBoxB-M
86QuaGra-8
86SevCoi-C5
86SevCoi-E5
86SevCoi-S5
86SevCoi-W5
86Spo-5
86Spo-62
86Spo-179
86Spo-183
86SpoDecG-67
86StaMur-1
86StaMur-2
86StaMur-3
86StaMur-4
86StaMur-5
86StaMur-6
86StaMur-7
86StaMur-8
86StaMur-9
86StaMur-10
86StaMur-11
86StaMur-12
86Top-456
86Top-600
86Top-705
86Top3-D-16
86TopGaloC-8
86TopGloA-18
86TopGloS-37
86TopMinL-37
86TopSti-35
86TopSti-145
86TopSti-149
86TopSup-39
86TopTat-2
86TopTif-456
86TopTif-600
86TopTif-705
86TopWaxBC-M
86TruVal-10
86Woo-23
87BoaandB-3
87BraSmo-14
87ClaGam-37
87ClaUpdY-106
87Don-3
87Don-78
87DonAll-14
87DonOpeD-40
87DonP-14
87DonSupD-3
87DonWaxBC-PC10
87Dra-13
87Fle-522
87FleAwaW-26
87FleBasA-29
87FleGamW-30
87FleGlo-522
87FleHotS-28
87FleLimE-30
87FleMin-74
87FleRecS-23
87FleSlu-28
87FleStiC-83
87FleWaxBC-C8
87GenMilB-6F
87HosSti-7
87K-M-29
87KayB-21
87KraFoo-2
87Lea-3
87Lea-141
87MandMSL-9
87MSAIceTD-15
87MSAJifPD-2
87OPC-359
87RedFolSB-47
87SmoNatL-2A
87SmoNatL-2B
87Spo-3
87Spo-155
87Spo-159
87SpoDeaP-3
87SpoSupD-5
87SpoTeaP-24
87StuPan-2
87Top-490
87TopCoi-37
87TopGloA-7
87TopGloS-6
87TopMinL-2
87TopSti-36
87TopSti-161
87TopTif-490
88CheBoy-17
88ClaBlu-201
88ClaBlu-215
88ClaRed-156
88Don-78
88DonAll-46
88DonBasB-113
88DonBonM-BC14
88Dra-15
88Fle-544
88Fle-639
88FleAwaW-27
88FleBasA-27
88FleBasM-25
88FleExcS-28
88FleGlo-544
88FleGlo-639
88FleHotS-29
88FleLeaL-29
88FleMin-65
88FleRecS-27
88FleSlu-28
88FleStiC-77
88FleSup-25
88FleTeaL-24
88FleWaxBC-C6
88GreBasS-72
88K-M-18
88KayB-20
88KinDis-2
88Lea-83
88MSAFanSD-13
88MSAIceTD-14
88Nes-2
88OPC-90
88PanSti-251
88RedFolSB-59
88Sco-450
88ScoGlo-450
88Spo-170
88StaLinAl-19
88StaLinBra-12
88Top-90
88Top-549
88TopBig-14
88TopCoi-48
88TopGloS-26
88TopMinL-41
88TopRitTM-1
88TopSti-45
88TopStiB-18
88TopTif-90
88TopTif-549
88TopUKM-52
88TopUKMT-52
89Bow-276
89BowTif-276
89BraDub-18
89ClaTraO-124
89Don-104
89DonBasB-29
89Fle-596
89FleExcS-33
89FleGlo-596
89FleLeaL-28
89KayB-22
89MSAIceTD-20
89OPC-210
89PanSti-45
89RedFolSB-84
89Sco-30
89ScoHot1S-66
89ScoSco-15
89Spo-110
89Top-210
89TopAme2C-21
89TopBasT-66
89TopBig-172
89TopCapC-11
89TopCoi-19
89TopHeaUT-23
89TopHilTM-21
89TopMinL-1
89TopSti-32
89TopTif-210
89TopUKM-55
89TVSpoM-58
89UppDec-357A
89UppDec-357B
89UppDec-672
90BasWit-38
90Bow-19
90BowTif-19
90BraDubP-20
90BraDubS-23
90ClaUpd-T36
90Don-168
90DonBesN-62
90Fle-591
90Fle-623
90FleBasM-28
90FleCan-591
90FleCan-623
90FleUpd-46
90Hot50PS-29
90KayB-20
90KinDis-11
90Lea-243
90OPC-750
90PanSti-222
90Pos-18
90PubSti-117
90RedFolSB-67
90RicBra2ATI-17
90Sco-66
90Sco100S-64
90ScoRoo-31T
90Spo-189
90Top-750
90TopAmeA-11
90TopBig-40
90TopCoi-53
90TopHilHM-16
90TopSti-25
90TopTif-750
90UppDec-533
90VenSti-359
90Woo-15
91Bow-486
91Cla1-T96
91ClaGam-148
91Don-484
91Don-744
91Fle-409
91JimDea-3
91Lea-412
91MajLeaCP-62
91OPC-545
91OPCBoxB-J
91OPCPre-85
91PanFreS-109
91PanSti-104
91PetSta-14
91PhiMed-31
91Sco-650
91Sco100S-35
91Sev3DCN-13
91SevCoi-NE13
91StaClu-243
91Stu-220
91Top-545
91TopDesS-545
91TopMic-545
91TopTif-545
91TopTriH-N8
91TopWaxBC-J
91Ult-270
91UppDec-447
91Woo-14
92Bow-684
92ClaGam-65
92DenHol-18
92Don-146
92Fle-541
92HitTheBB-24
92Lea-527
92Mr.TurS-17
92OPC-680
92PanSti-246
92PhiMed-23
92Pin-124
92Pin-284
92Sco-80
92Sco100S-40
92StaClu-280
92Stu-79
92Top-680
92TopGol-680
92TopGolW-680
92TopMcD-30
92TopMic-680
92TriPla-158
92TriPla-260
92Ult-249
92UppDec-127
92UppDecF-33
92UppDecFG-33
93Don-646
93Fle-496
93PacSpa-432
93Pin-479
93Pin-503
93PinCoo-5
93PinCooD-5
93RocUSPC-3C
93RocUSPC-10S
93Sco-597
93Sel-103
93StaClu-259
93StaCluFDI-572
93StaCluMOP-572
93Top-445
93TopGol-445
93TopInaM-445
93TopMic-445
93Ult-353
93UppDec-32
93UppDec-706
93UppDecGold-32
93UppDecGold-706

Murphy, Daniel

82TulDriT-17
83TulDriT-21
84OklCit8T-23
84TulDriTI-16
85MidAngT-9

Murphy, Daniel F.

03BreE10-108
08AmeCarE-16
08AmeCarE-55
08RosComP-61
09ColChiE-209
09RamT20-85
09T206-259
09T206-260
10CouT21-198
10DomDisP-90
10E101-35
10E102-19
10E12AmeCDC-27
10LuxCigPP-18
10MelMinE-35
10NadCarE-38
10NadE1-43
10PeoT21-42A
10PeoT21-42B
10RedCroT-57
10RedCroT-142
10RedCroT-229
10SweCapPP-48
11A'sFirT20-14
11S74Sil-33
11SpoLifCW-264
11SpoLifM-101
11T205-126
12ColRedB-209
12ColTinT-209
12HasTriFT-25C
14CraJacE-140
14PieStaT-43
15AmeCarE-31
15CraJacE-140
16FleBreD-69
61Top-214
62Top-119
62TopVen-119
63Top-272
70OPC-146
70Top-146

Murphy, Daniel Lee

86ElPasDP-16
87ElPasDP-22
89BlaYNPRWL-128
89BlaYNPRWLU-69
89LasVegSC-7
89LasVegSP-2
90CMC-511
90LasVegSC-8
90LasVegSP-117
90OPC-649
90ProAAAF-5
90Top-649
90TopDeb89-86
90TopTif-649

Murphy, Dwayne

79Top-711
80Top-461
81A'sGraG-21
81AllGamPI-61
81Don-359
81Fle-590
81OPC-341
81Top-341
81TopSti-119
82A'sGraG-11
82Don-239
82Fle-101
82FleSta-122
82Kel-57
82OPC-29
82Top-29
82TopSti-227
83A'sGraG-21
83AllGamPI-64
83Don-161
83Fle-528
83FleSta-135
83FleSti-189
83OPC-184
83Top-598
83TopSti-107
84A'sMot-4
84AllGamPI-154
84Don-3
84Don-3A
84Don-101
84Fle-456
84FunFooP-93
84Nes792-103
84OPC-103
84Top-103
84TopSti-332
84TopTif-103
85A'sMot-6
85AllGamPI-65
85Don-420
85Fle-432
85FleStaS-30
85GenMilS-20
85Lea-74
85Top-231

85TopSti-323
85TopTif-231
86A'sMot-6
86Don-176
86Fle-428
86FleMin-90
86OPC-8
86Top-8
86Top-216
86TopSti-171
86TopTat-20
86TopTif-8
86TopTif-216
86TruVal-27
87A'sSmoC-9
87Don-379
87DonOpeD-27
87Fle-400
87FleGlo-400
87OPC-121
87SpoTeaP-23
87Top-743
87TopSti-170
87TopTif-743
88Don-405
88Fle-287
88FleGlo-287
88OPC-334
88PanSti-176
88Sco-455
88ScoGlo-455
88Top-424
88TopTif-424
89PhiTas-23
89Sco-545
89Top-667
89TopAme2C-22
89TopTif-667
90Fle-569
90FleCan-569

Murphy, Eddie
11DiaGumP-22
14FatPlaT-35
15CraJacE-165
15SpoNewM-127
16BF2FP-15
16SpoNewM-130
16TanBraE-15
21E121So8-65
22AmeCarE-49
22W575-88
48SmiClo-24
75WhiSox1T-18
92Man191BSR-18

Murphy, Frank
88AllandGN-13

Murphy, Gary
86AshTouP-21
88BenBucL-31
89QuaCitAB-16
89QuaCitAGS-19

Murphy, Harriett
08AllLadBC-3

Murphy, Isaac
88GooN16-29
88KimN18-28

Murphy, James
88GenCubP-1638
89ChaWheB-10
89ChaWheP-1745
89FayGenP-1586
90PeoChiUTI-U7
90WinSpiTI-14

Murphy, Jeff
91PriRedC-18
91PriRedP-3511
92BenMusSP-21
92BilMusF-3352
92HamRedC-25
92HamRedF-1595
93PriRedC-21
93PriRedF-4177
93SavCarC-19
93SavCarF-688
94St.PetCC-20
94St.PetCF-2588
96ArkTraB-22

Murphy, John
88KimN18-29

Murphy, John Edward
91ConTSN-84

Murphy, John J.
80ArkTraT-21

Murphy, John Joseph
34BatR31-154
41DouPlaR-109
75YanDyn1T-34
80YanGreT-11
92YanWIZA-52
94ConTSN-1057

Murphy, John V.
87LouRedTI-21
87St.PetCP-13
88LouRedBC-16
88LouRedBP-429
88LouRedBTI-36
88SprCarB-22

Murphy, Johnny
43YanSta-20
88AllandGN-14
88ConSer3-20
94ConTSNB-1057

Murphy, Kent
86WatIndP-17
87BufBisP-2
88WilBilP-1305

Murphy, Matt
93HelBreF-4090
93HelBreSP-15
95AusFut-59

Murphy, Micah
89GenCubP-1880
90HunCubP-3291

Murphy, Michael
86WatIndP-18
92BatCliC-2
95KinIndTI-20

Murphy, Miguel
87KenTwiP-25
88FayGenP-1100

Murphy, Mike
77ArkTraT-6
87BufBisP-17
90MarPhiP-3198
91AubAstC-14
91AubAstP-4278
91MarPhiC-1
91MarPhiP-3470
92BatCliF-3278
93SouAtlLAGF-53
93SpaPhiC-20
93SpaPhiF-1069
94ClaGolF-164
94DunBluJC-21
94DunBluJF-2570

Murphy, Nate
96BoiHawB-20

Murphy, Neil
93BatCliC-22
93BatCliF-3149

Murphy, P.L.
87OldJudN-364

Murphy, Pat
89WesPalBES-25
92BurAstC-21
92BurAstF-541
93QuaCitRBC-14
93QuaCitRBF-97
94CarLeaAF-CAR3
94LynRedSC-20
94LynRedSF-1901

Murphy, Patrick J.
87OldJudN-365
89SFHaCN-12

Murphy, Pete
87MacPirP-11
87WatPirP-24
88SalBucS-14
89HarSenP-308
89HarSenS-12
90HarSenP-1190
90HarSenS-12
91CarMudLD-113
91CarMudP-1084
91LinDriAA-113

Murphy, Quinn
94BurIndC-16
94BurIndF-3803

Murphy, Red
20WalMaiW-36

Murphy, Rob
82CedRapRT-2
83CedRapRF-24
83CedRapRT-13
87ClaGam-70
87Don-452
87Fle-206
87FleGlo-206
87RedKah-46
87SpoTeaP-4
87Top-82
87TopTif-82
88Don-82
88DonBasB-230
88Fle-241
88FleGlo-241
88RedKah-46
88Sco-559
88ScoGlo-559
88StaLinRe-13
88Top-603
88TopTif-603
89Bow-22
89BowTif-22
89ClaTraP-183
89Don-139
89DonBasB-196
89DonTra-15
89Fle-165
89FleGlo-165
89FleUpd-10
89OPC-182
89Sco-141
89ScoRoo-8T
89Top-446
89TopTif-446
89TopTra-86T
89TopTraT-86T
89UppDec-372
89UppDec-759
90Bow-269
90BowTif-269
90CedRapRDGB-13
90Don-186
90Fle-281
90FleCan-281
90Lea-183
90OPC-268
90PubSti-461
90RedSoxP-13
90Sco-181
90Top-268
90TopBig-297
90TopSti-261
90TopTif-268
90TopTVRS-14
90UppDec-461
90VenSti-360
91Don-250
91Fle-104
91OPC-542
91Sco-183
91ScoRoo-33T
91Top-542
91TopDesS-542
91TopMic-542
91TopTif-542
91UppDec-683
91UppDec-707
92AstMot-21
92Don-329
92Fle-288
92OPC-706
92Sco-492
92StaClu-663
92Top-706
92TopGol-706
92TopGolW-706
92TopMic-706
92Ult-493
92UppDec-639
93CarPol-10
93Don-588
93Fle-439
93FleFinE-128
93StaClu-250
93StaCluCa-21
93StaCluFDI-250
93StaCluMOP-250
94CarPol-10
94Fle-637
94StaCluT-318
94StaCluTFDI-318

Murphy, Sean
96AshTouB-26

Murphy, Shaun
91MidLeaAP-MWL46
91RocExpC-24
91RocExpP-2059
92WesPalBEC-13
92WesPalBEF-2099

Murphy, Steve
85RedWinA-20
86RedWinA-5
91WasVia-3
93ClaFS7-226
93RocRoyC-20
93RocRoyF-728
93StaCluM-100
94WilBluRC-16
94WilBluRF-313
95WicWraTI-3

Murphy, Tim
74GasRanT-12

Murphy, Tom A.
69AngJacitB-9
69Top-474
70OPC-351
70Top-351
71OPC-401
71Top-401
71TopTat-39
72MilBra-248
72OPC-354
72Top-354
73OPC-539
73Top-539
74OPC-496
74Top-496
74TopTra-496T
75OPC-28
75Top-28
76OPC-219
76SSP-227
76Top-219
77Top-396
78BluJayP-19
78OPC-193
78Top-103
79OPC-308
79Top-588
89PacSenL-122
89TopSenL-28
94BreMilB-340

Murphy, Tommy
11TurRedT-59

Murphy, Wayne
87WinHavRSP-18

Murphy, William E.
66Top-574
91MetWIZ-286

Murphy, Yale (William Henry)
95May-22

Murray, Bill
88SalLakCTTI-29
89SalLakTTI-29
90CarLeaA-8
91RenSilSCLC-27
93WatDiaC-30
96ButCopKB-2

Murray, Brian
88SalLakCTTI-2

Murray, Calvin
92Bow-652
92TopTra-78T
92TopTraG-78T
93ClaYouG-YG14
93ShrCapF-2773
93StaCluM-34
93UppDec-421
93UppDec-432
93UppDecGold-421
93UppDecGold-432
94Cla-153
94ExcFS7-293
94ShrCapF-1620
94UppDecML-140
94UppDecML-261
94UppDecMLPotYF-PY11

Murray, Dale
75OPC-568
75Top-568
76ExpRed-23
76OPC-18
76SSP-350
76Top-18
77Top-252
78SSP270-131
78Top-149
79OPC-198
79Top-379
80ExpPos-18
80OPC-274
80Top-559
81SyrChiT-7
81SyrChiTI-15
83Don-381
83Fle-437
83OPC-42
83Top-42
83TopTra-79T
84Don-577
84Fle-134
84Nes792-697
84OPC-281
84Top-697
84TopTif-697
85Fle-137
85OklCit8T-27
85Top-481
85TopTif-481
86OPC-197
91MetWIZ-287
92YanWIZ8-130
93RanKee-275

Murray, Dan
95PitMetTI-29
96HilStaHWB-38
96StLucMTI-4

Murray, Dave
86SalRedBP-21

Murray, Eddie
78Hos-31
78Kel-25
78OPC-154
78RCColC-75
78Top-36
79Hos-115
79OPC-338
79Top-640
79TopCom-1
80Kel-24
80OPC-88
80Top-160
80TopSup-28
81AllGamPI-8
81Don-112
81Dra-6
81Fle-184
81FleStiC-117
81Kel-18
81MSAMinD-23
81OPC-39
81Squ-15
81Top-490
81TopScr-9
81TopSti-34
82Don-483
82Dra-25
82Fle-174
82FleSta-151
82Kel-64
82OPC-390
82PerCreC-22
82PerCreCG-22
82Top-162
82Top-163
82Top-390
82Top-426
82TopSti-4
82TopSti-6
82TopSti-145
83AllGamPI-5
83Don-405
83DonActA-1
83Dra-19
83Fle-67
83FleSta-136
83FleSti-202
83Kel-11
83OPC-141
83OriPos-17
83PerCreC-29
83PerCreCG-29
83Top-21
83Top-530
83TopGloS-37
83TopSti-29
84AllGamPI-96
84Don-22
84Don-22A
84Don-47
84DonActAS-50
84DonCha-19
84Dra-23
84Fle-14
84FleSti-23
84FleSti-38
84FunFooP-119

84Nes792-240
84Nes792-397
84NesDreT-1
84OCoandSI-23
84OPC-240
84OPC-291
84OriEng-9
84OriTeal-18
84RalPur-1
84SevCoi-C6
84SevCoi-E6
84SevCoi-W6
84Top-240
84Top-397
84TopCer-1
84TopGloS-4
84TopRubD-28
84TopSti-26
84TopSti-195
84TopSti-203
84TopStiB-12
84TopSup-25
84TopTif-240
84TopTif-397
85AllGamPI-7
85Don-47
85DonActA-9
85DonHig-34
85Dra-21
85Fle-184
85FleLimE-23
85FleStaS-20
85FleStaS-62
85FleStaS-63
85FleStaS-64
85FleStaS-65
85FleStaS-66
85FleStaS-67
85GenMilS-21
85Lea-203
85OPC-221
85OriHea-13
85SevCoi-E1
85SevCoi-G4
85SevCoi-W4
85Top-700
85Top-701
85Top3-D-2
85TopGloS-28
85TopMin-700
85TopRubD-28
85TopSti-196
85TopSup-18
85TopTif-700
85TopTif-701
86BasStaB-77
86BurKinA-14
86Don-88
86DonAll-13
86DonPop-13
86DorChe-12
86Dra-25
86Fle-282
86FleLimE-32
86FleMin-58
86FleSlu-25
86FleStiC-81
86Lea-83
86MSAJifPD-10
86OPC-30
86QuaGra-27
86SevCoi-E13
86Spo-4
86Spo-73
86Spo-145
86SpoDecG-70
86SpoRoo-48
86Top-30
86Top3-D-19
86TopGloA-2
86TopGloS-33
86TopMinL-1
86TopSti-158
86TopSti-227
86TopSup-40
86TopTat-13
86TopTif-30
86TruVal-3
86Woo-24
87BoaandB-2
87ClaGam-51
87Don-48
87DonAll-31
87DonHig-37
87DonOpeD-136
87Dra-24
87Fle-476
87Fle-636
87FleGlo-476
87FleGlo-636
87FleLeaL-32
87FleLimE-31
87FleMin-75
87FleRecS-24
87FleStiC-84
87GenMilB-2G
87HosSti-18
87K-M-30
87KayB-22
87KraFoo-1
87Lea-110
87OPC-120
87OriFreB-33
87RalPur-8
87RedFolSB-66
87SevCoi-M12
87Spo-6
87Spo-75
87Spo-159
87SpoDeaP-2
87SpoTeaP-21
87StuPan-14
87Top-120
87TopCoi-19
87TopGloS-12
87TopMinL-39
87TopSti-224
87TopTif-120
88Don-231
88DonBasB-142
88Dra-21
88Fle-567
88FleBasA-28
88FleGlo-567
88FleMin-1
88FleStiC-2
88Lea-172
88MSAJifPD-13
88OPC-4
88OriFreB-33
88PanSti-8
88PanSti-203
88PanSti-442
88Sco-18
88ScoGlo-18
88Spo-59
88StaLinAl-20
88StaLinO-10
88Top-4
88Top-4A
88Top-51
88Top-495
88TopBig-215
88TopCoi-22
88TopSti-11
88TopSti-233
88TopTif-4
88TopTif-51
88TopTif-495
88TopUKM-53
88TopUKMT-53
88Woo-5
89Bow-346
89BowTif-346
89ClaTraP-160
89DodMot-2
89DodPol-21
89DodStaSV-11
89Don-96
89DonBasB-92
89DonTra-12
89Fle-611
89FleGlo-611
89FleUpd-92
89KayB-23
89KinDis-2
89OPC-148
89PanSti-260
89RedFolSB-85
89Sco-94
89ScoHot1S-83
89ScoRoo-31T
89Spo-147
89Top-625
89TopBasT-89
89TopBatL-11
89TopBig-319
89TopCapC-15
89TopCoi-20
89TopHilTM-22
89TopMinL-44
89TopSti-238
89TopTif-625
89TopTra-87T
89TopTraT-87T
89TopUKM-56
89UppDec-275
89UppDec-763
90Bow-101
90BowTif-101
90ClaUpd-T37
90DodMot-5
90DodPol-33
90DodTar-563
90Don-77
90DonBesN-78
90Fle-404
90FleCan-404
90Hot50PS-30
90KayB-21
90Lea-181
90OPC-305
90PanSti-273
90PubSti-14
90RedFolSB-68
90Sco-80
90SunSee-24
90Top-305
90TopAmeA-7
90TopBatL-17
90TopBig-29
90TopHilHM-13
90TopMinL-60
90TopSti-57
90TopTif-305
90UppDec-277
90VenSti-361
90Woo-16
91BasBesHRK-15
91Bow-376
91Bow-614
91Cla1-T51
91Cla3-T65
91ClaGam-112
91DenHol-15
91DodMot-5
91DodPol-33
91Don-405
91Don-502
91DonBonC-BC18
91DonPre-12
91Fle-214
91Lea-126
91MajLeaCP-53
91OPC-397
91OPC-590
91OPCBoxB-K
91OPCPre-86
91OriCro-321
91PanCanT1-2
91PanFreS-55
91PanSti-53
91PosCan-11
91RedFolS-68
91Sco-310
91Sco100S-52
91SevCoi-SC10
91StaClu-177
91StaCluP-27
91StaPinB-34
91Stu-185
91Top-397
91Top-590
91TopCraJ2-1
91TopDesS-397
91TopDesS-590
91TopMic-397
91TopMic-590
91TopTif-397
91TopTif-590
91TopTriH-N5
91TopWaxBC-K
91Ult-166
91UppDec-237
91UppDecSS-SS6
91USPlaCA-2S
91Woo-15
92Bow-433
92ClaGam-162
92DodStaTA-30
92Don-392
92DonUpd-U8
92Fle-466
92Hig5-54
92Lea-396
92MetColP-8
92MetKah-33
92OPC-780
92OPCPre-193
92PanSti-192
92Pin-424
92Sco-195
92Sco100S-78
92ScoRoo-11T
92SpollIFK1-398
92SpoStaCC-35
92StaClu-795
92StaCluD-128
92StaCluMO-8
92StaCluMO-23
92StaCluMO-24
92Stu-68
92Top-780
92TopGol-780
92TopGolW-780
92TopKid-50
92TopMic-780
92TopTra-79T
92TopTraG-79T
92Ult-532
92UppDec-32
92UppDec-265
92UppDec-728
92UppDec-753
93Bow-454
93ClaGam-69
93DenHol-15
93DiaMar-78
93Don-278
93DonDiaK-DK25
93DonEli-21
93DonEliS-3
93DonMVP-10
93DonPre-7
93Fin-122
93FinRef-122
93Fla-94
93Fle-91
93FleFruotL-48
93FunPac-128
93JimDea-17
93Lea-167
93LeaHeaftH-4
93MetColP-41
93MetKah-33
93OPC-280
93PacSpa-545
93PanSti-247
93Pin-18
93Pin-292
93PinCoo-27
93PinCooD-27
93PinHomRC-35
93Sco-77
93Sel-29
93SP-152
93StaClu-50
93StaCluFDI-50
93StaCluMO-17
93StaCluMOP-50
93Top-430
93TopGol-430
93TopInaM-430
93TopMic-430
93TriPla-41
93Ult-78
93UppDec-115
93UppDec-484
93UppDecGold-115
93UppDecGold-484
93UppDecSH-HI13
93UppDecTAN-TN14
94Bow-467
94BowBes-R2
94BowBesR-R2
94ColC-595
94ColChoGS-595
94ColChoSS-595
94Don-386
94ExtBas-64
94Fin-317
94FinRef-317
94Fla-286
94Fle-573
94FleUpd-34
94FleUpdDT-8
94FUnPac-85
94Lea-313
94LeaL-29
94OPC-184
94Pac-413
94PanSti-221
94Pin-495
94PinArtP-495
94PinMusC-495
94ProMag-40
94Sco-36
94ScoGolR-36
94ScoRoo-RT5
94ScoRooGR-RT5
94ScoRooS-RT5
94Sel-329
94SP-100
94SPDieC-100
94SpoRoo-91
94SpoRooAP-91
94StaClu-542
94StaClu-674
94StaCluFDI-542
94StaCluFDI-674
94StaCluGR-542
94StaCluGR-674
94StaCluMOP-542
94StaCluMOP-674
94Stu-94
94Top-65
94TopGol-65
94TopSpa-65
94TopTra-60T
94TriPla-117
94Ult-347
94UppDec-341
94UppDecED-341
95Baz-78
95Bow-392
95BowBes-R60
95BowBesR-R60
95ClaPhoC-21
95ColCho-265
95ColCho-526
95ColChoGS-265
95ColChoGS-526
95ColChoSE-116
95ColChoSEGS-116
95ColChoSESS-116
95ColChoSS-265
95ColChoSS-526
95Don-435
95DonPreP-435
95DonTopotO-62
95Emb-114
95EmbGolI-114
95Emo-36
95Fin-112
95FinRef-112
95Fla-33
95Fle-141
95Lea-265
95LeaLim-39
95LeaLimIBP-19
95Pac-125
95PanSti-96
95Pin-342
95PinArtP-342
95PinMusC-342
95Sco-257
95ScoGolR-257
95ScoHaloG-HG34
95ScoPlaTS-257
95SelCer-14
95SelCer-32
95SelCerMG-14
95SelCerMG-32
95SP-27
95SP-148
95SPCha-98
95SPCha-142
95SPCha-144
95SPChaDC-98
95SPChaDC-142
95SPChaDC-144
95SPPlaP-PP14
95SPSil-27
95SPSil-148
95StaClu-186
95StaCluFDI-186
95StaCluMOP-186
95StaCluMOP-RL6
95StaCluRL-RL6
95StaCluSTDW-I186

95StaCluSTMP-17
95StaCluSTWS-186
95StaCluVR-96
95Stu-142
95Sum-101
95SumNthD-101
95Top-370
95TopCyb-196
95Ult-39
95UltGolM-39
95UppDec-341
95UppDecED-341
95UppDecEDG-341
95UppDecSE-24
95UppDecSEG-24
95Zen-43
96Bow-69
96BowBes-42
96BowBesAR-42
96BowBesR-42
96Cir-4
96CirRav-4
96ColCho-124
96ColCho-364
96ColCho-389T
96ColChoGS-124
96ColChoGS-364
96ColChoSS-124
96ColChoSS-364
96ColChoYMtP-28
96ColChoYMtP-28A
96ColChoYMtPGS-28
96ColChoYMtPGS-28A
96Don-105
96Don-220
96DonDiaK-29
96DonHitL-16
96DonPreP-105
96DonPreP-220
96EmoXL-53
96Fin-B21
96FinLan-4
96FinRef-B21
96Fla-71
96FlaDiaC-7
96Fle-92
96FleGolM-7
96FleInd-9
96FleTif-92
96FleUpd-7
96Lea-102
96LeaLim-67
96LeaLimG-67
96LeaPre-68
96LeaPreP-68
96LeaPrePB-102
96LeaPrePG-102
96LeaPrePS-102
96LeaSig-116
96LeaSigPPG-116
96LeaSigPPP-116
96MetMod-7
96MetUni-50
96MetUniP-50
96Pac-294
96PacMil-M8
96PacPri-P97
96PacPriFB-FB12
96PacPriG-P97
96PanSti-177
96Pin-117
96Pin-154
96Pin-280
96PinAfi-28
96PinAfiAP-28
96PinAfiFPP-28
96PinAfiSP-32
96PinArtP-46
96PinArtP-81
96PinArtP-180
96PinEssotG-17
96PinFoil-280
96PinPow-17
96PinSlu-14
96PinSta-46
96PinSta-81
96PinSta-180
96ProMagDM-11
96ProSta-58
96SchDis-8
96Sco-79
96Sco-366
96ScoAll-20
96ScoBigB-19
96ScoDiaA-22
96ScoDugC-A65
96ScoDugC-B91
96ScoDugCAP-A65
96ScoDugCAP-B91
96Sel-60
96SelArtP-60
96SelCer-10
96SelCerAP-10
96SelCerCB-10
96SelCerCR-10
96SelCerMB-10
96SelCerMG-10
96SelCerMR-10
96SelClaTF-20
96SP-69
96Spo-26
96Spo-119
96SpoArtP-26
96SpoArtP-119
96SpoPowS-23
96SPSpeFX-34
96SPSpeFXDC-34
96SPx-20
96SPxGol-20
96StaClu-224
96StaClu-293
96StaCluEPB-290
96StaCluEPG-290
96StaCluEPS-290
96StaCluMO-28
96StaCluMOP-224
96StaCluMOP-293
95StaCluVRMC-96
96Stu-96
96StuPrePB-96
96StuPrePG-96
96StuPrePS-96
96Sum-53
96SumAbo&B-53
96SumArtP-53
96SumFoi-53
96Top-125
96TopChr-34
96TopChrMotG-3
96TopChrMotGR-3
96TopChrR-34
96TopGal-167
96TopGalPG-PG1
96TopGalPPI-167
96TopLas-74
96TopMasotG-3
96Ult-51
96UltCaltH-6
96UltCaltHGM-6
96UltGolM-51
96UltRes-5
96UltResGM-5
96UltThu-14
96UltThuGM-14
96UppDec-2
96UppDec-105
96UppDec-316
96UppDec-382
96UppDec-415
96UppDecDD-DD8
96UppDecDDG-DD8
96UppDecDDS-DD8
96UppDecRCJ-22
96UppDecRipC-22
96Zen-49
96ZenArtP-49
97Bow-32
97BowInt-32
97Cir-33
97CirRav-33
97CirRavR-8
97ColCho-40
97ColCho-250
97ColChoPP-PP20
97ColChoPPG-PP20
97ColChoTBS-8
97ColChoTBSWH-8
97Don-115
97Don-267
97Don-298
97DonEli-25
97DonEliGS-25
97DonLim-7
97DonLim-75
97DonLim-197
97DonLimFotG-34
97DonLimLE-7
97DonLimLE-75
97DonLimLE-197
97DonPre-60
97DonPreCttC-60
97DonPreP-115
97DonPreP-267
97DonPreP-298
97DonPrePGold-115
97DonPrePGold-267
97DonPrePGold-298
97DonPrePM-12
97DonTea-8
97DonTeaSPE-8
97Fin-235
97FinRef-235
97FlaSho-A100
97FlaSho-B100
97FlaSho-C100
97FlaShoLC-100
97FlaShoLC-B100
97FlaShoLC-C100
97FlaShoLCM-A100
97FlaShoLCM-B100
97FlaShoLCM-C100
97Fle-9
97Fle-550
97FleDecoE-9
97FleDecoERT-9
97FleDiaT-8
97FleGolM-6
97FleGouG-9
97FleGouGF-9
97FleHea-14
97FleTif-9
97FleTif-550
97Lea-124
97Lea-224
97Lea-364
97LeaFraM-124
97LeaFraM-224
97LeaFraM-364
97LeaFraMDC-124
97LeaFraMDC-224
97LeaFraMDC-364
97LeaGolS-34
97MetUni-5
97NewPin-139
97NewPinAP-139
97NewPinMC-139
97NewPinPP-139
97Pac-25
97PacCar-3
97PacCarM-3
97PacFirD-3
97PacGolCD-4
97PacLigB-25
97PacPri-9
97PacPriGotD-GD12
97PacPriLB-9
97PacPriP-9
97PacSil-25
97Pin-65
97PinArtP-65
97PinCer-66
97PinCerMBlu-66
97PinCerMG-66
97PinCerMR-66
97PinCerR-66
97PinIns-93
97PinInsCE-93
97PinInsDE-93
97PinMusC-65
97PinTotCPB-66
97PinTotCPG-66
97PinTotCPR-66
97PinX-P-14
97PinX-PMoS-14
97Sco-46
97Sco-328
97Sco-421
97ScoHigZ-18
97ScoHobR-421
97ScoOri-2
97ScoOriPI-2
97ScoOriPr-2
97ScoPreS-46
97ScoPreS-328
97ScoResC-421
97ScoShoS-46
97ScoShoS-328
97ScoShoS-421
97ScoShoSAP-46
97ScoShoSAP-328
97ScoShoSAP-421
97SkyE-X-3
97SkyE-XC-3
97SkyE-XEC-3
97SkyE-XHoN-3
97SP-16
97SpollI-48
97SpollIEE-48
97SPSpeF-41
97SPSpxF-9
97SPSPxFA-9
97SPx-1
97SPxBro-1
97SPxCorotG-8
97SPxGraF-1
97SPxSil-1
97SPxSte-1
97StaClu-36
97StaCluI-I1
97StaCluMat-36
97StaCluMOP-36
97StaCluMOP-I1
97Stu-44
97StuPrePG-44
97StuPrePS-44
97Top-333
97Top-462
97TopChr-110
97TopChr-163
97TopChrR-113
97TopChrR-163
97TopGal-44
97TopGalPG-PG3
97TopGalPPI-44
97Ult-6
97Ult-398
97UltFamGam-18
97UltGolME-6
97UltGolME-398
97UltHitM-16
97UltPlaME-6
97UltPlaME-398
97UltTop3-23
97UltTop3GM-23
97UppDec-220
97UppDec-521
97UppDecAG-AG19
97UppDecU-20

Murray, Feg
85FegMurCG-1

Murray, Frank
76DalCon-8

Murray, George
36GouWidPPR-D20

Murray, Glenn
90JamExpP-9
91MidLeaAP-MWL47
91RocExpC-25
91RocExpP-2060
92Bow-289
92ClaFS7-214
92ProFS7-265
92UppDecML-302
92WesPalBEC-19
92WesPalBEF-2100
93ClaGolF-139
93HarSenF-279
94Cla-118
94ExcFS7-228
94PawRedSDD-15
94PawRedSF-956
94Top-616
94TopGol-616
94TopSpa-616
94UppDecML-133
95Bow-98
95Exc-12
95PawRedSDD-20
95PawRedTI-34
95SigRoo-38
95SigRooSig-38
96ScrRedBB-20

Murray, Heath
94SigRooDP-56
94SigRooDPS-56
94SpoIndF-3323
94StaCluDP-74
94StaCluDPFDI-74
95RanCucQT-28
96Bow-310
96MemChiB-25
97Bow-407
97BowCerBIA-CA56
97BowCerGIA-CA56
97BowChr-270
97BowChrI-270
97BowChrIR-270
97BowChrR-270
97BowInt-407
97ColCho-466
97Top-493

Murray, Jack
11TurRedT-48
14PieStaT-44
15SpoNewM-128

Murray, James
12ImpTobC-5

Murray, Jed
80SanJosMJitB-14
81LynSaiT-8
82LynSaiT-6
83SalLakCGT-9
84SalLakCGC-177
86CalCanP-17
87TolMudHP-13
87TolMudHT-18

Murray, Jeremiah
87OldJudN-194
87OldJudN-366

Murray, Jim
75CliPilT-11

Murray, Jooph
52Par-99

Murray, Keith
90ButCopKSP-16
91GasRanC-25
91GasRanP-2702

Murray, Larry
76SSP-449
80Top-284
92YanWIZ7-120

Murray, Matt
90Bes-285
90BurBraB-2
90BurBraP-2346
90BurBraS-19
90MidLeaASGS-45
91DurBulC-4
91DurBulP-1540
94DurBulC-12
94DurBulF-325
94DurBulTI-13
94UppDecML-28
95BowBes-B13
95BowBesR-B13
95RicBraRC-14
95RicBraTI-11
96RicBraUB-19
96ScrRedBB-21

Murray, Mike
87MyrBeaBJP-1442
88MyrBeaBJP-1179
89KinMetS-28

Murray, Pat
91JohCitCC-4
91JohCitCP-3985

Murray, Ray
50IndNumN-17
50IndTeal-18
52Bow-118
52Top-299
53BowBW-6
53IndPenCBP-22
53Top-234
54Bow-83
54OriEss-27
54Top-49
83TopRep5-299
91OriCro-322
91TopArc1-234
94TopArc1-49
94TopArc1G-49

Murray, Red (John Joseph)
08AmeCarE-56
08RosComP-169
09BriE97-24
09ColChiE-210A
09ColChiE-210B
09RamT20-86
09T206-261
09T206-262
10CouT21-199
10CouT21-200
10CouT21-201
10DomDisP-91
10E12AmeCDC-28
10NadE1-44
10RedCroT-58
10RedCroT-143
10RedCroT-230

10SweCapPP-121
10W555-52
11E94-26
11S74Sil-92
11SpoLifCW-265
11SpoLifM-214
11T205-127
12ColRedB-210A
12ColRedB-210B
12ColRedB-211
12ColTinT-210A
12ColTinT-210B
12ColTinT-211
12HasTriFT-48I
12PhiCarE-24
13PolGroW-21
14B18B-70
14FatPlaT-36
94ConTSN-1049
94ConTSNB-1049
Murray, Rich
76CedRapGT-17
77CedRapGT-1
78PhoGiaC-18
79PhoGiaVNB-18
80PhoGiaVNB-19
81Fle-452
81PhoGiaVNB-24
81Top-195
82ChaChaT-16
83PhoGiaBHN-6
84PhoGiaC-6
85OmaRoyT-8
Murray, Richard
80VenLeaS-63
82WicAerTI-11
Murray, Scott
86St.PetCP-21
88SanJosGCLC-125
88SanJosGP-113
Murray, Steve
84BeaGolGT-7
87SalSpuP-22
88SanBerSCLC-29
89WauTimGS-20
90SanBerSB-19
90SanBerSCLC-113
90SanBerSP-2651
91SanBerSC-12
91SanBerSP-2005
Murray, Venice
78CedRapGT-19
Murrell, Ivan
67Ast-21
68Top-569
69Top-333
70OPC-179
70Top-179
71MLBOffS-232
71OPC-569
71Top-569
72MilBra-249
72PadTeal-19
72Top-677
73OPC-409
73Top-409
74OPC-628
74Top-628
87WilBilP-11
89PacSenL-131
89TopSenL-7
Murrell, Michael
90GeoColC-22
Murrell, Rodney
86LitFalMP-20
87ColMetP-22
88ColMetGS-17
89PenPilS-16
Murtaugh, Danny
43PhiTeal-17
47PM1StaP1-146
49Bow-124A
49Bow-124B
49EurSta-168
49Lea-142
50Bow-203
50PirTeal-16
51Bow-273
52NatTeaL-19
59Top-17
59TopVen-17
60KeyChal-35
60PirJayP-10
60Top-223
61PirJayP-9
61Top-138
61Top-567
62Top-503
63PirIDL-15
63PirJayP-10
63Top-559
64PirKDK-21
64Top-141
64Top-268
64TopVen-141
64TopVen-268
70OPC-532
70Top-532
71OPC-437
71Top-437
74OPC-489
74Top-489
75OPC-304
75Top-304
76OPC-504
76SSP-586
76Top-504
81TCM60I-393
84OCoandSI-182
86PirGreT-12
Murtaugh, Tim
75ShrCapT-12
76ShrCapT-NNO
77ColCliT-13
77ShrCapT-14
Murtha, Brian
82CliGiaF-20
Muscat, Scott
89HelBreSP-24
90BelBreB-10
90BelBreS-15
Muser, Tony
73OPC-238
73Top-238
74OPC-286
74Top-286
75OPC-348
75SSP18-4
75Top-348
76OPC-537
76SSP-390
76Top-537
77Top-251
78SpoIndC-8
78Top-418
79TCMJapPB-4
81ElPasDT-23
82ElPasDT-23
84VanCanC-27
85BrePol-NNO
86BrePol-35
87BrePol-NNO
88BrePol-NNO
88Top-639
88TopTif-639
89BrePol-NNO
90El PasDAGTI-17
91DenZepLD-149
91DenZepP-137
91LinDriAAA-149
91OriCro-323
92DenZepF-2655
92DenZepS-149
93CubMar-19
94BreMilB-341
Musgrave, Scott
96LowSpiB-21
Musgraves, Dennis
77FriOneYW-47
81TCM60I-398
91MetWIZ-288
Musial, Stan
46SeaSLP-39
46SpoExcW-7-2
47Exh-164A
47Exh-164B
47HomBon-35
47PM1StaP1-147
47PM1StaP1-148
47PM1StaP1-149
48Bow-36
49Bow-24
49EurSta-191
49Lea-4
50RoyDes-1
51BerRos-B1
51R42SmaS-72
51Whe-4
52BerRos-45
52Bow-196
52RedMan-NL16
52RoyPre-7
52StaCalL-81E
52StaCalL-81F
52StaCalS-93A
52Whe-22A
52Whe-22B
53BowC-32
53CarHunW-16
53ExhCan-57
53RedMan-NL26
53SpoMagP-6
54CarHunW-14
54RedHeaF-23
55BigLeaIS-14
55CarHunW-15
55DaiQueS-14
55DonWin-34
55RawMus-1
55RawMus-1A
55RawMus-2
55RawMus-2A
55RawMus-3
55RawMus-4
56YelBasP-23
58CarJayP-11
58HarSta-6
58JayPubA-14
58Top-476
59Top-150
59Top-470
59TopVen-150
60CarJayP-8
60KeyChal-36
60NuHi-21
60RawGloT-22
60Top-250
60TopTat-39
60TopTat-94
61CarJayP-10
61NuSco-421
61Raw-7
61SevElev-16
61Top-290
61TopDicG-11
61TopStal-92
62CarJayP-10
62ExhStaB-28
62Top-50
62Top-317
62TopBuc-63
62TopStal-189
62TopVen-50
63BasMagM-61
63Baz-21
63CarJayP-15
63ExhStaB-48
63Top-1
63Top-138
63Top-250
63TopStil-30
66CarCoi-2
67TopVen-157
69EquSpoHoF-BB14
72LauGreF-24
73HalofFPP-12
74LauAllG-55
76GalBasGHoF-20
76JerJonPC-4
76RowExh-3
76ShaPiz-112
76TayBow4-2
77GalGloG-16
77GalGloG-237
77ShaPiz-25
77Spo-2116
79BasGre-68
79DiaGre-158
79TCM50-9
80MarExh-21
80PacLeg-8
80PerHaloFP-114
80SSPHOF-114
81SanDieSC-13
82BasCarN-3
82DiaCla-46
82GSGalAG-1
83CarGreT-7
83DonHOFH-32
83MLBPin-29
83Oco& SSBG-12
83TCMPla1942-26
83TigAIKS-67
84OCoandSI-40
84OCoandSI-200
84OCoandSI-228
84SpoDesPW-11
84WilMay-30
85CirK-15
85DalNatCC-1
85DonHOFS-5
85MusTTC-1
85MusTTC-2
85MusTTC-3
85MusTTC-4
85MusTTC-5
85MusTTC-6
85MusTTC-7
85MusTTC-8
85Woo-27
86SpoDecG-30
86TCM-9
86TCMSupS-34
87HygAllG-34
87LeaSpeO*-H4
87NesDreT-23
87SpoRea-18
88Don-641
88GreBasS-7
88HouSho-4
88Lea-263
88PacLegI-6
88Top-665
88TopTif-665
88WilMulP-18
89HOFStiB-30
89PerCelP-33
89TopBasT-27
90BasWit-36
90HOFStiB-51
90PerGreM-11
91TopEasCN-3
91USGamSBL-8C
91USGamSBL-8D
91USGamSBL-8H
91USGamSBL-8S
92AFUMus-1
92AFUMus-2
92AFUMus-3
92AFUMus-4
92AFUMus-5
92CarMcD-22
92PinMan-24
92ScoFra-1
92ScoFra-4
92ScoFra-AU1
92ScoFra-AU4
92SpoIIFK1-320
93Yoo-11
Musolino, Mike
87SalAngP-23
88PalSprACLC-105
88QuaCitAGS-30
89QuaCitAB-20
89QuaCitAGS-15
92PalSprAC-22
92PalSprAF-844
Musselman, Jeff
86VenGulP-16
87BluJayFS-25
87Don-591
87DonRoo-53
87FleUpd-84
87FleUpdG-84
87SpoRooI-15
87TopTra-83T
87TopTraT-83T
88BluJayFS-25
88Don-630
88Fle-121
88FleGlo-121
88Lea-234
88OPC-229
88Sco-478
88ScoGlo-478
88ScoYouS2-30
88StaLinBJ-17
88Top-229
88TopBig-69
88TopRoo-22
88TopSti-308
88TopTif-229
88ToyRoo-20
89BluJayFS-22
89Bow-240
89BowTif-240
89Don-656
89Fle-243
89FleGlo-243
89MetKah-U3
89OPC-362
89Sco-558
89Top-591
89TopTif-591
89UppDec-41
90Don-623
90Fle-212
90FleCan-212
90MetColP-21
90MetKah-13
90OPC-382
90Sco-525
90Top-382
90TopTif-382
90TopTVM-15
90UppDec-585
91LinDriAAA-542
91MetWIZ-289
91Sco-294
91TacTigLD-542
91TacTigP-2301
92TacTigF-2498
92TacTigS-540
Musselman, Ron
80LynSaiT-23
81SpoIndT-17
82SalLakCGT-14
83OklCit8T-14
85BluJayFS-25
85FleUpd-83
86SyrChiP-20
87PorBeaP-21
Musselwhite, Darren
90KenTwiB-16
90KenTwiS-28
91VisOakC-6
91VisOakP-1740
Musselwhite, Jim
93OneYanF-3500
94Bow-27
94FloStaLAF-FSL24
94TamYanC-19
94TamYanF-2381
95Exc-100
95NorNavTI-25
Musser, Andy
84PhiTas-7
88PhiTas-39
90PhiTas-35
Musset, Jose
92QuaCitRBC-12
92QuaCitRBF-806
93MidAngF-321
94Bow-221
94ColCliF-2951
94ExcFS7-28
95ColCliMCTI-6
95NorNagUTI-45
97MidAngOHP-20
Mussina, Mike
90ClaDraP-20
90RocRedWGC-12
90TopMag-83
91Bow-97
91Cla1-T17
91ClaGam-146
91LeaGolR-BC12
91LinDriAAA-462
91RocRedWLD-462
91RocRedWP-1899
91Sco-383
91UltUpd-4
91UppDec-65
92Bow-612
92Cla1-T67
92Cla2-T14
92Cla2-NNO
92ClaDraP-95
92ClaDraPFB-BC20
92ClaGam-148
92ColAllG-15
92ColAllP-15
92Don-632
92Fle-20
92Lea-13
92LeaBlaG-13
92OPC-242
92OPCPre-87
92Pin-204
92PinTea2-1

92ProFS7-1
92Sco-755
92ScoImpP-48
92SpoIllFK1-311
92StaClu-225
92Stu-127
92Top-242
92TopDeb91-130
92TopGol-242
92TopGolW-242
92TopMic-242
92TriPla-237
92Ult-9
92UppDec-675
93Bow-633
93ClaGam-70
93ColAllG-17
93DiaMar-79
93Don-427
93Fin-157
93FinRef-157
93Fla-154
93Fle-172
93FunPac-134
93HumDumC-2
93JimDea-27
93Lea-343
93LeaFas-4
93MSABenSPD-13
93OPC-214
93PacSpa-21
93PanSti-69
93Pin-44
93PinTea2-3
93PinTeaP-1
93Sco-27
93Sel-92
93SelAce-20
93SelStaL-81
93SelStaL-87
93SP-160
93StaClu-77
93StaCluFDI-77
93StaCluM-145
93StaCluMOP-77
93Stu-202
93StuSupoC-4
93Top-710
93TopComotH-2
93TopGol-710
93TopInaM-710
93TopMic-710
93Toy-37
93TriPla-13
93Ult-144
93UltAllS-20
93UppDec-233
93UppDec-463
93UppDecGold-233
93UppDecGold-463
93USPlaCA-8S
94Bow-627
94BowBes-R54
94BowBesR-R54
94ColC-475
94ColChoGS-475
94ColChoSS-475
94Don-331
94DonDiaK-DK26
94DonSpeE-331
94ExtBas-9
94ExtBasPD-4
94Fin-66
94FinPre-66P
94FinRef-66
94Fla-255
94Fle-12
94Fle-708
94FleAllS-18
94FleSmo'nH-8
94FUnPac-148
94Lea-105
94LeaL-3
94OPC-82
94OriPro-70
94OriUSPC-1D
94OriUSPC-9S
94Pac-38
94PanSti-21
94Pin-295
94PinArtP-295
94PinMusC-295
94ProMag-9
94RedFolMI-22
94Sco-9
94ScoDreT-1
94ScoGolR-9
94Sel-36
94SP-124
94SPDieC-124
94Spo-44
94SpoFanA-AS9
94StaClu-488
94StaCluFDI-488
94StaCluGR-488
94StaCluMOP-488
94StaCluT-279
94StaCluTFDI-279
94Stu-125
94StuHer-8
94Top-598
94TopGol-598
94TopSpa-598
94TriPla-157
94Ult-307
94UppDec-44
94UppDec-102
94UppDecAJ-19
94UppDecAJG-19
94UppDecED-44
94UppDecED-102
95Baz-10
95Bow-334
95ClaPhoC-6
95ColCho-340
95ColChoGS-340
95ColChoSE-157
95ColChoSEGS-157
95ColChoSESS-157
95ColChoSS-340
95Don-9
95DonDom-1
95DonMouM-3
95DonPreP-9
95DonTopotO-13
95Emb-93
95EmbGolI-93
95Emo-6
95Fin-48
95FinRef-48
95Fla-6
95FlaTodS-8
95Fle-15
95FleAllS-20
95FlePro-1
95FleTeaL-1
95Kra-9
95Lea-387
95LeaLim-70
95Pac-27
95PacPri-8
95PanSti-13
95Pin-14
95PinArtP-14
95PinMusC-14
95PinPin-2
95PinPinR-2
95PinTeaP-TP1
95RedFol-10
95Sco-415
95ScoGolR-415
95ScoHaloG-HG85
95ScoPlaTS-415
95ScoRul-SR30
95ScoRulJ-SR30
95Sel-19
95SelArtP-19
95SelCer-9
95SelCerMG-9
95SP-119
95SPCha-117
95SPChaDC-117
95Spo-60
95SpoArtP-60
95SPSil-119
95StaClu-426
95StaCluMOP-426
95StaCluSTWS-426
95StaCluVR-223
95Stu-29
95StuGolS-29
95Sum-102
95Sum-192
95SumNthD-102
95SumNthD-192
95Top-50
95TopCyb-37
95UC3-5
95UC3ArtP-5
95Ult-6
95UltGolM-6
95UppDec-130
95UppDecED-130
95UppDecEDG-130
95UppDecSE-186
95UppDecSEG-186
95USPlaCMLA-6S
95Zen-75
96Baz-81
96Bow-93
96BowBes-54
96BowBesAR-54
96BowBesMI-9
96BowBesMIAR-9
96BowBesMIR-9
96BowBesR-54
96Cir-5
96CirRav-5
96ColCho-6
96ColCho-465
96ColChoGS-6
96ColChoGS-465
96ColChoSS-6
96ColChoSS-465
96Don-518
96DonDiaK-28
96DonPreP-518
96DonSho-5
96EmoXL-6
96Fin-G90
96FinRef-G90
96Fla-9
96Fle-17
96FleOri-11
96FleTif-17
96Lea-191
96LeaLim-30
96LeaLimG-30
96LeaPre-36
96LeaPreP-36
96LeaPrePB-191
96LeaPrePG-191
96LeaPrePS-191
96LeaPreSG-49
96LeaPreSte-49
96LeaSig-19
96LeaSigPPG-19
96LeaSigPPP-19
96MetUni-6
96MetUniP-6
96MLBPin-22
96Pac-243
96PacPri-P75
96PacPriFT-FT2
96PacPriG-P75
96PanSti-125
96PanSti-127
96Pin-34
96PinAfi-83
96PinAfiAP-83
96PinAfiFPP-83
96PinArtP-16
96PinSta-16
96ProSta-79
96Sco-197
96Sco-301
96ScoDugC-B26
96ScoDugCAP-B26
96ScoRef-17
96Sel-30
96SelArtP-30
96SelCer-12
96SelCerAP-12
96SelCerCB-12
96SelCerCR-12
96SelCerIP-16
96SelCerMB-12
96SelCerMG-12
96SelCerMR-12
96SelTeaN-20
96SP-33
96SPMarM-MM17
96SPMarMDC-17
96Spo-74
96SpoArtP-74
96StaClu-6
96StaCluEPB-6
96StaCluEPG-6
96StaCluEPS-6
96StaCluMO-29
96StaCluMOP-6
95StaCluVRMC-223
96Stu-128
96StuPrePB-128
96StuPrePG-128
96StuPrePS-128
96Sum-119
96SumAbo&B-119
96SumArtP-119
96SumFoi-119
96Top-65
96Top-228
96TopChr-23
96TopChr-88
96TopChrR-23
96TopChrR-88
96TopClaC-CC12
96TopGal-159
96TopGalPPI-159
96TopLas-125
96Ult-9
96UltGolM-9
96UppDec-281
96UppDecPHE-H16
96UppDecPreH-H16
96Zen-52
96ZenArtP-52
96ZenMoz-8
97Bow-44
97BowBes-54
97BowBesAR-54
97BowBesR-54
97BowChr-35
97BowChrI-35
97BowChrIR-35
97BowChrR-35
97BowInt-44
97Cir-375
97CirRav-375
97ColCho-271
97ColChoNF-NF39
97Don-119
97Don-432
97DonEli-29
97DonEliGS-29
97DonLim-155
97DonLim-160
97DonLimLE-155
97DonLimLE-160
97DonPre-132
97DonPreCttC-132
97DonPreP-119
97DonPreP-432
97DonPrePGold-119
97DonPrePGold-432
97DonTea-34
97DonTeaSPE-34
97Fin-95
97FinRef-95
97FlaSho-A53
97FlaSho-B53
97FlaSho-C53
97FlaShoLC-53
97FlaShoLC-B53
97FlaShoLC-C53
97FlaShoLCM-A53
97FlaShoLCM-B53
97FlaShoLCM-C53
97Fle-10
97FleTif-10
97Lea-146
97LeaFraM-146
97LeaFraMDC-146
97LeaGet-8
97MetUni-6
97NewPin-128
97NewPinAP-128
97NewPinMC-128
97NewPinPP-128
97Pac-26
97PacGolCD-3
97PacLigB-26
97PacPri-10
97PacPriLB-10
97PacPriP-10
97PacPriSH-SH1B
97PacSil-26
97Pin-155
97PinArtP-155
97PinCar-9
97PinCer-43
97PinCerLI-20
97PinCerMBlu-43
97PinCerMG-43
97PinCerMR-43
97PinCerR-43
97PinIns-122
97PinInsCE-122
97PinInsDD-18
97PinInsDE-122
97PinMusC-155
97PinTotCPB-43
97PinTotCPG-43
97PinTotCPR-43
97PinX-P-74
97PinX-PMoS-74
97ProMag-45
97ProMagML-45
97Sco-154
97Sco-519
97ScoHobR-519
97ScoOri-8
97ScoOriPl-8
97ScoOriPr-8
97ScoPreS-154
97ScoResC-519
97ScoShoS-154
97ScoShoS-519
97ScoShoSAP-154
97ScoShoSAP-519
97Sel-82
97SelArtP-82
97SelRegG-82
97SelToootT-23
97SelToootTMB-23
97SkyE-X-6
97SkyE-XC-6
97SkyE-XEC-6
97SP-31
97SpoIll-125
97SpoIllEE-125
97SPSpeF-21
97StaClu-21
97StaCluMat-21
97StaCluMOP-21
97Stu-39
97StuPrePG-39
97StuPrePS-39
97Top-375
97TopChr-128
97TopChrR-128
97TopChrSB-19
97TopChrSBR-19
97TopGal-112
97TopGalPPI-112
97TopSeaB-SB19
97TopSta-70
97TopStaAM-70
97Ult-7
97UltGolME-7
97UltPlaME-7
97UppDec-22
97UppDec-67
97Zen-33

Mustad, Eric
80HawIslT-5
81TacTigT-4
82TacTigT-7
83WicAerDS-14
84IndIndTI-11
84IndIndTI-18

Mustaikis, Alex
79RedSoxEF-6

Mustari, Frank
88VerBeaDS-16

Muth, Bill
77WauMetT-12

Mutis, Jeff
87PanAmTURB-16
88BurIndP-1792
89KinIndS-13
90Bes-290
90CanIndB-22
90CanIndP-1291
90CanIndS-13
90CMC-834
91CanIndLD-90
91CanIndP-979
91Cla/Bes-24
91LinDriAA-90
92ColSprSSF-749
92ColSprSSS-92
92Don-411
92ProFS7-52
92SkyAA F-296
92SkyAAAF-40
92TopDeb91-131
93Bow-586
93IndWUA-21
93OPCPre-122

93Ult-543
94Fle-114
94Pac-178
94StaCluT-88
94StaCluTFDI-88
95ChaKniTI-18
96LouRedB-23
87PanAmTUBI-8
Mutrie, James
86OldJudN-10
87OldJudN-367
88GandBCGCE-28
89SFHaCN-13
Mutz, Frank
87SalAngP-16
88QuaCitAGS-12
88RenSilSCLC-276
89QuaCitAB-13
89QuaCitAGS-22
Mutz, Tommy
77IndIndTI-16
78IndIndTI-10
79IndIndTI-8
80OmaRoyP-19
Myaer, Jeff
86BenPhiC-153
Myatt, George
35GouPuzR-5B
35GouPuzR-6B
35GouPuzR-11K
35GouPuzR-13B
60BraLaktL-17
60BraSpiaS-15
60Top-464
62TigPosCF-12
79DiaGre-69
Myatt, Glenn
25Exh-84
26Exh-83
27Exh-43
28Exh-42
32R33So2-417
33Gou-10
33GouCanV-10
34DiaMatCSB-139
34DiaStaR-58
35DiaMatCS3T1-113
36GouWidPPR-D21
36WorWidGV-26
91ConTSN-187
Myer, Buddy (Charles M.)
28W56PlaC-C6A
29ExhFou-32
31Exh-32
31SenTealPW-25
33Gou-153
33GouCanV-78
34BatR31-19
34BatR31-133
34DiaStaR-4
35ExhFou-16
35GouPuzR-8H
35GouPuzR-9H
36ExhFou-16
36GouWidPPR-A78
36NatChiFPR-57
36NatChiFPR-95
36WorWidGV-132
37ExhFou-16
37KelPepS-BB11
37OPCBatUV-114
38ExhFou-16
39PlaBal-100
40PlaBal-17
41DouPlaR-73
60SenUniMC-14
69SCFOldT-14
92ConTSN-503
Myerchin, Mike
82BelBreF-12
Myers, Aaron
96PorRocB-24
Myers, Adrian
96HudValRB-11
Myers, Al
87BucN28-115
87OldJudN-369
88WG1CarG-68
89EdgR.WG-16
Myers, Brad
88CapCodPPaLP-135
Myers, Chris
88HagSunS-13
89FreKeyS-19
90Bes-34
90Bow-250
90BowTif-250
90CMC-792
90HagSunB-18
90HagSunDGB-18
90HagSunP-1412
90HagSunS-19
91LinDriAAA-463
91RocRedWLD-463
91RocRedWP-1900
92HarSenF-459
Myers, Dave
77CedRapGT-15
83WauTimF-12
86ChaLooP-21
87ChaLooB-20
87SouLeaAJ-11
88VerMarP-952
91BelMarC-27
91BelMarP-3683
92BelMarF-1461
93RivPilCLC-28
94RivPilCLC-29
95PorCitRTI-15
96TacRaiB-1
Myers, Ed
84AlbA'sT-18
86VanCanP-18
Myers, Elmer
16ColE13-124
22E120-8
22W573-90
Myers, Eric
90SouOreAB-27
90SouOreAP-3444
91MadMusC-12
91MadMusP-2129
Myers, George
87OldJudN-368
Myers, George I.
40WheM4-8A
40WheM4-8B
41WheM5-21
Myers, Glen
87VisOakP-2
Myers, Greg
86VenGulP-17
87SyrChiP-1931
87SyrChiT-10
88Don-624
88Fle-644
88FleGlo-644
88SyrChiC-18
88SyrChiP-821
89BluJayFS-23
90BluJayFS-22
90Bow-520
90BowTif-520
90Don-706
90Lea-527
90OPC-438
90Top-438
90TopTif-438
90UppDec-718
91BluJayFS-19
91BluJayFS-22
91BluJayS-12
91Don-494
91Fle-182
91Lea-256
91OPC-599
91PanFreS-346
91Sco-88
91Sco100RS-75
91StaClu-289
91Top-599A
91Top-599B
91TopDesS-599
91TopMic-599
91TopTif-599
91UltUpd-62
91UppDec-259
92Don-342
92Fle-338
92Lea-192
92OPC-203
92Pin-324
92Sco-471
92StaClu-468
92Top-203
92TopGol-203
92TopGolW-203
92TopMic-203
92Ult-150
92UppDec-407
93AngMot-16
93AngPol-18
93BluJayD4-42
93Don-269
93FleFinE-185
93Lea-318
93OPC-241
93PacSpa-370
93Sco-468
93StaClu-490
93StaCluAn-11
93StaCluFDI-490
93StaCluMOP-490
93Top-637
93TopGol-637
93TopInaM-637
93TopMic-637
93UppDec-789
93UppDecGold-789
94AngAdoF-4
94AngLAT-19
94AngMot-23
94ColC-461
94ColChoGS-461
94ColChoSS-461
94Don-198
94Fla-25
94Fle-65
94Lea-33
94Pac-85
94PanSti-40
94Pin-156
94PinArtP-156
94PinMusC-156
94Sco-121
94ScoGolR-121
94StaClu-468
94StaCluFDI-468
94StaCluGR-468
94StaCluMOP-468
94Top-171
94TopGol-171
94TopSpa-171
94UppDec-334
94UppDecED-334
95AngCHP-11
95AngMot-11
95Don-426
95DonPreP-426
95DonTopotO-38
95Sco-184
95ScoGolR-184
95ScoPlaTS-184
96Don-96
96DonPreP-96
96Fle-52
96FleTif-52
96LeaSigEA-135
96StaClu-206
96StaCluMOP-206
97Don-148
97DonPreP-148
97DonPrePGold-148
97Fle-152
97FleTif-152
97Pac-143
97PacLigB-143
97PacSil-143
97Pin-5
97PinArtP-5
97PinMusC-5
97Top-97
97Ult-91
97UltGolME-91
97UltPlaME-91
Myers, Hy (Henry)
10CouT21-50
10CouT21-51
10CouT21-308
10CouT21-309
15SpoNewM-129
16ColE13-125
16SpoNewM-131
17HolBreD-72
21E121So1-69A
21E121So1-69B
21E121So8-66
21Exh-115
22AmeCarE-50
22E120-145
22W575-89
90DodTar-564
Myers, Jason
94Bow-163
94Bow-352
94CliLumF-1978
94Top-754
94TopGol-754
94TopSpa-754
95BurBeeTI-14
96SanJosGB-20
96WesOahCHWB-43
94CliLumC-17
Myers, Jeff
92EveGiaC-12
92EveGiaF-1685
93CliGiaF-2487
Myers, Jim
87PocGiaTB-16
88PocGiaP-2076
89CliGiaP-886
90Bes-223
90ProAaA-146
90SanJosGB-15
90SanJosGCLC-49
90SanJosGP-2008
90SanJosGS-16
91LinDriAA-314
91ShrCapLD-314
91ShrCapP-1819
92PhoFirS-390
92SkyAAAF-178
93PhoFirF-1514
93ShrCapF-2756
94MemChiF-355
95RocRedWTI-26
96FleUpd-U6
96FleUpdTC-U6
96LeaSigEA-136
96RocRedWB-20
97Ult-8
97UltGolME-8
97UltPlaME-8
Myers, L.E.
88AllandGN-40
88KimN18-30
Myers, Linwood
39PlaBal-134
Myers, Matt
93BoiHawC-20
93BoiHawF-3913
Myers, Michael Stanley
88CapCodPPaLP-158
89CedRapRB-5
Myers, Mike (Michael R.)
87SpoIndP-24
88ChaRaiP-1199
89CedRapRP-918
89CedRapRS-14
90EveGiaB-9
90EveGiaP-3125
91Cla/Bes-323
91CliGiaP-831
91MidLeaAP-MWL5
93Bow-150
93StaClu-437
93StaCluFDI-437
93StaCluMarI-22
93StaCluMOP-437
94Bow-488
95ChaKniTI-19
96LeaSigEA-137
97PacPriGotD-GD43
Myers, Randy
86MetColP-22
86MetTCM-9
86MetWorSC-20
86TidTidP-22
87Don-29
87FleUpd-85
87FleUpdG-85
87Lea-29
87MetColP-18
87SpoTeaP-2
87Top-213
87TopTif-213
88Don-620
88DonBasB-265
88DonTeaBM-620
88Fle-146
88FleGlo-146
88MetColP-8
88MetFanC-48
88MetKah-48
88Sco-336
88ScoGlo-336
88Top-412
88TopRoo-12
88TopTif-412
88ToyRoo-21
89Bow-374
89BowTif-374
89ClaTraP-197
89Don-336
89DonBasB-153
89Fle-46
89FleGlo-46
89MetColP-15
89MetKah-19
89OPC-104
89PanSti-135
89Sco-306
89ScoYouSI-41
89Top-610
89TopBasT-121
89TopDouM-9
89TopSti-97
89TopStiB-66
89TopTif-610
89TVSpoM-7
89UppDec-634
90Bow-47
90BowTif-47
90ClaBlu-107
90ClaYel-T18
90Don-336
90DonBesN-88
90Fle-213
90FleCan-213
90Lea-149
90OPC-105
90PanSti-307
90PubSti-142
90RedFolSB-63
90RedKah-17
90Sco-351
90ScoRoo-16T
90Top-105
90TopSti-100
90TopTif-105
90TopTra-78T
90TopTraT-78T
90UppDec-581
90UppDec-797
90USPlaCA-WCO
90VenSti-362
91BasBesAotM-12
91Bow-666
91Cla2-T32
91ClaGam-114
91Don-209
91Fle-73
91Lea-504
91MajLeaCP-73
91MetWIZ-290
91MSAHolD-8
91OPC-780
91PanCanT1-82
91PanFreS-135
91PanSti-121
91RedKah-28
91RedPep-13
91Sco-501
91Sco-662
91Sco-885
91Sco100S-79
91StaClu-275
91Top-780A
91Top-780B
91TopDesS-780
91TopMic-780
91TopTif-780
91Ult-97
91UppDec-371
91Woo-23
92Bow-154
92Don-624
92Fle-413
92FleUpd-123
92OPC-24
92OPCPre-104
92PadCarJ-15
92PadMot-11
92PadSmo-21
92Sco-155
92ScoRoo-12T
92StaClu-805
92StaCluNC-805
92Top-24
92TopGol-24

92TopGolW-24
92TopMic-24
92TopTra-80T
92TopTraG-80T
92Ult-579
92UppDec-278
92UppDec-741
93Bow-32
93CubMar-18
93CubRol-1
93DiaMar-80
93Fin-182
93FinRef-182
93Fla-19
93Fle-522
93FleFinE-10
93FunPac-83
93Lea-358
93MSABenSPD-9
93OPC-215
93OPCPre-33
93Pin-549
93Sco-607
93Sel-215
93SelRoo-25T
93SelStaL-71
93SP-87
93StaClu-44
93StaClu-667
93StaCluCu-16
93StaCluFDI-44
93StaCluFDI-667
93StaCluMOP-44
93StaCluMOP-667
93Top-302
93TopGol-302
93TopInaM-302
93TopMic-302
93TopTra-65T
93TriPla-142
93Ult-317
93UppDec-283
93UppDec-483
93UppDec-667
93UppDecGold-283
93UppDecGold-483
93UppDecGold-667
94Bow-194
94BowBes-R58
94BowBesR-R58
94ColC-308
94ColC-460
94ColChoGS-308
94ColChoGS-460
94ColChoSS-308
94ColChoSS-460
94Don-399
94ExtBas-221
94Fin-357
94FinRef-357
94Fla-139
94Fle-392
94FUnPac-28
94Lea-396
94OPC-119
94Pac-105
94PanSti-16
94PanSti-155
94Pin-271
94PinArtP-271
94PinMusC-271
94RedFolMI-11
94Sco-534
94ScoGolR-534
94Sel-22
94SP-70
94SPDieC-70
94StaClu-162
94StaCluFDI-162
94StaCluGR-162
94StaCluMO-36
94StaCluMOP-162
94StaCluT-350
94StaCluTFDI-350
94Top-394
94Top-575
94TopBlaG-40
94TopGol-394
94TopGol-575
94TopSpa-394
94TopSpa-575
94TriPla-76
94Ult-462
94UltFir-6
94UppDec-257
94UppDecED-257
95Baz-14
95Bow-295
95ColCho-215
95ColChoGS-215
95ColChoSE-81
95ColChoSEGS-81
95ColChoSESS-81
95ColChoSS-215
95Don-429
95DonPreP-429
95DonTopotO-201
95Emo-112
95Fin-162
95FinRef-162
95Fla-114
95Fle-420
95FleAllS-24
95Lea-151
95LeaLim-101
95Pac-75
95PacPri-24
95Pin-255
95PinArtP-255
95PinMusC-255
95RedFol-13
95Sco-11
95ScoGolR-11
95ScoPlaTS-11
95SP-37
95SPCha-28
95SPChaDC-28
95SPSil-37
95StaClu-235
95StaCluFDI-235
95StaCluMOP-235
95StaCluSTWS-235
95StaCluVR-119
95Top-330
95TopCyb-180
95Ult-361
95UltGolM-361
95UppDec-66
95UppDecED-66
95UppDecEDG-66
95UppDecSE-259
95UppDecSEG-259
96Baz-123
96Cir-6
96CirRav-6
96ColCho-9
96ColCho-85
96ColChoGS-9
96ColChoGS-85
96ColChoSS-9
96ColChoSS-85
96Don-99
96DonPreP-99
96EmoXL-7
96Fin-B204
96FinRef-B204
96Fla-10
96Fle-323
96FleOri-12
96FleTif-323
96FleUpd-U7
96FleUpdTC-U7
96MetUni-7
96MetUniP-7
96MLBPin-23
96Pac-19
96PanSti-43
96PanSti-119
96Sco-161
96ScoDugC-A94
96ScoDugCAP-A94
96SP-34
96StaClu-15
96StaClu-265
96StaCluEPB-15
96StaCluEPG-15
96StaCluEPS-15
96StaCluMO-30
96StaCluMOP-15
96StaCluMOP-265
95StaCluVRMC-119
96Top-198
96TopChr-66
96TopChrR-66
96TopGal-62
96TopGalPPI-62
96TopLas-126
96Ult-308
96UltGolM-308
96UppDec-481U
97Cir-92
97CirRav-92
97ColCho-42
97Don-207
97Don-299
97DonPreP-207
97DonPreP-299
97DonPrePGold-207
97DonPrePGold-299
97DonTea-37
97DonTeaSPE-37
97Fin-91
97FinRef-91
97Fle-11
97FleTif-11
97Pac-27
97PacLigB-27
97PacSil-27
97Sco-190
97ScoOri-10
97ScoOriPl-10
97ScoOriPr-10
97ScoPreS-190
97ScoShoS-190
97ScoShoSAP-190
97StaClu-272
97StaCluMOP-272
97Top-133
97TopSta-80
97TopStaAM-80
97Ult-9
97UltGolME-9
97UltPlaME-9
97UppDec-18

Myers, Richard
52MotCoo-58
53MotCoo-15

Myers, Rod
91AppFoxP-1713
92LetMouSP-23
93MidLeaAGF-19
93RocRoyC-19
93RocRoyC-21
93RocRoyF-714
93RocRoyF-729
94WilBluRC-17
94WilBluRC-18
94WilBluRF-297
94WilBluRF-314
95OmaRoyTI-24
95WicWraTI-7
96FleUpd-U115
96FleUpdTC-U115
96LeaSigA-165
96LeaSigAG-165
96LeaSigAS-165
96Ult-455
96UltGolM-455
97Bow-348
97BowInt-348
97ColCho-128
97NewPin-166
97NewPinAP-166
97NewPinMC-166
97NewPinPP-166
97PinCer-126
97PinCerMBlu-126
97PinCerMG-126
97PinCerMR-126
97PinCerR-126
97PinTotCPB-126
97PinTotCPG-126
97PinTotCPR-126
97Sco-479
97ScoHobR-479
97ScoResC-479
97ScoShoS-479
97ScoShoSAP-479
97Sel-114
97SelArtP-114
97SelRegG-114
97UppDec-277

Myers, Ron
89AncBucTI-24

Myers, Runner
88GooN16-30

Myers, Thomas
92MadMusC-21
92MadMusF-1231
92RenSilSCLC-50
93ModA'sC-14
93ModA'sF-796
94FreKeyF-2611

Myers, William
35GouPuzR-8D
35GouPuzR-9D
38CinOraW-21
39OrcPhoAP-17
39PlaBal-38
40PlaBal-80
41CubTeal-14
41HarHarW-18

Myles, Rick
81CedRapRT-4
82LynMetT-17
84JacMetT-2

Myllykangas, Lauri
36GouWidPPR-D22
36WorWidGV-82

Myres, Doug
88St.LucMS-17

Myrick, Robert
77MetDaiPA-18
77Top-627
78MetDaiPA-19
78TidTidT-15
78Top-676
79TucTorT-21
80VenLeaS-163
91MetWIZ-291

Myrow, John
94CenValRC-13
94CenValRF-3216
95NewHavRTI-8
96NewHavRB-18

Mysel, David
92FroRowDP-32
92NiaFalRC-12
92NiaFalRF-3321
93FayGenC-17
93FayGenF-127
93StaCluM-48
94Bow-537
94TreThuF-2119
94UppDecML-188
95SigRooOJ-25
95SigRooOJP-25
95SigRooOJPS-25
95SigRooOJS-25

Na'te, Nikko (Jeff)
90BelBreB-21
90BelBreS-26

Nabekawa, Tom
87SanJosBP-13

Naber, Bob
83CliGiaF-13

Nabholz, Chris
89RocExpLC-19
90Bes-300
90FleUpd-30
90JacExpB-21
90JacExpP-1371
90ProAaA-37
91Bow-459
91ClaGam-74
91Don-667
91ExpPos-15
91Fle-240
91Lea-416
91OPC-197
91OPCPre-87
91Sco-804
91StaClu-326
91Top-197
91TopDeb90-112
91TopDesS-197
91TopMic-197
91TopRoo-21
91TopTif-197
91ToyRoo-21
91UppDec-538
92Don-170
92ExpDonD-13
92ExpPos-23
92Fle-487
92Lea-327
92OPC-32
92OPCPre-26
92Pin-360
92Sco-140
92StaClu-318
92Top-32
92TopGol-32
92TopGolW-32
92TopMic-32
92Ult-521
92UppDec-579
93Don-114
93ExpPosN-17
93Fle-78
93HumDumC-40
93Lea-73
93OPC-315
93PacSpa-536
93Pin-373
93Sco-477
93StaClu-469
93StaCluFDI-469
93StaCluMOP-469
93Top-278
93TopGol-278
93TopInaM-278
93TopMic-278
93Ult-69
93UppDec-404
93UppDecGold-404
94ColC-527
94ColChoGS-527
94ColChoSS-527
94Don-589
94Fin-420
94FinRef-420
94Fle-546
94Pin-60
94PinArtP-60
94PinMusC-60
94StaClu-31
94StaClu-619
94StaCluFDI-31
94StaCluFDI-619
94StaCluGR-31
94StaCluGR-619
94StaCluMOP-31
94StaCluMOP-619
94Top-656
94TopGol-656
94TopSpa-656
94Ult-348
95Fle-34

Naccarato, Stan
81TacTigT-30
82TacTigT-22
83TacTigT-19
88TacTigP-620
89TacTigP-1566

Nace, Todd
88MisStaB-23
91PitMetC-5
91PitMetP-3435

Nadeau, Michael
94BluOriC-15
94BluOriF-3569

Nader, John
93OneYanC-30

Naehring, Mark
78KnoKnoST-15
79KnoKnoST-1

Naehring, Tim
88ElmPioC-17
89LynRedSS-15
89TriA AAC-30
90CMC-268
90FleUpd-73
90PawRedSC-17
90PawRedSDD-16
90PawRedSP-469
90ProAAAF-441
90ScoRoo-87T
90TopTra-79T
90TopTraT-79T
90TopTVRS-54
90TriAAAC-30
90TriAllGP-AAA16
91Bow-127
91Cla1-T20
91Don-367
91Fle-105
91Lea-150
91OPC-702
91OPCPre-88
91RedSoxP-13
91Sco-356
91Sco100RS-77
91ScoAllF-5
91ScoRoo-30
91StaClu-83
91Stu-16
91Top-702
91TopDeb90-113
91TopDesS-702

91TopMic-702
91TopRoo-22
91TopTif-702
91ToyRoo-22
91Ult-36
91UppDec-527
92Bow-416
92Don-742
92Lea-235
92OPC-758
92OPCPre-37
92Pin-242
92PinTea2-15
92RedSoxDD-20
92Sco-259
92StaClu-854
92Stu-134
92Top-758
92TopGol-758
92TopGolW-758
92TopMic-758
92Ult-317
92UppDec-523
93Don-399
93OPC-304
93Pin-382
93RedSoxWHP-19
93Sco-452
93Top-24
93TopGol-24
93TopInaM-24
93TopMic-24
93Toy-50
93Ult-153
93UppDec-583
93UppDecGold-583
94ColC-452
94ColChoGS-452
94ColChoSS-452
94ExtBas-21
94Fla-264
94FleUpd-13
94Lea-201
94Pac-60
94Pin-65
94PinArtP-65
94PinMusC-65
94Sco-429
94ScoGolR-429
94Sel-151
94StaClu-131
94StaCluFDI-131
94StaCluGR-131
94StaCluMOP-131
94Top-474
94TopGol-474
94TopSpa-474
94Ult-315
94UppDec-337
94UppDecED-337
95ColCho-418
95ColChoGS-418
95ColChoSS-418
95Don-188
95DonPreP-188
95DonTopotO-23
95Emo-14
95Fin-184
95FinRef-184
95Fla-229
95Fle-35
95Lea-186
95LeaLim-125
95Pac-42
95Pin-105
95PinArtP-105
95PinMusC-105
95Sco-355
95ScoGolR-355
95ScoPlaTS-355
95SP-124
95SPCha-123
95SPChaDC-123
95SPSil-124
95StaClu-395
95StaCluMOP-395
95StaCluSTDW-RS395
95StaCluSTWS-395
95Sum-138
95SumNthD-138
95Top-329
95TopCyb-179
95Ult-12
95UltGolM-12
95UppDec-398
95UppDecED-398
95UppDecEDG-398
95Zen-101
96Cir-12
96CirRav-12
96ColCho-66
96ColChoGS-66
96ColChoSS-66
96Don-217
96DonPreP-217
96EmoXL-16
96Fin-B19
96FinRef-B19
96Fla-22
96Fle-31
96FleRedS-10
96FleTif-31
96Lea-7
96LeaPrePB-7
96LeaPrePG-7
96LeaPrePS-7
96MetUni-17
96MetUniP-17
96Pac-249
96PanSti-142
96Pin-100
96Sco-90
96ScoDugC-A70
96ScoDugCAP-A70
96SP-37
96StaClu-144
96StaCluEPB-144
96StaCluEPG-144
96StaCluEPS-144
96StaCluMOP-144
96Top-63
96Ult-19
96UltGolM-19
96UppDec-21
97Cir-127
97CirRav-127
97ColCho-279
97Don-179
97DonPreP-179
97DonPrePGold-179
97DonTea-50
97DonTeaSPE-50
97Fin-267
97FinRef-267
97FlaSho-A59
97FlaSho-B59
97FlaSho-C59
97FlaShoLC-59
97FlaShoLC-B59
97FlaShoLC-C59
97FlaShoLCM-A59
97FlaShoLCM-B59
97FlaShoLCM-C59
97Fle-27
97FleTif-27
97Lea-39
97LeaFraM-39
97LeaFraMDC-39
97MetUni-23
97NewPin-56
97NewPinAP-56
97NewPinMC-56
97NewPinPP-56
97Pac-43
97PacLigB-43
97PacSil-43
97PinX-PSfF-8
97PinX-PSfFU-8
97Sco-196
97ScoPreS-196
97ScoRedS-14
97ScoRedSPl-14
97ScoRedSPr-14
97ScoShoS-196
97ScoShoSAP-196
97SP-38
97Spolll-140
97SpollIEE-140
97StaClu-269
97StaCluMOP-269
97Top-230
97Ult-16
97UltGolME-16
97UltPlaME-16
97UppDec-27

Nagano, Cary
87HawRai-4

Nagano, Tetsuya
90IBAWorA-28

Nagasaki, Keiichi
79TCMJapPB-57

Nagashima, Kazushige
92VerBeaDC-28

Nagashima, Shigeo
79TCMJapPB-55

Nagel, Bill (William T.)
41DouPlaR-49

Nagelson, Rusty (Russell C.)
70OPC-7
70Top-7
71OPC-708
71Top-708

Nagle, Mike
77St.PetCT-NNO

Nagle, Tom (Thomas E.)
87OldJudN-370

Nago, Garrett
83ElPasDT-12
84ElPasDT-25
85VanCanC-223
86ElPasDP-17
87ElPasDP-5
88IndIndC-22
88IndIndP-515
89ColMudB-3
89ColMudP-146
89ColMudS-18

Nagurski, Bronko
38DixLid-6
38DixLidP-6
74NewYorNTDiS-35

Nagy, Charles
88TopTra-74T
88TopTraT-74T
89Bow-73
89BowTif-73
89KinIndS-14
89Sta-77
89Sta-178
89TopBig-217
90Bes-244
90Bes-323
90CanIndB-27
90CanIndP-1292
90CanIndS-14
90CMC-833
90EasLeaAP-EL37
90ProAaA-9
90Sco-611
91Bow-65
91Don-592
91DonRoo-18
91FleUpd-20
91IndFanC-20
91OPC-466
91Sco-75
91Sco100RS-47
91ScoAllF-8
91StaClu-472
91Top-466
91TopDeb90-114
91TopDesS-466
91TopMic-466
91TopTif-466
91UltUpd-20
91UppDec-19
92Bow-203
92Bow-566
92ClaGam-138
92Don-315
92Fle-118
92Hig5-45
92IndFanC-18
92Lea-115
92OPC-299
92OPCPre-138
92Pin-383
92Pin-609
92PinTea2-19
92Sco-330
92Sco100RS-26
92ScoImpP-19
92StaClu-389
92Top-299
92TopDaiQTU-12
92TopGol-299
92TopGolW-299
92TopMic-299
92Ult-351
92UppDec-178
92UppDecTMH-37
93Bow-149
93Don-141
93DurPowP2-11
93Fin-58
93FinRef-58
93Fle-219
93FleFruotL-49
93FunPac-110
93IndWUA-22
93Lea-171
93OPC-278
93PacSpa-415
93PanSti-46
93Pin-65
93PinTea2-22
93Sco-29
93Sco-538
93ScoGolDT-7
93Sel-70
93SelAce-12
93SelStaL-63
93SP-125
93StaClu-551
93StaCluFDI-551
93StaCluM-88
93StaCluMOP-551
93Stu-203
93Top-730
93TopComotH-6
93TopGol-730
93TopInaM-730
93TopMic-730
93TriPla-49
93Ult-189
93UppDec-243
93UppDecGold-243
94Bow-251
94ColC-578
94ColChoGS-578
94ColChoSS-578
94Don-239
94ExtBas-65
94Fin-104
94FinRef-104
94Fla-42
94Fle-115
94Lea-297
94OPC-254
94Pac-179
94PanSti-59
94Pin-385
94PinArtP-385
94PinMusC-385
94Sco-333
94ScoGolR-333
94Sel-264
94Spo-130
94StaClu-478
94StaCluFDI-478
94StaCluGR-478
94StaCluMOP-478
94Top-330
94TopGol-330
94TopSpa-330
94TriPla-118
94Ult-349
94UppDec-394
94UppDecED-394
95ColCho-277
95ColChoGS-277
95ColChoSS-277
95Don-134
95DonPreP-134
95DonTopotO-63
95Emb-67
95EmbGolI-67
95Fin-211
95FinRef-211
95Fla-34
95Fle-142
95Lea-311
95Pac-126
95Pin-89
95PinArtP-89
95PinMusC-89
95Sco-371
95ScoGolR-371
95ScoPlaTS-371
95Sel-64
95SelArtP-64
95StaClu-14
95StaCluFDI-14
95StaCluMOP-14
95StaCluSTWS-14
95StaCluVR-9
95Top-76
95TopCyb-53
95Ult-281
95UltGolM-281
95UppDec-91
95UppDecED-91
95UppDecEDG-91
96Cir-36
96CirRav-36
96ColCho-531
96ColChoGS-531
96ColChoSS-531
96Don-182
96DonPreP-182
96EmoXL-54
96Fla-72
96Fle-93
96FleInd-10
96FleTif-93
96LeaPre-102
96LeaPreP-102
96LeaSig-91
96LeaSigPPG-91
96LeaSigPPP-91
96MetUni-51
96MetUniP-51
96Pin-18
96ProSta-60
96SchDis-4
96Sco-350
96ScoDugC-B75
96ScoDugCAP-B75
95StaCluVRMC-9
96Top-326
96Ult-343
96UltGolM-343
96UppDec-317
96UppDecA-13
97Cir-357
97CirRav-357
97ColCho-89
97Don-242
97DonEli-133
97DonEliGS-133
97DonLim-43
97DonLimLE-43
97DonPre-11
97DonPreCttC-11
97DonPreP-242
97DonPrePGold-242
97DonTea-82
97DonTeaSPE-82
97Fin-7
97FinRef-7
97FlaSho-A141
97FlaSho-B141
97FlaSho-C141
97FlaShoLC-141
97FlaShoLC-B141
97FlaShoLC-C141
97FlaShoLCM-A141
97FlaShoLCM-B141
97FlaShoLCM-C141
97Fle-84
97FleTif-84
97Lea-56
97LeaFraM-56
97LeaFraMDC-56
97MetUni-85
97NewPin-136
97NewPinAP-136
97NewPinMC-136
97NewPinPP-136
97Pac-77
97PacLigB-77
97PacSil-77
97Pin-3
97PinArtP-3
97PinCar-20
97PinCer-29
97PinCerMBlu-29
97PinCerMG-29
97PinCerMR-29
97PinCerR-29
97PinIns-105
97PinInsCE-105
97PinInsDE-105
97PinMusC-3
97PinTotCPB-29
97PinTotCPG-29
97PinTotCPR-29
97PinX-P-41
97PinX-PMoS-41
97Sco-177

97Sco-526
97ScoHobR-526
97ScoInd-10
97ScoIndPl-10
97ScoIndPr-10
97ScoIndU-10
97ScoIndUTC-10
97ScoPreS-177
97ScoResC-526
97ScoShoS-177
97ScoShoS-526
97ScoShoSAP-177
97ScoShoSAP-526
97Sel-85
97SelArtP-85
97SelRegG-85
97SP-59
97SpoIll-49
97SpoIllEE-49
97StaClu-6
97StaCluMat-6
97StaCluMOP-6
97Stu-136
97StuPrePG-136
97StuPrePS-136
97Top-88
97TopChr-34
97TopChrR-34
97TopSta-81
97TopStaAM-81
97Ult-53
97UltGolME-53
97UltPlaME-53
97UppDec-49

Nagy, Jeff
92BenMusSP-25
92BilMusF-3371
93WesVirWC-20
93WesVirWF-2879

Nagy, Mike
70OPC-39
70RedSoxCPPC-9
70Top-39
71MLBOffS-325
71OPC-363
71Top-363
72OPC-488
72Top-488
81RedSoxBG2S-98

Nagy, Steve
49SomandK-7

Nahem, Sam
41CarW75-20
77TCMTheWY-19
90DodTar-565

Nahorodny, Bill (William G.)
76OklCit8TI-19
78SSP270-156
78Top-702
79Top-169
80OPC-286
80Top-552
81BraPol-15
81Fle-254
81Top-296
82ChaChaT-11
82Ind-26
82IndTeal-25
83Fle-416
83Top-616
84SalLakCGC-181
85PorBeaC-39

Nail, Charlie
82BirBarT-21
83EvaTriT-6
84WicAerRD-6

Naismith, James
87SpoCubG-1

Najera, Noe
92WatIndC-12
92WatIndF-3230
94WatIndC-21
94WatIndF-3934
96CarLeaA1B-6
96CarLeaA2B-6
96KenIndB-19

Naka, Toshio
79TCMJapPB-79

Nakabayashi, Debbie
91HawWomS-9
91HawWomS-10

Nakagawa, Shinya
93BriTigF-3646

Nakamoto, Brian
75LynRanT-17
76SanAntBTI-15

Nakamura, Hector
87SanJosBP-2

Nakamura, Katsuhiro
79TCMJapPB-84

Nakanose, Yukiyasu
96HilStaHWB-15

Nakashima, Toni
95GreFalDTI-6
96SavSanB-22

Nakashima, Yoshi
86SanJosBP-14

Nakatsuka, Masayuki
79TCMJapPB-6

Nalepka, Keith
91GulCoaRSP-3
92ButCopKSP-27

Nalley, Jerry
81BatTroT-14
82WatIndF-6
82WatIndT-21

Nallin, Dick
94ConTSN-1199
94ConTSNB-1199

Nalls, Gary
86QuaCitAP-25
87PalSprP-32
88PalSprACLC-106
88PalSprAP-1454
89CalLeaA-36
89RenSilSCLC-250
90RenSilSCLC-274

Nalls, Kevin
92IdaFalGF-3518
92IdaFalGSP-3

Nandin, Bob
81BirBarT-14
83SyrChiT-18
84SyrChiT-13
86ElPasDP-18

Nanni, Tito
80SanJosMJitB-15
81LynSaiT-23
82LynSaiT-15
83SalLakCGT-13
84SalLakCGC-174
85MidAngT-1

Nantel, Pierre
52LavPro-97

Nape, John
94LetMouF-3877
94LetMouSP-15

Napier, Jim
61UniOil-SD7
79QuaCitCT-22
80QuaCitCT-30
82IowCubT-25
83IowCubT-26
84IowCubT-11
86MaiGuiP-12

Naples, Brandon
96PitMetB-16

Napoleon, Danny (Daniel)
65Top-533
66OPC-87
66Top-87
66TopVen-87
81TCM60I-472
91MetWIZ-292

Napoleon, Ed
77ForLauYS-31
78TacYanC-8
79WesHavYT-2
80NasSouTI-16
83IndPos-24
83IndWhe-23
84Ind-22
84IndWhe-NNO
85Ind-22
85IndPol-NNO
88RoySmo-2
89AstLenH-14
89AstMot-27
89AstSmo-29
90AstMot-27
94RocRedWF-1015
95RanCra-19
96RanMot-28

Napp, Larry
55Bow-250

Naragon, Hal (Harold R.)
55Bow-129
55IndGolS-19
56Top-311
57Top-347
58Top-22
59Ind-13
59SenTealW-11
59Top-376
60Top-231
61Top-92
61TwiCloD-19
61TwiPetM-8
62Top-164
62TopVen-164

Naranjo, Cholly
57JetPos-13
58JetPos-12

Narcisse, Ron
85LitFalMT-14
86LitFalMP-21

Narcisse, Tyrone
93AshTouC-15
93AshTouF-2274
94OscAstC-18
94OscAstF-1137
95JacGenTI-7
96JacGenB-21

Narleski, Bill
88WatIndP-674

Narleski, Ray
55Bow-96
55IndGolS-9
55Top-160
56Top-133
57IndSoh-10
57Top-144
58Hir-22
58Top-439
59Top-442
60TigJayP-11
60Top-161
60TopVen-161
86IndGreT-11

Narleski, Steve
76BatTroTI-15
77WatIndT-15
81ChaLooT-5
82ChaLooT-19

Narron, Jerry (Jerry A.)
75ForLauYS-30
76ForLauYS-3
77WesHavYT-17
78TacYanC-38
79YanPicA-27
80Top-16
81Don-405
81MarPol-12
81OPC-249
81Top-637
82Don-433
82Fle-513
82SpoIndT-12
82Top-719
84AngSmo-20
85AngSmo-10
85Don-643
85Top-234
85TopTif-234
86AngSmo-10
86Don-451
86Top-543
86TopTif-543
87CalCanP-2329
87Don-603
87Top-474
87TopTif-474
88RocRedWC-14
88RocRedWGCP-17
88RocRedWP-216
88RocRedWTI-15
89FreKeyS-25
90HagSunB-29
90HagSunP-1431
90HagSunS-26
91HagSunLD-249
91HagSunP-2471
91LinDriAA-249
92RocRedWF-1955
92RocRedWS-474
92YanWIZ7-121
95RanCra-20
96RanMot-28

Narron, Johnny
75AppFoxT-19

Narron, Sam
49EurSta-44
60Top-467
63PirIDL-16
77TCMTheWY-1

Narum, Buster (L.F.)
64Top-418
65OPC-86
65Top-86
66Top-274
66TopVen-274
78TCM60I-44
91OriCro-324

Nash, Billy (William M.)
87OldJudN-371
88AugBecN-19
88WG1CarG-7
89N526N7C-10
94DukCabN-3
95May-23

Nash, Cotton (Charles F.)
71OPC-391
71Top-391
78QuaCitAT-15

Nash, Dave
86EveGiaC-184
86EveGiaPC-18
88FreSunCLC-13
88FreSunP-1228

Nash, Jim
67CokCapA-7
67CokCapAAm-30
67CokCapAt-1
67DexPre-150
67OPC-90
67Top-90
67TopVen-263
68Top-324
68TopVen-324
69MilBra-198
69MLBOffS-89
69Top-546
69TopSta-219
69TopTeaP-21
70MLBOffS-9
70OPC-171
70Top-171
71MLBOffS-18
71OPC-306
71Top-306
72MilBra-250
72OPC-401
72Top-401
73OPC-509
73Top-509

Nash, Rob
91BatCliC-1
91BatCliP-3498

Nastu, Phil
77CedRapGT-7
78PhoGiaC-19
79PhoGiaVNB-6
80PhoGiaVNB-7
80Top-686
80VenLeaS-75

Natal, Rob (Bob)
87JamExpP-2555
88FloStaLAS-14
88WesPalBES-20
89JacExpB-17
89JacExpP-176
90JacExpB-2
90JacExpP-1378
91HarSenLD-266
91HarSenP-630
91LinDriAA-266
92DonRoo-84
92IndIndF-1863
92IndIndS-189
92ProFS7-261
92SkyAAAF-93
92TriA AAS-189
93Bow-558
93Don-744
93EdmTraF-1141
93Fle-428
93FleFinE-67
93LinVenB-130
93LinVenB-277
93LinVenB-288
93MarPub-17
93MarUSPC-10S
93PacSpa-468
93StaClu-737
93StaCluFDI-737
93StaCluMOP-737
93TopTra-108T
94EdmTraF-2878
94Fle-472
94Pac-248
94Pin-173
94PinArtP-173
94PinMusC-173
94StaClu-291
94StaCluFDI-291
94StaCluGR-291
94StaCluMOP-291
94StaCluT-75
94StaCluTFDI-75
94Top-437
94TopGol-437
94TopSpa-437
94Ult-198
95ChaKniTI-20
95Top-192
96LeaSigEA-138
97PacPriGotD-GD146

Nate, Scott
95BelBreTI-22

Natera, Luis
85LitFalMT-20
86LitFalMP-22
87ColMetP-14

Nathan, Joseph
95BelGiaTI-11

Nation, Carrie
08AllLadBC-4

Nationals, New York
94OriofB-91

Nations, Joel
95SpoIndTI-15

Nattile, Sam
85PawRedST-10
86NewBriRSP-19

Nattress, Natty (William W.)
09ColChiE-212
09T206-450
12ColRedB-212
12ColTinT-212
12ImpTobC-8

Natupsky, Hal
79ElmPioRST-20

Naughton, Danny
87ColMetP-19
87LitFalMP-2405
88ColMetGS-23
89St.LucMS-18

Naulty, Dan
89AlaGol-2
92KenTwiF-600
93ForMyeMC-17
93ForMyeMF-2651
94ForMyeMC-16
94ForMyeMF-1167
96Fin-B358
96FinRef-B358
96FleUpd-U57
96FleUpdTC-U57
96LeaSigEA-139
96Ult-378
96UltGolM-378
97Cir-26
97CirRav-26
97ColCho-382
97Fle-153
97FleTif-153
97Ult-92
97UltGolME-92
97UltPlaME-92
97UppDec-106

Naumann, Rick
80AppFoxT-5
81AppFoxT-6

Nava, Lipso
91SanBerSC-19
91SanBerSP-1996
92PenPilC-4
92PenPilF-2940
93JacSunF-2717
93LinVenB-123
94VenLinU-204
95LinVen-39

Nava, Marlon
92EliTwiC-11
92EliTwiF-3687
92KenTwiC-13
93ForWayWC-21
93ForWayWF-1975

93LinVenB-78
94VenLinU-264
95ForMyeMTI-20
95LinVen-205
Navarro, Emilio
95NegLeaL2-27
Navarro, Jaime
88BlaYNPRWL-171
88StoPorCLC-182
88StoPorP-736
89BlaYNPRWL-147
89ElPasDGS-13
89FleUpd-39
90Bow-388
90BowTif-388
90BreMilB-16
90BrePol-31
90ClaUpd-T38
90Don-640
90El PasDAGTI-23
90Fle-331
90FleCan-331
90Lea-85
90Sco-569
90TopDeb89-87
90UppDec-646
91Bow-42
91BreMilB-18
91BrePol-16
91Don-216
91Fle-592
91Lea-409
91OPC-548
91Sco-102
91StaClu-436
91Top-548
91TopDesS-548
91TopMic-548
91TopTif-548
91UltUpd-31
91UppDec-476
92Bow-167
92BrePol-16
92Don-705
92Fle-183
92Lea-144
92OPC-222
92Pin-212
92Sco-231
92StaClu-87
92Stu-195
92Top-222
92TopGol-222
92TopGolW-222
92TopMic-222
92TriPla-188
92Ult-82
92UppDec-633
93Bow-647
93BrePol-18
93Don-281
93Fle-255
93Lea-296
93OPC-247
93PacBeiA-9
93PacSpa-161
93PanSti-35
93Pin-343
93Sco-218
93Sel-260
93SP-68
93StaClu-621
93StaCluFDI-621
93StaCluMOP-621
93Top-369
93TopGol-369
93TopInaM-369
93TopMic-369
93TriPla-233
93UppDec-237
93UppDecGold-237
94Bow-121
94BreMilB-57
94BrePol-19
94ColC-531
94ColChoGS-531
94ColChoSS-531
94Don-621
94Fin-129
94FinRef-129
94Fle-185
94Lea-439
94OPC-14
94Pac-336
94Sco-145
94ScoGolR-145
94StaClu-592
94StaCluFDI-592
94StaCluGR-592
94StaCluMOP-592
94StaCluMOP-ST22
94StaCluST-ST22
94Top-679
94TopGol-679
94TopSpa-679
94TriPla-56
94UppDec-426
94UppDecED-426
95ColCho-544T
95DonTopotO-202
95Fin-242
95FinRef-242
95FleUpd-127
95Pac-237
95SP-36
95SPSil-36
95StaClu-343
95StaClu-537
95StaCluMOP-343
95StaCluMOP-537
95StaCluSTWS-343
95StaCluSTWS-537
95Top-93
95TopTra-80T
95UppDec-459T
96ColCho-86
96ColChoGS-86
96ColChoSS-86
96Don-441
96DonPreP-441
96EmoXL-157
96Fla-221
96Fle-324
96FleCub-13
96FleTif-324
96MetUni-143
96MetUniP-143
96Pac-29
96PacEstL-EL22
96PacPri-P12
96PacPriG-P12
96PanSti-46
96Pin-22
96ProSta-39
96Sco-39
96SP-55
96StaClu-37
96StaClu-254
96StaCluMOP-37
96StaCluMOP-254
96Top-381
96Ult-456
96UltGolM-456
96UppDec-298
97Cir-388
97CirRav-388
97ColCho-294
97Don-254
97Don-297
97DonPreP-254
97DonPreP-297
97DonPrePGold-254
97DonPrePGold-297
97DonTea-71
97DonTeaSPE-71
97Fin-259
97FinRef-259
97Fle-281
97Fle-572
97FleTif-281
97FleTif-572
97Lea-52
97LeaFraM-52
97LeaFraMDC-52
97MetUni-13
97Pac-254
97PacLigB-254
97PacPri-87
97PacPriLB-87
97PacPriP-87
97PacSil-254
97Pin-60
97PinArtP-60
97PinMusC-60
97Sco-15
97Sco-348
97ScoHobR-348
97ScoPreS-15
97ScoResC-348
97ScoShoS-15
97ScoShoS-348
97ScoShoSAP-15
97ScoShoSAP-348
97StaClu-258
97StaCluMOP-258
97Top-21
97Ult-420
97UltGolME-420
97UltPlaME-420
Navarro, Julio
60Top-140
60TopVen-140
63Top-169
64Top-489
65Top-563
66Top-527
Navarro, Norberto
89PitMetS-18
Navarro, Rick
89SanDieSAS-19
92FroRowDP-48
92NiaFalRC-8
93FayGenC-18
93FayGenF-128
94LakTigC-17
94LakTigF-3034
Navarro, Tito
90ColMetGS-13
90ColMetPPI-6
90SouAtlLAS-37
90StaFS7-100
91ColMetPI-32
91LinDriAA-639
91WilBilLD-639
91WilBilP-302
92Bow-139
92ProFS7-281
92UppDecML-91
93NorTidF-2576
94Pac-414
94St.LucMF-1203
94StaClu-473
94StaCluFDI-473
94StaCluGR-473
94StaCluMOP-473
Navas, Francisco
76VenLeaS-64
Navas, Silverio
93LinVenB-88
93OneYanC-16
93OneYanF-3512
94VenLinU-193
95LinVen-104
Naveda, Edgar
86KenTwiP-17
87KenTwiP-5
88VisOakCLC-156
88VisOakP-103
89OrlTwiB-18
89OrlTwiP-1347
90CMC-567
90OrlSunRB-5
90PorBeaC-15
90PorBeaP-187
90ProAAAF-257
91LinDriAAA-413
91PorBeaLD-413
91PorBeaP-1580
92PorBeaF-2680
92PorBeaS-414
92SkyAAAF-189
93LinVenB-25
94VenLinU-8
95LinVen-74
Naveda, Yonni
93LinVenB-19
Navilliat, James
86SpoIndC-157
87ChaRaiP-11
Navratilova, Martina
82MonNew-10
Naworski, Andy
86BakDodP-21
86TriTriC-187
87Ft.MyeRP-9
Naylor, Earl
90DodTar-566
Naylor, Roleine C.
21Exh-116
22E120-86
22W572-69
22W573-91
Nazabal, Robert
85BenPhiC-17
Nazario, Victor Horatio
85DomLeaS-178
Neagle, Denny (Dennis)
88CapCodPPaLP-53
89EliTwiS-22
90CalLeaACLC-24
90CMC-862
90OrlSunRS-13
90ProAaA-142
90VisOakP-2150
91Bow-323
91Lea-466
91LinDriAAA-414
91PorBeaLD-414
91PorBeaP-1563
91TriA AAGP-AAA36
91Ult-383
91UppDecFE-34F
92Bow-485
92Cla1-T68
92Cla2-T66
92Don-605
92Fle-213
92LeaGolR-BC22
92OPC-592
92OPCPre-165
92Pin-556
92PinRoo-19
92PirNatI-17
92ProFS7-89
92ScoRoo-89T
92StaClu-724
92Stu-87
92Top-592
92TopDeb91-132
92TopGol-592
92TopGolW-592
92TopMic-592
92TopTra-81T
92TopTraG-81T
92Ult-556
92UppDec-426
92UppDec-748
92UppDecSR-SR17
93Don-226
93Fle-503
93Lea-42
93PacSpa-590
93PirHil-10
93PirNatI-22
93Sco-350
93Sel-299
93StaClu-241
93StaCluFDI-241
93StaCluMOP-241
93Top-244
93TopGol-244
93TopInaM-244
93TopMic-244
93Ult-454
93UppDec-415
93UppDecGold-415
94ColC-562
94ColChoGS-562
94ColChoSS-562
94ExtBas-350
94Fin-195
94FinRef-195
94Fla-425
94Fle-616
94Pac-504
94PirQui-19
94StaClu-232
94StaCluFDI-232
94StaCluGR-232
94StaCluMOP-232
94Top-129
94TopGol-129
94TopSpa-129
95BowBes-R7
95BowBesR-R7
95ClaPhoC-45
95ColCho-388
95ColChoGS-388
95ColChoSS-388
95Don-111
95DonPreP-111
95DonTopotO-322
95Emo-178
95Fla-188
95Fle-486
95Lea-400
95Pac-349
95PirFil-23
95Sco-513
95ScoGolR-513
95ScoPlaTS-513
95SP-94
95SPCha-80
95SPChaDC-80
95SPSil-94
95StaClu-474
95StaCluMOP-474
95StaCluSTWS-474
95StaCluVR-260
95Top-445
95TopCyb-241
95Ult-425
95UltGolM-425
95UppDec-386
95UppDecED-386
95UppDecEDG-386
96Baz-29
96ColCho-266
96ColChoGS-266
96ColChoSS-266
96Don-501
96DonPreP-501
96EmoXL-260
96Fin-B63
96FinRef-B63
96Fla-353
96Fle-530
96FleTif-530
96Lea-96
96LeaPrePB-96
96LeaPrePG-96
96LeaPrePS-96
96LeaSigA-166
96LeaSigAG-166
96LeaSigAS-166
96MetUni-220
96MetUniP-220
96Pac-178
96PanSti-72
96Pin-220
96PinAfi-130
96PinAfiAP-130
96PinArtP-120
96PinFoil-220
96PinSta-120
96ProSta-95
96Sco-168
96Sel-99
96SelArtP-99
96SelTeaN-3
96SP-146
96StaClu-242
96StaCluMOP-242
95StaCluVRMC-260
96Stu-119
96StuPrePB-119
96StuPrePG-119
96StuPrePS-119
96TeaOut-58
96Top-421
96TopGal-42
96TopGalPPI-42
96Ult-269
96UltGolM-269
96UppDec-177
97Cir-304
97CirRav-304
97ColCho-36
97Don-20
97DonLim-34
97DonLimLE-34
97DonPreP-20
97DonPrePGold-20
97DonTea-17
97DonTeaSPE-17
97Fin-80
97FinRef-80
97FlaSho-A132
97FlaSho-B132
97FlaSho-C132
97FlaShoLC-132
97FlaShoLC-B132
97FlaShoLC-C132
97FlaShoLCM-A132
97FlaShoLCM-B132
97FlaShoLCM-C132
97Fle-266
97FleTif-266
97Lea-282
97LeaFraM-282

97LeaFraMDC-282
97NewPin-83
97NewPin-187
97NewPinAP-83
97NewPinAP-187
97NewPinMC-83
97NewPinMC-187
97NewPinPP-83
97NewPinPP-187
97Pac-242
97PacLigB-242
97PacSil-242
97Sco-397
97ScoHobR-397
97ScoResC-397
97ScoShoS-397
97ScoShoSAP-397
97StaClu-246
97StaCluMat-246
97StaCluMOP-246
97Top-445
97TopChr-157
97TopChrR-157
97TopSta-98
97TopStaAM-98
97Ult-265
97Ult-319
97UltGolME-265
97UltGolME-319
97UltPlaME-265
97UltPlaME-319
97UppDec-303
Neal, Billy
96VerBeaDB-21
Neal, Bob
80PenPilBT-25
80PenPilCT-9
88AubAstP-1964
89AubAstP-2178
Neal, Bryan
82DurBulT-6
83DurBulT-10
Neal, Charlie (Charles Lenard)
47Exh-165
55Bow-278
56Dod-19
56Top-299
57Top-242
58DodJayP-8
58Hir-54
58Top-16
59DodMor-8
59DodTeal-18
59Top-427
60DodJayP-10
60DodMor-8
60DodPos-7
60DodTeal-13
60DodUniO-13
60Top-155
60Top-385
60Top-386
60Top-556
60TopTat-40
60TopVen-155
61DodBelB-43
61DodJayP-7
61DodUniO-14
61Pos-157A
61Pos-157B
61Top-423
62Jel-102
62MetJayP-9
62Pos-102
62PosCan-102
62SalPlaC-102A
62SalPlaC-102B
62ShiPlaC-102
62Top-365
63BasMagM-62
63ExhStaB-49
63Jel-195
63MetJayP-8
63Pos-195
63Top-511
64Top-436
74MetOriEB-12
81TCM60I-482
82MetGal62-3
89DodSmoG-66
90DodTar-567
91MetWIZ-293
91RinPosBD4-4
94UppDecAH-64
94UppDecAH1-64
95TopArcBD-139
95TopArcBD-163
Neal, Dave
88BenBucL-19
89PalSprACLC-49
89PalSprAP-474
90QuaCitAGS-5
Neal, Edwin
80ChaO'sP-13
80ChaO'sW-14
Neal, Len
57SeaPop-26
Neal, Mike
92LSUTigM-7
93LSUTigM-8
93WatIndC-19
93WatIndF-3570
94ExcFirYPF-5
94ExcFS7-46
94KinIndC-14
94KinIndF-2652
94LSUTigMP-11
94Top-158
94TopGol-158
94TopSpa-158
96CanIndB-19
Neal, Rob
96BoiHawB-21
Neal, Scott
85PriWilPT-2
86HawIsIP-18
87HarSenP-9
Neal, Willie
81ChaRoyT-25
82ChaRoyT-22
Neale, Greasy (Alfred Earle)
16ColE13-126
17HolBreD-73
19W514-6
20NatCarE-66
20RedWorCP-14
21E121So1-70
21Exh-117
22E120-176
22W575-90
23W501-51
23WilChoV-111
81ConTSN-29
88ConSer4-20
88PacEigMO-88
92ConTSN-401
94ConTSN-1028
94ConTSNB-1028
Nealeigh, Rod
83MemChiT-13
Nebraska, David
89BurIndS-18
Necciai, Ron
77FriOneYW-9
93UppDecAH-101
94UppDecAH-203
94UppDecAH1-203
Nedeau, John
93BoiHawC-21
93BoiHawF-3914
Nedin, Tim
89EliTwiS-23
89Sta-152
90Bes-306
90KenTwiB-22
90KenTwiP-2291
90KenTwiS-16
91Cla/Bes-185
91VisOakC-7
92Ft.MyeMCB-14
Nee, John
11T205-195
Needham, Kevin
96BilMusTI-23
Needham, Tom (Thomas J.)
09MaxPubP-20
09T206-265
10CouT21-202
10DomDisP-92
10JuJuDE-31
10SweCapPP-85
11BasBatEU-30
11S74Sil-65
11SpoLifCW-267
11SpoLifM-175
11T205-128
12HasTriFT-53
12T207-138
14PieStaT-45
15VicT21-22
Needle, Chad
96StCatSB-21
Neel, Troy
88MidLeaAGS-21
88WatIndP-681
89CanIndB-25
89CanIndP-1324
89CanIndS-17
89EasLeaAP-7
89EasLeaDDP-DD37
89Sta-155
90CMC-469
90ColSprSSC-17
90ColSprSSP-45
90ProAAAF-226
91HunStaTI-14
91LinDriAAA-543
91TacTigLD-543
91TacTigP-2318
92DonRoo-85
92FleUpd-50
92SkyAAAF-241
92TacTigF-2517
92TacTigS-541
93AthMot-15
93Bow-541
93Don-308
93FleFinE-259
93FleMajLP-A18
93LeaGolR-R9
93OPCPre-85
93PacSpa-571
93Pin-246
93Sco-326
93ScoBoyoS-6
93SelRoo-68T
93StaClu-429
93StaCluAt-28
93StaCluFDI-429
93StaCluMOP-429
93TacTigF-3048
93Top-807
93TopGol-807
93TopInaM-807
93TopMic-807
93Ult-260
93UppDec-767
93UppDecGold-767
94A'sMot-15
94Bow-464
94ColC-215
94ColChoGS-215
94ColChoSS-215
94Don-520
94ExtBas-154
94ExtBasSYS-14
94Fin-13
94FinJum-13
94FinRef-13
94Fla-95
94Fle-270
94FleRooS-13
94Lea-6
94LeaL-62
94OPC-249
94Pac-459
94PanSti-111
94Pin-150
94PinArtP-150
94PinMusC-150
94Sco-248
94ScoGolR-248
94Sel-68
94StaClu-40
94StaCluFDI-40
94StaCluGR-40
94StaCluMOP-40
94Stu-5
94Top-493
94TopGol-493
94TopSpa-493
94TriPla-6
94Ult-112
94UppDec-391
94UppDecED-391
94USPlaCR-11H
94USPlaCR-12C
95Baz-29
95ColCho-123
95Don-112
95DonPreP-112
95Fle-250
95Lea-106
95Pac-317
95Pin-81
95PinArtP-81
95PinMusC-81
95Sco-469
95ScoGolR-469
95ScoPlaTS-469
95StaClu-277
95StaCluMOP-277
95StaCluSTWS-277
95StaCluVR-141
95Top-157
95TopCyb-94
95Ult-95
95UltGolM-95
95StaCluVRMC-141
Neely, Jeff
89AugPirP-495
89SouAtlLAGS-7
91BufBisLD-40
91BufBisP-539
91LinDriAAA-40
Neeman, Cal (Calvin A.)
57Top-353
58Top-33A
58Top-33B
59Top-367
60Top-337
79TCM50-142
Neese, Joshua
93NiaFalRF-3384
94ExcFirYPF-10
94ExcFS7-58
Neff, Marty
91WelPirC-16
91WelPirP-3588
92AugPirC-16
92AugPirF-253
93Bow-274
93ClaFS7-287
93ClaGolF-179
93SalBucC-18
93SalBucF-446
93SouAtlLAPI-27
Neff, Paul
85FreGiaP-28
Nega, Chris
93DunBluJC-30
Negray, Ron
56Top-7
56TopPin-20
57Top-254
60MapLeaSF-15
61MapLeaBH-15
90DodTar-568
Negrette, Richard
95LinVen-140
95WatIndTI-22
96BurIndB-8
Negron, Miguel
80LynSaiT-10
83ChaLooT-10
Nehf, Art N.
16ColE13-127
16FleBreD-70
17HolBreD-74
20GasAmeMBD-30
20NatCarE-67
21E121So1-71
21E121So8-67
21Exh-118
21KoBreWSI-17
21Nei-93
22E120-189
22W572-70
22W575-91
22WilPatV-41
23W501-70
23W501-119
23W503-12
23W515-22
25Exh-37
27AmeCarE-59
28W502-43
28Yue-43
61Fle-65
75FlePio-28
76ISCHooHA-11
92ConTSN-492
94ConTSN-1246
94ConTSNB-1246
20W516-17
Nehf, Robert
20NatCarE-67
Neibauer, Gary
69Top-611
70OPC-384
70Top-384
71OPC-668
71RicBraTI-15
71Top-668
72OPC-149
72Top-149
Neidinger, Joe
89BriTigS-18
91FayGenC-6
91FayGenP-1166
Neidlinger, Jim
85PriWilPT-10
86NasPirP-19
87HarSenP-20
88HarSenP-842
89AlbDukC-9
89AlbDukP-71
90AlbDukC-10
90AlbDukP-343
90AlbDukT-23
90CMC-412
90DodPol-39
90ProAAAF-64
91AlbDukLD-16
91AlbDukP-1139
91Cla1-T53
91DodPol-31
91Don-713
91Fle-215
91LinDriAAA-16
91OPC-392
91Sco-794
91Top-39
91TopDeb90-115
91TopDesS-39
91TopMic-39
91TopTif-39
91UppDec-632
92AlbDukF-718
92AlbDukS-18
93PorBeaF-2382
94LouRedF-2980
Neier, Chris
93BenRocC-19
93BenRocF-3266
94AshTouC-18
94AshTouF-1778
95NewHavRTI-28
96NewHavRB-19
Neiger, Al
61Top-202
89ChaLooLITI-20
Neighbors, Bob
95ConTSN-1345
Neill, Mike
91Cla/Bes-415
91FroRowDP-9
91FroRowDPP-2
91SouOreAC-15
91SouOreAP-3864
92Bow-266
92CalLeaACL-4
92ProFS7-135
92RenSilSCLC-35
92StaCluD-129
92UppDecML-26
92UppDecML-52
92UppDecML-273
93Bow-217
93ClaFS7-227
93StaCluAt-30
93UppDec-424
93UppDecGold-424
94SigRoo-20
94SigRooS-20
95ModA'sTI-20
96ModA'sB-23
Neill, Scott
89WatIndS-16
90KinIndTI-24
91CarLeaAP-CAR18
91KinIndC-9
91KinIndP-321
Neilson, Mike
92WatIndC-11
92WatIndF-3231
93WatIndC-20

93WatIndF-3559
Neiper, Jim
80VenLeaS-167
Neis, Bernie (Bernard E.)
20NatCarE-68
26Exh-6
27Exh-44
90DodTar-569
Neisen, Gertrude
48BabRutS-7
Neitzel, R.A.
90BatCliP-3073
91ClePhiC-19
91ClePhiP-1630
92ReaPhiF-581
92ReaPhiS-536
Nelloms, Skip
88OneYanP-2048
89Ft.LauYS-18
90Ft.LauYS-13
Nelson, Andre
92HunCubC-5
92HunCubF-3163
Nelson, Battling
11TurRedT-57
Nelson, Bob (Robert S.)
56Top-169
91OriCro-325
Nelson, Brian
90NiaFalRP-22
91BriTigC-22
91BriTigP-3600
96EveAquB-16
Nelson, Bryant
94AubAstC-8
94AubAstF-3766
94QuaCitRBC-14
94QuaCitRBF-543
96BesAutS-65
96Bow-279
96KisCobB-19
Nelson, Byron
40WheM4-7A
40WheM4-7B
40WheM4-7C
41WheM5-17
74NewYorNTDiS-2
Nelson, Charlie
92Min-15
93BazTeaU-5
93TopTra-57T
94YakBeaC-10
94YakBeaF-3863
95VerBeaDTI-17
Nelson, Chester
77NewCoPT-24
Nelson, Chris
96MidLeaAB-58
96WesMicWB-18
Nelson, Darren
87EriCarP-25
88St.PetCS-19
Nelson, Dave (David Earl)
69MilBra-199
69Top-579
70OPC-112
70Top-112
71MLBOffS-547
71OPC-241
71SenTeaIW-18
71Top-241
72Top-529
73LinPor-179
73OPC-111
73Top-111
74GreHeroBP-5
74OPC-355
74Top-355
74TopDecE-4
74TopSta-238
75OPC-435
75ShrCapT-13
75SSP42-18
75Top-435
76OPC-535
76ShrCapT-10
76SSP-273
76Top-535
78Roy-15
84WhiSoxTV-8
92IndFanC-30
93IndWUA-33
93RanKee-30
94RanAllP-1
Nelson, Doug
75ShrCapT-14
76ShrCapT-4
77ColCliT-14
77ShrCapT-15
Nelson, Doug P.
87EugEmeP-2657
88AppFoxP-141
89BasCitRS-19
90MemChiB-24
90MemChiP-1004
90MemChiS-21
Nelson, Earl
93IdaFalBF-4027
93IdaFalBSP-5
Nelson, Eric
89WelPirP-19
Nelson, Frank
47SunBre-13
49RemBre-19
50RemBre-18
Nelson, Gene
79AshTouT-28
81TopTra-809
82Don-513
82Fle-45
82Top-373
82TopTra-80T
83Don-55
83Top-106
85Don-615
85Fle-522
85TopTifT-86T
85TopTra-86T
85WhiSoxC-30
86Don-501
86Fle-213
86Lea-245
86Top-493
86TopTif-493
86WhiSoxC-30
87Don-580
87Fle-504
87FleGlo-504
87FleUpd-86
87FleUpdG-86
87Top-273
87TopTif-273
87TopTra-84T
87TopTraT-84T
88A'sMot-25
88Don-133
88DonTeaBA-133
88Fle-288
88FleGlo-288
88Sco-588
88ScoGlo-588
88Top-621
88TopTif-621
89A'sMot-26
89Bow-185
89BowTif-185
89Don-540
89Fle-18
89FleGlo-18
89OPC-318
89Sco-434
89Top-581
89TopTif-581
89UppDec-643
89Woo-16
90A'sMot-22
90Don-540
90Fle-17
90FleCan-17
90Lea-477
90OPC-726
90Sco-441
90Top-726
90TopTif-726
90UppDec-80
90VenSti-363
91A'sMot-22
91A'sSFE-10
91Don-385
91Fle-19
91Lea-328
91OPC-316
91Sco-478
91StaClu-359
91Top-316
91TopDesS-316
91TopMic-316
91TopTif-316
91UppDec-403
92AthMot-22
92Don-696
92Fle-264
92OPC-62
92Pin-443
92Sco-383
92StaClu-414
92Top-62
92TopGol-62
92TopGolW-62
92TopMic-62
92Ult-426
92UppDec-508
92YanWIZ8-131
93AngMot-17
93FleFinE-186
93RanKee-416
93StaCluAn-22
94Sco-274
94ScoGolR-274
Nelson, Jackson
87BucN28-61
87OldJudN-372
90KalBatN-42
Nelson, Jamie
83SalLakCGT-16
84Nes792-166
84Top-166
84TopTif-166
84VanCanC-43
85VanCanC-221
87MemChiB-26
87MemChiP-8
88ColCliC-12
88ColCliP-23
88ColCliP-305
89EdmTraC-19
89EdmTraP-569
90CMC-565
90PorBeaC-13
90PorBeaP-180
90ProAAAF-250
Nelson, Jeff
86BakDodP-22
87SalSpuP-27
88SanBerSB-23
88SanBerSCLC-48
89WilBilP-637
89WilBilS-15
90WilBilB-17
90WilBilP-1056
90WilBilS-18
91JacSunLD-339
91JacSunP-147
91LinDriAA-339
92Don-408
92FleUpd-57
92MarMot-19
93Don-685
93Fle-311
93MarMot-19
93Sco-272
93StaClu-467
93StaCluFDI-467
93StaCluMOP-467
93Top-493
93TopGol-493
93TopInaM-493
93TopMic-493
94ColC-609
94ColChoGS-609
94ColChoSS-609
94Don-492
94Fle-296
94HelBreSP-29
94MarMot-25
94Pac-578
94Sco-302
94ScoGolR-302
94Top-24
94TopGol-24
94TopSpa-24
95Don-438
95DonPreP-438
95Fla-84
95FleUpd-76
95MarMot-25
95MarPac-37
95Top-564
95TopCyb-340
96BelSnaTI-24
96Don-108
96DonPreP-108
96Fle-191
96FleTif-191
96FleUpd-U65
96FleUpdTC-U65
96LeaSigEA-140
96Ult-391
96UltGolM-391
97Fle-173
97FleTif-173
97PacPriGotD-GD75
Nelson, Jerome
86ModA'sC-16
86ModA'sP-20
87ModA'sC-12
87ModA'sP-5
88HunStaTI-13
89ChaLooB-23
89ChaLooGS-19
90ChaLooGS-23
91RicBraBC-31
92HarSenF-472
Nelson, Jim
81LynSaiT-13
82LynSaiT-9
Nelson, Jim (James Lorin)
71OPC-298
71Top-298
Nelson, Joe
96EugEmeB-16
Nelson, Kim
79WisRapTT-11
Nelson, Lindsey
89RinPosM1-34
95TenVolW-14
Nelson, Lynn (Lynn B.)
34DiaMatCSB-140
34Gou-60
39PlaBal-118
40PlaBal-135
Nelson, Mel
60DarFar-11
61UniOil-P10
63Top-522
64Top-273
64TopVen-273
65Top-564
66Top-367
66TopVen-367
69OPC-181
69Top-181
69TopFou-11
81TCM60I-346
Nelson, Michael
89PeoChiTI-34
90PeoChiTI-3
91PeoChiTI-30
Nelson, Pat
78AshTouT-20
79AshTouT-19
Nelson, Red (Albert)
09ColChiE-213A
09ColChiE-213B
12ColRedB-213A
12ColRedB-213B
12ColTinT-213A
12ColTinT-213B
12T207-139
Nelson, Rick
84Don-636
84Fle-615
84Nes792-672
84Top-672
84TopSti-347
84TopTif-672
85CalCanC-91
85EveGiaC-11A
85EveGiaC-11B
85Top-296
85TopTif-296
86CalCanP-18
86CliGiaP-16
87TidTidP-16
88ShrCapP-1294
90ShrCapP-1455
90ShrCapS-16
Nelson, Rob
83IdaFalAT-22
84MadMusP-11
85HunStaJ-41
86TacTigP-15
87Don-595
87DonOpeD-25
87Fle-653
87FleGlo-653
87SpoTeaP-23
88Don-574
88LasVegSC-16
88LasVegSP-237
89LasVegSC-16
89LasVegSP-24
90Bow-213
90BowTif-213
90UppDec-51
91LinDriAAA-642
91VanCanLD-642
91VanCanP-1604
92PorBeaS-415
Nelson, Rocky (Glenn Richard)
52Par-61
52Top-390
53ExhCan-49
54Top-199
59Top-446
60KeyChal-37
60Lea-127
60Top-157
60TopVen-157
61Kah-29
61Pos-137
61Raw-8
61Top-304
61TopStal-68
82OhiHaloF-59
83TopRep5-390
90DodTar-570
94TopArc1-199
94TopArc1G-199
95TopArcBD-30
Nelson, Rod
79CliDodT-20
Nelson, Rodney
95SprSulTI-18
Nelson, Roger
68Top-549
69MLBOffS-61
69RoySol-11
69RoyTeal-9
69Top-279
69TopSta-186
69TopSup-23
69TopTeaP-7
70MLBOffS-225
70Top-633
71OPC-581
71Top-581
73OPC-251
73Top-251
74OPC-491
74Top-491
75OPC-572
75Top-572
75TucTorC-20
75TucTorTI-13
76OmaRoyTT-16
78ColCliT-17
81TCM60I-396
91OriCro-326
Nelson, Ron
87SpaPhiP-12
Nelson, Scott
88CliGiaP-698
89SalSpuCLC-127
89SalSpuP-1824
Nelson, Spike
49EurSta-192
Nelson, Tom (Thomas C.)
47SunBre-14
Nelson, Tracie
96BelSnaTI-25
Nelson, Travion
92GulCoaYF-3704
Nelson, Tray
92HigSchPLS-21
94OneYanC-16
94OneYanF-3804
Nemeth, Carey
86EriCarP-20
87SavCarP-16
Nemeth, Joe
79WauTimT-9
80AshTouT-12
81TulDriT-11
82ReaPhiT-17
82TulDriT-24
83TulDriT-19
Nen, Dick (Richard LeRoy)
64Top-14
64TopVen-14

65Top-466
66OPC-149
66Top-149
66TopVen-149
67CokCapS-11
67DexPre-151
67Top-403
68Top-591
69MilBra-200
90DodTar-571
Nen, Robb
88ButCopKSP-5
88GasRanP-1003
89GasRanP-1003
89GasRanS-16
89Sta-139
90Bow-487
90BowTif-487
90ChaRanS-15
91Bow-270
91Cla/Bes-240
91LinDriAA-589
91TulDriLD-589
91TulDriP-2769
91TulDriTI-20
92ClaFS7-288
92SkyAA F-271
92TulDriF-2692
92TulDriS-612
92UppDecML-84
93FleFinE-281
93MarPub-18
93PacSpa-643
93Pin-586
93RanKee-417
93StaCluR-24
93Ult-633
93UppDec-687
93UppDecGold-687
94ColC-604
94ColChoGS-604
94ColChoSS-604
94Don-625
94FleUpd-138
94Lea-212
94Pin-279
94PinArtP-279
94PinMusC-279
94StaClu-45
94StaCluFDI-45
94StaCluGR-45
94StaCluMOP-45
94StaCluT-80
94StaCluTFDI-80
94Top-284
94TopGol-284
94TopSpa-284
95ColCho-308
95ColChoGS-308
95ColChoSS-308
95Don-149
95DonPreP-149
95DonTopotO-245
95Fin-206
95FinRef-206
95Fla-140
95Fle-338
95FleTeaL-19
95Lea-170
95Pac-174
95Pin-439
95PinArtP-439
95PinMusC-439
95Sco-187
95ScoGolR-187
95ScoPlaTS-187
95StaClu-159
95StaCluFDI-159
95StaCluMOP-159
95StaCluSTWS-159
95StaCluVR-84
95Top-528
95TopCyb-313
95Ult-382
95UltGolM-382
95UppDec-114
95UppDecED-114
95UppDecEDG-114
96ColCho-151
96ColChoGS-151
96ColChoSS-151
96Don-159
96DonPreP-159
96Fla-265
96Fle-390
96FleTif-390
96LeaSigA-167
96LeaSigAG-167
96LeaSigAS-167
96Pac-68
96Sco-486
96StaClu-161
96StaCluEPB-161
96StaCluEPG-161
96StaCluEPS-161
96StaCluMOP-161
95StaCluVRMC-84
96Top-69
96Ult-202
96UltGolM-202
96UppDec-337
97Bow-17
97BowChr-13
97BowChrI-13
97BowChrIR-13
97BowChrR-13
97BowInt-17
97Cir-151
97CirRav-151
97ColCho-117
97Don-307
97DonPreP-307
97DonPrePGold-307
97Fin-242
97FinRef-242
97Fle-333
97FleTif-333
97Lea-258
97LeaFraM-258
97LeaFraMDC-258
97MetUni-177
97NewPin-26
97NewPinAP-26
97NewPinMC-26
97NewPinPP-26
97Pac-303
97PacLigB-303
97PacSil-303
97PinCer-60
97PinCerMBlu-60
97PinCerMG-60
97PinCerMR-60
97PinCerR-60
97PinTotCPB-60
97PinTotCPG-60
97PinTotCPR-60
97Sco-266
97ScoPreS-266
97ScoShoS-266
97ScoShoSAP-266
97StaClu-321
97StaCluMOP-321
97Top-79
97TopChr-29
97TopChrR-29
97TopGal-120
97TopGalPPI-120
97Ult-200
97UltGolME-200
97UltPlaME-200
97UppDec-361
Nenad, David
82CliGiaF-9
Neneviller, Tom
93ClaFS7-230
Nerat, Dan
91SouOreAC-27
91SouOreAP-3841
92ModA'sF-3897
Neri, Frank
52LavPro-4
Nerone, Phil
75AppFoxT-20
76AppFoxT-16
Nesmoe, Davey
80QuaCitCT-31
Nestor, Don
94BoiHawC-20
94BoiHawF-3352
Nettles, Dru
93Sou-14
Nettles, Graig
69OPC-99
69Top-99A
69Top-99B
70Ind-9
70OPC-491
70Top-491
71MLBOffS-380
71OPC-324
71Top-324
72Top-590
73LinPor-134
73NewYorN-12
73OPC-498
73SyrChiTI-21
73Top-498
73Yan-4
74OPC-251
74SyrChiTI-20
74Top-251
74TopSta-217
75Hos-24
75HosTwi-24
75OPC-160
75SyrChiTI-14
75Top-160
75YanSSP-20
76Hos-81
76OPC-169
76SSP-437
76Top-169
77BurCheD-174
77Hos-116
77OPC-2
77OPC-217
77Top-2
77Top-20
77YanBurK-15
78Hos-132
78OPC-10
78RCColC-88
78SSP270-25
78Top-250
78WifBalD-54
78YanBurK-14
78YanSSPD-25
79Hos-110
79OPC-240
79Top-460
79YanBurK-15
79YanPicA-28
80Kel-18
80OPC-359
80Top-710
80TopSup-21
81AllGamPI-36
81Don-105
81Fle-87A
81Fle-87B
81FleStiC-72
81OPC-365
81Top-365
81TopSupHT-69
82Don-335
82Dra-26
82Fle-46
82FleSta-119
82FleSta-238
82LouSlu-4
82OPC-21
82OPC-62
82Top-505
82Top-506
82TopSti-215
82TopStiV-215
83AllGamPI-36
83Don-83
83Fle-391
83FleSta-137
83FleSti-38
83OPC-207
83OPC-293
83Top-635
83Top-636
83TopFol-2
83TopSti-13
83YanRoyRD-7
84AllGamPI-33
84Don-518
84DonCha-12
84Fle-135
84FleUpd-82
84FunFooP-66
84Nes792-175
84Nes792-712
84Nes792-713
84OCoandSI-196
84OPC-175
84PadMot-22
84Top-175
84Top-712
84Top-713
84TopSti-326
84TopTif-175
84TopTif-712
84TopTif-713
84TopTra-83T
84TopTraT-83T
85AllGamPI-123
85Don-234
85Fle-42
85Lea-177
85OPC-35
85PadMot-4
85Top-35
85TopSti-155
85TopTif-35
86Don-478
86DonAll-6
86DonPop-6
86Fle-332
86GenMilB-5E
86OPC-151
86SevCoi-W11
86Spo-91
86Top-450
86TopGloA-15
86TopSti-106
86TopSti-151
86TopTat-7
86TopTif-450
87BraSmo-15
87Fle-426
87FleGlo-426
87OPC-205
87RedFolSB-87
87Top-205
87TopTif-205
87TopTra-85T
87TopTraT-85T
88AlaGolAA'TI-4
88ExpPos-14
88SanDieSAAG-13
88Sco-440
88ScoGlo-440
88ScoRoo-25T
88ScoRooG-25T
88Top-574
88TopTif-574
89PacSenL-115
89PacSenL-132
89PacSenL-158
89SanDieSAG-12
89Sco-277
89T/MSenL-82
89TopSenL-25
90EliSenL-43
91FouBal-25
91LinDri-26
91SweBasG-67
92KodCelD-3
92MCIAmb-6
92MVP-7
92MVP2H-19
92YanWIZ7-122
92YanWIZA-53
93ActPacA-162
93MCIAmb-13
93TedWil-68
93UppDecS-11
93UppDecS-13
93Yoo-13
94UppDecAH-148
94UppDecAH1-148
95PadMot-28
95SonGre-10
Nettles, Jim (James W.)
71OPC-74
71Top-74
72OPC-131
72Top-131
73TacTwiC-16
73OPC-358
73Top-358
75OPC-497
75Top-497
77ColCliT-15
80ColCliP-28
80ColCliT-12
81TacTigT-12
82TacTigT-17
83IdaFalAT-30
83TacTigT-20
84IdaFalATI-18
85MadMusP-20
85MadMusT-23
86MadMusP-24
86MadMusP-15
87MadMusP-22
87MadMusP-4
88MadMusP-16
88SanDieSAAG-14
89MadMusS-17
89PacSenL-126A
89PacSenL-126B
89SanDieSAG-13
90EliSenL-44
90PenPilS-25
91JacSunLD-349
91JacSunP-166
91LinDriAA-349
92MedHatBJF-3222
92MedHatBJSP-29
93HagSunC-25
93HagSunF-1895
94DunBluJC-27
94DunBluJF-2572
95DunBluJTI-16
Nettles, Morris
74SalLakCAC-95
75OPC-632
75Top-632
76OPC-434
76SSP-202
76Top-434
76TopTra-434T
Nettles, Robert
86EriCarP-21
Nettnin, Rodney
91MiaMirC-3
Neubart, Garrett
96AshTouB-27
97Bow-361
97BowInt-361
Neuendorff, Tony
83DurBulT-11
84DurBulT-16
Neuenschwander, Doug
80WatRedT-4
81WatRedT-5
Neufang, Gerry
82TulDriT-20
83TulDriT-23
Neun, Johnny
76TayBow4-75
91ConTSN-204
Neuzil, Jeff
84MemChiT-10
Nevers, Ernie
92ConTSN-394
Nevers, Tom
90AshTouC-16
90ClaDraP-21
91AshTouP-577
91Bow-542
91Cla/Bes-201
91Sco-387
91SouAtlLAGP-SAL2
92Bow-226
92ClaFS7-208
92OscAstC-1
92OscAstF-2539
92ProFS7-234
92UppDec-53
92UppDecML-250
93Bow-68
93ClaFS7-228
93ClaGolF-67
93ExcFS7-49
93JacGenF-2116
94JacGenF-225
95JacGenTI-24
96HarCitRCB-22
Nevill, Glenn
91BatCliC-19
91BatCliP-3482
92BatCliC-14
92BatCliF-3262
Neville, Dan
65Top-398
Neville, David
89BenBucL-13
Neville, Eddie
94CarLeaA-DJ31
Neville, Frank
92BluOriC-25
93BluOriC-27
Nevin, Phil
91TopGolS-3

91TopTra-83T
91TopTraT-83T
92Bow-670
92ClaDraP-1
92ClaDraPFB-BC1
92ClaDraPP-BB1
92ClaDraPP-2
92DEL-BB1
92StaCluD-130
92StaCluFDP-3
92TopTra-82T
92TopTraG-82T
93ClaFS7-AU6
93ClaYouG-YG15
93StaCluM-83
93TucTorF-3069
94ActPac-14
94ActPac-61
94ActPac2G-7G
94Cla-90
94ClaCreotC-C20
94ClaGolA-SH4
94ClaGolF-16
94ExcFS7-207
94SigRoo-37
94SigRooFCS-AU9
94SigRooHP-S8
94SigRooS-37
94TucTorF-771
94UppDecML-156
94UppDecML-230
94UppDecMLT1PJF-TP6
94UppDecMLT1PMF-6
95ActPacF-14
95AstMot-13
95ColCho-9
95ColChoGS-9
95ColChoSS-9
95Fin-295
95FinRef-295
95SP-62
95SPCha-51
95SPChaDC-51
95SPSil-62
95StaCluCB-CB4
95StaCluMOP-CB4
95TusTorTI-18
95UppDecML-22
96ColCho-548
96ColChoGS-548
96ColChoSS-548
96Don-506
96DonPreP-506
96Fin-B138
96FinRef-B138
96JacSunB-22
96Pac-311
96Pin-172
96PinAfi-119
96PinAfiAP-119
96PinArtP-98
96PinSta-98
96ProSta-122
96Sco-465
96SelTeaN-13
96Spo-50
96SpoArtP-50
96StaClu-60
96StaCluMOP-60
96Top-348
96UppDec-69
97Cir-289
97CirRav-289
97ColCho-103
97Fle-102
97FleTif-102
97Pac-92
97PacLigB-92
97PacSil-92
97Sco-407
97ScoHobR-407
97ScoResC-407
97ScoShoS-407
97ScoShoSAP-407
97Top-369
97Ult-547
97UltGolME-547
97UltPlaME-547
95UppDecMLFS-22

Newberg, Tom
87SalSpuP-24
88VerMarP-955
90MarMot-28

Newby, Mike
90HamRedB-11
90HamRedS-17

Newcomb, Chris
92ButCopKSP-14

Newcomb, Joe Dean
89KnoBluJB-19
89KnoBluJP-1135
89KnoBluJS-15

Newcombe, Don (Donald)
47Exh-166A
47Exh-166B
47Exh-166C
47PM1StaP1-150
47PM1StaP1-151
47PM1StaP1-152
47PM1StaP1-153
47StaPinP2-30
49EurSta-45
50Bow-23
51Bow-6
51R42SmaS-74
52BerRos-46
52Bow-128
52StaCalL-79D
53Bri-38
53ExhCan-16
54Bow-154
54NewYorJA-12
54StaMey-10
55Bow-143
55DodGolS-2
55RobGouS-21
55RobGouW-21
55StaMey-9
56Dod-20
56Dod-21
56Top-235
56YelBasP-24
57Top-130
58DodJayP-9
58Hir-13
58Top-340
59DodVol-10
59RedEnq-15
59RedShiBS-14
59Top-312
60Kah-28
60Lea-19
60RawGloT-23
60RedJayP-6
60Top-345
60TopTat-41
61Top-483
75OPC-194
75Top-194
77GalGloG-17
79TCM50-182
86SpoDecG-39
87Dod195T-7
88PacLegI-33
88RinPosD1-3A
89DodSmoG-55
89SweBasG-122
90DodTar-572
90PacLeg-64
90SweBasG-76
91SweBasG-68
91TopArc1-320
92ActPacA-51
92BazQua5A-2
93MetIma-14
93TedWil-15
93TedWil-139
94UppDecAH-72
94UppDecAH1-72
95DodROY-2
95TopArcBD-36
95TopArcBD-62
95TopArcBD-88
95TopArcBD-129
95TopArcBD-158

Newcomer, Breen
77BriRedST-13

Newell, Brandon
93PitMetC-15
93PitMetF-3707
94CapCitBC-15
94CapCitBF-1749
95StLucMTI-24

Newell, Brett
94DanBraC-20
94DanBraF-3542
95MacBraTI-21
96GreBraB-22
96GreBraTI-15

Newell, Paul
93MisStaB-33

Newell, Tom
86ClePhiP-18
87MaiGuiP-20
87MaiGuiT-6
87PhiTas-50
88Don-604
88Fle-648
88FleGlo-648
88MaiPhiC-8
88MaiPhiP-293
90AlbYanB-4
90Ft.LauYS-14
91AlbYanLD-16
91AlbYanP-1005
91LinDriAA-16
96BurBeeTI-29

Newfield, Marc
90ClaDraP-6
90ClaYel-T89
91Bow-698
91CalLeLA-1
91Cla/Bes-4
91ClaGam-62
91ClaGolB-BC2
91ClaPro-1
91OPC-529
91SanBerSC-23
91SanBerSP-2000
91Sco-391
91Top-529
91TopDesS-529
91TopMic-529
91TopTif-529
91UppDecFE-18F
92Bow-406
92ClaFS7-142
92JacSunF-3722
92JacSunS-365
92ProFS7-144
92SkyAA F-157
92UppDec-51
92UppDec-64
92UppDecML-36
92UppDecML-263
93Bow-51
93Bow-372
93ClaFisN-7
93ClaYouG-YG16
93ExcFS7-229
93JacSunF-2722
93Lea-490
93SP-283
93StaCluMari-19
93UppDec-434
93UppDecGold-434
94ActPac-30
94Bow-417
94CalCanF-802
94Cla-95
94ColC-14
94ColChoGS-14
94ColChoSS-14
94Don-574
94FleMajLP-26
94FUnPac-173
94LeaLimR-67
94Pac-579
94Pin-250
94PinArtP-250
94PinMusC-250
94PinRooTP-8
94Sco-584
94ScoBoyoS-46
94ScoGolR-584
94ScoRoo-RT155
94ScoRooGR-RT155
94ScoRooSR-SU10
94Sel-377
94Spo-165
94StaClu-357
94StaCluFDI-357
94StaCluGR-357
94StaCluMOP-357
94Top-262
94TopGol-262
94TopSpa-262
94TriPla-295
94Ult-122
94UppDec-22
94UppDecED-22
95ActPac2GF-2G
95ActPacF-15
95ActPacF-63
95Bow-259
95BowBes-B80
95BowBesR-B80
95BowGolF-259
95ColCho-282
95ColChoGS-282
95ColChoSS-282
95Don-478
95DonPreP-478
95Emo-81
95Fin-320
95FinRef-320
95Pin-197
95PinArtP-197
95PinMusC-197
95Sco-587
95ScoAi-AM3
95ScoGolR-587
95ScoPlaTS-587
95Sel-45
95SelArtP-45
95SigRooOJ-26
95SigRooOJP-26
95SigRooOJPS-26
95SigRooOJS-26
95Spo-155
95SpoArtP-155
95StaClu-180
95StaCluFDI-180
95StaCluMOP-180
95StaCluSTWS-180
95TacRaiTI-13
95Ult-329
95UltGolM-329
95UppDec-113
95UppDecED-113
95UppDecEDG-113
96Cir-51
96CirRav-51
96ColCho-697
96ColChoGS-697
96ColChoSS-697
96Don-364
96DonPreP-364
96Fla-379
96Fle-574
96FleTif-574
96LeaLim-14
96LeaLimG-14
96LeaPre-9
96LeaPreP-9
96LeaSig-4
96LeaSigA-168
96LeaSigAG-168
96LeaSigAS-168
96LeaSigPPG-4
96LeaSigPPP-4
96Pac-191
96PadMot-14
96Pin-51
96PinAfi-131
96PinAfiAP-131
96Sco-349
96ScoDugC-B74
96ScoDugCAP-B74
96ScoFutF-14
96Sel-33
96SelArtP-33
96SelCer-15
96SelCerAP-15
96SelCerCB-15
96SelCerCR-15
96SelCerMB-15
96SelCerMG-15
96SelCerMR-15
96SelTeaN-22
96Spo-33
96SpoArtP-33
96StaClu-115
96StaCluMOP-115
96Sum-116
96SumAbo&B-116
96SumArtP-116
96SumFoi-116
96Ult-561
96UltGolM-561
96Zen-8
96ZenArtP-8
97Cir-318
97CirRav-318
97ColCho-373
97Don-13
97DonEli-92
97DonEliGS-92
97DonPreP-13
97DonPrePGold-13
97Fle-136
97FleTif-136
97Lea-95
97LeaFraM-95
97LeaFraMDC-95
97MetUni-68
97NewPin-86
97NewPinAP-86
97NewPinMC-86
97NewPinPP-86
97PacPriGotD-GD56
97Pin-22
97PinArtP-22
97PinIns-7
97PinInsCE-7
97PinInsDE-7
97PinMusC-22
97Sco-65
97ScoPreS-65
97ScoSnoS-65
97ScoShoSAP-65
97Sel-45
97SelArtP-45
97SelRegG-45
97Stu-142
97StuPrePG-142
97StuPrePS-142
97Top-436
97Ult-81
97UltGolME-81
97UltPlaME-81
97UppDec-407

Newhan, Dave
96ModA'sB-17

Newhauser, Don
74OPC-33
74Top-33

Newhouse, Andre
92AppFoxC-3
92AppFoxF-998
93RocRoyC-22
93RocRoyF-730
94SouBenSHC-14
94SouBenSHF-609
95PriWilCTI-3

Newhouser, Hal
39ExhSal-46
46SpoExcW-7-1B
47Exh-167
49Lea-98
51R42SmaS-73
52StaCalL-72B
52StaCalS-86A
53ExhCan-12
53Top-228
55Top-24
55TopDouH-109
60Fle-68
61Fle-66
61NuSco-446
72TopTes5-5
76TayBow4-33
77TCMTheWY-30
79DiaGre-395
80PerHaloFP-214
80TigGreT-8
81TigDetN-116
81TigSecNP-20
83DiaClaS2-87
83TCMPla1944-6
83TigAlKS-31
83TigAlKS-39
86SpoDecG-19
86TigSpoD-9
90HOFStiB-42
90PerGreM-81
91TopArc1-228
92BazQua5A-8
92ConTSN-445
92PhoFilHoF-2
93ActPacA-111
93ActPacA2-45G
93FroRowN-1
93FroRowN-2
93FroRowN-3
93FroRowN-4
93FroRowN-5
94ConTSN-1009
94ConTSNB-1009
94ConTSNCI-24

97TopStaHRR-9
97TopStaHRRA-9
Newkirk, Craig
90Bes-234
90GasRanB-22
90GasRanP-2529
90GasRanS-16
91ChaRanC-19
91ChaRanP-1323
92ChaRanC-6
92ChaRanF-2234
Newlin, Jim
90Bes-259
90CalLeaACLC-23
90SanBerSB-23
90SanBerSCLC-89
90SanBerSP-2630
91JacSunLD-340
91JacSunP-148
91LinDriAA-340
92CalCanF-3728
92CalCanS-72
92SkyAAAF-29
93JacSunF-2709
93LinVenB-216
94PorSeaDF-675
94PorSeaDTI-23
95BowBayTI-34
Newman, Al
84BeaGolGT-4
85ExpPos-13
85IndIndTI-14
86DonRoo-9
86ExpPos-9
86ExpProPa-18
86FleUpd-80
87Don-426
87Fle-327
87FleGlo-327
87OPC-323
87Top-323
87TopTif-323
87TopTra-86T
87TopTraT-86T
88BlaYNPRWL-94
88Don-645
88Fle-17
88FleGlo-17
88SanDieSAAG-15
88SanDieSAAG-16
88Sco-252
88ScoGlo-252
88StaLinTw-14
88Top-648
88TopTif-648
88TwiSmoC-11
88TwiTeal-17
89Bow-156
89BowTif-156
89Don-436
89Fle-122
89FleGlo-122
89SanDieSAG-14
89SanDieSAG-15
89Sco-493
89Top-503
89TopTif-503
89UppDec-197
90Bow-419
90BowTif-419
90Don-506
90Fle-382
90FleCan-382
90Lea-347
90OPC-19
90PanSti-110
90PubSti-334
90Sco-128
90Top-19
90TopBig-53
90TopSti-293
90TopTif-19
90UppDec-199
90VenSti-364
91Don-208
91Fle-621
91Lea-446
91OPC-748
91PanFreS-301
91Sco-424
91StaClu-146
91Top-748
91TopDesS-748
91TopMic-748
91TopTif-748
91Ult-193
91UppDec-413
91VisOakC-8
92Don-339
92Fle-214
92Lea-511
92OPC-146
92RanMot-25
92RanTeal-13
92Sco-357
92ScoRoo-49T
92StaClu-821
92Top-146
92TopGol-146
92TopGolW-146
92TopMic-146
92UppDec-293
93Fle-685
93RanKee-276
95ForMyeMTI-30
96HarCitRCB-2
Newman, Alan
90Bes-39
90KenTwiB-23
90KenTwiP-2202
90KenTwiS-17
90MidLeaASGS-17
90ProAaA-112
90StaFS7-56
91CalLeLA-13
92Bow-221
92ClaFS7-202
92OrlSunRS-514
92SkyAA F-222
92UppDecML-240
93Bow-129
93ClaFS7-229
93NasXprF-402
Newman, Bruce
93IdaFalBF-4046
93IdaFalBSP-19
94DanBraC-21
94DanBraF-3546
Newman, Damon
94SouOreAC-21
95WesMicWTI-19
Newman, Danny
88AshTouP-1071
Newman, Doug
91MisStaB-33
92MisStaB-30
Newman, Eric
95IdaFalBTI-30
96CliLumKTI-20
Newman, Fred
63Top-496
64Top-569
65OPC-101
65Top-101
66Top-213
66TopRubI-70
66TopVen-213
67CokCapDA-24
67Top-451
69Top-543
81TCM60I-374
Newman, Jeff
76TucTorCa-19
76TusTorCr-12
76VenLeaS-20
77Top-204
78Top-458
79OPC-319
79Top-604
80Kel-7
80OPC-18
80Top-34
81A'sGraG-5
81Don-477
81Fle-577
81Top-587
81TopSti-120
82A'sGraG-12
82Don-517
82Fle-102
82Top-187
83Don-635
83Fle-529
83Top-784
83TopTra-80T
84Don-249
84Fle-404
84Nes792-296
84Top-296
84TopTif-296
85Top-376
85TopTif-376
86A'sMot-27
87A'sMot-19
88ModA'sCLC-81
88ModA'sTI-1
89HunStaB-20
89SouLeaAJ-25
90HunStaB-24
91LinDriAAA-549
91TacTigLD-549
91TacTigP-2321
92IndFanC-30
93IndWUA-33
Newman, Mark
82ForMyeRT-20
Newman, Randy
83WauTimF-25
86CalCanP-19
Newman, Ray
72Top-667
73OPC-568
73Top-568
04BreMilB-58
Newman, Rob
92IdaFalGF-3519
92IdaFalGSP-17
Newman, Todd
87AubAstP-17
87BriYouC-2
Newman, Tom
89IdaFalBP-2036
90IdaFalBP-3243
90SumBraB-14
Newsom, Bobo (Louis Norman)
33ButCanV-37
35ExhFou-15
36ExhFou-16
36GouBWR-22
36GouWidPPR-A79
36GouWidPPR-C20
36NatChiFPR-61
36WheBB3-10
37ExhFou-16
37OPCBatUV-139
38ExhFou-15
39ExhSal-47
39ExhSal-48
39GouPreR303A-34
39WorWidGTP-34
41DouPlaR-51
43DodTeal-19
53Top-15
54OriEss-28
55OriEss-21
60Fle-70
61Fle-67
81TigDetN-64
83DiaClaS2-71
83TCMPla1942-21
88ChaLooLTI-24
90DodTar-573
91ConTSN-230
91TopArc1-15
92BazQua5A-10
92ConTSN-364
93ConTSN-760
93DiaStaES-148
Newsom, Gary
83VerBeaDT-19
85VerBeaDT-4
86AlbDukP-18
87DurBulP-9
Newsome, Dick
42RedSoxTI-17
43RedSoxTI-17
Newsome, Skeeter (Lamar A.)
36NatChiFPR-60
39PlaBal-84
42RedSoxTI-18
43RedSoxTI-18
76TayBow4-60
83TCMPla1945-18
Newson, Warren
86SpoIndC-174
88CalLeaACLC-45
88RivRedWCLC-225
88RivRedWP-1416
89TexLeaAGS-8
89WicChaR-2
89WicChaR-8
89WicChaR-12
89WicChaR-13
89WicStaR-2
89WicUpdR-7
89WicUpdR-17
89WicWraR-24
90CMC-518
90LasVegSC-15
90LasVegSP-136
90ProAAAF-24
91DonRoo-15
91FleUpd-14
91LinDriAAA-643
91UltUpd-17
91VanCanLD-643
91VanCanP-1608
92Don-668
92Fle-91
92OPC-355
92OPCPre-76
92Sco-398
92StaClu-512
92Top-355
92TopDeb91-133
92TopGol-355
92TopGolW-355
92TopMic-355
92UppDec-621
92WhiSoxK-24
93Don-463
93StaCluWS-7
94Fle-90
94StaCluT-138
94StaCluTFDI-138
94WhiSoxK-23
95ColCho-501
95ColChoGS-501
95ColChoSS-501
95MarPac-38
95Sco-547
95ScoGolR-547
95ScoPlaTS-547
95WhiSoxK-22
96LeaSigEA-141
96RanMot-15
97Sco-252
97ScoPreS-252
97ScoRan-15
97ScoRanPl-15
97ScoRanPr-15
97ScoShoS-252
97ScoShoSAP-252
Newstrom, Doug
93YakBeaC-18
93YakBeaF-3889
94ExcFirYPF-4
94ExcFS7-219
94FloStaLAF-FSL48
94VerBeaDC-12
94VerBeaDF-80
95SanBerSTI-13
96HigDesMB-21
Newton, Chris
94JamJamC-18
94JamJamF-3961
Newton, Doc (Eustace)
08RosComP-51
09RamT20-87
11SpoLifCW-268
90DodTar-574
Newton, Geronimo
94BelMarC-20
94BelMarF-3230
96PorCitRB-21
Newton, Kimani
96YakBeaTI-26
Newton, Marty
86EveGiaC-15
86EveGiaPC-19
Newton, Newt (Warren)
87ChaRaiP-16
Newton, Steve
87LitFalMP-2390
88LitFalMP-18
89ColMetB-18
89ColMetGS-17
90St.LucMS-18
91ChaRaiC-9
Nezelek, Andy
88GreBraB-19
89BlaYNPRWL-62
89Don-616
89RicBraBC-19
89RicBraC-6
89RicBraP-839
89RicBraTI-17
90Bow-3
90BowTif-3
90CMC-281
90Don-523A
90Don-523B
90ProAAAF-401
90RicBraBC-13
90RicBraC-5
90RicBraP-256
90RicBraTI-24
91RicBraBC-11
92GreBraS-242
93ClaGolF-19
Niarhos, Gus (Constantine)
48BluTin-25
48YanTeal-19
49Bow-181
50Bow-154
51Bow-124
52Bow-129
52Top-121
53RedSoxTI-21
53Top-63
83TopRep5-121
91TopArc1-63
Nicastro, Steve
79NewCoPT-2
Nice, Bill
80AndBraT-14
Nicely, Roy M.
48SomandK-24
49SomandK-13
Nicely, Tony
78ChaPirT-16
Nichioka, Tsuyoshi
91SalSpuC-18
Nicholas, Darrell
94HelBreF-3626
94HelBreSP-18
94SigRooBS-7
94StaCluDPFDI-49
96El PasDB-21
Nicholas, Franci
36GouWidPPR-D23
Nicholls, Simon B.
08AmeCarE-17
08RosComP-62
09BriE97-25
09RamT20-88
09T206-266
09T206-267
10NadE1-45
10W555-53
Nichols, Brian
88BilMusP-1819
89BilMusP-2043
90BilMusP-3224
90CedRapRP-2326
90ChaWheB-13
Nichols, Carl
83SanJosBC-20
85ChaO'sT-9
86ChaOriW-18
87RocRedWP-11
87RocRedWT-10
88Don-477
88DonRoo-39
88RocRedWGCP-18
89Fle-612
89FleGlo-612
89TriAAP-AAA45
89TucTorC-15
89TucTorJP-18
89TucTorP-185
90CMC-613
90ProAAAF-195
90TucTorC-11
90TucTorP-205
91AstMot-22
91Lea-217
91OPC-119
91OriCro-327
91StaClu-440
91Top-119
91TopDesS-119
91TopMic-119
91TopTif-119
Nichols, Chet
52Bow-120
52Top-288
53BraSpiaS7-9
54BraJohC-16

54BraSpiaSP-14
55Bow-72
55BraGolS-5
55BraJohC-17
55BraSpiaSD-13
56Top-278
61Top-301
62Top-403
63Top-307
83TopRep5-288
89BluOriS-30
90WauTimP-2144
90WauTimS-28
Nichols, Dolan
59Top-362A
59Top-362B
Nichols, Fred
74GasRanT-13
Nichols, Gary
88SprCarB-23
90CMC-125
90LouRedBC-25
Nichols, Howard
86ReaPhiP-19
87ReaPhiP-14
88PhiTas-27
88ReaPhiP-879
89IowCubC-18
89IowCubP-1712
Nichols, James
96AppLeaAB-7
96BriWhiSB-26
Nichols, Kevin
96MarPhiB-18
Nichols, Kid (Charles A.)
06FanCraNL-33
36PC7AlbHoF-58
50CalHOFW-56
61Fle-129
76ShaPiz-58
80PerHaloFP-58
80SSPHOF-58
86BraGreT-10
87OldJudN-373
94ConTSN-1012
94ConTSNB-1012
94OriofB-78
95May-24
98CamPepP-58
Nichols, Lance
82RocRedWT-20
83RocRedWT-1
Nichols, Reid (Thomas Reid)
81Top-689
82Don-632
82Fle-300
82RedSoxC-12
82Top-124
83Don-460
83Fle-189
83Top-446
84Don-614
84Fle-405
84Nes792-238
84Top-238
84TopTif-238
85Don-636
85Fle-164
85Top-37
85TopTif-37
86Don-574
86Fle-214
86Lea-224
86Top-364
86TopTif-364
86WhiSoxC-20
87DonOpeD-87
87ExpPos-18
87FleUpd-89
87FleUpdG-89
87Top-539
87TopTif-539
87TopTra-87T
87TopTraT-87T
88Fle-191
88FleGlo-191
88OPC-261
88Top-748
88TopTif-748
Nichols, Rod
86WatIndP-20
87KinIndP-24
89Don-649
89IndTeal-20
89Top-443
89TopTif-443
90Don-546
90Fle-497
90FleCan-497
90IndTeal-29
90OPC-108
90Top-108
90TopTif-108
90UppDec-572
91IndFanC-21
92Don-194
92Fle-119
92IndFanC-19
92OPC-586
92Pin-525
92Sco-559
92StaClu-534
92Top-586
92TopGol-586
92TopGolW-586
92TopMic-586
92Ult-352
92UppDec-212
93AlbDukF-1457
93Don-521
93Fle-597
93PacSpa-99
93Top-372
93TopGol-372
93TopInaM-372
93TopMic-372
95RicBraTI-12
96RicBraB-22
96RicBraRC-16
96RicBraUB-20
Nichols, Samuel
87OldJudN-374
Nichols, Scott
87SavCarP-6
89St.PetCS-21
90LouRedBLBC-28
90LouRedBP-404
90ProAAAF-518
91LouRedP-2917
91LouRedTI-29
Nichols, Todd
95AusFut-48
Nichols, Ty
85NewOriT-3
86HagSunP-13
88ChaKniTI-22
89HagSunB-28
89HagSunP-279
89HagSunS-13
90HagSunB-8
90HagSunP-1425
90HagSunS-20
Nicholson, Bill (William B.)
41CubTeal-15
43CubTeal-17
44CubTeal-17
48BluTin-11
49Bow-76
49EurSta-142
49PhiBul-41
49PhiLumPB-7
50Bow-228
51Bow-113
52Top-185
53BowBW-14
76ChiGre-14
76TayBow4-89
77TCMTheWY-39
79DiaGre-111
83DiaClaS2-76
83TCMPla1943-36
83TopRep5-185
Nicholson, Carl
78WatIndT-15
79TacTugT-18
Nicholson, Dave (David L.)
61Top-182
62Top-577
63Top-234
63WhiSoxJP-9
63WhiSoxTS-18
64Top-31
64TopCoi-32
64TopSta-26
64TopTatI-57
64TopVen-31
64WhiSoxTS-17
65OPC-183
65Top-183
65WhiSoxJP-5
66Top-576
67OPC-113
67Top-113
69Top-298
69TopTeaP-7
78TCM60I-99
87AstShoSTw-11
91OriCro-328
Nicholson, J.W.
87OldJudN-375
Nicholson, John
97Top-482
Nicholson, Keith
87LakTigP-2
88FayGenP-1079
Nicholson, Larry
80BufBisT-14
Nicholson, Rick
77NewCoPT-25
78HolMilT-17
Nicholson, Thomas
87OldJudN-376
Nichting, Chris
87PanAmTURB-8
88FloStaLAS-15
88VerBeaDS-18A
89SanAntMB-22
92AlbDukF-719
92SanAntMS-572
94SanAntMF-2464
95RanCra-21
96LeaSigEA-142
87PanAmTUBI-27
Nickell, Jackie
92BelMarC-16
92BelMarF-1441
93AppFoxC-18
93AppFoxF-2458
93ClaFS7-246
94ExcFS7-126
94RivPilCLC-19
95PorCitRTI-16
Nickerson, Drew
74GasRanT-14
75AndRanT-57
77CedRapGT-12
Nickerson, Jim
77SpaPhiT-4
Nicol, Hugh (Hugh N.)
87BucN28-101
87LonJacN-9
87OldJudN-377A
87OldJudN-377B
87OldJudN-378
Nicolas, Darrell
94StaCluDP-49
Nicolau, Travis
91DaiDolF-16
Nicolet, Don
80WatIndT-22
Nicoll, Sam
88GandBCGCE-29
Nicolosi, Chris
59DarFar-13
60DarFar-1
Nicolosi, Sal
85VisOakT-5
86VisOakP-13
Nicometi, Tony
86JacExpT-1
Nicosia, Steve (Steven R.)
75ShrCapT-15
76VenLeaS-162
77ColCliT-16
78ColCliT-18
80Top-519
81Don-373
81Fle-371
81OPC-212
81Top-212
82Don-45
82Fle-488
82Top-652
83Don-528
83Fle-314
83Top-462
84GiaPos-19
84Nes792-98
84Top-98
84TopTif-98
85ExpPos-14
85Fle-618
85Top-191
85TopTif-191
85TopTifT-87T
85TopTra-87T
89EriOriS-15
Nied, David
88SumBraP-413
89DurBullS-16
89DurBulTI-16
90DurBulTI-17
91DurBulC-3
91DurBulP-1541
92Bow-504
92DonRoo-86
92FleUpd-68
92LeaGolR-BC10
92ProFS7-188
92RicBraBB-22
92RicBraF-373
92RicBraRC-13
92RicBraS-435
92SkyAAAF-200
92TriA AAS-435
93Bow-148
93Don-792
93DonDiaK-DK28
93Fin-198
93FinRef-198
93Fla-43
93Fle-9
93FleFinE-36
93FunPac-178
93HumDumC-30
93JimDeaR-7
93Lea-390
93OPC-49
93OPCPre-107
93PacSpa-433
93Pin-238
93PinExpOD-1
93RocUSPC-1S
93RocUSPC-2D
93Sco-553
93ScoBoyoS-23
93ScoFra-28
93ScoProaG-10
93SelRoo-78T
93StaClu-718
93StaCluFDI-718
93StaCluI-A3
93StaCluI-C1
93StaCluMOP-718
93StaCluMOP-MA3
93StaCluMOP-MC1
93StaCluMP-28
93StaCluRoc-1
93Stu-74
93Top-444
93TopGol-444
93TopInaM-444
93TopMic-444
93TopMic-P444
93TriPla-105
93TriPlaG-GS10
93Ult-354
93UltAllR-6
93UltPer-7
93UppDec-27
93UppDec-478
93UppDec-834
93UppDecDG-23
93UppDecGold-27
93UppDecGold-478
93UppDecGold-834
93UppDecSH-HI14
93USPlaCR-6S
94Bow-470
94ColC-576
94ColChoGS-576
94ColChoSS-576
94Don-106
94ExtBas-251
94ExtBasSYS-15
94Fin-282
94FinRef-282
94Fla-376
94Fle-447
94Lea-312
94OPC-208
94Pac-202
94Pin-43
94PinArtP-43
94PinMusC-43
94ProMag-45
94RocPol-19
94Sco-528
94ScoBoyoS-15
94ScoGolR-528
94Sel-113
94SP-168
94SPDieC-168
94StaClu-153
94StaCluFDI-153
94StaCluGR-153
94StaCluMOP-153
94StaCluT-111
94StaCluTFDI-111
94Top-135
94TopGol-135
94TopSpa-135
94TriPla-229
94Ult-486
94UppDec-70
94UppDecED-70
95Bow-396
95ColCho-438
95ColChoGS-438
95ColChoSE-208
95ColChoSEGS-208
95ColChoSESS-208
95ColChoSS-438
95Don-120
95DonPreP-120
95Emb-35
95EmbGolI-35
95Fin-77
95FinRef-77
95Fla-132
95Fle-525
95Lea-192
95Pac-142
95Pin-95
95PinArtP-95
95PinMusC-95
95Sco-139
95ScoGolR-139
95ScoPlaTS-139
95Spo-10
95SpoArtP-10
95StaClu-428
95StaCluMOP-428
95StaCluSTWS-428
95StaCluVR-224
95Top-594
95TopCyb-366
95Ult-376
95UltGolM-376
95UppDec-173
95UppDecED-173
95UppDecEDG-173
95UppDecSE-241
95UppDecSEG-241
96ColCho-134
96ColChoGS-134
96ColChoSS-134
96ColSprSSTI-24
96Fle-369
96FleTif-369
95StaCluVRMC-224
97RicBraBC-7
Niedenfuer, Tom
82AlbDukT-7
82DodPol-49
82DodPos-6
82DodUniOV-14
82Fle-16
83DodPol-49
83DodPos-11
83Don-536
83Fle-214
83Top-477
84DodPol-49
84DodSmo-2
84Don-128
84Fle-108
84Nes792-112
84Top-112
84TopTif-112
85DodCokP-22
85Don-153
85Fle-378
85OPC-281
85Top-782
85TopMin-782
85TopSti-80
85TopTif-782
86DodCokP-21

86DodPol-49
86DodUniOP-14
86Don-397
86Fle-139
86Lea-186
86Top-56
86TopTif-56
87DodMot-14
87DodPol-26
87Don-218
87Fle-448
87FleGlo-448
87Lea-204
87OPC-43
87OriFreB-49
87Top-538
87TopTif-538
87TopTra-88T
87TopTraT-88T
88Don-294
88DonBasB-321
88Fle-568
88FleGlo-568
88OPC-242
88OriFreB-49
88Sco-261A
88Sco-261B
88ScoGlo-261A
88ScoGlo-261B
88StaLinO-11
88Top-242
88TopSti-232
88TopTif-242
89Bow-204
89BowTif-204
89Don-282
89DonTra-54
89Fle-613
89FleGlo-613
89MarMot-12
89OPC-14
89PanSti-254
89Sco-252
89Top-651
89TopSti-236
89TopTif-651
89UppDec-488
90CarSmo-16
90DodTar-575
90LouRedBLBC-29
90OPC-306
90PubSti-438
90Top-306
90TopTif-306
90VenSti-365
91Fle-639
91OriCro-329
91Sco-217

Niedermaier, Brad
96ForWayWB-17

Niehaus, Dave
95MarPac-17

Niehoff, Bert (John Albert)
14CraJacE-125
15CraJacE-125
15SpoNewM-130
16ColE13-128
16SpoNewM-132
91ConTSN-151

Niekro, Joe
67Top-536
68Top-475
69OPC-43
69Top-43
70OPC-508
70Top-508
71MLBOffS-400
71OPC-695
71Top-695
72MilBra-251
72OPC-216
72Top-216
73OPC-585
73TigJew-14
73Top-585
74OPC-504
74Top-504
75IowOakT-12
75OPC-595
75Top-595
76OPC-273
76SSP-50
76Top-273
77Spo-8321
77Top-116
78AstBurK-5
78Top-306
79AstTeal-9
79Top-68
80OPC-226
80Top-205
80Top-437
81AllGamPI-171
81CokTeaS-66
81Don-380
81Fle-54
81OPC-102
81Top-722
81TopSti-26
81TopSti-174
82AstAstI-8
82Don-167
82Fle-221
82FleSta-45
82OPC-74
82Top-611
83Don-10
83Don-470
83Don-613
83DonActA-51
83Fle-457
83FleSta-138
83FleSti-210
83OPC-221
83Top-221
83Top-441
83TopFol-1
83TopSti-240
84AstMot-2
84Don-110
84Fle-234
84FunFooP-128
84Nes792-586
84OPC-384
84Top-586
84TopSti-69
84TopTif-586
85AstHouP-11
85AstMot-6
85Don-182
85Fle-355
85FleStaS-88
85Lea-189
85OPC-295
85Top-295
85TopSti-69
85TopTif-295
86AstMot-17
86Don-601
86Don-645
86Lea-243
86OPC-135
86Top-135
86TopTif-135
86YanTCM-10
87ClaUpdY-120
87Don-217
87Fle-106
87FleGlo-106
87FleUpd-87
87FleUpdG-87
87Top-344A
87Top-344B
87TopTif-344A
87TopTif-344B
87TopTra-89T
87TopTraT-89T
88Fle-18
88FleGlo-18
88OPC-233
88Sco-237
88ScoGlo-237
88Top-5
88Top-473
88TopTif-5
88TopTif-473
88TwiTeal-24
92BenRocC-25
92BenRocF-1490
92UppDecS-8
92YanWIZ8-132
95ColSilB-21

Niekro, John
95ColSilB-22
96ColSilB-21

Niekro, Phil
64Top-541
65Top-461
66OPC-28
66Top-28
66TopVen-28
67Top-456
68DexPre-58
68OPC-7
68Top-7
68Top-257
68TopVen-7
68TopVen-257
69MilBra-201
69MLBOffS-116
69Top-355
69TopTeaP-2
70MilBra-20
70MLBOffS-10
70OPC-69
70OPC-160
70Top-69
70Top-160
70TopPos-2
70TopSup-15
71MLBOffS-19
71OPC-30
71Top-30
71TopCoi-37
72MilBra-252
72Top-620
73Kel2D-29
73OPC-503
73Top-503
74BraPhoC-5
74OPC-29
74Top-29
74TopSta-9
75Hos-99
75OPC-130
75OPC-310
75Top-130
75Top-310
76Hos-3
76HosTwi-3
76OPC-435
76SSP-5
76Top-435
77BurCheD-209
77Hos-111
77OPC-43
77Spo-7410
77Spo-8321
77Top-615
78BraCok-11
78Hos-122
78OPC-6
78OPC-155
78RCColC-89
78Top-10
78Top-206
79Hos-62
79Kel-28
79OPC-313
79Top-595
79TopCom-19
80BurKinPHR-6
80Kel-51
80OPC-130
80Top-205
80Top-245
80TopSup-46
81BraPol-35
81Don-328
81Fle-242
81FleStiC-23
81Kel-12
81OPC-201
81Top-387
81TopSti-148
82BraBurKL-19
82BraPol-35
82Don-10
82Don-475
82Fle-444
82FleSta-68
82Kel-36
82OPC-185
82Top-185
82TopSti-20
83BraPol-35
83Don-97
83Don-613
83DonActA-12
83Fle-143
83FleSta-139
83FleSti-91
83OPC-94
83OPC-316
83Top-410
83Top-411
83Top-502
83TopFol-1
83TopSti-218
84Don-188
84DonCha-34
84Fle-187
84FleUpd-83
84FunFooP-115
84Nes792-650
84OCoandSI-234
84OPC-29
84Top-650
84TopSti-31
84TopTif-650
84TopTra-84T
84TopTraT-84T
85Don-458
85DonActA-49
85DonHig-50
85Fle-138
85FleStaS-93
85Lea-138
85OPC-40
85PolMet-Y2
85SevCoi-S11
85Top-40
85TopGloS-32
85TopSti-309
85TopTif-40
86Don-580
86Don-645
86Fle-112
86Fle-630
86FleLeaL-28
86FleStiC-82
86FleUpd-81
86IndOhH-35
86IndTeal-27
86Lea-243
86OPC-246
86QuaGra-28
86Spo-53
86Spo-135
86Spo-163
86Spo-182
86Top-204
86Top-790
86TopSti-7
86TopTat-8
86TopTif-204
86TopTif-790
86TopTra-77T
86TopTraT-77T
87Don-465
87Fle-254
87Fle-626
87FleGlo-254
87FleGlo-626
87FleRecS-25
87IndGat-35
87Lea-181
87OPC-6
87Spo-147
87SpoRea-22
87SpoTeaP-3
87Top-694
87TopTif-694
88ClaRed-198
88ClaRed-199
88ClaRed-200
88Sco-555
88ScoGlo-555
88Top-5
88TopTif-5
89PacLegI-212
89SweBasG-22
90BraDubS-24
90PacLeg-96
91LinDriAAA-449
91RicBraBC-38
91RicBraLD-449
91RicBraP-2583
91RicBraTI-4
92KelAll-6
92YanWIZ8-133
92YanWIZA-54
93MCIAmb-4
93NabAllA-4
94ColSilBC-6
95ColSilB-23
95ColSilB9-1
96ColSilB-22

Nielsen, Dan
88WatPirP-9

Nielsen, Jerry (Gerald)
88OneYanP-2062
89PriWilCS-14
89Sta-91
91Ft.LauYC-10
91Ft.LauYP-2423
92AlbYanS-14
93Don-359
93Fle-654
93Sco-268
93StaCluAn-28
93Top-594
93TopGol-594
93TopInaM-594
93TopMic-594
93VanCanF-2593
94MidAngF-2436
94MidAngOHP-20

Nielsen, Kevin
89SanDieSAS-20
90SanDieSA3-6
91SprCarC-19
91SprCarP-740
92St.PetCC-13
92St.PetCF-2026

Nielsen, Scott
84NasSouTI-15
85AlbYanT-9
87Don-597
87HawIsIP-15
87Top-57
87TopTif-57
88ColCliC-3
88ColCliP-6
88ColCliP-310
88TriAAAP-11
89ColCliC-2
89ColCliP-7
89ColCliP-754
89Fle-261
89FleGlo-261
90AlbDecGB-9
90CMC-359
90ProAAAF-272
90TidTidC-8
90TidTidP-541
90TopTVM-52
92YanWIZ8-134

Nielsen, Steve
78AshTouT-21
79TulDriT-9
80TulDriT-19
81TulDriT-9
82BurRanF-30
82BurRanT-26
83TulDriT-18
85BurRanT-11

Nielson, Gerald
90PriWilCTI-16
92AlbYanF-2225
92DonRoo-87

Nieman, Bob (Robert C.)
53TigGle-23
55Bow-145
56Top-267
57Top-14
58Hir-26
58OriJayP-7
58Top-165
59OriJayP-4
59Top-375
60CarJayP-9
60Top-149
60TopVen-149
61Top-178
62IndJayP-9
62Top-182
62TopVen-182
79TCM50-211
91OriCro-330

Niemann, Art
82AppFoxF-23

Niemann, Randy
76ForLauYS-28
80Top-469
81Don-143
81Fle-77
81Top-148
82Don-473
82PorBeaT-6

83Top-329
85TidTidT-7
86FleUpd-82
86MetTCM-31
86MetWorSC-26
86TopTra-78T
86TopTraT-78T
87Fle-18
87FleGlo-18
87PorBeaP-3
87Top-147
87TopTif-147
88TidTidCa-24
88TidTidCM-10
89PacSenL-127
90PitMetP-26
91MetWIZ-294
91St.LucMC-28
91St.LucMP-729
92BinMetF-534
92BinMetS-75
93BinMetF-2350
94BinMetF-722
95StLucMTI-2

Niemann, Tom
83ButCopKT-14
85Ft.MyeRT-6

Niemeier, Todd
95EveAqaTI-14
96LanJetB-21

Nieporte, Jay
85SpoIndC-16

Nieson, Chuck
77FriOneYW-26

Niethammer, Darren
88ChaRanS-17
90ChaRanS-16
91ChaRanC-13
91ChaRanP-1317
91FloStaLAP-FSL5
92TulDriF-2698
92TulDriS-613

Niethammer, Marc
94BurBeeC-17
94BurBeeF-1090
96HudValRB-14

Nieto, Andy
87DayBeaAP-23

Nieto, Rene
80VenLeaS-149

Nieto, Roy
92AshTouC-11
93OscAstC-17
93OscAstF-625

Nieto, Tom (Thomas Andrew)
82ArkTraT-12
83LouRedR-9
84Car5x7-19
84LouRedR-8
85CarTeal-24
85Don-596
85Fle-235
85OPC-294
85Top-294
85TopTif-294
86CarKASD-12
86CarTeal-30
86Don-327
86ExpPos-10
86Fle-43
86IndIndTI-30
86Top-88
86TopTif-88
87DonOpeD-220
87FleUpd-88
87FleUpdG-88
87OPC-124
87Top-416
87TopTif-416
87TopTra-90T
87TopTraT-90T
88Don-612
88Top-317
88TopTif-317
89PhiTas-24
90ProAAAF-305
90ScrRedBP-603
92ChaLooF-3835
92ChaLooS-200
93WesVirWC-25
94ChaWheF-2718
95NorNavTI-50
96GreBatB-2

Nieto, Tony
94BilMusF-3666
94BilMusSP-18

Nieves, Adelberto
81BatTroT-10
81WatIndT-30

Nieves, Ernie (Ernesto)
90BilMusP-3219
90ChaWheB-5
90ChaWheP-2237
91ChaWheC-7
91ChaWheP-2884
92ChaWheF-8
92ChaWVWC-5
93SouAtlLAPI-28
95MidAngOHP-24

Nieves, Fionel
90AshTouC-7
91AshTouP-565

Nieves, Jose
96RocCubTI-22

Nieves, Juan
86BrePol-20
86Don-40
86DonRoo-12
86FleUpd-83
86SpoRoo-5
86TopTra-79T
86TopTraT-79T
87BrePol-20
87BreTeal-9
87ClaUpdY-136
87Don-90
87DonHig-1
87Fle-352
87FleGlo-352
87OPC-79
87SpoTeaP-19
87Top-79
87TopRoo-11
87TopTif-79
88BrePol-20
88Don-126
88Fle-170
88FleGlo-170
88OPC-104
88PanSti-117
88PanSti-431
88RedFolSB-60
88Sco-513
88Sco-655
88ScoGlo-513
88ScoGlo-655
88ScoYouS2-33
88Spo-180
88Spo-211
88StaLinBre-12
88Top-515
88TopBig-190
88TopTif-515
89BimBreD-10
89Bow-131
89BowTif-131
89BreGar-10
89BrePol-20
89BreYea-20
89Don-575
89Sco-410
89Top-287
89TopTif-287
89UppDec-646
90BrePol-20
90OPC-467
90PubSti-501
90Top-467
90TopTif-467
90UppDec-648
90VenSti-366
92BreUSO-3
93BreSen-2
93OneYanC-29
93OneYanF-3522
94BreMilB-59
94BreSen-6
94BreUSO-3
94GreBatF-493
95NorNavTI-49
96GreBatB-3
97GreBatC-28

Nieves, Mel (Melvin)
89BlaYNPRWL-81
89PulBraP-1893
90Bes-219
90ProAaA-105
90SumBraB-15
90SumBraP-2447
91DurBulP-1560
92Bow-143
92ClaFS7-94
92DurBulC-22
92DurBulTI-21
92GreBraF-1165
93Bow-662
93ClaFS7-56
93Don-320
93FleMajLP-A1
93OPC-246
93PacSpa-10
93Pin-248
93PinRooTP-10
93PinTea2-5
93RicBraBB-5
93RicBraF-199
93RicBraP-21
93RicBraRC-16
93RicBraRC-22
93Sco-248
93ScoBoyoS-7
93ScoProaG-4
93StaClu-89
93StaCluB-28
93StaCluFDI-89
93StaCluMOP-89
93Top-658
93TopGol-658
93TopInaM-658
93TopMic-658
93Toy-20
93UppDec-21
93UppDecGold-21
94Bow-176
94Bow-365
94BowBes-X105
94BowBesR-X105
94Cla-154
94Fin-432
94FinJum-432
94FinRef-432
94Fle-671
94LasVegSF-881
94LeaLimR-3
94Pac-531
94Pin-478
94PinArtP-478
94PinMusC-478
94ScoBoyoS-40
94ScoRoo-RT150
94ScoRooGR-RT150
94Sel-415
94SpoRoo-40
94SpoRooAP-40
94StaClu-567
94StaCluFDI-567
94StaCluGR-567
94StaCluMOP-567
94Top-307
94TopGol-307
94TopSpa-307
94UppDec-256
94UppDecED-256
95Baz-130
95Bow-79
95ColCho-356
95ColChoGS-356
95ColChoSS-356
95Don-482
95DonPreP-482
95Emo-189
95Fla-421
95FleUpd-187
95Lea-15
95PadMot-26
95Pin-376
95PinArtP-376
95PinMusC-376
95PinUps-US14
95Sco-579
95ScoAi-AM13
95ScoGolR-579
95ScoPlaTS-579
95SPSpeF-47
95StaClu-438
95StaCluMOP-438
95StaCluSTWS-438
95Top-243
95TopCyb-137
95Ult-440
95UltGolM-440
95UppDec-372
95UppDecED-372
95UppDecEDG-372
95UppDecSE-132
95UppDecSEG-132
96Cir-41
96CirRav-41
96Don-152
96DonPreP-152
96Fle-575
96FleTif-575
96FleUpd-U35
96FleUpdTC-U35
96LeaPre-110
96LeaPreP-110
96LeaSigEA-143
96Pac-186
96PacPri-P62
96PacPriG-P62
96Sco-149
96SelCer-92
96SelCerAP-92
96SelCerCB-92
96SelCerCR-92
96SelCerMB-92
96SelCerMG-92
96SelCerMR-92
96SP-82
96Sum-121
96SumAbo&B-121
96SumArtP-121
96SumFoi-121
96Ult-349
96UltGolM-349
96UppDec-189
96Zen-59
96ZenArtP-59
97Cir-214
97CirRav-214
97ColCho-340
97Don-53
97DonPreP-53
97DonPrePGold-53
97FlaSho-A36
97FlaSho-B36
97FlaSho-C36
97FlaShoLC-36
97FlaShoLC-B36
97FlaShoLC-C36
97FlaShoLCM-A36
97FlaShoLCM-B36
97FlaShoLCM-C36
97Fle-103
97FleTif-103
97Lea-232
97LeaFraM-232
97LeaFraMDC-232
97MetUni-112
97Pac-93
97PacLigB-93
97PacPri-33
97PacPriLB-33
97PacPriP-33
97PacSil-93
97Sco-383
97ScoHobR-383
97ScoResC-383
97ScoShoS-383
97ScoShoSAP-383
97SP-73
97StaClu-169
97StaCluMOP-169
97Top-304
97Ult-61
97UltGolME-61
97UltPlaME-61
97UppDec-356

Nieves, Raul
76DubPacT-24

Niggeling, Johnny
41BroW75-23
93ConTSN-954

Niles, Harry (Harry Clyde)
08AmeCarE-88
08RosComP-52
09RamT20-89
09T206-268
10E12AmeCDC-29
11SpoLifCW-269
11SpoLifM-49
11TurRedT-111

Niles, Thomas
91WinHavRSP-485
92ElmPioC-10
92ElmPioF-1383
93LynRedSC-21
93LynRedSF-2517

Nill, George
08AmeLeaPC-13
11SpoLifCW-270

Nilsson, Anna Q.
28BabRCCE-4

Nilsson, Bob
91Cla/Bes-146
91DaiDolF-1
91DaiDolF-10

Nilsson, Dave
88BelBreGS-19
89StoPorB-1
89StoPorCLC-162
89StoPorP-374
89StoPorS-21
90ProAaA-151
90StoPorB-2
90StoPorCLC-187
90StoPorP-2186
91Cla/Bes-227
91ClaGolB-BC11
91DaiDolF-1
91DaiDolF-19
91ElPasDLD-194
91ElPasDP-2751
91LinDriAA-194
91UppDecFE-25F
92Bow-653
92DenZepS-142
92Don-4
92FleUpd-37
92OPC-58
92Pin-568
92PinRoo-27
92ProFS7-83
92ScoRoo-94T
92SkyAAAF-69
92Top-58
92TopGol-58
92TopGolW-58
92TopMic-58
92TopTra-83T
92TopTraG-83T
92UppDec-57
92UppDecSR-SR18
93Bow-591
93BrePol-19
93Don-235
93Fle-631
93Lea-327
93OPC-272
93PacSpa-162
93Pin-61
93Sco-344
93Sel-283
93StaClu-709
93StaCluFDI-709
93StaCluMOP-709
93Top-316
93TopGol-316
93TopInaM-316
93TopMic-316
93Toy-31
93Ult-222
93UppDec-795
93UppDecGold-795
94BreMilB-60
94BrePol-20
94ColC-216
94ColChoGS-216
94ColChoSS-216
94Don-204
94ExtBas-106
94Fin-268
94FinRef-268
94Fla-307
94Fle-186
94Lea-302
94LeaL-46
94Pac-337
94PanSti-84
94Pin-210
94PinArtP-210
94PinMusC-210
94Sco-533
94ScoGolR-533
94Sel-339
94StaClu-376
94StaCluFDI-376
94StaCluGR-376
94StaCluMOP-376

94Stu-46
94Top-548
94TopGol-548
94TopSpa-548
94TriPla-57
94Ult-80
94UppDec-359
94UppDecED-359
95AusFut-1
95AusFut-90
95AusFut-98
95Baz-79
95Bow-296
95ColCho-182
95ColChoGS-182
95ColChoSE-71
95ColChoSEGS-71
95ColChoSESS-71
95ColChoSS-182
95D3-49
95Don-288
95DonPreP-288
95DonTopotO-100
95Emb-33
95EmbGolI-33
95Fin-183
95FinRef-183
95Fla-54
95Fle-186
95Lea-73
95LeaLim-110
95Pac-238
95PacPri-76
95PanSti-30
95Pin-320
95PinArtP-320
95PinMusC-320
95RedFol-23
95Sco-120
95ScoGolR-120
95ScoHaloG-HG37
95ScoPlaTS-120
95Sel-69
95SelArtP-69
95Spo-22
95SpoArtP-22
95StaClu-140
95StaCluFDI-140
95StaCluMOP-140
95StaCluSTWS-140
95StaCluVR-72
95Stu-102
95Sum-128
95SumNthD-128
95Top-17
95TopCyb-15
95Ult-298
95UltGolM-298
95UppDec-301
95UppDecED-301
95UppDecEDG-301
95UppDecSE-234
95UppDecSEG-234
96Cir-52
96CirBos-11
96CirRav-52
96ColCho-325
96ColCho-594
96ColChoGS-325
96ColChoGS-594
96ColChoSS-325
96ColChoSS-594
96Don-356
96DonPreP-356
96EmoXL-76
96Fin-B110
96FinRef-B110
96Fla-105
96Fle-154
96FleTif-154
96Lea-209
96LeaPrePB-209
96LeaPrePG-209
96LeaPrePS-209
96LeaSigA-169
96LeaSigAG-169
96LeaSigAS-169
96MetUni-71
96MetUniP-71
96Pac-343
96PanSti-194
96Pin-94
96PinAfi-135
96PinAfi-155
96PinAfiAP-135
96PinAfiAP-155
96Sco-297
96ScoDugC-B22
96ScoDugCAP-B22
96Sel-134
96SelArtP-134
96StaClu-372
96StaCluMOP-372
95StaCluVRMC-72
96Stu-134
96StuPrePB-134
96StuPrePG-134
96StuPrePS-134
96Sum-135
96SumAbo&B-135
96SumArtP-135
96SumFoi-135
96Top-302
96TopGal-74
96TopGalPPI-74
96Ult-82
96UltGolM-82
96UppDec-119
97Cir-130
97CirRav-130
97ColCho-150
97Don-331
97DonEli-113
97DonEliGS-113
97DonLim-38
97DonLimLE-38
97DonPre-68
97DonPreCttC-68
97DonPreP-331
97DonPrePGold-331
97Fin-24
97FinRef-24
97FlaSho-A164
97FlaSho-B164
97FlaSho-C164
97FlaShoLC-164
97FlaShoLC-B164
97FlaShoLC-C164
97FlaShoLCM-A164
97FlaShoLCM-B164
97FlaShoLCM-C164
97Fle-137
97FleTif-137
97Lea-316
97LeaFraM-316
97LeaFraMDC-316
97MetUni-69
97Pac-127
97PacLigB-127
97PacPri-41
97PacPriLB-41
97PacPriP-41
97PacSil-127
97PinIns-84
97PinInsCE-84
97PinInsDE-84
97PinX-P-70
97PinX-PMoS-70
97PinX-PMP-13
97PinX-PSfF-28
97PinX-PSfFU-28
97Sco-122
97ScoPreS-122
97ScoShoS-122
97ScoShoSAP-122
97SP-99
97SpoIll-50
97SpoIllEE-50
97StaClu-153
97StaCluMOP-153
97Top-183
97TopGal-97
97TopGalPPI-97
97Ult-82
97UltGolME-82
97UltPlaME-82
97UppDec-181
97UppDec-404

Nilsson, Gary
91DaiDolF-1
91DaiDolF-7

Nimura, Kaoru
96HonShaHWB-33

Nina, Robin
89SalDodTI-19
90VerBeaDS-20

Nipp, Mark
80AlbDukT-21

Nipper, Al
85Don-614
85Fle-165
85Top-424
85TopTif-424
86Don-538
86Fle-356
86Top-181
86TopTif-181
87Don-297
87Fle-39
87FleGlo-39
87OPC-64
87Top-617
87TopTif-617
88CubDavB-45
88Don-523
88DonBasB-250
88DonTeaBC-NEW
88Fle-358
88FleGlo-358
88Sco-527
88ScoGlo-527
88Top-326
88TopTif-326
88TopTra-75T
88TopTraT-75T
89Don-394
89Fle-433
89FleGlo-433
89Sco-532
89Top-86
89TopTif-86
89UppDec-494
90IndTeal-30
91LinDriAAA-241
91LouRedLD-241
91LouRedP-2911
94SarRedSC-30
95TreThuTI-2

Nipper, Mike
85DurBulT-28
86DurBulP-20

Nipper, Ronald
87GreBraB-6

Nippert, Merlin
77FriOneYW-93

Nischwitz, Ron
62TigPosCF-13
62Top-591
63Top-152
66OPC-38
66Top-38
66TopVen-38
81TCM60I-380

Nishi, Masafumi
90IBAWorA-26

Nishijima, Takayuki
92SalSpuC-7
92SalSpuF-3771

Nishimura, Hioetsugu
88VerBeaDS-19

Nishioka, Tsuyoshi
91SalSpuP-2241

Nitcholas, Otho
90DodTar-576

Nitkowski, C.J.
94ClaUpdCotC-CC8
94SigRooDP-9
94SigRooDPS-9
94StaCluDP-2
94StaCluDPFDI-2
95ActPacF-61
95Bow-53
95BowBes-B71
95BowBesR-B71
95ColCho-43
95ColChoGS-43
95ColChoSS-43
95Exc-179
95Fin-301
95FinRef-301
95Pin-168
95PinArtP-168
95PinMusC-168
95RedKah-20
95ScoDraP-DP4
95SP-24
95SPChaDC-6
95SPSil-24
95StaClu-114
95StaCluFDI-114
95StaCluMOP-114
95StaCluSTWS-114
95Top-84
95UppDecML-192
95UppDecMLOP-OP7
96ColCho-545
96ColChoGS-545
96ColChoSS-545
96Don-467
96DonPreP-467
96Fin-S127
96FinRef-S127
96Fle-118
96FleTif-118
96Pin-174
96Sco-506
96TolMudHB-21
96Top-398
96UppDec-331
97Top-313
95UppDecMLFS-192

Nitschke, Bear
94MarPhiC-14
94MarPhiF-3296

Nitschke, Buzz (David)
75IntLeaASB-19
75PacCoaLAB-19
75TucTorC-5
75TucTorTI-14

Nittoli, Mike
86SanJosBP-15

Nitz, Rick
74AlbDukTI-11
75AlbDukC-16
75IntLeaASB-20
75PacCoaLAB-20

Niura, Hisao
79TCMJapPB-64

Nivens, Toby
87OrlTwiP-12
88OrlTwiB-6
89JacMetGS-6
90JacMetGS-17
91LinDriAA-640
91WilBilLD-640
91WilBilP-289

Nix, Dave
81AppFoxT-21
82AppFoxF-15
83GleFalWST-8
86MadMusP-15
86MadMusP-16
86HumStaDS-12

Nix, James
92PriRedC-16
92PriRedF-3087
93WesVirWC-21
93WesVirWF-2865
94WinSpiC-18
94WinSpiF-268
95ChaLooTI-16
96ChaLooB-22

Nix, John
75CedRapGT-11

Nixon, Al
90DodTar-577

Nixon, Donell
81WauTimT-17
82WauTimF-9
84ChaLooT-10
87CalCanP-2327
87DonOpeD-114
87MarMot-19
87SpoTeaP-25
88CalCanC-11
88Fle-382
88FleGlo-382
88FleUpd-129
88FleUpdG-129
88Sco-436
88ScoGlo-436
88Top-146
88TopTif-146
89Bow-477
89BowTif-477
89Fle-337
89FleGlo-337
89GiaMot-25
89Sco-481
89Top-447
89TopBig-214
89TopTif-447
90CMC-314
90Don-571
90Fle-66
90FleCan-66
90MLBBasB-25
90OPC-658
90ProAAAF-472
90PubSti-78
90RocRedWC-11
90RocRedWGC-8
90RocRedWP-715
90Sco-538
90Top-658
90TopTif-658
90VenSti-367
91OriCro-331
92ColSprSSF-765
92ColSprSSS-93
94ChaKniF-911

Nixon, Jason
90AugPirP-2467

Nixon, Otis
81NasSouTI-11
83ColCliT-25
84Ind-23
85Ind-23
85IndPol-20
86Fle-591
86IndOhH-20
86IndTeal-28
86TopTra-80T
86TopTraT-80T
87Fle-255
87FleGlo-255
87IndGat-20
87Top-486
87TopTif-486
88BlaYNPRWLU-19
88ExpPos-15
88IndIndC-14
88IndIndP-518
88StaLinMa-11
89Bow-366
89BowTif-366
89Fle-387
89FleGlo-387
89OPC-54
89Sco-451
89Top-674
89TopBig-234
89TopMinL-23
89TopTif-674
89UppDec-480
90Don-456
90ExpPos-25
90Fle-356
90FleCan-356
90OPC-252
90PubSti-183
90Sco-241
90Top-252
90TopBig-279
90TopMag-89
90TopTif-252
90UppDec-379
90VenSti-368
91Bow-571
91BraDubP-20
91BraSubS-27
91Don-626
91Fle-241
91FleUpd-75
91Lea-395
91OPC-558
91OPCPre-89
91PanFreS-152
91Sco-431
91ScoRoo-29T
91StaClu-174
91StaClu-392
91Top-558
91TopDesS-558
91TopMic-558
91TopTif-558
91TopTra-84T
91TopTraT-84T
91UltUpd-69
91UppDec-520
91UppDecFE-58F
92Bow-669
92BraLykP-20
92BraLykS-24
92Don-33
92Don-41
92FleUpd 69
92Lea-358
92OPC-340
92Pin-519

92Sco-429
92Sco-443
92Sco100S-73
92StaClu-882
92StaCluNC-882
92Top-340
92TopGol-340
92TopGolW-340
92TopKid-35
92TopMic-340
92TopPreS-174
92Ult-461
92UppDec-451
92YanWIZ8-135
93BluJayDM-22
93Bow-310
93BraLykP-21
93BraLykS-26
93ClaGam-71
93Don-262
93Fin-181
93FinRef-181
93Fle-10
93Lea-180
93OPC-271
93PacSpa-337
93PanSti-186
93Pin-35
93Sco-87
93Sel-159
93StaClu-678
93StaCluB-16
93StaCluFDI-678
93StaCluM-92
93StaCluMOP-678
93Stu-216
93Top-333
93TopGol-333
93TopInaM-333
93TopMic-333
93Ult-310
93UppDec-292
93UppDecGold-292
94Bow-91
94ColC-579
94ColChoGS-579
94ColChoSS-579
94Don-232
94ExtBas-22
94Fin-274
94FinRef-274
94Fla-265
94Fle-369
94FleUpd-14
94Lea-375
94OPC-188
94Pac-19
94Pin-498
94PinArtP-498
94PinMusC-498
94ProMag-15
94Sco-106
94ScoGolR-106
94ScoRoo-RT26
94ScoRooCP-CP5
94ScoRooGR-RT26
94Sel-228
94SpoRoo-36
94SpoRooAP-36
94StaClu-106
94StaClu-597
94StaCluFDI-106
94StaCluFDI-597
94StaCluGR-106
94StaCluGR-597
94StaCluMOP-106
94StaCluMOP-597
94Stu-163
94Top-52
94TopGol-52
94TopSpa-52
94TopTra-40T
94Ult-316
94UppDec-497
94UppDecED-497
94USPlaCA-7H
95ColCho-396
95ColChoGS-396
95ColChoSS-396
95Don-213
95DonPreP-213
95DonTopotO-163
95Fin-186
95FinRef-186
95Fla-308
95Fle-36
95FleUpd-85
95Lea-376
95Pac-43
95Pin-106
95PinArtP-106
95PinMusC-106
95RanCra-22
95StaClu-262
95StaClu-552
95StaCluFDI-262
95StaCluMOP-262
95StaCluMOP-552
95StaCluSTWS-262
95StaCluSTWS-552
95StaCluVR-130
95Top-148
95TopCyb-91
95TopLeaL-LL17
95TopTra-101T
95Ult-13
95UltGolM-13
95UppDec-155
95UppDecED-155
95UppDecEDG-155
95USPlaCMLA-12H
96BluJayB-3
96BluJayOH-21
96ColCho-343
96ColCho-746
96ColChoGS-343
96ColChoGS-746
96ColChoSS-343
96ColChoSS-746
96Don-402
96DonPreP-402
96EmoXL-135
96Fin-B269
96FinRef-B269
96Fla-189
96Fle-255
96FleTif-255
96FleUpd-U98
96FleUpdTC-U98
96MetUni-124
96MetUniP-124
96Pac-434
96PanSti-238
96Sco-113
96StaClu-113
96StaCluMOP-113
95StaCluVRMC-130
96Top-178
96Ult-433
96UltGolM-433
96UppDec-472
97BluJayS-16
97Cir-320
97CirRav-320
97ColCho-502
97Don-318
97DonPreP-318
97DonPrePGold-318
97Fin-8
97FinRef-8
97Fle-245
97FleTif-245
97Lea-290
97LeaFraM-290
97LeaFraMDC-290
97PacPriGotD-GD104
97Sco-408
97ScoHobR-408
97ScoResC-408
97ScoShoS-408
97ScoShoSAP-408
97StaClu-163
97StaCluMOP-163
97Top-170
97TopChrSB-23
97TopChrSBR-23
97TopSeaB-SB23
97Ult-147
97UltGolME-147
97UltPlaME-147
97UppDec-212

Nixon, Russ (Russell E.)
57IndSoh-11
58Top-133
59Ind-14
59Kah-25
59Top-344
60IndJayP-6
60Kah-29
60MacSta-17
60Top-36
60TopVen-36
61Pos-52A
61Pos-52B
61Top-53
61TopStaI-115
62RedSoxJP-7
62Top-523
62TopStaI-16
63Top-168
64Top-329
64TopVen-329
65OPC-162
65Top-162
66Top-227
66TopVen-227
67Top-446
68DexPre-59
68Top-515
69Top-363
80RedEnq-2
81RedSoxBG2S-99
83RedYea-7
83Top-756
84ExpPos-20
84ExpStu-5
84ExpStu-38
84Nes792-351
84Top-351
84TopTif-351
86BraPol-2
88TopTra-76T
88TopTraT-76T
89BraDub-19
89Top-564
89TopTif-564
90BraDubP-21
90OPC-171
90Top-171
90TopTif-171
91LinDriAAA-424
91PorBeaLD-424
91PorBeaP-1581
92MarMot-27
93LasVegSF-960
94LasVegSF-883

Nixon, Trot
94ActPac-2
94ActPac-65
94ActPac2G-11G
94ActPacP-1
94CarLeaAF-CAR4
94Cla-10
94ClaBonB-BB1
94ClaCreotC-C1
94ClaGolF-3
94ClaGolN1PLF-LP9
94ClaGolREF-RE9
94ClaTriF-T7
94ColC-25
94ColChoGS-25
94ColChoSS-25
94LynRedSC-1
94LynRedSF-1907
94Pin-270
94PinArtP-270
94PinMusC-270
94Sco-486
94ScoGolR-486
94SP-11
94SPDieC-11
94SPHol-28
94SPHolDC-28
94UppDec-543
94UppDecAHNIL-9
94UppDecED-543
94UppDecML-4
94UppDecML-270
95ActPacF-2
95Bes-6
95Bow-152
95BowBes-B39
95BowBesR-B39
95Exc-13
95SPML-21
95UppDecML-17
96Bow-211
96Exc-15
96TreThuB-28
97Cir-204
97CirRav-204
97Lea-178
97LeaFraM-178
97LeaFraMDC-178
97UppDec-282
95UppDecMLFS-17

Nixon, Willard
51Bow-270
52Top-269
53BowBW-2
53RedSoxTI-22
53Top-30
54Bow-114
55Bow-177
56Top-122
57Top-189
58Hir-47
58Top-395
59Top-361
79DiaGre-247
83TopRep5-269
91TopArc1-30

Nobis, Tommy
78AtlCon-19

Noble, Jeff
85CloHSS-29

Noble, Ray
85UtiBluST-20
86TucTorP-17

Noble, Ray (Rafael Miguel)
50RemBre-19
51Bow-269
52BerRos-47
75Gia195T-22
95NegLeaL2-14

Nobles, Jim
79LodDodT-10

Noboa, Junior (Milicades A.)
81BatTroT-15
82WatIndF-28
82WatIndT-18
83WatIndF-8
84BufBisT-4
85DomLeaS-186
85MaiGuiT-20
86IndTeal-29
86MaiGuiP-13
87BufBisP-8
87IndGat-17
88EdmTraP-564
88StaLinI-16
88Top-503
88TopTif-503
89IndIndC-20
89IndIndP-1235
89TriA AAC-3
89TriAAP-AAA8
90ExpPos-26
90TopTra-80T
90TopTraT-80T
90TriAAAC-3
91Don-726
91ExpPos-16
91Fle-242
91Lea-255
91OPC-182
91Sco-423
91Top-182
91TopDesS-182
91TopMic-182
91TopTif-182
91Ult-207
92Don-765
92Lea-403
92MetColP-25
92MetKah-3
92OPCPre-187
92StaClu-709
92StaCluNC-709
92Ult-533
93LimRocDWB-22
95RocRedWTI-27

Nocas, Luke
87AppFoxP-25
89AppFoxP-877

Nocciolo, Mark
80SalLakCGT-5
81HolMilT-18

Noce, Doug
90GatCitPP-3356
90GatCitPSP-18
91SumFlyC-14
91SumFlyP-2337

Noce, John
93GenCubC-30
94HunCubF-3571
94HunCubC-30

Noce, Paul
83MiaMarT-17
84MidCubT-21
85IowCubT-5
86IowCubP-20
87DonRoo-51
87IowCubTI-11
88Don-315
88DonTeaBC-315
88Fle-428
88FleGlo-428
88IowCubC-16
88IowCubP-538
88RedFolSB-61
88Sco-329
88ScoGlo-329
88Top-542
88TopTif-542
89CalCanC-16
89CalCanP-539
90CMC-139
90NasSouC-14
90NasSouP-241
90ProAAAF-553
91PhoFirP-72

Noch, Douglas
88VerBeaDS-20
89VerBeaDS-19

Nodell, Ray
83MiaMarT-12

Nodine, Rob
96LanJetB-4

Nodine, Robert
93RivPilCLC-31
94RivPilCLC-32

Noel, Jay
92PulBraC-3
92PulBraF-3192
93MacBraC-16
93MacBraF-1414

Noel, Mike
89FreStaBS-15
91FreStaBS-8

Noel, Todd
96BesAutS1RP-FR7
97Bow-383
97BowInt-383
97Top-269

Noelke, Michael
88LitFalMP-7
89ColMetB-9
89ColMetGS-18

Noffke, Andy
96MicBatCB-17

Noggle, Anne
75TopPho-85

Nogowski, Brandon
96EveAquB-17

Noguchi, Shigeki
94CenValRC-14
94CenValRF-3200

Nokes, David
91WasVia-4

Nokes, Matt
82CliGiaF-4
84ShrCapFB-14
86NasSouTI-18
87ClaUpdY-129
87DonRoo-12
87FleUpd-90
87FleUpdG-90
87SpoRooI-16
87TopTra-91T
87TopTraT-91T
88ClaBlu-207
88ClaRed-166
88Don-152
88DonAll-16
88DonBasB-237
88Fle-66
88Fle-638
88FleAll-1
88FleBasA-29
88FleExcS-29
88FleGlo-66
88FleGlo-638
88FleMin-23
88FleStiC-27
88FleSup-26
88Lea-60
88MSAIceTD-5

88Nes-41
88OPC-266
88PanSti-88
88RedFolSB-62
88Sco-15
88Sco-648
88ScoGlo-15
88ScoGlo-648
88ScoYouSI-5
88Spo-6
88SpoGam-18
88StaLinTi-16
88StaNok-1
88StaNok-2
88StaNok-3
88StaNok-4
88StaNok-5
88StaNok-6
88StaNok-7
88StaNok-8
88StaNok-9
88StaNok-10
88StaNok-11
88TigPep-33
88TigPol-9
88Top-393
88Top-645
88TopBig-185
88TopGloS-59
88TopRoo-8
88TopSti-269
88TopSti-311
88TopStiB-56
88TopTif-393
88TopTif-645
88TopUKM-54
88TopUKMT-54
88ToyRoo-22
89Bow-101
89BowTif-101
89ClaTraO-113
89Don-116
89DonBasB-181
89Fle-140
89FleGlo-140
89MSAHolD-13
89Nis-13
89OPC-116
89PanSti-339
89RedFolSB-86
89Sco-23
89Spo-203
89TigMar-33
89TigPol-33
89Top-445
89TopBig-303
89TopSti-280
89TopTif-445
89TVSpoM-70
89UppDec-150
90ClaBlu-141
90ClaYel-T15
90Don-178
90DonBesA-11
90Fle-611
90FleCan-611
90FleUpd-115
90Lea-192
90Lea-314
90MLBBasB-86
90OPC-131
90PubSti-479
90RedFolSB-69
90Sco-55
90ScoRoo-38T
90TigCok-14
90Top-131
90TopTif-131
90TopTra-81T
90TopTraT-81T
90UppDec-226
90UppDec-744
90VenSti-369
90YanScoNW-24
91Bow-164
91ClaGam-32
91Don-170
91Fle-674
91Lea-89
91OPC-336
91Sco-551
91StaClu-64
91StaCluP-28
91Top-336
91TopDesS-336
91TopMic-336
91TopTif-336
91UltUpd-42
91UppDec-673
92Bow-540
92DenHol-21
92Don-126
92DonCraJ2-34
92Fle-239
92Lea-102
92OPC-748
92PanSti-134
92Pin-72
92Sco-573
92StaClu-111
92Stu-217
92Top-404
92Top-748
92TopGol-404
92TopGol-748
92TopGolW-404
92TopGolW-748
92TopMic-404
92TopMic-748
92TriPla-178
92Ult-107
92UppDec-295
92UppDecHRH-HR22
92UppDecS-1
93Bow-334
93Don-239
93Fla-250
93Fle-283
93Lea-352
93OPC-177
93PacSpa-209
93PanSti-146
93Pin-82
93Sco-192
93Sel-368
93StaClu-189
93StaCluFDI-189
93StaCluMOP-189
93StaCluY-3
93Top-561
93TopGol-561
93TopInaM-561
93TopMic-561
93Ult-247
93UppDec-116
93UppDecGold-116
94Don-564
94ExtBas-135
94Fla-85
94Fle-242
94Pac-432
94Sco-196
94ScoGolR-196
94StaClu-23
94StaCluFDI-23
94StaCluGR-23
94StaCluMOP-23
94StaCluT-206
94StaCluTFDI-206
94Top-59
94TopGol-59
94TopSpa-59
94Ult-402
95Pin-417
95PinArtP-417
95PinMusC-417
95Top-238

Nokes, Wesley
89CarNewE-1

Nolan, Bob
75PhoGiaCK-4
77SalLakCGC-15

Nolan, Darin
91St.CatBJC-22
91St.CatBJP-3393
92MyrBeaHC-17

Nolan, Gary
68OPC-196
68Top-196
68TopVen-196
69MLBOffS-133
69Top-581
69TopTeaP-20
70DayDaiNM-14
70Kel-53
70MLBOffS-33
70OPC-484
70Top-484
71Kel-36A
71Kel-36B
71Kel-36C
71MLBOffS-66
71OPC-75
71Top-75
71TopTat-31
72MilBra-253
72OPC-475
72Top-475
73Kel2D-30
73OPC-260
73Top-260
73TopCanL-36
74OPC-277
74Top-277
75OPC-562
75Top-562
76OPC-444
76RedIceL-10
76RedKro-13
76RedPos-12
76SSP-29
76Top-444
77BurCheD-203
77Hos-113
77OPC-70
77PepGloD-51
77Top-121
78Top-115
92UppDecS-14

Nolan, Joseph W. Jr.
78Top-617
79Top-464
80Top-64
81Don-302
81Fle-212
81OPC-149
81Top-149
81TopSupHT-39
82Don-62
82Fle-77
82Top-327
82TopTra-81T
83Don-79
83Fle-68
83OriPos-18
83Top-242
84Don-489
84Fle-15
84Nes792-553
84OriTeal-19
84Top-553
84TopTif-553
85Don-594
85Fle-185
85Top-652
85TopTif-652
86Top-781
86TopTif-781
91MetWIZ-295
91OriCro-332

Noland, J.D.
89WatDiaP-1778
89WatDiaS-22
90Bes-238
90CMC-700
90MidLeaASGS-46
90WatDiaB-13
90WatDiaP-2390
91CalLeLA-18
91HigDesMC-27
91HigDesMP-2410
92ClaFS7-311
92ProFS7-337
92SkyAA F-284
92WicWraS-642
94NewHavRF-1563
95LinVen-271
95TacRaiTI-14

Nold, Dick
68OPC-96
68Top-96
68TopVen-96

Noles, Dickie
80Top-682
81Don-568
81Fle-12
81OklCit8T-14
81Top-406
82CubRedL-48
82Fle-253
82Top-530
82TopTra-82T
83CubThoAV-48
83Don-426
83Fle-504
83OPC-99
83Top-99
84Don-266
84Fle-500
84Nes792-618
84RanJarP-36
84Top-618
84TopTif-618
85AllGamPI-82
85OPC-149
85RanPer-36
85Top-149
85TopTif-149
86Don-587
86Fle-567
86IndOhH-48
86IndTeal-30
86Top-388
86TopTif-388
87CubCan-23
87CubDavB-47
87Fle-256
87FleGlo-256
87FleUpd-91
87FleUpdG-91
87Top-244
87TopTif-244
87TopTra-92T
87TopTraT-92T
88RocRedWC-8
88RocRedWGCP-19
88RocRedWP-219
88RocRedWTI-16
88Top-768
88TopTif-768
89ColCliC-3
89ColCliP-8
89ColCliP-749
90CMC-231
90ScrRedBC-5
91OriCro-333
93RanKee-277

Nolte, Bruce
96PitMetB-30

Nolte, Eric
85SpoIndC-17
86ChaRaiP-19
87WicPilRD-12
88Don-534
88Fle-593
88FleGlo-593
88PadSmo-20
88Sco-568
88ScoGlo-568
88Top-694
88TopTif-694
89LasVegSC-8
89LasVegSP-12
90CMC-508
90LasVegSC-5
90LasVegSP-118
90ProAAAF-6
92DenZepF-2639
92DenZepS-143
93NewOrlZF-970
93RanKee-278
94SanBerSC-13
94SanBerSF-2753

Nomo, Hideo
92SpoIllFK1-470
95BakBlaTI-4
95BakBlaTI-29
95Bow-238
95BowBes-R83
95BowBesJR-5
95BowBesR-R83
95BowGolF-238
95ClaPhoC-32
95ColCho-547T
95DodMot-13
95DodPol-16
95DonTopotO-269
95Emo-144
95EmoRoo-9
95Fin-228
95FinRef-228
95Fla-368
95FlaWavotF-10
95FleUpd-175
95FleUpdRU-7
95Lea-267
95LeaLim-64
95NatPac2-6
95Sel-251S
95SelArtP-251S
95SelCer-98
95SelCerF-3
95SelCerMG-98
95SelCerPU-10
95SelCerPU9-10
95SP-14
95SPCha-1
95SPChaDC-1
95SPChaDFC-6
95SPChaFCDC-6
95SPSil-14
95StaClu-556
95StaCluMOP-556
95StaCluSTDW-D556
95StaCluSTWS-556
95Sum-141
95SumNthD-141
95TopTra-40T
95TopTra-124T
95TopTra-164T
95UC3-97
95UC3ArtP-97
95UC3CleS-CS3
95UltGolMR-M17
95UppDec-226
95UppDecED-226
95UppDecEDG-226
95UppDecPAW-H38
95UppDecPAWE-H38
95UppDecSE-168
95UppDecSEG-168
95Zen-48
95Zen-149
95ZenAllS-7
95ZenRooRC-7
96Baz-98
96Bow-5
96BowBes-1
96BowBesAR-1
96BowBesC-8
96BowBesCAR-8
96BowBesCR-8
96BowBesP-BBP26
96BowBesPAR-BBP26
96BowBesPR-BBP26
96BowBesR-1
96Cir-144
96CirAcc-20
96CirBos-38
96CirRav-144
96Cla7/1PC-3
96ColCho-7
96ColCho-180
96ColCho-270
96ColCho-332
96ColCho-359
96ColCho-705
96ColChoGS-7
96ColChoGS-180
96ColChoGS-270
96ColChoGS-332
96ColChoGS-359
96ColChoGS-705
96ColChoNS-1
96ColChoNS-2
96ColChoNS-3
96ColChoNS-4
96ColChoNS-5
96ColChoSS-7
96ColChoSS-180
96ColChoSS-270
96ColChoSS-332
96ColChoSS-359
96ColChoSS-705
96ColChoYMtP-29
96ColChoYMtP-29A
96ColChoYMtPGS-29
96ColChoYMtPGS-29A
96DenHol-10
96DodMot-3
96DodPol-25
96Don-390
96DonDiaK-27
96DonEli-62
96DonFreF-4
96DonPreP-390
96DonSam-3
96DonSho-1
96EmoRarB-8
96EmoXL-213

96Fin-G33
96Fin-G232
96Fin-S59
96FinRef-G33
96FinRef-G232
96FinRef-S59
96Fla-297
96Fle-442
96FleDod-13
96FleRooS-12
96FleSmo'H-8
96FleTif-442
96FleTomL-8
96FleUpd-U234
96FleUpdH-14
96FleUpdTC-U234
96Kin-19
96Lea-148
96LeaGolS-7
96LeaHatO-6
96LeaLim-65
96LeaLimG-65
96LeaPre-64
96LeaPreP-64
96LeaPrePB-148
96LeaPrePG-148
96LeaPrePS-148
96LeaPreSG-11
96LeaPreSte-11
96LeaSig-51
96LeaSigPPG-51
96LeaSigPPP-51
96LeaStaS-5
96MetUni-186
96MetUniMFG-9
96MetUniP-186
96MetUniPP-7
96Pac-100
96Pac-117
96PacGolCD-DC19
96PacHom-HP19
96PacOctM-OM16
96PacPri-P37
96PacPriFT-FT5
96PacPriG-P37
96PanSti-92
96PanSti-117
96PanSti-239
96Pin-131
96Pin-132
96Pin-256
96PinAfi-132
96PinAfi-151
96PinAfiAP-132
96PinAfiAP-151
96PinAfiSP-11
96PinArtP-54
96PinArtP-156
96PinEssotG-9
96PinFan-6
96PinFoil-256
96PinSky-12
96PinSta-54
96PinSta-156
96PinTeaT-5
96ProMagA-11
96ProMagDM-15
96ProSta-45
96Sco-195
96Sco-320
96ScoAll-12
96ScoDiaA-1
96ScoDugC-B45
96ScoDugCAP-B45
96ScoFutF-13
96ScoGolS-24
96ScoNumG-10
96ScoRef-18
96Sel-73
96SelArtP-73
96SelCer-13
96SelCer-143
96SelCerAP-13
96SelCerAP-143
96SelCerCB-13
96SelCerCB-143
96SelCerCR-13
96SelCerCR-143
96SelCerIP-1
96SelCerMB-13
96SelCerMB-143
96SelCerMG-13
96SelCerMG-143
96SelCerMR-13
96SelCerMR-143
96SelCerSF-12
96SelClaTF-10
96SelEnF-25
96SelTeaN-11
96SP-106
96SP-186
96SPBasH-86
96SPMarM-MM2
96SPMarMDC-2
96Spo-48
96SpoArtP-48
96SpoDouT-5
96SpoPro-9
96SPSpeFX-5
96SPSpeFXDC-5
96SPx-35
96SPxGol-35
96StaClu-1
96StaClu-247
96StaCluEPB-1
96StaCluEPG-1
96StaCluEPS-1
96StaCluMeg-MH3
96StaCluMM-MM1
96StaCluMO-31
96StaCluMO-46
96StaCluMOP-1
96StaCluMOP-247
96StaCluMOP-MH3
96StaCluMOP-MM1
96StaCluMOP-PS2
96StaCluMOP-TSCA6
96StaCluPS-PS2
96StaCluTA-6
96Stu-55
96StuPrePB-55
96StuPrePB-63
96StuPrePG-55
96StuPrePG-63
96StuPrePS-55
96StuPrePS-63
96StuStaGS-9
96Sum-40
96SumAbo&B-40
96SumArtP-40
96SumFoi-40
96SumPos-6
96TeaOut-59
96Top-136
96TopBigC-6
96TopBroLL-3
96TopChr-37
96TopChrR-37
96TopGal-92
96TopGalE-7
96TopGalPPI-92
96TopLas-60
96TopLasBS-15
96TopMysF-M1
96TopMysF-M22
96TopMysFR-M1
96TopMysFR-M22
96TopPro-NL18
96Ult-223
96UltDiaP-6
96UltDiaPGM-6
96UltFreF-8
96UltFreFGM-8
96UltGolM-223
96UltRisS-8
96UltRisSGM-8
96UltSeaC-7
96UltSeaCGM-7
96UppDec-95
96UppDec-150
96UppDecBCP-BC1
96UppDecDD-DD22
96UppDecDDG-DD22
96UppDecDDS-DD22
96UppDecG-GF9
96UppDecHC-HC2
96UppDecNomH-1
96UppDecNomH-2
96UppDecNomH-3
96UppDecNomH-4
96UppDecNomH-5
96UppDecNRJ-1
96UppDecPHE-H46
96UppDecPreH-H46
96UppDecVJLS-VJ2
96Zen-84
96Zen-140
96ZenArtP-84
96ZenArtP-140
96ZenMoz-13
96ZenZ-10
97Bow-4
97BowBes-78
97BowBesAR-78
97BowBesR-78
97BowChr-3
97BowChrI-3
97BowChrIR-3
97BowChrR-3
97BowInt-4
97BowIntB-BBI5
97BowIntBAR-BBI5
97BowIntBR-BBI5
97Cir-15
97CirRav-15
97ColCho-141
97ColChoAC-45
97ColChoNF-NF3
97ColChoNF-NF4
97ColChoTBS-27
97ColChoTBSWH-27
97Don-36
97Don-427
97DonDom-10
97DonEli-32
97DonEli-150
97DonEliGS-32
97DonEliGS-150
97DonLim-43
97DonLim-53
97DonLim-137
97DonLimLE-43
97DonLimLE-53
97DonLimLE-137
97DonPre-28
97DonPre-194
97DonPreCttC-28
97DonPreCttC-194
97DonPreP-36
97DonPreP-427
97DonPrePGold-36
97DonPrePGold-427
97DonPreS-16
97DonPreTB-14
97DonPreTBG-14
97DonPreTF-14
97DonPreTP-14
97DonPreTPG-14
97DonTea-107
97DonTeaSPE-107
97Fin-143
97Fin-345
97FinEmb-143
97FinEmb-345
97FinEmbR-143
97FinEmbR-345
97FinPro-143
97FinRef-143
97FinRef-345
97FlaSho-A16
97FlaSho-B16
97FlaSho-C16
97FlaShoLC-16
97FlaShoLC-B16
97FlaShoLC-C16
97FlaShoLCM-A16
97FlaShoLCM-B16
97FlaShoLCM-C16
97Fle-368
97Fle-710
97FleGolM-7
97FleMilDM-16
97FleTif-368
97FleTif-710
97Lea-99
97Lea-360
97LeaFraM-99
97LeaFraM-360
97LeaFraMDC-99
97LeaFraMDC-360
97LeaGet-9
97LeaGolS-14
97MetUni-104
97NewPin-29
97NewPinAP-29
97NewPinIE-8
97NewPinKtP-16
97NewPinMC-29
97NewPinPP-29
97NewPinPP-I8B
97NewPinPP-K16
97Pac-336
97PacCar-30
97PacCarM-30
97PacCerCGT-18
97PacFirD-16
97PacGolCD-30
97PacLigB-336
97PacPri-114
97PacPriGA-GA25
97PacPriGotD-GD160
97PacPriLB-114
97PacPriP-114
97PacPriSH-SH11B
97PacSil-336
97Pin-192
97PinArtP-192
97PinCar-7
97PinCer-63
97PinCer-149
97PinCerCMGT-18
97PinCerCT-18
97PinCerMBlu-63
97PinCerMBlu-149
97PinCerMG-63
97PinCerMG-149
97PinCerMR-63
97PinCerMR-149
97PinCerR-63
97PinCerR-149
97PinIns-5
97PinInsC-20
97PinInsCE-5
97PinInsDD-18
97PinInsDE-5
97PinMin-12
97PinMinB-12
97PinMinCB-12
97PinMinCG-12
97PinMinCGR-12
97PinMinCN-12
97PinMinCS-12
97PinMinG-12
97PinMinS-12
97PinMusC-192
97PinPasttM-21
97PinTotCPB-63
97PinTotCPB-149
97PinTotCPG-63
97PinTotCPG-149
97PinTotCPR-63
97PinTotCPR-149
97PinX-P-10
97PinX-P-150
97PinX-PMoS-10
97PinX-PMoS-150
97PinX-PMP-11
97ProMag-22
97ProMagML-22
97Sco-159
97Sco-522
97ScoDod-15
97ScoDodPl-15
97ScoDodPr-15
97ScoHobR-522
97ScoPreS-159
97ScoResC-522
97ScoShoS-159
97ScoShoS-522
97ScoShoSAP-159
97ScoShoSAP-522
97ScoStaaD-14
97Sel-29
97SelArtP-29
97SelRegG-29
97SkyE-X-81
97SkyE-XC-81
97SkyE-XEC-81
97SP-92
97SpoIll-64
97SpoIll-116
97SpoIll-176
97SpoIllEE-64
97SpoIllEE-116
97SpoIllEE-176
97SPSpeF-27
97SPSpxF-7
97SPSPxFA-7
97SPx-29
97SPxBro-29
97SPxGraF-29
97SPxSil-29
97SPxSte-29
97StaClu-212
97StaCluI-I10
97StaCluMat-212
97StaCluMOP-212
97StaCluMOP-I10
97Stu-73
97StuMasS-18
97StuMasS8-18
97StuPor8-19
97StuPrePG-73
97StuPrePS-73
97Top-440
97Top-464
97TopChr-156
97TopChrDD-DD8
97TopChrDDR-DD8
97TopChrR-156
97TopGal-139
97TopGalPPI-139
97TopScr-16
97TopSta-71
97TopStaAM-71
97TopStaASGM-ASM8
97Ult-221
97UltDouT-15
97UltGolME-221
97UltPlaME-221
97UltTop3-21
97UltTop3GM-21
97UppDec-70
97UppDec-94
97UppDec-192
97UppDec-321
97UppDecHC-HC18
97UppDecP-17
97UppDecU-27
97Zen-18
97Zen8x1-18
97Zen8x1D-18

Nomura, Katsuya
79TCMJapPB-13

Nonnenkamp, Red (Leo W.)
40PlaBal-196

Noonan, Dennis
90CarLeaA-33
90KinIndTI-29

Noonan, Jim
78WauMetT-20

Noonan, Pete
11SpoLifCW-271

Noonan, Todd
87SalLakTTT-10

Noore, Daryl
89BluOriS-27

Nops, Jerry
90DodTar-578

Norbert, Ted
45CenFlo-18

Nordbrook, Tim (Timothy C.)
76OPC-252
76SSP-391
76Top-252
78OPC-139
78Top-369
79VanCanT-6
80VanCanT-10
83BelBreF-16
91OriCro-334
94BreMilB-157

Nordhagen, Wayne O.
76OklCit8TI-22
78SSP270-162
78Top-231
79Kel-4
79Top-351
80OPC-253
80Top-487
81CokTeaS-35
81Don-401
81Fle-348
81Top-186
81TopSti-59
81TopSupHT-21
82Don-67
82Fle-355
82OPC-139
82Top-597
83Fle-438
83OPC-47
83Top-714
89PacSenL-154
89TopSenL-47
90EliSenL-45

Nordstrom, Burt
72CedRapCT-18

Nordstrom, Carl
88BilMusP-1831
88CedRapRP-1158
89GreHorP-429
Nored, Mike
76AppFoxT-17
Noren, Irv (Irving Arnold)
47StaPinP2-31
49W72HolS-12
50Bow-247
51Bow-241
51FisBakL-20
51TopBluB-38
52Bow-63
52Top-40
53BowBW-45
53Dor-132
53Top-35
54NewYorJA-55
55Bow-63
55RedMan-AL9
56Top-253
57Top-298
58Top-114
59Top-59
59TopVen-59
60Lea-101
60Top-433
73OPC-179
73Top-179A
73Top-179B
83TopRep5-40
83YanASFY-31
89SweBasG-102
90DodTar-579
91TopArc1-35
92YanWIZA-55
Noriega, Kevin
93LinVenB-148
95LinVen-115
96BelSnaTI-26
Noriega, Ray
96SouOreTI-11
Noriega, Rey
90Ft.LauYS-15
91FloStaLAP-FSL17
91Ft.LauYC-22
91Ft.LauYP-2435
92AlbYanS-15
92Ft.LauYF-2628
92ProFS7-118
92SkyAA F-9
Norko, Tom
80UtiBluJT-7
Norman, Bill (H. Willis)
53Top-245
91TopArc1-245
Norman, Bull
83TamTarT-30
Norman, Dan (Daniel E.)
77IndIndTI-10
78TidTidT-16
79TidTidT-11
79Top-721
80Top-681
81Fle-337
81TidTidT-28
82ExpHygM-14
82ExpPos-24
83Fle-289
83OPC-237
83Top-237
84MidCubT-17
89KinMetS-27
90KinMetB-27
91MetWIZ-296
91PacSenL-64
92ColRedC-28
93CarLeaAGF-33
93KinIndC-28
93KinIndF-2265
93KinIndTI-28
94KinIndC-25
96RanCucQB-3
Norman, Fred
64Top-469
65Top-386
70OPC-427
70Top-427
71MLBOffS-280
71OPC-348
71Top-348
72OPC-194
72PadTeal-20
72Top-194
73OPC-32
73Top-32
74OPC-581
74Top-581
75OPC-396
75Top-396
76OPC-609
76RedKro-14
76RedPos-13
76SSP-30
76Top-609
77Kel-8
77OPC-181
77PadSchC-42A
77PadSchC-42B
77PepGloD-56
77Top-139
78Pep-20
78SSP270-109
78Top-273
79OPC-20
79Top-47
80ExpPos-19
80OPC-362
80Top 714
81Don-92
81Fle-158
81OPC-183
81Top-497
90DodTar-580
Norman, Greg
83BirBarT-13
Norman, Kenny
91EliTwiP-4313
92EliTwiC-17
92EliTwiF-3696
92KenTwiC-15
93ForMyeMC-18
93ForMyeMF-2670
94ForMyeMC-17
Norman, Les
91EugEmeC-13
91EugEmeP-3739
92AppFoxC-14
92AppFoxF-999
92MemChiF-2432
92UppDecML-100
93Bow-673
93ExcFS7-176
93MemChiF-390
94ClaGolF-121
94ExcFS7-69
94ForMyeMF-1181
94OmaRoyF-1236
94UppDecML-34
96ColCho-576
96ColChoGS-576
96ColChoSS-576
96Don-537
96DonPreP-537
96RoyPol-19
96Sco-262
96SigRooOJ-24
96SigRooOJS-24
97PacPriGotD-GD48
Norman, Nelson A.
77ShrCapT-16
78TucTorC-4
80ChaChaT-4
80OPC-270
80Top-518
81Don-509
82PorBeaT-16
83LynPirT-15
84HawIslC-133
85DomLeaS-187
85RocRedWT-7
86JacExpT-22
87IndIndTI-29
88IndIndP-517
89IndIndP-1227
93RanKee-279
95MacBraTI-22
96DanBraB-3
Norman, Rob
88MisStaB-24
89MisStaB-28
90MisStaB-28
91MisStaB-34
Norman, Ron
75SpoIndC-21
76SanAntBTI-16
Norman, Scott
83CliGiaF-3
87SprCarB-28
89TenTecGE-19
93BriTigC-16
94FayGenC-18
94FayGenF-2142
96JacSunB-23
Norman, Terry
80BatTroT-2
Normand, Guy
85AncGlaPTI-21
86AubAstP-17
87AshTouP-13
88OscAstS-18
89OscAstS-13
Norrid, Tim
76WilTomT-16
79TacTugT-22
79Top-705
80TacTigT-2
81ChaChaT-9
82ChaChaT-12
83ChaChaT-14
Norris, Allen
59DarFar-14
60DarFar-23
Norris, Bill
91CarLeaAP-CAR25
91LynRedSC-17
91LynRedSP-1207
92NewBriRSF-442
92NewBriRSS-491
92SkyAA F-211
93NewBriRSF-1229
94NewBriRSF-659
Norris, David
90JohCitCS-19
91SprCarC-20
91SprCarP-741
Norris, Dax
96EugEmeB-17
Norris, Jim (James Frances)
75OklCit8TI-17
76VenLeaS-45
78Top-484
79Top-611
80Top-333
81Don-388
81Fle-634
81Top-264
93RanKee-280
Norris, Joe
91SumFlyC-9
91SumFlyP-2332
92RocExpC-22
92RocExpF-2113
93WesPalBEC-16
93WesPalBEF-1337
94NasXprF-383
95HarCitRCTI-17
Norris, MacKenzie
96HelBreTI-16
Norris, Mike
76OPC-653
76SSP-487
76Top-653
77BurCheD-113
77Top-284
78Top-434
79Top-191
80Top-599
81A'sGraG-17
81AllGamPI-88
81Don-118
81Fle-573
81FleStiC-6
81MSAMinD-24
81OPC-55
81Top-55
81TopScr-53
81TopSti-2
81TopSti-4
81TopSti-6
81TopSti-122
82A'sGraG-13
82Don-19
82Don-197
82Fle-103
82FleSta-125
82Kel-59
82OPC-370
82Top-370
82TopSti-222
83A'sGraG-17
83AllGamPI-82
83Don-139
83Fle-530
83OPC-276
83Top-620
84Fle-457
84Nes792-493
84OPC-49
84Top-493
84TopTif-493
85Top-246
85TopTif-246
87A'sMot-22
90A'sMot-19
90HelBreSP-26
91PacSenL-107
91RenSilSCLC-15
Norris, Niles
93MisStaB-34
Norris, Scott
75ForLauYS-1
Norris, Steve
96JohCitCTI-24
Norris, Wade
92MedHatBJF-3216
92MedHatBJSP-13
Norsetter, Howard
91MelBusF-16
North, Billy (William Alex)
73OPC-234
73Top-234
74GreHeroBP-1
74GreHeroBP-5
74OPC-345
74Top-345
74TopSta-228
75A'sPos-65
75GreHeroBP-5
75Kel-23
75OPC-121
75OPC-309
75Top-121
75Top-309
76GreHeroBP-1
76GreHeroBP-5
76OPC-33
76SSP-491
76Top-33
77BurCheD-116
77Hos-33
77Kel-22
77MSADis-47
77OPC-4
77OPC-106
77Top-4
77Top-551
78Hos-76
78TasDis-13
78Top-163
79GiaPol-36
79OPC-351
79Top-668
80BurKinPHR-31
80GiaEurFS-7
80GiaPol-36
80OPC-213
80Top-408
81Don-76
81Fle-441
81OPC-47
81Top-713
86A'sGreT-7
90DodTar-581
94MCIAmb-11
North, Jay
85SprCarT-21
86St.PetCP-22
87St.PetCP-25
88St.PetCS-20
89SavCarP-343
90St.PetCS-26
91St.PetCC-11
91St.PetCP-2293
North, Mark
87GenCubP-3
88PeoChiTI-22
89KenTwiP-1061
89KenTwiS-18
North, Roy
80AndBraT-18
81DurBulT-21
North, Tim
92EriSaiC-6
92EriSaiF-1632
93HigDesMC-14
93HigDesMF-50
Northam, J.J.
90AriWilP-14
Northeimer, James
94BatCliC-15
94BatCliF-3450
95PiePhiF-189
95TenVolW-8
Northern, Hubbard
12T207-140
90DodTar-1144
Northey, Ron (Ronald J.)
43PhiTeal-18
47Exh-168
49Bow-79
50Bow-81
51Bow-70
52Top-204
57Top-31
63PirIDL-17
76TayBow4-77
77TCMTheWY-40
83TCMPla1942-44
83TopRep5-204
Northey, Scott (Scott R.)
70OPC-241
70Top-241
71OPC-633
71Top-633
Northrup, George
09ColChiE-214
12ColTinT-214
Northrup, Jim (James T.)
65OPC-259
65Top-259
66Top-554
67CokCapTi-8
67Top-408
68CokCapT-8
68OPC-78
68TigDetFPB-16
68Top-78
68TopVen-78
69MilBra-202
69MLBOffS-53
69OPC-3
69OPC-167
69TigFarJ-1
69TigTeal-9
69Top-3
69Top-167
69Top-580
69TopSta-178
69TopTeaP-1
70DayDaiNM-126
70MLBOffS-213
70OPC-177
70Top-177
71Kel-63
71MLBOffS-401
71OPC-265
71Top-265
71TopCoi-82
71TopGreM-21
71TopSup-55
72MilBra-254
72OPC-408
72Top-408
73LinPor-75
73OPC-168
73TigJew-15
73Top-168
74OPC-266
74Tig-8
74Top-266
75OPC-641
75Top-641
76SSP-399
78TigDeaCS-18
81TigDetN-52
83TigAlKS-52
86TigSpoD-16
88TigDom-17
90SweBasG-78
91OriCro-335
93UppDecS-26
Northrup, Kevin
92JamExpC-24
92JamExpF-1514
93WesPalBEC-17
93WesPalBEF-1355
94HarSenF-2106

95Exc-223
96ColCliB-23
Norton, Andy
95BelGiaTI-25
Norton, Chris
94SavCarC-22
94SavCarF-510
Norton, Doug
83BelBreF-11
86StoPorP-19
Norton, Greg
94SouBenSHC-15
94SouBenSHF-601
94Top-758
94TopGol-758
94TopSpa-758
96BirBarB-7
96Bow-234
97Fle-67
97FleTif-67
97PacPriGotD-GD31
97Sel-135
97SelArtP-135
97SelRegG-135
97UppDec-280
Norton, Rick
91SouOreAC-8
91SouOreAP-3856
92SouOreAF-3421
93ModA'sC-15
93ModA'sF-803
Norton, Tom
73TacTwiC-17
Norwood, Aaron
89BluOriS-19
Norwood, Steve
78NewWayCT-31
79BurBeeT-24
80BurBeeT-15
81BurBeeT-4
Norwood, Willie
76TacTwiDQ-14
76VenLeaS-23
77TacTwiDQ-8B
78Top-705
78TwiFriP-13
79Top-274
79TwiFriP-19
80TolMudHT-10
80Top-432
81Don-516A
81Don-516B
Nosek, Randy
88LakTigS-18
89LonTigP-1377
90CMC-383
90ProAAAF-375
90Sco-607
90TolMudHC-6
90TolMudHP-145
90TopDeb89-88
90UppDec-2
91LinDriAAA-594
91TolMudHLD-594
91TolMudHP-1930
Nossek, Joe (Joseph R.)
64Top-532
65Top-597
66OPC-22
66Top-22
66TopVen-22
67CokCapAt-12
67DexPre-152
67Top-209
69OPC-143
69Top-143
69TopFou-25
73OPC-646
73Top-646
74Top-99
78TwiFri-39
83Roy-18
84WhiSoxTV-8
90WhiSoxC-30
91WhiSoxK-NNO
92WhiSoxK-NNO
93WhiSoxK-30
94WhiSoxK-30
95WhiSoxK-31
Nossek, Scott
84AriWilP-14
Nottebart, Don
60Top-351
61SevElev-29
61Top-29
62Top-541
63Top-204
64Top-434
64TopCoi-119
65Top-469
66OPC-21
66Top-21
66TopVen-21
67AstTeal2-18
67Top-269
68OPC-171
68Top-171
68TopVen-171
69Top-593
78TCM60I-72
87AstSer1-18
92YanWIZ6-94
Nottle, Ed
74GasRanT-15
75AndRanT-NNO
76SacSolC-14
77TucTorC-27
79WatA'sT-9
80WesHavWCT-20A
81TacTigT-6
82TacTigT-19
84TacTigC-90
86PawRedSP-16
87IntLeaAT-9
87PawRedSP-72
87PawRedST-21
88PawRedSC-24
88PawRedSP-469
88TriAAAP-52
89PacSenL-51
89PawRedSC-25
89PawRedSP-677
89PawRedSP-678
89PawRedSTI-18
90CMC-261
90PawRedSC-10
90PawRedSDD-17
90PawRedSP-477
90ProAAAF-449
90TopTVRS-34
Nova, Pascual
96IdaFalB-18
Novak, Dave
92HamRedF-1609
Novak, Tom
87TamTarP-11
Novak, Troy
95OdgRapTI-20
Novick, Walter
52Par-77
Novikoff, Lou
41CubTeal-16
43CubTeal-18
43MPR302-1-18
44CubTeal-18
47CenFlo-16
47SigOil-82
83TCMPla1942-41
88LitSunMLL-4
Novoa, Rafael
88CapCodPPaLP-36
89BlaYNPRWLU-8
90Bes-89
90CliGiaB-24
90CliGiaP-2541
90CMC-843
90MidLeaASGS-57
90ProAaA-116
91Cla1-T9
91LinDriAAA-386
91PhoFirLD-386
91PhoFirP-62
91Sco-366
91TopDeb90-116
91UppDec-674
92ElPasDF-3918
93NewOrlZF-971
94BreMilB-257
94IowCubF-1274
94Pac-338
94StaCluT-343
94StaCluTFDI-343
94Top-623
94TopGol-623
94TopSpa-623
Novosel, Frank
52LavPro-102
Novotney, Rube
49EurSta-65
49W725AngTI-22
Nowak, Matt
88HagSunS-14
Nowak, Rick
90MyrBeaBJP-2774
Nowak, Steve
93BriTigF-3647
94FayGenF-2143
94JamJamF-3962
Nowlan, Bill
81BurBeeT-28
82BelBreF-25
83BelBreF-13
Nowlin, Jim (James)
87SumBraP-25
88BurBraP-15
Noworyta, Steve
83AppFoxF-9
Nozling, Paul
88BriTigP-1890
89FayGenP-1591
Nugent, Barney
86ReaPhiP-20
87MaiGuiP-10
88MaiPhiC-3
88MaiPhiP-299
89ScrRedBC-2
89ScrRedBP-712
90CMC-251
90ScrRedBC-25
Nuismer, Jack
80WatIndT-8
81ChaLooT-7
82ChaChaT-8
Nunamaker, Les (Leslie G.)
12T207-141
14CraJacE-132
15CraJacE-132
15SpoNewM-131
19W514-7
21E121So1-72
22E120-38
22W573-92
23W501-116
77Ind192T-14
95ConTSN-1361
Nuneviller, Tom
90BatCliP-3082
91ClePhiC-22
91ClePhiP-1633
92ClaFS7-233
92ReaPhiF-589
92ReaPhiS-537
92SkyAA F-233
92UppDecML-112
93ExcFS7-87
94ReaPhiF-2076
Nunex, Nelson
87WytCubP-11
Nunez, Abraham
96StCatSB-22
97Bow-362
97BowBes-164
97BowBesAR-164
97BowBesR-164
97BowChr-242
97BowChrI-242
97BowChrIR-242
97BowChrR-242
97BowInt-362
Nunez, Alex
90KenTwiB-11
90KenTwiP-2303
90KenTwiS-18
91VisOakC-18
91VisOakP-1750
Nunez, Bernie (Bernardino)
88MyrBeaBJP-1169
89DunBluJS-12
90CMC-772
90KnoBluJB-14
90KnoBluJP-1256
90KnoBluJS-13
91KnoBluJLD-363
91KnoBluJP-1781
91LinDriAA-363
93DayCubC-14
93DayCubF-870
93FloStaLAF-32
94ClaGolF-51
Nunez, Clemente
92Bow-417
92UppDec-701
93ElmPioC-1
93ElmPioF-3821
93Top-599
93TopGol-599
93TopInaM-599
93TopMic-599
94BreCouMC-10
95Bes-72
95BreCouMF-244
95SPML-58
96Exc-165
96PorSeaDB-20
Nunez, Dario
86PalSprAP-25
86PalSprAP-24
87PalSprP-22
88PalSprAP-1448
Nunez, Edwin
80WauTimT-6
81WauTimT-4
83SalLakCGT-1
84Don-435
84SalLakCGC-183
85Don-484
85Fle-496
85MarMot-24
85Top-34
85TopTif-34
86Don-145
86Fle-470
86Lea-66
86MarMot-24
86OPC-364
86SevCoi-W15
86Top-511
86TopSti-223
86TopTat-8
86TopTif-511
87Don-243
87FleUpd-92
87FleUpdG-92
87MarMot-11
87Top-427
87TopTif-427
88Don-445
88DonRoo-36
88Fle-383
88FleGlo-383
88MarMot-11
88OPC-258
88PanSti-182
88StaLinMa-12
88Top-258
88TopSti-216
88TopTif-258
89BlaYNPRWL-121
89BlaYNPRWLU-67
89MetColP-46
89TolMudHP-773
90Don-563
90FleUpd-98
90Lea-397
90OPC-586
90TigCok-15
90Top-586
90TopTif-586
91Bow-40
91BreMilB-19
91BrePol-17
91Don-620
91Fle-345
91FleUpd-32
91Lea-352
91MetWIZ-297
91OPC-106
91StaClu-595
91Top-106
91TopDesS-106
91TopMic-106
91TopTif-106
92BrePol-17
92Don-541
92Fle-184
92OPC-352
92RanTeal-14
92Sco-676
92StaClu-776
92StaCluECN-776
92Top-352
92TopGol-352
92TopGolW-352
92TopMic-352
92Ult-387
93AthMot-24
93Fle-686
93FleFinE-260
93RanKee-281
93Top-19
93TopGol-19
93TopInaM-19
93TopMic-19
93Ult-611
94BreMilB-342
94Fle-271
94Pac-460
94Sco-296
94ScoGolR-296
Nunez, Isaias
94JohCitCC-23
94JohCitCF-3711
95PeoChiTI-33
96PeoChiB-23
Nunez, Jose
96AriBlaDB-23
Nunez, Jose Jiminez
85Ft.MyeRT-13
87BluJayFS-26
87FleUpd-93
87FleUpdG-93
88Don-611
88Fle-122
88FleGlo-122
88OPC-28
88Sco-312
88ScoGlo-312
88SyrChiC-4
88SyrChiP-820
88Top-28
88TopTif-28
89BluJayFS-24
89SyrChiC-2
89SyrChiMB-16
89SyrChiP-806
90Don-467
90TopTVCu-13
90UppDec-716
91IowCubP-1057
92CalCanS-65
92SkyAAAF-30
93LimRocDWB-11
Nunez, Juan
96ChaRivTI-9624
Nunez, Mauricio
86St.PetCP-23
87St.PetCP-6
88ArkTraGS-10
89SavCarP-357
89SouAtlLAGS-38
90CMC-669
90LouRedBC-26
90LouRedBLBC-30
90LouRedBP-417
90ProAAAF-531
90TopTVCa-57
91St.PetCC-28
93GleFalRC-30
93LimRocDWB-37
Nunez, Maximo
95HagSunF-66
96HicCraB-12
Nunez, Primivito
94AugGreC-14
Nunez, Ramon
84IdaFalATI-19
94DurBulC-13
94DurBulF-335
Nunez, Raymond
92PulBraC-8
92PulBraF-3185
93MacBraC-17
93MacBraF-1410
93SouAtlLAGF-41
94DurBulTI-14
95BreBtaTI-8
95DurBulTI-23
96DurBulBrB-15
Nunez, Rogelio
90UtiBluSP-4
91Cla/Bes-277
91MidLeaAP-MWL11
91SouBenWSC-22
91SouBenWSP-2859
92ClaFS7-150
92ProFS7-46
92SarWhiSCB-3
92SarWhiSF-208

93BirBarF-1196
94BirBarC-17
94BirBarF-624
95TulDriTI-17
Nunez, Sergio
95Bow-235
95BowBes-B35
95BowBesR-B35
95BowGolF-235
95SPML-72
95UppDecML-185
95WilBluRTI-35
96BesAutS-66
96BesAutSA-49
96ColCho-436
96ColChoGS-436
96ColChoSS-436
96Exc-65
96UppDec-263
96WilBluRB-10
95UppDecMLFS-185
Nunez, Vladimir
96AriBlaDB-24
97Bow-154
97BowChr-154
97BowChrI-154
97BowChrIR-154
97BowChrR-154
97BowInt-154
97Top-250
Nunley, Angelo
85SprCarT-22
86TamTarP-14
87VerRedP-13
88ChaLooB-25
88ChaLooB-26
Nunn, Howard
59Top-549
61Top-346
62Top-524
Nunn, Wally
77SpaPhiT-6
Nunnally, Jon (Jonathan)
92ClaDraP-51
92FroRowDP-15
92WatIndC-17
92WatIndF-3248
93ClaFS7-231
93ColRedC-17
93ColRedF-606
93ExcFS7-161
93SouAtlLAGF-14
93StaCluM-7
94CarLeaAF-CAR35
94KinIndC-15
94KinIndF-2658
95ARuFalLS-15
95Bow-176
95BowBes-R79
95BowBesR-R79
95Emo-51
95Fin-260
95FinRef-260
95Fla-266
95FleUpd-47
95FleUpdRU-8
95SelCer-111
95SelCerF-9
95SelCerMG-111
95SP-158
95SPCha-4
95SPChaDC-4
95SPSil-158
95StaClu-587
95StaCluMOP-587
95StaCluSTWS-587
95Sum-121
95SumNthD-121
95TopTra-15T
95TopTra-133T
95UltGolMR-M18
95UppDec-258
95UppDecED-258
95UppDecEDG-258
95Zen-145
96ColCho-175
96ColCho-657
96ColChoGS-175
96ColChoGS-657
96ColChoSS-175
96ColChoSS-657
96ColChoYMtP-30
96ColChoYMtP-30A
96ColChoYMtPGS-30
96ColChoYMtPGS-30A
96Don-269
96DonPreP-269
96EmoXL-69
96Fla-93
96Fle-136
96FleTif-136
96Lea-106
96LeaPrePB-106
96LeaPrePG-106
96LeaPrePS-106
96LeaSigA-170
96LeaSigAG-170
96LeaSigAS-170
96MetUni-67
96MetUniP-67
96MetUniProS-67
96OmaRoyB-21
96Pac-331
96PanSti-186
96ProSta-119
96RoyPol-20
96Sco-17
96ScoDugC-A16
96ScoDugCAP-A16
96StaClu-229
96StaCluMOP-229
96Top-137
96TopGal-103
96TopGalPPI-103
96Ult-75
96UltGolM-75
96UppDec-91
97PacPriGotD-GD49
Nurre, Peter
90KisDodD-19
Nussbeck, Mark
96NewJerCB-20
Nutt, Steven
92MarPhiC-28
92MarPhiF-3055
93SpaPhiC-21
93SpaPhiF-1055
94SpaPhiF-1719
94SparPhiC-16
Nuttall, Todd
94OgdRapSP-28
Nutting, Robert
92Bow-85
92HunCubC-2
92HunCubF-3154
Nuttle, Jamison
93WelPirC-16
93WelPirF-3353
Nuxhall, Joe
52Top-406
53BowC-90
53Top-105
54Bow-76
55Bow-194
55Kah-4
56Kah-12
56RedBurB-15
56Top-218
57Kah-23
57RedSoh-15
57Top-103
58Kah-21
58RedEnq-27
58Top-63
59Kah-26
59RedBurBP-11
59RedEnq-16
59RedShiBS-15
59Top-389
60Kah-30
60RawGloT-24
60RedJayP-7
60Top-282
61A'sTeal-14
61AthJayP-14
61Top-444
63GadFunC-10
63Kah-22
63RedEnq-21
63RedFreBC-14
63Top-194
64Kah-19
64RedJayP-7
64Top-106
64TopVen-106
65Kah-31
65RedEnq-19
65Top-312
66Kah-23
66Top-483
67CokCapR-15
67OPC-44
67Top-44
78TCM60I-65
79DiaGre-274
82OhiHaloF-63
83TopRep5-406
89PacLegI-161
89SweBasG-53
90BasWit-105
91TopArc1-105
91UppDecS-9
93RedKah-4
97FleMilDM-15
Nyari, Pete
94BatCliC-16
94BatCliF-3442
95PiePhiF-186
Nybo, Tim
86RedWinA-17
Nyce, Frederick
87OldJudN-379
Nye, Rich
67Top-608
68Top-339
68TopVen-339
69CubJewT-11
69MilBra-203
69OPC-88
69Top-88
70OPC-139
70Top-139
71ExpLaPR-7
72MilBra-255
78TCM60I-281
Nye, Ryan
94BatCliC-17
94BatCliF-3443
94SigRooDP-49
94SigRooDPS-49
94StaCluDP-29
94StaCluDPFDI-29
95Bow-95
95ClePhiF-216
95Exc-244
95Top-421
96Bow-243
96Exc-211
96ReaPhiB-10
97Bow-358
97BowCerBIA-CA57
97BowCerGIA-CA57
97BowInt-358
Nyman, Chris (Christopher C.)
78KnoKnoST-16
79IowOakP-12
80IowOakP-9
81EdmTraRR-7
82EdmTraT-5
84Nes792-382
84Top-382
84TopTif-382
86BufBisP-20
86NasSouTI-19
Nyman, Gerald
69OPC-173
69Top-173
69TopFou-21
70Top-644
71MLBOffS-233
71OPC-656
71Top-656
89SalSpuCLC-147
89SalSpuP-1820
90JamExpP-10
90WelPirP-33
91WelPirP-3592
94DanBraF-3549
95EugEmeTI-30
96EugEmeB-27
Nyman, Nyls (Nyls W.)
75OPC-619
75Top-619
76OPC-258
76SSP-149
76Top-258
78SprRedWK-6
Nyquist, Mike
89SalLakTTI-5
Nyssen, Dan
87AubAstP-13
87HawRai-14
88OscAstS-19
89OscAstS-14
90OscAstS-21
O'Berry, Mike (Preston M.)
77BriRedST-14
80Top-662
82Don-538
82Fle-78
82RedCok-15
82Top-562
84ColCliP-16
84ColCliT-20
84Nes792-184
84Top-184
84TopTif-184
84TopTra-86T
84TopTraT-86T
85ColCliT-12
92BluOriC-23
92YanWIZ8-137
93AlbPolC-23
93AlbPolF-2042
94FreKeyF-2630
94FreKeyC-25
O'Bradovich, Jim (James T.)
78ChaChaT-10
O'Brien, Billy (William S.)
36GouWidPPR-D24
87BucN28-116
88WG1CarG-69
O'Brien, Brian
93EliTwiC-17
93EliTwiF-3415
94ForWayWC-17
94ForWayWF-2008
95ForMyeMTI-21
O'Brien, Buck (Thomas Joseph)
12T207-143
O'Brien, Charlie
83AlbA'sT-10
86VanCanP-19
87DenZepP-24
88BrePol-11
88DenZepC-15
88DenZepP-1268
88Top-566
88TopTif-566
89BrePol-22
89Fle-194
89FleGlo-194
89Sco-606
89Top-214
89TopTif-214
90BreMilB-17
90BrePol-22
90Don-410
90El PasDAGTI-30
90Fle-332
90FleCan-332
90Lea-375
90OPC-106
90PubSti-502
90Top-106
90TopTif-106
90UppDec-650
90VenSti-370
90WicStaSGD-28
91Bow-473
91Don-623
91Lea-122
91MetColP-41
91MetKah-5
91MetWIZ-298
91OPC-442
91Sco-829
91StaClu-157
91Top-442
91TopDesS-442
91TopMic-442
91TopTif-442
91UppDec-420
92Don-777
92Fle-514
92MetColP-17
92MetKah-22
92OPC-56
92Pin-488
92Sco-621
92StaClu-154
92Top-56
92TopGol-56
92TopGolW-56
92TopMic-56
92Ult-534
92UppDec-381
93Don-698
93Fle-478
93MetColP-42
93MetKah-22
93PacSpa-546
93StaClu-128
93StaCluFDI-128
93StaCluMOP-128
93Top-242
93TopGol-242
93TopInaM-242
93TopMic-242
93Ult-431
93UppDec-209
93UppDecGold-209
94BraLykP-25
94BraLykS-24
94BraUSPC-5S
94BreMilB-61
94Don-242
94Fle-574
94FleUpd-103
94Sco-195
94ScoGolR-195
94StaCluT-34
94StaCluTFDI-34
94Top-671
94TopGol-671
94TopSpa-671
94TopTra-92T
94Ult-448
95Don-437
95DonPreP-437
95Fle-315
95Sco-537
95ScoGolR-537
95ScoPlaTS-537
95StaClu-258
95StaCluFDI-258
95StaCluMOP-258
95StaCluSTWS-258
95Top-379
95Ult-132
95UltGolM-132
96BluJayOH-22
96ColCho-378T
96Fle-304
96FleTif-304
96FleUpd-U99
96FleUpdTC-U99
96LeaSigEA-144
97BluJayS-15
97ColCho-504
97Fle-246
97FleTif-246
97Pac-223
97PacLigB-223
97PacSil-223
97Top-353
97Ult-148
97UltGolME-148
97UltPlaME-148
97UppDec-517
O'Brien, Dan
77St.PetCT-11
78ArkTraT-18
80RicBraT-10
80Top-684
81RicBraT-18
O'Brien, Darby (William D.)
87OldJudN-384
90DodTar-1104
O'Brien, Eddie (Edward J.)
53Top-249
54Top-139
56Top-116
57JetPos-14
57Top-259
69PilPos-34
91TopArc1-249
94TopArc1-139
94TopArc1G-139
O'Brien, FB QB (Davey)
40WheM4-6A
40WheM4-6C
O'Brien, Jack (John Joseph)
11SpoLifCW-272
11TurRedT-75

90DodTar-584
O'Brien, Jack (John K.)
87OldJudN-381
87OldJudN-385
O'Brien, Joe
94BatCliC-18
94BatCliF-3456
95PiePhiF-194
O'Brien, John
91HamRedC-18
91HamRedP-4047
92SprCarC-21
92SprCarF-875
93SavCarC-20
93SavCarF-693
93SouAtlLAGF-49
94ClaGolF-159
O'Brien, Johnny (John Thomas)
53Top-223
54Top-139
55Top-135
56Top-65
56TopPin-44
58Top-426
59Top-499
60HenHouW-4
91TopArc1-223
94TopArc1-139
94TopArc1G-139
O'Brien, Kelly
91SalLakTSP-29
O'Brien, Mark
91GulCoaRSP-8
92ButCopKSP-19
92StaCluD-131
93EriSaiC-18
93EriSaiF-3114
94HudValRF-3382
94HudValRC-16
O'Brien, Pete (Peter James)
09T206-452
11SpoLifCW-273
O'Brien, Pete (Peter M.)
80AshTouT-13
81TulDriT-16B
83RanAffF-9
83TopTra-81T
84Don-281
84Fle-423
84Nes792-534
84OPC-71
84RanJarP-9
84Top-534
84TopSti-357
84TopTif-534
85AllGamPI-8
85Don-178
85Fle-563
85Lea-201
85OPC-196
85RanPer-9
85Top-196
85TopSti-344
85TopTif-196
86BasStaB-78
86Don-99
86Fle-568
86FleMin-112
86OPC-328
86RanPer-9
86Top-328
86TopSti-236
86TopTat-19
86TopTif-328
87ClaUpdY-138
87Don-259
87DonOpeD-174
87Fle-132
87FleGamW-31
87FleGlo-132
87FleMin-76
87HosSti-30
87Lea-186
87OPC-17
87RanMot-9
87RanSmo-12
87Spo-52
87SpoTeaP-1
87StuPan-26
87Top-17
87TopMinL-72
87TopSti-239
87TopTif-17
88Don-284
88DonBasB-167
88Fle-475
88FleGlo-475
88FleStiC-67
88GreBasS-6
88Lea-132
88OPC-381
88PanSti-200
88RanMot-9
88RanSmo-2
88RedFolSB-63
88Sco-29
88ScoGlo-29
88Spo-145
88StaLinRa-10
88Top-201
88Top-721
88TopBig-227
88TopSti-240
88TopTif-201
88TopTif-721
89Bow-84
89BowTif-84
89ClaTraP-184
89Don-107
89DonBasB-5
89DonTra-16
89Fle-529
89FleGlo-529
89FleUpd-29
89IndTeal-21
89OPC-314
89PanSti-452
89RedFolSB-87
89Sco-22
89ScoRoo-6T
89Spo-8
89Top-629
89TopBig-115
89TopSti-248
89TopTif-629
89TopTra-88T
89TopTraT-88T
89TopUKM-57
89UppDec-54
89UppDec-800
90Bow-475
90BowTif-475
90ClaYel-T38
90Don-24
90Don-202
90DonBesA-98
90DonSupD-24
90Fle-498
90FleCan-498
90Lea-9
90MarMot-17
90OPC-265
90PanSti-55
90PubSti-565
90Sco-175
90ScoRoo-23T
90Spo-92
90Top-265
90TopSti-218
90TopTif-265
90TopTra-82T
90TopTraT-82T
90TulDriDGB-4
90UppDec-110
90UppDec-719
90VenSti-371
91Bow-259
91Don-119
91Fle-459
91Lea-244
91MarCouH-8
91OPC-585
91PanFreS-228
91Sco-509
91StaClu-285
91Top-585
91TopDesS-585
91TopMic-585
91TopTif-585
91Ult-342
91UppDec-459
92Bow-313
92Don-86
92Fle-289
92Lea-260
92MarMot-8
92OPC-455
92PanSti-55
92Pin-125
92Sco-141
92StaClu-192
92Stu-238
92Top-455
92TopGol-455
92TopGolW-455
92TopMic-455
92Ult-128
92UppDec-388
93DiaMar-81
93Don-613
93Fle-678
93Lea-412
93MarMot-3
93PacSpa-625
93PanSti-59
93Pin-151
93RanKee-282
93Sco-460
93StaClu-378
93StaCluFDI-378
93StaCluMari-26
93StaCluMOP-378
93Top-125
93TopGol-125
93TopInaM-125
93TopMic-125
93UppDec-627
93UppDecGold-627
O'Brien, Robert
72OPC-198
72Top-198
90DodTar-583
O'Brien, Sid (Sydney L.)
69RedSoxAO-8
69Top-628
70OPC-163
70Top-163
71MLBOffS-353
71OPC-561
71Top-561
72OPC-289
72Top-289
72TopCloT-25
94BreMilB-62
O'Brien, William Smith
87OldJudN-382
O'Connell, Danny (Daniel F.)
47PM1StaP1-154
50JJKCopP-12
51Bow-93
53BraSpiaS3-18
53BraSpiaS7-10
53Top-107
54Bow-160
54BraJohC-4
54BraMer-3
54BraSpiaSP-15
54DixLid-11
55Bow-44
55BraGolS-24
55BraJohC-4
55BraSpiaSD-14
56Top-272
57BraSpiaS4-15
57Top-271
58GiaArmT-2
58GiaJayP-8
58GiaSFCB-18
58Hir-19
58Top-166
59Top-87
59TopVen-87
60TacBan-11
60Top-192
60TopVen-192
61SenJayP-7
61Top-318
62SalPlaC-221
62ShiPlaC-221
62Top-411
62TopBuc-64
62TopStal-99
91TopArc1-107
O'Connell, Jimmy (James J.)
20WalMaiW-37
23W503-8
23W515-13
O'Connell, Mark
81CliGiaT-11
O'Connell, P.J.
87OldJudN-386
O'Connell, Shawn
91BluOriC-23
91BluOriP-4126
92KanCouCC-19
92KanCouCF-91
O'Conner, Tim
86KenTwiP-18
87VisOakP-17
88OrlTwiB-2
O'Connor, Ben
90YakBeaTI-16
91YakBeaC-15
91YakBeaP-4246
O'Connor, Bill
85VisOakT-4
86VisOakP-14
O'Connor, Bob
82CliGiaF-25
84ShrCapFB-15
O'Connor, Brian
93MarPhiC-20
93MarPhiF-3471
96AugGreB-20
96EriSeaB-17
O'Connor, Buddy
43ParSpo-58
O'Connor, Jack (John J.)
03BreE10-109
11SpoLifM-113
87OldJudN-387
98CamPepP-59
O'Connor, Jack William
82Don-539
82Fle-557
82TolMudHT-5
82Top-353
82TwiPos-22
83Don-51
83Fle-621
83FleSti-134
83TolMudHT-29
83Top-33
83TwiTeal-22
84Nes792-268
84TolMudHT-15
84Top-268
84TopTif-268
85ExpPos-15
85IndIndTI-22
86CalCanP-20
87RocRedWP-20
87RocRedWT-7
88Sco-434
88ScoGlo-434
88SyrChiC-10
88SyrChiP-805
89SyrChiC-15
89SyrChiMB-17
89SyrChiP-812
91OriCro-336
O'Connor, James
91St.CatBJC-14
91St.CatBJP-3394
O'Connor, Kevin
90IdaFalBP-3257
91MacBraC-25
91MacBraP-878
92DurBulC-14
92DurBulTI-12
93GreBraF-363
94GreBraF-425
94GreBraTI-17
95AusFut-35
95RicBraRC-15
95RicBraTI-13
O'Connor, Nick
81BirBarT-18
O'Connor, Paddy (Patrick F.)
09AmeCarE-84
10PirTipTD-21
11SpoLifM-257
O'Connor, Richard
95MarPhiTI-18
96PieBolWB-18
O'Connor, William
88AllandGN-47
O'Day, Hank (Henry Francis)
87OldJudN-388
88SpoTimM-7
94ConTSN-1201
94ConTSNB-1201
O'Dea, Ken (James Kenneth)
35DiaMatCS3T1-114
36DiaMatCS3T2-18
36SandSW-43
40PlaBal-214
77TCMTheWY-24
83TCMPla1945-27
92ConTSN-497
O'Dell, Bill
47Exh-169
55Top-57
55TopDouH-7
57Top-316
58OriJayP-8
58Top-84
59OriJayP-5
59Top-250
60Top-303
61Pos-155
61Top-96
61Top-383
61TopStal-83
62Top-429
63ExhStaB-50
63Fle-66
63GiaJayP-9
63Jel-111
63Pos-111
63Top-7
63Top-9
63Top-235
64GiaJayP-9
64Top-18
64TopCoi-115
64TopVen-18
65Top-476
66Top-237
66TopVen-237
67OPC-162
67Top-162
67TopPirS-17
91OriCro-337
O'Dell, Jake
96SouOreTI-23
O'Dell, Jim (James Wesley)
85OscAstTI-20
86ColAstP-20
87BirBarB-4
88ChaKniTI-7
O'Donnell, Erik
91BelMarC-10
91BelMarP-3659
92PenPilC-5
92PenPilF-2929
93AppFoxC-19
94CenValRC-15
94CenValRF-3201
O'Donnell, George
58JetPos-13
60DarFar-15
O'Donnell, Glen
86ElmPioRSP-14
O'Donnell, Stephen P.
88CapCodPB-18
88CapCodPPaLP-41
89GreFalDSP-25
90BakDodCLC-248
91VerBeaDC-23
91VerBeaDP-784
92VerBeaDC-19
92VerBeaDF-2886
O'Donnell, T.J.
93UtiBluSC-17
93UtiBluSF-3542
94SarRedSC-20
94SarRedSF-1960
O'Donoghue, John
90LSUTigP-15
91FreKeyC-6
91FreKeyP-2361
92FreKeyF-1824
92HagSunF-2552
92HagSunS-267
92SkyAA F-111
93Bow-197
93FleFinE-162
93RocRedWF-235
93TriAAAGF-29
94ColC-217
94ColChoGS-217

94ColChoSS-217
94OriPro-73
94OriUSPC-3H
94Pin-253
94PinArtP-253
94PinMusC-253
94RocRedWF-996
94RocRedWTI-17
94Sco-593
94ScoGolR-593
94StaClu-86
94StaCluFDI-86
94StaCluGR-86
94StaCluMOP-86
94StaCluT-297
94StaCluTFDI-297
94Top-763
94TopGol-763
94TopSpa-763
96BowBayB-22
96TulDriTI-20
O'Donoghue, John Sr.
64Top-388
65OPC-71
65Top-71
66Top-501
66TopRubI-71
67CokCapI-5
67OPC-127
67Top-127
68CokCapO-6
68Top-456
70BreMcD-23
70BreMil-18
70OPC-441
70Top-441
71ExpLaPR-8
71ExpPS-18
71MLBOffS-136
71OPC-743
71Top-743
72MilBra-257
81TCM60I-377
83Pil69G-13
91FreKeyC-27
91OriCro-338
93BowBayF-2204
94BowBayF-2428
94BreMilB-63
O'Dougherty, Pat
43YanSta-21
O'Doul, Lefty (Francis J.)
28PorandAR-A26
28PorandAR-B26
29ExhFou-11
29PorandAR-66
30W554-11
31Exh-3
31W517-33
32OrbPinNP-31A
32OrbPinNP-31B
32OrbPinUP-48
32USCar-24
33DelR33-10
33DouDisP-33
33ExhFou-2
33GeoCMil-23
33Gou-58
33Gou-232
33GouCanV-58
33NatLeaAC-6
33RitCE-3C
33TatOrb-48
34DiaMatCSB-142
46SpoExcW-5-5
48SomandK-1
49SomandK-1
51R42SmaS-75
52MotCoo-25
53MotCoo-9
57HygMea-9
60Fle-37
61Fle-130
72FleFamF-34
75ShaPiz-17
76BooProC-10
77GalGloG-47
77GalGloG-219
80LauFamF-31
80PacLeg-29
82DiaCla-52
88ConSer5-23
90DodTar-585
91ConTSN-165
92ConTSN-447
93ConTSN-681
O'Dowd, ,Tom
80UtiBluJT-22
O'Farrell, Bob (Robert A.)
20NatCarE-70
21Nei-76
22E120-164
22W572-72
22W573-93
23WilChoV-113
26Exh-62
27Exh-31
27YorCarE-12A
27YorCarE-12B
28PorandAR-A27
28PorandAR-B27
28W502-12
28Yue-12
31Exh-10
33ButCre-19
33ExhFou-5
33Gou-34
33GouCanV-34
34DiaMatCSB-143
34ButPreR-48
35GouPuzR-4F
35GouPuzR-7F
35GouPuzR-12F
36WorWidGV-115
61Fle-131
76GrePlaG-29
91ConTSN-175
91ConTSN-316
92CarMcD-13
92ConTSN-621
93ConTSN-862
O'Flynn, Gardner
94HudValRF-3383
95ChaRivTI-12
94HudValRC-17
O'Halloran, Greg
89St.CatBJP-2079
90DunBluJS-14
90FloStaLAS-38
90StaFS7-66
91Cla/Bes-30
91DunBluJC-14
91DunBluJP-211
92ClaFS7-157
92KnoBluJF-2993
92KnoBluJS-389
92SkyAA F-164
93LinVenB-236
93LinVenB-288
93SyrChiF-1001
94PorSeaDF-682
94PorSeaDTI-24
94SpoRoo-52
94SpoRooAP-52
95Bow-293
95ScoGolR-293
95ScoPlaTS-293
O'Halloran, Mike
91MedHatBJP-4098
91MedHatBJSP-23
92MedHatBJF-3207
92MedHatBJSP-20
O'Hara, Duane
88CapCodPPaLP-73
O'Hara, Pat
82MadMusF-27
O'Hara, William A.
09RamT20-90
09T206-270
09T206-271
10E101-36
10MelMinE-36
10NadCarE-39
10PeoT21-44
11SpoLifM-286
12ImpTobC-1
O'Hearn, Bob
85BurRanT-16
86SalRedBP-22
O'Hearn, Paul
94OgdRapF-3736
94OgdRapSP-23
95OdgRapTI-21
O'Keeffe, Richard
80VenLeaS-253
80WatRedT-11
81WatRedT-6
82SyrChiT-27B
82SyrChiTI-17
O'Laughlin, Chad
76BurBeeT-24
92BelBreC-11
94SanBerSF-2754
O'Laughlin, Silk (Francis H)
09SpoNewSM-38
O'Leary, Bill
84ButCopKT-20
O'Leary, Charley (Charles T.)
07TigACDPP-10
08RosComP-38
09AmeCarE-85
09RamT20-91
09T206-274
09T206-275
09TigTaCP-14
09WolNewDTPP-12
09WolNewDTPP-16
10NadE1-46
10RedCroT-60
10RedCroT-146
10RedCroT-233
10SweCapPP-29
11SpoLifCW-275
11SpoLifM-66
11T205-131
12HasTriFT-2
12HasTriFT-37
21E121So1-74
21KoBreWSI-43
22W575-93
32CubTeal-19
91ConTSN-116
93UppDecTR-7
93UppDecTR-8
O'Leary, Daniel
88KimN18-32
O'Leary, Mike
92BluOriF-2375
O'Leary, Troy
89BelBreIS-19
89HelBreSP-11
89Sta-6
90BelBreB-5
90BelBreS-16
90Bes-98
91CalLeLA-36
91Cla/Bes-160
91DaiDolF-17
91StoPorC-17
91StoPorP-3046
92ClaFS7-98
92ElPasDF-3936
92ElPasDS-220
92SkyAA F-96
92UppDecML-268
92UppDecMLPotY-PY6
93Bow-344
93ClaGolF-215
93ClaMVPF-4
93ExcFS7-193
93ExcLeaLF-17
93FleFinE-231
93LinVenB-204
93NewOrlZF-985
93TopTra-59T
93TriAAAGF-45
94BreMilB-159
94Don-459
94Fle-187
94LeaLimR-21
94NewOrlZF-1482
94Pac-339
94Pin-424
94PinArtP-424
94PinMusC-424
94ScoRoo-RT114
94ScoRooGR-RT114
94SpoRoo-133
94SpoRooAP-133
94StaClu-347
94StaCluFDI-347
94StaCluGR-347
94StaCluMOP-347
94Top-770
94TopGol-770
94TopSpa-770
94Ult-81
95ColCho-169
95ColChoGS-169
95ColChoSS-169
95Don-273
95DonPreP-273
95DonTopotO-24
95FleUpd-12
95Sco-593
95ScoGolR-593
95ScoPlaTS-593
95SigRoo-39
95SigRooSig-39
95StaClu-600
95StaCluMOP-600
95StaCluSTDW-RS600
95StaCluSTWS-600
95Top-496
95TopCyb-286
95UppDec-51
95UppDec-485T
95UppDecED-51
95UppDecEDG-51
96ColCho-68
96ColChoGS-68
96ColChoSS-68
96Don-246
96DonPreP-246
96EmoXL-17
96Fla-23
96Fle-32
96FleRedS-11
96FleTif-32
96LeaSigA-172
96LeaSigAG-172
96LeaSigAS-172
96MetUni-18
96MetUniP-18
96Pac-252
96Sco-134
96ScoDugC-A85
96ScoDugCAP-A85
96StaClu-92
96StaCluMOP-92
96Top-91
96Ult-20
96UltGolM-20
96UppDec-22
97Cir-384
97CirRav-384
97ColCho-281
97Don-321
97DonPreP-321
97DonPrePGold-321
97DonTea-58
97DonTeaSPE-58
97Fle-28
97FleTif-28
97Pac-44
97PacLigB-44
97PacSil-44
97Sco-251
97ScoPreS-251
97ScoRedS-15
97ScoRedSPl-15
97ScoRedSPr-15
97ScoShoS-251
97ScoShoSAP-251
97SP-39
97StaClu-168
97StaCluMOP-168
97Top-54
97Ult-17
97UltGolME-17
97UltPlaME-17
97UppDec-315
O'Loughlin, Silk
94ConTSN-1187
94ConTSNB-1187
O'Malley, Mike
81VerBeaDT-13
O'Malley, Paul
94AubAstC-9
94AubAstF-3754
94SigRooBS-8
94StaCluDP-51
94StaCluDPFDI-51
96QuaCitRB-21
O'Malley, Tom (Thomas P.)
81ShrCapT-4
83Don-96
83Fle-271
83GiaMot-10
83Top-663
84Don-601
84Fle-384
84Nes792-469
84PhoGiaC-11
84Top-469
84TopSti-170
84TopTif-469
86RocRedWP-14
87Fle-477
87FleGlo-477
87OklCit8P-20
87Top-154
87TopTif-154
88OklCit8C-19
88OklCit8P-48
88RanSmo-1
88Sco-534
88ScoGlo-534
88StaLinRa-11
88Top-77
88TopTif-77
88TriAAAP-28
88TriAAC-4
89TidTidC-15
89TidTidP-1965
89TriA AAC-20
89TriAAP-AAA13
90MetColP-43
90MetKah-27
90OPC-504
90Top-504
90TopTif-504
90TopTVM-28
90TriAAAC-20
91Fle-157
91MetWIZ-299
91OPC-257
91OriCro-339
91Sco-439
91Top-257
91TopDesS-257
91TopMic-257
91TopTif-257
93GolCar-2
93RanKee-284
82PhoGiaVNB-23
O'Malley, Walter
88RinPosD1-10B
O'Mara, Ollie (Oliver E.)
15SpoNewM-133
16FleBreD-72
16SpoNewM-134
O'Neal, Doug
92AlbPolF-2318
93BurBeeC-14
93BurBeeF-171
O'Neal, Kelley
89BriTigS-19
90NiaFalRP-8
91FayGenC-21
91FayGenP-1180
91SouAtlLAGP-SAL20
92ClaFS7-167
92LakTigC-7
92LakTigF-2287
93LakTigC-20
93LakTigF-1319
94TreThuF-2128
O'Neal, Mark
90SavCarP-2084
95LouRedF-294
96LouRedB-4
O'Neal, Randy
82BirBarT-8
83EvaTriT-7
84EvaTriT-17
85Fle-645
86Don-394
86Fle-233
86TigCaiD-13
86Top-73
86TopTif-73
87BraSmo-3
87Don-584
87Fle-159
87FleGlo-159
87Top-196
87TopTif-196
88LouRedBC-4
88LouRedBP-430
88LouRedBTI-37
89PhiTas-25
89ScrRedBC-10
89ScrRedBP-726
90GiaMot-23
91Fle-268
O'Neal, Shaquille

93StaCluMO-36
O'Neal, Troy
96BelSnaTI-27
O'Neil, Buck (John Jordan)
49W72HolS-14
50W720HolS-22
86NegLeaF-45
87NegLeaPD-20
92NegLeaRLI-45
93NegLeaRL2-48
93UppDecS-17
94TedWil-109
94UppDecTAE-61
94UppDecTAELD-LD11
95NegLeaL2-31
96NegLeaBMKC-7
O'Neil, Johnny
47CenFlo-17
O'Neil, Mickey (George M.)
21Exh-121
22E120-132
23WilChoV-116
25Exh-8
26Exh-14
90DodTar-591
O'Neil, Richard
91IdaFalBSP-7
O'Neil, William John
04RedSoxUP-10
09T206-453
O'Neill, Dan
87FayGenP-3
88LakTigS-19
89LakTigS-16
90NewBriRSP-1317
90ProAaA-6
91LinDriAAA-362
91PawRedSDD-14
91PawRedSLD-362
91PawRedSP-37
O'Neill, Douglas
91JamExpC-11
91JamExpP-3559
92RocExpC-12
94OgdRapF-3748
94OgdRapSP-17
96PorSeaDB-21
O'Neill, Emmett (Robert Emmett)
77TCMTheWY-36
O'Neill, J.F.
21Exh-123
O'Neill, Jack (John Joseph)
11SpoLifCW-276
O'Neill, John (John J.)
47SigOil-83
O'Neill, Mike
06FanCraNL-34
11SpoLifCW-277
O'Neill, Paul
80IndIndTI-12
O'Neill, Paul Andrew
82CedRapRT-21
83TamTarT-19
86Don-37
86Fle-646
87FleUpd-94
87FleUpdG-94
87RedKah-21
87SpoRool-17
87SpoTeaP-4
88Don-433
88FleUpd-85
88FleUpdG-85
88RedFolSB-64
88RedKah-21
88Sco-304
88ScoGlo-304
88StaLinRe-14
88Top-204
88TopTif-204
89Bow-313
89BowTif-313
89Don-360
89DonBasB-230
89Fle-166
89FleGlo-166
89OPC-187
89PanSti-77
89RedKah-21
89Sco-206
89ScoYouS2-5
89Top-604
89TopBig-39
89TopTif-604
89TVSpoM-44
89UppDec-428
90Bow-49
90BowTif-49
90CedRapRDGB-5
90ClaBlu-117
90Don-198
90DonBesN-39
90Fle-427
90FleCan-427
90Lea-70
90OPC-332
90PanSti-245
90PubSti-36
90RedFolSB-71
90RedKah-20
90Sco-295
90Sco100S-17
90Spo-4
90Top-332
90TopBig-30
90TopSti-141
90TopTif-332
90UppDec-161
90VenSti-375
91Bow-685
91Don-583
91Fle-76
91Lea-219
91OPC-122
91PanFreS-133
91PanSti-120
91RedKah-21
91RedPep-15
91Sco-227
91StaClu-218
91Stu-169
91Top-122
91TopDesS-122
91TopMic-122
91TopTif-122
91Ult-100
91UppDec-133
91USPlaCA-2C
92Bow-267
92DenHol-11
92Don-63
92Fle-415
92Lea-99
92OPC-61
92PanSti-266
92Pin-154
92RedKah-21
92Sco-57
92Sco100S-58
92ScoImpP-66
92SpoIllFK1-391
92StaClu-175
92StaCluD-135
92Stu-25
92Top-61
92TopGol-61
92TopGolW-61
92TopKid-41
92TopMic-61
92TriPla-162
92Ult-194
92UppDec-464
92UppDecHRH-HR15
93Bow-75
93Don-696
93Fin-170
93FinRef-170
93Fla-251
93Fle-39
93FleFinE-250
93Lea-379
93OPC-218
93OPCPre-14
93PacSpa-560
93PanSti-151
93Pin-446
93Sco-439
93Sel-86
93SelRoo-21T
93SP-266
93StaClu-717
93StaCluFDI-717
93StaCluMOP-717
93StaCluY-14
93Stu-140
93Top-276
93TopGol-276
93TopInaM-276
93TopMic-276
93TopTra-84T
93Ult-599
93UppDec-796
93UppDecGold-796
93UppDecHRH-HR27
94Bow-249
94BowBes-R31
94BowBesR-R31
94ColC-218
94ColChoGS-218
94ColChoSS-218
94Don-50
94DonSpeE-50
94ExtBas-136
94Fin-69
94FinRef-69
94Fla-86
94Fle-243
94FUnPac-67
94Lea-108
94LeaL-57
94OPC-229
94Pac-433
94PanSti-103
94Pin-280
94PinArtP-280
94PinMusC-280
94Sco-15
94ScoGolR-15
94Sel-8
94SP-199
94SPDieC-199
94Spo-147
94StaClu-74
94StaCluFDI-74
94StaCluGR-74
94StaCluMOP-74
94StaCluT-199
94StaCluTFDI-199
94Stu-216
94StuEdiC-7
94Top-546
94TopGol-546
94TopSpa-546
94TriPla-277
94Ult-99
94UppDec-186
94UppDecED-186
95Baz-45
95BazRedH-RH10
95Bow-356
95BowBes-R66
95BowBesR-R66
95ClaPhoC-39
95ColCho-72
95ColChoGS-72
95ColChoSE-243
95ColChoSEGS-243
95ColChoSESS-243
95ColChoSS-72
95D3-26
95Don-284
95DonDiaK-DK7
95DonDom-9
95DonEli-50
95DonPreP-284
95DonTopotO-122
95Emb-72
95EmbGolI-72
95Emo-64
95Fin-181
95FinRef-181
95Fla-67
95Fle-78
95FleAllS-18
95FleLeaL-1
95Kra-10
95Lea-80
95LeaChe-4
95LeaLim-76
95Pac-301
95PacPri-98
95PanSti-89
95PanSti-122
95Pin-245
95PinArtP-245
95PinMusC-245
95PinPer-PP17
95PosCan-7
95Sco-41
95ScoGolR-41
95ScoHaloG-HG26
95ScoPlaTS-41
95ScoRul-SR21
95ScoRulJ-SR21
95Sel-131
95SelArtP-131
95SelCer-65
95SelCerMG-65
95SP-178
95SPCha-173
95SPChaDC-173
95Spo-58
95SpoArtP-58
95SPSil-178
95StaClu-124
95StaClu-519
95StaCluCC-CC22
95StaCluFDI-124
95StaCluMO-35
95StaCluMOP-124
95StaCluMOP-519
95StaCluMOP-CC22
95StaCluMOP-RL20
95StaCluMOP-SS13
95StaCluRL-RL20
95StaCluSS-SS13
95StaCluSTWS-124
95StaCluSTWS-519
95StaCluVR-63
95Stu-162
95Sum-77
95SumNthD-77
95Top-426
95TopCyb-224
95TopLeaL-LL26
95UC3-68
95UC3ArtP-68
95Ult-84
95UltAllS-14
95UltAllSGM-14
95UltGolM-84
95UltLeaL-1
95UltLeaLGM-1
95UltOnBL-9
95UltOnBLGM-9
95UppDec-208
95UppDecED-208
95UppDecEDG-208
95UppDecPLL-R24
95UppDecPLLE-R24
95UppDecSE-141
95UppDecSEG-141
95USPlaCMLA-12D
95Zen-80
96Baz-128
96Bow-34
96BowBes-37
96BowBesAR-37
96BowBesR-37
96Cir-67
96CirAcc-10
96CirBos-17
96CirRav-67
96ColCho-635
96ColChoGS-635
96ColChoSS-635
96Don-404
96DonPreP-404
96EmoXL-92
96Fin-B93
96Fin-S182
96Fin-S242
96FinBro-5
96FinRef-B93
96FinRef-S182
96FinRef-S242
96Fla-133
96Fle-192
96FleTif-192
96Lea-13
96LeaLim-44
96LeaLimG-44
96LeaPre-50
96LeaPreP-50
96LeaPrePB-13
96LeaPrePG-13
96LeaPrePS-13
96LeaSig-31
96LeaSigPPG-31
96LeaSigPPP-31
96MetUni-91
96MetUniP-91
96MLBPin-24
96Pac-384
96PacPri-P121
96PacPriG-P121
96PanSti-154
96Pin-237
96PinAfi-17
96PinAfiAP-17
96PinAfiFPP-17
96PinArtP-137
96PinFoil-237
96PinSta-137
96ProSta-138
96Sco-296
96ScoDugC-B21
96ScoDugCAP-B21
96Sel-92
96SelArtP-92
96SelCer-49
96SelCerAP-49
96SelCerCB-49
96SelCerCR-49
96SelCerIP-21
96SelCerMB-49
96SelCerMG-49
96SelCerMR-49
96SP-132
96Spo-81
96SpoArtP-81
96StaClu-212
96StaClu-272
96StaCluEPB-272
96StaCluEPG-272
96StaCluEPS-272
96StaCluMOP-212
96StaCluMOP-272
95StaCluVRMC-63
96Stu-110
96StuPrePB-110
96StuPrePG-110
96StuPrePS-110
96Sum-104
96SumAbo&B-104
96SumArtP-104
96SumFoi-104
96Top-284
96TopChr-114
96TopChrR-114
96TopGal-153
96TopGalPPI-153
96TopLas-75
96TopPro-AL7
96Ult-103
96UltGolM-103
96UppDec-155
96Zen-45
96ZenArtP-45
96ZenMoz-22
97Bow-260
97BowChr-82
97BowChrI-82
97BowChrIR-82
97BowChrR-82
97BowInt-260
97Cir-359
97CirRav-359
97ColCho-401
97Don-35
97DonLim-125
97DonLim-182
97DonLimLE-125
97DonLimLE-182
97DonPre-64
97DonPreCttC-64
97DonPreP-35
97DonPrePGold-35
97DonTea-122
97DonTeaSPE-122
97Fin-87
97FinRef-87
97FlaSho-A121
97FlaSho-B121
97FlaSho-C121
97FlaShoLC-121
97FlaShoLC-B121
97FlaShoLC-C121
97FlaShoLCM-A121
97FlaShoLCM-B121
97FlaShoLCM-C121
97Fle-174
97FleTif-174
97Lea-92
97LeaFraM-92
97LeaFraMDC-92
97MetUni-120

97NewPin-8
97NewPinAP-8
97NewPinMC-8
97NewPinPP-8
97Pac-155
97PacLigB-155
97PacSil-155
97PinX-P-43
97PinX-PMoS-43
97Sco-150
97ScoPreS-150
97ScoShoS-150
97ScoShoSAP-150
97ScoYan-9
97ScoYanPl-9
97ScoYanPr-9
97StaClu-32
97StaCluMat-32
97StaCluMOP-32
97Stu-117
97StuPrePG-117
97StuPrePS-117
97Top-247
97TopChr-88
97TopChrR-88
97TopGal-45
97TopGalPPI-45
97TopSta-83
97TopSta1AS-AS18
97TopStaAM-83
97Ult-339
97UltGolME-339
97UltPlaME-339
97UppDec-126

O'Neill, Steve F.
09ColChiE-218
12ColRedB-218
12ColTinT-218
14B18B-8A
14B18B-8B
15CraJacE-48
15SpoNewM-134
16ColE13-129
16SpoNewM-135
17HolBreD-75
19W514-26
20NatCarE-72
20WalMaiW-39
21E121So1-75
21E121So8-68
21Exh-122
21Nei-22
22AmeCarE-51
22E120-39
22W572-73
22W573-94
22W575-94
23W501-117
23WilChoV-117
34BatR31-160
34DiaStaR-87
36GouWidPPR-A119
36GouWidPPR-B17
36NatChiFPR-62
36R31Pre-L10
36WorWidGV-67
46SpoExcW-6-5
49IndTeal-29
51Bow-201
54Top-127
77Ind192T-15
80TigGreT-9
81TigDetN-11
88ConSer3-21
91ConTSN-186
91TopArc1-307
93ConTSN-826
93ConTSN-876
94TopArc1-127
94TopArc1G-127
95ConTSN-1356

O'Neill, Ted
76WauMetT-21
77LynMetT-21

O'Neill, Tip (James E.)
76SSP188WS-7
87BucN28-102
87LonJacN-10
87OldJudN-390A
87OldJudN-390B
87ScrDC-7
88GandBCGCE-30
88KimN18-33
90HOFStiB-7

O'Neill, Tom
92CliGiaF-3605
92EveGiaC-19
92EveGiaF-1698
93CliGiaC-17
93CliGiaF-2496

O'Quinn, James
95BoiHawTI-25
96CedRapKTI-18

O'Quinn, Steven
87ChaWheP-21

O'Rear, John
77RocRedWM-14
79AlbDukT-12
80AlbDukT-7

O'Regan, Dan
82OneYanT-5

O'Reilly, Jim
89ChaWheB-26
89ChaWheP-1746
90PeoChiTI-33
91PeoChiC-24
91PeoChiTI-3
92PeoChiC-30
92PeoChiTI-18
93PeoChiC-26
93PeoChiTI-18
96DayCubB-29

O'Reilly, John
96OgdRapTI-46

O'Reilly, Tom
90JamExpP-31
91JamExpC-29

O'Riley, Don
70Top-552
71OPC-679
71Top-679

O'Rourke, Frank (Francis J.)
25Exh-93
26Exh-94
29ExhFou-30
31Exh-29
33Gou-87
34GouCanV-43
79DiaGre-376
90DodTar-594
92ConTSN-604

O'Rourke, James
36PC7AlbHoF-37
50CalHOFW-57
73FleWilD-24
76ShaPiz-37
80PerHaloFP-37
80SSPHOF-37
84GalHaloFRL-37
86OldJudN-11
87BucN28-71A
87BucN28-71B
87OldJudN-392
88AugBecN-20A
88AugBecN-20B
88GandBCGCE-31
88WG1CarG-42
90BasWit-58
90KalBatN-43
94OriofB-29

O'Rourke, Patsy (Joseph Leo) Sr.
08RosComP-170

O'Rourke, Tom (Thomas J.)
87OldJudN-393

O'Shaughnessy, Jay
96YakBeaTI-31

O'Toole, Bobby
96BluOriB-21

O'Toole, Dennis
73OPC-604
73Top-604

O'Toole, Jack
85AncGlaPTI-24
86AncGlaPTI-27
87AncGlaP-23
89AncGlaP-18

O'Toole, Jim
56RedBurB-16
58RedEnq-28
59RedBurBP-12
59RedBurBP-13
59RedShiBS-16
59Top-136
59TopVen-136
60Kah-31
60RedJayP-8
60Top-32
60Top-325
60TopVen-32
61Kah-30
61Pos-189A
61Pos-189B
61Top-328
61TopStal-21
62Jel-126
62Kah-28
62Pos-126
62PosCan-126
62RedEnq-24
62RedJayP-9
62Top-56
62Top-58
62Top-60
62Top-450
62TopBuc-65
62TopStal-118
62TopVen-56
62TopVen-58
62TopVen-60
63Jel-136
63Kah-23
63Pos-136
63RedEnq-22
63RedFreBC-16
63RedJayP-8
63Top-70
64ChatheY-39
64RedJayP-8
64Top-185
64TopCoi-85
64TopSta-55
64TopStaU-53
64TopVen-185
64WheSta-32
65Baz-6
65ChaTheY-40
65Kah-33
65OPC-60
65RedEnq-20
65Top-60
65TopTral-22
66Top-389
67CokCapWS-12
67DexPre-157
67Top-467
78TCM60I-92
89PacLegI-147

O'Toole, Martin J.
09MaxPubP-9
09SpoNewSM-70
11L1L-112
11PloCanE-53
11S81LarS-87
12T207-146
13NatGamW-33
13TomBarW-31
14B18B-81A
14B18B-81B
14CraJacE-54
14TexTomE-37
15CraJacE-54

Oakes, Rebel (Ennis T.)
09AmeCarE-83
09ColChiE-215
09PC7HHB-32
09T206-269
10CouT21-203
10DomDisP-93
10PeoT21-43
10RedCroT-59
10RedCroT-144
10RedCroT-231
10SweCapPP-151A
10SweCapPP-151B
11S74Sil-122
11SpoLifM-276
11T205-129
12ColRedB-215
12ColTinT-215
12HasTriFT-11
12T207-142
14CraJacE-139
14PieStaT-46
15AmeCarE-32
16CraJacE-139
15VicT21-23

Oakes, Todd
85FreGiaP-26
87CliGiaP-18
88SanJosGCLC-143
88SanJosGP-122
89CalLeaA-50
89SanJosGB-29
89SanJosGCLC-236
89SanJosGP-455
89SanJosGS-26
90ShrCapP-1460
90ShrCapS-26
91LinDriAA-325
91ShrCapP-1839
92PhoFirF-2838
93SanJosGC-28
93SanJosGF-29
94SanJosGC-28
94SanJosGF-2835

Oakland, Mike
92BenRocC-19
93CenValRC-20
93CenValRF-2900
94CenValRC-16
94CenValRF-3211

Oakley, Annie
87AllandGN-41
88KimN18-31

Oana, Prince (Henry)
34DiaMatCSB-141

Oates, Johnny (Johnny Lane)
72OPC-474
72Top-474
73OPC-9
73Top-9
74BraPhoC-6
74OPC-183
74Top-183
74TopSta-10
75OPC-319
75Top-319
76OPC-62
76SSP-468
76Top-62
77Top-619
78SSP270-72
78Top-508
79Top-104
80DodPol-5
80Top-228
81Fle-99
81Top-303
82Fle-47
82NasSouTI-28
83ColCliT-1
84CubChiT-20
84CubSev-NNO
85CubSev-NNO
86CubGat-NNO
87CubCan-24
87CubDavB-NNO
88RocRedWC-24
88RocRedWGCP-30
88RocRedWP-211
88RocRedWTI-17
89OriFreB-46
90DodTar-582
91OriCro-340
91TopTra-85T
91TopTraT-85T
92OPC-579
92Top-579
92TopGol-579
92TopGolW-579
92TopMic-579
92YanWIZ8-136
93Top-501
93TopGol-501
93TopInaM-501
93TopMic-501
95RanCra-23
96RanMot-1

Obal, Dave
76BatRouCT-16

Obando, Sherman
89OneYanP-2102
90PriWilCTI-17
91Cla/Bes-116
91PriWilCC-28
91PriWilCP-1438
92AlbYanF-2232
92AlbYanS-1
92SkyAA F-10
93Bow-29
93FleFinE-161
93Lea-446
93LinVenB-157
93OPCPre-63
93PacJugC-11
93PacSpa-347
93SelRoo-70T
93StaClu-715
93StaCluFDI-715
93StaCluMOP-715
93TopTra-23T
93Ult-497
94OriPro-71
94OriUSPC-10S
94Pac-39
94RocRedWF-1010
94RocRedWTI-16
94Sco-597
94ScoGolR-597
94StaCluT-274
94StaCluTFDI-274
94TriAAF-AAA14
95FleUpd-6
96FleUpd-U149
96FleUpdTC-U149
96Ult-506
96UltGolM-506
97Fle-573
97FleTif-573
97Pac-348
97PacLigB-348
97PacSil-348

Obardovich, Jim
74TacTwiC-1

Oberdank, Jeff
88BenBucL-4
89QuaCitAB-5
89QuaCitAGS-20
90PalSprACLC-206
90PalSprAP-2585
91MelBusF-5
91QuaCitAC-20
91QuaCitAP-2639

Oberkfell, Ken (Kenneth R.)
76ArkTraT-7
78SprRedWK-1
79Car5-19
80Top-701
81AllGamPI-123
81Car5x7-18
81Car5x7-19
81CokTeaS-126
81Don-583
81Fle-532
81OPC-32
81Top-32
81TopSti-222
82Don-404
82Fle-123
82FleSta-21
82OPC-121
82Top-474
82TopSti-89
82TopStiV-89
83AllGamPI-124
83Car-20
83Don-246
83Fle-17
83FleSta-140
83FleSti-8
83OPC-206
83Top-206
83TopSti-287
84AllGamPI-34
84Don-504
84Fle-330
84FleUpd-84
84Nes792-102
84OPC-102
84Top-102
84TopSti-148
84TopStiB-2
84TopTif-102
84TopTra-85T
84TopTraT-85T
85BraHos-17
85BraPol-24
85Don-432
85Fle-336
85Lea-141
85OPC-307
85Top-569
85TopMin-569
85TopSti-32
85TopTif-569

86BraPol-24
86Don-531
86Fle-523
86OPC-334
86Top-334
86TopSti-38
86TopTif-334
87BraSmo-16
87Don-437
87DonOpeD-46
87Fle-523
87FleGlo-523
87Lea-171
87OPC-1
87RedFolSB-99
87SpoTeaP-24
87Top-627
87TopSti-38
87TopTif-627
88Don-67
88DonBasB-226
88Fle-545
88FleGlo-545
88OPC-67
88PanSti-244
88Sco-245
88ScoGlo-245
88Spo-165
88StaLinBra-13
88Top-67
88TopSti-37
88TopTif-67
89Bow-418
89BowTif-418
89Don-506
89OPC-97
89PirVerFJ-14
89Sco-139
89Top-751
89TopTif-751
89UppDec-313
90AstMot-16
90Bow-74
90BowTif-74
90Don-494
90Fle-67
90FleCan-67
90Lea-294
90OPC-488
90Sco-422
90ScoRoo-58T
90Top-488
90TopTif-488
90UppDec-360
91AstMot-16
91Don-109
91Fle-511
91OPC-286
91Sco-214
91StaClu-414
91Top-286
91TopDesS-286
91TopMic-286
91TopTif-286
92EdmTraF-3547

Oberlander, Hartman
87OldJudN-380

Oberlin, Frank
09T206-451
10SenWasT-4

Oblesbee, Mike
86EugEmeC-29

Obregon, Francisco
60HenHouW-3
60UniOil-4

Obregon, T.
76VenLeaS-182

Ocasio, Fredy
92OklStaC-22
95AshTouUTI-18

Ocasio, Javier
88BlaYNPRWL-75
88SouBenWSGS-3
89BlaYNPRWL-82
89SarWhiSS-16
90FloStaLAS-37
90SarWhiSS-17
91BirBarLD-69
91BirBarP-1463
91Cla/Bes-234
91LinDriAA-69

Oceak, Frank
57JetPos-15
60Top-467
63PirIDL-18

Ochiai, Hiro
87JapPlaB-13

Ochoa, Alex
91FroRowDP-29
92Bow-250
92KanCouCC-13
92KanCouCF-106
92KanCouCTI-23
92MidLeaATI-30
92StaCluD-132
92UppDecML-59
92UppDecML-254
93Bow-521
93BurBeeC-29
93CarLeaAGF-4
93ClaFS7-83
93ClaGolF-73
93ExcFS7-125
93FreKeyC-18
93FreKeyF-1040
94ActPac-11
94ActPac-59
94ActPac2G-5G
94AriFalLS-14
94Bow-103
94Bow-367
94BowBayF-2425
94BowBes-B52
94BowBesR-B52
94Cla-120
94ColC-646
94ColChoGS-646
94ColChoSS-646
94ExcFS7-13
94OriPro-72
94SigRoo-19
94SigRooHP-S9
94SigRooS-19
94SP-12
94SPDieC-12
94StaCluT-296
94StaCluTFDI-296
94UppDec-538
94UppDecAHNIL-10
94UppDecED-538
94UppDecML-20
94UppDecML-258
94UppDecMLPotYF-PY16
94UppDecMLT1PJF-TP7
94UppDecMLT1PMF-7
94WesPalBEC-30
95ActPacF-29
95Bow-248
95BowBes-B63
95BowBesR-B63
95BowGolF-248
95ColChoSE-8
95ColChoSEGS-8
95ColChoSESS-8
95Exc-8
95HarSenTI-NNO
95PinETA-2
95RocRedWTI-28
95Sum-132
95SumNthD-132
95UppDecML-3
95UppDecML-102
95UppDecMLMLA-8
95UppDecMLOP-OP2
96Bow-169
96BowBes-93
96BowBesAR-93
96BowBesR-93
96BowMinLP-9
96Cir-160
96CirRav-160
96ColCho-618
96ColChoGS-618
96ColChoSS-618
96Don-451
96DonPreP-451
96FlePro-7
96HarSenB-3
96Lea-214
96LeaLimR-1
96LeaLimRG-1
96LeaPrePB-214
96LeaPrePG-214
96LeaPrePS-214
96LeaSig-102
96LeaSigEA-145
96LeaSigEACM-21
96LeaSigPPG-102
96LeaSigPPP-102
96MetKah-24
96MetUniMFG-10
96NorTidB-21
96Pac-148
96Pin-164
96PinArtP-91
96PinSta-91
96Sco-494
96ScoFutF-5
96SelCer-129
96SelCerAP-129
96SelCerCB-129
96SelCerCR-129
96SelCerMB-129
96SelCerMG-129
96SelCerMR-129
96Spo-130
96SpoArtP-130
96StaClu-381
96StaCluMOP-381
96Top-339
96TopChr-133
96TopChrR-133
96TopGal-136
96TopGalPPI-136
96UppDec-232
96UppDecFSP-FS10
96Zen-123
96ZenArtP-123
97Cir-308
97CirEmeA-308
97CirEmeAR-AU3
97CirRav-308
97ColCho-398
97Don-345
97DonEli-56
97DonEliGS-56
97DonEliTotC-15
97DonEliTotCDC-15
97DonPre-136
97DonPreCttC-136
97DonPreP-345
97DonPrePGold-345
97Fin-200
97FinRef-200
97FlaSho-A66
97FlaSho-B66
97FlaSho-C66
97FlaShoLC-66
97FlaShoLC-B66
97FlaShoLC-C66
97FlaShoLCM-A66
97FlaShoLCM-B66
97FlaShoLCM-C66
97Fle-402
97FleRooS-9
97FleTif-402
97Lea-9
97LeaFraM-9
97LeaFraMDC-9
97MetUni-197
97MetUniEAR-AU3
97NewPin-148
97NewPinAP-148
97NewPinMC-148
97NewPinPP-148
97Pac-371
97PacLigB-371
97PacPri-126
97PacPriLB-126
97PacPriP-126
97PacSil-371
97Pin-184
97PinArtP-184
97PinCer-72
97PinCerMBlu-72
97PinCerMG-72
97PinCerMR-72
97PinCerR-72
97PinIns-94
97PinInsCE-94
97PinInsDE-94
97PinMusC-184
97PinTotCPB-72
97PinTotCPG-72
97PinTotCPR-72
97PinX-P-106
97PinX-PMoS-106
97Sco-120
97ScoPreS-120
97ScoShoS-120
97ScoShoSAP-120
97Sel-22
97SelArtP-22
97SelRegG-22
97SelRooR-9
97SelToootT-9
97SelToootTMB-9
97SkyE-X-87
97SkyE-XC-87
97SkyE-XEAR-AU3
97SkyE-XEC-87
97StaClu-198
97StaCluM-M23
97StaCluMat-198
97StaCluMOP-198
97StaCluMOP-M23
97Stu-107
97StuPrePG-107
97StuPrePS-107
97Top-103
97Top-298
97TopAwel-AI12
97TopGal-171
97TopGalPPI-171
97Ult-244
97UltAutE-1
97UltDouT-17
97UltGolME-244
97UltPlaME-244
97UltRooR-7
97UppDec-118
95UppDecMLFS-3
95UppDecMLFS-102
97UppDecRSF-RS14
97UppDecTTS-TS4

Ochoa, Levy
76VenLeaS-206
80VenLeaS-105

Ochoa, Rafael
90UtiBluSP-5
91UtiBluSC-29
91UtiBluSP-3254
92SouBenWSF-190

Ochs, Kevin
84ButCopKT-19

Ochs, Tony
89JohCitCS-16
90CMC-841
90SavCarP-2070
91St.PetCC-22
91St.PetCP-2285

Ochsenfeld, Chris
95GreFalDTI-15
96SavSanB-14

Oda, Yoshito
79TCMJapPB-66

Oddo, Ron
80ElmPioRST-23

Odekirk, Rick
88OklCit8C-10
88OklCit8P-29
91RenSilSCLC-8

Odgers, Steve
95WhiSoxK-24

Odierno, Scott
88CapCodPPaLP-60

Odle, Page
86PriWilPP-18

Odman, Matt
86RedWinA-15

Odom, Blue Moon (John)
65Top-526
67CokCapAt-5
67Top-282
68Top-501
69A'sJacitB-11
69MilBra-204
69MLBOffS-90
69OPC-195
69Top-195
69TopFou-12
69TopSta-220
69TopTeaP-21
69TraSta-8
70DayDaiNM-113
70Kel-38
70MLBOffS-263
70OPC-55
70Top-55
70TraSta-15A
71MLBOffS-523
71OPC-523
71Top-523
72'sA'sPos-13
72MilBra-256
72Top-557
72Top-558
73A'sPos-27
73OPC-207
73OPC-315
73Top-207
73Top-315
74OPC-461
74Top-461
75OPC-69
75Top-69
76OPC-651
76Top-651
77SanJosMC-3
78TCM60I-68
87A'sMot-3

Odom, Joe
84MadMusP-6
85ModA'sC-25

Odom, Tim
87Ft.MyeRP-10
88AppFoxP-150
89AugPirP-493

Odor, Rouglas
88BurIndP-1780
89KinIndS-15
89WatIndS-17
90CarLeaA-41
90KinIndTI-3
91CanIndLD-91
91CanIndP-988
91LinDriAA-91
92KinIndC-9
92KinIndF-2485
93CanIndF-2847
93LinVenB-181
94CanIndF-3125
94VenLinU-259
95LinVen-203

Odwell, Fred (Frederick W.)
09ColChiE-216
11MecDFT-37
12ColRedB-216
12ColTinT-216

Oedewaldt, Larry
89StoPorB-15
89StoPorCLC-167
89StoPorP-375
89StoPorS-2

Oehrlein, David
92HamRedF-1590
93ExcFS7-104
93SprCarC-20
93SprCarF-1849
94SavCarC-23
94SavCarF-504
94SouAtlLAF-SAL53
95ArkTraTI-22

Oelkers, Bryan
83TolMudHT-28
83TwiTeal-12
84Don-486
86IndTeal-31
86MaiGuiP-14
87BufBisP-18
87Don-596
87Fle-257
87FleGlo-257
87Top-77
87TopTif-77
89LouRedBP-1244
89LouRedBTI-29

Oelschlager, Ron
92AriWilP-11

Oertel, Chuck
91OriCro-341

Oertli, Chuck
86GenCubP-20

Oeschger, Joe
20NatCarE-69
20WalMaiW-38
21E121So1-73
21Exh-119
21Nei-98
22E120-131
22W572-71
22W575-92
22WilPatV-6
23W501-93
23W503-40
23WilChoV-112
61Top-403
72FleFamF-19
72LauGreF-37

90DodTar-586
Oester, Ron (Ronald John)
77IndIndTI-6
78IndIndTI-6
79IndIndTI-3
79Top-717
80RedEnq-16
81AllGamPI-105
81CokTeaS-45
81Don-423
81Fle-218
81OPC-21
81Top-21
81TopSupHT-40
82Don-500
82Fle-79
82FleSta-20
82RedCok-16
82Top-427
82TopSti-34
83AllGamPI-105
83Don-526
83Fle-598
83OPC-269
83RedYea-16
83Top-269
83TopSti-230
84AllGamPI-13
84Don-62
84DonActAS-46
84Fle-475
84Nes792-526
84Nes792-756
84OPC-99
84RedBor-16
84RedEnq-3
84Top-526
84Top-756
84TopSti-53
84TopTif-526
84TopTif-756
85Don-81
85Fle-542
85IndIndTI-30
85OPC-314
85RedYea-10
85Top-314
85TopSti-54
85TopTif-314
86BasStaB-79
86Don-81
86Fle-183
86Lea-78
86OPC-264
86RedTexG-16
86SevCoi-S14
86Top-627
86TopSti-138
86TopTif-627
87Don-206
87DonOpeD-195
87Fle-207
87FleGlo-207
87OPC-172
87RedKah-16
87Top-172
87TopSti-141
87TopTif-172
88Don-246
88Fle-242
88FleGlo-242
88OPC-17
88Sco-183
88ScoGlo-183
88Top-17
88TopSti-144
88TopTif-17
89Bow-310
89BowTif-310
89Don-553
89RedKah-16
89Sco-615
89Top-772
89TopBig-229
89TopTif-772
89UppDec-287
90Don-317
90OPC-492
90PubSti-35
90RedKah-18
90Sco-59
90Top-492
90TopBig-55
90TopTif-492
90UppDec-118
90VenSti-372
91Don-628
91Fle-74
91Sco-651
91UppDec-611
92ChaLooF-3833
Oestreich, Mark
89BurIndS-28
Offerman, Jose
88GreFalDTI-22
89BakDodCLC-194
89BasAmeAPB-AA25
89CalLeaA-1
89SanAntMB-27
90AlbDukC-19
90AlbDukP-354
90AlbDukT-24
90Bow-92
90BowTif-92
90ClaBlu-45
90CMC-421
90FleUpd-24
90Lea-464
90ProAAAF-75
90TopMag-39
90TriAllGP-AAA31
90UppDec-46
91AlbDukLD-17
91AlbDukP-1149
91Baz-6
91Bow-182
91Cla2-T37
91ClaGam-145
91DodPol-30
91Don-33
91Fle-216
91LinDriAAA-17
91MajLeaCP-51
91OPC-587
91OPCPre-90
91RedFolS-110
91Sco-343
91Sco100RS-99
91ScoHotR-10
91ScoRoo-26
91SevCoi-F12
91SevCoi-SC11
91StaClu-340
91StaCluCM-22
91Stu-186
91Top-587
91TopDeb90-117
91TopDesS-587
91TopMic-587
91TopRoo-23
91TopTif-587
91ToyRoo-23
91Ult-167
91UppDec-356
92Bow-304
92ClaGam-36
92DodMot-8
92DodPol-30
92DodSmo-10292
92Don-721
92Fle-467
92Lea-322
92OPC-493
92OPCPre-123
92Pin-153
92PinTea2-25
92ProFS7-237
92Sco-699
92Sco100RS-31
92StaClu-378
92Stu-47
92Top-493
92TopGol-493
92TopGolW-493
92TopMic-493
92TriPla-153
92Ult-215
92UppDec-532
93Bow-294
93DodMot-5
93DodPol-18
93Don-376
93Fle-66
93FunPac-91
93Lea-17
93LimRocDP-P1
93LimRocDWB-77
93LimRocDWB-P1
93OPC-299
93PacSpa-153
93PanSti-216
93Pin-345
93Sco-129
93Sel-197
93SP-97
93StaClu-129
93StaCluD-17
93StaCluFDI-129
93StaCluMOP-129
93Stu-182
93Top-776
93TopGol-776
93TopInaM-776
93TopMic-776
93Ult-59
93UppDec-225
93UppDec-464
93UppDecGold-225
93UppDecGold-464
94Bow-182
94ColC-219
94ColChoGS-219
94ColChoSS-219
94DodMot-5
94DodPol-20
94Don-623
94ExtBas-292
94Fin-23
94FinPre-23P
94FinRef-23
94Fla-180
94Fle-519
94Lea-123
94OPC-104
94Pac-317
94PacAll-5
94PanSti-202
94Pin-190
94PinArtP-190
94PinMusC-190
94Sco-340
94ScoGolR-340
94Sel-246
94StaClu-282
94StaCluFDI-282
94StaCluGR-282
94StaCluMOP-282
94Stu-71
94Top-241
94TopGol-241
94TopSpa-241
94TriPla-87
94Ult-217
94UppDec-236
94UppDecED-236
95ColCho-221
95ColChoGS-221
95ColChoSS-221
95DodMot-8
95DodPol-17
95Don-77
95DonPreP-77
95DonTopotO-270
95Fin-281
95FinRef-281
95Fla-369
95FleUpd-176
95Lea-260
95LeaLim-108
95Pac-223
95Pin-312
95PinArtP-312
95PinMusC-312
95StaClu-595
95StaCluMOP-595
95StaCluSTWS-595
95Top-152
95Zen-58
96ColCho-775
96Don-546
96DonPreP-546
96FleUpd-U42
96FleUpdTC-U42
96Pac-109
96RoyPol-21
96Sco-172
96Top-89
96Ult-359
96UltGolM-359
97Cir-136
97CirRav-136
97ColCho-359
97Don-189
97DonPreP-189
97DonPrePGold-189
97Fle-118
97FleTif-118
97Lea-142
97LeaFraM-142
97LeaFraMDC-142
97Pac-107
97PacLigB-107
97PacPri-38
97PacPriLB-38
97PacPriP-38
97PacSil-107
97Pin-37
97PinArtP-37
97PinMusC-37
97RoyPol-16
97Sco-302
97ScoPreS-302
97ScoShoS-302
97ScoShoSAP-302
97StaClu-309
97StaCluMOP-309
97Top-164
97Ult-69
97UltGolME-69
97UltPlaME-69
97UppDec-391
Office, Rowland J.
75OPC-262
75Top-262
76OPC-256
76SSP-20
76Top-256
77Top-524
78BraCok-12
78Top-632
79OPC-62
79Top-132
80ExpPos-20
80Top-39
81Don-213
81Fle-147
81OPC-319
81Top-319
82ExpHos-28
82Fle-198
82OkICit8T-2
82OPC-165
82Top-479
83ColCliT-27
92YanWIZ8-138
Officer, Jim
76QuaCitAT-25
Ofstun, John
90NebCor-20
Ogawa, Kuni
79VanCanT-15
80HolMilT-8
Ogawa, Toru
79TCMJapPB-46
Ogden, Charles
88CarLeaAS-33
88KinIndS-18
89CanIndB-27
Ogden, Curly (Warren)
33Gou-174
Ogden, Jamie
92ClaFS7-149
92KenTwiC-1
92KenTwiF-619
93ForMyeMC-19
93ForMyeMF-2671
94ForMyeMC-18
94ForMyeMF-1182
95HarCitRCTI-18
92UtiBluSC-8
Ogden, Jason
93SarWhiSC-20
94SouBenSHC-16
94SouBenSHF-591
Ogden, John M.
28Exh-58
33Gou-176
Ogden, Todd
89CanIndP-1322
89CanIndS-18
Ogea, Chad
90LSUTigA-6
90LSUTigP-8
91LSUTigP-15
92ClaFS7-154
92KinIndC-25
92KinIndF-2473
92StaCluD-133
92UppDecML-296
92UppDecMLPotY-PY12
93Bow-289
93ChaKniF-540
93ClaFS7-232
93ClaGolF-21
93ExcFS7-162
93ExcLeaLF-16
94Bow-607
94BowBes-B72
94BowBesR-B72
94ChaKniF-894
94Cla-124
94ExcFS7-47
94Fla-287
94FleUpd-35
94Top-316
94TopGol-316
94TopSpa-316
94Ult-350
94UppDecML-202
95BowBes-B6
95BowBesR-B6
95ColCho-7
95ColChoGS-7
95ColChoSS-7
95Fin-293
95FinRef-293
95Pin-412
95PinArtP-412
95PinMusC-412
95Sel-186
95SelArtP-186
95StaClu-479
95StaCluMOP-479
95StaCluSTWS-479
95Top-47
95UppDec-343
95UppDecED-343
95UppDecEDG-343
96ColCho-524
96ColChoGS-524
96ColChoSS-524
96Don-545
96DonPreP-545
96Fle-94
96FleTif-94
96LeaSigA-171
96LeaSigAG-171
96LeaSigAS-171
96Sco-407
96StaClu-27
96StaCluMOP-27
96Top-358
96Ult-52
96UltGolM-52
96UppDec-318
97Cir-39
97CirRav-39
97ColCho-311
97Fle-85
97FleTif-85
97PacPriGotD-GD37
97Sco-403
97ScoHobR-403
97ScoIndU-4
97ScoIndUTC-4
97ScoResC-403
97ScoShoS-403
97ScoShoSAP-403
97Top-367
97Ult-477
97UltGolME-477
97UltPlaME-477
97UppDec-346
Ogier, Moe
68Top-589
Ogiwara, Mitsuru
88MiaMarS-17
Oglesbee, Mike
85AncGlaPTI-22
87AshTouP-22
Oglesby, Luke
93EugEmeC-20
93EugEmeF-3870
94RocRoyC-17
94RocRoyF-577
95WilBluRTI-1
Oglesby, Ron
88RivRedWCLC-232
88RivRedWP-1407
89ChaRaiP-978

90WatDiaB-20
90WatDiaP-2394
Ogliaruso, Mike
89MyrBeaBJP-1464
90MyrBeaBJP-2775
90ProAaA-90
90SouAtlLAS-38
91Cla/Bes-133
91DunBluJC-9
91DunBluJP-205
92DunBluJF-1998
92KnoBluJF-2989
92KnoBluJS-388
Oglivie, Ben (Benjamin A.)
72Top-761
73LinPor-76
73OPC-388
73Top-388
74Tig-9
75OPC-344
75Top-344
76OPC-659
76SSP-359
76Top-659
77BurCheD-91
77OPC-236
77Top-122
78Top-286
79Top-519
80Top-53
81AllGamPI-62
81Don-446
81Fle-508
81FleStiC-14
81Kel-20
81OPC-340
81PerCreC-30
81Squ-3
81Top-2
81Top-415
81TopScr-7
81TopSti-11
81TopSti-14
81TopSti-92
82BrePol-24
82Don-484
82Fle-151
82FleSta-138
82OPC-280
82Top-280
82TopSti-197
83AllGamPI-65
83BreGar-14
83BrePol-24
83Don-384
83Dra-20
83Fle-43
83Fle-640
83FleSta-141
83FleSti-15
83FleSti-146
83OPC-91
83Top-750
83TopSti-82
84AllGamPI-156
84BreGar-15
84BrePol-24
84Don-229
84DonCha-6
84Fle-210
84FunFooP-67
84Nes792-190
84OPC-190
84Top-190
84TopRubD-31
84TopSti-296
84TopTif-190
85AllGamPI-66
85BreGar-15
85BrePol-24
85Don-333
85Fle-590
85Lea-123
85OPC-332
85Top-681
85TopRubD-29
85TopSti-292
85TopTif-681
86BrePol-24
86Don-333
86Fle-497
86Lea-199
86OPC-372
86Top-372
86TopSti-200
86TopTat-24
86TopTif-372
86Woo-25
87Don-419
87Fle-353
87FleGlo-353
87FleRecS-26
87FleStiC-85
87JapPlaB-19
87RedFolSB-100
87Top-586
87TopTif-586
91UppDecS-10
92BreCarT-18
92UppDecS-9
93ElPasDF-2968
94BreMilB-158
94BreMilB-343
94TedWil-44
Ogrodowski, Bruce
40SolHug-15
48SomandK-21
Oh, Sadaharu
79TCMJapPB-1
87JapPlaB-2
93UppDecS-22
Ohba, Toyokazu
96HonShaHWB-3
Ohishi, Tomoyoshi
94CenValRC-28
94CenValRF-3221
Ohlms, Mark
89PriWilCS-15
89Sta-92
90Ft.LauYS-16
91CarLeaAP-CAR35
91PriWilCC-8
91PriWilCP-1424
92KnoBluJF-2990
92KnoBluJS-390
92SkyAA F-165
93LinVenB-57
93SyrChiF-998
94KnoSmoF-1302
Ohman, Ed
89ChaRanS-18
89Sta-9
Ohman, Shawn
93LetMouF-4148
93LetMouSP-15
Ohme, Kevin
95HarCitRCTI-19
96HarCitRCB-23
Ohnoutka, Brian
85EveGialC-13
86ShrCapP-20
87ShrCapP-12
88PhoFirC-7
88PhoFirP-79
90CMC-524
90LasVegSC-21
90LasVegSP-119
90ProAAAF-7
Ohsubo, Kukio
91SalSpuC-16
Ohta, Katsumasa
91SalSpuC-14
91SalSpuP-2242
Ohtsubo, Yukio
91SalSpuP-2243
Ohtsuka, Ken (Kenichi)
90SalSpuP-2716
Ohtsuka, Yoshiki
90SalSpuP-2722
Oiler, David
93EliTwiC-18
93EliTwiF-3416
Ojala, Kirt
90OneYanP-3380
90ProAaA-178
91PriWilCC-9
91PriWilCP-1425
92AlbYanF-2226
93ColCliF-1111
93ColCliP-6
94ColCliF-2952
94ColCliP-21
94TriAAF-AAA4
95ColCliMCTI-10
95ColCliP-19
95ColCliTI-19
96IndIndB-17
Ojea, Alex
87SprCarB-3
88SprCarB-17
Ojeda, Bob
81PawRedST-5
82Don-540
82Fle-301
82RedSoxC-13
82Top-274
83Don-260
83Fle-190
83Top-654
84Don-538
84Fle-406
84Nes792-162
84Nes792-786
84OPC-162
84Top-162
84Top-786
84TopTif-162
84TopTif-786
85Don-371
85Fle-166
85OPC-329
85Top-477
85TopTif-477
86BasStaB-80
86Don-636
86Fle-357
86FleUpd-84
86MetColP-25
86MetTCM-10
86MetWorSC-16
86OPC-11
86Top-11
86TopTif-11
86TopTra-81T
86TopTraT-81T
87ClaGam-73
87Don-364
87DonOpeD-127
87Fle-19
87FleBasA-30
87FleGamW-32
87FleGlo-19
87FleMin-77
87FleStiC-86
87Lea-94
87MetColP-14
87MetFanC-6
87OPC-83
87Spo-36
87SpoTeaP-2
87Top-746
87TopGloS-36
87TopMinL-25
87TopSti-99
87TopTif-746
87Woo-24
88Don-632
88DonBasB-238
88DonTeaBM-632
88Fle-147
88FleGlo-147
88MetColP-41
88MetKah-19
88Sco-563
88ScoGlo-563
88Top-558
88TopBig-234
88TopTif-558
89Bow-371
89BowTif-371
89Don-218
89DonBasB-209
89Fle-47
89FleGlo-47
89MetColP-16
89MetKah-20
89OPC-333
89Sco-116
89Top-333
89TopTif-333
89UppDec-386
90Don-117
90Fle-214
90FleCan-214
90MetColP-22
90MetKah-19
90OPC-207
90PubSti-143
90Sco-53
90Top-207
90TopBig-131
90TopTif-207
90TopTVM-16
90UppDec-204
90VenSti-373
91Bow-591
91DodMot-13
91DodPol-17
91Don-584
91Fle-156
91FleUpd-95
91Lea-476
91MetWIZ-300
91OPC-601
91OPCPre-91
91Sco-321
91ScoRoo-79T
91SimandSMLBL-31
91StaClu-449
91Stu-187
91Top-601
91TopDesS-601
91TopMic-601
91TopTif-601
91TopTra-86T
91TopTraT-86T
91UltUpd-89
91UppDec-179
91UppDec-715
92Bow-379
92DodMot-23
92DodPol-17
92DodSmo-10392
92Don-157
92Fle-468
92Lea-345
92OPC-123
92Pin-512
92Sco-527
92StaClu-537
92Top-123
92TopGol-123
92TopGolW-123
92TopMic-123
92TriPla-21
92Ult-509
92UppDec-666
93Don-614
93Fle-452
93IndWUA-23
93Pin-537
93Sco-589
93Sel-263
93SelRoo-121T
93Top-338
93TopGol-338
93TopInaM-338
93TopMic-338
93UppDec-808
93UppDecGold-808
94Fle-116
94Pac-180
94Pin-507
94PinArtP-507
94PinMusC-507
94Top-93
94TopGol-93
94TopSpa-93
Ojeda, Erick
94VenLinU-4
95LinVen-98
Ojeda, Jorge
89BlaYNPRWL-148
Ojeda, Luis
82ArkTraT-16
83ArkTraT-16
86MiaMarP-19
87MiaMarP-26
88BlaYNPRWLU-20
Ojeda, Miguel
94WelPirC-21
94WelPirF-3499
Ojeda, Ray
86BelBreP-17
87BelBreP-22
88BlaYNPRWL-172
Ojeta, Erick
93LinVenB-4
Oka, Yukitoshi
91SalSpuC-15
91SalSpuP-2244
Okajima, Hideki
96HonShaHWB-8
Okamoto, Yoshi
90SalSpuCLC-147
Okerlund, Ron
85AncGlaPTI-39
Okubo, Dave
86SanJosBP-16
Olah, Bob
87LitFalMP-2401
89ColMetB-7
89ColMetGS-19
89SouAtlLAGS-18
90St.LucMS-19
Olajuwon, Hakeem
93StaCluMO-35
Olander, Jim
85PorBeaC-36
86ReaPhiP-21
87MaiGuiP-1
87MaiGuiT-18
87PhiTas-38
88MaiPhiC-21
88MaiPhiP-277
89ScrRedBC-15
89ScrRedBP-723
90CMC-619
90ProAAAF-206
90TucTorC-17
90TucTorP-216
91DenZepLD-147
91DenZepP-135
91LinDriAAA-147
91TriA AAGP-AAA11
92Bow-575
92DenZepS-144
92Don-766
92OPC-7
92Sco-839
92SkyAAAF-70
92SkyAAAF-293
92StaClu-274
92Top-7
92TopDeb91-134
92TopGol-7
92TopGolW-7
92TopMic-7
93ColSprSSF-3099
94BreMilB-160
94IndIndF-1822
Olden, Paul
82SpoIndT-6
Oldham, J.C.
23WilChoV-114
Oldham, Robert
94BurIndC-17
94BurIndF-3790
Oldis, Bob (Robert Carl)
53Bri-14
53Top-262
54Top-91
55Top-169
60KeyChal-38
60Top-361
61Top-149
62Top-269
63Top-404
89ChaLooLITI-22
91TopArc1-262
94TopArc1-91
94TopArc1G-91
Oldring, Rube (Reuben Henry)
08AmeCarE-18
08RosComP-63
09ColChiE-217
09T206-272
09T206-273
10CouT21-204
10CouT21-205
10DomDisP-94
10E12AmeCDC-30
10JuJuDE-32
10NadE1-47
10RedCroT-145
10RedCroT-232
10SweCapPP-49
11A'sFirT20-15
11BasBatEU-31
11MecDFT-38
11PloCanE-52
11S74Sil-34
11SpoLifCW-274
11SpoLifM-102
11T205-130
12ColRedB-217
12ColTinT-217
12HasTriFT-57
12HasTriFT-60

12T207-144
14CraJacE-8
14FatPlaT-37
15CraJacE-8
15SpoNewM-132
16BF2FP-39
16FleBreD-71
16SpoNewM-133
93ConTSN-788
Oleksak, Mike
79NewCoPT-8
Oleksik, George
96AriBlaDB-25
Olerud, John
90BluJayFS-23
90Bow-510
90BowTif-510
90ClaBlu-35
90ClaYel-T96
90Don-711
90DonBesA-100
90DonRoo-2
90FleUpd-128
90Lea-237
90Sco-589
90Sco100RS-39
90ScoMcD-17
90ScoYouS2-5
90TopBig-199
90TopDeb89-89
90TopMag-16
90TopTra-83T
90TopTraT-83T
90UppDec-56
91BluJayFS-20
91BluJayFS-23
91BluJayS-18
91Bow-7
91Cla1-T1
91Cla2-T24
91ClaGam-116
91Don-530
91Fle-183
91KinDis-7
91Lea-125
91MajLeaCP-27
91OPC-168
91OPCPre-92
91PanFreS-348
91PanSti-159
91PosCan-17
91Sco-625
91Sco-860
91Sco100RS-100
91StaClu-482
91Stu-136
91Top-168
91TopDesS-168
91TopMic-168
91TopRoo-24
91TopTif-168
91ToyRoo-24
91Ult-367
91UppDec-145
92Bow-644
92Don-98
92Fle-339
92Hig5-119
92Lea-60
92LeaBlaG-60
92OPC-777
92PanSti-25
92Pin-78
92PinTea2-65
92Sco-345
92Sco100S-71
92ScoImpP-41
92ScoProP-16
92SpoIllFK1-281
92StaClu-531
92Stu-258
92Top-777
92TopGol-777
92TopGolW-777
92TopMic-777
92TriPla-110
92Ult-151
92UppDec-375
93BluJayCP1-9
93BluJayD-10
93BluJayD4-10
93BluJayDM-27
93BluJayDWS-6
93BluJayFS-22
93Bow-659
93ColAllG-13
93DiaMar-82
93DiaMarA-5
93Don-483
93DonEliD-9
93Fin-13
93FinRef-13
93Fla-293
93Fle-339
93FunPac-60
93HumDumC-19
93Lea-47
93LeaGolA-U3
93OPC-188
93OPCPre-52
93OPCWorC-12
93PacJugC-12
93PacSpa-327
93PanSti-26
93Pin-86
93PinHomRC-29
93Sco-68
93Sel-124
93SP-6
93StaClu-649
93StaCluFDI-649
93StaCluMOP-649
93Stu-195
93Top-240
93TopFulS-10
93TopGol-240
93TopInaM-240
93TopMic-240
93TriPla-222
93Ult-291
93UppDec-344
93UppDecGold-344
94BluJayP-7
94BluJayUSPC-1C
94BluJayUSPC-6H
94BluJayUSPC-7D
94Bow-169
94BowBes-R62
94BowBes-X110
94BowBesR-R62
94BowBesR-X110
94ColC-600
94ColChoGS-600
94ColChoSS-600
94Don-354
94DonDiaK-DK24
94DonEli-43
94DonMVP-28
94DonPro-3
94DonSpeE-354
94DonSpiotG-1
94ExtBas-193
94ExtBasGB-21
94Fin-221
94FinJum-221
94FinRef-221
94Fla-120
94FlaHotN-6
94Fle-340
94Fle-707
94FleAllS-19
94FleLeaL-1
94FlePro-2
94FleSun-19
94FUnPac-99
94KinDis-13
94Lea-378
94LeaGolS-12
94LeaL-79
94OPC-130
94OPCAllR-16
94OPCJumA-16
94OPCWorC-5
94Pac-650
94PacSilP-6
94PanSti-5
94PanSti-141
94Pin-5
94PinArtP-5
94PinMusC-5
94PinRunC-RC1
94PinSam-5
94PinTheN-24
94Pos-24
94PosCan-4
94PosCanG-4
94ProMag-140
94RedFolMI-1
94Sco-2
94ScoCyc-TC6
94ScoGolR-2
94ScoGolS-37
94ScoSam-2
94ScoSam-2GR
94Sel-239
94SelCroC-CC8
94SP-45
94SPDieC-45
94Spo-75
94StaClu-110
94StaClu-228
94StaCluFDI-110
94StaCluFDI-228
94StaCluGR-110
94StaCluGR-228
94StaCluMO-9
94StaCluMOP-110
94StaCluMOP-228
94StaCluMOP-ST28
94StaCluST-ST28
94StaCluT-172
94StaCluTFDI-172
94Stu-30
94TomPiz-24
94Top-10
94TopBlaG-15
94TopGol-10
94TopSpa-10
94TopSupS-32
94TriPla-36
94TriPlaM-3
94TriPlaN-5
94Ult-141
94UltAllS-9
94UltHitM-8
94UltLeaL-1
94UltOnBL-10
94UltRisS-8
94UppDec-48
94UppDec-99
94UppDecAJ-24
94UppDecAJG-24
94UppDecED-48
94UppDecED-99
94USPlaCA-13D
95Baz-41
95BluJayP-5
95BluJayUSPC-1C
95BluJayUSPC-7D
95Bow-359
95ColCho-139
95ColChoGS-139
95ColChoSE-57
95ColChoSEGS-57
95ColChoSESS-57
95ColChoSS-139
95Don-433
95DonPreP-433
95DonTopotO-176
95Emb-52
95EmbGolI-52
95Emo-97
95Fin-59
95FinRef-59
95Fla-100
95Fle-102
95Lea-41
95LeaLim-179
95Pac-448
95PacPri-144
95Pin-94
95PinArtP-94
95PinMusC-94
95RedFol-36
95Sco-60
95ScoGolR-60
95ScoHaloG-HG29
95ScoPlaTS-60
95Sel-84
95SelArtP-84
95SelCer-7
95SelCerMG-7
95Spo-61
95SpoArtP-61
95StaClu-448
95StaCluMOP-448
95StaCluMOP-RL28
95StaCluRL-RL28
95StaCluSTWS-448
95StaCluVR-239
95Stu-195
95Sum-55
95SumNthD-55
95Top-499
95TopCyb-289
95UC3-3
95UC3ArtP-3
95Ult-342
95UltGolM-342
95UppDec-41
95UppDecED-41
95UppDecEDG-41
95UppDecPLL-R54
95UppDecPLLE-R54
95Zen-55
96Baz-78
96BluJayB-4
96BluJayOH-23
96Bow-70
96Cir-96
96CirRav-96
96ColCho-750
96ColChoGS-750
96ColChoSS-750
96Don-382
96DonPreP-382
96EmoXL-136
96Fin-B98
96FinRef-B98
96Fla-190
96Fle-280
96FleTif-280
96Lea-181
96LeaPrePB-181
96LeaPrePG-181
96LeaPrePS-181
96MetUni-125
96MetUniP-125
96Pac-442
96PanSti-166
96Pin-50
96Pin-225
96PinAfi-82
96PinAfiAP-82
96PinAfiFPP-82
96PinArtP-125
96PinFoil-225
96PinSta-125
96ProSta-19
96Sco-413
96Sel-57
96SelArtP-57
96StaClu-277
96StaCluEPB-277
96StaCluEPG-277
96StaCluEPS-277
96StaCluMOP-277
95StaCluVRMC-239
96Sum-138
96SumAbo&B-138
96SumArtP-138
96SumFoi-138
96TeaOut-60
96Top-264
96TopChr-106
96TopChrR-106
96TopGal-87
96TopGalPPI-87
96TopLas-87
96Ult-150
96UltGolM-150
96UppDec-475
97BluJayS-48
97Bow-240
97BowBes-31
97BowBesAR-31
97BowBesR-31
97BowChr-66
97BowChrI-66
97BowChrIR-66
97BowChrR-66
97BowInt-240
97Cir-9
97CirRav-9
97ColCho-392
97Don-69
97Don-350
97DonLim-20
97DonLimLE-20
97DonPreP-69
97DonPreP-350
97DonPrePGold-69
97DonPrePGold-350
97Fin-84
97FinRef-84
97FlaSho-A149
97FlaSho-B149
97FlaSho-C149
97FlaShoLC-149
97FlaShoLC-B149
97FlaShoLC-C149
97FlaShoLCM-A149
97FlaShoLCM-B149
97FlaShoLCM-C149
97Fle-247
97Fle-651
97FleTif-247
97FleTif-651
97Lea-278
97LeaFraM-278
97LeaFraMDC-278
97MetUni-188
97Pac-224
97PacLigB-224
97PacSil-224
97Sco-76
97Sco-336
97ScoHobR-336
97ScoPreS-76
97ScoResC-336
97ScoShoS-76
97ScoShoS-336
97ScoShoSAP-76
97ScoShoSAP-336
97StaClu-301
97StaCluMOP-301
97Top-426
97TopChr-151
97TopChrR-151
97TopGal-88
97TopGalPPI-88
97TopSta-36
97TopStaAM-36
97Ult-149
97Ult-436
97UltGolME-149
97UltGolME-436
97UltPlaME-149
97UltPlaME-436
97UppDec-541
Olexa, Mike
93HelBreF-4104
93HelBreSP-11
Olin, Steve
88MidLeaAGS-30
88WatIndP-688
89ColSprSSP-252
89TriA AAC-42
89TriAAP-AAA34
90Bow-326
90BowTif-326
90Don-438
90Fle-499
90FleCan-499
90IndTeal-31
90OPC-433
90PanSti-375
90Sco-590
90ScoYouS2-23
90Spo-178
90Top-433
90TopDeb89-90
90TopTif-433
90TriAAAC-42
90UppDec-553
91Don-339
91Fle-374
91IndFanC-22
91Lea-94
91OPC-696
91Sco-496
91Sco100RS-86
91StaClu-336
91Top-696
91TopDesS-696
91TopMic-696
91TopTif-696
91Ult-116
91UppDec-118
92Bow-236
92Don-151
92Fle-120
92IndFanC-20
92Lea-141
92OPC-559
92Pin-120
92Sco-644
92StaClu-169
92Top-559
92TopGol-559

92TopGolW-559
92TopMic-559
92TriPla-156
92Ult-53
92UppDec-215
93Don-567
93Fle-220
93OPC-349
93Pin-410
93Sco-388
93Sel-377
93Top-167
93TopGol-167
93TopInaM-167
93TopMic-167
93TriPla-204
93UppDec-206
93UppDecGold-206
Olinde, Chad
94WilCubC-17
94WilCubF-3772
95RocCubTI-14
Oliphant, John
87NewOriP-5
Oliva, Jose
89ButCopKSP-12
90GasRanB-21
90GasRanP-2530
90GasRanS-17
91ChaRanC-20
91ChaRanP-1324
92Bow-55
92ClaFS7-289
92SkyAA F-272
92TulDriF-2703
92TulDriS-614
92UppDecML-283
93Bow-282
93ExcFS7-235
93LimRocDWB-25
93LimRocDWB-146
93RicBraBB-16
93RicBraF-193
93RicBraP-7
93RicBraRC-7
93RicBraRC-23
93UppDec-426
93UppDecGold-426
94BraLykP-26
94FleUpd-104
94LeaLimR-48
94RicBraF-2855
94SpoRoo-144
94SpoRooAP-144
94StaCluT-48
94StaCluTFDI-48
95ActPac2GF-7G
95ActPacF-30
95ActPacF-68
95Baz-131
95Bow-438
95ColCho-166
95ColChoGS-166
95ColChoSE-64
95ColChoSEGS-64
95ColChoSESS-64
95ColChoSS-166
95Don-124
95DonPreP-124
95Fin-22
95FinRef-22
95Fla-107
95Fle-316
95Lea-349
95LeaGolR-7
95Pac-14
95PacLatD-25
95Pin-140
95PinArtP-140
95PinMusC-140
95Sco-295
95ScoAi-AM4
95ScoGolR-295
95ScoPlaTS-295
95ScoRooDT-RDT4
95Sel-181
95SelArtP-181
95SelCer-109
95SelCerMG-109
95Spo-147
95SpoArtP-147
95StaClu-332
95StaCluMOP-332
95StaCluSTWS-332
95StaCluVR-172
95Sum-119
95SumNthD-119
95Top-451
95TopCyb-247
95UC3-113
95UC3ArtP-113
95Ult-352
95UltGolM-352
95UppDec-214
95UppDecED-214
95UppDecEDG-214
95UppDecPAW-H19
95UppDecPAWE-H19
95UppDecSE-17
95UppDecSEG-17
95UppDecSoaD-SD4
96ColCho-689
96ColChoGS-689
96ColChoSS-689
96Don-417
96DonPreP-417
96Fle-550
96FleTif-550
96LouRedB-24
96Sco-138
95StaCluVRMC-172
Oliva, Steve
77QuaCitAT-22
78QuaCitAT-16
Oliva, Tony (Antonio Pedro)
63Top-228
64Top-116
64TopGia-44
64TopVen-116
64TwiJayP-8
65Baz-4
65MacSta-7
65OPC-1
65Top-1
65Top-340
65TopTral-60
66Baz-41
66Top-216
66Top-220
66Top-450
66TopRubI-72
66TopVen-216
66TopVen-220
66TwiFaiG-10
67Baz-41
67CokCapA-12
67CokCapAAm-27
67CokCapTw-17
67DexPre-153
67OPC-50
67OPCPapI-18
67Top-50
67Top-239
67TopPos-18
67TopTesF-17
67TopVen-230
68AtlOilPBCC-31
68Baz-9
68DexPre-60
68OPC-165
68Top-165
68Top-371
68Top-480
68TopActS-11A
68TopVen-165
69MilBra-205
69MLBOffS-69
69MLBPin-20
69NabTeaF-17
69OPC-1
69Top-1
69Top-427
69Top-582A
69Top-582B
69Top-600
69TopDecl-32
69TopSta-196
69TopSup-20
69TopTeaP-15
69TraSta-7
69TwiTealC-8
70DayDaiNM-30
70Kel-63
70MLBOffS-235
70OPC-62
70OPC-510
70Top-62
70Top-510
70TopBoo-8
70TopSup-26
70TraSta-13B
71BazNumT-36
71Kel-12
71MatMin-11
71MatMin-12
71MilDud-20
71MLBOffS-468
71OPC-61
71OPC-290
71Top-61
71Top-290
71TopCoi-128
71TopGreM-11
71TopSup-11
71TopTat-133
72EssCoi-10
72Kel-25
72MilBra-258
72OPC-86
72OPC-400
72Top-86
72Top-400
72TopPos-7
73Kel2D-4
73OPC-80
73Top-80
74OPC-190
74Top-190
74TopDecE-62
74TopSta-210
75Hos-20
75HosTwi-20
75OPC-325
75SSP42-20
75Top-325
76Hos-10
76HosTwi-10
76OPC-35
76SSP-217
76Top-35
77GalGloG-257
78TCM60I-71
78TwiFri-15
80WisRapTT-27
82CraJac-7
83FraBroR-27
83MLBPin-13
84OCoandSI-35
84OCoandSI-167
85TwiTeal-3
86SpoDecG-51
86TwiGreT-7
86TwiTeal-4
88PacLegI-59
88TwiTeal-3
89SweBasG-12
89Top-665A
89Top-665B
89TopTif-665
92ActPacA-60
92UppDecS-8
92UppDecS-29
93TedWil-50
93UppDecS-15
94UppDecAH-85
94UppDecAH-209
94UppDecAH1-85
94UppDecAH1-209
Olivares, Ed (Edward B.)
62Col45'HC-12
62Top-598
Olivares, Jose
89MyrBeaBJP-1473
90MyrBeaBJP-2776
Olivares, Mako
93LinVenB-316
Olivares, O.
76VenLeaS-163
78ColCliT-19
79PorBeaT-2
93LinVenB-125
Olivares, Omar
87ChaRaiP-13
88BlaYNPRWL-47
88ChaRaiP-1210
88SouAtlLAGS-10
89BlaYNPRWL-48
89TexLeaAGS-11
89WicChaR-18
89WicStaR-11
89WicUpdR-4
89WicWraR-26
90CMC-120
90LouRedBC-20
90LouRedBLBC-31
90LouRedBP-400
90ProAAAF-514
90TopTVCa-58
91Don-503
91LinDriAAA-237
91LouRedLD-237
91LouRedP-2912
91LouRedTI-3
91OPC-271
91Sco-748
91ScoRoo-5
91Top-271
91TopDeb90-118
91TopDesS-271
91TopMic-271
91TopTif-271
91UltUpd-108
91UppDec-463
92Bow-420
92CarPol-12
92ClaGam-22
92Don-481
92Fle-584
92Lea-282
92OPC-193
92OPCPre-38
92Pin-186
92ProFS7-316
92Sco-334
92StaClu-386
92Top-193
92TopGol-193
92TopGolW-193
92TopMic-193
92Ult-266
92UppDec-478
93Bow-432
93CarPol-11
93Don-388
93Fle-512
93Lea-438
93LinVenB-276
93OPC-206
93PacSpa-297
93Pin-394
93StaClu-489
93StaCluCa-24
93StaCluFDI-489
93StaCluMOP-489
93Top-490
93TopGol-490
93TopInaM-490
93TopMic-490
93Ult-465
93UppDec-194
93UppDecGold-194
94CarPol-11
94Don-120
94Fle-638
94LouRedF-2981
94Pac-595
94StaClu-425
94StaCluFDI-425
94StaCluGR-425
94StaCluMOP-425
94StaCluT-302
94StaCluTFDI-302
94Top-689
94TopGol-689
94TopSpa-689
95Pac-410
96LeaSigEA-146
97ColCho-337
97UppDec-354
Olivaros, Ed
77ReaPhiT-18
Olivas, Rich
86AncGlaPTI-25
Oliver, Al (Albert)
69OPC-82
69PirJacitB-7
69Top-82
70MLBOffS-105
70OPC-166
70PirTeal-5
70Top-166
71MLBOffS-210
71OPC-388
71PirActP-21
71PirArc-8
71Top-388
72Top-575
73LinPor-151
73OPC-225
73Top-225
74OPC-52
74Top-52
74TopSta-85
75Hos-81
75Kel-15
75OPC-555
75Top-555
76CraDis-43
76Hos-112
76OPC-620
76SSP-576
76Top-620
77BurCheD-189
77Hos-45
77Kel-46
77OPC-203
77PirPosP-17
77RCColC-47
77Top-130
77TopCloS-34
78OPC-97
78RanBurK-17
78RCColC-30
78SSP270-108
78Top-430
78WifBalD-55
79Hos-80
79OPC-204
79Top-391
79TopCom-16
80OPC-136
80Top-260
80TopSup-35
81AllGamPI-63
81Don-387
81Dra-24
81Fle-626
81FleStiC-64
81Kel-4
81OPC-70
81Squ-22
81Top-70
81TopScr-4
81TopSti-131
81TopSti-246
81TopSupHT-93
82Don-116
82ExpHygM-15
82ExpPos-25
82ExpPos-26
82ExpPos-27
82FBIDis-13
82Fle-326
82FleSta-178
82Kel-61
82OPC-22
82OPC-326
82Top-36
82Top-590
82Top-591
82TopSti-239
82TopTra-83T
83AllGamPI-97
83Don-140
83DonActA-6
83Dra-21
83ExpStu-6
83Fle-290
83FleSta-142
83FleSti-143
83FleSti-268
83OPC-5
83OPC-111
83OPC-311
83PerAll-13
83PerAllG-13
83PerCreC-10
83PerCreCG-10
83Top-111
83Top-420
83Top-421
83Top-701
83Top-703
83TopFol-2
83TopFol-3
83TopGloS-30
83TopLeaS-3
83TopSti-174
83TopSti-205

83TopSti-206
83TopSti-251
84AllGamPI-8
84Don-9
84Don-9A
84Don-177
84DonCha-30
84Dra-24
84Fle-280
84Fle-632
84FleSti-27
84FleUpd-85
84GiaPos-20
84MilBra-18
84Nes792-516
84Nes792-620
84Nes792-704
84OPC-307
84OPC-332
84Top-516
84Top-620
84Top-704
84TopGloA-13
84TopGloS-21
84TopSti-87
84TopStiB-1
84TopTif-516
84TopTif-620
84TopTif-704
84TopTra-87T
84TopTraT-87T
85DodCokP-23
85Don-598
85Fle-262
85FleUpd-84
85Lea-67
85OPC-130
85Top-130
85TopSti-118
85TopTif-130
85TopTifT-88T
85TopTra-88T
86Don-485
86Fle-69
86OPC-114
86RanGreT-9
86Spo-126
86Spo-140
86Spo-164
86Top-775
86TopSti-14
86TopTif-775
86Woo-26
89PacSenL-142
89T/MSenL-83
89TopSenL-36
90DodTar-587
90EliSenL-46
91UppDecS-13
92ActPacA-68
92Nab-21
92UppDecS-12
92UppDecS-30
93ExpDonM-16
93MCIAmb-11
93RanKee-283
93TedWil-79
93TedWilM-12
93UppDecAH-102
94RanAllP-8
94RanAllP-9
94UppDecAH-82
94UppDecAH1-82

Oliver, Bob (Robert Lee)
69RoySol-12
69RoyTeal-10
69Top-662
69TopSta-187
70MLBOffS-226
70RoyTeal-25
70Top-567
71MLBOffS-423
71OPC-470
71Top-470
71TopCoi-48
71TopTat-91
72MilBra-259
72OPC-57
72Top-57
73LinPor-33
73OPC-289
73Top-289
74OPC-243
74Top-243
74TopSta-143
75OPC-657
75SSP18-16
75Top-657
76OklCit8TI-30
76VenLeaS-53
77ColCliT-17
79QuaCitCT-26
91OriCro-342
92YanWIZ7-123
93UppDecS-4

Oliver, Brent
92DavLipB-20

Oliver, Bruce
79CedRapGT-11
81CliGiaT-5

Oliver, Darren
89GasRanP-1021
89GasRanS-17
89SouAtlLAGS-24
90ChaRanS-17
91ChaRanC-7
91ChaRanP-1311
92ChaRanC-19
92UppDecML-308
93RanKee-418
93TulDriF-2733
94Bow-513
94FleMajLP-27
94Pin-233
94PinArtP-233
94PinMusC-233
94ScoRoo-RT113
94ScoRooGR-RT113
94Sel-203
95ColCho-399
95ColChoGS-399
95ColChoSS-399
95Fla-90
95Lea-185
95Pin-262
95PinArtP-262
95PinMusC-262
95RanCra-24
95Sel-57
95SelArtP-57
95Top-403
95TopCyb-204
95UppDec-153
95UppDecED-153
95UppDecEDG-153
96ColCho-734
96ColChoGS-734
96ColChoSS-734
96RanMot-27
97Cir-302
97CirRav-302
97ColCho-237
97Don-107
97DonPreP-107
97DonPrePGold-107
97Fle-228
97FleTif-228
97Lea-160
97LeaFraM-160
97LeaFraMDC-160
97Pac-206
97PacLigB-206
97PacSil-206
97Pin-131
97PinArtP-131
97PinMusC-131
97Sco-129
97ScoPreS-129
97ScoRan-6
97ScoRanPl-6
97ScoRanPr-6
97ScoShoS-129
97ScoShoSAP-129
97Top-303
93TulDriTI-21
97Ult-305
97UltGolME-305
97UltPlaME-305
97UppDec-209

Oliver, Dave (David Jacob)
78Top-704
79TacTugT-12
79Top-705
80TacTigT-15
81BatTroT-27
83TriTriT-26
85OklCit8T-15
86OklCit8P-15
87RanMot-28
87RanSmo-30
88RanMot-27
89RanMot-27
89RanSmo-23
90RanMot-27
91RanMot-28
92RanMot-28
93RanKee-439

Oliver, Edward
49W72HolS-13

Oliver, Gene (Eugene George)
59Top-135
59TopVen-135
60Top-307
61Top-487
62CarJayP-11
62Top-561
63Fle-62
63Jel-164
63Pos-164
63Top-172
64Top-316
64TopVen-316
65Kah-32
65OPC-106
65Top-106
66Top-541
67CokCapB-4
67DexPre-154
67OPC-18
67Top-18
68CokCapRS-9
68Top-449
69MilBra-206
69Top-247
78AtlCon-20
81QuaCitCT-31
81RedSoxBG2S-100

Oliver, Harry
82RedPioT-19

Oliver, Joe
84CedRapRT-14
87VerRedP-19
88NasSouC-17
88NasSouP-483
89NasSouC-12
89NasSouP-1283
89NasSouTI-17
89ScoRoo-104T
90Bow-54
90BowTif-54
90CedRapRDGB-8
90ClaYel-T98
90Don-586
90DonBesN-15
90Fle-426
90FleCan-426
90Hot50RS-33
90Lea-453
90OPC-668
90PanSti-378
90RedKah-19
90Sco-576
90Sco100RS-26
90ScoYouSI-10
90Spo-71
90Top-668
90TopBig-281
90TopDeb89-91
90TopTif-668
90UppDec-568
91Bow-671
91Don-381
91Fle-75
91Lea-73
91OPC-517
91PanFreS-126
91RedKah-9
91RedPep-14
91Sco-620
91StaClu-68
91Top-517
91TopDesS-517
91TopMic-517
91TopTif-517
91Ult-99
91UppDec-279
91Woo-28
92Bow-594
92Don-261
92Fle-414
92Lea-7
92OPC-304
92PanSti-261
92Pin-331
92RedKah-9
92Sco-370
92StaClu-306
92Top-304
92TopGol-304
92TopGolW-304
92TopMic-304
92Ult-193
92UppDec-101
93Bow-6
93CadDis-43
93DenHol-22
93Don-586
93Fla-30
93Fle-38
93Lea-263
93OPC-260
93PacSpa-86
93PanSti-290
93Pin-190
93RedKah-17
93Sco-125
93Sel-235
93SP-212
93StaClu-96
93StaCluFDI-96
93StaCluMOP-96
93StaCluMP-5
93Stu-187
93Top-138
93TOPBLAG-14
93TopGol-138
93TopInaM-138
93TopMic-138
93TriPla-220
93Ult-32
93UppDec-234
93UppDecGold-234
94Bow-298
94ColC-220
94ColChoGS-220
94ColChoSS-220
94Don-249
94ExtBas-236
94Fin-37
94FinRef-37
94Fle-418
94Lea-146
94OPC-189
94Pac-153
94PanSti-166
94Pin-402
94PinArtP-402
94PinMusC-402
94RedKah-21
94Sco-444
94ScoGolR-444
94Sel-149
94StaClu-7
94StaCluFDI-7
94StaCluGR-7
94StaCluMOP-7
94Top-485
94TopGol-485
94TopSpa-485
94TriPla-217
94Ult-174
94UppDec-134
94UppDecED-134
95ColCho-539T
95DonTopotO-101
95Emo-54
95Fin-328
95FinRef-328
95Fla-274
95FleUpd-55
95LinVen-155
95Sco-418
95ScoGolR-418
95ScoPlaTS-418
95SP-168
95SPSil-168
95StaClu-549
95StaCluMOP-549
95StaCluSTWS-549
95TopTra-23T
95UppDec-297
95UppDecED-297
95UppDecEDG-297
96ColCho-194
96ColChoGS-194
96ColChoSS-194
96Don-299
96DonPreP-299
96Fle-155
96FleTif-155
96LeaSigEA-147
96MetUni-72
96MetUniP-72
96Pac-339
96PanSti-198
96Sco-477
96StaClu-387
96StaCluMOP-387
96Top-108
97Fle-300
97FleTif-300
97Pac-273
97PacLigB-273
97PacSil-273

Oliver, John
96AppLeaAB-30
96BesAutS1RP-FR11
97Top-269

Oliver, Nate (Nathaniel)
63Top-466
65DodTeal-11
65OPC-59
65Top-59
66Top-364
66TopVen-364
68OPC-124
68Top-124
68TopVen-124
69Top-354
70OPC-223
70Top-223
81TCM60I-389
88RenSilSCLC-291
89MidAngGS-2
90DodTar-588
90PalSprACLC-228
90PalSprAP-2594
91PalSprAP-2033
92MidAngF-4041
92MidAngOHP-17
92MidAngS-475
92YanWIZ6-95
93MidAngF-338
94AlbDukF-860
97MidAngOHP-21

Oliver, Rick
76WilTomT-17
80SalLakCGT-10

Oliver, Scott
82DanSunF-16
83RedPioT-20
85EdmTraC-5

Oliver, Thomas
36GouWidPPR-D25
36WorWidGV-119
54OriEss-29
54Top-207
79RedSoxEF-3
79RedSoxEF-23
94TopArc1-207
94TopArc1G-207

Oliver, Warren
82ForMyeRT-5

Oliveras, David
88BlaYNPRWLU-51
88BurIndP-1789
89KinIndS-16
90KinIndTI-17

Oliveras, Francisco
81MiaOriT-10
85ChaO'sT-15
86ChaOriW-20
87ChaO'sW-12
88BlaYNPRWL-48
88OrlTwiB-24
89BlaYNPRWL-49
89DonRoo-9
89PorBeaC-9
89PorBeaP-229
90CMC-560
90Lea-515
90PorBeaC-8
90PorBeaP-176
90ProAAAF-246
90TopDeb89-92
91Don-469
91GiaPacGaE-24
91GiaPos-2
91LinDriAAA-387

91OPC-52
91PhoFirLD-387
91PhoFirP-63
91Sco-635
91Top-52
91TopDesS-52
91TopMic-52
91TopTif-52
92Don-702
92Fle-645
92PhoFirS-391
92Sco-295
92StaClu-347
92UppDec-49
93Fle-534
93OklCit8F-1624
93PacSpa-276
Oliveras, Herbie
84ChaO'sT-27
Oliveras, Mako
89BlaYNPRWL-2
Oliveras, Max
75ShrCapT-16
86FloStaLAP-37
87MidAngP-15
88BlaYNPRWL-129
88MidAngGS-1
89MidAngGS-1
90CMC-502
90EdmTraC-2
90EdmTraP-531
90ProAAAF-107
91EdmTraLD-174
91EdmTraP-1531
91LinDriAAA-174
91TriA AAGP-AAA14
92EdmTraF-3553
92EdmTraS-174
93VanCanF-2613
94AngMot-28
Oliveras, Ossie
77SalPirT-16A
77SalPirT-16B
80VenLeaS-146
Oliverio, Steve
85CedRapRT-10
86VerRedP-14
87VerRedP-14
88NasSouC-9
88NasSouP-482
88NasSouTI-18
89CalCanC-4
89CalCanP-543
89ColMudB-24
94BilMusF-3686
94BilMusSP-24
95BilRedTI-28
96BilMusTI-24
Oliveros, Leonardo
94MarPhiC-15
94MarPhiF-3297
95MarPhiTI-19
96BatCliTI-15
Olivier, Richard
96GreBatB-17
Olivo, Chi-Chi (Frederico)
66Top-578
81TCM60I-349
84OCoandSI-127
Olivo, Mike
70OPC-381
70Top-381
Olker, Joe
84EveGiaC-4
86FreGiaP-12
88ShrCapP-1282
88TexLeaAGS-8
89PhoFirC-8
89PhoFirP-1497
91RenSilSCLC-25
Ollar, Rick
78CliDodT-25
Oller, Jeff
86JamExpP-18
87BurExpP-1074
88WesPalBES-21
90ChaRanS-18
Ollison, Ron
92ClePhiF-2064
94ClePhiC-21
94ClePhiF-2536
Ollison, Scott
91BenBucC-20
91BenBucP-3702
Ollom, James
67OPC-137
67Top-137
68OPC-91
68Top-91
68TopVen-91
81TCM60I-378
Ollom, Mike
84AriWilP-15
87PenWhiSP-9
88TamTarS-19
89BirBarB-2
89BirBarP-95
Olmeda, Jose
89IdaFalBP-2015
90Bes-183
90SumBraB-16
90SumBraP-2444
91MacBraP-874
91SouAtlLAGP-SAL35
92ClaFS7-95
92DurBulTI-13
92GreBraF-1162
93GreBraF-358
94RicBraF-2856
95RicBraRC-16
95RicBraTI-14
95TopTra-146T
96ChaKniB-21
Olmo, Luis
77TCMTheWY-35
90DodTar-589
91RinPosBD4-10
Olmstead, Fred
11T205-132
Olmstead, Nate
94ButCopKSP-4
95CedRapKTI-30
Olmstead, Reed
87EriCarP-4
87SavCarP-17
88SavCarP-346
89SpaPhiP-1048
89SpaPhiS-19
90Bes-257
90CMC-754
90OrlSunRB-7
90OrlSunRP-1092
90OrlSunRS-14
90StaFS7-46
91LinDriAA-490
91OrlSunRLD-490
91OrlSunRP-1860
Olmsted, Alan
80ArkTraT-11
81HawIslT-13
81Top-244
82LouRedE-21
Olsen, Al
86VenGulP-18
87MidAngP-9
88EdmTraP-584
89PalSprACLC-61
89PalSprAP-480
Olsen, Christopher
94SpaPhiF-1720
Olsen, D.C.
96DelShoB-24
Olsen, Jason
96MidLeaAB-54
96SouBenSHS-21
Olsen, John
52LavPro-113
Olsen, Lefty
52MotCoo-23
Olsen, Lew
75WatRoyT-21
76OmaRoyTT-17
77JacSunT-16
Olsen, Rick
78NewWayCT-32
79HolMilT-9
80VanCanT-22
81VanCanT-13
82VanCanT-15
Olsen, Steve
92SarWhiSCB-21
92SarWhiSF-202
92UppDecML-208
93BirBarF-1190
93Bow-691
93ClaFS7-84
93ClaGolF-77
93ExcFS7-153
94BirBarC-18
94BirBarF-621
96WicWraB-20
Olsen, Vern
41CubTeal-17
79DiaGre-112
Olsen, Walter
49W72HolS-15
Olsen, Zoe Ann
63GadFunC-79
Olson, Brad
93EliTwiC-24
Olson, Dan
89BoiHawP-1995
96HicCraB-13
Olson, Dean
77VisOakT-9
Olson, Greg
83LynMetT-8
84JacMetT-NNO
86JacMetT-12
87MetColP-42
87TidTidP-19
87TidTidT-11
88TidTidCa-6
88TidTidCM-13
88TidTidP-1597
89PorBeaC-13
89PorBeaP-225
90BraDubP-22
90BraDubS-25
90ClaYel-T19
90DonBesN-25
90DonRoo-46
90FleUpd-5
90Lea-323
90RedFolSB-70
90ScoRoo-69T
90TopBig-241
90TopTra-84T
90TopTraT-84T
90USPlaCA-2D
91Bow-577
91BraDubP-21
91BraSubS-28
91Don-285
91Fle-698
91Lea-158
91OPC-673
91PanFreS-18
91PanSti-25
91PetSta-2
91Sco-56
91Sco100RS-15
91StaClu-288
91StaCluP-29
91Top-673
91TopDesS-673
91TopMic-673
91TopTif-673
91Ult-9
91UppDec-303
92BraLykP-21
92BraLykS-25
92Don-386
92Fle-365
92Lea-226
92OPC-39
92PanSti-161
92Pin-149
92Sco-474
92ScoProP-18
92StaClu-675
92StaCluD-134
92StaCluNC-675
92Stu-7
92Top-39
92TopGol-39
92TopGolW-39
92TopMic-39
92TriPla-54
92Ult-166
92UppDec-189
93BraFloA-7
93BraLykP-22
93BraLykS-27
93Don-530
93Fle-11
93Lea-357
93OPC-296
93PacSpa-338
93PanSti-180
93Pin-173
93Sco-209
93Sel-46
93Sel-233
93StaClu-450
93StaCluB-7
93StaCluFDI-450
93StaCluMOP-450
93Top-708
93TopGol-708
93TopInaM-708
93TopMic-708
93Ult-10
93UppDec-187
93UppDecGold-187
94ColC-221
94ColChoGS-221
94ColChoSS-221
94Don-382
94Fle-370
94MetShuST-7
94Sco-442
94ScoGolR-442
94Top-346
94TopGol-346
94TopSpa-346
Olson, Gregg
87PanAmTURB-12
89Bow-6
89BowTif-6
89ClaTraO-132
89Don-46
89DonBasB-322
89DonRoo-35
89OriFreB-30
89ScoRoo-96T
89StaWal/O-1
89StaWal/O-3
89StaWal/O-5
89StaWal/O-7
89StaWal/O-9
89StaWal/O-11
89Top-161
89TopAwaW-3
89TopTif-161
89TopTra-89T
89TopTraT-89T
89UppDec-723
90Baz-11
90Bow-249
90BowIns-7
90BowInsT-7
90BowTif-249
90BowTif-A7
90ClaBlu-3
90Col-32
90Don-377
90DonBesA-43
90DonLeaS-27
90Fle-184
90FleAwaW-24
90FleCan-184
90FleLeaL-28
90GooHumICBLS-14
90HagSunDGB-19
90Hot50RS-34
90KinDis-23
90Lea-7
90MLBBasB-114
90MSAHolD-20
90OPC-655
90PanSti-2
90PubSti-581
90Sco-63
90Sco100RS-32
90ScoYouSI-4
90Spo-215
90Top-655
90TopCoi-3
90TopDeb89-93
90TopDou-48
90TopGaloC-6
90TopGloS-29
90TopHeaU-10
90TopRoo-22
90TopSti-10
90TopSti-238
90TopStiB-65
90TopTif-655
90TopTVA-30
90ToyRoo-21
90UppDec-604
90UppDecS-4
90USPlaCA-4C
90VenSti-374
90Woo-5
91BasBesAotM-13
91Bow-92
91Cla3-T70
91Don-23
91Don-111
91Don-393
91DonSupD-23
91Fle-486
91Lea-519
91OPC-10
91OPCPre-93
91OriCro-343
91PanCanT1-88
91PanFreS-248
91PanSti-193
91RedFolS-69
91Sco-490
91Sco100S-27
91SevCoi-A10
91SimandSMLBL-32
91StaClu-156
91StaCluMO-10
91StaCluP-30
91Stu-8
91Top-10
91TopCraJ2-22
91TopDesS-10
91TopMic-10
91TopTif-10
91TopTriH-A1
91Ult-21
91UppDec-47
91UppDec-326
92Bow-577
92Bow-629
92Bow-677
92Don-110
92DonCraJ2-25
92Fle-21
92Fle-701
92Hig5-3
92Lea-277
92OPC-350
92OPCPre-101
92PanSti-72
92Pin-61
92PinTea2-13
92Sco-71
92Sco-427
92Sco100S-91
92ScoImpP-87
92StaClu-293
92Stu-128
92Top-350
92TopGol-350
92TopGolW-350
92TopKid-66
92TopMic-350
92TriPla-13
92Ult-307
92UppDec-227
92UppDecTMH-38
93Bow-465
93Don-117
93Fin-121
93FinRef-121
93Fla-155
93Fle-173
93Lea-23
93MSABenSPD-17
93OPC-281
93PacSpa-22
93Pin-97
93Sco-80
93SP-161
93StaClu-418
93StaCluFDI-418
93StaCluMOP-418
93Top-246
93TopGol-246
93TopInaM-246
93TopMic-246
93TriPla-135
93Ult-145
93UppDec-674
93UppDecGold-674
94Bow-461
94BraLykP-27
94BraLykS-25
94ColC-368
94ColChoGS-368
94ColChoSS-368
94Don-8
94DonSpeE-8

94Fin-246
94FinRef-246
94Fle-13
94FleUpd-105
94Pac-40
94Pin-277
94PinArtP-277
94PinMusC-277
94Sco-525
94ScoGolR-525
94SpoRoo-29
94SpoRooAP-29
94StaClu-196
94StaClu-602
94StaCluFDI-196
94StaCluFDI-602
94StaCluGR-196
94StaCluGR-602
94StaCluMOP-196
94StaCluMOP-602
94Top-723
94TopGol-723
94TopSpa-723
94TopTra-118T
94UppDec-393
94UppDecED-393
87PanAmTUBI-31
Olson, James Vincent
87BurExpP-1068
Olson, Jimmy
86AubAstP-18
87AshTouP-9
Olson, Karl (Karl Arthur)
52Top-72
54Top-186
55Top-72
55TopDouH-35
56Top-322
57Top-153
83TopRep5-72
94TopArc1-186
94TopArc1G-186
Olson, Ken
91SalSpuP-2240
Olson, Kurt
88CapCodPPaLP-47
90YakBeaTI-6
Olson, Mike
81ChaRoyT-4
Olson, Mitch
80AppFoxT-18
Olson, Ollie (Ivan M.)
12T207-145
14B18B-7A
14B18B-7B
19W514-70
20NatCarE-71
21Exh-120
22E120-146
23WilChoV-115
90DodTar-590
Olson, Phil
96StLucMTI-9
Olson, Terry
75AndRanT-17
Olson, Warren
86BelBreP-18
88WinHavRSS-17
Olsson, Dan
86TulDriTI-19
Olszewski, Eric
94IdaFalBF-3582
94IdaFalBSP-20
95MacBraTI-23
96DurBulBIB-5
96DurBulBrB-6
Olszewski, John
53SpoMagP-7
Olszewski, Tim
96HigDesMB-22
Olszta, Ed
75AppFoxT-21
76AppFoxT-18
77AppFoxT-17
Olwine, Ed
83NasSouTI-13
84TidTidT-11
85TidTidT-12
86RicBraP-14
87BraSmo-6
87Don-560
87Fle-524
87FleGlo-524
87RicBraBC-16
87Top-159
87TopTif-159
88BlaYNPRWLU-41
88Sco-379
88ScoGlo-379
88Top-353
88TopTif-353
89OmaRoyC-8
89OmaRoyP-1725
89UppDec-435
90CMC-282
90ProAAAF-402
90RicBraBC-1
90RicBraC-6
90RicBraP-257
90RicBraTI-25
Omachi, George
88FreSunP-1246
Omo, Bob
78CedRapGT-20
Oms, Alejandro
91PomBlaBPB-9
Ongarato, Mike
81PawRedST-21
Onichuk, Sergei
89EasLeaDDP-DD11
Onis, Curly
90DodTar-1045
Onley, Shawn
96AppLeaAB-13
96DanBraB-15
Onofrei, Tim
96JohCitCTI-25
Onslow, Eddie
82OhiHalof-28
Ontiveros, Art
94LetMouF-3878
94LetMouSP-16
Ontiveros, Steve
83AlbA'sT-7
84TacTigC-83
85TacTigC-142
86A'sMot-22
86Don-589
86Fle-429
86SevCoi-W16
86Top-507
86TopTif-507
87Don-221
87DonHig-15
87Fle-401
87FleGlo-401
87Top-161
87TopTif-161
88A'sMot-13
88Don-467
88DonTeaBA-467
88Fle-289
88FleGlo-289
88Sco-511
88ScoGlo-511
88StaLinAs-11
88Top-272
88TopTif-272
89Don-596
89DonTra-11
89PhiTas-26
89Sco-337
89Top-692
89TopTif-692
89TopTra-90T
89TopTraT-90T
90AlbDecGB-7
90Bow-145
90BowTif-145
91Sco-832
94A'sMot-18
95AthMot-18
95ColCho-122
95ColChoGS-122
95ColChoSS-122
95Don-177
95DonPreP-177
95DonTopotO-140
95Emo-73
95Fla-294
95Fle-251
95Lea-389
95Pac-318
95Sco-38
95ScoGolR-38
95ScoPlaTS-38
95SelCer-19
95SelCerMG-19
95Top-593
95TopCyb-365
95Ult-320
95UltGolM-320
95UppDec-32
95UppDecED-32
95UppDecEDG-32
95USPlaCMLA-13S
95Zen-100
96ColCho-244
96ColChoGS-244
96ColChoSS-244
96Don-329
96DonPreP-329
96Fle-214
96FleTif-214
96MetUni-102
96MetUniP-102
96Pac-398
96Pin-75
96Sco-178
96StaClu-388
96StaCluEPB-388
96StaCluEPG-388
96StaCluEPS-388
96StaCluMOP-388
96Top-176
96UppDec-161
Ontiveros, Steve (Steven Robert)
74OPC-598
74Top-598
75Gia-7
75OPC-483
75Top-483
76OPC-284
76SSP-104
76Top-284
77CubJewT-12
78Kel-44
78SSP270-250
78Top-76
79OPC-150
79Top-299
80OPC-268
80Top-514
89TopSenL-79
90EliSenL-117
Ootsuka, Kenichi
90SalSpuCLC-120
Ootsuka, Yoshiki
90SalSpuCLC-141
Opatkiewicz, Ryan
94HunCubF-3562
94HunCubC-21
Opdyke, Paul
88IdaFalBP-1854
Opie, James
83AleDukT-6
85HawIslC-226
86NasPirP-20
87JacExpP-441
Oppenheimer, Jose
77BurBeeT-20
Oppenheimer, Juan
78CedRapGT-21
79CedRapGT-26
Opperman, Dan
88GreFalDTI-10
89VerBeaDS-20
90SanAntMGS-19
91AlbDukP-1140
91Bow-606
91Cla2-T83
91Ult-384
92AlbDukF-720
Oquendo, Ismael
84RocRedWT-8
Oquendo, Jorge
82IdaFalAT-27
Oquendo, Jose (Jose Manuel)
82TidTidT-15
83TidTidT-29
84Don-643
84Fle-592
84Nes792-208
84OPC-208
84Top-208
84TopSti-112
84TopTif-208
85Fle-88
85LouRedR-15
85Top-598
85TopTif-598
86CarSchM-17
86CarTeal-32
86TopTra-82T
86TopTraT-82T
87CarSmo-18
87Don-510
87Fle-305
87FleGlo-305
87Top-133
87TopTif-133
88CarSmo-16
88Don-234
88DonBasB-313
88Fle-44
88FleGlo-44
88Sco-248
88ScoGlo-248
88StaLinCa-15
88Top-83
88TopSti-18
88TopTif-83
89BimBreD-5
89Bow-438
89BowTif-438
89CarSmo-15
89Don-319
89DonBasB-100
89Fle-459
89FleGlo-459
89MSAIceTD-19
89OPC-69
89PanSti-184
89Sco-529
89ScoYouS2-16
89Top-442
89TopBig-77
89TopSti-45
89TopTif-442
89UppDec-514
90Bow-200
90BowTif-200
90CarSmo-17
90Don-161
90DonBesN-108
90Fle-255
90FleCan-255
90Lea-129
90MLBBasB-59
90OPC-645
90PanSti-341
90PubSti-223
90Sco-68
90Spo-85
90Top-645
90TopBig-65
90TopSti-44
90TopTif-645
90TopTVCa-27
90UppDec-319
90VenSti-376
91Bow-395
91CarPol-11
91Don-281
91Fle-640
91Lea-58
91MetWIZ-301
91OPC-343
91PanFreS-32
91PanSti-30
91Sco-622
91StaClu-190
91StaCluP-31
91Stu-236
91Top-343
91TopDesS-343
91TopMic-343
91TopTif-343
91Ult-292
91UppDec-193
92CarPol-13
92Don-280
92Fle-585
92Lea-289
92OPC-723
92PanSti-173
92Pin-239
92Sco-305
92StaClu-571
92Top-723
92TopGol-723
92TopGolW-723
92TopMic-723
92TriPla-118
92Ult-267
92UppDec-283
93CarPol-12
93Don-46
93Fle-513
93Lea-26
93PacBeiA-28
93PacSpa-298
93PacSpaGE-7
93Pin-316
93Sco-163
93StaCluCa-4
93Top-535
93TopGol-535
93TopInaM-535
93TopMic-535
93TriPla-228
93UppDec-84
93UppDecGold-84
94CarPol-12
94Fle-639
94Pac-596
94StaCluT-313
94StaCluTFDI-313
94Top-406
94TopGol-406
94TopSpa-406
94Ult-268
95DonTopotO-333
95Fla-193
95Pac-411
95Sco-218
95ScoGolR-218
95ScoPlaTS-218
95Top-291
96Don-234
96DonPreP-234
96Fle-551
96FleTif-551
96Pac-228
96Sco-143
Oquist, Mike
89EriOriS-16
90CarLeaA-2
90FreKeyTI-22
91Cla/Bes-188
91HagSunLD-241
91HagSunP-2455
91LinDriAA-241
92RocRedWF-1938
92RocRedWS-461
92SkyAAAF-210
93Bow-74
93RocRedWF-236
94ExtBas-10
94Fla-256
94FleUpd-4
94OriPro-74
94OriUSPC-2D
94Pin-224
94PinArtP-224
94PinMusC-224
94ScoRoo-RT129
94ScoRooGR-RT129
94SpoRoo-66
94SpoRooAP-66
94StaCluT-276
94StaCluTFDI-276
94Top-763
94TopGol-763
94TopSpa-763
95ColCho-343
95ColChoGS-343
95ColChoSS-343
95Fla-7
95Fle-16
95Sco-200
95ScoGolR-200
95ScoPlaTS-200
95UppDecSE-47
95UppDecSEG-47
96LasVegSB-19
Oram, Jon
93WatIndC-21
93WatIndF-3571
94WatIndC-22
94WatIndF-3946
Oramas, Victor
94VenLinU-162
Oravetz, Ernie (Ernest E.)
56Top-51
57Top-179
89ChaLooLITI-23
Orbit, Mascot

94MasMan-9
Ordaz, Luis
93PriRedC-22
93PriRedF-4188
94ChaWheC-18
94ChaWheF-2713
94PriRedC-19
94PriRedF-3270
95LinVen-199
96StPetCB-22
97Bow-215
97BowInt-215
Ordonez, Magglio
93HicCraC-17
93HicCraF-1292
94HicCraC-17
94HicCraF-2189
94SouAtlLAF-SAL25
94VenLinU-149
95LinVen-151
95PriWilCTI-4
96BirBarB-5
Ordonez, Rey
92SpollFK1-513
94Cla-199
94FloStaLAF-FSL40
94St.LucMC-1
94St.LucMF-1204
95Bes-85
95Bow-140
95BowBes-B33
95BowBesR-B33
95Exc-233
95ExcFirYP-5
95NorTidTI-19
95SPML-96
95SPMLA-19
95Top-571
95UppDecML-19
95UppDecML-110
96Bow-349
96BowBes-17
96BowBesAR-17
96BowBesP-BBP5
96BowBesPAR-BBP5
96BowBesPR-BBP5
96BowBesR-17
96Cir-161
96CirAcc-24
96CirBos-42
96CirRav-161
96ColCho-429
96ColChoGS-429
96ColChoSS-429
96EmoXL-237
96Fin-B276
96Fin-G338
96FinRef-B276
96FinRef-G338
96Fla-325
96FlaWavotF-18
96FleUpd-U160
96FleUpd-U248
96FleUpdNH-19
96FleUpdSL-8
96FleUpdTC-U160
96FleUpdTC-U248
96LeaLimR-9
96LeaLimRG-9
96LeaPre-117
96LeaPreP-117
96LeaSig-58
96LeaSigA-173
96LeaSigAG-173
96LeaSigAS-173
96LeaSigPPG-58
96LeaSigPPP-58
96MetKah-25
96Pin-380
96PinAfi-159
96PinAfi-191
96PinAfiAP-159
96PinAfiAP-191
96PinFoil-380
96Sel-173
96SelArtP-173
96SelCer-112
96SelCerAP-112
96SelCerCB-112
96SelCerCR-112
96SelCerIP-6
96SelCerMB-112
96SelCerMG-112
96SelCerMR-112
96SP-1
96SPMarM-MM4
96SPMarMDC-3
96SPSpeFX-46
96SPSpeFXDC-46
96SPx-42
96SPxGol-42
96Stu-14
96StuPrePB-14
96StuPrePG-14
96StuPrePS-14
96Sum-153
96Sum-162
96SumAbo&B-153
96SumAbo&B-162
96SumArtP-153
96SumArtP-162
96SumFoi-153
96SumFoi-162
96TeaOut-61
96Top-427
96TopGal-140
96TopGalPPI-140
96TopLas-76
96TopLasBS-5
96Ult-514
96UltGolM-514
96UppDec-245
96UppDecDD-DD29
96UppDecDDG-DD29
96UppDecDDS-DD29
96UppDecPHE-H59
96UppDecPreH-H59
96Zen-118
96ZenArtP-118
97Bow-42
97BowInt-42
97Cir-253
97CirRav-253
97ColCho-167
97ColChoTBS-32
97ColChoTBSWH-32
97Don-232
97DonEli-59
97DonEliGS-59
97DonLim-10
97DonLimLE-10
97DonPre-108
97DonPreCttC-108
97DonPreP-232
97DonPrePGold-232
97Fin-22
97FinRef-22
97FlaSho-A50
97FlaSho-B50
97FlaSho-C50
97FlaShoLC-50
97FlaShoLC-B50
97FlaShoLC-C50
97FlaShoLCM-A50
97FlaShoLCM-B50
97FlaShoLCM-C50
97Fle-403
97FleRooS-10
97FleTif-403
97Lea-41
97LeaFraM-41
97LeaFraMDC-41
97MetUni-198
97MetUniPP-7
97Pac-372
97PacLatotML-34
97PacLigB-372
97PacPri-127
97PacPriGotD-GD175
97PacPriLB-127
97PacPriP-127
97PacSil-372
97Pin-105
97PinArtP-105
97PinCer-32
97PinCerMBlu-32
97PinCerMG-32
97PinCerMR-32
97PinCerR-32
97PinIns-133
97PinInsCE-133
97PinInsDE-133
97PinMusC-105
97PinPasttM-20
97PinTotCPB-32
97PinTotCPG-32
97PinTotCPR-32
97PinX-P-24
97PinX-PMoS-24
97PinX-PMP-20
97ProMag-28
97ProMagML-28
97Sco-100
97Sco-543
97ScoHobR-543
97ScoPreS-100
97ScoResC-543
97ScoShoS-100
97ScoShoS-543
97ScoShoSAP-100
97ScoShoSAP-543
97SelRooR-6
97SelToootT-24
97SelToootTMB-24
97SkyE-X-86
97SkyE-XC-86
97SkyE-XEC-86
97SP-116
97Spolll-65
97SpollIEE-65
97SPSpxF-6
97SPVinAu-22
97SPVinAu-23
97StaClu-48
97StaCluC-CO8
97StaCluM-M12
97StaCluMat-48
97StaCluMOP-48
97StaCluMOP-M12
97StaCluMOP-PL11
97StaCluPL-PL11
97Stu-92
97StuPrePG-92
97StuPrePS-92
97Top-180
97TopAwel-AI13
97TopChr-70
97TopChrR-70
97TopGal-141
97TopGalPPI-141
97Ult-245
97UltDouT-17
97UltFieC-14
97UltGolME-245
97UltPlaME-245
97UltRooR-8
97UppDec-114
97UppDec-149
97UppDec-184
97UppDecGJ-GJ3
95UppDecMLFS-19
95UppDecMLFS-110
97UppDecRSF-RS2
97UppDecTTS-TS3
97UppDecU-49
97UppDecUGN-GN4
Ordway, Jeff
90SpolndSP-2
Ordway, Kirk
93NiaFalRF-3398
Orellano, Rafael
93UtiBluSC-18
93UtiBluSF-3531
94SarRedSC-21
94SarRedSF-1947
95Bes-2
95Bow-89
95SPML-24
95TreThuTI-12
96Bow-167
96ColCho-442
96ColChoGS-442
96ColChoSS-442
96Exc-16
96PawRedSDD-20
96Top-428
96UppDec-268
Orengo, Joe (Joseph C.)
41DouPlaR-29
47SunBre-15
79DiaGre-163
90DodTar-592
Orensky, Herb
80PenPilBT-23
81ReaPhiT-11
82OklCit8T-20
Orhan, Hugh
47SunBre-16
Orie, Kevin
93PeoChiTI-19
94Bow-166
94BowBes-B71
94BowBes-X94
94BowBesR-B71
94BowBesR-X94
94DayCubC-18
94DayCubF-2361
94Top-762
94TopGol-762
94TopSpa-762
95Bow-94
95Top-571
96BowBes-180
96BowBesAR-180
96BowBesR-180
96OrlCubB-18
97Bow-146
97BowBes-195
97BowBesAR-195
97BowBesR-195
97BowCerBIA-CA58
97BowCerGIA-CA58
97BowChr-151
97BowChrI-151
97BowChrIR-151
97BowChrR-151
97BowChrSHR-SHR5
97BowChrSHRR-SHR5
97BowInt-146
97BowScoHR-5
97ColCho-460
97ColChoNF-NF23
97ColChoNF-NF24
97Don-365
97DonLim-5
97DonLimLE-5
97DonPre-159
97DonPreCttC-159
97DonPreP-365
97DonPrePGold-365
97Fin-307
97FinEmb-307
97FinEmbR-307
97FinRef-307
97FlaSho-A15
97FlaSho-B15
97FlaSho-C15
97FlaShoLC-15
97FlaShoLC-B15
97FlaShoLC-C15
97FlaShoLCM-A15
97FlaShoLCM-B15
97FlaShoLCM-C15
97Fle-523
97FleNewH-10
97FleTif-523
97Lea-320
97LeaFraM-320
97LeaFraMDC-320
97NewPin-159
97NewPinAP-159
97NewPinMC-159
97NewPinPP-159
97PinCer-108
97PinCerMBlu-108
97PinCerMG-108
97PinCerMR-108
97PinCerR-108
97PinTotCPB-108
97PinTotCPG-108
97PinTotCPR-108
97PinX-P-125
97PinX-PMoS-125
97Sco-492
97ScoHobR-492
97ScoResC-492
97ScoShoS-492
97ScoShoSAP-492
97Sel-131
97SelArtP-131
97SelRegG-131
97SP-2
97Spolll-18
97SpollIEE-18
97Top-204
97TopStaFAS-FAS10
97Ult-455
97UltGolME-455
97UltGolP-5
97UltPlaME-455
97UppDec-274
Orioles, 19th C. (Baltimore)
86JosHalC-1
90KalTeaN-2
Orioles, Baltimore
56Top-100A
56Top-100B
56Top-100C
57Top-251
58Top-408A
58Top-408B
59Top-48
59TopVen-48
60Top-494
60TopTat-64
61Top-159
61TopMagR-8
62GuyPotCP-1
62Top-476
63Top-377
64Top-473
64TopTatI-1
65Top-572
66Top-348
66TopRubI-101
66TopVen-348
67Top-302
68LauWorS-63
68Top-334
68TopVen-334
69FleCloS-2
69FleCloS-36
69TopStaA-2
70FleWorS-63
70FleWorS-66
70OPC-387
70Top-387
71FleWorS-64
71FleWorS-67
71FleWorS-68
71OPC-1
71Top-1
71TopTat-86
72Top-731
73OPC-278
73OPCBTC-2
73Top-278
73TopBluTC-2
74OPC-16
74OPCTC-2
74Top-16
74TopStaA-2
74TopTeaC-2
78Top-96
81Ori6F-2
83FleSta-226
83FleSti-NNO
87SpoTeaL-21
87Top-506
87TopTif-506
88PanSti-455
88RedFolSB-109
90FleWaxBC-C24
90PubSti-648
90RedFolSB-108
90VenSti-516
93TedWilPC-3
94ImpProP-1
94Sco-317
94ScoGolR-317
95PanSti-147
96FleOri-19
96PanSti-131
Orman, Richard
90MedHatBJB-7
Ormonde, Troy
94HunCubF-3550
95RocCubTI-35
94HunCubC-22
Ormsby, Red
94ConTSN-1207
94ConTSNB-1207
Oropesa, Eddie
95SanAntMTI-54
96SanBerSB-19
Oropeza, Clemente
82IdaFalAT-20
Oropeza, Dave
89RocExpLC-20
Oropeza, Igor
94VenLinU-73
94WatIndC-23
94WatIndF-3935
95KinIndTI-21
95LinVen-248
Oropeza, Willie
95LinVen-221
96VerExpB-20
Orosco, Jesse

79TidTidT-23
80Top-681
80VenLeaS-210
81TidTidT-20
82Don-646
82MetPhoA-16
83Don-434
83Fle-550
83Top-369
84AllGamPI-84
84Don-197
84Fle-593
84FleSti-60
84JacMetF-9
84MetFanC-5
84Nes792-54
84Nes792-396
84OPC-54
84OPC-396
84Top-54
84Top-396
84TopGloS-33
84TopRubD-15
84TopSti-104
84TopTif-54
84TopTif-396
85AllGamPI-173
85Don-22
85Don-75
85DonSupD-22
85Fle-89
85FleStaS-106
85Lea-22
85MetColP-21
85MetTCM-15
85OPC-250
85ThoMcAD-37
85Top-250
85TopGloS-2
85TopMin-250
85TopRubD-13
85TopSti-101
85TopSup-54
85TopTif-250
86BasStaB-81
86Don-646
86Fle-90
86MetColP-8
86MetTCM-11
86MetWorSC-27
86OPC-182
86Top-465
86TopTat-5
86TopTif-465
87ClaGam-75
87Don-439
87Fle-20
87FleGlo-20
87FleMin-78
87FleRecS-27
87FleStiC-87
87Lea-175
87MetColP-19
87OPC-148
87RedFolSB-84
87Spo-76A
87Spo-76B
87Top-704
87TopTif-704
88DodMot-13
88DodPol-47
88Don-192
88DonBasB-234
88Fle-148
88FleGlo-148
88FleUpd-96
88FleUpdG-96
88Sco-495
88ScoGlo-495
88ScoRoo-64T
88ScoRooG-64T
88Spo-89
88StaLinD-12
88StaLinMe-16
88Top-105
88TopTif-105
88TopTra-77T
88TopTraT-77T
89Bow-81
89BowTif-81
89Don-228
89DonTra-26
89Fle-68
89FleGlo-68
89IndTeal-22
89Sco-356
89Top-513
89TopTif-513
89TopTra-91T
89TopTraT-91T
89UppDec-87
90DodTar-593
90Don-154
90Fle-500
90FleCan-500
90IndTeal-32
90Lea-101
90OPC-636
90PubSti-566
90Sco-353
90Top-636
90TopTif-636
90UppDec-588
90VenSti-377
91Bow-72
91Don-171
91Fle-375
91IndFanC-23
91MetWIZ-302
91OPC-346
91Sco-578
91StaClu-322
91Top-346
91TopDesS-346
91TopMic-346
91TopTif-346
91UppDec-240
92BrePol-18
92Don-473
92Fle-121
92Lea-524
92OPC-79
92Sco-547
92Top-79
92TopGol-79
92TopGolW-79
92TopMic-79
92UppDec-580
93BrePol-20
93Fle-632
93PacBeiA-10
93PacSpa-163
93StaClu-37
93StaCluFDI-37
93StaCluMOP-37
93Top-289
93TopGol-289
93TopInaM-289
93TopMic-289
93Ult-223
94BreMilB-258
94BrePol-21
94ColC-616
94ColChoGS-616
94ColChoSS-616
94Fle-188
94Pac-340
94Pin-473
94PinArtP-473
94PinMusC-473
94Sco-299
94ScoGolR-299
94Top-492
94TopGol-492
94TopSpa-492
95Pac-239
96Fle-18
96FleOri-13
96FleTif-18
96Pac-234
97PacPriGotD-GD13

Oroz, Felix Andres
83LasVegSBHN-16
84LasVegSC-233

Orphal, John
47CenFlo-18

Orr, Bobby
74NewYorNTDiS-34

Orr, David L.
87BucN28-62
87OldJudN-394A
87OldJudN-394B
89EdgR.WG-10
89SFHaCN-14
90KalBatN-44

Orr, Geoff
90IdaFalBP-3252
91MacBraC-22
91MacBraP-875

Orr, Jimmy
52LavPro-42

Orr, Johnny
89TenTecGE-20

Orr, William
14FatPlaT-38

Orsag, Jim
86GreHorP-15
87WinHavRSP-28
88CarLeaAS-13
88LynRedSS-16
89NewBriRSP-610
89NewBriRSS-12
89Sta-128
90Bes-269
90CanIndB-9

Orsatti, Ernie (Ernesto R.)
33ButCanV-38
33Gou-201
34DiaMatCSB-144
35DiaMatCS3T1-115
35GouPuzR-1A
35GouPuzR-2A
35GouPuzR-16A
35GouPuzR-17A
74Car193T-20
92ConTSN-650

Orsino, Johnny (John Joseph)
61TacBan-14
61UniOil-T25
62Top-377
63Top-418
64OriJayP-7
64Top-63
64TopCoi-3
64TopVen-63
65Top-303
65TopEmbl-51
66OPC-77
66Top-77
66TopRubl-73
66TopVen-77
67Top-207
81TCM60I-375
91OriCro-344

Orsulak, Joe
82AleDukT-22
85FleUpd-85
85TopTifT-89T
85TopTra-89T
86Don-444
86Fle-615
86FleLeaL-29
86FleMin-118
86FleStiC-83
86Lea-218
86Spo-177
86Top-102
86TopSti-132
86TopTif-102
87Don-291
87Fle-615
87FleGlo-615
87FleRecS-28
87SpoTeaP-18
87Top-414
87TopSti-132
87TopTif-414
88DonBasB-310
88FleUpd-2
88FleUpdG-2
88OriFreB-6
88ScoRoo-41T
88ScoRooG-41T
88TopTra-78T
88TopTraT-78T
89Don-287
89DonBasB-310
89Fle-614
89FleGlo-614
89OriFreB-6
89PanSti-263
89Sco-247
89Top-727
89TopBig-181
89TopTif-727
89UppDec-429
90Bow-252
90BowTif-252
90ClaYel-T50
90Don-287
90DonBesA-129
90Fle-185
90FleCan-185
90Lea-355
90OPC-212
90PanSti-5
90PubSti-582
90Sco-41
90Spo-38
90Top-212
90TopBig-318
90TopSti-234
90TopTif-212
90UppDec-270
90VenSti-378
91Bow-84
91Don-654
91Fle-487
91Lea-152
91OPC-521
91OriCro-345
91PanFreS-246
91PanSti-200
91RedFolS-70
91Sco-508
91Sco100S-8
91StaClu-191
91Top-521
91TopDesS-521
91TopMic-521
91TopTif-521
91Ult-22
91UppDec-506
92Bow-432
92Don-475
92Fle-22
92Hig5-4
92Lea-36
92OPC-325
92PanSti-71
92Pin-362
92Sco-551
92StaClu-135
92Top-325
92TopGol-325
92TopGolW-325
92TopMic-325
92UppDec-207
93Don-751
93Fla-95
93Fle-549
93FleFinE-104
93Lea-337
93MetColP-43
93MetKah-6
93OPC-303
93OPCPre-55
93PacSpa-23
93PanSti-77
93Pin-501
93Sco-590
93Sel-234
93SelRoo-131T
93StaClu-92
93StaCluFDI-92
93StaCluMOP-92
93Top-28
93TopGol-28
93TopInaM-28
93TopMic-28
93Ult-432
93UppDec-260
93UppDec-712
93UppDecGold-260
93UppDecGold-712
94Bow-72
94ColC-419
94ColChoGS-419
94ColChoSS-419
94Don-270
94Fin-45
94FinRef-45
94Fle-575
94Lea-124
94MetColP-20
94MetShuST-2
94Pac-415
94Pin-92
94PinArtP-92
94PinMusC-92
94Sco-398
94ScoGolR-398
94Sel-94
94StaClu-384
94StaCluFDI-384
94StaCluGR-384
94StaCluMOP-384
94Top-643
94TopGol-643
94TopSpa-643
94TriPla-147
94Ult-240
95ColCho-321
95ColChoGS-321
95ColChoSS-321
95Don-266
95DonPreP-266
95DonTopotO-296
95Fla-174
95Fle-378
95Lea-96
95Pac-285
95Sco-129
95ScoGolR-129
95ScoPlaTS-129
95StaClu-351
95StaCluMOP-351
95StaCluSTWS-351
95Top-128
95Ult-414
95UltGolM-414
96Don 322
96DonPreP-322
96Fle-391
96FleTif-391
96MetKah-24
96Pac-143
97Pac-304
97PacLigB-304
97PacSil-304

Orta, Jorge (Jorge Nunez)
72WhiSox-10
72WhiSoxTI1-9
73LinPor-51
73OPC-194
73Top-194
74OPC-376
74Top-376
74TopSta-159
75Hos-122
75HosTwi-122
75Kel-14
75OPC-184
75Top-184
76Hos-57
76HosTwi-57
76Kel-45A
76Kel-45B
76OPC-560
76SSP-144
76Top-560
77BurCheD-74
77Top-109
77WhiSoxJT-11
78Hos-105
78OPC-77
78SSP270-142
78Top-42
78WifBalD-56
79Hos-126
79OPC-333
79Top-631
80Top-442
81AllGamPI-64
81Don-439
81Fle-388
81OPC-222
81Top-222
82DodPol-31
82DodUniOV-15
82Don-211
82Fle-376
82OPC-26
82Top-26
82TopSti-175
82TopTra-84T
83Don-388
83Fle-215
83Top-722
83TopTra-82T
84Don-317
84Fle-166
84FleUpd-86
84Nes792-312
84OPC-312
84Top-312
84TopTif-312
84TopTra-88T
84TopTraT-88T

85Don-130
85Fle-209
85Lea-226
85Top-164
85TopSti-273
85TopTif-164
86Don-339
86Fle-17
86Lea-205
86OPC-44
86RoyKitCD-6
86RoyNatP-3
86Top-541
86TopTif-541
87Don-348
87Fle-376
87FleGlo-376
87OPC-63
87Top-738
87TopTif-738
90DodTar-595
Ortega, Dan
80AppFoxT-14
81AppFoxT-7
Ortega, Eduardo
89BatCliP-1939
90SpaPhiB-17
90SpaPhiP-2499
90SpaPhiS-16
91SalLakTP-3219
91SalLakTSP-18
92SalLakTSP-19
Ortega, Hector
90GatCitPP-3341
91SumFlyC-17
91SumFlyP-2342
92RocExpC-16
92RocExpF-2126
93LinVenB-217
94VenLinU-84
95LinVen-226
96BesAutS-67
96El PasDB-22
Ortega, Kirk
81CliGiaT-16
Ortega, Pablo
97Bow-183
97BowInt-183
97Top-253
Ortega, Phil
59DarFar-15
62Top-69
62TopVen-69
63Top-467
64Top-291
64TopVen-291
65OPC-152
65Top-152
66SenTeal-10
66Top-416
66TopRubI-74
67CokCapS-16
67DexPre-155
67SenTeal-9
67Top-493
68SenTeal-9
68Top-595
69MilBra-207
69SenTeal8-15
69Top-406
81TCM60I-390
90DodTar-596
Ortega, Randy
94WesMicWC-19
94WesMicWF-2301
95ModA'sTI-21
96WesMicWB-19
Ortega, Raul
76VenLeaS-4
80VenLeaS-4
Ortega, Roberto
92BriTigC-19
92BriTigF-1420
Ortegon, Ronnie
89PalSprACLC-35
89PalSprAP-478
90QuaCitAGS-22
Orteig, Ray
48SomandK-25
52MotCoo-50
53MotCoo-31
57HygMea-10
Ortenzio, Frank
75OmaRoyTI-12
76OmaRoyTT-18
79TCMJapPB-69
Orth, Al (Albert Lewis)
03BreE10-110
08RosComP-53
09ColChiE-220A
09ColChiE-220B
09T206-505
11SpoLifCW-278
12ColRedB-220A
12ColRedB-220B
12ColTinT-220A
12ColTinT-220B
94ConTSN-1192
94ConTSNB-1192
Ortiz, Alfredo
76VenLeaS-11
86VenGulP-19
89JohCitCS-25
93LinVenB-62
Ortiz, Andy
83WatIndF-5
84BufBisT-15
Ortiz, Angel
88BlaYNPRWLU-35
88WatIndP-667
89KinIndS-17
92CliGiaC-3
92CliGiaF-3596
Ortiz, Asbel
96ChaRivTI-9625
Ortiz, Bo (Basilio)
91BluOriC-9
91BluOriP-4140
92FreKeyC-16
92FreKeyF-1820
93FreKeyC-19
93FreKeyF-1041
94BowBayF-2426
94OriPro-75
95MidAngOHP-25
95MidAngTI-22
96MidAngB-25
96MidAngOHP-21
96TexLeaAB-34
Ortiz, Danny
93HunCubC-22
93HunCubF-3235
Ortiz, Darrell
80TulDriT-23
Ortiz, David Arias
96MidLeaAB-2
96WisTimRB-6
97FlaShoWotF-11
97Fle-512
97FleTif-512
97Ult-518
97UltGolME-518
97UltPlaME-518
Ortiz, Hector
89SalDodTI-20
89VerBeaDS-21
90YakBeaTI-11
91VerBeaDC-16
91VerBeaDP-777
92BakDodCLC-18
92CalLeaACL-44
93SanAntMF-3008
94AlbDukF-845
96OrlCubB-19
95OrlCubF-14
Ortiz, Javier
84TulDriTI-31
85TulDriTI-31
86TulDriTI-17
87OklCit8P-15
88BlaYNPRWL-187
88SanAntMB-22
89AlbDukC-25
89AlbDukP-84
89TriAAP-AAA46
90CMC-617
90FleUpd-16
90ProAAAF-207
90TucTorC-15
90TucTorP-217
91Bow-562
91Don-643
91LinDriAAA-617
91TopDeb90-119
91TucTorLD-617
91TucTorP-2226
92Don-551
92OPC-362
92Sco-403
92Top-362
92TopGol-362
92TopGolW-362
92TopMic-362
92UppDec-657
94NasSouF-1262
Ortiz, Joe
86AncGlaPTI-26
88AshTouP-1066
88CalLeaACLC-22
88RenSilSCLC-285
89BelBreIS-20
89OscAstS-15
90ColMudS-18
90ModA'sCLC-158
90ModA'sP-2216
Ortiz, Jorge
81WisRapTT-7
Ortiz, Jose
73WicAerKSB-11
Ortiz, Junior (Adalberto)
77ChaPatT-10
77ShrCapT-17
78ChaPirT-17
79AshTouT-14
80BufBisT-9
81PorBeaT-19
82PorBeaT-11
84Don-319
84Fle-594
84Nes792-161
84Top-161
84TopSti-114
84TopTif-161
85Pir-14
85ThoMcAD-38
85Top-439
85TopTif-439
86Don-508
86Top-682
86TopTif-682
87Don-449
87DonOpeD-164
87Fle-616
87FleGlo-616
87Top-583
87TopTif-583
88BlaYNPRWL-111
88Don-168
88Fle-335
88FleGlo-335
88PanSti-341
88Sco-404
88ScoGlo-404
88StaLinPi-15
88Top-274
88TopTif-274
89BlaYNPRWL-11
89Don-387
89DonBasB-269
89Fle-215
89FleGlo-215
89PirVerFJ-0
89Sco-402
89Top-769
89TopBig-66
89TopTif-769
89UppDec-86
90Fle-475
90FleCan-475
90FleUpd-108
90OPC-322
90PubSti-160
90Sco-143
90ScoRoo-66T
90Top-322
90TopTif-322
90TopTra-85T
90TopTraT-85T
90UppDec-389
90VenSti-379
91Bow-328
91Don-659
91Fle-622
91Lea-498
91MetWIZ-303
91OPC-72
91Sco-438
91StaClu-13
91Top-72
91TopDesS-72
91TopMic-72
91TopTif-72
91Ult-194
91UppDec-170
92Don-684
92Fle-215
92IndFanC-21
92OPC-617
92Sco-473
92StaClu-727
92StaCluNC-727
92Top-617
92TopGol-617
92TopGolW-617
92TopMic-617
92TopTra-84T
92TopTraG-84T
92Ult-353
92UppDec-109
93Don-699
93Fle-598
93IndWUA-24
93LinVenB-310
93PacBeiA-6
93PacSpa-416
93Top-199
93TopGol-199
93TopInaM-199
93TopMic-199
93Ult-544
93Ult-650
93UppDec-603
93UppDecGold-603
94Don-425
94Fle-117
94Pac-181
94Sco-262
94ScoGolR-262
94StaClu-15
94StaCluFDI-15
94StaCluGR-15
94StaCluMOP-15
94StaCluP-15
94Top-423
94TopGol-423
94TopSpa-423
95NasSouTI-15
95Pac-431
95Sco-64
95ScoGolR-64
95ScoPlaTS-64
Ortiz, Leo
85DomLeaS-188
Ortiz, Lou
55Top-114
55TopDouH-91
Ortiz, Luis
92Bow-306
92LynRedSC-11
92LynRedSF-2916
92UppDecML-114
93Bow-523
93ClaFS7-57
93ExcFS7-135
93LimRocDWB-35
93LimRocDWB-144
93PawRedSDD-20
93PawRedSF-2416
93PawRedSTI-18
94Bow-119
94Cla-155
94ColC-15
94ColChoGS-15
94ColChoSS-15
94FleMajLP-28
94PawRedSDD-16
94PawRedSF-952
94Pin-243
94PinArtP-243
94PinMusC-243
94PinRooTP-4
94Sco-602
94ScoGolR-602
94Top-369
94TopGol-369
94TopSpa-369
94TriAAF-AAA12
94UppDec-109
94UppDecED-109
95BowBes-B16
95BowBesR-B16
95Fin-324
95FinRef-324
95Pin-19
95PinArtP-19
95PinMusC-19
95Sco-276
95ScoGolR-276
95ScoPlaTS-276
95Sel-217
95SelArtP-217
96ColCho-737
96ColChoGS-737
96ColChoSS-737
96Don-191
96DonPreP-191
96Fle-256
96FleTif-256
96OklCit8B-14
97PacPriGotD-GD98
Ortiz, Miguel
80UtiBluJT-21
Ortiz, Nick
93ForLauRSC-19
93ForLauRSFP-1606
93UtiBluSC-19
93UtiBluSF-3543
96MicBatCB-18
Ortiz, Ramon
89BurIndS-19
90BurIndP-3022
92SavCarC-24
92SavCarF-680
93SavCarC-27
94SavCarC-30
94SavCarF-524
Ortiz, Ray
90CMC-864
90ProAaA-153
90VisOakCLC-70
90VisOakP-2169
91LinDriAA-491
91OrlSunRLD-491
91OrlSunRP-1863
92OrlSunRF-2861
92OrlSunRS-515
93ClaFS7-233
93PorBeaF-2395
94PhoFirF-1527
95PhoFirTI-29
Ortiz, Russ
95BelGiaTI-20
96BesAutS-68
96BesAutSA-50
96Bow-360
96SanJosGB-13
96WesOahCHWB-36
97Bow-373
97BowCerBIA-CA59
97BowCerGIA-CA59
97BowInt-373
Ortiz, Steve
94BurIndC-18
94BurIndF-3791
Ortman, Benjamin
93BenRocC-20
93BenRocF-3282
94CenValRC-17
94CenValRF-3217
Ortman, Doug
87MadMusP-13
87MadMusP-9
Orton, John
85AncGlaPTI-23
87SalAngP-6
88PalSprACLC-107
88PalSprAP-1433
89MidAngGS-25
90Bow-298
90BowTif-298
90ClaYel-T61
90DonRoo-54
90Fle-647
90FleCan-647
90FleUpd-79
90Lea-511
90Sco-582
90Sco100RS-64
90ScoYouS2-30
90Spo-132
90TopDeb89-94
90UppDec-672
91AngSmo-20
91Don-714
91Fle-320
91Lea-191
91OPC-176
91Sco-467
91StaClu-591
91Top-176

91TopDesS-176
91TopMic-176
91TopTif-176
92EdmTraS-155
92Fle-65
92OPC-398
92Sco-712
92StaClu-263
93AngMot-10
93AngPol-16
93Don-431
93Fle-195
93Lea-385
93PacSpa-371
93Pin-197
93Sco-453
93StaClu-459
93StaCluAn-17
93StaCluFDI-459
93StaCluMOP-459
93TriPla-131
93Ult-167
93UppDec-317
93UppDecGold-317
94RicBraF-2949
95NorTidTI-20
Oruna, Roland
83ChaRoyT-11
Osaka, Rocky
87SanJosBP-7
Osborn, Bob
93ConTSN-947
Osborn, Dan
76OPC-282
76SSP-135
76Top-282
Osborn, Don
47SigOil-31
74OPC-489
74Top-489
Osborn, Pat
75SacSolC-21
94BreMilB-344
Osborn, Wilfred
08RosComP-144
09ColChiE-221
12ColRedB-221
12ColTinT-221
Osborne, Bobo (Lawrence S.)
59Top-524
60Top-201
61Top-208
62TigPosCF-14
62Top-583
63Top-514
81TCM60I-463
Osborne, Donovan
90ClaDraP-13
90HamRedB-1
91ArkTraLD-40
91ArkTraP-1283
91Bow-406
91Cla/Bes-27
91LinDriAA-40
91Sco-677
92Bow-96
92Cla2-T94
92DonRoo-88
92FleUpd-120
92JimDeaRS-7
92LeaGolR-BC19
92Pin-541
92PinRoo-20
92ProFS7-317
92ScoRoo-90T
92Stu-95
92TopTra-85T
92TopTraG-85T
92Ult-570
92UltAllR-10
92UppDec-702
92UppDec-770
92UppDec-777
92UppDecSR-SR19
93Bow-376
93CarPol-13
93ClaGam-72
93Don-178
93Fla-123
93Fle-129
93FleRooS-RSA10
93Lea-62
93OPC-248
93PacSpa-634
93PanSti-199
93Pin-370
93Sco-349
93Sel-276
93SelChaR-7
93StaClu-586
93StaCluCa-16
93StaCluFDI-586
93StaCluMOP-586
93Top-662
93TopGol-662
93TopInaM-662
93TopMic-662
93Toy-41
93Ult-109
93UppDec-347
93UppDecGold-347
93USPlaCR-11H
94ColC-222
94ColChoGS-222
94ColChoSS-222
94Don-149
94Fle-640
94Pac-597
94Pin-209
94PinArtP-209
94PinMusC-209
94Sco-63
94ScoGolR-63
94StaCluT-304
94StaCluTFDI-304
94Top-501
94TopGol-501
94TopSpa-501
94Ult-269
95FleUpd-162
95TopTra-42T
96CarPol-20
96Fla-365
96Fle-552
96FleTif-552
96Pac-218
96Sco-115
97Cir-288
97CirRav-288
97ColCho-441
97Don-147
97DonPreP-147
97DonPrePGold-147
97Fle-450
97FleTif-450
97PacPriGotD-GD202
97Sco-144
97ScoPreS-144
97ScoShoS-144
97ScoShoSAP-144
97StaClu-91
97StaCluMOP-91
97Top-451
97UppDec-487
Osborne, Jeff
89AugPirP-494
89SouAtlLAGS-46
90CMC-786
90HarSenP-1200
90HarSenS-13
Osborne, Tiny
90DodTar-1046
Osentowski, Jared
92KinMetC-3
92StaCluD-136
93CapCitBC-15
93CapCitBF-469
94CapCitBC-16
94CapCitBF-1757
94PitMetC-16
94PitMetF-3530
Osentowski, Ozzie
92KinMetF-1541
Oshima, Yasuroni
79TCMJapPB-75
Osik, Keith
90LSUTigA-4
90LSUTigP-5
91SalBucC-2
91SalBucP-956
92CarMudF-1184
92CarMudS-138
93CarMudF-2058
93CarMudTI-2
94BufBisF-1840
Osilka, Garrett
96HelBreTI-17
Osinski, Dan
63AngJayP-11
63Top-114
64Top-537
65OPC-223
65Top-223
66OPC-168
66Top-168
66TopVen-168
67Top-594
68Top-331
68TopVen-331
69Top-622
81RedSoxBG2S-101
Osinski, Glenn
90MadMusB-8
90SouOreAB-28
91ModA'sC-10
91ModA'sP-3098
Osmon, Scott
89IdaFalBP-2032
Osofsky, Aaron
52LavPro-86
Osofsky, Alvin
75DubPacT-32
Osorio, Sam
93PriRedC-23
93PriRedF-4196
Osowski, Tom
83ButCopKT-33
84ButCopKT-6
85EveGiaC-12
86PalSprAP-1
Osteen, Claude
55DonWin-35
59RedEnq-17
59Top-224
60Top-206
61RedJayP-10
62Top-501
63Jel-100
63Pos-100
63Top-374
64Top-28
64TopCoi-13
64TopSta-74
64TopStaU-52
64TopTatI-58
64TopVen-28
65DodJayP-9
65DodTeal-12
65MacSta-8
65Top-570
66Top-270
66TopVen-270
67CokCapA-16
67CokCapD-15
67CokCapDA-15
67CokCapNLA-22
67DexPre-156
67Top-330
67TopVen-302
68AtlOilPBCC-32
68OPC-9
68Top-9
68Top-440
68TopActS-1C
68TopActS-16C
68TopGamI-12
69MilBra-208
69MLBOffS-150
69Top-528
69TopSta-47
69TopTeaP-22
70DayDaiNM-20
70MLBOffS-54
70OPC-260
70Top-260
70TopScr-15
70TopSup-1
71BazNumT-39
71BazUnn-12
71DodTic-12
71Kel-70A
71Kel-70B
71Kel-70C
71MilDud-56
71MLBOffS-110
71OPC-10
71Top-10
71TopCoi-45
71TopSup-27
72Kel-34A
72Kel-34B
72MilBra-260
72OPC-297
72OPC-298
72Top-297
72Top-298
73Kel2D-49
73OPC-490
73Top-490
74AstFouTIP-2
74OPC-42
74Top-42
74TopDecE-38
74TopSta-48
74TopTra-42T
75OPC-453
75Top-453
76OPC-488
76SSP-137
76Top-488
77Car5-17
77CarTeal-17
78CarTeal-14
78TCM60I-273
79Car5-20
84PhiTas-12
85PhiTas-5
85PhiTas-8
86PhiTas-3
87AstShoSTw-12
87DodSmoA-25
87PhiTas-xx0
88PhiTas-29
89DodSmoG-73
89PacLegI-132
89SanAntMB-26
89SweBasG-17
90AlbDukC-28
90AlbDukP-363
90AlbDukT-25
90CMC-658
90DodTar-597
90ProAAAF-83
91AlbDukP-1159
91LinDriAAA-25
92AlbDukF-740
92DodStaTA-9
93RanKee-440
95RocRedWTI-42
96SanAntMB-29
Osteen, Dave
87St.PetCP-1
88ArkTraGS-23
89ArkTraGS-15
89TexLeaAGS-23
90ArkTraGS-22
90CMC-107
90LouRedBC-7
90LouRedBLBC-32
90LouRedBP-401
90ProAAAF-515
90TexLeaAGS-34
91LinDriAAA-242
91LouRedLD-242
91LouRedP-2913
96YakBeaTI-NNO
Osteen, Gavin
89MedAthB-29
90CMC-692
90MadMusB-21
90MadMusP-2268
91HunStaC-16
91HunStaLD-290
91HunStaP-1792
91HunStaTI-15
91LinDriAA-290
92HunStaF-3947
92SkyAAAF-242
92TacTigS-542
93HunStaF-2081
94TacTigF-3171
Osteen, M. Darrell
66Top-424
67Top-222
68Top-199
68TopVen-199
Oster, Dave
88GenCubP-1659
Oster, Mike
92Min-21
Oster, Paul
88OklSoo-18
89OklSoo-21
89OneYanP-2127
90PriWilCTI-18
91PriWilCC-21
91PriWilCP-1439
93AlbYanF-2175
Osterkamp, Ken
93ForLauRSC-20
93ForLauRSFP-1596
Ostermeyer, Bill
90SpoIndSP-6
91ChaRaiP-105
91Cla/Bes-196
91SouAtlLAGP-SAL5
92ChaRaiF-130
92HigDesMC-19
Ostermueller, Fritz (Fred)
34DiaMatCSB-145
34DiaStaR-73
34Gou-93
35DiaMatCS3T1-116
35GouPuzR-8G
35GouPuzR-9G
36GouWidPPR-A80
39PlaBal-27
40PlaBal-33
41BroW75-24
41Gou-12
47TipTop-144
49Bow-227
76TayBow4-57
79RedSoxEF-4
90DodTar-598
91ConTSN-99
Osting, Jimmy
95DanBraTI-20
96EugEmeB-18
97Bow-318
97BowInt-318
Ostopowicz, Rich
89KinMetS-18
Ostrosser, Brian (Brian L.)
75OklCit8TI-14
91MetWIZ-304
Ostrowski, Joe P.
52BerRos-48
52Top-206
53MotCoo-2
83TopRep5-206
Ostrowski, John (John T.)
47SigOil-32
49W725AngTI-23
50RoyDes-20
Osugi, Katsuo
79TCMJapPB-19
Osuna, Al
87AubAstP-22
88OscAstS-20
89OscAstS-16
90Bes-312
90ColMudB-19
90ColMudP-1344
90ColMudS-19
90ProAaA-43
91AstMot-20
91DonRoo-52
91Lea-492
91OPC-149
91ScoRoo-89T
91Top-149
91TopDeb90-120
91TopDesS-149
91TopMic-149
91TopTif-149
91UppDec-752
92AstMot-20
92Bow-639
92Don-318
92Fle-442
92Lea-209
92OPC-614
92OPCPre-121
92Pin-347
92Sco-452
92Sco100RS-83
92StaClu-68
92Top-614
92TopGol-614
92TopGolW-614
92TopMic-614
92Ult-207
92UppDec-259
93Don-216
93Fle-440
93LinVenB-76
93Sco-475
93StaClu-236

93StaCluAs-11
93StaCluFDI-236
93StaCluMOP-236
93Top-63
93TopGol-63
93TopInaM-63
93TopMic-63
93Ult-45
94AlbDukF-840
94DodMot-23
94Don-541
94Fle-497
94Pac-271
94StaClu-293
94StaCluFDI-293
94StaCluGR-293
94StaCluMOP-293
94Top-277
94TopGol-277
94TopSpa-277
94VenLinU-23
95DodPol-18
95NorTidTI-21
Osuna, Antonio
91KisDodP-4181
94Bow-678
95Bow-18
95DodMot-22
95DodPol-19
95Exc-215
95Fla-370
95FleUpd-177
95SelCer-133
95SelCerMG-133
95SP-6
95SPSil-6
95StaClu-524
95StaCluMOP-524
95StaCluSTWS-524
95Sum-161
95SumNthD-161
95TopTra-111T
95UppDec-232
95UppDecED-232
95UppDecEDG-232
95Zen-142
96ColCho-583
96ColChoGS-583
96ColChoSS-583
96DodMot-19
96DodPol-26
96Don-293
96DonPreP-293
96Fle-443
96FleDod-14
96FleTif-443
96Pac-116
96Sco-221
96StaClu-419
96StaCluMOP-419
97Fle-369
97FleTif-369
97Lea-126
97LeaFraM-126
97LeaFraMDC-126
97Pac-337
97PacLigB-337
97PacSil-337
97StaClu-329
97StaCluMOP-329
97Top-240
Osuna, Pedro
92ProFS7-252
94SanAntMF-2465
Oswald, Steve
86BirBarTI-1
Otanez, Willis
91GreFalDSP-14
92ClaFS7-356
92UppDecML-102
92VerBeaDC-8
92VerBeaDF-2887
93BakDodCLC-21
93LimRocDWB-76
94FloStaLAF-FSL49
94VerBeaDC-13
94VerBeaDF-81
95Bow-11
95Exc-216
95UppDecML-212
95VerBeaDTI-18
96BowBayB-23
95UppDecMLFS-212
Otero, Reggie (Regino J.)
47SigOil-33
60Top-459
63RedFreBC-15
Otero, Ricky
91KinMetC-8
91KinMetP-3826
92ColMetC-12
92ColMetF-309
92ColMetPI-24
92ColMetPIISPI-6
92ProFS7-288
92UppDecML-236
93BinMetF-2347
93ClaGolF-158
93ExcFS7-77
93SouAtlLAIPI-9
93SouAtlLAPI-29
94BinMetF-718
95Bow-40
95Exc-234
95FleUpd-117
95NorTidTI-22
95Sum-155
95SumNthD-155
96Cir-168
96CirBos-43
96CirRav-168
96MetKah-25
96Sco-235
96ScrRedBB-22
97Cir-219
97CirRav-219
97Don-233
97DonPreP-233
97DonPrePGold-233
97Fle-417
97FleTif-417
97Lea-36
97LeaFraM-36
97LeaFraMDC-36
97MetUni-204
97Pac-383
97PacLigB-383
97PacPri-130
97PacPriLB-130
97PacPriP-130
97PacSil-383
97StaClu-328
97StaCluMOP-328
97Top-106
97Ult-254
97UltGolME-254
97UltPlaME-254
97UppDec-134
Otey, William
09T206-506
Otis, Amos (Amos Joseph)
69OPC-31
69Top-31
70DayDaiNM-114
70OPC-354
70RoyTeal-26
70Top-354
71BazNumT-42
71BazUnn-36
71Kel-38
71MLBOffS-424
71OPC-610
71Top-610
71TopCoi-96
71TopSup-45
71TopTat-32
72Kel-2
72OPC-10
72Top-10
72TopPos-6
73Kel2D-1
73LinPor-88
73OPC-510
73Top-510
73TopCanL-37
74GreHeroBP-5
74Kel-17
74OPC-65
74OPC-337
74Top-65
74Top-337
74TopDecE-1
74TopSta-185
75Hos-50
75OPC-520
75SSP42-22
75Top-520
76Hos-51
76HosTwi-51
76OPC-198
76OPC-510
76SSP-177
76Top-198
76Top-510
77BurCheD-65
77Hos-92
77OPC-141
77PepGloD-33
77RCColC-48
77Top-290
78OPC-16
78RCColC-55
78Roy-16
78SSP270-227
78Top-490
79Hos-132
79OPC-185
79RoyTeal-7
79Top-360
80OPC-72
80Top-130
80TopSup-50
81AllGamPI-65
81CokTeaS-78
81Don-104
81Fle-32A
81Fle-32B
81Fle-483A
81Fle-483B
81FleStiC-28
81OPC-288
81RoyPol-7
81Top-585
82Don-70
82Fle-419
82FleSta-211
82OPC-162
82OPC-350
82Roy-14
82Top-725
82Top-726
82TopSti-194
83AllGamPI-66
83Don-364
83Fle-120
83FleSta-143
83FleSti-99
83OPC-75
83Roy-19
83RoyPol-5
83Top-75
83TopFol-5
83TopSti-72
84AllGamPI-63
84Fle-351
84FleUpd-87
84Nes792-655
84OPC-53
84Top-655
84TopTif-655
84TopTra-89T
84TopTraT-89T
86RoyGreT-6
88PadSmo-21
89PacSenL-83
89T/MSenL-84
89TidTidC-4
89TopSenL-81
90EliSenL-74
90PadMag-22
91MetWIZ-305
91PacSenL-26
93RoySta2-8
94ColSprSSF-750
94TedWil-38
Otis, David
86MadMusP-17
Ott, Ed (Nathan Edward)
76OPC-594
76Top-594
77PirPosP-18
77Top-197
78OPC-161
78Top-28
79Hos-31
79OPC-289
79Top-561
80OPC-200
80Top-383
81CokTeaS-116
81Don-133
81Fle-365
81LonBeaPT-18
81OPC-246
81Top-246
81TopSti-214
81TopTra-810
82Don-192
82Fle-470
82OPC-225
82Top-469
83Fle-98
83Top-131
84EdmTraC-120
85PriWilPT-23
86WatPirP-16
89AstLenH-14
89AstMot-27
89AstSmo-30
91AstMot-28
92AstMot-27
93AstMot-28
Ott, Mel (Melvin Thomas)
29ExhFou-9
29PorandAR-67
30W554-12
31Exh-10
31W517-30
33GeoCMil-24
33Gou-127
33Gou-207
33RitCE-4C
34DiaMatCSB-146
34BatR31-27
34ButPreR-49
34DiaStaR-50
34ExhFou-5
35DiaMatCS2-17
35DiaMatCS3T1-117
35ExhFou-5
35GouPreR-14
35GouPuzR-4A
35GouPuzR-7A
35GouPuzR-12A
35WheBB1-22
36DiaMatCS4-12
36ExhFou-5
36PC7AlbHoF-60
36SandSW-44
36WheBB4-8
36WheBB5-7A
36WheBB5-7B
37ExhFou-5
37GouFliMR-3A
37GouFliMR-3B
37GouThuMR-3
37WheBB14-12
38ExhFou-5
38OurNatGPP-22
39ExhSal-49A
39ExhSal-49B
39GouPreR303A-35
39GouPreR303B-20
39PlaBal-51
39WheBB12-8
39WorWidGTP-35
40PlaBal-88
40WheM4-2B
41DouPlaR-31
41DouPlaR-89
41Gou-33
41PlaBal-8
43MPR302-1-19
48BluTin-18A
48BluTin-18B
50CalHOFW-58
51R42SmaS-76
52MotCoo-32
60ExhWriH-18
60Fle-36
60NuHi-58
61Fle-68
61GolPre-1
61NuSco-458
61SevElev-28
63BasMagM-63
63BazA-36
67TopVen-149
68LauWorS-30
69Baz-8
69Baz-11
70FleWorS-30
72FleFamF-25
73FleWilD-17
75SpoHobBG-6
76GalBasGHoF-21
76JerJonPC-2
76RowExh-12
76ShaPiz-60
76TayBow4-43
77GalGloG-50
77GalGloG-256
77TCMTheWY-17
80GiaGreT-9
80Lau300-12
80LauFamF-14
80PacLeg-35
80PerHaloFP-60
80SSPHOF-60
81ConTSN-85
82DiaCla-50
83DonHOFH-40
83TCMPla1942-32
85CirK-12
85FegMurCG-14
86BigLeaC-11
86ConSer1-36
86SpoDecG-8
86SpoDecGS-2
87HygAllG-35
88ConSer4-21
88GreBasS-58
89HOFStiB-49
89PacLegI-189
90SweBasG-55
91ConTSN-7
91ConTSN-225
91SweBasG-144
92ConTSNCI-11
92St.VinHHS-7
92TVSpoMF5HRC-10
93ActPacA-102
93ActPacA2-36G
93ConTSN-834
93UppDecAH-103
93UppDecAH-136
94ConTSN-1097
94ConTSN-1254
94ConTSNB-1097
94ConTSNB-1254
94TedWil-55
94UppDecAH-45
94UppDecAH-171
94UppDecAH1-45
94UppDecAH1-171
95ConTSNGJ-5
Ott, William
65Top-354
Ottavinia, Paul
94SigRooDP-69
94SigRooDPS-69
94StaCluDP-41
94StaCluDPFDI-41
96WesPalBEB-30
Otten, Brian
86GenCubP-21
87PeoChiP-15
88WinSpiS-13
Otten, Jim
75OPC-624
75Top-624
77Top-493
81Car5x7-20
Ottmers, Marc
93GleFalRC-22
93GleFalRF-4001
94MadHatC-19
94MadHatF-129
Otto, Dave
86MadMusP-16
87MadMusP-14
88Fle-652
88FleGlo-652
89ScoHot1R-60
89TacTigC-10
89TacTigP-1547
89Top-131
89TopTif-131
89UppDec-4
90Bow-448
90BowTif-448
90CMC-584
90ProAAAF-136
90ScoRoo-101T
90TacTigC-7
90TacTigP-89
91ColSprSSLD-93
91ColSprSSP-2180
91Fle-20
91IndFanC-24

91LinDriAAA-93
92Bow-619
92Don-730
92IndFanC-22
92Lea-218
92OPC-499
92Pin-316
92StaClu-461
92Top-499
92TopGol-499
92TopGolW-499
92TopMic-499
92Ult-354
92UppDec-698
93PirNatI-23

Otto, Mascot
95SpoIndTI-16

Otto, Steve
88EugEmeB-4
89AppFoxP-876
90BasCitRS-17

Ouellette, Phil
82CliGiaF-5
84PhoGiaC-1
85PhoGiaC-182
86PhoFirP-19
88CalCanC-12
88CalCanP-801
88TriAAAP-7
90CMC-390
90ProAAAF-383
90TolMudHC-13
90TolMudHP-153

Outen, Chink
90DodTar-1049

Outlaw, Jimmy (James Paulus)
39PlaBal-155
46SpoExcW-2-6
47TipTop-39
79DiaGre-253
83TCMPla1944-4

Overall, Orval
06FanCraNL-35
07CubA.CDPP-8
07CubGFGCP-8
08AmeCarE-19
08AmeCarE-57
08RosComP-105
09AmeCarE-86
09ColChiE-222
09SpoNewSM-30
09T206-276
09T206-277
09T206-278
10ChiE-7
10SepAnoP-20
10SweCapPP-86
11DiaGumP-23
11S74Sil-66
11SpoLifCW-279
11SpoLifM-176
11T205-133
11TurRedT-32
12ColRedB-222
12ColTinT-222
12HasTriFT-13C
12HasTriFT-36C
87Cub190T-5

Overeem, Steve
88JamExpP-1914

Overholser, Drew
91SpoIndC-14
91SpoIndP-3947

Overman, Dan
93PocPosSP-26
94OgdRapSP-26
95ForWayWTI-29

Overmire, Stubby (Frank)
47TipTop-40
49Lea-17
51Bow-280
52Top-155
83TopRep5-155

Overton, Jeff
82AppFoxF-2

Overton, Mike
79NewCoPT-5

Overy, Mike
76SalLakCGC-3
77SalLakCGC-24
77Top-489
79SalLakCGT-9
80SalLakCGT-26
78STLakCGC-24

Oviedo, Gelso
52LavPro-104

Oviedo, Igor
93LinVenB-241

Owchinko, Bob
77PadSchC-43
78PadFamF-20
78Top-164
79OPC-257
79Top-488
80OPC-44
80Top-79
81Don-563A
81Don-563B
81Top-536
81TopTra-811
82Don-287
82Fle-104
82Top-243
83Don-265
83Fle-531
83Top-338
84FleUpd-88
84RedEnq-21
85Don-506
85Fle-543
85TacTigC-144
85Top-752
85TopTif-752
86IndIndTI-9
91PacSenL-83

Owen, Andy
95YakBeaTI-24
96VerBeaDB-22

Owen, Billy
04FanCraAL-38

Owen, Dave
83IowCubT-18
84CubChiT-21
84CubSev-19
84IowCubT-18
85Don-483
85IowCubT-6
85Top-642
85TopTif-642
86OklCit8P-16
87OklCit8P-3
88OmaRoyC-16
88OmaRoyP-1510
89IowCubC-19
89IowCubP-1694
89LynRedSS-16
90NewBriRSB-18
90NewBriRSP-1318
90NewBriRSS-13
90ProAaA-7
91Bow-110
92WinHavRSF-1774

Owen, Frank Malcomb
09T206-279

Owen, Larry (Lawrence T.)
79RicBraT-5
82RicBraT-11
82Top-502
83BraPol-24
84RicBraT-8
85IntLeaAT-9
85RicBraT-12
86RicBraT-8
88OmaRoyC-18
88OmaRoyP-1516
88Sco-230
88ScoGlo-230
88StaLinRo-10
89Top-87
89TopTif-87
89UppDec-528
90RicBra2ATI-18

Owen, Marv (Marvin James)
34BatR31-168
34DiaStaR-67
35TigFreP-14
36GouWidPPR-A81
36GouWidPPR-B18
36WorWidGV-69
38GouHeaU-263
38GouHeaU-287
39GouPreR303A-36
39WorWidGTP-36
76TigOldTS-16
81TigSecNP-24
93ConTSN-941

Owen, Mickey (Arnold Malcolm)
39PlaBal-135
40PlaBal-111
41DouPlaR-15
42DodTeaI-15
43DodTeaI-20
50Bow-78
51Bow-174
60NuHi-15
61NuSco-475
68LauWorS-38
77TCMTheWY-3
83TCMPla1944-43
88RinPosD1-8C
89DodSmoG-44
90DodTar-599
91UppDecS-4

Owen, Spike D.
83SalLakCGT-23
84Don-313
84Fle-616
84MarMot-6
84Nes792-413
84Top-413
84TopSti-349
84TopTif-413
85AllGamPI-24
85Don-435
85DonActA-4
85Fle-497
85Lea-167
85MarMot-7
85Top-84
85TopSti-339
85TopTif-84
86Don-362
86Fle-471
86MarMot-20
86OPC-248
86Top-248
86TopSti-224
86TopTif-248
87Don-633
87DonOpeD-185
87Fle-40
87FleGlo-40
87Lea-87
87RedSoxSAP-9
87Top-591
87TopTif-591
88Don-544
88DonTeaBRS-544
88Fle-359
88FleGlo-359
88OPC-188
88PanSti-30
88Sco-372
88ScoGlo-372
88StaLinRS-14
88Top-21
88Top-733
88TopTif-21
88TopTif-733
89Bow-363
89BowTif-363
89Don-593
89DonBasB-236
89DonTra-14
89ExpPos-23
89Fle-93
89FleGlo-93
89FleUpd-98
89Sco-218
89ScoRoo-13T
89Top-123
89TopBig-221
89TopTif-123
89TopTra-92T
89TopTraT-92T
89UppDec-161
89UppDec-717
90Bow-116
90BowTif-116
90Don-102
90DonBesN-6
90ExpPos-27
90Fle-357
90FleCan-357
90Lea-186
90OPC-674
90PanSti-285
90PubSti-184
90Sco-247
90Top-674
90TopBig-25
90TopSti-73
90TopTif-674
90UppDec-291
90VenSti-380
91Bow-454
91Don-251
91Fle-243
91Lea-36
91OPC-372
91PanFreS-142
91PanSti-62
91Sco-452
91StaClu-236
91Top-372
91TopDesS-372
91TopMic-372
91TopTif-372
91Ult-208
91UppDec-189
92Bow-121
92Don-518
92ExpDonD-14
92ExpPos-24
92Fle-488
92Lea-455
92OPC-443
92PanSti-205
92Pin-234
92Sco-323
92StaClu-221
92Stu-58
92TexLon-30
92Top-443
92TopGol-443
92TopGolW-443
92TopMic-443
92Ult-224
92UppDec-206
93Bow-483
93Don-732
93Fle-463
93FleFinE-251
93Lea-405
93OPC-327
93OPCPre-8
93PacSpa-561
93Pin-499
93Sco-554
93Sel-239
93SelRoo-109T
93StaClu-677
93StaCluFDI-677
93StaCluMOP-677
93StaCluY-15
93Stu-79
93Top-42
93TopGol-42
93TopInaM-42
93TopMic-42
93TopPreS-8
93Ult-600
93UppDec-548
93UppDecGold-548
94AngLAT-24
94AngMot-11
94ColC-591
94ColChoGS-591
94ColChoSS-591
94Don-80
94Fin-264
94FinRef-264
94Fle-244
94FleUpd-20
94Pac-434
94Pin-492
94PinArtP-492
94PinMusC-492
94Sco-507
94ScoGolR-507
94ScoRoo-RT66
94ScoRooGR-RT66
94Sel-325
94Top-297
94TopGol-297
94TopSpa-297
95AngCHP-6
95AngMot-12
95ColChoGS-93
95ColChoSS-93
95Don-32
95DonPreP-32
95DonTopotO-39
95Fla-20
95Fle-231
95Sco-88
95ScoGolR-88
95ScoPlaTS-88
95Top-520
95TopCyb-307
95Ult-271
95UltGolM-271
96ColCho-74
96ColChoGS-74
96ColChoSS-74
96Don-321
96DonPreP-321

Owen, Tim
85BurRanT-14
86DayBealP-20

Owen, Tommy
90IdaFalBP-3248
91JamExpC-13
91JamExpP-3549
96BreCouMB-23

Owens, Bill (William John)
95NegLeaL2-7

Owens, Billy
90AriWilP-15
92AriWilP-12
92ClaDraP-53
92FroRowDP-2
92KanCouCTI-24
93AlbPolC-1
93AlbPolF-2034
93ClaFS7-85
93SouAtlLAGF-4
93StaCluM-146
94ClaGolF-7
94FreKeyF-2624
94OriPro-76
95BowBayTI-26
95RocRedWTI-29
96Exc-6
96RocRedWB-21
96Top-425

Owens, Brad
92HamRedC-28
92HamRedF-1602

Owens, Brick
94ConTSN-1211
94ConTSNB-1211

Owens, Eric
92BenMusSP-16
92BilMusF-3366
92ClaDraP-121
92FroRowDP-88
93ClaFS7-288
93StaCluM-109
93WinSpiC-16
93WinSpiF-1577
94ChaLooF-1365
94ExcFS7-180
94UppDecML-162
95Bow-219
95IndIndF-102
95SigRoo-40
95SigRooSig-40
96BesAutS-69
96Bow-373
96ColCho-519
96ColChoGS-519
96ColChoSS-519
96Fin-B227
96FinRef-B227
96Fle-348
96FleTif-348
96IndIndB-18
96LeaPre-134
96LeaPreP-134
96Pin-384
96PinFoil-384
96SelCer-119
96SelCerAP-119
96SelCerCB-119
96SelCerCR-119
96SelCerMB-119
96SelCerMG-119
96SelCerMR-119
96Sum-181
96SumAbo&B-181
96SumArtP-181
96SumFoi-181
96Top-103
96Top-104
96TopGal-129
96TopGalPPI-129

96Ult-464
96UltGolM-464
96Zen-126
96ZenArtP-126
97Don-348
97DonLim-113
97DonLimLE-113
97DonPreP-348
97DonPrePGold-348
97Pac-274
97PacLigB-274
97PacSil-274
97StaClu-103
97StaCluMOP-103
97Top-266

Owens, Farrell
79NasSouTI-18

Owens, Frank (Frank Walter)
07WhiSoxGWH-8
09ColChiE-223
11SpoLifCW-280
12ColRedB-223
12ColTinT-223
14CraJacE-74
15CraJacE-74

Owens, J. (Jayhawk)
90Bes-224
92OrlSunRF-2849
92OrlSunRS-516
92SkyAA F-223
93FleFinE-37
93Lea-505
93Top-606
93TopGol-606
93TopInaM-606
93TopMic-606
94ColC-223
94ColChoGS-223
94ColChoSS-223
94ColSprSSF-737
94Don-278
94Fle-448
94Pac-203
94Pin-418
94PinArtP-418
94PinMusC-418
94StaClu-512
94StaCluFDI-512
94StaCluGR-512
94StaCluMOP-512
94StaCluT-100
94StaCluTFDI-100
95Sco-588
95ScoGolR-588
95ScoPlaTS-588
96FleRoc-10
96FleUpd-U129
96FleUpdTC-U129
96LeaSigA-174
96LeaSigAG-174
96LeaSigAS-174
96RocPol-14
96SigRooOJ-25
96SigRooOJS-25
96Ult-471
96UltGolM-471
97Pac-284
97PacLigB-284
97PacSil-284
97Sco-224
97ScoPreS-224
97ScoRoc-12
97ScoRocPl-12
97ScoRocPr-12
97ScoShoS-224
97ScoShoSAP-224

Owens, Jesse
51BerRos-C18
62PC7HFGSS-5

Owens, Jim
55Top-202
55TopDouH-121
56Top-114
59Top-503
60Lea-39
60PhiJayP-9
60Top-185
60TopVen-185
61Pos-116A
61Pos-116B
61Top-341
62Top-212
63RedEnq-23
63RedFreBC-17
63Top-483
64Top-241
64TopVen-241
65Top-451
66Top-297
66TopVen-297
67Ast-22
67AstTeal2-19
67Top-582
67TopVen-304
73OPC-624
73Top-624
87AstSer1-27
87AstShowSTh-17
87AstShowSTh-26

Owens, Larry
88CapCodPPaLP-52
90PulBraB-7
90PulBraP-3102

Owens, Mark (Markus)
87EveGiaC-30
87HawRai-19
88CliGiaP-704
88MidLeaAGS-1
89ShrCapP-1849
90ShrCapP-1446
90ShrCapS-17

Owens, Marty
88GenCubP-1658

Owens, Michael
88BatCliP-1675
89BatCliP-1930
90BatCliP-3074
91SpaPhiC-10
91SpaPhiP-895

Owens, Paul
84Fle-643
84Fle-648
84FleSti-123
84Nes792-229
84PhiTas-8
84Top-229
84TopTif-229
85Top-92
85TopGloA-1
85TopTif-92

Owens, Steve
87GenCubP-26
88ChaWheB-8

Owens, Tom
79WauTimT-25
81WatIndT-12
82ChaLooT-9
83BufBisT-6

Owens, Walter
94BurIndC-19
94BurIndF-3811
95WatIndTI-23

Owens-Bragg, Luke
96HudValRB-15
96WesOahCHWB-2

Ownbey, Rick
82MetPhoA-27
82TidTidT-1
83Fle-551
83Top-739
84LouRedR-23
85LouRedR-26
86CarSchM-18
86CarTeal-31
86FleUpd-85
91MetWIZ-306

Oxner, Stan
83ButCopKT-15

Oyama, Randy
87HawRai-26

Oyas, Danny
92PriRedC-26
92PriRedF-3101
93BilMusF-3959
93BilMusSP-8
94ChaWheC-19
94ChaWheF-2716
94SouAtlLAF-SAL42

Oyler, Ray (Raymond F.)
65OPC-259
65Top-259
66OPC-81
66Top-81
66TopVen-81
67Top-352
68CokCapT-1
68TigDetFPB-17
68Top-399
69MilBra-209
69MLBOffS-97
69OPC-178
69PilPos-3
69Top-178
69TopFou-13
69TopSta-228
69TopTeaP-9
70MLBOffS-264
70Top-603
72MilBra-261
81TCM60I-379
81TigDetN-30
83Pil69G-29
88TigDom-18

Oyster, Jeff
87ArkTraP-18
88ArkTraGS-24
88LouRedBTI-38
89ArkTraGS-16
90SprCarDGB-11

Ozario, Claudio
91SumFlyC-18
91SumFlyP-2343
92AlbPolC-4
92AlbPolF-2319
93WesPalBEC-18
93WesPalBEF-1356

Ozario, Yudith
94PitMetF-3535

Ozark, Danny
73OPC-486
73Top-486A
73Top-486B
74OPC-119
74Top-119
75OPC-46
75Top-46
76OPC-384
76SSP-476
76Top-384
77Top-467
78PhiSSP-50
78SSP270-50
78Top-631
79PhiBurK-1
79Top-112
81DodPol-NNO
84GiaPos-21
85Top-365
85TopTif-365
86PhiGreT-8

Ozawa, Kouichi
89VisOakCLC-114
89VisOakP-1422

Oziomiela, Rich
77ModA'sC-16

Ozorio, Claudio
94WesPalBEC-18
94WesPalBEF-57

Ozorio, Yudith
94PitMetC-28
96StPetCB-23

Ozuna, Gabriel
89SavCarP-345
89SouAtlLAGS-37
90ArkTraGS-23
91ArkTraLD-41
91ArkTraP-1284
91LinDriAA-41
92ArkTraF-1127
92ArkTraS-40
92SkyAA F-17
93LimRocDWB-63
93LouRedF-212
94ArkTraF-3088

Ozuna, Mateo
89SavCarP-359
90SavCarP-2077
91Cla/Bes-244
91SprCarC-21
91SprCarP-749
92ClaFS7-281
92St.PetCC-18
92St.PetCF-2036
93LimRocDWB-85
93WinSpiC-17
93WinSpiF-1578

Ozuna, Rafael
95GreFalDTI-28
96SavSanB-28
96VerBeaDB-23

Ozzie, Mascot
91KanCouCTI-27
92KanCouCTI-25
94KanCouCTI-20
95KanCouCTI-NNO
96KanCouCTI-19

Paasch, Steve
94BatCliC-19
94BatCliF-3444

Paccito, Fred
52LavPro-85

Pace, Jim
88RenSilSCLC-288

Pace, Scott
94ElmPioF-3470
95HagSunF-67
96DunBluJB-19
96DunBluJTI-22
94ElmPioC-14

Pace, Tubby
85CedRapRT-23

Pacella, John
78TidTidT-17
79TidTidT-2
81ColCliP-30
81ColCliT-22
81Top-414
82ColCliP-17
82ColCliT-1
83Don-130
83Fle-622
83Top-166
85NasSouTI-17
87TolMudHP-8
87TolMudHT-14
91MetWIZ-307
91OriCro-346
92YanWIZ8-139

Pacheco, Al
89JohCitCS-17
90CMC-706
90SavCarP-2067

Pacheco, Alex
90WelPirP-24
92JamExpC-5
92JamExpF-1499
93JamExpC-15
93JamExpF-3323
94BurBeeC-18
94BurBeeF-1080
95HarSenTI-16

Pacheco, Antonio
90IBAWorA-10
90IBAWorA-48

Pacheco, Delvis
96DanBraB-16

Pacheco, Melcher
94VenLinU-19
95LinVen-94

Pacheco, Tony
74OPC-521
74Top-521

Pacheco, Yogi
92PeoChiC-15

Pacheo, Jose
91HunCubC-16
91HunCubP-3332
92HunCubC-15
92HunCubF-3147

Pacho, Juan
81WatIndT-24
83ChaChaT-11
89GreBraB-8
89GreBraP-1155
89GreBraS-16

Pacholec, Joe
87WatPirP-23
88AugPirP-373
89SalBucS-16

Pachot, John
94BurBeeC-19
94BurBeeF-1085
94MidLeaAF-MDW33
96WesPalBEB-20

Pacillo, Pat
85Top-402
85TopTif-402
87NasSouTI-16
87RedKah-35
87TopTra-93T
87TopTraT-93T
88Don-536
88NasSouC-10
88NasSouP-472
88Top-288
88TopTif-288
89IndIndC-4
89IndIndP-1236
90CalCanC-1
90CalCanP-649
90CMC-428
90ProAAAF-114

Paciorek, Jim
83ElPasDT-4
85VanCanC-213
86VanCanP-20
87BrePol-14
87FleUpd-95
87FleUpdG-95
90El PasDAGTI-11
93GolCar-4
94BreMilB-64

Paciorek, John
77FriOneYW-95

Paciorek, Peter S.
96IdaFalB-19

Paciorek, Tom (Thomas M.)
71OPC-709
71Top-709
73OPC-606
73Top-606
74OPC-127
74Top-127
75OPC-523
75Top-523
76OPC-641
76SSP-88
76Top-641
77BurCheD-215
77Top-48
78Top-322
79OPC-65
79Top-141
80Top-481
81Don-408
81Fle-614
81MarPol-11
81OPC-228
81Top-228
81TopScr-23
81TopSti-124
82Don-253
82Fle-514
82FleSta-224
82OPC-371
82Top-336
82Top-678
82TopSti-236
82TopStiV-236
82TopTra-85T
83AllGamPI-6
83Don-243
83Fle-248
83FleSta-144
83FleSti-157
83OPC-72
83Top-72
83TopSti-47
83WhiSoxTV-44
84AllGamPI-97
84Don-282
84Fle-70
84Nes792-777
84OPC-132
84Top-777
84TopSti-246
84TopTif-777
84WhiSoxTV-25
85Don-488
85Fle-523
85OPC-381
85SpoIndGC-15
85Top-572
85TopTif-572
85WhiSoxC-44
86BasStaB-82
86Fle-91
86FleUpd-86
86RanPer-44
86Top-362
86TopTif-362
86TopTra-83T
86TopTraT-83T
87Fle-133
87FleGlo-133
87OPC-21
87RanMot-8
87RanSmo-14

87Top-729
87TopTif-729
88Sco-531
88ScoGlo-531
89PacSenL-204
89T/MSenL-85
89TopSenL-107
90DodTar-600
90EliSenL-60
90PacLeg-97
91MetWIZ-308
93RanKee-285
93UppDecS-14
Pack, Steve
94KinMetC-14
94KinMetF-3820
96StLucMTI-14
Packard, Bob
94SprSulC-30
Packard, Eugene
14CraJacE-142
15CraJacE-142
Packel, Steve
89AncBucTI-27
Packer, Bill
83EriCarT-6
84SavCarT-17
Pactwa, Joe
76OPC-589
76Top-589
81TCM60I-376
Padden, Dick (Richard J.)
03BreE10-111
Padden, Tom (Thomas F.)
35GouPuzR-8K
35GouPuzR-9K
36GouWidPPR-A82
36NatChiFPR-63
43PhiTeal-19
92ConTSN-607
Paddy, Marco
88IdaFalBP-1835
Padget, Chris
86ChaOriW-21
86SouLeaAJ-7
87IntLeaAT-31
87RocRedWP-6
87RocRedWT-12
88RocRedWC-13
88RocRedWGCP-20
88RocRedWP-204
88RocRedWTI-18
89RocRedWC-14
89RocRedWP-1644
90CMC-317
90ProAAAF-473
90RocRedWC-17
90RocRedWGC-21
90RocRedWP-716
Padgett, Don (Don W.)
39PlaBal-157
40PlaBal-109
41CarW75-21
49RemBre-20
50RemBre-20
90DodTar-601
93ConTSN-716
Padgett, Ernie (Ernest)
21Exh-124
91ConTSN-206
Padia, Steve
83CedRapRF-25
83CedRapRT-12
86OrlTwiP-14
Padilla, Freddy
88BriTigP-1873
89FayGenP-1595
Padilla, Livio
87WinHavRSP-3
88FloStaLAS-46
88WinHavRSS-18
89NewBriRSP-620
89NewBriRSS-13
Padilla, Paul
79AlbDukT-23
80AlbDukT-24
Padilla, Roy
95ButCopKtI-16
96MicBatCB-19
96MidLeaAB-45
Padres, San Diego
69TopStaA-21
70Top-657
71OPC-482
71Top-482
71TopTat-70
72OPC-262
72Top-262
73OPC-316
73OPCBTC-21
73Top-316
73TopBluTC-21
74OPC-226
74OPCTC-21
74Top-226A
74Top-226B
74TopStaA-21
74TopTeaC-21
78Top-192
83FleSta-246
83FleSti-NNO
87SpoTeaL-16
88PanSti-479
88RedFolSB-107
90PubSti-625
90RedFolSB-119
90VenSti-536
94ImpProP-27
94Sco-659
94ScoGolR-659
95PanSti-134
96PanSti-101
Padron, Jesus
76VenLeaS-9
Padron, Oscar
95LinVen-91
Paduano, Donato
72Dia-139
Padula, Jim
78NewWayCT-33
79BurBeeT-23
Paepke, Dennis (Dennis Rae)
70Top-552
Paepke, Jack
49W72HolS-16
50W720HolS-23
Paez, Israel
95ForWayWTI-19
96ForWayWB-18
Paez, Raul
93WelPirC-17
93WelPirF-3368
94SalBucF-2329
Pafko, Andy (Andrew)
39ExhSal-50A
39ExhSal-50B
39ExhSal-50C
44CubTeal-19
46SpoExcW-3-6
47HomBon-36
47PM1StaP1-155
47TipTop-114
49Bow-63
49EurSta-66
49Lea-125
49MPR302-2-108
50Bow-60
50RoyDes-6A
50RoyDes-6B
51Bow-103
51FisBakL-21
51R42SmaS-82
51TopBluB-27
52Bow-204
52RoyPre-8
52TipTop-28
52Top-1
53BowBW-57
53BraJohC-24
53BraSpiaS3-19
53BraSpiaS7-11
53RedMan-NL9
54Bow-112
54BraJohC-48
54BraMer-4
54BraSpiaSP-16
54RedMan-NL8
54Top-79
54Wil-13
55Bow-12
55BraGolS-20
55BraJohC-48
55BraSpiaSD-15
56Top-312
57BraSpiaS4-16
57Top-143
58BraJayP-10
58Top-223
59Top-27
59TopVen-27
60BraLaktL-18
60BraSpiaS-16
60Top-464
76TayBow4-5
78BraTCC-10
79DiaGre-97
79TCM50-181
83Bra53F-48
83TopRep5-1
88RinPosD1-4B
89PacLegI-123
89SweBasG-74
90DodTar-602
92CubOldS-18
94TopArc1-79
94TopArc1G-79
95TopArcBD-1
Pagan, Angel
94AlbPolC-18
94AlbPolF-2244
94BluOriC-16
94BluOriF-3570
Pagan, Dave
74SyrChiTI-21
75IntLeaAT-9
75OPC-648
75SyrChiTI-15
75Top-648
76SSP-432
77Hos-132
77OPC-151
77Top-508
77TopCloS-35
78ColCliT-20
91OriCro-347
92YanWIZ7-124
Pagan, Felix
83IdaFalAT-23
Pagan, Jose (Jose Antonio)
60TacBan-12
60Top-67
60TopVen-67
61Top-279
62Jel-132
62Pos-132
62PosCan-132
62SalPlaC-200
62ShiPlaC-200
62Top-565
63GiaJayP-10
63Jel-103
63Pos-103
63Top-545
64GiaJayP-10
64Top-123
64TopVen-123
65Top-575
66OPC-54
66PirEasH-11
66Top-54
66TopVen-54
67CokCapPi-11
67PirTeal-15
67Top-322
67TopPirS-18
68PirKDK-11
68PirTeal-15
68Top-482
69MilBra-210
69OPC-192
69PirJacitB-8
69Top-192
69TopFou-18
70Top-643
71MLBOffS-211
71OPC-282
71PirActP-9
71Top-282
72MilBra-262
72Top-701
72Top-702
73OPC-659
73Top-659
77PirPosP-19
78TCM60I-102
79OgdA'sT-6
80OgdA'sT-23
Pagano, Scott
92NiaFalRC-3
92NiaFalRF-3341
95DurBulTI-24
96BinBeeB-21
Page, Greg
90SalSpuCLC-126
90SalSpuP-2714
Page, High Jumper
88GooN16-31
Page, Joe
46SpoExcW-7-8
47Exh-170
47PM1StaP1-156
47TipTop-54
48Bow-29
48YanTeal-21
49Bow-82
50Bow-12
50Dra-27
51BerRos-C5
51Bow-217
51FisBakL-22
51TopBluB-10
52Top-48A
52Top-48B
79TCM50-197
83TopRep5-48
85TCMPla1-7
92YanWIZA-56
Page, Kelvin
85LitFalMT-7
Page, Ken
81SpoIndT-21
Page, Marc J.
82WisRapTF-24
Page, Mike
77FriOneYW-75
85BurRanT-2
Page, Mitchell (Mitchell Otis)
75ShrCapT-17
76VenLeaS-152
78Hos-38
78Kel-47
78OPC-75
78PapGinD-39
78Top-55
79Hos-17
79OPC-147
79Top-295
79TopCom-14
80OPC-307
80Top-586
81A'sGraG-6
81Don-480
81Fle-580
81Top-35
82Fle-105
82OPC-178
82TacTigT-36
82Top-633
83Top-737
84Nes792-414
84Top-414
84TopTif-414
85HawIslC-234
92TacTigF-2519
92TacTigS-550
93TacTigF-3049
Page, Phil
49EurSta-91
Page, Phillip
92MisStaB-50
Page, Sean
90JohCitCS-20
91SavCarC-20
91SavCarP-1661
Page, Ted
78LauLonABS-16
86NegLeaF-2
86NegLeaF-4
88NegLeaD-15
Page, Thane
91MarPhiC-19
91MarPhiP-3452
92BatCliC-21
92BatCliF-3263
Page, Vance
39CubTeal-18
41CubTeal-18
41DouPlaR-1
Page, W.B.
88AllandGN-43
Page, William Byrd
88KimN18-34
Pagee, Shawn
94JamJamC-19
94JamJamF-3969
96FayGenB-3
Pagel, Dave
81QuaCitCT-1
Pagel, Karl (Karl Douglas)
79Top-716
80Top-676
80WicAerT-1
81ChaChaT-18
82ChaChaT-21
82Ind-27
83ChaChaT-12
83IndPos-25
84MaiGuiT-16
Pageler, Michael
96BelGiaTI-22
Pages, Javier
92AlbPolC-11
92AlbPolF-2310
93BurBeeC-15
93BurBeeF-162
93MidLeaAGF-31
94WesPalBEC-19
94WesPalBEF-44
Pagliari, Armando
88St.CatBJP-2005
89St.CatBJP-2092
91MyrBeaHC-30
Pagliaroni, Jim (James V.)
60DarFar-2
61Top-519
62Jel-63
62Pos-63
62PosCan-63
62SalPlaC-81
62ShiPlaC-81
62Top-81
62TopVen-81
63PirIDL-19
63Top-159
64Kah-20
64PirKDK-22
64Top-392
64TopCoi-62
65Kah-34
65OPC-265
65Top-265
66Kah-24
66OPC-33
66PirEasH-10
66Top-33
66TopVen-33
67CokCapPi-9
67DexPre-158
67Kah-27
67OPC-183
67PirTeal-16
67Top-183
67TopPirS-19
68Top-586
69MilBra-211
69Top-302
69TopTeaP-21
78TCM60I-91
83Pil69G-35
Pagliarulo, Mike
83NasSouTI-14
84ColCliP-17
84ColCliT-1
85DomLeaS-184
85Don-539
85Fle-139
85Top-638
85TopSti-317
85TopTif-638
86Don-152
86Fle-113
86Lea-80
86OPC-327
86Spo-177
86Top-327
86TopTif-327
86YanTCM-26
87ClaGam-22
87Don-298
87DonOpeD-239
87Fle-107
87FleGlo-107
87FleLeaL-33
87Lea-189
87OPC-195
87SevCoi-E6
87SmoAmeL-9

87Spo-55
87SpoTeaP-7
87Top-195
87TopGloS-56
87TopSti-300
87TopTif-195
88Don-105
88DonBasB-105
88DonReaBY-105
88Fle-216
88FleGlo-216
88FleStiC-49
88OPC-109
88PanSti-156
88Sco-170
88ScoGlo-170
88Spo-121
88SpoGam-23
88StaLinY-10
88Top-435
88TopBig-138
88TopSti-295
88TopTif-435
89Bow-175
89BowTif-175
89Don-127
89Fle-262
89FleGlo-262
89OPC-211
89PanSti-406
89Sco-189
89ScoRoo-11T
89Spo-153
89Top-211
89TopBig-28
89TopDouM-20
89TopSti-311
89TopTif-211
89UppDec-569
89YanScoNW-13
90Bow-219
90BowTif-219
90Don-364
90DonBesN-137
90Fle-163
90FleCan-163
90Lea-320
90OPC-63
90PadCok-12
90PadMag-3
90PubSti-542
90Sco-494
90Top-63
90TopBig-226
90TopSti-106
90TopTif-63
90UppDec-329
90VenSti-381
91Bow-339
91Don-140
91Fle-537
91FleUpd-40
91Lea-339
91OPC-547
91PanFreS-93
91Sco-199
91ScoRoo-42T
91StaClu-522
91Top-547
91TopDesS-547
91TopMic-547
91TopTif-547
91TopTra-87T
91TopTraT-87T
91UppDec-206
91UppDec-709
92Bow-685
92Don-62
92Fle-216
92Lea-346
92OPC-721
92PanSti-117
92Pin-246
92Sco-173
92StaClu-152
92StaCluD-137
92Top-721
92TopGol-721
92TopGolW-721
92TopMic-721
92Ult-96
92UppDec-509
92YanWIZ8-140
93Don-707
93Fla-241
93Fle-641
93Lea-474
93PacSpa-176
93Pin-508
93SelRoo-115T
93Stu-191
93Top-336
93TopGol-336
93TopInaM-336
93TopMic-336
93Ult-587
93UppDec-306
93UppDecGold-306
94ColC-224
94ColChoGS-224
94ColChoSS-224
94Don-243
94Fle-14
94Pac-41
94Sco-489
94ScoGolR-489
95RanCra-25
96Fle-257
96FleTif-257

Paglino, Joseph J.
82AppFoxF-16

Pagnozzi, Tom
83EriCarT-20
86LouRedTI-21
87CarSmo-12
87LouRedTI-22
88BlaYNPRWLU-27
88CarSmo-12
88Don-577
88Sco-358
88ScoGlo-358
88Top-689
88TopTif-689
89BlaYNPRWL-96
89CarSmo-16
89Don-399
89Sco-483
89Top-208
89TopTif-208
89UppDec-602
90CarSmo-18
90Don-591
90Lea-498
90OPC-509
90PubSti-224
90SprCarDGB-35
90Top-509
90TopTif-509
90TopTVCa-23
90VenSti-382
91Bow-389
91CarPol-19
91Don-337
91Fle-641
91Lea-72
91OPC-308
91PanFreS-30
91Sco-797
91StaClu-223
91Top-308
91TopDesS-308
91TopMic-308
91TopTif-308
91Ult-293
91UppDec-91
92Bow-241
92CarPol-14
92Cla1-T69
92Don-254
92Fle-586
92Fre-9
92Lea-359
92OPC-448
92PanSti-171
92Pin-69
92Sco-136
92StaClu-162
92Stu-96
92Top-448
92TopGol-448
92TopGolW-448
92TopMic-448
92Ult-268
92UltAllS-15
92UltAwaW-8
92UppDec-379
93Bow-220
93CarPol-14
93DiaMar-83
93Don-360
93Fla-124
93Fle-130
93FleFruotL-50
93Lea-136
93OPC-273
93PacSpa-299
93PanSti-191
93Pin-62
93Sco-135
93Sel-37
93SP-77
93StaClu-399
93StaCluCa-6
93StaCluFDI-399
93StaCluM-72
93StaCluMOP-399
93Stu-198
93Top-92
93TopGol-92
93TopInaM-92
93TopMic-92
93TriPla-194
93Ult-110
93UltAwaW-2
93UppDec-405
93UppDecGold-405
94Bow-320
94CarPol-13
94ColC-464
94ColChoGS-464
94ColChoSS-464
94Don-177
94ExtBas-361
94Fin-384
94FinRef-384
94Fla-430
94Fle-641
94Lea-7
94OPC-103
94Pac-598
94PanSti-246
94Pin-439
94PinArtP-439
94PinMusC-439
94Sco-466
94ScoGolR-466
94Sel-98
94StaClu-122
94StaCluFDI-122
94StaCluGR-122
94StaCluMOP-122
94StaCluP-122
94StaCluT-319
94StaCluTFDI-319
94Stu-53
94Top-719
94TopGol-719
94TopSpa-719
94TriPla-65
94Ult-567
94UppDec-106
94UppDecED-106
95Bow-338
95ColCho-193
95ColChoGS-193
95ColChoSS-193
95Don-102
95DonPreP-102
95DonTopotO-334
95Emb-56
95EmbGolI-56
95Fin-143
95FinRef-143
95Fla-194
95Fle-504
95Lea-31
95PanSti-23
95Pin-37
95PinArtP-37
95PinMusC-37
95Sco-69
95ScoGolR-69
95ScoPlaTS-69
95StaClu-69
95StaClu-316
95StaCluFDI-69
95StaCluMOP-69
95StaCluMOP-316
95StaCluSTWS-69
95StaCluSTWS-316
95Top-111
95TopCyb-72
95Ult-224
95UltAwaW-10
95UltAwaWGM-10
95UltGolM-224
95UppDec-306
95UppDecED-306
95UppDecEDG-306
96CarPol-21
96ColCho-686
96ColChoGS-686
96ColChoSS-686
96Don-278
96DonPreP-278
96EmoXL-270
96Fin-B53
96FinRef-B53
96Fla-366
96Fle-553
96FleTif-553
96LeaSigA-175
96LeaSigAG-175
96LeaSigAS-175
96MLBPin-25
96Pac-221
96Pin-65
96ProSta-33
96Sco-403
96StaClu-403
96StaCluEPB-403
96StaCluEPG-403
96StaCluEPS-403
96StaCluMOP-403
96Top-131
96Ult-277
96UltGolM-277
96UppDec-439
97Cir-205
97CirRav-205
97ColCho-443
97Don-118
97DonPreP-118
97DonPrePGold-118
97DonTea-155
97DonTeaSPE-155
97Fle-451
97FleTif-451
97MetUni-234
97Pac-415
97PacLigB-415
97PacSil-415
97ProMag-36
97ProMagML-36
97ScoPreS-273
97StaClu-374
97StaCluMOP-374
97Top-2
97UppDec-484

Paiement, Wilfred
82MonNew-11

Paige, Carey
92ClaDraP-67
92FroRowDP-20
92HigSchPLS-9
93DanBraC-17
93DanBraF-3616
94MacBraC-16
94MacBraF-2201
94SouAtlLAF-SAL45
95Bes-54
95DurBulTI-25
95Top-429
96BesAutSA-51

Paige, Pat (George L.)
09T206-507

Paige, Satchel (LeRoy)
47Exh-171
47PM1StaP1-157
48IndTeal-24
49Bow-224
49IndTeal-19
49IndVisEI-13
49Lea-8
52BroPenCB-2
53Top-220
60RawGloT-25
67TopVen-177
72TopTes5-1
73HalofFPP-13
74LauOldTBS-15
76GalBasGHoF-22
76LauIndC-21
76ShaPiz-125
76TulOilGP-23
77GalGloG-22
77GalGloG-258
77SerSta-18
79BasGre-76
80PacLeg-60
80PerHaloFP-125
80SSPHOF-125
82BasCarN-19
82DiaCla-31
82OhiHaloF-33
83ConMar-52
83DonHOFH-11
83MLBPin-14
84OCoandSI-91
86NegLeaF-10
86NegLeaF-21
87NegLeaPD-21
88ConNegA-10
88NegLeaD-11
89BowInsT-8
89BowRepI-8
89BowTif-R8
90BasWit-64
90NegLeaS-20
90PerGreM-20
90SweBasG-115
91HomCooC-2
91LinDri-47
91PomBlaBPB-8
91SweBasG-133
91TopArc1-220
91USGamSBL-5C
91USGamSBL-5D
91USGamSBL-5H
91USGamSBL-5S
92BazQua5A-18
92Sco-882
92St.VinHHS-8
93ActPacA-115
93ActPacA2-49G
93DiaStaES-N3
93Hoy-5
93LegFoi-8
93LegFoiP-1
93SpeHOFI-3
93TedWil-112
93TedWil-131
93TedWilLC-5
93TedWilP-115
94UppDecTAE-40
94UppDecTAEGM-6
95UppDecSHoB-20
96NoiSatP-1
96NoiSatP-2
96NoiSatP-3
96NoiSatP-4
96NoiSatP-5
96NoiSatP-6
96NoiSatP-7
96NoiSatP-8
96NoiSatP-9
96NoiSatP-10
96NoiSatP-11
96NoiSatP-12
97St.VinHHS-13

Pailthorpe, Bob
95ElmPioTI-21
95ElmPioUTI-21
96KanCouCTI-20

Paine, Phil
54BraJohC-11
55BraJohC-11
58Top-442
59DarFar-16

Painter, Chris
89GeoColC-21

Painter, Gary
91Cla/Bes-129
91FloStaLAP-FSL45
91WinHavRSC-6
91WinHavRSP-486
92NewBriRSF-430
92NewBriRSS-492
93NewBriRSF-1216
94SarRedSC-22
94SarRedSF-1948

Painter, Lance
90SpoIndSP-21
91Cla/Bes-352
91WatDiaC-7
91WatDiaP-1254
92ClaFS7-313
92ProFS7-339
92SkyAA F-285
92WicWraF-3657

92WicWraS-643
93Bow-89
93ColSprSSF-3084
93FleFinE-38
93SelRoo-48T
93Top-738
93TopGol-738
93TopInaM-738
93TopMic-738
93TriAAAGF-10
94ColSprSSF-731
94Don-474
94ScoBoyoS-29
94SpoRoo-135
94SpoRooAP-135
94StaClu-77
94StaCluFDI-77
94StaCluGR-77
94StaCluMOP-77
94StaCluT-119
94StaCluTFDI-119
94Top-229
94TopGol-229
94TopSpa-229
95ColCho-449
95ColChoGS-449
95ColChoSS-449
95UppDec-408
95UppDecED-408
95UppDecEDG-408
95UppDecSE-103
95UppDecSEG-103
96LeaSigEA-148
96RocPol-15
Painton, Tim
80CliGiaT-15
89FreStaBS-16
91FreStaBS-16
Paiva, Nelson
76VenLeaS-167
Paixao, Paulino
85UtiBluST-4
Pakele, Louis
90BoiHawP-3309
91PalSprAP-2010
Palacios, Peter
85CloHSS-30
Palacios, Rey
86GleFalTP-17
87IntLeaAT-11
87TolMudHP-15
87TolMudHT-1
88BlaYNPRWLU-28
88TolMudHC-18
88TolMudHP-605
88TriAAAP-43
89BlaYNPRWL-83
89Fle-648
89FleGlo-648
89UppDec-21
90Bow-381
90BowTif-381
91OPC-148
91Top-148
91TopDesS-148
91TopMic-148
91TopTif-148
93RocRedWF-243
Palacios, Vicente
87VanCanP-1619
88ClaRed-191
88Don-45
88Fle-336
88FleGlo-336
88Lea-45
88Sco-643
88ScoGlo-643
88Spo-224
88Top-322
88TopTif-322
89Fle-216
89FleGlo-216
89ScoHot1R-2
90BufBisC-7
90BufBisP-370
90BufBisTI-18
90CMC-7
90ProAAAF-485
91Don-732
91FleUpd-113
91Lea-442
91OPC-438
91StaClu-443
91Top-438
91TopDesS-438
91TopMic-438
91TopTif-438
91UppDecFE-71F
92Don-365
92OPC-582
92Pin-386
92Sco-109
92StaClu-486
92Top-582
92TopGol-582
92TopGolW-582
92TopMic-582
92Ult-557
93Pin-130
94FleUpd-181
95Don-254
95DonPreP-254
95Fle-505
95Pac-412
95Ult-225
95UltGolM-225
Palafox, Juan
85MexCitTT-12
Palat, Ed
74TacTwiC-26
75TacTwiK-20
Palermo, Pete
86HagSunP-14
87HagSunP-17
88HagSunS-16
Palermo, Steve
88T/MUmp-29
89T/MUmp-27
90T/MUmp-26
Palica, Alex
45CenFlo-19
Palica, Ambrose
46RemBre-22
47RemBre-10
47SmiClo-12
Palica, Erv
51Bow-189
52Top-273
54NewYorJA-13
55Bow-195A
55Bow-195B
56Top-206
60HenHouW-21
61UniOil-S7
79TCM50-233
83TopRep5-273
90DodTar-603
91OriCro-348
91RinPosBD2-8
95TopArcBD-16
95TopArcBD-134
Palica, John
81WisRapTT-22
83OrlTwiT-8
Pall, Donn Steven
86AppFoxP-17
87BirBarB-15
88BlaYNPRWL-27
88TriAAAP-45
88VanCanC-9
88VanCanP-759
89DonRoo-7
89Fle-505
89FleGlo-505
89ScoRoo-102T
89Top-458
89TopTif-458
89WhiSoxC-18
90BirBarDGB-26
90Don-606
90Fle-543
90FleCan-543
90Lea-392
90OPC-219
90PubSti-397
90Sco-304
90Sco100RS-7
90Top-219
90TopRoo-23
90TopTif-219
90UppDec-386
90VenSti-383
90WhiSoxC-18
91Don 215
91Fle-130
91Lea-468
91OPC-768
91Sco-132
91Top-768
91TopDesS-768
91TopMic-768
91TopTif-768
91UppDec-603
91WhiSoxK-22
92Bow-380
92Don-56
92Fle-92
92OPC-57
92Sco-484
92StaClu-184
92Top-57
92TopGol-57
92TopGolW-57
92TopMic-57
92Ult-41
92UppDec-592
92WhiSoxK-22
93Don-667
93Fle-586
93PacSpa-393
93StaClu-240
93StaCluFDI-240
93StaCluMOP-240
93StaCluWS-21
93Top-707
93TopGol-707
93TopInaM-707
93TopMic-707
93WhiSoxK-21
94StaCluT-200
94StaCluTFDI-200
94Top-328
94TopGol-328
94TopSpa-328
95NasSouTI-16
Pallas, Ted
82BelBreF-27
Pallino, John
94LetMouF-3891
94LetMouSP-3
Pallone, Dave
88T/MUmp-37
89T/MUmp-35
91FouBal-18
Palma, Brian
89RenSilSCLC-258
91SalSpuC-12
91SalSpuP-2258
Palma, Jay
83AndBraT-22
Palmeiro, Orlando
91BoiHawC-9
91BoiHawP-3895
92MidLeaATI-31
92QuaCitRBC-3
92QuaCitRBF-823
93Bow-637
93ClaFS7-234
93ExcFS7-145
93MidAngF-333
94ExcFS7-29
94VanCanF-1876
95SigRoo-41
95SigRooSig-41
96ColCho-37
96Don-361
96DonPreP-361
96Fle-53
96FleTif-53
96Pac-266
96UppDec-32
96VanCanB-20
97MidAngOHP-22
97Pac-11
97PacLigB-11
97PacPri-4
97PacPriLB-4
97PacPriP-4
97PacSil-11
Palmeiro, Rafael
86PitCubP-18
87Don-43
87DonRoo-47
87IowCubTI-24
87Lea-43
87Spo-158
87SpoRoo2-32
87SpoRooP-2
87SpoTeaP-22
87Top-634
87TopRoo-12
87TopTif-634
88CubDavB-25
88Don-324
88DonBasB-93
88DonTeaBC-324
88Fle-429
88FleGlo-429
88FleSluBC-C4
88OPC-186
88PanSti-268
88PeoChiTI-23
88Sco-186
88ScoGlo-186
88Top-186
88TopTif-186
89Bow-237
89BowTif-237
89ClaTraP-163
89Don-49
89DonAll-53
89DonBasB-88
89DonTra-6
89Fle-434
89Fle-631
89FleGlo-434
89FleGlo-631
89FleUpd-66
89OPC-310
89PanSti-60
89RanMot-5
89RanSmo-24
89RedFolSB-88
89Sco-199
89ScoHot1S-56
89ScoRoo-1T
89ScoYouSI-35
89Spo-30
89SpoIllFKI-268
89Top-310
89TopBig-257
89TopCoi-47
89TopMinL-5
89TopSti-47
89TopStiB-52
89TopTif-310
89TopTra-93T
89TopTraT-93T
89TopUKM-58
89UppDec-235
89UppDec-772
90Bow-496
90BowTif-496
90ClaBlu-74
90Don-225
90DonBesA-41
90Fle-308
90FleCan-308
90Lea-100
90OPC-755
90PanSti-164
90PubSti-418
90RanMot-9
90RedFolSB-72
90Sco-405
90Sco100S-58
90Spo-9
90Top-755
90TopBig-127
90TopHeaU-12
90TopSti-250
90TopTif-755
90UppDec-335
90VenSti-384
91Bow-286
91Cla1-T85
91Cla3-T71
91ClaGam-115
91Don-19
91Don-394
91Don-521
91DonSupD-19
91Fle-295
91Lea-347
91MisStaB-35
91OPC-295
91PanCanT1-7
91PanCanT1-29
91PanFreS-252
91PanSti-211
91PepSup-14
91RanMot-9
91Sco-216
91Sco100S-56
91SevCoi-T10
91StaClu-502
91Stu-127
91Top-295
91TopDesS-295
91TopMic-295
91TopTif-295
91Ult-350
91UppDec-30
91UppDec-474
91USPlaCA-6D
92Bow-610
92Cla2-T62
92ClaGam-69
92Don-46
92Fle-311
92FleAll-17
92FleTeaL-12
92Hig5-113
92Lea-296
92OPC-55
92PanSti-75
92Pin-35
92RanMot-9
92RanTeal-15
92Sco-55
92Sco100S-27
92ScoCokD-17
92ScoImpP-68
92ScoProP-14
92StaClu-516
92StaCluD-138
92Stu-244
92Top-55
92TopGol-55
92TopGolW-55
92TopKid-130
92TopMic-55
92TriPla-183
92Ult-136
92UppDec-223
92UppDecF-34
92UppDecFG-34
93Bow-137
93Don-365
93Fin-52
93FinRef-52
93Fla-283
93Fle-687
93FunPac-157
93KinDis-20
93Lea-49
93MilBonSS-8
93OPC-171
93PacBeiA-14
93PacSpa-314
93PacSpaGE-17
93PanSti-81
93Pin-220
93RanKee-419
93Sco-74
93Sel-162
93SP-196
93StaClu-115
93StaCluFDI-115
93StaCluMOP-115
93StaCluR-26
93Stu-185
93Top-305
93TopGol-305
93TopInaM-305
93TopMic-305
93TriPla-71
93Ult-281
93UppDec-52
93UppDec-574
93UppDecGold-52
93UppDecGold-574
94Bow-515
94BowBes-R51
94BowBesR-R51
94ColC-605
94ColChoGS-605
94ColChoSS-605
94Don-26
94DonSpeE-26
94ExtBas-11
94Fin-227
94FinJum-227
94FinRef-227
94Fla-257
94FlaInfP-6
94Fle-313
94Fle-710
94FleLeaL-3
94FleLumC-8

94FleUpd-5
94FUnPac-154
94Lea-289
94LeaL-4
94LeaMVPC-A10
94LeaMVPCG-A10
94OPC-25
94OriPro-77
94OriUSPC-7D
94OriUSPC-13C
94Pac-622
94PacAll-16
94PacGolP-5
94PacSilP-3
94PanSti-130
94Pin-493
94PinArtP-493
94PinMusC-493
94PinRunC-RC5
94RanAllP-19
94Sco-495
94ScoGolR-495
94ScoGolS-59
94ScoRoo-RT8
94ScoRooCP-CP2
94ScoRooGR-RT8
94ScoRooS-CP2
94Sel-317
94SP-125
94SPDieC-125
94Spo-144
94SpoRoo-26
94SpoRooAP-26
94StaClu-112
94StaClu-208
94StaClu-265
94StaClu-557
94StaCluFDI-112
94StaCluFDI-208
94StaCluFDI-265
94StaCluFDI-557
94StaCluGR-112
94StaCluGR-208
94StaCluGR-265
94StaCluGR-557
94StaCluMO-6
94StaCluMOP-112
94StaCluMOP-208
94StaCluMOP-265
94StaCluMOP-557
94StaCluT-295
94StaCluTFDI-295
94Stu-126
94Top-470
94TopBlaG-16
94TopGol-470
94TopSpa-470
94TopSupS-33
94TopTra-76T
94TriPla-158
94TriPlaM-3
94Ult-308
94UltHomRK-5
94UltLeaL-2
94UppDec-34
94UppDec-340
94UppDecED-34
94UppDecED-340
94USPlaCA-6C
95Baz-23
95Bow-385
95BowBes-R39
95BowBesR-R39
95ColCho-330
95ColChoGS-330
95ColChoSE-153
95ColChoSEGS-153
95ColChoSESS-153
95ColChoSS-330
95D3-45
95DenHol-19
95Don-357
95DonDiaK-DK23
95DonPreP-357
95DonTopotO-14
95Emb-126
95EmbGolI-126
95Emo-7
95Fin-177
95FinRef-177
95Fla-224
95FlaInfP-6
95Fle-17
95Lea-129
95LeaLim-86
95LeaLimIBP-14
95Pac-28
95PacGolCDC-3
95PacGolP-18
95PacLatD-26
95PacPri-9
95Pin-293
95Pin-398
95PinArtP-293
95PinArtP-398
95PinMusC-293
95PinMusC-398
95PinPer-PP16
95RedFol-10
95Sco-419
95ScoGolR-419
95ScoHaloG-HG89
95ScoPlaTS-419
95Sel-121
95SelArtP-121
95SelCer-26
95SelCerMG-26
95SP-120
95SPCha-118
95SPChaDC-118
95Spo-84
95SpoArtP-84
95SPSil-120
95StaClu-30
95StaCluCC-CC6
95StaCluCT-17
95StaCluFDI-30
95StaCluMO-36
95StaCluMOP-30
95StaCluMOP-CC6
95StaCluMOP-PZ10
95StaCluPZ-PZ10
95StaCluSTWS-30
95StaCluVR-20
95Stu-49
95StuGolS-49
95Sum-5
95SumBigB-BB16
95SumNthD-5
95Top-80
95TopCyb-56
95TopFin-11
95UC3-25
95UC3-147
95UC3ArtP-25
95UC3ArtP-147
95UC3CycS-CS16
95Ult-7
95UltGolM-7
95UppDec-366
95UppDecED-366
95UppDecEDG-366
95UppDecPLL-R33
95UppDecPLL-R44
95UppDecPLLE-R33
95UppDecPLLE-R44
95UppDecSE-50
95UppDecSEG-50
95Zen-82
95ZenZ-16
96Baz-102
96Bow-30
96BowBes-32
96BowBesAR-32
96BowBesR-32
96Cir-7
96CirRav-7
96ColCho-470
96ColChoCtG-CG3
96ColChoCtG-CG3B
96ColChoCtG-CG3C
96ColChoCtGE-CR3
96ColChoCtGG-CG3
96ColChoCtGG-CG3B
96ColChoCtGG-CG3C
96ColChoCtGGE-CR3
96ColChoGS-470
96ColChoSS-470
96Don-357
96DonPreP-357
96EmoXL-8
96Fin-B287
96Fin-S68
96FinRef-B287
96FinRef-S68
96Fla-11
96Fle-19
96FleOri-14
96FleTif-19
96Lea-174
96LeaLim-84
96LeaLimG-84
96LeaPre-47
96LeaPreP-47
96LeaPrePB-174
96LeaPrePG-174
96LeaPrePS-174
96LeaPreSG-15
96LeaPreSte-15
96LeaSig-75
96LeaSigEA-149
96LeaSigEACM-22
96LeaSigPPG-75
96LeaSigPPP-75
96LeaTotB-3
96MetUni-8
96MetUniML-6
96MetUniP-8
96MLBPin-26
96Pac-239
96PacEstL-EL23
96PacPri-P76
96PacPriG-P76
96PanSti-129
96Pin-146
96Pin-250
96PinAfi-3
96PinAfiAP-3
96PinAfiFPP-3
96PinArtP-73
96PinArtP-150
96PinFoil-250
96PinSlu-17
96PinSta-73
96PinSta-150
96ProSta-80
96Sco-31
96Sco-363
96ScoDugC-A30
96ScoDugC-B88
96ScoDugCAP-A30
96ScoDugCAP-B88
96ScoGolS-26
96ScoNumG-29
96ScoPowP-10
96ScoTitT-10
96Sel-58
96SelArtP-58
96SP-35
96Spo-29
96Spo-110
96SpoArtP-29
96SpoArtP-110
96SpoPowS-14
96SPSpeFX-28
96SPSpeFXDC-28
96SPx-7
96SPxGol-7
96StaClu-343
96StaCluEPB-343
96StaCluEPG-343
96StaCluEPS-343
96StaCluMO-32
96StaCluMOP-343
96StaCluMOP-PC6
96StaCluMOP-PS8
96StaCluPC-PC6
96StaCluPS-PS8
95StaCluVRMC-20
96Stu-9
96StuPrePB-9
96StuPrePG-9
96StuPrePS-9
96Sum-123
96SumAbo&B-123
96SumArtP-123
96SumFoi-123
96Top-395
96TopChr-158
96TopChrR-158
96TopGal-89
96TopGalPPI-89
96TopLas-88
96TopPro-AL19
96Ult-10
96UltGolM-10
96UltHitM-6
96UltHitMGM-6
96UltPowP-5
96UltPowPGM-5
96UltThu-15
96UltThuGM-15
96UppDec-15
96UppDecPD-PD11
96UppDecPHE-H3
96UppDecPRE-R6
96UppDecPreH-H3
96UppDecPreR-R6
96UppDecRunP-RP13
97Bow-239
97BowBes-85
97BowBesAR-85
97BowBesMI-MI7
97BowBesMIAR-MI7
97BowBesMIARI-MI7
97BowBesMII-MI7
97BowBesMIR-MI7
97BowBesMIRI-MI7
97BowBesR-85
97BowChr-65
97BowChrI-65
97BowChrIR-65
97BowChrR-65
97BowInt-239
97BowIntB-BBI10
97BowIntBAR-BBI10
97BowIntBR-BBI10
97Cir-198
97CirRav-198
97ColCho-272
97ColChoCtG-5A
97ColChoCtG-5B
97ColChoCtG-5C
97ColChoCtGIW-CG5
97ColChoPP-PP17
97ColChoPPG-PP17
97ColChoTBS-7
97ColChoTBSWH-7
97Don-56
97Don-440
97DonDom-18
97DonEli-35
97DonEliGS-35
97DonLim-130
97DonLimFotG-19
97DonLimLE-130
97DonPre-47
97DonPreCttC-47
97DonPreP-56
97DonPreP-440
97DonPrePGold-56
97DonPrePGold-440
97DonTea-33
97DonTeaSPE-33
97Fin-60
97Fin-156
97Fin-278
97FinEmb-156
97FinEmb-278
97FinEmbR-156
97FinEmbR-278
97FinRef-60
97FinRef-156
97FinRef-278
97FlaSho-A71
97FlaSho-B71
97FlaSho-C71
97FlaShoLC-71
97FlaShoLC-B71
97FlaShoLC-C71
97FlaShoLCM-A71
97FlaShoLCM-B71
97FlaShoLCM-C71
97Fle-12
97FleTif-12
97Lea-43
97Lea-388
97LeaFraM-43
97LeaFraM-388
97LeaFraMDC-43
97LeaFraMDC-388
97LeaGolS-35
97MetUni-7
97NewPin-84
97NewPinAP-84
97NewPinMC-84
97NewPinPP-84
97Pac-28
97PacLatotML-3
97PacLigB-28
97PacPri-11
97PacPriLB-11
97PacPriP-11
97PacPriSL-SL1B
97PacSil-28
97PacTriCD-2
97Pin-43
97PinArtP-43
97PinCer-61
97PinCerMBlu-61
97PinCerMG-61
97PinCerMR-61
97PinCerR-61
97PinIns-17
97PinInsCE-17
97PinInsDD-14
97PinInsDE-17
97PinMusC-43
97PinPasttM-19
97PinTotCPB-61
97PinTotCPG-61
97PinTotCPR-61
97PinX-P-20
97PinX-PMoS-20
97PinX-PMP-12
97PinX-PSfF-21
97PinX-PSfFU-21
97Sco-45
97Sco-497
97ScoHeaotO-10
97ScoHobR-497
97ScoOri-1
97ScoOriPl-1
97ScoOriPr-1
97ScoPreS-45
97ScoResC-497
97ScoShoS-45
97ScoShoS-497
97ScoShoSAP-45
97ScoShoSAP-497
97Sel-31
97SelArtP-31
97SelRegG-31
97SkyE-X-7
97SkyE-XC-7
97SkyE-XEC-7
97SP-30
97SPx-10
97SPxBro-10
97SPxGraF-10
97SPxSil-10
97SPxSte-10
97StaClu-56
97StaCluMat-56
97StaCluMOP-56
97Stu-128
97StuPrePG-128
97StuPrePS-128
97Top-140
97TopChr-54
97TopChrR-54
97TopChrSB-15
97TopChrSBR-15
97TopGal-36
97TopGalPPI-36
97TopSeaB-SB15
97TopSta-20
97TopStaAM-20
97TopSweS-SS11
97TopTeaT-TT8
97UppDec-21
97UppDec-185
97UppDecLDC-LD14
97UppDecPP-PP3
97UppDecPPJ-PP3
97UppDecRP-RP9
97UppDecU-17

Palmer, Bob
75AppFoxT-22
82HolMilT-11

Palmer, Brett
93BurIndC-20
93BurIndF-3296
94BurIndC-20

Palmer, David
79ExpPos-18
80ExpPos-21
80OPC-21
80Top-42
81Don-451
81Fle-160
81OPC-243
81Top-607
82ExpPos-29
82Fle-199
82OPC-292
82Top-292
83Don-68
83ExpPos-16
83Fle-291

83OPC-164
83Top-164
84ExpPos-21
84ExpStu-23
85Don-341
85ExpPos-16
85Fle-404
85Fle-643
85Lea-105
85OPC-211
85OPCPos-3
85Top-526
85TopMin-526
85TopTif-526
86BraPol-46
86Don-254A
86Don-254B
86Fle-255
86FleUpd-87
86OPC-143
86Top-421
86TopTif-421
86TopTra-84T
86TopTraT-84T
87BraSmo-4
87Don-325
87Fle-525
87FleGlo-525
87SpoTeaP-24
87Top-324
87TopSti-45
87TopTif-324
88Don-266
88Fle-546
88FleGlo-546
88FleUpd-111
88FleUpdG-111
88PhiTas-17
88Sco-457
88ScoGlo-457
88Top-732
88TopTif-732
88TopTra-79T
88TopTraT-79T
89Don-133
89Fle-577
89FleGlo-577
89OPC-67
89Sco-544
89TolMudHC-4
89TolMudHP-789
89Top-67
89TopTif-67
89UppDec-515

Palmer, Dean

87GasRanP-8
88ChaRanS-18
88FloStaLAS-47
89BasAmeAPB-AA27
89TexLeaAGS-32
89TulDriGS-19
89TulDriTI-17
90ClaUpd-T39
90Don-529
90Hot50RS-35
90OklCit8P-441
90ProAAAF-687
90Sco-594
90Sco100RS-38
90Spo-225
90TopDeb89-95
90TulDriDGB-5
90TulDriP-1170
90UppDec-74
91Bow-288
91Cla3-T72
91DonRoo-48
91FleUpd-61
91LinDriAAA-314
91OklCit8LD-314
91OklCit8P-187
91Sco100RS-28
91TopTra-88T
91TopTraT-88T
91UltUpd-56
91UppDecFE-74F
92Bow-107
92Don-177
92Fle-312
92Lea-225
92LeaGolP-28
92OPC-567
92OPCPre-112
92PanSti-77
92Pin-351
92PinTea2-64
92ProFS7-148
92RanMot-26
92RanTeal-16
92Sco-392
92Sco100RS-60
92StaClu-211
92StaPal-1
92StaPal-2
92StaPal-3
92StaPal-4
92StaPal-5
92StaPal-6
92StaPal-7
92StaPal-8
92StaPal-9
92StaPal-10
92StaPal-11
92Stu-245
92Top-567
92TopGol-567
92TopGolW-567
92TopMic-567
92Ult-137
92UppDec-465
93Bow-81
93Don-339
93Fin-159
93FinRef-159
93Fla-284
93Fle-325
93FunPac-158
93FunPac-217
93Lea-159
93OPC-258
93PacSpa-315
93PanSti-84
93Pin-161
93PinHomRC-25
93PinTea2-28
93RanKee-420
93Sco-138
93Sel-248
93SP-197
93SPPlaP-PP14
93StaClu-22
93StaCluFDI-22
93StaCluMOP-22
93StaCluR-11
93Stu-210
93Top-545
93TopGol-545
93TopInaM-545
93TopMic-545
93TriPla-111
93Ult-282
93UppDec-241
93UppDec-465
93UppDecGold-241
93UppDecGold-465
94Bow-213
94ColC-580
94ColChoGS-580
94ColChoSS-580
94Don-355
94DonLonBL-2
94DonSpeE-355
94ExtBas-183
94Fin-177
94FinPre-177P
94FinRef-177
94Fla-345
94Fle-314
94FUnPac-71
94Lea-311
94LeaL-73
94OPC-152
94Pac-623
94PacGolP-7
94PanSti-131
94Pin-101
94PinArtP-101
94PinMusC-101
94PinPowS-PS25
94PinTeaP-3
94PinTheN-20
94Sco-389
94ScoGolR-389
94Sel-223
94SP-150
94SPDieC-150
94Spo-85
94SpoSha-SH8
94StaClu-112
94StaClu-336
94StaCluFDI-112
94StaCluFDI-336
94StaCluGR-112
94StaCluGR-336
94StaCluMOP-112
94StaCluMOP-336
94StaCluMOP-ST27
94StaCluST-ST27
94StaCluT-269
94StaCluTFDI-269
94Stu-156
94Top-136
94TopGol-136
94TopSpa-136
94TriPla-197
94Ult-130
94UppDec-180
94UppDecAJ-22
94UppDecAJG-22
94UppDecED-180
94UppDecMLS-MM14
94UppDecMLSED-MM14
95Baz-75
95Bow-380
95ColCho-395
95ColChoGS-395
95ColChoSE-187
95ColChoSEGS-187
95ColChoSESS-187
95ColChoSS-395
95D3-46
95Don-19
95DonPreP-19
95DonTopotO-164
95Emb-41
95EmbGolI-41
95Emo-87
95Fin-91
95FinRef-91
95Fla-91
95Fle-292
95Lea-21
95LeaCor-5
95LeaLim-127
95Pac-432
95PanSti-60
95Pin-192
95PinArtP-192
95PinMusC-192
95RanCra-26
95Sco-245
95ScoGolR-245
95ScoPlaTS-245
95Sel-88
95SelArtP-88
95SelCer-44
95SelCerMG-44
95SP-197
95Spo-92
95SpoArtP-92
95SPSil-197
95StaClu-31
95StaCluFDI-31
95StaCluMOP-31
95StaCluSTWS-31
95StaCluVR-21
95Stu-59
95Sum-83
95SumNthD-83
95Top-365
95TopCyb-193
95Ult-336
95UltGolM-336
95UppDec-154
95UppDecED-154
95UppDecEDG-154
95UppDecSE-176
95UppDecSEG-176
95Zen-25
96Baz-94
96Bow-13
96Cir-90
96CirRav-90
96ColCho-735
96ColChoGS-735
96ColChoSS-735
96Don-45
96DonPreP-45
96EmoXL-125
96Fin-B173
96FinRef-B173
96Fla-176
96Fle-258
96FleRan-12
96FleTif-258
96Lea-188
96LeaLim-82
96LeaLimG-82
96LeaPre-96
96LeaPreP-96
96LeaPrePB-188
96LeaPrePG-188
96LeaPrePS-188
96LeaSig-83
96LeaSigA-176
96LeaSigAG-176
96LeaSigAS-176
96LeaSigPPG-83
96LeaSigPPP-83
96MetUni-115
96MetUniP-115
96Pac-426
96PacPri-P137
96PacPriG-P137
96PanSti-237
96Pin-159
96Pin-227
96PinAfi-88
96PinAfiAP-88
96PinAfiFPP-88
96PinArtP-86
96PinArtP-127
96PinFoil-227
96PinSlu-16
96PinSta-86
96PinSta-127
96ProSta-100
96RanMot-6
96Sco-179
96ScoDugC-A100
96ScoDugCAP-A100
96ScoRef-19
96Sel-146
96SelArtP-146
96SelCer-80
96SelCerAP-80
96SelCerCB-80
96SelCerCR-80
96SelCerMB-80
96SelCerMG-80
96SelCerMR-80
96SP-179
96StaClu-40
96StaCluEPB-40
96StaCluEPG-40
96StaCluEPS-40
96StaCluMOP-40
95StaCluVRMC-21
96Sum-144
96SumAbo&B-144
96SumArtP-144
96SumFoi-144
96Top-379
96TopChr-152
96TopChrR-152
96TopGal-81
96TopGalPPI-81
96TopLas-28
96Ult-423
96UltGolM-423
96UppDec-469
96Zen-32
96ZenArtP-32
97Bow-228
97BowBes-42
97BowBesAR-42
97BowBesR-42
97BowInt-228
97Cir-184
97CirRav-184
97ColCho-242
97ColChoBS-11
97ColChoBSGS-11
97Don-62
97DonEli-74
97DonEliGS-74
97DonLim-194
97DonLimLE-194
97DonPre-100
97DonPreCttC-100
97DonPreP-62
97DonPrePGold-62
97Fin-105
97Fin-270
97FinEmb-105
97FinEmbR-105
97FinRef-105
97FinRef-270
97FlaSho-A61
97FlaSho-B61
97FlaSho-C61
97FlaShoLC-61
97FlaShoLC-B61
97FlaShoLC-C61
97FlaShoLCM-A61
97FlaShoLCM-B61
97FlaShoLCM-C61
97Fle-229
97FleTif-229
97FleZon-12
97Lea-257
97LeaFraM-257
97LeaFraMDC-257
97MetUni-166
97NewPin-93
97NewPinAP-93
97NewPinMC-93
97NewPinPP-93
97Pac-207
97PacLigB-207
97PacPri-70
97PacPriLB-70
97PacPriP-70
97PacPriSL-SL7B
97PacSil-207
97PinCer-19
97PinCerMBlu-19
97PinCerMG-19
97PinCerMR-19
97PinCerR-19
97PinIns-50
97PinInsCE-50
97PinInsDE-50
97PinTotCPB-19
97PinTotCPG-19
97PinTotCPR-19
97PinX-P-72
97PinX-PMoS-72
97PinX-PSfF-13
97PinX-PSfFU-13
97Sco-175
97Sco-516
97ScoHobR-516
97ScoPreS-175
97ScoRan-9
97ScoRanPl-9
97ScoRanPr-9
97ScoResC-516
97ScoShoS-175
97ScoShoS-516
97ScoShoSAP-175
97ScoShoSAP-516
97Sel-41
97SelArtP-41
97SelRegG-41
97SP-173
97SpoIll-162
97SpoIllEE-162
97StaClu-225
97StaCluMat-225
97StaCluMOP-225
97Stu-24
97StuPrePG-24
97StuPrePS-24
97Top-393
97TopChr-136
97TopChrR-136
97TopGal-63
97TopGalPPI-63
97Ult-138
97UltGolME-138
97UltPlaME-138
97UppDec-210
97UppDecP-29

Palmer, Denzil

76CliPilT-25

Palmer, Donald

87BufBisP-28

Palmer, Doug

85VisOakT-2
86OrlTwiP-15
87OrlTwiP-17
88NewBriRSP-892

Palmer, Jim

66OPC-126
66Top-126
66TopVen-126
67CokCapO-5
67DexPre-159
67OPC-152

67Top-152
67Top-475
68CokCapO-5
68Top-575
69Top-573
70DayDaiNM-82
70OPC-68
70OPC-449
70Ori-9
70Top-68
70Top-449
71Kel-60
71MilDud-21
71MLBOffS-306
71OPC-67
71OPC-197
71OPC-570
71Ori-11
71Top-67
71Top-197
71Top-570
71TopCoi-90
71TopTat-23
72Kel-13A
72Kel-13B
72MilBra-263
72OPC-92
72OPC-270
72Top-92
72Top-270
73Kel2D-17
73LinPor-12
73OPC-160
73OPC-341
73OriJohP-22A
73OriJohP-22B
73Top-160
73Top-341
73TopCanL-38
73TopCom-13
73TopPin-13
74Kel-6
74OPC-40
74OPC-206
74Top-40
74Top-206
74TopDecE-45
74TopPuz-8
74TopSta-128
75Hos-126
75OPC-335
75SSP42-5
75SSPPuzB-19
75Top-335
76CraDis-44
76Hos-56
76HosTwi-56
76Kel-37
76OPC-200
76OPC-202
76OPC-450
76OriEngCL-3
76SSP-380
76Top-200
76Top-202
76Top-450
77BurCheD-42
77Hos-1
77OPC-5
77OPC-80
77PepGloD-20
77RCColC-49
77Spo-2615
77Top-5
77Top-600
77TopCloS-36
78Hos-116
78OPC-5
78OPC-179
78PapGinD-31
78Pep-36
78RCColC-45
78TasDis-2
78Top-160
78Top-205
78WifBalD-57
79Hos-11
79Kel-5
79OPC-174
79Top-340
80BurKinPHR-7
80Kel-15
80OPC-310
80PerHaloFP-206
80Top-590
80TopSup-4
81Don-353
81Don-473
81Fle-169
81FleStiC-124
81Kel-2
81OPC-210
81Ori6F-25
81PerCreC-28
81Top-210
81TopScr-50
81TopSti-39
81TopSupN-9
82Don-231
82Fle-175
82FleSta-143
82Kel-42
82OPC-80
82OPC-81
82Top-80
82Top-81
82TopSti-146
83Don-4
83Don-77
83Fle-69
83FleSta-145
83FleSti-200
83Kel-39
83OPC-299
83OPC-328
83OriPos-19
83Top-21
83Top-490
83Top-491
83TopFol-1
83TopGloS-19
83TopSti-23
83TopSti-175
83TopStiB-5
84Don-576
84DonCha-35
84Fle-16
84FleSti-102
84Nes792-715
84Nes792-717
84Nes792-750
84OCoandSI-157
84OPC-194
84OriEng-10
84OriTeal-20
84RalPur-23
84Top-715
84Top-717
84Top-750
84TopCer-23
84TopGaloC-8
84TopRubD-31
84TopSti-21
84TopSti-211
84TopTif-715
84TopTif-717
84TopTif-750
86OriGreT-3
86SpoDecG-58
86TCMSupS-33
87K-M-17
89SweBasG-105
90AGFA-17
90BasWit-33
90PerGreM-85
90TopMag-14
91OriCro-349
92KelAll-3
93ActPacA-127
93ActPacA2-61G
93FroRowP-1
93FroRowP-2
93FroRowP-3
93FroRowP-4
93FroRowP-5
93OriCroASU-2
93UppDecS-18
94NabAllA-2

Palmer, Ken
76BatRouCT-17

Palmer, Lowell
70OPC-252
70Top-252
71OPC-554
71Top-554
72Top-746
77ColCliT-18A
77ColCliT-18B
89PacSenL-174
89T/MSenL-86

Palmer, Mickey
82ForMyeRT-8

Palmer, Mike
81QuaCitCT-33

Palmieri, John
82ReaPhiT-5

Palmquist, Ed
60DarFar-7
90DodTar-604

Paluk, Brian
96YakBeaTI-47

Paluk, Jeff
94YakBeaC-11
94YakBeaF-3843
95SanBerSTI-14
96SanBerSB-20

Palumbo, Richard
92SalLakTSP-21

Palva, Nelson
80VenLeaS-150

Palyan, Vince
89EveGiaS-23
90CliGiaB-26
90CliGiaP-2564

Palys, Stan (Stanley F.)
58RedEnq-29
58Top-126

Pancoski, Tracey
88FreSunCLC-7
88FreSunP-1240

Panetta, Mario
83QuaCitCT-4

Paniagua, Jose
94Bow-32
94Cla-169
94ClaTriF-T49
94WesPalBEC-20
94WesPalBEF-35
96Bow-152
96FleUpd-U150
96FleUpdTC-U150
96HarSenB-21
96Ult-507
96UltGolM-507
97ColCho-19
97Don-165
97DonPreP-165
97DonPrePGold-165
97Pac-349
97PacLigB-349
97PacSil-349
97Pin-173
97PinArtP-173
97PinMusC-173
97StaClu-296
97StaCluMOP-296
97UppDec-239

Panick, Frank
77SalLakCGC-19

Pankovits, Jim (James F.)
77CocAstT-16
80TucTorT-19
81TucTorT-17
82HawIsIT-4
83TucTorT-16
84TucTorC-61
85AstHouP-14
85AstMot-25
85Don-502
86AstMilL-15
86AstPol-1
86Don-450
86Fle-307
86Top-618
86TopTif-618
87AstMot-22
87AstPol-25
87Don-605
87Fle-64
87FleGlo-64
87Top-249
87TopTif-249
88AstMot-22
88AstPol-16
88StaLinAst-11
88Top-487
88TopBig-109
88TopTif-487
89BufBisC-18
89BufBisP-1664
89Fle-363
89FleGlo-363
89Sco-192
89Top-153
89TopTif-153
89UppDec-100
90CMC-269
90PawRedSC-18
90PawRedSDD-18
90PawRedSP-470
90ProAAAF-442
90TopTVRS-55
91LinDriAAA-363
91PacSenL-89
91PawRedSDD-15
91PawRedSLD-363
91PawRedSP-48
92NewBriRSF-449
92NewBriRSS-499
93NewBriRSF-1237
94NewBriRSF-665
95QuaCitRBTI-17
96QuaCitRB-1

Panther, Jim
93RanKee-31

Pantoja, Jhonny
94AbaYanF-1437
95NorNavTI-27

Papa, John
77FriOneYW-77
91OriCro-350

Papagellin, Donna
94TulDriTI-29
93TulDriTI-22

Papageorge, Greg
88VirGenS-17
89PenPilS-17

Papai, Al
50Bow-245

Papajohn, Mike
87LSUTigP-7

Paparella, Joe (Joseph J.)
55Bow-235

Paparesta, Nick
96WatIndTI-22

Pape, Ken (Kenneth Wayne)
75SpoIndC-7
77TucTorC-5
78SyrChiT-15
79SpoIndT-8
92TexLon-31
93RanKee-286

Pape, Lawrence
09ColChiE-224
12ColRedB-224
12ColTinT-224

Papi, Stan (Stanley Gerard)
78ExpPos-9
79OPC-344
79RedSoxTI-3
79Top-652
81Don-246
81Fle-480A
81Fle-480B
81Top-273
82Don-333
82Fle-280
82Top-423

Papish, Frank
48WhiSoxTI-21
49IndTeal-20

Papke, William
11TurRedT-64

Pappageorgas, Bob
77WauMetT-13

Pappalau, John
98CamPepP-60

Pappas, Erik
86PalSprAP-6
86PalSprAP-25
87PalSprP-23
88MidAngGS-14
89ChaKniTI-12
90CMC-92
90IowCubC-17
90IowCubP-321
90ProAAAF-628
90TopTVCu-55
90TriAllGP-AAA34
91Bow-432
91CubVinL-20
91ScoRoo-95T
92OmaRoyF-2964
92OmaRoyS-340
92StaClu-442
92TopDeb91-135
93Fla-125
93FleFinE-129
93Lea-535
93LouRedF-219
93TopTra-5T
94CarPol-14
94ColC-593
94ColChoGS-593
94ColChoSS-593
94Don-205
94Fin-287
94FinRef-287
94Fle-642
94Pac-599
94Sco-188
94ScoBoyoS-30
94ScoGolR-188
94StaClu-448
94StaCluFDI-448
94StaCluGR-448
94StaCluMOP-448
94StaCluT-323
94StaCluTFDI-323
94Top-234
94TopGol-234
94TopSpa-234
94Ult-270
94USPlaCR-4H
95ChaKniTI-21
96OklCit8B-15

Pappas, Milt
47Exh-172
58Top-457
59OriJayP-6
59Top-391
60Baz-5
60Lea-57
60OriJayP-5
60Top-12
60Top-399
60TopTat-42
60TopVen-12
61Pos-71A
61Pos-71B
61Top-48
61Top-295
61TopStaI-103
62Baz-28
62ExhStaB-29
62Jel-34
62Pos-34
62PosCan-34
62SalPlaC-98
62ShiPlaC-98
62Top-55
62Top-75
62TopStaI-7
62TopVen-55
62TopVen-75
63ExhStaB-51
63Fle-3
63Jel-65
63Pos-65
63SalMetC-43
63Top-358
64ChatheY-40
64OriJayP-8
64Top-45
64TopCoi-70
64TopGia-5
64TopSta-4
64TopTatI-59
64TopVen-45
65ChaTheY-41
65OPC-270
65Top-270
65TopEmbI-20
65TopTraI-61
66Baz-29
66Kah-25
66OPC-105
66Top-105
66TopRubI-75
66TopVen-105
67CokCapR-1
67DexPre-160
67Top-254
68AtlOilPBCC-33
68OPC-74
68Top-74
68TopVen-74
69MilBra-212

69MLBOffS-117
69OPC-79
69Top-79
69TopSta-8
69TopTeaP-2
70DayDaiNM-123
70MLBOffS-11
70Top-576
71MilDud-57
71MLBOffS-39
71OPC-441
71Top-441
72CubChi-5
72CubTeal-9
72MilBra-264
72OPC-208
72Top-208
73OPC-70
73Top-70
74OPC-640
74Top-640
78TCM60I-56
89PacLegI-204
89SweBasG-113
90SweBasG-107
91OriCro-351
91SweBasG-69
92UppDecS-26

Paquette, Craig
89MedAthB-22
90CMC-846
90ModA'sC-22
90ModA'sP-2222
91Bow-236
91HunStaTI-16
92Bow-94
92ClaFS7-138
92HunStaF-3957
92HunStaS-316
92OPC-473
92SkyAA F-135
92Top-473
92TopGol-473
92TopGolW-473
92TopMic-473
92UppDecML-122
93Bow-329
93ClaFS7-235
93FleFinE-261
93Lea-506
93SelRoo-57T
93SP-42
93TopTra-38T
94ColC-225
94ColChoGS-225
94ColChoSS-225
94Don-532
94Fle-272
94Pac-461
94Pin-328
94PinArtP-328
94PinMusC-328
94Sco-567
94ScoGolR-567
94StaClu-328
94StaCluFDI-328
94StaCluGR-328
94StaCluMOP-328
94TacTigF-3184
94Top-46
94TopGol-46
94TopSpa-46
94TriPla-7
94Ult-113
94UppDec-262
94UppDecED-262
94USPlaCR-5C
95AthMot-22
96ColCho-644
96ColChoGS-644
96ColChoSS-644
96Don-530
96DonPreP-530
96Fle-215
96FleTif-215
96OmaRoyB-22
96Pac-390
97Cir-191
97CirRav-191
97ColCho-132
97Don-253
97DonPreP-253
97DonPrePGold-253
97Fle-119
97FleTif-119
97MetUni-96
97PacPriGotD-GD50
97Pin-58
97PinArtP-58
97PinMusC-58
97RoyPol-17
97Top-417
97UppDec-393

Paquette, Darryl
78WauMetT-21

Paragin, Billy
92PulBraC-22
92PulBraF-3181
93DanBraC-18
93DanBraF-3621

Paramo, Paul
91GulCoaRSP-9

Parascand, Steve
87FayGenP-4
88FayGenP-1088

Pardo, Al
81MiaOriT-2
83RocRedWT-12
84ChaO'sT-7
85RocRedWT-2
86Don-489
86RocRedWP-15
86Top-279
86TopTif-279
88TidTidP-1594
89ScrRedBC-21
89ScrRedBP-711
90HagSunDGB-20
91OriCro-352

Pardo, Bed
89EugEmeB-8

Pardo, Larry
86DayBealP-21
87QuaCitAP-6
88QuaCitAGS-6
89QuaCitAB-12
89QuaCitAGS-24
90CMC-710
90PalSprAP-2575

Pardue, Roy
93DavLipB-23
94DavLipB-20
95DavLipB-18

Paredes, Carlos
96LanLugB-18

Paredes, German
91KanCouCC-24
91KanCouCP-2672

Paredes, Jesus
87JamExpP-2543
88RocExpLC-26
89RocExpLC-21
90CMC-71
90IndIndC-21

Paredes, Johnny
86JacExpT-2
87IndIndTI-20
88DonRoo-29
88IndIndC-11
88IndIndP-516
88TriAAC-3
89Don-570
89Fle-388
89FleGlo-388
89OPC-367
89ScoHot1R-27
89Top-367
89TopTif-367
89UppDec-477
90IndIndP-303
90ProAAAF-586
91LinDriAAA-595
91TolMudHLD-595
91TolMudHP-1941
92TolMudHF-1056
93LinVenB-190
93LinVenB-313
93TolMudHF-1660
94VenLinU-150
95LinVen-227

Paredes, Roberto
96HelBreTI-18

Parent, Eric
82WauTimF-11
83WauTimF-10
84GreHorT-16

Parent, Freddy (Frederick A.)
03BreE10-112
04FanCraAL-39
04RedSoxUP-11
08RosComP-16
09ColChiE-225A
09ColChiE-225B
09T206-280
10DomDisP-95
10SweCapPP-13
11S74Sil-7
11SpoLifCW-281
11SpoLifM-26
11T205-134
12ColRedB-225A
12ColRedB-225B
12ColTinT-225A
12ColTinT-225B
12ImpTobC-44
14PieStaT-47

Parent, Gerald
95HelBreTI-30
96BelSnaTI-28
96Exc-73
96OgdRapTI-27

Parent, Mark
82AmaGolST-10
83BeaGolGT-13
84BeaGolGT-8
85LasVegSC-105
86LasVegSP-12
88DonRoo-8
88FleUpd-125
88FleUpdG-125
88PadCok-27
88PadSmo-22
88TopTra-80T
88TopTraT-80T
89Don-420
89FleUpd-125
89PadCok-11
89Sco-576
89Top-617
89TopTif-617
89UppDec-492
90Don-229
90Fle-164
90FleCan-164
90Lea-497
90OPC-749
90PadCok-13
90PadMag-7
90PubSti-55
90Sco-119
90Top-749
90TopTif-749
90UppDec-569
90VenSti-385
91Don-506
91Fle-538
91OPC-358
91Sco-213
91Top-358
91TopDesS-358
91TopMic-358
91TopTif-358
91UppDec-470
92RocRedWF-1942
92RocRedWS-462
92StaClu-623
92StaCluECN-623
92TriA AAS-462
93RanKee-287
93RocRedWF-244
94StaCluT-349
94StaCluTFDI-349
95DonTopotO-323
95PirFil-24
96Fle-325
96FleTif-325
96FleUpd-U36
96FleUpdTC-U36
96LeaSigEA-150
96Sco-173
96Ult-350
96UltGolM-350
96UppDec-329
97Ult-465
97UltGolME-465
97UltPlaME-465

Parese, Billy
89St.CatBJP-2082
90MyrBeaBJP-2786
91DunBluJC-18
91DunBluJP-216

Parfrey, Brian
82RedPioT-26

Parham, Bill
89BakDodCLC-191

Paris, Juan
85SpoIndC-18
86ChaRaiP-20
87GreHorP-12
88WinHavRSS-19
89LynRedSS-17
90NewBriRSB-17
90NewBriRSP-1331
90NewBriRSS-14
91LinDriAA-467
91NewBriRSLD-467
91NewBriRSP-366
92PawRedSF-936
92PawRedSS-361
97DunDonPPS-16

Paris, Kelly (Kelly Jay)
77St.PetCT-1
78St.PetCT-19
80ArkTraT-22
82LouRedE-22
84Don-384
84Fle-476
84HawIsIC-123
84Nes792-113
84Top-113
84TopTif-113
85IntLeaAT-28
85RocRedWT-8
86RocRedWP-16
88VanCanC-12
89Fle-506
89FleGlo-506
89UppDec-192
89VanCanC-11
89VanCanP-594
91OriCro-353

Paris, Porfino
85DomLeaS-93

Paris, Zacarias
82TucTorT-14
83ColAstT-17
86VenGulP-20

Parish, Jack
76CliPiIT-26

Parisi, Michael
94ElmPioF-3471
95KanCouCTI-18
96BreCouMB-24
94ElmPioC-15

Parisotto, Barry
89GreFalDSP-20
90BakDodCLC-242
92SalLakTSP-5
93HigDesMC-15
93HigDesMF-38

Parisse, Tony (Louis Peter)
77TCMTheWY-25

Park, Chan Ho
94ActPac-3
94ActPac-56
94ActPac2G-2G
94Bow-98
94BowBes-B25
94BowBesR-B25
94Cla-20
94ClaCreotC-C16
94DodPol-14
94ExtBas-293
94ExtBasRS-15
94Fin-426
94FinJum-426
94FinRef-426
94Fla-181
94FlaWavotF-A8
94FleUpd-151
94LeaLimR-78
94Pin-527
94PinArtP-527
94PinMusC-527
94SanAntMF-2466
94ScoRoo-RT136
94ScoRooGR-RT136
94Sel-177
94SelRooS-RS13
94SP-13
94SPDieC-13
94SpoRoo-122
94SpoRooAP-122
94SpoRooRS-TR13
94StaClu-521
94StaCluFDI-521
94StaCluGR-521
94StaCluMOP-521
94TopTra-70T
94Ult-520
94UltAllR-9
94UltAllRJ-9
94UppDec-520
94UppDecED-520
95ActPacF-4
95ARuFalLS-11
95Bow-432
95BowBes-B4
95BowBesR-B4
95ColCho-232
95ColChoGS-232
95ColChoSE-25
95ColChoSEGS-25
95ColChoSESS-25
95ColChoSS-232
95DodPol-20
95Don-175
95DonPreP-175
95Fle-546
95LeaGolR-12
95PacGolCDC-11
95Sco-582
95ScoGolR-582
95ScoPlaTS-582
95Sel-6
95SelArtP-6
95Spo-146
95SpoArtP-146
95Stu-152
95Sum21C-TC6
95Ult-398
95UltGolM-398
95UppDecSE-36
95UppDecSEG-36
96Bow-136
96BowBes-74
96BowBesAR-74
96BowBesR-74
96Cir-145
96CirRav-145
96ColCho-29
96ColCho-658
96ColChoGS-658
96ColChoSS-658
96DodMot-18
96Don-481
96DonPreP-481
96EmoXL-214
96Fin-S296
96FinRef-S296
96Fle-444
96FleDod-15
96FleTif-444
96Lea-18
96LeaPre-135
96LeaPreP-135
96LeaPrePB-18
96LeaPrePG-18
96LeaPrePS-18
96LeaSig-118
96LeaSigPPG-118
96LeaSigPPP-118
96Pin-386
96PinAfi-156
96PinAfi-188
96PinAfiAP-156
96PinAfiAP-188
96PinFoil-386
96Sco-514
96Sel-179
96SelArtP-179
96SelCer-120
96SelCerAP-120
96SelCerCB-120
96SelCerCR-120
96SelCerMB-120
96SelCerMG-120
96SelCerMR-120
96SP-107
96Spo-128
96SpoArtP-128
96StaClu-416
96StaCluMOP-416
96Stu-15
96StuPrePB-15
96StuPrePG-15
96StuPrePS-15
96Sum-176

96SumAbo&B-176
96SumArtP-176
96SumFoi-176
96Ult-499
96UltGolM-499
96UppDec-94
96UppDecFSP-FS16
96Zen-124
96ZenArtP-124
97Cir-278
97CirRav-278
97ColCho-367
97Don-194
97DonEli-115
97DonEliGS-115
97DonEliTotC-19
97DonEliTotCDC-19
97DonLim-53
97DonLimLE-53
97DonPre-33
97DonPreCttC-33
97DonPreP-194
97DonPrePGold-194
97DonTea-113
97DonTeaSPE-113
97FlaSho-A161
97FlaSho-B161
97FlaSho-C161
97FlaShoLC-161
97FlaShoLC-B161
97FlaShoLC-C161
97FlaShoLCM-A161
97FlaShoLCM-B161
97FlaShoLCM-C161
97Fle-370
97FleTif-370
97Lea-48
97LeaFraM-48
97LeaFraMDC-48
97Pac-338
97PacLigB-338
97PacSil-338
97Pin-31
97PinArtP-31
97PinIns-92
97PinInsCE-92
97PinInsDE-92
97PinMusC-31
97PinPasttM-23
97Sco-148
97ScoDod-5
97ScoDodPl-5
97ScoDodPr-5
97ScoPreS-148
97ScoShoS-148
97ScoShoSAP-148
97Sel-7
97SelArtP-7
97SelRegG-7
97StaClu-69
97StaCluMOP-69
97Stu-64
97StuPrePG-64
97StuPrePS-64
97Top-338
97Ult-222
97UltGolME-222
97UltPlaME-222
97UppDec-194
97UppDec-397
Park, Ji Chol
96WesOahCHWB-39
Parke, Jim
77ChaPatT-11
Parker, Ace (Clarence McKay)
79DiaGre-327
Parker, Allan
95TenVolW-9
96LakElsSB-20
Parker, Billy (William David)
72OPC-213
72Top-213
73OPC-354
73Top-354
75SyrChiTI-16
Parker, Billy Ray
76CedRapGT-18
Parker, Bob
85OscAstTI-21
86ColAstP-21
Parker, Brad
89AncBucTI-12
92ClaFS7-178
92MadMusC-17
92MadMusF-1245
Parker, Carrol
86EriCarP-22
87SavCarP-14
Parker, Christian
96VerExpB-21
Parker, Clay
86WauTimP-18
88ColCliC-2
88ColCliP-7
88ColCliP-309
88Fle-649
88FleGlo-649
89ColCliC-4
89ColCliP-9
89ColCliP-751
89DonBasB-164
89DonRoo-52
89ScoRoo-94T
89TopTra-94T
89TopTraT-94T
89YanScoNW-30
90Don-363
90Fle-451
90FleCan-451
90LSUTigGM-11
90OPC-511
90PubSti-543
90Sco-316
90Sco100RS-17
90ScoYouSI-8
90Top-511
90TopTif-511
90TopTVY-15
90VenSti-386
91Don-605
91Fle-346
91OPC-183
91TacTigP-2302
91Top-183
91TopDesS-183
91TopMic-183
91TopTif-183
92Bow-366
92CalCanS-67
92MarMot-25
92StaClu-631
92StaCluECN-631
92Ult-435
92YanWIZ8-141
93StaClu-45
93StaCluFDI-45
93StaCluMOP-45
Parker, Corey
92NiaFalRC-13
92NiaFalRF-3334
93FayGenC-19
93FayGenF-137
94FayGenC-19
94FayGenF-2157
Parker, Darrell
75WatRoyT-22
76WatRoyT-20
77JacSunT-17
Parker, Dave (David Gene)
74OPC-252
74Top-252
74TopSta-86
75OPC-29
75Pir-4
75SSPPuzB-20
75Top-29
76CraDis-45
76Hos-133
76Kel-15
76OPC-185
76SSP-572
76Top-185
76VenLeaS-180
77BurCheD-187
77Kel-19
77OPC-242
77PirPosP-20
77RCColC-50
77Spo-4208
77Top-270
78Hos-135
78Kel-52
78OPC-1
78OPC-60
78RCColC-35
78Top-201
78Top-560
78WifBalD-58
79Hos-53
79Kel-21
79OPC-223
79Top-1
79Top-430
79TopCom-29
80BurKinPHR-19
80Kel-23
80OPC-163
80Top-310
80TopSup-17
81AllGamPI-158
81CokTeaS-117
81Don-136
81Dra-4
81Fle-360
81FleStiC-26
81Kel-13
81MSAMinD-25
81OPC-178
81PerAll-6
81PerCreC-13
81Squ-10
81Top-640
81TopScr-59
81TopSti-210
81TopSti-257
81TopSupN-10
82Don-12
82Don-95
82FBIDis-14
82Fle-489
82Fle-638
82FleSta-71
82FleSta-241
82K-M-34
82Kel-48
82OPC-40
82OPC-41
82OPC-343
82Top-40
82Top-41
82Top-343
82TopSti-87
82TopSti-127
83AllGamPI-156
83Don-473
83Fle-315
83FleSta-146
83FleSti-72
83OPC-205
83PerCreC-11
83PerCreCG-11
83Top-205
83TopFol-3
83TopSti-280
84AllGamPI-64
84Don-288
84DonCha-57
84Fle-258
84FleUpd-89
84FunFooP-80
84Nes792-701
84Nes792-775
84OPC-31
84RedBor-39
84RedEnq-12
84Top-701
84Top-775
84TopSti-130
84TopTif-701
84TopTif-775
84TopTra-90T
84TopTraT-90T
85AllGamPI-155
85Don-62
85DonActA-35
85DonHig-13
85Dra-22
85Fle-544
85Lea-169
85OPC-175
85RedYea-11
85Top-175
85TopSti-47
85TopSup-42
85TopTif-175
86BasStaB-83
86Don-203
86DonAll-24
86Dra-4
86Fle-184
86Fle-640
86FleAll-6
86FleLeaL-30
86FleLimE-33
86FleMin-39
86FleStiC-84
86GenMilB-5F
86Lea-135
86OPC-287
86QuaGra-9
86RedTexG-39
86SevCoi-C4
86SevCoi-E4
86SevCoi-S4
86SevCoi-W4
86Spo-23
86Spo-58
86Spo-181
86Spo-183
86Top-595
86Top3-D-18
86TopGloS-13
86TopMinL-41
86TopSti-135
86TopSup-41
86TopTat-9
86TopTif-595
86Woo-27
87BoaandB-20
87ClaGam-33
87Don-388
87DonAll-34
87DonOpeD-198
87Dra-18
87Fle-208
87Fle-639
87FleAwaW-27
87FleGlo-208
87FleGlo-639
87FleMin-80
87FleSlu-29
87FleStiC-88
87FleWaxBC-C10
87GenMilB-6G
87KayB-23
87Lea-79
87OPC-352
87RalPur-7
87RedFolSB-90
87RedKah-39
87Spo-35
87Spo-117
87SpoTeaP-4
87StuPan-4
87Top-600
87Top-691
87TopCoi-38
87TopGloS-17
87TopMinL-6
87TopSti-145
87TopTif-600
87TopTif-691
88A'sMot-5
88Don-388
88DonBasB-190
88DonTeaBA-NEW
88Fle-243
88FleGlo-243
88FleMin-47
88FleUpd-55
88FleUpdG-55
88KayB-21
88OPC-315
88PanSti-277
88PanSti-284
88Sco-17
88ScoGlo-17
88ScoRoo-50T
88ScoRooG-50T
88Spo-101
88StaLinAs-12
88StaLinRe-15
88Top-315
88TopBig-242
88TopGloS-34
88TopMinL-48
88TopSti-136
88TopStiB-19
88TopTif-315
88TopTra-81T
88TopTraT-81T
88TopUKM-55
88TopUKMT-55
89A'sMot-4
89Bow-202
89BowTif-202
89Don-150
89DonBasB-336
89Fle-19
89FleGlo-19
89OPC-199
89PanSti-424
89Sco-108
89Spo-49
89Top-475
89TopAme2C-23
89TopBasT-116
89TopBatL-13
89TopBig-144
89TopSti-169
89TopTif-475
89UppDec-605
90Bow-398
90BowTif-398
90BreMilB-18
90BrePol-39
90ClaBlu-95
90ClaYel-T10
90Don-328
90DonBesA-51
90DonLeaS-33
90Fle-18
90FleCan-18
90FleUpd-106
90FleWorS-9
90FleWorS-10
90KayB-22
90Lea-190
90OPC-45
90OPCBoxB-J
90PubSti-312
90Sco-135
90ScoRoo-12T
90Top-45
90TopAmeA-6
90TopBatL-13
90TopBig-227
90TopHilHM-21
90TopSti-179
90TopTif-45
90TopTra-86T
90TopTraT-86T
90TopWaxBC-J
90UppDec-192
90UppDec-766
90USPlaCA-12S
90VenSti-387
90WinDis-1
91AngSmo-4
91Bow-199
91Bow-375
91ClaGam-34
91DenHol-5
91Don-6
91Don-142
91Don-390
91DonSupD-6
91Fle-593
91FleUpd-10
91Lea-334
91OPC-235
91OPCBoxB-L
91OPCPre-94
91PanFreS-210
91PanSti-171
91Sco-484
91Sco100S-44
91StaClu-75
91StaPinB-35
91StuPre-3
91Top-235
91TopCraJI-11
91TopDesS-235
91TopMic-235
91TopTif-235
91TopTra-89T
91TopTraT-89T
91TopWaxBC-L
91UltUpd-10
91UppDec-48
91UppDec-274
91UppDec-733
91UppDecSS-SS14
91Woo-16
92UppDec-522
93ActPacA-165
94BreMilB-65
94CarLeaA-DJ25

95MClAmb-13
Parker, Don
92AriWilP-13
92KinMetF-1543
Parker, Harry
73LinPor-121
74OPC-106
74Top-106
75OPC-214
75SSP18-1
75Top-214
91MetWIZ-309
Parker, James
87ChaLooB-4
89GeoColC-22
90GeoColC-23
Parker, Jarrod
89PulBraP-1906
90ColMetGS-4
90ColMetPPI-2
90PitMetP-7
Parker, Joel
81BurBeeT-27
Parker, Mark
80WicAerT-4
82lowCubT-21
Parker, Michael
95PitMetTI-33
Parker, Mike
89IdaFalBP-2035
Parker, Olen
87ClePhiP-5
Parker, Richard
85BenPhiC-18
87ClePhiP-1
88ReaPhiP-878
89BenBucL-14
89EasLeaAP-25
89ReaPhiB-9
89ReaPhiP-660
89ReaPhiS-19
90ClaYel-T72
90FleUpd-63
90Lea-398
90PalSprACLC-210
90PalSprAP-2581
90PhoFirP-26
90ProAAAF-52
90ScoRoo-77T
90TopTra-87T
90TopTraT-87T
90UppDec-732
91Fle-269
91GiaPacGaE-26
91OPC-218
91PhoFirP-73
91Sco-58
91Sco100RS-11
91Top-218
91TopDeb90-121
91TopDesS-218
91TopMic-218
91TopTif-218
92Sco-601
92StaClu-769
92StaCluECN-769
92TucTorF-500
92TucTorS-616
93AstMot-13
93StaCluAs-27
93TucTorF-3075
94NorTidF-2934
94Pac-272
95DodMot-27
Parker, Rob
87ColAstP-10
Parker, Salty (Francis James)
60Top-469
67Ast-23
73OPC-421
73Top-421A
73Top-421B
74OPC-276
74Top-276
76CedRapGT-19
87BelMarTI-28
Parker, Stacy
89ButCopKSP-1
91BenBucC-21
91BenBucP-3706
91ClePhiC-23
91ClePhiP-1634
Parker, Steve
87PeoChiP-24
88PitCubP-1369
89WinSpiS-13
90CMC-80
90lowCubC-5
90lowCubP-316
90ProAAAF-623
90TopTVCu-56
Parker, Tim
90GenCubP-3049
90GenCubS-18
90ProAaA-174
91ChaKniLD-137
91ChaKniP-1686
91LinDriAA-137
92ChaKniS-163
92ClaFS7-62
92SkyAA F-75
Parker, Wes (Maurice W.)
64Top-456
65DodJayP-10
65DodTeal-13
65Top-344
66OPC-134
66Top-134
66TopVen-134
67CokCapD-13
67CokCapDA-13
67DexPre-161
67Top-218
68Top-533
69MilBra-213
69MLBOffS-151
69Top-493A
69Top-493B
70DayDaiNM-127
70MLBOffS-55
70OPC-5
70Top-5
71DodTic-13
71MLBOffS-111
71OPC-430
71Top-430
71TopCoi-121
71TopGreM-30
71TopSup-14
71TopTat-66
72Kel-17
72MilBra-265
72OPC-265
72Top-265
73OPC-151
73Top-151
81TCM60I-365
84OCoandSI-189
88DodSmo-10
90DodTar-605
Parkins, Rob
86WinHavRSP-19
93CalCanF-1164
94SanBerSC-14
94SanBerSF-2755
Parkinson, Eric
89PriPirS-14
90AugPirP-2460
90CMC-726
91SalBucC-17
91SalBucP-947
92SalBucC-4
92SalBucF-62
93CarMudF-2052
93CarMudTI-8
Parkinson, Frank J.
22E120-203
22W572-74
23WilChoV-118
Parks, Art
90DodTar-1048
Parks, Danny
81PawRedST-6
Parks, Derek
87KenTwiP-19
88BasAmeAAB-12
88OrlTwiB-1
88SouLeaAJ-12
89OrlTwiB-19
89OrlTwiP-1350
90Bow-422
90BowTif-422
90ClaUpd-T40
90CMC-566
90PorBeaC-14
90PorBeaP-181
90ProAAAF-251
91Cla/Bes-159
91LinDriAA-492
91OrlSunRLD-492
91OrlSunRP-1852
92PorBeaF-2670
92PorBeaS-416
92SkyAAAF-190
93Don-237
93Pin-267
93PorBeaF-2386
93Sco-245
93StaClu-74
93StaCluFDI-74
93StaCluMOP-74
93TriAAAGF-47
94ColC-378
94ColChoGS-378
94ColChoSS-378
94Don-477
94Fle-216
94Pac-364
94ScoRoo-RT97
94ScoRooGR-RT97
94SpoRoo-79
94SpoRooAP-79
94Top-649
94TopGol-649
94TopSpa-649
94Ult-393
95Sco-375
95ScoGolR-375
95ScoPlaTS-375
95Top-151
Parks, Jack
55Top-23
55TopDouH-67
Parks, Jeff
85SpoIndC-19
Parmalee, LeRoy
36R31PasP-19
Parmelee, Roy (LeRoy Earl)
33Gou-239
34DiaMatCSB-147
34BatR31-94
35DiaMatCS3T1-118
36DiaMatCS3T2-19
36WorWidGV-20
91ConTSN-85
94ConTSN-1062
94ConTSNB-1062
Parmenter, Gary
86lowCubP-21
87lowCubTI-7
88PitCubP-1378
Parmenter, Ross
96OgdRapTI-9
Parnell, Mark
89AppFoxP-875
90BasCitRS-18
90StaFS7-44
91Cla/Bes-301
91LinDriAA-410
91MemChiLD-410
91MemChiP-648
92MemChiF-2416
92MemChiS-440
92SkyAA F-186
Parnell, Mel
47PM1StaP1-158
48RedSoxTI-19
50Bow-1
51FisBakL-23
51R42SmaS-77
51TopRedB-10
52BerRos-49
52Bow-241
52DixLid-14
52DixPre-14
52StaCalL-71A
52StaCalS-85B
52Top-30
53BowC-66
53DixLid-14
53DixPre-14
53NorBreL-20
53RedMan-AL25
53RedSoxFNSMS-3
53RedSoxTI-23
53Top-19
54DixLid-12
54RedMan-AL8
54Top-40
55RobGouS-28
55RobGouW-28
55Top-140
55TopDouH-119
56TopHocF-A18
57Top-313
63MilSau-5
79DiaGre-242
79TCM50-58
82GSGalAG-21
83TopRep5-30
83YanYealT-6
90PacLeg-98
91SweBasG-118
91TopArc1-19
92ActPacA-21
92BazQua5A-14
93TedWil-4
93UppDecAH-104
94TopArc1-40
94TopArc1G-40
Paronto, Chad
96BluOriB-22
Parotte, Frisco
95GreBatTI-19
96GreBatB-18
Parra, Franklin
91ButCopKSP-20
92ButCopKSP-13
92GasRanC-17
93ChaRaiF-1922
94ChaRanF-2505
95TulDriTI-18
Parra, Jose
90KisDodD-20
91GreFalDSP-6
92BakDodCLC-19
93LimRocDWB-56
93SanAntMF-3002
94AlbDukF-841
94Bow-42
95Sum-170
95SumNthD-170
95TopTra-58T
96ChaRivTI-9626
96Don-380
96DonPreP-380
96Fle-171
96FleTif-171
Parra, Julio
95VerBeaDTI-19
Parra, Luis
92GulCoaYF-3790
Parrett, Jeff
86ExpPos-11
86ExpProPa-25
86FleUpd-88
87ExpPos-19
87IndIndTI-17
88Don-406
88ExpPos-16
88FleUpd-102
88FleUpdG-102
88OPC-144
88Top-588
88TopTif-588
89Bow-390
89BowTif-390
89Don-334
89DonBasB-296
89DonTra-55
89Fle-389
89FleGlo-389
89FleUpd-112
89OPC-176
89PhiTas-27
89Sco-377
89ScoRoo-33T
89ScoYouSI-18
89Top-176
89TopSti-73
89TopTif-176
89TopTra-95T
89TopTraT-95T
89UppDec-398
89UppDec-741
90Bow-149
90BowTif-149
90Don-369
90Fle-570
90FleCan-570
90Lea-210
90OPC-439
90PanSti-312
90PhiTas-25
90PubSti-248
90Top-439
90TopSti-119
90TopTif-439
90UppDec-92
90VenSti-388
91BraDubP-22
91BraSubS-29
91Don-660
91Fle-699
91OPC-56
91RicBraBC-32
91Sco-565
91StaClu-544
91Top-56
91TopDesS-56
91TopMic-56
91TopTif-56
91UppDec-417
92AthMot-16
92Lea-520
92StaClu-834
93Don-241
93Fle-297
93FleFinE-39
93PacSpa-434
93Pin-431
93RocUSPC-7S
93RocUSPC-12D
93Sco-180
93Sel-396
93StaClu-99
93StaClu-414
93StaCluFDI-99
93StaCluFDI-414
93StaCluMOP-99
93StaCluMOP-414
93StaCluRoc-9
93Top-209
93TopGol-209
93TopInaM-209
93TopMic-209
93TopTra-46T
93Ult-261
93Ult-355
93UppDec-311
93UppDec-529
93UppDecGold-311
93UppDecGold-529
94Fle-449
96Don-542
96DonPreP-542
96FleUpd-U193
96FleUpdTC-U193
Parrill, Marty
78RocRedWT-13
Parris, Clyde
58MonRoyF-16
Parris, Steve
88CapCodPPaLP-43
89BatCliP-1923
90BatCliP-3065
91ClePhiC-7
91ClePhiP-1618
92ReaPhiF-572
92ReaPhiS-538
93ScrRedBTI-20
95CarMudF-152
96ColCho-267
96ColChoGS-267
96ColChoSS-267
96Don-59
96DonPreP-59
96Fle-531
96FleTif-531
96LeaSigEA-151
96StaClu-76
96StaCluMOP-76
Parrish, Lance M.
77EvaTriT-22
78Top-708
79Top-469
80Kel-54
80OPC-110
80Top-196
81AllGamPI-42
81CokTeaS-55
81Don-366
81Fle-467
81OPC-8
81TigDetN-90
81Top-392
81TopScr-14
81TopSti-73

82Don-281
82Fle-276
82FleSta-152
82OPC-214
82Top-535
82TopSti-188
83AllGamPl-42
83Don-407
83DonActA-50
83Fle-337
83FleSta-147
83FleSti-255
83Kel-40
83OPC-285
83PerCreC-30
83PerCreCG-30
83Tig-21
83Top-4
83Top-285
83TopGloS-27
83TopSti-63
83TopSti-193
83TopSti-194
84AllGamPl-131
84Don-15
84Don-15A
84Don-49
84DonActAS-34
84Fle-88
84Fle-637
84FunFooP-2
84Nes792-640
84NesDreT-8
84OPC-158
84TigFarJ-11
84TigWavP-28
84Top-640
84TopGloS-2
84TopRubD-14
84TopSti-265
84TopTif-640
85AllGamPl-42
85Don-49
85DonActA-53
85Dra-23
85Fle-19
85FleStaS-31
85Lea-41
85OPC-160
85SevCoi-C13
85SevCoi-D14
85TigCaiD-15
85TigWen-17
85Top-160
85Top-708
85TopGloA-20
85TopMin-160
85TopRubD-12
85TopSti-189
85TopSti-259
85TopSup-55
85TopTif-160
85TopTif-708
86Don-334
86Fle-234
86FleLeaL-31
86FleMin-49
86FleStiC-85
86GenMilB-1F
86Lea-201
86MSAJifPD-3
86OPC-147
86SevCoi-C12
86Spo-92
86SpoDecG-72
86TigCaiD-14
86Top-36
86Top-740
86TopGloS-8
86TopMinL-15
86TopSti-273
86TopTat-22
86TopTif-36
86TopTif-740
87BoaandB-19
87ClaGam-50
87Don-91
87DonAll-9
87DonOpeD-153
87DonP-9
87Fle-160
87FleAwaW-28
87FleGlo-160
87FleUpd-96
87FleUpdG-96
87Lea-107
87MSAIceTD-19
87MSAJifPD-13
87OPC-374
87PhiTas-13
87RedFolSB-36
87Spo-101
87Spo-154
87Top-613
87Top-791
87TopGloA-20
87TopGloS-58
87TopSti-149
87TopSti-269
87TopTif-613
87TopTif-791
87TopTra-94T
87TopTraT-94T
88Don-359
88DonBasB-184
88Fle-310
88FleGlo-310
88KayB-22
88Lea-130
88OPC-95
88PanSti-355
88PhiTas-18
88RedFolSB-65
88Sco-131
88ScoGlo-131
88Spo-143
88StaLinPh-12
88Top-95
88Top-669
88TopBig-45
88TopSti-123
88TopTif-95
88TopTif-669
89Bow-45
89BowTif-45
89Don-278
89DonAll-55
89DonBasB-59
89Fle-578
89FleGlo-578
89FleUpd-15
89OPC-114
89Sco-95
89ScoRoo-36T
89Spo-59
89Top-470
89TopBig-250
89TopTif-470
89TopTra-96T
89TopTraT-96T
89UppDec-240
89UppDec-775
90AngSmo-13
90Bow-295
90BowTif-295
90Don-213
90DonBesA-59
90DonLeaS-41
90Fle-141
90FleCan-141
90Lea-195
90MLBBasB-94
90OPC-575
90PanSti-38
90PubSti-376
90RedFolSB-73
90Sco-35
90Top-575
90TopBig-323
90TopSti-170
90TopTif-575
90UppDec-674
90USPlaCA-2C
90VenSti-389
91AngSmo-5
91Bow-188
91Bow-374
91CadEllD-40
91Don-135
91Don-388
91Fle-321
91Lea-368
91MooSna-20
91OPC-210
91PanFreS-179
91PanSti-133
91Sco-37
91StaClu-166
91Stu-29
91Top-210
91TopDesS-210
91TopMic-210
91TopTif-210
91Ult-51
91UppDec-552
91UppDecSS-SS11
92Don-166
92Fle-66
92Lea-269
92OPC-360
92PanSti-4
92Pin-105
92Sco-298
92StaClu-94
92Stu-149
92Top-360
92TopGol-360
92TopGolW-360
92TopMic-360
92TriPla-169
92TriPla-234
92Ult-28
92UppDec-431
93AlbDukF-1464
93DodPol-19
93Don-85
93Fle-679
93Sco-587
93Sel-388
93StaClu-252
93StaCluFD-252
93StaCluMOP-252
93Top-609
93TopGol-609
93TopInaM-609
93TopMic-609
93UppDec-117
93UppDecGold-117
95ColCho-377
95ColChoGS-377
95ColChoSS-377
95DonTopotO-177
95Fle-487
95Sco-550
95ScoGolR-550
95ScoPlaTS-550
95StaClu-604
95StaCluMOP-604
95StaCluSTWS-604
96ColCho-349
96ColChoGS-349
96ColChoSS-349
96UppDec-104

Parrish, Larry A.

76ExpRed-24
76Hos-126
76OPC-141
76SSP-326
76Top-141
77BurCheD-161
77ExpPos-24
77OPC-72
77Top-526
78ExpPos-10
78OPC-153
78Top-294
79OPC-357
79Top-677
80ExpPos-22
80OPC-182
80Top-345
80TopSup-53
81AllGamPl-124
81Don-89
81Fle-146
81FleStiC-69
81OPC-15
81OPCPos-4
81Top-15
81TopScr-89
81TopSti-183
82Don-466
82Fle-200
82FleSta-34
82OPC-353
82OPCPos-15
82Top-445
82TopSti-64
82TopTra-86T
83Don-467
83Fle-574
83FleSta-148
83FleSti-168
83OPC-2
83RanAffF-15
83Top-776
83TopSti-120
84AllGamPl-155
84Don-21
84Don-21A
84Don-422
84DonActAS-42
84Fle-424
84Nes792-169
84OPC-169
84RanJarP-15
84Top-169
84TopRubD-26
84TopSti-354
84TopTif-169
85AllGamPl-67
85Don-300
85DonActA-29
85Fle-564
85FleStaS-38
85Lea-96
85OPC-203
85RanPer-15
85Top-548
85TopRubD-26
85TopSti-346
85TopTif-548
86Don-178
86Fle-569
86FleStiC-86
86Lea-110
86OPC-238
86RanLit-4
86RanPer-15
86Top-238
86TopSti-240
86TopTat-19
86TopTif-238
87ClaGam-25
87Don-469
87DonHig-10
87DonOpeD-173
87Fle-134
87FleGamW-33
87FleGlo-134
87FleLeaL-34
87FleMin-81
87FleRecS-29
87FleStiC-89
87GenMilB-3H
87Lea-209
87RanMot-5
87RanSmo-18
87RedFolSB-104
87Spo-174
87SpoTeaP-1
87StuPan-26
87Top-629
87TopSti-234
87TopTif-629
88CheBoy-9
88Don-347
88DonAll-21
88DonBasB-334
88Fle-476
88FleGlo-476
88FleMin-57
88FleRecS-28
88FleStiC-68
88FleTeaL-25
88FleUpd-7
88FleUpdG-7
88KinDis-21
88Lea-119
88OPC-226
88PanSti-205
88RanMot-5
88RanSmo-14
88RedFolSB-66
88Sco-191
88ScoGlo-191
88ScoRoo-65T
88ScoRooG-65T
88Spo-49
88StaLinRa-12
88Top-490
88TopSti-243
88TopTif-490
88TopUKM-56
88TopUKMT-56
89Fle-94
89FleGlo-94
89Sco-495
89Top-354
89TopTif-354
89UppDec-36
91UppDecS-23
92Nab-17
92NiaFalRC-27
92NiaFalRF-3342
93ExpDonM-17
93NiaFalRF-3406
93RanKee-288
94RanAllP-15

Parrot, Pirate

93FunPacM-2
93PirNatl-24
93TriPla-164
94MasMan-12
94PirQui-20

Parrot, Steve

83ElPasDT-16

Parrott, Mike

77RocRedWM-4
79OPC-300
79Top-576
80Top-443
81MarPol-10
81Top-187
82Don-226
82Top-358
83OmaRoyT-7
84OmaRoyT-11
85OklCit8T-12
86OklCit8P-17
88RocExpLC-27
89RocExpLC-22
91OriCro-354
91WesPalBEP-1246
92HarSenF-476
92HarSenS-300
95ChaKniTI-3
96ChaKniB-3

Parrotte, Brian

89BilMusP-2050

Parry, Bob

86AncGlaPTI-28
88MadMusP-17
89ModA'sC-31
89ModA'sCLC-286
90ModA'sC-23
90ModA'sP-2228

Parsons, Bill

59DarFar-17
71BreTeal-10
72Kel-5
72OPC-281
72Top-281
73OPC-231
73Top-231
74OPC-574
74Top-574
75OPC-613
75Top-613
94BreMilB-66

Parsons, Bob

78SalPirT-11

Parsons, Casey (Casey R.)

78PhoGiaC-20
79PhoGiaVNB-17
80PhoGiaVNB-13
81SpoIndT-26
82Fle-515
82SalLakCGT-15
85DomLeaS-91
85LouRedR-27
86LouRedTI-22
87BufBisP-9
88MemChiB-9
90MadMusB-25
90MadMusP-2283
90MidLeaASGS-26
91HunStaC-22
91HunStaLD-299
91HunStaP-1811
91HunStaTI-25
91LinDriAA-299
92HunStaF-3964
92HunStaS-324
93HunStaF-2097
94TacTigF-3190

Parsons, Charles

87OldJudN-395

Parsons, Jason

95BilRedTI-14

Parsons, Jeff
95PitMetTI-9
96PitMetB-17
Parsons, Scott
87LasVegSP-5
Parsons, Thomas
62Top-326
65Top-308
91MetWIZ-310
Parsons, William Raymond
75TulOil7-10
Partee, Roy (Roy Robert)
43RedSoxTI-19
46RedSoxTI-17
47TipTop-10
49Bow-149
49SomandK-10
60RawGloT-26
77TCMTheWY-21
79DiaGre-231
83TCMPla1943-20
Partin, Billy
89SumBraP-1089
Partley, Calvin
74CedRapAT-9
Partlow, Roy
87NegLeaPD-18
Partrick, Dave
88BenBucL-11
89QuaCitAB-24
89QuaCitAGS-9
90BoiHawP-3327
90PalSprACLC-212
90PalSprAP-2591
91PalSprAP-2030
92BoiHawC-6
92BoiHawF-3621
Partridge, Glenn
77BurBeeT-21
Partridge, Jay
90DodTar-606
Pascarella, Andy
79NewCoPT-24
Paschal, Ben
91ConTSN-107
Paschall, Bill
77JacSunT-18
80OmaRoyP-20
80Top-667
81OmaRoyT-11
Pascual, Camilo
83IdaFalAT-10
Pascual, Camilo Alberto
47Exh-173
55Top-84
55TopDouH-103
56Top-98
57Top-211
58SenJayP-7
58Top-219
59SenTealW-12
59Top-291
59Top-316A
59Top-316B
59Top-413
60Baz-14
60Lea-4
60SenJayP-11
60Top-483
60Top-569
60TopTat-43
61NuSco-411
61Pos-99A
61Pos-99B
61Top-235
61TopDicG-12
61TopStaI-183
61TwiCloD-20
61TwiJayP-10
61TwiPetM-23
61TwiUniMC-11
62Jel-91
62Pos-91
62PosCan-91
62SalPlaC-78
62ShiPlaC-78
62Top-59
62Top-230
62TopBuc-66
62TopStaI-78
62TopVen-59
63BasMagM-64
63Baz-13
63ExhStaB-52
63Jel-9
63Pos-9
63SalMetC-36
63Top-8
63Top-10
63Top-220
63TopStil-31
63TwiJayP-8
64Baz-13
64Top-2
64Top-4
64Top-6
64Top-500
64TopCoi-76
64TopCoi-137
64TopGia-32
64TopSta-92
64TopStaU-54
64TopTatI-60
64TopVen-2
64TopVen-4
64TopVen-6
64TwiJayP-9
65OPC-11
65OPC-255
65Top-11
65Top-255
65TopTraI-23
66Top-305
66TopVen-305
66TwiFaiG-11
67CokCapS-5
67OPC-71
67SenTeal-10
67Top-71
67TopVen-243
68SenTeal-10
68Top-395
69MilBra-214
69MLBOffS-107
69SenTeal-12
69SenTeal8-16
69Top-513
69TopDecI-33
69TopSta-240
69TopSup-31
69TopTeaP-23
69TraSta-27
70OPC-254
70Top-254
76VenLeaS-76
78TCM60I-32
78TwiFri-16
79TwiFriP-20
80VenLeaS-2
90DodTar-607
94TopArc1-255
94TopArc1G-255
Pascual, Carlos
80VenLeaS-1
Pascual, Jorge
76VenLeaS-2
89SalDodTI-21
90MarPhiP-3203
90MiaMirIS-19
90MiaMirIS-20
Pashnick, Larry
81EvaTriT-5
83Don-233
83EvaTriT-8
83Fle-338
83Tig-22
84Don-394
84MinTwiP-22
84TwiTeal-14
Pasillas, Andy
77AppFoxT-18
78KnoKnoST-17
79KnoKnoST-20
80GleFalWSBT-15
80GleFalWSCT-6
81GleFalWST-10
Paskert, Dode (George H.)
08RosComP-122
09ColChiE-226A
09ColChiE-226B
09RamT20-92
09T206-281
10CouT21-52
10CouT21-206
10CouT21-207
10CouT21-310
10DomDisP-96
10RedCroT-61
10RedCroT-147
10RedCroT-234
10SweCapPP-130A
10SweCapPP-130B
11S74Sil-103
11SpoLifCW-282
11SpoLifM-238
11T205-135
11TurRedT-112
12ColRedB-226A
12ColRedB-226B
12ColTinT-226A
12ColTinT-226B
12HasTriFT-17
12T207-147
14PieStaT-48
15SpoNewM-135
16BF2FP-91
16ColE13-130
16FleBreD-73
16SpoNewM-136
17HolBreD-76
19W514-55
20NatCarE-73
23WilChoV-119
93ConTSN-922
Paskievitch, Tom
91EriSaiC-21
91EriSaiP-4067
92WatDiaC-13
92WatDiaF-2141
93RanCucQC-22
93RanCucQF-832
94KanCouCF-159
94KanCouCTI-21
94PorSeaDTI-25
Pasley, Kevin (Kevin P.)
74AlbDukTI-69
74AlbDukTI-12
75IntLeaASB-21
75PacCoaLAB-21
77Top-476
78Top-702
80SyrChiT-3
80SyrChiTI-16
81SyrChiT-8
82BirBarT-17
90DodTar-608
Pasqua, Dan
84NasSouTI-16
85ColCliP-17
85ColCliT-21
85Don-637
85FleUpd-86
86ColCliP-15
86ColCliP-17
86Don-417
86Fle-114
86KayB-22
86Lea-195
86Top-259
86TopGloS-20
86TopTif-259
86YanTCM-35
87ClaGam-13
87Don-474
87DonOpeD-244
87Fle-108
87FleGlo-108
87FleMin-79
87OPC-74
87Spo-143
87SpoTeaP-7
87Top-74
87TopSti-297
87TopTif-74
88Don-463
88DonBasB-137
88Fle-217
88FleGlo-217
88FleUpd-18
88FleUpdG-18
88OPC-207
88PanSti-159
88Sco-196
88ScoGlo-196
88ScoRoo-56T
88ScoRooG-56T
88StaLinWS-14
88Top-691
88TopBig-164
88TopTif-691
88TopTra-82T
88TopTraT-82T
88WhiSoxC-19
89Bow-67
89BowTif-67
89Don-294
89DonBasB-123
89Fle-507
89FleGlo-507
89OPC-31
89PanSti-313
89Sco-338
89Top-558
89TopBig-44
89TopSti-301
89TopTif-558
89TVSpoM-116
89UppDec-204
89WhiSoxC-19
90Bow-313
90BowTif-313
90Don-176
90Fle-544
90FleCan-544
90Lea-274
90OPC-446
90PubSti-398
90Sco-306
90Top-446
90TopBig-144
90TopSti-306
90TopSti-309
90TopTif-446
90UppDec-286
90VenSti-390
90WhiSoxC-19
91Bow-361
91Don-103
91Fle-131
91Lea-428
91OPC-364
91Sco-85
91StaClu-214
91Top-364
91TopDesS-364
91TopMic-364
91TopTif-364
91Ult-79
91UppDec-605
91WhiSoxK-44
92Don-142
92Fle-93
92Lea-369
92OPC-107
92Pin-227
92Sco-237
92StaClu-794
92StaCluNC-794
92Top-107
92TopGol-107
92TopGolW-107
92TopMic-107
92Ult-339
92UppDec-281
92WhiSoxK-44
92YanWIZ8-142
93Don-491
93Fle-587
93Lea-20
93PacSpa-394
93Pin-354
93Sco-210
93StaClu-94
93StaCluFDI-94
93StaCluMOP-94
93StaCluWS-11
93Top-204
93TopGol-204
93TopInaM-204
93TopMic-204
93UppDec-649
93UppDecGold-649
93WhiSoxK-22
94ColC-617
94ColChoGS-617
94ColChoSS-617
94Fle-91
94Pac-139
94StaClu-375
94StaCluFDI-375
94StaCluGR-375
94StaCluMOP-375
94StaCluT-149
94StaCluTFDI-149
94TopGol-792
94WhiSoxK-24
95Sco-188
95ScoGolR-188
95ScoPlaTS-188
Pasquale, Jeff
91HamRedC-8
91HamRedP-4037
Pasquali, Jeff
83EriCarT-13
Pasqualicchio, Mike
95HelBreTI-31
96StoPorB-4
Passalacqua, Ricky
76WatRoyT-21
Passeau, Claude W.
39CubTeal-19
39ExhSal-51
41CubTeal-19
43CubTeal-19
76ChiGre-15
93ConTSN-720
95ConTSN-1407
95ConTSN-1418
Passero, Joe
45CenFlo-20
Passini, Brian
96HelBreTI-19
Passmore, Jay
76BurBeeT-25
77BurBeeT-22
Pastore, Frank
78IndIndTI-23
80RedEnq-35
80Top-677
81Fle-204
81OPC-1
81Top-499
82Don-122
82Fle-80
82FleSta-13
82RedCok-17
82Top-128
83Don-62
83Fle-599
83OPC-119
83RedYea-35
83Top-658
84Don-164
84Fle-477
84Nes792-87
84OPC-87
84RedEnq-23
84Top-87
84TopTif-87
85Don-550
85Fle-545
85OPC-292
85Top-727
85TopTif-727
86Fle-185
86Top-314
86TopTif-314
86TopTra-85T
86TopTraT-85T
87OklCit8P-4
87Top-576
87TopTif-576
89PAORelT-4
Pastorius, James
03WilCarE-25
09AmeCarE-87
09T206-282
10StaCarE-23
10W555-54
11SpoLifCW-283
90DodTar-1047
Pastornicky, Cliff
81ChaRoyT-16
82ChaRoyT-21
83OmaRoyT-17
84OmaRoyT-21
94RocRoyC-30
94RocRoyF-583
Pastors, Greg
82BufBisT-5
83LynPirT-16
Pastrovich, Steve
80AppFoxT-13
80GleFalWSBT-1
80GleFalWSCT-16
81AppFoxT-8
82AppFoxF-11
83GleFalWST-18
Paszek, John

52LavPro-31
Patchett, Hal
45CenFlo-21
Patchin, Steve
75WatDodT-15
76OmaRoyTT-19
76VenLeaS-130
80EvaTriT-22
Pate, Bobby (Robert Wayne)
81Don-545
81OPC-136
81Top-479
83TucTorT-21
87BurExpP-1089
Patek, Freddie Joe
69PirJacitB-9
69Top-219
70OPC-94
70Top-94
71MLBOffS-425
71OPC-626
71Top-626
72MilBra-266
72Top-531
73LinPor-89
73OPC-334
73Top-334
74GreHeroBP-5
74OPC-88
74Top-88
74TopSta-186
75Hos-32
75HosTwi-32
75OPC-48
75Top-48
76OPC-167
76SSP-170
76Top-167
77BurCheD-67
77Hos-109
77Kel-36
77OPC-244
77RCColC-51
77Spo-5409
77Top-422
78Hos-48
78OPC-4
78OPC-91
78RCColC-63
78Roy-17
78SSP270-234
78Top-204
78Top-274
79Hos-46
79Kel-36
79OPC-273
79Top-525
80OPC-356
80Top-705
81Don-170
81Fle-283
81LonBeaPT-21
81Top-311
82Don-241
82Fle-471
82Top-602
86RoyGreT-3
92UppDecS-20
93RoySta2-9
94StoPorC-29
94StoPorF-1710
Patel, Manish
93BelMarC-21
93BelMarF-3220
94AppFoxC-15
94AppFoxF-1062
96PorCitRB-22
Patellis, Anthony
96BilMusTI-25
Patenaude, Alain
85MiaHur-11
Paterson, Jeff
92CalLeaACL-27
Paterson, Pat
86NegLeaF-106
Patino, Benny
85CloHSS-31
Patino, Leonardo
96BoiHawB-22
Patino, Victor
76VenLeaS-63
Patkin, Max
76OmaRoyTT-20
89BulDurOS-4
95ActPacF-80
95ActPacF-81
95ActPacF-82
Patof, Patof
72Dia-145
Patornicky, Cliff
86WatIndP-19
Patrick, Bronswell
89MadMusS-18
90CMC-666
90MadMusB-22
90ModA'sC-24
90ModA'sCLC-155
90ModA'sP-2211
91ModA'sC-11
91ModA'sP-3085
92HunStaF-3948
92HunStaS-317
93TacTigF-3027
94HunStaF-1327
94TacTigF-3172
95TusTorTI-19
96TusTorB-19
Patrick, Dan
96SelEnF-16
Patrick, Hisel
59DarFar-18
Patrick, James
49W725AngTI-24
85CloHSS-32
Patrick, Lynn
40WheM4-1A
40WheM4-1B
Patrick, Otis
87BelMarL-27
87BelMarTI-17
Patrick, Ron
77AshTouT-16
Patrick, Tim
90VerBeaDS-21
90YakBeaTI-14
91VerBeaDC-10
91VerBeaDP-771
Patrizi, Mike
91KinMetC-4
91KinMetP-3816
92ColMetC-4
92ColMetF-300
92ColMetPI-23
93CapCitBC-16
93CapCitBF-463
Pattee, Harry (Harry Ernest)
09T206-283
Patten, Bill
75AndRanT-39
Patten, Case
04FanCraAL-40
08RosComP-82
Patten, Eric
90HelBreSP-18
Patterson, Bob
83BeaGolGT-7
84LasVegSC-221
85LasVegSC-117
86HawIsIP-19
87DonOpeD-166
87SpoTeaP-18
88BufBisC-7
88BufBisP-1467
88Fle-337
88FleGlo-337
88Top-522
88TopTif-522
89BlaYNPRWLU-30
89BufBisP-1684
90Bow-168
90BowTif-168
90FleUpd-49
90TopTra-88T
90TopTraT-88T
91Don-345
91Fle-45
91OPC-479
91Sco-636
91StaClu-594
91Top-479
91TopDesS-479
91TopMic-479
91TopTif-479
92Don-590
92Fle-562
92OPC-263
92PirNatl-18
92Sco-548
92StaClu-876
92StaCluECN-876
92Top-263
92TopGol-263
92TopGolW-263
92TopMic-263
92Ult-558
93Don-174
93Fle-118
93RanKee-421
93SelRoo-120T
93Top-299
93TopGol-299
93TopInaM-299
93TopMic-299
93UppDec-412
93UppDecGold-412
94AngLAT-23
94AngMot-15
94Don-218
94Pac-624
94Sco-292
94ScoGolR-292
95AngMot-15
95Fle-232
96Fle-54
96FleTif-54
96LeaSigEA-152
Patterson, Casey
95PitMetTI-30
96PitMetB-18
Patterson, Danny
91GulCoaRSP-11
92GasRanC-24
92GasRanF-2253
93ChaRanC-18
93ChaRanF-1939
94TulDriTI-18
95TulDriTI-19
96OklCit8B-16
97Bow-213
97BowInt-213
97Fle-504
97FleTif-504
97NewPin-174
97NewPinAP-174
97NewPinMC-174
97NewPinPP-174
97PinCer-110
97PinCerMBlu-110
97PinCerMG-110
97PinCerMR-110
97PinCerR-110
97PinTotCPB-110
97PinTotCPG-110
97PinTotCPR-110
97Sco-320
97ScoPreS-320
97ScoShoS-320
97Sel-107
97SelArtP-107
97SelRegG-107
Patterson, Daryl
68OPC-113
68TigDetFPB-19
68Top-113
68TopVen-113
69OPC-101
69Top-101
70Top-592
71MLBOffS-402
71OPC-481
71Top-481
88TigDom-19
Patterson, Dave
86EveGiaPC-20
87CliGiaP-3
88CalLeaACLC-1
88SanJosGCLC-126
88SanJosGP-111
90ProAaA-73
90ShrCapP-1453
90ShrCapS-18
90TexLeaAGS-22
91Cla/Bes-253
91LinDriAA-315
91ShrCapLD-315
91ShrCapP-1831
92PhoFirF-2829
92PhoFirS-392
Patterson, Dave (David Glenn)
77LodDodT-11
79AlbDukT-6
80AlbDukT-10
80Top-679
81AlbDukT-2
82TacTigT-8
86EveGiaC-12
89ShrCapP-1843
90DodTar-609
Patterson, Gil
76VenLeaS-57
77Top-472
92MadMusC-27
92MadMusF-1253
92YanWIZ7-125
93MadMusC-28
93MadMusF-1839
94WesMicWC-27
94WesMicWF-2313
Patterson, Glenn
87GasRanP-2
88GasRanP-1021
Patterson, Greg
87LSUTigP-8
88WinSpiS-14
89GenCubP-1882
90LSUTigGM-14
Patterson, Ham
09PC7HHB-33
Patterson, Jake
94EliTwiC-16
94EliTwiF-3741
95Exc-87
95ForWayWTI-20
95MidLeaA-38
96Exc-79
Patterson, Jarrod
94KinMetC-15
94KinMetF-3832
96Bow-326
96Exc-190
96StLucMTI-20
Patterson, Jeff
89MarPhiS-23
90ClePhiS-17
91SpaPhiC-11
91SpaPhiP-896
92ClePhiC-7
92ReaPhiF-573
93ScrRedBF-2544
93ScrRedBTI-21
94ScrRedBF-921
95ColCliP-20
95ColCliTI-20
Patterson, Jim
91FreStaBS-9
92EriSaiC-28
92EriSaiF-1619
93HigDesMC-16
93HigDesMF-39
94SanBerSC-15
94SanBerSF-2756
Patterson, Jimmy
52Whe-23A
52Whe-23B
Patterson, John
97Bow-297
97BowChr-205
97BowChrI-205
97BowChrIR-205
97BowChrR-205
97BowInt-297
97Top-477
Patterson, John Allen
90Bes-202
90ProAaA-155
90SanJosGB-9
90SanJosGCLC-33
90SanJosGP-2017
90SanJosGS-17
91Cla/Bes-314
91LinDriAA-316
91ShrCapLD-316
91ShrCapP-1832
92Bow-67
92DonRoo-89
92PhoFirF-2830
92PhoFirS-379
92Pin-532
92ProFS7-345
92Ult-593
92UppDec-778
93Don-193
93Fle-535
93Lea-160
93Pin-413
93PinRooTP-5
93Sco-279
93ScoBoyoS-13
93Top-573
93TopGol-573
93TopInaM-573
93TopMic-573
93Toy-32
93USPlaCR-4C
94Fle-697
94GiaAMC-16
94GiaMot-11
94GiaUSPC-2C
94GiaUSPC-8H
94ScoRoo-RT96
94ScoRooGR-RT96
94Sel-189
94SpoRoo-118
94SpoRooAP-118
94StaClu-381
94StaCluFDI-381
94StaCluGR-381
94StaCluMOP-381
94StaCluT-18
94StaCluTFDI-18
94Ult-590
95ColCho-252
95ColChoGS-252
95ColChoSS-252
95Don-319
95DonPreP-319
95DonTopotO-354
95Fle-585
95GiaMot-9
95Lea-165
95Pac-382
95Sco-151
95ScoGolR-151
95ScoPlaTS-151
95StaClu-42
95StaCluFDI-42
95StaCluMOP-42
95StaCluSTWS-42
95Top-574
95TopCyb-348
95Ult-445
95UltGolM-445
96ColCho-721
96ColChoGS-721
96ColChoSS-721
96Fle-593
96FleTif-593
Patterson, Ken
82ChaRoyT-16
84IdaFalATI-20
86Ft.LauYP-17
87Ft.LauYP-30
88VanCanC-6
88VanCanP-757
89DonRoo-37
89Fle-508
89FleGlo-508
89ScoHot1R-61
89ScoRoo-97T
89Top-434
89TopTif-434
89WhiSoxC-20
90Don-371
90Fle-545
90FleCan-545
90OPC-156
90Sco-207
90Sco100RS-89
90ScoYouSI-27
90Top-156
90TopTif-156
90WhiSoxC-20
91Don-522
91Fle-132
91OPC-326
91Top-326
91TopDesS-326
91TopMic-326
91TopTif-326
91UppDec-283
91WhiSoxK-34
92CubMar-34
92Don-457
92Fle-94
92Lea-509
92OPC-784
92PeoChiTI-19

92Sco-347
92StaClu-289
92Top-784
92TopGol-784
92TopGolW-784
92TopMic-784
92Ult-472
92UppDec-440
93AngMot-24
93Don-742
93Fle-381
93StaClu-162
93StaCluFDI-162
93StaCluMOP-162
94Fle-66
94Ult-25
Patterson, Larry
80LynSaiT-2
81SpoIndT-23
82HolMilT-12
83NasAngT-11
Patterson, Michael L.
77ModA'sC-11
79OgdA'sT-24
79WatA'sT-14
80WesHavWCT-15
82ColCliP-14
82ColCliT-20
83ColCliT-22
92YanWIZ8-143
Patterson, Pat
78LauLonABS-18
Patterson, Reggie
80GleFalWSBT-9
80GleFalWSCT-18
81EdmTraRR-22
82EdmTraT-15
82Top-599
83IowCubT-7
84IowCubT-31
86Fle-376
Patterson, Rick
77WauMetT-14
88UtiBluSP-26
89SouBenWSGS-2
90SouBenWSB-24
90SouBenWSGS-27
91SarWhiSC-27
91SarWhiSP-1129
92SarWhiSCB-27
92SarWhiSF-224
94IowCubF-1290
Patterson, Rob
92MedHatBJSP-25
93MedHatBJF-3733
93MedHatBJSP-21
Patterson, Rod
77ModA'sC-13
Patterson, Roy
03BreE10-113
07WhiSoxGWH-9
11SpoLifCW-284
Patterson, Scott
80AndBraT-9
81DurBulT-22
82ColCliP-11
82ColCliT-19
83NasSouTI-15
84ColCliP-18
84ColCliT-14
85AlbYanT-10
86ColCliP-16
86ColCliP-18
Patterson, Shane
90ButCopKSP-14
Patterson, Steve
91PocPioP-3779
91PocPioSP-15
Patterson, Tony
89CarNewE-14
Pattin, Jon
90CliGiaB-28
90CliGiaP-2552
91SanJosGC-3
91SanJosGP-14
Pattin, Marty
69PilPos-18
69Top-563
70BreMcD-24
70BreMil-19
70OPC-31
70SunPin-14
70Top-31
71BreTeal-11
71MLBOffS-447
71OPC-579
71Top-579
72OPC-144
72Top-144
73LinPor-28
73OPC-415
73Top-415
74OPC-583
74Top-583
74TopSta-187
75OPC-413
75Top-413
76OPC-492
76SSP-162
76Top-492
77Top-658
78Roy-18
78SSP270-231
78Top-218
79Top-129
80Top-26
81Don-343
81Fle-37
81Top-389
83Pil69G-28
94BreMilB-67
Pattison, James
36GouWidPPR-D26
90DodTar-1050
Patton, Eric
89HelBreSP-20
Patton, Greg
95MicBatCTI-18
96SarRedSB-25
Patton, Jack
88BakDodCLC-266
89RenSilSCLC-263
90RenSilSCLC-292
Patton, Jeff
84PriWilPT-17
Patton, Melvin
51BerRos-B18
Patton, Owen
87OldJudN-396
Patton, Scott
92FroRowDP-16
92HigSchPLS-12
93HicCraC-18
93HicCraF-1293
93StaCluM-16
Patton, Tom
91OriCro-355
Patzke, Jeff
92HigSchPLS-26
92MedHatBJSP-23
93MedHatBJF-3746
93MedHatBJSP-12
93StaCluM-104
93Top-529
93TopGol-529
93TopInaM-529
93TopMic-529
94HagSunC-18
94HagSunF-2740
95DunBluJTI-17
96Exc-117
96KnoSmoB-19
Paugh, Rick
94WelPirC-15
94WelPirF-3492
96LynHilB-17
Paul VI, Pope
90RinPosYMP-9
Paul, Andy
94StoPorC-18
94StoPorF-1692
96El PasDB-23
Paul, Corey
87BelMarTI-31
89BelMarL-27
90SalSpuP-2733
Paul, Gabe
82OhiHaloF-51
Paul, Josh
96HicCraB-14
97Bow-97
97BowInt-97
Paul, Kortney
94EugEmeC-15
94EugEmeF-3716
Paul, Mike
69Top-537
70Top-582
71MLBOffS-381
71OPC-454
71Top-454
72MilBra-267
72Top-577
73OPC-58
73Top-58
74OPC-399
74Top-399
85VanCanC-208
86VanCanP-21
88A'sMot-27
89MarMot-27
90MarMot-27
93RanKee-32
Paul, Ron
81TCM60I-381
Paul, Stu
93SalBucC-30
Paula, Carlos (Carlos C.)
55Top-97
56Top-4
56TopPin-58
58UniOil-6
79TCM50-205
Paulin, Randy
95SpoIndTI-17
Paulino, Arturo
96WesMicWB-20
Paulino, Dario
91IdaFalBP-4338
91IdaFalBSP-23
92MacBraC-6
92ProFS7-198
Paulino, Elvin
87PeoChiP-17
87WytCubP-10
88PeoChiTI-24
89PeoChiTI-24
90CarLeaA-48
90WinSpiTI-24
91ChaKniLD-138
91ChaKniP-1697
91LinDriAA-138
92Bow-95
92IowCubS-214
92ProFS7-201
92SkyAAAF-103
93LimRocDWB-90
Paulino, Jose
77ForLauYS-12
96SouOreTI-24
Paulino, Luis
87HagSunP-14
88HagSunS-15
89FreKeyS-20
Paulino, Nelson
92PulBraC-26
92PulBraF-3186
93MacBraC-18
93MacBraF-1411
94DurBulC-14
94DurBulF-336
94DurBulTI-15
Paulino, Richard
92MacBraF-281
Paulino, Victor
84SavCarT-19
Paulis, George
89WatDiaS-28
Pauls, Matt
95ChaRivTI-3
Paulsen, Axel
88AllandGN-33
88KimN18-35
Paulsen, Troy
88AlaGolTI-13
91ClePhiC-20
91ClePhiP-1631
91FloStaLAP-FSL8
92ProFS7-300
92ReaPhiF-582
92ReaPhiS-539
92SkyAA F-234
Paustian, Mike
85CloHSS-33
Pautt, Juan
83PawRedST-23
84PawRedST-12
Pavano, Carl
95MicBatCTI-19
95MidLeaA-39
96Bow-259
96TreThuB-12
97Bow-161
97BowBes-120
97BowBesAR-120
97BowBesR-120
97BowCerBIA-CA60
97BowCerGIA-CA60
97BowChr-159
97BowChrI-159
97BowChrIR-159
97BowChrR-159
97BowInt-161
97Top-493
97TopSta-109
97TopStaAM-109
Paveloff, David
91KanCouCC-8
91KanCouCP-2656
91KanCouCTI-15
92FreKeyC-3
92FreKeyF-1802
93FreKeyC-20
93FreKeyF-1025
94BowBayF-2412
94OriPro-78
Pavicich, Paul
94EliTwiC-17
94EliTwiF-3728
95ForWayWTI-9
96FtMyeMB-15
Pavlas, Dave
86WinSpiP-18
87PitCubP-15
88TexLeaAGS-21
88TulDriTI-23
89OklCit8C-8
89OklCit8P-1529
90CMC-81
90IowCubC-6
90IowCubP-317
90ProAAAF-624
90TopTVCu-57
91IowCubLD-213
91IowCubP-1058
91LinDriAAA-213
91Sco-378
91TopDeb90-122
93LinVenB-55
95ColCliP-21
95ColCliTI-21
96ColCliB-24
Pavletich, Don (Donald S.)
59RedEnq-18
59Top-494
62RedEnq-25
62Top-594
63RedEnq-24
63RedFreBC-18
63RedJayP-9
65RedEnq-21
65Top-472
66OPC-196
66Top-196
66TopVen-196
67CokCapR-9
67Kah-28
67Top-292
68OPC-108
68Top-108
68TopVen-108
69MilBra-215
69OPC-179
69Top-179
69TopFou-4
70OPC-504
70Top-504
71MLBOffS-326
71OPC-409
71Top-409
72OPC-359
72Top-359
81TCM60I-333
Pavlick, Greg
78TidTidT-18
79TidTidT-20
84JacMetT-10
86MetTCM-40
88MetColP-52
88MetKah-52
89MetColP-47
89MetKah-21
90MetColP-44
90MetKah-52
90TopTVM-5
91MetColP-42
91MetKah-52
96MetKah-26
Pavlik, John
84PriWilPT-9
Pavlik, Roger
87GasRanP-15
88GasRanP-1020
89ChaRanS-19
90ChaRanS-19
90TulDriTI-18
91LinDriAAA-315
91OklCit8LD-315
91OklCit8P-174
92DonRoo-90
92FleUpd-62
92OklCit8F-1914
92OklCit8S-317
93Don-113
93Fle-688
93Lea-550
93OklCit8F-1625
93RanKee-422
93Sco-325
93StaClu-193
93StaCluFDI-193
93StaCluMOP-193
93StaCluR-5
93Top-223
93TopGol-223
93TopInaM-223
93TopMic-223
93Ult-283
94ColC-226
94ColChoGS-226
94ColChoSS-226
94Don-527
94Fin-155
94FinRef-155
94Fle-315
94Pac-625
94Pin-469
94PinArtP-469
94PinMusC-469
94RanMagM-12
94Sco-365
94ScoGolR-365
94Sel-333
94StaClu-178
94StaCluFDI-178
94StaCluGR-178
94StaCluMOP-178
94StaCluT-263
94StaCluTFDI-263
94Top-22
94TopGol-22
94TopSpa-22
94TriPla-198
94Ult-131
94UppDec-418
94UppDecED-418
95Don-375
95DonPreP-375
95Fle-293
95Lea-20
95RanCra-27
95StaClu-120
95StaCluFDI-120
95StaCluMOP-120
95StaCluSTWS-120
95Top-436
95TopCyb-233
95Ult-112
95UltGolM-112
96Cir-91
96CirRav-91
96ColCho-738
96ColChoGS-738
96ColChoSS-738
96Don-143
96DonPreP-143
96EmoXL-126
96Fla-177
96Fle-259
96FleRan-13
96FleTif-259
96LeaSigA-177
96LeaSigAG-177
96LeaSigAS-177
96Pac-432
96RanMot-19
96Sco-461
96StaClu-306
96StaCluMOP-306
96Top-79

96Ult-138
96UltGolM-138
96UppDec-209
97Cir-18
97CirRav-18
97ColCho-486
97Don-109
97DonPreP-109
97DonPrePGold-109
97Fin-81
97FinRef-81
97Fle-230
97FleTif-230
97Lea-309
97LeaFraM-309
97LeaFraMDC-309
97MetUni-167
97Pac-208
97PacLigB-208
97PacSil-208
97Sco-161
97ScoPreS-161
97ScoRan-8
97ScoRanPl-8
97ScoRanPr-8
97ScoShoS-161
97ScoShoSAP-161
97SP-171
97StaClu-133
97StaCluMOP-133
97Top-43
97Ult-139
97UltGolME-139
97UltPlaME-139
97UppDec-208
Pavlovich, Tony
96BelSnaTI-29
Pawling, Eric
86CliGiaP-17
86TriTriC-193
Pawlowski, John
86PenWhiSP-19
87BirBarB-17
88BlaYNPRWL-123
88Don-457
88WhiSoxC-20
89VanCanC-7
89VanCanP-595
90CMC-637
90ProAAAF-165
90Sco-617
90VanCanC-10
90VanCanP-487
92EdmTraF-3538
92EdmTraS-164
Paxson, Jeff
94BelBreC-30
95BelBreTI-27
Paxson, Jeffrey
96BelSnaTI-30
Paxton, Darrin
90WicStaSGD-29
92AlbPolC-3
92AlbPolF-2302
93BurBeeC-16
93BurBeeF-153
94HigDesMC-1
94HigDesMF-2786
95HarSenTI-28
Paxton, Greg
90RenSilSCLC-282
Paxton, Mike
78Top-216
79OPC-54
79Top-122
80TacTigT-27
80Top-388
81ChaChaT-5
81Fle-401
Payne, Chad
90GeoColC-24
Payne, Fred (Frederick T.)
07TigACDPP-11
09T206-284
09WolNewDTPP-13
10ChiE-16
11MecDFT-39
11S74Sil-8
11SpoLifCW-285
11SpoLifM-27
11T205-136
12HasTriFT-22A
12HasTriFT-22B
Payne, Harley
90DodTar-610
Payne, Jeff
90HamRedB-25
Payne, Jim
79WauTimT-24
80QuaCitCT-18
81WisRapTT-17
Payne, Joe
50WorWidGV-15
Payne, Larry
76IndIndTI-2
77IndIndTI-7
78IndIndTI-13
Payne, Mike
80AndBraT-15
81DurBulT-23
82DurBulT-19
85RicBraT-6
87JacExpP-444
Payne, Stan
92SouOreAC-25
92SouOreAF-3415
Paynter, Billy
88WytCubP-1983
89PeoChiTI-13
90GenCubP-3040
90GenCubS-19
90PeoChiTI-5
Payton, Dave
87EriCarP-21
88SprCarB-15
89SprCarB-15
Payton, Jay
94PitMetC-1
94PitMetF-3536
94SigRooDP-28
94SigRooDPS-28
94StaCluDP-17
94StaCluDPFDI-17
95Bes-84
95Bes-107
95Bes-AU3
95BinMetTI-24
95Bow-240
95BowBes-B62
95BowBesR-B62
95BowGolF-240
95Exc-235
95ExcFirYP-8
95SPML-9
95SPML-95
95SPMLA-20
95SPMLDtS-DS20
95Top-443
95UppDecML-195
96BesAutSA-52
96Bow-241
96BowBes-111
96BowBesAR-111
96BowBesR-111
96Exc-191
96ExcAll-8
96ExcCli-7
96NorTidB-22
96Top-350
96TopChr-141
96TopChrR-141
97Bow-151
97BowCerBIA-CA61
97BowCerGIA-CA61
97BowInt-151
97ColCho-475
97Sel-137
97SelArtP-137
97SelRegG-137
97Top-342
95UppDecMLFS-195
Payton, Ray
88MidLeaAGS-49
88SouBenWSGS-6
89SarWhiSS-17
90SarWhiSS-18
Paz, Richard
96BluOriB-23
Pazik, Mike
73SyrChiTI-22
74TacTwiC-8
75TacTwiK-14
76OPC-597
76SSP-212
76TacTwiDQ-15
76Top-597
77Top-643
80GleFalWSBT-24
80GleFalWSCT-21
82AppFoxF-30
88ChaKniTI-14
89FreKeyS-26
90FreKeyTI-2
Peacock, Johnny (John Gaston)
39PlaBal-16
40PlaBal-34
42RedSoxTI-19
43RedSoxTI-20
79DiaGre-304
90DodTar-611
Pearce, Chris
94LSUTig-13
Pearce, Jeff
90SpoIndSP-17
91ChaRaiC-23
91ChaRaiP-109
92WatDiaC-23
92WatDiaF-2153
93RanCucQC-23
93RanCucQF-844
96LanJetB-22
Pearce, Jim
55Top-170
Pearce, Steve
77CedRapGT-24
Pearlman, David
93St.CatBJC-19
93St.CatBJF-3974
Pearn, Joe
87PorChaRP-27
88GasRanP-1006
Pearsall, J.J.
95YakBeaTI-25
96SavSanB-17
Pearse, Steve
88RocExpLC-28
Pearsey, Les
81HolMilT-19
82SpoIndT-18
Pearson, Albie (Albert G.)
47Exh-174
58SenJayP-8
58Top-317
59Top-4
59TopVen-4
60Top-241
61AngJayP-9
61Top-288
62AngJayP-8
62Jel-78
62Pos-78
62PosCan-78
62SalPlaC-63A
62SalPlaC-63B
62ShiPlaC-63
62Top-343
62TopStal-67
63AngJayP-12
63AngJayP-13
63BasMagM-65
63Fle-19
63Jel-29
63Pos-29
63Top-182
64Top-110
64TopCoi-111
64TopCoi-132
64TopGia-23
64TopSta-42
64TopStaU-55
64TopTatl-61
64TopVen-110
64WheSta-33
65Top-358
66OPC-83
66Top-83
66TopVen-83
78TCM60I-16
79DiaGre-73
85AngStrH-10
86AngGreT-6
91OriCro-356
Pearson, Cory
92ClaDraP-82
92GulCoaRSP-22
93EriSaiC-19
93EriSaiF-3129
94ChaRivC-15
94ChaRivF-2686
95ChaRivUTIS-34
Pearson, Darren
85EveGiaC-13A
85EveGiaC-13B
86CliGiaP-18
Pearson, Don
77WauMetT-15
78WauMetT-22
Pearson, Donna
88OklSoo-19
Pearson, Eddie
92ClaFS7-409
92UppDecML-15
93ClaFS7-86
93ClaGolF-200
93HicCraC-1
93HicCraF-1286
94Bow-427
94BowBes-B14
94BowBesR-B14
94CarLeaAF-CAR10
94Cla-129
94ClaGolF-93
94ClaTriF-T16
94PriWilCC-18
94PriWilCF-1930
94UppDec-549
94UppDecED-549
94UppDecML-128
95Bow-141
96BirBarB-1
96BowBes-158
96BowBesAR-158
96BowBesR-158
Pearson, Frank
92NegLeaRLI-46
Pearson, George
89GeoColC-23
Pearson, Ike
47CenFlo-19
48WhiSoxTI-22
79DiaGre-303
Pearson, Kevin
87TamTarP-6
88GreHorP-1560
89ChaLooB-18
89ChaLooGS-20
89NasSouTI-18
90CMC-142
90NasSouC-17
90NasSouP-242
90ProAAAF-554
91LinDriAAA-269
91NasSouLD-269
91NasSouP-2167
92FroRowDP-31
93StaCluM-25
94EliTwiC-18
94EliTwiF-3744
95ForWayWTI-24
Pearson, Lennie
91PomBlaBPB-19
Pearson, Monte
34ButPreR-50
35DiaMatCS3T1-119
36WorWidGV-114
37OPCBatUV-131
39PlaBal-71
40PlaBal-5
75YanDyn1T-35
92ConTSN-369
92YanWIZA-57
93ConTSN-748
Pearson, Steve
87SalLakTTT-14
Pechek, Wayne
76CedRapGT-20
81PhoGiaVNB-19
Peck, Hal
47IndTeal-21
47IndVanPP-20
48IndTeal-25
49Bow-182
49IndTeal-21
83TCMPla1945-21
90DodTar-612
Peck, Steve
90MadMusP-2269
90ModA'sC-25
91PalSprAP-2011
92MidAngF-4026
92MidAngOHP-18
92MidAngS-467
93VanCanF-2594
94ElPasDF-3143
Peck, Tom
96HagSunB-16
Peckinpaugh, Roger
14B18B-26
14CraJacE-91
15CraJacE-91
15SpoNewM-136
16ColE13-131
16SpoNewM-137
17HolBreD-77
19W514-44
20NatCarE-74
20WalMaiW-40
21E121So8-69A
21E121So8-69B
21Exh-125
21Exh-126
21KoBreWSI-44
22AmeCarE-52
22E120-114
22W575-95
23MapCriV-23
23WilChoV-120
27YorCarE-56
28W502-56
28Yue-56
60SenUniMC-15
61Fle-132
69SCFOldT-21
77GalGloG-163
82OhiHaloF-20
86ConSer1-37
91ConTSN-308
94ConTSN-1258
94ConTSNB-1258
20W516-20
Pecorilli, Aldo
92JohCitCC-10
92JohCitCF-3119
93SavCarC-1
93SavCarF-689
93SouAtlLAGF-50
94ClaGolF-172
94ExcFS7-272
94St.PetCC-21
94St.PetCF-2595
95Bes-53
95BreBtaTI-15
95RicBraRC-17
96RicBraB-23
96RicBraRC-2
96RicBraUB-21
Pecota, Bill
82ForMyeRT-21
84MemChiT-24
85OmaRoyT-29
86OmaRoyP-17
86OmaRoyT-12
87FleUpd-97
87FleUpdG-97
88Don-466
88Fle-264
88FleGlo-264
88RoySmo-22
88Sco-377
88ScoGlo-377
88StaLinRo-11
88Top-433
88TopTif-433
89Fle-289
89FleGlo-289
89OmaRoyC-15
89Sco-339
89Top-148
89TopBig-292
89TopTif-148
89UppDec-507
90Bow-377
90BowTif-377
90CMC-191
90OmaRoyC-16
91Don-672
91Fle-565
91OPC-754
91PanFreS-277
91RoyPol-17
91Sco-513
91Top-754
91TopDesS-754
91TopMic-754
91TopTif-754
91UltUpd-28
92Don-361
92Fle-165
92Lea-244

92MetColP-26
92MetKah-32
92OPC-236
92OPCPre-149
92PanSti-96
92Pin-319
92Sco-252
92ScoRoo-52T
92StaClu-811
92Top-236
92TopGol-236
92TopGolW-236
92TopMic-236
92TopTra-86T
92TopTraG-86T
92Ult-535
92UppDec-240
92UppDec-793
93BraLykP-23
93BraLykS-28
93Don-248
93Fle-92
93PacSpa-339
93Sco-365
93StaClu-148
93StaCluB-2
93StaCluFDI-148
93StaCluMOP-148
93Top-517
93TopGol-517
93TopInaM-517
93TopMic-517
94BraLykP-28
94BraLykS-26
94BraUSPC-5H
94BraUSPC-11D
94Fle-371
94Sco-144
94ScoGolR-144
94StaClu-486
94StaCluFDI-486
94StaCluGR-486
94StaCluMOP-486
94StaCluT-57
94StaCluTFDI-57
94Top-414
94TopGol-414
94TopSpa-414
95Sco-215
95ScoGolR-215
95ScoPlaTS-215

Peden, Les
53Top-256
91TopArc1-256

Pedersen, Don
89NiaFalRP-1
90FayGenP-2414

Pedersen, Mark
81WauTimT-6

Pederson, Stu
82VerBeaDT-24
85AlbDukC-167
86AlbDukP-19
87AlbDukP-29
88BlaYNPRWLU-42
89SyrChiC-16
89SyrChiMB-18
89SyrChiP-798
90CMC-349
90DodTar-613
90ProAAAF-366
90SyrChiC-23
90SyrChiMB-18
90SyrChiP-586
91LinDriAAA-512
91SyrChiLD-512
91SyrChiMB-17
91SyrChiP-2495
92SyrChiF-1983
92SyrChiMB-15
92SyrChiS-513
86STaoftFt-16

Pedraza, Nelson
83WatIndF-7
85WatIndT-1

Pedraza, Rodney
91Cla/Bes-425
91FroRowDP-16
91JamExpC-27
91JamExpP-3543
92AlbPolC-6
92AlbPolF-2303
92StaCluD-139
93SanBerSC-1
93SanBerSF-767
94Cla-53
94NewHavRF-1546
95Top-648
96NewHavRB-20
96NewHavRUSTI-19

Pedre, Jorge
87EugEmeP-2668
88AppFoxP-137
88MidLeaAGS-37
89BasCitRS-20
90Bes-139
90MemChiB-2
90MemChiP-1013
90MemChiS-22
90StaFS7-87
91LinDriAA-411
91MemChiLD-411
91MemChiP-658
92IowCubF-4054
92IowCubS-215
92Sco-844
92TopDeb91-136
93IowCubF-2137
94PawRedSDD-17

Pedrique, Al (Alfredo)
80VenLeaS-207
82JacMetT-16
84JacMetT-23
85IntLeaAT-14
85TidTidT-24
86TidTidP-24
87MetColP-43
88Don-361
88Fle-338
88FleGlo-338
88PanSti-375
88Sco-301
88ScoGlo-301
88StaLinPi-16
88Top-294
88TopRoo-17
88TopSti-128
88TopSti-304
88TopTif-294
88ToyRoo-23
89Bow-104
89BowTif-104
89Sco-614
89TigMar-17
89Top-566
89Top-699
89TopTif-566
90CMC-596
90ProAAAF-149
90TacTigC-19
90TacTigP-102
91LinDriAAA-565
91MetWIZ-311
91TidTidLD-565
91TidTidP-2519
92OmaRoyF-2971
92OmaRoyS-341
93EdmTraF-1144
93LinVenB-275
94EdmTraF-2881
94VenLinU-170
95SpoIndTI-18

Pedro, Blanco
92EliTwiC-13

Pedrosa, Alex
96BluOriB-24

Peek, Timothy
87UtiBluSP-24
88SpaPhiP-1027
88SpaPhiS-15
90MadMusB-23
91HunStaC-18
91HunStaLD-291
91HunStaP-1793
91HunStaTI-17
91LinDriAA-291
92ProFS7-130
92SkyAAAF-243
92TacTigF-2499
92TacTigS-543
93TacTigF-3028
94MemChiF-356

Peel, Homer
34Gou-88

Peel, Jack
87ChaWheP-24
88TamTarS-20
89SarWhiSS-18
90ChaRanS-20

Peeples, James
87OldJudN-397

Peeples, Mike
96Exc-118
96HagSunB-17

Peer, Jeff
94VerExpC-25
94VerExpF-3918

Peever, Lloyd
92FroRowDP-37
92LSUTigM-8
93StaCluM-171
94NewHavRF-1547
95Exc-190

Peguero, Americo
96BluOriB-25

Peguero, Jerry
87ModA'sP-17
88HunStaTI-14
90SalSpuCLC-135

Peguero, Jose
86ModA'sC-17
87ModA'sC-13
89BelBreIS-21
90SalSpuP-2726
94SanBerSC-16
94SanBerSF-2768
95StCatSTI-11

Peguero, Julio
87MacPirP-16
88CarLeaAS-14
88SalBucS-15
89HarSenP-294
89HarSenS-13
90CMC-763
90EasLeaAP-EL24
90HarSenP-1206
90HarSenS-14
91LinDriAAA-492
91ScrRedBLD-492
91ScrRedBP-2553
92ScrRedBF-2460
92ScrRedBS-498
92Ult-547
93LimRocDWB-26
95PorCitRTI-17
96TacRaiB-19

Peguero, Pablo
75AlbDukC-15
77LodDodT-12
79AlbDukT-1
80AlbDukT-3
85DomLeaS-88

Pegues, Steve
88FayGenP-1081
89FayGenP-1594
90CMC-836
90LonTigP-1282
91Cla/Bes-126
91LinDriAA-393
91LonTigLD-393
91LonTigP-1891
92LasVegSF-2806
92LasVegSS-236
92SkyAAAF-115
93Bow-166
93LasVegSF-958
93LinVenB-226
93TriAAAGF-25
94IndIndF-1823
94VenLinU-74
95PirFil-25
95Top-655
96RicBraRC-22
96RicBraUB-22

Peitz, Henry
03BreE10-114
09ColChiE-227
12ColRedB-227
12ColTinT-227
95ConTSN-1352
98CamPepP-61

Pelatowski, Keith
94WilCubC-18
94WilCubF-3762

Pelka, Brian
93WelPirC-18
93WelPirF-3354
94WelPirC-16
94WelPirF-3493

Pellagrini, Ed
46RedSoxTI-18
49Bow-172
51Bow-292
52Top-405
53Top-28
79DiaGre-239
83TopRep5-405
91TopArc1-28

Pellant, Gary
80LynSaiT-14
82WauTimF-23
83WauTimF-3

Pellegrino, Tony
86SpoIndC-172
88ChaRaiP-1194
89WicStaR-3
89WicWraR-12

Pelletier, Michel
72Dia-125

Pellot, Victor
93JohCitCC-15
93JohCitCF-3696

Pellow, Kit
96SpoIndB-20

Pells, Harry
76QuaCitAT-24
76QuaCitAT-26
77QuaCitAT-23
78QuaCitAT-17

Pelmmons, Scott
90ChaWheB-6

Peltier, Dan
89ButCopKSP-27
90CMC-804
90ProAaA-71
90TopMag-2
90TulDriP-1168
90TulDriTI-19
91Bow-266
91Bow-288
91Cla2-T23
91ClaGam-176
91LinDriAAA-316
91OklCit8LD-316
91OklCit8P-192
91UppDec-69
92DonRoo-91
92OklCit8F-1927
92OklCit8S-318
92OPC-618
92SkyAAAF-146
92Top-618
92TopGol-618
92TopGolW-618
92TopMic-618
93Don-473
93Lea-443
93OklCit8F-1638
93PacSpa-644
93Pin-605
93RanKee-423
93Sco-240
93SelRoo-147T
93StaClu-242
93StaCluFDI-242
93StaCluMOP-242
93StaCluR-30
94Don-515
94Fle-316
94OklCit8F-1507
94Sco-569
94ScoGolR-569
94StaClu-457
94StaCluFDI-457
94StaCluGR-457
94StaCluMOP-457
94StaCluT-254
94StaCluTFDI-254
94Top-441
94TopGol-441
94TopSpa-441
96PhoFirB-22

Pelton, Brad
96BurIndB-13

Pelty, Barney
09PC7HHB-34
09RamT20-93
09T206-285
09T206-286
10DomDisP-97
10JuJuDE-33
10RedCroT-62
10RedCroT-148
10RedCroT-235
10SweCapPP-54
11S74Sil-35
11SpoLifCW-286
11SpoLifM-114
11T205-137
12HasTriFT-1B
12T207-148

Peltz, Peter
79WatIndT-25
81GleFalWST-14
82GleFalWST-9

Peltzer, Kurt
90EveGiaB-10
90EveGiaP-3126
91CliGiaC-7
91CliGiaP-832
92CliGiaC-12
93SanJosGC-19
93SanJosGF-5
94Bow-107
94ShrCapF-1602

Pemberton, Brock
75TidTidTI-17
91MetWIZ-312

Pemberton, Jose
87ElmPio(C-26

Pemberton, Rudy
89BriTigS-20
90FayGenP-2421
90SouAtlLAS-17
91Cla/Bes-181
91LakTigC-26
91LakTigP-280
92ClaFS7-168
92LakTigC-26
92LakTigF-2292
92OPC-656
92Top-656
92TopGol-656
92TopGolW-656
92TopMic-656
93ClaGolF-164
93LonTigF-2321
95Fla-260
95FleAllR-M8
95Sum-153
95SumNthD-153
95TolMudHTI-22
95UppDec-249
95UppDecED-249
95UppDecEDG-249
96PawRedSDD-21
96Sco-260
97Don-347
97DonPreP-347
97DonPrePGold-347
97DonTea-59
97DonTeaSPE-59
97FlaSho-A75
97FlaSho-B75
97FlaSho-C75
97FlaShoLC-75
97FlaShoLC-B75
97FlaShoLC-C75
97FlaShoLCM-A75
97FlaShoLCM-B75
97FlaShoLCM-C75
97Fle-547
97FleTif-547
97Lea-346
97LeaFraM-346
97LeaFraMDC-346
97Sco-471
97ScoHobR-471
97ScoResC-471
97ScoShoS-471
97ScoShoSAP-471
97Ult-520
97UltGolME-520
97UltPlaME-520

Pena, Abelino
75BurBeeT-19
76BurBeeT-26

Pena, Adelis
96EriSeaB-18

Pena, Adriano
81WisRapTT-8
85DomLeaS-163

Pena, Alejandro
79CliDodT-9
81AlbDukT-4
82DodPol-26
83AllGamPI-171
83DodPol-26
83TopTra-83T
84AllGamPI-85

84DodPol-26
84Don-250
84Fle-109
84Nes792-324
84Top-324
84TopSti-82
84TopTif-324
85DodCokP-24
85Don-337
85Fle-379
85FleStaS-94
85Lea-64
85OPC-110
85SevCoi-W15
85Top-110
85TopGloS-33
85TopSti-73
85TopSup-17
85TopTif-110
86DodCokP-22
86DodPol-26
86Fle-140
86Top-665
86TopTif-665
87DodMot-18
87DodPol-13
87Fle-449
87FleGlo-449
87OPC-363
87Top-787
87TopTif-787
88DodMot-18
88DodPol-26
88Don-598
88FleUpd-97
88FleUpdG-97
88StaLinD-13
88Top-277
88TopTif-277
89DodMot-18
89DodPol-10
89DodStaSV-9
89Don-557
89Fle-69
89FleGlo-69
89Sco-389
89Top-57
89TopTif-57
89UppDec-137
90Bow-124
90BowTif-124
90DodTar-614
90Don-664
90Fle-405
90FleCan-405
90FleUpd-38
90Lea-403
90MetColP-23
90MetKah-26
90OPC-483
90PubSti-15
90Sco-39
90ScoRoo-32T
90Top-483
90TopTif-483
90TopTra-89T
90TopTraT-89T
90TopTVM-17
90UppDec-279
90UppDec-703
90VenSti-391
91Don-566
91Fle-158
91Lea-70
91MetColP-43
91MetKah-26
91MetWIZ-313
91OPC-544
91Sco-204
91StaClu-583
91StaCluMO-30
91Top-544
91TopDesS-544
91TopMic-544
91TopTif-544
91UppDec-388
92BraLykP-22
92BraLykS-26
92Cla1-T18
92Don-616
92Don-772
92Fle-700
92FleUpd-70
92Lea-489
92OPC-337
92Pin-528
92Sco-691
92Sco-787
92StaClu-833
92Top-337
92TopGol-337
92TopGolW-337
92TopMic-337
92Ult-462
92UppDec-694
93Fle-369
93OPC-311
93Sco-625
93StaClu-205
93StaCluFDI-205
93StaCluMOP-205
93Top-198
93TopGol-198
93TopInaM-198
93TopMic-198
94ColC-458
94ColChoGS-458
94ColChoSS-458
95Pac-350
Pena, Alex
94BluOriC-17
94BluOriF-3561
96AugGreB-21
Pena, Angel
95GreFalDTI-18
Pena, Antonio
91SanBerSC-10
91SanBerSP-1986
Pena, Arturo
85DomLeaS-69
93LimRocDWB-88
Pena, Bert
80ColAstT-8
81TucTorT-7
82AstAstI-3
82TucTorT-1
83TucTorT-17
84TucTorC-67
86TucTorP-18
87AstMot-24
87TucTorP-16
88BlaYNPRWL-11
88ColCliC-13
88ColCliP-16
88ColCliP-322
89BlaYNPRWL-182
Pena, Dan
87VerBeaDP-4
88BakDodCLC-257
Pena, Elvis
95AshTouTI-2
96SalAvaB-21
Pena, George
73OPC-601
73Top-601
74TacTwiC-16
75IowOakT-13
Pena, Geronimo
87SavCarP-4
88FloStaLAS-16
88St.PetCS-21
90CMC-119
90FleUpd-52
90LouRedBC-19
90LouRedBLBC-33
90LouRedBP-412
90ProAAAF-526
90TopTVCa-59
91CarPol-7
91Don-712
91FleUpd-118
91OPC-636
91Sco-717
91ScoRoo-17
91Top-636
91TopDeb90-123
91TopDesS-636
91TopMic-636
91TopTif-636
91UppDec-20
92CarPol-15
92Don-533
92Fle-587
92OPC-166
92Pin-487
92Sco-516
92Sco100RS-12
92StaClu-466
92Top-166
92TopGol-166
92TopGolW-166
92TopMic-166
92UppDec-596
93Bow-604
93CarPol-15
93Don-310
93Fla-126
93Fle-131
93Lea-118
93LimRocDWB-78
93OPC-238
93PacBeiA-30
93PacSpa-300
93PacSpaGE-8
93PanSti-193
93Pin-174
93Sco-161
93Sel-372
93StaClu-215
93StaCluCa-20
93StaCluFDI-215
93StaCluMOP-215
93Top-312
93TopGol-312
93TopInaM-312
93TopMic-312
93Ult-466
93UppDec-331
93UppDec-466
93UppDec-482
93UppDecGold-331
93UppDecGold-466
93UppDecGold-482
94CarPol-15
94ColC-457
94ColChoGS-457
94ColChoSS-457
94Don-234
94Fin-315
94FinRef-315
94Fle-643
94Lea-172
94Pac-600
94Pin-214
94PinArtP-214
94PinMusC-214
94Sel-148
94StaClu-523
94StaCluFDI-523
94StaCluGR-523
94StaCluMOP-523
94StaCluT-307
94StaCluTFDI-307
94Top-444
94TopGol-444
94TopSpa-444
95ColCho-186
95ColChoGS-186
95ColChoSS-186
95Don-422
95DonPreP-422
95Fin-218
95FinRef-218
95Fle-506
95Lea-263
95LeaLim-119
95Pac-413
95Pin-348
95PinArtP-348
95PinMusC-348
95Sco-463
95ScoGolR-463
95ScoPlaTS-463
95Sel-100
95SelArtP-100
95StaClu-427
95StaCluMOP-427
95StaCluSTWS-427
95Ult-226
95UltGolM-226
95UppDec-61
95UppDecED-61
95UppDecEDG-61
96SP-136
Pena, Hipolito
85DomLeaS-39
86NasPirP-21
87VanCanP-1615
88ColCliC-7
88ColCliP-8
88ColCliP-315
89ColCliC-5
89ColCliP-10
89ColCliP-744
89Don-598
89Fle-263
89FleGlo-263
89Top-109
89TopTif-109
90CMC-206
90ColCliC-6
91ColCliLD-114
91ColCliP-597
91LinDriAAA-114
92YanWIZ8-144
93LimRocDWB-64
Pena, Jaime
89EriOriS-17
Pena, James
86EveGiaC-14
86EveGiaPC-21
87CliGiaP-19
89SanJosGB-16
89SanJosGCLC-216
89SanJosGP-445
89SanJosGS-21
90ShrCapP-1442
90ShrCapS-19
90TexLeaAGS-35
91LinDriAA-317
91ShrCapLD-317
91ShrCapP-1820
92DonRoo-92
92FleUpd-129
92PhoFirF-2819
92PhoFirS-393
93Bow-54
93Don-628
93Fle-536
93LasVegSF-942
93Sco-288
94SanBerSC-17
94SanBerSF-2757
Pena, Jesus
96EriSeaB-19
Pena, Jose
85DomLeaS-79
86CliGiaP-19
88ShrCapP-1292
88UtiBluSP-23
89ShrCapP-1848
Pena, Jose G.
69Top-339
70OPC-523
70Top-523
71MLBOffS-112
71OPC-693
71Top-693
72OPC-322
72Top-322
90DodTar-615
Pena, Juan
96MicBatCB-20
96MidLeaAB-46
Pena, Luis
86MacPirP-18
87NewOriP-29
Pena, Manny
83OrlTwiT-13
Pena, Orlando
59RedEnq-19
59Top-271
60RedJayP-9
63Top-214
64AthJayP-10
64Top-124
64TopVen-124
65Top-311
66Top-239
66TopVen-239
67Top-449
67TopVen-232
68Top-471
69TopSta-97
73OriJohP-27
74OPC-393
74Top-393
75OPC-573
75Top-573
75TucTorTI-15
76ForLauYS-18
76VenLeaS-184
91OriCro-357
Pena, Pedro
89MedAthB-11
90MadMusP-2270
90MidLeaASGS-56
90ModA'sC-26
91SanJosGC-19
91SanJosGP-8
Pena, Porfirio
90BatCliP-3068
91MarPhiC-15
91MarPhiP-3456
Pena, R. Roberto
65Top-549
66Top-559
69OPC-184
69Top-184
69TopFou-15
69TopTeaP-12
70OPC-44
70Top-44
71BreTeal-12
71MLBOffS-448
71OPC-334
71Top-334
94BreMilB-161
Pena, Ramon
86GleFalTP-18
87GleFalTP-20
88TolMudHC-6
88TolMudHP-610
89TigMar-18
89TolMudHC-2
89TolMudHP-779
90TopDeb89-96
Pena, Tony
77SalPirT-17
79BufBisT-5
80PorBeaT-24
81Top-551
82Don-124
82Fle-490
82FleSta-72
82Top-138
83AllGamPI-133
83Don-59
83DonActA-35
83Fle-316
83FleSta-149
83FleSti-74
83OPC-133
83Top-590
83TopSti-281
84AllGamPI-43
84Don-186
84DonActAS-3
84Fle-259
84FunFooP-88
84Nes792-645
84NesDreT-19
84OPC-152
84SevCoi-E18
84Top-645
84TopRubD-32
84TopSti-129
84TopTif-645
85AllGamPI-132
85Don-24
85Don-64
85DonActA-10
85DonSupD-24
85Fle-472
85FleLimE-24
85Lea-24
85OPC-358
85Pir-15
85Top-358
85TopMin-358
85TopRubD-32
85TopSti-124
85TopTif-358
86BurKinA-1
86Don-64
86DonAll-22
86Fle-616
86FleLimE-34
86FleMin-119
86FleStiC-87
86Lea-58
86OPC-260
86SevCoi-C12
86Spo-165
86SpoDecG-72
86Top-260
86TopSti-125
86TopTat-5
86TopTif-260
87BurKinA-15

87CarSmo-11
87ClaGam-34
87Don-115
87DonAll-46
87DonOpeD-64
87Fle-617
87FleBasA-31
87FleGlo-617
87FleLeaL-35
87FleLimE-32
87FleStiC-90
87FleUpd-98
87FleUpdG-98
87HosSti-14
87KraFoo-12
87Lea-256
87MandMSL-2
87MSAlceTD-5
87OPC-60
87RedFolSB-25
87Spo-93
87Spo-151
87SpoTeaP-18
87Top-60
87Top-131
87TopCoi-39
87TopSti-129
87TopTif-60
87TopTif-131
87TopTra-95T
87TopTraT-95T
88CarSmo-13
88Don-170
88DonBasB-156
88Fle-45
88FleGlo-45
88FleWorS-5
88Lea-95
88OPC-117
88PanSti-387
88PanSti-447
88PanSti-449
88RedFolSB-67
88Sco-48
88ScoGlo-48
88ScoSam-48
88Spo-142
88StaLinCa-16
88Top-351
88Top-410
88TopSti-52
88TopTif-351
88TopTif-410
89Bow-435
89BowTif-435
89CadEllD-38
89CarSmo-17
89Don-163
89DonBasB-299
89Fle-460
89FleGlo-460
89K-M-30
89OPC-94
89PanSti-180
89Sco-36
89Top-715
89TopSti-38
89TopTif-715
89UppDec-330
90Bow-271
90BowTif-271
90ClaYel-T67
90Don-181
90DonBesA-44
90Fle-256
90FleCan-256
90FleUpd-74
90Lea-104
90MLBBasB-34
90OPC-115
90PubSti-225
90PubSti-269
90RedSoxP-14
90Sco-122
90ScoRoo-7T
90Top-115
90TopBig-290
90TopTif-115
90TopTra-90T
90TopTraT-90T
90TopTVRS-20
90UppDec-276
90UppDec-748
90VenSti-392
90VenSti-393
91Bow-124
91CadEllD-41
91Don-456
91Fle-106
91Lea-33
91OPC-375
91PanFreS-263
91PanSti-219
91RedSoxP-14
91Sco-790
91StaClu-505
91Stu-17
91Top-375
91TopDesS-375
91TopMic-375
91TopTif-375
91Ult-37
91UppDec-652
92Bow-364
92Don-208
92Fle-43
92Fre-9
92HitTheBB-25
92Lea-323
92OPC-569
92PanSti-84
92Pin-33
92RedSoxDD-21
92Sco-446
92StaClu-706
92StaCluNC-706
92Stu-135
92Top-569
92TopGol-569
92TopGolW-569
92TopMic-569
92TriPla-48
92Ult-18
92UltAwaW-17
92UppDec-252
93Bow-439
93CadDis-44
93Don-297
93Fle-563
93FunPac-165
93Lea-43
93LimRocDWB-105
93LinVenB-298
93OPC-316
93PacSpa-34
93PanSti-91
93Pin-506
93RedSoxWHP-23
93Sco-261
93Sel-148
93StaClu-164
93StaCluFDI-164
93StaCluMOP-164
93Top-618
93TopGol-618
93TopInaM-618
93TopMic-618
93TriPla-85
93Ult-154
93UppDec-33
93UppDec-185
93UppDecGold-33
93UppDecGold-185
94Don-191
94Fle-37
94FleUpd-36
94Pac-61
94PanSti-32
94Sco-363
94ScoGolR-363
94ScoRoo-RT59
94ScoRooGR-RT59
94StaClu-71
94StaCluFDI-71
94StaCluGR-71
94StaCluMOP-71
94Top-85
94TopGol-85
94TopSpa-85
94TopTra-119T
95Don-454
95DonPreP-454
95DonTopotO-64
95Fle-143
95Pac-127
95Sco-495
95ScoGolR-495
95ScoPlaTS-495
95Top-284
96ColCho-366T
96ColCho-527
96ColChoGS-527
96ColChoSS-527
96Don-370
96DonPreP-370
96Fla-73
96Fle-95
96FleInd-11
96FleTif-95
96LeaSigEA-153
96Pac-304
96Sco-460
96UppDec-218
97PacPriGotD-GD38

Penafeather, Pat
88AubAstP-1952

Penalver, Luis
80VenLeaS-97

Pencavitch, Kevin
93VerBeaDF-2216

Pender, Shawn
92WatIndC-26
92WatIndF-3250

Pendergast, Steve
19W514-117

Pendergrass, Tyrone
96DanBraB-17

Pendleton, Jim
52Par-69
53BraJohC-25
53BraSpiaS3-20
53Top-185
54BraJohC-3
54Top-165
55BraGolS-26
55BraJohC-3
55Top-15
55TopDouH-33
55TopTesS-8
57Top-327
58Top-104
59RedEnq-20
59Top-174
59TopVen-174
62Col.45B-15
62Col45'HC-13
62Top-432
63Col45'JP-7
83Bra53F-53
89AstCol4S-25
91TopArc1-185
94TopArc1-165
94TopArc1G-165

Pendleton, Terry
83ArkTraT-15
84Car5x7-20
84LouRedR-15
84OCoandSI-219
85AllGamPI-124
85CarTeal-25
85Don-534A
85Don-534B
85Fle-236
85OPC-346
85Top-346
85TopTif-346
86CarIGAS-10
86CarKASD-14
86CarSchM-19
86CarTeal-33
86Don-205
86Fle-44
86KayB-23
86Lea-137
86OPC-321
86Top-528
86TopSti-53
86TopTat-17
86TopTif-528
87CarSmo-16
87Don-183
87DonOpeD-62
87Fle-306
87FleGlo-306
87Lea-124
87OPC-8
87SpoTeaP-12
87Top-8
87TopSti-54
87TopTif-8
88CarSmo-17
88Don-454
88DonBasB-187
88Fle-46
88FleAwaW-28
88FleGlo-46
88FleStiC-119
88FleSup-27
88Lea-246
88OPC-105
88PanSti-392
88RedFolSB-68
88Sco-190
88ScoGlo-190
88Spo-159
88StaLinCa-17
88Top-635
88TopBig-53
88TopSti-49
88TopStiB-7
88TopTif-635
89Bow-437
89BowTif-437
89CarSmo-18
89Don-230
89DonBasB-156
89Fle-461
89FleGlo-461
89OPC-375
89PanSti-185
89Sco-137
89Spo-99
89Top-375
89TopBig-151
89TopSti-42
89TopTif-375
89UppDec-131
90Bow-197
90BowTif-197
90CarSmo-19
90Don-299
90DonBesN-34
90Fle-257
90FleCan-257
90Lea-260
90OPC-725
90PanSti-337
90PubSti-226
90Sco-208
90Spo-174
90Top-725
90TopBig-135
90TopMag-69
90TopSti-40
90TopTif-725
90TopTVCa-28
90UppDec-469
90VenSti-394
91Bow-570
91BraDubP-23
91BraSubS-30
91Don-446
91Fle-642
91FleUpd-76
91Lea-304
91OPC-485
91OPCPre-95
91Sco-230
91ScoRoo-50T
91SimandSMLBL-33
91StaClu-327
91StaCluMO-23
91StaCluMO-24
91Stu-148
91Top-485
91TopDesS-485
91TopMic-485
91TopTif-485
91TopTra-90T
91TopTraT-90T
91Ult-10
91UppDec-484
91UppDec-708
92Bow-254
92BraLykP-23
92BraLykS-27
92CarMcD-40
92Cla1-T70
92ClaGam-182
92ColAllG-8
92ColAllP-8
92Don-237
92DonBonC-BC2
92DonCraJ1-26
92DonEli-16
92Fle-366
92Fle-691
92FleAll-15
92FleCitTP-15
92Fre-3
92Hig5-25
92KinDis-1
92Lea-245
92MSABenSHD-14
92New-20
92OPC-115
92OPCPre-195
92PanSti-148
92PanSti-164
92Pin-18
92Pos-22
92Sco-18
92Sco-789
92Sco100S-45
92ScoCokD-18
92ScoProaG-13
92ScoProP-1
92SpollIFK1-24
92StaClu-510
92Stu-8
92SunSee-7
92Top-115
92TopGol-115
92TopGolW-115
92TopKid-33
92TopMcD-7
92TopMic-115
92TriPla-139
92Ult-167
92UltAwaW-4
92UppDec-229
92UppDecTMH-2
92UppDecTMH-39
93Bow-254
93BraFloA-8
93BraLykP-24
93BraLykS-29
93ClaGam-73
93DenHol-5
93DiaMar-84
93Don-234
93DonMVP-7
93DurPowP1-8
93Fin-101
93FinJum-101
93FinRef-101
93Fla-9
93Fle-12
93FleAtl-17
93FleFruotL-51
93FleTeaL-NL2
93FunPac-66
93FunPacA-AS5
93Hos-9
93Kra-26
93Lea-387
93LeaGolA-R6
93MetBak-34
93OPC-322
93PacSpa-340
93PanSti-184
93Pin-60
93Pin-473
93Pos-17
93PosCan-18
93Sco-36
93ScoFra-15
93Sel-17
93SelStaL-10
93SelStaL-18
93SelStaL-35
93SP-61
93StaClu-338
93StaCluB-21
93StaCluFDI-338
93StaCluM-102
93StaCluMOP-338
93Stu-117
93Top-650
93TOPBLAG-15
93TopGol-650
93TopInaM-650
93TopMic-650
93TriPla-147
93Ult-11
93UltAwaW-5
93UppDec-163
93UppDecCP-R16
93UppDecDG-5
93UppDecGold-163

93UppDecHRH-HR18
93USPlaCA-3D
94Bow-573
94BraLykP-29
94BraLykS-27
94BraUSPC-3C
94BraUSPC-10H
94BraUSPC-13D
94ColC-372
94ColChoGS-372
94ColChoSS-372
94Don-556
94ExtBas-212
94Fin-118
94FinRef-118
94Fla-356
94Fle-372
94Lea-189
94OPC-38
94Pac-20
94PanSti-149
94Pin-371
94PinArtP-371
94PinMusC-371
94ProMag-1
94Sco-72
94ScoGolR-72
94Sel-34
94StaClu-313
94StaCluFDI-313
94StaCluGR-313
94StaCluMOP-313
94StaCluMOP-ST1
94StaCluST-ST1
94StaCluT-40
94StaCluTFDI-40
94Stu-41
94SucSav-3
94Top-735
94TopGol-735
94TopSpa-735
94TriPla-48
94TriPlaM-10
94Ult-449
94UppDec-95
94UppDecAJ-33
94UppDecAJG-33
94UppDecED-95
95Bow-371
95ColCho-559T
95ColCho-TC4
95Don-394
95DonPreP-394
95DonTopotO-246
95Fin-239
95FinRef-239
95Fla-355
95Fle-317
95FleUpd-98
95Lea-338
95LeaLim-85
95Pin-404
95PinArtP-404
95PinMusC-404
95Sco-339
95ScoGolR-339
95ScoPlaTS-339
95ScoYouTE-339T
95Sel-177
95SelArtP-177
95SP-57
95SPSil-57
95StaClu-66
95StaClu-613
95StaCluFDI-66
95StaCluMOP-66
95StaCluMOP-613
95StaCluMOP-RL34
95StaCluRL-RL34
95StaCluSTDW-B1T
95StaCluSTWS-66
95StaCluSTWS-613
95StaCluVR-40
95Stu-125
95Top-242
95TopCyb-134
95TopTra-105T
95Ult-353
95UltGolM-353
95UppDec-469T
95UppDec-TC2
95UppDecSE-249
95UppDecSEG-249
96ColCho-156
96ColChoGS-156
96ColChoSS-156
96Don-345
96DonPreP-345
96EmoXL-188
96Fin-B8
96FinRef-B8
96Fla-266
96Fle-392
96FleTif-392
96Lea-57
96LeaPrePB-57
96LeaPrePG-57
96LeaPrePS-57
96Pac-78
96Pin-240
96PinArtP-140
96PinFoil-240
96PinSta-140
96ProSta-68
96Sco-49
96ScoDugC-A42
96ScoDugCAP-A42
96StaClu-119
96StaCluEPB-119
96StaCluEPG-119
96StaCluEPS-119
96StaCluMOP-119
95StaCluVRMC-40
96Top-170
96TopGal-71
96TopGalPPI-71
96Ult-203
96UltGolM-203
96UppDec-78
97Don-63
97DonPreP-63
97DonPrePGold-63
97Fle-267
97FleTif-267
97Pin-138
97PinArtP-138
97PinMusC-138
97Sco-62
97ScoBra-3
97ScoBraPl-3
97ScoBraPr-3
97ScoPreS-62
97ScoShoS-62
97ScoShoSAP-62
97Top-319
97Ult-535
97UltGolME-535
97UltPlaME-535
Penigar, C.L.
86CliGiaP-20
88MidAngGS-17
89BirBarB-23
89BirBarP-115
90CMC-636
90ProAAAF-180
90VanCanC-9
90VanCanP-502
Penix, Troy
92ClaFS7-441
92FroRowDP-68
92SouOreAC-1
92SouOreAF-3427
93MadMusC-21
93MadMusF-1830
93MidLeaAGF-14
Penland, Ken
88ButCopKSP-6
Penn, Shannon
90ButCopKSP-24
91GasRanC-21
91GasRanP-2698
92NiaFalRC-16
92NiaFalRF-3335
93LonTigF-2316
94ExcFS7-59
94TolMudHF-1033
95Exc-51
95FleUpd-22
95Sum-160
95SumNthD-160
95TolMudHTI-23
95Top-636
96Sco-247
96TolMudHB-22
Penn, Trevor
88RocExpLC-29
89WesPalBES-21
90JacExpB-11
90JacExpP-1386
Penner, Ira
94DayCubC-30
Penniall, David
77St.PetCT-23
78ArkTraT-19
80ArkTraT-10
Pennington, Art
86NegLeaF-53
92NegLeaRLI-47
95NegLeaL2-24
Pennington, Brad
89BluOriS-18
90Bes-65
90WauTimB-8
90WauTimP-2121
90WauTimS-18
91Cla/Bes-390
91KanCouCC-9
91KanCouCP-2657
92Bow-136
92ClaFS7-108
92FreKeyC-20
92UppDecML-198
93Bow-361
93Bow-661
93ExcFS7-126
93FlaWavotF-11
93FleFinE-163
93Lea-526
93RocRedWF-237
93SelRoo-75T
93Top-797
93TopGol-797
93TopInaM-797
93TopMic-797
93Ult-498
93UppDec-437
93UppDecGold-437
94Bow-243
94ColC-227
94ColChoGS-227
94ColChoSS-227
94Don-317
94Fle-15
94Lea-177
94OriPro-79
94OriUSPC-3D
94OriUSPC-10C
94RocRedWF-997
94RocRedWTI-18
94Sco-258
94ScoGolR-258
94StaClu-17
94StaCluFDI-17
94StaCluGR-17
94StaCluMOP-17
94StaCluT-286
94StaCluTFDI-286
94Top-271
94TopGol-271
94TopSpa-271
94Ult-7
94UppDec-227
94UppDecED-227
95RedKah-21
96VanCanB-21
Pennington, Ken
87SumBraP-23
88DurBulS-16
89DurBulS-17
89DurBulTI-17
89Sta-72
90Bes-177
90CMC-757
90EasLeaAP-EL16
90WilBilB-18
90WilBilP-1065
90WilBilS-19
91JacSunLD-341
91JacSunP-159
91LinDriAA-341
92SanBerSF-970
Pennock, Herb
20NatCarE-75
22E120-9
22W573-95
22WilPatV-50
23MapCriV-27
23W503-51
23WilChoV-121
27YorCarE-8
28PorandAR-A28
28PorandAR-B28
28StaPlaCE-50
28W502-8
28W513-68
28W56PlaC-JOK
28Yue-8
29PorandAR-68
30W554-13
31Exh-25
33ExhFou-13
33Gou-138
34GouCanV-16
36PC7AlbHoF-54
46SpoExcW-7-5
50CalHOFW-59
51R42SmaS-84
60ExhWriH-19
60Fle-35
61Fle-133
63BazA-5
71FleWorS-21
76RowExh-16
76ShaPiz-54
77GalGloG-106
79RedSoxEF-15
79RedSoxEF-24
80LauFamF-2
80PacLeg-111
80PerHaloFP-54
80SSPHOF-54
86ConSer1-51
87Yan192T-2
89HOFStiB-67
90PerGreM-54
91ConTSN-120
91ConTSN-143
92ConTSN-465
92ConTSN-594
92MegRut-123
92YanWIZH-25
95ConTSN-1331
Penny, Brad
97Bow-199
97BowInt-199
Pennye, Darwin
88WatPirP-23
89AugPirP-504
90CarLeaA-24
90SalBucS-15
91CarMudLD-114
91CarMudP-1098
91LinDriAA-114
92HarSenF-473
92HarSenS-294
92SkyAA F-124
Pennyfeather, William
89WelPirP-1
90AugPirP-2477
90SouAtlLAS-39
91Bow-517
91Cla/Bes-158
91SalBucC-11
91SalBucP-965
92Bow-17
92BufBisF-334
92BufBisS-37
92DonRoo-93
92SkyAAAF-16
93BufBisF-530
93ClaFS7-143
93Don-702
93FleFinE-116
93LinVenB-227
93Sco-301
93StaClu-447
93StaCluFDI-447
93StaCluMOP-447
93Top-819
93TopGol-819
93TopInaM-819
93TopMic-819
94Don-485
94Ult-558
96VanCanB-22
Penrod, Jack
88PocGiaP-2102
Pensiero, Russ
80ChaO'sP-14
80ChaO'sW-15
Penson, Paul
54Top-236
94TopArc1-236
94TopArc1G-236
Pentland, Jeff
93ElmPioF-3841
95PorSeaDTI-19
96ChaKniB-2
Pentz, Gene
77Top-308
78AstBurK-11
78Top-64
79PorBeaT-12
80PorBeaT-25
81PhoGiaVNB-20
Penvose, Randy
86GenCubP-22
Peoples, Danny
96BesAutS1RP-FR14
96WatIndTI-23
97Bow-410
97BowChr-272
97BowChrI-272
97BowChrIR-272
97BowChrR-272
97BowInt-410
97Top-478
Peoples, James
87BucN28-15
Peoples, Nathaniel
92NegLeaRLI-48
Peopping, Mike
76TacTwiDQ-16
Pepin, Bob (Robert)
43ParSpo-60
Pepitone, Joe
47PM1StaP1-159
62Top-596
63Top-183
63YanJayP-9
64ChatheY-19
64Top-360
64TopCoi-121
64TopSta-22
64TopVen-360
64WheSta-34
64YanJayP-9
64YanReqKP-12
65ChaTheY-17
65OPC-245
65Top-245
66OPC-79
66Top-79
66TopVen-79
66YanTeal-9
67CokCapA-13
67CokCapAAm-28
67CokCapYM-V13
67DexPre-162
67DexPre-163
67OPCPapI-22
67Top-340
67TopPos-22
67TopVen-209
68AtlOilPBCC-34
68Baz-5
68OPC-195
68Top-195
68TopActS-3A
68TopActS-16A
68TopVen-195
69MilBra-216
69MLBOffS-76
69MLBPin-21
69Top-589
69TopSta-206
69TopTeaP-19
70AstTeal-9
70DayDaiNM-124
70Kel-59
70MLBOffS-45
70SunPin-7
70Top-598
71MLBOffS-40
71OPC-90
71Top-90
71TopGreM-53
72CubChi-6
72CubTeal-10
72MilBra-268
72OPC-303
72OPC-304
72Top-303
72Top-304
73OPC-580
73Top-580
76HawIslC-11
78TCM60I-6
81TCM60I-477
83YanASFY-32

86TCMSupS-36
87AstShowSTh-18
91UppDecS-16
91UppDecS-19
92YanWIZ6-96
92YanWIZA-58

Pepper, (Mascot)
93AlbPolC-30

Pepper, Laurin (Hugh)
55Top-147
56Top-108
58JetPos-14

Pepper, Ray
35DiaMatCS3T1-120
36GouWidPPR-A83

Pepper, Stu
91PacSenL-73

Pepper, Tony
75IntLeaASB-22
75PacCoaLAB-22
75PhoGiaC-4
75PhoGiaCK-18

Peppers, Devin
90EliTwiS-15

Pequignot, Jon
86VerBeaDP-19
87SanAntDTI-19

Peralta, Amado
85MexCitTT-21

Peralta, Martin
88SalLakCTTI-22

Peraza, Luis
86AppFoxP-18

Peraza, Oswald
86KnoBluJP-18
87KnoBluJP-1511
88OriFreB-23
88ScoRoo-77T
88ScoRooG-77T
89Bow-1
89BowTif-1
89Don-524
89Fle-615
89FleGlo-615
89Sco-571
89Top-297
89TopBig-219
89TopTif-297
89UppDec-651
90HagSunB-27
91HagSunLD-242
91HagSunP-2456
91LinDriAA-242
91OriCro-358
93LinVenB-66
94VenLinU-112

Percibal, Bill
93BluOriC-19
93BluOriF-4122
94AlbPolC-19
94AlbPolF-2235
94OriPro-80
95SPML-17
96BesAutS-70
96Exc-7

Percival, Troy
90BoiHawP-3335
91BoiHawC-23
91BoiHawP-3875
92Bow-290
92MidAngOHP-19
92ProFS7-38
92UppDecML-134
93Bow-363
93Bow-609
93ClaFS7-236
93FleFinE-187
93StaClu-681
93StaCluAn-9
93StaCluFDI-681
93StaCluMOP-681
93Ult-522
93UppDec-507
93UppDecGold-507
93VanCanF-2595
94UppDecML-227
94VanCanF-1864
95AngCHP-7
95AngMot-25
95Bow-69
95BowBes-B52
95BowBesR-B52
95DonTopotO-40
95Exc-23
95Fla-237
95Fle-233
95Pin-423
95PinArtP-423
95PinMusC-423
95Sel-219
95SelArtP-219
95Top-633
96AngMot-13
96Bow-6
96Cir-21
96CirRav-21
96ColCho-72
96ColChoGS-72
96ColChoSS-72
96Don-524
96DonPreP-524
96EmoXL-29
96Fin-B156
96FinRef-B156
96Fla-40
96Fle-55
96FleRooS-13
96FleTif-55
96Lea-76
96LeaPrePB-76
96LeaPrePG-76
96LeaPrePS-76
96LeaSigA-178
96LeaSigAG-178
96LeaSigAS-178
96MetUni-30
96MetUniP-30
96Pin-298
96PinFoil-298
96Sco-169
96StaClu-328
96StaCluEPB-328
96StaCluEPG-328
96StaCluEPS-328
96StaCluMOP-328
96Stu-37
96StuPrePB-37
96StuPrePG-37
96StuPrePS-37
96TeaOut-62
96Top-43
96TopChr-16
96TopChrR-16
96TopGal-99
96TopGalPPI-99
96Ult-32
96UltGolM-32
96UppDec-289
97Cir-222
97CirRav-222
97ColCho-251
97Don-212
97DonEli-131
97DonEliGS-131
97DonPre-120
97DonPreCttC-120
97DonPreP-212
97DonPrePGold-212
97DonTea-5
97DonTeaSPE-5
97Fin-65
97FinRef-65
97FlaSho-A162
97FlaSho-B162
97FlaSho-C162
97FlaShoLC-162
97FlaShoLC-B162
97FlaShoLC-C162
97FlaShoLCM-A162
97FlaShoLCM-B162
97FlaShoLCM-C162
97Fle-49
97FleTif-49
97Lea-240
97LeaFraM-240
97LeaFraMDC-240
97LeaGet-10
97MetUni-42
97NewPin-80
97NewPinAP-80
97NewPinKtP-13
97NewPinMC-80
97NewPinPP-80
97NewPinPP-K13
97Pac-12
97PacLigB-12
97PacSil-12
97Pin-119
97PinArtP-119
97PinCer-50
97PinCerMBlu-50
97PinCerMG-50
97PinCerMR-50
97PinCerR-50
97PinIns-102
97PinInsCE-102
97PinInsDE-102
97PinMusC-119
97PinTotCPB-50
97PinTotCPG-50
97PinTotCPR-50
97PinX-P-113
97PinX-PMoS-113
97Sco-253
97Sco-523
97ScoHobR-523
97ScoPreS-253
97ScoResC-523
97ScoShoS-253
97ScoShoS-523
97ScoShoSAP-253
97ScoShoSAP-523
97Sel-79
97SelArtP-79
97SelRegG-79
97SelToootT-22
97SelToootTMB-22
97StaClu-232
97StaCluMat-232
97StaCluMOP-232
97Stu-7
97StuPrePG-7
97StuPrePS-7
97Top-156
97TopChr-60
97TopChrR-60
97TopGal-140
97TopGalPPI-140
97Ult-29
97UltBasR-7
97UltGolME-29
97UltPlaME-29
97UppDec-29

Perconte, Jack
77LodDodT-13
79AlbDukT-13
80AlbDukT-16
80VenLeaS-22
81AlbDukT-17
81Top-302
82Ind-28
82IndTeal-26
82IndWhe-27
82TopTra-87T
83ChaChaT-13
83Don-463
83Fle-417
83IndPos-26
83Top-569
84FleUpd-90
84MarMot-15
85Don-74A
85Don-74B
85Fle-498
85Lea-221
85MarMot-11
85Top-172
85TopSti-341
85TopTif-172
86Fle-472
86Top-146
86TopTat-1
86TopTif-146
87AlbDukP-20
90DodTar-616

Perdomo, Felix
83GreHorT-21
86ColMetP-19
87LynMetP-12
88JacMetGS-24

Perdue, Alphie
77SalPirT-18

Perdue, Doran
81ShrCapT-15

Perdue, Hub (Herbert R.)
09T206-508
10CouT21-53
12RedSoxBASP-2
12T207-149
14B18B-53A
14B18B-53B
14CraJacE-121
14FatPlaT-39
15CraJacE-121

Pereira, Ray
84LitFalMT-8

Perez, Alex
88KenTwiP-1385

Perez, Beban
89QuaCitAB-28
89QuaCitAGS-23
90PalSprACLC-213
90PalSprAP-2592
91PalSprAP-2031
92BoiHawF-3622
92QuaCitRBC-8
92QuaCitRBF-807
93PalSprAC-16
93PalSprAF-66

Perez, Benny
75ForLauYS-3
76ForLauYS-24
78DunBluJT-17

Perez, Carlos Gross
75QuaCitAT-16
79SalLakCGT-18A
80SalLakCGT-13
91Cla/Bes-92
91SumFlyP-2333
92RocExpC-15
93BurBeeC-17
93BurBeeF-154
93LimRocDWB-57
94HarSenF-2088
95Bow-113
95BowBes-R72
95BowBesR-R72
95ClaPhoC-36
95ColCho-550T
95DonTopotO-283
95Emo-154
95Exc-224
95Fin-296
95FinRef-296
95Fla-377
95FleUpd-108
95LeaLim-103
95SelCer-92
95SelCerMG-92
95SP-19
95SPCha-15
95SPChaDC-15
95SPSil-19
95StaClu-542
95StaCluMOP-542
95StaCluSTWS-542
95Sum-114
95SumNthD-114
95Top-652
95TopTra-150T
95UltGolMR-M19
95UppDec-244
95UppDecED-244
95UppDecEDG-244
95Zen-124
95ZenRooRC-16
96Baz-84
96ColCho-212
96ColChoGS-212
96ColChoSS-212
96Don-317
96DonPreP-317
96DonSho-8
96EmoXL-224
96ExpDis-14
96Fin-S109
96FinRef-S109
96Fla-311
96Fle-463
96FleTif-463
96Lea-8
96LeaPrePB-8
96LeaPrePG-8
96LeaPrePS-8
96LeaSigA-179
96LeaSigAG-179
96LeaSigAS-179
96MetUni-193
96MetUniP-193
96MetUniPP-8
96Pac-130
96PacEstL-EL24
96PanSti-22
96Pin-319
96PinFoil-319
96Sco-132
96ScoDugC-A83
96ScoDugCAP-A83
96StaClu-278
96StaCluMOP-278
96Top-174
96TopGal-98
96TopGalPPI-98
96Ult-234
96UltGolM-234
96UppDec-396
97ColCho-386
78STLakCGC-26
97Fle-502
97FleTif-502
97Lea-260
97LeaFraM-260
97LeaFraMDC-260
97Sco-381
97ScoHobR-381
97ScoResC-381
97ScoShoS-381
97ScoShoSAP-381
97Ult-357
97UltGolME-357
97UltPlaME-357

Perez, Cesar
90GreHorB-9
90GreHorP-2661
90GreHorS-15
90OneYanP-3369
91GreHorP-3056
92ForLauYC-7
92ForLauYTI-22
92Ft.LauYF-2613
93KinIndC-21
93KinIndF-2246
93KinIndTI-21
94CanIndF-3119
94ExcFS7-48

Perez, Danny
91OklStaC-18
92HelBreF-1729
92HelBreSP-23
93BelBreC-17
93BelBreF-1723
93MidLeaAGF-3
94ElPasDF-3159
94StoPorC-19
95Exc-73

Perez, Dario
91AppFoxC-8
91AppFoxP-1714
92BasCitRC-17
92BasCitRF-3844
93LimRocDWB-125
93WilBluRC-19
93WilBluRF-1996
94Bow-87
94WilBluRC-19
94WilBluRF-298

Perez, David
89ButCopKSP-2
90ChaRanS-21
90FloStaLAS-39
90StaFS7-25
91LinDriAA-590
91TulDriLD-590
91TulDriP-2770
91TulDriTI-21
92ChaRanF-2224
92TulDriS-615
94OklCit8F-1495
93TulDriTI-23

Perez, Dick
83Don-654A
83Don-654B
85DonSupD-NNO
92DonDiaK-DK27

Perez, Eddie
91DurBulC-12
91DurBulP-1548
93GreBraF-353
93IdaFalBF-4047
93IdaFalBSP-2
94RicBraF-2850
95RicBraRC-18
95RicBraTI-15
95Top-480
96BurIndB-22
96FleBra-14
96LeaSigEA-154
96Ult-444
96UltGolM-444
97Fle-268

97FleTif-268
97Pac-243
97PacLigB-243
97PacSil-243
Perez, Eduardo
88BurBraP-23
89SumBraP-1112
90SumBraB-17
90SumBraP-2438
91BoiHawC-8
91BoiHawP-3896
91Cla/Bes-424
91ClaDraP-13
91ClaGolB-BC20
92CalLeaACL-48
92ClaFS7-211
92GreBraF-1157
92GreBraS-243
92MidAngOHP-20
92PalSprAC-1
92PalSprAF-849
92ProFS7-39
92UppDec-52
92UppDecML-24
92UppDecML-271
93Bow-441
93ClaFisN-10
93ClaGolF-32
93ClaYouG-YG17
93ExcFS7-146
93Lea-483
93LinVenB-184
93SelRoo-50T
93SP-284
93StaCluAn-6
93Top-494
93TopGol-494
93TopInaM-494
93TopMic-494
93TriAAAGF-32
93UppDec-467
93UppDecGold-467
93VanCanF-2605
94AngLAT-25
94Bow-291
94Cla-188
94ColC-228
94ColChoGS-228
94ColChoSS-228
94Don-227
94Fin-73
94FinRef-73
94Fla-26
94Fle-67
94FUnPac-121
94Lea-341
94OPC-36
94Pac-86
94PacAll-18
94Pin-202
94PinArtP-202
94PinMusC-202
94ProMag-20
94Sco-307
94ScoBoyoS-12
94ScoGolR-307
94Sel-360
94Spo-61
94StaClu-189
94StaCluFDI-189
94StaCluGR-189
94StaCluMOP-189
94Stu-14
94Top-721
94TopGol-721
94TopSpa-721
94TriPla-18
94Ult-26
94UppDec-124
94UppDecAJ-10
94UppDecAJG-10
94UppDecED-124
94VenLinU-194
95ActPacF-33
95AngMot-14
95ColCho-94
95ColChoGS-94
95ColChoSS-94
95Don-214
95DonPreP-214
95Fin-202
95FinRef-202
95Fle-234
95Lea-145
95LinVen-118
95LinVen-269
95LinVen-281
95LinVen-286
95Pac-63
95Pin-258
95PinArtP-258
95PinMusC-258
95Sel-65
95SelArtP-65
95SelCer-4
95SelCerMG-4
95StaClu-195
95StaCluFDI-195
95StaCluMOP-195
95StaCluSTWS-195
95Sum-93
95SumNthD-93
95Top-126
95TopCyb-79
95UppDec-266
95UppDecED-266
95UppDecEDG-266
95UppDecSE-125
95UppDecSEG-125
96ColCho-487
96ColChoGS-487
96ColChoSS-487
96Fle-305
96FleTif-305
96IndIndB-19
96MLBPin-27
96Pac-269
97Don-221
97DonPreP-221
97DonPrePGold-221
Perez, Erick
95LinVen-180
Perez, Eulogio
88MarPhiS-27
89MarPhiS-24
90BatCliP-3075
90SpaPhiP-2500
90SpaPhiS-17
91SpaPhiC-17
91SpaPhiP-901
Perez, Felix
93LinVenB-77
94VenLinU-159
Perez, Francisco
86EriCarP-23
89AshTouP-963
89AubAstP-2174
90AshTouP-2745
Perez, Fred
85UtiBluST-21
Perez, George
93GreFalDSP-13
Perez, Gil
92WelPirC-19
92WelPirF-1321
93WelPirC-19
93WelPirF-3355
94WelPirC-17
94WelPirF-3494
Perez, Gorky
87AshTouP-26
87AubAstP-15
88AshTouP-1062
89OscAstS-17
Perez, Hector
82MadMusF-32
83MadMusF-29
84LitFalMT-17
86LynMetP-16
87LynMetP-10
88St.LucMS-18
89PenPilS-18
93ForLauRSFP-1597
Perez, Hilario
93ForLauRSC-21
93UtiBluSC-20
93UtiBluSF-3532
94UtiBluSC-22
94UtiBluSF-3819
Perez, Jayson
92GulCoaDF-3564
93YakBeaF-3882
Perez, Jesse
96OgdRapTI-30
Perez, Jhonny
95SPML-68
96KisCobB-20
Perez, Joe
90WatIndS-15
91ColIndC-3
91ColIndP-1501
95ChaRivTI-7
Perez, Joel
77AppFoxT-19
79KnoKnoST-16
Perez, Jose
89SalDodTI-22
90KisDodD-21
90YakBeaTI-34
Perez, Juan
95WesMicWTI-11
96ModA'sB-26
Perez, Juan Carlos
96BluOriB-27
Perez, Julian
89BlaYNPRWL-122
Perez, Julio
75WesPalBES-1
78MemChiBC-7
79MemChiT-4
80GleFalWSBT-16
80GleFalWSCT-10
81EdmTraRR-17
83ReaPhiT-16
86MacPirP-19
87MacPirP-14
88MiaMarS-18
89HarSenP-307
89HarSenS-14
90HarSenP-1201
90HarSenS-15
94BurIndF-3792
96KenIndB-20
Perez, Junior
88BlaYNPRWL-112
90GreFalDSP-16
Perez, Leo
89StoPorB-13
89StoPorCLC-158
89StoPorP-373
89WytCubS-23
90CMC-865
90StoPorB-24
90StoPorCLC-186
90StoPorP-2185
91GenCubC-14
91GenCubP-4211
91WinSpiC-8
91WinSpiP-2827
92GulCoaRSP-10
Perez, Leonardo
88BelBreGS-18
Perez, Luis
92GulCoaRSP-5
94HudValRF-3384
94HudValRC-18
Perez, Manuel R.
48SomandK-17
49SomandK-8
Perez, Mario
85BenPhiC-19
87UtiBluSP-1
Perez, Martin
76DubPacT-25
Perez, Marty
71OPC-529
71Top-529
72OPC-119
72Top-119
73OPC-144
73Top-144
74OPC-374
74Top-374
75OPC-499
75Top-499
76Hos-65
76Kel-26
76OPC-177
76Top-177
77BurCheD-100
77Gia-18
77OPC-183
77RCColC-53
77Top-438
78RCColC-53
78TidTidT-19
78Top-613
92YanWIZ7-126
Perez, Melido
86BurExpP-17
88Don-589
88DonBasB-179
88DonRoo-21
88Fle-265
88FleGlo-265
88FleUpd-19
88FleUpdG-19
88ScoRoo-108T
88ScoRooG-108T
88TopTra-83T
88TopTraT-83T
88WhiSoxC-21
89Bow-59
89BowTif-59
89ClaLigB-88
89Don-58
89DonBasB-179
89Fle-509
89FleGlo-509
89OPC-88
89PanSti-300
89RedFolSB-89
89Sco-386
89ScoHot1R-79
89ScoYouSI-7
89Spo-118
89Top-786
89TopBig-235
89TopRoo-16
89TopSti-296
89TopTif-786
89ToyRoo-21
89UppDec-243
89WhiSoxC-21
90Bow-310
90BowTif-310
90Don-101
90DonBesA-18
90Fle-546
90FleCan-546
90Lea-36
90OPC-621
90PanSti-42
90PubSti-399
90PubSti-602
90Sco-311
90Top-621
90TopBig-195
90TopSti-304
90TopTif-621
90UppDec-525
90VenSti-395
90VenSti-396
90WhiSoxC-21
90WhiSoxK-2
91Bow-344
91Don-164
91DonBonC-BC13
91Fle-133
91FleWaxBC-7
91OPC-499
91PanCanT1-96
91PanFreS-358
91PanSti-7
91Sco-179
91Sco-705
91StaClu-232
91StaCluCM-23
91Top-499
91TopDesS-499
91TopMic-499
91TopTif-499
91Ult-80
91UppDec-623
91WhiSoxK-33
92Bow-365
92Don-509
92Fle-95
92Lea-479
92OPC-129
92OPCPre-10
92Pin-322
92Sco-29
92ScoProP-10
92ScoRoo-36T
92StaClu-869
92StaCluNC-869
92Stu-218
92Top-129
92TopGol-129
92TopGolW-129
92TopMic-129
92TopTra-87T
92TopTraG-87T
92Ult-42
92Ult-413
92UppDec-190
92UppDec-799
93Bow-19
93Don-709
93DurPowP2-2
93Fle-284
93Lea-74
93LimRocDWB-127
93OPC-231
93PacSpa-210
93Pin-109
93Sco-86
93Sel-116
93SelAce-22
93SelStaL-63
93SelStaL-74
93StaClu-465
93StaCluFDI-465
93StaCluMOP-465
93StaCluY-6
93Top-304
93TopComotH-11
93TopGol-304
93TopInaM-304
93TopMic-304
93Ult-248
93UppDec-326
93UppDecGold-326
94Bow-605
94ColC-432
94ColChoGS-432
94ColChoSS-432
94Don-476
94ExtBas-137
94Fla-87
94Fle-245
94Lea-190
94Pac-435
94Pin-168
94PinArtP-168
94PinMusC-168
94Sco-479
94ScoGolR-479
94StaClu-554
94StaCluFDI-554
94StaCluGR-554
94StaCluMOP-554
94StaCluT-188
94StaCluTFDI-188
94Top-31
94TopGol-31
94TopSpa-31
94Ult-100
94UppDec-471
94UppDecED-471
95ColCho-511
95ColChoGS-511
95ColChoSE-244
95ColChoSEGS-244
95ColChoSESS-244
95ColChoSS-511
95Don-397
95DonPreP-397
95DonTopotO-123
95Fla-68
95Fle-79
95Pin-23
95PinArtP-23
95PinMusC-23
95Sco-144
95ScoGolR-144
95ScoPlaTS-144
95StaClu-303
95StaCluMOP-303
95StaCluSTWS-303
95StaCluVR-159
95Top-511
95TopCyb-299
95Ult-313
95UltGolM-313
95UppDec-440
95UppDecED-440
95UppDecEDG-440
95UppDecSE-7
95UppDecSEG-7
96ColCho-634
96ColChoGS-634
96ColChoSS-634
96Fle-193
96FleTif-193
96Pac-377
96Sco-488
95StaCluVRMC-159
96Ult-392

96UltGolM-392
97PacPriGotD-GD76
Perez, Mike (Michael Irvin)
87SprCarB-15
88ArkTraGS-21
88BlaYNPRWL-173
89ArkTraGS-17
89BlaYNPRWL-149
89TexLeaAGS-24
90CMC-108
90LouRedBC-8
90LouRedBLBC-34
90LouRedBP-402
90ProAAAF-516
90SprCarDGB-25
90TopTVCa-60
90TriAllGP-AAA29
91Don-615
91Fle-643
91LouRedTI-12
91OPC-205
91Sco-758
91Top-205
91TopDeb90-124
91TopDesS-205
91TopMic-205
91TopTif-205
91UppDec-728
92DonRoo-94
92Fle-588
92Pin-565
92ScoRoo-95T
92StaClu-798
92StaCluNC-798
92TopTra-88T
92TopTraG-88T
92Ult-571
93CarPol-16
93Don-256
93Fle-132
93FleRooS-RSA9
93OPC-298
93PacSpa-635
93Pin-162
93Sco-345
93Sel-319
93StaClu-202
93StaCluCa-5
93StaCluFDI-202
93StaCluMOP-202
93Top-229
93TopGol-229
93TopInaM-229
93TopMic-229
93Toy-15
93Ult-111
93UppDec-204
93UppDecGold-204
94CarPol-16
94ColC-229
94ColChoGS-229
94ColChoSS-229
94Don-599
94ExtBas-362
94Fin-124
94FinRef-124
94Fla-227
94Fle-644
94Lea-130
94Pac-601
94PanSti-247
94Pin-182
94PinArtP-182
94PinMusC-182
94Sco-84
94ScoGolR-84
94Sel-108
94StaClu-175
94StaCluFDI-175
94StaCluGR-175
94StaCluMOP-175
94StaCluT-320
94StaCluTFDI-320
94Top-567
94TopGol-567
94TopSpa-567
94Ult-271
94UppDec-357
94UppDecED-357
95ColCho-199
95ColChoGS-199
95ColChoSS-199
95FleUpd-128
95Pac-414
95PacPri-132
95StaClu-150
95StaClu-558
95StaCluFDI-150
95StaCluMOP-150
95StaCluMOP-558
95StaCluSTWS-150
95StaCluSTWS-558
95TopTra-52T
96Don-254
96DonPreP-254
96Fle-326
96FleTif-326
96Pac-25
97Pac-255
97PacLigB-255
97PacSil-255
Perez, Neifi
93BenRocC-21
93BenRocF-3279
94Bow-282
94CenValRC-18
94CenValRF-3212
94Cla-63
94ExcFS7-186
94UppDec-545
94UppDecED-545
94UppDecML-196
95Bow-102
95NewHavRTI-3
95SPML-51
95UppDecML-101
95UppDecML-117
96Bow-323
96BowBes-168
96BowBesAR-168
96BowBesMI-4
96BowBesMIAR-4
96BowBesMIR-4
96BowBesR-168
96ColSprSSTI-25
96Top-427
97Bow-220
97BowBes-118
97BowBesAR-118
97BowBesR-118
97BowCerBIA-CA62
97BowCerGIA-CA62
97BowChr-197
97BowChrI-197
97BowChrIR-197
97BowChrR-197
97BowInt-220
97Cir-7
97CirRav-7
97ColCho-17
97Don-264
97DonLim-131
97DonLimLE-131
97DonPreP-264
97DonPrePGold-264
97DonTea-98
97DonTeaSPE-98
97Fin-58
97FinRef-58
97Fle-313
97FleRooS-17
97FleTif-313
97Lea-334
97LeaFraM-334
97LeaFraMDC-334
97MetUniMfG-8
97Pin-178
97PinArtP-178
97PinIns-147
97PinInsCE-147
97PinInsDE-147
97PinMusC-178
97Sel-127
97SelArtP-127
97SelRegG-127
97SkyE-XSD2-10
97StaClu-174
97StaCluM-M40
97StaCluMOP-174
97StaCluMOP-M40
97Top-474
97TopAwel-AI14
97TopGal-162
97TopGalPPI-162
97UppDec-269
95UppDecMLFS-101
95UppDecMLFS-117
Perez, Nelson
95ButCopKtl-17
Perez, Odalis
96EugEmeB-19
Perez, Onesimo
80VenLeaS-67
Perez, Ozzie
90HamRedB-18
90HamRedS-18
91SavCarC-21
91SavCarP-1662
Perez, Paco
77LynMetT-22
79JacMetT-1
Perez, Pascual
77ChaPatT-12
79PorBeaT-20
80PorBeaT-7
81PorBeaT-20
81Top-551
82Fle-491
82PorBeaT-7
82Top-383A
82Top-383B
83AllGamPI-172
83BraPol-27
83Don-557A
83Don-557B
83Fle-144
83TopTra-84T
84BraPol-27
84Don-507
84Fle-188
84FleSti-59
84Nes792-675
84OPC-1
84Top-675
84TopSti-36
84TopTif-675
85BraHos-18
85BraPol-27
85Don-507
85DonActA-18
85Fle-337
85Lea-55
85OPC-106
85Top-106
85TopTif-106
86Fle-524
86Top-491
86TopTif-491
87DonHig-50
87IndIndTI-26
88Don-591
88DonBasB-236
88ExpPos-17
88Fle-192
88FleGlo-192
88Lea-248
88OPC-237
88Sco-459
88ScoGlo-459
88Top-647
88TopBig-196
88TopTif-647
89Bow-354
89BowTif-354
89ClaLigB-85
89Don-248
89DonBasB-302
89Fle-390
89FleGlo-390
89OPC-73
89PanSti-115
89Sco-299
89Top-73
89TopSti-71
89TopTif-73
89UppDec-498
90Bow-430
90BowTif-430
90Don-342
90DonBesA-80
90Fle-358
90FleCan-358
90FleUpd-116
90OPC-278
90PanSti-282
90PubSti-185
90Sco-486
90ScoRoo-5T
90Top-278
90TopBig-291
90TopTif-278
90TopTra-91T
90TopTraT-91T
90TopTVY-16
90UppDec-487
90UppDec-769
90VenSti-397
90YanScoNW-11
91Fle-675
91FouBal-28
91Lea-293
91OPC-701
91StaClu-485
91Top-701
91TopDesS-701
91TopMic-701
91TopTif-701
91UppDec-671
92Don-695
92Fle-240
92OPC-503
92Pin-182
92Sco-88
92Top-503
92TopGol-503
92TopGolW-503
92TopMic-503
Perez, Pastor
74CedRapAT-21
76VenLeaS-137
Perez, Paulino
93ChaRaiC-15
93ChaRaiF-1908
Perez, Pedro
89SalDodTI-23
90VerBeaDS-22
91GenCubC-15
91GenCubP-4212
91PeoChiP-1340
92WinSpiF-1206
Perez, Pedro Julio
90YakBeaTI-36
Perez, Pitcher (Carlos)
85DomLeaS-158
Perez, Ralph
92SpoIndC-24
92SpoIndF-1307
Perez, Ramon
73CedRapAT-2
75IowOakT-14
78ChaChaT-11
79ChaChaT-9
Perez, Raul
80VenLeaS-197
94VenLinU-80
Perez, Richard
91HunCubC-17
91HunCubP-3342
92HunCubC-6
92HunCubF-3155
93PeoChiC-16
93PeoChiF-1093
93PeoChiTI-20
94DayCubC-19
94DayCubF-2362
94VenLinU-235
95LinVen-56
96OrlCubB-20
96RocCubTI-23
Perez, Robert
90St.CatBJP-3456
91DunBluJC-22
91DunBluJP-220
92ClaFS7-161
92KnoBluJF-3003
92KnoBluJS-391
92ProFS7-168
92SkyAA F-166
93LinVenB-262
93SyrChiF-1011
94ExcFS7-147
94LeaLimR-77
94SyrChiF-985
94SyrChiTI-19
94TriAAF-AAA19
94VenLinU-125
95LinVen-168
95LinVen-272
95Pac-449
95Sco-578
95ScoGolR-578
95ScoPlaTS-578
95SyrChiTI-19
96BluJayOH-24
96ColCho-747
96ColChoGS-747
96ColChoSS-747
96FleUpd-U100
96FleUpdTC-U100
96LeaSigA-180
96LeaSigAG-180
96LeaSigAS-180
96Pac-446
96Pin-173
96PinArtP-99
96PinSta-99
96Sco-491
96Sel-180
96SelArtP-180
96Ult-434
96UltGolM-434
97Fle-248
97FleTif-248
97Lea-158
97LeaFraM-158
97LeaFraMDC-158
97MetUni-189
97Pac-225
97PacLigB-225
97PacSil-225
97Sco-229
97ScoPreS-229
97ScoShoS-229
97ScoShoSAP-229
97Top-72
97Ult-150
97UltGolME-150
97UltPlaME-150
Perez, Santiago
95FayGenTI-19
96LakTigB-18
Perez, Segio
85DomLeaS-125
86ClePhiP-19
Perez, Tomas
94BurBeeC-20
94BurBeeF-1091
94MidLeaAF-MDW34
95LinVen-200
95StaClu-588
95StaCluMOP-588
95StaCluSTWS-588
95TopTra-24T
95UppDec-253
95UppDecED-253
95UppDecEDG-253
96ColCho-744
96ColChoGS-744
96ColChoSS-744
96Don-169
96DonPreP-169
96Pac-441
96Top-106
96UppDec-213
97BluJayS-56
97Don-161
97DonPreP-161
97DonPrePGold-161
97Lea-128
97LeaFraM-128
97LeaFraMDC-128
97Pac-226
97PacLigB-226
97PacSil-226
Perez, Tony
65RedEnq-22
65Top-581
66OPC-72
66Top-72
66TopVen-72
67CokCapR-8
67Kah-29
67Top-476
67TopVen-327
68Baz-12
68Kah-B27
68OPC-130
68Top-130
68Top3-D-7
68TopActS-12C
68TopVen-130
69Kah-A3
69Kah-B16
69MilBra-217
69MLBOffS-134
69Top-295
69TopSta-28
69TopTeaP-20
69TraSta-50

70DayDaiNM-11
70MLBOffS-34
70OPC-63
70OPC-380
70Top-63
70Top-380
70TopScr-16
71Kel-58
71MilDud-58
71MLBOffS-67
71OPC-64
71OPC-66
71OPC-580
71Top-64
71Top-66
71Top-580
71TopCoi-105
71TopGreM-14
71TopSup-6
71TopTat-76
72Dia-37
72EssCoi-11
72MilBra-269
72OPC-80
72Top-80
73LinPor-58
73OPC-205
73OPC-275
73Top-205
73Top-275
74OPC-230
74Top-230
74TopDecE-54
74TopSta-29
75Hos-127
75OPC-560
75Top-560
76CraDis-46
76Hos-86
76LinSup-92
76OPC-195
76OPC-325
76RedIceL-11
76RedKro-15
76RedPos-14
76SSP-39
76Top-195
76Top-325
77BurCheD-160
77ExpPos-25
77MSADis-48
77OPC-135
77RCColC-54
77Top-655
77TopCloS-37
78Hos-4
78OPC-90
78RCColC-14
78Top-15
78WifBalD-59
79ExpPos-19
79OPC-261
79Top-495
80OPC-69
80Top-125
81AllGamPI-6
81CokTeaS-8
81Don-334
81Fle-241
81FleStiC-66
81Kel-17
81OPC-231
81Top-575
81TopScr-8
81TopSti-44
81TopSupHT-7
82Don-408
82Fle-302
82FleSta-170
82OPC-255
82OPC-256
82RedSoxC-14
82Top-255
82Top-256
82TopSti-152
83Don-578
83Fle-191
83OPC-74
83OPC-355
83PhiTas-22
83Top-715
83Top-716
83TopFol-2
83TopSti-8
83TopTra-85T
84Don-503
84DonCha-29
84Fle-44
84Fle-636
84FleUpd-91
84FunFooP-99
84Nes792-385
84Nes792-702
84Nes792-703
84Nes792-704
84OPC-385
84RedBor-24
84RedEnq-1
84Top-385
84Top-702
84Top-703
84Top-704
84TopSti-126
84TopTif-385
84TopTif-702
84TopTif-703
84TopTif-704
84TopTra-91T
84TopTraT-91T
85CirK-28
85DonHig-9
85Fle-546
85OPC-212
85Top-675
85TopTif-675
86Don-15
86Don-428
86DonSupD-15
86Fle-186
86GenMilB-5G
86Lea-15
86OPC-85
86RedTexG-24
86Spo-138
86Top-85
86Top-205
86TopSti-8
86TopSti-143
86TopTat-16
86TopTif-85
86TopTif-205
87Fle-209
87FleGlo-209
87RedKah-NNO
88RedKah-NNO
89RedKah-xx
90RedKah-27
91RedKah-NNO
91UppDecS-9
92KelAll-2
92Nab-7
92RedKah-NNO
93TedWilM-19
93Top-503
93TopGol-503
93TopInaM-503
93TopMic-503
93UppDecS-28
96Red76K-3
96Red76K-10

Perez, Victor
90BilMusP-3236

Perez, Vladimir
87SpaPhiP-23
88LitFalMP-19
89ColMetB-2
89ColMetGS-20
90St.LucMS-20
92BasCitRC-20
92MemChiF-2417
93LimRocDWB-65
93MemChiF-373
94MemChiF-357

Perez, William
89ModA'sC-14

Perez, Yorkis
86KenTwiP-19
87WesPalBEP-667
88JacExpB-11
88JacExpP-973
89WesPalBES-17
90JacExpB-22
90JacExpP-1372
91LinDriAAA-436
91RicBraBC-12
91RicBraLD-436
91RicBraP-2564
91RicBraTI-16
92Don-754
92TopDeb91-137
93HarSenF-268
93LimRocDP-P4
93LimRocDWB-68
93LimRocDWB-P4
94Bow-439
94SpoRoo-63
94SpoRooAP-63
94Ult-495
95ColCho-297
95ColChoGS-297
95ColChoSS-297
95Fle-339
95Pac-175
95PacLatD-27
95Top-600
95TopCyb-371
95Ult-165
95UltGolM-165
96ChaKniB-22
96Don-154
96DonPreP-154
96LeaSigEA-155
96Pac-81
97Fle-588
97FleTif-588
97Pac-305
97PacLigB-305
97PacSil-305

Perezchica, Tony
84EveGiaC-30B
86FreGiaP-20
87ShrCapP-6
88PhoFirC-16
88PhoFirP-75
88TriAAAP-32
89Fle-338
89FleGlo-338
89PhoFirC-14
89PhoFirP-1502
89ScoHot1R-50
90Bow-235
90BowTif-235
90CMC-547
90PhoFirC-20
91DonRoo-10
91GiaPacGaE-30
91LinDriAAA-388
91PhoFirLD-388
91PhoFirP-74
91Sco-735
92ColSprSSF-759
92IndFanC-23
92Sco-702
92StaClu-454
92TopGol-366
92TopGolW-366
92Ult-355
94AbaYanF-1450
95ColCliMCTI-16
95ColCliP-22
95ColCliTI-22

Perigny, Don
91SouBenWSC-19
91SouBenWSP-2855
92SarWhiSCB-12
92SarWhiSF-203
93BirBarF-1191
94PorSeaDF-676
94PorSeaDTI-26

Perisho, Matt
94Bow-419
94CedRapKC-19
94CedRapKF-1107
96LakElsSB-9

Perkins, Bill
86NegLeaF-94

Perkins, Broderick
78PadFamF-21
79Top-725
80HawIsIT-22
81Don-525
81Fle-498
81Top-393
81TopSti-226
82Don-397
82Fle-579
82FleSta-103
82OPC-192
82Top-192
82TopSti-98
83Don-121
83Fle-368
83IndPos-27
83IndWhe-24
83Top-593
83TopSti-292
83TopTra-86T
84Don-276
84Fle-548
84Ind-24
84IndWhe-15
84Nes792-212
84Top-212
84TopTif-212
85Top-609
85TopTif-609

Perkins, Cecil
81TCM60I-471
92YanWIZ6-97

Perkins, Charlie
90DodTar-617

Perkins, Craig
75OmaRoyTI-13
76OmaRoyTT-21

Perkins, Cy (Ralph)
20NatCarE-76
21Exh-127
21Nei-11
21OxfConE-12
22E120-87
22W572-75
22W573-96
23WilChoV-122
25Exh-110
26Exh-110
27YorCarE-29
34DiaMatCSB-148
35TigFreP-15
36WorWidGV-24
49PhiBul-42
76TigOldTS-17
91ConTSN-185
94ConTSN-1157
94ConTSNB-1157
96NoiSatP-1

Perkins, Dan
93EliTwiC-1
93EliTwiF-3417
94EliTwiC-19
94EliTwiF-3729
94ExcFS7-97
94ForWayWC-18
94ForWayWF-2009
95ForWayWTI-10
96FtMyeMB-6

Perkins, David
90MisStaB-29
91MisStaB-36
92MisStaB-31
93MisStaB-30

Perkins, Harold
82VerBeaDT-19
83VerBeaDT-20
89RocRedWC-18
89RocRedWP-1643

Perkins, Paul
91PenPilC-9
91PenPilP-375
92SanBerC-24
92SanBerSF-951
93JacSunF-2710
94Bow-33
95LynHilTI-18

Perkins, Ray
82AubAstT-5
86FloStaLAP-38
86MiaMarP-20

Perkins, Scott
94HelBreF-3613
94HelBreSP-11

Perkins, Tom
75CliPilT-22

Perkowski, Harry
52Bow-202
52Top-142
53BowC-87
53Top-236
54Bow-44
54Top-125
55Top-184
83TopRep5-142
91TopArc1-236
94TopArc1-125
94TopArc1G-125

Perlman, Jon
83IowCubT-8
84IowCubT-6
85IowCubT-19
86PhoFirP-20
87PhoFirP-13
88ColSprSSC-6
88ColSprSSP-1542
88Fle-93
88FleGlo-93
88FleUpd-22
88FleUpdG-22
89Sco-591
89Top-476
89TopTif-476

Perlozzo, Sam
77TacTwiDQ-4
78Top-704
79HawIsIC-5
79HawIsIT-11
79Top-709
81TidTidT-22
83LynMetT-11
84JacMetT-16
86TidTidP-23
87MetColP-44
88MetColP-43
88MetKah-34
89MetColP-48
89MetKah-22
90RedKah-27
91RedKah-NNO
92RedKah-NNO
93MarMot-28
94MarMot-28
95MarMot-28

Perna, Bobby
90BilMusP-3230
91ChaWheC-18
91ChaWheP-2895
91SouAtlLAGP-SAL9
92ChaWheF-16
92ChaWVWC-21
92ClaFS7-56
93ClaFS7-237
93ExcFS7-26
93SouAtlLAPI-30
93WinSpiC-18
93WinSpiF-1579
94ChaLooF-1366

Perno, Donn
87EveGiaC-23

Pernoll, H. Hub
11SpoLifM-67

Perodin, Ron
80CliGiaT-21

Perona, Joe
92Bow-246
92ClaFS7-169
92LakTigC-5
92LakTigF-2282
92UppDecML-90
93LonTigF-2310
94Bow-453
94TreThuF-2123

Perozo, Danny
88BilMusP-1813
89BilMusP-2058
89GreHorP-409
90ChaWheB-23
90ChaWheP-2254
91CedRapRC-23
91CedRapRP-2733

Perozo, Ed
89ElmPioP-13
90LynRedSTI-3
91ColMetPI-6
91ColMetPPI-4
92ColMetC-15
92ColMetF-310
92ColMetPI-9
93ForLauRSC-22
93ForLauRSFP-1607
93LinVenB-266
94VenLinU-217
95LinVen-54

Perpetuo, Nelson
91BriTigC-28
91BriTigP-3601
95ChaRivTI-19

Perranoski, Ron
61DodUniO-15
61Top-525
62DodBelB-16
62Top-297
63Top-403

64ChatheY-41
64DodHea-8
64Top-30
64TopCoi-64
64TopSta-46
64TopTatI-62
64TopVen-30
64WheSta-35
65ChaTheY-42
65DodTeal-14
65Top-484
66Top-555
67CokCapD-16
67CokCapDA-16
67DexPre-164
67Top-197
68Top-435
69OPC-77
69Top-77A
69Top-77B
69TopSta-197
70DayDaiNM-116
70MLBOffS-237
70OPC-226
70Top-226
71MLBOffS-469
71OPC-475
71Top-475
71TopCoi-104
72OPC-367
72Top-367
78TwiFri-40
81DodPol-NNO
83DodPol-NNO
84DodPol-NNO
85DodCokP-25
86DodCokP-23
86DodPol-NNO
87DodMot-27
87DodPol-29
88DodMot-28
89DodMot-27
89DodPol-1
90DodMot-28
90DodPol-NNO
90DodTar-618
91DodMot-28
91DodPol-NNO
92DodMot-28
92DodPol-NNO
93DodMot-28
93DodPol-30
94DodMot-28
94DodPol-30

Perrier, Hip
87OldJudN-399

Perring, George
08AmeLeaPC-14
09T206-287
11SpoLifM-287
14CraJacE-119
15CraJacE-119

Perritt, Pol (William D.)
16ColE13-132
17HolBreD-78
92ConTSN-488

Perry, Alonzo
49RemBre-21

Perry, Bob
86KenTwiP-20

Perry, Bob (Melvin)
60TacBan-13
61TacBan-16
64Top-48
64TopVen-48

Perry, Chan
94BurIndC-21
94BurIndF-3804
96KenIndB-21

Perry, David
89BoiHawP-1981

Perry, Eric
87WytCubP-9
88ChaWheB-7
88GenCubP-1633
89PeoChiTI-19

Perry, Gaylord
47PM1StaP1-160
61TacBan-15
61UniOil-T29
62Top-199
63Top-169
64Top-468
65GiaTeal-9
65OPC-193
65Top-193
66Top-598
67CokCapA-26
67CokCapG-15
67CokCapNLA-31
67DexPre-165
67Top-236
67Top-320
67TopVen-312
68DexPre-61
68OPC-11
68OPC-85
68Top-11
68Top-85
68TopVen-11
68TopVen-85
69MilBra-218
69MLBOffS-207
69Top-485A
69Top-485B
69TopSta-110
69TopTeaP-14
70Gia-11
70Kel-20
70MLBOffS-132
70Top-560
71GiaTic-10
71Kel-6
71MilDud-59
71MLBOffS-261
71OPC-70
71OPC-140
71Top-70
71Top-140
71TopCoi-73
71TopSup-2
72MilBra-270
72OPC-285
72Top-285
73Kel2D-38
73LinPor-65
73OPC-66
73OPC-346
73OPC-400
73Top-66
73Top-346
73Top-400
73TopCanL-39
73TopCom-14
73TopPin-14
74OPC-35
74Top-35
74TopSta-168
75Hos-84
75Kel-45
75OPC-530
75SSP18-9
75SSP42-30
75Top-530
76Hos-4
76HosTwi-4
76OPC-55
76OPC-204
76Top-55
76Top-204
77BurCheD-20
77Hos-73
77OPC-149
77RCColC-52
77Spo-1920
77Top-152
78Hos-139
78PadFamF-22
78Top-686
78WifBalD-60
79Hos-83
79Kel-49
79OPC-161
79Top-5
79Top-321
80OPC-148
80PerHaloFP-210
80Top-280
81BraPol-46
81Don-471
81Fle-91
81Top-582
81TopTra-812
82Don-543
82Fle-445
82FleSta-67
82OPC-115
82Top-115
82TopTra-88T
83Don-307
83DonActA-28
83Fle-483
83Fle-630
83FleSta-150
83FleSti-181
83MarNal-4
83OPC-96
83OPC-159
83Top-463
83Top-464
83TopFol-1
83TopGayP-1
83TopGayP-2
83TopGayP-3
83TopGayP-4
83TopGayP-5
83TopGayP-6
83TopSti-114
84Don-A
84DonCha-32
84Fle-352
84Fle-638
84Fle-641
84FleSti-98
84GiaMot-4
84Nes792-4
84Nes792-6
84OCoandSI-214
84Top-4
84Top-6
84TopTif-4
84TopTif-6
86PadGreT-9
86RanGreT-1
88GreBasS-39
88HouSho-3
89PacLegI-152
89PadMag-24
89TopBasT-18
90BasWit-40
90PacLeg-43
90PerGreM-79
90SweBasG-66
91FouBal-20
91Kel3D-1
91PadMag-25
91SweBasG-70
91UppDecHoB-H2
91UppDecHoB-AU2
91UppDecS-5
91UppDecS-15
91UppDecS-18
91UppDecS-20
92GiaCheHoFP-3
92MVP-8
92MVP2H-9
92UppDecF-49
92UppDecFG-49
92UppDecHH-HI6
92UppDecS-34
92YanWIZ8-145
92YanWIZH-26
93ActPacA-125
93ActPacA2-59G
93ActPacAC-9
93MetIma-15
93RanKee-289
93TedWil-94
93Yoo-12
96AriLot-2
97TopStaHRR-10
97TopStaHRRA-10

Perry, Gerald
82ArkTraT-6
82RicBraT-14
83RicBraT-14
84BraPol-28
84Don-263
84FleUpd-92
84TopTra-92T
84TopTraT-92T
85BraHos-19
85BraPol-28
85Don-443
85Fle-338
85Top-219
85TopTif-219
86Don-165
86Fle-525
86RicBraP-16
86Top-557
86TopTif-557
87BraSmo-17
87Top-639
87TopTif-639
88Don-437
88DonBasB-58
88Fle-547
88FleGlo-547
88Lea-216
88PanSti-242
88Sco-136
88ScoGlo-136
88StaLinBra-14
88Top-39
88TopBig-40
88TopTif-39
89Bow-273
89BowTif-273
89BraDub-20
89CadEllD-39
89ClaTraO-118
89Don-22
89Don-239
89DonAll-57
89DonBasB-291
89DonBonM-BC24
89DonSupD-22
89Fle-597
89Fle-638
89FleBasA-31
89FleBasM-31
89FleGlo-597
89FleHeroB-30
89OPC-130
89PanSti-40
89RedFolSB-90
89Sco-101
89ScoHot1S-20
89Spo-164
89Top-130
89TopBasT-150
89TopBig-279
89TopCoi-21
89TopMinL-2
89TopSti-33
89TopTif-130
89TopUKM-59
89TVSpoM-57
89UppDec-431
90Bow-383
90BowTif-383
90ClaYel-T48
90Don-153
90Fle-592
90FleCan-592
90FleUpd-103
90Lea-441
90OPC-792
90PubSti-118
90RicBra2ATI-19
90Sco-249
90ScoRoo-28T
90Top-792
90TopSti-27
90TopTif-792
90TopTra-92T
90TopTraT-92T
90UppDec-101
90UppDec-707
90VenSti-398
91Bow-405
91CarPol-21
91Don-130
91Fle-566
91FleUpd-119
91Lea-272
91OPC-384
91PanSti-230
91Sco-286
91ScoRoo-63T
91StaClu-379
91Top-384
91TopDesS-384
91TopMic-384
91TopTif-384
91UltUpd-109
91UppDec-219
92CarPol-16
92Don-634
92Fle-589
92Lea-122
92OPC-498
92Sco-491
92StaClu-338
92Top-498
92TopGol-498
92TopGolW-498
92TopMic-498
92Ult-572
92UppDec-690
93CarPol-17
93Don-468
93Fle-514
93PacSpa-301
93Top-597
93TopGol-597
93TopInaM-597
93TopMic-597
94CarPol-17
94Fle-645
94Pac-602
94Sco-120
94ScoGolR-120
94StaCluT-329
94StaCluTFDI-329
94Top-263
94TopGol-263
94TopSpa-263
95Fle-507
95Pac-415
95Sco-111
95ScoGolR-111
95ScoPlaTS-111

Perry, Herb Edward Jr
93ExcFS7-163
94Bow-551
94BowBes-B76
94BowBesR-B76
94ChaKniF-904
94TriAAF-AAA2
94UppDec-519
94UppDecML-12
95ColCho-272
95ColChoGS-272
95ColChoSE-15
95ColChoSEGS-15
95ColChoSESS-15
95ColChoSS-272
95Top-635
96ColCho-532
96ColChoGS-532
96Don-124
96DonPreP-124
96Fle-96
96FleInd-12
96FleTif-96
96Sco-469
96Top-355
97Top-141

Perry, Herbert Scott
12ColRedB-228
12ColTinT-228
20NatCarE-77
91Cla/Bes-428
91FroRowDP-51
91WatIndC-21
91WatIndP-3376
92KinIndC-23
92KinIndF-2486
92UppDecML-190
94SigRoo-18
94SigRooS-18
94UppDecED-519
96BufBisB-16
96ColChoSS-532

Perry, Jason
92SpoIndC-30

Perry, Jeff
84SavCarT-14
87VisOakP-7

Perry, Jim
59Ind-15
59Kah-27
59Top-542
60Kah-32
60Lea-49
60Top-324
61Baz-22
61Kah-31
61Pos-59A
61Pos-59B
61Top-48
61Top-385
61Top-584
61TopStaI-138
62Jel-43
62Kah-29
62Pos-43
62PosCan-43

62SalPlaC-32
62ShiPlaC-32
62Top-37
62Top-405
62TopBuc-67
62TopStal-37
62TopVen-37
63Top-535
64Top-34
64TopVen-34
65Top-351
66Top-283
66TopVen-283
66TwiFaiG-12
67CokCapTw-5
67Top-246
67TopVen-247
68Top-393
69MilBra-219
69OPC-146
69Top-146
69TopFou-14
69TopTeaP-15
70DayDaiNM-45
70Kel-64
70MLBOffS-236
70OPC-70
70Top-70
70Top-620
71Kel-3
71MilDud-22
71MLBOffS-470
71OPC-69
71OPC-500
71Top-69
71Top-500
71TopCoi-12
71TopGreM-10
71TopSup-24
71TopTat-112
72MilBra-271
72OPC-220
72OPC-497
72Top-220
72Top-497
73LinPor-66
73OPC-385
73Top-385
74OPC-316
74Top-316
75OPC-263
75Top-263
78TCM60I-105
78TigDeaCS-10
78TwiFri-17
81TacTigT-31
86TwiGreT-9
88PacLegI-18
89SweBasG-37
90BasWit-44
Perry, Master (Ray)
88KimN18-36
Perry, Parnell
86GenCubP-23
87PeoChiP-22
Perry, Pat
83ColAstT-18
84ArkTraT-18
85LouRedR-18
86CarSchM-20
86CarTeal-34
86Don-596
86FleUpd-89
87CarSmo-4
87Don-430
87Fle-307
87FleGlo-307
87Top-417
87TopTif-417
88CubDavB-37
88Don-626
88Fle-244
88FleGlo-244
88Sco-557
88ScoGlo-557
88Top-282
88TopTif-282
89Don-404
89Fle-435
89FleGlo-435
89Sco-364
89Top-186
89TopBig-329
89TopTif-186
89UppDec-345
90OPC-541
90PubSti-199
90Sco-436
90SprCarDGB-17
90Top-541
90TopTif-541
90VenSti-399
91Sco-527
Perry, Ron
80GleFalWSBT-17
80GleFalWSCT-1
81GleFalWST-15
Perry, Shawn
83TacTigT-33
Perry, Steve
79LodDodT-8
81VerBeaDT-14
83AlbDukT-9
84AlbDukC-154
90OneYanP-3370
Perschke, Greg
89UtiBluSP-17
90SarWhiSS-19
90StaFS7-59
91LinDriAAA-644
91VanCanLD-644
91VanCanP-1593
92Bow-282
92SkyAAAF-288
92VanCanF-2720
92VanCanS-645
93AlbDukF-1458
94OrlCubF-1382
Persing, Tim
90EliTwiS-16
91Cla/Bes-371
91KenTwiC-8
91KenTwiP-2070
91MidLeaAP-MWL38
92Ft.MyeMF-2743
92VisOakC-7
92VisOakF-1013
Person, Carl
75QuaCitAT-9
Person, Robert
90KinIndTI-23
91BenBucC-9
91BenBucP-3694
91KinIndC-10
91KinIndP-322
92SarWhiSF-204
93HigDesMC-17
93HigDesMF-40
94BinMetF-702
95BinMetTI-16
95Bow-24
95UppDec-263
95UppDecED-263
95UppDecEDG-263
96Bow-317
96ColCho-39
96Fle-486
96FleTif-486
96LeaSigEA-156
96MetKah-27
96NorTidB-23
96Ult-515
96UltGolM-515
97Cir-180
97CirRav-180
97ColCho-168
97Fle-404
97Fle-511
97FleTif-404
97FleTif-511
97Top-116
97Ult-533
97UltGolME-533
97UltPlaME-533
Person, Wilton
94IdaFalBF-3600
94IdaFalBSP-4
95EugEmeTI-13
Persons, Archie
09T206-509
10CouT21-54
Pertica, William
22E120-235
23W503-60
Perusek, Bill
96FayGenB-24
Perzanowski, Stan
75IntLeaASB-23
75PacCoaLAB-23
76OPC-388
76Top-388
77SalLakCGC-17
93RanKee-290
Pesavento, Mike
85VerBeaDT-22
Pesavento, Patrick
90FayGenP-2415
90SouAtlLAS-18
Pesky, Johnny
42RedSoxTI-20
46RedSoxTI-19
46SpoExcW-7-3
47Exh-175
47HomBon-37
47PM1StaP1-161
47TipTop-11
48RedSoxTI-20
49Bow-86
49Lea-121
49MPR302-2-121
50AmeNut&CCP-13
50Bow-137
50Dra-32
51Bow-15
51TopBluB-5
52Bow-45
52Top-15
53BowC-134
53TigGle-24
54Bow-135
54Top-63
55Bow-241
61UniOil-S8
63Top-343
64Top-248
64TopVen-248
67TopPirS-20
76SSP-625
76TayBow4-6
83TopRep5-15
84TCMPla1-3
87RedSox1T-4
91TopArc1-315
91UppDecS-4
92BazQua5A-13
94TedWil-5
94TopArc1-63
94TopArc1G-63
Pesut, Nick
47SunBre-17
Petagine, Roberto
91BurAstC-17
91BurAstP-2811
92Bow-31
92ClaFS7-205
92JacGenF-4008
92OscAstC-23
92OscAstF-2540
92UppDecML-313
93Bow-644
93JacGenF-2117
93LinVenB-234
94Bow-342
94Bow-530
94BowBes-B42
94BowBesR-B42
94Cla-184
94ClaGolF-100
94ColC-581
94ColChoGS-581
94ColChoSS-581
94ExcAllF-2
94ExcFS7-208
94Lea-365
94Sel-406
94SpoRoo-113
94SpoRooAP-113
94Top-448
94TopGol-448
94TopSpa-448
94TucTorF-772
94Ult-510
94UppDecML-9
94UppDecML-268
94UppDecMLPotYF-PY2
94VenLinU-50
95Don-230
95DonPreP-230
95Fin-226
95FinRef-226
95Fla-422
95FleUpd-188
95LinVen-27
95LinVen-265
95Pac-192
95PadCHP-8
95PadMot-9
95Pin-145
95PinArtP-145
95PinMusC-145
95Sco-305
95ScoGolR-305
95ScoPlaTS-305
95Sel-152
95SelArtP-152
95SelCer-132
95SelCerMG-132
95Spo-165
95SpoArtP-165
95StaClu-591
95StaCluMOP-591
95StaCluSTWS-591
95Sum-158
95SumNthD-158
95Top-650
95TopTra-147T
95UC3-100
95UC3ArtP-100
95Zen-138
96ColCho-297
96ColCho-358
96ColChoGS-297
96ColChoGS-358
96ColChoSS-297
96ColChoSS-358
96Don-63
96DonPreP-63
96NorTidB-24
96Pac-183
96Sco-352
96ScoDugC-B77
96ScoDugCAP-B77
97PacPriGotD-GD176
Petcka, Joe
92FroRowDP-91
92PitMetF-3291
93CapCitBC-17
93CapCitBF-458
93StaCluM-59
94St.LucMF-1193
95StLucMTI-25
Pete, Pioneer
83RedPioT-32
Peterek, Jeff
86StoPorP-20
87ElPasDP-23
88ElPasDB-21
89DenZepC-8
89DenZepP-46
90CMC-26
90DenZepC-1
90DenZepP-623
90Don-530
90Fle-333
90FleCan-333
90ProAAAF-648
90TopDeb89-97
94BreMilB-162
Peterman, Ernie
95StCatSTI-13
Peters, Anthony
96BelSnaTI-31
Peters, Brannon
95ForWayWTI-11
Peters, Chris
93WelPirC-20
93WelPirF-3356
94AugGreC-15
94AugGreF-3005
95LynHilTI-19
96CarMudB-6
96Exc-221
97PacPriGotD-GD194
Peters, Dan
88BelBreGS-20
Peters, Donald
90ClaDraP-26
90ClaYel-T83
90ProAaA-161
90SouOreAB-25
90SouOreAP-3424
91Bow-224
91Cla/Bes-288
91Cla1-T77
91HunStaC-19
91HunStaLD-292
91HunStaP-1794
91HunStaTI-18
91LinDriAA-292
91Sco-381
92Bow-244
Peters, Doug
90EugEmeGS-22
91LinDriAA-412
91MemChiLD-412
91MemChiP-649
Peters, Francis
68Top-409
81TCM60I-400
Peters, Gary
47Exh-176
60Top-346
60Top-407
61Top-303
62WhiSoxTS-15
63Top-522
63WhiSoxJP-10
64Baz-27
64Top-2
64Top-130
64TopCoi-71
64TopCoi-140
64TopGia-1
64TopSta-56
64TopStaU-56
64TopTatI-63
64TopVen-2
64TopVen-130
64WhiSoxTS-18
65Baz-27
65OldLonC-32
65OPC-9
65Top-9
65Top-430
65TopEmbI-18
65TopTraI-62
65WhiSoxJP-6
66OPC-111
66Top-111
66TopVen-111
66WhiSoxTI-10
67Baz-9
67CokCapWS-1
67ProPizC-12
67Top-233
67Top-310
67TopGiaSU-2
67TopVen-196
68Baz-14
68Kah-B28
68OPC-8
68Top-8
68Top-210
68Top-379
68TopActS-10C
68TopGamI-13
68TopPla-10
68TopPos-13
68TopVen-8
68TopVen-210
69Kah-B17
69MilBra-220
69MLBOffS-34
69OPC-34
69Top-34
69TopSta-157
69WhiSoxTI-11
70DayDaiNM-134
70MLBOffS-161
70OPC-540
70RedSoxCPPC-10
70Top-540
71MLBOffS-327
71OPC-225
71RedSoxA-7
71RedSoxTI-7
71Top-225
71TopTat-84
72MilBra-272
72OPC-503
72Top-503
85WhiSoxC-40
89PacLegI-159
Peters, Jack (John)
21Nei-63
22E120-204
94EliTwiC-20
94EliTwiF-3730
Peters, Jay
79SalLakCGT-20A

80SalLakCGT-11
Peters, Jimmy
43ParSpo-61
Peters, Ken
76SeaRaiC-11
Peters, Oscar
12T207-150
Peters, Ray
94BreMilB-163
Peters, Reed
87SalAngP-13
88PalSprACLC-108
88PalSprAP-1439
89MidAngGS-26
90CMC-494
90EdmTraC-17
90EdmTraP-529
90ProAAAF-105
91EdmTraLD-168
91EdmTraP-1529
91LinDriAAA-168
92PhoFirF-2834
92ShrCapF-3883
92ShrCapS-588
93PhoFirF-1530
Peters, Rex
89SalDodTI-24
90VerBeaDS-23
91BakDodCLC-6
91CalLeLA-19
Peters, Ricky (Richard D.)
81Don-10
81Fle-470
81Top-177
81TopSti-77
82Don-155
82Fle-277
82OPC-269
82Top-504
83TacTigT-29A
84Fle-458
84Nes792-436
84Top-436
84TopTif-436
85TacTigC-130
86A'sMot-24
90AubAstP-3417
91PacSenL-117
92BurAstC-28
Peters, Rusty
94ConTSN-1296
94ConTSNB-1296
Peters, Steve
77ForLauYS-20
87ArkTraP-9
87TexLeaAF-19
88CarSmo-23
88DonRoo-22
88LouRedBTI-39
88TopTra-84T
88TopTraT-84T
89Fle-462
89FleGlo-462
89LouRedBC-9
89LouRedBP-1247
89LouRedBTI-30
89Top-482
89TopTif-482
89UppDec-771
90CMC-504
90LasVegSC-2
90LasVegSP-120
90ProAAAF-8
90SprCarDGB-20
91LinDriAAA-317
91OklCit8LD-317
91OklCit8P-175
Peters, Tim
86AncGlaPTI-29
87SalLakTTT-25
88MidLeaAGS-47
89JacExpB-13
89JacExpP-154
90JacExpP-1373
96ForWayWB-19
Peters, Tom
87BelMarTI-10
91BakDodCLC-28
Petersen, Andy
89SanDieSAS-21
Petersen, Chris
92FroRowDP-58
92GenCubF-1568
93DayCubC-15
96OrlCubB-21
95OrlCubF-20
Petersen, Matt
92EriSaiF-1620
93KanCouCC-14
93KanCouCF-914
93Top-497
93TopGol-497
93TopInaM-497
93TopMic-497
94BreCouMC-11
94BreCouMF-8
94FloStaLAF-FSL28
95OrlCubF-7
Peterson, Adam C.
86PenWhiSP-20
87BirBarB-13
87SouLeaAJ-20
88Fle-646
88FleGlo-646
88VanCanC-7
88VanCanP-776
89Don-619
89TriA AAC-45
89VanCanC-2
89VanCanP-589
90BirBarDGB-27
90Bow-307
90BowTif-307
90CMC-629
90OPC-299
90ProAAAF-166
90Top-299
90TopTif-299
90TriAAAC-45
90VanCanC-2
90VanCanP-488
91Fle-134
91LasVegSLD-290
91LasVegSP-233
91LinDriAAA-290
91OPC-559
91PadSmo-25
91Sco-604
91Sco100RS-94
91Top-559
91TopDesS-559
91TopMic-559
91TopTif-559
92LasVegSF-2794
92LasVegSS-237
92UppDec-602
Peterson, Art
76SeaRaiC-12
Peterson, Bart
91KenTwiC-14
91KenTwiP-2071
92Ft.MyeMCB-17
92Ft.MyeMF-2744
Peterson, Brian
90MemChiB-28
90MemChiP-1027
91LinDriAA-425
91MemChiLD-425
91MemChiP-671
92SalLakTSP-29
93KanCouCC-28
93KanCouCF-933
94KanCouCC-28
94KanCouCF-180
94KanCouCTI-22
95KanCouCTI-19
96KanCouCTI-21
93KanCouCTI-14
Peterson, Buddy (Carl)
52MotCoo-29
53MotCoo-8
91OriCro-359
Peterson, Cap (Charles Andrew)
64Top-568
65Top-512
66Top-349
66TopVen-349
67Top-387
68OPC-188
68SenTeal-11
68Top-188
68TopVen-188
69SenTeal8-17
69Top-571
Peterson, Charles
94AugGreC-16
94AugGreF-3021
94Bow-658
94ClaGolF-75
94ClaGolN1PLF-LP10
94ClaGolREF-RE10
94Top-207
94TopGol-207
94TopSpa-207
94UppDecML-211
95LynHilTI-20
95SPML-133
96BesAutS-71
96BesAutSA-53
96Bow-277
96CarMudB-24
96Exc-222
96Top-438
Peterson, Chris
92GenCubC-9
93DayCubF-865
94OrlCubF-1392
Peterson, D. Scott
77AshTouT-17
78AshTouT-22
Peterson, Dave
85GreHorT-19
86NewBriRSP-20
Peterson, Dean
95TreThuTI-13
96SarRedSB-26
Peterson, Dennis
76SeaRaiC-13
Peterson, Doug
76SeaRaiC-14
Peterson, Erik
80WatIndT-19
81NasSouTI-12
82NasSouTI-17
83NasSouTI-16
84NasSouTI-17
Peterson, Fritz
64YanReqKP-11
66Top-584
67CokCapYM-V16
67DexPre-166
67Top-495
68Top-246
68TopVen-246
69MLBOffS-77
69OPC-46
69Top-46
69TopTeaP-19
70DayDaiNM-128
70MLBOffS-248
70OPC-142
70Top-142
70YanCliDP-4
71MilDud-23
71MLBOffS-499
71OPC-460
71Top-460
71TopCoi-138
71TopGreM-44
71TopSup-13
71YanArcO-10
71YanCliDP-14
72ProStaP-33
72Top-573
72Top-574
73OPC-82
73SyrChiTI-23
73Top-82
73Yan-5
74OPC-229
74SyrChiTI-22
74Top-229
75OPC-62
75Top-62
76Hos-32
76HosTwi-32
76OPC-255
76SSP-511
76Top-255
81TCM60I-450
83YanASFY-33
90SweBasG-79
92YanWIZ6-98
92YanWIZ7-127
92YanWIZA-59
93RanKee-291
Peterson, Geoff
86Ft.MyeRP-21
Peterson, Harding
57JetPos-16
58Top-322
Peterson, Jayson
94ClaUpdCotC-CC13
94HunCubF-3551
94SigRooDP-15
94SigRooDPS-15
94StaCluDP-11
94StaCluDPFDI-11
95Bow-44
95Exc-168
95Pin-176
95PinArtP-176
95PinMusC-176
95ScoDraP-DP14
95StaClu-112
95StaCluFDI-112
95StaCluMOP-112
95StaCluSTWS-112
95Top-437
95UppDecML-196
96RocCubTI-24
94HunCubC-1
95UppDecMLFS-196
Peterson, Jerry
75WatRoyT-23
76WatRoyT-22
Peterson, Jim
77CliDodT-19
90DodTar-619
Peterson, Kent
49EurSta-92
49Lea-42
51Bow-215
Peterson, Mark
92EveGiaC-15
92EveGiaF-1686
93SanJosGC-20
93SanJosGF-6
94SanJosGC-19
94SanJosGF-2814
Peterson, Matt
92EriSaiC-2
93KanCouCTI-15
Peterson, Nate
93AubAstC-18
93AubAstF-3448
94QuaCitRBC-15
94QuaCitRBF-537
96JacGenB-22
Peterson, Pat
75ForLauYS-11
Peterson, Rick
78SalPirT-12
82BufBisT-17
88ColSprSSP-1530
89BirBarB-28
89BirBarP-99
89PacSenL-153
89TopSenL-104
90BirBarB-25
91BirBarLD-75
91BirBarP-1471
91LinDriAA-75
91PacSenL-49
93NasSouF-586
94NasSouF-1267
94WhiSoxK-30
Peterson, Ricky (Eric)
77ChaPatT-13
Peterson, Rob
89WelPirP-20
90WelPirP-18
Peterson, Robert A.
09ColChiE-229
12ColRedB-229
12ColTinT-229
Peterson, Tim
76CedRapGT-21
Petestio, Doug
84MidCubT-12
Petillo, Bruce
93BatCliC-23
93BatCliF-3150
Petit, Doug
92EriSaiF-1621
Petit, Ricardo
91IdaFalBP-4326
91PulBraC-25
91PulBraP-4002
Petitt, Steven
86St.PetCP-24
Petke, Jonathan
96WatIndTI-24
Petkovsek, Mark
88ChaRanS-19
89TexLeaAGS-36
89TulDriGS-20
89TulDriTI-18
90CMC-155
90OklCit8C-5
90OklCit8P-432
90ProAAAF-678
91LinDriAAA-318
91OklCit8LD-318
91OklCit8P-177
92BufBisBS-14
92BufBisF-321
92BufBisS-38
92SkyAAAF-17
92TexLon-32
92TopDeb91-138
93BufBisF-514
93RanKee-292
94Fle-617
94TucTorF-760
96CarPol-22
96ColCho-694
96ColChoGS-694
96ColChoSS-694
96Don-483
96DonPreP-483
96Fle-554
96FleTif-554
96LeaSigEA-157
96Pac-224
96Sco-448
96SigRooOJ-26
96SigRooOJS-26
96Ult-278
96UltGolM-278
96UppDec-182
97Fle-533
97FleTif-533
Petralli, Geno (Eugene J.)
80KnoBluJT-2
81SyrChiT-9
81SyrChiTI-16
82SyrChiT-13
82SyrChiTI-18
83Don-623
83Fle-439
83SyrChiT-15
85Ind-24
85MaiGuiT-16
85OklCit8T-5
86RanPer-12
86Top-296
86TopTif-296
87Don-619
87Fle-135
87FleGlo-135
87RanMot-20
87RanSmo-8
87Top-388
87TopTif-388
88Don-506
88Fle-477
88FleGlo-477
88Lea-241
88RanMot-20
88RanSmo-3
88Sco-373
88ScoGlo-373
88StaLinRa-13
88Top-589
88TopTif-589
89Don-343
89DonBasB-312
89Fle-530
89FleGlo-530
89OPC-137
89PanSti-451
89RanMot-11
89RanSmo-25
89Sco-526
89Top-137
89TopBig-12
89TopStiB-24
89TopTif-137
89UppDec-482
90Bow-495
90BowTif-495
90Don-56
90DonBesA-27
90Fle-309
90FleCan-309
90Lea-73
90OPC-706
90PanSti-161

90PubSti-419
90RanMot-7
90Sco-153
90Top-706
90TopTif-706
90UppDec-633
90VenSti-400
91Bow-284
91Don-137
91Fle-296
91Lea-148
91OPC-78
91PacRyaTEI-68
91PanFreS-251
91RanMot-7
91Sco-191
91StaClu-10
91Top-78
91TopDesS-78
91TopMic-78
91TopTif-78
91Ult-351
91UppDec-492
92Don-550
92Fle-313
92Lea-357
92OPC-409
92RanMot-7
92RanTeal-17
92Sco-283
92StaClu-3
92Top-409
92TopGol-409
92TopGolW-409
92TopMic-409
92Ult-138
92UppDec-599
93Don-319
93Fle-689
93RanKee-424
93StaClu-232
93StaCluFDI-232
93StaCluMOP-232
93StaCluR-22
93Top-332
93TopGol-332
93TopInaM-332
93TopMic-332
93UppDec-83
93UppDecGold-83
94Don-247
94Fle-317
94Sco-137
94ScoGolR-137

Petrick, Ben
96AshTouB-28
96Bow-252
96MauStiHWB-6
97Bow-206
97BowInt-206

Petrizzo, Tom
86DayBealP-22

Petrocella, Chris
92HelBreF-1713
92HelBreSP-14

Petrocelli, Rico
47PM1StaP1-162
65OPC-74
65Top-74
66Top-298
66TopVen-298
67CokCapRS-11
67DexPre-167
67Top-528
67TopRedSS-13
67TopVen-204
68Baz-5
68CokCapRS-11
68DexPre-62
68OPC-156
68Top-156
68Top-430
68TopVen-156
69CitMetC-8
69MilBra-221
69MLBOffS-15
69OPC-215
69RedSoxAO-9
69RedSoxTI-8
69Top-215
69TopFou-25
69TopSta-136
69TopTeaP-3
69TraSta-21
70DayDaiNM-10
70Kel-54
70MilBra-21
70MLBOffS-162
70OPC-457
70RedSoxCPPC-11
70Top-457
70Top-680
70TopBoo-2
70TopSup-14
70TraSta-15C
71BazNumT-10
71BazUnn-28
71MilDud-24
71MLBOffS-328
71OPC-340
71RedSoxTI-8
71Top-340
71TopCoi-30
71TopGreM-39
71TopSup-19
71TopTat-92
72MilBra-273
72OPC-30
72Top-30
73LinPor-29
73OPC-365
73Top-365
74OPC-609
74Top-609
75Hos-132
75OPC-356
75Top-356
76LinSup-106
76OPC-445
76RedSox-6
76RedSoxSM-12
76SSP-413
76Top-445
77Top-111
79DiaGre-250
81RedSoxBG2S-102
81TCM60I-335
87BirBarB-1
87SouLeaAJ-23
88BirBarB-8
88SouLeaAJ-38
89SweBasG-123
90BirBarDGB-28
90PacLeg-64
90SweBasG-56
91LinDri-31
91SweBasG-71
92PawRedSF-939
92PawRedSS-374
94CarLeaA-DJ26
94TedWil-6
94TedWilM-M35
94UppDecAH-42
94UppDecAH1-42
95TreThuTI-3
96PawRedSDD-22
97DunDonPPS-17

Petroff, Dan
94BoiHawC-21
94BoiHawF-3353
95CedRapKTI-39
96CedRapKTI-19

Petrulis, Paul
91MisStaB-37
92MisStaB-32
93MisStaB-35
93PitMetC-16
93PitMetF-3718
94CapCitBC-17
94CapCitBF-1758
95StLucMTI-26

Petry, Dan
80Top-373
81Don-128
81Fle-468
81Top-59
82Don-133
82Fle-278
82Top-211
82Top-666
83AllGamPI-83
83Don-359
83Fle-339
83OPC-79
83Tig-23
83Top-261
83Top-638
83TopSti-70
84AllGamPI-175
84Don-105
84Fle-89
84FunFooP-60
84Nes792-147
84OPC-147
84TigFarJ-12
84TigWavP-29
84Top-147
84TopSti-269
84TopTif-147
85AllGamPI-83
85Don-334
85Fle-20
85FleStaS-83
85Lea-188
85OPC-392
85SevCoi-D7
85TigCaiD-16
85TigWen-18
85Top-435
85TopGloS-25
85TopSti-264
85TopTif-435
86Don-212
86DonAll-42
86Fle-235
86Lea-144
86OPC-216
86TigCaiD-15
86Top-540
86TopSti-270
86TopTif-540
87Don-373
87Fle-161
87FleGlo-161
87Lea-228
87OPC-27
87SevCoi-D9
87SpoTeaP-15
87TigCaiD-15
87TigCok-12
87Top-752
87TopTif-752
88AngSmo-8
88Don-476
88DonBasB-139
88Fle-67
88FleGlo-67
88Sco-461
88ScoGlo-461
88ScoRoo-26T
88ScoRooG-26T
88Top-78
88TopTif-78
88TopTra-85T
88TopTraT-85T
89Don-344
89Fle-486
89FleGlo-486
89Sco-122
89TopBig-178
89UppDec-552
90Fle-142
90FleCan-142
90Lea-508
90OPC-363
90PubSti-377
90Sco-211
90ScoRoo-39T
90TigCok-16
90Top-363
90TopTif-363
90TopTra-93T
90TopTraT-93T
90UppDec-690
90VenSti-401
91Bow-146
91Don-675
91Fle-347
91PanFreS-295
91PanSti-240
91RedFolS-71
91Sco-434
91TigCok-46
91TigPol-8
91Ult-125
91UppDec-316
92Sco-705

Pett, Jose
93Bow-139
94SyrChiTI-20
95Bes-48
95Exc-140
95KnoSmoF-41
95SPML-165
95UppDecML-111
96KnoSmoB-20
96SyrChiTI-22
95UppDecMLFS-111

Pettaway, Ike
78GreBraT-18
83DurBulT-22

Pettee, Patrick E.
87OldJudN-400
87OldJudN-401

Pettengill, Tim
88NebCor-9
89SavCarP-352

Pettersen, Andy
90SanDieSA3-7

Pettibone, Jay
80AshTouT-17
82OrlTwiT-22
83OrlTwiT-14
84TolMudHT-24

Pettibone, Jim
82CedRapRT-10
83WatRedT-6
84CedRapRT-3
85CedRapRT-11

Pettiford, Cecil
89BurIndS-20
90CalLeaACLC-55
90RenSilSCLC-279
91KinIndC-11
91KinIndP-323
92SalLakTSP-15
93LakTigC-21
93LakTigF-1307
94TreThuF-2120

Pettiford, Torrey
94BatCliC-20
95BatCliTI-25
96PieBolWB-19

Pettini, Joe
78MemChiBC-8
80PhoGiaVNB-20
81Fle-453
81PhoGiaVNB-21
81Top-62
82Fle-398
82Top-568
83Top-143
84Nes792-449
84PhoGiaC-13
84Top-449
84TopTif-449
85LouRedR-12
86LouRedTI-23
87LouRedTI-2
88LouRedBC-24
88LouRedBP-435
88LouRedBTI-2
89HamRedS-27
90St.PetCS-26
91ArkTraLD-49
91ArkTraP-1302
91LinDriAA-49
92ArkTraF-1144
92ArkTraS-49
93ArkTraF-2827
94LouRedF-2996
95LouRedF-291
96LouRedB-1

Pettipiece, Paul
95StCatSTI-32

Pettis, Gary
81HolMilT-20
82SpoIndT-23
84AngSmo-21
84Don-647
84Fle-526
84TopTra-93T
84TopTraT-93T
85AngSmo-9
85Don-499
85Fle-308
85FleStaS-57
85OPC-39
85Top-497
85TopSti-226
85TopTif-497
86AngSmo-9
86Don-158
86Fle-165
86FleMin-33
86FleStiC-88
86Lea-84
86OPC-323
86Top-604
86TopMinL-7
86TopTif-604
87AngSmo-20
87ClaUpdY-134
87Don-160
87DonOpeD-10
87Fle-90
87FleAwaW-29
87FleGlo-90
87Lea-152
87OPC-278
87SevCoi-W7
87Spo-157
87SpoTeaP-11
87Top-278
87TopMinL-47
87TopSti-16
87TopSti-175
87TopTif-278
88Don-210
88DonBasB-203
88FleUpd-29
88FleUpdG-29
88OPC-71
88PanSti-48
88Sco-255
88ScoGlo-255
88ScoRoo-38T
88ScoRooG-38T
88StaLinAn-16
88TigPep-24
88Top-71
88TopSti-178
88TopTif-71
88TopTra-86T
88TopTraT-86T
89Don-60
89Fle-141
89FleGlo-141
89OPC-146
89PanSti-345
89Sco-26
89TigMar-24
89Top-146
89TopMinL-53
89TopSti-279
89TopTif-146
89UppDec-117
90Bow-498
90BowTif-498
90Don-661
90DonBesA-126
90Fle-612
90FleAwaW-25
90FleCan-612
90Lea-469
90OPC-512
90PanSti-78
90PubSti-480
90RanMot-12
90Sco-136
90ScoRoo-6T
90Spo-202
90Top-512
90TopBig-311
90TopMinL-14
90TopSti-283
90TopTif-512
90TopTra-94T
90TopTraT-94T
90UppDec-385
90UppDec-770
90VenSti-402
91Bow-276
91Don-512
91Fle-297
91OPC-314
91PanCanT1-115
91PanFreS-256
91RanMot-12
91Sco-182
91StaClu-141
91StuPre-9
91Top-314
91TopDesS-314
91TopMic-314
91TopTif-314
91Ult-352
91UppDec-229
92Fle-314
92Lea-466

92OPC-756
92PadSmo-22
92PanSti-80
92Sco-308
92StaClu-548
92Top-756
92TopGol-756
92TopGolW-756
92TopMic-756
92Ult-580
92UppDec-179
93RanKee-293
93Sco-442
Pettis, Lynn
85OPC-39
85Top-497
85TopTif-497
Pettis, Stacey
84PriWilPT-34
86PalSprAP-26
Pettit, Bob
60Pos-8
87OldJudN-402
88WG1CarG-13
Pettit, Doug
92EriSaiC-19
93KanCouCC-15
93KanCouCF-915
94BreCouMC-12
94BreCouMF-9
94FloStaLAF-FSL29
95PorSeaDTI-20
93KanCouCTI-16
Pettit, Paul
60HenHouW-15
77FriOneYW-13
Pettit, Thomas
88AllandGN-27
Pettitte, Andy
92ClaFS7-286
92GreHorC-1
92GreHorF-777
92SpollFK1-561
93Bow-103
93ClaGolF-117
93ExcFS7-214
93PriWilCC-19
93SouAtlLAPI-31
94AbaYanF-1438
94Bow-493
94Cla-28
94ExcFS7-111
95Bow-257
95BowBes-B50
95BowBesR-B50
95BowGolF-257
95ColCliMCTI-12
95ColCliP-23
95ColCliTI-23
95Emo-65
95Exc-101
95Fla-287
95FleUpd-27
95Sel-163
95SelArtP-163
95SelCer-96
95SelCerMG-96
95StaClu-565
95StaCluMOP-565
95StaCluSTWS-565
95Sum-168
95SumNthD-168
95Top-640
95UppDec-493T
95UppDecML-176
96BowBes-24
96BowBesAR-24
96BowBesR-24
96Cir-68
96CirRav-68
96ColCho-234
96ColChoGS-234
96ColChoSS-234
96Don-74
96DonPreP-74
96EmoXL-93
96Fin-B122
96FinRef-B122
96Fla-134
96Fle-194
96FleRooS-14
96FleTif-194
96Lea-185
96LeaLim-81
96LeaLimG-81
96LeaPre-72
96LeaPreP-72
96LeaPrePB-185
96LeaPrePG-185
96LeaPrePS-185
96LeaSig-54
96LeaSigA-181
96LeaSigAG-181
96LeaSigAS-181
96LeaSigEA-158
96LeaSigEACM-23
96LeaSigPPG-54
96LeaSigPPP-54
96MetUni-92
96MetUniMFG-11
96MetUniP-92
96Pac-371
96PanSti-152
96PanSti-242
96Pin-103
96Pin-291
96PinFoil-291
96Sco-396
96Sel-103
96SelArtP-103
96SelCer-91
96SelCerAP-91
96SelCerCB-91
96SelCerCR-91
96SelCerMB-91
96SelCerMG-91
96SelCerMR-91
96SP-130
96StaClu-436
96StaCluEPB-436
96StaCluEPG-436
96StaCluEPS-436
96StaCluMO-50
96StaCluMOP-436
96TeaOut-63
96Top-378
96TopGal-104
96TopGalPPI-104
96Ult-104
96UltGolM-104
96UppDec-144
96Zen-88
96ZenArtP-88
97Bow-248
97BowBes-21
97BowBesAR-21
97BowBesR-21
97BowChr-72
97BowChrI-72
97BowChrIR-72
97BowChrR-72
97BowInt-248
97Cir-149
97CirFasT-6
97CirRav-149
97ColCho-60
97ColCho-404
97ColChoAC-18
97ColChoTBS-35
97ColChoTBSWH-35
97ColChoTotT-T20
97Don-82
97Don-424
97DonEli-14
97DonEliGS-14
97DonLim-34
97DonLim-135
97DonLim-177
97DonLimLE-34
97DonLimLE-135
97DonLimLE-177
97DonPre-20
97DonPreCttC-20
97DonPreP-82
97DonPreP-424
97DonPrePGold-82
97DonPrePGold-424
97DonTea-126
97DonTeaSPE-126
97Fin-287
97FinEmb-287
97FinEmbR-287
97FinRef-287
97FlaSho-A46
97FlaSho-B46
97FlaSho-C46
97FlaShoLC-46
97FlaShoLC-B46
97FlaShoLC-C46
97FlaShoLCM-A46
97FlaShoLCM-B46
97FlaShoLCM-C46
97Fle-175
97Fle-711
97FleMilDM-48
97FleTeaL-10
97FleTif-175
97FleTif-711
97FleZon-13
97Lea-136
97Lea-198
97LeaFraM-136
97LeaFraM-198
97LeaFraMDC-136
97LeaFraMDC-198
97LeaGet-3
97LeaGolS-12
97MetUni-121
97MetUniPP-8
97NewPin-24
97NewPinAP-24
97NewPinKtP-15
97NewPinMC-24
97NewPinPP-24
97NewPinPP-K15
97Pac-156
97PacCar-14
97PacCarM-14
97PacCerCGT-17
97PacCraC-4
97PacFirD-8
97PacGolCD-12
97PacLigB-156
97PacPri-53
97PacPriGA-GA10
97PacPriLB-53
97PacPriP-53
97PacPriSH-SH5B
97PacSil-156
97Pin-14
97PinArtP-14
97PinCar-5
97PinCer-92
97PinCerCMGT-17
97PinCerCT-17
97PinCerMBlu-92
97PinCerMG-92
97PinCerMR-92
97PinCerR-92
97PinIns-52
97PinInsC-12
97PinInsCE-52
97PinInsDD-16
97PinInsDE-52
97PinMusC-14
97PinTeaP-9
97PinTeaP-10
97PinTotCPB-92
97PinTotCPG-92
97PinTotCPR-92
97PinX-P-2
97PinX-PMoS-2
97PinX-PMW-17
97PinX-PMWG-17
97PinX-PMWS-17
97ProMag-66
97ProMagML-66
97Sco-82
97Sco-518
97ScoAllF-17
97ScoHobR-518
97ScoPreS-82
97ScoResC-518
97ScoShoS-82
97ScoShoS-518
97ScoShoSAP-82
97ScoShoSAP-518
97ScoStaaD-10
97ScoYan-5
97ScoYanPl-5
97ScoYanPr-5
97Sel-58
97SelArtP-58
97SelRegG-58
97SelToootT-2
97SelToootTMB-2
97SkyE-X-34
97SkyE-XC-34
97SkyE-XEC-34
97SkyE-XSD2-3
97SP-128
97Spolll-66
97Spolll-130
97SpollIEE-66
97SpollIEE-130
97SPSpeF-34
97SPx-35
97SPxBro-35
97SPxGraF-35
97SPxSil-35
97SPxSte-35
97StaClu-46
97StaCluC-CO1
97StaClul-I13
97StaCluMat-46
97StaCluMOP-46
97StaCluMOP-I13
97Stu-5
97StuMasS-6
97StuMasS8-6
97StuPrePG-5
97StuPrePS-5
97Top-60
97TopAll-AS17
97TopChr-20
97TopChrAS-AS17
97TopChrR-20
97TopChrSAR-AS17
97TopChrSB-17
97TopChrSBR-17
97TopGal-160
97TopGalPG-PG14
97TopGalPPI-160
97TopSeaB-SB17
97Ult-102
97UltDouT-7
97UltFamGam-13
97UltGolME-102
97UltPlaME-102
97UltSeaC-7
97UltTop3-15
97UltTop3GM-15
97UppDec-68
97UppDec-122
97UppDec-254
97UppDec-266
97UppDec-380
97UppDecAWJ-9
97UppDecBCP-BC17
95UppDecMLFS-176
97UppDecRSF-RS9
97UppDecU-54
97UppDecUGN-GN12
97Zen-21
Petty, Brian
85EveGiaC-14
Petty, Jesse
33Gou-90
34GouCanV-42
90DodTar-620
Petway, Bruce
78LauLonABS-7
90NegLeaS-31
Pevey, Marty
86LouRedTI-24
89IndIndC-15
89IndIndP-1217
90OPC-137
90Top-137
90TopDeb89-98
90TopTif-137
90UppDec-628
91LinDriAAA-513
91SyrChiLD-513
91SyrChiMB-18
91SyrChiP-2483
92TolMudHF-1046
94SyrChiF-973
94SyrChiTI-21
96MedHatBJTI-22
Peyton, Byron
82CedRapRT-17
Peyton, Eric
82ElPasDT-1
83ElPasDT-2
84VanCanC-41
Peyton, Mickey
88AugPirP-362
Pezzoni, Ron
90PenPilS-14
91CarLeaAP-CAR29
91PenPilC-20
91PenPilP-390
92ClaFS7-247
92SanBerC-2
92SanBerSF-971
93SanJosGC-21
93SanJosGF-26
94Bow-219
94ShrCapF-1621
Pfaff, Bob
86SumBraP-21
87DurBulP-4
89BurBraP-1606
89BurBraS-16
Pfaff, Jason
92LakTigC-18
92LakTigF-2276
93Bow-503
93LonTigF-2305
95LynHilTI-21
Pfaff, Rich
89BelBrelS-22
89BelBrelS-23
Pfeffer, Big Jeff (Francis)
11SpoLifCW-287
11SpoLifM-177
Pfeffer, Jeff (Edward)
09T206-288
15SpoNewM-137
16ColE13-133
17HolBreD-79
19W514-58
20GasAmeMBD-36
20NatCarE-78
21E121So8-70
21E121So8-71
22AmeCarE-53
22W575-97
22W575-98
23WilChoV-123
90DodTar-621
Pfeffer, Kurt
90EliTwiS-17
91KenTwiC-11
91KenTwiP-2090
Pfeffer, Nathaniel F.
06FanCraNL-36
87BucN28-22
87OldJudN-403
88SpoTimM-19
88WG1CarG-14
89EdgR.WG-17
95May-25A
95May-25B
Pfeil, Bobby
70OPC-99
70Top-99
72Top-681
89RinPosM1-23
91MetWIZ-314
94Met69CCPP-26
94Met69CS-25
94Met69T-27
Pfiester, John
07CubA.CDPP-9
07CubGFGCP-9
09ColChiE-230
09RamT20-94
09T206-289
09T206-290
10SweCapPP-87
11SpoLifCW-288
11SpoLifM-178
11T205-138
11TurRedT-33
12ColRedB-230
12ColTinT-230
12PhiCarE-25
Pfirman, Charles
94ConTSN-1204
94ConTSNB-1204
Pfister, Dan
62Top-592
63Top-521
64Top-302
64TopVen-302
Phair, Kelly
95OdgRapTI-22
96OgdRapTI-7
Phanatic, Phillie
83PhiTas-30
84PhiTas-3
87PhiTas-xx
88PhiTas-30
90PhiTas-33
92PhiMed-33
92TriPla-133
93FunPacM-1
93PhiMed-25

94MasMan-11
96PhiTeal-25
96PinFan-PP1
Phelan, Art
11SpoLifM-200
12ImpTobC-35
12T207-151
14FatPlaT-40
Phelan, James D.
87OldJudN-404
Phelan, James F.
09T206-454
11T205-197
Phelan, John
89SpoIndSP-6
Phelps, Babe (Ernest Gordon)
36NatChiFPR-64
37ExhFou-2
38ExhFou-2
39PlaBal-96
40DodTeal-18
40PlaBal-66
41DodTeal-5
89DodSmoG-41
90DodTar-622
94ConTSN-1125
94ConTSNB-1125
Phelps, Edward
09AmeCarE-88
09PC7HHB-35
09T206-291
10DomDisP-98
10NadCarE-40
10SweCapPP-152
11SpoLifCW-289
11SpoLifM-277
11T205-139
12ImpTobC-36
Phelps, Joshua
96MedHatBJTI-23
Phelps, Ken
76WatRoyT-23
77DayBealT-15
77JacSunT-19
80OmaRoyP-21
82Fle-420
82WicAerTI-12
85Don-318
85Fle-499
85Lea-129
85MarMot-18
85OPC-322
85Top-582
85TopTif-582
86MarMot-18
86Top-34
86TopTif-34
87Don-317
87DonOpeD-118
87Fle-593
87FleGamW-34
87FleGlo-593
87FleSlu-30
87MarMot-7
87SpoTeaP-25
87Top-333
87TopSti-222
87TopTif-333
88Don-489
88DonBasB-248
88Fle-384
88FleGlo-384
88FleSlu-29
88FleStiC-61
88MarMot-7
88OPC-182
88RedFolSB-69
88Sco-256
88ScoGlo-256
88StaLinMa-13
88Top-182
88TopBig-189
88TopTif-182
89Bow-177
89BowTif-177
89Don-363
89DonBasB-276
89Fle-264
89FleGlo-264
89Sco-242
89Top-741
89TopBig-293
89TopDouM-24
89TopTif-741
89UppDec-167
89YanScoNW-10
90A'sMot-14
90Bow-462
90BowTif-462
90Don-675
90OPC-411
90PubSti-544
90Top-411
90TopTif-411
90VenSti-403
91PhoFirP-75
92YanWIZ8-146
Phelps, Ray
35DiaMatCS3T1-121
Phelps, Tom
93BurBeeC-18
93BurBeeF-155
94BurBeeC-21
96BesAutSA-54
96Bow-339
Phelps, Tommy
93JamExpC-16
93JamExpF-3324
96WesPalBEB-12
Phifer, Phil
91RinPosBD2-12
Philley, Dave
47Exh-177
48WhiSoxTI-23
49Bow-44
49Lea-85
50Bow-127
51Bow-297
51R42SmaS-8C
52NatTeaL-20
52Top-226
53Top-64
54Bow-163A
54Bow-163B
54RedMan-AL9A
54RedMan-AL9B
54Top-159
55IndGolS-25
56Top-222
57Top-124
58Hir-12
58Top-116
59Top-92
59TopVen-92
60Top-52
60TopVen-52
61Top-369
62Top-542
72LauGreF-46
79DiaGre-347
79TCM50-192
83TopRep5-226
85TCMPla1-13
90HOFStiB-55
91OriCro-360
91TopArc1-64
94TopArc1-159
94TopArc1G-159
Phillies, Philadelphia
13FatT20-14
38BasTabP-40
48ExhTea-5
51TopTea-7
56Top-72A
56Top-72B
56Top-72C
57Top-214
58Top-134
59Top-8
59TopVen-8
60Top-302
60TopTat-60
61Top-491
61TopMagR-14
62GuyPotCP-15
62Top-294
63Top-13
64Top-293
64TopTatl-16
64TopVen-293
65Top-338
66Top-463
66TopRubl-116
67OPC-102
67Top-102
68LauWorS-47
68Top-477
69FleCloS-18
69FleCloS-37
69TopStaA-18
70FleWorS-47
70OPC-436
70Top-436
71OPC-268
71Top-268
71TopTat-24
72OPC-397
72Top-397
73FleWilD-1
73OPC-536
73OPCBTC-19
73Top-536
73TopBluTC-19
74OPC-383
74OPCTC-19
74Top-383
74TopStaA-19
74TopTeaC-19
78Top-381
83FleSta-243
83FleSti-NNO
84PhiTas-2
85PhiTas-47
87FleStiWBC-S6
87PhiTas-xx
87SpoTeaL-6
88PanSti-476
88PhiTas-28
88RedFolSB-106
90KalTeaN-5
90PubSti-634
90RedFolSB-129
90VenSti-533
91PanCanT1-127
92PhiMed-34
94ImpProP-24
94PhiMel-26
94Sco-656
94ScoGolR-656
94SparPhiC-29
95PanSti-138
95Phi-36
96PanSti-37
Phillies, Reading
95ReaPhiELC-NNO
Phillip, Jim
86WinSpiP-19
Phillippe, Deacon (Charles)
03BreE10-115
06FanCraNL-37
08AmeCarE-89
08RosComP-154
09ColChiE-231
09T206-292
10DomDisP-99
10NadE1-48
10PirAmeCE-9
10PirTipTD-12
10StaCarE-24
10SweCapPP-143
10W555-55
11S74Sil-114
11SpoLifCW-290
11SpoLifM-258
11T205-140
12ColRedB-231
12ColTinT-231
12HasTriFT-14C
12HasTriFT-30E
68LauWorS-1
72FleFamF-37
Phillips, Adolfo
66OPC-32
66Top-32
66TopVen-32
67CokCapC-8
67CubProPS-10
67DexPre-168
67OPC-148
67Top-148
68Top-202
68TopVen-202
69MilBra-222
69Top-372
69TopSta-17
69TopTeaP-4
70Top-666
71ExpLaPR-9
71ExpPS-19
71MLBOffS-137
71OPC-418
71Top-418
Phillips, Anthony
92SanBerSF-952
Phillips, Bill
11SpoLifCW-291
63GadFunC-56
83ChaRoyT-8
86PeoChiP-19
87BucN28-16
Phillips, Bubba (John)
55Bow-228
57Top-395
58Top-212
59Top-187
59TopVen-187
60IndJayP-7
60Top-243
61Kah-32
61Top-101
61TopStal-140
62IndJayP-10
62Jel-39
62Kah-30
62Pos-39
62PosCan-39
62SalPlaC-74
62ShiPlaC-74
62Top-511
62TopStal-38
63Jel-70
63Pos-70
63Top-177
64TigLid-11
64Top-143
64TopVen-143
65Top-306
78TCM60I-192
Phillips, Charlie
77LodDodT-14
80ElPasDT-24
80SalLakCGT-8
88BenBucL-35
Phillips, Chris
83KnoBluJT-6
93SanBerSC-24
94ForMyeMC-19
94ForMyeMF-1174
Phillips, Crystal
94SanBerSC-28
Phillips, Damon
77TCMTheWY-45
Phillips, Dave
88T/MUmp-9
89T/MUmp-7
90T/MUmp-7
Phillips, Dick (Richard E.)
60TacBan-14
61TacBan-17
61UniOil-T12
63Top-544
64Top-559
78TCM60I-179
79HawIslC-24
79HawIslT-6
Phillips, Eddie
93ConTSN-980
Phillips, Gary
93EveGiaC-20
93EveGiaF-3777
94CliLumF-1988
94MidLeaAF-MDW40
94CliLumC-18
Phillips, Horace
87OldJudN-406
Phillips, J.R.
89QuaCitAB-22
89QuaCitAGS-7
90BoiHawP-3319
90PalSprACLC-207
90PalSprAP-2586
91PalSprAP-2025
92Bow-59
92ClaFS7-342
92MidAngOHP-21
92MidAngS-468
92SkyAA F-199
92UppDecML-228
93PhoFirF-1524
93StaCluG-7
93TriAAAGF-27
94ActPac-15
94Bow-247
94Cla-166
94ClaCreotC-C9
94Don-588
94Fin-429
94FinJum-429
94FinRef-429
94GiaUSPC-9H
94LeaLimR-9
94OPC-148
94PhoFirF-1528
94Pin-419
94PinArtP-419
94PinMusC-419
94PinNewG-NG13
94PinRooTP-2
94ScoRoo-RT118
94ScoRooGR-RT118
94Sel-396
94SigRooBS-P4
94Spo-164
94StaClu-158
94StaCluFDI-158
94StaCluGR-158
94StaCluMOP-158
94StaCluT-4
94StaCluTFDI-4
94Top-790
94TopGol-790
94TopSpa-790
94TriPla-294
94UppDec-116
94UppDecED-116
95Baz-132
95Bow-247
95BowGolF-247
95ColCho-27
95ColChoGS-27
95ColChoSS-27
95Don-138
95DonPreP-138
95DonTopotO-355
95Fin-93
95FinRef-93
95Fla-427
95Fle-586
95GiaMot-20
95Lea-380
95LeaCor-6
95Pin-63
95PinArtP-63
95PinMusC-63
95PinNewB-NB9
95Sco-303
95ScoAi-AM10
95ScoGolR-303
95ScoPlaTS-303
95ScoRooDT-RDT1
95Sel-82
95Sel-234
95SelArtP-82
95SelArtP-234
95Spo-149
95SpoArtP-149
95StaClu-337
95StaCluMOP-337
95StaCluSTWS-337
95Stu-112
95Sum-16
95SumNthD-16
95Top-590
95UC3-99
95UC3ArtP-99
95UC3CleS-CS11
95Ult-446
95UltGolM-446
95UppDec-334
95UppDecED-334
95UppDecEDG-334
95UppDecSE-203
95UppDecSEG-203
96ColCho-714
96ColChoGS-714
96ColChoSS-714
96Don-276
96DonPreP-276
96Fle-594
96FleTif-594
96GiaMot-10
96LeaSigEA-159
96Pac-211
96PacPri-P66
96PacPriG-P66
96Sco-119
96Ult-297
96UltGolM-297

Phillips, Jack Dorn
50PirTeal-17
52Top-240
53MotCoo-57
57Top-307
83TopRep5-240
Phillips, Jason
93WelPirC-21
93WelPirF-3357
94AugGreC-17
94AugGreF-3006
96AugGreB-22
Phillips, Jim
87PitCubP-12
89MarPhiS-25
Phillips, Jon
94AubAstC-10
94AubAstF-3755
95AubAstTI-19
Phillips, Lanny
77HolMilT-19
78SpoIndC-6
Phillips, Lefty
70OPC-376
70Top-376
71AngJacitB-8
71OPC-279
71Top-279
Phillips, Lonnie
87EveGiaC-5
88CliGiaP-720
89SanJosGB-5
89SanJosGCLC-217
89SanJosGP-452
91RenSilSCLC-3
Phillips, Marc
94EugEmeC-16
94EugEmeF-3709
95SprSulTI-19
96WilBluRB-25
Phillips, Mike
74OPC-533
74Top-533
75MetSSP-18
75OPC-642
75Top-642
76OPC-93
76SSP-540
76Top-93
77Car5-18
77MetDaiPA-19
77Top-352
78CarTeal-15
78Top-88
79Car5-21
79Top-258
80Top-439
81Don-188
81ExpPos-8
81Fle-538
81Top-113
81TopTra-813
82ExpPos-30
82Fle-201
82OPC-263
82Top-762
83ExpPos-17
91MetWIZ-315
Phillips, Montie
87EugEmeP-2670
88CalLeaACLC-8
89SanJosGB-12
89SanJosGP-433
89SanJosGS-22
91FloStaLAP-FSL26
91OscAstC-8
91OscAstP-680
Phillips, Randy
90PulBraB-27
90PulBraP-3113
92MedHatBJF-3208
92MedHatBJSP-11
93DunBluJF-1794
93FloStaLAF-9
94ClaGolF-56
94KnoSmoF-1303
95PhoFirTI-26
Phillips, Robbie
84CedRapRT-1
Phillips, Steve
85LynMetT-16
86LynMetP-17
87JacMetF-18
91OneYanP-4167
92GreHorC-12
92GreHorF-794
94SanBerSC-18
94SanBerSF-2771
95NorNavTI-28
Phillips, Thomas G.
22E120-115
22W573-97
Phillips, Tony
91Cla3-T73
91TopTra-91T
91TopTraT-91T
92StaCluD-140
92TopDaiQTU-29
93RivPilCLC-13
94CalCanF-786
94Cla-158
95TacRaiTI-15
96TacRaiB-20
Phillips, Tony (Keith Anthony)
80MemChiT-16
81WesHavAT-14
82TacTigT-32
83TopTra-87T
84A'sMot-23
84Don-278
84Fle-459
84Nes792-309
84Top-309
84TopTif-309
85Don-101
85Fle-433
85Top-444
85TopSti-329
85TopTif-444
86A'sMot-19
86Don-542
86Fle-430
86Top-29
86TopTif-29
87A'sSmoC-10
87Don-103
87DonOpeD-26
87Fle-402
87FleGlo-402
87SpoTeaP-23
87Top-188
87TopTif-188
88A'sMot-12
88Don-221
88DonTeaBA-221
88Fle-290
88FleGlo-290
88OPC-12
88PanSti-168
88Sco-294
88ScoGlo-294
88StaLinAs-13
88Top-673
88TopSti-165
88TopTif-673
89A'sMot-11
89DonBasB-211
89FleUpd-56
89Sco-156
89Top-248
89TopTif-248
89UppDec-267
90Bow-359
90BowTif-359
90ClaYel-T79
90Don-91
90DonBesA-20
90Fle-19
90FleCan-19
90FleUpd-99
90Lea-324
90OPC-702
90Sco-84
90ScoRoo-14T
90TigCok-17
90Top-702
90TopBig-239
90TopTif-702
90TopTra-95T
90TopTraT-95T
90UppDec-154
90UppDec-768
91Bow-137
91Don-286
91Fle-348
91Lea-4
91OPC-583
91PanFreS-290
91Sco-38
91StaClu-41
91StaCluP-32
91TigCok-4
91TigPol-9
91Top-583
91TopDesS-583
91TopMic-583
91TopTif-583
91TopTriH-A6
91Ult-126
91UppDec-131
92Bow-272
92Don-328
92DonDiaK-DK25
92Fle-143
92Hig5-48
92Lea-40
92OPC-319
92Pin-243
92Sco-453
92StaClu-488
92Stu-176
92Top-319
92TopGol-319
92TopGolW-319
92TopKid-79
92TopMic-319
92TriPla-99
92TriPla-218
92Ult-62
92UppDec-184
93Bow-419
93DiaMar-85
93Don-701
93Fin-75
93FinRef-75
93Fla-207
93Fle-233
93FunPac-188
93Lea-126
93OPC-262
93PacSpa-113
93PanSti-115
93Pin-406
93Sco-614
93Sel-218
93SelStaL-37
93SP-239
93StaClu-5
93StaCluFDI-5
93StaCluMOP-5
93Stu-213
93TigGat-22
93Top-189
93TopGol-189
93TopInaM-189
93TopMic-189
93TriPla-176
93Ult-203
93UppDec-195
93UppDecGold-195
94Bow-397
94ColC-230
94ColChoGS-230
94ColChoSS-230
94Don-445
94ExtBas-79
94Fin-178
94FinRef-178
94Fla-52
94Fle-142
94FUnPac-64
94Lea-160
94OPC-192
94Pac-227
94PanSti-67
94Pin-330
94PinArtP-330
94PinMusC-330
94PinRunC-RC11
94Sco-103
94ScoCyc-TC5
94ScoGolR-103
94ScoGolS-54
94Sel-215
94SP-179
94SPDieC-179
94Spo-56
94StaClu-553
94StaCluFDI-553
94StaCluGR-553
94StaCluMO-37
94StaCluMOP-553
94StaCluMOP-ST20
94StaCluST-ST20
94Top-48
94TopGol-48
94TopSpa-48
94TriPla-247
94Ult-59
94UltOnBL-11
94UppDec-56
94UppDecED-56
95AngCHP-14
95AngMot-7
95Bow-422
95ColCho-473
95ColCho-531T
95ColChoGS-473
95ColChoSE-223
95ColChoSEGS-223
95ColChoSESS-223
95ColChoSS-473
95Don-407
95DonPreP-407
95DonTopotO-41
95Emb-79
95EmbGolI-79
95Fin-212
95Fin-223
95FinRef-212
95FinRef-223
95Fla-41
95Fla-238
95Fle-59
95FleUpd-67
95Lea-331
95LeaLim-3
95Pac-158
95PacPri-50
95Pin-209
95PinArtP-209
95PinMusC-209
95Sco-49
95ScoGolR-49
95ScoHaloG-HG50
95ScoPlaTS-49
95SP-136
95Spo-97
95SpoArtP-97
95SPSil-136
95StaClu-208
95StaClu-607
95StaCluFDI-208
95StaCluMO-37
95StaCluMOP-208
95StaCluMOP-607
95StaCluSTWS-208
95StaCluSTWS-607
95StaCluVR-109
95Stu-175
95Top-541
95TopCyb-322
95TopTra-44T
95Ult-50
95UltGolM-50
95UppDec-267
95UppDecED-267
95UppDecEDG-267
95UppDecSE-97
95UppDecSEG-97
96Cir-28
96CirRav-28
96Don-232
96DonPreP-232
96EmoXL-40
96Fin-B225
96FinRef-B225
96Fla-56
96Fle-56
96FleTif-56
96FleUpd-U26
96FleUpdTC-U26
96FleWhiS-13
96MetUni-31
96MetUniP-31
96Pac-273
96Sco-165
96SP-58
96StaClu-195
96StaClu-434
96StaCluEPB-434
96StaCluEPG-434
96StaCluEPS-434
96StaCluMO-33
96StaCluMOP-195
96StaCluMOP-434
95StaCluVRMC-109
96Top-199
96TopLas-12
96Ult-334
96UltGolM-334
96UppDec-305
97Cir-215
97CirRav-215
97ColCho-72
97Don-218
97DonPreP-218
97DonPrePGold-218
97DonTea-3
97DonTeaSPE-3
97Fin-215
97FinRef-215
97Fle-68
97FleTif-68
97Lea-227
97LeaFraM-227
97LeaFraMDC-227
97MetUni-60
97Pac-61
97PacLigB-61
97PacSil-61
97Sco-214
97ScoPreS-214
97ScoShoS-214
97ScoShoSAP-214
97ScoWhiS-14
97ScoWhiSPI-14
97ScoWhiSPr-14
97StaClu-27
97StaCluMat-27
97StaCluMOP-27
97Stu-114
97StuPrePG-114
97StuPrePS-114
97Top-165
97TopChr-66
97TopChrR-66
97TopGal-25
97TopGalPPI-25
97Ult-43
97UltGolME-43
97UltPlaME-43
97UppDec-38
Phillips, Vince
89PriWilCS-16
90AlbYanB-22
90AlbYanP-1046
90AlbYanS-12
90CMC-782
90TopTVY-57
91AlbYanLD-12
91AlbYanP-1021
91LinDriAA-12
Phillips, W. Taylor
57Top-343
58Top-159
59Top-113
59TopVen-113
60Top-211
Phillips, Wade
87FayGenP-9
87LakTigP-15
88LakTigSP-20
Phillips, William
87OldJudN-405
Philyaw, Dino
91PocPioP-3798
91PocPioSP-25
Philyaw, Thad
75WatDodT-16
Phipps, Brian
93HunCubC-30
Phipps, Chris
93MarPhiC-21
93MarPhiF-3472
94MarPhiC-16
94MarPhiF-3290
Phipps, Ron
83PeoSunF-26
Phoebus, Tom
67CokCapO-18
67Top-204
68CokCapO-18
68DexPre-63
68OPC-97
68Top-97
68TopActS-2C
68TopActS-13C
68TopVen-97

69MilBra-223
69MLBOffS-6
69OPC-185
69Top-185
69Top-532
69TopFou-18
69TopSta-127
69TopTeaP-5
70MLBOffS-152
70Top-717
71MLBOffS-234
71OPC-611
71Top-611
72MilBra-274
72OPC-477
72Top-477
91OriCro-361

Phoenix, Steve

91ModA'sP-3086
92HunStaF-3949
92HunStaS-318
93TacTigF-3029
94HunStaF-1328
95EdmTraTI-18
95Top-369
96CarMudB-7

Piatt, Bruce

83ButCopKT-32

Piatt, Doug

88BurIndP-1790
89KinIndS-18
89Sta-184
89WatIndS-18
90WesPalBES-17
91IndIndLD-191
91IndIndP-459
91LinDriAAA-191
91TopTra-92T
91TopTraT-92T
92ClaFS7-118
92Don-640
92HarSenF-460
92HarSenS-295
92OPC-526
92ProFS7-253
92Sco-422
92SkyAA F-125
92StaClu-408
92Top-526
92TopDeb91-139
92TopGol-526
92TopGolW-526
92TopMic-526
93MemChiF-374

Piatt, Wiley

03BreE10-116

Piazza, Anthony

87EveGiaC-4

Piazza, Mike

89SalDodTI-25
90TopMag-107
90VerBeaDS-24
91BakDodCLC-7
91CalLeLA-6
92AlbDukF-723
92Bow-461
92ClaBluBF-BC16
92ClaFS7-345
92ClaRedB-BC16
92DonRooP-BC9
92FleUpd-92
92SanAntMS-573
92SkyAA F-251
92SpoIllFK1-313
93Bow-646
93ClaGam-74
93ColAllG-24
93ColPosP-1
93ColPosP-2
93ColPosP-3
93ColPosP-4
93ColPosP-5
93ColPosP-6
93ColPosP-7
93ColPosP-8
93DiaMar-86
93DodMot-4
93DodPol-20
93Don-209
93DonEliD-8
93Fin-199
93FinRef-199
93Fla-75
93FlaWavotF-12
93FleMajLP-A13
93FunPac-6
93JimDeaR-8
93Lea-35
93LeaGolR-U4
93OPC-314
93OPCPre-26
93PacJugC-34
93PacSpa-502
93Pin-252
93PinHomRC-26
93PinRooTP-3
93Sco-286
93ScoBoyoS-5
93Sel-347
93SelRoo-ROY2
93SelRooAR-5
93SP-98
93SPPlaP-PP15
93StaClu-585
93StaCluD-6
93StaCluFDI-585
93StaCluMO-18
93StaCluMO-19
93StaCluMOP-585
93Stu-201
93StuSil-9
93Top-701
93TopFulS-6
93TopGol-701
93TopInaM-701
93TopMic-701
93TopTra-24T
93Toy-22
93TriPla-55
93Ult-60
93Ult-300
93UltAllR-7
93UppDec-2
93UppDecDG-34
93UppDecGold-2
94Bow-387
94Bow-510
94BowBes-R81
94BowBes-X104
94BowBesR-R81
94BowBesR-X104
94BowPre-2
94ChuHomS-14
94ChuHomSG-14
94ColC-310
94ColC-318
94ColC-336
94ColC-400
94ColC-637
94ColChoGS-310
94ColChoGS-318
94ColChoGS-336
94ColChoGS-400
94ColChoGS-637
94ColChoHRA-HA8
94ColChoSS-310
94ColChoSS-318
94ColChoSS-336
94ColChoSS-400
94ColChoSS-637
94ColChoT-11
94DenHol-18
94DodMot-2
94DodPol-21
94Don-2
94DonAwaWJ-3
94DonDiaK-DK15
94DonEli-46
94DonLonBL-7
94DonMVP-7
94DonPro-5
94DonSpeE-2
94DonSpiotG-4
94ExtBas-294
94ExtBasGB-22
94ExtBasSYS-16
94Fin-1
94FinJum-1
94FinRef-1
94Fla-182
94FlaHotN-7
94FlaInfP-7
94Fle-520
94Fle-713
94FleAllS-47
94FleAwaW-6
94FlePro-8
94FleRooS-14
94FleSun-20
94FleTeaL-21
94FUnPac-31
94FUnPac-185
94FUnPac-203
94FUnPac-208
94FUnPac-220
94FUnPac-231
94FUnPac-238
94KinDis-19
94Kra-27
94Lea-436
94LeaGam-12
94LeaL-120
94LeaLimGA-16
94LeaMVPC-N11
94LeaMVPCG-N11
94LeaPowB-6
94LeaPro-6
94LeaSli-2
94LeaStaS-4
94MotPia-1
94MotPia-2
94MotPia-3
94MotPia-4
94MotPia-1
94MotPia-2
94MotPia-3
94MotPia-4
94MotPia-BLUE
94MotPia-RED
94OPC-147
94OPCAllR-9
94OPCDiaD-1
94OPCJumA-9
94OscMayR-27
94Pac-318
94Pac-658
94PacGolP-16
94PacPro-P6
94PacSilP-29
94PanSti-203
94Pin-28
94PinArtP-28
94PinMusC-28
94PinNewG-NG2
94PinPowS-PS17
94PinRunC-RC28
94PinTeaP-5
94PinTheN-19
94PinTri-TR7
94Pos-1
94PosCan-14
94PosCanG-14
94ProMag-70
94RedFolMI-20
94RemUltP-1
94RemUltP-2
94RemUltP-3
94RemUltP-4
94RemUltP-5
94RemUltP-6
94RemUltPP-1
94RemUltPP-2
94Sco-476
94Sco-636
94ScoBoyoS-6
94ScoGolR-476
94ScoGolR-636
94ScoGolS-13
94Sel-4
94SelCroC-CC9
94SP-80
94SPDieC-80
94SPHol-29
94SPHolDC-29
94Spo-67
94Spo-189
94SpoFanA-AS5
94SpoRooGGG-GG5
94SpoSha-SH11
94SPPre-WR4
94StaClu-140
94StaClu-266
94StaCluDD-DD1
94StaCluF-F8
94StaCluFDI-140
94StaCluFDI-266
94StaCluGR-140
94StaCluGR-266
94StaCluMO-28
94StaCluMOP-140
94StaCluMOP-266
94StaCluMOP-F8
94StaCluMOP-DD1
94StaCluMOP-ST7
94StaCluST-ST7
94Stu-72
94StuEdiC-8
94StuSerS-6
94SucSav-17
94TomPiz-15
94Top-1
94Top-391
94TopBlaG-41
94TopGol-1
94TopGol-391
94TopSpa-1
94TopSpa-391
94TopSupS-34
94TopTraFI-2
94TriPla-88
94TriPlaP-6
94Ult-218
94UltAllS-11
94UltAwaW-25
94UltHitM-9
94UltHomRK-12
94UltRBIK-10
94UltRisS-9
94UltSecYS-9
94UppDec-33
94UppDec-47
94UppDec-273
94UppDec-500
94UppDecAJ-31
94UppDecAJG-31
94UppDecDC-W9
94UppDecED-33
94UppDecED-47
94UppDecED-273
94UppDecED-500
94UppDecMLS-MM15
94UppDecMLSED-MM15
94UppDecNG-13
94UppDecNGED-13
94USDepoT-1
94USPlaCA-4C
94USPlaCA-4D
94USPlaCR-1C
94USPlaCR-13H
95Baz-77
95BazRedH-RH15
95Bow-310
95BowBes-R36
95BowBesJR-6
95BowBesR-R36
95ClaFanFPCP-5
95ClaPhoC-33
95ColCho-80
95ColCho-87
95ColChoCtA-6
95ColChoCtAG-6
95ColChoCtG-CG15
95ColChoCtG-CG15B
95ColChoCtG-CG15C
95ColChoCtGE-15
95ColChoCtGG-CG15
95ColChoCtGG-CG15B
95ColChoCtGG-CG15C
95ColChoCtGGE-15
95ColChoGS-80
95ColChoGS-87
95ColChoSE-90
95ColChoSE-253
95ColChoSEGS-90
95ColChoSEGS-253
95ColChoSESS-90
95ColChoSESS-253
95ColChoSS-80
95ColChoSS-87
95D3-27
95DenHol-20
95DodMot-2
95DodPol-21
95DodROY-13
95Don-5
95DonAll-NL2
95DonDom-2
95DonEli-52
95DonLonBL-5
95DonPreP-5
95DonTopotO-271
95Emb-110
95EmbGolI-110
95Emo-145
95EmoN-8
95Fin-113
95FinPowK-PK6
95FinRef-113
95Fla-155
95FlaHotN-7
95FlaInfP-7
95FlaTodS-9
95Fle-547
95FleAllF-1
95FleAllS-1
95FleTeaL-21
95FleUpdH-15
95FleUpdSS-8
95KinDis-16
95Kra-26
95Lea-218
95Lea300C-3
95LeaGolS-11
95LeaLim-79
95LeaLimG-16
95LeaLimIBP-10
95LeaLimL-6
95LeaOpeD-5
95NatPac-5
95Pac-224
95PacGolCDC-13
95PacGolP-17
95PacPri-72
95PanSti-24
95Pin-237
95Pin-300
95Pin-448
95Pin-450
95PinArtP-237
95PinArtP-300
95PinArtP-448
95PinArtP-450
95PinFan-23
95PinGatA-GA5
95PinMusC-237
95PinMusC-300
95PinMusC-448
95PinMusC-450
95PinPer-PP9
95PinPin-3
95PinPinR-3
95PinRedH-RH5
95PinTeaP-TP2
95PinUps-US3
95PinWhiH-WH5
95Pos-12
95RedFol-22
95Sco-17
95Sco-558
95ScoDreT-DG5
95ScoGolR-17
95ScoGolR-558
95ScoHaloG-HG10
95ScoPlaTS-17
95ScoPlaTS-558
95ScoRul-SR3
95ScoRulJ-SR3
95Sel-17
95Sel-248
95Sel-250
95SelArtP-17
95SelArtP-248
95SelArtP-250
95SelBigS-BS4
95SelCer-39
95SelCer-80
95SelCerC-5
95SelCerGT-5
95SelCerMG-39
95SelCerMG-80
95SelCerS-39
95SP-70
95SPCha-57
95SPCha-60
95SPChaDC-57
95SPChaDC-60
95SPChaDFC-4
95SPChaFCDC-4
95Spo-83
95Spo-167
95SpoArtP-83
95SpoArtP-167
95SpoDet-DE5
95SpoDouT-7
95SpoHamT-HT4
95SpoPro-PM5
95SPPlaP-PP6
95SPSil-70
95SPSpeF-43
95StaClu-149

95StaClu-320
95StaClu-502
95StaCluCC-CC1
95StaCluFDI-149
95StaCluMO-38
95StaCluMOP-149
95StaCluMOP-320
95StaCluMOP-502
95StaCluMOP-CC1
95StaCluSTDW-D7T
95StaCluSTDW-D149
95StaCluSTWS-149
95StaCluSTWS-320
95StaCluSTWS-502
95StaCluVR-78
95Stu-4
95StuGolS-4
95StuPlaS-4
95Sum-88
95Sum-178
95Sum-198
95SumBigB-BB5
95SumNthD-88
95SumNthD-178
95SumNthD-198
95Top-391
95Top-466
95TopCyb-261
95TopLeaL-LL40
95TopPre-PP2
95TopTra-6T
95TopTra-163T
95TopTraPB-6
95UC3-39
95UC3-126
95UC3ArtP-39
95UC3ArtP-126
95UC3CycS-CS6
95UC3InM-IM4
95Ult-399
95UltAllS-15
95UltAllSGM-15
95UltGolM-399
95UltHitM-9
95UltHitMGM-9
95UltRBIK-10
95UltRBIKGM-10
95UltRisS-8
95UltRisSGM-8
95UppDec-320
95UppDecED-320
95UppDecEDG-320
95UppDecPAW-H8
95UppDecPAWE-H8
95UppDecPLL-R18
95UppDecPLL-R37
95UppDecPLL-R60
95UppDecPLLE-R18
95UppDecPLLE-R37
95UppDecPLLE-R60
95UppDecSE-35
95UppDecSEG-35
95UppDecSoaD-SD1
95Zen-76
95ZenAllS-3
95ZenZ-5
96Baz-8
96Bow-27
96BowBes-26
96BowBesAR-26
96BowBesC-9
96BowBesCAR-9
96BowBesCR-9
96BowBesMI-8
96BowBesMIAR-8
96BowBesMIR-8
96BowBesP-BBP7
96BowBesPAR-BBP7
96BowBesPR-BBP7
96BowBesR-26
96Cir-146
96CirAcc-21
96CirBos-39
96CirRav-146
96ColCho-185
96ColCho-272
96ColCho-406
96ColChoCtG-CG21
96ColChoCtG-CG21B
96ColChoCtG-CG21C
96ColChoCtGE-CR21
96ColChoCtGG-CG21
96ColChoCtGG-CG21B
96ColChoCtGG-CG21C
96ColChoCtGGE-CR21
96ColChoGS-185
96ColChoGS-272
96ColChoGS-406
96ColChoSS-185
96ColChoSS-272
96ColChoSS-406
96ColChoYMtP-31
96ColChoYMtP-31A
96ColChoYMtPGS-31
96ColChoYMtPGS-31A
96DenHolGS-3
96DenHolGSAP-3
96DodMot-2
96DodPol-27
96Don-424
96DonFreF-8
96DonHitL-4
96DonPreP-424
96DonPurP-5
96DonRouT-7
96DonSam-7
96DonSho-5
96EmoLegoB-6
96EmoXL-215
96Fin-B113
96Fin-B275
96Fin-S11
96FinRef-B113
96FinRef-B275
96FinRef-S11
96Fla-298
96FlaDiaC-8
96FlaHotG-7
96FlaPow-6
96Fle-445
96FleChe-5
96FleDod-16
96FleLumC-6
96FleRoaW-5
96FleTeaL-21
96FleTif-445
96FleUpd-U235
96FleUpdH-15
96FleUpdSS-7
96FleUpdTC-U235
96FleZon-9
96Kin-16
96Lea-200
96LeaAllGMC-2
96LeaAllGMCG-2
96LeaGolS-5
96LeaLim-13
96LeaLimG-13
96LeaLimL-8
96LeaLimLB-8
96LeaPicP-10
96LeaPre-25
96LeaPre-150
96LeaPreP-25
96LeaPreP-150
96LeaPrePB-200
96LeaPrePG-200
96LeaPrePS-200
96LeaPreSG-51
96LeaPreSP-5
96LeaPreSta-12
96LeaPreSte-51
96LeaSig-1
96LeaSigPPG-1
96LeaSigPPP-1
96MetUni-187
96MetUniHM-6
96MetUniP-187
96MetUniT-6
96Pac-103
96PacBaeS-2
96PacCraC-CC7
96PacGolCD-DC7
96PacHom-HP1
96PacOctM-OM17
96PacPri-P38
96PacPriFB-FB13
96PacPriG-P38
96PacPriRHS-RH4
96PanSti-95
96Pin-4
96Pin-132
96Pin-138
96Pin-198
96Pin-265
96Pin-322
96Pin-398
96Pin-399
96PinAfi-124
96PinAfi-198
96PinAfiAP-124
96PinAfiAP-198
96PinAfiR-12
96PinAfiR-13
96PinAfiR-15
96PinAfiR-16
96PinAfiR-17
96PinAfiR-19
96PinAfiR-21
96PinAfiSP-1
96PinArtP-4
96PinArtP-65
96PinArtP-165
96PinArtP-197
96PinEssotG-10
96PinFan-10
96PinFoil-265
96PinFoil-322
96PinFoil-398
96PinFoil-399
96PinPow-7
96PinSam-4
96PinSky-7
96PinSlu-7
96PinSta-4
96PinSta-65
96PinSta-165
96PinSta-197
96PinTeaP-8
96PinTeaS-4
96Pro-10
96ProMagA-16
96ProMagDM-16
96ProSta-41
96RemUltPP-1
96RemUltPP-2
96RemUltPP-3
96RemUltPP-4
96RemUltPP-5
96RemUltPP-6
96RemUltPP-7
96RemUltPP-8
96RemUltPP-9
96Sco-270
96Sco-317
96ScoBigB-5
96ScoDiaA-10
96ScoDreT-5
96ScoDugC-B42
96ScoDugCAP-B42
96ScoGolS-5
96ScoNumG-4
96ScoPowP-7
96ScoRef-12
96ScoTitT-11
96Sel-22
96Sel-155
96Sel-199
96SelArtP-22
96SelArtP-155
96SelArtP-199
96SelCer-30
96SelCer-138
96SelCerAP-30
96SelCerAP-138
96SelCerCB-30
96SelCerCB-138
96SelCerCR-30
96SelCerCR-138
96SelCerIP-4
96SelCerMB-30
96SelCerMB-138
96SelCerMG-30
96SelCerMG-138
96SelCerMR-30
96SelCerMR-138
96SelCerSF-10
96SelClaTF-12
96SelEnF-11
96SelTeaN-11
96SP-105
96SPBasH-87
96SPMarM-MM6
96SPMarMDC-6
96Spo-10
96Spo-102
96SpoArtP-10
96SpoArtP-102
96SpoDouT-7
96SpoHitP-4
96SpoPowS-6
96SpoPro-5
96SPPreF-6
96SPSpeFX-3
96SPSpeFXDC-3
96SPx-33
96SPx-MP1
96SPx-MPAU
96SPxBoufG-10
96SPxGol-33
96StaClu-216
96StaClu-442
96StaCluEPB-442
96StaCluEPG-442
96StaCluEPS-442
96StaCluEWB-EW2
96StaCluEWG-EW2
96StaCluEWS-EW2
96StaCluMM-MM2
96StaCluMO-34
96StaCluMOP-216
96StaCluMOP-442
96StaCluMOP-MM2
96StaCluMOP-PC7
96StaCluMOP-PP4
96StaCluPC-PC7
96StaCluPP-PP4
96StaCluVRMC-78
96Stu-80
96StuHitP-6
96StuMas-2
96StuPrePB-80
96StuPrePG-80
96StuPrePS-80
96StuStaGS-6
96Sum-1
96Sum-156
96SumAbo&B-1
96SumAbo&B-156
96SumArtP-1
96SumArtP-156
96SumBal-11
96SumBigB-8
96SumBigBM-8
96SumFoi-1
96SumFoi-156
96SumHitI-13
96SumPos-5
96TeaOut-64
96TeaOut-C98
96Top-2
96Top-246
96TopChr-2
96TopChr-93
96TopChrR-2
96TopChrR-93
96TopChrWC-WC12
96TopChrWCR-WC12
96TopClaC-CC10
96TopGal-166
96TopGalE-1
96TopGalPPI-166
96TopLas-89
96TopLasPC-4
96TopMysF-M12
96TopMysF-M24
96TopMysFR-M12
96TopMysFR-M24
96TopPowB-2
96TopPro-NL7
96TopRoaW-RW12
96TopWreC-WC12
96Ult-224
96Ult-587
96UltChe-A6
96UltCheGM-A6
96UltDiaP-7
96UltDiaPGM-7
96UltGolM-224
96UltGolM-587
96UltHitM-7
96UltHitMGM-7
96UltOn-L-7
96UltOn-LGM-7
96UltPowP-6
96UltPowPGM-6
96UltPriL-10
96UltPriLGM-10
96UltRaw-8
96UltRawGM-8
96UppDec-145
96UppDec-360
96UppDec-383
96UppDecA-14
96UppDecDD-DD23
96UppDecDDG-DD23
96UppDecDDS-DD23
96UppDecG-GF6
96UppDecHC-HC14
96UppDecPD-PD12
96UppDecPHE-H38
96UppDecPRE-R36
96UppDecPRE-R46
96UppDecPRE-R59
96UppDecPreH-H38
96UppDecPreR-R36
96UppDecPreR-R46
96UppDecPreR-R59
96UppDecRunP-RP14
96UppDecVJLS-VJ17
96Zen-12
96Zen-138
96ZenArtP-12
96ZenArtP-138
96ZenDiaC-4
96ZenDiaCP-4
96ZenMoz-13
96ZenZ-8
97Bow-266
97BowBes-5
97BowBesAR-5
97BowBesBC-BC8
97BowBesBCAR-BC8
97BowBesBCR-BC8
97BowBesMI-MI4
97BowBesMIAR-MI4
97BowBesMIARI-MI4
97BowBesMII-MI4
97BowBesMIR-MI4
97BowBesMIRI-MI4
97BowBesR-5
97BowChr-85
97BowChrI-85
97BowChrIR-85
97BowChrR-85
97BowInt-266
97Cir-356
97Cir-399
97CirBos-13
97CirIco-8
97CirLimA-11
97CirRav-356
97CirRav-399
97CirRavR-9
97CirSupB-13
97ColCho-365
97ColChoAC-26
97ColChoBS-18
97ColChoBSGS-18
97ColChoCtG-20A
97ColChoCtG-20B
97ColChoCtG-20C
97ColChoCtGIW-CG20
97ColChoNF-NF9
97ColChoNF-NF10
97ColChoPP-PP19
97ColChoPPG-PP19
97ColChoS-13
97ColChoTBS-28
97ColChoTBSWH-28
97ColChoTotT-T15
97Don-134
97Don-402
97DonDiaK-7
97DonDiaKC-7
97DonDom-13
97DonEli-7
97DonEli-11
97DonEliGS-7
97DonFraFea-9
97DonLim-9
97DonLim-26
97DonLim-82
97DonLimFotG-11
97DonLimLE-9
97DonLimLE-26
97DonLimLE-82
97DonLonL-9
97DonPowA-5
97DonPowADC-5
97DonPre-107
97DonPre-171
97DonPreCttC-107
97DonPreCttC-171
97DonPreP-134
97DonPreP-402
97DonPrePGold-134
97DonPrePGold-402
97DonPrePM-20
97DonPreS-5

97DonPreTB-15
97DonPreTBG-15
97DonPreTF-15
97DonPreTP-15
97DonPreTPG-15
97DonPreXP-9A
97DonRocL-4
97DonTea-111
97DonTeaSMVP-2
97DonTeaSPE-111
97Fin-50
97Fin-151
97Fin-292
97FinEmb-151
97FinEmb-292
97FinEmbR-151
97FinEmbR-292
97FinRef-50
97FinRef-151
97FinRef-292
97FlaSho-A31
97FlaSho-B31
97FlaSho-C31
97FlaShoDC-12
97FlaShoHG-11
97FlaShoLC-31
97FlaShoLC-B31
97FlaShoLC-C31
97FlaShoLCM-A31
97FlaShoLCM-B31
97FlaShoLCM-C31
97Fle-371
97Fle-497
97Fle-712
97Fle-734
97FleBleB-6
97FleDiaT-9
97FleGolM-8
97FleGouG-10
97FleGouGF-10
97FleHea-15
97FleLumC-13
97FleMilDM-14
97FleNig&D-6
97FleSoaS-10
97FleTeaL-21
97FleTif-371
97FleTif-497
97FleTif-712
97FleTif-734
97FleZon-14
97Lea-191
97Lea-203
97Lea-373
97LeaDrefS-8
97LeaFraM-191
97LeaFraM-203
97LeaFraM-373
97LeaFraMDC-191
97LeaFraMDC-203
97LeaFraMDC-373
97LeaGet-3
97LeaGolS-24
97LeaKnoG-5
97LeaLeaotN-5
97LeaStaS-8
97MetUni-105
97MetUniBF-9
97MetUniML-8
97MetUniT-7
97NewPin-45
97NewPin-191
97NewPinAP-45
97NewPinAP-191
97NewPinIE-5
97NewPinKtP-18
97NewPinMC-45
97NewPinMC-191
97NewPinPP-45
97NewPinPP-191
97NewPinPP-I5A
97NewPinPP-K18
97NewPinPP-MP1
97NewPinPP-MP2
97NewPinPP-MP3
97NewPinPP-MP4
97NewPinPP-MP5
97NewPinPP-MP6
97NewPinS-MP1
97NewPinS-MP2
97NewPinS-MP3
97NewPinS-MP4
97NewPinS-MP5
97NewPinS-MP6
97Pac-339
97PacCar-31
97PacCarM-31
97PacCerCGT-10
97PacCraC-9
97PacFirD-17
97PacGolCD-31
97PacLigB-339
97PacPri-115
97PacPriGA-GA26
97PacPriGotD-GD161
97PacPriLB-115
97PacPriP-115
97PacPriSH-SH11A
97PacPriSL-SL11A
97PacSil-339
97PacTriCD-18
97Pin-103
97PinArtP-103
97PinCar-1
97PinCer-26
97PinCerCMGT-10
97PinCerCT-10
97PinCerMBlu-26
97PinCerMG-26
97PinCerMR-26
97PinCerR-26
97PinHom-5
97PinHom-6
97PinIns-27
97PinInsC-19
97PinInsCE-27
97PinInsDD-4
97PinInsDE-27
97PinMin-7
97PinMinB-7
97PinMinCB-7
97PinMinCG-7
97PinMinCGR-7
97PinMinCN-7
97PinMinCS-7
97PinMinG-7
97PinMinS-7
97PinMusC-103
97PinPasttM-5
97PinSha-8
97PinTeaP-5
97PinTeaP-10
97PinTotCPB-26
97PinTotCPG-26
97PinTotCPR-26
97PinX-P-16
97PinX-P-146
97PinX-PF&A-7
97PinX-PMoS-16
97PinX-PMoS-146
97PinX-PMW-7
97PinX-PMWG-7
97PinX-PMWS-7
97PinX-PSfF-39
97PinX-PSfFU-39
97ProMag-23
97ProMagML-23
97Sco-22
97Sco-501
97Sco-550
97ScoAllF-16
97ScoBla-9
97ScoDod-2
97ScoDodPl-2
97ScoDodPr-2
97ScoFra-5
97ScoFraG-5
97ScoHeaotO-22
97ScoHigZ-5
97ScoHobR-501
97ScoHobR-550
97ScoPreS-22
97ScoResC-501
97ScoResC-550
97ScoShoS-22
97ScoShoS-501
97ScoShoS-550
97ScoShoSAP-22
97ScoShoSAP-501
97ScoShoSAP-550
97ScoStaaD-13
97ScoSteS-9
97ScoTitT-2
97Sel-32
97Sel-147
97SelArtP-32
97SelArtP-147
97SelRegG-32
97SelRegG-147
97SelToootT-4
97SelToootTMB-4
97SkyE-X-82
97SkyE-XC-82
97SkyE-XEC-82
97SkyE-XHoN-15
97SP-95
97SPGamF-GF5
97SPInsI-16
97SPMarM-MM5
97SpoIll-112
97SpoIll-174
97SpoIllEE-112
97SpoIllEE-174
97SpoIllGS-15
97SPSpeF-5
97SPSpxF-7
97SPSPxFA-7
97SPx-30
97SPxBoufG-12
97SPxBro-30
97SPxCorotG-7
97SPxGraF-30
97SPxSil-30
97SPxSte-30
97StaClu-31
97StaClu-383
97StaCluFR-F10
97StaCluMat-31
97StaCluMOP-31
97StaCluMOP-383
97StaCluMOP-FB10
97StaCluMOP-PG18
97StaCluPG-PG18
97Stu-21
97StuHarH-10
97StuMasS-14
97StuMasS8-14
97StuPor8-7
97StuPrePG-21
97StuPrePS-21
97Top-20
97Top-104
97TopChr-9
97TopChrDD-DD8
97TopChrDDR-DD8
97TopChrR-9
97TopGal-133
97TopGalGoH-GH7
97TopGalP-PP3
97TopGalPG-PG11
97TopGalPMS-10
97TopGalPMSSS-7
97TopGalPPI-133
97TopHobM-HM12
97TopIntF-ILM2
97TopIntFR-ILM2
97TopScrSI-3
97TopSta-7
97TopSta1AS-AS6
97TopStaAM-7
97TopStaASGM-ASM3
97TopSweS-SS12
97TopTeaT-TT16
97Ult-223
97UltBasR-8
97UltChe-A6
97UltChe-B6
97UltDiaP-8
97UltDouT-15
97UltFamGam-5
97UltGolME-223
97UltHitM-6
97UltHRK-8
97UltPlaME-223
97UltPowP-A7
97UltPowP-B5
97UltSeaC-8
97UltStaR-6
97UltThu-9
97UltTop3-6
97UltTop3GM-6
97UppDec-95
97UppDecAG-AG20
97UppDecHC-HC13
97UppDecLDC-LD16
97UppDecMM-6
97UppDecP-18
97UppDecPP-PP15
97UppDecPPJ-PP15
97UppDecRP-RP15
97UppDecU-18
97UppDecUMA-MA7
97Zen-6
97Zen Z-Z-5
97Zen8x1-5
97Zen8x1D-5
97ZenV-2-4

Picano, John
92WesPalBEC-29

Picciolo, Dustin
87SpoIndP-25

Picciolo, Rob
76TucTorCa-1
76TusTorCr-9
78Top-528
79Top-378
80Top-158
81A'sGraG-8
81Don-357A
81Don-357B
81Fle-582
81Top-604
82A'sGraG-14
82Don-465
82Fle-106
82Top-293
82TopTra-89T
83BrePol-8
83Don-456
83Top-476
84AngSmo-22
84Don-455
84Nes792-88
84Top-88
84TopTif-88
84TopTra-94T
84TopTraT-94T
85A'sMot-13
85Top-756
85TopTif-756
85TopTifT-90T
85TopTra-90T
86Don-497
86OPC-3
86SpoIndC-177
86Top-672
86TopTif-672
87LasVegSP-26
87SpoIndP-26
91PadSmo-26
92PadMot-27
92PadPolD-15
92PadPolD-28
92PadSmo-23
93PadMot-28
94BreMilB-164
94PadMot-28
95PadMot-28
96PadMot-28

Picciuto, Nick
77TCMTheWY-16

Pichardo, Francisco
90EliTwiS-18
90KenTwiB-12
90KenTwiP-2309
90KenTwiS-19

Pichardo, Hipolito
90BasCitRS-19
91Cla/Bes-296
91LinDriAA-413
91MemChiLD-413
91MemChiP-650
92DonRoo-95
92FleUpd-32
92ScoRoo-103T
92TopTra-89T
92TopTraG-89T
93Don-571
93Fle-246
93LimRocDWB-128
93OPC-390
93PacSpa-493
93PacSpaPl-18
93Pin-450
93RoyPol-24
93Sco-336
93Sel-312
93StaClu-211
93StaCluFDI-211
93StaCluMOP-211
93StaCluRoy-8
93Top-349
93TopGol-349
93TopInaM-349
93TopMic-349
93Toy-89
93Ult-567
93UppDec-72
93UppDecGold-72
94ColC-231
94ColChoGS-231
94ColChoSS-231
94Don-391
94Fin-194
94FinRef-194
94Fle-171
94Lea-327
94Pac-299
94Pin-275
94PinArtP-275
94PinMusC-275
94Sco-218
94ScoGolR-218
94StaClu-223
94StaCluFDI-223
94StaCluGR-223
94StaCluMOP-223
94Top-482
94TopGol-482
94TopSpa-482
94Ult-71
95Don-376
95DonPreP-376
95Fle-171
95Pac-211
95StaClu-55
95StaCluFDI-55
95StaCluMOP-55
95StaCluSTWS-55
95Top-172
96Don-46
96DonPreP-46
96LeaSigEA-160
96Pac-327
96RoyPol-22
97Pac-108
97PacLigB-108
97PacSil-108
97RoyPol-18
97Sco-399
97ScoHobR-399
97ScoResC-399
97ScoShoS-399
97ScoShoSAP-399

Pichardo, Nelson
77WesHavYT-18

Pichardo, Sandy
92GulCoaMF-3492
93KinMetC-18
93KinMetF-3804
94CapCitBC-18
94CapCitBF-1759
94SouAtlLAF-SAL37
95StLucMTI-27
96TamYanY-20

Piche, Ron
61Top-61
62Top-582
63Top-179
65Top-464
76ExpRed-25

Picinich, Val J.
20NatCarE-79
21Exh-128
21Exh-129
22E120-116
22W573-98
25Exh-67
29ExhFou-7
33Gou-118
34GouCanV-3
90DodTar-623
92ConTSN-479
93ConTSN-875

Pickens, Kevin
87EugEmeP-2676
89BasCitRS-21

Pickens, Ritchie
86DavLipB-17

Pickering, Calvin
96BluOriB-26
97Bow-184
97BowChr-174
97BowChrI-174
97BowChrIR-174
97BowChrR-174
97BowInt-184

Pickering, Oliver
03BreE10-117
09ColChiE-232A

09ColChiE-232B
09ColChiE-232C
09T206-455
12ColRedB-232A
12ColRedB-232B
12ColRedB-232C
12ColTinT-232A
12ColTinT-232B
12ColTinT-232C
Pickering, Urbane
79RedSoxEF-14
Pickett, Antoine
87EugEmeP-2649
88ModA'sTI-28
Pickett, Bob
92WinHavRSC-19
Pickett, Danny
90ChaRaiB-18
90ChaRaiP-2033
Pickett, Eric
94StaCluDP-47
94StaCluDPFDI-47
95DanBraTI-21
96EugEmeB-20
Pickett, John
87OldJudN-407
Pickett, Rich
83LynMetT-21
84TidTidT-12
Pickett, Ricky
92BenMusSP-7
92BilMusF-3353
94ChaWheC-20
94ChaWheF-2701
95ChaLooTI-17
96PhoFirB-23
Pickett, Tony
87AppFoxP-23
Picketts, William
90SouOreAB-7
90SouOreAP-3435
91MadMusC-26
91MadMusP-2141
92RenSilSCLC-51
Pickford, Kevin
94ClaGolF-76
94WelPirC-18
94WelPirF-3495
96LynHilB-18
Pickich, Jeff
93WelPirC-22
93WelPirF-3358
94AugGreC-18
94AugGreF-3007
Pickle, V.H.
95DavLipB-19
Pico, Brandon
92ClaDraP-107
92FroRowDP-14
92HunCubC-1
92HunCubF-3164
94MidLeaAF-MDW50
94PeoChiC-21
94PeoChiF-2281
96DayCubB-19
Pico, Jeff
86WinSpiP-20
87PitCubP-19
88CubDavB-41
88FleUpd-80
88FleUpdG-80
88IowCubC-3
88IowCubP-546
88PeoChiTI-25
88ScoRoo-94T
88ScoRooG-94T
88TopTra-87T
88TopTraT-87T
89CubMar-41
89Don-513
89Fle-436
89FleGlo-436
89PanSti-50
89PeoChiTI-28
89Sco-13
89Top-262
89TopTif-262
89ToyRoo-22
89UppDec-491
90CMC-82
90CubMar-15
90Don-585
90Fle-39
90FleCan-39
90IowCubC-7
90OPC-613
90PubSti-200
90Sco-428
90Top-613
90TopTif-613
90TopTVCu-14
90VenSti-404
91Fle-428
91LinDriAAA-537
91OPC-311
91Sco-326
91TacTigLD-537
91TacTigP-2303
91Top-311
91TopDesS-311
91TopMic-311
91TopTif-311
Picollo, John
94OneYanC-17
94OneYanF-3794
Picota, Leny (Len)
87SavCarP-23
88St.PetCS-22
89ArkTraGS-18
90ArkTraGS-24
91LinDriAAA-243
91LouRedLD-243
91LouRedP-2914
92HarSenF-461
92HarSenS-296
93LinVenB-208
93OttLynF-2433
94VenLinU-239
Piechota, Al
77TCMTheWY-42
Piechowski, Tim
88JamExpP-1902
Piela, D.
88PulBraP-1765
Pieratt, Dan
91QuaCitAC-25
92QuaCitRBC-30
Pierce, Ben
87EugEmeP-2658
89AppFoxP-874
90BasCitRS-20
Pierce, Billy
47Exh-178
47PM1StaP1-163
51Bow-196
51TopBluB-45
52Bow-54
52RedMan-AL16
52StaCalL-73B
52StaCalS-87C
52Top-98
52WhiSoxH-6
53BowC-73
53Dor-121
53RedMan-AL16
53Top-143
54Bow-102
54RedHeaF-24
54RedMan-AL10
55Bow-214
55RobGouS-27
55RobGouW-27
56Top-160
57SwiFra-4
57Top-160
58JayPubA-15
58Top-50A
58Top-50B
58Top-334
58WhiSoxJP-8
59Baz-18
59Top-156
59Top-410
59Top-466
59Top-572
59TopVen-156
59WilSpoG-5
60Top-150
60Top-571
60TopTat-44
60TopTat-95
60TopVen-150
60WhiSoxTS-15
61Pos-21A
61Pos-21B
61Top-205
61TopStal-126
61WhiSoxTS-12
62GiaJayP-12
62Jel-54
62Pos-54
62PosCan-54
62SalPlaC-2
62ShiPlaC-2
62Top-260
63GiaJayP-11
63Top-50
63Top-147
63Top-331
64Top-222
64TopVen-222
76ChiGre-16
76WhiSoxTAG-8
77GalGloG-30
79TCM50-16
80MarExh-22
80WhiSoxGT-5
83TopRep5-98
83YanYealT-2
85WhiSoxC-46
88WhiSoxC-22
89PacLegI-134
89SweBasG-57
90PacLeg-82
91TopArc1-143
92ActPacA-38
92BazQua5A-16
94UppDecAH-133
94UppDecAH1-133
Pierce, Chris
86PriWilPP-19
Pierce, Dominic
88ButCopKSP-16
89GasRanP-1001
89GasRanS-18
89Sta-38
Pierce, Don Diego
82WauTimF-24
Pierce, Ed (Eddie)
89EugEmeB-9
91LinDriAA-414
91MemChiLD-414
91MemChiP-651
92MemChiF-2418
92MemChiS-442
92SkyAA F-187
93Don-147
93Fle-623
93MemChiF-375
93Top-803
93TopGol-803
93TopInaM-803
93TopMic-803
94MemChiF-358
Pierce, George
15SpoNewM-138
Pierce, Jeff
91UtiBluSC-13
91UtiBluSP-3255
92MidLeaATI-32
92SouBenWSC-5
92SouBenWSF-175
93BirBarF-1192
93LinVenB-224
94ExcFS7-39
94NewBriRSF-647
Pierce, Jim
85CloHSS-34
Pierce, Kirk
95BatCliTI-26
96PieBolWB-20
Pierce, L. Jack
76OPC-162
76SSP-368
76Top-162
78SanJosMMC-23
79SpoIndT-7
Pierce, Marvin
94BurIndF-3793
Pierce, Rob
92MadMusC-22
92MadMusF-1232
92RenSilSCLC-52
94HunStaF-1329
95HunStaTI-20
Pierce, Tony
67Top-542
68OPC-38
68Top-38
68TopVen-38
81TCM60I-401
Pierce, Walter
83ArkTraT-5
84ArkTraT-24
Piercy, Bill
21Exh-130
21Exh-131
21KoBreWSI-45
Pieretti, Chick (Marino)
47SenGunBP-8
49Bow-217
50Bow-181
50IndNumN-18
50IndTeal-19
52MotCoo-12
53MotCoo-35
Pierorazio, Wes
83WatIndF-23
85VisOakT-19
86VisOakP-15
87OrlTwiP-22
Pierre, Shape (Rogers)
93NegLeaRL2-29
Pierre-Louis, Danton
93MarPhiC-22
93MarPhiF-3484
94MarPhiC-17
94MarPhiF-3303
Piersall, Jim
47Exh-179
47PM1StaP1-164
51Bow-306
52Bow-189
53BowBW-36
53RedSoxTI-24
54Bow-66B
54Bow-210
54ColMeaPP-1
54ColMeaPP-2
54RedMan-AL11
55Bow-16
55RedMan-AL21
56Top-143
57Top-75
58RedSoxJP-7
58Top-280
59Ind-16
59RedSoxJP-7
59Top-355
60IndJayP-8
60Top-159
60TopVen-159
61Top-345
61TopStal-139
61WilSpoGH828-3
61WilSpoGH828-1-5
62Baz-36
62SalPlaC-88A
62SalPlaC-88B
62SenNewLP-1
62ShiPlaC-88
62Top-51
62Top-90
62TopBuc-68
62TopStal-100
62TopVen-51
62TopVen-90
63BasMagM-66
63ExhStaB-53
63Fle-29
63Top-443
64Top-586
65OPC-172
65Top-172
66Top-565
67Top-584
77Spo-10224
79TCM50-188
80MarExh-23
87CubCan-25
87SpoRea-14
89PacLegI-182
89SweBasG-83
90PacLeg-44
90SweBasG-92
91LinDri-20
91MetWIZ-316
91SweBasG-72
91TopArc1-286
92ActPacA-49
93RanKee-294
93TedWil-5
93UppDecAH-105
94UppDecAH-13
94UppDecAH-61
94UppDecAH1-13
94UppDecAH1-61
Pierson, Jason
93MidLeaAGF-26
93SouBenWSC-17
93SouBenWSF-1429
94CarLeaAF-CAR11
94PriWilCC-19
94PriWilCF-1919
95PriWilCTI-21
96BinBeeB-22
92UtiBluSC-2
Pierson, John
96RocCubTI-25
Pierson, Larry
88St.PetCS-23
89St.PetCS-22
90ArkTraGS-25
Pierzynski, A.J.
94SigRooDP-61
94SigRooDPS-61
95ForWayWTI-14
96BesAutS-72
96Bow-344
96Exc-80
96ForWayWB-20
Pict, Tony
33Gou-228
34BatR31-70
34BatR31-142
34DiaStaR-72
34ExhFou-4
34Gou-8
34GouCanV-63
35GouPuzR-1H
35GouPuzR-3F
35GouPuzR-14F
35GouPuzR-15F
36GouWidPPR-A84
36WorWidGV-95
83ConMar-28
88ConNatA-16
92ConTSN-524
Pietroburgo, Rob
79SpoIndT-18
80TacTigT-1
81ChaChaT-23
82ChaChaT-9
Pifer, Gary
87ChaWheP-10
88LakTigS-21
Pifferini, Raeann
91FreStaLBS-8
Piggot, Rusty
81QuaCitCT-4
Pignatano, Joe
58Top-373
59DodMor-7
59DodTeal-19
59Top-16
59TopVen-16
60DodBelB-10
60Lea-126
60Top-292
60Top-442
61A'sTeal-15
61AthJayP-15
61Top-74
62Jel-97
62Pos-97
62PosCan-97
62SalPlaC-45
62ShiPlaC-45
62Top-247
73OPC-257
73Top-257A
73Top-257B
74OPC-179
74Top-179
79TCM50-204
81TCM60I-407
82BraPol-52
83BraPol-52
84BraPol-52
89RinPosM1-30
90DodTar-624
91MetWIZ-317
94Met69CCPP-5
94Met69CS-4
94Met69T-31
95ColSilB-24
96ColSilB-23
Pike, David
92IdaFalGF-3510
92IdaFalGSP-12

94ChaRanF-2495
Pike, Mark
87WatIndP-6
88WatIndP-683
89KinIndS-19
Pilarcik, Al
57Top-311
58Hir-76
58HirTes-8
58OriJayP-9
58Top-259
59Top-7
59TopVen-7
60Top-498
61A'sTeal-16
61Top-62
79TCM50-212
91OriCro-362
Pilkington, Eric
86CliGiaP-21
88SanJosGCLC-136
88SanJosGP-127
Pilkinton, Lem
86ElmPioRSP-15
87GreHorP-23
89PenPilS-19
89Sta-107
90CarLeaA-44
90PenPilS-15
91JacSunP-168
91LinDriAA-350
92BelMarF-1462
92SanBerC-29
Pill, Mike
78ChaPirT-18
Pilla, Tony
82OrlTwiT-11
83OrlTwiT-2
Pillette, Duane
51Bow-316
52Top-82
53BowBW-59
53Top-269
54Bow-133
54OriEss-30
54Top-107
55Bow-244
55OriEss-22
55Top-168
79DiaGre-199
79TCM50-191
83TopRep5-82
91OriCro-363
91TopArc1-269
94TopArc1-107
94TopArc1G-107
Pillette, Herman
21Exh-132
21Nei-19
22E120-57
22W572-76
22W573-99
46SunBre-15
Pilots, Seattle
69FleCloS-22
69FleCloS-38
69TopStaA-23
70Top-713
Pimentel, Ed
90Ft.LauYS-17
Pimentel, Jose
96SavSanB-24
Pimentel, Rafael D.
81ArkTraT-13
82ArkTraT-5
85DomLeaS-190
86MidAngP-19
Pimentel, Wander
90HamRedB-16
90HamRedS-19
91SavCarC-22
91SavCarP-1663
92SprCarC-8
92SprCarF-876
93ArkTraF-2820
94St.PetCC-22
94St.PetCF-2596
Pina, Horacio
71MLBOffS-548
71OPC-497
71SenTealW-19
71Top-497
72Top-654
73OPC-138
73Top-138
74OPC-516
74Top-516
74TopTra-516T
75OPC-139
75Top-139
93RanKee-33
Pina, Mickey
87ElmPio(C-33
88ElmPio1C-3
88LynRedSS-17
89NewBriRSP-619
89NewBriRSS-14
89Sta-129
89TriA AAC-27
90Bow-270
90BowTif-270
90CMC-271
90PawRedSC-20
90PawRedSDD-19
90PawRedSP-473
90ProAAAF-445
90ScoRoo-104T
90TopTVRS-56
90TriAAAC-27
90UppDec-764
91LinDriAAA-364
91PawRedSDD-16
91PawRedSLD-364
91PawRedSP-50
Pina, Rafael
91EliTwiP-4298
92EliTwiC-12
92EliTwiF-3680
Pinales, Aquiles
96MacBraB-10
Pinango, Simon
93LinVenB-231
94VenLinU-143
Pincavitch, Kevin
92GreFalDSP-12
93YakBeaC-19
93YakBeaF-3883
94BakDodC-19
95AusFut-42
95VerBeaDTI-20
96Exc-181
96MauStiHWB-10
Pinckes, Mike
90BurIndP-3016
91ColIndC-5
91ColIndP-1494
Pinder, Chris
88HagSunS-17
89HagSunB-27
89HagSunP-268
90KinIndTI-20
Pineda, Gabriel
90EugEmeGS-21
91AppFoxC-9
91AppFoxP-1715
Pineda, Jose
91Ft.LauYC-17
91Ft.LauYP-2430
92ForLauYC-6
92ForLauYTI-23
92GreHorF-781
93AlbYanF-2166
Pineda, Lionel
95KanCouCTI-27
Pineda, Rafael
87QuaCitAP-15
87SalAngP-21
Pineiro, Michael
92BoiHawC-8
92BoiHawF-3632
93BenRocC-22
93BenRocF-3272
94CenValRC-19
94CenValRF-3207
Pinelli, Babe (Ralph)
20WalMaiW-41
21Nei-78
22E120-177
22W572-77
22W573-100
26SpoComoA-31
55Bow-307
87ConSer2-20
88ConSer4-22
92ConTSN-476
94ConTSN-1197
94ConTSNB-1197
Pinelli, Willie
87BakDodP-29
Pinero, Hugo
95LinVen-61
Pinhey, Lon
95TolMudHTI-4
Piniella, Lou
64Top-167
64TopVen-167
68OPC-16
68Top-16
68TopVen-16
69PilPos-25
69RoySol-13
69Top-394
70DayDaiNM-76
70MLBOffS-227
70OPC-321
70RoyTeal-27
70Top-321
70TopScr-17
70TopSup-32
71MLBOffS-426
71OPC-35
71Top-35
71TopCoi-152
71TopGreM-38
71TopSup-62
71TopTat-77
72MilBra-275
72OPC-491
72Top-491
72Top-580
73Kel2D-24
73LinPor-135
73OPC-140
73Top-140
73TopCanL-40
73TopCom-15
73TopPin-15
74OPC-390
74Top-390
74TopSta-188
74TopTra-390T
75Kel-34
75OPC-217
75Top-217
75YanSSP-11
76OPC-453
76SSP-445
76Top-453
77Kel-48
77Top-96
77YanBurK-23
78OPC-82
78RCColC-90
78SSP270-3
78Top-159
78YanBurK-18
78YanSSPD-3
79Hos-69
79OPC-342
79Top-648
79YanBurK-18
79YanPicA-29
80OPC-120
80Top-225
81Don-109
81Fle-85
81FleStiC-45
81OPC-306
81Top-724
82Don-135
82Fle-48
82FleSta-114
82OPC-236
82Top-538
83Don-335
83Fle-392
83FleSta-151
83FleSti-45
83OPC-307
83Top-307
83YanRoyRD-8
84Don-274
84Fle-136
84Nes792-408
84OPC-351
84Top-408
84TopTif-408
86RoyGreT-5
86TopTra-86T
86TopTraT-86T
86YanTCM-38
87Top-168
87TopTif-168
88Top-44
88TopTif-44
90PacLeg-99
90RedKah-21
90TopTra-96T
90TopTraT-96T
91OPC-669
91OriCro-364
91RedKah-41
91RedPep-16
91Top-669
91TopDesS-669
91TopMic-669
91TopTif-669
92OPC-321
92RedKah-41
92Top-321
92TopGol-321
92TopGolW-321
92TopMic-321
92YanWIZ7-128
92YanWIZ8-147
93MarMot-1
93Top-512
93TopGol-512
93TopInaM-512
93TopMic-512
94MarMot-1
95MarMot-1
95MarPac-15
95MarPac-50
96MarMot-1
Pinkerton, Wayne
76AshTouT-9
76AshTouT-11
76SanAntBTI-17
77TucTorC-6
78TucTorC-9
79TucTorT-12
80ChaChaT-3
Pinkham, Bill
72CedRapCT-1
83KnoBluJT-8
Pinkney, Alton
90KisDodD-22
91GreFalDSP-30
92VerBeaDC-4
92YakBeaC-3
92YakBeaF-3465
93VerBeaDF-2233
Pinkney, George
87OldJudN-408
90DodTar-625
Pinkston, Lal
52LavPro-62
55JetPos-12
Pinkus, Jeff
77SalPirT-19
Pinnell, Lance
89SanDieSAS-22
Pino, Rolando
83AppFoxF-12
86BirBarTI-12
87BirBarB-19
89KenTwiP-1082
89KenTwiS-19
90GreBraB-20
92St.CatBJC-30
92St.CatBJF-3402
93St.CatBJC-26
93St.CatBJF-3990
94St.CatBJC-29
95DunBluJTI-18
96DunBluJB-29
96DunBluJTI-23
Pinol, Juan
87TamTarP-7
Pinoni, Scott
94EugEmeC-17
94EugEmeF-3722
Pinson, Chris
90ArkRaz-32
Pinson, Tom
92KinMetC-1
92KinMetF-1529
Pinson, Vada
47Exh-180
56RedBurB-17
58Top-420
59Kah-28
59RedBurBP-14
59RedBurBP-15
59RedBurBP-16
59RedShiBS-17
59Top-448
60ArmCoi-17
60Kah-33
60RedJayP-10
60Top-32
60Top-176
60TopVen-32
60TopVen-176
61Kah-33
61Pos-181A
61Pos-181B
61RedJayP-11
61Top-25
61Top-110
61TopStal-22
62Baz-3
62ExhStaB-30
62Jel-121
62Kah-31
62Pos-121
62PosCan-121
62RedEnq-26
62RedJayP-10
62SalPlaC-118
62ShiPlaC-118
62Top-52
62Top-80
62TopBuc-69
62TopStal-119
62TopVen-52
62TopVen-80
63BasMagM-67
63ExhStaB-54
63Fle-34
63Jel-130
63Kah-24
63Pos-130
63RedEnq-25
63RedFreBC-19
63RedJayP-10
63Top-265
64Kah-21
64RedJayP-9
64Top-80
64Top-162
64TopCoi-45
64TopCoi-152
64TopGia-56
64TopSta-2
64TopStaU-57
64TopVen-80
64TopVen-162
65Kah-35
65OldLonC-16
65RedEnq-23
65Top-355
65TopEmbl-42
65TopTral-24
66Kah-26
66OPC-180
66Top-180
66TopVen-180
67CokCapA-29
67CokCapNLA-33
67CokCapR-11
67DexPre-169
67Kah-30
67Top-550
67TopVen-285
68AtlOilPBCC-35
68Baz-9
68Kah-A10
68Kah-B29
68OPC-90
68Top-90
68TopActS-10A
68TopVen-90
69MilBra-224
69OPC-160
69Top-160
69TopFou-4
69TopSta-119
69TopTeaP-18
70Ind-10
70MLBOffS-202
70OPC-445
70Top-445
70TopBoo-5
70TopSup-31
71Ind-10
71MLBOffS-382
71OPC-275
71Top-275

71TopCoi-18
71TopGreM-12
71TopTat-40
72MilBra-276
72OPC-135
72Top-135
73OPC-75
73Top-75
74OPC-490
74Top-490
74TopSta-144
75OPC-295
75SSP42-9
75Top-295
76OPC-415
76SSP-178
76Top-415
77Spo-2109
77Top-597
78TCM60I-146
82Don-445
82OhiHaloF-52
83DiaClaS2-92
86RedGreT-6
88TigPep-NNO
89TigMar-NNO
90TigCok-28
91TigCok-NNO
93MarPub-28
94TedWil-23
94TedWil-140
Pinto, Gustavo
89NiaFalRP-19
93LinVenB-64
94VenLinU-69
95LinVen-245
Pinto, Mauro
80VenLeaS-171
Pinto, Rene
95LinVen-119
96GreBatB-19
Pioneer, Old
90ElmPioP-27
Pioneers, Elmira
88ElmPio1C-10
88ElmPio1C-11
88ElmPio1C-12
94ElmPioC-29B
94ElmPioC-30
Piotrowicz, Brian
90GreFalDSP-23
91BakDodCLC-8
92VerBeaDC-14
92VerBeaDF-2872
93SanAntMF-3003
Pipgras, Ed
90DodTar-626
Pipgras, George
28PorandAR-A29
28PorandAR-B29
28W56PlaC-S4A
32R33So2-404
33DouDisP-34
33Gou-12
33GouCanV-12
35DiaMatCS3T1-122
61Fle-134
76GrePlaG-33
79DiaGre-6
91ConTSN-123
Piphus, Ben
83WatIndF-3
Pipik, Gary
89JamExpP-2138
Pipp, Wally
15SpoNewM-139
16BF2FP-35
16ColE13-134
16SpoNewM-138
19W514-84
20GasAmeMBD-14
20NatCarE-80
20WalMaiW-42
21E121So8-72
21Exh-133
21Nei-48
22AmeCarE-54
22E120-70
22W572-78
22W573-101
22W575-99
22WilPatV-45
23W503-4
23W515-39
23W551-6
23WilChoV-124
25Exh-99
26Exh-29
26SpoComoA-32
27Exh-14
63GadFunC-62
91ConTSN-157
Pippen, Cotton (Henry)
39PlaBal-8
40PlaBal-136
46RemBre-24
47RemBre-13
47SigOil-51
47SmiClo-9
Pippin, Craig
83LynPirT-7
86IndTeal-32
86MaiGuiP-15
87OmaRoyP-15
Pirates, Pittsburgh
09SpoNewSM-18
10E-UOraBSC-1
13FatT20-15
36R31Pre-G26
38BasTabP-41
56Top-121
57Top-161
58Top-341
59Top-528
60Top-484
60TopTat-61
61Top-554
61TopMagR-11
62GuyPotCP-16
62Top-409
63Top-151
64Top-373
64TopTatI-17
65OPC-209
65Top-209
66Top-404
66TopRubI-117
67Top-492
68LauWorS-24
68LauWorS-57
68Top-308
68TopVen-308
69FleCloS-19
69FleCloS-39
69TopStaA-19
70FleWorS-1
70FleWorS-24
70FleWorS-57
70Top-608
71FleWorS-7
71FleWorS-25
71FleWorS-58
71OPC-603
71Top-603
71TopTat-110
72OPC-1
72Top-1
73OPC-26
73OPCBTC-20
73Top-26
73TopBluTC-20
74OPC-626
74OPCTC-20
74Top-626
74TopStaA-20
74TopTeaC-20
78Top-606
83FleSta-244
83FleSti-NNO
87SpoTeaL-18
88PanSti-477
88RedFolSB-111
89FleWaxBC-C23
89TopTif-699
90KalTeaN-6
90PubSti-630
90RedFolSB-116
90VenSti-534
92OPCBoxB-1
93TedWilPC-19
94ImpProP-25
94Sco-657
94ScoGolR-657
95PanSti-136
96PanSti-70
98CamPepP-88
Pirkl, Greg
87BelMarL-7
89BelMarL-1
90Bes-233
90CMC-860
90SanBerSB-14
90SanBerSCLC-105
90SanBerSP-2637
91PenPilC-1
91SanBerSC-14
91SanBerSP-1990
92Bow-654
92CalCanF-3736
92ClaFS7-143
92DonRoo-96
92JacSunF-3710
92JacSunS-367
92SkyAA F-158
93Bow-571
93CalCanF-1173
93Don-589
94Fin-291
94FinRef-291
94MarMot-21
94ScoRoo-RT107
94ScoRooGR-RT107
94ScoRooSR-SU13
94Sel-414
94SpoRoo-98
94SpoRooAP-98
94StaClu-578
94StaCluFDI-578
94StaCluGR-578
94StaCluMOP-578
94Top-448
94TopGol-448
94TopSpa-448
95Bow-425
95ColCho-294
95ColChoGS-294
95ColChoSS-294
95Fle-274
95MarPac-39
95Sco-302
95ScoGolR-302
95ScoPlaTS-302
95Sel-48
95SelArtP-48
95Spo-156
95SpoArtP-156
95StaClu-396
95StaCluMOP-396
95StaCluSTWS-396
95TacRaiTI-16
95Ult-330
95UltGolM-330
96TacRaiB-21
Pirruccello, Mark
83ChaRoyT-1
84MemChiT-23
Pirtle, Jerry
79RocRedWT-12
79Top-720
89PacSenL-198
Pisacreta, Mike
89PulBraP-1890
Pisarkiewicz, Mike
77St.PetCT-19
78St.PetCT-20
Piscetta, Rob
89BakDodCLC-187
Pisciotta, Marc
91WelPirP-3570
92AugPirF-236
92ProFS7-314
93AugPirC-14
93AugPirF-1540
94CarLeaAF-CAR42
94SalBucC-15
94SalBucF-2321
94UppDecML-192
95CarMudF-153
Pisciotta, Scott
92JamExpC-9
92JamExpF-1500
92StaCluD-141
92UppDecML-149
93BurBeeC-19
93BurBeeF-156
94BurBeeC-22
94WesPalBEC-21
94WesPalBEF-36
96HarSenB-22
Pisel, Ron
78CedRapGT-22
83PhoGiaBHN-19
Pisker, Don
76DubPacT-26
78ChaChaT-12
79SyrChiT-8
79SyrChiTI-7
79Top-718
80SyrChiT-23
80SyrChiTI-17
81SalLakCGT-24
Piskol, Pete
84PriWilPT-8
Piskor, Kirk
90ArkRaz-21
Piskor, Steve
88LitFalMP-9
89PitMetS-19
Pisoni, Jim
57Top-402
59Top-259
92YanWIZ6-99
Pitcher, Scott
87BelMarL-19
89WauTimGS-8
90SanBerSB-17
90SanBerSCLC-95
90SanBerSP-2631
91SanBerSC-11
91SanBerSP-1987
92JacSunF-3706
92PenPilC-9
Pitler, Jake
49EurSta-46
52Top-395
55DodGolS-28
56Dod-22
79TCM50-187
83TopRep5-395
95TopArcBD-32
Pitlock, Skip (Lee)
71OPC-19
71Top-19
75OPC-579
75Top-579
75TucTorC-19
76SalLakCGC-16
76TusTorCr-44
Pittaro, Chris
85FleUpd-87
85NasSouTI-18
85TopTifT-91T
85TopTra-91T
86Don-150
86Top-393
86TopTif-393
86TwiTeal-1
87PorBeaP-6
88PorBeaC-19
88PorBeaP-653
92SouOreAC-28
Pittenger, Clark A.
21Nei-42
22E120-10
22W573-102
29ExhFou-8
Pittinger, Charley
06FanCraNL-38
Pittman, Charles
92JohCitCC-14
92JohCitCF-3117
Pittman, Doug
87SalBucP-27
88KenTwiP-1388
Pittman, James
88OrlTwiB-8
Pittman, Joe
76DubPacT-27
77OrlTwiT-16
80TucTorT-3
81TucTorT-3
82Don-218
82Fle-222
82Top-119
82TopTra-90T
83Don-247
83Don-422
83Fle-369
83LasVegSBHN-17
83Top-346
85NasSouTI-19
89PacSenL-38
89TopSenL-19
90EliSenL-101
91PacSenL-151
96QuaCitRB-2
Pittman, Mike
82SprCarF-5
83SprCarF-20
Pittman, Park
87VisOakP-11
89OrlTwiB-20
89OrlTwiP-1334
90Bow-408
90BowTif-408
90CMC-561
90FleUpd-109
90PorBeaC-9
90PorBeaP-177
90ProAAAF-247
Pitts, Gaylen
75TucTorC-4
75TucTorTI-16
76TucTorCa-14
76TusTorCr-42
81ArkTraT-21
82ArkTraT-22
82LouRedE-23
83LouRedR-2
84LouRedR-2
87SprCarB-1
89ArkTraGS-1
89TexLeaAGS-19
90CMC-678
90LouRedBC-27
90LouRedBLBC-3
90LouRedBP-419
90ProAAAF-533
90SprCarDGB-27
90TopTVCa-61
Pitts, Jon
91HigSchPLS-28
92GulCoaRSP-3
93ButCopKSP-21
94ChaRanF-2501
Pitts, Kevin
93YakBeaC-20
93YakBeaF-3900
94VerBeaDC-14
94VerBeaDF-88
Pitts, Rick
96SpoIndB-21
Pittsley, Jim
92ClaDraP-80
92ClaFS7-405
92UppDecML-93
93ClaGolF-202
93RocRoyC-23
93RocRoyF-715
94BowBes-B48
94BowBesR-B48
94CarLeaAF-CAR21
94Cla-23
94ExcFS7-70
94StaClu-712
94StaCluFDI-712
94StaCluGR-712
94StaCluMOP-712
94WilBluRC-20
94WilBluRF-299
95Bow-100
95ColCho-31
95ColChoGS-31
95ColChoSS-31
95Exc-61
95ExcLeaL-12
95SelCer-95
95SelCerMG-95
95SigRooOJ-27
95SigRooOJP-27
95SigRooOJPS-27
95SigRooOJS-27
95SP-17
95SPSil-17
95Sum21C-TC4
95UppDecML-23
96ColCho-570
96ColChoGS-570
96ColChoSS-570
96Pin-183
96PinAfi-169
96PinAfiAP-169
96Sco-261
96Sel-184
96SelArtP-184
96SelCer-124
96SelCerAP-124
96SelCerCB-124
96SelCerCR-124
96SelCerMB-124

96SelCerMG-124
96SelCerMR-124
96Spo-125
96SpoArtP-125
96Sum-190
96SumAbo&B-190
96SumArtP-190
96SumFoi-190
97Bow-413
97BowChr-274
97BowChrI-274
97BowChrIR-274
97BowChrR-274
97BowInt-413
95UppDecMLFS-23

Pitz, Michael
87BakDodP-28
88SanAntMB-3
89SanAntMB-23
90SanAntMGS-20
91JacSunLD-342
91JacSunP-149
91LinDriAA-342

Pivaral, Hugo
94FloStaLAF-FSL50
94VerBeaDF-68
95Bow-16
95SanBerSTI-15
95UppDecML-73
96BesAutSA-55
96SigRooOJ-27
96SigRooOJS-27
95UppDecMLFS-73

Pivnick, Phil
85AlbYanT-31

Pizarro, Germain
52LavPro-78

Pizarro, Juan
57Top-383
59Top-188
59TopVen-188
60BraLaktL-19
60BraSpiaS-17
60Lea-51
60Top-59
60TopVen-59
61Pos-112
61Top-227
61WhiSoxTS-13
62Top-59
62Top-255
62TopBuc-70
62TopStal-28
62TopVen-59
62WhiSoxJP-9
62WhiSoxTS-16
63Jel-44
63Pos-44
63Top-10
63Top-160
63WhiSoxJP-11
63WhiSoxTS-19
64Top-2
64Top-430
64TopCoi-14
64TopGia-53
64TopSta-31
64TopStaU-58
64TopVen-2
64WheSta-36
65OPC-9
65OPC-125
65Top-9
65Top-125
65TopTral-25
65WhiSoxJP-7
66Top-335
66TopVen-335
67PirTeal-17
67Top-602
67TopPirS-5
67TopVen-272
68OPC-19
68PirKDK-29
68PirTeal-16
68Top-19
68TopVen-19
69Top-498
71MLBOffS-41
71OPC-647
71Top-647
72OPC-18
72Top-18A
72Top-18B
78TCM60I-79
81RedSoxBG2S-103
84OCoandSI-197
89BlaYNPRWL-165

Pizarro, Melvin
95MarPhiTI-20

Pizarro, Miguel
78AshTouT-23

Pizzitola, Vince
52LavPro-112

Place, Michael
90PulBraP-3106
91IdaFalBSP-2
92MacBraC-21
93MacBraC-19

Place, Mike
90PulBraB-8
92MacBraF-264
93MacBraF-1397
96PriWilCB-20

Placeres, Benigno
88St.CatBJP-2009

Pladson, Gordy
75DubPacT-23
76DubPacT-28
77CocAstT-17
79ChaChaT-13
80TucTorT-18
81Top-491
81TucTorT-18
82TucTorT-21
83TucTorT-7

Plainte, Brandon
80ElmPioRST-15

Plamondon, Gerry
43ParSpo-59

Plamondon, Jerry
43ParSpo-62

Plank, Ed
76PheGiaCr-28
76PhoGiaCa-18
76PhoGiaCC-18
76PhoGiaVNB-19
77GalGloG-156
77PhoGiaCC-19
77PhoGiaCP-19
77PhoGiaVNB-19
78PhoGiaC-21
79PhoGiaVNB-8
80PhoGiaVNB-6

Plank, Edward A.
03BreE10-118
04FanCraAL-41
08AmeCarE-20
08AmeCarE-58
08RosComP-64
09AmeCarE-89
09PhiCarE-20
09RamT20-95
09SpoNewSM-39
09T206-293
10E-UOraBSC-19
10E12AmeCDC-31
10LuxCigPP-19
10NadE1-49
10PeoT21-45
10SepAnoP-21
10StaCarE-25
10W555-56
11A'sFirT20-16
11DiaGumP-24
11SpoLifCW-292
11SpoLifM-103
13PolGroW-22
14CraJacE-6
14TexTomE-38
15AmeCarE-33
15CraJacE-6
36PC7AlbHoF-46
48ExhHoF-24
50CalHOFW-60
60Fle-46
61Fle-135
63BazA-9
69SCFOldT-26
72FleFamF-26
76ShaPiz-46
77BobParHoF-38
81ConTSN-82
80Lau300-22
80MarExh-24
80PerHaloFP-46
80SSPHOF-46
84GalHaloFRL-44
84OCoandSI-173
87ConSer2-49
88ConSer3-22
88FriBasCM-5
89HOFStiB-78
92ConTSN-463
93CraJac-19
94ConTSN-1002
94ConTSNB-1002
96PitPosH-10

Plante, Bill
85ElmPioT-16
86GreHorP-16

Plantenberg, Erik
89SanDieSAS-23
90ElmPioP-19
90SanDieSA3-8
91CarLeaAP-CAR26
91LynRedSC-6
91LynRedSP-1195
92LynRedSC-13
92LynRedSF-2904
93JacSunF-2711
94Don-647
94Fle-297
94JacSunF-1410
94StaClu-518
94StaCluFDI-518
94StaCluGR-518
94StaCluMOP-518
94Top-774
94TopGol-774
94TopSpa-773
96CanIndB-20

Plantier, Phil
87ElmPio(C-34
88WinHavRSS-20
89LynRedSS-18
89Sta-170
90CMC-272
90PawRedSC-21
90PawRedSDD-20
90PawRedSP-474
90ProAAAF-446
90TopMag-67
90TopTVRS-57
91Bow-117
91Cla1-T22
91Cla2-T66
91ClaGam-128
91Don-41
91Fle-107
91LinDriAAA-365
91OPC-474
91PawRedSDD-17
91PawRedSLD-365
91PawRedSP-51
91RedSoxP-15
91Sco-348
91StaClu-459
91Stu-18
91Top-474
91TopDeb90-125
91TopDesS-474
91TopMic-474
91TopTif-474
91TriA AAGP-AAA31
91Ult-38
91UppDec-2
92Bow-459
92Cla1-T71
92ClaGam-111
92Don-488
92DonCraJ2-28
92Fle-44
92FleRooS-19
92Hig5-8
92Lea-50
92LeaGolP-14
92LeaPre-14
92OPC-782
92OPCPre-74
92Pin-51
92PinTea2-2
92ProFS7-14
92RedSoxDD-22
92Sco-406
92Sco100RS-86
92ScoImpP-20
92ScoProP-15
92StaClu-760
92StaCluNC-760
92StaPla-1
92StaPla-2
92StaPla-3
92StaPla-4
92StaPla-5
92StaPla-6
92StaPla-7
92StaPla-8
92StaPla-9
92StaPla-10
92StaPla-11
92Stu-136
92Top-782
92TopGol-782
92TopGolW-782
92TopMic-782
92TriPla-120
92Ult-318
92UppDec-425
92UppDecF-7
92UppDecFG-7
92UppDecWB-T18
93Bow-278
93Don-3
93Fla-136
93Fle-564
93FleFinE-144
93FunPac-140
93Lea-275
93OPC-332
93OPCPre-10
93PacSpa-599
93PadMot-8
93PanSti-99
93Pin-539
93Sco-176
93Sel-242
93SelRoo-128T
93SP-171
93StaClu-282
93StaClu-614
93StaCluFDI-282
93StaCluFDI-614
93StaCluMOP-282
93StaCluMOP-614
93Top-592
93TopGol-592
93TopInaM-592
93TopMic-592
93TopTra-42T
93Ult-475
93UppDec-274
93UppDec-474
93UppDec-774
93UppDecGold-274
93UppDecGold-474
93UppDecGold-774
94Bow-616
94ChuHomS-22
94ChuHomSG-22
94ColC-232
94ColChoGS-232
94ColChoSS-232
94Don-566
94ExtBas-376
94Fin-84
94FinPre-84P
94FinRef-84
94Fla-235
94Fle-672
94FUnPac-62
94Lea-59
94LeaL-153
94OPC-65
94Pac-532
94PacGolP-18
94PadMot-11
94PanSti-258
94Pin-80
94PinArtP-80
94PinMusC-80
94PinPowS-PS21
94ProMag-118
94Sco-404
94ScoGolR-404
94Sel-120
94SP-132
94SPDieC-132
94Spo-64
94StaClu-115
94StaCluFDI-115
94StaCluGR-115
94StaCluMOP-115
94Stu-135
94Top-13
94TopGol-13
94TopSpa-13
94TriPla-170
94Ult-583
94UppDec-145
94UppDecAJ-17
94UppDecAJG-17
94UppDecED-145
94USPlaCA-2C
95AstMot-15
95ColCho-120
95ColChoGS-120
95ColChoSE-164
95ColChoSEGS-164
95ColChoSESS-164
95ColChoSS-120
95Don-135
95DonPreP-135
95Emo-140
95Fin-275
95FinRef-275
95Fla-363
95Fle-566
95FleUpd-143
95Lea-308
95LeaLim-155
95Pac-368
95Pin-214
95PinArtP-214
95PinMusC-214
95Sco-430
95ScoGolR-430
95ScoPlaTS-430
95Sel-223
95SelArtP-223
95Spo-124
95SpoArtP-124
95StaClu-412
95StaClu-608
95StaCluMOP-412
95StaCluMOP-608
95StaCluSTWS-412
95StaCluSTWS-608
95StaCluVR-211
95Stu-108
95Top-176
95TopCyb-102
95TopTra-149T
95Ult-390
95UltGolM-390
95UppDec-273
95UppDec-474T
95UppDecED-273
95UppDecEDG-273
95UppDecSE-177
95UppDecSEG-177
96A'sMot-15
96ColCho-358
96ColChoGS-358
96ColChoSS-358
96Don-528
96DonPreP-528
96Fle-119
96FleTif-119
96FleUpd-U75
96FleUpdTC-U75
96LeaSigA-182
96LeaSigAG-182
96LeaSigAS-182
96PacPri-P63
96PacPriG-P63
96Pin-29
96Sco-454
95StaCluVRMC-211
96Ult-287
96Ult-403
96UltGolM-287
96UltGolM-403
96UppDec-333

Plants, Dan
84ElPasDT-17

Plaskett, Elmo
63Top-549

Plasse, Michel
72Dia-96
72Dia-97

Plaster, Allen
91BluOriC-19
91BluOriP-4127
92FreKeyC-12
92FreKeyF-1803
93ModA'sC-16
93ModA'sF-797
94ModA'sC-19
94ModA'sF-3063

95HunStaTI-21
Platel, Mark
79AppFoxT-22
80GleFalWSBT-5
80GleFalWSCT-9
81AppFoxT-9
Platt, Mizell
49Bow-89
49Lea-159
Platts, Jim
87SpaPhiP-1
88SpaPhiP-1048
Plautz, Rick
82ForMyeRT-9
Plaza, Ron
62KahAtl-16
69PilPos-33
80RedEnq-11
83Pil69G-23
86A'sMot-27
Pleasac, Joe
86ChaRaiP-21
Pledger, Kinnis
88SouBenWSGS-9
89SouBenWSGS-19
90SarWhiSS-20
91BirBarLD-70
91BirBarP-1467
91LinDriAA-70
92BirBarS-91
92SarWhiSF-221
92SkyAA F-44
93BirBarF-1205
96NorNavB-18
Pleicones, Johnnie
86Ft.LauYP-18
Plein, Ronald
93CedRapKC-30
Pleis, Scott
83EriCarT-14
Pleis, William
62Top-124
62TopVen-124
63Top-293
64Top-484
65OPC-122
65Top-122
78TCM60I-135
78TwiFri-41
Plemel, Lee
88HamRedP-1726
89SprCarB-11
90St.PetCS-18
91ArkTraLD-42
91ArkTraP-1285
91LinDriAA-42
92ArkTraF-1128
92ArkTraS-41
Plemmons, Ron
89UtiBluSP-18
90Bes-36
90SouBenWSB-7
90SouBenWSGS-13
91SarWhiSC-24
91SarWhiSP-1125
92SarWhiSF-222
Plemmons, Scott
90Bes-299
90ChaWheP-2238
92CedRapRC-22
92CedRapRF-1072
Plesac, Dan
86BrePol-37
86DonRoo-14
86FleUpd-90
86SpoRoo-10
86TopTra-87T
86TopTraT-87T
87BrePol-37
87BreTeal-10
87Don-214
87Fle-354
87FleGlo-354
87SpoTeaP-19
87Top-279
87TopSti-201
87TopTif-279
87ToyRoo-22
88BrePol-37
88Don-109
88DonAll-18
88DonBasB-221
88Fle-171
88Fle-625
88FleGlo-171
88FleGlo-625
88FleMin-32
88FleStiC-39
88OPC-317
88PanSti-118
88RedFolSB-70
88Sco-77
88ScoGlo-77
88ScoYouS2-32
88Spo-191
88StaLinBre-13
88Top-670
88TopMinL-20
88TopSti-203
88TopStiB-65
88TopTif-670
89Bow-133
89BowTif-133
89BreGar-8
89BrePol-37
89BreYea-37
89CadEllD-40
89Don-382
89DonAll-22
89DonBasB-165
89Fle-195
89FleGlo-195
89FleLeaL-29
89FleSup-32
89OPC-167
89PanSti-367
89Sco-320
89ScoHot1S-32
89Spo-128
89Top-740
89TopBasT-131
89TopSti-197
89TopTif-740
89UppDec-630
90Bow-386
90BowTif-386
90BreMilB-19
90BrePol-37
90Don-175
90DonBesA-36
90El PasDAGTI-5
90Fle-334
90FleBasA-28
90FleCan-334
90FleLeaL-29
90K-M-30
90Lea-216
90MLBBasB-85
90OPC-490
90PanSti-95
90PubSti-503
90RedFolSB-74
90Sco-86
90Sco100S-86
90Spo-102
90Top-490
90TopBig-33
90TopMinL-21
90TopSti-200
90TopTif-490
90TopTVA-31
90UppDec-477
90VenSti-405
91Bow-34
91BreMilB-20
91BrePol-18
91ClaGam-33
91Don-104
91Fle-594
91Lea-287
91OPC-146
91PanFreS-212
91PanSti-163
91RedFolS-72
91Sco-275
91StaClu-7
91Top-146
91TopDesS-146
91TopMic-146
91TopTif-146
91Ult-179
91UppDec-322
92BrePol-19
92Don-682
92Fle-185
92OPC-303
92Pin-162
92Sco-567
92StaClu-532
92Top-303
92TopGol-303
92TopGolW-303
92TopMic-303
92Ult-388
92UppDec-550
93CubMar-20
93Don-677
93Fle-633
93Lea-388
93OPC-297
93PacSpa-381
93Pin-433
93Sco-456
93StaClu-24
93StaCluCu-6
93StaCluFDI-24
93StaCluMOP-24
93Top-16
93TopGol-16
93TopInaM-16
93TopMic-16
93TriPla-142
93Ult-318
93UppDec-804
93UppDecGold-804
94BreMilB-165
94Don-641
94Fle-393
94StaClu-256
94StaCluFDI-256
94StaCluGR-256
94StaCluMOP-256
94StaCluT-355
94StaCluTFDI-355
94Top-215
94TopGol-215
94TopSpa-215
95DonTopotO-324
95Fle-421
95FleUpd-151
95PirFil-26
96Fle-532
96FleTif-532
96Ult-537
96UltGolM-537
97BluJayS-9
Pless, Rance
56Top-339
79TCM50-176
Pletsch, John
93SanJosGC-29
Plews, Herb
57Top-169
58SenJayP-9
58Top-109
59Top-373
60MapLeaSF-16
61MapLeaBH-16
Plinski, Paul
79CedRapGT-17
Plitt, Norman
90DodTar-1051
Ploeger, Tim
91SpoIndC-13
91SpoIndP-3948
92SpoIndC-22
92SpoIndF-1292
93PocPosF-4208
93PocPosSP-17
94HigDesMC-20
94HigDesMF-2787
Plonk, Chad
92GulCoaYF-3791
Plonk, Chris
92HunCubC-23
92HunCubF-3156
Plooy, Eric
96BoiHawB-23
Ploucher, George
77CocAstT-18
Plumb, Dave
87SumBraP-13
88CarLeaAS-34
88DurBulS-17
89GreBraB-25
89GreBraP-1164
89GreBraS-17
89RicBraBC-20
90GreBraB-2
90GreBraP-1133
90GreBraS-15
Plumlee, Chris
93WatIndC-22
93WatIndF-3560
94ButCopKSP-18
Plummer, Bill
73OPC-177
73Top-177
74OPC-524
74Top-524
75OPC-656
75Top-656
76OPC-627
76SSP-32
76Top-627
77Top-239
78SanJosMMC-19
78Top-106
79OPC-208
79SpoIndT-10
79Top-396
80SanJosMJitB-1
81WauTimT-29
84ChaLooT-8
86CalCanP-21
87CalCanP-2312
88CalCanC-24
88CalCanP-800
88TriAAAP-49
89MarMot-27
90MarMot-27
92MarMot-1
92OPC-171
92Top-171
92TopGol-171
92TopGolW-171
92TopMic-171
94RocPol-27
95JacSunTI-23
96JacSunB-2
Plummer, Dale
88LitFalMP-20
89JacMetGS-28
89St.LucMS-19
89Sta-23
90CMC-360
90ProAAAF-273
90TidTidC-9
90TidTidP-542
90TopTVM-53
91LinDriAAA-566
91TidTidLD-566
91TidTidP-2507
92TidTidF-894
92TidTidS-568
93NorTidF-2568
95PawRedSDD-21
95PawRedTI-19
Plunk, Eric
85HunStaJ-33
86DonRoo-40
86Fle-649
86TacTigP-16
87Don-178
87Fle-403
87FleGlo-403
87Top-587
87TopTif-587
88A'sMot-20
88Don-503
88DonBasB-267
88DonTeaBA-503
88Fle-291
88FleGlo-291
88Sco-614
88ScoGlo-614
88Top-173
88TopTif-173
89A'sMot-16
89Bow-191
89BowTif-191
89Don-125
89DonBasB-49
89Fle-20
89FleGlo-20
89OPC-141
89Sco-392
89Top-448
89TopTif-448
89UppDec-353
90Don-196
90Fle-452
90FleCan-452
90Lea-504
90OPC-9
90PubSti-313
90Top-9
90TopTif-9
90TopTVY-17
90UppDec-630
90VenSti-406
90YanScoNW-20
91Don-593
91Fle-676
91OPC-786
91Sco-428
91StaClu-529
91Top-786
91TopDesS-786
91TopMic-786
91TopTif-786
91Ult-241
91UppDec-695
92Don-554
92Fle-241
92OPC-672
92Sco-379
92Top-672
92TopGol-672
92TopGolW-672
92TopMic-672
92UppDec-608
92YanWIZ8-148
93Fla-198
93Fle-599
93IndWUA-25
93PacSpa-417
93Sco-594
93StaClu-486
93StaCluFDI-486
93StaCluMOP-486
93UppDec-713
93UppDecGold-713
94Don-267
94Fla-288
94Fle-118
94Pac-182
94Pin-366
94PinArtP-366
94PinMusC-366
94Sco-131
94ScoGolR-131
94Top-577
94TopGol-577
94TopSpa-577
94Ult-47
95Don-396
95DonPreP-396
95DonTopotO-65
95Fle-144
95Sco-542
95ScoGolR-542
95ScoPlaTS-542
95Top-256
95Ult-40
95UltGolM-40
96Don-479
96DonPreP-479
96Fle-97
96FleInd-13
96FleTif-97
96LeaSigEA-161
97Fle-86
97FleTif-86
97ScoIndU-14
97ScoIndUTC-14
Plunkett, Wilson
75ForLauYS-23
Plympton, Jeff
88LynRedSS-18
89NewBriRSP-622
89NewBriRSS-16
90Bes-242
90EasLeaAP-EL33
90NewBriRSB-20
90NewBriRSP-1319
90NewBriRSS-15
90ProAaA-8
91LinDriAAA-366
91PawRedSDD-18
91PawRedSLD-366
91PawRedSP-38
92PawRedSF-920
92PawRedSS-362
92ProFS7-19
92Sco-823
92Sco100RS-13
92SkyAAAF-164
92StaClu-481
92TopDeb91-140

92UppDec-71
93PawRedSDD-21
93RedSoxWHP-21
97DunDonPPS-18
Poat, Ray
48Bow-42
Pocekay, Walter
53MotCoo-10
Poche, Gerry
76BatRouCT-18
Pocoroba, Biff
76OPC-103
76SSP-15
76Top-103
77Top-594
78BraCok-13
78Hos-99
78Top-296
79OPC-285
79Top-555
80OPC-73
80Top-132
81BraPol-4
81Fle-257
81Top-326
82BraBurKL-20
82BraPol-4
82Fle-446
82Top-88
83BraPol-4
83Don-436
83Fle-145
83OPC-367
83Top-676
84Don-77
84Fle-189
84Nes792-438
84Top-438
84TopTif-438
Podbielan, Bud (Clarence)
50WorWidGV-12
52Top-188
53BowBW-21
53Top-237
54Top-69
55Top-153
56Top-224
57SeaPop-27
83TopRep5-188
90DodTar-627
91RinPosBD2-7
91TopArc1-237
94TopArc1-69
94TopArc1G-69
95TopArcBD-10
Podesednik, Scott
96BreCouMB-25
Podgajny, Johnny
93ConTSN-948
Podjan, Jim
96OgdRapTI-45
Podres, Johnny
47PM1StaP1-165
47StaPinP2-32
52Par-76
53Top-263
54Top-166
55Bow-97
55DodGolS-4
55Top-25
55TopDouH-111
56Dod-23
56Top-173
57SwiFra-1
57Top-277
58DodBelB-7
58DodJayP-10
58Hir-42
58Top-120
59ArmCoi-13
59DodMor-9
59DodTeal-20
59DodVol-11
59Top-262
59Top-495
60DodBelB-19
60DodJayP-11
60DodMor-9
60DodPos-8
60DodTeal-14
60DodUniO-14
60NuHi-2
60Top-425
61DodBelB-22
61DodJayP-8
61DodUniO-16
61NuSco-474
61Pos-169
61Top-109
61Top-207
61TopStal-31
62DodBelB-22
62DodJayP-8
62Jel-108
62Pos-108
62PosCan-108
62SalPlaC-172
62ShiPlaC-172
62Top-280
62TopBuc-71
62TopStal-138
63DodJayP-9
63SalMetC-9
63Top-150
63Top-412
64ChatheY-42
64Top-580
65ChaTheY-43
65DodTeal-15
65Top-387
66Top-468
67CokCapTi-15
67DexPre-170
67TigDexP-7
67Top-284
68LauWorS-52
69PadVol-6
69Top-659
70FleWorS-52
73OPC-12
73Top-12A
73Top-12B
78TCM60I-156
79TCM50-239
79TCM50-267
82Don-566
82TwiPos-23
83TwiTeal-30
83TwiTeal-34
84MinTwiP-23
84TwiTeal-31
85TwiTeal-33
87DodSmoA-26
88PacLegI-105
88RinPosD1-6A
89DodSmoG-63
90DodTar-628
90PacLeg-45
90SweBasG-104
91PhiMed-32
91SweBasG-73
91TopArc1-263
92DodStaTA-1
92PhiMed-24
93PhiMed-26
93TedWilM-8
93UppDecAH-106
94PhiMed-25
94TopArc1-166
94TopArc1G-166
94UppDecAH-63
94UppDecAH1-63
95Phi-23
95TopArcBD-56
95TopArcBD-77
95TopArcBD-93
95TopArcBD-120
95TopArcBD-127
95TopArcBD-153
96PhiTeal-26
Podsednik, Scott
95HudValRTI-2
Poe, Bill
72CedRapCT-28
Poe, Charles
90HigSchPLS-6
91SouBenWSC-10
91SouBenWSP-2870
92ClaFS7-261
92SouBenWSF-191
93SarWhiSC-21
93SarWhiSF-1384
94PriWilCC-20
94PriWilCF-1935
95SPML-34
96BesAutS-73
96BirBarB-25
96Exc-35
96HunStaTI-20
Poe, Rick
82JacMetT-13
Poehl, Michael
86WatIndP-21
87KinIndP-9
88EasLeaAP-42
88WilBilP-1325
91LinDriAA-415
91MemChiLD-415
91MemChiP-652
Poepping, Mike
75TacTwiK-21
Poff, John William
81EdmTraRR-2
94BreMilB-166
Poffenberger, Boots
79DiaGre-389
90DodTar-629
Pohl, Jeff
96BelGiaTI-21
Pohle, Rich
88IdaFalBP-1861
Pohle, Walt
85BelBreT-2
86StoPorP-21
87ElPasDP-19
Poholsky, Tom
52Top-242
54CarHunW-15
54Top-142
55Bow-76
55CarHunW-16
56Top-196
57Top-235
83TopRep5-242
94TopArc1-142
94TopArc1G-142
Poindexter, Mike
81BatTroT-5
83WatIndF-24
Pointer, Aaron
67CokCapAs-11
67Top-564
Pointer, Corey
94SigRooDP-41
94SigRooDPS-41
94StaCluDP-89
94StaCluDPFDI-89
94TopTra-98T
95DanBraTI-22
96EugEmeB-1
Pointer-Jones, Carl
88BurBraP-2
Poissant, Rod
86LakTigP-17
87GleFalTP-16
89SanBerSCLC-75
90PenPilS-16
90StaFS7-78
Poisson, The Fish (Gilles)
72Dia-126
Polak, Rich
90PriWilCTI-19
91Ft.LauYC-11
91Ft.LauYP-2424
92PriWilCC-17
92PriWilCF-144
93AlbYanF-2161
93LinVenB-267
Polakowski, Ted
84IdaFalATI-21
Polanco, Carlos
91BoiHawC-21
91BoiHawP-3888
91QuaCitAC-21
91QuaCitAP-2640
Polanco, Felipe
94AugGreC-19
94AugGreF-3018
94WelPirC-19
94WelPirF-3503
Polanco, Giovanni
91BelMarC-26
91BelMarP-3660
92LetMouSP-3
Polanco, Juan
96SouOreTI-6
Polanco, Nicholas
89KinMetS-19
90KinMetB-12
90KinMetS-19
Polanco, Placido
95PeoChiTI-10
96StPetCB-24
Polanco, Radhames
87LitFalMP-2402
88LitFalMP-10
89ColMetB-21
89ColMetGS-21
Polanco, Roger
75DubPacT-12
76VenLeaS-56
Poland, Philip
09T206-456
Polasek, John
89AncGlaP-19
90JamExpP-24
91WesPalBEC-9
91WesPalBEP-1225
92FreKeyC-14
92FreKeyF-1804
92HagSunF-2553
93FreKeyC-21
93FreKeyF-1026
Polcovich, Kevin
92WelPirF-1332
93AugPirC-15
93AugPirF-1553
94CarMudF-1587
95CarMudF-168
Poldberg, Brian
81NasSouTI-13
82NasSouTI-18
83OmaRoyT-11
84OmaRoyT-23
85OmaRoyT-31
87AppFoxP-17
88AppFoxP-162
89AppFoxP-872
90BasCitRS-28
91LinDriAAA-350
91OmaRoyLD-350
91OmaRoyP-1051
92MemChiF-2435
92MemChiS-449
94EugEmeC-28
95SprSulTI-20
96LanLugB-1
Pole, Dick
74OPC-596
74Top-596
75OPC-513
75Top-513
76OPC-326
76Top-326
77Top-187
78Top-233
80PorBeaT-11
81BirBarT-19
83QuaCitCT-3
86PitCubP-19
87IowCubTI-21
88CubDavB-NNO
89CubMar-NNO
90CubMar-28
90TopTVCu-5
91CubVinL-21
92PawRedSF-941
92PawRedSS-375
93GiaMot-28
93GiaPos-27
94GiaMot-28
95GiaMot-28
96GiaMot-28
97DunDonPPS-19
Polemil, Miguel
85DomLeaS-102
Poles, Spot
74LauOldTBS-21
Polese, Joe
77NewCoPT-26
Polewski, Steve
90WelPirP-7
91AugPirC-17
91AugPirP-813
Polhemus, Mark
87BucN28-45
Polidor, Gus
80VenLeaS-185
81HolMilT-21
82HolMilT-18
83NasAngT-14
85EdmTraC-12
86EdmTraP-22
86Fle-650
87AngSmo-18
87Don-579
88AngSmo-6
88Don-356
88Fle-501
88FleGlo-501
88Sco-341
88ScoGlo-341
88Top-708
88TopTif-708
89BrePol-14
90BrePol-14
90Don-412
90OPC-313
90Top-313
90TopTif-313
90UppDec-480
92TacTigF-2511
92TacTigS-544
93EdmTraF-1145
93LinVenB-225
94BreMilB-167
94VenLinU-64
95LinVen-241
95LinVen-330
Polidor, Wil
93HicCraC-19
93HicCraF-1287
93LinVenB-158
93SouBenWSC-18
94SouBenSHC-17
94SouBenSHF-602
94VenLinU-136
95LinVen-147
95PriWilCTI-10
Poling, Mark
88CliGiaP-699
Polinski, Bob
76VenLeaS-65
78TacYanC-43
79ColCliT-15
Polis, Pete
92MedHatBJF-3211
92MedHatBJSP-16
93MedHatBJF-3741
Politte, Cliff
96MidLeaAB-21
96PeoChiB-24
97Bow-419
97BowChr-279
97BowChrI-279
97BowChrIR-279
97BowChrR-279
97BowInt-419
Polk, Riley
87WatIndP-24
Polk, Ron
88MisStaB-25
89MisStaB-29
90MisStaB-30
91MisStaB-38
91TopTra-93T
91TopTraT-93T
92MisStaB-33
93MisStaB-36
Polk, Steve
88MisStaB-26
89MisStaB-30
90MisStaB-31
Polka, Fritz
86LitFalMP-23
87ColMetP-21
88FloStaLAS-17
88St.LucMS-19
Pollack, Chris
87JamExpP-2679
88RocExpLC-30
90WesPalBES-18
91HarSenLD-267
91HarSenP-624
91LinDriAA-267
92HarSenF-462
92HarSenS-297
Pollack, Rick
88BirBarB-15
Pollard, Damon
90EugEmeGS-23
91AppFoxC-10
91AppFoxP-1716
92BasCitRC-6
92BasCitRF-3845
95HarSenTI-2
Pollard, Jim
52Whe-24A
52Whe-24B
Pollard, Nathaniel

93NegLeaRL2-30
Pollet, Howie (Howard)
39ExhSal-52A
39ExhSal-52B
46SeaSLP-40
46SpoExcW-8-2
49Bow-95
49EurSta-193
50Bow-72
51Bow-263
51R42SmaS-83
51TopRedB-7
52Bow-83
52Top-63
53NorBreL-21
53Top-83
54Top-89
55Top-76
55TopDouH-31
56Top-262
60Top-468
67AstTeal2-20
76TayBow4-37
77TCMTheWY-41
83TopRep5-63
87AstSer1-30
91TopArc1-83
92BazQua5A-4
92CarMcD-49
94TopArc1-89
94TopArc1G-89
Polley, Dale
89GreBraB-15
89GreBraP-1160
89GreBraS-18
90CMC-279
90ProAAAF-403
90RicBraBC-14
90RicBraC-3
90RicBraP-258
90RicBraTI-26
90TriAllGP-AAA4
91LinDriAAA-437
91RicBraBC-13
91RicBraLD-437
91RicBraP-2565
91RicBraTI-23
92RicBraBB-17
92RicBraF-374
92RicBraRC-14
92RicBraS-436
93GreBraF-344
95RicBraTI-16
96ColCliB-25
97RicBraBC-17
Polley, Dave
88GreBraB-12
95RicBraRC-19
Polli, Crip (Lou)
36GouWidPPR-D27
36WorWidGV-84
Pollock, Elton
96AugGreB-23
Pollock, Jason
93PocPosF-4220
93PocPosSP-13
94OgdRapF-3749
94OgdRapSP-18
96NewJerCB-21
Pollock, Syd
76LauIndC-6
76LauIndC-23
Pollock, Wayne
91MelBusF-17
Polly, Nick
90DodTar-630
Poloni, John
76SanAntBTI-18
77TucTorC-35
80KnoBluJT-3
83WauTimF-2
87MyrBeaBJP-1451
88KnoBluJB-23
89KnoBluJB-29
89KnoBluJP-1147
89KnoBluJS-25
90KnoBluJB-19
90KnoBluJP-1261
90KnoBluJS-26
91LinDriAAA-522
91SyrChiLD-522
91SyrChiMB-19
91SyrChiP-2497
92SyrChiF-1987
92SyrChiMB-16
92SyrChiS-525
93RanKee-295
93SyrChiF-1014
94SyrChiF-987
94SyrChiTI-22
95DunBluJTI-19
Polonia, Luis
84MadMusP-7
85DomLeaS-56
85HunStaJ-11
86TacTigP-17
87DonRoo-25
87FleUpd-99
87FleUpdG-99
87SpoRooI-18
87TopTra-96T
87TopTraT-96T
88Don-425
88DonTeaBA-425
88Fle-292
88FleGlo-292
88Lea-256
88OPC-238
88PanSti-177
88RedFolSB-71
88Sco-64
88ScoGlo-64
88ScoYouSI-22
88Spo-71
88StaLinAs-14
88TacTigC-16
88TacTigP-638
88Top-238
88TopBig-65
88TopRoo-14
88TopSti-172
88TopTif-238
88ToyRoo-24
89A'sMot-17
89Don-386
89Fle-21
89FleGlo-21
89OPC-386
89PanSti-425
89Sco-380
89ScoRoo-38T
89Spo-133
89Top-424
89TopTif-424
89UppDec-162
89YanScoNW-4
90Don-547
90DonBesA-116
90FleUpd-80
90Lea-295
90OPC-634
90PubSti-314
90Sco-442
90ScoRoo-46T
90Top-634
90TopTif-634
90TopTra-97T
90TopTraT-97T
90TopTVY-32
90UppDec-316
90VenSti-407
91AngSmo-1
91Bow-209
91Don-93
91DonGraS-10
91Fle-322
91FouBal-16
91KinDis-10
91Lea-81
91OPC-107
91Sco-587
91StaClu-144
91Top-107
91TopDesS-107
91TopMic-107
91TopTif-107
91UltUpd-11
91UppDec-187
92AngPol-15
92Bow-582
92DenHol-12
92Don-252
92Fle-67
92Lea-45
92OPC-37
92PanSti-10
92Pin-166
92Sco-68
92StaClu-528
92Top-37
92TopGol-37
92TopGolW-37
92TopMic-37
92TriPla-99
92Ult-29
92UppDec-147
92UppDecTMH-40
92YanWIZ8-149
93AngMot-15
93AngPol-15
93Bow-413
93Don-461
93DonDiaK-DK26
93DonMVP-1
93DonSpiotG-SG7
93Fla-176
93Fle-196
93FunPac-41
93KinDis-7
93Lea-399
93LimRocDWB-111
93LinVenB-308
93LinVenB-320
93OPC-266
93PacBeiA-2
93PacSpa-50
93PacSpaPI-19
93PanSti-8
93Pin-31
93Sco-39
93Sel-74
93SP-24
93StaClu-100
93StaCluAn-19
93StaCluFDI-100
93StaCluMOP-100
93Stu-170
93Top-760
93TopGol-760
93TopInaM-760
93TopMic-760
93TriPla-12
93TriPla-190
93Ult-168
93UppDec-178
93UppDecGold-178
93USPlaCA-10H
94Bow-409
94ColC-504
94ColChoGS-504
94ColChoSS-504
94Don-255
94ExtBas-138
94Fin-365
94FinRef-365
94Fla-323
94Fle-68
94FleUpd-70
94Lea-390
94OPC-128
94Pac-87
94PanSti-41
94Pin-512
94PinArtP-512
94PinMusC-512
94ProMag-89
94Sco-45
94ScoGolR-45
94ScoRoo-RT9
94ScoRooGR-RT9
94Sel-251
94SpoRoo-10
94SpoRooAP-10
94StaClu-11
94StaClu-639
94StaCluFDI-11
94StaCluFDI-639
94StaCluGR-11
94StaCluGR-639
94StaCluMO-39
94StaCluMOP-11
94StaCluMOP-639
94StaCluT-208
94StaCluTFDI-208
94Top-566
94TopGol-566
94TopSpa-566
94TopTra-20T
94Ult-403
94UppDec-496
94UppDecED-496
94USPlaCA-11H
95ColCho-516
95ColChoGS-516
95ColChoSS-516
95Don-514
95DonPreP-514
95DonTopotO-124
95Fle-80
95Lea-162
95Pac-302
95PacPri-99
95Pin-445
95PinArtP-445
95PinMusC-445
95Sco-462
95ScoGolR-462
95ScoPlaTS-462
95StaClu-171
95StaCluFDI-171
95StaCluMOP-171
95StaCluSTWS-171
95StaCluVR-89
95Top-323
95TopCyb-176
95Ult-85
95UltGolM-85
96ColCho-390T
96Fle-306
96FleTif-306
96Sco-489
95StaCluVRMC-89
Polverini, Steve
87AubAstP-9
Pomeranz, Mike
89KenTwiP-1081
89KenTwiS-20
90CarLeaA-20
90SalBucS-16
Pomierski, Joe
93ClaGolF-145
94BelMarC-21
94BelMarF-3245
95EveAqaTI-15
96HudValRB-1
Pomorski, John
36WorWidGV-92
Ponce, Carlos
81BurBeeT-22
83ElPasDT-19
84VanCanC-34
85VanCanC-224
86Don-595
87JapPlaB-5
90El PasDAGTI-10
91SumFlyC-28
91SumFlyP-2353
93HigDesMC-28
93HigDesMF-59
94BreCouMC-26
94BreMilB-259
Pond, Simon
96VerExpB-22
Ponder, Charles Elmer
20WalMaiW-43
23WilChoV-125
Ponder, Kevin
88ColMetGS-10
89MiaMirIS-16
90MiaMirIS-21
Ponder, Marcus
92LetMouSP-13
Pone, Vince
78NewWayCT-34
79BurBeeT-22
80BurBeeT-11
81BurBeeT-2
Ponio, Mike
89OklSoo-22
Ponson, Sidney
97Bow-74
97BowBes-130
97BowBesAR-130
97BowBesR-130
97BowCerBIA-CA63
97BowCerGIA-CA63
97BowChr-102
97BowChrI-102
97BowChrIR-102
97BowChrR-102
97BowInt-74
Pont, Jon
94BelBreC-29
94BelBreF-120
95BelBreTI-28
96El PasDB-3
Pontbriant, Matt
93AugPirC-16
93AugPirF-1541
94AugGreC-20
94AugGreF-3008
94SouAtlLAF-SAL35
95LynHilTI-22
96CarMudB-8
Ponte, Edward
90OscAstS-22
91OscAstC-9
91OscAstP-681
92JacGenS-344
92ProFS7-229
93QuaCitRBC-15
93QuaCitRBF-98
Pontes, Blossom
91HawWomS-11
Pontes, Dan
93GleFalRC-23
93GleFalRF-4002
95PeoChiTI-27
96StPetCB-25
Pontiff, Wally
74GasRanT-16
Pool, Bruce
92OneYanC-23
93GreHorC-18
93GreHorF-884
Pool, Harlin
36GouWidPPR-D28
Pool, Matt
94BenRocF-3591
95SalAvaTI-23
96SalAvaB-22
97BenRocC-19
Poole, Ed
03BreE10-119
03BreE10-120
11SpoLifCW-293
Poole, Jimmy (James)
87PanAmTURB-13
88TopTra-88T
88TopTraT-88T
89TopBig-263
89VerBeaDS-22
90SanAntMGS-21
91Cla1-T54
91Don-655
91Fle-217
91LinDriAAA-319
91OklCit8LD-319
91OklCit8P-176
91Sco-357
91TopDeb90-126
92Don-600
92Fle-23
92OPC-683
92ProFS7-150
92Sco-693
92StaClu-412
92Top-683
92TopGol-683
92TopGolW-683
92TopMic-683
93Don-295
93FleFinE-164
93PacSpa-348
93RanKee-296
93Top-793
93TopGol-793
93TopInaM-793
93TopMic-793
94Don-427
94Fla-7
94Fle-16
94OriPro-81
94OriUSPC-4S
94OriUSPC-9D
94Pac-42
94Sco-112
94ScoGolR-112
94StaCluT-293
94StaCluTFDI-293
94Top-449
94TopGol-449
94TopSpa-449
94Ult-8
95Pac-29
95Top-107
96Fle-98
96FleInd-14
96FleTif-98
96LeaSigEA-162

97PacPriGotD-GD219
87PanAmTUBI-23
Poole, Mark
83KinBluJTI-15
85SyrChiT-17
86SyrChiP-21
86TulDriTI-1
Poole, Stine
81BirBarT-20
82EvaTriT-13
83TolMudHT-12
Poor, Jeff
95BurBeeTI-15
95MidLeaA-40
96BurBeeTI-12
Poorman, Thomas
87OldJudN-409
90KalBatN-45
Pope, Dave
55Bow-198
55IndGolS-24
56Top-154
57Top-249
61MapLeaBH-17
91OriCro-365
Pope, Greg
81WatIndT-13
Pope, Matt
85CloHSS-35
Pope, Mike
78St.PetCT-21
Pope, Willie
95NegLeaL2-13
Popham, Art
80TacTigT-22
81TacTigT-3
82TacTigT-21
83TacTigT-23
Poplawski, Misty
91FreStaLBS-9
Popoff, Jim
92PitMetF-3292
93ExcFS7-78
93ExcLeaLF-10
Popov, Andrey
89EasLeaDDP-DD21
Popovich, Nick
77SpaPhiT-10
Popovich, Paul
67Top-536
68Top-266
68TopVen-266
69CubJewT-12
69OPC-47
69Top-47A
69Top-47B
69TopSta-48
69TopTeaP-22
70OPC-258
70Top-258
71MLBOffS-42
71OPC-726
71Top-726
72OPC-512
72Top-512
73OPC-309
73Top-309
74OPC-14
74Top-14
75OPC-359
75Top-359
79CliDodT-8
90DodTar-631
Popowski, Eddie
73OPC-131
73Top-131A
73Top-131B
74OPC-403
74Top-403
87ElmPio(C-32
Popplewell, Tom
87OneYanP-9
88PriWilYS-19
89Ft.LauYS-19
90FloStaLAS-40
90Ft.LauYS-18
91AlbYanLD-13
91AlbYanP-1006
91LinDriAA-13
92AlbYanF-2227
92AlbYanS-16
93AlbYanF-2162
94ElPasDF-3144
Poquette, Tom
75OPC-622
75Top-622
77BurCheD-66
77Kel-24
77OPC-66
77Top-93
78OPC-197
78Roy-19
78SSP270-239
78Top-357
79Top-476
80Top-597
81Top-153
82Roy-15
82Top-657
86RoyGreT-7
88OmaRoyP-1495
89OmaRoyC-25
89OmaRoyP-1741
90CMC-198
90OmaRoyC-23
90OmaRoyP-81
90ProAAAF-616
92AppFoxC-27
92AppFoxF-1001
93MemChiF-391
93RanKee-297
94OmaRoyF-1240
95OmaRoyTI-25
Porcelli, Joe
90GenCubP-3038
90GenCubS-20
91WinSpiC-10
91WinSpiP-2828
Portales, Nelson
94VenLinU-240
Porte, Carlos
80CedRapRT-6
83WatRedT-12
85CedRapRT-18
Porter, Andy
86NegLeaF-15
92NegLeaK-14
92NegLeaRLI-49
93UppDecS-17
95NegLeaL2-28
Porter, Bo
96DayCubB-20
96RocCubTI-26
Porter, Bob
78GreBraT-19
79SavBraT-22
81RicBraT-7
82RicBraT-21
83RicBraT-20
85DurBulT-16
Porter, Brad
84EveGiaC-22A
Porter, Brian
89AubAstP-2169
90AubAstB-21
Porter, Carlos
80VenLeaS-17
Porter, Chuck
76QuaCitAT-27
79SalLakCGT-19A
81VanCanT-2
82Top-333
82VanCanT-21
84BrePol-43
84Don-333
84Fle-211
84Nes792-452
84Top-452
84TopTif-452
85BreGar-16
85Don-115
85Fle-591
85Top-32
85TopTif-32
86Top-292
86TopTif-292
86VanCanP-22
94BreMilB-260
78STLakCGC-17
Porter, Darrell
72OPC-162
72Top-162
73OPC-582
73Top-582
74OPC-194
74Top-194
74TopSta-198
75Hos-62
75OPC-52
75Top-52
76BreA&P-10
76Hos-117
76OPC-645
76SSP-232
76Top-645
77OPC-116
77Top-214
78Hos-130
78OPC-66
78Roy-20
78SSP270-221
78Top-19
79Hos-4
79Kel-25
79OPC-295
79Top-571
80Kel-12
80OPC-188
80Top-360
80TopSup-39
81AllGamPI-133
81Car5x7-21
81CokTeaS-127
81Don-505
81Fle-36
81Top-610
81TopSti-224
81TopTra-814
82Don-498
82Fle-124
82FleSta-29
82OPC-98
82OPC-348
82Top-447
82Top-448
82TopSti-93
82TopStiV-93
83AllGamPI-134
83Car-21
83CarColBP-1
83Don-278
83Fle-18
83FleSta-152
83FleSti-3
83OPC-103
83PerCreC-12
83PerCreCG-12
83Top-103
83TopSti-148
83TopSti-149
83TopSti-182
83TopSti-183
84AllGamPI-44
84Car-22
84Car5x7-21
84Don-303
84Fle-331
84MilBra-19
84Nes792-285
84OPC-285
84Top-285
84TopRubD-31
84TopSti-143
84TopTif-285
85AllGamPI-133
85CarTeal-26
85Don-353
85Fle-237
85Lea-258
85OPC-246
85Top-525
85TopRubD-29
85TopSti-140
85TopTif-525
86BasStaB-84
86BreGreT-8
86CarKASD-16
86CarTeal-35
86Don-290
86Fle-45
86FleUpd-91
86OPC-84
86RanLit-5
86RanPer-17
86Spo-148
86Top-757
86TopTif-757
86TopTra-88T
86TopTraT-88T
87Don-593
87Fle-136
87FleGlo-136
87OPC-213
87RanMot-10
87RanSmo-10
87RedFolSB-52
87Top-689
87TopTif-689
88Sco-537
88ScoGlo-537
93RanKee-298
93RoySta2-10
94BreMilB-261
Porter, Dick
32OrbPinNP-36
32OrbPinUP-49
33TatOrb-49
34Gou-43
34GouCanV-88
93ConTSN-778
Porter, Eric
82WisRapTF-20
92Min-16
Porter, Griggy
73WicAerKSB-12
74WicAerODF-118
Porter, Henry
87BucN28-17
87OldJudN-410
88GandBCGCE-32
88SpoTimM-20
Porter, J.W.
53Top-211
55Top-49
55TopDouH-9
58Top-32A
58Top-32B
59SenTealW-13
59Top-246
91TopArc1-211
Porter, Jeff
83MemChiT-22
84IndIndTI-31
Porter, Merle
93NegLeaRL2-31
Porter, Mike
79SpoIndT-3
92BluOriC-5
92BluOriF-2359
93BluOriC-20
93BluOriF-4123
Porterfield, Bob (Erwin)
47Exh-181
49Bow-3
50Bow-216
51R42SmaS-81
52Bow-194
52RedMan-AL17
52TipTop-29
52Top-301
53BowC-22
53Bri-15
53RedMan-AL19
53Top-108
54Bow-24
54RedMan-AL18
55Bow-104
55DonWin-4
55RedMan-AL10
55RobGouS-7
55RobGouW-7
56Top-248
56YelBasP-25
57Top-118
58Top-344
59Top-181
59TopVen-181
79TCM50-284
83TopRep5-301
91TopArc1-108
Porterfield, Ron
88AubAstP-1954
90ColMudS-26
95TusTorTI-20
96TusTorB-29
Portillo, Alex
95LinVen-142
96PriWilCB-21
Portillo, Luis
93LinVenB-105
94VenLinU-230
Portillo, Ramon
96MarPhiB-19
Portocarrero, Arnie (Arnold)
54Top-214
55A'sRodM-25
55A'sRodM-26
55Top-77
55TopDouH-11
56Top-53
58Top-465
59Top-98
59TopVen-98
60Top-254
76A'sRodMC-17
79TCM50-196
91OriCro-366
94TopArc1-214
94TopArc1G-214
Portugal, Mark
82WisRapTF-14
83VisOakF-24
85TolMudHT-10
86DonRoo-44
87Don-566
87Fle-548
87FleGlo-548
87Top-419
87TopTif-419
88PorBeaC-5
88PorBeaP-658
89Bow-318
89BowTif-318
89Fle-123
89FleGlo-123
89Sco-482
89Top-46
89TopTif-46
89TucTorJP-19
89UppDec-358
90AstLenH-17
90AstMot-10
90Bow-63
90BowTif-63
90ClaBlu-121
90Don-542
90Lea-399
90OPC-253
90Sco-552
90Top-253
90TopTif-253
90UppDec-502
91AstMot-10
91Bow-552
91Don-268
91Fle-512
91Lea-63
91OPC-647
91Sco-319
91StaClu-320
91Top-647
91TopDesS-647
91TopMic-647
91TopTif-647
91Ult-138
91UppDec-250
92AstMot-10
92Bow-656
92Don-188
92Fle-443
92OPC-114
92Pin-189
92Sco-243
92StaClu-126
92Top-114
92TopGol-114
92TopGolW-114
92TopMic-114
92Ult-494
92UppDec-448
93AstMot-11
93Don-612
93Fle-441
93Lea-467
93OPC-318
93PacSpa-126
93Pin-366
93StaClu-426
93StaCluAs-30
93StaCluFDI-426
93StaCluMOP-426
93Top-335
93TopGol-335
93TopInaM-335
93TopMic-335
93Ult-394
93UppDec-99
93UppDecGold-99
94Bow-303

94ColC-568
94ColChoGS-568
94ColChoSS-568
94Don-199
94ExtBas-391
94Fin-413
94FinRef-413
94Fla-246
94Fle-498
94FleUpd-195
94GiaAMC-17
94GiaMot-10
94Lea-429
94OPC-42
94Pac-273
94Pin-506
94PinArtP-506
94PinMusC-506
94Sco-193
94ScoGolR-193
94ScoRoo-RT64
94ScoRooGR-RT64
94Sel-316
94SpoRoo-62
94SpoRooAP-62
94StaClu-644
94StaCluFDI-644
94StaCluGR-644
94StaCluMOP-644
94StaCluT-20
94StaCluTFDI-20
94Top-734
94TopGol-734
94TopSpa-734
94TopTra-22T
94Ult-591
94UppDec-386
94UppDecED-386
94USPlaCA-11S
95ColCho-258
95ColChoGS-258
95ColChoSE-107
95ColChoSEGS-107
95ColChoSESS-107
95ColChoSS-258
95Don-268
95DonPreP-268
95DonTopotO-217
95Emo-196
95Fin-322
95FinRef-322
95Fla-210
95Fle-587
95GiaMot-8
95Lea-153
95Pac-383
95Pin-87
95PinArtP-87
95PinMusC-87
95Sco-446
95ScoGolR-446
95ScoPlaTS-446
95SP-117
95SPSil-117
95StaClu-378
95StaCluMOP-378
95StaCluSTWS-378
95Top-155
95Ult-243
95UltGolM-243
95UppDec-336
95UppDecED-336
95UppDecEDG-336
95UppDecSE-69
95UppDecSEG-69
96ColCho-99
96ColChoGS-99
96ColChoSS-99
96Don-540
96DonPreP-540
96EmoXL-167
96Fla-236
96Fle-349
96FleTif-349
96Pac-47
96Sco-458
96StaClu-417
96StaCluEPB-417
96StaCluEPG-417
96StaCluEPS-417
96StaCluMOP-417
96Top-328
96Ult-181
96UltGolM-181
96UppDec-309
97ColCho-421
97Fle-301
97Fle-684
97FleTif-301
97FleTif-684
97MetUni-49
97PacPriGotD-GD128
97Top-33
97Ult-179
97Ult-466
97UltGolME-179
97UltGolME-466
97UltPlaME-179
97UltPlaME-466

Portwood, Craig
94DavLipB-21

Porzio, Mike
95OdgRapTI-23

Posada, Jorge
91OneYanP-4156
92GreHorC-7
92GreHorF-782
93CarLeaAGF-23
93PriWilCC-20
93PriWilCF-660
94Bow-38
94BowBes-B29
94BowBes-X106
94BowBesR-B29
94BowBesR-X106
94ColCliF-2955
94ColCliP-22
94ExcFS7-112
95Bow-56
95ColCliMCTI-2
95ColCliP-24
95ColCliTI-24
96ColCho-636
96ColChoGS-636
96ColChoSS-636
96ColCliB-26
96UppDec-159
97FlaSho-A117
97FlaSho-B117
97FlaSho-C117
97FlaShoLC-117
97FlaShoLC-B117
97FlaShoLC-C117
97FlaShoLCM-A117
97FlaShoLCM-B117
97FlaShoLCM-C117
97FlaShoWotF-16
97Fle-522
97FleTif-522
97PinCer-125
97PinCerMBlu-125
97PinCerMG-125
97PinCerMR-125
97PinCerR-125
97PinTotCPB-125
97PinTotCPG-125
97PinTotCPR-125
97Sco-481
97ScoHobR-481
97ScoResC-481
97ScoShoS-481
97ScoShoSAP-481
97Ult-536
97UltGolME-536
97UltPlaME-536

Posada, Leo
61A'sTeal-17
61AthJayP-16
61Top-39
62Jel-96
62Pos-96
62PosCan-96
62SalPlaC-62
62ShiPlaC-62
62Top-168
62TopStal-55
62TopVen-168
73CedRapAT-25
74CedRapAT-25
75ForLauYS-25
76VenLeaS-38
78DayBeaAT-21
80VenLeaS-49

Pose, Scott
89BilMusP-2063
90Bes-91
90ChaWheB-24
90ChaWheP-2255
90CMC-696
90ProAaA-103
90SouAtlLAS-19
91ChaLooLD-164
91ChaLooP-1972
91LinDriAA-164
92ChaLooF-3831
92ChaLooS-192
92ClaFS7-442
92SkyAA F-85
92UppDecML-97
93Bow-318
93ClaGolF-54
93ExcFS7-27
93ExcLeaLF-13
93FleFinE-68
93Lea-272
93MarUSPC-5D
93PacSpa-469
93Pin-576
93PinExpOD-8
93StaClu-584
93StaCluFDI-584
93StaCluMarl-21
93StaCluMOP-584
93TopTra-113T
93Ult-384
93UppDec-762
93UppDecGold-762
94NewOrlZF-1481
96SyrChiTI-23

Posedel, Bill
39PlaBal-121
40PlaBal-58
41Gou-19
47CenFlo-20
49EurSta-169
52Top-361
54CarHunW-16
55CarHunW-17
60Top-469
74PadDea-21
79DiaGre-221
83TopRep5-361
90DodTar-632
95ConTSN-1343

Posey, Bob
85DurBulT-29
86DurBulP-21

Posey, Cum
88NegLeaD-3

Posey, Gary
90ButCopKSP-6

Posey, John
87HagSunP-13
88ChaKniTI-11
89HagSunB-26
89HagSunS-14
89RocRedWC-12
90ChaKniTI-8

Posey, Marty
91GasRanC-26
91GasRanP-2703
91SouAtlLAGP-SAL24

Poss, David
87SalLakTTT-27

Post, David
92ClaDraP-103
92FroRowDP-70
92HigSchPLS-16
93YakBeaC-21
93YakBeaF-3890
94YakBeaC-12
94YakBeaF-3858
95VerBeaDTI-21
96WesPalBEB-27

Post, Jeff
92SouOreAC-16
92SouOreAF-3416
93PocPosF-4209
93PocPosSP-21

Post, John
88ElmPioC-28

Post, Wally
52Top-151
55Bow-32
55Kah-5
56Kah-13
56RedBurB-18
56Top-158
57Kah-24
57RedSoh-16
57Top-157
58Hir-14
58Kah-22
58Top-387
59HomRunD-15
59Top-398
60PhiJayP-10
60Top-13
60TopVen-13
61Kah-34
61Top-378
61TopStal-23
62Jel-128
62Kah-32
62Pos-128
62PosCan-128
62RedEnq-27
62RedJayP-11
62Top-148
62TopVen-148
63RedEnq-26
63Top-462
64Top-253
64TopVen-253
79DiaGre-273
82OhiHaloF-53
83TopRep5-151
91TopArc1-294

Postema, Andy
90EriSaiS-18
91RenSilSCLC-9

Postier, Paul
87GasRanP-16
88TulDriTI-24
89TulDriGS-21
89TulDriTI-19
90TulDriP-1164
90TulDriTI-20
91LinDriAAA-320
91OklCit8LD-320
91OklCit8P-188
92OklCit8S-319

Postiff, J.P.
90HunCubP-3292
91WinSpiP-2838
92PeoChiC-20
92PeoChiTI-20
93PocPosF-4217
93PocPosSP-7

Poston, Mark
85BeaGolGT-16
86BeaGolGP-20
87LasVegSP-10

Pote, Lou
92ShrCapF-3867
92ShrCapS-589
93ShrCapF-2757
94Bow-547
94ShrCapF-1603
95UppDecML-177
96HarSenB-23
95UppDecMLFS-177

Potenziano, Benjamin
95BelGiaTI-NNO
96SanJosGB-30

Potestio, Doug
86IowCubP-22
87IowCubTI-6
86STaoftFt-6

Potestio, Frank
87DayBeaAP-17
88SprCarB-10
89ArkTraGS-19
89LouRedBTI-31

Pott, Larry
85TulDriTI-17

Potter, Lonnie
90BenBucL-9

Potter, Mike
76TulOilGP-15
78SprRedWK-3

Potter, Nelson
41DouPlaR-129
46SeaSLP-41
47TipTop-70
49EurSta-16
79DiaGre-193
93ConTSN-717
96Bro194F-7

Potter, Scott
89EasLeaDDP-DD48

Potthoff, Michael
89GreFalDSP-4
90BakDodCLC-240

Pottinger, Mark
86ClePhiP-20
87LakTigP-20

Potts, Dave
86AubAstP-19
87OscAstP-16
88OscAstS-21
89OscAstS-18

Potts, Mike
92DurBulC-21
92DurBulF-1096
92DurBulTI-5
93GreBraF-345
94BraUSPC-4S
94RicBraF-2845
95RicBraRC-20
95RicBraTI-17
96LeaSigA-183
96LeaSigAG-183
96LeaSigAS-183

Pough, Pork Chop (Clyde)
89BurIndS-21
90RenSilSCLC-264
90WatIndS-16
91KinIndC-18
91KinIndP-330
92KinIndC-20
92KinIndF-2487
92UppDecML-199
93KinIndC-22
93KinIndF-2256
93KinIndTI-22
94CanIndF-3126
95Bes-5
95TreThuTI-22
96Exc-17
96PawRedSDD-23

Poulin, Jim
88BelBreGS-3
89StoPorB-25
89StoPorCLC-178
89StoPorP-387
89StoPorS-27

Poulis, George
90WatDiaB-21
91WatDiaC-27
96MemChiB-3

Poulsen, Ken
77FriOneYW-23

Pound, John
78QuaCitAT-18

Pounders, Brad
87TexLeaAF-5
87WicPilRD-8
88LasVegSC-15
88LasVegSP-247
89Fle-642
89FleGlo-642

Poupart, Melvin
96PitMetB-19

Poveda, Crispin
90IBAWorA-14

Powell, Alonzo
83CliGiaF-14
86SouLeaAJ-15
86WesPalBEP-24
87DonOpeD-93
87ExpPos-20
87IndIndTI-33
87SpoRooP-8
87SpoTeaP-20
88IndIndC-15
88IndIndP-520
88StaLinE-12
89IndIndP-1210
89WesPalBES-18
90PorBeaP-193
90ProAAAF-263
91CalCanLD-69
91CalCanP-529
91FleUpd-55
91Lea-521
91LinDriAAA-69
92CalCanS-66
92Don-213
92Fle-290
92OPC-295
92Sco-413
92StaClu-547
92Top-295
92TopGol-295
92TopGolW-295
92TopMic-295

Powell, Boog (John)
47Exh-182
62Top-99

62TopVen-99
63Jel-62
63Pos-62
63Top-398
64OriJayP-9
64Top-89
64TopCoi-104
64TopSta-36
64TopStaU-59
64TopTatI-64
64TopVen-89
65Baz-11
65OldLonC-33
65OPC-3
65Top-3
65Top-560
65TopEmbl-29
65TopTraI-63
66OPC-167
66Top-167
66TopVen-167
67CokCapO-11
67DexPre-171
67OPCPapI-1
67Top-230
67Top-241
67Top-243
67Top-521
67TopPos-1
67TopTesF-18
67TopVen-199
68AtlOilPBCC-36
68CokCapO-11
68DexPre-64
68Top-381
68Top3-D-8
69MilBra-225
69MLBOffS-7
69MLBPin-22
69OPC-15
69OPCDec-17
69Top-15
69TopDec-2
69TopSta-128
69TopTeaP-5
70DayDaiNM-34
70Kel-19
70MilBra-22
70MLBOffS-153
70OPC-64
70OPC-200
70OPC-201
70OPC-410
70OPC-451
70Ori-10
70Top-64
70Top-200
70Top-201
70Top-410
70Top-451
70TopScr-18
70TopSup-38
70TraSta-11C
71AllBasA-18
71Kel-20
71MilDud-25
71MLBOffS-307
71MLBOffS-570
71OPC-63
71OPC-195
71OPC-327
71OPC-700
71Top-63
71Top-195
71Top-327
71Top-700
71TopCoi-74
71TopSup-5
71TopTat-56
71TopTat-57
72MilBra-277
72OPC-250
72OriPol-7
72ProStaP-34
72Top-250
73OPC-325
73OriJohP-26
73Top-325
74OPC-460
74Top-460
75OPC-208
75OPC-625
75Top-208
75Top-625
76Hos-75
76Kel-50
76OPC-45
76SSP-524
76Top-45
77Top-206
78TCM60I-80
81Ori6F-26
82K-M-17
83FraBroR-22
83FraBroR-23
83FraBroR-26
83YanYealT-16
86OriGreT-11
90BasWit-9
90DodTar-633
90PacLeg-46
90SweBasG-16
91Kel3D-13
91MDAA-12
91OriCro-367
91SweBasG-74
91UppDecS-3
91UppDecS-5
92ActPacA-80
92MDAMVP-7
92MVP2H-18
93MetIma-16
93OriCroASU-11
93TedWil-84
93TedWil-143
94UppDecAH-195
94UppDecAH1-195
95MrTurBG-4

Powell, Brian
96LakTigB-19
96Top-244

Powell, Charlie
78ChaPirT-19

Powell, Colin
91Bow-533

Powell, Corey
91MidLeaAP-MWL48
91RocExpC-10
91RocExpP-2045
92WesPalBEC-17
92WesPalBEF-2088
93BurBeeC-20
93BurBeeF-172
94OscAstC-19
94OscAstF-1146

Powell, Dante
93BazTeaU-2
93TopTra-45T
94ClaUpdCotC-CC19
94EveGiaF-3669
94SigRooDP-22
94SigRooDPS-22
95Exc-292
95ExcFirYP-9
95SPML-148
95UppDecML-100
95UppDecMLOP-OP25
96BesAutS-74
96BesAutSA-56
96Bow-201
96Exc-246
96TexLeaAB-13
97Bow-166
97BowBes-148
97BowBesAR-148
97BowBesR-148
97BowChr-162
97BowChrI-162
97BowChrIR-162
97BowChrR-162
97BowInt-166
97FlaSho-A79
97FlaSho-B79
97FlaSho-C79
97FlaShoLC-79
97FlaShoLC-B79
97FlaShoLC-C79
97FlaShoLCM-A79
97FlaShoLCM-B79
97FlaShoLCM-C79
97Fle-644
97FleTif-644
97SpoIll-19
97SpoIllEE-19
97Top-206
97Ult-467
97UltGolME-467
97UltPlaME-467
97UppDec-544
95UppDecMLFS-100

Powell, Dennis
85AlbDukC-154
86DodCokP-24
86DodPol-48
86Don-250
87CalCanP-2314
87Don-499
87Fle-450
87FleGlo-450
87Top-47
87TopTif-47
88CalCanC-4
88CalCanP-796
88Top-453
88TopTif-453
89FleUpd-61
89TopTra-97T
89TopTraT-97T
90BreMilB-20
90CMC-47
90DenZepC-22
90DenZepP-624
90DodTar-634
90Fle-521
90FleCan-521
90ProAAAF-649
90Sco-308
90UppDec-229
91CalCanLD-68
91CalCanP-521
91LinDriAAA-68
92Bow-426
92MarMot-12
93CalCanF-1165
93Fle-312
93MarMot-23
93StaClu-108
93StaCluFDI-108
93StaCluMOP-108
94BreMilB-345
94NasSouF-1250

Powell, Gordon
90HelBreSP-12
91BelBreC-15
91BelBreP-2111
92BelBreC-22
92BelBreF-414

Powell, Grover
64Top-113
64TopVen-113
76Met63 S-11
91MetWIZ-318

Powell, Hosken
77TacTwiDQ-6
78TwiFriP-14
79OPC-346
79Top-656
79TwiFriP-21
80Top-471
81Don-567
81Fle-559
81Top-137
82Don-228
82Fle-558
82Top-584
82TopSti-206
82TopStiV-206
82TopTra-91T
83Don-644
83Fle-440
83FleSta-153
83FleSti-106
83OPC-77
83Top-77
84VanCanC-38

Powell, Jake (Alvin Jacob)
38OurNatGPP-23
39PlaBal-1
40PlaBal-11
75YanDyn1T-36
75YanDyn1T-51
91ConTSN-83

Powell, James E.
87OldJudN-411

Powell, Jay
91MisStaB-39
92MisStaB-34
93MisStaB-31
94Bow-655
94Cla-179
94ClaGolF-8
94ClaGolN1PLF-LP11
94ClaGolREF-RE11
94ClaTriF-T4
94ExcFS7-14
94FreKeyF-2612
94OriPro-82
94Pin-435
94PinArtP-435
94PinMusC-435
94Sco-575
94ScoGolR-575
94SigRoo-36
94SigRooS-36
94Top-745
94TopGol-745
94TopSpa-745
95PorSeaDTI-21
96Bow-170
96BowBes-103
96BowBesAR-103
96BowBesR-103
96ColCho-559
96ColChoGS-559
96ColChoSS-559
96Pin-381
96PinAfi-167
96PinAfiAP-167
96PinFoil-381
96Sel-186
96SelArtP-186
96SelCer-128
96SelCerAP-128
96SelCerCB-128
96SelCerCR-128
96SelCerMB-128
96SelCerMG-128
96SelCerMR-128
94FreKeyC-19
97StaClu-366
97StaCluMOP-366
97Top-339

Powell, Jeremy
94SigRooBS-9
96DelShoB-25

Powell, John
93BazTeaU-16
93TopTra-131T
94TopTra-59T
95TulDriTI-20
96TulDriTI-21

Powell, John GA
89GeoColC-24

Powell, John J.
03BreE10-121
03BreE10-122
08RosComP-71
09RamT20-96
09T206-294
10DarChoE-25
11SpoLifCW-294
11SpoLifM-115
98CamPepP-62

Powell, Kelly
87OldJudN-282
89SanDieSAS-24

Powell, Kenny
90Bes-275
90GasRanB-5
90GasRanP-2534
90GasRanS-18
91ChaRanC-24
91ChaRanP-1328
92ClaFS7-112
92GasRanF-2266
93ChaRanF-1953
93ClaFS7-111

Powell, Paul Ray
74AlbDukTI-75
74AlbDukTI-13
76SSP-82
90DodTar-635

Powell, Ray
21Exh-134
21Exh-135
21Nei-95
22E120-133
22W572-79
23WilChoV-126

Powell, Robert LeRoy
56Top-144

Powell, Ross
89CedRapRS-30
90CedRapRDGB-31
90ChaLooGS-24
91LinDriAAA-270
91NasSouLD-270
91NasSouP-2155
93IndIndF-1486
94IndIndF-1808
94Pin-401
94PinArtP-401
94PinMusC-401
94Sco-589
94ScoBoyoS-56
94ScoGolR-589
94TopTra-84T
94TucTorF-761
96IndIndB-20

Powell, William
93NegLeaRL2-32

Power, John
86WatIndP-22

Power, Ted
80AlbDukT-22
80VenLeaS-28
81AlbDukT-5
82Fle-17
84Don-447
84Fle-478
84Nes792-554
84RedEnq-22
84Top-554
84TopTif-554
85Don-286
85Fle-547
85RedYea-12
85Top-342
85TopSti-50
85TopTif-342
86Don-408
86Fle-187
86OPC-108
86RedTexG-48
86SevCoi-S12
86Spo-166
86Top-108
86TopSti-140
86TopTif-108
87Don-536
87Fle-210
87FleGlo-210
87RedKah-48
87Top-437
87TopTif-437
88Don-142
88Fle-245
88FleGlo-245
88FleUpd-33
88FleUpdG-33
88OPC-236
88PanSti-272
88RoySmo-14
88Sco-242
88ScoGlo-242
88StaLinRe-16
88Top-236
88TopTif-236
88TopTra-89T
88TopTraT-89T
89Don-153
89Fle-142
89FleGlo-142
89LouRedBC-10
89LouRedBP-1249
89LouRedBTI-32
89OPC-331
89Sco-348
89Top-777
89TopTif-777
90DodTar-636
90Don-653
90Fle-258
90FleCan-258
90FleUpd-50
90Lea-473
90OPC-59
90PirHomC-23
90Top-59
90TopTif-59
90UppDec-340
91Bow-688
91Don-608
91Fle-46
91FleUpd-85
91OPC-621
91RedKah-48
91Sco-255
91SimandSMLBL-34
91Top-621

91TopDesS-621
91TopMic-621
91TopTif-621
91UppDec-450
92Don-586
92Fle-416
92IndFanC-24
92Sco-113
92StaClu-812
92UppDec-680
93Don-766
93Fle-600
93IndWUA-26
93Lea-61
93PacSpa-418
93StaClu-82
93StaCluFDI-82
93StaCluMOP-82
94StaClu-163
94StaCluFDI-163
94StaCluGR-163
94StaCluMOP-163
94Top-319
94TopGol-319
94TopSpa-319
94Ult-123
Power, Vic
54Top-52
55A'sRodM-27
55A'sRodM-28
55Top-30
55TopDouH-29
56A'sRodM-7
56Top-67
56TopPin-14
57Top-167
58A'sJayP-7
58Top-406
59Ind-17
59Kah-29
59Top-229
60Baz-16
60IndJayP-9
60Kah-34
60Lea-65
60Top-75
60TopVen-75
61Kah-35
61Pos-63A
61Pos-63B
61Top-255
61TwiCloD-21
62Jel-37
62Kah-33A
62Kah-33B
62Pos-37
62PosCan-37
62SalPlaC-44
62ShiPlaC-44
62Top-445
62TopBuc-72
62TopStal-39
63Fle-23
63Jel-1
63Pos-1
63Top-40
63TwiJayP-9
64PhiPhiB-18
64Top-355
64TopVen-355
65Top-442
66OPC-192
66Top-192
66TopVen-192
76A'sRodMC-18
78TCM60I-196
79TCM50-147
81SanDieSC-5
84OCoandSI-114
90HOFStiB-56
94TopArc1-52
94TopArc1G-52
Powers, Jack
89AncBucTI-28
Powers, John
57JetPos-17
58Kah-23
58Top-432
59RedEnq-21
59Top-489
60Top-422
91OriCro-368
Powers, Larry
79LodDodT-11
Powers, Michael Riley
03BreE10-123
09T206-295
82OhiHaloF-9
Powers, Randy
90BoiHawP-3305
90ProAaA-159
91PalSprAP-2012
92SalSpuC-5
Powers, Robert
92HelBreF-1722
92HelBreSP-11
93HelBreF-4105
93HelBreSP-1
Powers, Scott
87ElmPio(C-12
88LynRedSS-19
89LynRedSS-19
90LynRedSTI-7
91LinDriAA-468
91NewBriRSLD-468
91NewBriRSP-359
Powers, Steve
75QuaCitAT-20
77SalPirT-20A
77SalPirT-20B
90AshTouC-8
90AubAstB-11
90AubAstP-3407
91AshTouP-566
92BurAstC-13
92BurAstF-542
93OscAstC-18
93OscAstF-626
Powers, Tad
89PenPilS-20
90RenSilSCLC-285
91SalLakTP-3209
91SalLakTSP-3
91SydWavF-12
Powers, Terry
91WinHavRSC-7
91WinHavRSP-487
92ClaFS7-192
92WinHavRSC-10
92WinHavRSF-1775
93WesPalBEC-19
93WesPalBEF-1338
94WesPalBEC-22
94WesPalBEF-37
Powers, Thomas
87OldJudN-412
Powis, Carl
91OriCro-369
Pozo, Arquimedez
92SanBerSF-967
93RivPilCLC-14
94Bow-9
94BowBes-B78
94BowBes-X103
94BowBesR-B78
94BowBesR-X103
94Cla-198
94JacSunF-1419
94UppDec-535
94UppDecED-535
94UppDecML-131
95ActPacF-41
95Exc-120
95MarPac-40
95TacRaiTI-17
95Top-540
95UppDecML-74
95UppDecMLOP-OP26
96ColCho-729
96ColChoGS-23
96ColChoGS-729
96ColChoSS-23
96ColChoSS-729
96TacRaiB-22
96UppDec-224
96UppDecFSP-FS17
96UppDecPHE-H26
96UppDecPreH-H26
97Sco-312
97ScoPreS-312
97ScoRedS-13
97ScoRedSPl-13
97ScoRedSPr-13
97ScoShoS-312
97ScoShoSAP-312
95UppDecMLFS-74
Pozo, Joel
94VenLinU-249
Pozo, Melanio
85DomLeaS-193
Pozo, Yohel
94BenRocF-3598
95AshTouTI-33
Prado, Jose
91MiaHurBB-10
94BakDodC-20
95SanAntMTI-55
Prager, Howard
88CapCodPPaLP-175
89AubAstP-2175
90OscAstS-23
91OscAstP-694
92JacGenF-4009
92JacGenS-345
92SkyAA F-144
93ArkTraF-2825
94LouRedF-2989
95LouRedF-284
Prall, Wilford
74WicAerODF-111
Pramesa, John
47PM1StaP1-166
51Bow-324
52Bow-247
52Top-105
79DiaGre-270
83TopRep5-105
Prappas, Jim
52LavPro-99
Prater, Andy
93ElmPioC-15
93ElmPioF-3826
94KanCouCC-19
94KanCouCF-165
94KanCouCTI-23
95BreCouMF-249
97Top-482
Prater, Pete
94EveGiaC-23
94EveGiaF-3652
95BurBeeTI-16
Prather, Mark
93Tex-5
Prats, Jean
52LavPro-27
Prats, Mario
91AshTouP-567
Pratt, Cressy (Crestwell)
82WatRedT-22
83TamTarT-20
Pratt, Del (Derrill)
14B18B-33A
14B18B-33B
14CraJacE-93
15CraJacE-93
15SpoNewM-140
16ColE13-135
16SpoNewM-139
17HolBreD-80
20NatCarE-81
21E121So1-76
21Exh-136
21Exh-137
21OxfConE-13
22E120-11
22W573-103
23W501-11
23WilChoV-127
91ConTSN-162
Pratt, Evan
93SouAtlLAPI-32
Pratt, Louis A.
79SavBraT-21
81ArkTraT-20
Pratt, Rich
94HicCraF-2175
95Exc-30
95PriWilCTI-22
96BirBarB-18
Pratt, Steve
89CliGiaP-908
Pratt, Todd
85ElmPioT-17
86GreHorP-17
87WinHavRSP-29
88EasLeaAP-22
88NewBriRSP-906
89NewBriRSP-624
89NewBriRSS-15
90NewBriRSP-1321
90NewBriRSS-16
91LinDriAAA-367
91PawRedSDD-19
91PawRedSLD-367
91PawRedSP-41
92ReaPhiS-540
92ScrRedBF-2450
92SkyAA F-235
93Don-620
93Fle-497
93LinVenB-9
93LinVenB-288
93PhiMed-27
93Pin-598
93Sco-276
93Top-479
93TopGol-479
93TopInaM-479
93TopMic-479
93Ult-444
94Don-188
94Fle-598
94Pac-484
94PhiMed-26
94PhiMel-18
94PhiUSPC-3S
94PhiUSPC-9D
94StaClu-84
94StaCluFDI-84
94StaCluGR-84
94StaCluMOP-84
94StaCluT-227
94StaCluTFDI-227
94Top-597
94TopGol-597
94TopSpa-597
94VenLinU-135
95Pac-336
Pratt, Wes
94AubAstC-11
94AubAstF-3771
95AubAstTI-10
95QuaCitRBTI-18
96AubDouB-3
Pratte, Evan
91NiaFalRC-12
91NiaFalRP-3643
92FayGenC-22
92FayGenF-2178
93LonTigF-2317
Pratts, Tato (Alberto)
88ElmPioC-2
89WinHavRSS-17
90LynRedSTI-20
90NewBriRSB-22
91ElmPioC-26
91ElmPioP-3271
Preikszas, Dave
91HelBreSP-14
Premack, Clayton
94LetMouF-3879
94LetMouSP-17
Prempas, Lyle
96HelBreTI-20
Prendergast, Jim
50WorWidGV-39
Prensi, Dagoberto
94MedHatBJF-3694
94MedHatBJSP-7
95HagSunF-81
Preqenger, John
77FriOneYW-92
Prescott, George
60TacBan-15
61UniOil-H3
Preseren, Ken
76BatTroTI-16
Presko, Joe
52Bow-62
52Top-220
53CarHunW-17
54Bow-190
54CarHunW-17
54Top-135
79TCM50-178
83TopRep5-220
94TopArc1-135
94TopArc1G-135
Presley, Billy
80ChaO'sP-15
80ChaO'sW-16
Presley, Jim
80WauTimT-13
81WauTimT-20
82LynSaiT-13
84SalLakCGC-184
85DomLeaS-150
85Don-240
85Fle-500
85MarMot-20
85TopTifT-92T
85TopTra-92T
86Don-313
86Fle-473
86FleMin-98
86FleStiC-89
86KayB-24
86Lea-183
86MarMot-7
86OPC-228
86SevCoi-W14
86Spo-40
86Top-598
86TopSti-219
86TopTat-12
86TopTif-598
87ClaGam-48
87Don-23
87Don-120
87DonAll-29
87DonOpeD-123
87DonSupD-23
87Fle-594
87FleGlo-594
87FleLimE-33
87FleMin-82
87FleStiC-91
87Lea-23
87Lea-154
87MarMot-4
87OPC-45
87RedFolSB-19
87Spo-179
87SpoTeaP-25
87Top-45
87TopSti-214
87TopTif-45
88Don-366
88DonBasB-219
88Fle-385
88FleGlo-385
88MarMot-4
88OPC-285
88PanSti-189
88Sco-46
88ScoGlo-46
88Spo-54
88StaLinMa-14
88Top-285
88TopBig-90
88TopSti-217
88TopTif-285
89Bow-214
89BowTif-214
89ChaLooLITI-24
89Don-379
89DonBasB-331
89Fle-555
89FleGlo-555
89MarMot-4
89OPC-112
89PanSti-437
89Sco-73
89Spo-7
89Top-112
89TopBig-75
89TopSti-223
89TopTif-112
89UppDec-642
90Bow-18
90BowTif-18
90BraDubP-23
90BraDubS-26
90ClaYel-T21
90Don-497
90DonBesN-37
90Fle-522
90FleCan-522
90FleUpd-6
90Lea-277
90OPC-346
90PubSti-439
90Sco-34
90ScoRoo-36T
90Top-346
90TopBig-304
90TopSti-224
90TopTif-346
90TopTra-98T
90TopTraT-98T

90UppDec-315
90UppDec-760
90VenSti-408
91Bow-646
91Don-173
91Fle-700
91OPC-643
91PadMag-23A
91PanFreS-21
91PanSti-24
91RedFolS-73
91Sco-771
91Top-643
91TopDesS-643
91TopMic-643
91TopTif-643
91UppDec-282
91UppDec-791
92OklCit8F-1924
92OklCit8S-320
96AriBlaDB-3
Presley, Kirk
94ActPac-8
94Bow-324
94BowBes-B26
94BowBesR-B26
94Cla-50
94Cla-AU6
94ClaBonB-BB2
94ClaCreotC-C2
94ColC-26
94ColChoGS-26
94ColChoSS-26
94Pin-436
94PinArtP-436
94PinMusC-436
94PitMetC-17
94PitMetF-3521
94Sco-518
94ScoGolR-518
94SigRoo-45
94SigRooS-45
94SP-14
94SPDieC-14
94Top-740
94TopGol-740
94TopSpa-740
94UppDecAHNIL-11
94UppDecML-TC2
95Bow-164
95Exc-236
95UppDecML-30
96PitMetB-20
95UppDecMLFS-30
Press, Greg
94ElmPioF-3472
95KanCouCTI-26
95MidLeaA-41
96BreCouMB-26
94ElmPioC-16
Pressnell, Tot (Forest)
39PlaBal-134
40DodTeal-19
40PlaBal-146
41CubTeal-20
90DodTar-637
Presto, Nick
96BilMusTI-26
Preston, Dayton
88ColAstB-24
Preston, Doyle
94PriRedF-3271
95BilRedTI-22
Preston, George
94BelBreC-19
94BelBreF-97
94HelBreSP-8
Preston, Steve
88EugEmeB-20
89AppFoxP-861
Prevost, Eric
78WisRapTT-15
Prewitt, Larry
80PhoGiaVNB-5
Price, Al
81ElPasDT-24
82ElPasDT-24
83ElPasDT-18
85VanCanC-225
87DenZepP-3
Price, Bill
81WisRapTT-18
Price, Bryan
85MidAngT-2
86PalSprAP-15
86PalSprAP-27
88VerMarP-940
89CalCanC-9
89CalCanP-540
89WilBilS-16
91PenPilP-396
92BelMarF-1463
93RivPilCLC-29
94BelMarF-3233
95EveAqaTI-16
96PorCitRB-3
Price, Chris
95SprSulTI-21
Price, Corey
96BilMusTI-27
Price, Harris
75AppFoxT-23
76AppFoxT-19
Price, Jamey
96WesMicWB-21
Price, Jimmie
67OPC-123
67Top-123
68TigDetFPB-18
68Top-226
68TopVen-226
69Top-472
70OPC-129
70Top-129
71MLBOffS-403
71OPC-444
71Top-444
72MilBra-278
88TigDom-20
Price, Joe
79NaSouTI-19
80IndIndTI-5
81Fle-210
81Top-258
82Don-481
82Fle-81
82RedCok-18
82Top-492
83Don-481
83Fle-600
83RedYea-49
83Top-191
84Don-506
84Fle-479
84Nes792-686
84OPC-159
84RedEnq-17
84Top-686
84TopSti-58
84TopTif-686
85Don-627
85Fle-548
85OPC-82
85RedYea-13
85Top-82
85TopMin-82
85TopSti-56
85TopTif-82
86Don-506
86Fle-188
86RedTexG-49
86Top-523
86TopTif-523
87Fle-211
87FleGlo-211
87PhoFirP-17
87Top-332
87TopTif-332
88Don-655
88GiaMot-26
88Top-786
88TopTif-786
89Don-376
89Fle-339
89FleGlo-339
89GiaMot-26
89Sco-444
89Top-217
89TopTif-217
89UppDec-505
90Bow-245
90BowTif-245
90Fle-282
90FleCan-282
90OPC-473
90Top-473
90TopTif-473
91Fle-488
91LinDriAAA-464
91OPC-127
91OriCro-370
91RocRedWLD-464
91Top-127
91TopDesS-127
91TopMic-127
91TopTif-127
Price, John Thomas
46RemBre-16
Price, Kevin
82DanSunF-9
83RedPioT-21
86JacExpT-14
86SouLeaAJ-25
87JacExpP-448
87SouLeaAJ-17
88ChaKniTI-4
Price, Phil
87SpaPhiP-25
88VirGenS-18
Price, Ray
77ColCliT-19
Price, Tom
94GreFalDSP-25
95SanBerSTI-16
Prichard, Brian
91BriTigC-8
91BriTigP-3608
Pricher, John
92BoiHawC-18
92BoiHawF-3623
93ClaFS7-238
93ExcFS7-147
93PalSprAC-17
93PalSprAF-67
94ClaGolF-139
94ExcFS7-30
94MidAngF-2437
94MidAngOHP-21
Priddy, Jerry (Gerald)
41DouPlaR-109
49Bow-4A
49Bow-4B
49Lea-111
50Bow-212
51Bow-71
51R42SmaS-79
51TopBluB-46
52Bow-139
52NatTeaL-21
52Top-28
53DixLid-15
53DixPre-15
53NorBreL-22
53TigGle-25
53Top-113
67OPC-26
77TCMTheWY-33
79TCM50-213
83TopRep5-28
91TopArc1-113
Priddy, Robert
64Top-74
64TopVen-74
65Top-482
66Top-572
67Top-26A
67Top-26B
68Top-391
69Top-248
70Top-687
71MLBOffS-20
71OPC-147
71Top-147
Pride, Charley
73A'sPos-31
73A'sPos-32
Pride, Curtis
89PitMetS-20
91FloStaLAP-FSL33
91St.LucMC-2
91St.LucMP-725
92BinMetF-530
92BinMetS-65
92ClaFS7-159
92SkyAA F-30
93HarSenF-280
94ActPac-33
94AriFalLS-15
94Cla-197
94ColC-233
94ColChoGS-233
94ColChoSS-233
94Don-646
94FleMajLP-29
94Pac-387
94Pin-230
94PinArtP-230
94PinMusC-230
94Spo-167
94Top-237
94TopGol-237
94TopSpa-237
94UppDec-250
94UppDecED-250
95ActPacF-45
96Fle-464
96FleTif-464
96LeaSig-137
96LeaSigA-184
96LeaSigAG-184
96LeaSigAS-184
96LeaSigPPG-137
96LeaSigPPP-137
96TolMudHB-23
97Cir-331
97CirRav-331
97ColCho-107
97Don-192
97DonEli-145
97DonEliGS-145
97DonPreP-192
97DonPrePGold-192
97Fle-104
97FleTif-104
97Lea-143
97LeaFraM-143
97LeaFraMDC-143
97Pac-94
97PacLigB-94
97PacSil-94
97PinIns-123
97PinInsCE-123
97PinInsDE-123
97Sco-217
97ScoPreS-217
97ScoShoS-217
97ScoShoSAP-217
97Top-376
97Ult-62
97UltGolME-62
97UltPlaME-62
Pridy, Todd
92EriSaiC-20
92EriSaiF-1633
93ClaFS7-112
93ExcFS7-39
93KanCouCC-16
93KanCouCF-924
93Top-441
93TopGol-441
93TopInaM-441
93TopMic-441
94BreCouMC-13
94BreCouMF-20
95SigRoo-42
95SigRooSig-42
93KanCouCTI-17
Pries, Jeff
86AlbYanT-15
86ColCliP-17
86ColCliP-19
87AlbYanP-18
Priessman, Kraig
83SanJosBC-17
Priest, Adam
95TenVolW-10
Priest, Chris
94LetMouF-3892
94LetMouSP-4
Priest, Eddie
94BilMusF-3667
94BilMusSP-19
94StaCluDP-45
94StaCluDPFDI-45
95Exc-180
95Top-316
Prieto, Alejandro
94VenLinU-72
95SprSulTI-22
96WilBluRB-22
Prieto, Ariel
95A'sCHP-8
95AthMot-29
95LeaLim-121
95SPCha-10
95SPChaDC-10
95UppDec-453T
96Bow-56
96ColCho-14
96ColChoGS-14
96ColChoSS-14
96Don-231
96DonPreP-231
96EmoXL-106
96Fla-152
96Fle-216
96FleTif-216
96Lea-84
96LeaPrePB-84
96LeaPrePG-84
96LeaPrePS-84
96LeaSigA-185
96LeaSigAG-185
96LeaSigAS-185
96Pac-392
96Pin-316
96PinFoil-316
96Sco-127
96ScoDugC-A79
96ScoDugCAP-A79
96SP-138
96TopGal-137
96TopGalPPI-137
96Ult-116
96UltGolM-116
96UppDec-164
97Cir-153
97CirRav-153
97ColCho-186
97Fle-659
97FleTif-659
97Pac-174
97PacLigB-174
97PacSil-174
97Sco-351
97ScoHobR-351
97ScoResC-351
97ScoShoS-351
97ScoShoSAP-351
97Top-279
97Ult-368
97UltGolME-368
97UltPlaME-368
97UppDec-446
Prieto, Arnie
88MiaMarS-19
89MiaMirIS-23
Prieto, Chris
93SpoIndC-16
93SpoIndF-3604
94RanCucQC-22
94RanCucQF-1650
95RanCucQT-1
96RanCucQB-22
Prieto, Omar
80VenLeaS-241
Prieto, Pete (Pedro)
76DubPacT-29
77CocAstT-19
Prieto, Rick
93WatIndC-23
93WatIndF-3572
94ColRedC-16
94ColRedF-457
95BakBlaTI-7
95KinIndTI-22
Prihoda, Steve
95SpoIndTI-19
96CarLeaA1B-5
96CarLeaA2B-5
96WilBluRB-5
Prim, Ray
43CubTeal-20
47SigOil-34
Primmante, Val
80ColAstT-2
Prince, Bicyclist
88GooN16-32
Prince, Don
77FriOneYW-55
Prince, Doug
75TopPho-119
Prince, Ray
77DayBealT-16
Prince, Tom
86PriWilPP-20
87HarSenP-3
88BufBisC-19
88BufBisP-1488
88Don-538

88TriAAAP-5
89Don-527
89Fle-217
89FleGlo-217
89Sco-626
89ScoHot1R-45
89Top-453
89TopTif-453
89UppDec-311
90Bow-176
90BowTif-176
90BufBisC-14
90BufBisP-376
90BufBisTI-19
90CMC-14
90ProAAAF-491
90PubSti-161
90VenSti-409
92BufBisBS-15
92Sco-618
92StaClu-332
92Ult-559
93PacSpa-591
93PirHil-11
93PirNatl-25
94DodPol-22
94Fle-618
94Pac-505
97PacPriGotD-GD162

Prinz, Paul
87BriYouC-21

Prioleau, Laney
86LakTigP-18

Prior, Dan
80CarMudF-20
81ReaPhiT-5
82ReaPhiT-6

Pritchard, Buddy (Harold)
58Top-151

Pritchard, Michael
94HelBreF-3622
94HelBreSP-2

Pritchett, Anthony
91BenBucC-18
91BenBucP-3707

Pritchett, Chris
91BoiHawC-2
91BoiHawP-3889
91Cla/Bes-445
91FroRowDP-54
92MidLeaATI-33
92QuaCitRBC-26
92QuaCitRBF-820
92StaCluD-142
92UppDecML-152
93Bow-665
93ExcFS7-148
93MidAngF-330
94ExcFS7-31
94MidAngF-2446
94MidAngOHP-22
96Top-103
96VanCanB-23
97MidAngOHP-23

Pritikin, James
86BelMarC-113
88WauTimGS-12
89SanBerSB-14
89SanBerSCLC-86

Probst, Alan
92AubAstC-16
92AubAstF-1356
93AshTouC-16
93AshTouF-2279
94MidLeaAF-MDW53
94QuaCitRBC-16
94QuaCitRBF-538
95QuaCitRBTI-19
96JacGenB-23

Probst, Thomas
92BenRocC-27

Procopio, Jim
87IdaFalBP-16
88IdaFalBP-1853
92LetMouSP-26

Procter, Craig
88SpoIndP-1944

Proctor, Bill
94SouBenSHC-18
94SouBenSHF-592

Proctor, Dave
88LitFalMP-21
89Bow-378
89BowTif-378
89St.LucMS-20
90JacMetGS-14
91Cla/Bes-257
91St.LucMP-707
92St.LucMF-1745

Proctor, Jim
60Top-141
60TopVen-141

Proctor, Murph
89AncGlaP-20
91YakBeaC-5
91YakBeaP-4254
92BakDodCLC-20
92CalLeaACL-30
92ProFS7-248
93SanAntMF-3014
94CanIndF-3127

Proctor, Steve
93SavCarC-28
94MadHatC-29

Prodanov, Peter
92OklStaC-23

Proffitt, Mike
72CedRapCT-19

Proffitt, Steve
89HigSchPLS-9

Prohaska, Tim
89NiaFalRP-28

Prokopee, Luke
95GreFalDTI-16
96SavSanB-7

Proly, Michael
75TulOil7-14
76TulOilGP-16
77TacTwiDQ-17
79Top-514
80Top-399
81Don-596
81Fle-358
81Top-83
81TopTra-815
82CubRedL-36
82Don-345
82Fle-254
82IowCubT-22
82Top-183
82TopTra-92T
83CubThoAV-36
83Don-225
83Fle-505
83Top-597
84Don-320
84Fle-501
84Nes792-437
84SyrChiT-16
84Top-437
84TopTif-437

Prospero, Teo
95BelGiaTI-2
96BelGiaTI-8

Prothro, Doc
93ConTSN-964

Provence, Todd
86VenGulP-21
87KnoBluJP-1504
88MyrBeaBJP-1192
89MyrBeaBJP-1455
90MyrBeaBJP-2790

Prts, Mario
90AshTouC-9

Pruett, Hub (Hubert)
23W503-45
73FleWilD-34
87ConSer2-50
88ConSer5-24
92MegRut-100
93ConTSN-904

Pruiett, Tex
08RosComP-5

Pruitt, Darrell Ray
86PenWhiSP-21
87BirBarB-21
88ChaLooB-11
88SouLeaAJ-6
89GreBraB-3
89GreBraP-1171
89GreBraS-19

Pruitt, Donald
90HelBreSP-20
91BelBreC-6
91BelBreP-2101
91MidLeaAP-MWL34
92BelBreC-9
92BelBreF-403
93StoPorC-19
93StoPorF-744

Pruitt, Ed
86JacMetT-8
87JacMetF-14

Pruitt, Jason
91ClaDraP-26
91FroRowDP-26
91HigSchPLS-31
92AppFoxC-26
92AppFoxF-983
92ClaFS7-358
92EugEmeC-21
92EugEmeF-3028
92OPC-246
92StaCluD-143
92Top-246
92TopGol-246
92TopGolW-246
92TopMic-246

Pruitt, Ron
75SpoIndC-11
77Top-654
78Top-198
79Top-226
80Top-13
81Top-442
83PorBeaT-21
89PacSenL-103
89TopSenL-74
93RanKee-299
82PhoGiaVNB-13

Pruitt, Russell
79ElmPioRST-12

Prusia, Greg
89AppFoxP-858

Prybylinski, Bruce
88OneYanP-2061
89PriWilCS-17
90PriWilCTI-20
91Ft.LauYC-12
91Ft.LauYP-2425
92PriWilCC-1
92PriWilCF-145
92ProFS7-117

Prybylinski, Don
91ArkTraLD-43
91ArkTraP-1289
91LinDriAA-43
92ArkTraF-1133
92ArkTraS-42
92ClaFS7-333
92SkyAA F-18
92StaClu-748

Pryce, Ken
81QuaCitCT-22
83MidCubT-11
84IowCubT-1
85IowCubT-20
86IowCubP-23

Pryor, Buddy
83CedRapRF-2
83CedRapRT-14
86VerRedP-15
87NasSouTI-17
89TacTigC-15
89TacTigP-1558

Pryor, Greg
76SacSolC-10
78SSP270-145
79Top-559
80OPC-91
80Top-164
81Don-278
81Fle-359
81Top-608
82Don-521
82Fle-356
82Roy-16
82Top-76
82TopTra-93T
83Don-264
83Fle-121
83Roy-20
83Top-418
84Don-374
84Fle-353
84Nes792-317
84Top-317
84TopTif-317
85Don-277
85Fle-210
85Top-188
85TopTif-188
86Don-344
86RoyNatP-4
86Top-773
86TopTif-773
87Don-378
87OPC-268
87Top-761
87TopTif-761
93RanKee-300

Pryor, Jim
76CedRapGT-22
77CedRapGT-13

Pryor, Pete
96HicCraB-15

Pryor, Randy
88CapCodPPaLP-107

Przybylinski, Rodney
89TenTecGE-21

Psaltis, Spiro
82ChaRoyT-19
85MidAngT-16

Puccinelli, George
36ExhFou-14
36WorWidGV-127
38ExhFou-1

Puchales, Javier
90KisDodD-23
91GreFalDSP-29
93VerBeaDC-20
93VerBeaDF-2234
94SanAntMF-2484
95SanAntMTI-33

Puchkov, Evgeny
89EasLeaDDP-DD6
93Top-633
93TopGol-633
93TopInaM-633
93TopMic-633

Puckett, Kirby
83VisOakF-6
84FleUpd-93
84OCoandSI-243
85AllGamPI-68
85Don-438
85Fle-286
85FleStaS-122
85Lea-107
85OPC-10
85Top-536
85TopSti-307
85TopSti-376
85TopTif-536
85Twi7-1
85TwiTeal-24
86Don-72
86DonHig-7
86Fle-401
86FleLeaL-32
86FleMin-85
86FleSluBC-M5
86FleStiC-90
86KayB-25
86Lea-69
86OPC-329
86Spo-93
86Top-329
86TopSti-285
86TopTat-13
86TopTat-22
86TopTif-329
86TwiTeal-24
86WilGloT-2
87ClaGam-55
87ClaUpdY-112
87Don-19
87Don-149
87DonAll-4
87DonHig-30
87DonOpeD-221
87DonP-4
87DonSupD-19
87Dra-19
87Fle-549
87Fle-633
87FleAll-5
87FleAwaW-30
87FleBasA-32
87FleGlo-549
87FleGlo-633
87FleLeaL-36
87FleMin-83
87FleSlu-31
87FleStiC-92
87FleWaxBC-C11
87GenMilB-3I
87HosSti-26
87KayB-24
87KraFoo-27
87Lea-19
87Lea-56
87MandMSL-15
87OPC-82
87RedFolSB-23
87SmoAmeL-8
87Spo-7
87Spo-198
87SpoSupD-11
87SpoTeaP-17
87StuPan-22
87Top-450
87Top-611
87TopCoi-20
87TopGloA-19
87TopGloS-57
87TopMinL-63
87TopSti-146
87TopSti-274
87TopTif-450
87TopTif-611
88Daz-14
88CheBoy-13
88ClaRed-164
88Don-368
88DonAll-15
88DonBasB-186
88DonBonM-BC15
88Dra-19
88Fle-19
88Fle-638
88FleAwaW-29
88FleBasA-30
88FleBasM-26
88FleExcS-30
88FleGlo-19
88FleGlo-638
88FleGlo-WS8
88FleHotS-30
88FleLeaL-30
88FleMin-36
88FleRecS-29
88FleSlu-30
88FleStiC-45
88FleSup-28
88FleTeaL-26
88FleWaxBC-C7
88FleWorS-8
88GreBasS-43
88KayB-23
88KinDis-3
88Lea-144
88MSAFanSD-1
88MSAIceTD-6
88Nes-39
88OPC-120
88PanSti-144
88PanSti-444
88RedFolSB-72
88Sco-24
88Sco-653
88ScoGlo-24
88ScoGlo-653
88Spo-8
88Spo-180
88StaLinAl-21
88StaLinTw-15
88StaPuc-1
88StaPuc-2
88StaPuc-3
88StaPuc-4
88StaPuc-5
88StaPuc-6
88StaPuc-7
88StaPuc-8
88StaPuc-9
88StaPuc-10
88StaPuc-11
88Top-120
88Top-391
88TopBig-36
88TopCoi-23
88TopGloS-27
88TopMinL-23
88TopRevLL-21
88TopRitTM-21
88TopSti-283
88TopStiB-52
88TopTif-120
88TopTif-391

88TopUKM-57
88TopUKMT-57
88TwiMasBD-8
88TwiSmoC-12
88TwiTeal-23
88Woo-31
89Bow-162
89BowTif-162
89CadEllD-41
89CerSup-8
89ClaLigB-15
89ClaTraP-176
89Don-182
89DonAll-23
89DonBasB-130
89DonBonM-BC1
89Fle-124
89Fle-639
89FleBasA-32
89FleBasM-32
89FleExcS-34
89FleGlo-124
89FleGlo-639
89FleHeroB-31
89FleLeaL-30
89FleSup-33
89FleWaxBC-C20
89K-M-16
89KayB-24
89MasBreD-2
89MSAHolD-8
89MSAIceTD-12
89Nis-8
89OPC-132
89PanSti-247
89PanSti-393
89Sco-20
89ScoHot1S-11
89ScoSco-19
89Spo-156
89SpollIFKI-167
89Top-403
89Top-650
89TopAme2C-24
89TopBasT-46
89TopBatL-4
89TopBig-167
89TopCapC-20
89TopCoi-48
89TopDouA-7
89TopGloS-1
89TopHeaUT-20
89TopHilTM-23
89TopMinL-62
89TopSti-293
89TopStiB-19
89TopTif-403
89TopTif-650
89TopUKM-60
89TVSpoM-102
89UppDec-376
90AllBasT-12
90Baz-7
90Bow-424
90BowTif-424
90ClaBlu-28
90Col-33
90Don-269
90Don-683A
90Don-683B
90DonBesA-23
90DOnBonM-BC8
90DonLeaS-46
90DonPre-12
90Fle-383
90Fle-635
90FleAll-7
90FleAwaW-26
90FleBasA-29
90FleBasM-29
90FleCan-383
90FleCan-635
90FleLeaL-30
90FleWaxBC-C22
90GooHumICBLS-15
90Hot50PS-31
90K-M-22
90KayB-23
90KinDis-21
90Lea-123
90MLBBasB-98
90MSAHolD-17
90MSAIceTD-13
90NikMin-2
90OPC-391
90OPC-700
90PanSti-105
90PanSti-183
90PanSti-199
90Pos-3
90PubSti-292
90PubSti-335
90RedFolSB-75
90Sco-400
90Sco-690
90Sco100S-1
90Spo-11
90SunSee-5
90SupActM-4
90Top-391
90Top-700
90TopAmeA-24
90TopBatL-3
90TopBig-2
90TopCoi-4
90TopDou-49
90TopGaloC-7
90TopGloA-18
90TopGloS-48
90TopHeaU-20
90TopHilHM-27
90TopMag-24
90TopMinL-23
90TopSti-157
90TopSti-286
90TopStiB-52
90TopTif-391
90TopTif-700
90TopTVA-6
90UppDec-48
90UppDec-236
90USPlaCA-8S
90VenSti-410
90VenSti-411
90WinDis-2
90WonBreS-9
91BasBesHM-15
91Bow-320
91CadEllD-42
91Cla1-T57
91Cla3-T74
91ClaGam-111
91Col-7
91Don-490
91Fle-623
91FlePro-1
91JimDea-11
91KinDis-23
91Lea-208
91LeaPre-21
91MajLeaCP-12
91MooSna-2
91OPC-300
91OPCPre-96
91PanFreS-305
91PanSti-248
91PepSup-13
91PetSta-17
91Pos-28
91PosCan-30
91RedFolS-74
91Sco-200
91Sco-855
91Sco-891
91Sco100S-7
91SevCoi-A11
91SevCoi-F13
91SimandSMLBL-35
91StaClu-110
91StaPinB-36
91Stu-90
91Top-300
91TopCraJI-34
91TopDesS-300
91TopMic-300
91TopTif-300
91TopTriH-A9
91Ult-195
91UltGol-8
91UppDec-544
91USPlaCA-4D
92Bow-80
92Cla1-T72
92Cla2-T90
92ClaGam-101
92ColAllG-9
92ColAllP-9
92Don-617
92DonCraJ2-32
92DonEli-17
92DonMcD-21
92Fle-217
92Fle-704
92FleAll-22
92FleCitTP-11
92FleTeaL-5
92Fre-7
92Hig5-84
92HitTheBB-26
92KinDis-20
92Lea-98
92LeaBlaG-98
92MooSna-6
92Mr.TurS-18
92MSABenSHD-7
92OPC-575
92OPCBoxB-4
92OPCPre-102
92PanSti-120
92PepDieM-27
92Pin-20
92Pin-289
92PinSlu-13
92Pos-7
92PosCan-17
92RevSup1-10
92RevSup1-11
92RevSup1-12
92Sco-600
92Sco-796
92Sco-886
92Sco100S-7
92ScoFacl-B6
92ScoProaG-6
92ScoProP-4
92SevCoi-18
92SpollIFK1-29
92SpoStaCC-36
92StaClu-500
92StaCluD-144
92StaCluD-145
92StaPuc-1
92StaPuc-2
92StaPuc-3
92StaPuc-4
92StaPuc-5
92StaPuc-6
92StaPuc-7
92StaPuc-8
92StaPuc-9
92StaPuc-10
92StaPuc-11
92Stu-209
92StuHer-BC14
92StuPre-2
92SunSee-5
92Top-575
92TopGol-575
92TopGolW-575
92TopKid-109
92TopMcD-19
92TopMic-575
92TriPla-202
92TriPlaP-7
92Ult-97
92UltAllS-8
92UltAwaW-23
92UppDec-254
92UppDecF-35
92UppDecFG-35
92UppDecTMH-41
92UppDecWB-T9
93Bow-325
93CadDis-45
93ClaGam-75
93ColAllG-5
93DenHol-26
93DiaMar-87
93DiaMarP-6
93Don-607
93DonDiaK-DK4
93DonMasotG-13
93DonMVP-18
93DurPowP1-5
93Fin-112
93FinJum-112
93FinRef-112
93Fla-242
93Fle-273
93Fle-355
93FleAll-AL9
93FleAtl-18
93FleFruotL-52
93FleTeaL-AL1
93FunPac-191
93FunPac-195
93FunPacA-AS9
93Hos-29
93HumDumC-11
93JimDea-13
93Kra-11
93Lea-378
93LeaGolA-R17
93LeaGolA-U7
93LeaHeaftH-9
93MetBak-16
93OPC-306
93OPCPreSP-11
93OPCPreSPF-11
93PacSpa-177
93PanSti-130
93Pin-426
93PinCoo-12
93PinCooD-12
93PinSlu-16
93PinTeaP-9
93Pos-3
93PosCan-8
93Sco-505
93Sco-533
93Sco-550
93Sco-606
93ScoFra-9
93ScoGolDT-2
93Sel-4
93SelChaS-18
93SelStaL-2
93SelStaL-7
93SP-7
93StaClu-283
93StaClu-597
93StaCluFDI-283
93StaCluFDI-597
93StaCluM-28
93StaCluMMP-7
93StaCluMO-20
93StaCluMOP-283
93StaCluMOP-597
93StaCluMP-6
93Stu-214
93Top-200
93Top-406
93TOPBLAG-40
93TopGol-200
93TopGol-406
93ToplnaM-200
93ToplnaM-406
93TopMic-200
93TopMic-406
93TopMic-P200
93TriPla-260
93TriPlaA-20
93Ult-236
93UltAllS-18
93UltAwaW-17
93UppDec-34
93UppDec-50
93UppDec-565
93UppDecCP-R17
93UppDecDG-26
93UppDecFH-61
93UppDecGold-34
93UppDecGold-50
93UppDecGold-565
93UppDecHRH-HR24
93UppDecIC-WI24
93UppDecICJ-WI24
93UppDecOD-D19
93UppDecTriCro-TC6
93USPlaCA-12D
94Bow-460
94BowBes-R75
94BowBesR-R75
94ChuHomS-5
94ChuHomSG-5
94ColC-319
94ColC-353
94ColC-425
94ColC-638
94ColChoGS-319
94ColChoGS-353
94ColChoGS-425
94ColChoGS-638
94ColChoSS-319
94ColChoSS-353
94ColChoSS-425
94ColChoSS-638
94ColChoT-12
94Don-343
94DonAwaWJ-5
94DonDom-B5
94DonMVP-23
94DonSpeE-343
94ExtBas-123
94ExtBasGB-23
94Fin-204
94FinJum-204
94FinRef-204
94Fla-77
94FlaHotG-7
94FlaOutP-8
94Fle-217
94Fle-712
94FleAllS-20
94FleSun-21
94FleTeaL-9
94FleUpdDT-9
94FUnPac-34
94FUnPac-206
94FUnPac-232
94KinDis-12
94Kra-9
94Lea-294
94LeaGam-9
94LeaL-51
94LeaLimGA-9
94LeaMVPC-A11
94LeaMVPCG-A11
94OPC-93
94OPCAllR-17
94OPCJumA-17
94OscMayR-10
94Pac-365
94PacSilP-11
94PanSti-96
94Pin-21
94PinArtP-21
94PinMusC-21
94PinRunC-RC20
94PinTheN-11
94Pos-4
94PosCan-18
94PosCanG-18
94ProMag-77
94RedFolMI-21
94Sco-21
94ScoGolR-21
94ScoGolS-52
94Sel-17
94SelSam-17
94SP-186
94SPDieC-186
94SPHol-30
94SPHolDC-30
94Spo-42
94SpoFanA-AS8
94SpoMov-MM4
94SPPre-CR3
94StaClu-359
94StaCluFDI-359
94StaCluGR-359
94StaCluMOP-359
94StaCluMOP-DD5
94StaCluMOP-ST23
94StaCluST-ST23
94Stu-200
94TomPiz-25
94Top-100
94Top-607
94TopBlaG-17
94TopGol-100
94TopGol-607
94TopSpa-100
94TopSpa-607
94TopSupS-35
94TriPla-258
94TriPlaM-11
94Ult-394
94UppDec-289
94UppDec-325
94UppDecAJ-14
94UppDecAJG-14
94UppDecDC-C4
94UppDecED-289
94UppDecED-325
94UppDecNG-14
94UppDecNGED-14
95Baz-113
95Bow-280
95BowBes-R27

95BowBesR-R27
95ClaPhoC-35
95ColCho-77
95ColChoGS-77
95ColChoSE-230
95ColChoSEGS-230
95ColChoSESS-230
95ColChoSS-77
95D3Zon-2
95DenHol-21
95Don-330
95Don-380
95DonAll-AL9
95DonDiaK-DK19
95DonDom-9
95DonEli-57
95DonPreP-330
95DonPreP-380
95DonTopotO-113
95Emb-71
95EmbGolI-71
95Emo-58
95Fin-167
95FinRef-167
95Fla-62
95FlaOutP-8
95Fle-212
95FleAllS-8
95FleLeaL-3
95FleTeaL-9
95FleUpdH-16
95KinDis-17
95Kra-11
95Lea-183
95Lea300C-17
95LeaGolS-13
95LeaGreG-12
95LeaHeaftH-5
95LeaLim-122
95LeaLimG-11
95LeaLimIBP-16
95LeaLimL-7
95LeaStaS-6
95Pac-255
95PacGolCDC-14
95PacGolP-26
95PacPri-82
95PanSti-82
95PanSti-124
95Pin-296
95Pin-340
95PinArtP-296
95PinArtP-340
95PinFan-5
95PinGatA-GA7
95PinMusC-296
95PinMusC-340
95PinPer-PP14
95PinPin-18
95PinPinR-18
95PinRedH-RH9
95PinTeaP-TP9
95PinWhiH-WH9
95Pos-6
95PosCan-9
95RedFol-24
95Sco-237
95Sco-559
95ScoDouGC-GC11
95ScoGolR-237
95ScoGolR-559
95ScoHaloG-HG11
95ScoPlaTS-237
95ScoPlaTS-559
95ScoRul-SR12
95ScoRulJ-SR12
95Sel-79
95SelArtP-79
95SelCer-33
95SelCerGT-11
95SelCerMG-33
95SP-170
95SPCha-111
95SPCha-167
95SPCha-170
95SPChaCP-CP8
95SPChaCPDC-CP8
95SPChaDC-111
95SPChaDC-167
95SPChaDC-170
95Spo-25
95SpoArtP-25
95SpoDouT-11
95SpoHamT-HT12
95SpoPro-PM12
95SPSil-170
95SPSpeF-13
95StaClu-319
95StaClu-450
95StaClu-518
95StaCluCC-CC12
95StaCluCT-2
95StaCluMO-39
95StaCluMOP-319
95StaCluMOP-450
95StaCluMOP-518
95StaCluMOP-CC12
95StaCluMOP-RL24
95StaCluRL-RL24
95StaCluSTWS-319
95StaCluSTWS-450
95StaCluSTWS-518
95StaCluVR-241
95Stu-22
95StuGolS-22
95StuPlaS-22
95Sum-32
95Sum-184
95SumBigB-BB11
95SumNthD-32
95SumNthD-184
95TomPiz-13
95Top-390
95Top-534
95TopCyb-319
95TopFin-13
95TopLeaL-LL12
95TopTra-162T
95UC3-33
95UC3-138
95UC3ArtP-33
95UC3ArtP-138
95UC3CycS-CS8
95UC3InM-IM7
95Ult-76
95UltAllS-16
95UltAllSGM-16
95UltGolM-76
95UltRBIK-1
95UltRBIKGM-1
95UppDec-430
95UppDecED-430
95UppDecEDG-430
95UppDecPAW-H4
95UppDecPAWE-H4
95UppDecPC-MLB12
95UppDecPLL-R14
95UppDecPLL-R55
95UppDecPLLE-R14
95UppDecPLLE-R55
95UppDecSE-85
95UppDecSEG-85
95Zen-65
95ZenAllS-4
96Baz-24
96Bow-98
96BowBes-78
96BowBesAR-78
96BowBesR-78
96Cir-59
96CirAcc-9
96CirBos-14
96CirRav-59
96ColCho-200
96ColChoGS-200
96ColChoSS-200
96ColChoYMtP-32
96ColChoYMtP-32A
96ColChoYMtPGS-32
96ColChoYMtPGS-32A
96DenHol-11
96DenHolGS-10
96DenHolGSAP-10
96Don-50
96Don-330
96DonDiaK-22
96DonHitL-8
96DonPreP-50
96DonPreP-330
96EmoXL-85
96Fin-B271
96Fin-G18
96Fin-S79
96FinRef-B271
96FinRef-G18
96FinRef-S79
96Fla-120
96Fle-172
96FleTeaL-9
96FleTif-172
96Kin-7
96Lea-77
96LeaAllGMC-16
96LeaAllGMCG-16
96LeaLim-70
96LeaLimG-70
96LeaPre-63
96LeaPreP-63
96LeaPrePB-77
96LeaPrePG-77
96LeaPrePS-77
96LeaPreSG-41
96LeaPreSte-41
96LeaSig-99
96LeaSigEA-163
96LeaSigEACM-24
96LeaSigPPG-99
96LeaSigPPP-99
96LeaTotB-5
96MetUni-80
96MetUniP-80
96Pac-365
96PacGolCD-DC25
96PacHom-HP17
96PacPri-P117
96PacPriFB-FB14
96PacPriG-P117
96PacPriRHS-RH9
96PanSti-200
96Pin-155
96Pin-203
96Pin-268
96Pin-318
96PinAfi-24
96PinAfiAP-24
96PinAfiFPP-24
96PinAfiSP-28
96PinArtP-82
96PinArtP-103
96PinArtP-168
96PinArtP-196
96PinEssotG-8
96PinFan-14
96PinFirR-6
96PinFoil-203
96PinFoil-268
96PinFoil-318
96PinSky-14
96PinSta-82
96PinSta-103
96PinSta-168
96PinSta-196
96Pro-11
96ProMagDM-17
96ProSta-127
96Sco-52
96Sco-358
96ScoDugC-A45
96ScoDugC-B83
96ScoDugCAP-A45
96ScoDugCAP-B83
96Sel-64
96SelArtP-64
96SelCer-62
96SelCerAP-62
96SelCerCB-62
96SelCerCR-62
96SelCerIP-15
96SelCerMB-62
96SelCerMG-62
96SelCerMR-62
96SelClaTF-17
96SelEnF-14
96SelTeaN-19
96SP-115
96Spo-6
96SpoArtP-6
96SpoDouT-10
96SpoHitP-10
96SPSpeFX-16
96SPSpeFXDC-16
96SPx-36
96SPxGol-36
96StaClu-23
96StaCluEPB-23
96StaCluEPG-23
96StaCluEPS-23
96StaCluMM-MM9
96StaCluMO-35
96StaCluMOP-23
96StaCluMOP-MM9
95StaCluVRMC-241
96Stu-74
96StuHitP-5
96StuPrePB-74
96StuPrePG-74
96StuPrePS-74
96Sum-77
96SumAbo&B-77
96SumArtP-77
96SumBal-17
96SumFoi-77
96Top-50
96Top-221
96TopChr-19
96TopChr-81
96TopChrMotG-15
96TopChrMotGR-15
96TopChrR-19
96TopChrR-81
96TopClaC-CC4
96TopGal-152
96TopGalE-4
96TopGalPG-PG11
96TopGalPPI-152
96TopLas-109
96TopLasSS-7
96TopMasotG-15
96TopMysF-M8
96TopMysFR-M8
96Ult-92
96UltDiaP-8
96UltDiaPGM-8
96UltGolM-92
96UltPriL-8
96UltPriLGM-8
96UltRes-6
96UltResGM-6
96UltThu-16
96UltThuGM-16
96UppDec-130
96UppDec-384
96UppDecDD-DD24
96UppDecDDG-DD24
96UppDecDDS-DD24
96UppDecHC-HC7
96Zen-90
96Zen-149
96ZenArtP-90
96ZenArtP-149
96ZenMoz-19
96ZenZ-17
97ColCho-151
97ColChoS-26
97ColChoTBS-30
97ColChoTBSWH-30
97DonEli-95
97DonEliGS-95
97DonEliPtT-4
97DonEliPtT-6
97DonEliPtTA-4
97DonEliPtTA-6
97Fle-154
97FleTif-154
97PacPriGotD-GD64
97SpoIllAM-3
97SpoIllCC-10
97Ult-93
97UltGolME-93
97UltPlaME-93
97UppDec-105
97UppDec-214
97UppDec-414
97UppDecAG-AG13
97UppDecHC-HC20
97UppDecU-40

Pudlo, Scott

91EriSaiC-22
91EriSaiP-4068

Pueschner, Craig

90ChaRaiB-19
90ChaRaiP-2052
90SouAtlLAS-40
91Cla/Bes-366
91WatDiaC-22
91WatDiaP-1269
92CedRapRC-21
92CedRapRF-1086
93WinSpiC-19
93WinSpiF-1582

Puetz, Matt

86AncGlaPTI-30

Puffer, Aaron

93BoiHawC-22
93BoiHawF-3915

Pugh, Scott

91SpoIndC-5
91SpoIndP-3958
92WatDiaC-4
92WatDiaF-2151
93RanCucQC-24
93RanCucQF-841
94WicWraF-200

Pugh, Tim

89BilMusP-2064
90Bes-186
90ChaWheB-7
90ChaWheP-2239
90CMC-694
90ProAaA-92
91ChaLooLD-165
91ChaLooP-1958
91Cla/Bes-299
91LinDriAA-165
92MarPhiC-17
92MarPhiF-3056
92NasSouF-1832
92NasSouS-289
92SkyAAAF-135
93BatCliC-24
93BatCliF-3144
93Bow-442
93Don-162
93Fle-40
93Lea-331
93OPCPre-75
93Pin-270
93RedKah-18
93Sco-247
93StaClu-265
93StaCluFDI-265
93StaCluMOP-265
93Top-702
93TopGol-702
93TopInaM-702
93TopMic-702
93Ult-332
93UppDec-26
93UppDecGold-26
94ColC-234
94ColChoGS-234
94ColChoSS-234
94Don-277
94Fin-67
94FinRef-67
94Fle-419
94Lea-91
94Pac-154
94Pin-481
94PinArtP-481
94PinMusC-481
94RedKah-22
94StaClu-243
94StaCluFDI-243
94StaCluGR-243
94StaCluMOP-243
94Top-95
94TopGol-95
94TopSpa-95
94UppDec-481
94UppDecED-481
94USPlaCR-5S
95RedKah-22
95TopTra-120T
95UppDec-403
95UppDecED-403
95UppDecEDG-403

Puhl, Terry

75DubPacT-2
78AstBurK-19
78Top-553
79AstTeal-10
79Kel-33
79Top-617
80OPC-82
80Top-147
81AllGamPI-159
81CokTeaS-67
81Don-24
81Fle-62
81Kel-42
81OPC-64
81Top-411
81TopScr-88
81TopSti-171
81TopSupHT-100
82AstAstI-5
82Don-370
82Fle-223
82FleSta-44

82OPC-277
82Top-277
82TopSti-42
83AllGamPl-157
83Don-167
83Fle-458
83FleSti-209
83OPC-39
83Top-39
83TopSti-239
84AllGamPl-65
84AstMot-10
84Don-476
84Fle-235
84Nes792-383
84OPC-383
84Top-383
84TopSti-67
84TopTif-383
85AllGamPl-156
85AstHouP-7
85AstMot-7
85Don-426
85Fle-356
85GenMilS-6
85Lea-80
85OPC-283
85SevCoi-C14
85ThoMcAD-39
85Top-613
85TopMin-613
85TopSti-67
85TopTif-613
86AstMilL-16
86AstMot-16
86AstPol-21
86AstTeal-11
86BasStaB-85
86Don-206
86Fle-308
86Lea-138
86OPC-161
86Top-763
86TopTif-763
87AstMot-7
87AstPol-15
87Don-431
87Fle-65
87FleGlo-65
87OPC-227
87Top-693
87TopTif-693
88AstMot-7
88AstPol-17
88Don-533
88FleUpd-90
88FleUpdG-90
88Sco-282
88ScoGlo-282
88StaLinAst-12
88Top-587
88TopTif-587
89AstLenH-22
89AstMot-6
89AstSmo-31
89Don-472
89DonBasB-294
89Fle-364
89FleGlo-364
89Sco-567
89Top-119
89TopTif-119
90AstLenH-18
90AstMot-9
90Don-354
90Fle-233
90FleCan-233
90MLBBasB-60
90OPC-494
90PanSti-256
90PubSti-98
90Sco-473
90Top-494
90TopTif-494
90UppDec-201
90VenSti-412
91MetColP-44
91SimandSMLBL-36

Puig, Benny
89BlaYNPRWL-183
94OttLynF-2899

Puig, Ed
87StoPorP-27
88BlaYNPRWL-12
88ElPasDB-22
88TexLeaAGS-31
89ElPasDGS-14
90CMC-27
90DenZepC-2
90DenZepP-625
90ElPasDGS-24
90ProAAAF-650
91DenZepLD-148
91DenZepP-123
91LinDriAAA-148
92MemChiF-2419
92MemChiS-443

Puig, Rich
91MetWIZ-319

Puikunas, Ed
85FreGiaP-15
86ShrCapP-21
87ShrCapP-15
88PhoFirC-11
88PhoFirP-74
88ShrCapP-1301
89PhoFirC-2
89PhoFirP-1492

Pujals, Denis
96ButCopKB-25

Pujols, Luis
73CedRapAT-11
74CedRapAT-11
75DubPacT-21
78ChaChaT-13
79ChaChaT-14
79Top-139
81Don-379A
81Don-379B
81Fle-68
81Top-313
82AstAstI-8
82Don-576
82Fle-224
82Top-582
83Don-642
83Fle-459
83OPC-112
83Top-752
83TucTorT-13
84Fle-236
84Nes792-446
84Top-446
84TopTif-446
84TucTorC-71
85DomLeaS-22
85RanPer-8
86OklCit8P-18
87IndIndTI-6
89PacSenL-167
89TopSenL-130
89WesPalBES-26
93ExpPosN-18
93RanKee-301

Pujols, Ruben
88VirGenS-19
89BasCitRS-22

Pulchinski, Thomas
77WatIndT-16
78WatIndT-16

Puleo, Charles
80KnoBluJT-21
81TidTidT-13
82MetPhoA-17
82TopTra-94T
83Don-128
83Fle-552
83OPC-358
83RedYea-25
83Top-549
83TopTra-88T
84Don-530
84Fle-480
84Nes792-273
84Top-273
84TopTif-273
84WicAerRD-1
86RicBraP-17
87BraSmo-2
88Don-537
88Fle-548
88FleGlo-548
88Sco-454
88ScoGlo-454
88Top-179
88TopTif-179
89Bow-263
89BowTif-263
89Don-286
89Fle-598
89FleGlo-598
89RicBraBC-21
89Sco-448
89Top-728
89TopTif-728
89UppDec-589
90PubSti-119
90VenSti-413
91MetWIZ-320
92BluOriF-2376
93AlbPolC-24
93AlbPolF-2043
94BluOriC-24
94BluOriF-3580
96BluOriB-3

Pulford, Don
47CenFlo-21

Pulido, Alfonso
84HawIslC-121
85ColCliP-18
85ColCliT-8
86ColCliP-18
86ColCliP-20
87ColCliP-20
87ColCliT-7
87TopTif-642
92YanWIZ8-150
86STaoftFt-3

Pulido, Carlos
85Don-34
87Top-642
90KenTwiB-24
90KenTwiP-2293
90KenTwiS-20
91VisOakC-9
92OrlSunRF-2848
92OrlSunRS-517
92SkyAA F-224
93PorBeaF-2383
94Bow-328
94ColC-611
94ColChoGS-611
94ColChoSS-611
94FleUpd-64
94Sel-410
94SpoRoo-126
94SpoRooAP-126
95Don-353
95DonPreP-353
95Pac-256
96IowCubB-21

Pulido, Juan Carlos
93LinVenB-85
94VenLinU-22
95LinVen-93

Pulido, Phil
77DayBealT-17

Pull, Elizabeth
08AllLadBC-5

Pullen, Shane
94MarPhiC-18
94MarPhiF-3309
95Exc-245
95PiePhiF-195
95Top-237
96PieBolWB-21

Pulli, Frank
88T/MUmp-14
89T/MUmp-12
89T/MUmp-60
90T/MUmp-12

Pulliam, Harry C.
06FanCraNL-39

Pulliam, Harvey
88BasCitRS-19
89MemChiB-15
89MemChiP-1204
89MemChiS-19
89SouLeaAJ-1
90CMC-192
90OmaRoyC-17
90OmaRoyP-78
90ProAAAF-613
91Bow-303
91LinDriAAA-344
91OmaRoyLD-344
91OmaRoyP-1048
92DonRoo-97
92Fle-166
92OmaRoyS-342
92OPC-687
92Pin-279
92Sco-761
92ScoRoo-22
92SkyAAAF-156
92StaClu-428
92Top-687
92TopDeb91-141
92TopGol-687
92TopGolW-687
92TopMic-687
92UppDec-457
93PacSpa-494
93StaCluRoy-28
94LasVegSF-882
96ColSprSSTI-26

Pullins, Jimmie
89IdaFalBP-2011
90PulBraB-23
90PulBraP-3110

Pulsipher, Bill
92PitMetC-1
92PitMetF-3293
92StaClu-676
92StaCluECN-676
94ActPac-36
94BinMetF-703
94Bow-212
94Bow-361
94BowBes-B3
94BowBes-X109
94BowBesR-B3
94BowBesR-X109
94Cla-110
94ClaCreotC-C19
94ClaTriF-T52
94ExcFS7-237
94ExtBas-322
94ExtBasMLH-7
94MetShuST-1
94Top-785
94TopGol-785
94TopSpa-785
94Ult-532
94UppDecML-205
94UppDecMLPotYF-PY15
95Bow-270
95BowBes-B61
95BowBesR-B61
95BowGolF-270
95ColCho-35
95ColChoGS-35
95ColChoSE-4
95ColChoSEGS-4
95ColChoSESS-4
95ColChoSS-35
95Emo-161
95Exc-237
95ExcLeaL-13
95Fin-294
95FinRef-294
95Fle-379
95NorTidTI-23
95Sel-212
95SelArtP-212
95SelCer-125
95SelCerMG-125
95SP-84
95SPCha-5
95SPChaDC-5
95SPSil-84
95StaCluCB-CB13
95StaCluMOP-CB13
95Top-156
95UppDec-2
95UppDecED-2
95UppDecEDG-2
95UppDecML-4
95UppDecML-106
95UppDecMLOP-OP18
95UppDecMLT1PF-5
95UppDecSE-59
95UppDecSEG-59
95Zen-130
95ZenRooRC-6
96Baz-127
96ColCho-223
96ColChoGS-223
96ColChoSS-223
96Don-100
96DonPreP-100
96EmoXL-238
96Fin-S38
96FinRef-S38
96Fla-326
96Fle-487
96FleTif-487
96Lea-173
96LeaPrePB-173
96LeaPrePG-173
96LeaPrePS-173
96LeaSig-129
96LeaSigA-186
96LeaSigAG-186
96LeaSigAS-186
96LeaSigPPG-129
96LeaSigPPP-129
96MetKah-27
96MetKah-28
96MetUni-205
96MetUniP-205
96Pac-137
96PanSti-30
96Pin-2
96PinArtP-2
96PinSam-2
96PinSta-2
96Sco-43
96ScoDiaA-12
96ScoDugC-A38
96ScoDugCAP-A38
96ScoFutF-12
96Sel-4
96SelArtP-4
96SelTeaN-21
96SigRooOJMR-M5
96Spo-52
96SpoArtP-52
96StaClu-18
96StaCluEPB-18
96StaCluEPG-18
96StaCluEPS-18
96StaCluMOP-18
96Top-144
96TopGal-94
96TopGalPPI-94
96Ult-247
96UltGolM-247
96UppDec-139
96UppDecBCP-BC4
97Cir-116
97CirRav-116
97Don-131
97DonEli-80
97DonEliGS-80
97DonPre-18
97DonPreCttC-18
97DonPreP-131
97DonPrePGold-131
97Lea-230
97LeaFraM-230
97LeaFraMDC-230
97LeaGet-15
97NewPin-131
97NewPinAP-131
97NewPinMC-131
97NewPinPP-131
97PinIns-73
97PinInsCE-73
97PinInsDE-73
97Sco-130
97ScoPreS-130
97ScoShoS-130
97ScoShoSAP-130
97Sel-43
97SelArtP-43
97SelRegG-43
97Stu-40
97StuPrePG-40
97StuPrePS-40
97Top-408
95UppDecMLFS-4
95UppDecMLFS-106

Pumphrey, Kenny
96BesAutS-75
96PitMetB-21

Purcell, Gary
77BriRedST-15

Purcell, William
87BucN28-4
87OldJudN-413
94OriofB-32

Purcey, Walter
36GouWidPPR-D29

Purdin, John
65DodTeal-16
65Top-331
68Top-336
68TopVen-336
69OPC-161

69Top-161
69TopFou-9
71OPC-748
71Top-748
85SpoIndGC-16
90DodTar-638
Purdy, Alan
93WelPirC-23
94SalBucC-16
94SalBucF-2330
Purdy, Pid (Everett V.)
28StaPlaCE-51
29ExhFou-8
92ConTSN-406
Purdy, Shawn
91BoiHawC-12
91BoiHawP-3876
91Cla/Bes-447
91MiaHurBB-11
92ClaFS7-212
92PalSprAC-16
92PalSprAF-836
94LakElsSC-13
94LakElsSF-1660
94MidAngF-2438
97MidAngOHP-24
Purkey, Bob
54Top-202
55Top-118
55TopDouH-113
56RedBurB-19
57Top-368
58Kah-24
58RedEnq-30
58RedJayP-10
58Top-311
59Kah-30
59RedBurBP-17
59RedBurBP-18
59RedShiBS-18
59Top-506
60Kah-35
60Lea-67
60RedJayP-11
60Top-4
60TopVen-4
61Kah-36
61Pos-184A
61Pos-184B
61SevElev-4
61Top-9
62Jel-123
62Kah-34A
62Kah-34B
62Pos-123
62PosCan-123
62RedEnq-28
62SalPlaC-153
62ShiPlaC-153
62Top-120
62Top-263
62TopBuc-73
62TopStal-120
62TopVen-120
63Baz-26
63Fle-35
63Jel-134
63Kah-25
63Pos-134
63RedEnq-27
63RedFreBC-20
63RedJayP-11
63SalMetC-6
63Top-5
63Top-7
63Top-350
63TopStil-32
64Kah-22
64RedJayP-10
64Top-480
65CarJayP-7
65CarTeal-18
65OPC-214
65Top-214
66Top-551
79TCM50-260
88PacLegI-77
94TopArc1-202
94TopArc1G-202
Purnell, Byron
76LauIndC-18
Purpura, Dan
82AmaGolST-8
83BeaGolGT-10
Purpura, Joe
78CliDodT-26
Pursell, Joe
83KinBluJTI-16
Purtell, William
09ColChiE-233A
09ColChiE-233B
09ColChiE-233C
09T206-296
10ChiE-17
10CouT21-208
10RedCroT-149
10RedCroT-236
11SpoLifCW-295
11SpoLifM-28
12ColRedB-233A
12ColRedB-233B
12ColRedB-233C
12ColTinT-233A
12ColTinT-233B
12ColTinT-233C
12ImpTobC-30
Purvis, Glenn
75AndRanT-10
76AshTouT-21
77VisOakT-10
Puryear, Nate
76BatTroTI-17
77WatIndT-17
79TacTugT-17
81ChaChaT-22
82ChaLooT-1
Pust, John
87VisOakP-21
Putman, Ed
80EvaTriT-7
80Top-59
81RocRedWW-13
81RocRedWT-13
Putnam, Pat
75LynRanT-21
76AshTouT-15
77TucTorC-51
78Top-706
78TucTorC-32
79Top-713
80OPC-8
80Top-22
81Don-265
81Fle-630
81OPC-302
81Top-498
82Don-520
82Fle-327
82FleSta-180
82OPC-149
82Top-149
82TopSti-241
82TopStiV-241
83TopTra-89T
84Don-145
84Fle-617
84MarMot-16
84Nes792-336
84Nes792-636
84OPC-226
84Top-336
84Top-636
84TopRubD-23
84TopSti-339
84TopTif-336
84TopTif-636
85Fle-287
85OmaRoyT-9
85Top-535
85TopTif-535
86MarGreT-1
87JapPlaB-31
89PacSenL-85
89T/MSenL-87
90EliSenL-75
93RanKee-302
Putrich, Josh
94HunCubF-3552
94HunCubC-23
Puttman, Ambrose
05RotCP-1
09T206-457
11SpoLifCW-296
Puttman, Shannon
94WelPirC-20
94WelPirF-3496
Puzey, James W.
86St.PetCP-25
87SprCarB-5
88ArkTraGS-22
88LouRedBTI-40
89LouRedBC-12
89LouRedBP-1243
89LouRedBTI-33
Pyburn, James
57Top-276
91OriCro-371
Pyburn, Jeff
82HawIsIT-12
Pyc, David
92GreFalDSP-9
94SanAntMF-2467
95SanAntMTI-57
96SanAntMB-17
Pye, Eddie
88GreFalDTI-9
89BakDodCLC-198
89CalLeaA-19
90SanAntMGS-22
90TexLeaAGS-2
91AlbDukLD-18
91AlbDukP-1150
91LinDriAAA-18
92AlbDukF-729
92AlbDukS-9
93AlbDukF-1471
94AlbDukF-852
95DodPol-22
Pyfrom, Joel
82MiaMarT-6
Pyle, John
94HudValRF-3389
94HudValRC-19
Pyle, Scott
81WesHavAT-23
82WesHavAT-28
83TacTigT-26
Pyrtle, Joe
95PitMetTI-25
Pytlak, Frank A.
33TatOrbSDR-180
34DiaMatCSB-149
34ExhFou-11
35DiaMatCS3T1-123
36GouWidPPR-A85
36GouWidPPR-A119
36OveCanR-36
37ExhFou-11
38GouHeaU-245
38GouHeaU-269
39GouPreR303A-37
39WorWidGTP-37
39WorWidGV-20
41DouPlaR-107
91ConTSN-280
Pyznarski, Tim
82WesHavAT-17
83AlbA'sT-13
84TacTigC-87
85LasVegSC-122
86LasVegSP-13
87DenZepP-2
87Don-654
87Spo-158
87SpoTeaP-19
87Top-429
87TopTif-429
88DenZepC-11
88DenZepP-1273
88RocRedWGCP-21
88TriAAAP-13
89OmaRoyP-1726
Quackenbush, Bill
51BerRos-A18
Quade, Mike
82AleDukT-10
83AleDukT-28
86MacPirP-20
87JacExpP-455
89RocExpLC-23
90RocExpLC-19
90RocExpP-2710
91HarSenLD-274
91HarSenP-642
91LinDriAA-274
92HarSenF-475
92HarSenS-299
93OttLynF-2449
94ScrRedBF-935
95ScrRedBTI-22
96WesMicWB-1
Quade, Scott
93JamExpC-17
93JamExpF-3335
Quakes, Rancho Cucamanga
96RanCucQB-30
Qualls, Jim
69CubJewT-13
69Top-602
70OPC-192
70Top-192
71OPC-731
71Top-731
88BoiHawP-1610
Qualls, Kent
95PawRedSDD-22
95PawRedTI-NNO
Qualters, Tom
54Top-174
55Top-33
55TopDouH-107
58Top-453
59Top-341
94TopArc1-174
94TopArc1G-174
Quantrill, Paul
89ElmPioP-31
90WinHavRSS-21
91LinDriAA-469
91NewBriRSLD-469
91NewBriRSP-351
91PawRedSDD-20
92Bow-23
92PawRedSF-921
92PawRedSS-363
92SkyAAAF-165
93Don-327
93Fle-181
93Lea-544
93PacSpa-362
93Pin-175
93RedSoxWHP-11
93Sco-221
93SelRoo-46T
93Top-528
93TopGol-528
93TopInaM-528
93TopMic-528
93Ult-155
94Don-644
94Fle-38
94FleUpd-169
94Pac-63
94PhiMel-19
94Sco-583
94ScoGolR-583
94Top-417
94TopGol-417
94TopSpa-417
94Ult-317
94USPlaCR-2S
95FleUpd-124
95Phi-24
95PhiMel-18
95StaClu-577
95StaCluMOP-577
95StaCluSTWS-577
95TopTra-127T
96BluJayOH-26
96ColCho-248
96ColChoGS-248
96ColChoSS-248
96Don-348
96DonPreP-348
96Fla-191
96Fle-281
96FleTif-281
96FleUpd-U101
96FleUpdTC-U101
96LeaSigEA-164
96Pac-158
96ProSta-89
96Ult-258
96Ult-435
96UltGolM-258
96UltGolM-435
97BluJayS-21
97DunDonPPS-20
Quarles, Melvin
78QuaCitAT-19
Quatraro, Matt
96ButCopKB-26
97Top-252
Quatrine, Mike
90ElmPioP-26
Quealey, Steve
82BirBarT-20
Queckberner, C.A.J.
88AllandGN-44
Queen, Mel D.
64Top-33
64TopVen-33
66Top-556
67Top-374A
67Top-374B
67TopVen-296
68Top-283
68TopVen-283
69OPC-81
69Top-81
71MLBOffS-354
71OPC-736
71Top-736
72OPC-196
72Top-196
79WatIndT-23
80TacTigT-7
81ChaChaT-21
82Ind-29
82IndBurK-8
82IndBurK-9
82IndTeal-27
82IndWhe-17
87SyrChiT-28
96BluJayOH-25
97BluJayS-27
Queen, Mel J.
47TipTop-55
50PirTeal-18
51Bow-309
52Bow-171
Querecuto, Juan
90St.CatBJP-3453
92St.CatBJC-4
92St.CatBJF-3390
93LinVenB-180
93St.CatBJC-20
93St.CatBJF-3978
94DunBluJC-22
94DunBluJF-2566
94VenLinU-113
95DunBluJTI-20
95LinVen-173
Quero, Juan
91ChaRanC-8
91ChaRanP-1312
94VenLinU-66
Quesada, Ed
89EveGiaS-24
Quezada, Edward
96VerExpB-23
Quezada, Rafael
80AndBraT-29
Quezada, Silvano
75LafDriT-21
76PheGiaCr-32
76PhoGiaCa-4
76PhoGiaCC-19
76PhoGiaVNB-20
85DomLeaS-41
Quick, Gene
76CliPilT-27
Quick, Jim
88T/MUmp-26
89T/MUmp-24
90T/MUmp-23
Quick, Ron
81ShrCapT-17
Quigley, Donald
96SpoIndB-22
Quigley, Ernest
34DiaMatCSB-150
94ConTSN-1206
94ConTSNB-1206
Quigley, Jerry
76QuaCitAT-28
Quijada, Ed
90AshTouP-2758
90CMC-662
92BurAstC-14
92BurAstF-543
Quiles, Henry
91BriTigP-3602
Quiles, Victor
87WytCubP-8
Quilici, Frank
66Top-207
66TopVen-207
66TwiFaiG-13

68Top-557
69MilBra-226
69Top-356
70Top-572
71MLBOffS-471
71OPC-141
71Top-141
72MilBra-279
73OPC-49
73Top-49A
73Top-49B
74OPC-447
74Top-447
75OPC-443
75Top-443
78TwiFri-18
Quillin, Lee
09T206-458
Quillin, Ty
91KinMetC-7
91KinMetP-3827
92PitMetC-4
92PitMetF-3307
94PitMetC-18
94PitMetF-3522
Quilty, John
43ParSpo-65
Quinlan, Craig
91St.CatBJC-10
91St.CatBJP-3399
Quinlan, Tom
87MyrBeaBJP-1445
88KnoBluJB-25
89KnoBluJB-20
89KnoBluJP-1123
89KnoBluJS-16
90Bes-247
90CMC-773
90KnoBluJB-22
90KnoBluJP-1252
90KnoBluJS-14
90ProAaA-62
91LinDriAAA-514
91SyrChiLD-514
91SyrChiMB-20
91SyrChiP-2487
91TopDeb90-127
92SkyAAAF-230
92SyrChiF-1977
92SyrChiMB-17
92SyrChiS-514
93BluJayD4-27
93BluJayFS-23
93Don-161
93Sco-309
93SyrChiF-1006
94ScrRedBF-928
94SpoRoo-67
94SpoRooAP-67
95Pac-337
96LeaSigEA-165
97PacPriGotD-GD65
Quinn, Bob
79RedSoxEF-22
94ConTSN-1111
94ConTSNB-1111
Quinn, Frank W.
51Bow-276
Quinn, Jack (John Picus)
09T206-297
10CouT21-209
10CouT21-210
10CouT21-311
10DomDisP-100
10RedCroT-63
10RedCroT-237
10SweCapPP-37
11S74Sil-24
11T205-141
12HasTriFT-4
12T207-152
15VicT21-24
20GasAmeMBD-15
21E121So8-73
21KoBreWSI-46
22E120-12
22W572-80
22W575-100
25Exh-68
26Exh-68
27AmeCarE-14
31Exh-4
31W517-17
33Gou-78
33GouCanV-53
81ConTSN-93
87ConSer2-51
88ConSer3-23
90DodTar-639
91ConTSN-287
93ConTSN-709
94ConTSN-1148
94ConTSNB-1148
Quinn, James
77NewCoPT-27
Quinn, Joseph J.
87OldJudN-415
89N526N7C-11
Quinn, Mark
95SpoIndTI-20
96LanLugB-19
96MidLeaAB-39
Quinn, Mike
92BriTigC-29
Quinn, Thomas G.
87OldJudN-414
Quinn, Tom
90MisStaB-32
91MisStaB-40
92MisStaB-35
Quinones, Elliot
90BilMusP-3234
90ProAaA-197
91ChaWheC-25
91ChaWheP-2900
92ChaWheF-22
92ChaWVWC-11
93ClaGolF-188
93SouAtlLAPI-33
Quinones, Hector
83BelBreF-26
86FreGiaP-18
Quinones, Luis
83AlbA'sT-14
84MaiGuiT-20
85MaiGuiT-21
86FleUpd-92
86PhoFirP-21
87IowCubTI-20
87Top-362
87TopTif-362
88BlaYNPRWL-76
88Don-365
88NasSouC-14
88NasSouP-490
88NasSouTI-19
88Top-667
88TopTif-667
89BlaYNPRWL-84
89NasSouC-17
89NasSouP-1272
90ClaBlu-132
90Don-595
90Fle-428
90FleCan-428
90OPC-176
90RedKah-22
90Sco-499
90Top-176
90TopTif-176
90UppDec-593
91Don-459
91Fle-77
91Lea-233
91OPC-581
91RedKah-10
91Sco-822
91Top-581
91TopDesS-581
91TopMic-581
91TopTif-581
91UltUpd-77
92Fle-417
92OPC-356
92PorBeaF-2676
92PorBeaS-405
92Sco-638
92StaClu-151
92Top-356
92TopGol-356
92TopGolW-356
92TopMic-356
93TucTorF-3070
94CalCanF-798
Quinones, Rene
77BurBeeT-23
79HolMilT-1
80VanCanT-16
81VanCanT-18
83BufBisT-18
83ElPasDT-8
84BufBisT-5
93WinSpiC-20
93WinSpiF-1569
94WinSpiC-19
94WinSpiF-269
Quinones, Rey F.
86DonRoo-48
86FleUpd-93
86PawRedSP-17
86TopTra-89T
86TopTraT-89T
87Don-638
87DonOpeD-121
87Fle-595
87FleGlo-595
87MarMot-20
87Top-561
87TopTif-561
88Don-198
88DonBasB-275
88Fle-386
88FleGlo-386
88MarMot-20
88OPC-358
88PanSti-186
88PanSti-190
88Sco-192
88ScoGlo-192
88StaLinMa-15
88Top-358
88TopSti-215
88TopTif-358
89BimBreD-4
89BlaYNPRWL-150
89Bow-213
89BowTif-213
89Don-330
89DonBasB-185
89Fle-556
89FleGlo-556
89OPC-246
89PanSti-438
89Sco-361
89Top-246
89TopSti-224
89TopTif-246
89TopTra-98T
89TopTraT-98T
89UppDec-508
89UppDec-750
Quintana, Al
86WatPirP-17
Quintana, Carlos
85ElmPioT-18
86GreHorP-18
87NewBriRSP-12
88PawRedSC-20
88PawRedSP-453
88TriAAC-22
89ClaTraO-133
89Don-37
89Fle-95
89FleGlo-95
89PawRedSC-13
89PawRedSP-688
89PawRedSTI-19
89Sco-623
89ScoHot1R-13
89Top-704
89TopBig-142
89TopTif-704
89UppDec-26
90ClaYel-T44
90Don-517
90DonBesA-140
90Fle-283
90FleCan-283
90Hot50RS-36
90Lea-394
90OPC-18
90RedSoxP-15
90Sco-658
90Sco100RS-49
90ScoYouS2-42
90Top-18
90TopBig-273
90TopTif-18
90TopTVRS-32
90UppDec-465
91Bow-126
91Cla3-T75
91Don-568
91Fle-108
91Lea-473
91OPC-206
91PanFreS-264
91PanSti-221
91RedSoxP-16
91Sco-149
91StaClu-12
91Top-206
91TopDesS-206
91TopMic-206
91TopTif-206
91Ult-39
91UppDec-232
92Cla1-T73
92Don-609
92Fle-45
92OPC-127
92PanSti-85
92Pin-358
92RedSoxDD-23
92Sco-189
92StaClu-25
92Top-127
92TopGol-127
92TopGolW-127
92TopMic-127
92Ult-19
92UppDec-421
93Bow-227
93FleFinE-176
93Lea-437
93LinVenB-269
93PacJugC-13
93PacSpa-35
93Pin-564
93SP-203
93StaClu-605
93StaCluFDI-605
93StaCluMOP-605
93Ult-514
93UppDec-747
93UppDecGold-747
94Don-219
94Fle-39
94Pac-62
94Pin-175
94PinArtP-175
94PinMusC-175
94Sco-499
94ScoGolR-499
94StaClu-290
94StaCluFDI-290
94StaCluGR-290
94StaCluMOP-290
94Top-349
94TopGol-349
94TopPre-294
94TopSpa-349
94VenLinU-233
95LinVen-42
Quintana, Luis
75SalLakCC-16
76SalLakCGC-17
77SalLakCGC-16
80ChaO'sP-16
80ChaO'sW-17
82WicAerTI-13
83WicAerDS-15
Quintana, Urbano
96MarPhiB-20
Quintana, Willibaldo
76VenLeaS-94
80VenLeaS-96
Quintell, John
91OneYanP-4157
92AlbYanS-17
92Ft.LauYF-2615
Quintero, Frank
77VisOakT-11
78OrlTwiT-16
Quinzer, Paul
86SpoIndC-165
88WicPilRD-23
89WicUpdR-16
89WicWraR-27
90LasVegSP-121
90ProAAAF-9
Quirico, Rafael
90Bes-147
90GreHorB-10
90GreHorP-2662
90GreHorS-16
90OneYanP-3371
91GreHorP-3057
91SouAtlLAGP-SAL29
92PriWilCF-146
92ProFS7-126
92UppDecML-229
93AlbYanF-2163
93LimRocDWB-13
94ColCliF-2953
94ColCliP-23
95ColCliMCTI-3
95ColCliP-25
95ColCliTI-25
96ReaPhiB-11
Quirk, Art
62Top-591
63Top-522
91OriCro-372
Quirk, Jamie
75OmaRoyTI-14
76OPC-598
76Top-598
77Top-463
78SpoIndC-5
78Top-95
79Top-26
80Top-248
81Don-341
81Fle-50
81Top-507
82Don-212
82Fle-421
82Roy-17
82Top-173
83Car-22
83Top-264
83TopTra-90T
84Fle-332
84Nes792-671
84Top-671
84TopTif-671
85OmaRoyT-16
87Fle-377
87FleGlo-377
87Top-354
87TopTif-354
88Don-404
88Fle-266
88FleGlo-266
88PanSti-103
88RoySmo-19
88Sco-577
88ScoGlo-577
88StaLinRo-12
88Top-477
88TopTif-477
89Bow-173
89BowTif-173
89Fle-290
89FleGlo-290
89Sco-461
89Top-702
89TopTif-702
89UppDec-620
90A'sMot-15
91A'sMot-15
91Don-588
91Fle-21
91Lea-431
91OPC-132
91OriCro-373
91StaClu-573
91Top-132
91TopDesS-132
91TopMic-132
91TopTif-132
92AthMot-15
92Don-472
92Fle-265
92OPC-19
92Sco-526
92StaClu-83
92Top-19
92TopGol-19
92TopGolW-19
92TopMic-19
92YanWIZ8-151
93Fle-667
94BreMilB-68
Quirk, John
94HicCraC-18
94HicCraF-2176
96PriWilCB-22
Quiros, Gus

79VanCanT-11
80VanCanT-4
80VenLeaS-252
81VanCanT-11
Quiroz, Juan
76VenLeaS-24
Quisenberry, Dan
75WatRoyT-24
76WatRoyT-24
77JacSunT-20
79RoyTeal-8
80Top-667
81CokTeaS-79
81Don-222
81Fle-31
81FleStiC-24
81OPC-206
81Top-8
81Top-493
81TopSti-7
82Don-112
82Fle-422
82FleSta-204
82Roy-18
82Top-264
83AllGamPI-84
83Don-70
83Fle-122
83FleSta-154
83FleSti-100
83Kel-32
83OPC-155
83OPC-396
83Roy-21
83RoyPol-6
83Top-155
83Top-396
83Top-708
83TopFol-4
83TopLeaS-6
83TopSti-22
83TopSti-74
83TopSti-165
84Don-583
84DonActAS-56
84Fle-354
84Fle-635
84FleSti-73
84FunFooP-25
84Nes792-3
84Nes792-138
84Nes792-407
84Nes792-570
84Nes792-718
84NesDreT-11
84OPC-69
84OPC-273
84RalPur-25
84SevCoi-C24
84Top-3
84Top-138
84Top-407
84Top-570
84Top-718
84TopCer-25
84TopGloS-38
84TopRubD-10
84TopSti-9
84TopSti-10
84TopSti-279
84TopSti-290
84TopSup-9
84TopTif-3
84TopTif-138
84TopTif-407
84TopTif-570
84TopTif-718
85AllGamPI-84
85Don-6
85Don-95
85DonActA-8
85DonSupD-6
85Dra-39
85Fle-211
85FleLimE-25
85FleStaS-99
85KASDis-9
85KitCloD-9
85Lea-6
85OPC-270
85SevCoi-C15
85ThoMcAD-16
85Top-270
85Top-711
85Top3-D-24
85TopGaloC-8
85TopGloS-35
85TopRubD-10
85TopSti-173
85TopSti-269
85TopSup-8
85TopTif-270
85TopTif-711
85Woo-28
86BasStaB-86
86Don-541
86Fle-18
86FleAll-9
86FleMin-2
86FleStiC-91
86GenMilB-2H
86Lea-208
86OPC-50
86QuaGra-29
86RoyKitCD-8
86RoyNatP-29
86SevCoi-C7
86SevCoi-E7
86SevCoi-S7
86SevCoi-W7
86Spo-55
86Spo-118
86Spo-186
86Top-50
86Top-722
86Top3-D-21
86TopGaloC-9
86TopGloS-35
86TopSti-257
86TopSup-5
86TopTat-3
86TopTif-50
86TopTif-722
87Don-177
87Fle-378
87FleBasA-33
87FleGlo-378
87FleMin-84
87FleStiC-93
87GenMilB-3J
87OPC-15
87RedFolSB-7
87Spo-167
87SpoTeaP-13
87Top-714
87TopSti-257
87TopTif-714
88Don-471
88Fle-267
88FleGlo-267
88GreBasS-80
88OPC-195
88PanSti-101
88RoySmo-15
88Sco-290
88ScoGlo-290
88ScoRoo-18T
88ScoRooG-18T
88Spo-76
88StaLinAl-22
88StaLinRo-13
88Top-195
88TopSti-256
88TopTif-195
89CarSmo-19
89FleUpd-120
89OPC-13
89Sco-520
89Top-612
89TopTif-612
89UppDec-533
90Don-437
90Fle-259
90FleCan-259
90OPC-312
90PubSti-227
90Sco-475
90Top-312
90TopTif-312
90UppDec-659
90VenSti-414
92KelAll-9
93RoySta2-11
Ra, Michael
93AubAstC-30
94AubAstC-26
Raabe, Brian
91CalLeLA-8
91VisOakC-19
91VisOakP-1751
92Ft.MyeMCB-8
92Ft.MyeMF-2755
93ClaGolF-165
93NasXprF-410
94SalLakBF-824
94TriAAF-AAA17
97Sco-326
97ScoShoS-326
97ScoShoSAP-326
Raasch, Glen
91PenPilP-382
93PeoChiTI-21
Rabb, John
79CedRapGT-5
81ShrCapT-2
83PhoGiaBHN-1
84Don-143
84GiaPos-22
84Nes792-228
84Top-228
84TopTif-228
85DomLeaS-97
85Don-236
85IntLeaAT-12
85PhoGiaC-183
85RicBraT-22
85Top-696
85TopTif-696
86RicBraP-18
87RicBraBC-17
87RicBraC-20
87RicBraT-20
91RenSilSCLC-1
82PhoGiaVNB-5
Rabbit, Dodger
95GreFalDTI-38
Rabe, Charles
57SeaPop-28
58Kah-25
58RedEnq-31
58Top-376
59RedEnq-22
Rabouin, Andre
88AppFoxP-159
89AppFoxP-871
90AppFoxBS-20
90AppFoxP-2113
Raccoon, Rocky
95ChaLooTI-30
Rackley, Keifer
93BelMarC-22
93BelMarF-3223
94RivPilCLC-13
95PorCitRTI-18
96WilBluRB-21
Rackley, Marv
43ParSpo-81
47TipTop-103
90DodTar-640
Racobaldo, Mike
90KisDodD-24
Raczka, Mike
86ChaOriW-22
87ChaO'sW-10
88RocRedWGCP-22
89RocRedWC-5
89RocRedWP-1648
92ModA'sC-18
92TacTigF-2500
93Don-183
93Pin-277
93TacTigF-3030
94NewBriRSF-648
95LouRedF-276
Radachowsky, Gregg
90NiaFalRP-13
91NiaFalRP-3637
Radar, Keith
91SalLakTSP-1
Radatz, Dick
47PM1StaP1-167
62Top-591
63Top-363
64ChatheY-43
64Top-170
64TopCoi-30
64TopGia-40
64TopSta-41
64TopVen-170
64WheSta-37
65Baz-10
65ChaTheY-44
65OldLonC-34
65Top-295
65TopEmbl-48
65TopTral-64
66Top-475
66TopRubl-76
67CokCapl-16
67OPC-174
67Top-174
69Top-663
74LauAllG-63
78TCM60I-76
81RedSoxBG2S-104
86RedSoxGT-11
89PacLegl-122
89SweBasG-46
Radbourn, Hoss (Charles)
36PC7AlbHoF-24
50CalHOFW-61
63GadFunC-8
75FlePio-5
75TCMAllG-26
76ShaPiz-25
80PerHaloFP-24
80SSPHOF-24
84GalHaloFRL-25
87BucN28-11A
87BucN28-11B
87OldJudN-416A
87OldJudN-416B
89N526N7C-12
90BasWit-92
90HOFStiB-2
94OriofB-42
Radcliff, Rip (Ray)
36GouWidPPR-A86
36NatChiFPR-102
36OveCanR-37
36SandSW-45
37OPCBatUV-125
37WheBB14-13
37WheBB7-29H
38BasTabP-24
38GouHeaU-261
38GouHeaU-285
91ConTSN-98
Radcliffe, Alex
91PomBlaBPB-5
Radcliffe, Double-Duty (Ted)
78LauLonABS-36
86NegLeaF-64
91NegLeaRL-25
92NegLeaK-7
92NegLeaRLI-50
93UppDecS-17
94TedWil-110
95NegLeaL2-6
95NegLeaLI-25
Radcliffe, Ernest
87EriCarP-9
88VirGenS-20
Rader, Dave
72OPC-232
72Top-232
73OPC-121
73Top-121
74OPC-213
74Top-213
74TopSta-108
75Gia-8
75OPC-31
75Top-31
76Hos-21
76HosTwi-21
76OPC-54
76SSP-101
76Top-54
77Car5-19
77CarTeal-18
77Top-427
78SSP270-246
78Top-563
79OPC-369
79Top-489
79Top-693
80Top-296
81Don-512
81OPC-359
81Top-378
Rader, Doug
67Ast-24
67Top-412
68CokCapA-11
68Top-332
68TopVen-332
69MilBra-227
69MLBOffS-142
69OPC-119
69Top-119
69TopFou-15
69TopSta-37
69TopTeaP-6
70AstTeal-10
70MLBOffS-46
70OPC-355
70Top-355
71AstCok-9
71MLBOffS-90
71OPC-425
71Top-425
71TopCoi-17
72Kel-14
72MilBra-280
72Top-536
73OPC-76
73Top-76
74AstFouTIP-2
74OPC-395
74Top-395
74TopDecE-14
74TopSta-35
75Hos-89A
75Hos-89B
75OPC-165
75Top-165
76OPC-44
76SSP-59
76Top-44
76TopTra-44T
77BurCheD-128
77PadSchC-44
77Top-9
78OPC-166
78Top-651
80HawIsIT-2
81HawIsIT-21
82AstAstI-2
82HawIsIT-23
83RanAffF-11
83TopTra-91T
84Nes792-412
84RanJarP-11
84Top-412
84TopTif-412
85Top-519
85TopTif-519
86AstGreT-4
87AstSer1-26
87AstShoSO-19
87AstShoSTw-24
87AstShoSTw-27
87AstShowSTh-25
89TopTra-99T
89TopTraT-99T
90OPC-51
90Top-51
90TopTif-51
91OPC-231
91Top-231
91TopDesS-231
91TopMic-231
91TopTif-231
92AthMot-28
93MarPub-28
93RanKee-303
Rader, Keith
91SalLakTP-3220
Radford, Paul
87OldJudN-417
Radinsky, Scott
87PenWhiSP-12
89SouBenWSGS-7
90Bow-308
90BowTif-308
90ClaYel-T5
90DonRoo-40
90FleUpd-86
90Lea-484
90ScoRoo-90T
90TopTra-99T
90TopTraT-99T
90UppDec-725
90WhiSoxC-22
90WhiSoxC-28
91Baz-22
91Bow-365
91Don-332

91Fle-135
91Lea-463
91OPC-299
91Sco-62
91Sco100RS-83
91StaClu-311
91Top-299
91TopDeb90-128
91TopDesS-299
91TopMic-299
91TopRoo-25
91TopTif-299
91ToyRoo-25
91UltUpd-18
91UppDec-621
91WhiSoxK-31
92Don-299
92Fle-96
92Lea-281
92OPC-701
92Pin-389
92PinTea2-46
92PinTeaP-12
92Sco-444
92Top-701
92TopGol-701
92TopGolW-701
92TopMic-701
92Ult-340
92UppDec-594
92WhiSoxK-31
93Don-169
93Fle-208
93PacSpa-74
93Pin-451
93Sco-182
93StaClu-275
93StaCluFDI-275
93StaCluMOP-275
93StaCluWS-19
93Top-550
93TopGol-550
93TopInaM-550
93TopMic-550
93Ult-177
93UppDec-298
93UppDecGold-298
93WhiSoxK-23
94ColC-235
94ColChoGS-235
94ColChoSS-235
94Don-230
94Fle-92
94Pac-135
94Pin-135
94PinArtP-135
94PinMusC-135
94Sco-276
94ScoGolR-276
94StaClu-434
94StaCluFDI-434
94StaCluGR-434
94StaCluMOP-434
94StaCluT-125
94StaCluTFDI-125
94Top-421
94TopGol-421
94TopSpa-421
95TopTra-71T
95WhiSoxK-25
96DodMot-22

Radison, Dan
88HamRedP-1732
89BlaYNPRWL-97
89SprCarB-29
91AlbYanLD-24
91AlbYanP-1023
91LinDriAA-24
92AlbYanF-2348
92AlbYanS-24
93PadMot-28
94PadMot-28

Radke, Brad
92KenTwiC-22
92KenTwiF-601
93ForMyeMC-20
93ForMyeMF-2652
94Cla-88
94NasXprF-384
95Exc-88
95Fla-281
95FleUpd-62
95StaClu-560
95StaCluMOP-560
95StaCluSTWS-560
95TopTra-79T
95UppDec-257
95UppDecED-257
95UppDecEDG-257
96ColCho-201
96ColChoGS-201
96ColChoSS-201
96Don-10
96DonPreP-10
96EmoXL-86
96Fla-121
96Fle-173
96FleTif-173
96Lea-131
96LeaPrePB-131
96LeaPrePG-131
96LeaPrePS-131
96LeaSigA-187
96LeaSigAG-187
96LeaSigAS-187
96MetUni-81
96MetUniP-81
96MetUniProS-81
96Pac-356
96Pin-37
96Sco-77
96ScoDugC-A63
96ScoDugCAP-A63
96SP-114
96StaClu-163
96StaCluMOP-163
96Sum-6
96SumAbo&B-6
96SumArtP-6
96SumFoi-6
96Top-163
96Ult-93
96UltGolM-93
96UppDec-126
97Cir-389
97CirRav-389
97ColCho-380
97Fle-155
97FleTif-155
97StaClu-265
97StaCluMOP-265
97Top-257
97Ult-345
97UltGolME-345
97UltPlaME-345
97UppDec-413

Radloff, Scott
83CedRapRF-21
83CedRapRT-15

Radlosky, Rob
95ForWayWTI-12
96FtMyeMB-7

Radmanovich, Ryan
94ForWayWC-19
94ForWayWF-2016
94MidLeaAF-MDW14
95ForMyeMTI-22
96HarCitRCB-24

Radtke, Jack
90DodTar-641

Radziewicz, Doug
91JohCitCC-8
91JohCitCP-3986
92SprCarC-5
92SprCarF-877
93St.PetCC-20
93St.PetCF-2636
94ArkTraF-3103
94ExcFS7-273

Raeside, John
82LynMetT-23

Raether, Peter
90ArkRaz-22

Raether, Richard
85MiaHur-12
86TulDriTI-22
87PorChaRP-9
88BlaYNPRWL-28
88TulDriTI-26
90TulDriDGB-10

Raffensberger, Ken
49Bow-176
49EurSta-93
51Bow-48
52Bow-55
52TipTop-30
52Top-118
53BowC-106
53Top-276
54Bow-92
54Top-46
83TopRep5-118
91TopArc1-276
94TopArc1-46
94TopArc1G-46
95ConTSN-1414

Raffo, Greg
91BriTigC-16
91BriTigP-3603
92NiaFalRC-26
92NiaFalRF-3322
93LakTigF-1308

Raffo, Thomas
88CapCodPB-9
88CapCodPPaLP-79
88MisStaB-27
89MisStaB-31
90MiaMirIS-20
90MisStaB-33
91ChaWheC-19
91ChaWheP-2896
91Cla/Bes-261
91SouAtlLAGP-SAL10
92CedRapRC-5
92CedRapRF-1080

Ragan, Pat (Don C.P.)
12T207-153
16FleBreD-74
16SpoNewM-140
75WhiSox1T-19
90DodTar-642

Raggio, Brady
94NewJerCF-3418
95MidLeaA-42
95PeoChiTI-37
96ArkTraB-23
96TexLeaAB-14
97Bow-306
97BowInt-306
97Fle-584
97FleTif-584
97Ult-519
97UltGolME-519
97UltPlaME-519

Ragland, Tom
72OPC-334
72Top-334
74OPC-441
74Top-441
93RanKee-34

Ragland, Trace
91WelPirC-14
91WelPirP-3589
93SalBucC-19
93SalBucF-447

Ragni, John
52MotCoo-34

Ragsdale, Jerry
83AndBraT-27

Rahan, Johnny
52LavPro-67

Raich, Eric
76OPC-484
76Top-484
77Top-62

Raifstanger, John
94UtiBluSC-23
96MicBatCB-21

Raimondi, Bill
46RemBre-25
47RemBre-1
47SigOil-52
47SmiClo-2
48SigOil-19
48SmiClo-1
49BowPCL-18
49RemBre-22
53MotCoo-36

Raimondo, Pasquale
81VerBeaDT-15

Rain, Steve
94HunCubF-3553
95MidLeaA-43
95RocCubTI-28
96OrlCubB-22
97Bow-189
97BowChr-177
97BowChrI-177
97BowChrIR-177
97BowChrR-177
97BowInt-189
94HunCubC-24

Rainbolt, Ray
74GasRanT-17
75LynRanT-22
76SanAntBTI-19
79TulDriT-8

Rainbows, Charlestown
89ChaRaiP-970

Rainer, Rick
84JacMetT-11
85TidTidT-28
86TidTidP-25
87TidTidP-30
87TidTidT-25

Raineri, Joe
92OklStaC-24

Raines, Kenneth
94IdaFalBF-3583
94IdaFalBSP-21
95DanBraTI-23
95DurBulTI-26
96HudValRB-9

Raines, Larry
58Top-243

Raines, Mike
81CedRapRT-5

Raines, Ned
79CedRapGT-21

Raines, Rock (Tim)
79MemChiT-20
81Don-538
81ExpPos-9
81OPC-136
81Top-479
81TopTra-816
82Don-214
82ExpHygM-16
82ExpPos-31
82ExpZel-3
82FBIDis-15
82Fle-202
82Fle-207
82FleSta-31
82Kel-53
82OPC-70
82OPCPos-17
82PerAll-13
82PerAllG-13
82PerCreC-6
82PerCreCG-6
82Top-3
82Top-70
82Top-164
82TopSti-7
82TopSti-62
82TopSti-116
83AllGamPI-158
83Don-540
83ExpStu-9
83Fle-292
83FleSta-155
83FleSti-265
83OPC-227
83OPC-352
83PerAll-14
83PerAllG-14
83Top-403
83Top-595
83Top-704
83TopSti-210
83TopSti-253
84AllGamPI-66
84Don-299
84ExpPos-22
84ExpStu-20
84ExpStu-36
84ExpStu-37
84Fle-281
84Fle-631
84FleSti-51
84FleSti-88
84FunFooP-41
84Nes792-134
84Nes792-370
84Nes792-390
84NesDreT-17
84OPC-370
84OPC-390
84SevCoi-E20
84Top-134
84Top-370
84Top-390
84TopGloA-17
84TopGloS-37
84TopRubD-23
84TopSti-91
84TopSti-179
84TopSti-201
84TopStiB-4
84TopTif-134
84TopTif-370
84TopTif-390
85AllGamPI-157
85Don-299
85DonActA-1
85Dra-24
85ExpPos-17
85Fle-405
85FleLimE-26
85FleStaS-42
85FleStaS-58
85Lea-218
85Lea-252
85OPC-277
85OPCPos-7
85SevCoi-S12
85Top-630
85Top3-D-17
85TopMin-630
85TopRubD-9
85TopSti-82
85TopSti-282
85TopSup-15
85TopTif-630
86Don-177
86DonAll-20
86Dra-15
86ExpProPa-7
86ExpProPo-1
86Fle-256
86Fle-632
86FleLeaL-33
86FleMin-54
86FleStiC-92
86GenMilB-6E
86Lea-108
86OPC-280
86QuaGra-10
86SevCoi-E12
86Spo-11
86Spo-127
86Spo-144
86SpoDecG-74
86Top-280
86TopGloS-15
86TopMinL-49
86TopSti-75
86TopSup-42
86TopTat-17
86TopTif-280
87BoaandB-24
87ClaGam-29
87Don-56
87DonAll-36
87DonHig-7
87DonHig-16
87ExpPos-21
87Fle-328
87Fle-642
87FleAll-12
87FleBasA-34
87FleExcS-34
87FleGlo-328
87FleGlo-642
87FleMin-85
87FleRecS-30
87FleSlu-32
87FleStiC-94
87GenMilB-5E
87KayB-25
87Lea-149
87OPC-30
87RedFolSB-39
87Spo-34
87Spo-152
87Spo-197
87Spo-199
87SpoDeaP-1
87SpoSupD-15
87StaRai-1
87StaRai-2
87StaRai-3
87StaRai-4
87StaRai-5
87StaRai-6
87StaRai-7
87StaRai-8
87StaRai-9
87StaRai-10

87StaRai-11
87StaRai-12
87StuPan-7
87Top-30
87TopGaloC-8
87TopGloS-48
87TopMinL-17
87TopSti-85
87TopTif-30
87Woo-11
88Baz-15
88ClaRed-168
88Don-2
88Don-345
88DonAll-57
88DonAll-62
88DonBasB-180
88DonBonM-BC18
88DonSupD-2
88Dra-2
88ExpPos-18
88Fle-193
88Fle-631
88FleAwaW-30
88FleBasA-31
88FleBasM-27
88FleExcS-31
88FleGlo-193
88FleGlo-631
88FleHea-6
88FleHotS-31
88FleLeaL-31
88FleMin-90
88FleRecS-30
88FleStiC-97
88FleSup-29
88FleTeaL-27
88GreBasS-51
88K-M-19
88KayB-24
88Lea-2
88Lea-114
88Lea-211
88MSAFanSD-16
88MSAHosD-11
88MSAJifPD-14
88Nes-31
88OPC-243
88PanSti-325
88PanSti-330
88Sco-3
88Sco-649
88ScoGlo-3
88ScoGlo-649
88Spo-2
88StaLinAl-23
88StaLinE-13
88Top-403
88Top-720
88TopBig-116
88TopCoi-49
88TopGloS-12
88TopMinL-57
88TopRevLL-5
88TopRitTM-6
88TopSti-76
88TopStiB-20
88TopTif-403
88TopTif-720
88TopUKM-58
88TopUKMT-58
89Bow-369
89BowTif-369
89CerSup-6
89ClaLigB-42
89Don-97
89DonBasB-258
89ExpPos-24
89Fle-391
89FleGlo-391
89K-M-27
89KayB-25
89OPC-87
89PanSti-125
89RedFolSB-91
89Sco-40
89ScoHot1S-95
89Spo-150
89SpoIllFKI-178
89Top-81
89Top-560
89TopBasT-80
89TopBatL-7
89TopBig-73
89TopCoi-22
89TopGloS-53
89TopSti-77
89TopTif-81
89TopTif-560
89TopUKM-61
89TVSpoM-13
89UppDec-402
89UppDecS-2
90Bow-118
90BowTif-118
90ClaBlu-118
90Don-216
90DonBesN-104
90DOnBonM-BC7
90ExpPos-28
90Fle-359
90FleBasM-30
90FleCan-359
90GooHumICBLS-16
90Hot50PS-32
90KayB-24
90KinDis-6
90Lea-212
90MSAHolD-2
90OPC-180
90PanSti-283
90PubSti-186
90Sco-409
90Sco100S-75
90Spo-69
90StaLonJS-23
90StaLonJS-39
90SunSee-14
90SupActM-16
90Top-180
90TopAmeA-17
90TopBatL-7
90TopBig-154
90TopCoi-54
90TopDou-50
90TopGloS-38
90TopMinL-63
90TopSti-69
90TopStiB-18
90TopTif-180
90TopTVA-55
90UppDec-29
90UppDec-177
90VenSti-415
91BasBesHM-16
91Bow-362
91Cla2-T9
91ClaGam-174
91DenHol-26
91Don-457
91Fle-244
91FleUpd-15
91Lea-413
91OPC-360
91OPCPre-97
91PanFreS-143
91PanSti-63
91RedFolS-75
91Sco-35
91Sco100S-89
91ScoRoo-10T
91StaClu-523
91StaPro-4
91Stu-37
91StuPre-4
91Top-360
91TopCraJI-3
91TopDesS-360
91TopMic-360
91TopTif-360
91TopTra-94T
91TopTraT-94T
91Ult-81
91UppDec-143
91UppDec-773
91WhiSoxK-30
92Bow-204
92ClaGam-99
92Don-312
92Fle-97
92Lea-37
92OPC-426
92PanSti-131
92Pin-178
92Pin-605
92Sco-635
92StaClu-426
92Stu-156
92Top-426
92TopGol-426
92TopGolW-426
92TopKid-104
92TopMic-426
92TriPla-107
92Ult-43
92UppDec-575
92WhiSoxK-30
93Bow-499
93Don-565
93ExpDonM-6
93Fin-183
93FinRef-183
93Fle-209
93FunPac-201
93Lea-420
93OPC-290
93PacSpa-75
93PanSti-140
93Pin-53
93Sco-658
93Sel-236
93SP-259
93StaClu-43
93StaCluFDI-43
93StaCluMOP-43
93StaCluWS-5
93Stu-215
93Top-675
93TopGol-675
93TopInaM-675
93TopMic-675
93TriPla-108
93Ult-178
93UppDec-597
93UppDecGold-597
93USPlaCA-6H
93WhiSoxK-24
94Bow-127
94ColC-385
94ColChoGS-385
94ColChoSS-385
94Don-220
94Don-258
94ExtBas-52
94Fin-192
94FinRef-192
94Fla-35
94Fle-93
94Lea-116
94LeaL-23
94OPC-228
94Pac-136
94Pin-462
94PinArtP-462
94PinMusC-462
94ProMag-27
94Sco-379
94ScoGolR-379
94Sel-92
94StaClu-350
94StaClu-525
94StaCluFDI-350
94StaCluFDI-525
94StaCluGR-350
94StaCluGR-525
94StaCluMOP-350
94StaCluMOP-525
94StaCluT-136
94StaCluTFDI-136
94Stu-208
94SucSav-4
94Top-243
94TopGol-243
94TopSpa-243
94TriPla-268
94Ult-341
94UppDec-254
94UppDecAJ-42
94UppDecAJG-42
94UppDecED-254
94WhiSoxK-25
95Bow-291
95ColCho-495
95ColChoGS-495
95ColChoSS-495
95Don-75
95DonPreP-75
95DonTopotO-53
95Emb-130
95EmbGolI-130
95Emo-28
95Fin-187
95FinRef-187
95Fla-248
95Fle-127
95Lea-208
95LeaLim-94
95Pac-95
95Sco-112
95ScoGolR-112
95ScoPlaTS-112
95SP-139
95SPCha-139
95SPChaDC-139
95SPSil-139
95StaClu-302
95StaClu-410
95StaCluMOP-302
95StaCluMOP-410
95StaCluMOP-RL12
95StaCluRL-RL12
95StaCluSTWS-302
95StaCluSTWS-410
95StaCluVR-158
95Stu-148
95Top-77
95TopCyb-54
95Ult-33
95UltGolM-33
95UppDec-198
95UppDecED-198
95UppDecEDG-198
95UppDecSE-157
95UppDecSEG-157
95WhiSoxK-26
96ColCho-95
96ColCho-779
96ColChoGS-95
96ColChoSS-95
96Don-384
96DonPreP-384
96EmoXL-94
96Fin-B224
96FinRef-B224
96Fla-135
96Fle-75
96FleTif-75
96FleUpd-U66
96FleUpdTC-U66
96LeaSig-136
96LeaSigPPG-136
96LeaSigPPP-136
96MetUni-93
96MetUniP-93
96MLBPin-28
96Pac-284
96PanSti-174
96Pin-364
96PinFoil-364
96Sco-449
96StaClu-418
96StaCluEPB-418
96StaCluEPG-418
96StaCluEPS-418
96StaCluMOP-418
95StaCluVRMC-158
96Stu-59
96StuPrePB-59
96StuPrePG-59
96StuPrePS-59
96Top-272
96TopChrMotG-7
96TopChrMotGR-7
96TopMasotG-7
96Ult-43
96Ult-393
96UltGolM-43
96UltGolM-393
96UppDec-111
96UppDec-409
97Cir-292
97CirRav-292
97ColCho-182
97Fle-503
97FleTif-503
97Lea-274
97LeaFraM-274
97LeaFraMDC-274
97Pac-157
97PacLigB-157
97PacSil-157
97Sco-391
97ScoHobR-391
97ScoResC-391
97ScoShoS-391
97ScoShoSAP-391
97Top-334
97Ult-461
97UltGolME-461
97UltPlaME-461
97UppDec-443

Rainey, Chuck
80Top-662
81Top-199
82Fle-303
82RedSoxC-15
82Top-522
83CubThoAV-30
83Don-334
83Fle-192
83Top-56
83TopTra-92T
84Don-76
84Fle-502
84Nes792-334
84OPC-334
84Top-334
84TopSti-47
84TopTif-334
85Don-618

Rainey, Scott
83CliGiaF-9
87WicPilRD-16

Rainout, Chief
87PeoChiPW-6

Raisanen, Keith
87WatPirP-8
88SalBucS-16
89AugPirP-506
89SouAtlLAGS-9
90SalBucS-17

Rajotte, Jason
95WesMicWTI-20
96ModA'sB-10

Rajsich, Dave
75ForLauYS-7
78TacYanC-28
79Top-710
80Top-548
81Don-267
83OklCit8T-15
85RocRedWT-21
86LouRedTI-25
88LouRedBC-9
88LouRedBP-443
88LouRedBTI-41
89PacSenL-3
91BelBreC-26
91BelBreP-2120
91PacSenL-154
91PacSenL-160
92AugPirF-256
92YanWIZ7-129
93RanKee-304
93SalBucC-27
93SalBucF-449
94SalBucC-27
94SalBucF-2341
95CarMudF-174

Rajsich, Gary
77CocAstT-20
80TucTorT-16
81TidTidT-9
82MetPhoA-18
83Don-599
83Fle-553
83TidTidT-8
83Top-317
84LouRedR-6
85GiaMot-24
85GiaPos-25
87JapPlaB-14
89PacSenL-7
89TopSenL-124
90EliSenL-12
91MetWIZ-321
91PacSenL-156
91PacSenL-160

Rakers, Jason
95WatIndTI-24

Rakow, Ed
58MonRoyF-18
60Top-551
61AthJayP-17
61Top-147
62Top-342
63Jel-90
63Pos-90
63Top-82
64TigJayP-9

64TigLid-12
64Top-491
65Top-454
90DodTar-643
Raleigh, Matt (Matthew)
92JamExpC-23
92JamExpF-1508
93JamExpC-18
94BurBeeC-1
94BurBeeF-1092
95Bow-135
95Exc-225
95UppDecML-210
96FreKeyB-19
95UppDecMLFS-210
Raley, Dan
89LakTigS-17
90LakTigS-20
91LinDriAA-400
91LonTigLD-400
91LonTigP-1894
92LakTigC-29
92LakTigF-2295
93LonTigF-2324
94LakTigC-29
94LakTigF-3053
Raley, Tim
88BelBreGS-5
89StoPorB-20
89StoPorCLC-169
89StoPorP-401
89StoPorS-9
90StoPorB-13
90StoPorCLC-198
90StoPorP-2198
91HagSunLD-243
91HagSunP-2469
91LinDriAA-243
Rally, Mascot
90BraDubS-27
92BraLykS-28
93BraLykS-30
94MasMan-13
95NewHavRTI-NNO
Ralph, Curtis
90PriWilCTI-21
91PriWilCC-10
91PriWilCP-1426
92ForLauYC-12
92ForLauYTI-24
92PriWilCC-25
92PriWilCF-147
93PriWilCC-21
93PriWilCF-654
94AbaYanF-1439
Ralston, Bill
74TacTwiC-19
75TacTwiK-5
Ralston, Bobby (Robert)
84AriWilP-16
85OrlTwiT-10
86TolMudHP-18
87OrlTwiP-6
88PorBeaC-21
88PorBeaP-657
89PorBeaC-15
89PorBeaP-232
90HunStaB-18
Ralston, Kris
93EugEmeC-21
93EugEmeF-3854
94CarLeaAF-CAR22
94ExcFS7-71
94WilBluRC-21
94WilBluRF-300
95WicWraTI-35
96OmaRoyB-23
96SigRooOJTP-T9
Rama, Shelby
94SpaPhiF-1721
94SparPhiC-17
Ramanouchi, Kenichi
91SalSpuC-7
91SalSpuP-2254
Ramazzotti, Bob
49EurSta-67
51Bow-247
52Top-184
53BowBW-41
83TopRep5-184
90DodTar-644
Rambadt, Charles
90HelBreSP-22
Rambis, Randy
79WatIndT-17
Rambo, Dan
90Bes-123
90CalLeaACLC-53
90CMC-717
90ProAaA-145
90SanJosGB-23
90SanJosGCLC-44
90SanJosGP-2006
90SanJosGS-18
91LinDriAA-318
91ShrCapLD-318
91ShrCapP-1821
92PhoFirF-2820
92ShrCapF-3868
92ShrCapS-590
92SkyAA F-260
93LinVenB-86
93PhoFirF-1515
Rambo, Matt
87UtiBluSP-26
88SpaPhiP-1025
88SpaPhiS-16
89ClePhiS-17
91Cla/Bes-53
91OscAstC-10
91OscAstP-682
92JacGenS-346
92SkyAA F-145
Rametta, Steve
75SanAntBT-16
Ramey, Jeff
92BenMusSP-17
92BilMusF-3358
93PriRedC-24
93PriRedF-4189
Ramharter, Steve
89AncGlaP-21
90ButCopKSP-17
Ramie, Vern
82KnoBluJT-17
83SyrChiT-23
Ramirez, Alex
76VenLeaS-165
80OrlTwiT-18
80VenLeaS-142
Ramirez, Alex (Alexander)
93BurIndC-21
93BurIndF-3313
94Bow-335
94ColRedC-17
94ColRedF-458
94VenLinU-104
95BakBlaTI-3
95LinVen-156
96CanIndB-21
Ramirez, Allan (D. Allan)
80ChaO'sP-17
80ChaO'sW-18
82RocRedWT-5
83OriPos-20
83RocRedWT-7
84Don-332
84Nes792-347
84OriTeal-21
84RocRedWT-16
84Top-347
84TopTif-347
85ChaO'sT-25
91OriCro-374
Ramirez, Angel
93MedHatBJF-3750
93MedHatBJSP-3
94HagSunC-19
94HagSunF-2744
95DunBluJTI-21
96BesAutS-76
96BesAutSA-57
Ramirez, Aramis
96EriSeaB-20
97Bow-310
97BowChr-214
97BowChrI-214
97BowChrIR-214
97BowChrR-214
97BowInt-310
Ramirez, Daniel
91KanCouCC-19
91KanCouCP-2666
91KanCouCTI-16
92FreKeyC-27
92FreKeyF-1814
93FreKeyC-22
93FreKeyF-1036
96PitMetB-22
Ramirez, Fausto
86BelMarC-125
87BelMarTI-27
88WauTimGS-3
Ramirez, Francisco
91EliTwiP-4304
Ramirez, Frank
87IdaFalBP-23
Ramirez, Hector
91KinMetC-19
91KinMetP-3811
92ColMetC-2
92ColMetF-293
92ColMetPI-27
94St.LucMC-19
94St.LucMF-1194
95BinMetTI-31
96BinBeeB-23
Ramirez, J.D.
89SalLakTTI-11
90RocExpLC-20
90RocExpP-2703
91WesPalBEC-23
91WesPalBEP-1238
94MidAngF-2447
94MidAngOHP-23
95MidAngOHP-26
95MidAngTI-23
Ramirez, Jack
79TulDriT-12
Ramirez, Joel
94BelMarC-22
94BelMarF-3246
95EveAqaTI-17
96MidLeaAB-5
96WisTimRB-17
Ramirez, Jose
96FayGenB-25
Ramirez, Juan
94KinMetC-16
94KinMetF-3837
Ramirez, Julio
96BesAutS-77
Ramirez, Leo
93MacBraC-20
93MacBraF-1398
93SouAtlLAGF-42
94ClaGolF-116
Ramirez, Luis
78NewWayCT-35
92GulCoaYF-3792
Ramirez, Manny
91BurIndP-3316
91ClaDraP-10
91FroRowDP-47
91HigSchPLS-7
92Bow-532
92Bow-676
92ClaFS7-155
92DonRoo-98
92KinIndF-2488
92OPC-156
92Pin-295
92ProFS7-62
92Sco-800
92StaCluD-146
92Top-156
92TopGol-156
92TopGolW-156
92TopMic-156
92UppDec-63
92UppDecML-35
92UppDecML-55
92UppDecML-146
93Bow-365
93Bow-669
93CanIndF-2849
93ClaGolF-124
93ClaYouG-YG18
93ExcFS7-164
93FlaWavotF-13
93FleFinE-204
93SP-285
93Ult-545
93UppDec-433
93UppDecGold-433
94Bow-55
94Bow-371
94BowBes-R88
94BowBes-X107
94BowBesR-R88
94BowBesR-X107
94ColC-16
94ColChoGS-16
94ColChoSS-16
94Don-322
94ExtBas-66
94ExtBasRS-16
94Fin-430
94FinJum-430
94FinRef-430
94Fla-43
94Fle-119
94FUnPac-1
94LeaGolR-6
94LeaL-30
94LeaLimRP-9
94OPC-121
94OPCHotP-6
94Pac-183
94Pin-244
94PinArtP-244
94PinMusC-244
94PinNewG-NG17
94PinPowS-PS13
94PinRooTP-6
94ProMag-39
94Sco-645
94ScoBoyoS-38
94ScoGolR-645
94ScoRoo-RT72
94ScoRooGR-RT72
94ScoRooS-SU2
94ScoRooSR-SU2
94Sel-181
94SelRooS-RS10
94SP-101
94SPDieC-101
94SPHol-31
94SPHolDC-31
94Spo-151
94SpoRoo-RO1
94SpoRooRS-TR2
94SpoSha-SH12
94SPPre-CR4
94StaClu-320
94StaClu-627
94StaCluFDI-320
94StaCluFDI-627
94StaCluGR-320
94StaCluGR-627
94StaCluMOP-320
94StaCluMOP-627
94Stu-95
94Top-216
94TopGol-216
94TopSpa-216
94TopSupS-36
94TopTraFI-8
94TriPla-286
94Ult-351
94UppDec-23
94UppDecDC-C5
94UppDecED-23
94UppDecMLS-MM16
94UppDecMLSED-MM16
94UppDecNG-15
94UppDecNGED-15
95Baz-109
95Bow-352
95BowBes-R12
95BowBes-X2
95BowBesR-R12
95BowBesR-X2
95ClaPhoC-18
95ColCho-275
95ColChoCtA-7
95ColChoCtAG-7
95ColChoCtG-CG16
95ColChoCtG-CG16B
95ColChoCtG-CG16C
95ColChoCtGE-16
95ColChoCtGG-CG16
95ColChoCtGG-CG16B
95ColChoCtGG-CG16C
95ColChoCtGGE-16
95ColChoGS-275
95ColChoSE-117
95ColChoSEGS-117
95ColChoSESS-117
95ColChoSS-275
95Don-370
95DonPreP-370
95DonTopotO-66
95Emb-136
95EmbGolI-136
95Emo-37
95EmoN-9
95Fin-4
95FinPowK-PK5
95FinRef-4
95Fla-35
95FlaTodS-10
95Fle-145
95FlePro-6
95FleRooS-14
95Lea-280
95LeaLim-66
95LeaLimG-23
95LeaLimIBP-7
95LeaLimL-14
95Pac-128
95PacGolCDC-8
95PacGolP-32
95PacLatD-28
95PacPri-41
95PanSti-105
95Pin-287
95Pin-350
95PinArtP-287
95PinArtP-350
95PinMusC-287
95PinMusC-350
95PinPer-PP13
95PinRedH-RH15
95PinUps-US11
95PinWhiH-WH15
95Sco-445
95Sco-568
95ScoAi-AM15
95ScoGolR-445
95ScoGolR-568
95ScoHaloG-HG38
95ScoPlaTS-445
95ScoPlaTS-568
95ScoRul-SR24
95ScoRulJ-SR24
95Sel-81
95SelArtP-81
95SelCanM-CM5
95SelCer-48
95SelCerC-7
95SelCerMG-48
95SelCerPU-2
95SelCerPU9-2
95SigRooMR-MR4
95SigRooMRS-MR4
95SigRooOJSS-10
95SigRooOJSSS-10
95SP-151
95SPCha-150
95SPChaDC-150
95Spo-105
95SpoArtP-105
95SpoHamT-HT13
95SpoSam-105
95SPPlaP-PP15
95SPSil-151
95SPSpeF-11
95StaClu-264
95StaCluFDI-264
95StaCluMO-46
95StaCluMOP-264
95StaCluSTDW-I264
95StaCluSTMP-18
95StaCluSTWS-264
95StaCluVR-132
95Stu-32
95StuGolS-32
95Sum-18
95SumNewA-NA2
95SumNthD-18
95Top-577
95TopCyb-351
95UC3-48
95UC3-134
95UC3ArtP-48
95UC3ArtP-134
95UllHomRK-8
95Ult-41
95UltAllR-9
95UltAllRGM-9
95UltGolM-41
95UltSecYS-11
95UltSecYSGM-11
95UppDec-97
95UppDecED-97
95UppDecEDG-97
95UppDecPLL-R35
95UppDecPLLE-R35
95UppDecSE-161

95UppDecSEG-161
95Zen-69
95ZenAllS-5
95ZenZ-10
96Baz-106
96Bow-85
96BowBes-52
96BowBesAR-52
96BowBesC-10
96BowBesCAR-10
96BowBesCR-10
96BowBesR-52
96Cir-37
96CirAcc-7
96CirBos-10
96CirRav-37
96ColCho-125
96ColCho-329
96ColCho-382T
96ColChoCtG-CG12
96ColChoCtG-CG12B
96ColChoCtG-CG12C
96ColChoCtGE-CR12
96ColChoCtGG-CG12
96ColChoCtGG-CG12B
96ColChoCtGG-CG12C
96ColChoCtGGE-CR12
96ColChoGS-125
96ColChoGS-329
96ColChoSS-125
96ColChoSS-329
96Don-40
96DonDiaK-3
96DonEli-67
96DonPowA-9
96DonPowADC-9
96DonPreP-40
96DonPurP-7
96DonSam-6
96DonSho-8
96EmoLegoB-7
96EmoRarB-9
96EmoXL-55
96EmoXL-P55
96Fin-B298
96Fin-S95
96FinRef-B298
96FinRef-S95
96Fla-74
96FlaPow-7
96Fle-99
96FleChe-6
96FleInd-15
96FleLumC-7
96FleRoaW-6
96FleTif-99
96FleTomL-9
96FleUpd-U236
96FleUpdH-16
96FleUpdSS-8
96FleUpdTC-U236
96Lea-38
96LeaAllGMC-13
96LeaAllGMCG-13
96LeaGolS-14
96LeaLim-8
96LeaLimG-8
96LeaPicP-4
96LeaPre-5
96LeaPreP-5
96LeaPrePB-38
96LeaPrePG-38
96LeaPrePS-38
96LeaPreSG-77
96LeaPreSte-77
96LeaSig-11
96LeaSigA-188
96LeaSigAG-188
96LeaSigAS-188
96LeaSigPPG-11
96LeaSigPPP-11
96MetUni-52
96MetUniML-7
96MetUniP-52
96MetUniPP-9
96Pac-301
96PacCraC-CC9
96PacEstL-EL25
96PacGolCD-DC6
96PacHom-HP9
96PacOctM-OM18
96PacPri-P98
96PacPriG-P98
96PacPriRHS-RH14
96PanSti-176
96Pin-46
96Pin-149
96Pin-278
96PinAfi-109
96PinAfiAP-109
96PinAfiSP-13
96PinArtP-18
96PinArtP-76
96PinArtP-178
96PinChrBC-11
96PinFan-24
96PinFirR-14
96PinFoil-278
96PinPow-16
96PinProS-14
96PinSky-17
96PinSlu-13
96PinSta-18
96PinSta-76
96PinSta-178
96PinTeaT-4
96ProSta-59
96SchDis-6
96Sco-305
96ScoAll-19
96ScoBigB-11
96ScoDiaA-16
96ScoDreT-8
96ScoDugC-B30
96ScoDugCAP-B30
96ScoFutF-6
96ScoGolS-30
96ScoNumG-12
96ScoPowP-14
96ScoRef-6
96ScoTitT-15
96Sel-8
96SelArtP-8
96SelCer-51
96SelCerAP-51
96SelCerCB-51
96SelCerCR-51
96SelCerIP-8
96SelCerMB-51
96SelCerMG-51
96SelCerMR-51
96SelCerSF-14
96SelEnF-24
96SelTeaN-1
96SP-74
96SPBasH-88
96Spo-30
96Spo-113
96SpoArtP-30
96SpoArtP-113
96SpoDouT-11
96SpoPowS-17
96SpoPro-15
96SPSpeFX-43
96SPSpeFXDC-43
96SPx-21
96SPxBoufG-8
96SPxGol-21
96StaClu-215
96StaClu-368
96StaCluEPB-368
96StaCluEPG-368
96StaCluEPS-368
96StaCluMO-36
96StaCluMOP-215
96StaCluMOP-368
95StaCluVRMC-132
96Stu-114
96StuMas-4
96StuPrePB-114
96StuPrePG-114
96StuPrePS-114
96StuStaGS-11
96Sum-85
96SumAbo&B-85
96SumArtP-85
96SumBigB-10
96SumBigBM-10
96SumFoi-85
96SumHitI-10
96SumPos-9
96TeaOut-65
96Top-400
96TopChr-161
96TopChrR-161
96TopGal-126
96TopGalPPI-126
96TopLas-13
96TopMysF-M10
96TopMysFR-M10
96TopRoaW-RW13
96Ult-53
96Ult-599
96UltChe-A7
96UltCheGM-A7
96UltFreF-9
96UltFreFGM-9
96UltGolM-53
96UltGolM-599
96UltHomRKGM-8
96UltHomRKR-8
96UltPowP-7
96UltPowPGM-7
96UltRBIK-6
96UltRBIKGM-6
96UltRisS-9
96UltRisSGM-9
96UppDec-55
96UppDecBCP-BC20
96UppDecDD-DD17
96UppDecDDG-DD17
96UppDecDDS-DD17
96UppDecHC-HC6
96UppDecPD-PD13
96UppDecPRE-R17
96UppDecPreR-R17
96UppDecRunP-RP15
96Zen-34
96Zen-142
96ZenArtP-34
96ZenArtP-142
96ZenMoz-18
96ZenZ-12
97Bow-34
97BowBes-62
97BowBesAR-62
97BowBesR-62
97BowChr-29
97BowChrI-29
97BowChrIR-29
97BowChrR-29
97BowInt-34
97Cir-280
97CirBos-14
97CirRav-280
97CirSupB-14
97ColCho-310
97ColChoAC-15
97ColChoCtG-11A
97ColChoCtG-11B
97ColChoCtG-11C
97ColChoCtGIW-CG11
97ColChoNF-NF27
97ColChoS-6
97ColChoTBS-19
97ColChoTBSWH-19
97ColChoTotT-T13
97Don-11
97Don-412
97DonEli-18
97DonEliGS-18
97DonEliLaL-9
97DonLim-8
97DonLim-117
97DonLim-142
97DonLimFotG-9
97DonLimLE-8
97DonLimLE-117
97DonLimLE-142
97DonPowA-13
97DonPowADC-13
97DonPre-38
97DonPre-180
97DonPreCttC-38
97DonPreCttC-180
97DonPreP-11
97DonPreP-412
97DonPrePGold-11
97DonPrePGold-412
97DonPreTB-16
97DonPreTBG-16
97DonPreTF-16
97DonPreTP-16
97DonPreTPG-16
97DonPreXP-1A
97DonRocL-12
97DonTea-76
97DonTeaSPE-76
97Fin-138
97Fin-265
97Fin-349
97FinEmb-138
97FinEmb-349
97FinEmbR-138
97FinEmbR-349
97FinRef-138
97FinRef-265
97FinRef-349
97FlaSho-A33
97FlaSho-B33
97FlaSho-C33
97FlaShoDC-14
97FlaShoLC-33
97FlaShoLC-B33
97FlaShoLC-C33
97FlaShoLCM-A33
97FlaShoLCM-B33
97FlaShoLCM-C33
97Fle-87
97Fle-713
97Fle-728
97FleNig&D-7
97FleTif-87
97FleTif-713
97FleTif-728
97Lea-105
97Lea-359
97LeaFraM-105
97LeaFraM-359
97LeaFraMDC-105
97LeaFraMDC-359
97LeaWarT-7
97MetUni-86
97NewPin-42
97NewPinAP-42
97NewPinMC-42
97NewPinPP-42
97Pac-78
97PacLatotML-9
97PacLigB-78
97PacPriSL-SL3B
97PacSil-78
97Pin-196
97PinArtP-196
97PinCar-9
97PinCer-68
97PinCerLI-19
97PinCerMBlu-68
97PinCerMG-68
97PinCerMR-68
97PinCerR-68
97PinIns-67
97PinInsC-4
97PinInsCE-67
97PinInsDD-13
97PinInsDE-67
97PinMin-14
97PinMinB-14
97PinMinCB-14A
97PinMinCB-14B
97PinMinCG-14
97PinMinCGR-14
97PinMinCN-14
97PinMinCS-14
97PinMinG-14
97PinMinS-14
97PinMusC-196
97PinPasttM-16
97PinTotCPB-68
97PinTotCPG-68
97PinTotCPR-68
97PinX-P-61
97PinX-PF&A-17
97PinX-PMoS-61
97PinX-PMP-5
97PinX-PMW-18
97PinX-PMWG-18
97PinX-PMWS-18
97ProMag-54
97ProMagML-54
97Sco-162
97Sco-496
97ScoHeaotO-13
97ScoHobR-496
97ScoInd-8
97ScoIndPl-8
97ScoIndPr-8
97ScoIndU-8
97ScoIndUTC-8
97ScoPreS-162
97ScoResC-496
97ScoShoS-162
97ScoShoS-496
97ScoShoSAP-162
97ScoShoSAP-496
97ScoStaaD-17
97Sel-4
97SelArtP-4
97SelRegG-4
97SelTooot-12
97SelToootTMB-12
97SkyE-X-17
97SkyE-XACA-8
97SkyE-XC-17
97SkyE-XEC-17
97SP-60
97SPInsI-12
97SPMarM-MM11
97SpoIll-67
97SpoIllEE-67
97SPSpeF-30
97SPSpxF-8
97SPSPxFA-8
97SPx-21
97SPxBoufG-9
97SPxBro-21
97SPxGraF-21
97SPxSil-21
97SPxSte-21
97StaClu-244
97StaCluMat-244
97StaCluMOP-244
97Stu-32
97StuMasS-13
97StuMasS8-13
97StuPor8-16
97StuPrePG-32
97StuPrePS-32
97Top-318
97TopChr-106
97TopChrDD-DD4
97TopChrDDR-DD4
97TopChrR-106
97TopGal-116
97TopGalPPI-116
97TopSta-35
97TopStaAM-35
97Ult-54
97UltGolME-54
97UltHitM-13
97UltPlaME-54
97UltTop3-18
97UltTop3GM-18
97UppDec-188
97UppDec-345
97UppDecAG-AG16
97UppDecBCP-BC4
97UppDecHC-HC14
97UppDecLDC-LD19
97UppDecMM-5
97UppDecPPJ-PP14
97UppDecPPJ-PP14
97UppDecRP-RP16
97UppDecRSF-RS10
97UppDecTTS-TS20
97UppDecU-51
97UppDecUGN-GN20

Ramirez, Mario
76WauMetT-22
77LynMetT-23
78TidTidT-20
79TidTidT-12
81HawIslT-23
84Fle-309
84Nes792-94
84PadMot-23
84Top-94
84TopTif-94
85PadMot-16
85Top-427
85TopTif-427
86Don-568
86TolMudHP-19
86Top-262
86TopTif-262
91MetWIZ-322

Ramirez, Milt
71MLBOffS-281
71OPC-702
71Top-702
76VenLeaS-120
77SanJosMC-5
80OgdA'sT-14

Ramirez, Nelson
90HunCubP-3280

Ramirez, Nick
88ChaWheB-26
88GenCubP-1634

Ramirez, Omar
91WatIndC-27

91WatIndP-3382
92KinIndC-4
93CanIndF-2850
93ExcFS7-165
93LimRocDP-P3
93LimRocDWB-113
93LimRocDWB-149
93LimRocDWB-P3
94ChaKniF-908
94Cla-59
94ExcFS7-49
94UppDecML-172
94UppDecMLPotYF-PY12

Ramirez, Orlando
76SSP-197
77Top-131

Ramirez, Pete
96BurBeeTI-13

Ramirez, Rafael
78GreBraT-20
79SavBraT-23
80RicBraT-2
81BraPol-16
81Fle-266
81Top-192
82BraBurKL-21
82BraPol-16
82Don-546
82Fle-447
82Top-536
83AllGamPI-112
83BraPol-16
83Don-310
83Fle-146
83FleSta-156
83FleSti-85
83Top-439
84AllGamPI-23
84BraPol-16
84Don-589
84Fle-190
84FleSti-26
84Nes792-234
84OPC-234
84Top-234
84TopSti-33
84TopTif-234
85AllGamPI-113
85BraHos-20
85BraPol-16
85Don-141
85Fle-339
85Lea-86
85OPC-232
85Top-647
85TopSti-27
85TopTif-647
86BraPol-16
86Don-263
86Fle-526
86OPC-107
86Top-107
86TopSti-42
86TopTat-11
86TopTif-107
87BraSmo-18
87Don-202
87Fle-526
87FleGlo-526
87Top-31
87Top-76
87TopSti-42
87TopTif-31
87TopTif-76
88AstMot-17
88AstPol-18
88Don-448
88FleUpd-91
88FleUpdG-91
88OPC-379
88PanSti-247
88Sco-426
88ScoGlo-426
88ScoRoo-12T
88ScoRooG-12T
88StaLinAst-13
88Top-379
88TopTif-379
88TopTra-90T
88TopTraT-90T
89AstLenH-16
89AstMot-16
89AstSmo-32
89Bow-330
89BowTif-330
89Don-509
89DonBasB-64
89Fle-365
89FleGlo-365
89OPC-261
89PanSti-90
89Sco-113
89Top-749
89TopBig-268
89TopSti-17
89TopTif-749
89UppDec-341
90AstLenH-19
90AstMot-19
90Don-241
90DonBesN-77
90Fle-234
90FleCan-234
90Lea-135
90OPC-558
90PanSti-266
90PubSti-99
90Sco-42
90Top-558
90TopBig-183
90TopSti-18
90TopTif-558
90UppDec-144
90VenSti-416
91AstMot-19
91Bow-564
91Don-586
91Fle-513
91OPC-423
91PanFreS-10
91Sco-305
91StaClu-107
91StaCluP-33
91Top-423
91TopDesS-423
91TopMic-423
91TopTif-423
91Ult-139
91UppDec-210
92AstMot-19
92Sco-388
92StaClu-451
92Ult-495
92UppDec-582
93PacSpa-127

Ramirez, Randy
84ChaLooT-21

Ramirez, Ray
86OrlTwiP-16
87OklCit8P-24
88OklCit8P-51
89OklCit8P-1533
90CMC-174
90OklCit8C-24

Ramirez, Rich
95ModA'sTI-22
96ModA'sB-29

Ramirez, Richard
87GasRanP-23
93BurIndC-22
93BurIndF-3307

Ramirez, Roberto
91CliGiaP-848
91EveGiaC-27
91EveGiaP-3922
91WelPirC-24
91WelPirP-3571
92SouOreAF-3422
94CarMudF-1578
94RivPilCLC-20
95PorCitRTI-19
96PorCitRB-23

Ramirez, Russell
78NewWayCT-36
79BurBeeT-2

Ramirez, Victor
85DomLeaS-75
92ButCopKSP-30
92KinIndF-2489

Ramon, Julio
87OneYanP-16

Ramon, Ray
86ReaPhiP-22

Ramos, Bobby (Roberto)
75WesPalBES-7
79SalLakCGT-21B
80ExpPos-23
81ExpPos-10
81Fle-162
81OPC-136
81Top-479
82ColCliP-31
82ColCliT-18
82Fle-203
82OPC-354
82Top-354
83ExpPos-18
83ExpStu-20
83TopTra-93T
84Don-209
84ExpPos-23
84ExpStu-9
84Fle-282
84Nes792-32
84OPC-32
84Top-32
84TopTif-32
85EdmTraC-15
85OPC-269
85Top-407
85TopTif-407
86IowCubP-24
87OmaRoyP-21
88PhoFirC-13
88PhoFirP-69
89ColMudB-20
89ColMudP-121
89ColMudS-24
89PacSenL-65
89TopSenL-18
90OscAstS-29
91OscAstC-20
92YanWIZ8-152
93AshTouC-25
93AshTouF-2293

Ramos, Cesar
93BurIndC-23
93BurIndF-3297
94ColRedC-18
94ColRedF-441

Ramos, Domingo
76ForLauYS-9
77WesHavYT-19
78TacYanC-17
79SyrChiT-6
79SyrChiTI-1
80SyrChiT-22
81SyrChiTI-17
82SalLakCGT-16
84Don-440
84MarMot-18
84Nes792-194
84Top-194
84TopTif-194
85DomLeaS-146
85MarMot-12
85Top-349
85TopTif-349
86MarMot-12
86Top-462
86TopTif-462
87MarMot-21
87Top-641
87TopTif-641
88ColSprSSC-16
88ColSprSSP-1534
88Don-622
88FleUpd-23
88FleUpdG-23
88Sco-362
88ScoGlo-362
88Top-206
88TopTif-206
89CubMar-15
90CubMar-16
90Don-491
90Lea-440
90OPC-37
90Sco-489
90Top-37
90TopTif-37
90TopTVCu-24
90UppDec-150
91Fle-429
91OPC-541
91Top-541
91TopDesS-541
91TopMic-541
91TopTif-541
91UppDec-85
92YanWIZ7-130

Ramos, Eddie
91Cla/Bes-440
91ClaDraP-45
91FroRowDP-33
92AshTouC-15
92ClaFS7-382
92StaCluD-147
93QuaCitRBC-16
93QuaCitRBF-109
94QuaCitRBC-17
94QuaCitRBF-544

Ramos, Edgar
94QuaCitRBC-18
94QuaCitRBF-531
95QuaCitRBTI-20
96KisCobB-21
97Fle-649
97FleTif-649

Ramos, George
78GreBraT-21

Ramos, Jairo
91MedHatBJP-4116
91MedHatBJSP-8
93LinVenB-27
94VenLinU-89
95LinVen-223

Ramos, John
87PriWilYP-28
88CarLeaAS-15
88PriWilYS-20
89AlbYanB-13
89AlbYanP-336
89AlbYanS-15
89EasLeaAP-22
89Sta-100
90AlbYanB-12
90AlbYanP-1177
90AlbYanS-13
90Bes-152
90EasLeaAP-EL42
91AlbYanCB-4
91ColCliLD-115
91ColCliP-15
91ColCliP-599
91LinDriAAA-115
91Ult-385
92ColCliF-356
92ColCliP-14
92ColCliS-113
92Don-15
92Fle-242
92ProFS7-105
92Sco-818
92ScoRoo-8
92SkyAAAF-53
92TopDeb91-142
92TopGol-658
92TopGolW-658
94LasVegSF-875
95SyrChiTI-20
96SyrChiTI-24

Ramos, Jorge
90SouBenWSB-8
90SouBenWSGS-14
91SouBenWSC-4
91SouBenWSP-2864

Ramos, Jose
87FayGenP-2
88FayGenP-1086
89LonTigP-1387
90CMC-384
90ProAAAF-376
90TolMudHC-7
90TolMudHP-146
90WicStaSGD-30
91LinDriAA-394
91LonTigLD-394
91LonTigP-1877
92LonTigS-414
93LinVenB-73
95LinVen-243

Ramos, Ken
88NebCor-14
90CarLeaA-43
90KinIndTI-9
91CanIndLD-97
91CanIndP-991
91LinDriAA-97
92CanIndF-702
92CanIndS-115
93Bow-473
93ChaKniF-558
93ClaFS7-239
93ClaGolF-7
93ExcFS7-166
93ExcLeaLF-20
94TucTorF-776
94VenLinU-224
95TusTorTI-21
96TusTorB-21

Ramos, Luis
90IBAWorA-19

Ramos, Papo
92EveGiaC-17
92EveGiaF-1704
93CliGiaC-18

Ramos, Pedro
56Top-49
57Top-326
58SenJayP-10
58Top-331
59SenTealW-14
59Top-78
59Top-291
59TopVen-78
60Lea-21
60SenJayP-12
60Top-175
60TopVen-175
61Pos-98A
61Pos-98B
61Top-50
61Top-528
61TopStal-184
61TwiCloD-22
61TwiPetM-3
61TwiUniMC-12
62IndJayP-11
62Top-485
62TopBuc-74
62TopStal-79
63Top-14
64IndJayP-9
64Kah-23
64Top-562
64YanReqKP-13
65ChaTheY-18
65OPC-13
65Top-13
66Top-439
67OPC-187
67Top-187
78TCM60I-38
89PacSenL-68
89PacSenL-217
92YanWIZ6-100

Ramos, Richard
82WicAerTI-14
83WicAerDS-16

Ramos, Wolf
80ElmPioRST-24
80VenLeaS-12

Ramppen, Frank
83VisOakF-7

Ramsdell, Willie (J. Willard)
49W72HolS-17
51Bow-251
52Bow-22
52Top-114
53MotCoo-3
79TCM50-279
83TopRep5-114
90DodTar-645

Ramsey, Bill
47SigOil-66
47SigOil-84
47SunBre-18

Ramsey, Fernando
87GenCubP-10
88ChaWheB-22
89PeoChiTI-21
89PeoChiTI-25
90WinSpiTI-11
91ChaKniLD-139
91ChaKniP-1701
91LinDriAA-139
92IowCubF-4061
92IowCubS-216
92ProFS7-203
92SkyAAAF-104
93Don-539
93IowCubF-2145
93LinVenB-174
93Pin-273
93StaCluCu-29
93UppDec-382
93UppDecGold-382
95NasSouTI-17

96NasSouB-17
Ramsey, Jeff
90RocExpLC-21
90RocExpP-2707
Ramsey, Matthew
89MisStaB-32
90MisStaB-34
Ramsey, Mike (Michael James)
87AlbDukP-30
88AlbDukC-14
88AlbDukP-267
88BlaYNPRWLU-43
88Sco-267
88ScoGlo-267
89EdmTraC-16
89EdmTraP-561
90DodTar-646
91SprCarP-759
Ramsey, Mike (Michael Jeffery)
76ArkTraT-8
77ArkTraT-7A
77ArkTraT-7B
78SprRedWK-5
81Fle-549
81Top-366
82Don-316
82Fle-125
82Top-574
83Car-23
83Don-568
83Fle-19
83Top-128
84Don-382
84Fle-333
84Nes792-467
84Top-467
84TopTif-467
85Fle-406
85OPC-62
85Top-62
85TopTif-62
86TamTarP-15
87DodMot-11
87DonOpeD-80
87EdmTraP-2066
90DodTar-647
91PacSenL-18
91SprCarC-11
92SavCarC-23
92SavCarF-679
93SprCarC-28
93SprCarF-1868
94St.PetCC-28
94St.PetCF-2602
95ArkTraTI-23
96CliLumKTI-21
Ramsey, Thomas
87OldJudN-418
88SpoTimM-21
89EdgR.WG-18
Ramstack, Curt
76AppFoxT-20
Rand, Dick
54CarHunW-19
58JetPos-15
58Top-218
Rand, Ian
95BelGiaTI-24
96BelGiaTI-7
Rand, Kevin
85AlbYanT-27
89EasLeaDDP-DD49
Randa, Joe
91EugEmeC-14
91EugEmeP-3736
92AppFoxC-1
92AppFoxF-995
92BasCitRF-3852
92Bow-560
92ClaFS7-11
92MidLeaATI-34
92ProFS7-78
92UppDecML-325
93Bow-237
93ClaFS7-240
93ClaGolF-5
93ExcFS7-177
93MemChiF-383
93StaCluRoy-20
94AriFalLS-16
94Bow-199
94Cla-89
94ExcFS7-72
94OmaRoyF-1231
94UppDecML-75
94UppDecML-96
95ColCho-14
95ColChoGS-14
95ColChoSS-14
95Exc-62
95FleUpd-48
95Sel-180
95SelArtP-180
95SelCer-121
95SelCerMG-121
95SigRoo-43
95SigRooSig-43
95StaClu-532
95StaCluMOP-532
95StaCluSTWS-532
95Sum-139
95SumNthD-139
95Top-637
95UC3-107
95UC3ArtP-107
95UppDec-243
95UppDecED-243
95UppDecEDG-243
95UppDecML-31
96Cir-47
96CirRav-47
96ColCho-577
96ColCho-652
96ColChoGS-577
96ColChoGS-652
96ColChoSS-577
96ColChoSS-652
96FleUpd-U43
96FleUpdTC-U43
96LeaSigA-189
96LeaSigAG-189
96LeaSigAS-189
96RoyPol-23
96Sco-268
96StaClu-450
96StaCluMOP-450
96UppDec-353
97Cir-61
97CirRav-61
97ColCho-133
97ColCho-429
97Don-349
97DonLim-50
97DonLimLE-50
97DonPreP-349
97DonPrePGold-349
97Fle-120
97Fle-680
97FleTif-120
97FleTif-680
97Lea-15
97LeaFraM-15
97LeaFraMDC-15
97NewPin-90
97NewPinAP-90
97NewPinMC-90
97NewPinPP-90
97Pac-109
97PacLigB-109
97PacSil-109
97SP-143
97StaClu-271
97StaCluMOP-271
97Top-216
97Ult-399
97UltGolME-399
97UltPlaME-399
97UppDec-89
95UppDecMLFS-31
Randahl, Rick
81TacTigT-2
Randall, Bob
74AlbDukTI-78
74AlbDukTI-14
75AlbDukC-6
75IntLeaASB-24
75PacCoaLAB-24
77BurCheD-52
77Top-578
78Top-363
78TwiFriP-15
79Top-58
79TwiFriP-22
80OPC-90
80TolMudHT-2
80Top-162
Randall, Mark
89MarPhiS-26
90ClePhiS-18
91SpaPhiC-12
91SpaPhiP-897
92ClePhiF-2057
92SpaPhiC-14
93ClePhiC-18
93ClePhiF-2682
Randall, Newton
09T206-459
Randall, Sap (James)
82RedPioT-8
83NasAngT-18
84EdmTraC-101
85EdmTraC-10
86MidAngP-20
87EdmTraP-2076
88BlaYNPRWL-29
88TriAAAP-46
88VanCanC-20
88VanCanP-765
Randall, Scott
96AshTouB-29
97Bow-379
97BowInt-379
Randle, Carl
88ButCopKSP-7
89GasRanP-1005
89GasRanS-19
90GasRanB-3
90GasRanP-2519
90GasRanS-19
91ChaRanC-9
91ChaRanP-1313
Randle, Len
71SenTealW-20
72Top-737
73OPC-378
73Top-378
74OPC-446
74Top-446
75OPC-259
75Top-259
76OPC-31
76SSP-266
76Top-31
76VenLeaS-90
77BurCheD-21
77Top-196
78Hos-102
78Kel-22
78MetDaiPA-20
78OPC-132
78Top-544
79OPC-236
79Top-454
81Don-485
81Fle-301
81MarPol-9
81Top-692
81TopTra-817
82Don-307
82Fle-516
82OPC-312
82Top-312
82TopSti-230
86RanGreT-8
87WatIndP-27
89PacSenL-11
89T/MSenL-88
89TopSenL-38
90EliSenL-13
90OrlSunRB-11
90SweBasG-53
91FouBal-13
91MetWIZ-323
91PacSenL-116
92YanWIZ7-131
93RanKee-35
Randle, Michael
87KenTwiP-3
88CalLeaACLC-37
88VisOakCLC-147
88VisOakP-85
89OrlTwiB-21
89OrlTwiP-1339
90OrlSunRP-1097
90OrlSunRS-15
Randle, Randy
86OscAstP-20
87OscAstP-5
88ModA'sCLC-77
89NewBriRSP-618
89NewBriRSS-17
90NewBriRSB-19
90NewBriRSP-1328
90NewBriRSS-17
91LinDriAA-470
91NewBriRSLD-470
91NewBriRSP-360
Randolph, Bob
81LynSaiT-26
83ChaLooT-13
Randolph, Carl
94OneYanC-30
Randolph, Ed
96WisTimRB-18
Randolph, Scott
87SalAngP-29
Randolph, Steve
96GreBatB-20
Randolph, Tommy
86DavLipB-18
Randolph, Willie
76OPC-592
76SSP-584
76Top-592
76TopTra-592T
77BurCheD-175
77OPC-110
77Top-359
77YanBurK-13
78Hos-89
78OPC-228
78SSP270-27
78Top-411
78Top-620
78YanBurK-13
78YanSSPD-27
79OPC-125
79RawActT-1
79Top-250
79YanBurK-13
79YanPicA-30
80OPC-239
80Top-460
81AllGamPI-15
81Don-345
81Fle-109
81FleStiC-107
81OPC-60
81PerAll-16
81Top-60
81TopScr-36
81TopSti-108
81TopSti-242
81TopSupHT-70
82Don-461
82Fle-49
82FleSta-121
82OPC-37
82OPC-159
82OPC-213
82Top-548
82Top-569
82Top-570
82TopSti-219
83AllGamPI-14
83Don-283
83Fle-393
83FleSta-157
83FleSti-44
83OPC-140
83Top-140
83TopSti-95
83YanRoyRD-9
84AllGamPI-105
84Don-417
84Fle-137
84FunFooP-20
84Nes792-360
84OPC-360
84Top-360
84TopSti-324
84TopTif-360
85AllGamPI-15
85Don-92
85Fle-140
85Lea-83
85OPC-8
85PolMet-Y1
85Top-765
85TopSti-312
85TopTif-765
86BasStaB-87
86Don-16
86Don-92
86DonSupD-16
86Fle-115
86Lea-16
86OPC-332
86Top-276
86Top-455
86TopSti-305
86TopTat-15
86TopTif-276
86TopTif-455
86YanTCM-27
87Don-154
87DonOpeD-246
87Fle-109
87FleBasA-35
87FleGlo-109
87Lea-58
87OPC-377
87RedFolSB-2
87SpoTeaP-7
87Top-701
87TopSti-302
87TopTif-701
88Don-228
88DonAll-3
88DonBasB-108
88DonPop-3
88DonReaBY-228
88Dra-18
88Fle-218
88FleBasA-32
88FleBasM-28
88FleGlo-218
88FleMin-42
88FleStiC-50
88Lea-162
88Nes-22
88OPC-210
88PanSti-153
88PanSti-228
88Sco-266
88ScoBoxC-3
88ScoGlo-266
88Spo-47
88SpoGam-6
88StaLinAl-24
88StaLinY-11
88Top-210
88Top-387
88Top-459
88TopBig-76
88TopGloA-3
88TopGloS-42
88TopMinL-28
88TopSti-162
88TopSti-294
88TopStiB-37
88TopTif-210
88TopTif-387
88TopTif-459
88TopUKM-59
88TopUKMT-59
89Bow-344
89BowTif-344
89DodMot-10
89DodPol-8
89DodSmoG-57
89DodStaSV-11
89Don-395
89DonBasB-148
89DonTra-8
89Fle-265
89FleGlo-265
89FleUpd-93
89OPC-244
89PanSti-405
89RedFolSB-92
89Sco-45
89ScoRoo-41T
89Top-519
89Top-635
89TopBig-244
89TopSti-309
89TopTif-519
89TopTif-635
89TopTra-100T
89TopTraT-100T
89UppDec-237
89UppDec-777
90Bow-90
90BowTif-90
90ClaBlu-122
90ClaYel-T71
90DodPol-12

90DodTar-648
90Don-19
90Don-250
90DonBesA-110
90DonSupD-19
90Fle-406
90FleCan-406
90Lea-345
90OPC-25
90PanSti-279
90PubSti-16
90Sco-395
90Sco100S-4
90ScoRoo-51T
90Spo-175
90Top-25
90TopBig-43
90TopCoi-55
90TopSti-66
90TopTif-25
90TopTra-100T
90TopTraT-100T
90UppDec-183
90UppDec-704
90VenSti-417
91Bow-46
91BreMilB-21
91BrePol-19
91Don-217
91Don-766
91Fle-22
91FleUpd-33
91Lea-419
91OPC-525
91PanFreS-193
91Sco-194
91ScoRoo-35T
91StaClu-545
91Stu-74
91Top-525
91TopDesS-525
91TopMic-525
91TopTif-525
91TopTra-95T
91TopTraT-95T
91TopTriH-A10
91UltUpd-32
91UppDec-421
91UppDec-720
92Bow-681
92Cla1-T74
92ClaGam-169
92DodStaTA-28
92Don-625
92Fle-186
92Lea-240
92MetColP-9
92MetKah-12
92OPC-116
92OPCPre-67
92PanSti-36
92Pin-382
92Sco-30
92ScoRoo-35T
92StaClu-890
92Top-116
92TopGol-116
92TopGolW-116
92TopMic-116
92TopTra-90T
92TopTraG-90T
92Ult-536
92UppDec-211
92UppDec-795
92YanWIZ7-132
92YanWIZ8-153
92YanWIZA-60
93Don-644
93Fle-479
93PacSpa-200
93Sco-613
93Sel-195
93Top-324
93TopGol-324
93TopInaM-324
93TopMic-324
93UppDec-419
93UppDecGold-419
94BreMilB-69
96MetMod-8

Ranew, Merritt
62Top-156
62TopVen-156
63Col45'JP-8
64Top-78
64TopVen-78
66OPC-62
66Top-62A
66Top-62B
66TopVen-62
83Pil69G-31
89AstCol4S-11

Ranger, Rowdy
91GasRanC-30

Rangers, Texas
69FleCloS-23
69FleCloS-40
72Top-668
73OPC-7
73OPCBTC-24
73Top-7
73TopBluTC-24
74OPC-184
74OPCTC-24
74Top-184
74TopStaA-24
74TopTeaC-24
78Top-659
83FleSta-249
83FleSti-NNO
87SpoTeaL-1
88PanSti-467
88RedFolSB-123
90PubSti-640
90RedFolSB-106
90VenSti-539
93RanKee-SP1
94ImpProP-13
94Sco-329
94ScoGolR-329
95PanSti-153
96FleRan-19
96PanSti-235
94HudValRC-29

Rannow, John
86EveGiaC-19
86EveGiaPC-22
87CliGiaP-10

Ransom, Gene
82MadMusF-9
83MadMusF-18

Ransom, Jeff
81PhoGiaVNB-22
83PhoGiaBHN-5
87TolMudHP-24
87TolMudHT-11

Rantz, Mike
83IdaFalAT-24

Raper, Ron
88CapCodPPaLP-37

Rapp, Craig
91IdaFalBP-4327
91IdaFalBSP-20

Rapp, Earl
49RemBre-23
50RemBre-21
53MotCoo-30
75Gia195T-23

Rapp, Goldie (Joe)
20NatCarE-82
21Exh-138
21Nei-104
22E120-205
22W572-81
22W573-104
23WilChoV-128

Rapp, Pat (Patrick)
90CliGiaB-23
90CliGiaP-2547
90ProAaA-117
91CalLeLA-39
91Cla/Bes-275
91SanJosGC-20
91SanJosGP-9
92DonRoo-99
92PhoFirF-2821
92PhoFirS-394
92SkyAAAF-180
93ClaFS7-247
93EdmTraF-1134
93Fle-429
93MarPub-19
93Top-791
93TopGol-791
93TopInaM-791
93TopMic-791
94ColC-236
94ColChoGS-236
94ColChoSS-236
94Fle-473
94Pin-189
94PinArtP-189
94PinMusC-189
94Sco-310
94ScoGolR-310
94StaClu-606
94StaCluFDI-606
94StaCluGR-606
94StaCluMOP-606
94StaCluT-65
94StaCluTFDI-65
94Top-227
94TopGol-227
94TopSpa-227
94Ult-496
95ColCho-304
95ColChoGS-304
95ColChoSE-131
95ColChoSEGS-131
95ColChoSESS-131
95ColChoSS-304
95Don-121
95DonPreP-121
95Fle-340
95Lea-142
95Pac-176
95Pin-198
95PinArtP-198
95PinMusC-198
95Sco-492
95ScoGolR-492
95ScoPlaTS-492
95StaClu-364
95StaCluMOP-364
95StaCluSTWS-364
95StaCluVR-191
95Top-497
95TopCyb-287
95Ult-166
95UltGolM-166
95UppDec-356
95UppDecED-356
95UppDecEDG-356
96ColCho-558
96ColChoGS-558
96ColChoSS-558
96Don-392
96DonPreP-392
96EmoXL-189
96Fla-267
96Fle-393
96FleTif-393
96LeaSigA-190
96LeaSigAG-190
96LeaSigAS-190
96MetUni-168
96MetUniP-168
96Pac-72
96Sco-481
96StaClu-41
96StaClu-248
96StaCluMOP-41
96StaCluMOP-248
95StaCluVRMC-191
96Top-54
96Ult-480
96UltGolM-480
96UppDec-338
97ColCho-346
97Fle-334
97FleTif-334
97Sco-441
97ScoHobR-441
97ScoResC-441
97ScoShoS-441
97ScoShoSAP-441

Rapp, Vern
77Car5-20
77CarTeal-19
77Top-183
78Top-324
79ExpPos-20
80ExpPos-24
82ExpPos-32
83ExpPos-19
83ExpStu-3
84RedEnq-32
84TopTra-95T
84TopTraT-95T

Rappoli, Paul
91ElmPioC-12
91ElmPioP-3285
92LynRedSC-10
92LynRedSF-2922
93NewBriRSF-1235
94SarRedSC-23
94SarRedSF-1967
96TreThuB-25

Rariden, Bill (William A.)
09ColChiE-234
12ColRedB-234
12ColTinT-234
14CraJacE-137
15CraJacE-137
15SpoNewM-141
16ColE13-136
16FleBreD-75
16SpoNewM-141
17HolBreD-81
20RedWorCP-15
88PacEigMO-86
94ConTSN-1024
94ConTSNB-1024

Raschi, Vic (Victor)
47Exh-183
47PM1StaP1-168
48BluTin-32
48YanTeal-22
49Bow-35
50Bow-100
51BerRos-C4
51Bow-25
52BerRos-50
52Bow-37
52StaCalL-70D
52StaCalS-84A
53BowC-27
53ExhCan-5
54Bow-33A
54Bow-33B
54CarHunW-18
55A'sRodM-29
55Bow-185
55CarHunW-18
74LauAllG-48
75JohMiz-20
76A'sRodMC-19
79TCM50-186
83YanASFY-34
88PacLegI-70
90BasWit-53
92YanWIZA-61

Rascon, Rene
95ElmPioTI-22
95ElmPioUTI-22
96KanCouCTI-22

Rash, Joshua
93GreFalDSP-7
94YakBeaC-13
94YakBeaF-3864

Rashid, Ralph
93PeoChiC-27

Rasmus, Tony
86TriTriC-191
87SalAngP-14

Rasmussen, Dennis
81HolMilT-25
83ColCliT-8
84ColCliP-19
84ColCliT-25
84Don-446
85Don-518
85Fle-141
85Lea-48
85Top-691
85TopTif-691
86Don-336
86Top-301
86TopTif-301
86YanTCM-12
87ClaGam-87
87Don-175
87DonOpeD-247
87Fle-110
87FleExcS-35
87FleGamW-35
87FleGlo-110
87FleMin-86
87FleStiC-95
87Lea-260
87OPC-364
87Spo-71A
87Spo-71B
87SpoTeaP-7
87Top-555
87TopMinL-66
87TopSti-303
87TopTif-555
88Don-575
88Fle-246
88FleGlo-246
88FleUpd-126
88FleUpdG-126
88Sco-560
88ScoGlo-560
88StaLinRe-17
88Top-135
88TopSti-145
88TopTif-135
88TopTra-91T
88TopTraT-91T
89Bow-450
89BowTif-450
89ClaLigB-86
89Don-559
89Fle-314
89FleGlo-314
89OPC-32
89PadCok-12
89PadMag-17
89PanSti-195
89Sco-562
89Spo-212
89Top-32
89TopTif-32
89UppDec-645
90Bow-205
90BowTif-205
90Don-420
90Fle-165
90FleCan-165
90Lea-471
90OPC-449
90PadCok-14
90PadMag-4
90PubSti-56
90Sco-129
90Top-449
90TopTif-449
90UppDec-594
90VenSti-418
91Don-458
91Fle-539
91OPC-774
91PadMag-2
91PadSmo-27
91Sco-457
91StaClu-169
91StaCluP-34
91Top-774
91TopDesS-774
91TopMic-774
91TopTif-774
91Ult-309
91UppDec-230
92Don-245
92Fle-617
92OPC-252
92RocRedWS-463
92Sco-536
92StaClu-749
92StaCluECN-749
92Top-252
92TopGol-252
92TopGolW-252
92TopMic-252
92UppDec-439
92YanWIZ8-154
93Don-778
93Sco-392
93StaCluRoy-12
94PhoFirF-1518
96ButCopKB-5

Rasmussen, Eric (Harold)
75TulOil7-11
76OPC-182
76SSP-296
76Top-182
77Car5-21
77CarTeal-20
77Top-404
78PadFamF-23
78Top-281
79Top-57
80Top-531
81Don-123
81Fle-497
81Top-342
83Car-24
83Top-594

84Nes792-724
84OPC-377
84Top-724
84TopTif-724
84TucTorC-49
86MiaMarP-21
86RocRedWP-17
87RocRedWP-8
87RocRedWT-8
88WatIndP-686
89CanIndB-11
89CanIndP-1308
89CanIndS-2
89PacSenL-107
90EliSenL-76
96FtMyeMB-3
Rasmussen, Jim
81OklCit8T-25
82OklCit8T-16
82OklCit8T-18
82ReaPhiT-7
84NasSouTI-18
87HawIsIP-11
Rasmussen, Mark
87HawRai-3
Rasmussen, Nate
94GreFalDSP-18
95YakBeaTI-26
Rasmussen, Neil
73CedRapAT-10
75BurBeeT-20
77HolMilT-20
78HolMilT-18
Rasp, Ronnie
88WytCubP-2001
89ChaWheB-17
89ChaWheP-1764
90PeoChiTI-27
90WinSpiTI-13
Ratekin, Mark
91BoiHawC-28
91BoiHawP-3877
92QuaCitRBC-4
92QuaCitRBF-808
92StaCluD-148
93PalSprAC-18
93PalSprAF-68
94Bow-647
94MidAngOHP-24
95MidAngOHP-27
97MidAngOHP-25
Rath, Fred
96ForWayWB-21
96MidLeaAB-31
Rath, Fred Helsher
77FriOneYW-35
Rath, Gary
92MisStaB-36
93MisStaB-37
94StaCluDP-20
94StaCluDPFDI-20
95BowBes-B58
95BowBesR-B58
95SanAntMTI-19
95SPML-78
95TopTra-88T
96BesAutS-78
96BesAutSA-58
96Bow-290
96Top-429
Rath, Maurice
09ColChiE-235
12ColRedB-235
12ColTinT-235
12T207-155
19W514-57
20RedWorCP-16
88PacEigMO-85
Rathbun, Jason
94GreBatF-471
95TamYanYI-21
97GreBatC-16
Rather, Dody
86FloStaLAP-39
86OscAstP-21
87ColAstP-17
Rathjen, Dennis
80CliGiaT-2
Ratliff, Chris
95BurBeeTI-18
Ratliff, Danny
86StoPorP-22
Ratliff, Daryl
89PriPirS-15
90AugPirP-2478
90CMC-724
91CarLeaAP-CAR36
91SalBucC-12
91SalBucP-966
92Bow-71
92CarMudF-1194
92CarMudS-139
92SkyAA F-65
93CarMudF-2069
93CarMudTI-16
93ClaFS7-289
94SalBucC-17
Ratliff, Jon
93GenCubC-1
93GenCubF-3172
94Bow-334
94Cla-65
94ClaGolF-52
94ClaGolN1PLF-LP12
94ClaGolREF-RE12
94ClaTriF-T13
94DayCubC-20
94DayCubF-2350
94ExcFS7-166
94Pin-437
94PinArtP-437
94PinMusC-437
94Sco-454
94ScoGolR-454
94Top-739
94TopGol-739
94TopSpa-739
94UppDecML-231
95SPML-31
96BesAutS-79
96IowCubB-30
95OrlCubF-8
Ratliff, Kelly Eugene
65Top-553
67AstTeal2-21
Ratliff, Paul
63Top-549
70OPC-267
70Top-267
71OPC-607
71Top-607
94BreMilB-70
Ratto, Len
49SolSunP-9
Ratzer, Steve
81ExpPos-11
82TidTidT-21
Rau, Doug
73OPC-602
73Top-602
74OPC-64
74Top-64
75OPC-269
75Top-269
76LinSup-119
76OPC-124
76SSP-71
76Top-124
77BurCheD-149
77Kel-11
77OPC-128
77Top-421
78OPC-24
78SSP270-78
78Top-641
79DodBlu-10
79Kel-56
79OPC-178
79Top-347
80DodPol-31
80Top-527
81Fle-133
81RedPioT-9
81Top-174
81TopTra-818
90DodTar-649
Raub, Tommy
11SpoLifCW-297
Raubolt, Art
86LakTigP-19
Rauch, Bob
91MetWIZ-324
Rauch, Rocky (Al)
78WatIndT-17
Rauer, Troy
96SouOreTI-4
96WesMicWB-22
Rauth, Chris
85LitFalMT-8
86ColMetP-20
87LynMetP-15
89JacMetGS-24
90KnoBluJB-16
92TidTidF-895
92TidTidS-569
Rautzhan, Lance (Clarence G.)
75WatDodT-17
78Top-709
79HolMilT-25
79OPC-193
79Top-373
80VanCanT-9
90DodTar-650
94BreMilB-71
Ravelo, Graciano
76VenLeaS-110
80VenLeaS-183
93LinVenB-72
Raven, Luis
91BoiHawC-3
91BoiHawP-3897
92PalSprAC-15
92PalSprAF-850
93MidAngF-334
94MidAngF-2448
94MidAngOHP-25
94VenLinU-9
95Exc-24
95LinVen-82
95MidAngOHP-28
95UppDecML-76
96SigRooOJTP-T4
97MidAngOHP-26
95UppDecMLFS-76
Ravitz, David
93YakBeaC-22
93YakBeaF-3891
Rawdon, Chris
86ElmPioRSP-16
Rawitzer, Kevin
93EugEmeF-3855
94ExcFS7-73
94MidLeaAF-MDW24
94RocRoyC-18
94RocRoyF-562
95WilBluRTI-36
96WicWraB-10
Rawley, Billy
83CedRapRT-6
Rawley, Shane
75WesPalBES-21
79OPC-30
79Top-74
80OPC-368
80Top-723
81Don-167
81MarPol-16
81OPC-51
81Top-423
81TopSti-129
82Don-352A
82Don-352B
82Fle-517
82Top-197
82TopTra-95T
83AllGamPI-85
83Don-513
83Fle-394
83Top-592
84Don-295
84Fle-138
84FleUpd-94
84Nes792-254
84OPC-254
84Top-254
84TopTif-254
85AllGamPI-174
85Don-599
85DonHig-39
85Fle-263
85Lea-31
85OPC-169
85PhiCIG-15
85PhiTas-9
85PhiTas-22
85Top-636
85TopTif-636
86BasStaB-88
86Don-233
86Fle-446
86Lea-109
86OPC-361
86PhiCIG-6
86PhiTas-28
86Top-361
86TopSti-123
86TopTif-361
87Don-83
87DonAll-56
87DonOpeD-159
87Fle-180
87FleGlo-180
87FleRecS-31
87FleStiC-96
87Lea-139
87OPC-239
87PhiTas-28
87RedFolSB-124
87Spo-181
87SpoTeaP-6
87StuPan-9
87Top-771
87TopSti-120
87TopTif-771
88Don-13
88Don-83
88DonBasB-240
88DonSupD-13
88Fle-311
88FleGlo-311
88FleHotS-32
88FleMin-100
88FleStiC-109
88FleSupBC-C4
88FleWaxBC-C8
88Lea-13
88Lea-92
88OPC-66
88PanSti-352
88PhiTas-19
88Sco-375
88ScoGlo-375
88Spo-51
88StaLinPh-13
88Top-66
88Top-406
88TopGloS-45
88TopMinL-65
88TopSti-121
88TopTif-66
88TopTif-406
89Bow-151
89BowTif-151
89Don-251
89Fle-579
89FleGlo-579
89FleUpd-44
89OPC-24
89Sco-170
89Top-494
89TopSti-118
89TopTif-494
89TopTra-101T
89TopTraT-101T
89UppDec-427
89UppDec-786
90Don-537
90Fle-384
90FleCan-384
90OPC-101
90PubSti-336
90Sco-71
90Top-101
90TopTif-101
90UppDec-438
90VenSti-419
92YanWIZ8-155
Rawlings, John
20GasAmeMBD-31
21E121So1-77
21E121So8-74
21KoBreWSI-18
22E120-190
22W573-105
22W575-101
23W501-61
23W503-26
23WilChoV-129
93ConTSN-699
Ray, Art
83AleDukT-9
Ray, Bregg
84ButCopKT-21
Ray, Glenn
81ChaRoyT-7
Ray, Jay
86BakDodP-23
88VerBeaDS-21
Ray, Jim F.
67Ast-25
68DexPre-37
68Top-539
69Top-257
70MLBOffS-124
70OPC-113
70Top-113
71MLBOffS-91
71MLBOffS-249
71OPC-242
71Top-242
72MilBra-135
72Top-603
73OPC-313
73Top-313
74OPC-458
74Tig-10
74Top-458
74TopTra-458T
75CedRapGT-16
75OPC-89
75Top-89
82AstAstI-2
87AstShowSTh-19
Ray, Johnny
80ColAstT-7
81TucTorT-10
82Don-528
82Fle-492
82Top-291
82TopTra-96T
83AllGamPI-106
83Don-437
83Fle-317
83FleSta-158
83FleSti-76
83Kel-24
83OPC-149
83Top-149
83TopSti-327
84AllGamPI-14
84Don-308
84Fle-260
84FunFooP-69
84Nes792-387
84Nes792-537
84NesDreT-13
84OPC-323
84OPC-387
84Top-387
84Top-537
84TopGloS-5
84TopRubD-9
84TopSti-134
84TopSti-186
84TopStiB-7
84TopTif-387
84TopTif-537
85AllGamPI-103
85Don-186
85DonActA-50
85Fle-473
85FleStaS-43
85GenMilS-7
85Lea-212
85OPC-96
85Pir-16
85ThoMcAD-40
85Top-96
85TopMin-96
85TopRubD-5
85TopSti-130
85TopTif-96
86Don-19
86Don-186
86DonHig-9
86DonSupD-19
86Fle-617
86FleStiC-93
86Lea-19
86OPC-37
86Top-615
86TopSti-124
86TopTat-4
86TopTif-615
87Don-144
87DonOpeD-162
87DonOpeD-163A
87Fle-618
87FleAwaW-31

87FleExcS-36
87FleGlo-618
87FleMin-87
87FleStiC-97
87KraFoo-14
87Lea-147
87OPC-291
87RedFolSB-51
87SmoNatL-8
87Spo-116
87Spo-121
87SpoTeaP-18
87StuPan-10
87Top-747
87TopGloS-55
87TopSti-135
87TopTif-747
88AngSmo-2
88Don-428
88DonBasB-171
88Fle-502
88FleGlo-502
88FleSlu-31
88Lea-260
88OPC-115
88Sco-254
88ScoGlo-254
88Spo-186
88StaLinAn-17
88Top-115
88TopBig-97
88TopTif-115
89AngSmo-20
89Bow-49
89BowTif-49
89CadEllD-42
89Don-12
89Don-331
89DonAll-25
89DonBasB-195
89DonSupD-12
89Fle-487
89FleBasA-33
89FleGlo-487
89FleHeroB-32
89OPC-109
89PanSti-292
89RedFolSB-93
89Sco-14
89ScoHot1S-99
89Spo-195
89Top-455
89TopBatL-18
89TopBig-7
89TopCoi-49
89TopHilTM-24
89TopMinL-50
89TopSti-182
89TopTif-455
89TopUKM-62
89TVSpoM-111
89UppDec-481
90AngSmo-14
90Bow-302
90BowTif-302
90ChaWheB-8
90ChaWheP-2240
90Don-234
90DonBesA-73
90Fle-143
90FleCan-143
90Lea-208
90OPC-334
90PanSti-33
90PubSti-378
90Sco-293
90Spo-82
90Top-334
90TopBatL-18
90TopBig-95
90TopSti-174
90TopTif-334
90UppDec-509
90VenSti-420
91ChaWheC-8
91ChaWheP-2885
91Don-622
91Fle-323
91OPC-273
91PanFreS-181
91PanSti-138
91Sco-31
91Top-273
91TopDesS-273
91TopMic-273
91TopTif-273
91UppDec-678
92CedRapRC-4
92ChaLooF-3817
92ChaLooS-193
92SkyAA F-86
93ChaLooF-2361
Ray, Ken
94RocRoyC-19
94RocRoyF-563
95Bow-38
95Exc-63
95WilBluRTI-24
96WicWraB-11
Ray, Larry
82TucTorT-10
83TucTorT-20
84TucTorC-70
86ColAstP-22
86SouLeaAJ-11
87VanCanP-1617
Ray, Rick
89UtiBluSP-31
91UtiBluSC-25
Ray, Steve
83GreHorT-11
Ray, T.
88AllandGN-34
Raybon, Shannon
86VisOakP-16
87VisOakP-27
88OrlTwiB-25
Raydon, Curt
59Top-305
60Top-49
60TopVen-49
Rayford, Floyd
78AngFamF-29
78SSP270-200
79SalLakCGT-20B
80RocRedWT-18
81RocRedWT-14
81RocRedWW-14
81Top-399
83RocRedWT-13
83Top-192
84Fle-334
84FleUpd-95
84Nes792-514
84Top-514
84TopTif-514
84TopTra-96T
84TopTraT-96T
85Don-576
85Fle-186
85OriHea-14
85Top-341
85TopTif-341
86Don-332
86Fle-283
86Lea-197
86Top-623
86TopTif-623
87OriFreB-6
87Top-426
87TopTif-426
88Sco-359
88ScoGlo-359
88Top-296
88TopTif-296
89ScrRedBC-22
89ScrRedBP-727
90CMC-248
90El PasDAGTI-39
90ScrRedBC-22
91LinDriAAA-500
91OriCro-375
91ScrRedBLD-500
91ScrRedBP-2556
92BatCliC-29
92BatCliF-3284
94BatCliC-28
94BatCliF-3464
Raymer, Fred
11SpoLifCW-298
Raymer, Greg
83MiaMarT-9
86JacExpT-12
Raymond, Bugs (Arthur)
09ColChiE-236
09RamT20-97
09SpoNewSM-35
09T206-298
11S74Sil-93
11SpoLifM-216
11T205-142
11TurRedT-113
12ColRedB-236
12ColTinT-236
12HasTriFT-69
Raymond, Claude
63Top-519
64Top-504
65OPC-48
65Top-48
66Top-586
67AstTeal2-22
67CokCapAs-4
67Top-364
68OPC-166
68Top-166
68TopVen-166
69Top-446
70DayDaiNM-132
70ExpPin-12
70MLBOffS-68
70OPC-268
70Top-268
71ExpPS-20
71MLBOffS-138
71OPC-202
71OPC-536
71Top-536
78TCM60I-46
86AstMot-4
87AstSer1-19
87AstShoSTw-13
92Nab-23
92UppDecS-21
93ExpDonM-26
Raymond, Paul
43ParSpo-63
Raymondi, Michael
96HudValRB-21
Raynor, Mark
95BatCliTI-27
96PieBolWB-22
Raynor, Tom
92ForLauYTI-25
93PriWilCC-30
Raziano, Barry
75IntLeaASB-25
75PacCoaLAB-25
75SalLakCC-15
Raziano, Michael S.
88SprCarB-16
Razjigaev, Rudy
93BoiHawC-23
93BoiHawF-3916
93Top-633
93TopGol-633
93TopInaM-633
93TopMic-633
Razook, Mark
87AncGlaP-24
89WauTimGS-12
89WilBilS-17
90CMC-756
90WilBilB-19
90WilBilP-1066
90WilBilS-20
Razorback, The
90ArkRaz-11
Razorbacks, Arkansas
90ArkRaz-31
Rea, Clarke
91NiaFalRC-8
91NiaFalRP-3638
92LetMouSP-10
93FayGenC-20
93FayGenF-133
Rea, Shayne
90EugEmeGS-24
91AppFoxC-11
91AppFoxP-1717
91Cla/Bes-250
92AppFoxC-17
92AppFoxF-984
Read, James
88PacEigMO-11
Reade, Bill
80UtiBluJT-30
Reade, Curtis
81VerBeaDT-16
Ready, Jerry
78TucTorC-48
Ready, Randy
81BurBeeT-17
82ElPasDT-7
84BrePol-2
84TopTra-97T
84TopTraT-97T
85BrePol-2
85Fle-592
86BrePol-2
86Don-481
86Fle-498
86Top-209
86TopTif-209
87FleUpd-100
87FleUpdG-100
87PadBohHB-5
87TopTra-97T
87TopTraT-97T
88Don-264
88Fle-594
88FleGlo-594
88OPC-151
88PadCok-5
88PadSmo-23
88PanSti-407
88Sco-512
88ScoGlo-512
88StaLinPa-10
88Top-426
88TopBig-102
88TopTif-426
89Don-365
89DonBasB-215
89Fle-315
89FleGlo-315
89OPC-82
89PadCok-13
89PanSti-201
89PhiTas-45
89Sco-426
89ScoRoo-60T
89Top-551
89TopSti-106
89TopTif-551
89TopTra-102T
89TopTraT-102T
89UppDec-474
90Don-396
90El PasDAGTI-13
90Fle-571
90FleCan-571
90Lea-500
90OPC-356
90PanSti-311
90PhiTas-26
90PubSti-57
90Sco-376
90Top-356
90TopBig-150
90TopSti-120
90TopTif-356
90UppDec-404
90VenSti-421
91Bow-495
91Don-148
91Fle-410A
91Fle-410B
91Lea-82
91OPC-137
91PanFreS-104
91PhiMed-33
91Sco-615
91StaClu-265
91Top-137
91TopDesS-137
91TopMic-137
91TopTif-137
91Ult-271
91UppDec-540
92AthMot-25
92Don-179
92Fle-542
92Lea-246
92OPC-63
92Sco-59
92ScoProP-13
92Stu-228
92Top-63
92TopGol-63
92TopGolW-63
92TopMic-63
92Ult-427
92UppDec-408
94BreMilB-72
94Fle-547
95Phi-25
95PhiMel-19
Reagan, Edward
09T206-510
10CouT21-55
Reagan, Kyle
89BilMusP-2047
Reagan, Ronald
84WilMay-39
86TopRos-88
Reagans, Javan
88JamExpP-1917
Reames, Britt
95NewJerCTI-23
96MidLeaAB-22
96PeoChiB-25
Reames, Jay
96NewJerCB-22
Reams, Ronald
90MedHatBJB-22
91MyrBeaHC-25
91MyrBeaHP-2959
92MyrBeaHC-9
92MyrBeaHF-2212
93KnoSmoF-1264
Reardon, Beans
94ConTSN-1188
94ConTSNB-1188
Reardon, Jeff
77LynMetT-24
79TidTidT-5
81Don-156
81ExpPos-12
81Fle-335
81OPC-79
81Top-456
81TopTra-819
82Don-547
82ExpHygM-17
82ExpPos-33
82Fle-204
82FleSta-37
82OPC-123
82OPCPos-23
82Top-667
83Don-194
83ExpPos-20
83ExpStu-5
83Fle-293
83FleSta-159
83FleSti-267
83OPC-290
83Top-290
83TopSti-254
84Don-279
84ExpPos-24
84ExpStu-13
84Fle-283
84FleSti-71
84JacMetF-10
84Nes792-595
84OPC-116
84Top-595
84TopSti-89
84TopTif-595
85Don-331
85Fle-407
85Lea-126
85OPC-375
85OPCPos-12
85Top-375
85TopMin-375
85TopSti-85
85TopTif-375
86Don-209
86DonAll-33
86DonHig-14
86ExpProPa-13
86ExpProPo-11
86Fle-257
86FleLimE-35
86FleSlu-26
86FleStiC-94
86GenMilB-6F
86Lea-214
86OPC-35
86SevCoi-E10
86Spo-119
86Top-35
86Top-711
86Top3-D-20
86TopGaloC-10
86TopGloS-55
86TopSti-76

86TopSup-6
86TopTat-22
86TopTif-35
86TopTif-711
87ClaGam-94
87Don-98
87DonAll-52
87DonWaxBC-PC11
87Fle-329
87FleGlo-329
87FleLimE-34
87FleMin-88
87FleSlu-33
87FleStiC-98
87FleUpd-101
87FleUpdG-101
87KraFoo-40
87Lea-143
87OPC-165
87RedFolSB-65
87Spo-77
87SpoTeaP-17
87Top-165
87TopGloS-15
87TopMinL-18
87TopSti-81
87TopTif-165
87TopTra-98T
87TopTraT-98T
88Don-122
88DonBasB-242
88Fle-20
88FleAwaW-31
88FleBasA-33
88FleGlo-20
88FleMin-37
88FleSlu-32
88FleStiC-46
88FleTeaL-28
88Nes-27
88OPC-99
88PanSti-133
88RedFolSB-73
88Sco-91
88ScoGlo-91
88Spo-53
88StaLinTw-16
88Top-425
88TopBig-10
88TopMinL-24
88TopRitTM-28
88TopSti-14
88TopSti-280
88TopTif-425
88TwiMasBD-4
88TwiSmoC-4
88TwiTeal-26
89Bow-148
89BowTif-148
89CadEllD-43
89Don-155
89DonAll-24
89DonBasB-242
89Fle-125
89FleGlo-125
89FleSup-34
89OPC-86
89PanSti-382
89RedFolSB-94
89Sco-305
89ScoHot1S-24
89Spo-168
89Top-775
89TopBasT-136
89TopGloS-54
89TopMinL-63
89TopSti-8
89TopSti-284
89TopStiB-33
89TopTif-775
89UppDec-596
89Woo-17
90Bow-265
90BowTif-265
90ClaBlu-101
90ClaYel-T55
90Don-119
90DonBesA-72
90Fle-385
90FleCan-385
90FleUpd-75
90Lea-276
90OPC-235
90OPCBoxB-K
90PanSti-108
90PubSti-293
90PubSti-337
90RedFolSB-76
90RedSoxP-16
90Sco-522
90ScoRoo-17T
90Spo-37
90Top-235
90TopBig-285
90TopMag-93
90TopSti-6
90TopSti-289
90TopTif-235
90TopTra-101T
90TopTraT-101T
90TopTVRS-15
90TopWaxBC-K
90UppDec-417
90UppDec-729
90VenSti-422
90VenSti-423
90Woo-17
91Bow-107
91Don-369
91Fle-109
91Lea-252
91MetWIZ-325
91OPC-605
91OPCBoxB-M
91OPCPre-98
91PanFreS-272
91PanSti-218
91RedFolS-76
91RedSoxP-17
91Sco-164
91StaClu-354
91StaCluMO-25
91Stu-19
91Top-605
91TopDesS-605
91TopMic-605
91TopTif-605
91TopWaxBC-M
91Ult-40
91UppDec-418
91USPlaCA-5D
91Woo-17
92Bow-475
92Don-89
92DonUpd-U9
92Fle-46
92FleUpd-71
92FleUpdH-3
92Hig5-9
92Lea-151
92OPC-3
92OPC-182
92PepDieM-8
92Pin-158
92RedSoxDD-24
92Sco-58
92Sco100S-5
92ScoRoo-46T
92StaClu-657
92StaCluD-149
92StaCluNC-657
92Stu-137
92SunSee-1
92Top-3
92Top-182
92TopGol-3
92TopGol-182
92TopGolW-3
92TopGolW-182
92TopMic-3
92TopMic-182
92Ult-20
92UppDec-501
93Don-739
93ExpDonM-11
93Fle-370
93FleFinE-18
93Lea-389
93OPC-342
93Pin-535
93RedKah-19
93Sco-514
93Sco-564
93Sel-362
93SelRoo-135T
93StaClu-161
93StaClu-602
93StaCluFDI-161
93StaCluFDI-602
93StaCluMO-21
93StaCluMOP-161
93StaCluMOP-602
93Top-475
93TopGol-475
93TopInaM-475
93TopMic-475
93Ult-333
93UppDec-541
93UppDecGold-541
93UppDecSH-HI15
94ColC-592
94ColChoGS-592
94ColChoSS-592
94Fle-420
94Pac-155
94Pin-521
94PinArtP-521
94PinMusC-521
94Sco-251
94ScoGolR-251
Reardon, Kenny
43ParSpo-66
Reaves, Scott
87UtiBluSP-20
88ClePhiS-20
88SpaPhiS-1
89ClePhiS-18
Reavis, Kelly
91OklStaC-19
Reay, Billy
43ParSpo-64
Reberger, Frank
69Top-637
70Gia-12
70MLBOffS-117
70OPC-103
70Top-103
71MLBOffS-262
71OPC-251
71Top-251
72Top-548
83NasAngT-21
84EdmTraC-242
85EdmTraC-23
86EdmTraP-23
87EdmTraP-2077
92SanJosGC-28
93MarPub-28
96VanCanB-2
Reboulet, James
83EriCarT-4
84SavCarT-10
86FloStaLAP-40
86St.PetCP-26
87ArkTraP-23
88BufBisC-17
88BufBisP-1470
88BufBisTI-7
Reboulet, Jeff
87OrlTwiP-15
88OrlTwiB-19
89OrlTwiP-1345
90LSUTigGM-4
90OrlSunRB-27
90OrlSunRP-1093
90OrlSunRS-16
91LinDriAAA-415
91PorBeaLD-415
91PorBeaP-1572
92DonRoo-100
92PorBeaS-417
93Don-179
93Fle-642
93PacSpa-525
93Sco-233
93StaClu-146
93StaCluFDI-146
93StaCluMOP-146
93Top-172
93TopGol-172
93TopInaM-172
93TopMic-172
93UppDec-733
93UppDecGold-733
94Don-85
94Fle-218
94Pac-366
94StaClu-183
94StaCluFDI-183
94StaCluGR-183
94StaCluMOP-183
94TopTra-123T
95ColCho-488
95ColChoGS-488
95ColChoSS-488
95Don-432
95DonPreP-432
95Fle-213
95Sco-545
95ScoGolR-545
95ScoPlaTS-545
95StaClu-137
95StaCluFDI-137
95StaCluMOP-137
95StaCluSTWS-137
95Top-359
96ColCho-607
96ColChoGS-607
96ColChoSS-607
96Don-512
96DonPreP-512
96Fle-174
96FleTif-174
96LeaSigEA-166
96Sco-440
97Pac-144
97PacLigB-144
97PacSil-144
Rech, Ed
82LynMetT-8
Rector, Bobby
95BurBeeTI-17
96SanJosGB-25
Red Birds, Columbus
36R31Pre-G22
38BasTabP-42
Red Sox, Boston
09MaxPubP-22
09SpoNewSM-82
13FatT20-1
35GouPreR-1
36R31Pre-G19A
36R31Pre-G19B
38BasTabP-43
46SpoExcW-10-3
51TopTea-1
56Top-111
57Top-171
58Top-312
59Top-248
60Top-537
60TopTat-65
61Top-373
61TopMagR-5
62GuyPotCP-2
62Top-334
63GadFunC-14
63Top-202
64Top-579
64TopTatI-2
65Top-403
66Top-259
66TopRubI-102
66TopVen-259
67Top-604
68LauWorS-9
68LauWorS-15
69FleCloS-3
69FleCloS-42
69TopStaA-3
70FleWorS-1
70FleWorS-9
70FleWorS-15
70FleWorS-64
70Top-563
71FleWorS-10
71FleWorS-14
71FleWorS-65
71OPC-386
71Top-386
71TopTat-15
72OPC-328
72Top-328
72TopCloT-26
73OPC-596
73OPCBTC-3
73Top-596
73TopBluTC-3
74OPC-567
74OPCTC-3
74Top-567
74TopStaA-3
74TopTeaC-3
78Top-424
83FleSta-227
83FleSti-NNO
87FleWaxBC-C5
87SpoTeaL-9
88PanSti-456
88RedFolSB-119
89FleWaxBC-C17
90PubSti-642
90RedFolSB-109
90VenSti-517
91PanCanT1-122
91PanCanT1-125
94ImpProP-2
94Sco-318
94ScoGolR-318
95PanSti-149
96FleRedS-19
96PanSti-139
Red Sox, Memphis
92NegLeaRLI-89
92NegLeaRLI-90
93NegLeaRL2-54
93NegLeaRL2-74
Red Sox, Pawtucket
87IntLeaAT-41
89PawRedSTI-30
90PawRedSDD-31
91PawRedSDD-31
93PawRedSDD-31
94PawRedSDD-31
95PawRedSDD-31
96PawRedSDD-30
97DunDonPPS-31
Red Stockings, Cincinnati
63GadFunC-16
90BasWit-90
94OriofB-19
94UppDecAH-101
94UppDecAH1-101
94UppDecAJ-43
94UppDecAJG-43
94UppDecMPC-NNO
Red Wings, Rochester
81RocRedWW-20
87IntLeaAT-44
88RocRedWGCP-1
88RocRedWGCP-33
88RocRedWGCP-34
88RocRedWGCP-35
88RocRedWGCP-36
Redd, Rick R.
88HarSenP-840
Redd, Ricky Joe
91MisStaB-41
92MisStaB-37
93MisStaB-38
Redd, Ulysses A.
93NegLeaRL2-33
Redding, Cannonball (Dick)
74LauOldTBS-25
86NegLeaF-112
90NegLeaS-3
Redding, Corey
95DavLipB-20
Redding, Mike
86KenTwiP-21
87VisOakP-16
88VisOakCLC-160
88VisOakP-93
89OrlTwiB-22
89OrlTwiP-1333
90OrlSunRB-19
90OrlSunRP-1081
90OrlSunRS-17
90StaFS7-47
Reddish, Mike
83NasSouTI-17
85ChaO'sT-10
86RocRedWP-18
Redfern, Pete
77Top-249
78Top-81
78TwiFriP-16
79Top-113
79TwiFriP-23
80Top-403
81Don-548
81Fle-560
81Top-714
82Don-51
82Fle-559
82Top-309
82TwiPos-24
83Don-256
83Fle-623

83Top-559
88AlaGolAA'TI-14
Redfield, Joe
86ChaOriW-23
87MidAngP-13
87TexLeaAF-12
88EdmTraC-20
88EdmTraP-555
89ScrRedBC-20
89ScrRedBP-731
90CMC-34
90DenZepC-9
90DenZepP-634
90ProAAAF-659
90TriAllGP-AAA25
91BufBisLD-41
91BufBisP-549
91LinDriAAA-41
92Bow-438
92BufBisBS-16
92BufBisF-335
92BufBisS-39
92Fle-563
92Sco-412
Redick, Kevin
86EveGiaC-6
86EveGiaPC-23
87CliGiaP-13
Redington, Thomas
88SumBraP-412
89BurBraP-1610
89BurBraS-17
90Bes-75
90GreBraB-5
90GreBraP-1137
90GreBraS-16
90StaFS7-95
91Cla/Bes-327
91LinDriAA-615
91WicWraLD-615
91WicWraP-2605
91WicWraRD-15
92BirBarF-2593
92BirBarS-87
92ClaFS7-32
92OPC-473
92Top-473
92TopGol-473
92TopGolW-473
92TopMic-473
94LakElsSC-14
94LakElsSF-1673
95AusFut-80
95LakElsSTI-19
Redman, Mark
95Bes-132
95BowBes-X2
95BowBesR-X2
95ForMyeMTI-9
95SPML-109
96BesAutSA-59
96Bow-382
96Exc-81
96FtMyeMB-8
96HarCitRCB-25
96Top-14
96TopPowB-14
97Bow-126
97BowBes-161
97BowBesAR-161
97BowBesR-161
97BowInt-126
97Top-494
Redman, Tim
87EriCarP-29
88HamRedP-1729
89HamRedS-22
90St.PetCS-19
91ArkTraP-1290
92LouRedF-1890
95NewJerCTI-24
Redmon, Glenn
74PhoGiaC-83
75PhoGiaC-8
75PhoGiaCK-13
76WilTomT-19
Redmond, Andre
89PriPirS-16
90WelPirP-25
91AugPirP-805
Redmond, Dan
87WatIndP-28
89CanIndB-9
Redmond, H. Wayne
71OPC-728
71Top-728
Redmond, Mike
93KanCouCC-17
93KanCouCF-919
94KanCouCC-20
94KanCouCF-166
94KanCouCTI-24
95PorSeaDTI-22
96PorSeaDB-22
93KanCouCTI-18
Reds, Cincinnati
09MaxPubP-24
13FatT20-12
20RedWorCP-25
38BasTabP-44
41HarHarW-30
41HarHarW-31
51TopTea-4
56Top-90A
56Top-90B
56Top-90C
57Top-322
58Top-428A
58Top-428B
59Top-111
59TopVen-111
60Top-164
60TopTat-57
60TopVen-164
61Top-249
61TopMagR-15
62GuyPotCP-5
62Top-465
63Top-63
64Top-403
64TopTatI-6
65Top-316
66OPC-59
66Top-59
66TopRubI-106
66TopVen-59
67Top-407
68LauWorS-16
68LauWorS-37
68Top-574
69FleCloS-7
69FleCloS-41
69TopStaA-7
70FleWorS-16
70FleWorS-36
70FleWorS-37
70OPC-544
70Top-544
71FleWorS-17
71FleWorS-37
71FleWorS-38
71FleWorS-68
71OPC-357
71Top-357
71TopTat-52
72Top-651
73OPC-641
73OPCBTC-7
73Top-641
73TopBluTC-7
74OPC-459
74OPCTC-7
74Top-459
74TopStaA-7
74TopTeaC-7
78Top-526
83FleSta-231
83FleSti-NNO
86JosHalC-5
87SpoTeaL-4
88PanSti-269
88PanSti-471
88RedFolSB-130
90PubSti-624
90RedFolSB-107
90TopMag-37
90VenSti-521
91FleWorS-8
91PanCanT1-117
91PanCanT1-128
91PanCanT1-131
91Woo-32
93TedWilPC-6
94ImpProP-17
94Sco-649
94ScoGolR-649
95PanSti-131
96PanSti-53
Redus, Gary
81WatRedT-15
82IndIndTI-17
83RedYea-2
83TopTra-94T
84AllGamPI-67
84Don-184
84DonActAS-16
84Fle-481
84Nes792-475
84OPC-231
84RedBor-2
84RedEnq-9
84Top-475
84TopRubD-20
84TopSti-52
84TopTif-475
85Don-306
85Fle-549
85IndIndTI-34
85Lea-47
85OPC-146
85Top-146
85TopRubD-20
85TopSti-49
85TopTif-146
86Don-306
86Fle-189
86FleUpd-94
86OPC-342
86PhiCIG-12
86PhiKel-3
86PhiTas-22
86Top-342
86TopTif-342
86TopTra-90T
86TopTraT-90T
87Don-288
87DonOpeD-229
87Fle-181
87FleGlo-181
87FleUpd-102
87FleUpdG-102
87OPC-42
87Top-42
87TopSti-119
87TopTif-42
87TopTra-99T
87TopTraT-99T
87WhiSoxC-24
88Don-370
88Fle-408
88FleGlo-408
88OPC-332
88PanSti-64
88Sco-443
88ScoGlo-443
88StaLinWS-15
88Top-657
88TopMinL-9
88TopTif-657
88WhiSoxC-24
89Bow-425
89BowTif-425
89Don-605
89Fle-218
89FleGlo-218
89OPC-281
89PirVerFJ-2
89Sco-177
89Top-281
89TopBig-131
89TopTif-281
89UppDec-419
90Bow-180
90BowTif-180
90Don-597
90Fle-476
90FleCan-476
90Lea-209
90OPC-507
90PanSti-331
90PirHomC-24
90PubSti-162
90Sco-14
90Top-507
90TopBig-52
90TopSti-127
90TopTif-507
90UppDec-248
90VenSti-424
91Bow-516
91Don-587
91Fle-47
91Lea-254
91OPC-771
91Sco-226
91StaClu-486
91Top-771
91TopDesS-771
91TopMic-771
91TopTif-771
91Ult-285
91UppDec-38
92Don-67
92Fle-564
92Lea-223
92OPC-453
92PirNatI-19
92Sco-303
92StaClu-524
92Top-453
92TopGol-453
92TopGolW-453
92TopMic-453
92Ult-560
92UppDec-519
93Don-516
93Fle-504
93Lea-426
93PacSpa-250
93RanKee-425
93StaCluR-14
93Ult-634
94Don-275
94Fle-318
94Lea-387
94Pac-626
94Sco-191
94ScoGolR-191
94StaClu-514
94StaCluFDI-514
94StaCluGR-514
94StaCluMOP-514
94StaCluT-264
94StaCluTFDI-264
94Top-108
94TopGol-108
94TopSpa-108
95Sco-103
95ScoGolR-103
95ScoPlaTS-103
Reece, Bob
78ExpPos-11
83WicAerDS-17
Reece, Jeff
86StoPorP-23
87WicPilRD-14
Reece, John
93DanBraC-19
93DanBraF-3633
Reece, Thad
83MadMusF-9
84AlbA'sT-5
85TacTigC-135
86TacTigP-18
87TacTigP-10
88MemChiB-24
90AlbDecGB-35
90CMC-195
90OmaRoyC-20
90OmaRoyP-74
90ProAAAF-609
Reed, Billy
89HigSchPLS-23
89WatDiaP-1788
89WatDiaS-23
90Bes-314
90WatDiaB-14
90WatDiaP-2379
91HigDesMC-9
91HigDesMP-2392
95HudValRTI-5
Reed, Bob E.
70OPC-207
70Top-207
71MLBOffS-404
71OPC-732
71Top-732
Reed, Bobby
88MisStaB-28
88MisStaB-33
90MisStaB-35
91LinDriAA-591
91TulDriLD-591
91TulDriP-2771
91TulDriTI-22
92Bow-522
92UppDecML-232
Reed, Brandon
94BriTigC-20
94BriTigF-3500
95Bes-19
95Bes-110
95FayGenTI-20
96Exc-52
96ExcSeaC-7
96JacSunB-24
96Top-431
97Bow-325
97BowInt-325
Reed, Brian
94ButCopKSP-8
95PeoChiTI-21
96StPetCB-26
Reed, Chris
91PriRedC-6
91PriRedP-3512
92BenMusSP-15
92BilMusF-3354
94ChaWheC-21
94ChaWheF-2702
96ChaLooB-23
Reed, Curt
82AppFoxF-12
83GleFalWST-9
Reed, Curtis
81HawIsIT-10
Reed, Darren
86AlbYanT-23
87AlbYanP-16
88MetColP-44
88TidTidCa-17
88TidTidCM-16
88TidTidP-1603
89MetColP-49
89TidTidC-17
89TidTidP-1957
90AlbDecGB-20
90CMC-376
90FleUpd-39
90MetColP-45
90ProAAAF-288
90TidTidC-25
90TidTidP-557
90TopTVM-54
91Fle-159
91MetColP-20
91MetWIZ-326
91Sco-368
91TopDeb90-129
92Bow-537
92DonRoo-101
92StaClu-824
92TopTra-91T
92TopTraG-91T
93Don-105
93MetColP-44
93MetKah-21
93Top-482
93TopGol-482
93TopInaM-482
93TopMic-482
94BufBisF-1850
95RicBraTI-18
Reed, Dennis
87AncGlaP-25
90AshTouC-10
91AshTouP-568
92BurAstC-11
92BurAstF-544
Reed, Howard
60Lea-84
61UniOil-SP9
65DodTeal-17
65Top-544
66Top-387
70Top-548
71ExpLaPR-10
71ExpPS-21
71OPC-398
71Top-398
90DodTar-651
Reed, Jack
61Yan61RL-36
91RinPos1Y2-10
92YanWIZ6-101
Reed, Jamie
84ChaO'sT-14
85RocRedWT-28
87RocRedWP-22
88RocRedWGCP-31

88RocRedWP-214
Reed, Jason
94YakBeaC-14
94YakBeaF-3844
95GreFalDTI-19
95VerBeaDTI-22
Reed, Jeff
81WisRapTT-14
83OrlTwiT-5
84MinTwiP-24
84TolMudHT-2
84TwiTeal-7
85Don-30
85IntLeaAT-38
85TolMudHT-14
85TwiTeal-7
86FleUpd-95
86TwiTeal-7
87DonOpeD-92
87ExpPos-22
87Fle-550
87FleGlo-550
87Top-247
87TopTif-247
87TopTra-100T
87TopTraT-100T
88Don-88
88Fle-194
88FleGlo-194
88OPC-176
88Sco-408
88ScoGlo-408
88StaLinE-14
88Top-176
88TopTif-176
89Don-469
89Fle-167
89FleGlo-167
89RedKah-34
89Sco-99
89Top-626
89TopBig-158
89TopTif-626
89UppDec-276
90Don-351
90Fle-429
90FleCan-429
90Lea-505
90OPC-772
90PubSti-37
90RedKah-23
90Sco-147
90Top-772
90TopTif-772
90UppDec-165
90VenSti-425
91Don-741
91Fle-78
91Lea-102
91OPC-419
91RedKah-34
91RedPep-17
91StaClu-534
91Top-419
91TopDesS-419
91TopMic-419
91TopTif-419
91Ult-101
92Don-451
92Fle-418
92OPC-91
92RedKah-34
92Sco-311
92StaClu-487
92Top-91
92TopGol-91
92TopGolW-91
92TopMic-91
92Ult-195
92UppDec-299
93Fle-397
93FleFinE-154
93GiaMot-25
93GiaPos-28
93PacSpa-87
93StaCluG-13
93Ult-488
94Fle-698
94GiaAMC-18
94GiaMot-21
94GiaTarBCI-6
94GiaUSPC-4C
94GiaUSPC-10H
94Pac-552
94StaClu-504
94StaCluFDI-504
94StaCluGR-504
94StaCluMOP-504
94StaCluT-17
94StaCluTFDI-17
94Top-291
94TopGol-291
94TopSpa-291
95GiaMot-21
95Top-181
96FleUpd-U130
96FleUpdTC-U130
96LeaSigEA-167
97DonTea-103
97DonTeaSPE-103
97Fle-314
97FleTif-314
97Pac-285
97PacLigB-285
97PacPriGotD-GD137
97PacSil-285
97Top-486
97Ult-188
97UltGolME-188
97UltPlaME-188
Reed, Jerry M.
80VenLeaS-247
81ReaPhiT-1
82OklCit8T-9
83ChaChaT-4
83IndPos-28
84MaiGuiT-2
85IndPol-35
85MaiGuiT-8
86CalCanP-22
86Fle-592
86Top-172
86TopTif-172
87MarMot-22
87Top-619
87TopTif-619
88Don-517
88Fle-387
88FleGlo-387
88MarMot-22
88Sco-488
88ScoGlo-488
88StaLinMa-16
88Top-332
88TopTif-332
89Don-657
89Fle-557
89FleGlo-557
89MarMot-22
89Sco-427
89Top-441
89TopTif-441
89UppDec-529
90Don-614
90Fle-523
90FleCan-523
90FleUpd-76
90Lea-368
90OPC-247
90PubSti-440
90Sco-492
90Top-247
90TopTif-247
90TopTVRS-58
90UppDec-210
90VenSti-426
91Fle-110
91PacSenL-141
Reed, Jody
86NewBriRSP-21
87IntLeaAT-21
87PawRedSP-56
87PawRedST-17
88Don-41
88DonBasB-196
88DonRoo-44
88DonTeaBRS-41
88Fle-360
88FleGlo-360
88Lea-41
88Sco-625
88ScoGlo-625
88Spo-225
88StaLinRS-15
88Top-152
88TopBig-202
88TopTif-152
89Bow-30
89BowTif-30
89Don-305
89DonBasB-289
89Fle-96
89FleGlo-96
89OPC-232
89PanSti-268
89RedFolSB-95
89Sco-486
89ScoHot1R-85
89ScoYouSI-2
89Spo-210
89Top-321
89Top-734
89TopBig-97
89TopGloS-60
89TopTif-321
89TopTif-734
89ToyRoo-23
89UppDec-370
90Bow-272
90BowTif-272
90ClaYel-T54
90Don-398
90DonBesA-16
90Fle-284
90FleCan-284
90Lea-150
90OPC-96
90PanSti-25
90PubSti-462
90RedSoxP-17
90Sco-11
90Top-96
90TopBig-167
90TopMinL-6
90TopTif-96
90TopTVRS-25
90UppDec-321
90VenSti-427
91Bow-120
91Don-123
91Fle-111
91Lea-69
91OPC-247
91PanFreS-265
91PanSti-220
91RedSoxP-18
91Sco-173
91StaClu-33
91Top-247
91TopDesS-247
91TopMic-247
91TopTif-247
91Ult-41
91UppDec-184
92Bow-642
92Don-47
92Fle-47
92Lea-413
92OPC-598
92PanSti-86
92Pin-222
92RedSoxDD-25
92Sco-85
92ScoProP-24
92StaClu-816
92StaCluNC-816
92Stu-138
92Top-598
92TopGol-598
92TopGolW-598
92TopMic-598
92TriPla-25
92Ult-21
92UppDec-404
93Bow-506
93DodMot-9
93DodPol-21
93Don-165
93Fla-76
93FlaPro-6
93Fle-182
93FleFinE-83
93Lea-299
93OPC-357
93OPCPre-115
93PacSpa-503
93Pin-519
93Sco-414
93Sel-120
93SelRoo-93T
93StaClu-612
93StaCluD-3
93StaCluFDI-612
93StaCluMOP-612
93Stu-177
93Top-103
93TopGol-103
93TopInaM-103
93TopMic-103
93TriPla-253
93Ult-403
93UppDec-96
93UppDec-568
93UppDecGold-96
93UppDecGold-568
94BreMilB-346
94BrePol-22
94ColC-564
94ColChoGS-564
94ColChoSS-564
94Don-236
94ExtBas-107
94Fin-346
94FinRef-346
94Fla-308
94Fle-521
94FleUpd-56
94Lea-376
94Pac-319
94Pin-519
94PinArtP-519
94PinMusC-519
94Sco-368
94ScoGolR-368
94ScoRoo-RT49
94ScoRooGR-RT49
94Sel-336
94StaClu-13
94StaClu-642
94StaCluFDI-13
94StaCluFDI-642
94StaCluGR-13
94StaCluGR-642
94StaCluMOP-13
94StaCluMOP-642
94Top-325
94TopGol-325
94TopSpa-325
94TopTra-57T
94Ult-377
94UppDec-473
94UppDecED-473
95ColCho-171
95ColCho-565T
95ColChoGS-171
95ColChoSS-171
95Don-414
95DonPreP-414
95DonTopotO-344
95Fin-50
95FinRef-50
95Fle-187
95FleUpd-189
95Pac-240
95PadCHP-13
95PadMot-13
95Sco-176
95ScoGolR-176
95ScoPlaTS-176
95StaClu-38
95StaCluFDI-38
95StaCluMOP-38
95StaCluSTWS-38
95StaCluVR-27
95Top-418
95TopCyb-218
96ColCho-298
96ColChoGS-298
96ColChoSS-298
96Don-336
96DonPreP-336
96EmoXL-282
96Fla-380
96Fle-576
96FleTif-576
96Pac-195
96PadMot-10
96ProSta-85
96StaClu-352
96StaCluMOP-352
95StaCluVRMC-27
96Ult-288
96UltGolM-288
96UppDec-446
97Fle-468
97FleTif-468
97Pac-431
97PacLigB-431
97PacSil-431
97StaClu-285
97StaCluMOP-285
97Top-109
Reed, Ken
86BirBarTI-3
87DayBeaAP-7
Reed, Kenny
93BluOriF-4129
93BluOriC-21
94AlbPolC-20
94AlbPolF-2245
94MarPhiC-19
94MarPhiF-3291
95MarPhiTI-21
Reed, Marty
86KinEagP-18
87MidAngP-27
87TexLeaAF-15
88EdmTraC-9
88EdmTraP-562
Reed, Patrick
91GreFalDSP-27
92YakBeaC-7
92YakBeaF-3466
93WelPirC-24
93WelPirF-3375
Reed, Rick (Richard Allen)
87MacPirP-10
88SalBucS-17
89BlaYNPRWL-160
89BlaYNPRWLU-66
89BlaYNPRWLU-68
89BlaYNPRWLU-70
89BufBisC-9
89BufBisP-1675
90BufBisC-8
90BufBisP-371
90CMC-8
90Don-527
90Fle-477
90FleCan-477
90Lea-427
90ProAAAF-486
90Sco-544
90Sco100RS-8
90UppDec-89A
91BufBisLD-42
91BufBisP-540
91LinDriAAA-42
91Sco-584
91TriA AAGP-AAA4
92OmaRoyS-1
92OmaRoyS-343
92Sco100RS-73
92SkyAAAF-295
92StaClu-434
93OmaRoyF-1678
93RanKee-426
93Top-212
93TopGol-212
93TopInaM-212
93TopMic-212
93TriAAAGF-42
94RanMagM-13
96NorTidB-25
Reed, Rick A.
88T/MUmp-48
89T/MUmp-46
90T/MUmp-44
Reed, Ron
68OPC-76
68Top-76
68TopVen-76
69OPC-177
69Top-177
69TopFou-8
69TopSta-9
70MLBOffS-12
70OPC-546
70Top-546
71MLBOffS-21
71OPC-359
71Top-359
72MilBra-281
72Top-787
73OPC-72
73Top-72
74OPC-346
74Top-346
75OPC-81
75Top-81

76OPC-58
76Top-58
76TopTra-58T
77Top-243
78PhiSSP-30
78SSP270-30
78Top-472
79OPC-84
79PhiBurK-7
79Top-177
80OPC-318
80PhiBurK-21
80Top-609
81Don-44
81Fle-11
81Top-376
82Don-399
82Fle-255
82Top-581
83Don-567
83Fle-169
83FleSta-160
83FleSti-172
83PhiPosGPaM-13
83PhiTas-23
83Top-728
83TopFol-4
84Don-529
84Fle-45
84FleUpd-96
84Nes792-43
84Top-43
84TopTif-43
84TopTra-98T
84TopTraT-98T
84WhiSoxTV-26
85Don-282
85Fle-524
85Top-221
85TopTif-221
90RicBra2ATI-20
Reed, Sean
88WytCubP-1981
89ChaWheB-16
89ChaWheP-1762
Reed, Steve
78BurBeeT-22
79HolMilT-21
80HolMilT-18
88PocGiaP-2082
90ShrCapP-1443
90ShrCapS-20
91LinDriAA-319
91ShrCapLD-319
91ShrCapP-1822
92PhoFirF-2822
92ShrCapF-3869
92ShrCapS-591
92SkyAA F-261
93Don-375
93Fle-414
93FleFinE-40
93PacSpa-435
93Pin-584
93RocUSPC-5H
93RocUSPC-11D
93Sco-573
93Sel-351
93StaClu-674
93StaCluFDI-674
93StaCluMOP-674
93StaCluRoc-26
93Top-461
93TopGol-461
93TopInaM-461
93TopMic-461
93Ult-356
93UppDec-752
93UppDecGold-752
94Don-438
94Fle-450
94Pac-204
94RocPol-20
94Sco-170
94ScoGolR-170
94StaClu-475
94StaCluFDI-475
94StaCluGR-475
94StaCluMOP-475
94StaCluT-112
94StaCluTFDI-112
94Top-627
94TopGol-627
94TopSpa-627
94Ult-187
94USPlaCR-3S
95Don-123
95DonPreP-123
95DonTopotO-230
95Fle-526
95Pac-143
95StaClu-64
95StaCluFDI-64
95StaCluMOP-64
95StaCluSTWS-64
95Top-321
95Ult-156
95UltGolM-156
96ColCho-539
96ColChoGS-539
96ColChoSS-539
96Don-146
96DonPreP-146
96Fla-249
96Fle-370
96FleRoc-11
96FleTif-370
96JohCitCTI-26
96LeaSigEA-168
96Pac-51
96RocPol-16
96Ult-472
96UltGolM-472
96UppDec-66
97Cir-360
97CirRav-360
97Fle-315
97FleTif-315
Reed, Steven Vincnet
89CliGiaP-906
Reed, Tom
84VisOakT-13
Reed, Toncie
89AubAstP-2167
90OscAstS-24
Reeder, Bill E.
49EurSta-194
52MotCoo-48
Reeder, Jim
96AubDouB-16
Reeder, Mike
87GenCubP-14
88ChaWheB-5
Reelhorn, John
81OklCit8T-15
82OklCit8T-19
Rees, Robert
90KinMetB-14
90KinMetS-20
91ColMetPI-8
91ColMetPPI-4
92ColMetF-294
93QuaCitRBC-17
93QuaCitRBF-99
Rees, Sean
89AlaGol-11
92PenPilC-7
92PenPilF-2930
92StaCluD-150
93RivPilCLC-15
Reese, Andrew
28PorandAR-A30
28PorandAR-B30
29ExhFou-9
Reese, Calvin
91Cla/Bes-412
91ClaDraP-16
91FroRowDP-23
91PriRedC-15
91PriRedP-3523
92Bow-86
92ChaWheF-17
92ChaWVWC-1
92ClaFS7-59
92OPC-714
92ProFS7-220
92StaCluD-151
92Top-714
92TopGol-714
92TopGolW-714
92UppDecML-70
92UppDecML-226
93Bow-146
93ChaLooF-2369
93ClaFS7-248
93ClaGolF-189
93ExcFS7-28
93SouAtlLAIPI-10
93SouAtlLAPI-34
94ActPac-49
94Bow-270
94Bow-355
94BowBes-B9
94BowBesR-B9
94Cla-108
94SigRoo-44
94SigRooS-44
94Top-278
94TopGol-278
94TopSpa-278
94UppDecML-117
95ActPacF-47
95Bes-63
95Bow-264
95BowBes-B24
95BowBesR-B24
95BowGolF-264
95SPML-38
95Top-171
95UppDecML-28
96Bow-200
96BowBes-98
96BowBesAR-98
96BowBesP-BBP12
96BowBesPAR-BBP12
96BowBesPR-BBP12
96BowBesR-98
97Bow-155
97BowBes-119
97BowBesAR-119
97BowBesR-119
97BowCerBIA-CA64
97BowCerGIA-CA64
97BowChr-155
97BowChrI-155
97BowChrIR-155
97BowChrR-155
97BowInt-155
97DonLim-49
97DonLim-116
97DonLimLE-49
97DonLimLE-116
97PinCer-119
97PinTotCPB-119
97PinTotCPG-119
97PinTotCPR-119
97TopStaFAS-FAS11
95UppDecMLFS-28
Reese, Chip
83AndBraT-10
89BoiHawP-1979
Reese, Jason
90MedHatBJB-2
91PocPioP-3780
91PocPioSP-11
Reese, Jimmie
31Exh-26
73OPC-421
73Top-421A
73Top-421B
74OPC-276
74Top-276
76SSP-630
78AngFamF-30
91Bow-186
91Stu-21
92UppDecS-13
93AngMot-28
93AngPol-12
93ConTSN-690
93PacRya2S-245
94UppDecAH-199
94UppDecAH1-199
Reese, Kyle
86EriCarP-24
87Ft.MyeRP-27
88VirGenS-21
89MemChiB-16
89MemChiP-1206
89MemChiS-20
90MemChiB-12
90MemChiP-1011
90MemChiS-23
Reese, Matt
93SouOreAC-21
93SouOreAF-4079
94WesMicWC-20
94WesMicWF-2311
95ModA'sTI-23
Reese, Pee Wee (Harold H.)
40DodTeal-20
41DouPlaR-23
41PlaBal-54
41WheM5-18
42DodTeal-16
43MPR302-1-20
46SpoExcW-4-6
47Exh-184A
47Exh-184B
47HomBon-38
47PM1StaP1-169
47PM1StaP1-170
47PM1StaP1-171
47PM1StaP1-172
48SweSpoT-18
49Bow-36
49EurSta-47
49MPR302-2-106
50AmeNut&CCP-14
50Bow-21
50Dra-19
50RoyDes-2
51Bow-80
51R42SmaS-86
52BerRos-51
52Bow-8
52CokTip-7
52RedMan-NL17
52RoyPre-9
52StaCalL-79B
52StaCalS-91A
52Top-333
53BowC-33
53Dor-127
53ExhCan-21
53RedMan-NL10
53Top-76
54Bow-58
54NewYorJA-14
54RedMan-NL15
55ArmCoi-15
55BigLeaIS-15
55Bow-37
55DaiQueS-15
55DodGolS-16
55RedMan-NL17
56Dod-24
56Top-260
56YelBasP-26
57Top-30
58DodBelB-8
58DodJayP-11
58Hir-23
58Top-375
59DodTeal-21
59DodVol-12
60NuHi-37
61NuSco-437
69EquSpoHoF-BB15
76SSP-594
76SSPYanOD-8
76TayBow4-16
77GalGloG-31
79DiaGre-90
79TCM50-84
80DodGreT-3
80PacLeg-52
80PerHaloFP-189
80SSPHOF-188
82DiaCla-16
82GSGalAG-11
83TCMPla1942-28
83TopRep5-333
84FifNatCT-13
84OCoandSI-48
86SpoDecG-21
86TCMSupS-16
87Dod195T-6
87LeaSpeO*-H8
88PacLegI-21
88RinPosD1-5A
89DodSmoG-23
89PerCelP-34
90DodTar-652
90PerGreM-26
90PerGreM-91
91TopArc1-76
92BazQua5A-15
92Zip-6
95TopArcBD-24
95TopArcBD-43
95TopArcBD-89
95TopArcBD-123
95TopArcBD-159
Reese, Pokey
92TopMic-714
94ChaLooF-1367
94ColC-666
94ColChoGS-666
94ColChoSS-666
94UppDec-544
94UppDecED-544
95ARuFalLS-16
95Exc-181
95IndIndF-103
95Sum21C-TC2
96IndIndB-21
97ColCho-308
97Don-369
97DonFraFea-14
97DonLimFotG-39
97DonPre-157
97DonPreCttC-157
97DonPreP-369
97DonPrePGold-369
97Fle-686
97FleTif-686
97Lea-323
97LeaFraM-323
97LeaFraMDC-323
97PinCerMBlu-119
97PinCerMG-119
97PinCerMR-119
97PinCerR-119
97SpoIll-20
97SpoIllEE-20
97Ult-460
97UltGolME-460
97UltPlaME-460
Reese, Rich
65Top-597
67Top-486
68OPC-111
68Top-111
68TopVen-111
69MilBra-228
69OPC-56
69Top-56
70DayDaiNM-120
70MLBOffS-238
70OPC-404
70Top-404
71MLBOffS-472
71OPC-349
71Top-349
71TopCoi-72
72MilBra-282
72Top-611
78TwiFri-19
89PacLegI-112
Reese, Stan
79AshTouT-27
Reeser, Jeffery
89PeoChiTI-34
Reeve, Bob
85AncGlaPTI-41
Reeves, Dave
91BilMusP-3751
91BilMusSP-22
Reeves, Glenn
94KanCouCC-21
94KanCouCF-177
94KanCouCTI-25
95BreCouMF-259
96BreCouMB-27
Reeves, Jim
78St.PetCT-22
Reeves, Matt
79CliDodT-5
82VerBeaDT-10
Reeves, Mel
47SmiClo-24
Reeves, Mickey
91HunCubC-18
91HunCubP-3348
92HunCubC-12
92HunCubF-3165
Reeves, Robert E.
29ExhFou-17
31Exh-17
Regalado, Rudy
55Bow-142
60HenHouW-14
Regalado, Uvaldo
82DayBeaAT-6
83DayBeaAT-9
85DomLeaS-103
Regan, Frank
79WatIndT-7

80WatIndT-24
Regan, Michael J.
09ColChiE-237
12ColRedB-237
12ColTinT-237
Regan, Phil
61Top-439
62Jel-24
62Pos-24
62PosCan-24
62TigPosCF-15
62Top-366
63Top-494
64TigJayP-10
64TigLid-13
64Top-535
65OPC-191
65Top-191
66Top-347
66TopVen-347
67Baz-29
67CokCapD-1
67CokCapDA-1
67DexPre-172
67OPC-130
67Top-130
68OPC-88
68Top-88
68TopVen-88
69CubJewT-14
69CubPho-9
69CubTealC-7
69MilBra-229
69MLBOffS-124
69Top-535
69TopSta-18
70DayDaiNM-129
70MLBOffS-21
70OPC-334
70Top-334
71MLBOffS-43
71OPC-634
71Top-634
72MilBra-283
72OPC-485
72Top-485
84CubUno-9
85DomLeaS-177
85MarMot-27
86MarMot-28
87DodSmoA-27
88DodSmo-9
89DodSmoG-72
90DodTar-653
92DodStaTA-5
93LinVenB-205
94VenLinU-58
95LinVen-37
Regan, William W.
28StaPlaCE-52
29ExhFou-18
29PorandAR-69
93ConTSN-813
Reger, Roy
85CloHSS-36
Reggins, Mark
92LouRedS-275
Regira, Gary
89JamExpP-2154
90RocExpLC-22
90RocExpP-2688
91WesPalBEC-10
91WesPalBEP-1226
Rehbaum, Chris
80BatTroT-27
80WatIndT-16
81BatTroT-23
82WatIndF-17
82WatIndT-22
Rehkopf, Rob
94WilCubC-19
94WilCubF-3763
Rehm, Vic
60Lea-61
Rehwinkel, Pat
89HelBreSP-4
Reiber, Frank
36WorWidGV-111
39WorWidGV-21
Reiber, Lee
93LetMouF-4153
93LetMouSP-21
Reich, Andy
89ColMetB-19
89ColMetGS-22
89SouAtlLAGS-16
90St.LucMS-21
91St.LucMC-18
91St.LucMP-708
92BinMetF-513
93BinMetF-2331
Reich, Frank
92StaCluMO-40
Reich, Herman
49EurSta-68
Reich, Steve
93BazTeaU-4
93TopTra-85T
Reichard, Bud (Clyde)
78WisRapTT-16
85TulDriTI-37
89PenPilS-21
89PenPilS-26
Reichardt, Kevin
87BelMarTI-5
Reichardt, Rick
65OPC-194
65Top-194
66AngDexP-4
66Top-321
66TopVen-321
67Baz-1
67OPC-40
67Top-40
67TopVen-202
68Top-570
68TopActS-3C
68TopActS-14C
69AngJacitB-10
69MilBra-230
69MLBOffS-25
69MLBPin-23
69OPC-205
69Top-205
69TopDecI-34
69TopFou-7
69TopSta-147
69TopSup-8
69TopTeaP-17
69TraSta-18
70Kel-18
70MLBOffS-177
70Top-720
70TraSta-12C
71OPC-643
71Top-643
71TopCoi-102
72MilBra-284
72WhiSoxTI1-10
73LinPor-52
81TCM60I-337
86AngGreT-7
Reichel, Tom
87PenWhiSP-19
Reichenbach, Eric
91PitMetC-24
91PitMetP-3420
92ClaFS7-81
92ColMetC-23
92ColMetF-295
92ColMetPI-17
93CapCitBC-18
93CapCitBF-459
Reichle, Darrin
87SpoIndP-2
88ChaRaiP-1208
88SouAtlLAGS-11
89RivRedWB-14
89RivRedWCLC-15
89RivRedWP-1393
90Bes-151
90CMC-853
90RivRedWB-24
90RivRedWCLC-23
90RivRedWP-2607
91LinDriAA-616
91WicWraLD-616
91WicWraP-2596
91WicWraRD-7
Reichler, Joe
90LitSunW-7
Reichow, Robert
96BurIndB-14
Reichstein, Derek
95ElmPioTI-23
95ElmPioUTI-23
Reid, Derek
90EveGiaB-26
90EveGiaP-3142
90ProAaA-172
91Cla/Bes-273
91SanJosGC-28
91SanJosGP-25
92ShrCapF-3884
92UppDecML-87
94SanBerSC-19
94SanBerSF-2772
95BurBeeTI-19
96SanJosGB-9
Reid, Gregory
91MadMusC-19
91MadMusP-2143
92MadMusC-5
92MadMusF-1250
Reid, Jessie
84ShrCapFB-16
85FreGiaP-18
86PhoFirP-22
87PhoFirP-16
88Fle-643
88FleGlo-643
89TacTigC-17
89TacTigP-1549
86STaoftFt-36
Reid, John
91NiaFalRC-20
92FayGenC-4
92FayGenF-2166
92LakTigF-2277
Reid, Rayon
96AugGreB-24
Reid, Scott D.
70OPC-56
70Top-56
71OPC-439
71Top-439
Reid, Terry
91MelBusF-15
Reidy, Bill
11SpoLifCW-299
90DodTar-654
Reilley, John
88SumBraP-394
89WauTimGS-5
90SalSpuP-2720
90SalSpuCLC-129
Reilly, Charles T.
87OldJudN-421
Reilly, Ed
83DayBeaAT-10
Reilly, John
94St.CatBJC-17
94St.CatBJF-3647
95StCatSTI-15
Reilly, John G.
87OldJudN-420
88SpoTimM-22
89EdgR.WG-13
Reilly, Mike
88T/MUmp-33
89T/MUmp-31
90T/MUmp-30
Reilly, Neil
85BurRanT-6
Reilly, Thomas H.
09ColChiE-238
09ColChiE-239
09RamT20-98
12ColRedB-238
12ColRedB-239
12ColTinT-238
12ColTinT-239
Reimer, Kevin
86SalRedBP-23
87PorChaRP-26
88TulDriTI-25
89Fle-641
89FleGlo-641
89OklCit8C-19
89OklCit8P-1527
89ScoHot1R-59
90CMC-169
90Fle-310
90FleCan-310
90OklCit8C-19
90OklCit8P-446
90ProAAAF-692
90TulDriDGB-30
91Don-80
91Fle-298
91OPC-304
91RanMot-15
91Sco-836
91Top-304
91TopDesS-304
91TopMic-304
91TopTif-304
91UltUpd-57
91UppDec-494
92Bow-115
92Don-251
92Fle-315
92Lea-93
92OPC-737
92Pin-340
92RanMot-15
92RanTeal-18
92Sco-152
92StaClu-57
92Top-737
92TopGol-737
92TopGolW-737
92TopMic-737
92Ult-444
92UppDec-201
93Bow-479
93BrePol-21
93BreSen5-4
93Don-55
93Fla-228
93Fle-326
93FleFinE-232
93Lea-377
93OPC-284
93OPCPre-131
93PacSpa-515
93PanSti-43
93Pin-531
93RanKee-305
93Sco-628
93Sel-268
93SelRoo-101T
93SP-69
93StaClu-699
93StaCluFDI-699
93StaCluMOP-699
93Top-87
93TopGol-87
93TopInaM-87
93TopMic-87
93Ult-576
93UppDec-578
93UppDecGold-578
94BreMilB-168
94ColC-237
94ColChoGS-237
94ColChoSS-237
94Don-233
94Fle-189
94PanSti-85
94Sco-477
94ScoGolR-477
94Top-585
94TopGol-585
94TopSpa-585
94Ult-82
Reimer, Matt
93AlbPolC-18
Reimer, Robin
86EveGiaPC-25
Reimers, Tom
96HicCraB-16
Reimink, Robert
89NiaFalRP-20
90LakTigS-21
91LinDriAA-395
91LonTigLD-395
91LonTigP-1887
92LonTigF-641
92LonTigS-415
93TolMudHF-1661
Reimsnyder, Brian
90EriSaiS-19
Rein, Fred
77ChaPatT-14
77SalPirT-21
Reinbach, Mike
75IntLeaAT-5
79TCMJapPB-81
91OriCro-376
Reincke, Corey
91FayGenC-7
91FayGenP-1167
91NiaFalRC-28
91NiaFalRP-3631
93NiaFalRF-3385
Reinebold, Jim
88SouBenWSGS-16
89SouBenWSGS-3
90SouBenWSB-29
90SouBenWSGS-29
91SouBenWSP-2876
92SouBenWSF-196
93SouBenWSC-27
93SouBenWSF-1449
94SouBenSHC-27
94SouBenSHF-612
Reinert, Greg
91IdaFalBSP-9
Reinhart, Art
91ConTSN-242
Reinheimer, Christian
94JohCitCC-24
94JohCitCF-3701
Reinholtz, Eric
87SalAngP-10
Reinisch, Paul
90BriTigP-3170
90BriTigS-19
Reinke, Jeff
75CliPilT-30
Reis, Bobby (Robert)
36GouWidPPR-A87
90DodTar-655
Reis, Dave
88PulBraP-1757
89BurBraP-1619
89BurBraS-18
90Bes-195
90BurBraB-7
90BurBraP-2347
90BurBraS-20
90MidLeaASGS-47
Reis, Paul
88PulBraP-1759
89SumBraP-1090
90BurBraB-17
90BurBraP-2359
90BurBraS-21
Reis, Tom
47CenFlo-22
Reiser, James
86MedA'sC-52
87MadMusP-15
87MadMusP-10
88MadMusP-18
Reiser, Pete
36OveCanR-38
39ExhSal-53A
39ExhSal-53B
41DouPlaR-17
42DodTeal-17
43MPR302-1-21
46SpoExcW-8-3
47PM1StaP1-173
48Bow-7
48SweSpoT-2
49Bow-185
49EurSta-17
49Lea-146
50Bow-193
51Bow-238
52Top-189
60DodTeal-15
60DodUniO-23
60Top-463
73OPC-81
73Top-81A
73Top-81B
80MarExh-25
80PacLeg-88
83TopRep5-189
86TCMSupS-44
87SpoRea-34
88WilMulP-7
89DodSmoG-47
90DodTar-656
91RinPosBD3-8
Reish, Steve
83KinBluJTI-17
84MemChiT-17
Reisling, Doc (Frank)
11SpoLifM-131
90DodTar-1052
Reiter, Gary
81DurBulT-24
82DurBulT-20
83RicBraT-8
84RicBraT-15
85RicBraT-7

Reitmeister, Ben
87HawRai-27
Reitsma, Chris
97Bow-219
97BowChr-196
97BowChrI-196
97BowChrIR-196
97BowChrR-196
97BowInt-219
97Top-273
Reitz, Ken
73OPC-603
73Top-603
74OPC-372
74Top-372
75OPC-27
75Top-27
76OPC-158
76SSP-280
76Top-158
76TopTra-158T
77BurCheD-13
77Car5-22
77CarTeal-21
77Kel-38A
77Kel-38B
77Top-297
78CarTeal-16
78Hos-106
78Top-692
79Hos-23
79OPC-307
79Top-587
80OPC-103
80Top-182
81AllGamPI-125
81CokTeaS-19
81Don-307
81Fle-530
81OPC-316
81Top-441
81TopScr-101
81TopSti-158
81TopSupHT-28
81TopTra-820
82Don-277
82Fle-602
82FleSta-91
82OPC-245
82Top-245
82TopSti-26
85TulDriTI-1
86SanJosBP-17
87SanJosBP-3
89PacSenL-213
89T/MSenL-89
89TopSenL-35
90EliSenL-61
91PacSenL-33
91SweBasG-119
92CarMcD-41
Reitzel, Mark
87HawRai-18
Reitzel, Mike
90MiaMirIS-22
Rekar, Bryan
93BenRocC-1
93BenRocF-3267
94Bow-554
94CenValRC-20
94CenValRF-3202
94ExcFS7-187
95Bow-160
95BowBes-B76
95BowBesR-B76
95NewHavRTI-35
96ColCho-542
96ColChoGS-542
96ColChoSS-542
96ColSprSSTI-27
96Don-444
96DonPreP-444
96Fin-B119
96FinRef-B119
96Fle-371
96FleTif-371
96LeaSigA-191
96LeaSigAG-191
96LeaSigAS-191
96Pac-61
96PacPri-P22
96PacPriG-P22
96Pin-48
96RocPol-17
96Sco-463
96StaClu-107
96StaCluMOP-107
96Top-416
96Ult-473
96UltGolM-473
96UppDec-64
97Pac-286
97PacLigB-286
97PacSil-286
Relaford, Desi
92ClaFS7-387
92PenPilC-8
92PenPilF-2941
92StaCluD-152
93Bow-163
93ClaFS7-249
93ExcFS7-230
93JacSunF-2718
93StaCluMari-2
94AriFalLS-17
94Bow-529
94JacSunF-1420
94RivPilCLC-3
94UppDecML-186
95Bes-40
95Bow-153
95BowBes-B89
95BowBesR-B89
95PorCitRTI-20
95SPML-152
95Top-642
95UppDecML-77
96Bow-186
96BowBes-166
96BowBesAR-166
96BowBesMI-2
96BowBesMIAR-2
96BowBesMIR-2
96BowBesR-166
96Exc-106
96SigRooOJTP-T5
96TacRaiB-23
96Top-426
97Don-397
97DonPreP-397
97DonPrePGold-397
97Lea-171
97LeaFraM-171
97LeaFraMDC-171
97Sco-298
97ScoPreS-298
97ScoShoS-298
97ScoShoSAP-298
95UppDecMLFS-77
Relaford, Winnie
88SumBraP-400
89SumBraP-1103
Relaigh, Matt
93JamExpF-3336
Rembielak, Rick
82MiaMarT-16
Remington, Jake
95IdaFalBTI-21
96CliLumKTI-22
Remlinger, Mike
87EveGiaC-31
88ShrCapP-1296
89ShrCapP-1832
90Bow-227
90BowTif-227
90ShrCapP-1444
90ShrCapS-21
91DonRoo-37
91GiaPacGaE-27
91LinDriAAA-390
91PhoFirLD-390
91PhoFirP-64
91UppDecFE-36F
92CalCanF-3729
92CalCanS-68
92Don-336
92Fle-646
92Sco-410
92Sco100RS-49
92SkyAAAF-31
92TopDeb91-143
92UppDec-585
93CalCanF-1166
94FleUpd-159
94NorTidF-2919
96IndIndB-22
Remmerswaal, Win
77BriRedST-16
81Don-98
81PawRedST-7
81Top-38
Remo, Bryon
91OklStaC-20
Remo, Jeff
82QuaCitCT-16
Remy, Jerry
76OPC-229
76SSP-198
76Top-229
77BurCheD-121
77Kel-44
77Top-342
78Hos-66
78PapGinD-2
78SSP270-186
78Top-478
79OPC-325
79Top-618
80OPC-85
80Top-155
81Don-215
81Fle-238
81OPC-131
81Top-549
82Don-156
82Fle-304
82FleSta-171
82OPC-25
82RedSoxC-16
82Squ-2
82Top-25
82TopSti-132
82TopSti-149
83AllGamPI-15
83Don-74
83Fle-193
83FleSti-68
83OPC-295
83Top-295
83TopSti-33
84AllGamPI-106
84Don-172
84Fle-407
84Nes792-445
84OPC-58
84Top-445
84TopRubD-21
84TopSti-215
84TopTif-445
85Fle-167
85OPC-173
85Top-761
85TopRubD-21
85TopSti-218
85TopTif-761
Rende, Sal
79TacTugT-11
80TacTigT-14
81ChaLooT-17
82ChaLooT-11
83BufBisT-13
87ChaLooB-1
88ChaLooLTI-25
88MemChiB-26
89OmaRoyC-23
89OmaRoyP-1740
89TriAAP-AAA37
90CMC-200
90OmaRoyC-25
90OmaRoyP-80
90ProAAAF-615
91LinDriAAA-349
91OmaRoyLD-349
91OmaRoyP-1049
91TriA AAGP-AAA27
93EdmTraF-1152
94EdmTraF-2890
95ChaKniTI-1
96ChaKniB-1
Rendell, Ed
96PinFan-ER1
Rendina, Mike
88BriTigP-1877
89BriTigS-21
89FayGenP-1584
90FayGenP-2416
90SouAtlLAS-20
91LakTigC-22
91LakTigP-275
92LakTigC-2
92LakTigF-2288
93LonTigF-2318
94TreThuF-2129
Renegade, Rookie the
96HudValRB-29
Renfroe, Chad
93UtiBluSC-21
93UtiBluSF-3533
94LynRedSC-21
94LynRedSF-1891
95MicBatCTI-22
96SigRooOJ-28
96SigRooOJS-28
Renfroe, Chico
92NegLeaRLI-51
Renfroe, Laddie (Cohen)
86WinSpiP-21
87PitCubP-8
88IowCubC-4
88IowCubP-551
89ChaKniTI-1
90CMC-83
90IowCubC-8
90IowCubP-318
90ProAAAF-625
90TopTVCu-58
91IowCubLD-214
91IowCubP-1059
91LinDriAAA-214
91TriA AAGP-AAA19
92IowCubF-4050
92IowCubS-217
92Sco-875
92SkyAAAF-105
92TopDeb91-144
Renfroe, Marshall
60Lea-99
60TacBan-16
Renick, Rick
68Top-301
68TopVen-301
69MilBra-231
70OPC-93
70Top-93
71MLBOffS-473
71OPC-694
71Top-694
72MilBra-285
72OPC-459
72Top-459
73TacTwiC-18
74TacTwiC-20
75TacTwiK-8
76TacTwiDQ-17
78TwiFri-42
83MemChiT-23
85ExpPos-18
86ExpProPa-28
88TwiTeal-29
92VanCanF-2734
92VanCanS-649
93NasSouF-583
94NasSouF-1265
95NasSouTI-18
96NasSouB-1
Reniff, Hal
61Yan61RL-25
62Top-139B
62Top-139C
62Top-159
62TopVen-159
63Top-546
64ChatheY-20
64Top-36
64TopVen-36
65ChaTheY-19
65Top-413
66OPC-68
66Top-68
66TopVen-68
67CokCapYM-V10
67Top-201
78TCM60I-106
91MetWIZ-327
91RinPos1Y2-7
92YanWIZ6-102
Renko, Steve
69ExpPin-6
70OPC-87
70Top-87
71ExpPS-22
71MLBOffS-139
71OPC-209
71Top-209
72Dia-38
72OPC-307
72OPC-308
72ProStaP-10
72Top-307
72Top-308
73OPC-623
73Top-623
74ExpWes-8
74OPC-49
74Top-49
74TopSta-58
75Hos-69
75OPC-34
75Top-34
76OPC-264
76Top-264
77Top-586
78Top-493
79Top-352
80Top-184
81Don-337
81Fle-231
81LonBeaPT-24
81Top-63
81TopTra-821
82Don-38
82Fle-472
82Top-702
83Don-393
83Fle-99
83FleSti-24
83OPC-236
83Roy-22
83Top-236
83TopTra-95T
84Fle-355
84Nes792-444
84Top-444
84TopTif-444
91WesPalBEC-11
91WesPalBEP-1227
92WinHavRSF-1776
93ExpDonM-27
93HagSunC-21
93HagSunF-1878
94WicWraF-188
96CedRapKTI-28
Renna, Bill
54Top-112
55A'sRodM-30
55A'sRodM-31
55Top-121
55TopDouH-99
56Top-82
57SeaPop-29
58Top-473
59Top-72
59TopVen-72
76A'sRodMC-20
94TopArc1-112
94TopArc1G-112
Renneau, Charlie
77VisOakT-12
Rennert, Dutch
88T/MUmp-18
89T/MUmp-18
90T/MUmp-16
Rennhack, Mike
92HigSchPLS-4
93AshTouC-17
93AshTouF-2291
94QuaCitRBC-19
94QuaCitRBF-548
95QuaCitRBTI-21
96StoPorB-15
Rennicke, Dean
83AlbDukT-5
84AlbDukC-160
85AlbDukC-151
Renninger, Bob
74CedRapAT-1
Rennspies, Dustin
92GreFalDSP-21
Rensa, Tony
34DiaMatCSB-151
93ConTSN-950
Renteria, David
92GulCoaYF-3799
93OneYanC-17
93OneYanF-3513
94GreBatF-485
95NorNagUTI-2
97GreBatC-17
Renteria, Ed (Edison)
87AubAstP-23

88AshTouP-1058
89OscAstS-19
90ColMudB-23
90ColMudP-1355
90ColMudS-20
91OscAstC-21
91OscAstP-695
Renteria, Edgar
93ClaYouG-YG19
93KanCouCC-18
93KanCouCF-925
94Bow-94
94BowBes-B63
94BowBesR-B63
94BreCouMC-1
94BreCouMF-21
94Cla-111
94ClaTriF-T31
94FloStaLAF-FSL30
94PorSeaDF-688
95Bes-70
95Bes-104
95BesFra-F7
95Bow-120
95KanCouCLTI-12
95PorSeaDTI-23
95SPML-62
95UppDecML-186
96Bow-377
96BowBes-130
96BowBesAR-130
96BowBesR-130
96ChaKniB-23
96ColCho-446
96ColChoGS-446
96ColChoSS-446
96Exc-166
96Fin-B332
96FinRef-B332
96LeaPre-142
96LeaPreP-142
96LeaSig-96
96LeaSigPPG-96
96LeaSigPPP-96
96SP-9
96UppDec-256
96Zen-115
96ZenArtP-115
97Bow-2
97BowBes-65
97BowBesAR-65
97BowBesR-65
97BowInt-2
97Cir-10
97CirRav-10
97ColCho-116
97Don-326
97DonLim-13
97DonLimLE-13
97DonPre-134
97DonPreCttC-134
97DonPreP-326
97DonPrePGold-326
97DonRatR-19
97Fin-17
97FinRef-17
97FlaSho-A60
97FlaSho-B60
97FlaSho-C60
97FlaShoLC-60
97FlaShoLC-B60
97FlaShoLC-C60
97FlaShoLCM-A60
97FlaShoLCM-B60
97FlaShoLCM-C60
97Fle-335
97FleRooS-11
97FleTif-335
93KanCouCTI-19
97Lea-8
97LeaFraM-8
97LeaFraMDC-8
97MetUni-178
97MetUniMF-7
97MetUniPP-9
97NewPin-111
97NewPinAP-111
97NewPinMC-111
97NewPinPP-111
97Pac-306
97PacGolCD-27
97PacLigB-306
97PacPri-103
97PacPriLB-103
97PacPriP-103
97PacSil-306
97Pin-182
97PinArtP-182
97PinCer-103
97PinCerMBlu-103
97PinCerMG-103
97PinCerMR-103
97PinCerR-103
97PinIns-140
97PinInsCE-140
97PinInsDE-140
97PinMusC-182
97PinTotCPB-103
97PinTotCPG-103
97PinTotCPR-103
97PinX-P-90
97PinX-PMoS-90
97PinX-PMP-17
97Sco-50
97ScoPreS-50
97ScoShoS-50
97ScoShoSAP-50
97SelRooR-4
97SkyE-X-73
97SkyE-XC-73
97SkyE-XEC-73
97SP-77
97SpoIll-68
97SpoIllEE-68
97StaClu-154
97StaCluM-M17
97StaCluMOP-154
97StaCluMOP-M17
97Stu-138
97StuPrePG-138
97StuPrePS-138
97Top-211
97TopAwel-AI15
97TopChr-79
97TopChrR-79
97TopGal-142
97TopGalPPI-142
97Ult-201
97UltGolME-201
97UltPlaME-201
97UltRooR-9
97UppDec-77
97UppDec-183
97UppDecBCP-BC11
95UppDecMLFS-186
97UppDecU-43
97UppDecUGN-GN7
Renteria, Rich
82AleDukT-27
83LynPirT-17
85MexCitTT-22
86HawIsIP-20
87MarMot-23
88MarMot-23
89Bow-212
89BowTif-212
89MarMot-20
89Sco-142
89TopBig-109
89UppDec-547
93Bow-10
93FleFinE-69
93MarFloA-7
93MarPub-20
93MarUSPC-6D
93MarUSPC-13H
93PacSpa-470
93TopTra-2T
93Ult-385
94Don-499
94Fle-474
94PanSti-184
94StaClu-87
94StaCluFDI-87
94StaCluGR-87
94StaCluMOP-87
94StaCluT-63
94StaCluTFDI-63
94Top-681
94TopGol-681
94TopSpa-681
95Top-340
Rentschuler, Tom
83PeoSunF-16
83RedPioT-22
Renwick, Richard
80QuaCitCT-9
Renz, Kevin
86PenWhiSP-22
87PenWhiSP-2
88BirBarB-28
Replogle, Andy
77ArkTraT-8A
77ArkTraT-8B
79Top-427
79VanCanT-8
81VanCanT-16
94BreMilB-169
Repoz, Craig
85LitFalMT-21
86ColMetP-21
87LynMetP-1
88St.LucMS-20
89JacMetGS-4
90WicWraRD-17
Repoz, Jeff
90PriPatD-16
Repoz, Roger
66OPC-138
66Top-138
66TopVen-138
67CokCapAt-13
67DexPre-173
67Top-416
68Top-587
69MilBra-232
69MLBOffS-26
69OPC-103
69Top-103
69TopSta-148
69TopTeaP-17
70MLBOffS-178
70OPC-397
70Top-397
71MLBOffS-355
71OPC-508
71Top-508
72MilBra-286
72Top-541
81TCM60I-458
92YanWIZ6-103
Repulski, Rip
53Top-172
54Bow-46
54CarHunW-20
54RedMan-NL17
54Top-115
55Bow-205
55CarHunW-19
55Top-55
55TopDouH-125
56Top-201
57Top-245
58Hir-15
58PhiJayP-8
58Top-14
59DodTeal-22
59DodVol-13
59Top-195
59TopVen-195
60DodBelB-5
60Lea-86
60Top-265
61Top-128
90DodTar-657
91TopArc1-172
94TopArc1-115
94TopArc1G-115
Rescigno, Xavier
47SigOil-13
49BowPCL-5
Resendez, Oscar
91BurIndP-3302
92ColRedF-2389
92ProFS7-61
92WatIndC-7
92WatIndF-3232
93ColRedC-19
93ColRedF-594
94HigDesMC-21
94HigDesMF-2788
Resetar, Gary
89KenTwiP-1075
89KenTwiS-21
90Bes-174
90OrlSunRB-12
90OrlSunRP-1087
90OrlSunRS-18
91CanIndLD-92
91CanIndP-982
91LinDriAA-92
Resnikoff, Bob
88SouBenWSGS-24
89SarWhiSS-19
90SarWhiSS-21
90StaFS7-60
91OscAstP-683
Respondek, Mark
91WavRedF-11
92AlbPolC-12
92AlbPolF-2304
93JamExpC-19
93JamExpF-3325
95AusFut-77
95AusFut-91
Restilli, Dino
48SomandK-12
49SomandK-17
50Bow-123
Restin, Eric
76BurBeeT-27
77BurBeeT-24
Resz, Greg
93OneYanC-18
93OneYanF-3501
94GreBatF-472
96TamYanY-21
Retes, Lorenzo
85MexCitTT-10
Rettenmund, Merv
69OPC-66
69Top-66
70DayDaiNM-143
70Ori-11
70Top-629
71MLBOffS-308
71OPC-393
71Top-393
72Kel-11
72MilBra-287
72OPC-86
72OPC-235
72OriPol-9
72ProStaP-35
72Top-86
72Top-235
73OPC-56
73OriJohP-14
73Top-56
74OPC-585
74Top-585
74TopTra-585T
75OPC-369
75Top-369
76OPC-283
76SSP-46
76Top-283
77PadSchC-45
77Top-659
78AngFamF-31
78Top-566
79Top-48
80Top-402
83RanAffF-NNO
84RanJarP-NNO
89A'sMot-27
90A'sMot-27
91OriCro-377
91PadSmo-28
92PadMot-27
92PadPolD-27
92PadPolD-28
92PadSmo-24
93PadMot-28
93RanKee-306
94PadMot-28
95PadMot-28
96PadMot-28
Retzer, Ed
83MadMusF-10
83TacTigT-31
Retzer, Ken
55DonWin-36
61SenJayP-8
62Top-594
63Jel-94
63Pos-94
63Top-471
64Top-277
64TopVen-277
65OPC-278
65Top-278
Reucor, Randy
72CedRapCT-16
Reulbach, Ed
06FanCraNL-40
07CubA.CDPP-10
07CubGFGCP-10
08AmeCarE-21
08AmeCarE-59
08RosComP-106
09ColChiE-240
09PhiCarE-21
09RamT20-101
09T206-299
09T206-300
10CouT21-211
10CouT21-212
10CouT21-213
10CouT21-312
10DomDisP-101
10JuJuDE-34
10RedCroT-64
10RedCroT-150
10RedCroT-238
10SweCapPP-88
11S74Sil-67
11SpoLifCW-300
11SpoLifM-179
11T205-143
12ColRedB-240
12ColTinT-240
12HasTriFT-36D
12T207-156
14CraJacE-80
14FatPlaT-41
15CraJacE-80
69Baz-12
72FleFamF-29
87Cub190T-3
90DodTar-658
90HOFStiB-12
92ConTSN-549
Reuschel, Paul
73WicAerKSB-13
74WicAerODF-112
76VenLeaS-170
77CubJewT-13
77Top-333
77Top-634
78SSP270-247
78Top-663
79Top-511
Reuschel, Rick
73OPC-482
73Top-482
74OPC-136
74Top-136
74TopSta-18
75Hos-51
75OPC-153
75Top-153
76Hos-17
76HosTwi-17
76OPC-359
76SSP-301
76Top-359
77BurCheD-193
77Hos-103
77OPC-214
77Spo-4307
77Top-530
77Top-634
78Hos-131
78Kel-45
78OPC-56
78RCColC-91
78SSP270-245
78Top-50
79Hos-67
79Kel-47
79OPC-123
79Top-240
80OPC-99
80Top-175
81CokTeaS-20
81Don-561
81Fle-293
81FleStiC-93
81OPC-205
81Top-645
81TopSti-157
81TopSupHT-29
81TopTra-822
82Don-157
82Fle-50
82OPC-204
82Top-405
84CubChiT-22
84CubSev-47

85Fle-63
85FleUpd-88
85HawIsIC-230
85OPC-306
85Top-306
85TopMin-306
85TopTif-306
85TopTifT-93T
85TopTra-93T
86Don-532
86Fle-618
86FleSlu-27
86FleStiC-95
86Lea-207
86Top-779
86TopMinL-57
86TopSti-126
86TopTat-7
86TopTif-779
87Don-188
87Fle-619
87FleGlo-619
87OPC-154
87RedFolSB-129
87Top-521
87TopSti-128
87TopTif-521
88Don-613
88DonAll-52
88DonBasB-218
88Fle-94
88FleGlo-94
88FleLeaL-32
88FleStiC-130
88GiaMot-15
88Lea-219
88OPC-278
88Sco-519
88ScoGlo-519
88Spo-136
88StaLinG-14
88Top-660
88TopBig-188
88TopMinL-76
88TopRevLL-13
88TopRitTM-30
88TopTif-660
89Bow-466
89BowTif-466
89Don-11
89Don-335
89DonBasB-162
89DonSupD-11
89Fle-340
89FleGlo-340
89GiaMot-15
89OPC-65
89PanSti-210
89Sco-5
89ScoHot1S-22
89Spo-72
89Top-65
89TopBasT-83
89TopMinL-42
89TopSti-79
89TopTif-65
89TopUKM-63
89TVSpoM-50
89UppDec-194
90Bow-223
90BowTif-223
90Don-112
90Don-663A
90Don-663B
90Fle-68
90FleCan-68
90GiaMot-8
90KayB-25
90MLBBasB-23
90OPC-190
90OPCBoxB-L
90PanSti-206
90PanSti-370
90PubSti-79
90RedFolSB-77
90Sco-465
90Sco100S-7
90Spo-161
90Top-190
90TopBig-328
90TopGloA-10
90TopGloS-18
90TopMinL-87
90TopSti-89
90TopSti-154
90TopStiB-26
90TopTif-190
90TopWaxBC-L
90UppDec-696
90VenSti-428
90Woo-18
91Don-518
91Fle-270
91GiaMot-14
91OPC-422
91Sco-544
91Top-422
91TopDesS-422
91TopMic-422
91TopTif-422
91UppDec-249
92CubOldS-19
92YanWIZ8-156

Reuss, Jerry
70OPC-96
70Top-96
71CarTeal-30
71OPC-158
71Top-158
72Top-775
73LinPor-83
73OPC-446
73Top-446
74OPC-116
74Top-116
74TopSta-38
75OPC-124
75Pir-5
75Top-124
76CraDis-47
76Hos-29
76HosTwi-29
76Kel-43
76OPC-60
76SSP-562
76Top-60
77BurCheD-181
77Hos-119
77MSADis-49
77OPC-97
77PepGloD-65
77PirPosP-21
77Top-645
78Top-255
79Top-536
80DodPol-41
80Top-318
81Dod-9
81DodPol-41
81Don-417
81Fle-118
81LonBeaPT-9
81OPC-153
81Top-440
81TopScr-103
81TopSti-181
81TopSupHT-50
82DodPol-41
82DodUniOV-16
82DogBuiE-6
82Don-284
82Fle-18
82FleSta-7
82OPC-278
82Top-710
82TopSti-56
82TopSti-259
83AllGamPI-173
83DodPol-41
83DodPos-12
83Don-158
83Fle-216
83FleSta-161
83FleSti-123
83OPC-90
83Top-90
83TopFol-1
83TopSti-247
84DodPol-41
84DodUniOP-6
84Don-418
84Fle-110
84Nes792-170
84OPC-170
84Top-170
84TopSti-81
84TopTif-170
85DodCokP-26
85Don-226
85Fle-380
85OPC-66
85Top-680
85TopTif-680
86BasStaB-89
86DodCokP-25
86DodPol-41
86DodUniOP-15
86Don-104
86Fle-141
86OPC-236
86Spo-53
86Top-577
86TopSti-66
86TopTif-577
87AstShowSTh-20
87AstShowSTh-26
87DodPol-21
87DodSmoA-28
87Fle-451
87FleGlo-451
87OPC-373
87Top-682
87TopTif-682
88DodSmo-6
88Sco-270
88ScoGlo-270
88ScoRoo-61T
88ScoRooG-61T
88Top-216
88TopTif-216
88WhiSoxC-23
89Bow-57
89BowTif-57
89Don-413
89DonBasB-305
89Fle-510
89FleGlo-510
89Sco-489
89Top-357
89TopTif-357
89UppDec-151
89WhiSoxC-22
90DodTar-659
90Don-528
90Fle-335
90FleCan-335
90KayB-26
90OPC-424
90PubSti-400
90Top-424
90TopTif-424
90UppDec-96
90VenSti-429
91DodUno7P-4
92DodStaTA-19
94BreMilB-170

Reuteman, AGM (R.C.)
88TidTidCa-26

Reutter, Derrick
83KinBluJTI-18

Revak, Ray
86GreHorP-19

Reveira, Frank
60TacBan-17
61TacBan-18

Revelle, Dutch (R.H.)
09T206-511

Revenig, Todd
90SouOreAB-8
90SouOreAP-3445
91MadMusP-2130
92Bow-198
92HunStaF-3950
92HunStaS-319
92SkyAA F-136
93StaCluAt-26
93Top-766
93TopGol-766
93TopInaM-766
93TopMic-766
95EdmTraTI-19

Revering, Dave
76IndIndTI-7
77IndIndTI-4
78Top-706
79Hos-139
79OPC-113
79Top-224
80OPC-227
80Top-438
80TopSup-58
81A'sGraG-13
81Don-117
81Fle-576
81FleStiC-4
81OPC-57
81Top-568
81TopScr-22
81TopSti-117
81TopTra-823
82Don-234
82Fle-51
82OPC-109
82Top-109
82TopTra-97T
83Fle-484
83OPC-291
83Top-677
85IndIndTI-29
92YanWIZ8-157

Revson, Peter
74NewYorNTDiS-16

Rex, Mike
76CedRapGT-23
79PhoGiaVNB-23
80PhoGiaVNB-18
81PhoGiaVNB-11
82PhoGiaVNB-26

Rexrode, Jackie
97Top-469

Rey, Everett
80WatIndT-25
81ChaLooT-9
82ChaLooT-3
83BufBisT-12

Reyan, Julio
87BelMarL-8
89BelMarL-2
91BelMarP-3661

Reyes, Alberto
92AlbPolC-19
92AlbPolF-2305
93BurBeeC-21
93BurBeeF-157
93LimRocDWB-2
93MidLeaAGF-33
94HarSenF-2089
95Exc-226
95Fin-308
95Fla-275
95FleUpd-56
96ColCho-196
96ColChoGS-196
96ColChoSS-196
96Fle-156
96FleTif-156
97PacPriGotD-GD57

Reyes, Amner
90BenBucL-24

Reyes, Basilo
84IdaFalATI-22

Reyes, Carlos
86AshTouP-22

Reyes, Carlos Alberto
92MacBraC-20
92MacBraF-265
93GreBraF-346
94A'sMot-20
94Bow-492
94Fin-302
94FinRef-302
94Fla-332
94FleUpd-77
94Lea-296
94ScoRoo-RT117
94ScoRooGR-RT117
94SpoRoo-97
94SpoRooAP-97
94TopTra-128T
94Ult-410
95AthMot-20
95FinRef-308
95Fle-252
95Pac-319
95Sco-489
95ScoGolR-489
95ScoPlaTS-489
95Top-72
96A'sMot-21
96Fle-217
96FleTif-217
96LeaSigEA-169
96Pac-394
97Pac-175
97PacLigB-175
97PacSil-175

Reyes, Dennis
94GreFalDSP-26
94VerBeaDC-15
94VerBeaDF-69
96SanBerSB-21
97Bow-391
97BowChr-258
97BowChrI-258
97BowChrIR-258
97BowChrR-258
97BowInt-391
97DonLim-60
97DonLimLE-60

Reyes, Freddy
96AppLeaAB-18

Reyes, Gilberto
85AlbDukC-170
86AlbDukP-20
86Don-581
87AlbDukP-17
87DodPol-7
88AlbDukC-21
88AlbDukP-257
89IndIndC-11
89IndIndP-1240
90DodTar-1053
91Bow-447
91ExpPos-17
91FleUpd-99
91Lea-451
91UltUpd-92
92Don-381
92Fle-489
92OPC-286
92PanSti-201
92Pin-428
92Sco-229
92StaClu-173
92Top-286
92TopGol-286
92TopGolW-286
92TopMic-286
92Ult-225
92UppDec-230
93ColSprSSF-3089
93LimRocDWB-71

Reyes, Giovanny
86QuaCitAP-26
86SalAngC-77
87QuaCitAP-5
88PalSprACLC-109

Reyes, Jesus
73CedRapAT-8
74CedRapAT-3
76VenLeaS-187

Reyes, Jimmy
93HicCraC-20
93HicCraF-1288
94SouBenSHC-19
94SouBenSHF-603

Reyes, Jose
77CliDodT-20
80OrlTwiT-7
82OrlTwi8SCT-22
84MemChiT-21
85DomLeaS-189
86OmaRoyP-18
90BenBucL-13
91CliGiaC-9
91CliGiaP-833
96AugGreB-25

Reyes, Joselito
85KinBluJT-18

Reyes, Juan
86BelBreP-19
89BenBucL-6
89BriTigS-22

Reyes, Michael
94ElmPioF-3488
95KanCouCTI-13
94ElmPioC-17

Reyes, Nap
83TCMPla1945-35

Reyes, Orlando
76VenLeaS-191

Reyes, Pablo
85KinBluJT-9
86VenGulP-22

Reyes, Rafael
91RocExpC-11
91RocExpP-2046

Reyes, Sergio
91HunCubC-19
91HunCubP-3349

Reyes, Steve
88BilMusP-1810
Reyes, Victor
90ButCopKSP-20
Reyes, Wascar
78ChaPirT-20
Reyes, Winston
94MarPhiC-20
94MarPhiF-3304
Reyna, Dion
88MadMusP-19
Reyna, Luis
86VenGulP-23
87KnoBluJP-1502
88SyrChiC-12
88SyrChiP-810
Reynolds, Allie
47StaPinP2-33
47TipTop-56
48BluTin-21
48Bow-14
48YanTeal-23
49Bow-114
50Bow-138
50Dra-28
51BerRos-C3
51Bow-109
51R42SmaS-89
51TopRedB-6
52BasPho-4
52BerRos-52
52DixLid-15
52DixPre-15
52StaCalL-70A
52StaCalS-84A
52TipTop-31
52Top-67
53BowC-68
53DixLid-16
53DixPre-16
53Dor-109
53NorBreL-23
53SpoMagP-8
53Top-141
54Bow-113
54NewYorJA-56
55ArmCoi-16
55Bow-201
590klTodML-6
61Fle-69
68LauWorS-46
69EquSpoHoF-BB16
70FleWorS-46
71FleWorS-48
75JohMiz-13
75SheGrePG-5
76GrePlaG-5
77GalGloG-33
79TCM50-185
83TopRep5-67
83YanASFY-35
83YanYealT-12
84FifNatCT-14
85TCMPla1-8
88PacLegI-41
89SweBasG-101
91TopArc1-141
92BazQua5A-5
92UppDecS-16
92YanWIZA-62
93ActPacA-135
Reynolds, Archie
71MLBOffS-356
71OPC-664
71Top-664
72Top-672
94BreMilB-171
Reynolds, Carl
28PorandAR-C4
29ExhFou-20
30ChiEveAP-19
31Exh-20
32OrbPinNP-2
32OrbPinUP-50
33ButCanV-39
33CraJacP-18
33GeoCMil-25
33Gou-120
33TatOrb-50
34BatR31-49
34BatR31-95
34ButPreR-51
34GouCanV-12
35GouPuzR-6E
35GouPuzR-11G
35GouPuzR-13E
35GouPuzR-15E
39CubTeal-20
91ConTSN-80
Reynolds, Chance
93EveGiaC-21
93EveGiaF-3772
96CarMudB-15
Reynolds, Charles
87OldJudN-422
Reynolds, Craig
76OPC-596
76SSP-582
76Top-596
76VenLeaS-158
77Top-474
78Top-199
79AstTeal-11
79Kel-51
79OPC-251
79Top-482
80OPC-71
80Top-129
81Don-378
81Fle-74
81OPC-12
81Top-617
82AstAstI-4
82Don-344
82Fle-225
82OPC-57
82Top-57
82TopSti-46
83Don-317
83Fle-460
83Top-328
84AstMot-26
84Don-405
84Fle-237
84Nes792-776
84Top-776
84TopTif-776
85AllGamPI-114
85AstHouP-8
85AstMot-14
85Don-328
85Fle-357
85OPC-156
85Top-156
85TopMin-156
85TopSti-65
85TopTif-156
86AstMilL-17
86AstMot-18
86AstPol-13
86AstTeal-12
86Don-232
86Fle-309
86Lea-107
86OPC-298
86Top-298
86TopTif-298
87AstMot-19
87AstPol-10
87Don-384
87DonOpeD-19
87Fle-66
87FleGlo-66
87OPC-298
87Top-779
87TopTif-779
88AstMot-19
88AstPol-19
88Don-209
88Fle-454
88FleGlo-454
88Lea-205
88OPC-18
88PanSti-297
88Sco-207
88ScoGlo-207
88StaLinAst-14
88Top-557
88TopBig-219
88TopTif-557
89AstLenH-15
89AstMot-18
89AstSmo-33
89Bow-328
89BowTif-328
89Don-477
89Fle-366
89FleGlo-366
89PAORelT-5
89Sco-468
89Top-428
89TopBig-312
89TopTif-428
89UppDec-284
90OPC-637
90PubSti-100
90Top-637
90TopTif-637
90VenSti-430
Reynolds, Dave
86AppFoxP-19
87PenWhiSP-11
88TamTarS-21
89SarWhiSS-20
90BirBarB-21
90BirBarP-1109
Reynolds, Don
78PadFamF-24
79HawIsIT-13
79Top-292
80HawIsIT-23
87BelMarL-29
88SanBerSB-2
88SanBerSCLC-55
91JacGenLD-575
91JacGenP-941
91LinDriAA-575
92JacGenF-4016
94JacGenF-232
95TusTorTI-22
96TusTorB-27
Reynolds, Doug
89EriOriS-18
90FreKeyTI-9
91FreKeyC-14
91FreKeyP-2368
91KanCouCTI-17
Reynolds, Harold
81WauTimT-18
82LynSaiT-17
83SalLakCGT-22
84SalLakCGC-185
85MarMot-23
86CalCanP-23
86Don-484
86Top-769
86TopTif-769
87Don-489
87DonOpeD-117
87Fle-596
87FleGlo-596
87MarMot-10
87Top-91
87TopSti-216
87TopTif-91
88Don-563
88DonAll-13
88DonBasB-304
88Fle-388
88FleAwaW-32
88FleGlo-388
88FleMin-53
88FleRecS-31
88FleStiC-62
88Lea-227
88MarMot-10
88OPC-7
88PanSti-188
88PanSti-219
88Sco-277
88ScoGlo-277
88Spo-127
88StaLinMa-17
88Top-485
88Top-519
88TopBig-142
88TopMinL-35
88TopRevLL-19
88TopSti-221
88TopTif-485
88TopTif-519
88TopUKM-60
88TopUKMT-60
89Bow-210
89BowTif-210
89ClaTraO-147
89Don-21
89Don-93
89DonAll-27
89DonBasB-51
89DonSupD-21
89Fle-558
89FleBasA-34
89FleGlo-558
89FleHeroB-33
89FleLeaL-31
89K-M-13
89MarMot-10
89OPC-208
89PanSti-436
89RedFolSB-96
89Sco-310
89ScoHot1S-82
89Spo-165
89Top-580
89TopBasT-143
89TopBig-2
89TopMinL-74
89TopSti-226
89TopStiB-5
89TopTif-580
89TVSpoM-123
89UppDec-249
90Bow-478
90BowTif-478
90ClaBlu-128
90Don-227
90DonBesA-138
90Fle-524
90FleAwaW-27
90FleCan-524
90Hot50PS-33
90Lea-140
90MarMot-6
90MLBBasB-118
90OPC-161
90PanSti-144
90PubSti-294
90PubSti-441
90Sco-167
90Sco100S-43
90Spo-119
90Top-161
90TopBig-321
90TopDou-51
90TopHeaU-17
90TopMinL-34
90TopSti-221
90TopTif-161
90UppDec-179
90VenSti-431
90VenSti-432
91Bow-252
91ClaGam-47
91Don-175
91Fle-460
91Lea-297
91MarCouH-3
91OPC-260
91PanCanT1-55
91PanCanT1-111
91PanFreS-229
91PanSti-191
91Sco-48
91SevCoi-NW13
91StaClu-217
91Stu-119
91Top-260
91TopDesS-260
91TopMic-260
91TopTif-260
91TopTriH-A12
91Ult-343
91UppDec-32
91UppDec-148
92Bow-503
92Don-239
92Fle-291
92Hig5-110
92HitTheBB-27
92Lea-38
92MarMot-3
92OPC-670
92PanSti-56
92Pin-59
92Sco-250
92StaClu-181
92Stu-239
92Top-670
92TopGol-670
92TopGolW-670
92TopKid-123
92TopMic-670
92TriPla-203
92Ult-129
92UppDec-314
93Bow-57
93Don-639
93Fin-50
93FinRef-50
93Fla-156
93Fle-680
93FleFinE-165
93Lea-370
93OPC-279
93OPCPre-89
93PacSpa-349
93Pin-530
93Sco-559
93Sel-134
93SelRoo-14T
93StaClu-23
93StaClu-668
93StaCluFDI-23
93StaCluFDI-668
93StaCluMOP-23
93StaCluMOP-668
93Stu-129
93Top-757
93TopGol-757
93TopInaM-757
93TopMic-757
93Ult-499
93UppDec-35
93UppDec-803
93UppDecGold-35
93UppDecGold-803
94AngLAT-22
94AngMot-12
94ColC-384
94ColChoGS-384
94ColChoSS-384
94Don-271
94ExtBas-38
94Fla-273
94Fle-17
94FleUpd-21
94Lea-428
94Pac-43
94PanSti-22
94Pin-475
94PinArtP-475
94PinMusC-475
94Sco-441
94ScoGolR-441
94ScoRoo-RT20
94ScoRooGR-RT20
94Sel-313
94StaClu-625
94StaCluFDI-625
94StaCluGR-625
94StaCluMOP-625
94Top-355
94TopGol-355
94TopSpa-355
94Ult-332
94UppDec-423
94UppDecED-423
95ColCho-93
95Top-69
Reynolds, Jeff
83SyrChiT-19
86JacExpT-21
87IndIndTI-16
88TolMudHC-15
88TolMudHP-585
89NasSouTI-19
Reynolds, Ken
71OPC-664
71Top-664
72OPC-252
72Top-252
73OPC-638
73Top-638
75TulOil7-4
76HawIsIC-14
76SSP-292
78SyrChiT-16
79SyrChiT-19
79SyrChiTI-15
87GenCubP-6
89GenCubP-1885
94BreMilB-173
Reynolds, Larry
80TulDriT-9
81TulDriT-7
82ArkTraT-21
83ArkTraT-22
84ArkTraT-9
Reynolds, Mark

85OscAstTI-14
Reynolds, Mike
79RicBraT-2
82RicBraT-18
84RicBraT-1
85DurBulT-30
86DurBulP-22
Reynolds, Neil
87SalLakTTT-5
Reynolds, R.J. (Robert J.)
81VerBeaDT-17
84AlbDukC-148
84FleUpd-97
85DodCokP-27
85DomLeaS-24
85Don-128
85Fle-381
85Top-369
85TopTif-369
86Don-552
86Fle-619
86FleMin-120
86Lea-212
86OPC-306
86Top-417
86TopTif-417
87Don-65
87Fle-620
87FleGlo-620
87GenMilB-5F
87OPC-109
87RedFolSB-77
87SpoTeaP-18
87StuPan-10
87Top-109
87TopSti-134
87TopTif-109
88Don-65
88DonBasB-201
88Fle-339
88FleGlo-339
88OPC-27
88PanSti-379
88Sco-34
88ScoGlo-34
88StaLinPi-17
88Top-27
88TopTif-27
89Don-134
89DonBasB-257
89Fle-219
89FleGlo-219
89PirVerFJ-23
89Sco-91
89Top-658
89TopTif-658
89UppDec-315
90DodTar-660
90Don-447
90Fle-478
90FleCan-478
90Lea-381
90OPC-592
90PirHomC-25
90PubSti-163
90Sco-469
90Top-592
90TopSti-126
90TopTif-592
90UppDec-540
91Don-101
91Fle-48
91OPC-198
91Sco-273
91Top-198
91TopDesS-198
91TopMic-198
91TopTif-198
91UppDec-150
Reynolds, Randy
76AshTouT-2
Reynolds, Robert
71OPC-664
71Top-664
72OPC-162
72Top-162
73OPC-612
73OriJohP-34
73Top-612
74OPC-259
74Top-259
75OPC-142
75Top-142
82IowCubT-28
91OriCro-378
94BreMilB-172
Reynolds, Ronn
82JacMetT-11
84TidTidT-25
85MetColP-30
85MetTCM-20
86Fle-92
86PhiTas-29
86PorBeaP-19
86Top-649
86TopTif-649
87PhiTas-29
87Top-471
87TopTif-471
87TucTorP-20
88DenZepC-16
88DenZepP-1262
89UppDec-627A
90CMC-515
90LasVegSC-12
90LasVegSP-127
90ProAAAF-15
91MetWIZ-328
91PacSenL-109
Reynolds, Shane
89AubAstP-2161
90ColMudB-12
90ColMudP-1345
91Cla/Bes-67
91JacGenLD-572
91JacGenP-926
91LinDriAA-572
92Bow-327
92DonRoo-102
92SkyAAAF-275
92TucTorF-485
92TucTorS-617
93Don-164
93Pin-254
93Sco-282
93Top-522
93TopGol-522
93TopInaM-522
93TopMic-522
93TucTorF-3058
94AstMot-22
94ExtBas-280
94Fla-392
94FleUpd-147
94LeaLimR-41
94Sco-586
94ScoGolR-586
94ScoRoo-RT86
94ScoRooGR-RT86
94Sel-196
94SpoRoo-123
94SpoRooAP-123
94StaClu-558
94StaCluFDI-558
94StaCluGR-558
94StaCluMOP-558
94Ult-511
95AstMot-21
95ColCho-117
95ColChoGS-117
95ColChoSS-117
95Don-307
95DonPreP-307
95DonTopotO-260
95Fla-364
95Fle-467
95FleRooS-15
95Lea-245
95Pac-193
95Sco-538
95ScoGolR-538
95ScoPlaTS-538
95StaClu-270
95StaCluFDI-270
95StaCluMOP-270
95StaCluSTWS-270
95StaCluVR-135
95Top-257
95Ult-176
95UltGolM-176
95UppDec-23
95UppDecED-23
95UppDecEDG-23
95USPlaCMLA-7S
96AstMot-13
96Cir-139
96CirRav-139
96ColCho-164
96ColChoGS-164
96ColChoSS-164
96Don-411
96DonPreP-411
96EmoXL-203
96Fin-B31
96FinRef-B31
96Fla-284
96Fle-418
96FleTif-418
96LeaSigA-192
96LeaSigAG-192
96LeaSigAS-192
96MetUni-180
96MetUniP-180
96Pac-95
96PanSti-60
96ProSta-15
96Sco-212
96StaClu-110
96StaCluEPB-110
96StaCluEPG-110
96StaCluEPS-110
96StaCluMOP-110
95StaCluVRMC-135
96Top-169
96TopChr-49
96TopChrR-49
96TopGal-66
96TopGalPPI-66
96TopLas-61
96Ult-214
96UltGolM-214
96UppDec-79
97Cir-44
97CirRav-44
97ColCho-124
97Don-59
97DonEli-132
97DonEliGS-132
97DonLim-109
97DonLimLE-109
97DonPreP-59
97DonPrePGold-59
97Fin-258
97FinRef-258
97Fle-353
97FleTif-353
97Lea-70
97LeaFraM-70
97LeaFraMDC-70
97MetUni-140
97PacPri-109
97PacPriLB-109
97PacPriP-109
97PacPriSH-SH10B
97Pin-130
97PinArtP-130
97PinIns-103
97PinInsCE-103
97PinInsDE-103
97PinMusC-130
97ProMag-19
97ProMagML-19
97Sco-284
97ScoPreS-284
97ScoShoS-284
97ScoShoSAP-284
97SP-83
97SpoIll-69
97SpoIllEE-69
97StaClu-45
97StaCluMat-45
97StaCluMOP-45
97Stu-58
97StuPrePG-58
97StuPrePS-58
97Top-430
97Ult-211
97UltGolME-211
97UltPlaME-211
97UppDec-369
Reynolds, Tim
83CedRapRF-1
83CedRapRT-9
Reynolds, Tommie (Thomas D.)
64Top-528
65Top-333
67Top-487
69A'sJacitB-12
69Top-467
70OPC-259
70Top-259
71OPC-676
71Top-676
74SacSolC-46
75IntLeaASB-26
75PacCoaLAB-26
75SacSolC-3
76SpoIndC-16
77SpoIndC-15
78SpoIndC-15
86ModA'sC-25
86ModA'sP-21
87ModA'sC-23
87ModA'sP-23
88HunStaTI-15
89A'sMot-27
90A'sMot-27
91A'sMot-28
91MetWIZ-329
92AthMot-28
93AthMot-27
94A'sMot-28
94BreMilB-174
95AthMot-28
Reynolds, Walker
95DanBraTI-24
Reynolds, William
86MedA'sC-56
Reynoso, Armando
91BraSubS-31
91LinDriAAA-438
91RicBraBC-14
91RicBraLD-438
91RicBraP-2566
91RicBraTI-1
91TriA AAGP-AAA38
92Fle-367
92OPC-631
92RicBraBB-7
92RicBraF-375
92RicBraRC-15
92RicBraS-437
92Sco-877
92SkyAAAF-201
92SkyAAAF-296
92StaClu-763
92StaCluECN-763
92Top-631
92TopDeb91-145
92TopGol-631
92TopGolW-631
92TopMic-631
92UppDec-674
93Don-752
93FleFinE-41
93Lea-454
93PacJugC-35
93PacSpa-436
93SelRoo-38T
93SP-224
93StaClu-652
93StaCluFDI-652
93StaCluMOP-652
93TopTra-116T
93UppDec-793
93UppDecGold-793
94Bow-198
94ColC-238
94ColChoGS-238
94ColChoSS-238
94Don-497
94ExtBas-252
94Fin-14
94FinJum-14
94FinRef-14
94Fla-157
94Fle-451
94FleRooS-15
94Lea-148
94OPC-114
94Pac-205
94Pin-220
94PinArtP-220
94PinMusC-220
94RocPol-21
94Sco-227
94ScoGolR-227
94Sel-344
94StaClu-332
94StaCluFDI-332
94StaCluGR-332
94StaCluMOP-332
94StaCluT-103
94StaCluTFDI-103
94Top-49
94TopGol-49
94TopSpa-49
94TriPla-230
94Ult-188
94UppDec-348
94UppDecED-348
94USPlaCR-12S
95Pac-144
95Sco-497
95ScoGolR-497
95ScoPlaTS-497
95Top-349
96ColCho-536
96ColChoGS-536
96ColChoSS-536
96Pac-57
96RocPol-18
96Ult-191
96UltGolM-191
96UppDec-321
97Cir-237
97CirRav-237
97ColCho-96
97Fle-316
97Fle-673
97FleTif-316
97FleTif-673
97Pac-287
97PacLigB-287
97PacSil-287
97RicBraBC-2
97Sco-204
97ScoPreS-204
97ScoRoc-11
97ScoRocPl-11
97ScoRocPr-11
97ScoShoS-204
97ScoShoSAP-204
97Top-217
97Ult-506
97UltGolME-506
97UltPlaME-506
Reynoso, Ben
96IdaFalB-20
Reynoso, Gabriel
92MedHatBJF-3209
92MedHatBJSP-21
Reynoso, Henry
90BelBreB-19
90BelBreS-17
Reynoso, Querbin
92GulCoaRSP-23
93ChaRaiC-16
93ChaRaiF-1909
94ChaRivC-16
94ChaRivF-2670
Reznik, Brad
89BirBarB-30
Rhawn, Bobby
52Par-2
Rhea, Allen
90St.CatBJP-3469
Rhea, Chip
96AriBlaDB-26
Rhein, Jeff
92AubAstC-7
92AubAstF-1367
93QuaCitRBC-18
93QuaCitRBF-113
Rhem, Flint (Charles)
28W56PlaC-S3A
33DouDisP-35
33Gou-136
34GouCanV-5
35GouPuzR-8L
35GouPuzR-9L
74Car193T-21
87ConSer2-52
88ConSer4-23
91ConTSN-325
Rhiel, William
36GouWidPPR-D30
36WorWidGV-81
90DodTar-661
Rhine, Kendall
93AubAstC-19
93AubAstF-3441
94AubAstC-12
94AubAstF-3756
94ClaGolF-17
95HagSunF-68
96DunBluJB-20
96DunBluJTI-24
Rhinehart, Dallas

92BoiHawF-3624
Rhines, Billy
98CamPepP-63
Rhoades, James
88AugPirP-387
Rhoads, Robert
05IndSouPSoCP-15
08RosComP-29
09T206-301
09T206-302
10CouT21-56
11SpoLifCW-301
11TurRedT-114
Rhoda, Gary
93HelBreF-4091
93HelBreSP-22
Rhodas, Kevin
83MiaMarT-10
Rhoden, Rick
74AlbDukTI-15
75OPC-618
75Top-618
76LinSup-124
76OPC-439
76SSP-72
76Top-439
77BurCheD-148
77OPC-57
77Top-245
78OPC-159
78SSP270-59
78Top-605
79OPC-66
79Top-145
80PorBeaT-27
80Top-92
81AllGamPI-172
81Fle-377
81OPC-312
81Top-312
82Don-423
82Fle-493
82Top-513
82TopSti-82
83Don-250
83Fle-318
83FleSta-162
83OPC-181
83Top-781
84Don-552
84Fle-261
84Nes792-485
84Nes792-696
84OPC-46
84Top-485
84Top-696
84TopTif-485
84TopTif-696
85Don-552
85Fle-474
85FleStaS-97
85Lea-63
85OPC-53
85Pir-17
85Top-695
85TopSti-127
85TopTif-695
86Don-166
86DonHig-20
86Fle-620
86OPC-232
86Top-232
86Top-756
86TopSti-130
86TopTat-9
86TopTif-232
86TopTif-756
87DodSmoA-29
87Don-10
87Don-435
87DonAll-24
87DonSupD-10
87Fle-621
87FleGlo-621
87FleUpd-103
87FleUpdG-103
87Lea-10
87OPC-365
87RedFolSB-103
87Spo-129
87SpoTeaP-7
87Top-365
87TopMinL-31
87TopSti-130
87TopTif-365
87TopTra-101T
87TopTraT-101T
88Don-128
88DonBasB-161
88DonReaBY-128
88Fle-219
88FleGlo-219
88FleStiC-51
88FleSup-30
88Lea-98
88OPC-185
88PanSti-149
88RedFolSB-74
88Sco-74
88ScoGlo-74
88Spo-104
88SpoGam-16
88StaLinY-12
88Top-185
88TopBig-108
88TopSti-298
88TopTif-185
89AstLenH-3
89AstMot-24
89AstSmo-34
89Bow-323
89BowTif-323
89DodSmoG-87
89Don-429
89DonTra-40
89Fle-266
89FleGlo-266
89FleUpd-89
89OPC-18
89PanSti-399
89Sco-317
89Top-18
89TopBig-237
89TopDouM-23
89TopTif-18
89UppDec-56
90DodTar-662
90Fle-235
90FleCan-235
90OPC-588
90PubSti-101
90Top-588
90TopTif-588
90UppDec-504
92DodStaTA-15
92YanWIZ8-158
Rhodes, Art (Arthur Lee)
89EriOriS-19
90FreKeyTI-29
91Bow-95
91Cla/Bes-335
91ClaGolB-BC14
91HagSunLD-244
91HagSunP-2457
91LeaGolR-BC6
91LinDriAA-244
91UppDecFE-13F
92Bow-631
92Cla1-T75
92ClaGam-146
92Don-727
92Fle-24
92Lea-394
92OPC-771
92Pin-251
92ProFS7-6
92RocRedWF-1939
92RocRedWS-464
92Sco-736
92ScoImpP-35
92ScoRoo-7
92SkyAAAF-211
92StaClu-641
92StaCluECN-641
92Top-771
92TopDeb91-146
92TopGol-771
92TopGolW-771
92TopMic-771
92UppDec-17
93Bow-169
93Don-133
93Fle-174
93FleRooS-RSB8
93Lea-397
93OPC-329
93PacSpa-350
93Pin-326
93Sco-360
93Sel-300
93SelChaR-14
93StaClu-560
93StaCluFDI-560
93StaCluMOP-560
93Top-554
93TopGol-554
93TopInaM-554
93TopMic-554
93Toy-28
93Ult-500
93UppDec-384
93UppDecGold-384
93USPlaCR-6C
94ColC-373
94ColChoGS-373
94ColChoSS-373
94Don-299
94Fin-335
94FinRef-335
94Fle-18
94OPC-17
94OriPro-83
94OriUSPC-5C
94OriUSPC-10H
94RocRedWTI-19
94StaClu-129
94StaCluFDI-129
94StaCluGR-129
94StaCluMOP-129
94StaCluT-280
94StaCluTFDI-280
94Top-477
94TopGol-477
94TopSpa-477
94Ult-309
95Fla-8
95Fle-18
95StaClu-453
95StaCluMOP-453
95StaCluSTWS-453
95Top-289
95TopCyb-156
95Ult-257
95UltGolM-257
95UppDec-369
95UppDecED-369
95UppDecEDG-369
96LeaSigA-193
96LeaSigAG-193
96LeaSigAS-193
97PacPriGotD-GD14
97Top-53
97Ult-10
97UltGolME-10
97UltPlaME-10
Rhodes, Charles
09PC7HHB-37
09T206-303
Rhodes, Dusty
89HelBreSP-27
91HelBreSP-29
Rhodes, Dusty (James L.)
54NewYorJA-34
54Top-170
55GiaGolS-23
55RedMan-NL22
55StaMey-10
55Top-1
55TopDouH-27
56Top-50
56TopHocF-A4
56TopHocF-B6
57Top-61
60TacBan-18
61TacBan-19
61UniOil-T26
68LauWorS-51
79TCM50-190
84FifNatCT-15
91TopArc1-299
94TedWilM-M23
94TopArc1-170
94TopArc1G-170
Rhodes, Gordon
35DiaMatCS3T1-124
93ConTSN-983
Rhodes, Harry(Lefty)
93NegLeaRL2-34
Rhodes, Jeff
83CedRapRF-15
83CedRapRT-24
Rhodes, Joey
96HigDesMB-23
Rhodes, Mike
83ArkTraT-1
86ArkTraP-17
89Ft.LauYS-20
89Sta-79
90GreHorB-24
90GreHorP-2676
90GreHorS-17
Rhodes, Ricky
89OneYanP-2123
90Bes-249
90CMC-823
90GreHorB-11
90GreHorP-2663
90GreHorS-18
90ProAaA-86
91Cla/Bes-235
91PriWilCC-11
91PriWilCP-1427
92ForLauYC-22
92ForLauYTI-26
92Ft.LauYF-2610
Rhodes, Tuffy (Karl)
87AshTouP-1
88FloStaLAS-18
88OscAstS-22
89ColMudB-22
89ColMudP-142
89ColMudS-19
90Bow-79
90BowTif-79
90CMC-620
90ProAAAF-208
90TucTorC-18
90TucTorP-218
91AstMot-14
91Bow-544
91ClaGam-72
91Don-698
91Fle-514
91Lea-195
91OPC-516
91Sco-365
91ScoRoo-32
91StaClu-52
91Top-516
91TopDeb90-130
91TopDesS-516
91TopMic-516
91TopTif-516
91UppDec-466
91UppDec-702
92StaClu-241
92TucTorS-618
93LinVenB-229
93OmaRoyF-1694
93TriAAAGF-43
93Ult-395
94Bow-222
94ColC-489
94ColChoGS-489
94ColChoSS-489
94ExtBas-222
94Fin-330
94FinRef-330
94Fla-140
94FleUpd-110
94Lea-356
94Pac-106
94Pin-497
94PinArtP-497
94PinMusC-497
94Sco-447
94ScoGolR-447
94Sel-141
94StaClu-608
94StaCluFDI-608
94StaCluGR-608
94StaCluMOP-608
94StaCluT-344
94StaCluTFDI-344
94Stu-62
94Top-657
94TopGol-657
94TopSpa-657
94Ult-463
94UppDec-492
94UppDecED-492
94VenLinU-87
95Don-334
95DonPreP-334
95Fla-115
95Fle-422
95Pac-76
95Pin-213
95PinArtP-213
95PinMusC-213
95Sco-121
95ScoGolR-121
95ScoPlaTS-121
95StaClu-369
95StaCluMOP-369
95StaCluSTWS-369
95Top-178
95Ult-362
95UltGolM-362
Rhodriguez, Rory
91PriRedC-22
91PriRedP-3513
96WesPalBEB-13
Rhomberg, Kevin
78WatIndT-18
80TacTigT-20
80VenLeaS-255
81ChaLooT-23
82ChaChaT-17
83ChaChaT-17
83IndPos-29
84Ind-25
85PhoGiaC-193
88ChaLooLTI-26
Rhone, O.J.
93EugEmeC-22
93EugEmeF-3871
94RocRoyC-20
94RocRoyF-578
Rhubarb, Mascot
95TacRaiTI-30
96TacRaiB-30
Rhyne, Hal
29ExhFou-18
31Exh-18
33ExhFou-9
91ConTSN-195
Ribant, Dennis
65OPC-73
65Top-73
66Top-241
66TopVen-241
67Kah-31
67PirTeal-18
67Top-527
67TopPirS-3
68CokCapT-13
68Top-326
68TopVen-326
69Top-463
81TCM60I-443
91MetWIZ-330
Ribbie, Mascot
85WhiSoxC-NNO
86WhiSoxC-NNO
87WhiSoxC-25
88WhiSoxC-25
Ricabal, Dan
94YakBeaC-15
94YakBeaF-3845
95Exc-217
95SanBerSTI-17
96HilStaHWB-NNO
96SavSanB-13
Ricanelli, John
76QuaCitAT-29
78STLakCGC-11
Riccelli, Frank
74OPC-599
74Top-599A
74Top-599B
74Top-599C
75LafDriT-15
76PheGiaCr-30
76PhoGiaCa-7
76PhoGiaCC-20
76PhoGiaVNB-21
77Gia-19
77PhoGiaCC-20
77PhoGiaCP-20
77PhoGiaVNB-20
78SprRedWK-17
80Top-247
81BufBisT-24
82SyrChiT-6
89PacSenL-59
91PacSenL-67
Ricci, Chuck
89WatDiaP-1783
89WatDiaS-24

91FreKeyC-7
91FreKeyP-2362
92HagSunF-2554
93BowBayF-2186
94ReaPhiF-2061
95ScrRedBTI-23
96PawRedSDD-24
Ricci, Frank
81NasSouTI-15
82NasSouTI-19
83BeaGolGT-17
Ricciardi, J.P.
88SouOreAP-1714
Riccitant, Chuck
90FreKeyTI-26
Rice, Andy
94Top-208
94TopGol-208
94TopSpa-208
Rice, Charles
94ClaGolF-77
96AugGreB-26
96EriSeaB-21
96Exc-223
Rice, David
89BenBucL-9
Rice, Del
46SeaSLP-42
47Exh-185
47TipTop-161
49EurSta-195
49MPR302-2-112
50Bow-125
51Bow-156
51R42SmaS-87
52Bow-107
52Top-100
53BowC-53
53CarHunW-18
53Top-68
54Bow-30
54CarHunW-21
54RedMan-NL9
55Bow-106
55CarHunW-20
57Top-193
58Top-51
59Top-104
59TopVen-104
60Top-248
61Top-448
72Top-718
83TopRep5-100
91OriCro-379
91TopArc1-68
Rice, Gary
91AdeGiaF-2
Rice, Grantland
90LitSunW-5
92MegRut-163
92MegRutP-138
Rice, Gregory
51BerRos-D17
Rice, Hal
51Bow-300
52Top-398
53CarHunW-19
53Top-93
54Bow-219
54Top-95
55Bow-52
83TopRep5-398
91TopArc1-93
94TopArc1-95
94TopArc1G-95
Rice, Harry F.
29ExhFou-23
29PorandAR-70
31SenTealPW-26
34DiaMatCSB-152
91ConTSN-216
Rice, Jim
57JetPos-18
75OPC-616
75SSPPuzB-21
75Top-616
76Hos-127
76Kel-10
76LinSup-113
76OPC-340
76RedSox-7
76RedSoxSM-13
76SSP-405
76Top-340
77BurCheD-29
77Hos-23
77OPC-62
77Spo-3810
77Top-60
78Hos-45
78Kel-49
78OPC-2
78OPC-163
78PapGinD-14
78RCColC-77
78SSP270-189
78Top-202
78Top-670
78WifBalD-61
79Hos-2
79Kel-15
79OPC-210
79SpaGloT-1
79Top-2
79Top-3
79Top-400
79TopCom-2
80BurKinPHR-20
80Kel-44
80OPC-112
80Top-200
80TopSup-5
80WilGloT-5
80WilGloT-6
81AllGamPI-66
81CokTeaS-9
81Don-338
81Dra-8
81Fle-222
81FleStiC-53
81Kel-9
81OPC-68
81PerCreC-23
81Squ-7
81Top-500
81TopScr-13
81TopSti-41
81TopSupHT-8
81TopSupN-11
82Don-200
82Dra-27
82FBIDis-16
82Fle-305
82FleSta-163
82K-M-33
82OPC-366
82RedSoxC-17
82Top-750
82TopSti-150
82WilSpoG-6
83AllGamPI-67
83Don-208
83Dra-22
83Fle-194
83FleSta-163
83FleSti-66
83Kel-13
83Oco& SSBG-13
83OPC-30
83PerAll-4
83PerAllG-4
83PerCreC-31
83PerCreCG-31
83Top-30
83Top-381
83TopFol-2
83TopFol-3
83TopSti-37
84AllGamPI-157
84Don-50
84DonActAS-52
84DonCha-4
84Dra-25
84Fle-408
84FleSti-20
84FleSti-37
84FunFooP-5
84Nes792-132
84Nes792-133
84Nes792-401
84Nes792-550
84NesDreT-5
84OCoandSI-31
84OPC-184
84OPC-364
84RalPur-9
84SevCoi-E15
84Top-132
84Top-133
84Top-401
84Top-550
84TopCer-9
84TopGloA-6
84TopGloS-22
84TopRubD-16
84TopSti-102A
84TopSti-189
84TopSti-200B
84TopSti-217
84TopSup-5
84TopTif-132
84TopTif-133
84TopTif-401
84TopTif-550
85AllGamPI-69
85Don-15
85Don-50
85DonActA-27
85DonSupD-15
85Dra-25
85Fle-168
85FleLimE-27
85FleStaS-13
85FleStaS-23
85GenMilS-22
85Lea-15
85OPC-150
85SevCoi-E4
85SevCoi-W2
85SpoSam-1
85Top-150
85Top3-D-6
85TopGloS-6
85TopMin-150
85TopRubD-14
85TopSti-208
85TopSup-50
85TopTif-150
86BasStaB-90
86BurKinA-8
86Don-213
86DonAll-16
86DonPop-16
86DorChe-20
86Dra-13
86Fle-358
86FleMin-76
86FleStiC-96
86GenMilB-1G
86Lea-146
86MeaGolSB-14
86MSAJifPD-1
86OPC-320
86QuaGra-30
86SevCoi-C5
86SevCoi-E5
86SevCoi-S5
86SevCoi-W5
86Spo-17
86Spo-52
86Spo-61
86Spo-139
86Spo-146
86SpoDecG-57
86StaRic-1
86StaRic-2
86StaRic-3
86StaRic-4
86StaRic-5
86StaRic-6
86StaRic-7
86StaRic-8
86StaRic-9
86StaRic-10
86StaRic-11
86StaRic-12
86Top-320
86Top3-D-23
86TopGloA-6
86TopGloS-36
86TopSti-161
86TopSti-246
86TopSup-43
86TopTat-20
86TopTif-320
86TruVal-7
86WilGloT-2
86Woo-28
87BoaandB-5
87BurKinA-16
87ClaGam-59
87Don-92
87DonAll-45
87DonOpeD-182
87Dra-15
87Fle-41
87Fle-633
87FleExcS-37
87FleGlo-41
87FleGlo-633
87FleHea-6
87FleLimE-35
87FleMin-89
87FleStiC-99
87K-M-18
87KayB-26
87KraFoo-5
87Lea-247
87MSAJifPD-19
87OPC-146
87OPCBoxB-F
87RedFolSB-44
87RedSoxSAP-10
87SevCoi-E14
87SevCoi-M14
87Spo-80
87Spo-97
87SpoDeaP-3
87SpoTeaP-9
87Top-480
87Top-610
87TopCoi-21
87TopGloS-42
87TopMinL-44
87TopSti-17
87TopSti-248
87TopTif-480
87TopTif-610
87TopWaxBC-F
87Woo-5
87Woo-27
88CheBoy-21
88Don-399
88DonBasB-28
88DonTeaBRS-399
88Fle-361
88FleGlo-361
88Lea-215
88OPC-61
88PanSti-33
88Sco-14
88ScoGlo-14
88Spo-158
88StaLinRS-16
88Top-662
88Top-675
88TopBig-181
88TopSti-247
88TopTif-662
88TopTif-675
89Bow-33
89BowTif-33
89Don-122
89Fle-97
89FleGlo-97
89OPC-245
89OPCBoxB-I
89PanSti-281
89Sco-85
89Spo-173
89Top-245
89TopBasT-112
89TopBatL-9
89TopBig-18
89TopSti-256
89TopTif-245
89TopWaxBC-I
89UppDec-413
90KayB-27
90MLBBasB-70
90OPC-785
90OPCBoxB-M
90PubSti-463
90Top-785
90TopAmeA-3
90TopBatL-9
90TopHilHM-8
90TopTif-785
90TopWaxBC-M
90UppDec-373
91PacSenL-148
92KelAll-8
92MDAMVP-12
93ActPacA-166
93Yoo-14
Rice, Lance
88GreFalDTI-7
89BakDodCLC-192
89CalLeaA-5
90SanAntMGS-23
91LinDriAA-539
91SanAntMLD-539
91SanAntMP-2979
92SanAntMF-3978
94HarSenF-2108
96BowBayB-24
Rice, Pat
87WauTimP-24
88SanBerSB-6
88SanBerSCLC-43
89WilBilP-646
89WilBilS-18
90CalCanC-4
90CalCanP-650
90CMC-431
90ProAAAF-115
91CalCanLD-70
91CalCanP-515
91Cla3-T76
91LinDriAAA-70
92CalCanF-3730
92CalCanS-69
92Fle-658
92Sco-423
92SkyAAAF-32
92TopDeb91-147
96WisTimRB-2
Rice, Pete
83AleDukT-8
85NasPirT-19
86NasPirP-22
87SalBucP-7
88TolMudHC-23
88TolMudHP-598
Rice, Rich
86ChaOriW-24
Rice, Sam (Edgar)
16ColE13-137
17HolBreD-82
19W514-79
20NatCarE-83
20WalMaiW-44
21E121So1-78
21E121So8-75
21Exh-140
22AmeCarE-55
22E120-117
22W572-83
22W575-102
23W501-14
23WilChoV-130
26SpoComoA-34
26SpoNewSM-7
27AmeCarE-29
27YorCarE-36
28W502-36
28Yue-36
29ExhFou-32
29PorandAR-71
31Exh-32
31SenTealPW-27
33DouDisP-36
33Gou-134
34DiaStaR-32
34GouCanV-18
60Fle-34
60SenUniMC-16
61Fle-70
75TCMAllG-27
76RowExh-10
76ShaPiz-93
77GalGloG-108
80PerHaloFP-93
80SSPHOF-93
81SpoHaloF-19
82DiaCla-11
91ConTSN-54
92ConTSN-436
93ConTSN-887
94ConTSN-1256
94ConTSNB-1256
Rice, Tim
86WinSpiP-22
87PitCubP-24
88BasCitRS-20
Rice, Woolsey
83BelBreF-2
Rich, Bart
94KanCouCC-22
Rich, Ted

93SouBenWSC-19
92UtiBluSC-10
Rich, Woody
39GouPreR303A-38
39WorWidGTP-38
Richard, Bee Bee (Lee)
72OPC-476
72Top-476
75OPC-653
75Top-653
76OPC-533
76SSP-145
76Top-533
Richard, Chris
95NewJerCTI-25
96StPetCB-27
Richard, Henri
72Dia-98
72Dia-99
Richard, J.R.
72OPC-101
72Top-101
74OPC-522
74Top-522
74TopSta-36
75OPC-73
75Top-73
76Hos-110
76OPC-625
76Top-625
77BurCheD-1
77Hos-112
77OPC-227
77RCColC-55
77Spo-7103
77Top-260
78AstBurK-4
78Hos-92
78OPC-149
78RCColC-49
78Top-470
79AstTeal-12
79Hos-29
79Kel-19
79OPC-310
79Top-6
79Top-203
79Top-590
79TopCom-23
80BurKinPHR-8
80Kel-58
80OPC-28
80Top-50
80Top-206
80Top-207
80TopSup-25
81CokTeaS-68
81Don-140
81Fle-56
81FleStiC-44
81Kel-16
81MSAMinD-26
81OPC-350
81Top-350
82Fle-226
82OPC-190
82Top-190
86AstGreT-9
86AstMot-21
87AstShoSO-20
87AstShowSTh-26
88HouSho-18
92UppDecS-26
93UppDecS-11
Richard, Maurice
43ParSpo-67
43ParSpo-68
Richard, Ray
79WatIndT-32
Richard, Ron
91YakBeaC-4
91YakBeaP-4255
Richardi, Rick
85MiaHur-13
87MiaMarP-8
88MiaMarS-20
Richards, Bob
68AtlOil-9
Richards, Dave
78LodDodT-13
81AlbDukT-8
82HawIslT-2
Richards, Dave T.
88FayGenP-1095
89LakTigS-18
90LonTigP-1267
91JacSunLD-343
91JacSunP-150
91LinDriAA-343
92ArkTraF-1129
92ElPasDF-3919
93ElPasDF-2949
Richards, Fuzzy (Fred)
53MotCoo-50
Richards, Gene (Eugene)
76HawIslC-13
77PadSchC-46A
77PadSchC-46B
77Top-473
78PadFamF-25
78Top-292
79Top-364
80OPC-323
80Top-616
81AllGamPI-160
81Don-4
81Fle-486
81FleStiC-17
81OPC-171
81Top-171
81TopScr-86
81TopSti-225
82Don-499
82Fle-580
82FleSta-104
82OPC-253
82Top-708
82TopSti-103
83AllGamPI-159
83Don-271
83Fle-370
83OPC-7
83Top-7
83TopSti-294
84Don-429
84Fle-310
84FleUpd-98
84GiaPos-23
84Nes792-594
84Top-594
84TopTif-594
84TopTra-99T
84TopTraT-99T
85Fle-619
85Top-434
85TopTif-434
86PadGreT-5
89PacSenL-48
89T/MSenL-90
89TopSenL-63
90EliSenL-102
91LinDriAA-450
91MidAngOHP-21
91MidAngP-450
92CalLeaACL-52
92PalSprAC-29
92PalSprAF-857
93PalSprAC-27
93PalSprAF-88
Richards, Kevin
81TulDriT-22
82TulDriT-8
Richards, Nicky
83ChaRoyT-2
Richards, Paul
33Gou-142
51Bow-195
52Bow-93
52Top-305
53BowC-39
54Wil-14
55Bow-225
58OriJayP-10
60Lea-112
60OriJayP-6
60Top-224
61Top-131
61Top-566
62Col.45B-16
62Col45'JP-10
63BasMagM-68
79DiaGre-383
81TigDetN-40
83TCMPla1944-5
83TopRep5-305
88ConSer5-25
90DodTar-663
91TopArc1-322
93ConTSN-765
Richards, Rowan
96HudValRB-3
Richards, Rusty
87SumBraP-8
89RicBraBC-22
89RicBraC-7
89RicBraP-829
89RicBraTI-18
90CMC-280
90ProAAAF-404
90RicBraBC-17
90RicBraC-4
90RicBraP-259
90RicBraTI-27
90TopDeb89-99
91LinDriAAA-439
91RicBraBC-4
91RicBraLD-439
91RicBraTI-9
92OrlSunRS-518
92SkyAA F-225
92TexLon-33
Richards, Ryan
91OklStaC-21
Richards, Todd
80BatTroT-4
81BatTroT-6
Richardson, A.J.
88VisOakCLC-157
88VisOakP-87
89OrlTwiB-23
89OrlTwiP-1346
Richardson, Bobby
47Exh-186
57Top-286
58Top-101A
58Top-101B
59Top-76
59Top-237
59TopVen-76
60Top-405
61NuSco-415
61Pos-8A
61Pos-8B
61Top-180
61Top-308
61TopDicG-13
61Yan61RL-2
61YanJayP-10
62AmeTraS-43A
62AmeTraS-43B
62AmeTraS-43C
62AmeTraS-43D
62Jel-2
62Pos-2
62PosCan-2
62SalPlaC-64
62ShiPlaC-64
62Top-65
62TopStaI-90
62TopVen-65
62YanJayP-11
63Fle-25
63Jel-13
63Kah-26
63Pos-13
63SalMetC-52
63Top-173
63Top-420
63TopStiI-33
63YanJayP-10
64ChatheY-21
64Top-190
64TopCoi-72
64TopCoi-123
64TopSta-12
64TopStaU-60
64TopVen-190
64WheSta-38
64YanJayP-10
64YanReqKP-14
65ChaTheY-20
65MacSta-9
65OPC-115
65Top-115
65TopEmbI-65
65TopTraI-26
66Top-490
66TopRubI-77
66YanTeal-10
70FleWorS-61
77GalGloG-247
78TCM60I-112
81TCM60I-477
83FraBroR-16
83YanASFY-36
84OCoandSI-210
87Yan196T-3
88PacLegI-74
89SweBasG-49
90HOFStiB-61
90PacLeg-100
91LinDri-4
91RinPos1Y1-11
91SweBasG-75
91UppDecS-16
92ActPacA-31
92YanWIZ6-104
92YanWIZA-63
93UppDecAH-107
94TedWil-63
94TedWilM-M28
94UppDecAH-131
94UppDecAH1-131
94UppDecS-2
97FleMilDM-27
Richardson, Brad
96OgdRapTI-28
Richardson, Brian
92GulCoaDF-3575
93GreFalDSP-28
94VerBeaDC-16
94VerBeaDF-82
94YakBeaC-16
94YakBeaF-3859
95SanBerSTI-18
Richardson, C.N.
29ExhFou-24
Richardson, Danny (Daniel)
86OldJudN-12
87BucN28-72A
87BucN28-72B
87OldJudN-275
87OldJudN-424
88AugBecN-21
88GandBCGCE-33
88WG1CarG-43
89SFHaCN-15
90DodTar-664
90KalBatN-46
Richardson, David
89SprCarB-16
90LouRedBLBC-35
90St.PetCS-20
91LinDriAAA-244
91LouRedLD-244
91LouRedP-2915
Richardson, Don
86WinSpiP-23
Richardson, Eric
92StaCluD-153
93HicCraC-21
93HicCraF-1294
94HicCraC-19
94HicCraF-2190
Richardson, Gordon
66OPC-51
66Top-51
66TopVen-51
81TCM60I-460
91MetWIZ-331
Richardson, Hardy (A.H.)
76SSP188WS-17
87BucN28-33A
87BucN28-33B
87OldJudN-423
87ScrDC-15
88WG1CarG-23
89N526N7C-14
Richardson, James
88KinIndS-19
Richardson, Jeff
85LitFalMT-9
86LynMetP-18
87LynMetP-24
87TamTarP-12
88ChaLooB-22
88PalSprACLC-92
88PalSprAP-1463
89NasSouC-18
89NasSouP-1291
89NasSouTI-20
89PalSprAP-469
90BufBisC-12
90BufBisP-382
90BufBisTI-20
90CMC-12
90ProAAAF-497
91BufBisLD-43
91BufBisP-550
91LinDriAAA-43
92BufBisBS-17
92BufBisF-328
92BufBisS-40
92SkyAAAF-18
93PawRedSF-2417
93SouOreAF-4080
94LouRedF-2990
94SouOreAC-22
94SouOreAF-3639
95LynHilTI-23
96EriSeaB-1
Richardson, Jeffrey Scott
89PalSprACLC-51
90TopDeb89-100
91Bow-198
91TopDeb90-131
93SouOreAC-22
93TopTra-81T
Richardson, Jesse
95HelBreTI-28
Richardson, Jim
87WatIndP-3
88AlaGolTI-14
89KinIndS-20
Richardson, Jon
78RicBraT-12
79RicBraT-7
Richardson, Kasey
96ForWayWB-22
Richardson, Keith
88WatPirP-1
89SalBucS-17
89Sta-95
90HarSenP-1191
90HarSenS-16
Richardson, Kenny
78NewWayCT-37
Richardson, Kerry
87KinIndP-23
88WilBilP-1328
Richardson, Lenny
88CapCodPPaLP-5
Richardson, Mike
89EriOriS-20
90FreKeyTI-6
93NiaFalRF-3386
Richardson, Milt
88EugEmeB-27
89EugEmeB-18
Richardson, Ron
83MidCubT-18
Richardson, Ronnie
87ElmPio(C-27
88ElmPio1C-4
88LynRedSS-20
89LynRedSS-28
Richardson, Scott
92HelBreF-1723
92HelBreSP-21
93BelBreC-18
93BelBreF-1720
94StoPorC-20
94StoPorF-1706
95ElPasDTI-20
96SanBerSB-22
Richardson, Tim
86HagSunP-15
87HagSunP-19
90HagSunDGB-21
Richardson, Tracey
90WatIndS-28
Richardt, Mike
79AshTouT-26
80ChaChaT-8
83Don-368
83Fle-575
83FleSta-164
83RanAffF-2
83Top-371
84Nes792-641
84Top-641
84TopTif-641
93RanKee-307
Richartz, Scott
75AppFoxT-24
76AppFoxT-21
Richbourg, Lance
29ExhFou-2
29PorandAR-72

31Exh-2
33ExhFou-1
93ConTSN-701
Richeal, Ryan
94BurBeeC-29
95BurBeeTI-22
Richer, Troy
92CalLeaACL-35
Richert, Pete
62Top-131
62TopVen-131
63Top-383
64Top-51
64TopVen-51
65OPC-252
65Top-252
66Baz-43
66OPC-95
66SenTeal-11
66Top-95
66TopRubI-78
66TopVen-95
67Baz-43
67CokCapS-4
67DexPre-174
67SenTeal-11
67Top-590
68CokCapO-12
68Top-354
68TopVen-354
69MLBPin-24
69OPC-86
69Top-86
70Top-601
71MLBOffS-311
71OPC-273
71Ori-12
71Top-273
72Top-649
73OPC-239
73Top-239
74OPC-348
74Top-348
74TopTra-348T
88ModA'sCLC-82
88ModA'sTI-2
89ModA'sC-2
89ModA'sCLC-287
90DodTar-665
90ModA'sC-34
90ModA'sCLC-172
90ModA'sP-2230
91ModA'sC-18
91ModA'sP-3107
91OriCro-380
92CalLeaACL-22
92ModA'sC-26
92ModA'sF-3911
93ModA'sC-27
93ModA'sF-816
94ModA'sC-27
94ModA'sF-3079
95EdmTraTI-20
Richey, Jeff
92EveGiaC-20
92EveGiaF-1687
93CliGiaC-19
93CliGiaF-2488
94ExcFS7-294
94SanJosGC-20
94SanJosGF-2815
95Exc-293
Richey, Mikal
96GreFalDB-22
96GreFalDTI-30
Richey, Rodney
88IdaFalBP-1838
89SumBraP-1104
90DurBulTI-24
Richie, Bennie
83VisOakF-19
84VisOakT-1
Richie, Lewis
09AmeCarE-90
10DomDisP-102
10SweCapPP-89
11SpoLifM-180
11T205-144
12HasTriFT-53
Richie, Rob
88BasAmeAAB-3
88EasLeaAP-11
88GleFalTP-925
89TolMudHP-765
89TriA AAC-29
90OPC-146
90Top-146
90TopDeb89-101
90TopTif-146
90TriAAAC-29
90UppDec-76
Richman, Arthur
88MetColP-54
Richmond, Bob
69PilPos-24
87CliGiaP-25
Richmond, Clarence
91KisDodP-4203
92GulCoaDF-3582
Richmond, Don
50WorWidGV-43
51Bow-264
Richmond, Ryan
89PitMetS-21
89Sta-161
90ColMetGS-18
90ColMetPPI-3
Richter, Francis C.
90LitSunW-4
Richter, Mike
93StaCluMO-57
Rick, Dean
78SalPirT-13
Ricken, Ray
94OneYanC-18
94OneYanF-3790
94StaCluDP-60
94StaCluDPFDI-60
95Bes-36
95GreBatTI-20
95TamYanYI-22
96Bow-327
96Exc-92
96ExcCli-8
96NorNavB-19
96Top-428
97Bow-209
97BowCerBIA-CA65
97BowCerGIA-CA65
97BowInt-209
Ricker, Drew
86EveGiaC-9
86EveGiaPC-24
87CliGiaP-22
Ricker, Troy
85UtiBluST-22
86JamExpP-19
87JamExpP-2550
88RocExpLC-31
89WesPalBES-19
90JamExpP-25
90RocExpLC-23
90RocExpP-2708
91WesPalBEC-28
91WesPalBEP-1242
92ClaFS7-297
92VisOakC-22
92VisOakF-1027
93ClaFS7-250
93ExcFS7-35
Rickert, Marv
47TipTop-115
52Top-50
83TopRep5-50
84TCMPla1-31
Rickert, Rick
49EurSta-18
Ricketts, Chad
96RocCubTI-27
Ricketts, Dave
65Top-581
67Top-589
68OPC-46
68Top-46
68TopVen-46
69MilBra-233
69Top-232
70Top-626
72MilBra-288
73OPC-517
73Top-517A
73Top-517B
78CarTeal-17
79Car5-22
81Car5x7-22
83Car-25
84Car-23
84Car5x7-22
85CarTeal-27
86CarTeal-36
90TopTVCa-4
Ricketts, Dick
59Top-137
59TopVen-137
60Top-236
Rickey, Ralph
73WicAerKSB-14
Rickey, W. Branch
14CraJacE-133
15CraJacE-133
23WilChoV-131
41CarW75-22
60Fle-55
76ShaPiz-106
77GalGloG-124
80PerHaloFP-105
80SSPHOF-105
82OhiHaloF-29
88RinPosD1-6B
88WilMulP-9
89HOFStiB-91
90BasWit-101
90PerGreM-84
92YanWIZH-27
93CraJac-12
94UppDecTAE-55
95ConTSN-1399
Rickman, Andy
88GreHorP-1568
89CedRapRB-13
89CedRapRP-932
89CedRapRS-15
Ricks, Ed
89MadMusS-19
Rico, Alfredo
70Top-552
Rico, Carlos
92AriWilP-14
Rico, Ron
92HelBreF-1714
92HelBreSP-19
Riconda, Harry
90DodTar-666
Riddle, David
89EriOriS-21
89SanDieSAS-25
90Bes-317
90CMC-693
90WauTimB-12
90WauTimP-2125
90WauTimS-19
91FreKeyC-8
91FreKeyP-2363
Riddle, Elmer
41HarHarW-19
49EurSta-170
79DiaGre-261
83TCMPla1943-28
84OCoandSI-166
Riddle, Johnny (John L.)
53Top-274
54CarHunW-22
54Top-147
55CarHunW-21
55Top-98
58RedEnq-32
75CedRapGT-6
83TCMPla1945-42
91TopArc1-274
94TopArc1-147
94TopArc1G-147
Riddleberger, Dennis
71OPC-93
71SenTealW-21
71Top-93
72Top-642
73OPC-157
73Top-157
Riddoch, Greg
88PadSmo-24
90PadMag-22
90TopTra-102T
90TopTraT-102T
91OPC-109
91PadCok-7
91PadMag-1
91PadSmo-29
91Top-109
91TopDesS-109
91TopMic-109
91TopTif-109
92OPC-351
92PadCarJ-16
92PadMot-1
92PadPolD-17
92PadSmo-25
92Top-351
92TopGol-351
92TopGolW-351
92TopMic-351
Riddoch, Rory
92SanBerC-30
Rideau, Greg
92BurIndC-14
92BurIndF-1654
Ridenour, Dana
87Ft.LauYP-9
88AlbYanP-1342
88EasLeaAP-4
89WilBilP-647
90Bes-55
90EasLeaAP-EL18
90WilBilB-20
90WilBilP-1057
90WilBilS-21
91IndIndLD-192
91IndIndP-460
91LinDriAAA-192
91TriA AAGP-AAA16
92IndIndF-1856
92IndIndS-190
93ColSprSSF-3085
94EdmTraF-2875
Ridenour, Ryan
90BatCliP-3069
Ridzik, Steve
53BowBW-48
54Bow-223
55Bow-111
57Top-123
60MapLeaSF-17
60Top-489
61MapLeaBH-18
64Top-92
64TopVen-92
65OPC-211
65Top-211
66Top-294
66TopVen-294
Riebe, Harvey
95PacHarR-1
Riedling, John
94BilMusF-3668
95BilRedTI-15
Rieger, Elmer
09PC7HHB-36
Riegert, Tim
96JohCitCTI-27
Riel, Franich
40SolHug-16
Riemer, Matt
92BluOriC-17
92BluOriF-2368
93BluOriC-1
93BluOriF-4134
94AlbPolC-21
94AlbPolF-2246
94OriPro-84
Riemer, Robin
86EveGiaC-183
Riemer, Tim
89WatIndS-19
Riesgo, Nikco
88SpoIndP-1936
89ChaRaiP-995
90FloStaLAS-16
90St.LucMS-22
90StaFS7-10
91Bow-536
91ReaPhiP-1375
92ProFS7-298
92TopDeb91-148
Riewerts, Tom
82AubAstT-15
Rife, Jackie
93MarPhiC-23
93MarPhiF-3473
94MarPhiC-21
94MarPhiF-3292
Riffle, Brian
78QuaCitAT-20
Rigby, Bob
82MonNew-12
Rigby, Brad
94SigRooDP-34
94SigRooDPS-34
94StaCluDP-28
94StaCluDPFDI-28
95ModA'sTI-24
95SPML-124
96BesAutS-80
96Bow-321
96Exc-100
96HunStaTI-21
97Bow-354
97BowCerBIA-CA66
97BowCerGIA-CA66
97BowChr-239
97BowChrI-239
97BowChrIR-239
97BowChrR-239
97BowInt-354
Rigby, Kevin
81DurBulT-3
Rigdon, Paul
96WatIndTI-25
Riggan, Jerrod
96BoiHawB-24
96HilStaHWB-24
Riggar, Butch
77ForLauYS-28
79HolMilT-18
Riggert, Joe
90DodTar-667
Riggin, Ailleen
28W512-40
Riggins, Mark A.
81ArkTraT-14
82ArkTraT-7
83St.PetCT-11
86ArkTraP-18
87SprCarB-2
89BlaYNPRWL-98
89LouRedBC-24
89LouRedBP-1254
90CMC-679
90LouRedBC-28
90LouRedBLBC-4
90LouRedBP-420
90ProAAAF-534
90TopTVCa-62
91LinDriAAA-250
91LouRedLD-250
91LouRedP-2933
91LouRedTI-31
92LouRedF-1903
94LouRedF-2997
Riggleman, James D.
75WatDodT-18
77ArkTraT-9A
77ArkTraT-9B
79ArkTraT-5
80ArkTraT-4
81ArkTraT-19
83St.PetCT-29
86ArkTraP-19
87ArkTraP-7
88ArkTraGS-4
89BlaYNPRWL-69
90TopTVCa-5
91LasVegSLD-299
91LasVegSP-253
91LinDriAAA-299
92LasVegSF-2809
92LasVegSS-249
93PadMot-1
93Top-513
93TopGol-513
93TopInaM-513
93TopMic-513
94PadMot-1
Riggs, Adam
94GreFalDSP-19
95Bes-78
95SanBerSTI-19
95SPML-4
95SPML-75
95SPMLA-21
95SPMLDtS-DS6
96BesAutSA-60
96Bow-319
96Exc-182
96ExcAll-3
96ExcSeaTL-8
96SanAntMB-18
96Top-426
97Bow-85
97BowCerBIA-CA67
97BowCerGIA-CA67
97BowInt-85

97ColCho-474
Riggs, Jim
82OneYanT-2
83GreHorT-22
85AlbYanT-18
86AlbYanT-1
Riggs, Kevin
90BilMusP-3231
91CedRapRC-19
91CedRapRP-2728
92CedRapRC-18
92CedRapRF-1081
92MidLeaATI-35
93StoPorC-20
93StoPorF-753
94ClaGolF-176
94ElPasDF-3154
94ExcFS7-84
94UppDecML-234
95NorNavTI-41
96NorNavB-20
Riggs, Lew
34DiaStaR-96
36GouWidPPR-A88
37ExhFou-4
38CinOraW-22
38ExhFou-4
39OrcPhoAP-19
39PlaBal-77
40PlaBal-78
41DodTeal-6
41DouPlaR-141
41HarHarW-20
42DodTeal-18
77TCMTheWY-78
90DodTar-668
92ConTSN-567
Riggs, Tony
92GulCoaRSP-26
93NewOrlZF-983
Righetti, Dave
79WesHavYT-21
80ColCliP-24
80ColCliT-17
81ColCliP-24
81ColCliT-9
82Don-73
82Fle-52
82Top-439
83Don-199
83Fle-395
83OPC-176
83Top-81
83Top-176
84Don-10
84Don-10A
84Don-103
84DonActAS-59
84Fle-139
84Fle-639
84FleSti-86
84FunFooP-116
84Nes792-5
84Nes792-635
84OPC-277
84Top-5
84Top-635
84TopGloS-28
84TopRubD-24
84TopSti-287B
84TopSti-315
84TopTif-5
84TopTif-635
85AllGamPI-85
85Don-336
85DonHig-37
85Dra-40
85Fle-142
85FleStaS-102
85Lea-219
85OPC-260
85PolMet-Y5
85SevCoi-E13
85Top-260
85TopRubD-24
85TopSti-314
85TopSup-58
85TopTif-260
86BasStaB-91
86Don-214
86DonHig-52
86Fle-116
86FleMin-25
86FleStiC-97
86GenMilB-1H
86Lea-89
86OPC-34
86SevCoi-E10
86Spo-41
86Spo-72
86Spo-141
86SpoRoo-48
86Top-560
86TopSti-303
86TopSup-44
86TopTat-11
86TopTif-560
86YanTCM-13
87ClaGam-86
87Don-128
87DonAll-55
87Fle-111
87Fle-627
87FleAwaW-32
87FleGlo-111
87FleGlo-627
87FleHotS-31
87FleMin-90
87FleRecS-32
87FleSlu-34
87FleStiC-100
87FleWaxBC-C12
87KayB-27
87Lea-53
87MSAIceTD-20
87OPC-40
87SevCoi-E9
87Spo-57
87Spo-119
87Spo-194
87SpoTeaP-7
87Top-5
87Top-40
87Top-616
87TopCoi-22
87TopGaloC-9
87TopGloS-24
87TopMinL-67
87TopSti-8
87TopSti-9
87TopSti-299
87TopTif-5
87TopTif-40
87TopTif-616
87Woo-14
88Baz-16
88Don-93
88DonAll-29
88DonBasB-164
88DonReaBY-93
88Fle-220
88Fle-625
88FleAwaW-33
88FleGlo-220
88FleGlo-625
88FleMin-43
88FleRecS-32
88FleSlu-33
88FleStiC-52
88FleTeaL-29
88K-M-20
88Lea-57
88Nes-28
88OPC-155
88PanSti-150
88RedFolSB-75
88Sco-351
88ScoGlo-351
88Spo-135
88SpoGam-19
88StaLinAl-25
88StaLinY-13
88Top-790
88TopGaloC-10
88TopMinL-29
88TopSti-300
88TopStiB-66
88TopTif-790
88Woo-16
89Bow-167
89BowTif-167
89Don-78
89DonBasB-76
89Fle-267
89FleGlo-267
89OPC-335
89PanSti-400
89RedFolSB-97
89Sco-225
89ScoHot1S-37
89Spo-158
89Top-335
89TopBasT-73
89TopDouM-18
89TopSti-307
89TopTif-335
89TVSpoM-84
89UppDec-59
89YanScoNW-6
90Bow-426
90BowTif-426
90ClaBlu-41
90Don-311
90DonBesA-136
90DonLeaS-14
90Fle-453
90FleCan-453
90OPC-160
90PanSti-124
90PubSti-545
90RedFolSB-79
90Sco-194
90Sco100S-39
90Spo-88
90Top-160
90TopBig-102
90TopTif-160
90TopTVY-18
90UppDec-479
90YanScoNW-16
91BasBesRB-12
91Bow-632
91ClaGam-87
91Don-21
91Don-275
91DonSupD-21
91Fle-677
91FleUpd-131
91GiaMot-8
91GiaPacGaE-15
91GiaSFE-12
91Lea-301
91OPC-410
91OPCPre-99
91PanFreS-332
91PanSti-266
91RedFolS-77
91Sco-24
91Sco100S-68
91ScoRoo-53T
91StaClu-356
91Stu-258
91Top-410
91TopDesS-410
91TopMic-410
91TopTif-410
91TopTra-96T
91TopTraT-96T
91UppDec-448
91UppDec-778
92Bow-324
92ClaGam-43
92Don-174
92Fle-647
92GiaMot-8
92GiaPacGaE-30
92Lea-135
92OPC-35
92PanSti-219
92Pin-82
92Sco-260
92StaClu-107
92Top-35
92TopGol-35
92TopGolW-35
92TopKid-62
92TopMic-35
92TriPla-23
92Ult-594
92UppDec-171
92UppDecTMH-42
92YanWIZ7-133
92YanWIZ8-159
92YanWIZA-64
93Don-552
93Fle-537
93GiaMot-10
93GiaPos-29
93PacSpa-614
93StaClu-431
93StaCluFDI-431
93StaCluG-2
93StaCluMOP-431
93Top-310
93TopGol-310
93TopInaM-310
93TopMic-310
93UppDec-579
93UppDecGold-579
94Pac-553
95NasSouTI-19
Righetti, Lou
57SeaPop-30
Righetti, Steve
78AshTouT-24
79AshTouT-15
Rightnowar, Ron
87FayGenP-24
88LakTigS-22
89LonTigP-1369
90LonTigP-1268
91TolMudHP-1931
92TolMudHF-1043
93TolMudHF-1654
94NewOrlZF-1466
94TriAAF-AAA8
Riginos, Tom
88CapCodPPaLP-58
Rigler, Cy
21Exh-141
94ConTSN-1202
94ConTSNB-1202
Rigney, Bill (William J.)
47PM1StaP1-174
48Bow-32
49Bow-170
49EurSta-123
50Bow-117
50JJKCopP-13
51Bow-125
52BerRos-53
52NatTeaL-22
52Top-125
53BowBW-3
58GiaSFCB-19
58PacBel-6
60MacSta-18
60Top-7
60Top-225
60TopVen-7
61AngJayP-10
61Top-225
62AngJayP-9
62Top-549
63AngJayP-14
63Top-294
64Top-383
65OPC-66
65Top-66
66Top-249
66TopVen-249
67Top-494
68Top-416
69OPC-182
69Top-182
70OPC-426
70Top-426
71OPC-532
71Top-532
72OPC-389
72Top-389
75Gia195T-24
78TwiFri-20
79DiaGre-41
81TCM60I-457
83TopRep5-125
84TCMPla1-43
86AngGreT-12
89AngSmo-1
91TopArc1-328
92BazQua5A-19
Rigney, John D.
39WhiSoxTI-14
41DouPlaR-71
47TipTop-26
79DiaGre-133
94ConTSN-1225
94ConTSNB-1225
Rigney, Topper (Emory E.)
21Exh-142
21Nei-17
22E120-58
22W572-84
22W573-106
25Exh-94
26Exh-69
26SpoComoA-35
27YorCarE-38
93ConTSN-728
Rigoli, Joe
79NewCoPT-3
83EriCarT-2
85LouRedR-2
86EriCarP-25
87EriCarP-3
96PhiTeal-27
Rigos, John
83EriCarT-3
85SprCarT-1
86St.PetCP-27
87SalBucP-14
88HarSenP-834
Rigsby, Rickey
88PulBraP-1761
89IdaFalBP-2013
Rigsby, Tim
90MiaMirIS-21
90MiaMirIS-26
91KinIndC-19
91KinIndP-331
92SalLakTSP-6
Rijo, Jose
84FleUpd-99
84TopTra-100T
84TopTraT-100T
85DomLeaS-35
85Don-492
85Fle-143
85TacTigC-133
85Top-238
85TopTif-238
86A'sMot-13
86Don-522
86DonHig-2
86Fle-431
86Top-536
86TopTif-536
87Don-55
87Fle-404
87FleGlo-404
87Lea-119
87SpoTeaP-23
87Top-34
87TopTif-34
88Don-548
88FleUpd-86
88FleUpdG-86
88RedKah-27
88Sco-392
88ScoGlo-392
88ScoRoo-27T
88ScoRooG-27T
88Top-316
88TopTif-316
88TopTra-92T
88TopTraT-92T
89Bow-300
89BowTif-300
89ClaTraO-141
89Don-375
89DonBasB-278
89Fle-168
89FleGlo-168
89OPC-135
89PanSti-68
89RedKah-27
89Sco-552A
89Sco-552B
89ScoYouSI-31
89SpoIllFKI-240
89Top-135
89TopMinL-12
89TopSti-140
89TopTif-135
89UppDec-619
90Bow-45
90BowTif-45
90Don-115
90Fle-430
90FleCan-430
90Lea-282
90OPC-627
90PanSti-243
90PubSti-38
90RedKah-24
90Sco-511
90Top-627
90TopBig-257
90TopSti-137
90TopTif-627

90UppDec-216
91Bow-681
91Cla1-T97
91Cla2-T31
91ClaGam-109
91Col-27
91Don-722
91Don-742
91Fle-79
91FleWorS-7
91KinDis-24
91Lea-326
91OPC-493
91PanFreS-134
91PepSup-5
91RedKah-27
91RedPep-18
91Sco-658
91StaClu-11
91Top-493
91TopCraJI-9
91TopDesS-493
91TopMic-493
91TopTif-493
91Ult-102
91UppDec-298
91Woo-31
91Woo-33
92Bow-680
92ClaGam-77
92Don-223
92Fle-419
92Hig5-34
92Lea-139
92MooSna-3
92OPC-220
92PanSti-269
92Pin-508
92RedKah-27
92Sco-232
92Sco100S-43
92ScoImpP-83
92StaClu-800
92Stu-26
92Top-220
92TopGol-220
92TopGolW-220
92TopKid-42
92TopMic-220
92Ult-196
92UppDec-258
92UppDec-712
92UppDecTMH-43
92YanWIZ8-160
93Bow-62
93DiaMar-88
93Don-454
93Fin-24
93FinRef-24
93Fla-31
93Fle-41
93FleFruotL-53
93HumDumC-29
93KinDis-8
93Lea-411
93MSABenSPD-15
93OPC-286
93PacBeiA-21
93PacSpa-88
93PacSpaGE-9
93PacSpaPI-5
93PanSti-289
93Pin-77
93RedKah-20
93Sco-105
93Sel-163
93SP-213
93StaClu-233
93StaCluFDI-233
93StaCluMOP-233
93Stu-211
93Top-165
93TopComotH-20
93TopGol-165
93TopInaM-165
93TopMic-165
93Ult-33
93UppDec-226
93UppDec-473
93UppDecGold-226
93UppDecGold-473
93USPlaCA-6S
94Bow-402
94BowBes-R56
94BowBesR-R56
94ColC-239
94ColChoGS-239
94ColChoSS-239
94DenHol-19
94Don-361
94DonMVP-3
94DonSpeE-361
94ExtBas-237
94ExtBasPD-7
94Fin-308
94FinRef-308
94Fla-148
94Fle-421
94FleSmo'nH-9
94FUnPac-84
94Lea-340
94OPC-50
94OscMayR-28
94Pac-156
94PacAll-10
94PanSti-15
94PanSti-167
94Pin-322
94PinArtP-322
94PinMusC-322
94ProMag-33
94RedFolMI-35
94RedKah-23
94Sco-52
94ScoGolR-52
94Sel-40
94SP-161
94SPDieC-161
94Spo-112
94StaClu-596
94StaClu-715
94StaCluFDI-596
94StaCluFDI-715
94StaCluGR-596
94StaCluGR-715
94StaCluMO-40
94StaCluMOP-596
94StaCluMOP-715
94Stu-171
94Top-705
94TopGol-705
94TopSpa-705
94TriPla-218
94TriPlaM-14
94Ult-476
94UltLeaL-10
94UltStrK-4
94UppDec-143
94UppDecAJ-26
94UppDecAJG-26
94UppDecED-143
94USPlaCA-13S
95Baz-88
95Bow-374
95ColCho-434
95ColChoGS-434
95ColChoSE-197
95ColChoSEGS-197
95ColChoSESS-197
95ColChoSS-434
95D3-38
95Don-292
95DonPreP-292
95DonTopotO-218
95Emb-26
95EmbGolI-26
95Fin-35
95FinFlaT-FT7
95FinRef-35
95Fla-122
95Fle-443
95FleTeaL-17
95Lea-102
95LeaLim-130
95Pac-111
95PacLatD-29
95PacPri-35
95Pin-223
95PinArtP-223
95PinMusC-223
95PinSam-223
95RedFol-15
95RedKah-23
95Sco-270
95ScoGolR-270
95ScoHaloG-HG30
95ScoPlaTS-270
95Sel-138
95SelArtP-138
95SP-46
95Spo-40
95SpoArtP-40
95SPSil-46
95StaClu-300
95StaCluMOP-300
95StaCluSTDW-RE300
95StaCluSTWS-300
95StaCluVR-157
95Stu-85
95Top-529
95TopCyb-314
95TopLeaL-LL47
95Ult-147
95UltGolM-147
95UltStrK-6
95UltStrKGM-6
95UppDec-407
95UppDecED-407
95UppDecEDG-407
95UppDecSE-28
95UppDecSEG-28
95USPlaCMLA-5S
95Zen-57
96AubDouB-10
96ColCho-113
96ColChoGS-113
96ColChoSS-113
96Don-500
96DonPreP-500
96Fin-B150
96FinRef-B150
96Fla-237
96Fle-350
96FleTif-350
96PacPriFT-FT6
96Pin-44
96ProSta-104
96Sco-208
96Sel-43
96SelArtP-43
96StaClu-428
96StaCluEPB-428
96StaCluEPG-428
96StaCluEPS-428
96StaCluMOP-428
95StaCluVRMC-157
96Top-120
96Ult-465
96UltGolM-465
96UppDec-307
97Pac-275
97PacLigB-275
97PacSil-275
97Top-373
Rijo, Rafael
89SalDodTI-26
90YakBeaTI-13
91VerBeaDC-25
91VerBeaDP-790
92RocExpC-27
92RocExpF-2128
Riker, Robert
90BriTigP-3161
90BriTigS-20
Riles, Earnest
83ElPasDT-21
84VanCanC-35
85FleUpd-89
85VanCanC-207
86BrePol-1
86Don-359
86Fle-499
86FleLeaL-34
86FleMin-102
86FleStiC-98
86KayB-26
86Lea-161
86MSAJayPCD-14
86SevCoi-C13
86Spo-16
86Top-398
86TopGloS-40
86TopSti-310
86TopTif-398
87BrePol-1
87Don-151
87Fle-355
87FleGamW-36
87FleGlo-355
87FleMin-91
87Lea-66
87OPC-318
87SpoTeaP-19
87Top-523
87TopSti-203
87TopTif-523
88BlaYNPRWL-124
88BrePol-1
88Don-478
88Fle-172
88FleGlo-172
88FleUpd-130
88FleUpdG-130
88Sco-349
88ScoGlo-349
88ScoRoo-57T
88ScoRooG-57T
88StaLinBre-14
88Top-88
88TopTif-88
88TopTra-93T
88TopTraT-93T
89Bow-475
89BowTif-475
89BreGar-14
89ClaLigB-87
89Don-625
89DonBasB-50
89Fle-341
89FleGlo-341
89GiaMot-16
89Sco-458
89Top-676
89TopTif-676
89UppDec-497
90Bow-239
90BowTif-239
90Don-131
90El PasDAGTI-9
90Fle-69
90FleCan-69
90GiaMot-15
90GiaSmo-16
90OPC-732
90PubSti-80
90Sco-447
90Top-732
90TopSti-81
90TopTif-732
90UppDec-378
91A'sMot-16
91Bow-217
91Don-461
91Fle-271
91FleUpd-51
91Lea-358
91OPC-408
91Sco-626
91ScoRoo-55T
91StaClu-432
91Top-408
91TopDesS-408
91TopMic-408
91TopTif-408
91TopTra-97T
91TopTraT-97T
91UltUpd-47
91UppDec-780
92OPC-187
92Sco-222
92Top-187
92TopGol-187
92TopGolW-187
92TopMic-187
92TucTorF-498
92UppDec-494
94BreMilB-175
94Fle-40
94VanCanF-1871
Riley, Cash
96GreFalDB-23
96GreFalDTI-31
Riley, Darren
85CedRapRT-24
86FloStaLAP-41
86TamTarP-16
87VerRedP-25
88ChaLooB-24
91ParPatF-5
94ButCopKSP-22
Riley, Ed
89ElmPioP-14
90WinHavRSS-22
91LynRedSC-7
91LynRedSP-1196
92NewBriRSF-431
92NewBriRSS-493
92SkyAA F-212
93ClaGolF-29
93ExcFS7-136
93NewBriRSF-1217
94NewBriRSF-649
Riley, George
80WicAerT-20
81Don-588
81Top-514
83ReaPhiT-8
84PorBeaC-206
86ExpPos-12
Riley, Jim
92EveGiaC-16
92EveGiaF-1688
Riley, Marquis
92BoiHawC-1
92BoiHawF-3644
92ClaDraP-48
92FroRowDP-26
93ClaFS7-113
93PalSprAC-1
93PalSprAF-83
93StaCluM-199
94Bow-263
94ExcFS7-32
94MidAngF-2451
94MidAngOHP-26
94UppDecML-33
94UppDecMLPotYF-PY1
95Bow-188
Riley, Mike
79WisRapTT-3
82CedRapRT-6
96BelGiaTI-18
Riley, P.J.
89AubAstP-2180
Riley, Randy
84NewOriT-1
Riley, Tim
77DayBealT-18
Riley, Tom
83CedRapRF-5
83CedRapRT-16
84CedRapRT-15
85CedRapRT-31
Rima, Tom
74CedRapAT-5
75DubPacT-4
Rincon, Andy (Andrew)
80ArkTraT-9
81Top-244
82LouRedE-24
82Top-135
83LouRedR-17
89ArkTraGS-20
Rincon, Ricardo
97Fle-519
97FleTif-519
97SpoIll-51
97SpoIllEE-51
Rincones, Hector
80VenLeaS-6
81WatRedT-16
83WatRedT-13
84WicAerRD-3
85AlbDukC-157
86MemChiSTOS-22
86MemChiTOS-22
93LinVenB-189
Rinderknecht, Bob
93BluOriF-4124
Rineer, Jeff
78RocRedWT-14
79RocRedWT-16
80RocRedWT-8
91OriCro-381
Rinehart, Dallas
92BoiHawC-21
93CedRapKC-14
93PalSprAC-19
93PalSprAF-69
Rinehart, Robert
86ColMetP-22
Riner, Willard
89GeoColC-25
90GeoColC-25
Rines, Doug
89TenTecGE-22
Ring, Dave
90ElmPioP-20
Ring, James J.
19W514-98

20NatCarE-84
20RedWorCP-17
21Exh-143
21Nei-120
22E120-206
22W575-103
23W503-47
23WilChoV-132
26Exh-39
27AmeCarE-24
28Exh-22
88PacEigMO-87
92ConTSN-614
20W516-11

Ringgold, Keith
90EveGiaB-27
90EveGiaP-3143
91BenBucC-19
91BenBucP-3708

Ringkamp, Mark
92Ft.MyeMCB-9
92Ft.MyeMF-2745

Ringler, Tim
88KnoBluJB-22
89KnoBluJB-30
89KnoBluJP-1122

Ringo, Frank
87OldJudN-425

Riopelle, Rip (Howie)
43ParSpo-69

Rios, Armando
92LSUTigM-9
93LSUTigM-4
94CliLumF-1995
94LSUTigMP-12
94CliLumC-19

Rios, Carlos Rafael
77AppFoxT-20
78ChaPirT-21
81BufBisT-19
82KnoBluJT-15
85IntLeaAT-5
85RicBraT-15
86GreBraTI-15
88BlaYNPRWL-139
88RicBraC-18
88RicBraP-8
89BlaYNPRWL-12
89RicBraBC-23
89RicBraC-13
89RicBraP-842
89RicBraTI-19
88RicBraBC-3

Rios, Coronel (Carlos)
87GreBraB-5

Rios, Danny
95TamYanYI-23
96NorNavB-21
97GreBatC-18

Rios, Eddie
95Bow-49
95SanAntMTI-21

Rios, Eduardo
93GreFalDSP-10
94VenLinU-44
94VerBeaDC-17
94VerBeaDF-83
95LinVen-20
96SanAntMB-19

Rios, Enrique
87KenTwiP-29
88CarLeaAS-16
88LynRedSS-21

Rios, Jesus
85MexCitTT-1

Rios, Juan
69RoyTeal-11
69Top-619
70OPC-89
70Top-89
72MilBra-289

Ripken, Bill
86ChaOriW-25
86SouLeaAJ-1
87DonRoo-16
87IntLeaAT-27
87OriFreB-3
87RocRedWP-12
87RocRedWT-13
87SpoRoo2-28
88ClaRed-163
88Don-336
88Don-625
88DonBasB-254
88Fle-569
88Fle-640
88FleGlo-569
88FleGlo-640
88Lea-134
88MSAIceTD-7
88OPC-352
88OriFreB-7
88PanSti-9
88Sco-200
88ScoGlo-200
88ScoYouSI-20
88Spo-216
88StaLinO-12
88Top-352
88TopRoo-1
88TopSti-227
88TopTif-352
88ToyRoo-25
89Bow-12
89BowTif-12
89Don-259
89DonBasB-318
89Fle-616A
89Fle-616B
89Fle-616C
89Fle-616D
89FleGlo-616
89OPC-22
89OriFreB-3
89PanSti-261
89RedFolSB-98
89Sco-18
89Top-571
89TopBig-27
89TopTif-571
89TVSpoM-92
89UppDec-283
90Bow-256
90BowTif-256
90Don-164
90Fle-186
90FleCan-186
90HagSunDGB-22
90Lea-271
90MLBBasB-113
90OPC-468
90PanSti-3
90PubSti-583
90Sco-174
90Top-468
90TopBig-244
90TopSti-235
90TopTif-468
90UppDec-184
91Bow-87
91Don-167
91Fle-489
91Lea-7
91OPC-677
91OriCro-382
91PanFreS-241
91Sco-487
91SevCoi-A12
91StaClu-222
91StaCluP-35
91StaPinB-37
91Top-677
91TopDesS-677
91TopMic-677
91TopTif-677
91Ult-23
91UppDec-550
92Bow-373
92Don-734
92Fle-25
92Lea-184
92OPC-752
92PanSti-66
92Pin-336
92Sco-97
92StaClu-533
92Top-752
92TopGol-752
92TopGolW-752
92TopMic-752
92Ult-10
92UppDec-82
92UppDec-250
93Bow-517
93Don-59
93Fle-550
93FleFinE-282
93Lea-435
93OPCPre-59
93PacSpa-645
93PanSti-72
93Pin-153
93RanKee-427
93StaClu-603
93StaCluFDI-603
93StaCluMOP-603
93StaCluR-29
93Ult-635
93UppDec-181
93UppDec-511
93UppDecGold-181
93UppDecGold-511
94Fin-339
94FinRef-339
94FleUpd-95
94StaClu-369
94StaCluFDI-369
94StaCluGR-369
94StaCluMOP-369
94StaCluT-268
94StaCluTFDI-268
95Fle-294
95Sco-499
95ScoGolR-499
95ScoPlaTS-499
97PacPriGotD-GD15

Ripken, Cal Jr.
80ChaO'sP-18
80ChaO'sW-19
81RocRedWT-15
81RocRedWW-1
82Don-405
82Fle-176
82Top-21
82TopTra-98T
83AllGamPI-23
83Don-279
83DonActA-52
83Dra-23
83Fle-70
83FleSta-165
83FleSti-198
83OPC-163
83OriPos-21
83Top-163
83TopSti-26
83TopSti-315
84AllGamPI-113
84Don-106
84DonActAS-20
84DonCha-48
84Dra-26
84Fle-17
84FleSti-15
84FleSti-29
84FunFooP-118
84MilBra-20
84Nes792-400
84Nes792-426
84Nes792-490
84NesDreT-4
84OCoandSI-9
84OCoandSI-82
84OCoandSI-222
84OPC-2
84OPC-363
84OriEng-11
84OriTeal-22
84RawGloT-2
84SevCoi-E14
84Top-400
84Top-426
84Top-490
84TopRubD-30
84TopSti-24
84TopSti-197
84TopSti-204
84TopStiB-13
84TopSup-1
84TopTif-400
84TopTif-426
84TopTif-490
85AllGamPI-25
85Don-14
85Don-169
85DonActA-7
85DonSupD-14
85Dra-26
85Fle-187
85Fle-626
85Fle-641
85FleLimE-28
85FleStaS-41
85KASDis-10
85KitCloD-10
85Lea-14
85OPC-30
85OriHea-15
85SevCoi-E14
85ThoMcAD-17
85Top-30
85Top-704
85Top3-D-16
85TopGloA-16
85TopGloS-24
85TopRubD-31
85TopSti-185
85TopSti-197
85TopSup-48
85TopTif-30
85TopTif-704
86BasStaB-92
86BurKinA-15
86Don-210
86DonAll-14
86DonPop-14
86DorChe-4
86Dra-11
86Fle-284
86Fle-633
86FleAll-5
86FleLeaL-35
86FleLimE-36
86FleMin-59
86FleSlu-28
86FleStiC-99
86GenMilB-1I
86Lea-142
86MeaGolBB-11
86MeaGolM-8
86MeaGolSB-11
86MSAJifPD-9
86OPC-340
86QuaGra-31
86SevCoi-C3
86SevCoi-E3
86SevCoi-S3
86SevCoi-W3
86Spo-8
86Spo-54
86Spo-57
86Spo-69
86Spo-73
86Spo-128
86SpoDecG-73
86SpoRoo-48
86Top-340
86Top-715
86TopGloA-5
86TopGloS-14
86TopMinL-2
86TopSti-159
86TopSti-226
86TopSup-45
86TopTat-4
86TopTif-340
86TopTif-715
86TruVal-22
87BoaandB-22
87ClaGam-52
87Don-89
87DonAll-5
87DonHig-38
87DonOpeD-133
87DonP-5
87Dra-6
87Fle-478
87FleAwaW-33
87FleBasA-36
87FleGamW-37
87FleGlo-478
87FleMin-92
87FleSlu-35
87FleStiC-101
87KraFoo-3
87Lea-98
87MandMSL-13
87MSAIceTD-14
87MSAJifPD-8
87OPC-312
87OriFreB-8
87RalPur-12
87RedFolSB-118
87SevCoi-M16
87Spo-9
87Spo-113
87SpoDeaP-4
87SpoSupD-8
87SpoTeaP-21
87StuPan-14
87Top-609
87Top-784
87TopCoi-23
87TopGloA-16
87TopGloS-37
87TopMinL-40
87TopSti-151
87TopSti-233
87TopTif-609
87TopTif-784
88Baz-17
88CheBoy-7
88ClaRed-176
88Don-26
88Don-171
88Don-625
88DonAll-5
88DonBasB-198
88DonBonM-BC1
88DonPop-5
88DonSupD-26
88Dra-25
88Fle-570
88Fle-635
88Fle-640
88FleGlo-570
88FleGlo-635
88FleGlo-640
88FleRecS-33
88FleSlu-34
88FleStiC-3
88FleSup-31
88FleTeaL-30
88GreBasS-74
88K-M-21
88KayB-25
88KinDis-24
88Lea-26
88Lea-100
88OPC-74
88OriFreB-8
88PanSti-11
88PanSti-13
88PanSti-230
88RedFolSB-76
88Sco-550
88Sco-651
88ScoBoxC-5
88ScoGlo-550
88ScoGlo-651
88Spo-152
88StaLinAl-26
88StaLinO-13
88Top-51
88Top-650
88TopBig-62
88TopCoi-24
88TopGloA-5
88TopGloS-6
88TopRitTM-13
88TopSti-160
88TopSti-228
88TopStiB-44
88TopTif-51
88TopTif-650
88TopUKM-61
88TopUKMT-61
89Bow-9
89Bow-260
89BowTif-9
89BowTif-260
89CadElID-44
89ClaLigB-56
89Don-51
89DonAll-5
89DonAll-32
89DonBasB-142
89DonBonM-BC15
89DonPop-5
89Fle-617
89FleBasA-35
89FleGlo-617
89FleHeroB-34
89FleLeaL-32
89K-M-15
89MasBreD-12
89MSAIceTD-16
89OPC-250
89OPCBoxB-J
89OriFreB-8

89PanSti-241
89PanSti-262
89RedFolSB-99
89Sco-15
89ScoHot1S-77
89ScoSco-3
89Spo-66
89SpollIFKI-69
89Top-250
89TopBasT-77
89TopBig-286
89TopCapC-6
89TopCoi-50
89TopGloA-5
89TopGloS-47
89TopSti-150
89TopSti-237
89TopStiB-11
89TopTif-250
89TopUKM-64
89TopWaxBC-J
89TVSpoM-89
89UppDec-467
89UppDec-682
89UppDecS-2
90AllBasT-4
90Bow-255
90BowTif-255
90ClaBlu-24
90Don-96
90Don-676
90Don-676A
90DonBesA-57
90DOnBonM-BC18
90DonLeaS-19
90Fle-187
90Fle-624A
90Fle-624B
90Fle-634
90FleAll-8
90FleBasA-30
90FleBasM-31
90FleCan-187
90FleCan-624
90FleCan-634
90Hot50PS-34
90K-M-16
90K-M-20
90Lea-197
90MLBBasB-112
90OPC-8
90OPC-388
90OPC-570
90OPCBoxB-N
90PanSti-7
90PanSti-202
90PanSti-388
90Pos-21
90PubSti-584
90RedFolSB-78
90Sco-2
90Sco100S-66
90Spo-100
90StaRip-1
90StaRip-2
90StaRip-3
90StaRip-4
90StaRip-5
90StaRip-6
90StaRip-7
90StaRip-8
90StaRip-9
90StaRip-10
90StaRip-11
90SunSee-23
90SupActM-10
90Top-8
90Top-388
90Top-570
90TopAmeA-15
90TopBig-327
90TopCoi-24
90TopDou-52
90TopGloA-16
90TopGloS-51
90TopHilHM-32
90TopMag-49
90TopSti-5
90TopSti-160
90TopSti-231
90TopStiB-44
90TopTif-8
90TopTif-388
90TopTif-570
90TopTVA-19
90TopWaxBC-N
90UppDec-266
90USPlaCA-6S
90WinDis-9
90Woo-19
91BasBesRB-13
91Bow-104
91CadEllD-43
91Cla2-T3
91Cla3-T77
91Cla3-NNO
91ClaGam-110
91Col-2
91DenHol-20
91Don-52
91Don-223
91DonBonC-BC17
91Fle-490
91JimDea-15
91Lea-430
91MajLeaCP-29
91MooSna-14
91MSAHolD-20
91OPC-5
91OPC-150
91OPCPre-100
91OriCro-383
91PanFreS-170
91PanFreS-243
91PanSti-192
91PepSup-8
91PetSta-1
91Pos-19
91PosCan-22
91RedFolS-78
91RedFolS-124
91Sco-95
91Sco-849
91Sco100S-21
91SevCoi-A13
91SilHol-4
91StaClu-430
91StaCluMO-26
91StaPinB-38
91Stu-9
91Top-5
91Top-150
91TopCraJI-13
91TopDesS-5
91TopDesS-150
91TopGloA-5
91TopMic-5
91TopMic-150
91TopSta-28
91TopTif-5
91TopTif-150
91TopTriH-A1
91Ult-24
91UppDec-347
91UppDecFE-85F
91USPlaCA-13D
91Woo-18
92Bow-400
92Cla1-T76
92Cla2-T56
92ClaGam-190
92ColAllG-5
92ColAllP-5
92DenHol-9
92Don-22
92Don-35
92DonBonC-BC1
92DonCraJ1-13
92DonDiaK-DK5
92DonEli-S2
92DonMcD-1
92DonPre-10
92Fle-26
92Fle-703
92Fle-711
92FleAll-20
92FleCitTP-5
92FleLumC-L7
92FleTeaL-17
92Fre-13
92Hig5-5
92Hig5S-24
92HitTheBB-28
92JimDeaLL-5
92KinDis-12
92Lea-52
92Lea-199
92LeaBlaG-52
92LeaGolP-13
92LeaPre-13
92MooSna-23
92Mr.TurS-19
92MSABenSHD-6
92New-21
92OPC-40
92OPCPre-137
92PanSti-68
92PanSti-275
92PepDieM-17
92Pin-200
92PinRool-11
92PinSlu-14
92PinTeaP-7
92Pos-9
92PosCan-15
92Sco-433
92Sco-540
92Sco-788
92Sco-794
92Sco-884
92Sco100S-89
92ScoProaG-5
92SevCoi-9
92SpollIFK1-132
92SpollIFK1-455
92SpoStaCC-37
92StaClu-1
92StaClu-595
92StaCluD-154
92StaCluMP-10
92Stu-129
92StuHer-BC7
92StuPre-5
92SunSee-9
92Top-40
92Top-400
92TopGol-40
92TopGol-400
92TopGolPS-40
92TopGolW-40
92TopGolW-400
92TopKid-63
92TopMcD-13
92TopMic-40
92TopMic-400
92TriPla-199
92TriPla-253
92TriPlaG-GS11
92Ult-11
92UltAllS-3
92UltAwaW-5
92UltAwaW-21A
92UltAwaW-21B
92UppDec-82
92UppDec-165
92UppDec-645
92UppDecF-36
92UppDecFG-36
92UppDecHRH-HR4
92UppDecTMH-1
92UppDecTMH-44
93Bow-225
93CadDis-46
93ClaGam-76
93ColAllG-9
93ColPosRJ-1
93ColPosRJ-2
93ColPosRJ-3
93ColPosRJ-4
93ColPosRJ-5
93ColPosRJ-6
93ColPosRJ-7
93DenHol-16
93DiaMar-89
93Don-559
93DonEliD-19
93DonMasotG-6
93DonMVP-14
93DonPre-12
93DurPowP2-1
93Fin-96
93FinJum-96
93FinRef-96
93Fla-157
93Fle-551
93FleAtl-19
93FleFruotL-54
93FunPac-32
93FunPac-130
93FunPac-135
93FunPac-218
93FunPacA-AS6
93Hos-26
93HumDumC-1
93JimDea-3
93KinDis-3
93Kra-12
93Lea-431
93LeaGolA-R14
93LeaGolA-U6
93LeaHeaftH-5
93MetBak-17
93MilBonSS-12
93OPC-352
93OPCPre-125
93OriCroASU-7
93PacSpa-24
93PanSti-73
93Pin-20
93Pin-305
93Pin-471
93PinCoo-17
93PinCooD-17
93PinHomRC-47
93Pos-9
93PosCan-7
93Sco-6
93ScoFra-1
93Sel-18
93SelChaS-15
93SelDufIP-10
93SP-8
93StaClu-40
93StaCluFDI-40
93StaCluM-141
93StaCluMOP-40
93StaCluMP-7
93Stu-80
93Top-300
93TopFulS-11
93TopGol-300
93TopInaM-300
93TopMic-300
93TriPla-3
93TriPlaA-17
93TriPlaP-3
93Ult-501
93UltAllS-14
93UltAwaW-15
93UppDec-36
93UppDec-44
93UppDec-585
93UppDecDG-16
93UppDecGold-36
93UppDecGold-44
93UppDecGold-585
93UppDecIC-WI15
93UppDecICJ-WI15
93UppDecTAN-TN4
93UppDecTriCro-TC7
93USPlaCA-WCO
94Bow-75
94BowBes-R71
94BowBes-X94
94BowBesR-R71
94BowBesR-X94
94BurKinR-1
94BurKinR-2
94BurKinR-3
94BurKinR-4
94BurKinR-5
94BurKinR-6
94BurKinR-7
94BurKinR-8
94BurKinR-9
94BurKinRG-1
94BurKinRG-2
94BurKinRG-3
94BurKinRG-4
94BurKinRG-5
94BurKinRG-6
94BurKinRG-7
94BurKinRG-8
94BurKinRG-9
94ChuHomS-7
94ChuHomSG-7
94ClaUpdCotC-CR1
94ClaUpdCotC-AU1
94ColC-240
94ColC-343
94ColChoGS-240
94ColChoGS-343
94ColChoSS-240
94ColChoSS-343
94ColChoT-13
94DenHol-20
94Don-40
94Don-140
94DonAnn8-6
94DonMVP-15
94DonSpeE-40
94ExtBas-12
94ExtBasGB-24
94Fin-235
94FinJum-235
94FinRef-235
94Fla-8
94FlaHotG-8
94FlaHotN-8
94FlaInfP-8
94Fle-19
94FleAllS-21
94FleTeaL-1
94FleUpdDT-10
94FUnPac-108
94FUnPac-180
94FUnPac-219
94Kra-10
94Lea-1
94LeaL-5
94LeaLimGA-7
94LeaMVPC-A12
94LeaMVPCG-A12
94LeaPro-7
94LeaStaS-10
94OPC-185
94OPCAllR-15
94OPCJumA-15
94OriPro-85
94OriUSPC-1H
94OriUSPC-9C
94OscMayR-11
94Pac-44
94PacSilP-15
94PanSti-23
94Pin-50
94PinArtP-50
94PinMusC-50
94PinTeaP-4
94PinTheN-23
94PinTri-TR13
94Pos-25
94PosCan-13
94PosCanG-13
94ProMag-8
94RedFolMI-22
94Sco-85
94ScoGolR-85
94ScoGolS-36
94Sel-249
94Sel-SS1
94SP-126
94SPDieC-126
94SPHol-32
94SPHolDC-32
94Spo-69
94Spo-179
94SpoFanA-AS4
94SPPre-ER5
94StaClu-373
94StaCluDD-DD4
94StaCluFDI-373
94StaCluGR-373
94StaCluMOP-373
94StaCluMOP-DD4
94StaCluMOP-ST15
94StaCluST-ST15
94StaCluT-271
94StaCluTF-8
94StaCluTFDI-271
94Stu-127
94StuSerS-7
94SucSav-15
94TomPiz-26
94Top-200
94Top-387
94Top-604
94TopBlaG-18
94TopGol-200
94TopGol-387
94TopGol-604
94TopSpa-200
94TopSpa-387
94TopSpa-604
94TopSupS-37
94TriPla-159
94TriPlaM-7
94TriPlaN-6
94Ult-9
94UltAllS-4

94UltCarA-3
94UppDec-281
94UppDec-425
94UppDecAJ-15
94UppDecAJG-15
94UppDecDC-E9
94UppDecED-281
94UppDecED-425
94USDepoT-2
95Baz-2
95BazRedH-RH2
95Bow-413
95BowBes-R10
95BowBesJR-7
95BowBesR-R10
95ClaFanFPCP-6
95ClaPhoC-5
95ColCho-85
95ColChoGS-85
95ColChoSE-155
95ColChoSE-263
95ColChoSEGS-155
95ColChoSEGS-263
95ColChoSESS-155
95ColChoSESS-263
95ColChoSS-85
95D3-2
95Don-83
95DonAll-AL6
95DonDom-6
95DonPreP-83
95DonTopotO-15
95Emb-113
95EmbGolI-113
95Emo-8
95Emo-P8
95EmoMas-8
95EmoR-1
95EmoR-2
95EmoR-3
95EmoR-4
95EmoR-5
95EmoR-6
95EmoR-7
95EmoR-8
95EmoR-9
95EmoR-10
95EmoR-11
95EmoR-12
95EmoR-13
95EmoR-14
95EmoR-15
95Fin-120
95FinRef-120
95Fla-9
95FlaHotG-9
95FlaHotN-8
95FlaRip-1
95FlaRip-2
95FlaRip-3
95FlaRip-4
95FlaRip-5
95FlaRip-6
95FlaRip-7
95FlaRip-8
95FlaRip-9
95FlaRip-10
95FlaRip-11
95FlaRip-12
95FlaRip-13
95FlaRip-14
95FlaRip-15
95Fle-19
95FleAllF-4
95FleAllS-5
95FleTeaL-1
95FleUpdSL-8
95KinDis-18
95Kra-12
95Lea-134
95LeaGreG-14
95LeaHeaftH-6
95LeaLim-97
95LeaLimG-7
95LeaLimL-16
95LeaOpeD-6
95LeaSli-4A
95LeaSli-4B
95LeaStaS-7
95MetImpRi-1
95MetImpRi-2
95MetImpRi-3
95MetImpRi-4
95MetImpRi-5
95MetImpRi-6
95MetImpRi-7
95MetImpRi-8
95MetImpRi-9
95MetImpRi-10
95NatPac-10
95Pac-30
95PacGolCDC-4
95PacGolP-9
95PacPri-10
95PanSti-68
95Pin-204
95Pin-305
95PinArtP-204
95PinArtP-305
95PinFan-1
95PinGatA-GA3
95PinMusC-204
95PinMusC-305
95PinPin-10
95PinPinR-10
95PinRedH-RH1
95PinTeaP-TP5
95PinWhiH-WH1
95Pos-8
95PosCan-18
95RedFol-7
95Sco-3
95Sco-556
95ScoDouGC-GC12
95ScoDreT-DG3
95ScoGolR-3
95ScoGolR-556
95ScoHaloG-HG6
95ScoPlaTS-3
95ScoPlaTS-556
95ScoRul-SR18
95ScoRulJ-SR18
95ScoSam-HG5
95Sel-1
95Sel-245
95SelArtP-1
95SelArtP-245
95SelBigS-BS3
95SelCer-72
95SelCer-2131
95SelCerC-3
95SelCerGT-3
95SelCerMG-72
95SelCerMG-2131
95SelCerS-3
95SP-1
95SPCha-99
95SPCha-115
95SPCha-120
95SPCha-CR1
95SPChaDC-99
95SPChaDC-115
95SPChaDC-120
95Spo-122
95Spo-170
95SpoArtP-122
95SpoArtP-170
95SpoDouT-5
95SpoHamT-HT5
95SpoPro-PM3
95SpoSam-122
95SPPlaP-PP16
95SPSil-1
95SPSpeF-16
95StaClu-1
95StaClu-239
95StaClu-314
95StaClu-510
95StaCluCT-20
95StaCluFDI-1
95StaCluFDI-239
95StaCluMO-40
95StaCluMOP-1
95StaCluMOP-239
95StaCluMOP-314
95StaCluMOP-510
95StaCluMOP-RL27
95StaCluRL-RL27
95StaCluSTWS-1
95StaCluSTWS-239
95StaCluSTWS-314
95StaCluSTWS-510
95StaCluVR-1
95StaRip-1
95StaRip-2
95StaRip-3
95StaRip-4
95StaRip-5
95StaRip-6
95StaRip-7
95StaRip-8
95StaRip-9
95StaRip-10
95StaRip-11
95StaRip-12
95StaRip-13
95StaRip-14
95StaRip-15
95StaRip-16
95StaRip-17
95StaRip-18
95StaRip-19
95StaRip-20
95StaRip-21
95StaRip-22
95StaRip-23
95StaRip-24
95StaRip-25
95StaRip-26
95StaRip-27
95StaRip-28
95StaRip-29
95StaRip-30
95StaRip-31
95StaRip-32
95StaRip-33
95StaRip-34
95StaRip-35
95StaRip-36
95StaRip-37
95StaRip-38
95StaRip-39
95StaRip-40
95StaRip-41
95StaRip-42
95StaRip-43
95StaRip-44
95StaRip-45
95StaRip-46
95StaRip-47
95StaRip-48
95StaRip-49
95StaRip-50
95StaRip-51
95StaRip-52
95StaRip-53
95StaRip-54
95StaRip-55
95StaRip-56
95StaRip-57
95StaRip-58
95StaRip-59
95StaRip-60
95StaRip-61
95StaRip-62
95StaRip-63
95StaRip-64
95StaRip-65
95StaRip-66
95StaRip-67
95StaRip-68
95StaRip-69
95StaRip-70
95StaRip-71
95StaRip-72
95StaRip-73
95StaRip-74
95StaRip-75
95StaRip-76
95StaRip-77
95StaRip-78
95StaRip-79
95StaRip-80
95Stu-8
95StuGolS-8
95StuPlaS-8
95Sum-79
95Sum-176
95Sum-196
95SumBigB-BB3
95SumNthD-79
95SumNthD-176
95SumNthD-196
95SumSam-79
95TomPiz-14
95Top-387
95Top-588
95TopCyb-360
95TopTra-5T
95TopTra-159T
95TopTraPB-5
95UC3-75
95UC3-123
95UC3ArtP-75
95UC3ArtP-123
95UC3CycS-CS4
95UC3InM-IM1
95Ult-258
95UltAllS-17
95UltAllSGM-17
95UltGolM-258
95UppDec-365
95UppDecED-365
95UppDecEDG-365
95UppDecPAW-H21
95UppDecPAWE-H21
95UppDecPC-MLB13
95UppDecSE-46
95UppDecSEG-46
95Zen-12
95ZenAllS-1
95ZenAllS-18
95ZenZ-1
96Baz-15
96Bow-1
96BowBes-3
96BowBesAR-3
96BowBesC-11
96BowBesCAR-11
96BowBesCR-11
96BowBesMI-4
96BowBesMIAR-4
96BowBesMIR-4
96BowBesP-BBP28
96BowBesPAR-BBP28
96BowBesPR-BBP28
96BowBesR-3
96Cir-8
96Cir-199
96CirAcc-1
96CirBos-2
96CirBos-P2
96CirRav-8
96CirRav-199
96Cla7/1PC-1
96ColCho-1
96ColCho-362
96ColCho-421
96ColChoCtG-CG4
96ColChoCtG-CG4B
96ColChoCtG-CG4C
96ColChoCtGE-CR4
96ColChoCtGG-CG4
96ColChoCtGG-CG4B
96ColChoCtGG-CG4C
96ColChoCtGGE-CR4
96ColChoGS-1
96ColChoGS-362
96ColChoGS-421
96ColChoSS-1
96ColChoSS-362
96ColChoSS-421
96ColChoYMtP-33
96ColChoYMtP-33A
96ColChoYMtPGS-33
96ColChoYMtPGS-33A
96CUIMCR-1
96CUIMCR-2
96CUIMCR-3
96CUIMCR-4
96CUIMCR-NNO
96DenHol-2
96DenHolGS-1
96DenHolGSAP-1
96Don-110
96Don-145
96DonDiaK-30
96DonEli-61
96DonFreF-3
96DonPreP-110
96DonPreP-145
96DonRouT-8
96DonSam-5
96DonSho-6
96EmoN-8
96EmoXL-9
96EmoXLD-8
96Fin-B281
96Fin-G25
96Fin-S165
96FinLan-3
96FinRef-B281
96FinRef-G25
96FinRef-S165
96Fla-12
96FlaDiaC-9
96FlaHotG-8
96Fle-20
96Fle-P20
96FleChe-7
96FleGolM-8
96FleOri-15
96FleTeaL-1
96FleTif-20
96FleUpd-U237
96FleUpd-8
96FleUpdH-17
96FleUpdSL-9
96FleUpdTC-U237
96Kin-22
96Lea-21
96LeaAllGMC-4
96LeaAllGMCG-4
96LeaGolS-8
96LeaHatO-1
96LeaLim-15
96LeaLimG-15
96LeaLimL-3
96LeaLimLB-3
96LeaLimPC-2
96LeaPicP-2
96LeaPre-22
96LeaPreP-22
96LeaPrePB-21
96LeaPrePG-21
96LeaPrePS-21
96LeaPreSG-17
96LeaPreSP-4
96LeaPreSta-7
96LeaPreSte-17
96LeaSig-15
96LeaSigPPG-15
96LeaSigPPP-15
96LeaStaS-1
96MetUni-9
96MetUniML-8
96MetUniP-9
96MetUniT-7
96MLBPin-29
96Pac-230
96PacCraC-CC3
96PacGolCD-DC15
96PacHom-HP6
96PacMil-M10
96PacPri-P77
96PacPriFB-FB15
96PacPriG-P77
96PacPriRHS-RH19
96PanSti-128
96Pin-136
96Pin-196
96Pin-214
96Pin-258
96Pin-393
96Pin-399
96Pin-CR1
96PinAfi-18
96PinAfiAP-18
96PinAfiFPP-18
96PinAfiMN-8
96PinAfiR-2
96PinAfiR-3
96PinAfiR-5
96PinAfiR-7
96PinAfiR-10
96PinAfiR-12
96PinAfiSP-2
96PinArtP-63
96PinArtP-114
96PinArtP-158
96PinEssotG-1
96PinFan-1
96PinFoil-214
96PinFoil-258
96PinFoil-393
96PinFoil-399
96PinSky-4
96PinSta-63
96PinSta-114
96PinSta-158
96PinTeaP-4
96PinTeaS-5
96Pro-12
96ProMagA-5
96ProMagDM-4
96ProSta-76
96SchDis-13
96Sco-60
96Sco-274
96Sco-356

96Sco-NNO
96ScoAll-4
96ScoBigB-1
96ScoDiaA-5
96ScoDreT-1
96ScoDugC-A52
96ScoDugC-B81
96ScoDugCAP-A52
96ScoDugCAP-B81
96ScoGolS-25
96ScoNumG-1
96ScoRef-1
96Sel-19
96Sel-153
96Sel-200
96SelArtP-19
96SelArtP-153
96SelArtP-200
96SelCer-53
96SelCer-139
96SelCerAP-53
96SelCerAP-139
96SelCerCB-53
96SelCerCB-139
96SelCerCR-53
96SelCerCR-139
96SelCerIP-14
96SelCerMB-53
96SelCerMB-139
96SelCerMG-53
96SelCerMG-139
96SelCerMR-53
96SelCerMR-139
96SelCerSF-5
96SelClaTF-1
96SelEnF-3
96SelTeaN-20
96SP-30
96SP-187
96SPMarM-MM9
96SPMarMDC-9
96Spo-54
96Spo-100
96Spo-144
96SpoArtP-54
96SpoArtP-100
96SpoArtP-144
96SpoDouT-1
96SpoHitP-2
96SpoPowS-4
96SpoPro-1
96SPSpeFX-20
96SPSpeFXDC-20
96SPx-5
96SPxBoufG-4
96SPxGol-5
96StaClu-198
96StaClu-424
96StaCluEPB-424
96StaCluEPG-424
96StaCluEPS-424
96StaCluMet-M7
96StaCluMM-MM6
96StaCluMOP-198
96StaCluMOP-424
96StaCluMOP-M7
96StaCluMOP-MM6
96StaCluMOP-TSCA1
96StaCluTA-1
95StaCluVRMC-1
96Stu-1
96StuMas-5
96StuPrePB-1
96StuPrePG-1
96StuPrePS-1
96StuStaGS-1
96Sum-19
96Sum-154
96Sum-200
96SumAbo&B-19
96SumAbo&B-154
96SumAbo&B-200
96SumArtP-19
96SumArtP-154
96SumArtP-200
96SumBal-1
96SumBigB-6
96SumBigBM-6
96SumFoi-19
96SumFoi-200
96SumHitI-9
96SumPos-4
96TeaOut-66
96TeaOut-C99
96Top-96
96Top-200
96Top-222
96TopBigC-7
96TopChr-28
96TopChr-67
96TopChr-82
96TopChrMotG-9
96TopChrMotGR-9
96TopChrR-28
96TopChrR-67
96TopChrR-82
96TopClaC-CC2
96TopGal-168
96TopGalPG-PG3
96TopGalPPI-168
96TopLas-90
96TopLasSS-8
96TopMasotG-9
96TopMysF-M7
96TopMysF-M23
96TopMysFR-M7
96TopMysFR-M23
96TopPro-AL8
96Ult-11
96Ult-588
96UltCalttH-7
96UltCalttHGM-7
96UltChe-A8
96UltChe-B9
96UltCheGM-A8
96UltCheGM-B9
96UltDiaP-9
96UltDiaPGM-9
96UltGolM-11
96UltGolM-588
96UltPriL-4
96UltPriLGM-4
96UltPro-3
96UltRaw-9
96UltRawGM-9
96UltRes-7
96UltResGM-7
96UltSeaC-8
96UltSeaCGM-8
96UltThu-17
96UltThuGM-17
96UppDec-1
96UppDec-115
96UppDec-280
96UppDec-385
96UppDecA-15
96UppDecDD-DD6
96UppDecDDG-DD6
96UppDecDDS-DD6
96UppDecG-GF5
96UppDecHC-HC15
96UppDecPHE-H6
96UppDecPreH-H6
96UppDecRCJ-1
96UppDecRCJ-2
96UppDecRCJ-3
96UppDecRCJ-4
96UppDecRCJ-5
96UppDecRCJ-6
96UppDecRCJ-7
96UppDecRCJ-8
96UppDecRCJ-9
96UppDecRCJ-10
96UppDecRCJ-11
96UppDecRCJ-12
96UppDecRCJ-13
96UppDecRCJ-14
96UppDecRCJ-15
96UppDecRCJ-16
96UppDecRCJ-17
96UppDecRCJ-18
96UppDecRCJ-19
96UppDecRCJ-20
96UppDecRCJ-21
96UppDecRCJ-22
96UppDecRipC-1
96UppDecRipC-2
96UppDecRipC-3
96UppDecRipC-4
96UppDecRipC-5
96UppDecRipC-6
96UppDecRipC-7
96UppDecRipC-8
96UppDecRipC-9
96UppDecRipC-10
96UppDecRipC-11
96UppDecRipC-12
96UppDecRipC-13
96UppDecRipC-14
96UppDecRipC-15
96UppDecRipC-16
96UppDecRipC-17
96UppDecRipC-18
96UppDecRipC-19
96UppDecRipC-20
96UppDecRipC-21
96UppDecRipC-22
96UppDecRipC-NNO
96Zen-76
96Zen-132
96ZenArtP-76
96ZenArtP-132
96ZenDiaC-5
96ZenDiaCP-5
96ZenMoz-8
96ZenZ-3
97Bow-18
97BowBes-64
97BowBesAR-64
97BowBesBC-BC4
97BowBesBCAR-BC4
97BowBesBCR-BC4
97BowBesP-7
97BowBesPAR-7
97BowBesPR-7
97BowBesR-64
97BowChr-14
97BowChrI-14
97BowChrIR-14
97BowChrR-14
97BowInt-18
97Cir-8
97Cir-398
97CirBos-15
97CirIco-9
97CirLimA-12
97CirRav-8
97CirRav-398
97CirRavR-10
97CirSupB-15
97ColCho-41
97ColChoAC-13
97ColChoBS-8
97ColChoBSGS-8
97ColChoCtG-6A
97ColChoCtG-6B
97ColChoCtG-6C
97ColChoCtGIW-CG6
97ColChoNF-NF35
97ColChoS-20
97ColChoTBS-5
97ColChoTBSWH-5
97ColChoTotT-T7
97Don-121
97Don-400
97Don-448
97DonArmaD-8
97DonDiaK-2
97DonDiaKC-2
97DonDom-4
97DonEli-6
97DonEli-9
97DonEliGS-6
97DonEliLaL-6
97DonEliPtT-1
97DonEliPtT-3
97DonEliPtTA-1
97DonEliPtTA-3
97DonFraFea-13
97DonLim-5
97DonLim-36
97DonLim-37
97DonLimFotG-1
97DonLimFotG-43
97DonLimLE-5
97DonLimLE-36
97DonLimLE-37
97DonPowA-3
97DonPowADC-3
97DonPre-98
97DonPre-169
97DonPreCttC-98
97DonPreCttC-169
97DonPreP-121
97DonPreP-400
97DonPreP-448
97DonPrePGold-121
97DonPrePGold-400
97DonPrePGold-448
97DonPrePM-18
97DonPreS-4
97DonPreTB-17
97DonPreTBG-17
97DonPreTF-17
97DonPreTP-17
97DonPreTPG-17
97DonPreXP-5B
97DonRipOWIK-1
97DonRipOWIK-2
97DonRipOWIK-3
97DonRipOWIK-4
97DonRipOWIK-5
97DonRipOWIK-6
97DonRipOWIK-7
97DonRipOWIK-8
97DonRipOWIK-9
97DonRipOWIK-10
97DonRipOWIK-10A
97DonRocL-15
97DonTea-35
97DonTeaSMVP-9
97DonTeaSPE-35
97Fin-135
97Fin-252
97Fin-334
97FinEmb-135
97FinEmb-334
97FinEmbR-135
97FinEmbR-334
97FinRef-135
97FinRef-252
97FinRef-334
97FlaSho-A8
97FlaSho-B8
97FlaSho-C8
97FlaShoDC-15
97FlaShoHG-12
97FlaShoLC-8
97FlaShoLC-B8
97FlaShoLC-C8
97FlaShoLCM-A8
97FlaShoLCM-B8
97FlaShoLCM-C8
97Fle-13
97Fle-498
97Fle-714
97Fle-723
97FleDecoE-10
97FleDecoERT-10
97FleDiaT-10
97FleGolM-9
97FleGouG-11
97FleGouGF-11
97FleHea-16
97FleMilDM-8
97FleTeaL-1
97FleTif-13
97FleTif-498
97FleTif-714
97FleTif-723
97Lea-188
97Lea-218
97Lea-370
97LeaDrefS-2
97LeaFraM-188
97LeaFraM-218
97LeaFraM-370
97LeaFraMDC-188
97LeaFraMDC-218
97LeaFraMDC-370
97LeaGet-15
97LeaGolS-21
97LeaKnoG-8
97LeaLeaotN-2
97LeaStaS-9
97MetUni-8
97MetUniMF-8
97MetUniML-9
97MetUniT-8
97NewPin-91
97NewPin-178
97NewPinAP-91
97NewPinAP-178
97NewPinIE-4
97NewPinKtP-14
97NewPinMC-91
97NewPinMC-178
97NewPinPP-91
97NewPinPP-178
97NewPinPP-I4A
97NewPinPP-K14
97NewPinPP-CR1
97NewPinPP-CR2
97NewPinPP-CR3
97NewPinPP-CR4
97NewPinPP-CR5
97NewPinPP-CR6
97NewPinS-CR1
97NewPinS-CR2
97NewPinS-CR3
97NewPinS-CR4
97NewPinS-CR5
97NewPinS-CR6
97Pac-29
97PacCar-4
97PacCarM-4
97PacCerCGT-7
97PacFirD-4
97PacGolCD-5
97PacLigB-29
97PacPri-12
97PacPriGA-GA3
97PacPriGotD-GD16
97PacPriLB-12
97PacPriP-12
97PacPriSH-SH1A
97PacPriSL-SL1A
97PacSil-29
97Pin-191
97PinArtP-191
97PinCar-3
97PinCer-28
97PinCer-146
97PinCerCMGT-7
97PinCerCT-7
97PinCerLI-1
97PinCerMBlu-28
97PinCerMBlu-146
97PinCerMG-28
97PinCerMG-146
97PinCerMR-28
97PinCerMR-146
97PinCerR-28
97PinCerR-146
97PinHom-21
97PinHom-22
97PinIns-23
97PinInsC-22
97PinInsCE-23
97PinInsDD-1
97PinInsDE-23
97PinMin-4
97PinMinB-4
97PinMinCB-4
97PinMinCG-4
97PinMinCGR-4
97PinMinCN-4
97PinMinCS-4
97PinMinG-4
97PinMinS-4
97PinMusC-191
97PinPasttM-4
97PinSha-5
97PinTotCPB-28
97PinTotCPB-146
97PinTotCPG-28
97PinTotCPG-146
97PinTotCPR-28
97PinTotCPR-146
97PinX-P-57
97PinX-PMoS-57
97PinX-PMP-18
97PinX-PMW-6
97PinX-PMWG-6
97PinX-PMWS-6
97PinX-PSfF-18
97PinX-PSfFU-18
97ProMag-46
97ProMagIM-3
97ProMagML-46
97Sco-151
97Sco-546
97ScoFra-3
97ScoFraG-3
97ScoHeaotO-12
97ScoHigZ-15
97ScoHobR-546
97ScoOri-7
97ScoOriPl-7
97ScoOriPr-7
97ScoPitP-1
97ScoPitP-3
97ScoPreS-151
97ScoResC-546
97ScoShoS-151
97ScoShoS-546
97ScoShoSAP-151
97ScoShoSAP-546
97ScoStaaD-23
97Sel-71

97SelArtP-71
97SelRegG-71
97SelToootT-3
97SelToootTMB-3
97SkyE-X-8
97SkyE-XC-8
97SkyE-XEC-8
97SkyE-XHoN-4
97SP-34
97SPGamF-GF4
97SPInsI-8
97SPMarM-MM14
97SpoIll-33
97SpoIll-124
97SpoIll-177
97SpoIllAM-2
97SpoIllEE-33
97SpoIllEE-124
97SpoIllEE-177
97SpoIllGS-7
97SPSpeF-8
97SPx-12
97SPxBoufG-5
97SPxBro-12
97SPxCorotG-8
97SPxGraF-12
97SPxSil-12
97SPxSte-12
97StaClu-8
97StaCluMat-8
97StaCluMOP-8
97StaCluMOP-PG16
97StaCluPG-PG16
97Stu-51
97StuHarH-6
97StuMasS-11
97StuMasS8-11
97StuPor8-5
97StuPrePG-51
97StuPrePS-51
97Top-400
97TopAll-AS9
97TopChr-140
97TopChrAS-AS9
97TopChrDD-DD7
97TopChrDDR-DD7
97TopChrR-140
97TopChrSAR-AS9
97TopGal-4
97TopGalGoH-GH5
97TopGalPMS-7
97TopGalPMSSS-8
97TopGalPPI-4
97TopHobM-HM2
97TopIntF-ILM12
97TopIntFR-ILM12
97TopScr-17
97TopScrSI-4
97TopSta-3
97TopSta1AS-AS7
97TopStaAM-3
97TopStaASGM-ASM1
97Ult-11
97UltBasR-9
97UltChe-A7
97UltChe-B5
97UltDiaP-9
97UltDouT-1
97UltFamGam-4
97UltFieC-15
97UltGolME-11
97UltGolME-NNO
97UltHitM-5
97UltLeaS-3
97UltPlaME-11
97UltPowP-A8
97UltPowP-B4
97UltStaR-5
97UltTop3-5
97UltTop3GM-5
97UppDec-20
97UppDec-147
97UppDecAG-AG15
97UppDecHC-HC8
97UppDecMM-3
97UppDecP-7
97UppDecU-25
97UppDecUMA-MA8
97Zen-35
97Zen Z-Z-6
97Zen8x1-19
97Zen8x1D-19
97ZenV-2-6

Ripken, Cal Sr.
88Don-579
83OriPos-22
84OriTeal-23
85Fle-641
87OriFreB-7
87TopTra-102T
87TopTraT-102T
88Don-625
88Top-444
88TopTif-444
89Bow-260
89BowTif-260
89OriFreB-7

Ripley, Allen
78PapGinD-1
78SSP270-188
79Top-702
80Top-413
81Fle-454
81Top-144
82CubRedL-33
82Don-125
82Fle-399
82Top-529
82TopTra-99T
83Don-57
83Fle-506
83Top-73

Ripley, Walter
79RedSoxEF-6

Rippelmeyer, Brad
91IdaFalBP-4333
91IdaFalBSP-3
92DurBulC-13
92DurBulF-1105
92DurBulTI-15
93GreBraF-354
94DurBulC-15
94DurBulF-331
94DurBulTI-16
95BreBtaTI-9

Rippelmeyer, Ray
60HenHouW-28
60UniOil-10
61Top-276
62Top-271
73OPC-486
73Top-486A
73Top-486B
74OPC-119
74Top-119
78PhiSSP-36
78SSP270-36
89NasSouC-24
89NasSouP-1280
89NasSouTI-29
90CMC-150
90NasSouC-25
90NasSouP-250
90ProAAAF-562

Ripple, Charles
47CenFlo-23
47SigOil-67

Ripple, Jimmy
36WorWidGV-28
38ExhFou-5
38OurNatGPP-24
39PlaBal-66
41DouPlaR-11
41DouPlaR-95
41HarHarW-21
44CenFlo-18
90DodTar-669
91ConTSN-86

Rippley, Steve
88T/MUmp-49
89T/MUmp-47
90T/MUmp-45

Ripslager, Charles
87OldJudN-426

Ris, Greg
78QuaCitAT-21

Risberg, Swede (Charles)
19W514-105
75WhiSox1T-20
88PacEigMO-16
88PacEigMO-26
88PacEigMO-70
88PacEigMO-103
92Man191BSR-19
94ConTSN-1032
94ConTSNB-1032

Riscen, Fred
88SalLakCTTI-21

Risley, Bill (William)
88GreHorP-1551
89CedRapRB-6
89CedRapRP-912
89CedRapRS-16
90CedRapRB-14
90CedRapRP-2313
90ProAaA-121
91ChaLooLD-166
91ChaLooP-1959
91LinDriAA-166
92DonRoo-103
92IndIndF-1857
93Bow-44
93FleFinE-96
93OttLynF-2434
94CalCanF-787
94ExtBas-171
94Fla-339
94FleUpd-85
95Don-205
95DonPreP-205
95DonTopotO-154
95Fla-302
95Fle-275
95FleRooS-16
95MarMot-27
95MarPac-41
95Top-448
95TopCyb-244
95Ult-105
95UltGolM-105
95UltSecYS-12
95UltSecYSGM-12
96BluJayOH-27
96Don-438
96DonPreP-438
96Fla-192
96Fle-242
96FleTif-242
96FleUpd-U102
96FleUpdTC-U102
96LeaSigEA-170
96Ult-436
96UltGolM-436

Ritch, Harry
85VerBeaDT-13

Ritchey, Claude
03BreE10-124
06FanCraNL-41
08RosComP-92
09ColChiE-241
09RamT20-99
09T206-304
11SpoLifCW-303
12ColRedB-241
12ColTinT-241
98CamPepP-64

Ritchey, Larry
86MedA'sC-60

Ritchie, Dave
89EugEmeB-11

Ritchie, Gregg
86EveGiaC-5
86EveGiaPC-26
87CliGiaP-4
88SanJosGCLC-127
88SanJosGP-131
89ShrCapP-1841
90CMC-541
90PhoFirC-14
90PhoFirP-25
90ProAAAF-51
91LinDriAAA-391
91PhoFirLD-391
91PhoFirP-81
92PhoFirF-2835
92PhoFirS-395
96BriWhiSB-2

Ritchie, Jay
65Top-494

Ritchie, Lewis
09SpoNewSM-87
14PieStaT-49

Ritchie, Todd
90ClaDraP-12
90EliTwiS-19
91Bow-332
91Cla/Bes-319
91Cla1-T58
91KenTwiC-22
91KenTwiP-2072
91MidLeaAP-MWL39
91Sco-678
92Bow-524
92ClaFS7-298
92ProFS7-99
92UppDecML-106
92VisOakC-23
92VisOakF-1014
93ClaFS7-251
93ClaGolF-44
93NasXprF-403
94Bow-272
94NasXprF-385
94SigRoo-17
94SigRooS-17
94UppDecML-167
95HarCitRCTI-20
96HarCitRCB-26

Ritchie, Wally
86ClePhiP-21
87FleUpd-104
87FleUpdG-104
87MaiGuiP-17
87TopTra-103T
87TopTraT-103T
88BlaYNPRWLU-9
88Don-555
88Fle-312
88FleGlo-312
88OPC-322
88PhiTas-20
88Sco-526
88ScoGlo-526
88Top-494
88TopTif-494
89ScrRedBC-9
89ScrRedBP-715
90CMC-232
90ProAAAF-300
90ScrRedBC-6
90ScrRedBP-598
91LinDriAAA-493
91ScrRedBLD-493
91ScrRedBP-2536
92Don-631
92Fle-543
92Lea-443
92PhiMed-25
92Sco-619
92StaClu-324
93TolMudHF-1655
93TriAAAGF-39
94ClaGolF-179

Ritter, Chris
86PriWilPP-21
87HarSenP-25
88HarSenP-845

Ritter, Darren
89PulBraP-1905
90Bes-47
90BurBraB-25
90BurBraP-2348
90BurBraS-22
91DurBulUP-6
91MacBraC-7
91MacBraP-861
92DurBulC-9
92DurBulF-1097
92DurBulTI-31

Ritter, Jason
94EugEmeC-18
94EugEmeF-3710
95SpoIndTI-21
96LanLugB-20

Ritter, Ken
89MedAthB-15

Ritter, Lawrence
90LitSunW-12

Ritter, Lou (Louis)
09ColChiE-242
09T206-460
11SpoLifCW-304
12ColRedB-242
12ColTinT-242
90DodTar-670

Ritter, Reggie
83WatIndF-15
85WatIndT-11
86IndOhH-53
86MaiGuiP-16
87BufBisP-19
88ColSprSSC-7
88ColSprSSP-1540
89BlaYNPRWLU-4

Ritter, Ryan
95HelBreTI-15
96BelSnaTI-32

Ritter, William
16ColE13-138

Rittman, Alvin
89BelMarL-24
90SprCarB-2

Rittwage, James
65Top-501

Rittweger, Bill
82JacMetT-18

Ritz, Kevin
87GleFalTP-6
88GleFalTP-926
89TolMudHC-7
89TolMudHP-786
90Bow-350
90BowTif-350
90ClaBlu-131
90CMC-385
90Don-415
90Fle-613
90FleCan-613
90Hot50RS-37
90OPC-237
90ProAAAF-377
90Sco-572
90Sco100RS-11
90Spo-29
90TigCok-18
90TolMudHC-8
90TolMudHP-147
90Top-237
90TopDeb89-102
90TopTif-237
90UppDec-98
91LinDriAAA-596
91TigCok-31
91TolMudHLD-596
91TolMudHP-1932
92Bow-419
92Lea-386
92StaClu-337
92Ult-368
93Don-99
93Fle-415
93Top-771
93TopGol-771
93TopInaM-771
93TopMic-771
94ColSprSSF-732
94FleUpd-130
95Fle-527
95StaClu-576
95StaCluMOP-576
95StaCluSTWS-576
95TopTra-115T
95Ult-157
95UltGolM-157
96ColCho-137
96ColChoGS-137
96ColChoSS-137
96Don-383
96DonPreP-383
96EmoXL-176
96Fla-250
96Fle-372
96FleRoc-12
96FleTif-372
96LeaSigEA-171
96Pac-52
96RocPol-19
96Sco-45
96StaClu-377
96StaCluMOP-377
96Ult-192
96UltGolM-192
96UppDec-324
97Cir-220
97CirRav-220
97ColCho-97
97Fle-317
97FleTif-317
97Lea-96
97LeaFraM-96
97LeaFraMDC-96
97MetUni-75
97Pac-288
97PacLigB-288
97PacSil-288
97Sco-29
97ScoPreS-29
97ScoRoc-2
97ScoRocPl-2
97ScoRocPr-2

97ScoShoS-29
97ScoShoSAP-29
97StaClu-158
97StaCluMOP-158
97Top-233
97Ult-189
97UltGolME-189
97UltPlaME-189
97UppDec-58
Ritz, Trey
92HamRedC-17
92HamRedF-1603
93GleFalRC-24
93GleFalRF-4014
Rivard, John
89MiaMirlS-17
Rivas, Hector
80VenLeaS-213
Rivas, Javier
91PulBraC-15
91PulBraP-4019
Rivas, Limbert
90AshTouP-2746
Rivas, Martin
77ChaPatT-15
85DomLeaS-160
Rivas, Oscar
89BelMarL-12
90PenPilS-17
91SanBerSP-1988
Rivas, Rafael
80UtiBluJT-31
Rivas, Ralph
83KinBluJTI-19
Rivas, Rene
85DomLeaS-159
Rivell, Robert
88CapCodPPaLP-72
91WatDiaC-19
91WatDiaP-1266
River Rascal, Crash the
94WesMicWC-28
95WesMicWTI-99
96WesMicWB-4
Rivera, Angel
88JamExpP-1900
Rivera, Ben
88SumBraP-410
89DurBullS-18
89DurBulTI-18
90DurBulUTI-4
90GreBraB-6
90GreBraP-1126
90GreBraS-17
91Bow-579
91GreBraC-3
91GreBraLD-214
91GreBraP-2997
91LinDriAA-214
92DonRoo-104
92FleUpd-111
92PhiMed-45
92Pin-554
92Ult-463
93Don-412
93Fle-107
93Lea-393
93LimRocDWB-44
93OPC-330
93PacSpa-580
93PhiMed-28
93Pin-437
93Sco-242
93Sel-329
93StaClu-654
93StaCluFDI-654
93StaCluMOP-654
93StaCluP-20
93Top-622
93TopGol-622
93ToplnaM-622
93TopMic-622
93Ult-93
93UppDec-389
93UppDecGold-389
94ColC-626
94ColChoGS-626
94ColChoSS-626
94Don-216
94Fla-211
94Fle-599
94Lea-213
94Pac-485
94PhiMed-27
94PhiUSPC-5H
94PhiUSPC-12C
94Pin-178
94PinArtP-178
94PinMusC-178
94Sco-293
94ScoGolR-293
94StaClu-252
94StaCluFDI-252
94StaCluGR-252
94StaCluMOP-252
94StaCluT-232
94StaCluTFDI-232
94Top-352
94TopGol-352
94TopSpa-352
94Ult-252
95Top-239
Rivera, Bombo (Jesus)
76ExpRed-26
77OPC-54
77Top-178
78Top-657
78TwiFriP-17
79Top-449
79TwiFriP-24
80OPC-22
80Top-43
81Don-593
81Fle-556
81OmaRoyT-23
81Top-256
82OmaRoyT-20
83OmaRoyT-19
88BlaYNPRWL-14
Rivera, Carlos
87FayGenP-14
88ElmPioC-11
88WinHavRSS-21
89BlaYNPRWLU-17
89ElmPioP-15
Rivera, Charlie
95NegLeaL2-21
Rivera, Dave
76AshTouT-4
77AshTouT-18
82ChaChaT-22
Rivera, David
88BlaYNPRWL-113
89BlaYNPRWL-184
91KenTwiC-6
91KenTwiP-2084
92VisOakC-18
92VisOakF-1023
93NasXprF-411
Rivera, Elvin
86QuaCitAP-27
87QuaCitAP-16
88RenSilSCLC-269
Rivera, Ernesto
92OklStaC-25
Rivera, German
78CliDodT-27
83AlbDukT-17
84DodPol-25
85AlbDukC-162
85Don-638
85Fle-382
85Top-626
85TopTif-626
86NasSouTI-20
87TolMudHP-4
87TolMudHT-3
88BlaYNPRWL-13
88DenZepC-12
88DenZepP-1253
88TriAAAP-14
88TriAAC-9
90DodTar-671
90IndIndP-305
90ProAAAF-588
90TriAllGP-AAA9
Rivera, Hector
89WesPalBES-20
90CMC-670
90GatCitPP-3349
90GatCitPSP-20
90JacExpB-23
90JacExpP-1374
91Bow-444
91HarSenLD-261
91HarSenP-625
91LinDriAA-261
Rivera, Jim (Manuel J.)
53Top-156
54Top-34
55Top-58
55TopDouH-89
56Top-70
56TopHocF-A11
56TopHocF-B13
56TopPin-35
57Top-107
58Top-11A
58Top-11B
58WhiSoxJP-9
59Top-213
60Lea-55
60Top-116
60TopVen-116
60WhiSoxTS-16
61Pos-33A
61Pos-33B
61Top-367
83AndBraT-14
84DurBulT-26
91TopArc1-156
94TopArc1-34
94TopArc1G-34
Rivera, Jose
83GreHorT-23
83QuaCitCT-23
87MemChiB-4
87MemChiP-23
88BlaYNPRWL-15
88MemChiB-25
89BlaYNPRWL-151
Rivera, Lino
88BlaYNPRWL-74
88ChaRanS-20
89BlaYNPRWL-85
89FayGenP-1573
89SouAtlLAGS-21
90LakTigS-22
90StaFS7-37
91LakTigC-11
91LakTigP-266
92ArkTraS-43
Rivera, Luis
83VerBeaDT-13
86IndIndTI-28
87ExpPos-23
87Fle-330
87FleGlo-330
87IndIndTI-27
88BlaYNPRWL-77
88ExpPos-19
88StaLinE-15
88TopBig-223
88TopTra-94T
88TopTraT-94T
89BlaYNPRWL-86
89Bow-29
89BowTif-29
89Don-578
89Fle-392
89FleGlo-392
89OPC-257
89PawRedSC-20
89PawRedSP-697
89PawRedSTI-20
89Sco-169
89Top-431
89TopSti-68
89TopTif-431
89UppDec-423
90Don-421
90Fle-285
90FleCan-285
90Lea-283
90OPC-601
90RedSoxP-18
90Top-601
90TopTif-601
90TopTVRS-26
90UppDec-482
91Don-234
91Fle-112
91Lea-408
91OPC-338
91PanFreS-267
91RedSoxP-19
91Sco-271
91StaClu-55
91Top-338
91TopDesS-338
91TopMic-338
91TopTif-338
91Ult-42
91UppDec-182
92Bow-355
92Don-332
92Fle-48
92Lea-355
92OPC-97
92PanSti-88
92Pin-346
92RedSoxDD-26
92Sco-159
92StaClu-255
92Top-97
92TopGol-97
92TopGolW-97
92TopMic-97
92Ult-22
92UppDec-308
93Don-591
93Fle-565
93PacSpa-36
93PanSti-94
93Pin-159
93RedSoxWHP-24
93StaClu-533
93StaCluFDI-533
93StaCluMOP-533
93Top-296
93TopGol-296
93ToplnaM-296
93TopMic-296
93TriPla-246
93Ult-515
93UppDec-602
93UppDecGold-602
94MetColP-21
94Pac-64
94StaCluMOP-ST16
94StaCluST-ST16
95Pac-286
95StaCluSTDW-RS1T
96NorTidB-26
Rivera, Mariano
90TamYanD-17
91GreHorP-3058
92Bow-302
92Ft.LauYF-2611
93Bow-327
94TamYanC-20
94TamYanF-2382
95Bow-165
95Exc-102
95StaClu-592
95StaCluMOP-592
95StaCluSTWS-592
95TopTra-130T
96ColCho-19
96ColChoGS-19
96ColChoSS-19
96Don-67
96DonPreP-67
96Fle-195
96FleTif-195
96LeaSig-107
96LeaSigA-194
96LeaSigAG-194
96LeaSigAS-194
96LeaSigPPG-107
96LeaSigPPP-107
96Pac-382
96Pin-189
96Sco-225
96StaClu-411
96StaCluMOP-411
96Ult-105
96UltGolM-105
97Bow-27
97BowBes-32
97BowBesAR-32
97BowBesR-32
97BowChr-23
97BowChrI-23
97BowChrIR-23
97BowChrR-23
97BowInt-27
97BowIntB-BBI9
97BowIntBAR-BBI9
97BowIntBR-BBI9
97Cir-3
97CirFasT-7
97CirRav-3
97ColCho-405
97ColChoBS-7
97ColChoBSGS-7
97Don-133
97DonEli-118
97DonEliGS-118
97DonLim-134
97DonLimLE-134
97DonPre-123
97DonPreCttC-123
97DonPreP-133
97DonPrePGold-133
97DonTea-128
97DonTeaSPE-128
97Fin-117
97FinEmb-117
97FinEmbR-117
97FinRef-117
97FlaSho-A142
97FlaSho-B142
97FlaSho-C142
97FlaShoLC-142
97FlaShoLC-B142
97FlaShoLC-C142
97FlaShoLCM-A142
97FlaShoLCM-B142
97FlaShoLCM-C142
97Fle-176
97FleTif-176
97Lea-147
97LeaFraM-147
97LeaFraMDC-147
97LeaGet-16
97MetUni-122
97NewPin-87
97NewPinAP-87
97NewPinMC-87
97NewPinPP-87
97Pac-158
97PacGolCD-13
97PacLatotML-14
97PacLigB-158
97PacPri-54
97PacPriLB-54
97PacPriP-54
97PacSil-158
97Pin-128
97PinArtP-128
97PinCar-14
97PinCer-62
97PinCerMBlu-62
97PinCerMG-62
97PinCerMR-62
97PinCerR-62
97PinIns-113
97PinInsCE-113
97PinInsDD-17
97PinInsDE-113
97PinMusC-128
97PinTotCPB-62
97PinTotCPG-62
97PinTotCPR-62
97PinX-P-25
97PinX-PMoS-25
97Sco-116
97Sco-527
97ScoHobR-527
97ScoPreS-116
97ScoResC-527
97ScoShoS-116
97ScoShoS-527
97ScoShoSAP-116
97ScoShoSAP-527
97ScoStaaD-12
97ScoYan-7
97ScoYanPI-7
97ScoYanPr-7
97Sel-87
97SelArtP-87
97SelRegG-87
97SelRooR-18
97SP-127
97SpollI-132
97SpollIEE-132
97StaClu-11
97StaCluMat-11
97StaCluMOP-11
97Stu-104
97StuPrePG-104
97StuPrePS-104
97Top-256
97TopAwel-AI16
97TopChr-89
97TopChrR-89
97TopGal-158
97TopGalPPI-158
97TopSta-94

97TopStaAM-94
97Ult-103
97UltGolME-103
97UltPlaME-103
97UppDec-69
97UppDec-439
Rivera, Maximo
93WelPirC-25
93WelPirF-3369
Rivera, Miguel
94JohCitCC-25
94JohCitCF-3712
96PeoChiB-26
Rivera, Oscar
92BelMarC-15
92BelMarF-1442
94AppFoxC-16
94AppFoxF-1053
95GreFalDTI-5
Rivera, Pablo
89BlaYNPRWL-13
89ChaKniTI-25
Rivera, Rafael
91SalSpuC-2
91SalSpuP-2247
92SalSpuC-9
92SalSpuF-3759
96EveAquB-18
Rivera, Ricardo
82AubAstT-17
83DayBeaAT-22
Rivera, Roberto
89BurlndS-22
90WatIndS-17
91ColIndC-15
91ColIndP-1482
92KinIndC-15
92KinIndF-2474
93CanIndF-2837
94PeoChiC-22
94PeoChiF-2266
96IowCubB-22
96Pac-32
95OrlCubF-9
Rivera, Ruben
92GulCoaYF-3705
93OneYanC-1
93OneYanF-3518
94AriFalLS-18
94Bow-348
94BowBes-X99
94BowBesR-X99
94Cla-73
94ExcFS7-113
94GreBatF-489
94SouAtlLAF-SAL16
95ActPac2GF-10G
95ActPacF-31
95ActPacF-71
95Bow-231
95BowBes-B42
95BowBes-X9
95BowBesR-B42
95BowBesR-X9
95BowGolF-231
95ColCho-28
95ColChoGS-28
95ColChoSS-28
95ColCliP-26
95ColCliTI-26
95Emo-66
95Exc-103
95ExcAll-8
95NorNagUTI-24
95NorNavTI-24
95SigRooFD-FD4
95SigRooFDS-FD4
95SigRooOJ-36
95SigRooOJHP-HP4
95SigRooOJHPS-HP4
95SigRooOJSS-1
95SigRooOJSSS-1
95SP-10
95SPCha-9
95SPChaDC-9
95SPSil-10
95StaCluCB-CB12
95StaCluMOP-CB12
95Sum21C-TC5
95Top-640
95UppDec-1
95UppDecED-1
95UppDecEDG-1
95UppDecML-8
95UppDecML-112
95UppDecMLOP-OP19
95UppDecMLT1PF-4
95UppDecSE-144
95UppDecSEG-144
96Bow-168
96BowBes-96
96BowBesAR-96
96BowBesC-12
96BowBesCAR-12
96BowBesCR-12
96BowBesMI-5
96BowBesMIAR-5
96BowBesMIR-5
96BowBesP-BBP19
96BowBesPAR-BBP19
96BowBesPR-BBP19
96BowBesR-96
96BowMinLP-11
96Cir-69
96CirRav-69
96ColCho-20
96ColChoGS-20
96ColChoSS-20
96ColCliB-27
96Don-397
96DonPreP-397
96EmoXL-95
96Fin-B340
96FinRef-B340
96Fla-136
96FlaWavotF-19
96FlePro-8
96FleUpd-U67
96FleUpdTC-U67
96Lea-215
96LeaLimR-3
96LeaLimRG-3
96LeaPre-137
96LeaPreP-137
96LeaPrePB-215
96LeaPrePG-215
96LeaPrePS-215
96LeaSig-92
96LeaSigPPG-92
96LeaSigPPP-92
96MLBPin-30
96PacPri-P122
96PacPriG-P122
96Pin-165
96PinArtP-92
96PinSam-165
96PinSta-92
96PinTeaT-1
96Sco-263
96Sco-381
96ScoDugC-A109
96ScoDugC-B106
96ScoDugCAP-A109
96ScoDugCAP-B106
96ScoFutF-8
96SelCer-134
96SelCerAP-134
96SelCerCB-134
96SelCerCR-134
96SelCerMB-134
96SelCerMG-134
96SelCerMR-134
96Spo-109
96Spo-126
96SpoArtP-109
96SpoArtP-126
96SpoDouT-4
96SpoPowS-13
96SpoPro-19
96StaClu-258
96StaCluMOP-258
96Top-346
96TopChr-138
96TopChrR-138
96Ult-394
96Ult-600
96UltGolM-394
96UltGolM-600
96UltGolP-10
96UltGolPGM-10
96UppDec-230
96UppDecBCP-BC9
96Zen-111
96ZenArtP-111
96ZenDiaC-15
96ZenDiaCP-15
97Bow-118
97BowBes-142
97BowBesAR-142
97BowBesP-14
97BowBesPAR-14
97BowBesPR-14
97BowBesR-142
97BowCerBIA-CA68
97BowCerGIA-CA68
97BowInt-118
97BowIntB-BBI15
97BowIntBAR-BBI15
97BowIntBR-BBI15
97Cir-312
97CirRav-312
97ColCho-178
97Don-106
97DonEli-27
97DonEliGS-27
97DonEliTotC-18
97DonEliTotCDC-18
97DonPreP-106
97DonPrePGold-106
97Fin-280
97FinEmb-280
97FinEmbR-280
97FinRef-280
97FlaShoWotF-17
97Fle-177
97FleTif-177
97GreBatC-1
97Lea-30
97LeaFraM-30
97LeaFraMDC-30
97Pac-159
97PacLatotML-15
97PacLigB-159
97PacSil-159
97PinIns-130
97PinInsCE-130
97PinInsDE-130
97PinPasttM-25
97Sco-114
97ScoPreS-114
97ScoShoS-114
97ScoShoSAP-114
97ScoYan-6
97ScoYanPI-6
97ScoYanPr-6
97Sel-110
97SelArtP-110
97SelRegG-110
97SelRooR-15
97SelToootT-14
97SelToootTMB-14
97SkyE-X-35
97SkyE-XC-35
97SkyE-XEC-35
97StaClu-90
97StaCluMOP-90
97Stu-158
97StuPrePG-158
97StuPrePS-158
97Top-403
97TopAwel-AI17
97TopChr-141
97TopChrR-141
97TopGal-159
97TopGalPPI-159
97Ult-104
97UltGolME-104
97UltGolP-9
97UltPlaME-104
97UppDec-121
97UppDec-199
97UppDec-381
97UppDecBCP-BC18
95UppDecMLFS-8
95UppDecMLFS-112
97UppDecTTS-TS6
97UppDecU-53
97UppDecUGN-GN16
Rivera, Santiago
93SpoIndC-17
94SprSulC-19
94SprSulF-2046
95RanCucQT-26
Rivera, Willie
94UtiBluSC-24
94UtiBluSF-3834
96MicBatCB-22
RiverDog, Charlie the
94ChaRivC-30
95ChaRivTI-30
96ChaRivTI-9605
RiverDog, Shamrock the
96ChaRivTI-9604
Riverdogs, Charleston
95ChaRivUTIS-39
96ChaRivTI-9631
Rivero, Marty
87GenCubP-13
88PeoChiTI-26
89WinSpiS-14
Rivers, Jonathan
94MedHatBJF-3695
94MedHatBJSP-8
95HagSunF-82
96DunBluJB-21
96DunBluJTI-25
Rivers, Ken
87DunBluJP-949
88KnoBluJB-14
89KnoBluJB-21
89KnoBluJP-1132
89KnoBluJS-17
90MyrBeaBJP-2779
91LinDriAA-441
91MidAngLD-441
91MidAngOHP-22
91MidAngP-437
Rivers, Mickey
88ElmPioC-23
89WinHavRSS-18
90LynRedSTI-4
91Cla/Bes-90
91WinHavRSC-24
91WinHavRSP-503
Rivers, Mickey Sr.
72OPC-272
72Top-272
73OPC-597
73Top-597
74OPC-76
74Top-76
75GreHeroBP-1
75Hos-22
75HosTwi-22
75OPC-164
75Top-164
76Hos-102
76Kel-41A
76Kel-41B
76OPC-85
76OPC-198
76SSP-203
76Top-85
76Top-198
76TopTra-85T
77BurCheD-180
77Kel-55
77OPC-69
77Top-305
77YanBurK-18
78Hos-110
78Kel-17
78OPC-182
78SSP270-13
78Top-690
78YanBurK-20
78YanSSPD-13
79OPC-24
79Top-60
79YanBurK-20
80OPC-251
80Top-485
81AllGamPI-67
81Don-496
81Fle-617
81FleStiC-32
81OPC-145
81Top-145
81TopScr-31
81TopSti-132
81TopSupHT-94
82Don-242
82Fle-328
82FleSta-174
82OPC-51
82OPC-356
82Top-704
82Top-705
82TopSti-243
83Don-394
83Fle-576
83OPC-224
83RanAffF-17
83Top-224
83TopFol-5
84Don-465
84Fle-425
84Nes792-504
84OPC-269
84RanJarP-17
84Top-504
84TopSti-361
84TopTif-504
85Don-465
85Fle-565
85Lea-35
85OPC-371
85Top-371
85TopSti-355
85TopTif-371
86RanGreT-10
89PacSenL-163
89T/MSenL-91
89TopSenL-115
90EliSenL-28
92YanWIZ7-134
92YanWIZA-65
93RanKee-308
Rives, Sherron
95FayGenTI-21
Rivette, Scott
96WesMicWB-23
Rixey, Eppa
15SpoNewM-142
16ColE13-139
16SpoNewM-142
17HolBreD-83
21E121So1-79A
21E121So1-79B
21E121So8-76
21Exh-144
22AmeCarE-56
22E120-178
22W572-85
22W575-104
23W501-54
23WilChoV-133
25Exh-30
26Exh-30
27Exh-15
27YorCarE-16
28StaPlaCE-53
28W502-16
28Yue-16
33Gou-74
34GouCanV-32
61Fle-71
76RowExh-6
76ShaPiz-94
77BobParHoF-39
77GalGloG-99
80PerHaloFP-94
80SSPHOF-94
82OhiHaloF-41
86RedGreT-4
89HOFStiB-69
91ConTSN-39
93ConTSN-906
95ConTSN-1327
Rizza, Jerry
88SouOreAP-1715
90EriSaiS-20
Rizzo, Johnny
39ExhSal-54
39PlaBal-11
40PlaBal-108
41DouPlaR-123
42DodTeal-19
47SigOil-68
47SunBre-19
90DodTar-672
93ConTSN-944
Rizzo, Mike
83PeoSunF-14
Rizzo, Rick
81ChaRoyT-23
82ForMyeRT-1
84MemChiT-3
Rizzo, Todd
92YakBeaC-16
92YakBeaF-3447
95PriWilCTI-23
Rizzo, Tom
88PulBraP-1754
89SumBraP-1087
90IdaFalBP-3246
Rizzuto, Phil
41DouPlaR-61
41DouPlaR-63
46SpoExcW-5-6

47Exh-187A
47Exh-187B
47HomBon-39
47PM1StaP1-175
47StaPinP2-34
47TipTop-57
48Bow-8
48YanTeal-24
49Bow-98A
49Bow-98B
49Lea-11
50AmeNut&CCP-15
50Bow-11
50Dra-25
50RoyDes-11
51BerRos-A3
51Bow-26
51R42SmaS-90
51TopCurA-9
51TopRedB-5
52BerRos-54A
52BerRos-54B
52Bow-52
52RoyPre-10
52StaCalL-70F
52StaCalS-84C
52TipTop-32
52TipTop-33
52Top-11
52Whe-25A
52Whe-25B
53BowC-9
53BowC-93
53Bri-39
53Dor-101
53Dor-101A
53ExhCan-25
53RedMan-AL10
53StaMey-7
53Top-114
54Bow-1
54DanDee-19
54NewYorJA-57
54RedMan-AL17
54StaMey-11
54Top-17
55Bow-10
55StaMey-11
55Top-189
56Top-113
56TopPin-29
60NuHi-45
61NuSco-445
61Top-471
67TopVen-186
77GalGloG-37
79TCM50-144
80PacLeg-82
80PerHaloFP-219
80YanGreT-4
82DiaCla-45
82GSGalAG-10
83MLBPin-15
83TopRep5-11
83YanASFY-37
83YanYealT-3
84OCoandSI-54
84TCMPla1-7
86SpoDecG-22
86TCMSupS-9
86TCMSupS-19
88PacLegI-10
89SweBasG-111
89YanCitAG-4
90PacLeg-101
90RinPosYMP-5
91TopArc1-114
92BazQua5A-2
92UppDecS-16
92YanWIZA-66
93Yoo-15
94TopArc1-17
94TopArc1G-17
94Yoo-12
95ComIma-6
95ComImaP-1

Roa, Hector
90PulBraB-17
90PulBraP-3097
91MiaMirC-23
91MiaMirP-417
92DurBulC-5
92DurBulF-1110
92DurBulTI-2
93Bow-2
93GreBraF-359
93LimRocDWB-50
94GreBraF-422
94GreBraTI-18
95RicBraRC-21
95RicBraTI-19

Roa, Joe
90PulBraB-9
90PulBraP-3107
91MacBraC-8
91MacBraP-862
92St.LucMCB-10
92St.LucMF-1746
93BinMetF-2332
96BufBisB-17
97Fle-583
97FleTif-583
97PacPriGotD-GD39
97SpoIII-21
97SpoIIIEE-21

Roa, Pedro
89BelMarL-19
90BenBucL-27

Roach, Brett
88BriTigP-1884
89FayGenP-1589

Roach, John
87OldJudN-427

Roach, Kevin
89CarNewE-4

Roach, Mel
54Top-181
55BraGolS-28
55Top-117
59Top-54
59TopVen-54
60BraLaktL-20
60BraSpiaS-18
60Top-491
61Pos-163
61Top-217
62Top-581
94TopArc1-181
94TopArc1G-181

Roach, Petie
92EveGiaC-2
92EveGiaF-1699
93CliGiaC-20
93CliGiaF-2501
93EveGiaC-22
93EveGiaF-3778
94YakBeaF-3846
95SanBerSTI-20
96SanAntMB-20
96VerBeaDB-24

Roadcap, Steve
83QuaCitCT-16
86PitCubP-20
88WytCubP-1991
89WytCubS-29
90HunCubP-3303
91HunCubC-30
91HunCubP-3353
92PeoChiC-28
92PeoChiTI-21
93PeoChiF-1100
93PeoChiTI-22
94PeoChiC-26
94PeoChiF-2283
95RocCubTI-NNO
96RocCubTI-28

Roarke, Mike
61Top-376
62TigPosCF-16
62Top-87
62TopVen-87
63Top-224
64TigJayP-11
64Top-292
64TopVen-292
74WicAerODF-109
83PawRedST-26
84Car-24
84Car5x7-23
85CarTeal-28
86CarTeal-37
90TopTVCa-6
91PadSmo-30
92PadMot-27
92PadPolD-28
92PadSmo-26
93PadMot-28

Roarke, Tom
82AubAstT-1

Robarge, Dennis
88ElmPioC-29
89ElmPioP-26
94SalBucC-29

Robbe, Fletcher
53MotCoo-5

Robbins, Bruce
80EvaTriT-18
80Top-666
80VenLeaS-104
81BirBarT-6
81Don-129
81Fle-477
81Top-79
82EvaTriT-6
83BirBarT-10

Robbins, Doug
88TopTra-95T
88TopTraT-95T
89TopBig-49
90Bes-53
90HagSunB-3
90HagSunP-1416
90HagSunS-21
91HagSunLD-245
91HagSunP-2460
91LinDriAA-245
92OPC-58
92RocRedWF-1943
92RocRedWS-465
92Top-58
92TopGol-58
92TopGolW-58
92TopMic-58
93TacTigF-3036

Robbins, Jake
96GreBatB-21

Robbins, Jason
93PriRedC-25
93PriRedF-4178
94BilMusF-3669
94BilMusSP-20
95Exc-182
95SPML-42
95UppDecML-104
96ChaLooB-24
95UppDecMLFS-104

Robbins, Johnny Lee
79CliDodT-3

Robbins, Lance
95CedRapKTI-15

Robbins, Leroy
79WatA'sT-7
80WesHavWCT-3

Robbins, Mike
96LanLugB-21

Robbins, Tim
88BulDurM-2

Robbins, Wes
81NasSouTI-16

Robbs, Bill
92SpoIndC-5
92SpoIndF-1308
93RanCucQC-25
93RanCucQF-845

Robbs, Don
87HawRai-30

Roberge, Al
50WorWidGV-46
95ConTSN-1341

Roberge, Bert
77CocAstT-21
80Top-329
80TucTorT-23
81TucTorT-21
82AstAstI-3
82AstAstI-10
82TucTorT-15
83Don-496
83Fle-461
83Top-611
83TucTorT-8
85ExpPos-19
85Fle-525
85Top-388
85TopTif-388
85TopTifT-94T
85TopTra-94T
86Don-575
86ExpProPa-16
86Fle-258
86OPC-154
86Top-154
86TopTif-154

Roberge, J.P.
94GreFalDSP-20
95SanBerSTI-21
96SanAntMB-21

Roberson, Gerald
94IdaFalBF-3593
94IdaFalBSP-18

Roberson, Kevin
88WytCubP-1978
89ChaWheB-7
89ChaWheP-1747
90WinSpiTI-10
91ChaKniLD-140
91ChaKniP-1702
91Cla/Bes-2
91LinDriAA-140
92IowCubF-4062
92IowCubS-218
92SkyAAAF-106
92UppDecML-124
93Bow-60
93ClaFS7-14
93ExcFS7-12
93Lea-458
93SelRoo-89T
93SP-88
93TriAAAGF-5
94ColC-241
94ColChoGS-241
94ColChoSS-241
94Don-235
94Fin-77
94FinRef-77
94Fle-394
94IowCubF-1287
94Pac-107
94Sco-604
94ScoBoyoS-9
94ScoGolR-604
94StaClu-383
94StaCluFDI-383
94StaCluGR-383
94StaCluMOP-383
94StaCluT-348
94StaCluTFDI-348
94Top-119
94TopGol-119
94TopSpa-119
94Ult-165
94UppDec-199
94UppDecED-199
95ColCho-211
95ColChoGS-211
95ColChoSS-211
95Pac-77
95UppDec-311
95UppDecED-311
95UppDecEDG-311
95UppDecSE-122
95UppDecSEG-122
96FleUpd-U161
96FleUpdTC-U161
96LeaSigEA-172

Roberson, Sid
93StoPorC-21
93StoPorF-745
94ElPasDF-3145
94ExcFS7-85
95Bow-109
95BowBes-B40
95BowBesR-B40
95Exc-74
95TopTra-97T
96ColCho-189
96ColChoGS-189
96ColChoSS-189
96Don-26
96DonPreP-26
96Pac-351
96Top-47

Robert, Yvon
72Dia-127
72Dia-128

Roberts, Bill
76DubPacT-30

Roberts, Bip (Leon)
86DonRoo-33
86FleUpd-96
86TopTra-91T
86TopTraT-91T
87Don-114
87Fle-427
87FleGlo-427
87LasVegSP-23
87Top-637
87TopTif-637
88LasVegSC-14
88LasVegSP-245
89FleUpd-126
89PadCok-14
89TopTra-103T
89TopTraT-103T
90Bow-222
90BowTif-222
90Don-347
90DonBesN-60
90Fle-166
90FleCan-166
90Lea-233
90OPC-307
90PadCok-15
90PadMag-26
90PanSti-359
90Sco-51
90ScoYouSI-23
90Spo-116
90Top-307
90TopBig-149
90TopSti-103
90TopTif-307
90UppDec-303
91Bow-654
91Don-195
91Fle-540
91Lea-478
91OPC-538
91PadCok-8
91PadMag-9
91PadMag-23B
91PadSmo-31
91PanFreS-96
91PanSti-97
91Sco-28
91StaClu-18
91Stu-248
91Top-538
91TopCraJ2-31
91TopDesS-538
91TopMic-538
91TopTif-538
91Ult-310
91UppDec-271
92Bow-525
92ClaGam-192
92Don-371
92Fle-618
92FleUpd-82
92Lea-252
92OPC-20
92OPCPre-69
92PanSti-233
92Pin-404
92RedKah-10
92Sco-123
92ScoRoo-79T
92StaClu-48
92StaClu-645
92StaCluMO-25
92StaCluNC-645
92Stu-27
92Top-20
92TopGol-20
92TopGolPS-20
92TopGolW-20
92TopKid-56
92TopMic-20
92TopPreS-20
92TopTra-92T
92TopTraG-92T
92Ult-485
92UppDec-141
92UppDec-763
93Bow-582
93ClaGam-77
93Don-106
93DonDiaK-DK11
93DonMVP-23
93DonSpiotG-SG9
93DurPowP1-18
93Fin-15
93FinRef-15
93Fla-32
93Fle-42
93FleGolM-B2
93FunPac-172
93Lea-414
93OPC-305

93PacSpa-89
93PanSti-292
93Pin-358
93RedKah-21
93Sco-85
93Sco-516
93Sel-111
93SelStaL-60
93SP-214
93StaClu-30
93StaCluFDI-30
93StaCluM-30
93StaCluMOP-30
93StaCluMP-8
93Stu-135
93Top-219
93TOPBLAG-16
93TopGol-219
93TopInaM-219
93TopMic-219
93TriPla-88
93Ult-34
93UppDec-112
93UppDecGold-112
93UppDecSH-HI16
93USPlaCA-4H
93USPlaCA-9D
94Bow-64
94ColC-476
94ColC-479
94ColChoGS-476
94ColChoGS-479
94ColChoSS-479
94Don-304
94ExtBas-377
94Fin-363
94FinRef-363
94Fla-440
94Fle-422
94FleUpd-189
94FUnPac-110
94Lea-299
94LeaL-154
94OPC-111
94Pac-157
94PadMot-4
94Pin-500
94PinArtP-500
94PinMusC-500
94ProMag-120
94Sco-108
94ScoGolR-108
94ScoRoo-RT46
94ScoRooGR-RT46
94Sel-218
94SP-133
94SPDieC-133
94StaClu-186
94StaClu-698
94StaCluFDI-186
94StaCluFDI-698
94StaCluGR-186
94StaCluGR-698
94StaCluMOP-186
94StaCluMOP-698
94Top-733
94TopGol-733
94TopSpa-733
94TopTra-81T
94Ult-584
94UppDec-382
94UppDecED-382
95Baz-56
95Bow-343
95ColCho-352
95ColChoGS-352
95ColChoSE-166
95ColChoSEGS-166
95ColChoSESS-166
95ColChoSS-352
95D3-47
95Don-450
95DonPreP-450
95DonTopotO-345
95Emb-57
95EmbGolI-57
95Fin-85
95FinRef-85
95Fla-205
95Fle-567
95Lea-92
95LeaLim-113
95Pac-369
95PacPri-118
95PadCHP-7
95PadMot-4
95Pin-388
95PinArtP-388
95PinMusC-388
95Sco-40
95ScoGolR-40
95ScoPlaTS-40
95SP-110
95SPCha-92
95SPChaDC-92
95SPSil-110
95StaClu-344
95StaCluMOP-344
95StaCluSTWS-344
95StaCluVR-182
95Stu-118
95Top-265
95TopCyb-144
95Ult-441
95UltGolM-441
95UppDec-136
95UppDecED-136
95UppDecEDG-136
96Cir-48
96CirRav-48
96ColCho-295
96ColCho-774
96ColChoGS-295
96ColChoSS-295
96Don-120
96DonPreP-120
96EmoXL-70
96Fin-B259
96FinRef-B259
96Fla-94
96Fle-577
96FleTif-577
96FleUpd-U44
96FleUpdTC-U44
96Pac-189
96Pin-325
96PinFoil-325
96RoyPol-24
96Sco-38
96ScoDugC-A36
96ScoDugCAP-A36
96SP-99
96StaClu-90
96StaCluEPB-90
96StaCluEPG-90
96StaCluEPS-90
96StaCluMOP-90
95StaCluVRMC-182
96Stu-10
96StuPrePB-10
96StuPrePG-10
96StuPrePS-10
96Top-288
96Ult-360
96UltGolM-360
96UppDec-188
96UppDec-350
96UppDec-417
97Cir-315
97CirRav-315
97ColCho-361
97Don-311
97DonLim-79
97DonLimLE-79
97DonPreP-311
97DonPrePGold-311
97Fin-92
97FinRef-92
97Fle-121
97FleTif-121
97Lea-285
97LeaFraM-285
97LeaFraMDC-285
97Pac-110
97PacLigB-110
97PacSil-110
97RoyPol-19
97Sco-396
97ScoHobR-396
97ScoResC-396
97ScoShoS-396
97ScoShoSAP-396
97StaClu-339
97StaCluMOP-339
97Top-55
97TopGal-24
97TopGalPPI-24
97Ult-70
97UltGolME-70
97UltPlaME-70
97UppDec-394

Roberts, Bobby
89TenTecGE-23

Roberts, Brent
88BurIndP-1772

Roberts, Brett
93ForMyeMC-21
93ForMyeMF-2653
94ForMyeMC-20
94ForMyeMF-1168
95HarCitRCTI-21

Roberts, Brian
91ButCopKSP-25
92Ft.MyeMCB-4
92Ft.MyeMF-2750

Roberts, Chris
91TopTra-98T
91TopTraT-98T
92Bow-569
92ClaDraP-13
92ClaDraPFB-BC12
92FroRowDP-50
92StaCluD-155
92TopDaiQTU-25
92TopTra-93T
92TopTraG-93T
93ClaFS7-252
93FloStaLAF-41
93Pin-467
93Sco-499
93Sel-297
93St.LucMC-20
93StaCluM-4
93StaCluM-170
93StaCluMMP-8
94BinMetF-704
94Bow-596
94Cla-156
94ClaGolF-124
94ExcFS7-238
94MetShuST-4
94UppDecML-80
95Bow-28
95Exc-238
95NorTidTI-24
95Top-653
95UppDecML-80
93StLucMF-2920
95UppDecMLFS-80

Roberts, Cliff
77DayBealT-19

Roberts, Curt
54DanDee-20
54Top-242
55Top-107
55TopDouH-11
56Top-306
58MonRoyF-19
60DarFar-6
61UniOil-SP10
94TopArc1-242
94TopArc1G-242

Roberts, Dale
72Dia-129
92YanWIZ6-105

Roberts, Dave A.
69Top-536
70OPC-151
70Top-151
71MLBOffS-235
71OPC-448
71Top-448
72Kel-15A
72Kel-15B
72OPC-91
72OPC-360
72Top-91
72Top-360
73LinPor-84
73OPC-39
73Top-39
74AstFouTIP-1
74OPC-177
74Top-177
74TopSta-37
75OPC-301
75Top-301
76OPC-649
76Top-649
76TopTra-649T
77Hos-101
77OPC-38
77Top-363
79GiaPol-25
79Top-473
80Top-212
81Don-501
81Fle-636
81Top-431
86AstGreT-10
87AstShoSTw-14
87AstShowSTh-26
91MetWIZ-332

Roberts, Dave L.
63Top-158
66Top-571

Roberts, Dave W.
73LinPor-156
73OPC-133
73Top-133
74OPC-309
74PadDea-22
74PadMcDD-11
74Top-309A
74Top-309B
74TopSta-99
75HawIslC-5
75IntLeaASB-27
75PacCoaLAB-27
75OPC-558
75Top-558
76HawIslC-5
76OPC-107
76Top-107
77OPC-193
77PadSchC-47
77Top-537
78PadFamF-26
78SSP270-266
78Top-501
79Top-342
80Top-93
81Don-490A
81Don-490B
81Fle-607
81Top-57
81TopTra-824
82Don-625
82Fle-227
82Top-218
83Don-273
83Top-148
86PadGreT-4
93RanKee-309
82PhoGiaVNB-8

Roberts, David
94JamJamC-20
94JamJamF-3981
95Bes-17

Roberts, Drex
85KinBluJT-20

Roberts, Grant
97Bow-299
97BowChr-207
97BowChrI-207
97BowChrIR-207
97BowChrR-207
97BowInt-299

Roberts, James Newsom
90DodTar-673

Roberts, James Wilfred
72Dia-100
72Dia-101

Roberts, Jay
83AndBraT-31

Roberts, Jeff
86WauTimP-19

Roberts, John
87GreHorP-8
88EasLeaAP-23
88NewBriRSP-894
89PawRedSC-21
89PawRedSP-693
89PawRedSTI-21
92ChaRaiC-7
92ChaRaiF-134
93WatDiaC-24
93WatDiaF-1782
94SprSulC-20
94SprSulF-2051
95RanCucQT-23
96RanCucQB-23

Roberts, Keith
90BriTigP-3150
90BriTigS-21

Roberts, Leon (Leon K.)
75OPC-620
75Top-620
76OPC-292
76SSP-362
76Top-292
76TopTra-292T
77BurCheD-3
77Top-456
79Hos-37
79OPC-81
79Top-166
79TopCom-15
80OPC-266
80Top-507
81Don-48
81Fle-608
81Top-368
81TopTra-825
82Don-415
82Fle-329
82OPC-186
82Top-688
83OPC-89
83Roy-23
83Top-89
83TopTra-96T
84Don-399
84Fle-356
84Nes792-784
84PriWilPT-1
84Top-784
84TopTif-784
85NasPirT-20
85NasSouTI-20
85Top-217
85TopTif-217
86MarGreT-5
86NasSouTI-21
87TolMudHP-20
87TolMudHT-21
88FayGenP-1104
89PacSenL-30
89T/MSenL-92
89TopSenL-113
90EliSenL-103
91PacSenL-97
92DurBulC-25
92DurBulF-1115
92DurBulTI-7
93DurBulC-26
93DurBulF-503
93DurBulTI-1
93RanKee-310
94MacBraC-27
94MacBraF-2222

Roberts, Lonell
90MedHatBJB-9
91Cla/Bes-99
91MyrBeaHC-26
91MyrBeaHP-2960
92St.CatBJC-17
92St.CatBJF-3399
93HagSunC-22
93HagSunF-1894
94DunBluJC-23
94DunBluJF-2571
95AusFut-70
95Bow-182
95KnoSmoF-52
96BesAutSA-61
96KnoSmoB-21

Roberts, Mark
96HicCraB-17

Roberts, Mel
77ReaPhiT-19
88SouAtlLAGS-2
88SpaPhiP-1033
88SpaPhiS-6
89SpaPhiP-1050
89SpaPhiS-26
90SpaPhiB-25
90SpaPhiP-2508
90SpaPhiS-27
91SpaPhiC-28
91SpaPhiP-913
92PhiMed-26
93PhiMed-29
94PhiMed-28
95Phi-26
96GreBraB-3
96GreBraTI-30

Roberts, Mike
80TulDriT-5
81TulDriT-17

Roberts, Norman
86HagSunP-16
Roberts, Pete
88LasVegSC-5
88LasVegSP-228
89LasVegSC-9
89LasVegSP-13
90CMC-510
90LasVegSC-7
90LasVegSP-122
90ProAAAF-10
Roberts, Ray
94EugEmeC-19
94EugEmeF-3711
95SprSulTI-23
Roberts, Robin
47Exh-188A
47Exh-188B
47PM1StaP1-176
47PM1StaP1-177
49Bow-46
49EurSta-143
49OlmStu-5
49PhiBul-43
49PhiLumPB-8
50Bow-32
50JJKCopP-14
51BerRos-D8
51Bow-3
51TopCurA-10
52BerRos-55
52Bow-4
52NatTeaL-23
52RedMan-NL18
52TipTop-34
52Top-59
53BowC-65
53MacSta-3
53RedMan-NL11
53SpoMagP-9
54Bow-95
54RedMan-NL18
55Bow-171
56Top-180
56YelBasP-27
57Top-15
58JayPubA-16
58PhiJayP-9
58Top-90
59Top-156
59Top-352
59TopVen-156
60Baz-26
60KeyChal-39
60MacSta-19
60NuHi-44
60PhiJayP-11
60Top-264
60TopTat-45
61NuSco-444
61Pos-117A
61Pos-117B
61Top-20
61TopStal-58
62Jel-198
62Pos-198
62PosCan-198
62Top-243
63Jel-66
63Pos-66
63Top-6
63Top-125
64OriJayP-10
64Top-285
64TopVen-285
65OPC-15
65Top-15
66Top-530
69EquSpoHoF-BB17
74NewYorNTDiS-19
76GalBasGHoF-23
76JerJonPC-8
76RowExh-6
76ShaPiz-157
76ShaPiz-158
77GalGloG-4
78ReaRem-16
79BasGre-67
79DiaGre-317
79PhiTeal-7
79TCM50-4
80PacLeg-56
80PerHaloFP-157
80SSPHOF-157
81TCM60I-459
82CraJac-14
83DiaClaS2-108
83DonHOFH-41
83MLBPin-30
83PhiPosGM-8
83PhiPosGPaM-2
83TopRep5-59
84OCoandSI-64
86PhiTas-36
86SpoDecG-39
86SpoDesJM-21
86TCMSupS-26
87AstShowSTh-24
87Phi195T-9
88PacLegI-15
89TopBasT-40
90PacLeg-47
90PerGreM-17
90PhiTas-31
90SweBasG-11
91LinDri-33
91OriCro-384
91SweBasG-77
91TopArc1-288
91UppDecS-3
92ActPacA-12
92ActPacA2-12G
92BazQua5A-21
92UppDecF-54
92UppDecFG-54
92UppDecHH-HI7
92UppDecS-35
93ActPacAC-12
93TedWil-73
93UppDecAH-108
94UppDecAH-36
94UppDecAH-223
94UppDecAH1-36
94UppDecAH1-223
97TopStaHRR-11
97TopStaHRRA-11
Roberts, Scott
84VanCanC-42
85VanCanC-218
86IndTeal-33
86MaiGuiP-17
87BufBisP-20
Roberts, Tim
91EriSaiC-23
91EriSaiP-4069
Roberts, Willis
93BriTigC-17
94BriTigC-21
94BriTigF-3501
95FayGenTI-22
96LakTigB-20
Robertson, Andre
81ColCliP-2
81ColCliT-3
82ColCliP-2
82ColCliT-17
82Top-83
83Don-387
83Fle-396
83Top-281
83TopSti-316
83YanRoyRD-10
84ColCliP-20
84ColCliT-9
84Don-347
84Fle-140
84Nes792-592
84OPC-282
84Top-592
84TopSti-323
84TopTif-592
85Fle-144
85Top-354
85TopTif-354
86ColCliP-19
86ColCliP-21
86Don-469
86Fle-117
86Top-738
86TopTif-738
86YanTCM-28
87ChaLooB-25
88HunStaTI-16
88TacTigC-19
88TacTigP-634
89OklCit8C-14
89OklCit8P-1514
92TexLon-34
92YanWIZ8-161
86STaoftFt-5
Robertson, Bill
90BelBreB-2
90BelBreS-18
Robertson, Bob E.
68OPC-36
68Top-36
68TopVen-36
69PirJacitB-10
69Top-468A
69Top-468B
69TopTeaP-16
70PirTeal-6
70Top-664
71Kel-4
71MLBOffS-212
71OPC-255
71Pir-5
71PirActP-22
71PirArc-9
71Top-255
72Kel-45
72OPC-429
72OPC-430
72Top-429
72Top-430
73OPC-422
73Top-422
74OPC-540
74Top-540
75OPC-409
75Top-409
76OPC-449
76SSP-578
76Top-449
77Top-176
79OPC-158
79Top-312
89SweBasG-107
90AshTouC-28
91AshTouP-586
92AshTouC-27
93OscAstC-27
93OscAstF-645
Robertson, Bryant
85LitFalMT-27
Robertson, Charles
21Exh-145
21Nei-10
22E120-26
22W573-107
22W575-105
23W503-54
75WhiSox1T-21
92ConTSN-354
93ConTSN-815
Robertson, Dale
81PawRedST-13
84PawRedST-4
Robertson, Daryl
77FriOneYW-19
Robertson, David A.
15SpoNewM-143
16ColE13-140
16FleBreD-76
16SpoNewM-143
17HolBreD-84
23W503-3
23WilChoV-134
Robertson, Doug
85EveGialC-14
86CliGiaP-22
87CliGiaP-1
88CalLeaACLC-6
88SanJosGCLC-137
88SanJosGP-115
89ShrCapP-1851
90CMC-457
90ColSprSSC-5
90ColSprSSP-32
90IndTeal-33
90ProAAAF-213
91LinDriAA-442
91MidAngLD-442
91MidAngOHP-23
91MidAngP-433
96SouOreTI-9
Robertson, Gene (Eugene E.)
92ConTSN-386
Robertson, Jason
89HigSchPLS-14
90Bes-288
90GreHorB-25
90GreHorP-2677
90GreHorS-19
91PriWilCC-22
91PriWilCP-1440
92ClaFS7-225
92PriWilCC-24
92PriWilCF-163
92ProFS7-123
93AlbYanF-2176
94AbaYanF-1456
95NorNagUTI-22
95NorNavTI-22
96ChaKniB-24
Robertson, Jay
78DunBluJT-18
80SyrChiT-6
80SyrChiTI-18
Robertson, Jenny
88BulDurM-3
Robertson, Jerry L.
69Top-284
70Top-661
71OPC-651
71Top-651
Robertson, Jim (Alfred J.)
54Bow-211
54Top-149
55A'sRodM-32
55Bow-5
55Top-177
94TopArc1-149
94TopArc1G-149
Robertson, Michael
86JamExpP-20
Robertson, Mike
87St.PetCP-5
88ArkTraGS-20
89ArkTraGS-21
92Bow-687
92ClaFS7-375
92SarWhiSCB-20
92SarWhiSF-215
92StaCluD-156
92UppDecML-48
92UppDecML-156
93BirBarF-1200
93Bow-315
93ClaFS7-87
93ClaGolF-78
93UppDec-448
93UppDecGold-448
94BirBarC-19
94BirBarF-634
94Bow-43
94UppDecML-40
94VenLinU-147
95LinVen-150
95NasSouTI-20
96NasSouB-18
Robertson, Rich
69OPC-16
69Top-16
70OPC-229
70Top-229
71MLBOffS-263
71OPC-443
71Top-443
72Top-618
91SalBucC-18
91SalBucP-948
92CarMudF-1178
93Bow-123
93BufBisF-515
93FleFinE-117
94BufBisF-1834
94TriAAF-AAA27
96Fle-175
96FleTif-175
96LeaSigEA-173
96Ult-379
96UltGolM-379
97PacPriGotD-GD66
Robertson, Richard P.
90WelPirP-26
Robertson, Robby
93AppFoxC-20
93AppFoxF-2475
Robertson, Rod (Roderick)
86BenPhiC-130
88SpaPhiP-1034
88SpaPhiS-2
89ClePhiS-19
90ReaPhiB-18
90ReaPhiP-1228
90ReaPhiS-21
91LinDriAA-515
91ReaPhiLD-515
91ReaPhiP-1376
92LonTigF-642
92LonTigS-416
93TolMudHF-1662
94OrlCubF-1393
95RocRedWTI-30
Robertson, Ryan
96KanCouCTI-23
Robertson, Shawn
91SpoIndC-10
91SpoIndP-3961
92WatDiaC-18
92WatDiaF-2154
Robertson, Sherry
47SenGunBP-9
50Bow-161
51Bow-95
52Top-245
83TopRep5-245
Robertson, Stan
92AlbPolC-23
92AlbPolF-2320
92JamExpF-1515
Robertson, Tommy
92SanBerC-10
92SanBerSF-972
93RivPilCLC-16
95LynHilTI-24
Robicheaux, Randy
86WatPirP-18
Robidoux, Billy Jo
83BelBreF-21
86BrePol-13
86Don-515
86Fle-652
86FleUpd-97
86Spo-178
86SpoRoo-28
86TopTra-92T
86TopTraT-92T
87BrePol-13
87BreTeal-11
87Don-240
87DonOpeD-51
87Fle-356
87FleGlo-356
87SpoTeaP-19
87Top-401
87TopRoo-13
87TopSti-202
87TopTif-401
88DenZepC-13
88DenZepP-1267
88Sco-334
88ScoGlo-334
88StaLinBre-15
89WhiSoxC-23
90TopTVRS-27
90UppDec-782
94BreMilB-262
Robinette, Gary
81AppFoxT-22
Robinson, Aaron
46SpoExcW-9-3
47HomBon-40
47TipTop-58
48WhiSoxTI-24
49Bow-133
50Bow-95
51Bow-142
53MotCoo-6
92YanWIZA-67
Robinson, Admiral (David Maurice)
93StaCluMO-38
Robinson, Alan
92HamRedC-21
92HamRedF-1608
Robinson, Bill
87SalAngP-8
88QuaCitAGS-8
Robinson, Bill H.
67Top-442
68Top-337
68Top3-D-9
68TopVen-337
69MilBra-234
69MLBOffS-78
69Top-313
69TopSta-207

69TopTeaP-19
70MLBOffS-249
70OPC-23
70Top-23
72MilBra-290
73OPC-37
73Top-37
74OPC-174
74PhiJohP-24
74Top-174
74TopSta-78
75OPC-501
75Top-501
76OPC-137
76SSP-577
76Top-137
77BurCheD-183
77PirPosP-22
77Top-335
78OPC-128
78Top-455
79OPC-336
79Top-637
80OPC-138
80Top-264
81Don-137
81Fle-373
81Top-51
82Don-402
82Fle-494
82Top-543
82TopTra-100T
83Fle-170
83PhiTas-24
83Top-754
85MetTCM-3
85PolMet-M1
86MetTCM-34
87MetColP-45
88MetColP-45
88MetKah-28
89MetColP-50
89MetKah-23
90SweBasG-114
92ShrCapF-3887
92ShrCapS-599
92YanWIZ6-106
94ReaPhiF-2080
95ReaPhiELC-30
96ReaPhiB-26
Robinson, Bob
92VisOakC-10
92VisOakF-1015
93ForMyeMC-22
Robinson, Bobby
86NegLeaF-65
91NegLeaRL-12
92NegLeaRLI-52
95NegLeaL2-7
95NegLeaLI-12
Robinson, Brad
88GreHorP-1557
Robinson, Brett
87GenCubP-2
88PeoChiTI-27
89PeoChiTI-7
90ChaKniTI-17
Robinson, Brian
85CedRapRT-19
86VerRedP-16
87CedRapRP-17
Robinson, Brooks
47Exh-189
47PM1StaP1-178
55DonWin-37
57Top-328
58Top-307
59OriJayP-7
59Top-439
60Lea-27
60OriJayP-7
60Top-28
60TopVen-28
61Pos-75A
61Pos-75B
61Raw-9
61Top-10
61Top-572
61TopDicG-14
61TopStaI-104
62Pos-29
62PosCan-29
62SalPlaC-40
62ShiPlaC-40
62Top-45
62Top-468
62TopBuc-75
62TopStaI-8
62TopVen-45
63BasMagM-69
63Baz-30
63ExhStaB-55
63Fle-4
63Jel-59
63Pos-59
63SalMetC-53
63Top-345
63TopStil-34
64Baz-30
64OriJayP-11
64Raw-5
64Top-230
64TopCoi-18
64TopCoi-125
64TopGia-50
64TopSta-21
64TopStaU-61
64TopVen-230
64WheSta-39
65Baz-30
65OldLonC-35
65OPC-1
65OPC-5
65OPC-150
65Top-1
65Top-5
65Top-150
65TopEmbI-16
65TopTraI-65
66Baz-34
66Top-390
66TopRubI-79
67Baz-34
67CokCapA-3
67CokCapAAm-21
67CokCapO-10
67DexPre-175
67DexPre-176
67OPC-1
67OPC-154
67OPCPapI-3
67Top-1
67Top-154
67Top-531
67Top-600
67TopPos-3
67TopTesF-19
67TopVen-211
68AtlOilPBCC-37
68Baz-8
68CokCapO-10
68DexPre-65
68OPC-20
68Top-20
68Top-365
68Top-530
68TopActS-12C
68TopGamI-9
68TopVen-20
68TopVen-365
69EquSpoHoF-BB18
69MilBra-235
69MLBOffS-8
69MLBPin-25
69NabTeaF-18
69OPCDec-18
69Top-421
69Top-504
69Top-550
69TopDec-1
69TopSta-129
69TopSup-3
69TopTeaP-5
69TraSta-13
70DayDaiNM-154
70Kel-21
70MLBOffS-154
70OPC-230
70OPC-455
70Top-230
70Top-455
71AllBasA-19
71BazNumT-22
71BazUnn-31
71MilDud-26
71MLBOffS-309
71MLBOffS-571
71OPC-300
71OPC-331
71Ori-13
71Top-300
71Top-331
71TopCoi-114
71TopGreM-9
71TopSup-59
71TopTat-6
71TopTat-7
72MilBra-291
72OPC-222
72OPC-498
72OriPol-8
72ProStaP-36
72Top-222
72Top-498
72Top-550
73LinPor-13
73OPC-90
73OriJohP-5A
73OriJohP-5B
73Top-90
73TopCanL-41
73TopCom-16
73TopPin-16
74LauAllG-66
74OPC-160
74OPC-334
74Top-160
74Top-334
74TopDecE-25
74TopSta-129
75Hos-144
75Kel-18
75OPC-50
75OPC-202
75SSP42-6
75Top-50
75Top-202
76CraDis-48
76Hos-36
76HosTwi-36
76LauDiaJ-11
76OPC-95
76SSP-392
76Top-95
77BurCheD-43
77MSADis-50
77Spo-1607
77Top-285
78OPC-239
78TCM60I-190
78Top-4
80MarExh-26
80PacLeg-54
80PerHaloFP-184
80SSPHOF-181
81Ori6F-27
82CraJac-8
82K-M-5
83DiaClaS2-67
83FraBroR-1
83FraBroR-2
83FraBroR-3
83FraBroR-4
83FraBroR-5
83FraBroR-6
83FraBroR-7
83FraBroR-8
83FraBroR-9
83FraBroR-10
83FraBroR-11
83FraBroR-12
83FraBroR-13
83FraBroR-14
83FraBroR-15
83FraBroR-16
83FraBroR-17
83FraBroR-18
83FraBroR-19
83FraBroR-20
83FraBroR-21
83FraBroR-22
83FraBroR-23
83FraBroR-24
83FraBroR-25
83FraBroR-26
83FraBroR-27
83FraBroR-28
83FraBroR-29
83FraBroR-30
83FraBroR-31
83FraBroR-32
83FraBroR-33
83FraBroR-34
83FraBroR-35
83FraBroR-36
83FraBroR-37
83FraBroR-38
83FraBroR-39
83FraBroR-40
83MLBPin-16
83TigAlKS-69
83TopTraBP-9
84OCoandSI-33
84OCoandSI-76
84SpoDesPW-7
85DalNatCC-4
86OriGreT-10
86SpoDecG-45
86SpoDesJM-10
86TCM-13
86TCMSupS-30
87HygAllG-36
87K-M-9
87LeaSpeO*-H9
87NesDreT-14
88GreBasS-21
88HouSho-1
88PacLegI-3
89KahCoo-9
89PacLegI-129
89PerCelP-35
89SweBasG-134
89TopBasT-10
90AGFA-13
90BasWit-17
90PacLeg-102
90PerGreM-39
91MDAA-14
91MDAA-NNO
91OriCro-385
91SweBasG-146
91UppDecS-3
91UppDecS-11
92FroRowBR-1
92FroRowBR-2
92FroRowBR-3
92FroRowBR-4
92FroRowBR-5
92KodCelD-4
92MDAMVP-4
92PMGol-1
92PMGol-2
92UppDecF-51
92UppDecFG-51
92UppDecHH-HI8
92UppDecS-17
92UppDecS-26
92UppDecS-34
92Zip-5
93ActPacA-120
93ActPacA2-54G
93CouTimLBR-1
93CouTimLBR-2
93CouTimLBR-3
93CouTimLBR-4
93CouTimLBR-5
93CouTimLBR-6
93CouTimLBR-7
93NabAllA-5
93OriCroASU-3
93TedWilBR-1
93TedWilBR-2
93TedWilBR-3
93TedWilBR-4
93TedWilBR-5
93TedWilBR-6
93TedWilBR-7
93TedWilBR-8
93TedWilBR-9
93UppDecS-18
93Yoo-16
94TedWil-10
94Yoo-13
95MCIAmb-15
95TopLegot6M-10
96AriLot-3
97FleMilDM-5
97JimDea-2
97SpollICC-8
97TopStaHRR-12
97TopStaHRRA-12
Robinson, Bruce
79ColCliT-16
79Top-711
80ColCliP-26
80ColCliT-15
81Top-424
84TacTigC-73
92YanWIZ7-135
92YanWIZ8-162
Robinson, Chris
91BoiHawC-27
91BoiHawP-3878
92PalSprAC-4
92PalSprAF-837
Robinson, Clifford
93StaCluMO-37
Robinson, Clyde
09ColChiE-243
11SpoLifCW-305
12ColRedB-243
Robinson, Connie
83FraBroR-10
Robinson, Craig
74OPC-23
74Top-23
74TopTra-23T
75OPC-367
75Top-367
76SSP-12
76VenLeaS-51
81RicBraT-23
82RicBraT-29
83RicBraT-24
Robinson, Daniel
93KanCouCC-19
93KanCouCF-928
93Top-599
93TopGol-599
93TopInaM-599
93TopMic-599
94BreCouMC-14
94BreCouMF-24
95BreCouMF-260
93KanCouCTI-20
Robinson, Darek
93JohCitCC-16
93JohCitCF-3689
94NewJerCC-20
94NewJerCF-3425
95PeoChiTI-3
Robinson, Darryl
87EugEmeP-2648
88AppFoxP-144
88MidLeaAGS-38
89AppFoxP-860
90BasCitRS-21
91LinDriAA-416
91MemChiLD-416
91MemChiP-663
92MemChiF-2428
92MemChiS-444
Robinson, David
88SanDieSAAG-17
89SanDieSAG-16
95BatCliTI-28
96PieBolWB-23
Robinson, David T.
71OPC-262
71Top-262
Robinson, Dewey
78AppFoxT-15
79IowOakP-13
80IowOakP-10
80Top-664
81Top-487
82Top-176
87PenWhiSP-7
93WhiSoxK-30
Robinson, Don
77ShrCapT-18
79Top-264
80Top-719
81CedRapRT-6
81Don-375
81Fle-366
81OPC-168
81Top-168
82Fle-495
82OPC-332
82Top-332
83Don-171
83Fle-319
83OPC-44
83Top-44
83TopSti-277
84Don-532
84Fle-262
84Nes792-616
84OPC-22

84Top-616
84TopTif-616
85Don-264
85Fle-475
85OPC-129
85Pir-18
85Top-537
85TopTif-537
86Don-357
86Fle-621
86Lea-159
86Top-731
86TopTif-731
87Don-608
87Fle-622
87FleGlo-622
87OPC-387
87Top-712
87TopTif-712
88Don-573
88Fle-95
88FleGlo-95
88FleMin-120
88FleStiC-131
88FleTeaL-31
88GiaMot-22
88Sco-619
88ScoGlo-619
88Spo-90
88StaLinG-15
88Top-52
88TopSti-94
88TopTif-52
89Bow-463
89BowTif-463
89Don-571
89DonBasB-191
89Fle-342
89FleBasA-36
89FleGlo-342
89GiaMot-22
89PanSti-211
89Sco-440
89Top-473
89TopSti-86
89TopTif-473
89UppDec-523
90Don-258
90Fle-70
90FleCan-70
90GiaMot-20
90GiaSmo-17
90Lea-267
90OPC-217
90PubSti-81
90Sco-112
90Top-217
90TopBig-193
90TopSti-84
90TopTif-217
90UppDec-616
91Bow-384
91Bow-619
91Don-581
91Fle-272
91GiaMot-20
91GiaPacGaE-21
91GiaSFE-13
91Lea-188
91OPC-104
91PanFreS-73
91PanSti-74
91PulBraC-13
91PulBraP-4020
91Sco-639
91StaClu-167
91Top-104
91TopDesS-104
91TopMic-104
91TopTif-104
91Ult-327
91UppDec-402
91UppDecSS-SS16
92MacBraC-24
92MacBraF-282
92OPC-373
92PhiMed-46
92Pin-463
92ProFS7-192
92StaClu-729
92StaCluNC-729
92Top-373
92TopGol-373
92TopGolW-373
92TopMic-373
92Ult-329
93DurBulC-14
93DurBulF-498
93DurBulTI-32
94GreBraF-426
94GreBraTI-19

Robinson, Dwight

91PitMetC-3
91PitMetP-3432
92ColMetC-20
92ColMetF-305
92ColMetPI-22
93CapCitBC-19
93CapCitBF-470
94ClaGolF-24
94St.LucMC-20
94St.LucMF-1205

Robinson, Earl

60DarFar-20
61Top-343
62Top-272
78TCM60I-81
90DodTar-674
91OriCro-386

Robinson, Eddie (William E.)

47Exh-190
47IndTeal-22
47IndVanPP-21
48IndTeal-26
50Bow-18
50RoyDes-22
51Bow-88
51TopRedB-51
52BerRos-56
52Bow-77
52NatTeaL-24
52RedMan-AL18
52RoyPre-11
52StaCalL-73C
52StaCalS-87A
52Top-32
52WhiSoxH-7
53BowBW-20
53Dor-135
53MotCoo-59
53RedMan-AL11
53Top-73
54Bow-193
54NewYorJA-58
54Top-62
55Bow-153
56Top-302
57Top-238
60Top-455
76WhiSoxTAG-9
79DiaGre-298
79TCM50-283
80WhiSoxGT-12
83FraBroR-11
83TopRep5-32
91OriCro-387
91TopArc1-73
94TopArc1-62
94TopArc1G-62

Robinson, Eli

91PriRedC-17
91PriRedP-3524
92PriRedC-2
92PriRedF-3096
93BilMusF-3955
93BilMusSP-11

Robinson, Emmett

86KinEagP-19

Robinson, Floyd

47Exh-191
62SalPlaC-214
62ShiPlaC-214
62Top-454
62TopBuc-76
62TopStal-29
62WhiSoxJP-10
62WhiSoxTS-17
63Baz-24
63Jel-39
63Pos-39
63Top-2
63Top-405
63TopStil-35
63WhiSoxTS-20
64Baz-24
64Top-195
64TopCoi-39
64TopSta-18
64TopStaU-62
64TopVen-195
64WhiSoxTS-20
65Top-345
65WhiSoxJP-8
66OPC-8
66Top-8
66Top-199
66TopRubl-80
66TopVen-8
66TopVen-199
67CokCapR-16
67OPC-120
67Top-120
68Top-404

Robinson, Frank

47Exh-192
56Kah-14
56RedBurB-20
57Kah-25
57RedSoh-17
57SwiFra-16
57Top-35
58Kah-26
58RedEnq-33
58RedJayP-11
58Top-285
58Top-386
58Top-484
59ArmCoi-14
59HomRunD-16
59Kah-31
59RedBurBP-19
59RedBurBP-20
59RedShiBS-19
59Top-435
60Baz-29
60Kah-36
60MacSta-20
60RedJayP-12
60Top-352
60Top-490
60TopTat-46
61Baz-31
61Kah-37
61Pos-182A
61Pos-182B
61RedJayP-12
61Top-25
61Top-360
61Top-581
61TopDicG-15
61TopStal-24
62AurRec-14
62Baz-26
62Jel-122
62Kah-35
62Pos-122
62PosCan-122
62RedEnq-29
62RedJayP-12
62SalPlaC-165
62ShiPlaC-165
62Top-54
62Top-350
62Top-396
62TopBuc-77
62TopStal-121
62TopVen-54
63BasMagM-70
63Baz-31
63ExhStaB-56
63Jel-131
63Kah-27
63Pos-131A
63Pos-131B
63RedEnq-28
63RedFreBC-22
63RedJayP-12
63SalMetC-29
63Top-1
63Top-3
63Top-400
63TopStil-36
64Baz-31
64Kah-24
64RedJayP-11
64Top-260
64TopCoi-37
64TopCoi-154
64TopGia-29
64TopSta-15
64TopStaU-63
64TopTatl-65
64TopVen-260
65Baz-31
65Kah-36
65OldLonC-17
65OPC-120
65RedEnq-24
65Top-120
65TopEmbl-22
65TopTral-66
66Baz-32
66Top-219
66Top-310
66TopRubl-81
66TopVen-219
66TopVen-310
67AshOil-8
67Baz-32
67CokCapA-23
67CokCapAAm-32
67CokCapO-4
67DexPre-177
67DexPre-178
67OPC-1
67OPC-62
67OPC-100
67OPCPapl-19
67Top-1
67Top-62
67Top-100
67Top-239
67Top-241
67Top-243
67TopGiaSU-3
67TopPos-19
67TopTesF-20
67TopVen-194
68AtlOilPBCC-38
68Baz-3
68CokCapO-4
68DexPre-66
68OPC-2
68OPC-4
68Top-2
68Top-4
68Top-373
68Top-454A
68Top-454B
68Top-500
68Top-530
68TopActS-3B
68TopActS-4A
68TopActS-13A
68TopActS-15B
68TopGamI-7
68TopPla-11
68TopPos-24
68TopVen-2
68TopVen-4
68TopVen-6
69MilBra-236
69MLBOffS-9
69MLBPin-26
69NabTeaF-19
69Top-250
69TopDecl-35
69TopSta-130
69TopSup-2
69TopTeaP-5
69TraSta-16
70DayDaiNM-5
70Kel-15
70MilBra-23
70MLBOffS-155
70OPC-463
70Ori-12
70Top-463
70Top-700
70TopPos-12
70TopSup-37
70TraSta-12A
71AllBasA-20
71BazNumT-2
71Kel-15
71MatMin-13
71MatMin-14
71MilDud-27
71MLBOffS-310
71MLBOffS-572
71OPC-63
71OPC-329
71OPC-640
71Ori-14
71Top-329
71Top-640
71TopCoi-50
71TopTat-93
72MilBra-292
72OPC-88
72OPC-100
72OPC-228
72ProStaP-20
72Top-88
72Top-100
72Top-228
72Top-754
73LinPor-34
73OPC-175
73Top-175
73TopCanL-42
74LauAllG-59
74OPC-55
74SupBlaB-11
74Top-55
74TopDecE-66
74TopSta-145
75OPC-199
75OPC-204
75OPC-331
75OPC-580
75SSP42-8
75Top-199
75Top-204
75Top-331
75Top-580
76CraDis-49
76LauDiaJ-5
76OPC-477
76SSP-525
76Top-477
77Spo-5920
77Top-18
78RocRedWT-15
78TCM60I-140
80Lau300-23
80PacLeg-123
80PerHaloFP-180
80SSPHOF-178
81Ori6F-28
82Don-424
82K-M-9
82OhiHaloF-30
83Don-564
83Don-648
83DonHOFH-19
83FraBroR-23
83FraBroR-24
83FraBroR-25
83GiaMot-1
83Oco& SSBG-14
83Top-576
83TopSti-4
84DonCha-43
84GiaPos-24
84Nes792-171
84OCoandSI-70
84Top-171
84TopTif-171
85CirK-4
85DonHOFS-8
85Woo-29
86BigLeaC-4
86OriGreT-7
86RedGreT-5
86SpoDecG-41
86Top-404
86TopTif-404
87K-M-10
87NesDreT-16
87OriFreB-20
88GreBasS-57
88OriFreB-20
88TopTra-96T
88TopTraT-96T
89AngSmo-8
89DodSmoG-24
89OriFreB-20
89Top-774
89TopTif-774
90BasWit-48
90DodTar-675
90OPC-381
90PerGreM-94
90Top-381
90TopTif-381
91OPC-639
91OriCro-388
91Top-639

91TopDesS-639
91TopEasCN-4
91TopMic-639
91TopTif-639
91UppDecS-3
92TVSpoMF5HRC-11
93OriCroASU-4
93SelTriC-3
93UppDecS-18
94NabAllA-3
94UppDecS-10
94UppDecTAE-68
95BalParF-2
95TopLegot6M-5
95UppDecA-5
97FleMilDM-11
97SpollIAM-5
97SpollICC-12
97St.VinHHS-14

Robinson, Gladys

28W512-31

Robinson, Hank

14B18B-87A
14B18B-87B

Robinson, Hassan

94AubAstC-13
94AubAstF-3772
95AubAstTI-27
96QuaCitRB-22

Robinson, Henry

86Ft.MyeRP-22

Robinson, Humberto

52LavPro-91
55Top-182
59Top-366
60Lea-70
60Top-416

Robinson, Jackie R.

47BonBreR-1
47BonBreR-2
47BonBreR-3
47BonBreR-4
47BonBreR-5
47BonBreR-6
47BonBreR-7
47BonBreR-8
47BonBreR-9
47BonBreR-10
47BonBreR-11
47BonBreR-12
47BonBreR-13
47Exh-193
47HomBon-41
47PM1StaP1-179
47PM1StaP1-180
47PM1StaP1-181
47PM1StaP1-182
47PM1StaP1-183
47PM1StaP1-184
47PM1StaP1-185
47PM1StaP1-186
47StaPinP2-33A
48BluTin-36
48SweSpoT-3
49Bow-50
49EurSta-48
49Lea-79
50Bow-22
50JJKCopP-15
51R42SmaS-91
52BerRos-57
52StaCalL-79G
52StaCalS-91B
52Top-312
53ExhCan-19
53Top-1
54NewYorJA-15
54Top-10
55DodGolS-15
55Top-50
55TopDouH-25
56Dod-25
56Top-30
56TopHocF-A14
56TopPin-51
60NuHi-53
60RawGloT-27
61NuSco-428
63BasMagM-71
67TopVen-184
72TopTes5-2
73HalofFPP-14
74LauAllG-49
75TCMAllG-28
76GalBasGHoF-24
76LauDiaJ-26
76ShaPiz-88
76TayBow4-17
77BobParHoF-40
77GalGloG-20
77GalGloG-228
77Spo-923
79BasGre-77
79TCM50-291
80DodGreT-4
80LauFamF-18
80PacLeg-15
80PerHaloFP-89
80SSPHOF-89
81SanDieSC-6
81SpoHaloF-18
82BasCarN-13
82BHCRSpoL-7
82DiaCla-48
82GSGalAG-24
83DonHOFH-6
83MLBPin-31
83TopRep5-312
83TopTraBP-8
84FifNatCT-16
84OCoandSI-97
84OCoandSI-135
84SpoDesPW-1
85TCMPla1-27
86NegLeaF-11
86NegLeaF-25
86SpoDecG-28
86TCM-7
86TCMSupS-21
86TCMSupS-48
87Dod195T-3
87HygAllG-37
87NegLeaPD-33
87NesDreT-24
87SpoRea-35
88GreBasS-19
88PacLegI-40
88RinPosD1-3C
88RinPosD1-6B
88WilMulP-10
89BowInsT-9
89BowRepl-9
89BowTif-R9
89DodSmoG-25
89HOFStiB-12
89SpollIFKI-212
89USPLegSC-3
90BasWit-52
90DodTar-676
90PerGreM-3
90PerGreM-91
91PomBlaBPB-2
91TopArc1-1
92BazQua5A-14
94TopArc1-10
94TopArc1G-10
94UppDecTAE-50
94UppDecTAEGM-7
94UppDecTAELD-LD9
95DodROY-1
95TopArcBD-18
95TopArcBD-37
95TopArcBD-66
95TopArcBD-95
95TopArcBD-117
95TopArcBD-142
97ColCho-55
97FleMilDM-17
97LeaJacRR-1
97LeaJacRSNWG-1
97St.VinHHS-17
97Top-42
97TopChr-42
97TopChrR-42
97UppDec-1
97UppDec-2
97UppDec-3
97UppDec-4
97UppDec-5
97UppDec-6
97UppDec-7
97UppDec-8
97UppDec-9

Robinson, Jeff (Jeffrey D.)

84FleUpd-100
84GiaPos-25
84TopTra-101T
84TopTraT-101T
85Don-201
85Fle-620
85OPC-5
85Top-592
85TopMin-592
85TopTif-592
86GiaMot-15
86TopTra-93T
86TopTraT-93T
87Don-559
87Fle-283
87FleGlo-283
87GiaMot-25
87Top-389
87TopTif-389
88Don-558
88DonBasB-241
88OPC-244
88Sco-439
88ScoGlo-439
88StaLinPi-18
88Top-244
88TopBig-123
88TopSti-133
88TopTif-244
89Bow-410
89BowTif-410
89Don-370
89DonBasB-129
89Fle-220
89FleGlo-220
89OPC-351
89PanSti-164
89PirVerFJ-49
89Sco-309
89Top-681
89TopBig-45
89TopSti-129
89TopTif-681
89TVSpoM-72
89UppDec-332
90Bow-427
90BowTif-427
90Don-134
90Fle-479
90FleCan-479
90Lea-412
90OPC-723
90PubSti-164
90Sco-333
90Top-723
90TopTif-723
90TopTraT-103T
90TopTVY-19
90UppDec-403
90YanScoNW-23
91AngSmo-18
91Bow-193
91Don-291
91Fle-678
91Lea-307
91OPC-19
91Sco-192
91StaClu-542
91Top-19
91TopDesS-19
91TopMic-19
91TopTif-19
91TopTra-99T
91TopTraT-99T
92CubMar-38
92Don-59
92IowCubS-219
92OPC-137
92Sco-186
92StaClu-756
92Top-137
92TopGol-137
92TopGolW-137
92TopMic-137
93Fle-382

Robinson, Jeff (Jeffrey M.)

85PhoGiaC-184
86NasSouTI-22
87DonRoo-13
87FleUpd-105
87FleUpdG-105
87SpoRoo2-46
87TopTra-104T
87TopTraT-104T
88Don-296
88Fle-68A
88Fle-68B
88FleGlo-68
88Sco-549
88ScoGlo-549
88TigPep-44
88TigPol-10
88Top-449
88TopTif-449
89Bow-97
89BowTif-97
89ClaLigB-93
89Don-18
89Don-470
89DonSupD-18
89Fle-143
89FleGlo-143
89FleLeaL-33
89OPC-267
89PanSti-335
89Sco-284
89ScoHot1S-34
89ScoYouS2-8
89Spo-193
89TigMar-44
89TigPol-44
89Top-267
89TopBig-274
89TopTif-267
89UppDec-472
90Don-417
90Fle-614
90FleCan-614
90Lea-429
90OPC-42
90PubSti-481
90PubSti-603
90TigCok-19
90Top-42
90TopSti-284
90TopTif-42
90TopTra-103T
90UppDec-552
91Bow-90
91Don-245
91Fle-349
91Lea-464
91OPC-766
91OriCro-500
91Sco-129
91StaClu-441
91Top-766
91TopDesS-766
91TopMic-766
91TopTif-766
91TopTra-100T
91TopTraT-100T
91UppDec-676
91UppDec-796
92Don-77
92Pin-516
92RanMot-16
92Sco-274
92StaClu-715
92UppDec-320
93RanKee-311

Robinson, Jerry

63Top-466

Robinson, Jim

78NewWayCT-38
79BurBeeT-9
88MisStaB-29
89MisStaB-34
90MisStaB-36
90PeoChiUTI-U2
91GenCubC-16
91GenCubP-4222
92ChaKniF-2774
92ChaKniS-164
92ProFS7-211
93OrlCubF-2789

Robinson, Ken

91MedHatBJP-4099
92MyrBeaHF-2196
93HagSunC-23
93HagSunF-1879
94HagSunC-20
94HagSunF-2728
95SyrChiTI-21
96Fle-282
96FleTif-282
96SyrChiTI-25

Robinson, Kerry

96MidLeaAB-23
96PeoChiB-27
97Bow-382
97BowChr-252
97BowChrI-252
97BowChrIR-252
97BowChrR-252
97BowInt-382

Robinson, Kevin

87EriCarP-20
88HamRedP-1730

Robinson, Larry

72Dia-102
72Dia-103

Robinson, Lee

74AlbDukTI-74
74AlbDukTI-16
75AlbDukC-4

Robinson, Lynn

88BurBraP-1

Robinson, M.C.

87OldJudN-429

Robinson, Marteese

88MadMusP-20
89MadMusS-27
89ModA'sCLC-285
90Bes-280

Robinson, Marty

96GreBatB-22

Robinson, Mike

83EriCarT-24
85SprCarT-25
86ArkTraP-20
87ArkTraP-2
88ArkTraGS-19
88LouRedBTI-42

Robinson, Napoleon

89SalDodTI-27
90BakDodCLC-233
91GreBraC-4
91GreBraLD-215
91GreBraP-2998
91LinDriAA-215
92Bow-34
92ProFS7-184
92RicBraBB-20
92RicBraF-376
92RicBraRC-16
92RicBraS-438
92SkyAAAF-202
93ExcFS7-5
93RicBraBB-4
93RicBraF-183
93RicBraP-15
93RicBraRC-3
93RicBraRC-24
97RicBraBC-18

Robinson, Randall

87ChaWheP-27

Robinson, Randy

83ButCopKT-9
88SouBenWSGS-25

Robinson, Raul

91MacBraC-26
91MacBraP-879

Robinson, Rhett

89GeoColC-26
89GeoColC-28

Robinson, Rogers

64TulOil-6

Robinson, Ron

82WatRedT-4
84WicAerRD-8
85Don-649
85Fle-650
86Don-121
86Fle-190
86RedTexG-33
86Top-442
86TopTif-442
87Don-310
87Fle-212
87FleGamW-38
87FleGlo-212
87FleMin-93
87RedKah-33
87Top-119
87TopTif-119
88Don-166
88DonBasB-308
88Fle-247
88FleGlo-247
88FleMin-75
88OPC-342
88RedKah-33
88Sco-476
88ScoGlo-476
88Top-81

88Top-517
88TopTif-81
88TopTif-517
89Bow-303
89BowTif-303
89Don-308
89Fle-169
89FleGlo-169
89OPC-16
89RedKah-33
89Sco-559
89Top-16
89TopBig-132
89TopTif-16
89UppDec-187
90BreMilB-21
90CedRapRDGB-14
90Don-553
90Fle-431
90FleCan-431
90Lea-467
90OPC-604
90Sco-495
90Top-604
90TopTif-604
90TopTra-104T
90TopTraT-104T
91Bow-39
91BreMilB-22
91BrePol-20
91Don-254
91Fle-595
91Lea-14
91OPC-313
91Sco-517
91StaClu-296
91Stu-75
91Top-313
91TopDesS-313
91TopMic-313
91TopTif-313
91UppDec-620
92BrePol-20
92Fle-187
92OPC-395
92StaClu-739
92StaCluECN-739
92UppDec-198
93Fle-634
94BreMilB-263
Robinson, Scott
90BilMusP-3220
91CedRapRC-11
91CedRapRP-2718
92ChaLooF-3818
92ChaWVWC-18
93ChaLooF-2362
93SouAtlLAIPI-7
93SouAtlLAPI-35
94PhoFirF-1519
95AusFut-66
95PhoFirTI-14
Robinson, Sugar (Ray)
51BerRos-B13
Robinson, Terry
91PocPioP-3799
91PocPioSP-5
Robinson, Tony
96LynHilB-19
Robinson, Wilbert
15SpoNewM-144
16SpoNewM-144
21E121So1-80
22W575-106
23W501-97
23W515-53
27YorCarE-43
36PC7AlbHoF-38
50CalHOFW-62
60Fle-33
63BazA-27
72FleFamF-10
72LauGreF-30
75TCMAllG-29
76ShaPiz-38
77GalGloG-162
77Ind192T-22
80PerHaloFP-38
80SSPHOF-38
84GalHaloFRL-38
87OldJudN-428
89DodSmoG-104
89HOFStiB-86
90DodTar-677A
90KalBatN-47
90KalBatN-48
93ConMasC-8
93ConTSN-846
94DukCabN-4
95May-36
Robinson, Yank (William H.)
76SSP188WS-15
87BucN28-103
87LonJacN-11
87OldJudN-430A
87OldJudN-430B
87ScrDC-8
Robitaille, Martin
88JamExpP-1921
92JamExpC-28
92JamExpF-1518
Robledo, Nilson
91SouBenWSC-24
91SouBenWSP-2860
92SarWhiSF-209
93FloStaLAF-24
93SarWhiSC-22
93SarWhiSF-1371
94SouBenSHC-20
94SouBenSHF-597
95MidLeaA-44
96Exc-36
96PriWilCB-23
Robles, Gabby (Gabriel)
86KinEagP-20
87WinSpiP-18
Robles, Greg
82IdaFalAT-21
83MadMusF-22
84AlbA'sT-25
Robles, Javier
91BurIndP-3309
Robles, Jorge
89BlaYNPRWL-50
89WauTimGS-19
90PenPilS-18
Robles, Josman
90DurBulTI-18
Robles, Juan
96LanLugB-22
96SpoIndB-23
Robles, Oscar
94SigRooDP-66
94SigRooDPS-66
94StaCluDP-38
94StaCluDPFDI-38
95AubAstTI-12
96KisCobB-22
Robles, Rafael
69Top-592
70Top-573
71OPC-408
71Top-408
72PadTeal-21
94NewJerCC-21
94NewJerCF-3426
Robles, Ruben
83TucTorT-26
84TucTorC-66
85DomLeaS-82
Robles, Scott
90KenTwiB-25
90KenTwiP-2294
90KenTwiS-21
Robles, Sergio
73OPC-601
73Top-601
74OPC-603
74Top-603
75TulOil7-21
90DodTar-678B
91OriCro-389
Robles, Silvano
75AppFoxT-25
76AppFoxT-22
76CliPilT-28
Robson, David
92NiaFalRC-2
92NiaFalRF-3327
Robson, Gary
88BelBreGS-2
Robson, Tom
74SpoIndC-38
75IntLeaASB-28
75PacCoaLAB-28
75SpoIndC-1
79WauTimT-16
80AshTouT-2
86RanPer-NNO
87RanMot-28
87RanSmo-21
88RanMot-27
89RanMot-27
89RanSmo-26
90RanMot-27
91RanMot-28
92RanMot-28
93RanKee-312
Roby, Ellis
86SumBraP-22
87DurBulP-10
88DurBulS-18
89GreBraB-9
89GreBraP-1159
89GreBraS-20
Roca, Gilbert
86MacPirP-21
87SalBucP-16
88HarSenP-851
89JacMetGS-17
90TopTVM-55
94VenLinU-144
Rocco, Mickey (Michael)
47CenFlo-24
47SigOil-85
48SomandK-26
49SomandK-14
Rocha, Juan
95SprSulTI-24
96LanLugB-23
96MidLeaAB-40
Roche, Marlon
96QuaCitRB-23
Roche, Rod
86VerBeaDP-20
87BakDodP-17
Roche, Steve
80WauTimT-7
81ChaLooT-8
82ChaLooT-15
82WatIndF-10
Roche, Tim
77CliDodT-21
78LodDodT-14
Roche, Titi
87LitFalMP-2406
88LitFalMP-11
89St.LucMS-21
89Sta-24
Rochelli, Lou
90DodTar-1055
Rochford, Mike
84PawRedST-21
86PawRedSP-18
87PawRedSP-59
87PawRedST-9
88PawRedSC-2
88PawRedSP-447
89Fle-650
89FleGlo-650
89PawRedSC-6
89PawRedSP-700
89PawRedSTI-22
90Bow-264
90BowTif-264
90CMC-254
90PawRedSC-3
90PawRedSDD-21
90PawRedSP-460
90ProAAAF-432
90TopTVRS-16
90UppDec-694
91Sco-739
Rochon, Henri
43ParSpo-89
Rock Cats, Hardware City
96HarCitRCB-1
Rock, Bob
77ChaPatT-16
78SalPirT-14
80BufBisT-12
81BufBisT-10
Rock, Royal
09ColChiE-244
12ColRedB-244
12ColTinT-244
12ImpTobC-10
Rockenfeld, Isaac B.
09T206-512
10CouT21-57
Rocker, John
94DanBraC-22
94DanBraF-3530
95EugEmeTI-17
95MacBraTI-24
96MacBraB-11
Rockett, Pat
78Top-502
79RicBraT-20
80SyrChiT-5
80SyrChiTI-19
Rockey, Jim
86DurBulP-23
Rockhill, Ron
75LynRanT-23
Rockies, Colorado
83KelCerB-3
92DonBonC-BC7
92HitTheBB-11
94ImpProP-18
94Sco-650
94ScoGolR-650
95PanSti-135
96FleRoc-19
96PanSti-85
96TopGalPG-PG14
Rockman, Marv
88GasRanP-995
89TulDriGS-22
89TulDriTI-20
90TulDriP-1152
90TulDriTI-21
Rockmore, Thurston
94LetMouF-3893
94LetMouSP-5
Rockne, Knute
87SpoCubG-1
Rockweiler, Dean
86JamExpP-21
Rodarte, Raul
92PenPilC-10
92PenPilF-2942
93RivPilCLC-17
94JacSunF-1421
95LynHilTI-25
96GreBraB-23
96GreBraTI-9
96RicBraRC-20
96RicBraUB-23
Rodas, Rick (Richard)
82AlbDukT-9
83AlbDukT-6
84AlbDukC-147
84DodPol-56
85AlbDukC-174
90DodTar-678
Roddy, Phil
77AshTouT-19
Rode, Don
48SomandK-30
Rodgers, Andre
57Top-377
59Top-216
60Lea-42
60Top-431
61Pos-153A
61Pos-153B
61Top-183
62Jel-185
62Pos-185
62PosCan-185
62SalPlaC-155A
62SalPlaC-155B
62ShiPlaC-155
62Top-477
63CubJayP-10
63Jel-173
63Pos-173
63Top-193
64CubJayP-10
64Top-336
64TopVen-336
65Top-536
66PirEasH-16
66Top-592
67PirTeal-19
67Top-554
78TCM60I-52
Rodgers, Bob
84IndIndTI-2
85IndIndTI-36
96LowSpiB-22
Rodgers, Bobby
97Top-200
Rodgers, Buck (Robert L.)
47Exh-195
62Top-431
62TopStal-68
63AngJayP-15
63Baz-2
63Fle-20
63Jel-31
63Pos-31
63Top-280
63TopStiI-37
64Top-61
64Top-426
64TopVen-61
65Top-342
65TopTral-27
66AngDexP-5
66Top-462
67CokCapDA-26
67Top-281
68Top-433
69MilBra-237
69MLBOffS-27
69OPC-157
69Top-157
69TopFou-16
69TopSta-149
69TopTeaP-17
73OPC-49
73Top-49A
73Top-49B
74OPC-447
74Top-447
78TCM60I-63
81Don-327
81Top-668
82BrePol-NNO
82Don-232
85ExpPos-20
85TopTifT-95T
85TopTra-95T
86AngGreT-8
86ExpProPa-3
86ExpProPo-4
86OPC-141
86Top-171
86TopTif-171
87ExpPos-24
87OPC-293
87Top-293
87TopTif-293
88ExpPos-20
88OPC-134
88Top-504
88TopTif-504
89ExpPos-25
89OPC-193
89Top-474
89TopTif-474
90El PasDAGTI-19
90ExpPos-29
90OPC-81
90Top-81
90TopTif-81
91OPC-321
91Top-321
91TopDesS-321
91TopMic-321
91TopTif-321
92OPC-21
92Top-21
92TopGol-21
92TopGolW-21
92TopMic-21
93AngMot-1
93AngPol-3
93ExpDonM-32
93Top-503
93TopGol-503
93TopInaM-503
93TopMic-503
92Top-21
92TopGol-21
92TopGolW-21
92TopMic-21
Rodgers, Charlie
91MiaMirC-11
Rodgers, Darrell
85EveGialC-15
86FreGiaP-15
88MidLeaAGS-13
89ChaLooB-15
89ChaLooGS-21
92PriRedC-28
Rodgers, Doc

91PriRedP-3532
92PriRedF-3103
Rodgers, John
93PeoChiTI-23
Rodgers, Paul
87MyrBeaBJP-1464
88DunBluJS-14
89DunBluJS-13
90KnoBluJB-12
90KnoBluJP-1255
90KnoBluJS-15
91Cla/Bes-3
91KnoBluJLD-364
91KnoBluJP-1782
91LinDriAA-364
Rodgers, Tim
83KinBluJTI-20
84SyrChiT-17
86TulDriTI-7
87OklCit8P-17
Rodgers, William
16FleBreD-77
Rodiles, Jose
85Ft.MyeRT-30
86MemChiSTOS-23
86MemChiTOS-23
87ColAstP-18
Rodiles, Steve
85IowCubT-36
Rodrigues, Rynee
91HawWomS-12
Rodriguez, A.
86AshTouP-23
Rodriguez, Abimael
90JamExpP-4
91SumFlyC-19
91SumFlyP-2344
Rodriguez, Adam
93BriTigF-3648
94FayGenC-20
94FayGenF-2150
96LakTigB-21
Rodriguez, Adriano
85DomLeaS-181
Rodriguez, Ahmed
89JohCitCS-18
89SavCarP-353
90HamRedB-17
90HamRedS-20
91SprCarC-22
91SprCarP-750
92SprCarF-878
Rodriguez, Al
91EveGiaC-3
91EveGiaP-3923
92CliGiaC-18
93LinVenB-223
Rodriguez, Alex (Alexander E.)
92SpollIFK1-543
93ClaCP-1
94ActPac-1
94ActPac-55
94ActPac2G-1G
94AppFoxC-1
94AppFoxF-1063
94Cla-51
94Cla-100
94Cla-151
94Cla-AU1
94ClaBonB-BB3
94ClaCreotC-C11
94ClaTriF-T73
94ColC-647
94ColChoGS-647
94ColChoSS-647
94Fla-340
94FlaWavotF-B8
94FleUpd-86
94LeaLimRP-10
94MidLeaAF-MDW5
94ScoRoo-HC1
94SP-15
94SPDieC-15
94SPHol-33
94SPHolDC-33
94SpoRoo-148
94SpoRooAP-148
94SpoRooRS-TR11
94UppDec-24
94UppDec-298
94UppDec-A298
94UppDecED-24
94UppDecED-298
94UppDecML-TC1
94UppDecMLT1PMF-8
94UppDecNG-16
94UppDecNGED-16
95ColCho-5
95ColCho-527
95ColChoCtG-CG17
95ColChoCtG-CG17B
95ColChoCtG-CG17C
95ColChoCtGE-17
95ColChoCtGG-CG17
95ColChoCtGG-CG17B
95ColChoCtGG-CG17C
95ColChoCtGGE-17
95ColChoGS-5
95ColChoGS-527
95ColChoSE-1
95ColChoSEGS-1
95ColChoSESS-1
95ColChoSS-5
95ColChoSS-527
95Don-114
95DonPreP-114
95DonTopotO-155
95Emo-82
95EmoRoo-10
95Fla-85
95FleMajLP-10
95FleUpd-77
95FleUpdRU-9
95Lea-313
95LeaGolR-1
95LeaLim-14
95LeaLimG-19
95MarMot-7
95MarPac-42
95NatPac-12
95Pac-402
95PacGolCDC-17
95PacLatD-30
95PacPri-129
95Pin-132
95Pin-283
95PinArtP-132
95PinArtP-283
95PinMusC-132
95PinMusC-283
95PinNewB-NB1
95PinSam-132
95Sco-312
95Sco-569
95ScoAi-AM17
95ScoConR-AD1
95ScoGolR-312
95ScoGolR-569
95ScoHaloG-HG41
95ScoPlaTS-312
95ScoPlaTS-569
95ScoRooDT-RDT3
95ScoRul-SR5
95ScoRulJ-SR5
95Sel-203
95Sel-241
95SelArtP-203
95SelArtP-241
95SelCanM-CM10
95SelCer-118
95SelCerF-10
95SelCerMG-118
95SelCerPU-20
95SelCerPU9-20
95SelSam-241
95SigRooMR-MR5
95SigRooMRS-MR5
95SP-188
95SPCha-184
95SPChaDC-184
95Spo-141
95SpoArtP-141
95SpoDouT-6
95SPSil-188
95SPSpeF-20
95Stu-18
95StuGolS-18
95StuPlaS-18
95Sum-133
95SumNewA-NA4
95SumNthD-133
95TacRaiTI-18
95UC3-115
95UC3ArtP-115
95UC3CleS-CS1
95Ult-331
95UltGolM-331
95UltGolP-9
95UltGolPGM-9
95UppDec-215
95UppDec-J215
95UppDecED-215
95UppDecEDG-215
95UppDecPAW-H15
95UppDecPAWE-H15
95UppDecSE-120
95UppDecSEG-120
95Zen-146
95ZenRooRC-1
96Cir-81
96CirRav-81
96ColCho-316
96ColChoGS-316
96ColChoSS-316
96ColChoYMtP-34
96ColChoYMtP-34A
96ColChoYMtPGS-34
96ColChoYMtPGS-34A
96Don-8
96DonPreP-8
96EmoXL-117
96Fla-164
96Fle-243
96FleTif-243
96Lea-24
96LeaLim-31
96LeaLimG-31
96LeaLimL-5
96LeaLimLB-5
96LeaLimPC-8
96LeaPre-35
96LeaPreP-35
96LeaPrePB-24
96LeaPrePG-24
96LeaPrePS-24
96LeaPreSG-8
96LeaPreSta-2
96LeaPreSte-8
96LeaSig-16
96LeaSigA-195
96LeaSigAG-195
96LeaSigAS-195
96LeaSigEA-174
96LeaSigEACM-25
96LeaSigPPG-16
96LeaSigPPP-16
96MarMot-9
96MetUni-110
96MetUniP-110
96MetUniProS-110
96Pac-416
96PacEstL-EL26
96PanSti-224
96Pin-275
96PinAfi-136
96PinAfiAP-136
96PinAfiSP-20
96PinArtP-175
96PinFirR-5
96PinFoil-275
96PinProS-5
96PinSta-175
96PinTeaT-8
96ProMagA-10
96ProSta-65
96Sco-20
96Sco-361
96ScoDiaA-15
96ScoDugC-A19
96ScoDugC-B86
96ScoDugCAP-A19
96ScoDugCAP-B86
96ScoFutF-4
96ScoNumG-30
96ScoRef-2
96Sel-45
96SelArtP-45
96SelCer-6
96SelCerAP-6
96SelCerCB-6
96SelCerCR-6
96SelCerMB-6
96SelCerMG-6
96SelCerMR-6
96SelEnF-21
96SigRooOJMR-M1
96SP-171
96Spo-20
96SpoArtP-20
96SpoDouT-9
96SPx-57
96SPxGol-57
96Stu-65
96StuPrePB-65
96StuPrePG-65
96StuPrePS-65
96Sum-84
96SumAbo&B-84
96SumArtP-84
96SumFoi-84
96SumPos-4
96TeaOut-67
96TeaOut-C99
96Ult-130
96UltGolM-130
96UppDec-202
96UppDecBCP-BC15
96UppDecDD-DD38
96UppDecDDG-DD38
96UppDecDDS-DD38
96Zen-99
96ZenArtP-99
96ZenDiaC-9
96ZenDiaCP-9
96ZenMoz-5
97Cir-100
97Cir-397
97Cir-P100
97CirBos-16
97CirEmeA-100
97CirEmeAR-AU4
97CirFasT-8
97CirIco-10
97CirLimA-13
97CirRav-100
97CirRav-397
97CirRavR-11
97CirSupB-16
97ColCho-56
97ColCho-235
97ColCho-332
97ColChoAC-4
97ColChoBS-5
97ColChoBSGS-5
97ColChoCtG-29A
97ColChoCtG-29B
97ColChoCtG-29C
97ColChoCtGIW-CG29
97ColChoNF-NF1
97ColChoPP-PP18
97ColChoPPG-PP18
97ColChoS-3
97ColChoTBS-41
97ColChoTBSWH-41
97ColChoTotT-T28
97Don-44
97Don-404
97DonArmaD-6
97DonDom-5
97DonEli-2
97DonEli-6
97DonEliGS-2
97DonEliLaL-2
97DonEliPtT-2
97DonEliPtT-3
97DonEliPtTA-2
97DonEliPtTA-3
97DonEliTotC-1
97DonEliTotCDC-1
97DonFraFea-3
97DonLim-13
97DonLim-69
97DonLim-122
97DonLimLE-13
97DonLimLE-69
97DonLimLE-122
97DonPowA-7
97DonPowADC-7
97DonPre-92
97DonPre-167
97DonPreCttC-92
97DonPreCttC-167
97DonPreP-44
97DonPreP-404
97DonPrePGold-44
97DonPrePGold-404
97DonPrePM-15
97DonPreS-1
97DonPreTB-18
97DonPreTBG-18
97DonPreTF-18
97DonPreTP-18
97DonPreTPG-18
97DonPreXP-7B
97DonTea-137
97DonTeaSMVP-7
97DonTeaSPE-137
97FlaSho-A3
97FlaSho-B3
97FlaSho-C3
97FlaShoARR-AR1
97FlaShoDC-16
97FlaShoHG-13
97FlaShoLC-3
97FlaShoLC-B3
97FlaShoLC-C3
97FlaShoLCM-A3
97FlaShoLCM-B3
97FlaShoLCM-C3
97Fle-213
97Fle-499
97Fle-715
97FleBleB-7
97FleDiaT-11
97FleGouG-12
97FleGouGF-12
97FleHea-17
97FleLumC-14
97FleMilDM-28
97FleNig&D-8
97FleSoaS-11
97FleTif-213
97FleTif-499
97FleTif-715
97FleZon-15
97Lea-16
97Lea-350
97Lea-368
97LeaBanS-5
97LeaDrefS-11
97LeaFraM-16
97LeaFraM-350
97LeaFraM-368
97LeaFraMDC-16
97LeaFraMDC-350
97LeaFraMDC-368
97LeaGet-5
97LeaGolS-2
97LeaLeaotN-12
97LeaStaS-4
97MetUni-149
97MetUni-P149
97MetUniBF-10
97MetUniEAR-AU4
97MetUniMF-9
97MetUniML-10
97MetUniPP-10
97MetUniT-9
97NewPin-81
97NewPin-180
97NewPin-190
97NewPinAP-81
97NewPinAP-180
97NewPinAP-190
97NewPinIE-8
97NewPinKtP-5
97NewPinMC-81
97NewPinMC-180
97NewPinMC-190
97NewPinPP-81
97NewPinPP-180
97NewPinPP-190
97NewPinPP-I8A
97NewPinPP-K5
97NewPinPP-AR1
97NewPinPP-AR2
97NewPinPP-AR3
97NewPinPP-AR4
97NewPinS-AR1
97NewPinS-AR2
97NewPinS-AR3
97NewPinS-AR4
97Pac-192
97PacCar-18
97PacCarM-18
97PacCerCGT-5
97PacCraC-6
97PacFirD-12
97PacGolCD-18
97PacLatotML-20
97PacLigB-192
97PacPri-65
97PacPriGA-GA15
97PacPriGotD-GD91
97PacPriLB-65
97PacPriP-65
97PacPriSH-SH7A
97PacPriSL-SL6B
97PacSil-192

97PacTriCD-10
97Pin-92
97PinArtP-92
97PinCar-19
97PinCer-22
97PinCer-144
97PinCerCMGT-5
97PinCerCT-5
97PinCerLI-12
97PinCerMBlu-22
97PinCerMBlu-144
97PinCerMG-22
97PinCerMG-144
97PinCerMR-22
97PinCerMR-144
97PinCerR-22
97PinCerR-144
97PinHom-11
97PinHom-12
97PinIns-8
97PinInsC-5
97PinInsCE-8
97PinInsDD-1
97PinInsDE-8
97PinMin-3
97PinMinB-3
97PinMinCB-3
97PinMinCG-3
97PinMinCGR-3
97PinMinCN-3
97PinMinCS-3
97PinMinG-3
97PinMinS-3
97PinMusC-92
97PinPasttM-6
97PinSha-10
97PinTeaP-4
97PinTeaP-10
97PinTotCPB-22
97PinTotCPB-144
97PinTotCPG-22
97PinTotCPG-144
97PinTotCPR-22
97PinTotCPR-144
97PinX-P-15
97PinX-P-147
97PinX-PF&A-18
97PinX-PMoS-15
97PinX-PMoS-147
97PinX-PMP-7
97PinX-PMP-P7
97PinX-PMW-4
97PinX-PMWG-4
97PinX-PMWS-4
97ProMag-73
97ProMagIM-4
97ProMagML-73
97Sco-95
97Sco-507
97ScoAllF-5
97ScoBla-12
97ScoHeaotO-7
97ScoHigZ-10
97ScoHobR-507
97ScoMar-3
97ScoMarPl-3
97ScoMarPr-3
97ScoPitP-2
97ScoPitP-3
97ScoPreS-95
97ScoResC-507
97ScoShoS-95
97ScoShoS-507
97ScoShoSAP-95
97ScoShoSAP-507
97ScoStaaD-6
97ScoSteS-8
97ScoTitT-17
97Sel-53
97Sel-141
97SelArtP-53
97SelArtP-141
97SelRegG-53
97SelRegG-141
97SelToootT-24
97SelTooотTMB-24
97SkyE-X-43
97SkyE-X-S43
97SkyE-X-NNO
97SkyE-XACA-3
97SkyE-XC-43
97SkyE-XEAR-AU4
97SkyE-XEC-43
97SkyE-XHoN-9
97SkyE-XSD2-1
97SP-166
97SPGamF-GF1
97SPInsI-10
97SPMarM-MM8
97SpoIll-70
97SpoIll-158
97SpoIll-170
97SpoIll-179
97SpoIllAM-1
97SpoIllEE-70
97SpoIllEE-158
97SpoIllEE-170
97SpoIllEE-179
97SpoIllGS-23
97SPSpeF-10
97SPSpeF-49
97SPSpxF-6
97SPSPxFA-6
97SPVinAu-24
97SPVinAu-25
97SPVinAu-26
97SPx-46
97SPxBoufG-18
97SPxBoufGSS-4
97SPxBro-46
97SPxCorotG-10
97SPxGraF-46
97SPxSil-46
97SPxSte-46
97Stu-43
97Stu-165
97StuHarH-8
97StuMasS-8
97StuMasS8-8
97StuPor8-3
97StuPrePG-43
97StuPrePG-165
97StuPrePS-43
97StuPrePS-165
97Ult-126
97UltAutE-5
97UltChe-B4
97UltDiaP-10
97UltDouT-9
97UltFamGam-3
97UltFieC-16
97UltGolME-126
97UltHitM-4
97UltLeaS-2
97UltPlaME-126
97UltPowP-A9
97UltPowP-B3
97UltSeaC-9
97UltStaR-4
97UltThu-6
97UltTop3-4
97UltTop3GM-4
97UppDec-319
97UppDec-422
97UppDec-500
97UppDecAG-AG3
97UppDecAWJ-1
97UppDecBCP-BC20
97UppDecHC-HC1
97UppDecLDC-LD15
97UppDecMM-10
97UppDecP-27
97UppDecRP-RP10
97UppDecRSF-RS1
97UppDecTTS-TS10
97UppDecU-50
97UppDecUGN-GN1
97UppDecUMA-MA10
97Zen-22
97Zen Z-Z-4
97Zen8x1-13
97Zen8x1D-13
97ZenV-2-5

Rodriguez, Alexander
75BurBeeT-21

Rodriguez, Amando
91IdaFalBSP-4

Rodriguez, Andres
90PriWilCTI-22
91Ft.LauYC-23
91Ft.LauYP-2436
92ForLauYC-5
92ForLauYTI-27
92Ft.LauYF-2621

Rodriguez, Andy
75SanAntBT-17
78QuaCitAT-22

Rodriguez, Angel
85BelBreT-10
87StoPorP-10
88BlaYNPRWL-16
88ElPasDB-23
88StoPorCLC-198
88StoPorP-742

Rodriguez, Anthony
91KisDodP-4189
92GulCoaDF-3569

Rodriguez, Armando
90PulBraB-24
90PulBraP-3109
91IdaFalBP-4340

Rodriguez, Aurelio
69AngJacitB-11
69SenTeal-13
69Top-653
70MLBOffS-179
70OPC-228
70SenPolY-8
70Top-228
71MLBOffS-405
71OPC-464
71Top-464
71TopCoi-124
72MilBra-293
72OPC-319
72Top-319
72TopCloT-27
73LinPor-77
73OPC-218
73TigJew-16
73Top-218
74OPC-72
74Top-72
74TopSta-179
75OPC-221
75Top-221
76OPC-267
76SSP-366
76Top-267
77BurCheD-93
77Hos-120
77OPC-136
77Top-574
78OPC-64
78TigBurK-14
78Top-342
79OPC-83
79Top-176
80OPC-245
80Top-468
81Fle-105
81TigDetN-47
81Top-34
82Fle-53
82OPCPos-10
82Top-334
82TopTra-101T
83Don-369
83Fle-249
83Top-758
83TopTra-97T
84Nes792-269
84Top-269
84TopTif-269
88ColSprSSC-25
88ColSprSSP-1536
90CMC-402
90ProAAAF-396
90TolMudHC-25
90TolMudHP-166
91OriCro-390
92UppDecS-30
92YanWIZ8-163
96BurIndB-23

Rodriguez, Beto
90JohCitCS-21
91SprCarC-23
91SprCarP-751

Rodriguez, Buena
89JamExpP-2131
90RocExpLC-24
90RocExpP-2705

Rodriguez, Carlos
76VenLeaS-50
88Ft.LauYS-18
89Ft.LauYS-21
90AlbYanP-1178
90AlbYanS-14
90ColCliP-683
90ProAAAF-333
90TopTVY-58
91ColCliLD-116
91ColCliP-16
91ColCliP-604
91DonRoo-41
91LinDriAAA-116
92AlbYanF-2233
92AlbYanS-18
92Sco-411
92TopDeb91-149
92UppDec-77
93ColCliF-1117
93ColCliP-15
94PawRedSDD-18
94PawRedSF-953
94SpoRoo-61
94SpoRooAP-61
95ColCho-407
95ColChoGS-407
95ColChoSS-407
95Don-144
95DonPreP-144
95Fle-37
95Pac-44
95PacLatD-32
95PacPri-15
95Sco-453
95ScoGolR-453
95ScoPlaTS-453
95Top-562
95TopCyb-338

Rodriguez, Cecil
93ExcFS7-194

Rodriguez, Chris
91HunCubC-20
91HunCubP-3333
92GenCubC-8
92GenCubF-1559
93PeoChiC-17
93PeoChiF-1083
94DayCubC-21
94DayCubF-2351
96WatIndTI-26

Rodriguez, Dave
83TacTigT-30B
92BriTigC-14
92BriTigF-1409
93NiaFalRF-3387

Rodriguez, Eddie
83PeoSunF-28
87QuaCitAP-18
87SalAngP-1
88QuaCitAGS-1
89QuaCitAB-2
89QuaCitAGS-1
92GreFalDSP-15

Rodriguez, Eddy Alberto
89BriTigS-23
90NiaFalRP-23
91FayGenC-8
91FayGenP-1168
92LakTigC-25
92LakTigF-2278

Rodriguez, Edgal Antonio
87QuaCitAP-3
88BlaYNPRWL-17
88QuaCitAGS-7
89PalSprACLC-41
89PalSprAP-465
90QuaCitAGS-28
91PalSprAP-2032

Rodriguez, Eduardo
71MLBOffS-449
74OPC-171
74Top-171
75OPC-582
75Top-582
76OPC-92
76SSP-228
76Top-92
77BurCheD-86
77Top-361
78Top-623
79Top-108
80Top-273
81HolMilT-1
86QuaCitAP-28
90MidAngGS-1
94BreMilB-264

Rodriguez, Edwin
83ColCliT-18
84LasVegSC-240
85LasVegSC-108
86LasVegSP-14
87LasVegSP-19
92YanWIZ8-164

Rodriguez, Eligio
88GenCubP-1646

Rodriguez, Ellie (Eliseo)
69OPC-49
69RoySol-14
69Top-49A
69Top-49B
69TopTeaP-7
70OPC-402
70RoyTeal-28
70Top-402
71BreTeal-13
71OPC-344
71Top-344
72MilBra-294
72OPC-421
72Top-421
73Kel2D-2
73OPC-45
73Top-45
73TopCanL-43
74OPC-405
74Top-405
74TopSta-146
75Hos-34
75HosTwi-34
75OPC-285
75Top-285
76OPC-512
76SSP-193
76Top-512
77Top-448
81TCM60I-421
89BlaYNPRWL-166
90DodTar-679
92YanWIZ6-107
93UppDecS-4
94BreMilB-265

Rodriguez, Ernesto
91Cla/Bes-40
91MyrBeaHC-22
91MyrBeaHP-2956
91SouAtlLAGP-SAL39
92DunBluJC-19
92DunBluJF-2008

Rodriguez, Ernie
85BenPhiC-20
88ButCopKSP-28
89ButCopKSP-28
93PocPosF-4222
93PocPosSP-24

Rodriguez, F. Boi
87JamExpP-2544
88WesPalBES-22
89JacExpB-16
89JacExpP-177
90JacExpB-8
91GreBraC-24
91GreBraLD-216
91LinDriAA-216
91RicBraBC-35
92RicBraBB-25
92RicBraF-385
92RicBraRC-17
92RicBraS-439
92SkyAAAF-203
93RicBraBB-24
93RicBraF-194
93RicBraP-20
93RicBraRC-4
93RicBraRC-25
97RicBraBC-11

Rodriguez, Felix
76VenLeaS-178
77ShrCapT-19
80VenLeaS-144
91KisDodP-4190
92GreFalDSP-6
93VerBeaDC-21
93VerBeaDF-2217
94SanAntMF-2468
95Bow-81
95BowBes-B27
95BowBesR-B27
95TopTra-63T
96Bow-286
96ColCho-587
96ColChoGS-587
96ColChoSS-587
96Fle-446
96FleTif-446

Rodriguez, Fernando
88BlaYNPRWL-18
89BlaYNPRWLU-37

Rodriguez, Frank (Francisco)
91Cla/Bes-397
91ClaDraP-NNO
91ClaGolB-BC17
91ElmPioC-14
91ElmPioP-3279
91FroRowDP-1
91FroRowFR-1
91FroRowFR-2
91FroRowFR-3
91FroRowFR-4
91UppDecFE-21F
92Bow-45
92ClaBluBF-BC20
92ClaFS7-391
92ClaRedB-BC20
92LynRedSC-1
92LynRedSF-2905
92ProFS7-23
92UppDecML-43
92UppDecML-54
92UppDecML-266
92UppDecMLTPHF-TP6
93Bow-143
93Bow-362
93ClaGolF-22
93ClaYouG-YG20
93ExcFS7-137
93HelBreSP-2
93NewBriRSF-1218
93UppDec-442
93UppDecGold-442
94ActPac-22
94ActPac-AU1
94Bow-368
94Bow-615
94BowBes-B30
94BowBesR-B30
94Cla-94
94ClaCreotC-C23
94ClaGolA-SH5
94ClaGolF-112
94PawRedSDD-19
94PawRedSF-947
94StoPorC-21
94StoPorF-1693
94Top-112
94TopGol-112
94TopSpa-112
94UppDecML-115
94UppDecML-262
94UppDecMLPotYF-PY21
95ActPac2GF-16G
95ActPacF-26
95ActPacF-77
95Bow-126
95ElPasDTI-21
95Exc-14
95Fla-230
95FleAllR-M9
95PawRedSDD-23
95PawRedTI-30
95Sel-166
95SelArtP-166
95SelCer-123
95SelCerMG-123
95SelCerPU-13
95SelCerPU9-13
95StaClu-580
95StaCluMOP-580
95StaCluSTWS-580
95Sum-131
95SumNewA-NA13
95SumNthD-131
95Top-244
95UC3-109
95UC3ArtP-109
95UppDec-236
95UppDec-492T
95UppDecED-236
95UppDecEDG-236
95UppDecML-24
96ColCho-25
96ColChoGS-25
96ColChoSS-25
96Don-23
96DonPreP-23
96Fin-S153
96FinRef-S153
96Fla-122
96Fle-176
96FleTif-176
96LeaSigA-196
96LeaSigAG-196
96LeaSigAS-196
96PinAfi-138
96PinAfiAP-138
96Sco-155
96ScoDugC-A90
96ScoDugCAP-A90
96Sel-130
96SelArtP-130
96StaClu-379
96StaCluMOP-379
96Sum-117
96SumAbo&B-117
96SumArtP-117
96SumFoi-117
96Top-254
96Ult-380
96UltGolM-380
96UppDec-368
97Cir-122
97CirRav-122
97ColCho-158
97Don-247
97DonPreP-247
97DonPrePGold-247
97Fin-33
97FinRef-33
97Fle-156
97FleTif-156
97Lea-61
97LeaFraM-61
97LeaFraMDC-61
97MetUni-213
97Pin-89
97PinArtP-89
97PinMusC-89
97Sco-108
97ScoPreS-108
97ScoShoS-108
97ScoShoSAP-108
97SP-107
97StaClu-179
97StaCluMOP-179
97Top-77
97Ult-94
97UltGolME-94
97UltPlaME-94
97UppDec-107
95UppDecMLFS-24
Rodriguez, Frankie
93HelBreF-4092
94ExcFS7-21
Rodriguez, Gabriel
87GenCubP-15
88BlaYNPRWL-114
88Ft.LauYS-19
88PeoChiTI-28
89BlaYNPRWL-123
89Ft.LauYS-22
89Sta-80
89WinSpiS-NNO
90GenCubS-21
90OscAstS-25
Rodriguez, Gary
96WatIndTI-27
Rodriguez, Guillermo
96BelGiaTI-2
Rodriguez, Hector
91AugPirC-18
91AugPirP-814
94NewJerCC-22
94NewJerCF-3427
96BoiHawB-25
Rodriguez, Hector (Antonio H.)
52WhiSoxH-8
53BowC-98
Rodriguez, Henry
89VerBeaDS-23
90SanAntMGS-24
90TexLeaAGS-8
91AlbDukLD-19
91AlbDukP-1156
91Bow-185
91Cla2-T51
91LeaGolR-BC8
91LinDriAAA-19
91Ult-386
91UppDec-21
92AlbDukF-735
92AlbDukS-19
92Bow-108
92DonRoo-105
92Fle-661
92OPC-656
92ProFS7-241
92SkyAAAF-10
92SpolllFK1-505
92StaClu-268
92Top-656
92TopGol-656
92TopGolW-656
92TopMic-656
92TriA AAS-19
93AlbDukF-1477
93DodPol-22
93Don-218
93Fle-453
93LimRocDWB-84
93Pin-182
93Sco-244
93Sel-404
93StaClu-226
93StaCluFDI-226
93StaCluMOP-226
93Top-284
93TopGol-284
93TopInaM-284
93TopMic-284
93Toy-38
93UppDec-391
93UppDecGold-391
94UlC-596
94ColChoGS-596
94ColChoSS-596
94DodMot-8
94DodPol-23
94Don-264
94ExtBas-295
94Fla-399
94Fle-522
94Lea-385
94LeaL-121
94Pac-320
94Sel-320
94StaClu-176
94StaCluFDI-176
94StaCluGR-176
94StaCluMOP-176
94Top-727
94TopGol-727
94TopSpa-727
94Ult-521
94UppDec-436
94UppDecED-436
95ColCho-224
95ColCho-551T
95ColChoGS-224
95ColChoSS-224
95DodPol-23
95Don-280
95DonPreP-280
95Fle-548
95Lea-36
95Pac-225
95PacPri-73
95Sco-52
95ScoGolR-52
95ScoPlaTS-52
95StaClu-491
95StaCluMOP-491
95StaCluSTWS-491
95StaCluVR-270
95Top-400
95TopCyb-201
95Ult-184
95UltGolM-184
96Bow-82
96BowBes-18
96BowBesAR-18
96BowBesR-18
96Cir-151
96CirAcc-23
96CirBos-41
96CirRav-151
96ColCho-616
96ColChoGS-616
96ColChoSS-616
96ExpDis-15
96Fin-B325
96FinRef-B325
96FleUpd-U151
96FleUpdTC-U151
96LeaLim-85
96LeaLimG-85
96LeaPre-97
96LeaPreP-97
96LeaSig-35
96LeaSigPPG-35
96LeaSigPPP-35
96Pac-127
95StaCluVRMC-270
96Ult-508
96UltGolM-508
96Zen-50
96ZenArtP-50
96ZenMoz-17
97Bow-47
97BowInt-47
97Cir-293
97CirRav-293
97ColCho-160
97Don-10
97DonDiaK-6
97DonDiaKC-6
97DonEli-100
97DonEliGS-100
97DonLim-150
97DonLim-164
97DonLimLE-150
97DonLimLE-164
97DonPre-40
97DonPreCttC-40
97DonPreP-10
97DonPrePGold-10
97DonRocL-13
97Fin-232
97FinRef-232
97FlaSho-A101
97FlaSho-B101
97FlaSho-C101
97FlaShoLC-101
97FlaShoLC-B101
97FlaShoLC-C101
97FlaShoLCM-A101
97FlaShoLCM-B101
97FlaShoLCM-C101
97Fle-384
97Fle-737
97FleTeaL-22
97FleTif-384
97FleTif-737
97Lea-71
97LeaFraM-71
97LeaFraMDC-71
97MetUni-159
97NewPin-110
97NewPinAP-110
97NewPinMC-110
97NewPinPP-110
97Pac-350
97PacFirD-18
97PacLatotML-32
97PacLigB-350
97PacPri-120
97PacPriGotD-GD170
97PacPriLB-120
97PacPriP-120
97PacSil-350
97PinCer-91
97PinCerMBlu-91
97PinCerMG-91
97PinCerMR-91
97PinCerR-91
97PinIns-38
97PinInsCE-38
97PinInsDE-38
97PinMin-26
97PinMinB-26
97PinMinCB-26
97PinMinCG-26
97PinMinCGR-26
97PinMinCN-26
97PinMinCS-26
97PinMinG-26
97PinMinS-26
97PinPasttM-18
97PinTotCPB-91
97PinTotCPG-91
97PinTotCPR-91
97PinX-P-76
97PinX-PMoS-76
97PinX-PSfF-38
97PinX-PSfFU-38
97ProMag-25
97ProMagML-25
97Sco-228
97Sco-517
97ScoHobR-517
97ScoPreS-228
97ScoResC-517
97ScoShoS-228
97ScoShoS-517
97ScoShoSAP-228
97ScoShoSAP-517
97ScoSteS-15
97Sel-40
97SelArtP-40
97SelRegG-40
97SkyE-X-84
97SkyE-XC-84
97SkyE-XEC-84
97SP-114
97Spolll-85
97SpolllEE-85
97StaClu-28
97StaCluMat-28
97StaCluMOP-28
97Stu-27
97StuPrePG-27
97StuPrePS-27
97Top-210
97TopChr-78
97TopChrR-78
97TopGal-131
97TopGalPPI-131
97TopIntF-ILM11
97Ult-233
97UltDouT-16
97UltGolME-233
97UltPlaME-233
97UppDec-109
Rodriguez, Iggy
86WesPalBEP-25
Rodriguez, Inocencio
90IBAWorA-12
Rodriguez, Ismael
93LinVenB-7
Rodriguez, Ivan Minors
78BurBeeT-23
80HolMilT-6
81VanCanT-8
Rodriguez, Javier
95EveAqaTI-18
Rodriguez, Jonis
84GreHorT-20
Rodriguez, Jose
79WisRapTT-21
81BufBisT-13
82JacMetT-8
82PorBeaT-21
83LynPirT-22
83St.PetCT-23
86ArkTraP-21
86BurExpP-18
87AppFoxP-20
89BriTigS-24
89PriPirS-17
93IdaFalBSP-17
94IdaFalBF-3589
94IdaFalBSP-25
Rodriguez, Joshua
90MidAngGS-NNO
Rodriguez, Juan
77DayBealT-20
96BoiHawB-26
Rodriguez, Julian
76BatTroTI-18
Rodriguez, Larry
96AriBlaDB-27
97Bow-137
97BowInt-137
97Top-250
Rodriguez, Leo
58JetPos-16
Rodriguez, Liu
96HicCraB-18
Rodriguez, Luis
95BelGiaTI-15
95StCatSTI-14
96HagSunB-18
Rodriguez, Luis E.
81OklCit8T-16
Rodriguez, Manuel
90JohCitCS-22
91JohCitCC-24
91JohCitCP-3976
Rodriguez, Marcos
79CliDodT-15
Rodriguez, Maximo
95KanCouCTI-11
96BreCouMB-28
Rodriguez, Miguel
80UtiBluJT-32
Rodriguez, Pudge (Ivan Torres)

89BlaYNPRWL-51
89GasRanP-1006
89GasRanS-20
89SouAtlLAGS-26
90ChaRanS-22
90FloStaLAS-41
90StaFS7-26
91Bow-272
91Cla/Bes-136
91ClaGolB-BC7
91Cla2-T82
91Cla3-T78
91DonRoo-33
91FleUpd-62
91LinDriAA-592
91ScoRoo-82T
91TopTra-101T
91TopTraT-101T
91TulDriLD-592
91TulDriP-2776
91TulDriTI-23
91UltUpd-58
91UppDecFE-55F
92Bow-1
92Cla1-T77
92Cla2-T69
92ClaGam-159
92ColAllG-23
92ColAllP-23
92Don-289
92DonCraJ1-27
92Fle-316
92FleRooS-12
92Lea-194
92OPC-78
92OPCPre-55
92PanSti-74
92Pin-156
92PinTea2-8
92PinTeaP-3
92ProFS7-153
92RanMot-5
92RanTeal-19
92Sco-700
92Sco100RS-77
92ScoImpP-5
92SpoIllFK1-518
92StaClu-415
92Stu-246
92Top-78
92TopDeb91-150
92TopGol-78
92TopGolW-78
92TopMcD-41
92TopMic-78
92TriPla-51
92Ult-139
92UppDec-245
92UppDecF-2
92UppDecFG-2
93Bow-489
93ClaGam-78
93ColAllG-11
93DiaMar-90
93Don-187
93Fin-47
93FinRef-47
93Fla-285
93Fle-327
93Fle-355
93FunPac-159
93FunPacA-AS2
93HumDumC-17
93Lea-5
93LeaFas-15
93LeaGolA-R1
93LeaGolA-U2
93OPC-331
93PacBeiA-4
93PacBeiA-16
93PacJugC-14
93PacSpa-316
93PacSpaPI-20
93PanSti-80
93Pin-21
93Pin-301
93PinTea2-29
93PinTeaP-3
93RanKee-428
93Sco-25
93Sco-507
93Sco-537
93ScoGolDT-6
93Sel-136
93SelChaS-17
93SP-9
93StaClu-524
93StaClu-592
93StaCluFDI-524
93StaCluFDI-592
93StaCluM-175
93StaCluMOP-524
93StaCluMOP-592
93StaCluR-10
93Stu-133
93Top-360
93TopGol-360
93TopInaM-360
93TopMic-360
93Toy-33
93ToyMasP-10
93TriPla-16
93Ult-284
93UltAllS-11
93UltAwaW-11
93UppDec-52
93UppDec-123
93UppDec-450
93UppDec-468
93UppDecFA-A12
93UppDecFAJ-A12
93UppDecGold-52
93UppDecGold-123
93UppDecGold-450
93UppDecGold-468
93UppDecS-19
94Bow-101
94ChuHomS-27
94ChuHomSG-27
94ColC-625
94ColChoGS-625
94ColChoSS-625
94Don-376
94DonDiaK-DK10
94DonSpeE-376
94ExtBas-184
94Fin-126
94FinPre-126P
94FinRef-126
94Fla-346
94Fle-319
94FleAllS-22
94FUnPac-70
94FUnPac-176
94Lea-338
94LeaL-74
94LeaLimGA-15
94OPC-87
94Pac-627
94PacAll-13
94PanSti-132
94Pin-349
94PinArtP-349
94PinMusC-349
94PinTeaP-5
94ProMag-135
94RanAllP-20
94RanAllP-21
94RanAllP-22
94Sco-31
94ScoGolR-31
94ScoGolS-58
94Sel-214
94SelSki-SK8
94SP-151
94SPDieC-151
94Spo-88
94SpoFanA-AS5
94StaClu-116
94StaCluFDI-116
94StaCluGR-116
94StaCluMOP-116
94StaCluMOP-ST27
94StaCluST-ST27
94StaCluT-265
94StaCluTFDI-265
94Stu-157
94Top-165
94TopGol-165
94TopSpa-165
94TriPla-199
94Ult-132
94UltAwaW-1
94UppDec-245
94UppDecAJ-34
94UppDecAJG-34
94UppDecED-245
95Baz-16
95Bow-344
95BowBes-X1
95BowBesR-X1
95ClaPhoC-55
95ColCho-391
95ColChoGS-391
95ColChoSE-188
95ColChoSEGS-188
95ColChoSESS-188
95ColChoSS-391
95D3-32
95Don-423
95DonAll-AL2
95DonDom-2
95DonPreP-423
95DonTopotO-165
95Emb-54
95EmbGolI-54
95Emo-88
95Fin-109
95FinRef-109
95Fla-92
95FlaHotG-10
95Fle-295
95FleAllS-1
95FleUpdSL-9
95KinDis-19
95Kra-13
95Lea-107
95LeaGreG-16
95LeaLim-131
95Pac-433
95PacLatD-31
95PacPri-137
95PanSti-28
95Pin-122
95PinArtP-122
95PinFan-10
95PinMusC-122
95PinSam-122
95RanCra-28
95Sco-367
95ScoConR-AD2
95ScoGolR-367
95ScoHaloG-HG74
95ScoPlaTS-367
95Sel-63
95SelArtP-63
95SelCer-77
95SelCerMG-77
95SP-198
95SPCha-192
95SPChaDC-192
95Spo-33
95SpoArtP-33
95SPSil-198
95StaClu-197
95StaCluFDI-197
95StaCluMOP-197
95StaCluSTWS-197
95StaCluVR-103
95Stu-117
95Sum-82
95SumNthD-82
95TomPiz-15
95Top-543
95TopCyb-324
95TopTra-163T
95UC3-82
95UC3ArtP-82
95Ult-113
95UltAllS-18
95UltAllSGM-18
95UltAwaW-1
95UltAwaWGM-1
95UltGolM-113
95UppDec-391
95UppDecED-391
95UppDecEDG-391
95UppDecSE-41
95UppDecSEG-41
95Zen-39
95ZenAllS-12
96Baz-104
96Bow-3
96BowBes-30
96BowBesAR-30
96BowBesMI-8
96BowBesMIAR-8
96BowBesMIR-8
96BowBesR-30
96Cir-92
96CirRav-92
96Cla7/1PC-8
96ColCho-345
96ColChoGS-345
96ColChoSS-345
96DenHol-21
96Don-350
96DonPreP-350
96EmoXL-127
96EmoXLD-9
96Fin-B258
96Fin-S3
96FinRef-B258
96FinRef-S3
96Fla-178
96FlaHotG-9
96Fle-260
96FleRan-14
96FleTif-260
96Kin-21
96Lea-151
96LeaLim-1
96LeaLimG-1
96LeaPre-21
96LeaPreP-21
96LeaPrePB-151
96LeaPrePG-151
96LeaPrePS-151
96LeaSig-40
96LeaSigEA-175
96LeaSigEACM-26
96LeaSigPPG-40
96LeaSigPPP-40
96MetUni-116
96MetUniP-116
96MetUniProS-116
96Pac-420
96PacEstL-EL27
96PacGolCD-DC24
96PacPri-P138
96PacPriG-P138
96PanSti-234
96Pin-59
96PinAfi-69
96PinAfiAP-69
96PinAfiFPP-69
96PinArtP-23
96PinFan-22
96PinSta-23
96PinTeaP-8
96ProMagA-7
96ProSta-99
96RanMot-4
96Sco-302
96ScoDugC-B27
96ScoDugCAP-B27
96ScoGolS-22
96ScoNumG-24
96Sel-9
96SelArtP-9
96SelCer-35
96SelCerAP-35
96SelCerCB-35
96SelCerCR-35
96SelCerMB-35
96SelCerMG-35
96SelCerMR-35
96SelTeaN-14
96SP-180
96Spo-11
96SpoArtP-11
96SpoDouT-7
96StaClu-380
96StaCluEPB-380
96StaCluEPG-380
96StaCluEPS-380
96StaCluMM-MM2
96StaCluMOP-380
96StaCluMOP-MM2
95StaCluVRMC-103
96Stu-139
96StuPrePB-139
96StuPrePG-139
96StuPrePS-139
96Sum-12
96SumAbo&B-12
96SumArtP-12
96SumFoi-12
96SumPos-5
96TeaOut-68
96Top-140
96Top-227
96TopChr-39
96TopChr-87
96TopChrR-39
96TopChrR-87
96TopGal-52
96TopGalPPI-52
96TopLas-91
96Ult-139
96UltGolM-139
96UltPriL-1
96UltPriLGM-1
96UppDec-210
96Zen-7
96ZenArtP-7
96ZenMoz-2
97BowBes-84
97BowBesAR-84
97BowBesMI-MI4
97BowBesMIAR-MI4
97BowBesMIARI-MI4
97BowBesMII-MI4
97BowBesMIR-MI4
97BowBesMIRI-MI4
97BowBesR-84
97Cir-259
97CirRav-259
97ColCho-243
97ColChoAC-8
97Don-31
97Don-438
97DonArmaD-4
97DonDiaK-8
97DonDiaKC-8
97DonEli-13
97DonEliGS-13
97DonEliLaL-5
97DonLim-44
97DonLim-171
97DonLimLE-44
97DonLimLE-171
97DonPowA-20
97DonPowADC-20
97DonPre-49
97DonPre-186
97DonPreCttC-49
97DonPreCttC-186
97DonPreP-31
97DonPreP-438
97DonPrePGold-31
97DonPrePGold-438
97DonPrePM-8
97DonPreS-20
97DonPreTF-19
97DonPreTP-19
97DonPreXP-3A
97Fin-90
97Fin-152
97Fin-289
97FinEmb-152
97FinEmb-289
97FinEmbR-152
97FinEmbR-289
97FinRef-90
97FinRef-152
97FinRef-289
97FlaSho-A57
97FlaSho-B57
97FlaSho-C57
97FlaShoHG-14
97FlaShoLC-57
97FlaShoLC-B57
97FlaShoLC-C57
97FlaShoLCM-A57
97FlaShoLCM-B57
97FlaShoLCM-C57
97Fle-231
97FleTif-231
97Bow-261
97BowChr-83
97BowChrI-83
97BowChrIR-83
97BowChrR-83
97BowInt-261
97DonLim-28
97DonLimFotG-3
97DonLimLE-28
97DonPreTBG-19
97DonTeaSMVP-1
97Lea-221
97Lea-384
97Lea-194
97LeaDrefS-16
97LeaFraM-194
97LeaFraM-221
97LeaFraM-384
97LeaFraMDC-221
97LeaFraMDC-194
97LeaFraMDC-384

97LeaGolS-9
97LeaGet-12
97LeaLeaotN-5
97MetUni-168
97NewPin-61
97NewPin-185
97NewPinAP-61
97NewPinAP-185
97NewPinIE-5
97NewPinKtP-3
97NewPinMC-61
97NewPinMC-185
97NewPinPP-I5B
97NewPinPP-61
97NewPinPP-185
97NewPinPP-K3
97NewPinPP-IR1
97NewPinPP-IR2
97NewPinPP-IR3
97NewPinPP-IR4
97NewPinPP-IR5
97NewPinS-IR1
97NewPinS-IR2
97NewPinS-IR3
97NewPinS-IR4
97NewPinS-IR5
97Pac-209
97PacCar-20
97PacCarM-20
97PacCerCGT-9
97PacGolCD-20
97PacLatotML-22
97PacLigB-209
97PacPri-71
97PacPriLB-71
97PacPriP-71
97PacPriSL-SL7C
97PacSil-209
97Pin-47
97PinArtP-47
97PinCar-13
97PinCer-79
97PinCerCMGT-9
97PinCerCT-9
97PinCerMBlu-79
97PinCerMG-79
97PinCerMR-79
97PinCerR-79
97PinIns-48
97PinInsC-17
97PinInsCE-48
97PinInsDD-4
97PinInsDE-48
97PinMin-25
97PinMinB-25
97PinMinCB-25
97PinMinCG-25
97PinMinCGR-25
97PinMinCN-25
97PinMinCS-25
97PinMinG-25
97PinMinS-25
97PinMusC-47
97PinPastM-12
97PinTeaP-5
97PinTeaP-10
97PinTotCPB-79
97PinTotCPG-79
97PinTotCPR-79
97PinX-P-35
97PinX-P-141
97PinX-PMoS-35
97PinX-PMoS-141
97PinX-PMP-10
97ProMag-76
97ProMagML-76
97Sco-203
97Sco-547
97ScoAllF-15
97ScoHeaotO-2
97ScoHobR-547
97ScoPitP-5
97ScoPreS-203
97ScoRan-12
97ScoRanPl-12
97ScoRanPr-12
97ScoResC-547
97ScoShoS-203
97ScoShoS-547
97ScoShoSAP-203
97ScoShoSAP-547
97Sel-25
97SelArtP-25
97SelRegG-25
97SelToootT-20
97SelToootTMB-20
97SkyE-X-47
97SkyE-XC-47
97SkyE-XEC-47
97SP-170
97SpoIll-71
97SpoIllEE-71
97SPSpeF-18
97SPSpxF-8
97SPSPxFA-8
97SPx-49
97SPxBro-49
97SPxCorotG-7
97SPxGraF-49
97SPxSil-49
97SPxSte-49
97StaClu-200
97StaCluMat-200
97StaCluMOP-200
97StaCluMOP-PL1
97StaCluPL-PL1
97Stu-108
97StuHarH-1
97StuPrePG-108
97StuPrePS-108
97Top-340
97TopAll-AS1
97TopChr-114
97TopChrAS-AS1
97TopChrDD-DD6
97TopChrDDR-DD6
97TopChrR-114
97TopChrSAR-AS1
97TopGal-111
97TopGalPPI-111
97TopSta-16
97TopSta1AS-AS5
97TopStaAM-16
97Ult-140
97UltFieC-17
97UltGolME-140
97UltPlaME-140
97UppDec-138
97UppDec-203
97UppDec-211
97UppDecRSF-RS11
97UppDecU-28
97Zen-15
97Zen8x1-9
97Zen8x1D-9
Rodriguez, Ramon
85SpoIndC-20
86ChaRaiP-22
Rodriguez, Rich (Richard A.)
84LitFalMT-25
86LynMetP-19
87LynMetP-19
88Fle-293
88FleGlo-293
88FleUpd-24
88FleUpdG-24
88JacMetGS-13
88MetColP-46
88Top-166
88TopTif-166
89WicChaR-4
89WicStaR-19
89WicWraR-29
90CMC-512
90LasVegSC-9
90LasVegSP-123
90ProAAAF-11
91Don-769
91Fle-541
91Lea-448
91OPC-573
91PadMag-16
91Sco-593
91StaClu-565
91Top-573
91TopDeb90-132
91TopDesS-573
91TopMic-573
91TopTif-573
91UppDec-640
92Don-388
92Fle-619
92Lea-319
92OPC-462
92PadCarJ-17
92PadMot-22
92PadPolD-29
92PadSmo-27
92Sco-149
92StaClu-712
92StaCluNC-712
92Top-462
92TopGol-462
92TopGolW-462
92TopMic-462
92Ult-581
92UppDec-568
93Don-338
93Fle-145
93Lea-368
93MarPub-21
93PacSpa-262
93PadMot-11
93Sco-466
93StaClu-137
93StaCluFDI-137
93StaCluMOP-137
93Top-693
93TopGol-693
93TopInaM-693
93TopMic-693
93TopTra-71T
93Ult-120
93UppDec-330
93UppDecGold-330
94Don-635
94Fle-475
94FleUpd-182
94Sco-295
94ScoGolR-295
94StaCluT-76
94StaCluTFDI-76
94Top-312
94TopGol-312
94TopSpa-312
95Fle-508
95Top-601
95TopCyb-372
96OmaRoyB-24
Rodriguez, Richard
77ChaPatT-17
Rodriguez, Rick
85ModA'sC-18
86TacTigP-19
88ColSprSSC-8
88ColSprSSP-1549
89VanCanC-8
89VanCanP-580
91LinDriAAA-392
91PhoFirLD-392
91PhoFirP-65
91PocPioP-3801
91PocPioSP-29
93SouOreAC-29
95ModA'sTI-25
96ModA'sB-25
Rodriguez, Rigo
85BeaGolGT-10
Rodriguez, Roberto
68Top-199
68TopVen-199
69Top-358
71MLBOffS-44
71OPC-424
71Top-424
74WicAerODF-104
Rodriguez, Roman
89PriPirS-18
90AugPirP-2474
91SalBucC-7
91SalBucP-961
92CarMudS-140
94StoPorC-22
94StoPorF-1703
95LynHilTI-26
Rodriguez, Rosario
88GreHorP-1567
90CedRapRDGB-24
90ChaLooGS-25
90NasSouP-231
90ProAAAF-543
90TopDeb89-103
91BufBisLD-44
91BufBisP-541
91LinDriAAA-44
91OPC-688
91Sco-373
91Top-688
91TopDesS-688
91TopMic-688
91TopTif-688
92Bow-498
92BufBisBS-18
92BufBisS-34
92Don-748
92Fle-565
92SkyAAAF-19
92StaClu-697
92StaCluNC-697
Rodriguez, Ruben
83AleDukT-26
85DomLeaS-57
85NasPirT-21
86NasPirP-23
87SalLakTTT-7
87VanCanP-1620
88SalLakCTTI-3
89BoiHawP-1992
89DenZepC-18
89DenZepP-34
89SalLakTTI-3
90EriSaiS-21
91LinDriAA-396
91LonTigLD-396
91LonTigP-1881
92PawRedSF-926
92PawRedSS-364
93LimRocDWB-47
93PawRedSDD-22
93PawRedSF-2411
93PawRedSTI-19
94PawRedSDD-20
94PawRedSF-949
Rodriguez, Sammy
96PitMetB-23
Rodriguez, Steve
91TopTra-102T
91TopTraT-102T
92ClaDraP-112
92FroRowDP-84
92StaCluD-157
92TopDaiQTU-26
92TopTra-94T
92TopTraG-94T
93ClaFS7-114
93LynRedSC-22
93LynRedSF-2525
93StaCluM-10
93StaCluM-50
94NewBriRSF-660
94PawRedSDD-21
94UppDecML-66
95Bow-59
95FleUpd-13
95PawRedSDD-24
95PawRedTI-7
95Sum-152
95SumNthD-152
95UppDec-246
95UppDecED-246
95UppDecEDG-246
96ColCho-544
96ColChoGS-544
96ColChoSS-544
96Pac-320
96Sco-254
96StaClu-445
96StaCluMOP-445
96TolMudHB-24
Rodriguez, Tomas
88BilMusP-1816
89BilMusP-2044
89BlaYNPRWL-152
Rodriguez, Tony
91ElmPioC-13
91ElmPioP-3280
92LynRedSC-7
92LynRedSF-2917
93NewBriRSF-1230
94PawRedSDD-22
94SarRedSC-24
94SarRedSF-1961
95PawRedSDD-25
95PawRedTI-2
96PawRedSDD-25
96SarRedSB-27
Rodriguez, Victor
82RocRedWT-16
85Don-535
85LasVegSC-101
87LouRedTI-26
88BlaYNPRWL-115
88PorBeaC-20
88PorBeaP-649
89BlaYNPRWL-52
89PorBeaC-17
89PorBeaP-210
89TriAAP-AAA40
90CMC-564
90PorBeaC-12
90PorBeaP-188
90ProAAAF-258
91LinDriAAA-416
91OriCro-391
91PorBeaLD-416
91PorBeaP-1573
92ScrRedBF-2454
93ScrRedBF-2550
93ScrRedBTI-22
94EdmTraF-2882
95KanCouCLTI-13
95KanCouCTI-24
95MidLeaA-45
95UppDecML-214
96BreCouMB-29
96SarRedSB-3
96SigRooOJ-29
96StCatSB-24
95UppDecMLFS-214
Rodriques, Cecil
92HelBreF-1730
92HelBreSP-20
93BelBreC-19
93BelBreF-1724
94BelBreC-20
94BelBreF-117
96El PasDB-24
Roe, Preacher
47Exh-194
47PM1StaP1-187
47TipTop-145
49Bow-162
50Bow-167
50Dra-1
51Bow-118
51TopRedB-16
52BerRos-58
52Bow-168
52DixLid-16
52DixPre-16
52NatTeaL-25
52StaCalL-79F
52StaCalS-91C
52Top-66
52Whe-26A
52Whe-26B
53BowBW-26
53DixLid-17
53DixPre-17
53ExhCan-1
53NorBreL-24
53Top-254
54Bow-218
54DixLid-13
54NewYorJA-16
54Top-14
55Bow-216
68LauWorS-46
70FleWorS-46
71FleWorS-47
79DiaGre-87
79TCM50-145
79TCM50-239
83TCMPla1945-32
83TopRep5-66
88RinPosD1-9C
89DodSmoG-56
90DodTar-680
91TopArc1-254
92BazQua5A-9
94TopArc1-14
94TopArc1G-14
95TopArcBD-8
95TopArcBD-53
95TopArcBD-67
Roe, Rocky
88T/MUmp-42
89T/MUmp-40
90T/MUmp-38
Roebig, Stuart
91BriBanF-9
Roebuck, Ed
52LaPat-14
52Par-75
53ExhCan-41
55DodGolS-24
55Top-195
56Dod-26
56Top-58

58Top-435
60DodBelB-13
60DodUniO-15
60Top-519
61DodBelB-37
61Pos-170
61Top-6
61TopStal-32
62DodBelB-37
62Top-535
63Top-295
64PhiPhiB-19
64Top-187
64TopCoi-20
64TopSta-35
64TopStaU-64
64TopVen-187
65OPC-52
65Top-52
78TCM60I-165
87Dod195T-8
90DodTar-681
91RinPosBD3-12
95TopArcBD-106
95TopArcBD-144

Roebuck, Joe
89HelBreSP-13
90EriSaiS-22
91RenSilSCLC-13
92ChaRanC-8
92ChaRanF-2239

Roebuck, Ron
86AshTouP-24
86AubAstP-20

Roebuck, Scott
83WauTimF-20

Roeder, Jack
82WauTimF-3

Roeder, Steve
90WelPirP-27
91WelPirC-19
92PulBraC-23
92PulBraF-3175

Roenicke, Gary
76SSP-338
80Top-568
81Don-116
81Fle-187
81OPC-37
81Top-37
82Don-509
82Fle-177
82Top-204
83Don-27
83Fle-71
83OPC-382
83OriPos-23
83Top-605
84Don-392
84Fle-18
84Nes792-372
84OPC-372
84OriEng-12
84OriTeal-24
84Top-372
84TopSti-205
84TopTif-372
85Don-123
85Fle-188
85OPC-109
85Top-109
85TopMin-109
85TopTif-109
86Don-472
86Fle-285
86FleUpd-98
86OPC-183
86Top-494
86TopTif-494
86TopTra-94T
86TopTraT-94T
86YanTCM-37
87BraSmo-23
87DonOpeD-47
87Fle-112
87FleGlo-112
87OPC-283
87Top-683
87TopTif-683
87TopTra-105T
87TopTraT-105T
88PanSti-252
88Sco-482
88ScoGlo-482
88StaLinBra-15
88Top-523
88TopTif-523
91OriCro-392
91PacSenL-85
91PacSenL-104
92YanWIZ8-165
95IdaFalBTI-19

Roenicke, Ron
78LodDodT-15
80AlbDukT-6
81AlbDukT-9
82DodPol-40
82DodUniOV-17
82Fle-19
82Top-681
83DodPol-40
83Don-327
83Fle-217
83FleSta-166
83Top-113
84Don-484
84Fle-618
84LasVegSC-237
84Nes792-647
84Top-647
84TopTif-647
86FleUpd-99
86Top-63
86TopTif-63
87Don-412
87Fle-182
87FleGlo-182
87PhiTas-17
87Top-329
87TopTif-329
88NasSouC-21
88NasSouP-475
88NasSouTI-20
88Sco-566
88ScoGlo-566
88Top-783
88TopTif-783
89OklCit8C-16
89OklCit8P-1519
90DodTar-682
91PacSenL-85
91PacSenL-106
91SanAntMP-2993
92DodMot-28
92DodPol-NNO
93DodMot-28
93DodPol-30
94GreFalDSP-30
95SanBerSTI-31

Roesch, John
77NewCoPT-28
78NewWayCT-39

Roesler, Mike
86CedRapRT-8
87TamTarP-5
88NasSouC-11
88NasSouP-492
89BlaYNPRWL-161
89NasSouC-7
89NasSouP-1282
89NasSouTI-21
90BufBisTI-21
90Fle-645
90FleCan-645
90OPC-203
90Sco-648
90Top-203
90TopDeb89-104
90TopTif-203
91CarMudLD-115
91CarMudP-1085
91LinDriAA-115
92BufBisBS-19
92BufBisF-322
92BufBisS-41

Roessler, Pat
90BirBarB-29
90BirBarP-1399
91BirBarP-1472
91LinDriAA-75
92BirBarF-2599
93SarWhiSF-1388

Roetter, Randy
82QuaCitCT-28
88WauTimGS-28
89WilBilP-634
90CalCanC-25
90CMC-452
96TacRaiB-4

Roettgen, Mark
96PeoChiB-28

Roettger, Oscar F.L.
78HalHalR-14
81ConTSN-94
90DodTar-683

Roettger, Wally (Walter H.)
31Exh-8
33ButCanV-40
34DiaMatCSB-153
81ConTSN-95
92ConTSN-653

Rogaliner, Chris
90NiaFalRP-30

Rogalski, Wayne
86AshTouP-25

Rogan, Bullet (Wilbur)
74LauOldTBS-19
86NegLeaF-32
87NegLeaPD-34
90NegLeaS-29
94TedWil-111

Rogan, Pat
65Top-486

Rogascozv, Boris
89EasLeaDDP-DD12

Rogell, William
33Gou-11
33GouCanV-11
34DiaMatCSB-154
34BatR31-177
34DiaStaR-76
35GolMedFR-11
35GouPuzR-1D
35GouPuzR-2D
35GouPuzR-16D
35GouPuzR-17D
35TigFreP-16
36GouWidPPR-A89
36NatChiFPR-65
36WorWidGV-52
76TigOldTS-18
80TigGreT-2
81TigDetN-16
81TigSecNP-29
83TigAlKS-39
86TigSpoD-7
94ConTSN-1236
94ConTSNB-1236

Rogers, Brad
88BatCliP-1691

Rogers, Bryan
90St.LucMS-23
91LinDriAA-641
91WilBilLD-641
91WilBilP-290
92BinMetF-514
92BinMetS-66
93BinMetF-2333
94NorTidF-2920
95NorTidTI-25

Rogers, Charlie
90MiaMirIS-22
90MiaMirIS-27
91Cla/Bes-375
91MiaMirP-407
92StoPorC-11
92StoPorF-35
93ElPasDF-2950
94ExcFS7-86
94NewOrlZF-1467

Rogers, Danny
87SumBraP-22
88CedRapRP-1162
90NiaFalRP-1
91Cla/Bes-379
91FayGenC-22
91FayGenP-1181

Rogers, Dave
77SalPirT-22

Rogers, Dennis
86NasPirP-24
87MacPirP-24

Rogers, Doug
89IdaFalBP-2027

Rogers, Dusty
86TamTarP-17
87CedRapRP-11

Rogers, Jason
94BluOriC-18
94BluOriF-3562
96FreKeyB-18

Rogers, Jesse
96NegLeaBMKC-8

Rogers, Jimmy
88MyrBeaBJP-1190
88SouAtlLAGS-22
89KnoBluJB-22
89KnoBluJP-1133
89KnoBluJS-18
90Bes-176
90CMC-815
90KnoBluJB-2
90KnoBluJP-1241
90KnoBluJS-16
91KnoBluJLD-365
91KnoBluJP-1764
91LinDriAA-365
94SyrChiF-970
94SyrChiTI-23
95SyrChiTI-22
96SyrChiTI-26

Rogers, Kenny
88TulDriTI-28
89DonBasB-315
89DonRoo-13
89RanMot-21
89RanSmo-27
89ScoRoo-107T
89TopTra-104T
89TopTraT-104T
90Don-283
90Fle-311
90FleCan-311
90Lea-311
90OPC-683
90RanMot-22
90Sco-301
90Sco100RS-46
90ScoYouSI-21
90Spo-216
90Top-683
90TopDeb89-105
90TopRoo-24
90TopTif-683
90ToyRoo-22
90UppDec-606
91Bow-290
91Don-258
91Fle-299
91Lea-105
91OPC-332
91RanMot-22
91Sco-155
91StaClu-258
91Top-332
91TopDesS-332
91TopMic-332
91TopTif-332
91Ult-353
91UppDec-606
92Don-368
92Fle-317
92Lea-173
92OPC-511
92Pin-482
92RanMot-22
92RanTeal-20
92Sco-101
92StaClu-311
92Top-511
92TopGol-511
92TopGolW-511
92TopMic-511
92Ult-445
92UppDec-651
93Don-509
93Fle-328
93Lea-92
93OPC-356
93PacSpa-646
93Pin-381
93RanKee-429
93Sco-204
93StaClu-55
93StaCluFDI-55
93StaCluMOP-55
93StaCluR-19
93Top-169
93TopGol-169
93TopInaM-169
93TopMic-169
93Ult-285
93UppDec-92
93UppDecGold-92
94Bow-429
94ColC-242
94ColChoGS-242
94ColChoSS-242
94Don-410
94ExtBas-185
94Fin-94
94FinRef-94
94Fla-347
94Fle-320
94Lea-293
94Pac-628
94Pin-221
94PinArtP-221
94PinMusC-221
94Sco-212
94ScoGolR-212
94Sel-297
94StaClu-467
94StaCluFDI-467
94StaCluGR-467
94StaCluMOP-467
94StaCluT-252
94StaCluTFDI-252
94Stu-158
94Top-413
94TopGol-413
94TopSpa-413
94TriPla-200
94Ult-133
94UppDec-457
94UppDecED-457
95Bow-289
95BowBes-R61
95BowBesR-R61
95ColCho-65
95ColCho-398
95ColChoGS-65
95ColChoGS-398
95ColChoSE-183
95ColChoSE-264
95ColChoSEGS-183
95ColChoSEGS-264
95ColChoSESS-183
95ColChoSESS-264
95ColChoSS-65
95ColChoSS-398
95Don-531
95DonPreP-531
95DonTopotO-166
95Emo-89
95Fin-178
95FinRef-178
95Fla-309
95Fle-296
95FleTeaL-13
95Lea-222
95LeaLim-136
95Pin-327
95PinArtP-327
95PinMusC-327
95RanCra-29
95Sco-315
95Sco-425
95ScoGolR-315
95ScoGolR-425
95ScoPlaTS-315
95ScoPlaTS-425
95SP-199
95SPCha-193
95SPChaDC-193
95SPSil-199
95StaClu-67
95StaCluFDI-67
95StaCluMOP-67
95StaCluSTWS-67
95StaCluVR-41
95Top-13
95TopCyb-11
95UppDec-394
95UppDecC-4A
95UppDecED-394
95UppDecEDG-394
95UppDecSE-38
95UppDecSEG-38
95Zen-40
96Baz-22
96ColCho-781
96Don-163
96DonPreP-163
96EmoXL-96
96Fin-B195
96FinRef-B195
96Fla-137
96Fle-261

96FleTif-261
96FleUpd-U68
96FleUpdTC-U68
96MetUni-94
96MetUniP-94
96Pac-427
96PanSti-233
96Pin-31
96Pin-341
96PinAfi-47
96PinAfiAP-47
96PinAfiFPP-47
96PinFoil-341
96Sco-319
96ScoDugC-B44
96ScoDugCAP-B44
96Spo-80
96SpoArtP-80
96StaClu-143
96StaClu-238
96StaCluEPB-143
96StaCluEPG-143
96StaCluEPS-143
96StaCluMOP-143
96StaCluMOP-238
95StaCluVRMC-41
96Sum-54
96SumAbo&B-54
96SumArtP-54
96SumFoi-54
96Top-130
96TopGal-72
96TopGalPPI-72
96TopLas-127
96Ult-140
96Ult-395
96UltGolM-140
96UltGolM-395
96UppDec-504U
96UppDecPHE-H18
96UppDecPreH-H18
97ColCho-407
97Fle-178
97FleTif-178
97Pac-160
97PacLigB-160
97PacSil-160
97Sco-225
97ScoPreS-225
97ScoShoS-225
97ScoShoSAP-225
97ScoYan-14
97ScoYanPl-14
97ScoYanPr-14
97StaClu-98
97StaCluMOP-98
97Top-372
97Ult-105
97UltGolME-105
97UltPlaME-105

Rogers, Kevin
88PocGiaP-2091
89CliGiaP-891
90Bes-76
90CalLeaACLC-50
90CMC-716
90SanJosGB-24
90SanJosGCLC-51
90SanJosGP-2003
90SanJosGS-19
91Bow-638
91Cla/Bes-221
91LinDriAA-320
91ShrCapLD-320
91ShrCapP-1823
92Bow-415
92ShrCapF-3870
92ShrCapS-593
92SkyAA F-262
93Bow-576
93FleFinE-155
93FleMajLP-A10
93GiaMot-24
93GiaPos-30
93LeaGolR-R11
93PacSpa-615
93Pin-613
93PinRooTP-2
93Sco-319
93SelRoo-64T
93StaCluG-8
93Top-822
93TopGol-822
93TopInaM-822
93TopMic-822
93Ult-489
93UppDec-8
93UppDecGold-8
94ColC-243
94ColChoGS-243
94ColChoSS-243
94Don-508
94Fle-699
94GiaAMC-19
94GiaUSPC-3S
94GiaUSPC-9D
94Pac-554
94Pin-365
94PinArtP-365
94PinMusC-365
94Sco-581
94ScoGolR-581
94StaClu-459
94StaCluFDI-459
94StaCluGR-459
94StaCluMOP-459
94StaCluT-23
94StaCluTFDI-23
94Top-3
94TopGol-3
94TopSpa-3
94Ult-592
95Fla-211
95Top-219

Rogers, Lamarr
93CenValRF-2901
93Top-746
93TopGol-746
93TopInaM-746
93TopMic-746
94NewHavRF-1558
95NewHavRTI-5

Rogers, Lee
39WorWidGV-22
79RedSoxEF-6
90DodTar-684

Rogers, Mac
85DurBulT-9
86DurBulP-24

Rogers, Marte
85ElmPioT-19

Rogers, Packy
88ElmPio1C-5
90DodTar-685

Rogers, Randy
78TidTidT-21
83AndBraT-15

Rogers, Robbie
88RenSilSCLC-283

Rogers, Roy
75JohMiz-14

Rogers, Steve
72Dia-39
73ExpPos-6
74OPC-169
74Top-169
74TopDecE-65
74TopSta-59
75OPC-173
75Top-173
76CraDis-50
76ExpRed-27
76OPC-71
76SSP-349
76Top-71
77BurCheD-159
77ExpPos-26
77Hos-22
77OPC-153
77Top-316
78OPC-9
78Top-425
78WifBalD-62
79ExpPos-21
79OPC-120
79Top-235
80ExpPos-25
80Kel-8
80OPC-271
80Top-520
81Don-330A
81Don-330B
81ExpPos-13
81Fle-143
81FleStiC-57
81OPC-340
81OPCPos-9
81Top-725
81TopScr-106
81TopSti-190
82Don-36
82ExpHygM-18
82ExpPos-34
82ExpZel-2
82FBIDis-17
82Fle-205
82FleSta-36
82OPC-52
82OPCPos-20
82PerAll-15
82PerAllG-15
82Top-605
82TopSti-59
83AllGamPI-174
83Don-219
83Don-320
83ExpStu-10
83Fle-294
83FleSta-167
83FleSti-260
83OPC-106
83OPC-111
83OPC-320
83Top-111
83Top-320
83Top-405
83Top-707
83TopSti-208
83TopSti-256
84Don-219
84DonActAS-48
84ExpPos-25
84ExpStu-19
84ExpStu-36
84Fle-284
84Nes792-80
84Nes792-394
84Nes792-708
84OPC-80
84OPC-394
84SevCoi-W20
84Top-80
84Top-394
84Top-708
84TopGloS-3
84TopRubD-30
84TopSti-88
84TopSti-182
84TopTif-80
84TopTif-394
84TopTif-708
85Don-219
85Fle-408
85Lea-192
85OPC-205
85OPCPos-11
85Top-205
85TopMin-205
85TopRubD-31
85TopSti-89
85TopTif-205
86ExpGreT-9
88GreBasS-34
91UppDecS-23
92Nab-33
92UppDecS-21
93ExpDonM-28
93UppDecS-27
94TedWil-51

Rogers, Stu
85BurRanT-23

Rogers, Thomas
21E121So1-81
21KoBreWSI-47
22W575-107
23W501-28

Roggenburk, Garry
63Top-386
64Top-258
64TopVen-258
66Top-582
67Top-429
68Top-581
81TCM60I-336
91ElmPioC-28
91ElmPioP-3288
92ElmPioC-25
92ElmPioF-1397
93UtiBluSC-26
93UtiBluSF-3549
94UtiBluSC-29
94UtiBluSF-3837

Roggendorf, Kip
93St.CatBJC-21
93St.CatBJF-3983
94St.CatBJC-28
94St.CatBJF-3653

Rogodzinski, Mike
74OPC-492
74Top-492
76SSP-607

Rogovin, Saul
47PM1StaP1-188
52Bow-165
52RedMan-AL19
52TipTop-35
52Top-159
53BowC-75
54Bow-140
57Top-129
91OriCro-393

Rogow, Mark
96CarMudB-28
96HonShaHWB-NNO

Rogozenski, Karl
83St.PetCT-28

Rohan, Tony
85NewOriT-7
87MiaMarP-9
88MiaMarS-22

Rohde, Brad
86BelMarC-112
86WauTimP-20

Rohde, Dave
86AriWilP-12
86AubAstP-21
87OscAstP-29
88ColAstB-11
89ColMudB-21
89ColMudP-123
89ColMudS-20
89Sta-2
89TucTorJP-20
90AstLenH-20
90Bow-75
90BowTif-75
90CMC-621
90FleUpd-17
90TucTorC-19
91AstMot-18
91Bow-558
91Don-743
91Lea-424
91OPC-531
91Sco100RS-69
91StaClu-137
91Top-531
91TopDeb90-133
91TopDesS-531
91TopMic-531
91TopTif-531
91UppDec-662
92ColSprSSF-760
92StaClu-753
92StaCluECN-753
93BufBisF-526
93PacSpa-100
94BufBisF-1844
95TusTorTI-23

Rohde, Dr. Richard
63RedFreBC-21

Rohe, George
11SpoLifCW-306

Rohlfing, Wayne
79QuaCitCT-6
80QuaCitCT-24

Rohlof, Scott
86VisOakP-17

Rohm, Dave
78DunBluJT-19

Rohn, Andy
87EveGiaC-7

Rohn, Dan
80VenLeaS-115
80WicAerT-6
82IowCubT-8
83IowCubT-19
84CubChiT-23
84IowCubT-8
85IntLeaAT-36
85MaiGuiT-22
86IndOhH-15
86IndTeal-34
87TacTigP-16
88OklCit8C-20
88OklCit8P-31
89OklCit8C-15
89OklCit8P-1530
91PacSenL-21
92Ft.MyeMCB-26
92Ft.MyeMF-2760
94SalLakBF-833
95ForWayWTI-26
96ForWayWB-27

Rohr, Les
68Top-569
91MetWIZ-333

Rohr, William
67Top-547
68Top-314
68TopVen-314

Rohrmeier, Dan
88FloStaLAS-48
88TamTarS-22
89SarWhiSS-21
90ProAaA-70
90TexLeaAGS-29
90TulDriP-1169
90TulDriTI-22
91LinDriAA-593
91TulDriLD-593
91TulDriP-2787
91TulDriTI-24
92MemChiF-2433
92MemChiS-445
93ClaGolF-26
93ExcFS7-178
93OmaRoyF-1695
94MemChiF-371
95ChaLooTI-18
96MemChiB-26

Rohrwild, Shawn
90IdaFalBP-3266
91MacBraC-9
91MacBraP-863

Roig, Tony
59DarFar-19
60DarFar-16
61UniOil-SD8
77FriOneYW-12

Rois, Luis
80GleFalWSBT-6
80GleFalWSCT-17
81GleFalWST-20

Rojano, Rafael
95GreBatTI-32

Rojas, Christian
94PriRedC-20
94PriRedF-3272
95BilRedTI-6
96Exc-149

Rojas, Cookie
62RedEnq-30
63Top-221
64PhiPhiB-20
64PhiTeaS-4
64Top-448
65Top-474
66OPC-170
66PhiTeal-10
66Top-170
66TopRubI-82
66TopVen-170
67CokCapPh-11
67DexPre-179
67PhiPol-11
67Top-595
68OPC-39
68Top-39
68TopVen-39
69MilBra-238
69MLBOffS-176
69PhiTeal-7
69Top-507
69TopSta-77
69TopSup-55
69TopTeaP-8
69TraSta-55
70DayDaiNM-131
70MLBOffS-142
70RoyTeal-29
70Top-569
71MLBOffS-427
71OPC-118
71Top-118
72Kel-39A
72Kel-39B
72MilBra-295
72OPC-415
72Top-415

73LinPor-90
73OPC-188
73Top-188
74Kel-42
74OPC-278
74Top-278
74TopSta-189
75Hos-2
75HosTwi-2
75OPC-169
75Top-169
76OPC-311
76SSP-171
76Top-311
77Top-509
83PhiPosGPaM-8
85DomLeaS-179
86RoyGreT-2
88AngSmo-1
88TopTra-97T
88TopTraT-97T
93MarPub-28
93UppDecS-28
94TopSpa-L9
Rojas, Francisco
78CedRapGT-23
Rojas, Freddy
93KinMetC-19
93KinMetF-3805
Rojas, Homar
85MexCitTT-17
87SanAntDTI-21
88FloStaLAS-19
88VerBeaDS-22
89SanAntMB-21
90SanAntMGS-25
Rojas, Jeff
85VisOakT-18
Rojas, Luis
82WesHavAT-24
Rojas, Mel (Melquiades)
87BurExpP-1093
89JacExpB-28
89JacExpP-156
89SouLeaAJ-20
90Bow-108
90BowTif-108
90IndIndP-302
90ProAAAF-585
90UppDec-772
91Don-681
91ExpPos-18
91Fle-245
91OPC-252
91OPCPre-101
91Sco-729
91ScoRoo-1
91Top-252
91TopDeb90-134
91TopDesS-252
91TopMic-252
91TopTif-252
91UppDec-357
92Don-435
92ExpPos-25
92Fle-490
92IndIndS-191
92OPC-583
92OPCPre-124
92Sco-725
92StaClu-489
92Top-583
92TopGol-583
92TopGolW-583
92TopMic-583
92UppDec-683
93Don-408
93ExpColP7-6
93ExpPosN-19
93Fle-79
93Lea-364
93LimRocDWB-14
93OPC-347
93PacSpa-537
93Pin-419
93Sco-363
93StaClu-553
93StaCluFDI-553
93StaCluMOP-553
93Top-341
93TopGol-341
93TopInaM-341
93TopMic-341
93Ult-70
93UppDec-190
93UppDecGold-190
94ColC-244
94ColChoGS-244
94ColChoSS-244
94Don-491
94ExtBas-310
94Fla-403
94Fle-548
94Lea-47
94Pac-388
94Pin-176
94PinArtP-176
94PinMusC-176
94Sco-162
94ScoGolR-162
94StaClu-14
94StaCluFDI-14
94StaCluGR-14
94StaCluMOP-14
94Top-78
94TopGol-78
94TopSpa-78
94Ult-525
94UppDec-366
94UppDecED-366
95Baz-67
95ColCho-248
95ColChoGS-248
95ColChoSS-248
95Don-322
95DonPreP-322
95DonTopotO-284
95Fla-378
95Fle-357
95Lea-237
95Pac-272
95Pin-59
95PinArtP-59
95PinMusC-59
95Sco-488
95ScoGolR-488
95ScoPlaTS-488
95StaClu-266
95StaCluFDI-266
95StaCluMOP-266
95StaCluSTWS-266
95Top-74
95TopCyb-51
95Ult-193
95UltGolM-193
96ColCho-216
96ColChoGS-216
96ColChoSS-216
96Don-156
96DonPreP-156
96EmoXL-225
96ExpDis-16
96Fin-B132
96FinRef-B132
96Fla-312
96Fle-465
96FleTif-465
96LeaSigA-197
96LeaSigAG-197
96LeaSigAS-197
96Pac-119
96PacPri-P43
96PacPriG-P43
96Sco-431
96StaClu-167
96StaCluEPB-167
96StaCluEPG-167
96StaCluEPS-167
96StaCluMOP-167
96Top-186
96TopGal-47
96TopGalPPI-47
96Ult-235
96UltGolM-235
96UppDec-393
97Bow-61
97BowInt-61
97Cir-306
97CirRav-306
97ColCho-289
97Fin-274
97FinRef-274
97FlaSho-A84
97FlaSho-B84
97FlaSho-C84
97FlaShoLC-84
97FlaShoLC-B84
97FlaShoLC-C84
97FlaShoLCM-A84
97FlaShoLCM-B84
97FlaShoLCM-C84
97Fle-385
97Fle-665
97FleTif-385
97FleTif-665
97Lea-82
97LeaFraM-82
97LeaFraMDC-82
97Pac-351
97PacLigB-351
97PacSil-351
97Sco-460
97ScoHobR-460
97ScoResC-460
97ScoShoS-460
97ScoShoSAP-460
97SP-42
97StaClu-148
97StaCluMOP-148
97Top-26
97Ult-312
97UltGolME-312
97UltPlaME-312
97UppDec-527
Rojas, Mike
83IdaFalAT-17
93BirBarF-1210
Rojas, Minnie
67CokCapDA-33
67OPC-104
67Top-104
68Top-305
68TopVen-305
69Top-502
Rojas, Olinto
76VenLeaS-172
80VenLeaS-139
Rojas, Ricky
86Ft.MyeRP-23
87Ft.MyeRP-20
88EasLeaAP-36
88VerMarP-959
89WilBilS-19
90Bes-73
90WilBilB-21
90WilBilP-1058
90WilBilS-22
91CalCanLD-71
91CalCanP-516
91LinDriAAA-71
92LonTigF-631
92LonTigS-417
93LinVenB-81
Rojas, Roberto
92BriTigF-1428
93FayGenC-21
93FayGenF-143
93LimRocDWB-38
93SouAtlLAGF-17
94LakTigC-18
94LakTigF-3050
Rojas, Wilberto
90St.CatBJP-3478
Rojek, Stan
47PM1StaP1-189
49Bow-135
49EurSta-171
50Bow-86
50PirTeal-19
50RoyDes-15A
50RoyDes-15B
51Bow-166
52Bow-137
52NatTeaL-26
52Top-163
83TopRep5-163
90DodTar-686
Rokosz, Keith
77AppFoxT-21
Roland, James
63Top-522
64Top-341
64TopVen-341
65OPC-171
65Top-171
68Top-276
68TopVen-276
69Top-336
70Top-719
71MLBOffS-524
71OPC-642
71Top-642
72OPC-464
72Top-464
78TwiFri-43
92YanWIZ7-136
93RanKee-36
Roland, William
95SpoIndTI-22
Roldan, Sal
88MiaMarS-21
88SalLakCTTI-27
Rolen, Scott
94ClaGolF-120
94SpaPhiF-1731
94SparPhiC-1
95Bes-89
95Bes-105
95Bow-271
95BowBes-B87
95BowBesR-B87
95BowGolF-271
95Exc-246
95ReaPhiELC-31
95SPML-130
95SPMLA-22
95SPMLDtS-DS13
95UppDecML-78
95UppDecMLOP-OP21
96BesAutSA-62
96Bow-114
96BowBes-145
96BowBesAR-145
96BowBesMI-3
96BowBesMIAR-3
96BowBesMIR-3
96BowBesR-145
96Exc-212
96ExcCli-9
96LeaSig-122
96LeaSigPPG-122
96LeaSigPPP-122
96ReaPhiB-21
96Top-434
97Bow-294
97BowBes-194
97BowBesA-194
97BowBesAAR-194
97BowBesAR-194
97BowBesBC-BC15
97BowBesBCAR-BC15
97BowBesBCR-BC15
97BowBesP-12
97BowBesPAR-12
97BowBesPR-12
97BowBesR-194
97BowCerBIA-CA70
97BowCerGIA-CA70
97BowChr-202
97BowChrI-202
97BowChrIR-202
97BowChrR-202
97BowChrSHR-SHR11
97BowChrSHRR-SHR11
97BowInt-294
97BowScoHR-11
97Cir-283
97CirEmeA-283
97CirEmeAR-AU5
97CirFasT-9
97CirRav-283
97ColCho-15
97ColChoBS-4
97ColChoBSGS-4
97ColChoNF-NF39
97ColChoNF-NF40
97ColChoTotT-T23
97Don-357
97DonEli-57
97DonEliGS-57
97DonEliTotC-5
97DonEliTotC-P5
97DonEliTotCDC-5
97DonFraFea-13
97DonLim-36
97DonLim-72
97DonLimFotG-63
97DonLimLE-36
97DonLimLE-72
97DonPre-160
97DonPre-198
97DonPreCttC-160
97DonPreCttC-198
97DonPreP-357
97DonPrePGold-357
97DonRatR-3
97DonRooDK-3
97DonRooDKC-3
97Fin-133
97FinEmb-133
97FinEmbR-133
97FinRef-133
97FlaSho-A6
97FlaSho-B6
97FlaSho-C6
97FlaShoLC-6
97FlaShoLC-B6
97FlaShoLC-C6
97FlaShoLCM-A6
97FlaShoLCM-B6
97FlaShoLCM-C6
97FlaShoWotF-19
97Fle-418
97FleNewH-11
97FleRooS-18
97FleTif-418
97Lea-174
97LeaFraM-174
97LeaFraMDC-174
97LeaGolS-29
97LeaLeaotN-13
97MetUni-205
97MetUniEAR-AU5
97MetUniMfG-9
97NewPin-172
97NewPin-200
97NewPinAP-172
97NewPinAP-200
97NewPinMC-172
97NewPinMC-200
97NewPinPP-172
97NewPinPP-200
97PacPriGotD-GD186
97PinCer-112
97PinCerMBlu-112
97PinCerMG-112
97PinCerMR-112
97PinCerR-112
97PinIns-132
97PinInsCE-132
97PinInsDE-132
97PinTotCPB-112
97PinTotCPG-112
97PinTotCPR-112
97PinX-P-134
97PinX-PMoS-134
97Sco-474
97ScoHobR-474
97ScoResC-474
97ScoShoS-474
97ScoShoSAP-316
97ScoShoSAP-474
97Sel-102
97SelArtP-102
97SelRegG-102
97SelRooR-13
97SelToootT-17
97SelToootTMB-17
97SkyE-X-89
97SkyE-XC-89
97SkyE-XEAR-AU5
97SkyE-XEC-89
97SkyE-XSD2-11
97SP-135
97SPInsI-18
97SpoIll-22
97SpoIllEE-22
97SPSpeF-46
97SPSpxF-10
97SPSPxFA-10
97SPx-39
97SPxBro-39
97SPxGraF-39
97SPxSil-39
97SPxSte-39
97StaClu-172
97StaClu-193
97StaCluC-CO4
97StaCluM-M38
97StaCluMOP-172
97StaCluMOP-193
97StaCluMOP-M38
97Stu-155
97StuAut-2
97StuHarH-22
97StuPor8-24
97StuPrePG-155
97StuPrePS-155
97Top-268
97TopAwel-AI18

97TopChr-96
97TopChrR-96
97TopGal-154
97TopGalPPI-154
97TopStaFAS-FAS4
97Ult-255
97UltAutE-3
97UltGolME-255
97UltPlaME-255
97UltRooR-10
97UppDec-229
97UppDecBCP-BC3
95UppDecMLFS-78
97UppDecU-58
97UppDecUGN-GN19
97Zen-49
97Zen8x1-24
97Zen8x1D-24
Rolen, Steve
90CliGiaB-25
90CliGiaP-2559
91Cla/Bes-112
91SanJosGC-11
91SanJosGP-20
92SanJosGC-3
Rolfe, Red (Robert)
34BatR31-22
34BatR31-181
34DiaStaR-29
34DiaStaR-104
34Gou-94
35GouPuzR-8E
35GouPuzR-9E
36GouWidPPR-A90
36OveCanR-39
36WorWidGV-38
41DouPlaR-65
42GilRazL-1
46SpoExcW-8-12
51Bow-319
52Top-296
71FleWorS-34
72FleFamF-22
75YanDyn1T-37
75YanDyn1T-52
80YanGreT-3
83TopRep5-296
87SpoCubG-2
92ConTSN-576
92YanWIZA-68
Rolish, Chad
94SouOreAC-23
94SouOreAF-3621
Rolison, Nate
96KanCouCTI-24
96KanCouCUTI-11
96MauStiHWB-29
97Bow-197
97BowChr-184
97BowChrI-184
97BowChrIR-184
97BowChrR-184
97BowInt-197
Rolland, Dave
82BirBarT-13
86DayBealP-23
87SanJosBP-15
Rollin, Rondal
84EvaTriT-3
86BirBarTI-28
87BirBarB-7
87SouLeaAJ-2
90BirBarDGB-29
Rollings, Bill
79TulDriT-23
Rollings, Red (William R.)
33Gou-88
34GouCanV-40
Rollins, Jimmy
96AppLeaAB-25
96MarPhiB-21
Rollins, Michael
92DavLipB-21
93DavLipB-18
Rollins, Pep (Patrick)
91UtiBluSC-28
91UtiBluSP-3250
Rollins, Rich
47Exh-196
61TwiCloD-23
62Top-596
63Fle-24
63Jel-4
63Pos-4
63SalMetC-49
63Top-110
63TwiJayP-10
64Baz-10
64ChatheY-44
64Top-8
64Top-270
64TopCoi-51
64TopSta-52
64TopStaU-65
64TopVen-8
64TopVen-270
64TwiJayP-10
65ChaTheY-45
65OPC-90
65Top-90
66Top-473
66TwiFaiG-14
67CokCapTw-8
67DexPre-180
67OPC-98
67Top-98
68DexPre-67
68Top-243
68TopVen-243
69MilBra-239
69MLBOffS-98
69PilPos-10
69Top-451A
69Top-451B
69TopSta-229
69TopTeaP-9
70BreMcD-25
70BreMil-20
70MLBOffS-276
70Top-652
72MilBra-296
78TCM60I-119
83Pil69G-16
89PacLegI-169
94BreMilB-266
Rolls, Damian
96BesAutS1RP-FR10
96YakBeaTI-29
Rolls, David
88EugEmeB-12
90EugEmeGS-25
91SalLakTP-3213
91SalLakTSP-9
92ChaRanC-13
92ChaRanF-2228
93TulDriF-2736
94TulDriF-247
94TulDriTI-19
93TulDriTI-24
Rolocut, Brian
93GreFalDSP-12
94YakBeaC-17
94YakBeaF-3847
95SanBerSTI-22
96VerBeaDB-25
Romagna, Randy
83KinBluJTI-21
85KinBluJT-14
86KinEagP-21
Roman, Bob
77SpaPhiT-20
Roman, Dan
87OneYanP-7
88Ft.LauYS-20
89Ft.LauYS-23
92EriSaiC-11
92EriSaiF-1622
93LetMouF-4149
93LetMouSP-16
93Top-782
93TopGol-782
93TopInaM-782
93TopMic-782
Roman, Jose
81BatTroT-3
82WatIndF-24
83WatIndF-12
84BufBisT-8
85Fle-646
85MaiGuiT-13
86IndTeal-35
86MaiGuiP-18
87BufBisP-21
87TidTidP-23
87TidTidT-29
88MetColP-47
88TidTidCa-25
88TidTidCM-9
88TidTidP-1601
Roman, Junior
77WatIndT-18
78WauMetT-23
92GulCoaMF-3497
Roman, Luis
85DomLeaS-107
Roman, Melvin
94EveGiaC-24
94EveGiaF-3661
Roman, Miguel
81BatTroT-26
83WatIndF-13
86IndTeal-36
86WatIndP-20
87WilBilP-13
88JacMetGS-17
Roman, Ray
87ReaPhiP-11
88ReaPhiP-885
Roman, Vince
90AshTouC-22
90AubAstB-10
90AubAstP-3405
91AshTouP-580
92OscAstC-24
92OscAstF-2544
93QuaCitRBC-19
93QuaCitRBF-114
Roman, William A.
65Top-493
Romanick, Ron
81RedPioT-5
82HolMilT-8
83NasAngT-6
84AngSmo-23
84FleUpd-101
84TopTra-102T
84TopTraT-102T
85AngSmo-11
85Don-451
85Fle-309
85OPC-280
85Top-579
85TopSti-231
85TopTif-579
86AngSmo-11
86Don-85
86Fle-166
86FleMin-34
86FleStiC-100
86Lea-81
86OPC-76
86Top-733
86TopSti-180
86TopTif-733
87ColCliP-21
87ColCliP-23
87ColCliT-8
87OPC-136
87Top-136
87TopTif-136
88StoPorCLC-176
88StoPorP-731
94RivPilCLC-30
95PorCitRTI-22
Romano, Andy
89MajLeaM-5
89MajLeaM-11
Romano, James
52Par-73
90DodTar-1056
Romano, Jason
97TopSta-111
97TopStaAM-111
Romano, John
59Top-138
59TopVen-138
60IndJayP-10
60Top-323
61Kah-38
61Pos-67A
61Pos-67B
61SevElev-6
61Top-5
61TopMagR-19
61TopStal-142
62Baz-31
62IndJayP-12
62Jel-42
62Kah-36
62Pos-42
62PosCan-42
62SalPlaC-94
62ShiPlaC-94
62Top-330
62TopBuc-78
62TopStal-40
63Baz-18
63IndJayP-11
63Jel-76
63Pos-76
63SalMetC-46
63Top-72
63Top-392
63TopStil-38
64Baz-18
64IndJayP-10
64Kah-25
64Top-515
64TopCoi-9
64TopGia-59
64TopSta-48
64TopStaU-66
64TopTatl-66
65OPC-17
65Top-17
65TopEmbl-10
65WhiSoxJP-9
66Top-199
66Top-413
66TopVen-199
67OPC-196
67Top-196
Romano, Mike
94HagSunC-21
94HagSunF-2729
94SouAtlLAF-SAL18
95DunBluJTI-22
96KnoSmoB-22
Romano, Scott
90Bes-270
90GreHorB-18
90GreHorP-2670
90GreHorS-20
90OneYanP-3373
91GreHorP-3067
92ForLauYC-15
92ForLauYTI-28
92Ft.LauYF-2622
93GreHorC-19
93GreHorF-896
94FloStaLAF-FSL25
94TamYanC-21
94TamYanF-2395
95AusFut-12
95NorNavTI-34
95SPML-116
95UppDecML-94
95UppDecMLFS-94
Romano, Thomas
82MadMusF-28
83AlbA'sT-19
84TacTigC-77
85TacTigC-131
86IndIndTI-7
87IndIndTI-14
88BlaYNPRWLU-10
88BufBisC-13
88BufBisP-1485
88BufBisTI-4
89BufBisC-21
89BufBisP-1670
Romanoli, Paul
92SprCarC-7
92SprCarF-864
93St.PetCC-21
93St.PetCF-2626
Romanov, Vitalyi
89EasLeaDDP-DD2
Romanovsky, Mike
86PalSprAP-10
86PalSprAP-28
87MidAngP-22
Romay, Willie
89BelMarL-28
91PenPilC-17
91PenPilP-391
94BreCouMF-25
Rombard, Rich
91FayGenP-1187
Romberger, Al
55JetPos-13
Romboli, Curt
96MicBatCB-23
96MidLeaAB-47
Romero, Al
83NasAngT-19
85EdmTraC-25
86EdmTraP-24
Romero, Brian
89ButCopKSP-6
90Bes-301
90GasRanB-7
90GasRanP-2520
90GasRanS-20
90ProAaA-79
90SouAtlLAS-21
90StaFS7-97
91LinDriAA-594
91TulDriLD-594
91TulDriP-2772
91TulDriTI-25
92SkyAA F-265
92TulDriF-2693
92TulDriS-601
93TulDriF-2734
93TulDriTI-25
Romero, Charlie
88QuaCitAGS-24
89PalSprACLC-36
89PalSprAP-470
94CedRapKC-25
94CedRapKF-1126
96CedRapKTI-29
Romero, Ed
76BurBeeT-28
77HolMilT-21
78SpolndC-10
79Top-708
79VanCanT-17
80VanCanT-13
81Top-659
82BrePol-11
82Don-536
82Top-408
83BreGar-15
83BrePol-11
83Don-584
83Fle-44
83Top-271
84BreGar-16
84BrePol-11
84Don-89
84Fle-212
84Nes792-146
84Top-146
84TopTif-146
85BreGar-17
85BrePol-11
85Don-515
85Fle-593
85ThoMcAD-18
85Top-498
85TopTif-498
86Don-455
86Fle-500
86OPC-317
86Top-317
86TopTif-317
86TopTra-95T
86TopTraT-95T
87Don-606
87Fle-42
87FleGlo-42
87OPC-158
87Top-675
87TopTif-675
88BlaYNPRWL-174
88Don-623
88DonTeaBRS-623
88Fle-362
88FleGlo-362
88Sco-259
88ScoGlo-259
88StaLinRS-17
88Top-37
88TopTif-37
89TopTra-105T
89TopTraT-105T
89UppDec-40
90Bow-361
90BowTif-361
90TigCok-20
91LasVegSLD-291
91LasVegSP-244
91LinDriAAA-291
92BreCarT-19
92SpolndC-27
92SpolndF-1310
93WatDiaC-28
93WatDiaF-1784

94BreMilB-267
94SprSulC-28
94SprSulF-2052
96MemChiB-1
Romero, Elbi
87SpaPhiP-19
Romero, Elvis
86BenPhiC-140
87KenTwiP-23
Romero, Esmyel
82RedPioT-9
Romero, Jonathan
92MidAngF-4034
92PalSprAC-6
Romero, Mandy
89AugPirP-498
89SouAtlLAGS-10
90CarLeaA-21
90SalBucS-18
91CarMudLD-103
91CarMudP-1090
91LinDriAA-103
92CarMudF-1185
92CarMudS-141
92ClaFS7-326
92SkyAA F-66
93BufBisF-521
94BufBisF-1841
95WicWraTI-29
96Exc-66
96MemChiB-27
Romero, Philip
91FreStaBS-10
92MarPhiC-9
92MarPhiF-3066
93SpaPhiC-22
93SpaPhiF-1063
Romero, Ramon
78WatIndT-19
79WauTimT-14
80WatIndT-6
81AppFoxT-23
81WatIndT-14
82AppFoxF-6
82WatIndT-9
83BufBisT-9
83GleFalWST-10
83IndPos-30
84BufBisT-16
84MaiGuiT-1
85BufBisT-11
85Ind-25
85IndPol-50
86Don-495
86TolMudHP-20
86Top-208
86TopTif-208
90HagSunDGB-23
Romero, Richard
93LinVenB-244
95LinVen-178
Romero, Robinson
96BriWhiSB-27
Romero, Ronaldo
89GasRanP-1016
89GasRanS-21
90GasRanB-2
90GasRanP-2521
90GasRanS-21
Romero, Tony
87ElmPio(C-21
88ElmPio1C-6
Romero, Willie
93GreFalDSP-20
93LinVenB-243
94BakDodC-21
94VerBeaDC-18
94VerBeaDF-89
95LinVen-15
95SanAntMTI-35
96SanAntMB-22
Romine, Jason
96PorRocB-25
Romine, Kevin
84PawRedST-13
85PawRedST-11
86PawRedSP-19
87PawRedSP-54
87PawRedST-18
87Top-121
87TopTif-121
88DonTeaBRS-NEW
88Fle-363
88FleGlo-363
88Sco-644
88ScoGlo-644
88StaLinRS-18
89Fle-98A
89Fle-98B
89FleGlo-98
89PawRedSC-18
89PawRedSP-682
89PawRedSTI-23
89Sco-541
89UppDec-524
90Bow-273
90BowTif-273
90Don-476
90Fle-286
90FleCan-286
90Lea-414
90RedSoxP-19
90Sco-458
90TopTra-105T
90TopTraT-105T
90TopTVRS-33
90UppDec-441
91Don-290
91Fle-113
91OPC-652
91Sco-116
91ScoPro-116
91Top-652
91TopDesS-652
91TopMic-652
91TopTif-652
Rommel, Ed
20WalMaiW-45
21E121So1-82A
21E121So1-82B
21Exh-146
21Nei-9
22E120-88
22W572-86
22W573-108
22W575-108
23W501-1
23W515-5
23WilChoV-135
25Exh-111
26Exh-111
27YorCarE-55
28W502-55
28Yue-55
29PorandAR-73
30W554-14
33ButCre-20
34DiaMatCSB-155
55Bow-239
77GalGloG-196
87ConSer2-19
94ConTSN-1156
94ConTSNB-1156
Rommell, Rick
23W501-103
80ElPasDT-6
81HolMilT-26
Romo, Enrique
78OPC-186
78Top-278
79OPC-281
79Top-548
80Top-332
81Don-255
81Fle-385
81OPC-28
81Top-28
82Don-59
82Fle-496
82Top-106
83Fle-320
83Top-226
Romo, Robert
87AubAstP-16
Romo, Vicente
69Top-267
70MLBOffS-163
70OPC-191
70Top-191
71MLBOffS-329
71OPC-723
71Top-723
72MilBra-297
72OPC-499
72Top-499
73OPC-381
73Top-381
74OPC-197
74PadDea-23
74Top-197A
74Top-197B
75OPC-274
75Top-274
81RedSoxBG2S-105
83Fle-218
83Top-633
90DodTar-687
Romonosky, John
59SenTealW-15
59Top-267
60Top-87
60TopVen-87
Ronan, Kernan
82CliGiaF-16
83PhoGiaBHN-10
84ShrCapFB-17
89PalSprACLC-62
89PalSprAP-481
90PalSprACLC-229
90PalSprAP-2595
91LinDriAA-450
91MidAngLD-450
91MidAngOHP-24
91MidAngP-451
92MidAngF-4042
93MidAngF-339
94MidAngF-2455
94MidAngOHP-27
95MidAngOHP-29
95MidAngTI-24
96MidAngB-2
96MidAngOHP-22
Ronan, Marc
88AlaGolTI-15
89AlaGol-15
90HamRedB-14
91Cla/Bes-5
91SavCarC-14
91SavCarP-1654
92ClaFS7-270
92SprCarC-2
92SprCarF-872
93St.PetCC-22
93St.PetCF-2630
94LouRedF-2984
95LouRedF-278
96ChaKniB-25
Ronca, Joe
90WelPirP-14
91AugPirC-22
91AugPirP-821
92SalBucF-77
Rondon, Alberto
76DubPacT-31
Rondon, Alex
95WesMicWTI-28
96SouOreTI-17
96WesMicWB-24
Rondon, Alfie
89PacSenL-173
91PacSenL-68
91PacSenL-78
Rondon, Gil (Gilbert)
89PacSenL-196
90KinMetB-26
90KinMetS-27
91MedHatBJP-4118
91MedHatBJSP-24
91PacSenL-11
92MedHatBJSP-28
Rondon, Isidro
86TamTarP-18
Ronk, Jeff
82AmaGolST-7
83BeaGolGT-14
84BeaGolGT-25
Ronning, Al
52Par-49
53ExhCan-56
Ronson, Tod
86EveGiaC-21
86EveGiaPC-27
87CliGiaP-8
88SanJosGCLC-128
88SanJosGP-126
89SalSpuCLC-143
89SalSpuP-1821
Roobarb, Mascot
85WhiSoxC-NNO
86WhiSoxC-NNO
87WhiSoxC-25
88WhiSoxC-25
Rood, Nelson
86TucTorP-19
87TucTorP-15
88TucTorC-13
88TucTorJP-19
88TucTorP-191
90CMC-491
90EdmTraC-14
90EdmTraP-525
90ProAAAF-101
92CliGiaC-27
92CliGiaF-3613
Roof, Gene (Eugene L.)
78St.PetCT-23
79ArkTraT-22
80VenLeaS-118
82Don-615
82LouRedE-25
82Top-561
83Fle-20
83LouRedR-5
84LouRedR-5
85RicBraT-20
86NasSouTI-23
87TolMudHP-22
87TolMudHT-22
88TolMudHP-599
89FayGenP-1577
90FayGenP-2423
90SouAtlLAS-23
91LinDriAA-399
91LonTigLD-399
91LonTigP-1892
93TigGat-28
Roof, Phil
63Top-324
64Top-541
65Top-537
66Top-382
67CokCapAt-9
67DexPre-181
67OPC-129
67Top-129
68Top-484
69MilBra-240
69Top-334
70BreMcD-26
70BreMil-21
70BreTeal-10
70OPC-359
70SunPin-15
70Top-359
71BreTeal-14
71MLBOffS-450
71OPC-22
71Top-22
72MilBra-298
72OPC-201
72Top-201
73OPC-598
73Top-598
74OPC-388
74Top-388
75OPC-576
75Top-576
76OPC-424
76SSP-224
76Top-424
77OPC-121
77Top-392
78PadFamF-27
83OrlTwiT-1
84MarMot-27
85MarMot-27
86MarMot-28
87MarMot-28
90CubMar-28
90TopTVCu-6
91CubMar-NNO
91CubVinL-22
92OrlSunRF-2862
92OrlSunRS-524
93NasXprF-417
94BreMilB-347
94NasXprF-401
Rooker, Dave
83ButCopKT-26
86PriWilPP-22
87HarSenP-4
Rooker, Jim
69Top-376
70OPC-222
70RoyTeal-30
70Top-222
71MLBOffS-428
71OPC-730
71Top-730
71TopCoi-32
72Top-742
74OPC-402
74Top-402
75OPC-148
75Top-148
76OPC-243
76SSP-566
76Top-243
77OPC-161
77PirPosP-23
77Top-82
78Top-308
79Top-584
80Top-694
81Fle-368
93PirNatl-26
Rooker, Michael
88PacEigMO-9
Rookie, Ray the
96MauStiHWB-NNO
Rooks, George
87BucN28-51
87OldJudN-431
Roomes, Rolando
82QuaCitCT-24
83QuaCitCT-27
86WinSpiP-24
87PitCubP-25
88BlaYNPRWLU-36
88TriAAC-7
89Don-577
89Fle-644
89FleGlo-644
89FleUpd-86
89NasSouC-22
89NasSouP-1286
89RedKah-36
89ScoHot1R-37
89ScoRoo-109T
89UppDec-6
90Bow-56
90BowTif-56
90ClaBlu-38
90Don-360
90Fle-432
90FleCan-432
90OPC-364
90PanSti-254
90Sco-417
90Sco100RS-92
90ScoYouSI-22
90Top-364
90TopBig-87
90TopSti-143
90TopTif-364
90UppDec-170
91DenZepP-136
Rooney, Jim
84NewOriT-16
Rooney, Pat
79MemChiT-22
80MemChiT-17
82WicAerTI-15
83WicAerDS-18
84ColCliP-21
84ColCliT-3
85SyrChiT-16
Roosevelt, Franklin Delano
94UppDecTAE-47
Rooster, Rowdy the
95PorCitRTI-21
96PorCitRB-29
Root, Charley H.
28Exh-11
28StaPlaCE-54
29ExhFou-6
29PorandAR-74
30ChiEveAP-8
30SchR33-44
31CubTeal-18
31Exh-6
32CubTeal-20
32OrbPinUP-51
33ButCre-21
33ExhFou-3
33Gou-226
33TatOrb-51
33TatOrbSDR-190
34DiaMatCSB-156
35DiaMatCS3T1-125

36DiaMatCS3T2-20
39CubTeal-21
39GouPreR303A-39
39WorWidGTP-39
41CubTeal-21
60Top-457
77GalGloG-59
80CubGreT-2
88ConSer3-24
91ConTSN-93
92CubOldS-20
Root, Derek
95AubAstTI-3
96QuaCitRB-24
Root, Mitch
91HunCubC-21
91HunCubP-3343
92HunCubC-19
92HunCubF-3157
94JamJamC-21
94JamJamF-3975
95MidLeaA-46
Roper, Brian
89ButCopKSP-3
Roper, Chad
92ClaDraP-46
92FroRowDP-60
92HigSchPLS-22
93ClaFS7-15
93ForMyeMC-1
93ForMyeMF-2665
93StaCluM-177
94Bow-572
94BowBes-B53
94BowBesR-B53
94FloStaLAF-FSL12
94ForMyeMC-21
94ForMyeMF-1175
94UppDecML-243
95HarCitRCTI-22
96HarCitRCB-27
Roper, John
91ChaWheC-9
91ChaWheP-2886
91Cla/Bes-276
91SouAtlLAGP-SAL11
92Bow-528
92ChaLooF-3819
92ChaLooS-194
92ClaFS7-72
92ProFS7-218
92SkyAA F-87
92UppDecML-44
92UppDecML-233
93Bow-34
93ClaFS7-16
93ClaGolF-55
93ExcFS7-29
93FlaWavotF-14
93FleFinE-19
93IndIndF-1487
93SelRoo-34T
93Ult-334
94BowBes-B34
94BowBesR-B34
94Cla-114
94ColC-245
94ColChoGS-245
94ColChoSS-245
94Don-551
94Fla-369
94Fle-423
94IndIndF-1809
94Pin-137
94PinArtP-137
94PinMusC-137
94RedKah-24
94Sco-623
94ScoGolR-623
94StaClu-476
94StaCluFDI-476
94StaCluGR-476
94StaCluMOP-476
94Top-581
94TopGol-581
94TopSpa-581
94Ult-175
94UppDec-68
94UppDecED-68
95ColCho-437
95ColChoGS-437
95ColChoSS-437
95Don-442
95DonPreP-442
95Fin-141
95FinRef-141
95Fla-123
95Fle-444
95Lea-286
95RedKah-24
95Sco-356
95ScoGolR-356
95ScoPlaTS-356
95StaClu-269
95StaCluFDI-269
95StaCluMOP-269
95StaCluSTWS-269
95Top-604
95TopCyb-375
95Ult-369
95UltGolM-369
95UppDec-171
95UppDecED-171
95UppDecEDG-171
96ChaLooB-25
Roque, Francisco
96HelBreTI-21
Roque, Jorge
96NewJerCB-23
Roque, Jorge Vargas
72OPC-316
72Top-316
73OPC-606
73Top-606
Roque, Rafael
92GulCoaMF-3479
93KinMetC-20
93KinMetF-3794
95StLucMTI-28
96BinBeeB-24
Rorex, Troy
92DavLipB-22
93DavLipB-19
Rosa, Julio
88BriTigP-1869
89FayGenP-1587
Rosado, Ed (Edwin)
88MarPhiS-28
89BatCliP-1944
89BlaYNPRWL-124
89SpaPhiP-1029
89SpaPhiS-20
90ClePhiS-19
91LinDriAA-516
91ReaPhiLD-516
91ReaPhiP-1373
92ReaPhiF-579
92ReaPhiS-541
93ReaPhiF-298
Rosado, Jose
95WilBluRTI-26
96Bow-229
96OmaRoyB-25
96WicWraB-12
97BowBes-106
97BowBesAR-106
97BowBesR-106
97Cir-11
97CirRav-11
97ColCho-354
97Don-366
97DonLim-172
97DonLimLE-172
97DonPre-89
97DonPreCttC-89
97DonPreP-366
97DonPrePGold-366
97Fin-268
97FinRef-268
97Fle-122
97FleTif-122
97MetUni-97
97RoyPol-20
97Sco-286
97ScoPreS-286
97ScoShoS-286
97ScoShoSAP-286
97SpoIll-72
97SpoIllEE-72
97StaClu-83
97StaCluM-M26
97StaCluMOP-83
97StaCluMOP-M26
97Top-409
97TopChr-144
97TopChrR-144
97TopGal-174
97TopGalPPI-174
97TopSta-97
97TopStaAM-97
97Ult-71
97UltGolME-71
97UltPlaME-71
97UppDec-388
Rosado, Juan
96VerExpB-24
Rosado, Papo (Luis)
78TidTidT-22
79SyrChiT-18
79SyrChiTI-2
80TidTidT-22
84RocRedWT-12
85RocRedWT-3
91MetWIZ-334
Rosar, Buddy (Warren)
41Gou-4
46SpoExcW-6-6
48BluTin-19
48Bow-10
49Bow-138
49Lea-128
49PhiBul-44
50Bow-136
51Bow-236
63GadFunC-29
75YanDyn1T-38
76TayBow4-83
79DiaGre-15
84TCMPla1-23
92YanWIZA-69
Rosar, Greg
94ButCopKSP-9
Rosario, Alfonso
78CedRapGT-24
85DomLeaS-207
Rosario, David
87PeoChiP-16
88BlaYNPRWL-140
88WinSpiS-15
89BlaYNPRWL-14
89BlaYNPRWLU-55
89ChaKniTI-13
91IowCubLD-215
91IowCubP-1060
91LinDriAAA-215
92ColCliF-349
92ColCliP-8
92ColCliS-114
92SkyAAAF-54
Rosario, Eliezel
90AshTouP-2747
95IdaFalBTI-2
Rosario, Felix
94MedHatBJF-3696
94MedHatBJSP-9
95StCatSTI-23
Rosario, Francisco
88SavCarP-358
90MarPhiP-3194
Rosario, Gabriel
91MedHatBJP-4108
91MedHatBJSP-15
92MyrBeaHC-22
92MyrBeaHF-2205
93DunBluJC-18
93DunBluJFFN-20
Rosario, Jimmy (Angel)
72OPC-366
72Top-366
74PhoGiaC-87
75SacSolC-12
76SpoIndC-2
94BreMilB-348
Rosario, Jose
78DunBluJT-20
Rosario, Jossy
87WytCubP-7
89ChaWheB-8
89ChaWheP-1750
Rosario, Julio
86ElmPioRSP-17
87ElmPio(C-8
88ElmPio1C-7
88ElmPioC-18
88WinHavRSS-22
89ElmPioP-16
93GreFalDSP-8
Rosario, Liriano
94KnoSmoF-1311
Rosario, Maximo
83AndBraT-16
Rosario, Mel
97Bow-420
97BowChr-280
97BowChrI-280
97BowChrIR-280
97BowChrR-280
97BowInt-420
Rosario, Melvin
86KinEagP-22
87Ft.LauYP-26
88AlbYanP-1343
88BlaYNPRWL-49
89BlaYNPRWL-53
89Ft.LauYS-24
90ChaLooGS-26
92SpoIndC-14
92SpoIndF-1297
93SpoIndC-18
93SpoIndF-3596
93WatDiaC-25
93WatDiaF-1778
96HigDesMB-24
Rosario, Ruben
96JohCitCTI-28
Rosario, Sal
75BurBeeT-22
Rosario, Santiago
77FriOneYW-108
Rosario, Simon
76DubPacT-32
77CocAstT-22
78DayBeaAT-22
80ColAstT-14
81TucTorT-8
84DurBulT-1
85DomLeaS-201
85GreBraTI-14
Rosario, Victor
85ElmPioT-20
86GreHorP-21
87GreHorP-19
88MarPhiS-29
89ReaPhiS-20
89ScrRedBC-23
89ScrRedBP-710
90CMC-241
90ProAAAF-309
90ScrRedBC-15
90ScrRedBP-607
91Fle-701
91LinDriAAA-440
91RicBraBC-21
91RicBraLD-440
91RicBraP-2577
91RicBraTI-11
91TopDeb90-135
92SkyAAAF-267
92TolMudHF-1051
92TolMudHS-595
93LimRocDWB-135
Roscoe, Greg
88WatIndP-691
89KinIndS-21
89WatIndS-20
90CanIndB-23
90CanIndP-1308
90CanIndS-15
91CanIndLD-93
91CanIndP-980
91LinDriAA-93
92ColSprSSF-750
92ColSprSSS-94
Rose, Bobby (Robert)
86QuaCitAP-29
88MidLeaAGS-23
88QuaCitAGS-14
89MidAngGS-27
89TexLeaAGS-3
90Bow-293
90BowTif-293
90ClaUpd-T41
90CMC-492
90EdmTraC-15
90EdmTraP-526
90Fle-651
90FleCan-651
90ProAAAF-102
90Sco-604
90TopDeb89-106
90UppDec-77
91Bow-206
91EdmTraLD-169
91EdmTraP-1524
91Fle-324
91LinDriAAA-169
92AngPol-16
92Don-90
92Fle-68
92Lea-250
92OPC-652
92OPCPre-169
92Sco-558
92StaClu-79
92Top-652
92TopGol-652
92TopGolW-652
92TopMic-652
92Ult-330
92UppDec-611
Rose, Brian
94BenRocF-3592
94StaCluDP-35
94StaCluDPFDI-35
95AshTouUTI-8
95MicBatCTI-23
96Bow-357
96TreThuB-13
97Bow-105
97Bow98ROY-ROY14
97BowBes-144
97BowBesAR-144
97BowBesR-144
97BowChr-125
97BowChr1RC-ROY14
97BowChr1RCR-ROY14
97BowChrI-125
97BowChrIR-125
97BowChrR-125
97BowInt-105
97BenRocC-20
Rose, Carl
86WatPirP-19
Rose, Don
73OPC-178
73Top-178
75PhoGiaC-21
75PhoGiaCK-7
91MetWIZ-335
Rose, Guy
71RicBraTI-16
Rose, Heath
92BurAstF-545
93QuaCitRBC-20
Rose, Kevin
79NewCoPT-20
Rose, Mark
91OneYanP-4169
92GreHorC-27
92GreHorF-798
93GreHorF-905
94OneYanC-27
Rose, Mike
96AubDouB-23
Rose, Pete
56RedBurB-21
63RedEnq-32
63RedFreBC-23
63Top-537
64Kah-26
64RedJayP-12
64Top-125
64TopCoi-82
64TopVen-125
65Kah-37
65OPC-207
65RedEnq-25
65Top-207
66Baz-38
66Kah-27
66OPC-30
66Top-30
66TopRubI-83
66TopVen-30
67Baz-38
67CokCapA-2
67CokCapNLA-30
67CokCapR-13
67DexPre-182
67Kah-32
67Top-430
67TopGiaSU-1
67TopVen-270
68AtlOilPBCC-39
68Baz-6
68Baz-15
68Top-230
68TopActS-5C
68TopGamI-30
68TopPla-21

68TopPos-23
68TopVen-230
69CitMetC-14
69KelPin-15
69MilBra-241
69MLBOffS-135
69MLBPin-55
69NabTeaF-20
69OPC-2
69OPC-120
69Top-2
69Top-120
69Top-424
69TopDec-21
69TopDecI-36
69TopFou-19
69TopSta-29
69TopSup-41
69TopTeaP-20
69TraSta-54
70DayDaiNM-1
70Kel-2
70MilBra-24
70MLBOffS-35
70OPC-61
70OPC-458
70Top-61
70Top-458
70Top-580
70TopBoo-15
70TopSup-34
70TraSta-1A
71AllBasA-21
71BazNumT-32
71BazUnn-5
71Kel-65
71MilDud-60
71MLBOffS-68
71MLBOffS-573
71OPC-100
71Top-100
71Top-511
71TopCoi-101
71TopGreM-15
71TopSup-20
71TopTat-113
72Dia-63
72Kel-6
72MilBra-299
72ProStaP-21
72Top-559
72Top-560
72TopPos-11
73Kel2D-6
73LinPor-59
73OPC-130
73Top-130
73TopCanL-44
74Kel-38
74NewYorNTDiS-22
74OPC-201
74OPC-300
74OPC-336
74Top-201
74Top-300
74Top-336
74TopDecE-16
74TopSta-30
75BlaBacD-5
75Hos-29
75HosTwi-29
75Kel-11
75OPC-211
75OPC-320
75SSPPuzB-22
75Top-211
75Top-320
76CraDis-51
76Hos-66
76Kel-55
76LinSup-97
76OPC-240
76RedIceL-12
76RedKro-16
76RedPos-15
76SafSupLB-4
76SafSupLB-6
76SafSupLB-10
76SafSupLB-13
76SafSupLB-15
76SSP-41
76Top-240
77BurCheD-204
77Hos-8
77Kel-20
77MSADis-51
77OPC-240
77PepGloD-43
77RCColC-56
77Spo-804
77Top-277
77Top-450
77TopCloS-38
78Hos-128
78OPC-100
78OPC-240
78Pep-21
78RCColC-3
78SSP270-132
78Top-5
78Top-20
78WifBalD-63
79Hos-144
79Kel-22
79OPC-343
79PhiBurK-13
79PhiTeaI-8
79Top-204
79Top-650
79TopCom-28
80BurKinPHR-21
80Kel-35
80OPC-282
80PhiBurK-4
80Top-4
80Top-540
80TopSup-19
81AllGamPI-98
81CokTeaS-104
81Don-131
81Don-131B
81Don-251
81Don-371
81Dra-3
81Fle-1
81Fle-645
81Fle-645B
81FleStiC-43
81FleStiC-74
81Kel-63
81MSAMinD-27
81OPC-180
81PerAll-7
81PerCreC-5
81Squ-11
81Top-180
81Top-205
81TopScr-62
81TopSti-200
81TopSupHT-86
81TopSupN-12
82Don-1
82Don-168
82Don-585
82Dra-28
82FBIDis-18
82Fle-256
82Fle-640
82FleSta-51
82FleSta-107
82FleSta-109
82K-M-24
82K-M-44
82Kel-18
82MonNew-13
82OPC-24
82OPC-337
82OPC-361
82PerAll-16
82PerAllG-16
82PerCreC-9
82PerCreCG-9
82Squ-12
82Top-4
82Top-337
82Top-636
82Top-780
82Top-781
82TopSti-78
82TopSti-117
82TopSti-121
83AllGamPI-98
83Don-42
83DonActA-31
83Dra-24
83Fle-171
83Fle-634
83FleSta-168
83FleSti-143
83FleSti-145
83FleSti-174
83Kel-6
83Oco& SSBG-15
83OPC-100
83OPC-101
83OPC-373
83PerCreC-13
83PerCreCG-13
83PhiPosGM-13
83PhiPosGPaM-7
83PhiTas-25
83Top-100
83Top-101
83Top-397
83TopFol-3
83TopGloS-14
83TopSti-272
83TopStiB-7
83TopTraBP-3
84AllGamPI-68
84Don-61
84DonActAS-54
84DonCha-27
84Dra-27
84ExpPos-26
84ExpStu-17
84Fle-46
84Fle-636
84FleSti-99
84FleSti-119
84FleUpd-102
84FunFooP-4
84MilBra-21
84Nes792-300
84Nes792-701
84Nes792-702
84OCoandSI-30
84OCoandSI-108
84OCoandSI-125
84OCoandSI-134
84OCoandSI-184
84OPC-300
84RalPur-4
84SevCoi-C22
84Top-300
84Top-701
84Top-702
84TopCer-4
84TopGaloC-9
84TopGloS-1
84TopRubD-24
84TopSti-115
84TopTif-300
84TopTif-701
84TopTif-702
84TopTra-103T
84TopTraT-103T
85AllGamPI-98
85Don-254
85Don-641
85DonHig-10
85DonHig-40
85Fle-550
85Fle-640
85FleLimE-29
85FleStaS-1
85FleStaS-2
85FleStaS-3
85Lea-144
85OPC-116
85RedYea-14
85SevCoi-G10
85SpoSam-43
85Top-6
85Top-547
85Top-600
85Top3-D-5
85TopGloS-10
85TopRubD-24
85TopSti-57
85TopSup-32
85TopTif-6
85TopTif-547
85TopTif-600
85Woo-30
86BasStaB-93
86BurKinA-4
86Don-62
86Don-644
86Don-653
86DonAll-34
86DonSupD-27
86Dra-22
86Fle-191
86Fle-628
86Fle-638
86FleFutHoF-1
86FleLeaL-36
86FleLimE-37
86FleMin-40
86FleSlu-29
86FleStiC-101
86Lea-53
86Lea-209
86Lea-260
86MeaGolBB-12
86MeaGolM-9
86MeaGolSB-8
86MSAJifPD-11
86OPC-1
86OPCBoxB-N
86QuaGra-11
86RedTexG-14A
86RedTexG-14B
86RedTexG-14C
86SevCoi-C2
86SevCoi-E2
86SevCoi-S2
86SevCoi-S16
86SevCoi-W2
86Spo-50
86Spo-51
86Spo-56
86Spo-58
86Spo-69
86Spo-130
86Spo-138
86Spo-181
86Spo-182
86SpoDecG-60
86SpoRoo-46
86Top-1
86Top-2
86Top-3
86Top-4
86Top-5
86Top-6
86Top-7
86Top-206
86Top-741
86Top3-D-22
86TopGaloC-11
86TopGloS-51
86TopRos-1
86TopRos-2
86TopRos-3
86TopRos-4
86TopRos-5
86TopRos-6
86TopRos-7
86TopRos-8
86TopRos-9
86TopRos-10
86TopRos-11
86TopRos-12
86TopRos-13
86TopRos-14
86TopRos-15
86TopRos-16
86TopRos-17
86TopRos-18
86TopRos-19
86TopRos-20
86TopRos-21
86TopRos-22
86TopRos-23
86TopRos-24
86TopRos-25
86TopRos-26
86TopRos-27
86TopRos-28
86TopRos-29
86TopRos-30
86TopRos-31
86TopRos-32
86TopRos-33
86TopRos-34
86TopRos-35
86TopRos-36
86TopRos-37
86TopRos-38
86TopRos-39
86TopRos-40
86TopRos-41
86TopRos-42
86TopRos-43
86TopRos-44
86TopRos-45
86TopRos-46
86TopRos-47
86TopRos-48
86TopRos-49
86TopRos-50
86TopRos-51
86TopRos-52
86TopRos-53
86TopRos-54
86TopRos-55
86TopRos-56
86TopRos-57
86TopRos-58
86TopRos-59
86TopRos-60
86TopRos-61
86TopRos-62
86TopRos-63
86TopRos-64
86TopRos-65
86TopRos-66
86TopRos-67
86TopRos-68
86TopRos-69
86TopRos-70
86TopRos-71
86TopRos-72
86TopRos-73
86TopRos-74
86TopRos-75
86TopRos-76
86TopRos-77
86TopRos-78
86TopRos-79
86TopRos-80
86TopRos-81
86TopRos-82
86TopRos-83
86TopRos-84
86TopRos-85
86TopRos-86
86TopRos-87
86TopRos-88
86TopRos-89
86TopRos-90
86TopRos-91
86TopRos-92
86TopRos-93
86TopRos-94
86TopRos-95
86TopRos-96
86TopRos-97
86TopRos-98
86TopRos-99
86TopRos-100
86TopRos-101
86TopRos-102
86TopRos-103
86TopRos-104
86TopRos-105
86TopRos-106
86TopRos-107
86TopRos-108
86TopRos-109
86TopRos-110
86TopRos-111
86TopRos-112
86TopRos-113
86TopRos-114
86TopRos-115
86TopRos-116
86TopRos-117
86TopRos-118
86TopRos-119
86TopRos-120
86TopSti-1
86TopSti-2
86TopSti-134
86TopSup-46
86TopTat-6
86TopTif-1
86TopTif-2
86TopTif-3
86TopTif-4
86TopTif-5
86TopTif-6
86TopTif-7
86TopTif-206
86TopTif-741
86TopWaxBC-N
86TruVal-4
86Woo-29

87ClaGam-1
87ClaUpdY-103
87Don-186
87Fle-213
87FleBasA-37
87FleExcS-38
87FleGlo-213
87FleHotS-32
87FleLeaL-37
87FleLimE-36
87FleRecS-33
87FleStiC-102
87K-M-19
87KraFoo-34
87Lea-129
87OPC-200
87RedFolSB-64
87RedKah-NNO
87Spo-25
87SpoRea-19
87SpoRea-22
87SpoSupD-17
87SpoTeaP-4
87Top-200
87Top-281
87Top-393
87TopGloS-41
87TopSti-139
87TopTif-200
87TopTif-281
87TopTif-393
88ClaBlu-226
88GreBasS-79
88K-M-22
88RedKah-14
88Top-475
88TopTif-475
89ClaLigB-71
89KahComC-1
89RedKah-14
89Top-505
89TopBasT-34
89TopTif-505
90HOFStiB-84
91FouBal-5
91TopRut-7
92DynRos-1
92DynRos-2
92DynRos-3
92DynRos-4
92DynRos-5
92DynRos-6
92DynRos-7
92DynRos-8
92DynRos-9
92DynRos-10
92DynRos-11
92DynRos-12
92DynRos-13
92DynRos-14
93Yoo-17
94UppDecTAE-77
96Red76K-3

Rose, Pete Jr.
82Fle-640
86TopRos-5
86TopRos-83
89EriOriS-22
89FreKeyS-27
89Sta-175
90ClaBlu-75
90FreKeyTI-20
91SarWhiSC-18
91SarWhiSP-1120
92ColRedC-1
92ColRedF-2420
93ClaFS7-17
93KinIndC-1
93KinIndF-2257
93KinIndTI-23
94HicCraC-20
94HicCraF-2185
95MidLeaA-47
96BirBarB-12

Rose, Scott
91ModA'sC-13
91ModA'sP-3087
92MadMusC-23
92MadMusF-1233
93SanBerSF-768
94HunStaF-1330
95HunStaTI-22

Rose, Tyler
86TopRos-56

Roseboro, Jaime
86LitFalMP-24
87ColMetP-6
88ColMetGS-24
89St.LucMS-22
89Sta-117
90Bow-134
90BowTif-134
90JacMetGS-10
90TopTVM-56
91TidTidP-2525
92HarSenF-474

Roseboro, Johnny
58Top-42
59DodMor-10
59DodTeal-23
59Top-441
60DodBelB-7
60DodJayP-12
60DodMor-10
60DodTeal-16
60DodUniO-16
60MacSta-21
60Top-88
60Top-292
60TopVen-88
61DodBelB-8
61DodJayP-9
61DodUniO-17
61Pos-166A
61Pos-166B
61Top-363
61TopStal-33
62DodBelB-8
62DodJayP-9
62Jel-107
62Pos-107
62PosCan-107
62SalPlaC-133
62ShiPlaC-133
62Top-32
62Top-397
62TopStal-139
62TopVen-32
63Jel-120
63Pos-120
63SalMetC-12
63Top-487
64DodHea-9
64Top-88
64TopVen-88
65DodJayP-11
65DodTeal-18
65Top-405
65TopTral-28
66OPC-189
66Top-189
66TopRubl-84
66TopVen-189
67CokCapD-9
67CokCapDA-9
67Top-365
67TopVen-268
68Baz-7
68DexPre-68
68OPC-65
68Top-65
68TopVen-65
69MilBra-242
69MLBOffS-70
69OPC-218
69Top-218
69TopFou-9
69TopSta-198
69TopTeaP-15
70MLBOffS-285
70SenPolY-9
70Top-655
72MilBra-300
73OPC-421
73Top-421A
73Top-421B
74OPC-276
74Top-276
78TCM60I-185
87DodSmoA-30
88DodSmo-2
89DodSmoG-64
90DodTar-688
90MetColP-46
91RinPosBD2-2
92DodStaTA-1

Roselli, Bob
56Top-131
61Top-529
61WhiSoxTS-14
62Top-363
62WhiSoxTS-18

Rosello, Dave
73WicAerKSB-15
74OPC-607
74Top-607
76OPC-546
76Top-546
77Top-92
78Top-423
80Top-122
81Don-79
82ChaChaT-18
82Don-617
82Fle-377
82Top-724

Roseman, James
87BucN28-63
87FouBasHN-8
87OldJudN-432
88AugBecN-22
88GandBCGCE-34
90KalBatN-49

Rosen, Al
47PM1StaP1-190
49IndTeal-22
50Bow-232
50IndNumN-19
50IndTeal-20
51BerRos-A1
51Bow-187
51R42SmaS-85
51TopRedB-35
52Bow-151
52IndNumN-10
52NatTeaL-27
52StaCalL-74B
52StaCalS-88C
52Top-10
53BowC-8
53IndPenCBP-23
53NorBreL-25
53RedMan-AL24
53Top-135
54DanDee-21
54DixLid-14
54RedHeaF-25
54RedMan-AL12
54Top-15
55ArmCoi-17
55BigLealS-16
55DaiQueS-16
55Ind-7
55IndCarBL-7
55IndGolS-14
55RedMan-AL11
55Top-70
55TopDouH-1
56Top-35
56TopHocF-A8
56TopPin-10
61Top-474
72TopTes5-4
74LauAllG-54
75OPC-191
75Top-191
77GalGloG-35
79TCM50-175
82OhiHaloF-60
83DiaClaS2-73
83TopRep5-10
86IndGreT-4
90PacLeg-78
90SweBasG-39
91SweBasG-78
91TopArc1-135
92ActPacA-70
92BazQua5A-20
93UppDecAH-109
94TedWil-28
94TopArc1-15
94TopArc1G-15
94UppDecAH-67
94UppDecAH1-67

Rosen, David
85OscAstTI-30

Rosen, Goody (Goodwin)
39PlaBal-76
83TCMPla1945-31
90DodTar-689
91RinPosBD2-4

Rosenbalm, Marc
92SanBerC-9

Rosenberg, Charlie Phil
28W513-99

Rosenberg, Steve
87AlbYanP-1
88BlaYNPRWL-30
88VanCanC-3
88VanCanP-754
89Don-219
89FleUpd-22
89Top-616
89TopTif-616
89UppDec-715
89WhiSoxC-24
90AlbDecGB-30
90CMC-638
90Don-253
90Fle-547
90FleCan-547
90OPC-379
90ProAAAF-167
90Sco-523
90Top-379
90TopTif-379
90UppDec-522
90VanCanC-11
90VanCanP-489
91LasVegSLD-292
91LasVegSP-234
91LinDriAAA-292
91PadSmo-32

Rosenbohm, Jim
92ClaDraP-30
92FroRowDP-92
93CliGiaC-1
93CliGiaF-2489
93MidLeaAGF-41
93Top-667
93TopGol-667
93TopInaM-667
93TopMic-667
94CliLumF-1979
95AubAstTI-16
96PitMetB-24
94CliLumC-20

Rosenfeld, Max
90DodTar-1057

Rosenfield, Dave
88TidTidCa-5

Rosengren, John
92BriTigC-9
93NiaFalRF-3388
94ExcFS7-60
94FloStaLAF-FSL14
94LakTigC-19
94LakTigF-3035
95JacSunTI-24
96JacSunB-25

Rosengren, Rosey (John)
92BriTigF-1410
95Exc-52

Rosenkranz, Terry
92ButCopKSP-12

Rosenthal, Larry
39WhiSoxTI-15
40WhiSoxL-15
79DiaGre-130
94ConTSN-1309
94ConTSNB-1309

Rosenthal, Todd
92SalLakTSP-11

Rosenthal, Wayne
87GasRanP-18
88ChaRanS-21
89ChaRanS-20
89TulDriTI-21
90TulDriP-1153
91LinDriAAA-321
91OklCit8LD-321
91OklCit8P-178
92Fle-318
92OklCit8F-1915
92OklCit8S-304
92OPC-584
92OPCPre-30
92Sco-749
92SkyAAAF-147
92StaClu-658
92Top-584
92TopDeb91-151
92TopGol-584
92TopGolW-584
92TopMic-584
92Ult-446
93RanKee-313

Rosfelder, Chris
89ElmPioP-17

Rosinski, Brian
80WicAerT-17

Roskom, Bryan
89KenTwiP-1069
89KenTwiS-22
90KenTwiB-15
90KenTwiS-29

Roskos, John
94ClaGolF-74
94ElmPioF-3479
95KanCouCTI-22
95MidLeaA-48
96PorSeaDB-23
94ElmPioC-18

Roslund, John
75QuaCitAT-21

Roso, Jimmy (James)
89BluOriS-17
89Sta-115
90CMC-870
90WauTimB-16
90WauTimP-2129
90WauTimS-20
91KanCouCC-13
91KanCouCP-2660
91KanCouCTI-18
92FreKeyC-24
92FreKeyF-1808
93BowBayF-2191

Ross, Bob (Floyd Robert)
52Top-298
54Top-189
57SeaPop-31
83TopRep5-298
94TopArc1-189
94TopArc1G-189

Ross, Brandi
91HawWomS-13

Ross, Broadswordman
88GooN16-33

Ross, Chelcie
89MajLeaM-6

Ross, Chester
41Gou-31

Ross, Chuck
76BurBeeT-29
77BurBeeT-25
78HolMilT-19

Ross, Dan
89LonTigP-1361

Ross, David
89MarPhiS-27
90BatCliP-3066
91PeoChiC-1
91PeoChiP-1341
91PeoChiTI-12

Ross, Don
47RoyMon-3
49BowPCL-20
83TCMPla1945-13
90DodTar-690

Ross, Duncan C.
88AllandGN-17
88KimN18-37

Ross, Gary Douglas
69Top-404
70Top-694
71MLBOffS-236
71OPC-153
71Top-153
72PadTeal-22
73OPC-112
73Top-112
75HawIslC-16
75IntLeaASB-29
75PacCoaLAB-29
77Top-544
78Top-291
90BenBucL-26
91MadMusP-2131

Ross, Jackie
92HelBreF-1731
92HelBreSP-13
93BelBreC-20
93BelBreF-1725

Ross, Jason
96DanBraB-18

Ross, Jeremy
95ElmPioTI-24
95ElmPioUTI-24

Ross, Joe

89OneYanP-2125
Ross, Mark
82TucTorT-3
84TucTorC-68
85TucTorC-54
86TucTorP-20
87VanCanP-1602
88SyrChiC-5
88SyrChiP-824
89SyrChiC-4
89SyrChiMB-19
89SyrChiP-814
90BufBisC-9
90BufBisP-372
90BufBisTI-22
90CMC-9
90ProAAAF-487
91LinDriAAA-441
91RicBraBC-15
91RicBraLD-441
91RicBraP-2567
91RicBraTI-28
92GreBraF-1169
93IdaFalBF-4052
94IdaFalBSP-29
96MacBraB-28
Ross, Michael
88HamRedP-1727
89SprCarB-10
90ArkTraGS-26
90IBAWorA-37
91LinDriAAA-245
91LouRedLD-245
91LouRedP-2931
92ArkTraF-1139
92ArkTraS-44
Ross, Ron
89NiaFalRP-27
Ross, Sean
87SumBraP-27
88BurBraP-20
89DurBullS-19
89DurBulTI-19
91Cla/Bes-156
91GreBraC-22
91GreBraLD-217
91GreBraP-3017
91LinDriAA-217
92RicBraBB-19
92RicBraF-389
92RicBraRC-18
92RicBraS-440
93ColSprSSF-3100
93PawRedSF-2422
93PawRedSTI-20
97RicBraBC-5
Ross, Tony
94AubAstC-14
94AubAstF-3773
95MidLeaA-49
95QuaCitRBTI-23
96KisCobB-24
Ross, Wallace
87AllandGN-28
Rosselli, Joe
90EveGiaB-11
90EveGiaP-3127
90ProAaA-165
91CliGiaC-6
92CalLeaACL-17
92ClaFS7-250
92SanJosGC-2
92UppDecML-295
92UppDecMLPotY-PY11
93Bow-632
93ClaFS7-58
93ClaGolF-68
94Bow-575
94ShrCapF-1604
94Ult-593
95Bow-107
95Exc-294
95Fla-428
95Fle-588
95GiaMot-17
95StaClu-570
95StaCluMOP-570
95StaCluSTWS-570
95Sum-157
95SumNthD-157
95Top-272
95UppDec-231
95UppDecED-231
95UppDecEDG-231
95UppDecML-79
96ColCho-307
96ColChoGS-307
96ColChoSS-307
96Sco-239
96VanCanB-24
95UppDecMLFS-79
Rossen, Bob
77LynMetT-25
Rosser, Rex
75OklCit8TI-24
Rossi, Joe
52Top-379
53Top-74
83TopRep5-379
91TopArc1-74
Rossi, Tom
83EriCarT-21
Rossiter, Mike
91ClaDraP-34
91FroRowDP-14
91HigSchPLS-21
92ClaFS7-374
92MadMusC-20
92MadMusF-1234
92MidLeaATI-36
92OPC-474
92StaCluD-158
92Top-474
92TopGol-474
92TopGolW-474
92TopMic-474
92UppDecML-214
93ModA'sC-17
93ModA'sF-798
95ModA'sTI-26
96HunStaTI-22
Rossler, Ross (Brett)
91KinMetC-12
91KinMetP-3817
92PitMetC-9
92PitMetF-3300
Rossman, Claude
07TigACDPP-12
08RosComP-39
09BriE97-26
09BusBroBPP-13
09T206-305
09TigMorPenWBPP-10
09WolNewDTPP-14
10CouT21-58
11SpoLifCW-307
12PhiCarE-26
Rossum, Floyd
85BenPhiC-21
Rossy, Elem
86MiaMarP-22
88BlaYNPRWL-141
89BlaYNPRWL-15
Rossy, Rico
85NewOriT-14
86ChaOriW-26
87ChaO'sW-5
88BufBisC-18
88BufBisP-1471
89HarSenP-289
89HarSenS-15
90GreBraP-1138
90RicBraBC-19
91LinDriAAA-442
91RicBraBC-22
91RicBraLD-442
91RicBraP-2578
91RicBraTI-3
92Bow-390
92DonRoo-106
92Fle-676
92OmaRoyS-2
92OmaRoyS-344
92Sco-817
92StaClu-629
92StaCluECN-629
92TopDeb91-152
92Ult-376
93OmaRoyF-1687
93OPCPre-123
93PacSpa-495
93StaClu-106
93StaCluFDI-106
93StaCluMOP-106
94Fle-172
94Pac-300
94TriAAF-AAA11
96LasVegSB-20
Rostel, Bud
86AncGlaPTI-31
87AncGlaP-26
Rotblatt, Marv
51Bow-303
Roth, Bob F.
15SpoNewM-145
16ColE13-141
16SpoNewM-145
17HolBreD-85
19W514-47
20GasAmeMBD-16
21E121So8-77
21KoBreWSI-48
22W575-109
Roth, Frank
11SpoLifCW-308
Roth, Greg
89SouBenWSGS-26
90BirBarB-8
90BirBarP-1115
91BirBarLD-71
91BirBarP-1464
91LinDriAA-71
92BirBarS-92
92HagSunF-2564
92RocRedWS-466
Roth, Kris
86PeoChiP-20
87WinSpiP-22
88PitCubP-1376
Rothan, Bill
76TulOilGP-17
78SprRedWK-19
Rothermal, Russ
75IowOakT-15
79ChaChaT-3
Rothey, Mark
81CedRapRT-7
82CedRapRT-1
83WatRedT-7
Rothford, Jim
81ShrCapT-19
Rothrock, Brian
77OrlTwiT-17
Rothrock, John
28StaPlaCE-55
29ExhFou-17
31Exh-17
34DiaMatCSB-157
34ExhFou-8
35DiaMatCS3T1-126
74Car193T-22
79DiaGre-153
79RedSoxEF-3
79RedSoxEF-14
93ConTSN-851
Rothschild, Larry
77IndIndTI-17
79IndIndTI-9
80IndIndTI-14
81EvaTriT-6
82EvaTriT-7
83LasVegSBHN-18
85IowCubT-21
89CedRapRB-26
89CedRapRP-933
90RedKah-27
91RedKah-NNO
92RedKah-NNO
Rothstein, Arnold
88PacEigMO-28
Roundtree, Brian
92MisStaB-38
Rounsifer, Aaron
92ClaDraP-99
Rountree, Brian
89BriTigS-25
90FayGenP-2405
Rountree, Jerrold
91SpoIndC-11
91SpoIndP-3962
Rountree, Mike
86WatIndP-23
88RenSilSCLC-284
Rouse, Chuck
77ChaPatT-18
Rouse, Randy
76DubPacT-33
77CocAstT-23
78DayBeaAT-23
Rousey, Steve
87WesPalBEP-676
Roush, Edd
15CraJacE-161
15SpoNewM-146
16ColE13-142
16FleBreD-78
16SpoNewM-146
17HolBreD-86
19W514-85
20NatCarE-85
20RedWorCP-18
21E121So1-83
21E121So8-78
21Nei-79
21OxfConE-14
22E120-179
22W572-87
22W575-110
22WilPatV-1
23MapCriV-28
23W501-53
23W515-57
23WilChoV-136
25Exh-31
26Exh-31
27YorCarE-53
28Exh-20
28W502-53
28W513-61
28Yue-53
29PorandAR-75
31W517-3
38CinOraW-23
61Fle-72
76ISCHooHA-1
76RowExh-8
76ShaPiz-90
77BobParHoF-41
77GalGloG-93
77SerSta-19
79DiaGre-251
80PacLeg-70
80PerHaloFP-90
80SSPHOF-90
82DiaCla-44
82OhiHaloF-10
84OCoandSI-155
86RedGreT-11
87ConSer2-54
88PacEigMO-84
89PacLegI-216
89SweBasG-35
90SweBasG-35
91ConTSN-55
91SweBasG-134
93ActPacA-93
93ActPacA2-27G
94ConTSN-993
94ConTSN-1023
94ConTSNB-993
94ConTSNB-1023
20W516-29
Rovasio, Dom
89KenTwiP-1066
Rover, Vince
83CedRapRF-19
83CedRapRT-21
Rowan, John Albert
09ColChiE-245A
09ColChiE-245B
10DomDisP-103
10JuJuDE-35
10SweCapPP-131
11S74Sil-104
11SpoLifCW-309
11SpoLifM-201
11T205-145
12ColRedB-245A
12ColRedB-245B
12ColTinT-245A
12ColTinT-245B
12HasTriFT-13D
14PieStaT-50
Rowdie, Mascot
96IndIndB-29
Rowdon, Wade
82AppFoxF-5
83WatRedT-14
84WicAerRD-21
85Don-642
87IowCubTI-19
87Top-569
87TopTif-569
88Fle-430
88FleGlo-430
88RocRedWGCP-23
91OriCro-394
Rowe, Bicyclist
88GooN16-34
Rowe, Butch (Harold)
78WisRapTT-17
Rowe, Davis E.
87OldJudN-433
Rowe, Don
57SeaPop-32
58JetPos-17
63Top-562
83RedPioT-28
84VanCanC-243
87HawIslP-10
91DenZepP-139
91LinDriAAA-150
91MetWIZ-336
92BrePol-30
Rowe, Jim
85BelBreT-4
86BelBreP-20
87BelBreP-11
88ElPasDB-11
94PawRedSDD-23
Rowe, John Charles
76SSP188WS-5
87OldJudN-434
87ScrDC-16
88WG1CarG-24
Rowe, Ken
63Top-562
65Top-518
82RocRedWT-22
89ColCliC-24
89ColCliP-24
89ColCliP-755
90CMC-224
90ColCliC-24
90ColCliP-1
90ColCliP-693
90DodTar-691
90ProAAAF-343
91OriCro-395
92CanIndF-708
92CanIndS-125
93CanIndF-2854
94CanIndF-3135
95WatIndTI-25
96KenIndB-29
Rowe, Matt
86SumBraP-23
Rowe, Mike
76BatTroTI-19
Rowe, Pete
78DunBluJT-21
80KnoBluJT-4
82AleDukT-14
83LynPirT-13
90SalSpuCLC-146
90SalSpuP-2737
91DunBluJC-27
Rowe, Ralph
73OPC-49
73Top-49A
73Top-49B
74OPC-447
74Top-447
76SSP-603
83OriPos-24
84OriTeal-25
89SumBraP-1091
90SumBraP-2453
Rowe, Schoolboy (Lynwood)
34BatR31-184
34DiaStaR-33
34DiaStaR-98
34WarBakSP-7
35ExhFou-12
35GouPreR-15
35GouPuzR-8F
35GouPuzR-9F
35TigFreP-17
36ExhFou-12
36GouWidPPR-A91
36GouWidPPR-C21
36NatChiFPR-66
36OveCanR-40
36R31PasP-49
36R31Pre-G13
36WheBB4-9
36WorWidGV-44
37ExhFou-12
37OPCBatUV-134

38BasTabP-25
39PlaBal-60
42DodTeal-20
43PhiTeal-20
49Bow-216
49EurSta-144
49PhiBul-45
49PhiLumPB-9
54Top-197
61Fle-73
76TayBow4-50
76TigOldTS-19
77GalGloG-83
78TigDeaCS-3
80LauFamF-17
81TigDetN-93
81TigSecNP-21
83TCMPla1942-15
86TigSpoD-8
90DodTar-692
91ConTSN-256
93ConTSN-718
94TopArc1-197
94TopArc1G-197
95MegRut-24

Rowe, Tom A.
80RocRedWT-9
81RocRedWT-16
81RocRedWW-6
84ChaLooT-19
85IntLeaAT-42
85MaiGuiT-9
86MaiGuiP-19

Rowe, William A.
88AllandGN-22
88KimN18-38

Rowell, Carvel
41DouPlaR-43
47TipTop-83

Rowell, Pedestrian
88GooN16-35

Rowen, Rob
87SanAntDTI-6
88FreSunCLC-19
88FreSunP-1244

Rowland, Donnie
85MiaHur-14
86FloStaLAP-42
86LakTigP-20
87LakTigP-6
88TolMudHC-22
88TolMudHP-589
89LonTigP-1363

Rowland, Mike
78PhoGiaC-22
79PhoGiaVNB-3
80PhoGiaVNB-4
81PhoGiaVNB-10
81Top-502
82PhoGiaVNB-4

Rowland, Pants (Clarence)
15SpoNewM-147
16BF2FP-16
16ColE13-143
16SpoNewM-147
92ConTSN-485
92Man191BSR-20

Rowland, Rich
88BriTigP-1872
89FayGenP-1578
90LonTigP-1271
91Cla2-T95
91LinDriAAA-597
91TolMudHLD-597
91TolMudHP-1936
91TopDeb90-136
92OPC-472
92SkyAAAF-268
92StaClu-508
92TolMudHF-1047
92TolMudHS-596
92Top-472
92TopGol-472
92TopGolW-472
92TopMic-472
93Don-77
93Fle-610
93Pin-264
93Sco-283
93ScoBoyoS-30
93StaClu-519
93StaCluFDI-519
93StaCluMOP-519
93TolMudHF-1656
93TriAAAGF-40
94Don-645
94Pac-228
94Sco-228
94ScoGolR-228
94ScoRoo-RT98
94ScoRooGR-RT98
94Sel-392
94SpoRoo-105
94SpoRooAP-105
94Top-588
94TopGol-588
94TopSpa-588
94TopTra-122T
95Don-505
95DonPreP-505
95Fle-38
95Lea-57
95Sco-62
95ScoGolR-62
95ScoPlaTS-62
95StaClu-483
95StaCluMOP-483
95StaCluSTWS-483
95Top-272
95Ult-14
95UltGolM-14
96SyrChiTI-27

Rowley, Bill
87IndIndTI-36

Rowley, Steve
89ButCopKSP-10
90ChaRanS-24
91ChaRanC-10
91ChaRanP-1314
91TulDriTI-26
92SkyAA F-273
92TulDriS-617
94TulDriF-243
94TulDriTI-20

Rowson, James
96EveAquB-19

Roy, Jean-Pierre
43ParSpo-82
50W720HolS-24
52Par-90

Roy, Kevin
83WauTimF-13

Roy, Luther
90DodTar-693

Roy, Norman
51Bow-278

Roy, Pat
76CedRapGT-24
95FRIAAG-168

Roy, Patrick
91StaCluMO-50
93StaCluMO-58

Roy, Walt
90BurBraB-14
90BurBraP-2349
90BurBraS-23
91DurBulP-1542

Royals, Kansas City
69FleCloS-11
69FleCloS-43
69TopStaA-11
70OPC-422
70Top-422
71OPC-742
71Top-742
71TopTat-33
72Top-617
73OPC-347
73OPCBTC-11
73Top-347
73TopBluTC-11
74OPC-343
74OPCTC-11
74Top-343
74TopStaA-11
74TopTeaC-11
78Top-724
83FleSta-236
83FleSti-NNO
86FleWaxBC-C1
87SpoTeaL-13
88PanSti-461
88RedFolSB-112
90FleWaxBC-C23
90PubSti-637
90RedFolSB-126
90VenSti-525
94ImpProP-7
94Sco-323
94ScoGolR-323
95PanSti-145
96PanSti-187

Royals, Montreal
43ParSpo-83

Royalty, Doug
87AubAstP-26
88AshTouP-1065

Royer, Stan
88SouOreAP-1701
89Bow-195
89BowTif-195
89CalLeaA-31
89ModA'sC-25
89ModA'sCLC-276
90Bes-240
90HunStaB-19
90LouRedBLBC-36
91LinDriAAA-246
91LouRedLD-246
91LouRedP-2924
91LouRedTI-22
92Don-602
92LouRedF-1894
92LouRedS-268
92Pin-263
92Sco-822
92SkyAAAF-129
92StaClu-286
92TopDeb91-153
93CarPol-18
93Don-680
93FleFinE-130
93LouRedF-224
93PacSpa-636
93Top-820
93TopGol-820
93TopInaM-820
93TopMic-820
94CarPol-18
94Pac-603
94ScoRoo-RT140
94ScoRooGR-RT140
94SpoRoo-119
94SpoRooAP-119
94StaCluT-311
94StaCluTFDI-311

Royster, Aaron
94MarPhiC-22
94MarPhiF-3310
95PiePhiF-198

Royster, Jerry
74AlbDukTI-76
74AlbDukTI-17
75AlbDukC-3
75IntLeaASB-30
75PacCoaLAB-30
76OPC-592
76Top-592
77BurCheD-212
77Hos-38
77OPC-251
77Top-549
78BraCok-14
78Top-187
79Top-344
80OPC-241
80Top-463
81BraPol-1
81Don-339
81Fle-250
81Top-268
82BraBurKL-22
82BraPol-1
82Don-555
82Fle-448
82Top-608
83BraPol-1
83Don-425
83Fle-147
83FleSta-169
83FleSti-92
83Top-26
84BraPol-1
84Don-531
84Fle-191
84Nes792-572
84Top-572
84TopSti-37
84TopTif-572
85Fle-340
85FleUpd-90
85PadMot-18
85Top-776
85TopTif-776
85TopTifT-96T
85TopTra-96T
86Don-446
86Fle-333
86OPC-118
86Top-118
86TopTif-118
87Don-534
87Fle-428
87FleGlo-428
87OPC-324
87Top-403
87TopTif-403
87TopTra-106T
87TopTraT-106T
87WhiSoxC-26
88Don-660
88Fle-221
88FleGlo-221
88StaLinY-14
88Top-257
88TopTif-257
89UppDec-433
90DodTar-694
90EliSenL-47
90YakBeaTI-23
91VerBeaDC-30
91VerBeaDP-791
92SanAntMF-3988
92SanAntMS-574
92YanWIZ8-166
94JacSunF-1428
95MemChiTI-1
96LasVegSB-2

Royster, Willie
79RocRedWT-5
80ChaO'sP-19
80ChaO'sW-20
82RocRedWT-11
83EvaTriT-12
91OriCro-396

Rozek, Richard
50IndTeal-21
52IndNumN-11
52Top-363
83TopRep5-363

Rozema, Dave
75CliPilT-2
77TigBurK-3
78Hos-36
78Kel-21
78OPC-38
78TigBurK-5
78Top-124
79OPC-12
79Top-33
80OPC-151
80Top-288
81Don-9
81Fle-464
81Top-614
82Don-259
82Fle-279
82FleSta-153
82Top-319
83Don-133
83Fle-340
83Tig-24
83Top-562
84Don-272
84Fle-90
84Nes792-457
84OPC-133
84TigFarJ-13
84TigWavP-30
84Top-457
84TopTif-457
85Don-125
85Fle-21
85FleUpd-91
85RanPer-30
85SevCoi-D5
85Top-47
85TopTif-47
85TopTifT-97T
85TopTra-97T
86Don-343
86Fle-570
86Lea-154
86OPC-208
86Top-739
86TopTif-739
91PacSenL-135
93RanKee-314

Rozman, Richard
88SouOreAP-1694

Roznovsky, Ron
75IowOakT-16

Roznovsky, Vic
65Top-334
66Top-467
67OPC-163
67Top-163
68Top-428
69Top-368
81Ori6F-29
91OriCro-397

Rub, Jerry
88PriWilYS-21
89AlbYanB-12
89AlbYanP-328
89AlbYanS-16
90AlbYanP-1035
90AlbYanS-15
90CMC-781
91AlbYanLD-14
91AlbYanP-1007
91LinDriAA-14

Rub, Ron
87Ft.LauYP-15

Rubel, John
83ButCopKT-27

Rubel, Mike
82TulDriT-28
83TulDriT-15
84OklCit8T-14
85OklCit8T-22
87PhoFirP-27
90TulDriDGB-12

Rubeling, Albert
52Par-82
79DiaGre-336

Ruberto, Sonny (John E.)
76IndIndTI-11
77Car5-23
77CarTeal-22
78CarTeal-18
80ArkTraT-5

Rubio, Jorge
77FriOneYW-34

Ruby, J. Gary
87QuaCitAP-20
88CalLeaACLC-36
88PalSprACLC-114
88PalSprAP-1435
89MidAngGS-3
90MidAngGS-2
91EdmTraP-1532
91LinDriAAA-175
92EdmTraF-3554
93VanCanF-2614
94VanCanF-1879

Ruch, Rob
94EliTwiC-21
94EliTwiF-3731

Rucker, Dave
80EvaTriT-9
80VenLeaS-122
82EvaTriT-8
82Top-261
83Don-641
83EvaTriT-9
83Fle-341
83Tig-25
83Top-304
84Car-25
84Car5x7-24
84Don-260
84Nes792-699
84Top-699
84TopTif-699
85Don-260
85Fle-238
85FleUpd-92
85PorBeaC-26
85Top-421
85TopTif-421
85TopTifT-98T
85TopTra-98T
86Don-448
86Fle-447
86PhiTas-39
86Top-39
86TopTif-39
87OklCit8P-27
88BufBisC-8

88BufBisP-1472
89BufBisC-5
89BufBisP-1662
89UppDec-436
Rucker, Johnny
40PlaBal-213
41DouPlaR-137
47CenFlo-25
49BowPCL-7
Rucker, Nap (George)
03WilCarE-26
08RosComP-98
09ColChiE-246
09RamT20-100
09SpoNewSM-10
09T206-306
09T206-307
10CouT21-214
10CouT21-215
10CouT21-313
10DomDisP-104
10RedCroT-65
10RedCroT-151
10RedCroT-239
10SweCapPP-75A
10SweCapPP-75B
11L1L-117
11MecDFT-14
11PloCanE-54
11S74Sil-54
11S81LarS-92
11SpoLifM-162
11T205-146
11TurRedT-34
12ColRedB-246
12ColTinT-246
12HasTriFT-3B
12PhiCarE-27
12T207-157
13NatGamW-34
13PolGroW-23
13TomBarW-32
14B18B-60
14CraJacE-51
15CraJacE-51
15SpoNewM-148
16BF2FP-63
16FleBreD-79
16SpoNewM-148
83DiaClaS2-104
90DodTar-695
92ConTSN-333
94ConTSN-1263
94ConTSNB-1263
Ruckman, Scott
86BenPhiC-133
87UtiBluSP-5
88SpaPhiP-1037
88SpaPhiS-3
Rudi, Joe
69Top-587
70OPC-102
70Top-102
71MLBOffS-525
71OPC-407
71Top-407
72OPC-209
72Top-209
73A'sPos-41
73Kel2D-36
73OPC-360
73Top-360
74A'sPos-50
74OPC-264
74Top-264
74TopSta-229
75Hos-40
75HosTwi-40
75Kel-28
75OPC-45
75OPC-465
75Top-45
75Top-465
76Kel-7
76OPC-475
76SSP-490
76Top-475
77BurCheD-125
77Hos-146
77MSADis-52
77OPC-206
77RCColC-57
77Spo-2105
77Top-155
77TopCloS-39
78AngFamF-32
78Hos-114
78OPC-28
78RCColC-40
78SSP270-214
78Top-635
78WifBalD-64
79Hos-84
79OPC-134
79Top-267
80OPC-289
80Top-556
81Don-174
81Fle-272
81FleStiC-113
81OPC-362
81Top-701
81TopTra-826
82Don-586
82Fle-306
82OPC-388
82Top-388
82TopTra-102T
83Don-287
83Fle-532
83Top-87
84OCoandSI-190
86A'sGreT-5
87A'sMot-9
87ModA'sC-A2
91UppDecS-19
93MCIAmb-7
Rudison, Karl
90PulBraB-18
90PulBraP-3094
Rudolph, Blaine
88BriTigP-1879
89FayGenP-1579
90DunBluJS-15
Rudolph, F. Don
58Top-347
59Top-179
59TopVen-179
60HenHouW-33
60UniOil-17
62Top-224
63Top-291
64Top-427
Rudolph, Greg
92St.PetCC-25
92St.PetCF-2037
93SprCarC-21
93SprCarF-1864
Rudolph, Jeremi
96MedHatBJTI-24
Rudolph, Ken
70OPC-46
70Top-46
71MLBOffS-45
71OPC-472
71Top-472
72OPC-271
72Top-271
73OPC-414
73Top-414
74OPC-584
74Top-584
75OPC-289
75Top-289
76OPC-601
76SSP-287
76Top-601
78SprRedWK-24
91OriCro-398
Rudolph, Mason
90KinMetB-6
90KinMetS-21
91ColMetPI-25
91ColMetPPI-2
92St.LucMCB-16
92St.LucMF-1749
93St.LucMC-21
95PorSeaDTI-24
93StLucMF-2925
Rudolph, Richard
09ColChiE-247A
09ColChiE-247B
09T206-461
10CouT21-216
10CouT21-314
12ColRedB-247A
12ColRedB-247B
12ColTinT-247A
12ColTinT-247B
12ImpTobC-22
15CraJacE-154
15SpoNewM-149
16BF2FP-56
16ColE13-144
16FleBreD-80
16SpoNewM-149
19W514-13
55DonWin-38
93ConTSN-704
20W516-15
Rudstrom, Tom
89BenBucL-15
Ruebel, Matt
90OklSoo-18
91WelPirC-20
91WelPirP-3572
92AugPirC-12
92AugPirF-237
92ClaFS7-19
93SalBucC-20
93SalBucF-430
93SouAtlLAPI-36
94CarMudF-1579
95Bes-94
95CarMudF-154
96BowBes-122
96BowBesAR-122
96BowBesR-122
96Top-430
97Fle-435
97FleTif-435
97StaClu-340
97StaCluMOP-340
97Ult-266
97UltGolME-266
97UltPlaME-266
Ruel, Muddy (Harold)
21E121So1-84
21Exh-147
22E120-13
22W573-109
22W575-111
23MapCriV-24
23W501-10
23WilChoV-137
25Exh-128
26Exh-128
27AmeCarE-25
27Exh-63
28Exh-64
28StaPlaCE-56
29ExhFou-31
29PorandAR-76
33ButCre-22
33DouDisP-37
33ExhFou-12
33Gou-18
33GouCanV-18
35DiaMatCS3T1-127
35GouPuzR-5A
35GouPuzR-6A
35GouPuzR-11J
35GouPuzR-13A
40PlaBal-127
48IndTeal-27
49IndTeal-29
79RedSoxEF-21
91ConTSN-284
93ConTSN-865
Ruess, Matt
94JamJamC-22
94JamJamF-3963
Rueter, Kirk
92RocExpC-13
92RocExpF-2114
93HarSenF-269
93SelRoo-88T
94Bow-60
94ColC-246
94ColChoGS-246
94ColChoSS-246
94Don-237
94ExtBas-311
94ExtBasSYS-17
94Fin-9
94FinJum-9
94FinRef-9
94Fla-194
94Fle-549
94FleRooS-16
94FUnPac-142
94Lea-8
94OPC-255
94OPCDiaD-8
94Pac-389
94Pin-382
94PinArtP-382
94PinMusC-382
94Sco-312
94ScoBoyoS-11
94ScoGolR-312
94Sel-172
94StaClu-302
94StaCluFDI-302
94StaCluGR-302
94StaCluMOP-302
94Top-628
94TopGol-628
94TopSpa-628
94TriPla-98
94Ult-231
94UltRisS-10
94UppDec-171
94UppDecED-171
94USPlaCR-9S
95ColCho-249
95ColChoGS-249
95ColChoSS-249
95Don-486
95DonPreP-486
95Fla-165
95Fle-358
95Lea-241
95Sco-171
95ScoGolR-171
95ScoPlaTS-171
95StaClu-139
95StaCluFDI-139
95StaCluMOP-139
95StaCluSTWS-139
95Top-344
95TopCyb-186
95Ult-406
95UltGolM-406
95UppDec-330
95UppDecED-330
95UppDecEDG-330
96ColCho-611
96ColChoGS-611
96ColChoSS-611
96Fle-466
96FleTif-466
96Ult-509
96UltGolM-509
97Ult-478
97UltGolME-478
97UltPlaME-478
Ruether, Dutch (Walter)
19W514-108
20RedWorCP-19
21E121So1-85
21Exh-139
21Nei-64
22E120-147
22W572-82
22W573-110
23W501-99
23W503-56
23W515-40
26SpoComoA-33
27YorCarE-2
28W502-2
28Yue-2
88PacEigMO-83
90DodTar-696
91ConTSN-104
Ruff, Anthony
93IdaFalBSP-8
94DanBraC-23
Ruff, Dan
91BriTigC-24
91BriTigP-3616
92LakTigC-4
92LakTigF-2289
93LakTigC-22
93LakTigF-1325
Ruffcorn, Scott
91Cla/Bes-409
91ClaDraP-21
91FroRowDP-4
91FroRowDPP-3
92Bow-88
92ClaBluBF-BC18
92ClaFS7-373
92ClaRedB-BC18
92OPC-36
92Pin-300
92SarWhiSCB-1
92SarWhiSF-205
92Sco-806
92StaCluD-159
92Top-36
92TopGol-36
92TopGolW-36
92TopMic-36
92UppDecML-246
93BirBarF-1193
93Bow-443
93ClaFisN-16
93ClaGolF-79
93ClaYouG-YG21
93ExcFS7-154
93FleFinE-197
94ActPac-20
94Bow-595
94BowBes-B36
94BowBes-X100
94BowBesR-B36
94BowBesR-X100
94Cla-102
94ClaCreotC-C21
94ClaGolREF-RE2
94ColC-247
94ColChoGS-247
94ColChoSS-247
94Don-619
94Fin-440
94FinJum-440
94FinRef-440
94LeaGolR-5
94LeaLimR-10
94NasSouF-1251
94Pin-255
94PinArtP-255
94PinMusC-255
94PinNewG-NG16
94Sco-611
94ScoGolR-611
94SigRooTPD-T1
94SigRooTPS-T1
94Spo-169
94StaCluT-127
94StaCluTFDI-127
94Top-356
94TopGol-356
94TopSpa-356
94TriAAF-AAA7
94UppDec-25
94UppDecED-25
95ActPac2GF-17G
95ActPacF-12
95ActPacF-78
95Bow-423
95ColCho-2
95ColChoGS-2
95ColChoSS-2
95Don-504
95DonPreP-504
95FleUpd-37
95Lea-273
95Pin-256
95PinArtP-256
95PinMusC-256
95Sel-178
95Sel-232
95SelArtP-178
95SelArtP-232
95SelCer-94
95SelCerMG-94
95SelCerPU-4
95SelCerPU9-4
95Spo-157
95SpoArtP-157
95StaClu-480
95StaCluMOP-480
95StaCluSTWS-480
95Sum-118
95SumNthD-118
95Top-488
95UC3-96
95UC3ArtP-96
95Ult-276
95UltGolM-276
95UppDec-199
95UppDecED-199
95UppDecEDG-199
95UppDecPAW-H33
95UppDecPAWE-H33
95Zen-121
96NasSouB-19

96Sco-163
97Fle-530
97FleTif-530
97Ult-483
97UltGolME-483
97UltPlaME-483
Ruffin, Bruce
86ReaPhiP-23
86SpoRoo-29
87Don-555
87Fle-183
87FleGlo-183
87FleHotS-33
87Lea-168
87PhiTas-47
87SpoTeaP-6
87Top-499
87TopRoo-14
87TopSti-123
87TopSti-312
87TopTif-499
87ToyRoo-23
88Don-165
88Fle-313
88FleGlo-313
88OPC-268
88PanSti-353
88PhiTas-21
88Sco-492
88ScoGlo-492
88StaLinPh-14
88Top-268
88TopSti-119
88TopTif-268
89Bow-393
89BowTif-393
89Don-515
89Fle-580
89FleGlo-580
89OPC-222
89PanSti-148
89PhiTas-28
89Sco-328
89ScrRedBP-728
89Top-518
89TopSti-122
89TopTif-518
89UppDec-319
90Fle-572
90FleCan-572
90Lea-151
90OPC-22
90PhiTas-27
90Top-22
90TopTif-22
90UppDec-580
91Fle-411
91LinDriAAA-494
91OPC-637
91Sco-524
91ScrRedBLD-494
91ScrRedBP-2537
91StaClu-89
91Top-637
91TopDesS-637
91TopMic-637
91TopTif-637
91UppDec-410
92Bow-354
92BrePol-21
92Don-680
92Fle-544
92Lea-414
92OPC-307
92Sco-161
92ScoRoo-71T
92StaClu-867
92TexLon-35
92Top-307
92TopGol-307
92TopGolW-307
92TopMic-307
92TopTra-95T
92TopTraG-95T
92UppDec-309
93FleFinE-42
93PacSpa-437
93RocUSPC-7D
93RocUSPC-12S
93StaClu-270
93StaCluFDI-270
93StaCluMOP-270
93StaCluRoc-15
93Ult-357
93UppDec-670
93UppDecGold-670
94BreMilB-349
94ColC-407
94ColChoGS-407
94ColChoSS-407
94Don-305
94ExtBas-253
94Fin-199
94FinRef-199
94Fla-158
94Fle-452
94Pac-206
94RocPol-22
94StaCluT-101
94StaCluTFDI-101
94Top-407
94TopGol-407
94TopSpa-407
94Ult-189
95ColCho-451
95ColChoGS-451
95ColChoSS-451
95Don-476
95DonPreP-476
95DonTopotO-231
95Fla-133
95Fle-528
95FleTeaL-18
95Lea-296
95Pac-145
95Sco-189
95ScoGolR-189
95ScoPlaTS-189
95StaClu-5
95StaCluFDI-5
95StaCluMOP-5
95StaCluSTWS-5
95Top-625
95TopCyb-392
95Ult-158
95UltGolM-158
96Don-367
96DonPreP-367
96Fle-373
96FleTif-373
96LeaSigEA-176
96RocPol-20
96Ult-474
96UltGolM-474
97Cir-65
97CirRav-65
97ColCho-321
97DonTea-100
97DonTeaSPE-100
97Fle-318
97FleTif-318
97Pac-289
97PacLigB-289
97PacSil-289
97Sco-332
97ScoHobR-332
97ScoResC-332
97ScoRoc-14
97ScoRocPl-14
97ScoRocPr-14
97ScoShoS-332
97ScoShoSAP-332
97Top-136
97Ult-340
97UltGolME-340
97UltPlaME-340
Ruffin, Johnny
89UtiBluSP-19
90SouBenWSGS-15
91Bow-347
91Cla/Bes-95
91SarWhiSC-9
91SarWhiSP-1112
92BirBarS-93
92Bow-451
92ClaFS7-33
92DonRoo-107
92LeaGolR-BC13
92ProFS7-43
92SarWhiSF-206
92SkyAA F-45
92UppDecML-224
93BirBarF-1194
93Bow-147
93ClaFS7-88
93StaCluWS-26
94Bow-102
94ColC-17
94ColChoGS-17
94ColChoSS-17
94Don-135
94ExtBas-238
94Fin-283
94FinRef-283
94Fla-370
94Fle-424
94Lea-305
94LeaLimR-18
94Pin-410
94PinArtP-410
94PinMusC-410
94RedKah-25
94ScoRoo-RT144
94ScoRooGR-RT144
94Sel-394
94SpoRoo-96
94SpoRooAP-96
94Top-779
94TopGol-779
94TopSpa-779
94Ult-176
94UppDec-170
94UppDecED-170
95ColChoGS-435
95ColChoSS-435
95Don-287
95DonPreP-287
95Fle-445
95FleRooS-17
95IndIndF-93
95Lea-109
95Pac-112
95RedKah-25
95Sco-67
95ScoGolR-67
95ScoPlaTS-67
95StaClu-276
95StaCluMOP-276
95StaCluSTWS-276
95Top-270
95TopCyb-146
95Ult-148
95UltGolM-148
Ruffing, Red (Charles H.)
25Exh-69
26Exh-70
29ExhFou-17
29PorandAR-77
32USCar-20
33CraJacP-19
33GeoCMil-26
33Gou-56
34ButPreR-52
34DiaStaR-60
34GouCanV-48
35GouPuzR-4D
35GouPuzR-7D
35GouPuzR-12D
36ExhFou-13
36NatChiFPR-92
36R31PasP-20
36R31Pre-L11
36WorWidGV-102
37OPCBatUV-136
37WheBB6-2
38OurNatGPP-25
39PlaBal-3
40PlaBal-10
40WheM4-1A
40WheM4-1B
41DouPlaR-67
41DouPlaR-85
41PlaBal-20
43MPR302-1-22
47PM1StaP1-191
60Fle-63
61Fle-74
69EquSpoHoF-BB19
75YanDyn1T-39
76GrePlaG-35
76RowExh-1
76ShaPiz-105
77GalGloG-54
80PacLeg-109
80PerHaloFP-106
80SSPHOF-106
80YanGreT-9
82MetGal62-31
82OhiHaloF-11
83DiaClaS2-107
83DonHOFH-31
86SpoDecG-14
89HOFStiB-83
91ConTSN-13
91ConTSN-227
92YanWIZA-70
92YanWIZH-28
93ConTSN-882
94ConTSN-1078
94ConTSNB-1078
Ruffner, Mark
89ReaPhiB-24
Rugg, Rusty
89HelBreSP-6
91HelBreSP-19
Ruhl, Dan
92LetMouSP-4
Ruhle, Vern
75OPC-614
75Top-614
76Hos-46
76HosTwi-46
76OPC-89
76Top-89
77OPC-212
77Top-311
78ChaChaT-14
78Top-456
79Top-49
80Top-234
81Don-261A
81Don-261B
81Fle-53
81Top-642
82AstAstI-7
82Don-293
82Fle-228
82Top-539
83Don-627
83Fle-462
83Top-172
84AstMot-23
84Don-564
84Fle-238
84Nes792-328
84Top-328
84TopTif-328
85Don-380
85Fle-358
85FleUpd-93
85Ind-26
85IndPol-48
85Top-426
85TopTif-426
85TopTifT-99T
85TopTra-99T
86Fle-593
86Top-768
86TopTif-768
87Fle-91
87FleGlo-91
87Top-221
87TopTif-221
90SweBasG-128
91SweBasG-76
Ruiz, Augie
79LodDodT-2
81BirBarT-23
82EvaTriT-9
83RicBraT-9
Ruiz, Benny
86GleFalTP-19
87GleFalTP-14
88TolMudHC-16
88TolMudHP-602
Ruiz, Cecilio
83LasVegSBHN-19
Ruiz, Cesar
94BriTigC-22
94BriTigF-3512
96FayGenB-26
Ruiz, Chico (Hiraldo S.)
62RedEnq-31
63Top-407
64Top-356
64TopVen-356
65RedEnq-26
65Top-554
66OPC-159
66Top-159
66TopVen-159
67CokCapR-12
67Top-339
67TopVen-305
68Kah-B30
68Top-213
68TopVen-213
69MilBra-243
69Top-469
70Top-606
71MLBOffS-357
71OPC-686
71Top-686
72MilBra-301
77SerSta-20
78TCM60I-35
Ruiz, Chico (Manuel)
78RicBraT-13
79RicBraT-13
81RicBraT-9
82RicBraT-15
83RicBraT-15
90RicBra2ATI-21
Ruiz, Estuar
92KanCouCTI-26
Ruiz, Mauricio
93LinVenB-240
95LinVen-141
Ruiz, Nelson
80BatTroT-29
Ruiz, Rafael
96HicCraB-19
Ruiz, Stewart
91BluOriC-3
91BluOriP-4136
92KanCouCF-102
94VenLinU-161
Rujff, Anthony
93IdaFalBF-4048
Ruling, Stephen
77SpoIndC-8
78SpoIndC-11
Rumer, Tim
90TamYanD-18
91Ft.LauYC-13
91Ft.LauYP-2426
92ClaFS7-224
92PriWilCC-13
92PriWilCF-148
94AbaYanF-1440
95ColCliMCTI-4
95ColCliP-27
95ColCliTI-27
96NorNavB-22
Rumfield, Toby
91Cla/Bes-413
91FroRowDP-35
91PriRedC-13
91PriRedP-3518
92BenMusSP-6
92BilMusF-3359
93WesVirWF-2869
94CarLeaAF-CAR50
94WinSpiC-20
94WinSpiF-282
95ChaLooTI-19
96ChaLooB-26
Rumler, William G.
16ColE13-145
Rumsey, Dan
91CliGiaP-849
92MidAngF-4039
92PalSprAC-26
93MidAngF-335
97MidAngOHP-27
Rumsey, Derrell
91VisOakC-23
91VisOakP-1755
92ClaFS7-371
92Ft.MyeMCB-12
92Ft.MyeMF-2757
Rundels, Matt
92JamExpC-6
92JamExpF-1509
93BurBeeC-22
93BurBeeF-167
94HarSenF-2100
95HarSenTI-4
96SigRooOJ-30
96SigRooOJS-30
Rundles, Gary
89CarNewE-21
Runge, Ed
55Bow-277
90T/MUmp-64
Runge, Paul
87RicBraBC-18
87RicBraC-12
87RicBraT-14
88StaLinBra-16

89LasVegSC-21
90CMC-343
90ProAAAF-359
90SyrChiC-17
90SyrChiMB-19
90SyrChiP-579
96MacBraB-26
Runge, Paul E.
88T/MUmp-17
89T/MUmp-17
90T/MUmp-17
90T/MUmp-64
Runge, Paul W.
81RicBraT-10
82RicBraT-16
83RicBraT-16
84RicBraT-24
85BraPol-12
85TopTifT-100T
85TopTra-100T
86RicBraP-19
86Top-409
86TopTif-409
88FleUpd-71
88FleUpdG-71
89Top-38
89TopBig-23
89TopTif-38
89UppDec-55
93IdaFalBF-4050
93IdaFalBSP-30
94DanBraC-30
94DanBraF-3548
95EugEmeTI-29
Runge, Scott
86WatPirP-20
87WatPirP-5
88AugPirP-376
89SanBerSB-19
89WilBilP-638
Runion, Jeff
92GulCoaRSP-24
93ChaRaiC-17
93ChaRaiF-1910
93ClaGolF-108
94ChaRivC-17
94ChaRivF-2671
95ChaRivTI-17
Runion, Tony
94ColRedC-19
95KinIndTI-23
96KenIndB-22
Runnells, Tom
81PhoGiaVNB-23
83PhoGiaBHN-9
84WicAerRD-11
86Don-569
87VerRedP-16
88ChaLooB-14
89ChaLooLITI-25
89IndIndC-25
89IndIndP-1220
90ExpPos-30
91ExpPos-19
91TopTra-103T
91TopTraT-103T
92ExpDonD-15A
92ExpPos-26
92OPC-51
92Top-51
92TopGol-51
92TopGolW-51
92TopMic-51
93LonTigF-2322
94TreThuF-2134
95TolMudHTI-1
96TolMudHB-2
82PhoGiaVNB-21
Runnels, Pete (James E.)
47Exh-197
52Top-2
53BowC-139
53Bri-16
53Top-219
54Top-6
55Bow-255
55RedMan-AL20
56Top-234
57Top-64
58Hir-38
58RedSoxJP-8
58Top-265
59Top-370
59Top-519
59WilSpoG-6
60KeyChal-40
60RedSoxJP-8
60Top-15
60TopTat-47
60TopVen-15
61Baz-32
61NuSco-407
61Pos-47A
61Pos-47B
61SevElev-11
61Top-42
61Top-210
61TopMagR-29
61TopStal-116
62Jel-57
62Pos-57
62PosCan-57
62RedSoxJP-8
62SalPlaC-47A
62SalPlaC-47B
62ShiPlaC-47
62Top-3
62TopBuc-79
62TopStal-17
62TopVen-3
63BasMagM-72
63Col45"P-12
63Col45"P-18
63Col45'JP-9
63ExhStaB-57
63Jel-77
63Pos-77
63SalMetC-61
63Top-2
63Top-230
64Col.45JP-6
64Top-121
64TopVen-121
80MarExh-27
83TopRep5-2
90PacLeg-103
91TopArc1-219
94TopArc1-6
94TopArc1G-6
Runyan, Paul
94PriRedC-21
94PriRedF-3261
Runyan, Sean
92FroRowDP-41
92HigSchPLS-14
93Bow-616
93ClaGolF-161
93StaCluM-89
94AubAstC-15
94AubAstF-3757
96QuaCitRB-25
Runyon, Curt
75AndRanT-16
Runzi, Andy
93BoiHawF-3917
Ruocchio, James
91BoiHawC-6
91BoiHawP-3890
Rupcich, Mike
89FreStaBS-17
91FreStaBS-16
Rupe, Brian
83VisOakF-25
Rupkey, Rich
90HamRedB-12
90HamRedS-21
Rupp, Brian
93Bow-700
93ClaFS7-115
93SavCarC-21
93SavCarF-694
93SouAtlLAGF-51
94ClaGolF-160
94ExcFS7-274
94St.PetCC-23
94St.PetCF-2598
94UppDecML-184
96ArkTraB-24
Rupp, Chad
93EliTwiC-19
93EliTwiF-3422
94ForWayWC-20
94ForWayWF-2017
95ForMyeMTI-23
96HarCitRCB-28
Rupp, Mark
89EriOriS-23
90HelBreSP-21
Rupp, Terry
89SpoIndSP-9
90WatDiaB-15
90WatDiaP-2386
Ruppert, Colonel (Jacob)
75YanDyn1T-33
89CMCRut-15
90RinPosYMP-10
95ConTSN-1398
Rusch, Glendon
94RocRoyC-21
94RocRoyF-564
95Bes-23
95Exc-64
95SPML-70
95WilBluRTI-18
96BesAutSA-63
96Bow-289
96BowBes-105
96BowBesAR-105
96BowBesR-105
96Exc-67
96ExcSeaC-8
96OmaRoyB-26
97Bow-415
97BowBes-126
97BowBesAR-126
97BowBesR-126
97BowInt-415
97ColCho-461
97Don-370
97DonPre-148
97DonPreCttC-148
97DonPreP-370
97DonPrePGold-370
97Fle-567
97FleTif-567
97PinCer-123
97PinCerMBlu-123
97PinCerMG-123
97PinCerMR-123
97PinCerR-123
97PinTotCPB-123
97PinTotCPG-123
97PinTotCPR-123
97PinX-P-126
97PinX-PMoS-126
97Sco-476
97ScoHobR-476
97ScoResC-476
97ScoShoS-476
97ScoShoSAP-476
97SpoIll-23
97SpoIllEE-23
97StaClu-191
97StaCluMOP-191
97Top-207
97Ult-475
97UltGolME-475
97UltPlaME-475
Rusciano, Chris
92IdaFalGF-3511
92IdaFalGSP-4
93IdaFalBF-4028
93IdaFalBSP-15
94IdaFalBF-3584
94IdaFalBSP-22
94MacBraC-17
94MacBraF-2202
Rush, Andy
89ElmPioP-18
90DodTar-1058
90WinHavRSS-23
91LynRedSC-28
91LynRedSP-1197
92LynRedSC-14
92LynRedSF-2906
93RanCucQF-833
Rush, Bob
49EurSta-69
50Bow-61
51Bow-212
52NatTeaL-28
52StaCalL-80D
52StaCalS-92C
52Top-153
53BowC-110
54Bow-77
55Bow-182
55RobGouS-13
55RobGouW-13
56Top-214
57Top-137
58Top-313
59Top-396
60BraJayP-9
60BraLaktL-21
60BraSpiaS-19
60Top-404
79DiaGre-115
79TCM50-164
83TopRep5-153
Rush, Eddie (Edward)
88CedRapRP-1155
89GreHorP-418
90CedRapRB-6
90CedRapRP-2329
91CedRapRP-2729
91MidLeaAP-MWL23
Rush, Larry
79HolMilT-20
80VanCanT-1
81VanCanT-12
82VanCanT-7
Rush, Rod
84EveGiaC-13B
Rush, Tony
94OneYanF-3791
Rushing, Will
96FtMyeMB-9
Rushworth, Jim
92JamExpC-22
92JamExpF-1501
93BurBeeC-23
93BurBeeF-158
94WesPalBEC-23
94WesPalBEF-38
Rusie, Amos
75FlePio-12
76ISCHooHA-5
80PerHaloFP-162
80SSPHOF-162
81ConTSN-72
86IndIndTI-8
87ConSer2-53
87OldJudN-435
92ConTSN-535
94OriofB-68
95May-26A
95May-26B
95NewN566-175
Rusin, Dave
91PerHeaF-4
Rusk, Mike
75ForLauYS-28
Rusk, Troy
90PriPatD-17
91SpaPhiC-15
91SpaPhiP-902
92ClePhiF-2065
92SpaPhiC-4
92SpaPhiF-1272
93ClePhiC-19
93ClePhiF-2687
94ReaPhiF-2066
Ruskey, Jason
94BelMarC-23
94BelMarF-3231
Ruskin, Scott
87MacPirP-22
88SalBucS-18
89BlaYNPRWLU-31
89SalBucS-18
90Bow-167
90BowTif-167
90DonRoo-27
90Lea-512
90TopTra-106T
90TopTraT-106T
90UppDec-713
91Don-612
91ExpPos-20
91Fle-246
91OPC-589
91Sco-799
91Top-589
91TopDeb90-137
91TopDesS-589
91TopMic-589
91TopRoo-26
91TopTif-589
91Ult-209
91UppDec-383
92Don-394
92Fle-491
92FleUpd-83
92Lea-521
92OPC-692
92RedKah-28
92Sco-121
92ScoRoo-57T
92StaClu-777
92StaCluNC-777
92Top-692
92TopGol-692
92TopGolW-692
92TopMic-692
92TopTra-96T
92TopTraG-96T
92UppDec-384
93Fle-398
93IndIndF-1488
93StaClu-199
93StaCluFDI-199
93StaCluMOP-199
93Top-328
93TopGol-328
93TopInaM-328
93TopMic-328
93TriAAAGF-9
Russ, Kevin
84IdaFalATI-23
86MadMusP-18
Russell, Alan
91BoiHawC-30
93BoiHawC-30
Russell, Allen
23WilChoV-138
Russell, Bill E.
70MLBOffS-56
70OPC-304
70Top-304
71DodTic-14
71MLBOffS-113
71OPC-226
71Top-226
72Top-736
73LinPor-96
73OPC-108
73Top-108
74OPC-239
74Top-239
74TopDecE-40
74TopSta-49
75Hos-91
75OPC-23
75Top-23
76LinSup-116
76OPC-22
76Top-22
77Top-322
78SSP270-56
78Top-128
79DodBlu-11
79Top-546
80DodPol-18
80OPC-40
80Top-75
81AllGamPI-113
81DodPol-18
81Don-57
81Fle-117
81FleStiC-68
81LonBeaPT-3
81OPC-20
81Top-465
81TopSti-179
81TopSupHT-51
82DodPol-18
82DodUniOV-18
82Don-453
82Fle-20
82FleSta-8
82Top-279
83AllGamPI-113
83DodPol-18
83DodPos-13
83Don-210
83Fle-219
83FleSti-116
83OPC-123
83Top-661
83TopSti-249
84AllGamPI-24
84DodPol-18
84Don-587
84Fle-111
84Nes792-792
84OPC-14
84Top-792
84TopRubD-21
84TopSti-77

84TopTif-792
85AllGamPI-115
85DodCokP-28
85Don-93
85Fle-383
85Lea-232
85OPC-343
85SpoIndGC-17
85Top-343
85TopMin-343
85TopRubD-21
85TopSti-76
85TopTif-343
86DodCokP-26
86DodPol-18
86DodUniOP-16
86Don-153
86Fle-142
86Top-506
86Top-696
86TopTif-506
86TopTif-696
87DodMot-27
87DodPol-29
87DodSmoA-31
87Fle-452
87FleGlo-452
87Top-116
87TopTif-116
88DodMot-28
88DodSmo-13
88DodSmo-15
89DodMot-27
89DodPol-1
89DodSmoG-81
90DodMot-28
90DodPol-NNO
90DodTar-697
91DodMot-28
91DodPol-NNO
91DodUno7P-1
92AlbDukF-737
92AlbDukS-24
92DodStaTA-15
92UppDecS-15
93AlbDukF-1478
93TriAAAGF-15
94DodMot-28
94DodPol-30
95DodMot-28
95DodPol-30
96DodMot-28
96DodPol-8

Russell, Dan
88ModA'sTI-25

Russell, Fred
88EugEmeB-15
89EugEmeB-19
90AppFoxBS-21
90AppFoxP-2103
90CMC-698
91BasCitRC-20
91BasCitRP-1406
91Cla/Bes-122

Russell, Jack Erwin
29PorandAR-78
33Gou-123
33Gou-167
34DiaMatCSB-158
39CubTeal-23
79DiaGre-67
94ConTSN-1048
94ConTSNB-1048

Russell, Jake
94MarPhiC-23
94MarPhiF-3305
95BatCliTI-29

Russell, Jeff
82WatRedT-8
83IndIndTI-14
84Don-569
84Nes792-270
84RedBor-46
84RedEnq-16
84Top-270
84TopTif-270
85Don-487
85Fle-551
85RedYea-15
85Top-651
85TopTif-651
86Don-586
86OklCit8P-19
86RanPer-40
87Don-550
87Fle-137
87FleGlo-137
87RanMot-26
87RanSmo-32
87Top-444
87TopTif-444
88Don-531
88Fle-478
88FleGlo-478
88RanMot-26
88RanSmo-17
88Sco-514
88ScoGlo-514
88StaLinRa-14
88Top-114
88TopTif-114
89Bow-226
89BowTif-226
89Don-403
89DonAll-26
89DonBasB-200
89Fle-531
89FleGlo-531
89OPC-166
89PanSti-447
89RanMot-6
89RanSmo-28
89Sco-438
89Top-565
89TopBig-309
89TopSti-243
89TopTif-565
89UppDec-461
90Bow-485
90BowTif-485
90Don-284
90DonBesA-99
90Fle-312
90Fle-633
90FleAwaW-28
90FleCan-312
90FleCan-633
90Lea-152
90Lea-442
90OPC-80
90OPC-395
90PanSti-159
90PubSti-420
90RanMot-8
90RedFolSB-80
90Sco-263
90Sco100S-23
90Spo-192
90Top-80
90Top-395
90TopBig-15
90TopGaloC-8
90TopMinL-38
90TopSti-252
90TopStiB-66
90TopTif-80
90TopTif-395
90UppDec-638
91Bow-267
91Don-202
91Fle-300
91Lea-291
91OPC-344
91RanMot-8
91Sco-277
91StaClu-421
91Top-344
91TopDesS-344
91TopMic-344
91TopTif-344
91Ult-354
91UppDec-648
92Bow-218
92Don-129
92Fle-319
92Lea-90
92OPC-257
92Pin-209
92RanMot-8
92RanTeal-21
92Sco-124
92StaClu-28
92Stu-247
92Top-257
92TopGol-257
92TopGolW-257
92TopMic-257
92Ult-140
92UppDec-695
93Bow-115
93Don-711
93Fla-167
93Fle-668
93FleFinE-177
93Lea-494
93OPCPre-9
93Pin-444
93RanKee-315
93Sco-413
93Sel-365
93SelRoo-7T
93SP-204
93StaClu-635
93StaCluFDI-635
93StaCluMOP-635
93Top-736
93TopGol-736
93TopInaM-736
93TopMic-736
93TopTra-25T
93Ult-516
93UppDec-702
93UppDecGold-702
94ColC-583
94ColChoGS-583
94ColChoSS-583
94Don-248
94ExtBas-23
94Fin-90
94FinPre-90P
94FinRef-90
94Fle-41
94Lea-336
94OPC-113
94Pac-65
94Pin-46
94PinArtP-46
94PinMusC-46
94RanAllP-16
94RanAllP-17
94Sco-529
94ScoGolR-529
94Sel-272
94StaClu-710
94StaCluFDI-710
94StaCluGR-710
94StaCluMOP-710
94Top-55
94TopGol-55
94TopSpa-55
94TriPla-206
94Ult-17
94UppDec-213
94UppDecED-213
95ColCho-271
95ColChoGS-271
95ColChoSS-271
95DonTopotO-167
95Fla-310
95Fle-146
95FleUpd-86
95RanCra-30
95TopTra-89T
96ColCho-344
96ColChoGS-344
96ColChoSS-344
96Don-201
96DonPreP-201
96Fle-262
96FleTif-262
96Pac-430
97PacPriGotD-GD99

Russell, Jim
47TipTop-146
49Bow-235
49EurSta-20
50Bow-223
52MotCoo-52
52Top-51
83TCMPla1944-27
83TopRep5-51
90DodTar-698
95TopArcBD-6

Russell, Joe
75AndRanT-46
76AshTouT-1
79TulDriT-2
81TulDriT-27

Russell, John
83PorBeaT-17
84PhiTas-42
84PorBeaC-208
85Don-648
85Fle-653
85PhiTas-11
85PhiTas-31
86Don-82
86Fle-448
86PhiCIG-14
86PhiTas-6
86Top-392
86TopTif-392
87Don-207
87Fle-184
87FleGlo-184
87PhiTas-6
87Top-379
87TopTif-379
88MaiPhiC-12
88MaiPhiP-285
88PhiTas-37
88Top-188
88TopTif-188
89BraDub-21
89UppDec-532
90CMC-161
90DodTar-699
90Don-458
90OklCit8C-11
90OklCit8P-436
90ProAAAF-682
90PubSti-120
90RanMot-26
90TopTra-107T
90TopTraT-107T
91Fle-301
91OPC-734
91RanMot-26
91Sco-802
91StaClu-474
91Top-734
91TopDesS-734
91TopMic-734
91TopTif-734
91UppDec-191
92Sco-339
92StaClu-846
92StaCluECN-846
92TulDriF-2699
92TulDriS-618
93PacSpa-647
93RanKee-430
93StaCluR-23
96FtMyeMB-1

Russell, LaGrande
91BelMarC-28
92PenPilC-12
92PenPilF-2931
93Bow-403
93JacSunF-2712
95PorCitRTI-23
96PorCitRB-24

Russell, Larry
88CapCodPPaLP-28

Russell, Leonard
91StaCluMO-33

Russell, Matt
89BenBucL-25
90BenBucL-31

Russell, Mike
94StaCluDP-7
94StaCluDPFDI-7

Russell, Reb (Ewell A.)
13PolGroW-24
14CraJacE-15
15CraJacE-15
15SpoNewM-150
16BF2FP-17
16ColE13-146A
16ColE13-146B
16SpoNewM-150
75WhiSox1T-22
92ConTSN-482
92Man191BSR-21

Russell, Richard
91BelMarP-3662

Russell, Rip (Glen David)
39CubTeal-22
39ExhSal-55
46RedSoxTI-20
47TipTop-12
93ConTSN-727

Russell, Rob
85PriWilPT-7
86PriWilPP-23
87HarSenP-12
88HarSenP-858
89HarSenP-303
89HarSenS-16

Russell, Ron
86DayBealP-24

Russell, Todd
90BenBucL-14
91MadMusC-1

Russell, Tony
83GreHorT-26
85AlbYanT-21
86AlbYanT-10
87AlbYanP-2

Russo, Marius
41DouPlaR-111
43YanSta-22
75YanDyn1T-40
79DiaGre-14
83YanASFY-38
89SweBasG-101
92YanWIZA-71

Russo, Pat
91KenTwiC-15
91KenTwiP-2073

Russo, Paul
90EliTwiS-20
91Bow-695
91Cla/Bes-344
91KenTwiP-2085
92ClaFS7-203
92OPC-473
92OrlSunRF-2856
92OrlSunRS-519
92SkyAA F-226
92Top-473
92TopGol-473
92TopGolW-473
92TopMic-473
93ClaFS7-18
93ClaGolF-94
93PorBeaF-2390
94SalLakBF-825
95MemChiTI-27
96LasVegSB-21

Russo, Tony
87EriCarP-16
88SavCarP-333
89St.PetCS-23

Rust, Brian
95EugEmeTI-8
96EugEmeB-22

Rusteck, Dick
77FriOneYW-43
81TCM60I-420
91MetWIZ-337

Ruszkowski, Hank
47IndTeal-23
47IndVanPP-22

Ruth, Babe (George Herman)
15SpoNewM-151
16ColE13-147
16SpoNewM-151
17HolBreD-87
19W514-2
20NatCarE-86
21E121So1-86A
21E121So1-86B
21E121So1-86C
21E121So1-86D
21E121So1-86E
21E121So8-79A
21E121So8-79B
21E121So8-79C
21Exh-148
21Exh-149
21KoBreWSI-49
21Nei-37
21OxfConE-15
22AmeCarE-57
22E120-71
22W572-88
22W573-111
22W575-112
22WilPatV-25
23MapCriV-8
23W501-49
23W503-32
23W515-3
23W515-47
23W551-7
23WilChoV-139
24MrsShePP-7
25Exh-100

26Exh-102
26SpoComoA-36
26SpoNewSM-2
27AmeCarE-38
27Exh-52
27YorCarE-6
28BabRCCE-1
28BabRCCE-2
28BabRCCE-3
28BabRCCE-4
28BabRCCE-5
28BabRCCE-6
28Exh-51
28FroJoy-1
28FroJoy-2
28FroJoy-3
28FroJoy-4
28FroJoy-5
28FroJoy-6
28PorandAR-A31
28PorandAR-B31
28StaPlaCE-57
28W502-6
28W512-6
28W56PlaC-JOK
28Yue-6
29ExhFou-26
29PorandAR-79
30SchR33-26
30SchR33-42
30W554-15
31Exh-26
31W517-4
31W517-20
32R33So2-402
32USCar-32
33ButCanV-41
33ButCre-23
33ExhFou-13
33Gou-53
33Gou-144
33Gou-149
33Gou-181
33GouCanV-80
33GouCanV-93
33RitCE-1S
33RitCE-13C
33SpoKin-2
34ButPreR-53
34ExhFou-13
34GouCanV-28
34GouPreR-4
35ClaBreD3-4
35ExhFou-1
35GouPuzR-1J
35GouPuzR-3A
35GouPuzR-14A
35GouPuzR-15A
36NatChiFPR-84
36PC7AlbHoF-4
38QuaOatR-1
46SpoExcW-8-4
47PM1StaP1-192
48BabRutS-1
48BabRutS-25
48BabRutS-26
48BabRutS-27
48BabRutS-28
48ExhHoF-25A
48ExhHoF-25B
48SweSpoT-12
49Lea-3
49LeaPre-7
50CalHOFW-63
50H80FouMH-3
51R42SmaS-92
51TopConMA-9
56TopHocF-B1
58HarSta-2
59FleWil-2
59FleWil-75
60ExhWriH-20
60Fle-3
60KeyChal-41
60NuHi-1
60NuHi-16
60NuHi-47
60RawGloT-28
61Fle-75
61GolPre-3
61NuSco-447
61NuSco-455
61Top-401
62Top-135
62Top-136
62Top-137
62Top-138
62Top-139A
62Top-140
62Top-141
62Top-142
62Top-143
62Top-144
62TopVen-135
62TopVen-136
62TopVen-137
62TopVen-138
62TopVen-139
62TopVen-140
62TopVen-141
62TopVen-142
62TopVen-143
62TopVen-144
63BasMagM-73
63BazA-17
63GadFunC-1
63GadFunC-34
63HalofFB-16
66AurSpoMK-4
67TopVen-147
68AtlOil-10
68LauWorS-12
68LauWorS-13
68LauWorS-20
68LauWorS-25
68LauWorS-29
68SpoMemAG-11
69Baz-5
69Baz-9
69Baz-10
69Baz-11
69EquSpoHoF-BB20
69SCFOldT-1
70FleWorS-12
70FleWorS-13
70FleWorS-20
70FleWorS-25
70FleWorS-29
71FleWorS-16
71FleWorS-30
72FleFamF-20
72KelATG-6
72KelATG-14
72LauGreF-32
73HalofFPP-15
73OPC-1
73OPC-474
73SyrChiTI-24
73Top-1
73Top-474
74LauAllG-33
74SyrChiTI-23
75SyrChiTI-17
75TCMAllG-30
75TCMAllG-31
76BooProC-11
76BooProC-17
76GalBasGHoF-25
76LauDiaJ-32
76MotOldT-9
76OPC-345
76RowExh-16
76ShaPiz-2
76TayBow4-3
76TayBow4-49
76TayBow4-113
76Top-345
77BobParHoF-42
77GalGloG-69
77GalGloG-91
77GalGloG-165
77GalGloG-193
77GalGloG-227
77SerSta-21
77ShaPiz-20
77Spo-511
77Spo-6818
79Pew-5
80FraBabR-1
80FraBabR-2
80FraBabR-3
80FraBabR-4
80FraBabR-5
80FraBabR-6
80FraBabR-7
80FraBabR-8
80FraBabR-9
80FraBabR-10
80FraBabR-11
80FraBabR-12
80FraBabR-13
80FraBabR-14
80FraBabR-15
80FraBabR-16
80FraBabR-17
80FraBabR-18
80FraBabR-19
80FraBabR-20
80FraBabR-21
80FraBabR-22
80FraBabR-23
80FraBabR-24
80FraBabR-25
80FraBabR-26
80FraBabR-27
80FraBabR-28
80FraBabR-29
80FraBabR-30
80FraBabR-31
80FraBabR-32
80FraBabR-33
80FraBabR-34
80FraBabR-35
80FraBabR-36
80FraBabR-37
80FraBabR-38
80FraBabR-39
80FraBabR-40
80FraBabR-41
80FraBabR-42
80FraBabR-43
80FraBabR-44
80FraBabR-45
80FraBabR-46
80FraBabR-47
80FraBabR-48
80FraBabR-49
80FraBabR-50
80FraBabR-51
80FraBabR-52
80FraBabR-53
80FraBabR-54
80FraBabR-55
80FraBabR-56
80FraBabR-57
80FraBabR-58
80FraBabR-59
80FraBabR-60
80FraBabR-61
80FraBabR-62
80FraBabR-63
80FraBabR-64
80FraBabR-65
80FraBabR-66
80FraBabR-67
80FraBabR-68
80FraBabR-69
80FraBabR-70
80FraBabR-71
80FraBabR-72
80FraBabR-73
80FraBabR-74
80FraBabR-75
80FraBabR-76
80FraBabR-77
80FraBabR-78
80FraBabR-79
80FraBabR-80
80Lau300-2
80LauFamF-16
80PacLeg-1
80PerHaloFP-4
80SSPHOF-1
80YanGreT-5
81ConTSN-4
81SpoHaloF-3
82BasCarN-20
82BHCRSpoL-2
82DiaCla-13
83ConMar-17
83TopSti-2
84DonCha-1
84GalHaloFRL-2
84OCoandSI-90
85CirK-2
85DonHOFS-1
85FegMurCG-15
85FegMurCG-16
85GeoSteM-8
85UltBasC-3
85Woo-31
86BigLeaC-2
86ConSer1-13
86ConSer1-20
86ConSer1-48
86ConSer1-50
86ConSer1-54
86SpoDecG-1
86TCM-12
86TCMSupS-2
86TCMSupS-9
86TCMSupS-14
86TCMSupS-42
86TCMSupS-43
86TopRos-87
87HygAllG-38
87NesDreT-5
87SpoCubG-1
87SpoRea-2
87Yan192T-9
88ConAmeA-21
88ConSer3-25
88GreBasS-81
88WilMulP-5
89CadEllD-45
89CMCBasG-4
89CMCRut-1
89CMCRut-2
89CMCRut-3
89CMCRut-4
89CMCRut-5
89CMCRut-6
89CMCRut-7
89CMCRut-8
89CMCRut-9
89CMCRut-10
89CMCRut-11
89CMCRut-12
89CMCRut-13
89CMCRut-14
89CMCRut-15
89CMCRut-16
89CMCRut-17
89CMCRut-18
89CMCRut-19
89CMCRut-20
89CMCRut-P1
89DodSmoG-26
89HOFStiB-47
89PacLegI-176
89SpollIFKI-216
89SweBasG-1
89TopBasT-20
89USPLegSC-4
89YanCitAG-5
90BasWit-86
90Col-10
90HOFStiB-25
90PerGreM-1
90RinPosYMP-2
90SweBasG-10
91CadEllD-44
91ConTSN-110
91ConTSN-145
91ConTSNP-145
91DenBal-3
91HomCooC-1
91SweBasG-124
91USGamSBL-2C
91USGamSBL-2D
91USGamSBL-2H
91USGamSBL-2S
92ConTSN-426
92ConTSN1N-663
92ConTSNAP-663G
92ConTSNCI-4
92DelRut-1
92GolEntR-1
92GolEntR-2
92GolEntR-3
92GolEntR-4
92GolEntR-5
92MegRut-1
92MegRut-2
92MegRut-3
92MegRut-4
92MegRut-5
92MegRut-6
92MegRut-7
92MegRut-8
92MegRut-9
92MegRut-10
92MegRut-11
92MegRut-12
92MegRut-13
92MegRut-14
92MegRut-15
92MegRut-16
92MegRut-17
92MegRut-18
92MegRut-19
92MegRut-20
92MegRut-21
92MegRut-22
92MegRut-23
92MegRut-24
92MegRut-25
92MegRut-26
92MegRut-27
92MegRut-28
92MegRut-29
92MegRut-30
92MegRut-31
92MegRut-32
92MegRut-33
92MegRut-34
92MegRut-35
92MegRut-36
92MegRut-37
92MegRut-38
92MegRut-39
92MegRut-40
92MegRut-41
92MegRut-42
92MegRut-43
92MegRut-44
92MegRut-45
92MegRut-46
92MegRut-47
92MegRut-48
92MegRut-49
92MegRut-50
92MegRut-51
92MegRut-52
92MegRut-53
92MegRut-54
92MegRut-55
92MegRut-56
92MegRut-57
92MegRut-58
92MegRut-59
92MegRut-60
92MegRut-61
92MegRut-62
92MegRut-63
92MegRut-64
92MegRut-65
92MegRut-66
92MegRut-67
92MegRut-68
92MegRut-69
92MegRut-70
92MegRut-71
92MegRut-72
92MegRut-73
92MegRut-74
92MegRut-75
92MegRut-76
92MegRut-77
92MegRut-78
92MegRut-79
92MegRut-80
92MegRut-81
92MegRut-82
92MegRut-83
92MegRut-84
92MegRut-85
92MegRut-86
92MegRut-87
92MegRut-88
92MegRut-89
92MegRut-90
92MegRut-91
92MegRut-92
92MegRut-93
92MegRut-94
92MegRut-95
92MegRut-96
92MegRut-97
92MegRut-98
92MegRut-99
92MegRut-100
92MegRut-101
92MegRut-102
92MegRut-103
92MegRut-104
92MegRut-105
92MegRut-106
92MegRut-107
92MegRut-108

92MegRut-109
92MegRut-110
92MegRut-111
92MegRut-112
92MegRut-113
92MegRut-114
92MegRut-115
92MegRut-116
92MegRut-117
92MegRut-118
92MegRut-119
92MegRut-120
92MegRut-121
92MegRut-122
92MegRut-123
92MegRut-124
92MegRut-125
92MegRut-126
92MegRut-127
92MegRut-128
92MegRut-129
92MegRut-130
92MegRut-131
92MegRut-132
92MegRut-133
92MegRut-134
92MegRut-135
92MegRut-136
92MegRut-137
92MegRut-138
92MegRut-139
92MegRut-140
92MegRut-141
92MegRut-142
92MegRut-143
92MegRut-144
92MegRut-145
92MegRut-146
92MegRut-147
92MegRut-148
92MegRut-149
92MegRut-150
92MegRut-151
92MegRut-152
92MegRut-153
92MegRut-154
92MegRut-155
92MegRut-156
92MegRut-157
92MegRut-158
92MegRut-159
92MegRut-160
92MegRut-161
92MegRut-162
92MegRut-163
92MegRutP-14
92MegRutP-31
92MegRutP-75
92MegRutP-106
92MegRutP-124
92MegRutP-129
92MegRutP-134
92MegRutP-138
92MegRutP-154
92PMGolRP-1
92Sco-879
92St.VinHHS-9
92TVSpoMF5HRC-12
92WhiLegtL-3
92WhiPro-3
92YanWIZA-72
92YanWIZH-29
93ActPacA-94
93ActPacA2-28G
93CadDis-47
93ConMasB-2
93ConMasC-5
93ConTSN-663
93ConTSN-888
93ConTSNP-888
93Hoy-6
93LegFoi-9
93LegFoiHI-1
93SpeHOFI-1
93TedWil-121
93TedWilLC-6
93UppDecAH-110
93UppDecAH-131
93UppDecAH-133
93UppDecAH-134
93UppDecAH-146
93UppDecAH-149
93UppDecAH-151
93UppDecAH-152
94ConTSN-1080
94ConTSNB-1080
94ConTSNCI-33
94ConTSNCI-35
94MegRutS-1
94MegRutS-2
94MegRutS-3
94MegRutS-4
94MegRutS-5
94TedWil5C-6
94TedWilTfB-T1
94TedWilTfB-T2
94TedWilTfB-T3
94TedWilTfB-T4
94TedWilTfB-T5
94TedWilTfB-T6
94TedWilTfB-T7
94TedWilTfB-T8
94TedWilTfB-T9
94UppDecAH-60
94UppDecAH-110
94UppDecAH-165
94UppDecAH1-60
94UppDecAH1-110
94UppDecAH1-165
94UppDecAJ-45
94UppDecAJG-45
94UppDecTAE-30
94UppDecTAE-BC1
94UppDecTAEGM-8
95ConTSN-1405
95ConTSN-NNO
95ConTSNGJ-1
95ConTSNP-3C
95ConTSNP-1535
95MegRut-1
95MegRut-2
95MegRut-3
95MegRut-4
95MegRut-5
95MegRut-6
95MegRut-7
95MegRut-8
95MegRut-9
95MegRut-10
95MegRut-11
95MegRut-12
95MegRut-13
95MegRut-14
95MegRut-15
95MegRut-16
95MegRut-17
95MegRut-18
95MegRut-19
95MegRut-20
95MegRut-21
95MegRut-22
95MegRut-23
95MegRut-24
95MegRut-25
95Top-3
95UppDecRH-73
95UppDecRH-74
95UppDecRH-75
95UppDecRH-76
95UppDecRH-77
95UppDecRH-78
95UppDecRH-79
95UppDecRH-80
95UppDecRH-81
95UppDecRH-NNO
95UppDecSHoB-3
96ColCho-500
96ColChoGS-500
96ColChoSS-500
97FleMilDM-3
20W516-1

Ruth, Claire
92MegRut-121

Ruth, Dorothy
92MegRut-151

Ruth, Helen
92MegRut-120

Ruth, Julia
92MegRut-152
92MegRut-153

Ruth, Pat
85CloHSS-37
89FreStaBS-18
91BatCliC-4
91BatCliP-3486
92ClaFS7-265
92SpaPhiF-1277
93SpaPhiC-23

Rutherford, Daryl
96IdaFalB-21

Rutherford, John
52Top-320
53Top-137
83TopRep5-320
90DodTar-700
91TopArc1-137
95TopArcBD-21
95TopArcBD-48

Ruthven, Dick
74OPC-47
74Top-47
75OPC-267
75Top-267
76OPC-431
76SSP-477
76Top-431
77BurCheD-208
77Hos-74
77Top-575
78Top-75
79PhiBurK-6
79Top-419
80PhiBurK-19
80Top-136
81AllGamPI-173
81Don-153
81Fle-16
81OPC-285
81Top-691
81TopSupHT-87
82Don-525
82Fle-257
82FleSta-52
82OPC-317
82Top-317
83CubThoAV-44
83Don-497
83Fle-172
83OPC-313
83PhiTas-26
83Top-484
83TopTra-98T
84CubChiT-24
84CubSev-44
84Don-510
84Fle-503
84Nes792-736
84OPC-156
84Top-736
84TopSti-49
84TopTif-736
85CubLioP-18
85CubSev-44
85Fle-64
85OPC-268
85Top-563
85TopMin-563
85TopTif-563
86Don-564
86Fle-377
86Top-98
86TopTif-98

Rutkay, Gary
52LavPro-38

Rutledge, Jeff
82QuaCitCT-19
86PitCubP-21

Rutledge, Trey
93PriRedC-26
93PriRedF-4179
94ChaWheC-22
94ChaWheF-2703
94LSUTigMP-13

Rutter, Sam
92BelBreC-5
92BelBreF-404

Rutz, Ryan
94HudValRF-3393
95ChaRivTI-13
95ChaRivUTIS-36
94HudValRC-20

Ruyak, Craig
90JohCitCS-23

Ruyak, Todd
92PriRedC-12
92PriRedF-3088
93WesVirWC-22
93WesVirWF-2866
94KinIndC-16
94KinIndF-2640

Ruzek, Don
77LodDodT-15
78LodDodT-16
83AppFoxF-27

Ryal, Mark
82OmaRoyT-21
83OmaRoyT-20
84OmaRoyT-24
85BufBisT-15
86EdmTraP-25
87AngSmo-14
87Don-583
88Fle-503
88FleGlo-503
88LouRedBTI-43
88Top-243
88TopTif-243
89BlaYNPRWL-162
89PhiTas-29
90BufBisC-20
90BufBisP-383
90BufBisTI-23
90CMC-20
90ProAAAF-498
93EdmTraF-1149

Ryan, Bill
20GasAmeMBD-32
21E121So1-87
21E121So8-80
23W503-5

Ryan, Blondy (John C.)
33ButCanV-42
34DiaMatCSB-159
34DiaStaR-40
34ExhFou-5
34Gou-32
34GouCanV-73
35ExhFou-6
81ConTSN-25
93ConTSN-694

Ryan, Bobby
90WatIndS-18
91RocExpC-12
91RocExpP-2047
92SalLakTSP-22

Ryan, Colin
88CapCodPPaLP-71
89EugEmeB-13
90AppFoxBS-22
90AppFoxP-2098
91BasCitRC-15
91BasCitRP-1401
91Cla/Bes-130

Ryan, Connie
47TipTop-84
49EurSta-19
51Bow-216
52Bow-164
52DixLid-17
52DixPre-17
52Top-107
53BowC-131
53NorBreL-26
53Top-102
54Top-136
74OPC-634
74Top-634
79DiaGre-222
83TCMPla1944-40
83TopRep5-107
91JesHSA-3
91TopArc1-102
93RanKee-316
94TopArc1-136
94TopArc1G-136

Ryan, Craig
79VanCanT-5
80VanCanT-15
80VenLeaS-124

Ryan, Dan
89SalLakTTI-8

Ryan, Duffy
81RedPioT-11

Ryan, Ellis
50IndTeal-22

Ryan, Jack
14TexTomE-39
90DodTar-701
90DodTar-1059
98CamPepP-65

Ryan, James E.
03BreE10-125
87BucN28-23
87OldJudN-436
88AllandGN-6
88AugBecN-23
88GandBCGCE-35
88WG1CarG-15
95May-37

Ryan, Jason
95Bow-12
95Exc-169
96Bow-256
96OrlCubB-23

Ryan, Jody
86BelMarC-117
87WauTimP-3
88SanBerSB-7
88SanBerSCLC-42
89SanBerSB-21
89SanBerSCLC-67

Ryan, John Budd
09ColChiE-248
09ColChiE-249
12ColRedB-248
12ColRedB-249
12ColTinT-248
12ColTinT-249
12T207-158
34ButPreR-54

Ryan, Ken (Kenneth Frederick)
86ElmPioRSP-18
87GreHorP-6
88LynRedSS-22
89WinHavRSS-19
90LynRedSTI-21
91WinHavRSC-8
91WinHavRSP-488
92NewBriRSF-432
92NewBriRSS-494
92SkyAA F-213
93Bow-3
93Don-383
93FleMajLP-B18
93LeaGolR-R13
93OPCPre-41
93PawRedSDD-23
93Pin-278
93Sco-329
93SelRoo-65T
93Top-786
93TopGol-786
93TopInaM-786
93TopMic-786
93TopTra-103T
93Ult-517
93UppDec-772
93UppDecGold-772
94ColC-248
94ColChoGS-248
94ColChoSS-248
94Don-276
94ExtBas-24
94Fla-266
94Fle-42
94SarRedSC-25
94Sco-592
94ScoGolR-592
94StaClu-404
94StaCluFDI-404
94StaCluGR-404
94StaCluMOP-404
94Top-264
94TopGol-264
94TopSpa-264
95ColCho-417
95ColChoGS-417
95ColChoSS-417
95Don-44
95DonPreP-44
95DonTopotO-25
95Emb-60
95EmbGolI-60
95Fle-39
95Lea-217
95Pin-353
95PinArtP-353
95PinMusC-353
95Sco-498
95ScoGolR-498
95ScoPlaTS-498
95StaClu-81
95StaCluFDI-81
95StaCluMOP-81
95StaCluSTWS-81
95Top-63
95TopCyb-45
95Ult-15
95UltGolM-15

95UppDec-401
95UppDecED-401
95UppDecEDG-401
95UppDecSE-79
95UppDecSEG-79
96FleUpd-U169
96FleUpdTC-U169
96LeaSigA-198
96LeaSigAG-198
96LeaSigAS-198
96PhiTeal-28
97Fle-419
97FleTif-419
97Top-144
Ryan, Kevin
85AncGlaPTI-26
91BluOriC-17
91BluOriP-4128
92FreKeyC-26
92FreKeyF-1805
93BowBayF-2187
94BowBayF-2413
94OriPro-86
95BowBayTI-40
95RocRedWTI-31
Ryan, Matt
94AugGreC-21
94AugGreF-3009
95CarMudF-155
Ryan, Mike
65Top-573
66Top-419
67CokCapRS-9
67Top-223
67TopRedSS-14
68Top-306
68TopVen-306
69MLBOffS-177
69OPC-28
69PhiTeal-8
69Top-28
69TopTeaP-8
70MLBOffS-93
70Top-591
71MLBOffS-186
71OPC-533
71Top-533
72MilBra-302
72OPC-324
72Top-324
73OPC-467
73Top-467
74OPC-564
74Top-564
81RedSoxBG2S-106
84PhiTas-13
85PhiTas-6
85PhiTas-8
86PhiTas-5
87PhiTas-xx0
88PhiTas-29
88Top-669
88TopTif-669
89PhiTas-30
90PhiTas-34
92PhiMed-27
93PhiMed-30
94PhiMed-29
95Phi-27
Ryan, Nolan
68OPC-177
68Top-177
68TopVen-177
69MetNewYDN-15
69Top-533
70MetTra-24A
70MLBOffS-81
70OPC-197
70OPC-198
70Top-197
70Top-198
70Top-712
71MLBOffS-162
71OPC-513
71Top-355
71Top-513
72Top-595
73Kel2D-16
73LinPor-35
73MetAllEB-9
73OPC-67
73OPC-220
73Top-67
73Top-220
73TopCanL-45
73TopCom-17
73TopPin-17
74Kel-8
74NewYorNTDiS-15
74OPC-20
74OPC-207
74Top-20
74Top-207
74TopDecE-41
74TopPuz-9
74TopSta-147
75Hos-58
75HosTwi-58
75Kel-26
75OPC-5
75OPC-7
75OPC-312
75OPC-500
75SSP42-10
75Top-5
75Top-7
75Top-312
75Top-500
76BooProC-18
76CraDis-52
76Hos-79
76LauDiaJ-1
76OPC-330
76SSP-187
76SSP-593A
76SSP-593B
76Top-330
77BurCheD-123
77Hos-81
77MSADis-53
77OPC-6
77OPC-65
77OPC-264
77PepGloD-24
77Spo-216
77Spo-2304
77Top-6
77Top-234
77Top-650
77TopCloS-40
78AngFamF-33
78Hos-83
78Kel-51
78OPC-6
78OPC-105
78OPC-241
78Pep-37
78RCColC-93
78SSP270-203
78Top-6
78Top-206
78Top-400
78WifBalD-65
79Hos-101
79OPC-51
79Top-6
79Top-115
79Top-417
79TopCom-4
80BurKinPHR-9
80Kel-20
80OPC-303
80Top-206
80Top-580
80TopSup-20
81AllGamPI-174
81CokTeaS-69
81Don-260
81Fle-57
81FleStiC-108
81Kel-6
81OPC-240
81PerCreC-26
81Top-240
81TopSti-30
81TopSti-173
81TopSupHT-101
82AstAstI-7
82Don-13
82Don-419
82FBIDis-19
82Fle-229
82FleSta-42
82FleSta-242
82Kel-11
82OPC-90
82Top-5
82Top-66
82Top-90
82Top-167
82TopSti-13
82TopSti-41
82TopStiV-41
83AllGamPI-175
83Don-118
83DonActA-23
83Fle-463
83FleSta-170
83FleSti-141
83FleSti-207
83Kel-31
83KelCerB-2
83OPC-360
83OPC-361
83Top-360
83Top-361
83TopFol-1
83TopGloS-28
83TopSti-235
84AllGamPI-86
84AstMot-1
84Don-60
84DonActAS-14
84DonCha-39
84Fle-239
84FleSti-82
84FunFooP-109
84Nes792-4
84Nes792-66
84Nes792-470
84Nes792-707
84OCoandSI-7
84OCoandSI-211
84OCoandSI-244
84OPC-66
84RalPur-14
84RawGloT-3
84SevCoi-W13
84Top-4
84Top-66
84Top-470
84Top-707
84TopCer-14
84TopGaloC-10
84TopGloS-15
84TopPewB-7
84TopRubD-26
84TopSti-66
84TopSup-28
84TopTif-4
84TopTif-66
84TopTif-470
84TopTif-707
85AllGamPI-175
85AngStrH-11
85AstHouP-3
85AstMot-2
85Don-60
85DonActA-20
85DonHig-22
85Fle-359
85FleLimE-30
85FleStaS-115
85Lea-216
85OPC-63
85SevCoi-C1
85SevCoi-S3
85StaRya-1
85StaRya-2
85StaRya-3
85StaRya-4
85StaRya-5
85StaRya-6
85StaRya-7
85StaRya-8
85StaRya-9
85StaRya-10
85StaRya-11
85StaRya-12
85Top-7
85Top-760
85TopMin-760
85TopRubD-26
85TopSti-58
85TopSup-23
85TopTif-7
85TopTif-760
85Woo-32
86AstMilL-18
86AstMot-23
86AstPol-2
86AstTeal-13
86BasStaB-94
86Don-258
86DonAll-21
86Dra-33
86Fle-310
86FleFutHoF-5
86FleMin-65
86FleSlu-30
86FleStiC-102
86Lea-132
86MSAJifPD-13
86OPC-100
86QuaGra-12
86SevCoi-C8
86SevCoi-E8
86SevCoi-S8
86SevCoi-W8
86Spo-43
86Spo-141
86Spo-143
86Spo-182
86SpoDecG-63
86Top-100
86TopGloS-45
86TopMinL-43
86TopSti-9
86TopSti-24
86TopSup-47
86TopTat-24
86TopTif-100
86TruVal-26
87AstMot-8
87AstPol-16
87ClaGam-82
87Don-138
87DonHig-53
87Dra-32
87Fle-67
87FleBasA-38
87FleGlo-67
87FleStiC-103
87K-M-20
87KraFoo-48
87Lea-257
87MandMSL-22
87OPC-155
87RalPur-1
87RedFolSB-121
87Spo-125
87SpoRea-22
87SpoTeaP-8
87StuPan-5
87Top-757
87TopCoi-40
87TopSti-27
87TopTif-757
88AstMot-8
88AstPol-20
88ClaRed-179
88Don-61
88DonBasB-232
88Fle-455
88FleBasA-34
88FleGlo-455
88FleMin-79
88FleStiC-88
88GreBasS-22
88HouSho-12
88K-M-23
88Lea-77
88Nes-43
88OPC-250
88OPCBoxB-N
88PanSti-288
88PanSti-435
88Sco-575
88ScoGlo-575
88Spo-39
88StaLinAl-27
88StaLinAst-15
88Top-6
88Top-250
88Top-661
88TopBig-29
88TopCoi-50
88TopGaloC-11
88TopMinL-50
88TopRevLL-8
88TopSti-7
88TopTif-6
88TopTif-250
88TopTif-661
88TopUKM-62
88TopUKMT-62
88TopWaxBC-N
88Woo-6
89AngSmo-7
89BesWesR-NNO
89Bow-225
89BowTif-225
89CadEllD-46
89ClaTraP-164
89Don-154
89DonBasB-55
89DonTra-19
89Fle-368
89FleGlo-368
89FleUpd-67
89KinDis-10
89OPC-366
89OPCBoxB-K
89PanSti-83
89PanSti-226
89RanMot-2
89RanSmo-29
89RedFolSB-100
89RinPosM1-24
89Sco-300
89ScoHot1S-64
89ScoRoo-2T
89ScoSco-5
89Spo-115
89SpoIllFKI-81
89Top-530
89TopBasT-70
89TopMinL-14
89TopSti-20
89TopTif-530
89TopTra-106T
89TopTraT-106T
89TopWaxBC-K
89UppDec-145
89UppDec-669
89UppDec-774
90AllBasT-16
90BasWit-55
90Bow-486
90BowIns-8
90BowInsT-8
90BowTif-486
90BowTif-A8
90ClaBlu-1
90ClaUpd-T26
90ClaYel-T84
90ClaYel-T91
90ClaYel-NNO0
90Col-14
90Don-166
90Don-659
90Don-659A
90Don-665
90Don-665A
90Don-665C
90DonBesA-49
90DonLeaS-24
90DonPre-7
90DonSupD-NNO
90Fle-313
90Fle-636
90FleAwaW-29
90FleCan-313
90FleCan-636
90FleLeaL-31
90FleUpd-131
90GooHumICBLS-17
90HOFStiB-77
90Hot50PS-35
90K-M-25
90KayB-28
90KinDis-22
90Lea-21
90Lea-264
90Lea-265
90MotRya-1
90MotRya-2
90MotRya-3
90MotRya-4
90MSAIceTD-20
90OPC-1
90OPC-2
90OPC-3
90OPC-4
90OPC-5
90OPCBoxB-O
90PanSti-160
90PanSti-185
90PanSti-387
90Pos-11

90PubSti-421
90RanMot-2
90RedFolSB-81
90RinPosR1-1
90RinPosR1-2
90RinPosR1-3
90RinPosR1-4
90RinPosR1-5
90RinPosR1-6
90RinPosR1-7
90RinPosR1-8
90RinPosR1-9
90RinPosR1-10
90RinPosR1-11
90RinPosR1-12
90RinPosR2-1
90RinPosR2-2
90RinPosR2-3
90RinPosR2-4
90RinPosR2-5
90RinPosR2-6
90RinPosR2-7
90RinPosR2-8
90RinPosR2-9
90RinPosR2-10
90RinPosR2-11
90RinPosR2-12
90RyaArlYP-1
90Sco-250
90Sco-696
90Sco100S-44
90ScoSpoR-NNO
90Spo-8
90StaLonJS-13
90StaLonJS-26
90StaRya-1
90StaRya-2
90StaRya-3
90StaRya-4
90StaRya-5
90StaRya-6
90StaRya-7
90StaRya-8
90StaRya-9
90StaRya-10
90StaRya-11
90SupActM-5
90Top-1
90Top-2
90Top-3
90Top-4
90Top-5
90TopBig-171
90TopCoi-25
90TopDou-53
90TopGaloC-9
90TopGloS-2
90TopMag-10
90TopMag-109
90TopMag-110
90TopMag-111
90TopMag-112
90TopMinL-39
90TopSti-3
90TopSti-242
90TopStiB-58
90TopTif-1
90TopTif-2
90TopTif-3
90TopTif-4
90TopTif-5
90TopTVA-9
90TopWaxBC-O
90UppDec-34
90UppDec-544
90UppDec-734A
90UppDec-734B
90UppDecS-1
90UppDecS-2
90WonBreS-16
90Woo-20
91BasBesRB-14
91BlePro-3
91BlePro-4
91BlePro-5
91BlePro-6
91BlePro-7
91Bow-280
91CadEllD-45
91Cla1-T86
91Cla2-T80
91Cla2-T97
91Cla3-T79
91Cla3-T98
91ClaGam-196
91ClaNolR1-1
91ClaNolR1-2
91ClaNolR1-3
91ClaNolR1-4
91ClaNolR1-5
91ClaNolR1-6
91ClaNolR1-7
91ClaNolR1-8
91ClaNolR1-9
91ClaNolR1-10
91Col-3
91Don-89
91DonBonC-BC3
91DonBonC-BC15
91DonEli-L1
91DonPre-7
91Fle-302
91FleWaxBC-3
91JimDea-24
91Lea-423
91LeaGolR-BC25
91LeaPre-25
91MajLeaCP-35
91MetWIZ-338
91MotNolR-1
91MotNolR-2
91MotNolR-3
91MotNolR-4
91MSAHolD-19
91OPC-1
91OPC-6
91OPCBoxB-N
91OPCPre-102
91PacRya7N-1
91PacRya7N-2
91PacRya7N-3
91PacRya7N-4
91PacRya7N-5
91PacRya7N-6
91PacRya7N-7
91PacRyaI8-1
91PacRyaI8-2
91PacRyaI8-3
91PacRyaI8-4
91PacRyaI8-5
91PacRyaI8-6
91PacRyaI8-7
91PacRyaI8-8
91PacRyaTEI-1
91PacRyaTEI-2
91PacRyaTEI-3
91PacRyaTEI-4
91PacRyaTEI-5
91PacRyaTEI-6
91PacRyaTEI-7
91PacRyaTEI-8
91PacRyaTEI-9
91PacRyaTEI-10
91PacRyaTEI-11
91PacRyaTEI-12
91PacRyaTEI-13
91PacRyaTEI-14
91PacRyaTEI-15
91PacRyaTEI-16
91PacRyaTEI-17
91PacRyaTEI-18
91PacRyaTEI-19
91PacRyaTEI-20
91PacRyaTEI-21
91PacRyaTEI-22
91PacRyaTEI-23
91PacRyaTEI-24
91PacRyaTEI-25
91PacRyaTEI-26
91PacRyaTEI-27
91PacRyaTEI-28
91PacRyaTEI-29
91PacRyaTEI-30
91PacRyaTEI-31
91PacRyaTEI-32
91PacRyaTEI-33
91PacRyaTEI-34
91PacRyaTEI-35
91PacRyaTEI-36
91PacRyaTEI-37
91PacRyaTEI-38
91PacRyaTEI-39
91PacRyaTEI-40
91PacRyaTEI-41
91PacRyaTEI-42
91PacRyaTEI-43
91PacRyaTEI-44
91PacRyaTEI-45
91PacRyaTEI-46
91PacRyaTEI-47
91PacRyaTEI-48
91PacRyaTEI-49
91PacRyaTEI-50
91PacRyaTEI-51
91PacRyaTEI-52
91PacRyaTEI-53
91PacRyaTEI-54
91PacRyaTEI-55
91PacRyaTEI-56
91PacRyaTEI-57
91PacRyaTEI-58
91PacRyaTEI-59
91PacRyaTEI-60
91PacRyaTEI-61
91PacRyaTEI-62
91PacRyaTEI-63
91PacRyaTEI-64
91PacRyaTEI-65
91PacRyaTEI-66
91PacRyaTEI-67
91PacRyaTEI-68
91PacRyaTEI-69
91PacRyaTEI-70
91PacRyaTEI-71
91PacRyaTEI-72
91PacRyaTEI-73
91PacRyaTEI-74
91PacRyaTEI-75
91PacRyaTEI-76
91PacRyaTEI-77
91PacRyaTEI-78
91PacRyaTEI-79
91PacRyaTEI-80
91PacRyaTEI-81
91PacRyaTEI-82
91PacRyaTEI-83
91PacRyaTEI-84
91PacRyaTEI-85
91PacRyaTEI-86
91PacRyaTEI-87
91PacRyaTEI-88
91PacRyaTEI-89
91PacRyaTEI-90
91PacRyaTEI-91
91PacRyaTEI-92
91PacRyaTEI-93
91PacRyaTEI-94
91PacRyaTEI-95
91PacRyaTEI-96
91PacRyaTEI-97
91PacRyaTEI-98
91PacRyaTEI-99
91PacRyaTEI-100
91PacRyaTEI-101
91PacRyaTEI-102
91PacRyaTEI-103
91PacRyaTEI-104
91PacRyaTEI-105
91PacRyaTEI-106
91PacRyaTEI-107
91PacRyaTEI-108
91PacRyaTEI-109
91PacRyaTEI-110
91PanCanT1-77
91PanFreS-259
91PanFreS-354
91PanSti-3
91PanSti-205
91PetSta-25
91Pos-17
91PosCan-27
91RanMot-2
91RedFolS-79
91Sco-4
91Sco-417
91Sco-686
91Sco-701
91Sco100S-25
91ScoCoo-B7
91ScoRyaLaT-1
91ScoRyaLaT-2
91ScoRyaLaT-3
91ScoRyaLaT-4
91SevCoi-A14
91SevCoi-F14
91SevCoi-T11
91SevCoi-NC8
91SevCoi-NW14
91SevCoi-SC12
91SilHol-2
91StaClu-200
91StaCluCM-24
91StaCluCM-25
91StaCluCM-NNO
91StaCluMO-7
91StaCluMO-27
91StaCluP-36
91StaPinB-39
91StaRya-1
91StaRya-2
91StaRya-3
91StaRya-4
91StaRya-5
91StaRya-6
91StaRya-7
91StaRya-8
91StaRya-9
91StaRya-10
91StaRya-11
91Stu-128
91SunSee-20
91Top-1
91Top-6
91TopCraJI-1
91TopDesS-1
91TopDesS-6
91TopMic-1
91TopMic-6
91TopSta-29
91TopTif-1
91TopTif-6
91TopTriH-A13
91TopWaxBC-N
91Ult-355
91Ult-395
91Ult-400
91UppDec-345
91UppDec-SP2
91UppDecCBP-1
91UppDecCBP-3
91UppDecRH-10
91UppDecRH-11
91UppDecRH-12
91UppDecRH-13
91UppDecRH-14
91UppDecRH-15
91UppDecRH-16
91UppDecRH-17
91UppDecRH-18
91UppDecRH-AU2
91Woo-19
92Ble23KR-1
92Ble23KR-2
92Ble23KR-3
92Bow-222
92Cla1-T78
92Cla1-NNO
92Cla2-T67
92ClaBluBF-BC1
92ClaFS7-1
92ClaGam-183
92ClaRedB-BC1
92ColPro-12
92ColRya-1
92ColRya-2
92ColRya-3
92ColRya-4
92ColRya-5
92ColRya-6
92ColRya-7
92ColRya-8
92ColRya-9
92ColRya-10
92ColRya-11
92ColRya-12
92ConTSNGI-934G
92DEL-AU3
92Don-154
92Don-555
92Don-707
92DonCokR-1
92DonCokR-2
92DonCokR-3
92DonCokR-4
92DonCokR-5
92DonCokR-6
92DonCokR-7
92DonCokR-8
92DonCokR-9
92DonCokR-10
92DonCokR-11
92DonCokR-12
92DonCokR-13
92DonCokR-14
92DonCokR-15
92DonCokR-16
92DonCokR-17
92DonCokR-18
92DonCokR-19
92DonCokR-20
92DonCokR-21
92DonCokR-22
92DonCokR-23
92DonCokR-24
92DonCokR-25
92DonCokR-26
92DonCraJ1-15
92DonMcD-5
92DonPre-11
92Fle-320
92Fle-682
92Fle-710
92FleCitTP-1
92FleSmo'nH-S5
92Hig5-114
92Hig5S-25
92Hig5S-34
92JimDeaLL-6
92KinDis-7
92Lea-41
92Lea-133
92LeaBlaG-41
92LeaGolP-25
92LeaPre-25
92MooSna-20
92MotRya7N-1
92MotRya7N-2
92MotRya7N-3
92MotRya7N-4
92MotRya7N-5
92MotRya7N-6
92MotRya7N-7
92MotRya7N-8
92Mr.TurS-20
92New-22
92OPC-1
92OPC-4
92OPCPre-81
92PacRyaG-1
92PacRyaG-2
92PacRyaG-3
92PacRyaG-4
92PacRyaG-5
92PacRyaG-6
92PacRyaG-7
92PacRyaG-8
92PacRyaL-1
92PacRyaL-2
92PacRyaL-3
92PacRyaL-4
92PacRyaL-5
92PacRyaL-6
92PacRyaM6-1
92PacRyaM6-2
92PacRyaM6-3
92PacRyaM6-4
92PacRyaM6-5
92PacRyaM6-6
92PacRyaTEI-111
92PacRyaTEI-112
92PacRyaTEI-113
92PacRyaTEI-114
92PacRyaTEI-115
92PacRyaTEI-116
92PacRyaTEI-117
92PacRyaTEI-118
92PacRyaTEI-119
92PacRyaTEI-120
92PacRyaTEI-121
92PacRyaTEI-122
92PacRyaTEI-123
92PacRyaTEI-124
92PacRyaTEI-125
92PacRyaTEI-126
92PacRyaTEI-127
92PacRyaTEI-128
92PacRyaTEI-129
92PacRyaTEI-130
92PacRyaTEI-131
92PacRyaTEI-132
92PacRyaTEI-133
92PacRyaTEI-134
92PacRyaTEI-135
92PacRyaTEI-136
92PacRyaTEI-137
92PacRyaTEI-138
92PacRyaTEI-139
92PacRyaTEI-140
92PacRyaTEI-141
92PacRyaTEI-142

92PacRyaTEI-143
92PacRyaTEI-144
92PacRyaTEI-145
92PacRyaTEI-146
92PacRyaTEI-147
92PacRyaTEI-148
92PacRyaTEI-149
92PacRyaTEI-150
92PacRyaTEI-151
92PacRyaTEI-152
92PacRyaTEI-153
92PacRyaTEI-154
92PacRyaTEI-155
92PacRyaTEI-156
92PacRyaTEI-157
92PacRyaTEI-158
92PacRyaTEI-159
92PacRyaTEI-160
92PacRyaTEI-161
92PacRyaTEI-162
92PacRyaTEI-163
92PacRyaTEI-164
92PacRyaTEI-165
92PacRyaTEI-166
92PacRyaTEI-167
92PacRyaTEI-168
92PacRyaTEI-169
92PacRyaTEI-170
92PacRyaTEI-171
92PacRyaTEI-172
92PacRyaTEI-173
92PacRyaTEI-174
92PacRyaTEI-175
92PacRyaTEI-176
92PacRyaTEI-177
92PacRyaTEI-178
92PacRyaTEI-179
92PacRyaTEI-180
92PacRyaTEI-181
92PacRyaTEI-182
92PacRyaTEI-183
92PacRyaTEI-184
92PacRyaTEI-185
92PacRyaTEI-186
92PacRyaTEI-187
92PacRyaTEI-188
92PacRyaTEI-189
92PacRyaTEI-190
92PacRyaTEI-191
92PacRyaTEI-192
92PacRyaTEI-193
92PacRyaTEI-194
92PacRyaTEI-195
92PacRyaTEI-196
92PacRyaTEI-197
92PacRyaTEI-198
92PacRyaTEI-199
92PacRyaTEI-200
92PacRyaTEI-201
92PacRyaTEI-202
92PacRyaTEI-203
92PacRyaTEI-204
92PacRyaTEI-205
92PacRyaTEI-206
92PacRyaTEI-207
92PacRyaTEI-208
92PacRyaTEI-209
92PacRyaTEI-210
92PacRyaTEI-211
92PacRyaTEI-212
92PacRyaTEI-213
92PacRyaTEI-214
92PacRyaTEI-215
92PacRyaTEI-216
92PacRyaTEI-217
92PacRyaTEI-218
92PacRyaTEI-219
92PacRyaTEI-220
92PacSea-82
92PacSea-85
92PanSti-82
92Pin-50
92Pin-281
92Pin-294
92Pin-618
92PinRool-12
92Pos-27
92RanMot-2
92RanTeal-22
92Sco-2
92Sco-425
92Sco100S-50
92ScoProP-1
92ScoProP-14
92SevCoi-11
92SpollIFK1-168
92SpoStaCC-38
92StaClu-605
92StaClu-770
92StaCluECN-605
92StaCluMO-26
92StaCluMO-27
92StaCluMP-11
92Stu-248
92Top-1
92Top-4
92TopGol-1
92TopGol-4
92TopGolPS-1
92TopGolW-1
92TopGolW-4
92TopKid-127
92TopMcD-24
92TopMic-1
92TopMic-4
92TopMic-G1
92TriPla-22
92Ult-141
92UppDec-92
92UppDec-655
92UppDecF-37
92UppDecFG-37
92UppDecS-13
92UppDecTMH-45
93BlePro-4
93BlePro-5
93BlePro-6
93BlePro-7
93BlePro-8
93BlePro-9
93BleRya6-1
93BleRya6-2
93BleRya6-3
93BleRya6-4
93BleRya6-5
93BleRya6-6
93Bow-405
93CadDis-48
93ClaGam-79
93ConMasC-3
93ConTSN-928
93ConTSN-929
93ConTSN-930
93ConTSN-931
93ConTSN-932
93ConTSN-933
93ConTSN-934
93ConTSN-935
93ConTSNP-934
93DiaMar-91
93DiaMarA-6
93Don-423
93DonEliD-10
93DonEliD-AU10
93DonEliS-20
93DonMasotG-2
93DurPowP1-20
93Fin-107
93FinJum-107
93FinPro-107
93FinProR-107
93FinRef-107
93Fla-286
93FlaPro-7
93Fle-690
93FleAtl-20
93FleFinEDT-6
93FleFruotL-55
93FunPac-18
93FunPac-26
93FunPac-33
93FunPac-160
93FunPac-214
93HumDumC-16
93JimDea-16
93KinDis-17
93Kra-13
93Lea-115
93LeaGolA-R19
93LeaHeaftH-1
93MetBak-35
93MotRyaF-1
93MotRyaF-2
93MotRyaF-3
93MotRyaF-4
93MotRyaF-5
93MotRyaF-6
93MotRyaF-7
93MotRyaF-8
93MotRyaF-9
93MotRyaF-10
93OPC-229
93OPCPreSP-20
93OPCPreSPF-20
93PacJugC-15
93PacRya2S-221
93PacRya2S-222
93PacRya2S-223
93PacRya2S-224
93PacRya2S-225
93PacRya2S-226
93PacRya2S-227
93PacRya2S-228
93PacRya2S-229
93PacRya2S-230
93PacRya2S-231
93PacRya2S-232
93PacRya2S-233
93PacRya2S-234
93PacRya2S-235
93PacRya2S-236
93PacRya2S-237
93PacRya2S-238
93PacRya2S-239
93PacRya2S-240
93PacRya2S-241
93PacRya2S-242
93PacRya2S-243
93PacRya2S-244
93PacRya2S-245
93PacRya2S-246
93PacRya2S-247
93PacRya2S-248
93PacRya2S-249
93PacRya2S-250
93PacRyaFM-1
93PacRyaFM-2
93PacRyaFM-3
93PacRyaFM-4
93PacRyaFM-5
93PacRyaFM-6
93PacRyaFM-7
93PacRyaFM-8
93PacRyaFM-9
93PacRyaFM-10
93PacRyaFM-11
93PacRyaFM-12
93PacRyaFM-13
93PacRyaFM-14
93PacRyaFM-15
93PacRyaFM-16
93PacRyaFM-17
93PacRyaFM-18
93PacRyaFM-19
93PacRyaFM-20
93PacRyaL-7
93PacRyaL-8
93PacRyaL-9
93PacRyaL-10
93PacRyaL-11
93PacRyaL-12
93PacRyaPI-1
93PacRyaPI-2
93PacRyaPI-3
93PacRyaPI-4
93PacRyaPI-5
93PacRyaPI-6
93PacRyaPI-7
93PacRyaPI-8
93PacRyaPI-9
93PacRyaPI-10
93PacRyaPI-11
93PacRyaPI-12
93PacRyaPI-13
93PacRyaPI-14
93PacRyaPI-15
93PacRyaPI-16
93PacRyaPI-17
93PacRyaPI-18
93PacRyaPI-19
93PacRyaPI-20
93PacSpa-317
93PanSti-87
93PhoFilR-1
93PhoFilR-2
93PhoFilR-3
93PhoFilR-4
93PhoFilR-5
93PhoFilR-6
93PhoFilR-7
93Pin-75
93Pin-290
93PinCoo-1
93PinCooD-1
93PinTri-6
93PinTri-7
93PinTri-8
93PinTri-9
93PinTri-10
93Pos-20
93RanDrP-3
93RanKee-431
93Sco-59
93Sel-90
93SelRoo-NR1
93SP-198
93SpeRya1-1
93SpeRya1-2
93SpeRya1-3
93SpeRya1-4
93SpeRya1-5
93SpeRya1-6
93SpeRya1-7
93SpeRya1-8
93SpeRya1-9
93SpeRya1-10
93SpeRya2-1
93SpeRya2-2
93SpeRya2-3
93SpeRya5-1
93SpeRya5-2
93SpeRya5-3
93SpeRya5-4
93SpeRya5-5
93SpeRyaTS-1
93StaClu-353
93StaCluFDI-353
93StaCluMOP-353
93StaCluMP-21
93StaCluR-1
93Stu-71
93StuSil-10
93TexSupRS-1
93TexSupRS-2
93TexSupRS-3
93TexSupRS-4
93TexSupRS-5
93TexSupRS-6
93TexSupRS-7
93TexSupRS-8
93TexSupRS-9
93TexSupRS-10
93TexSupRS-11
93TexSupRS-12
93TexSupRS-13
93TexSupRS-14
93TexSupRS-15
93TexSupRS-16
93TexSupRS-17
93TexSupRS-18
93TexSupRS-19
93TexSupRS-20
93TexSupRS-21
93TexSupRS-22
93TexSupRS-23
93TexSupRS-24
93TexSupRS-25
93TexSupRS-26
93TexSupRS-27
93TexSupRS-28
93TexSupRS-29
93TexSupRS-30
93Top-700
93TopGol-700
93TopInaM-700
93TopMagJRC-4
93TopMic-700
93TopMic-P700
93TriPla-96
93TriPlaN-7
93Ult-636
93UltStrK-4
93UppDec-37
93UppDec-155
93UppDec-SP6
93UppDecDG-30
93UppDecFA-A5
93UppDecFAJ-A5
93UppDecGold-37
93UppDecGold-155
93UppDecIC-WI19
93UppDecICJ-WI19
93UppDecOD-D20
93UppDecS-19
93UppDecSH-HI17
93UppDecTAN-TN5
93WhaRya-1
93WhaRya-2
93WhaRya-3
93WhaRya-4
93WhaRya-5
93WhaRya-6
93WhaRya-7
93WhaRya-8
93WhaRya-9
93WhaRya-10
94ColC-249
94ColC-320
94ColChoGS-249
94ColChoGS-320
94ColChoSS-249
94ColChoSS-320
94ConTSNCI-30
94Don-1
94DonAnn8-5
94DonSpeE-1
94Fle-321
94FleGolM-7
94FleSmo'nH-10
94HarStaR-1
94LegPosR-1
94Met69CCPP-27
94Met69CS-26
94Met69T-7
94RanAllP-17
94RyaSSC-1
94RyaSSC-2
94RyaSSC-3
94RyaSSC-4
94RyaSSC-5
94RyaSSC-6
94RyaSSC-7
94RyaSSC-8
94RyaSSC-9
94RyaSSC-10
94RyaSSC-11
94RyaSSC-12
94SigRooFCS-AU7
94SigRooFCS-AU8
94StaClu-34
94StaCluFDI-34
94StaCluGR-34
94StaCluMOP-34
94Top-34
94TopGol-34
94TopPorP-700
94TopPre-700
94TopSpa-34
94UppDecAH-15
94UppDecAH-34
94UppDecAH-120
94UppDecAH-125
94UppDecAH1-15
94UppDecAH1-34
94UppDecAH1-120
94UppDecAH1-125
94UppDecTAE-79
95ColCho-46
95ColCho-52
95ColChoGS-46
95ColChoGS-52
95ColChoSS-46
95ColChoSS-52
95EagBalL-1
95FanRya-1
95FanRya-2
95FanRya-3
95FanRya-4
95FanRya-5
95SP-2
95SPChaCP-CP2
95SPChaCPDC-CP2
95SPSil-2
95UppDec-448
95UppDecED-448
95UppDecEDG-448
95UppDecSE-175
95UppDecSEG-175
95UppDecSHoB-6
96MetImpRy-1
96MetImpRy-2
96MetImpRy-3
96MetImpRy-4
96MetImpRy-5
96MetImpRy-6
96MetImpRy-7
96MetImpRy-8
96MetImpRy-9
96MetImpRy-10
96PacNolR-1

96PacNolR-2
96PacNolR-3
96PacNolR-4
96PacNolR-5
96PacNolR-6
96PacNolR-7
96PacNolR-8
96PacNolR-9
96PacNolR-10
96PacNolR-11
96PacNolR-12
96PacNolR-13
96PacNolR-14
96PacNolR-15
96PacNolR-16
96PacNolR-17
96PacNolR-18
96PacNolR-19
96PacNolR-20
96PacNolR-21
96PacNolR-22
96PacNolR-23
96PacNolR-24
96PacNolR-25
96PacNolR-26
96PacNolR-27
96PacNolR-A
96PacNolR-B
96Pro-13
Ryan, Ray
09T206-513
Ryan, Reese
92PacRyaTEI-149
Ryan, Reid
90ClaYel-T91
94HudValRF-3385
94SigRooFCD-4
94SigRooFCS-AU7
94SigRooFCS-AU8
94TopTra-101T
95ChaRivTI-1
95ColCho-45
95ColChoGS-45
95ColChoSS-45
95Exc-131
95UppDec-15
95UppDecED-15
95UppDecEDG-15
94HudValRC-21
Ryan, Rob
94LetMouF-3887
94LetMouSP-14
96AriBlaDB-28
Ryan, Rosy (Wilfred)
21KoBreWSI-19
22W575-113
23W501-75
23WilChoV-140
90DodTar-702
93ConTSN-746
Ryan, Sean
90BatCliP-3076
91Cla/Bes-117
91LinDriAA-517
91ReaPhiLD-517
91ReaPhiP-1377
92ClaFS7-234
92ReaPhiF-583
92ReaPhiS-542
92SkyAA F-236
92UppDecML-120
93ScrRedBF-2551
93ScrRedBTI-23
Ryba, Mike (Dominic)
42RedSoxTI-21
43RedSoxTI-21
46RedSoxTI-21
54CarHunW-23
54Top-237
83TCMPla1944-11
94TopArc1-237
94TopArc1G-237
95ConTSN-1401
Rychel, Kevin
90AugPirP-2461
91SalBucC-19
91SalBucP-949
92AugPirC-9
92SalBucF-63
93SalBucC-21
93SalBucF-431
94CarMudF-1580
95CarMudF-156
96CarMudB-9
Ryder, Brian
80NasSouTI-17
81ColCliP-35
81ColCliT-14
82IndIndTI-11
83IndIndTI-11
Ryder, Derek
95CedRapKTI-20
96CedRapKTI-20
Ryder, Scott
90IdaFalBP-3245
91PulBraC-26
91PulBraP-4003
92DurBulC-4
92DurBulF-1098
92DurBulTI-26
93DurBulC-15
93DurBulF-484
Ryder, Steve
94HunCubF-3563
94HunCubC-25
Ryerson, Gary
75SalLakCC-14
94BreMilB-350
Rymer, Carlos
80AndBraT-16
Rypien, Mark
91StaCluMO-34
Ryun, Jim
74NewYorNTDiS-8
Saa, Humberto
90HunCubP-3293
91GenCubC-17
91GenCubP-4227
Saatzer, Michael
82RedPioT-10
83NasAngT-7
86QuaCitAP-30
Saavedra, Ed
78WatIndT-20
79WatIndT-21
81WatIndT-27
82ChaLooT-4
83BufBisT-20
84BufBisT-22
Saavedra, Justo
80BatTroT-23
Sabel, Erik
96AriBlaDB-29
Saberhagen, Bret
84FleUpd-103
84TopTra-104T
84TopTraT-104T
85Don-222
85DonHig-26
85Fle-212
85FleStaS-124
85OPC-23
85Top-23
85TopTif-23
86BasStaB-95
86Don-11
86Don-100
86DonSupD-11
86Dra-29
86Fle-19
86FleLeaL-37
86FleLimE-38
86FleMin-3
86FleSlu-31
86FleStiC-103
86GenMilB-2I
86KayB-27
86Lea-11
86OPC-249
86OPCBoxB-O
86QuaGra-19
86RoyKitCD-3
86RoyNatP-31
86SevCoi-C6
86SevCoi-E6
86SevCoi-S6
86SevCoi-W6
86Spo-10
86Spo-176
86Spo-185
86Spo-186
86Top-487
86Top-720
86Top3-D-25
86TopGaloC-12
86TopGloS-27
86TopMinL-20
86TopSti-17
86TopSti-260
86TopSup-3
86TopTat-2
86TopTif-487
86TopTif-720
86TopWaxBC-O
87ClaGam-88
87ClaUpdY-116
87Don-132
87DonHig-6
87Fle-379
87FleAwaW-34
87FleGlo-379
87FleLimBC-C5
87FleSlu-36
87Lea-261
87OPC-140
87Spo-145
87SpoTeaP-13
87StuPan-20
87Top-140
87TopTif-140
88ClaRed-172
88Don-96
88DonAll-8
88DonBasB-231
88DonPop-8
88Fle-268
88Fle-626
88FleGlo-268
88FleGlo-626
88FleLeaL-33
88FleMin-26
88FleStiC-32
88FleTeaL-32
88GreBasS-53
88Lea-68
88MSAJifPD-15
88Nes-11
88OPC-5
88PanSti-102
88PanSti-106
88PanSti-107
88PanSti-229
88RedFolSB-77
88RoySmo-16
88Sco-89
88ScoBoxC-9
88ScoGlo-89
88ScoYouS2-17
88Spo-15
88StaLinRo-14
88Top-141
88Top-540
88TopBig-94
88TopCoi-25
88TopGloA-10
88TopMinL-14
88TopSti-163
88TopSti-254
88TopStiB-60
88TopTif-141
88TopTif-540
88TopUKM-63
88TopUKMT-63
89Bow-111
89BowTif-111
89ClaLigB-62
89Don-144
89DonBasB-95
89Fle-291
89FleGlo-291
89OPC-157
89PanSti-352
89RoyTasD-11
89Sco-251
89Spo-109
89Top-750
89TopAwaW-4
89TopBasT-92
89TopBig-6
89TopSti-263
89TopTif-750
89UppDec-37
90StaSab-1
90StaSab-2
90StaSab-4
90StaSab-6
90StaSab-8
90StaSab-10
90BasWit-21
90Baz-4
90Bow-364
90BowIns-9
90BowInsT-9
90BowTif-364
90BowTif-A9
90ClaBlu-139
90ClaUpd-NNO
90Col-30
90Don-89
90DonBesA-21
90Fle-116
90FleAwaW-30
90FleBasA-31
90FleBasM-32
90FleCan-116
90FleLeaL-32
90GooHumICBLS-18
90Hot50PS-36
90K-M-26
90Lea-72
90MSAHolD-5
90MSAIceTD-17
90OPC-350
90OPC-393
90PanSti-81
90PubSti-354
90Sco-195A
90Sco-195B
90Spo-94
90StaLonJS-19
90StaLonJS-36
90Top-350
90Top-393
90TopBig-21
90TopCoi-2
90TopDou-54
90TopGaloC-10
90TopGloS-13
90TopHeaU-7
90TopMag-5
90TopMinL-17
90TopSti-266
90TopStiB-59
90TopTif-350
90TopTif-393
90TopTVA-15
90UppDec-326
90USPlaCA-3C
90WinDis-4
90Woo-3
91BasBesAotM-14
91Bow-291
91CadEllD-46
91Cla3-T80
91ClaGam-36
91Don-88
91Fle-567
91Lea-118
91OPC-280
91PanFreS-283
91PanSti-225
91RedFolS-80
91RoyPol-18
91Sco-6
91Sco100S-59
91SimandSMLBL-37
91StaClu-38
91StaCluMO-28
91StaPinB-40
91Stu-69
91Top-280
91TopCraJ2-14
91TopDesS-280
91TopMic-280
91TopTif-280
91TopTriH-A7
91Ult-154
91UppDec-33
91UppDec-435
92Bow-586
92ClaGam-175
92Don-128
92Don-434
92Fle-167
92Hig5-65
92Lea-376
92MetColP-5
92MetKah-18
92New-23
92OPC-75
92OPCPre-82
92PanSti-101
92Pin-442
92Sco-6
92Sco-786
92Sco100S-11
92ScoRoo-20T
92SpoStaCC-39
92StaClu-755
92Stu-69
92Top-75
92TopGol-75
92TopGolW-75
92TopKid-107
92TopMic-75
92TopTra-97T
92TopTraG-97T
92Ult-537
92UppDec-233
92UppDec-751
93Bow-510
93CadDis-49
93Don-222
93Fin-53
93FinRef-53
93Fla-96
93Fle-93
93FunPac-129
93Lea-93
93MetColP-25
93MetKah-18
93OPC-302
93PacSpa-201
93Pin-185
93RoySta2-12
93Sco-115
93Sel-123
93SP-153
93StaClu-335
93StaCluFDI-335
93StaCluMOP-335
93Stu-112
93Top-600
93TopGol-600
93TopInaM-600
93TopMic-600
93TriPla-124
93Ult-79
93UppDec-282
93UppDecGold-282
94Bow-16
94ColC-250
94ColChoGS-250
94ColChoSS-250
94Don-298
94ExtBas-323
94ExtBasPD-8
94Fin-419
94FinRef-419
94Fla-409
94Fle-576
94Lea-437
94LeaL-132
94MetColP-22
94MetShuST-3
94OPC-46
94Pac-416
94PanSti-222
94Pin-203
94PinArtP-203
94PinMusC-203
94ProMag-95
94Sco-92
94ScoGolR-92
94Sel-101
94SP-120
94SPDieC-120
94StaClu-368
94StaCluFDI-368
94StaCluGR-368
94StaCluMOP-368
94Stu-119
94Top-245
94TopGol-245
94TopSpa-245
94TriPla-148
94Ult-533
94UppDec-428
94UppDecED-428
95Baz-86
95Bow-322
95BowBes-R40
95BowBesR-R40
95ColCho-325
95ColChoGS-325
95ColChoSE-150
95ColChoSE-251
95ColChoSEGS-150
95ColChoSEGS-251
95ColChoSESS-150

95ColChoSESS-251
95ColChoSS-325
95DenHol-22
95Don-431
95DonMouM-4
95DonPreP-431
95DonTopotO-232
95Emb-124
95EmbGolI-124
95Emo-162
95Fin-166
95FinFlaT-FT8
95FinRef-166
95Fla-175
95Fle-380
95FleTeaL-23
95Kra-27
95Lea-74
95LeaLim-173
95Pac-287
95PanSti-7
95Pin-355
95PinArtP-355
95PinMusC-355
95RedFol-26
95Sco-21
95ScoGolR-21
95ScoHaloG-HG43
95ScoPlaTS-21
95Sel-128
95SelArtP-128
95SelCer-46
95SelCerMG-46
95SP-85
95SPCha-72
95SPChaCP-CP9
95SPChaCPDC-CP9
95SPChaDC-72
95Spo-38
95SpoArtP-38
95SPSil-85
95SPSpeF-45
95StaClu-45
95StaClu-138
95StaCluFDI-45
95StaCluFDI-138
95StaCluMOP-45
95StaCluMOP-138
95StaCluSTWS-45
95StaCluSTWS-138
95StaCluVR-71
95Stu-99
95Sum-106
95SumNthD-106
95TomPiz-28
95Top-459
95TopCyb-254
95TopLeaL-LL49
95UC3-46
95UC3ArtP-46
95Ult-415
95UltGolM-415
95UppDec-120
95UppDec-490T
95UppDecED-120
95UppDecEDG-120
95UppDecSE-195
95UppDecSEG-195
95USPlaCMLA-12S
95Zen-10
96Baz-114
96ColCho-130
96ColChoGS-130
96ColChoSS-130
96Don-53
96DonPreP-53
96Fla-251
96Fle-374
96FleRoc-13
96FleTif-374
96Lea-29
96LeaPrePB-29
96LeaPrePG-29
96LeaPrePS-29
96LeaSigA-199
96LeaSigAG-199
96LeaSigAS-199
96MetKah-28
96MetMod-9
96MetUni-157
96MetUniP-157
96Pac-63
96PanSti-82
96Pin-251
96PinArtP-151
96PinFoil-251
96PinSta-151
96RocPol-21
96Sco-292
96ScoDugC-B17
96ScoDugCAP-B17
96StaClu-55
96StaCluMOP-55
95StaCluVRMC-71
96Top-292
96TopChrMotG-14
96TopChrMotGR-14
96TopMasotG-14
96Ult-475
96UltGolM-475
96UppDec-61
Sabino, Miguel
87SumBraP-3
88GreBraB-7
89GreBraB-27
89GreBraP-1170
89GreBraS-21
90CanIndB-15
90CanIndP-1305
90CanIndS-16
90CMC-721
91CanIndLD-94
91CanIndP-992
91LinDriAA-94
93LimRocDWB-36
Sable, Luke
88GasRanP-1002
89ChaRanS-21
90ChaRanS-25
91LinDriAA-595
91TulDriLD-595
91TulDriP-2782
91TulDriTI-27
92TulDriF-2704
92TulDriS-619
93OklCit8F-1634
Sabo, Chris
87NasSouTI-18
88DonBasB-278
88DonRoo-30
88FleSlu-35
88FleUpd-87
88FleUpdG-87
88RedKah-17
88ScoRoo-100T
88ScoRooG-100T
88Top-288
88TopTra-98T
88TopTraT-98T
89Baz-18
89Bow-309
89BowTif-309
89ClaLigB-53
89Don-4
89Don-317
89DonAll-59
89DonBasB-222
89DonSupD-4
89Fle-170
89Fle-637
89FleBasM-33
89FleExcS-35
89FleGlo-170
89FleGlo-637
89FleSup-35
89FleWaxBC-C21
89K-M-3
89KinDis-7
89OPC-156
89PanSti-64
89PanSti-476
89RedKah-17
89Sco-104
89ScoHot1R-76
89ScoYouSI-10
89Spo-13
89SpoIllFKI-48
89Top-490
89TopBasT-140
89TopBig-251
89TopCoi-3
89TopGaloC-9
89TopGloS-40
89TopMinL-13
89TopRoo-17
89TopSti-142
89TopSti-325
89TopTif-490
89TopUKM-65
89TovRoo-24
89TVSpoM-38
89TVSpoM-139
89UppDec-180
89UppDec-663
89Woo-6
90Bow-53
90BowTif-53
90CedRapRDGB-4
90ClaUpd-T43
90Don-242
90DonBesN-64
90Fle-433
90FleCan-433
90KinDis-10
90Lea-146
90MLBBasB-19
90MSAIceTD-3
90OPC-737
90PanSti-248
90PubSti-39
90RedKah-25
90Sco-70
90StaLonJS-20
90StaLonJS-25
90SupActM-12
90Top-737
90TopBig-121
90TopMag-18
90TopSti-140
90TopTif-737
90UppDec-181
90USPlaCA-5H
91Bow-674
91CadEIID-47
91Cla1-T26
91ClaGam-108
91Don-153
91Don-412
91Don-440
91Fle-80
91FleWorS-5
91Lea-65
91MooSna-21
91OPC-45
91PanFreS-129
91PanFreS-160
91PanSti-127
91Pos-13
91PosCan-10
91RedFolS-81
91RedFolS-125
91RedKah-17
91RedPep-19
91Sco-462
91Sco-795
91Sco100S-28
91SimandSMLBL-38
91StaClu-165
91StaPinB-41
91Stu-170
91Top-45
91TopCraJ2-29
91TopDesS-45
91TopGloA-15
91TopMic-45
91TopTif-45
91TopTriH-N3
91Ult-103
91UltGol-9
91UppDec-77
91UppDec-135
91UppDecFE-94F
91USPlaCA-12C
91Woo-29
92Bow-595
92ClaGam-79
92Don-50
92Don-424
92DonCraJ2-16
92Fle-420
92FleTeaL-3
92Fre-14
92Hig5-35
92HitTheBB-29
92JimDea-6
92KinDis-2
92Lea-271
92LeaGolP-3
92LeaPre-3
92Mr.TurS-21
92OPC-485
92OPCPre-23
92PanSti-264
92PanSti-283
92Pin-135
92RedKah-17
92Sco-70
92StaClu-273
92StaCluD-160
92Stu-28
92SunSee-10
92Top-485
92TopGol-485
92TopGolW-485
92TopKid-39
92TopMic-485
92TriPla-90
92Ult-197
92UppDec-123
92UppDecF-38
92UppDecFG-38
93Bow-286
93CadDis-50
93Don-58
93Fin-39
93FinRef-39
93Fla-33
93Fle-43
93Lea-418
93OPC-333
93PacSpa-90
93PanSti-294
93Pin-47
93RedKah-22
93Sco-149
93Sel-135
93SP-215
93StaClu-286
93StaCluFDI-286
93StaCluMOP-286
93Stu-73
93Top-245
93TopGol-245
93TopInaM-245
93TopMic-245
93TriPla-184
93Ult-35
93UppDec-147
93UppDecGold-147
94Bow-187
94ColC-485
94ColChoGS-485
94ColChoSS-485
94Don-330
94ExtBas-13
94Fin-418
94FinRef-418
94Fla-9
94Fle-425
94FleUpd-6
94Lea-324
94OPC-136
94OriPro-87
94OriUSPC-6D
94Pac-158
94PanSti-168
94Pin-490
94PinArtP-490
94PinMusC-490
94Sco-360
94ScoGolR-360
94ScoRoo-RT17
94ScoRooGR-RT17
94Sel-314
94SpoRoo-51
94SpoRooAP-51
94StaClu-676
94StaCluFDI-676
94StaCluGR-676
94StaCluMOP-676
94StaCluT-291
94StaCluTFDI-291
94Top-542
94TopGol-542
94TopSpa-542
94TopTra-125T
94TriPla-160
94Ult-310
94UppDec-347
94UppDecED-347
95ColCho-333
95ColChoGS-333
95ColChoSS-333
95Fle-20
95FleUpd-38
95Lea-314
95Pin-405
95PinArtP-405
95PinMusC-405
95Sco-385
95ScoGolR-385
95ScoPlaTS-385
95Top-137
95TopCyb-84
95UppDec-433
95UppDecED-433
95UppDecEDG-433
95UppDecSE-152
95UppDecSEG-152
96FleUpd-U125
96FleUpdTC-U125
96Ult-466
96UltGolM-466
Sabo, Scott
84IdaFalATI-24
85MadMusP-21
85MadMusT-1
86MadMusP-17
86MadMusP-19
87WilBilP-20
Sabol, Tony
46RemBre-13
47RemBre-15
47SigOil-53
47SmiClo-13
Saccavino, Craig
92EliTwiC-3
92EliTwiF-3681
93ForMyeMC-23
93ForMyeMF-2654
94ForMyeMC-22
94ForMyeMF-1169
Saccomanno, Joseph
89BurBraP-1600
89BurBraS-19
Sachen, Bob
85RedWinA-8
86RedWinA-7
Sachse, Matt
95Bow-96
95EveAqaTI-19
96BesAutSA-64
96EveAquB-20
Sacka, Frank
89ChaLooLITI-26
Sackinsky, Brian
92ClaDraP-28
92ClaFS7-420
93AlbPolF-2025
93ClaFS7-59
93StaCluM-160
93Top-647
93TopGol-647
93TopInaM-647
93TopMic-647
94BowBayF-2414
94ExcFS7-15
94OriPro-88
94UppDecML-191
95Bow-8
95RocRedWTI-32
95Top-429
95UppDecML-134
96RocRedWB-23
95UppDecMLFS-134
Saddler, Sandy
51BerRos-D12
Sadecki, Ray
60Top-327
61Top-32
62Top-383
62TopStal-190
63CarJayP-16
63CarJayP-17
63Top-486
64CarTeal-7
64Top-147
64TopVen-147
65CarTeal-19
65OPC-10
65OPC-230
65Top-10
65Top-230
66OPC-26
66Top-26
66TopVen-26
67CokCapG-14
67Top-409
67TopVen-323
68DexPre-69

68Top-494
69MilBra-244
69OPC-125
69Top-125
69TopFou-17
70Top-679
71MLBOffS-163
71OPC-406
71Top-406
72MilBra-303
72Top-563
72Top-564
73OPC-283
73Top-283
74MetDaiPA-13
74OPC-216
74Top-216
75OPC-349
75SSP18-14
75Top-349
77MetDaiPA-20
77Top-26
91MetWIZ-339
92PeoChiTI-22
94BreMilB-73
Sadecki, Steve
92ChaRanF-2225
92ClaFS7-113
92GasRanC-2
93ChaRanC-19
93ChaRanF-1940
94TulDriF-244
94TulDriTI-21
Sadek, Mike
74PhoGiaC-81
74OPC-577
74Top-577
75PhoGiaCK-3
76OPC-234
76Top-234
77Gia-20
77Top-129
78Top-8
79GiaPol-3
79Top-256
80GiaPol-3
80OPC-240
80Top-462
81Don-498
81Top-384
96GiaMot-28
Sadler, Alan
85BelBreT-21
86StoPorP-24
87ElPasDP-24
88StoPorCLC-181
88StoPorP-726
89BlaYNPRWLU-22
89DenZepC-9
89DenZepP-44
90CMC-44
90DenZepC-19
90DenZepP-626
90ProAAAF-651
93BelBreC-21
93BelBreF-1708
Sadler, Donnie
95Bes-7
95Bow-191
95MicBatCTI-24
95MidLeaA-50
96BesAutSA-65
96Bow-376
96BowBes-165
96BowBesAR-165
96BowBesMI-6
96BowBesMIAR-6
96BowBesMIR-6
96BowBesR-165
96Exc-18
96TreThuB-29
97Bow-140
97BowBes-193
97BowBesAR-193
97BowBesMI-MI8
97BowBesMIAR-MI8
97BowBesMIARI-MI8
97BowBesMII-MI8
97BowBesMIR-MI8
97BowBesMIRI-MI8
97BowBesR-193
97BowCerBIA-CA72
97BowCerGIA-CA72
97BowChr-148
97BowChrI-148
97BowChrIR-148
97BowChrR-148
97BowInt-140
Sadler, Sean
90NiaFalRP-14
91FayGenC-15
91FayGenP-1173
Sadowski, Ed
59Top-139
59TopVen-139
60Lea-113
60Top-403
61Top-163
62AngJayP-10
62Top-569
63AngJayP-16
63Top-527
64Top-61
64TopVen-61
Sadowski, Jim
76VenLeaS-92
Sadowski, Robert
61TopStal-174
62KahAtl-17
62Top-595
63Top-568
64BraJayP-10
64Top-271
64TopVen-271
65OPC-156
65Top-156
66Top-523
78TCM60I-167
Sadowski, Ted
61Top-254
61TwiCloD-24
Sadowsky, Clinton
91BriTigC-17
91BriTigP-3604
Saeki, Kazushi
79TCMJapPB-36
Saenz, Olmedo
92SouBenWSC-13
92SouBenWSF-187
93SarWhiSC-23
93SarWhiSF-1379
94BowBes-B84
94BowBesR-B84
94ExcFS7-40
94NasSouF-1259
95ColCho-497
95ColChoGS-497
95ColChoSS-497
95LinVen-152
95NasSouTI-21
95Pac-96
95Top-634
96Bow-313
96NasSouB-20
Saetre, Damon
90PenPilS-19
91PenPilC-16
91PenPilP-392
Saferight, Harry
75ShrCapT-18
76ShrCapT-18
77ShrCapT-20
78ColCliT-21
79PorBeaT-21
80RicBraT-16
80Top-683
81RicBraT-24
82TolMudHT-10
Saffell, Tom
49PorBeaP-3
51Bow-130
52MotCoo-36
59DarFar-20
Saffer, Jeffery
96GreBatB-23
Saffer, Jon
93ClaGolF-140
93JamExpC-20
93JamExpF-3339
93StaCluM-166
94VerExpC-19
94VerExpF-3922
96HarSenB-24
Safly, Joel
90VisOakCLC-82
92VisOakC-26
93ForMyeMC-28
Sagawa, Kiyoshi
89VisOakCLC-103
89VisOakP-1434
Sage, Henry
87OldJudN-437
87OldJudN-438
Sagedal, Brent
95HudValRTI-25
Sager, A.J.
88SpoIndP-1933
89ChaRaiP-971
90WicWraRD-18
91LinDriAA-617
91WicWraLD-617
91WicWraP-2597
91WicWraRD-8
92LasVegSF-2795
92LasVegSS-238
94Bow-474
94PadMot-18
95Pac-370
96TolMudHB-25
97Fle-105
97FleTif-105
97PacPriGotD-GD44
Sagmoen, Marc
93EriSaiC-20
93EriSaiF-3130
94ChaRanF-2509
96TulDriTI-22
97Fle-586
97FleTif-586
97Ult-537
97UltGolME-537
97UltPlaME-537
Saier, Matt
95SpoIndTI-23
96WilBluRB-26
Saier, Vic
12T207-159
14CraJacE-104
14FatPlaT-42
15CraJacE-104
15SpoNewM-152
16BF2FP-68
16ColE13-148
16SpoNewM-152
Sailors, Jamie
93JohCitCC-17
93JohCitCF-3674
94MadHatC-20
94MadHatF-130
Sain, Joe
83WisRapTF-5
Sain, Johnny
46SpoExcW-7-6
47Exh-198
47HomBon-42
47TipTop-85
48Bow-12
49Bow-47
49EurSta-21
49MPR302-2-122
50AmeNut&CCP-16
51Bow-314
51FisBakL-24
51TopBluB-9
52BerRos-59
52Top-49A
52Top-49B
53BowBW-25
53Dor-116
53Dor-116A
53Top-119
54Top-205
55A'sRodM-33
55Top-193
61Yan61RL-39
68TigDetFPB-20
73OPC-356
73Top-356
74OPC-221
74Top-221
75SSP42-2
76A'sRodMC-21
76BooProC-12
76TayBow4-40
78AtlCon-21
78RicBraT-14
79RicBraT-3
80RicBraT-9
81RicBraT-1
81TCM60I-481
82RicBraT-28
83ASASpa-4
83RicBraT-25
83TopRep5-49
83YanASFY-40
84RicBraT-26
84TCMPla1-35
85BraPol-33
86BraPol-33
89SweBasG-121
91TopArc1-119
92BazQua5A-15
92YanWIZA-73
93ActPacA-136
94TopArc1-205
94TopArc1G-205
Sain, Tom
76TacTwiDQ-18
77TacTwiDQ-7
78OrlTwiT-17
79TolMudHT-15
Saints, St Paul
38BasTabP-45
Saipe, Mike
94BenRocF-3593
95SalAvaTI-19
96NewHavRB-21
97BenRocC-21
Saitoh, Takayuki
96HonShaHWB-4
Saitta, Pat
87DunBluJP-951
Saitta, Rich
96YakBeaTI-4
Saitz, Robbie
91FreStaBS-11
92ClaFS7-361
92PalSprAC-2
92PalSprAF-838
Sajonia, Brian
88JamExpP-1907
Sak, James
96CliLumKTI-23
96RanCucQB-24
Sakamoto, Toshizo
79TCMJapPB-3
Sakata, Lenn
76SpoIndC-19
77SpoIndC-11
79VanCanT-22B
80Top-668
81Don-499
81Fle-194
81Top-287
82Don-644
82Fle-178
82Top-136
83Don-205
83Fle-72
83OriPos-25
83Top-319
84Don-620
84Fle-19
84Nes792-578
84OriTeal-26
84Top-578
84TopTif-578
85Fle-189
85Top-81
85TopTif-81
86TacTigP-20
86Top-446
86TopTif-446
88SouOreAP-1717
88Top-716
88TopTif-716
89ModA'sCLC-288
91EdmTraLD-175
91EdmTraP-1533
91LinDriAAA-175
91OriCro-399
91PacSenL-91
92EdmTraF-3555
92EdmTraS-175
92YanWIZ8-167
93VanCanF-2615
94BreMilB-74
94VanCanF-1880
Sakowski, Vince
83TriTriT-19
Sakumoto, Masahiro
96MauStiHWB-16
Sakurai, Teruhide
79TCMJapPB-65
Sala, David J.
87SprCarB-16
89SavCarP-367
Salado, Jose
74SacSolC-56
Salado, Tim
94OgdRapF-3737
94OgdRapSP-21
Salaiz, David
89ColMudB-5
89ColMudP-138
Salamon, John
91MarPhiC-18
91MarPhiP-3453
93AugPirC-17
93AugPirF-1542
94BelBreC-21
94BelBreF-98
94MidLeaAF-MDW10
95AusFut-46
Salas, Jose
76VenLeaS-127
Salas, Mark
82ArkTraT-11
82NasSouTI-20
83ArkTraT-12
84Car-26
84LouRedR-27
85Don-547
85FleUpd-94
85TopTifT-101T
85TopTra-101T
85TwiTeal-9
86Don-316
86Fle-402
86FleStiC-104
86KayB-28
86Lea-185
86OPC-43
86Spo-177
86Spo-178
86Top-537
86TopSti-278
86TopSti-315
86TopTat-17
86TopTif-537
86TwiTeal-8
87Fle-551
87FleGlo-551
87FleUpd-106
87FleUpdG-106
87OPC-87
87SpoTeaP-17
87Top-87
87TopTif-87
87TopTra-107T
87TopTraT-107T
88Sco-232
88ScoGlo-232
88ScoRoo-52T
88ScoRooG-52T
88StaLinWS-16
88TopTra-99T
88TopTraT-99T
88WhiSoxC-26
89ColSprSSC-20
89ColSprSSP-240
89Fle-511
89FleGlo-511
89Sco-542
89Top-384
89TopTif-384
89UppDec-460
90TigCok-21
91Don-65
91Fle-350
91OPC-498
91StaClu-456
91TigCok-27
91TigPol-10
91Top-498
91TopDesS-498
91TopMic-498
91TopTif-498
91Ult-127
91UppDec-205
92Don-512
92Fle-144
92Sco-394
92YanWIZ8-168
93HicCraC-29
93HicCraF-1297
95WhiSoxK-31
Salava, Randy
82ReaPhiT-18
83ReaPhiT-19

84PorBeaC-203
85PhiTas-45
85PorBeaC-37
Salazar, Angel (Argenis)
80VenLeaS-209
83WicAerDS-19
84Don-33
84ExpPos-27
84ExpStu-31
85Don-523
85OPC-154
85Top-154
85TopMin-154
85TopTif-154
86FleUpd-100
86TopTra-96T
86TopTraT-96T
87Don-624
87Fle-380
87FleGlo-380
87Top-533
87TopSti-259
87TopTif-533
88CubDavB-18
88Don-502
88DonTeaBC-NEW
88Fle-269
88FleGlo-269
88OPC-29
88PanSti-109
88Sco-330
88ScoGlo-330
88Top-29
88TopTif-29
89Sco-527
89Top-642
89TopTif-642
89UppDec-222
Salazar, Carlos
90SouOreAB-19
90SouOreAP-3436
91ModA'sP-3099
92ModA'sC-19
92ModA'sF-3907
Salazar, Jeff
83PeoSunF-17
Salazar, Julian
91BelBreC-16
91BelBreP-2112
92StoPorF-42
93PocPosF-4218
93PocPosSP-22
Salazar, Lazerio
86NegLeaF-93
Salazar, Luis Ernesto
76VenLeaS-134
77SalPirT-23
78SalPirT-15
79BufBisT-16
80PorBeaT-9
80VenLeaS-200
81Fle-501
81Top-309
81TopSti-228
82Don-472
82Fle-581
82OPC-133
82Top-366
82Top-662
82TopSti-101
82TopStiV-101
83Don-548
83Fle-371
83OPC-156
83Top-533
84Don-356
84Fle-311
84Nes792-68
84OPC-68
84PadMot-24
84PadSmo-20
84Top-68
84TopSti-159
84TopTif-68
85Don-568
85Fle-43
85FleUpd-95
85Top-789
85TopTif-789
85TopTifT-102T
85TopTra-102T
85WhiSoxC-5
86Don-302
86Fle-215
86Top-103
86TopTif-103
87Top-454
87TopTif-454
87TopTra-108T
87TopTraT-108T
88Fle-595
88FleGlo-595
88FleUpd-30
88FleUpdG-30
88OPC-276
88Sco-284
88ScoGlo-284
88ScoRoo-13T
88ScoRooG-13T
88TigPep-12
88Top-276
88TopTif-276
88TopTra-100T
88TopTraT-100T
89ClaLigB-72
89Don-352
89Fle-144
89FleGlo-144
89OPC-122
89PadCok-15
89PanSti-342
89Sco-316
89Top-553
89TopSti-276
89TopTif-553
89TopTra-107T
89TopTraT-107T
89UppDec-136
90Bow-40
90BowTif-40
90BriTigP-3164
90BriTigS-22
90CubMar-17
90Don-513
90FleUpd-9
90Lea-388
90OPC-378
90Sco-92
90Top-378
90TopBig-182
90TopTif-378
90TopTVCu-25
90UppDec-6
91Bow-428
91CubMar-10
91CubVinL-24
91Don-372
91Fle-430
91Lea-185
91OPC-614
91PanFreS-45
91Sco-207
91StaClu-94
91Top-614
91TopDesS-614
91TopMic-614
91TopTif-614
91Ult-67
91UppDec-311
92CubMar-10
92Don-152
92OPC-67
92PanSti-184
92Pin-372
92Sco-508
92StaClu-21
92Top-67
92TopGol-67
92TopGolW-67
92TopMic-67
92Ult-179
92UppDec-638
93Fle-383
93LinVenB-1
93PacSpa-60
93StaClu-549
93StaCluFDI-549
93StaCluMOP-549
93Top-21
93TopGol-21
93TopInaM-21
93TopMic-21
96BelSnaTI-33
Salazar, Luis R.
88St.CatBJP-2006
93LinVenB-207
93LinVenB-343
94VenLinU-60
94VenLinU-255
95LinVen-210
95LinVen-252
96StoPorB-10
Salazar, Mike
93NiaFalRF-3389
94FayGenC-21
94FayGenF-2144
96LakTigB-22
Salazar, Terry
81BufBisT-21
Salcedo, Edwin
90TamYanD-19
92PriWilCC-14
92PriWilCF-153
94TamYanF-2387
Salcedo, Jose
91KisDodP-4182
94StoPorC-23
94StoPorF-1694
Salcedo, Luis
87MadMusP-16
87MadMusP-24
Salcedo, Ron
84ChaO'sT-4
85ChaO'sT-11
86ChaOriW-27
87RocRedWP-4
87RocRedWT-19
88RocRedWC-16
88RocRedWGCP-24
88RocRedWP-200
88RocRedWTI-19
89ScrRedBC-16
89ScrRedBP-707
90HagSunDGB-24
Salcedo, Yamil
94TamYanC-22
95NorNavTI-45
Salery, Johnny
82WisRapTF-9
83WisRapTF-13
Saleski, Stan
77ForLauYS-24
Salfran, Francisco
52LavPro-110
Salinas, Manual V.
86BirBarTI-2
87BirBarB-23
88JacMetGS-18
88TexLeaAGS-14
89JacMetGS-13
89TidTidP-1951
Salinas, Trey
96ButCopKB-27
Salisbury, Jim
86SumBraP-24
87DurBulP-24
Salkeld, Bill
49Bow-88A
49Bow-88B
49EurSta-22
50Bow-237
Salkeld, Roger
89BelMarL-13
90Bes-14
90Bow-465
90BowTif-465
90CalLeaACLC-21
90CMC-858
90OPC-44
90ProAaA-135
90SanBerSB-1
90SanBerSCLC-87
90SanBerSP-2632
90Sco-674
90Top-44
90TopMag-75
90TopTif-44
91Bow-262
91Cla/Bes-106
91Cla2-T59
91JacSunLD-344
91JacSunP-151
91LeaGolR-BC19
91LinDriAA-344
91UppDec-63
92Bow-369
92CalCanS-51
92Don-7
92OPC-676
92ProFS7-140
92SkyAAAF-33
92Top-676
92TopGol-676
92TopGolW-676
92TopMic-676
92UppDec-15
92UppDecML-257
94Bow-145
94CalCanF-788
94ColC-589
94ColChoGS-589
94ColChoSS-589
94ExtBas-172
94Fin-318
94FinRef-318
94Fla-341
94FleMajLP-30
94FleUpd-87
94LeaLimR-79
94Pac-580
94Pin-393
94PinArtP-393
94PinMusC-393
94Sco-644
94ScoGolR-644
94ScoRoo-RT79
94ScoRooGR-RT79
94Sel-388
94SpoRoo-131
94SpoRooAP-131
94StaClu-495
94StaCluFDI-495
94StaCluGR-495
94StaCluMOP-495
94Top-376
94TopGol-376
94TopSpa-376
94Ult-424
94UppDec-164
94UppDecED-164
95Don-107
95DonPreP-107
95Fle-276
95Lea-189
95Pin-345
95PinArtP-345
95PinMusC-345
95Sco-458
95ScoGolR-458
95ScoPlaTS-458
96Fin-B331
96FinRef-B331
96FleUpd-U126
96FleUpdTC-U126
97Fle-302
97FleTif-302
97PacPriGotD-GD129
97Top-178
Sallee, Andy
91MarPhiC-7
91MarPhiP-3464
92BatCliC-28
92BatCliF-3274
93SpaPhiC-24
93SpaPhiF-1064
Sallee, H. Slim
09ColChiE-250
09PC7HHB-38
09RamT20-102
10DarChoE-26
11PloCanE-55
11SpoLifCW-310
11SpoLifM-278
11TurRedT-37
12ColRedB-250
12ColTinT-250
14B18B-88A
14B18B-88B
14CraJacE-123
14FatPlaT-43
15CraJacE-123
15SpoNewM-153
16BF2FP-96
16ColE13-149
16SpoNewM-153
17HolBreD-88
17HolBreD-89
19W514-86
20RedWorCP-20
21E121So8-81A
21E121So8-81B
21KoBreWSI-20
22AmeCarE-58
22W575-114
23WilChoV-141
88ConSer4-24
88PacEigMO-82
93ConTSN-780
94ConTSN-1020
94ConTSNB-1020
Salles, John
89PeoChiTI-8
90CarLeaA-47
90WinSpiTI-3
91ChaKniLD-141
91ChaKniP-1687
91LinDriAA-141
92IowCubS-220
92SkyAAAF-107
93ClaFS7-19
93OrlCubF-2782
Salmon, Chico
64Top-499
65OPC-105
65Top-105
66Top-594
67CokCapI-11
67OPC-43
67Top-43
68Top-318
68TopVen-318
69MilBra-245
69MLBOffS-99
69OPC-62
69PilPos-8
69Top-62
69TopSta-230
69TopTeaP-9
70MLBOffS-156
70OPC-301
70Ori-13
70Top-301
71MLBOffS-312
71OPC-249
71Top-249
72MilBra-304
72Top-646
91OriCro-400
Salmon, Fabian
93HelBreF-4093
93HelBreSP-13
94BelBreC-22
94BelBreF-99
Salmon, Tim
88CapCodPPaLP-176
89BenBucL-23
90CMC-854
90PalSprACLC-215
90PalSprAP-2593
90TopMag-104
91Bow-203
91Cla/Bes-329
91Cla3-T81
91LinDriAA-443
91MidAngLD-443
91MidAngOHP-25
91MidAngP-447
92Bow-259
92DonRooP-BC10
92EdmTraF-3551
92EdmTraS-165
92FleUpd-10
92ProFS7-32
92ScoRoo-93T
92SkyAAAF-81
92TriA AAS-165
93AngAdoFD-3
93AngMot-7
93AngPol-20
93Bow-229
93Bow-341
93DiaMar-92
93Don-176
93DonEliD-7
93Fin-163
93FinRef-163
93Fla-177
93FlaWavotF-15
93Fle-197
93FunPac-7
93FunPac-37
93JimDeaR-9
93Lea-445
93LeaGolR-R10
93OPC-292
93OPCPre-37
93PacSpa-51
93Pin-276
93Pin-303
93PinHomRC-42

93PinRooTP-8
93PinTea2-20
93Sco-346
93ScoBoyoS-2
93Sel-339
93SelChaR-11
93SelRoo-ROY1
93SelRooAR-8
93SP-25
93SPPlaP-PP16
93StaClu-249
93StaCluAn-13
93StaCluFDI-249
93StaCluMO-22
93StaCluMOP-249
93Stu-114
93Top-20
93TopFulS-9
93TopGol-20
93TopInaM-20
93TopMic-20
93TopMic-P20
93Toy-67
93TriPla-37
93Ult-523
93UltAllR-8
93UppDec-1
93UppDec-25
93UppDec-812
93UppDecDG-1
93UppDecFA-A15
93UppDecFAJ-A15
93UppDecGold-1
93UppDecGold-25
93UppDecGold-812
93UppDecIC-WI1
93UppDecICJ-WI1
93UppDecOD-D21
93UppDecS-19
94AngLAT-21
94AngMot-5
94Bow-395
94BowBes-R25
94BowBes-X102
94BowBesR-R25
94BowBesR-X102
94ChuHomS-9
94ChuHomSG-9
94ColC-251
94ColC-328
94ColC-639
94ColChoGS-251
94ColChoGS-328
94ColChoGS-639
94ColChoSS-251
94ColChoSS-328
94ColChoSS-639
94ColChoT-10
94DenHol-21
94Don-353
94DonAwaWJ-8
94DonDiaK-DK4
94DonEli-39
94DonMVP-17
94DonPro-6
94DonSpeE-353
94DonSpiotG-7
94ExtBas-39
94ExtBasGB-25
94ExtBasSYS-18
94Fin-18
94FinJum-18
94FinRef-18
94Fla-27
94FlaHotG-9
94FlaOutP-9
94Fle-69
94Fle-P69
94FleAwaW-5
94FleRooS-17
94FleSal-1
94FleSal-2
94FleSal-3
94FleSal-4
94FleSal-5
94FleSal-6
94FleSal-7
94FleSal-8
94FleSal-9
94FleSal-10
94FleSal-11
94FleSal-12
94FleSal-13
94FleSal-14
94FleSal-15
94FleSal-AU0
94FleSun-22
94FleTeaL-3
94FUnPac-15
94FUnPac-203
94FUnPac-239
94KinDis-7
94Lea-109
94LeaL-18
94LeaSli-8
94MotPia-1
94MotPia-2
94MotPia-3
94MotPia-4
94MotPia-BLUE
94MotPia-RED
94MotSal-1
94MotSal-2
94MotSal-3
94MotSal-4
94OPC-194
94OPCAllR-10
94OPCDiaD-11
94OPCJumA-10
94OscMayR-12
94Pac-88
94Pac-659
94PacGolP-9
94PacPro-P7
94PacSilP-12
94PanSti-42
94Pin-9
94PinArtP-9
94PinMusC-9
94PinNewG-NG1
94PinPowS-PS4
94PinRunC-RC13
94PinTeaP-8
94PinTheN-9
94Pos-26
94ProMag-18
94RedFolMI-23
94Sco-539
94Sco-635
94ScoBoyoS-24
94ScoGolR-539
94ScoGolR-635
94ScoGolS-44
94Sel-309
94SP-26
94SPDieC-26
94SPHol-34
94SPHolDC-34
94Spo-89
94SpoRooGGG-GG7
94SpoSha-SH2
94SPPre-WR5
94StaClu-36
94StaClu-181
94StaCluDD-DD8
94StaCluF-F9
94StaCluFDI-36
94StaCluFDI-181
94StaCluGR-36
94StaCluGR-181
94StaCluMO-47
94StaCluMOP-36
94StaCluMOP-181
94StaCluMOP-F9
94StaCluMOP-DD8
94StaCluMOP-ST17
94StaCluP-36
94StaCluST-ST17
94Stu-15
94StuEdiC-6
94TedWil-158
94TedWil-159
94TedWil-160
94TedWil-161
94TomPiz-27
94Top-397
94TopBlaG-19
94TopGol-397
94TopSpa-397
94TopSupS-38
94TriPla-19
94TriPlaP-7
94Ult-27
94UltAwaW-24
94UltRisS-11
94UltSecYS-4
94UppDec-54
94UppDec-111
94UppDec-283
94UppDecAJ-10
94UppDecAJG-10
94UppDecDC-W10
94UppDecED-54
94UppDecED-111
94UppDecED-283
94UppDecMLS-MM17
94UppDecMLSED-MM17
94UppDecNG-17
94UppDecNGED-17
94USPlaCR-6H
94USPlaCR-13C
94USPlaCR-JK
95AngCHP-1
95AngMot-4
95Baz-119
95Bow-353
95BowBes-R33
95BowBesR-R33
95ClaPhoC-10
95ColCho-100
95ColChoGS-100
95ColChoSE-35
95ColChoSEGS-35
95ColChoSESS-35
95ColChoSS-100
95D3-16
95DenHol-23
95Don-403
95DonPreP-403
95DonTopotO-42
95Emb-108
95EmbGolI-108
95Emo-21
95Fin-79
95FinRef-79
95Fla-21
95FlaTodS-11
95Fle-235
95FlePro-5
95FleTeaL-3
95FleUpdH-17
95FleUpdSS-9
95Lea-264
95LeaLim-30
95LeaLimG-13
95LeaLimIBP-20
95NatPac-8
95Pac-64
95PacGolP-5
95PacPri-21
95PanSti-88
95Pin-286
95Pin-391
95PinArtP-286
95PinArtP-391
95PinFan-12
95PinMusC-286
95PinMusC-391
95PinPer-PP8
95PinRedH-RH19
95PinUps-US8
95PinWhiH-WH19
95RedFol-12
95Sco-420
95ScoGolR-420
95ScoHaloG-HG78
95ScoPlaTS-420
95ScoRul-SR20
95ScoRulJ-SR20
95Sel-59
95SelArtP-59
95SelCer-17
95SelCerMG-17
95SP-135
95SPCha-135
95SPChaDC-135
95Spo-68
95SpoArtP-68
95SpoHamT-HT18
95SPPlaP-PP17
95SPSil-135
95SPSpeF-4
95StaClu-473
95StaClu-512
95StaCluMOP-473
95StaCluMOP-512
95StaCluMOP-SS7
95StaCluSS-SS7
95StaCluSTWS-473
95StaCluSTWS-512
95StaCluVR-259
95Stu-13
95StuGolS-13
95StuPlaS-13
95Sum-35
95SumBigB-BB19
95SumNthD-35
95Top-200
95TopCyb-114
95UC3-14
95UC3ArtP-14
95UC3CycS-CS18
95UllHomRK-9
95Ult-23
95UltGolM-23
95UppDec-270
95UppDecED-270
95UppDecEDG-270
95UppDecPLL-R36
95UppDecPLLE-R36
95UppDecSE-126
95UppDecSEG-126
95Zen-102
96AngMot-4
96Baz-111
96Bow-43
96BowBes-9
96BowBesAR-9
96BowBesC-13
96BowBesCAR-13
96BowBesCR-13
96BowBesP-BBP6
96BowBesPAR-BBP6
96BowBesPR-BBP6
96BowBesR-9
96Cir-22
96CirAcc-3
96CirBos-5
96CirRav-22
96ColCho-75
96ColCho-416
96ColChoCtG-CG8
96ColChoCtG-CG8B
96ColChoCtG-CG8C
96ColChoCtGG-CG8
96ColChoCtGG-CG8B
96ColChoCtGG-CG8C
96ColChoGS-75
96ColChoGS-416
96ColChoSS-75
96ColChoSS-416
96ColChoYMtP-35
96ColChoYMtP-35A
96ColChoYMtPGS-35
96ColChoYMtPGS-35A
96DenHol-16
96Don-477
96DonDiaK-7
96DonEli-65
96DonHitL-13
96DonPowA-5
96DonPowADC-5
96DonPreP-477
96DonRouT-4
96EmoLegoB-8
96EmoXL-30
96Fin-B97
96Fin-G249
96Fin-S22
96FinRef-B97
96FinRef-G249
96FinRef-S22
96Fla-41
96Fle-57
96FleLumC-8
96FleRoaW-7
96FleTif-57
96FleUpd-U238
96FleUpdH-18
96FleUpdTC-U238
96Lea-45
96LeaAllGMC-10
96LeaAllGMCG-10
96LeaGolS-6
96LeaLim-17
96LeaLimG-17
96LeaPre-28
96LeaPreP-28
96LeaPrePB-45
96LeaPrePG-45
96LeaPrePS-45
96LeaPreSG-25
96LeaPreSte-25
96LeaSig-9
96LeaSigA-200
96LeaSigAG-200
96LeaSigAS-200
96LeaSigPPG-9
96LeaSigPPP-9
96MetUni-32
96MetUniML-9
96MetUniP-32
96Pac-264
96PacGolCD-DC12
96PacPri-P86
96PacPriFB-FB16
96PacPriG-P86
96PacPriRHS-RH5
96PanSti-209
96Pin-26
96Pin-142
96Pin-276
96PinAfi-122
96PinAfiAP-122
96PinAfiSP-29
96PinArtP-12
96PinArtP-69
96PinArtP-176
96PinEssotG-14
96PinFoil-276
96PinPow-14
96PinSta-12
96PinSta-69
96PinSta-176
96PinTeaP-5
96ProMagDM-7
96ProSta-2
96Sco-328
96ScoAll-13
96ScoDiaA-30
96ScoDugC-B53
96ScoDugCAP-B53
96ScoGolS-4
96ScoPowP-16
96ScoTitT-8
96Sel-10
96SelArtP-10
96SelCer-37
96SelCerAP-37
96SelCerCB-37
96SelCerCR-37
96SelCerIP-17
96SelCerMB-37
96SelCerMG-37
96SelCerMR-37
96SelEnF-22
96SelTeaN-23
96SP-45
96SPMarM-MM5
96SPMarMDC-5
96Spo-2
96Spo-106
96SpoArtP-2
96SpoArtP-106
96SpoPowS-10
96SpoPro-18
96SPSpeFX-42
96SPSpeFXDC-42
96SPx-12
96SPxGol-12
96StaClu-213
96StaClu-405
96StaCluEPB-405
96StaCluEPG-405
96StaCluEPS-405
96StaCluMO-37
96StaCluMOP-213
96StaCluMOP-405
96StaCluMOP-PP9
96StaCluMOP-PS13
96StaCluPP-PP9
96StaCluPS-PS13
95StaCluVRMC-259
96Stu-56
96StuHitP-9
96StuPrePB-56
96StuPrePG-56
96StuPrePS-56
96Sum-81
96Sum-160
96SumAbo&B-81
96SumAbo&B-160
96SumArtP-81
96SumArtP-160
96SumBal-16
96SumBigB-11
96SumBigBM-11
96SumFoi-81
96SumFoi-160
96SumHitI-3

96TeaOut-69
96Top-319
96TopChr-126
96TopChrR-126
96TopGal-154
96TopGalPPI-154
96TopLas-110
96TopLasPC-5
96TopPro-AL20
96TopRoaW-RW14
96Ult-33
96Ult-589
96UltGolM-33
96UltGolM-589
96UltHitM-8
96UltHitMGM-8
96UltHomRKGM-9
96UltHomRKR-9
96UltOn-L-8
96UltOn-LGM-8
96UltPowP-8
96UltPowPGM-8
96UltPriL-9
96UltPriLGM-9
96UppDec-290
96UppDecHC-HC16
96UppDecPD-PD14
96UppDecPHE-H5
96UppDecPRE-R7
96UppDecPRE-R28
96UppDecPreH-H5
96UppDecPreR-R7
96UppDecPreR-R28
96UppDecRunP-RP16
96UppDecVJLS-VJ16
96Zen-39
96ZenArtP-39
96ZenMoz-7
97Bow-5
97BowBes-98
97BowBesA-98
97BowBesAAR-98
97BowBesAR-98
97BowBesR-98
97BowChr-4
97BowChrI-4
97BowChrIR-4
97BowChrR-4
97BowInt-5
97Cir-5
97CirRav-5
97ColCho-260
97ColChoNF-NF9
97ColChoTBS-13
97ColChoTBSWH-13
97Don-76
97Don-447
97DonEli-23
97DonEliGS-23
97DonLim-75
97DonLim-142
97DonLimFotG-46
97DonLimLE-75
97DonLimLE-142
97DonPre-51
97DonPreCttC-51
97DonPreP-76
97DonPreP-447
97DonPrePGold-76
97DonPrePGold-447
97DonPreXP-6A
97DonTea-2
97DonTeaSPE-2
97Fin-144
97Fin-246
97FinEmb-144
97FinEmbR-144
97FinRef-144
97FinRef-246
97FlaSho-A30
97FlaSho-B30
97FlaSho-C30
97FlaShoLC-30
97FlaShoLC-B30
97FlaShoLC-C30
97FlaShoLCM-A30
97FlaShoLCM-B30
97FlaShoLCM-C30
97Fle-50
97Fle-721
97FleTif-50
97FleTif-721
97Lea-129
97LeaFraM-129
97LeaFraMDC-129
97MetUni-43
97NewPin-20
97NewPinAP-20
97NewPinMC-20
97NewPinPP-20
97Pac-13
97PacLigB-13
97PacPri-5
97PacPriLB-5
97PacPriP-5
97PacSil-13
97Pin-53
97PinArtP-53
97PinCer-23
97PinCerMBlu-23
97PinCerMG-23
97PinCerMR-23
97PinCerR-23
97PinIns-85
97PinInsCE-85
97PinInsDE-85
97PinMin-24
97PinMinB-24
97PinMinCB-24
97PinMinCG-24
97PinMinCGR-24
97PinMinCN-24
97PinMinCS-24
97PinMinG-24
97PinMinS-24
97PinMusC-53
97PinTotCPB-23
97PinTotCPG-23
97PinTotCPR-23
97PinX-P-49
97PinX-PMoS-49
97PinX-PSfF-22
97PinX-PSfFU-22
97ProMag-42
97ProMagML-42
97Sco-149
97Sco-494
97ScoBla-18
97ScoHeaotO-32
97ScoHobR-494
97ScoPitP-7
97ScoPreS-149
97ScoResC-494
97ScoShoS-149
97ScoShoS-494
97ScoShoSAP-149
97ScoShoSAP-494
97Sel-44
97SelArtP-44
97SelRegG-44
97SelToootT-13
97SelToootTMB-13
97SP-20
97SPMarM-MM6
97SpoIll-163
97SpoIllEE-163
97SPSpeF-32
97SPx-3
97SPxBro-3
97SPxGraF-3
97SPxSil-3
97SPxSte-3
97StaClu-7
97StaCluMat-7
97StaCluMOP-7
97Stu-67
97StuHarH-16
97StuPrePG-67
97StuPrePS-67
97Top-320
97TopChr-107
97TopChrR-107
97TopGal-102
97TopGalPPI-102
97TopIntF-ILM2
97TopIntFR-ILM2
97Ult-30
97UltDouT-3
97UltGolME-30
97UltPlaME-30
97UppDec-290
97UppDecPP-PP12
97UppDecPPJ-PP12
97UppDecRP-RP19
97UppDecU-22

Saltzgaber, Brian
90NiaFalRP-9
91FayGenC-16
91FayGenP-1174
91SouAtlLAGP-SAL21
92LakTigC-10
92LakTigF-2283
93LonTigF-2311
94TreThuF-2133

Saltzgaver, Jack
35DiaMatCS3T1-128
75YanDyn1T-41
93ConTSN-972

Salva, Elias
80WauTimT-8

Salveson, John
33ButCanV-43
49W72HolS-18
50W720HolS-25

Salvior, Troy
90HamRedB-10
90HamRedS-22
91Cla/Bes-310
91St.PetCC-10
91St.PetCP-2274
92St.PetCF-2027

Salvo, Manny
94ConTSN-1294
94ConTSNB-1294

Salyer, Ron
75SanAntBT-18

Salzano, Jerry
93HelBreF-4106
93HelBreSP-10
94BelBreC-23
94BelBreF-112
94WilCubC-20
94WilCubF-3773
96LakTigB-23

Samaniego, Art
79ElmPioRST-5

Sambel, Arnie
90EugEmeGS-26

Sambito, Joe
74CedRapAT-6
77Top-227
78AstBurK-10
78Top-498
79AstTeal-13
79Top-158
80Top-571
81CokTeaS-70
81Don-21
81Fle-65
81OPC-334
81Top-385
81TopSti-172
82AstAstl-4
82Don-65
82Fle-230
82FleSta-47
82Top-34
83Don-244
83Fle-464
83OPC-296
83Top-662
85Don-572
85Fle-360
85FleUpd-96
85Top-264
85TopTif-264
85TopTifT-103T
85TopTra-103T
86AstMot-19
86FleUpd-101
86TopTra-97T
86TopTraT-97T
87Don-421
87Fle-43
87FleGlo-43
87OPC-262
87Top-451
87TopTif-451
88Fle-364
88FleGlo-364
88Sco-314
88ScoGlo-314
88Top-784
88TopTif-784
88TucTorJP-20
89PacSenL-18
89T/MSenL-93
89TopSenL-95
91MetWIZ-340
91PacSenL-157
93UppDecAH-111

Sambo, Ramon
87VerRedP-7
88CedRapRP-1149
89ElPasDGS-28
89TexLeaAGS-15
90CMC-642
90ProAAAF-181
90VanCanC-15
90VanCanP-503
91LinDriAA-444
91MidAngLD-444
91MidAngOHP-26
91MidAngP-448
93LimRocDWB-122

Samboy, Alvaro
91SpoIndC-25
91SpoIndP-3949

Samboy, Javier
96AriBlaDB-30

Samboy, Nelson
96KisCobB-25

Samcoff, Ed
48SmiClo-19
49RemBre-24

Samford, Ron
59SenTealW-16
59Top-242
60Top-409
76DalCon-9
79TCM50-102

Sammons, Lee
90BenBucL-22
91MadMusC-28
91TacTigP-2319
92JacGenF-4013
92JacGenS-347
92SkyAA F-146

Samonds, Shereen
89OrlTwiB-28
94ColSilBC-7
95ColSilB9-2

Sampen, Bill
86WatPirP-21
87SalBucP-21
89HarSenP-290
89HarSenS-17
90Bow-104
90BowTif-104
90DonRoo-12
90ExpPos-31
90FleUpd-31
90ScoRoo-79T
90TopTra-108T
90TopTraT-108T
90UppDec-724
91Don-351
91Fle-247
91Lea-318
91OPC-649
91PanFreS-149
91Sco-68
91Sco100RS-64
91StaClu-249
91StaCluP-37
91Stu-199
91Top-649
91TopDeb90-138
91TopDesS-649
91TopMic-649
91TopTif-649
91ToyRoo-26
91UppDec-661
92Bow-348
92Don-571
92ExpDonD-3A
92ExpPos-27
92Fle-492
92OPC-566
92Sco-166
92StaClu-277
92Top-566
92TopGol-566
92TopGolW-566
92TopMic-566
92TriPla-221
92Ult-522
93Don-337
93Fle-624
93OmaRoyF-1679
93PacSpa-188
93StaCluRoy-22
94AngLAT-10

Sample, Billy
78TucTorC-19
79Top-713
80Top-458
81Don-268
81Fle-637
81OPC-283
81Top-283
82Don-69
82Fle-330
82OPC-112
82Top-112
83Don-242
83Fle-577
83FleSti-166
83RanAffF-5
83Top-641
84Don-403
84Fle-426
84Nes792-12
84OPC-12
84RanJarP-5
84Top-12
84TopSti-352
84TopTif-12
85Don-464
85Fle-566
85FleUpd-97
85Top-337
85TopSti-351
85TopTif-337
86BraPol-5
86Don-539
86Fle-118
86FleUpd-102
86Top-533
86TopTif-533
86TopTra-98T
86TopTraT-98T
87Don-143
87Fle-527
87FleGlo-527
87Top-104
87TopTif-104
90SweBasG-118
91SweBasG-79
92YanWIZ8-169
93RanKee-317

Sample, Deron
89KinMetS-20
90ColMetGS-10
90ColMetPPI-1
90SouAtlLAS-41
91St.LucMC-17
91St.LucMP-709
92EriSaiC-7
92EriSaiF-1623

Sample, Frank
91HunCubC-22
91HunCubP-3334

Samples, Todd
90JamExpP-11
91SouAtlLAGP-SAL47
91SumFlyC-24
91SumFlyP-2349
92RocExpC-25
92RocExpF-2129
93StoPorC-22
93StoPorF-758
94ElPasDF-3160
94StoPorC-24
94StoPorF-1707

Samplinski, Rich
88CapCodPPaLP-104
89OklSoo-23
90OklSoo-7

Sampson, Benj
94ForWayWC-1
94ForWayWF-2010
95ForMyeMTI-24
96BesAutS-81

Sampson, Mark
86SpoIndC-166

Sampson, Michael
89VerBeaDS-24
90YakBeaTI-3
91VerBeaDC-11
91VerBeaDP-772

Sampson, Tommy
92NegLeaK-15
92NegLeaRLI-53
95NegLeaL2-20

Sams, Andre
78GreBraT-22

Samson, Fred (Frederic)
87PorChaRP-14
89TulDriGS-23

89TulDriTI-22
90ChaRanS-26
90FloStaLAS-42
90StaFS7-27
91LinDriAA-596
91TulDriLD-596
91TulDriP-2783
91TulDriTI-28
Samson, William
52Par-51
53ExhCan-54
Samuel, Amado
62Top-597
64Top-129
64TopVen-129
91MetWIZ-341
Samuel, Cody
94OneYanC-19
94OneYanF-3803
96GreBatB-24
Samuel, Juan
83PorBeaT-2
83ReaPhiT-17
84Fle-47
84FunFooP-68
84PhiTas-32
84TopTra-105T
84TopTraT-105T
85AllGamPI-104
85Don-23
85Don-183
85DonActA-56
85DonSupD-23
85Dra-27
85Fle-264
85Fle-634
85FleStaS-44
85FleStaS-59
85Lea-23
85OPC-265
85PhiCIG-1
85PhiTas-11
85PhiTas-32
85SevCoi-E15
85Top-8
85Top-265
85TopGloS-31
85TopRubD-16
85TopSti-114
85TopSti-369
85TopSup-28
85TopTif-8
85TopTif-265
86BurKinA-10
86Don-326
86DonHig-37
86Fle-449
86FleLeaL-38
86FleLimE-39
86FleMin-93
86FleStiC-105
86KayB-29
86Lea-196
86OPC-237
86PhiCIG-1
86PhiKel-4
86PhiTas-8
86SevCoi-E12
86Spo-94
86Top-475
86TopMinL-54
86TopSti-121
86TopTat-15
86TopTif-475
87Don-165
87DonOpeD-156
87Fle-185
87Fle-642
87FleBasA-39
87FleGlo-185
87FleGlo-642
87FleLeaL-38
87FleMin-94
87FleStiC-104
87Lea-132
87OPC-255
87PhiCha-3
87PhiTas-8
87Spo-123
87SpoTeaP-6
87StuPan-9
87Top-255
87Top-481
87TopMinL-29
87TopSti-125
87TopTif-255
87TopTif-481
88Baz-18
88Don-288
88Don-576
88DonAll-55
88DonBasB-215
88Dra-20
88Fle-314
88FleAll-10
88FleBasA-35
88FleGlo-314
88FleMin-101
88FleStiC-110
88FleTeaL-33
88KayB-26
88Lea-146
88Nes-16
88OPC-19
88PanSti-359
88PhiTas-22
88Sco-32
88ScoGlo-32
88Spo-96
88SpoGam-12
88StaLinPh-15
88Top-398
88Top-705
88TopBig-67
88TopCoi-51
88TopGloS-43
88TopMinL-66
88TopRevLL-7
88TopSti-120
88TopStiB-5
88TopTif-398
88TopTif-705
88TopUKM-64
88TopUKMT-64
89Bow-405
89BowTif-405
89CadEllD-47
89ClaTraO-146
89Don-76
89DonBasB-238
89Fle-581
89FleGlo-581
89FleUpd-102
89MetKah-24
89OPC-372
89PanSti-152
89PhiTas-31
89RedFolSB-101
89Sco-255
89ScoHot1S-26
89ScoRoo-21T
89Spo-17
89Top-575
89TopAme2C-25
89TopBasT-95
89TopBig-321
89TopCoi-23
89TopGloS-13
89TopHilTM-25
89TopMinL-29
89TopSti-117
89TopStiB-37
89TopTif-575
89TopTra-108T
89TopTraT-108T
89TopUKM-66
89TVSpoM-29
89UppDec-336
90Bow-91
90BowTif-91
90ClaYel-T45
90DodMot-7
90DodPol-10
90Don-53
90DonBesN-29
90Fle-215
90FleCan-215
90FleUpd-25
90Lea-226
90OPC-85
90PubSti-249
90Sco-198
90ScoRoo-33T
90Top-85
90TopAmeA-25
90TopBig-283
90TopMinL-68
90TopTif-85
90TopTra-109T
90TopTraT-109T
90UppDec-583
90UppDec-795
91Bow-596
91Cla3-T82
91DodMot-7
91DodPol-10
91Don-62
91Fle-218
91Lea-10
91MetWIZ-342
91OPC-645
91OPCBoxB-O
91PanFreS-56
91Sco-446
91StaClu-495
91Stu-188
91Top-645
91TopDesS-645
91TopMic-645
91TopTif-645
91TopWaxBC-O
91Ult-168
91UppDec-117
91USPlaCA-8C
92Bow-253
92ClaGam-37
92DodMot-24
92DodPol-10
92DodSmo-10492
92DodStaTA-30
92Don-105
92Fle-469
92Lea-125
92OPC-315
92PanSti-193
92Pin-99
92Sco-73
92ScoProP-16
92StaClu-11
92StaCluD-161
92Top-315
92TopGol-315
92TopGolW-315
92TopMic-315
92TriPla-73
92TriPla-125
92Ult-216
92UppDec-195
93PacBeiA-21
93PacSpa-404
93RedKah-23
93Sco-611
93Sel-237
93SelRoo-129T
93Ult-335
93UppDec-527
93UppDecGold-527
94Fle-426
94FleUpd-46
94Pac-159
94StaClu-679
94StaCluFDI-679
94StaCluGR-679
94StaCluMOP-679
95Don-506
95DonPreP-506
95Fle-60
95Pac-159
95Sco-527
95ScoGolR-527
95ScoPlaTS-527
96BluJayOH-28
96Fle-137
96FleTif-137
96FleUpd-U103
96FleUpdTC-U103
96LeaSigEA-177
96Pac-323
97Pac-227
97PacLigB-227
97PacSil-227
Samuel, Mike
81BurBeeT-19
82BelBreF-19
84ElPasDT-9
85BelBreT-1
Samuels, Geoff
91BenBucC-10
91BenBucP-3695
92SalSpuC-3
92SalSpuF-3752
Samuels, Roger
86ColAstP-23
88BlaYNPRWL-125
88FleUpd-131
88FleUpdG-131
88PhoFirC-8
88PhoFirP-70
90CMC-370
90ProAAAF-274
90TidTidC-19
90TidTidP-543
90TopTVM-57
Samuels, Scott
92ClaFS7-443
92EriSaiC-13
92EriSaiF-1639
94BreCouMC-15
94BreCouMF-26
95Bes-59
96OrlCubB-24
Sanborn, Kyle
88CapCodPPaLP-112
Sanchez, Adam
92PeoChiTI-31
93PocPosSP-25
Sanchez, Adrian
90HunCubP-3281
91HunCubC-23
91HunCubP-3335
92MidLeaATI-37
92PeoChiC-18
92PeoChiTI-23
93PeoChiTI-24
Sanchez, Alejandro
81ReaPhiT-22
82OklCit8T-7
83PorBeaT-22
84PhoGiaC-8
85Don-43
85Fle-648
85FleUpd-98
86Don-415
86Fle-236
86Top-563
86TopTif-563
86TwiTeal-13
87TacTigP-20
Sanchez, Alex
97BluJayS-36
97Bow-333
97BowBes-200
97BowBesAR-200
97BowBesR-200
97BowChr-229
97BowChrI-229
97BowChrIR-229
97BowChrR-229
97BowInt-333
97Top-252
Sanchez, Alex Anthony
88BasAmeAAB-13
88KnoBluJB-1
88OPC-194
88SouLeaAJ-26
88TacTigC-17
88TacTigP-637
89Bow-245
89BowTif-245
89Don-47
89FleUpd-71
89SyrChiC-10
89SyrChiMB-20
89SyrChiP-813
89TopTra-109T
89TopTraT-109T
89TriA AAC-25
90BluJayFS-24
90CMC-327
90Don-45
90Fle-92
90FleCan-92
90OPC-563
90ProAAAF-350
90SyrChiC-1
90SyrChiMB-20
90SyrChiP-570
90Top-563
90TopDeb89-107
90TopTif-563
90ToyRoo-23
90TriAAAC-25
90UppDec-757
91LinDriAAA-515
91SyrChiK-3
91SyrChiLD-515
91SyrChiMB-21
91SyrChiP-2479
92BasCitRF-3846
93MemChiF-376
94CalCanF-789
Sanchez, Arturo
80VenLeaS-53
Sanchez, Carlos
88PocGiaP-2077
Sanchez, Celerino
73OPC-103
73SyrChiTI-25
73Top-103
74OPC-623
74SyrChiTI-24
74Top-623
92YanWIZ7-137
Sanchez, Daniel
90GreHorB-19
90GreHorP-2671
90GreHorS-21
91PriWilCC-19
91PriWilCP-1436
Sanchez, Francisco
87GasRanP-28
Sanchez, Frank
78WauMetT-24
Sanchez, Geraldo
86HagSunP-17
87HagSunP-28
88BlaYNPRWL-175
89BlaYNPRWL-54
Sanchez, Gordon
92FroRowDP-38
92OneYanC-6
93ColCliF-1114
93ColCliP-12
94TamYanC-23
94TamYanF-2388
95NorNavTI-48
Sanchez, Israel
83ChaRoyT-22
85Ft.MyeRT-15
86MemChiSTOS-24
86MemChiTOS-24
87OmaRoyP-18
88FleUpd-34
88FleUpdG-34
88OmaRoyC-11
88OmaRoyP-1496
89Don-474
89Top-452
89TopTif-452
89UppDec-326
90UppDec-384
91LinDriAAA-465
91RocRedWLD-465
91RocRedWP-1901
92RocRedWS-467
Sanchez, Jesus
94KinMetC-17
94KinMetF-3821
96StLucMTI-26
Sanchez, Jose
93AppFoxC-21
93AppFoxF-2459
Sanchez, Juan
87ClePhiP-22
Sanchez, Leo
84PriWilPT-28
85DomLeaS-51
85NasPirT-22
Sanchez, Luis
73CedRapAT-15
74CedRapAT-13
Sanchez, Luis M.
76VenLeaS-139
80VenLeaS-196
81LonBeaPT-16
82Top-653
83Don-519
83Fle-100
83Top-623
84AngSmo-24
84Don-597
84Fle-527
84Nes792-258
84OPC-258
84Top-258
84TopSti-233
84TopTif-258
85AngSmo-16
85Don-352
85Fle-310

85OPC-42
85Top-42
85TopTif-42
86Top-124
86TopTif-124
87JapPlaB-11
93LinVenB-98
94VenLinU-138
95LinVen-132
Sanchez, Marcos
80VenLeaS-227
95IdaFalBTI-34
96CliLumKTI-24
Sanchez, Martin
96MacBraB-12
Sanchez, Mike
95YakBeaTI-27
96GreFalDB-24
96GreFalDTI-12
96SanBerSB-23
Sanchez, Omar
94St.CatBJC-18
94St.CatBJF-3657
94VenLinU-118
95DunBluJTI-23
95LinVen-174
95StCatSTI-25
96DunBluJUTI-11
96HagSunB-19
Sanchez, Orlando
81Car5x7-23
82Don-636
82Fle-126
82LouRedE-26
82Top-604
83LouRedR-24
85MaiGuiT-23
88BlaYNPRWL-176
91OriCro-401
Sanchez, Ozzir (Osvaldo)
87SpoIndP-1
88ChaRaiP-1200
89BlaYNPRWL-153
89WatDiaP-1786
89WatDiaS-25
90Bes-281
90CMC-701
90WatDiaB-16
90WatDiaP-2391
91HigDesMC-28
91HigDesMP-2411
92DurBulC-6
92DurBulF-1111
92DurBulTI-17
93ClaFS7-290
93DurBulC-16
93DurBulF-499
Sanchez, Pedro
75BurBeeT-23
85DomLeaS-104
86AubAstP-22
87AshTouP-27
88OscAstS-23
89ColMudB-6
89ColMudP-127
89ColMudS-21
90CMC-624
90ProAAAF-197
90TucTorC-22
90TucTorP-207
Sanchez, Perry
90GatCitPP-3360
90GatCitPSP-21
91WesPalBEC-17
91WesPalBEP-1233
Sanchez, Raul
57Top-393
60Top-311
61MapLeaBH-19
Sanchez, Rey
88BlaYNPRWLU-21
88ChaRanS-NNO
89BlaYNPRWL-16
89OklCit8C-18
89OklCit8P-1511
91IowCubLD-216
91IowCubP-1067
91LinDriAAA-216
91TriA AAGP-AAA20
92CubMar-6
92Don-412
92FleUpd-75
92IowCubS-221
92Pin-550
92ProFS7-200
92StaClu-308
92TopDeb91-154
92TopTra-98T
92TopTraG-98T
92Ult-180
92UppDec-562
93Bow-496
93CubMar-22
93Don-424
93Fle-24
93Lea-88
93PacBeiA-18
93PacSpa-61
93Pin-317
93Sco-324
93StaClu-36
93StaCluCu-24
93StaCluFDI-36
93StaCluMOP-36
93Top-292
93TopGol-292
93TopInaM-292
93TopMic-292
93Toy-60
93Ult-319
93Ult-648
93UppDec-612
93UppDecGold-612
93USPlaCR-8H
94ColC-558
94ColChoGS-558
94ColChoSS-558
94Don-383
94ExtBas-223
94Fin-249
94FinRef-249
94Fla-362
94Fle-395
94Pac-108
94Sco-482
94ScoGolR-482
94StaClu-104
94StaCluFDI-104
94StaCluGR-104
94StaCluMOP-104
94StaCluT-338
94StaCluTFDI-338
94Top-422
94TopGol-422
94TopSpa-422
95ColCho-202
95ColChoGS-202
95ColChoSS-202
95D3-53
95Don-173
95DonPreP-173
95DonTopotO-203
95Emb-59
95EmbGolI-59
95Fin-66
95FinRef-66
95Fla-116
95Fle-423
95Lea-160
95Pac-78
95PacPri-25
95Pin-315
95PinArtP-315
95PinMusC-315
95Sco-63
95ScoGolR-63
95ScoPlaTS-63
95StaClu-21
95StaCluFDI-21
95StaCluMOP-21
95StaCluSTWS-21
95StaCluVR-15
95Top-57
95Ult-138
95UltGolM-138
95UppDec-63
95UppDecED-63
95UppDecEDG-63
96ColCho-496
96ColChoGS-496
96ColChoSS-496
96Don-111
96DonPreP-111
96EmoXL-158
96Fla-222
96Fle-327
96FleCub-14
96FleTif-327
96LeaSigA-201
96LeaSigAG-201
96LeaSigAS-201
96MetUni-144
96MetUniP-144
96Pac-27
96Sco-395
96StaClu-389
96StaCluMOP-389
95StaCluVRMC-15
96Top-287
96Ult-169
96UltGolM-169
96UppDec-296
97ColCho-68
97Pac-256
97PacLigB-256
97PacSil-256
97Sco-429
97ScoHobR-429
97ScoResC-429
97ScoShoS-429
97ScoShoSAP-429
97StaClu-349
97StaCluMOP-349
97Top-179
97UppDec-32
Sanchez, Sammye
88LitFalMP-12
Sanchez, Sergio
93ElmPioC-16
93ElmPioF-3831
Sanchez, Stan
87SanBerSP-6
89SanBerSB-26
89SanBerSCLC-91
Sanchez, Victor
94AubAstC-16
94AubAstF-3763
95QuaCitRBTI-24
96JacGenB-24
Sanchez, Yuri
92BriTigC-20
92BriTigF-1421
92ClaDraP-39
92ClaFS7-427
93ClaFS7-116
93FayGenC-1
93FayGenF-138
94Cla-4
94LakTigC-20
94LakTigF-3045
94UppDecML-129
95JacSunTI-25
95UppDecML-206
95UppDecMLFS-206
Sanchez, Zoilo
86LynMetP-20
87JacMetF-6
87MetColP-46
88JacMetGS-2
89JacMetGS-15
90CMC-377
90ProAAAF-289
90TidTidC-26
90TidTidP-558
90TopTVM-58
Sand, Heinie (John Henry)
21Exh-150
25Exh-47
26Exh-47
28Exh-23
33Gou-85
34GouCanV-27
92ConTSN-615
Sandberg, Chuck
81BriRedST-11
Sandberg, Jared
97Top-470
Sandberg, Ryne
80CarMudF-22
81OklCit8T-17
82CubRedL-23
83AllGamPI-107
83CubThoAV-23
83Don-277
83Fle-507
83OPC-83
83Top-83
83Top-282
83TopSti-328
84AllGamPI-15
84CubChiT-25
84CubSev-23
84CubUno-2
84CubUno-3
84CubUno-7
84CubUno-12
84CubUno-15
84Don-311
84DonActAS-43
84Fle-504
84FunFooP-13
84Nes792-596
84OCoandSI-102
84OCoandSI-202
84OPC-64
84Top-596
84TopSti-45
84TopTif-596
85AllGamPI-105
85CubLioP-19
85CubSev-23
85Don-1
85Don-67
85DonActA-24
85DonSupD-1
85DonWaxBC-PC2
85Dra-28
85Fle-65
85Fle-630
85FleLimE-31
85FleStaS-11
85FleStaS-45
85GenMilS-8
85KASDis-11
85KitCloD-11
85Lea-1
85OPC-296
85SevCoi-G11
85ThoMcAD-41
85Top-460
85Top-713
85Top3-D-7
85TopGaloC-9
85TopGloA-3
85TopGloS-21
85TopRubD-9
85TopSti-34
85TopSti-175
85TopSup-1
85TopTif-460
85TopTif-713
86BasStaB-96
86CubGat-23
86CubUno-15
86Don-67
86DonAll-32
86DorChe-14
86Dra-19
86Fle-378
86FleLeaL-39
86FleLimE-40
86FleMin-80
86FleSlu-32
86FleStiC-106
86GenMilB-4G
86Lea-62
86MeaGolBB-13
86MeaGolM-10
86MeaGolSB-12
86MSAJayPCD-15
86MSAJifPD-12
86OPC-19
86QuaGra-13
86SevCoi-C9
86Spo-20
86Spo-51
86Spo-127
86Top-690
86TopGloS-34
86TopMinL-39
86TopSti-55
86TopSup-48
86TopTat-8
86TopTif-690
86TruVal-14
87BoaandB-30
87BurKinA-18
87ClaGam-35
87CubCan-26
87CubDavB-23
87Don-77
87DonAll-13
87DonOpeD-75
87DonP-13
87Dra-21
87Fle-572
87Fle-639
87FleAwaW-35
87FleGlo-572
87FleGlo-639
87FleLeaL-39
87FleMin-95
87FleStiC-105
87FleWaxBC-C14
87GenMilB-5G
87HosSti-8
87KayB-28
87KraFoo-8
87Lea-234
87MandMSL-4
87MSAJifPD-1
87OPC-143
87RalPur-15
87RedFolSB-16
87SevCoi-C14
87SevCoi-M11
87Spo-8
87Spo-116
87Spo-197
87SpoSupD-3
87SpoTeaP-22
87Top-680
87TopCoi-41
87TopGloA-3
87TopSti-61
87TopSti-156
87TopTif-680
88Baz-19
88CarSmo-16
88CheBoy-11
88ClaRed-169
88CubDavB-23
88Don-242
88DonAll-35
88DonBasB-116
88DonPop-13
88DonTeaBC-242
88Fle-431
88Fle-628
88FleBasM-29
88FleExcS-32
88FleGlo-431
88FleGlo-628
88FleMin-70
88FleStiC-80
88FleSupBC-C5
88FleWaxBC-C10
88GreBasS-49
88Lea-207
88OPC-10
88PanSti-234
88PanSti-260
88Sco-26
88ScoBoxC-12
88ScoGlo-26
88Spo-12
88StaLinAl-28
88StaLinCu-9
88Top-10
88TopBig-16
88TopCoi-52
88TopGloA-14
88TopGloS-14
88TopSti-57
88TopSti-147
88TopStiB-6
88TopTif-10
88TopUKM-65
88TopUKMT-65
89Bow-290
89BowTif-290
89CadEllD-48
89ClaLigB-99
89CubMar-23
89Don-105
89DonAll-35
89DonBasB-26
89DonPop-35
89Fle-437
89FleGlo-437
89FleHeroB-35
89K-M-24
89KayB-26
89KinDis-5
89OPC-360
89PanSti-56
89PanSti-233
89Sco-35
89ScoHot1S-54
89ScoSco-23

89Spo-201
89SpoIllFKI-121
89Top-360
89Top-387
89TopAme2C-26
89TopBasT-69
89TopBig-212
89TopDouA-14
89TopGloA-14
89TopGloS-34
89TopHeaUT-9
89TopSti-55
89TopSti-155
89TopStiB-38
89TopTif-360
89TopTif-387
89TopUKM-67
89TVSpoM-18
89UppDec-120
89UppDec-675
90AllBasT-19
90Bow-30
90BowTif-30
90ClaBlu-27
90ClaYel-T86
90Col-29
90CubMar-18
90Don-105
90Don-692A
90Don-692B
90DonBesN-26
90DOnBonM-BC10
90DonLeaS-11
90Fle-40
90Fle-625
90Fle-639
90FleAll-9
90FleAwaW-31
90FleBasA-32
90FleBasM-33
90FleCan-40
90FleCan-625
90FleCan-639
90FleLeaL-33
90GooHumICBLS-19
90Hot50PS-37
90K-M-2
90Lea-98
90Lea-528
90MLBBasB-47
90MSAIceTD-12
90OPC-210
90OPC-398
90OPCBoxB-P
90PanSti-212
90PanSti-231
90Pos-9
90PubSti-201
90PubSti-270
90Sco-90
90Sco-561A
90Sco-561B
90Sco-691
90Sco100S-32
90ScoMcD-8
90Spo-54
90StaSan-1
90StaSan-2
90StaSan-3
90StaSan-4
90StaSan-5
90StaSan-6
90StaSan-7
90StaSan-8
90StaSan-9
90StaSan-10
90StaSan-11
90SunSee-20
90SupActM-20
90Top-210
90Top-398
90TopBig-75
90TopCoi-56
90TopDou-55
90TopGloA-3
90TopGloS-1
90TopHeaU-9
90TopMag-25
90TopMinL-51
90TopSti-12
90TopSti-46
90TopSti-152
90TopStiB-6
90TopTif-210
90TopTif-398
90TopTVA-51
90TopTVCu-26
90TopWaxBC-P
90UppDec-324
90UppDecS-5
90USPlaCA-4H
90WonBreS-20
90Woo-21
91BasBesHM-17
91BasBesRB-15
91Baz-9
91Bow-377
91Bow-416
91CadElID-48
91Cla1-T29
91Cla1-NNO
91Cla2-T67
91ClaGam-107
91Col-15
91ColPosS-1
91ColPosS-2
91ColPosS-3
91ColPosS-4
91ColPosS-5
91ColPosS-6
91ColPosS-7
91ColPosS-8
91ColSan-1
91ColSan-2
91ColSan-3
91ColSan-4
91ColSan-5
91ColSan-6
91ColSan-7
91ColSan-8
91ColSan-9
91ColSan-10
91ColSan-11
91ColSan-12
91ColSan-xx
91CubMar-23
91CubVinL-23
91CubVinL-36
91Don-14
91Don-404
91Don-433
91Don-504
91DonBonC-BC7
91DonEli-S1
91DonPre-9
91DonSupD-14
91Fle-431
91Fle-709
91Fle-713
91FleAll-1
91FlePro-F3
91JimDea-6
91KinDis-19
91Lea-207
91LeaPre-2
91LinDriS-1
91LinDriS-2
91LinDriS-3
91LinDriS-4
91LinDriS-5
91LinDriS-6
91LinDriS-7
91LinDriS-8
91LinDriS-9
91LinDriS-10
91LinDriS-11
91LinDriS-12
91LinDriS-13
91LinDriS-14
91LinDriS-15
91LinDriS-16
91LinDriS-17
91LinDriS-18
91LinDriS-19
91LinDriS-20
91MajLeaCP-68
91MooSna-5
91MSAHoID-6
91OPC-7
91OPC-398
91OPC-740
91OPCPre-103
91PacPro-1
91PanCanT1-9
91PanCanT1-27
91PanCanT1-34
91PanCanT1-49
91PanCanT1-101
91PanFreS-44
91PanFreS-159
91PanSti-40
91PepSup-3
91PetSta-4
91Pos-16
91RedFolS-82
91RedFolS-126
91Sco-3
91Sco-665
91Sco-815
91Sco-862
91Sco100S-60
91SevCoi-M11
91SevCoi-T12
91SevCoi-NW8
91StaClu-230
91StaCluCM-26
91StaPinB-42
91Stu-158
91Top-7
91Top-398
91Top-740
91TopCraJI-6
91TopDesS-7
91TopDesS-398
91TopDesS-740
91TopGaloC-10
91TopGloA-14
91TopMic-7
91TopMic-398
91TopMic-740
91TopSta-30
91TopTif-7
91TopTif-398
91TopTif-740
91TopTriH-N2
91Ult-66
91UltGol-10
91UppDec-132
91UppDec-725
91UppDecFE-79F
91UppDecFE-93F
91UppDecSS-SS8
91USPlaCA-12S
91Woo-20
92Bow-300
92Cla1-T79
92Cla2-T29
92Cla2-NNO
92ClaGam-131
92ColAllG-4
92ColAllP-4
92ColPro-13
92CubMar-23
92DenHol-10
92Don-429
92Don-576
92DonCraJ1-28
92DonMcD-6
92Fle-389
92FleAll-14
92FleCitTP-3
92FleLumC-L4
92Fre-12
92Hig5-30
92Hig5S-26
92HitTheBB-30
92JimDea-18
92KinDis-19
92Lea-317
92Lea-331
92LeaBlaG-317
92LeaGolP-2
92LeaPre-2
92Mr.TurS-22
92MSABenSHD-19
92New-24
92OPC-110
92OPCPre-34
92PanSti-183
92PanSti-282
92PepDieM-16
92Pin-10
92Pin-617
92PinRool-13
92PinSlu-9
92PinTeaP-5
92Pos-2
92PosCan-4
92RevSup1-7
92RevSup1-8
92RevSup1-9
92Sco-200
92Sco-442
92Sco-774
92Sco100S-85
92ScoProaG-12
92ScoProP-4
92ScoSam-5
92SevCoi-15
92StaClu-50
92StaClu-600
92StaCluD-162
92StaSan-1
92StaSan-2
92StaSan-3
92StaSan-4
92StaSan-5
92StaSan-6
92StaSan-7
92StaSan-8
92StaSan-9
92StaSan-10
92StaSan-11
92Stu-18
92StuHer-BC1
92StuPre-3
92Top-110
92Top-387
92TopGol-110
92TopGol-387
92TopGolW-110
92TopGolW-387
92TopKid-1
92TopMcD-5
92TopMic-110
92TopMic-387
92TriPla-229
92Ult-181
92UltAllS-12
92UltAwaW-25
92UppDec-145
92UppDecF-39
92UppDecFG-39
92UppDecTMH-46
93Ble23KS-1
93Ble23KS-2
93Ble23KS-3
93BlePro-10
93BlePro-11
93BlePro-12
93BlePro-13
93Bow-200
93CadDis-51
93ClaGam-80
93ColAllG-10
93CubMar-21
93DenHol-8
93DiaMar-93
93DiaMarP-7
93Don-344
93DonDiaK-DK2
93DonEli-20
93DonEliD-1
93DonEliS-2
93DonLonBL-LL15
93DonMasotG-5
93DonMVP-22
93DonPre-2
93DonSpiotG-SG14
93DurPowP2-13
93Fin-105
93FinJum-105
93FinRef-105
93Fla-20
93Fle-25
93Fle-356
93FleAtl-21
93FleFruotL-56
93FleTeaL-NL6
93FunPac-19
93FunPac-80
93FunPac-84
93FunPacA-AS4
93Hos-2
93JimDea-25
93KinDis-22
93Kra-27
93Lea-224
93LeaGolA-R4
93LeaGolA-U4
93LeaHeaftH-8
93MetBak-18
93OPC-274
93OPCPreSP-4
93OPCPreSPF-4
93PacSpa-62
93PanSti-204
93Pin-15
93PinCoo-8
93PinCooD-8
93PinHomRC-12
93PinSlu-27
93Pos-13
93PosCan-14
93Sco-4
93Sco-530
93ScoFra-16
93Sel-97
93SelChaS-2
93SelDufIP-11
93SelStaL-11
93SP-17
93SPPlaP-PP17
93StaClu-366
93StaClu-600
93StaCluCu-1
93StaCluFDI-366
93StaCluFDI-600
93StaCluI-B3
93StaCluM-44
93StaCluMMP-9
93StaCluMOP-366
93StaCluMOP-600
93StaCluMOP-MB3
93Stu-176
93Top-3
93Top-402
93TOPBLAG-17
93TopGol-3
93TopGol-402
93TopInaM-3
93TopInaM-402
93TopMic-3
93TopMic-402
93TopPos-1
93TriPla-10
93TriPlaA-4
93TriPlaN-3
93TriPlaP-10
93Ult-320
93UltAllS-3
93UppDec-38
93UppDec-175
93UppDec-483
93UppDec-735
93UppDecCP-R18
93UppDecDG-8
93UppDecGold-38
93UppDecGold-175
93UppDecGold-483
93UppDecGold-735
93UppDecHRH-HR11
93UppDecOD-D22
93UppDecTAN-TN6
94Bow-250
94Bow-388
94ChuHomS-16
94ChuHomSG-16
94ColC-335
94ColC-555
94ColChoGS-335
94ColChoGS-555
94ColChoSS-335
94ColChoSS-555
94ColChoT-14
94DenHol-22
94Don-18
94Don-110
94DonAnn8-9
94DonSpeE-18
94Fin-210
94FinJum-210
94FinRef-210
94Fla-141
94FlaHotN-9
94Fle-396
94FleAllS-48
94FleTeaL-16
94FUnPac-60
94KinDis-22
94Lea-425
94LeaPro-8
94LeaSli-4
94OPC-16
94OPCAllR-7
94OPCJumA-7
94OscMayR-29
94Pac-109
94PacSilP-26
94PanSti-156

94Pin-6
94PinArtP-6
94PinMusC-6
94PinTheN-14
94RedFolMI-36
94Sco-20
94ScoGolR-20
94Sel-32
94SP-71
94SPDieC-71
94Spo-45
94SpoFanA-AS2
94SpoMov-MM2
94StaClu-397
94StaClu-719
94StaCluFDI-397
94StaCluFDI-719
94StaCluGR-397
94StaCluGR-719
94StaCluMOP-397
94StaCluMOP-719
94StaCluT-331
94StaCluTF-9
94StaCluTFDI-331
94Stu-63
94StuHer-5
94Top-300
94Top-602
94TopGol-300
94TopGol-602
94TopSpa-300
94TopSpa-602
94TopSupS-39
94TopTra-130T
94TopTra-131T
94TriPla-77
94TriPlaM-6
94TriPlaN-2
94Ult-166
94UltAllS-13
94UltCarA-4
94UppDec-92
94UppDecAJ-5
94UppDecAJG-5
94UppDecDC-C6
94UppDecED-92
94Yoo-14
95ColCho-48
95ColChoGS-48
95ColChoSS-48
95UppDec-447
95UppDecED-447
95UppDecEDG-447
95UppDecSE-258
95UppDecSEG-258
96Bow-51
96BowBes-8
96BowBesAR-8
96BowBesR-8
96Cir-111
96CirBos-29
96CirRav-111
96ColCho-495
96ColChoGS-495
96ColChoSS-495
96DenHol-9
96EmoXL-159
96Fin-G39
96Fin-S234
96FinRef-G39
96FinRef-S234
96Fla-223
96Fle-328
96FleCub-15
96FleTif-328
96FleUpd-U239
96FleUpd-U249
96FleUpdTC-U239
96FleUpdTC-U249
96LeaLim-77
96LeaLimG-77
96LeaPre-91
96LeaPreP-91
96LeaPreSG-66
96LeaPreSte-66
96LeaSig-84
96LeaSigPPG-84
96LeaSigPPP-84
96MetUni-145
96MetUniML-10
96MetUniP-145
96Pin-342
96PinAfi-16
96PinAfiAP-16
96PinAfiFPP-16
96PinAfiSP-16
96PinFan-12
96PinFoil-342
96Sel-140
96SelArtP-140
96SelCer-28
96SelCerAP-28
96SelCerCB-28
96SelCerCR-28
96SelCerIP-19
96SelCerMB-28
96SelCerMG-28
96SelCerMR-28
96SelTeaN-15
96SP-53
96SPx-14
96SPxGol-14
96Stu-6
96StuPrePB-6
96StuPrePG-6
96StuPrePS-6
96Sum-70
96SumAbo&B-70
96SumArtP-70
96SumBal-10
96SumFoi-70
96SumHitI-15
96TeaOut-70
96Top-356
96TopBigC-8
96TopChr-144
96TopChrR-144
96TopGal-38
96TopGalPPI-38
96TopLas-48
96TopLasSS-15
96Ult-457
96UltCalttH-8
96UltCalttHGM-8
96UltGolM-457
96UltRes-8
96UltResGM-8
96UltThu-18
96UltThuGM-18
96UppDec-486U
96Zen-16
96ZenArtP-16
96ZenMoz-6
97Bow-22
97BowBes-8
97BowBesAR-8
97BowBesR-8
97BowChr-18
97BowChrI-18
97BowChrIR-18
97BowChrR-18
97BowInt-22
97Cir-23
97CirRav-23
97ColCho-66
97ColChoAC-29
97ColChoNF-NF15
97ColChoNF-NF16
97Don-72
97DonEli-70
97DonEliGS-70
97DonLim-30
97DonLim-68
97DonLimFotG-47
97DonLimLE-30
97DonLimLE-68
97DonPre-96
97DonPreCttC-96
97DonPreP-72
97DonPrePGold-72
97DonPreTBG-20
97DonPreTF-20
97DonPreTP-20
97Fin-2
97Fin-303
97FinEmb-303
97FinEmbR-303
97FinRef-2
97FinRef-303
97FlaSho-A23
97FlaSho-B23
97FlaSho-C23
97FlaShoLC-23
97FlaShoLC-B23
97FlaShoLC-C23
97FlaShoLCM-A23
97FlaShoLCM-B23
97FlaShoLCM-C23
97Fle-282
97Fle-716
97Fle-725
97FleDecoE-11
97FleDecoERT-11
97FleGouG-13
97FleGouGF-13
97FleHea-18
97FleTif-282
97FleTif-716
97FleTif-725
97Lea-196
97Lea-205
97LeaFraM-196
97LeaFraM-205
97LeaFraMDC-196
97LeaFraMDC-205
97LeaGolS-32
97MetUni-14
97NewPin-140
97NewPinAP-140
97NewPinMC-140
97NewPinPP-140
97Pac-257
97PacCar-25
97PacCarM-25
97PacGolCD-25
97PacLigB-257
97PacPri-88
97PacPriGA-GA20
97PacPriGotD-GD121
97PacPriLB-88
97PacPriP-88
97PacSil-257
97Pin-99
97PinArtP-99
97PinCer-4
97PinCerLI-18
97PinCerMBlu-4
97PinCerMG-4
97PinCerMR-4
97PinCerR-4
97PinIns-37
97PinInsCE-37
97PinInsDE-37
97PinMusC-99
97PinTotCPB-4
97PinTotCPG-4
97PinTotCPR-4
97PinX-P-45
97PinX-PMoS-45
97ProMag-6
97ProMagML-6
97Sco-94
97Sco-537
97ScoAllF-4
97ScoHobR-537
97ScoPreS-94
97ScoResC-537
97ScoShoS-94
97ScoShoS-537
97ScoShoSAP-94
97ScoShoSAP-537
97Sel-33
97SelArtP-33
97SelRegG-33
97SelToootT-18
97SelToootTMB-18
97SkyE-X-62
97SkyE-XC-62
97SkyE-XEC-62
97SkyE-XHoN-5
97SP-43
97SpoIll-95
97SpoIllEE-95
97SpoIllGS-11
97SPSpeF-36
97SPx-15
97SPxBro-15
97SPxCorotG-6
97SPxGraF-15
97SPxSil-15
97SPxSte-15
97StaClu-229
97StaCluMat-229
97StaCluMOP-229
97Stu-41
97StuPor8-23
97StuPrePG-41
97StuPrePS-41
97Top-167
97TopChr-67
97TopChrR-67
97TopGal-29
97TopGalPPI-29
97TopSta-59
97TopStaAM-59
97Ult-168
97UltFamGam-16
97UltGolME-168
97UltHitM-15
97UltLeaS-9
97UltPlaME-168
97UltTop3-20
97UltTop3GM-20
97UppDec-325
97Zen-42

Sander, Mike
87NewOriP-12
88HagSunS-18
89EasLeaDDP-DD40
89HagSunB-25
89HagSunP-275
89HagSunS-15
90HagSunB-21
90HagSunDGB-25
90HagSunP-1413
90HagSunS-22

Sander, Rick
77LodDodT-16

Sanderlin, Rick
77PhoGiaCC-21
77PhoGiaCP-21
77PhoGiaVNB-21
78PhoGiaC-23
79PhoGiaVNB-21

Sanders, Adam
90UtiBluSP-6

Sanders, Al
88ElmPioC-10
89ElmPioP-19
89WinHavRSS-20
90StaFS7-5
90WinHavRSS-24
91LinDriAA-471
91NewBriRSLD-471
91NewBriRSP-352
92NewBriRSF-433
92NewBriRSS-495

Sanders, Alexander
87OldJudN-441

Sanders, Allen
95SpoIndTI-24
96SpoIndB-24

Sanders, Anthony
93MedHatBJF-3751
93MedHatBJSP-16
94St.CatBJC-19
94St.CatBJF-3658
95HagSunF-83
96DunBluJB-22
96DunBluJTI-26
96DunBluJUTI-12
96MauStiHWB-18
97Bow-127
97BowChr-139
97BowChrI-139
97BowChrIR-139
97BowChrR-139
97BowInt-127

Sanders, Barry
91AreHol-4
91StaCluCM-37
91StaCluMO-35

Sanders, Craig
95SpoIndTI-25
96LanLugB-24

Sanders, Deion
89AlbYanB-1
89AlbYanP-338
89AlbYanS-23
89ClaTraP-200
89DonRoo-6
89FleUpd-53
89Sta-150
89TopTra-110T
89TopTraT-110T
89YanScoNW-22
90AlbDecGB-1
90ClaBlu-21A
90ClaBlu-21B
90Don-427
90Fle-454
90FleCan-454
90Hot50RS-38
90Lea-359
90OPC-61
90Sco-586
90Sco100RS-40
90ScoYouS2-27
90Spo-221
90Top-61
90TopDeb89-108
90TopMag-82
90TopTif-61
90TopTVY-33
90UppDec-13
90YanScoNW-22
91Bow-588
91BraDubP-24
91BraSubS-32
91Lea-436
91RicBraBC-37
91Sco100RS-6
91ScoRoo-34T
91StaClu-442
91UppDec-352
91UppDec-743
92Bow-160
92BraKryPS-1
92BraLykP-24
92BraLykS-29
92Cla1-T80
92Cla2-T13
92ClaGam-127
92Don-564
92Fle-368
92Lea-448
92LeaGolP-27
92OPC-645
92OPCPre-91
92Pin-170
92PinTea2-31
92Sco-571
92StaClu-15
92StaCluMP-12
92Stu-9
92Top-645
92TopGol-645
92TopGolW-645
92TopMic-645
92TriPla-186
92Ult-464
92UltAllS-17
92UppDec-247
92UppDec-SP3
92YanWIZ8-170
93BluJayDM-17
93Bow-438
93BraLykP-25
93BraLykS-31
93ClaGam-81
93DiaMar-94
93Don-158
93DonMasotG-16
93DurPowP2-7
93Fin-141
93FinRef-141
93Fla-10
93Fle-13
93FunPac-34
93FunPac-67
93FunPac-219
93Lea-222
93OPC-372
93OPCPreSP-10
93OPCPreSPF-10
93PacSpa-11
93PanSti-188
93Pin-4
93Sco-123
93Sel-84
93SelStaL-22
93SP-62
93StaClu-408
93StaCluB-22
93StaCluFDI-408
93StaCluMOP-408
93Top-795
93TopGol-795
93TopInaM-795
93TopMic-795
93Toy-82
93TriPla-162
93TriPlaA-9
93TriPlaN-8
93Ult-12
93UppDec-166
93UppDecGold-166
94Bow-301
94BowBes-R38
94BowBesR-R38

94BraLykS-28
94BraUSPC-7C
94BraUSPC-9S
94BraUSPC-13H
94ColC-575
94ColChoGS-575
94ColChoSS-575
94Don-430
94ExtBas-239
94Fin-22
94FinPre-22P
94FinRef-22
94Fla-371
94Fle-373
94FleUpd-121
94FUnPac-164
94Lea-101
94LeaL-98
94LeaMVPC-N12
94LeaMVPCG-N12
94OPC-118
94Pac-21
94PanSti-150
94Pin-174
94PinArtP-174
94PinMusC-174
94RedKah-26
94Sco-496
94ScoGolR-496
94ScoGolS-6
94ScoRoo-RT57
94ScoRooCP-CP10
94ScoRooGR-RT57
94Sel-305
94SP-162
94SPDieC-162
94Spo-108
94SpoRoo-25
94SpoRooAP-25
94SpoRooS-25
94StaClu-472
94StaCluFDI-472
94StaCluGR-472
94StaCluMOP-472
94StaCluT-54
94StaCluTFDI-54
94Stu-172
94Top-375
94TopGol-375
94TopSpa-375
94TopTra-103T
94TriPla-49
94Ult-156
94UppDec-85
94UppDecED-85
95Baz-115
95Bow-277
95BowBes-X3
95BowBesR-X3
95ClaPhoC-49
95ColCho-425
95ColChoGS-425
95ColChoSE-199
95ColChoSEGS-199
95ColChoSESS-199
95ColChoSS-425
95Don-415
95DonPreP-415
95DonTopotO-356
95Emb-12
95EmbGolI-12
95Emo-118
95Fin-205
95FinRef-205
95Fla-340
95Fle-446
95Lea-94
95LeaLim-90
95LeaLim-98
95LeaLimG-24
95NatPac-17
95Pac-113
95PacPri-36
95PanSti-80
95Pin-341
95PinArtP-341
95PinFan-19
95PinMusC-341
95PinRedH-RH22
95PinUps-US25
95PinWhiH-WH22
95RedKah-26
95Sco-266
95ScoGolR-266
95ScoHaloG-HG27
95ScoPlaTS-266
95Sel-116
95SelArtP-116
95SelCer-8
95SelCerMG-8
95SP-43
95SPCha-93
95SPChaDC-93
95Spo-77
95SpoArtP-77
95SPSil-43
95StaClu-122
95StaCluFDI-122
95StaCluMO-41
95StaCluMOP-122
95StaCluMOP-SS8
95StaCluMOP-VRE8
95StaCluSS-SS8
95StaCluSTWS-122
95StaCluVE-VRE8
95StaCluVR-61
95Stu-20
95StuGolS-20
95StuPlaS-20
95Sum-36
95SumNthD-36
95Top-508
95TopCyb-297
95TopLeaL-LL19
95UC3-4
95UC3ArtP-4
95Ult-149
95UltGolM-149
95UppDec-170
95UppDec-465T
95UppDecED-170
95UppDecEDG-170
95UppDecSE-165
95UppDecSEG-165
95USPlaCMLA-10H
95Zen-26
96Baz-130
96ColCho-306
96ColChoGS-306
96ColChoSS-306
96Don-405
96DonPreP-405
96Fle-595
96FleTif-595
96Lea-34
96LeaPrePB-34
96LeaPrePG-34
96LeaPrePS-34
96MetUni-245
96MetUniP-245
96Pac-200
96PacGolCD-DC30
96PacPri-P67
96PacPriG-P67
96PanSti-110
96Pin-25
96PinArtP-11
96PinSta-11
96ProSta-53
96Sco-18
96ScoDugC-A17
96ScoDugCAP-A17
96Spo-83
96SpoArtP-83
96StaClu-11
96StaCluEPB-11
96StaCluEPG-11
96StaCluEPS-11
96StaCluMeg-MH9
96StaCluMOP-11
96StaCluMOP-MH9
95StaCluVRMC-61
96Top-315
96Ult-298
96UltGolM-298
96UppDec-192
97Bow-70
97BowBes-44
97BowBesAR-44
97BowBesR-44
97BowChr-51
97BowChrI-51
97BowChrIR-51
97BowChrR-51
97BowInt-70
97Cir-81
97CirRav-81
97ColCho-305
97ColChoBS-9
97ColChoBSGS-9
97ColChoNF-NF21
97ColChoNF-NF22
97Don-304
97DonLim-42
97DonLim-61
97DonLim-181
97DonLimFotG-16
97DonLimLE-42
97DonLimLE-61
97DonLimLE-181
97DonPreP-304
97DonPrePGold-304
97Fin-299
97FinEmb-299
97FinEmbR-299
97FinRef-299
97FlaSho-A47
97FlaSho-B47
97FlaSho-C47
97FlaShoLC-47
97FlaShoLC-B47
97FlaShoLC-C47
97FlaShoLCM-A47
97FlaShoLCM-B47
97FlaShoLCM-C47
97Fle-650
97FleTif-650
97Lea-209
97Lea-397
97LeaFraM-209
97LeaFraM-397
97LeaFraMDC-209
97LeaFraMDC-397
97LeaGolS-8
97LeaLeaotN-9
97LeaWarT-16
97NewPin-125
97NewPinAP-125
97NewPinMC-125
97NewPinPP-125
97ProMag-9
97ProMagML-9
97Sco-431
97ScoHobR-431
97ScoResC-431
97ScoShoS-431
97ScoShoSAP-431
97SkyE-X-65
97SkyE-XC-65
97SkyE-XEC-65
97SP-53
97SpoIll-97
97SpoIllEE-97
97SpoIllGS-12
97SPx-20
97SPxBro-20
97SPxGraF-20
97SPxSil-20
97SPxSte-20
97Stu-134
97StuPrePG-134
97StuPrePS-134
97Ult-346
97UltGolME-346
97UltPlaME-346
97UppDec-528
97Zen-34

Sanders, Doug
95TacRaiTI-19

Sanders, Earl
87DunBluJP-946
88DunBluJS-15
89DunBluJS-14
90KnoBluJB-23
90KnoBluJP-1245
90KnoBluJS-17
91GreBraC-5
91GreBraLD-218
91GreBraP-2999
91LinDriAA-218

Sanders, Ken
66Top-356
66TopVen-356
70SunPin-16
71BreTeal-15
71MLBOffS-451
71OPC-116
71Top-116
72OPC-391
72Top-391
73OPC-246
73Top-246
74OPC-638
74Top-638
75OPC-366
75Top-366
76OPC-291
76SSP-550
76Top-291
77SpoIndC-20
77Top-171
91MetWIZ-343
94BreMilB-75

Sanders, Lance
89UtiBluSP-20
93MarPhiC-25
93MarPhiF-3474
94SpaPhiF-1722
94SparPhiC-18

Sanders, Matt
91BluOriC-16
91BluOriP-4129
92KanCouCC-7
92KanCouCF-92
92KanCouCTI-27

Sanders, Pat
93SouOreAC-23
93SouOreAF-4073
94SouOreAC-24
94SouOreAF-3633
95WesMicWTI-26

Sanders, Paul
91EugEmeC-8
91EugEmeP-3729

Sanders, Ray
47TipTop-86
79DiaGre-167
83TCMPla1944-23

Sanders, Reggie (Reginald Jerome)
74OPC-600
74Top-600
75OPC-617
75Top-617
78SSP270-149

Sanders, Reggie (Reginald Laverne)
88BilMusP-1822
89GreHorP-415
89SouAtlLAGS-23
90CedRapRB-11
90CedRapRP-2334
90CMC-655
90MidLeaASGS-48
90ProAaA-128
90TopMag-66
91Bow-537
91ChaLooLD-167
91ChaLooP-1973
91Cla/Bes-41
91ClaGam-70
91ClaGolB-BC4
91LeaGolR-BC10
91LinDriAA-167
91LinDriP-167
91UppDec-71
91UppDecFE-1F
91UppDecFE-11F
92Bow-118
92Cla1-T81
92Cla2-T72
92Cla2-NNO
92ClaGam-141
92Don-415
92DonCraJ2-15
92Fle-421
92JimDeaRS-5
92Lea-360
92LeaGolP-33
92OPC-283
92OPCPre-25
92Pin-440
92PinRoo-22
92PinRooI-1
92PinTea2-70
92ProFS7-214
92RedKah-16
92Sco-829
92ScoImpP-76
92ScoRoo-35
92StaClu-865
92StaCluNC-865
92Stu-29
92Top-283
92TopDeb91-155
92TopGol-283
92TopGolW-283
92TopMic-283
92TriPla-109
92Ult-486
92UltAllR-8
92UppDec-27
92UppDecSR-SR20
93Bow-666
93ClaGam-82
93DiaMar-95
93Don-402
93Fin-20
93FinRef-20
93Fla-34
93Fle-44
93FleRooS-RSA7
93Lea-428
93OPC-358
93PacSpa-405
93PanSti-298
93Pin-158
93PinTea2-24
93RedKah-24
93Sco-171
93Sel-274
93SelChaR-3
93SP-216
93StaClu-471
93StaCluFDI-471
93StaCluMOP-471
93Top-83
93TopGol-83
93TopInaM-83
93TopMic-83
93Toy-27
93Ult-36
93UppDec-354
93UppDec-469
93UppDecGold-354
93UppDecGold-469
93USPlaCR-10C
94Bow-242
94ColC-252
94ColChoGS-252
94ColChoSS-252
94Don-436
94ExtBas-240
94Fin-43
94FinPre-43P
94FinRef-43
94Fla-149
94Fle-427
94FUnPac-116
94Lea-106
94LeaL-99
94OPC-207
94Pac-160
94PanSti-169
94Pin-360
94PinArtP-360
94PinMusC-360
94PinPowS-PS10
94ProMag-34
94RedFolMI-15
94RedKah-27
94Sco-394
94ScoGolR-394
94Sel-71
94SP-163
94SPDieC-163
94StaClu-136
94StaCluFDI-136
94StaCluGR-136
94StaCluMOP-136
94StaCluMOP-ST3
94StaCluST-ST3
94Stu-173
94Top-647
94TopGol-647
94TopSpa-647
94TriPla-219
94Ult-177
94UppDec-222
94UppDecED-222
95Bow-312
95ClaPhoC-16
95ColCho-431
95ColChoGS-431
95ColChoSE-202
95ColChoSEGS-202
95ColChoSESS-202
95ColChoSS-431
95Don-204
95DonPreP-204

95DonTopotO-219
95Emo-119
95Fin-127
95FinRef-127
95Fla-124
95Fle-447
95Lea-47
95LeaLim-160
95Pac-114
95Pin-76
95PinArtP-76
95PinMusC-76
95RedKah-27
95Sco-366
95ScoGolR-366
95ScoHaloG-HG69
95ScoPlaTS-366
95Sel-104
95SelArtP-104
95SelCer-2
95SelCerMG-2
95SelCerS-2
95SP-41
95SPCha-34
95SPChaDC-34
95Spo-112
95SpoArtP-112
95SPSil-41
95SPSpeF-33
95StaClu-333
95StaCluMOP-333
95StaCluSTDW-RE3T
95StaCluSTDW-RE333
95StaCluSTWS-333
95StaCluVR-173
95Stu-88
95Sum-110
95Top-411
95TopCyb-211
95Ult-370
95UltGolM-370
95UppDec-404
95UppDecED-404
95UppDecEDG-404
95UppDecSE-30
95UppDecSEG-30
95Zen-86
96Baz-4
96Bow-58
96BowBes-35
96BowBesAR-35
96BowBesR-35
96Cir-118
96CirBos-32
96CirRav-118
96ColCho-115
96ColChoGS-115
96ColChoSS-115
96Don-219
96DonDiaK-10
96DonEli-63
96DonPowA-3
96DonPowADC-3
96DonPreP-219
96EmoXL-168
96Fin-B196
96Fin-S86
96FinRef-B196
96FinRef-S86
96Fla-238
96Fle-351
96FleTif-351
96FleUpd-U240
96FleUpdTC-U240
96Lea-146
96LeaAllGMC-6
96LeaAllGMCG-6
96LeaLim-6
96LeaLimG-6
96LeaPre-4
96LeaPreP-4
96LeaPrePB-146
96LeaPrePG-146
96LeaPrePS-146
96LeaPreSG-73
96LeaPreSte-73
96LeaSig-25
96LeaSigPPG-25
96LeaSigPPP-25
96MetUni-151
96MetUniP-151
96Pac-44
96PacGolCD-DC21
96PacOctM-OM19
96PacPri-P17
96PacPriG-P17
96PanSti-52
96Pin-20
96Pin-143
96Pin-264
96PinAfi-96
96PinAfiAP-96
96PinAfiFPP-96
96PinAfiSP-17
96PinArtP-10
96PinArtP-70
96PinArtP-164
96PinEssotG-6
96PinFoil-264
96PinPow-6
96PinSlu-12
96PinSta-10
96PinSta-70
96PinSta-164
96PinTeaP-6
96ProSta-102
96Sco-311
96ScoAll-16
96ScoBigB-18
96ScoDiaA-18
96ScoDugC-B36
96ScoDugCAP-B36
96ScoGolS-3
96ScoNumG-18
96ScoRef-11
96Sel-24
96SelArtP-24
96SelCer-24
96SelCerAP-24
96SelCerCB-24
96SelCerCR-24
96SelCerIP-8
96SelCerMB-24
96SelCerMG-24
96SelCerMR-24
96SelClaTF-9
96SelEnF-10
96SelTeaN-25
96SP-65
96Spo-35
96Spo-107
96SpoArtP-35
96SpoArtP-107
96SpoPowS-11
96SpoPro-17
96StaClu-214
96StaClu-435
96StaCluB&B-BB3
96StaCluEPB-435
96StaCluEPG-435
96StaCluEPS-435
96StaCluMO-38
96StaCluMOP-214
96StaCluMOP-435
96StaCluMOP-BB3
95StaCluVRMC-173
96Stu-48
96StuPrePB-48
96StuPrePG-48
96StuPrePS-48
96Sum-4
96SumAbo&B-4
96SumArtP-4
96SumFoi-4
96Top-330
96TopChr-132
96TopChrR-132
96TopClaC-CC7
96TopGal-151
96TopGalE-17
96TopGalPPI-151
96TopLas-77
96TopPro-NL8
96TopRoaW-RW15
96Ult-182
96UltGolM-182
96UltPowP-9
96UltPowPGM-9
96UltRBIK-7
96UltRBIKGM-7
96UppDec-45
96UppDecPD-PD15
96UppDecPRE-R47
96UppDecPreR-R47
96Zen-63
96ZenArtP-63
96ZenMoz-10
97Bow-233
97BowBes-76
97BowBesAR-76
97BowBesR-76
97BowChr-60
97BowChrI-60
97BowChrIR-60
97BowChrR-60
97BowInt-233
97Cir-284
97CirRav-284
97ColCho-78
97ColCho-306
97Don-100
97DonLim-154
97DonLimLE-154
97DonPre-23
97DonPreCttC-23
97DonPreP-100
97DonPrePGold-100
97Fin-14
97FinRef-14
97FlaSho-A55
97FlaSho-B55
97FlaSho-C55
97FlaShoLC-55
97FlaShoLC-B55
97FlaShoLC-C55
97FlaShoLCM-A55
97FlaShoLCM-B55
97FlaShoLCM-C55
97Fle-303
97FleTif-303
97Lea-228
97LeaFraM-228
97LeaFraMDC-228
97MetUni-50
97NewPin-22
97NewPinAP-22
97NewPinMC-22
97NewPinPP-22
97Pac-276
97PacLigB-276
97PacPri-94
97PacPriLB-94
97PacPriP-94
97PacSil-276
97ProMag-10
97ProMagML-10
97Sco-19
97ScoPreS-19
97ScoShoS-19
97ScoShoSAP-19
97SkyE-X-66
97SkyE-XC-66
97SkyE-XEC-66
97SP-52
97SpoIll-98
97SpoIllEE-98
97StaClu-34
97StaCluMat-34
97StaCluMOP-34
97Stu-103
97StuPrePG-103
97StuPrePS-103
97Top-80
97TopChr-30
97TopChrR-30
97TopGal-108
97TopGalPPI-108
97Ult-180
97UltGolME-180
97UltPlaME-180
97UppDec-46
Sanders, Rod
92PriRedC-21
92PriRedF-3097
93PriRedC-27
93PriRedF-4197
94PriRedC-22
94PriRedF-3273
Sanders, Satch
81MiaOriT-9
Sanders, Scott
90SpoIndSP-14
91Cla/Bes-338
91WatDiaC-8
91WatDiaP-1255
92SkyAA F-286
92WicWraS-644
93Bow-110
93ClaFS7-253
93LasVegSF-943
93Ult-476
94ColC-528
94ColChoGS-528
94ColChoSS-528
94Don-489
94ExtBas-378
94Fla-441
94FleMajLP-31
94FleUpd-190
94Lea-37
94PadMot-17
94Pin-381
94PinArtP-381
94PinMusC-381
94ScoRoo-RT122
94ScoRooGR-RT122
94Top-789
94TopGol-789
94TopSpa-789
94Ult-282
94UppDec-362
94UppDecED-362
95ColCho-359
95ColChoGS-359
95ColChoSS-359
95Don-528
95DonPreP-528
95Emo-190
95Fle-568
95Lea-203
95PadCHP-6
95PadMot-22
95Sco-508
95ScoGolR-508
95ScoPlaTS-508
95StaClu-260
95StaCluFDI-260
95StaCluMOP-260
95StaCluSTWS-260
95StaCluVR-128
95Top-33
95TopCyb-25
95Ult-237
95UltGolM-237
96ColCho-703
96ColChoGS-703
96ColChoSS-703
96Don-6
96DonPreP-6
96Fle-578
96FleTif-578
96LeaSigA-202
96LeaSigAG-202
96LeaSigAS-202
96PadMot-6
95StaCluVRMC-128
96Top-58
97Cir-47
97CirRav-47
97ColCho-459
97DonTea-149
97DonTeaSPE-149
97Fle-469
97Fle-595
97FleTif-469
97FleTif-595
97MetUni-224
97NewPin-48
97NewPinAP-48
97NewPinMC-48
97NewPinPP-48
97PacPriGotD-GD209
97Top-362
97Ult-400
97UltGolME-400
97UltPlaME-400
Sanders, Stan
82OneYanT-7
Sanders, Tracy
90BurIndP-3023
90ProAaA-188
91CarLeaAP-CAR19
91Cla/Bes-202
91KinIndC-27
91KinIndP-339
92Bow-42
92CanIndF-703
92CanIndS-116
92ClaFS7-40
92ProFS7-53
92SkyAA F-54
92UppDecML-127
93Bow-9
93CanIndF-2851
93ClaFS7-20
93ExcFS7-167
93Top-616
93TopGol-616
93TopInaM-616
93TopMic-616
93WicWraF-2992
94BinMetF-719
95NorTidTI-26
96MidAngB-26
96TulDriTI-23
Sanderski, John
86WinHavRSP-20
87GreHorP-24
Sanderson, David
94KinMetC-18
94KinMetF-3838
Sanderson, Scott
79ExpPos-22
79Top-720
80ExpPos-26
80OPC-301
80Top-578
81AllGamPI-175
81Don-450
81ExpPos-14
81Fle-166
81OPC-235
81OPCPos-12
81Top-235
82Don-288
82ExpHygM-19
82ExpPos-35
82ExpZel-17
82Fle-206
82FleSta-40
82OPC-7
82OPCPos-22
82Top-7
82TopSti-63
83Don-446
83ExpPos-21
83ExpStu-17
83Fle-295
83FleSti-259
83OPC-54
83Top-717
84CubChiT-26
84CubSev-24
84Don-341
84Fle-285
84FleUpd-104
84Nes792-164
84OPC-164
84Top-164
84TopTif-164
84TopTra-106T
84TopTraT-106T
85CubLioP-20
85CubSev-21
85Don-266
85Fle-66
85Lea-194
85OPC-373
85Top-616
85TopSti-40
85TopTif-616
86BasStaB-97
86CubGat-21
86CubUno-16
86Don-442
86Fle-379
86Top-406
86TopTif-406
87CubCan-27
87CubDavB-21
87Don-447
87Fle-573
87FleGlo-573
87SpoTeaP-22
87Top-534
87TopSti-60
87TopTif-534
88AlaGolAA'TI-21
88CubDavB-21
88Don-646
88DonTeaBC-646
88Fle-432
88FleGlo-432
88Sco-544
88ScoGlo-544
88StaLinCu-10
88Top-311
88TopTif-311
89CubMar-21
89Don-629

89FleUpd-78
89Top-212
89TopTif-212
89UppDec-342
90A'sMot-11
90Bow-447
90BowTif-447
90Don-647
90Fle-41
90FleCan-41
90FleUpd-118
90Lea-194
90OPC-67
90PubSti-202
90Sco-488
90ScoRoo-61T
90Top-67
90TopTif-67
90TopTra-110T
90TopTraT-110T
90UppDec-39
90UppDec-739
91Bow-177
91Don-533
91Fle-23
91Lea-169
91OPC-728
91OPCPre-104
91Sco-118
91ScoPro-118
91ScoRoo-78T
91Stu-99
91Top-728
91TopDesS-728
91TopMic-728
91TopTif-728
91TopTra-104T
91TopTraT-104T
91UltUpd-43
91UppDec-582
91UppDec-750
91USPlaCA-3D
92Don-227
92DonDiaK-DK10
92Fle-243
92Lea-152
92OPC-480
92PanSti-142
92Pin-337
92Pin-587
92Sco-211
92Sco100S-59
92StaClu-496
92StaCluD-163
92Stu-219
92Top-480
92TopGol-480
92TopGolW-480
92TopMic-480
92TriPla-39
92TriPla-77
92Ult-414
92UppDec-415
92UppDecTMH-47
92YanWIZA-74
93AngMot-9
93AngPol-9
93Don-726
93Fla-178
93Fle-655
93FleFinE-188
93Lea-419
93OPCPre-100
93PacSpa-211
93PanSti-145
93Pin-574
93Sco-618
93Sel-261
93StaClu-679
93StaCluAn-7
93StaCluFDI-679
93StaCluMOP-679
93Stu-15
93Top-525
93TopGol-525
93TopInaM-525
93TopMic-525
93Ult-524
93UppDec-734
93UppDecGold-734
94Don-266
94Fle-700
94FleUpd-30
94Lea-406
94Sco-401
94ScoGolR-401
94ScoRoo-RT54
94ScoRooGR-RT54
94StaClu-551
94StaCluFDI-551
94StaCluGR-551
94StaCluMOP-551
94WhiSoxK-26
95AngMot-24
95ColCho-498
95ColChoGS-498
95ColChoSS-498
95Don-521
95DonPreP-521
95Sco-53
95ScoGolR-53
95ScoPlaTS-53
96AngMot-24
96ColCho-488
96ColChoGS-488
96ColChoSS-488

Sanderson, Shaun
89SalLakTTI-17
90EriSaiS-23

Sandillo, Bill
96HarCitRCB-5

Sandling, Bob
80ElmPioRST-14

Sandlock, Mike
49W72HolS-19
50W720HolS-26
53Top-247
54Top-104
79DiaGre-217
90DodTar-703
91TopArc1-247
94TopArc1-104
94TopArc1G-104

Sandoval, Dennis
77WauMetT-16

Sandoval, Guillermo
89BelBreIS-24
90StoPorB-22
90StoPorCLC-183
90StoPorP-2183
91StoPorC-10

Sandoval, Jesus
86AppFoxP-20

Sandoval, Jhensy
97Top-468

Sandoval, Jose
76VenLeaS-42
93Bow-78
93BufBisF-527

Sandoval, Mike
87WatPirP-31
90HarSenS-25
92BufBisBS-20
96AugGreB-3

Sandry, Bill
83AppFoxF-28

Sands, Charlie
71PirActP-23
72Top-538
74OPC-381
74Top-381
75OPC-548
75Top-548
75TucTorTI-17
76TucTorCa-20
76TusTorCr-39
92YanWIZ6-108

Sandt, Tommy
75TucTorC-2
75TucTorTI-18
76VenLeaS-21
77Top-616
78SyrChiT-17
79PorBeaT-6
80PorBeaT-8
81PorBeaT-21
82BufBisT-18
83LynPirT-23
84HawIslC-137
85HawIslC-233
86HawIslP-6
89PirVerFJ-31
90PirHomC-26
93PirNatl-27
94PirQui-21

Sandy, Tim
90KinMetB-17
90KinMetS-22
91PitMetC-8
91PitMetP-3436
92St.LucMCB-3
92St.LucMF-1762
93BinMetF-2348
93StLucMF-2935

Saneaux, Francisco
92BluOriC-7
92BluOriF-2360
94AlbPolC-22
94AlbPolF-2236
94OriPro-89

Sanford, Chance
92WelPirC-20
92WelPirF-1333
93SalBucC-22
93SalBucF-442
94CarLeaAF-CAR43
94SalBucC-18
94SalBucF-2331
96CarMudB-21

Sanford, Ed
82ArkTraT-8

Sanford, Jack (John S.)
47PM1StaP1-193
57Top-387
58Hir-39
58PhiJayP-10
58Top-264
59Top-275
60GiaJayP-11
60Lea-54
60Top-165
60TopVen-165
61Pos-154
61Top-258
61Top-383
61TopStaI-84
62Jel-141
62Pos-141
62PosCan-141
62Top-538
63GiaJayP-12
63Jel-110
63Pos-110
63Top-7
63Top-143
63Top-325
63TopStil-39
64GiaJayP-11
64Top-414
65OPC-228
65Top-228
66OPC-23
66Top-23
66TopVen-23
67CokCapDA-27
67Top-549
79TCM50-125

Sanford, John F.
47TipTop-71
49Bow-236
50Bow-156
51BerRos-D3
51Bow-145
52MotCoo-53

Sanford, Mo (Meredith)
89GreHorP-423
89SouAtlLAGS-31
90CedRapRB-23
90CedRapRP-2321
90MidLeaASGS-49
90ProAaA-120
91ChaLooLD-168
91ChaLooP-1960
91Cla/Bes-47
91FleUpd-86
91LinDriAA-168
92Bow-281
92Cla1-T82
92ClaGam-197
92Don-417
92NasSouS-290
92OPC-674
92OPCPre-17
92Pin-254
92PinTea2-77
92ProFS7-215
92Sco-769
92ScoRoo-40
92SkyAAAF-136
92StaClu-336
92Top-674
92TopDeb91-156
92TopGol-674
92TopGolW-674
92TopMic-674
92UppDec-45
92UppDecML-253
93ColSprSSF-3086
93Don-760
93Pin-230
93SelRoo-33T
93Top-634
93TopGol-634
93TopInaM-634
93TopMic-634
94Fle-453
94SalLakBF-815
94Sco-253
94ScoGolR-253
94Top-343
94TopGol-343
94TopSpa-343
96OklCit8B-17

Sangeado, Juan
95GreFalDTI-8

Sanguillen, Manny
68PirKDK-35
68PirTeal-17
68Top-251
68TopVen-251
69PirJacitB-11
69Top-509
70DayDaiNM-148
70MLBOffS-106
70OPC-188
70PirTeal-7
70Top-188
71Kel-13
71MilDud-61
71MLBOffS-213
71OPC-62
71OPC-480
71PirActP-10
71PirArc-10
71Top-62
71Top-480
71TopTat-41
72EssCoi-12
72Kel-19
72MilBra-305
72OPC-60
72OPC-225
72OPC-228
72Top-60
72Top-225
72Top-228
73Kel2D-42
73LinPor-152
73OPC-250
73Top-250
73TopCanL-46
74Kel-15
74OPC-28
74Top-28
74TopDecE-22
74TopSta-87
75Hos-21
75HosTwi-21
75OPC-515
75Top-515
76CraDis-53
76Hos-72
76Kel-42
76OPC-191
76OPC-220
76SSP-571
76Top-191
76Top-220
77BurCheD-111
77MSADis-54
77OPC-231
77PepGloD-4
77Top-61
78Hos-58
78Top-658
78WifBalD-66
79Top-447
80Top-148
81Don-14
81Fle-376
81Top-226
86PirGreT-8
89SweBasG-29
90PacLeg-75
90SweBasG-126
91KelLey-10
91SweBasG-80
93MCIAmb-9
93TedWil-80
93TedWilM-13
93UppDecAH-112
94MCIAmb-9
94MCIAmb-S4
94UppDecAH-29
94UppDecAH-224
94UppDecAH1-29
94UppDecAH1-224

Sanjurjo, Jose
91BriTigC-11
91BriTigP-3620
93BriTigC-18
93BriTigF-3665

Sankey, Ben
36GouWidPPR-D31
36WorWidGV-83

Sankey, Brian
96YakBeaTI-17

Sanner, Dale
75TucTorC-7
75TucTorTI-19
76TusTorCr-14

Sano, Motokuni
88MiaMarS-23

Santa, Roberto
94HudValRF-3394
95ChaRivTI-22
94HudValRC-22

SantaCruz, Nick
88BatCliP-1678
89SpaPhiP-1043
89SpaPhiS-21
90SpaPhiB-18
90SpaPhiP-2501
90SpaPhiS-18

Santaella, Alexis
90TamYanD-20
94GreBatF-473
94VenLinU-195
95LinVen-127
97GreBatC-19

SantaMaria, Silverio
90ElmPioP-21
91WinHavRSC-9
91WinHavRSP-489
92WinHavRSC-13
93ForLauRSC-23
93ForLauRSFP-1598
94SarRedSF-1949

Santamaria, William
96BesAutSA-66

Santana, Andres
87PocGiaTB-23
88CliGiaP-705
88MidLeaAGS-2
89SanJosGB-1
89SanJosGCLC-226
89SanJosGP-450
89SanJosGS-23
89Sta-87
90Bow-230
90BowTif-230
90ShrCapP-1449
90ShrCapS-22
90TexLeaAGS-23
91LinDriAAA-393
91PhoFirLD-393
91PhoFirP-76
91Sco-762
91TopDeb90-139
91TriA AAGP-AAA34
91Ult-328
91UppDec-87
92PhoFirF-2831
92Sco100RS-32
92StaClu-491

Santana, Ernesto
87MacPirP-1
88WatPirP-10
89St.CatBJP-2087
90UtiBluSP-22

Santana, Jose
89AubAstP-2165
90AshTouP-2763
90BoiHawP-3318
92AubAstC-11
92AubAstF-1363
93AshTouC-19
93AshTouF-2285
94OscAstC-20
94OscAstF-1147

95QuaCitRBTI-25
Santana, Julio
94ChaRivC-18
94ChaRivF-2672
94Cla-6
94SouAtlLAF-SAL5
95Bes-45
95BowBes-B26
95BowBesR-B26
95Exc-132
95SPML-160
95TulDriTI-2
95UppDecML-211
95UppDecMLOP-OP27
96Bow-130
96BowBes-144
96BowBesAR-144
96BowBesR-144
96OklCit8B-18
97ColCho-488
97Fle-691
97FleTif-691
97Sco-490
97ScoHobR-490
97ScoResC-490
97ScoShoS-490
97ScoShoSAP-490
95UppDecMLFS-211
Santana, Manuel
93AugPirC-18
93AugPirF-1543
94SalBucC-19
94SalBucF-2322
Santana, Marino
93BelMarC-23
93BelMarF-3206
94BelMarC-24
94BelMarF-3232
95Bes-44
95Exc-121
95MidLeaA-51
96Bow-198
96Exc-107
96LanJetB-23
Santana, Miguel
88FloStaLAS-20
88VerBeaDS-23
90JacExpB-12
90JacExpP-1387
93LimRocDWB-59
Santana, Rafael
80NasSouTI-18
82LouRedE-27
83Car-26
84TidTidT-16
85DomLeaS-148
85Don-610
85Fle-90
85MetTCM-29
85Top-67
85TopTif-67
86Don-319
86Fle-93
86MetTCM-22
86MetWorSC-7
86OPC-102
86Top-587
86TopSti-102
86TopTif-587
87Don-569
87DonOpeD-126
87Fle-21
87FleGlo-21
87Lea-167
87Top-378
87TopTif-378
88Don-633
88DonBasB-273
88DonReaBY-NEW
88Fle-149
88FleGlo-149
88FleUpd-50
88FleUpdG-50
88PanSti-344
88Sco-316
88ScoGlo-316
88ScoRoo-54T
88ScoRooG-54T
88StaLinMe-17
88Top-233
88TopBig-246
88TopTif-233
88TopTra-101T
88TopTraT-101T
89Bow-174
89BowTif-174
89Don-309
89Fle-268
89FleGlo-268
89PanSti-407
89Sco-296
89Top-792
89TopBig-192
89TopDouM-21
89TopSti-313
89TopTif-792
89UppDec-216
89YanScoNW-11
90OPC-651
90PubSti-546
90Top-651
90TopTif-651
91MetWIZ-344
92BasCitRC-25
92BasCitRF-3861
92YanWIZ8-171
93WilBluRC-29
93WilBluRF-2015
94EugEmeC-30
95SprSulTI-25
Santana, Ralph
80KnoBluJT-11
Santana, Raul
91SumFlyC-15
91SumFlyP-2338
92RocExpC-3
92RocExpF-2120
93WesPalBEC-20
93WesPalBEF-1345
94HigDesMC-22
94HigDesMF-2793
Santana, Rodolfo
80ElmPioRST-43
Santana, Ruben
85MetColP-2
87MetColP-20
90PenPilS-20
91SanBerSC-20
91SanBerSP-1997
92ClaFS7-215
92PenPilC-14
92PenPilF-2943
93ClaFS7-254
93ExcFS7-231
93JacSunF-2719
93LimRocDWB-23
93LimRocDWB-148
94ClaGolF-102
94ColC-667
94ColChoGS-667
94ColChoSS-667
94ExcFS7-127
94JacSunF-1422
94Top-527
94TopGol-527
94TopSpa-527
94UppDec-88
94UppDecED-88
94UppDecML-95
94UppDecML-173
94UppDecMLPotYF-PY13
95ChaLooTI-20
96ChaLooB-27
Santana, Simon
77ChaPatT-19
Santangelo, F.P.
88CapCodPPaLP-156
89JamExpP-2132
90WesPalBES-19
91HarSenLD-268
91HarSenP-636
91LinDriAA-268
92IndIndF-1869
92IndIndS-192
93OttLynF-2447
94OttLynF-2906
96Fle-467
96FleTif-467
96Pac-124
96Pin-388
96PinFoil-388
96Sco-256
97Cir-31
97CirRav-31
97ColCho-389
97Don-225
97DonLim-97
97DonLimLE-97
97DonPreP-225
97DonPrePGold-225
97Fle-386
97FleTif-386
97Lea-317
97LeaFraM-317
97LeaFraMDC-317
97Pac-352
97PacLigB-352
97PacPri-121
97PacPriLB-121
97PacPriP-121
97PacSil-352
97Pin-157
97PinArtP-157
97PinCer-70
97PinCerMBlu-70
97PinCerMG-70
97PinCerMR-70
97PinCerR-70
97PinMusC-157
97PinTotCPB-70
97PinTotCPG-70
97PinTotCPR-70
97Sco-276
97ScoPreS-276
97ScoShoS-276
97ScoShoSAP-276
97SelRooR-7
97StaClu-290
97StaCluMOP-290
97Top-17
97UppDec-429
Santarelli, Cal
85WatIndT-9
86WatIndP-21
Santiago, Angelo
90GatCitPP-3354
90GatCitPSP-16
Santiago, Arnold
94BurIndC-22
94BurIndF-3805
Santiago, Benny (Benito)
83MiaMarT-20
84OCoandSI-238
85BeaGolGT-21
86Fle-644
86LasVegSP-15
87ClaUpdY-132
87Don-31
87DonHig-45
87DonHig-55
87DonOpeD-148
87DonRoo-44
87Fle-429
87FleGlo-429
87Lea-31
87PadBohHB-9
87PadFirPTB-4
87Spo-118
87SpoRooI-19
87SpoRooP-9
87SpoTeaP-16
87TopTra-109T
87TopTraT-109T
88Baz-20
88ClaBlu-219
88ClaRed-160
88Don-3
88Don-114
88DonBasB-301
88DonSupD-3
88Fle-596
88FleAwaW-34
88FleBasM-30
88FleExcS-33
88FleGlo-596
88FleHotS-33
88FleLeaL-34
88FleMin-115
88FleRecS-34
88FleStiC-125
88FleSup-32
88GreBasS-59
88K-M-24
88Lea-3
88Lea-58
88MSAIceTD-15
88Nes-12
88OPC-86
88PadCok-9
88PadSmo-25
88PanSti-402
88PanSti-405
88PanSti-433
88RedFolSB-78
88Sco-25
88Sco-654
88ScoGlo-25
88ScoGlo-654
88ScoYouSI-2
88Spo-22
88Spo-222
88SpoGam-10
88StaLinPa-11
88Top-7
88Top-404
88Top-693
88Top-699
88TopBig-12
88TopCoi-35
88TopGaloC-12
88TopGloS-30
88TopRoo-18
88TopSti-2
88TopSti-112
88TopTif-7
88TopTif-404
88TopTif-693
88TopTif-699
88TopUKM-66
88TopUKMT-66
88ToyRoo-26
88Woo-14
89BimBreD-3
89Bow-453
89BowTif-453
89CadEllD-49
89ClaLigB-73
89Don-205
89Fle-316
89FleGlo-316
89MSAIceTD-9
89OPC-256
89PadCok-16
89PadMag-11
89PanSti-199
89RedFolSB-102
89Sco-4
89ScoHot1S-47
89Spo-22
89StaSan-1
89StaSan-2
89StaSan-3
89StaSan-4
89StaSan-5
89StaSan-6
89StaSan-7
89StaSan-8
89StaSan-9
89StaSan-10
89StaSan-11
89Top-256
89TopBasT-148
89TopBig-134
89TopCoi-24
89TopGloS-15
89TopSti-101
89TopStiB-57
89TopTif-256
89TopUKM-68
89TVSpoM-46
89TVSpoM-138
89UppDec-165
90Bow-218
90BowTif-218
90ClaUpd-T44
90Don-465
90Don-708A
90Don-708B
90DonBesN-121
90DonLeaS-4
90Fle-167
90FleAwaW-32
90FleCan-167
90GooHumICBLS-20
90HOFStiB-92
90Lea-207
90MLBBasB-58
90OPC-35
90PadCok-16
90PadMag-2
90PadMag-21
90PanSti-213
90PanSti-358
90PubSti-58
90PubSti-271
90RedFolSB-82
90Sco-454
90Sco100S-63
90ScoMcD-15
90Spo-115
90SupActM-15
90Top-35
90TopBig-125
90TopDou-56
90TopGloA-9
90TopSti-110
90TopSti-153
90TopStiB-23
90TopTif-35
90UppDec-12
90UppDec-325
90USPlaCA-10H
91Bow-383
91Bow-656
91CadEllD-49
91Cla2-T43
91ClaGam-175
91DenHol-18
91Don-449
91Fle-542
91FleAll-9
91KinDis-20
91Lea-432
91OPC-760
91OPCPre-105
91PadMag-26
91PadSmo-33
91PanCanT1-99
91PanFreS-90
91PanFreS-157
91PanSti-93
91PosCan-13
91RedFolS-83
91Sco-416
91Sco-663
91Sco-810
91Sco-870
91Sco-893
91Sco100S-61
91SevCoi-SC13
91StaClu-105
91StaPinB-43
91Stu-249
91Top-760
91TopCraJI-33
91TopDesS-760
91TopMic-760
91TopTif-760
91TopTriH-N10
91Ult-311
91UppDec-467
91UppDecFE-91F
91UppDecSS-SS17
91USPlaCA-11S
92Bow-395
92ClaGam-62
92ColAllG-14
92ColAllP-14
92Don-40
92Don-430
92Fle-620
92Fre-10
92Hig5-125
92Lea-321
92New-25
92OPC-185
92OPCPre-154
92PadCarJ-18
92PadMot-6
92PadPolD-18
92PadSmo-28
92PanSti-231
92PanSti-280
92Pin-2
92Pin-601
92Pin-615
92PinTeaP-3
92PosCan-2
92Sco-245
92Sco100S-36
92ScoCokD-19
92ScoImpP-58
92ScoProaG-10
92StaClu-130
92StaCluD-164
92StaPro-8
92Stu-107
92Top-185
92TopGol-185
92TopGolW-185

92TopKid-54
92TopMcD-2
92TopMic-185
92TriPla-70
92Ult-283
92UppDec-253
92UppDecF-40
92UppDecFG-40
93Bow-178
93CadDis-52
93DenHol-14
93DiaMar-96
93Don-522
93DurPowP2-10
93Fin-138
93FinRef-138
93Fla-53
93Fle-523
93FleFinE-70
93FunPac-117
93FunPac-121
93Hos-21
93HumDumC-31
93JimDea-21
93KinDis-6
93Lea-410
93MarFloA-4
93MarPub-22
93MarUSPC-1H
93MarUSPC-2S
93OPC-353
93OPCPre-43
93PacBeiA-23
93PacSpa-263
93PacSpa-471
93PacSpaGE-10
93PacSpaPI-6
93Pin-502
93PinExpOD-2
93Sco-591
93Sel-269
93SelRoo-26T
93SP-142
93StaClu-274
93StaClu-319
93StaCluFDI-274
93StaCluFDI-319
93StaCluM-5
93StaCluMarI-12
93StaCluMOP-274
93StaCluMOP-319
93Stu-127
93Top-220
93TopGol-220
93TopInaM-220
93TopMic-220
93TopPos-2
93TopPos-3
93TopTra-44T
93TriPla-210
93TriPlaG-GS9
93Ult-386
93UppDec-776
93UppDecDG-14
93UppDecGold-776
94Bow-122
94ColC-374
94ColChoGS-374
94ColChoSS-374
94Don-348
94DonSpeE-348
94ExtBas-265
94Fin-366
94FinRef-366
94Fla-384
94Fle-476
94Lea-96
94LeaL-108
94OPC-150
94Pac-249
94PacAll-1
94PanSti-185
94Pin-305
94PinArtP-305
94PinMusC-305
94ProMag-53
94Sco-40
94ScoGolR-40
94Sel-354
94Spo-13
94StaClu-143
94StaCluFDI-143
94StaCluGR-143
94StaCluMOP-143
94StaCluT-79
94StaCluTFDI-79
94Stu-111
94SucSav-6
94Top-370
94TopGol-370
94TopSpa-370
94TriPla-139
94Ult-497
94UppDec-397
94UppDecED-397
95ColCho-306
95ColCho-577T
95ColChoGS-306
95ColChoSE-136
95ColChoSEGS-136
95ColChoSESS-136
95ColChoSS-306
95Don-484
95DonPreP-484
95Fla-341
95Fle-341
95FleUpd-135
95Lea-257
95Pac-177
95PanSti-25
95Pin-400
95PinArtP-400
95PinMusC-400
95RedFol-19
95RedKah-28
95Sco-158
95ScoGolR-158
95ScoPlaTS-158
95StaClu-23
95StaClu-566
95StaCluFDI-23
95StaCluMOP-23
95StaCluMOP-566
95StaCluSTDW-RE566
95StaCluSTWS-23
95StaCluSTWS-566
95Top-160
95TopCyb-95
95TopTra-34T
95Ult-383
95UltGolM-383
95UppDec-486T
95UppDec-TC3
95UppDecSE-167
95UppDecSEG-167
96ColCho-116
96ColCho-669
96ColChoGS-116
96ColChoGS-669
96ColChoSS-116
96ColChoSS-669
96Don-493
96DonPreP-493
96EmoXL-248
96Fin-S277
96FinRef-S277
96Fla-337
96Fle-352
96FleTif-352
96FleUpd-U170
96FleUpdTC-U170
96Pac-49
96PacPri-P18
96PacPriG-P18
96PhiTeaI-29
96Pin-327
96PinFoil-327
96ProSta-103
96Sco-126
96SP-143
96StaClu-56
96StaCluEPB-56
96StaCluEPG-56
96StaCluEPS-56
96StaCluMOP-56
96TeaOut-71
96Top-394
96Ult-523
96UltGolM-523
96UppDec-432
97BluJayS-5
97Cir-235
97CirRav-235
97Don-71
97Don-280
97DonPreP-71
97DonPreP-280
97DonPrePGold-71
97DonPrePGold-280
97Fin-247
97FinRef-247
97FlaSho-A62
97FlaSho-B62
97FlaSho-C62
97FlaShoLC-62
97FlaShoLC-B62
97FlaShoLC-C62
97FlaShoLCM-A62
97FlaShoLCM-B62
97FlaShoLCM-C62
97Fle-420
97Fle-687
97FleTif-420
97FleTif-687
97Lea-296
97LeaFraM-296
97LeaFraMDC-296
97MetUni-206
97Pac-384
97PacLigB-384
97PacPri-131
97PacPriLB-131
97PacPriP-131
97PacSil-384
97Sco-455
97ScoHobR-455
97ScoResC-455
97ScoShoS-455
97ScoShoSAP-455
97StaClu-178
97StaCluMOP-178
97Top-82
97TopSta-88
97TopStaAM-88
97Ult-306
97UltGolME-306
97UltPlaME-306

Santiago, Cedric
90ElmPioP-22

Santiago, Delvy
89BlaYNPRWLU-32
89PriPirS-19
90AugPirP-2462
91CollndC-16
91CollndP-1483

Santiago, Gus
91SumFlyC-20
91SumFlyP-2345

Santiago, Jorge
91BurIndP-3310

Santiago, Jose
95SpoIndTI-26
96LanLugB-25

Santiago, Jose G.
56Top-59

Santiago, Jose R.
65Top-557
66Top-203
66TopVen-203
67CokCapRS-4
67DexPre-183
67Top-473
67TopRedSS-15
67TopVen-240
68AtlOilPBCC-40
68CokCapRS-10
68OPC-123
68Top-123
68TopVen-123
69MilBra-246
69MLBOffS-16
69OPC-21
69Top-21
69TopSta-137
69TopTeaP-3
70Top-708
81RedSoxBG2S-107

Santiago, Mike
85DurBulT-11
86JacMetT-9
87JacMetF-25
88JacMetGS-9

Santiago, Norm
86Ft.LauYP-19
87JacExpP-431
88WesPalBES-23

Santiago, Rafael
90ChaRaiB-20
90ChaRaiP-2031

Santiago, Sandi
90TamYanD-21
91OneYanP-4153
92OneYanC-13
93GreHorC-20
93GreHorF-885
94SanBerSC-20
94SanBerSF-2758
95TamYanYI-24

Santini, Aaron
94ForWayWC-21
94ForWayWF-2018

Santo, Jose
96ChaRivTI-9627

Santo, Ron
47Exh-199
61Baz-3
61CubJayP-10
61Pos-196A
61Pos-196B
61Top-35
61WilSpoGH828-1-6
62Baz-34
62CubJayP-9
62Jel-184
62Pos-184
62PosCan-184
62SalPlaC-136
62ShiPlaC-136
62Top-170
62TopStaI-109
62TopVen-170
63BasMagM-74
63CubJayP-11
63ExhStaB-58
63Fle-32
63Jel-170
63Pos-170
63Top-113
63Top-252
64ChatheY-45
64CubJayP-11
64Top-375
64TopCoi-68
64TopCoi-146
64TopGia-58
64TopSta-33
64TopStaU-67
64WheSta-40
65Baz-28
65ChaTheY-46
65CubJayP-10
65OPC-6
65OPC-110
65Top-6
65Top-110
65TopEmbI-28
65TopTraI-67
66Baz-39
66CubTeaI-11
66Top-290
66TopRubI-85
66TopVen-290
67AshOil-9
67Baz-39
67CokCapA-6
67CokCapC-11
67CokCapNLA-23
67CubProPS-11
67DexPre-184
67DexPre-185
67OPC-70
67OPCPapI-26
67ProPizC-13
67Top-70
67TopGiaSU-22
67TopPos-26
67TopTesF-21
67TopVen-309
68AtlOilPBCC-41
68Baz-6
68Baz-15
68Kah-B31
68OPC-5
68Top-5
68Top-235
68Top-366
68TopActS-4B
68TopActS-5A
68TopActS-16B
68TopGamI-19
68TopPla-22
68TopPos-21
68TopVen-5
68TopVen-235
68TopVen-366
69CitMetC-13
69CubJewT-15
69CubPho-10
69CubTeaIC-8
69Kah-B18
69KelPin-16
69MilBra-247
69MLBOffS-125
69MLBPin-56
69NabTeaF-21
69OPC-4
69OPCDec-19
69Top-4
69Top-420
69Top-570
69TopDec-19
69TopDecI-37
69TopSta-19
69TopSup-38
69TopTeaP-4
69TraSta-42
70CubDunD-5
70DayDaiNM-121
70Kel-42
70MilBra-25
70MLBOffS-22
70OPC-63
70OPC-454
70SunPin-8
70Top-63
70Top-454
70Top-670
70TopPos-5
70TopSup-21
70TraSta-2A
71MilDud-62
71MLBOffS-46
71OPC-220
71Top-220
71TopCoi-95
71TopSup-35
71TopTat-108
72CubChi-7
72CubTeaI-11
72MilBra-306
72Top-555
72Top-556
73Kel2D-54
73LinPor-44
73OPC-115
73Top-115
74Kel-7A
74Kel-7B
74OPC-270
74OPC-334
74Top-270
74Top-334
74TopSta-19
74TopTra-270T
75OPC-35
75Top-35
78TCM60I-22
80CubGreT-3
83MLBPin-32
84CubUno-2
84CubUno-7
84OCoandSI-232
88PacLegI-97
89SweBasG-36
90BasWit-14
90PacLeg-48
90SweBasG-64
91LinDri-5
91MDAA-5
91SweBasG-81
91UppDecS-21
92ActPacA-39
92CubOldS-21
92UppDecS-28
93TedWil-23
93UppDecAH-113
94UppDecAH-201
94UppDecAH1-201

SantoDomingo, Rafael
78IndIndTI-17
79NaSouTI-20
80IndIndTI-22

Santop, Louis
74LauOldTBS-16
90NegLeaS-33

Santora, Steve
85EveGiaC-15
85EveGiaIC-16

Santorini, Al
69PadVol-7

69Top-592
70OPC-212
70Top-212
71CarTeal-31
71MLBOffS-237
71OPC-467
71Top-467
72Top-723
73OPC-24
73Top-24
Santoro, Gary
95ElmPioTI-25
95ElmPioUTI-25
96KanCouCTI-25
Santos, Don
86WatIndP-24
87WatIndP-20
Santos, Ed
77LodDodT-17
Santos, Eddie
83KinBluJTI-22
Santos, Faustoe
85MadMusP-22
85MadMusT-2
Santos, Henry
92BriTigC-10
92BriTigF-1411
93NiaFalRF-3390
94FayGenC-22
94FayGenF-2145
96El PasDB-25
Santos, Jerry (Gerald)
91JohCitCC-21
91JohCitCP-3977
92MidLeaATI-38
92ProFS7-329
92SprCarC-24
92SprCarF-865
93ArkTraF-2812
93ExcFS7-105
94ArkTraF-3089
94Bow-452
Santos, Juan
93EugEmeC-23
93EugEmeF-3856
Santos, Leigh
94ButCopKSP-10
Santos, Luis
80WisRapTT-2
Santos, Matthew
95ModA'sTI-27
Santovenia, Nelson
83MemChiT-8
86JacExpT-8
87JacExpP-433
87SouLeaAJ-5
88ExpPos-21
88FleUpd-103
88FleUpdG-103
88IndIndC-18
88IndIndP-500
88ScoRoo-96T
88ScoRooG-96T
88TopTra-102T
88TopTraT-102T
89Bow-361
89BowTif-361
89Don-366
89DonBasB-146
89ExpPos-26
89Fle-393
89FleGlo-393
89OPC-228
89PanSti-112
89Sco-346
89ScoHot1R-71
89Top-228
89TopBig-98
89TopRoo-18
89TopSti-78
89TopTif-228
89ToyRoo-25
89UppDec-380
90Don-224
90ExpPos-32
90Fle-360
90FleCan-360
90Lea-502
90OPC-614
90PanSti-289
90PubSti-187
90Sco-451
90Spo-162
90Top-614
90TopTif-614
90UppDec-432
91ExpPos-21
91Fle-248
91OPC-744
91Sco-777
91StaClu-416
91Top-744
91TopDesS-744
91TopMic-744
91TopTif-744
92OPC-732
92Top-732
92TopGol-732
92TopGolW-732
92TopMic-732
92VanCanF-2726
92VanCanS-646
93OmaRoyF-1682
94OmaRoyF-1227
Santoya, Cristobal
91IdaFalBSP-18
Santucci, Steve
93GleFalRC-25
93GleFalRF-4020
94MadHatC-21
94MadHatF-148
94NewJerCC-23
94NewJerCF-3432
96StPetCB-28
Sapienza, Rich
87TamTarP-29
88CedRapRP-1148
Sapp, Damian
96MicBatCB-24
97Bow-195
97BowInt-195
Sarandon, Susan
88BulDurM-4
Sarazen, Gene
32USCar-9
41WheM5-19
Sarbaugh, Mike
90CalLeaACLC-46
91KinIndC-20
91KinIndP-332
92CanIndF-699
92CanIndS-117
94CanIndF-3128
95KinIndTI-24
Sarcia, Joe
91GenCubC-18
91GenCubP-4228
Sardinha, Ed
86ElmPioRSP-19
96DelShoB-3
Sarmiento, Danny
92GulCoaDF-3565
93GreFalDSP-17
Sarmiento, Manny
76IndIndTI-16
76VenLeaS-174
77IndIndTI-25
77Top-475
78Pep-22
78SSP270-122
78Top-377
79IndIndTI-21
79OPC-69
79Top-149
80SpoIndT-12
80Top-21
80VenLeaS-151
81PawRedST-10
81Top-649
82PorBeaT-8
83Don-502
83Fle-321
83FleSta-171
83FleSti-75
83Top-566
84Don-200
84Fle-263
84Nes792-209
84Top-209
84TopTif-209
85HawIslC-248
Sarmiento, Oscar
93LinVenB-75
94VenLinU-133
Sarmiento, Wally
80TolMudHT-12
81TolMudHT-8
Sarmiento, Wilfredo
80VenLeaS-7
Sarni, Bill
54Top-194
55Bow-30
55CarHunW-22
55RedMan-NL9
56Top-247
57Top-86
79TCM50-106
94TopArc1-194
94TopArc1G-194
Sarrett, Daniel
80WatRedT-17
Sartain, Dave
91EliTwiP-4299
92ClaFS7-152
92KenTwiC-4
92KenTwiF-602
92ProFS7-100
94HigDesMC-23
94HigDesMF-2789
Sasaki, Kenichi
94CenValRC-21
94CenValRF-3203
Sasaki, Kyosuke
79TCMJapPB-48
Sasaki, Shigehi
90SalSpuCLC-118
90SalSpuP-2719
Sass, James
90StoPorB-10
90StoPorCLC-195
90StoPorP-2195
91BelBreC-9
91BelBreP-2118
Sasser, Don
75CedRapGT-12
76CedRapGT-26
Sasser, Mackey
85FreGiaP-8
86ShrCapP-22
87PhoFirP-20
88Don-28
88DonRoo-51
88DonTeaBM-NEW
88FleUpd-106
88FleUpdG-106
88Lea-28
88MetKah-2
88Sco-642
88ScoGlo-642
88ScoRoo-30T
88ScoRooG-30T
88TopTra-103T
88TopTraT-103T
89ClaLigB-26
89Don-454
89Fle-48
89FleGlo-48
89MetColP-17
89MetKah-25
89Sco-303
89ScoHot1R-82
89ScoYouSI-38
89Top-457
89TopRoo-19
89TopTif-457
89ToyRoo-26
89UppDec-561
90ClaBlu-78
90Don-471
90Fle-216
90FleCan-216
90Lea-435
90MetColP-24
90MetKah-2
90OPC-656
90PubSti-144
90Sco-510
90Top-656
90TopTif-656
90TopTVM-22
90UppDec-185
91ClaGam-37
91Don-136
91Fle-160
91Lea-361
91MetColP-21
91MetKah-2
91MetTro-8
91MetWIZ-345
91OPC-382
91PanFreS-78
91Sco-307
91Sco100S-75
91StaClu-172
91Top-382
91TopDesS-382
91TopMic-382
91TopTif-382
91Ult-226
91UppDec-103
92Don-256
92Fle-515
92Lea-108
92MetColP-18
92MetKah-2
92OPC-533
92Pin-447
92Sco-472
92StaClu-249
92Top-533
92TopGol-533
92TopGolW-533
92TopMic-533
92Ult-237
93Don-512
93Fle-480
93FleFinE-274
93MarMot-22
93OPC-328
93StaCluMari-11
93Top-788
93TopGol-788
93TopInaM-788
93TopMic-788
94Fle-298
94MarMot-22
94Pac-581
94Sco-439
94ScoGolR-439
94StaClu-510
94StaCluFDI-510
94StaCluGR-510
94StaCluMOP-510
94Ult-124
94VenLinU-120
Sasser, Robert
94IdaFalBF-3594
94IdaFalBSP-24
95DanBraTI-25
95EugEmeTI-26
96MacBraB-19
Sassone, Mike
87St.PetCP-4
88ArkTraGS-18
Satnat, Dave
86SalRedBP-24
Sato, Shin-Ichi
90IBAWorA-23
90IBAWorA-45
90IBAWorA-52
Satoh, Hideki
96HonShaHWB-16
Satoh, Hiroyuki
90GatCitPP-3340
90GatCitPSP-19
Satre, Jason
89GreHorP-414
90Bes-42
90ChaWheB-9
90ChaWheP-2241
90CMC-707
91CedRapRC-12
91CedRapRP-2719
92ChaLooF-3820
93BowBayF-2188
94OriPro-90
94RocRedWF-998
94RocRedWTI-20
94VenLinU-234
Satriano, Gina
94ColSilBC-8
95ColSilB-25
95ColSilB9-4
Satriano, Tom
63Top-548
64Top-521
65OPC-124
65Top-124
66Top-361
66TopVen-361
67Top-343
68Top-238
68TopVen-238
69MilBra-248
69OPC-78
69Top-78
69TopSta-150
70MLBOffS-164
70Top-581
71MLBOffS-330
71OPC-557
71Top-557
72MilBra-307
Satterfield, Cory
88HamRedP-1731
89SprCarB-18
90St.PetCS-21
Satterfield, Jeremy
96MedHatBJTI-25
Sattler, Bill
82WicAerTI-16
83WicAerDS-20
84IndIndTI-19
84IndIndTI-21
Saturnino, Sherton
92IdaFalGF-3528
92IdaFalGSP-11
93DanBraC-20
93DanBraF-3634
94MacBraC-18
94MacBraF-2220
Saturria, Luis
96AppLeaAB-21
96JohCitCTI-29
Satzinger, Jeff
86MacPirP-22
87KenTwiP-17
88OrlTwiB-13
89OrlTwiB-24
89OrlTwiP-1330
90CMC-158
90OklCit8C-8
90OklCit8P-433
90ProAAAF-679
Saucier, Kevin
77ReaPhiT-20
80PhiBurK-22
80Top-682
81Fle-24A
81Fle-24B
81Fle-24C
81Top-53
81TopTra-827
82Don-485
82Fle-275
82FleSta-158
82OPC-238
82Top-238
83Top-373
Sauer, Ed
44CubTeal-20
47SigOil-35
49EurSta-196
Sauer, Hank (Henry)
47Exh-200
47PM1StaP1-194
48Bow-45
49Bow-5
49Lea-20
49MPR302-2-113
50Bow-25
50JJKCopP-16
51Bow-22
51TopBluB-49
52DixLid-18
52DixPre-18
52NatTeaL-29
52StaCalL-80E
52StaCalS-92C
52Top-35
53BowC-48
53DixLid-18
53DixPre-18
53ExhCan-7
53NorBreL-27
53RedMan-NL16
53Top-111
54RedHeaF-26
54Top-4
54Wil-15
55Top-45
55TopDouH-103
56Top-41
56TopHocF-A3
56TopPin-6
57Top-197
58GiaJayP-9
58GiaSFCB-20
58Hir-49
58PacBel-7

58Top-378
59Top-404
61Top-481
74LauAllG-52
75OPC-190
75Top-190
76ChiGre-17
77GalGloG-27
77Gia-21
79DiaGre-125
79TCM50-70
82GSGalAG-19
83TopRep5-35
84CubUno-3
88PacLegI-23
91TopArc1-111
92BazQua5A-2
92CubOldS-22
94TopArc1-4
94TopArc1G-4

Sauerbeck, Scott
94PitMetC-19
94PitMetF-3523
95StLucMTI-29
96StLucMTI-32

Saugel, Rich
96HicCraB-20

Saugstad, Mark
92EveGiaC-1
92EveGiaF-1700
93CliGiaC-21
93EveGiaC-23
93EveGiaF-3767
94HigDesMC-24
94HigDesMF-2790

Saul, Jim
62KahAtl-18
80ElPasDT-7
81HolMilT-2
82PorBeaT-23
83NasSouTI-18
84NasSouTI-19
85AlbYanT-25
86AlbYanT-16
89BurBraP-1615
89BurBraS-27
90BurBraB-28
90BurBraP-2365
90BurBraS-27
96EugEmeB-25

Saulter, Kevin
91PulBraC-29
91PulBraP-4004
92MacBraC-14
92MacBraF-266

Saunders, Chris
92PitMetF-3305
93ClaFS7-21
93ClaGolF-168
93St.LucMC-22
94BinMetF-712
95BinMetTI-35
96BinBeeB-25
93StLucMF-2930

Saunders, Dennis
71OPC-423
71Top-423

Saunders, Doug
89ColMetB-20
89ColMetGS-23
90St.LucMS-24
91St.LucMC-5
91St.LucMP-721
92BinMetF-525
92BinMetS-67
93FleFinE-105
93NorTidF-2577
93TopTra-43T
94BinMetF-713

Saunders, Henri
90LSUTigA-16

Saunders, Mark
79ElmPioRST-28

Saunders, Tony
94BreCouMC-16
94BreCouMF-10
96PorSeaDB-24
97Bow-123
97BowCerBIA-CA71
97BowCerGIA-CA71
97BowChr-137
97BowChrI-137
97BowChrIR-137
97BowChrR-137
97BowInt-123
97Fle-581
97FleTif-581

Saunier, Randy
82CliGiaF-12

Sauritch, Chris
94BluOriF-3571
96HigDesMB-25

Sauve, Erik
94HudValRF-3395
94HudValRC-23

Sauve, Jeff
96MicBatCB-25

Sauveur, Rich
84PriWilPT-23
85NasPirT-23
86NasPirP-25
87HarSenP-24
88JacExpB-3
88JacExpP-986
89IndIndP-1228
90MiaMirIS-23
91LinDriAAA-567
91TidTidLD-567
91TidTidP-2508
92OmaRoyF-2962
92OmaRoyS-345
93TopGol-396
94IndIndF-1810
95IndIndF-94
96NasSouB-21
97PacSil-62

Savage, Ashleigh
89AncGlaP-22

Savage, Jack
86BakDodP-24
87SanAntDTI-22
87TexLeaAF-34
88Fle-650
88FleGlo-650
88MetColP-48
88TidTidCa-27
88TidTidCM-1
88TidTidP-1583
89Don-618
89MetColP-51
89TidTidC-5
89TidTidP-1971
90DodTar-1060
90TopTra-111T
90TopTraT-111T
91LinDriAAA-417
91OPC-357
91PorBeaLD-417
91PorBeaP-1564
91Top-357
91TopDesS-357
91TopMic-357
91TopTif-357

Savage, Jim
90BatCliP-3077
91BenBucC-13
91BenBucP-3703
91SpaPhiC-18
91SpaPhiP-903

Savage, John
88RenSilSCLC-275

Savage, John Robert
49Bow-204

Savage, Reggie
92StaCluMO-48

Savage, Ted
62Top-104
62TopVen-104
63PirIDL-20
63Top-508
64Top-62
64TopVen-62
67Top-552
68OPC-119
68Top-119
68TopVen-119
69Top-471A
69Top-471B
70BreMcD-27
70BreMil-22
70BreTeal-11
70SunPin-17
70Top-602
71BreTeal-16
71MLBOffS-434
71OPC-76
71Top-76
71TopCoi-44
71TopSup-3
71TopTat-58
72MilBra-308
81TCM60I-343
90DodTar-704
94BreMilB-76

Savard, Serge
72Dia-104
72Dia-105

Savarino, Bill (William)
86MedA'sC-51
87ModA'sC-14
87ModA'sP-2
88ModA'sCLC-75
89CalLeaA-44
89HunStaB-4
89ModA'sC-21

Savary, Scott
94BilMusF-3683
94BilMusSP-12

Saverine, Bob
63Top-158
64Top-221
64TopVen-221
65Top-427
66Top-312
66TopVen-312
67CokCapS-13
67DexPre-186
67OPC-27
67Top-27
68OPC-149
68Top-149
68TopVen-149
78TCM60I-14
91OriCro-402

Saverino, Mike
82DanSunF-23
83PeoSunF-27

Savinon, Odalis
89JohCitCS-19
91SprCarC-24
91SprCarP-757
92St.PetCC-21
93ArkTraF-2826

Savoy, Annie
89BulDurOS-5

Sawatski, Carl
47Exh-201A
47Exh-201B
47Exh-201C
53Top-202
54Top-198
55Top-122
55TopDouH-93
58Top-234
59Top-56
59TopVen-56
60Lea-120
60Top-545
61Top-198
62Jel-162
62Pos-162
62PosCan-162
62SalPlaC-119
62ShiPlaC-119
62Top-106
62TopVen-106
63Top-267
64Top-24
64TopVen-24
89TexLeaAGS-40
91TopArc1-202
94TopArc1-198
94TopArc1G-198

Sawatski, John
72CedRapCT-6

Sawkiw, Warren
88CapCodPPaLP-3
90NiaFalRP-10
91LakTigC-27
91LakTigP-276
92LakTigC-24
95KnoSmoF-53

Sawyer, Eddie
49EurSta-145
49PhiBul-46
50Bow-225
51Bow-184
60PhiJayP-12
60Top-226
79DiaGre-325
83PhiPosGPaM-11
87Phi195T-1

Sawyer, Rick
75SyrChiTI-18
76SSP-426
77PadSchC-48
77Top-268
92YanWIZ7-138

Sawyer, Zach
93MadMusC-22
93MadMusF-1821
94WesMicWC-21
94WesMicWF-2294
95ModA'sTI-28

Sax, Dave
79CliDodT-18
82AlbDukT-13
83DodPol-23
84AlbDukC-152
84Don-519
85PawRedST-15
86Top-307
86TopTif-307
87Don-647
87PawRedST-25
88BufBisC-22
88BufBisP-1483
89ColCliC-26
89ColCliP-756
90CMC-219
90ColCliC-19
90ColCliP-7
90ColCliP-680
90DodTar-705
90ProAAAF-330
90TopTVY-59
91ColCliLD-117
91ColCliP-17
91ColCliP-600
91LinDriAAA-117
91PacSenL-34
92ColCliF-357
92ColCliP-15
92ColCliS-115

Sax, Steve
79CliDodT-10
82DodPol-52
82DodPos-7
82DodUniOV-19
82DogBuiE-7
82Don-624
82Fle-21
82Top-681
82TopTra-103T
83AllGamPI-108
83DodPol-3
83DodPos-14
83Don-336
83Fle-220
83FleSta-172
83FleSti-118
83OPC-245
83PerAll-15
83PerAllG-15
83SevCoi-2
83Top-245
83TopSti-329
84AllGamPI-16
84DodPol-3
84DodSmo-3
84Don-104
84Fle-112
84Fle-633
84FleSti-90
84FunFooP-45
84MilBra-22
84Nes792-610
84OPC-144
84SevCoi-W22
84Top-610
84TopGloA-14
84TopRubD-19
84TopSti-78
84TopTif-610
85AllGamPI-106
85DodCokP-29
85Don-418
85Fle-384
85FleLimE-32
85Lea-90
85OPC-369
85Top-470
85TopMin-470
85TopRubD-18
85TopSti-77
85TopTif-470
86BasStaB-98
86DodCokP-27
86DodPol-3
86DodUniOP-17
86Don-540
86DonHig-50
86Fle-143
86GenMilB-5H
86OPC-175
86Spo-56
86Spo-95
86SpoRoo-48
86Top-175
86TopSti-72
86TopTat-21
86TopTif-175
87ClaGam-20
87DodMot-3
87DodPol-2
87DodSmoA-32
87Don-26
87Don-278
87DonAll-28
87DonOpeD-85
87DonSupD-26
87Dra-25
87Fle-453
87FleAll-4
87FleGamW-39
87FleGlo-453
87FleHotS-34
87FleMin-96
87FleRecS-34
87FleStiC-106
87GenMilB-6H
87KraFoo-38
87Lea-26
87Lea-203
87MandMSL-21
87OPC-254
87SevCoi-W10
87SmoNatL-1
87Spo-12
87SpoTeaP-14
87Top-596
87Top-769
87TopCoi-42
87TopMinL-15
87TopSti-70
87TopTif-596
87TopTif-769
88DodMot-3
88DodPol-3
88DodSmo-25
88Don-176
88DonBasB-204
88Fle-523
88FleGlo-523
88FleMin-85
88FleStiC-93
88Lea-185
88OPC-305
88PanSti-311
88Sco-35
88ScoGlo-35
88StaLinAl-29
88StaLinD-14
88Top-305
88TopBig-46
88TopSti-74
88TopTif-305
89Bow-178
89BowTif-178
89CadEllD-50
89ClaTraP-179
89DodSmoG-99
89Don-84
89DonBasB-20
89DonTra-23
89Fle-70
89FleGlo-70
89FleGlo-WS9
89FleUpd-52
89FleWorS-9
89OPC-40
89PanSti-106
89RedFolSB-103
89Sco-69
89ScoHot1S-33
89ScoRoo-20T
89Spo-58
89Top-40
89TopBasT-100
89TopBig-111

89TopDouM-19
89TopMinL-19
89TopSti-57
89TopStiB-39
89TopTif-40
89TopTra-111T
89TopTraT-111T
89TopUKM-69
89UppDec-53
89UppDec-748
89YanScoNW-2
90Bow-442
90BowTif-442
90ClaBlu-149
90DodTar-706
90Don-2
90Don-78
90DonBesA-24
90DOnBonM-BC22
90DonSupD-2
90Fle-455
90FleBasA-33
90FleCan-455
90FleLeaL-34
90Hot50PS-38
90Lea-96
90LeaPre-1
90MLBBasB-62
90MSAHolD-16
90MSAIceTD-19
90OPC-560
90PanSti-129
90PubSti-547
90RedFolSB-83
90Sco-125
90Sco100S-2
90ScoMcD-22
90Spo-12
90Top-560
90TopBig-141
90TopCoi-26
90TopDou-57
90TopGloS-8
90TopMinL-25
90TopSti-310
90TopStiB-38
90TopTif-560
90TopTVA-18
90TopTVY-26
90UppDec-18
90UppDec-172
90USPlaCA-4S
90WinDis-7
90YanScoNW-3
91Bow-170
91CadEllD-50
91Cla2-T17
91ClaGam-106
91Don-48
91Don-163
91Fle-679
91Lea-220
91OPC-290
91PanCanT1-46
91PanFreS-168
91PanFreS-325
91PanSti-271
91RedFolS-84
91RedFolS-127
91Sco-32
91Sco100S-72
91StaClu-204
91StaCluP-38
91StaPinB-44
91Stu-100
91Top-290
91TopCraJ2-30
91TopDesS-290
91TopGloA-3
91TopMic-290
91TopTif-290
91TopTriH-A10
91Ult-242
91UppDec-462
92Bow-469
92ClaGam-195
92DodStaTA-25
92Don-729
92Fle-244
92Hig5-90
92Lea-217
92OPC-430
92OPCPre-43
92PanSti-136
92Pin-328
92Sco-475
92ScoRoo-4T
92SpoStaCC-40
92StaClu-635
92StaCluNC-635
92Stu-157
92Top-430
92TopGol-430
92TopGolW-430
92TopKid-85
92TopMic-430
92TopTra-99T
92TopTraG-99T
92TriPlaG-GS4
92Ult-108
92Ult-341
92UppDec-358
92UppDec-743
92WhiSoxK-7
92YanWIZ8-172
92YanWIZA-75
93CadDis-53
93Don-123
93Fle-588
93Lea-107
93OPC-307
93PacSpa-395
93PanSti-137
93Pin-335
93Sco-418
93Sel-160
93StaClu-482
93StaCluFDI-482
93StaCluMOP-482
93Top-367
93TopGol-367
93TopInaM-367
93TopMic-367
93TriPla-47
93Ult-179
93UppDec-369
93UppDecGold-369
93WhiSoxK-25
94Don-286
94Fle-94
94Lea-210
94Pac-137
94Sco-254
94ScoGolR-254
94StaCluT-128
94StaCluTFDI-128
94Top-662
94TopGol-662
94TopSpa-662
95DodROY-11

Sayers, Gale
68AtlOil-11

Sayers, Keith
95OdgRapTI-24
96OgdRapTI-NNO

Sayler, Barry
83St.PetCT-24

Sayles, Bill
90DodTar-707

Sayles, Steve
83MiaMarT-24

Sbrocco, Jon
94CliLumF-1989
96SanJosGB-3
94CliLumC-21

Scafa, Bob
93BazTeaU-17
93TopTra-120T
94YakBeaC-18
95BakBlaTI-19

Scaglione, Tony
88WatIndP-690
89KinIndS-22

Scala, Dominic
77ModA'sC-4

Scala, Jerry
50WorWidGV-28

Scales, George
78LauLonABS-26

Scales, Matthew
92LetMouSP-19

Scalzitti, Will
92BenRocC-20
92BenRocF-1476
93CenValRC-21
93CenValRF-2895
93Top-476
93TopGol-476
93TopInaM-476
93TopMic-476
94CenValRC-22
94CenValRF-3208
95NewHavRTI-15

Scanlan, Bob
86ClePhiP-22
87PhiTas-39B
87ReaPhiP-20
88MaiPhiC-9
88MaiPhiP-294
89ReaPhiB-8
89ReaPhiP-652
89ReaPhiS-21
90CMC-233
90ProAAAF-301
90ScrRedBC-7
90ScrRedBP-599
91CubMar-30
91IowCubLD-223
91IowCubP-1061
91Lea-520
91LinDriAAA-223
91ScoRoo-102T
91TopTra-105T
91TopTraT-105T
91UppDecFE-48F
92CubMar-30
92Don-454
92FleUpd-76
92Lea-437
92OPC-274
92OPCPre-14
92Sco-285
92Sco100RS-59
92StaClu-112
92Top-274
92TopDeb91-157
92TopGol-274
92TopGolW-274
92TopMic-274
92Ult-473
93CubMar-23
93Don-292
93Fle-26
93Lea-13
93OPC-325
93Pin-417
93Sco-361
93StaClu-444
93StaCluCu-22
93StaCluFDI-444
93StaCluMOP-444
93Top-47
93TopGol-47
93TopInaM-47
93TopMic-47
93Ult-22
93UppDec-617
93UppDecGold-617
94BreMilB-351
94BrePol-23
94Don-263
94Fin-310
94FinRef-310
94Fle-397
94FleUpd-57
94Top-451
94TopGol-451
94TopSpa-451
95Don-56
95DonPreP-56
95Fle-188

Scanlan, Doc (William)
10DomDisP-105A
10DomDisP-105B
10SweCapPP-76
11S74Sil-55
11SpoLifM-163
11T205-147
12HasTriFT-43
12T207-160

Scanlin, Michael
87GasRanP-19
88TulDriTI-1

Scanlon, Ken
80AndBraT-23
81DurBulT-4
82DurBulT-7
83DurBulT-12

Scanlon, Pat (James P.)
76SSP-332
78Top-611

Scanlon, Steve
88VisOakCLC-161
88VisOakP-94

Scannell, Larry
87ElmPio(C-5
88ElmPioC-24
89WinHavRSS-21

Scantlebury, Pat
60MapLeaSF-18
61MapLeaBH-20
86NegLeaF-35

Scarbery, Randy
77SanJosMC-18
80Top-291

Scarborough, Carey
75BurBeeT-24

Scarborough, Ray
47SenGunBP-10
49Bow-140
50Bow-108
50Dra-29
50RoyDes-14A
50RoyDes-14B
50RoyDes-14C
51Bow-39
51TopRedB-42
52Bow-140
52RoyPre-12
52TipTop-36
52Top-43
53Dor-108
53Top-213
79DiaGre-72
79TCM50-208
83TopRep5-43
91TopArc1-213

Scarce, Mac
73OPC-6
73Top-6
74OPC-149
74Top-149
75OPC-527
75Top-527
76IndIndTI-22
77IndIndTI-15
91MetWIZ-346

Scarpace, Ken
81CedRapRT-17
82WatRedT-19

Scarpetta, Dan
83BelBreF-25
87DenZepP-15
88ElPasDB-3
88TexLeaAGS-6
89SanAntMB-18

Scarpitti, Jeff
94EugEmeC-20
94EugEmeF-3712

Scarsella, Les
36GouWidPPR-D32
38CinOraW-24
39OrcPhoAP-20
46RemBre-26
47RemBre-2
47SigOil-54
47SmiClo-3
48SigOil-20
48SmiClo-6
49BowPCL-25
49RemBre-25

Scarsone, Steve (Stephen)
86BenPhiC-135
87ChaWheP-5
88ClePhiS-22
89EasLeaDDP-DD25
89ReaPhiB-4
89ReaPhiP-665
89ReaPhiS-22
89ReaPhiS-27
90ClePhiS-20
91LinDriAA-518
91ReaPhiLD-518
91ScrRedBP-2548
91TriA AAGP-AAA41
92DonRoo-108
92ScrRedBF-2455
92ScrRedBS-492
92SkyAAAF-222
92TriA AAS-492
93Don-381
93StaCluG-21
94Fle-701
94GiaAMC-20
94GiaMot-9
94GiaTarBCI-7
94GiaUSPC-4H
94GiaUSPC-11S
94Pac-555
94Sco-596
94ScoGolR-596
94StaClu-3
94StaCluFDI-3
94StaCluGR-3
94StaCluMOP-3
94StaCluT-9
94StaCluTFDI-9
94Top-729
94TopGol-729
94TopSpa-729
95Don-462
95DonPreP-462
95DonTopotO-357
95FleUpd-196
95GiaMot-13
95StaClu-603
95StaCluMOP-603
95StaCluSTWS-603
96ColCho-718
96ColChoGS-718
96ColChoSS-718
96Don-387
96DonPreP-387
96Fle-596
96FleTif-596
96GiaMot-18
96LeaSigA-203
96LeaSigAG-203
96LeaSigAS-203
96Ult-570
96UltGolM-570
97Pac-447
97PacLigB-447
97PacSil-447

Scavo, Vinny
94BreCouMC-27
95BreCouMF-264
87PanAmTUBI-NNO

Schaaf, Bob
94YakBeaC-19
94YakBeaF-3860
95SanBerSTI-23
96VerBeaDB-26

Schaal, Paul
65Top-517
66AngDexP-6
66Top-376
67CokCapDA-21
67OPC-58
67Top-58
68Top-474
69MilBra-249
69MLBOffS-62
69Top-352
69TopSta-188
70MLBOffS-228
70OPC-338
70RoyTeal-31
70Top-338
71MLBOffS-429
71OPC-487
71Top-487
72MilBra-309
72OPC-177
72OPC-178
72Top-177
72Top-178
73OPC-416
73Top-416
74OPC-514
74Top-514
86RoyGreT-4

Schacht, Al
31SenTeaIPW-28
34DiaMatCSB-160
36GouWidPPR-A92
36NatChiFPR-98
36R31PasP-40
36WorWidGV-29
39PlaBal-113
40PlaBal-116
79RedSoxEF-15
87ConSer2-9
92ConTSN-559
93ConTSN-920

Schaefer, Billiards
88GooN16-36

Schaefer, Bob
82TidTidT-22
84TidTidT-10

85IntLeaAT-1
85TidTidT-27
86GleFalTP-20
87MemChiB-1
87MemChiP-10
88RoySmo-2
91RoyPol-26
Schaefer, Chris
88CapCodPPaLP-31
89EugEmeB-1
90AppFoxBS-23
90AppFoxP-2093
Schaefer, Doug
79PhoGiaVNB-1
80PhoGiaVNB-3
81PhoGiaVNB-7
Schaefer, Germany (Herman)
07TigACDPP-13
08RosComP-40
09AmeCarE-91
09BusBroBPP-14
09RamT20-103
09T206-308
09T206-309
09TigMorPenWBPP-11
09WolNewDTPP-15
09WolNewDTPP-16
10CouT21-217
10CouT21-218
10CouT21-219
10CouT21-315
10DomDisP-106
10E101-37
10E102-20
10MelMinE-37
10NadCarE-41
10PeoT21-46A
10PeoT21-46B
10RedCroT-66
10RedCroT-152
10RedCroT-153
10RedCroT-240
10SepAnoP-10
10SweCapPP-63
11S74Sil-40
11SpoLifCW-311
11SpoLifM-132
11T205-148
12HasTriFT-58
12HasTriFT-59
12T207-161
14PieStaT-51
15AmeCarE-34
15SpoNewM-154
16TanBraE-16
77GalGloG-167
81TigDetN-102
95ConTSN-1372
Schaefer, Jacob
87AllandGN-45
88KimN18-39
Schaefer, Jeff
84RocRedWT-10
85ChaO'sT-12
85UtiBluST-14
86MidAngP-21
87SanAntDTI-1
88VanCanC-21
88VanCanP-753
89VanCanC-24
89WhiSoxC-25
90CalCanP-660
90FleUpd-120
90ProAAAF-125
90TopDeb89-109
91FleUpd-56
91MarCouH-2
91OPC-681
91Top-681
91TopDesS-681
91TopMic-681
91TopTif-681
92Don-525
92Lea-513
92MarMot-24
92OPC-391
92Sco-629
92StaClu-108
93ChaKniF-552
Schaefer, Jim
80AshTouT-6
88RoySmo-2
Schaefer, Steve
79ElmPioRST-15
Schaeffer, Harry
78ReaRem-17
Schaeffer, Mark
72PadTeal-23
Schafer, Bill
90SumBraB-18
90SumBraP-2430
Schafer, Brett
95SpoIndTI-27
96LanLugB-26
Schafer, Dennis
81CliGiaT-13
Schafer, Randy
79MemChiT-11
Schaffer, Jim
61UniOil-P11
62Top-579
63Top-81
64Top-359
64TopVen-359
65Top-313
68Top-463
78TCM60I-152
78TCM60I-169
78TCM60I-184
79TulDriT-13
83Roy-24
91MetWIZ-347
93RanKee-318
Schaffer, Jimmie
89HagSunB-10
89HagSunP-282
89HagSunS-22
Schaffer, John
86RedWinA-9
Schaffernoth, Joe
61Top-58
63Top-463
Schaffner, Eric
96GreBatB-25
Schaffrath, Pam
95ColSilB-26
96ColSilB-24
Schaive, John
82BufBisT-6
83LynPirT-18
Schaive, John Sr.
61Top-259
62Top-529
63Top-356
Schalk, Ray
09ColChiE-251
09SpoNewSM-96
12ColRedB-251
12ColTinT-251
14CraJacE-61
15CraJacE-61
15SpoNewM-155
16BF2FP-18
16ColE13-150
16SpoNewM-154
17HolBreD-90
19W514-60
21E121So1-88A
21E121So1-88B
21E121So8-82
21Exh-151
21OxfConE-16
22AmeCarE-59
22E120-27
22W572-89
22W573-112
22W575-115
22WilPatV-16
23MapCriV-3
23W501-43
23W515-51
25Exh-78
26Exh-78
26SpoComoA-37
27AmeCarE-8
27Exh-40
27YorCarE-23
28W502-23
28Yue-23
31CubTeal-20
36WorWidGV-124
50CalHOFW-64
60Fle-56
61Fle-136
75SheGrePG-24
75WhiSox1T-23
75WhiSox1T-24
76GrePlaG-24
76MotOldT-6
76ShaPiz-79
76WhiSoxTAG-10
77GalGloG-177
80PacLeg-85
80PerHaloFP-78
80SSPHOF-78
80WhiSoxGT-9
85WhiSoxC-72
87ConSer2-55
88PacEigMO-43
88PacEigMO-45
88PacEigMO-50
88PacEigMO-51
88PacEigMO-52
88PacEigMO-100
89WhiSoxK-3
91ConTSN-48
92Man191BSR-22
93ConTSN-879
94ConTSN-1033
94ConTSNB-1033
94ConTSNCI-38
95ConTSN-1384
20W516-4
Schall, Gene
91BatCliC-2
91BatCliP-3493
91FroRowDP-6
92ClaFS7-266
92SpaPhiF-1278
92StaCluD-165
93Bow-512
93ReaPhiF-304
93StaCluP-18
94Bow-280
94Cla-113
94ExcFS7-248
94ScrRedBF-929
94Top-786
94TopGol-786
94TopSpa-786
94TriAAF-AAA44
94UppDecML-193
95Exc-247
95ScrRedBTI-24
95Top-79
95UppDecML-82
96ColCho-32
96ColChoGS-32
96ColChoSS-32
96Don-453
96DonPreP-453
96Fle-506
96FleTif-506
96ScrRedBB-23
96Ult-524
96UltGolM-524
97Pac-385
97PacLigB-385
97PacSil-385
97Pin-54
97PinArtP-54
97PinMusC-54
95UppDecMLFS-82
Schallock, Art
49W72HolS-20
50W720HolS-28
91OriCro-403
Schammel, Bill
83MidCubT-1
Schang, Wally (Walter H.)
14CraJacE-58
14FatPlaT-44
15CraJacE-58
15SpoNewM-156
16BF2FP-40
16ColE13-151
16FleBreD-81
16SpoNewM-155
17HolBreD-91
19W514-99
20GasAmeMBD-17
20NatCarE-87
21E121So1-89
21E121So8-83
21Exh-152
21Exh-157
21KoBreWSI-50
21Nei-20
22AmeCarE-60
22E120-72
22W572-90
22W573-113
22W575-116
22WilPatV-11
23W501-27
23W503-2
23W515-17
23WilChoV-142
25Exh-101
28Exh-59
28StaPlaCE-58
29ExhFou-29
31Exh-24
69SCFOldT-25
91ConTSN-249
92ConTSN-448
93ConTSN-872
94ConTSN-1231
94ConTSNB-1231
Schanz, Charley
52MotCoo-41
53MotCoo-40
79DiaGre-311
83TCMPla1944-44
Schanz, Scott
91PenPilC-10
91PenPilP-376
92SanBerC-12
92SanBerSF-953
93JacSunF-2713
94JacSunF-1411
Schardt, Bill (Wilbur)
09ColChiE-252A
09ColChiE-252B
12ColRedB-252A
12ColRedB-252B
12ColTinT-252A
12ColTinT-252B
12T207-162
90DodTar-708
Scharein, George
47SigOil-86
Scharff, Tony
91SouOreAC-19
91SouOreAP-3842
92MadMusC-24
Scharrer, Jim
95TopTra-126T
96AppLeaAB-14
96DanBraB-19
96Top-21
96TopPowB-21
Schattinger, Jeff
80OmaRoyP-22
81OmaRoyT-12
82EdmTraT-25
Schatz, Dan
87VisOakP-25
Schatzeder, Dan
77ExpPos-27
78ExpPos-13
78Top-709
79OPC-56
79Top-124
80OPC-140
80Top-267
81Don-248
81Fle-482
81OPC-112
81Top-417
82Don-385
82ExpPos-36
82Fle-281
82OPC-106
82Top-691
82TopTra-104T
83ExpPos-22
83ExpStu-22
83Fle-296
83OPC-189
83Top-189
84Don-132
84ExpPos-28
84ExpStu-7
84Fle-286
84Nes792-57
84OPC-57
84Top-57
84TopTif-57
85Don-543
85Fle-409
85Lea-59
85OPC-293
85Top-501
85TopMin-501
85TopTif-501
86ExpPos-13
86ExpProPa-12
86Fle-259
86OPC-324
86Top-324
86TopTif-324
87Don-482
87ExpPos-25
87Fle-186
87FleGlo-186
87OPC-168
87PhiTas-35
87Top-789
87TopTif-789
88Fle-21A
88Fle-21B
88FleGlo-21
88IndGat-31
88StaLinTw-17
88Top-218
88TopTif-218
88TwiTeal-20
89AstLenH-9
89AstSmo-35
89FleUpd-90
89TucTorC-10
89TucTorJP-21
89TucTorP-198
90AstLenH-21
90AstMot-18
90Bow-69
90BowTif-69
90Don-594
90Fle-236
90FleCan-236
90Sco-418
91Don-497
91MetWIZ-348
Schaub, Greg
96HelBreTI-22
Schauer, Rube (A.J.)
16FleBreD-82
Scheckla, Roddy
88AubAstP-1960
89AshTouP-946
Scheckter, Jody
72Dia-142
Scheer, Greg
95EveAqaTI-20
96WisTimRB-19
Scheer, Ron
83WisRapTF-2
84VisOakT-21
86PenWhiSP-23
87PenWhiSP-17
Scheetz, Brian
90ButCopKSP-19
Scheetz, Rick
82WisRapTF-11
Scheffer, Aaron
95EveAqaTI-21
96WisTimRB-20
Scheffer, Lawrence
95OdgRapTI-25
Scheffing, Bob
41CubTeal-22
49Bow-83A
49Bow-83B
49EurSta-71
49Lea-160
50Bow-168
54Top-76
60BraLaktL-22
60BraSpiaS-20
60Top-464
61TigJayP-12
61Top-223
62TigJayP-11
62Top-72
62Top-416
62TopVen-72
63TigJayP-10
63Top-134
79DiaGre-114
85TCMPla1-29
94TopArc1-76
94TopArc1G-76
Scheffler, Craig
93GreFalDSP-9
94VerBeaDC-19
94VerBeaDF-70
94YakBeaC-20
94YakBeaF-3848

95BakBlaTI-20
96VerBeaDB-27
Scheffler, Jim
90PitMetP-21
91PitMetC-17
91PitMetP-3421
Schefsky, Steve
84BeaGolGT-13
85BeaGolGT-11
Scheib, Carl
49Bow-25
49OlmStu-6
49PhiBul-47
50Bow-213
51Bow-83
52Bow-46
52Top-116
53BowC-150
53Top-57
54Bow-67
54Top-118
60RawGloT-29
76TayBow4-109
79DiaGre-338
83TopRep5-116
91TopArc1-57
94TopArc1-118
94TopArc1G-118
Scheibe, Britton
92SpoIndC-3
92SpoIndF-1309
93SpoIndC-19
93SpoIndF-3605
Scheibeck, Frank
87OldJudN-442
Scheid, Rich
87Ft.LauYP-18
88PitCubP-1372
89IowCubC-9
89IowCubP-1713
90Bes-175
90BirBarB-22
90BirBarP-1110
91LinDriAAA-645
91VanCanLD-645
91VanCanP-1594
92VanCanF-2721
92VanCanS-647
93EdmTraF-1135
93Top-646
93TopGol-646
93TopInaM-646
93TopMic-646
94EdmTraF-2876
94TriAAF-AAA30
95ChaKniTI-22
95FleUpd-99
Scheinblum, Richie
65Top-577
68OPC-16
68Top-16
68TopVen-16
69Top-479
70OPC-161
70Top-161
71OPC-326
71Top-326
72OPC-468
72Top-468
73OPC-78
73Top-78
74OPC-323
74Top-323
74TopSta-148
Schell, Danny (Clyde)
55Top-79
55TopDouH-81
Scheller, Rod
77LodDodT-18
78LodDodT-17A
78LodDodT-17B
Schellhasse, Albert
87OldJudN-443
Schelzo, Phil
96VerExpB-6
Schemer, Mike
47SunBre-20
Schenbeck, Tom
92HelBreF-1715
92HelBreSP-22
93BelBreC-22
93BelBreF-1709
94StoPorC-25
94StoPorF-1695
Schenck, Bruce
91PocPioP-3781
91PocPioSP-6
Schenck, Larry
89GeoColC-27
90GeoColC-26
90GeoColC-33
Schenkle, William
87OldJudN-444
Schenz, Henry
50PirTeal-20
52MotCoo-30
Scherer, Doug
84ModA'sC-20
85ModA'sC-23
85TacTigC-141
87HunStaTI-20
88KnoBluJB-11
86HumStaDS-40
Scherger, George
73OPC-296
73Top-296
74OPC-326
74Top-326
79NaSouTI-21
81WatRedT-22
82IndIndTI-2
84RedEnq-29
86RedTexG-NNO
Scherger, Joe
82AmaGolST-4
Scherman, Fred
71MLBOffS-406
71OPC-316
71Top-316
72OPC-6
72Top-6
73LinPor-78
73OPC-660
73TigJew-17
73Top-660
74OPC-186
74Top-186
74TopTra-186T
75OPC-252
75SSP18-10
75Top-252
76ExpRed-28
76OPC-188
76SSP-343
76Top-188
77ColCliT-20
87AstShoSTw-15
Scherrer, Bill
80WatRedT-7
81WatRedT-7
84Don-203
84Fle-482
84Nes792-373
84RedEnq-18
84Top-373
84TopSti-62
84TopTif-373
85Fle-22
85TigCaiD-17
85TigWen-19
85Top-586
85TopTif-586
86Don-516
86Fle-237
86Top-217
86TopTif-217
87Top-98
87TopTif-98
88RocRedWC-9
88RocRedWP-209
88RocRedWTI-20
89OklCit8C-3
89TidTidP-1955
91OriCro-404
Schettler, Louis
11SpoLifM-239
Scheuer, Chris
89AugPirP-520
Scheznayder, Wade
78QuaCitAT-23
81RedPioT-12
Schiefelbein, Mike
92AriWilP-15
94EveGiaC-25
94EveGiaF-3653
95BelGiaTI-30
Schiel, Rob
90KenTwiB-13
90KenTwiP-2304
90KenTwiS-22
Schiller, Jon
89EveGiaS-25
Schilling, Chuck
47PM1StaP1-195
47PM1StaP1-196
61Top-499
62Baz-21
62Jel-56
62Pos-56
62PosCan-56
62RedSoxJP-9
62Top-345
62Top-467
62TopStal-18
63Top-52
64Top-182
64Top-481
64TopCoi-103
64TopVen-182
65OPC-272
65Top-272
66OPC-6
66Top-6
66TopVen-6
78TCM60I-183
81RedSoxBG2S-108
Schilling, Curt
86ElmPioRSP-20
87GreHorP-2
88NewBriRSP-908
89Don-635
89RocRedWC-7
89RocRedWP-1655
90Bow-246
90BowTif-246
90CMC-306
90Don-667
90FleUpd-68
90OPC-97
90ProAAAF-458
90RocRedWC-5
90RocRedWGC-14
90RocRedWP-701
90Sco-581
90Sco100RS-94
90Spo-133
90Top-97
90TopTif-97
91AstMot-15
91Bow-560
91Don-556
91Fle-491
91Lea-292
91OPC-569
91OriCro-405
91Sco-788
91ScoRoo-80T
91Stu-179
91Top-569
91TopDesS-569
91TopMic-569
91TopTif-569
91UppDec-528
92Don-757
92FleUpd-112
92Lea-516
92OPC-316
92PhiMed-28
92Sco-671
92ScoRoo-25T
92StaClu-279
92Top-316
92TopGol-316
92TopGolW-316
92TopMic-316
92TopTra-100T
92TopTraG-100T
92Ult-208
92Ult-548
93Bow-680
93Don-118
93Fin-10
93FinRef-10
93Fla-107
93Fle-108
93Lea-4
93OPC-354
93PacSpa-581
93PanSti-268
93PhiMed-31
93Pin-402
93Sco-52
93Sel-229
93SelStaL-65
93SP-178
93StaClu-422
93StaCluFDI-422
93StaCluMO-23
93StaCluMOP-422
93StaCluP-14
93Stu-131
93Top-421
93TopComotH-25
93TopGol-421
93TopInaM-421
93TopMic-421
93TriPla-129
93TriPla-230
93Ult-445
93UppDec-67
93UppDecGold-67
93USPlaCA-12S
94Bow-308
94ColC-253
94ColChoGS-253
94ColChoSS-253
94Don-577
94ExtBas-341
94ExtBasPD-6
94Fin-150
94FinRef-150
94Fla-417
94Fle-600
94FleSmo'nH-11
94FUnPac-38
94Lea-320
94OPC-66
94Pac-486
94PanSti-230
94PhiMed-30
94PhiMel-20
94PhiUSPC-7C
94PhiUSPC-12H
94Pin-105
94PinArtP-105
94PinMusC-105
94ProMag-105
94Sco-88
94ScoGolR-88
94Sel-161
94Spo-51
94StaClu-289
94StaCluFDI-289
94StaCluGR-289
94StaCluMOP-289
94StaCluT-229
94StaCluTFDI-229
94Top-142
94TopGol-142
94TopSpa-142
94TriPla-179
94Ult-554
94UppDec-460
94UppDecED-460
95ColCho-374
95ColChoGS-374
95ColChoSS-374
95Don-21
95DonPreP-21
95DonTopotO-309
95Emo-170
95Fla-395
95Fle-403
95Lea-205
95Phi-28
95PhiMel-20
95Pin-100
95PinArtP-100
95PinMusC-100
95Sco-163
95ScoGolR-163
95ScoPlaTS-163
95SP-91
95SPSil-91
95StaClu-4
95StaCluFDI-4
95StaCluMOP-4
95StaCluSTWS-4
95Top-297
95TopCyb-160
95Ult-209
95UltGolM-209
95UppDec-381
95UppDecED-381
95UppDecEDG-381
96Cir-169
96CirRav-169
96ColCho-672
96ColChoGS-672
96ColChoSS-672
96Don-309
96DonPreP-309
96EmoXL-249
96Fla-338
96Fle-507
96FleTif-507
96LeaSigA-204
96LeaSigAG-204
96LeaSigAS-204
96Sco-153
96StaClu-292
96StaCluMOP-292
96Top-128
96Ult-525
96UltGolM-525
97Bow-232
97BowChr-59
97BowChrI-59
97BowChrIR-59
97BowChrR-59
97BowInt-232
97Cir-338
97CirRav-338
97ColCho-197
97Don-306
97DonLim-114
97DonLimLE-114
97DonPreP-306
97DonPrePGold-306
97Fin-104
97FinEmb-104
97FinEmbR-104
97FinRef-104
97FlaSho-A138
97FlaSho-B138
97FlaSho-C138
97FlaShoLC-138
97FlaShoLC-B138
97FlaShoLC-C138
97FlaShoLCM-A138
97FlaShoLCM-B138
97FlaShoLCM-C138
97Fle-421
97Fle-741
97FleTeaL-24
97FleTif-421
97FleTif-741
97Lea-252
97LeaFraM-252
97LeaFraMDC-252
97MetUni-207
97Pac-386
97PacLigB-386
97PacSil-386
97Pin-9
97PinArtP-9
97PinMusC-9
97Sco-416
97ScoHobR-416
97ScoResC-416
97ScoShoS-416
97ScoShoSAP-416
97SP-137
97SpoIll-91
97SpoIllEE-91
97StaClu-152
97StaCluMOP-152
97Top-368
97TopGal-54
97TopGalPPI-54
97TopSta-84
97TopStaAM-84
97Ult-256
97UltGolME-256
97UltPlaME-256
97UppDec-156
Schilling, Jarrett
85CloHSS-38
Schimdt, Eric
77CliDodT-22
88ColCliC-8
Schimming, Mark
84IowCubT-13
Schimpf, Rex
82DayBeaAT-7
83DayBeaAT-11
Schiraldi, Calvin
84JacMetT-4
85Don-38
85FleUpd-99

85MetTCM-16
85TidTidT-5
86Don-652
86PawRedSP-20
86SpoRoo-44
86Top-210
86TopTif-210
87Don-641
87Fle-44
87FleGlo-44
87Lea-137
87SpoTeaP-9
87Top-94
87TopTif-94
87Woo-20
88CubDavB-32
88Don-375
88DonBasB-194
88DonTeaBC-NEW
88Fle-365
88FleGlo-365
88OPC-62
88Sco-218
88ScoGlo-218
88ScoRoo-39T
88ScoRooG-39T
88StaLinCu-11
88Top-599
88TopTif-599
88TopTra-104T
88TopTraT-104T
89CubMar-32
89Don-285
89DonBasB-82
89Fle-438
89FleGlo-438
89OPC-337
89Sco-321
89Top-337
89TopSti-56
89TopTif-337
89UppDec-82
90Don-672
90Fle-168
90FleCan-168
90OPC-693
90PadCok-17
90PadMag-13
90PubSti-203
90Top-693
90TopTif-693
90UppDec-643
91Don-308
91Fle-543
91LinDriAAA-610
91MetWIZ-349
91OPC-424
91PadMag-15A
91Sco-611
91Top-424
91TopDesS-424
91TopMic-424
91TopTif-424
91TucTorLD-610
91TucTorP-2212
92TexLon-36
93RanKee-319
Schirm, George
09ColChiE-254A
09ColChiE-254B
09T206-462
12ColRedB-254A
12ColRedB-254B
12ColTinT-254A
12ColTinT-254B
12ImpTobC-29
Schlafly, Harry
09ColChiE-255
09T206-463
12ColRedB-255
12ColTinT-255
Schlei, Admiral (George)
09BriE97-27
09RamT20-105
09T206-310
09T206-311
09T206-312
10CouT21-220
10CouT21-221
10E101-38
10MelMinE-38
10NadCarE-42
10NadE1-50
10PeoT21-47
11S74Sil-94
11SpoLifCW-312
11SpoLifM-217
11T205-149
11TurRedT-115
Schleighoffer, Mike
86AlbDukP-21
Schlesinger, Bill
65Top-573
68Top-258
68TopVen-258
Schley, Van
88SalLakCTTI-16
89SalLakTTI-18
Schlicher, B.J.
96AppLeaAB-26
96MarPhiB-22
Schlichting, John
85VerBeaDT-3
86VerBeaDP-21
Schlitzer, Victor
09AmeCarE-92
Schlomann, Brett
95GreBatTI-21
96TamYanY-22
Schlopy, Butch
86WatPirP-22
88AugPirP-374
89SalBucS-19
90SalBucS-19
Schloss, M.
88KimN18-40
Schlutt, Jason
93SpoIndC-20
93SpoIndF-3591
94SprSulC-21
94SprSulF-2035
95RanCucQT-27
Schlyder, Brett
95AusFut-54
Schmack, Brian
96HicCraB-21
Schmakel, Jim
84TigWavP-31
Schmandt, Ray
20NatCarE-88
22E120-148
22W573-114
23WilChoV-143
90DodTar-1062
Schmees, George
50W720HolS-29
50WorWidGV-20
52Bow-245
53MotCoo-13
Schmelz, Al
91MetWIZ-350
Schmelz, Heinrich
87OldJudN-446
Schmid, Michael
82BurRanF-18
82BurRanT-8
Schmidt, Augie
83KnoBluJT-12
84SyrChiT-8
85PhoGiaC-194
Schmidt, Bill
40SolHug-17
91OneYanP-4170
92OneYanC-28
93OneYanC-28
93OneYanF-3523
Schmidt, Bob (Robert B.)
58GiaJayP-10
58GiaSFCB-21
58Top-468
59Top-109
59TopVen-109
60GiaJayP-12
60Top-501
61GiaJayP-12
61Pos-151
61Top-31
62SalPlaC-179
62ShiPlaC-179
62Top-262
63Top-94
65Top-582
79TCM50-246
84GiaMot-14
92YanWIZ6-109
Schmidt, Boss (Charles)
07TigACDPP-14
08RosComP-41
09T206-313
09T206-314
09TigMorPenWBPP-12
09TigTaCP-15
09WolNewDTPP-17
10CouT21-59
10CouT21-222
10DomDisP-107
10E101-39
10E102-21
10MelMinE-39
10NadCarE-43
10PeoT21-48
10SweCapPP-30A
10SweCapPP-30B
11PloCanE-56
11SpoLifCW-313
11SpoLifM-68
11T205-150
11TurRedT-116
15SpoNewM-157
Schmidt, Butcher (Charles John)
12ImpTobC-12
14CraJacE-127
15CraJacE-127
Schmidt, Curtis
92JamExpC-18
92JamExpF-1502
93WesPalBEC-21
93WesPalBEF-1339
94HarSenF-2090
Schmidt, Dave
96NewJerCB-24
Schmidt, Dave (David F.)
80TulDriT-22
82Top-418
87FleUpdG-107
91OPC-136
Schmidt, Dave (David J.)
80AshTouT-25
83Don-321
83Fle-578
83RanAffF-24
83Top-116
84Don-586
84Fle-427
84Nes792-584
84RanJarP-24
84Top-584
84TopTif-584
85Don-586
85Fle-567
85OPC-313
85RanPer-24
85Top-313
85TopMin-313
85TopTif-313
86Don-378
86Fle-571
86FleUpd-103
86OPC-79
86Top-79
86TopTif-79
86TopTra-99T
86TopTraT-99T
86WhiSoxC-24
87Don-182
87Fle-505
87FleGlo-505
87FleUpd-107
87OPC-372
87OriFreB-24
87Top-703
87TopTif-703
87TopTra-110T
87TopTraT-110T
88Don-371
88DonBasB-333
88Fle-571
88FleGlo-571
88FleMin-2
88OPC-214
88OriFreB-24
88PanSti-6
88Sco-103
88ScoGlo-103
88StaLinO-14
88Top-214
88TopSti-226
88TopTif-214
89Bow-5
89BowTif-5
89Don-13
89Don-215
89DonSupD-13
89Fle-618
89FleGlo-618
89OPC-231
89OriFreB-24
89PanSti-255
89Sco-292
89Top-677
89TopBig-130
89TopTif-677
89UppDec-447
90Bow-110
90BowTif-110
90Don-524
90ExpPos-33
90Fle-188
90FleCan-188
90FleUpd-32
90Lea-457
90OPC-497
90PubSti-585
90Sco-30
90Top-497
90TopTif-497
90TopTra-112T
90TopTraT-112T
90UppDec-641
91Fle-249
91OriCro-406
91Sco-156
91Top-136
91TopDesS-136
91TopMic-136
91TopTif-136
91UppDec-684
92CalCanS-70
93LynRedSF-2526
93RanKee-320
Schmidt, David M.
92WinHavRSC-4
92WinHavRSF-1787
Schmidt, Donnie
96PorRocB-26
Schmidt, Eric
78LodDodT-18
79CliDodT-12
86AlbYanT-21
87AlbYanP-4
88ColCliP-9
88ColCliP-313
Schmidt, Gregg
86Ft.MyeRP-24
Schmidt, Haven
58RedEnq-34
Schmidt, Henry M.
90DodTar-1063
Schmidt, J.D.
89BoiHawP-1978
Schmidt, Jason
92ClaFS7-260
92MacBraC-25
92MacBraF-267
93ClaFS7-22
93DurBulC-17
93DurBulF-485
93DurBulTI-29
94GreBraF-411
94GreBraTI-20
94TopTra-56T
94UppDecML-67
95Bow-194
95BowBes-B31
95BowBesR-B31
95Fla-329
95FleUpd-93
95RicBraRC-22
95RicBraTI-20
95SigRoo-44
95SigRooSig-44
96Bow-53
96ColCho-48
96ColChoGS-48
96ColChoSS-48
96EmoXL-148
96Fin-B268
96FinRef-B268
96Fla-209
96Fle-307
96FleBra-15
96FleTif-307
96Lea-213
96LeaPre-126
96LeaPreP-126
96LeaPrePB-213
96LeaPrePG-213
96LeaPrePS-213
96LeaSigA-205
96LeaSigAG-205
96LeaSigAS-205
96Pin-371
96PinAfi-162
96PinAfiAP-162
96PinChrBC-9
96PinFoil-371
96RicBraB-24
96RicBraUB-24
96Sco-228
96Sel-164
96SelArtP-164
96SelCer-110
96SelCerAP-110
96SelCerCB-110
96SelCerCR-110
96SelCerMB-110
96SelCerMG-110
96SelCerMR-110
96SP-20
96Spo-138
96SpoArtP-138
96StaClu-112
96StaCluMOP-112
96Stu-127
96StuPrePB-127
96StuPrePG-127
96StuPrePS-127
96Sum-184
96SumAbo&B-184
96SumArtP-184
96SumFoi-184
96TopLasBS-6
96Ult-445
96UltGolM-445
96UppDec-250
96UppDecBCP-BC16
96Zen-116
96ZenArtP-116
97Cir-203
97CirRav-203
97ColCho-436
97Fle-436
97FleTif-436
97Sco-446
97ScoHobR-446
97ScoResC-446
97ScoShoS-446
97ScoShoSAP-446
97SP-144
97Top-383
97Ult-414
97UltGolME-414
97UltPlaME-414
97UppDec-463
Schmidt, Jeff
92BoiHawC-27
92BoiHawF-3625
92ClaDraP-21
92ClaFS7-413
92FroRowDP-57
93CedRapKC-15
93CedRapKF-1734
93Pin-469
93Sco-501
93StaCluM-113
94ClaGolF-99
94LakElsSC-15
94LakElsSF-1661
95MidAngOHP-30
95MidAngTI-25
96VanCanB-25
97Fle-51
97FleTif-51
97PacPriGotD-GD7
97Ult-31
97UltGolME-31
97UltPlaME-31
Schmidt, Keith
89BluOriS-20
90WauTimB-27
90WauTimP-2141
90WauTimS-21
91Cla/Bes-59
91KanCouCC-25
91KanCouCP-2673
92KanCouCC-15
92KanCouCF-107
92KanCouCTI-28
93AlbPolF-2039

94DurBulC-16
94DurBulF-341
94DurBulTI-17
Schmidt, Mike
73OPC-615
73Top-615
74OPC-283
74PhiJohP-20
74Top-283
75Hos-133
75Kel-56
75OPC-70
75OPC-307
75Top-70
75Top-307
76CraDis-54
76Hos-84
76OPC-193
76OPC-480
76SSP-470
76Top-193
76Top-480
77BurCheD-168
77Hos-43
77MSADis-55
77OPC-2
77OPC-245
77PepGloD-70
77RCColC-58
77Spo-3402
77Spo-8124
77Top-2
77Top-140
77TopCloS-41
78Hos-113
78Kel-3
78OPC-225
78PhiSSP-46
78RCColC-18
78SSP270-46
78Top-360
78WifBalD-67
79Hos-9
79OPC-323
79PhiBurK-16
79PhiTeal-9
79Top-610
80Kel-2
80OPC-141
80PerHaloFP-223
80PhiBurK-6
80Top-270
80TopSup-2
81AllGamPI-126
81CokTeaS-105
81Don-11
81Don-590
81Dra-7
81Fle-5
81Fle-640
81Fle-640B
81Fle-645
81Fle-645B
81FleStiC-9
81FleStiC-43
81FleStiC-128
81Kel-5
81MSAMinD-28
81OPC-207
81PerAll-8
81PerCreC-2
81Squ-8
81Top-2
81Top-3
81Top-206
81Top-540
81TopScr-60
81TopSti-19
81TopSti-21
81TopSti-199
81TopSti-254
81TopSupHT-88
81TopSupN-13
82Don-294
82Don-585
82Dra-29
82FBIDis-20
82Fle-258
82Fle-637
82Fle-641
82FleSta-53
82K-M-39
82K-M-41
82Kel-16
82MonNew-14
82OPC-100
82OPC-101
82OPC-339
82PerAll-17
82PerAllG-17
82PerCreC-3
82PerCreCG-3
82Squ-14
82Top-100
82Top-101
82Top-162
82Top-163
82Top-339
82TopSti-3
82TopSti-5
82TopSti-74
82TopSti-123
83AllGamPI-125
83Don-168
83DonActA-57
83Dra-25
83Fle-173
83FleSta-173
83FleSti-145
83FleSti-170
83Kel-58
83OPC-300
83OPC-301
83OPC-342
83PerAll-16
83PerAllG-16
83PerCreC-14
83PerCreCG-14
83PhiPosGM-5
83PhiPosGPaM-10
83PhiTas-27
83StaSch-1
83StaSch-2
83StaSch-3
83StaSch-4
83StaSch-5
83StaSch-6
83StaSch-7
83StaSch-8
83StaSch-9
83StaSch-10
83StaSch-11
83StaSch-12
83StaSch-13
83StaSch-14
83StaSch-15
83Top-300
83Top-301
83Top-399
83TopFol-2
83TopGloS-8
83TopSti-10
83TopSti-172
83TopSti-270
83TopStiB-3
84AllGamPI-35
84Don-23
84Don-23A
84Don-183
84DonActAS-57
84DonCha-11
84Dra-28
84Fle-48
84FleSti-16
84FleSti-35
84FleSti-48
84FraGloT-1
84FunFooP-11
84MilBra-23
84Nes792-132
84Nes792-388
84Nes792-700
84Nes792-703
84NesDreT-14
84OCoandSI-69
84OCoandSI-87
84OPC-361
84OPC-388
84PhiTas-6
84PhiTas-33
84RalPur-22
84SevCoi-C4
84SevCoi-E4
84SevCoi-W4
84Top-132
84Top-388
84Top-700
84Top-703
84TopCer-22
84TopGaloC-11
84TopGloA-15
84TopGloS-39
84TopRubD-23
84TopSti-101
84TopSti-117
84TopSti-188
84TopSup-6
84TopTif-132
84TopTif-388
84TopTif-700
84TopTif-703
85AllGamPI-125
85CirK-19
85Don-61
85DonActA-17
85Dra-29
85Fle-265
85Fle-627
85Fle-630
85FleLimE-33
85FleStaS-17
85FleStaS-34
85FleStaS-74
85FleStaS-75
85FleStaS-76
85FleStaS-77
85FleStaS-78
85FleStaS-79
85GenMilS-9
85KASDis-12
85KitCloD-12
85Lea-205
85OPC-67
85PhiCIG-4
85PhiTas-11
85PhiTas-33
85SevCoi-C4
85SevCoi-E16
85SevCoi-W1
85SpoPro-2
85SpoSam-1
85ThoMcAD-42
85Top-500
85Top-714
85Top3-D-1
85TopGaloC-10
85TopGloA-4
85TopGloS-23
85TopMin-500
85TopRubD-9
85TopSti-94
85TopSti-111
85TopSti-193
85TopSup-12
85TopTif-500
85TopTif-714
86BasStaB-99
86BurKinA-5
86Don-61
86DonHig-4
86DonHig-36
86DorChe-8
86Dra-26
86Fle-450
86FleLimE-41
86FleMin-94
86FleSlu-33
86FleStiC-107
86FraGloT-4
86FraGloT-5
86GenMilB-4H
86Lea-51
86MeaGolBB-14
86MeaGolM-11
86MeaGolSB-16
86MSAJifPD-17
86OPC-200
86PhiCIG-10
86PhiKel-5
86PhiTas-20
86QuaGra-14
86SevCoi-C5
86SevCoi-E5
86SevCoi-S5
86SevCoi-W5
86Spo-44
86Spo-62
86Spo-68
86Spo-139
86Spo-148
86SpoDecG-55
86Top-200
86Top3-D-24
86TopGloS-17
86TopMinL-55
86TopSti-114
86TopSup-49
86TopTat-7
86TopTif-200
86TruVal-28
86Woo-30
87BoaandB-1
87BurKinA-17
87ClaGam-62
87ClaUpdY-101
87Don-139
87DonAll-17
87DonHig-2
87DonOpeD-160
87DonP-17
87Dra-23
87Fle-187
87FleAll-6
87FleAwaW-36
87FleBasA-40
87FleGamW-40
87FleGlo-187
87FleHotS-35
87FleLeaL-40
87FleLimE-37
87FleMin-97
87FleRecS-35
87FleSlu-37
87FleStiC-107
87FleWaxBC-C15
87GenMilB-5H
87HosSti-13
87K-M-31
87KayB-29
87KraFoo-30
87Lea-122
87MandMSL-3
87MSAIceTD-11
87MSAJifPD-16
87OPC-396
87PhiCha-4
87PhiTas-20
87RalPur-14
87RedFolSB-46
87Spo-30
87Spo-115
87Spo-156
87SpoDeaP-1
87SpoSupD-4
87SpoTeaP-6
87StuPan-9
87Top-430
87Top-597
87TopCoi-43
87TopGaloC-10
87TopGloA-4
87TopGloS-28
87TopMinL-30
87TopSti-116
87TopSti-160
87TopTif-430
87TopTif-597
87Woo-8
88CheBoy-14
88ClaRed-167
88Don-330
88DonAll-39
88DonBasB-271
88DonBonM-BC4
88DonPop-17
88Dra-8
88Fle-315
88Fle-636
88FleAwaW-35
88FleBasA-36
88FleBasM-31
88FleExcS-34
88FleGlo-315
88FleGlo-636
88FleHotS-34
88FleLeaL-35
88FleMin-102
88FleRecS-35
88FleSlu-36
88FleStiC-111
88FleSup-33
88FleTeaL-34
88FleWaxBC-C11
88GreBasS-23
88K-M-25
88KayB-27
88KinDis-1
88Lea-124
88MSAFanSD-19
88MSAIceTD-16
88Nes-6
88OPC-321
88OPCBoxB-O
88PanSti-234
88PanSti-360
88PanSti-429
88PhiTas-23
88RedFolSB-79
88Sco-16
88Sco-657
88ScoBoxC-13
88ScoGlo-16
88ScoGlo-657
88Spo-35
88Spo-180
88SpoGam-21
88StaLinAl-30
88StaLinPh-16
88StaMat/S-1
88StaMat/S-2
88StaMat/S-4
88StaMat/S-6
88StaMat/S-8
88StaMat/S-10
88Top-600
88TopBig-88
88TopCoi-53
88TopGloA-15
88TopGloS-3
88TopMinL-67
88TopRitTM-8
88TopSti-9
88TopSti-125
88TopSti-149
88TopStiB-8
88TopTif-600
88TopUKM-67
88TopUKMT-67
88TopWaxBC-O
88Woo-7
89Bow-402
89BowTif-402
89CadEllD-51
89CerSup-4
89ClaLigB-48
89ClaTraP-153
89Don-193
89Fle-582
89FleGlo-582
89FleSup-36
89FleUpd-131
89KayB-27
89OPC-100
89OPCBoxB-L
89PanSti-3
89PanSti-153
89PhiTas-32
89RedFolSB-104
89Sco-149
89ScoHot1S-76
89Spo-21
89SpollIFKI-90
89Top-100
89Top-489
89TopAme2C-27
89TopBasT-72
89TopBig-220
89TopCapC-16
89TopHeaUT-24
89TopSti-120
89TopTif-100
89TopTif-489
89TopUKM-70
89TopWaxBC-L
89TVSpoM-32
89UppDec-406
89UppDec-684
90AGFA-21
90BasWit-39
90Don-643
90HOFStiB-94
90OPC-662
90PhiTas-32
90PhiTas-36
90PubSti-250
90Top-662
90TopTif-662
90UppDec-20
91BasBesRB-16
91Cla/Bes-1

91Cla/Bes-AU1
91ClaGolB-BC1
91UppDecS-2
92ClaFS7-100
92DEL-AU4
92KelAll-10
92PhiDaiN-7
92TVSpoMF5HRC-13
93UppDecS-12
94TedWil-75
94TedWil-141
94TedWil-151
94TedWil5C-7
94TedWilMS-MS1
94TedWilMS-MS2
94TedWilMS-MS3
94TedWilMS-MS4
94TedWilMS-MS5
94TedWilMS-MS6
94TedWilMS-MS7
94TedWilMS-MS8
94Yoo-15
95ColCho-50
95ColChoGS-50
95ColChoSS-50
95JimDeaAG-4
95Phi-29
95SP-4
95SPCha-112
95SPChaDC-112
95SPSil-4
95UppDec-450
95UppDecC-5B
95UppDecED-450
95UppDecEDG-450
95UppDecSE-208
95UppDecSEG-208
95UppDecSHoB-5

Schmidt, Milt
43ParSpo-3

Schmidt, Pete
87BelMarL-10

Schmidt, Todd
96BesAutSA-67

Schmidt, Tom
92BenRocC-21
92BenRocF-1482
93CenValRC-22
93CenValRF-2902
93Top-433
93TopGol-433
93TopInaM-433
93TopMic-433
94Bow-114
94CenValRC-23
94CenValRF-3213
95NewHavRTI-34
96JacSunB-26

Schmidt, Walter
20WalMaiW-46
21Nei-113
22E120-223
22W572-91
22W573-115
92ConTSN-571

Schmidt, Willard
53CarHunW-20
53Top-168
56Top-323
57Top-206
58RedEnq-35
58Top-214
59RedEnq-23
59Top-171
59TopVen-171
62KahAtl-19
79TCM50-153
91TopArc1-168

Schmitt, Chris
93HelBreF-4094
93HelBreSP-23
94BelBreC-24
94BelBreF-100
96DurBulBIB-19
96DurBulBrB-20

Schmitt, Todd
92SpoIndC-7
92SpoIndF-1293
93WatDiaC-26
93WatDiaF-1768
94RanCucQC-23
94RanCucQF-1639
95Exc-287
95MemChiTI-20

Schmittou, Larry
79NaSouTI-22
89NasSouTI-28
95NasSouTI-22

Schmittou, Mike
89TenTecGE-24

Schmitz, Dan
79WesHavYT-5
80NasSouTI-19
81ColCliP-6
82ColCliP-6
82ColCliT-16
82NasSouTI-21
83TidTidT-17
84TolMudHT-7
85VisOakT-25
86VisOakP-18

Schmitz, John
47Exh-202
47TipTop-116
49Bow-52
49EurSta-70
49Lea-48
50Bow-24
51Bow-69
51TopBluD-41
52Bow-224
52NatTeaL-30
52Top-136
53Bri-17
54Top-33
55Bow-105
55Top-159
56Top-298
56TopHocF-A16
56TopHocF-B18
79DiaGre-113
83TopRep5-136
85TCMPla1-30
90DodTar-709
91OriCro-407
94TopArc1-33
94TopArc1G-33
95TopArcBD-9

Schmitz, Mike
93OneYanC-19
93OneYanF-3514
94GreBatF-486
97GreBatC-20

Schmutz, Charlie
90DodTar-1064

Schnacke, Ken
92ColCliP-1
93ColCliP-25

Schneck, Dave
76IndIndTI-15
91MetWIZ-351

Schneider, Brian
95TopTra-122T

Schneider, Dan
94EveGiaC-26
94EveGiaF-3654
95BurBeeTI-20

Schneider, Dan Louis
63Top-299
64Top-351
64TopVen-351
65Top-366
67Top-543
68OPC-57
68Top-57
68TopVen-57
69Top-656
87AstShoSTw-29

Schneider, Herm
95WhiSoxK-27

Schneider, Jeff
80RocRedWT-10
81RocRedWW-7
82SpoIndT-7
82Top-21
83SyrChiT-11
91OriCro-408
94St.CatBJC-20
94St.CatBJF-3642

Schneider, Paul
83WauTimF-19
86ChaLooP-22
86SouLeaAJ-20
87CalCanP-2316
88CalCanC-2
88CalCanP-793

Schneider, Pete
16FleBreD-83

Schneider, Phil
93BenRocC-23
93BenRocF-3268
94NewHavRF-1548
95NewHavRTI-18
95Top-648

Schneider, Tom
93JamExpC-21
93JamExpF-3326
94BurBeeC-23
94BurBeeF-1081

Schnittker, Dick
51BerRos-A12

Schnoor, Chuck
82LynMetT-14

Schnur, Curt
95DanBraTI-26

Schnurbusch, Chris
88FayGenP-1097
89CedRapRB-16
89CedRapRP-934
89CedRapRS-17

Schober, Dave
84MadMusP-3
85MadMusP-23
85MadMusT-25
86MadMusP-25
86MadMusP-20
87MadMusP-23
87MadMusP-2
89HunStaB-19

Schoch, R.F.
87OldJudN-447

Schock, Will (William)
88HunStaTI-17
88MadMusP-21
88MidLeaAGS-54
89HunStaB-2
90Bes-197
90HunStaB-9
91LinDriAAA-544
91TacTigLD-544
91TacTigP-2304

Schockman, Mark
85NewOriT-16

Schoen, Jerry
69PilPos-19
91BenBucC-14
91BenBucP-3704

Schoendienst, Kevin
81QuaCitCT-10

Schoendienst, Red (Albert)
46SeaSLP-43
47Exh-203A
47Exh-203B
47Exh-203C
48Bow-38
49Bow-111
49EurSta-197
50Bow-71
50JJKCopP-17
51Bow-10
51FisBakL-25
51R42SmaS-97
51TopBluB-6
52BasPho-5
52BerRos-60
52Bow-30
52DixLid-19
52DixPre-19
52RedMan-NL19
52StaCalL-81A
52StaCalS-93B
52TipTop-37
52Top-91
53BowC-101
53CarHunW-21
53DixLid-19
53DixPre-19
53MacSta-4
53NorBreL-28
53RedMan-NL12
53Top-78
54Bow-110
54CarHunW-24
54DanDee-22
54DixLid-15
54RedHeaF-27
54RedMan-NL10
54Wil-16
55Bow-29
55CarHunW-23
55RedMan-NL18
55RobGouS-3
55RobGouW-3
56Top-165
56YelBasP-28
57BraSpiaS4-17
57Top-154
58BraJayP-11
58Top-190
59Top-480
60BraJayP-10
60BraLaktL-23
60BraSpiaS-21
60MacSta-22
60NuHi-25
60Top-335
61NuSco-425
61Pos-111
61Top-505
62SalPlaC-151
62ShiPlaC-151
62Top-575
65CarJayP-8
65CarTeal-20
65Top-556
66CarCoi-12
66CarTeal-9
66OPC-76
66Top-76
66TopVen-76
67Top-512
67TopVen-297
68Top-294
68TopVen-294
69Top-462
70CarTeal-10
70OPC-346
70Top-346
71CarTeal-32
71OPC-239
71Top-239
72OPC-67
72Top-67
73OPC-497
73Top-497A
73Top-497B
74LauAllG-50
74OPC-236
74Top-236
75OPC-246
75Top-246
76GrePlaG-32
76OPC-581
76SSP-300
76Top-581
78BraTCC-11
79Car5-24
79TCM50-94
80PerHaloFP-203
81Car5x7-24
81Don-431
81TCM60I-395
83Car-27
83CarGreT-12
83TopRep5-91
84Car-27
84Car5x7-25
84TCMPla1-24
85CarTeal-29
86CarTeal-38
87Bra195T-5
88PacLegI-2
88ScoBoxC-T5
88Top-351
88TopTif-351
90PerGreM-55
90TopTra-113T
90TopTraT-113T
91TopArc1-78
91UppDecS-14
92BazQua5A-11
92CarMcD-21
92UppDecS-11
93ActPacA-114
93ActPacA2-48G
93ActPacAC-4
94TedWil-83
96IllLot-4

Schoeneck, Jumbo (Louis N.)
87OldJudN-448

Schoeneweis, Scott
96LakElsSB-11
97Bow-370
97BowInt-370

Schoenhaus, Ted
76CedRapGT-27

Schoenvogel, Chad
91FroRowDP-3
91FroRowDPP-4
92ClaFS7-325
92StaCluD-166
92WinHavRSC-16
92WinHavRSF-1777

Schofield, Andy
96NewJerCB-25

Schofield, Dick (Richard C.)
54CarHunW-25
55CarHunW-24
58Top-106
59Top-68
59TopVen-68
60KeyChal-42
60Top-104
60TopVen-104
61Kah-39
61Top-453
62Top-484
63PirIDL-21
63Top-34
64PirKDK-23
64Top-284
64TopVen-284
65OPC-218
65Top-218
66OPC-156
66Top-156
66Top-474
67Top-381
68Top-588
69OPC-18
69Top-18
70OPC-251
70Top-251
71MLBOffS-282
71OPC-396
71Top-396
72MilBra-310
78TCM60I-199
81RedSoxBG2S-109
82DanSunF-27
84AllGamPI-114
84AngSmo-25
84Don-35
84FleUpd-105
84TopTra-107T
84TopTraT-107T
85AngSmo-13
85Don-329
85Fle-311
85Top-138
85Top-629
85TopTif-138
85TopTif-629
86AngSmo-13
86Don-133
86Fle-167
86OPC-311
86Top-311
86TopTif-311
87AngSmo-15
87Don-283
87DonOpeD-4
87Fle-92
87FleGlo-92
87OPC-54
87SevCoi-W9
87Top-502
87TopSti-176
87TopTif-502
88AngSmo-16
88Don-233
88DonBasB-195
88Fle-504
88FleGlo-504
88Lea-178
88OPC-43
88PanSti-45
88RedFolSB-80
88Sco-274
88ScoGlo-274
88StaLinAn-18
88Top-43
88TopBig-204
88TopSti-177
88TopTif-43
89Bow-46
89BowTif-46
89Don-108

89DonBasB-251
89Fle-488
89FleGlo-488
89OPC-286
89PanSti-294
89Sco-16
89Top-477
89TopBig-53
89TopSti-174
89TopTif-477
89UppDec-201
90AngSmo-15
90Bow-291
90BowTif-291
90DodTar-710
90Don-288
90DonBesA-131
90Fle-144
90FleCan-144
90Lea-419
90OPC-189
90PubSti-379
90Sco-44
90Top-189
90TopBig-211
90TopTif-189
90UppDec-669
91AngSmo-14
91Bow-191
91Don-262
91Fle-325
91Lea-59
91OPC-736
91PanFreS-183
91Sco-776
91StaClu-59
91Top-736
91TopDesS-736
91TopMic-736
91TopTif-736
91Ult-52
91UppDec-169
92Don-44
92Fle-69
92FleUpd-105
92Lea-419
92MetKah-11
92OPC-230
92PanSti-8
92Pin-338
92Sco-552
92ScoRoo-26T
92StaClu-16
92StaClu-738
92Top-230
92TopGol-230
92TopGolW-230
92TopMic-230
92TopTra-101T
92TopTraG-101T
92Ult-30
92Ult-538
92UppDec-269
92UppDec-791
92YanWIZ6-110
93BluJayD-23
93BluJayDM-30
93BluJayFS-24
93Fle-94
93Lea-382
93OPCPre-129
93PacSpa-202
93Top-79
93TopGol-79
93TopInaM-79
93TopMic-79
93Ult-646
93UppDec-768
93UppDecGold-768
94BluJayUSPC-10S
94BreMilB-77
94ColC-569
94ColChoGS-569
94ColChoSS-569
94Fle-341
94Lea-211
94StaClu-234
94StaCluFDI-234
94StaCluGR-234
94StaCluMOP-234
94StaCluT-160
94StaCluTFDI-160
94TopArc1-191
94TopArc1G-191
95ColCho-153
95ColChoGS-153
95ColChoSS-153
95Fle-103
96AngMot-27

Schofield, Ducky (John R.)
54Top-191
55Top-143
66TopVen-156
85Top-138
85TopTif-138

Schofield, John
86KinEagP-23
87PorChaRP-2

Scholan, Jarrod
96DayCubB-30

Scholzen, Jeffrey
91PocPioP-3791
91PocPioSP-22

Schooler, Aaron
94EliTwiC-22
94EliTwiF-3732

Schooler, Mike (Michael)
86WauTimP-21
87ChaLooB-8
88CalCanC-9
88CalCanP-795
88ScoRoo-91T
88ScoRooG-91T
88TopTra-105T
88TopTraT-105T
89ChaLooLITI-27
89Don-637
89Fle-559
89FleGlo-559
89MarMot-25
89Sco-528
89ScoHot1R-73
89ScoYouS2-34
89Top-199
89TopTif-199
89ToyRoo-27
89UppDec-28
90Bow-470
90BowTif-470
90ClaBlu-79
90Don-330
90DonBesA-82
90Fle-525
90FleCan-525
90Lea-258
90MarMot-21
90OPC-681
90PanSti-151
90RedFolSB-84
90Sco-149
90Spo-187
90Top-681
90TopBig-235
90TopMinL-35
90TopSti-228
90TopTif-681
90UppDec-214
91Bow-241
91Don-302
91Fle-461
91Lea-230
91MarCouH-25
91OPC-365
91PanFreS-236
91PanSti-184
91RedFolS-85
91Sco-489
91SevCoi-NW15
91StaClu-508
91Top-365
91TopDesS-365
91TopMic-365
91TopTif-365
91UppDec-638
92Bow-336
92Don-444
92Fle-292
92MarMot-10
92OPC-28
92Pin-171
92Sco-654
92StaClu-313
92Top-28
92TopGol-28
92TopGolW-28
92TopMic-28
92UppDec-405
93Don-449
93Fle-313
93OklCit8F-1626
93OPC-350
93RanKee-432
93Sco-544
93Sel-392
93StaClu-198
93StaCluFDI-198
93StaCluMOP-198
93Top-258
93TopGol-258
93TopInaM-258
93TopMic-258
93Ult-271
94WicWraF-189
95MidAngOHP-31
95MidAngTI-26

Schoon, Peter
90IBAWorA-7

Schoonmaker, Jerry
56Top-216
57Top-334

Schoonover, Gary
87BriYouC-19
88IdaFalBP-1836
89BurBraP-1602
89BurBraS-20

Schoppee, Dave
81BriRedST-9
83PawRedST-10

Schorr, Bill
88ButCopKSP-8

Schorr, Bradley
91KinMetC-22
91KinMetP-3812
92ColMetC-5
92ColMetF-296
92ColMetPI-20
93St.LucMC-23
94St.LucMC-21
94St.LucMF-1195
93StLucMF-2921

Schorzman, Steve
96BriWhiSB-28

Schott, Arthur Eugene
36R31PasP-21
38CinOraW-25

Schott, Marge
93RedKah-25

Schottzie, Schottzie
91RedKah-0
92RedKah-2
94RedKah-28
95RedKah-29

Schourek, Pete
88LitFalMP-22
89ColMetB-14
89ColMetGS-24
90MetColP-47
90St.LucMS-25
90TexLeaAGS-33
90TopTVM-59
91Bow-482
91FleUpd-104
91LeaGolR-BC15
91MetColP-45
91MetKah-48
91OPCPre-106
91ScoRoo-87T
91TopTra-106T
91TopTraT-106T
91UppDec-766
92Don-535
92Fle-516
92Lea-176
92MetColP-27
92OPC-287
92OPCPre-58
92Pin-141
92Sco-332
92Sco100RS-20
92SkyAAAF-255
92StaClu-521
92TidTidS-570
92Top-287
92TopDeb91-158
92TopGol-287
92TopGolW-287
92TopMic-287
92Ult-539
92UppDec-673
93Don-198
93Fle-95
93MetColP-45
93MetKah-48
93PacSpa-203
93Pin-324
93StaClu-238
93StaCluFDI-238
93StaCluMOP-238
93Top-352
93TopGol-352
93TopInaM-352
93TopMic-352
93Ult-433
93UppDec-658
93UppDecGold-658
94Don-652
94Fle-577
94MetShuST-6
94RedKah-29
94StaClu-439
94StaCluFDI-439
94StaCluGR-439
94StaCluMOP-439
94Top-699
94TopGol-699
94TopSpa-699
94TriPla-149
95ColCho-423
95ColChoGS-423
95ColChoSS-423
95DonTopotO-220
95Emo-120
95Fla-125
95Fle-448
95Pin-430
95PinArtP-430
95PinMusC-430
95RedKah-30
95Top-484
95TopCyb-276
95Ult-371
95UltGolM-371
95UppDec-167
95UppDecED-167
95UppDecEDG-167
96ColCho-114
96ColCho-372T
96ColChoGS-114
96ColChoSS-114
96Don-85
96DonPreP-85
96EmoXL-169
96Fin-B137
96FinRef-B137
96Fla-239
96Fle-353
96FleTif-353
96Lea-86
96LeaPrePB-86
96LeaPrePG-86
96LeaPrePS-86
96MetUni-152
96MetUniP-152
96Pac-43
96PanSti-50
96Pin-70
96Pin-216
96PinAfi-74
96PinAfiAP-74
96PinAfiFPP-74
96PinArtP-94
96PinArtP-116
96PinFoil-216
96PinSta-94
96PinSta-116
96Sco-190
96Sel-84
96SelArtP-84
96SP-64
96Spo-86
96SpoArtP-86
96StaClu-396
96StaCluEPB-396
96StaCluEPG-396
96StaCluEPS-396
96StaCluMOP-396
96Sum-42
96SumAbo&B-42
96SumArtP-42
96SumFoi-42
96Top-112
96TopGal-49
96TopGalPPI-49
96Ult-183
96UltGolM-183
96UppDec-46
96UppDecPHE-H47
96UppDecPreH-H47
97Cir-161
97CirRav-161
97ColCho-83
97Fin-49
97FinRef-49
97Fle-304
97FleTif-304
97Sco-458
97ScoHobR-458
97ScoResC-458
97ScoShoS-458
97ScoShoSAP-458
97StaClu-323
97StaCluMOP-323
97Top-349
97UppDec-47

Schramka, Paul
77FriOneYW-14

Schramm, Carl
91GenCubC-27
91GenCubP-4213
92PeoChiC-8
92PeoChiTI-24
93DayCubC-16
93DayCubF-856
96SanJosGB-23

Schreckengost, Ossie
03BreE10-126
04FanCraAL-42
08AmeCarE-23
08RosComP-65
09T206-464

Schreiber, Bruce
89PriPirS-20
89Sta-174
90CarLeaA-23
90SalBucS-20
90StaFS7-1
91CarMudLD-116
91CarMudP-1094
91Cla/Bes-225
91LinDriAA-116
92CarMudF-1189
92SalBucC-5
93CarMudF-2064
93CarMudTI-5
94CarMudF-1588

Schreiber, Hank
20RedWorCP-21

Schreiber, Marty
84DurBulT-27
85DurBulT-12
86OscAstP-22

Schreiber, Paul
92CalLeaACL-24

Schreiber, Paul Frederick
54Top-217
75YanDyn1T-42
94TopArc1-217
94TopArc1G-217

Schreiber, Stan
96AugGreB-27

Schreiber, Ted
76Met63 S-12
77FriOneYW-103
91MetWIZ-352

Schreimann, Eric
94MarPhiF-3298
95MarPhiTI-22
96PieBolWB-24

Schreiner, John
91BasCitRC-21
91BasCitRP-1407

Schreiser, Andre
52LavPro-82

Schrenk, Steve
88SouBenWSGS-26
89SouBenWSGS-15
90Bes-104
90SouBenWSB-16
90SouBenWSGS-16
92SarWhiSCB-15
92SarWhiSF-207
93ExcFS7-155
94NasSouF-1252
95Bow-47
96NasSouB-22

Schriver, Pop (William)
63GadFunC-13
87OldJudN-449
98CamPepP-66

Schroder, Bob

65Top-589
Schroeck, Bob
82ElPasDT-16
83ElPasDT-24
84ElPasDT-3
Schroeder, Bill (Alfred W.)
81ElPasDT-13
82VanCanT-3
84BrePol-21
84Don-515
84Nes792-738
84Top-738
84TopTif-738
85BreGar-18
85BrePol-21
85Don-124
85Fle-594
85Top-176
85TopTif-176
86BrePol-21
86Don-211
86Fle-501
86Top-662
86TopTif-662
87BrePol-21
87BreTeal-12
87Don-486
87DonOpeD-49
87Fle-357
87FleGlo-357
87Top-302
87TopTif-302
88BrePol-21
88Don-419
88Fle-173
88FleGlo-173
88Sco-311
88ScoGlo-311
88StaLinBre-16
88Top-12
88TopTif-12
89Bow-44
89BowTif-44
89Don-644
89Top-563
89TopTif-563
89UppDec-627A
89UppDec-627B
90Don-567
90El PasDAGTI-18
90OPC-244
90Sco-362
90Top-244
90TopTif-244
90UppDec-149
91OPC-452
91Top-452
91TopDesS-452
91TopMic-452
91TopTif-452
94BreMilB-176
Schroeder, Jay
83KinBluJTI-23
Schroeder, John
94SigRooDP-85
94SigRooDPS-85
96ForWayWB-23
Schroeder, Scott A.
96IdaFalB-22
Schroeder, Todd
91WelPirC-3
91WelPirP-3582
92AugPirC-6
92SalBucC-20
92SalBucF-72
Schroeffel, Scott
96PorRocB-27
Schroll, Al
55Bow-319
57SeaPop-33
59Top-546
60Lea-95
60Top-357
62Top-102
62TopVen-102
Schrom, Dave
80VenLeaS-78
Schrom, Ken
77QuaCitAT-24
80SalLakCGT-7
81Fle-425
81OPC-238
81SyrChiT-21
81SyrChiTI-18
81Top-577
82SyrChiT-7
82SyrChiTI-19
83TolMudHT-9
84Don-72
84Fle-572
84MinTwiP-25
84Nes792-11
84Nes792-322
84OPC-322
84Top-11
84Top-322
84TopSti-308
84TopTif-11
84TopTif-322
84TwiTeal-13
85Don-486
85Fle-288
85OPC-161
85Top-161
85TopTif-161
85TwiTeal-13
86Don-635
86Fle-403
86FleUpd-104
86IndOhH-18
86IndTeal-37
86OPC-71
86Top-71
86TopTif-71
86TopTra-100T
86TopTraT-100T
87Don-403
87DonAll-53
87Fle-258
87FleGlo-258
87FleMin-98
87IndGat-18
87OPC-171
87Spo-107
87SpoTeaP-3
87Top-635
87TopSti-204
87TopTif-635
88Don-501
88Fle-614
88FleGlo-614
88OPC-256
88Sco-574
88ScoGlo-574
88StaLinI-17
88Top-256
88TopTif-256
90El PasDAGTI-36
Schu, Rick
84PorBeaC-209
85Don-448
85FleUpd-100
85PhiTas-43
85PorBeaC-34
85TopTifT-104T
85TopTra-104T
86Don-570
86Fle-451
86OPC-16
86PhiTas-15
86SevCoi-E9
86Top-16
86TopSti-122
86TopTif-16
87Don-509
87Fle-188
87FleGlo-188
87PhiTas-15
87Top-209
87TopTif-209
88Don-432
88Fle-316
88FleGlo-316
88OriFreB-25
88Sco-448
88ScoGlo-448
88StaLinPh-17
88Top-731
88TopBig-122
88TopTif-731
89Don-406
89Fle-619
89FleGlo-619
89OPC-352
89RedFolSB-105
89RocRedWC-23
89RocRedWP-1642
89Sco-452
89TigMar-35
89Top-352
89TopBig-164
89TopTif-352
89TopTra-112T
89TopTraT-112T
89UppDec-490
90Don-599
90OPC-498
90Top-498
90TopTif-498
91Fle-326
91LinDriAAA-495
91OriCro-409
91ScrRedBLD-495
91ScrRedBP-2547
92ScrRedBF-2456
92ScrRedBS-493
92SkyAAAF-223
92TriA AAS-493
Schubert, Brian
90NiaFalRP-24
Schuble, Henry
32R33So2-411
33Gou-4
33GouCanV-4
35GouPuzR-5F
35GouPuzR-6F
35GouPuzR-11H
35GouPuzR-13F
35TigFreP-18
76TigOldTS-20
Schuckert, Wayne
81AppFoxT-12
82AppFoxF-18
83GleFalWST-19
Schueler, Ron
73OPC-169
73Top-169
74OPC-544
74PhiJohP-37
74Top-544
74TopTra-544T
75OPC-292
75Top-292
76OPC-586
76Top-586
77Top-337
78SSP270-138
78Top-409
79Top-686
84A'sMot-27
Schueler, Russ
87BurExpP-1080
Schuerholz, John
82Roy-19
83Roy-25
Schuermann, Lance
91ButCopKSP-16
92Ft.MyeMCB-24
92Ft.MyeMF-2746
93ChaRanC-20
93ChaRanF-1941
94TulDriF-245
94TulDriTI-22
96BowBayB-25
Schugel, Jeff
84VisOakT-14
85VisOakT-6
Schula, Kevin
92IdaFalGF-3516
Schuler, Dave
77WatIndT-19
79SalLakCGT-17A
80SalLakCGT-6
81SalLakCGT-11
82OmaRoyT-8
83OmaRoyT-9
85RicBraT-8
86OmaRoyP-19
86OmaRoyT-19
87DenZepP-11
88VerMarP-941
90Ft.LauYS-24
91PriWilCC-25
91PriWilCP-1443
92PriWilCF-166
93AlbYanF-2179
94AbaYanF-1459
96SanJosGB-29
78STLakCGC-20
Schuler, David
89Ft.LauYS-29
96WesOahCHWB-17
Schulhofer, Adam
92GenCubC-7
92GenCubF-1560
93PeoChiC-18
93PeoChiF-1084
Schullstrom, Erik
88AlaGolTI-16
89FreStaBS-19
92ClaFS7-121
92HagSunF-2555
92HagSunS-268
92SkyAA F-112
93BowBayF-2189
94NasXprF-386
95Ult-306
95UltGolM-306
96Pac-359
96PawRedSDD-26
96TreThuB-15
Schulmerich, Wes
34DiaMatCSB-161
34ExhFou-6
34Gou-54
83ConMar-30
88ConNatA-17
Schult, Art
53Top-167
58Top-58A
58Top-58B
60Lea-123
60Top-93
60TopVen-93
79TCM50-253
91TopArc1-167
Schulte, Fred
28Exh-60
29ExhFou-30
29PorandAR-80
31Exh-29
33Gou-112
33Gou-190
34BatR31-50
35DiaMatCS3T1-129
35ExhFou-16
79DiaGre-52
91ConTSN-286
91ConTSN-304
Schulte, Joe
86AshTouP-26
87OscAstP-14
Schulte, John
90HigSchPLS-12
90WelPirP-9
92AugPirC-15
92AugPirF-254
Schulte, John C.
33Gou-186
40PlaBal-12
43YanSta-23
75YanDyn1T-43
94ConTSN-1046
94ConTSNB-1046
Schulte, Len
96Bro194F-8
Schulte, Mark
84ArkTraT-13
86ArkTraP-22
87Ft.MyeRP-12
Schulte, Rich
91AubAstC-10
91AubAstP-4287
92BurAstC-24
92BurAstF-559
93OscAstC-19
93OscAstF-640
Schulte, Todd
83BurRanF-2
83BurRanT-10
Schulte, Troy
93AubAstC-21
93AubAstF-3442
94AubAstC-17
94AubAstF-3758
95AubAstTI-17
Schulte, Wildfire (Frank)
07CubA.CDPP-11
07CubGFGCP-11
08AmeCarE-24
08AmeCarE-61
08RosComP-107
09ColChiE-256
09MaxPubP-10
09MaxPubP-21
09RamT20-106
09SpoNewSM-66
09T206-315
09T206-316
10ChiE-8
10CouT21-223
10CouT21-316
10DomDisP-108
10RedCroT-67
10RedCroT-154
10RedCroT-241
10SweCapPP-90
11BasBatEU-32
11S74Sil-68
11SpoLifCW-314
11SpoLifM-181
11T205-151
11TurRedT-117
12ColRedB-256
12ColTinT-256
12HasTriFT-66
12T207-163
13PolGroW-25
14CraJacE-101
14FatPlaT-45
15CraJacE-101
15SpoNewM-158
15VicT21-25
16BF2FP-69
16ColE13-152
16SpoNewM-156
19W514-10
87Cub190T-7
Schultea, Chris
92SalLakTSP-12
Schultea, Matt
95OdgRapTI-26
Schultz, Barney (George)
62CubJayP-10
62Top-89
62TopStal-110
62TopVen-89
63Top-452
65OPC-28
65Top-28
71CarTeal-33
73OPC-497
73Top-497A
73Top-497B
74OPC-236
74Top-236
78TCM60I-15
Schultz, Bob D.
52Top-401
53Top-144
54Bow-59
83TopRep5-401
91TopArc1-144
Schultz, Bobby
77Car5-24
91BurIndP-3317
Schultz, Buddy (Charles)
77CarTeal-23
78CarTeal-19
78Top-301
79Car5-25
79Top-532
80Top-601
82ArkTraT-9
Schultz, Carl
93DanBraF-3617
94CarLeaAF-CAR30
Schultz, Greg
83AlbDukT-18
84AlbDukC-157
85PhoGiaC-196
Schultz, Howie
90DodTar-711
Schultz, Joseph C. Jr.
46SeaSLP-47
47TipTop-72
62KahAtl-20
65CarTeal-21
69Top-254
70RoyTeal-32
83Pil69G-2
89PacLegI-162
93ConTSN-790
96Bro194F-18
Schultz, Joseph C. Sr.
21Nei-114
22E120-236
22W572-92
22W573-116
90DodTar-1065

Schultz, Scott
87LakTigP-5
92LSUTigM-6
93LSUTigM-16
94LSUTig-9
94LSUTigMP-15
95WatIndTI-26
Schultz, Ted
76AppFoxT-23
Schulz, Harry
75CliPilT-25
Schulz, Jeff
83ButCopKT-28
86OmaRoyP-20
86OmaRoyT-6
87OmaRoyP-23
88OmaRoyC-15
88OmaRoyP-1508
89OmaRoyC-22
89OmaRoyP-1736
90CMC-193
90OmaRoyC-18
90OmaRoyP-79
90ProAAAF-614
90TopDeb89-110
91BufBisLD-45
91BufBisP-554
91Don-687
91Fle-568
91LinDriAAA-45
91Sco-336
91Sco100RS-25
91UppDec-607
92IowCubF-4063
92NasSouS-291
Schulz, Pat
93WatIndC-24
93WatIndF-3578
Schulze, Don
81QuaCitCT-29
83IowCubT-9
84IndWhe-37
84IowCubT-22
85AllGamPI-86
85Don-639
85Fle-454
85Ind-27
85Top-93
85TopTif-93
86IndOhH-37
86IndTeal-38
86Top-542
86TopTif-542
87BufBisP-22
87Fle-259
87FleGlo-259
87TidTidP-25
87TidTidT-26
87Top-297
87TopTif-297
88TolMudHC-3
88TolMudHP-604
88Top-131
88TopTif-131
89ColCliC-6
89ColCliP-11
89ColCliP-753
89TidTidC-11
91MetWIZ-353
92YanWIZ8-173
93RocRedWF-238
Schumacher, Hal
33Gou-129
33Gou-240
33NatLeaAC-14
34BatR31-52
34BatR31-110
35GouPuzR-1K
35GouPuzR-3B
35GouPuzR-14B
35GouPuzR-15B
35WheBB1-23
36WorWidGV-23
38OurNatGPP-26
39PlaBal-73
40PlaBal-85
48SweSpoT-7
61Fle-137
77GalGloG-221
83ConMar-46
88ConNatA-18
94ConTSN-1127
94ConTSNB-1127
Schumacher, Roy
81AppFoxT-11
Schumaker, Mark
94FreKeyC-29
Schuman, Rich
87AriWilP-11
Schumate, Jack
79WisRapTT-22
Schunk, Jerry
87DunBluJP-947
88DunBluJS-16
89KnoBluJB-23
89KnoBluJP-1142
89KnoBluJS-19
90KnoBluJB-25
90KnoBluJP-1250
90KnoBluJS-18
90StaFS7-89
91BluJayS-34
91Bow-20
91LinDriAAA-516
91SyrChiLD-516
91SyrChiMB-22
91SyrChiP-2488
92SkyAAAF-231
92SyrChiF-1978
92SyrChiMB-18
92SyrChiS-515
93PorBeaF-2391
94PorSeaDTI-27
95ChaKniTI-23
Schupp, Ferdie
16ColE13-153
16FleBreD-84
21E121So1-90
21E121So8-84A
21E121So8-84B
22AmeCarE-61
22AmeCarE-62
22W575-117
90DodTar-712
Schurman, Ryan
96DanBraB-20
Schurr, Wayne
64Top-548
65OPC-149
65Top-149
Schuster, Bill
44CubTeal-21
47SigOil-36
49W725AngTI-25
Schuster, Frank
74TacTwiC-9
Schuster, Mark
79HolMilT-7
80HolMilT-3
81VanCanT-5
82ElPasDT-8
84PhoGiaC-7
85PhoGiaC-185
Schutz, Carl
93DanBraC-21
94DurBulC-17
94DurBulF-326
94DurBulTI-18
95BreBtaTI-49
95Exc-156
96RicBraB-25
96RicBraRC-6
96RicBraUB-25
Schwab, Chris
94Bow-556
94BurBeeC-24
94BurBeeF-1096
94ClaGolF-73
94ClaGolN1PLF-LP13
94ClaGolREF-RE13
94UppDecML-178
96DelShoB-26
Schwab, Ken
80CliGiaT-8
Schwabe, Mike
88GleFalTP-927
89BlaYNPRWL-27
89FleUpd-32
89LonTigP-1375
90CMC-386
90ProAAAF-378
90TolMudHC-9
90TolMudHP-148
90TopDeb89-111
91Fle-351
92PorBeaF-2665
92PorBeaS-418
Schwall, Don
62Baz-37
62Jel-64
62Pos-64
62PosCan-64
62RedSoxJP-10
62SalPlaC-210
62ShiPlaC-210
62Top-35
62TopBuc-80
62TopStal-19
62TopVen-35
63Top-344
64PirKDK-24
64Top-558
65Top-362
66OPC-144
66Top-144
66TopVen-144
67CokCapB-15
67Top-267
78TCM60I-118
81RedSoxBG2S-110
Schwanke, Jim
91OklStaC-22
92OklStaC-5
Schwankl, Darren
92Min-17
Schwarber, Mike
80BatTroT-10
81WatIndT-15
82ChaLooT-10
Schwarber, Tom
91BriTigC-23
91BriTigP-3605
92FayGenC-19
92FayGenF-2167
93LakTigF-1309
93LonTigF-2306
Schwartz, Dave
91EliTwiP-4300
Schwartz, Randy
67OPC-33
67Top-33
Schwarz, Jeff
88WinSpiS-19
89HagSunB-24
89HagSunP-263
89HagSunS-16
91ElPasDLD-195
91ElPasDP-2748
91LinDriAA-195
92BirBarF-2581
92BirBarS-94
92VanCanF-2722
93FleFinE-198
93WhiSoxK-26
94Fle-95
94Sco-588
94ScoGolR-588
94StaClu-482
94StaCluFDI-482
94StaCluGR-482
94StaCluMOP-482
94StaCluT-137
94StaCluTFDI-137
94Top-33
94TopGol-33
94TopSpa-33
94Ult-38
Schwarz, Tom
86VisOakP-19
87OrlTwiP-18
88ReaPhiP-863
Schweighoffer, Mike
85VerBeaDT-18
87SanAntDTI-13
88SanAntMB-10
Schweitzer, Al
09PC7HHB-39
10JHDABE-15
11SpoLifCW-315
11SpoLifM-116
Schweitzer, Tim
92AriWilP-16
Schwenke, Matt
94BakDodC-22
96LasVegSB-22
96RanCucQB-25
Schwerman, Brian
77ChaPatT-20
78ChaPirT-22
Sciortino, Michael
90PitMetP-15
91PitMetC-9
91PitMetP-3433
Scioscia, Mike
77CliDodT-23
79AlbDukT-10
80AlbDukT-26
81DodPol-14
81Fle-131
81LonBeaPT-8
81Top-302
82DodPol-14
82DodPos-8
82DodUniOV-20
82Don-598
82Fle-22
82OPC-173
82Top-642
83DodPol-14
83DodPos-15
83Don-75
83Fle-221
83Top-352
84DodPol-14
84Fle-113
84Nes792-64
84Top-64
84TopTif-64
85AllGamPI-134
85DodCokP-30
85Don-459
85Fle-385
85Lea-118
85Top-549
85TopSti-79
85TopTif-549
86DodCokP-28
86DodPol-14
86DodUniOP-18
86Don-93
86Fle-144
86Lea-87
86OPC-111
86Spo-167
86Top-468
86TopMinL-46
86TopSti-68
86TopTat-19
86TopTif-468
87DodMot-10
87DodPol-6
87Don-130
87DonOpeD-82
87Fle-454
87FleGlo-454
87Lea-123
87OPC-144
87SevCoi-W12
87Spo-67
87Spo-151
87SpoTeaP-14
87Top-144
87TopSti-73
87TopTif-144
88DodMot-10
88DodPol-14
88Don-106
88DonBasB-260
88Fle-524
88FleGlo-524
88Lea-97
88OPC-225
88PanSti-307
88Sco-53
88ScoGlo-53
88Spo-110
88StaLinD-15
88Top-225
88TopBig-72
88TopSti-67
88TopTif-225
89Bow-342
89BowTif-342
89DodMot-3
89DodPol-9
89DodSmoG-31
89DodStaSV-12
89Don-77
89DonBasB-66
89Fle-71
89FleAll-9
89FleGlo-71
89FleGlo-WS4
89FleWorS-4
89OPC-7
89PanSti-104
89Sco-121
89Spo-138
89Top-755
89TopBig-281
89TopSti-58
89TopTif-755
89TVSpoM-36
89UppDec-116
90Bow-89
90BowTif-89
90DodMot-4
90DodPol-14
90DodTar-713
90Don-316
90DonBesN-5
90DonGraS-7
90Fle-407
90FleCan-407
90Lea-49
90OPC-605
90PanSti-276
90PubSti-17
90Sco-398
90Sco100S-48
90Spo-163
90Top-605
90TopBig-67
90TopDou-58
90TopGloS-34
90TopSti-64
90TopStiB-24
90TopTif-605
90UppDec-298
90USPlaCA-2H
91Bow-613
91DodMot-4
91DodPol-14
91Don-112
91Don-436A
91Don-436B
91Fle-219
91Lea-24
91OPC-305
91OPC-404
91PanFreS-54
91PanSti-57
91RedFolS-128
91Sco-520
91StaClu-19
91StaCluP-39
91StaPinB-45
91Stu-189
91Top-305
91Top-404
91TopDesS-305
91TopDesS-404
91TopGloA-20
91TopMic-305
91TopMic-404
91TopTif-305
91TopTif-404
91Ult-169
91UppDec-139
92Bow-368
92DodMot-9
92DodPol-14
92DodSmo-5192
92DodStaTA-29
92Don-480
92Fle-470
92HitTheBB-31
92Lea-165
92New-26
92OPC-13
92PanSti-191
92Pin-210
92Sco-226
92Sco-782
92SpoStaCC-41
92StaClu-140
92Stu-48
92Top-13
92TopGol-13
92TopGolW-13
92TopMic-13
92TriPla-191
92Ult-217
92UppDec-152
93Don-508
93Fle-67
93OPC-326
93PadMot-23
93PanSti-213
93Pin-498

93Sco-623
93Sel-69
93StaClu-46
93StaCluFDI-46
93StaCluMOP-46
93StaCluMP-9
93Top-202
93TopGol-202
93TopInaM-202
93TopMic-202
93TriPla-196
93UppDec-688
93UppDecGold-688
94StaCluT-255
94StaCluTFDI-255
Scoble, Troy
91AdeGiaF-15
95AusFutSFP-SFFP1
Scolaro, Don
94AubAstC-18
94AubAstF-3767
95AubAstTI-6
Sconiers, Daryl
78QuaCitAT-24
80ElPasDT-14
81SalLakCGT-20
82Top-653
83Don-141
83TopTra-99T
84AngSmo-26
84Don-451
84Fle-528
84FleSti-112
84Nes792-27
84Top-27
84TopTif-27
85Don-620
85Fle-312
85OPC-256
85Top-604
85TopTif-604
86Fle-168
86SanJosBP-18
86Top-193
86TopTif-193
87SanJosBP-28
88VanCanC-22
88VanCanP-766
91LinDriAA-445
91MidAngLD-445
91MidAngP-443
Scooch, Mascot
92SyrChiMB-19
Scopio, Joe
94WilCubC-21
94WilCubF-3780
Scoras, John
78MemChiBC-9
79MemChiT-17
Score, Herb
47Exh-204A
47Exh-204B
55IndCarBL-8
55IndGolS-7
56Top-140
57IndSoh-12
57Top-50
58Top-352
58Top-495
59Ind-18
59Kah-32
59Top-88
59TopVen-88
60Kah-37
60Top-360
60TopTat-48
61Top-185
61Top-337
61UniOil-SD9
61WhiSoxTS-15
62Top-116
62TopVen-116
62WhiSoxTS-19
76SSP-595
77SerSta-22
78ReaRem-18
79DiaGre-300
79TCM50-134
80MarExh-28
86IndIndTI-24
87SpoRea-16
89PacLegI-126
89SweBasG-114
90PacLeg-49
90SweBasG-32
91SweBasG-82
92ActPacA-79
94TopArc1-256
94TopArc1G-256
94UppDecAH-56
94UppDecAH1-56
Scott, Andrew
91AdeGiaF-16
Scott, Barbara Ann
43ParSpo-90
Scott, Charles
86WatIndP-25
88ColSprSSC-9
88ColSprSSP-1529
89ColSprSSC-8
90CMC-559
90PorBeaC-7
90PorBeaP-178
90ProAAAF-248
91LinDriAAA-419
91PorBeaLD-419
91PorBeaP-1565
Scott, Craig
89KinMetS-21
Scott, Dale
88T/MUmp-58
89T/MUmp-56
90T/MUmp-54
Scott, Darryl
88CapCodPPaLP-34
90BoiHawP-3313
91QuaCitAC-10
91QuaCitAP-2627
92MidAngF-4027
92MidAngOHP-22
92MidAngS-469
92ProFS7-35
92SkyAA F-200
93FleFinE-189
93StaCluAn-26
93TriAAAGF-33
93VanCanF-2596
94Pin-225
94PinArtP-225
94PinMusC-225
96BufBisB-18
Scott, Death Valley (James)
11SpoLifM-29
11T205-152
14CraJacE-26
15CraJacE-26
92Man191BSR-23
Scott, Dick
92MadMusF-1252
Scott, Dick (Richard E.)
82ColCliT-15
85AlbYanT-19
87ColCliP-13
88AlbYanP-1350
89TacTigC-20
89TacTigP-1554
90CMC-601
90ProAAAF-150
90TacTigC-24
90TacTigP-103
90TopDeb89-112
92MadMusC-26
93SouOreAC-28
93SouOreAF-4081
94ModA'sC-26
94ModA'sF-3078
95HunStaTI-23
96HunStaTI-23
Scott, Dick (Richard L.)
77FriOneYW-38
90DodTar-714
Scott, Donnie
84OklCit8T-19
95BilRedTI-27
Scott, Donnie (Donald M.)
80AshTouT-21
81TulDriT-13
82TulDriT-11
83OklCit8T-23
84RanJarP-43
85CalCanC-81
85Don-544
85Fle-568
85Top-496
85TopTif-496
85TopTifT-105T
85TopTra-105T
86Fle-474
86RocRedWP-19
86Top-568
86TopTif-568
87ElPasDP-3
88ElPasDB-2
89DenZepC-6
89DenZepP-52
90CMC-137
90NasSouC-12
90NasSouP-237
90ProAAAF-549
91LinDriAAA-271
91NasSouLD-271
91NasSouP-2160
92BenMusSP-30
92BilMusF-3373
93BilMusF-3962
93BilMusSP-27
93RanKee-321
94BilMusF-3685
94BilMusSP-23
Scott, Gary
88CapCodPPaLP-88
89GenCubP-1877
90CarLeaA-49
90TopMag-54
90WinSpiTI-1
91Bow-535
91Cla2-T88
91CubVinL-25
91FleUpd-80
91IowCubP-1068
91LeaGolR-BC4
91OPCPre-107
91ScoAllF-3
91ScoRoo-90T
91StaClu-596
91Stu-159
91TopTra-107T
91TopTraT-107T
91UltUpd-72
91UppDec-58
92Bow-128
92Lea-6
92Pin-269
92PinRoo-15
92PinTea2-73
92Sco100RS-81
92StaClu-708
92Stu-19
92TopDeb91-159
92TopTra-102T
92TopTraG-102T
92Ult-474
93Don-750
93IndIndF-1498
93Sco-547
93Top-656
93TopGol-656
93TopInaM-656
93TopMic-656
93TriPla-84
94PhoFirF-1529
95PhoFirTI-21
Scott, George C.
92ElmPioC-1
92ElmPioF-1392
93LynRedSC-23
93LynRedSF-2532
Scott, George Charles
47PM1StaP1-197
66Top-558
67CokCapA-34
67CokCapAAm-22
67CokCapRS-12
67DexPre-187
67OPC-75
67Top-75
67TopRedSS-16
67TopVen-200
68AtlOilPBCC-42
68Baz-7
68CokCapRS-12
68DexPre-70
68Top-233
68TopActS-2C
68TopActS-13C
68TopGamI-22
68TopVen-233
69MLBOffS-17
69RedSoxAO-10
69RedSoxTI-9
69Top-574
69TopSta-138
69TopTeaP-3
70MLBOffS-165
70OPC-385
70RedSoxCPPC-12
70Top-385
71MilDud-28
71MLBOffS-331
71OPC-9
71RedSoxA-8
71RedSoxTI-9
71Top-9
71TopCoi-98
72MilBra-311
72Top-585
73LinPor-103
73OPC-263
73Top-263
73TopCanL-47
73TopCom-18
73TopPin-18
74OPC-27
74Top-27
74TopDecE-30
74TopSta-199
75Hos-26
75HosTwi-26
75OPC-360
75Top-360
76BreA&P-11
76Hos-54
76HosTwi-54
76Kel-21
76OPC-15
76OPC-194
76OPC-196
76RedSox-8
76SSP-237
76Top-15
76Top-194
76Top-196
77Hos-148
77OPC-210
77Top-255
78Hos-24
78OPC-12
78PapGinD-15
78SSP270-183
78Top-125
79OPC-340
79Top-645
80Top-414
80VenLeaS-77
81RedSoxBG2S-66
81RedSoxBG2S-111
86BreGreT-1
92UppDecS-6
92YanWIZ7-139
94BreMilB-177
Scott, Jeff
75LynRanT-24
77AshTouT-20
79AshTouT-22
87UtiBluSP-11
Scott, Jim
09T206-317
12T207-164
13PolGroW-26
15SpoNewM-159
16BF2FP-19
16SpoNewM-158
63GadFunC-51
86VerRedP-17
92ConTSN-341
Scott, Joe
86NegLeaF-58
92NegLeaRLI-54
92NegLeaRLI-55
Scott, John H.
75OPC-616
75Top-616
76HawIsIC-7
76SSP-131
77OPC-94
77Top-473
78SprRedWK-4
78Top-547
79TCMJapPB-21
Scott, John William
23W503-63
23W515-25
91ConTSN-97
Scott, Kelly
83NasSouTI-19
84ColCliP-22
84ColCliT-19
85ColCliP-19
85ColCliT-9
Scott, Kevin
89AubAstP-2183
90AshTouP-2752
91Cla/Bes-37
91OscAstC-28
91OscAstP-689
92OscAstC-14
92OscAstF-2534
93OscAstC-20
93OscAstF-632
Scott, L. Everett
15SpoNewM-160
16ColE13-154
16SpoNewM-157
17HolBreD-92
19W514-90
20NatCarE-89
21E121So1-91
21E121So8-85
21Exh-153
21Exh-154
22AmeCarE-63
22E120-73
22W575-118
22W575-119
23W501-30
23W515-46
23WilChoV-144
28W512-7
91ConTSN-149
Scott, Mark
59HomRunD-17
80ChaChaT-2
Scott, Marty (Martin)
79TucTorT-10
80VenLeaS-27
81TulDriT-4
82BurRanF-28
82BurRanT-25
83TulDriT-25
90TulDriDGB-34
Scott, Michael Wm.
87GreBraB-28
87SprCarB-19
Scott, Mickey (Ralph)
70Top-669
72Top-724
73OPC-553
73Top-553
76OPC-276
76Top-276
77Top-401
78ColCliT-22
91OriCro-410
Scott, Mike (Michael Warren)
76VenLeaS-188
78TidTidT-23
79TidTidT-15
80TidTidT-23
80Top-681
81Don-37
81Top-109
82Don-128
82Fle-535
82MetPhoA-19
82Top-246
82Top-432
83Fle-554
83Top-679
83TopTra-100T
84AstMot-14
84Don-136
84Fle-240
84Nes792-559
84Top-559
84TopTif-559
85AstHouP-16
85AstMot-18
85Don-258
85Fle-361
85OPC-17
85Top-17
85TopMin-17
85TopTif-17
86AstMilL-19
86AstPol-3
86AstTeal-14
86Don-476
86DonHig-46

86Fle-311
86FleMin-66
86FleStiC-108
86GreBraTI-16
86Lea-235
86SevCoi-S11
86Spo-195
86Top-268
86TopSti-27
86TopTat-23
86TopTif-268
87AstMot-2
87AstPol-11
87ClaGam-81
87ClaUpdY-123
87Don-18
87Don-163
87DonAll-32
87DonAllB-PC13
87DonOpeD-15
87DonSupD-18
87Dra-33
87Fle-68
87Fle-630
87FleAwaW-37
87FleGlo-68
87FleGlo-630
87FleLimE-38
87FleMin-99
87FleRecS-36
87FleSlu-38
87FleStiC-108
87GenMilB-6I
87HosSti-10
87KayB-30
87KraFoo-4
87Lea-18
87Lea-258
87MandMSL-18
87MSAJifPD-18
87OPC-330
87SmoNatL-5
87Spo-19
87Spo-119
87Spo-120
87SpoSupD-2
87SpoTeaP-8
87StuPan-5
87Top-330
87TopCoi-44
87TopGaloC-11
87TopMinL-11
87TopSti-15
87TopSti-35
87TopTif-330
87Woo-18
88AstMot-2
88AstPol-21
88CheBoy-19
88ClaBlu-221
88Don-112
88DonAll-40
88DonBasB-206
88DonBonM-BC12
88DonPop-18
88Fle-456
88Fle-632
88FleAwaW-36
88FleBasA-37
88FleBasM-32
88FleExcS-35
88FleGlo-456
88FleGlo-632
88FleHotS-35
88FleLeaL-36
88FleMin-80
88FleRecS-36
88FleSlu-37
88FleStiC-89
88FleSup-34
88FleTeaL-35
88GreBasS-50
88K-M-26
88KinDis-13
88Lea-54
88OPC-227
88PanSti-233
88PanSti-289
88RedFolSB-81
88Sco-335
88ScoBoxC-18
88ScoGlo-335
88Spo-66
88StaLinAl-31
88StaLinAst-16
88StaSco-1
88StaSco-2
88StaSco-3
88StaSco-4
88StaSco-5
88StaSco-6
88StaSco-7
88StaSco-8
88StaSco-9
88StaSco-10
88StaSco-11
88Top-760
88TopBig-140
88TopCoi-54
88TopGloA-21
88TopGloS-5
88TopMinL-51
88TopRitTM-4
88TopSti-30
88TopSti-154
88TopStiB-26
88TopTif-760
88TopUKM-68
88TopUKMT-68
89AstLenH-4
89AstMot-2
89AstSmo-36
89Bow-322
89BowTif-322
89ClaLigB-23
89Don-69
89DonBasB-94
89DonBonM-BC2
89Fle-367
89FleBasM-34
89FleGlo-367
89FleLeaL-34
89FleSup-37
89OPC-180
89PanSti-84
89RedFolSB-106
89Sco-550
89ScoHot1S-60
89ScoSco-4
89Spo-120
89SpoIllFKI-144
89Top-180
89TopBasT-50
89TopBig-51
89TopMinL-15
89TopSti-15
89TopTif-180
89TVSpoM-53
89UppDec-295
90AstLenH-22
90AstMot-4
90BasWit-12
90Bow-71
90BowTif-71
90ClaBlu-29
90Don-207
90DonBesN-16
90DonLeaS-50
90Fle-237
90Fle-636
90FleAll-10
90FleAwaW-33
90FleCan-237
90FleCan-636
90FleLeaL-35
90GooHumICBLS-21
90Hot50PS-39
90K-M-9
90KinDis-1
90Lea-4
90MLBBasB-43
90OPC-405
90OPC-460
90PanSti-262
90Pos-20
90PubSti-102
90RedFolSB-85
90Sco-40
90Sco-692
90Sco100S-97
90Spo-55
90SunSee-22
90Top-405
90Top-460
90TopBig-249
90TopDou-59
90TopGloS-14
90TopMag-8
90TopMinL-56
90TopSti-19
90TopStiB-27
90TopTif-405
90TopTif-460
90TopTVA-42
90UppDec-88
90UppDec-125
91AstMot-4
91BasBesAotM-15
91Bow-546
91ClaGam-38
91Don-483
91Fle-515
91MetWIZ-354
91OPC-240
91PanFreS-14
91PanSti-16
91PetSta-8
91RedFolS-86
91Sco-46
91SevCoi-T9
91StaClu-209
91Stu-180
91Top-240
91TopDesS-240
91TopMic-240
91TopTif-240
91Ult-140
91UppDec-531
94TedWil-36

Scott, Pete (Floyd John)
33Gou-70
34GouCanV-33
92ConTSN-578

Scott, Phaintin (Phil)
28W513-93

Scott, Philip
90PitMetP-1
91GreHorP-3068

Scott, Rennie
90LynRedSTI-22
91LynRedSC-8
91LynRedSP-1198

Scott, Rodney
72Dia-40
76SSP-172
78Top-191
79ExpPos-23
79ExpPos-24
79Top-86
80ExpPos-27
80OPC-360
80Top-712
81AllGamPI-106
81Don-209
81Fle-155
81OPC-227
81OPCPos-2
81Top-204
81Top-539
81TopSti-185
82Don-240
82ExpPos-37
82Fle-207
82FleSta-38
82OPC-259
82OPCPos-14
82Top-259
89PacSenL-177
89T/MSenL-94
89TopSenL-29
90EliSenL-29
91PacSenL-69
92Nab-13
92YanWIZ8-174
93ExpDonM-18

Scott, Ron
93JohCitCC-18
93JohCitCF-3675
94SavCarC-24
94SavCarF-505
95PeoChiTI-19

Scott, Sean
92SouOreAC-26
92SouOreAF-3435

Scott, Shawn
90St.CatBJP-3480
91DunBluJC-23
91DunBluJP-221
92KnoBluJF-3004
92KnoBluJS-392
93SyrChiF-1012

Scott, Steve
87SalLakTTT-26

Scott, Tary
85GreHorT-3
86FloStaLAP-43
86WinHavRSP-21
87NewBriRSP-22

Scott, Tim
83CedRapRF-3
83CedRapRT-8
87HawIsIP-14
87SanAntDTI-4
88BakDodCLC-258
89SanAntMB-24
90AlbDukC-9
90AlbDukP-344
90AlbDukT-26
90CMC-411
90ProAAAF-65
91LasVegSLD-293
91LasVegSP-235
91LinDriAAA-293
92BenRocC-22
92BenRocF-1483
92Bow-454
92DonRoo-109
92LasVegSF-2796
92LasVegSS-239
92PadPolD-29
92StaClu-881
92StaCluECN-881
92TopDeb91-160
93Don-362
93Fle-524
93Lea-174
93PacSpa-600
93PadMot-27
93SanBerSC-14
93SanBerSF-779
93Sco-251
93StaClu-76
93StaCluFDI-76
93StaCluMOP-76
93Top-166
93TopGol-166
93TopInaM-166
93TopMic-166
93Ult-477
93UppDec-662
93UppDecGold-662
94Don-265
94Fle-550
94Lea-219
94Top-373
94TopGol-373
94TopSpa-373
95Don-208
95DonPreP-208
95DonTopotO-285
95Fla-166
95Fle-359
95TopTra-62T
95Ult-407
95UltGolM-407
96ColCho-609
96ColChoGS-609
96ColChoSS-609
96Don-162
96DonPreP-162
96ExpBoo-4
96ExpDis-17
96Fle-468
96FleTif-468
96LeaSigEA-178

Scott, Tom
95BilRedTI-18

Scott, Tony
76SSP-339
77Car5-25
77CarTeal-24
78CarTeal-20
78Top-352
79Car5-23
79Top-143
80OPC-17
80Top-33
81CokTeaS-128
81Don-191
81Fle-531
81Top-165
81TopSti-223
81TopTra-828
82AstAstI-9
82Don-522
82Fle-231
82FleSta-46
82Top-698
83Don-293
83Fle-465
83Top-507
84AstMot-20
84Don-527
84Fle-241
84Nes792-292
84Top-292
84TopTif-292
85OPC-367
85Top-733
85TopTif-733
89TopSenL-91
90EliSenL-104
91BatCliP-3502
91PacSenL-121
92SpaPhiC-23
92SpaPhiF-1282
93SpaPhiC-26
93SpaPhiF-1073
94SpaPhiF-1740
94SparPhiC-27

Scott, Tyrone
90AubAstB-19
90AubAstP-3402
91BurAstC-8
91BurAstP-2799
92BurAstC-9
92BurAstF-546

Scranton, Jim
84OmaRoyT-27
85OmaRoyT-17
86OmaRoyP-21
86OmaRoyT-7

Scripture, Billy
78ChaPirT-23

Scrivener, Chuck (Churck)
77Top-173
78Top-94
79SyrChiTI-3

Scruggs, Ron
86AppFoxP-21
87PenWhiSP-25

Scruggs, Tony
88ChaRanS-22
89TulDriGS-24
89TulDriTI-23
90Bes-19
90CMC-654
90GasRanB-1
90GasRanP-2535
90GasRanS-22
90ProAaA-98
90SouAtlLAS-22
90StaFS7-98
91Bow-289
91LinDriAAA-304
91OklCit8LD-304
92OklCit8F-1928
92OklCit8S-321
92TopDeb91-161
93JacSunF-2723
93RanKee-322

Scudder, Bill
83VerBeaDT-10
85AlbDukC-166

Scudder, Scott
87CedRapRP-7
88CedRapRP-1157
88MidLeaAGS-14
89FleUpd-87
89NasSouC-8
89NasSouP-1293
89NasSouTI-22
89ScoRoo-99T
90Bow-46
90BowTif-46
90CedRapRDGB-15
90CMC-135
90Don-435
90Fle-434
90FleCan-434
90Hot50RS-39
90Lea-413
90NasSouC-10
90NasSouP-232
90OPC-553
90ProAAAF-544
90Sco-518
90Sco100RS-65
90Top-553
90TopDeb89-113

90TopTif-553
90UppDec-164
91Don-265
91Fle-81
91Lea-183
91OPC-713
91RedKah-47
91Sco-642
91Top-713
91TopDesS-713
91TopMic-713
91TopTif-713
91UppDec-615
92Bow-571
92ClaGam-180
92Don-306
92Fle-422
92IndFanC-25
92Lea-429
92OPC-48
92OPCPre-181
92Pin-480
92Sco-209
92ScoRoo-67T
92StaClu-644
92StaCluNC-644
92Top-48
92TopGol-48
92TopGolW-48
92TopMic-48
92Ult-356
92UppDec-485
92UppDec-787
93Don-653
93Fle-601
93IndWUA-27
93PacSpa-101
93StaClu-243
93StaCluFDI-243
93StaCluMOP-243
93Top-248
93TopGol-248
93TopInaM-248
93TopMic-248
93Ult-190
93UppDec-208
93UppDecGold-208
94BufBisF-1835
Scull, Angel
53Bri-18
54Top-204
94TopArc1-204
94TopArc1G-204
Scully, Vin
59DodVol-14
60DodUniO-22
61DodUniO-24
71DodTic-20
82DodUniOV-21
Scurry, Rod
76ShrCapT-7
77ShrCapT-21
78ColCliT-23
79PorBeaT-22
81Fle-380
81Top-194
82Don-185
82Fle-497
82Top-207
83AllGamPI-177
83Don-376
83Fle-322
83Top-537
84Don-235
84Fle-264
84Nes792-69
84Top-69
84TopTif-69
85Don-142
85Fle-476
85Pir-19
85Top-641
85TopTif-641
86Top-449
86TopTif-449
86YanTCM-14
87Don-374
87Fle-113
87FleGlo-113
87OPC-393
87Top-665
87TopTif-665
88CalCanC-10
88CalCanP-779
89Sco-516
89UppDec-208
92YanWIZ8-175
Scutero, Brian
95BoiHawTI-26
96CedRapKTI-21
Sea Dogs, Portland
94PorSeaDTI-2
95PorSeaDTI-30
Seabury, Jaron
96MedHatBJTI-26
Seal, Mike
88OklSoo-23
89MyrBeaBJP-1462
Seale, Johnnie
77FriOneYW-87
Sealer, Joel
88NebCor-15
Seals, Joey
89GreFalDSP-15
91GreFalDSP-10
Sealy, Randy
75ShrCapT-19
76ShrCapT-12
80WesHavWCT-23B
Sealy, Scot
92GasRanF-2256
93ChaRaiC-18
93ChaRaiF-1914
93ClaGolF-206
96LanJetB-24
Seaman, Kim
77WauMetT-17
81HawIslT-16
82HawIslT-22
82WicAerTI-17
Seamon, Jonathan
86DavLipB-19
Seanez, Rudy
87WatIndP-18
88WatIndP-692
89KinIndS-23
90Bes-164
90CanIndB-24
90CanIndP-1293
90CMC-832
90Fle-640
90FleCan-640
90IndTeal-34
90Lea-417
90ProAaA-10
90TopDeb89-114
91ColSprSSLD-89
91ColSprSSP-2181
91Don-218
91Fle-376
91LinDriAAA-89
91UppDec-358
92Don-552
92Fle-122
92SanAntMS-575
92Sco-696
92StaClu-713
92StaCluECN-713
93Don-758
93OPC-391
93StaCluRoc-16
93Top-676
93TopGol-676
93TopInaM-676
93TopMic-676
94AlbDukF-842
95DodMot-24
95DodPol-24
95Fla-156
95Fle-549
95TopTra-143T
Searage, Ray
77St.PetCT-7
79ArkTraT-20
81TidTidT-24
82ChaChaT-10
82Top-478
84VanCanC-30
85BrePol-41
85Fle-595
86Don-536
86Fle-502
86Top-642
86TopTif-642
86VanCanP-23
87Fle-506
87FleGlo-506
87Top-149
87TopTif-149
87WhiSoxC-27
88AlbDukC-4
88AlbDukP-262
88Don-429
88Fle-409
88FleGlo-409
88StaLinWS-17
88Top-788
88TopTif-788
89DodMot-22
89DodPol-30
89DodStaSV-13
89FleUpd-94
90DodMot-22
90DodPol-59
90DodTar-1066
90Don-649
90Fle-408
90FleCan-408
90OPC-84
90Top-84
90TopTif-84
91Fle-220
91LinDriAAA-496
91MetWIZ-355
91ScrRedBLD-496
91ScrRedBP-2538
92EdmTraF-3539
94BreMilB-178
94MadHatC-28
94MadHatF-150
95PeoChiTI-39
96PeoChiB-2
Search, Michael
90BoiHawP-3316
90PalSprACLC-223
90PalSprAP-2576
Searcy, Steve
86GleFalTP-21
87TolMudHP-2
87TolMudHT-16
88TolMudHC-4
88TolMudHP-609
88TriAAC-25
89Bow-95
89BowTif-95
89ClaLigB-78
89Don-29
89Fle-145
89FleGlo-145
89Sco-627
89ScoHot1R-47
89ScoYouS2-27
89Top-167
89TopTif-167
89UppDec-764
90CMC-387
90Fle-615
90FleCan-615
90Hot50RS-40
90OPC-487
90ProAAAF-379
90Sco100RS-97
90TolMudHC-10
90TolMudHP-149
90Top-487
90TopTif-487
90TriAllGP-AAA20
90UppDec-575
91Don-549
91Lea-187
91OPC-369
91Sco-649
91Sco100RS-76
91StaClu-352
91TigCok-49
91Top-369
91TopDesS-369
91TopMic-369
91TopTif-369
91UppDec-338
92Fle-545
92OPC-599
92PhiMed-29
92Sco-698
92ScrRedBF-2445
92StaClu-648
92Top-599
92TopGol-599
92TopGolW-599
92TopMic-599
93RocRedWF-239
Searles, Bob
87CubCan-28
Sears, Allen
83DurBulT-23
91BoiHawC-20
Sears, Jimmy
91BoiHawP-3891
Sears, Ken
43YanSta-24
46SeaSLP-44
Sears, Mike
86FloStaLAP-44
86WinHavRSP-22
87WinHavRSP-19
Sears, R.D.
88AllandGN-28
88GooN16-37
Seaton, Billy
91GulCoaRSP-13
92GulCoaRSP-13
Seaton, Tom
14CraJacE-100
15CraJacE-100
15SpoNewM-161
16SpoNewM-159
Seats, Dean
81CedRapRT-13
Seats, Tom
49BowPCL-35
90DodTar-715
Seaver, Anne
92PacSea-63
Seaver, Mark
96MauStiHWB-36
Seaver, Nancy
92PacSea-63
Seaver, Tom
67Top-581
68Baz-1
68OPC-45
68Top-45
68TopActS-3C
68TopActS-14C
68TopVen-45
69MetBoyS-1
69MetCit-8
69MetNewYDN-16
69MilBra-250
69MLBOffS-170
69NabTeaF-22
69Top-480
69TopDecI-38
69TopSta-68
69TopSup-52
69TopTeaP-24
69TraSta-48
70DayDaiNM-8
70Kel-7
70MetTra-21C
70MilBra-26
70MLBOffS-82
70OPC-69
70OPC-195
70OPC-300
70Top-69
70Top-195
70Top-300
70TopScr-19
70TopSup-5
70TraSta-4C
71AllBasA-22
71BazNumT-35
71Kel-2
71MatMin-15
71MatMin-16
71MilDud-63
71MLBOffS-164
71MLBOffS-574
71OPC-68
71OPC-72
71OPC-160
71Top-68
71Top-72
71Top-160
71TopCoi-127
71TopSup-53
71TopTat-114
71TopTat-115
72Kel-1A
72Kel-1B
72MilBra-312
72OPC-91
72OPC-93
72OPC-95
72OPC-347
72OPC-445
72OPC-446
72ProStaP-22
72Top-91
72Top-93
72Top-95
72Top-347
72Top-445
72Top-446
72TopPos-13
73Kel2D-46
73LinPor-122
73MetAllEB-10
73NewYorN-3
73OPC-350
73Top-350
73TopCanL-48
73TopCom-19
73TopPin-19
74Kel-52
74LauAllG-68
74MetDaiPA-9
74MetJapEB-9
74NewYorNTDiS-13
74OPC-80
74OPC-206
74OPC-207
74Top-80
74Top-206
74Top-207
74TopDecE-9
74TopPuz-10
74TopSta-70
75BlaBacD-6
75Hos-75
75MetSSP-12
75OPC-370
75SSP42-15
75SSPPuzB-23
75SSPSam-6
75Top-370
76CraDis-55
76Hos-35
76HosTwi-35
76Kel-32A
76Kel-32B
76MetMSAP-1
76OPC-5
76OPC-199
76OPC-201
76OPC-203
76OPC-600
76SafSupLB-5
76SafSupLB-9
76SafSupLB-12
76SafSupLB-14
76SafSupLB-15
76SSP-551
76Top-5
76Top-199
76Top-201
76Top-203
76Top-600
77BurCheD-142
77Hos-7
77MetDaiPA-21
77MSADis-56
77OPC-6
77OPC-205
77PepGloD-67
77RCColC-59
77Spo-121
77Spo-2922
77Top-6
77Top-150
77TopCloS-42
78Hos-149
78Kel-27
78OPC-120
78Pep-23
78RCColC-36
78SSP270-116
78TasDis-10
78Top-450
78WifBalD-68
79Hos-65
79Kel-29
79OPC-44
79SpaGloT-2
79Top-100
79TopCom-22
80BurKinPHR-10
80Kel-49
80OPC-260

80PerHaloFP-215
80RawActTS-1
80RedEnq-41
80Top-500
80TopSup-15
81AllGamPI-176
81CokTeaS-46
81Don-422
81Don-425
81Fle-200
81FleStiC-49
81Kel-38
81MSAMinD-29
81OPC-220
81PerCreC-11
81Top-220
81TopScr-107
81TopSti-165
81TopSupHT-41
81TopSupN-14
82Don-16
82Don-148
82Don-628
82FBIDis-21
82Fle-82
82Fle-634
82Fle-645
82FleSta-11
82Kel-8
82OPC-30
82OPC-31
82OPC-346
82PerCreC-2
82PerCreCG-2
82RedCok-19
82Squ-21
82Top-30
82Top-31
82Top-165
82Top-346
82Top-346B
82Top-756
82TopSti-9
82TopSti-36
83AllGamPI-176
83Don-122
83Fle-601
83FleSta-174
83FleSti-218
83Oco& SSBG-16
83OPC-52
83OPC-354
83Top-580
83Top-581
83TopFol-1
83TopSti-233
83TopTra-101T
84Don-116
84DonActAS-53
84DonCha-40
84Fle-595
84FleUpd-106
84FunFooP-15
84Nes792-246
84Nes792-706
84Nes792-707
84Nes792-708
84Nes792-740
84OCoandSI-105
84OCoandSI-164
84OPC-261
84RalPur-8
84SevCoi-E8
84Top-246
84Top-706
84Top-707
84Top-708
84Top-740
84TopCer-8
84TopGaloC-12
84TopPewB-1
84TopRubD-17
84TopSti-106
84TopTif-246
84TopTif-706
84TopTif-707
84TopTif-708
84TopTif-740
84TopTra-108T
84TopTraT-108T
84WhiSoxTV-27
85AllGamPI-87
85Don-424A
85Don-424B
85DonHig-1
85DonHig-30
85Dra-41
85Fle-526
85FleLimE-34
85FleStaS-68
85FleStaS-69
85FleStaS-70
85FleStaS-71
85FleStaS-72
85FleStaS-73
85KASDis-13
85KitCloD-13
85Lea-101
85OPC-1
85SevCoi-G12
85SpoSam-45
85ThoMcAD-19
85Top-670
85Top3-D-30
85TopMin-670
85TopSti-235
85TopSup-31
85TopTif-670
85WhiSoxC-41
86Don-609
86Don-609B
86Fle-216
86Fle-630
86FleFutHoF-3
86FleLeaL-40
86FleMin-46
86FleSlu-34
86FleStiC-109
86Lea-234
86MSAJayPCD-16
86OPC-390
86QuaGra-32
86SevCoi-C8
86SevCoi-E8
86SevCoi-S8
86SevCoi-W8
86Spo-25
86Spo-60
86Spo-67
86Spo-70
86Spo-134
86Spo-135
86Spo-142
86Spo-182
86SpoDecG-52
86SpoRoo-47
86StaSea-1
86StaSea-2
86StaSea-3
86StaSea-4
86StaSea-5
86StaSea-6
86StaSea-7
86StaSea-8
86StaSea-9
86StaSea-10
86StaSea-11
86StaSea-12
86Top-390
86Top-402
86TopGloS-22
86TopSti-10
86TopSti-287
86TopSup-50
86TopTat-10
86TopTif-390
86TopTif-402
86TopTra-101T
86TopTraT-101T
86TruVal-12
86WhiSoxC-41
87Don-375
87Fle-45
87FleGlo-45
87K-M-21
87Lea-263
87OPC-49
87Spo-28
87SpoRea-22
87Top-306
87Top-425
87TopSti-246
87TopTif-306
87TopTif-425
88AlaGolAA'TI-3
89Met196C-11
89RinPosM1-26
89TopBasT-15
90AGFA-14
90BasWit-46
90HOFStiB-76
90MetHaloF-4
90PacLeg-60
90PerGreM-73
90SouCalS-11
90SweBasG-1
91MetWIZ-356
91SweBasG-107
91UppDecRH-10
92FroRowAH-3
92FroRowSe-1
92FroRowSe-2
92FroRowSe-3
92FroRowSe-4
92FroRowSe-5
92KelAll-5
92PacSea-1
92PacSea-2
92PacSea-3
92PacSea-4
92PacSea-5
92PacSea-6
92PacSea-7
92PacSea-8
92PacSea-9
92PacSea-10
92PacSea-11
92PacSea-12
92PacSea-13
92PacSea-14
92PacSea-15
92PacSea-16
92PacSea-17
92PacSea-18
92PacSea-19
92PacSea-20
92PacSea-21
92PacSea-22
92PacSea-23
92PacSea-24
92PacSea-25
92PacSea-26
92PacSea-27
92PacSea-28
92PacSea-29
92PacSea-30
92PacSea-31
92PacSea-32
92PacSea-33
92PacSea-34
92PacSea-35
92PacSea-36
92PacSea-37
92PacSea-38
92PacSea-39
92PacSea-40
92PacSea-41
92PacSea-42
92PacSea-43
92PacSea-44
92PacSea-45
92PacSea-46
92PacSea-47
92PacSea-48
92PacSea-49
92PacSea-50
92PacSea-51
92PacSea-52
92PacSea-53
92PacSea-54
92PacSea-55
92PacSea-56
92PacSea-57
92PacSea-58
92PacSea-59
92PacSea-60
92PacSea-61
92PacSea-62
92PacSea-63
92PacSea-64
92PacSea-65
92PacSea-66
92PacSea-67
92PacSea-68
92PacSea-69
92PacSea-70
92PacSea-71
92PacSea-72
92PacSea-73
92PacSea-74
92PacSea-75
92PacSea-76
92PacSea-77
92PacSea-78
92PacSea-79
92PacSea-80
92PacSea-81
92PacSea-82
92PacSea-83
92PacSea-84
92PacSea-85
92PacSea-86
92PacSea-87
92PacSea-88
92PacSea-89
92PacSea-90
92PacSea-91
92PacSea-92
92PacSea-93
92PacSea-94
92PacSea-95
92PacSea-96
92PacSea-97
92PacSea-98
92PacSea-99
92PacSea-100
92PacSea-101
92PacSea-102
92PacSea-103
92PacSea-104
92PacSea-105
92PacSea-106
92PacSea-107
92PacSea-108
92PacSea-109
92PacSea-110
92PacSeaI6-1
92PacSeaI6-2
92PacSeaI6-3
92PacSeaI6-4
92PacSeaI6-5
92PacSeaI6-6
92PacSeaI6-AU1
92PhoFilHoF-3
92PhoFilHoF-4
93ActPacA-129
93ActPacA2-63G
93ActPacSP-TS1
93ActPacSP-TS2
93ActPacSP-TS3
93ActPacSP-TS4
93ActPacSP-TS5
93PacRya2S-241
93PacRya2S-250
93SpeGolSS-1
93Yoo-18
94Met69CCPP-28
94Met69CS-27
94Met69SP-P1
94Met69SP-P3
94Met69T-3
94Met69T-42
94Met69T-52
94UppDecAH-120
94UppDecAH-177
94UppDecAH-180
94UppDecAH1-120
94UppDecAH1-177
94UppDecAH1-180
94UppDecTAE-70
95EagBalL-3
95UppDecSHoB-9

Seay, Dick
78LauLonABS-14

Seay, Mark
87SanJosBP-16

Sebach, Kyle
92BoiHawF-3626
92QuaCitRBC-20
92QuaCitRBF-809
93CedRapKC-16
93CedRapKF-1735
94LakElsSC-16
94LakElsSF-1662
94MidAngOHP-28
96LakElsSB-10
96MidAngB-27

Seberino, Ronnie
97Top-253

Sebra, Bob
83TriTriT-1
85OklCit8T-19
86IndIndTI-23
87Don-468
87ExpPos-26
87Fle-331
87FleGlo-331
87Lea-213
87OPC-314
87Top-479
87TopTif-479
88Don-458
88Fle-195
88FleGlo-195
88IndIndC-3
88IndIndP-511
88OPC-93
88Sco-337
88ScoGlo-337
88Top-93
88TopTif-93
88TriAAAP-17
89BlaYNPRWL-163
89ScrRedBC-4
89ScrRedBP-718
90BreMilB-22
90CMC-136
90NasSouC-11
90NasSouP-233
90ProAAAF-545
90TulDriDGB-8
92IowCubF-4051
92OklCit8S-322
92SkyAAAF-148
93LouRedF-213
93RanKee-323
94BreMilB-179

Sebring, James
09RamT20-107
90DodTar-716

Sebring, Jeff
96PorRocB-28

Secoda, Jason
96SouBenSHS-22

Secory, Frank
55Bow-286

Secrest, Charlie
59Top-140
59TopVen-140

Secrist, Don
69Top-654

Secrist, Reed
93AugPirC-19
93AugPirF-1554
94SalBucC-20
94SalBucF-2332
95LynHilTI-27
96Exc-224

Seda, Israel
91PenPilC-22
91PenPilP-387

Sedar, Ed
83AppFoxF-18
86PenWhiSP-24
87DayBeaAP-19
88SouBenWSGS-17
91PocPioP-3802
91PocPioSP-28

See, Charles
20RedWorCP-22

See, Larry
82VerBeaDT-20
84AlbDukC-162
86AlbDukP-22
87AlbDukP-21
89TolMudHC-14
89TolMudHP-784
90DodTar-717
93RanKee-324

Seeburger, John
88OneYanP-2050
89Ft.LauYS-25

Seeds, Robert Ira
32OrbPinUP-52
33ExhFou-10
33TatOrb-52
36GouWidPPR-D33
36WorWidGV-27
39PlaBal-32
40PlaBal-91
75YanDyn1T-44

Seefried, Tate
90TamYanD-22
91OneYanP-4163
92ClaFS7-307
92GreHorC-25
92GreHorF-789
93CarLeaAGF-24
93PriWilCC-1
93PriWilCF-666

94AbaYanF-1451
94AlbYanTI-3
94Bow-661
94BowBes-B20
94BowBesR-B20
94Cla-174
94ExcFS7-114
94UppDecML-87
95Bow-139
95Exc-104
95NorNagUTI-31
95SigRooOJ-29
95SigRooOJP-29
95SigRooOJPS-29
95SigRooOJS-29
95UppDecML-96
96Bow-141
96NorNavB-23
95UppDecMLFS-96
Seeger, Mark
81AppFoxT-24
Seegers, Pat
78NewWayCT-40
79BurBeeT-3
Seelbach, Christopher
92ClaFS7-252
92MacBraC-22
92MacBraF-268
92StaCluD-167
92UppDecML-94
93ClaFS7-255
93DurBulC-18
93DurBulF-486
93DurBulTI-31
94GreBraF-412
94GreBraTI-21
94UppDecML-78
95Exc-157
95RicBraRC-23
95RicBraTI-21
96ChaKniB-26
Seelbach, Chuck
73OPC-51
73Top-51
74OPC-292
74Tig-11
74Top-292
Seerey, James Pat
47IndTeal-24
47IndVanPP-23
49Lea-73
77TCMTheWY-13
94TedWil-152
Seery, John Emmett
87BucN28-46A
87BucN28-46B
87OldJudN-450
88WG1CarG-35
Sees, Eric
96SpoIndB-25
Seesz, Brian
92GulCoaRSP-21
93ChaRaiC-19
93ChaRaiF-1915
Sefcik, Kevin
93BatCliC-25
93BatCliF-3155
94ClePhiC-22
94ClePhiF-2537
95ReaPhiELC-32
95ReaPhiTI-9
96Bow-262
96FleUpd-U171
96FleUpdTC-U171
96LeaSigEA-179
96ScrRedBB-24
96Ult-526
96UltGolM-526
97Fle-422
97FleTif-422
97Pac-387
97PacLigB-387
97PacSil-387
Sefly, Joel
91VisOakC-27
Segelke, Herman
82IowCubT-23
83PhoGiaBHN-13
84PhoGiaC-10
Segrist, Kal
58UniOil-7
91OriCro-411
Segui, Daniel
89PitMetS-25
89Sta-166
90VisOakCLC-77
90VisOakP-2164
Segui, David
88HagSunS-19
89FreKeyS-21
90Bow-251A
90Bow-251B
90BowTif-251A
90BowTif-251B
90FleUpd-69
90HagSunDGB-26
90RocRedWGC-2
90ScoRoo-95T
90TriAllGP-AAA54
90UppDec-773
91Bow-102
91Cla1-T15
91Don-730
91Fle-492
91LinDriAAA-466
91MajLeaCP-30
91OPC-724
91OriCro-412
91RocRedWLD-466
91RocRedWP-1910
91Sco-362
91Sco100RS-61
91ScoRoo-31
91SevCoi-A15
91StaClu-50
91StaCluP-40
91Stu-10
91Top-724
91TopDeb90-140
91TopDesS-724
91TopMic-724
91TopTif-724
91Ult-25
91UppDec-342
92Don-321
92Fle-27
92OPC-447
92OPCPre-153
92Pin-185
92ProFS7-5
92Sco-554
92Sco100RS-33
92StaClu-783
92StaCluNC-783
92Top-447
92TopGol-447
92TopGolW-447
92TopMic-447
92Ult-308
92UppDec-316
93Don-397
93Fle-175
93Lea-306
93PacSpa-25
93Pin-325
93Sco-610
93SP-162
93StaClu-479
93StaCluFDI-479
93StaCluMOP-479
93Top-82
93TopGol-82
93TopInaM-82
93TopMic-82
93Toy-45
93TriPla-12
93TriPlaP-12
93Ult-146
93UppDec-792
93UppDecGold-792
94ColC-254
94ColC-529
94ColChoGS-254
94ColChoGS-529
94ColChoSS-254
94ColChoSS-529
94Don-624
94ExtBas-324
94Fin-103
94FinRef-103
94Fla-410
94Fle-20
94FleUpd-160
94Lea-352
94MetColP-23
94OriPro-91
94OriUSPC-7C
94OriUSPC-12H
94Pac-45
94PanSti-24
94Pin-131
94PinArtP-131
94PinMusC-131
94Sco-361
94ScoGolR-361
94ScoRoo-RT35
94ScoRooGR-RT35
94Sel-322
94StaClu-95
94StaClu-696
94StaCluFDI-95
94StaCluFDI-696
94StaCluGR-95
94StaCluGR-696
94StaCluMOP-95
94StaCluMOP-696
94StaCluT-285
94StaCluTFDI-285
94Top-571
94TopGol-571
94TopSpa-571
94TopTra-94T
94Ult-534
94UppDec-421
94UppDecED-421
95ColCho-313
95ColChoGS-313
95ColChoSS-313
95Don-242
95DonPreP-242
95DonTopotO-286
95Fle-381
95Lea-262
95Pac-288
95Pin-313
95PinArtP-313
95PinMusC-313
95Sco-388
95ScoGolR-388
95ScoPlaTS-388
95StaClu-83
95StaCluFDI-83
95StaCluMOP-83
95StaCluSTWS-83
95Top-101
95TopCyb-65
95Ult-416
95UltGolM-416
95UppDec-358
95UppDec-464T
95UppDecED-358
95UppDecEDG-358
95UppDecSE-57
95UppDecSEG-57
96Baz-110
96Cir-152
96CirRav-152
96ColCho-210
96ColChoGS-210
96ColChoSS-210
96Don-78
96DonPreP-78
96EmoXL-226
96ExpBoo-5
96ExpDis-18
96ExpDis-19
96Fin-B36
96FinRef-B36
96Fla-313
96Fle-469
96FleTif-469
96Lea-162
96LeaPrePB-162
96LeaPrePG-162
96LeaPrePS-162
96LeaSigA-206
96LeaSigAG-206
96LeaSigAS-206
96MetUni-194
96MetUniP-194
96Pac-121
96PacEstL-EL28
96PacPri-P44
96PacPriG-P44
96PanSti-23
96Pin-39
96ProSta-48
96Sco-133
96ScoDugC-A84
96ScoDugCAP-A84
96StaClu-28
96StaCluMOP-28
96Stu-77
96StuPrePB-77
96StuPrePG-77
96StuPrePS-77
96Top-151
96TopChr-44
96TopChrR-44
96TopGal-45
96TopGalPPI-45
96Ult-236
96UltGolM-236
96UppDec-131
97Cir-181
97CirRav-181
97ColCho-159
97Don-187
97DonPreP-187
97DonPrePGold-187
97Fin-131
97FinEmb-131
97FinEmbR-131
97FinRef-131
97Fle-387
97FleTif-387
97Pac-353
97PacLigB-353
97PacSil-353
97Pin-59
97PinArtP-59
97PinMusC-59
97Sco-420
97ScoHobR-420
97ScoResC-420
97ScoShoS-420
97ScoShoSAP-420
97StaClu-64
97StaCluMOP-64
97Top-36
97Ult-421
97UltGolME-421
97UltPlaME-421
97UppDec-113
Segui, Diego
61UniOil-H4
63Top-157
64A's-14
64AthJayP-11
64Top-508
64TopCoi-24
65OPC-197
65Top-197
65TopEmbl-24
65TopTral-68
66Top-309
66TopVen-309
68Top-517
69PilPos-11
69Top-511A
69Top-511B
70OPC-2
70Top-2
71MLBOffS-526
71OPC-67
71OPC-215
71Top-67
71Top-215
72Top-735
73OPC-383
73Top-383
74OPC-151
74Top-151
74TopTra-151T
75OPC-232
75Top-232
76SSP-423
76VenLeaS-83
77Top-653
80VenLeaS-16
83Pil69G-25
87PocGiaTB-30
88PocGiaP-2100
89EveGiaS-31
90EveGiaP-3146
90PacLeg-104
Seguignol, Fernando
94OneYanC-20
94OneYanF-3805
96DelShoB-27
Segura, Angel
89CarNewE-19
Segura, Jose
85DomLeaS-135
85KinBluJT-10
86KnoBluJP-19
87SyrChiP-1936
87SyrChiT-7
88FleUpd-20
88FleUpdG-20
88WhiSoxC-27
89VanCanC-6
89VanCanP-591
90CMC-639
90ProAAAF-168
90VanCanC-12
90VanCanP-490
91LinDriAAA-394
91PhoFirLD-394
91PhoFirP-66
92NasSouS-292
92Sco-278
93LimRocDWB-69
Segura, Juan
93LetMouF-4157
93LetMouSP-20
94AugGreC-22
94SalBucC-21
94SalBucF-2333
Sehorn, Jason
90HunCubP-3302
Seibert, Gib
85PorBeaC-27
87MaiGuiP-15
87MaiGuiT-16
Seibert, Kurt
80TolMudHT-20
81TolMudHT-14
Seibert, Mal
90FayGenP-2406
Seibert, Rick
89PenPilS-22
Seibold, Socks (Harry)
29PorandAR-84
33DouDisP-38
93ConTSN-975
Seidel, Dick
83GreHorT-12
Seidel, Ryan
96RocCubTI-29
Seidensticker, Andy
88VisOakCLC-172
88VisOakP-106
Seidholz, Don
78KnoKnoST-18
79KnoKnoST-9
Seifert, Keith
87WatIndP-21
88WatIndP-678
Seiler, Keith
90TamYanD-23
91GreHorP-3059
92PriWilCC-20
92PriWilCF-149
93PriWilCC-22
93PriWilCF-655
94AbaYanF-1441
95NorNavTI-20
Seilheimer, Rick
80GleFalWSBT-7
80GleFalWSCT-8
81GleFalWST-9
82EdmTraT-21
86BirBarTI-14
Seip, Rod
92GulCoaRSP-1
93EriSaiC-21
93EriSaiF-3115
94ChaRivC-19
94ChaRivF-2673
Seitz, Charles
09T206-514
Seitz, David
86SumBraP-25
Seitzer, Brad
91BluOriC-8
91BluOriP-4137
91KanCouCTI-19
92ClaFS7-146
92FreKeyC-11
92FreKeyF-1815
93FreKeyC-23
93FreKeyF-1037
96El PasDB-26
97Top-490
Seitzer, Kevin
83ButCopKT-20
85Ft.MyeRT-9
86OmaRoyP-22
86OmaRoyT-3

87ClaUpdY-139
87DonHig-26
87DonHig-47
87DonOpeD-207
87DonRoo-15
87Fle-652
87FleGlo-652
87FleSlu-39
87FleUpd-108
87FleUpdG-108
87Spo-158
87SpoRool-20
87SpoTeaP-13
87TopTra-111T
87TopTraT-111T
88ClaBlu-218
88ClaRed-159
88Don-280
88DonAll-27
88DonBasB-175
88DonBonM-BC17
88Fle-270
88FleAwaW-37
88FleBasA-38
88FleBasM-33
88FleExcS-36
88FleGlo-270
88FleHotS-36
88FleLeaL-37
88FleMin-27
88FleRecS-37
88FleSlu-38
88FleStiC-33
88FleSup-35
88FleTeaL-36
88FleWaxBC-C12
88K-M-27
88Lea-105
88MSAIceTD-8
88OPC-275
88PanSti-108
88PanSti-436
88RoySmo-21
88Sco-6
88ScoGlo-6
88ScoYouSI-10
88Spo-17
88SpoGam-13
88StaLinRo-15
88StaSei-1
88StaSei-2
88StaSei-3
88StaSei-4
88StaSei-5
88StaSei-6
88StaSei-7
88StaSei-8
88StaSei-9
88StaSei-10
88StaSei-11
88Top-275
88TopBig-115
88TopGloS-9
88TopMinL-15
88TopRevLL-22
88TopRitTM-19
88TopRoo-9
88TopSti-261
88TopSti-306
88TopTif-275
88TopUKM-69
88TopUKMT-69
88ToyRoo-27
89Bow-123
89BowTif-123
89CadEllD-52
89ClaLigB-65
89Don-10
89Don-238
89DonBasB-207
89DonSupD-10
89Fle-292
89FleExcS-36
89FleGlo-292
89FleHeroB-36
89FleWaxBC-C22
89MSAHolD-9
89Nis-9
89OPC-58
89PanSti-357
89RedFolSB-107
89RoyTasD-2
89Sco-55
89ScoHot1S-17
89Spo-55
89Top-670
89TopBasT-120
89TopBig-313
89TopSti-264
89TopTif-670
89TVSpoM-106
89UppDec-510
89UppDecS-3
90Bow-380
90BowTif-380
90Don-85
90DonBesA-91
90Fle-117
90FleCan-117
90Lea-230
90MLBBasB-102
90OPC-435
90PanSti-86
90PubSti-355
90RedFolSB-86
90Sco-199
90Sco100S-88
90Spo-46
90Top-435
90TopBig-76
90TopMinL-18
90TopSti-267
90TopTif-435
90UppDec-363
91Bow-305
91ClaGam-40
91Don-73
91Fle-569
91KinDis-2
91Lea-133
91OPC-695
91PanFreS-278
91PanSti-227
91RoyPol-19
91Sco-279
91Sco100S-97
91SimandSMLBL-39
91StaClu-88
91StuPre-5
91Top-695
91TopDesS-695
91TopMic-695
91TopTif-695
91Ult-155
91UppDec-433
92Bow-126
92BrePol-22
92Don-577
92DonUpd-U15
92Fle-168
92FleUpd-38
92Lea-399
92OPC-577
92OPCPre-27
92Pin-11
92RoyPol-24
92Sco-310
92ScoProP-5
92ScoRoo-2T
92StaClu-285
92StaClu-820
92Top-577
92TopGol-577
92TopGolW-577
92TopMic-577
92TopTra-103T
92TopTraG-103T
92Ult-389
92UppDec-327
92UppDec-783
93AthMot-21
93Bow-597
93Don-603
93Fle-256
93FleFinE-262
93Lea-353
93OPC-312
93OPCPre-121
93PacSpa-164
93PanSti-40
93Pin-117
93Sco-571
93Sel-87
93StaClu-57
93StaClu-657
93StaCluAt-5
93StaCluFDI-57
93StaCluFDI-657
93StaCluMOP-57
93StaCluMOP-657
93Stu-169
93Top-44
93TopGol-44
93TopInaM-44
93TopMic-44
93Ult-612
93UppDec-295
93UppDec-616
93UppDecGold-295
93UppDecGold-616
94BreMilB-180
94BrePol-24
94ColC-379
94ColChoGS-379
94ColChoSS-379
94Don-261
94ExtBas-108
94Fin-314
94FinRef-314
94Fla-70
94Fle-190
94Lea-339
94Pac-341
94PanSti-86
94ProMag-72
94Sco-519
94ScoGolR-519
94Sel-355
94StaClu-90
94StaCluFDI-90
94StaCluGR-90
94StaCluMOP-90
94Stu-47
94Top-411
94TopGol-411
94TopSpa-411
94Ult-378
94UppDec-378
94UppDecED-378
95BowBes-R67
95BowBesR-R67
95ColCho-172
95ColChoGS-172
95ColChoSS-172
95Don-10
95DonDiaK-DK13
95DonPreP-10
95DonTopotO-102
95Emo-55
95Fin-210
95FinRef-210
95Fla-276
95Fle-189
95Lea-86
95LeaLim-61
95Pin-46
95PinArtP-46
95PinMusC-46
95Sco-45
95ScoGolR-45
95ScoPlaTS-45
95SP-166
95SPCha-165
95SPChaDC-165
95SPSil-166
95StaClu-435
95StaCluMOP-435
95StaCluSTWS-435
95StaCluVR-230
95Stu-145
95TomPiz-16
95Top-309
95TopCyb-166
95Ult-68
95UltGolM-68
95UppDec-302
95UppDecED-302
95UppDecEDG-302
95Zen-64
96Baz-46
96Cir-53
96CirRav-53
96ColCho-190
96ColChoGS-190
96ColChoSS-190
96DenHol-26
96Don-503
96DonPreP-503
96EmoXL-77
96Fin-B70
96FinRef-B70
96Fla-106
96Fle-157
96FleTif-157
96Lea-74
96LeaPre-89
96LeaPreP-89
96LeaPrePB-74
96LeaPrePG-74
96LeaPrePS-74
96LeaSigA-207
96LeaSigAG-207
96LeaSigAS-207
96MetUni-73
96MetUniP-73
96PanSti-197
96Pin-231
96PinAfi-7
96PinAfiAP-7
96PinAfiFPP-7
96PinArtP-131
96PinFan-19
96PinFoil-231
96PinSta-131
96ProSta-26
96Sco-59
96Sel-28
96SelArtP-28
96SelTeaN-28
96SP-109
96Spo-93
96SpoArtP-93
96StaClu-33
96StaCluMOP-33
95StaCluVRMC-230
96Stu-84
96StuPrePB-84
96StuPrePG-84
96StuPrePS-84
96Sum-10
96SumAbo&B-10
96SumArtP-10
96SumFoi-10
96TeaOut-72
96Top-111
96TopChr-30
96TopChrR-30
96Ult-83
96UltGolM-83
96UppDec-365
96ZenMoz-14
97Cir-152
97CirRav-152
97ColCho-316
97Don-324
97DonEli-139
97DonEliGS-139
97DonPreP-324
97DonPrePGold-324
97DonTea-88
97DonTeaSPE-88
97Fin-231
97FinRef-231
97Fle-88
97FleTif-88
97Lea-286
97LeaFraM-286
97LeaFraMDC-286
97Pin-79
97PinArtP-79
97PinMusC-79
97Sco-207
97ScoInd-11
97ScoIndPl-11
97ScoIndPr-11
97ScoIndU-11
97ScoIndUTC-11
97ScoPreS-207
97ScoShoS-207
97ScoShoSAP-207
97StaClu-305
97StaCluMOP-305
97Stu-72
97StuPrePG-72
97StuPrePS-72
97Top-421
97UppDec-341

Seja, Aaron

91FayGenP-1184
91NiaFalRC-7
91NiaFalRP-3648

Selak, Ron**

76VenLeaS-59
78SprRedWK-21

Selanne, Teemu

92StaCluMO-49
92StaCluMO-50
93StaCluMO-59

Selbach, Kip (Albert)

03BreE10-127
11SpoLifCW-317

Selby, Bill

92ElmPioC-19
92ElmPioF-1393
92FroRowDP-49
93LynRedSC-24
93LynRedSF-2527
94CarLeaAF-CAR5
94LynRedSC-22
94LynRedSF-1902
95Bow-63
95Exc-15
95TreThuTI-23
95UppDecML-187
96BowBes-173
96BowBesAR-173
96BowBesR-173
96Exc-19
96PawRedSDD-27
97Ult-18
97UltGolME-18
97UltPlaME-18
95UppDecMLFS-187

Sele, Aaron

91Cla/Bes-437
91ClaDraP-19
91FroRowDP-2
92Bow-311
92ClaBluBF-BC11
92ClaFS7-175
92ClaRedB-BC11
92LynRedSC-16
92LynRedSF-2907
92OPC-504
92Sco-809
92StaCluD-168
92Top-504
92TopGol-504
92TopGolW-504
92TopMic-504
92UppDecML-291
92UppDecMLPotY-PY20
93Bow-255
93ClaFisN-8
93ClaFS7-23
93ClaGolF-23
93ExcAllF-7
93ExcFS7-138
93FlaWavotF-16
93FleFinE-178
93Lea-518
93PawRedSDD-24
93PawRedSF-2408
93PawRedSTI-21
93SelRoo-86T
93SP-205
93TopTra-3T
94Bow-643
94BowBes-R44
94BowBesR-R44
94ColC-255
94ColChoGS-255
94ColChoSS-255
94Don-303
94ExtBas-25
94ExtBasPD-4
94ExtBasSYS-19
94Fin-6
94FinJum-6
94FinRef-6
94Fla-15
94Fla-P15
94Fle-43
94FleRooS-18
94FUnPac-36
94Lea-199
94LeaL-11
94OPC-89
94OPCDiaD-17
94Pac-66
94Pin-95
94PinArtP-95
94PinMusC-95
94PinNewG-NG5
94Sco-561
94ScoBoyoS-2
94ScoGolR-561
94Sel-337
94SP-156
94SPDieC-156

94Spo-37
94StaClu-179
94StaClu-678
94StaCluFDI-179
94StaCluFDI-678
94StaCluGR-179
94StaCluGR-678
94StaCluMOP-179
94StaCluMOP-678
94Stu-164
94Top-445
94TopGol-445
94TopSpa-445
94TriPla-207
94Ult-18
94UltRisS-12
94UltSecYS-5
94UppDec-45
94UppDec-80
94UppDecAJ-21
94UppDecAJG-21
94UppDecED-45
94UppDecED-80
94USPlaCR-8S
95Bow-314
95ColCho-406
95ColChoGS-406
95ColChoSE-191
95ColChoSEGS-191
95ColChoSESS-191
95ColChoSS-406
95Don-17
95DonPreP-17
95DonTopotO-26
95Emo-15
95Fin-201
95FinRef-201
95Fla-13
95Fle-40
95Lea-7
95LeaLim-137
95Pac-45
95Pin-259
95PinArtP-259
95PinMusC-259
95PinUps-US18
95RedFol-11
95Sco-335
95ScoGolR-335
95ScoPlaTS-335
95Sel-29
95SelArtP-29
95SP-129
95Spo-57
95SpoArtP-57
95SPSil-129
95StaClu-464
95StaCluMOP-464
95StaCluSTDW-RS464
95StaCluSTWS-464
95StaCluVR-253
95Stu-150
95Top-301
95TopCyb-162
95UC3-16
95UC3ArtP-16
95Ult-264
95UltGolM-264
95UppDec-162
95UppDecED-162
95UppDecEDG-162
96ColCho-476
96ColChoGS-476
96ColChoSS-476
96Don-157
96DonPreP-157
96Fla-24
96Fle-33
96FleRedS-12
96FleTif-33
96Lea-202
96LeaPrePB-202
96LeaPrePG-202
96LeaPrePS-202
96Sco-416
95StaCluVRMC-253
96Top-332
96Ult-319
96UltGolM-319
96UppDec-284
97Cir-19
97CirRav-19
97ColCho-49
97Don-319
97DonPreP-319
97DonPrePGold-319
97DonTea-57
97DonTeaSPE-57
97Fle-662
97FleTif-662
97Lea-302
97LeaFraM-302
97LeaFraMDC-302
97PacPriGotD-GD25
97Sco-395
97ScoHobR-395
97ScoResC-395
97ScoShoS-395
97ScoShoSAP-395
97StaClu-177
97StaCluMOP-177
97Top-243
97Ult-539
97UltGolME-539
97UltPlaME-539
Selee, Frank
87OldJudN-439
Selig, Bud
96PinFan-BS1
Selkirk, George
34DiaStaR-88
35DiaMatCS3T1-130
36WorWidGV-11
37KelPepS-BB12
37OPCBatUV-108
38OurNatGPP-27
39PlaBal-25
40PlaBal-8
75YanDyn1T-45
75YanDyn1T-51
79DiaGre-7
83YanASFY-41
92ConTSN-388
92YanWIZA-76
Sell, Chip
94YakBeaC-21
94YakBeaF-3865
95VerBeaDTI-23
96SanBerSB-24
Sellas, Marcelino
88CapCodPPaLP-91
Selleck, Tom
92UppDec-SP4
Sellers, Jeff
86DonRoo-29
86PawRedSP-21
87Don-544
87Fle-46
87FleGlo-46
87Lea-158
87Top-12
87TopTif-12
88Don-585
88DonTeaBRS-585
88Fle-366
88FleGlo-366
88Sco-541
88ScoGlo-541
88Top-653
88TopTif-653
89Bow-299
89BowTif-299
89Don-517
89NasSouP-1270
89Sco-491
89Top-544
89TopTif-544
92TulDriF-2694
Sellers, Rick
89NiaFalRP-21
90FayGenP-2412
91LakTigC-16
92LonTigF-637
92LonTigS-418
93LonTigF-2312
95ChaLooTI-21
Sellheimer, Rick
85BufBisT-5
Sellick, John
88SavCarP-347
88SouAtlLAGS-25
89SprCarB-14
90St.PetCS-22
91ArkTraLD-44
91ArkTraP-1296
91LinDriAA-44
92ArkTraF-1140
92ArkTraS-45
92SkyAA F-19
Sellner, Scott
88BilMusP-1807
89CedRapRB-17
89CedRapRP-925
89CedRapRS-18
90ChaLooGS-27
91ChaLooLD-169
91ChaLooP-1968
91LinDriAA-169
Sells, Dave
74OPC-37
74Top-37
90DodTar-718
Sells, George
88CapCodPPaLP-117
90HamRedB-9
90HamRedS-23
91St.PetCP-2275
Selma, Dick
66OPC-67
66Top-67
66TopVen-67
67Top-386
68Top-556
69CubJewT-16
69MLBOffS-195
69OPC-197
69Top-197
69TopDecl-39
69TopFou-6
69TopSta-98
69TopSup-62
69TopTeaP-12
70MLBOffS-23
70OPC-24
70Top-24
71Kel-21
71MLBOffS-187
71OPC-705
71PhiArcO-10
71Top-705
72Top-726
73OPC-632
73Top-632
75AlbDukC-11
91MetWIZ-357
94BreMilB-181
Selmo, Feliberto
93DanBraC-15
93DanBraF-3625
Seltzer, Randy
76AppFoxT-24
77AppFoxT-22
Semall, Paul
79ColCliT-3
80WicAerT-15
83OklCit8T-16
84HawIslC-125
85HawIslC-232
Sember, Mike
79SyrChiT-10
79SyrChiTI-10
Sembera, Carroll
66Top-539
67OPC-136
67Top-136
68Top-207
68TopVen-207
69Top-351
Sementelli, Chris
89SpaPhiP-1049
Semerano, Bob
77ChaPatT-21
Seminara, Frank
88OneYanP-2071
89OneYanP-2121
89PriWilCS-18
90CarLeaA-14
90PriWilCTI-23
91Cla/Bes-382
91LinDriAA-618
91WicWraLD-618
91WicWraP-2598
91WicWraRD-9
92Bow-561
92Don-10
92DonRooP-BC17
92FleUpd-124
92LasVegSS-240
92PadPolD-19
92PadSmo-29
92PinRoo-25
92ProFS7-334
92ScoRoo-97T
92SkyAAAF-116
92TopTra-104T
92TopTraG-104T
93Bow-222
93ClaGam-83
93Don-550
93Fle-146
93Lea-64
93OPC-282
93PacSpa-601
93PadMot-16
93Pin-561
93Sco-342
93Sel-305
93StaClu-438
93StaCluFDI-438
93StaCluMOP-438
93Top-247
93TopGol-247
93TopInaM-247
93TopMic-247
93Toy-57
93Ult-121
93UppDec-307
93UppDecGold-307
93USPlaCR-10D
94Fle-673
94MetShuST-8
94NorTidF-2921
94Pac-533
94Ult-283
95RocRedWTI-33
Seminick, Andy
47Exh-205
47PM1StaP1-198
49Bow-30
49EurSta-146
49PhiBul-48
49PhiLumPB-10
50Bow-121
50RoyDes-7A
50RoyDes-7B
51BerRos-C7
51Bow-51
51TopRedB-45
52DixLid-20
52DixPre-20
52RoyPre-13
52Top-297
53BowBW-7
53Top-153
54Bow-172
55Bow-93
56Top-296
76TayBow4-51
79DiaGre-315
83PhiPosGPaM-3
83TCMPla1945-43
83TopRep5-297
91TopArc1-153
Seminoff, Rich
93ElmPioC-17
93ElmPioF-3832
94ElmPioF-3484
Semore, Enos
88OklSoo-6
89OklSoo-1
Semprini, John
82JacMetT-9
84ChaLooT-11
Semproch, Roman
58Top-474
59Top-197
60Top-286
61Top-174
61TopStaI-206
Sempsprott, Ed
75WatRoyT-25
Sempsrott, Ed
76WatRoyT-25
77DayBeaIT-21
Sena, Sean
90YakBeaTI-22
Senators, Washington
13FatT20-8
24SenWri&D-1
35GouPreR-3
38BasTabP-39
51TopTea-9
56Top-146
57Top-270
58Top-44
59Top-397
60Top-43
60TopTat-71
60TopVen-43
61TopMagR-4
62GuyPotCP-19
62Top-206
63Top-131
64Top-343
64TopTatI-20
64TopVen-343
65OPC-267
65Top-267
66OPC-194
66Top-194
66TopRubI-120
66TopVen-194
67Top-437
68LauWorS-21
69FleCloS-24
69FleCloS-44
69TopStaA-24
70Top-676
71OPC-462
71Top-462
71TopTat-94
Sencion, Pablo
96MedHatBJTI-27
Sendoh, Mikio
79TCMJapPB-42
Seninger, Glenn
88SalLakCTTI-4
Senior, Shawn
94LynRedSC-23
94LynRedSF-1892
95Bow-169
95SigRooOJ-30
95SigRooOJP-30
95SigRooOJPS-30
95SigRooOJS-30
95TreThuTI-14
96Bow-118
96TreThuB-14
Senkowitz, Mark
92ElmPioC-17
92ElmPioF-1385
93UtiBluSC-22
93UtiBluSF-3536
Senn, Terry
75TidTidTI-18
Senne, Michael
86AriWilP-13
87St.PetCP-9
88ArkTraGS-25
89ShrCapP-1840
Senne, Tim
86VisOakP-20
87VisOakP-14
Senteney, Steve
82SyrChiT-8
82SyrChiTI-20
83Don-52
83TidTidT-10
Sentlinger, Rick
77QuaCitAT-25
Seo, Yoshihiro
96HonShaHWB-27
Seoane, Manny (Manuel)
76OklCit8TI-26
76VenLeaS-215
80WicAerT-21
81BirBarT-4
81EvaTriT-7
Seoane, Mitch
84GreHorT-25
86PalSprAP-24
87MidAngP-20
88QuaCitAB-25
89QuaCitAGS-2
90QuaCitAGS-3
91QuaCitAC-27
91QuaCitAP-2645
92QuaCitRBC-27
92QuaCitRBF-826
93CedRapKC-26
93CedRapKF-1754
94LakElsSC-26
94LakElsSF-1680
95LakElsSTI-20
96LakElsSB-26
Seok, Tae
96HilStaHWB-29
Sepanek, Rob
86Ft.LauYP-20
87PriWilYP-10

88AlbYanP-1332
89AlbYanB-9
89AlbYanP-330
89AlbYanS-17
89EasLeaAP-8
90AlbDecGB-29
90CMC-221
90ColCliC-21
90ColCliP-22
90ColCliP-684
90ProAAAF-334
Sepeda, Jamie
92BatCliC-1
92BatCliF-3264
93ClaGolF-152
93ClePhiC-20
93ClePhiF-2683
94ClePhiC-23
94ClePhiF-2526
Sepela, Thom
86ElmPioRSP-21
87ElmPio(C-20
Septimo, Felix
90MedHatBJB-11
91St.CatBJP-3409
Sepulveda, Jorge
86VerBeaDP-22
Serad, William
87OldJudN-451
Serafin, Ricardo
95MarPhiTI-23
96MarPhiB-23
Serafini, Dan
92ClaBluBF-BC28
92ClaDraP-20
92ClaFS7-411
92UppDecML-104
93Bow-397
93ClaFS7-256
93ClaGolF-114
93ForWayWC-1
93ForWayWF-1968
93Pin-465
93Sco-497
93Sel-352
93StaCluM-43
93Top-307
93TopGol-307
93TopInaM-307
93TopMic-307
94Cla-132
94ClaGolF-67
94ExcFS7-98
94ForMyeMC-23
94UppDecML-108
95Bes-29
95HarCitRCTI-23
95SPML-89
96Bow-139
96ColCho-777
96Exc-82
96UppDec-264
Serafini, Rudy
83QuaCitCT-14
Serbalik, Mike
92YakBeaF-3460
Serbin, Scott
90SarWhiSS-30
Serena, Bill
50Bow-230
51Bow-246
52Top-325
53BowC-122
54Bow-93
55Bow-233
83TopRep5-325
Serna, Joe
93WelPirC-26
Serna, Paul
81LynSaiT-18
82Don-567
83ChaLooT-2
83Top-492
84ChaLooT-12
85CalCanC-79
86WauTimP-23
Serna, Ramon
87ElPasDP-25
88ElPasDB-7
Serra, Armando
88St.CatBJP-2037
Serra, Jose
92BluOriC-8
92BluOriF-2369
93AlbPolC-19
93AlbPolF-2035
94AlbPolC-23
94AlbPolF-2247
94OriPro-92
Serrano, Andy
79ElmPioRST-17
Serrano, Marty
77DayBealT-22
Serrano, Nestor
93BelMarC-24
93BelMarF-3224
94BelMarC-25
94BelMarF-3247
Serrato, Jacob
93HunCubC-23
93HunCubF-3239
Serrell, Barney
95NegLeaL2-11
Serritella, John
83ButCopKT-10
83ChaRoyT-23
Serum, Gary
77OrlTwiT-18
77TacTwiDQ-16A
78TwiFriP-18
79Top-627
79TwiFriP-25
80TolMudHT-5
80Top-61
82OrlTwi8SCT-23
Servais, Scott
87PanAmTURB-3
88TopTra-106T
88TopTraT-106T
89OscAstS-20
89Sta-17
89TopBig-291
90CMC-623
90ProAAAF-196
90TucTorC-21
90TucTorP-206
91LinDriAAA-618
91TucTorLD-618
91TucTorP-2216
91UppDecFE-68F
92AstMot-17
92Bow-463
92Don-763
92Fle-444
92Lea-121
92OPC-437
92Pin-255
92Sco-816
92ScoRoo-36
92StaClu-509
92Top-437
92TopDeb91-162
92TopGol-437
92TopGolW-437
92TopMic-437
92Ult-496
92UppDec-561
93AstMot-6
93Don-108
93Fle-442
93Lea-33
93OPC-339
93PacSpa-480
93StaClu-363
93StaCluAs-13
93StaCluFDI-363
93StaCluMOP-363
93Top-36
93TopGol-36
93TopInaM-36
93TopMic-36
93Ult-396
93UppDec-613
93UppDecGold-613
93USPlaCR-8C
94AstMot-19
94ColC-256
94ColChoGS-256
94ColChoSS-256
94Don-381
94ExtBas-281
94Fin-135
94FinRef-135
94Fla-175
94Fle-499
94Lea-332
94Pac-274
94Pin-134
94PinArtP-134
94PinMusC-134
94Sco-257
94ScoGolR-257
94StaClu-150
94StaCluFDI-150
94StaCluGR-150
94StaCluMOP-150
94Top-674
94TopGol-674
94TopSpa-674
94Ult-209
94UppDec-404
94UppDecED-404
95AstMot-6
95ColCho-113
95ColChoGS-113
95ColChoSS-113
95Don-313
95DonPreP-313
95DonTopotO-204
95Fle-468
95Lea-39
95Sco-486
95ScoGolR-486
95ScoPlaTS-486
95StaClu-163
95StaCluFDI-163
95StaCluMOP-163
95StaCluSTWS-163
95Top-342
95TopCyb-185
95Ult-177
95UltGolM-177
96ColCho-493
96ColChoGS-493
96ColChoSS-493
96Don-4
96DonPreP-4
96Fla-224
96Fle-329
96FleCub-16
96FleTif-329
96LeaSigA-208
96LeaSigAG-208
96LeaSigAS-208
96Pac-20
96StaClu-309
96StaCluMOP-309
96TeaOut-73
96Ult-170
96UltGolM-170
96UppDec-297
97ColCho-64
97Don-186
97DonPreP-186
97DonPrePGold-186
97Fle-283
97FleTif-283
97Lea-66
97LeaFraM-66
97LeaFraMDC-66
97Pac-258
97PacLigB-258
97PacSil-258
87PanAmTUBI-28
97Pin-126
97PinArtP-126
97PinMusC-126
97Sco-290
97ScoPreS-290
97ScoShoS-290
97ScoShoSAP-290
97StaClu-279
97StaCluMOP-279
97Top-284
97UppDec-33
Servello, Dan
91EugEmeC-12
91EugEmeP-3740
92AppFoxC-20
92AppFoxF-1000
Service, Scott
88ReaPhiP-868
89Fle-653
89FleGlo-653
89ReaPhiB-6
89ReaPhiP-657
89ReaPhiS-23
90Bow-143
90BowTif-143
90CMC-234
90ProAAAF-302
90ScrRedBC-8
90ScrRedBP-600
90UppDec-35
91IndIndLD-193
91IndIndP-461
91LinDriAAA-193
92IndIndS-193
93IndIndF-1489
94Fle-428
94IndIndF-1811
94Top-306
94TopGol-306
94TopSpa-306
95IndIndF-95
96IndIndB-23
Servoss, Bob
76WilTomT-18
Sessi, Walter
46SeaSLP-45
Sevcik, John
65Top-597
Severeid, Henry
12T207-165
16ColE13-155
17HolBreD-93
21E121So8-86
21Exh-155
21Nei-25
22AmeCarE-64
22E120-99
22W572-93
22W573-117
22W575-120
23WilChoV-145
25Exh-116
93ConTSN-855
Severino, Eddy
96MedHatBJTI-28
Severino, Jose
93BriTigC-19
95NewJerCTI-26
Severinsen, Al
70OPC-477
70Top-477
71MLBOffS-238
71OPC-747
71Top-747
72OPC-274
72Top-274
72TopCloT-28
91OriCro-413
Severns, Bill
77HolMilT-22
78SpolndC-7
79VanCanT-21
80VanCanT-8
Severson, Rich
71MLBOffS-430
71OPC-103
71Top-103
Seward, Ed
87OldJudN-452
Sewell, Joe
91AubAstC-9
91AubAstP-4273
92BurAstC-7
92BurAstF-547
93OscAstC-21
93OscAstF-627
Sewell, Joe (Joseph W.)
20NatCarE-90
20WalMaiW-47
21E121So1-92
21Exh-156
21Nei-12
22E120-40
22W572-94
22W573-118
22W575-121
23MapCriV-12
23W501-16
23WilChoV-146
25Exh-85
26Exh-84
26SpoComoA-38
27YorCarE-10
28Exh-43
28StaPlaCE-59
28W502-10
28Yue-10
29ExhFou-21
29PorandAR-81
31W517-46
32OrbPinNP-116
33Gou-165
33GouCanV-89
61Fle-76
72LauGreF-40
77GalGloG-107
77Ind192T-16
79DiaGre-5
80PerHaloFP-163
80SSPHOF-163
81ConTSN-53
82OhiHaloF-42
83DiaClaS2-97
83YanYealT-13
89HOFStiB-22
89PacLegI-125
89PerCelP-36
90HOFStiB-33
90PacLeg-67
90PerGreM-68
91ConTSN-40
91ConTSN-275
92YanWIZH-30
93ConTSN-786
94ConTSN-992
94ConTSN-1175
94ConTSNB-992
94ConTSNB-1175
95ConTSN-1363
Sewell, Luke
23W503-61
28StaPlaCE-60
28W56PlaC-H5
29ExhFou-22
29PorandAR-82
31Exh-22
33ExhFou-11
33Gou-114
33Gou-163
33GouCanV-91
34BatR31-155
35GouPuzR-1I
35GouPuzR-2F
35GouPuzR-16F
35GouPuzR-17F
36GouWidPPR-A93
36NatChiFPR-103
36NatChiFPR-115
36R31PasP-43
36WorWidGV-62
38ExhFou-10
39PlaBal-5
40PlaBal-48
41BroW75-25
46SeaSLP-46
46SpoExcW-8-5
49EurSta-94
51Bow-322
52Bow-94
61Fle-138
79DiaGre-65
81ConTSN-54
82OhiHaloF-12
83DiaClaS2-99
91ConTSN-193
94ConTSN-996
94ConTSN-1175
94ConTSNB-996
94ConTSNB-1175
96Bro194F-17
Sewell, T. Rip
34DiaMatCSB-162
46SpoExcW-6-1A
47Exh-206
47TipTop-147
49Bow-234
49EurSta-172
77TCMTheWY-20
79DiaGre-363
83TCMPla1943-34
89PacLegI-202
Sexauer, Elmer
90DodTar-1067
Sexson, Richie
93BurlndC-24
93BurIndF-3308
94ColRedC-20
94ColRedF-451
94SouAtlLAF-SAL10
95Bes-15
95BowBes-B10
95BowBesR-B10
95KinIndTI-25
95SPML-46
95TopTra-122T
96BesAutSA-68

96Bow-335
96BowBes-138
96BowBesAR-138
96BowBesMI-1
96BowBesMIAR-1
96BowBesMIR-1
96BowBesP-BBP24
96BowBesPAR-BBP24
96BowBesPR-BBP24
96BowBesR-138
96CanIndB-22
96Exc-46
96ExcSeaC-9
96Top-425
97Bow-160
97BowCerBIA-CA73
97BowCerGIA-CA73
97BowChr-158
97BowChrI-158
97BowChrIR-158
97BowChrR-158
97BowInt-160
97ColCho-463
97FlaShoWotF-8
97Fle-529
97FleTif-529
97Sel-136
97SelArtP-136
97SelRegG-136
97Ult-485
97UltGolME-485
97UltPlaME-485

Sexton, Billiards
88GooN16-38

Sexton, Chris
93BilMusF-3956
93BilMusSP-2
94ChaWheC-2
94ChaWheF-2714
94Top-527
94TopGol-527
94TopSpa-527
94UppDecML-213
95SalAvaTI-9
96NewHavRB-22
96NewHavRUSTI-16

Sexton, Jeff
94WatIndC-24
94WatIndF-3936
96CanIndB-23

Sexton, Jimmy
75ShrCapT-20
76ShrCapT-8
77SanJosMC-22
79Top-232
80Top-11
80TucTorT-2
81TacTigT-15
82TacTigT-38
83Don-449
83Fle-533
83Top-709

Sexton, Twink (Wayne)
79JacMetT-4

Sexton, William
87AllandGN-46

Seybold, Socks (Ralph)
03BreE10-128
08AmeCarE-25
08RosComP-66

Seyfried, Gordon
64Top-499

Seymour, Bob
82VerBeaDT-25

Seymour, Cy (James B.)
06FanCraNL-42
08AmeCarE-26
08AmeCarE-62
08RosComP-130
09ColChiE-259A
09ColChiE-259B
09T206-318
09T206-319
09T206-320
10E12AmeCDC-32
10NadE1-51
11BasBatEU-33
11MecDFT-18
11SpoLifCW-318
11SpoLifM-218
12ColRedB-259A
12ColRedB-259B
12ColTinT-259A
12ColTinT-259B
12ImpTobC-38

Seymour, Harold
90LitSunW-16

Seymour, Paul
81BatTroT-29

Seymour, Steve
91KinMetC-20
91KinMetP-3813
92PitMetC-7
92PitMetF-3294

Seymour, Winston
89SalBucS-20
89WelPirP-21
90AugPirP-2475

Seys, John
31CubTeal-21

Sferrazza, Matt
86JacExpT-13
87GleFalTP-13

Sferrazza, Vince
86FreGiaP-3
87ShrCapP-23
88ShrCapP-1284
89SprCarB-26

Shaab, Doug
85OscAstTI-12

Shabazz, Basil
91JohCitCC-15
91JohCitCP-3990
92JohCitCC-1
92JohCitCF-3131
92StaCluD-169
93Bow-108
93ExcFS7-106
93MidLeaAGF-53
93SprCarC-22
93SprCarF-1865
93StaCluCa-23
94Bow-292
94Cla-26
94ClaTriF-T76
94FloStaLAF-FSL44
94St.PetCC-24
94St.PetCF-2599
94UppDecML-244
95SigRoo-45

Shabosky, Brian
88CapCodPB-7
88CapCodPPaLP-186

Shackelford, Brett
93DavLipB-25

Shackle, Richard
89JohCitCS-20
89Sta-167
90SavCarP-2068
90SouAtlLAS-42
91FloStaLAP-FSL35
91St.PetCC-12
91St.PetCP-2276
92ArkTraF-1130
92ArkTraS-46
93ArkTraF-2813

Shadburne, Adam
96BatCliTI-12

Shaddy, Chris
83KnoBluJT-14
86KnoBluJP-20
87KnoBluJP-1495
88SyrChiC-22
88SyrChiP-833
89RicBraBC-24
89RicBraC-22
89RicBraP-824
89RicBraTI-20

Shade, Mick (Mike)
83SprCarF-11
85LouRedR-24
87JacExpP-442
88JacExpB-2
88JacExpP-985

Shade, Steve
86EriCarP-26

Shafer, Bill
92PulBraC-24
92PulBraF-3176
93DanBraC-22
93DanBraF-3618
94MacBraC-19
94MacBraF-2203
95BreBtaTI-28

Shafer, Frank T.
87OldJudN-454

Shafer, George
87OldJudN-453

Shafer, Tillie (Arthur Joseph)
11SpoLifM-219

Shaffer, Duane
78KnoKnoST-19
79AppFoxT-21
80GleFalWSBT-25
80GleFalWSCT-24

Shaffer, Travis
92KinMetC-4
92KinMetF-1530
93PitMetC-17
93PitMetF-3708
94St.LucMC-22
94St.LucMF-1196

Shagena, Randy
94ElmPioF-3473
94ElmPioC-19

Shambaugh, Mike
86AncGlaPTI-32
88BoiHawP-1611

Shamblin, Bill
87KinIndP-1
88RenSilSCLC-272

Shamburg, Ken
90FreKeyTI-17
90RocRedWGC-31
91HagSunLD-246
91HagSunP-2465
91LinDriAA-246
92RocRedWF-1947
92RocRedWS-468
92SkyAAAF-212

Shamsky, Art
65RedEnq-27
65Top-398
66OPC-119
66Top-119
66TopVen-119
67CokCapR-17
67DexPre-188
67Kah-33
67OPC-96
67Top-96
68Kah-B32
68Top-292
68TopVen-292
69MetBoyS-4
69MetNewYDN-17
69MilBra-251
69Top-221
69TopSta-69
70DayDaiNM-69
70MetTra-23A
70OPC-137
70Top-137
71MLBOffS-165
71OPC-445
71Top-445
71TopCoi-43
72MilBra-313
72OPC-353
72Top-353
72TopCloT-29
78TCM60I-278
89RinPosM1-27
91MetWIZ-358
93UppDecS-3
94Met69CCPP-29
94Met69CS-28
94Met69T-11
96Met69Y-7

Shanahan, Bill
92ColMetPI-35

Shanahan, Chris
91PitMetC-16
91PitMetP-3422
92St.LucMCB-4
92St.LucMF-1747
93CapCitBC-20
93CapCitBF-460

Shanahan, Damien
95AusFut-76

Shanahan, Greg (Paul)
74AlbDukTI-73
74AlbDukTI-18
74OPC-599
74Top-599A
74Top-599B
74Top-599C
75AlbDukC-12
76VenLeaS-196
90DodTar-719

Shanahan, Jason
95ElmPioTI-26
95ElmPioUTI-26
96BreCouMB-30

Shaner, Wally
94ConTSN-1292
94ConTSNB-1292

Shankle, Ron
93BluOriC-22
93BluOriF-4135
94LetMouF-3888
94LetMouSP-21

Shankman, Herbert
52LavPro-9

Shanks, Cliff
95ButCopKtI-18

Shanks, Hank (Howard S.)
14B18B-46
15SpoNewM-162
16ColE13-156
16SpoNewM-160
21Exh-157
22E120-118
23WilChoV-147
93ConTSN-729

Shanks, Willie
85KinBluJT-11
86VenGulP-24

Shannon, Dan
89HamRedS-23
90SpaPhiB-21
90SpaPhiP-2504
90SpaPhiS-19

Shannon, Daniel
87OldJudN-455

Shannon, Maurice J.
20NatCarE-91

Shannon, Mike
90LitSunW-24

Shannon, Mike (Thomas Michael)
61UniOil-P12
62KahAtl-21
64Top-262
64TopVen-262
65CarJayP-9
65CarTeal-22
65OPC-43
65OPC-132
65Top-43
65Top-132
66Top-293
66TopVen-293
67Top-605
67TopVen-266
68Top-445
69MilBra-252
69MLBOffS-215
69OPC-110
69Top-110
69TopFou-18
69TopSta-120
69TopTeaP-18
70CarTeal-11
70MLBOffS-143
70Top-614
71MLBOffS-283
71OPC-735
71Top-735
72MilBra-314
78TCM60I-275
91UppDecS-14
92CarMcD-31

Shannon, Robert
86JamExpP-22

Shannon, Scott
91St.CatBJC-24
92St.CatBJC-29
93St.CatBJC-29
96KnoSmoB-3

Shannon, Spike (William P.)
08RosComP-131
09T206-465
11SpoLifCW-319

Shannon, Thomas L.
87NewOriP-26
88RocExpLC-32

Shannon, Wally
60Lea-93

Shannon, William
52LavPro-63

Shantz, Bobby
47PM1StaP1-199
47PM1StaP1-200
49PhiBul-49
50Bow-234
51Bow-227
52DixLid-21
52DixPre-21
52RedMan-AL20
52StaCalL-76C
52Top-219
53BowC-11
53DixLid-20
53DixPre-20
53Dor-114
53NorBreL-29
53RedMan-AL20
53SpoMagP-10
53Top-225
54Bow-19
54Top-21
55A'sRodM-34
55A'sRodM-35
55Bow-139
55Bow-140
56A'sRodM-8
56Top-261
57Top-272
58Top-289
58Top-419
58YanJayP-9
59Top-222
60RawGloT-30
60Top-315
61Pos-15
61Top-379
61Top-473
61TopStal-198
62Col.45B-17
62Col45'HC-14
62SalPlaC-188
62ShiPlaC-188
62Top-177
62TopBuc-81
62TopStal-128
62TopVen-177
63Top-533
64PhiPhiB-21
64Top-278
64TopVen-278
75OPC-190
75Top-190
76A'sRodMC-22
79DiaGre-349
79TCM50-171
81TCM60I-456
83TopRep5-219
83YanASFY-42
84OCoandSI-49
84OCoandSI-218
88PacLegI-61
89AstCol4S-7
89SweBasG-131
90PacLeg-105
91SweBasG-83
91TopArc1-225
92ActPacA-78
92BazQua5A-3
92YanWIZ6-112
92YanWIZA-77
93TedWil-69
94TopArc1-21
94TopArc1G-21

Shantz, Wilmer
55A'sRodM-36
55A'sRodM-37
55Bow-139
55Bow-175
76A'sRodMC-23
92YanWIZ6-111

Shapiro, Tony
95ButCopKtI-19

Shapley, Joe
90NebCor-21

Sharitt, Kelly
89OneYanP-2108
90SouAtlLAS-25

Sharkey, Jack
28W513-87
32USCar-25

Sharkey, Tom
98CamPepP-67

Sharko, Gary
89CliGiaP-887
90SanJosGB-19
90SanJosGCLC-46
90SanJosGP-2005

90SanJosGS-20
91CalLeLA-35
91SanJosGC-21
91SanJosGP-10
92ProFS7-352
Sharman, Bill
51BerRos-D11
Sharon, Dick
74OPC-48
74Tig-12
74Top-48
75OPC-293
75Top-293
Sharp, Bill
74OPC-519
74Top-519
75OPC-373
75Top-373
76BreA&P-12
76OPC-244
76SSP-246
76Top-244
77SpoIndC-6
94BreMilB-182
Sharp, Gary
82BurRanF-19
82BurRanT-9
Sharp, Mike
91YakBeaC-26
91YakBeaP-4247
92BakDodCLC-21
92CalLeaACL-34
92ProFS7-251
Sharp, Scott
94PriRedC-23
94PriRedF-3265
Sharpe, Bayard
09T206-466
11SpoLifM-143
11T205-153
12ImpTobC-31
Sharpe, Grant
96AppLeaAB-10
96BurIndB-24
Sharpe, Ken
91ParPatF-1
Sharpe, Sterling
93StaCluMO-50
Sharperson, Mike
83KinBluJTI-24
85SyrChiT-19
86SyrChiP-22
87BluJayFS-27
87Don-565
87DonOpeD-31
88AlbDukC-16
88AlbDukP-253
88DodPol-27
88Fle-525
88FleGlo-525
89AlbDukC-14
89AlbDukP-59
89Bow-348
89BowTif-348
89DodPol-17
89DodStaSV-14
89Fle-72
89FleGlo-72
89Sco-602
90DodMot-20
90DodPol-27
90DodTar-720
90Don-603
90Lea-490
90OPC-117
90Top-117
90TopTif-117
91Bow-602
91DodMot-20
91DodPol-27
91Don-168
91Fle-221
91OPC-53
91Sco-546
91StaClu-541
91Top-53
91TopDesS-53
91TopMic-53
91TopTif-53
91Ult-170
91UppDec-598
92DodMot-25
92DodPol-27
92DodSmo-10592
92DodStaTA-31
92Don-526
92FleUpd-93
92Lea-318
92OPC-627
92Pin-167
92Sco-592
92StaClu-93
92Stu-49
92Top-627
92TopGol-627
92TopGolW-627
92TopMic-627
92Ult-218
93DodMot-14
93DodPol-23
93Don-166
93Fle-68
93OPC-346
93PacSpa-154
93PanSti-217
93Pin-37
93Sco-429
93Sel-157
93StaClu-307
93StaCluD-9
93StaCluFDI-307
93StaCluM-164
93StaCluMOP-307
93Top-526
93TopGol-526
93TopInaM-526
93TopMic-526
93Ult-404
93UppDec-316
93UppDecGold-316
94Fle-523
94Sco-287
94ScoGolR-287
95RicBraRC-24
95RicBraTI-22
96LasVegSB-1
Sharpnack, Bob
86ModA'sC-18
86ModA'sP-22
87MadMusP-17
87MadMusP-25
88HunStaTI-18
89HunStaB-11
Sharrott, George
90DodTar-1068
Sharsig, William J.
87OldJudN-456
Sharts, Scott
91WatIndC-22
91WatIndP-3377
92WatIndC-4
92WatIndF-3233
93ColRedC-20
93ColRedF-595
Sharts, Stephen
85BenPhiC-22
87ClePhiP-16
88ReaPhiP-865
89ReaPhiB-5
89ReaPhiP-651
90CMC-235
90ProAAAF-303
90ScrRedBC-9
90ScrRedBP-601
Shatley, Andy
96StCatSB-25
Shaughnessy, Shag (Francis)
09T206-515
36GouWidPPR-D34
36WorWidGV-78
Shaute, Joe
28StaPlaCE-61
90DodTar-721
93ConTSN-857
Shave, Jon
88MisStaB-30
89MisStaB-35
90ButCopKSP-26
90MisStaB-38
91Cla/Bes-380
91GasRanC-22
91GasRanP-2699
92ClaFS7-445
92SkyAA F-274
92TulDriF-2705
92TulDriS-620
92UppDecML-312
93Bow-59
93ClaGolF-9
93ExcFS7-236
93FleFinE-283
93OklCit8F-1635
93RanKee-433
93StaClu-725
93StaCluFDI-725
93StaCluMOP-725
93Top-451
93TopGol-451
93TopInaM-451
93TopMic-451
93TopTra-78T
94OklCit8F-1501
94Pac-629
94Pin-422
94PinArtP-422
94PinMusC-422
94PinRooTP-3
94StaClu-199
94StaCluFDI-199
94StaCluGR-199
94StaCluMOP-199
94StaCluT-247
94StaCluTFDI-247
94Top-775
94TopGol-775
94TopSpa-775
95Top-643
96OklCit8B-19
Shaver, Jeff
86MadMusP-18
86MadMusP-21
87HunStaTI-21
88TacTigC-8
88TacTigP-619
89TacTigC-11
89TacTigP-1559
Shaver, Tony
95QuaCitRBTI-26
96KisCobB-26
Shaw, Al
09T206-321
Shaw, Bob
58Top-206
59TigGraASP-14
59Top-159
59TopVen-159
60Lea-83
60Top-380
60WhiSoxJP-9
60WhiSoxTS-17
61Pos-23
61Top-352
61TopStaI-127
61WhiSoxTS-16
62Top-109
62TopStaI-56
62TopVen-109
63BraJayP-9
63Jel-154
63Pos-154A
63Pos-154B
63SalMetC-7
63Top-5
63Top-255
64GiaJayP-12
64Top-328
64TopVen-328
65Top-428
65TopEmbI-57
66Top-260
66TopVen-260
67CokCapYM-V25
67DexPre-189
67Kah-34
67MetTeal-10
67Top-470
73OPC-646
73Top-646
79DiaGre-149
91MetWIZ-359
Shaw, Brian
93StaCluMO-39
Shaw, Cedric
88ButCopKSP-9
89ChaRanS-22
90TulDriP-1154
90TulDriTI-23
91LinDriAA-597
91TulDriLD-597
91TulDriP-2773
91TulDriTI-29
92SkyAA F-275
92TulDriF-2695
92TulDriS-621
93OklCit8F-1627
Shaw, Curtis (Malcolm)
90ProAaA-164
90SouOreAB-17
90SouOreAP-3427
91MadMusC-14
92Bow-174
92CalLeaACL-19
92ClaFS7-190
92ModA'sC-2
92ModA'sF-3898
93Bow-513
93ClaFS7-257
93ClaGolF-75
93ExcFS7-218
93HunStaF-2082
94Bow-52
94Cla-119
94ClaTriF-T58
94HunStaF-1331
94TacTigF-3173
94UppDecML-26
95EdmTraTI-21
96ModA'sB-14
Shaw, Don
67Top-587
68Top-521
69OPC-183
69Top-183
70ExpPos-2
70OPC-476
70Top-476
71CarTeal-34
71OPC-654
71Top-654
72OPC-479
72Top-479
81TCM60I-449
88SanDieSAAG-18
89SanDieSAG-17
91MetWIZ-360
Shaw, Jeff
87WatIndP-16
88WilBilP-1309
89CanIndB-3
89CanIndP-1298
89CanIndS-19
90Bow-329
90BowTif-329
90ColSprSSP-33
90DonRoo-53
90IndTeal-35
90ProAAAF-214
91ColSprSSLD-95
91ColSprSSP-2182
91LinDriAAA-95
91Sco-746
91TopDeb90-141
92Bow-410
92ColSprSSF-751
92ColSprSSS-95
92Don-595
92Sco-624
92SkyAAAF-41
92StaClu-843
92StaCluNC-843
92UppDec-660
93ExpPosN-20
93FleFinE-97
94Fle-551
94Top-469
94TopGol-469
94TopSpa-469
94VenLinU-38
95Fla-167
95Fle-360
95StaClu-478
95StaCluMOP-478
95StaCluSTWS-478
95Ult-408
95UltGolM-408
96LeaSigEA-180
Shaw, John W.
87OldJudN-458
Shaw, Kerry
88SalLakCTTI-17
89SalSpuCLC-144
89SalSpuP-1803
90SanJosGB-2
90SanJosGCLC-29
90SanJosGP-2020
90SanJosGS-21
Shaw, Kevin
88AppFoxP-140
89BasCitRS-8
89Sta-63
90BasCitRS-22
91BasCitRC-11
91BasCitRP-1398
91FloStaLAP-FSL3
92BasCitRC-2
92BasCitRF-3847
93WinSpiC-21
93WinSpiF-1570
Shaw, Rick
82AmaGolST-22
Shaw, Robert
12ImpTobC-83
Shaw, Royal N.
09T206-467
Shaw, Samuel E.
87OldJudN-457
Shaw, Scott
86Ft.LauYP-21
87Ft.LauYP-7
88AlbYanP-1345
89AlbYanB-4
89AlbYanP-317
89AlbYanS-18
Shaw, Shelby
92ChaRanC-22
92ChaRanF-2226
Shaw, Theo
81ChaRoyT-8
84OmaRoyT-17
85Ft.MyeRT-20
86OmaRoyP-23
86OmaRoyT-20
87MemChiB-12
87MemChiP-15
88WilBilP-1318
89ColSprSSP-259
90CalCanC-20
90CMC-447
94EugEmeC-29
Shawkey, J. Bob
09ColChiE-260
12ColRedB-260
12ColTinT-260
15CraJacE-164
15SpoNewM-163
16ColE13-157
16SpoNewM-161
17HolBreD-94
19W514-29
20NatCarE-92
21E121So1-93
21E121So8-87
21KoBreWSI-51
21Nei-39
22E120-74
22W572-95
22W573-119
22W575-122
23W501-31
23W515-9
25Exh-102
26Exh-103
27AmeCarE-37
27YorCarE-59
28PorandAR-A32
28PorandAR-B32
61Fle-139
79DiaGre-4
88ConSer5-26
91ConTSN-156
95ConTSN-1328
Shay, Dan
08AmeCarE-27
11SpoLifCW-320
Shea, Bill
90BasWit-27
Shea, Ed
87WatPirP-4
Shea, John
87MyrBeaBJP-1452
88KnoBluJB-3
89KnoBluJB-24
89KnoBluJP-1140
89KnoBluJS-20
90CMC-334
90ProAAAF-351
90SyrChiC-8
90SyrChiMB-21
90SyrChiP-571

91LinDriAAA-517
91SyrChiLD-517
91SyrChiMB-23
91SyrChiP-2480
92SyrChiF-1965
92SyrChiMB-20
92SyrChiS-516
93NewBriRSF-1219
94ElPasDF-3146
95RocRedWTI-34
Shea, Kevin
87VerBeaDP-29
Shea, Kurt
88BriTigP-1887
89FayGenP-1582
Shea, Mervyn D.J.
29ExhFou-24
35AlDemDCR3-13
35DiaMatCS3T1-131
90DodTar-722
92ConTSN-412
Shea, Red (Patrick)
20GasAmeMBD-33
20WalMaiW-48
21E121So1-94
21E121So8-88A
21E121So8-88B
21KoBreWSI-21
22W575-123
23W501-63
Shea, Spec (Frank)
47PM1StaP1-201
48BluTin-13
48Bow-26
48YanTeal-25
49Bow-49
50Bow-155
52Bow-230
52Top-248
53BowC-141
53Bri-19
53Top-164
54Bow-104
55Bow-207
83TopRep5-248
83YanASFY-43
91TopArc1-164
92YanWIZA-78
Shea, Steven F.
69Top-499
Sheaffer, Danny
85PawRedST-12
86PawRedSP-22
87PawRedST-8
89ColSprSSC-21
89ColSprSSP-241
90BufBisC-15
90BufBisP-377
90BufBisTI-24
90CMC-15
90ProAAAF-492
91LinDriAAA-418
91PorBeaLD-418
91PorBeaP-1568
92PorBeaF-2671
92PorBeaS-419
92SkyAAAF-191
93FleFinE-43
93RocUSPC-6C
93RocUSPC-9H
93StaCluRoc-28
93TopTra-39T
93Ult-358
94Don-610
94Fle-454
94RocPol-23
94Sco-197
94ScoGolR-197
94StaClu-185
94StaCluFDI-185
94StaCluGR-185
94StaCluMOP-185
94StaCluT-96
94StaCluTFDI-96
94Top-314
94TopGol-314
94TopSpa-314
96Fle-555
96FleTif-555
96LeaSigEA-181
Shean, David
09AmeCarE-94
10E101-41
10E102-22
10JuJuDE-36
10MelMinE-41
10NadCarE-45
10PeoT21-49
11S74Sil-46
11SpoLifCW-321
11SpoLifM-144
11T205-154A
11T205-154B
12HasTriFT-13E
Shean, Larry
19W514-116
Shearer, Ray
58Top-283
Sheary, Kevin
85MiaHur-15
88RocExpLC-33
Sheckard, James
03BreE10-129
06FanCraNL-43
07CubA.CDPP-12
07CubGFGCP-12
08AmeCarE-22
08AmeCarE-60
08RosComP-108
09AmeCarE-95
09ColChiE-253
09RamT20-104
09T206-322
09T206-323
10ChiE-9
10DarChoE-27
10DomDisP-109
10JHDABE-14
10RedCroT-68
10RedCroT-242
10SweCapPP-91
11BasBatEU-34
11PloCanE-57
11S74Sil-69
11SpoLifCW-322
11SpoLifM-182
11T205-155
12ColRedB-253
12ColTinT-253
12HasTriFT-66
16ColE13-158
90DodTar-723
93ConTSN-900
Sheehan, Chris
92EugEmeC-22
92EugEmeF-3029
93RocRoyC-24
93RocRoyF-716
94ExcFS7-74
95WicWraTI-36
95WilBluRTI-38
Sheehan, Jack
90DodTar-724
Sheehan, John
87AshTouP-28
88OscAstS-24
89OscAstS-21
90ColMudB-18
90ColMudP-1346
90ColMudS-21
Sheehan, Terry
76SeaRaiC-15
78OrlTwiT-18
79TolMudHT-10
80OrlTwiT-16
Sheehan, Tommy
08RosComP-99
78HalHalR-8
90DodTar-1069
Sheehy, Mark
84AlbDukC-246
87BakDodP-16
88SanAntMB-25
Sheely, Earl Homer
21E121So1-95
21Exh-158
21Nei-34
22E120-28
22W572-96
22W573-120
22W575-124
23W501-46
23WilChoV-148
25Exh-79
26Exh-79
27YorCarE-37
28W502-37
28Yue-37
29ExhFou-13
31Exh-2
33ExhFou-1
46SunBre-16
47CenFlo-26
92ConTSN-515
Sheen, Charlie
88PacEigMO-10
89MajLeaM-7
89MajLeaM-10
Sheets, Andy
92LSUTigM-10
93RivPilCLC-18
94RivPilCLC-16
95TacRaiTI-20
96TacRaiB-24
97PacPriGotD-GD92
Sheets, Larry
84RocRedWT-1
85Don-36
85FleUpd-101
85OriHea-16
85TopTifT-106T
85TopTra-106T
86Don-350
86Fle-286
86SevCoi-E9
86Spo-177
86Top-147
86TopGloS-50
86TopSti-308
86TopTat-7
86TopTif-147
87Don-248
87Fle-479
87FleGlo-479
87FleHotS-36
87OriFreB-18
87SmoAmeL-10
87SpoTeaP-21
87Top-552
87TopSti-229
87TopTif-552
88ClaRed-188
88Don-273
88DonBasB-286
88Dra-23
88Fle-572
88FleAwaW-38
88FleBasM-34
88FleExcS-37
88FleGlo-572
88FleHotS-37
88FleLeaL-38
88FleMin-3
88FleStiC-4
88OPC-327
88OriFreB-18
88PanSti-16
88Sco-219
88ScoGlo-219
88Spo-161
88StaLinO-15
88Top-327
88TopBig-26
88TopSti-230
88TopTif-327
88TopUKM-70
88TopUKMT-70
89Bow-16
89BowTif-16
89Don-333
89Fle-620
89FleGlo-620
89OPC-98
89OriFreB-19
89PanSti-264
89Sco-81
89Top-98
89Top-381
89TopBig-113
89TopSti-239
89TopTif-98
89TopTif-381
89TVSpoM-91
89UppDec-254
90Don-495
90Fle-189
90FleCan-189
90FleUpd-100
90HagSunDGB-27
90Lea-350
90OPC-708
90PubSti-586
90Sco-111
90ScoRoo-65T
90TigCok-22
90Top-708
90TopTif-708
90UppDec-287
91Fle-352
91OPC-281
91OriCro-414
91Sco-176
91Top-281
91TopDesS-281
91TopMic-281
91TopTif-281
91UppDec-340
93NewOrlZF-980
Sheff, Chris
92ClaDraP-101
92FroRowDP-59
93Bow-642
93KanCouCC-20
93KanCouCF-929
93MidLeaAGF-10
94BreCouMF-27
95PorSeaDTI-25
95SigRooOJ-28
95SigRooOJP-28
95SigRooOJPS-28
95SigRooOJS-28
96Bow-284
96Exc-167
96PorSeaDB-25
93KanCouCTI-21
Sheffer, Chad
95EveAqaTI-22
96WisTimRB-21
Sheffield, Gary
87StoPorP-1
88BasAmeAAB-22
88ElPasDB-1
88TexLeaAGS-26
88TriAAC-14
89Baz-19
89Bow-142
89BowTif-142
89BrePol-1
89BreYea-1
89ClaTraO-101
89Don-31
89DonBasB-113
89DonRoo-1
89Fle-196
89FleGlo-196
89PanSti-364
89Sco-625
89ScoHot1R-10
89ScoYouSI-25
89Spo-41
89Spo-223
89Top-343
89TopBig-55
89TopHeaUT-13
89TopRoo-20
89TopTif-343
89ToyRoo-28
89UppDec-13
89UppDec-13A
90Baz-16
90Bow-391
90BowTif-391
90BreMilB-23
90BrePol-11
90ClaBlu-14
90Don-501
90DonBesA-121
90El PasDAGTI-27
90Fle-336
90FleCan-336
90Hot50RS-41
90Lea-157
90OPC-718
90PubSti-504
90PubSti-604
90Sco-97
90Sco100RS-20
90ScoMcD-12
90Spo-52
90Top-718
90TopBig-163
90TopCoi-27
90TopGloS-10
90TopHeaU-13
90TopMag-91
90TopRoo-25
90TopSti-202
90TopSti-326
90TopTif-718
90ToyRoo-24
90UppDec-157
90VenSti-433
91Bow-52
91BreMilB-23
91BrePol-20
91CadEllD-51
91Cla2-T13
91ClaGam-103
91Don-751
91Fle-596
91JimDea-7
91Lea-173
91OPC-68
91PanFreS-206
91PanSti-170
91Pos-15
91Sco-473
91Sco100S-30
91StaClu-95
91Stu-76
91Top-68
91TopDesS-68
91TopMic-68
91TopTif-68
91Ult-180
91UppDec-266
92Bow-214
92Cla2-T59
92ColAllG-20
92ColAllP-20
92Don-192
92DonUpd-U11
92Fle-188
92FleUpd-125
92Lea-446
92OPC-695
92PadCarJ-19
92PadMot-3
92PadPolD-20
92PadPolD-30
92PadSmo-30
92Pin-235
92PinTea2-59
92Sco-589
92ScoRoo-1T
92StaClu-309
92StaClu-766
92StaCluECN-766
92StaCluMO-12
92StaCluMO-28
92StaCluMO-29
92Stu-108
92Top-695
92TopGol-695
92TopGolW-695
92TopMic-695
92TopTra-105T
92TopTraG-105T
92TriPla-53
92Ult-83
92Ult-582
92UltAllS-14
92UppDec-84
92UppDec-234
92UppDec-745
93Bow-490
93CadDis-54
93ClaGam-84
93ClaGolF-216
93ClaGolF-AU2
93DenHol-17
93DiaMar-97
93Don-444
93DonDiaK-DK21
93DonEli-28
93DonEliS-10
93DonLonBL-LL16
93DonMasotG-3
93DonMVP-26
93DonPre-10
93DonSpiotG-SG12
93DurPowP2-18
93Fin-31
93FinRef-31
93Fla-54
93Fle-147
93Fle-351
93Fle-356
93Fle-704
93FleAll-NL3

93FleAtl-22
93FleFinE-71
93FleFruotL-57
93FlePro-A3
93FleTeaL-NL5
93FunPac-20
93FunPac-25
93FunPac-141
93Hos-6
93JimDea-18
93Kra-28
93Lea-307
93LeaGolA-R15
93LeaGolA-U5
93MarPub-23
93OPC-317
93OPCPreSP-6
93OPCPreSPF-6
93PacSpa-264
93PadMot-2
93PanSti-158
93PanSti-261
93Pin-1
93Pin-300
93PinHomRC-6
93PinSlu-7
93PinTeaP-6
93Pos-11
93PosCan-16
93Sco-2
93Sco-531
93Sco-534
93ScoFra-25
93ScoGolDT-3
93Sel-41
93SelChaS-4
93SelRoo-4T
93SelSam-41
93SelStaL-4
93SelStaL-30
93SelStaL-47
93SP-18
93SPPlaP-PP18
93StaClu-300
93StaClu-618
93StaCluFDI-300
93StaCluFDI-618
93StaCluM-17
93StaCluMMP-10
93StaCluMOP-300
93StaCluMOP-618
93Stu-207
93Top-140
93Top-403
93TOPBLAG-18
93TopFulS-18
93TopGol-140
93TopGol-403
93TopInaM-140
93TopInaM-403
93TopMic-140
93TopMic-403
93TopTra-51T
93Toy-64
93ToyMasP-11
93TriPla-6
93TriPlaA-10
93TriPlaLL-L6
93TriPlaP-6
93Ult-122
93UltAllS-5
93UltAwaW-25
93UltHomRK-8
93UltPer-8
93UppDec-222
93UppDec-474
93UppDec-492
93UppDec-494
93UppDec-828
93UppDecFA-A2
93UppDecFAJ-A2
93UppDecGold-222
93UppDecGold-474
93UppDecGold-492
93UppDecGold-494
93UppDecGold-828
93UppDecS-19
93UppDecTriCro-TC8
93USPlaCA-7C
93USPlaCA-13D
94Bow-290
94BowBes-R13
94BowBesR-R13
94BreMilB-268
94ChuHomS-18
94ChuHomSG-18
94ColC-257
94ColC-341
94ColChoGS-257
94ColChoGS-341
94ColChoSS-257
94ColChoSS-341
94ColChoT-6
94DenHol-23
94Don-5
94DonDiaK-DK25
94DonPro-10
94DonSpeE-5
94ExtBas-266
94ExtBasGB-26
94Fin-225
94FinJum-225
94FinRef-225
94Fla-166
94Fle-477
94FleAllS-49
94FleTeaL-19
94FUnPac-10
94Kra-28
94Lea-319
94LeaL-109
94LeaMVPC-N13
94LeaMVPCG-N13
94OPC-45
94Pac-250
94PanSti-186
94Pin-88
94PinArtP-88
94PinMusC-88
94PinPowS-PS15
94PinTheN-18
94PinTheN-P18
94Pos-5
94ProMag-54
94RedFolMI-24
94Sco-100
94ScoGolR-100
94ScoGolS-20
94Sel-256
94SP-114
94SPDieC-114
94SPHol-35
94SPHolDC-35
94Spo-28
94SpoFanA-AS8
94SpoRooGGG-GG1
94SpoRooS-GG1
94StaClu-4
94StaClu-180
94StaCluFDI-4
94StaCluFDI-180
94StaCluGR-4
94StaCluGR-180
94StaCluMOP-4
94StaCluMOP-180
94StaCluT-67
94StaCluTF-10
94StaCluTFDI-67
94Stu-112
94Top-560
94TopGol-560
94TopSpa-560
94TopSupS-40
94TriPla-140
94TriPlaM-10
94TriPlaN-3
94Ult-199
94UppDec-50
94UppDec-271
94UppDec-475
94UppDecAJ-3
94UppDecAJG-3
94UppDecDC-E10
94UppDecED-50
94UppDecED-271
94UppDecED-475
94UppDecNG-18
94UppDecNGED-18
95Baz-44
95Bow-325
95BowBes-R5
95BowBesR-R5
95ColCho-300
95ColChoCtG-CG18
95ColChoCtG-CG18B
95ColChoCtG-CG18C
95ColChoCtGE-18
95ColChoCtGG-CG18
95ColChoCtGG-CG18B
95ColChoCtGG-CG18C
95ColChoCtGGE-18
95ColChoGS-300
95ColChoSE-130
95ColChoSEGS-130
95ColChoSESS-130
95ColChoSS-300
95DenHol-24
95Don-168
95DonPreP-168
95DonTopotO-247
95Emb-2
95EmbGolI-2
95Emo-132
95Fin-119
95FinPowK-PK14
95FinRef-119
95Fla-141
95FlaOutP-9
95Fle-342
95KinDis-21
95Lea-182
95LeaLim-126
95Pac-178
95PacPri-57
95PanSti-74
95Pin-119
95PinArtP-119
95PinFan-29
95PinMusC-119
95PinSam-119
95RedFol-19
95Sco-340
95ScoGolR-340
95ScoHaloG-HG61
95ScoPlaTS-340
95Sel-62
95SelArtP-62
95SelCer-28
95SelCerMG-28
95SP-55
95SPCha-47
95SPChaDC-47
95Spo-46
95SpoArtP-46
95SPSil-55
95SPSpeF-37
95StaClu-90
95StaClu-500
95StaCluCC-CC13
95StaCluFDI-90
95StaCluMOP-90
95StaCluMOP-500
95StaCluMOP-CC13
95StaCluMOP-RL15
95StaCluRL-RL15
95StaCluSTWS-90
95StaCluSTWS-500
95StaCluVR-56
95Stu-181
95Sum-43
95SumNthD-43
95Top-440
95TopCyb-236
95UC3-28
95UC3ArtP-28
95Ult-167
95UltGolM-167
95UppDec-355
95UppDecED-355
95UppDecEDG-355
95UppDecPC-MLB14
95UppDecPLL-R40
95UppDecPLLE-R40
95UppDecSE-115
95UppDecSEG-115
95Zen-35
96Baz-132
96Bow-42
96BowBes-53
96BowBesAR-53
96BowBesR-53
96Cir-131
96CirAcc-18
96CirBos-36
96CirRav-131
96ColCho-399
96ColCho-560
96ColChoCtG-CG18
96ColChoCtG-CG18B
96ColChoCtG-CG18C
96ColChoCtGE-CR18
96ColChoCtGG-CG18
96ColChoCtGG-CG18B
96ColChoCtGG-CG18C
96ColChoCtGGE-CR18
96ColChoGS-399
96ColChoGS-560
96ColChoSS-399
96ColChoSS-560
96ColChoYMtP-36
96ColChoYMtP-36A
96ColChoYMtPGS-36
96ColChoYMtPGS-36A
96DenHol-12
96Don-36
96DonPreP-36
96EmoXL-190
96Fin-B309
96Fin-S60
96Fin-S337
96FinRef-B309
96FinRef-S60
96FinRef-S337
96Fla-268
96Fle-394
96FleTif-394
96FleUpd-U241
96FleUpdTC-U241
96Lea-14
96LeaLim-3
96LeaLimG-3
96LeaPre-27
96LeaPreP-27
96LeaPrePB-14
96LeaPrePG-14
96LeaPrePS-14
96LeaPreSG-19
96LeaPreSte-19
96LeaSig-30
96LeaSigPPG-30
96LeaSigPPP-30
96MetUni-169
96MetUniP-169
96Pac-83
96PacPri-P27
96PacPriG-P27
96PanSti-15
96Pin-123
96Pin-271
96PinAfi-94
96PinAfiAP-94
96PinAfiFPP-94
96PinArtP-32
96PinArtP-171
96PinFan-17
96PinFirR-7
96PinFoil-271
96PinSky-11
96PinSlu-11
96PinSta-32
96PinSta-171
96ProSta-66
96Sco-281
96ScoDugC-B6
96ScoDugCAP-B6
96ScoGolS-7
96ScoPowP-6
96ScoTitT-16
96Sel-29
96SelArtP-29
96SelCer-3
96SelCerAP-3
96SelCerCB-3
96SelCerCR-3
96SelCerIP-16
96SelCerMB-3
96SelCerMG-3
96SelCerMR-3
96SelCerSF-15
96SelEnF-17
96SelTeaN-16
96SP-86
96Spo-45
96Spo-108
96SpoArtP-45
96SpoArtP-108
96SpoHitP-12
96SpoPowS-12
96SPSpeFX-11
96SPSpeFXDC-11
96SPx-27
96SPxGol-27
96StaClu-400
96StaCluEPB-400
96StaCluEPG-400
96StaCluEPS-400
96StaCluEWB-EW9
96StaCluEWG-EW9
96StaCluEWS-EW9
96StaCluMOP-400
95StaCluVRMC-56
96Stu-64
96StuPrePB-64
96StuPrePG-64
96StuPrePS-64
96Sum-100
96SumAbo&B-100
96SumArtP-100
96SumFoi-100
96SumPos-9
96TeaOut-74
96Top-80
96TopChr-27
96TopChrR-27
96TopGal-177
96TopGalE-9
96TopGalPPI-177
96TopLas-78
96TopPro-NL19
96Ult-481
96UltGolM-481
96UppDec-340
96UppDecDD-DD20
96UppDecDDG-DD20
96UppDecDDS-DD20
96Zen-21
96Zen-143
96ZenArtP-21
96ZenArtP-143
96ZenDiaC-14
96ZenDiaCP-14
96ZenMoz-16
96ZenZ-13
97Bow-231
97BowBes-35
97BowBesAR-35
97BowBesMI-MI6
97BowBesMIAR-MI6
97BowBesMIARI-MI6
97BowBesMII-MI6
97BowBesMIR-MI6
97BowBesMIRI-MI6
97BowBesP-9
97BowBesPAR-9
97BowBesPR-9
97BowBesR-35
97BowChr-58
97BowChrI-58
97BowChrIR-58
97BowChrR-58
97BowInt-231
97Cir-299
97CirRav-299
97ColCho-345
97ColChoAC-34
97ColChoCtG-17A
97ColChoCtG-17B
97ColChoCtG-17C
97ColChoCtGIW-CG17
97ColChoNF-NF31
97ColChoNF-NF32
97ColChoPP-PP10
97ColChoPPG-PP10
97ColChoS-17
97ColChoTBS-22
97ColChoTBSWH-22
97Don-159
97Don-403
97DonDom-20
97DonEli-43
97DonEliGS-43
97DonFraFea-11
97DonLim-3
97DonLim-24
97DonLim-127
97DonLimFotG-29
97DonLimFotG-67
97DonLimLE-3
97DonLimLE-24
97DonLimLE-127
97DonPowA-17
97DonPowADC-17
97DonPre-101
97DonPre-191
97DonPreCttC-101
97DonPreCttC-191
97DonPreP-159
97DonPreP-403
97DonPrePGold-159
97DonPrePGold-403

97DonPreS-17
97DonPreTB-21
97DonPreTBG-21
97DonPreTF-21
97DonPreTP-21
97DonPreTPG-21
97DonRocL-10
97Fin-109
97Fin-176
97Fin-326
97FinEmb-109
97FinEmb-326
97FinEmbR-109
97FinEmbR-326
97FinRef-109
97FinRef-176
97FinRef-326
97FlaSho-A38
97FlaSho-B38
97FlaSho-C38
97FlaShoLC-38
97FlaShoLC-B38
97FlaShoLC-C38
97FlaShoLCM-A38
97FlaShoLCM-B38
97FlaShoLCM-C38
97Fle-336
97Fle-731
97FleLumC-15
97FleTeaL-19
97FleTif-336
97FleTif-731
97FleZon-16
97Lea-49
97Lea-357
97LeaDrefS-6
97LeaFraM-49
97LeaFraM-357
97LeaFraMDC-49
97LeaFraMDC-357
97LeaLeaotN-11
97LeaWarT-10
97MetUni-179
97NewPin-94
97NewPin-186
97NewPinAP-94
97NewPinAP-186
97NewPinMC-94
97NewPinMC-186
97NewPinPP-94
97NewPinPP-186
97Pac-307
97PacCar-27
97PacCarM-27
97PacCerCGT-16
97PacLigB-307
97PacPri-104
97PacPriLB-104
97PacPriP-104
97PacSil-307
97PinCar-11
97PinCer-44
97PinCerCMGT-16
97PinCerCT-16
97PinCerMBlu-44
97PinCerMG-44
97PinCerMR-44
97PinCerR-44
97PinIns-45
97PinInsCE-45
97PinInsDE-45
97PinInsFS-15
97PinMin-23
97PinMinB-23
97PinMinCB-23
97PinMinCG-23
97PinMinCGR-23
97PinMinCN-23
97PinMinCS-23
97PinMinG-23
97PinMinS-23
97PinSha-4
97PinTeaP-8
97PinTeaP-10
97PinTotCPB-44
97PinTotCPG-44
97PinTotCPR-44
97PinX-P-80
97PinX-PF&A-10
97PinX-PMoS-80
97PinX-PSfF-49
97PinX-PSfFU-49
97ProMag-16
97ProMagML-16
97Sco-184
97Sco-515
97ScoBla-13
97ScoHobR-515
97ScoPreS-184
97ScoResC-515
97ScoShoS-184
97ScoShoS-515
97ScoShoSAP-184
97ScoShoSAP-515
97ScoSteS-17
97ScoTitT-16
97Sel-11
97SelArtP-11
97SelRegG-11
97SelTooot-12
97SelToootTMB-12
97SkyE-X-74
97SkyE-XC-74
97SkyE-XEC-74
97SP-75
97SPMarM-MM16
97SpoIll-83
97SpoIllEE-83
97SPSpeF-22
97SPSpxF-4
97SPSPxFA-4
97SPVinAu-27
97SPVinAu-28
97SPVinAu-29
97SPVinAu-30
97SPx-26
97SPxBoufG-10
97SPxBoufGSS-5
97SPxBro-26
97SPxGraF-26
97SPxSil-26
97SPxSte-26
97StaClu-2
97StaClu-381
97StaCluMat-2
97StaCluMOP-2
97StaCluMOP-381
97StaCluMOP-PG9
97StaCluPG-PG9
97StaCluPP-PP3
97Stu-2
97StuMasS-21
97StuMasS8-21
97StuPor8-22
97StuPrePG-2
97StuPrePS-2
97Top-264
97TopAll-AS16
97TopChr-94
97TopChrAS-AS16
97TopChrR-94
97TopChrSAR-AS16
97TopGal-55
97TopGalPG-PG10
97TopGalPPI-55
97TopIntF-ILM14
97TopIntFR-ILM14
97TopSta-53
97TopStaAM-53
97TopSweS-SS13
97TopTeaT-TT13
97Ult-202
97UltGolME-202
97UltPlaME-202
97UppDec-215
97UppDec-360
97UppDecLDC-LD10
97UppDecP-16
97UppDecPP-PP11
97UppDecPPJ-PP11
97UppDecRP-RP12
97UppDecU-10
97Zen-29
Sheffield, Tony
92ClaDraP-40
92ClaFS7-428
92FroRowDP-17
92HigSchPLS-5
93StaCluM-85
93Top-687
93TopGol-687
93TopInaM-687
93TopMic-687
94UtiBluSC-25
94UtiBluSF-3835
Sheffield, Travis
86DayBeaIP-25
Sheffler, Jim
89KinMetS-22
Shehan, Brian
88CapCodPPaLP-38
Shelby, Anthony
95GreBatTI-22
96GreBatB-26
Shelby, John
80ChaO'sP-20
80ChaO'sW-21
82RocRedWT-17
83TopTra-102T
84Don-291
84Fle-20
84FleSti-114
84Nes792-86
84Top-86
84TopTif-86
85Don-472
85Fle-190
85OPC-264
85OriHea-17
85RocRedWT-13
85Top-508
85TopSti-204
85TopTif-508
86Don-643
86Fle-287
86FleMin-60
86Top-309
86TopTif-309
87Don-354
87DonOpeD-139
87Fle-480
87FleGlo-480
87FleUpd-109
87FleUpdG-109
87Top-208
87TopTif-208
87TopTra-112T
87TopTraT-112T
88DodMot-14
88DodPol-31
88Don-352
88DonBasB-290
88Fle-526
88FleGlo-526
88OPC-307
88PanSti-316
88Sco-286
88ScoGlo-286
88StaLinD-16
88Top-428
88TopBig-218
88TopTif-428
89Bow-349
89BowTif-349
89DodMot-14
89DodPol-20
89DodStaSV-15
89Don-314
89Fle-73
89FleGlo-73
89OPC-175
89PanSti-109
89Sco-103
89Top-175
89TopSti-63
89TopTif-175
89UppDec-75
90DodMot-25
90DodPol-31
90DodTar-725
90PubSti-18
90VenSti-434
91Don-563
91Fle-353
91OPC-746
91OriCro-415
91Sco-609
91TigCok-25
91TigPol-11
91Top-746
91TopDesS-746
91TopMic-746
91TopTif-746
91UppDec-201
92PawRedSF-937
92PawRedSS-365
93ButCopKSP-22
94BakDodC-27
95SanAntMTI-31
96SanAntMB-30
97DunDonPPS-21
Sheldon, Bob
74SacSolC-63
75OPC-623
75SacSolC-8
75Top-623
76OPC-626
76SpoIndC-1
76SSP-256
76Top-626
77SpoIndC-12
94BreMilB-269
Sheldon, Dave
86AppFoxP-22
Sheldon, Roland
61Top-541
61Yan61RL-23
62Top-185
62TopVen-185
63Top-507
65OPC-254
65Top-254
66OPC-18
66Top-18
66TopVen-18
69Top-413
91RinPos1Y3-7
92YanWIZ6-113
Sheldon, Scott
91SouOreAC-13
91SouOreAP-3857
92ClaFS7-179
92MadMusC-15
92MadMusF-1246
92MidLeaATI-39
93MadMusC-23
93MadMusF-1831
93MidLeaAGF-15
94HunStaF-1337
95EdmTraTI-22
Sheldon, Shane
95HelBreTI-24
Sheldon-Collins, Mathew
91WavRedF-9
Sheldon-Collins, Simon
95AusFut-75
Shell, Scott
91EliTwiP-4308
Shellenback, Frank
75Gia195T-33
75WhiSox1T-24
88LitSunMLL-7
Shellenback, Jim
67Top-592
68PirTeal-18
69Top-567
70OPC-389
70Top-389
71MLBOffS-549
71OPC-351
71SenTealW-22
71Top-351
74SpoIndC-31
74OPC-657
74Top-657
75HawIsIC-14
76HawIsIC-2
84TolMudHT-21
85TolMudHT-27
87OrlTwiP-7
88PorBeaC-25
88PorBeaP-644
89PorBeaC-25
89PorBeaP-226
90CMC-573
90PorBeaC-21
90PorBeaP-194
90ProAAAF-264
91LinDriAA-496
91OrlSunRLD-496
91OrlSunRP-1867
92OrlSunRF-2864
93ForMyeMC-27
93ForMyeMF-2673
93RanKee-37
Shelley, Jason
93DanBraC-23
93DanBraF-3635
Shelton, Andrew
12ColRedB-261
12ColTinT-261
Shelton, Barry
96HicCraB-22
Shelton, Ben
88AugPirP-370
89AugPirP-511
90SalBucS-21
91ParPatF-3
91SalBucC-8
91SalBucP-962
92Bow-568
92CarMudF-1190
92CarMudS-142
92ClaFS7-45
92SkyAA F-67
92UppDecML-282
93BufBisF-528
93FleFinE-118
Shelton, Derek
92OneYanC-10
Shelton, Harry
86GenCubP-24
87PeoChiP-19
88ChaWheB-21
89PeoChiTI-26
90MiaMirIS-24
90MiaMirIS-23
Shelton, Mike
86ReaPhiP-24
87ReaPhiP-9
88MaiPhiC-7
88MaiPhiP-282
88TriAAAP-25
Shelton, Ron
90LitSunW-17
Shenk, Larry
93AlbPolC-26
93AlbPolF-2026
94FreKeyF-2613
94OriPro-93
94FreKeyC-20
Shepard, Bert Robert
77TCMTheWY-43
Shepard, David
96BilMusTI-28
Shepard, Greg
96SouBenSHS-23
Shepard, Jack
55Top-73
55TopDouH-23
79TCM50-112
Shepard, Kelvin
87JamExpP-2549
89RocExpLC-24
Shepard, Ken
88GenCubP-1656
Shepard, Larry
68PirKDK-7
68PirTeal-19
68Top-584
69PirGre-7
69Top-384
73OPC-296
73Top-296
74OPC-326
74Top-326
79GiaPol-8
Shepard, Laurie
96ColSilB-25
Shepherd, Alvie
96BesAutSA-69
96Bow-325
96FreKeyB-1
96Top-234
Shepherd, Brian
94EveGiaF-3655
Shepherd, Keith
87WatPirP-15
88AugPirP-375
89BasCitRS-23
90RenSilSCLC-276
90WatIndS-19
91SouBenWSC-20
91SouBenWSP-2856
92BirBarF-2582
92BirBarS-95
93Don-332
93Fle-109
93FleFinE-44
93Top-447
93TopGol-447
93TopInaM-447
93TopMic-447
94ColSprSSF-733
94Pac-207
96RocRedWB-24
Shepherd, Mike
90PulBraB-10
90PulBraP-3105
Shepherd, Ron

82KnoBluJT-20
83SyrChiT-24
84SyrChiT-5
85FleUpd-102
86SyrChiP-23
87IndIndTI-12
87OPC-117
87Top-643
87TopTif-643
88IndIndC-16
88IndIndP-524
89LouRedBC-22
89LouRedBP-1261
89LouRedBTI-34
Sheppard, Don
89HigSchPLS-22
91SouBenWSC-11
91SouBenWSP-2871
92SalSpuC-13
92SalSpuF-3772
93DunBluJC-19
93DunBluJFFN-21
94KnoSmoF-1317
Sheppard, Phillip
84VisOakT-8
Shepperd, Richard
90BoiHawP-3329
91SalSpuC-13
91SalSpuP-2259
Shepston, Mike
79QuaCitCT-24
Sherdel, Bill
21Nei-100
22E120-237
22W572-97
25Exh-63
26Exh-63
27AmeCarE-12
28W56PlaC-C8A
31W517-6
91ConTSN-194
92ConTSN-619
Sheridan, Bobby
87SpoIndP-13
89RivRedWCLC-19
89RivRedWP-1418
89SpoIndSP-22
Sheridan, John
94ConTSN-1198
94ConTSNB-1198
Sheridan, Neil
52Par-16
Sheridan, Pat
81OmaRoyT-24
82OmaRoyT-22
83OmaRoyT-21
84Don-588
84Fle-357
84Nes792-121
84Top-121
84TopSti-286
84TopTif-121
85Don-339
85Fle-213
85Top-359
85TopSti-272
85TopTif-359
86Don-155
86Fle-20
86OPC-240
86RoyKitCD-11
86Top-743
86TopTif-743
87Fle-162
87FleGlo-162
87TigCaiD-18
87TigCok-6
87Top-234
87TopTif-234
88Don-522
88Fle-69
88FleGlo-69
88PanSti-97
88Sco-171
88ScoGlo-171
88StaLinTi-17
88TigPep-15
88Top-514
88TopTif-514
89Bow-107
89BowTif-107
89Don-417
89Fle-146
89FleGlo-146
89Sco-204
89ScoRoo-71T
89TigMar-15
89TigPol-15
89Top-288
89TopBig-150
89TopTif-288
89UppDec-652A
89UppDec-652B
90Don-367
90Fle-71
90FleCan-71
90OPC-422
90PubSti-482
90Sco-509
90Top-422
90TopTif-422
90UppDec-460
90VenSti-435
91ColCliP-610
Sheridan, Shane
89AncGlaP-23
Sheriff, Dave
81LynSaiT-9
82IdaFalAT-33
83IdaFalAT-34
84IdaFalATI-25
Sherlock, Glenn
85OscAstTI-15
86OscAstP-23
87ColCliP-22
87ColCliP-3
87ColCliT-25
88ColCliP-304
89AlbYanB-7
89AlbYanP-339
90AlbYanP-1183
90AlbYanS-26
90TamYanD-28
91Ft.LauYC-3
91Ft.LauYP-2443
Sherlock, Vince
90DodTar-726
Sherman, Claire
51BerRos-C17
Sherman, Darrell
89SpoIndSP-26
90Bes-286
90CalLeaACLC-10
90CMC-719
90ProAaA-147
90RivRedWB-17
90RivRedWCLC-3
90RivRedWP-2620
91Cla/Bes-153
91LinDriAA-619
91WicWraLD-619
91WicWraP-2613
91WicWraRD-23
92ClaFS7-347
92SkyAA F-287
92UppDecML-61
92UppDecML-249
92WicWraS-645
93Bow-602
93LeaGolR-R20
93OPCPre-118
93PacSpa-602
93PadMot-15
93Pin-619
93StaClu-739
93StaCluFDI-739
93StaCluMOP-739
93Top-576
93TopGol-576
93TopInaM-576
93TopMic-576
93Ult-478
93UppDec-784
93UppDecGold-784
94ColSprSSF-746
94RocPol-24
94Sco-595
94ScoBoyoS-54
94ScoGolR-595
94StaCluT-94
94StaCluTFDI-94
95TacRaiTI-21
Sherman, Jack
47SigOil-14
Sherman, Jim
83ColAstT-5
86TucTorP-21
Sherman, Steve
76CedRapGT-28
77CedRapGT-17
Sherman, Tyril
92GulCoaMF-3480
Shermet, Dave
86AriWilP-14
87AriWilP-12
88AriWilP-11
88AubAstP-1958
89AshTouP-948
Shermeyer, Keith
77WauMetT-18
78WauMetT-25
Sherow, Dennis
79MemChiT-19
80MemChiT-18
81WesHavAT-19
82TacTigT-18
82WesHavAT-25
83TacTigT-27
Sherrill, Dennis
79ColCliT-19
80ColCliP-12
80ColCliT-23
92YanWIZ8-176
Sherrill, Tim
88SavCarP-334
89St.PetCS-24
90CMC-122
90LouRedBC-22
90LouRedBLBC-37
90LouRedBP-403
90ProAAAF-517
90TopTVCa-63
91LinDriAAA-247
91LouRedLD-247
91LouRedTI-6
91OPC-769
91Top-769
91TopDeb90-142
91TopDesS-769
91TopMic-769
91TopTif-769
92LouRedF-1887
92LouRedS-269
92Sco-404
92Sco100RS-90
92StaClu-822
92StaCluECN-822
Sherry, Larry
59WilSpoG-7
60Baz-17
60DodJayP-13
60DodMor-11
60DodPos-9
60DodTeaI-17
60DodUniO-17
60Top-105
60TopVen-105
61DodBelB-51
61DodJayP-10
61DodUniO-18
61NuSco-431
61Pos-161A
61Pos-161B
61Top-412
61Top-521
61TopStaI-34
62DodBelB-51
62Jel-111
62Pos-111
62PosCan-111
62Top-435
63Top-565
64Top-474
65Top-408
66Top-289
66TopVen-289
67CokCapTi-1
67Top-571
68LauWorS-56
68Top-468
77PirPosP-24
87AstShowSTh-21
90DodTar-727
90HOFStiB-59
Sherry, Norm
59DarFar-21
60DodUniO-18
60Top-529
61DodBelB-34
61DodUniO-19
61Top-521
62DodBelB-34
62Top-238
63Top-316
74SalLakCAC-97
75IntLeaASB-31
75PacCoaLAB-31
75SalLakCC-20
76Met63 S-13
77Top-34
78ExpPos-12
79ExpPos-25
80ExpPos-28
84PadMot-27
84PadSmo-21
85SpoIndC-21
86GiaMot-28
87GiaMot-27
88GiaMot-27
89GiaMot-28
90DodTar-728
90GiaMot-21
90GiaSmo-18
91GiaMot-27
91MetWIZ-361
92EveGiaC-30
92EveGiaF-1706
Shetrone, Barry
60Top-348
63Top-276
91OriCro-416
Shevlin, Jim
90SalSpuCLC-138
90SalSpuP-2727
Shibata, Kazuya
96HonShaHWB-25
Shibata, Keith
87EugEmeP-2659
88AppFoxP-153
88EugEmeB-29
Shibata, Osao
79TCMJapPB-60
Shidawara, Cliff
86PhoFirP-23
87PhoFirP-19
88PhoFirP-66
Shields, Doug
88CapCodPPaLP-40
90EugEmeGS-27
91BasCitRC-27
91BasCitRP-1413
92MemChiF-2434
Shields, Mike
79SavBraT-9
Shields, Steve
81BriRedST-17
83PawRedST-11
84RicBraT-17
85RicBraT-9
86Fle-527
86RicBraP-20
87TopTra-113T
87TopTraT-113T
88ColCliC-6
88ColCliP-10
88ColCliP-314
88DonReaBY-NEW
88Sco-396
88ScoGlo-396
88ScoRoo-47T
88ScoRooG-47T
88Top-632
88TopTif-632
89Fle-269
89FleGlo-269
89PorBeaC-4
89PorBeaP-218
89Sco-578
89Top-484
89TopTif-484
90PubSti-338
90VenSti-436
92YanWIZ8-177
Shields, Tom
86WatPirP-23
88HarSenP-836
89EasLeaDDP-DD26
89HarSenP-298
89HarSenS-18
89Sta-20
90BufBisC-21
90BufBisP-384
90BufBisTI-25
90CMC-21
90ProAAAF-499
91LinDriAAA-467
91RocRedWLD-467
91RocRedWP-1911
92RocRedWF-1948
92RocRedWS-469
93Bow-228
93PacSpa-382
93Ult-321
94IowCubF-1283
94Pac-110
94StaCluT-336
94StaCluTFDI-336
Shiell, Jason
96DanBraB-21
Shiera, Norman
76VenLeaS-210
80VenLeaS-223
Shifflett, Steve
90AppFoxBS-24
90AppFoxP-2094
91LinDriAA-417
91MemChiLD-417
91MemChiP-653
92DonRoo-110
92OmaRoyF-2961
92OmaRoyS-346
92SkyAAAF-158
93Don-73
93Fle-625
93OmaRoyF-1680
93Sco-266
93StaClu-84
93StaCluFDI-84
93StaCluMOP-84
93Top-735
93TopGol-735
93TopInaM-735
93TopMic-735
93Ult-216
94OmaRoyF-1223
Shiflett, Chris
88GasRanP-1001
89ButCopKSP-14
90TulDriP-1155
91LinDriAA-598
91TulDriLD-598
91TulDriP-2774
Shiflett, Mark
83NasSouTI-20
84NasSouTI-20
87MemChiB-13
87MemChiP-6
90AlbYanS-27
90OneYanP-3391
91GreHorP-3077
91SouAtlLAGP-SAL30
92ForLauYC-24
92ForLauYTI-29
92Ft.LauYF-3010
93PriWilCC-29
93PriWilCF-675
Shiflett, Matt
87JamExpP-2562
89RocExpLC-25
91DurBulC-1
91DurBulP-1543
Shikles, Larry
86GreHorP-22
87WinHavRSP-4
88NewBriRSP-899
89NewBriRSP-613
89NewBriRSS-18
90CMC-255
90PawRedSC-4
90PawRedSDD-22
90PawRedSP-461
90ProAAAF-433
90TopTVRS-59
91LinDriAAA-368
91PawRedSDD-21
91PawRedSLD-368
91PawRedSP-39
92PawRedSF-922
92PawRedSS-366
92SkyAAAF-166
93TacTigF-3031
97DunDonPPS-22
Shillinglaw, Dave
86MadMusP-26
86MadMusP-22
Shimp, Tommy Joe
80MemChiT-19
83MemChiT-10
84TulDriTI-37
85OklCit8T-13

86OklCit8P-20
Shinall, Zakary
88BakDodCLC-259
89VerBeaDS-25
90SanAntMGS-26
91Bow-612
91Cla/Bes-384
91LinDriAA-540
91SanAntMLD-540
91SanAntMP-2972
92AlbDukF-721
92AlbDukS-20
93ChaKniF-541
Shindle, William
87OldJudN-459
90DodTar-729
95May-38
98CamPepP-68
Shines, Razor
83MemChiT-21
84IndIndTI-17
84IndIndTI-26
85Don-401
85ExpPos-21
85Lea-164
86OPC-132
86Top-132
86TopTif-132
87IndIndTI-8
88IndIndC-12
88IndIndP-514
89IndIndC-12
89IndIndP-1219
91IndIndLD-194
91IndIndP-471
91LinDriAAA-194
91PacSenL-128
92IndIndF-1870
92IndIndS-194
93IndIndF-1505
Shingledecker, Gary
89EriOriS-24
90WauTimB-19
90WauTimP-2132
Shinholster, Vince
87SanBerSP-12
Shinjyo, Tsuyoshi
96HilStaHWB-1
Shinners, Ralph
22E120-191
22W573-121
23WilChoV-149
Shiotani, Kazu
94BriTigC-23
Shiozaki, Kenny
88ButCopKSP-11
Shipanoff, Dave
83KnoBluJT-7
84SyrChiT-25
85PorBeaC-28
86Don-34
86Fle-452
86Lea-29
86PhiTas-33
86PorBeaP-20
87EdmTraP-2065
Shipke, William
08RosComP-84
09RamT20-108
09T206-324
Shipley, Craig
85AlbDukC-155
86AlbDukP-23
87AlbDukP-22
88JacMetGS-12
89MetColP-52
89TidTidC-22
89TidTidP-1961
90DodTar-730
90TopTVM-60
91LasVegSP-245
91MetWIZ-362
92Don-667
92Fle-621
92OPC-308
92OPCPre-33
92PadCarJ-20
92PadMot-25
92PadPolD-21
92PadSmo-31
92Sco-856
92StaClu-374
92Top-308
92TopGol-308
92TopGolW-308
92TopMic-308
92Ult-583
93Don-206
93Lea-395
93PacSpa-603
93PadMot-20
93PanSti-260
93StaClu-258
93StaCluFDI-258
93StaCluMOP-258
93Stu-130
93Top-601
93TopGol-601
93TopInaM-601
93TopMic-601
93Ult-123
93UppDec-788
93UppDecGold-788
94Don-516
94Fle-674
94Pac-534
94PadMot-14
94PanSti-259
94StaClu-460
94StaCluFDI-460
94StaCluGR-460
94StaCluMOP-460
94Top-184
94TopGol-184
94TopSpa-184
95AstMot-20
95Don-534
95DonPreP-534
95Fle-569
95FleUpd-144
95Pin-187
95PinArtP-187
95PinMusC-187
95Top-328
96ColCho-358
96ColChoGS-358
96ColChoSS-358
96FleUpd-U199
96FleUpdTC-U199
96LeaSigEA-182
96PadMot-15
96Sco-211
97Pac-432
97PacLigB-432
97PacSil-432
Shipley, Joe
59Top-141
59TopVen-141
60Top-239
Shipley, Mark
91SydWavF-1
95AusFut-79
Shipman, Mike
92MarPhiC-19
92MarPhiF-3061
93MarPhiC-26
93MarPhiF-3479
94BatCliC-21
94BatCliF-3451
Shipp, Skip
96EriSeaB-22
Shippy, Greg
75CliPilT-20
Shirahata, Hiro
83SanJosBC-10
Shireman, Jeff
89SprCarB-12
90St.PetCS-23
91ArkTraLD-45
91ArkTraP-1297
91LinDriAA-45
92LouRedF-1895
92LouRedS-270
93ArkTraF-2821
93LouRedF-225
94ArkTraF-3097
94ClaGolF-14
95ArkTraTI-24
96ArkTraB-2
Shires, Art (Charles A.)
28PorandAR-C5
29PorandAR-83
30ChiEveAP-20
31W517-43
92ConTSN-608
Shirley, Al
91ClaDraP-14
91FroRowDP-43
91HigSchPLS-2
92KinMetC-9
92KinMetF-1544
92OPC-306
92Pin-297
92Sco-802
92StaCluD-170
92Top-306
92TopGol-306
92TopGolW-306
92TopMic-306
93Bow-566
93CapCitBC-1
93CapCitBF-472
93ClaFS7-117
93ExcFS7-79
94CapCitBC-19
94CapCitBF-1764
94MetShuST-7
95AusFut-14
95StLucMTI-30
96WilBluRB-17
Shirley, Bart
66Top-591
67Top-287
69Top-289
90DodTar-731
91MetWIZ-363
92TexLon-37
Shirley, Bob
77PadSchC-49
78PadFamF-28
78Top-266
79Top-594
80OPC-248
80Top-476
81Car5x7-25
81Don-242
81Fle-495
81OPC-49
81Top-49
81TopTra-829
82Don-120
82Fle-127
82OPC-33
82Top-749
82TopTra-105T
83Fle-602
83Top-112
83TopTra-103T
84Don-214
84Fle-141
84Nes792-684
84Top-684
84TopTif-684
85Don-370
85Fle-145
85Top-328
85TopTif-328
86Don-458
86Fle-119
86Top-213
86TopTif-213
86YanTCM-15
87Don-463
87Fle-114
87FleGlo-114
87Top-524
87TopTif-524
88SyrChiC-7
88SyrChiP-827
89PacSenL-207
89St.CatBJP-2095
89T/MSenL-95
89TopSenL-6
90CMC-333
90ProAAAF-369
90SyrChiC-7
90SyrChiMB-22
90SyrChiP-589
92YanWIZ8-179
Shirley, Mike
91BurIndP-3318
92Ft.MyeMCB-7
92Ft.MyeMF-2758
Shirley, Steve
77LodDodT-19
78LodDodT-19
81AlbDukT-3
85HawIslC-235
85NasSouTI-21
86AlbDukP-24
87OmaRoyP-14
88IndIndC-4
88IndIndP-505
90DodTar-732
Shirley, Tex (Alvis)
46SeaSLP-48
96Bro194F-24
Shirley, Tom
82AlbDukT-8
Shive, Chuck
89MarPhiS-28
Shoals, Leo
94CarLeaA-DJ18
Shoch, George
87OldJudN-460
88WG1CarG-70
90DodTar-1071
Shocker, Urban
20NatCarE-93
21E121So1-96
21Exh-159
21Nei-40
22E120-100
22W572-98
22W573-122
22W575-125
23W501-2
23W503-55
23W515-48
23WilChoV-150
25Exh-103
26Exh-104
26SpoComoA-39
27AmeCarE-36
28Exh-52
91ConTSN-114
93ConTSN-711
Shockey, Greg
92BelMarC-2
92BelMarF-1459
93ClaGolF-192
93RivPilCLC-19
95LakElsSTI-21
95SPML-29
96BesAutS-82
96MidAngB-28
96MidAngOHP-23
96TexLeaAB-35
Shockey, Richard
90ModA'sC-27
Shockey, Scott
88CapCodPPaLP-63
89MedAthB-2
90CMC-659
90MadMusP-2278
91Cla/Bes-237
91HunStaC-21
91HunStaLD-293
91HunStaP-1805
91HunStaTI-19
91LinDriAA-293
93ModA'sC-18
93ModA'sF-809
94ClaGolF-127
94HunStaF-1338
Shockley, Costen (John Costen)
65OPC-107
65Top-107
88ChaLooLTI-27
Shockley, Keith
96MarPhiB-24
Shoebridge, Terry
77BurBeeT-26
78BurBeeT-24
80HolMilT-9
81ElPasDT-5
Shoemaker, Charlie
77FriOneYW-89
Shoemaker, John
78LodDodT-20
81VerBeaDT-26
82VerBeaDT-29
83VerBeaDT-26
85VerBeaDT-27
86VerBeaDP-23
87VerBeaDP-30
88FloStaLAS-1
88VerBeaDS-18B
89SanAntMB-25
90SanAntMGS-1
91LinDriAA-549
91SanAntMLD-549
91SanAntMP-2991
92GulCoaDF-3583
93YakBeaC-28
93YakBeaF-3901
94VerBeaDC-29
95GreFalDTI-31
96SavSanB-1
Shoemaker, Steve
92MadMusC-12
92MadMusF-1235
93SanBerSC-15
93SanBerSF-769
94HunStaF-1332
94OneYanC-21
94OneYanF-3792
94SigRooDP-79
94SigRooDPS-79
94StaCluDP-52
94StaCluDPFDI-52
95GreBatTI-23
95HunStaTI-24
96BesAutS-83
96BesAutSA-70
96SalAvaB-24
Shoen, Gerry
77FriOneYW-20
Shoeneck, Lewis
88WG1CarG-36
Shoffner, Milburn
39OrcPhoAP-21
39PlaBal-87
40PlaBal-149
41HarHarW-22
93ConTSN-925
Shofner, Frank S.
48SomandK-9
49SomandK-15
Sholl, Derek
87EugEmeP-2663
88EugEmeB-25
Sholton, Craig
91WelPirC-15
Shombert, Otto
87BucN28-47
87OldJudN-461
Shook, Wes
92ButCopKSP-9
93EriSaiC-1
93EriSaiF-3121
94ExcFS7-137
Shoop, Brian
88MisStaB-31
89MisStaB-42
Shopay, Tom
70OPC-363
70Top-363
72OPC-418
72Top-418
76SSP-401
78ColCliT-24
89PacSenL-71
91OriCro-417
92YanWIZ6-114
Shore, Ernie (Ernest)
15SpoNewM-164
16ColE13-159
16FleBreD-85
16SpoNewM-162
73FleWilD-31
86WinSpiP-5
86WinSpiP-6
87ConSer2-56
90HOFStiB-15
91ConTSN-141
92ConTSN-351
Shore, Jeff
89ChaRanS-23
Shore, Ray
52Par-18
63RedFreBC-24
Shores, Brad
86BurExpP-19
89AppFoxP-869
91AppFoxC-21
Shores, Scott
94BatCliC-22
94BatCliF-3460
94SigRooBS-10
94StaCluDP-61
94StaCluDPFDI-61
95ClePhiF-230
96ReaPhiB-25
Shores, William
31W517-7
94ConTSN-1145
94ConTSNB-1145
Short, Barry

96StLucMTI-5
Short, Ben
91OneYanP-4154
92GreHorC-9
92GreHorF-778
Short, Bill
60Top-142
60TopVen-142
61Top-252
62Top-221
67Top-577
68Top-536
69Top-259
91MetWIZ-364
91OriCro-418
92YanWIZ6-115
Short, Chris
47StaPinP2-35
64PhiJayP-9
64PhiPhiB-22
64PhiTeaS-5
65PhiJayP-9
66PhiTeal-11
67CokCapPh-15
67DexPre-190
67PhiPol-12
67Top-395
67TopVen-329
68OPC-7
68OPC-139
68Top-7
68Top-139
68TopActS-9C
68TopVen-7
68TopVen-9
68TopVen-139
69MilBra-253
69MLBOffS-178
69PhiTeal-9
69Top-395
69TopDecl-40
69TopSta-78
69TopSup-54
69TopTeaP-8
70Kel-41
70MLBOffS-94
70OPC-270
70PhiTeal-10
70Top-270
71Kel-75
71MLBOffS-188
71OPC-511
71PhiArcO-11
71Top-511
72MilBra-315
72Top-665
83PhiPosGPaM-9
84OCoandSI-229
86PhiGreT-6
94BreMilB-270
94CarLeaA-DJ15
Short, Rick
94BluOriC-19
94BluOriF-3572
96FreKeyB-21
Shorten, Chick (Charles)
16ColE13-160
22E120-101
23W503-41
91ConTSN-136
Shotkoski, David
88HunStaTI-19
88ModA'sCLC-57
88ModA'sTI-31
89HunStaB-15
91LinDriAA-446
91MidAngLD-446
91MidAngOHP-27
91MidAngP-434
Shotton, Burt
14B18B-34A
14B18B-34B
14CraJacE-86
15CraJacE-86
15SpoNewM-165
16ColE13-161
16SpoNewM-163
17HolBreD-96
19W514-78
49EurSta-49
60RawGloT-31
90DodTar-733
91ConTSN-152
Shotton, Craig
91WelPirP-3590
92WelPirC-21
Shoulders, Bob
87NewOriP-13
Shoun, Clyde
36DiaMatCS3T2-21
41CarW75-23
50RemBre-22
51R42SmaS-99
92ConTSN-379
Shoup, Eric
88BriTigP-1876
Shouppe, Jamey
83DayBeaAT-12
Shourds, Jeff
77CedRapGT-23
Shouse, Brian
90WelPirP-28
91AugPirC-11
92CarMudF-1179
92CarMudS-143
93BufBisF-516
94BufBisF-1836
95CarMudF-157
Show, Eric
81HawIsIT-19
82TopTra-106T
83AllGamPI-178
83Don-439
83Fle-372
83FleSta-175
83FleSti-225
83OPC-68
83Top-68
83TopSti-330
84AllGamPI-87
84Don-406
84Fle-312
84Nes792-532
84OPC-238
84PadMot-4
84PadSmo-22
84Top-532
84TopRubD-27
84TopSti-162
84TopTif-532
85Don-202
85DonActA-59
85Fle-44
85Lea-137
85OPC-118
85PadMot-9
85Top-118
85TopRubD-27
85TopSti-156
85TopTif-118
86Don-234
86Fle-334
86Lea-111
86OPC-209
86Top-762
86TopTif-762
87Don-164
87DonOpeD-149
87Fle-430
87FleGlo-430
87FleHotS-37
87OPC-354
87PadBohHB-30
87Top-730
87TopSti-112
87TopTif-730
88Don-387
88Fle-597
88FleGlo-597
88PadCok-30
88PadSmo-26
88PanSti-400
88Sco-338
88ScoGlo-338
88StaLinPa-12
88Top-303
88TopTif-303
89Bow-446
89BowTif-446
89Don-482
89Fle-317
89FleGlo-317
89OPC-147
89PadCok-17
89PadMag-7
89PanSti-196
89Sco-254
89Top-427
89TopBig-35
89TopTif-427
89UppDec-171
90Bow-209
90BowTif-209
90Don-559
90Fle-169
90FleCan-169
90Lea-115
90OPC-239
90PadCok-18
90PadMag-5
90PubSti-59
90Sco-493
90Top-239
90TopBig-71
90TopSti-111
90TopTif-239
90UppDec-587
90VenSti-437
91A'sMot-23
91A'sSFE-11
91Bow-223
91Fle-544
91Lea-354
91OPC-613
91Sco-563
91ScoRoo-64T
91StaClu-138
91Stu-108
91Top-613
91TopDesS-613
91TopMic-613
91TopTif-613
91UppDec-293
91UppDec-798
92OPC-132
92Sco-662
92Top-132
92TopGol-132
92TopGolW-132
92TopMic-132
Showalter, Buck (William N.)
77ForLauYS-10
79WesHavYT-7
80NasSouTI-20
81ColCliP-11
81ColCliT-20
81NasSouTI-17
82NasSouTI-22
83NasSouTI-21
88FloStaLAS-27
89AlbYanB-8
89AlbYanP-326
89AlbYanS-22
89EasLeaAP-26
92OPC-201
92Top-201
92TopGol-201
92TopGolW-201
92TopMic-201
93Top-510
93TopGol-510
93TopInaM-510
93TopMic-510
96StaClu-356
96StaCluMOP-356
96UppDec-476
Showalter, J.R.
90BoiHawP-3326
91PalSprAP-2026
Shreimann, Eric
94MarPhiC-24
Shrev, Ben
88WytCubP-1992
Shreve, Leven
87OldJudN-462
88GenCubP-1652
Shrum, Dennis
94AubAstC-19
94AubAstF-3759
Shuba, George
52Top-326
53BowC-145
53Top-34
54Bow-202
54NewYorJA-17
55Bow-66
55DodGolS-26
79TCM50-277
82Bow195E-267
83TopRep5-326
88RinPosD1-5B
90DodTar-734
91TopArc1-34
95TopArcBD-23
95TopArcBD-41
95TopArcBD-90
95TopArcBD-126
Shubert, Rich
74GasRanT-18
76SanAntBTI-20
77HolMilT-23
Shucks, Mr.
95CedRapKTI-NNO
Shuey, Paul
91TopTra-108T
91TopTraT-108T
92ClaBluBF-BC21
92ClaDraP-2
92ClaDraPFB-BC2
92ClaDraPP-BB2
92ClaFS7-401
92ColRedF-2390
92DEL-BB2
92StaCluD-171
92TopDaiQTU-32
92UppDecML-142
93CanIndF-2838
93ClaFisN-19
93ClaFS7-1
93ClaFS7-AU7
93ClaGolF-14
93ExcFS7-168
94Cla-160
94ClaGolF-107
94ExtBas-67
94Fla-289
94FleUpd-37
94KinIndF-2641
94LeaLimR-7
94ScoRoo-RT109
94ScoRooGR-RT109
94Sel-411
94SigRoo-42
94SigRooS-42
94SpoRoo-46
94SpoRooAP-46
94TopTra-78T
94UppDec-522
94UppDecED-522
94UppDecML-47
95Bow-252
95BowBes-B86
95BowBesR-B86
95BowGolF-252
95ColCho-26
95ColChoGS-26
95ColChoSE-22
95ColChoSEGS-22
95ColChoSESS-22
95ColChoSS-26
95Don-479
95DonPreP-479
95Fle-147
95Lea-91
95Pin-155
95PinArtP-155
95PinMusC-155
95Sco-138
95ScoGolR-138
95ScoPlaTS-138
95StaClu-288
95StaCluMOP-288
95StaCluSTWS-288
95TopTra-112T
96BufBisB-19
97Fle-607
97FleTif-607
97StaClu-302
97StaCluMOP-302
97Top-16
Shuffield, Jack
83ChaRoyT-12
Shugars, Shawn
94HudValRF-3401
95ChaRivTI-27
94HudValRC-24
Shuler, Dave
92PriWilCC-27
Shull, Mike
87PalSprP-10
90PalSprACLC-222
Shulleeta, Mike
82QuaCitCT-11
Shulock, John
88T/MUmp-39
89T/MUmp-37
90T/MUmp-35
Shultea, Chris
91SalLakTSP-19
Shultis, Chris
86EveGiaC-22
86EveGiaPC-28
88BoiHawP-1613
Shumake, Brooks
86VerRedP-18
Shumaker, Anthony
95BatCliTI-30
95MarPhiTI-24
96PieBolWB-25
Shumate, Jacob
94DanBraC-1
94DEL-1
94DEL-26
94SigRooDP-26
94SigRooDPS-26
94StaCluDP-1
94StaCluDPFDI-1
94TopTra-13T
95Exc-158
95MacBraTI-27
95Pin-172
95PinArtP-172
95PinMusC-172
95ScoDraP-DP9
95StaClu-99
95StaCluFDI-99
95StaCluMOP-99
95StaCluSTWS-99
95Top-6
95UppDecML-191
95UppDecMLFS-191
Shumpert, Derek
94OneYanC-22
94OneYanF-3806
96GreBatB-27
Shumpert, Terry
87EugEmeP-2674
88AppFoxP-142
89BlaYNPRWLU-9
89OmaRoyC-18
89OmaRoyP-1721
90ClaYel-T65
90DonBesA-134
90DonRoo-55
90FleUpd-104
90Lea-409
90ScoRoo-110T
90TopTra-114T
90TopTraT-114T
90UppDec-733
91Bow-314
91Don-297
91Fle-570
91Lea-104
91MajLeaCP-22
91OPC-322
91OPCPre-108
91RoyPol-20
91Sco-349
91Sco100RS-3
91ScoAllF-9
91ScoRoo-27
91SevCoi-F15
91StaClu-111
91Top-322
91TopDeb90-143
91TopDesS-322
91TopMic-322
91TopTif-322
91Ult-156
91UppDec-521
92Bow-157
92Cla1-T83
92Don-562
92Fle-169
92Lea-347
92OmaRoyF-2972
92OPC-483
92PanSti-95
92Pin-203
92RoyPol-25
92Sco-248
92Sco100RS-44
92StaClu-165
92Top-483
92TopGol-483
92TopGolW-483
92TopMic-483
92UppDec-348

93Don-601
93OmaRoyF-1688
93PacSpa-141
93TriAAAGF-44
94FleUpd-51
94VenLinU-88
95Don-176
95DonPreP-176
95Fle-172
95Sco-523
95ScoGolR-523
95ScoPlaTS-523
95Top-87
95Ult-61
95UltGolM-61
96IowCubB-23
97PacPriGotD-GD122

Shupe, Wilford
20WalMaiW-49

Shutt, Steve
72Dia-106
72Dia-107

Shwan, Dan
88SalLakCTTI-3
89SalLakTTI-3
91SalLakTP-3229
91SalLakTSP-27

Shy, Jason
95EugEmeTI-15
96DanBraB-22

Siberz, Bo
90OneYanP-3381
91GreHorP-3060

Siblerud, Daniel
86ColMetP-23

Siciliano, Jess
96EriSeaB-23

Sick, David
94BoiHawC-22
94BoiHawF-3354
95CedRapKTI-28
96CedRapKTI-22

Siddall, Joe
88JamExpP-1908
89RocExpLC-26
90WesPalBES-20
91HarSenLD-269
91HarSenP-631
91LinDriAA-269
92HarSenF-464
92HarSenS-298
93OttLynF-2439
94OttLynF-2901
94Pac-390
97PacPriGotD-GD147

Sides, Craig
92BurIndC-5
92BurIndF-1655

Siebern, Norm
47Exh-207
58Top-54
59Top-308
60A's-9
60A'sJayP-8
60A'sTeal-14
60Top-11
60TopVen-11
61A'sTeal-18
61AthJayP-18
61AthJayP-19
61Pos-82A
61Pos-82B
61Top-119
61Top-267
61TopDicG-16
61TopStal-165
62Baz-33
62ExhStaB-31
62Jel-92
62Pos-92
62PosCan-92
62SalPlaC-85
62ShiPlaC-85
62Top-127
62Top-275
62TopBuc-82
62TopStal-57
62TopVen-127
63AthJayP-9
63BasMagM-75
63Baz-4
63ExhStaB-59
63Fle-17
63Jel-85
63Pos-85
63SalMetC-51
63Top-2
63Top-430
63TopStil-40
64OriJayP-12
64Top-145
64TopCoi-49
64TopSta-14
64TopStaU-68
64TopTatl-67
64TopVen-145
64WheSta-41
65Top-455
66OPC-14
66Top-14
66TopVen-14
67CokCapG-5
67DexPre-191
67Top-299
68CokCapRS-15
68Top-537
78TCM60I-178
79TCM50-223
81RedSoxBG2S-112
83FraBroR-18
91OriCro-419

Siebert, Dick
40PlaBal-192
41DouPlaR-127
77TCMTheWY-22
83TCMPla1943-23
90DodTar-735
93ConTSN-926

Siebert, Mac
89BriTigS-26

Siebert, Paul
75IowOakT-17
75OPC-614
75Top-614
76VenLeaS-138
78MetDaiPA-21
89PacSenL-212
91MetWIZ-365

Siebert, Rick
86DurBulP-25
87DurBulP-18
88SumBraP-402

Siebert, Sonny
64Top-552
65OPC-96
65Top-96
66Kah-28
66Top-197
66Top-222
66Top-226
66TopVen-197
66TopVen-222
66TopVen-226
67CokCapI-8
67Kah-35
67OPC-95
67Top-95
67Top-463
67TopVen-246
68OPC-8
68Top-8
68Top-295
68TopVen-8
68TopVen-295
69MLBOffS-43
69Top-455
69TopSta-167
69TopTeaP-13
70MLBOffS-166
70RedSoxCPPC-13
70Top-597
71Kel-24
71MLBOffS-332
71OPC-710
71RedSoxA-9
71RedSoxTI-10
71Top-710
71TopCoi-122
72Kel-36
72OPC-290
72Top-290
73OPC-14
73Top-14
74OPC-548
74Top-548
75OPC-328
75Top-328
76SSP-484
81RedSoxBG2S-113
85LasVegSC-121
87LasVegSP-6
88LasVegSC-25
88LasVegSP-248
91WatDiaC-26
91WatDiaP-1274
92WicWraS-650
93RanKee-325
93WicWraF-2994
94PadMot-28
95PadMot-28
96ColSprSSTI-28

Siebert, Steve
90SpoIndSP-13
91UtiBluSC-15
91UtiBluSP-3251

Siebler, Dwight
64Top-516
65Top-326
66Top-546
67OPC-164
67Top-164
78TCM60I-126

Siegel, Bob
86WauTimP-24

Siegel, Dan
94PriRedC-29

Siegel, Justin
96HudValRB-16

Siegel, Lanny
89AncBucTI-26

Siegle, John H.
09AmeCarE-93
10E101-40
10MelMinE-40
10NadCarE-44
10PeoT21-50

Sieradzki, Al
89BluOriS-21

Sierra, Candy (Ulises)
85BeaGolGT-9
86BeaGolGP-21
87WicPilRD-20
88NasSouTI-21
89BlaYNPRWL-154
89Fle-171
89FleGlo-171
89Top-711
89TopTif-711
90RivRedWB-23
90RivRedWP-2609

Sierra, Ernie
89SanJosGB-30

Sierra, Ruben
85TulDriTI-12
86DonRoo-52
86FleUpd-105
86OklCit8P-21
86RanPer-3
86SpoRoo-16
87ClaUpdY-149
87Don-346
87DonOpeD-172
87Fle-138
87FleGlo-138
87FleMin-100
87Lea-225
87RanMot-13
87RanSmo-17
87SpoTeaP-1
87Top-6
87Top-261
87TopRoo-15
87TopSti-10
87TopTif-6
87TopTif-261
87ToyRoo-24
88BlaYNPRWLU-52
88ClaRed-180
88Don-223
88DonBasB-200
88DonBonM-BC26
88Fle-479
88FleExcS-38
88FleGlo-479
88FleHotS-38
88FleLeaL-39
88FleMin-58
88FleStiC-69
88FleSup-36
88KayB-28
88Lea-206
88OPC-319
88PanSti-209
88RanMot-10
88RanSmo-9
88Sco-113
88ScoGlo-113
88ScoYouSI-36
88Spo-113
88StaLinRa-15
88Top-771
88TopCoi-26
88TopGloS-4
88TopRitTM-25
88TopSti-234
88TopTif-771
88TopUKM-71
88TopUKMT-71
89BimBreD-6
89Bow-235
89BowTif-235
89ClaTraP-162
89Don-48
89DonBasB-111
89DonBonM-BC26
89Fle-532
89FleBasA-37
89FleBasM-35
89FleExcS-37
89FleGlo-532
89FleHeroB-37
89OPC-53
89PanSti-457
89RanMot-7
89RanSmo-30
89RedFolSB-108
89Sco-43
89ScoSco-31
89Spo-189
89SpoIllFKI-165
89Top-53
89TopBig-82
89TopCoi-51
89TopHilTM-26
89TopSti-242
89TopTif-53
89TopUKM-71
89TulDriTI-27
89TVSpoM-117
89UppDec-416
89UppDec-686
90Bow-490
90BowTif-490
90ClaBlu-7
90ClaBlu-59A
90ClaBlu-59B
90ClaYel-T77
90Col-7
90Don-3A
90Don-3B
90Don-174
90Don-673A
90Don-673B
90DonBesA-143
90DonSupD-3
90Fle-314
90FleAll-11
90FleAwaW-34
90FleBasA-34
90FleBasM-34
90FleCan-314
90FleLeaL-36
90FleWaxBC-C25
90Hot50PS-40
90Lea-257
90OPC-185
90OPC-390
90PanSti-162
90PanSti-203
90PubSti-422
90PubSti-605
90RanMot-3
90Sco-420
90Sco100S-85
90Spo-188
90StaLonJS-8
90StaLonJS-33
90Top-185
90Top-390
90TopAmeA-32
90TopBig-175
90TopCoi-28
90TopDou-60
90TopGloA-19
90TopGloS-26
90TopHilHM-20
90TopMag-4
90TopMinL-40
90TopSti-161
90TopSti-244
90TopStiB-53
90TopTif-185
90TopTif-390
90TopTVA-7
90TulDriDGB-35
90UppDec-355
90UppDecS-1
90VenSti-438
90VenSti-439
91BasBesHRK-16
91Bow-283
91CadEllD-52
91Cla3-T83
91ClaGam-41
91DenHol-21
91Don-567
91Fle-303
91FlePro-3
91KinDis-9
91Lea-97
91MooSna-16
91OPC-535
91OPCPre-109
91PanFreS-257
91PanSti-202
91RanMot-3
91RedFolS-87
91Sco-495
91Sco-859
91Sco100S-12
91SevCoi-T13
91StaClu-123
91StaPinB-46
91Stu-129
91Top-535
91TopCraJ2-18
91TopDesS-535
91TopMic-535
91TopTif-535
91Ult-356
91UniWayS-1
91UppDec-455
91USPlaCA-9H
92Bow-225
92Cla2-T65
92ClaGam-151
92DenHol-25
92Don-298
92DonCraJ2-26
92Fle-321
92FleCitTP-18
92FleUpd-51
92Hig5-115
92HitTheBB-32
92Lea-383
92OPC-700
92OPCPre-66
92PanSti-79
92Pin-14
92Pin-616
92PinSlu-10
92PinTeaP-10
92RanMot-3
92RanTeal-23
92Sco-437
92Sco-490
92Sco100S-87
92ScoImpP-46
92ScoRoo-63T
92StaClu-387
92StaCluD-172
92Stu-249
92StuPre-1
92Top-403
92Top-700
92TopGol-403
92TopGol-700
92TopGolW-403
92TopGolW-700
92TopKid-128
92TopMic-403
92TopMic-700
92TopMic-G403
92TriPla-238
92Ult-142
92UppDec-176
92UppDecF-41
92UppDecFG-41
92UppDecTMH-48
92UppDecWB-T10

93AthMot-5
93Bow-245
93ClaGam-85
93DiaMar-98
93Don-637
93DurPowP2-6
93Fin-158
93FinRef-158
93Fla-262
93Fle-298
93FunPac-52
93Lea-29
93OPC-243
93PacSpa-225
93PacSpaGE-18
93PanSti-21
93Pin-200
93PinHomRC-46
93PinSlu-12
93RanKee-326
93Sco-608
93Sel-366
93SP-43
93StaClu-580
93StaCluAt-10
93StaCluFDI-580
93StaCluM-47
93StaCluMOP-580
93StaCluMP-22
93Stu-113
93Top-440
93TopGol-440
93TopInaM-440
93TopMic-440
93TriPla-60
93Ult-613
93UppDec-49
93UppDec-145
93UppDecGold-49
93UppDecGold-145
94A'sMot-7
94Bow-24
94BowBes-R57
94BowBesR-R57
94ChuHomS-3
94ChuHomSG-3
94ColC-258
94ColChoGS-258
94ColChoSS-258
94Don-33
94DonDiaK-DK18
94DonMVP-25
94DonSpeE-33
94ExtBas-155
94Fin-371
94FinRef-371
94Fla-333
94Fle-273
94FUnPac-141
94Lea-67
94LeaL-63
94OPC-195
94OscMayR-13
94Pac-462
94PacAll-12
94PanSti-112
94Pin-61
94PinArtP-61
94PinMusC-61
94ProMag-98
94RanAllP-17
94RanAllP-19
94RanAllP-20
94Sco-409
94ScoGolR-409
94Sel-45
94SP-37
94SPDieC-37
94Spo-73
94StaClu-307
94StaClu-536
94StaCluFDI-307
94StaCluFDI-536
94StaCluGR-307
94StaCluGR-536
94StaCluMOP-307
94StaCluMOP-536
94Stu-6
94TomPiz-28
94Top-680
94TopGol-680
94TopSpa-680
94TriPla-8
94Ult-411
94UppDec-380
94UppDecAJ-2
94UppDecAJG-2
94UppDecED-380
95AthMot-7
95Baz-100
95Bow-360
95BowBes-R8
95BowBesR-R8
95ColCho-135
95ColChoGS-135
95ColChoSE-50
95ColChoSEGS-50
95ColChoSESS-50
95ColChoSS-135
95D3-3
95Don-406
95DonDiaK-DK5
95DonPreP-406
95DonTopotO-125
95Emb-14
95EmbGolI-14
95Emo-74
95Fin-208
95FinRef-208
95Fla-295
95FlaOutP-10
95Fle-253
95FleTeaL-11
95Lea-243
95LeaLim-56
95Pac-320
95PacPri-103
95PanSti-87
95Pin-45
95PinArtP-45
95PinMusC-45
95Sco-351
95ScoGolR-351
95ScoHaloG-HG84
95ScoPlaTS-351
95Sel-15
95SelArtP-15
95SP-184
95SPCha-180
95SPChaDC-180
95Spo-86
95SpoArtP-86
95SPSil-184
95SPSpeF-17
95StaClu-96
95StaClu-520
95StaCluCC-CC2
95StaCluCT-14
95StaCluFDI-96
95StaCluMOP-96
95StaCluMOP-520
95StaCluMOP-CC2
95StaCluMOP-RL29
95StaCluRL-RL29
95StaCluSTWS-96
95StaCluSTWS-520
95StaCluVR-59
95Stu-111
95Sum-108
95SumNthD-108
95TomPiz-17
95Top-310
95TopCyb-167
95UC3-86
95UC3ArtP-86
95Ult-96
95UltGolM-96
95UppDec-280
95UppDec-494T
95UppDecED-280
95UppDecEDG-280
95UppDecPLL-R46
95UppDecPLLE-R46
95UppDecSE-110
95UppDecSEG-110
95Zen-95
96ColCho-630
96ColChoGS-630
96ColChoSS-630
96Don-171
96DonPreP-171
96EmoXL-97
96Fin-B169
96FinRef-B169
96Fla-138
96Fle-196
96FleTif-196
96Lea-168
96LeaPrePB-168
96LeaPrePG-168
96LeaPrePS-168
96MetUni-95
96MetUniP-95
96Pac-379
96PacEstL-EL29
96Pin-116
96PinAfi-40
96PinAfiAP-40
96PinAfiFPP-40
96Sco-342
96ScoDugC-B67
96ScoDugCAP-B67
96Sel-118
96SelArtP-118
96SP-133
96StaClu-354
96StaCluEPB-354
96StaCluEPG-354
96StaCluEPS-354
96StaCluMOP-354
95StaCluVRMC-59
96Stu-69
96StuPrePB-69
96StuPrePG-69
96StuPrePS-69
96Sum-58
96SumAbo&B-58
96SumArtP-58
96SumFoi-58
96Top-290
96TopGal-14
96TopGalPPI-14
96Ult-106
96UltGolM-106
96UppDec-158
97Cir-247
97CirRav-247
97Don-259
97DonEli-66
97DonEliGS-66
97DonPre-44
97DonPreCttC-44
97DonPreP-259
97DonPrePGold-259
97Fle-106
97FleTif-106
97NewPin-145
97NewPinAP-145
97NewPinMC-145
97NewPinPP-145
97Pac-95
97PacLigB-95
97PacSil-95
97Pin-39
97PinArtP-39
97PinIns-21
97PinInsCE-21
97PinInsDE-21
97PinMusC-39
97PinPreP-4
97Sco-143
97Sco-342
97ScoHobR-342
97ScoPreS-143
97ScoResC-342
97ScoShoS-143
97ScoShoS-342
97ScoShoSAP-143
97ScoShoSAP-342
97StaClu-277
97StaCluMOP-277
97Stu-26
97StuPrePG-26
97StuPrePS-26
97Top-452
97Ult-422
97UltGolME-422
97UltPlaME-422

Siever, Edward
03BreE10-130
07TigACDPP-15
09WolNewDTPP-18
11SpoLifCW-323

Sievers, Jason
90EveGiaB-15
90EveGiaP-3131
92EveGiaF-1694
93ButCopKSP-2
94CliLumF-1984
94CliLumC-22

Sievers, Roy
47Exh-208A
47Exh-208B
47Exh-208C
47Exh-208D
47StaPinP2-36
50Bow-16
51Bow-67
51FisBakL-26
51TopRedB-9
52Top-64
53Top-67
54Top-245
55DonWin-5
55Top-16
55TopDouH-79
56Top-75
56TopPin-59
57Top-89
58SenJayP-11
58Top-250
59ArmCoi-15
59Baz-19
59Top-74
59Top-340
59Top-465
59Top-566
59TopVen-74
60NuHi-23
60SenUniMC-17
60Top-25
60TopVen-25
60WhiSoxJP-10
60WhiSoxTS-18
61NuSco-423
61Pos-26A
61Pos-26B
61SevElev-9
61Top-470
61TopStal-128
61WhiSoxTS-17
62Jel-46
62Pos-46
62PosCan-46
62SalPlaC-66
62ShiPlaC-66
62Top-220
62TopBuc-83
62TopStal-58
62TopStal-169
63BasMagM-76
63Jel-177
63Pos-177
63Top-283
64PhiTeaS-6
64Top-43
64TopVen-43
65Top-574
76GrePlaG-36
77GalGloG-43
78TCM60I-242
79DiaGre-75
79TCM50-206
83TopRep5-64
83YanYeaIT-9
88PacLegI-26
89SweBasG-47
91TopArc1-67
94TopArc1-245
94TopArc1G-245

Sievert, Mark
93MedHatBJF-3735
93MedHatBJSP-15
94St.CatBJC-21
94St.CatBJF-3643
95HagSunF-69
95SPML-164
96BowBes-123
96BowBesAR-123
96BowBesR-123
96Exc-119
96KnoSmoB-23

Sigler, Allen
85CedRapRT-25
86CedRapRT-22

Sigler, Brad
93HunCubC-24
93HunCubF-3246

Siglin, Paddy (W.)
20WalMaiW-50

Sigman, Lee
78BurBeeT-25
80HolMilT-25
83ElPasDT-25

Sigmund, John
63GadFunC-68

Sigwart, Clete
93SpaPhiC-28
94ClePhiC-30
95ClePhiF-234

Sikes, Jason
94MarPhiC-25
94MarPhiF-3293
94SigRooDP-78
94SigRooDPS-78
94StaCluDP-53
94StaCluDPFDI-53
95MarPhiTI-25
96PieBolWB-26

Sikes, Ken
93GreFalDSP-14
94YakBeaC-22
94YakBeaF-3849
95Exc-218
95VerBeaDTI-26
96SanBerSB-25

Sikorski, Brian
95AubAstTI-14
96BesAutSA-71
96MidLeaAB-28
96QuaCitRB-26

Silch, Edward
87OldJudN-463

Silcox, Rusty
90SpoIndSP-3
91HigDesMC-10
91HigDesMP-2393
92HigDesMC-1
93BinMetF-2334

Siler, Jeff
96LakTigB-24

Siler, Mike
87BakDodP-26

Silicato, Tom
77ReaPhiT-21

Silkwood, Joe
83SprCarF-12
84ArkTraT-20

Silva, Carlos
96MarPhiB-25

Silva, Freddie
82SprCarF-6
83St.PetCT-12

Silva, Herman
76VenLeaS-52

Silva, Ildemero
80VenLeaS-60

Silva, Jose
93HagSunC-24
93HagSunF-1880
94ActPac-47
94ActPac-62
94ActPac2G-8G
94BowBes-B86
94BowBesR-B86
94Cla-3
94ClaTriF-T82
94ColC-648
94ColChoGS-648
94ColChoSS-648
94DunBluJC-24
94DunBluJF-2556
94ExcFS7-148
94ExcLeaLF-16
94SP-16
94SPDieC-16
94TedWil-130
94UppDec-526
94UppDecAHNIL-12
94UppDecED-526
94UppDecML-50
94UppDecML-254
94UppDecMLT1PJF-TP9
94UppDecMLT1PMF-9
95ActPacF-16
95ColChoSE-16
95ColChoSEGS-16
95ColChoSESS-16
95Exc-141
95UppDecML-29
95UppDecML-113
95UppDecMLOP-OP28
95UppDecMLT1PF-6
95UppDecMLFS-29
95UppDecMLFS-113

Silva, Luis
95LinVen-68
95WesMicWTI-24

Silva, Mark
83NasSouTI-22

85ColCliP-20
85ColCliT-24
85DomLeaS-200
86ColCliP-20
86ColCliP-22
Silva, Natalio
80VenLeaS-100
Silva, Ryan
86BenPhiC-149
Silva, Ted
95ChaRivUTIS-32
Silvas, Brian
81BatTroT-7
Silver, Chad
89CarNewE-12
90PriPatD-18
Silver, Keith
84EveGiaC-10A
86ShrCapP-23
Silver, Larry
78St.PetCT-24
Silver, Long Ball
94SalBucC-30
Silver, Roy
86St.PetCP-28
87ArkTraP-12
87TexLeaAF-2
88LouRedBC-22
88LouRedBP-431
88LouRedBTI-44
89ArkTraGS-22
89BlaYNPRWL-87
89BlaYNPRWLU-53
89TexLeaAGS-38
90CMC-116
90LouRedBC-16
90LouRedBLBC-38
90LouRedBP-418
90ProAAAF-532
90TopTVCa-64
91SavCarC-2
91SavCarP-1669
92SprCarC-28
92SprCarF-886
94NewJerCC-29
95PeoChiTI-38
96PeoChiB-1
Silvera, Al
56Top-137
Silvera, Charlie
52Bow-197
52Top-168
53Dor-119
53Top-242
54Top-96
55Top-188
57Top-255
73OPC-323
73Top-323
74OPC-379
74Top-379
79TCM50-266
83TopRep5-168
91TopArc1-242
93RanKee-327
94TopArc1-96
94TopArc1G-96
Silverio, Francisco
86TamTarP-19
87CedRapRP-23
Silverio, Luis
75WatRoyT-26
76WatRoyT-26
77JacSunT-21
82OmaRoyT-23
85DomLeaS-53
88FloStaLAS-30
89BasCitRS-27
Silverio, Nelson
86MadMusP-19
86MadMusP-23
88ChaRaiP-1220
Silverio, Tom
72OPC-213
72Top-213
Silverio, Victor
91QuaCitAC-11
91QuaCitAP-2628
92PalSprAC-5
92PalSprAF-839
93LimRocDWB-3
Silverman, Aaron
52Par-3
Silverman, Bob
80KnoBluJT-9
Silverman, Don
85IowCubT-27
Silverman, Eric
50WorWidGV-19
Silverstein, Allan
88MyrBeaBJP-1187
89DunBluJS-15
90DunBluJS-16
Silvestri, David
87PanAmTURB-24
88TopTra-107T
88TopTraT-107T
89OscAstS-22
89Sta-18
89TopBig-141
90PriWilCTI-24
91AlbYanLD-15
91AlbYanP-1016
91LinDriAA-15
92Bow-87
92Cla2-T95
92ColCliF-361
92ColCliP-19
92ColCliS-116
92DonRoo-111
92LeaGolR-BC20
92Pin-531
92ProFS7-111
92SkyAAAF-55
93ClaFS7-291
93ColCliF-1118
93ColCliP-16
93FleFinE-252
93FleMajLP-B5
93Pin-180
93Sco-252
93Top-529
93TopGol-529
93TopInaM-529
93TopMic-529
94ColCliF-2960
94ColCliP-24
94StaCluT-191
94StaCluTFDI-191
95Sco-298
95ScoGolR-298
95ScoPlaTS-298
96LeaSigEA-183
97Pac-354
97PacLigB-354
97PacSil-354
87PanAmTUBI-5
Silvestri, Ken
39WhiSoxTI-16
40WhiSoxL-16
49EurSta-147
49PhiBul-50
51Bow-256
52Bow-200
60Top-466
73OPC-237
73Top-237A
73Top-237B
74OPC-634
74Top-634
78KnoKnoST-20
87PorBeaP-23
89WatIndS-26
90WatIndS-25
Silvey, Jeff
90GeoColC-27
Silvey, Jim
72CedRapCT-21
Silvia, Brian
92PriRedC-18
92PriRedF-3090
93PriRedC-28
93PriRedF-4183
94NewJerCC-24
94NewJerCF-3420
Sima, Al
52Top-93
53Bri-20
53Top-241
54Top-216
83TopRep5-93
88ChaLooLTI-28
91TopArc1-241
94TopArc1-216
94TopArc1G-216
Simas, Bill
92BoiHawC-29
92BoiHawF-3627
93CedRapKC-17
93CedRapKF-1736
94LakElsSC-17
94LakElsSF-1663
95Bow-197
95NasSouTI-23
96Bow-175
96FleUpd-U27
96FleUpdTC-U27
96Ult-335
96UltGolM-335
Simcox, Larry
82DayBeaAT-23
83ColAstT-7
Simmermacher, Bret
86BelMarC-114
Simmons, Al (Aloysius)
21Exh-160
26SpoComoA-40
26SpoNewSM-8
28Exh-56
28PorandAR-A33
28PorandAR-B33
28W56PlaC-C11
29PorandAR-85
30SchR33-1
30W554-16
31Exh-27
31W517-40
32OrbPinNP-39
32OrbPinUP-53
32R33So2-415
32USCar-17
33ButCanV-44
33ButCre-24
33CraJacP-20
33DelR33-2
33DouDisP-39
33ExhFou-14
33GeoCMil-27
33Gou-35
33GouCanV-35
33RitCE-9D
33TatOrb-53
33TatOrbSDR-154
34BatR31-34
34ButPreR-55
34DiaStaR-2A
34DiaStaR-2B
34ExhFou-10
34ExhFou-14
35AlDemDCR3-14
35AlDemDCR3-16
35ExhFou-10
35GouPuzR-5A
35GouPuzR-6A
35GouPuzR-11J
35GouPuzR-13A
35WheBB1-24
36GouWidPPR-A94
36GouWidPPR-B19
36NatChiFPR-67
36NatChiFPR-90
36OveCanR-41
36WorWidGV-77
38BasTabP-26
38OurNatGPP-28
39GouPreR303A-40
39GouPreR303B-21
39WorWidGTP-40
43RedSoxTI-22
49PhiBul-51
50CalHOFW-65
51R42SmaS-102
60ExhWriH-21
60Fle-32
61Fle-77
61GolPre-20
63BazA-21
67TopVen-170
69Baz-2
69Baz-9
75SheGrePG-8
76GrePlaG-8
76RowExh-13
76ShaPiz-64
76WhiSoxTAG-11
77BobParHoF-43
77GalGloG-58
77GalGloG-190
80LauFamF-3
80PacLeg-119
80PerHaloFP-68
80SSPHOF-68
80WhiSoxGT-8
81ConTSN-81
82DiaCla-9
83ConMar-4
83MiaMarT-16
85FegMurCG-17
86SpoDecG-5
87HygAllG-39
88ConAmeA-22
88ConSer4-25
91ConTSN-49
91ConTSN-311
91TopArc1-326
92ConTSN-423
92ConTSN-554
92ConTSNCI-13
93ConTSN-666
94ConTSN-1084
94ConTSN-1136
94ConTSNB-1084
94ConTSNB-1136
94TedWil-70
95ConTSN-1375
95MegRut-3
Simmons, Brad
77DayBealT-23
Simmons, Brian
96MidLeaAB-55
96SouBenSHS-24
Simmons, Carlos
96ChaRivTI-9628
Simmons, Chris
94OgdRapF-3750
94OgdRapSP-19
Simmons, Curt
47Exh-209
47PM1StaP1-202
49Bow-14
49EurSta-148
49PhiBul-52
49PhiLumPB-11
50Bow-68
50JJKCopP-18
50PhiPhil-3
51BerRos-D9
51Bow-111
52Bow-184
52StaCalL-77C
52Top-203
53BowC-64
54Bow-79
54RedMan-NL12
55ArmCoi-18
55Bow-64
55RedMan-NL24
55RobGouS-6
55RobGouW-6
56Top-290
57Top-158
58Hir-28
58PhiJayP-11
58Top-404
59Top-382
60Top-451
61Top-11
61TopStal-93
62CarJayP-11
62Jel-167
62Pos-167
62PosCan-167
62Top-56
62Top-285
62TopVen-56
63CarJayP-18
63CarJayP-19
63Top-22
64Top-385
65CarTeal-23
65Top-373
66CarTeal-10
66Top-489
67CokCapC-16
67OPC-39
67Top-39
79DiaGre-319
79TCM50-54
83PhiPosGPaM-9
83TopRep5-203
87Phi195T-2
91TopArc1-318
Simmons, Deon
86AncGlaPTI-41
Simmons, Enoch
89MedAthB-26
90MadMusB-10
90MadMusP-2281
91Cla/Bes-256
91ModA'sC-23
91ModA'sP-3105
92CalLeaACL-11
92RenSilSCLC-53
93HunStaF-2096
94TacTigF-3189
Simmons, George
11T205-156
12ImpTobC-75
Simmons, Greg
85BelBreT-17
86BelBreP-21
Simmons, Gus
63GadFunC-77
Simmons, Hack
11DiaGumP-25
Simmons, Jason
93IdaFalBF-4029
93IdaFalBSP-10
Simmons, John
92IdaFalGF-3512
92IdaFalGSP-1
93MacBraC-21
93MacBraF-1399
94DurBulC-18
94DurBulF-327
94DurBulTI-19
95BreBtaTI-50
Simmons, John Earl
50WorWidGV-5
52Par-62
53ExhCan-35
Simmons, Josh
92HunCubC-10
92HunCubF-3158
93PeoChiTI-25
Simmons, Mark
92BoiHawC-7
92BoiHawF-3639
93BoiHawF-3931
93CedRapKC-18
93CedRapKF-1748
94CedRapKC-20
94CedRapKF-1118
95LakElsSTI-22
Simmons, Mitch
92AlbPolF-2315
Simmons, Nelson
83BirBarT-16
84EvaTriT-9
85DomLeaS-138
85FleUpd-103
85NasSouTI-22
86Don-272
86Fle-238
86RocRedWP-21
86TigCaiD-16
86Top-121
86TopTif-121
87RocRedWP-18
88CalCanC-19
88CalCanP-802
89BlaYNPRWLU-10
89Don-212
90HunStaB-22
91LinDriAAA-545
91OriCro-420
91TacTigLD-545
91TacTigP-2320
93LinVenB-315
Simmons, Randy
88PulBraP-1768
89SouAtlLAGS-44
89SumBraP-1110
90Bes-81
90BurBraB-24
90BurBraP-2364
90BurBraS-24
91DurBulP-1561
Simmons, Scott
91HamRedP-4038
92ClaFS7-271
92MidLeaATI-40
92SprCarC-22
92SprCarF-866
93St.PetCC-23
93St.PetCF-2627
94ArkTraF-3090
95ArkTraTI-25
95Exc-274
96LouRedB-25

Simmons, Ted
71CarTeal-35
71CarTeal-36
71OPC-117
71Top-117
72OPC-154
72Top-154
73LinPor-169
73OPC-85
73Top-85
74Kel-21
74OPC-260
74Top-260
74TopDecE-10
74TopSta-116
75Hos-95
75OPC-75
75Top-75
76CraDis-56
76Hos-113
76Kel-57
76OPC-191
76OPC-290
76Spo-5
76SSP-274
76Top-191
76Top-290
77BurCheD-16
77Car5-26
77CarTeal-25
77Hos-61
77OPC-196
77Top-470
77TopCloS-43
78CarTeal-21
78Hos-65
78OPC-150
78Pep-38
78Top-380
78WifBalD-69
79Car5-26
79Hos-44
79Kel-2
79OPC-267
79Top-510
79TopCom-30
80Kel-45
80OPC-47
80Top-85
80TopSup-36
81AllGamPI-43
81Don-308
81Fle-528
81FleStiC-120
81OPC-352
81PerCreC-17
81Top-705
81TopScr-63
81TopSti-94
81TopSupN-15
81TopTra-830
82BrePol-23
82Don-106
82Fle-152
82FleSta-137
82OPC-150
82Top-150
82TopSti-201
82TopStiV-201
83AllGamPI-43
83BreGar-16
83BrePol-23
83Don-332
83Fle-45
83FleSta-176
83FleSti-22
83OPC-33
83OPC-284
83PerAll-5
83PerAllG-5
83Top-450
83Top-451
83TopSti-85
84AllGamPI-133
84BreGar-17
84BrePol-23
84Don-473
84DonActAS-58
84Fle-213
84FunFooP-124
84MilBra-24
84Nes792-404
84Nes792-630
84Nes792-713
84Nes792-726
84OPC-94
84OPC-122
84RalPur-3
84SevCoi-C21
84Top-404
84Top-630
84Top-713
84Top-726
84TopCer-3
84TopGloA-9
84TopGloS-18
84TopSti-193
84TopSti-293
84TopStiB-2
84TopTif-404
84TopTif-630
84TopTif-713
84TopTif-726
85BreGar-19
85BrePol-23
85Don-414
85Fle-596
85Lea-104
85OPC-318
85Top-318
85TopSti-294
85TopTif-318
86BasStaB-100
86BraPol-23
86Don-292
86Fle-503
86FleUpd-106
86Lea-167
86Spo-196
86SpoDecG-62
86Top-237
86TopSti-199
86TopTat-4
86TopTif-237
86TopTra-102T
86TopTraT-102T
87BraSmo-13
87Don-537
87Fle-528
87FleGlo-528
87Top-516
87TopTif-516
88Don-560
88Fle-549
88FleGlo-549
88Lea-222
88Sco-285
88ScoGlo-285
88StaLinBra-17
88Top-791
88TopTif-791
89Fle-599
89FleGlo-599
89Sco-611
89UppDec-570
91MDAA-2
92BreCarT-20
92CarMcD-35
93PirNatI-28
94BreMilB-352
94BreMilB-353

Simmons, Todd
86BeaGolGP-22
87LasVegSP-11
88Fle-650
88FleGlo-650
88LasVegSC-6
88LasVegSP-240
89DenZepC-10
89DenZepP-30
89Fle-318
89FleGlo-318

Simms, Mike (Michael)
87AshTouP-17
88FloStaLAS-21
88OscAstS-25
89ColMudB-7
89ColMudP-141
89ColMudS-22
89Sta-3
90CMC-622
90ProAAAF-198
90TucTorC-20
90TucTorP-208
91Bow-551
91Cla2-T90
91Fle-516
91LinDriAAA-619
91OPC-32
91Sco-766
91StaClu-281
91Top-32
91TopDeb90-144
91TopDesS-32
91TopMic-32
91TopTif-32
91TucTorLD-619
91TucTorP-2221
91UppDec-664
92Don-747
92Fle-445
92OPC-463
92PanSti-156
92Sco-632
92SkyAAAF-276
92StaClu-262
92Top-463
92TopGol-463
92TopGolW-463
92TopMic-463
92TucTorF-501
92TucTorS-619
92UppDec-584
93Don-32
93LasVegSF-953
93PacSpa-128
94BufBisF-1845
95TusTorTI-24
96AstMot-24
96ColCho-566
96ColChoGS-566
96ColChoSS-566
96Don-499
96DonPreP-499

Simon, Ben
96YakBeaTI-41

Simon, Michael
75TopPho-30

Simon, Michael Edward
10PirHerP-10
10PirTipTD-19
11MecDFT-40
11SpoLifM-259
12T207-166
14CraJacE-25
15CraJacE-25

Simon, Randall
93DanBraC-24
93DanBraF-3626
94MacBraC-20
94MacBraF-2216
95DurBulTI-27
96BesAutSA-72
96GreBraB-24
96GreBraTI-18
97Bow-131
97BowChr-143
97BowChrI-143
97BowChrIR-143
97BowChrR-143
97BowInt-131
97FlaShoWotF-3
97Fle-653
97FleTif-653
97Ult-508
97UltGolME-508
97UltPlaME-508

Simon, Richie (Richard)
86AubAstP-23
87AubAstP-25
88AshTouP-1069
89OscAstS-23
90ColMudB-13
90ColMudP-1347
90ColMudS-22
91JacGenLD-573
91JacGenP-927
91LinDriAA-564
91LinDriAA-573
92JacGenF-4000
92JacGenS-343
92SkyAA F-147
92TucTorF-486
93ShrCapF-2758
94ShrCapF-1605

Simon, Rick
74GasRanT-19

Simon, Willie
76WauMetT-23

Simond, Rob
80LynSaiT-6
81LynSaiT-10

Simonds, Dan
88FreSunCLC-6
88FreSunP-1230
89EasLeaDDP-DD29
89FreKeyS-22
89HagSunB-23
90HagSunB-2
90HagSunP-1417
91IowCubLD-217
91IowCubP-1064
91LinDriAAA-217
93CubMar-24
96BluOriB-2
96BowBayB-3

Simoneaux, Wayne
91IdaFalBSP-19

Simons, Doug
89CalLeaA-17
89VisOakCLC-95
89VisOakP-1435
90CMC-749
90OrlSunRB-21
90OrlSunRP-1082
90OrlSunRS-19
91Bow-463
91Cla2-T86
91DonRoo-26
91MetColP-46
91MetKah-43
91OPCPre-110
91ScoRoo-91T
91TopTra-109T
91TopTraT-109T
91UppDecFE-63F
92Don-688
92IndIndF-1858
92MetColP-28
92OPC-82
92Sco-479
92Sco100RS-91
92Top-82
92TopDeb91-163
92TopGol-82
92TopGolW-82
92TopMic-82
93Don-276
93OttLynF-2435
94OmaRoyF-1224
96JacGenB-25
96TexLeaAB-15

Simons, Mitchel
91JamExpC-12
91JamExpP-3555
91OklStaC-23
92AlbPolC-25
93WesPalBEC-22
93WesPalBEF-1350

Simons, Neil
82DayBeaAT-15

Simonson, Bob
85BelBreT-6
86BelBreP-22
88BelBreGS-9
93ChaRaiC-20
93ChaRaiF-1925

Simontacchi, Jason
96SpoIndB-26

Simonton, Benji
92ClaDraP-55
92EveGiaC-9
92EveGiaF-1705
93Bow-112
93CliGiaF-2502
93StaCluM-60
94CliLumF-1996
94MidLeaAF-MDW41
95Exc-295
95ExcLeaL-14
95UppDecML-55
94CliLumC-1
95UppDecMLFS-55

Simonton, Cy
95EveAqaTI-23
96EveAquB-21

Simpson, Danny
83TriTriT-22

Simpson, Dick
63Top-407
64Top-127
64TopVen-127
65Top-374
66Top-311
66TopVen-311
67CokCapR-18
67OPC-6
67Top-6
68Top-459
69MilBra-254
69Top-608
87AstShowSTh-22
92YanWIZ6-116

Simpson, Greg
86CedRapRT-9
87VerRedP-6
88CedRapRP-1137

Simpson, Herb
92NegLeaRLI-56

Simpson, Jay
92BoiHawC-10
93PalSprAC-20
93PalSprAF-84
94LakElsSC-18
94LakElsSF-1677

Simpson, Jeramie
96StLucMTI-10

Simpson, Joe
75AlbDukC-2
75IntLeaASB-32
75PacCoaLAB-32
79Top-719
80Top-637
81Don-168
81Fle-616
81MarPol-15
81Top-116
82Don-55
82Fle-518
82Top-382
83Fle-485
83Roy-26
83Top-567
83TopTra-104T
84Don-496
84EdmTraC-115
84Fle-358
84Nes792-219
84Top-219
84TopTif-219
89CarNewE-9
90DodTar-736

Simpson, O.J.
74NewYorNTDiS-32

Simpson, Shelton
90WelPirP-29

Simpson, Suitcase (Harry)
52Bow-223
52IndNumN-17
52Top-193
53BowC-86
53Top-150
55A'sRodM-38
56A'sRodM-9
56Top-239
57Top-225
58Top-299
59Top-333
60Lea-81
60Top-180
60TopVen-180
61UniOil-SD10
76A'sRodMC-24
79TCM50-79
83TopRep5-193
84OCoandSI-123
86NegLeaF-92
91TopArc1-150

Simpson, Wayne
70DayDaiNM-68
70Top-683
71Kel-1
71MilDud-64
71MLBOffS-69
71OPC-68
71OPC-339
71Top-68
71Top-339
71TopCoi-53
72Top-762
73OPC-428
73Top-428
76SalLakCGC-14
76SSP-599

Simpson, William
77AshTouT-21
78AshTouT-25

Sims, Daniel
89IdaFalBP-2018
90SumBraB-20

90SumBraP-2448
Sims, Duke (Duane)
66OPC-169
66Top-169
66TopVen-169
67OPC-3
67Top-3
68Top-508
69MilBra-255
69Top-414
69TopSta-168
69TopTeaP-13
70MLBOffS-203
70OPC-275
70Top-275
71DodTic-15
71MLBOffS-114
71OPC-172
71Top-172
71TopCoi-66
72MilBra-316
72OPC-63
72Top-63
73OPC-304
73Top-304
74OPC-398
74Top-398
86AppFoxP-23
89SweBasG-128
90DodTar-737
92YanWIZ7-140
93RanKee-328
Sims, Greg
66Top-596
89AugPirP-517
89SouAtlLAGS-5
90SalBucS-22
91VisOakP-1756
Sims, Harry
52LavPro-33
Sims, Joe Beely
86JamExpP-23
87JamExpP-2545
Sims, Kinney
88RenSilSCLC-278
Sims, Mark
87SpaPhiP-6
88ClePhiS-21
89ClePhiS-20
90Bes-182
90EasLeaAP-EL22
90ReaPhiB-10
90ReaPhiP-1220
90ReaPhiS-22
91LinDriAA-519
91ReaPhiLD-519
91ReaPhiP-1370
92ScrRedBF-2446
92ScrRedBS-494
93PorBeaF-2384
94ButCopKSP-28
Sims, Mike
83TamTarT-29
86VerRedP-19
93ElmPioC-18
93ElmPioF-3827
94BreCouMC-17
94BreCouMF-15
95BreCouMF-250
Sims, Wesley
93EriSaiC-22
93EriSaiF-3125
94ChaRanF-2506
Simunic, Doug
79MemChiT-7
80MemChiT-22
83ChaChaT-7
84BufBisT-6
84MaiGuiT-5
89AubAstP-2184
89PacSenL-35
89TopSenL-84
90EliSenL-105
91KisDodP-4205
91PacSenL-55
92GulCoaDF-3586
Sinacori, Chris
91GreFalDSP-21
92VerBeaDC-16
92VerBeaDF-2873
93VerBeaDC-22
93VerBeaDF-2218
94VerBeaDC-20
94VerBeaDF-71
95DunBluJTI-24
Sinatro, Greg
77SanJosMC-8
Sinatro, Matt
81RicBraT-20
82Don-149
82RicBraT-12
83Don-622
83RicBraT-11
85GreBraTI-15
87TacTigP-9
88TacTigC-18
88TacTigP-616
89BlaYNPRWLU-38
89TucTorC-11
89TucTorP-201
90CalCanC-13
90CalCanP-654
90CMC-440
90ProAAAF-119
90TopTra-115T
90TopTraT-115T
91OPC-709
91Top-709
91TopDesS-709
91TopMic-709
91TopTif-709
92Bow-462
92MarMot-18
92StaClu-872
95MarMot-28
96MarMot-28
Sinclair, John
87BriYouC-12
Sinclair, Ken
84SavCarT-25
Sinclair, Steve
91MedHatBJP-4100
91MedHatBJSP-12
93MedHatBJF-3736
93MedHatBJSP-2
94HagSunC-22
94HagSunF-2730
95DunBluJTI-25
96DunBluJB-23
96DunBluJTI-27
Siner, Hosea John
09ColChiE-262
12ColRedB-262
12ColTinT-262
Singer, Bill
66Top-288
66TopVen-288
67OPC-12
67Top-12
68Top-249
68TopVen-249
69MLBOffS-152
69OPC-12
69Top-12
69Top-575
69TopSta-49
69TopTeaP-22
70Kel-17
70MLBOffS-57
70OPC-71
70OPC-490
70Top-71
70Top-490
70TopBoo-17
71DodTic-16
71MLBOffS-115
71OPC-145
71Top-145
72MilBra-317
72OPC-25
72Top-25
73LinPor-36
73OPC-570
73Top-570
74Kel-12
74OPC-210
74Top-210
74TopSta-149
75Hos-82
75HosTwi-82
75OPC-40
75Top-40
76OPC-411
76SSP-188
76Top-411
76TopTra-411T
77Hos-139
77MSADis-57
77OPC-85
77RCColC-60
77Top-346
77TopCloS-44
78RCColC-2
84DodUniOP-6
87DodSmoA-33
88DodSmo-6
89DodSmoG-75
90DodTar-738
91DodUno7P-4
92DodStaTA-8
92Nab-18
93RanKee-329
Singer, Tom
90St.CatBJP-3457
91MyrBeaHC-10
91MyrBeaHP-2944
92DunBluJC-16
92DunBluJF-1999
93DunBluJC-20
93DunBluJF-1795
93DunBluJFFN-22
94DunBluJC-25
94DunBluJF-2557
Singletary, Chico
87SavCarP-15
Singleton, Bert Elmer
49Bow-147
49SomandK-25
52MotCoo-17
57Top-378
59Top-548
63MilSau-6
Singleton, Chris
94Cla-176
94ClaGolF-63
94ClaTriF-T70
94SanJosGC-21
94SanJosGF-2829
96Cir-194
96CirRav-194
96FleUpd-U209
96FleUpdTC-U209
96TexLeaAB-16
96UltGolP-15
96UltGolPHGM-15
97Ult-298
97UltGolME-298
97UltPlaME-298
Singleton, Duane
92Bow-679
92ClaFS7-285
92StoPorC-7
92UppDecML-196
93Bow-43
93ClaGolF-100
93ElPasDF-2965
94Bow-533
94BreMilB-354
95Bow-255
95BowGolF-255
95Pin-150
95PinArtP-150
95PinMusC-150
95Sco-581
95ScoGolR-581
95ScoPlaTS-581
95Sel-218
95SelArtP-218
95Spo-159
95SpoArtP-159
95Top-638
95Ult-299
95UltGolM-299
96Don-549
96DonPreP-549
96TolMudHB-26
97PacPriGotD-GD45
Singleton, Ken
71OPC-16
71Top-16
72OPC-425
72OPC-426
72ProStaP-11
72Top-425
72Top-426
73OPC-232
73Top-232
74ExpWes-9
74Kel-48
74OPC-25
74Top-25
74TopSta-60
75Kel-40
75OPC-125
75Top-125
76Hos-76
76Kel-12
76OPC-175
76SSP-400
76Top-175
77BurCheD-41
77Hos-107
77OPC-19
77Top-445
78Hos-75
78Kel-55
78OPC-80
78Top-65
79Hos-135
79OPC-324
79Top-615
80Kel-30
80OPC-178
80Top-340
80TopSup-11
81AllGamPI-68
81Don-115
81Dra-12
81Fle-188
81FleStiC-103
81Kel-39
81OPC-281
81PerAll-17
81Top-570
81TopScr-17
81TopSti-33
82Don-24
82Don-105
82Dra-30
82FBIDis-22
82Fle-179
82FleSta-150
82Kel-58
82OPC-2
82OPC-290
82Top-290
82Top-552
82TopSti-136
82TopSti-144
83AllGamPI-68
83Don-257
83Dra-26
83Fle-73
83FleSta-177
83FleSti-195
83OPC-85
83Top-85
83TopSti-28
84AllGamPI-159
84Don-610
84Fle-21
84FleSti-46
84FleSti-55
84Nes792-165
84OPC-165
84OriEng-13
84OriTeal-27
84Top-165
84TopRubD-29
84TopSti-206
84TopStiB-8
84TopTif-165
85Fle-191
85OPC-326
85Top-755
85TopMin-755
85TopSti-201
85TopTif-755
86ExpGreT-5
86OriGreT-8
89SweBasG-26
91MetWIZ-366
91OriCro-421
92Nab-3
93ExpDonM-19
93OriCroASU-12
Singleton, Scott
94SpoIndC-22
94SpoIndF-3324
Singley, Joe
87PenWhiSP-6
89UtiBluSP-21
90SouBenWSB-9
90SouBenWSGS-25
Sington, Fred
39PlaBal-68
90DodTar-739
Sinner, Greg
92BurIndC-13
92BurIndF-1656
93WatIndC-25
93WatIndF-3561
Sinnes, David
94HagSunC-23
94HagSunF-2731
94SouAtlLAF-SAL19
95Exc-142
95WilBluRTI-23
Sinnett, Lou
85AncGlaPTI-40
Sipe, Pat
87WesPalBEP-659
88JacExpB-20
88JacExpP-981
89JacExpB-8
89JacExpP-165
Sipin, John
79TCMJapPB-59
Sipple, John
89ChaRanS-24
Siracusa, John
75OklCit8TI-11
Sirak, Kenny
88NebCor-26
91SpaPhiC-19
91SpaPhiP-904
92ClePhiC-10
92ClePhiF-2066
93ClePhiC-21
93ClePhiF-2692
Siriano, Rick
82DurBulT-8
83DurBulT-13
Sirotka, Mike
92LSUTigM-11
93LSUTigM-5
94LSUTigMP-14
94MidLeaAF-MDW28
94SouBenSHC-21
94SouBenSHF-593
95Exc-31
95NasSouTI-24
96BirBarB-26
96Fle-76
96FleTif-76
96NasSouB-23
Sisco, Mike
87BelMarTI-21
Sisco, Steve
92EugEmeC-23
92EugEmeF-3039
93MidLeaAGF-18
93RocRoyC-25
93RocRoyF-725
95WicWraTI-26
96WicWraB-22
Sisk, Doug
82JacMetT-10
83TopTra-105T
84Don-615
84Fle-596
84JacMetF-11
84Nes792-599
84OPC-21
84Top-599
84TopTif-599
85Don-441
85Fle-91
85Lea-187
85MetColP-5
85MetFanC-7
85MetTCM-17
85OPC-315
85Top-315
85TopSti-103
85TopTif-315
86Fle-94
86MetTCM-12
86MetWorSC-9
86TidTidP-26
86Top-144
86TopTif-144
87Fle-22
87FleGlo-22
87MetColP-47
87Top-404
87TopTif-404
88Don-642
88Fle-150
88FleGlo-150

88FleUpd-3
88FleUpdG-3
88Sco-227
88ScoGlo-227
88Top-763
88TopTif-763
89Fle-621
89FleGlo-621
89Sco-264
89Top-13
89TopTif-13
89UppDec-261
90IndTeal-36
91BraDubP-25
91MetWIZ-367
91OriCro-422

Sisk, Kevin
91ButCopKSP-21

Sisk, Tommie
63Top-169
64PirKDK-25
64Top-224
64TopVen-224
65Top-558
66PirEasH-25
66Top-441
67OPC-84
67PirTeal-20
67Top-84
67TopPirS-21
68PirKDK-25
68PirTeal-20
68Top-429
69MLBOffS-196
69OPC-152
69Top-152
69TopFou-11
70MLBOffS-118
70OPC-374
70Top-374

Sisler, Dave
57Top-56
58Hir-40
58Top-59
59RedSoxJP-8
59Top-346
59Top-384
60Lea-64
60Top-186
60TopVen-186
61Pos-44
61SevElev-1
61Top-239
61TopStal-155
62RedEnq-32
62Top-171
62TopVen-171
63RedEnq-29
63Top-284

Sisler, Dick
46SeaSLP-49
47Exh-210
47TipTop-162
49Bow-205
49EurSta-149
49Lea-143
49PhiBul-53
50Bow-119
50Dra-10
50RoyDes-19A
50RoyDes-19B
51BerRos-C8
51Bow-52
51TopBluB-8
52Bow-127
52RoyPre-14
52TipTop-38
52Top-113
53BowBW-10
53CarHunW-22
53ExhCan-62
60HenHouW-8
63RedFreBC-25
64Top-162
64TopVen-162
65OPC-158
65RedEnq-28
65Top-158
66CarCoi-4
74NewYorNTDiS-26
75PadDea-4
76SSP-622
79DiaGre-170
79TCM50-152
83PhiPosGM-2
83TopRep5-113
84TCMPla1-25
87Phi195T-8
89JohCitCS-24

Sisler, George
80ColCliP-NNO
80ColCliT-27
81ColCliP-NNO
81ColCliT-27
82ColCliP-NNO
82ColCliT-26
84ColCliP-23
84ColCliT-24
85ColCliP-21
85ColCliT-29
86ColCliP-21
87ColCliP-23
89ColCliP-25

Sisler, George Sr.
15SpoNewM-166
16BF2FP-44
16ColE13-162
16SpoNewM-164
17HolBreD-97
19W514-101
20NatCarE-94
20WalMaiW-51
21E121So1-97A
21E121So1-97B
21E121So8-89A
21E121So8-89B
21Exh-161
21Nei-32
21OxfConE-17
22AmeCarE-65
22AmeCarE-66
22E120-102
22W572-99
22W573-123
22W575-126
22WilPatV-4
23W501-4
23W503-13
23W515-11
23W551-8
23WilChoV-151
24MrsShePP-8
25Exh-117
26Exh-118
26SpoComoA-41
27AmeCarE-49
27Exh-59
27YorCarE-54
28StaPlaCE-62
28W502-54
28Yue-54
29ExhFou-1
36PC7AlbHoF-25
40PlaBal-179
48ExhHoF-26
50CalHOFW-66
51R42SmaS-103
60Fle-13
61Fle-78
61Fle-89
61GolPre-13
67TopVen-154
72KelATG-5
72LauGreF-5
73FleWilD-12
74NewYorNTDiS-22
75TCMAllG-32
76RowExh-2
76ShaPiz-20
77GalGloG-94
77SerSta-23
77ShaPiz-11
79Top-411
80Lau300-24
80LauFamF-9
80PacLeg-108
80PerHaloFP-25
80SSPHOF-25
81ConTSN-83
81SpoHaloF-21
82OhiHaloF-31
84GalHaloFRL-20
85Woo-33
87ConSer2-58
87HygAllG-40
88ConSer4-26
90HOFStiB-23
91ConTSN-66
92ConTSN-595
93ConTSN-798
93ConTSN-836

Sismondo, Ron
83WauTimF-24

Sisney, Lorenzo
88WauTimGS-5

Sisson, Doug
91ButCopKSP-27
92ChaRanC-28
92ChaRanF-2241
93EriSaiC-27
93EriSaiF-3131
94HudValRF-3402
96DelShoB-21
94HudValRC-26

Sisti, Sibby
41DouPlaR-41
46SpoExcW-9-12
47TipTop-87
49Bow-201
49EurSta-23
50Bow-164
50JJKCopP-19
51Bow-170
52Bow-100
52Top-293
53BraJohC-13
53Top-124
54BraJohC-13
58UniOil-8
79DiaGre-219
83Bra53F-13
83Pil69G-22
83TopRep5-293
91TopArc1-124

Sitko, Emil
51BerRos-B15

Siuda, Matt
85AncGlaPTI-33
88MadMusP-22

Sivik, Mike
77AppFoxT-23
78AppFoxT-16
79AppFoxT-13

Siwa, Joe
90KenTwiB-14
90KenTwiP-2298
90KenTwiS-23
91LinDriAA-493
91OrlSunRLD-493
91OrlSunRP-1853
92OrlSunRF-2850
92OrlSunRS-520

Siwy, Jim
81AppFoxT-10
82EdmTraT-3
85Ind-28
85MaiGuiT-12
86LasVegSP-16
87LasVegSP-25

Sizemore, Bill
93LetMouF-4166
93LetMouSP-26
94LetMouF-3896
94LetMouSP-28
95ElmPioTI-27
95ElmPioUTI-27

Sizemore, Ted
69Top-552
70MLBOffS-58
70OPC-174
70Top-174
71CarTeal-37
71MLBOffS-284
71OPC-571
71Top-571
71TopCoi-65
72OPC-514
72Top-514
73OPC-128
73Top-128
74OPC-209
74Top-209
74TopSta-117
75Hos-71
75OPC-404
75Top-404
76Hos-70
76LinSup-125
76OPC-522
76SSP-284
76Top-522
77Top-366
78OPC-118
78PhiSSP-39
78SSP270-39
78Top-136
79OPC-148
79Top-297
80OPC-46
80Top-81
85SpoIndGC-18
90DodTar-740
95DodROY-7

Skaalen, Jim
87PorChaRP-24
88TulDriTI-10
89OklCit8C-23
89OklCit8P-1508
90TulDriDGB-29
93AppFoxC-29

Skadan, Scott
93AlbPolC-27
94AlbPolC-30

Skaff, Frank (Francis)
52Par-91
54OriEss-31
90DodTar-741

Skaggs, David
78Top-593
79Top-367
80Top-211
81Top-48
91OriCro-423
91PacSenL-100

Skaggs, Steve
80CedRapRT-14

Skalisky, Rocky
77ReaPhiT-22

Skalski, Joe
87WilBilP-27
88ColSprSSC-10
88ColSprSSP-1533
89ColSprSSC-9
89IndTeal-23
89UppDec-716
90Bow-323
90BowTif-323
90CMC-455
90ColSprSSC-3
90ColSprSSP-34
90IndTeal-37
90ProAAAF-215
90Sco-618A
90Sco-618B
90TopDeb89-115

Skaugstad, Dave
58RedEnq-36

Skeels, Andy
87SpoIndP-7
88RivRedWCLC-226
88RivRedWP-1425
89CalLeaA-20
89RivRedWB-15
89RivRedWCLC-12
89RivRedWP-1414
90AlbYanB-13
90AlbYanP-1038
90AlbYanS-16
91AlbYanP-1012
92SalSpuF-3760

Skeels, David
96EveAquB-22

Skeels, Mark
92EriSaiC-8
92EriSaiF-1627
93HigDesMC-18
93HigDesMF-45
93Top-558
93TopGol-558
93TopInaM-558
93TopMic-558
94BreCouMF-16

Skeen, Archie
63MilSau-7
64Top-428

Skeete, Rafael
87HagSunP-22
88ChaKniTI-15
89HagSunB-22
89HagSunP-278
89HagSunS-17
90ElPasDGS-25

Skelton, Bryan
93DavLipB-20
94DavLipB-22
95DavLipB-21

Skelton, John
87KenTwiP-28
88KenTwiP-1400

Skett, Will
96StCatSB-26

Skiba, Daniel
77WatIndT-20

Skidmore, Roe (Robert)
71OPC-121
71Top-121

Skiff, Bill (William)
20WalMaiW-52
43CenFlo-21
44CenFlo-20
45CenFlo-22

Skillicorn, Dirk
90NebCor-22

Skinner, Bob
47Exh-221A
55Top-88
55TopDouH-55
56Top-297
57Top-209
58Hir-30
58JayPubA-17
58Kah-27
58Top-94
59ArmCoi-16
59Kah-33
59Top-320
59Top-543
60Kah-38
60KeyChal-43
60PirJayP-11
60PirTag-4
60Top-113
60TopVen-113
61Kah-40
61PirJayP-10
61Pos-131A
61Pos-131B
61Top-204
61TopStal-69
62Jel-174
62Pos-174
62PosCan-174
62SalPlaC-143
62ShiPlaC-143
62Top-115
62TopVen-115
63Jel-141
63PirJayP-11
63Pos-141
63RedFreBC-26
63Top-18
63Top-215
64Top-377
65CarTeal-24
65Top-591
66Top-471
69PhiTeal-10
69Top-369
73OPC-12
73Top-12A
73Top-12B
74OPC-489
74Top-489
77PadSchC-50
78AngFamF-34
79DiaGre-373
79TCM50-248
85Top-139
85TopTif-139
86BraPol-4
87Pir196T-5
89TucTorC-25
89TucTorP-203
90CMC-627
90ProAAAF-209
90SweBasG-129
90TucTorC-25
90TucTorP-219
91LinDriAAA-624
91TriA AAGP-AAA53
91TucTorLD-624
91TucTorP-2228
92TucTorF-503
92TucTorS-624

Skinner, Joel
82GleFalWST-10
84Don-27
85BufBisT-6
85Don-574
85Fle-646

85Top-139
85Top-488
85TopTif-139
85TopTif-488
85WhiSoxC-22
86Don-330
86Top-239
86TopTif-239
86WhiSoxC-22
87Don-545
87DonOpeD-240
87Fle-115
87FleGlo-115
87SpoTeaP-7
87Top-626
87TopTif-626
88Don-474
88DonBasB-300
88DonReaBY-474
88Sco-532
88ScoGlo-532
88Top-109
88TopTif-109
89Don-427
89DonBasB-224
89DonTra-22
89Fle-270
89FleGlo-270
89IndTeal-24
89OPC-127
89Sco-447
89ScoRoo-76T
89Top-536
89TopTif-536
89UppDec-328
90Don-73
90Fle-501
90FleCan-501
90IndTeal-38
90Lea-286
90OPC-54
90PubSti-567
90Top-54
90TopTif-54
90UppDec-369
90VenSti-440
91Don-120
91Fle-377
91IndFanC-25
91Lea-211
91OPC-783
91Sco-809
91StaClu-561
91Top-783
91TopDesS-783
91TopMic-783
91TopTif-783
91UppDec-121
92Don-99
92Fle-123
92IndFanC-26
92Lea-181
92OPC-378
92Sco-227
92StaClu-278
92Top-378
92TopGol-378
92TopGolW-378
92TopMic-378
92UppDec-199
92YanWIZ8-180
93IndWUA-28
95WatIndTI-27

Skinner, John
82AppFoxF-14

Skinner, Matt
85NewOriT-23

Skinner, Mike
86RocRedWP-22
87RocRedWP-5
87RocRedWT-9

Skizas, Lou
57Top-83
58Top-319
59Top-328
60UniOil-15

Skjerpen, Trevor
94WelPirC-22
94WelPirF-3497

Sklar, Joel
86LitFalMP-25

Skodny, Joe
86EugEmeC-48
87AppFoxP-11
88BasCitRS-21

Skoglund, Brad
83WisRapTF-23

Skok, Craig
76SacSolC-4
79Top-363
80RicBraT-20
80VenLeaS-20
93RanKee-330

Skoog, Jack
89SanDieSAS-26

Skorochocki, John
77NewCoPT-29
78BurBeeT-26
80HolMilT-2
81ElPasDT-4
82VanCanT-6

Skowron, Bill
47Exh-211A
47Exh-211B
47StaPinP2-37
53Dor-140
54Top-239
55Bow-160
55Top-22
55TopDouH-21
56Top-61
56TopPin-30
57Top-135
57YanJayP-10
58JayPubA-18
58Top-240
58Top-477
58YanJayP-10
59Top-90
59Top-554
59TopVen-90
59Yoo-6
60MacSta-23
60Top-370
60Top-553
60YanJayP-10
61Pos-3A
61Pos-3B
61Top-42
61Top-371
61Top-568
61Yan61RL-5
61YanJayP-11
62Jel-1
62Pos-1
62PosCan-1
62SalPlaC-59
62ShiPlaC-59
62Top-110
62TopStal-91
62TopVen-110
62YanJayP-12
63DodJayP-11
63Jel-12
63Pos-12
63Top-180
64ChatheY-46
64Top-445
64TopGia-60
65OPC-70
65Top-70
65TopEmbl-5
65TopTral-69
65WhiSoxJP-10
66Baz-33
66Top-199
66Top-590
66TopRubl-86
66TopVen-199
67CokCapWS-13
67DexPre-192
67Top-357
70FleWorS-60
78TCM60I-230
79TCM50-210
81TCM60I-474
83MLBPin-17
83TigAlKS-18
83YanASFY-44
85WhiSoxC-23
87Yan196T-1
88PacLegI-82
90DodTar-742
91RinPos1Y1-3
92ActPacA-35
92YanWIZ6-117
92YanWIZA-79
93MetIma-17
93UppDecAH-114
94TedWil-64
94TopArc1-239
94TopArc1G-239
94UppDecAH-66
94UppDecAH1-66

Skripko, Joseph
85GreHorT-8

Skripko, Scott
86WinHavRSP-23
87NewBriRSP-10
89LynRedSS-25

Skrmetta, Matt
93BriTigC-20
94JamJamC-23
94JamJamF-3964
95FayGenTI-23
96LakTigB-25
96WesOahCHWB-23

Skryd, Chris
89SalLakTTI-19

Skube, Bob
81ElPasDT-15
82VanCanT-1
83BrePol-26
85VanCanC-214
94BreMilB-271

Skurla, John
86FreGiaP-23
88ShrCapP-1297
88TexLeaAGS-15
89PhoFirC-23
89PhoFirP-1496
90CMC-489
90EdmTraC-12
90EdmTraP-530
90ProAAAF-106

Skurski, Andy
47SigOil-15
49W72HolS-21

Skuse, Nick
94BoiHawC-23
94BoiHawF-3355
95CedRapKTI-38
96CedRapKTI-23

Skyta, Damon
86EveGiaPC-29

Slack, Bill
85GreBraTI-16
86GreBraTI-17
87DurBulP-15
89GreBraB-18
89GreBraP-1168
89GreBraS-25
90GreBraP-1144
91GreBraC-26
91GreBraP-3020
91LinDriAA-225
92GreBraF-1170
93GreBraF-366
94CarLeaA-DJ37
94DurBulC-28
94DurBulF-347
94DurBulTI-20
95DurBulTI-28
96GreBraB-2
96GreBraTI-27

Slade, Gordon
34DiaMatCSB-163
35DiaMatCS2-18
90DodTar-743

Slade, Shawn
93BoiHawC-24
93BoiHawF-3918
94CedRapKC-21
94CedRapKF-1108
95CedRapKTI-9

Slagle, Eric
92Min-18

Slagle, James J.
07CubA.CDPP-14
07CubGFGCP-13
08AmeCarE-28
08RosComP-109
09T206-468
11SpoLifCW-324

Slagle, Lee
92JamExpC-29
93WesPalBEC-28
94VerExpC-23

Slagle, Roger
76ForLauYS-22
77WesHavYT-20
78TacYanC-10
80ColCliP-18
80ColCliT-2
80NasSouTI-21
81NasSouTI-18
82NasSouTI-23
91PacSenL-17
92YanWIZ7-141

Slamka, John
94SigRooDP-84
94SigRooDPS-84
95AshTouUTI-28

Slater, Bob
76QuaCitAT-30
79SalLakCGT-21A
79Top-703

Slater, Vernon
90EugEmeGS-28
91AppFoxC-7
91EugEmeC-10
91EugEmeP-3741

Slaton, Jim
72Top-744
73OPC-628
73Top-628
74OPC-371
74Top-371
74TopSta-200
75OPC-281
75Top-281
76BreA&P-13
76OPC-163
76SSP-229
76Top-163
77BurCheD-83
77Hos-105
77OPC-29
77Top-604
78Hos-14
78OPC-146
78TigBurK-7
78Top-474
79Top-541
80OPC-10
80Top-24
81Don-447
81Fle-518
81Top-357
82BrePol-41
82Don-80
82Fle-153
82Top-221
83AllGamPI-86
83BreGar-17
83BrePol-41
83Don-330A
83Don-330B
83Fle-46
83OPC-114
83Top-114
84AngSmo-27
84Don-481
84Fle-214
84FleUpd-107
84Nes792-772
84OPC-104
84Top-772
84TopSti-302
84TopTif-772
84TopTra-109T
84TopTraT-109T
85AllGamPI-88
85AngSmo-17
85Don-545
85Fle-313
85Top-657
85TopTif-657
86AngSmo-17
86Don-402
86Fle-169
86Top-579
86TopTif-579
87Fle-163
87FleGlo-163
87Top-432
87TopTif-432
89PacSenL-110
89T/MSenL-96
91SouOreAP-3867
92BreCarT-21
92RenSilSCLC-61
92SouOreAC-29
94BreMilB-272
96DayCubB-27

Slattery, Chris
88CapCodPPaLP-161

Slattery, Don
92JohCitCC-17
92JohCitCF-3125

Slattery, Jack
11SpoLifCW-325

Slattery, Kevin
75CliPilT-17

Slattery, Mike
87OldJudN-464
89SFHaCN-16

Slaught, Don
82OmaRoyT-12
83Don-196
83Fle-123
83Roy-27
84Don-419
84Fle-359
84Nes792-196
84Top-196
84TopTif-196
85Don-496
85Fle-214
85FleUpd-104
85OPC-159
85RanPer-4
85Top-542
85TopSti-279
85TopTif-542
85TopTifT-107T
85TopTra-107T
86BasStaB-101
86Don-281
86Fle-572
86Lea-155
86OPC-24
86RanLit-6
86RanPer-4
86Top-761
86TopSti-243
86TopTif-761
87Don-136
87DonOpeD-176
87Fle-139
87FleGlo-139
87OPC-308
87RanMot-12
87RanSmo-9
87Spo-32
87Spo-154
87SpoTeaP-1
87Top-308
87TopSti-241
87TopTif-308
88AlaGolAA'TI-13
88DonBasB-188
88DonReaBY-NEW
88FleUpd-51
88FleUpdG-51
88Sco-268
88ScoGlo-268
88ScoRoo-19T
88ScoRooG-19T
88StaLinRa-16
88StaLinY-15
88Top-462
88TopTif-462
88TopTra-108T
88TopTraT-108T
89Bow-172
89BowTif-172
89Don-190
89DonBasB-105
89Fle-271
89FleGlo-271
89OPC-238
89PanSti-403
89Sco-561
89Spo-218
89Top-611
89TopBig-138
89TopTif-611
89UppDec-178
89YanScoNW-12
90Bow-182
90BowTif-182
90Don-277
90Fle-456
90FleCan-456
90FleUpd-51
90Lea-354
90MLBBasB-65
90OPC-26
90PirHomC-27

90PubSti-548
90Sco-79
90ScoRoo-13T
90Top-26
90TopSti-318
90TopTif-26
90TopTra-116T
90TopTraT-116T
90UppDec-152
90VenSti-441
91Bow-532
91Don-213
91Fle-49
91Lea-29
91OPC-221
91Sco-610
91SimandSMLBL-40
91StaClu-358
91Stu-228
91Top-221
91TopDesS-221
91TopMic-221
91TopTif-221
91Ult-286
91UppDec-181
92Don-653
92Fle-566
92Lea-124
92OPC-524
92Pin-416
92PirNatl-20
92Sco-280
92StaClu-545
92Top-524
92TopGol-524
92TopGolW-524
92TopMic-524
92Ult-258
92UppDec-540
92YanWIZ8-181
93Bow-430
93Don-438
93Fla-116
93Fle-119
93Lea-6
93PacSpa-251
93Pin-188
93PirNatl-29
93RanKee-331
93Sco-181
93Sel-171
93SP-187
93StaClu-127
93StaCluFDI-127
93StaCluMOP-127
93Stu-209
93Top-778
93TopGol-778
93TopInaM-778
93TopMic-778
93Ult-455
93UppDec-743
93UppDecGold-743
94Bow-602
94ColC-259
94ColChoGS-259
94ColChoSS-259
94Don-217
94ExtBas-351
94Fin-127
94FinRef-127
94Fla-219
94Fle-619
94Lea-135
94Pac-506
94PanSti-238
94Pin-217
94PinArtP-217
94PinMusC-217
94PirQui-22
94ProMag-108
94Sco-86
94ScoGolR-86
94Sel-65
94StaClu-137
94StaCluFDI-137
94StaCluGR-137
94StaCluMOP-137
94Stu-149
94SucSav-9
94Top-405
94TopGol-405
94TopSpa-405
94TriPla-188
94Ult-260
94UppDec-479
94UppDecED-479
95ColCho-387
95ColChoGS-387
95ColChoSS-387
95Don-498
95DonPreP-498
95Fin-43
95FinRef-43
95Fla-189
95Fle-488
95Lea-136
95Pac-351
95Pin-322
95PinArtP-322
95PinMusC-322
95PirFil-27
95Sco-73
95ScoGolR-73
95ScoPlaTS-73
95StaClu-299
95StaCluMOP-299
95StaCluSTWS-299
95StaCluVR-156
95Top-345
95TopCyb-187
95Ult-219
95UltGolM-219
95UppDec-387
95UppDecED-387
95UppDecEDG-387
96AngMot-25
96Don-335
96DonPreP-335
96Fle-533
96FleTif-533
96FleUpd-U21
96FleUpdTC-U21
96LeaSigA-209
96LeaSigAG-209
96LeaSigAS-209
95StaCluVRMC-156
97Ult-515
97UltGolME-515
97UltPlaME-515
Slaughter, Enos
41CarW75-24
41DouPlaR-39
46SeaSLP-50
46SpoExcW-9-2
47Exh-212
47HomBon-43
47PM1StaP1-203
47StaPinP2-38
47TipTop-163
48BluTin-34
48Bow-17
49Bow-65
49EurSta-198
49Lea-127
50AmeNut&CCP-17
50Bow-35
50Dra-36
51Bow-58
51R42SmaS-96
51TopBluB-30
52Bow-232
52DixLid-22
52DixPre-22
52NatTeaL-31
52RedMan-NL20
52StaCalL-81D
52StaCalS-93B
52TipTop-39
52Top-65
53BowC-81
53CarHunW-23
53DixLid-21
53DixPre-21
53Dor-133
53NorBreL-30
53RedMan-NL13
53Top-41
54Bow-62
54CarHunW-26
54DixLid-16
54RedHeaF-28
54RedMan-NL19A
54Wil-17
55A'sRodM-39
55Bow-60
56A'sRodM-10
56Top-109
57Top-215
58Top-142
59Top-155
59TopVen-155
66CarCoi-11
68LauWorS-43
70FleWorS-43
71FleWorS-44
74LauAllG-53
75JohMiz-16
76A'sRodMC-25
76TayBow4-18
77GalGloG-40
79DiaGre-166
79TCM50-240
80PacLeg-32
80PerHaloFP-191
80SSPHOF-194
82DiaCla-2
83TopRep5-65
84OCoandSI-51
85DalNatCC-6
85UltBasC-15
86SpoDecG-18
88HouSho-16
88PacLegl-84
89PacLegl-137
89PerCelP-37
89SweBasG-65
90PacLeg-50
90PerGreM-29
90SweBasG-54
91ConTSN-56
91SweBasG-84
91TopArc1-41
92ActPacA-15
92ActPacA2-15G
92BazQua5A-13
92CarMcD-23
92ConTSN-642
92UppDecS-11
92YanWIZH-31
93ActPacAC-15
93TedWil-92
93TedWilLC-7
93UppDecAH-115
94ConTSNCI-27
94UppDecAH-14
94UppDecAH-134
94UppDecAH1-14
94UppDecAH1-134
97TopStaHRR-13
97TopStaHRRA-13
Slaughter, Garland
89WelPirP-22
Slaughter, Sterling
64Top-469
65Top-314
Slavic, Joseph
86LakTigP-21
88LakTigS-23
Slavin, Dave
88PocGiaP-2094
89CliGiaP-909
Slavin, Tim
83WauTimF-8
Slayback, Bill
73OPC-537
73Top-537
Slaymaker, Joe
75BurBeeT-25
Sleater, Lou
52Top-306
53Top-224
55A'sRodM-40
58Top-46A
58Top-46B
59TigGraASP-15
76A'sRodMC-26
83TopRep5-306
91OriCro-424
91TopArc1-224
Slettvet, Doug
75QuaCitAT-22
76QuaCitAT-31
77QuaCitAT-26
Slezak, Robert
82VerBeaDT-11
83VerBeaDT-12
Slider, Mascot
93IndWUA-34
94MasMan-14
95StLucMTI-36
96StLucMTI-29
Slider, Rac (Rachel)
61UniOil-H5
85IntLeaAT-45
85PawRedST-14
90TopTVRS-6
Slifko, Paul
86NewBriRSP-22
87WinHavRSP-20
Sline, Fred
12ImpTobC-9
Slininger, Dennis
91JohCitCC-20
91JohCitCP-3978
92SprCarC-15
92SprCarF-867
93MidLeaAGF-54
93SprCarC-23
93SprCarF-1850
94ClaGolF-26
Sliwinski, Kevin
86KnoBluJP-21
87KnoBluJP-1503
88HunStaTI-20
88TacTigC-20
88TacTigP-626
Sloan, Dave
76SeaRaiC-16
Sloan, Shae
95ColSilB-27
96ColSilB-26
Sloat, Lefty (Dwain)
90DodTar-744
Slocum, Ron
70Top-573
71MLBOffS-239
71OPC-274
71Top-274
Slocumb, H.W.
88AllandGN-29
Slocumb, Heathcliff
86LitFalMP-26
87WinSpiP-7
88WinSpiS-16
89PeoChiTI-9
90ChaKniTI-6
91Bow-421
91Cla3-T84
91CubMar-51
91CubVinL-26
91DonRoo-25
91FleUpd-81
91Lea-370
91ScoRoo-84T
91UltUpd-73
91UppDec-767
92Don-334
92Fle-390
92OPC-576
92Sco-213
92Sco100RS-28
92StaClu-382
92Top-576
92TopDeb91-164
92TopGol-576
92TopGolW-576
92TopMic-576
92UppDec-569
93Don-664
93IowCubF-2132
93Top-783
93TopGol-783
93TopInaM-783
93TopMic-783
94FleUpd-170
94PhiMed-31
94PhiMel-21
94StaClu-681
94StaCluFDI-681
94StaCluGR-681
94StaCluMOP-681
94StaCluT-231
94StaCluTFDI-231
94TopTra-43T
95Don-263
95DonPreP-263
95DonTopotO-310
95Emo-171
95Fin-264
95FinRef-264
95Fla-396
95Fle-404
95Lea-132
95Phi-30
95PhiMel-21
95SP-92
95SPCha-77
95SPChaDC-77
95SPSil-92
95StaClu-610
95StaCluMOP-610
95StaCluSTWS-610
95Top-88
95Ult-210
95UltGolM-210
95UppDec-477T
96Baz-16
96ColCho-257
96ColChoGS-257
96ColChoSS-257
96Don-65
96DonPreP-65
96Fin-B125
96Fin-B318
96FinRef-B125
96FinRef-B318
96Fla-25
96Fle-508
96FleRedS-13
96FleTif-508
96FleUpd-U17
96FleUpdTC-U17
96MetUni-213
96MetUniP-213
96Pac-165
96PanSti-35
96StaClu-82
96StaCluEPB-82
96StaCluEPG-82
96StaCluEPS-82
96StaCluMOP-82
96Top-11
96Top-385
96TopChr-11
96TopChrR-11
96TopGal-13
96TopGalPPI-13
96TopPowB-11
96Ult-259
96Ult-320
96UltGolM-259
96UltGolM-320
96UppDec-172
96UppDec-287
97Cir-171
97CirRav-171
97ColCho-46
97Fin-228
97FinRef-228
97Fle-29
97FleTif-29
97Pac-45
97PacLigB-45
97PacSil-45
97StaClu-354
97StaCluMOP-354
97Top-379
97Ult-19
97UltGolME-19
97UltPlaME-19
97UppDec-310
Slominski, Rich
86WauTimP-22
Slomkowski, Rich
89WatDiaP-1798
89WatDiaS-19
90FreKeyTI-8
Sloniger, Chris
88SalLakCTTI-5
89MiaMirIS-17
Slosson, Bill
91SumFlyC-29
95AshTouTI-NNO
96AshTouB-5
97BenRocC-30
Slosson, Billiards
88GooN16-39
Slosson, George
87AllandGN-47
Slotnick, Joe
86BurExpP-20
Slowik, Tad
86PeoChiP-21
87WinSpiP-11
93AubAstC-29
93AubAstF-3461
Sluggerr, Mascot
94PorSeaDTI-21
96PorSeaDB-5

97RoyPol-23
Slusarski, Joe
87PanAmTURB-20
88TopTra-109T
88TopTraT-109T
89ModA'sC-15
89ModA'sCLC-266
89TopBig-213
90Bes-203
90HunStaB-10
91Bow-233
91Cla3-T85
91ScoRoo-105T
91TacTigP-2305
91UppDec-777
92AthMot-19
92Bow-58
92Don-626
92Fle-266
92Lea-431
92OPC-651
92Pin-187
92Sco-309
92Sco100RS-18
92StaClu-782
92StaCluECN-782
92Top-651
92TopDaiQTU-14
92TopDeb91-165
92TopGol-651
92TopGolW-651
92TopMic-651
92UppDec-663
93StaClu-376
93StaCluFDI-376
93StaCluMOP-376
93TacTigF-3032
87PanAmTUBI-24
Sly, Kian
92PulBraC-4
92PulBraF-3193
93MacBraC-22
93MacBraF-1415
Smajstra, Craig
83AppFoxF-10
86WatIndP-22
87BufBisP-10
88TucTorC-23
88TucTorJP-21
88TucTorP-168
89TucTorC-12
89TucTorJP-22
89TucTorP-200
90CMC-611
90ProAAAF-199
90TriAllGP-AAA40
90TucTorC-9
90TucTorP-209
91IowCubLD-205
91IowCubP-1069
91LinDriAAA-205
Smaldone, Ed
89GenCubP-1859
89GenCubP-1861
Small, Aaron
90MyrBeaBJP-2777
91Cla/Bes-361
91DunBluJC-10
91DunBluJP-206
92ClaFS7-162
92KnoBluJF-2991
92KnoBluJS-393
92SkyAA F-167
93Bow-631
93KnoSmoF-1251
94BowBes-B83
94BowBesR-B83
94KnoSmoF-1304
94SpoRoo-88
94SpoRooAP-88
95Pin-141
95PinArtP-141
95PinMusC-141
95Sco-592
95ScoGolR-592
95ScoPlaTS-592
96LeaSigEA-184
Small, Andru
93ElmPioC-19
93ElmPioF-3833
Small, Chris
88AubAstP-1949
Small, Hank
78RicBraT-15
Small, Jeff
86PeoChiP-22
87WinSpiP-24
90CMC-95
90IowCubC-20
90IowCubP-325
90ProAAAF-632
90TopTVCu-59
90TriAllGP-AAA35
91IowCubLD-218
91IowCubP-1070
91LinDriAAA-218
92NasSouF-1841
92NasSouS-293
93EdmTraF-1146
Small, Jim
56Top-207
57Top-33
61UniOil-H6
Small, Lefty (Nataniel)
76LauIndC-7
Small, Mark
89AubAstP-2188
90AshTouP-2748
91OscAstC-11
91OscAstP-684
92OscAstC-12
92OscAstF-2530
93JacGenF-2109
94JacGenF-217
95TusTorTI-25
96AstMot-27
96TusTorB-22
Small, Robert
89JamExpP-2133
Smalley, Dave
84GreHorT-13
Smalley, Roy
75SpoIndC-6
76OPC-70
76OPC-657
76SSP-267
76Top-70
76Top-657
77Hos-66
77Spo-8504
77Top-66
78Hos-118
78Top-471
78TwiFriP-19
79Hos-60
79OPC-110
79Top-219
79TwiFriP-26
80Kel-13
80OPC-296
80Top-570
80TopSup-40
81AllGamPI-23
81Don-487
81Fle-551
81FleStiC-55
81MSAMinD-30
81OPC-115
81Top-115
81TopScr-43
81TopSti-100
82Don-22
82Don-573
82Fle-560
82FleSta-228
82OPC-197
82Top-767
82TopSti-207
82TopTra-107T
83AllGamPI-24
83Don-209
83Fle-397
83FleSta-178
83FleSti-37
83OPC-38
83Top-460
83TopSti-96
83YanRoyRD-11
84Don-225
84Fle-142
84Nes792-305
84OPC-305
84Top-305
84TopTif-305
85Don-622
85Fle-527
85FleUpd-105
85OPC-26
85Top-26
85Top-140
85TopSti-237
85TopTif-26
85TopTif-140
85TopTifT-108T
85TopTra-108T
85Twi7-6
85TwiTeal-2
86Don-486
86Fle-404
86Lea-237
86OPC-156
86Top-613
86TopTif-613
86TwiTeal-3
87Don-443
87Fle-552
87FleGlo-552
87OPC-47
87SpoTeaP-17
87Top-744
87TopSti-282
87TopTif-744
88Don-566
88Fle-22
88FleGlo-22
88Lea-233
88Sco-606
88ScoGlo-606
88StaLinTw-18
88Top-239
88TopTif-239
88TwiTeal-2
90SouCalS-12
92YanWIZ8-182
93RanKee-332
Smalley, Roy Sr.
47PM1StaP1-204
49EurSta-72
49Lea-77
50Bow-115
51Bow-44
51FisBakL-27
51TopBluB-17
52Bow-64
52Top-173
53BowBW-56
54Bow-109
54Top-231
55Bow-252
55BraJohC-30
57Top-397
60DarFar-3
76OPC-70
76Top-70
79DiaGre-116
83TopRep5-173
85Top-140
85TopTif-140
91TopArc1-297
94TopArc1-231
94TopArc1G-231
Smalls, Roberto
88WytCubP-1986
89ChaWheB-15
89ChaWheP-1761
90GenCubP-3052
90GenCubS-22
Smallwood, Kevin
90ArkRaz-29
Smallwood, Woody (DeWitt)
93NegLeaRL2-35
Smart, J.D.
95TopTra-49T
96DelShoB-28
Smedes, Mike
89AncGlaP-24
Smelko, Mark
82RedPioT-11
83RedPioT-23
Smelser, Don
80ElPasDT-15
Smetana, Steve
96LowSpiB-23
Smiley, John
85PriWilPT-22
86PriWilPP-24
87DonRoo-39
87FleUpd-110
87FleUpdG-110
87SpoRooI-21
87SpoRooP-7
87SpoTeaP-18
87TopTra-114T
87TopTraT-114T
88Don-449
88DonBasB-257
88Fle-340
88FleGlo-340
88RedFolSB-82
88Sco-287
88ScoGlo-287
88StaLinPi-19
88Top-423
88TopTif-423
88ToyRoo-28
89Bow-413
89BowTif-413
89ClaTraP-191
89Don-329
89DonBasB-157
89Fle-221
89FleGlo-221
89OPC-322
89PanSti-167
89PirVerFJ-57
89Sco-409
89ScoYouSI-37
89Top-322
89TopBig-85
89TopSti-132
89TopTif-322
89UppDec-516
90ClaBlu-126
90Don-17
90Don-54
90DonBesN-21
90DonSupD-17
90Fle-480
90FleCan-480
90Lea-328
90OPC-568
90PanSti-323
90PirHomC-30
90PubSti-165
90Sco-334
90Sco100S-65
90Spo-191
90Top-568
90TopBig-79
90TopSti-132
90TopTif-568
90UppDec-387
90VenSti-442
91Bow-509
91Cla3-T86
91Don-664
91Fle-50
91Lea-123
91OPC-143
91Sco-465
91StaClu-471
91Stu-229
91Top-143
91TopDesS-143
91TopMic-143
91TopTif-143
91UltUpd-102
91UppDec-669
91USPlaCA-3C
92Bow-257
92Cla2-T88
92ClaGam-156
92Don-331
92Fle-567
92FleUpd-41
92Fre-5
92Hig5-93
92Hig5S-27
92Lea-526
92MooSna-12
92OPC-232
92OPCPre-2
92Pin-184
92Sco-659
92Sco100S-3
92ScoImpP-79
92ScoRoo-22T
92StaClu-380
92StaClu-625
92StaCluD-173
92StaCluNC-625
92Stu-210
92SunSee-17
92Top-232
92TopGol-232
92TopGolW-232
92TopMic-232
92TopTra-106T
92TopTraG-106T
92TriPla-52
92Ult-259
92Ult-400
92UppDec-467
92UppDec-785
93Bow-230
93ClaGam-86
93Don-475
93Fin-14
93FinRef-14
93Fle-643
93FleFinE-20
93Lea-433
93OPC-335
93OPCPre-56
93PacSpa-406
93Pin-543
93PinTeaP-2
93RedKah-26
93Sco-624
93Sel-75
93SelAce-13
93SelRoo-100T
93SelSam-75
93StaClu-190
93StaCluFDI-190
93StaCluMOP-190
93Top-363
93TopComotH-10
93TopGol-363
93TopInaM-363
93TopMic-363
93Ult-336
93UppDec-268
93UppDec-694
93UppDecGold-268
93UppDecGold-694
94ColChoSS-473
94Don-105
94ExtBas-241
94Fin-179
94FinRef-179
94Fla-150
94Fle-429
94Lea-24
94Pac-161
94Pin-99
94PinArtP-99
94PinMusC-99
94ProMag-31
94RedKah-30
94Sco-424
94ScoGolR-424
94Sel-169
94StaClu-487
94StaCluFDI-487
94StaCluGR-487
94StaCluMOP-487
94Stu-174
94Top-12
94TopGol-12
94TopSpa-12
94TriPla-220
94Ult-178
94UppDec-327
94UppDecED-327
95ColCho-436
95ColChoGS-436
95ColChoSS-436
95Don-11
95DonPreP-11
95DonTopotO-221
95Emo-121
95Fla-126
95Fle-449
95Lea-343
95Pin-51
95PinArtP-51
95PinMusC-51
95RedKah-31
95Sco-471
95ScoGolR-471
95ScoPlaTS-471
95SPCha-38
95SPChaDC-38
95StaClu-416
95StaCluMOP-416
95StaCluSTDW-RE416
95StaCluSTWS-416
95StaCluVR-214

95Top-56
95TopCyb-41
95Ult-372
95UltGolM-372
95UppDec-402
95UppDecED-402
95UppDecEDG-402
96Cir-119
96CirRav-119
96ColCho-522
96ColChoGS-522
96ColChoSS-522
96Don-139
96DonPreP-139
96EmoXL-170
96Fla-240
96Fle-354
96FleTif-354
96MetUni-153
96MetUniP-153
96Pac-38
96PanSti-51
96Sco-94
96SP-66
96StaClu-124
96StaClu-244
96StaCluEPB-124
96StaCluEPG-124
96StaCluEPS-124
96StaCluMOP-124
96StaCluMOP-244
95StaCluVRMC-214
96Top-257
96Ult-184
96UltGolM-184
96UppDec-47
97Cir-351
97CirRav-351
97ColCho-82
97Fin-89
97FinRef-89
97Fle-305
97FleTif-305
97MetUni-51
97PacPriGotD-GD130
97Sco-388
97ScoHobR-388
97ScoResC-388
97ScoShoS-388
97ScoShoSAP-388
97StaClu-150
97StaCluMOP-150
97Top-119
97Ult-181
97UltGolME-181
97UltPlaME-181
97UppDec-338

Smiley, Reuben
88PocGiaP-2087
89CliGiaP-894
90Bes-310
90CalLeaACLC-45
90SanJosGB-3
90SanJosGCLC-30
90SanJosGP-2024
90SanJosGS-22
90SanJosGS-26
91LinDriAA-321
91ShrCapLD-321
91ShrCapP-1836
92ShrCapF-3885
92ShrCapS-594
93PhoFirF-1531
94PhoFirF-1534

Smith, Ackroyd
52LavPro-77

Smith, Adam
88PocGiaP-2092

Smith, Al (Alfred J.)
33ButCanV-45
46SunBre-17
47SigOil-69
47SunBre-21
54Top-248
55Bow-20
55IndCarBL-9
55IndGolS-17
55Top-197
56Top-105
56TopPin-11
57IndSoh-13
57Top-145
58Top-177
58WhiSoxJP-10
59Top-22
59TopVen-22
60Top-428
60WhiSoxJP-11
60WhiSoxTS-19
61Pos-24A
61Pos-24B
61Top-42
61Top-170
61TopStal-129
61WhiSoxTS-18
62Jel-48
62Pos-48
62PosCan-48
62SalPlaC-29
62ShiPlaC-29
62Top-410
62WhiSoxJP-11
62WhiSoxTS-20
63Jel-38
63Pos-38
63Top-16
64IndJayP-11
64Top-317
64TopVen-317
76GrePlaG-38
83TCMPla1943-8
84OCoandSI-206
91OriCro-425
92ConTSN-580
93DiaStaES-149
94TopArc1-248
94TopArc1G-248

Smith, Alex
87DurBulP-14
88RicBraC-13
88RicBraP-25
89RicBraBC-25
89RicBraP-841
89RicBraTI-21
96OklCit8B-20
88RicBraBC-16

Smith, Andy
94SouOreAC-25
94SouOreAF-3622
95WesMicWTI-31
96WesMicWB-25

Smith, Anthony
09RamT20-109

Smith, Archie
87EugEmeP-2655

Smith, Ballard
77PadSchC-51

Smith, Ben
89KinMetS-29
90KinMetS-30

Smith, Bernie
71OPC-204
71Top-204
83RedPioT-29
94BreMilB-273

Smith, Bill
83AppFoxF-1

Smith, Bill (William Garland)
60MapLeaSF-19
61MapLeaBH-21

Smith, Billy
85EveGiaIC-17

Smith, Billy Edward
76SalLakCGC-9
76SSP-199
78Top-666
79Top-237
80Top-367
82Fle-400
82Top-593
91OriCro-426

Smith, Billy Franklin
84BluJayFS-27
85BluJayFS-26
86BluJayFS-28
87BluJayFS-28
88BluJayFS-26

Smith, Billy Lavern
78DayBeaAT-24
80TucTorT-11
81TucTorT-24
82Top-441
82TucTorT-18

Smith, Bob
52LavPro-13
60MapLeaSF-20
61MapLeaBH-22

Smith, Bob (Robert Eldridge)
21Exh-166
29ExhFou-2
29PorandAR-86
31CubTeal-19
32CubTeal-21
33Gou-185
34BatR31-47
34DiaMatCSB-164
91ConTSN-217
34DiaMatCSB-164

Smith, Bob Gilchrist
58Top-226
59Top-83
59TopVen-83
91MetWIZ-368

Smith, Bob W.
58Top-445

Smith, Bobby
94DurBulF-337
95BreBtaTI-2
97Sel-123
97SelArtP-123
97SelRegG-123

Smith, Bobby Gene
57Top-384
58Top-402
59Top-162
59TopVen-162
60Top-194
60TopVen-194
61Top-316
62Jel-196
62Pos-196
62PosCan-196
62SalPlaC-176A
62SalPlaC-176B
62ShiPlaC-176
62Top-531

Smith, Bobby Glen
78BurBeeT-27
79HolMilT-6
80VanCanT-5
81VanCanT-19

Smith, Brad
88ClePhiS-23

Smith, Brandon
94PitMetC-20

Smith, Brent
93EveGiaC-24
93EveGiaF-3768

Smith, Brett
94OgdRapF-3738
94OgdRapSP-11

Smith, Brian
94MedHatBJF-3679
94MedHatBJSP-19
95HagSunF-70
96KnoSmoB-24

Smith, Brick
84ChaLooT-4
86ChaLooP-23
86SouLeaAJ-17
87CalCanP-2320
87SpoRooP-5
88CalCanP-803
89ChaLooLITI-28
89TucTorC-17
89TucTorJP-23
89TucTorP-193

Smith, Broadway (Alexander B.)
90DodTar-1072
98CamPepP-69

Smith, Brook
93EveGiaC-25
93EveGiaF-3769
95BurBeeTI-28

Smith, Bryan
80VenLeaS-250
86BakDodP-25
87VerBeaDP-24
90AubAstB-12
90AubAstP-3406
90VenSti-443
91BurAstC-22
91BurAstP-2816
91Cla/Bes-313

Smith, Bryn
79MemChiT-5
80MemChiT-20
82ExpHygM-20
82ExpPos-38
82OPC-118
82Top-118
83Don-88A
83Don-88B
83ExpPos-23
83ExpStu-29
83Fle-297
83OPC-234
83Top-447
84AllGamPI-88
84Don-453
84ExpPos-29
84ExpStu-21
84Fle-287
84Nes792-656
84OPC-77
84Top-656
84TopTif-656
85AllGamPI-176
85Don-209
85ExpPos-22
85Fle-410
85Lea-171
85OPC-88
85Top-88
85TopMin-88
85TopSti-90
85TopTif-88
86Don-299
86ExpPos-14
86ExpProPa-19
86ExpProPo-2
86Fle-260
86FleMin-55
86FleSlu-35
86FleStiC-110
86GenMilB-6G
86Lea-174
86OPC-299
86Spo-120
86Top-299
86TopSti-79
86TopSup-51
86TopTat-22
86TopTif-299
87Don-159
87ExpPos-27
87Fle-332
87FleGlo-332
87GenMilB-4F
87Lea-60
87OPC-281
87StuPan-8
87Top-505
87TopSti-83
87TopTif-505
88Don-335
88DonBasB-202
88ExpPos-22
88Fle-196
88FleGlo-196
88Lea-129
88OPC-161
88PanSti-320
88Sco-356
88ScoGlo-356
88StaLinE-16
88Top-161
88TopBig-250
88TopTif-161
89Bow-353
89BowTif-353
89Don-216
89DonBasB-124
89ExpPos-27
89Fle-394
89FleGlo-394
89OPC-131
89PanSti-116
89Sco-428
89Top-464
89TopBig-47
89TopTif-464
89UppDec-78
90Bow-184
90BowTif-184
90CarSmo-20
90Don-25
90Don-106
90DonBesN-10
90DonSupD-25
90Fle-361
90FleCan-361
90Lea-393
90OPC-352
90PubSti-188
90Sco-419
90ScoRoo-55T
90Top-352
90TopSti-78
90TopTif-352
90TopTra-117T
90TopTraT-117T
90TopTVCa-18
90UppDec-579
90UppDec-794
91Bow-407
91CarPol-36
91Don-113
91Fle-644
91Lea-226
91OPC-743
91Sco-444
91StaClu-17
91Top-743
91TopDesS-743
91TopMic-743
91TopTif-743
91Ult-294
91UppDec-307
92CarPol-17
92Don-323
92Fle-590
92Lea-157
92OPC-31
92Pin-474
92Sco-529
92StaClu-368
92Top-31
92TopGol-31
92TopGolW-31
92TopMic-31
92Ult-269
92UppDec-591
93Fle-515
93Lea-409
93PacSpa-438
93RocUSPC-5D
93RocUSPC-8H
93StaCluRoc-4
93Ult-359
93UppDec-723
93UppDecGold-723

Smith, Bubba (Charles)
91BelMarC-12
91BelMarP-3675
91Cla/Bes-446
92ClaFS7-216
92PenPilC-1
92PenPilF-2944
92UppDecML-170
93Bow-346
93ClaGolF-34
93ClaMVPF-1
93ExcFS7-232
93ExcLeaLF-2
93JacSunF-2720
93Top-423
93TopGol-423
93TopInaM-423
93TopMic-423
94Bow-344
94ChaLooF-1368
95ForMyeMTI-25
95HarCitRCTI-24
96TexLeaAB-17
96TulDriTI-24

Smith, C.L.
90RocExpLC-25

Smith, Calvin
91HunCubC-24
91HunCubP-3344

Smith, Cameron
93BriTigC-1
94FayGenC-23
94FayGenF-2146
95FayGenTI-24
96Bow-182
96LakTigB-26
96WesOahCHWB-16

Smith, Carlos
09T206-516

Smith, Chad
88BurBraP-4
89SumBraP-1108
90DurBulTI-23
90MiaMirIS-25
92HamRedC-3

92HamRedF-1591
93SprCarC-24
93SprCarF-1851
Smith, Charles Edwin
08RosComP-85
09SenBarP-8
11SpoLifCW-326
11SpoLifM-145
Smith, Charles M.
11TurRedT-118
Smith, Charles W.
60DarFar-12
61SevElev-26
62SalPlaC-135A
62SalPlaC-135B
62ShiPlaC-135
62Top-283
62WhiSoxTS-21
63Top-424
63WhiSoxTS-21
64Top-519
65OPC-22
65Top-22
66CarTeal-11
66Top-358
66TopVen-358
67CokCapYM-V11
67DexPre-193
67Top-257
68Top-596
69Top-538
78TCM60I-289
90DodTar-745
91MetWIZ-369
92YanWIZ6-118
94CarLeaA-DJ14
Smith, Chris
92BoiHawC-26
92BoiHawF-3640
92ClaDraP-33
92ClaFS7-423
93CedRapKC-19
93CedRapKF-1749
93MidLeaAGF-36
93StaCluM-132
94Bow-154
94Cla-41
94MidAngF-2449
94MidAngOHP-29
96LakElsSB-21
Smith, Chris W.
80MemChiT-21
82WicAerTI-18
83PhoGiaBHN-22
84Don-46
87SalAngP-33
Smith, Chuck
92AshTouC-23
93QuaCitRBC-21
93QuaCitRBF-100
94OscAstC-21
94OscAstF-1138
96PriWilCB-24
Smith, Clay
79CliDodT-2
Smith, Cleo
75AlbDukC-9
Smith, Coleman
92HunCubC-17
92HunCubF-3166
94PeoChiC-23
94PeoChiF-2282
Smith, Coley
74TacTwiC-10
75TacTwiK-17
Smith, Corey
87UtiBluSP-30
Smith, Craig
93HelBreSP-5
94StoPorC-26
94StoPorF-1704
Smith, D.L.
86ChaOriW-28
87RocRedWP-14
88RocRedWP-195
88RocRedWTI-21
89BelMarL-29
89ElPasDGS-24
89TexLeaAGS-16
90CMC-35
90DenZepC-10
90DenZepP-635
90ProAAAF-660
90SanBerSCLC-99
90SanBerSP-2647
91DenZepLD-126
91DenZepP-132
91LinDriAAA-126
92ColSprSSS-96
Smith, D.W. (David Wayne)
82HolMilT-10
83NasAngT-8
84EdmTraC-103
84NewOriT-11
85EdmTraC-16
86EdmTraP-26
Smith, Dan
75CedRapGT-17
78TidTidT-24
79JacMetT-17
86BakDodP-26
87OrlTwiP-3
91RocExpC-21
Smith, Dan (Daniel Scott)
90ButCopKSP-7
90ClaDraP-16
91Bow-275
91LinDriAAA-322
91OklCit8LD-322
91OklCit8P-179
91PacRyaTEI-61
91Sco-384
92Bow-391
92ClaFS7-291
92SkyAA F-276
92TulDriF-2696
92TulDriS-622
93Bow-109
93ClaGolF-10
93DayCubC-17
93DayCubF-866
93Don-374
93Fle-329
93PacSpa-648
93Pin-603
93RanKee-333
93StaCluR-6
93Top-607
93TopGol-607
93TopInaM-607
93TopMic-607
93Toy-68
93Ult-637
93UppDec-7
93UppDecGold-7
94ChaRivC-20
94ChaRivF-2674
94DayCubC-22
94DayCubF-2363
94SigRoo-43
94SigRooS-43
94SpoRoo-33
94SpoRooAP-33
94UppDecML-174
95Pac-434
95Top-127
Smith, Dana
86HagSunP-18
88ChaKniTI-21
89HagSunB-21
89HagSunP-286
89HagSunS-18
Smith, Danny
85CedRapRT-12
86VerRedP-20
Smith, Daryl
80AshTouT-19
83TulDriT-7
86WatIndP-23
87WilBilP-12
88BirBarB-19
90MemChiS-24
91LinDriAAA-345
91OmaRoyLD-345
91OmaRoyP-1035
91TopDeb90-145
Smith, Dave
76BurBeeT-30
77HolMilT-24
78HolMilT-20
79ChaChaT-11A
79ChaChaT-11B
80SpoIndT-2
81LynSaiT-11
83WauTimF-27
94SarRedSC-26
94SarRedSF-1962
Smith, Dave (David S.)
77CocAstT-24
81Don-23A
81Don-23B
81Fle-71
81OPC-287
81Top-534
82AstAstI-5
82Don-191
82Fle-232
82OPC-297
82Top-761
83Don-370
83Fle-466
83OPC-247
83Top-247
84AstMot-13
84Don-548
84Fle-242
84Nes792-361
84Top-361
84TopTif-361
85AstHouP-13
85AstMot-21
85Don-548
85Fle-362
85Top-123
85TopTif-123
86AstMilL-20
86AstPol-11
86Don-328
86Fle-312
86FleStiC-111
86OPC-222
86SevCoi-S12
86Top-408
86TopSti-31
86TopTif-408
87AstMot-20
87AstPol-17
87ClaGam-66
87Don-308
87DonAll-30
87Fle-69
87FleGlo-69
87FleHotS-38
87FleStiC-109
87Lea-224
87OPC-50
87Spo-77
87Spo-94
87SpoTeaP-8
87Top-50
87TopMinL-12
87TopTif-50
88AlaGolAA'TI-24
88AstMot-20
88AstPol-22
88Don-410
88DonBasB-262
88Fle-457
88FleGlo-457
88FleHotS-39
88FleMin-81
88FleStiC-90
88FleTeaL-37
88OPC-73
88PanSti-290
88SanDieSAAG-19
88Sco-365
88ScoGlo-365
88Spo-208
88StaLinAst-17
88Top-520
88TopSti-26
88TopTif-520
89AstLenH-19
89AstMot-19
89AstSmo-37
89Bow-317
89BowTif-317
89ClaLigB-22
89Don-272
89DonBasB-232
89Fle-369
89FleBasA-38
89FleGlo-369
89OPC-305
89PanSti-87
89SanDieSAG-18
89Sco-245
89Top-305
89TopSti-13
89TopTif-305
89UppDec-302
90AstLenH-23
90AstMot-17
90Bow-62
90BowTif-62
90ClaBlu-94
90Don-88
90DonBesN-40
90Fle-238
90FleCan-238
90Lea-122
90OPC-746
90PanSti-257
90PubSti-103
90RedFolSB-87
90Sco-45
90Sco100S-19
90Spo-140
90Top-746
90TopBig-145
90TopSti-16
90TopSti-190
90TopTif-746
90TopTVA-49
90UppDec-448
90USPlaCA-8D
90VenSti-444
91Bow-425
91Cla3-T87
91CubMar-42
91CubVinL-27
91Don-212
91Fle-517
91FleUpd-82
91Lea-456
91OPC-215
91OPCPre-111
91PanSti-12
91Sco-314
91ScoRoo-9T
91StaClu-345
91Stu-160
91Top-215
91TopDesS-215
91TopMic-215
91TopTif-215
91TopTra-110T
91TopTraT-110T
91UppDec-513
91UppDec-704
92Bow-333
92ClaGam-31
92CubMar-42
92Don-53
92Fle-391
92Lea-30
92OPC-601
92Pin-94
92Sco-98
92StaClu-219
92Top-601
92TopGol-601
92TopGolW-601
92TopMic-601
92Ult-475
92UppDec-549
94SpoIndF-3341
95RanCucQT-37
Smith, David
95MicBatCTI-25
Smith, David (Marvin David)
88KenTwiP-1391
89VisOakCLC-117
89VisOakP-1448
90SanBerSB-20
Smith, David A.
82HolMilT-9
Smith, Del Roy
85IowCubT-35
Smith, Demond
91KinMetC-2
91KinMetP-3828
92PitMetC-2
92PitMetF-3308
93CapCitBF-473
94BoiHawC-24
94BoiHawF-3369
94LakElsSC-19
94LakElsSF-1678
95CedRapKTI-24
95MidLeaA-52
96BesAutS-84
96Exc-101
96HunStaTI-24
96Top-437
Smith, Dick (Richard Arthur)
53MotCoo-39
55Bow-288
64Top-398
65Top-579
76Met63 S-14
90DodTar-746
91MetWIZ-370
Smith, Don
84AlbDukC-155
85AlbDukC-171
Smith, Duke (John)
82MadMusF-5
Smith, Dwight
86PeoChiP-23
87PitCubP-26
88BlaYNPRWL-188
88IowCubC-21
88IowCubP-530
88TriAAAP-19
89Bow-297
89BowTif-297
89CubMar-18
89DonBasB-205
89DonRoo-32
89FleUpd-79
89IowCubC-22
89IowCubP-1708
89Sco-642
89ScoHot1R-64
89TopTra-113T
89TopTraT-113T
89UppDec-780
90Bow-32
90BowTif-32
90ClaBlu-30
90CubMar-19
90Don-393
90DonBesN-63
90Fle-42
90FleBasM-35
90FleCan-42
90FleSoaS-12
90Hot50RS-42
90Lea-255
90OPC-311
90PanSti-235
90PubSti-204
90Sco-240
90Sco100RS-4
90ScoYouSI-2
90Spo-152
90Top-311
90TopBig-151
90TopCoi-57
90TopDeb89-116
90TopHeaU-23
90TopRoo-26
90TopSti-52
90TopTif-311
90TopTVCu-33
90ToyRoo-25
90UppDec-376
90VenSti-445
91CubMar-18
91CubVinL-28
91Don-559
91Fle-432
91OPC-463
91PanFreS-47
91Sco-301
91StaClu-181
91Top-463
91TopDesS-463
91TopMic-463
91TopTif-463
91Ult-68
91UppDec-452
92CubMar-18
92Don-561
92Fle-392
92OPC-168
92Pin-293
92Sco-612
92StaClu-196
92Top-168
92TopGol-168
92TopGolW-168
92TopMic-168
93CubMar-25
93Don-476

93Fla-21
93Fle-384
93Lea-547
93PacSpa-63
93Sco-637
93StaClu-278
93StaCluCu-11
93StaCluFDI-278
93StaCluMOP-278
93Top-688
93TopGol-688
93TopInaM-688
93TopMic-688
93TriPla-172
93Ult-23
94AngLAT-12
94AngMot-8
94ColC-582
94ColChoGS-582
94ColChoSS-582
94Don-570
94Fle-398
94FleUpd-7
94Pac-111
94PanSti-157
94Pin-66
94PinArtP-66
94PinMusC-66
94Sco-408
94ScoGolR-408
94Top-536
94TopGol-536
94TopSpa-536
94TopTra-52T
95ColCho-336
95ColChoGS-336
95ColChoSS-336
95Top-261
96ColCho-451
96ColChoGS-451
96ColChoSS-451
96FleUpd-U106
96FleUpdTC-U106
96MLBPin-31

Smith, Earl L.
22W573-124
23WilChoV-152
28Exh-26
28W502-48
28Yue-48

Smith, Earl S.
20GasAmeMBD-34
20NatCarE-95
21E121So1-98
21E121So8-90
21Exh-162
21Exh-163
21KoBreWSI-22
22E120-119
22E120-192
22W572-100
22W573-125
22W575-128
23W501-71
23W503-28
23WilChoV-153
25Exh-54
26Exh-54
27Exh-27
91ConTSN-74

Smith, Ed
88SouBenWSGS-5
89SouBenWSGS-28
90SarWhiSS-22
91SarWhiSC-19
91SarWhiSP-1121
92ElPasDF-3932
92StoPorC-4
92StoPorF-43
93ElPasDF-2959
94OrlCubF-1394

Smith, Eddie (Edgar)
39WhiSoxTI-17
40WhiSoxL-17
79DiaGre-129
84TCMPla1-13

Smith, Elmer E.
87OldJudN-467
88SpoTimM-23
98CamPepP-70

Smith, Elmer John
16ColE13-163
21E121So1-99
21Exh-164
22E120-14
22W572-101
22W575-127
23W501-110
69SCFOldT-8
77Ind192T-17
95ConTSN-1367

Smith, Emmitt
91StaCluMO-36
92StaCluMO-41
93StaCluMO-51

Smith, Eric
92BatCliC-12
92BatCliF-3265
94ClePhiC-24
94ClePhiF-2527
95AubAstTI-15
96QuaCitRB-27

Smith, F.C.
87OldJudN-468

Smith, Frank
90KisDodD-25
91GreFalDSP-1
92GreFalDSP-27
93BakDodCLC-22
94VerBeaDC-21
94VerBeaDF-84
95SanBerSTI-24

Smith, Frank T.
52Bow-186
52Top-179
53Top-116
54Bow-188
54Top-71
55CarHunW-25
55Top-204
83TopRep5-179
91TopArc1-116
94TopArc1-71
94TopArc1G-71

Smith, Fred
92WatIndC-13
92WatIndF-3234
93ColRedC-21
93ColRedF-596

Smith, Freddie
81MiaOriT-3

Smith, Garry J.
77WesHavYT-21
78TacYanC-39B
79ColCliT-5
80ColCliP-15
80ColCliT-5
81ColCliP-13
82ColCliP-13
82ColCliT-14
82NasSouTI-24

Smith, Gary
81ColCliT-21

Smith, Gene
81BurBeeT-5

Smith, George A.
23WilChoV-154
90DodTar-747

Smith, George C.
65Top-483
66Top-542
67CokCapRS-13
67DexPre-194
67Top-444
67TopRedSS-18

Smith, George H.
09ColChiE-265
09T206-469
12ColRedB-265
12ColTinT-265

Smith, Germany (George J.)
87OldJudN-469
90DodTar-748
95May-39
98CamPepP-71

Smith, Glenn
75LynRanT-25

Smith, Greg
81VerBeaDT-18
86EriCarP-27
87EriCarP-11
87OklCit8P-19
88SpoIndP-1932
91AlbDukLD-20
91AlbDukP-1151

Smith, Greg (Gregory A.)
85BeaGolGT-6
86LasVegSP-17
87PeoChiP-14
88CarLeaAS-35
88WinSpiS-17
89ChaKniTI-11
89ChaRaiP-979
89SouLeaAJ-11
90Bow-31
90BowTif-31
90CMC-88
90Fle-643
90FleCan-643
90IowCubC-13
90IowCubP-326
90ProAAAF-633
90RivRedWB-18
90RivRedWCLC-2
90RivRedWP-2621
90Sco-614
90TopDeb89-117
90TopTVCu-27
90UppDec-738
91Bow-594
91Don-574
91Fle-433
91LinDriAAA-20
91OPC-560
91StaClu-554
91Top-560
91TopDesS-560
91TopMic-560
91TopTif-560
92TolMudHF-1052
92TolMudHS-597
93IowCubF-2142
94NewOrlZF-1477

Smith, Hal R.
56Top-283
57Top-111
58CarJayP-12
58Top-273
59Top-497
60CarJayP-10
60Lea-94
60Top-84
60TopVen-84
61CarJayP-11
61Pos-180A
61Pos-180B
61Top-549
61TopStal-70
61TopStal-94
62SalPlaC-190
62ShiPlaC-190

Smith, Hal W.
55OriEss-23
55Top-8
56Top-62
56TopHocF-A15
56TopPin-3
57Top-41
58A'sJayP-8
58Top-257
59Top-227
60KeyChal-44
60Lea-58
60Lea-94
60Lea-119
60Top-48
60TopVen-48
61Kah-41
61Pos-139
61Top-242
62Col.45B-18
62Col45'HC-15
62Col45'JP-11
62Jel-181
62Pos-181
62PosCan-181
62Top-492
62TopBuc-84
62TopStal-129
63Col45'JP-10
63Top-153
64Top-233
64TopVen-233
79TCM50-127
89AstCol4S-12
91OriCro-427

Smith, Hamlin
94LetMouSP-27

Smith, Hap (Henry J.)
09T206-328
10DomDisP-110
10SweCapPP-77
90DodTar-1073

Smith, Harold
33ButCanV-46
89TenTecGE-25

Smith, Harry Thomas
03BreE10-131
11SpoLifCW-329
11SpoLifM-146

Smith, Herb
91PomBlaBPB-23

Smith, Hilton
78LauLonABS-34
86NegLeaF-27
87NegLeaPD-27

Smith, Hut
92ClaDraP-75
92HigSchPLS-18
93StaCluM-95
94AlbPolC-24
94AlbPolF-2237

Smith, Indiana (Mike)
92FroRowDP-78
92GasRanF-2262
93ChaRanC-21
93ChaRanF-1950
93StaCluM-101

Smith, Ira
90GreFalDSP-28
92BakDodCLC-22
93RanCucQC-26
93RanCucQF-846
94ClaGolF-143
94ExcFS7-286
94WicWraF-203
95Exc-288
95MemChiTI-9
96LasVegSB-23

Smith, Jack
20WalMaiW-53
21Exh-165
21Nei-75
22E120-238
22W572-102
22W573-126
27AmeCarE-51
81BirBarT-15
82WesHavAT-9
83ColAstT-20
92ConTSN-507

Smith, Jack (Jack Everett)
86TamTarP-20
87TamTarP-14
88GreHorP-1569
89EasLeaAP-20
89WilBilP-643
89WilBilS-20
91JacSunLD-345
91JacSunP-160
91LinDriAA-345
92OrlSunRS-521
92TacTigF-2512
93CalCanF-1174

Smith, Jack H.
63Top-496
90DodTar-749

Smith, Jackie
78AppFoxT-17
79KnoKnoST-17

Smith, Jason
92ElmPioC-6
92ElmPioF-1386
93BenRocC-24
93BenRocF-3273
94AshTouC-19
94AshTouF-1786
94SouAtlLAF-SAL30
95AshTouTI-30

Smith, Jed
82LouRedE-28
83LouRedR-30
84LouRedR-10
85LouRedR-10
86LouRedTI-29

Smith, Jeff
75DubPacT-3
76DubPacT-34
81RedPioT-6
82RedPioT-12
86BelBreP-23
87LitFalMP-2391
91EugEmeC-20
91EugEmeP-3727
92AppFoxC-21
92AppFoxF-1091
93CarLeaAGF-16
93WilBluRC-20
93WilBluRF-1997
94WilBluRC-22
94WilBluRF-301
96ForWayWB-24

Smith, Jem
87AllandGN-18
88KimN18-41

Smith, Jim
77ChaPatT-22
79BufBisT-17
79RocRedWT-13
80RocRedWT-17
88EugEmeB-8
91LinDriAA-418
91MemChiLD-418
91MemChiP-654

Smith, Jimmy (James Lorne)
14FatPlaT-46
20RedWorCP-23
80TidTidT-20
81PorBeaT-22
83Don-402
83Fle-323
83Top-122

Smith, Joe
92BakDodCLC-23

Smith, Joel
88SouOreAP-1697
89RocExpLC-27
90WesPalBES-22
92BoiHawC-4
92BoiHawF-3633
93PalSprAC-21
93PalSprAF-79
95LakElsSTI-23

Smith, John
58RedEnq-37
78CedRapGT-25
89UtiBluSP-22
90UtiBluSP-23
92PitMetF-3309
93St.LucMC-24
94SouOreAC-26
94SouOreAF-3623
94St.LucMC-23
94St.LucMF-1208
95BelBreTI-3
93StLucMF-2936

Smith, John Francis
87OldJudN-466A
87OldJudN-466B

Smith, John W.
20NatCarE-96
23WilChoV-155

Smith, JoJo
91YakBeaC-27
91YakBeaP-4248

Smith, Julie
91FreStaLBS-10

Smith, Justin
94PriRedC-24
94PriRedF-3262
95BatCliTI-31

Smith, Keilan
94St.CatBJC-22
94St.CatBJF-3644
95DunBluJTI-26
96DunBluJUTI-13

Smith, Keith L.
74GasRanT-20
76SacSolC-2
77TucTorC-11
78Top-710
78TucTorC-15B
81Don-539
81Fle-534
83NasSouTI-23
84NasSouTI-21
85ColCliP-22
85ColCliT-19
86ColCliP-22
86ColCliP-23
87DenZepP-25
88BlaYNPRWLU-29
88DenZepC-14
88DenZepP-1261
89VanCanC-13
89VanCanP-578
90CMC-646
90ProAAAF-174

90VanCanC-19
90VanCanP-496
92RicBraBB-3
92RicBraF-386
92RicBraRC-20
92RicBraS-441
92YanWIZ8-183
93RanKee-334
94BriTigF-3513
95PeoChiTI-30

Smith, Kelly
82PhoGiaVNB-20

Smith, Kelvin
83CliGiaF-20

Smith, Ken
79SavBraT-24
80RicBraT-18
81RicBraT-4
82BraBurKL-23
82RicBraT-23
83BraPol-11
83Fle-148
84RicBraT-3
85RicBraT-16
86RocRedWP-23
88SavCarP-332
89St.PetCS-25

Smith, Kevin
91KisDodP-4183
92GulCoaDF-3566
93AubAstC-22
93AubAstF-3443

Smith, Kielan
93MedHatBJF-3737

Smith, Lance
90AshTouC-20
91AshTouP-572
92BurAstC-10
92BurAstF-551

Smith, Larry
83IdaFalAT-11
85HunStaJ-30
87SanBerSP-2
89WelPirP-31
93WelPirC-29
94WelPirC-30
94WelPirF-3512
96EriSeaB-2

Smith, Larry (Lawrence)
89MiaMirIS-18

Smith, Lee Arthur
80WicAerT-12
82CubRedL-46
82Don-252
82Fle-603
82Fle-603B
82Top-452
83CubThoAV-46
83Don-403
83Fle-508
83Top-699
84AllGamPI-89
84CubChiT-27
84CubSev-46
84CubUno-9
84Don-289
84Fle-505
84FleSti-67
84FunFooP-108
84Nes792-176
84OPC-176
84Top-176
84TopSti-44
84TopTif-176
85AllGamPI-177
85CubLioP-21
85CubSev-46
85Don-311
85Fle-67
85FleStaS-105
85Lea-128
85OPC-43
85Top-511
85TopMin-511
85TopSti-41
85TopTif-511
86BasStaB-102
86CubGat-46
86CubUno-17
86Don-144
86DonAllB-PC8
86Fle-380
86FleLeaL-41
86FleLimE-42
86FleStiC-112
86GenMilB-4I
86Lea-64
86MSAJayPCD-17
86OPC-355
86SevCoi-C11
86Spo-45
86Spo-55
86Top-355
86Top-636
86TopSti-56
86TopSup-52
86TopTat-1
86TopTif-355
86TopTif-636
87CubCan-29
87CubDavB-46
87Don-292
87Fle-574
87FleExcS-39
87FleGlo-574
87FleLimE-39
87FleMin-101
87FleStiC-110
87Lea-80
87OPC-23
87RedFolSB-42
87SevCoi-C16
87SevCoi-M15
87Spo-104
87SpoTeaP-22
87Top-23
87TopMinL-3
87TopSti-56
87TopTif-23
88Don-292
88DonAll-60
88DonBasB-252
88DonTeaBRS-NEW
88Fle-433
88FleGlo-433
88FleMin-9
88FleUpd-8
88FleUpdG-8
88OPC-240
88PanSti-256
88Sco-31
88ScoGlo-31
88ScoRoo-20T
88ScoRooG-20T
88Spo-179
88StaLinCu-12
88StaLinRS-19
88Top-240
88TopGloS-56
88TopMinL-44
88TopSti-64
88TopStiB-33
88TopTif-240
88TopTra-110T
88TopTraT-110T
89Bow-19
89BowTif-19
89Don-66
89DonBasB-84
89Fle-99
89FleGlo-99
89OPC-149
89PanSti-272
89RedFolSB-109
89Sco-150
89ScoHot1S-18
89Spo-148
89SpollIFKI-294
89Top-760
89TopBasT-144
89TopSti-251
89TopTif-760
89TVSpoM-68
89UppDec-521
90Bow-263
90BowTif-263
90CarSmo-21
90ClaBlu-137
90Don-110
90DonBesN-120
90Fle-287
90FleCan-287
90FleUpd-53
90Lea-524
90OPC-495
90PanSti-14
90PubSti-464
90Sco-37
90ScoRoo-48T
90Top-495
90TopMag-71
90TopSti-262
90TopTif-495
90TopTra-118T
90TopTraT-118T
90TopTVRS-17
90UppDec-393
90VenSti-446
91Bow-387
91CarPol-47
91Don-169
91Don-403
91Fle-645
91Lea-44
91OPC-660
91PanCanT1-83
91PanFreS-39
91PanSti-38
91Sco-81
91StaClu-42
91Stu-237
91Top-660
91TopDesS-660
91TopMic-660
91TopTif-660
91Ult-295
91UppDec-348
91USPlaCA-10C
92Bow-505
92CarMcD-53
92CarPol-18
92Cla2-T28
92ClaGam-23
92Don-112
92DonCraJ2-4
92Fle-591
92Fle-697
92FleAll-8
92FleSmo'nH-S1
92Fre-6
92Hig5-98
92Lea-254
92OPC-565
92OPCPre-190
92PanSti-179
92Pin-195
92Sco-630
92Sco-781
92Sco100S-28
92StaClu-180
92StaCluD-174
92StaCluMO-30
92Stu-97
92Top-396
92Top-565
92TopGol-396
92TopGol-565
92TopGolW-396
92TopGolW-565
92TopKid-28
92TopMic-396
92TopMic-565
92TriPla-62
92Ult-270
92UppDec-376
92UppDecTMH-49
93Bow-600
93CarPol-19
93ClaGam-87
93CubRol-2
93Don-548
93Fin-95
93FinJum-95
93FinRef-95
93Fla-127
93Fle-133
93FleAll-NL12
93FleFinEDT-7
93FunPac-77
93Kra-29
93Lea-154
93OPC-324
93PacSpa-303
93PanSti-160
93PanSti-192
93Pin-416
93Sco-103
93Sco-529
93Sel-83
93SelChaS-12
93SelDufIP-12
93SelRoo-31T
93SelStaL-70
93SP-78
93StaClu-462
93StaCluCa-13
93StaCluFDI-462
93StaCluM-128
93StaCluMO-24
93StaCluMOP-462
93Stu-147
93Top-12
93Top-411
93TOPBLAG-19
93TopGol-12
93TopGol-411
93TopInaM-12
93TopInaM-411
93TopMic-12
93TopMic-411
93TriPla-83
93Ult-112
93UltAllS-10
93UppDec-82
93UppDecGold-82
94Bow-299
94BowBes-R5
94BowBesR-R5
94ColC-260
94ColC-556
94ColChoGS-260
94ColChoGS-556
94ColChoSS-260
94ColChoSS-556
94Don-650
94ExtBas-14
94Fin-351
94FinRef-351
94Fla-258
94Fle-246
94FleUpd-8
94Lea-357
94LeaL-6
94OriPro-94
94Pac-436
94Pin-499
94PinArtP-499
94PinMusC-499
94PinTri-TR18
94Sco-245
94Sco-627
94ScoGolR-245
94ScoGolR-627
94ScoRoo-RT2
94ScoRooCP-CP8
94ScoRooGR-RT2
94ScoRooS-RT2
94Sel-217
94SP-127
94SPDieC-127
94SpoRoo-38
94SpoRooAP-38
94StaClu-543
94StaClu-605
94StaCluFDI-543
94StaCluFDI-605
94StaCluGR-543
94StaCluGR-605
94StaCluMOP-543
94StaCluMOP-605
94Stu-128
94Top-110
94TopGol-110
94TopSpa-110
94TopTra-100T
94Ult-311
94UppDec-505
94UppDecED-505
95AngCHP-15
95AngMot-13
95Baz-3
95Bow-330
95BowBes-R59
95BowBesR-R59
95ColCho-57
95ColCho-105
95ColChoGS-57
95ColChoGS-105
95ColChoSE-144
95ColChoSE-152
95ColChoSEGS-144
95ColChoSEGS-152
95ColChoSESS-144
95ColChoSESS-152
95ColChoSS-57
95ColChoSS-105
95Don-133
95DonPreP-133
95DonTopotO-43
95Emo-22
95Fin-172
95Fin-241
95FinRef-172
95FinRef-241
95Fla-239
95Fle-21
95FleAllS-24
95FleUpd-68
95Lea-346
95LeaLim-189
95Pac-31
95PacPri-11
95PanSti-17
95PanSti-128
95Pin-64
95PinArtP-64
95PinMusC-64
95Sco-91
95ScoDreT-DG12
95ScoGolR-91
95ScoHaloG-HG40
95ScoPlaTS-91
95SPCha-130
95SPChaDC-130
95StaClu-12
95StaClu-627
95StaCluFDI-12
95StaCluMO-42
95StaCluMOP-12
95StaCluMOP-627
95StaCluSTWS-12
95StaCluSTWS-627
95StaCluVR-7
95Stu-92
95Top-394
95Top-425
95Top-659
95Top-660
95TopCyb-223
95TopTra-66T
95Ult-272
95UltGolM-272
95UltLeaL-5
95UltLeaLGM-5
95UppDec-16
95UppDecED-16
95UppDecEDG-16
95UppDecSE-261
95UppDecSEG-261
96AngMot-11
96Baz-60
96ColCho-77
96ColChoGS-77
96ColChoSS-77
96ColChoYMtP-37
96ColChoYMtP-37A
96ColChoYMtPGS-37
96ColChoYMtPGS-37A
96Don-291
96DonPreP-291
96EmoXL-31
96Fin-S142
96FinRef-S142
96Fla-42
96Fle-58
96FleTif-58
96Lea-110
96LeaPrePB-110
96LeaPrePG-110
96LeaPrePS-110
96MetUni-33
96MetUniP-33
96Pac-270
96Pin-222
96PinAfi-43
96PinAfiAP-43
96PinAfiFPP-43
96PinArtP-122
96PinFoil-222
96PinSta-122
96Sco-150
96ScoDugC-A88
96ScoDugCAP-A88
96Sel-141
96SelArtP-141
96StaClu-66
96StaCluEPB-66
96StaCluEPG-66
96StaCluEPS-66
96StaCluMOP-66

95StaCluVRMC-7
96Stu-91
96StuPrePB-91
96StuPrePG-91
96StuPrePS-91
96Sum-89
96SumAbo&B-89
96SumArtP-89
96SumFoi-89
96Top-251
96TopChr-98
96TopChrMotG-8
96TopChrMotGR-8
96TopChrR-98
96TopGal-46
96TopGalPPI-46
96TopMasotG-8
96Ult-34
96UltGolM-34
96UppDec-113
96UppDec-288
96UppDecPHE-H19
96UppDecPreH-H19
97Cir-242
97CirRav-242
97ColCho-85
97ColCho-390
97Fle-685
97FleTif-685
97PacPriGotD-GD131
97Sco-379
97ScoHobR-379
97ScoResC-379
97ScoShoS-379
97ScoShoSAP-379
97Ult-446
97UltGolME-446
97UltPlaME-446
97UppDec-48

Smith, Lillian
88KimN18-42

Smith, Lonnie
76OklCit8TI-4
79Top-722
80PhiBurK-14
81CokTeaS-106
81Don-295
81Fle-15
81OPC-317
81Top-317
82Don-606
82Fle-259
82Fle-641
82FleSta-60
82OPC-127
82Top-127
82TopTra-108T
83AllGamPI-160
83Car-28
83Don-91
83DonActA-34
83Fle-21
83Fle-636
83FleSta-179
83FleSti-4
83Kel-30
83OPC-273
83PerCreC-15
83PerCreCG-15
83Top-465
83Top-561
83TopFol-3
83TopSti-283
84AllGamPI-70
84Car-28
84Car5x7-26
84Don-231
84Don-625
84DonCha-23
84Fle-335
84FleSti-7
84Nes792-186
84Nes792-580
84OPC-113
84SevCoi-C14
84Top-186
84Top-580
84TopRubD-1
84TopSti-140
84TopStiB-5
84TopTif-186
84TopTif-580
85AllGamPI-158
85Don-231
85Fle-239
85FleStaS-61
85FleUpd-106
85Lea-225
85OPC-255
85Top-255
85TopMin-255
85TopRubD-1
85TopSti-139
85TopTif-255
85TopTifT-109T
85TopTra-109T
86BasStaB-103
86Don-399
86Fle-21
86FleMin-4
86Lea-188
86OPC-7
86RoyKitCD-1
86RoyNatP-21
86Spo-186
86Top-617
86TopMinL-21
86TopSti-264
86TopTif-617
87Don-225
87Fle-381
87FleGlo-381
87FleLimE-40
87FleStiC-111
87SpoTeaP-13
87Top-69
87TopSti-262
87TopTif-69
88BlaYNPRWL-154
88Don-527
88PanSti-111
88RicBraC-14
88RicBraP-1
88Sco-263
88ScoGlo-263
88Top-777
88TopTif-777
88TriAAC-24
89Bow-278
89BowTif-278
89BraDub-22
89DonBasB-114
89FleUpd-74
89TopBig-242
89TopTra-114T
89TopTraT-114T
89UppDec-731
90Bow-12
90BowTif-12
90BraDubP-24
90BraDubS-28
90ClaBlu-52
90Don-222
90DonBesN-86
90Fle-593
90FleAwaW-35
90FleCan-593
90FleLeaL-37
90GooHumICBLS-22
90Lea-217
90OPC-152
90PanSti-227
90PubSti-121
90RedFolSB-88
90Sco-399
90Sco100S-82
90Spo-65
90Top-152
90TopBatL-19
90TopBig-7
90TopCoi-58
90TopDou-61
90TopMinL-46
90TopSti-24
90TopStiB-19
90TopTif-152
90UppDec-215
90VenSti-447
91Bow-567
91BraDubP-26
91BraSubS-33
91Don-364
91Fle-702
91Lea-13
91OPC-306
91PanFreS-24
91PanSti-22
91Sco-543
91SimandSMLBL-41
91StaClu-97
91Top-306A
91Top-306B
91TopDesS-306
91TopMic-306
91TopTif-306
91Ult-11
91UppDec-305
92BraLykP-25
92BraLykS-30
92Don-517
92Fle-369
92Lea-480
92OPC-467
92PanSti-168
92Pin-465
92Sco-13
92ScoFacI-B4
92ScoProP-1
92StaClu-282
92Top-467
92TopGol-467
92TopGolW-467
92TopMic-467
92TriPla-40
92Ult-168
92UppDec-301
93Don-658
93Fle-371
93FleFinE-119
93Lea-394
93Pin-454
93PirNatl-30
93Sco-431
93StaClu-658
93StaCluFDI-658
93StaCluM-182
93StaCluMOP-658
93Ult-456
93UppDec-716
93UppDecGold-716
94OriPro-95
94Sco-462
94ScoGolR-462
94StaClu-643
94StaCluFDI-643
94StaCluGR-643
94StaCluMOP-643
95Sco-75
95ScoGolR-75
95ScoPlaTS-75
88RicBraBC-5

Smith, Mandy
81WisRapTT-19

Smith, Mark
83BirBarT-7
83RocRedWT-8

Smith, Mark Edward
88CapCodPPaLP-146
90HamRedB-7
90HamRedS-24
91ClaDraP-6
91St.PetCC-13
92Bow-556
92ClaDraP-91
92ClaFS7-122
92HagSunF-2569
92HagSunS-269
92SkyAA F-113
92SprCarC-14
92SprCarF-868
92UppDec-66
92UppDecML-38
92UppDecML-281
92UppDecMLPotY-PY15
93Bow-253
93ClaFS7-89
93ClaGolF-59
93ExcFS7-127
93FreKeyC-24
93FreKeyF-1027
93RocRedWF-254
93TriAAAGF-30
94Bow-47
94Cla-99
94ClaGolF-145
94LeaLimR-64
94OriPro-96
94RocRedWF-1011
94RocRedWTI-21
94ScoRoo-RT108
94ScoRooGR-RT108
94Sel-408
94TopTra-4T
94UppDecML-232
95Don-372
95DonPreP-372
95Pac-32
95Pin-166
95PinArtP-166
95PinMusC-166
95RocRedWTI-35
95Sco-284
95ScoGolR-284
95ScoPlaTS-284
95Top-631
96RocRedWB-25
96Sco-236
96ScoDugC-A105
96ScoDugCAP-A105
96StaClu-395
96StaCluMOP-395
97PacPriGotD-GD17

Smith, Mason
94MedHatBJF-3680
94MedHatBJSP-20

Smith, Matt
94ClaUpdCotC-CC14
94DEL-4
94DEL-16
94SigRooDP-16
94SigRooDPS-16
94StaCluDP-4
94StaCluDPFDI-4
94TopTra-116T
95Bow-210
95ScoDraP-DP16
95SPML-73
95SprSulTI-26
95StaClu-110
95StaCluFDI-110
95StaCluMOP-110
95StaCluSTWS-110
95Top-53
95UppDec-12
95UppDecED-12
95UppDecEDG-12
95UppDecML-180
95UppDecSE-56
95UppDecSEG-56
96BesAutSA-73
96HonShaHWB-23
96WilBluRB-1
95UppDecMLFS-180

Smith, Mayo (Edward)
55Top-130
55TopDouH-69
56Top-60
56TopHocF-A9
56TopPin-21
58PhiJayP-12
59RedEnq-24
67Top-321
68TigDetFPB-21
68Top-544
69OPC-40
69TigTeal-10
69Top-40
70OPC-313
70Top-313
78TigDeaCS-11
81TigDetN-35

Smith, Mike
76AppFoxT-25
82RicBraT-26
94HigDesMC-25
94HigDesMF-2797
95TulDriTI-21

Smith, Milt
61UniOil-H7

Smith, Mississippi (Michael A.)
87IndIndTI-23
88IndIndC-7
88IndIndP-509
89RocRedWC-8
89RocRedWP-1634
89RocRedWP-1637
90OPC-552
90TamYanD-24
90Top-249
90Top-552
90TopTif-552

Smith, Myrl
77RocRedWM-20
79TucTorT-2

Smith, Nate
91OriCro-429

Smith, Nick
87OldJudN-471

Smith, Nig (Frank Elmer)
07WhiSoxGWH-10
08RosComP-17
09T206-325
09T206-326
09T206-327
10ChiE-18
10CouT21-224
10E101-42
10E102-23
10MelMinE-42
10NadCarE-46
10RedCroT-69
10RedCroT-155
10RedCroT-156
10RedCroT-243
11SpoLifCW-328
11SpoLifM-30
12T207-168
14CraJacE-90
15CraJacE-90

Smith, Ottis
91PitMetC-15
91PitMetP-3423
92ColMetC-3
92ColMetPI-19
93St.LucMC-25
94OrlCubF-1383
93StLucMF-2922
95OrlCubF-10

Smith, Ozzie
78PadFamF-29
79Hos-102
79OPC-52
79Top-116
80OPC-205
80Top-393
81AllGamPI-114
81Don-1
81Fle-488
81OPC-254
81Top-207
81Top-254
81TopScr-68
81TopSti-230
82Don-21
82Don-94
82Fle-582
82FleSta-101
82Kel-6
82OPC-95
82Top-95
82TopSti-104
82TopTra-109T
83AllGamPI-114
83Car-29
83Don-120
83Fle-22
83Fle-636
83FleSta-180
83FleSti-10
83Kel-21
83OPC-14
83PerAll-17
83PerAllG-17
83PerCreC-16
83PerCreCG-16
83Top-540
83TopSti-168
83TopSti-180
83TopSti-186
83TopSti-288
84AllGamPI-25
84Car-29
84Car5x7-27
84Don-59
84Don-625
84Fle-336
84FunFooP-71
84MilBra-25
84Nes792-130
84Nes792-389
84NesDreT-15
84OPC-130
84OPC-389
84RalPur-2
84RawGloT-4
84SevCoi-C19
84Top-130
84Top-389
84TopCer-2

84TopGloA-16
84TopGloS-17
84TopRubD-28
84TopSti-144
84TopSti-187
84TopTif-130
84TopTif-389
85AllGamPI-116
85CarTeal-30
85Don-59
85DonActA-28
85Fle-240
85Fle-631
85FleLimE-35
85GenMilS-10
85KASDis-14
85KitCloD-14
85Lea-60
85OPC-191
85SevCoi-C16
85Top-605
85Top-715
85TopGloA-5
85TopRubD-28
85TopSti-137
85TopSti-181
85TopSup-47
85TopTif-605
85TopTif-715
86BasStaB-104
86CarIGAS-11
86CarKASD-7
86CarSchM-21
86CarTeal-39
86Don-59
86DonAll-8
86DonPop-8
86Fle-46
86FleLeaL-42
86FleMin-10
86FleStiC-113
86GenMilB-4J
86Lea-47
86OPC-297
86QuaGra-15
86SevCoi-S10
86Spo-121
86Top-704
86Top-730
86TopGloA-16
86TopGloS-46
86TopSti-11
86TopSti-46
86TopSti-153
86TopSup-53
86TopTat-16
86TopTif-704
86TopTif-730
86TruVal-9
87BurKinA-14
87CarSmo-17
87ClaGam-32
87Don-5
87Don-60
87DonAll-15
87DonOpeD-65
87DonP-15
87DonSupD-5
87Fle-308
87FleAwaW-38
87FleBasA-41
87FleGlo-308
87FleMin-102
87FleStiC-112
87GenMilB-5I
87HosSti-15
87KraFoo-16
87Lea-5
87Lea-108
87MandMSL-24
87MSAJifPD-7
87OPC-107
87RalPur-13
87RedFolSB-112
87SmoNatL-9
87Spo-79
87Spo-142
87SpoTeaP-12
87StuPan-11
87Top-598
87Top-749
87TopCoi-45
87TopGloA-5
87TopGloS-23
87TopSti-46
87TopSti-162
87TopTif-598
87TopTif-749
88ActPacT-6
88CarSmo-18
88CheBoy-5
88ClaBlu-210
88Don-263
88DonAll-37
88DonAll-63
88DonBasB-243
88DonBonM-BC22
88DonPop-15
88Fle-47
88Fle-628
88FleAwaW-39
88FleBasA-39
88FleBasM-35
88FleGlo-47
88FleGlo-628
88FleGlo-WS4
88FleHotS-40
88FleMin-109
88FleRecS-38
88FleStiC-120
88FleTeaL-38
88FleWorS-4
88GreBasS-35
88K-M-28
88KinDis-4
88Lea-115
88MSAFanSD-11
88Nes-5
88OPC-39
88PanSti-235
88PanSti-393
88Sco-12
88ScoBoxC-14
88ScoGlo-12
88Spo-68
88StaLinAl-32
88StaLinCa-18
88Top-400
88Top-460
88TopBig-228
88TopCoi-55
88TopGloA-16
88TopGloS-47
88TopMinL-72
88TopSti-53
88TopSti-153
88TopStiB-12
88TopTif-400
88TopTif-460
88TopUKM-72
88TopUKMT-72
89Bow-436
89BowTif-436
89CadElID-53
89CarSmo-20
89CerSup-1
89ClaLigB-58
89ColPosOS-1
89ColPosOS-2
89ColPosOS-3
89ColPosOS-4
89ColPosOS-5
89ColPosOS-6
89ColPosOS-7
89ColPosOS-8
89Don-63
89DonAll-37
89DonAll-62
89DonBasB-44
89DonBonM-BC14
89DonPop-37
89Fle-463
89FleExcS-38
89FleGlo-463
89FleLeaL-35
89KayB-28
89MSAHolD-3
89OPC-230
89PanSti-186
89PanSti-235
89RedFolSB-110
89Sco-80
89ScoHot1S-88
89ScoSco-27
89Spo-105
89SpoIllFKI-43
89Top-230
89Top-389
89TopBasT-45
89TopBig-110
89TopCoi-25
89TopDouA-16
89TopGloA-16
89TopGloS-42
89TopHeaUT-17
89TopMinL-37
89TopSti-44
89TopSti-161
89TopStiB-45
89TopTif-230
89TopTif-389
89TopUKM-72
89TVSpoM-25
89UppDec-265
89UppDec-674
90AllBasT-10
90BasWit-41
90Bow-195
90BowTif-195
90CarSmo-22
90ClaBlu-18
90Col-5
90Don-201
90Don-710A
90Don-710B
90DonBesN-83
90DonLeaS-9
90Fle-260
90FleAwaW-36
90FleBasA-35
90FleBasM-36
90FleCan-260
90GooHumICBLS-23
90Hot50PS-41
90K-M-4
90KayB-29
90KinDis-4
90Lea-142
90Lea-364
90LeaPre-12
90MLBBasB-30
90OPC-400
90OPC-590
90PanSti-206
90PanSti-338
90Pos-6
90PubSti-228
90PubSti-272
90RedFolSB-89
90Sco-285
90Sco100S-6
90ScoMcD-24
90Spo-16
90Top-400
90Top-590
90TopBig-203
90TopDou-62
90TopGloA-5
90TopGloS-16
90TopMag-57
90TopSti-42
90TopSti-145
90TopStiB-12
90TopTif-400
90TopTif-590
90TopTVA-52
90TopTVCa-29
90UppDec-225
90USPlaCA-6H
90VenSti-448
90VenSti-449
90WonBreS-5
91BasBesRB-17
91Bow-398
91CadElID-53
91CarPol-1
91ClaGam-39
91Don-240
91Don-437
91Fle-646
91JimDea-20
91Lea-80
91MajLeaCP-49
91MooSna-8
91OPC-130
91OPCPre-112
91PanCanT1-103
91PanFreS-34
91PanFreS-161
91PanSti-39
91PepSup-12
91PetSta-18
91PosCan-8
91RedFolS-129
91Sco-825
91Sco100S-18
91SevCoi-M12
91StaClu-154
91StaPinB-47
91Stu-238
91SunSee-1
91Top-130
91TopCraJ2-27
91TopDesS-130
91TopGloA-16
91TopMic-130
91TopSta-31
91TopTif-130
91TopTriH-N12
91Ult-296
91UppDec-162
91UppDecFE-95F
91USPlaCA-13S
92Bow-675
92CarMcD-38
92CarPol-19
92Cla1-T51
92Cla2-T26
92ClaGam-24
92ColAllG-6
92ColAllP-6
92Don-423
92Don-432
92DonCraJ1-6
92DonMcD-26
92Fle-592
92Fre-13
92Hig5-99
92HitTheBB-33
92JimDeaLL-3
92Lea-400
92LeaBlaG-400
92Mr.TurS-23
92New-27
92OPC-760
92OPCPre-84
92PanSti-175
92PanSti-284
92PepDieM-19
92Pin-6
92Pin-285
92PinRool-15
92Pos-8
92PosCan-6
92Sco-590
92Sco100S-47
92ScoCokD-20
92ScoFacI-B9
92ScoProaG-14
92ScoProP-5
92SevCoi-14
92SpoStaCC-42
92StaClu-680
92StaCluD-175
92StaCluMO-9
92StaCluMO-10
92StaCluMO-31
92StaCluMO-32
92StaCluMO-33
92StaCluNC-680
92Stu-98
92StuPre-20
92Top-760
92TopGol-760
92TopGolW-760
92TopKid-25
92TopMcD-11
92TopMic-760
92TriPla-244
92Ult-271
92UltAwaW-9
92UppDec-177
92UppDec-716
92UppDecF-42
92UppDecFG-42
92UppDecTMH-50
93Bow-460
93CadDis-55
93CarPol-20
93ClaGam-88
93ColAllG-16
93DiaMar-99
93Don-520
93DurPowP1-11
93Fin-28
93FinRef-28
93Fla-128
93FleFinE-131
93FleFinEDT-8
93FunPac-35
93FunPac-74
93FunPac-78
93FunPac-215
93FunPacA-AS6
93HumDumC-50
93KinDis-12
93Lea-328
93LeaHeaftH-10
93MetBak-36
93OPC-313
93PacSpa-302
93PanSti-194
93Pin-329
93PinCoo-9
93PinCooD-9
93PinTeaP-7
93Pos-26
93PosCan-17
93Sco-522
93Sco-532
93Sco-562
93ScoGolDT-1
93Sel-15
93SelChaS-3
93SP-79
93StaClu-548
93StaCluCa-1
93StaCluFDI-548
93StaCluM-147
93StaCluMOP-548
93Stu-217
93StuHer-6
93Top-40
93TOPBLAG-20
93TopGol-40
93TopInaM-40
93TopMic-40
93TriPla-122
93TriPlaA-3
93TriPlaN-9
93Ult-113
93UltAwaW-6
93UppDec-146
93UppDec-482
93UppDecDG-31
93UppDecGold-146
93UppDecGold-482
93UppDecIC-WI7
93UppDecICJ-WI7
93UppDecTAN-TN7
93USPlaCA-3H
94Bow-424
94BowBes-R3
94BowBesR-R3
94CarPol-19
94ChuHomS-26
94ChuHomSG-26
94ColC-334
94ColC-545
94ColChoGS-334
94ColChoGS-545
94ColChoSS-334
94ColChoSS-545
94ColChoT-14
94DenHol-24
94Don-35
94DonSpeE-35
94ExtBas-363
94Fin-136
94FinPre-136P
94FinRef-136
94Fla-228
94Fle-646
94FlePro-5
94FUnPac-101
94Kra-29
94Lea-409
94LeaL-147
94LeaLimGA-8
94OPC-181
94Pac-604
94PanSti-248
94Pin-389
94PinArtP-389
94PinMusC-389
94PinTri-TR10
94ProMag-114
94RedFolMI-14
94Sco-384
94ScoGolR-384

94Sel-30
94SP-65
94SPDieC-65
94SPHol-36
94SPHolDC-36
94Spo-41
94SpoFanA-AS4
94StaClu-417
94StaClu-541
94StaCluFDI-417
94StaCluFDI-541
94StaCluGR-417
94StaCluGR-541
94StaCluMOP-417
94StaCluMOP-541
94StaCluT-301
94StaCluTF-11
94StaCluTFDI-301
94Stu-54
94SucSav-8
94Top-320
94TopGol-320
94TopSpa-320
94TriPla-66
94Ult-568
94UppDec-278
94UppDec-360
94UppDecDC-C7
94UppDecED-278
94UppDecED-360
95Baz-28
95Bow-370
95ClaFanFPCP-7
95ClaPhoC-52
95ColCho-200
95ColChoGS-200
95ColChoSE-75
95ColChoSEGS-75
95ColChoSESS-75
95ColChoSS-200
95D3-58
95DenHol-25
95Don-50
95DonAll-NL6
95DonPreP-50
95DonTopotO-335
95Emb-75
95EmbGolI-75
95Emo-183
95Fin-217
95FinRef-217
95Fla-195
95Fle-509
95FleAllS-5
95KinDis-20
95Kra-28
95Lea-212
95LeaGreG-13
95LeaLim-62
95Pac-416
95PacPri-133
95PanSti-63
95Pin-282
95Pin-333
95PinArtP-282
95PinArtP-333
95PinFan-18
95PinMusC-282
95PinMusC-333
95PinPin-9
95PinPinR-9
95PinTeaP-TP5
95RedFol-31
95Sco-26
95ScoGolR-26
95ScoHaloG-HG24
95ScoPlaTS-26
95Sel-123
95SelArtP-123
95SelCer-55
95SelCerMG-55
95SP-100
95SPCha-83
95SPCha-85
95SPChaCP-CP7
95SPChaCPDC-CP7
95SPChaDC-83
95SPChaDC-85
95Spo-108
95SpoArtP-108
95SpoDouT-5
95SPSil-100
95StaClu-65
95StaCluFDI-65
95StaCluMOP-65
95StaCluMOP-RL3
95StaCluRL-RL3
95StaCluSTWS-65
95StaCluVR-39
95Stu-41
95StuGolS-41
95Sum-40
95SumNthD-40
95TomPiz-29
95Top-347
95TopCyb-188
95TopTra-159T
95UC3-56
95UC3ArtP-56
95Ult-227
95UltGolM-227
95UppDec-60
95UppDecED-60
95UppDecEDG-60
95UppDecPC-MLB15
95UppDecSE-225
95UppDecSEG-225
95UppDecSoaD-SD8
95Zen-79
96CarPol-23
96Cir-181
96CirAcc-26
96CirBos-46
96CirRav-181
96ColCho-104
96ColCho-280
96ColCho-404
96ColCho-756
96ColChoGS-104
96ColChoGS-280
96ColChoGS-404
96ColChoGS-756
96ColChoSS-104
96ColChoSS-280
96ColChoSS-404
96ColChoSS-756
96ColChoYMtP-38
96ColChoYMtP-38A
96ColChoYMtPGS-38
96ColChoYMtPGS-38A
96DenHol-20
96Don-352
96DonPreP-352
96EmoXL-271
96Fla-367
96Fle-556
96FleTif-556
96FleUpd-9
96Lea-163
96LeaLim-66
96LeaLimG-66
96LeaPre-31
96LeaPreP-31
96LeaPrePB-163
96LeaPrePG-163
96LeaPrePS-163
96LeaSig-52
96LeaSigPPG-52
96LeaSigPPP-52
96MetUni-229
96MetUniP-229
96MLBPin-32
96Pac-226
96PacPri-P72
96PacPriG-P72
96PanSti-74
96Pin-104
96Pin-281
96PinAfi-5
96PinAfiAP-5
96PinAfiFPP-5
96PinArtP-39
96PinArtP-181
96PinFan-15
96PinFoil-281
96PinSta-39
96PinSta-181
96Pro-14
96ProSta-35
96Sco-61
96ScoDugC-A53
96ScoDugCAP-A53
96Sel-67
96SelArtP-67
96SelCer-50
96SelCerAP-50
96SelCerCB-50
96SelCerCR-50
96SelCerMB-50
96SelCerMG-50
96SelCerMR-50
96SelTeaN-2
96SP-155
96Spo-53
96SpoArtP-53
96SPx-48
96SPxGol-48
96StaCluMeg-MH4
96StaCluMOP-MH4
95StaCluVRMC-39
96Stu-22
96StuPrePB-22
96StuPrePG-22
96StuPrePS-22
96Sum-102
96Sum-153
96SumAbo&B-102
96SumAbo&B-153
96SumArtP-102
96SumArtP-153
96SumFoi-102
96SumFoi-154
96TeaOut-75
96TeaOut-C97
96Top-301
96TopChr-120
96TopChrMotG-5
96TopChrMotGR-5
96TopChrR-120
96TopMasotG-5
96Ult-279
96UltCalttH-9
96UltCalttHGM-9
96UltGolM-279
96UppDec-108
96UppDec-386
96UppDec-440
96UppDecDD-DD31
96UppDecDDG-DD31
96UppDecDDS-DD31
96Zen-2
96ZenArtP-2
96ZenMoz-11
97ColCho-200
97ColChoS-1
97ColChoTBS-38
97ColChoTBSWH-38
97Don-231
97DonEli-125
97DonEliGS-125
97DonEliPtT-10
97DonEliPtT-12
97DonEliPtTA-10
97DonEliPtTA-12
97DonPreP-231
97DonPrePGold-231
97Fle-452
97FleGolM-10
97FleTif-452
97Lea-152
97LeaFraM-152
97LeaFraMDC-152
97Pac-416
97PacLigB-416
97PacPri-141
97PacPriGA-GA29
97PacPriGotD-GD203
97PacPriLB-141
97PacPriP-141
97PacSil-416
97Pin-122
97PinArtP-122
97PinMusC-122
97ScoHigZ-13
97Ult-276
97UltGolME-276
97UltPlaME-276
97UppDec-148
97UppDec-161
97UppDec-214
97UppDecU-39

Smith, Paul
54DanDee-23
54Top-11
57Top-345
58Top-269
63MilSau-8
94TopArc1-11
94TopArc1G-11

Smith, Pete J.
63MilSau-9
64Top-428
86GreBraTI-18
87GreBraB-24
88Don-571
88DonBasB-197
88DonRoo-10
88Fle-647
88FleGlo-647
88FleUpd-73
88FleUpdG-73
88ScoRoo-84T
88ScoRooG-84T
88TopTra-111T
88TopTraT-111T
89Bow-269
89BowTif-269
89BraDub-23
89Don-263
89Fle-600
89FleGlo-600
89OPC-388
89PanSti-36
89Sco-207
89ScoHot1R-74
89ScoYouSI-19
89Top-537
89TopSti-31
89TopTif-537
89ToyRoo-29
89UppDec-412
90BraDubP-25
90BraDubS-29
90Don-499
90Fle-594
90FleCan-594
90Lea-144
90OPC-771
90PubSti-122
90Sco-225
90Top-771
90TopBig-161
90TopTif-771
90UppDec-613
90VenSti-450
91BraDubP-27
91BraSubS-34
91Fle-703
91OPC-383
91Sco-205
91StaClu-519
91Top-383
91TopDesS-383
91TopMic-383
91TopTif-383
91UppDec-622
92Fle-370
92OPC-226
92RicBraBB-18
92RicBraF-3014
92RicBraRC-21
92RicBraS-442
92Sco-464
92StaClu-632
92Top-226
92TopGol-226
92TopGolW-226
92TopMic-226
92TriA AAS-442
93BraLykP-26
93BraLykS-32
93Don-498
93Fle-372
93Lea-214
93OPC-222
93Pin-541
93Sco-408
93StaClu-237
93StaCluB-13
93StaCluFDI-237
93StaCluMOP-237
93Top-413
93TopGol-413
93TopInaM-413
93TopMic-413
93Ult-311
93UppDec-589
93UppDecGold-589
94Bow-624
94ColC-509
94ColChoGS-509
94ColChoSS-509
94Don-585
94ExtBas-325
94Fin-350
94FinRef-350
94Fle-374
94FleUpd-161
94Lea-419
94MetColP-24
94MetShuST-6
94ScoRoo-RT52
94ScoRooGR-RT52
94Sel-318
94SpoRoo-4
94SpoRooAP-4
94Top-658
94TopGol-658
94TopSpa-658
94Ult-535
94UppDec-419
94UppDecED-419
95Don-451
95DonPreP-451
95Fle-382
95FleUpd-136
95Top-43
96LasVegSB-24
97RicBraBC-10

Smith, Phil
82DayBeaAT-24

Smith, Pop (Charles Marvin)
87BucN28-91
87OldJudN-470
88WG1CarG-62

Smith, Pugilist
88GooN16-40

Smith, Ramon
94MedHatBJF-3681
94MedHatBJSP-21

Smith, Randy
76QuaCitAT-32
89IdaFalBP-2008
90IdaFalBP-3263
91IdaFalBP-4346
91RocExpP-2056
94St.CatBJC-23
94St.CatBJF-3645
95StCatSTI-8

Smith, Ray
77VisOakT-13
78OrlTwiT-19
79TolMudHT-22
80TolMudHT-16
82TolMudHT-11
83TwiTeal-3
83TwiTeal-32
84Fle-573
84Nes792-46
84TolMudHT-4
84Top-46
84TopTif-46
85LasVegSC-114
86TacTigP-21
89EliTwiS-29
90EliTwiS-24
91EliTwiP-4315
92EliTwiC-23
92EliTwiF-3697
93EliTwiF-3430
94EliTwiF-3746

Smith, Red
90LitSunW-8

Smith, Red (James C.)
11S74Sil-56
14B18B-61
15SpoNewM-167
16ColE13-164
16FleBreD-86
16SpoNewM-165
17HolBreD-98
90DodTar-1074

Smith, Reggie (Carl R.)
67Top-314
67TopRedSS-12
68OPC-61
68Top-61
68TopVen-61
69MilBra-256
69MLBOffS-18
69RedSoxAO-11
69RedSoxTI-10
69Top-660
69TopSta-139
69TopTeaP-3
70Kel-46
70MLBOffS-167
70OPC-62
70OPC-215

70RedSoxCPPC-14
70Top-62
70Top-215
70TopPos-20
71Kel-52
71MilDud-29
71MLBOffS-333
71OPC-305
71RedSoxA-10
71RedSoxTI-11
71Top-305
71TopCoi-78
71TopSup-1
71TopTat-67
72Kel-35
72MilBra-318
72OPC-88
72Top-88
72Top-565
72Top-566
73LinPor-170
73OPC-40
73Top-40
74OPC-285
74Top-285
74TopSta-118
75Hos-59
75Kel-3
75OPC-490
75Top-490
76BatTroTI-20
76CraDis-57
76Hos-30
76HosTwi-30
76OPC-215
76SSP-278
76Top-215
77BurCheD-152
77OPC-223
77Top-345
78Hos-30
78Kel-34
78OPC-57
78RCColC-95
78SSP270-58
78Top-168
78WifBalD-70
79Hos-72
79OPC-243
79Top-465
79TopCom-25
80DodPol-8
80OPC-350
80Top-695
81AllGamPI-161
81DodPol-8
81Don-59
81Fle-111
81FleStiC-87
81Kel-36
81LonBeaPT-17
81OPC-75
81RedSoxBG2S-114
81Top-75
81TopScr-57
81TopSti-178
81TopSupHT-52
82Don-488
82Fle-23
82OPC-5
82OPC-228
82Top-545
82Top-546
82TopTra-110T
83Don-611
83Fle-272
83FleSta-181
83FleSti-49
83OPC-282
83OPC-283
83Top-282
83Top-283
83TopSti-12
83TopSti-302
84DodUniOP-8
87DodSmoA-34
88DodSmo-21
89DodSmoG-88
90DodTar-750
91DodUno7P-5
92CarMcD-34
92DodStaTA-16
93ActPacA-159
94DodMot-28
94DodPol-30
95DodMot-28
95DodPol-30
96DodMot-28
96DodPol-8
Smith, Rhett
89OklSoo-24
Smith, Richard
90WauTimB-7
90WauTimP-2120
90WauTimS-22
96BelSnaTI-34
Smith, Rick
88BakDodCLC-267
95HelBreTI-12
Smith, Rob (Robert D.)
88StoPorCLC-192
88StoPorP-741
89StoPorB-23
89StoPorCLC-168
89StoPorP-394
89StoPorS-18
90BelBreS-19
Smith, Robbie
86OrlTwiP-17
87OrlTwiP-2
Smith, Robbie (Robert A.)
91CollndC-28
91CollndP-1495
92ColRedC-23
92ColRedF-2401
Smith, Robert
28Exh-3
94CarLeaAF-CAR31
94DurBulC-19
94DurBulTI-21
96BesAutS-85
96Bow-296
96ColCho-441
96ColChoGS-441
96ColChoSS-441
96Exc-133
96RicBraB-26
96RicBraRC-8
96RicBraUB-26
96UppDec-259
97Bow-86
97BowInt-86
Smith, Rod
95GreBatTI-25
96GreBatB-28
Smith, Rodriguez
94SigRooDP-50
94SigRooDPS-50
Smith, Rogers
91MisStaB-55
Smith, Ron
75BurBeeT-26
76BurBeeT-31
76WatRoyT-27
80PenPilBT-20
80PenPilCT-26
81ReaPhiT-15
Smith, Ronald
93HunCubC-25
93HunCubF-3247
Smith, Ronnie
47SigOil-70
Smith, Roosevelt
91EriSaiC-24
91EriSaiP-4070
Smith, Roy
80PenPilBT-12
80PenPilCT-4
81ReaPhiT-7
82ReaPhiT-8
83ChaChaT-5
84IndWhe-33
84MaiGuiT-3
85Don-611
85Fle-455
85Ind-29
85IndPol-33
85MaiGuiT-10
85Top-381
85TopTif-381
86Don-468
86Top-9
86TopTif-9
86TwiTeaI-14
87PorBeaP-8
88PorBeaC-6
88PorBeaP-645
88TriAAAP-33
90Don-273
90Fle-386
90FleCan-386
90Lea-400
90OPC-672
90PanSti-107
90Sco-568
90Top-672
90TopTif-672
90UppDec-284
91Don-470
91Fle-624
91OPC-503
91RocRedWP-1902
91Sco-151
91Top-503
91TopDesS-503
91TopMic-503
91TopTif-503
91UppDec-490
92Fle-28
92Sco-256
93BufBisF-517
93TriAAAGF-21
96WisTimRB-22
Smith, Ryan
92BelMarC-14
92BelMarF-1443
96PorCitRB-25
Smith, Samuel
87OldJudN-465
Smith, Scott
93EriSaiC-23
93EriSaiF-3116
94ChaRanF-2496
95TulDriTI-22
96MidLeaAB-6
96WisTimRB-23
Smith, Sean
92GreHorC-8
92GreHorF-779
93ClaGolF-150
93DanBraC-25
93DanBraF-3622
93StaCluM-152
94MacBraC-21
94MacBraF-2210
95DurBulTI-29
96DurBulBIB-23
96DurBulBrB-24
Smith, Shad
91GreHorP-3061
92PriWilCC-18
92PriWilCF-150
93ShrCapF-2759
94ShrCapF-1606
Smith, Shawn
94AubAstC-27
95AubAstTI-1
96BatCliTI-27
Smith, Sherry (Sherrod)
20NatCarE-97
21Exh-167
21Exh-168
22E120-149
23W503-48
25Exh-86
26Exh-85
27AmeCarE-22
27YorCarE-31
28W502-31
28Yue-31
90DodTar-751
92ConTSN-609
Smith, Sloan
94GreBatF-490
94OneYanC-23
94OneYanF-3807
94Top-748
94TopGol-748
94TopSpa-748
95TamYanYI-25
96NorNavB-24
97GreBatC-21
Smith, Snuffy (Donald)
47SmiClo-16
Smith, Stephen
96BilMusTI-29
Smith, Steve
84ShrCapFB-18
85FreGiaP-23
86FreGiaP-17
90MisStaB-41
90WicStaSGD-31
91MisStaB-42
92MisStaB-39
93MisStaB-39
Smith, Steve J.
79HawIslT-14
80HawIslT-18
81HawIslT-4
82HawIslT-3
86BeaGolGP-23
87TexLeaAF-13
87WicPilRD-9
88LasVegSC-24
88LasVegSP-244
89LasVegSC-24
89LasVegSP-25
89TriAAP-AAA50
90CMC-171
90OklCit8C-21
90OklCit8P-448
91PenPilP-394
93AppFoxF-2478
94CalCanF-804
95TacRaiTI-1
96MarMot-28
Smith, Syd
09T206-517
10CouT21-60
Smith, Tad
93PitMetC-18
93PitMetF-3719
Smith, Ted
77ModA'sC-1
Smith, Terry
86LakTigP-22
87LakTigP-11
90LakTigS-28
90PriPatD-19
96TreThuB-4
Smith, Texas (Michael A.)
86CedRapRT-10
87VerRedP-12
88ChaLooB-21
89RocRedWC-9
90CMC-309
90OPC-249
90ProAAAF-459
90RocRedWC-8
90RocRedWGC-23
90RocRedWP-702
90Sco-635
90TopDeb89-118
90TopTif-249
91OriCro-428
Smith, Tim
84NewOriT-14
90ElmPioP-23
91CarLeaAP-CAR27
91LynRedSC-9
91LynRedSP-1199
91SouOreAC-3
91SouOreAP-3843
92NewBriRSF-434
92NewBriRSS-496
92ProFS7-22
92RenSilSCLC-54
92SkyAA F-214
92StaCluD-176
93NewBriRSF-1220
93SanBerSC-16
93SanBerSF-770
94NewBriRSF-650
94TacTigF-3174
Smith, Tobe
87NegLeaPD-14
Smith, Toby
94RocRoyC-22
94RocRoyF-565
95WilBluRTI-34
96WicWraB-25
Smith, Todd
86MiaMarP-23
87SalBucP-26
89MedAthB-30
90ModA'sC-28
90ModA'sCLC-151
90ModA'sP-2212
91ModA'sC-14
91ModA'sP-3088
91OklStaC-24
92HunStaS-320
92ProFS7-132
92SkyAA F-137
Smith, Tom
52LavPro-70
81QuaCitCT-18
83PeoSunF-10
91AppFoxC-25
91AppFoxP-1730
92BasCitRC-7
92BasCitRF-3858
92Bow-383
92ClaFS7-145
93WilBluRC-21
93WilBluRF-2011
Smith, Tommy
75AndRanT-1
75LafDriT-5
80ChaO'sP-21
80ChaO'sW-22
80RocRedWT-19
Smith, Tommy A.
74OPC-606
74Top-606
75OklCit8TI-15
75OPC-619
75Top-619
76SSP-530
77OPC-92
77Top-14
78STLakCGC-1
Smith, Tony
11T205-157
12ImpTobC-32
90DodTar-1075
Smith, Tracy
88GenCubP-1647
89PeoChiTI-20
90WinSpiTI-21
Smith, Travis
95HelBreTI-11
96StoPorB-14
Smith, Vinnie
52MotCoo-59
Smith, Wallace H.
12T207-167
Smith, Ward
75AndRanT-47
76AshTouT-8
Smith, Wib
09PC7HHB-40
Smith, Willie
65OPC-85
65Top-85
66AngDexP-7
66DexPre-2
66Top-438
67Top-397
68Top-568
69CubJewT-17
69CubTealC-9
69MilBra-257
69OPC-198
69Top-198
69TopFou-23
70OPC-318
70Top-318
71OPC-457
71Top-457
72MilBra-319
90BatCliP-3070
91SalLakTSP-15
92SalLakTSP-9
Smith, Willie (William G.)
63Top-241
Smith, Willie Everett
88AugPirP-377
89SalBucS-21
90AlbYanB-7
90Bow-425
90BowTif-425
90CMC-207
90ColCliC-7
90ColCliP-14
90ColCliP-676
90ProAAAF-326
90TopTVY-60
91AlbYanCB-5
91AlbYanLD-17
91AlbYanP-1008
91Bow-160
91Cla/Bes-332
91LinDriAA-17
91SalLakTP-3214
92CanIndF-689
92CanIndS-120
92ColSprSSF-752
92ProFS7-113
94Bow-508

96SigRooOJ-31
96SigRooOJS-31
Smith, Woody
88WytCubP-1990
89PeoChiTI-22
90PeoChiTI-13
Smith, Woody (Forest)
75SanAntBT-19
77WatIndT-21
78WatIndT-21
81ChaLooT-24
Smith, Zane
83DurBulT-24
85BraPol-34
85Fle-651
86BraPol-34
86Don-565
86Fle-528
86Lea-222
86OPC-167
86Top-167
86TopTif-167
87BraSmo-1
87Don-167
87Fle-529
87FleGlo-529
87OPC-226
87RedFolSB-73
87SpoTeaP-24
87Top-544
87TopTif-544
88Don-167
88DonBasB-170
88Fle-550
88FleGlo-550
88FleMin-66
88FleStiC-78
88FleTeaL-39
88OPC-297
88PanSti-240
88Sco-410
88ScoGlo-410
88Spo-134
88StaLinBra-18
88Top-297
88TopBig-193
88TopMinL-42
88TopSti-40
88TopTif-297
88TopUKM-73
88TopUKMT-73
89Bow-262
89BowTif-262
89Don-499
89Fle-601
89FleGlo-601
89FleUpd-99
89OPC-339
89RedFolSB-111
89Sco-492
89ScoRoo-56T
89Top-688
89TopSti-27
89TopTif-688
89UppDec-71
90Don-460
90ExpPos-34
90Fle-362
90FleCan-362
90Lea-238
90OPC-48
90PubSti-123
90Sco-477A
90Sco-477B
90Top-48
90TopTif-48
90UppDec-607
90VenSti-451
91Bow-524
91ClaGam-82
91Don-532
91Fle-51
91Lea-495
91OPC-441
91PanCanT1-66
91Sco-845
91StaClu-260
91StaCluP-41
91Top-441
91TopDesS-441
91TopMic-441
91TopTif-441
91UppDec-759
92Bow-409
92Don-360
92Fle-568
92Hig5-94
92Lea-96
92OPC-345
92Pin-237
92PirNatl-21
92Sco-493
92StaClu-807
92StaCluD-177
92StaCluECN-807
92Top-345
92TopGol-345
92TopGolW-345
92TopMic-345
92Ult-260
92UppDec-486
93Don-94
93Fle-120
93FunPac-150
93Lea-152
93OPC-170
93PacSpa-252
93PanSti-278
93Pin-403
93PirNatl-31
93Sco-121
93Sel-231
93StaClu-343
93StaCluFDI-343
93StaCluMOP-343
93Top-560
93TopGol-560
93TopInaM-560
93TopMic-560
93Ult-101
93UppDec-349
93UppDecGold-349
94ColC-571
94ColChoGS-571
94ColChoSS-571
94Don-559
94Fin-381
94FinRef-381
94Fla-220
94Fle-620
94Lea-374
94Pac-507
94PanSti-239
94PirQui-23
94Sco-239
94ScoGolR-239
94StaClu-310
94StaCluFDI-310
94StaCluGR-310
94StaCluMOP-310
94Top-707
94TopGol-707
94TopSpa-707
94Ult-559
94UppDec-251
94UppDecED-251
95ColCho-389
95ColChoGS-389
95ColChoSE-176
95ColChoSEGS-176
95ColChoSESS-176
95ColChoSS-389
95Don-457
95DonPreP-457
95Fle-489
95FleTeaL-25
95Pac-352
95Sco-157
95ScoGolR-157
95ScoPlaTS-157
95StaClu-44
95StaCluFDI-44
95StaCluMOP-44
95StaCluSTWS-44
95TopTra-55T
95Ult-426
95UltGolM-426
95UppDec-147
95UppDecED-147
95UppDecEDG-147
96ColCho-63
96ColChoGS-63
96ColChoSS-63
96Fle-34
96FleTif-34
96FleUpd-U180
96FleUpdTC-U180
96LeaSigA-210
96LeaSigAG-210
96LeaSigAS-210
Smithberg, Roger
89BlaYNPRWLU-23
89LasVegSP-17
90Bow-203
90BowTif-203
90CMC-503
90LasVegSC-1
90LasVegSP-124
90ProAAAF-12
91HigDesMC-11
91HigDesMP-2394
91WicWraP-2599
93HunStaF-2083
94Don-421
94TacTigF-3175
94Top-652
94TopGol-652
94TopSpa-652
Smithson, Mike
80VenLeaS-165
81PawRedST-11
83RanAffF-48
83TopTra-106T
84AllGamPI-176
84Don-221
84Fle-428
84FleUpd-108
84MinTwiP-26
84Nes792-89
84Top-89
84TopTif-89
84TopTra-110T
84TopTraT-110T
84TwiTeal-32
85Don-316
85Fle-289
85OPC-359
85Top-483
85TopSti-301
85TopTif-483
85Twi7-11
85TwiTeal-34
86Don-147
86Fle-405
86Lea-73
86OPC-101
86Top-695
86TopMinL-24
86TopSti-282
86TopTat-10
86TopTif-695
86TwiTeal-33
87Don-245
87Fle-553
87FleGlo-553
87OPC-225
87Top-225
87TopSti-275
87TopTif-225
88DonTeaBRS-NEW
88Fle-23
88FleGlo-23
88FleUpd-9
88FleUpdG-9
88OPC-389
88ScoRoo-59T
88ScoRooG-59T
88Top-554
88TopTif-554
89Don-628
89Fle-100
89FleGlo-100
89Sco-403
89Top-377
89TopBig-222
89TopTif-377
89UppDec-38
90Don-464
90Fle-288
90FleCan-288
90OPC-188
90PubSti-465
90Sco-512
90Top-188
90TopTif-188
90UppDec-610
90VenSti-452
93RanKee-335
Smock, Greg
92RenSilSCLC-58
93MadMusC-24
94ModA'sC-20
Smokey, Mascot
95TenVolW-13
Smolen, Bruce
91BatCliC-11
91BatCliP-3494
Smoll, Clyde
87ElmPio(C-1
88ElmPioC-30
89ElmPioP-25
Smoltz, John
86LakTigP-23
87GleFalTP-24
88FleUpd-74
88FleUpdG-74
88RicBraC-3
88RicBraP-23
88TriAAC-30
89Bow-266
89BowTif-266
89BraDub-24
89ClaTraP-174
89Don-642
89DonBasB-85
89Fle-602
89FleGlo-602
89Sco-616
89Top-382
89TopBig-260
89TopTif-382
89UppDec-17
90Bow-10
90BowTif-10
90BraDubP-26
90BraDubS-30
90ClaBlu-13
90Don-8
90Don-121
90DonBesN-50
90DOnBonM-BC12A
90DOnBonM-BC12B
90DonSupD-8
90Fle-595
90FleBasA-36
90FleCan-595
90Hot50PS-42
90Lea-59
90OPC-535
90PanSti-228
90PubSti-124
90RedFolSB-90
90Sco-370
90Sco100S-35
90ScoYouSI-36
90Spo-61
90StaLonJS-14
90StaLonJS-34
90Top-535
90TopBig-306
90TopMinL-47
90TopSti-30
90TopTif-535
90UppDec-84
90UppDec-535
90VenSti-453
91Bow-580
91BraDubP-28
91BraSubS-35
91Cla2-T27
91ClaGam-180
91Don-75
91Fle-704
91Lea-27
91OPC-157
91PanFreS-26
91PanSti-26
91Sco-208
91StaClu-365
91Stu-149
91Top-157
91TopDesS-157
91TopMic-157
91TopTif-157
91Ult-12
91UppDec-264
92Bow-347
92BraLykP-26
92BraLykS-31
92ClaGam-18
92Don-442
92Fle-371
92Lea-191
92OPC-245
92Pin-191
92PinTea2-30
92Sco-287
92ScoImpP-30
92SpoIllFK1-503
92StaClu-459
92StaCluD-178
92Stu-10
92Top-245
92TopGol-245
92TopGolW-245
92TopMic-245
92TriPla-172
92Ult-169
92UppDec-322
93Bow-494
93BraLykP-27
93BraLykS-33
93ClaGam-89
93DiaMar-100
93Don-130
93Fin-166
93FinRef-166
93Fla-11
93Fle-14
93FunPac-68
93HumDumC-27
93Lea-104
93MSABenSPD-8
93OPC-364
93PacSpa-12
93Pin-143
93Pin-298
93Sco-61
93Sel-177
93SelAce-17
93SelStaL-66
93SelStaL-76
93SP-63
93StaClu-463
93StaClu-599
93StaCluB-12
93StaCluFDI-463
93StaCluFDI-599
93StaCluM-86
93StaCluM-135
93StaCluMOP-463
93StaCluMOP-599
93Stu-61
93Top-35
93TopComotH-30
93TopGol-35
93TopInaM-35
93TopMic-35
93TriPla-67
93Ult-312
93UltStrK-5
93UppDec-363
93UppDec-472
93UppDecCP-R19
93UppDecGold-363
93UppDecGold-472
94Bow-629
94BraLykP-30
94BraLykS-29
94BraUSPC-6D
94BraUSPC-12C
94ColC-420
94ColChoGS-420
94ColChoSS-420
94Don-260
94ExtBas-213
94Fin-100
94FinPre-100P
94FinRef-100
94Fla-357
94Fle-375
94FleAllS-50
94FleSmo'nH-12
94FUnPac-233
94Lea-309
94OPC-39
94Pac-22
94PanSti-151
94Pin-342
94PinArtP-342
94PinMusC-342
94Sco-366
94ScoGolR-366
94Sel-174
94Spo-136
94StaClu-405
94StaClu-714
94StaCluFDI-405
94StaCluFDI-714
94StaCluGR-405

94StaCluGR-714
94StaCluMO-7
94StaCluMOP-405
94StaCluMOP-714
94StaCluT-35
94StaCluTFDI-35
94Top-687
94TopGol-687
94TopSpa-687
94TriPla-50
94Ult-157
94UltStrK-5
94UppDec-87
94UppDecED-87
95ColCho-167
95ColChoGS-167
95ColChoSS-167
95Don-461
95DonPreP-461
95DonTopotO-193
95Emo-108
95Fin-313
95FinRef-313
95Fla-108
95Fle-318
95Lea-18
95Pac-15
95Pin-25
95PinArtP-25
95PinMusC-25
95Sco-468
95ScoGolR-468
95ScoHaloG-HG66
95ScoPlaTS-468
95Sel-189
95SelArtP-189
95StaClu-397
95StaCluMOP-397
95StaCluSTDW-B397
95StaCluSTMP-9
95StaCluSTWS-397
95Top-145
95Ult-133
95UltGolM-133
95UppDec-294
95UppDecED-294
95UppDecEDG-294
96BowBes-72
96BowBesAR-72
96BowBesR-72
96Cir-107
96CirAcc-15
96CirBos-28
96CirRav-107
96ColCho-49
96ColChoGS-49
96ColChoSS-49
96Don-363
96DonPreP-363
96EmoXL-149
96Fin-B124
96FinRef-B124
96Fla-210
96Fle-308
96FleBra-16
96FleSmo'H-9
96FleTif-308
96Lea-1
96LeaLim-74
96LeaLimG-74
96LeaPre-111
96LeaPreP-111
96LeaPrePB-1
96LeaPrePG-1
96LeaPrePS-1
96LeaSig-69
96LeaSigEA-185
96LeaSigEACM-27
96LeaSigPPG-69
96LeaSigPPP-69
96MetUni-136
96MetUniP-136
96Pac-10
96Pin-315
96PinAfi-79
96PinAfiAP-79
96PinAfiFPP-79
96PinFoil-315
96Sco-27
96Sco-200
96ScoDugC-A26
96ScoDugCAP-A26
96ScoRef-14
96Sel-125
96SelArtP-125
96SP-24
96StaClu-250
96StaCluMOP-250
96Stu-85
96StuPrePB-85
96StuPrePG-85
96StuPrePS-85
96TeaOut-76
96Top-189
96TopChr-59
96TopChrR-59
96TopGal-67
96TopGalPPI-67
96TopLas-62
96Ult-161
96UltGolM-161
96UppDec-271
96UppDecA-16
96UppDecDD-DD3
96UppDecDDG-DD3
96UppDecDDS-DD3
88RicBraBC-8
97Bow-53
97BowBes-95
97BowBesAR-95
97BowBesMI-MI3
97BowBesMIAR-MI3
97BowBesMIARI-MI3
97BowBesMII-MI3
97BowBesMIR-MI3
97BowBesMIRI-MI3
97BowBesR-95
97BowChr-41
97BowChrI-41
97BowChrIR-41
97BowChrR-41
97BowInt-53
97Cir-192
97CirBos-17
97CirRav-192
97CirSupB-17
97ColCho-60
97ColCho-61
97ColCho-221
97ColCho-265
97ColChoAC-27
97ColChoTBS-4
97ColChoTBSWH-4
97ColChoTotT-T4
97Don-104
97Don-425
97DonDom-12
97DonEli-49
97DonEliGS-49
97DonLim-16
97DonLim-81
97DonLim-161
97DonLimLE-16
97DonLimLE-81
97DonLimLE-161
97DonPre-112
97DonPre-188
97DonPreCttC-112
97DonPreCttC-188
97DonPreP-104
97DonPreP-425
97DonPrePGold-104
97DonPrePGold-425
97DonPrePTBG-22
97DonPreTF-22
97DonPreTP-22
97DonTea-20
97DonTeaSPE-20
97Fin-136
97Fin-350
97FinEmb-136
97FinEmb-350
97FinEmbR-136
97FinEmbR-350
97FinRef-136
97FinRef-350
97FlaSho-A98
97FlaSho-B98
97FlaSho-C98
97FlaShoLC-98
97FlaShoLC-B98
97FlaShoLC-C98
97FlaShoLCM-A98
97FlaShoLCM-B98
97FlaShoLCM-C98
97Fle-269
97Fle-717
97FleHea-19
97FleMilDM-34
97FleNig&D-9
97FleTif-269
97FleTif-717
97FleZon-17
97Lea-77
97Lea-367
97LeaBanS-12
97LeaFraM-77
97LeaFraM-367
97LeaFraMDC-77
97LeaFraMDC-367
97LeaGet-2
97LeaStaS-14
97MetUni-35
97NewPin-147
97NewPinAP-147
97NewPinMC-147
97NewPinPP-147
97Pac-244
97PacCerCGT-20
97PacCraC-8
97PacGolCD-24
97PacLigB-244
97PacPri-83
97PacPriLB-83
97PacPriP-83
97PacPriSH-SH9B
97PacSil-244
97Pin-112
97PinArtP-112
97PinCar-17
97PinCer-67
97PinCerCMGT-20
97PinCerCT-20
97PinCerLI-15
97PinCerMBlu-67
97PinCerMG-67
97PinCerMR-67
97PinCerR-67
97PinIns-68
97PinIns-149
97PinInsC-3
97PinInsCE-68
97PinInsCE-149
97PinInsDD-16
97PinInsDE-68
97PinInsDE-149
97PinMusC-112
97PinSha-3
97PinTeaP-9
97PinTeaP-10
97PinTotCPB-67
97PinTotCPG-67
97PinTotCPR-67
97PinX-P-52
97PinX-PMoS-52
97ProMag-4
97ProMagML-4
97Sco-117
97Sco-521
97ScoAllF-18
97ScoBra-6
97ScoBraPl-6
97ScoBraPr-6
97ScoFra-2
97ScoFraG-2
97ScoHobR-521
97ScoPreS-117
97ScoResC-521
97ScoShoS-117
97ScoShoS-521
97ScoShoSAP-117
97ScoShoSAP-521
97ScoStaaD-4
97ScoSteS-4
97Sel-12
97Sel-146
97SelArtP-12
97SelArtP-146
97SelRegG-12
97SelRegG-146
97SelToootT-23
97SelTooотTMB-23
97SkyE-X-59
97SkyE-XC-59
97SkyE-XEC-59
97SP-22
97SPInsI-11
97SpoIll-73
97SpoIllEE-73
97SpoIllGS-5
97SPSpeF-15
97SPSPxFA-5
97SPx-6
97SPxBro-6
97SPxGraF-6
97SPxSil-6
97SPxSte-6
97StaClu-29
97StaCluI-I15
97StaCluMat-29
97StaCluMOP-29
97StaCluMOP-I15
97Stu-56
97StuPrePG-56
97StuPrePS-56
97Top-157
97TopAll-AS20
97TopChr-61
97TopChrAS-AS20
97TopChrR-61
97TopChrSAR-AS20
97TopChrSB-16
97TopChrSBR-16
97TopGal-51
97TopGalPPI-51
97TopSeaB-SB16
97TopSta-41
97TopStaAM-41
97Ult-160
97UltChe-A8
97UltGolME-160
97UltLeaS-12
97UltPlaME-160
97UltSeaC-10
97UltTop3-25
97UltTop3GM-25
97UppDec-64
97UppDec-217
97UppDec-259
97UppDec-300
97UppDecAWJ-10
97UppDecAWJ-12
97UppDecAWJ-23
97UppDecHC-HC9
97UppDecP-5
97UppDecU-29
97Zen-26

Smoot, Allen
82CliGiaF-18

Smoot, Homer
11SpoLifCW-330

Smorol, Jason
96BatCliTI-34

Smotherman, Dick
75WatRoyT-27

Smyth, Gregg
95AubAstTI-21

Smythe, Harry
36GouWidPPR-D35
36WorWidGV-79
90DodTar-752

Snaith, Andy
82AleDukT-26

Snappers, Beloit
95BelBreTI-31
96BelSnaTI-36

Snead, Jay
89AugPirP-519

Snead, Sam
51Whe-5
52Whe-27A
52Whe-27B
59FleWil-67

Snead, Scott
91BilMusP-3764
91BilMusSP-3

Snedeker, Sean
88GreFalDTI-20
89BakDodCLC-181
89CalLeaA-21
91VerBeaDC-12
91VerBeaDP-773
96HicCraB-27

Snediker, Jim
86WinHavRSP-24

Snell, Dave
86WauTimP-25
87SalSpuP-3
88VerMarP-956

Snell, Nate
85FleUpd-107
85TopTifT-110T
85TopTra-110T
86Don-367
86Fle-288
86Lea-166
86Top-521
86TopTif-521
87Don-396
87Fle-481
87FleGlo-481
87Top-86
87TopTif-86
88Fle-70
88FleGlo-70
91OriCro-430

Snelling, Allen
96StCatSB-27

Snider, Duke
47Exh-213A
47Exh-213B
47PM1StaP1-205
47PM1StaP1-206
47PM1StaP1-207
47StaPinP2-39
49Bow-226
49EurSta-50
50Bow-77
50Dra-5
51Bow-32
51R42SmaS-95
51TopRedB-38
52BerRos-61
52Bow-116
52NatTeaL-32
52RedMan-NL21
52StaCalL-79E
52StaCalS-91C
52TipTop-40
52Top-37
53BowC-117
53Bri-40
53RedMan-NL14
53StaMey-8
54Bow-170
54DanDee-24
54NewYorJA-18
54RedHeaF-29
54RedMan-NL16
54StaMey-12
54Top-32
55ArmCoi-19
55BigLealS-17
55DaiQueS-17
55DodGolS-17
55RedMan-NL19
55StaMey-12
55Top-210
56Dod-27
56Top-150
56TopPin-52
56YelBasP-29
57Top-170
57Top-400
58DodBelB-9
58DodJayP-12
58HarSta-12
58Hir-61
58Top-88
58Top-314
58Top-436
59Baz-20
59DodMor-11
59DodTeal-24
59DodVol-15
59HomRunD-18
59Top-20
59Top-468
59TopVen-20
60DodBelB-2
60DodJayP-14
60DodMor-12
60DodPos-10
60DodTeal-18
60DodUniO-19
60KeyChal-45
60Lea-37
60NuHi-55
60RawGloT-32
60Top-493
61DodBelB-4
61DodUniO-20
61Pos-167A
61Pos-167B
61Raw-10
61Top-443
62DodBelB-4
62DodJayP-10
62Jel-114
62Pos-114

62PosCan-114
62SalPlaC-215
62ShiPlaC-215
62Top-500
62TopStaI-140
63BasMagM-77
63Jel-118
63MetJayP-9
63Pos-118
63Top-68
63Top-550
64ChatheY-47
64MetJayP-10
64Top-155
64TopVen-155
64WheSta-42
68LauWorS-49
70FleWorS-49
71FleWorS-53
71FleWorS-57
75ShaPiz-12
76GalBasGHoF-26
76Met63 S-15
76SSP-351
76SSP-591
77GalGloG-24
77Spo-10122
79DiaGre-94
79TCM50-43
79TCM50-72
80DodGreT-10
80PacLeg-19
80PerHaloFP-172
80SSPHOF-170
81SanDieSC-3
81TCM60I-363
82CraJac-15
82DiaCla-26
83DonHOFH-14
83MLBPin-33
83Oco& SSBG-17
83TopRep5-37
83TopTraBP-6
84Don-648
84FifNatCT-17
84OCoandSI-66
84SpoDesPW-24
84WilMay-13
85CirK-20
86SpoDecG-32
86SpoDesJM-20
86TCM-2
86TCMSupS-49
86TCMSupS-50
87Dod195T-1
87HygAllG-41
87LeaSpeO*-H6
87NesDreT-33
88HouSho-8
88PacLegI-55
88RinPosD1-4A
88WilMulP-15
89BowInsT-10
89BowRepl-10
89BowTif-R10
89DodSmoG-27
89PerCelP-38
89TopBasT-30
90DodTar-753
90PerGreM-33
90PerGreM-87
90PerMasW-16
90PerMasW-17
90PerMasW-18
90PerMasW-19
90PerMasW-20
91MetWIZ-371
91TopArc1-327
92BazQua5A-10
92UppDecS-21
93TedWil-16
93TedWilM-4
93Yoo-19
94NabAllA-4
94TopArc1-32
94TopArc1G-32
95TopArcBD-5
95TopArcBD-63
95TopArcBD-68
95TopArcBD-108
95TopArcBD-119
95TopArcBD-151

Snider, Kelly
77LodDodT-20
79AlbDukT-14
80AlbDukT-4
81TolMudHT-15
82TolMudHT-16

Snider, Mark
89GeoColC-29
90GeoColC-28

Snider, Van
83ChaRoyT-13
84MemChiT-9
86MemChiSTOS-25
86MemChiTOS-25
87OmaRoyP-4
88BlaYNPRWL-61
88NasSouC-22
88NasSouP-473
88NasSouTI-22
88TriAAC-8
89Don-586
89Fle-172
89FleGlo-172
89NasSouC-23
89NasSouP-1281
89NasSouTI-23
89Sco-640
89ScoHot1R-41
89Spo-177
89UppDec-23
90CMC-216
90ColCliC-16
90ColCliP-15
90ColCliP-692
90ProAAAF-342
90TopTVY-61
91ColCliLD-118
91ColCliP-18
91ColCliP-611
91LinDriAAA-118
92PawRedSF-938
92PawRedSS-367
93LouRedF-229
97DunDonPPS-23

Snipes, Wesley
89MajLeaM-8
89MajLeaM-10

Snitker, Brian
78GreBraT-23
79SavBraT-5
83DurBulT-28
84DurBulT-28
86SumBraP-26
87DurBulP-6
89BraDub-25
90BraDubS-31
91MacBraC-18
91MacBraP-883
92MacBraC-26
92MacBraF-284
93GreBraF-367
94DanBraF-3550
94GreBraF-431
94GreBraTI-3
95DurBulTI-30
96DanBraB-1

Snoddy, Chris
86DavLipB-20

Snodgrass, Fred
09ColChiE-266
09SpoNewSM-76
09T206-329
09T206-330
10DarChoE-28
10W555-57
11S74Sil-95
11SpoLifM-220
11T205-158
12ColRedB-266
12ColTinT-266
12HasTriFT-48I
12T207-169
14B18B-71
15SpoNewM-168
16ColE13-165
16FleBreD-87
16SpoNewM-166
60NuHi-54
61NuSco-454
88ConSer3-26
91ConTSN-168

Snook, Rob
94HelBreF-3617
94HelBreSP-14

Snopek, Chris
93Bow-259
93ClaFS7-145
93SarWhiSF-1380
93SouBenWSC-20
93SouBenWSF-1440
94AriFalLS-19
94BirBarC-20
94BirBarF-630
94Bow-539
94BowBes-B43
94BowBesR-B43
94Cla-33
95Bow-147
95NasSouTI-25
96Bow-180
96BowBes-104
96BowBesAR-104
96BowBesR-104
96ColCho-18
96ColChoGS-18
96ColChoSS-18
96Don-517
96DonPreP-517
96Fin-G243
96FinRef-G243
96Fla-57
96FlePro-9
96FleUpd-U28
96FleUpdTC-U28
96FleWhiS-14
96Lea-25
96LeaPre-141
96LeaPreP-141
96LeaPrePB-25
96LeaPrePG-25
96LeaPrePS-25
96Pac-280
96Pin-188
96PinAfi-164
96PinAfiAP-164
96Sco-499
96Sel-163
96SelArtP-163
96SelCer-126
96SelCerAP-126
96SelCerCB-126
96SelCerCR-126
96SelCerMB-126
96SelCerMG-126
96SelCerMR-126
96SP-11
96Spo-129
96SpoArtP-129
96StaClu-339
96StaCluMOP-339
96Sum-187
96SumAbo&B-187
96SumArtP-187
96SumFoi-187
96Top-345
96TopChr-137
96TopChrR-137
96TopGal-141
96TopGalPPI-141
96TopLasBS-7
96Ult-336
96UltGolM-336
96UppDec-231
96UppDecFSP-FS18
96UppDecPHE-H29
96UppDecPreH-H29
96Zen-128
96ZenArtP-128
97BowBes-141
97BowBesAR-141
97BowBesR-141
97ColCho-77
97Don-346
97DonLim-31
97DonLimLE-31
97DonPre-141
97DonPreCttC-141
97DonPreP-346
97DonPrePGold-346
97DonTea-72
97DonTeaSPE-72
97Fin-142
97FinEmb-142
97FinEmbR-142
97FinRef-142
97FlaSho-A72
97FlaSho-B72
97FlaSho-C72
97FlaShoLC-72
97FlaShoLC-B72
97FlaShoLC-C72
97FlaShoLCM-A72
97FlaShoLCM-B72
97FlaShoLCM-C72
97Fle-69
97FleTif-69
97NewPin-19
97NewPinAP-19
97NewPinMC-19
97NewPinPP-19
97Sco-419
97ScoHobR-419
97ScoResC-419
97ScoShoS-419
97ScoShoSAP-419
97StaClu-109
97StaCluM-M34
97StaCluMOP-109
97StaCluMOP-M34
97Top-137
97UppDec-42
92UtiBluSC-3

Snover, Colonel L.
22E120-207

Snover, Dan
87HawRai-10
89PulBraP-1896
90DurBulUTI-6

Snow, Casey
96GreFalDB-25
96GreFalDTI-19

Snow, Felton
91PomBlaBPB-2

Snow, J.T.
87AriWilP-13
88AriWilP-12
88CapCodPPaLP-125
89OneYanP-2112
90CarLeaA-17
90PriWilCTI-25
90TopMag-106
91AlbYanLD-18
91AlbYanP-1017
91Cla/Bes-279
91LinDriAA-18
92ColCliF-362
92ColCliP-20
92ColCliS-117
92ProFS7-114
92SkyAAAF-56
93AngAdoFD-4
93AngMot-4
93AngPol-10
93Bow-173
93Bow-340
93DiaMar-101
93Don-110
93Fin-156
93FinRef-156
93Fla-179
93FleFinE-190
93FleMajLP-A7
93FunPac-8
93Lea-500
93LeaGolR-R17
93OPCPre-70
93PacJugC-16
93PacSpa-372
93Pin-609
93PinHomRC-27
93PinRooTP-4
93Sco-260
93Sel-385
93SelRoo-44T
93SP-26
93StaClu-719
93StaCluAn-1
93StaCluFDI-719
93StaCluMOP-719
93StaCluMP-29
93Stu-58
93StuHer-11
93StuSil-6
93Top-422
93TopGol-422
93TopInaM-422
93TopMic-422
93TopTra-62T
93TriPlaG-GS8
93Ult-525
93UltAllR-9
93UltPer-9
93UppDec-23
93UppDec-785
93UppDecDG-35
93UppDecGold-23
93UppDecGold-785
94ActPac-42
94AngMot-3
94Bow-11
94DEL-99
94Don-283
94Fin-157
94FinPre-157P
94FinRef-157
94Fla-274
94Fle-70
94FleRooS-19
94FUnPac-106
94OPC-55
94OPCDiaD-9
94Pac-89
94PanSti-43
94Pin-68
94PinArtP-68
94PinMusC-68
94PinNewG-NG9
94PinPowS-PS5
94Sco-511
94ScoGolR-511
94SigRooDP-99
94SigRooDPS-99
94Spo-121
94SpoSha-SH10
94StaClu-181
94StaClu-447
94StaCluFDI-181
94StaCluFDI-447
94StaCluGR-181
94StaCluGR-447
94StaCluMO-49
94StaCluMOP-181
94StaCluMOP-447
94Top-293
94TopGol-293
94TopSpa-293
94TriPla-20
94Ult-28
94USPlaCR-10C
94VanCanF-1872
95AngCHP-13
95AngMot-3
95AngTeal-3
95ColCho-92
95ColChoGS-92
95ColChoSS-92
95Don-139
95DonPreP-139
95DonTopotO-44
95Emo-23
95Fla-22
95Fle-236
95Lea-223
95LeaLim-57
95LinVen-107
95Pac-65
95Pin-215
95PinArtP-215
95PinMusC-215
95Sco-164
95ScoGolR-164
95ScoPlaTS-164
95SelCer-71
95SelCerMG-71
95SP-131
95SPCha-134
95SPChaDC-134
95SPSil-131
95StaClu-482
95StaCluMOP-482
95StaCluSTWS-482
95StaCluVR-263
95Top-582
95TopCyb-355
95Ult-24
95UltGolM-24
95UppDec-272
95UppDecED-272
95UppDecEDG-272
95UppDecSE-262
95UppDecSEG-262
95Zen-41
96AngMot-8
96Baz-2
96Bow-16
96Cir-23
96CirRav-23
96ColCho-489

96ColChoGS-489
96ColChoSS-489
96Don-507
96DonPreP-507
96EmoXL-32
96Fin-B144
96FinRef-B144
96Fla-43
96Fle-59
96FleTif-59
96Lea-149
96LeaLim-89
96LeaLimG-89
96LeaPre-99
96LeaPreP-99
96LeaPrePB-149
96LeaPrePG-149
96LeaPrePS-149
96LeaPreSG-31
96LeaPreSte-31
96LeaSig-66
96LeaSigPPG-66
96LeaSigPPP-66
96MetUni-34
96MetUniP-34
96Pac-265
96PanSti-210
96Pin-249
96PinAfi-147
96PinAfiAP-147
96PinArtP-149
96PinFoil-249
96PinSta-149
96ProSta-3
96Sco-23
96ScoDugC-A22
96ScoDugCAP-A22
96ScoNumG-27
96ScoRef-5
96Sel-71
96SelArtP-71
96SelCer-19
96SelCerAP-19
96SelCerCB-19
96SelCerCR-19
96SelCerMB-19
96SelCerMG-19
96SelCerMR-19
96SP-49
96Spo-34
96SpoArtP-34
96StaClu-128
96StaCluEPB-128
96StaCluEPG-128
96StaCluEPS-128
96StaCluMOP-128
95StaCluVRMC-263
96Stu-24
96StuPrePB-24
96StuPrePG-24
96StuPrePS-24
96Sum-75
96SumAbo&B-75
96SumArtP-75
96SumFoi-75
96Top-59
96TopChr-21
96TopChrR-21
96TopGal-41
96TopGalE-2
96TopGalPPI-41
96TopLas-29
96Ult-327
96UltGolM-327
96UppDec-26
96Zen-97
96ZenArtP-97
97Cir-85
97CirRav-85
97Don-42
97Don-275
97DonEli-89
97DonEliGS-89
97DonLim-29
97DonLimLE-29
97DonPreP-42
97DonPreP-275
97DonPrePGold-42
97DonPrePGold-275
97Fin-237
97FinRef-237
97FlaSho-A153
97FlaSho-B153
97FlaSho-C153
97FlaShoLC-153
97FlaShoLC-B153
97FlaShoLC-C153
97FlaShoLCM-A153
97FlaShoLCM-B153
97FlaShoLCM-C153
97Fle-52
97Fle-537
97FleTif-52
97FleTif-537
97Lea-244
97LeaFraM-244
97LeaFraMDC-244
97MetUni-247
97NewPin-133
97NewPinAP-133
97NewPinMC-133
97NewPinPP-133
97Pac-14
97PacLigB-14
97PacPri-6
97PacPriLB-6
97PacPriP-6
97PacSil-14
97PinCer-75
97PinCerMBlu-75
97PinCerMG-75
97PinCerMR-75
97PinCerR-75
97PinIns-119
97PinInsCE-119
97PinInsDE-119
97PinTotCPB-75
97PinTotCPG-75
97PinTotCPR-75
97Sco-304
97Sco-365
97ScoHobR-365
97ScoPreS-304
97ScoResC-365
97ScoShoS-304
97ScoShoS-365
97ScoShoSAP-304
97ScoShoSAP-365
97SkyE-X-96
97SkyE-XC-96
97SkyE-XEC-96
97SP-159
97SpoIll-122
97SpoIllEE-122
97StaClu-238
97StaCluMat-238
97StaCluMOP-238
97Top-263
97Ult-359
97UltGolME-359
97UltPlaME-359
97UppDec-140
97UppDec-545

Snuder, Kendall
87KenTwiP-4

Snusz, Chris
95BatCliTI-32

Snyder, Ben
82DayBeaAT-8
83ColAstT-19

Snyder, Brett
90BelBreB-11
90BelBreS-20
90Bes-145

Snyder, Brian
80SanJosMJitB-16
81WauTimT-7
82SalLakCGT-17
83SalLakCGT-4
84SalLakCGC-178
84ShrCapFB-19
85CalCanC-92
86LasVegSP-18
86Top-174
86TopTif-174
87LasVegSP-15
88TacTigC-9
88TacTigP-629
89TacTigC-4
89TacTigP-1545
90CMC-301
90ProAAAF-405
90RicBraBC-4
90RicBraC-25
90RicBraP-260
90RicBraTI-28

Snyder, Charles N.
87OldJudN-472

Snyder, Chris
88CapCodPPaLP-9
90PriPatD-20

Snyder, Cory
85Top-403
85TopTif-403
85WatIndT-23
86Don-29
86DonRoo-15
86Fle-653
86IndTeal-39
86MaiGuiP-20
86SpoRoo-18
87ClaUpdY-110
87Don-526
87DonOpeD-106
87Fle-260
87FleExcS-40
87FleGlo-260
87FleHotS-39
87FleMin-103
87FleSluBC-M5
87FleStiC-113
87IndGat-28
87KraFoo-17
87Lea-157
87OPC-192
87Spo-24A
87Spo-24B
87Spo-24C
87SpoSupD-10
87SpoTeaP-3
87Top-192
87TopCoi-24
87TopGloS-9
87TopRoo-16
87TopSti-213
87TopTif-192
87ToyRoo-25
88StaSny-1
88StaSny-2
88StaSny-3
88StaSny-4
88StaSny-5
88StaSny-6
88StaSny-7
88StaSny-8
88StaSny-9
88StaSny-10
88StaSny-11
88ClaRed-184
88Don-350
88DonBasB-224
88Fle-615
88Fle-622
88FleGlo-615
88FleGlo-622
88FleStiC-21
88FleSup-37
88IndGat-28
88KinDis-10
88Lea-125
88OPC-169
88PanSti-80
88RedFolSB-83
88Sco-92
88ScoGlo-92
88ScoYouSI-40
88Spo-29
88StaLinI-18
88StaStiS-1
88StaStiS-2
88StaStiS-3
88StaStiS-4
88StaStiS-5
88StaStiS-6
88StaStiS-7
88StaStiS-8
88Top-620
88Top-789
88TopBig-43
88TopCoi-27
88TopGloS-23
88TopSti-208
88TopStiB-53
88TopTif-620
88TopUKM-74
88TopUKMT-74
89Bow-89
89BowTif-89
89ClaLigB-19
89Don-8
89Don-191
89DonBasB-168
89DonSupD-8
89Fle-412
89FleGlo-412
89FleSup-38
89IndTeal-25
89OPC-80
89PanSti-329
89Sco-52
89ScoHot1S-6
89Spo-196
89Top-80
89TopBasT-124
89TopBig-175
89TopSti-210
89TopTif-80
89TopUKM-73
89TVSpoM-87
89UppDec-170
89UppDec-679
90Bow-336
90BowTif-336
90Don-272
90DonBesA-47
90Fle-502
90FleCan-502
90GooHumICBLS-24
90IndTeal-39
90KinDis-12
90Lea-187
90OPC-770
90PanSti-56
90PubSti-568
90RedFolSB-91
90Sco-10
90Sco100S-28
90Spo-3
90SupActM-8
90Top-770
90TopBig-221
90TopSti-211
90TopTif-770
90UppDec-126
90VenSti-454
91Bow-357
91Cla2-T8
91ClaGam-188
91Don-288
91Fle-378
91Lea-506
91OPC-323
91OPCPre-113
91PanFreS-221
91RedFolS-88
91Sco-19
91Sco-695
91Sco100S-74
91ScoRoo-61T
91StaClu-488
91Top-323
91TopDesS-323
91TopMic-323
91TopTif-323
91TopTra-111T
91TopTraT-111T
91Ult-83
91UppDec-123
91UppDec-724
91WhiSoxK-28
92Bow-492
92DonUpd-U21
92FleUpd-130
92GiaMot-19
92GiaPacGaE-31
92Lea-188
92Pin-506
92Sco-598
92ScoRoo-48T
92StaClu-772
92StaCluECN-772
92TopTra-107T
92TopTraG-107T
92Ult-595
92UppDec-504
93DodMot-20
93DodPol-24
93Don-656
93Fle-160
93FleFinE-84
93Lea-436
93OPC-250
93PanSti-242
93Pin-529
93Sco-574
93Sel-71
93SelRoo-111T
93StaCluD-29
93Top-254
93TopGol-254
93TopInaM-254
93TopMic-254
93Ult-405
93UppDec-218
93UppDec-791
93UppDecGold-218
93UppDecGold-791
94ColC-261
94ColChoGS-261
94ColChoSS-261
94DodMot-20
94DodPol-24
94Don-535
94ExtBas-296
94Fla-183
94Fle-524
94Pac-321
94PanSti-204
94Pin-466
94PinArtP-466
94PinMusC-466
94Sco-80
94ScoGolR-80
94Sel-170
94StaClu-463
94StaCluFDI-463
94StaCluGR-463
94StaCluMOP-463
94Top-683
94TopGol-683
94TopSpa-683
94Ult-219
94UppDec-266
94UppDecED-266
95Sco-487
95ScoGolR-487
95ScoPlaTS-487

Snyder, Doug
86OscAstP-24
87OscAstP-9
88VisOakCLC-158
88VisOakP-100
89OrlTwiB-25
89OrlTwiP-1327

Snyder, Gene W.
59Top-522
90DodTar-1076

Snyder, Gerald
52Bow-246
54Bow-216
55Bow-74
57Top-22

Snyder, Jared
93GenCubC-24
93GenCubF-3178
96DayCubB-21

Snyder, Jim
76IndIndTI-1
77FriOneYW-102
81OklCit8T-23
87CubCan-30
87CubDavB-NNO
88TopTra-112T
88TopTraT-112T
89Top-44
89TopTif-44
91PadSmo-34
92PadMot-27
92PadPolD-28
92PadSmo-32
93RicBraF-204
93RicBraRC-4

Snyder, John
94LakElsSC-20
94LakElsSF-1664
95MidAngOHP-32
95MidAngTI-27
96BirBarB-17

Snyder, Matt
96HigDesMB-26
96MauStiHWB-19
97Bow-404
97BowChr-267
97BowChrI-267
97BowChrIR-267
97BowChrR-267
97BowInt-404

Snyder, Pancho (Frank)
20GasAmeMBD-35
20NatCarE-98A

20NatCarE-98B
21E121So1-100
21E121So8-91
21Exh-169
21KoBreWSI-23
21Nei-94
22E120-193
22W575-129
22WilPatV-33
23W501-66
23W503-7
23W515-44
25Exh-38
26Exh-35
40PlaBal-159
91ConTSN-232
93ConTSN-870
Snyder, Randy
89StoPorB-17
89StoPorCLC-170
89StoPorP-382
89StoPorS-16
90BelBreB-13
90BelBreS-21
90Bes-215
90MidLeaASGS-18
91StoPorC-14
91StoPorP-3035
92SalLakTSP-14
93HigDesMC-19
93HigDesMF-46
95SalAvaTI-1
Snyder, Russ
60A'sTeal-15
60Lea-102
60Top-81
60TopVen-81
61SevElev-7
61Top-143
62SalPlaC-206
62ShiPlaC-206
62Top-64
62TopVen-64
63Jel-63
63Pos-63
63Top-543
64Top-126
64TopVen-126
65OPC-204
65Top-204
66Top-562
67CokCapO-6
67DexPre-195
67Top-405
68Top-504
69MilBra-258
69OPC-201
69Top-201
69TopFou-13
69TopTeaP-13
70BreMcD-28
70BreMil-23
70OPC-347
70Top-347
71MLBOffS-452
71OPC-653
71Top-653
72MilBra-320
78TCM60I-136
81Ori6F-30
91OriCro-431
94BreMilB-274
Soar, Hank
55Bow-279
Soares, Todd
88JacExpP-978
91KisDodP-4196
Sobbe, William
81VerBeaDT-19
Sobczyk, Bob
88BelBreGS-11
89BoiHawP-1993
Sobik, Trad
94BriTigC-24
94BriTigF-3502
95FayGenTI-25
96LakTigB-27
Sobkoviak, Jeff
93BenRocC-25
93BenRocF-3269
94AshTouC-20
94AshTouF-1779
95SalAvaTI-3
Sobocienski, Adam
92Min-19
Sobolewski, Mark
92SouOreAC-5
92SouOreAF-3428
93ModA'sC-19
93ModA'sF-810
94HunStaF-1339
95HunStaTI-25
Socko, Mascot
96SarRedSB-30
Sodders, Mike
82TolMudHT-18
83OrlTwiT-9
88GenCubP-1642
89PeoChiTI-10
91ChaKniLD-142
91ChaKniP-1688
91LinDriAA-142
92ChaKniF-2770
92ChaKniS-165
Sodders, Randy
89WytCubS-24
Soden, Chad
95EveAqaTI-24
96WisTimRB-24
Soderholm, Dale
74TacTwiC-2
76TacTwiDQ-19
77OrlTwiT-19
Soderholm, Eric
73TacTwiC-19
73OPC-577
73Top-577
74OPC-503
74Top-503
75OPC-54
75Top-54
76Kel-28
76OPC-214
76SSP-223
76Top-214
77Top-273
77WhiSoxJT-12
78Hos-20
78Kel-32
78OPC-21
78SSP270-148
78Top-602
79Hos-103
79OPC-93
79Top-186
80Top-441
81Don-106
81Fle-92
81Top-383
90SweBasG-98
91LinDri-6
91SweBasG-85
92YanWIZ8-184
93RanKee-336
Soderstrom, Steve
91FreStaBS-12
94Cla-165
94ClaGolF-161
94ClaGolN1PLF-LP14
94ClaGolREF-RE14
94ColC-24
94ColChoGS-24
94ColChoSS-24
94SanJosGC-1
94SanJosGF-2816
94Ult-594
94UppDec-533
94UppDecED-533
94UppDecML-189
95SPML-147
96BesAutS-86
96Bow-155
96PhoFirB-24
97Bow-357
97BowInt-357
97UppDec-288
Sodowsky, Clint
92BriTigC-11
92BriTigF-1412
93FayGenC-22
93FayGenF-129
94FloStaLAF-FSL15
94LakTigC-21
94LakTigF-3036
95JacSunTI-26
96Fle-120
96FleTif-120
96TolMudHB-27
96Top-429
Soff, Ray
80QuaCitCT-7
81QuaCitCT-23
83MidCubT-22
84MidCubT-9
86ArkTraP-23
86LouRedTI-26
87CarSmo-1
87Don-631
87Fle-309
87FleGlo-309
87LouRedTI-27
87OPC-96
87Top-671A
87Top-671B
87TopTif-671A
87TopTif-671B
88PorBeaC-7
88PorBeaP-662
89PorBeaC-5
89PorBeaP-216
90CMC-361
90ProAAAF-275
90TidTidC-10
90TidTidP-544
90TopTVM-61
91LinDriAAA-568
91TidTidLD-568
91TidTidP-2509
92EdmTraS-166
Sofield, Rick
77VisOakT-14
79Top-709
80Top-669
80VenLeaS-32
81Don-592
81Fle-563
81OPC-278
81Top-278
82TolMudHT-21
82Top-42
96WesPalBEB-2
Softy, Mark
77ForLauYS-11
79WesHavYT-16
80WauTimT-9
Soh, Katsuo
87JapPlaB-20
Sohn, Young Chul
91KisDodP-4184
Sohns, Thomas
79NaSouTI-23
80WatRedT-16
Sojo, Luis
87MyrBeaBJP-1463
88MyrBeaBJP-1189
88SouAtlLAGS-18
89SyrChiC-22
89SyrChiMB-21
89SyrChiP-809
90Bow-517
90BowTif-517
90CMC-344
90FleUpd-129
90Lea-291
90OPC-594
90ProAAAF-360
90SyrChiC-18
90SyrChiMB-23
90SyrChiP-580
90Top-594
90TopTif-594
90TriAllGP-AAA3
91AngSmo-15
91Bow-197
91Don-579
91Fle-184
91Lea-367
91OPC-26
91OPCPre-114
91Sco-342
91Sco100RS-43
91ScoRoo-49T
91StaClu-507
91Top-26
91TopDeb90-146
91TopDesS-26
91TopMic-26
91TopTif-26
91TopTra-112T
91TopTraT-112T
91UltUpd-12
91UppDec-297
91UppDec-714
92Bow-418
92Don-302
92EdmTraS-167
92Fle-70
92Lea-5
92OPC-206
92PanSti-6
92Pin-223
92Sco-127
92StaClu-373
92Top-206
92TopGol-206
92TopGolW-206
92TopMic-206
92Ult-31
92UppDec-149
93BluJayD-24
93BluJayFS-25
93Don-137
93Fle-198
93LinVenB-100
93OPC-338
93PacSpa-655
93PanSti-28
93Sco-124
93Sel-77
93StaClu-27
93StaCluFDI-27
93StaCluMOP-27
93Top-347
93TopGol-347
93TopInaM-347
93TopMic-347
93UppDec-94
93UppDec-802
93UppDecGold-94
93UppDecGold-802
94CalCanF-799
94VenLinU-108
95ColCho-286
95ColChoGS-286
95ColChoSS-286
95Fle-277
95LinVen-164
95LinVen-284
95MarMot-20
95MarPac-3
95MarPac-43
95Sco-470
95ScoGolR-470
95ScoPlaTS-470
95Top-583
95TopCyb-356
96ColCho-728
96ColChoGS-728
96ColChoSS-728
96Don-409
96DonPreP-409
96Fle-244
96FleTif-244
96LeaSigEA-186
96MarMot-19
96Pac-411
96Sco-475
96StaClu-68
96StaCluMOP-68
96Ult-415
96UltGolM-415
96UppDec-462
Solaita, Tony
72Dia-41
75OPC-389
75Top-389
76OPC-121
76SSP-173
76Top-121
77Top-482
78AngFamF-35
78SSP270-215
78Top-557
79ExpPos-26
79Top-18
80OPC-212
80Top-407
92YanWIZ6-119
Solano, Fausto
94St.CatBJC-24
94St.CatBJF-3654
95DunBluJTI-27
95StCatSTI-21
96HagSunB-20
Solano, Julio
83TucTorT-11
84TucTorC-63
85AstMot-12
85DomLeaS-87
85Fle-363
85Top-353
85TopTif-353
86AstPol-16
87AstPol-18
88MarMot-24
89MarMot-26
Solano, Ramon
87FayGenP-6
Solarte, Jose
88JamExpP-1912
93LinVenB-95
94VenLinU-202
95LinVen-57
Solimine, Joe
90UtiBluSP-7
91SouBenWSP-2861
Solis, Julio
85MiaHur-16
Solis, Marcelino
59Top-214
Soliz, Steve
93WatIndC-26
93WatIndF-3566
94CarLeaAF-CAR36
94KinIndC-17
94KinIndF-2648
95BakBlaTI-26
96CanIndB-24
Sollecito, Gabe
93NiaFalRF-3391
94FayGenC-24
94FayGenF-2147
Solo, Julio
89PacSenL-50
Solomon, Buddy (Eddie)
74AlbDukTI-71
74AlbDukTI-19
75OPC-624
75Top-624
78Top-598
79OPC-74
79Top-156
80Top-346
81Don-16
81Fle-384
81Top-298
82Don-437
82Fle-498
82Top-73
82Top-696
90DodTar-754
Solomon, David
94BilMusF-3670
94BilMusSP-21
Solomon, Ray
93LetMouF-4150
93LetMouSP-19
Solomon, Steve
92BatCliC-17
92BatCliF-3279
93ClaGolF-153
94ClePhiC-25
94ClePhiF-2542
95ReaPhiELC-33
95ReaPhiTI-27
Solseth, David
89EugEmeB-12
90AppFoxBS-25
90AppFoxP-2099
91BasCitRC-16
91BasCitRP-1402
Soltero, Saul
87SpoIndP-4
88ChaRaiP-1215
89RivRedWB-16
89RivRedWCLC-31
89RivRedWP-1406
89WicStaR-23
89WicUpdR-9
92ChaRaiC-19
92ChaRaiF-120
94SprSulC-29
94SprSulF-2053
96RanCucQB-4
Solters, Moose (Julius)
34DiaMatCSB-165
34DiaStaR-85
34Gou-30
34GouCanV-77
36GouWidPPR-B20

36GouWidPPR-C22
38GouHeaU-255
38GouHeaU-279
39PlaBal-78
39WhiSoxTI-18
40PlaBal-126
40WhiSoxL-18
41DouPlaR-71
81ConTSN-34
91ConTSN-285
Soma, Katsuya
83SanJosBC-18
Somers, Charles A.
09SpoNewSM-100
Somers, P.T.
87OldJudN-473
Sommer, David
87WytCubP-6
89JamExpP-2144
90WesPalBES-21
91LinDriAA-642
91WilBilLD-642
91WilBilP-291
Sommer, Joseph J.
87OldJudN-474
Sommers, Denny (Dennis)
75LafDriT-30
82Ind-30
82IndBurK-10
82IndBurK-11
82IndBurK-12
82IndTeal-28
82IndWhe-28
83IndPos-31
83IndWhe-25
84Ind-27
84IndWhe-NNO
85Ind-30
85IndPol-NNO
88PadSmo-27
90PadMag-22
93GiaMot-28
94GiaMot-28
Sommers, Joseph A.
87OldJudN-475
Sommers, Scott
86ElmPioRSP-22
88LynRedSS-23
89NewBriRSP-623
89NewBriRSS-19
89Sta-130
Sonberg, Erik
85AlbDukC-159
89HagSunB-18
89HagSunP-267
Sondrini, Joe
91AugPirC-26
91AugPirP-815
92Bow-211
92ProFS7-310
92SalBucC-16
92SalBucF-73
93CarMudF-2065
Song, Koo Hong
90IBAWorA-38
Songer, Don
94ConTSN-1303
94ConTSNB-1303
Songini, Mike (Michael)
88BilMusP-1829
89GreHorP-421
90EriSaiS-24
91RenSilSCLC-21
Sonneberger, Steve
88HagSunS-20
Sontag, Alan
86OrlTwiP-18
87OrlTwiP-23
91MidAngOHP-28
91PalSprAP-2013
92SalSpuC-11
92SalSpuF-3753
Soo, Sang
96WesOahCHWB-26
Soos, Charles
87KinIndP-4
88KinIndS-20
Soper, Mike
83BurRanT-11
86ColCliP-23
86ColCliP-24
90CalLeaACLC-52
90RenSilSCLC-277
91CarLeaAP-CAR20
91KinIndC-12
91KinIndP-324
92CanIndS-118
92ProFS7-54
92SkyAA F-55
93CanIndF-2839
93LinVenB-84
94CarLeaA-DJ19
Soper, Steve
94MedHatBJF-3689
94MedHatBJSP-2
Sorakichi, Matsada
87AllandGN-37
Sorce, Sam
83BurRanF-3
83BurRanT-22
85OrlTwiT-11
86OrlTwiP-19
Sordo, Ed
96GreFalDTI-13
Sorel, Mike
81CedRapRT-14
Sorensen, Lary
77SpoIndC-19
78Top-569
79OPC-152
79Top-303
80OPC-84
80Top-154
81AllGamPI-177
81CokTeaS-129
81Don-325
81Fle-519
81Top-379
81TopTra-831
82Don-246
82Fle-128
82Ind-31
82IndTeal-29
82IndWhe-18
82OPC-136
82Top-689
82TopTra-111T
83Don-363
83Fle-418
83FleSti-244
83IndPos-32
83IndWhe-26
83OPC-48
83Top-48
84A'sMot-14
84Don-635
84Fle-549
84FleUpd-109
84Nes792-286
84Nes792-546
84OPC-286
84Top-286
84Top-546
84TopSti-259
84TopTif-286
84TopTif-546
84TopTra-111T
84TopTraT-111T
85CubLioP-22
85CubSev-42
85Don-131
85Fle-434
85FleUpd-108
86Fle-381
86Top-744
86TopTif-744
87ExpPos-28
87FleUpd-111
87FleUpdG-111
88ChaLooB-20
90SweBasG-63
94BreMilB-275
Sorensen, Todd
93KanCouCC-29
94PorSeaDTI-6
93KanCouCTI-22
Sorey, Ron
75WesPalBES-27
78DunBluJT-22
Sorg, Jay
94PriRedC-25
94PriRedF-3274
95BilRedTI-7
Soriano, Fred
94ModA'sC-21
94ModA'sF-3071
95WesMicWTI-6
96ModA'sB-2
Soriano, Hilario
77CliDodT-24
85DomLeaS-156
Soriano, Jose
94SouOreAC-27
95WesMicWTI-14
96WesMicWB-26
Soriano, Tony
47RemBre-24
Soroko, Mark
76AshTouT-23
77TucTorC-45
Sorrel, Mike
82ChaRoyT-3
Sorrell, Billy
66Top-254
66TopVen-254
67Top-341
70RoyTeal-33
71OPC-17
71Top-17
Sorrell, Vic
33Gou-15
33GouCanV-15
35TigFreP-19
36WorWidGV-21
76TigOldTS-21
92ConTSN-577
Sorrento, Paul
87PalSprP-11
88PalSprACLC-110
88PalSprAP-1450
89BasAmeAPB-AA19
89OrlTwiB-1
89OrlTwiP-1343
89SouLeaAJ-13
90Bow-421
90BowTif-421
90CMC-577
90Don-420
90PorBeaC-25
90PorBeaP-189
90ProAAAF-259
90Sco-647
90TopDeb89-119
90TopTra-119T
90TopTraT-119T
90UppDec-784
91Don-745
91LinDriAAA-420
91OPC-654
91PorBeaLD-420
91PorBeaP-1574
91Sco-796
91Sco100RS-44
91StaClu-408
91Top-654
91TopDesS-654
91TopMic-654
91TopTif-654
91UppDec-680
92Don-752
92Fle-218
92FleUpd-18
92IndFanC-27
92Lea-401
92OPC-546
92StaClu-707
92Stu-169
92Top-546
92TopGol-546
92TopGolW-546
92TopMic-546
92TopTra-108T
92TopTraG-108T
92Ult-357
93Bow-501
93Don-229
93Fla-199
93Fle-221
93IndWUA-29
93Lea-105
93PacBeiA-6
93PacSpa-102
93PanSti-55
93Pin-320
93Sco-194
93Sel-226
93SP-126
93StaClu-194
93StaCluFDI-194
93StaCluMOP-194
93Stu-67
93Top-264
93TopGol-264
93TopInaM-264
93TopMic-264
93Ult-191
93UppDec-196
93UppDecGold-196
94Bow-83
94ColC-262
94ColChoGS-262
94ColChoSS-262
94Don-536
94ExtBas-68
94Fin-185
94FinPre-185P
94FinRef-185
94Fla-44
94Fle-120
94Lea-361
94Pac-184
94PanSti-60
94Pin-308
94PinArtP-308
94PinMusC-308
94Sco-473
94ScoGolR-473
94Sel-358
94StaClu-636
94StaCluFDI-636
94StaCluGR-636
94StaCluMOP-636
94Stu-96
94Top-358
94TopGol-358
94TopSpa-358
94TriPla-119
94Ult-48
94UppDec-363
94UppDecED-363
95ColCho-267
95ColChoGS-267
95ColChoSS-267
95Don-510
95DonPreP-510
95DonTopotO-67
95Fin-270
95FinRef-270
95Fla-36
95Fle-148
95Lea-43
95LeaLim-168
95Pac-129
95Pin-84
95PinArtP-84
95PinMusC-84
95Sco-396
95ScoGolR-396
95ScoPlaTS-396
95StaClu-220
95StaCluFDI-220
95StaCluMOP-220
95StaCluSTWS-220
95StaCluVR-111
95Top-132
95TopCyb-82
95Ult-282
95UltGolM-282
96Cir-82
96CirRav-82
96ColCho-126
96ColCho-727
96ColChoGS-126
96ColChoGS-727
96ColChoSS-126
96ColChoSS-727
96Don-290
96DonPreP-290
96EmoXL-118
96Fin-B213
96FinRef-B213
96Fla-165
96Fle-100
96FleTif-100
96FleUpd-U84
96FleUpdTC-U84
96LeaSigA-211
96LeaSigAG-211
96LeaSigAS-211
96MarMot-17
96MetUni-111
96MetUniP-111
96Pac-306
96Pin-68
96Sco-189
96StaClu-135
96StaCluEPB-135
96StaCluEPG-135
96StaCluEPS-135
96StaCluMOP-135
95StaCluVRMC-111
96Top-373
96TopGal-37
96TopGalPPI-37
96Ult-416
96UltGolM-416
96UppDec-459
97Cir-294
97CirRav-294
97ColCho-483
97Don-123
97DonLim-102
97DonLimLE-102
97DonPreP-123
97DonPrePGold-123
97DonTea-140
97DonTeaSPE-140
97Fin-79
97FinRef-79
97Fle-214
97FleTif-214
97MetUni-150
97NewPin-99
97NewPinAP-99
97NewPinMC-99
97NewPinPP-99
97Pac-193
97PacLigB-193
97PacPri-66
97PacPriLB-66
97PacPriP-66
97PacSil-193
97Sco-136
97ScoMar-4
97ScoMarPl-4
97ScoMarPr-4
97ScoPreS-136
97ScoShoS-136
97ScoShoSAP-136
97StaClu-345
97StaCluMOP-345
97Top-423
97TopGal-78
97TopGalPPI-78
97UppDec-502
Sortedahl, John
96BelSnaTI-35
Sosa, Brian
93BelMarC-25
93BelMarF-3207
Sosa, Elias
72Dia-42
74OPC-54
74Top-54
74TopSta-109
75OPC-398
75Top-398
76OPC-364
76SSP-7
76Top-364
77Top-558
78Top-694
79ExpPos-27
79Top-78
80ExpPos-29
80OPC-153
80Top-293
81Don-599
81Fle-151
81OPC-181
81Top-181
82Don-446
82Fle-208
82OPC-116
82Top-414
82TopTra-112T
83Don-259
83Fle-342
83Top-753
83TopFol-4
83TopTra-107T
84Fle-313
84Nes792-503
84Top-503
84TopTif-503
87SanJosBP-18
89PacSenL-8
89SumBraP-1093
89T/MSenL-97
89TopSenL-45

90DodTar-755
90EliSenL-14
91PacSenL-137
92MClAmb-11
95BelGiaTI-34
96BelGiaTI-35

Sosa, Franklin
96FayGenB-27

Sosa, Helpis
95WesMicWTI-27

Sosa, Jose
90PriPatD-21
92AugPirC-19
92AugPirF-238
93AugPirC-20
93AugPirF-1544
94AugGreC-23
94AugGreF-3010

Sosa, Jose Y.
73CedRapAT-16
74CedRapAT-24
76OPC-591
76Top-591
78ChaChaT-15

Sosa, Juan
95YakBeaTI-28
96SavSanB-21

Sosa, Miguel
80AndBraT-24
81DurBulT-1
82DurBulT-9
85IntLeaAT-3
85RicBraT-17
86AlbYanT-4
86ColCliP-25

Sosa, Sammy
87GasRanP-29
88ChaRanS-23
89BasAmeAPB-AA29
89DonBasB-324
89TulDriGS-25
89TulDriTI-24
90Bow-312
90BowTif-312
90ClaBlu-140
90Don-489
90DonBesA-104
90Fle-548
90FleCan-548
90Hot50RS-43
90Lea-220
90OPC-692
90Sco-558
90Sco100RS-35
90ScoYouS2-25
90Spo-81
90StaFS7-61
90Top-692
90TopBig-286
90TopDeb89-120
90TopTif-692
90TulDriDGB-31
90UppDec-17
90WhiSoxC-23
91Bow-350
91ClaGam-60
91Don-147
91Fle-136
91Lea-321
91MajLeaCP-16
91OPC-414
91PanFreS-316
91Sco-256
91StaClu-6
91Stu-38
91Top-414
91TopDesS-414
91TopMic-414
91TopTif-414
91Ult-82
91UppDec-265
91WhiSoxK-25
92Bow-116
92Cla2-T27
92CubMar-21
92Don-740
92Fle-98
92FleUpd-77
92Lea-412
92OPC-94
92OPCPre-120
92PanSti-129
92Pin-369
92PinTea2-55
92Sco-258
92ScoRoo-23T
92StaClu-628
92Stu-20
92Top-94
92TopGol-94
92TopGolW-94
92TopMic-94
92TopTra-109T
92TopTraG-109T
92Ult-476
92UppDec-438
92UppDec-723
93Bow-636
93CubMar-26
93Don-186
93Fin-79
93FinRef-79
93Fla-22
93FlaPro-8
93Fle-27
93FunPac-85
93Lea-70
93LimRocDWB-31
93PacBeiA-19
93PacBeiA-20
93PacSpa-383
93PanSti-208
93Pin-145
93RanKee-337
93Sco-143
93Sel-165
93SP-89
93StaClu-531
93StaCluCu-2
93StaCluFDI-531
93StaCluMOP-531
93Stu-121
93Top-156
93TopGol-156
93TopInaM-156
93TopMic-156
93TriPla-151
93Ult-24
93UppDec-127
93UppDec-819
93UppDecGold-127
93UppDecGold-819
94Bow-82
94BowBes-R70
94BowBesR-R70
94ColC-263
94ColChoGS-263
94ColChoSS-263
94Don-337
94DonSpeE-337
94ExtBas-224
94Fin-236
94FinJum-236
94FinRef-236
94Fla-363
94Fle-399
94FUnPac-162
94Lea-98
94LeaL-92
94OPC-161
94Pac-112
94PacGolP-19
94PanSti-158
94Pin-3
94PinArtP-3
94PinMusC-3
94PinPowS-PS7
94PinSam-3
94ProMag-23
94Sco-510
94ScoGolR-510
94Sel-58
94SP-72
94SPDieC-72
94SPHol-37
94SPHolDC-37
94Spo-81
94SpoMov-MM7
94StaClu-80
94StaCluFDI-80
94StaCluGR-80
94StaCluMOP-80
94StaCluMOP-ST2
94StaCluST-ST2
94StaCluTFDI-347
94Stu-64
94Top-725
94TopBlaG-42
94TopGol-725
94TopSpa-725
94TriPla-78
94Ult-464
94UppDec-268
94UppDec-510
94UppDecAJ-30
94UppDecAJG-30
94UppDecED-268
94UppDecED-510
95Baz-4
95Bow-372
95BowBes-R35
95BowBesJR-8
95BowBesR-R35
95ClaPhoC-12
95ColCho-210
95ColChoGS-210
95ColChoSE-85
95ColChoSEGS-85
95ColChoSESS-85
95ColChoSS-210
95DenHol-26
95Don-122
95DonDiaK-DK14
95DonPreP-122
95DonTopotO-205
95Emo-113
95Fin-197
95FinPowK-PK12
95FinRef-197
95Fla-334
95Fle-424
95FleTeaL-16
95Kra-29
95Lea-272
95LeaLim-188
95Pac-79
95PacLatD-33
95PacPri-26
95Pin-230
95PinArtP-230
95PinFan-22
95PinMusC-230
95PinUps-US12
95Sco-34
95ScoGolR-34
95ScoHaloG-HG31
95ScoPlaTS-34
95Sel-126
95SelArtP-126
95SelCer-84
95SelCerMG-84
95SP-35
95SPCha-27
95SPCha-30
95SPChaDC-27
95SPChaDC-30
95Spo-52
95SpoArtP-52
95SPSil-35
95SPSpeF-30
95StaClu-174
95StaClu-238
95StaClu-497
95StaCluCC-CC17
95StaCluFDI-174
95StaCluFDI-238
95StaCluMOP-174
95StaCluMOP-238
95StaCluMOP-497
95StaCluMOP-CC17
95StaCluSTWS-174
95StaCluSTWS-238
95StaCluSTWS-497
95StaCluVR-91
95Stu-78
95Sum-44
95SumNthD-44
95TomPiz-30
95Top-11
95TopCyb-9
95UC3-91
95UC3ArtP-91
95Ult-139
95UltGolM-139
95UppDec-315
95UppDecED-315
95UppDecEDG-315
95UppDecSE-123
95UppDecSEG-123
95Zen-98
96Baz-20
96Bow-105
96BowBes-48
96BowBesAR-48
96BowBesR-48
96Cir-112
96CirAcc-16
96CirBos-30
96CirRav-112
96ColCho-106
96ColCho-277
96ColCho-403
96ColCho-490
96ColChoCtG-CG9
96ColChoCtG-CG9B
96ColChoCtG-CG9C
96ColChoCtGE-CR9
96ColChoCtGG-CG9
96ColChoCtGG-CG9B
96ColChoCtGG-CG9C
96ColChoCtGGE-CR9
96ColChoGS-106
96ColChoGS-277
96ColChoGS-403
96ColChoGS-490
96ColChoSS-106
96ColChoSS-277
96ColChoSS-403
96ColChoSS-490
96ColChoYMtP-39
96ColChoYMtP-39A
96ColChoYMtPGS-39
96ColChoYMtPGS-39A
96DenHolGS-5
96DenHolGSAP-5
96Don-334
96DonPreP-334
96EmoLegoB-9
96EmoXL-160
96Fin-B257
96Fin-G347
96Fin-S171
96FinRef-B257
96FinRef-G347
96FinRef-S171
96Fla-225
96FlaPow-8
96Fle-330
96FleCub-17
96FleGolM-2
96FleLumC-9
96FleTeaL-16
96FleTif-330
96FleUpd-U242
96FleUpdTC-U242
96Lea-112
96LeaAllGMC-3
96LeaAllGMCG-3
96LeaGolS-3
96LeaLim-5
96LeaLimG-5
96LeaLimL-2
96LeaLimLB-2
96LeaPre-17
96LeaPreP-17
96LeaPrePB-112
96LeaPrePG-112
96LeaPrePS-112
96LeaPreSG-32
96LeaPreSte-32
96LeaSig-24
96LeaSigEA-187
96LeaSigEACM-28
96LeaSigPPG-24
96LeaSigPPP-24
96MetUni-146
96MetUniHM-7
96MetUniP-146
96Pac-21
96PacBaeS-8
96PacEstL-EL30
96PacGolCD-DC14
96PacPri-P13
96PacPriFB-FB17
96PacPriG-P13
96PanSti-48
96Pin-92
96Pin-140
96Pin-263
96PinAfi-67
96PinAfi-158
96PinAfiAP-67
96PinAfiAP-158
96PinAfiFPP-67
96PinAfiMN-10
96PinArtP-53
96PinArtP-67
96PinArtP-163
96PinFoil-263
96PinPow-10
96PinSlu-10
96PinSta-53
96PinSta-67
96PinSta-163
96PinTeaP-7
96ProSta-40
96Sco-336
96ScoDugC-B61
96ScoDugCAP-B61
96ScoGolS-20
96ScoPowP-15
96ScoTitT-14
96Sel-26
96Sel-157
96SelArtP-26
96SelArtP-157
96SelCer-59
96SelCerAP-59
96SelCerCB-59
96SelCerCR-59
96SelCerIP-3
96SelCerMB-59
96SelCerMG-59
96SelCerMR-59
96SelCerSF-1
96SelClaTF-8
96SelEnF-9
96SelTeaN-15
96SP-51
96SPMarM-MM16
96SPMarMDC-16
96Spo-57
96Spo-104
96SpoArtP-57
96SpoArtP-104
96SpoDouT-11
96SpoHitP-9
96SpoPowS-8
96SPPreF-8
96SPSpeFX-33
96SPSpeFXDC-33
96SPx-13
96SPxGol-13
96StaClu-370
96StaCluB&B-BB1
96StaCluEPB-370
96StaCluEPG-370
96StaCluEPS-370
96StaCluMO-39
96StaCluMOP-370
96StaCluMOP-BB1
96StaCluMOP-PS10
96StaCluPS-PS10
95StaCluVRMC-91
96Stu-43
96StuPrePB-43
96StuPrePG-43
96StuPrePS-43
96Sum-87
96Sum-159
96SumAbo&B-87
96SumAbo&B-159
96SumArtP-87
96SumArtP-159
96SumBigB-13
96SumBigBM-13
96SumFoi-87
96SumFoi-159
96SumHitI-5
96SumPos-9
96TeaOut-77
96TeaOut-C95
96Top-252
96TopChr-99
96TopChrR-99
96TopGal-17
96TopGalE-12
96TopGalPPI-17
96TopLas-14
96TopLasPC-15
96TopMysF-M15
96TopMysFR-M15
96TopPro-NL9
96Ult-171
96UltGolM-171
96UltRBIK-8
96UltRBIKGM-8
96UppDec-35
96UppDecDD-DD13

96UppDecDDG-DD13
96UppDecDDS-DD13
96UppDecHC-HC17
96UppDecPD-PD16
96UppDecPRE-R37
96UppDecPRE-R48
96UppDecPreR-R37
96UppDecPreR-R48
96UppDecRunP-RP17
96Zen-100
96Zen-148
96ZenArtP-100
96ZenArtP-148
96ZenDiaC-12
96ZenDiaCP-12
96ZenMoz-6
96ZenZ-18
97Bow-52
97BowBes-83
97BowBesAR-83
97BowBesR-83
97BowChr-40
97BowChrI-40
97BowChrIR-40
97BowChrR-40
97BowInt-52
97BowIntB-BBI6
97BowIntBAR-BBI6
97BowIntBR-BBI6
97Cir-275
97CirRav-275
97ColCho-65
97ColChoAC-32
97ColChoCtG-8A
97ColChoCtG-8B
97ColChoCtG-8C
97ColChoCtGIW-CG8
97ColChoNF-NF19
97ColChoNF-NF20
97ColChoPP-PP13
97ColChoPPG-PP13
97ColChoS-21
97ColChoTBS-14
97ColChoTBSWH-14
97ColChoTotT-T9
97Don-15
97Don-442
97DonDom-14
97DonEli-31
97DonEli-3
97DonEliGS-31
97DonLim-59
97DonLim-68
97DonLim-195
97DonLimFotG-7
97DonLimLE-59
97DonLimLE-68
97DonLimLE-195
97DonLonL-11
97DonPowA-22
97DonPowADC-22
97DonPre-115
97DonPre-195
97DonPreCttC-115
97DonPreCttC-195
97DonPreP-15
97DonPreP-442
97DonPrePGold-15
97DonPrePGold-442
97DonPreTBG-23
97DonPreTF-23
97DonPreTP-23
97Fin-20
97Fin-168
97Fin-277
97FinEmb-168
97FinEmb-277
97FinEmbR-168
97FinEmbR-277
97FinRef-20
97FinRef-168
97FinRef-277
97FlaSho-A34
97FlaSho-B34
97FlaSho-C34
97FlaShoLC-34
97FlaShoLC-B34
97FlaShoLC-C34
97FlaShoLCM-A34
97FlaShoLCM-B34
97FlaShoLCM-C34
97Fle-284
97FleLumC-16
97FleTif-284
97Lea-121
97Lea-361
97LeaFraM-121
97LeaFraM-361
97LeaFraMDC-121
97LeaFraMDC-361
97LeaLeaotN-7
97LeaWarT-15
97MetUni-15
97NewPin-2
97NewPinAP-2
97NewPinMC-2
97NewPinPP-2
97Pac-259
97PacLatotML-25
97PacLigB-259
97PacPri-89
97PacPriGA-GA21
97PacPriLB-89
97PacPriP-89
97PacSil-259
97Pin-194
97PinArtP-194
97PinCar-8
97PinCer-35
97PinCerLI-7
97PinCerMBlu-35
97PinCerMG-35
97PinCerMR-35
97PinCerR-35
97PinIns-2
97PinInsCE-2
97PinInsDE-2
97PinInsFS-13
97PinMin-17
97PinMinB-17
97PinMinCB-17
97PinMinCG-17
97PinMinCGR-17
97PinMinCN-17
97PinMinCS-17
97PinMinG-17
97PinMinS-17
97PinMusC-194
97PinPasttM-15
97PinTotCPB-35
97PinTotCPG-35
97PinTotCPR-35
97PinX-P-73
97PinX-PF&A-11
97PinX-PMoS-73
97PinX-PMP-16
97PinX-PSfF-51
97PinX-PSfFU-51
97ProMag-7
97ProMagML-7
97Sco-244
97ScoBla-15
97ScoFra-8
97ScoFraG-8
97ScoHigZ-8
97ScoPreS-244
97ScoShoS-244
97ScoShoSAP-244
97ScoSteS-12
97ScoTitT-7
97Sel-14
97SelArtP-14
97SelRegG-14
97SelTooотT-14
97SelTooотTMB-14
97SkyE-X-63
97SkyE-XC-63
97SkyE-XEC-63
97SP-40
97SPInsI-13
97SPMarM-MM20
97SpoIll-94
97SpoIllEE-94
97SPSpeF-20
97SPSpxF-4
97SPSPxFA-4
97SPx-16
97SPxBro-16
97SPxGraF-16
97SPxSil-16
97SPxSte-16
97StaClu-40
97StaCluMat-40
97StaCluMOP-40
97Stu-37
97StuMasS-19
97StuMasS8-19
97StuPrePG-37
97StuPrePS-37
97Top-305
97TopChr-102
97TopChrR-102
97TopGal-84
97TopGalPPI-84
97TopHobM-HM19
97TopIntF-ILM5
97TopIntFR-ILM5
97TopScr-18
97TopSta-10
97TopStaAM-10
93TulDriTI-30
97Ult-169
97UltChe-A9
97UltDouT-12
97UltGolME-169
97UltHitM-17
97UltHRK-9
97UltPlaME-169
97UltPowP-A10
97UltRBIK-8
97UltSeaC-11
97UppDec-30
97UppDec-189
97UppDecAG-AG12
97UppDecLDC-LD13
97UppDecP-9
97UppDecPP-PP5
97UppDecPPJ-PP5
97UppDecRP-RP13
97UppDecU-15
97Zen-16
97Zen8x1-10
97Zen8x1D-10

Sosh, John
52LavPro-68

Sossamon, Tim (L. Timothy)
86BenPhiC-148
87ChaWheP-23
88ReaPhiP-870
90JacExpP-1375

Soth, Paul
77AppFoxT-24
78AppFoxT-18
79AppFoxT-1

Sothern, Denny
90DodTar-1077

Sothoron, Allen
21Exh-170
22E120-41
22W573-127
27AmeCarE-11
36R31PasP-35
92ConTSN-523

Soto, Ed
86DayBealP-26
87GasRanP-14

Soto, Emison
91ElmPioC-15
91ElmPioP-3286
92WinHavRSF-1782
93ForLauRSC-24
93ForLauRSFP-1601
93LinVenB-228
94VenLinU-216
95LinVen-38

Soto, Fernando
93LinVenB-164
94VenLinU-171

Soto, Jose
86GenCubP-25
89BluOriS-30

Soto, Juan
93HicCraF-1278

Soto, Mario
77IndIndTI-21
78IndIndTI-9
78SSP270-117
78Top-427
79IndIndTI-28
80RedEnq-36
80Top-622
81CokTeaS-47
81Don-63
81Fle-214
81Top-354
81TopSupHT-42
82Don-103
82Fle-83
82FleSta-19
82RedCok-20
82Top-63
83AllGamPI-179
83Don-248
83Fle-603
83FleSta-182
83FleSti-216
83OPC-215
83PerAll-18
83PerAllG-18
83RedYea-36
83Top-215
83Top-351
83TopSti-234
84AllGamPI-90
84Don-428
84Fle-483
84FleSti-79
84FunFooP-61
84Nes792-160
84Nes792-756
84OPC-160
84RedBor-36
84RedEnq-25
84SevCoi-C13
84Top-160
84Top-756
84TopGloA-21
84TopRubD-18
84TopSti-51
84TopTif-160
84TopTif-756
85AllGamPI-178
85Don-19
85Don-184
85DonActA-3
85DonSupD-19
85Fle-552
85FleLimE-36
85FleStaS-86
85FleStaS-116
85GenMilS-11
85IndIndTI-31
85Lea-19
85OPC-131
85RedYea-16
85SevCoi-G13
85Top-495
85TopGloS-37
85TopMin-495
85TopRubD-17
85TopSti-46
85TopSup-21
85TopTif-495
86BasStaB-105
86Don-184
86Fle-192
86FleMin-41
86FleSlu-36
86FleStiC-114
86Lea-119
86OPC-28
86RedTexG-36
86SevCoi-S11
86Spo-168
86Top-725
86TopMinL-42
86TopSti-136
86TopTat-12
86TopTif-725
87Don-82
87Fle-214
87FleGlo-214
87Lea-140
87OPC-11
87Top-517
87TopTif-517
88Top-666
88TopBig-120
88TopTif-666
89Sco-588

Soto, Max
86GleFalTP-22

Soto, Miguel
84SavCarT-24
91GulCoaRSP-27
92IdaFalGF-3517
92IdaFalGSP-23
93LinVenB-109
93MacBraC-23
93MacBraF-1403
94VenLinU-63
95LinVen-193

Soto, Ozzie
85CedRapRT-13
86TamTarP-21

Soto, Rafael
90HunCubP-3294
91PeoChiC-27
91PeoChiP-1351
91PeoChiTI-19
92WinSpiC-3
92WinSpiF-1216
93PeoChiC-19
93PeoChiF-1094
93PeoChiTI-26

Soto, Seferino
95YakBeaTI-29
96GreFalDB-26
96GreFalDTI-14

Soto, Tom
78NewWayCT-41
79HolMilT-10
81VanCanT-23

Sottile, Shaun
89PulBraP-1898
90SumBraB-21
90SumBraP-2431
91DurBulC-22

Souchock, Steve
52Bow-235
52Top-234
53BowC-91
53TigGle-26
54Bow-103
79DiaGre-393
83TopRep5-234

Soult, David
94CliLumF-1980

Sounds, Nashville
79NaSouTI-1

South, Carl
94GreFalDSP-27
95YakBeaTI-30
96SavSanB-23

Southard, Scott
93ElmPioC-20
93ElmPioF-3834
94KanCouCC-23
94KanCouCF-172
94KanCouCTI-26
95BreCouMF-256

Southland, Kip
87EveGiaC-8

Southworth, Bill
19W514-16
21E121So1-101
22E120-134
22W572-103
23W501-90
25Exh-39
27AmeCarE-10
27Exh-32
41CarW75-25
46SpoExcW-9-5
47TipTop-88
49EurSta-24
51Bow-207
80PacLeg-17
91ConTSN-89
92ConTSN-627
93ConTSN-839

Souza, Brian
90HelBreSP-25
91BelBreC-7
91BelBreP-2102
91HelBreSP-24
92BelBreC-8

Souza, Mark
75WatRoyT-28
76WatRoyT-28
77OrlTwiT-20
79OgdA'sT-17
80OgdA'sT-10
81TacTigT-22

Sovern, Jeff
76IndIndTI-8
78IndIndTI-25

Sowards, Ryan
94GreFalDSP-21
95VerBeaDTI-25

Sowards, Van
83CliGiaF-21
84ShrCapFB-20

Sowders, John
87OldJudN-477

Sowders, William J.
87OldJudN-476
88AugBecN-24
88GandBCGCE-36

89N526N7C-15
Sowell, Scott
90MidAngGS-25
96MidAngB-4
Spaan, Tony
90EliTwiS-21
Spade, Matt
94WelPirC-23
94WelPirF-3498
96LynHilB-20
Spade, Robert
09ColChiE-267A
09ColChiE-267B
09T206-331
11SpoLifM-202
12ColRedB-267A
12ColRedB-267B
12ColTinT-267A
12ColTinT-267B
Spagnola, Glen
83CedRapRF-16
83CedRapRT-5
86VerRedP-21
87VerRedP-18
88ColAstB-4
89CalCanC-10
89CalCanP-527
89EasLeaDDP-DD33
89WilBilS-21
Spagnuolo, Joe
87VerBeaDP-3
Spahn, Warren E.
46SpoExcW-9-9
47Exh-214A
47Exh-214B
47StaPinP2-40
47TipTop-89
48BluTin-20
48Bow-18
49Bow-33
49EurSta-25
49Lea-32
50AmeNut&CCP-18
50Bow-19
50Dra-14
50RoyDes-5
51BerRos-B2
51Bow-134
51TopRedB-30
52BasPho-6
52Bow-156
52NatTeaL-33
52RedMan-NL22
52RoyPre-15
52TipTop-41
52Top-33
53BowC-99
53BraJohC-10
53BraSpiaS3-22
53BraSpiaS7-12
53DixLid-22A
53DixLid-22B
53DixPre-22
53ExhCan-32
53MacSta-5
53NorBreL-31
53RedMan-NL19
53Top-147
54BraJohC-21
54BraMer-5
54BraSpiaSP-17
54RedHeaF-30
54RedMan-NL11
54Top-20
55ArmCoi-20
55BraGolS-3
55BraJohC-21
55BraSpiaSD-16
55RedMan-NL10
55Top-31
55TopDouH-127
56BraBilaBP-14
56Top-10
56TopHocF-A10
56TopHocF-B12
56TopPin-19
57BraSpiaS4-18
57Top-90
58BraJayP-12
58HarSta-7
58JayPubA-19
58Top-270
58Top-494
59OklTodML-5
59Top-40A
59Top-40B
59Top-40C
59Top-571
59TopVen-40
60Baz-19
60BraJayP-11
60BraLaktL-24
60BraSpiaS-22
60KeyChal-46
60NuHi-63
60RawGloT-33
60Top-230
60Top-445
60TopTat-49
61Baz-29
61ChePat-9
61NuSco-402
61NuSco-463
61Pos-101A
61Pos-101B
61Raw-11
61SevElev-15
61Top-47
61Top-200
61Top-589
61TopStal-47
62AurRec-15
62Baz-5
62BraJayP-9
62ExhStaB-32
62Top-56
62Top-58
62Top-100
62Top-312
62Top-399
62TopBuc-85
62TopStal-150
62TopVen-56
62TopVen-58
62TopVen-100
63BasMagM-78
63Baz-5
63BraJayP-10
63ExhStaB-60
63Fle-45
63SalMetC-8
63Top-320
63TopStil-41
64Baz-5
64BraJayP-11
64Raw-6
64Top-3
64Top-400
64TopCoi-88
64TopCoi-160
64TopGia-31
64TopSta-57
64TopStaU-69
64TopTatl-68
64TopVen-3
64WheSta-43
65MetJayP-11
65OPC-205
65Top-205
67TopVen-152
68SpoMemAG-4
69EquSpoHoF-BB21
73HalofFPP-16
73MetAllEB-11
73OPC-449
73Top-449A
73Top-449B
74NewYorNTDiS-21
75SSP42-36
76GalBasGHoF-27
76RowExh-14
76ShaPiz-139
76TayBow4-79
77GalGloG-38
77GalGloG-264
77Spo-2323
78AtlCon-22
78BraTCC-12
79BasGre-79
79DiaGre-225
79TCM50-3
80Lau300-15
80MarExh-29
80PacLeg-57
80PerHaloFP-139
80SSPHOF-139
81RedPioT-22
82CraJac-16
82DiaCla-30
82FleSta-108
83ASASpa-1
83ASASpa-2
83ASASpa-3
83ASASpa-4
83ASASpa-5
83ASASpa-6
83ASASpa-7
83ASASpa-8
83ASASpa-9
83ASASpa-10
83ASASpa-11
83ASASpa-12
83Bra53F-21
83MLBPin-34
83TopRep5-33
84OCoandSI-92
84SpoDesPW-19
85DalNatCC-5
85TCMPla1-33
86BraGreT-9
86SpoDecG-27
86TCMSupS-13
87Bra195T-8
87NesDreT-32
88GreBasS-63
88PacLegl-109
89Don-588
89HOFStiB-84
89PerCelP-39
90Col-24
90HOFStiB-68
90PacLeg-51
90PerGreM-14
90PerMasW-21
90PerMasW-22
90PerMasW-23
90PerMasW-24
90PerMasW-25
90SweBasG-12
91Kel3D-12
91MetWIZ-372
91SweBasG-86
91TopArc1-147
92ActPacA-16
92ActPacA2-16G
92ActPacAP-4
92BazQua5A-9
92Zip-1
93ActPacAC-16
93MetIma-18
93TedWil-48
93UppDecAH-116
93UppDecAH-144
94TopArc1-20
94TopArc1G-20
94UppDecAH-90
94UppDecAH-154
94UppDecAH1-90
94UppDecAH1-154
95MrTurBG-5
95SonGre-11
Spain, Dan
78OrlTwiT-20
Spalding, Albert G.
36PC7AlbHoF-26
50CalHOFW-67
63HalofFB-27
75FlePio-4
76ShaPiz-26
77BobParHoF-44
80PerHaloFP-26
80SSPHOF-26
84GalHaloFRL-26
94OriofB-26
94OriofB-62
94UppDecTAE-6
Spalding, Dick
41CubTeal-25
43CubTeal-25
Spalt, Paul
88WatPirP-24
Span, Brian
89ChaRaiP-975
89SpoIndSP-15
Spang, R.J.
92GulCoaMF-3481
Spangler, Al
60BraLaktL-25
60BraSpiaS-23
60Lea-38
60Top-143
60TopVen-143
61Pos-114
61Top-73
62Col.45B-19
62Col45'HC-16
62Col45'JP-12
62Jel-157
62Pos-157
62PosCan-157
62SalPlaC-196
62ShiPlaC-196
62Top-556
62TopStal-130
63Col45"P-13
63Col45"P-19
63Col45'JP-11
63Fle-39
63Jel-185
63Pos-185
63Top-77
64Col.45JP-7
64Top-406
65OPC-164
65Top-164
65TopEmbl-53
65TopTral-70
66OPC-173
66Top-173
66TopVen-173
68Top-451
69CubJewT-18
69CubPho-11
69MilBra-259
69Top-268
70Top-714
72MilBra-321
74OPC-354
74Top-354
78TCM60I-166
78TCM60I-171
87AstSer1-20
87AstSer1-28
87AstShoSO-21
89AstCol4S-23
Spann, Tookie
88BriTigP-1891
89LakTigS-19
90LakTigS-23
92ClaFS7-133
92HigDesMC-13
93WicWraF-2987
Spanswick, Bill
63MilSau-10
64Top-287
64TopVen-287
65Top-356
78TCM60I-147
81RedSoxBG2S-115
Sparesus, Brad
93AlbPolC-29
Sparks, Don
89PriWilCS-19
90AlbYanB-18
90AlbYanP-1042
90AlbYanS-17
90Bes-237
90CMC-736
90EasLeaAP-EL2
90StaFS7-53
91ColCliLD-119
91ColCliP-19
91ColCliP-605
91LinDriAAA-119
92AlbYanF-2234
92AlbYanS-19
92ClaFS7-7
93ClaFS7-25
93ClaGolF-4
93ColCliF-1119
93ColCliP-17
94ColCliF-2961
94ColCliP-25
95ColCliMCTI-24
95ColCliP-28
95ColCliTI-28
96BufBisB-20
Sparks, Greg
86ChaRaiP-23
88HunStaTI-21
89CalLeaA-48
89SalSpuP-1819
90AlbYanB-19
90AlbYanP-1043
90AlbYanS-18
90Bes-252
90EasLeaAP-EL14
91CarMudLD-117
91CarMudP-1095
91LinDriAA-117
92LonTigF-647
92LonTigS-419
93PawRedSDD-25
93PawRedSF-2418
93PawRedSTI-22
94NewHavRF-1559
Sparks, Joe
75IowOakT-18
80OmaRoyP-23
81OmaRoyT-1
82OmaRoyT-25
83OmaRoyT-24
84RedEnq-30
86IndIndTI-3
87IndIndTI-4
88IndIndC-24
88IndIndP-496
88TriAAAP-50
89ExpPos-28
90TopTVY-5
91LinDriAAA-599
91TolMudHLD-599
91TolMudHP-1946
92TolMudHF-1057
92TolMudHS-599
93TolMudHF-1667
94TolMudHF-1040
Sparks, Nathan
89BirBarB-30
Sparks, Rodney
94EugEmeC-21
94EugEmeF-3723
95SprSulTI-27
Sparks, Shane
92AugPirC-2
92AugPirF-239
Sparks, Steve
88BelBreGS-24
89StoPorB-8
89StoPorCLC-152
89StoPorP-390
89StoPorS-11
91ElPasDLD-196
91ElPasDP-2749
91LinDriAA-196
91StoPorP-3031
92ElPasDF-3920
92ElPasDS-221
93NewOrlZF-972
94NewOrlZF-1468
95FleUpd-57
96ColCho-192
96ColChoGS-192
96ColChoSS-192
96Don-3
96DonPreP-3
96Fla-107
96Fle-158
96FleTif-158
96LeaSigEA-188
96Pac-344
96Sco-474
96StaClu-156
96StaCluMOP-156
96Top-279
96Ult-84
96UltGolM-84
96UppDec-121
97ColCho-371
Sparks, Tully
03BreE10-132
08RosComP-145
09ColChiE-268A
09ColChiE-268B
10LuxCigPP-20
10NadE1-52
11SpoLifCW-331
11SpoLifM-240
12ColRedB-268A
12ColRedB-268B
12ColTinT-268A
12ColTinT-268B
Sparling, Don
85Ft.MyeRT-5
87MemChiB-14
87MemChiP-19
Sparma, Blase
92DurBulF-1099
92MacBraC-13
93GreBraF-347

94DurBulC-20
94DurBulF-328
94DurBulTI-22
Sparma, Joe
64Top-512
65Top-587
66Top-267
66TopVen-267
67CokCapTi-5
67DexPre-196
67OPC-13
67TigDexP-8
67Top-13
68CokCapT-5
68TigDetFPB-22
68Top-505
69TigFarJ-2
69TigTealC-8
69Top-488
70MLBOffS-69
70OPC-243
70Top-243
88TigDom-21
Sparrow, Chris
89IdaFalBP-2024
90UtiBluSP-8
Spaulding, Chad
94CarLeaAF-CAR23
Spaulding, Scott
95NewJerCTI-27
Speake, Bob
56Top-66
57Top-339
58Top-437
59Top-526
79DiaGre-124
Speaker, Tris
08AmeCarE-90
08RosComP-182
09AmeCarE-96
09ColChiE-269A
09ColChiE-269B
09MaxPubP-11
09SpoNewSM-21
09T206-332
10CouT21-225
10CouT21-317
10DarChoE-29
10DomDisP-111
10E-UOraBSC-20
10E12AmeCDC-33
10JuJuDE-37
10OrnOvaPP-12
10PeoT21-51
10RedCroT-71
10RedCroT-157
10RedCroT-244
10SepAnoP-22
10SweCapPP-6A
10SweCapPP-6B
11BasBatEU-35
11E94-27
11L1L-131
11MecDFT-22
11PloCanE-58
11S74Sil-3
11S81LarS-106
11SpoLifM-15
11T205-159
11TurRedT-36
12ColRedB-269A
12ColRedB-269B
12ColTinT-269A
12ColTinT-269B
12HasTriFT-23
12HasTriFT-35
12HasTriFT-62
12HasTriFT-63
12HasTriFT-64
12RedSoxBASP-3
12T207-170
13NatGamW-35
13PolGroW-27
13TomBarW-33
14CraJacE-65
14PieStaT-52
14TexTomE-41
15AmeCarE-35
15CraJacE-65
16ColE13-166
16FleBreD-88
17HolBreD-99
19W514-102
20NatCarE-99
21E121So1-102A
21E121So1-102B
21E121So8-92A
21E121So8-92B
21Exh-171
21OxfConE-18
22AmeCarE-67
22E120-42
22W572-104
22W573-128
22W575-130
22WilPatV-13
23W501-19
23W515-28
23W551-9
23WilChoV-156
24MrsShePP-9
25Exh-87
26Exh-86
26SpoComoA-42
27AmeCarE-27
27Exh-64
27YorCarE-28
28StaPlaCE-63
28W502-28
28W512-4
28Yue-28
33Gou-89
34GouCanV-29
36PC7AlbHoF-11
36R31PasP-37
37KelPepS-BB13
40PlaBal-170
48ExhHoF-27
50CalHOFW-68
51R42SmaS-104
51TopConMA-10
60ExhWriH-22
60Fle-10
61Fle-79
61GolPre-30
63BasMagM-79
63BazA-24
63HalofFB-18
67TopVen-156
68SpoMemAG-9
69Baz-4
69Baz-9
72FleFamF-32
72KelATG-11
75McCCob-15
75TCMAllG-33
76GalBasGHoF-28
76ShaPiz-7
76TayBow4-113
77BobParHoF-45
77GalGloG-96
77GalGloG-138
77GalGloG-268
77Ind192T-18
77Ind192T-22
77ShaPiz-22
79Pew-6
79RedSoxEF-17
80PerHaloFP-11
80SSPHOF-11
81ConTSN-14
81SpoHaloF-24
82OhiHaloF-13
83DiaClaS2-81
84GalHaloFRL-7
85Woo-34
86ConSer1-30
86IndGreT-6
86RedSoxGT-10
87HygAllG-42
87NesDreT-6
88ConSer3-27
89HOFStiB-41
90BasWit-72
90SweBasG-45
91ConTSN-44
91SweBasG-140
92ConTSN-422
92ConTSN-591
92ConTSNCI-18
93ActPacA-91
93ActPacA2-25G
93ConMasB-6
93ConTSN-795
93ConTSN-827
93CraJac-6
93TedWil-35
93TedWil-128
93UppDecAH-117
93UppDecAH-161
94ConTSN-1222
94ConTSNB-1222
95ConTSN-1357
95ConTSN-1423
95ConTSNGJ-7
95ConTSNP-1357
93UppDecTR-10
20W516-5
Speakes, Joey
88PocGiaP-2097
Speakman, Tim
85ElmPioT-21
Speakman, Willie
91BelMarC-14
91BelMarP-3669
92PenPilC-13
93BoiHawC-25
93BoiHawF-3920
Spear, Mike
88ButCopKSP-20
Spear, Russell
95IdaFalBTI-6
96CliLumKTI-25
Spearman, Vernon
91YakBeaC-1
91YakBeaP-4261
92ProFS7-249
92VerBeaDC-12
92VerBeaDF-2892
93ClaGolF-180
93ExcFS7-54
93SanAntMF-3019
94SanAntMF-2485
95SanBerSTI-25
96SanAntMB-23
Spearnock, Mike
86SalAngC-99
87PalSprP-1
Speck, R. Cliff
77LynMetT-26
80CarMudF-19
82RocRedWT-6
83RocRedWT-9
86RicBraP-21
87Don-571
87RicBraBC-19
87RicBraC-39
87RicBraT-25
87Top-269
87TopTif-269
88ColCliC-22
88ColCliP-11
88ColCliP-311
Speckenbach, Paul
64Top-548
Specyalski, Brian
88CapCodPPaLP-89
89BenBucL-19
90BoiHawP-3322
Speece, Byron
43CenFlo-22
44CenFlo-21
45CenFlo-23
Speed, Horace
75IntLeaASB-33
75PacCoaLAB-33A
75PacCoaLAB-33B
75PhoGiaC-3
75PhoGiaCK-22
76PheGiaCr-20
76PhoGiaCa-8
76PhoGiaCC-21
76PhoGiaVNB-22
76SSP-112
77PhoGiaCC-22
77PhoGiaCP-22
77PhoGiaVNB-22
79Top-438
80RicBraT-14
Speek, Frank
90JohCitCS-24
91SavCarC-11
91SavCarP-1652
92SprCarC-3
92SprCarF-869
Speer, Kid (George Nathan)
09TigTaCP-16
Speer, V. Floyd
46RemBre-18
47RemBre-14
47SigOil-55
48SigOil-21
48SmiClo-18
Spehr, Tim
90CMC-196
90OmaRoyC-21
90OmaRoyP-69
90ProAAAF-604
91Bow-298
91LinDriAAA-346
91OmaRoyLD-346
91OmaRoyP-1038
91TriA AAGP-AAA28
92Cla1-T84
92Don-689
92Fle-674
92OmaRoyF-2965
92OmaRoyS-347
92OPC-342
92Sco-416
92SkyAAAF-159
92StaClu-96
92Top-342
92TopDeb91-166
92TopGol-342
92TopGolW-342
92TopMic-342
93Don-15
93ExpPosN-21
93UppDec-669
93UppDecGold-669
94Fle-552
94StaClu-515
94StaCluFDI-515
94StaCluGR-515
94StaCluMOP-515
94Top-714
94TopGol-714
94TopSpa-714
94VenLinU-43
95Top-134
96ExpDis-20
96LeaSigEA-189
Speier, Chris
72Kel-28
72OPC-165
72OPC-166
72Top-165
72Top-166
73LinPor-164
73OPC-273
73OPC-345
73Top-273
73Top-345
73TopCanL-49
74Kel-40
74OPC-129
74OPC-335
74Top-129
74Top-335
74TopDecE-29
74TopSta-110
75Hos-73
75HosTwi-73
75OPC-505
75SSPPuzB-24
75Top-505
76Hos-82
76OPC-630
76SSP-105
76Top-630
77BurCheD-108
77ExpPos-28
77Gia-22
77OPC-53
77PepGloD-41
77Top-515
78ExpPos-14
78OPC-232
78Top-221
79OPC-221
79Top-426
80ExpPos-30
80OPC-168
80Top-319
81AllGamPI-115
81Don-329
81ExpPos-15
81Fle-153
81OPC-97
81OPCPos-3
81Top-97
81TopSti-189
82Don-366
82ExpHygM-21
82ExpPos-39
82ExpZel-8
82Fle-209
82FleSta-32
82OPC-198
82Top-198
82TopSti-58
83AllGamPI-115
83Don-266
83ExpStu-27
83Fle-298
83FleSta-183
83FleSti-257
83OPC-121
83Top-768
83TopSti-258
84Don-523
84ExpPos-30
84ExpStu-27
84Fle-288
84GiaMot-22
84Nes792-678
84OPC-328
84Top-678
84TopSti-95
84TopTif-678
85CubLioP-23
85CubSev-28
85FleUpd-109
85Top-577
85TopTif-577
85TopTifT-111T
85TopTra-111T
86CubGat-28
86Fle-382
86OPC-212
86Top-212
86TopTif-212
87Don-392
87Fle-575
87FleGlo-575
87FleUpd-112
87FleUpdG-112
87GiaMot-18
87Top-424
87TopTif-424
87TopTra-115T
87TopTraT-115T
88Don-239
88Fle-96
88FleGlo-96
88GiaMot-18
88Sco-493
88ScoGlo-493
88StaLinG-16
88Top-329
88TopTif-329
89Don-532
89Fle-343
89FleGlo-343
89GiaMot-18
89Sco-297
89Top-94
89TopTif-94
89UppDec-206
90Fle-72
90FleCan-72
90OPC-753
90PubSti-82
90Top-753
90TopTif-753
90VenSti-455
91UppDecS-23
96AriBlaDB-1
95OrlCubF-27
Speier, Justin
96DayCubB-22
96WesOahCHWB-36
Spence, J. Bob
71OPC-186
71Top-186
Spence, John
76BatTroTI-21
Spence, Michael
96TamYanY-23
Spence, Samuel
76BatTroTI-22
77WatIndT-22
78WatIndT-22
Spence, Stan
47Exh-215
48RedSoxTI-21
49Bow-102
60SenUniMC-18

76TayBow4-94
79DiaGre-232
83TCMPla1943-5
95ConTSN-1402
Spencer, Andrew
95AusFut-10
Spencer, Daryl
54Bow-185
56Top-277
57Top-49
58GiaJayP-11
58GiaSFCB-22
58Hir-51
58Top-68
59Top-443
60CarJayP-11
60Lea-129
60MacSta-24
60Top-368
61CarJayP-12
61DodUniO-21
61Pos-173A
61Pos-173B
61Top-357
61Top-451
61TopStaI-95
62DodBelB-20
62Jel-103
62Pos-103
62PosCan-103
62SalPlaC-178A
62SalPlaC-178B
62ShiPlaC-178
62Top-197
62TopStaI-141
63Jel-124
63Pos-124
63RedFreBC-27
63Top-502
79DiaGre-49
79TCM50-226
90DodTar-756
Spencer, George
52BerRos-62
52Top-346
53Top-115
55GiaGolS-11
63MilSau-11
75Gia195T-25
83TopRep5-346
91TopArc1-115
Spencer, Glenn Edward
33Gou-84
34DiaMatCSB-166
34GouCanV-37
Spencer, Jeff
96AppLeaAB-15
96DanBraB-23
Spencer, Jim
69AngJacitB-12
70OPC-255
70Top-255
70TopScr-20
71AngJacitB-9
71MLBOffS-358
71OPC-78
71Top-78
71TopCoi-4
72MilBra-322
72OPC-419
72Top-419
73OPC-319
73Top-319
74OPC-580
74Top-580
74TopSta-239
75OPC-387
75Top-387
76OPC-83
76SSP-268
76Top-83
76TopTra-83T
77BurCheD-79
77Hos-16
77OPC-46
77Top-648
77WhiSoxJT-13
78OPC-122
78Top-182
78YanBurK-16
79OPC-315
79Top-599
79YanBurK-17
79YanPicA-31
80OPC-147
80Top-278
81Don-226
81Fle-96
81OPC-209
81Top-435
81TopTra-832
82Don-265
82Fle-107
82FleSta-127
82OPC-88
82Top-729
82TopSti-223
92UppDecS-12
92YanWIZ7-142
92YanWIZ8-185
93RanKee-338
94RanAllP-1
Spencer, John
88ElmPioC-25
89ElmPioP-20
Spencer, Joseph B.
93NegLeaRL2-36
Spencer, Kyle
88ButCopKSP-10
89GasRanP-1002
89GasRanS-22
90ChaRanS-27
91ChaRanC-11
91ChaRanP-1315
Spencer, Robert
90NewBriRSB-27
Spencer, Roy
31Exh-31
31SenTeaIPW-29
33ExhFou-16
90DodTar-757
91ConTSN-320
Spencer, Shane
90TamYanD-25
92GreHorC-4
92GreHorF-795
93GreHorC-21
93GreHorF-900
94TamYanC-24
94TamYanF-2398
95SPML-121
95TamYanYI-26
96Bow-251
96Exc-93
96ExcSeaC-10
96NorNavB-25
96Top-436
Spencer, Stan
91Bow-441
91Cla/Bes-84
91HarSenLD-270
91HarSenP-626
91LinDriAA-270
93HigDesMC-20
93HigDesMF-41
94BreCouMF-11
95ChaKniTI-24
Spencer, Tom
89CedRapRB-25
89CedRapRP-917
89CedRapRS-24
91ChaWheC-24
92ChaWVWC-24
93WinSpiC-27
94CarLeaAF-CAR51
94WinSpiC-28
96BilMusTI-30
Spencer, Tom (Hubert Thomas)
76IndIndTI-6
78KnoKnoST-21
79KnoKnoST-25
80TucTorT-15
81TucTorT-13
86PitCubP-22
87GenCubP-4
88IndGat-2
89IndTeaI-28
89PacSenL-101
89TopSenL-24
90CedRapRB-13
90SanJosGB-29
90SanJosGCLC-53
90SanJosGP-2026
90SanJosGS-27
91MetColP-47
91MetKah-51
92AstMot-27
93AstMot-28
94ColCliF-2968
94ColCliP-3
Spencer, Troy
52LavPro-66
Spencer, Tubby (Edward)
08RosComP-72
09ColChiE-270
09RamT20-110
09T206-333
12ColRedB-270
12ColTinT-270
12ImpTobC-81
12PhiCarE-28
19W514-36
Spencer, Vernon
20NatCarE-100
Spenrath, Chris
94ButCopKSP-23
Sperring, Robert
74WicAerODF-116
76OPC-323
76SSP-320
76Top-323
78ChaChaT-16
78Top-514
79ChaChaT-16
Sperry, Chris
89SalDodTI-28
Spetter, Bryan
92PulBraC-19
92PulBraF-3187
Spicer, Len
79NewCoPT-22
Spicer, Robert
52MotCoo-61
Spiegel, Mike
96BurIndB-15
Spiegel, Rich
94DanBraC-24
94DanBraF-3536
Spiers, Bill
88StoPorCLC-197
88StoPorP-738
89BrePol-6
89DonRoo-5
89FleUpd-40
89ScoRoo-82T
89TopTra-115T
89TopTraT-115T
89UppDec-745
90Bow-402
90BowTif-402
90BreMilB-24
90ClaBlu-134
90Don-382
90El PasDAGTI-26
90Fle-337
90FleCan-337
90Lea-203
90OPC-538
90PanSti-376
90Sco-449A
90Sco-449B
90Sco100RS-55
90ScoYouSI-14
90Spo-206
90Top-538
90TopBig-88
90TopDeb89-121
90TopRoo-27
90TopTif-538
90ToyRoo-26
90UppDec-237
91BreMilB-24
91BrePol-21
91Don-310
91Fle-597
91Lea-111
91OPC-284
91PanFreS-207
91PanSti-162
91Sco-84
91StaClu-360
91Top-284
91TopDesS-284
91TopMic-284
91TopTif-284
91Ult-181
91UppDec-268
92Bow-536
92BrePol-23
92Don-364
92Fle-189
92Lea-106
92OPC-742
92PanSti-38
92Pin-177
92Sco-218
92StaClu-379
92Top-742
92TopGol-742
92TopGolW-742
92TopMic-742
92Ult-84
92UppDec-214
93BrePol-22
93Fla-229
93Fle-635
93Lea-403
93OPC-323
93PacSpa-516
93PanSti-38
93Pin-525
93Sco-88
93Sel-259
93StaClu-566
93StaCluFDI-566
93StaCluMOP-566
93Top-619
93TopGol-619
93TopInaM-619
93TopMic-619
93Ult-577
93UppDec-325
93UppDecGold-325
94BreMilB-276
94BrePol-25
94ColC-264
94ColChoGS-264
94ColChoSS-264
94Don-288
94Fle-191
94Pac-342
94Pin-370
94PinArtP-370
94PinMusC-370
94Sco-105
94ScoGolR-105
94StaClu-677
94StaCluFDI-677
94StaCluGR-677
94StaCluMOP-677
94Top-73
94TopGol-73
94TopSpa-73
95Don-182
95DonPreP-182
95Fle-190
95StaClu-49
95StaCluFDI-49
95StaCluMOP-49
95StaCluSTWS-49
95Top-188
96AstMot-16
96MetKah-29
97Pac-324
97PacLigB-324
97PacSil-324
Spiers, Mike
90SalSpuCLC-145
Spiezio, Ed
65Top-431
67OPC-128
67Top-128
68Top-349
68TopVen-349
69MLBOffS-197
69PadVol-8
69Top-249
69TopTeaP-12
70MLBOffS-119
70Top-718
71MLBOffS-240
71OPC-6
71Top-6
72MilBra-323
72OPC-504
72PadTeal-24
72Top-504
77PadSchC-52
Spiezio, Scott
93SouOreAC-24
93SouOreAF-4074
94Bow-413
94ModA'sC-22
94ModA'sF-3072
95Bes-39
95Exc-112
95HunStaTI-26
95SPML-123
95Top-641
95UppDecML-37
96BesAutSA-74
96ColCho-447
96ColChoGS-447
96ColChoSS-447
96FleUpd-U76
96FleUpdTC-U76
96Top-434
96Ult-404
96UltGolM-404
96UppDec-267
97Bow-142
97BowBes-185
97BowBesA-185
97BowBesAAR-185
97BowBesAR-185
97BowBesR-185
97BowCerBIA-CA74
97BowCerGIA-CA74
97BowChr-150
97BowChrI-150
97BowChrIR-150
97BowChrR-150
97BowInt-142
97Cir-216
97CirRav-216
97ColCho-187
97Don-359
97DonLim-48
97DonLim-54
97DonLimLE-48
97DonLimLE-54
97DonPre-153
97DonPreCttC-153
97DonPreP-359
97DonPrePGold-359
97Fin-272
97FinRef-272
97FlaShoWotF-18
97Fle-195
97FleNewH-12
97FleRooS-19
97FleTif-195
97Lea-325
97LeaFraM-325
97LeaFraMDC-325
97NewPin-164
97NewPinAP-164
97NewPinMC-164
97NewPinPP-164
97PacPriGotD-GD82
97PinCer-128
97PinCerMBlu-128
97PinCerMG-128
97PinCerMR-128
97PinCerR-128
97PinTotCPB-128
97PinTotCPG-128
97PinTotCPR-128
97PinX-P-128
97PinX-PMoS-128
97Sco-485
97ScoHobR-485
97ScoResC-485
97ScoShoS-485
97ScoShoSAP-485
97Sel-122
97SelArtP-122
97SelRegG-122
97SpoIll-24
97SpoIllEE-24
97Stu-148
97StuPrePG-148
97StuPrePS-148
97TopStaFAS-FAS9
97Ult-115
97UltGolME-115
97UltPlaME-115
97UppDec-449
95UppDecMLFS-37
Spikes, Charlie
73LinPor-67
73OPC-614
73Top-614
74OPC-58
74Top-58
74TopDecE-33
74TopSta-169
75OPC-135
75Top-135

76OPC-408
76SSP-531
76Top-408
77Top-168
78Top-459
80Top-294
81Fle-259
92YanWIZ7-143
Spikes, Mascot
96OrlCubB-29
95OrlCubF-29
Spiller, Derron
92SavCarC-22
92SavCarF-664
93SprCarC-25
93SprCarF-1852
94St.PetCC-25
94St.PetCF-2586
Spillner, Dan
74PadDea-24
75OPC-222
75PadDea-5
75Top-222
76OPC-557
76SSP-119
76Top-557
77PadSchC-53
77Top-182
78PadFamF-30
78Top-488
79Top-359
80Top-38
81Fle-392
81Top-276
82Don-411
82Fle-378
82Ind-32
82IndTeal-30
82IndWhe-29
82OPC-1
82Top-664
83Don-137
83Fle-419
83FleSta-184
83FleSti-243
83IndPos-33
83IndWhe-27
83OPC-278
83Top-725
83TopSti-59
84Don-582
84Fle-550
84Ind-26
84Nes792-91
84OPC-91
84Top-91
84TopTif-91
85Fle-528
85Top-169
85TopTif-169
85WhiSoxC-37
86Don-122
86Fle-217
86Top-423
86TopTif-423
91EveGiaP-3935
Spilman, Harry
78IndIndTI-5
79IndIndTI-5
79Top-717
80RedEnq-12
80Top-677
81Don-304
81Fle-209
81Top-94
81TopTra-833
82AstAstI-10
82Fle-233
82Top-509
82TucTorT-11
83Don-65
83Fle-467
83Top-193
84AstMot-12
84Don-258
84Nes792-612
84Top-612
84TopTif-612
85AstMot-19
85Top-482
85TopTif-482
86Top-352
86TopTif-352
87Fle-284
87FleGlo-284
87GiaMot-16
87Top-64
87TopTif-64
88Don-607
88Fle-97
88FleGlo-97
88GiaMot-16
88Sco-618
88ScoGlo-618
88StaLinG-17
88Top-217
88TopTif-217
89TucTorC-18
89TucTorJP-24
89TucTorP-199
90CMC-616
90ProAAAF-200
90TucTorC-14
90TucTorP-210
96BurIndB-30
Spinelli, Michael
96MicBatCB-26
Spinello, Joe
95PriWilCTI-15
Spingola, Don
94KinMetC-19
94KinMetF-3822
Spink, J.G. Taylor
94ConTSN-1111
94ConTSN-1112
94ConTSNB-1111
94ConTSNB-1112
Spink, Mrs. (J.G. Taylor)
94ConTSN-1111
94ConTSN-1112
94ConTSNB-1111
94ConTSNB-1112
Spinks, Scipio
70OPC-492
70Top-492
71CarTeal-38
71MLBOffS-92
71OPC-747
71Top-747
72OPC-202
72Top-202
73OPC-417
73Top-417
74OPC-576
74Top-576
74WicAerODF-125
75IowOakT-19
95IdaFalBTI-36
96CliLumKTI-26
Spino, Tom
79QuaCitCT-23
Spinosa, John
87WesPalBEP-679
92IndIndF-NNO
Spires, Tony
90EveGiaB-19
90EveGiaP-3135
91Cla/Bes-113
91SanJosGC-8
91SanJosGP-21
Spirits, Winston Salem
86WinSpiP-29
89WinSpiS-NNO
90WinSpiTI-30
Spitale, Ben
87BurExpP-1078
Spitaleri, Camille
96ColSilB-27
Spivey, Jim
90JohCitCS-25
91SavCarC-13
91SavCarP-1655
Splawn, Matt
96PitMetB-25
Split, Lickety
90WinSpiTI-26
Splitt, Steve
77BurBeeT-27
78HolMilT-21
79HolMilT-19
Splittorff, Jamie
96ForWayWB-1
Splittorff, Paul
71OPC-247
71Top-247
72OPC-315
72Top-315
73LinPor-91
73OPC-48
73Top-48
74OPC-225
74Top-225
74TopDecE-56
74TopSta-190
75OPC-340
75Top-340
76OPC-43
76SSP-163
76Top-43
77BurCheD-64
77OPC-41
77Top-534
78Hos-111
78RCColC-86
78Roy-21
78SSP270-230
78Top-638
79Kel-10
79OPC-90
79RoyTeal-9
79Top-183
80OPC-214
80Top-409
81Don-342A
81Don-342B
81Fle-30
81FleStiC-95
81Top-218
82Don-464
82Fle-423
82OPC-126
82Roy-20
82Top-759
83Don-286
83Fle-124
83Roy-28
83Top-316
83TopFol-1
84Don-521
84Fle-360
84Nes792-52
84Top-52
84TopSti-281
84TopTif-52
86RoyGreT-10
93RoySta2-13
Spohrer, Al
31Exh-1
33Gou-161
33GouCanV-94
34DiaMatCSB-167
34ButPreR-56
35DiaMatCS3T1-132
35GouPuzR-8L
35GouPuzR-9L
92ConTSN-602
Spokaneasurus, Otto the
96SpoIndB-30
Spoljaric, Paul
91St.CatBJC-20
91St.CatBJP-3395
92MyrBeaHC-23
92MyrBeaHF-2197
93Bow-279
93ClaFS7-118
93ClaGolF-130
93DunBluJC-21
93DunBluJFFN-23
93ExcFS7-245
93SouAtlLAIPI-14
93SouAtlLAPI-37
94Bow-581
94ColC-668
94ColChoGS-668
94ColChoSS-668
94LeaLimR-69
94Pin-539
94PinArtP-539
94PinMusC-539
94ScoRoo-RT137
94ScoRooGR-RT137
94SigRoo-16
94SigRooS-16
94StaCluT-175
94StaCluTFDI-175
94SyrChiTI-24
94Top-776
94TopGol-776
94TopSpa-776
94Ult-439
94UppDec-26
94UppDecED-26
94UppDecML-149
94UppDecML-210
95Sco-308
95ScoGolR-308
95ScoPlaTS-308
95SigRoo-46
95SigRooSig-46
95SyrChiTI-23
95Top-644
96SyrChiTI-28
97BluJayS-17
97PacPriGotD-GD105
Spoolstra, Scott
88ColMetGS-20
Spooner, Karl
55DodGolS-10
55Top-90
55TopDouH-19
55TopTesS-9
56Top-83
56TopHocF-B20
56TopPin-53
79TCM50-238
90DodTar-758
95TopArcBD-98
95TopArcBD-147
Sposito, Gus
76VenLeaS-197
80VenLeaS-236
85SpoIndGC-19
Spradlin, Jerry
88BilMusP-1821
89GreHorP-413
90CedRapRP-2322
90ChaWheB-10
91ChaLooLD-170
91ChaLooP-1961
91LinDriAA-170
92ChaLooF-3821
92ChaLooS-195
93ExcFS7-30
93IndIndF-1490
94Don-579
94Fle-430
94IndIndF-1812
94Pac-162
94StaClu-56
94StaCluFDI-56
94StaCluGR-56
94StaCluMOP-56
94StaCluP-56
94Top-779
94TopGol-779
94TopSpa-779
94Ult-179
95ChaKniTI-25
96IndIndB-24
Sprague, Charles
87OldJudN-478
Sprague, Ed
87PanAmTURB-22
88TopTra-113T
88TopTraT-113T
89Bow-252
89BowTif-252
89DunBluJS-16
89TopBig-40
90Bow-511
90BowTif-511
90CMC-345
90ProAAAF-361
90SyrChiC-19
90SyrChiMB-24
90SyrChiP-581
91BluJayS-26
91Bow-26
91Cla1-T90
91Cla3-T88
91DonRoo-14
91FleUpd-66
91Lea-485
91LinDriAAA-518
91ScoAllF-7
91ScoRoo-101T
91StaClu-387
91SyrChiK-4
91SyrChiLD-518
91SyrChiMB-24
91SyrChiP-2484
91UltUpd-63
91UppDecFE-47F
92Don-187
92Fle-340
92OPC-516
92ProFS7-162
92Sco-504
92Sco100RS-52
92SkyAAAF-232
92StaClu-445
92SyrChiF-1972
92SyrChiMB-21
92SyrChiS-517
92Top-516
92TopDaiQTU-15
92TopDeb91-167
92TopGol-516
92TopGolW-516
92TopMic-516
92TriA AAS-517
92UppDec-242
93BluJayD-8
93BluJayD4-11
93BluJayDM-14
93BluJayDM-29
93BluJayDWS-3
93BluJayFS-26
93Bow-491
93Don-219
93Fla-294
93Fle-698
93Lea-408
93OPC-203
93OPCWorC-13
93OPCWorSH-3
93PacSpa-328
93Pin-223
93Sco-214
93Sco-520
93SP-52
93StaClu-90
93StaCluFDI-90
93StaCluM-112
93StaCluMOP-90
93Stu-116
93Top-659
93TopGol-659
93TopInaM-659
93TopMic-659
93TriPla-238
93Ult-292
93UppDec-764
93UppDecGold-764
93UppDecSH-HI18
94BluJayP-8
94BluJayUSPC-5H
94BluJayUSPC-13C
94Bow-57
94ColC-423
94ColChoGS-423
94ColChoSS-423
94Don-84
94ExtBas-194
94Fin-160
94FinRef-160
94Fla-350
94Fle-342
94Lea-117
94OPC-265
94OPCWorC-7
94Pac-651
94Pin-459
94PinArtP-459
94PinMusC-459
94Sco-399
94ScoGolR-399
94Sel-135
94StaClu-418
94StaCluFDI-418
94StaCluGR-418
94StaCluMOP-418
94StaCluT-156
94StaCluTFDI-156
94Stu-31
94Top-426
94TopGol-426
94TopSpa-426
94TriPla-37
94Ult-142
94UppDec-241
94UppDecED-241
95BluJayUSPC-4H
95BluJayUSPC-11S
95ColCho-142
95ColChoGS-142
95ColChoSS-142
95Don-132
95DonPreP-132
95DonTopotO-178

95Fin-312
95FinRef-312
95Fla-318
95Fle-104
95Lea-70
95LeaLim-157
95Pin-112
95PinArtP-112
95PinMusC-112
95Sco-414
95ScoGolR-414
95ScoPlaTS-414
95StaClu-194
95StaCluFDI-194
95StaCluMOP-194
95StaCluSTWS-194
95StaCluVR-102
95Top-146
95TopCyb-90
95Ult-123
95UltGolM-123
95UppDec-286
95UppDecED-286
95UppDecEDG-286
95UppDecSE-64
95UppDecSEG-64
96BluJayB-5
96BluJayOH-29
96Cir-97
96CirRav-97
96ColCho-748
96ColChoGS-748
96ColChoSS-748
96Don-30
96DonPreP-30
96EmoXL-137
96Fla-193
96Fle-283
96FleTif-283
96Lea-203
96LeaPrePB-203
96LeaPrePG-203
96LeaPrePS-203
96Pac-437
96Pin-60
96ProSta-16
96Sco-111
96StaClu-386
96StaCluEPB-386
96StaCluEPG-386
96StaCluEPS-386
96StaCluMOP-386
95StaCluVRMC-102
96Top-295
96Ult-151
96UltGolM-151
96UppDec-471
97BluJayS-4
97Cir-60
97CirRav-60
97ColCho-493
97Don-239
97DonPreP-239
97DonPrePGold-239
97Fin-257
97FinRef-257
97Fle-249
97FleTif-249
97Lea-306
97LeaFraM-306
97LeaFraMDC-306
97MetUni-190
97Pac-228
97PacLigB-228
97PacPri-76
97PacPriLB-76
97PacPriP-76
97PacSil-228
87PanAmTUBI-33
97Pin-57
97PinArtP-57
97PinMusC-57
97Sco-275
97ScoPreS-275
97ScoShoS-275
97ScoShoSAP-275
97SP-178
97StaClu-25
97StaCluMat-25
97StaCluMOP-25
97Top-345
97TopChr-116
97TopChrR-116
97TopGal-122
97TopGalPPI-122
97Ult-408
97UltGolME-408
97UltPlaME-408
97UppDec-518
Sprague, Ed Sr.
69Top-638
72OPC-121
72Top-121
75OPC-76
75Top-76
76SSP-230
94BreMilB-277
Spratke, Ken
87ChaLooB-12
88MemChiB-23
89OmaRoyC-9
89OmaRoyP-1719
Spratt, Greg
91SouAtlLAGP-SAL31
95NorNavTI-NNO
96NorNavB-4
Spratt, Jack (Henry)
12T207-171
Sprick, Scott
91EriSaiC-9
91EriSaiP-4078
91FreKeyC-19
91FreKeyP-2373
Spridzans, Mark
95StCatSTI-29
Spriggs, George
67Top-472
68Top-314
68TopVen-314
69Top-662
71MLBOffS-431
71OPC-411
71Top-411
Spring, Jack
57SeaPop-34
62Top-257
63Top-572
64Top-71
64TopVen-71
85SpoIndGC-20
Spring, Joshua
93AubAstC-23
93AubAstF-3444
95DunBluJTI-28
Springer, Dennis
88BakDodCLC-260
89SanAntMB-20
89TexLeaAGS-18
90AlbDukC-12
90AlbDukT-27
90CMC-414
90SanAntMGS-27
90TexLeaAGS-15
91LinDriAA-541
91SanAntMLD-541
91SanAntMP-2973
92SanAntMF-3973
92SanAntMS-568
92SkyAA F-252
93AlbDukF-1459
95ScrRedBTI-25
Springer, Gary
83SanJosBC-6
Springer, Russell
87AncGlaP-27
88CapCodPPaLP-35
90LSUTigGM-15
91FloStaLAP-FSL18
91Ft.LauYC-14
91Ft.LauYP-2427
92Bow-308
92Cla2-T93
92ColCliF-350
92ColCliP-9
92ColCliS-118
92Pin-561
92SkyAAAF-57
93Bow-285
93Don-285
93FleFinE-191
93FleMajLP-A8
93Lea-549
93Sco-238
93Sel-337
93SP-27
93StaClu-736
93StaCluAn-24
93StaCluFDI-736
93StaCluMOP-736
93Top-686
93TopGol-686
93TopInaM-686
93TopMic-686
93VanCanF-2597
94Don-325
94Sco-562
94ScoGolR-562
94Top-113
94TopGol-113
94TopSpa-113
94VanCanF-1865
96LeaSigEA-190
96PhiTeal-30
Springer, Steve
90CMC-470
90ColSprSSC-18
90ColSprSSP-46
90ProAAAF-227
91CalCanLD-72
91CalCanP-524
91LinDriAAA-72
91TopDeb90-147
92TidTidF-907
92TidTidS-571
93NorTidF-2578
94TolMudHF-1034
Springer, Steve (Billy)
84JacMetT-22
85IntLeaAT-13
85TidTidT-16
85TidTidT-17
86TidTidP-27
87TidTidP-11
87TidTidT-18
88TidTidCa-12
88TidTidCM-21
88TidTidP-1598
89VanCanC-12
89VanCanP-592
Sprinz, Joseph C.
48SomandK-28
49SomandK-22
Sproat, Ed
87OldJudN-479
Sproesser, Mark
81RedPioT-18
82RedPioT-13
Sprout, Bob
77FriOneYW-109
Sproviero, Nick
91JamExpC-19
91JamExpP-3544
Sprowl, Bobby (Robert)
80TucTorT-6
80VenLeaS-264
81Top-82
82Top-441
82TucTorT-19
83ColAstT-21
Spry, Shane
93SarWhiSC-24
94HicCraC-21
94HicCraF-2191
Spurgeon, Fred
26Exh-87
Spurgeon, Scott
88AubAstP-1948
89AshTouP-958
Spurlock, Robert
90VisOakCLC-85
Spykstra, David
92ClaDraP-65
93StaCluM-150
93YakBeaC-23
93YakBeaF-3884
94YakBeaC-23
94YakBeaF-3850
96SavSanB-11
Squires, Mike
78SSP270-147
79Top-704
80Top-466
81Don-398
81Fle-349
81Top-292
82Don-39
82Fle-357
82FleSta-188
82Top-398
83Don-495
83Fle-250
83Top-669
83WhiSoxTV-25
84Don-404
84Fle-71
84Nes792-72
84Top-72
84TopTif-72
84WhiSoxTV-29
85Don-501
85Fle-529
85OPC-278
85Top-543
85TopTif-543
89BluJayFS-25
90BluJayFS-25
91BluJayFS-21
92WhiSoxK-NNO
St-Vincent, Claude
52LavPro-94
St. Onge, Paul
74WicAerODF-128
St.Clair, Dan
83OmaRoyT-8
84OmaRoyT-18
St.Claire, Ebba
52Bow-172
52Top-393
53BowBW-34
53BraJohC-16
53BraSpiaS3-21
53Top-91
54Bow-128
83Bra53F-42
83TopRep5-393
91TopArc1-91
St.Claire, Mark
92PulBraC-6
92PulBraF-3182
St.Claire, Randy
85Don-575
85ExpPos-23
85IndIndTI-19
86Don-463
86Fle-261
86IndIndTI-15
86Lea-229
86OPC-89
86Top-89
86TopTif-89
87ExpPos-29
87FleUpd-113
87FleUpdG-113
87OPC-366
87SpoTeaP-20
87Top-467
87TopTif-467
88Don-426
88Fle-197
88FleGlo-197
88OPC-279
88Sco-397
88ScoGlo-397
88Top-279
88TopTif-279
89PorBeaC-11
89PorBeaP-213
89Top-666
89TopTif-666
89UppDec-29
90CMC-607
90OPC-503
90ProAAAF-193
90Top-503
90TopTif-503
90TucTorC-5
90TucTorP-203
91LinDriAAA-443
91RicBraBC-16
91RicBraLD-443
91RicBraP-2568
91RicBraTI-10
92RicBraBB-14
92RicBraF-377
92RicBraRC-19
92RicBraS-443
92Sco-708
92SkyAAAF-204
93RicBraF-184
94SyrChiF-971
94SyrChiTI-25
96StoPorB-28
97RicBraBC-20
St.Claire, Steve
85UtiBluST-23
86JamExpP-24
87BurExpP-1077
St.John, Anthony
89SalLakTTI-16
St.John, Rich
89WatIndS-28
90RenSilSCLC-289
St.Laurent, Jim
85BurRanT-15
86DayBealP-27
87TexLeaAF-17
88OklCit8C-23
88OklCit8P-39
89OklCit8C-17
89OklCit8P-1524
90TulDriDGB-7
St.Peter, Bill (William)
88GenCubP-1650
89ChaWheB-6
89ChaWheP-1753
90ButCopKSP-18
90PeoChiTI-12
91ChaKniLD-143
91ChaKniP-1698
91LinDriAA-143
St.Pierre, Bob
96Exc-94
Staats, Todd
89GeoColC-30
Stabile, Ed
92WatIndC-28
Stablein, George
80HawIslT-15
81HawIslT-14
81Top-356
82HawIslT-15
Stabler, Ken
93Pin-477
Stacey, Al
89GenCubP-1874
90EriSaiS-25
Stachler, Eric
95AubAstTI-22
96KisCobB-27
Stack, Eddie (William Edward)
12T207-172
80PerHaloFP-D
80PerHaloFP-F
90DodTar-759
Stackhouse, Brian
86MacPirP-23
Stading, Greg
86PriWilPP-25
87SalBucP-6
Stadler, Jeff
78CedRapGT-26
79CedRapGT-7
Stadler, Mike
94BurIndC-23
94BurIndF-3799
Staehle, Marv
65OPC-41
65Top-41
66OPC-164
66Top-164
66TopVen-164
69PilPos-30
69Top-394
71ExpLaPR-11
71MLBOffS-140
71OPC-663
71Top-663
Stafford, Bill
61Top-213
61TopStal-199
61Yan61RL-13
62Jel-13
62Pos-13
62PosCan-13
62Top-55
62Top-570
62TopVen-55
63Jel-22
63Kah-28
63Pos-22
63Top-155
63Top-331
64ChatheY-22
64Top-299
64TopVen-299
64YanReqKP-15
65ChaTheY-21
65OPC-281
65Top-281

69PilPos-36
91RinPos1Y3-4
92YanWIZ6-120
Stafford, Gil
75BurBeeT-27
Stafford, Jerry
92EriSaiC-26
92EriSaiF-1624
93HigDesMC-21
93HigDesMF-42
93Top-683
93TopGol-683
93TopInaM-683
93TopMic-683
94BreCouMC-18
94BreCouMF-12
Stafford, Mitch
93EveGiaC-26
93EveGiaF-3779
Stagg, Bob
47CenFlo-27
Staggs, Ron
75WesPalBES-14
Staggs, Steve
75OmaRoyTI-15
76OmaRoyTT-22
76VenLeaS-129
78OPC-94
78Top-521
Stahl, Chick (Charles)
11SpoLifCW-332
Stahl, Jake (Garland)
03BreE10-133
04FanCraAL-43
04RedSoxUP-12
08AmeCarE-91
08RosComP-54
09AmeCarE-97
09ColChiE-271
09MaxPubP-12
09RamT20-111
09SpoNewSM-84
09T206-334
09T206-335
10E-UOraBSC-21
10E12AmeCDC-34
10RedCroT-72
10RedCroT-158
10RedCroT-245
11L1L-130
11S74Sil-4
11S81LarS-105
11SpoLifCW-333
11SpoLifM-16
11T205-160
11TurRedT-38
12ColRedB-271
12ColTinT-271
12HasTriFT-46
12HasTriFT-65
12HasTriFT-68A
12HasTriFT-68B
12RedSoxBASP-4
13NatGamW-36
14TexTomE-41
14TexTomE-62
Stahl, Larry
66OPC-107
66Top-107
66TopVen-107
69MilBra-260
69MLBOffS-198
69Top-271
69TopSta-99
70MLBOffS-120
70OPC-494
70Top-494
71OPC-711
71Top-711
72MilBra-324
72Top-782
73OPC-533
73Top-533
74OPC-507
74Top-507
91MetWIZ-373
Stahlhoefer, Larry
92WelPirC-22
92WelPirF-1327
93AugPirC-21
93AugPirF-1548
Stahoviak, Scott
91Cla/Bes-401
91ClaDraP-23
91FroRowDP-25
91VisOakUP-2
92Bow-360
92CalLeaACL-41
92ClaFS7-299
92OPC-66
92ProFS7-97
92StaCluD-179
92Top-66
92TopGol-66
92TopGolW-66
92TopMic-66
92UppDecML-320
92VisOakC-1
92VisOakF-1024
93ClaFS7-26
93ClaGolF-45
93ExcFS7-204
93NasXprF-412
94ColC-18
94ColChoGS-18
94ColChoSS-18
94Pin-248
94PinArtP-248
94PinMusC-248
94SalLakBF-826
94Spo-154
94StaClu-51
94StaCluFDI-51
94StaCluGR-51
94StaCluMOP-51
95Bow-46
95DonTopotO-114
95Fin-259
95FinRef-259
95FleUpd-63
95SP-171
95SPSil-171
95UppDec-229
95UppDecED-229
95UppDecEDG-229
96Cir-60
96CirRav-60
96ColCho-206
96ColChoGS-206
96ColChoSS-206
96Don-270
96DonPreP-270
96Fla-123
96Fle-177
96FleTif-177
96LeaSigA-212
96LeaSigAG-212
96LeaSigAS-212
96MetUni-82
96MetUniP-82
96Pac-358
96PanSti-204
96Sco-426
96StaClu-121
96StaCluMOP-121
96Ult-94
96UltGolM-94
97Cir-189
97CirRav-189
97ColCho-383
97Don-83
97DonPreP-83
97DonPrePGold-83
97Fle-157
97FleTif-157
97Lea-19
97LeaFraM-19
97LeaFraMDC-19
97Pac-145
97PacLigB-145
97PacSil-145
97Pin-45
97PinArtP-45
97PinMusC-45
97Sco-111
97ScoPreS-111
97ScoShoS-111
97ScoShoSAP-111
97StaClu-327
97StaCluMOP-327
97Top-9
Staiger, Roy
75TidTidTI-19
76OPC-592
76SSP-560
76Top-592
77MetDaiPA-22
77Top-281
78TacYanC-23
79ColCliT-2
80ColCliP-25
80ColCliT-9
89TidTidC-10
91MetWIZ-374
92YanWIZ7-144
Stainback, G. Tucker
34DiaMatCSB-168
34DiaStaR-52
35DiaMatCS3T1-133
36DiaMatCS3T2-22
43YanSta-25
47SigOil-37
79DiaGre-380
83TCMPla1945-10
90DodTar-760
95ConTSN-1393
Stairs, Matt
89JamExpP-2141
89WesPalBES-22
90WesPalBES-23
91HarSenLD-271
91HarSenP-637
91LinDriAA-271
92Bow-434
92Bow-602
92DonRoo-112
92ExpDonD-16B
92IndIndS-195
92LeaGolR-BC8
92Pin-583
92PinRoo-28
92ProFS7-259
92SkyAA F-293
92SkyAAAF-94
92TopTra-110T
92TopTraG-110T
92UppDec-786
93ClaFS7-27
93Don-460
93Fle-464
93OttLynF-2448
93Sco-232
93Sel-327
94NewBriRSF-664
95PawRedSDD-26
95PawRedTI-24
96LeaSigEA-191
97Pac-176
97PacLigB-176
97PacSil-176
Stajduhar, Marty
90RanMot-28
Staley, Gerry (Gerald)
46SunBre-18
51Bow-121
51R42SmaS-98
51TopBluB-7
52Bow-50
52NatTeaL-34
52StaCalL-81G
52Top-79
53BowC-17
53CarHunW-24
53RedMan-NL24
53Top-56
54Bow-14
54CarHunW-27
55Bow-155
57Top-227
58Top-412
59Top-426
60Top-57
60Top-510
60TopVen-57
60WhiSoxTS-20
61Pos-29
61Top-90
61TopStaI-130
61WhiSoxTS-19
76WhiSoxTAG-12
79TCM50-40
80WhiSoxGT-10
83TopRep5-79
89WhiSoxK-5
91TopArc1-56
Staley, Henry E.
87OldJudN-480
Stallard, Tracy
61Top-81
62Top-567
63Top-419
64Top-176
64TopVen-176
65CarJayP-10
65CarTeal-25
65OldLonC-18
65Top-491
66CarTeal-12
66OPC-7
66Top-7
66TopVen-7
76Met63 S-16
81RedSoxBG2S-116
91MetWIZ-375
Stallcup, Jeff
89TenTecGE-26
Stallcup, T. Virgil
49Bow-81
49EurSta-95
50Bow-116
51Bow-108
52Bow-6
52NatTeaL-35
52Top-69
53Top-180
83TopRep5-69
91TopArc1-180
Staller, George
73OPC-136
73Top-136A
73Top-136B
74OPC-306
74Top-306
Stallings, George T.
11SpoLifM-82
13NatGamW-37
13TomBarW-34
15CraJacE-162
15SpoNewM-169
16BF2FP-57
16FleBreD-89
16SpoNewM-167
90DodTar-761
90HOFStiB-21
Stalp, Joe
83CedRapRF-4
83CedRapRT-10
Stamison, Mike
94SouOreAC-28
94SouOreAF-3634
Stampel, Eric
86LynMetP-21
Stamps, Crandall
89GeoColC-31
90GeoColC-29
Stamps, Jerry
75CedRapGT-24
Stanage, Oscar
07TigACDPP-25
09AmeCarE-98
09T206-336
09TigTaCP-17
10PeoT21-52
10SweCapPP-31
11BasBatEU-36
11BasBatEU-37
11SpoLifM-69
11T205-161
12HasTriFT-5
12HasTriFT-26
12HasTriFT-55
12T207-173
14PieStaT-53
14TexTomE-42
15AmeCarE-36
15SpoNewM-170
16BF2FP-30
16ColE13-167
16SpoNewM-168
19W514-115
Stancel, Mark
86MedA'sC-54
88ModA'sCLC-65
88ModA'sTI-14
90HunStaB-11
Stanceu, Charles
77TCMTheWY-72
Stanczak, Jack
94ChaRanF-2507
Standaert, Jerry
90DodTar-762
Standart, Rich
75ShrCapT-21
76ShrCapT-2
77ColCliT-21
Standiford, Mark
86AncGlaPTI-33
87AncGlaP-28
89SalSpuCLC-139
89SalSpuP-1801
Standish, Scott
93OneYanC-20
93OneYanF-3502
94GreBatF-474
95AusFut-78
95Exc-105
95NorNavTI-38
97GreBatC-22
Standley, Don
75WatDodT-19
Standridge, Jason
97Bow-439
97BowChr-299
97BowChrI-299
97BowChrIR-299
97BowChrR-299
97BowInt-439
Stanek, Al
64Top-99
64TopVen-99
65Top-302
66Top-437
97TopSta-124
97TopStaAM-124
Stanfield, Kevin
77VisOakT-15
79TolMudHT-5
79Top-709
Stanfield, Mike
88CliGiaP-713
Stanford, Don
89PriWilCS-20
90AlbYanB-8
90AlbYanP-1036
90AlbYanS-19
90Bes-92
90ProAaA-21
91AlbYanLD-19
91AlbYanP-1009
91LinDriAA-19
92ColCliF-351
92ColCliP-10
92ColCliS-119
93ColCliF-1112
93ColCliP-7
Stanford, Larry
89OneYanP-2106
90FloStaLAS-43
90Ft.LauYS-19
90StaFS7-41
91AlbYanLD-20
91AlbYanP-1010
91LinDriAA-20
92ColCliF-352
92ColCliS-120
92ProFS7-116
92SkyAAAF-58
94NewHavRF-1549
Stange, Albert Lee
61TwiCloD-25
62Top-321
63Top-246
63TwiVol-8
64Top-555
65Top-448
66Top-371
67CokCapRS-1
67OPC-99
67Top-99
67TopRedSS-19
68CokCapRS-1
68Top-593
69MilBra-261
69OPC-148
69Top-148
69TopFou-19
70OPC-447
70RedSoxCPPC-15
70Top-447
71OPC-311
71Top-311
72MilBra-325
73OPC-131
73Top-131A
73Top-131B
74OPC-403
74Top-403
78TwiFri-44
81RedSoxBG2S-117
89PawRedSP-692

89PawRedSTI-24
90PawRedSDD-25
90PawRedSP-479
90ProAAAF-451
91WinHavRSC-16
92WinHavRSC-30
93ForLauRSC-29
93ForLauRSFP-1615
94CarLeaA-DJ7
Stange, Kurt
87SalLakTTT-1
88MidLeaAGS-58
88WauTimGS-10
89SanBerSB-13
Stange, Tim
88ElmPioC-9
90LynRedSTI-23
Stangel, Chris
84EveGiaC-18
Stanhope, Chuck (Chester D.)
86HagSunP-19
87ChaO'sW-31
88RocRedWGCP-25
89HagSunB-17
89HagSunP-269
89RocRedWC-2
90HagSunDGB-28
Stanhouse, Don
73OPC-352
73Top-352
75OPC-493
75Top-493
76ExpRed-29
77ExpPos-29
77Kel-32
77OPC-63
77Top-274
78OPC-162
78Top-629
79Top-119
80DodPol-29
80Top-517
81DodPol-26
81Don-557
81Fle-121
81OPC-24
81Top-24
90DodTar-763
91OriCro-432
93RanKee-38
Stanicek, Pete
86HagSunP-20
87ChaO'sW-1
87IntLeaAT-29
88Don-541
88DonBasB-294
88DonRoo-15
88Fle-573
88FleGlo-573
88OriFreB-17
88RocRedWC-18
88RocRedWP-205
88RocRedWTI-22
88Sco-628
88ScoGlo-628
88TopTra-114T
88TopTraT-114T
89Bow-14
89BowTif-14
89Don-169
89Fle-622
89FleGlo-622
89HagSunS-20
89OPC-317
89PanSti-265
89Sco-236
89Top-497
89TopCoi-52
89TopSti-232
89TopTif-497
89ToyRoo-30
89UppDec-592
90HagSunDGB-29
90ProAAAF-474
90RocRedWP-717
91OriCro-433
Stanicek, Steve
84ShrCapFB-21
86ElPasDP-19
87DenZepP-27
88DenZepC-22
88DenZepP-1266
88Fle-174
88FleGlo-174
88StaLinO-16
89ScrRedBC-12
89ScrRedBP-717
90CMC-242
90CMC-315
90ProAAAF-310
90RocRedWC-15
90ScrRedBC-16
90ScrRedBP-608
94BreMilB-355
Stanifer, Rob
94ElmPioF-3474
95BreCouMF-245
94ElmPioC-20
Staniland, Steve
77ArkTraT-10
Stanka, Joe
58UniOil-9
Stankiewicz, Andy
87Ft.LauYP-10
88AlbYanP-1330
88EasLeaAP-5
89AlbYanB-15
89AlbYanP-333
89AlbYanS-19
89BlaYNPRWLU-11
89EasLeaAP-2
90AlbDecGB-17
90CMC-210
90ColCliC-10
90ColCliP-24
90ColCliP-685
90ProAAAF-335
90TopTVY-62
91ColCliLD-120
91ColCliP-20
91ColCliP-606
91LinDriAAA-120
92Bow-482
92Cla2-T7
92DonRooP-BC11
92DonUpd-U2
92FleUpd-44
92JimDeaRS-1
92Lea-470
92OPC-179
92Pin-564
92PinRoo-6
92ScoRoo-100T
92StaClu-725
92StaCluECN-725
92Top-179
92TopGol-179
92TopGolW-179
92TopMic-179
92TopTra-111T
92TopTraG-111T
92Ult-415
92UltAllR-2
92UppDec-779
92UppDecSR-SR21
93ColCliF-1120
93ColCliP-18
93Don-213
93Fle-285
93Lea-9
93OPC-291
93PacSpa-212
93PanSti-149
93Pin-363
93Sco-338
93Sel-279
93SelChaR-17
93StaClu-105
93StaCluFDI-105
93StaCluMOP-105
93StaCluY-29
93Top-348
93TopGol-348
93TopInaM-348
93TopMic-348
93Toy-34
93TriPla-101A
93TriPla-101B
93Ult-249
93UppDec-257
93UppDecGold-257
93USPlaCR-12D
94AstMot-26
94Fin-253
94FinRef-253
94Pac-437
94StaClu-635
94StaCluFDI-635
94StaCluGR-635
94StaCluMOP-635
95StaClu-584
95StaCluMOP-584
95StaCluSTWS-584
96FleUpd-U152
96FleUpdTC-U152
96LeaSigEA-192
Stanky, Eddie
43CubTeal-21
44CubTeal-22
46SpoExcW-7-1A
47Exh-216A
47Exh-216B
48BluTin-31
49Bow-104
49EurSta-26
50Bow-29
50Dra-22
50JJKCopP-20
50JJKCopP-21
51Bow-13
51R42SmaS-105
51TopCurA-11
51TopRedB-48
52BerRos-63
52Bow-160
52RedMan-NL23
52Top-76
53BowC-49
53CarHunW-25
53ExhCan-9
54CarHunW-28
54Top-38
55Bow-238
55CarHunW-26
55Top-191
66Top-448
66WhiSoxTI-11
67OPC-81
67Top-81
68Top-564
75Gia195T-26
79TCM50-108
83TCMPla1944-41
83TopRep5-76
89DodSmoG-53
90DodTar-764
91RinPosBD2-3
91TopArc1-300
92BazQua5A-17
92TopMic-179
93RanKee-340
94TopArc1-38
94TopArc1G-38
Stanley, B.J.
94JohCitCC-26
94JohCitCF-3713
Stanley, Bob
78PapGinD-12
78SSP270-164
78Top-186
79OPC-314
79Top-597
80OPC-35
80Top-63
81CokTeaS-4
81Don-456
81Fle-234
81OPC-296
81Top-421
81TopSupHT-9
82Don-134
82Fle-307
82FleSta-169
82OPC-289
82RedSoxC-18
82Top-289
83AllGamPI-87
83Don-386
83Fle-195
83FleSta-185
83FleSti-65
83OPC-242
83Top-381
83Top-682
84Don-644
84Fle-409
84FleSti-74
84FunFooP-81
84Nes792-320
84OPC-320
84Top-320
84TopSti-220
84TopTif-320
85Don-91
85Dra-42
85Fle-169
85OPC-204
85Top-555
85TopSti-215
85TopTif-555
86Don-91
86Fle-359
86OPC-158
86SevCoi-E10
86Spo-169
86Top-785
86TopSti-253
86TopTif-785
87Don-216
87DonOpeD-180
87Fle-47
87FleGlo-47
87OPC-175
87RedFolSB-18
87Top-175
87TopSti-245
87TopTif-175
88Don-92
88DonTeaBRS-92
88Fle-367
88FleGlo-367
88OPC-369
88PanSti-23
88Sco-300
88ScoGlo-300
88StaLinRS-20
88Top-573
88TopTif-573
89Bow-25
89BowTif-25
89Don-421
89DonBasB-233
89Fle-101
89FleGlo-101
89Sco-383
89Top-37
89TopSti-258
89TopTif-37
89UppDec-411
90Fle-289
90FleCan-289
90PubSti-466
90UppDec-654
90VenSti-456
Stanley, Carl
90GenCubS-23
93SavCarC-22
93SavCarF-686
Stanley, Derek
92JohCitCC-2
92JohCitCF-3132
Stanley, Fred
72OPC-59
72Top-59
74OPC-423
74SyrChiTI-25
74Top-423
75OPC-503
75SyrChiTI-19
75Top-503
75YanSSP-13
76OPC-429
76SSP-442
76Top-429
77Top-123
77YanBurK-16
78SSP270-12
78Top-664
78YanBurK-17
78YanSSPD-12
79Top-16
79YanBurK-16
79YanPicA-32
80Top-387A
80Top-387B
81Don-585
81Fle-100
81Top-281
81TopTra-834
82A'sGraG-15
82Don-449
82Fle-108
82Top-787
83Don-197
83Fle-534
83Top-513
89T/MSenL-98
91BreMilB-32
91BrePol-NNO
91PacSenL-6
91PacSenL-133
92YanWIZ7-145
92YanWIZ8-186
94BreMilB-356
Stanley, Joe
11SpoLifCW-334
Stanley, Kevin
83ButCopKT-21
Stanley, Mickey
66Top-198
66TopVen-198
67Top-607
68CokCapT-4
68OPC-129
68TigDetFPB-23
68Top-129
68TopVen-129
69MilBra-262
69MLBOffS-54
69OPC-13
69TigTeal-11
69TigTealC-9
69Top-13
69TopSta-179
69TopTeaP-1
70MLBOffS-214
70OPC-383
70Top-383
71MLBOffS-407
71OPC-524
71Top-524
72MilBra-326
72OPC-385
72Top-385
73LinPor-79
73OPC-88
73TigJew-18
73Top-88
74OPC-530
74Top-530
74TopSta-180
75OPC-141
75Top-141
76OPC-483
76SSP-372
76Top-483
77TigBurK-4
77Top-533
78TigBurK-21
78Top-232
79OPC-368
79Top-692
81TigDetN-25
86TigSpoD-15
88TigDom-22
89SweBasG-104
Stanley, Mike
86TulDriTI-25
87Don-592
87DonRoo-28
87Fle-647
87FleGlo-647
87OklCit8P-8
87RanSmo-23
87SpoRoo2-44
87TopTra-116T
87TopTraT-116T
88Don-259
88DonBasB-223
88Fle-480
88FleGlo-480
88OPC-219
88PanSti-199
88RanMot-11
88RanSmo-11
88Sco-47
88ScoGlo-47
88StaLinRa-17
88Top-219
88TopSti-238
88TopTif-219
88ToyRoo-29
89Don-166
89Fle-533
89FleGlo-533
89OPC-123
89RanMot-22
89RanSmo-31
89Sco-241

89Top-587
89TopSti-244
89TopTif-587
89UppDec-579
90Don-579
90OPC-92
90RanMot-20
90Top-92
90TopTif-92
90TulDriDGB-6
91OPC-409
91PacRya7N-6
91RanMot-20
91Sco-92
91StaClu-526
91Top-409
91TopDesS-409
91TopMic-409
91TopTif-409
92Bow-370
92Don-582
92Lea-367
92PacRyaTEI-177
92Sco-549
92StaClu-741
92StaCluNC-741
92Ult-416
93Don-718
93Fla-252
93Fle-656
93Lea-184
93Pin-563
93RanKee-341
93SP-267
93StaClu-323
93StaCluFDI-323
93StaCluMOP-323
93StaCluY-12
93Top-359
93TopGol-359
93TopInaM-359
93TopMic-359
93Ult-601
94Bow-137
94ColC-265
94ColChoGS-265
94ColChoSS-265
94Don-202
94ExtBas-139
94Fin-76
94FinPre-76P
94FinRef-76
94Fla-324
94Fle-247
94Lea-295
94OPC-95
94Pac-438
94PanSti-104
94Pin-338
94PinArtP-338
94PinMusC-338
94Sco-451
94ScoDreT-10
94ScoGolR-451
94Sel-100
94Spo-2
94StaClu-271
94StaCluFDI-271
94StaCluGR-271
94StaCluMOP-271
94StaCluT-197
94StaCluTFDI-197
94Stu-217
94Top-391
94Top-695
94TopBlaG-20
94TopGol-391
94TopGol-695
94TopSpa-391
94TopSpa-695
94TriPla-278
94Ult-101
94UppDec-229
94UppDecED-229
95Baz-24
95BazRedH-RH5
95Bow-393
95ColCho-519
95ColChoGS-519
95ColChoSE-246
95ColChoSEGS-246
95ColChoSESS-246
95ColChoSS-519
95D3-23
95Don-62
95DonPreP-62
95DonTopotO-126
95Emb-77
95EmbGolI-77
95Emo-67
95Fin-171
95FinRef-171
95Fla-288
95Fle-81
95Lea-292
95LeaLim-156
95Pac-303
95PanSti-29
95Pin-263
95PinArtP-263
95PinMusC-263
95Sco-195
95ScoGolR-195
95ScoPlaTS-195
95StaClu-223
95StaCluFDI-223
95StaCluMOP-223
95StaCluSTWS-223
95StaCluVR-112
95Top-142
95Top-391
95TopCyb-86
95Ult-86
95UltGolM-86
95UppDec-443
95UppDecED-443
95UppDecEDG-443
95UppDecSE-6
95UppDecSEG-6
96Baz-6
96Bow-8
96ColCho-236
96ColCho-478
96ColChoGS-236
96ColChoGS-478
96ColChoSS-236
96ColChoSS-478
96Don-184
96DonPreP-184
96EmoXL-18
96Fin-B262
96FinRef-B262
96Fla-26
96Fle-197
96FleRedS-14
96FleTif-197
96FleUpd-U18
96FleUpdTC-U18
96LeaSigA-213
96LeaSigAG-213
96LeaSigAS-213
96MetUni-19
96MetUniP-19
96Pac-370
96Pin-366
96PinAfi-51
96PinAfiAP-51
96PinAfiFPP-51
96PinFoil-366
96Sco-467
96Sel-137
96SelArtP-137
96StaClu-217
96StaCluMOP-217
95StaCluVRMC-112
96Sum-34
96SumAbo&B-34
96SumArtP-34
96SumFoi-34
96TeaOut-78
96Top-135
96TopGal-82
96TopGalPPI-82
96TopLas-30
96Ult-321
96UltGolM-321
96UppDec-283
97Bow-43
97BowInt-43
97Cir-322
97CirRav-322
97ColCho-283
97Don-65
97DonPreP-65
97DonPrePGold-65
97DonTea-46
97DonTeaSPE-46
97Fin-134
97FinEmb-134
97FinEmbR-134
97FinRef-134
97Fle-30
97FleTif-30
97MetUni-24
97Pin-151
97PinArtP-151
97PinMusC-151
97Sco-164
97ScoPreS-164
97ScoRedS-6
97ScoRedSPI-6
97ScoRedSPr-6
97ScoShoS-164
97ScoShoSAP-164
97StaClu-165
97StaCluMOP-165
97Top-151
97TopGal-6
97TopGalPPI-6
97Ult-20
97UltGolME-20
97UltPlaME-20
97UppDec-312

Stanley, Scott
90AriWilP-16
92AriWilP-17

Stanley, Tim
87AncGlaP-29
88JamExpP-1919

Stanley, Todd
93MisStaB-40

Stantiago, Ramon
90GasRanB-29

Stanton, Duane
93JohCitCC-19
93JohCitCF-3676
94MadHatC-22
94MadHatF-131

Stanton, Gary
91IdaFalBSP-13

Stanton, Lee (Leroy)
72OPC-141
72Top-141
73LinPor-37
73OPC-18
73Top-18
74OPC-594
74Top-594
75Kel-12
75OPC-342
75Top-342
76Hos-39
76HosTwi-39
76OPC-152
76SSP-204
76Top-152
77Top-226
78Hos-60
78OPC-123
78Top-447
79OPC-275
79TCMJapPB-86
79Top-533
86MarGreT-6
87MyrBeaBJP-1443
88MyrBeaBJP-1180
89MyrBeaBJP-1451
90MyrBeaBJP-2794
91MetWIZ-376
91MyrBeaHC-29
91MyrBeaHP-2963
92MyrBeaHC-28
92MyrBeaHF-2215
93HagSunC-26
93HagSunF-1897
94HagSunC-28
94HagSunF-2748

Stanton, Mike (Michael Thomas)
73CedRapAT-14
75IowOakT-20
78SyrChiT-18
81Fle-400
82Don-285
82Fle-379
82Top-473
82TopTra-113T
83Don-433
83Fle-486
83Top-159
84Fle-619
84MarMot-20
84Nes792-694
84Top-694
84TopTif-694
85Don-562
85Fle-501
85MarMot-16
85Top-256
85TopSti-343
85TopTif-256

Stanton, Mike (William Michael)
88BurBraP-3
89GreBraB-14
89GreBraP-1166
89GreBraS-22
90Bow-4
90BowTif-4
90BraDubP-27
90ClaUpd-T45
90Don-508
90DonRoo-7
90Fle-596
90FleCan-596
90FleSoaS-2
90OPC-694
90Sco-609
90Sco100RS-29
90ScoYouS2-7
90Top-694
90TopDeb89-122
90TopTif-694
90UppDec-61
91BraDubP-29
91BraSubS-36
91Don-716
91Fle-705
91Lea-491
91OPC-514
91Sco-468
91StaClu-413
91Top-514
91TopDesS-514
91TopMic-514
91TopTif-514
91UppDec-749
92BraLykP-27
92BraLykS-32
92ClaGam-19
92Don-780
92Fle-372
92Lea-377
92OPC-788
92Pin-350
92Sco-498
92StaClu-344
92Top-788
92TopGol-788
92TopGolW-788
92TopMic-788
92Ult-170
92UppDec-653
93BraLykP-28
93BraLykS-34
93Don-474
93Fin-176
93FinRef-176
93Fla-12
93Fle-15
93Lea-398
93PacSpa-341
93Pin-569
93Sco-317
93StaClu-38
93StaCluB-17
93StaCluFDI-38
93StaCluMOP-38
93Top-88
93TopGol-88
93TopInaM-88
93TopMic-88
93Ult-13
93UppDec-90
93UppDecGold-90
94BraLykP-31
94BraLykS-30
94BraUSPC-2S
94BraUSPC-11H
94ColC-441
94ColChoGS-441
94ColChoSS-441
94Don-506
94Fla-358
94Fle-376
94Lea-20
94Pin-461
94PinArtP-461
94PinMusC-461
94Sco-205
94ScoGolR-205
94StaClu-471
94StaCluFDI-471
94StaCluGR-471
94StaCluMOP-471
94StaCluT-58
94StaCluTFDI-58
94Top-107
94TopGol-107
94TopSpa-107
94Ult-450
95Don-28
95DonPreP-28
95Fle-319
95Top-271
95Ult-354
95UltGolM-354
96LeaSigEA-193
96StaClu-426
96StaCluMOP-426
97Cir-134
97CirRav-134
97Fle-590
97FleTif-590
97Ult-430
97UltGolME-430
97UltPlaME-430

Stanton, Rob
96WatIndTI-28

Staples, Ken
81WisRapTT-1
82WisRapTF-3

Stapleton, Dave (David E.)
86ElPasDP-20
88BrePol-43
88Don-521
88DonRoo-4
89Sco-581
89UppDec-304
94BreMilB-357

Stapleton, Dave (David L.)
81CokTeaS-10
81Don-544
81Fle-236
81OPC-81
81Top-81
81TopScr-48
81TopSti-47
81TopSupHT-10
82Don-208
82Fle-308
82OPC-93
82RedSoxC-19
82Top-589
83Don-200
83Fle-196
83OPC-239
83Top-239
83TopSti-35
84Don-273
84Fle-410
84Nes792-653
84OPC-249
84Top-653
84TopSti-221
84TopTif-653
85Top-322
85TopTif-322
86Top-151
86TopTif-151
87Top-507
87TopTif-507

Star, Clucky
96HilStaHWB-NNO

Stare, Lonny
95BakBlaTI-1

Stargell, Tim
87BelMarL-11
89WauTimGS-26
90Bes-297
90CMC-859
90SanBerSB-24
90SanBerSCLC-108
90SanBerSP-2641
91Cla/Bes-109
91JacSunLD-346
91JacSunP-163
91LinDriAA-346

Stargell, Willie
63PirIDL-22

63Top-553
64PirKDK-26
64Top-342
64TopVen-342
65Kah-38
65Top-377
66Kah-29
66OPC-99
66PirEasH-8
66Top-99
66Top-255
66TopRubI-87
66TopVen-99
66TopVen-255
67CokCapA-11
67CokCapNLA-29
67CokCapPi-12
67DexPre-197
67Kah-36
67OPC-140
67PirTeal-21
67Top-140
67Top-266
67TopPirS-22
67TopPirS-31
67TopVen-280
68OPC-86
68PirKDK-8
68PirTeal-21
68Top-86
68TopVen-86
69MilBra-263
69MLBOffS-188
69PirGre-8
69PirJacitB-12
69Top-545
69TopSta-89
69TopTeaP-16
70DayDaiNM-156
70Kel-29
70MLBOffS-107
70OPC-470
70PirTeal-8
70Top-470
70TopScr-21
70TopSup-19
71Kel-68
71MatMin-17
71MatMin-18
71MLBOffS-214
71OPC-230
71PirActP-24
71PirArc-11
71Top-230
71TopCoi-123
71TopSup-43
71TopTat-68
72Dia-64
72Kel-53A
72Kel-53B
72MilBra-327
72OPC-87
72OPC-89
72OPC-343
72OPC-447
72OPC-448
72ProStaP-23
72Top-87
72Top-89
72Top-343
72Top-447
72Top-448
72TopPos-15
73Kel2D-25
73LinPor-153
73OPC-370
73Top-370
73TopCanL-50
73TopCom-20
73TopPin-20
74Kel-37
74LauAllG-65
74NewYorNTDiS-14
74OPC-100
74OPC-202
74OPC-203
74Top-100
74Top-202
74Top-203
74TopDecE-31
74TopPuz-11
74TopSta-88
75Hos-135
75OPC-100
75Pir-6
75Top-100
76CraDis-58
76Hos-49
76HosTwi-49
76Kel-22
76OPC-270
76SSP-573
76Top-270
77BurCheD-186
77Hos-27
77MSADis-58
77OPC-25
77PepGloD-64
77PirPosP-25
77Top-460
77TopCloS-45
78Hos-11
78TasDis-11
78Top-510
78WifBalD-71
79Hos-104
79OPC-22
79Top-55
80Kel-25
80OPC-319
80PerHaloFP-200
80Top-610
80TopSup-1
81AllGamPI-99
81CokTeaS-118
81Don-12
81Don-132
81Fle-363
81FleStiC-15
81Kel-11
81MSAMinD-31
81OPC-127
81PerCreC-14
81Top-380
81TopSti-215
82Don-639
82Fle-499
82FleSta-76
82FleSta-106
82K-M-37
82MonNew-15
82OPC-188
82OPC-372
82PerCreC-5
82PerCreCG-5
82Top-715
82Top-716
82TopSti-85
82TopStiV-85
83Don-8
83Don-610
83Fle-324
83Fle-634
83FleSta-186
83FleSti-81
83FraBroR-33
84OCoandSI-26
84OCoandSI-132
84SpoDesPW-6
85CirK-16
86BraPol-8
86PirGreT-1
86SpoDesJM-23
87K-M-22
89HOFStiB-27
89KahCoo-10
89PerCelP-40
89TopBasT-16
89TopGloA-22
90BasWit-4
90PerGreM-38
90PerMasW-36
90PerMasW-37
90PerMasW-38
90PerMasW-39
90PerMasW-40
91Don-702
91MDAA-3
91UppDecS-13
92ActPacA-17
92ActPacA2-17G
92ActPacAP-5
92FroRowSt-1
92FroRowSt-2
92FroRowSt-3
92FroRowSt-4
92FroRowSt-5
92KelAll-1
92MDAMVP-14
92Pin-588
93ActPacAC-17
93MetIma-19
93NabAllA-6
93TedWil-81
93TedWilM-14
93Yoo-20
94UppDecAH-95
94UppDecAH-172
94UppDecAH1-95
94UppDecAH1-172
94UppDecS-5
94UppDecTAE-76
95EagBalL-8
95StoPop-5
95UppDecSHoB-15
97FleMilDM-45
97SpoIllCC-9
97St.VinHHS-15
Stark, Clinton
61UniOil-P13
Stark, Dolly (Monroe)
09T206-518
34DiaMatCSB-169
39PlaBal-106
40PlaBal-117
90DodTar-765
94ConTSN-1191
94ConTSNB-1191
Stark, George
83TigAIKS-12
Stark, Greg
92PitMetC-13
92PitMetF-3295
93CapCitBC-21
93CapCitBF-461
Stark, Jeff
87SpaPhiP-4
88SpaPhiP-1024
Stark, Matt
86KnoBluJP-22
87BluJayFS-29
90Bes-99
90BirBarB-4
90BirBarP-1113
90CMC-746
90ProAaA-47
91Cla1-T30
91Don-747
91LinDriAAA-646
91Sco-751
91VanCanLD-646
91VanCanP-1597
92MidAngS-470
Stark, Richard
94StoPorC-30
96StoPorB-30
Stark, Zachary
95KanCouCTI-34
Starkey, Harold
63GadFunC-82
Starkey, Melveena
91HawWomS-14
Starkovich, Paul
75SanAntBT-20
Starks, Bob
76QuaCitAT-33
Starks, Fred
93HicCraC-23
93HicCraF-1279
Starling, Marcus
94EliTwiC-23
94EliTwiF-3733
Starr, Bart
68AtlOil-12
Starr, Charles
09T206-337
10CouT21-61
11MecDFT-41
Starr, Chris
91ButCopKSP-3
93ButCopKSP-4
Starr, Dick
50Bow-191
51Bow-137
Starr, Ray
77TCMTheWY-74
Starrette, Herm
64Top-239
64TopVen-239
65Top-539
74OPC-634
74Top-634
78TCM60I-194
84GiaPos-26
85BrePol-NNO
86BrePol-38
87CubCan-31
87CubDavB-NNO
88OriFreB-31
91OriCro-434
92RocExpC-29
93JamExpF-3344
Stars, New York
93NegLeaRL2-100
93TedWilPC-12
Stars, Philadelphia
92NegLeaRLI-96
93NegLeaRL2-83
93NegLeaRL2-84
93NegLeaRL2-85
93TedWilPC-13
Stars, St. Louis
91PomBlaBPB-28
93NegLeaRL2-79
Stasio, Chris
94EveGiaC-27
94EveGiaF-3662
95MicBatCTI-26
Statham, Cliff
52LavPro-2
Staton, Dave
88CapCodPPaLP-167
89SpoIndSP-1
90Bes-6
90CalLeaACLC-1
90ProAaA-148
90RivRedWB-1
90RivRedWCLC-1
90RivRedWP-2617
90TopMag-1
91Bow-645
91Cla2-T44
91ClaGam-182
91LasVegSLD-294
91LasVegSP-246
91LinDriAAA-294
91UppDec-66
92Bow-499
92LasVegSF-2807
92LasVegSS-241
92OPC-126
92PadSmo-33
92ProFS7-333
92SkyAAAF-117
92Top-126
92TopGol-126
92TopGolW-126
92TopMic-126
92TriA AAS-241
92UppDecML-191
93Don-325
93ExcFS7-111
94Bow-448
94ColC-266
94ColChoGS-266
94ColChoSS-266
94ExtBas-379
94Fin-428
94FinJum-428
94FinRef-428
94Fla-236
94FlaWavotF-A9
94FleMajLP-32
94Lea-349
94OPC-84
94PadMot-26
94Pin-396
94PinArtP-396
94PinMusC-396
94ScoRoo-RT128
94ScoRooGR-RT128
94Sel-200
94SpoRoo-69
94SpoRooAP-69
94Top-507
94TopGol-507
94TopSpa-507
94Ult-585
94UltAllR-10
94UltAllRJ-10
94UppDec-214
94UppDecED-214
95Sco-584
95ScoGolR-584
95ScoPlaTS-584
Staton, T.J.
94WelPirC-24
94WelPirF-3510
96CarMudB-25
97FlaShoWotF-22
97Fle-597
97FleTif-597
97Ult-497
97UltGolME-497
97UltPlaME-497
Statz, Jigger (Arnold)
21Exh-172
22E120-165
23MapCriV-16
23WilChoV-157
27AmeCarE-33
37WheBB7-29M
88LitSunMLL-9
90DodTar-766
93ConTSN-782
Staub, Rusty
69ExpPin-7
63Col45"P-14
63Col45"P-20
63Top-544
64Col.45JP-8
64Top-109
64TopCoi-96
64TopSta-88
64TopVen-109
65Top-321
66OPC-106
66Top-106
66Top-273
66TopVen-106
66TopVen-273
67Ast-26
67AstTeal1-11
67AstTeal2-23
67CokCapA-5
67CokCapAs-13
67CokCapNLA-32
67DexPre-198
67OPC-73
67Top-73
67TopGiaSU-17
67TopVen-292
68Baz-14
68CokCapA-13
68DexPre-71
68Top-300
68Top3-D-10
68TopActS-6C
68TopGamI-28
68TopPla-23
68TopPos-22
68TopVen-300
69CitMetC-15
69ExpFudP-11
69MilBra-264
69MLBOffS-161
69NabTeaF-23
69OPCDec-20
69Top-230
69TopDec-22A
69TopDecI-41
69TopSta-38
69TopSup-48
69TopTeaP-10
69TraSta-39
70DayDaiNM-38
70ExpPin-13
70ExpPos-11
70MLBOffS-70
70Top-585
70TopBoo-18
70TopSup-41
71AllBasA-23
71BazNumT-40
71BazUnn-34
71ExpLaPR-12
71ExpPS-23
71MilDud-65
71MLBOffS-141
71MLBOffS-575
71OPC-289
71OPC-560
71Top-560
71TopCoi-111
71TopGreM-35
71TopSup-9
71TopTat-59
72Dia-65
72MilBra-328
73LinPor-123

73NewYorN-20
74MetDaiPA-12
74OPC-475
74OPC-629
74Top-475
74Top-629
75Hos-129
75MetSSP-7
75OPC-90
75Top-90
76CraDis-59
76OPC-120
76SSP-537
76Top-120
76TopTra-120T
77BurCheD-96
77Hos-82
77MSADis-59
77OPC-88
77PepGloD-29
77RCColC-61
77Spo-6615
77Top-420
77TopCloS-46
78OPC-188
78TigBurK-22
78Top-370
78WifBalD-72
79ExpPos-28
79Hos-56
79OPC-228
79Top-440
79TopCom-7
80OPC-347
80Top-660
81CokTeaS-91
81Fle-629
81Top-80
81TopSupHT-76
81TopTra-835
82Don-56
82Fle-536
82FleSta-82
82MetPhoA-20
82OPC-270
82Top-270
83Don-350
83Fle-555
83FleSta-187
83FleSti-238
83OPC-1
83OPC-51
83Top-740
83Top-741
83TopFol-2
83TopSti-14
84Don-6
84Don-6A
84Don-554
84DonCha-28
84Fle-597
84FleSti-40
84FunFooP-84
84MetFanC-6
84Nes792-430
84Nes792-702
84Nes792-704
84OPC-224
84Top-430
84Top-702
84Top-704
84TopSti-287A
84TopTif-430
84TopTif-702
84TopTif-704
85Fle-92
85FleStaS-50
85MetColP-27
85OPC-190
85Top-190
85TopMin-190
85TopTif-190
86AstGreT-7
86AstMot-6
86ExpGreT-7
86Fle-95
86MetGreT-7
86Spo-138
86Top-570
86TopTif-570
87AstSer1-21
87AstSer1-28
87AstShoSO-22
87AstShoSO-26
87AstShoSTw-25
90MetHaloF-3
90PacLeg-52
90SweBasG-91
91JesHSA-6
91MetWIZ-377
91SweBasG-87
92ActPacA-81
92MVP2H-10
92Nab-25
92UppDecS-10
92UppDecS-21
93ExpDonM-20
93RanKee-342
93UppDecS-27
94TedWil-52
Staubach, Roger
74NewYorNTDiS-39
92Pin-589
Stauffacher, Stuart
86BurExpP-21
Staydohar, Dave
90BoiHawP-3328
92QuaCitRBC-25
92QuaCitRBF-824
Stearnes, Turkey
90NegLeaS-15
95NegLeaL2-7
Stearns, Bill
83OklCit8T-1
86TulDriTI-6
Stearns, Dan
87OldJudN-481
Stearns, Don
87SanBerSP-4
Stearns, John
75IntLeaAT-7
75MetSSP-8
76OPC-633
76SSP-546
76Top-633
77BurCheD-140
77MetDaiPA-23
77Top-119
78MetDaiPA-22
78Top-334
79Hos-124
79OPC-280
79Top-205
79Top-545
80Kel-37
80OPC-41
80Top-76
81AllGamPI-134
81Don-35
81Fle-317
81OPC-255
81Top-428
81TopScr-96
81TopSti-194
82Don-434
82Fle-537
82FleSta-89
82MetPhoA-21
82OPC-232
82Top-743
83AllGamPI-135
83Don-380
83DonActA-25
83Fle-556
83FleSti-234
83OPC-212
83Top-212
83TopSti-264
84Fle-598
90KnoBluJB-9
90KnoBluJP-1259
90KnoBluJS-24
91KnoBluJLD-374
91KnoBluJP-1784
91LinDriAA-374
91MetWIZ-378
94MCIAmb-2
94PriRedC-26
94PriRedF-3279
Stearns, Randy
87SanBerSP-5
96YakBeaTI-8
Stearns, Turkey (Norman)
78LauLonABS-4
87NegLeaPD-35
Stechschulte, Gene
96NewJerCB-26
Steck, Dave
76QuaCitAT-34
Stedman, Tom
75LafDriT-11
Steed, David
93GreFalDSP-15
94YakBeaC-24
94YakBeaF-3855
95VerBeaDTI-24
96SanBerSB-26
Steed, Rick
90St.CatBJP-3473
91MyrBeaHC-11
91MyrBeaHP-2945
91SouAtlLAGP-SAL40
92DunBluJC-18
92DunBluJF-2000
93DunBluJC-22
93DunBluJF-1796
93DunBluJFFN-24
95IndIndF-92
95KnoSmoF-42
96GreBraB-25
96GreBraTI-49
Steed, Scott
91PerHeaF-19
Steel, Ed
86NegLeaF-48
Steele, Bill (William)
12T207-174
14B18B-89A
14B18B-89B
90DodTar-1078
Steele, Don
75LafDriT-26
Steele, Steve
92KinMetC-11
92KinMetF-1535
Steele, Tim
75WatDodT-20
Steele, Walt
80BurBeeT-20
Steelman, Farmer
90DodTar-1080
Steels, James
82AmaGolST-11
83BeaGolGT-20
83LasVegSBHN-20
84BeaGolGT-3
85LasVegSC-125
86LasVegSP-19
87DonRoo-50
87PadBohHB-21
88Don-360
88FleUpd-64
88FleUpdG-64
88OklCit8C-24
88OklCit8P-38
88RanMot-21
88Top-117
88TopTif-117
90CMC-65
90IndIndC-15
90IndIndP-306
90ProAAAF-589
93RanKee-343
Steen, Mike
76SanAntBTI-21
Steen, Scott
86ClePhiP-23
Steenstra, Kennie
90WicStaSGD-32
91TopTra-113T
91TopTraT-113T
92GenCubC-6
92GenCubF-1561
92PeoChiTI-25
92StaCluD-180
92TopDaiQTU-23
93ClaFS7-258
93DayCubC-18
93DayCubF-857
93FloStaLAF-33
94ClaGolF-131
94ExcFS7-167
94OrlCubF-1384
94UppDecML-82
95IowCubTI-23
96IowCubB-24
Stefan, Todd
91SalLakTP-3221
91SalLakTSP-21
92PeoChiC-9
92PeoChiTI-26
Stefani, Mario
89BriTigS-27
90FayGenP-2407
Stefanik, Robert
92LetMouSP-25
Stefanski, Jim
82DurBulT-10
Stefanski, Mike
92BelBreC-16
92BelBreF-408
92ClaFS7-360
92MidLeaATI-41
93StoPorC-23
93StoPorF-748
94ElPasDF-3150
94ExcFS7-87
96LouRedB-26
Stefaro, John
84Don-622
85ChaO'sT-5
87Don-541
87ExpPos-30
87Fle-652
87FleGlo-652
87FleGlo-653
87Top-563
87TopTif-563
88ColSprSSC-11
88ColSprSSP-1522
90ChaKniTI-9
90HagSunDGB-30
91OriCro-435
Steffen, David
80EvaTriT-4
81Top-626
Steffens, Mark
90PriPatD-22
91SpaPhiC-27
91SpaPhiP-912
92ClePhiF-2071
92SpaPhiC-19
92SpaPhiF-1279
Steger, Chip
77TucTorC-NNO
Steger, Kevin
80SanJosMJitB-17
81WauTimT-1
83ChaLooT-22
Stegman, Dave
79Top-706
82ColCliP-23
82ColCliT-13
84Nes792-664
84Top-664
84TopTif-664
84WhiSoxTV-28
85SyrChiT-31
85Top-194
85TopTif-194
86ColCliP-24
92YanWIZ8-187
Steigerwald, John
75LafDriT-24
Stein, Bill
76OPC-131
76SSP-146
76Top-131
77Hos-136
77OPC-20
77Top-334
78Hos-39
78OPC-147
78Top-476
79Hos-18
79OPC-372
79Top-698
80OPC-121
80Top-226
81Don-543
81Fle-605
81Top-532
81TopTra-836
82Don-37
82Fle-331
82FleSta-179
82Top-402
82TopSti-118
83Don-594
83Fle-579
83RanAffF-1
83Top-64
84Fle-429
84Nes792-758
84RanJarP-1
84Top-758
84TopTif-758
85Don-621
85RanPer-1
85Top-171
85TopTif-171
86Don-403
86MarGreT-4
86Top-371
86TopTif-371
88LitFalMP-26
89ColMetB-22
89ColMetGS-1
89T/MSenL-99
90ColMetGS-1
90ColMetPPI-1
90SouAtlLAS-46
91BenBucC-28
91BenBucP-3710
92CliGiaC-26
92CliGiaF-3612
93RanKee-344
93ShrCapF-2777
Stein, Blake
94JohCitCC-27
94JohCitCF-3702
95PeoChiTI-34
96StPetCB-29
97Bow-204
97BowInt-204
Stein, Ethan
96SpoIndB-27
Stein, John
86AppFoxP-24
87BakDodP-9
89SalLakTTI-10
Stein, Jose
91BoiHawC-11
Stein, Kevin
96AubDouB-26
Stein, Ray
80WisRapTT-25
Stein, W. Randy
79Top-394
79VanCanT-16
80SpoIndT-13
80Top-613
81SpoIndT-24
82IowCubT-24
83IowCubT-10
94BreMilB-358
Steinbach, Terry
84MadMusP-10
85HunStaJ-16
86SouLeaAJ-10
87Don-34
87DonRoo-26
87Fle-405
87FleGlo-405
87Lea-34
87Spo-118
87SpoRooI-22
87SpoRooP-1
87SpoTeaP-23
87TopTra-117T
87TopTraT-117T
88A'sMot-4
88ClaRed-186
88Don-158
88DonBasB-78
88DonTeaBA-158
88Fle-294
88FleGlo-294
88OPC-44
88PanSti-166
88Sco-82
88ScoGlo-82
88ScoYouSI-16
88Spo-174
88StaLinAs-15
88Top-551
88TopBig-39A
88TopBig-39B
88TopCoi-28
88TopRoo-15
88TopTif-551
88ToyRoo-30
89A'sMot-3
89Bow-193
89BowTif-193
89CadEllD-54
89ClaLigB-69
89Don-268
89DonAll-9
89DonAll-31

89DonBasB-323
89DonPop-9
89Fle-22
89Fle-634
89FleGlo-22
89FleGlo-634
89K-M-19
89OPC-304
89PanSti-236
89PanSti-419
89Sco-365
89Spo-119
89Top-725
89TopBig-80
89TopGloA-9
89TopSti-152
89TopSti-165
89TopTif-725
89TVSpoM-97
89UppDec-256
90A'sMot-3
90Bow-456
90BowTif-456
90ClaUpd-T46
90Don-268
90Don-637A
90Don-637B
90DonBesA-137
90Fle-20
90FleBasA-38
90FleCan-20
90FleWorS-3
90FleWorS-7
90Lea-252
90MLBBasB-115
90OPC-145
90PanSti-143
90PanSti-205
90PubSti-315
90Sco-162
90Sco-693A
90Sco-693B
90Sco100S-55
90Spo-33
90Top-145
90TopBig-118
90TopGloA-20
90TopSti-163
90TopSti-186
90TopStiB-56
90TopTif-145
90UppDec-246
90VenSti-457
90Woo-28
91A'sMot-3
91A'sSFE-12
91Bow-216
91CadEIID-54
91Don-329
91Fle-24
91Lea-87
91OPC-625
91PanFreS-191
91Sco-780
91SevCoi-NC11
91StaClu-518
91Top-625
91TopDesS-625
91TopMic-625
91TopTif-625
91Ult-253
91UppDec-153
92AthMot-3
92Bow-392
92Don-104
92Fle-267
92Lea-501
92OPC-234
92PanSti-14
92Pin-76
92Sco-440
92Sco-633
92ScoProP-18
92StaClu-22
92Stu-229
92Top-234
92TopGol-234
92TopGolW-234
92TopMic-234
92TriPla-10
92Ult-116
92UppDec-473
93AthMot-3
93Bow-21
93DiaMar-102
93Don-505
93Fin-67
93FinRef-67
93Fla-263
93Fle-299
93FunPac-53
93Lea-7
93OPC-268
93PacSpa-226
93PanSti-14
93Pin-12
93Sco-626
93Sel-132
93SP-44
93StaClu-208
93StaCluAt-9
93StaCluFDI-208
93StaCluMOP-208
93Stu-57
93Top-18
93TopGol-18
93TopInaM-18
93TopMic-18
93TriPla-177
93Ult-262
93UppDec-278
93UppDecGold-278
94A'sMot-3
94Bow-408
94ColC-267
94ColChoGS-267
94ColChoSS-267
94Don-254
94ExtBas-156
94Fin-38
94FinRef-38
94Fla-96
94Fle-274
94Lea-178
94OPC-117
94Pac-463
94PanSti-113
94Pin-120
94PinArtP-120
94PinMusC-120
94ProMag-99
94Sco-47
94ScoGolR-47
94Sel-257
94SP-38
94SPDieC-38
94StaClu-346
94StaCluFDI-346
94StaCluGR-346
94StaCluMOP-346
94Stu-7
94Top-610
94TopGol-610
94TopSpa-610
94TriPla-9
94Ult-412
94UppDec-291
94UppDec-488
94UppDecED-291
94UppDecED-488
95A'sCHP-5
95AthMot-3
95Bow-308
95ColCho-132
95ColChoGS-132
95ColChoSE-49
95ColChoSEGS-49
95ColChoSESS-49
95ColChoSS-132
95Don-354
95DonPreP-354
95DonTopotO-141
95Emb-135
95EmbGolI-135
95Emo-75
95Fin-116
95FinRef-116
95Fla-296
95Fle-254
95Lea-148
95Pac-321
95PacPri-104
95Pin-354
95PinArtP-354
95PinMusC-354
95Sco-104
95ScoGolR-104
95ScoHaloG-HG48
95ScoPlaTS-104
95Sel-66
95SelArtP-66
95SelCer-3
95SelCerMG-3
95SP-183
95SPCha-179
95SPChaDC-179
95SPSil-183
95StaClu-463
95StaCluMOP-463
95StaCluSTWS-463
95StaCluVR-252
95Stu-113
95Sum-66
95SumNthD-66
95Top-442
95TopCyb-238
95Ult-97
95UltGolM-97
95UppDecSE-111
95UppDecSEG-111
96A'sMot-4
96Baz-18
96Bow-74
96Cir-74
96CirRav-74
96ColCho-241
96ColChoGS-241
96ColChoSS-241
96Don-24
96DonPreP-24
96EmoXL-107
96Fin-B32
96FinRef-B32
96Fla-153
96Fle-218
96FleTif-218
96Lea-160
96LeaPrePB-160
96LeaPrePG-160
96LeaPrePS-160
96LeaSigA-214
96LeaSigAG-214
96LeaSigAS-214
96MetUni-103
96MetUniP-103
96Pac-388
96PacPri-P127
96PacPriG-P127
96PanSti-221
96Pin-284
96PinFoil-284
96ProSta-7
96Sco-95
96SelTeaN-5
96SP-137
96StaClu-349
96StaCluEPB-349
96StaCluEPG-349
96StaCluEPS-349
96StaCluMOP-349
95StaCluVRMC-252
96TeaOut-79
96Top-267
96TopChr-107
96TopChrR-107
96TopGal-26
96TopGalPPI-26
96TopLas-31
96Ult-117
96UltGolM-117
96UppDec-411
97Bow-226
97BowInt-226
97Cir-75
97CirRav-75
97ColChoAC-17
97Don-110
86HumStaDS-16
97DonPreP-110
97DonPrePGold-110
97Fin-241
97FinRef-241
97Fle-196
97Fle-540
97FleTif-196
97FleTif-540
97Lea-270
97LeaFraM-270
97LeaFraMDC-270
97MetUni-214
97NewPin-151
97NewPinAP-151
97NewPinMC-151
97NewPinPP-151
97Pac-177
97PacLigB-177
97PacPri-60
97PacPriLB-60
97PacPriP-60
97PacSil-177
97Pin-107
97PinArtP-107
97PinIns-126
97PinInsCE-126
97PinInsDE-126
97PinMusC-107
97PinX-PSfF-26
97PinX-PSfFU-26
97Sco-146
97Sco-350
97ScoHobR-350
97ScoPreS-146
97ScoResC-350
97ScoShoS-146
97ScoShoS-350
97ScoShoSAP-146
97ScoShoSAP-350
97SP-109
97StaClu-130
97StaCluMOP-130
97Top-111
97TopChr-43
97TopChrR-43
97TopGal-28
97TopGalPPI-28
97TopSta-76
97TopStaAM-76
97Ult-351
97UltGolME-351
97UltPlaME-351
97UppDec-410
Steinbach, Tom
85BelBreT-9
Steinbacher, Hank
94ConTSN-1316
94ConTSNB-1316
Steinberg, David
83WisRapTF-8
Steinbrenner, George
91FouBal-14
Steiner, Brian
88GasRanP-1018
89ButCopKSP-18
90GasRanB-15
90GasRanP-2522
90GasRanS-23
91ChaRanC-12
91ChaRanP-1316
Steinert, Paul
84ButCopKT-22
Steinert, Rob
93St.CatBJC-22
93St.CatBJF-3975
94HagSunC-24
94HagSunF-2732
95DunBluJTI-29
95Exc-143
Steinfeldt, Harry
03BreE10-134
07CubA.CDPP-13
07CubGFGCP-14
08AmeCarE-29
08AmeCarE-63
08CubPos-4
08RosComP-110
09BriE97-28
09ColChiE-273
09RamT20-112
09T206-338
09T206-339
10ChiE-10
10RedCroT-73
10RedCroT-159
10RedCroT-246
10SweCapPP-92
10W555-58
11S74Sil-47
11S74Sil-70
11SpoLifCW-335
11SpoLifM-183
11T205-162
12ColRedB-273
12ColTinT-273
12HasTriFT-50D
12T207-175
84CubUno-7
87Cub190T-1
90BasWit-57
Steinitz, Chess
88GooN16-41
Steinkamp, Mike
89SalLakTTI-13
Steinke, Brock
96KisCobB-28
Steinmann, Scott
96EveAquB-23
Steinmetz, Earl
90Bes-136
90CMC-729
90SumBraB-22
90SumBraP-2432
91DurBulC-9
91DurBulP-1544
92DurBulC-12
92DurBulF-1100
92DurBulTI-23
Steinmetz, Kevin
83TamTarT-21
Steirer, Ricky
80ElPasDT-4
81SalLakCGT-12
82SpoIndT-8
84EdmTraC-102
Stela, Jose
91BoiHawP-3883
91QuaCitAC-13
91QuaCitAP-2631
92MidLeaATI-42
92QuaCitRBC-15
92QuaCitRBF-813
93CedRapKC-20
93PalSprAC-22
93PalSprAF-73
Stella, Jose
93LinVenB-136
94VenLinU-46
95LinVen-195
Stellern, Mike
82AubAstT-4
85OscAstTI-25
Stello, Dick
88T/MUmp-60
Stelmaszek, Rick
70Top-599
73OPC-601
73Top-601
74OPC-611
74Top-611
75OPC-338
75Top-338
77TucTorC-17
78WisRapTT-18
79WisRapTT-23
80WisRapTT-26
82TwiPos-25
83TwiTeal-28
83TwiTeal-34
84MinTwiP-27
84TwiTeal-29
85TwiTeal-32
86TwiTeal-30
88TwiTeal-28
93RanKee-345
Stember, Jeff
78CedRapGT-27
79CedRapGT-16
81PhoGiaVNB-5
82PhoGiaVNB-16
Stemberger, Brian
82KnoBluJT-9
Stemler, Andy
91WatIndC-11
91WatIndP-3366
Stemmyer, William
87OldJudN-482
Stengel, Casey (Charles Dillon)
14B18B-62
15SpoNewM-171
16ColE13-168
16FleBreD-90
16SpoNewM-169
17HolBreD-100
19W514-113
20NatCarE-101
21Exh-173
21KoBreWSI-24
22W575-131
22W575-132
23MapCriV-15

23W503-15
23W515-24
23W551-10
34DiaMatCSB-170
35DiaMatCS2-19
35DiaMatCS3T1-134
36NatChiFPR-68
36R31PasP-22
40PlaBal-141
46RemBre-10
47RemBre-8
47SigOil-56
47SmiClo-1
48SigOil-22
48SmiClo-20
50Bow-217
51Bow-181
51R42SmaS-93
52Bow-217
52RedMan-AL1
53BowBW-39
53Dor-113
53RedMan-AL1
57YanJayP-11
58JayPubA-20
58Top-475
59Top-383
59Top-552
60Top-227
60YanJayP-11
61NuSco-461
62MetJayP-10
62Top-29
62TopVen-29
63BasMagM-80
63MetJayP-10
63Top-43
63Top-233
64MetJayP-11
64Top-324
64Top-393
64TopVen-324
65MetJayP-12
65OPC-187
65Top-187
68LauWorS-50
72LauGreF-20
73HalofFPP-17
73MetAllEB-12
74MetOriEB-13
74NewYorNTDiS-17
75ShaPiz-8
76GrePlaG-39
76LauIndC-40
76Met63 S-17
76RowExh-14
76ShaPiz-104
77BobParHoF-46
77GalGloG-13
77GalGloG-253
77TCMTheWY-63
80LauFamF-20
80PacLeg-47
80PerHaloFP-103
80SSPHOF-103
80YanGreT-12
81ConTSN-71
81SpoHaloF-13
81TCM60I-422
81TCM60I-482
82MetGal62-26
83DiaClaS2-96
83DonHOFH-37
83TCMPla1942-42
83YanASFY-45
84OCoandSI-149
84OCoandSI-212
85FegMurCG-18
85UltBasC-6
86ConSer1-33
86SpoDesJM-12
86TCMSupS-9
86TCMSupS-47
88ConHar-5
88WilMulP-2
88WilMulP-11
89DodSmoG-28
89PacLegI-218
89SweBasG-130
89YanCitAG-6
90BasWit-85
90DodTar-767
90HOFStiB-60
90MetHaloF-1
90SweBasG-40
91ConTSN-37
91LinDri-46
91SweBasG-136
91TopArc1-325
92BazQua5A-21
92ConTSN-558
92ConTSNCI-5
92PinMan-27
92St.VinHHS-10
92YanWIZH-32
93ConTSN-829
93DiaStaES-150
93Hoy-7
93LegFoi-10
93SpeHOF2-5
94TedWilLC-LC16
94UppDecTAE-57
95ConTSN-1330

Stenholm, Richard A.
76ForLauYS-23
77WesHavYT-22
81ColCliP-15
81ColCliT-1

Stenhouse, Dave
55DonWin-39
60HenHouW-26
62Top-592
63Fle-30
63Jel-97
63Pos-97
63SalMetC-37
63Top-263
63TopStil-42
64Top-498
65Top-304
78TCM60I-141
84SyrChiT-26
85Top-141
85TopTif-141
86SyrChiP-24
87SyrChiP-1940
87SyrChiT-11

Stenhouse, Michael
82WicAerTI-19
83WicAerDS-21
84Don-29A
84Don-29B
84ExpPos-31
84ExpStu-26
84IndIndTI-30
85Don-376
85Fle-411
85FleUpd-110
85OPC-282
85Top-141
85Top-658
85TopTif-141
85TopTif-658
85TopTifT-112T
85TopTra-112T
85TwiTeal-23
86Fle-406
86OPC-17
86PawRedSP-23
86Top-17
86TopTif-17
87TolMudHP-19
87TolMudHT-5

Stennett, Matt
86AubAstP-24

Stennett, Rennie
72OPC-219
72Top-219
73OPC-348
73Top-348
74OPC-426
74Top-426
74TopSta-89
75Hos-131
75OPC-336
75Top-336
76CraDis-60
76Hos-9
76HosTwi-9
76OPC-6
76OPC-425
76SSP-575
76Top-6
76Top-425
77BurCheD-182
77Hos-100
77OPC-129
77PirPosP-26
77Top-35
78Hos-33
78OPC-25
78Top-165
79OPC-365
79Top-687
80GiaEurFS-8
80GiaPol-6
80Top-501
81AllGamPI-107
81Don-72A
81Don-72B
81Fle-438
81OPC-257
81Top-257
82Don-563
82Fle-401
82OPC-84
82Top-84
83WicAerDS-22
89PacSenL-79
89T/MSenL-100
89TopSenL-127
90EliSenL-89
90HOFStiB-82
94UppDecAH-137
94UppDecAH-217
94UppDecAH1-137
94UppDecAH1-217

Stenta, Jeff
91EriSaiC-10
91EriSaiP-4079

Stento, Bernie
87ElmPio(C-28

Stentz, Brent
96FayGenB-28

Stenz, Dan
90BoiHawP-3314

Stenzel, Jake
98CamPepP-72

Stepanov, Roman
89EasLeaDDP-DD16

Steph, Rodney
91PriRedC-9
91PriRedP-3514
92CedRapRC-13
92CedRapRF-1073
93WinSpiC-22
93WinSpiF-1571
94Bow-654
96RicBraB-27

Stephan, Todd
89PenPilS-23
90CarLeaA-3
90FreKeyTI-24
91HagSunLD-247
91HagSunP-2458
91LinDriAA-247
91PerHeaF-6
92RocRedWF-1940
92RocRedWS-470
92SkyAAAF-213
93LinVenB-271
93RocRedWF-240

Stephans, Russell
81ChaRoyT-13
83OmaRoyT-12
84OmaRoyT-26
85Don-42
86OmaRoyP-24
86OmaRoyT-10

Stephen, Buzz (Louis)
69PilPos-15
70OPC-533
70Top-533

Stephens, B.F.
87OldJudN-484

Stephens, Bill
91HigSchPLS-17
91KisDodP-4197
92GulCoaDF-3567

Stephens, Brian
91RenSilSCLC-24

Stephens, Bryan
46RemBre-19
47IndTeal-25
47IndVanPP-24
49W725AngTI-26
50WorWidGV-11

Stephens, Darryl
82RedPioT-14
83NasAngT-15

Stephens, Gene
53RedSoxTI-25
53Top-248
56Top-313
57Top-217
58Hir-72
58RedSoxJP-9
58Top-227
59Top-261
60RedSoxJP-9
60Top-363
61Top-102
61TopStal-105
62Jel-95
62Pos-95A
62Pos-95B
62PosCan-95
62SalPlaC-56
62ShiPlaC-56
62Top-38
62TopStal-59
62TopVen-38
64Top-308
64TopVen-308
64WhiSoxTS-21
65Top-498
79DiaGre-244
90HOFStiB-48
91OriCro-436
91TopArc1-248

Stephens, James W.
09PC7HHB-41
09RamT20-113
09T206-340
11MecDFT-42
11SpoLifM-117

Stephens, Joel
96BluOriB-28

Stephens, Mark
90HelBreSP-14
91BelBreC-8
91BelBreP-2103
91SalLakTP-3211
91SalLakTSP-20
92SalSpuF-3754

Stephens, Ray (Carl Ray)
87ArkTraP-22
87TexLeaAF-31
88LouRedBC-19
88LouRedBP-422
88LouRedBTI-45
89ArkTraGS-23
89TexLeaAGS-21
90CMC-113
90LouRedBC-13
90LouRedBLBC-39
90LouRedBP-405
90ProAAAF-519
90TopTVCa-65
91LinDriAAA-248
91LouRedLD-248
91LouRedP-2918
91LouRedTI-27
91Sco-743
91TopDeb90-148
91TriA AAGP-AAA22
92Don-764
92OklCit8F-1917
92ScrRedBS-495
93OklCit8F-1629
93RanKee-346

Stephens, Reggie
91SpoIndC-9
91SpoIndP-3963
91WatDiaC-23
91WatDiaP-1270

Stephens, Ron
88UtiBluSP-24
89SarWhiSS-22
89Sta-60
90Bes-50
90BirBarB-23
90BirBarP-1393
91LinDriAAA-647
91VanCanLD-647
91VanCanP-1595
92SkyAAAF-289
92VanCanF-2723
92VanCanS-648

Stephens, Seth
91FayGenC-5

Stephens, Shannon
95ElmPioTI-28
96KanCouCTI-26
96MidLeaAB-34

Stephens, Vern
46SeaSLP-51
46SpoExcW-9-10
47Exh-217A
47Exh-217B
47HomBon-44
47TipTop-73
48RedSoxTI-22
49Bow-71
49Lea-161
50AmeNut&CCP-19
50Bow-2
50Dra-34
51Bow-92
51R42SmaS-94
51TopRedB-4
52Bow-9
52RedMan-AL21
52StaCalL-71D
52StaCalS-85C
52TipTop-42
52Top-84
53Top-270
54Top-54
54Wil-18
55Bow-109
56YelBasP-30
76TayBow4-19
83TCMPla1942-8
83TopRep5-84
91OriCro-437
91TopArc1-270
94TopArc1-54
94TopArc1G-54
96Bro194F-9

Stephenson, Brian
94SigRooDP-43
94SigRooDPS-43
94WilCubC-22
94WilCubF-3764
95Bow-175
96Bow-348
96OrlCubB-25

Stephenson, Earl (Chester)
72OPC-61
72Top-61
74TacTwiC-11
75IntLeaAT-4
77RocRedWM-7
78RocRedWT-16
79TidTidT-25
86HagSunP-21
87NewOriP-4
89PacSenL-159
91OriCro-438
94BreMilB-359

Stephenson, Ed
76BatRouCT-19

Stephenson, Garrett
92BluOriC-1
92BluOriF-2361
93AlbPolC-20
93AlbPolF-2027
94FreKeyF-2614
94OriPro-97
95BowBayTI-36
96Bow-122
96Exc-8
96RocRedWB-26
97Fle-598
97FleTif-598
94FreKeyC-21

Stephenson, Gene
90WicStaSGD-44

Stephenson, J. Riggs
21Exh-174
22W575-133
23MapCriV-26
23WilChoV-158
28PorandAR-A34
28PorandAR-B34
28StaPlaCE-64
29PorandAR-87
30ChiEveAP-9
31CubTeal-22
31Exh-5
32CubTeal-22
32OrbPinNP-3
32OrbPinUP-54
33DelR33-15
33ExhFou-3
33Gou-204
33TatOrb-54
33TatOrbSDR-170
34DiaMatCSB-171

61Fle-140
76ChiGre-18
77GalGloG-51
80PacLeg-95
83ConMar-27
83DiaClaS2-106
88ConNatA-19
88ConSer4-27
91ConTSN-218
92ConTSN-441
92CubOldS-23
Stephenson, Jerry
65OPC-74
65Top-74
66Top-396
67TopRedSS-20
68Top-519
69OPC-172
69Top-172
71OPC-488
71Top-488
81RedSoxBG2S-118
90DodTar-768
92MetColP-38
Stephenson, John
64Top-536
66OPC-17
66Top-17
66TopVen-17
67CokCapYM-V26
67DexPre-199
67Top-522
68OPC-83
68Top-83
68TopVen-83
71OPC-421
71Top-421
91MetWIZ-379
91WhiSoxK-NNO
92MetKah-51
94KinMetC-27
94KinMetF-3841
Stephenson, Joseph
85GreHorT-11
Stephenson, Phil
83AlbA'sT-15
84TacTigC-88
85TacTigC-132
86PitCubP-23
87IowCubTI-18
88IowCubC-17
88IowCubP-540
89DonRoo-36
90AlbDecGB-14
90OPC-584
90Sco-642
90Top-584
90TopDeb89-123
90TopTif-584
90WicStaSGD-35
91Fle-545
91OPC-726
91PadSmo-35
91Sco-138
91StaClu-420
91Top-726
91TopDesS-726
91TopMic-726
91TopTif-726
92LasVegSF-2804
92PadPolD-22
92StaClu-684
92StaCluECN-684
93Top-357
93TopGol-357
93TopInaM-357
93TopMic-357
94LouRedF-2991
Stephenson, Walter
35DiaMatCS3T1-135
Stepka, Tom
96PorRocB-29
Sterling, J.C.
87OldJudN-485
Sterling, Randy
75TidTidTI-20
91MetWIZ-380
Stetson, Mike
91CalLeLA-52
Stevanus, Mike
86MacPirP-24
87SalBucP-22
88SalBucS-19
88WatPirP-11
89AugPirP-502
Steve, Harry
83SanJosBC-26
86SanJosBP-19
89SanJosGCLC-237
Stevens, Bicyclist
88GooN16-42
Stevens, Brian
90LSUTigA-11
Stevens, Charles
46SeaSLP-52
49W72HolS-22
50W720HolS-30
52MotCoo-39
53MotCoo-17
Stevens, Clay
96BriWhiSB-29
Stevens, Dale
91PocPioP-3782
91PocPioSP-17
Stevens, Dave
90HunCubP-3282
91GenCubP-4214
92ChaKniS-166
93Bow-116
93OrlCubF-2783
94BowBes-B70
94BowBesR-B70
94Cla-79
94FleUpd-65
94SalLakBF-816
94SpoRoo-71
94SpoRooAP-71
94TopTra-97T
94UppDecML-118
95ColCho-24
95ColChoGS-24
95ColChoSS-24
95Fle-214
95Pin-163
95PinArtP-163
95PinMusC-163
95Sco-536
95ScoGolR-536
95ScoPlaTS-536
95Top-516
95TopCyb-304
95Ult-77
95UltGolM-77
95UppDec-431
95UppDecED-431
95UppDecEDG-431
96ColCho-207
96ColChoGS-207
96ColChoSS-207
96Don-102
96DonPreP-102
96Fin-B103
96FinRef-B103
96Fle-178
96FleTif-178
96StaClu-94
96StaCluMOP-94
96Top-88
96Ult-95
96UltGolM-95
96UppDec-389
97Fle-158
97FleTif-158
97PacPriGotD-GD67
97StaClu-365
97StaCluMOP-365
97Top-439
Stevens, Donald
52LavPro-98
Stevens, Ed (Edward Lee)
47TipTop-104
49Bow-93
49EurSta-173
49Lea-43
52Par-25
90DodTar-769
Stevens, Jake
91PomBlaBPB-23
Stevens, John
89JohCitCS-21
Stevens, John W.
55Bow-258
Stevens, Kristopher
96AppLeaAB-27
96BatCliTI-5
96MarPhiB-26
Stevens, Lee
86SalAngC-96
87PalSprP-12
88MidAngGS-18
89EdmTraC-21
89EdmTraP-554
89FleUpd-16
89TriA AAC-44
90Bow-300
90BowTif-300
90CMC-490
90Don-449
90EdmTraC-13
90EdmTraP-527
90Fle-145
90FleCan-145
90ProAAAF-103
90TriAAAC-44
90TriAllGP-AAA42
91Cla1-T25
91Don-754
91EdmTraLD-170
91EdmTraP-1530
91Fle-327
91LinDriAAA-170
91MajLeaCP-24
91OPC-648
91Sco-67
91Sco100RS-82
91StaClu-293
91Top-648
91TopDeb90-149
91TopDesS-648
91TopMic-648
91TopTif-648
91TriA AAGP-AAA15
91Ult-53
91UppDec-573
92AngPol-17
92Bow-427
92Cla1-T85
92Don-460
92Fle-71
92Lea-361
92LeaPre-15
92OPC-702
92Pin-453
92ProFS7-28
92Sco-372
92StaClu-281
92Stu-150
92Top-702
92TopGol-702
92TopGolW-702
92TopMic-702
92TriPla-119
92Ult-331
92UppDec-634
93Don-65
93Fle-576
93PacSpa-52
93PanSti-9
93Pin-169
93StaClu-219
93StaCluFDI-219
93StaCluMOP-219
93SyrChiF-1007
93Top-467
93TopGol-467
93TopInaM-467
93TopMic-467
93TriAAAGF-54
94ClaGolF-177
96OklCit8B-21
97Don-288
97DonPreP-288
97DonPrePGold-288
97Sco-376
97ScoHobR-376
97ScoResC-376
97ScoShoS-376
97ScoShoSAP-376
97Ult-393
97UltGolME-393
97UltPlaME-393
Stevens, Matt
89BatCliP-1924
90SpaPhiB-8
90SpaPhiP-2489
90SpaPhiS-20
91ClePhiC-8
91ClePhiP-1619
92ReaPhiF-574
92ReaPhiS-543
92SkyAA F-237
93PorBeaF-2385
94SalLakBF-817
Stevens, Mike
85PriWilPT-24
86PriWilPP-26
87SalBucP-2
Stevens, Morris
65Top-521
78TCM60I-175
Stevens, Paul
77DayBealT-24
80WesHavWCT-7
Stevens, R.C.
58Top-470
59Top-282
61Top-526
Stevens, Scott
89UtiBluSP-23
90SouBenWSB-22
90SouBenWSGS-17
91SarWhiSC-10
91SarWhiSP-1113
92BasCitRC-22
Stevens, Tony
80ElmPioRST-22
Stevenson, Bill
85SpoIndC-22
86ChaRaiP-24
88WicPilRD-29
Stevenson, Chad
94BriTigC-25
94BriTigF-3507
Stevenson, Jason
94HunCubF-3554
95RocCubTI-26
96DayCubB-23
94HunCubC-26
Stevenson, Jeff
92AppFoxC-29
Stevenson, John
78NewWayCT-42
82AmaGolST-3
84ShrCapFB-22
Stevenson, Rich
70RoyTeal-34
Stevenson, Rodney
96VerExpB-25
Stevenson, Stevie
36WorWidGV-128
Stevenson, Tenoa
82IdaFalAT-12
Steverson, Todd
89AlaGol-9
92ClaBluBF-BC27
92ClaDraP-19
92ClaFS7-410
92FroRowDP-7
92St.CatBJC-1
92St.CatBJF-3400
92UppDecML-16
93ClaFS7-28
93ClaGolF-177
93DunBluJC-1
93DunBluJF-1810
93DunBluJFFN-25
93ExcFS7-246
93OPCPreTDP-4
93Pin-464
93Sco-496
93Sel-353
93SP-286
93StaCluM-129
93Top-269
93TopGol-269
93TopInaM-269
93TopMic-269
94ClaGolF-57
94KnoSmoF-1318
94UppDecML-45
95FleUpd-23
95Sum-166
95SumNthD-166
95TopTra-31T
96ColCho-546
96ColChoGS-546
96ColChoSS-546
96LasVegSB-25
96Pac-316
96Sco-244
Steward, Chuck (Charles)
88FayGenP-1092
89LakTigS-20
Steward, Hector
86NewBriRSP-23
Stewart, Andy
92BasCitRC-13
92BasCitRF-3849
93WilBluRC-22
93WilBluRF-2000
94CarLeaAF-CAR24
94WilBluRF-304
95SigRooOJ-31
95SigRooOJP-31
95SigRooOJPS-31
95SigRooOJS-31
95WicWraTI-28
96WicWraB-16
Stewart, Bill
55JetPos-14
Stewart, Brady
90EugEmeGS-29
91AppFoxC-20
91AppFoxP-1726
92BasCitRC-8
92BasCitRF-3853
93WilBluRC-23
93WilBluRF-2007
94MemChiF-367
Stewart, Bud (Edward P.)
49Bow-173
49Lea-104
50Bow-143
51Bow-159
52Bow-185
52Top-279
52WhiSoxH-9
83TopRep5-279
Stewart, Bunky (Vernon)
55Top-136
55TopDouH-75
Stewart, Carl
88BilMusP-1826
90BilMusP-3221
91ChaWheC-10
91ChaWheP-2887
92ChaWVWC-19
93WinSpiC-23
Stewart, Chris
93JohCitCC-20
93JohCitCF-3677
94SavCarC-25
94SavCarF-506
95Exc-275
Stewart, Dave
76SeaRaiC-17
77CliDodT-25
79AlbDukT-5
80AlbDukT-1
80VenLeaS-121
81DodPol-48
81LonBeaPT-24
82DodPol-48
82DodUniOV-22
82Don-410
82Fle-24
82Top-213
83DodPol-48
83DodPos-16
83Don-588
83Fle-222
83Top-532
84Don-343
84Fle-430
84Nes792-352
84OPC-352
84RanJarP-31
84Top-352
84TopSti-360
84TopTif-352
85Don-343
85Fle-569
85RanPer-48
85Top-723
85TopTif-723
86Don-619
86Fle-453
86PhiTas-48
86Top-689
86TopTif-689
87A'sSmoC-11
87Don-648
87Fle-406
87FleGlo-406
87Top-14
87TopSti-167
87TopTif-14
88A'sMot-3
88ClaRed-196
88Don-472

88DonBasB-99
88DonTeaBA-472
88Fle-295
88FleBasM-36
88FleGlo-295
88FleMin-48
88FleSlu-39
88FleStiC-57
88FleWaxBC-C14
88Lea-217
88OPC-353
88PanSti-164
88Sco-458
88ScoGlo-458
88Spo-162
88StaLinAs-16
88Top-476
88TopGloS-33
88TopMinL-32
88TopRevLL-29
88TopSti-168
88TopTif-476
88TopUKM-75
88TopUKMT-75
89A'sMot-6
89Bow-188
89BowTif-188
89CadEllD-55
89Don-214
89DonBasB-99
89Fle-23
89FleExcS-39
89FleGlo-23
89FleLeaL-36
89OPC-145
89PanSti-415
89RedFolSB-112
89Sco-32
89Sco-582
89ScoSco-14
89Spo-23
89SpollIFKI-133
89Top-145
89TopBig-101
89TopCoi-53
89TopGloS-45
89TopHilTM-27
89TopMinL-71
89TopSti-163
89TopStiB-27
89TopTif-145
89TopUKM-74
89TVSpoM-95
89UppDec-185
90A'sMot-5
90Bow-449
90BowTif-449
90ClaUpd-T47
90Col-18
90DodTar-770
90Don-6
90Don-150
90Don-703A
90Don-703B
90DonBesA-25
90DOnBonM-BC3
90DonLeaS-35
90DonPre-5
90DonSupD-6
90Fle-21
90FleAwaW-37
90FleBasA-39
90FleBasM-38
90FleCan-21
90FleWaxBC-C26
90FleWorS-8
90Lea-81
90MLBBasB-74
90MSAHolD-14
90OPC-270
90PanSti-141
90PanSti-198
90PubSti-295
90PubSti-316
90Sco-410
90Sco-700
90Sco100S-13
90ScoMcD-23
90Spo-194
90SunSee-16
90Top-270
90TopBig-64
90TopCoi-29
90TopDou-63
90TopGloA-21
90TopGloS-4
90TopMinL-32
90TopSti-164
90TopSti-185
90TopStiB-60
90TopTif-270
90TopTVA-16
90UppDec-272
90VenSti-458
90VenSti-459
90Woo-25
90Woo-33
91A'sMot-5
91A'sSFE-13
91BasBesAotM-16
91Bow-225
91CadEllD-55
91Cla2-T89
91ClaGam-102
91Col-32
91Don-102
91DonBonC-BC4
91Fle-25
91FlePro-F4
91FleWaxBC-4
91FleWorS-6
91FouBal-29
91Lea-417
91OPC-580
91OPCPre-115
91PanCanT1-62
91PanCanT1-71
91PanCanT1-93
91PanFreS-199
91PanFreS-355
91PanSti-4
91PanSti-144
91RedFolS-90
91Sco-150
91Sco-702
91Sco-883
91Sco100S-24
91SevCoi-NC12
91StaClu-1
91StaCluCM-27
91Stu-107
91Top-580
91TopCraJ2-10
91TopDesS-580
91TopMic-580
91TopSta-32
91TopTif-580
91Ult-254
91UppDec-28
91UppDec-127
91Woo-24
92A'sUno7P-3
92A'sUno7P-4
92AthMot-5
92Bow-280
92ClaGam-10
92Don-225
92Fle-268
92HitTheBB-34
92Lea-258
92OPC-410
92Pin-157
92Sco-580
92Sco100S-60
92SpoStaCC-43
92StaClu-390
92Stu-230
92Top-410
92TopGol-410
92TopGolW-410
92TopKid-117
92TopMic-410
92TriPla-88
92Ult-117
92UppDec-547
93BluJayCP1-14
93BluJayD-14
93BluJayFS-27
93CadDis-56
93DiaMar-103
93Don-611
93DurPowP1-10
93Fla-295
93Fle-669
93FleFinE-296
93Lea-294
93OPC-294
93OPCPre-45
93PacSpa-656
93PanSti-29
93Pin-442
93RanKee-347
93Sco-656
93Sel-240
93SelRoo-24T
93StaClu-629
93StaCluFDI-629
93StaCluMO-25
93StaCluMOP-629
93Top-290
93TopComotH-12
93TopGol-290
93TopInaM-290
93TopMic-290
93TopTra-114T
93Ult-647
93UppDec-39
93UppDec-546
93UppDecGold-39
93UppDecGold-546
94BluJayUSPC-3C
94BluJayUSPC-11H
94Bow-113
94ColC-371
94ColChoGS-371
94ColChoSS-371
94Don-257
94ExtBas-195
94Fin-134
94FinRef-134
94Fla-121
94Fle-343
94Lea-308
94OPC-12
94Pac-652
94Pin-374
94PinArtP-374
94PinMusC-374
94PosCan-5
94PosCanG-5
94Sco-133
94ScoGolR-133
94Sel-165
94StaClu-317
94StaCluFDI-317
94StaCluGR-317
94StaCluMOP-317
94StaCluT-179
94StaCluTFDI-179
94Top-455
94TopGol-455
94TopSpa-455
94TriPla-38
94Ult-143
94UppDec-89
94UppDecED-89
95AthMot-11
95BluJayUSPC-3D
95BluJayUSPC-10C
95ColCho-151
95ColCho-534T
95ColChoGS-151
95ColChoSS-151
95Don-374
95DonPreP-374
95Fla-297
95Fle-105
95FleUpd-72
95Pin-387
95PinArtP-387
95PinMusC-387
95SPCha-113
95SPChaDC-113
95StaClu-527
95StaCluMOP-527
95StaCluSTWS-527
95TopTra-154T
95Ult-343
95UltGolM-343
95UppDec-36
95UppDecED-36
95UppDecEDG-36
96ColCho-246
96ColChoGS-246
96ColChoSS-246
97BluJayS-47

Stewart, David
94BatCliC-23
94BatCliF-3445

Stewart, Ed
47Exh-218
83CliGiaF-23

Stewart, Gabby (Glen)
46RemBre-27
47SigOil-16
83TCMPla1943-41

Stewart, Gaye
43ParSpo-70

Stewart, Greg
80AppFoxT-19

Stewart, Hattie
88KimN18-43

Stewart, Hector
87PawRedSP-61
87PawRedST-10
88BlaYNPRWL-142
89BlaYNPRWL-55
89WinHavRSS-22

Stewart, Jack
51BerRos-B16

Stewart, James F.
64Top-408
65CubJayP-11
65Top-298
66OPC-63
66Top-63
66TopVen-63
67OPC-124
67Top-124
70Top-636
71MLBOffS-70
71OPC-644
71Top-644
72MilBra-329
72Top-747
73OPC-351
73Top-351
87AstShoSTw-26
87AstShowSTh-23

Stewart, Jef
87WicPilRD-17

Stewart, Joe
76AshTouT-25
77VisOakT-16

Stewart, John
87CedRapRP-21
87DurBulP-13
89SalLakTTI-30
91SalSpuC-19
91SalSpuP-2245

Stewart, Keith
96EveAquB-24

Stewart, Lee
89GeoColC-32

Stewart, Lefty (Walter C.)
31Exh-30
33Gou-121
33Gou-146
33GouCanV-75
33TatOrbSDR-179
34DiaMatCSB-172
35GouPuzR-8I
35GouPuzR-9I
91ConTSN-243

Stewart, Neb
43PhiTeal-21

Stewart, Paul
96OgdRapTI-47

Stewart, Paxton
96StCatSB-28

Stewart, Rachaad
94BluOriC-20
96Exc-9
96GreBraB-26
96GreBraTI-51

Stewart, Reggie
93WatDiaC-27
93WatDiaF-1783

Stewart, Richard
94BluOriF-3563

Stewart, Riley A.
93NegLeaRL2-37

Stewart, Sammy
79Top-206
79Top-701
80Top-119
81Don-474
81Fle-181
81OPC-262
81Top-262
82Don-457
82Fle-180
82OPC-279
82Top-426
82Top-679
83Don-203
83Fle-74
83OPC-347
83OriPos-26
83Top-347
84AllGamPI-177
84Don-514
84Fle-22
84Nes792-59
84OriTeal-28
84Top-59
84TopSti-25
84TopTif-59
85Don-148
85Fle-192
85Lea-98
85OPC-213
85Top-469
85TopTif-469
86Don-270
86Fle-289
86FleUpd-107
86OPC-172
86Top-597
86TopSti-235
86TopTif-597
86TopTra-103T
86TopTraT-103T
87Don-658
87Fle-48
87FleGlo-48
87Top-204
87TopTif-204
88Don-596
88Fle-616
88FleGlo-616
88Top-701
88TopTif-701
89PacSenL-27
89PacSenL-135
89T/MSenL-101
90EliSenL-48
91OriCro-439

Stewart, Scott
95ChaRivTI-2

Stewart, Shannon
92ClaBluBF-BC24
92ClaDraP-14
92ClaDraPFB-BC13
92ClaFS7-406
92UppDecML-10
93ClaGolF-174
93OPCPreTDP-2
93Pin-462
93Sco-494
93Sel-355
93St.CatBJC-1
93St.CatBJF-3988
93StaCluM-180
94Bow-309
94Cla-71
94ClaCreotC-C10
94ClaGolF-22
94ExcFS7-149
94HagSunC-1
94HagSunF-2745
94SouAtlLAF-SAL20
94UppDec-299
94UppDecED-299
94UppDecML-195
95Bow-55
95BowBes-B15
95BowBesR-B15
95KnoSmoF-54
95UppDecML-32
96Bow-177
96BowBes-142
96BowBesAR-142
96BowBesR-142
96ColCho-433
96ColChoGS-21
96ColChoGS-433
96ColChoSS-21
96ColChoSS-433
96FlePro-10
96Lea-123
96LeaPrePB-123
96LeaPrePG-123
96LeaPrePS-123
96Spo-140
96SpoArtP-140
96SyrChiTI-29
96Top-343
96UppDec-233
96UppDecFSP-FS19

96UppDecPHE-H28
96UppDecPreH-H28
97BluJayS-57
97Bow-320
97BowBes-171
97BowBesAR-171
97BowBesR-171
97BowChr-220
97BowChrI-220
97BowChrIR-220
97BowChrR-220
97BowInt-320
97Cir-105
97CirRav-105
97Don-262
97DonFraFea-12
97DonLim-79
97DonLimLE-79
97DonPre-162
97DonPreCttC-162
97DonPreP-262
97DonPrePGold-262
97FlaSho-A107
97FlaSho-B107
97FlaSho-C107
97FlaShoLC-107
97FlaShoLC-B107
97FlaShoLC-C107
97FlaShoLCM-A107
97FlaShoLCM-B107
97FlaShoLCM-C107
97Fle-546
97FleTif-546
97Lea-175
97LeaFraM-175
97LeaFraMDC-175
97NewPin-171
97NewPinAP-171
97NewPinMC-171
97NewPinPP-171
97PacPriGotD-GD106
97PinCer-135
97PinCerMBlu-135
97PinCerMG-135
97PinCerMR-135
97PinCerR-135
97PinTotCPB-135
97PinTotCPG-135
97PinTotCPR-135
97PinX-P-135
97PinX-PMoS-135
97StaClu-283
97StaCluMOP-283
97Stu-147
97StuPrePG-147
97StuPrePS-147
97Top-456
97Ult-471
97UltGolME-471
97UltPlaME-471
95UppDecMLFS-32

Stewart, Stanley
96TamYanY-24

Stewart, Stuffy (John F.)
90DodTar-771
94ConTSN-1132
94ConTSNB-1132

Stewart, Tito
88NewBriRSP-905
89NewBriRSS-5
89Sta-136
90CMC-252
90PawRedSC-1
90PawRedSDD-23
90PawRedSP-462
90ProAAAF-434
90TopTVRS-60
91IndIndLD-195
91IndIndP-462
91LinDriAAA-195

Stiboro, Tom
80BatTroT-13

Stickels, Bob
71MLBOffS-527

Stidham, Phil
90ArkRaz-23
92LakTigC-20
93FloStaLAF-19
93LakTigC-23
93LakTigF-1310
94ExcFS7-61
95NorTidTI-27

Stidham, Phillip
92LakTigF-2279
94Bow-204
94SpoRoo-39
94SpoRooAP-39
95Sco-594
95ScoGolR-594
95ScoPlaTS-594

Stieb, Dave
80OPC-42
80Top-77
81AllGamPI-89
81Don-582
81Fle-414
81OPC-5
81OPCPos-22
81Top-467
81TopSti-142
82Don-52
82FBIDis-23
82Fle-622
82FleSta-232
82OPC-53
82OPC-380
82OPCPos-6
82Top-380
82Top-606
82TopSti-250
83AllGamPI-88
83Don-9
83Don-507
83DonActA-48
83Fle-441
83FleSta-188
83FleSti-111
83Kel-36
83OPC-130
83OPC-202
83PerAll-6
83PerAllG-6
83Top-130
83Top-202
83TopGloS-25
83TopSti-127
84AllGamPI-178
84BluJayFS-28
84Don-71
84DonActAS-19
84Fle-167
84FleSti-85
84FunFooP-75
84MilBra-26
84Nes792-590
84Nes792-606
84OPC-134
84OPC-289
84SevCoi-E13
84Top-590
84Top-606
84TopGloA-10
84TopGloS-24
84TopRubD-8
84TopSti-368
84TopTif-590
84TopTif-606
85BluJayFS-27
85BluJayPLP-3
85Don-193
85DonHig-12
85Fle-117
85FleLimE-37
85FleStaS-91
85FleStaS-110
85GenMilS-23
85Lea-54
85Lea-251
85OPC-240
85OPCPos-22
85SevCoi-S14
85Top-240
85Top3-D-20
85TopGloA-21
85TopGloS-40
85TopRubD-22
85TopSti-191
85TopSti-356
85TopSup-22
85TopTif-240
86BluJayAF-22
86BluJayFS-29
86Don-146
86DonAll-55
86Dra-34
86Fle-70
86Fle-642
86FleLeaL-43
86FleMin-16
86FleSlu-37
86FleStiC-115
86GenMilB-3H
86Lea-68
86OPC-353
86SevCoi-E14
86Spo-96
86Top-650
86Top3-D-27
86TopGloS-43
86TopMinL-36
86TopSti-186
86TopSup-54
86TopTat-23
86TopTif-650
86TruVal-19
87BluJayFS-30
87Don-195
87Fle-238
87FleGlo-238
87GenMilB-1H
87Lea-72
87OPC-90
87RedFolSB-81
87SpoTeaP-5
87StuPan-28
87SyrChi1A-3
87Top-90
87TopTif-90
88BluJay5-10
88BluJayFS-27
88Don-148
88DonBasB-284
88Fle-123
88FleGlo-123
88GreBasS-2
88Lea-80
88MSAHosD-17
88OPC-153
88PanSti-215
88Sco-76
88ScoGlo-76
88StaLinBJ-18
88Top-775
88TopBig-172
88TopSti-191
88TopTif-775
89BluJayFS-26
89Bow-239
89BowTif-239
89ClaLigB-49
89Don-349
89DonAll-28
89DonBasB-143
89Fle-244
89FleBasA-40
89FleGlo-244
89OPC-4
89PanSti-463
89Sco-197
89Spo-35
89Top-460
89TopBig-128
89TopSti-194
89TopTif-460
89TVSpoM-78
89UppDec-383
90BluJayFS-26
90BluJayHS-6
90Bow-505
90BowTif-505
90ClaBlu-97
90Don-87
90DonBesA-127
90Fle-93
90FleCan-93
90Lea-79
90OPC-320
90PanSti-173
90PubSti-526
90Sco-201
90Sco100S-89
90Spo-26
90SunSee-7
90Top-320
90TopBig-112
90TopMinL-44
90TopTif-320
90UppDec-605
90USPlaCA-10C
90VenSti-460
91BasBesAotM-17
91BluJayFS-22
91BluJayFS-24
91BluJayS-5
91Bow-22
91Cla1-T89
91Don-1
91Don-551
91DonBonC-BC21
91DonSupD-1
91Fle-185
91FleWaxBC-9
91Lea-96
91LeaPre-26
91MajLeaCP-26
91MSAHolD-18
91OPC-460
91OPCPre-116
91PanCanT1-64
91PanFreS-344
91PanFreS-360
91PanSti-9
91PanSti-160
91PepSup-4
91PosCan-16
91RedFolS-89
91Sco-30
91Sco-707
91Sco100S-93
91StaClu-62
91StaCluCM-28
91StaPinB-48
91Stu-137
91Top-460
91TopCraJ2-32
91TopDesS-460
91TopMic-460
91TopTif-460
91Ult-368
91UppDec-106
92Bow-376
92ClaGam-13
92Don-724
92Fle-341
92Lea-291
92OPC-535
92PanSti-32
92Pin-108
92Sco-656
92Sco100S-37
92StaClu-97
92Top-535
92TopGol-535
92TopGolW-535
92TopKid-91
92TopMic-535
92TriPla-147
92Ult-152
92UppDec-99
92UppDec-136
93BluJayD4-29
93BluJayDM-8
93Don-708
93Fle-699
93OPC-235
93OPCPre-60
93PacSpa-396
93Pin-552
93Sco-630
93Sel-386
93StaClu-641
93StaCluFDI-641
93StaCluMOP-641
93StaCluWS-4
93Top-295
93TopGol-295
93TopInaM-295
93TopMic-295
93Ult-536
93UppDec-805
93UppDecGold-805
96BluJayOH-30
97BluJayS-33

Stiegele, Rob
89BluOriS-22
90FreKeyTI-23

Stieglitz, Al
60Top-144
60TopVen-144

Stigman, Dick
59Top-142
59TopVen-142
60Lea-85
60Top-507
61Top-77
61TwiCloD-26
62Top-37
62Top-532
62TopVen-37
63Top-89
63TwiJayP-11
64Top-6
64Top-245
64TopVen-6
64TopVen-245
64TwiJayP-11
65Top-548
66Top-512
78TCM60I-162
78TwiFri-45

Stigman, Lee
81VanCanT-20

Stiles, Will
84LitFalMT-1
86ColMetP-24
87LynMetP-16
88St.LucMS-21

Stillman, Royle
76OPC-594
76SSP-393
76Top-594
78Top-272
79OgdA'sT-14
79SpoIndT-2
80OgdA'sT-18
91OriCro-440

Stillwell, Kurt
84CedRapRT-17
86FleUpd-108
86RedTexG-11
86TopTra-104T
86TopTraT-104T
87ClaUpdY-142
87Don-123
87Fle-215
87FleGlo-215
87RedKah-11
87Top-623
87TopRoo-17
87TopTif-623
87ToyRoo-26
88Don-265
88DonBasB-207
88Fle-248
88FleGlo-248
88FleUpd-35
88FleUpdG-35
88PanSti-276
88RoySmo-23
88Sco-221
88ScoGlo-221
88ScoRoo-4T
88ScoRooG-4T
88StaLinRe-18
88StaLinRo-16
88Top-339
88TopBig-136
88TopTif-339
88TopTra-115T
88TopTraT-115T
89Bow-120
89BowTif-120
89ClaLigB-14
89Don-322
89DonAll-29
89DonBasB-63
89Fle-293
89FleGlo-293
89OPC-217
89RoyTasD-8
89Sco-162
89ScoYouS2-42
89Top-596
89TopBig-161
89TopSti-266
89TopTif-596
89UppDec-616
90Bow-376
90BowTif-376
90CedRapRDGB-6
90ClaYel-T29
90Don-120
90DonBesA-106
90Fle-118
90FleCan-118
90Lea-256
90MLBBasB-106
90OPC-222
90PanSti-79
90PubSti-356

90Sco-96
90Top-222
90TopBig-293
90TopSti-269
90TopTif-222
90UppDec-361
90VenSti-461
91Bow-307
91Don-24
91Don-520
91DonSupD-24
91Fle-571
91Lea-2
91OPC-478
91PanFreS-279
91RedFolS-91
91RoyPol-21
91Sco-295
91StaClu-189
91Stu-70
91Top-478
91TopDesS-478
91TopMic-478
91TopTif-478
91Ult-157
91UppDec-587
92Bow-135
92Don-440
92Fle-170
92Lea-142
92OPC-128
92OPCPre-177
92PadCarJ-21
92PadMot-5
92PadPolD-23
92PadSmo-34
92PanSti-97
92Pin-418
92Sco-236
92ScoRoo-19T
92StaClu-650
92StaCluNC-650
92Stu-109
92Top-128
92TopGol-128
92TopGolW-128
92TopMic-128
92TopTra-112T
92TopTraG-112T
92Ult-584
92UppDec-329
92UppDec-705
93Bow-434
93Don-258
93Fle-148
93Lea-138
93PacSpa-265
93PanSti-259
93Pin-154
93Sco-379
93Sel-193
93StaClu-568
93StaCluFDI-568
93StaCluMOP-568
93Top-84
93TopGol-84
93TopInaM-84
93TopMic-84
93TriPla-69
93Ult-124
93UppDec-152
93UppDecGold-152
94IndIndF-1819
94Pac-90
94Top-198
94TopGol-198
94TopSpa-198
95IndIndF-104
96RanMot-22
97Pac-210
97PacLigB-210
97PacSil-210

Stillwell, Rod
90AppFoxBS-26
90AppFoxP-2104

Stillwell, Ron
77FriOneYW-114

Stillwell, Steve
76SeaRaiC-18

Stimac, Craig
79HawIslC-14
79HawIslT-4
80HawIslT-6
81Top-356
82ChaChaT-13

Stine, Lee
35DiaMatCS3T1-136
36NatChiFPR-106

Stingley, Derek
93MarPhiC-27
93MarPhiF-3490
94SpaPhiF-1736
94SparPhiC-19
95PiePhiF-199

Stingrays, Maui
96MauStiHWB-NNO

Stinnett, Kelly
90WatIndS-20
91ColIndC-21
91ColIndP-1488
92CanIndF-694
92CanIndS-119
92SkyAA F-56
93ChaKniF-547
94Bow-653
94ExtBas-326
94Fin-369
94FinRef-369
94FleUpd-162
94MetColP-25
94Pin-538
94PinArtP-538
94PinMusC-538
94ScoRoo-RT151
94ScoRooGR-RT151
94Sel-195
94SpoRoo-110
94SpoRooAP-110
94StaClu-599
94StaCluFDI-599
94StaCluGR-599
94StaCluMOP-599
94Ult-536
94VenLinU-269
95ColCho-326
95ColChoGS-326
95ColChoSS-326
95Don-171
95DonPreP-171
95Fle-383
95Sco-137
95ScoGolR-137
95ScoPlaTS-137
95Top-71
95Ult-200
95UltGolM-200
96Fle-488
96FleTif-488
96LeaSigEA-194
96MetKah-30

Stinson, Bob (Gorrell R.)
70OPC-131
70Top-131
71MLBOffS-285
71OPC-594
71Top-594
72Top-679
74OPC-653
74Top-653
75OPC-471
75Top-471
76OPC-466
76SSP-166
76Top-466
77Top-138
78Top-396
79Hos-79
79OPC-126
79Top-252
80OPC-305
80Top-583
85SpoIndGC-21
86MarGreT-8
87AstShoSTw-17
87AstShowSTh-29
90DodTar-772

Stipetich, Mark
75QuaCitAT-32

Stirnweiss, Snuffy (George)
39ExhSal-56
43YanSta-26
47Exh-219
47TipTop-59
48Bow-35
48YanTeal-26
49Bow-165
49Lea-95
50Bow-249
51Bow-21
52NatTeaL-36
52Top-217
76TayBow4-46
83TCMPla1945-12
83TopRep5-217
92YanWIZA-80

Stitt, Jerry
84AriWilP-17
86AriWilP-15
87AriWilP-14
88AriWilP-13
90AriWilP-17
92AriWilP-18

Stitz, John
88WatIndP-669

Stitzel, Glenn
75IntLeaAT-19

Stivers, Pat
88IdaFalBP-1849

Stivetts, Jack
98CamPepP-73

Stobbs, Chuck
48RedSoxTI-23
52Top-62
53Bri-21
53Top-89
54Top-185
55DonWin-6
55Top-41
55TopDouH-43
56Top-68
56TopPin-60
57Top-101
58Top-239
59Top-26
59TopVen-26
60Top-432
61Pos-94A
61Top-431
61TopStal-185
61TwiCloD-27
61TwiPetM-4
62SalPlaC-90A
62SalPlaC-90B
62ShiPlaC-90
79DiaGre-62
79TCM50-101
80WatIndT-31
81ChaLooT-19
82ChaLooT-24
83TopRep5-62
91TopArc1-89
94TopArc1-185
94TopArc1G-185

Stober, Mark
80KnoBluJT-6

Stock, Kevin
83BurRanF-22
83BurRanT-23
85ModA'sC-1
92BelMarC-13
92BelMarF-1444

Stock, Milt
15SpoNewM-172
16ColE13-169
16SpoNewM-170
17HolBreD-101
20NatCarE-102A
20NatCarE-102B
21E121So1-103A
21E121So1-103B
21E121So8-93
21Exh-175
21Nei-56
22AmeCarE-68
22E120-239
22W572-105
22W575-134
23W501-77
23WilChoV-159
25Exh-14
52Top-381
83TopRep5-381
90DodTar-773

Stock, Sterling
89St.CatBJP-2089

Stock, Wes
60Top-481
61Top-26
62Top-442
63Top-438
64A's-15
64Top-382
65AthJayP-11
65OPC-117
65Top-117
67CokCapAt-4
67OPC-74
67Top-74
70BreMcD-29
73OPC-179
73Top-179A
73Top-179B
77Top-597
78TCM60I-139
78TCM60I-154
85A'sMot-27
86A'sMot-27
91OriCro-441

Stockam, Doug
88DurBulS-19
89GreBraB-16
89GreBraP-1165
89GreBraS-23
90GreBraB-15
90GreBraP-1127
90GreBraS-18

Stocker, Bob
86MadMusP-20
86MadMusP-24
87MadMusP-18
88MadMusP-23
89HunStaB-8

Stocker, Bruce
80WisRapTT-24

Stocker, Kevin
91FroRowDP-10
92ClaFS7-76
92ClePhiC-19
92StaCluD-181
92UppDecML-110
93Bow-104
93Bow-356
93ClaFS7-259
93Lea-523
93ScrRedBF-2552
93ScrRedBTI-24
93SelRoo-84T
93SelRooAR-4
93SP-179
93StaClu-682
93StaCluFDI-682
93StaCluMOP-682
93StaCluP-6
93UppDec-508
93UppDecGold-508
94Bow-252
94ColC-268
94ColChoGS-268
94ColChoSS-268
94Don-245
94ExtBas-342
94ExtBasSYS-20
94Fin-2
94FinJum-2
94FinRef-2
94Fla-212
94Fle-601
94FleRooS-20
94FUnPac-174
94Lea-417
94OPC-5
94OPCDiaD-4
94Pac-487
94PanSti-231
94PhiMed-32
94PhiMel-22
94PhiUSPC-5C
94PhiUSPC-9H
94Pin-460
94PinArtP-460
94PinMusC-460
94Sco-619
94ScoBoyoS-3
94ScoGolR-619
94Sel-52
94SP-139
94SPDieC-139
94StaClu-444
94StaCluFDI-444
94StaCluGR-444
94StaCluMOP-444
94StaCluT-240
94StaCluTFDI-240
94Stu-143
94Top-57
94TopGol-57
94TopSpa-57
94TriPla-180
94Ult-253
94UltSecYS-10
94UppDec-84
94UppDecED-84
94USPlaCR-1H
95ColCho-363
95ColChoGS-363
95ColChoSS-363
95Don-291
95DonPreP-291
95DonTopotO-311
95Fla-183
95Fle-405
95Lea-127
95Pac-338
95Phi-31
95PhiMel-22
95Pin-98
95PinArtP-98
95PinMusC-98
95Sco-405
95ScoGolR-405
95ScoPlaTS-405
95StaClu-346
95StaCluMOP-346
95StaCluSTWS-346
95Stu-173
95Top-533
95TopCyb-318
95Ult-422
95UltGolM-422
95UppDec-144
95UppDecED-144
95UppDecEDG-144
96ColCho-250
96ColChoGS-250
96ColChoSS-250
96Don-18
96DonPreP-18
96Fla-339
96Fle-509
96FleTif-509
96Lea-58
96LeaPrePB-58
96LeaPrePG-58
96LeaPrePS-58
96LeaSigA-215
96LeaSigAG-215
96LeaSigAS-215
96Pac-157
96PhiTeal-31
96Sco-414
96Top-44
96UppDec-173
97Cir-121
97CirRav-121
97ColCho-418
97Pac-388
97PacLigB-388
97PacSil-388
97Top-384
97UppDec-456

Stocksdale, Otis
95May-40

Stockstill, Dave
79WauTimT-5
81TulDriT-5
82TulDriT-15
83OklCit8T-17
84OklCit8T-8
85OklCit8T-23

Stockstill, Jason
96BoiHawB-27

Stockstill, John
80QuaCitCT-28

Stockton, John
93StaCluMO-40

Stockwell, Len
87OldJudN-486

Stoddard, Bob
80SpoIndT-1
81SpoIndT-18
82SalLakCGT-18
83Top-195
84Don-619
84Fle-620
84MarMot-22
84Nes792-439
84Top-439
84TopTif-439
85CalCanC-90

85Fle-502
85NasSouTI-23
86LasVegSP-20
87Fle-431
87FleGlo-431
87OmaRoyP-12
88TacTigC-10
88TacTigP-628
89DenZepC-11
89DenZepP-31
Stoddard, Tim
78RocRedWT-17
80Top-314
81Don-475
81Fle-176
81OPC-91
81Top-91
82Don-131
82Fle-181
82Top-457
83Don-581
83Fle-75
83OPC-217
83OriPos-27
83Top-217
84CubChiT-28
84CubSev-49
84Don-245
84Fle-23
84FleUpd-110
84Nes792-106
84Top-106
84TopTif-106
84TopTra-112T
84TopTraT-112T
85Don-144
85Fle-68
85FleUpd-111
85OPC-393
85PadMot-19
85Top-693
85TopTif-693
85TopTifT-113T
85TopTra-113T
86Don-406
86Fle-335
86Top-558
86TopTif-558
87Don-497
87Fle-116
87FleGlo-116
87OPC-321
87Top-788
87TopTif-788
88Don-497
88DonReaBY-497
88Fle-222
88FleGlo-222
88Sco-258
88ScoGlo-258
88StaLinY-16
88Top-359
88TopTif-359
89PacSenL-182
89T/MSenL-102
89TopSenL-37
90EliSenL-30
91OriCro-442
92YanWIZ8-188
Stoeckel, Jim
87SanAntDTI-3
Stoecklin, Tony
92IdaFalGF-3513
92IdaFalGSP-18
93IdaFalBF-4030
93IdaFalBSP-11
94DurBulC-21
94DurBulF-329
94DurBulTI-23
Stoerck, Scott
87BelMarL-21
87BelMarTI-26
88WauTimGS-23
89WauTimGS-14
Stofflet, Ty
78ReaRem-19
Stohr, Bill
90PriPatD-23
Stojsavljevic, Paul
92GenCubC-5
92GenCubF-1564
Stoker, J.W.
41WheM5-16
Stoker, Mike
87AshTouP-14
88DurBulS-20
89DurBullS-20
89DurBulTI-20
Stokes, Gus
81CliGiaT-15
82CliGiaF-27
83CliGiaF-1
Stokes, Randall
90BriTigS-23
91FayGenC-28
91FayGenP-1169
Stokke, Doug
80ColAstT-9
80TucTorT-24
Stoll, Pete
83SprCarF-1
84ArkTraT-23
85SprCarT-23
Stoll, Rich
85IndIndTI-4
86IndIndTI-4
Stoltenberg, Scott
79WisRapTT-12
Stone, Bill
76AshTouT-6
77VisOakT-17
Stone, Brian
87BelBreP-9
88StoPorCLC-178
88StoPorP-739
90ArkTraGS-27
91ArkTraLD-46
91LinDriAA-46
Stone, Craig
94MedHatBJF-3690
94MedHatBJSP-3
95AusFut-24
95AusFutGP-1
95HagSunF-76
96DunBluJUTI-14
96HagSunB-21
Stone, Dave
88WatPirP-25
Stone, Dean
54Top-114
55DonWin-7
55Top-60
55TopDouH-17
56Top-87
57Top-381
59Top-286
62Top-574
63Top-271
79TCM50-65
91OriCro-443
94TopArc1-114
94TopArc1G-114
Stone, Eric
89LakTigS-21
90Bow-348
90BowTif-348
90CMC-388
90ProAAAF-380
90TolMudHC-11
90TolMudHP-150
91LinDriAA-397
91LonTigLD-397
91LonTigP-1878
92KinIndC-19
92KinIndF-2476
93CanIndF-2840
Stone, Fred
04FanCraAL-44
Stone, George
86AppFoxP-25
Stone, George H.
69Top-627
70OPC-122
70Top-122
71MLBOffS-22
71OPC-507
71Top-507
72MilBra-330
72Top-601
73LinPor-124
73OPC-647
73Top-647
74MetDaiPA-4
74OPC-397
74Top-397
75MetSSP-13
75OPC-239
75Top-239
76OPC-567
76SSP-557
76Top-567
91MetWIZ-381
Stone, George R.
08RosComP-73
09AmeCarE-99
09AmeCarE-100
09ColChiE-274
09PC7HHB-42
09T206-341
10NadCarE-47
10SweCapPP-55
11S74Sil-36
11SpoLifCW-336
11SpoLifM-118
11T205-163
11TurRedT-119
12ColRedB-274
12ColTinT-274
12HasTriFT-66
Stone, H. Ron
66Top-568
68Top-409
69Top-576
70OPC-218
70Top-218
71MLBOffS-189
71OPC-366
71Top-366
72Top-528
Stone, Jeff
83ReaPhiT-20
84FleUpd-111
84PhiTas-43
84PorBeaC-197
85Don-624
85Fle-266
85FleStaS-119
85PhiCIG-8
85PhiTas-12
85PhiTas-39
85Top-476
85TopSti-116
85TopTif-476
86Don-259
86Fle-454
86KayB-30
86PhiTas-14
86PorBeaP-21
86Top-686
86TopTif-686
87Don-309
87Fle-189
87FleGlo-189
87MaiGuiP-11
87MaiGuiT-19
87PhiTas-14
87Top-532
87TopTif-532
88Don-482
88Fle-317
88FleGlo-317
88OPC-154
88RocRedWGCP-26
88Top-154
88TopBig-146
88TopTif-154
89OklCit8P-1510
89RanMot-26
89UppDec-486
90CMC-273
90PawRedSC-22
90PawRedSDD-24
90PawRedSP-475
90ProAAAF-447
90TopTVRS-61
91LinDriAAA-369
91OriCro-444
91PawRedSDD-22
91PawRedSLD-369
91PawRedSP-52
92NasSouF-1846
92NasSouS-294
93RanKee-348
Stone, Jerry
76HawIslC-8
Stone, John (John Thomas)
33ExhFou-12
34Gou-40
34GouCanV-89
35DiaMatCS3T1-137
35GouPuzR-8H
35GouPuzR-9H
36GouWidPPR-A95
37ExhFou-16
38ExhFou-16
81TigDetN-41
91ConTSN-289
Stone, Marcenia
94TedWil-112
Stone, Matthew
95MarPhiTI-26
Stone, Michael
77St.PetCT-9
78CliDodT-28
78LodDodT-21
Stone, Percy
88AllandGN-23
Stone, Ricky
94GreFalDSP-28
94StaCluDP-43
94StaCluDPFDI-43
95YakBeaTI-31
Stone, Rocky
75IntLeaASB-34
75PacCoaLAB-34
75TacTwiK-12
Stone, Shawn
84PriWilPT-21
Stone, Steve
82AmaGolST-17
90SweBasG-27
Stone, Steve (Steven M.)
72OPC-327
72Top-327
72TopCloT-30
72WhiSox-11
73LinPor-45
73OPC-167
73Top-167
74OPC-486
74Top-486
74TopTra-486T
75OPC-388
75Top-388
76OPC-378
76SSP-302
76Top-378
77Top-17
77WhiSoxJT-14
78OPC-46
78Top-153
79OPC-115
79Top-227
80Top-688
81Don-476
81Don-591
81Fle-170
81FleStiC-104
81Kel-58
81OPC-101
81Top-5
81Top-520
81TopScr-49
81TopSti-1
81TopSti-40
81TopSti-249
82Don-357
82Fle-182
82FleSta-144
82Top-419
90PacLeg-63
91OriCro-445
Stone, Toni
76LauIndC-27
Stonecipher, Eric
91EveGiaC-23
91EveGiaP-3911
92CliGiaC-11
93SanJosGC-23
93SanJosGF-7
Stoneham, Horace
84WilMay-12
Stoneman, Bill
69ExpPin-8
68OPC-179
68Top-179
68TopVen-179
69OPC-67
69Top-67
70ExpPos-4
70MLBOffS-71
70OPC-398
70Top-398
71ExpPS-24
71MLBOffS-142
71OPC-266
71Top-266
72Dia-43
72MilBra-331
72OPC-95
72ProStaP-12
72Top-95
72Top-610
73Kel2D-23
73OPC-254
73Top-254
74ExpWes-10
74OPC-352
74Top-352
92Nab-29
93ExpDonM-29
Stoner, Lil
92ConTSN-605
Stoner, Mike
96AriBlaDB-31
Stonikas, Bill
88AppFoxP-147
89BasCitRS-24
Stoops, Jim
95BelGiaTI-27
96BurBeeTI-10
Stoppello, Jason
93JohCitCC-21
93JohCitCF-3678
Storey, Harvey
49BowPCL-15
Storke, Alan
08AmeCarE-92
Storm, Bob
73TacTwiC-20
Storm, Lake Elsinore
95LakElsSTI-30
Storti, Lin
34DiaMatCSB-173
Story, Jonathan
91UtiBluSC-14
91UtiBluSP-3256
Stottlemyre, Jeff
80SanJosMJitB-18
81LynSaiT-27
81WauTimT-2
82LynSaiT-7
83ChaLooT-16
Stottlemyre, Mel Jr.
86OscAstP-25
87ColAstP-6
88MemChiB-1
89Bow-110
89Bow-261
89BowTif-110
89BowTif-261
90CMC-182
90Lea-310
90OmaRoyC-7
90OmaRoyP-66
90OPC-263
90ProAAAF-601
90Top-263
90TopTif-263
91Don-257
91OPC-58
91Sco-361
91Sco100RS-23
91Top-58
91TopDeb90-150
91TopDesS-58
91TopMic-58
91TopTif-58
Stottlemyre, Mel Sr.
64YanReqKP-16
65ChaTheY-22
65OPC-133
65Top-133
65Top-550
66Baz-5
66Top-224
66Top-350
66TopRubI-88
66TopVen-224
66TopVen-350
66YanTeal-11
67Baz-5
67CokCapYM-V1
67DexPre-200
67Top-225
67TopVen-242
68OPC-120
68Top-120
68Top3-D-11

68TopActS-1C
68TopActS-16C
68TopVen-120
69CitMetC-5
69MilBra-265
69MLBOffS-79
69MLBPin-27
69NabTeaF-24
69OPC-9
69OPCDec-21
69Top-470A
69Top-470B
69TopDec-13
69TopDecl-42
69TopSta-208
69TopSup-25
69TopTeaP-19
69TraSta-28
70DayDaiNM-39
70Kel-5
70MilBra-27
70MLBOffS-250
70OPC-70
70OPC-100
70Top-70
70Top-100
70TopScr-22
70TopSup-27
70TraSta-13C
70YanCliDP-12
71Kel-40
71MilDud-30
71MLBOffS-500
71OPC-615
71Top-615
71TopCoi-94
71TopSup-10
71TopTat-98
71YanArcO-11
71YanCliDP-15
72Kel-50
72MilBra-332
72OPC-325
72OPC-492
72Top-325
72Top-492
73LinPor-136
73NewYorN-4
73OPC-520
73SyrChiTI-26
73Top-520
74OPC-44
74SyrChiTI-26
74Top-44
74TopSta-218
75OPC-183
75SyrChiTI-20
75Top-183
81TCM60I-450
83YanASFY-46
85MetTCM-4
86MetTCM-27
87MetColP-48
88MetColP-49
88MetKah-30
88PacLegI-22A
88PacLegI-22B
89Bow-261
89BowTif-261
89MetColP-54
89MetKah-26
90BasWit-15A
90BasWit-15B
90MetColP-49
90MetKah-30
90TopTVM-6
91MetColP-48
91MetKah-30
92MetColP-29
92MetKah-30
92YanWIZ6-121
92YanWIZA-81
94AstMot-27
95AstMot-28

Stottlemyre, Todd

86VenGulP-25
87IntLeaAT-25
87SyrChiP-1938
87SyrChiT-8
88BluJayFS-28
88Don-658
88DonRoo-37
88FleUpd-68
88FleUpdG-68
88ScoRoo-90T
88ScoRooG-90T
88TopTra-116T
88TopTraT-116T
89BluJayFS-27
89Bow-242
89BowTif-242
89Don-620
89Fle-245
89FleGlo-245
89OPC-237
89PanSti-460
89Sco-453
89ScoHot1R-81
89ScoYouS2-20
89Top-722
89TopBig-298
89TopTif-722
89UppDec-362
90BluJayFS-27
90Don-669
90Fle-94
90FleCan-94
90Lea-475
90OPC-591
90PanSti-172
90PubSti-527
90Sco-554
90Top-591
90TopBig-240
90TopTif-591
90UppDec-692
90VenSti-462
91BluJayFS-23
91BluJayFS-25
91BluJayS-6
91Bow-10
91Cla3-T89
91Don-155
91Fle-186
91Lea-227
91OPC-348
91PanFreS-349
91Sco-39
91StaClu-564
91Top-348
91TopDesS-348
91TopMic-348
91TopTif-348
91UppDec-257
92Bow-18
92ClaGam-14
92Don-263
92Fle-342
92Lea-167
92OPC-607
92Pin-240
92Sco-74
92ScoProP-20
92StaClu-307
92Top-607
92TopGol-607
92TopGolW-607
92TopMic-607
92TriPla-58
92Ult-153
92UppDec-371
93BluJayCP1-10
93BluJayD-5
93BluJayD4-21
93BluJayFS-28
93Bow-111
93Don-585
93Fle-340
93Lea-25
93OPC-244
93OPCWorC-14
93PacSpa-329
93Pin-311
93Sco-186
93StaClu-409
93StaCluFDI-409
93StaCluMOP-409
93Top-23
93TopGol-23
93TopInaM-23
93TopMic-23
93Ult-293
93UppDec-413
93UppDecGold-413
94BluJayUSPC-4H
94BluJayUSPC-12C
94ColC-269
94ColChoGS-269
94ColChoSS-269
94Don-504
94ExtBas-196
94Fin-113
94FinRef-113
94Fla-122
94Fle-344
94Lea-28
94Pin-56
94PinArtP-56
94PinMusC-56
94Sco-149
94ScoGolR-149
94StaClu-563
94StaCluFDI-563
94StaCluGR-563
94StaCluMOP-563
94StaCluT-173
94StaCluTFDI-173
94Top-155
94TopGol-155
94TopSpa-155
94Ult-440
94UppDec-189
94UppDecED-189
95AthMot-14
95BluJayUSPC-2S
95BluJayUSPC-10H
95ColCho-152
95ColCho-535T
95ColChoGS-152
95ColChoSS-152
95Don-360
95DonPreP-360
95DonTopotO-142
95Fin-309
95FinRef-309
95Fla-298
95Fle-106
95FleUpd-73
95Sco-262
95ScoGolR-262
95ScoPlaTS-262
95SP-186
95SPSil-186
95StaClu-130
95StaCluFDI-130
95StaCluMOP-130
95StaCluSTWS-130
95StaCluVR-66
95Top-354
95TopTra-51T
95Ult-344
95UltGolM-344
95UppDec-278
95UppDecED-278
95UppDecEDG-278
95UppDecSE-244
95UppDecSEG-244
96CarPol-24
96Cir-182
96CirRav-182
96ColCho-688
96ColChoGS-688
96ColChoSS-688
96Don-226
96DonPreP-226
96EmoXL-272
96Fin-S239
96FinRef-S239
96Fla-368
96Fle-219
96FleSmo'H-10
96FleTif-219
96FleUpd-U194
96FleUpdTC-U194
96MetUni-230
96MetUniP-230
96MLBPin-33
96Pac-395
96PanSti-216
96Pin-357
96PinAfi-50
96PinAfiAP-50
96PinAfiFPP-50
96PinFoil-357
96ProSta-9
96Sco-69
96Sel-116
96SelArtP-116
96StaClu-404
96StaCluEPB-404
96StaCluEPG-404
96StaCluEPS-404
96StaCluMOP-404
95StaCluVRMC-66
96Sum-37
96SumAbo&B-37
96SumArtP-37
96SumFoi-37
96Top-114
96Ult-118
96Ult-553
96UltGolM-118
96UltGolM-553
96UppDec-505U
97Cir-84
97CirRav-84
97ColCho-198
97Don-340
97DonPreP-340
97DonPrePGold-340
97DonTea-160
97DonTeaSPE-160
97Fin-71
97FinRef-71
97FlaSho-A97
97FlaSho-B97
97FlaSho-C97
97FlaShoLC-97
97FlaShoLC-B97
97FlaShoLC-C97
97FlaShoLCM-A97
97FlaShoLCM-B97
97FlaShoLCM-C97
97Fle-453
97FleTif-453
97Lea-284
97LeaFraM-284
97LeaFraMDC-284
97MetUni-235
97Pac-417
97PacLigB-417
97PacSil-417
97Pin-83
97PinArtP-83
97PinMusC-83
97Sco-406
97ScoHobR-406
97ScoResC-406
97ScoShoS-406
97ScoShoSAP-406
97StaClu-315
97StaCluMOP-315
97Top-437
97TopChr-155
97TopChrR-155
97Ult-277
97UltGolME-277
97UltPlaME-277
97UppDec-486

Stotz, Carl

90BasWit-87

Stouffer, Blair

76SanAntBTI-22

Stoughton, Mark

92Ft.MyeMCB-28
93PitMetC-27

Stout, Allyn

33ButCanV-47
34DiaMatCSB-174

Stout, Jeff

89AugPirP-501

Stout, John

89TenTecGE-33

Stout, Tim

82CedRapRT-22

Stoval, Jerry

80CliGiaT-5

Stovall, DaRond

91JohCitCC-12
91JohCitCP-3991
92SavCarC-11
92SavCarF-676
93SprCarC-26
93SprCarF-1866
94FloStaLAF-FSL45
94St.PetCC-26
94St.PetCF-2600
96HarSenB-25
96Top-437
97Bow-390
97BowBes-160
97BowBesAR-160
97BowBesR-160
97BowInt-390

Stovall, George T.

05IndSouPSoCP-16
09AmeCarE-101
09ColChiE-275
09SpoNewSM-79
09T206-342
09T206-343
10CouT21-226
10DomDisP-112
10PeoT21-53
10SweCapPP-19A
10SweCapPP-19B
11MecDFT-43
11SpoLifCW-337
11SpoLifM-50
11T205-164
12ColRedB-275
12ColTinT-275
12HasTriFT-21
12HasTriFT-75C
12T207-176
13NatGamW-38
14CraJacE-11
15AmeCarE-37
15CraJacE-11
94ConTSN-1259
94ConTSNB-1259

Stovall, Jesse

11SpoLifCW-338

Stover, C.D.

96YakBeaTI-44

Stover, Mike

78QuaCitAT-25

Stovey, Harry

87OldJudN-487
88SpoTimM-24
90DodTar-774
90KalBatN-50
90KalBatN-51
90KalBatN-52

Stowe, Chris

97Bow-423
97BowChr-283
97BowChrI-283
97BowChrIR-283
97BowChrR-283
97BowInt-423
97TopSta-116
97TopStaAM-116

Stowe, Harold

62Top-291
92YanWIZ6-122

Stowell, Brad

91SouOreAP-3844
92MadMusC-18
92MadMusF-1236

Stowell, Steve

88KenTwiP-1384
89VisOakCLC-97
89VisOakP-1444
90Bes-304
90OrlSunRB-22
90OrlSunRP-1083
90OrlSunRS-20
91LinDriAA-494
91OrlSunRLD-494
91OrlSunRP-1848

Stowers, Chris

96VerExpB-26
97Bow-324
97BowInt-324

Stoyanovich, Pete

91StaCluCM-38

Strade, Sean

94MedHatBJF-3682
94MedHatBJSP-22

Strahler, Mike

71MLBOffS-116
71OPC-188
71Top-188
72OPC-198
72Top-198
73OPC-279
73Top-279
74AlbDukTI-20
90DodTar-775

Strain, Joe

78PhoGiaC-24
79PhoGiaVNB-9
79Top-726
80GiaPol-20
80OPC-280
80Top-538
81Don-73
81Fle-458
81Top-361

81TopTra-837
82IowCubT-9
82Top-436
83OklCit8T-21
85EveGialC-18
86EveGiaC-180
86EveGiaPC-30
87EveGiaC-12
89EveGiaS-30
Straker, Les
80CedRapRT-17
80VenLeaS-37
81WatRedT-8
83WatRedT-8
84AlbA'sT-19
85OrlTwiT-20
86TolMudHP-21
87DonRoo-21
87SpoRoo2-45
87TopTra-118T
87TopTraT-118T
88Don-73
88Fle-24
88FleGlo-24
88Sco-108
88ScoGlo-108
88StaLinTw-19
88Top-264
88TopTif-264
88TwiTeal-11
89PorBeaC-10
89PorBeaP-219
89Sco-244
89Top-101
89TopBig-90
89TopTif-101
89UppDec-83
93LinVenB-107
94VenLinU-189
95LinVen-126
Strampe, Bob
73OPC-604
73Top-604
75HawIslC-17
76SpoIndC-9
Strand, Paul
94ConTSN-1300
94ConTSNB-1300
Strang, Sammy Nicklin
03BreE10-135
06GiaUllAFS-11
09T206-470
11SpoLifCW-339
89ChaLooLITI-21
90DodTar-776
Strange, Alan
41BroW75-26
79DiaGre-178
Strange, Don
89PulBraP-1895
90Bes-305
90ProAaA-94
90SouAtlLAS-43
90SumBraB-24
90SumBraP-2433
91DurBulP-1545
92GreBraF-1152
92GreBraS-244
92ProFS7-189
92SkyAA F-102
93GreBraF-348
93LinVenB-83
93RicBraP-10
93RicBraRC-24
94ExcFS7-160
95WicWraTI-22
Strange, Doug
86FloStaLAP-45
86LakTigP-24
87GleFalTP-10
88TolMudHC-14
88TolMudHP-587
89BlaYNPRWL-63
89TolMudHC-13
89TolMudHP-782
90CMC-618
90Don-535
90OPC-641
90ProAAAF-201
90Sco100RS-63
90Top-641
90TopDeb89-124
90TopTif-641
90TopTVCu-60
90TucTorC-16
90TucTorP-211
91IowCubLD-219
91IowCubP-1071
91LinDriAAA-219
92Bow-322
92CubMar-1
92IowCubS-222
92Lea-476
93Don-136
93FleFinE-284
93Lea-542
93RanKee-434
93StaClu-132
93StaCluFDI-132
93StaCluMOP-132
94ColC-270
94ColChoGS-270
94ColChoSS-270
94Don-302
94Fin-353
94FinRef-353
94Fla-114
94Fle-322
94Lea-328
94Pac-630
94PanSti-133
94Pin-376
94PinArtP-376
94PinMusC-376
94Sco-163
94ScoGolR-163
94Sel-260
94StaClu-97
94StaCluFDI-97
94StaCluGR-97
94StaCluMOP-97
94StaCluT-267
94StaCluTFDI-267
94Top-591
94TopGol-591
94TopSpa-591
94Ult-134
94UppDec-317
94UppDecED-317
95Don-402
95DonPreP-402
95Fle-297
95MarMot-17
95MarPac-44
95Ult-114
95UltGolM-114
96FleUpd-U85
96FleUpdTC-U85
96LeaSigEA-195
96MarMot-22
Strange, Keith
90UtiBluSP-9
91SouBenWSC-5
91SouBenWSP-2865
92SarWhiSCB-5
92SarWhiSF-210
93SarWhiSC-25
Strange, Kurt
89SanBerSCLC-69
Strange, Mike
95HagSunF-77
96DunBluJUTI-15
Strangfeld, Aaron
96DanBraB-24
Stranghoner, Todd
96BriWhiSB-5
Stranski, Scott
80SanJosMJitB-19
81SpoIndT-3
82LynSaiT-8
85BufBisT-24
86ChaOriW-29
86HagSunP-22
87MemChiB-10
87MemChiP-14
90HagSunDGB-31
Strasser, John
96HicCraB-23
96PriWilCB-25
Strathairn, David
88PacEigMO-14
Stratton, C. Scott
87OldJudN-488
Stratton, Drew
87ModA'sC-22
88ModA'sCLC-69
88ModA'sTI-29
Stratton, John
93UtiBluSC-23
93UtiBluSF-3537
94LynRedSC-24
94LynRedSF-1896
Stratton, Kelly
95HudValRTI-18
Stratton, Monty
39WhiSoxTI-19
40WhiSoxL-19
77Spo-7708
79DiaGre-126
80PacLeg-103
95ConTSN-1417
Stratton, Rob
96BesAutS1RP-FR3
97Bow-374
97BowInt-374
97Top-270
Straus, Tim
94ColRedC-30
Strauss, Jon
94OneYanF-3795
94VenLinU-242
Strauss, Joseph
87BucN28-55
87OldJudN-489
Strauss, Julio
89WinSpiS-NNO
90WinSpiTI-23
91ChaKniLD-144
91ChaKniP-1689
91LinDriAA-144
92ChaKniS-167
92IowCubF-4052
93LinVenB-91
94VenLinU-33
95LinVen-124
Strawberry, Darryl
82JacMetT-21
82RegGloT-8
83TidTidT-28
83TopTra-108T
83TopTraBP-2
84AllGamPI-69
84Don-68
84Dra-29
84Fle-599
84FleSti-104
84FunFooP-8
84JacMetF-12
84MetFanC-7
84Nes792-182
84OCoandSI-29
84OCoandSI-104
84OCoandSI-240
84OPC-182
84SevCoi-E17
84StaStr-1
84StaStr-2
84StaStr-3
84StaStr-4
84StaStr-5
84StaStr-6
84StaStr-7
84StaStr-8
84StaStr-9
84StaStr-10
84StaStr-11
84StaStr-12
84TidTidT-NNO
84Top-182
84TopGloS-29
84TopRubD-7
84TopSti-385
84TopSup-12
84TopTif-182
85AllGamPI-159
85Don-312
85Dra-30
85Fle-93
85Fle-631
85FleLimE-38
85FleStaS-36
85Lea-159
85MetColP-22
85MetFanC-8
85MetTCM-35
85OPC-126
85PolMet-M6
85SevCoi-S13
85Top-278
85Top-570
85Top3-D-9
85TopGloA-8
85TopRubD-8
85TopSti-100
85TopSti-179
85TopSup-30
85TopTif-278
85TopTif-570
86BasStaB-106
86Don-197
86DonAll-5
86DonHig-24
86DonPop-5
86Dra-16
86Fle-96
86Fle-632
86FleMin-21
86FleSlu-38
86FleStiC-116
86KayB-31
86Lea-131
86MetColP-4
86MetFanC-8
86MetTCM-28
86MetWorSC-11
86OPC-80
86QuaGra-16
86SevCoi-E11
86Spo-56
86Spo-97
86SpoRoo-48
86Top-80
86Top3-D-26
86TopGloA-19
86TopGloS-11
86TopSti-95
86TopSti-150
86TopSup-55
86TopTat-18
86TopTif-80
87BoaandB-33
87BurKinA-19
87ClaGam-3
87ClaUpdY-122
87Don-4
87Don-118
87DonAll-12
87DonHig-42
87DonHig-49
87DonOpeD-128
87DonP-12
87DonSupD-4
87Dra-1
87Fle-23
87Fle-629
87Fle-638
87FleExcS-41
87FleGlo-23
87FleGlo-629
87FleGlo-638
87FleGlo-WS11
87FleLeaL-41
87FleSlu-40
87FleStiC-114
87FleWorS-11
87GenMilB-5J
87K-M-32
87KayB-31
87KraFoo-26
87Lea-4
87Lea-68
87MetColP-8
87MetFanC-7
87MSAIceTD-1
87MSAJifPD-17
87OPC-379
87RedFolSB-58
87SevCoi-E13
87Spo-20
87SpoTeaP-2
87StuPan-1
87Top-331
87Top-460
87Top-601
87TopCoi-46
87TopGloA-8
87TopGloS-32
87TopMinL-26
87TopSti-103
87TopSti-159
87TopTif-331
87TopTif-460
87TopTif-601
87Woo-29
88Baz-21
88ClaBlu-209
88Don-439
88DonAll-34
88DonBasB-182
88DonBonM-BC20
88DonPop-12
88DonTeaBM-439
88Dra-3
88Fle-151
88Fle-637
88FleAwaW-40
88FleBasA-40
88FleBasM-37
88FleExcS-39
88FleGlo-151
88FleGlo-637
88FleHea-4
88FleHotS-41
88FleLeaL-40
88FleMin-97
88FleRecS-39
88FleSlu-40
88FleStiC-106
88FleSup-38
88FleTeaL-40
88GreBasS-71
88K-M-29
88KayB-29
88KinDis-8
88Lea-220
88MetColP-9
88MetFanC-18
88MetKah-18
88MSAFanSD-17
88MSAIceTD-17
88Nes-18
88OPC-178
88OPCBoxB-L
88PanSti-236
88PanSti-342
88PanSti-347
88Sco-360
88ScoBoxC-17
88ScoGlo-360
88ScoYouS2-20
88Spo-155
88SpoGam-15
88StaLinAl-33
88StaLinMe-18
88StaStr-1
88StaStr-2
88StaStr-3
88StaStr-4
88StaStr-5
88StaStr-6
88StaStr-7
88StaStr-8
88StaStr-9
88StaStr-10
88StaStr-11
88Top-710
88TopBig-253
88TopCoi-56
88TopGloA-19
88TopGloS-22
88TopMinL-63
88TopRitTM-7
88TopSti-96
88TopSti-151
88TopStiB-21
88TopTif-710
88TopUKM-76
88TopUKMT-76
88TopWaxBC-L
89Baz-20
89Bow-387
89BowTif-387
89CadEllD-56
89CerSup-3
89ClaLigB-8
89ClaTraO-108
89ClaTraO-150
89Don-147
89DonAll-34
89DonBasB-40
89DonBonM-BC6
89DonPop-34
89Fle-49
89Fle-632
89FleAll-10
89FleBasA-39
89FleBasM-36
89FleExcS-40
89FleGlo-49
89FleGlo-632

89FleHeroB-38
89FleLeaL-37
89FleSup-39
89FleWaxBC-C25
89K-M-28
89KayB-29
89KinDis-15
89MetCol8-3
89MetCol8-33
89MetColP-2
89MetFanC-18
89MetKah-27
89MSAHolD-10
89MSAIceTD-5
89Nis-10
89OPC-300
89PanSti-140
89PanSti-223
89PanSti-231
89RedFolSB-113
89Sco-10
89ScoHot1S-50
89ScoSco-42
89Spo-205
89SpoIllFKI-20
89Top-291
89Top-300
89Top-390
89TopAme2C-28
89TopBasT-44
89TopBig-139
89TopCapC-7
89TopCoi-26
89TopDouA-18
89TopDouM-1
89TopGaloC-10
89TopGloA-19
89TopGloS-8
89TopHeaUT-6
89TopHilTM-28
89TopMinL-28
89TopSti-98
89TopSti-157
89TopStiB-53
89TopTif-291
89TopTif-300
89TopTif-390
89TopUKM-75
89TVSpoM-1
89TVSpoM-129
89UppDec-260
89UppDec-681
90Bow-141
90BowTif-141
90ClaBlu-33
90Col-20
90Don-235
90DonBesN-80
90Fle-217
90FleAwaW-38
90FleBasA-37
90FleBasM-37
90FleCan-217
90FleLeaL-38
90FleLeaS-3
90Hot50PS-43
90Lea-250
90MetColP-6
90MetFanC-18
90MetKah-18
90MLBBasB-13
90OPC-600
90PanSti-302
90Pos-10
90PubSti-145
90PubSti-273
90RedFolSB-92
90Sco-200
90Sco100S-15
90Spo-146
90StaLonJS-21
90StaLonJS-37
90SupActM-17
90Top-600
90TopAmeA-23
90TopBig-186
90TopDou-64
90TopGloS-7
90TopHilHM-4
90TopMag-33
90TopSti-91
90TopStiB-20
90TopTif-600
90TopTVA-56
90TopTVM-33
90UppDec-182
90USPlaCA-13H
90VenSti-463
90VenSti-464
90WonBreS-10
91BasBesHRK-17
91Bow-382
91Bow-609
91Cla1-T68
91Cla1-T99
91Cla2-T73
91ClaGam-177
91ColStr-1
91ColStr-2
91ColStr-3
91ColStr-4
91ColStr-5
91ColStr-6
91ColStr-7
91ColStr-8
91ColStr-9
91ColStr-10
91ColStr-11
91ColStr-12
91ColStr-xx
91DodMot-2
91DodPol-44
91Don-408
91Don-696
91DonGraS-13
91Fle-161
91FlePro-12
91FleUpd-96
91JimDea-5
91Lea-377
91Lea-444
91MetWIZ-382
91MLBKeyC-4
91MSAHolD-1
91OPC-200
91OPC-402
91OPCPre-117
91PanCanT1-10
91PanFreS-85
91PanFreS-164
91PanSti-88
91PlaStr-53
91PlaStr-54
91PlaStr-55
91PlaStr-56
91PlaStr-57
91PlaStr-58
91PlaStr-60
91Pos-7
91Sco-640
91Sco-691
91Sco-864
91Sco100S-62
91ScoRoo-16T
91Sev3DCN-14
91SevCoi-NE14
91SevCoi-SC14
91SilHol-8
91SimandSMLBL-42
91SpoNSP-1
91StaClu-301
91StaPinB-49
91StaPro-5
91StaStr-1
91StaStr-2
91StaStr-3
91StaStr-4
91StaStr-5
91StaStr-6
91StaStr-7
91StaStr-8
91StaStr-9
91StaStr-10
91StaStr-11
91Stu-190
91Top-200
91Top-402
91TopDesS-200
91TopDesS-402
91TopMic-200
91TopMic-402
91TopSta-33
91TopTif-200
91TopTif-402
91TopTra-114T
91TopTraT-114T
91TopTriH-N5
91Ult-171
91UppDec-245
91UppDecSS-SS9
92Bow-40
92Cla1-T86
92Cla2-T38
92ClaGam-132
92ColPro-14
92DodMot-10
92DodPol-44
92DodSmo-4692
92DodStaTA-30
92Don-559
92DonCraJ2-7
92DonMcD-7
92Fle-471
92FleCitTP-12
92FleLumC-L3
92FleTeaL-16
92Fre-17
92Hig5-55
92Hig5S-28
92Hig5S-35
92JimDea-9
92Lea-29
92LeaGolP-5
92LeaPre-5
92MooSna-11
92Mr.TurS-24
92New-28
92OPC-550
92OPCPre-179
92PanSti-196
92Pin-80
92Pin-308
92PinRool-16
92Pos-10
92PosCan-7
92RevSup1-1
92RevSup1-2
92RevSup1-3
92Sco-9
92Sco100S-55
92ScoImpP-59
92ScoProP-5
92ScoProP-19
92SevCoi-24
92SpoStaCC-44
92StaClu-560
92StaCluMP-13
92StaPro-9
92Stu-50
92StuHer-BC6
92SunSee-20
92Top-550
92TopGol-550
92TopGolW-550
92TopKid-47
92TopMic-550
92TriPla-187
92TriPlaP-2
92Ult-219
92UltAllS-18
92UppDec-174
92UppDecF-43
92UppDecFG-43
92UppDecHRH-HR16
92UppDecTMH-51
93Bow-126
93CadDis-57
93DenHol-9
93DiaMar-104
93DodMot-8
93DodPol-25
93Don-112
93DonLonBL-LL11
93DurPowP2-21
93Fin-89
93FinJum-89
93FinRef-89
93Fle-454
93FunPac-92
93FunPac-220
93Hos-7
93Lea-210
93MetBak-19
93OPC-375
93PacSpa-155
93PanSti-219
93Pin-64
93Pin-309
93PinSlu-19
93Sco-42
93Sel-21
93SP-99
93StaClu-398
93StaCluD-1
93StaCluFDI-398
93StaCluI-B4
93StaCluMOP-398
93StaCluMOP-MB4
93StaCluMP-23
93Stu-122
93Top-450
93TopGol-450
93TopInaM-450
93TopMic-450
93TriPla-187
93Ult-406
93UppDec-477
93UppDec-575
93UppDec-820
93UppDecDG-9
93UppDecGold-477
93UppDecGold-575
93UppDecGold-820
93UppDecOD-D23
93UppDecTAN-TN8
94ColC-366
94ColChoGS-366
94ColChoSS-366
94Don-292
94Fin-87
94FinRef-87
94Fla-444
94Fle-525
94FleUpd-196
94GiaMot-17
94Pac-322
94PanSti-205
94Pin-294
94PinArtP-294
94PinMusC-294
94Sco-428
94ScoGolR-428
94Sel-99
94SpoRoo-149
94SpoRooAP-149
94StaClu-335
94StaCluFDI-335
94StaCluGR-335
94StaCluMOP-335
94SucSav-12
94Top-640
94TopGol-640
94TopSpa-640
94TriPla-89
95ColCho-260
95ColChoSE-113
95ColChoSEGS-113
95ColChoSESS-113
95ColCliP-29
95ColCliTI-29
95Don-194
95DonPreP-194
95Fle-589
95Pac-384
95PacPri-121
95Sco-209
95ScoGolR-209
95ScoHaloG-HG36
95ScoPlaTS-209
95Sel-5
95SelArtP-5
95StaCluMOP-RL5
95StaCluRL-RL5
95TamYanYI-27
95Top-629
95TopCyb-395
95Ult-244
95UltGolM-244
95UppDec-89
95UppDecED-89
95UppDecEDG-89
96Don-215
96DonPreP-215
96Fle-198
96FleTif-198
96LeaSig-109
96LeaSigPPG-109
96LeaSigPPP-109
96Pin-43
96Sco-353
96ScoDugC-B78
96ScoDugCAP-B78
96Ult-107
96UltGolM-107
97Cir-221
97CirRav-221
97ColCho-399
97Don-261
97DonEli-110
97DonEliGS-110
97DonPre-41
97DonPreCttC-41
97DonPreP-261
97DonPrePGold-261
97DonTea-132
97DonTeaSPE-132
97Fle-179
97FleTif-179
97Lea-291
97LeaFraM-291
97LeaFraMDC-291
97MetUni-123
97Pac-161
97PacLigB-161
97PacSil-161
97Pin-35
97PinArtP-35
97PinIns-74
97PinInsCE-74
97PinInsDE-74
97PinMusC-35
97ProMag-65
97ProMagML-65
97Sco-79
97ScoPreS-79
97ScoShoS-79
97ScoShoSAP-79
97ScoYan-4
97ScoYanPl-4
97ScoYanPr-4
97StaClu-82
97StaCluMOP-82
97Stu-143
97StuPrePG-143
97StuPrePS-143
97Top-282
97TopChr-98
97TopChrR-98
97TopGal-12
97TopGalPPI-12
97Ult-106
97UltGolME-106
97UltPlaME-106
97UppDec-253
97UppDec-444
Strawn, Fla
79TucTorT-13
79TulDriT-5
80ChaChaT-14
Strebeck, Rick
90ModA'sC-29
91ModA'sC-15
92HunStaF-3951
92HunStaS-321
92SkyAA F-138
93ModA'sC-20
93ModA'sF-799
Street, Gabby (Charles)
08AmeCarE-93
09ColChiE-276
09RamT20-114
09SpoNewSM-40
09T206-344
09T206-345
10CouT21-62
10CouT21-227
10CouT21-228
10CouT21-318
10CouT21-319
10DomDisP-113A
10DomDisP-113B
10RedCroT-74
10RedCroT-75
10RedCroT-247
10SenWasT-5
10SepAnoP-23
10SweCapPP-64A
10SweCapPP-64B
11MecDFT-44
11S74Sil-41
11SpoLifM-133
11T205-165
11TurRedT-120
12ColRedB-276
12ColTinT-276
12HasTriFT-7
12T207-177
40PlaBal-169
73FleWilD-16
77GalGloG-85

88ConSer5-27
92ConTSN-652
93ConTSN-833
95ConTSN-1324
Street, John
15SpoNewP-5
96PinFan-JS1
Street, Mickey
85WatIndT-7
Streeter, Sam
88NegLeaD-13
Strehlow, Bobby
93JohCitCC-22
93JohCitCF-3697
Strelitz, Len
78ArkTraT-20
79ArkTraT-2
Stribling, Young
28W513-91
Stricek, Jim
86ModA'sP-23
90WinHavRSS-28
91WinHavRSC-27
92WinHavRSC-27
Stricker, John
87OldJudN-490
89EdgR.WG-16
Strickfaden, Dave
77WatIndT-23
Strickland, Bob
86GenCubP-26
87ChaWheP-18
89WinSpiS-15
Strickland, Chad
91AppFoxC-14
91AppFoxP-1720
92AppFoxC-4
92AppFoxF-988
92MidLeaATI-43
93CarLeaAGF-17
93WilBluRC-24
93WilBluRF-2001
94MemChiF-361
95WicWraTI-27
Strickland, Dedrick
90OneYanP-3372
Strickland, Erick
93ElmPioC-21
93ElmPioF-3838
Strickland, George
50PirTeal-21
52Bow-207
52Top-197
54Bow-36
54DanDee-25
55Bow-192
55Ind-8
55IndCarBL-10
55IndGolS-13
57IndSoh-14
57Top-263
58Top-102
59Ind-19
59Kah-34
59Top-207
60IndJayP-11
60Lea-30
60Top-63
60TopVen-63
70RoyTeal-35
79DiaGre-294
83TopRep5-197
Strickland, Jim
72Top-778
73TacTwiC-21
73OPC-122
73Top-122
75OklCit8TI-9
76SSP-512
Strickland, Rick
88CapCodPPaLP-49
89OneYanP-2116
91Ft.LauYC-28
91Ft.LauYP-2442
92AlbYanF-2239
92AlbYanS-20
Stricklett, Elmer
11SpoLifCW-340
90DodTar-777
Stricklin, Scott
93EliTwiC-20
93EliTwiF-3419
94ForWayWC-22
94ForWayWF-2013
94MidLeaAF-MDW15
95ForMyeMTI-26
96GreBraB-27
96GreBraTI-25
Strijek, Randy
87NewOriP-27
88CarLeaAS-17
88HagSunS-21
89HagSunB-20
89HagSunP-265
89HagSunS-19
90ShrCapP-1452
90ShrCapS-23
Striker, Jake
60Top-169
60TopVen-169
Strincevich, Nick
47TipTop-148
50WorWidGV-17
77TCMTheWY-52
79DiaGre-354
83TCMPla1944-28
Stringer, Lou
41CubTeal-23
47SigOil-38
49Bow-183
50Bow-187
52MotCoo-38
Stringfellow, Bean (Thornton)
86GreBraTI-19
87RicBraC-31
87RicBraT-7
88RicBraC-4
88RicBraP-13
88RicBraBC-2
Stripp, Joe
33GeoCMil-28
34DiaMatCSB-175
34DiaStaR-89
34Gou-46
34GouCanV-91
35GouPuzR-1G
35GouPuzR-3E
35GouPuzR-5E
35GouPuzR-14E
90DodTar-778
93ConTSN-809
Strittmatter, Mark
92BenRocC-23
92BenRocF-1477
93CenValRC-23
93CenValRF-2896
93Top-746
93TopGol-746
93TopInaM-746
93TopMic-746
94NewHavRF-1552
95NewHavRTI-19
96ColSprSSTI-29
Strobel, Craig
86HagSunP-23
87HagSunP-8
90SpaPhiB-30
90SpaPhiS-28
92ClePhiC-26
93ScrRedBTI-25
95ScrRedBTI-26
96ScrRedBB-4
Strode, Jim (Lester)
82ForMyeRT-19
84MemChiT-14
85OmaRoyT-7
86OmaRoyP-25
86OmaRoyT-18
88LouRedBTI-46
89WytCubS-29
90PeoChiTI-32
91PeoChiC-23
91PeoChiP-1360
91PeoChiTI-2
92WinSpiC-27
92WinSpiF-1224
93DayCubC-25
93DayCubF-874
Strohmayer, John
71ExpPS-25
71OPC-232
71Top-232
72Dia-44
72Top-631
73OPC-457
73Top-457
91MetWIZ-383
Strom, Brent
73OPC-612
73Top-612
74OPC-359
74Top-359
75HawIslC-12
75OPC-643
75Top-643
76OPC-84
76Top-84
77PadSchC-54
77Top-348
78Top-509
80TucTorT-20
81AlbDukT-12
82AlbDukT-27
83AlbDukT-13
87AlbDukP-3
88AlaGolAA'TI-11
88AlbDukP-251
89AlbDukP-60
90ProAAAF-210
90TucTorP-220
91LinDriAAA-622
91MetWIZ-384
91TucTorLD-622
91TucTorP-2230
92TucTorF-506
92TucTorS-625
93TucTorF-3078
94TucTorF-779
95TusTorTI-26
96AstMot-28
Stromer, Rick
83PeoSunF-11
85HunStaJ-43
Stromsborg, Ryan
96MedHatBJTI-29
Strong, Garret
75CedRapGT-30
Strong, Joe
85ModA'sC-9
86ModA'sP-24
88CalLeaACLC-20
88RenSilSCLC-274
89CalLeaA-41
89RenSilSCLC-245
93LasVegSF-944
94SanBerSC-21
94SanBerSF-2759
Strong, Kevin
91EliTwiP-4314
Strong, Shannon
90EugEmeGS-30
Strong, Steve
86AriWilP-16
87AriWilP-15
89LakTigS-22
Strong, Stewart
91GreFalDSP-13
Stroth, Scott
92EveGiaC-8
92EveGiaF-1689
Stroud, Derek
86AncGlaPTI-34
87WytCubP-5
88GenCubP-1649
89PeoChiTI-11
90WinSpiTI-9
92PalSprAF-840
93MidAngF-322
97MidAngOHP-28
Stroud, Ed
67Top-598
68OPC-31
68Top-31
68TopVen-31
69MilBra-266
69MLBOffS-108
69SenTeal-14
69Top-272
70MLBOffS-286
70OPC-506
70SenPolY-10
70Top-506
71MLBOffS-550
71OPC-217
71Top-217
72MilBra-333
Stroud, Ralph
11MecDFT-45
11SpoLifM-70
12ImpTobC-58
16FleBreD-91
Stroughter, Steve
80SpoIndT-23
81TolMudHT-22
82TopTra-114T
78STLakCGC-9
Strovink, Eric
91GulCoaRSP-5
Strube, Bob
86KenTwiP-22
87VisOakP-5
88VisOakCLC-162
88VisOakP-101
89VisOakCLC-99
89VisOakP-1429
Strucher, Mark
82DayBeaAT-25
83ColAstT-6
86RicBraP-22
87RicBraBC-20
87RicBraC-5
87RicBraT-15
Struck, J.O.
87OldJudN-491
Struek, Randy
87HagSunP-9
Strunk, Amos
09ColChiE-277
10NadE1-53
11A'sFirT20-17
11SpoLifM-104
12ColRedB-277
12ColTinT-277
12T207-178
14CraJacE-33
14FatPlaT-47
15CraJacE-33
15SpoNewM-173
16ColE13-170
16FleBreD-92
16SpoNewM-171
17HolBreD-102
20GasAmeMBD-4
21E121So1-104
21E121So8-94
22AmeCarE-69
22E120-29
22W573-129
22W575-135
23W501-44
Strus, George
93JohCitCC-23
93JohCitCF-3682
Stryffeler, Dan
82SprCarF-9
83SprCarF-21
84ArkTraT-3
86LouRedTI-27
Stryker, Dutch
90DodTar-1081
Stryker, Ed
90GreFalDSP-26
91BakDodCLC-5
92VerBeaDC-17
92VerBeaDF-2874
Stuart, Brad
90LSUTigA-7
Stuart, Dick (Richard L.)
47PM1StaP1-208
59HomRunD-19
59Kah-35
59Top-357
60ArmCoi-18
60Baz-6
60Kah-39
60KeyChal-47
60PirJayP-12
60PirTag-7
60Top-402
61Kah-42
61NuSco-409
61PirJayP-11
61Pos-127A
61Pos-127B
61Top-126
61TopStal-71
62Baz-24
62Jel-169
62Kah-37
62Pos-169
62PosCan-169
62SalPlaC-120
62ShiPlaC-120
62Top-160
62TopBuc-86
62TopStal-180
62TopVen-160
63BasMagM-81
63Jel-137
63Pos-137
63Top-18
63Top-285
64Top-10
64Top-12
64Top-410
64TopCoi-12
64TopCoi-122
64TopGia-42
64TopSta-51
64TopStaU-70
64TopTatl-69
64TopVen-10
64TopVen-12
65OPC-5
65OPC-280
65Top-5
65Top-280
65TopTral-29
66Top-480
66TopRubl-89
81RedSoxBG2S-119
81TCM60I-366
84WilMay-26
87Pir196T-1
90DodTar-779
91MetWIZ-385
Stuart, Marlin
52Bow-147
52Top-208
53BowC-120
54OriEss-32
83TopRep5-208
91OriCro-446
Stuart, Richard
96BoiHawB-28
Stubberfield, Chris
86EveGiaC-18
86EveGiaPC-31
Stubblefield, Dana
93StaCluMO-52
Stubbs, Franklin
83AlbDukT-1
84AlbDukC-151
85AlbDukC-175
85DomLeaS-25
85Don-348
85Fle-386
85Top-506
85TopTif-506
86DodPol-22
86DodUniOP-19
86Don-592
86TopTra-105T
86TopTraT-105T
87DodMot-13
87DodPol-10
87Don-299
87DonOpeD-83
87Fle-455
87FleGlo-455
87OPC-292
87SevCoi-W14
87SpoTeaP-14
87Top-292
87TopSti-72
87TopTif-292
88DodMot-11
88DodPol-22
88Don-218
88DonBasB-331
88Fle-527
88FleGlo-527
88Lea-182
88OPC-198
88PanSti-308
88RedFolSB-84
88Sco-147
88ScoGlo-147
88StaLinD-17
88Top-198
88TopBig-112
88TopSti-66
88TopTif-198
89DodMot-11
89DodPol-13
89DodStaSV-6
89Don-321
89DonGraS-9
89Fle-74

89FleGlo-74
89Sco-599
89Top-697A
89Top-697B
89TopBig-32
89TopTif-697
89UppDec-91
90AstLenH-24
90AstMot-14
90DodPol-22
90DodTar-780
90Don-615
90DonBesN-143
90Lea-425
90OPC-56
90PubSti-19
90Sco-478
90ScoRoo-40T
90Top-56
90TopTif-56
90TopTra-120T
90TopTraT-120T
90UppDec-550
90VenSti-465
91Bow-37
91BreMilB-25
91BrePol-22
91Don-99
91Fle-518
91FleUpd-34
91Lea-277
91OPC-732
91PanFreS-13
91Sco-308
91ScoRoo-59T
91StaClu-461
91Stu-77
91Top-732
91TopDesS-732
91TopMic-732
91TopTif-732
91TopTra-115T
91TopTraT-115T
91UppDec-168
91UppDec-718
92Bow-49
92BrePol-24
92Don-618
92Lea-328
92OPC-329
92PanSti-35
92Pin-320
92Sco-292
92StaClu-189
92Stu-196
92Top-329
92TopGol-329
92TopGolW-329
92TopMic-329
92Ult-390
92UppDec-396
93Don-177
93Fle-636
93PanSti-37
93PawRedSDD-26
93StaClu-168
93StaCluFDI-168
93StaCluMOP-168
93Top-124
93TopGol-124
93TopInaM-124
93TopMic-124
93UppDec-269
93UppDecGold-269
94BreMilB-360

Stubbs, Jerry
94VerExpC-20
94VerExpF-3909
96WesPalBEB-14

Stubing, Moose (Lawrence)
76QuaCitAT-35
77FriOneYW-72
80SalLakCGT-18
81SalLakCGT-25
82SpoIndT-24
84EdmTraC-97
89Top-444
89TopTif-444

Stuckeman, Al
75LafDriT-27

Stuckenschneider, Eric
94YakBeaC-25
94YakBeaF-3866
95Bow-138
95GreFalDTI-33
95SanBerSTI-26
96SavSanB-9
96SavSanB-29

Studeman, Dennis
87EugEmeP-2677
87Ft.MyeRP-13
89AppFoxP-851

Stull, Everett
92ClaDraP-52
92JamExpC-13
92JamExpF-1503
93ClaGolF-123
93StaCluM-41
94WesPalBEC-24
94WesPalBEF-39
95AusFutSFP-SFFP5
95Bow-203
95BowBes-B11
95BowBesR-B11
95Exc-227
95HarSenTI-29
96BesAutSA-75
96Bow-134
96HarSenB-26
97Bow-143
97BowCerBIA-CA75
97BowCerGIA-CA75
97BowInt-143

Stull, Walt
86BakDodP-27
87SanBerSP-18

Stumberger, Darren
94WatIndC-25
94WatIndF-3947

Stump, Jim
77FriOneYW-78

Stumpf, Brian
94MarPhiC-26
94MarPhiF-3294
95Exc-248
95PiePhiF-187
96Exc-213

Stumpf, George
78HalHalR-5

Stuper, John
82LouRedE-29
83Car-30
83Don-621
83Fle-23
83FleSti-9
83Top-363
84Car5x7-28
84Don-412
84Fle-337
84Nes792-49
84Nes792-186
84Top-49
84Top-186
84TopTif-49
84TopTif-186
85FleUpd-112
86Fle-193
86Top-497
86TopTif-497
91SavCarC-28
91SavCarP-1669
92St.PetCC-28

Stupur, Dan
89SalDodTI-29

Sturdivant, Dave
88BenBucL-15
89PalSprACLC-33
89PalSprAP-486
90PalSprACLC-211
90PalSprAP-2582

Sturdivant, Marcus
93BelMarC-26
93BelMarF-3225
94AppFoxC-17
94AppFoxF-1068
96LanJetB-25

Sturdivant, Tom
57Top-34
57YanJayP-12
58Top-127
58YanJayP-11
59OklTodML-4
59Top-471
60Top-487
61Top-293
62Top-179
62TopVen-179
63PirIDL-23
63Top-281
64Top-402
81RedSoxBG2S-120
91MetWIZ-386

Sturgeon, Bob
41CubTeal-24
47TipTop-117

Sturm, Johnny
41DouPlaR-113
77TCMTheWY-55
94ConTSN-1312
94ConTSNB-1312

Sturtze, Tanyon
91Cla/Bes-439
91MadMusC-2
91MadMusP-2133
91MidLeaAP-MWL44
92CalLeaACL-8
92ModA'sC-8
93Bow-569
93ClaFS7-260
93HunStaF-2084
95FleUpd-129
96IowCubB-25

Stutheit, Tim
92HunCubC-24
92HunCubF-3159
93ClaFS7-261
93DayCubF-867
93PeoChiC-20

Stutts, Angelo
93DanBraC-26
93DanBraF-3636

Stutts, Dennis
93JamExpC-22
93JamExpF-3327

Stutz, John
92JohCitCF-3126
93GleFalRC-26
93GleFalRF-4015

Stutz, Shawn
96ButCopKB-28

Stutzriem, Jerry
79WatIndT-6
79WauTimT-2

Stynes, Chris
92MyrBeaHC-10
92MyrBeaHF-2206
92StaCluD-182
93ClaFS7-292
93DunBluJC-23
93DunBluJF-1805
93DunBluJFFN-26
93FloStaLAF-10
94ClaGolF-58
94KnoSmoF-1312
95Bow-77
95BowBes-B51
95BowBesR-B51
95Exc-144
95OmaRoyTI-26
95SigRooOJA-AS5
95SigRooOJAS-AS5
95UppDecML-97
96BowBes-124
96BowBesAR-124
96BowBesR-124
96ColCho-578
96ColChoGS-578
96ColChoSS-578
96OmaRoyB-27
96Pin-191
96Sco-248
96Spo-141
96SpoArtP-141
97Pac-111
97PacLigB-111
97PacSil-111
97Pin-168
97PinArtP-168
97PinMusC-168
97Ult-72
97UltGolME-72
97UltPlaME-72
95UppDecMLFS-97

Su'a, Murphy
81BurBeeT-13

Suarez, Cesar
80VenLeaS-230

Suarez, Ken
66Top-588
68Top-218
68TopVen-218
69OPC-19
69Top-19
70Ind-11
70OPC-209
70Top-209
71Ind-11
71MLBOffS-383
71OPC-597
71Top-597
72MilBra-334
72OPC-483
72Top-483
74OPC-39
74Top-39
93RanKee-39

Suarez, Luis
81WisRapTT-9

Suarez, Nelson
81WisRapTT-23

Subbiondo, Joe
52LavPro-10

Subero, Carlos
93EugEmeC-24
93EugEmeF-3864
93LinVenB-166
94RocRoyC-23
94RocRoyF-575
94VenLinU-92
95LinVen-224

Such, Dick
70Top-599
71OPC-283
71Top-283
83RanAffF-NNO
84RanJarP-NNO
86TwiTeal-29
88TwiTeal-27
93RanKee-339

Sudakis, Bill
69Top-552
69TopTeaP-22
70OPC-341
70Top-341
71DodTic-17
71MLBOffS-117
71OPC-253
71Top-253
72Top-722
73OPC-586
73Top-586
74OPC-63
74Top-63
74TopSta-240
74TopTra-63T
75OPC-291
75Top-291
76OmaRoyTT-23
90DodTar-781
91MetWIZ-387
92YanWIZ7-146
93RanKee-349

Sudbury, Craig
90SouOreAB-9
90SouOreAP-3430
91MadMusC-3
91ModA'sC-3
91ModA'sP-3089
92ModA'sC-14
92ModA'sF-3899
93ModA'sC-21
93ModA'sF-800

Suder, Pete
48BluTin-15
49PhiBul-54
50Bow-140
51Bow-154
52Bow-179
52Top-256
53BowBW-8
54Bow-99
55Bow-6
76TayBow4-39
77TCMTheWY-79
79DiaGre-346
83TCMPla1942-24
83TopRep5-256

Sudgen, Joe
98CamPepP-75

Sudhoff, William
03BreE10-136
04FanCraAL-45
11SpoLifCW-341

Sudo, Bob
85UtiBluST-5
86BurExpP-22
87JacExpP-447
88SprCarB-11

Sued, Jose
93LimRocDWB-95

Sued, Nick
92ColRedC-17
92ColRedF-2394
93KinIndC-23
93KinIndF-2251
93KinIndTI-24
93SouAtlLAPI-38

Suehr, Scott
83PeoSunF-21
85MidAngT-21

Sueme, Hal
43CenFlo-23
44CenFlo-22
45CenFlo-24
47CenFlo-28
47SigOil-87

Suero, Ignacio
96HelBreTI-23

Suero, William (Williams)
88MyrBeaBJP-1186
88SouAtlLAGS-17
89DunBluJS-17
90Bes-44
90KnoBluJB-5
90KnoBluJP-1249
90KnoBluJS-19
90ProAaA-61
90StaFS7-90
91Bow-8
91LinDriAAA-519
91SyrChiLD-519
91SyrChiMB-25
91SyrChiP-2489
92Bow-181
92BrePol-25
92DenZepF-2650
92DonRoo-113
92Lea-475
92Ult-391
93BrePol-23
93LimRocDWB-109
93LinVenB-318
93Pin-271
93Sco-258
93StaClu-377
93StaCluFDI-377
93StaCluMOP-377
94BreMilB-361
94CarMudF-1589
94Pac-343

Suess, Ken
52LavPro-32

Suetsugu, Toshimitsu
87MiaMarP-25

Sugden, Joseph
03BreE10-137
11SpoLifCW-342
93ConTSN-937

Suggs, George
10DarChoE-30
10DomDisP-114
10SweCapPP-105
11SpoLifM-203
11T205-166
12HasTriFT-41B
14CraJacE-113
14PieStaT-54
15CraJacE-113

Sugiura, Toru
79TCMJapPB-22

Suhr, Gus
31Exh-13
33CraJacP-21
33ExhFou-7
33Gou-206
34DiaMatCSB-176
34BatR31-41
34BatR31-187
34ButPreR-57
34DiaStaR-56
35DiaMatCS3T1-138
35GouPuzR-8K
35GouPuzR-9K
36GouWidPPR-A96
37ExhFou-7
38ExhFou-7
39PlaBal-83
40PlaBal-94

Suigiura, Mamoru

87MiaMarP-27
Sukeforth, Clyde
52Bow-227
52Top-364
79DiaGre-89
83TopRep5-364
90DodTar-782
Sukla, Ed
66Top-417
74PhoGiaC-84
75PhoGiaC-18
75PhoGiaCK-6
Sularz, Guy
78PhoGiaC-25
79PhoGiaVNB-22
80PhoGiaVNB-21
81PhoGiaVNB-15
83Don-605
83Fle-273
83PhoGiaBHN-14
83Top-379
84PhoGiaC-22
91PacSenL-129
Sullivan, Adam
94DavLipB-23
95DavLipB-22
Sullivan, Brendan
96IdaFalB-23
Sullivan, Brian
89RenSilSCLC-246
90JohCitCS-26
90RocExpP-2690
91NiaFalRC-9
91NiaFalRP-3649
92FayGenF-2183
Sullivan, Carl
87DayBeaAP-2
88FloStaLAS-49
88TamTarS-23
89SarWhiSS-23
90SarWhiSS-23
91Cla/Bes-303
91SarWhiSC-25
91SarWhiSP-1126
Sullivan, Charlie
91ButCopKSP-19
92ButCopKSP-15
93PitMetC-19
93PitMetF-3720
Sullivan, Dan
86WinHavRSP-25
92PenPilC-22
92PenPilF-2932
93RivPilCLC-20
94RivPilCLC-18
Sullivan, Daniel C.
87WinHavRSP-9
Sullivan, Dave
87ElmPio(C-3
Sullivan, Frank
55Bow-15
55Top-106
55TopDouH-21
56Top-71
56TopPin-25
57Top-21
58Hir-58
58RedSoxJP-10
58Top-18
59RedSoxJP-9
59Top-323
60Top-280
61Pos-55A
61Pos-55B
61Top-281
62Top-352
63Top-389
79TCM50-57
Sullivan, Glenn
87GenCubP-25
88WinSpiS-18
89ChaKniTI-10
90ChaKniTI-11
90CMC-90
90IowCubC-15
90IowCubP-327
90ProAAAF-634
91IowCubLD-220
91IowCubP-1072
91LinDriAAA-220
Sullivan, Grant
91OneYanP-4155
92GreHorC-19
92GreHorF-780
93PriWilCC-23
93PriWilCF-656
94TamYanC-25
94TamYanF-2383
95NorNavTI-34
Sullivan, Haywood
57Top-336
58Top-197
59Top-416
60Top-474
61A'sTeal-19
61AthJayP-20
61AthJayP-21
61Pos-56A
61Pos-56B
61Top-212
62Jel-99
62Pos-99
62PosCan-99
62Top-184
62TopStal-60
62TopVen-184
63AthJayP-10
63Jel-92
63Pos-92
63Top-359
Sullivan, Jason
93PriRedC-29
93PriRedF-4180
Sullivan, Jim
75ForLauYS-12
98CamPepP-76
Sullivan, Joe
36GouWidPPR-A97
41Gou-22
Sullivan, John
75WatRoyT-29
76WatRoyT-29
Sullivan, John L.
23WilChoV-160
87AllandGN-19
88GooN16-43
88KimN18-44
Sullivan, John Paul
83TCMPla1944-21
84BluJayFS-29
85BluJayFS-28
86BluJayFS-30
87BluJayFS-31
88BluJayFS-29
89BluJayFS-28
90BluJayFS-28
91BluJayFS-24
91BluJayFS-26
93BluJayFS-29
Sullivan, John Peter
66Top-597
67Top-568
91MetWIZ-388
Sullivan, Marc
84PawRedST-20
86Don-614
86Top-529
86TopTif-529
87Don-643
87DonOpeD-187
87OPC-66
87Top-66
87TopTif-66
88Sco-271
88ScoGlo-271
88StaLinAst-18
88Top-354
88TopTif-354
Sullivan, Martin J.
12ColRedB-278A
12ColRedB-278B
12ColRedB-279
12ColTinT-278B
12ColTinT-280
87FouBasHN-9
87OldJudN-492
88GandBCGCE-37
88WG1CarG-16
Sullivan, Michael J.
87OldJudN-493
90SpaPhiB-9
90SpaPhiS-21
Sullivan, Mike
81WatRedT-9
89BatCliP-1929
90SpaPhiP-2490
91ClePhiC-9
91ClePhiP-1620
92ReaPhiF-575
92ReaPhiS-544
93ReaPhiF-295
Sullivan, Russell
53TigGle-27
55JetPos-15
57JetPos-19
Sullivan, Scott
93BilMusF-3944
93BilMusSP-17
94Bow-598
94ChaLooF-1358
94ExcFS7-181
94UppDecML-207
95Bow-154
95Exc-183
95FleUpd-137
95Sum-171
95SumNthD-171
95UppDecML-140
96Bow-213
96IndIndB-25
96Sco-251
95UppDecMLFS-140
Sullivan, Sport
88PacEigMO-27
Sullivan, Twin (Jack)
11TurRedT-56
Sullivan, William
92BenMusSP-26
92BilMusF-3355
Sullivan, William Joseph Jr.
34DiaMatCSB-177
36R31PasP-23
42DodTeal-21
61Fle-141
90DodTar-783
Sullivan, William Joseph Sr.
03BreE10-138
08RosComP-18
09BriE97-29A
09BriE97-29B
09ColChiE-278A
09ColChiE-278B
09ColChiE-279
09T206-346
11PloCanE-60
11SpoLifCW-343
11SpoLifM-31
11TurRedT-121
12ColTinT-278A
12ColTinT-279
12HasTriFT-67A
12HasTriFT-67B
12T207-179
15SpoNewM-174
16SpoNewM-172
87BucN28-24
Sultea, Chris
91SalLakTP-3210
Summa, Howard Homer
23MapCriV-6
25Exh-88
26Exh-88
29ExhFou-28
81ConTSN-100
91ConTSN-205
94ConTSN-1147
94ConTSNB-1147
Summers, Champ (John)
76OPC-299
76Top-299
78IndIndTI-12
78SSP270-125
78Top-622
79Top-516
80OPC-100
80Top-176
81CokTeaS-49
81Don-130
81Fle-466
81OPC-27
81Top-27
81TopScr-24
81TopSti-76
82Don-81
82Fle-282
82FleSta-154
82Top-369
82TopTra-115T
83Fle-274
83Top-428
84FleUpd-112
84Nes792-768
84PadMot-25
84Top-768
84TopTif-768
84TopTra-113T
84TopTraT-113T
85Top-208
85TopTif-208
86IndIndTI-32
87ColCliP-25
88ColCliP-24
88ColCliP-307
89ColCliC-24
89ColCliP-24
89PacSenL-96
89T/MSenL-103
90TopTVY-6
Summers, Craig
91ParPatF-13
Summers, Ed (Oron Edgar)
07TigACDPP-26
08RosComP-42
09AmeCarE-102
09BusBroBPP-15
09ColChiE-281
09T206-347
09TigMorPenWBPP-13
09TigTaCP-18
10CouT21-63
10CouT21-229
10NadE1-54
10RedCroT-160
10RedCroT-248
11MecDFT-29
11S74Sil-18
11SpoLifCW-344
11SpoLifM-71
11T205-167
12ColRedB-281
12ColTinT-281
12HasTriFT-26
81TigDetN-66
Summers, Jeff
83SanJosBC-22
84ChaO'sT-25
85ChaO'sT-16
Summers, Lonnie
92NegLeaRLI-57
Summers, Scott
87GreHorP-9
Summers, Tom
86TamTarP-22
Summers, William
55Bow-317
Summitt, Kerry
92DavLipB-24
Sumner, Chad
92JohCitCC-13
92JohCitCF-3127
93SavCarC-23
93SavCarF-695
Sumter, Kevin
95BoiHawTI-27
Sunday, Billy
87BucN28-25
87OldJudN-494
88AugBecN-25
88GandBCGCE-38
88WG1CarG-63
Sundberg, Jim
75Hos-100
75OPC-567
75Top-567
76Hos-68
76OPC-226
76SSP-260
76Top-226
77BurCheD-23
77Hos-110
77OPC-185
77Top-351
78Hos-79
78RanBurK-2
78SSP270-83
78Top-492
79Hos-97
79Kel-60
79OPC-53
79Top-120
80OPC-276
80Top-530
81AllGamPI-44
81Don-385
81Fle-619
81OPC-95
81Top-95
81TopSti-133
81TopSupHT-95
82Don-268
82Fle-332
82FleSta-181
82OPC-335
82Top-335
82TopSti-240
83AllGamPI-44
83Don-7
83Don-609
83DonActA-26
83Fle-580
83FleSta-189
83Kel-38
83OPC-158
83RanAffF-10
83Top-665
83TopSti-126
84AllGamPI-132
84BreGar-18
84BrePol-8
84Don-178
84Fle-431
84FleUpd-113
84Nes792-779
84OPC-251
84Top-779
84TopSti-355
84TopTif-779
84TopTra-114T
84TopTraT-114T
85AllGamPI-43
85Don-89
85Fle-597
85FleUpd-113
85Lea-78
85OPC-102
85Top-446
85TopMin-446
85TopSti-286
85TopTif-446
85TopTifT-114T
85TopTra-114T
86BasStaB-107
86Don-277
86Fle-22
86Lea-149
86OPC-245
86RoyKitCD-18
86RoyNatP-8
86Spo-186
86Top-245
86TopSti-15
86TopSti-259
86TopTif-245
87CubCan-32
87CubDavB-11
87Don-280
87Fle-382
87FleGlo-382
87FleUpd-114
87FleUpdG-114
87OPC-190
87Top-190
87TopSti-256
87TopTif-190
87TopTra-119T
87TopTraT-119T
88Don-488
88DonTeaBC-488
88Fle-434
88FleGlo-434
88Sco-244
88ScoGlo-244
88Top-516
88TopBig-100
88TopTif-516
89Bow-227
89BowTif-227
89RanMot-24
89RanSmo-32
89Top-78
89TopBig-103
89TopTif-78
89UppDec-331
90PubSti-423
90VenSti-466
91PacRyaTEI-93
92UppDecS-12
93RanKee-350

94BreMilB-362
94RanAllP-2
94RanAllP-6
94TedWil-87

Sundberg, Richard
82RedPioT-15

Sunderlage, Jeff
82LynMetT-9
83LynMetT-18

Sundgren, Scott
86BurExpP-23

Sundin, Gordie
91OriCro-447

Sundra, Steve
40PlaBal-122
75YanDyn1T-46
93ConTSN-902
96Bro194F-13

Sung, Pil
96WesOahCHWB-7

Sunkel, Mark
88AlaGolTI-17

Sunkel, Tom
39PlaBal-146
40PlaBal-110
90DodTar-784
95ConTSN-1422

Sunker, Steve
78CliDodT-29

Sunnen, Gene
88WatPirP-34

Sunny, Stacy
94ColSilBC-9
95ColSilB-28
95ColSilB9-8
96ColSilB-28

Suns, Jacksonville
91JacSunP-165

Suntop, Lionel
75TopPho-117

Suplee, Ray
92ClaDraP-113
92OneYanC-17
93GreHorC-22
93GreHorF-901
93SouAtlLAGF-23
94Bow-396
94ClaGolF-86
94TamYanC-26
94TamYanF-2399
95TamYanYI-28
96HigDesMB-27

Suppan, Jeff
94Bow-391
94Cla-183
94SarRedSC-1
94SarRedSF-1950
95Bow-65
95BowBes-B60
95BowBesR-B60
95Exc-16
95SPCha-17
95SPChaDC-17
95TreThuTI-15
95UppDecML-83
96Bow-236
96BowBes-153
96BowBesAR-153
96BowBesR-153
96ColCho-428
96ColChoGS-39
96ColChoGS-428
96ColChoSS-39
96ColChoSS-428
96Fla-27
96Fle-35
96FleRedS-15
96FleTif-35
96Lea-217
96LeaPre-138
96LeaPreP-138
96LeaPrePB-217
96LeaPrePG-217
96LeaPrePS-217
96LeaSigA-216
96LeaSigAG-216
96LeaSigAS-216
96PawRedSDD-28
96Pin-387
96PinAfi-194
96PinAfiAP-194
96PinFoil-387
96Sco-500
96SelCer-123
96SelCerAP-123
96SelCerCB-123
96SelCerCR-123
96SelCerMB-123
96SelCerMG-123
96SelCerMR-123
96SigRooOJTP-T10
96StaClu-444
96StaCluMOP-444
96Sum-178
96SumAbo&B-178
96SumArtP-178
96SumFoi-178
96Top-347
96TopChr-139
96TopChrR-139
96TopGal-144
96TopGalPPI-144
96Ult-322
96UltGolM-322
96UppDec-227
96UppDecFSP-FS20
96Zen-109
96ZenArtP-109
97Bow-300
97BowBes-159
97BowBesAR-159
97BowBesR-159
97BowChr-208
97BowChrI-208
97BowChrIR-208
97BowChrR-208
97BowInt-300
97ColCho-47
97Don-208
97Don-375
97DonLim-159
97DonLimLE-159
97DonPreP-208
97DonPreP-375
97DonPrePGold-208
97DonPrePGold-375
97DonTea-51
97DonTeaSPE-51
97Lea-340
97LeaFraM-340
97LeaFraMDC-340
97Sco-210
97ScoPreS-210
97ScoRedS-11
97ScoRedSPl-11
97ScoRedSPr-11
97ScoShoS-210
97ScoShoSAP-210
97Top-348
97UppDec-28
95UppDecMLFS-83

Surane, John
90IdaFalBP-3250

Surhoff, B.J.
86VanCanP-24
87BrePol-5
87BreTeal-13
87ClaUpdY-135
87Don-28
87DonRoo-17
87FleUpd-115
87FleUpdG-115
87Lea-28
87SpoRooI-23
87SpoRooP-6
87SpoTeaP-19
87Top-216
87TopTif-216
88BrePol-5
88ClaBlu-202
88Don-172
88DonBasB-277
88Fle-175
88FleGlo-175
88Lea-164
88OPC-174
88PanSti-120
88RedFolSB-85
88Sco-22
88ScoGlo-22
88ScoYouSI-8
88Spo-57
88StaLinBre-17
88Top-491
88TopBig-22
88TopGloS-49
88TopRoo-10
88TopSti-202
88TopStiB-57
88TopTif-491
88ToyRoo-31
89Bow-137
89BowTif-137
89BreGar-5
89BrePol-5
89BreYea-5
89ClaLigB-25
89Don-221
89DonBasB-221
89Fle-197
89FleGlo-197
89OPC-33
89PanSti-368
89Sco-154
89Spo-208
89Top-33
89TopSti-200
89TopTif-33
89UppDec-343
90Bow-393
90BowTif-393
90BreMilB-25
90Don-173
90DonBesA-78
90Fle-338
90FleCan-338
90Lea-290
90MLBBasB-84
90OPC-696
90PanSti-93
90PubSti-505
90Sco-74
90Top-696
90TopBig-198
90TopSti-203
90TopTif-696
90UppDec-159
90VenSti-467
91Bow-44
91BreMilB-26
91BrePol-23
91Don-460
91Fle-598
91Lea-42
91OPC-592
91PanFreS-203
91PanSti-169
91Sco-477
91StaClu-206
91StaCluP-42
91Stu-78
91Top-592
91TopDesS-592
91TopMic-592
91TopTif-592
91Ult-182
91UppDec-254
92Bow-481
92BrePol-26
92Don-70
92Fle-190
92Hig5-68
92Lea-212
92OPC-718
92PanSti-34
92Pin-118
92Sco-78
92StaClu-117
92Stu-197
92Top-718
92TopDaiQTU-7
92TopGol-718
92TopGolW-718
92TopKid-82
92TopMic-718
92TriPla-56
92Ult-85
92UppDec-120
93Bow-71
93BrePol-24
93BreSen5-3
93DiaMar-105
93Don-545
93Fin-8
93FinRef-8
93Fla-230
93Fle-257
93Lea-166
93OPC-343
93PacSpa-165
93PanSti-36
93Pin-87
93Sco-33
93Sel-62
93SP-70
93StaClu-711
93StaCluFDI-711
93StaCluMOP-711
93Stu-174
93Top-417
93TopGol-417
93TopInaM-417
93TopMic-417
93TriPla-248
93Ult-224
93UppDec-102
93UppDecGold-102
94BreMilB-363
94BrePol-26
94ColC-469
94ColChoGS-469
94ColChoSS-469
94Don-310
94Fin-344
94FinRef-344
94Fle-192
94Lea-369
94OPC-197
94Pac-344
94PanSti-87
94Pin-152
94PinArtP-152
94PinMusC-152
94ProMag-73
94Sco-77
94ScoGolR-77
94Sel-330
94SP-60
94SPDieC-60
94StaClu-215
94StaCluFDI-215
94StaCluGR-215
94StaCluMOP-215
94Top-102
94TopGol-102
94TopSpa-102
94TriPla-58
94Ult-379
94UppDec-369
94UppDecED-369
95ColCho-174
95ColChoGS-174
95ColChoSS-174
95Don-356
95DonPreP-356
95DonTopotO-103
95Fle-191
95Pin-352
95PinArtP-352
95PinMusC-352
95Sco-345
95ScoGolR-345
95ScoPlaTS-345
95Top-367
96ColCho-195
96ColCho-469
96ColChoGS-195
96ColChoGS-469
96ColChoSS-195
96ColChoSS-469
96Don-113
96DonDiaK-20
96DonPreP-113
96EmoXL-10
96Fin-B304
96FinRef-B304
96Fla-13
96Fle-159
96FleOri-16
96FleTeaL-8
96FleTif-159
96FleUpd-U8
96FleUpdTC-U8
96MetUni-10
96MetUniP-10
96MLBPin-34
96Pac-349
96PacPri-P110
96PacPriG-P110
96PanSti-191
96Pin-88
96Pin-351
96PinAfi-92
96PinAfiAP-92
96PinAfiFPP-92
96PinArtP-50
96PinFoil-351
96PinSta-50
96Sco-54
96ScoDugC-A47
96ScoDugCAP-A47
96Sel-133
96SelArtP-133
96Spo-43
96SpoArtP-43
96StaClu-332
96StaCluMOP-332
96Sum-35
96SumAbo&B-35
96SumArtP-35
96SumFoi-35
96Ult-85
96Ult-309
96UltGolM-85
96UltGolM-309
96UppDec-120
96UppDec-276
97Cir-277
97CirRav-277
97ColCho-43
97Don-245
97DonPreP-245
97DonPrePGold-245
97DonTea-38
97DonTeaSPE-38
97Fin-47
97FinRef-47
97Fle-14
97FleTif-14
97Lea-157
97LeaFraM-157
97LeaFraMDC-157
97MetUni-9
97Pac-30
97PacLigB-30
97PacSil-30
97Pin-142
97PinArtP-142
97PinMusC-142
97Sco-197
97ScoOri-11
97ScoOriPl-11
97ScoOriPr-11
97ScoPreS-197
97ScoShoS-197
97ScoShoSAP-197
97StaClu-79
97StaCluMOP-79
97Top-41
97Ult-423
97UltGolME-423
97UltPlaME-423
97UppDec-304

Surhoff, Rich
85PhiTas-46
85PorBeaC-49
86Don-42
86OklCit8P-22
88IowCubC-10
88IowCubP-529
93RanKee-351

Surico, Steve
89AncGlaP-25
90ButCopKSP-23

Suris, Jorge
85SpoIndC-23

Surkont, Max
46SeaSLP-53
52Bow-12
52Top-302
53BowC-156
53BraJohC-11
53BraSpiaS3-23
54Bow-75
54DanDee-26
55Bow-83
56Top-209
57Top-310
83Bra53F-36
83TopRep5-302

Surner, Ben
82HolMilT-26
83NasAngT-24

Surratt, Alfred
92NegLeaRLI-58
96NegLeaBMKC-9

Surratt, Jamie
93JohCitCC-24
93JohCitCF-3690

Susce, George

49IndTeal-29
55A'sRodM-41
55Bow-320
56Top-93
57Top-229
58Top-189
59Top-511
76A'sRodMC-27
93RanKee-43

Susce, Steve
83AleDukT-21

Sutch, Rick (Ray)
92MadMusC-19
92MadMusF-1237
93SanBerSC-17
93SanBerSF-771

Sutcliffe, Cy (Elmer Ellsworth)
87OldJudN-495

Sutcliffe, Rick
80DodPol-43
80Top-544
81DodPol-43
81Don-418
81Fle-125
81LonBeaPT-12
81OPC-191
81Top-191
82Fle-25
82Ind-33
82IndTeal-31
82IndWhe-30
82OPC-141
82Top-609
82TopTra-116T
83Don-72
83Fle-420
83FleSta-190
83FleSti-240
83IndPos-34
83IndWhe-28
83Top-141
83Top-497
83Top-707
83TopSti-20
83TopSti-61
84CubChiT-29
84CubSev-40
84CubUno-12
84CubUno-14
84Don-338
84Fle-551
84FleSti-87
84FleUpd-114
84FunFooP-32
84Ind-28
84Nes792-245
84OPC-245
84Top-245
84TopRubD-8
84TopSti-254
84TopTif-245
84TopTra-115T
84TopTraT-115T
85CubLioP-24
85CubSev-40
85Don-433
85Dra-43
85Fle-69
85FleLimE-39
85FleStaS-89
85KASDis-15
85KitCloD-15
85Lea-139
85OPC-72
85SevCoi-G14
85ThoMcAD-43
85Top-72
85Top-720
85Top3-D-29
85TopGaloC-11
85TopGloS-9
85TopMin-72
85TopRubD-14
85TopSti-35
85TopSti-97
85TopSup-3
85TopTif-72
85TopTif-720
86BasStaB-108
86CubGat-40
86CubUno-18
86Don-189
86DorChe-17
86Fle-383
86FleMin-81
86FleSlu-39
86Lea-122
86MeaGolSB-19
86MSAJayPCD-18
86OPC-330
86SevCoi-C10
86Spo-46
86Spo-60
86Spo-70
86Spo-72
86Spo-134
86Spo-149
86Top-330
86TopSti-61
86TopTat-21
86TopTif-330
86TruVal-18
87CubCan-33
87CubDavB-40
87Don-68
87DonOpeD-69
87Fle-576
87FleGlo-576
87FleSlu-41
87OPC-142
87Top-142
87TopTif-142
88ClaBlu-224
88CubDavB-40
88Don-68
88DonAll-43
88DonBasB-138
88DonTeaBC-68
88Dra-31
88Fle-435
88FleAwaW-41
88FleBasA-41
88FleBasM-38
88FleExcS-40
88FleGlo-435
88FleHotS-42
88FleLeaL-41
88FleMin-71
88FleRecS-40
88FleStiC-81
88FleSup-39
88FleTeaL-41
88K-M-30
88Lea-91
88OPC-372
88PanSti-257
88RedFolSB-86
88Sco-50
88ScoGlo-50
88Spo-27
88StaLinCu-13
88Top-740
88TopBig-128
88TopCoi-57
88TopMinL-45
88TopRevLL-9
88TopSti-61
88TopStiB-27
88TopTif-740
88TopUKM-77
88TopUKMT-77
89Bow-281
89BowTif-281
89CubMar-40
89Don-223
89DonBasB-138
89Fle-439
89FleGlo-439
89OPC-394
89PanSti-51
89Sco-407
89Spo-217
89Top-520
89TopBasT-75
89TopSti-52
89TopTif-520
89UppDec-303
90Bow-21
90BowTif-21
90CubMar-20
90DodTar-785
90Don-157
90Fle-43
90FleCan-43
90Lea-6
90MLBBasB-53
90OPC-640
90PanSti-233
90PubSti-205
90Sco-450
90Spo-181
90Top-640
90TopBig-38
90TopSti-55
90TopTif-640
90TopTVCu-15
90UppDec-109
90VenSti-468
91Bow-430
91CubMar-40
91CubVinL-29
91Don-462
91Fle-434
91OPC-415
91PeoChiTI-31
91Sco-785
91Top-415
91TopDesS-415
91TopMic-415
91TopTif-415
91UppDec-473
92Bow-106
92Cla2-T54
92Don-642
92DonUpd-U13
92Fle-393
92FleUpd-3
92Lea-508
92OPCPre-98
92Pin-398
92Sco-665
92ScoRoo-8T
92StaClu-700
92StaCluECN-700
92Stu-130
92TopTra-113T
92TopTraG-113T
92Ult-309
92UppDec-529
92UppDec-708
93Bow-113
93Don-719
93Fla-158
93Fle-552
93Lea-89
93OPC-381
93PacSpa-26
93Pin-532
93Sco-563
93Sel-182
93StaClu-246
93StaCluFDI-246
93StaCluMOP-246
93StaCluMP-10
93Top-274
93TopGol-274
93TopInaM-274
93TopMic-274
93TriPla-106
93Ult-502
93UppDec-80
93UppDecGold-80
94CarPol-20
94ColC-548
94ColChoGS-548
94ColChoSS-548
94Don-500
94Fle-21
94FleUpd-183
94Lea-315
94Sco-497
94ScoGolR-497
94ScoRoo-RT19
94ScoRooGR-RT19
94StaClu-691
94StaCluFDI-691
94StaCluGR-691
94StaCluMOP-691
94Top-91
94TopGol-91
94TopSpa-91
94Ult-569
95ColCho-194
95ColChoGS-194
95ColChoSS-194
95DodROY-8
95Sco-244
95ScoGolR-244
95ScoPlaTS-244
96IdaFalB-24

Sutcliffe, Terry
81VerBeaDT-20

Suter, Bill
81OklCit8T-18

Suter, Burke
77BriRedST-17

Sutey, John
91BriTigC-10
91BriTigP-3621
92BriTigC-26
92BriTigF-1429

Sutherland, Alex
92Bow-123
92SanBerSF-959
93AppFoxC-22
93AppFoxF-2464
93LinVenB-161
94AppFoxC-18
94AppFoxF-1058
95LinVen-52

Sutherland, Darrell
66OPC-191
66Top-191
66TopVen-191
68Top-551
91MetWIZ-389

Sutherland, Gary
67Top-587
68OPC-98
68Top-98
68TopVen-98
69ExpFudP-12
69Top-326
69TopSta-59
69TopTeaP-10
70ExpPos-7
70Top-632
71ExpLaPR-13
71ExpPS-26
71MLBOffS-143
71OPC-434
71Top-434
72MilBra-335
72OPC-211
72Top-211
73OPC-572
73Top-572
74OPC-428
74Top-428
74TopTra-428T
75Hos-146
75OPC-522
75Top-522
76OPC-113
76SSP-364
76Top-113
77PadSchC-55
77Top-307
94BreMilB-364

Sutherland, John
92OneYanC-12
93SanBerSC-18
93SanBerSF-772
94AbaYanF-1442
95NorNavTI-23
96NorNavB-26

Sutherland, Leo
77AppFoxT-25
78AppFoxT-19
79KnoKnoST-7
80IowOakP-11
81Don-42
81EdmTraRR-14
81Top-112
82EdmTraT-11
82Top-599

Sutherland, Matt
79CedRapGT-8

Sutherland, Suds (Harry)
20WalMaiW-54

Suthers, Gregory
91BriBanF-3

Sutko, Glenn
88BilMusP-1806
89GreHorP-420
90CedRapRB-2
91Bow-668
91ChaLooLD-171
91ChaLooP-1963
91Cla/Bes-216
91LinDriAA-171
91MajLeaCP-72
91Sco-767
91TopDeb90-151
92ChaLooF-3823
92ChaLooS-196
92Fle-423
92Sco100RS-98
92SkyAA F-88
92StaClu-559
95ElPasDTI-22

Sutryk, Tom
87PenWhiSP-15

Sutter, Bruce
77CubJewT-14
77Top-144
78Hos-5
78Kel-48
78OPC-196
78RCColC-96
78SSP270-254
78Top-325
79Hos-130
79Kel-1
79OPC-238
79Top-457
80BurKinPHR-11
80Kel-10
80OPC-4
80Top-17
80TopSup-32
80WilGloT-7
81AllGamPI-178
81CokTeaS-130
81Don-560
81Fle-294
81FleStiC-80
81Kel-56
81OPC-9
81PerCreC-24
81Top-590
81TopSti-32
81TopSti-221
81TopTra-838
82Don-372
82FBIDis-24
82Fle-129
82Fle-631
82FleSta-28
82Kel-17
82OPC-260
82OPC-347
82Squ-22
82Top-168
82Top-260
82Top-347
82TopSti-15
82TopSti-94
82TopSti-130
83AllGamPI-180
83Car-31
83Don-40
83DonActA-41
83Fle-24
83FleSta-191
83FleSti-1
83Kel-37
83OPC-150
83OPC-151
83OPC-266
83PerCreC-17
83PerCreCG-17
83Top-150
83Top-151
83Top-407
83Top-708
83TopFol-4
83TopGloS-40
83TopLeaS-8
83TopSti-166
83TopSti-187
83TopSti-209
83TopSti-284
84Car-30
84Car5x7-29
84CubUno-9
84Don-13
84Don-13A
84Don-534
84Fle-338
84FleSti-70
84FunFooP-14
84Nes792-709
84Nes792-730
84OPC-243
84RalPur-24
84SevCoi-C7
84Top-709
84Top-730

84TopCer-24
84TopRubD-22
84TopSti-145
84TopTif-709
84TopTif-730
85BraHos-21
85BraPol-40
85BraTBSAT-3
85Don-109
85Dra-44
85Fle-241
85FleStaS-104
85FleUpd-114
85KASDis-16
85KitCloD-16
85Lea-163
85OPC-370
85SevCoi-C5
85SevCoi-G5
85SevCoi-S4
85SpoPro-3
85ThoMcAD-44
85Top-9
85Top-370
85Top-722
85Top3-D-23
85TopGaloC-12
85TopGloS-22
85TopRubD-23
85TopSti-135
85TopSti-172
85TopSup-9
85TopTif-9
85TopTif-370
85TopTif-722
85TopTifT-115T
85TopTra-115T
86BasStaB-109
86BraPol-40
86Don-321
86Fle-529
86FleMin-106
86FleStiC-117
86GenMilB-5I
86Lea-192
86MeaGolSB-17
86OPC-133
86SevCoi-C7
86SevCoi-E7
86SevCoi-S7
86SevCoi-W7
86Spo-47
86Spo-65
86Top-620
86TopSti-37
86TopTat-10
86TopTif-620
86TruVal-15
87Fle-530
87FleGlo-530
87OPC-344
87RedFolSB-125
87Top-435
87TopTif-435
88Top-155
88TopTif-155
89Don-458
89Fle-603
89FleGlo-603
89OPC-11
89OPCBoxB-M
89PanSti-39
89RedFolSB-114
89Sco-425
89Top-11
89TopBasT-105
89TopBig-64
89TopSti-25
89TopTif-11
89TopWaxBC-M
89UppDec-414
90AGFA-19
90PubSti-125
92CarMcD-52
92CubOldS-24
93CubRol-3
94TedWil-18

Suttles, Mule
74LauOldTBS-30
86NegLeaF-115
90NegLeaS-21
91PomBlaBPB-22
91PomBlaBPB-25

Sutton, Daron
92BoiHawC-22
92BoiHawF-3628

Sutton, Derek
93KinMetC-21
93KinMetF-3795
94PitMetC-21
94PitMetF-3524

Sutton, Don
66Top-288
66TopVen-288
67CokCapD-5
67CokCapDA-5
67DexPre-201
67Top-445
67TopVen-317
68OPC-103
68Top-103
68TopVen-103
69MilBra-267
69MLBOffS-153
69OPC-216
69Top-216
69TopFou-19
69TopSta-50
70DayDaiNM-67
70Kel-8
70MLBOffS-59
70Top-622
71DodTic-18
71Kel-31
71MLBOffS-118
71OPC-361
71Top-361
71TopCoi-145
72MilBra-336
72Top-530
73Kel2D-5
73LinPor-97
73OPC-10
73Top-10
73TopCanL-51
73TopCom-21
73TopPin-21
74OPC-220
74Top-220
74TopDecE-12
74TopSta-50
75Hos-7
75HosTwi-7
75OPC-220
75Top-220
76CraDis-61
76Kel-13
76LinSup-120
76OPC-530
76SSP-73
76Top-530
77BurCheD-147
77Hos-70
77OPC-24
77PepGloD-62
77RCColC-62
77Top-620
77TopCloS-47
78Dim2GT-1
78Hos-70
78Kel-57
78OPC-96
78RCColC-1
78SSP270-80
78Top-310
79DodBlu-12
79Hos-92
79OPC-80
79Top-170
80DodPol-20
80OPC-228
80Top-440
81AllGamPI-179
81CokTeaS-71
81Dod-10
81Don-58
81Fle-112
81FleStiC-59
81Squ-16
81Top-7
81Top-605
81TopSti-27
81TopSupHT-102
81TopTra-839
82AstAstI-9
82Don-443
82Fle-234
82FleSta-43
82Kel-21
82OPC-305
82OPC-306
82Top-305
82Top-306
83BreGar-18
83BrePol-21
83Don-531A
83Don-531B
83Fle-47
83FleSta-192
83FleSti-16
83OPC-145
83OPC-146
83Top-145
83Top-146
83TopFol-1
84BreGar-19
84BrePol-20
84Don-414
84DonCha-41
84Fle-215
84FunFooP-86
84Nes792-35
84Nes792-715
84Nes792-716
84OPC-35
84Top-35
84Top-715
84Top-716
84TopSti-300
84TopTif-35
84TopTif-715
84TopTif-716
85A'sMot-3
85Don-16
85Don-107
85DonSupD-16
85Fle-598
85FleUpd-115
85Lea-16
85OPC-172
85Top-10
85Top-729
85TopMin-729
85TopSti-7
85TopSti-8
85TopSti-290
85TopTif-10
85TopTif-729
85TopTifT-116T
85TopTra-116T
86AngSmo-4
86Don-611
86DonHig-16
86Fle-170
86FleLimE-43
86FleMin-35
86Lea-236
86OPC-335
86Spo-135
86Spo-175
86Top-335
86TopTat-7
86TopTif-335
87AngSmo-2
87DodSmoA-35
87Don-181
87Fle-93
87Fle-626
87FleGlo-93
87FleGlo-626
87FleRecS-37
87FleStiC-115
87Lea-153
87OPC-259
87OPCBoxB-G
87RalPur-6
87SevCoi-W11
87Spo-99
87Spo-156
87SpoTeaP-11
87Top-673
87TopSti-183
87TopTif-673
87TopWaxBC-G
87Woo-6
88DodMot-9
88DodPol-20
88DodSmo-30
88Don-407
88Fle-505
88FleGlo-505
88PanSti-37
88Sco-105
88ScoGlo-105
88Spo-213
88StaLinD-18
88Top-575
88TopTif-575
89DodSmoG-78
89OPCBoxB-N
89Sco-400
89TopWaxBC-N
90DodTar-786
92BreCarT-22
92DodStaTA-11
94BreMilB-365
94BreSen-7

Sutton, Doug
89BluOriS-23

Sutton, Ezra
87BucN28-12
87OldJudN-496
88AugBecN-26
88GandBCGCE-39
88WG1CarG-8

Sutton, Jim
82AppFoxF-4

Sutton, Johnny
74GasRanT-21
76SacSolC-13
76VenLeaS-61
79IowOakP-14
79Top-676
80OgdA'sT-13

Sutton, Larry
92EugEmeC-24
92EugEmeF-3040
93Bow-697
93ClaMVPF-7
93ExcFS7-179
93RocRoyC-26
93RocRoyF-726
93Top-423
93TopGol-423
93TopInaM-423
93TopMic-423
94CarLeaAF-CAR25
94TopTra-56T
94WilBluRC-23
94WilBluRF-310
95Bow-228
95BowGolF-228
95Exc-65
95ExcLeaL-15
95WicWraTI-8
96WicWraB-5

Sutton, Mark
83BurRanF-21
83BurRanT-24

Sutton, Phil
79CedRapGT-30

Sutton, Rico
80UtiBluJT-33
83KinBluJTI-25

Suyat, Paulette
91HawWomS-15

Suzuki, Keiji
79TCMJapPB-45

Suzuki, Ken
88SanJosGCLC-129
88SanJosGP-121
90IBAWorA-17

Suzuki, Mac (Makato)
93SanBerSC-19
93SanBerSF-773
94ActPac-17
94Bow-313
94Bow-378
94BowBes-B59
94BowBesR-B59
94BowPre-9
94Cla-49
94ClaCreotC-C3
94ExcFS7-128
94ExtBas-173
94ExtBasMLH-8
94JacSunF-1412
94TedWil-131
94Ult-425
95ActPacF-24
95ARuFalLS-17
95Bow-199
95Fle-278
95Top-168
95UppDecML-84
95UppDecML-114
96LeaSig-121
96LeaSigPPG-121
96LeaSigPPP-121
96PorCitRB-26
97Bow-163
97BowInt-163
97DonRatR-22
97PacPriGotD-GD93
97PinPasttM-22
97Sco-318
97ScoMar-15
97ScoMarPl-15
97ScoMarPr-15
97ScoPreS-318
97ScoShoS-318
97ScoShoSAP-318
97UppDec-193
97UppDec-480
95UppDecMLFS-84
95UppDecMLFS-114

Suzuki, Yasu
89SalSpuCLC-135
89SalSpuP-1814

Sveum, Dale
84ElPasDT-24
85VanCanC-209
86DonRoo-37
86FleUpd-109
86SpoRoo-4
86TopTra-106T
86TopTraT-106T
86VanCanP-25
87BrePol-7
87BreTeal-14
87Don-542
87DonOpeD-55
87Fle-358
87FleGlo-358
87Lea-156
87SpoTeaP-19
87Top-327
87TopRoo-18
87TopSti-309
87TopTif-327
87ToyRoo-27
88BrePol-7
88Don-232
88DonBasB-305
88Fle-176
88FleGlo-176
88OPC-81
88PanSti-126
88Sco-120
88ScoGlo-120
88StaLinBre-18
88Top-592
88TopBig-44
88TopSti-199
88TopTif-592
89Bow-139
89BowTif-139
89BreGar-6
89BrePol-7
89BreYea-7
89Don-146
89Fle-198
89FleGlo-198
89OPC-12
89PanSti-374
89Sco-256
89ScoYouS2-24
89Top-12
89TopBig-126
89TopSti-206
89TopTif-12
89UppDec-421
90BreMilB-26
90BrePol-7
90El PasDAGTI-8
90OPC-739
90PubSti-506
90Top-739
90TopTif-739
90UppDec-499
91BreMilB-27
91BrePol-24
91Sco-814
92Bow-367
92Don-452
92Fle-191
92Lea-473
92OPC-478
92PhiMed-30
92Sco-181

92StaClu-687
92Top-478
92TopGol-478
92TopGolW-478
92TopMic-478
92UppDec-498
93AthMot-11
93BreSen-3
93PacSpa-572
93StaCluAt-29
94BreMilB-366
94CalCanF-800
Swacina, Harry
12ColRedB-282
12ColTinT-282
Swafford, Derek
94WelPirC-25
94WelPirF-3505
96Exc-225
96LynHilB-21
Swafford, J.C.
89TenTecGE-27
Swaggerty, Bill
82RocRedWT-7
83RocRedWT-10
84RocRedWT-17
85Don-392
85Fle-193
85RocRedWT-22
85Top-147
85TopTif-147
86Don-594
88OmaRoyC-9
88OmaRoyP-1498
91OriCro-448
Swaggerty, Glenn
80QuaCitCT-6
81QuaCitCT-25
Swail, Steve
89PulBraP-1914
90BurBraB-9
90BurBraP-2353
90BurBraS-25
91DurBulC-11
91DurBulP-1549
92DurBulF-1106
92MacBraC-7
93DurBulC-19
93DurBulF-489
93DurBulTI-28
94GreBraF-417
94GreBraTI-22
Swain, Rob
86WatIndP-26
87KinIndP-18
88CarLeaAS-36
88KinIndS-21
89CanIndB-26
89CanIndP-1303
89CanIndS-20
90CanIndB-11
90CanIndP-1301
92KinIndC-28
92KinIndF-2493
Swain, Steve
82AubAstT-16
Swain, Thayer
88ButCopKSP-21
90ChaRanS-28
Swaino, Shannon
96VerExpB-27
Swan, Craig
74OPC-602
74Top-602
75TidTidTI-21
76OPC-494
76SSP-558
76Top-494
77MetDaiPA-24
77Spo-7911
77Top-94
78MetDaiPA-23
78Top-621
79Hos-41
79OPC-170
79Top-7
79Top-334
79TopCom-27
80OPC-1
80Top-8
80TopSup-41
81CokTeaS-92
81Don-155
81Fle-319
81OPC-189
81Top-189
82Don-589
82Fle-538
82MetPhoA-22
82Top-592
83Don-254
83Fle-557
83FleSta-193
83FleSti-231
83OPC-292
83Top-292
83Top-621
83TopSti-262
84Don-441
84Fle-600
84FleUpd-115
84Nes792-763
84Top-763
84TopTif-763
84TopTra-116T
84TopTraT-116T
89TidTidC-9
91MetWIZ-391
Swan, Russ
86EveGiaC-8
88BlaYNPRWLU-44
88SanJosGCLC-138
88SanJosGP-118
89ShrCapP-1831
90Bow-224
90BowTif-224
90CMC-532
90PhoFirC-5
90TopDeb89-125
90TopTra-121T
90TopTraT-121T
91Don-621
91FleUpd-57
91MarCouH-22
91OPC-739
91StaClu-577
91Top-739
91TopDesS-739
91TopMic-739
91TopTif-739
92Bow-378
92Don-382
92Fle-293
92Lea-203
92MarMot-22
92OPC-588
92Pin-484
92Sco-281
92StaClu-472
92Top-588
92TopGol-588
92TopGolW-588
92TopMic-588
92UppDec-618
93Don-713
93Fle-314
93MarMot-16
93PacSpa-626
93StaClu-179
93StaCluFDI-179
93StaCluMari-14
93StaCluMOP-179
93Top-96
93TopGol-96
93TopInaM-96
93TopMic-96
93Ult-272
93UppDec-624
93UppDecGold-624
95EdmTraTI-23
96LasVegSB-26
Swan, Tyrone
93BatCliC-26
93BatCliF-3145
94SouAtlLAF-SAL56
94SpaPhiF-1723
94SparPhiC-20
Swank, Ken
82ChaRoyT-18
Swank, Randy
91EveGiaC-4
91EveGiaP-3924
Swann, Pedro
91IdaFalBP-4341
91IdaFalBSP-25
92PulBraC-21
92PulBraF-3194
93DurBulC-20
93DurBulF-500
93DurBulTI-15
94GreBraF-427
94GreBraTI-23
95BreBtaTI-16
96Exc-134
96RicBraRC-NNO
96RicBraUB-27
Swanson, Art
56Top-204
58JetPos-18
Swanson, Chad
88KenTwiP-1386
89KenTwiP-1078
90VisOakCLC-57
90VisOakP-2152
Swanson, Dave
92KinMetC-5
92KinMetF-1531
93PitMetC-20
93PitMetF-3709
94CapCitBC-20
94CapCitBF-1750
Swanson, Eric
82DayBeaAT-16
Swanson, Evar
33Gou-195
33TatOrbSDR-174
34ExhFou-10
35AlDemDCR3-12
63GadFunC-20
83ConMar-15
88ConAmeA-23
92ConTSN-393
94ConTSN-1239
94ConTSNB-1239
Swanson, John
91OklStaC-25
Swanson, Perry
82ChaRoyT-8
Swanson, Stan
72OPC-331
72Top-331
72TopCloT-31
Swartwood, Cyrus
87OldJudN-497
Swartz, Nick
84OmaRoyT-7
85OmaRoyT-3
86OmaRoyP-26
87OmaRoyP-5
88OmaRoyP-1500
Swartzbaugh, David
88CapCodPPaLP-66
89GenCubP-1866
90PeoChiTI-28
91PeoChiP-1342
91WinSpiP-2829
92ChaKniF-2771
92ChaKniS-168
92ClaFS7-63
92SkyAA F-76
94IowCubF-1275
94OrlCubF-1385
95IowCubTI-24
95OrlCubF-11
96IowCubB-26
97Fle-285
97FleTif-285
Swartzel, Parke
87OldJudN-498
Swartzlander, Keith
86MacPirP-25
Sweatt, George Alexander
86NegLeaF-117
87NegLeaPD-26
Sweeney, Bill
12ColRedB-284
12ColTinT-284
31Exh-18
Sweeney, Bill (William)
53MotCoo-23
Sweeney, D.B.
88PacEigMO-13
Sweeney, Dennis
91EliTwiP-4301
92KenTwiF-603
93ForMyeMC-24
93ForMyeMF-2655
94NasXprF-387
Sweeney, Ed
10CouT21-230
10CouT21-231
10CouT21-232
10CouT21-233
10CouT21-320
10JuJuDE-38
10PeoT21-54
11MecDFT-46
12ColTinT-283
14CraJacE-112
15CraJacE-112
15VicT21-26
Sweeney, Jeff
09AmeCarE-104
09ColChiE-283
09T206-348
10RedCroT-249
11SpoLifM-83
11T205-168
12ColRedB-283
12HasTriFT-38B
12HasTriFT-67B
12HasTriFT-68A
12HasTriFT-68B
14B18B-27
15AmeCarE-38
Sweeney, Jim
90PeoChiUTI-U6
Sweeney, Kevin
96AriBlaDB-32
96HonShaHWB-32
97Bow-356
97BowInt-356
97Top-249
Sweeney, Kim
89GenCubP-1873
Sweeney, Mark
88CapCodPPaLP-59
91BoiHawC-15
91BoiHawP-3898
92ClaFS7-228
92ColRedC-8
92KinIndF-2475
92QuaCitRBC-21
92QuaCitRBF-825
93PalSprAC-23
93PalSprAF-85
94Top-237
94TopGol-237
94TopSpa-237
94UppDecML-228
94VanCanF-1877
95TopTra-122T
96CarPol-25
96ColCho-281
96ColChoGS-281
96ColChoSS-281
96Fle-557
96FleTif-557
96LeaSigEA-196
97DonFraFea-9
97Fle-454
97FleTif-454
97MidAngOHP-29
97Pac-418
97PacLigB-418
97PacSil-418
97Pin-143
97PinArtP-143
97PinMusC-143
97Ult-278
97UltGolME-278
97UltPlaME-278
Sweeney, Michael
89IdaFalBP-2023
90IdaFalBP-3258
Sweeney, Mike
91HigSchPLS-5
92EugEmeC-25
92EugEmeF-3033
93EugEmeC-25
93EugEmeF-3859
94MidLeaAF-MDW25
94RocRoyC-24
94RocRoyF-569
95WilBluRTI-33
96Bow-334
96BowBes-164
96BowBesAR-164
96BowBesR-164
96BowMinLP-10
96ColCho-438
96ColChoGS-438
96ColChoSS-438
96Fle-138
96FleTif-138
96Pin-180
96Sco-492
96TexLeaAB-36
96UppDec-251
96WicWraB-1
97Bow-111
97BowBes-192
97BowBesAR-192
97BowBesR-192
97BowCerBIA-CA76
97BowCerGIA-CA76
97BowChr-131
97BowChrI-131
97BowChrIR-131
97BowChrR-131
97BowInt-111
97ColCho-131
97Don-235
97DonLim-171
97DonLimLE-171
97DonPre-139
97DonPreCttC-139
97DonPreP-235
97DonPrePGold-235
97Fin-88
97FinRef-88
97Fle-123
97FleTif-123
97Lea-333
97LeaFraM-333
97LeaFraMDC-333
97Pac-112
97PacLigB-112
97PacSil-112
97RoyPol-21
97Sco-262
97ScoPreS-262
97ScoShoS-262
97ScoShoSAP-262
97StaClu-274
97StaCluM-M31
97StaCluMOP-274
97StaCluMOP-M31
97Top-447
97TopGal-168
97TopGalPPI-168
97Ult-73
97UltGolME-73
97UltPlaME-73
Sweeney, Peter
87OldJudN-499
Sweeney, Robert
90KisDodD-26
91KisDodP-4185
92BakDodCLC-24
Sweeney, Roger
91YakBeaP-4262
92GreFalDSP-8
Sweeney, William John
09AmeCarE-103
09ColChiE-284
09RamT20-115
09T206-349
10CouT21-64
10RedCroT-76
10RedCroT-161
11SpoLifCW-345
11SpoLifM-147
12T207-180
13NatGamW-39
13TomBarW-35
14FatPlaT-48
14TexTomE-43
Sweet, Jonathan
94WelPirC-26
94WelPirF-3500
96LynHilB-22
Sweet, Richard
78PadFamF-31
78Top-702
79HawIslC-18
79HawIslT-3
79OPC-341
79Top-646
80HawIslT-20
81TidTidT-1
83Don-352
83Fle-487
83MarNal-5
83Top-437
84Don-196
84Fle-621
84MarMot-27
84Nes792-211
84Top-211

84TopTif-211
87BelMarTI-24
88WauTimGS-1
89OscAstS-27
90ColMudP-1361
90ColMudS-25
91JacGenLD-574
91JacGenP-940
91LinDriAA-574
91MetWIZ-392
92JacGenF-4014
92JacGenS-349
93LinVenB-215
93TucTorF-3076
94TucTorF-777
95TusTorTI-27
96AstMot-28

Sweetland, Lester L.
29ExhFou-12
31CubTeal-23

Sweezey, Gary
95GreFalDTI-17

Swenson, Mark
82CliGiaF-31

Swenson, Mickey
82CliGiaF-30
82CliGiaF-32

Swenson, Mike
95NewJerCTI-28

Swepson, Dobie
86CliGiaP-23
88PocGiaP-2095

Swepson, Lyle
84EveGiaC-2

Swetonic, Steve
34ButPreR-58
94ConTSN-1163
94ConTSNB-1163

Swiacki, Bill
79AlbDukT-4
80AlbDukT-5
81AlbDukT-6
82TacTigT-9

Swift, Bill
34Gou-57
36GouWidPPR-A98
36NatChiFPR-69
36R31PasP-24
39PlaBal-129
41DodTeal-7
85Top-404
85TopTif-404
86Don-562
86Fle-475
86MarMot-16
86Top-399
86TopTif-399
87Don-517
87Fle-597
87FleGlo-597
87Top-67
87TopTif-67
88FleUpd-61
88FleUpdG-61
88MarMot-25
88TopTra-117T
88TopTraT-117T
89Fle-560
89FleGlo-560
89MarMot-17
89OPC-198
89RedFolSB-115
89Sco-219
89Top-712
89TopSti-228
89TopTif-712
89UppDec-623
90DodTar-787
90Don-566
90Fle-526
90FleCan-526
90MarMot-11
90OPC-574
90PubSti-442
90Top-574
90TopTif-574
90UppDec-313
91Don-564
91Fle-462
91Lea-380
91MarCouH-12
91OPC-276
91Sco-123
91StaClu-372
91Top-276
91TopDesS-276
91TopMic-276
91TopTif-276
91UltUpd-53
91UppDec-498
92Bow-182
92Bow-611
92Cla2-T33
92Don-260
92DonUpd-U22
92Fle-294
92FleUpd-131
92GiaMot-3
92GiaPacGaE-32
92Lea-407
92OPC-144
92OPCPre-133
92Pin-448
92Sco-541
92ScoRoo-32T
92StaClu-243
92StaClu-855
92StaCluECN-855
92Stu-118
92Top-144
92TopGol-144
92TopGolW-144
92TopMic-144
92TopTra-114T
92TopTraG-114T
92Ult-596
92UppDec-620
92UppDec-736
93Bow-380
93Don-232
93DonDiaK-DK5
93Fla-146
93Fle-161
93Fle-708
93FleFruotL-58
93FunPac-102
93GiaMot-5
93GiaPos-31
93Lea-194
93MilBonSS-5
93OPC-277
93PacSpa-616
93PanSti-234
93Pin-347
93Sco-67
93Sel-51
93SelStaL-82
93SP-115
93StaClu-204
93StaCluFDI-204
93StaCluG-20
93StaCluMOP-204
93Top-755
93TopComotH-29
93TopGol-755
93TopInaM-755
93TopMic-755
93TriPla-262
93Ult-136
93UppDec-118
93UppDecGold-118
93USPlaCA-1S
94Bow-435
94BowBes-R49
94BowBesR-R49
94ColC-271
94ColChoGS-271
94ColChoSS-271
94Don-294
94ExtBas-392
94ExtBasPD-9
94Fin-151
94FinPre-151P
94FinRef-151
94Fla-445
94Fle-702
94FUnPac-26
94GiaAMC-21
94GiaMot-6
94GiaSFC-3
94GiaTeal-7
94GiaUSPC-1D
94GiaUSPC-8S
94Lea-288
94LeaL-159
94OPC-79
94Pac-556
94PanSti-266
94Pin-326
94PinArtP-326
94PinMusC-326
94Sco-430
94ScoGolR-430
94Sel-252
94SP-93
94SPDieC-93
94Spo-54
94StaClu-330
94StaCluFDI-330
94StaCluGR-330
94StaCluMOP-330
94StaCluT-16
94StaCluTFDI-16
94Stu-87
94Top-639
94TopGol-639
94TopSpa-639
94TriPla-108
94TriPlaM-14
94Ult-294
94UppDec-62
94UppDecED-62
94USPlaCA-10S
95Bow-327
95ColCho-259
95ColCho-575T
95ColChoGS-259
95ColChoSE-110
95ColChoSEGS-110
95ColChoSESS-110
95ColChoSS-259
95Don-387
95DonPreP-387
95DonTopotO-233
95Fin-255
95FinRef-255
95Fla-346
95Fle-590
95FleUpd-169
95Lea-368
95Pin-373
95PinArtP-373
95PinMusC-373
95RocPol-9
95Sco-491
95ScoGolR-491
95ScoPlaTS-491
95SP-49
95SPCha-41
95SPChaDC-41
95SPSil-49
95StaClu-365
95StaClu-554
95StaCluMOP-365
95StaCluMOP-554
95StaCluSTWS-365
95StaCluSTWS-554
95StaCluVR-192
95Top-433
95TopCyb-230
95TopTra-137T
95Ult-447
95UltGolM-447
95UppDec-414
95UppDecED-414
95UppDecEDG-414
95UppDecSE-237
95UppDecSEG-237
96ColCho-535
96ColChoGS-535
96ColChoSS-535
96Don-239
96DonPreP-239
96EmoXL-177
96Fin-B170
96FinRef-B170
96Fla-252
96Fle-375
96FleRoc-14
96FleTif-375
96LeaSigA-217
96LeaSigAG-217
96LeaSigAS-217
96MetUni-158
96MetUniP-158
96PanSti-87
96RocPol-22
96Sco-429
96StaClu-43
96StaCluMOP-43
95StaCluVRMC-192
96Top-401
96Ult-193
96UltGolM-193
96UppDec-325
97ColCho-318
97DonTea-104
97DonTeaSPE-104
97Fle-548
97FleTif-548
97Pin-26
97PinArtP-26
97PinMusC-26
97Sco-387
97ScoHobR-387
97ScoResC-387
97ScoShoS-387
97ScoShoSAP-387
97Ult-440
97UltGolME-440
97UltPlaME-440

Swift, Bob (Robert V.)
41BroW75-27
47TipTop-41
49Bow-148
50Bow-149
51Bow-214
52Bow-131
52Top-181
54Top-65
60Top-470
77TCMTheWY-50
81TigDetN-42
83TopRep5-181
85TCMPla1-5
94TopArc1-65
94TopArc1G-65

Swift, Scott
95BurBeeTI-29

Swift, Tim
96VerExpB-5

Swift, Weldon
78BurBeeT-28
79HolMilT-23
80HolMilT-11
81ElPasDT-19

Swim, Greg
91SalSpuC-29
91SalSpuP-2253

Swindell, Greg
86SpoRoo-30
87Don-32
87Fle-644
87FleGlo-644
87FleUpd-116
87FleUpdG-116
87IndGat-21
87Lea-32
87SpoTeaP-3
87Top-319
87TopTif-319
88Don-227
88DonBasB-280
88Fle-617
88FleGlo-617
88FleSlu-41
88IndGat-21
88Lea-158
88OPC-22
88PanSti-70
88Sco-154
88ScoGlo-154
88ScoYouS2-39
88StaLinI-19
88Top-22
88TopBig-156
88TopSti-210
88TopTif-22
89Bow-76
89BowTif-76
89ClaLigB-61
89ClaTraP-195
89Don-232
89DonBasB-112
89Fle-413
89FleGlo-413
89FleLeaL-38
89IndTeal-26
89OPC-315
89PanSti-320
89RedFolSB-116
89Sco-282
89Spo-4
89Top-315
89TopBig-68
89TopCoi-54
89TopMinL-52
89TopSti-213
89TopTif-315
89TopUKM-76
89TVSpoM-88
89UppDec-250
90Bow-325
90BowTif-325
90ClaUpd-T48
90Don-310
90DonBesA-6
90DOnBonM-BC24
90Fle-503
90FleAwaW-39
90FleBasM-39
90FleCan-503
90Hot50PS-44
90IndTeal-40
90Lea-206
90OPC-595
90PanSti-59
90PubSti-569
90PubSti-606
90RedFolSB-93
90Sco-230
90Sco100S-11
90Top-595
90TopBig-288
90TopDou-65
90TopSti-214
90TopStiB-63
90TopTif-595
90TopTVA-32
90UppDec-574
90WonBreS-15
91Bow-58
91Cla2-T10
91ClaGam-101
91Don-546
91Fle-379
91IndFanC-26
91Lea-6
91OPC-445
91Sco-110
91StaClu-428
91Stu-49
91Top-445
91TopDesS-445
91TopMic-445
91TopTif-445
91Ult-117
91UppDec-236
92Bow-46
92Bow-578
92ClaGam-193
92Don-483
92DonDiaK-DK23
92Fle-124
92FleUpd-84
92Lea-384
92OPC-735
92OPCPre-44
92PanSti-52
92Pin-327
92RedKah-29
92Sco-371
92ScoRoo-10T
92StaClu-673
92StaCluECN-673
92Stu-30
92TexLon-38
92Top-735
92TopGol-735
92TopGolW-735
92TopKid-72
92TopMic-735
92Ult-487
92UppDec-95
92UppDec-336
92UppDec-765
93AstMot-17
93Bow-320
93Don-634
93Fin-137
93FinRef-137
93Fla-67
93Fle-399
93FleFinE-80
93Lea-334
93OPC-392
93OPCPre-86
93PacSpa-481
93Pin-507
93Sco-566

93Sel-179
93SelAce-18
93SelRoo-99T
93StaClu-165
93StaClu-608
93StaCluAs-9
93StaCluFDI-165
93StaCluFDI-608
93StaCluMOP-165
93StaCluMOP-608
93Stu-59
93Top-515
93TopGol-515
93TopInaM-515
93TopMic-515
93TopTra-32T
93TriPla-232
93Ult-397
93UppDec-695
93UppDecGold-695
93USPlaCA-4S
94AstMot-15
94Bow-6
94ColC-526
94ColChoGS-526
94ColChoSS-526
94Don-228
94ExtBas-282
94Fin-99
94FinRef-99
94Fle-500
94Lea-379
94OPC-157
94Pac-275
94Pin-163
94PinArtP-163
94PinMusC-163
94Sco-502
94ScoGolR-502
94Sel-243
94SP-32
94SPDieC-32
94StaClu-113
94StaCluFDI-113
94StaCluGR-113
94StaCluMOP-113
94Top-125
94TopGol-125
94TopSpa-125
94Ult-210
94UppDec-484
94UppDecED-484
95AstMot-24
95ColCho-119
95ColChoGS-119
95ColChoSS-119
95Don-347
95DonPreP-347
95DonTopotO-261
95Fle-469
95Lea-282
95Pac-194
95Sco-201
95ScoGolR-201
95ScoPlaTS-201
95StaClu-275
95StaCluMOP-275
95StaCluSTWS-275
95StaCluVR-140
95Top-285
95TopCyb-155
95Ult-391
95UltGolM-391
96AstMot-15
96ColCho-569
96ColChoGS-569
96ColChoSS-569
96Don-484
96DonPreP-484
96Fla-285
96Fle-419
96FleTif-419
96LeaSigA-218
96LeaSigAG-218
96LeaSigAS-218
96Pac-86
96Sco-473
95StaCluVRMC-140
96Ult-490
96UltGolM-490
96UppDec-343
97Ult-362
97UltGolME-362
97UltPlaME-362
Swindle, Allen
83TamTarT-22
Swingle, Paul
89BenBucL-10
90BoiHawP-3312
91PalSprAP-2014
92ClaFS7-339
92MidAngF-4028
92MidAngOHP-23
92MidAngS-471
92SkyAA F-201
93VanCanF-2598
94Top-765
94TopGol-765
94TopSpa-765
96VanCanB-26
Swingle, Russ
52Par-94
Swinton, Jermaine
90AshTouC-23
91AshTouP-581
91Cla/Bes-77
92Bow-137
92BurAstC-5
92BurAstF-560
92UppDecML-316
93AshTouF-2286
96StoPorB-11
Swisher, Steve
74WicAerODF-123
75OPC-63
75Top-63
76OPC-173
76SSP-319
76Top-173
77OPC-23
77Top-419
78CarTeal-22
78Top-252
79Car5-27
79Top-304
80Top-163
81Top-541
81TopTra-840
82Top-764
83Don-633
83RicBraT-12
83Top-612
86WatIndP-27
87WilBilP-18
88ColSprSSC-24
88ColSprSSP-1546
89JacMetGS-20
90CMC-684
90ProAAAF-291
90TidTidC-27
90TidTidP-560
90TopTVM-62
91LinDriAAA-574
91TidTidLD-574
91TidTidP-2526
91TriA AAGP-AAA50
92BinMetF-532
92BinMetS-74
93BinMetF-2349
96MetKah-31
96MetKah-29
Switzer, Mike
89AncBucTI-8
Swob, Tim
87TamTarP-9
Swoboda, Ron
64YanReqKP-17
65Top-533
66OPC-35
66Top-35
66TopRubI-90
66TopVen-35
67CokCapA-28
67CokCapNLA-26
67CokCapYM-V27
67DexPre-202
67MetTeal-11
67OPC-186
67Top-186
67Top-264
67TopGiaSU-5
67TopVen-288
68AtlOilPBCC-43
68Baz-13
68OPC-114
68Top-114
68Top3-D-12
68TopActS-2A
68TopActS-15A
68TopPos-17
68TopVen-114
69CitMetC-18
69MetBoyS-5
69MetNewYDN-18
69MilBra-268
69MLBOffS-171
69MLBPin-57
69Top-585
69TopSta-70
69TopTeaP-24
69TraSta-44
70MetTra-25A
70MLBOffS-83
70OPC-431
70Top-431
71MLBOffS-166
71OPC-665
71Top-665
72MilBra-337
72OPC-8
72Top-8
73OPC-314
73Top-314
81TCM60I-322
84OCoandSI-153
89Met196C-12
89RinPosM1-25
91MetWIZ-390
91UppDecS-8
92YanWIZ7-147
94Met69CCPP-30
94Met69CS-29
94Met69T-9
96Met69Y-8
97FleMilDM-35
Swoope, Bill
77CliDodT-26
78CliDodT-30
79LodDodT-13
Swope, Mark
90ArkRaz-24
91Cla/Bes-74
91VisOakC-10
91VisOakP-1741
92Ft.MyeMCB-11
92Ft.MyeMF-2747
93ForMyeMF-2656
Sykes, Bob
77Top-491
79Car5-28
79Top-569
80Top-223
81Fle-533
81Top-348
82ColCliP-38
82ColCliT-12
82Don-640
82Fle-130
82JacMetT-24
82NasSouTI-25
82Top-108
83TidTidT-27
84TidTidT-17
89MetColP-53
90MetColP-48
Sylvester, John
77CedRapGT-4
Sylvester, Johnny
92MegRut-140
Sylvestri, Tony
93KanCouCC-21
93KanCouCF-926
94BreCouMC-19
94BreCouMF-22
93KanCouCTI-23
Sylvia, Dave
75BurBeeT-28
Sylvia, Ronald
81RedPioT-7
82RedPioT-16
83NasAngT-9
Symmonds, Maika
96LowSpiB-24
Syverson, Dain
85WatIndT-25
86IndTeal-40
86WatIndP-24
87WilBilP-11
Szarko, Andy
93MarPhiC-28
93MarPhiF-3475
Szczechowski, Dennis
92CliGiaF-3597
92EveGiaC-22
92EveGiaF-1690
Szczepanski, Joe
91GenCubC-20
91GenCubP-4215
92WinSpiC-22
92WinSpiF-1207
Szekely, Joe
83ChaRoyT-3
85VerBeaDT-6
87SanAntDTI-17
87TexLeaAF-35
89AlbDukC-19
89AlbDukP-77
90CMC-337
90ProAAAF-354
90SyrChiC-11
90SyrChiMB-25
90SyrChiP-574
91LinDriAAA-444
91RicBraBC-18
91RicBraLD-444
91RicBraP-2572
91RicBraTI-12
92RicBraBB-16
92RicBraF-381
92RicBraRC-22
92RicBraS-444
93MacBraC-28
93MacBraF-1419
Szeryk, Neil
91OklStaC-26
Szimanski, Tom
94BelMarC-26
94BelMarF-3234
94StaCluDP-9
94StaCluDPFDI-9
96LanJetB-26
Szotkiewicz, Ken
71OPC-749
71Top-749
Szymarek, Paul
81ShrCapT-12
82PhoGiaVNB-6
Szymborski, Thomas
96IdaFalB-25
Szymczak, Dave
83NasSouTI-24
84BufBisT-13
Szynal, Jon
89SpaPhiP-1031
89SpaPhiS-22
Tabacheck, Marty
50WorWidGV-23
Tabaka, Jeff
86JamExpP-25
87WesPalBEP-656
88WesPalBES-24
89ReaPhiB-7
89ReaPhiP-663
91LinDriAA-520
91ReaPhiLD-520
91ReaPhiP-1371
92ElPasDF-3921
92ElPasDS-222
93ClaGolF-154
93NewOrlZF-973
93Top-586
93TopGol-586
93TopInaM-586
93TopMic-586
94BufBisF-1837
95Fle-570
95Pac-371
95PadMot-15
96AstMot-23
96Fle-420
96FleTif-420
96LeaSigEA-197
96TusTorB-23
Tabb, Jerry
78Top-224
Tabeling, Bob
86VisOakP-21
Tabler, Pat
77ForLauYS-18
80NasSouTI-22
81ColCliP-25
81ColCliT-16
82Don-529
82IowCubT-10
83Don-552
83Fle-509
84Don-536
84Fle-552
84Ind-29
84IndWhe-10
84Nes792-329
84Top-329
84TopSti-252
84TopTif-329
85Don-460
85Fle-456
85Ind-31
85IndPol-10
85Lea-76
85OPC-158
85Top-158
85TopSti-250
85TopTif-158
86Don-129
86Fle-594
86IndOhH-10
86IndTeal-41
86Lea-52
86OPC-66
86Top-674
86TopSti-212
86TopTat-8
86TopTif-674
87Don-254
87DonOpeD-107
87Fle-261
87FleGlo-261
87FleSlu-42
87GenMilB-2H
87IndGat-10
87Lea-182
87OPC-77
87Spo-24A
87Spo-24B
87Spo-66
87SpoTeaP-3
87StuPan-18
87Top-575
87TopMinL-52
87TopSti-205
87TopTif-575
88Don-219
88DonAll-17
88Fle-618
88Fle-633
88FleGlo-618
88FleGlo-633
88FleHotS-43
88FleMin-20
88FleStiC-22
88FleUpd-36
88FleUpdG-36
88IndGat-10
88OPC-230
88PanSti-81
88RedFolSB-87
88Sco-23
88ScoGlo-23
88ScoRoo-22T
88ScoRooG-22T
88Spo-205
88StaLinI-20
88Top-230
88TopBig-173
88TopSti-204
88TopTif-230
88TopTra-118T
88TopTraT-118T
89Bow-125
89BowTif-125
89Don-326
89Fle-294
89FleGlo-294
89OPC-56
89PanSti-359
89RoyTasD-3
89Sco-391
89Spo-172
89Top-56
89TopBatL-19
89TopBig-67
89TopSti-6
89TopTif-56
89UppDec-233
89Woo-18
90Don-444
90Fle-119
90FleCan-119
90OPC-727
90PubSti-357

90Sco-242
90Spo-218
90Top-727
90TopBig-89
90TopTif-727
90UppDec-142
91BluJayFS-25
91BluJayFS-27
91BluJayS-19
91Bow-28
91FleUpd-67
91Lea-443
91MetWIZ-393
91OPC-433
91OPCPre-118
91Sco-811
91ScoRoo-22T
91Top-433
91TopDesS-433
91TopMic-433
91TopTif-433
92OPC-333
92Sco-312
92StaClu-333
92Top-333
92TopGol-333
92TopGolW-333
92TopMic-333
92UppDec-203
93BluJayD4-12
93Fle-700
93OPC-270
93StaClu-160
93StaCluFDI-160
93StaCluMOP-160
Tabor, Greg
82BurRanF-15
82BurRanT-10
84TulDriTI-19
85OklCit8T-28
86OklCit8P-23
87OklCit8P-21
88Fle-644
88FleGlo-644
88IowCubC-18
88IowCubP-548
93RanKee-352
Tabor, Jim
39GouPreR303A-41
39PlaBal-14
39WorWidGTP-41
40PlaBal-36
41DouPlaR-57
42RedSoxTI-22
43RedSoxTI-23
49BowPCL-33
49SolSunP-10
76TayBow4-99
92ConTSN-542
Tabor, Scott
83BirBarT-15
86OmaRoyP-27
86OmaRoyT-17
Taborn, Earl
93NegLeaRL2-38
95NegLeaL2-10
Tabuchi, Koichi
79TCMJapPB-12
Tackett, Gary
90NebCor-23
Tackett, Jeff (Jack)
85NewOriT-5
87ChaO'sW-9
88ChaKniTI-8
89RocRedWC-17
89RocRedWP-1645
90CMC-310
90ProAAAF-463
90RocRedWC-9
90RocRedWGC-13
90RocRedWP-706
91Bow-106
91LinDriAAA-469
91RocRedWLD-469
91RocRedWP-1906
92DonRoo-114
92Lea-411
92ScoRoo-86T
92StaClu-383
92TopDeb91-168
92TopTra-115T
92TopTraG-115T
92Ult-310
93Don-529
93Fle-553
93PacSpa-351
93Sco-355
93Sel-294
93StaClu-186
93StaCluFDI-186
93StaCluMOP-186
93Top-6
93TopGol-6
93TopInaM-6
93TopMic-6
93Ult-147
93UppDec-517
93UppDecGold-517
94OriPro-98
94OriUSPC-4C
94OriUSPC-9H
94Sco-136
94ScoGolR-136
94StaCluT-294
94StaCluTFDI-294
94Top-664
94TopGol-664
94TopPre-6
94TopSpa-664
94VenLinU-221
95StaClu-168
95StaCluFDI-168
95StaCluMOP-168
95StaCluSTWS-168
95TolMudHTI-24
95Top-375
96TolMudHB-28
Taco, Puffy
95SanAntMTI-NNO
Taczy, Craig
95GreFalDTI-11
96YakBeaTI-46
Tafoya, Dennis
88AshTouP-1070
88AubAstP-1951
89OscAstS-28
90ColMudB-24
90ColMudP-1348
90ColMudS-23
91CarMudLD-118
91CarMudP-1086
91LinDriAA-118
92CarMudS-144
93CarMudF-2053
Tafoya, Rod
89BoiHawP-1987
90EriSaiS-26
Taft, Brett
96SpoIndB-28
Taft, Dennie
83CliGiaF-24
Taft, Tim
88BenBucL-14
88ClePhiS-24
Taft, William Howard
77Spo-6715
90BasWit-107
Tagi, Anthony
88FreSunCLC-20
88FreSunP-1234
Tagle, Hank
91UtiBluSC-26
91UtiBluSP-3239
92SouBenWSC-23
92SouBenWSF-176
93SarWhiSF-1368
93SouBenWSC-21
94SouBenSHC-1
94SouBenSHF-594
95PriWilCTI-24
Tagliaferri, Gino
90FayGenP-2417
90NiaFalRP-11
Taguchi, Dragon
89SalSpuCLC-132
89SalSpuP-1809
Tahan, Kevin
90CMC-664
90SavCarP-2078
91SprCarC-25
91SprCarP-752
92SprCarC-20
92SprCarF-873
93ArkTraF-2815
Taitt, D.
29ExhFou-18
Tajima, Toni
94SanBerSC-22
94SanBerSF-2760
Takach, Dave
87SprCarB-14
88SalBucS-20
Takacs, John
77AshTouT-22
Takada, Shigeru
79TCMJapPB-62
Takagi, Morimichi
79TCMJapPB-74
Takagi, Yoshikazu
79TCMJapPB-56
Takagi, Yutaka
87JapPlaB-24
Takahashi, Kazumi
79TCMJapPB-35
Takahashi, Kurt
95BelGiaTI-35
96BelGiaTI-20
Takahashi, Shigeyuki
92NiaFalRC-28
92NiaFalRF-3344
93BriTigF-3667
94BriTigC-29
Takahashi, Yoshihiko
79TCMJapPB-29
87JapPlaB-10
Takao, Scott
92SouBenWSC-27
93SouBenWSC-30
94SouBenSHC-28
Takara, Steven
87HawRai-15
Takayoshi, Todd
93PocPosF-4211
93PocPosSP-15
94LakElsSC-21
94LakElsSF-1667
95LakElsSTI-24
96LakElsSB-13
Takenouci, Masashi
79TCMJapPB-82
Takeuchi, Yoshiya
96HilStaHWB-23
Talamantez, Greg
85NewOriT-4
86HagSunP-24
87ChaO'sW-35
88FloStaLAS-22
88St.LucMS-22
89JacMetGS-1
91LinDriAA-643
91WilBilLD-643
91WilBilP-292
Talanoa, Scott
92BelBreC-7
92BelBreF-415
92ClaFS7-362
92MidLeaATI-44
93BelBreC-23
93BelBreF-1721
93MidLeaAGF-4
94Bow-505
94Cla-78
94ClaTriF-T43
94ElPasDF-3155
94ExcFS7-88
95Exc-75
95Top-79
95UppDecML-144
95UppDecMLFS-144
Talbert, Louis
90AppFoxBS-27
90AppFoxP-2095
90CMC-699
91LinDriAA-419
91MemChiLD-419
91MemChiP-655
Talbot, Bob D.
52MotCoo-16
54Top-229
55Bow-137
94TopArc1-229
94TopArc1G-229
Talbot, Daniel
82MonNew-16
Talbot, Fred
64A's-16
65AthJayP-12
65OPC-58
65Top-58
66Top-403
66TopRubI-91
67CokCapYM-V5
67Top-517
68Top-577
69Top-332
70OPC-287
70Top-287
72MilBra-338
81TCM60I-467
83Pil69G-17
92YanWIZ6-123
Talbott, Rick
92HigSchPLS-17
Talbott, Shawn
86AshTouP-27
87AshTouP-18
Talford, Calvin
89MarPhiS-29
Tallent, Ron
91BoiHawC-16
91BoiHawP-3892
Tallis, Cedric
70RoyTeal-36
Tallman, Fan (Matt)
86Spo-182
Tallman, Troy
92KanCouCC-12
92KanCouCF-94
93FreKeyC-25
93FreKeyF-1030
Talton, Tim (Marion)
67Top-603
Tam, Andy
79AshTouT-8
Tam, Jeff
93PitMetC-21
93PitMetF-3710
94CapCitBC-21
94CapCitBF-1751
94SouAtlLAF-SAL38
95Exc-239
96BinBeeB-26
Tamarez, Adame
92CliGiaC-20
92CliGiaF-3606
Tamarez, Carlos
90MadMusP-2279
90SouOreAP-3437
Tamargo, John
76TulOilGP-11
78SprRedWK-10
79GiaPol-30
79Top-726
80ExpPos-31
80OPC-351
80Top-680
81Don-210
81Fle-152
81OPC-35
81Top-519
82MiaMarT-22
87LynMetP-22
89MetColP-55
91St.LucMC-26
91St.LucMP-727
92St.LucMCB-26
92St.LucMF-1763
93St.LucMC-26
94BinMetF-720
95BinMetTI-32
96BinBeeB-27
96PitMetB-26
93StLucMF-2937
Tambay, Patrick
72Dia-143
Tamulis, Vito
35GouPreR-16
36GouWidPPR-A99
36WorWidGV-101
39PlaBal-139
40DodTeal-21
40PlaBal-145
41DodTeal-8
41Gou-17
90DodTar-788
Tanabe, Collin
82BelBreF-13
Tanabe, Nori
86SanJosBP-20
Tanana, Frank
74OPC-605
74Top-605
75OPC-16
75Top-16
76Hos-101
76Kel-30A
76Kel-30B
76OPC-204
76OPC-490
76SSP-189
76Top-204
76Top-490
77BurCheD-122
77Hos-63
77Kel-45
77OPC-105
77Spo-2518
77Top-200
78AngFamF-36
78Hos-101
78Kel-54
78OPC-7
78OPC-65
78PapGinD-33
78RCColC-92
78SSP270-211
78TasDis-23
78Top-207
78Top-600
78WifBalD-73
79Hos-47
79Kel-55
79OPC-274
79Top-530
80OPC-57
80Top-105
81CokTeaS-7
81Don-171
81Fle-276
81OPC-369
81Top-369
81TopSti-56
81TopSupHT-11
81TopTra-841
82Don-326
82Fle-309
82OPC-4
82Top-792
82TopTra-117T
83Don-447
83Fle-581
83RanAffF-28
83Top-272
84Don-98
84Fle-432
84FunFooP-133
84Nes792-479
84OPC-276
84RanJarP-28
84Top-479
84TopTif-479
85AngStrH-12
85Don-9
85Don-220
85DonSupD-9
85Fle-570
85Lea-9
85OPC-55
85Top-55
85TopSti-348
85TopTif-55
86Don-491
86Fle-239
86Lea-241
86OPC-124
86TigCaiD-17
86Top-592
86TopTif-592
87Don-152
87Fle-164
87FleGlo-164
87FleHotS-40
87OPC-231
87SevCoi-D10
87SpoTeaP-15
87TigCaiD-20
87TigCok-5
87Top-726
87TopTif-726
88Don-461
88DonBasB-259
88Fle-71
88FleGlo-71
88FleSlu-42
88OPC-177
88PanSti-86
88Sco-490
88ScoGlo-490
88Spo-133
88StaLinTi-18

88TigPep-26
88TigPol-11
88Top-177
88TopSti-264
88TopTif-177
89AngSmo-9
89Bow-92
89BowTif-92
89Don-90
89DonBasB-91
89Fle-147
89FleGlo-147
89OPC-299
89PanSti-336
89RedFolSB-117
89Sco-112
89Spo-103
89TigMar-26
89TigPol-26
89Top-603
89Top-609
89TopBasT-158
89TopSti-275
89TopTif-603
89TopTif-609
89UppDec-391
90Bow-343
90BowTif-343
90ClaBlu-108
90Don-180
90DonBesA-48
90Fle-616
90FleCan-616
90KayB-30
90Lea-87
90OPC-343
90PanSti-72
90PubSti-483
90Sco-57
90TigCok-23
90Top-343
90TopBig-119
90TopSti-277
90TopTif-343
90UppDec-516
91Don-508
91Fle-354
91Lea-497
91OPC-236
91PacRyaTEI-32
91Sco-328
91StaClu-158
91Stu-57
91TigCok-26
91TigPol-12
91Top-236A
91Top-236B
91TopDesS-236
91TopMic-236
91TopTif-236
91Ult-128
91UppDec-369
92Don-111
92Fle-145
92Lea-21
92OPC-458
92Pin-198
92Sco-271
92StaClu-416
92Stu-177
92Top-458
92TopGol-458
92TopGolW-458
92TopMic-458
92TriPla-249
92UppDec-605
93Don-599
93Fle-611
93FleFinE-106
93Lea-365
93MetColP-46
93MetKah-29
93OPC-288
93PacSpa-547
93PanSti-120
93Pin-542
93RanKee-353
93Sco-652
93Sel-398
93SelRoo-127T
93StaClu-267
93StaCluFDI-267
93StaCluMOP-267
93Top-53
93TopGol-53
93TopInaM-53
93TopMic-53
93Ult-434
93UppDec-68
93UppDec-626
93UppDecGold-68
93UppDecGold-626
94Sco-538
94ScoGolR-538

Tanderys, Jeff
91HamRedC-12
91HamRedP-4039
92HamRedC-1
92HamRedF-1592

Tank, Travis
96HelBreTI-24

Tanks, Talmage
76BurBeeT-32

Tanksley, Scott
93MisStaB-41
96ForWayWB-25

Tannahill, Kevin
89HelBreSP-23
91ChaRanC-14
91ChaRanP-1318

Tannehill, Jesse
04RedSoxUP-13
09SenBarP-9
09T206-350
12HasTriFT-45

Tannehill, Lee Ford
08RosComP-19
09AmeCarE-105
09AmeCarE-106
09ColChiE-285
09T206-351
09T206-352
10RedCroT-77
10RedCroT-250
11S74Sil-9
11SpoLifCW-346
11SpoLifM-32
11T205-169
12ColRedB-285
12ColTinT-285
12HasTriFT-52
12T207-181

Tanner, Bruce
85BufBisT-25
85FleUpd-116
86BufBisP-21
86Fle-218
87TacTigP-8
88HunStaTI-22
89TacTigP-1540
90SpoIndSP-27
91ChaRaiC-25
91ChaRaiP-112
91SouAtlLAGP-SAL6
92HigDesMC-30
93RanCucQC-28
93RanCucQF-848
94AugGreC-29
94AugGreF-3025
96CarMudB-27

Tanner, Chuck
55BraJohC-18
55Top-161
56Top-69
57Top-392
58Top-91
59Top-234
60Lea-115
60Top-279
61MapLeaBH-23
71OPC-661
71Top-661
72OPC-98
72Top-98
72WhiSoxC-6
72WhiSoxTI1-11
73OPC-356
73Top-356
74OPC-221
74Top-221
75OPC-276
75Top-276
76OPC-656
76SSP-151
76Top-656
77PirPosP-27
77Top-354
78Top-494
79TCM50-63
79Top-244
80Top-551
81Don-257
81Fle-367
81Top-683
82Don-150
83Don-124
83Top-696
84Fle-657
84Nes792-291
84Top-291
84TopTif-291
85Pir-20
85Top-268
85TopTif-268
86BraPol-7
86Top-351
86TopTif-351
86TopTra-107T
86TopTraT-107T
87BraSmo-26
87Top-593
87TopTif-593
88Top-134
88TopTif-134
92UppDecS-5
92UppDecS-19
94UppDecS-5

Tanner, Eddie (Ed)
81BatTroT-16
82WatIndF-22
82WatIndT-19
83SprCarF-8
84ArkTraT-1
86ArkTraP-24
87NasSouTI-19
88NasSouTI-23
89NasSouC-19
89NasSouP-1287
89NasSouTI-24
90CMC-146
90NasSouC-21
90NasSouP-243
90ProAAAF-555
90SprCarDGB-6

Tanner, Joe
93DayCubC-26
94PeoChiC-28
94PeoChiF-2285

Tanner, Mark
74GasRanT-22
75LynRanT-26

Tanner, Paul
96JohCitCTI-30

Tanner, Roy
75WatRoyT-30
76WatRoyT-30
77DayBeaIT-25
82ChaRoyT-24
83ChaRoyT-24

Tanoue, Keisaburoh
96MauStiHWB-24

Tanzi, Bobby
79AshTouT-16
80WauTimT-12

Tanzi, Michael
82AppFoxF-25
83GleFalWST-20

Tao, Yasushi
79TCMJapPB-76

Taormina, Sal
60TacBan-19

Tapais, Luis
86KenTwiP-23

Tapani, Kevin
86MedA'sC-64
86ModA'sC-22
87ModA'sC-15
87ModA'sP-12
88JacMetGS-23
89MetColP-56
89TidTidC-10
89TidTidP-1972
90Bow-407
90BowTif-407
90ClaYel-T16
90Don-473
90DonBesA-93
90DonRoo-35
90FleUpd-110
90Lea-269
90OPC-227
90ScoRoo-82T
90ScoYouS2-31
90Top-227
90TopBig-225
90TopDeb89-126
90TopTif-227
90UppDec-87
91Bow-322
91ClaGam-42
91Don-116
91Fle-625
91Lea-128
91MajLeaCP-13
91MetWIZ-394
91OPC-633
91PanFreS-307
91PanSti-249
91Sco-60
91Sco100RS-52
91StaClu-161
91Top-633
91TopDesS-633
91TopMic-633
91TopRoo-27
91TopTif-633
91Ult-196
91UppDec-434
92Bow-552
92Cla1-T87
92ClaGam-104
92Don-236
92Fle-219
92Hig5-85
92Lea-14
92OPC-313
92Pin-176
92Sco-507
92StaClu-433
92Top-313
92TopGol-313
92TopGolW-313
92TopMic-313
92TriPla-98
92Ult-98
92UppDec-624
93Bow-269
93Don-443
93Fle-274
93Lea-404
93OPC-361
93PacSpa-178
93Pin-334
93Sco-45
93Sel-130
93SelAce-24
93StaClu-492
93StaCluFDI-492
93StaCluMOP-492
93Top-420
93TopGol-420
93TopInaM-420
93TopMic-420
93TriPla-240
93Ult-237
93UppDec-313
93UppDecGold-313
94Bow-628
94ColC-272
94ColChoGS-272
94ColChoSS-272
94Don-115
94ExtBas-124
94Fin-21
94FinRef-21
94Fla-317
94Fle-219
94Lea-52
94OPC-246
94Pac-367
94Pin-54
94PinArtP-54
94PinMusC-54
94ProMag-78
94Sco-351
94ScoGolR-351
94Sel-144
94StaClu-117
94StaCluFDI-117
94StaCluGR-117
94StaCluMOP-117
94Top-185
94TopGol-185
94TopSpa-185
94TriPla-259
94Ult-395
94UppDec-439
94UppDecED-439
95ColCho-482
95ColChoGS-482
95ColChoSE-229
95ColChoSEGS-229
95ColChoSESS-229
95ColChoSS-482
95Don-269
95DonPreP-269
95DonTopotO-272
95Emb-81
95EmbGolI-81
95Fin-75
95FinRef-75
95Fla-282
95Fle-215
95Lea-173
95Pac-257
95Pin-6
95PinArtP-6
95PinMusC-6
95Sco-347
95ScoGolR-347
95ScoPlaTS-347
95SP-172
95SPSil-172
95StaClu-93
95StaCluFDI-93
95StaCluMOP-93
95StaCluSTWS-93
95StaCluVR-58
95Top-37
95TopCyb-29
95Ult-78
95UltGolM-78
95UppDec-194
95UppDecED-194
95UppDecEDG-194
95UppDecSE-217
95UppDecSEG-217
96ColCho-768
96Don-488
96DonPreP-488
96Fla-58
96Fle-447
96FleTif-447
96FleUpd-U29
96FleUpdTC-U29
96FleWhiS-15
96LeaSigA-219
96LeaSigAG-219
96LeaSigAS-219
96Sco-218
95StaCluVRMC-58
96Ult-225
96Ult-337
96UltGolM-225
96UltGolM-337
96UppDec-489U
97Cir-53
97CirRav-53
97Fle-70
97Fle-608
97FleTif-70
97FleTif-608
97Pac-62
97PacLigB-62
97Sco-245
97ScoPreS-245
97ScoShoS-245
97ScoShoSAP-245
97ScoWhiS-13
97ScoWhiSPI-13
97ScoWhiSPr-13
97StaClu-270
97StaCluMOP-270
97Top-32
97Ult-502
97UltGolME-502
97UltPlaME-502

Tapia, Dagoberto
90MarPhiP-3208

Tapia, Elias
94GreFalDSP-24
95BakBlaTI-24
95YakBeaTI-32

Tapia, Jose
87QuaCitAP-7
87VerBeaDP-2
88PalSprACLC-93
88PalSprAP-1446

Tappe, Elvin
53MotCoo-48

55Bow-51
55Top-129
55TopDouH-93
58Top-184
60Top-457
Tarangelo, Joseph
84VisOakT-23
Tarasco, Tony
89PulBraP-1904
90Bes-100
90SumBraB-23
90SumBraP-2449
91DurBulC-21
91DurBulP-1675
92GreBraF-1166
92GreBraS-245
92SkyAA F-103
92UppDecML-82
93Bow-522
93BraLykP-29
93BraLykS-35
93ExcFS7-6
93FleFinE-5
93Lea-452
93RicBraBB-12
93RicBraF-200
93RicBraP-11
93RicBraRC-19
93StaClu-696
93StaCluB-29
93StaCluFDI-696
93StaCluMOP-696
93UppDec-623
93UppDecGold-623
94Bow-77
94BraLykP-32
94BraLykS-31
94BraUSPC-5D
94ColC-273
94ColChoGS-273
94ColChoSS-273
94Don-287
94ExtBas-214
94ExtBasRS-17
94Fin-422
94FinJum-422
94FinRef-422
94Fla-359
94FlaWavotF-B9
94Fle-377
94Lea-2
94LeaLimR-80
94Pac-23
94Pin-256
94PinArtP-256
94PinMusC-256
94Sco-617
94ScoGolR-617
94ScoRoo-RT90
94ScoRooGR-RT90
94ScoRooSR-SU16
94Sel-381
94SelRooS-RS11
94SpoRoo-82
94SpoRooAP-82
94SpoRooS-82
94StaClu-272
94StaCluFDI-272
94StaCluGR-272
94StaCluMOP-272
94StaCluT-51
94StaCluTFDI-51
94Top-442
94TopGol-442
94TopSpa-442
94Ult-451
94UppDec-206
94UppDecED-206
95ColCho-159
95ColCho-552T
95ColChoGS-159
95ColChoSS-159
95Don-468
95DonPreP-468
95DonTopotO-287
95Emo-155
95Fin-225
95FinRef-225
95Fla-109
95Fla-379
95Fle-320
95FleUpd-109
95Lea-365
95LeaLim-65
95Pac-16
95PacLatD-34
95PacPri-6
95Pin-212
95PinArtP-212
95PinMusC-212
95Sco-145
95ScoGolR-145
95ScoHaloG-HG110
95ScoHaloGYTE-HG110T
95ScoPlaTS-145
95Sel-43
95SelArtP-43
95SP-75
95SPCha-66
95SPChaDC-66
95SPSil-75
95StaClu-628
95StaCluMOP-628
95StaCluSTWS-628
95Top-32
95TopTra-60T
95UC3-11
95UC3ArtP-11
95Ult-355
95UltGolM-355
95UppDec-325
95UppDecED-325
95UppDecEDG-325
96ColCho-617
96ColChoGS-617
96ColChoSS-617
96Don-455
96DonPreP-455
96Fle-470
96FleOri-17
96FleTif-470
96FleUpd-U9
96FleUpdTC-U9
96Lea-85
96LeaPrePB-85
96LeaPrePG-85
96LeaPrePS-85
96MetUni-195
96MetUniP-195
96Pac-128
96PanSti-20
96Sco-106
96StaClu-323
96StaCluMOP-323
96Top-37
96Ult-237
96Ult-310
96UltGolM-237
96UltGolM-310
97Pac-31
97PacLigB-31
97PacSil-31
97Sco-382
97ScoHobR-382
97ScoResC-382
97ScoShoS-382
97ScoShoSAP-382
Tarbell, Steve
77BriRedST-18
Tarchione, Travis
88CapCodPPaLP-23
89SalLakTTI-6
Tardif, Marc
72Dia-108
Tarin, Fernando
77QuaCitAT-27
Tarjick, Dave
90PitMetP-29
Tarnow, Greg
81QuaCitCT-3
83AppFoxF-21
Tarrh, Jamey
90WicStaSGD-33
Tarrolly, Dave
83BelBreF-17
Tartabull, Danny
82WatRedT-14
83ChaLooT-6
84SalLakCGC-170
85CalCanC-94
85Don-27
85Fle-647
86Don-38
86DonRoo-45
86Fle-476
86FleMin-99
86MarMot-22
86Spo-178
86SpoRoo-22
86TopTra-108T
86TopTraT-108T
87ClaUpdY-145
87Don-147
87DonOpeD-200
87Fle-598
87FleGlo-598
87FleUpd-117
87FleUpdG-117
87Lea-250
87OPC-332
87RedFolSB-97
87Spo-23
87SpoTeaP-13
87Top-476
87TopCoi-25
87TopGloS-19
87TopRoo-19
87TopSti-223
87TopSti-306
87TopTif-476
87TopTra-120T
87TopTraT-120T
87ToyRoo-28
88ClaBlu-235
88Don-5
88Don-177
88DonBasB-287
88DonSupD-5
88Fle-271
88FleAwaW-42
88FleExcS-41
88FleGlo-271
88FleMin-28
88FleStiC-34
88FleSup-40
88KayB-30
88Lea-5
88Lea-190
88OPC-211
88PanSti-112
88RedFolSB-88
88RoySmo-4
88Sco-106
88ScoGlo-106
88ScoYouS2-5
88Spo-19
88StaLinRo-17
88Top-724
88TopBig-230
88TopCoi-29
88TopMinL-16
88TopRevLL-26
88TopSti-257
88TopTif-724
88TopUKM-78
88TopUKMT-78
89Bow-128
89BowTif-128
89ChaLooLITI-29
89Don-61
89DonBasB-39
89DonGraS-10
89Fle-295
89FleBasM-37
89FleGlo-295
89OPC-275
89PanSti-360
89RedFolSB-118
89RoyTasD-4
89Sco-105
89ScoHot1S-19
89Spo-46
89Top-275
89TopBig-107
89TopCoi-55
89TopSti-267
89TopTif-275
89TVSpoM-107
89UppDec-329
90Bow-375
90BowTif-375
90Don-322
90DonBesA-128
90Fle-120
90FleCan-120
90Lea-99
90OPC-540
90PanSti-90
90PubSti-358
90Sco-244
90Sco100S-72
90Spo-129
90Top-540
90TopAmeA-33
90TopBig-56
90TopHilHM-9
90TopMag-105
90TopSti-274
90TopTif-540
90UppDec-656
91Bow-294
91ClaGam-43
91DenHol-16
91Don-463
91Fle-572
91Lea-147
91OPC-90
91PanFreS-282
91RoyPol-22
91Sco-515
91StaClu-272
91Top-90
91TopDesS-90
91TopMic-90
91TopTif-90
91TopTriH-A7
91Ult-158
91UppDec-523
91UppDecFE-89F
91USPlaCA-JKO
92Bow-550
92Cla1-T88
92Cla2-T98
92ClaGam-167
92Don-26
92Don-676
92DonCraJ2-35
92DonUpd-U17
92Fle-171
92FleAll-12
92FleTeaL-18
92FleUpd-45
92KinDis-13
92Lea-406
92MSABenSHD-13
92OPC-145
92OPCPre-93
92PanSti-98
92Pin-309
92Pin-547
92PinTeaP-8
92Pos-30
92RemUltP-P13
92RemUltP-P14
92RemUltP-P15
92RemUltP-P16
92RemUltP-P18
92Sco-145
92Sco100S-90
92ScoImpP-64
92ScoRoo-3T
92SpoIllFK1-75
92StaClu-191
92StaClu-690
92StaCluD-183
92StaCluMP-14
92StaCluNC-690
92StaTar-1
92StaTar-2
92StaTar-3
92StaTar-4
92StaTar-5
92StaTar-6
92StaTar-7
92StaTar-8
92StaTar-9
92StaTar-10
92StaTar-11
92Stu-220
92Top-145
92TopGol-145
92TopGolW-145
92TopKid-106
92TopMcD-26
92TopMic-145
92TopTra-116T
92TopTraG-116T
92TriPlaG-GS5
92Ult-77
92Ult-417
92UppDec-88
92UppDec-237
92UppDec-746
92UppDecHRH-HR11
93Bow-299
93ClaGam-90
93DenHol-28
93DiaMar-106
93Don-549
93DonSpiotG-SG16
93Fin-167
93FinRef-167
93Fla-253
93Fle-286
93FleFruotL-59
93FunPac-209
93Lea-119
93MetBak-20
93OPC-308
93PacSpa-213
93PacSpaGE-19
93PanSti-153
93Pin-168
93Pin-478
93PinHomRC-33
93PinSlu-10
93Sco-35
93Sco-515
93Sel-12
93SelStaL-50
93SP-268
93StaClu-85
93StaCluFDI-85
93StaCluMOP-85
93StaCluMP-11
93StaCluY-4
93Top-330
93TopGol-330
93TopInaM-330
93TopMic-330
93TriPla-207
93Ult-602
93UppDec-242
93UppDec-839
93UppDecGold-242
93UppDecGold-839
93UppDecHRH-HR13
94Bow-577
94BowBes-R18
94BowBesR-R18
94ChuHomS-23
94ChuHomSG-23
94ColC-383
94ColChoGS-383
94ColChoSS-383
94Don-414
94ExtBas-140
94Fin-325
94FinRef-325
94Fla-88
94Fle-248
94FUnPac-145
94Kra-11
94Lea-353
94LeaCleC-6
94LeaL-58
94OPC-8
94Pac-439
94PacAll-11
94PacGolP-10
94PanSti-105
94Pin-81
94PinArtP-81
94PinMusC-81
94PinRunC-RC21
94ProMag-90
94Sco-373
94ScoGolR-373
94Sel-306
94SP-200
94SPDieC-200
94Spo-118
94StaClu-410
94StaCluFDI-410
94StaCluGR-410
94StaCluMOP-410
94StaCluT-209
94StaCluTFDI-209
94Stu-218
94Top-670
94TopGol-670
94TopSpa-670
94TriPla-279
94Ult-102
94UppDec-212
94UppDecED-212
95Baz-53
95Bow-347
95ColCho-518
95ColChoGS-518

95ColChoSE-247
95ColChoSEGS-247
95ColChoSESS-247
95ColChoSS-518
95Don-103
95DonPreP-103
95DonTopotO-143
95Emb-39
95EmbGolI-39
95Fin-90
95FinRef-90
95Fla-69
95Fle-82
95Lea-246
95LeaLim-170
95Pac-304
95PacPri-100
95PanSti-91
95Pin-273
95PinArtP-273
95PinMusC-273
95Sco-456
95ScoGolR-456
95ScoPlaTS-456
95Sel-9
95SelArtP-9
95Spo-117
95SpoArtP-117
95StaClu-156
95StaCluFDI-156
95StaCluMOP-156
95StaCluSTWS-156
95StaCluVR-82
95Stu-134
95Top-413
95TopCyb-213
95UC3-15
95UC3ArtP-15
95Ult-87
95UltGolM-87
95UppDec-444
95UppDec-452T
95UppDecED-444
95UppDecEDG-444
95UppDecSE-9
95UppDecSEG-9
95Zen-19
96ColCho-513
96ColChoGS-513
96ColChoSS-513
96Don-548
96DonPreP-548
96EmoXL-41
96Fla-59
96Fle-220
96FleTif-220
96FleUpd-U30
96FleUpdTC-U30
96FleWhiS-16
96LeaSigA-220
96LeaSigAG-220
96LeaSigAS-220
96PacPri-P128
96PacPriG-P128
96Pin-17
96Pin-356
96PinAfi-33
96PinAfiAP-33
96PinAfiFPP-33
96PinFoil-356
96ProSta-8
96Sco-339
96ScoDugC-B64
96ScoDugCAP-B64
96Sel-145
96SelArtP-145
96StaClu-310
96StaCluEPB-310
96StaCluEPG-310
96StaCluEPS-310
96StaCluMOP-310
95StaCluVRMC-82
96Ult-338
96UltGolM-338
96UppDec-302
97Don-97
97DonPreP-97
97DonPrePGold-97
97FlaSho-A94
97FlaSho-B94
97FlaSho-C94
97FlaShoLC-94
97FlaShoLC-B94
97FlaShoLC-C94
97FlaShoLCM-A94
97FlaShoLCM-B94
97FlaShoLCM-C94
97Fle-71
97Fle-614
97FleTif-71
97FleTif-614
97Pac-63
97PacLigB-63
97PacPri-21
97PacPriLB-21
97PacPriP-21
97PacSil-63
97Pin-140
97PinArtP-140
97PinMusC-140
97Sco-58
97Sco-448
97ScoHobR-448
97ScoPreS-58
97ScoResC-448
97ScoShoS-58
97ScoShoS-448
97ScoShoSAP-58
97ScoShoSAP-448
97ScoWhiS-3
97ScoWhiSPl-3
97ScoWhiSPr-3
97StaClu-134
97StaCluMOP-134
97Top-78
Tartabull, Jose
86BelMarC-108
87WauTimP-8
88SanBerSB-13
88SanBerSCLC-36
89SanBerSB-18
89SanBerSCLC-79
Tartabull, Jose Milages
62Top-451
63AthJayP-11
63Top-449
64A's-17
64AthJayP-12
64Top-276
64TopVen-276
66OPC-143
66Top-143
66TopVen-143
67CokCapRS-17
67DexPre-203
67OPC-56
67Top-56
67TopRedSS-21
68Top-555
69MilBra-269
69Top-287
70OPC-481
70Top-481
72MilBra-339
81RedSoxBG2S-121
81TCM60I-331
93Pin-478
Tarumi, Kanenori
88MiaMarS-11
Tarutis, Pete
91JamExpC-26
91JamExpP-3545
Tarver, LaSchelle
82LynMetT-2
84TidTidT-21
85IntLeaAT-6
85MetTCM-39
85TidTidT-13
86PawRedSP-24
87PawRedSP-60
87PawRedST-19
Tasby, Willie
59OriJayP-8
59Top-143
59TopVen-143
60Lea-100
60OriJayP-8
60Top-322
61Pos-51A
61Pos-51B
61SenJayP-9
61Top-458
61TopStaI-117
62Jel-70
62Pos-70
62PosCan-70
62SalPlaC-21
62ShiPlaC-21
62Top-462A
62Top-462B
91OriCro-449
Tashiro, Tomio
79TCMJapPB-54
Tasker, Paul
76BatTroTI-23
Tata, Terry
88T/MUmp-16
89T/MUmp-14
89T/MUmp-60
90T/MUmp-14
Tatar, Jason
94ForWayWC-23
94ForWayWF-2011
95ForMyeMTI-27
96FtMyeMB-10
Tatar, Kevin
90BilMusP-3222
91ChaWheC-11
91ChaWheP-2888
91Cla/Bes-294
92Bow-621
92ChaLooS-197
92ClaFS7-73
92SkyAA F-89
92UppDecML-306
Tatarian, Dean
89UtiBluSP-24
90UtiBluSP-10
91SarWhiSC-20
91SarWhiSP-1122
92BasCitRC-4
92BasCitRF-3854
92ClaFS7-139
Tate, Bennie
34DiaMatCSB-178
36GouWidPPR-D36
36WorWidGV-80
91ConTSN-220
Tate, Chuck
86EveGiaC-16
86EveGiaPC-32
Tate, Edward
87OldJudN-501
Tate, Henry
31Exh-20
Tate, Lee W.
59Top-544
Tate, Michael
88BoiHawP-1606
Tate, Randy L.
76OPC-549
76SSP-555
76Top-549
77LynMetT-27
78ColCliT-25
91MetWIZ-395
Tate, Stu (Stuart)
84EveGiaC-12
85FreGiaP-19
86ShrCapP-24
87ShrCapP-20
88ShrCapP-1295
89PhoFirC-9
89PhoFirP-1491
89TriAAP-AAA52
90Fle-643
90FleCan-643
90TopDeb89-127
91LinDriAAA-395
91PhoFirLD-395
91PhoFirP-67
Taterson, Gary
91WatIndC-12
Tatis, Bernie
83KinBluJTI-26
85DomLeaS-154
86KnoBluJP-23
87KnoBluJP-1509
87SouLeaAJ-4
88BufBisC-14
88BufBisP-1475
90CMC-170
90OklCit8C-20
90OklCit8P-447
90ProAAAF-693
90ProAAAF-694
91CanIndLD-95
91CanIndP-993
91ColSprSSP-2194
91LinDriAA-95
93LimRocDWB-96
Tatis, Fausto
90BakDodCLC-231
90YakBeaTI-33
91BakDodCLC-3
Tatis, Fernando
74CedRapAT-17
75DubPacT-16
95ChaRivTI-8
95ChaRivUTIS-36
95SPML-157
96BesAutS-87
96Exc-112
97Bow-198
97Bow98ROY-ROY15
97BowBes-145
97BowBesAR-145
97BowBesR-145
97BowCerBIA-CA77
97BowCerGIA-CA77
97BowChr-185
97BowChr1RC-ROY15
97BowChr1RCR-ROY15
97BowChrI-185
97BowChrIR-185
97BowChrR-185
97BowInt-198
97FlaShoWotF-24
97Fle-524
97FleTif-524
97Ult-538
97UltGolME-538
97UltPlaME-538
Tatis, Rafael
73CedRapAT-19
Tatis, Ramon
92GulCoaMF-3482
93KinMetC-22
93KinMetF-3796
94KinMetC-20
94KinMetF-3823
95PitMetTI-7
96StLucMTI-15
97Fle-568
97FleTif-568
Tatrow, Danny
93JohCitCC-25
93JohCitCF-3691
Tatsuno, Derek
82ElPasDT-22
87HawIslP-5
Tatterson, Gary
91WatIndP-3367
92KinIndC-8
Tatum, Goose (Reece)
76LauIndC-16
86NegLeaF-107
Tatum, Jarvis
70Top-642
71MLBOffS-334
71OPC-159
71Top-159
Tatum, Jim
85SpoIndC-24
86ChaRaiP-25
87ChaRaiP-19
88WicPilRD-18
90CanIndB-12
90CanIndP-1302
90CMC-774
91ElPasDLD-197
91ElPasDP-2757
91LinDriAAA-197
92DenZepF-2651
92DenZepS-145
92ProFS7-86
92SkyAAAF-71
92TriA AAS-145
93Bow-339
93Don-341
93Fle-416
93FleFinE-45
93PacSpa-439
93Pin-587
93RocUSPC-1C
93RocUSPC-2H
93StaClu-730
93StaCluFDI-730
93StaCluMOP-730
93StaCluRoc-25
93Top-691
93TopGol-691
93TopInaM-691
93TopMic-691
93Ult-360
93UppDec-13
93UppDec-761
93UppDecGold-13
93UppDecGold-761
94AriFalLS-20
94BreMilB-78
94ColSprSSF-747
94Fle-455
94Pac-208
94Sco-311
94ScoGolR-311
94StaCluT-120
94StaCluTFDI-120
Tatum, Ken
70MLBOffS-180
70Top-658
71MLBOffS-335
71OPC-601
71RedSoxA-11
71Top-601
72MilBra-340
72Top-772
73OPC-463
73Top-463
Tatum, Tommy
90DodTar-1082
Tatum, Willie
88ElmPioC-19
89WinHavRSS-23
90LynRedSTI-8
91LynRedSC-18
91LynRedSP-1208
92NewBriRSF-443
92NewBriRSS-497
92ProFS7-21
92SkyAA F-215
93PawRedSTI-23
Taubensee, Eddie (Edward)
88GreHorP-1558
88SouAtlLAGS-6
89CedRapRB-12
89CedRapRP-937
89CedRapRS-19
90Bes-184
90CedRapRB-3
90CedRapRDGB-11
90CedRapRP-2325
90CMC-876
90MidLeaASGS-50
91ColSprSSLD-76
91ColSprSSP-2187
91LinDriAAA-76
92AstMot-11
92Bow-697
92ClaGam-166
92Don-18
92DonRoo-115
92LeaGolR-BC9
92OPC-427
92OPCPre-136
92Pin-538
92Sco-871
92Sco100RS-29
92StaClu-790
92StaCluNC-790
92Stu-40
92Top-427
92TopDeb91-169
92TopGol-427
92TopGolW-427
92TopMic-427
92TopTra-117T
92TopTraG-117T
92Ult-497
92UppDec-757
93AstMot-18
93Bow-476
93Don-560
93Fle-55
93Lea-362
93PacSpa-482
93PanSti-169
93Pin-140
93Sco-108
93Sel-333
93StaClu-329
93StaCluAs-2
93StaCluFDI-329
93StaCluMOP-329
93Top-117
93TopGol-117
93TopInaM-117
93TopMic-117
93TriPla-17

93Ult-46
93UppDec-296
93UppDecGold-296
93USPlaCR-9S
94ColC-621
94ColChoGS-621
94ColChoSS-621
94Don-256
94Fle-501
94Pac-276
94RedKah-31
94Sco-456
94ScoGolR-456
94ScoRoo-RT34
94ScoRooGR-RT34
94Sel-334
94SpoRoo-19
94SpoRooAP-19
94StaClu-168
94StaCluFDI-168
94StaCluGR-168
94StaCluMOP-168
94Top-68
94TopGol-68
94TopSpa-68
95ColCho-432
95ColChoGS-432
95ColChoSS-432
95Don-323
95DonPreP-323
95DonTopotO-222
95Fle-450
95Lea-23
95Pin-434
95PinArtP-434
95PinMusC-434
95RedKah-32
95Sco-153
95ScoGolR-153
95ScoPlaTS-153
95StaClu-166
95StaCluFDI-166
95StaCluMOP-166
95StaCluSTWS-166
95Top-293
95Ult-150
95UltGolM-150
96ColCho-111
96ColChoGS-111
96ColChoSS-111
96Don-193
96DonPreP-193
96Fla-241
96Fle-355
96FleTif-355
96Ult-467
96UltGolM-467
96UppDec-312
97Cir-107
97CirRav-107
97ColCho-301
97Don-143
97DonPreP-143
97DonPrePGold-143
97Fin-59
97FinRef-59
97Fle-306
97FleTif-306
97Pac-277
97PacLigB-277
97PacSil-277
97Top-326
97Ult-182
97UltGolME-182
97UltPlaME-182
97UppDec-339

Tauer, Jay
85RedWinA-14
86RedWinA-3

Tauken, Daniel
87PenWhiSP-5

Taulbee, Andy
94SigRooDP-51
94SigRooDPS-51
94StaCluDP-31
94StaCluDPFDI-31
95Bow-14
96TexLeaAB-18

Taussig, Don
62Col45'HC-17
62SalPlaC-186
62ShiPlaC-186
62Top-44
62TopVen-44
89AstCol4S-22

Tavarez, Alfonso
85UtiBluST-15
86BurExpP-24

Tavarez, Davis
83CliGiaF-12
84EveGiaC-21

Tavarez, Hector
90MedHatBJB-27
91MedHatBJP-4109
91MedHatBJSP-6
92DunBluJC-21

Tavarez, Jesus
90PenPilS-21
91CalLeLA-11
91SanBerSC-24
91SanBerSP-2001
92ClaFS7-144
92JacSunF-3723
92JacSunS-368
92SkyAA F-159
93HigDesMC-22
93HigDesMF-56
93LimRocDWB-30
94BowBes-B85
94BowBesR-B85
94FleUpd-139
94LeaLimR-36
94PorSeaDF-691
94PorSeaDTI-28
94UppDecML-114
95ChaKniTI-26
95StaClu-379
95StaCluMOP-379
95StaCluSTWS-379
95UppDecSE-114
95UppDecSEG-114
96ColCho-26
96Don-366
96DonPreP-366
96Fle-395
96FleTif-395
96LeaSigEA-198
96Pac-79
96UppDec-58
97Pac-308
97PacLigB-308
97PacSil-308

Tavarez, Juan
93KinIndTI-25

Tavarez, Julian
92BurIndC-18
92BurIndF-1657
93CarLeaAGF-34
93KinIndC-24
93KinIndF-2247
93LimRocDWB-89
94Bow-279
94ChaKniF-895
94Cla-46
94ColC-274
94ColChoGS-274
94ColChoSS-274
94Don-627
94Pin-411
94PinArtP-411
94PinMusC-411
94SpoRoo-49
94SpoRooAP-49
94StaClu-128
94StaCluFDI-128
94StaCluGR-128
94StaCluMOP-128
94Top-767
94TopGol-767
94TopSpa-767
94TriAAF-AAA3
95ActPacF-44
95Bow-159
95BowBes-R87
95BowBesR-R87
95ColCho-6
95ColChoGS-6
95ColChoSS-6
95Emo-38
95Fla-251
95FleUpd-42
95FleUpdRU-10
95Sco-277
95ScoGolR-277
95ScoPlaTS-277
95ScoRooDT-RDT9
95Sel-204
95SelArtP-204
95SelCer-127
95SelCerMG-127
95StaClu-24
95StaCluFDI-24
95StaCluMOP-24
95StaCluSTWS-24
95Sum21C-TC7
95TopTra-119T
95UltGolMR-M20
95UppDec-221
95UppDecED-221
95UppDecEDG-221
95Zen-125
95ZenRooRC-11
96ColCho-118
96ColChoGS-118
96ColChoSS-118
96Don-297
96DonPreP-297
96Fla-75
96Fle-101
96FleInd-16
96FleTif-101
96Lea-75
96LeaPrePB-75
96LeaPrePG-75
96LeaPrePS-75
96LeaSigA-221
96LeaSigAG-221
96LeaSigAS-221
96MetUni-53
96MetUniP-53
96Pac-298
96PacEstL-EL31
96Pin-294
96PinAfi-112
96PinAfiAP-112
96PinFoil-294
96Sco-312
96ScoDugC-B37
96ScoDugCAP-B37
96Sel-95
96SelArtP-95
96Sum-113
96SumAbo&B-113
96SumArtP-113
96SumFoi-113
96Top-81
96Ult-344
96UltGolM-344
97Cir-224
97CirRav-224
97Fle-89
97Fle-693
97FleTif-89
97FleTif-693
97Pac-79
97PacLigB-79
97PacSil-79
97Sco-373
97ScoHobR-373
97ScoResC-373
97ScoShoS-373
97ScoShoSAP-373
97Top-234
97Ult-55
97Ult-424
97UltGolME-55
97UltGolME-424
97UltPlaME-55
97UltPlaME-424

Tavener, Jack
28Exh-46
28StaPlaCE-65
29ExhFou-21
92ConTSN-572

Taveras, Alex
74CedRapAT-10
75IowOakT-21
77Top-474
79AlbDukT-15
81AlbDukT-18
82AlbDukT-18
83AlbDukT-10
84AlbDukC-153
85BufBisT-12
89BelBrelS-26
89BelBrelS-25

Taveras, Frank
96BurIndB-25

Taveras, Frank Crisostomo
74OPC-607
74Top-607
75OPC-277
75OPC-460
75Top-277
76OPC-36
76SSP-583
76Top-36
77BurCheD-184
77PirPosP-28
77Top-538
78OPC-4
78Top-204
78Top-685
79OPC-79
79Top-165
80BurKinPHR-32
80OPC-237
80Top-456
81AllGamPI-116
81CokTeaS-93
81Don-154
81Fle-320
81OPC-343
81Top-343
81TopSti-196
81TopSupHT-77
82Don-98
82ExpHygM-22
82ExpPos-43
82Fle-539
82OPC-351
82Top-782
82TopTra-118T
91MetWIZ-396

Taveras, Marcos
88St.CatBJP-2028
89DunBluJS-18
90DunBluJS-17

Taveras, Ramon
89SalDodTI-30
90FloStaLAS-17
90StaFS7-21
90VerBeaDS-25
91LinDriAA-542
91SanAntMLD-542

Tawwater, Darren
91OklStaC-27
92OklStaC-26

Taylor, Aaron
89WytCubS-25
90HunCubP-3283
91PeoChiC-9
91PeoChiP-1343
91PeoChiTI-13
92WinSpiC-23
92WinSpiF-1208
93OrlCubF-2784
93Top-786
93TopGol-786
93TopInaM-786
93TopMic-786

Taylor, Adam
96WatIndTI-29

Taylor, Andrew
86LitFalMP-27
88SprCarB-8
89SavCarP-368

Taylor, Ben
78LauLonABS-12
90NegLeaS-10

Taylor, Bill (William Howell)
58Top-389
80AshTouT-18
82WauTimF-26
85TulDriTI-34
87OklCit8P-25
88OklCit8P-28
89LasVegSC-10
90MadMusB-24
90ModA'sCLC-154
90ModA'sP-2213
91GreBraC-6
91GreBraP-3000
92RicBraF-378
93RicBraBB-23
93RicBraF-185
93RicBraP-17
93RicBraRC-20
93RicBraRC-27
93TriAAAGF-4
94A'sMot-25
94Bow-276
94ExtBas-157
94Fla-97
94FleUpd-78
94ScoRoo-RT71
94Sel-391
94TopTra-2T
94Ult-413
95Don-377
95DonPreP-377
95Fle-255
95Sco-473
95ScoGolR-473
95ScoPlaTS-473
95Ult-321
95UltGolM-321
96A'sMot-24
97ColCho-414
97Fle-197
97FleTif-197

Taylor, Bill (William M.)
54Top-74
55GiaGolS-29
55Top-53
55TopDouH-7
94TopArc1-74
94TopArc1G-74

Taylor, Billy
75QuaCitAT-23
76QuaCitAT-36
83TulDriT-5
84TulDriTI-32
89LasVegSP-3
89MadMusS-20
92RicBraBB-12
92RicBraRC-23
92RicBraS-445
94ScoRooGR-RT71
97Cir-76
97CirRav-76
97RicBraBC-21
97Ult-425
97UltGolME-425
97UltPlaME-425

Taylor, Billy (William Henry)
90KalBatN-31

Taylor, Bob
58Top-164
61Top-446
62Top-406
63Top-481
64Top-381
69Top-239
76BatRouCT-20
91MetWIZ-399

Taylor, Bobbie
85AncGlaPTI-45

Taylor, Brien
90TopMag-79
91ClaDraP-1
91ClaDraPP-3
92Bow-124
92ClaBluBF-BC15
92ClaDraP-86
92ClaDraPFB-BC18
92ClaDraPP-3
92ClaFS7-300
92ClaRedB-BC15
92DEL-AU5
92ForLauYC-1
92ForLauYTI-30
92Ft.LauYF-2612
92OPC-6
92StaCluD-184
92StaCluFDP-2
92Top-6
92TopGol-6
92TopGol-793
92TopGolW-6
92TopMic-6
92UppDecML-49
92UppDecML-57
92UppDecML-265
92UppDecMLPotY-PY26
92UppDecMLTPHF-TP7
93AlbYanF-2164
93BluOriC-28
93Bow-370
93Bow-679
93CapCitBC-28
93ClaFisN-14
93ClaGolF-17
93ClaGolLF-2
93ClaGolP-3
93ClaYouG-YG22
93DayCubC-28
93EliTwiC-28

93EugEmeC-28
93ExcAllF-1
93ExcFS7-215
93PeoChiC-28
93PitMetC-28
93SanBerSC-28
93StaClu-689
93StaCluFDI-689
93StaCluMOP-689
93StaCluMP-30
93StaCluY-22
93Top-742
93TopGol-742
93TopInaM-742
93TopMic-742
93Toy-19
93UtiBluSC-28
93WesVirWC-28
93WinSpiC-28
94ActPac-41
94Bow-165
94Cla-80
94ClaGolA-SH1
94ClaGolF-1
94ExcFS7-115
94ExcLeaLF-17
94TedWil-132
94TedWilDGC-DG8
94Top-772
94TopGol-772
94TopSpa-772
94UppDecML-5
94UppDecML-251
95Bow-17
96NorNavB-27

Taylor, Bruce
77EvaTriT-23
78Top-701

Taylor, Byron
94NewJerCC-25
94NewJerCF-3433

Taylor, C.I. (Charles Isam)
87NegLeaPD-12

Taylor, Carl
68Top-559
69Top-357
70OPC-76
70Top-76
71MLBOffS-286
71MLBOffS-432
71OPC-353
71Top-353
71TopCoi-55
73OPC-99
73Top-99
74OPC-627
74Top-627
89PacSenL-160

Taylor, Charley
85OscAstTI-2
87AshTouP-11
88AshTouP-1067
89AshTouP-944
90ColMudB-21
90ColMudP-1362
90ColMudS-25
91JacGenP-942
91LinDriAA-575
92JacGenF-4015
92JacGenS-350
93JacGenF-2125
94JacGenF-233
95JacGenTI-26
96TusTorB-28

Taylor, Chuck (Charles Gilbert)
70OPC-119
70Top-119
71CarTeal-39
71OPC-606
71Top-606
72OPC-407
72Top-407
73OPC-176
73Top-176
74OPC-412
74Top-412
75OPC-58
75Top-58
76ExpRed-30
76SSP-346
86ColAstP-24
91MetWIZ-397
94BreMilB-79

Taylor, Dan
34DiaMatCSB-179
34BatR31-108
35ExhFou-2
36GouWidPPR-A100
36WorWidGV-72
90DodTar-789
93ConTSN-898

Taylor, Dave
87BelBreP-25
88StoPorCLC-195
88StoPorP-729
90MiaMirIS-24

Taylor, Dorn
83AleDukT-30
84PriWilPT-6
85NasPirT-24
86NasPirP-26
87FleUpd-118
87FleUpdG-118
87VanCanP-1621
88BlaYNPRWLU-45
88BufBisC-9
88BufBisP-1468
88BufBisTI-5
88TriAAC-11
89PirVerFJ-52
89TriAAP-AAA9
90BufBisC-10
90BufBisP-373
90BufBisTI-26
90CMC-10
90ProAAAF-488
90TriAllGP-AAA22
91OriCro-451

Taylor, Dummy (Luther H.)
03BreE10-139
05RotCP-9
06FanCraNL-45
08AmeCarE-30
08RosComP-132
09T206-471
11SpoLifCW-348
12ImpTobC-41

Taylor, Dwight
82WatIndT-23
83BufBisT-21
84MaiGuiT-18
85MaiGuiT-28
86OmaRoyT-11
87OmaRoyP-8
89ColSprSSC-19
89ColSprSSP-234
90ColSprSSP-51
90ProAAAF-232
92ChaLooS-198
92NasSouF-1847

Taylor, Eddie
45CenFlo-25
47CenFlo-29

Taylor, Edward
26Exh-7

Taylor, Gary
91HamRedC-14
91HamRedP-4055
92SavCarC-14
92SavCarF-677
93SprCarC-27
93SprCarF-1867

Taylor, Gene
91BilMusP-3769
91BilMusSP-16
92CedRapRC-2
92CedRapRF-1088

Taylor, Greg
96BatCliTI-22

Taylor, Harry
90DodTar-790
92TexLon-39

Taylor, Hawk (Robert D.)
65Top-329
68OPC-52
68Top-52
68TopVen-52
70RoyTeal-37
93LinVenB-199

Taylor, Herb
52LavPro-24

Taylor, Jack
06FanCraNL-44
07CubGFGCP-15
11SpoLifCW-347
90HOFStiB-13

Taylor, Jamie
92FroRowDP-27
92WatIndC-1
92WatIndF-3244
93Bow-205
93ClaFS7-262
93ColRedC-22
93ColRedF-607
93StaCluM-165
94KinIndC-18
94KinIndF-2653
96NewHavRB-23

Taylor, Jeff
81NasSouTI-19
83MemChiT-14
85GreBraTI-17
86OrlTwiP-20
88NebCor-16
88OneYanP-2070
89CarNewE-7
89OneYanP-2101

Taylor, Jerry
96KenIndB-23

Taylor, Joe
52LavPro-57
57HygMea-11
58Top-451
60HenHouW-22
60UniOil-13
61UniOil-SD11
91OriCro-450

Taylor, John
81CliGiaT-17
82AleDukT-1
82AppFoxF-8
83AleDukT-12

Taylor, John I.
09SpoNewSM-48

Taylor, John W.
09ColChiE-286
09ColChiE-287
12ColRedB-287
26Exh-8
27Exh-4
28Exh-4
63GadFunC-15

Taylor, Jonathon
92VerBeaDF-2880

Taylor, Joseph F.
54BraJohC-50
55BraJohC-51

Taylor, Kerry
89EliTwiS-25
89Sta-153
91KenTwiC-16
91KenTwiP-2074
92KenTwiC-14
92KenTwiF-604
93Bow-63
93FleFinE-145
93PadMot-26
94Don-244
94Fle-675
94LasVegSF-872

Taylor, Lawn Tennis
88GooN16-44

Taylor, Lawrence
91StaCluCM-39

Taylor, Mark
91SavCarC-15
91SavCarP-1656
96WatIndTI-30

Taylor, Michael Patrick
91BurIndP-3305
91MedHatBJSP-7
92EriSaiC-24
92EriSaiF-1628
92MedHatBJSP-22
92ProFS7-176

Taylor, Mike
80WatIndT-29
81WatIndT-28
82WatIndT-24
86BirBarTI-13
87HawIsIP-12

Taylor, Mike (David Michael)
86AriWilP-17
88GasRanP-998
89ChaRanS-25
90TulDriP-1156
90TulDriTI-24
94NewJerCC-26
94NewJerCF-3428

Taylor, Mike (Michael David)
88St.CatBJP-2032
89MyrBeaBJP-1463
90DunBluJS-18
91KnoBluJLD-366
91KnoBluJP-1776
91LinDriAA-366
92KnoBluJS-394

Taylor, Mike (Michael Larry)
90St.CatBJP-3474
91MedHatBJP-4101
92MyrBeaHC-20
93GleFalRC-27
93GleFalRF-4016

Taylor, Phil
86MiaMarP-24

Taylor, Randy
77SanJosMC-21

Taylor, Reggie
95Bes-117
95BowBes-X3
95BowBesR-X3
95MarPhiTI-27
95TopTra-108T
96Bow-271
96Exc-214
96PieBolWB-27
96SigRooOJPP-P7
96Top-240
97Bow-185
97BowChr-175
97BowChrI-175
97BowChrIR-175
97BowChrR-175
97BowInt-185

Taylor, Rob
90Bes-129
90CliGiaB-27
90CliGiaP-2544
90MidLeaASGS-51
91SanJosGC-22
91SanJosGP-11
92ShrCapF-3871
92ShrCapS-595
93PhoFirF-1516
94PhoFirF-1520
95IowCubTI-25

Taylor, Ron
62Top-591
63Top-208
64Top-183
64TopVen-183
65Top-568
66OPC-174
66Top-174
66TopVen-174
67Top-606
68Top-421
69MetNewYDN-19
69OPC-72
69Top-72
69TopSta-79
70OPC-419
70Top-419
71MLBOffS-167
71OPC-687
71Top-687
72OPC-234
72PadTeal-25
72Top-234
77Spo-7713
81TCM60I-449
81TCM60I-466
87Mct196T-7
89RinPosM1-28
91MetWIZ-398
94Met69CCPP-31
94Met69CS-30-
94Met69T-15

Taylor, Sam
60CubJayP-10
60Lea-131
61Pos-198A
61Pos-198B
62CubJayP-11
62Jel-189
62Pos-189
62PosCan-189
88CapCodPPaLP-121
89BatCliP-1937
91Cla/Bes-349
91ClePhiC-24
91ClePhiP-1635
92ReaPhiF-590
92ReaPhiS-545
92SkyAA F-238
93ReaPhiF-309
94BoiHawF-3370

Taylor, Sammy
58Top-281
59Top-193
59TopVen-193
60Top-162
60TopVen-162
61Top-253
61TopStaI-10
62SalPlaC-164
62ShiPlaC-164
62Top-274
63Top-273
82MetGal62-12
91MetWIZ-400
94BoiHawC-25

Taylor, Scott
87WytCubP-4

Taylor, Scott (Rodney Scott)
88ElmPioC-4
89LynRedSS-29
90LynRedSTI-24
91Bow-121
91Cla/Bes-83
91LinDriAA-472
91NewBriRSLD-472
91NewBriRSP-353
91PawRedSDD-23
92Bow-618
92PawRedSF-923
92PawRedSS-368
92SkyAAAF-167
92WinSpiC-8
92WinSpiF-1212
93Don-267
93FleMajLP-B13
93PawRedSDD-27
93PawRedSF-2409
93PawRedSTI-24
93RedSoxWHP-25
93Top-456
93TopGol-456
93TopInaM-456
93TopMic-456
96CarMudB-10
97DunDonPPS-24

Taylor, Scott Michael
88ChaWheB-4
88GenCubP-1651
89ChaWheB-5
89ChaWheP-1757
89SouAtlLAGS-13
89WauTimGS-11
90Bes-246
90SanBerSB-15
90SanBerSCLC-93
90SanBerSP-2633
90WinSpiTI-22
91CarLeaAP-CAR3
91ChaKniLD-145
91ChaKniP-1692
91DurBulP-1546
91GreBraLD-219
91LinDriAA-145
91LinDriAA-219
92ElPasDF-3922
92GreBraF-1153
92GreBraS-246
93ElPasDF-2951
94NewOrlZF-1469

Taylor, Steve
78TacYanC-25
79ColCliT-20
80NasSouTI-23
81NasSouTI-20
90EliTwiS-22
91KenTwiC-17
91KenTwiP-2075

Taylor, Ted
76TayBow4-NNO

Taylor, Terry
88CapCodPPaLP-137
89BenBucL-24
89BlaYNPRWL-194
90CalCanC-5
90PalSprACLC-208
90PalSprAP-2587
91Cla/Bes-328
91LinDriAA-420

91LinDriAA-447
91MemChiLD-420
91MemChiP-656
91MidAngLD-447
91MidAngOHP-29
91MidAngP-444
92MidAngF-4035
92MidAngOHP-24
92MidAngS-472
Taylor, Terry Derrell
83WauTimF-9
86ChaLooP-24
87CalCanP-2325
88CalCanP-781
89Fle-651
89FleGlo-651
89Top-597
89TopTif-597
90CalCanP-651
90CMC-432
90ProAAAF-116
Taylor, Tex
52LavPro-28
Taylor, Todd
91TopTra-116T
91TopTraT-116T
92EliTwiF-3683
92StaCluD-185
93ForWayWC-22
93ForWayWF-1969
Taylor, Tom
90CMC-871
90MidLeaASGS-19
90WauTimP-2122
92FreKeyF-1806
Taylor, Tommy (Thomas)
89BluOriS-24
90WauTimB-9
90WauTimS-23
91Cla/Bes-242
91KanCouCC-10
91KanCouCTI-20
92FreKeyC-22
93BowBayF-2190
94FreKeyF-2615
94FreKeyC-22
Taylor, Tony (Antonio S.)
58Top-411
59Top-62
59TopVen-62
60CubJayP-11
60Lea-44
60Top-294
61Pos-118A
61Pos-118B
61Top-411
61TopStal-59
62Jel-193
62Pos-193
62PosCan-193
62SalPlaC-156
62ShiPlaC-156
62Top-77
62TopBuc-87
62TopStal-170
62TopVen-77
63Jel-178
63Pos-178
63Top-366
64PhiJayP-10
64PhiPhiB-23
64Top-585
64TopCoi-113
64TopCoi-144
64TopSta-9
65PhiJayP-10
65Top-296
66Top-585
67CokCapPh-12
67DexPre-204
67OPC-126
67Top-126
67TopVen-314
68Top-327
68TopVen-327
69MilBra-270
69MLBOffS-179
69OPC-108
69PhiTeal-11
69Top-108
69TopTeaP-8
70DayDaiNM-139
70MilBra-28
70MLBOffS-95
70OPC-324
70PhiTeal-11
70Top-324
71Kel-67
71MLBOffS-190
71OPC-246
71PhiArcO-12
71Top-246
72MilBra-341
72OPC-511
72Top-511
73OPC-29
73TigJew-19
73Top-29
75OPC-574
75Top-574
76OPC-624
76SSP-474
76Top-624
78PhiSSP-41
78SSP270-41
78TCM60I-133
83PhiPosGM-4
83PhiPosGPaM-8
86PhiGreT-12
88PhiTas-29
89PhiTas-33
90ShrCapP-1459
90ShrCapS-27
91LinDriAA-325
91ShrCapLD-325
91ShrCapP-1840
92PhoFirS-400
Taylor, Wade
87BelMarTI-14
88Ft.LauYS-21
89PriWilCS-21
90AlbYanB-9
90AlbYanP-1176
90AlbYanS-20
90Bes-154
90CMC-778
90EasLeaAP-EL12
90ProAaA-20
90TopTVY-63
91AlbYanCB-2
91Bow-165
91Cla2-T87
91ColCliLD-121
91ColCliP-21
91ColCliP-598
91DonRoo-34
91FleUpd-48
91LeaGolR-BC16
91LinDriAAA-121
91OPCPre-119
91ScoRoo-100T
91TopTra-117T
91TopTraT-117T
92ClaGam-56
92ColCliF-353
92ColCliP-12
92ColCliS-121
92Don-527
92Fle-245
92OPC-562
92ProFS7-107
92Sco-631
92Sco100RS-45
92SkyAAAF-59
92StaClu-667
92Top-562
92TopDeb91-170
92TopGol-562
92TopGolW-562
92TopMic-562
92TriPla-96
Taylor, Will (William Christopher)
86SpoIndC-179
87ChaRaiP-6
88RivRedWCLC-227
88RivRedWP-1419
89RivRedWCLC-13
89RivRedWP-1402
91LasVegSLD-295
91LasVegSP-250
91LinDriAAA-295
92LasVegSS-243
92SkyAAAF-118
Taylor, William
89RivRedWB-17
90WicWraRD-19
Taylor, Zack (James)
31CubTeal-24
32CubTeal-23
33Gou-152
33GouCanV-79
41BroW75-28
46SeaSLP-54
46SpoExcW-10-12
51Bow-315
90DodTar-791
91ConTSN-210
94TedWil-113
Tayor, Fiona
85AncGlaPTI-38
Teachout, Bud
31CubTeal-25
Teague, Scott
89WytCubS-26
Teahan, Jim
83BelBreF-19
Teasley, Ronald
86NegLeaF-55
93NegLeaRL2-39
Tebbetts, Birdie (George)
47Exh-220
47HomBon-45
47TipTop-42
48RedSoxTI-24
50Dra-30
51Bow-257
52Bow-124
52IndNumN-3
52Top-282
53IndPenCBP-24
55Bow-232
58RedEnq-38
58RedJayP-12
58Top-386
62BraJayP-10
62Top-588
63IndJayP-12
63Top-48
64IndJayP-12
64Top-462
65Top-301
66IndTeal-10
66Top-552
76TayBow4-45
77TCMTheWY-6
79DiaGre-377
81TigDetN-92
82OhiHaloF-64
83TopRep5-282
Tebbetts, Scott
95MarPhiTI-28
Tebbetts, Steve
76QuaCitAT-37
77QuaCitAT-28
Tebbs, Nathan
94UtiBluSC-26
94UtiBluSF-3829
96Exc-20
96SarRedSB-28
Tebeau, Patsy (Oliver)
87OldJudN-502
98CamPepP-77
Techman, Marc
90AubAstB-22
91AubAstC-28
Tedder, Scott
89SarWhiSS-24
89Sta-61
90FloStaLAS-44
90SarWhiSS-24
91SarWhiSC-26
91SarWhiSP-1127
92BirBarF-2596
92BirBarS-96
93NasSouF-582
94BirBarC-21
94BirBarF-635
Teegarden, Travis
89BilMusP-2040
Teel, Garett
88CapCodPPaLP-171
90BakDodCLC-252
92VerBeaDF-2895
93VerBeaDC-29
Teemer, John
87AllandGN-29
Teemer, Oarsman
88GooN16-45
Teeters, Brian
92EugEmeC-26
92EugEmeF-3044
94EugEmeC-22
94EugEmeF-3727
95WilBluRTI-8
96WilBluRB-8
Tegtmeier, Doug
88NebCor-17
89AncBucTI-9
90NebCor-24
91PenPilC-11
91PenPilP-377
Teich, Mike
91WelPirC-27
91WelPirP-3573
92AugPirC-5
92AugPirF-240
93SalBucC-23
93SalBucF-432
Teising, John
76BatTroTI-24
78WatIndT-23
Teixeira, Joe
89BluOriS-25
90WauTimB-11
90WauTimP-2124
Teixeira, Vince
86MedA'sC-74
87MadMusP-19
87MadMusP-5
88ModA'sCLC-80
89VisOakCLC-113
89VisOakP-1423
Tejada, Alejandro
89JamExpP-2153
Tejada, Domingo
90MarPhiP-3206
Tejada, Eugenio
88UtiBluSP-10
89SouBenWSGS-25
90SouBenWSGS-18
Tejada, Francisco
88MarPhiS-30
90PriPatD-24
92SpaPhiC-8
92SpaPhiF-1266
Tejada, Joaquin
86ElmPioRSP-23
87ElmPio(C-25
Tejada, Leo
90SouBenWSB-6
91SarWhiSC-21
91SarWhiSP-1123
Tejada, Miguel
96CarLeaA2B-26
96CarLeaAIB-B10
96ModA'sB-1
96SouOreTI-1
97Bow-411
97BowBes-114
97BowBesAR-114
97BowBesP-18
97BowBesPAR-18
97BowBesPR-18
97BowBesR-114
97BowCerBIA-CA78
97BowCerGIA-CA78
97BowChr-273
97BowChrI-273
97BowChrIR-273
97BowChrR-273
97BowInt-411
Tejada, Wilfredo
85DomLeaS-134
86JacExpT-18
87Don-529
87IndIndTI-25
88IndIndC-19
88IndIndP-523
89Bow-468
89BowTif-468
89OPC-391
89PhoFirC-12
89PhoFirP-1489
89Top-747
89TopTif-747
91HunStaLD-294
91LinDriAA-294
93LimRocDWB-4
Tejcek, John
92AriWilP-19
94CalCanF-803
94RivPilCLC-15
Tejeda, Enrique
88BenBucL-16
Tejeda, Felix
86VerBeaDP-24
87SanAntDTI-15
Tejero, Fausto
90BoiHawP-3334
91QuaCitAC-14
91QuaCitAP-2632
92MidAngF-4031
92MidAngOHP-25
92MidAngS-454
93MidAngF-325
94MidAngF-2442
94MidAngOHP-30
95MidAngOHP-33
96VanCanB-27
97MidAngOHP-30
Tekulve, Kent
76OPC-112
76SSP-561
76Top-112
77PirPosP-29
77Top-374
78Top-84
79Top-223
80OPC-297
80Top-573
80TopSup-45
81CokTeaS-119
81Don-254
81Fle-362A
81Fle-362B
81FleStiC-21
81OPC-94
81Top-695
82Don-311
82Fle-500
82FleSta-73
82OPC-281
82Top-485
83Don-297
83Fle-326
83FleSta-194
83FleSti-73
83OPC-17
83OPC-18
83Top-17
83Top-18
83TopFol-4
84Don-410
84Fle-265
84FunFooP-12
84Nes792-754
84OPC-74
84Top-754
84TopRubD-12
84TopSti-132
84TopTif-754
85Don-479
85Fle-477
85FleUpd-117
85Lea-119
85OPC-125
85Top-125
85TopRubD-15
85TopSti-129
85TopTif-125
85TopTifT-117T
85TopTra-117T
86Don-111
86Fle-455
86OPC-326
86PhiCIG-4
86PhiTas-27
86Top-326
86TopTif-326
87Don-453
87Fle-190
87FleExcS-42
87FleGlo-190
87FleMin-104
87FleStiC-116
87OPC-86
87PhiTas-27
87SpoTeaP-6
87Top-684
87TopSti-118
87TopTif-684
88Don-535
88DonBasB-327
88Fle-318
88FleGlo-318
88OPCBoxB-P
88PanSti-354
88PhiTas-24
88Sco-425

88ScoGlo-425
88StaLinPh-18
88Top-543
88TopRevLL-10
88TopTif-543
88TopWaxBC-P
89Fle-583
89FleGlo-583
89OPCBoxB-O
89RedKah-43
89Sco-287
89TopTra-116T
89TopTraT-116T
89TopWaxBC-O
89UppDec-207
90PubSti-40
92UppDecS-19
93ActPacA-167
94CarLeaA-DJ23
Telemaco, Amaury
92HunCubC-27
92HunCubF-3148
93ClaFS7-119
93MidLeaAGF-42
93PeoChiC-21
93PeoChiF-1085
93PeoChiTI-27
94Bow-49
94Cla-77
94DayCubC-1
94DayCubF-2352
94ExcFS7-168
94FloStaLAF-FSL34
95Bes-61
95Bow-184
95SPML-32
96Bow-212
96BowBes-146
96BowBesAR-146
96BowBesR-146
96Exc-142
96IowCubB-27
96SigRooOJ-32
96SigRooOJS-32
97ColCho-292
97Don-172
97DonPreP-172
97DonPrePGold-172
97Fle-286
97FleTif-286
97MetUni-16
95OrlCubF-12
97PacPriGotD-GD123
97Pin-177
97PinArtP-177
97PinMusC-177
97StaClu-359
97StaCluMOP-359
97Top-316
97Ult-170
97UltGolME-170
97UltPlaME-170
97UppDec-31
Telford, Anthony
88HagSunS-22
89FreKeyS-23
90FreKeyTI-11
90HagSunS-23
91Cla1-T16
91Don-501
91Fle-493
91LinDriAAA-470
91OPC-653
91OriCro-452
91RocRedWLD-470
91RocRedWP-1903
91Sco-354
91StaClu-330
91Top-653
91TopDeb90-152
91TopDesS-653
91TopMic-653
91TopTif-653
91UppDec-304
92Don-623
92Fle-29
92RocRedWF-1941
92RocRedWS-471
92Sco-853
92ScoHotR-8
92SkyAAAF-214
92StaClu-557
93Don-789
93RocRedWF-241
94RicBraF-2846
Telgheder, Dave
89PitMetS-22
90ColMetGS-26
90ColMetPPI-1
91Cla/Bes-342
91LinDriAA-644
91WilBilLD-644
91WilBilP-293
92SkyAAAF-256
92TidTidF-896
92TidTidS-572
93FleFinE-107
93NorTidF-2569
93TopTra-89T
94Don-467
94Fle-578
94MetColP-26
94NorTidF-2922
94Pac-417
94Sco-599
94ScoGolR-599
94Top-402
94TopGol-402
94TopSpa-402
94Ult-537
94UppDec-69
94UppDecED-69
95NorTidTI-28
97ColCho-413
Telgheder, Jim
94SarRedSC-27
94SarRedSF-1951
95MicBatCTI-27
96WilBluRB-27
Tellechea, John
90LSUTigP-9
91LSUTigP-6
Tellers, David
90WelPirP-30
91CarLeaAP-CAR37
91SalBucC-20
91SalBucP-950
92CarMudF-1180
92SalBucC-7
94NewHavRF-1550
95NewHavRTI-12
Tellez, Alonzo
87SanAntDTI-5
Tellgren, Scott
83TolMudHT-25
85MaiGuiT-32
Tellmann, Tom
79HawIsIC-16
79HawIsIT-23
80HawIsIT-14
81HawIsIT-15
81Top-356
82HawIsIT-19
83BrePol-42
83TopTra-109T
84BreGar-20
84BrePol-42
84Don-149
84Fle-216
84Nes792-476
84Top-476
84TopSti-297
84TopTif-476
85BreGar-20
85Don-246
85Fle-599
85TacTigC-150
85Top-112
85TopTif-112
85TopTifT-118T
85TopTra-118T
86Top-693
86TopTif-693
94BreMilB-80
Telvin, Creighton
81SyrChiT-19
Temperly, Kevin
89CliGiaP-881
92CliGiaC-30
Temple, Jason
96LynHilB-23
Temple, Johnny
55Bow-31
55Kah-6
56Kah-15
56RedBurB-22
56Top-212
57Kah-26
57RedSoh-18
57Top-9
58Kah-28
58RedEnq-39
58Top-205
58Top-478
59Kah-36
59RedEnq-25
59RedShiBS-21
59Top-335
60IndJayP-12
60Kah-40
60MacSta-25
60RawGloT-34
60Top-500
60TopTat-50
61Kah-43
61Pos-61A
61Pos-61B
61SevElev-8
61Top-155
61TopStal-143
62Jel-38
62Pos-38
62PosCan-38
62SalPlaC-52A
62SalPlaC-52B
62ShiPlaC-52
62Top-34
62TopVen-34
63Col45"P-15
63Jel-189
63Pos-189
63Top-576
64Col.45JP-9
91OriCro-453
Temple, Ralph
88AllandGN-24
Templeton, Chuck
79TCM50-282
90DodTar-793
95TopArcBD-116
Templeton, Garry
76TulOilGP-18
77Car5-27
77CarTeal-26
77Hos-78
77OPC-84
77Spo-4001
77Top-161
78CarTeal-23
78Hos-43
78Kel-31
78OPC-51
78RCColC-94
78Top-32
79Car5-29
79Hos-127
79OPC-181
79Top-350
80OPC-308
80Top-5
80Top-587
80TopSup-37
81AllGamPI-117
81CokTeaS-131
81Don-187
81Fle-529
81FleStiC-125
81Kel-27
81MSAMinD-32
81OPC-144
81PerCreC-10
81Squ-12
81Top-485
81TopScr-82
81TopSti-217
81TopSti-255
82Don-545
82Fle-131
82FleSta-27
82OPC-288
82Top-288
82TopSti-96
82TopTra-119T
83AllGamPI-116
83Don-145
83Fle-373
83FleSti-227
83Kel-17
83OPC-336
83Top-505
83TopSti-291
84AllGamPI-26
84Don-185
84Fle-314
84Nes792-615
84OPC-173
84PadMot-8
84PadSmo-24
84Top-615
84TopSti-151
84TopTif-615
85AllGamPI-117
85Don-356
85Fle-45
85OPC-124
85PadMot-7
85Top-735
85TopSti-151
85TopTif-735
86Don-202
86DonAll-30
86Fle-336
86FleMin-71
86FleStiC-118
86Lea-133
86OPC-90
86Spo-170
86Top-90
86TopSti-110
86TopTat-19
86TopTif-90
87Don-141
87DonOpeD-150
87Fle-432
87FleGlo-432
87Lea-63
87OPC-325
87PadBohHB-1
87Top-325
87TopSti-110
87TopTif-325
88Don-649
88Fle-598
88FleGlo-598
88OPC-264
88PadCok-1
88PadSmo-28
88PanSti-409
88RedFolSB-89
88Sco-189
88ScoGlo-189
88Top-640
88TopSti-113
88TopTif-640
89Bow-455
89BowTif-455
89Don-483
89DonBasB-154
89Fle-319
89FleGlo-319
89PadCok-18
89PadMag-19
89PanSti-202
89Sco-176
89Top-121
89TopBig-328
89TopTif-121
89UppDec-297
90Bow-215
90BowTif-215
90Don-246
90DonBesN-133
90Fle-170
90FleCan-170
90Lea-102
90OPC-481
90PadCok-19
90PadMag-14
90PanSti-354
90PubSti-60
90Sco-336
90Top-481
90TopBig-177
90TopTif-481
90UppDec-288
91Don-252
91Fle-546
91OPC-253
91PanFreS-94
91Sco-117
91ScoPro-117
91ScoRoo-38T
91StaClu-72
91Top-253
91TopDesS-253
91TopMic-253
91TopTif-253
91TopTra-118T
91TopTraT-118T
91Ult-312
91UppDec-295
92OPC-772
92Sco-588
92Top-772
92TopGol-772
92TopGolW-772
92TopMic-772
92UppDec-411
Tena, Dario
94AugGreC-24
94AugGreF-3022
Tena, Paulino
90WatIndS-21
91KinIndC-21
91KinIndP-333
Tenace, Gene
70OPC-21
70Top-21
71MLBOffS-528
71OPC-338
71Top-338
72'sA'sPos-23
72OPC-189
72Top-189
73OPC-203
73OPC-206
73OPC-360
73OPC-524
73Top-203
73Top-206
73Top-360
73Top-524
74A'sPos-55
74OPC-79
74Top-79
74TopSta-230
75Hos-64
75HosTwi-64
75OPC-535
75Top-535
76Hos-122
76OPC-165
76SSP-493
76Top-165
77BurCheD-131
77Hos-141
77OPC-82
77PadSchC-56
77PepGloD-39
77RCColC-63
77Spo-5202
77Top-303
78Hos-125
78OPC-35
78PadFamF-32
78RCColC-4
78TasDis-20
78Top-240
78WifBalD-74
79Hos-19
79OPC-226
79Top-435
80OPC-355
80Top-704
81Car5x7-26
81Don-241
81Fle-489
81OPC-29
81Top-29
81TopTra-842
82Don-152
82Fle-132
82FleSta-26
82OPC-166
82Top-631
83Don-442
83Fle-25
83OPC-252
83Top-515
83TopTra-110T
84Don-264
84Fle-266
84Nes792-729
84Top-729
84TopTif-729
86A'sGreT-1
86AstPol-26
87A'sMot-14
87AstMot-27
87AstPol-26

90BluJayFS-29
91BluJayFS-26
91BluJayFS-28
93BluJayFS-30
96BluJayOH-31
97BluJayS-28
Tenacen, Francisco
86TamTarP-23
87VerRedP-4
88WinSpiS-20
89WinSpiS-16
Tenbarge, Jeffrey
92AubAstC-4
92AubAstF-1353
93AshTouC-20
93AshTouF-2275
Tenenini, Bob
79MemChiT-15
80MemChiT-23
83MemChiT-17
Tener, John
87OldJudN-503
89EdgR.WG-15
Tenhunfeld, Joe
88BatCliP-1679
90ClePhiS-21
Tennant, Mike
77LodDodT-21
79AlbDukT-2
Tenney, Fred
03BreE10-140
03WilCarE-27
06FanCraNL-46
08AmeCarE-31
08AmeCarE-64
08RosComP-133
09AmeCarE-107
09RamT20-116
09T206-353
10DarChoE-31
10E98-25
11SpoLifCW-349
11SpoLifM-221
11TurRedT-122
12HasTriFT-51
12HasTriFT-69
98CamPepP-78
Tenney, Mickey
81QuaCitCT-8
Tepedino, Frank
70Top-689
71OPC-342
71Top-342
73SyrChiTI-27
74OPC-526
74Top-526
75OPC-9
75Top-9
81TCM60I-469
92YanWIZ6-124
92YanWIZ7-148
94BreMilB-81
Tepper, Marc
89MiaMirIS-19
89Sta-185
89WatIndS-21
90KinIndTI-11
91KinIndC-22
91KinIndP-334
Teramae, Masao
96HonShaHWB-18
Terhune, Mike
96DanBraB-25
Terilli, Joey
91GenCubC-21
91GenCubP-4232
92MidLeaATI-45
92PeoChiC-6
92PeoChiTI-27
93DayCubC-19
93DayCubF-871
94DayCubC-23
94DayCubF-2367
Terlecky, Greg
75TulOil7-15
76SSP-299
77Top-487
78SprRedWK-20
Terpko, Jeff
72Dia-45
77ExpPos-30
77Top-137
93RanKee-354
Terrazas, Marc
82HolMilT-24
83RedPioT-31

Terrell, James
91BelMarC-6
91BelMarP-3681
92PenPilC-26
92PenPilF-2946
Terrell, Jerry
74OPC-481
74Top-481
75OPC-654
75TacTwiK-3
75Top-654
76OPC-159
76SSP-222
76Top-159
77Top-513
78Roy-22
78SSP270-243
78Top-525
79RoyTeal-10
79Top-273
80Top-98
87Ft.MyeRP-29
91PacSenL-8
Terrell, Matt
93PitMetC-22
93PitMetF-3725
94St.LucMC-24
94St.LucMF-1209
95StLucMTI-31
Terrell, Walt
81TulDriT-12
82TidTidT-24
83TidTidT-12
84Don-640
84Fle-601
84Nes792-549
84Top-549
84TopSti-110
84TopTif-549
85Don-597
85Fle-94
85FleUpd-118
85OPC-287
85Top-287
85TopMin-287
85TopSti-109
85TopTif-287
85TopTifT-119T
85TopTra-119T
86Don-247
86Fle-240
86Lea-123
86OPC-301
86TigCaiD-18
86Top-461
86TopMinL-16
86TopTif-461
87Don-275
87Fle-165
87FleGlo-165
87Lea-180
87OPC-72
87TigCaiD-16
87TigCok-3
87Top-72
87TopTif-72
88Don-91
88DonBasB-293
88Fle-72
88FleGlo-72
88FleMin-24
88FleStiC-28
88OPC-284
88PanSti-87
88RedFolSB-90
88Sco-538
88ScoGlo-538
88TigPep-35
88TigPol-12
88Top-668
88TopTif-668
89Bow-445
89BowTif-445
89Don-296
89DonBasB-245
89DonTra-28
89Fle-149
89FleGlo-149
89PadCok-19
89Sco-314
89ScoRoo-75T
89Top-127
89TopTif-127
89TopTra-117T
89TopTraT-117T
89UppDec-475
89UppDec-703
90Bow-165
90BowTif-165
90Don-309
90Fle-457
90FleCan-457
90OPC-611
90PirHomC-28
90PubSti-61
90Sco-463
90Top-611
90TopTif-611
90TulDriDGB-11
90UppDec-661
91Don-717
91MetWIZ-401
91OPC-328
91Sco-801
91StaClu-315
91TigCok-35
91Top-328
91TopDesS-328
91TopMic-328
91TopTif-328
91UppDec-320
92Don-565
92Fle-146
92OPC-722
92Pin-190
92Sco-355
92StaClu-139
92Top-722
92TopGol-722
92TopGolW-722
92TopMic-722
92UppDec-520
92YanWIZ8-189
93Don-772
93Fle-612
93StaClu-223
93StaCluFDI-223
93StaCluMOP-223
Terrill, James
87EveGiaC-19
88CliGiaP-702
89SanJosGB-4
89SanJosGCLC-218
89SanJosGP-449
89SanJosGS-24
91LinDriAA-543
91SanAntMLD-543
91SanAntMP-2974
Terrio, Tim
89BakDodCLC-208
89CalLeaA-26
Terris, Adam
89RocExpLC-28
90WesPalBES-24
Terry, Adonis (William H.)
87OldJudN-504
90DodTar-1084
98CamPepP-79
Terry, Bill (William Harold)
25Exh-40
26Exh-40
27YorCarE-46
28PorandAR-A35
28PorandAR-B35
28W502-46
28W513-67
28Yue-46
29ExhFou-9
29PorandAR-88
31Exh-10
31W517-23
32R33So2-405
32USCar-4
33ButCre-25
33CraJacP-22
33DelR33-4
33GeoCMil-29
33Gou-20
33Gou-125
33GouCanV-20
33NatLeaAC-16
33RitCE-10D
34BatR31-6
34DiaStaR-14
34ExhFou-5
34Gou-21
34GouCanV-53
35ExhFou-5
35GouPuzR-1K
35GouPuzR-3B
35GouPuzR-14B
35GouPuzR-15B
36ExhFou-5
36R31Pre-G14
36WorWidGV-7
37KelPepS-BB14
38OurNatGPP-29
50CalHOFW-69
60Fle-52
61Fle-142
61GolPre-5
67TopVen-161
76RowExh-12
76ShaPiz-73
77BobParHoF-47
77GalGloG-112
77GalGloG-204
77GalGloG-250
79DiaGre-30
80GiaGreT-7
80Lau300-7
80PacLeg-9
80PerHaloFP-73
80SSPHOF-73
81ConTSN-7
81SpoHaloF-17
82DiaCla-38
83ConMar-29
85FegMurCG-19
86ConSer1-31
87HygAllG-43
88ConNatA-20
88ConSer3-28
89HOFStiB-2
89PerCelP-41
91ConTSN-64
91ConTSNP-661
92ConTSN-588
92ConTSNAP-661G
93ConTSN-661
93ConTSN-841
94ConTSN-1100
94ConTSNB-1100
Terry, Brent
88SalLakCTTI-6
Terry, Brett
88UtiBluSP-3
Terry, Ralph
57Top-391
58A'sJayP-9
58Top-169
59Top-358
60Top-96
60TopVen-96
61Top-389
61Yan61RL-12
62Jel-10
62Pos-10
62PosCan-10
62SalPlaC-77
62ShiPlaC-77
62Top-48
62TopVen-48
63Baz-20
63Fle-26
63Jel-20
63Kah-29
63Pos-20
63SalMetC-38
63Top-8
63Top-10
63Top-148
63Top-315
63TopStil-43
63YanJayP-11
64ChatheY-23
64Top-458
64YanJayP-11
64YanReqKP-18
65Kah-39
65Top-406
66OPC-109
66Top-109
66TopRubl-92
66TopVen-109
67OPC-59
67Top-59
78TCM60I-168
81TCM60I-480
83YanASFY-47
88PacLegl-64
89SweBasG-31
91MetWIZ-402
91RinPos1Y2-6
92YanWIZ6-125
92YanWIZA-82
Terry, Scott Ray
81CedRapRT-18
82CedRapRT-23
83TamTarT-23
87NasSouTI-20
87Top-453
87TopTif-453
88CarSmo-8
88Don-647
88FleUpd-121
88FleUpdG-121
88LouRedBTI-47
88TopTra-119T
88TopTraT-119T
89CarSmo-21
89Don-397
89Fle-464
89FleGlo-464
89Sco-397
89Top-686
89TopBig-31
89TopTif-686
90CarSmo-23
90CedRapRDGB-7
90Don-418
90Fle-261
90FleCan-261
90Lea-234
90OPC-82
90PubSti-229
90Sco-235
90Top-82
90TopTif-82
90TopTVCa-19
90UppDec-260
91CarPol-37
91Fle-647
91OPC-539
91Sco-247
91StaClu-469
91Top-539
91TopDesS-539
91TopMic-539
91TopTif-539
92CarPol-20
92Don-655
92Fle-593
92OPC-117
92Sco-219
92StaClu-522
92Top-117
92TopGol-117
92TopGolW-117
92TopMic-117
92UppDec-688
96TulDriTI-25
Terry, Tony
94BilMusF-3684
94BilMusSP-13
94SigRooDP-38
94SigRooDPS-38
94StaCluDP-23
94StaCluDPFDI-23
95Bow-105
Terry, Yank
42RedSoxTI-23
43RedSoxTI-24
Terry, Zeb
16ColE13-171
17HolBreD-103
20GasAmeMBD-26
21E121So1-105
21E121So8-95
22W575-136
23W501-58
27YorCarE-46
Terwilliger, Wayne
49W725AngTI-27
50Bow-114
51Bow-175
51TopRedB-14
52Top-7
53Bri-22
53Top-159

54Top-73
55Top-34
55TopDouH-131
56Top-73
59Top-496
60Lea-134
60Top-26
60TopVen-26
75LynRanT-18
76AshTouT-20
77AshTouT-23
79AshTouT-5
80TulDriT-24
83RanAffF-NNO
83TopRep5-7
84RanJarP-NNO
85RanPer-NNO
86TwiTeal-32
88TwiTeal-30
90DodTar-794
91TopArc1-159
93RanKee-44
94TopArc1-73
94TopArc1G-73
95TopArcBD-2

Terzarial, Anthony
88BilMusP-1811
90CedRapRB-10
90CedRapRP-2333

Teske, David
92PitMetF-3296

Tesmer, Jim
87LitFalMP-2407
89PitMetS-28

Tesreau, Jeff (Charles)
09SpoNewSM-92
14B18B-72
14CraJacE-44
15CraJacE-44
15SpoNewM-175
16BF2FP-82
16ColE13-172
16FleBreD-96
16SpoNewM-173
81ConTSN-46
88ConSer3-29
92ConTSN-340

Tessicini, David
93EveGiaC-27
93EveGiaF-3780
94CliLumF-1990
94EveGiaC-28
94EveGiaF-3663
94CliLumC-23

Tessmer, Jay
96Exc-95
96TamYanY-25
97Bow-313
97BowInt-313

Teston, Phil
80PenPilBT-1
80PenPilCT-1

Teter, Craig
90SouBenWSB-11
90SouBenWSGS-26
90UtiBluSP-11

Teter, Doug
93FayGenC-28
94JamJamC-30
96LakTigB-4

Tettleton, Mickey
84AlbA'sT-22
85A'sMot-11
85FleUpd-119
85TopTifT-120T
85TopTra-120T
86A'sMot-11
86Don-345
86Fle-432
86Top-457
86TopTif-457
87Don-349
87DonOpeD-23
87Fle-407
87FleGlo-407
87Top-649
87TopTif-649
88Don-103
88OriFreB-14
88RocRedWC-21
88RocRedWP-202
88RocRedWTI-23
88Sco-269
88ScoGlo-269
88ScoRoo-31T
88ScoRooG-31T
88StaLinAs-17
88Top-143
88TopTif-143
88TopTra-120T
88TopTraT-120T
89Don-401
89DonBasB-86
89Fle-623
89FleGlo-623
89OriFreB-14
89PanSti-259
89Sco-358
89Top-521
89TopBig-198
89TopSti-231
89TopTif-521
89UppDec-553
89UppDecS-1
90AlbDecGB-31
90Bow-254
90BowTif-254
90ClaBlu-39
90Don-5
90Don-169
90DonBesA-15
90DonSupD-5
90Fle-190
90FleAll-12
90FleCan-190
90Hot50PS-45
90K-M-24
90Lea-65
90MLBBasB-111
90OPC-275
90PanSti-8
90PubSti-587
90RedFolSB-94
90Sco-322
90Sco100S-9
90Spo-171
90Top-275
90TopCoi-30
90TopGloS-57
90TopSti-237
90TopStiB-57
90TopTif-275
90TopTVA-24
90UppDec-60A
90UppDec-60B
90UppDec-297
91Bow-140
91CadEllD-56
91Cla2-T62
91Don-597
91Fle-494
91FleUpd-24
91Lea-322
91OPC-385
91OriCro-454
91PanFreS-239
91Sco-270
91ScoRoo-25T
91SimandSMLBL-43
91StaClu-412
91Stu-58
91TigCok-20
91Top-385
91TopDesS-385
91TopMic-385
91TopTif-385
91TopTra-119T
91TopTraT-119T
91UltUpd-24
91UppDec-296
91UppDec-729
92Bow-117
92ClaGam-89
92Don-85
92Fle-147
92FleAll-9
92FleLumC-L2
92Lea-285
92OPC-29
92PanSti-104
92Pin-226
92Sco-134
92StaClu-195
92Stu-178
92Top-29
92TopGol-29
92TopGolW-29
92TopMic-29
92TriPla-44
92Ult-63
92UltAllS-5
92UppDec-251
93Bow-615
93DiaMar-107
93Don-13
93DonSpiotG-SG10
93Fin-80
93FinRef-80
93Fla-208
93Fle-234
93FleFruotL-60
93FunPac-189
93Lea-213
93MetBak-37
93OPC-334
93PacSpa-114
93PanSti-113
93Pin-52
93PinHomRC-18
93PinSlu-22
93Sco-60
93Sel-60
93SP-240
93StaClu-31
93StaCluFDI-31
93StaCluMOP-31
93Stu-138
93TigGat-23
93Top-135
93TOPBLAG-41
93TopGol-135
93TopInaM-135
93TopMic-135
93TriPla-92
93Ult-554
93UppDec-46
93UppDec-86
93UppDecGold-46
93UppDecGold-86
93USPlaCA-6C
94Bow-125
94ChuShoS-10
94ColC-275
94ColChoGS-275
94ColChoSS-275
94Don-44
94DonSpeE-44
94ExtBas-80
94Fin-281
94FinRef-281
94Fla-295
94Fle-143
94FUnPac-20
94FUnPac-187
94Lea-279
94LeaL-33
94OPC-32
94Pac-229
94PacGolP-8
94PanSti-68
94Pin-67
94PinArtP-67
94PinMusC-67
94PinRunC-RC19
94ProMag-48
94Sco-51
94ScoGolR-51
94Sel-331
94SP-180
94SPDieC-180
94Spo-131
94StaClu-192
94StaCluFDI-192
94StaCluGR-192
94StaCluMOP-192
94Stu-193
94Top-495
94TopGol-495
94TopSpa-495
94TriPla-248
94TriPlaM-1
94TriPlaM-6
94Ult-357
94UppDec-301
94UppDecED-301
95Baz-101
95Bow-433
95ColCho-474
95ColCho-570T
95ColChoGS-474
95ColChoSE-221
95ColChoSEGS-221
95ColChoSESS-221
95ColChoSS-474
95Don-537
95DonPreP-537
95DonTopotO-168
95Emb-121
95EmbGolI-121
95Fin-107
95Fin-266
95FinRef-107
95FinRef-266
95Fla-311
95Fle-61
95FleAllS-15
95FleUpd-87
95Lea-363
95LeaLim-88
95Pac-160
95Pin-375
95PinArtP-375
95PinMusC-375
95RanCra-31
95Sco-78
95ScoGolR-78
95ScoHaloG-HG49
95ScoPlaTS-78
95Sel-222
95SelArtP-222
95SP-194
95Spo-137
95SpoArtP-137
95SPSil-194
95StaClu-34
95StaClu-540
95StaCluFDI-34
95StaCluMOP-34
95StaCluMOP-540
95StaCluSTWS-34
95StaCluSTWS-540
95StaCluVR-23
95Top-612
95TopCyb-380
95TopTra-50T
95UppDec-479T
96ColCho-346
96ColChoCtG-CG29
96ColChoCtG-CG29B
96ColChoCtG-CG29C
96ColChoCtGE-CR29
96ColChoCtGG-CG29
96ColChoCtGG-CG29B
96ColChoCtGG-CG29C
96ColChoCtGGE-CR29
96ColChoGS-346
96ColChoSS-346
96Don-72
96DonPreP-72
96EmoXL-128
96Fin-B166
96FinRef-B166
96Fla-179
96Fle-263
96FleRan-15
96FleTif-263
96Lea-167
96LeaPrePB-167
96LeaPrePG-167
96LeaPrePS-167
96MetUni-117
96MetUniP-117
96Pac-422
96PacPri-P139
96PacPriG-P139
96PanSti-236
96RanMot-7
96Sco-388
96SP-176
96StaClu-98
96StaCluEPB-98
96StaCluEPG-98
96StaCluEPS-98
96StaCluMOP-98
96StaCluVRMO-23
96Top-286
96TopGal-21
96TopGalPPI-21
96Ult-141
96UltGolM-141
96UppDec-465
97ColCho-490
97Don-84
97DonPreP-84
97DonPrePGold-84
97Fle-232
97FleTif-232
97Lea-62
97LeaFraM-62
97LeaFraMDC-62
97MetUni-169
97Pac-211
97PacLigB-211
97PacSil-211
97Sco-2
97ScoPreS-2
97ScoRan-1
97ScoRanPl-1
97ScoRanPr-1
97ScoShoS-2
97ScoShoSAP-2
97StaClu-297
97StaCluMOP-297
97Top-162
97TopChr-64
97TopChrR-64
97TopGal-27
97TopGalPPI-27
97Ult-389
97UltGolME-389
97UltPlaME-389
97UppDec-506

Teufel, Tim
82OrlTwi8SCT-9
82OrlTwiT-12
83TolMudHT-16
84Don-37
84Fle-574
84MinTwiP-28
84TopTra-117T
84TopTraT-117T
84TwiTeal-8
85AllGamPI-16
85Don-192
85Fle-290
85Lea-97
85OPC-239
85Top-239
85TopMin-239
85TopSti-303
85TopTif-239
85Twi7-10
85TwiTeal-8
86BasStaB-114
86Don-242
86Fle-407
86FleUpd-110
86MetColP-26
86MetTCM-23
86MetWorSC-25
86OPC-91
86Top-667
86TopSti-280
86TopTif-667
86TopTra-109T
86TopTraT-109T
87Don-581
87DonOpeD-131
87Fle-24
87FleGlo-24
87MetColP-21
87Top-158
87TopTif-158
88Don-648
88DonTeaBM-648
88Fle-152
88FleGlo-152
88MetColP-10
88MetKah-11
88PanSti-342
88Sco-128
88ScoGlo-128
88StaLinMe-19
88Top-508
88TopTif-508
89Bow-382
89BowTif-382
89Don-507
89Fle-50
89FleGlo-50
89MetColP-18
89MetKah-28
89Sco-58
89Top-9
89TopDouM-11
89TopTif-9
89UppDec-277
90Don-618
90Fle-218
90FleCan-218

90Lea-383
90MetColP-10
90MetKah-11
90OPC-764
90PubSti-146
90Sco-501
90Top-764
90TopTif-764
90TopTVM-29
90UppDec-492
91Don-370
91Fle-162
91FleUpd-127
91Lea-314
91MetColP-10
91MetKah-11
91MetWIZ-403
91OPC-302
91PadSmo-36
91Sco-427
91ScoRoo-67T
91StaClu-43
91Top-302
91TopDesS-302
91TopMic-302
91TopTif-302
91TopTra-120T
91TopTraT-120T
91UltUpd-114
91UppDec-370
92Don-171
92Fle-622
92Lea-261
92OPC-413
92PadCarJ-22
92PadMot-17
92PadPolD-24
92PadSmo-35
92Pin-313
92Sco-234
92StaClu-485
92Stu-110
92Top-413
92TopGol-413
92TopGolW-413
92TopMic-413
92TriPla-255
92Ult-585
92UppDec-349
93Don-98
93Fle-525
93Lea-10
93PacSpa-266
93PadMot-6
93Pin-183
93Sco-480
93StaClu-213
93StaCluFDI-213
93StaCluMOP-213
93Top-636
93TopGol-636
93TopInaM-636
93TopMic-636
93TriPla-183
93UppDec-61
93UppDecGold-61
94Don-272
94Fle-676
94Pac-535
94StaClu-46
94StaCluFDI-46
94StaCluGR-46
94StaCluMOP-46
94Top-254
94TopGol-254
94TopSpa-254

Teutsch, Mark
79AppFoxT-15
80GleFalWSBT-13
80GleFalWSCT-3
81EdmTraRR-24
82GleFalWST-23

Tevlin, Creighton J.
77RocRedWM-17
78SpoIndC-12
79VanCanT-23A
81SyrChiTI-19
82SyrChiT-22
82SyrChiTI-21

Tewell, Terry
90MarPhiP-3202
91ClePhiC-14
91ClePhiP-1625
92ClePhiC-15
92ClePhiF-2060

Tewksbury, Bob
84NasSouTI-22
85AlbYanT-11
86DonRoo-8
86FleUpd-111
86TopTra-110T
86TopTraT-110T
86YanTCM-16
87ColCliT-9
87Don-422
87Fle-117
87FleGlo-117
87SpoTeaP-7
87Top-254
87TopTif-254
88IowCubC-5
88IowCubP-534
88Top-593
88TopTif-593
89LouRedBC-11
89LouRedBP-1250
89LouRedBTI-35
90AlbDecGB-13
90Don-714
90Lea-406
90LouRedBLBC-40
90TopTra-122T
90TopTraT-122T
90TopTVCa-20
91Bow-394
91CarPol-39
91Don-183
91Fle-648
91Lea-460
91OPC-88
91PanSti-36
91Sco-499
91StaClu-417
91Top-88
91TopDesS-88
91TopMic-88
91TopTif-88
91UppDec-630
92CarPol-21
92Don-201
92Fle-594
92Lea-95
92OPC-623
92Pin-219
92Pin-288
92Sco-282
92StaClu-258
92Top-623
92TopGol-623
92TopGolW-623
92TopMic-623
92Ult-573
92UppDec-512
92YanWIZ8-190
93Bow-248
93CarPol-21
93ClaGam-91
93Don-204
93DonDiaK-DK22
93Fin-193
93FinRef-193
93Fla-129
93Fle-134
93FunPac-79
93Lea-44
93OPC-344
93PacSpa-304
93PanSti-190
93Pin-13
93Sco-34
93Sel-107
93SelAce-15
93SelStaL-83
93SelStaL-89
93SP-80
93StaClu-341
93StaCluCa-10
93StaCluFDI-341
93StaCluM-66
93StaCluMOP-341
93Top-285
93TopComotH-27
93TopGol-285
93TopInaM-285
93TopMic-285
93TriPla-156
93Ult-114
93UppDec-318
93UppDecGold-318
94Bow-264
94BowBes-R65
94BowBesR-R65
94CarPol-21
94ColC-468
94ColChoGS-468
94ColChoSS-468
94Don-262
94ExtBas-364
94ExtBasPD-8
94Fin-42
94FinRef-42
94Fla-431
94Fle-647
94FUnPac-58
94Lea-333
94OPC-217
94Pac-605
94PanSti-249
94Pin-452
94PinArtP-452
94PinMusC-452
94Sco-56
94ScoGolR-56
94Sel-83
94SP-66
94SPDieC-66
94StaClu-586
94StaCluFDI-586
94StaCluGR-586
94StaCluMOP-586
94StaCluT-312
94StaCluTFDI-312
94Stu-55
94Top-473
94TopGol-473
94TopSpa-473
94TriPla-67
94Ult-272
94UppDec-353
94UppDecED-353
95ColCho-187
95ColCho-571T
95ColChoGS-187
95ColChoSE-78
95ColChoSEGS-78
95ColChoSESS-78
95ColChoSS-187
95Don-480
95DonPreP-480
95DonTopotO-169
95Fin-280
95FinRef-280
95Fla-312
95Fle-510
95FleTeaL-26
95FleUpd-88
95Lea-392
95Pac-417
95Pin-236
95PinArtP-236
95PinMusC-236
95RanCra-32
95Sco-167
95ScoGolR-167
95ScoPlaTS-167
95StaClu-41
95StaClu-612
95StaCluFDI-41
95StaCluMOP-41
95StaCluMOP-612
95StaCluSTWS-41
95StaCluSTWS-612
95StaCluVR-30
95Top-195
95TopCyb-111
95TopTra-96T
95Ult-433
95UltGolM-433
95UppDec-57
95UppDecED-57
95UppDecEDG-57
96ColCho-347
96ColCho-782
96ColChoGS-347
96ColChoSS-347
96Don-423
96DonPreP-423
96EmoXL-283
96Fin-B292
96FinRef-B292
96Fla-381
96Fle-264
96FleTif-264
96FleUpd-U200
96FleUpdTC-U200
96Pac-428
96PadMot-11
96Sco-141
96StaCluVRMO-30
96Top-387
96Ult-562
96UltGolM-562
97ColCho-378
97Fle-470
97Fle-643
97FleTif-470
97FleTif-643
97StaClu-111
97StaCluMOP-111
97Top-219
97Ult-369
97UltGolME-369
97UltPlaME-369

Texidor, Esteban
78HolMilT-22

Texidor, Jose
91ButCopKSP-26
91ChaRanC-25
91ChaRanP-1329
92GasRanC-9
92GasRanF-2267
93ChaRanC-22
93ChaRanF-1954
94ChaRanF-2510
95TulDriTI-23
96BesAutS-88
96BesAutSA-76
96TulDriTI-26

Thacker, Moe
59Top-474
61CubJayP-11
61Top-12
62Top-546

Thatcher, Aaron
92FroRowDP-25

Thayer, Ernest
90BasWit-98

Thayer, Greg
75TacTwiK-15
77OrlTwiT-21
78TwiFriP-20
79TolMudHT-16

Thayer, Scott
78GreBraT-24

Thebo, Antonio
09T206-519

Thees, Michael
91SouOreAC-26
91SouOreAP-3845

Theil, Mark
77ForLauYS-5

Theilman, Harry
06FanCraNL-47

Theisen, Mike
86St.PetCP-29

Theiss, Duane
78RicBraT-16
79RicBraT-16
80AndBraT-3

Thelen, Jeffrey John
90Bes-149
90KenTwiB-26
90KenTwiP-2295
90KenTwiS-24
91KenTwiC-18
91KenTwiP-2076
92VisOakC-9
92VisOakF-1016
93ForMyeMC-25
93ForMyeMF-2657

Theobald, Ron
72OPC-77
72Top-77
94BreMilB-183

Theodile, Robert
94HicCraC-22
94HicCraF-2177
96PriWilCB-26

Theodore, George
73LinPor-125
74MetDaiPA-2
74MetJapEB-10
74OPC-99
74Top-8
75TidTidTI-22
89TidTidC-8
91MetWIZ-404

Theron, Greg
93BelMarC-27
93BelMarF-3208
94AppFoxC-19
94AppFoxF-1054

Therrien, Dominic
91IdaFalBP-4342
91PulBraP-4021
92MacBraF-277
93CarLeaAGF-39
93DurBulC-21
93DurBulF-494
93DurBulTI-13
94ExcFS7-161

Therrien, Ed
88CapCodPPaLP-4

Thevenow, Tom J.
28W56PlaC-S8
31Exh-13
33ExhFou-7
33Gou-36
33GouCanV-36
34DiaMatCSB-180
34ExhFou-7
35DiaMatCS2-20
35DiaMatCS3T1-139
35GouPuzR-4B
35GouPuzR-7B
35GouPuzR-12B
91ConTSN-69

Thibault, Ryan
90SpoIndSP-25
91WatDiaC-9
91WatDiaP-1256
92HigDesMC-21
93BelBreC-24
93BelBreF-1710

Thibert, John
90TamYanD-26
92GreHorC-10
92OneYanC-16
94LakElsSC-22
94LakElsSF-1665
95MidAngOHP-34

Thibodeau, John
69OPC-189
69Top-189
69TopFou-14

Thibodeaux, Keith
82BufBisT-8
83LynPirT-8

Thielen, D.J.
91EveGiaC-1
91EveGiaP-3925
92CliGiaC-21
92CliGiaF-3607
93Bow-224
93CliGiaC-22
93CliGiaF-2497
94CliLumF-1991
94SanJosGC-22
94SanJosGF-2830
94CliLumC-24

Thielker, Dave
85ChaO'sT-6

Thielman, John
09T206-472

Thienpont, Gregg
84ButCopKT-23

Thies, Dave
61UniOil-H8
77FriOneYW-53

Thies, Jake (Vernon)
55JetPos-16
55Top-12
55TopDouH-39

Thiessen, Tim
86WesPalBEP-26

Thigpen, Arthur
90NiaFalRP-25

Thigpen, Bobby
86BirBarTI-19
87Don-370
87Fle-507
87FleGlo-507
87SevCoi-C13
87SpoTeaP-26
87Top-61
87TopTif-61
87WhiSoxC-28
88Don-247
88DonBasB-235
88Fle-410

88FleGlo-410
88FleStiC-17
88FleTeaL-42
88Sco-307
88ScoGlo-307
88StaLinWS-18
88Top-613
88TopTif-613
88ToyRoo-32
88WhiSoxC-28
89Bow-55
89BowTif-55
89Don-266
89DonBasB-25
89Fle-512
89FleBasM-38
89FleGlo-512
89FleHeroB-39
89FleLeaL-39
89OPC-368
89PanSti-303
89Sco-399
89ScoHot1S-68
89ScoYouSI-29
89Spo-207
89SpoIllFKI-275
89Top-762
89TopSti-305
89TopTif-762
89TVSpoM-115
89UppDec-647
89WhiSoxC-26
89WhiSoxK-5
90BirBarDGB-30
90Bow-306
90BowTif-306
90ClaYel-T81
90Don-266
90DonBesA-32
90Fle-549
90FleBasA-40
90FleBasM-40
90FleCan-549
90FleLeaL-39
90Lea-175
90OPC-255
90PanSti-50
90PubSti-401
90RedFolSB-95
90Sco-335
90Sco-694
90Sco100S-87
90Spo-27
90Top-255
90TopBig-295
90TopMinL-12
90TopSti-297
90TopTif-255
90UppDec-269
90USPlaCA-9C
90WhiSoxC-24
91Bow-342
91Cla1-T31
91ClaGam-140
91Don-8
91Don-90
91Don-399
91DonBonC-BC20
91DonSupD-8
91Fle-137
91Fle-712
91Lea-336
91MajLeaCP-15
91MisStaB-43
91OPC-8
91OPC-396
91OPC-420
91OPCPre-120
91PanCanT1-85
91PanFreS-320
91PanSti-252
91PosCan-25
91RedFolS-92
91Sco-280
91Sco-401
91Sco-418
91Sco100S-95
91SevCoi-M13
91SimandSMLBL-44
91StaClu-256
91StaCluCM-29
91StaCluP-43
91Stu-39
91SunSee-22
91Top-8
91Top-396
91Top-420
91TopCraJI-32
91TopDesS-8
91TopDesS-396
91TopDesS-420
91TopGaloC-11
91TopMic-8
91TopMic-396
91TopMic-420
91TopTif-8
91TopTif-396
91TopTif-420
91Ult-84
91Ult-396
91UppDec-93
91UppDec-261
91WhiSoxK-37
91Woo-21
92Bow-36
92Cla2-T89
92ClaGam-100
92Don-708
92Fle-99
92Hig5-18
92Lea-210
92OPC-505
92PanSti-132
92Pin-214
92Sco-570
92Sco100S-54
92StaClu-224
92StaCluMO-34
92Stu-158
92Top-505
92TopGol-505
92TopGolW-505
92TopKid-101
92TopMic-505
92TriPla-32
92Ult-342
92UppDec-285
92WhiSoxK-37
93Bow-119
93Don-67
93Fle-589
93Lea-173
93OPC-336
93PacSpa-76
93Pin-452
93Sco-582
93Sel-232
93StaClu-575
93StaCluFDI-575
93StaCluMOP-575
93StaCluWS-20
93Top-645
93TopGol-645
93TopInaM-645
93TopMic-645
93Ult-180
93UppDec-671
93UppDecGold-671
93WhiSoxK-27
94ColC-516
94ColChoGS-516
94ColChoSS-516
94Don-273
96NasSouB-24

Thigpen, Len
89PenPilS-24

Thobe, J.J.
93ColRedC-23
93ColRedF-597
93SouAtlLAGF-15
94Bow-144
94ClaGolF-45
94ExcFS7-50
94HarSenF-2091
95SigRoo-47
95SigRooSig-47

Thobe, Steve
94WelPirC-27
94WelPirF-3504
96HonShaHWB-36
96LynHilB-24

Thobe, Tom
93MacBraC-24
93MacBraF-1400
94ClaGolF-117
94GreBraF-413
94GreBraTI-24
95RicBraRC-25
95RicBraTI-23
96RicBraB-28
96RicBraRC-17
96RicBraUB-28

Thoden, John
88CapCodPPaLP-106
89JamExpP-2157
90RocExpLC-26
90RocExpP-2686
91WesPalBEC-12
91WesPalBEP-1228
92SalLakTSP-18

Thoenen, Dick
68Top-348
68TopVen-348

Thoma, Ray
84AlbA'sT-26
85HunStaJ-19
87PitCubP-1
88PitCubP-1358
86HumStaDS-19

Thomas, Allen
96HicCraB-24

Thomas, Andres
83AndBraT-23
84DurBulT-14
85DomLeaS-175
85GreBraTI-18
86BraPol-14
86DonRoo-10
86FleUpd-112
86SpoRoo-14
86TopTra-111T
86TopTraT-111T
87BraSmo-20
87ClaGam-7
87Don-266
87DonOpeD-43
87Fle-531
87FleBasA-42
87FleGlo-531
87FleMin-105
87FleStiC-117
87SpoTeaP-24
87Top-296
87TopRoo-20
87TopSti-39
87TopSti-305
87TopTif-296
87ToyRoo-29
88Don-627
88Fle-551
88FleGlo-551
88OPC-13
88Sco-299
88ScoGlo-299
88StaLinBra-19
88Top-13
88TopBig-68
88TopSti-41
88TopTif-13
89Bow-272
89BowTif-272
89BraDub-26
89CadEllD-57
89ClaLigB-21
89Don-576
89DonBasB-197
89Fle-604
89FleGlo-604
89OPC-358
89PanSti-43
89Sco-406
89ScoYouS2-35
89Top-171
89Top-523
89TopSti-26
89TopTif-171
89TopTif-523
89UppDec-144
90BraDubP-28
90BraDubS-32
90Don-263
90Fle-597
90FleCan-597
90Lea-33
90OPC-358
90PanSti-229
90PubSti-126
90Sco-99
90Top-358
90TopSti-33
90TopTif-358
90UppDec-212
91Don-491
91Fle-706
91OPC-111
91Sco-613
91Top-111
91TopDesS-111
91TopMic-111
91TopTif-111
91UppDec-384
92PhoFirS-396

Thomas, Bill
83ArkTraT-7

Thomas, Brad
96GreFalDB-27
96GreFalDTI-15

Thomas, Brian
94ChaRanF-2511
94FloStaLAF-FSL4
95TulDriTI-24
96OklCit8B-22

Thomas, Bud (Luther)
39PlaBal-158
40PlaBal-42

Thomas, C.L.
88BilMusP-1823

Thomas, Carey
91Cla/Bes-281

Thomas, Carl
77FriOneYW-115
87KenTwiP-18

Thomas, Carlos
91YakBeaC-28
91YakBeaP-4249
92YakBeaF-3448
93BakDodCLC-23
94BakDodC-23
94SanAntMF-2469

Thomas, Chris
80WisRapTT-11
83VerBeaDT-11
92AubAstC-3
92AubAstF-1368
93HelBreSP-8

Thomas, Claude
12T207-182

Thomas, Clinton Cyrus
86NegLeaF-33
89RinPosNL1-3

Thomas, Corey
89MarPhiS-30
91SouAtlLAGP-SAL45
91SpaPhiC-20
91SpaPhiP-905
92ClePhiF-2067

Thomas, Danny
77FriOneYW-100
77Top-488
94BreMilB-184

Thomas, Dave
81HolMilT-5

Thomas, Delvin
90PenPilS-22
91SanBerSC-21
91SanBerSP-1998

Thomas, Dennis
82ReaPhiT-9
83ReaPhiT-9

Thomas, Deron
82SprCarF-21
83St.PetCT-19
84ArkTraT-4

Thomas, Derrel
72OPC-457
72PadTeal-26
72Top-457
73OPC-57
73Top-57
74OPC-518
74PadDea-25
74Top-518
75Gia-9
75OPC-378
75Top-378
76OPC-493
76SSP-106
76Top-493
77PadSchC-57A
77PadSchC-57B
77Top-266
78PadFamF-33
78Top-194
79OPC-359
79Top-679
80DodPol-30
80OPC-9
80Top-23
81Dod-11
81DodPol-30
81Don-419
81Fle-123
81LonBeaPT-18
81OPC-211
81Top-211
82DodPol-30
82DodUniOV-23
82Don-537
82Fle-26
82Top-348
83DodPol-30
83DodPos-17
83Fle-223
83Top-748
84Don-397
84ExpPos-32
84ExpStu-28
84Fle-114
84FleUpd-116
84Nes792-583
84Top-583
84TopTif-583
84TopTra-118T
84TopTraT-118T
85Fle-314
85OPC-317
85Top-448
85TopTif-448
85TopTifT-121T
85TopTra-121T
86Top-158
86TopTif-158
89PacSenL-64
89T/MSenL-104
89TopSenL-55
90DodTar-795
90EliSenL-90
91PacSenL-87

Thomas, Derrick
91StaCluCM-40

Thomas, Don
74GasRanT-23
75LynRanT-19
76SacSolC-16

Thomas, Don G.
76SanAntBTI-23

Thomas, Duane
92BluOriC-11
92BluOriF-2372
93AlbPolF-2040

Thomas, Eric
75AppFoxT-26

Thomas, Evan
96BatCliTI-10

Thomas, Fay
35DiaMatCS3T1-140
90DodTar-796

Thomas, Frank Edward
84OCoandSI-235
87PanAmTURB-23
88CapCodPB-14
88CapCodPPaLP-126
90Bes-1
90Bes-318
90BirBarB-1
90BirBarP-1116
90Bow-320
90BowTif-320
90ClaYel-T93
90CMC-818
90FleUpd-87
90Lea-300
90OPC-414
90ProAaA-46
90Sco-663
90ScoRoo-86T
90Top-414A
90Top-414B
90TopMag-48
90TopTif-414
90WhiSoxC-25
91AreHol-3
91Baz-7
91Ble23KT-1
91Ble23KT-2
91Ble23KT-3
91Bow-366
91Cla1-T32
91Cla2-T28
91ClaGam-181

91Don-477
91Fle-138
91JimDea-9
91Lea-281
91MajLeaCP-17
91OPC-79
91OPCPre-121
91RedFolS-111
91Sco-840
91Sco-874
91Sco100RS-78
91ScoHotR-4
91SevCoi-M14
91StaClu-57
91StaThoRG-1
91StaThoRG-2
91StaThoRG-3
91StaThoRG-4
91StaThoRG-5
91StaThoRG-6
91StaThoRG-7
91StaThoRG-8
91StaThoRG-9
91StaThoRG-10
91StaThoRG-11
91Stu-40
91Top-79
91TopCraJ2-20
91TopDeb90-153
91TopDesS-79
91TopMic-79
91TopRoo-28
91TopTif-79
91TopTriH-A4
91ToyRoo-27
91Ult-85
91UppDec-246
91WhiSoxK-35
91WhiSoxK-NNO
92Bow-114
92Bow-551
92Cla1-T89
92Cla2-T87
92ClaGam-106
92ColPro-15
92ColTho-1
92ColTho-2
92ColTho-3
92ColTho-4
92ColTho-5
92ColTho-6
92ColTho-7
92ColTho-8
92ColTho-9
92ColTho-10
92ColTho-11
92ColTho-12
92Don-592
92DonCraJ1-35
92DonDiaK-DK8
92DonEli-18
92DonMcD-2
92Fle-100
92Fle-701
92Fle-712
92FleAll-11
92FleCitTP-2
92FleRooS-1
92FroRowT-1
92FroRowT-2
92FroRowT-3
92FroRowT-4
92FroRowT-5
92FroRowT-6
92FroRowT-7
92FroRowTG-1
92FroRowTG-2
92FroRowTG-3
92Hig5-19
92Hig5S-29
92Hig5S-36
92JimDea-4
92KinDis-3
92Lea-67
92Lea-349
92LeaBlaG-349
92LeaGolP-16
92LeaPre-16
92MooSna-24
92MSABenSHD-11
92MTVRocnJ-2
92OPC-555
92OPCPre-59
92PanSti-125
92Pin-1
92PinSlu-11
92PinTea2-3
92PinTeaP-4
92Pos-24
92RevSup1-4
92RevSup1-5
92RevSup1-6
92Sco-505
92Sco-893
92Sco100S-51
92ScoImpP-43
92ScoProP-3
92SevCoi-16
92SpollIFK1-45
92SpollIFK1-343
92SpoStaCC-45
92StaClu-301
92StaClu-591
92StaCluMP-15
92StaPro-10
92Stu-159
92StuPre-18
92Top-555
92TopGol-555
92TopGolW-555
92TopKid-99
92TopMcD-25
92TopMic-555
92TriPla-206
92TriPlaG-GS12
92TriPlaP-6
92Ult-44
92UltAllS-9
92UppDec-87
92UppDec-166
92UppDec-SP4
92UppDecF-10
92UppDecFG-10
92UppDecHRH-HR8
92UppDecTMH-52
92UppDecWB-T19
92WhiSoxK-35
93Bow-555
93CadDis-58
93ClaGam-92
93DiaMar-108
93DiaMarA-7
93DiaMarP-8
93Don-7
93DonEliD-13
93DonEliS-19
93DonLonBL-LL10
93DonMasotG-1
93DonMVP-2
93DonPre-14
93DonSpiotG-SG6
93DonSpiotG-SG18
93DurPowP1-2
93Fin-102
93FinJum-102
93FinRef-102
93Fla-189
93Fle-210
93Fle-714
93FleAll-AL1
93FleAtl-23
93FleFruotL-61
93FleGolM-B3
93FleTeaL-AL5
93FunPac-21
93FunPac-27
93FunPac-36
93FunPac-197
93FunPac-202
93FunPac-225
93FunPacA-AS1
93Hos-13
93HumDumC-6
93JimDea-1
93KinDis-4
93Lea-195
93Lea-FT
93LeaFas-1
93LeaGolA-R12
93LeaTho-1
93LeaTho-2
93LeaTho-3
93LeaTho-4
93LeaTho-5
93LeaTho-6
93LeaTho-7
93LeaTho-8
93LeaTho-9
93LeaTho-10
93OPC-362
93OPCPreSP-1
93OPCPreSPF-1
93PacSpa-77
93PanSti-136
93Pin-108
93PinCoo-24
93PinCooD-24
93PinHomRC-17
93PinSlu-9
93PinTeaP-4
93Pos-14
93Sco-3
93Sco-510
93Sco-541
93ScoFra-4
93ScoGolDT-10
93Sel-6
93SelStaL-3
93SelStaL-13
93SelStaL-33
93SelStaL-38
93SelStaL-45
93SelStaL-49
93SP-260
93SPPlaP-PP19
93StaClu-200
93StaClu-746
93StaCluFDI-200
93StaCluFDI-746
93StaCluI-B3
93StaCluMO-26
93StaCluMOP-200
93StaCluMOP-746
93StaCluMOP-MB3
93StaCluWS-1
93Stu-139
93StuHer-8
93StuSil-1
93StuSupoC-6
93StuTho-1
93StuTho-2
93StuTho-3
93StuTho-4
93StuTho-5
93Top-150
93Top-401
93TOPBLAG-42
93TopFulS-1
93TopGol-150
93TopGol-401
93TopInaM-150
93TopInaM-401
93TopMic-150
93TopMic-401
93TopMic-P150
93TopPos-1
93TopPre-150
93Toy-66
93ToyMasP-12
93TriPla-26
93TriPla-77
93TriPlaA-21
93TriPlaN-1
93Ult-181
93UltAllS-19
93UltPer-10
93UppDec-51
93UppDec-105
93UppDec-555
93UppDecCP-R20
93UppDecDG-27
93UppDecFA-A14
93UppDecFAJ-A14
93UppDecFH-62
93UppDecGold-51
93UppDecGold-105
93UppDecGold-555
93UppDecIC-WI25
93UppDecICJ-WI25
93UppDecOD-D24
93UppDecS-19
93UppDecTriCro-TC9
93USPlaCA-8D
93WhiSoxK-28
94Bow-15
94BowBes-R55
94BowBes-X91
94BowBesR-R55
94BowBesR-X91
94BowPre-1
94ChuShoS-5
94ColC-327
94ColC-354
94ColC-500
94ColC-640
94ColChoGS-327
94ColChoGS-354
94ColChoGS-500
94ColChoGS-640
94ColChoSS-327
94ColChoSS-354
94ColChoSS-500
94ColChoSS-640
94ColChoT-1
94DenHol-25
94Don-341
94DonAwaWJ-6
94DonDiaK-DK28
94DonDom-B2
94DonEli-37
94DonLonBL-8
94DonMVP-18
94DonPro-4
94DonPro-4SE
94DonSpeE-341
94DonSpiotG-6
94ExtBas-53
94ExtBasGB-27
94Fin-203
94FinJum-203
94FinRef-203
94Fla-36
94FlaHotN-10
94FlaInfP-9
94Fle-96
94FleAllS-23
94FleAwaW-1
94FleGolM-9
94FleLumC-9
94FleSun-23
94FleTeaL-4
94FraThoC-NNO
94FUnPac-35
94FUnPac-177
94FUnPac-195
94FUnPac-204
94FUnPac-210
94FUnPac-236
94KinDis-14
94Kra-12
94Lea-400
94Lea-A300
94LeaGam-7
94LeaGolS-11
94LeaL-24
94LeaLimGA-1
94LeaMVPC-A13
94LeaMVPC-J400
94LeaMVPCG-A13
94LeaPowB-1
94LeaPro-9
94LeaSli-1
94LeaStaS-1
94OPC-127
94OPCAllR-1
94OPCJumA-1
94OscMayR-14
94Pac-138
94Pac-660
94PacGolP-3
94PacPro-P8
94PacSilP-13
94PanSti-51
94Pin-1
94PinArtP-1
94PinMusC-1
94PinPowS-PS6
94PinRunC-RC2
94PinTeaP-1
94PinTheN-1
94PinTri-TR14
94Pos-21
94PosCan-12
94PosCanG-12
94ProMag-28
94ProMagP-3
94RedFolMI-25
94Sco-41
94Sco-631
94ScoCyc-TC18
94ScoGolR-41
94ScoGolR-631
94ScoGolS-45
94Sel-6
94SelCroC-CC5
94SP-193
94SPDieC-193
94Spo-70
94Spo-176
94SpoFanA-AS1
94SpoRooGGG-GG6
94SPPre-CR5
94StaClu-267
94StaClu-285
94StaClu-528
94StaClu-718
94StaCluDD-DD9
94StaCluF-F10
94StaCluFDI-267
94StaCluFDI-285
94StaCluFDI-528
94StaCluFDI-718
94StaCluGR-267
94StaCluGR-285
94StaCluGR-528
94StaCluGR-718
94StaCluMO-29
94StaCluMOF-3
94StaCluMOP-267
94StaCluMOP-285
94StaCluMOP-528
94StaCluMOP-718
94StaCluMOP-F10
94StaCluMOP-DD9
94StaCluT-121
94StaCluTF-12
94StaCluTFDI-121
94Stu-209
94StuEdiC-2
94StuHer-2
94StuSerS-3
94TomPiz-29
94Top-270
94Top-384
94Top-601
94TopBlaG-21
94TopGol-270
94TopGol-384
94TopGol-601
94TopSpa-270
94TopSpa-384
94TopSpa-601
94TopSupS-41
94TopTraFI-7
94TriPla-269
94TriPlaBS-1
94TriPlaM-3
94TriPlaP-2
94Ult-39
94UltAllS-2
94UltAwaW-19
94UltHitM-10
94UltHomRK-3
94UltOnBL-12
94UltRBIK-2
94UppDec-55
94UppDec-284
94UppDec-300
94UppDecAJ-40
94UppDecAJG-40
94UppDecDC-C8
94UppDecED-55
94UppDecED-284
94UppDecED-300
94UppDecMLS-MM18
94UppDecMLSED-MM18
94USPlaCA-3D
94USPlaCA-11C
94WhiSoxK-27
95Baz-120
95BazRedH-RH22
95Bow-351
95BowBes-R65
95BowBes-X9
95BowBesJR-9
95BowBesR-R65
95BowBesR-X9
95ClaFanFPCP-8
95ClaPhoC-13
95ColCho-64
95ColCho-75
95ColCho-89
95ColChoCtA-8
95ColChoCtAG-8
95ColChoCtG-CG19
95ColChoCtG-CG19B
95ColChoCtG-CG19C
95ColChoCtGE-19
95ColChoCtGG-CG19
95ColChoCtGG-CG19B

95ColChoCtGG-CG19C
95ColChoCtGGE-19
95ColChoGS-64
95ColChoGS-75
95ColChoGS-89
95ColChoSE-29
95ColChoSE-235
95ColChoSEGS-29
95ColChoSEGS-235
95ColChoSESS-29
95ColChoSESS-235
95ColChoSS-64
95ColChoSS-75
95ColChoSS-89
95D3Zon-1
95Don-275
95DonAll-AL3
95DonBomS-2
95DonDiaK-DK1
95DonDom-3
95DonEli-55
95DonLonBL-1
95DonPreP-275
95DonTopotO-54
95Emb-100
95EmbGolI-100
95Emo-29
95EmoMas-9
95EmoN-10
95Fin-89
95FinPowK-PK9
95FinRef-89
95Fla-27
95FlaHotN-9
95FlaInfP-8
95FlaTodS-12
95Fle-128
95FleAllF-2
95FleAllS-2
95FleAwaW-1
95FleLumC-9
95FleTeaL-4
95FleUpdDT-9
95FleUpdH-18
95KinDis-22
95Kra-14
95Lea-1
95Lea300C-1
95LeaChe-3
95LeaCor-1
95LeaGolS-10
95LeaHeaftH-1
95LeaLim-1
95LeaLimG-1
95LeaLimIBP-1
95LeaLimL-9
95LeaOpeD-1
95LeaSli-2A
95LeaSli-2B
95LeaStaS-8
95LeaTho-1
95LeaTho-2
95LeaTho-3
95LeaTho-4
95LeaTho-5
95LeaTho-6
95NatPac-1
95Pac-97
95PacGolCDC-6
95PacGolP-19
95PacPri-31
95PanSti-39
95PanSti-113
95Pin-226
95Pin-302
95Pin-446
95Pin-450
95PinArtP-226
95PinArtP-302
95PinArtP-446
95PinArtP-450
95PinFan-13
95PinGatA-GA2
95PinMusC-226
95PinMusC-302
95PinMusC-446
95PinMusC-450
95PinPer-PP1
95PinPin-6
95PinPinR-6
95PinRedH-RH3
95PinTeaP-TP3
95PinUps-US1
95PinWhiH-WH3
95Pos-14
95PosCan-11
95RedFol-8
95Sco-1
95Sco-571
95ScoDouGC-GC1
95ScoDreT-DG1
95ScoGolR-571
95ScoHaloG-HG56
95ScoPlaTS-571
95ScoRul-SR2
95ScoRulJ-SR2
95Sel-22
95Sel-242
95Sel-250
95SelArtP-22
95SelArtP-242
95SelArtP-250
95SelBigS-BS1
95SelCer-5
95SelCerC-2
95SelCerGT-2
95SelCerMG-5
95SP-140
95SP-140A
95SPCha-136
95SPCha-140
95SPChaDC-136
95SPChaDC-140
95SPChaDFC-2
95SPChaFCDC-2
95Spo-20
95Spo-169
95SpoArtP-20
95SpoArtP-169
95SpoDet-DE4
95SpoDouT-1
95SpoHamT-HT2
95SpoPro-PM2
95SpoSam-20
95SPPlaP-PP18
95SPSil-140A
95SPSil-140B
95StaClu-47
95StaClu-236
95StaClu-318
95StaClu-400
95StaClu-513
95StaCluCC-CC4
95StaCluCT-3
95StaCluFDI-47
95StaCluFDI-236
95StaCluMO-43
95StaCluMOP-47
95StaCluMOP-236
95StaCluMOP-318
95StaCluMOP-400
95StaCluMOP-513
95StaCluMOP-CC4
95StaCluMOP-PZ11
95StaCluMOP-RL26
95StaCluMOP-VRE5
95StaCluPZ-PZ11
95StaCluRL-RL26
95StaCluSTWS-47
95StaCluSTWS-236
95StaCluSTWS-318
95StaCluSTWS-400
95StaCluSTWS-513
95StaCluVE-VRE5
95StaCluVR-209
95Stu-1
95StuGolS-1
95StuPlaS-1
95Sum-92
95Sum-175
95Sum-194
95SumBigB-BB2
95SumNthD-92
95SumNthD-175
95SumNthD-194
95TomPiz-1
95Top-1
95Top-384
95TopCyb-1
95TopFin-4
95TopLeaL-LL9
95TopLeaL-LL28
95TopLeaL-LL39
95TopTra-1T
95TopTra-156T
95TopTraPB-1
95UC3-1
95UC3-125
95UC3ArtP-1
95UC3ArtP-125
95UC3CycS-CS1
95UC3InM-IM3
95UllHomRK-10
95Ult-34
95UltAllS-19
95UltAllSGM-19
95UltAwaW-19
95UltAwaWGM-19
95UltGolM-34
95UltHitM-10
95UltHitMGM-10
95UltHomRK-2
95UltHomRKGM-2
95UltOnBL-10
95UltOnBLGM-10
95UltPowP-3
95UltPowPGM-3
95UltRBIK-4
95UltRBIKGM-4
95UltRisS-9
95UltRisSGM-9
95UppDec-105
95UppDec-435
95UppDecED-105
95UppDecED-435
95UppDecEDG-105
95UppDecEDG-435
95UppDecPAW-H5
95UppDecPAWE-H5
95UppDecPC-MLB3
95UppDecPLL-R5
95UppDecPLL-R15
95UppDecPLL-R25
95UppDecPLLE-R5
95UppDecPLLE-R15
95UppDecPLLE-R25
95UppDecSE-20
95UppDecSEG-20
95USPlaCMLA-10D
95USPlaCMLA-11C
95WhiSoxK-28
95WhiSoxK-29
95Zen-33
95ZenAllS-2
95ZenAllS-17
95ZenZ-3
96Baz-61
96Bow-54
96BowBes-13
96BowBesAR-13
96BowBesC-14
96BowBesCAR-14
96BowBesCR-14
96BowBesMI-1
96BowBesMIAR-1
96BowBesMIR-1
96BowBesP-BBP13
96BowBesPAR-BBP13
96BowBesPR-BBP13
96BowBesR-13
96Cir-29
96Cir-200
96CirAcc-4
96CirBos-6
96CirRav-29
96CirRav-200
96Cla7/1PC-2
96ColCho-90
96ColCho-105
96ColCho-412
96ColCho-759
96ColCho-764
96ColChoCtG-CG10
96ColChoCtG-CG10B
96ColChoCtG-CG10C
96ColChoCtGE-CR10
96ColChoCtGG-CG10
96ColChoCtGG-CG10B
96ColChoCtGG-CG10C
96ColChoCtGGE-CR10
96ColChoGS-90
96ColChoGS-105
96ColChoGS-412
96ColChoGS-759
96ColChoSS-90
96ColChoSS-105
96ColChoSS-412
96ColChoSS-759
96ColChoYMtP-40
96ColChoYMtP-40A
96ColChoYMtPGS-40
96ColChoYMtPGS-40A
96DenHol-3
96DenHolGS-2
96DenHolGSAP-2
96Don-1
96DonDiaK-1
96DonEli-69
96DonFreF-1
96DonHitL-9
96DonLonBL-8
96DonPowA-1
96DonPowADC-1
96DonPreP-1
96DonPurP-4
96DonRouT-9
96DonSam-1
96DonSho-1
96EmoLegoB-10
96EmoN-9
96EmoXL-42
96Fin-B48
96Fin-B322
96Fin-G186
96FinBro-6
96FinRef-B48
96FinRef-B322
96FinRef-G186
96Fla-60
96FlaDiaC-10
96FlaPow-9
96Fle-77
96FleChe-8
96FleGolM-9
96FleLumC-10
96FleRoaW-8
96FleTeaL-4
96FleTif-77
96FleUpd-U243
96FleUpd-U250
96FleUpd-10
96FleUpdH-19
96FleUpdSS-9
96FleUpdTC-U243
96FleUpdTC-U250
96FleWhiS-17
96FleZon-10
96Kin-14
96Lea-150
96LeaAllGMC-1
96LeaAllGMCG-1
96LeaGolS-1
96LeaHatO-3
96LeaLim-23
96LeaLimG-23
96LeaLimL-4
96LeaLimLB-4
96LeaLimPC-3
96LeaPicP-1
96LeaPre-13
96LeaPre-147
96LeaPreP-13
96LeaPreP-147
96LeaPrePB-150
96LeaPrePG-150
96LeaPrePS-150
96LeaPreSG-1
96LeaPreSP-8
96LeaPreSta-5
96LeaPreSte-1
96LeaSig-7
96LeaSig-150
96LeaSigA-222
96LeaSigA-NNO
96LeaSigAG-222
96LeaSigAS-222
96LeaSigEA-199
96LeaSigEA-NNO
96LeaSigEACM-29
96LeaSigPPG-7
96LeaSigPPP-7
96LeaStaS-3
96LeaThoGH-1
96LeaThoGH-2
96LeaThoGH-3
96LeaThoGH-4
96LeaThoGH-5
96LeaThoGH-6
96LeaThoGH-7
96LeaThoGH-8
96LeaTotB-1
96MetUni-40
96MetUniHM-8
96MetUniML-11
96MetUniP-40
96MetUniT-8
96Pac-287
96PacBaeS-4
96PacCraC-CC5
96PacGolCD-DC18
96PacHom-HP13
96PacPri-P91
96PacPriFB-FB18
96PacPriG-P91
96PacPriRHS-RH10
96PanSti-173
96Pin-135
96Pin-194
96Pin-201
96Pin-257
96Pin-323
96Pin-395
96Pin-399
96PinAfi-59
96PinAfi-200
96PinAfiAP-59
96PinAfiAP-200
96PinAfiFPP-59
96PinAfiMN-3
96PinAfiR-1
96PinAfiR-2
96PinAfiR-6
96PinAfiR-8
96PinAfiR-11
96PinAfiSP-5
96PinArtP-62
96PinArtP-101
96PinArtP-157
96PinArtP-198
96PinEssotG-3
96PinFan-4
96PinFirR-2
96PinFoil-201
96PinFoil-257
96PinFoil-323
96PinFoil-395
96PinFoil-399
96PinPow-1
96PinSky-2
96PinSlu-1
96PinSta-62
96PinSta-101
96PinSta-157
96PinSta-198
96PinTeaP-1
96PinTeaS-6
96Pro-15
96ProMagA-6
96ProMagDM-8
96ProSta-131
96SchDis-18
96Sco-21
96Sco-272
96Sco-373
96ScoAll-1
96ScoBigB-3
96ScoDiaA-4
96ScoDreT-2
96ScoDugC-A20
96ScoDugC-B98
96ScoDugCAP-A20
96ScoDugCAP-B98
96ScoGolS-2
96ScoNumG-2
96ScoPowP-4
96ScoRef-3
96ScoTitT-2
96Sel-11
96Sel-152
96Sel-196
96SelArtP-11
96SelArtP-152
96SelArtP-196
96SelCer-1
96SelCer-135
96SelCerAP-1
96SelCerAP-135
96SelCerCB-1
96SelCerCB-135
96SelCerCR-1
96SelCerCR-135
96SelCerIP-3
96SelCerMB-1
96SelCerMB-135
96SelCerMG-1
96SelCerMG-135
96SelCerMR-1
96SelCerMR-135
96SelCerSF-7
96SelClaTF-4

96SelEnF-2
96SelTeaN-27
96SP-60
96SPBasH-82
96SPMarM-MM15
96SPMarMDC-15
96Spo-13
96Spo-99
96SpoArtP-13
96SpoArtP-99
96SpoDouT-6
96SpoHitP-3
96SpoPowS-3
96SpoPro-7
96SPPreF-2
96SPSpeFX-35
96SPSpeFXDC-35
96SPx-16
96SPxBoufG-2
96SPxGol-16
96StaClu-182
96StaClu-285
96StaCluEPB-285
96StaCluEPG-285
96StaCluEPS-285
96StaCluMeg-MH1
96StaCluMet-M8
96StaCluMM-MM3
96StaCluMO-40
96StaCluMOP-182
96StaCluMOP-285
96StaCluMOP-M8
96StaCluMOP-MH1
96StaCluMOP-MM3
96StaCluMOP-PC8
96StaCluMOP-PP10
96StaCluMOP-PS6
96StaCluPC-PC8
96StaCluPP-PP10
96StaCluPS-PS6
96StaCluVRMO-209
96Stu-93
96StuHitP-3
96StuMas-6
96StuPrePB-93
96StuPrePG-93
96StuPrePS-93
96StuStaGS-3
96Sum-88
96Sum-157
96Sum-198
96SumAbo&B-88
96SumAbo&B-157
96SumAbo&B-198
96SumArtP-88
96SumArtP-157
96SumArtP-198
96SumBal-9
96SumBigB-1
96SumBigBM-1
96SumFoi-88
96SumFoi-157
96SumFoi-198
96SumHitI-6
96SumPos-1
96TeaOut-80
96TeaOut-C100
96Top-100
96Top-229
96TopBigC-9
96TopChr-29
96TopChr-89
96TopChrMotG-20
96TopChrMotGR-20
96TopChrR-29
96TopChrR-89
96TopChrWC-WC13
96TopChrWCR-WC13
96TopClaC-CC5
96TopGal-175
96TopGalPG-PG5
96TopGalPPI-175
96TopLas-92
96TopLasPC-6
96TopLasSS-16
96TopMasotG-20
96TopMysF-M21
96TopMysF-M26
96TopMysFR-M21
96TopMysFR-M26
96TopPro-AL9
96TopRoaW-RW16
96TopWreC-WC13
96Ult-44
96Ult-590
96UltCalttH-10
96UltCalttHGM-10
96UltChe-A9
96UltChe-B10
96UltCheGM-A9
96UltCheGM-B10
96UltDiaP-10
96UltDiaPGM-10
96UltGolM-44
96UltGolM-590
96UltHitM-9
96UltHitMGM-9
96UltHomRKGM-10
96UltHomRKR-10
96UltOn-L-9
96UltOn-LGM-9
96UltPowP-10
96UltPowPGM-10
96UltRBIK-9
96UltRBIKGM-9
96UltRes-9
96UltResGM-9
96UltSeaC-9
96UltSeaCGM-9
96UltThu-19
96UltThuGM-19
96UppDec-300
96UppDec-387
96UppDecA-17
96UppDecDD-DD14
96UppDecDDG-DD14
96UppDecDDS-DD14
96UppDecG-GF2
96UppDecHC-HC20
96UppDecPD-PD17
96UppDecPHE-H8
96UppDecPRE-R8
96UppDecPRE-R18
96UppDecPRE-R29
96UppDecPreH-H8
96UppDecPreR-R8
96UppDecPreR-R18
96UppDecPreR-R29
96UppDecRunP-RP18
96UppDecVJLS-VJ15
96Zen-22
96Zen-133
96ZenArtP-22
96ZenArtP-133
96ZenDiaC-8
96ZenDiaCP-8
96ZenMoz-3
96ZenZ-4
97Bow-290
97BowBes-38
97BowBesAR-38
97BowBesBC-BC3
97BowBesBCAR-BC3
97BowBesBCR-BC3
97BowBesMI-MI2
97BowBesMIAR-MI2
97BowBesMIARI-MI2
97BowBesMII-MI2
97BowBesMIR-MI2
97BowBesMIRI-MI2
97BowBesP-1
97BowBesPAR-1
97BowBesPR-1
97BowBesR-38
97BowChr-100
97BowChrI-100
97BowChrIR-100
97BowChrR-100
97BowInt-290
97BowIntB-BBI1
97BowIntBAR-BBI1
97BowIntBR-BBI1
97Cir-45
97Cir-396
97CirBos-18
97CirIco-11
97CirLimA-14
97CirRav-45
97CirRav-396
97CirRavR-12
97CirSupB-18
97ColCho-300
97ColCho-328
97ColChoAC-10
97ColChoBS-10
97ColChoBSGS-10
97ColChoCtG-10A
97ColChoCtG-10B
97ColChoCtG-10C
97ColChoCtGIW-CG10
97ColChoNF-NF15
97ColChoPP-PP12
97ColChoPPG-PP12
97ColChoS-30
97ColChoTBS-16
97ColChoTBSWH-16
97ColChoTotT-T11
97Don-138
97Don-398
97DonDiaK-9
97DonDiaKC-9
97DonDom-1
97DonEli-3
97DonEli-1
97DonEliGS-3
97DonEliLaL-3
97DonEliPtT-8
97DonEliPtT-9
97DonEliPtTA-8
97DonEliPtTA-9
97DonFraFea-2
97DonLim-4
97DonLim-78
97DonLim-100
97DonLimFotG-37
97DonLimFotG-60
97DonLimLE-4
97DonLimLE-78
97DonLimLE-100
97DonLonL-1
97DonPowA-1
97DonPowADC-1
97DonPre-1
97DonPre-168
97DonPreCttC-1
97DonPreCttC-168
97DonPreP-138
97DonPreP-398
97DonPrePGold-138
97DonPrePGold-398
97DonPrePM-1
97DonPreS-2
97DonPreTB-24
97DonPreTBG-24
97DonPreTF-24
97DonPreTP-24
97DonPreTPG-24
97DonPreXP-4B
97DonRocL-1
97DonTea-64
97DonTeaSMVP-3
97DonTeaSPE-64
97Fin-29
97Fin-160
97Fin-279
97FinEmb-160
97FinEmb-279
97FinEmbR-160
97FinEmbR-279
97FinRef-29
97FinRef-160
97FinRef-279
97FlaSho-A35
97FlaSho-B35
97FlaSho-C35
97FlaShoDC-17
97FlaShoHG-15
97FlaShoLC-35
97FlaShoLC-B35
97FlaShoLC-C35
97FlaShoLCM-A35
97FlaShoLCM-B35
97FlaShoLCM-C35
97Fle-72
97Fle-500
97Fle-718
97Fle-726
97FleBleB-8
97FleDiaT-12
97FleGouG-14
97FleGouGF-14
97FleHea-20
97FleLumC-17
97FleMilDM-32
97FleNig&D-10
97FleSoaS-12
97FleTeaL-4
97FleTif-72
97FleTif-500
97FleTif-718
97FleTif-726
97FleZon-18
97Lea-107
97Lea-348
97Lea-369
97LeaBanS-4
97LeaDrefS-4
97LeaFraM-107
97LeaFraM-348
97LeaFraM-369
97LeaFraMDC-107
97LeaFraMDC-348
97LeaFraMDC-369
97LeaGet-2
97LeaGolS-1
97LeaKnoG-3
97LeaLeaotN-7
97LeaStaS-5
97LeaThoC-1
97LeaThoC-2
97LeaThoC-3
97LeaThoC-4
97LeaThoC-5
97LeaThoC-6
97MetUni-61
97MetUniBF-11
97MetUniML-11
97MetUniT-10
97NewPin-118
97NewPin-197
97NewPinAP-118
97NewPinAP-197
97NewPinIE-10
97NewPinKtP-7
97NewPinMC-118
97NewPinMC-197
97NewPinPP-118
97NewPinPP-197
97NewPinPP-I10A
97NewPinPP-K7
97NewPinPP-FT1
97NewPinPP-FT2
97NewPinPP-FT3
97NewPinPP-FT4
97NewPinPP-FT5
97NewPinS-FT1
97NewPinS-FT2
97NewPinS-FT3
97NewPinS-FT4
97NewPinS-FT5
97Pac-64
97PacCar-7
97PacCarM-7
97PacCerCGT-1
97PacCraC-2
97PacFirD-5
97PacGolCD-7
97PacLigB-64
97PacPri-22
97PacPriGA-GA4
97PacPriGotD-GD32
97PacPriLB-22
97PacPriP-22
97PacPriSH-SH3A
97PacPriSL-SL2A
97PacSil-64
97PacTriCD-4
87PanAmTUBI-36
97Pin-102
97PinArtP-102
97PinCar-15
97PinCer-41
97PinCer-148
97PinCerCMGT-1
97PinCerCT-1
97PinCerLI-9
97PinCerMBlu-41
97PinCerMBlu-148
97PinCerMG-41
97PinCerMG-148
97PinCerMR-41
97PinCerMR-148
97PinCerR-41
97PinCerR-148
97PinHom-7
97PinHom-8
97PinIns-13
97PinInsC-2
97PinInsCE-13
97PinInsDD-8
97PinInsDE-13
97PinInsFS-16
97PinMin-2
97PinMinB-2
97PinMinCB-2
97PinMinCG-2
97PinMinCGR-2
97PinMinCN-2
97PinMinCS-2
97PinMinG-2
97PinMinS-2
97PinMusC-102
97PinPasttM-3
97PinSha-9
97PinTeaP-1
97PinTeaP-10
97PinTotCPB-41
97PinTotCPB-148
97PinTotCPG-41
97PinTotCPG-148
97PinTotCPR-41
97PinTotCPR-148
97PinX-P-5
97PinX-P-140
97PinX-PF&A-3
97PinX-PMoS-5
97PinX-PMoS-140
97PinX-PMP-8
97PinX-PMW-2
97PinX-PMWG-2
97PinX-PMWS-2
97PinX-PSfF-10
97PinX-PSfFU-10
97ProMag-51
97ProMagIM-2
97ProMagML-51
97Sco-26
97Sco-508
97Sco-549
97ScoAllF-1
97ScoFra-7
97ScoFraG-7
97ScoHeaotO-4
97ScoHigZ-1
97ScoHobR-508
97ScoHobR-549
97ScoPitP-10
97ScoPreS-26
97ScoResC-508
97ScoResC-549
97ScoShoS-26
97ScoShoS-508
97ScoShoS-549
97ScoShoSAP-26
97ScoShoSAP-508
97ScoShoSAP-549
97ScoStaaD-24
97ScoSteS-7
97ScoTitT-5
97ScoWhiS-1
97ScoWhiSPI-1
97ScoWhiSPr-1
97Sel-8
97Sel-144
97Sel-149
97SelArtP-8
97SelArtP-144
97SelArtP-149
97SelRegG-8
97SelRegG-144
97SelRegG-149
97SelToootT-19
97SelToootTMB-19
97SkyE-X-15
97SkyE-XACA-1
97SkyE-XC-15
97SkyE-XEC-15
97SkyE-XHoN-1
97SP-50
97SPGamF-GF2
97SPInsI-5
97SPMarM-MM19
97SpoIll-148
97SpoIll-178
97SpoIllEE-148
97SpoIllEE-178
97SpoIllGS-10
97SPSpeF-2
97SPSpxF-3
97SPSPxFA-3
97SPx-17
97SPxBoufG-7
97SPxBro-17
97SPxCorotG-2
97SPxGraF-17
97SPxSil-17
97SPxSte-17
97StaClu-213
97StaClu-378
97StaCluFR-F9

97StaCluMat-213
97StaCluMOP-213
97StaCluMOP-378
97StaCluMOP-FB9
97StaCluMOP-PG10
97StaCluPG-PG10
97Stu-1
97Stu-164
97StuHarH-5
97StuMasS-5
97StuMasS8-5
97StuPor8-2
97StuPrePG-1
97StuPrePG-164
97StuPrePS-1
97StuPrePS-164
97Top-108
97TopAll-AS3
97TopChr-41
97TopChrAS-AS3
97TopChrDD-DD10
97TopChrDDR-DD10
97TopChrR-41
97TopChrSAR-AS3
97TopChrSB-2
97TopChrSBR-2
97TopGal-90
97TopGalGoH-GH3
97TopGalPG-PG7
97TopGalPMS-6
97TopGalPMSSS-2
97TopGalPPI-90
97TopHobM-HM11
97TopIntF-ILM5
97TopIntFR-ILM5
97TopScr-19
97TopScrSI-5
97TopSeaB-SB2
97TopSta-13
97TopStaAM-13
97TopSweS-SS14
97TopTeaT-TT5
97Ult-44
97UltBasR-10
97UltChe-A10
97UltChe-B3
97UltDiaP-11
97UltDouT-4
97UltFamGam-2
97UltGolME-44
97UltHitM-3
97UltHRK-10
97UltPlaME-44
97UltPowP-A11
97UltPowP-B2
97UltRBIK-9
97UltSeaC-12
97UltStaR-3
97UltThu-10
97UltTop3-3
97UltTop3GM-3
97UppDec-40
97UppDec-418
97UppDecAG-AG10
97UppDecHC-HC4
97UppDecLDC-LD12
97UppDecMM-4
97UppDecP-11
97UppDecPP-PP20
97UppDecPPJ-PP20
97UppDecRP-RP5
97UppDecU-16
97UppDecUMA-MA5
97Zen-1
97Zen Z-Z-3
97Zen8x1-1
97Zen8x1D-1
97ZenV-2-3

Thomas, Frank J.
47Exh-221A
47Exh-221B
54Bow-155
54DanDee-27
55ArmCoi-21
55Bow-58
55RedMan-NL20
56RedBurB-23
56Top-153
57Kah-27
57Top-140
58Hir-27
58JayPubA-21
58Kah-29
58Top-409
59ArmCoi-17
59Kah-37
59RedEnq-26
59RedShiBS-20
59Top-17
59Top-490
59TopVen-17
60CubJayP-12
60Kah-41
60Top-95
60TopVen-95
61Pos-193A
61Pos-193B
61Top-382
62Jel-151
62MetJayP-11
62Pos-151
62PosCan-151
62SalPlaC-104
62ShiPlaC-104
62Top-7
62TopVen-7
63Jel-196
63MetJayP-11
63Pos-196
63SalMetC-59
63Top-495
64PhiPhiB-24
64Top-345
64TopCoi-73
64TopVen-345
65OPC-123
65Top-123
74MetOriEB-14
79TCM50-24
82MetGal62-19
89PacLegI-153
90SweBasG-113
91MetWIZ-405
91TopArc1-283
92ActPacA-77
93UppDecAH-118
94UppDecAH-126
94UppDecAH-218
94UppDecAH1-126
94UppDecAH1-218

Thomas, Frankie (Frank)
80HolMilT-5
81VanCanT-6
82VanCanT-2
83ElPasDT-22
84VanCanC-33

Thomas, Gene
93EveGiaC-28

Thomas, George
61Top-544
62Top-525
62TopStaI-69
63Jel-34
63Pos-30
63Pos-34
63Top-98
64Top-461
65OPC-83
65Top-83
66Top-277
66TopVen-277
67CokCapRS-18
67OPC-184
67Top-184
67TopRedSS-22
69Top-521
71OPC-678
71Top-678
78TCM60I-153
81RedSoxBG2S-122

Thomas, Gorman (James Gorman)
74SacSolC-48
74OPC-288
74Top-288
75OPC-532
75Top-532
76OPC-139
76SSP-243
76Top-139
77SpoIndC-13
77Top-439
79OPC-196
79Top-376
80Kel-11
80OPC-327
80Top-202
80Top-623
80TopSup-30
81AllGamPI-69
81Don-326A
81Don-326B
81Fle-507
81FleStiC-77
81OPC-135
81PerCreC-29
81Top-135
81TopSti-12
81TopSti-96
82BrePol-20
82Don-26
82Don-132
82Fle-154
82FleSta-134
82OPC-324
82Top-765
82TopSti-204
83AllGamPI-69
83BreGar-19
83BrePol-20
83Don-510
83Dra-27
83Fle-48
83FleSta-195
83FleSti-20
83Kel-47
83OPC-10
83PerCreC-32
83PerCreCG-32
83Top-10
83Top-702
83TopSti-17
83TopSti-84
83TopTra-111T
84AllGamPI-158
84Don-574
84DonCha-5
84Fle-553
84FleUpd-117
84FunFooP-56
84MarMot-7
84Nes792-515
84OPC-146
84Top-515
84TopSti-253
84TopTif-515
84TopTra-119T
84TopTraT-119T
85Fle-503
85MarMot-9
85OPC-202
85Top-202
85TopTif-202
86Don-440
86Fle-477
86FleAll-11
86FleStiC-119
86Lea-213
86MarMot-9
86OPC-347
86SevCoi-W9
86Top-750
86TopGloS-48
86TopMinL-31
86TopSti-216
86TopSup-56
86TopTat-22
86TopTif-750
86Woo-31
87Fle-359
87FleGlo-359
87Top-495
87TopTif-495
91UppDecS-10
92BreCarT-23
92UppDecS-9
94BreMilB-185
94BreMilB-367
94TedWil-45

Thomas, Greg
93WatIndC-27
93WatIndF-3573
94KinIndC-19
94KinIndF-2654
95KinIndTI-26
96CanIndB-25

Thomas, Ira
03WilCarE-28
08AmeCarE-65
09AmeCarE-108
09RamT20-117
09SpoNewSM-60
09T206-354
10CouT21-321
10DomDisP-115
10E12AmeCDC-35
10NadE1-55
10RedCroT-251
10SweCapPP-50A
10SweCapPP-50B
11A'sFirT20-18
11BasBatEU-38
11DiaGumP-26
11MecDFT-13
11PloCanE-60
11SpoLifCW-350
11SpoLifM-105
11T205-170
11TurRedT-123
12HasTriFT-19
12HasTriFT-70D
12PhiCarE-29
14CraJacE-34
14PieStaT-55
15CraJacE-34
19W514-97
87GreBraB-23

Thomas, Isiah
93StaCluMO-41

Thomas, Jason
93IdaFalBF-4031
93IdaFalBSP-21
94DanBraC-28
94DanBraF-3531
94MacBraC-22
94MacBraF-2204

Thomas, Jeff
85CloHSS-40

Thomas, Jim
76SanAntBTI-24
83DayBeaAT-23
84BeaGolGT-15
86TucTorP-22
87ColAstP-5
88MidAngGS-23
89EdmTraC-22
89EdmTraP-550

Thomas, John
90HamRedB-24
90HamRedS-25
91St.PetCC-5
92ArkTraS-47
92ClaFS7-14
92SkyAA F-20

Thomas, Juan
93HicCraC-24
93HicCraF-1289
94SouBenSHC-22
94SouBenSHF-604
95PriWilCTI-11
96Exc-37
96ExcSeaTL-9
96PriWilCB-27

Thomas, Keith
88GreHorP-1554
89ModA'sC-32
90MadMusB-11
90ModA'sCLC-161
90ModA'sP-2226
91MadMusP-2144
92SalBucC-10
92SalBucF-78
93CarMudF-2070
93CarMudTI-6
93ExcFS7-94
94WicWraF-204
95MemChiTI-10

Thomas, Keith Marshall
53BowBW-62
53Top-129
91TopArc1-129

Thomas, Kelvin
90PenPilS-23
91EriSaiC-11
91EriSaiP-4081
91PenPilC-3
91PenPilP-393

Thomas, Larry
91Cla/Bes-418
91UtiBluSC-20
91UtiBluSP-3240
92BirBarF-2583
92ClaFS7-323
92SarWhiSCB-22
92StaCluD-186
93Bow-35
93ExcFS7-156
93NasSouF-571
94BirBarC-22
94BirBarF-622
96BirBarB-27
96ColCho-512
96ColChoGS-512
96ColChoSS-512
96Fle-78
96FleTif-78
96LeaSigEA-200
96Pac-285
96Pin-192
96Sco-259
96StaClu-375
96StaCluMOP-375

Thomas, Lee (J. Leroy)
47Exh-222
61Top-464
61Yan61RL-34
62Baz-6
62Top-154
62TopBuc-88
62TopStaI-70
62TopVen-154
63AngJayP-17
63AngJayP-18
63BasMagM-82
63Baz-32
63ExhStaB-61
63Jel-30
63Pos-30
63Pos-34
63Top-441
63TopStiI-44
64Top-255
64TopSta-99
64TopStaU-71
64TopTatI-70
64TopVen-255
65OPC-111
65Top-111
66Top-408
67Ast-27
67CokCapC-12
67DexPre-205
67Top-458
68CokCapA-6
68Top-438
71CarTeal-40
78TCM60I-231
81RedSoxBG2S-123
91RinPos1Y2-4
92YanWIZ6-126

Thomas, Mark
87WatPirP-20
89AugPirP-507
89WelPirP-23
90ColMetGS-24
90ColMetPPI-4
91St.LucMC-1
91St.LucMP-726

Thomas, Mike (Mike Samuel)
91BluOriC-5
91BluOriP-4141
92BluOriC-3
92BluOriF-2373
92RocExpC-1
94SprSulC-22

Thomas, Mike (Mike Steven)
90PitMetP-18
91ColMetPI-16
91ColMetPI-31
91ColMetPPI-5
92RocExpF-2115
93WesPalBEC-23
93WesPalBEF-1340
94ElPasDF-3147

Thomas, Mitch
86SalRedBP-25
87PorChaRP-6
88TulDriTI-4
90TulDriP-1157

Thomas, Myles
91ConTSN-106

Thomas, Orlando
87EriCarP-18
89SavCarP-349
90SprCarB-15
91SprCarC-26
91SprCarP-745
92JohCitCC-27

92JohCitCF-3135
94NewJerCC-30
Thomas, Pinch (Chester David)
10CouT21-65
10CouT21-234
10CouT21-235
16ColE13-173
16FleBreD-93
17HolBreD-104
21E121So8-96
22AmeCarE-70
22W575-137
Thomas, Randy
78ArkTraT-21
79ArkTraT-18
Thomas, Ray
90DodTar-1085
Thomas, Ricky
81VerBeaDT-21
82IdaFalAT-28
Thomas, Rob
88BriTigP-1888
89Bow-358
89FayGenP-1571
92StaClu-885
92Ult-524
95BakBlaTI-23
Thomas, Rodney
91PriRedC-16
91PriRedP-3529
92PriRedC-19
92PriRedF-3102
93BilMusF-3960
93BilMusSP-19
94ChaWheC-23
94ChaWheF-2717
Thomas, Ron
88PulBraP-1769
89PulBraP-1889
90SumBraB-6
90SumBraP-2434
Thomas, Roy Allen
03BreE10-141
06FanCraNL-48
08RosComP-155
09AmeCarE-109
Thomas, Roy J.
78ChaChaT-17
78Top-711
79Car5-30
79Top-563
80Top-397
81TacTigT-20
82SalLakCGT-19
84Fle-622
84MarMot-25
84Nes792-181
84Top-181
84TopSti-348
84TopTif-181
85CalCanC-82
86Fle-478
86MarMot-26
86Top-626
86TopTif-626
87CalCanP-2321
89PacSenL-124
89TopSenL-121
90EliSenL-118
91PacSenL-130
Thomas, Royal
87UtiBluSP-22
88ClePhiS-25
88SpaPhiS-4
89ClePhiS-21
89ClePhiS-NNO
90Bes-248
90RivRedWB-25
90RivRedWCLC-21
90RivRedWP-2608
91BriBanF-18
91HigDesMC-12
91HigDesMP-2395
92WicWraF-3658
92WicWraS-646
93SanAntMF-3004
94GreBraF-414
94GreBraTI-25
95RicBraRC-26
95RicBraTI-24
Thomas, Ryan
96IdaFalB-26
Thomas, Skeets
91St.PetCP-2291
92ArkTraF-1143
92UppDecML-95
93LouRedF-230
94LouRedF-2994
95LouRedF-290
Thomas, Stan
76OPC-148
76Top-148
77Top-353
78TucTorC-22
92YanWIZ7-149
93RanKee-355
Thomas, Steve
90PitMetP-14
92ColMetC-9
92ColMetF-297
92ColMetPI-4
Thomas, Terrence
88St.PetCS-24
Thomas, Tim
90ArkRaz-25
90BurIndP-3017
91WatIndC-28
91WatIndP-3383
92BriTigC-21
92BriTigF-1422
93LakTigC-24
93LakTigF-1320
94FloStaLAF-FSL16
94LakTigC-22
94LakTigF-3046
Thomas, Todd
86ShrCapP-25
87ShrCapP-11
Thomas, Tom
75ShrCapT-22
86VisOakP-22
87VerBeaDP-14
96GreFalDTI-35
Thomas, Tommy (Alphonse)
26Exh-76
28StaPlaCE-66
29ExhFou-20
29PorandAR-89
33Gou-169
77ShrCapT-22
79DiaGre-54
92ConTSN-579
Thomas, Tony
77WauMetT-19
Thomas, Troy Gene
86BirBarTI-5
87BirBarB-25
88VanCanC-18
88VanCanP-775
Thomas, Valmy
58GiaSFCB-23
58Top-86
59Top-235
60Top-167
60TopVen-167
61Top-319
79TCM50-276
91OriCro-455
Thomas, Vern
80RocRedWT-3
81EdmTraRR-9
82GleFalWST-11
Thomas, Wayne
72Dia-109
72Dia-110
Thomason, Mel
76SSP-600
Thomasson, Gary
74OPC-18
74Top-18
75Gia-10
75OPC-529
75Top-529
76OPC-261
76SSP-107
76Top-261
77BurCheD-102
77Gia-23
77Top-496
78Top-648
79OPC-202
79Top-387
80DodPol-9
80OPC-70
80Top-127
81Don-534
81Fle-138
81Top-512
86KenTwiP-24
90DodTar-797
92YanWIZ7-150
Thomasson, Hal
75WatRoyT-31
76WatRoyT-31
77DayBeaIT-26
Thomasson, Shane
95EveAqaTI-25
Thome, Jim
90BurIndP-3018
90ProAaA-187
91Bow-68
91CanIndLD-96
91CanIndP-989
91Cla/Bes-195
91ClaGolB-BC9
91LinDriAA-96
91UppDecFE-17F
92Bow-460
92Cla1-T90
92ClaGam-139
92Don-406
92Fle-125
92IndFanC-28
92Lea-299
92LeaBlaG-299
92OPC-768
92Pin-247
92PinRool-13
92PinTea2-37
92ProFS7-50
92Sco-859
92ScoImpP-36
92ScoRoo-4
92StaClu-360
92Top-768
92TopDeb91-171
92TopGol-768
92TopGolW-768
92TopMcD-37
92TopMic-768
92Ult-54
92UppDec-1
92UppDec-5
92UppDecSR-SR22
93ChaKniF-553
93Don-171
93Fle-222
93IndWUA-30
93Pin-348
93Sco-364
93Sel-304
93StaClu-8
93StaCluFDI-8
93StaCluMOP-8
93Top-603
93TopGol-603
93TopInaM-603
93TopMic-603
93TriAAAGF-38
93Ult-192
93UppDec-45
93UppDecGold-45
94Bow-338
94ColC-624
94ColChoGS-624
94ColChoSS-624
94Don-523
94ExtBas-69
94Fin-102
94FinPre-102P
94FinRef-102
94Fla-45
94Fle-121
94Lea-382
94Pin-73
94PinArtP-73
94PinMusC-73
94Sco-167
94ScoGolR-167
94Sel-299
94Spo-98
94SpoSha-SH9
94StaClu-257
94StaCluFDI-257
94StaCluGR-257
94StaCluMOP-257
94Stu-97
94Top-612
94TopGol-612
94TopSpa-612
94TriPla-120
94Ult-49
94UppDec-352
94UppDecED-352
95ColCho-268
95ColChoGS-268
95ColChoSE-114
95ColChoSEGS-114
95ColChoSESS-114
95ColChoSS-268
95D3-15
95Don-200
95DonPreP-200
95DonTopotO-68
95Emo-39
95Fin-37
95FinRef-37
95Fla-252
95Fle-149
95Lea-348
95LeaLim-84
95Pac-130
95Pin-18
95PinArtP-18
95PinMusC-18
95Sco-229
95ScoGolR-229
95ScoHaloG-HG99
95ScoPlaTS-229
95Sel-32
95SelArtP-32
95SelCer-42
95SelCerMG-42
95SP-146
95SPCha-146
95SPChaDC-146
95Spo-85
95SpoArtP-85
95SPPlaP-PP19
95SPSil-146
95StaClu-147
95StaCluFDI-147
95StaCluMOP-147
95StaCluSTDW-I147
95StaCluSTMP-19
95StaCluSTWS-147
95StaCluVR-76
95Stu-193
95Sum-7
95SumNthD-7
95Top-312
95TopCyb-169
95UC3-37
95UC3ArtP-37
95Ult-42
95UltGolM-42
95UppDec-96
95UppDecED-96
95UppDecEDG-96
95UppDecSE-162
95UppDecSEG-162
95Zen-51
96Baz-21
96Bow-41
96BowBes-47
96BowBesAR-47
96BowBesC-15
96BowBesCAR-15
96BowBesCR-15
96BowBesR-47
96Cir-38
96CirRav-38
96ColCho-120
96ColCho-367T
96ColCho-392T
96ColChoCtG-CG13
96ColChoCtG-CG13B
96ColChoCtG-CG13C
96ColChoCtGE-CR13
96ColChoCtGG-CG13
96ColChoCtGG-CG13B
96ColChoCtGG-CG13C
96ColChoCtGGE-CR13
96ColChoGS-120
96ColChoSS-120
96Don-371
96DonPreP-371
96EmoXL-56
96Fin-B47
96FinRef-B47
96Fla-76
96Fle-102
96FleInd-17
96FlePosG-5
96FleTif-102
96Lea-169
96LeaLim-55
96LeaLimG-55
96LeaPre-57
96LeaPreP-57
96LeaPrePB-169
96LeaPrePG-169
96LeaPrePS-169
96LeaSig-71
96LeaSigA-223G
96LeaSigA-223S
96LeaSigAG-223
96LeaSigAS-223
96LeaSigPPG-71
96LeaSigPPP-71
96MetUni-54
96MetUniP-54
96Pac-302
96PacOctM-OM20
96Pin-238
96PinAfi-90
96PinAfiAP-90
96PinAfiFPP-90
96PinAfiSP-22
96PinArtP-138
96PinChrBC-14
96PinFoil-238
96PinSta-138
96PinTeaP-3
96SchDis-1
96Sco-6
96ScoDugC-A6
96ScoDugCAP-A6
96ScoRef-19
96ScoSam-6
96Sel-52
96SelArtP-52
96SelCer-69
96SelCerAP-69
96SelCerCB-69
96SelCerCR-69
96SelCerMB-69
96SelCerMG-69
96SelCerMR-69
96SP-68
96Spo-90
96SpoArtP-90
96StaClu-191
96StaClu-357
96StaCluEPB-357
96StaCluEPG-357
96StaCluEPS-357
96StaCluMO-41
96StaCluMOP-191
96StaCluMOP-357
96StaCluVRMO-76
96Sum-76
96SumAbo&B-76
96SumArtP-76
96SumFoi-76
96SumPos-3
96Top-253
96TopChr-100
96TopChrR-100
96TopGal-70
96TopGalPPI-70
96TopLas-79
96Ult-54
96UltGolM-54
96UltOn-L-10
96UltOn-LGM-10
96UppDec-54
96Zen-6
96ZenArtP-6
97Bow-246
97BowBes-22
97BowBesAR-22
97BowBesR-22
97BowChr-71
97BowChrI-71
97BowChrIR-71
97BowChrR-71
97BowInt-246
97Cir-391
97CirRav-391
97ColCho-94
97ColChoAC-3
97ColChoCtG-12A
97ColChoCtG-12B
97ColChoCtG-12C
97ColChoCtGIW-CG12
97ColChoNF-NF19
97ColChoS-18

97Don-105
97Don-441
97DonEli-50
97DonEliGS-50
97DonLim-38
97DonLim-157
97DonLimFotG-69
97DonLimLE-38
97DonLimLE-157
97DonPre-42
97DonPre-192
97DonPreCttC-42
97DonPreCttC-192
97DonPreP-105
97DonPreP-441
97DonPrePGold-105
97DonPrePGold-441
97DonPreXP-1B
97DonTea-78
97DonTeaSPE-78
97Fin-148
97Fin-190
97FinEmb-148
97FinEmbR-148
97FinRef-148
97FinRef-190
97FlaSho-A77
97FlaSho-B77
97FlaSho-C77
97FlaShoLC-77
97FlaShoLC-B77
97FlaShoLC-C77
97FlaShoLCM-A77
97FlaShoLCM-B77
97FlaShoLCM-C77
97Fle-90
97FleTif-90
97FleZon-19
97Lea-197
97Lea-223
97LeaFraM-197
97LeaFraM-223
97LeaFraMDC-197
97LeaFraMDC-223
97LeaGolS-19
97MetUni-87
97NewPin-82
97NewPinAP-82
97NewPinMC-82
97NewPinPP-82
97Pac-80
97PacLigB-80
97PacPri-27
97PacPriLB-27
97PacPriP-27
97PacSil-80
97PacTriCD-6
97Pin-36
97PinArtP-36
97PinCer-47
97PinCerMBlu-47
97PinCerMG-47
97PinCerMR-47
97PinCerR-47
97PinIns-72
97PinInsCE-72
97PinInsDD-7
97PinInsDE-72
97PinMusC-36
97PinTeaP-3
97PinTeaP-10
97PinTotCPB-47
97PinTotCPG-47
97PinTotCPR-47
97PinX-P-84
97PinX-PMoS-84
97PinX-PSfF-12
97PinX-PSfFU-12
97Sco-107
97Sco-514
97ScoAllF-7
97ScoHeaotO-15
97ScoHobR-514
97ScoInd-3
97ScoIndPl-3
97ScoIndPr-3
97ScoIndU-3
97ScoIndUTC-3
97ScoPreS-107
97ScoResC-514
97ScoShoS-107
97ScoShoS-514
97ScoShoSAP-107
97ScoShoSAP-514
97ScoStaaD-18
97Sel-35
97SelArtP-35
97SelRegG-35
97SelToootT-16
97SelTooo tTMB-16
97SkyE-X-18
97SkyE-XC-18
97SkyE-XEC-18
97SP-56
97SPMarM-MM17
97SpolII-144
97SpolIIEE-144
97SPSpeF-35
97SPx-22
97SPxBro-22
97SPxGraF-22
97SPxSil-22
97SPxSte-22
97StaClu-18
97StaCluMat-18
97StaCluMOP-18
97Stu-118
97StuHarH-9
97StuPrePG-118
97StuPrePS-118
97Top-105
97TopAll-AS7
97TopChr-40
97TopChrAS-AS7
97TopChrR-40
97TopChrSAR-AS7
97TopGal-115
97TopGalPPI-115
97TopScr-20
97TopSta-78
97TopStaAM-78
97Ult-380
97UltGolME-380
97UltPlaME-380
97UppDec-347
97UppDecP-13
97UppDecRP-RP21
97UppDecU-36

Thomforde, Jim
92OneYanC-9
93OneYanC-21
93OneYanF-3503
94GreBatF-475
97GreBatC-23

Thompson, Al
77AshTouT-24

Thompson, Andre
95HagSunF-78
96DunBluJB-24
96DunBluJTI-28
96LowSpiB-25

Thompson, Angelo
93JamExpC-23
93JamExpF-3340

Thompson, Averett
46SunBre-19

Thompson, Bill
85FreGiaP-29

Thompson, Bob
75CedRapGT-7
87LakTigP-19
92AlbYanS-25

Thompson, Bobby L.
74GasRanT-24
75LynRanT-20
76SanAntBTI-25
78RanBurK-22
79Top-336
93RanKee-356

Thompson, Brian
91AubAstC-21
91AubAstP-4288
92AubAstC-9
92AubAstF-1369

Thompson, Bruce
95BelGiaTI-8
96BurBeeTI-25

Thompson, Charles
52Par-52
90ChaRaiB-21
90ChaRaiP-2035
91ChaRaiC-10
91ChaRaiP-95

Thompson, Chris
96LowSpiB-26

Thompson, Dan
96HelBreTI-25

Thompson, Danny
71MLBOffS-474
71OPC-127
71Top-127
72OPC-368
72Top-368
73LinPor-109
73OPC-443
73Top-443
74Kel-35
74OPC-168
74Top-168
75OPC-249
75Top-249
76OPC-111
76SSP-225
76Top-111
78TwiFri-46
93RanKee-357

Thompson, Don
52LaPat-16
90DodTar-798

Thompson, Fay
75DubPacT-6
78DunBluJT-23

Thompson, Fletcher
90AubAstB-18
90AubAstP-3410
91BurAstC-18
91BurAstP-2812
91MidLeaAP-MWL17
92ProFS7-231
93JacGenF-2118
94JacGenF-226
95UppDecML-174
96BowBayB-26
96HigDesMB-28
95UppDecMLFS-174

Thompson, Forrest D.
47SenGunBP-4
49RemBre-26
50RemBre-23

Thompson, Frank
96GreFalDB-28
96GreFalDTI-16

Thompson, Greg
94YakBeaC-26
94YakBeaF-3851

Thompson, Hank
47PM1StaP1-209
50Bow-174
51Bow-89
51R42SmaS-107
51TopRedB-32
52BerRos-64
52Bow-249
52Top-3
53Top-20
54Bow-217
54NewYorJA-35
54Top-64
55Bow-94
55GiaGolS-18
55RedMan-NL11
55RobGouS-19
55RobGouW-19
56Top-199
57Top-109
75Gia195T-28
79TCM50-150
83TopRep5-3
84WilMay-4
86NegLeaF-98
91TopArc1-20
94TedWilM-M24
94TopArc1-64
94TopArc1G-64

Thompson, Jason Dolph
77BurCheD-99
77Hos-64
77OPC-64
77Top-291
78Hos-77
78OPC-212
78RCColC-97
78TigBurK-12
78Top-660
79Hos-96
79Kel-7
79OPC-33
79TigFreP-1
79Top-80
80Kel-17
80OPC-83
80Top-150
80TopSup-42
81Don-293
81Fle-278
81OPC-373
81Top-505
81TopTra-843
82Don-502
82Fle-501
82Top-295
83AllGamPI-99
83Don-95
83DonActA-8
83Dra-28
83Fle-325
83FleSta-196
83FleSti-79
83OPC-209
83Top-730
83TopSti-276
84AllGamPI-9
84Don-64
84Fle-267
84Nes792-355
84OPC-355
84Top-355
84TopRubD-27
84TopSti-128
84TopTif-355
85AllGamPI-99
85Don-322
85Fle-478
85Lea-89
85OPC-22
85Pir-21
85Top-490
85TopRubD-27
85TopSti-125
85TopSup-56
85TopTif-490
86Don-321
86ExpPos-15
86ExpProPa-15
86Fle-622
86FleUpd-113
86GenMilB-6H
86OPC-153
86Top-635
86TopSti-129
86TopTif-635
87GenMilB-4G
95Bes-99
95Exc-289
95SPML-143
95SPMLA-23
95UppDecML-85
96BowBes-178
96BowBesAR-178
96BowBesR-178
96Exc-239
96LeaPre-118
96LeaPreP-118
97ColCho-213
97DonRatR-1
97PacPriGotD-GD210
97Pin-180
97PinArtP-180
97PinMusC-180
97Sco-299
97ScoPreS-299
97ScoShoS-299
97ScoShoSAP-299
97Ult-287
97UltGolME-287
97UltPlaME-287
95UppDecMLFS-85

Thompson, Jason Michael
93SpoIndC-21
93SpoIndF-3598
94RanCucQC-24
94RanCucQF-1647
95MemChiTI-4
95SigRooOJHP-HP5
95SigRooOJHPS-HP5
96LasVegSB-27

Thompson, Jocko (John)
49Bow-161
50Bow-120
51Bow-294

Thompson, John
93BelMarC-28
93BelMarF-3209
94BelMarC-27
94BelMarF-3235
96LanJetB-27

Thompson, Junior (Eugene)
38CinOraW-26
39OrcPhoAP-22
41HarHarW-23
76TayBow4-88
77TCMTheWY-86

Thompson, Justin
91BriTigC-25
91BriTigP-3606
91Cla/Bes-405
91ClaDraP-28
91FroRowDP-31
91HigSchPLS-4
92Bow-543
92ClaFS7-105
92FayGenC-1
92FayGenF-2168
92ProFS7-71
92UppDecML-46
92UppDecML-161
93Bow-366
93Bow-587
93ClaGolF-53
93ClaYouG-YG23
93FloStaLAF-20
93LakTigC-1
93LakTigF-1311
94Bow-372
94Bow-649
94BowBes-B6
94BowBesR-B6
94ClaGolF-111
94ExcFS7-62
94SigRoo-25
94SigRooHP-S10
94SigRooS-25
94Top-313
94TopGol-313
94TopSpa-313
94UppDecML-43
95Bow-68
95SPML-55
96Bow-214
96Fin-B336
96FinRef-B336
96LeaPre-129
96LeaPreP-129
96SelCer-127
96SelCerAP-127
96SelCerCB-127
96SelCerCR-127
96SelCerMB-127
96SelCerMG-127
96SelCerMR-127
96SP-7
96TolMudHB-1
96Zen-127
96ZenArtP-127
97Bow-312
97BowBes-128
97BowBesAR-128
97BowBesR-128
97BowCerBIA-CA79
97BowCerGIA-CA79
97BowChr-216
97BowChrI-216
97BowChrIR-216
97BowChrR-216
97BowInt-312
97Cir-160
97CirRav-160
97ColCho-21
97Don-373
97DonEliTotC-12
97DonEliTotCDC-12
97DonLim-139
97DonLimLE-139
97DonPreP-373
97DonPrePGold-373
97DonRatR-23
97Fin-36
97FinRef-36
97Fle-107
97FleTif-107
97Lea-177
97LeaFraM-177
97LeaFraMDC-177
97MetUni-113
97PacPri-34
97PacPriGotD-GD46
97PacPriLB-34
97PacPriP-34
97Pin-169

97PinArtP-169
97PinMusC-169
97Sco-267
97ScoPreS-267
97ScoShoS-267
97ScoShoSAP-267
97StaClu-160
97StaCluM-M13
97StaCluMOP-160
97StaCluMOP-M13
97Top-163
97TopChr-65
97TopChrR-65
97TopGal-179
97TopGalPPI-179
97TopSta-100
97TopStaAM-100
97Ult-63
97UltGolME-63
97UltPlaME-63
97UppDec-224
Thompson, Karl
95EveAqaTI-26
96MidLeaAB-1
96WisTimRB-25
Thompson, Kelly
87AncGlaP-39
Thompson, Kirk
89EugEmeB-10
Thompson, L. Fresco
29ExhFou-11
29PorandAR-90
31Exh-3
33ButCanV-48
33Gou-13
33GouCanV-13
36GouWidPPR-D37
90DodTar-799
92ConTSN-493
Thompson, Leroy
92BurIndC-10
92BurIndF-1673
93BurIndC-25
93BurIndF-3314
94ColRedC-21
94ColRedF-459
Thompson, Mark Radford
92BenRocC-7
92BenRocF-1474
92ClaDraP-47
92ClaFS7-433
92FroRowDP-75
93Bow-8
93Bow-350
93CenValRC-1
93CenValRF-2893
93ClaYouG-YG24
93ColSprSSF-3087
93ExcFS7-36
93StaCluM-108
93StaCluRoc-20
93Top-419
93TopGol-419
93TopInaM-419
93TopMic-419
94Bow-170
94Cla-34
94ClaGolF-42
94ColSprSSF-734
94DanBraC-25
94DanBraF-3532
94ExcFS7-188
94ExtBas-254
94ExtBasMLH-9
94Top-286
94TopGol-286
94TopSpa-286
94Ult-487
94UppDecML-220
95Bow-15
95ColCho-11
95ColChoGS-11
95ColChoSE-14
95ColChoSEGS-14
95ColChoSESS-14
95ColChoSS-11
95Fla-347
95FleUpd-170
95MacBraTI-25
95Top-52
96LeaSigEA-201
96RocPol-23
96Sco-231
97ColCho-322
97Fle-624
97FleTif-624
97PacPriGotD-GD138
97Pin-147
97PinArtP-147
97PinMusC-147
97Sco-240
97ScoPreS-240
97ScoRoc-13
97ScoRocPl-13
97ScoRocPr-13
97ScoShoS-240
97ScoShoSAP-240
97StaClu-313
97StaCluMOP-313
97Top-441
97Ult-494
97UltGolME-494
97UltPlaME-494
97UppDec-348
Thompson, Marvin W.
75ForLauYS-13
78TacYanC-22
79ColCliT-12
80ColCliP-22
80ColCliT-24
81SyrChiT-20
81SyrChiTI-20
Thompson, Michael
88WinHavRSS-23
89BelMarL-36
89ElmPioP-28
89WinHavRSS-24
92MarPhiC-5
92MarPhiF-3074
93BatCliC-27
93BatCliF-3162
Thompson, Mike (Michael Wayne)
71SenTealW-23
73OPC-564
73Top-564
76IndIndTI-18
76OPC-536
76SSP-6
76Top-536
80QuaCitCT-1
Thompson, Milt
84RicBraT-25
85RicBraT-21
86Don-507
86Fle-530
86FleUpd-114
86PhiTas-24
86Top-517
86TopTif-517
86TopTra-112T
86TopTraT-112T
87Don-330
87DonOpeD-154
87Fle-191
87FleGlo-191
87PhiTas-24
87SpoTeaP-6
87Top-409
87TopTif-409
88Don-236
88DonBasB-296
88Fle-319
88FleGlo-319
88FleStiC-112
88OPC-298
88PanSti-363
88PhiTas-25
88Sco-115
88ScoGlo-115
88Spo-173
88StaLinPh-19
88Top-298
88TopBig-2
88TopTif-298
89Bow-441
89BowTif-441
89CarSmo-22
89Don-313
89DonBasB-212
89DonTra-43
89Fle-584
89FleGlo-584
89FleUpd-121
89OPC-128
89PanSti-157
89RedFolSB-119
89Sco-92
89ScoRoo-45T
89Spo-169
89Top-128
89TopTif-128
89TopTra-118T
89TopTraT-118T
89UppDec-317
90Bow-196
90BowTif-196
90CarSmo-24
90Don-82
90Fle-262
90FleCan-262
90Lea-308
90OPC-688
90PanSti-345
90PubSti-230
90Sco-49
90Top-688
90TopBig-126
90TopSti-37
90TopTif-688
90TopTVCa-36
90UppDec-278
91Bow-386
91CarPol-25
91Don-225
91Fle-649
91Lea-176
91OPC-63
91PanFreS-36
91Sco-54
91StaClu-66
91Stu-239
91Top-63
91TopDesS-63
91TopMic-63
91TopTif-63
91Ult-297
91UppDec-309A
91UppDec-309B
92CarPol-22
92Don-513
92Fle-595
92Lea-150
92OPC-323
92Pin-345
92Sco-114
92StaClu-447
92Top-323
92TopGol-323
92TopGolW-323
92TopMic-323
92Ult-272
92UppDec-397
93Don-775
93Lea-417
93OPCPre-74
93PacSpa-582
93PhiMed-32
93Pin-516
93Sco-397
93Sel-223
93SelRoo-125T
93StaClu-642
93StaCluFDI-642
93StaCluMOP-642
93StaCluP-28
93Ult-446
93UppDec-558
93UppDecGold-558
94ColC-472
94ColChoGS-472
94ColChoSS-472
94Don-301
94Fin-198
94FinRef-198
94Fla-213
94Fle-602
94Lea-22
94Pac-488
94PhiMed-33
94PhiMel-23
94PhiUSPC-3C
94PhiUSPC-11H
94Sco-158
94ScoGolR-158
94StaClu-355
94StaCluFDI-355
94StaCluGR-355
94StaCluMOP-355
94StaCluT-219
94StaCluTFDI-219
94Top-722
94TopGol-722
94TopSpa-722
94UppDec-184
94UppDecED-184
95AstMot-9
95Pin-83
95PinArtP-83
95PinMusC-83
95Sco-479
95ScoGolR-479
95ScoPlaTS-479
96DodMot-17
96DodPol-28
Thompson, Mitch
91MisStaB-54
92MisStaB-40
93MisStaB-42
Thompson, Nick
96MarPhiB-27
Thompson, Ray
76DubPacT-35
Thompson, Rich (Richard)
81WatIndT-16
82ChaLooT-5
83AndBraT-32
83BufBisT-7
84BufBisT-12
85Don-129
85FleUpd-120
85IndPol-41
85MaiGuiT-11
85TopTifT-122T
85TopTra-122T
86Fle-595
86OPC-242
86Top-242
86TopSti-215
86TopTif-242
86VanCanP-26
88MemChiB-2
89IndIndC-10
89IndIndP-1237
90CMC-59
90ExpPos-35
90IndIndC-9
90IndIndP-304
90OPC-474
90ProAAAF-587
90Top-474
90TopTif-474
90UppDec-597A
Thompson, Rick
82AubAstT-19
Thompson, Rob
94OneYanC-29
Thompson, Robby
86DonRoo-39
86FleUpd-115
86GiaMot-16
86SpoRoo-25
86TopTra-113T
86TopTraT-113T
87Don-145
87DonOpeD-101
87Fle-285
87FleAwaW-39
87FleGlo-285
87FleMin-106
87GiaMot-10
87Lea-64
87MSAIceTD-12
87Spo-46
87SpoTeaP-10
87StuPan-13
87Top-658
87TopGloS-40
87TopRoo-21
87TopSti-91
87TopSti-307
87TopTif-658
87ToyRoo-30
88Don-268
88DonBasB-274
88Fle-98
88FleGlo-98
88GiaMot-10
88Lea-120
88OPC-208
88PanSti-423
88Sco-146
88ScoGlo-146
88ScoYouSI-28
88Spo-24
88StaLinG-18
88Top-472
88TopBig-83
88TopSti-93
88TopTif-472
89Bow-473
89BowTif-473
89Don-98
89DonBasB-79
89Fle-344
89FleGlo-344
89GiaMot-10
89OPC-15
89PanSti-215
89RedFolSB-120
89Sco-172
89ScoHot1S-84
89Spo-78
89Top-15
89TopBig-163
89TopSti-87
89TopTif-15
89TVSpoM-52
89UppDec-172
90Bow-233
90BowTif-233
90Don-140
90DonBesN-73
90Fle-73
90FleCan-73
90GiaMot-10
90GiaSmo-19
90Lea-199
90MLBBasB-26
90OPC-325
90PanSti-371
90PubSti-83
90Sco-397
90Sco100S-21
90Spo-60
90Top-325
90TopBig-169
90TopCoi-59
90TopMinL-88
90TopSti-83
90TopTif-325
90UppDec-169
91Bow-623
91ClaGam-44
91Don-363
91Fle-273
91GiaMot-10
91GiaPacGaE-2
91GiaSFE-14
91Lea-107
91OPC-705
91PanFreS-68
91PanSti-77
91Sco-26
91StaClu-77
91StaCluMO-8
91Top-705
91TopDesS-705
91TopMic-705
91TopTif-705
91Ult-329
91UppDec-178
92Bow-448
92ClaGam-44
92Don-52
92Fle-648
92GiaMot-10
92GiaPacGaE-33
92Hig5-129
92Lea-109
92OPC-475
92PanSti-213
92Pin-143
92Sco-247
92StaClu-160
92Stu-119
92Top-475
92TopGol-475
92TopGolW-475
92TopMic-475
92TriPla-45
92Ult-295
92UppDec-286
93Bow-436
93Don-524
93Fla-147
93Fle-538
93FunPac-103
93GiaMot-14
93GiaPos-32

93Lea-30
93OPC-301
93PacSpa-277
93PanSti-237
93Pin-491
93Sco-593
93Sel-139
93SP-116
93StaClu-688
93StaCluFDI-688
93StaCluG-30
93StaCluMOP-688
93Stu-124
93Top-115
93TopGol-115
93TopInaM-115
93TopMic-115
93TriPla-81
93Ult-137
93UppDec-126
93UppDec-822
93UppDecGold-126
93UppDecGold-822
94Bow-407
94ColC-535
94ColChoGS-535
94ColChoSS-535
94Don-48
94DonSpeE-48
94ExtBas-393
94Fin-68
94FinRef-68
94Fla-446
94Fle-703
94FUnPac-74
94GiaAMC-22
94GiaMot-2
94GiaTeal-5
94GiaTeal-6
94GiaUSPC-1H
94GiaUSPC-8C
94Lea-30
94OPC-20
94Pac-557
94PacSilP-36
94PanSti-267
94Pin-315
94PinArtP-315
94PinMusC-315
94PinTeaP-2
94ProMag-123
94Sco-406
94ScoGolR-406
94ScoGolS-29
94Sel-240
94SP-94
94SPDieC-94
94Spo-46
94Spo-186
94StaClu-598
94StaCluFDI-598
94StaCluGR-598
94StaCluMOP-598
94StaCluT-5
94StaCluTFDI-5
94Stu-88
94Top-385
94Top-505
94TopBlaG-43
94TopGol-385
94TopGol-505
94TopSpa-385
94TopSpa-505
94TriPla-109
94Ult-595
94UltAwaW-12
94UppDec-193
94UppDecED-193
95ColCho-253
95ColChoGS-253
95ColChoSE-111
95ColChoSEGS-111
95ColChoSESS-111
95ColChoSS-253
95Don-405
95DonPreP-405
95DonTopotO-358
95Fla-429
95Fle-591
95GiaMot-2
95Lea-258
95LeaLim-151
95PanSti-41
95Pin-385
95PinArtP-385
95PinMusC-385
95Sco-243
95ScoGolR-243
95ScoPlaTS-243
95Sel-213
95SelArtP-213
95SP-116
95Spo-93
95SpoArtP-93
95SPSil-116
95StaClu-398
95StaCluMOP-398
95StaCluSTWS-398
95Stu-151
95Top-556
95Ult-245
95UltGolM-245
95UppDec-88
95UppDecED-88
95UppDecEDG-88
95UppDecSE-71
95UppDecSEG-71
96Cir-195
96CirRav-195
96ColCho-308
96ColChoGS-308
96ColChoSS-308
96Don-132
96DonPreP-132
96EmoXL-294
96Fin-B58
96FinRef-B58
96Fla-392
96Fle-597
96FleTif-597
96GiaMot-5
96Lea-90
96LeaPrePB-90
96LeaPrePG-90
96LeaPrePS-90
96Pac-207
96Pin-53
96Sco-351
96ScoDugC-B76
96ScoDugCAP-B76
96StaClu-359
96StaCluEPB-359
96StaCluEPG-359
96StaCluEPS-359
96StaCluMOP-359
96Top-391
96Ult-571
96UltGolM-571
96UppDec-456
97Don-101
97DonPreP-101
97DonPrePGold-101
97Lea-112
97LeaFraM-112
97LeaFraMDC-112
97Pac-448
97PacLigB-448
97PacSil-448
97Pin-71
97PinArtP-71
97PinMusC-71
97Sco-90
97ScoPreS-90
97ScoShoS-90
97ScoShoSAP-90

Thompson, Ryan
88St.CatBJP-2035
89St.CatBJP-2072
90DunBluJS-19
91KnoBluJLD-367
91KnoBluJP-1783
91LinDriAA-367
92FleUpd-106
92SyrChiF-1984
92SyrChiMB-22
92SyrChiS-518
93Bow-270
93Don-242
93Fle-481
93LeaGolR-R7
93MetColP-47
93MetKah-44
93NorTidF-2584
93OPC-351
93OPCPre-79
93PacSpa-548
93Pin-249
93PinRooTP-9
93Sco-227
93ScoBoyoS-9
93ScoProaG-6
93SelRoo-39T
93StaClu-542
93StaCluFDI-542
93StaCluMOP-542
93Top-547
93TopGol-547
93TopInaM-547
93TopMic-547
93Toy-17
93TriAAAGF-18
93Ult-435
93UppDec-373
93UppDecGold-373
94Bow-240
94ColC-276
94ColChoGS-276
94ColChoSS-276
94Don-157
94ExtBas-327
94Fin-39
94FinRef-39
94Fla-202
94Fle-579
94Lea-48
94LeaL-133
94MetColP-27
94MetShuST-2
94OPC-135
94Pac-418
94PanSti-223
94Pin-400
94PinArtP-400
94PinMusC-400
94Sco-576
94ScoGolR-576
94Sel-46
94StaClu-274
94StaCluFDI-274
94StaCluGR-274
94StaCluMOP-274
94Stu-120
94Top-98
94TopGol-98
94TopSpa-98
94TriPla-150
94Ult-241
94UppDec-160
94UppDecED-160
94USPlaCR-4C
95ColCho-319
95ColChoGS-319
95ColChoSE-148
95ColChoSEGS-148
95ColChoSESS-148
95ColChoSS-319
95Don-458
95DonPreP-458
95DonTopotO-297
95Emb-13
95EmbGolI-13
95Fin-191
95FinRef-191
95Fle-384
95Lea-138
95LeaLim-148
95Pac-289
95Pin-57
95PinArtP-57
95PinMusC-57
95Sco-81
95ScoGolR-81
95ScoPlaTS-81
95Spo-131
95SpoArtP-131
95StaClu-287
95StaCluMOP-287
95StaCluSTWS-287
95StaCluVR-149
95Stu-167
95Top-402
95TopCyb-203
95Ult-201
95UltGolM-201
95UppDec-362
95UppDecED-362
95UppDecEDG-362
95UppDecSE-62
95UppDecSEG-62
96BufBisB-21
96ColCho-623
96ColChoGS-623
96ColChoSS-623
96Don-458
96DonPreP-458
96Fle-489
96FleTif-489
96MetKah-32
96MetTeal-6
96Pac-145
96Sco-437
96StaClu-410
96StaCluMOP-410
96StaCluVRMO-149
96Top-77

Thompson, Sam
76ShaPiz-146
76SSP188WS-10
80PerHaloFP-146
80SSPHOF-146
87BucN28-34A
87BucN28-34B
87OldJudN-505
87ScrDC-17
88GandBCGCE-41
88SpoTimM-25
88WG1CarG-25
94OriofB-93

Thompson, Scot
79Top-716
80OPC-298
80Top-574
81CokTeaS-21
81Don-519
81Fle-296
81Top-395
82CubRedL-18
82IowCubT-11
83Don-378
83Top-481
84Don-167
84GiaPos-27
85Fle-621
85GiaMot-15
85GiaPos-26
85Top-646
85TopTif-646
86Fle-262
86FreGiaP-21
86OPC-93
86Top-93
86TopTif-93

Thompson, Sean
88PocGiaP-2079
90SalSpuCLC-137
90SalSpuP-2734

Thompson, Squeezer
88SpoIndP-1927
90ChaRaiP-2030

Thompson, Tim
80KnoBluJT-15
82KnoBluJT-12
83SyrChiT-20
84SyrChiT-30

Thompson, Tim (Charles Lemoine)
50WorWidGV-18
52LaPat-15
53ExhCan-40
54Top-209
57Top-142
58Top-57A
58Top-57B
59TigGraASP-16
60MapLeaSF-21
61MapLeaBH-24
90DodTar-800
94TopArc1-209
94TopArc1G-209
95TopArcBD-80

Thompson, Timothy
84VisOakT-11

Thompson, Tom
86BufBisP-22
87SanBerSP-23
91PacSenL-86

Thompson, Tommy
47SigOil-71
47SunBre-22
78ArkTraT-22
79ArkTraT-7
81DurBulT-5
82DurBulT-11
82ForMyeRT-3
85GreBraTI-19
86JacExpT-19
87HawIslP-9
87JacExpP-453
88BirBarB-10
88JacExpB-24
88JacExpP-971
88SouLeaAJ-39
89BirBarB-27
89BirBarP-104
89TulDriGS-1
89TulDriTI-25
90TulDriP-1172
90TulDriTI-25
90UtiBluSP-25
91LinDriAAA-324
91OklCit8LD-324
91OklCit8P-193
91SouBenWSC-27
91SouBenWSP-2873
92OklCit8F-1929
92OklCit8S-324
93ChaRanC-26
93ChaRanF-1955
94ChaRanF-2512
94ConTSN-1244
94ConTSNB-1244

Thompson, Tony
86LitFalMP-28

Thompson, William
90ChaRaiB-22
94LakTigC-23
94LakTigF-3040
96JacSunB-27

Thompson, Willie
78KnoKnoST-22
79KnoKnoST-26

Thomsen, Chris
91SouOreAC-7
91SouOreAP-3858
92SouOreAF-3429

Thomson, Bobby
47Exh-223
47HomBon-46
47PM1StaP1-210
48BluTin-41
48Bow-47
49Bow-18
49EurSta-124
50Bow-28
50Dra-9
50RoyDes-10
51Bow-126
52BerRos-65
52Bow-2
52CokTip-8
52CokTip-9
52RedMan-NL24
52RoyPre-16
52StaCalL-78A
52StaCalS-90C
52Top-313
53BraSpiaS3-24
53BraSpiaS7-13
53RedMan-NL25
53StaMey-9
54Bow-201
54BraJohC-34
54BraSpiaSP-18
55Bow-102
55BraGolS-22
55BraJohC-34
55BraSpiaSD-17
55RobGouS-23
55RobGouW-23
56Top-257
57BraSpiaS4-19
57Top-262
58GiaSFCB-24
58Hir-46
58Top-430
59Top-429
60NuHi-10
60RedSoxJP-10
60Top-153
60TopVen-153
61NuSco-480
75Gia195T-27
76LauDiaJ-29
76SSPYanOD-9
76TayBow4-20
77GalGloG-39
77GalGloG-255
77Spo-514
79TCM50-202
80GiaGreT-5

80PacLeg-115
82GSGalAG-20
83TopRep5-313
84FifNatC-5
85TCMPla1-43
88PacLegI-45
89SweBasG-133
89TopBasT-12
90HOFStiB-46
90PacLeg-106
90SweBasG-21
91Bow-410
91OriCro-456
91SweBasG-88
91TopArc1-330
92ActPacA-52
92BazQua5A-7
93UppDecAH-119
93UppDecAH-164
94MCIAmb-3
94TedWil-56
94UppDecAH-16
94UppDecAH-51
94UppDecAH-115
94UppDecAH1-16
94UppDecAH1-61
94UppDecAH1-115
94UppDecS-8
94UppDecTAE-58
94UppDecTAELD-LD10
95SkiBra-3
97FleMilDM-19

Thomson, Doug
78QuaCitAT-26

Thomson, John
94AshTouC-21
94AshTouF-1780
95Bow-67
95NewHavRTI-20
96NewHavRB-24
96NewHavRUSTI-23
97Bow-115
97BowChr-133
97BowChrI-133
97BowChrIR-133
97BowChrR-133
97BowInt-115

Thomson, Rob
88LakTigS-24
89EasLeaDDP-DD45
89LonTigP-1379
89UtiBluSP-25
90Ft.LauYS-25
91PriWilCC-26
91PriWilCP-1444
92AlbYanF-2350
93AlbYanF-2180

Thon, Dickie
76QuaCitAT-38
78AngFamF-37
80Top-663
81Don-290
81Fle-277
81Top-209
81TopTra-844
82AstAstI-6
82Fle-235
82Top-404
83AllGamPI-117
83Don-191
83Fle-468
83FleSta-197
83FleSti-204
83Top-558
84AllGamPI-27
84AstMot-7
84Don-304
84DonActAS-44
84Fle-243
84Fle-634
84FleSti-1
84Nes792-692
84OPC-344
84SevCoi-W23
84Top-692
84TopRubD-22
84TopSti-64
84TopTif-692
85AstHouP-15
85AstMot-9
85Fle-364
85OPC-44
85Top-44
85TopMin-44
85TopRubD-23
85TopSti-63
85TopTif-44
86AstMilL-21
86AstMot-26
86AstPol-17
86AstTeal-15
86Don-572
86Fle-313
86OPC-166
86Top-166
86TopSti-33
86TopTat-1
86TopTif-166
87AstMot-25
87AstPol-14
87Don-261
87Fle-70
87FleGlo-70
87Lea-196
87Top-386
87TopTif-386
88PadSmo-29
88ScoRoo-29T
88ScoRooG-29T
88TopTra-121T
88TopTraT-121T
89Bow-400
89BowTif-400
89Don-441
89Fle-320
89FleGlo-320
89OPC-181
89PhiTas-34
89Sco-234
89ScoRoo-55T
89Top-726
89TopTif-726
89TopTra-119T
89TopTraT-119T
89UppDec-258
89UppDec-704
90Bow-155
90BowTif-155
90Don-549
90DonBesN-81
90Fle-573
90FleCan-573
90Lea-105
90MLBBasB-4
90OPC-269
90PanSti-318
90PhiTas-28
90PubSti-251
90Sco-142
90Top-269
90TopBig-115
90TopSti-115
90TopTif-269
90UppDec-439
91Bow-499
91Don-91
91Fle-412
91Lea-60
91OPC-439
91PanFreS-106
91PanSti-106
91PhiMed-34
91Sco-103
91StaClu-184
91Top-439
91TopDesS-439
91TopMic-439
91TopTif-439
91Ult-272
91UppDec-449
92Bow-162
92Don-510
92Fle-546
92Lea-180
92OPC-557
92OPCPre-19
92PanSti-245
92Pin-394
92RanMot-12
92RanTeal-24
92Sco-24
92ScoProP-8
92ScoRoo-41T
92StaClu-868
92Stu-250
92Top-557
92TopGol-557
92TopGolW-557
92TopMic-557
92TopTra-118T
92TopTraG-118T
92Ult-447
92UppDec-150
92UppDec-769
93BrePol-25
93Lea-482
93LinVenB-305
93OPCPre-16
93PacSpa-318
93RanKee-358
93Ult-578
93UppDec-769
93UppDecGold-769
94BreMilB-278
94Fle-193
94Pac-345
94Sco-505
94ScoGolR-505
78STLakCGC-4

Thon, Frankie
78CedRapGT-28
80CliGiaT-17

Thoney, John
03BreE10-142
03BreE10-143
08RosComP-6
11MecDFT-47
11SpoLifCW-351
11SpoLifM-17

Thor, Audie
80MemChiT-30

Thorell, Billy
90NebCor-26

Thorell, Greg
90NebCor-25

Thorell, Mike
87AriWilP-16
88AriWilP-14

Thoren, Rick
77AppFoxT-26
78AppFoxT-20

Thormahlen, H.F.
90DodTar-801

Thormahlen, Herb
23WilChoV-161

Thormodsgard, Paul
78OPC-73
78Top-162
78TwiFriP-21
79TolMudHT-2
79Top-249

Thorn, John
90LitSunW-23

Thorn, Todd
96LanLugB-27
96MidLeaAB-41

Thorne, Gary
87MetColP-53
88MetColP-55

Thornhil, Chad
95WatIndTI-28

Thornton, Al
86ElmPioRSP-24
87ElmPio(C-13
88ElmPioC-20

Thornton, Andre
74OPC-604
74Top-604
75OPC-39
75Top-39
76CraDis-62A
76CraDis-62B
76ExpRed-31
76OPC-26
76Top-26
77Spo-5307
77Spo-8418
78OPC-114
78Top-148
79Hos-93
79OPC-140
79Top-280
79TopCom-6
80Kel-28
80OPC-278
80Top-534
80TopSup-43
81Don-198
81OPC-128
81Top-388
81TopSti-70
82Don-324
82Fle-380
82FleSta-201
82Ind-34
82IndTeal-32
82IndWhe-19
82OPC-161
82Top-746
82TopSti-174
83AllGamPI-7
83Don-211
83Fle-421
83Fle-635
83FleSta-198
83FleSti-241
83IndPos-35
83IndWhe-29
83Kel-26
83OPC-344
83Top-640
83TopGloS-3
83TopSti-55
84AllGamPI-98
84Don-25
84Don-25A
84Don-94
84DonActAS-15
84Fle-554
84FunFooP-125
84Ind-30
84IndWhe-29
84Nes792-115
84OPC-115
84Top-115
84TopRubD-22
84TopSti-255
84TopTif-115
85Don-468
85Fle-457
85FleStaS-32
85FleStaS-47
85Ind-32
85IndPol-29
85Lea-102
85OPC-272
85Top-475
85TopRubD-23
85TopSti-244
85TopTif-475
86Don-251
86Fle-596
86FleStiC-120
86IndOhH-29
86IndTeal-42
86Lea-129
86OPC-59
86Spo-171
86Top-59
86Top-336
86TopSti-208
86TopTat-3
86TopTif-59
86TopTif-336
87Don-279
87DonOpeD-108
87Fle-262
87FleGlo-262
87IndGat-29
87OPC-327
87Top-780
87TopTif-780
88RedFolSB-91
88Sco-231
88ScoGlo-231
89SweBasG-117
90SweBasG-47
93UppDecAH-120
93UppDecS-30

Thornton, Eric
89KinMetS-23
90PitMetP-3

Thornton, Lou
85BluJayFS-29
85FleUpd-121
86Fle-71
86OPC-18
86SyrChiP-25
86Top-488
86TopTif-488
87SyrChiP-1930
87SyrChiT-21
89BlaYNPRWLU-18
89BufBisC-22
89BufBisP-1669
89TidTidP-1954
90CMC-362
90MetColP-50
90MetKah-1
90ProAAAF-290
90TidTidC-11
90TidTidP-559
90TopTVM-34
91MetWIZ-406

Thornton, Paul
93ElmPioC-22
93ElmPioF-3822
94KanCouCC-24
94KanCouCF-160
94KanCouCTI-27
95BreCouMF-246
96PorSeaDB-26

Thornton, Woodie A.
09T206-520
10CouT21-66

Thorp, Bradley S.
81VerBeaDT-22

Thorpe, Bob (Benjamin R.)
52Top-367
53BraSpiaS3-25
57SeaPop-35
77FriOneYW-5
02Dow195E 258
83Bra53F-18
83TopRep5-367

Thorpe, Jim (James F.)
09ColChiE-288
09MaxPubP-13
12ColRedB-288
12ColTinT-288
15SpoNewM-176
33SpoKin-6
59FleWil-70
69SCFOldT-55
73FleWilD-3
76BooProC-13
81ConTSN-31
87ConSer2-59
87SpoCubG-1
87SpoRea-25
88ConSer4-28
88FriBasCM-7
92ConTSN-403
92ConTSNCI-22
93ConTSN-771

Thorpe, Michael
86BelMarC-111
87WauTimP-19

Thorpe, Paul
86HagSunP-25
87HagSunP-23
88ChaKniTI-17
89HagSunB-19
89HagSunP-285
89HagSunS-21
90EasLeaAP-EL10
90HagSunB-26
90HagSunP-1414
90HagSunS-24

Thorson, Doc (Brian)
79HolMilT-16
80BurBeeT-9
81VanCanT-7
82VanCanT-24
84AlbA'sT-9
85HunStaJ-NNO
88MadMusP-24
90HunStaB-26
91HunStaC-10
92MadMusC-28

Thorton, John
86ElPasDP-21

Thoutsis, Paul
87WinHavRSP-27
89St.PetCS-26
90ArkTraGS-28
92NewBriRSF-448
92NewBriRSS-498
93NewBriRSF-1236
94PawRedSDD-24
94PawRedSF-957
95ColCliP-30
95ColCliTI-30

Thrams, Jeff
89BoiHawP-1988

Threadgill, Chris
88BenBucL-12
89PalSprACLC-42
89PalSprAP-472

Threadgill, George

85BurRanT-8
86DayBealP-28
86FloStaLAP-46
88TulDriTI-2
89TulDriGS-26
90TulDriTI-26
92DurBulC-27
92DurBulF-1117
93ChaRaiC-28
93ChaRaiF-1929
94ChaRivC-28
94ChaRivF-2691
94ChaRivF-2692
95ButCopKtI-23
Threadgill, Henry
90QuaCitAGS-20
Threatt, Tony
83TamTarT-24
Thrift, Jim
87SalBucP-18
89PenPilS-26
90KinMetB-25
90KinMetS-26
91PitMetC-25
91PitMetP-3438
92PitMetC-18
92PitMetF-3310
93RocRoyC-30
93RocRoyF-733
94IndIndF-1826
95IndIndF-113
96IndIndB-3
Throneberry, M. Faye
52Top-376
53Top-49
55Top-163
57Top-356
59Top-534
60Lea-136
60Top-9
60TopVen-9
61AngJayP-11
61Top-282
83TopRep5-376
91TopArc1-49
Throneberry, Marv
58Top-175
59Top-326
60A'sJayP-9
60Top-436
61A'sTeal-20
61AthJayP-22
61Pos-85A
61Pos-85B
61Top-57
61TopStal-166
63Jel-194
63MetJayP-12
63Pos-194
63Top-78
74MetOriEB-15
79TCM50-173
82MetGal62-1
88PacLegI-48
90PacLeg-62
90SweBasG-77
91MetWIZ-407
91OriCro-457
91SweBasG-89
93UppDecAH-121
94UppDecAH-94
94UppDecAH1-94
Throop, George
75OmaRoyTI-16
76OmaRoyTT-24
76OPC-591
76Top-591
Thrower, Keith
84ModA'sC-21
85TacTigC-128
86TacTigP-22
Thurberg, Tom
77WauMetT-20
82ArkTraT-10
83LouRedR-25
Thurman, Gary
85Ft.MyeRT-18
86MemChiSTOS-26
86MemChiTOS-26
86SouLeaAJ-4
87OmaRoyP-6
88Don-44
88DonRoo-33
88Fle-272
88FleGlo-272
88FleMin-29
88Lea-44
88OmaRoyC-14
88OmaRoyP-1521
88RoySmo-6
88Sco-631
88ScoGlo-631
88ScoYouS2-25
88Spo-223
88StaLinRo-18
88Top-89
88TopTif-89
89Don-498
89Fle-296
89FleGlo-296
89PanSti-348
89ScoHot1R-24
89Top-323
89TopTif-323
89UppDec-347
90CMC-194
90Don-416
90Fle-121
90FleCan-121
90OmaRoyC-19
90OPC-276
90PubSti-359
90Top-276
90TopTif-276
91Bow-316
91Fle-573
91RoyPol-23
91StaClu-306
91UltUpd-29
92Don-346
92Fle-172
92OPC-494
92RoyPol-26
92Sco-512
92StaClu-131
92Top-494
92TopGol-494
92TopGolW-494
92TopMic-494
92UppDec-629
93Don-629
93Fle-626
93PacSpa-450
93StaClu-52
93StaCluFDI-52
93StaCluMOP-52
93TigGat-24
94NasSouF-1263
94Sco-268
94ScoGolR-268
95TacRaiTI-22
96NorTidB-27
Thurman, Mike
94SigRooDP-29
94SigRooDPS-29
94StaCluDP-81
94StaCluDPFDI-81
94TopTra-74T
94VerExpF-3910
95Top-259
96BesAutSA-77
96WesPalBEB-15
Thurman, Robert
52MotCoo-49
57Kah-28
57Top-279
58RedEnq-40
58Top-34
59RedEnq-27
59RedShiBS-22
59Top-541
86NegLeaF-60
87NegLeaPD-39
92NegLeaRLI-59
Thurmond, Mark
82HawIsIT-21
83LasVegSBHN-21
84Don-505
84Fle-315
84Nes792-481
84PadMot-26
84PadSmo-25
84Top-481
84TopTif-481
85Don-284
85Fle-46
85Lea-149
85OPC-236
85PadMot-21
85Top-236
85TopMin-236
85TopTif-236
86Don-261
86Fle-337
86Top-37
86TopTif-37
87Don-543
87Fle-166
87FleGlo-166
87TigCaiD-17
87Top-361
87TopTif-361
88Don-599
88Fle-73
88FleGlo-73
88Sco-382
88ScoGlo-382
88StaLinO-17
88Top-552
88TopTif-552
89OriFreB-21
89Top-152
89TopTif-152
89UppDec-571
90Don-612
90Fle-191
90FleCan-191
90OPC-758
90PubSti-588
90Sco-350
90Top-758
90TopTif-758
91Fle-274
91LinDriAAA-389
91OriCro-458
91PhoFirLD-389
Thurmond, Travis
94BoiHawC-26
94BoiHawF-3356
95BoiHawTI-28
95CedRapKTI-37
Thurston, Jerrey
91ChaRaiC-13
91ChaRaiP-98
91Cla/Bes-102
91SpoIndC-21
91SpoIndP-3952
92WatDiaC-11
92WatDiaF-2145
93WicWraF-2981
94WicWraF-193
Thurston, Sloppy (Hollis)
25Exh-80
26Exh-80
90DodTar-802
93ConTSN-735
94ConTSN-1264
94ConTSNB-1264
Tiamo, Jesus
80VenLeaS-148
Tiant, Luis
65Kah-40
65OPC-145
65Top-145
65TopTral-30
66IndTeal-11
66Top-285
66TopVen-285
67CokCapl-1
67DexPre-206
67Top-377
68Kah-B33
68Top-532
69Kah-B19
69MilBra-271
69MLBOffS-44
69MLBPin-28
69OPC-7
69OPC-9
69OPC-11
69OPCDec-22
69Top-7
69Top-9
69Top-11
69Top-560
69TopDec-7
69TopDecI-43
69TopSta-169
69TopSup-13
69TopTeaP-13
69TraSta-3
70DayDaiNM-70
70Kel-56
70MLBOffS-239
70OPC-231
70Top-231
71MLBOffS-475
71OPC-95
71Top-95
72MilBra-342
73LinPor-30
73OPC-65
73OPC-270
73Top-65
73Top-270
74OPC-167
74Top-167
74TopDecE-27
74TopSta-138
75Hos-102
75Kel-49
75OPC-430
75Top-430
76CraDis-63
76Hos-23
76HosTwi-23
76LinSup-108
76OPC-130
76RedSoxSM-14
76SSP-424
76Top-130
76Top-461
77BurCheD-34
77Hos-10
77OPC-87
77RCColC-64
77Spo-3709
77Top-258
77TopCloS-48
78OPC-124
78PapGinD-23
78SSP270-176
78Top-345
78WifBalD-75
79OPC-299
79Top-575
79YanBurK-8
79YanPicA-33
80OPC-19
80Top-35
81Don-231
81Fle-82
81PorBeaT-23
81Top-627
82OPC-160
82Top-160
83Don-542
83OPC-179
83Top-178
83Top-179
89PacSenL-77
89T/MSenL-105
89T/MSenL-118
90EliSenL-119
91LinDri-11
91SweBasG-90
92ActPacA-46
92GulCoaDF-3585
92YanWIZ7-151
92YanWIZ8-191
93MetIma-20
93TedWil-6
93UppDecAH-122
93UppDecS-28
93YakBeaC-29
93YakBeaF-3902
94GreFalDSP-29
94TedWilM-M36
94TopSpa-L10
94UppDecAH-87
94UppDecAH1-87
94UppDecTAE-73
Tibbs, Jay
82LynMetT-19
83LynMetT-16
84TidTidT-15
85Don-262
85Fle-553
85RedYea-17
85Top-573
85TopTif-573
86BasStaB-110
86Don-262
86ExpPos-16
86ExpProPa-8
86Fle-194
86FleUpd-116
86Top-176
86TopTif-176
86TopTra-114T
86TopTraT-114T
87Don-282
87ExpPos-31
87Fle-333
87FleGlo-333
87Lea-207
87OPC-9
87Top-9
87TopTif-9
88OPC-282
88OriFreB-53
88RocRedWC-10
88RocRedWP-201
88RocRedWTI-24
88Sco-608
88ScoGlo-608
88Top-464
88TopTif-464
89Fle-624
89FleGlo-624
89RocRedWP-1633
89Sco-262
89Top-271
89TopTif-271
89UppDec-655
90Fle-192
90FleCan-192
90OPC-677
90PubSti-589
90Sco-480
90Top-677
90TopTif-677
91OriCro-459
Tiburcio, Freddy
82DurBulT-12
83DurBulT-14
85DomLeaS-169
85GreBraTI-20
86GreBraTI-20
87TolMudHP-11
87TolMudHT-6
Tickell, Brian
95AubAstTI-23
Tides, Tidewater
87IntLeaAT-40
Tidrow, Dick
72OPC-506
72Top-506
73OPC-339
73Top-339
74OPC-231
74Top-231
74TopSta-170
75OPC-241
75Top-241
75YanSSP-23
76OPC-248
76SSP-428
76Top-248
77OPC-235
77Top-461
77YanBurK-9
78SSP270-10
78Top-179
78YanBurK-6
78YanSSPD-10
79OPC-37
79Top-89
80Top-594
81CokTeaS-22
81Don-551
81Fle-299
81Top-352
82CubRedL-41
82Don-477
82Fle-604
82FleSta-99
82OPC-249
82Top-699
82TopSti-27
83Fle-510
83FleSta-199
83FleSti-126
83Top-787
83TopSti-225
83TopTra-112T
83WhiSoxTV-41
84Fle-72
84Nes792-153
84Top-153

84TopTif-153
91MetWIZ-408
92YanWIZ7-152
93UppDecS-14
Tidwell, Danny
75AndRanT-25
76AshTouT-19
Tidwell, Jason
94BreCouMC-20
94BreCouMF-13
93KanCouCTI-24
Tidwell, Mike
91GenCubC-22
91GenCubP-4216
92PeoChiC-3
92PeoChiTI-28
93DayCubC-20
93DayCubF-858
Tiefenauer, Bob
55CarHunW-27
59Top-501
62Col45'HC-18
62Top-227
62TopStaI-131
64Top-522
65OPC-23
65Top-23
68Top-269
68TopVen-269
80PenPilBT-10
80PenPilCT-27
83ReaPhiT-24
85PorBeaC-47
86PorBeaP-22
87SpaPhiP-22
88BatCliP-1662
92YanWIZ6-127
Tiefenthaler, Verle
60TacBan-20
61TacBan-20
77FriOneYW-82
Tiernan, Mike
87OldJudN-506
88AugBecN-27
88GandBCGCE-40
88WG1CarG-44
89EdgR.WG-8
95NewN566-176
Tierney, Cotton (James A.)
20WalMaiW-55
21Exh-176
21Exh-177
22E120-224
22W572-106
22W573-130
23WilChoV-162
90DodTar-803
Tierney, Jake
89NiaFalRP-30
Tierney, Tom
91IdaFalBP-4343
Tietje, Les
35DiaMatCS3T1-141
94ConTSN-1283
94ConTSNB-1283
Tiger, Tacoma
81TacTigT-28
83TacTigT-24
Tigers, Cincinnati
92NegLeaRLI-100
93NegLeaRL2-90
Tigers, Detroit
07TigACDPP-29
09SpoNewSM-19
09TigHMTP-4
10E-UOraBSC-2
13FatT20-4
36R31Pre-G17
36R31Pre-L14
38BasTabP-46
56Top-213
57Top-198
58Top-397A
58Top-397B
59Top-329
60Top-72
60TopTat-68
60TopVen-72
61Top-51
61TopMagR-1
62GuyPotCP-7
62Top-24
62TopVen-24
63GadFunC-37
63Top-552
64Top-67
64TopTatI-8
64TopVen-67
65OPC-173
65Top-173
66Top-583
66TopRubI-108
67Top-378
68LauWorS-4
68LauWorS-32
68LauWorS-37
68Top-528
69FleCloS-9
69FleCloS-46
69TopStaA-9
70FleWorS-4
70FleWorS-31
70FleWorS-37
70FleWorS-65
70Top-579
71FleWorS-5
71FleWorS-7
71FleWorS-32
71FleWorS-38
71FleWorS-66
71OPC-336
71Top-336
71TopTat-78
72OPC-487
72Top-487
73OPC-191
73OPCBTC-9
73Top-191
73TopBluTC-9
74OPC-94
74OPCTC-9
74Top-94
74TopStaA-9
74TopTeaC-9
78Top-404
81TigDetN-7
81TigDetN-13
81TigDetN-22
81TigDetN-53
81TigDetN-61
81TigDetN-83
81TigDetN-95
81TigDetN-98
81TigDetN-108
81TigDetN-112
81TigSecNP-16
81TigSecNP-32
83FleSta-233
83FleSti-NNO
87FleStiWBC-S1
87SpoTeaL-15
87Top-631
87TopTif-631
88FleStiWBC-S8
88FleWaxBC-C13
88PanSti-460
88RedFolSB-110
89FleWaxBC-C13
90PubSti-643
90RedFolSB-112
90VenSti-523
91PanCanT1-123
94ImpProP-6
94Sco-322
94ScoGolR-322
95PanSti-152
96PanSti-147
Tigers, LSU
93LSUTigM-1
Tijerina, Tano
94HelBreF-3614
94HelBreSP-6
96HelBreTI-26
Tijerina, Tony
91PitMetC-1
91PitMetP-3426
92St.LucMCB-22
92St.LucMF-1750
93CapCitBC-22
93CapCitBF-464
94BinMetF-707
95BinMetTI-10
96StLucMTI-21
Tilden, Bill
28W512-36
37DixLid-6
37DixPre-6
Tiller, Brad
94BurIndC-24
94BurIndF-3806
96WatIndTI-31
96WesOahCHWB-25
Tillman, Bennie
94IdaFalBF-3601
94IdaFalBSP-5
Tillman, Darren
91HunCubC-25
91HunCubP-3350
92GenCubC-24
92GenCubF-1574
92PeoChiC-2
Tillman, J. Bob
61UniOil-S9
62Top-368
63Top-384
64Top-112
64TopVen-112
65OPC-222
65Top-222
66OPC-178
66Top-178
66TopVen-178
67CokCapRS-10
67DexPre-207
67OPC-36
67Top-36
67TopRedSS-23
68OPC-174
68Top-174
68TopVen-174
69MilBra-272
69Top-374
70Top-668
71MLBOffS-453
71OPC-244
71Top-244
72MilBra-343
78TCM60I-172
81RedSoxBG2S-124
92YanWIZ6-128
Tillman, Ken
81RedPioT-20
Tillman, Rusty
82TidTidT-11
83TidTidT-19
84TidTidT-9
85LasVegSC-102
86TacTigP-23
88PhoFirC-21
88PhoFirP-59
89PhoFirC-15
89PhoFirP-1479
91MetWIZ-409
Tillman, Tony (Tommy)
89BurIndS-23
90BurIndP-3008
Tillmon, Darrell
95MicBatCTI-28
Tillotson, Thad
67Top-553
81TCM60I-462
92YanWIZ6-129
Tilma, Tommy
90WicStaSGD-34
Tilmon, Pat
88BurBraP-6
89DurBullS-21
89DurBulTI-21
90DurBulTI-14
Tilton, Ira
96BatCliTI-20
Timberlake, Don
83PeoSunF-13
85MidAngT-12
86MidAngP-22
Timberlake, Gary
83Pil69G-4
Timbers, Wausau
82WauTimF-2
Timko, Andy
81MiaOriT-13
90HagSunDGB-32
Timko, John
92NiaFalRC-20
92NiaFalRF-3328
93BriTigC-21
Timlin, Mike
88MyrBeaBJP-1184
89DunBluJS-19
90DunBluJS-20
90FloStaLAS-45
90StaFS7-67
91BluJayFS-29
91BluJayS-7
91Bow-15
91Cla3-T90
91DonRoo-27
91FleUpd-68
91Lea-525
91OPCPre-122
91ScoRoo-85T
91TopTra-121T
91TopTraT-121T
91UppDec-785
92Don-301
92Fle-343
92FleRooS-8
92OPC-108
92OPCPre-172
92Sco-214
92Sco100RS-58
92StaClu-493
92SyrChiMB-23
92Top-108
92TopDeb91-172
92TopGol-108
92TopGolW-108
92TopMic-108
92UppDec-409
93BluJayD-25
93BluJayD4-22
93BluJayFS-31
93Don-87
93Fle-701
93Lea-465
93OPC-295
93PacSpa-657
93Sco-410
93StaClu-120
93StaCluFDI-120
93StaCluMOP-120
93Top-564
93TopGol-564
93TopInaM-564
93TopMic-564
93Toy-42
93Ult-294
93UppDec-322
93UppDecGold-322
94BluJayUSPC-2S
94BluJayUSPC-9D
94Fla-123
94Fle-345
94Sco-298
94ScoGolR-298
94StaClu-441
94StaCluFDI-441
94StaCluGR-441
94StaCluMOP-441
94StaCluT-180
94StaCluTFDI-180
94Top-333
94TopGol-333
94TopSpa-333
94Ult-144
95BluJayUSPC-3H
95BluJayUSPC-10S
95FleUpd-30
95Top-58
96BluJayOH-32
96Fle-284
96FleTif-284
96LeaSigEA-202
97BluJayS-19
97ColCho-494
97Fle-250
97FleTif-250
97Pac-229
97PacLigB-229
97PacSil-229
97Sco-411
97ScoHobR-411
97ScoResC-411
97ScoShoS-411
97ScoShoSAP-411
97StaClu-171
97StaCluMOP-171
97Top-23
97Ult-449
97UltGolME-449
97UltPlaME-449
97UppDec-519
Timmerman, Tom
70Top-554
71MLBOffS-408
71OPC-296
71Top-296
72OPC-239
72Top-239
73OPC-413
73TigJew-20
73Top-413
74OPC-327
74Top-327
Timmons, Ozzie
91GenCubC-23
91GenCubP-4233
92StaCluD-187
92UppDecML-162
92UppDecMLPotY-PY8
93Bow-552
93ClaFS7-29
93OrlCubF-2800
94ActPac-40
94Bow-466
94ExcFS7-169
94IowCubF-1288
94UppDecML-180
95ColCho-545T
95Exc-170
95Fla-335
95FleUpd-130
95SigRooOJ-32
95SigRooOJP-32
95SigRooOJPS-32
95SigRooOJS-32
95StaClu-605
95StaCluMOP-605
95StaCluSTWS-605
95Sum-154
95SumNthD-154
95Top-599
95UppDec-248
95UppDecED-248
95UppDecEDG-248
95UppDecML-213
96ColCho-88
96ColChoGS-88
96ColChoSS-88
96Don-28
96DonPreP-28
96Fla-226
96Fle-331
96FleTif-331
96Lea-59
96LeaPrePB-59
96LeaPrePG-59
96LeaPrePS-59
96LeaSigA-223
96LeaSigAG-224
96LeaSigAS-224
96Ult-172
96UltGolM-172
95UppDecMLFS-213
Timmons, Shayne
94St.CatBJC-25
94St.CatBJF-3648
Tincup, Frank
44CenFlo-23
Tingle, Darrel
87OneYanP-3
88PriWilYS-22
Tingley, Ron
82HawIsIT-1
83LasVegSBHN-22
85CalCanC-97
86RicBraP-23
87BufBisP-11
88ColSprSSC-12
88ColSprSSP-1532
89ColSprSSC-11
89ColSprSSP-257
89Fle-414
89FleGlo-414
89PanSti-316
89ScoHot1R-56
89Top-721
89TopBig-37
89TopTif-721
90CMC-500
90EdmTraC-23
90EdmTraP-520
90ProAAAF-96
91EdmTraLD-171
91EdmTraP-1519
91LinDriAAA-171
92Don-287
92OPC-388
92Sco-757
92StaClu-233

92TriPla-193
93AngMot-25
93Don-621
93Fle-577
93PacSpa-373
93PanSti-3
93StaClu-169
93StaCluAn-5
93StaCluFDI-169
93StaCluMOP-169
94Fle-71
94Pac-91

Tinker, Harold
88NegLeaD-19
92NegLeaRLI-60

Tinker, Joe
07CubA.CDPP-15
07CubGFGCP-16
08AmeCarE-32
08AmeCarE-66
08RosComP-111
09AmeCarE-110
09ColChiE-289A
09ColChiE-289B
09MaxPubP-14
09RamT20-118
09SpoNewSM-47
09T206-355
09T206-356
09T206-357
09T206-358
10ChiE-11
10CouT21-236
10CouT21-237
10CouT21-238
10CouT21-239
10CouT21-322
10DomDisP-116
10E101-43
10E102-24
10E98-26
10MelMinE-43
10NadCarE-48
10OrnOvaPP-13
10PeoT21-55A
10PeoT21-55B
10PeoT21-55C
10RedCroT-78
10RedCroT-79
10RedCroT-162
10RedCroT-252
10StaCarE-26
10SweCapPP-93A
10SweCapPP-93B
10W555-59
11BasBatEU-39
11DiaGumP-27
11L1L-122
11PloCanE-61
11S74Sil-71
11S81LarS-97
11SpoLifCW-352
11SpoLifM-184
11T205-171
11TurRedT-35
12ColRedB-289A
12ColRedB-289B
12ColTinT-289A
12ColTinT-289B
12HasTriFT-36E
12HasTriFT-42
12PhiCarE-30
12T207-183
13NatGamW-40
13TomBarW-36
14CraJacE-3
14PieStaT-56
15AmeCarE-39A
15AmeCarE-39B
15CraJacE-3
15SpoNewM-177
15VicT21-27
16BF2FP-70
16SpoNewM-174
16TanBraE-17
16TanBraE-19
36PC7AlbHoF-47
37KelPepS-BB15
48ExhHoF-28
50CalHOFW-70
60ExhWriH-23
60Fle-40
61Fle-143
63BazA-1
68LauWorS-5
69Baz-4
69Baz-11
70FleWorS-5
76ShaPiz-47
77GalGloG-160
80MarExhH-29
80PacLeg-42
80PerHaloFP-47
80SSPHOF-47
81ConTSN-12
84CubUno-7
84GalHaloFRL-43
87Cub190T-6
90PerGreM-40
92CubOldS-25
93ConTSN-817
93CraJac-16
93UppDecAH-123
93UppDecAH-147
94ConTSN-1164
94ConTSNB-1164
93UppDecTR-9
96PitPosH-11

Tinkey, Jim
86SanJosBP-21

Tinkey, Robert
87KenTwiP-13
88KenTwiP-1379

Tinkle, David
86EugEmeC-27
87Ft.MyeRP-5

Tinney, Roy
57SeaPop-36

Tinning, Lyle
32CubTeal-24
32OrbPinNP-17
32OrbPinUP-55
33TatOrb-55
34DiaMatCSB-181
34Gou-71

Tinoco, Luis
95EveAqaTI-27
95LinVen-209
96MidLeaAB-7
96WisTimRB-26

Tinsley, Charles
93MarPhiC-29
93MarPhiF-3491
94MarPhiC-27
94MarPhiF-3311

Tinsley, Lee
88SouOreAP-1706
89MadMusS-21
90CMC-868
90MadMusB-12
90MadMusP-2282
90MidLeaASGS-20
91Cla/Bes-207
91HunStaC-23
91HunStaLD-295
91HunStaP-1810
91HunStaTI-20
91LinDriAA-295
92CanIndF-704
92ColSprSSS-97
92OPC-656
92SkyAAAF-42
92Top-656
92TopGol-656
92TopGolW-656
92TopMic-656
93FleFinE-275
93Pin-604
93StaCluMari-12
93Ult-621
94ScoRoo-RT135
94ScoRooGR-RT135
94SpoRoo-130
94SpoRooAP-130
94StaClu-493
94StaCluFDI-493
94StaCluGR-493
94StaCluMOP-493
95DonTopotO-27
95Fin-289
95FinRef-289
95Fla-231
95FleUpd-14
95Lea-337
95Pac-46
95StaClu-160
95StaCluFDI-160
95StaCluMOP-160
95StaCluSTDW-RS160
95StaCluSTWS-160
95UppDec-397
95UppDecED-397
95UppDecEDG-397
96ColCho-67
96ColChoGS-67
96ColChoSS-67
96Don-413
96DonPreP-413
96Fle-36
96FleTif-36
96FleUpd-U172
96FleUpdTC-U172
96PhiTeal-32
96Sco-399
96StaClu-307
96StaCluMOP-307
96Top-359
96Ult-527
96UltGolM-527
97ColCho-478
97Pac-46
97PacLigB-46
97PacSil-46
97Ult-416
97UltGolME-416
97UltPlaME-416

Tippin, Greg
96MicBatCB-27

Tippitt, Brad
91KanCouCTI-21
92FreKeyC-5
92FreKeyF-1807

Tipton, Eric
79DiaGre-335
83TCMPla1944-29

Tipton, Gordon
88CapCodPPaLP-136
90GreFalDSP-20
91BakDodCLC-4
92BakDodCLC-25

Tipton, Jeff
82MadMusF-13

Tipton, Joe
48IndTeal-28
49Bow-103
49OlmStu-7
50Bow-159
51Bow-82
52Top-134
53BowBW-13
53Bri-23
53IndPenCBP-25
54Bow-180
83TopRep5-134

Tirado, Aristarco
86Ft.LauYP-22
88BlaYNPRWL-19
89AlbYanB-18
89AlbYanP-331
89AlbYanS-20
89BlaYNPRWL-185
95HarSenTI-36

Tirpack, Ken
92EliTwiC-9
92EliTwiF-3688
93ForWayWC-23
93ForWayWF-1976
93MidLeaAGF-7
94ExcFS7-99
94NasXprF-395

Tischinski, Tom
70OPC-379
70Top-379
71MLBOffS-476
71OPC-724
71Top-724
74AlbDukTI-65
74AlbDukTI-21

Tisdale, Freddie
78ArkTraT-23
79ArkTraT-11
80ArkTraT-18
81ArkTraT-5

Tisdale, Tom
90GasRanB-28
91GasRanC-28
92GulCoaRSP-27
95TulDriTI-25

Titcomb, Ledell
87OldJudN-507
89SFHaCN-17

Titus, Brian
94HelBreF-3615
94HelBreSP-21

Titus, John
08RosComP-146
09ColChiE-290A
09ColChiE-290B
09T206-359
10DomDisP-117
10LuxCigPP-21
10SweCapPP-132A
10SweCapPP-132B
11MecDFT-16
11PloCanE-62
11S74Sil-105
11SpoLifM-241
11T205-172
12ColRedB-290A
12ColRedB-290B
12ColTinT-290A
12ColTinT-290B
12HasTriFT-31C

Tjader, Jimmy
80AshTouT-11

Toale, John
85ElmPioT-22
86EveGiaC-7
86EveGiaPC-33
86GreHorP-23
87CliGiaP-2
87WinHavRSP-16
88St.LucMS-23
89LonTigP-1365
90CMC-732
90EasLeaAP-EL3
90LonTigP-1283
91AlbYanLD-21
91AlbYanP-1013
91LinDriAA-21
93HigDesMC-23
93HigDesMF-51
94ClaGolF-96
94ExcFS7-195

Tober, David
96BatCliTI-2

Tobey, Keith
90HigSchPLS-10

Tobias, Grayling
80MemChiT-24

Tobik, Dave
79Top-706
80Top-269
80VenLeaS-129
81Top-102
82Don-511
82Top-391
83Don-385
83Fle-343
83OPC-186
83RanAffF-41
83Top-691
83TopTra-113T
84Fle-433
84Nes792-341
84Top-341
84TopTif-341
85CalCanC-87
93RanKee-359

Tobin, Dan
90HigSchPLS-18
91BilMusP-3752
91BilMusSP-4
92BenMusSP-13
92BilMusF-3356

Tobin, Jack (John T.)
21Exh-178
21Nei-2
22E120-103
22W573-131
23W503-36
23WilChoV-163
25Exh-118
27AmeCarE-44
27AmeCarE-50
88ConSer5-28
94ConTSN-1168
94ConTSNB-1168

Tobin, James A.
39PlaBal-9
41Gou-30
83TCMPla1943-40
90HOFStiB-41
92ConTSN-372
94ConTSN-1257
94ConTSNB-1257

Tobin, John Patrick
48SomandK-16
49SomandK-27
53MotCoo-45

Tocchet, Rick
91UppDecS-2

Tocco, Todd
95EugEmeTI-27

Todd, Alfred
41Gou-28
43CubTeal-22
77TCMTheWY-7
79DiaGre-358
90DodTar-804
91ConTSN-239

Todd, Chuck
86WatIndP-28

Todd, Jackson
77MetDaiPA-25
78Top-481
79SyrChiT-13
79SyrChiTI-16
80SyrChiT-4
80SyrChiTI-20
81Don-31
81OPC-142
81Top-142
82Don-178
82Fle-623
82OPC-327
82SyrChiT-9
82SyrChiTI-22
82Top-565
86ElPasDP-22
87DenZepP-21
88DenZepP-1250
89DenZepC-24
89DenZepP-51
90CMC-672
90DenZepC-26
90DenZepP-642
90ProAAAF-667
91GasRanP-2706
91MetWIZ-410
92TulDriF-2711
94TulDriF-259
94TulDriTI-27
95TulDriTI-29
96MemChiB-2
93TulDriTI-26

Todd, Jim
73WicAerKSB-16
74WicAerODF-110
75OPC-519
75Top-519
76A'sPos-78
76OPC-221
76SSP-478
76Top-221
76VenLeaS-19
77Top-31
78Top-333
79OPC-46
79Top-103
80Top-629

Todd, Kyle
86PriWilPP-27
87HarSenP-13
88ColAstB-9

Todd, Theron
88CarLeaAS-37
88DurBulS-21
89DurBullS-22
89DurBulTI-22
89Sta-73
90DurBulTI-15
96StoPorB-29

Todt, Phil
25Exh-70
26Exh-71
27Exh-35
28Exh-36
29ExhFou-18
29PorandAR-91
33Gou-86
34GouCanV-39
92ConTSN-419

Toerner, Sean
81CliGiaT-20

Tofoya, Dennis
93CarMudTI-13

Toft, Marv
61UniOil-S10

Togher, Martin

91FreStaBS-13
Togneri, Paul
87BelMarTI-30
Tokheim, David
92ClaFS7-77
92ClePhiC-9
92ClePhiF-2072
93ClePhiC-22
93ClePhiF-2697
94ReaPhiF-2077
95ScrRedBTI-27
96ScrRedBB-25
Tolan, Bob
65CarTeal-26
65OPC-116
65Top-116
66OPC-179
66Top-179
66TopVen-179
67Top-474
68OPC-84
68Top-84
68TopVen-84
69MilBra-273
69Top-448
69TopSta-30
70DayDaiNM-25
70MLBOffS-36
70OPC-409
70Top-409
71MilDud-66
71MLBOffS-71
71OPC-190
71OPC-200
71Top-190
71Top-200
71TopCoi-81
71TopTat-99
72MilBra-344
72OPC-3
72Top-3
73Kel2D-32
73OPC-335
73Top-335
74GreHeroBP-6
74OPC-535
74PadDea-26
74PadMcDD-12
74Top-535
74TopDecE-23
75Hos-1
75HosTwi-1
75OPC-402
75Top-402
76Hos-42
76HosTwi-42
76OPC-56
76SSP-132
76Top-56
77PadSchC-58A
77PadSchC-58B
77PirPosP-30
77Top-188
80Top-708
84BeaGolGT-21
85BeaGolGT-25
87MarMot-28
89EriOriS-27
89PacSenL-1
89T/MSenL-106
89TopSenL-59
90EliSenL-2
91PacSenL-152
93UppDecS-8
Tolar, Kevin
90UtiBluSP-24
91Cla/Bes-114
91MidLeaAP-MWL12
91SouBenWSC-1
91SouBenWSP-2857
92SalSpuC-16
92SouBenWSF-177
93SarWhiSC-26
93SarWhiSF-1369
95LynHilTI-28
96CanIndB-26
Tolbert, Andrew
94IdaFalBF-3602
94IdaFalBSP-6
Tolbert, Mark
90SavCarP-2069
Tolentino, Jose
84ModA'sC-22
85TacTigC-127
86SouLeaAJ-6
87HunStaTI-22
87TacTigP-17
88OklCit8C-14
88OklCit8P-41
89TucTorC-13
89TucTorJP-25
89TucTorP-183
90CMC-615
90ProAAAF-202
90TucTorC-13
90TucTorP-212
91LinDriAAA-620
91TucTorLD-620
91TucTorP-2222
92BufBisBS-21
92BufBisF-329
92BufBisS-42
92Don-589
92OPC-541
92Top-541
92TopDeb91-173
92TopGol-541
92TopGolW-541
92TopMic-541
86HumStaDS-24
Tolentino, Reynaldo
91GulCoaRSP-25
Toler, Greg
85CedRapRT-15
86CedRapRT-11
Toliver, Fred
82CedRapRT-7
83IndIndTI-19
84WicAerRD-20
86Don-612
86Fle-647
86FleUpd-117
86PhiCIG-15
86PhiTas-43
86PorBeaP-23
87MaiGuiP-5
87MaiGuiT-7
87PhiTas-43
87Top-63
87TopTif-63
88PorBeaC-8
88PorBeaP-664
88Top-203
88TopTif-203
89Bow-147
89BowTif-147
89Don-510
89Fle-126
89FleGlo-126
89Sco-479
89Top-623
89TopTif-623
89UppDec-64
90OPC-423
90Top-423
90TopTif-423
92SalSpuF-3755
93CarMudF-2054
93CarMudTI-21
93FleFinE-120
Tollberg, Brian
95BelBreTI-15
Tolleson, Wayne
79TulDriT-1
80TulDriT-16
83Don-573
83RanAffF-3
83TopTra-114T
84Don-464
84Fle-434
84Nes792-557
84RanJarP-3
84Top-557
84TopSti-358
84TopTif-557
85Don-378
85Fle-571
85RanPer-3
85Top-247
85TopTif-247
86Don-134
86Fle-573
86FleUpd-118
86Lea-59
86Top-641
86TopTif-641
86TopTra-115T
86TopTraT-115T
86WhiSoxC-1
87Don-524
87DonOpeD-245
87Fle-118
87FleGlo-118
87OPC-224
87Top-224
87TopTif-224
88Don-154
88Fle-223
88FleGlo-223
88OPC-133
88PanSti-157
88Sco-117
88ScoGlo-117
88StaLinY-17
88Top-411
88TopTif-411
89Don-659
89Top-716
89TopTif-716
89YanScoNW-9
90PubSti-549
90Sco-386
90TopTra-123T
90TopTraT-123T
90TopTVY-27
90TulDriDGB-3
90UppDec-320
90YanScoNW-26
92YanWIZ8-192
93RanKee-360
Tollison, Dave
88CapCodPPaLP-141
89AncBucTI-14
90St.CatBJP-3471
91DunBluJC-19
91DunBluJP-217
92ClaFS7-163
92KnoBluJF-3000
92KnoBluJS-395
93ClaGolF-175
Tolliver, Jerome
91PitMetC-7
91PitMetP-3437
92ClaFS7-82
92ColMetC-1
92ColMetF-311
Tolly, Steve
92ColMetPI-14
94ElmPioC-26
Tolman, Tim
80ColAstT-3
81TucTorT-20
82AstAstI-3
82TucTorT-8
84TucTorC-57
85AstHouP-19
85AstMot-23
86NasSouTI-24
86Top-272
86TopTif-272
87TolMudHP-12
87TolMudHT-23
88TidTidCa-13
88TidTidCM-23
88TidTidP-1584
89SyrChiC-14
89SyrChiMB-22
89SyrChiP-815
90ProAAAF-211
90TucTorP-221
91BurAstC-27
91BurAstP-2817
92AshTouC-26
93OscAstC-26
93OscAstF-643
94OscAstC-26
94OscAstF-1154
94VenLinU-27
95JacGenTI-25
95LinVen-101
96TusTorB-26
Tom-E-Hawk, Mascot
84IndWhe-NNO
Toman, Tom
75AppFoxT-27
76AppFoxT-26
78AppFoxT-21
78KnoKnoST-23
Tomanek, Dick
58Top-123
59Top-369
Tomaselli, Chuck
84NasSouTI-23
Tomasello, John
92GasRanF-2263
93ButCopKSP-14
Tomashoff, Chris
94ButCopKSP-30
95ButCopKtI-25
96ButCopKB-7
Tomberlin, Andy
86SumBraP-27
88BurBraP-24
89DurBullS-23
89DurBulTI-23
89Sta-74
90Bes-265
90GreBraB-19
90GreBraP-1142
90GreBraS-19
90RicBraBC-20
91LinDriAAA-445
91RicBraBC-1
91RicBraLD-445
91RicBraTI-19
92RicBraBB-8
92RicBraF-390
92RicBraRC-24
92RicBraS-446
93BufBisF-531
94Don-329
94PawRedSDD-25
94PawRedSF-958
94Pin-227
94PinArtP-227
94PinMusC-227
94StaClu-70
94StaCluFDI-70
94StaCluGR-70
94StaCluMOP-70
95AthMot-24
96MetKah-30
96NorTidB-28
97PacPriGotD-GD177
97RicBraBC-16
Tomberlin, Rob
86SumBraP-28
Tomchek, Dave
93DurBulC-30
93DurBulTI-4
95BreBtaTI-TR
Tomita, Masaru
79TCMJapPB-40
Tomkins, Larry
91MisStaB-44
92MisStaB-41
93MisStaB-43
Tomko, Brett
96BesAutS-89
96BesAutSA-78
96Bow-227
96ChaLooB-28
96Top-26
96TopPowB-26
97Bow-76
97BowChr-104
97BowChrI-104
97BowChrIR-104
97BowChrR-104
97BowInt-76
97DonLim-74
97DonLimLE-74
97Fle-755
97FleTif-755
Tomlin, Dave
75OPC-578
75Top-578
76OPC-398
76SSP-627
76Top-398
77PadSchC-59
77Top-241
78Pep-24
78Top-86
79Top-674
80RedEnq-37
80Top-126
81SyrChiT-22
81SyrChiTI-21
82IndIndTI-25
84HawIsIC-126
85HawIsIC-241
86IndIndTI-31
87IndIndTI-7
89WesPalBES-28
94HarSenF-2109
Tomlin, Randy Leon
88WatPirP-12
89SalBucS-22
90HarSenP-1192
90HarSenS-17
90ProAaA-14
91Bow-518
91Cla1-T83
91Don-725
91Fle-52
91Lea-203
91OPC-167
91Sco-782
91StaClu-178
91Top-167A
91Top-167B
91TopDeb90-154
91TopDesS-167
91TopMic-167
91TopRoo-29
91TopTif-167
91ToyRoo-28
91UltUpd-103
91UppDecFE-76F
92Bow-495
92Don-367
92Fle-569
92Lea-256
92OPC-571
92Pin-213
92Pin-606
92PirNatl-22
92Sco-86
92StaClu-661
92StaCluECN-661
92Stu-88
92Top-571
92TopGol-571
92TopGolW-571
92TopMic-571
92Ult-261
92UppDec-537
93Bow-213
93Don-570
93Fle-121
93Lea-24
93OPC-257
93PacSpa-592
93Pin-74
93PirNatl-32
93Sco-101
93Sel-61
93StaClu-104
93StaCluFDI-104
93StaCluMOP-104
93Stu-219
93Top-416
93TopGol-416
93TopInaM-416
93TopMic-416
93TriPla-197
93Ult-102
93UppDec-284
93UppDecGold-284
94ColC-392
94ColChoGS-392
94ColChoSS-392
94Don-274
94Fin-156
94FinRef-156
94Fle-621
94Pac-508
94Pin-49
94PinArtP-49
94PinMusC-49
94StaClu-316
94StaCluFDI-316
94StaCluGR-316
94StaCluMOP-316
94Top-338
94TopGol-338
94TopSpa-338
94UppDec-368
94UppDecED-368
Tomlin, Rick
89EliTwiS-30
90EliTwiS-25
91EliTwiP-4317
92EliTwiC-24
92EliTwiF-3698
93ForWayWC-27
93ForWayWF-1985
94ForMyeMC-27
94ForMyeMF-1184

95ForMyeMTI-28
96NorNavB-3
Tomney, Phil
87OldJudN-508
Tomori, Denny
88ButCopKSP-12
Tompkins, Ron
66OPC-107
66Top-107
66TopVen-107
68Top-247
68TopVen-247
73WicAerKSB-17A
73WicAerKSB-17B
Toms, Tommy
75PhoGiaC-17
76PheGiaCr-33
76PhoGiaCa-12
76PhoGiaCC-22
76PhoGiaVNB-23
77Gia-24
77PhoGiaCC-23
77PhoGiaCP-23
77PhoGiaVNB-23
78SprRedWK-14
Tomsick, Troy
85DurBulT-13
Tomski, Jeffery
76BatTroTI-25
77WatIndT-24
81ChaLooT-22
Tomso, Matt
91SavCarC-12
91SavCarP-1653
Tonascia, Bruce
78GreBraT-25
Toney, Andy (Anthony)
88FayGenP-1082
88SouAtlLAGS-15
89LakTigS-23
Toney, Chris
88MarPhiS-31
Toney, Fred
15SpoNewM-178
16ColE13-174
16FleBreD-94
16SpoNewM-175
17HolBreD-105
21E121So1-106
21E121So8-97A
21E121So8-97B
21KoBreWSI-25
22E120-194
22W575-138
23W501-69
61Fle-80
69Baz-1
72FleFamF-14
72LauGreF-39
90HOFStiB-17
92ConTSN-347
Toney, Mike
93MedHatBJSP-9
94MedHatBJF-3683
94MedHatBJSP-23
95DunBluJTI-30
95Exc-145
Tonkin, Tonk (Wyatt)
78GreBraT-26
Tonnucci, Norm
86KnoBluJP-24
87KnoBluJP-1518
88SyrChiC-6
88SyrChiP-809
Tooch, Chuck
91WelPirP-3583
92WelPirC-23
92WelPirF-1334
93AugPirC-22
93AugPirF-1555
Toole, Matt
90WatDiaB-24
90WatDiaP-2387
Toole, Stephen John
87OldJudN-509
Tooley, Albert
12T207-184
90DodTar-805
Toolson, Earl
49RemBre-27
Toothman, Ken
57JetPos-20
Topaum, Tom
96BelGiaTI-6
Topham, Ryan
96SouBenSHS-25
Toporcer, Specs (George)
21E121So1-107
21Exh-179
21Nei-82
22E120-240
22W573-132
22W575-139
23W501-79
25Exh-64
26Exh-64
27AmeCarE-9
81ConTSN-35
88ConSer3-30
91ConTSN-176
92ConTSN-644
93ConTSN-893
Topping, Dan
95BelGiaTI-28
96BurBeeTI-14
Torassa, George
79CedRapGT-20
Torborg, Dale
94KinMetC-21
94KinMetF-3833
95GreBatTI-33
Torborg, Doug
85AncGlaPTI-27
87WatPirP-28
88SalBucS-21
89MiaMirIS-18
Torborg, Jeff
64Top-337
64TopVen-337
65Top-527
66Top-257
66TopVen-257
67CokCapD-10
67CokCapDA-10
67Top-398
68Top-492
69MilBra-274
69Top-353
70OPC-54
70Top-54
71MLBOffS-119
71OPC-314
71Top-314
72MilBra-345
72OPC-404
72Top-404
73OPC-154
73Top-154
78Top-351
79Top-96
86YanTCM-22
89TopTra-120T
89TopTraT-120T
89WhiSoxC-3
90DodTar-806
90OPC-21
90Top-21
90TopTif-21
90WhiSoxC-26
91OPC-609
91Top-609
91TopDesS-609
91TopMic-609
91TopTif-609
91WhiSoxK-10
92MetColP-19
92MetKah-10
92OPC-759
92Top-759
92TopGol-759
92TopGolW-759
92TopMic-759
93MetColP-48
93Top-509
93TopGol-509
93TopInaM-509
93TopMic-509
Torchia, Todd
87SpoIndP-21
88ChaRaiP-1209
Torchia, Tony
81BriRedST-8
83PawRedST-25
84PawRedST-3A
84PawRedST-3B
86NewBriRSP-24
87ChaRaiP-17
88RivRedWCLC-229
88RivRedWP-1413
89LasVegSC-25
89LasVegSP-27
89PacSenL-109
90CMC-527
90LasVegSC-24
90LasVegSP-139
90ProAAAF-27
91LasVegSP-255
91LasVegSP-256
91LinDriAAA-300
92LasVegSF-2810
92LasVegSS-250
94AshTouC-26
94AshTouF-1797
94SouAtlLAF-SAL31
95SalAvaTI-27
96ColSprSSTI-30
Torgeson, Earl
46SpoExcW-11-12
47Exh-224A
47Exh-224B
49Bow-17
50AmeNut&CCP-20
50Bow-163
50Dra-3
51Bow-99
51TopBluB-34
52Bow-72
52NatTeaL-37
52RedMan-NL25
52TipTop-43
52Top-97
54Bow-63
55Bow-210
56Top-147
57Top-357
58Top-138
59Top-351
60Lea-122
60Top-299
60WhiSoxTS-21
61Top-152
61Yan61RL-24
83TopRep5-97
85TCMPla1-32
91RinPos1Y2-8
92YanWIZ6-130
Torian, Van
92IdaFalGF-3520
92IdaFalGSP-13
Torino, Damian
93QuaCitRBC-22
93QuaCitRBF-104
Tornay, Nine
53MotCoo-11
57SeaPop-37
Torok, John
94BatCliF-3461
95PiePhiF-200
Torre, Frank
56BraBilaBP-15
56Top-172
57Top-37
58Top-117
59Top-65
59TopVen-65
60BraJayP-12
60BraLaktL-26
60BraSpiaS-24
60Top-478
62Top-303
63Top-161
90PacLeg-53
90SweBasG-74
91SweBasG-91
93TopGol-512
Torre, Joe
62BraJayP-11
62Jel-152
62Pos-152
62PosCan-152
62SalPlaC-152
62ShiPlaC-152
62Top-218
62Top-351
62TopStal-151
63BraJayP-11
63Jel-156
63Pos-156
63Top-347
64BraJayP-12
64Top-70
64TopCoi-118
64TopCoi-155
64TopGia-26
64TopSta-59
64TopStaU-72
64TopTatl-71
64TopVen-70
64WheSta-44
65Baz-16
65Kah-41
65OldLonC-19
65OPC-200
65Top-200
65TopEmbl-12
65TopTral-31
66Baz-36
66Kah-30
66OPC-130
66Top-130
66TopRubl-93
66TopVen-130
67AshOil-10
67Baz-36
67BraIrvD-4
67CokCapA-20
67CokCapB-9
67CokCapNLA-21
67DexPre-208
67DexPre-209
67Kah-37A
67Kah-37B
67OPCPapl-27
67Top-350
67TopPos-27
67TopTesF-22
67TopVen-324
68Baz-10
68CokCapB-9
68DexPre-73
68Kah-A11
68Kah-B34
68OPC-30
68Top-30
68TopActS-12A
68TopGamI-31
68TopVen-30
69CitMetC-11
69Kah-B20
69KelPin-17
69MilBra-275
69MLBOffS-216
69MLBPin-58
69Top-460
69TopSta-10
69TopSup-36
69TopTeaP-2
69TraSta-49
70CarTeal-12
70DayDaiNM-106
70MLBOffS-144
70OPC-190
70Top-190
70TraSta-3B
71CarTeal-41
71Kel-62
71MilDud-67
71MLBOffS-287
71OPC-62
71OPC-370
71Top-62
71Top-370
71TopCoi-11
71TopSup-61
71TopTat-85
72Kel-10
72MilBra-346
72OPC-85
72OPC-87
72OPC-341
72OPC-500
72ProStaP-24
72Top-85
72Top-87
72Top-341
72Top-500
72TopPos-16
73Kel2D-31
73LinPor-171
73OPC-450
73Top-450
73TopCanL-52
73TopCom-22
73TopPin-22
74MetJapEB-5
74MetJapEB-11
74OPC-15
74Top-15
74TopSta-119
75Hos-70
75MetSSP-20
75OPC-209
75OPC-565
75Top-209
75Top-565
76CraDis-64
76MetMSAP-2
76OPC-585
76SSP-541
76Top-585
77MetDaiPA-26
77Top-425
78AtlCon-23
78BraTCC-13
78MetDaiPA-1
78TCM60I-137
78Top-109
79Top-82
80Top-259
81Don-506
81Fle-325
81Top-681
82BraPol-9
82K-M-20
83BraPol-9
83Don-628
83Top-126
84BraPol-9
84Fle-654
84Nes792-502
84Top-502
84TopTif-502
85Top-438
85TopTif-438
86SpoDecG-49
90AGFA-4
90PacLeg-107
90SweBasG-130
91CarPol-9
91LinDri-2
91MetWIZ-411
91OPC-351
91StuPre-17
91SweBasG-92
91Top-351
91TopDesS-351
91TopMic-351
91TopTif-351
92CarMcD-39
92CarPol-23
92MVP-18
92MVP2H-17
92OPC-549
92Top-549
92TopGol-549
92TopGolW-549
92TopMic-549
93ActPacA-151
93CarPol-22
93TedWil-93
93Top-512
93TopInaM-512
93TopMic-512
94CarPol-22
94UppDecAH-186
94UppDecAH1-186
Torrealba, Pablo
76OPC-589
76Top-589
76VenLeaS-95
77Top-499
78Top-78
79Top-242
80VenLeaS-111
90RicBra2ATI-22
93LinVenB-152
Torrealba, Yolvit
95BelGiaTI-21
96BelGiaTI-5
Torres, Al
77ChaPatT-23
78SalPirT-16
79BufBisT-18
80BufBisT-13
80VenLeaS-140
81PorBeaT-24
82BufBisT-7
89MiaMirIS-19
Torres, Angel
78IndIndTI-18

80IndIndTI-27
Torres, David
76VenLeaS-68
Torres, Dilson
93LinVenB-93
93St.CatBJC-23
93St.CatBJF-3976
94CarLeaAF-CAR26
94VenLinU-111
95Exc-66
95Fla-267
95FleUpd-49
95LinVen-183
95TopTra-103T
95UppDec-259
95UppDecED-259
95UppDecEDG-259
96Pac-328
96WicWraB-14
Torres, Felix
62Top-595
63Jel-27
63Pos-27
63Top-482
Torres, Freddy
89FayGenP-1588
89NiaFalRP-22
90FayGenP-2418
93LinVenB-179
94VenLinU-81
Torres, Gil
77TCMTheWY-9
Torres, Hector
67Ast-28
69Top-526
70OPC-272
70Top-272
71MLBOffS-47
71OPC-558
71Top-558
72Dia-46
72Top-666
74CarHawI-103
76OPC-241
76SSP-128
76Top-241
77Spo-6917
78SyrChiT-19
80UtiBluJT-11
80VenLeaS-132
81TCM60I-342
82KnoBluJT-22
87AstShoSTw-16
87SyrChiP-1947
87SyrChiT-25
88SyrChiC-23
88SyrChiP-822
89SyrChiP-801
91BluJayFS-27
92DunBluJC-27
92DunBluJF-2014
94SyrChiF-988
94SyrChiTI-26
95SyrChiTI-24
96SyrChiTI-30
Torres, Jackson
95GreFalDTI-1
96SavSanB-16
Torres, Jaime
92GulCoaYF-3794
93GreHorC-23
93GreHorF-888
93LinVenB-193
93OneYanC-22
93OneYanF-3506
94GreBatF-479
94VenLinU-192
95LinVen-111
95TamYanYI-29
96ColCliB-28
96NorNavB-28
97GreBatC-24
Torres, Jessie
89PriPirS-21
90AugPirP-2468
91AugPirC-14
91AugPirP-808
92CarMudF-1186
92CarMudS-145
Torres, Jose
83ButCopKT-11
Torres, Leo (Leonardo)
89FayGenP-1569
90FayGenP-2408
91LakTigC-12
91LakTigP-267
92LonTigS-420
92SkyAA F-176
Torres, Loco (Antonio)
76VenLeaS-75
80VenLeaS-93
93LinVenB-132
Torres, Luis
96CliLumKTI-27
Torres, Martin
85MexCitTT-13
Torres, Miguel
88BlaYNPRWL-20
88OneYanP-2054
Torres, Nelson
80VenLeaS-36
Torres, Paul
89WytCubS-27
90GenCubP-3048
90GenCubS-7
90PeoChiTI-14
91Cla/Bes-174
91PeoChiC-13
91PeoChiTI-20
91WinSpiC-26
91WinSpiP-2843
92ClaFS7-318
92WinSpiC-7
92WinSpiF-1222
93DayCubC-21
93DayCubF-872
94OrlCubF-1399
96ArkTraB-25
95OrlCubF-23
Torres, Phil
87VerBeaDP-31
88SanAntMB-17
89ColMudB-27
Torres, Rafael
92HelBreF-1716
93BelBreC-25
93BelBreF-1711
Torres, Ramon
89BurIndS-24
90BurIndP-3024
91ColIndP-1502
Torres, Ray
79KnoKnoST-23
80GleFalWSBT-8
80GleFalWSCT-27
80IowOakP-12A
80IowOakP-12B
81AppFoxT-25
81GleFalWST-21
Torres, Ricky (Rick)
84GreHorT-17
87PriWilYP-4
88AlbYanP-1338
88BlaYNPRWL-50
88BlaYNPRWLU-11
89AlbYanB-11
89AlbYanP-335
89AlbYanS-21
89BlaYNPRWL-186
90AlbYanB-10
90AlbYanS-21
90CMC-218
90ColCliC-18
90ColCliP-677
90ProAAAF-327
90TopTVY-64
Torres, Rudy
83AndBraT-17
Torres, Rusty (Rosendo)
72OPC-124
72Top-124
73OPC-571
73Top-571
74OPC-499
74Top-499
75SalLakCC-1
77Top-224
78TucTorC-35
80Top-36
81PorBeaT-25
92YanWIZ7-153
Torres, Salomon
91Cla/Bes-324
91CliGiaC-8
91CliGiaP-834
91MidLeaAP-MWL6
92Bow-4
92Bow-584
92ClaBluBF-BC14
92ClaFS7-257
92ClaRedB-BC14
92DonRooP-BC18
92LeaGolR-BC11
92ProFS7-353
92ShrCapF-3872
92ShrCapS-596
92SkyAA F-263
92UppDecML-34
92UppDecML-261
93Bow-660
93ClaFS7-60
93ClaGolF-134
93ExcFS7-121
93LimRocDWB-66
93LimRocDWB-147
93ShrCapF-2760
93StaCluG-5
94Bow-366
94Bow-631
94ColC-19
94ColChoGS-19
94ColChoSS-19
94Don-327
94ExtBas-394
94Fin-439
94FinJum-439
94FinRef-439
94Fla-247
94FleMajLP-33
94FleUpd-197
94FUnPac-65
94GiaAMC-23
94GiaMot-14
94GiaUSPC-2S
94GiaUSPC-8D
94Lea-318
94LeaLimR-16
94OPC-165
94OPCHotP-3
94Pac-558
94Pin-261
94PinArtP-261
94PinMusC-261
94PinNewG-NG6
94PinRooTP-9
94Sco-641
94ScoBoyoS-39
94ScoGolR-641
94ScoRoo-RT88
94ScoRooGR-RT88
94Sel-182
94SelRooS-RS7
94Spo-156
94SpoSha-SH5
94StaClu-314
94StaCluFDI-314
94StaCluGR-314
94StaCluMOP-314
94StaCluT-10
94StaCluTFDI-10
94Top-298
94TopGol-298
94TopSpa-298
94TriPla-293
94Ult-295
94UppDec-27
94UppDecED-27
95ColCho-264
95ColChoGS-264
95ColChoSS-264
95Don-30
95DonPreP-30
95Lea-108
95MarPac-45
95Pac-385
95Pin-360
95PinArtP-360
95PinMusC-360
95Sco-528
95ScoGolR-528
95ScoPlaTS-528
95Sel-61
95SelArtP-61
95StaClu-436
95StaCluMOP-436
95StaCluSTWS-436
95TacRaiTI-23
96Sco-145
96TacRaiB-25
97Pac-194
97PacLigB-194
97PacSil-194
Torres, Sammy
80WatIndT-17
Torres, Tony
80HolMilT-24
81ElPasDT-18
92EriSaiC-29
92EriSaiF-1634
93HigDesMC-24
93HigDesMF-52
94BreCouMC-21
94BreCouMF-23
96PorSeaDB-27
Torrez, Mike
68OPC-162
68Top-162
68TopVen-162
69OPC-136
69Top-136
69TopFou-25
70OPC-312
70Top-312
71CarTeal-42
71MLBOffS-288
71OPC-531
71Top-531
72Dia-47
73ExpPos-7
73OPC-77
73Top-77
74OPC-568
74Top-568
75OPC-254
75Top-254
76A'sPos-71
76Hos-139
76OPC-25
76SSP-381
76Top-25
77BurCheD-110
77Hos-13
77OPC-144
77Top-365
77YanBurK-7
78Hos-127
78PapGinD-21
78RCColC-98
78SSP270-170
78Top-645
79Hos-22
79OPC-92
79RedSoxTI-4
79Top-185
80OPC-236
80Top-455
81Don-216
81Fle-233
81OPC-216
81Top-525
82Don-235
82Fle-310
82FleSta-166
82RedSoxC-20
82Top-225
82Top-786
82TopSti-151
82TopStiV-151
83Don-512
83Fle-197
83FleSti-62
83OPC-312
83Top-743
83TopFol-1
83TopTra-115T
84Don-556
84Fle-602
84Nes792-78
84OPC-78
84Top-78
84TopSti-113
84TopTif-78
85DomLeaS-14
89PacLegI-168
91MetWIZ-412
91OriCro-460
92YanWIZ7-154
93UppDecS-20
Torrez, Peter
80RocRedWT-21
84ChaO'sT-9
Torricelli, Tim
87StoPorP-22
88BelBreGS-14
89ElPasDGS-19
90CMC-33
90DenZepC-8
90DenZepP-629
90ProAAAF-654
92RocExpF-3012
93JamExpC-26
93JamExpF-3342
94JamJamC-29
Torrienti, Christobel
74LauOldTBS-18
90NegLeaS-19
Torti, Mike
96BatCliTI-14
Tortorice, Mark
86ModA'sC-19
86ModA'sP-25
88SouBenWSGS-27
Torve, Kelvin
83PhoGiaBHN-12
84ShrCapFB-23
85ChaO'sT-7
86RocRedWP-24
87RocRedWP-21
87RocRedWT-15
88PorBeaC-15
88PorBeaP-641
89PanSti-380
89PorBeaC-16
89PorBeaP-220
89TriA AAC-32
89UppDec-177
90CMC-373
90FleUpd-40
90ProAAAF-285
90TidTidC-22
90TidTidP-554
90TopTVM-63
90TriAAAC-32
90TriAllGP-AAA5
91Fle-163
91LinDriAAA-569
91MetColP-49
91MetWIZ-413
91Sco-754
91TidTidLD-569
91TidTidP-2520
Torve, Kenton Craig
87BirBarB-20
Tosar, Mike
91MiaHurBB-12
Tosca, Carlos
83GreHorT-27
84GreHorT-1
91BasCitRC-28
93KanCouCC-26
93KanCouCF-931
94PorSeaDF-692
94PorSeaDTI-3
95PorSeaDTI-26
96PorSeaDB-1
93KanCouCTI-25
Tosone, Joe
93JamExpC-24
93JamExpF-3341
Tost, Lou
49RemBre-28
50RemBre-24
Toth, Dave
91IdaFalBP-4334
91IdaFalBSP-15
92MacBraC-4
92MacBraF-271
93MacBraC-25
93MacBraF-1404
94DurBulC-22
94DurBulF-332
94DurBulTI-24
95DurBulTI-31
96GreBraB-28
96GreBraTI-42
Toth, Paul
62KahAtl-22
63Top-489
64Top-309
64TopVen-309
Toth, Robert
92AppFoxC-15
92AppFoxF-985
93CarLeaAGF-18
93WilBluRC-25
93WilBluRF-1998
94Bow-311
94ExcFS7-75
94MemChiF-359
95WicWraTI-13

96OmaRoyB-28
96SigRooOJ-33
96SigRooOJS-33
Totman, Jason
96CliLumKTI-28
Touch, Chuck
91WelPirC-11
Touchet, Sean
94ElmPioF-3475
94ElmPioC-21
Touchstone, Benny
28W513-94
Touma, Tim
87WesPalBEP-653
Toups, Tony
76BatTroTI-26
77WatIndT-25
Tourists, Asheville
95AshTouUTI-NNO
Tousignant, Lou
82MonNew-17
Toussaint, Daris
88PocGiaP-2088
Toutsis, Paul
86GreHorP-24
Touzzo, John
85LitFalMT-10
Tovar, Cesar
65OPC-201
65Top-201
66Top-563
67CokCapTw-11
67Top-317
67TopVen-191
68DexPre-72
68Top-420
69MilBra-276
69MLBOffS-71
69Top-530
69TopSta-199
69TopTeaP-15
69TraSta-9
69TwiTeaIC-9
70DayDaiNM-153
70MLBOffS-240
70OPC-25
70Top-25
71Kel-18
71MilDud-31
71MLBOffS-477
71OPC-165
71Top-165
71TopCoi-52
72MilBra-347
72OPC-275
72Top-275
73OPC-405
73Top-405
74OPC-538
74Top-538
74TopTra-538T
75OPC-178
75Top-178
76OPC-246
76Top-246
76VenLeaS-13
77Top-408
78TCM60I-174
78TwiFri-21
80VenLeaS-246
86TwiGreT-4
92YanWIZ7-155
93LinVenB-92
93RanKee-361
Tovar, Edgar
92JamExpC-21
92JamExpF-1510
93ExcFS7-62
93HarSenF-278
93LinVenB-141
94SanBerSC-23
94SanBerSF-2769
94VenLinU-180
95HarSenTI-13
95LinVen-112
Tovar, Gil
80VenLeaS-248
Tovar, Raul
82MiaMarT-18
83BirBarT-1
86MidAngP-23
93LinVenB-233
93LinVenB-276
Towers, Josh
96BluOriB-29
Towers, Kevin
84BeaGolGT-10
86ChaRaiP-26
88LasVegSC-8
88LasVegSP-242
89SpoIndSP-23
90SpoIndSP-28
Towers, Tony
82MonNew-18
Towey, Steve
88MyrBeaBJP-1185
89ModA'sC-16
Towle, Justin
92PriRedC-24
92PriRedF-3091
93BilMusF-3949
93BilMusSP-4
94ChaWheC-24
94ChaWheF-2706
97Bow-104
97BowCerBIA-CA80
97BowCerGIA-CA80
97BowChr-124
97BowChrI-124
97BowChrIR-124
97BowChrR-124
97BowInt-104
97FlaShoWotF-7
97Fle-544
97FleTif-544
97Ult-543
97UltGolME-543
97UltPlaME-543
Town, Randall
80WatRedT-6
81WatRedT-10
Towner, Kyle
94BelMarC-28
94BelMarF-3252
Townes, Jeremy
95DavLipB-23
Townley, Jason
88DunBluJS-17
88St.CatBJP-2027
90DunBluJS-21
90FloStaLAS-46
91KnoBluJLD-368
91KnoBluJP-1772
91LinDriAA-368
92ClaFS7-330
92KnoBluJF-2994
92KnoBluJS-396
94SyrChiF-974
94SyrChiTI-27
95LinVen-171
95SyrChiTI-25
Towns, Ryan
93EugEmeC-26
93EugEmeF-3857
94RocRoyC-25
94RocRoyF-566
95SprSulTI-28
Townsend, Chad
92BurIndC-25
92BurIndF-1665
93ClaFS7-263
93ColRedC-24
93ColRedF-608
94HigDesMC-26
94HigDesMF-2798
96SanBerSB-27
Townsend, George
87OldJudN-510
90KalBatN-53
90KalBatN-54
Townsend, Howard
85EveGiaC-16A
85EveGiaC-16B
86CliGiaP-24
87WauTimP-5
88SanBerSCLC-45
89VisOakCLC-100
89VisOakP-1421
Townsend, James
87SalAngP-15
88QuaCitAGS-17
89PalSprACLC-48
89PalSprAP-463
Townsend, John
03BreE10-144
Townsend, Ken
77CliDodT-27
78LodDodT-22
Townsend, Lee
88SanBerSB-3
Townsend, Mike
91MarPhiC-30
Townsend, Richard
92WelPirC-24
92WelPirF-1322
93AugPirC-23
93AugPirF-1545
94SalBucC-22
94SalBucF-2323
Toy, Tracy
86WatPirP-24
87MacPirP-2
88AugPirP-379
Toyotoshi, Chikada
89SalSpuCLC-131
Tozier, Pat
90OklSoo-9
Traber, Jim
85Don-45
85RocRedWT-9
86RocRedWP-25
86SpoRoo-32
87Don-477
87Fle-482
87FleGlo-482
87RocRedWP-26
87RocRedWT-20
87SpoTeaP-21
87Top-484
87TopSti-232
87TopTif-484
87ToyRoo-31
88OriFreB-28
88RocRedWTI-25
88Top-544
88TopTif-544
89Bow-13
89BowTif-13
89Fle-625
89FleGlo-625
89OPC-124
89OriFreB-28
89Sco-590
89Top-124
89TopSti-233
89TopTif-124
89UppDec-294
90Don-569
90Fle-193
90FleCan-193
90HagSunDGB-33
90PubSti-590
90UppDec-268
91OriCro-461
Trabous, Manuel
52LavPro-89
Tracewski, Dick
64Top-154
64TopVen-154
65DodTeal-19
65OPC-279
65Top-279
66Top-378
67CokCapTi-11
67Top-559
68CokCapT-11
68TigDetFPB-24
68Top-488
69MilBra-277
69OPC-126
69TigTeaIC-10
69Top-126
69TopFou-20
73OPC-323
73Top-323
81TCM60I-461
83Tig-26
84TigWavP-32
88TigDom-23
88TigPep-NNO
89TigMar-NNO
90DodTar-807
90TigCok-28
91TigCok-NNO
93TigGat-28
Trachsel, Steve
91GenCubP-4217
92ChaKniF-2772
92ChaKniS-169
92SkyAA F-77
92UppDecML-118
93Bow-172
93ClaFS7-264
93IowCubF-2133
94Bow-634
94Don-636
94ExtBas-225
94ExtBasRS-18
94Fin-296
94FinRef-296
94Fla-142
94FleMajLP-34
94FleUpd-111
94LeaGolR-19
94LeaLimR-25
94Pin-536
94PinArtP-536
94PinMusC-536
94ScoRoo-RT161
94ScoRooGR-RT161
94Sel-389
94SelRooS-RS18
94SP-73
94SPDieC-73
94StaClu-62
94StaClu-633
94StaCluFDI-62
94StaCluFDI-633
94StaCluGR-62
94StaCluGR-633
94StaCluMOP-62
94StaCluMOP-633
94StaCluT-345
94StaCluTFDI-345
94Top-778
94TopGol-778
94TopSpa-778
94Ult-465
94UppDec-28
94UppDecED-28
95Bow-409
95ColCho-212
95ColChoGS-212
95ColChoSE-86
95ColChoSEGS-86
95ColChoSESS-86
95ColChoSS-212
95Don-23
95DonPreP-23
95DonTopotO-206
95Emb-96
95EmbGolI-96
95Emo-114
95Fin-18
95FinRef-18
95Fla-117
95Fle-425
95FleRooS-18
95FleTeaL-16
95Lea-163
95Pac-80
95Pin-131
95PinArtP-131
95PinMusC-131
95Sco-337
95ScoGolR-337
95ScoPlaTS-337
95StaClu-80
95StaCluFDI-80
95StaCluMOP-80
95StaCluSTWS-80
95StaCluVR-50
95Stu-138
95Top-273
95TopCyb-147
95Ult-140
95UltAlIR-10
95UltAlIRGM-10
95UltGolM-140
95UltSecYS-13
95UltSecYSGM-13
95UppDec-67
95UppDecED-67
95UppDecEDG-67
95UppDecSE-124
95UppDecSEG-124
95USPlaCMLA-2S
96Cir-113
96CirRav-113
96ColCho-497
96ColChoGS-497
96ColChoSS-497
96Don-466
96DonPreP-466
96Fle-332
96FleCub-18
96FleTif-332
96LeaSigEA-203
96Sco-389
96StaCluVRMO-50
96TeaOut-81
96Ult-173
96UltGolM-173
96UppDec-294
97Cir-339
97CirRav-339
97ColCho-69
97Don-41
97DonPreP-41
97DonPrePGold-41
97Fin-132
97FinEmb-132
97FinEmbR-132
97FinRef-132
97Fle-287
97FleTif-287
97Lea-268
97LeaFraM-268
97LeaFraMDC-268
97MetUni-17
97PacPriGotD-GD124
97Pin-132
97PinArtP-132
97PinMusC-132
97Sco-456
97ScoHobR-456
97ScoResC-456
97ScoShoS-456
97ScoShoSAP-456
97StaClu-118
97StaCluMOP-118
97Top-154
97TopGal-92
97TopGalPPI-92
97Ult-171
97UltGolME-171
97UltPlaME-171
97UppDec-34
Tracy, Andy
96VerExpB-28
Tracy, Jack
81TCM60I-451
Tracy, Jim (James C.)
87MyrBeaBJP-1450
88DunBluJS-18
88PeoChiTI-29
90HarSenS-18
90ProAaA-13
92BufBisBS-22
92BufBisF-323
92BufBisS-43
93BufBisF-518
Tracy, Jim (James E.)
80WicAerT-2
81Don-520
81Fle-308
82Fle-605
82FleSta-97
82Top-403
82TucTorT-9
87PeoChiP-27
89ChaLooB-7
89ChaLooGS-1
89HarSenP-309
89HarSenS-19
90ChaLooGS-1
90EasLeaAP-EL27
90HarSenP-1193
91BufBisLD-46
91BufBisP-542
91ChaLooLD-174
91ChaLooP-1974
91LinDriAA-174
91LinDriAAA-46
91PacSenL-70
93HarSenF-284
Tracy, Rich
88BatCliP-1685
Tracy, Rick
87SanJosBP-20
Traen, Tom
86JacExpT-5
87WesPalBEP-671
Traffley, William
87OldJudN-511
Trafton, Todd
84AriWilP-18
86AriWilP-18
87DayBeaAP-1
88BirBarB-9

89BirBarB-19
89BirBarP-97
89SouLeaAJ-10
90CMC-647
90ProAAAF-175
90VanCanC-20
90VanCanP-497
91ChaLooLD-172
91ChaLooP-1969
91LinDriAA-172
92ChaLooF-3832
92NasSouF-1842
92NasSouS-295
93LinVenB-69

Tragresser, Walter
16FleBreD-95

Trail, Chet
81TCM60I-399

Tramble, Otis
82QuaCitCT-20

Trammell, Alan
78TigBurK-15
78Top-707
79OPC-184
79Top-358
80OPC-123
80Top-232
81AllGamPI-24
81CokTeaS-57
81Don-5
81Fle-461
81FleStiC-89
81Kel-51
81OPC-133
81TigDetN-68
81TigPepT-1
81Top-709
81TopScr-38
81TopSti-75
82Don-5
82Don-5A
82Don-76
82Don-76A
82Fle-283
82FleSta-155
82OPC-381
82Squ-4
82Top-475
82TopSti-181
82TopStiV-181
83AllGamPI-25
83Don-207
83Fle-344
83FleSti-253
83OPC-95
83Tig-27
83Top-95
83TopSti-66
84AllGamPI-115
84Don-293
84Dra-30
84Fle-91
84FleSti-14
84FunFooP-40
84Nes792-510
84OPC-88
84TigFarJ-14
84TigWavP-33
84Top-510
84TopRubD-25
84TopSti-266
84TopStiB-9
84TopTif-510
85AllGamPI-26
85Don-171
85DonActA-44
85Dra-31
85Fle-23
85FleLimE-40
85KASDis-17
85KitCloD-17
85Lea-158
85OPC-181
85SevCoi-D8
85SevCoi-G15
85ThoMcAD-20
85TigCaiD-18
85TigWen-20
85Top-690
85TopGloS-16
85TopRubD-25
85TopSti-18
85TopSti-20
85TopSti-258
85TopSup-25
85TopTif-690
86BasStaB-111
86Don-171
86DonAll-45
86Fle-241
86Fle-633
86FleMin-50
86FleStiC-121
86Lea-101
86OPC-130
86Spo-147
86Spo-172
86TigCaiD-19
86Top-130
86TopSti-267
86TopTat-10
86TopTif-130
87Don-127
87DonHig-51
87DonOpeD-216
87Fle-167
87FleGlo-167
87FleHotS-41
87FleMin-107
87FleRecS-38
87FleStiC-118
87Lea-126
87OPC-209
87RedFolSB-62
87SevCoi-D11
87Spo-188
87SpoTeaP-15
87StuPan-19
87TigCaiD-7
87TigCok-4
87Top-687
87TopMinL-56
87TopSti-270
87TopTif-687
88ClaBlu-231
88Don-4
88Don-230
88DonAll-22
88DonBasB-281
88DonBonM-BC11
88DonSupD-4
88Dra-13
88Fle-74
88Fle-635
88FleAll-9
88FleAwaW-43
88FleBasA-42
88FleBasM-39
88FleExcS-42
88FleGlo-74
88FleGlo-635
88FleHotS-44
88FleLeaL-42
88FleMin-25
88FleRecS-41
88FleStiC-29
88FleSup-41
88FleTeaL-43
88KayB-31
88Lea-4
88Lea-167
88MSAFanSD-6
88MSAJifPD-16
88Nes-35
88OPC-320
88PanSti-94
88PanSti-444
88Sco-37
88Sco-651
88ScoGlo-37
88ScoGlo-651
88Spo-25
88StaLinTi-19
88StaTra-1
88StaTra-2
88StaTra-3
88StaTra-4
88StaTra-5
88StaTra-6
88StaTra-7
88StaTra-8
88StaTra-9
88StaTra-10
88StaTra-11
88TigPep-2
88TigPol-13
88Top-320
88Top-389
88Top-429
88TopBig-8
88TopCoi-30
88TopGloS-37
88TopMinL-12
88TopRitTM-18
88TopSti-273
88TopStiB-45
88TopTif-320
88TopTif-389
88TopTif-429
88TopUKM-79
88TopUKMT-79
89Bow-105
89BowTif-105
89CadEllD-58
89CerSup-10
89ClaTraO-128
89Don-180
89DonBasB-13
89DonBonM-BC17
89Fle-148
89FleAll-11
89FleBasA-41
89FleBasM-39
89FleExcS-41
89FleGlo-148
89FleHeroB-40
89FleLeaL-40
89FleSup-40
89FleWaxBC-C26
89KayB-30
89KinDis-9
89MasBreD-4
89OPC-49
89PanSti-343
89RedFolSB-121
89Sco-110
89ScoHot1S-7
89Spo-215
89SpoIllFKI-56
89TigMar-3
89TigPol-3
89Top-400
89Top-770
89TopAme2C-29
89TopBasT-43
89TopBatL-22
89TopBig-123
89TopCapC-12
89TopCoi-56
89TopDouA-4
89TopGloS-25
89TopHilTM-29
89TopSti-281
89TopStiB-12
89TopTif-400
89TopTif-609
89TopTif-770
89TopUKM-77
89TVSpoM-69
89UppDec-290
89UppDec-690
90Bow-353
90BowTif-353
90ClaBlu-106
90Don-90
90DonBesA-7
90DOnBonM-BC26
90DonLeaS-20
90Fle-617
90FleBasA-41
90FleBasM-41
90FleCan-617
90GooHumICBLS-25
90Hot50PS-46
90Lea-218
90MLBBasB-88
90OPC-440
90PanSti-70
90Pos-28
90PubSti-296
90PubSti-484
90RedFolSB-96
90Sco-9
90Sco100S-41
90Spo-154
90StaLonJS-10
90StaLonJS-24
90SunSee-15
90TigCok-24
90Top-440
90TopBig-190
90TopCoi-31
90TopDou-66
90TopSti-281
90TopStiB-45
90TopTif-440
90UppDec-554
90USPlaCA-10S
90WonBreS-13
91Bow-154
91Bow-370
91CadEllD-57
91Cla2-T96
91ClaGam-97
91Don-118
91Fle-355
91Lea-351
91MajLeaCP-33
91MSAHolD-10
91OPC-275
91OPC-389
91OPCPre-123
91PanCanT1-8
91PanFreS-291
91PanSti-238
91RedFolS-93
91Sco-40
91Sco-852
91Sco100S-63
91SevCoi-M15
91StaClu-63
91StaCluP-44
91StaPinB-50
91Stu-59
91TigCok-3
91TigPol-13
91Top-275
91Top-389
91TopCraJ2-26
91TopDesS-275
91TopDesS-389
91TopMic-275
91TopMic-389
91TopTif-275
91TopTif-389
91TopTriH-A6
91Ult-129
91UppDec-223
91UppDecSS-SS2
92Bow-690
92ClaGam-90
92Don-164
92DonCraJ2-31
92Fle-148
92Hig5-49
92Lea-172
92OPC-120
92OPCPre-31
92PanSti-108
92Pin-113
92PinRool-17
92Sco-515
92SpoStaCC-46
92StaClu-850
92StaCluNC-850
92Stu-179
92Top-120
92TopGol-120
92TopGolW-120
92TopKid-75
92TopMic-120
92TriPla-176
92Ult-64
92UppDec-273
93Bow-391
93DiaMar-109
93Don-655
93Fin-18
93FinRef-18
93Fla-209
93Fle-613
93Lea-421
93MetBak-38
93OPC-360
93PacSpa-115
93Pin-353
93Sco-313
93Sel-230
93SP-241
93StaClu-416
93StaCluFDI-416
93StaCluMOP-416
93TigGat-25
93Top-660
93TopGol-660
93TopInaM-660
93TopMic-660
93TriPla-191
93Ult-204
93UppDec-532
93UppDecGold-532
94Bow-509
94ColChoSS-474
94Don-280
94ExtBas-81
94Fin-159
94FinPre-159P
94FinRef-159
94Fla-53
94Fle-144
94Fle-709
94FUnPac-103
94Lea-120
94LeaL-34
94OPC-72
94Pac-230
94PanSti-69
94Pin-429
94PinArtP-429
94PinMusC-429
94Sco-337
94ScoGolR-337
94Sel-285
94SP-181
94SPDieC-181
94Spo-93
94StaClu-331
94StaCluFDI-331
94StaCluGR-331
94StaCluMOP-331
94StaCluMOP-ST20
94StaCluST-ST20
94Stu-194
94Top-75
94TopGol-75
94TopSpa-75
94TriPla-249
94TriPlaM-7
94Ult-358
94UppDec-201
94UppDecED-201
95ColCho-471
95ColChoGS-471
95ColChoSS-471
95Don-502
95DonPreP-502
95DonTopotO-80
95Emo-46
95Fin-203
95FinRef-203
95Fla-261
95Fle-62
95Lea-224
95LeaLim-93
95Pac-161
95PacPri-51
95Pin-392
95PinArtP-392
95PinMusC-392
95Sco-383
95ScoGolR-383
95ScoPlaTS-383
95SP-154
95SPCha-114
95SPCha-153
95SPChaDC-114
95SPChaDC-153
95SPSil-154
95StaClu-298
95StaCluMOP-298
95StaCluSTWS-298
95StaCluVR-155
95Stu-98
95Top-474
95TopCyb-267
95UC3-12
95UC3ArtP-12
95Ult-51
95UltGolM-51
95UppDec-426
95UppDecED-426
95UppDecEDG-426
95UppDecSE-96
95UppDecSEG-96
96Cir-42
96CirRav-42
96ColCho-145
96ColChoGS-145
96ColChoSS-145
96Don-172

96DonPreP-172
96EmoXL-63
96Fla-85
96Fle-121
96FleGolM-10
96FleTif-121
96Lea-11
96LeaPrePB-11
96LeaPrePG-11
96LeaPrePS-11
96Pac-312
96PacPri-P103
96PacPriG-P103
96Pin-81
96PinArtP-52
96PinSta-52
96ProSta-124
96Sco-100
96ScoDugC-A72
96ScoDugCAP-A72
96SP-85
96StaClu-337
96StaCluEPB-337
96StaCluEPG-337
96StaCluEPS-337
96StaCluMOP-337
96StaCluVRMO-155
96Ult-65
96UltGolM-65
96UppDec-106
96UppDec-330
97ColCho-105
97Don-220
97DonPreP-220
97DonPrePGold-220
97Fle-108
97FleTif-108
97Pac-96
97PacLigB-96
97PacSil-96
97Pin-93
97PinArtP-93
97PinMusC-93
97Sco-106
97ScoPreS-106
97ScoShoS-106
97ScoShoSAP-106
97Ult-64
97UltGolME-64
97UltPlaME-64
97UppDec-75
Trammell, Bubba
94JamJamC-1
94JamJamF-3982
95SPML-56
95TenVolW-11
96Exc-53
96JacSunB-28
97Bow-71
97BowChr-101
97BowChrI-101
97BowChrIR-101
97BowChrR-101
97BowInt-71
97ColCho-468
97Don-364
97DonFraFea-5
97DonLim-200
97DonLimLE-200
97DonPre-150
97DonPreCttC-150
97DonPreP-364
97DonPrePGold-364
97Fin-249
97FinRef-249
97FlaSho-A18
97FlaSho-B18
97FlaSho-C18
97FlaShoLC-18
97FlaShoLC-B18
97FlaShoLC-C18
97FlaShoLCM-A18
97FlaShoLCM-B18
97FlaShoLCM-C18
97FlaShoWotF-9
97Fle-510
97FleNewH-13
97FleTif-510
97Lea-322
97LeaFraM-322
97LeaFraMDC-322
97NewPin-160
97NewPinAP-160
97NewPinMC-160
97NewPinPP-160
97PinCer-127
97PinCerMBlu-127
97PinCerMG-127
97PinCerMR-127
97PinCerR-127
97PinTotCPB-127
97PinTotCPG-127
97PinTotCPR-127
97PinX-P-120
97PinX-PMoS-120
97Sco-483
97ScoHobR-483
97ScoResC-483
97ScoShoS-483
97ScoShoSAP-483
97Sel-125
97SelArtP-125
97SelRegG-125
97SP-14
97SpoIll-25
97SpoIllEE-25
97Top-206
97Ult-527
97UltGolME-527
97UltPlaME-527
97UppDec-533
Trammell, Gary
94AubAstC-20
94AubAstF-3768
95MidLeaA-53
95QuaCitRBTI-27
96KisCobB-29
Trammell, Marcus
88UtiBluSP-11
Tramuta, Marc
91YakBeaC-3
91YakBeaP-4256
Tranbarger, Mark
92SprCarC-16
92SprCarF-870
93SavCarC-24
93SavCarF-687
94WinSpiC-21
94WinSpiF-270
95ChaLooTI-22
Tranberg, Mark
92BatCliC-22
92BatCliF-3266
93SouAtlLAGF-54
93SpaPhiC-1
93SpaPhiF-1056
94Bow-468
94ExcFS7-249
94ReaPhiF-2062
95ReaPhiTI-26
Trapaga, Julio
94DurBulC-23
94DurBulF-338
94DurBulTI-25
Trapp, Mike
87Ft.MyeRP-4
Trappers, Salt Lake
91SalLakTP-3230
Trachsel, Steve
94SpoRoo-83
94SpoRooAP-83
Trautman, Keith
92YakBeaC-19
Trautwein, Dave
87LitFalMP-2392
88St.LucMS-24
89JacMetGS-8
89TexLeaAGS-27
90CMC-363
90MetColP-51
90ProAAAF-276
90TidTidC-12
90TidTidP-545
90TopTVM-64
91LinDriAAA-570
91TidTidLD-570
91TidTidP-2510
92SalSpuC-4
92SalSpuF-3756
Trautwein, John
86JacExpT-7
87JacExpP-449
87SouLeaAJ-14
88BlaYNPRWL-155
88DonRoo-24
88DonTeaBRS-NEW
88FleUpd-10
88FleUpdG-10
89PawRedSC-9
89PawRedSP-685
89PawRedSTI-25
90CMC-253
90PawRedSC-2
90PawRedSDD-26
90PawRedSP-463
90ProAAAF-435
90TopTVRS-62
Travels, Darren
85UtiBluST-6
86JamExpP-26
Travers, Bill
75OPC-488
75SacSolC-20
75Top-488
76BreA&P-14
76OPC-573
76SSP-244
76Top-573
77BurCheD-90
77Hos-87
77Kel-9
77OPC-174
77Top-125
77TopCloS-49
78Top-355
79OPC-106
79Top-213
80Top-109
81Don-508
81Fle-514A
81Fle-514B
81Fle-525
81LonBeaPT-13
81Top-704
81TopTra-845
82Top-628
89PacSenL-118
89T/MSenL-107
89TopSenL-21
94BreMilB-279
Travers, Steve
82IdaFalAT-13
Travis, Cecil
34DiaMatCSB-182
36GouWidPPR-A101
36NatChiFPR-70
36OveCanR-42
37OPCBatUV-126
37WheBB14-14
37WheBB7-29B
37WheBB9-15
38WheBB10-2
39ExhSal-57
39GouPreR303A-42
39PlaBal-114
39WorWidGTP-42
39WorWidGV-23
40PlaBal-16
41DouPlaR-75
41PlaBal-48
46SpoExcW-9-7
77TCMTheWY-76
79DiaGre-53
83DiaClaS2-101
84TCMPla1-10
95ConTSN-1349
96NoiSatP-3
Trawick, Tim
95EveAqaTI-28
96LanJetB-28
Traxler, Brian
89SanAntMB-11
90AlbDukT-28
90DonRoo-38
91LinDriAA-544
91SanAntMLD-544
91SanAntMP-2984
91TopDeb90-155
92AlbDukF-730
92AlbDukS-21
93AlbDukF-1472
Traylor, Keith
84LitFalMT-9
Traynor, Pie (Harold)
22E120-225
22W572-107
23MapCriV-2
25Exh-55
26Exh-55
26SpoComoA-43
26SpoNewSM-9
27Exh-28
27YorCarE-14
28PorandAR-A36
28PorandAR-B36
28StaPlaCE-67
28W502-14
28W513-82
28Yue-14
29ExhFou-13
29PorandAR-92
30SchR33-23
31Exh-13
31W517-2
32R33So2-xx
33DelR33-12
33Gou-22
33GouCanV-22
33NatLeaAC-15
33RitCE-10C
34BatR31-14
34BatR31-100
34DiaStaR-27
34DiaStaR-99
34ExhFou-7
35ExhFou-7
35GouPuzR-4B
35GouPuzR-7B
35GouPuzR-12B
36ExhFou-7
36NatChiFPR-71
36PC7AlbHoF-55
36R31PasP-45
36R31Pre-G15
36SandSW-46
40PlaBal-224
50CalHOFW-71
60Fle-77
61Fle-89
61Fle-144
61GolPre-15
63HalofFB-19
67TopVen-144
68SpoMemAG-15
72KelATG-8
76OPC-343
76RowExh-15
76ShaPiz-55
76Top-343
77GalGloG-102
77GalGloG-205
77ShaPiz-17
80PacLeg-36
80PerHaloFP-55
80SSPHOF-55
81ConTSN-63
82DiaCla-40
83ConMar-40
86ConSer1-38
86PirGreT-4
86SpoDecG-11
86TCM-10
87HygAllG-44
87NesDreT-3
88ConNatA-21
91ConTSN-36
91ConTSN-268
91SweBasG-148
92ConTSN-434
93ActPacA-96
93ActPacA2-30G
93ConMasB-9
93ConTSN-670
93ConTSNP-1050
93LegFoi-11
94ConTSN-1050
94ConTSN-1093
94ConTSNB-1050
94ConTSNB-1093
94ConTSNCI-29
94TedWil-80
Treadgill, Chris
90QuaCitAGS-29
Treadway, Andre
82DurBulT-21
85GreBraTI-21
86RicBraP-24
Treadway, Doug
88WinHavRSS-24
Treadway, George
87OldJudN-512
90DodTar-1086
Treadway, Jeff
86VerRedP-22
87NasSouTI-21
88Don-29
88DonRoo-17
88Fle-249
88FleGlo-249
88FleMin-76
88Lea-29
88RedKah-15
88Sco-646
88ScoGlo-646
88ScoYouS2-26
88Spo-225
88StaLinRe-19
88TopBig-214
88TopTra-122T
88TopTraT-122T
89BraDub-27
89ClaLigB-54
89Don-351
89DonBasB-141
89Fle-173A
89Fle-173B
89FleGlo-173
89FleUpd-75
89OPC-61
89PanSti-73
89Sco-86
89ScoHot1R-84
89ScoRoo-18T
89Spo-107
89Top-685
89TopSti-139
89TopTif-685
89TopTra-121T
89TopTraT-121T
89ToyRoo-31
89UppDec-393
90BraDubP-29
90BraDubS-33
90ClaYel-T25
90Don-50
90DonBesN-123
90Fle-598
90FleCan-598
90Lea-455
90OPC-486
90PanSti-218
90Sco-95
90Spo-219
90Top-486
90TopSti-29
90TopTif-486
90UppDec-141
91Bow-586
91BraDubP-30
91BraSubS-37
91Don-117
91Fle-707
91Lea-246
91OPC-139
91PanFreS-20
91PanSti-28
91Sco-219
91Sco100S-31
91StaClu-497
91Stu-150
91Top-139
91TopDesS-139
91TopMic-139
91TopTif-139
91Ult-13
91UppDec-499
92BraLykP-28
92BraLykS-33
92Don-324
92Fle-373
92OPC-99
92Sco-142
92StaClu-82
92Top-99
92TopGol-99
92TopGolW-99
92TopMic-99
92Ult-171
92UppDec-389
93BoyScooAT-1
93Don-448
93FleFinE-205
93IndWUA-31
93Lea-480
93Sco-461
93Ult-546
94DodMot-14
94DodPol-25
94Don-295
94Fle-122

94Pac-185
94PanSti-61
94Sco-115
94ScoGolR-115
94ScoRoo-RT67
94ScoRooGR-RT67
94StaClu-30
94StaClu-694
94StaCluFDI-30
94StaCluFDI-694
94StaCluGR-30
94StaCluGR-694
94StaCluMOP-30
94StaCluMOP-694
95DodPol-25
95Sco-451
95ScoGolR-451
95ScoPlaTS-451

Treadway, Red (Thadford Lee)
77TCMTheWY-18

Treadway, Steven
88CapCodPPaLP-181

Treadwell, Jody
91LinDriAA-545
91SanAntMLD-545
91SanAntMP-2975
92SanAntMF-3974
93AlbDukF-1460
94AlbDukF-843

Treanor, Dean
88FreSunCLC-26
88FreSunP-1236
89MiaMirIS-25
90RenSilSCLC-288
91RenSilSCLC-28
92WatDiaC-27
92WatDiaF-2157
93WatDiaC-29
93WatDiaF-1785
94RanCucQC-27
94RanCucQF-1653
95MemChiTI-2
96DelShoB-2

Treanor, Matt
94SigRooDP-77
94SigRooDPS-77
95SprSulTI-29
96LanLugB-28

Trebelhorn, Tom
77ModA'sC-17
80PorBeaT-18
81PorBeaT-2
84BrePol-NNO
85VanCanC-215
86BrePol-42
87BrePol-42
87TopTra-121T
87TopTraT-121T
88BrePol-42
88Top-224
88TopTif-224
89BrePol-42
89BreYea-42
89Top-344
89TopTif-344
90BreMilB-27
90BrePol-42
90OPC-759
90Top-759
90TopTif-759
91BreMilB-28
91BrePol-25
91OPC-459
91Top-459
91TopDesS-459
91TopMic-459
91TopTif-459
92CubMar-NNO
93CubMar-27

Trechuck, Frank
50WorWidGV-6

Tredaway, Chad
92GenCubC-4
92GenCubF-1569
93ExcFS7-13
94OrlCubF-1395
95RanCucQT-9
96LasVegSB-28

Tredway, Ed
90MadMusB-2
90MadMusP-2273

Treece, Jack
44CenFlo-24

Treend, Pat
95ElmPioTI-28
95ElmPioUTI-28

Trella, Steve
75CliPilT-24

Tremark, Nick
90DodTar-808

Tremblay, Gary
86PawRedSP-25
87PawRedSP-70
87PawRedST-12
88PawRedSC-22
88PawRedSP-450
89PawRedSC-14
89PawRedSP-702
89PawRedSTI-26
90CMC-264
90PawRedSC-13
90PawRedSDD-27
90PawRedSP-466
90ProAAAF-438
90TopTVRS-63

Tremblay, Wayne
79ElmPioRST-25
85GreHorT-12

Trembley, Dave
86KinEagP-24
87HarSenP-2
88EasLeaAP-45
88HarSenP-846
89EasLeaDDP-DD46
89HarSenP-292
91ChaRaiC-24
91ChaRaiP-110
92ChaRaiC-22
92ChaRaiF-135
93WicWraF-2993
94OrlCubF-1401
96DayCubB-26

Tremel, William
55Top-52
55TopDouH-101
56Top-96
56TopPin-7

Tremie, Chris
93HicCraC-25
93HicCraF-1282
93SarWhiSF-1372
94BirBarC-1
94BirBarF-625
95NasSouTI-26
96NasSouB-25
92UtiBluSC-16

Tremper, Overton
90DodTar-1087

Trent, Ted (Theodore)
78LauLonABS-1
86NegLeaF-116
87NegLeaPD-3

Tresamer, Michael
86EugEmeC-49
87AppFoxP-9
88BasCitRS-22
89MemChiB-22
89MemChiP-1197
89MemChiS-21
89Sta-45
90OmaRoyP-65
90ProAAAF-600

Tresch, Dave
85LynMetT-3
86LynMetP-22

Tresh, Mickey
87PriWilYP-12
88PriWilYS-23
89PenPilS-25

Tresh, Mike (Michael)
39WhiSoxTI-20
40WhiSoxL-20
41DouPlaR-69
47TipTop-27
48KelPep*-BB3
48WhiSoxTI-25
49Bow-166
49IndTeal-23
50IndNumN-20
77TCMTheWY-53
83TCMPla1943-9
90LakTigS-24
90StaFS7-38

Tresh, Tom
61Yan61RL-38
62Top-31
62TopVen-31
63Jel-23
63Pos-23
63SalMetC-54
63Top-146
63Top-173
63Top-470
63YanJayP-12
64ChatheY-24
64Raw-7
64Top-395
64TopCoi-10
64WheSta-45
64YanJayP-12
64YanReqKP-19
65ChaTheY-23
65Top-440
66Baz-40
66Top-205
66TopRubI-94
66TopVen-205
66YanTeal-12
67Baz-40
67CokCapYM-V17
67DexPre-210
67Top-289
67TopVen-216
68AtlOilPBCC-44
68OPC-69
68Top-69
68TopVen-69
69MilBra-278
69MLBOffS-80
69OPC-212
69Top-212
69TopSta-209
69TopTeaP-19
70MLBOffS-215
70Top-698
72MilBra-348
76TayBow4-86
83FraBroR-17
83YanASFY-48
84WilMay-24
88PacLegI-25
89SweBasG-52
90SweBasG-17
91RinPos1Y1-2
91SweBasG-66
92YanWIZ6-131
92YanWIZA-83

Treuel, Ralph
80EvaTriT-15
89LakTigS-28
91LinDriAAA-600
91TolMudHP-1947
92TolMudHF-1059
96TreThuB-3

Trevino, Alex
77WauMetT-21
78TidTidT-25
80Top-537
81CokTeaS-94
81Fle-318
81Top-23
81TopSupHT-78
82Don-350
82Fle-540
82RedCok-21
82Top-368
82TopTra-120T
83Don-374
83Fle-604
83RedYea-29
83Top-632
83TopSti-232
84BraPol-25
84Don-286
84Fle-484
84FleUpd-118
84Nes792-242
84Top-242
84TopTif-242
84TopTra-120T
84TopTraT-120T
85Don-565
85Fle-341
85FleUpd-122
85OPC-279
85Top-747
85TopSti-30
85TopTif-747
85TopTifT-123T
85TopTra-123T
86DodCokP-29
86DodPol-29
86DodUniOP-20
86Fle-550
86FleUpd-119
86OPC-169
86Top-444
86TopTif-444
86TopTra-116T
86TopTraT-116T
87DodMot-23
87DodPol-15
87Don-546
87Fle-456
87FleGlo-456
87Top-173
87TopTif-173
88DodPol-29
88Don-376
88Sco-182
88ScoGlo-182
88StaLinD-19
88Top-512
88TopTif-512
88TucTorC-16
88TucTorJP-22
89AstLenH-6
89AstMot-17
89AstSmo-38
89Bow-326
89BowTif-326
89OPC-64
89Sco-574
89Top-64
89TopTif-64
89UppDec-262
90AstLenH-25
90AstMot-21
90DodTar-809
90Don-443
90Fle-239
90FleCan-239
90Lea-432
90OPC-342
90PubSti-104
90Top-342
90TopTif-342
90UppDec-205
91MetWIZ-414
92LouRedF-1891
92LouRedS-271

Trevino, Gerald
92IdaFalGF-3521
92IdaFalGSP-22

Trevino, Ricardo
94LetMouF-3880
94LetMouSP-18

Trevino, Ted
80QuaCitCT-15

Trevino, Tony
88BatCliP-1665
88SpaPhiP-1040
89ClePhiS-22
90ClePhiS-22
90FloStaLAS-18
90StaFS7-72
91LinDriAA-521
91ReaPhiLD-521
91ReaPhiP-1378
92ClePhiC-16
92ReaPhiF-584

Trevor, Claire
48BabRutS-3
48BabRutS-4
48BabRutS-9
48BabRutS-27
48BabRutS-28

Triandos, Gus
47Exh-225
47PM1StaP1-211
55OriEss-24
55Top-64
55TopDouH-81
56Top-80
56TopPin-4
57SwiFra-2
57Top-156
58JayPubA-22
58OriJayP-11
58Top-429
59ArmCoi-18
59Baz-21
59HomRunD-20
59OriJayP-9
59Top-330
59Top-568
60ArmCoi-19
60Baz-11
60OriJayP-9
60Top-60
60TopTat-51
60TopVen-60
61Baz-25
61Pos-69A
61Pos-69B
61Top-140
61TopStaI-106
62Jel-33
62Pos-33
62PosCan-33
62SalPlaC-93
62ShiPlaC-93
62Top-420
62TopBuc-89
62TopStaI-9
63TigJayP-11
63Top-475
64PhiJayP-11
64PhiPhiB-25
64Top-83
64TopVen-83
65OPC-248
65PhiJayP-11
65Top-248
79TCM50-75
86OriGreT-6
91OriCro-462

Tribble, Scott
93Sou-15

Tribolet, Scott
91MisStaB-45
92MisStaB-42
95AubAstTI-4

Trice, Robert Lee
47PM1StaP1-212
52LavPro-60
54Top-148
55A'sRodM-42
55JetPos-17
55Top-132
55TopDouH-123
86NegLeaF-43
94TopArc1-148
94TopArc1G-148

Trice, Wally (Walter)
88AubAstP-1950
89OscAstS-25
90Bes-205
90ColMudB-15
90ColMudP-1349
90ColMudS-24
91BurAstC-9
91BurAstP-2800
91Cla/Bes-326
91MidLeaAP-MWL18
92CanIndF-690
92ProFS7-232

Triche, Bryan
91MisStaB-46
92MisStaB-43
93MisStaB-44

Trickett, E.A.
87AllandGN-30

Triessl, Mike
94RivPilCLC-25

Trillo, Carlos
93LinVenB-213
94VenLinU-250
95LinVen-214

Trillo, Manny
74OPC-597
74Top-597
75OPC-617
75Top-617
76OPC-206
76SSP-316
76Top-206
76VenLeaS-89
76VenLeaS-223
76VenLeaS-227
76VenLeaS-241
77BurCheD-191
77CubJewT-15
77OPC-158
77PepGloD-59
77Top-395
78Hos-69
78OPC-217
78Top-123

78WifBalD-76
79OPC-337
79PhiBurK-14
79PhiTeal-10
79Top-639
80OPC-50
80PhiBurK-5
80Top-90
80WilGloT-8
81AllGamPI-108
81CokTeaS-107
81Don-22
81Fle-3
81FleStiC-96
81OPC-368
81Top-470
81TopSupHT-89
82Don-245
82Fle-260
82FleSta-59
82OPC-220
82PerAll-18
82PerAllG-18
82Top-220
82TopSti-76
82TopSti-122
83AllGamPI-16
83Don-294
83Fle-174
83Fle-631
83FleSta-200
83FleSti-175
83IndPos-36
83IndWhe-30
83OPC-73
83OPC-174
83PerAll-8
83PerAllG-8
83PhiPosGPaM-8
83Top-5
83Top-398
83Top-535
83TopSti-141
83TopSti-142
83TopSti-268
83TopTra-116T
84AllGamPI-17
84Don-575
84Fle-289
84Fle-627
84FleUpd-119
84FunFooP-57
84GiaPos-28
84Nes792-180
84OPC-180
84Top-180
84TopGloA-3
84TopSti-93
84TopTif-180
84TopTra-121T
84TopTraT-121T
85AllGamPI-107
85Don-431
85DonActA-31
85Fle-622
85GiaMot-5
85GiaPos-27
85OPC-310
85Top-310
85TopMin-310
85TopTif-310
86BasStaB-112
86CubGat-19
86CubUno-19
86Don-201
86Fle-551
86FleUpd-120
86OPC-142
86Top-655
86TopSti-88
86TopTif-655
86TopTra-117T
86TopTraT-117T
87CubCan-34
87CubDavB-19
87Don-570
87Fle-577
87FleGlo-577
87OPC-32
87Top-732
87TopTif-732
88CubDavB-19
88Don-516
88DonTeaBC-516
88Fle-436
88FleGlo-436
88Sco-524
88ScoGlo-524
88StaLinCu-14
88Top-171
88Top-287
88TopTif-171
88TopTif-287
89Bow-308
89BowTif-308
89Don-608
89Fle-440A
89Fle-440B
89FleGlo-440
89Sco-446
89Top-66
89TopBig-295
89TopTif-66
89UppDec-127
90PubSti-41
93LinVenB-192

Trimarco, Mike
93BluOriC-23
93BluOriF-4125
94AlbPolC-25
94AlbPolF-2238
96FreKeyB-22

Trimble, Rob
93OneYanC-23
94GreBatF-480
94OneYanC-24
97GreBatC-25

Trinidad, Hector
92GenCubC-3
92GenCubF-1562
93MidLeaAGF-43
93PeoChiC-22
93PeoChiF-1086
93PeoChiTI-28
94Bow-662
94ClaGolF-132
94DayCubC-24
94DayCubF-2353
94ExcFS7-170
94UppDecML-237
95HarCitRCTI-25
96BesAutSA-79
96HarCitRCB-29

Trinkle, Ken
47TipTop-133
49Bow-193
49EurSta-150
49PhiBul-55

Triplett, Alfred
93EriSaiC-24
93EriSaiF-3126

Triplett, Antonio
82BurRanF-6
82BurRanT-11
83BurRanF-6
83BurRanT-25
86TulDriTI-2
87SanBerSP-21
88FreSunCLC-1
88FreSunP-1243

Triplett, Coaker
41CarW75-26
43PhiTeal-22
50WorWidGV-16

Triplett, Hunter
92OklStaC-27

Tripodi, Max
89SalLakTTI-20

Tripp, Dave
90SouOreAB-23
90SouOreAP-3446

Trippy, Joe
95EugEmeTI-9
96MacBraB-25

Trisler, John
91HelBreSP-1
92BelBreF-405
93ClePhiC-23
93ClePhiF-2684
94ClePhiC-26
94ClePhiF-2528
95ReaPhiELC-34
95ReaPhiTI-39

Tritonenkov, Timur
89EasLeaDDP-DD19

Trlicek, Rick
87UtiBluSP-17
88BatCliP-1670
90DunBluJS-22
91KnoBluJLD-369
91KnoBluJP-1765
91LinDriAA-369
92Bow-76
92DonRoo-116
92LeaGolR-BC15
92ProFS7-166
92SyrChiF-1966
92SyrChiMB-24
93BluJayD4-37
93DodMot-27
93FleFinE-85
93PacSpa-504
93Pin-284
93Sco-318
93SelRoo-138T
93StaClu-218
93StaCluFDI-218
93StaCluMOP-218
93Ult-407
94Fle-526
94Sco-600
94ScoGolR-600
94Top-276
94TopGol-276
94TopSpa-276
95PhoFirTI-35
96NorTidB-29

Troconis, O.
76VenLeaS-132

Troedson, Rich
74OPC-77
74PadDea-27
74Top-77A
74Top-77B

Troglin, Mike
90ArkRaz-33

Troilo, Jason
94OneYanF-3796
96GreBatB-29
96TamYanY-26

Trombley, Mike
88CapCodPPaLP-75
90VisOakCLC-58
90VisOakP-2153
91LinDriAA-495
91OrlSunRLD-495
91OrlSunRP-1849
92Bow-102
92PorBeaF-2666
92PorBeaS-420
92SkyAAAF-192
93Bow-621
93Don-47
93Fle-644
93PacSpa-526
93Pin-578
93PinRooTP-1
93Sco-287
93SelRoo-52T
93StaClu-336
93StaCluFDI-336
93StaCluMOP-336
93Top-588
93TopGol-588
93TopInaM-588
93TopMic-588
93Toy-47
93Ult-588
93UppDec-28
93UppDecGold-28
94Don-620
94Fle-220
94Pac-368
94Sco-591
94ScoGolR-591
94StaClu-477
94StaCluFDI-477
94StaCluGR-477
94StaCluMOP-477
94Top-308
94TopGol-308
94TopSpa-308
94Ult-91
95DonTopotO-115
96ColCho-599
96ColChoGS-599
96ColChoSS-599
96Don-340
96DonPreP-340
96Ult-96
96UltGolM-96
97Fle-593
97FleTif-593

Troncoso, Nolberton
90YakBeaTI-25

Tronerud, Rick
79WatA'sT-2
80WesHavWCT-24
81WesHavAT-15
84AlbA'sT-8
85ModA'sC-27
89HunStaB-18
86HumStaDS-44

Trosky, Hal
34DiaStaR-70
34Gou-76
35ExhFou-11
35GouPuzR-1L
35GouPuzR-2E
35GouPuzR-16E
35GouPuzR-17E
36ExhFou-11
36GouWidPPR-A102
36GouWidPPR-B21
36GouWidPPR-C23
36OveCanR-43
37ExhFou-11
37OPCBatUV-113
37WheBB14-15
37WheBB7-29G
38ExhFou-11
38OurNatGPP-30
39GouPreR303A-43
39WorWidGTP-43
39WorWidGV-24
40PlaBal-50
40WheM4-13
41DouPlaR-79
41DouPlaR-87
41PlaBal-16
61Fle-145
75SheGrePG-4
76GrePlaG-4
77FriOneYW-15
79RedSoxEF-20
86IndGreT-1
92ConTSN-385

Trott, Sam
87OldJudN-513
87OldJudN-514

Trotter, Bill
39PlaBal-148
40PlaBal-54
41BroW75-29
77TCMTheWY-54
79DiaGre-189

Troup, James
89SalLakTTI-27

Trouppe, Quincy
78LauLonABS-33
91NegLeaRL-16
91PomBlaBPB-2
92NegLeaRLI-61
95NegLeaLI-16

Trout, Dizzy (Paul)
39ExhSal-58
39PlaBal-153
40PlaBal-44
46SpoExcW-8-6
47TipTop-43
48KelPep*-BB4
49Bow-208
49Lea-10
50AmeNut&CCP-21
50Bow-134
51TopBluB-23
52NatTeaL-38
52Top-39
53Top-169
76TayBow4-54
77TCMTheWY-5
81TigDetN-113
81TigSecNP-31
83TCMPla1945-2
83TopRep5-39
85Top-142
85TopTif-142
91OriCro-463
91TopArc1-169
95ConTSN-1415

Trout, Jeff
85OrlTwiT-12
86OrlTwiP-21

Trout, Steve
77AppFoxT-27
78KnoKnoST-24
80Top-83
81Don-400
81Fle-345
81OPC-364
81Top-552
82Don-243
82Fle-358
82OPC-299
82Top-299
82TopSti-169
83CubThoAV-34
83Don-417
83Fle-251
83Top-461
83TopTra-117T
84CubChiT-30
84CubSev-34
84Don-533
84Fle-506
84Nes792-151
84OPC-151
84Top-151
84TopTif-151
85AllGamPI-179
85CubLioP-25
85CubSev-34
85Don-198
85Fle-70
85Lea-243
85OPC-139
85Top-142
85Top-668
85TopSti-43
85TopTif-142
85TopTif-668
86CubGat-34
86CubUno-20
86Don-117
86Fle-384
86OPC-384
86Top-384
86TopSti-57
86TopTif-384
87CubCan-35
87CubDavB-34
87Don-201
87Fle-578
87FleGlo-578
87OPC-147
87Top-581
87Top-750
87TopTif-581
87TopTif-750
88Don-524
88MarMot-8
88Sco-342
88ScoGlo-342
88Top-584
88TopBig-107
88TopTif-584
89MarMot-24
89Sco-522
89Top-54
89TopTif-54
90LouRedBLBC-41
90PubSti-43
92YanWIZ8-193

Troutman, Keith
92YakBeaF-3449
93GreFalDSP-18
94VerBeaDC-22
94VerBeaDF-72
95SanAntMTI-36
96ReaPhiB-12

Trowbridge, Bob
57BraSpiaS4-20
58Top-252
59Top-239
60Top-66
60TopVen-66

Trower, Don
48SomandK-10

Truby, Chris
94AubAstC-21
94AubAstF-3769
94QuaCitRBC-21
94QuaCitRBF-545
95Bow-232
95BowGolF-232
95QuaCitRBTI-28
96QuaCitRB-28

Trucchio, Frank
83MadMusF-30

Trucks, Phil

76CliPilT-29
78AppFoxT-22
79KnoKnoST-2
Trucks, Virgil
47Exh-226
47TipTop-44
49Bow-219
49Lea-5
50Bow-96
50RoyDes-21A
50RoyDes-21B
51Bow-104
51R42SmaS-106
52DixLid-23
52DixPre-23
52Top-262
53BowBW-17
53DixLid-23A
53DixLid-23B
53DixPre-23
53Top-96
54Bow-198
55ArmCoi-22
55Bow-26
56Top-117
57Top-187
58A'sJayP-10
58Top-277
59Top-417
63PirIDL-24
76TayBow4-53
79DiaGre-198
79TCM50-85
81TigDetN-111
82Bow195E-264
83TopRep5-262
83YanYealT-14
84TCMPla1-6
87SpoRea-8
89PacLegI-120
89SweBasG-73
91TopArc1-96
92ActPacA-20
94TedWil-34
94UppDecAH-39
94UppDecAH1-39
Trudeau, Kevin
86WatIndP-29
87PorBeaP-15
88OrlTwiB-14
89MidAngGS-28
90MidAngGS-19
Trudo, Glenn
86WatPirP-25
87MacPirP-21
88AugPirP-384
True, Bryan
86DavLipB-21
Truesdale, Fred
12ImpTobC-53
Truitt, Bill
52LavPro-26
Trujillo, Jose
89HamRedS-24
89Sta-106
90St.PetCS-24
91St.PetCC-23
91St.PetCP-2286
92GenCubC-2
92GenCubF-1570
92PeoChiC-5
93PalSprAF-70
Trujillo, Louie
83CedRapRF-12
83CedRapRT-11
Trujillo, Mike
83AppFoxF-2
86Fle-360
86PawRedSP-26
86Top-687
86TopTif-687
87Don-613
87MarMot-25
87Top-402
87TopTif-402
88TolMudHC-7
88TolMudHP-593
88Top-307
88TopTif-307
89TolMudHC-3
89TolMudHP-776
89TriAAP-AAA25
Truman, Harry S.
94UppDecTAE-56
Trumbauer, Gary
72CedRapCT-15
Trumpour, Andy
94KinMetC-22
94KinMetF-3824
95PitMetTI-34
Trunk, Mascot
94MasMan-15
Truschke, Mike
88CapCodPPaLP-24
Trusky, Ken
89WelPirP-24
90AugPirP-2479
90SouAtlLAS-44
91SalBucC-13
91SalBucP-967
Tsamis, George
88CapCodPPaLP-80
90CalLeaACLC-16
90ProAaA-143
90VisOakCLC-65
90VisOakP-2154
91LinDriAAA-421
91PorBeaLD-421
91PorBeaP-1566
92PorBeaF-2667
92PorBeaS-421
92SkyAAAF-193
93Bow-509
93FleFinE-240
94Fle-221
94Pac-369
94Top-128
94TopGol-128
94TopSpa-128
Tschida, Tim
88T/MUmp-59
89T/MUmp-57
90T/MUmp-55
Tsitouris, John
60A'sTeal-16
60Lea-63
60Top-497
63RedEnq-30
63RedFreBC-28
63Top-244
64Kah-27
64Top-275
64TopVen-275
65Kah-42
65OPC-221
65RedEnq-29
65Top-221
66OPC-12
66Top-12
66TopVen-12
68Top-523
Tsitouris, Marc
90JamExpP-5
91SumFlyC-21
91SumFlyP-2346
Tsotsos, Pete
88CapCodPPaLP-26
Tsoukalas, John
91MedHatBJP-4110
91MedHatBJSP-4
92MyrBeaHC-2
92MyrBeaHF-2207
Tua, Franklin
76VenLeaS-66
80VenLeaS-65
Tubbs, Gregory Alan
86GreBraTI-21
87GreBraB-26
88RicBraC-15
88RicBraP-5
89BlaYNPRWL-28
89GreBraP-1152
89RicBraBC-26
89RicBraP-823
89TriA AAC-23
90TriAAAC-23
91BufBisLD-47
91BufBisP-555
91LinDriAAA-47
91LinDriP-47
92BufBisBS-23
92BufBisF-336
92BufBisS-44
93IndIndF-1502
94BufBisF-1851
97BobCamRB-19
Tucci, Pete
97Top-480
Tuck, Gary
82TucTorT-25
83TucTorT-24
84TucTorC-248
86OscAstP-26
87AubAstP-12
88AshTouP-1068
89ColCliC-24
Tucker, Benjamin
95BelGiaTI-40
96SanJosGB-24
Tucker, Bill
89BelMarL-34
95BelGiaTI-NNO
96BelGiaTI-32
Tucker, Bob
86VerBeaDP-25
Tucker, Brett
94CliLumF-1981
Tucker, Eddie
90Bes-274
90SanJosGB-13
90SanJosGP-2014
Tucker, Horace
87WytCubP-3
Tucker, Jon
95YakBeaTI-33
96GreFalDB-29
96GreFalDTI-26
Tucker, Julien
94AubAstC-22
94AubAstF-3760
95Exc-207
96KisCobB-30
Tucker, Lanning H.
92EliTwiC-25
94ForMyeMC-29
95ForMyeMTI-31
96HarCitRCB-6
Tucker, Michael
92Bow-682
92ClaDraP-7
92ClaDraPFB-BC7
92FroRowDP-44
92FroRowDPPS-44
92TopTra-119T
92TopTraG-119T
92UppDecML-1
92UppDecML-6
93ClaFS7-30
93Pin-466
93Sco-498
93Sel-291
93SP-287
93StaCluM-196
93UppDec-445
93UppDecGold-445
93WilBluRC-1
93WilBluRF-2008
94ActPac-24
94ActPac-60
94ActPac2G-6G
94Cla-150
94Cla-AU5
94ClaBonB-BB5
94ClaCreotC-C7
94ClaGolF-122
94ExcFS7-76
94ExcLeaLF-18
94OmaRoyF-1237
94SigRoo-41
94SigRooHP-S11
94SigRooS-41
94TedWil-133
94TedWilDGC-DG2
94Ult-369
94UppDecML-3
94UppDecML-260
94UppDecMLPotYF-PY24
94UppDecMLT1PJF-TP10
94UppDecMLT1PMF-10
95ActPacF-21
95ARuFalLS-18
95BowBes-B90
95BowBesR-B90
95ColCho-10
95ColChoGS-10
95ColChoSS-10
95Exc-67
95ExcLeaL-16
95Fla-268
95Fle-173
95LeaLim-92
95OmaRoyTI-27
95Pin-426
95PinArtP-426
95PinMusC-426
95Sel-201
95SelArtP-201
95SelCer-134
95SelCerF-9
95SelCerMG-134
95SelCerPU-19
95SelCerPU9-19
95SP-157
95SPSil-157
95Sum-143
95SumNewA-NA7
95SumNthD-143
95TopTra-99T
95UC3-98
95UC3ArtP-98
95UC3CleS-CS12
95UltGolP-10
95UltGolPGM-10
95UppDec-230
95UppDecED-230
95UppDecEDG-230
95UppDecML-2
95UppDecMLT1PF-9
95UppDecPAW-H34
95UppDecPAWE-H34
95UppDecSE-189
95UppDecSEG-189
95Zen-143
95ZenRooRC-13
96Bow-59
96ColCho-176
96ColCho-653
96ColChoGS-176
96ColChoGS-653
96ColChoSS-176
96ColChoSS-653
96Don-376
96DonPreP-376
96Fla-95
96Fle-139
96FleTif-139
96Lea-79
96LeaPre-93
96LeaPreP-93
96LeaPrePB-79
96LeaPrePG-79
96LeaPrePS-79
96LeaPreSG-58
96LeaPreSte-58
96LeaSig-79
96LeaSigA-224
96LeaSigAG-225
96LeaSigAS-225
96LeaSigPPG-79
96LeaSigPPP-79
96Pin-202
96PinAfi-111
96PinAfiAP-111
96PinArtP-102
96PinFirR-12
96PinFoil-202
96PinSta-102
96RoyPol-25
96Sco-241
96ScoDugC-A107
96ScoDugCAP-A107
96ScoSam-241
96Sel-149
96SelArtP-149
96SelCer-76
96SelCerAP-76
96SelCerCB-76
96SelCerCR-76
96SelCerMB-76
96SelCerMG-76
96SelCerMR-76
96SelTeaN-17
96SP-98
96Spo-44
96SpoArtP-44
96StaClu-439
96StaCluMOP-439
96Stu-130
96StuPrePB-130
96StuPrePG-130
96StuPrePS-130
96Sum-47
96SumAbo&B-47
96SumArtP-47
96SumFoi-47
96Top-92
96TopGal-133
96TopGalPPI-133
96Ult-361
96UltGolM-361
96UppDec-89
96UppDecBCP-BC6
96Zen-94
96ZenArtP-94
97Bow-279
97BowInt-279
97Cir-217
97CirRav-217
97ColCho-134
97Don-28
97Don-274
97DonEli-140
97DonEliGS-140
97DonLim-115
97DonLim-158
97DonLimLE-115
97DonLimLE-158
97DonPre-140
97DonPreCttC-140
97DonPreP-28
97DonPreP-274
97DonPrePGold-28
97DonPrePGold-274
97DonTea-23
97DonTeaSPE-23
97Fle-124
97Fle-580
97FleTif-124
97FleTif-580
97Lea-123
97LeaFraM-123
97LeaFraMDC-123
97MetUni-98
97NewPin-76
97NewPinAP-76
97NewPinMC-76
97NewPinPP-76
97PacPriGotD-GD51
97PinIns-116
97PinInsCE-116
97PinInsDE-116
97PinX-P-114
97PinX-PMoS-114
97ProMag-58
97ProMagML-58
97Sco-283
97Sco-468
97ScoHobR-468
97ScoPreS-283
97ScoResC-468
97ScoShoS-283
97ScoShoS-468
97ScoShoSAP-283
97ScoShoSAP-468
97Sel-95
97SelArtP-95
97SelRegG-95
97StaClu-164
97StaCluMOP-164
97Stu-122
97StuPrePG-122
97StuPrePS-122
97Top-453
97TopGal-167
97TopGalPPI-167
97Ult-341
97UltGolME-341
97UltPlaME-341
97UppDec-392
97UppDec-524
95UppDecMLFS-2
Tucker, Mike
81ShrCapT-8
82PhoGiaVNB-10
Tucker, Robert
91HelBreSP-22
93CedRapKC-21
93CedRapKF-1743
94LakElsSC-23
94LakElsSF-1668
Tucker, Scooter
89CliGiaP-897
90CalLeaACLC-37
90SanJosGCLC-37
90SanJosGS-23
91Cla/Bes-315
91LinDriAA-322
91ShrCapLD-322
91ShrCapP-1825
92DonRoo-117

92SkyAAAF-277
92TopTra-120T
92TopTraG-120T
92TucTorF-492
92TucTorS-620
93Don-60
93FleMajLP-B1
93Pin-245
93Sco-237
93StaClu-488
93StaCluFDI-488
93StaCluMOP-488
93Top-814
93TopGol-814
93TopInaM-814
93TopMic-814
93TucTorF-3062
93Ult-47
94TucTorF-765
96OmaRoyB-29
Tucker, T.J.
97Bow-431
97BowChr-291
97BowChrI-291
97BowChrIR-291
97BowChrR-291
97BowInt-431
Tucker, Thomas
87OldJudN-188
87OldJudN-515
89EdgR.WG-11
90DodTar-810
95May-27
Tucker, Thurman
47TipTop-28
48IndTeal-29
49IndTeal-24
50IndNumN-21
50IndTeal-23
51Bow-222
53IndPenCBP-26
76TayBow4-56
79DiaGre-141
83TCMPla1944-18
Tucker, Tuck (Stephen)
90GreHorB-12
90GreHorP-2664
90GreHorS-22
91PriWilCC-12
91PriWilCP-1428
Tucker, Vance
89ChaRaiP-972
Tucker, William
78GreBraT-27
Tuckerman, William
87OldJudN-516
Tudor, John
77BriRedST-19
81Don-457A
81Don-457B
81Top-14
82Don-260
82Fle-311
82RedSoxC-21
82Top-558
83Don-563
83Fle-198
83FleSta-201
83Top-318
84Don-416
84Fle-411
84FleUpd-120
84Nes792-601
84OPC-171
84Top-601
84TopSti-225
84TopTif-601
84TopTra-122T
84TopTraT-122T
85CarTeal-31
85Don-235
85DonHig-20
85Fle-479
85FleUpd-123
85OPC-214
85Top-214
85TopTif-214
85TopTifT-124T
85TopTra-124T
86BasStaB-113
86CarIGAS-12
86CarKASD-17
86CarSchM-22
86CarTeal-40
86Don-260
86Dra-30
86Fle-47
86FleAll-12
86FleMin-11
86FleSlu-40
86FleStiC-122
86Lea-134
86OPC-227
86SevCoi-S11
86Spo-122
86Spo-184
86Spo-185
86Top-474
86Top-710
86Top3-D-28
86TopGloS-53
86TopMinL-64
86TopSti-20
86TopSti-52
86TopSup-57
86TopTat-12
86TopTif-474
86TopTif-710
87CarSmo-3
87ClaGam-77
87Don-170
87DonOpeD-63
87Dra-30
87Fle-310
87FleGamW-41
87FleGlo-310
87FleMin-108
87FleRecS-39
87FleStiC-119
87KraFoo-22
87OPC-110
87RedFolSB-34
87Spo-173
87SpoTeaP-12
87Top-110
87TopSti-53
87TopTif-110
88CarSmo-9
88Don-553
88DonBasB-212
88Dra-33
88Fle-48
88FleGlo-48
88FleGlo-WS3
88FleMin-110
88FleStiC-121
88FleWorS-3
88Lea-212
88OPC-356
88Sco-275
88ScoGlo-275
88Spo-198
88StaLinCa-19
88Top-792
88TopRitTM-29
88TopSti-13
88TopSti-21
88TopTif-792
88Woo-23
89ClaLigB-63
89DodMot-9
89DodPol-19
89DodStaSV-13
89Don-195
89Fle-75
89FleGlo-75
89OPC-35
89PanSti-100
89RedFolSB-122
89Sco-560
89Spo-86
89Top-35
89TopBasT-71
89TopMinL-20
89TopSti-64
89TopTif-35
89UppDec-66
90Bow-188
90BowTif-188
90CarSmo-25
90ClaYel-T2
90DodTar-811
90FleUpd-54
90Lea-176
90PubSti-20
90TopBig-253
90TopTra-124T
90TopTraT-124T
90TopTVCa-21
90UppDec-396
91Fle-650
91RedFolS-94
91Sco-53
91Sco100S-47
91UppDec-329
92CarMcD-50
Tudor, Mark
81CliGiaT-29
82CliGiaF-26
Tufts, Bob
80PhoGiaVNB-2
81PhoGiaVNB-3
82OmaRoyT-9
82Top-171
Tufts, Glenn
95BelGiaTI-48
96BurBeeTI-27
94CliLumC-28
Tuggle, Eugene
90GeoColC-30
Tuholald, Tom
89WelPirP-25
Tukes, Stan
89ChaRaiP-977
89HamRedS-25
Tulacz, Mike
77AppFoxT-28
78AppFoxT-23
Tuller, Brian
83QuaCitCT-15
Tullier, Mike
86WinSpiP-25
87WinSpiP-19
88PitCubP-1365
89IowCubC-23
89IowCubP-1701
91BluOriC-24
91BluOriP-4143
Tullish, Bill
76CedRapGT-29
Tumbas, Dave
83AleDukT-15
84PriWilPT-27
85NasPirT-25
Tumpane, Bob
82DurBulT-13
83DurBulT-15
84DurBulT-12
85GreBraTI-22
85IntLeaAT-2
86GreBraTI-22
87RicBraBC-21
87RicBraC-9
87RicBraT-16
Tunison, Rich
89EugEmeB-16
90AppFoxBS-28
90AppFoxP-2105
90CMC-874
90MidLeaASGS-21
90ProAaA-125
91Cla/Bes-200
91LinDriAA-421
91MemChiLD-421
91MemChiP-664
92MemChiF-2429
92MemChiS-446
92SkyAA F-188
94ForMyeMC-24
94ForMyeMF-1176
Tunkin, Scott
91ParPatF-16
95AusFut-11
Tunnell, Lee
82PorBeaT-9
83TopTra-118T
84Don-592
84Fle-268
84FleSti-107
84Nes792-384
84Top-384
84TopTif-384
85Don-288
85Fle-480
85Fle-638
85Pir-22
85Top-21
85TopTif-21
86Fle-623
86HawIsIP-21
86Top-161
86TopTif-161
87FleUpd-119
87FleUpdG-119
88Fle-49
88FleGlo-49
88LouRedBTI-48
88Sco-587
88ScoGlo-587
89BlaYNPRWLU-19
89PorBeaC-6
89PorBeaP-217
90CMC-609
90ProAAAF-194
90TucTorC-7
90TucTorP-204
91LinDriAAA-621
91TucTorLD-621
91TucTorP-2213
Tunney, Gene
28W512-44
32USCar-15
87SpoCubG-2
Tuozzo, John
86ColMetP-25
Tupper, Craig
93BriTigC-22
Turang, Brian
88CapCodPB-20
88CapCodPPaLP-22
89BelMarL-20
90ProAaA-149
90SanBerSB-18
90SanBerSCLC-106
90SanBerSP-2642
91JacSunLD-347
91JacSunP-161
91LinDriAA-347
92JacSunF-3718
92JacSunS-358
93CalCanF-1175
93ExcFS7-233
93StaCluMari-27
94ColC-614
94ColChoGS-614
94ColChoSS-614
94Don-314
94Fle-299
94Pac-582
94Pin-377
94PinArtP-377
94PinMusC-377
94Sco-637
94ScoBoyoS-37
94ScoGolR-637
94StaClu-177
94StaCluFDI-177
94StaCluGR-177
94StaCluMOP-177
94Top-82
94TopGol-82
94TopSpa-82
95TacRaiTI-24
Turbeville, George
93ConTSN-979
Turco, Frank
91BenBucC-15
91BenBucP-3705
91RenSilSCLC-4
92ChaRanC-5
92ChaRanF-2235
93TulDriF-2744
94TulDriF-253
94TulDriTI-24
95TulDriTI-26
93TulDriTI-27
Turco, Steve F.
81ArkTraT-2
83St.PetCT-25
85SprCarT-18
91HamRedC-30
91HamRedP-4057
92JohCitCC-26
92JohCitCF-3134
93GleFalRF-4021
96JohCitCTI-31
Turek, Joseph
88GreHorP-1559
88SouAtlLAGS-8
89CedRapRB-7
89CedRapRP-920
89CedRapRS-20
90CedRapRB-18
91ChaLooP-1962
92CanIndF-691
92CanIndS-121
92SkyAA F-57
93CanIndF-2841
Turgeon, David
87OneYanP-12
88Ft.LauYS-22
89PriWilCS-22
90Ft.LauYS-20
Turgeon, Mike
80WicAerT-11
82PhoGiaVNB-17
Turgeon, Steve
83St.PetCT-26
85SprCarT-19
86EriCarP-28
Turlais, John
92FroRowDP-64
94KinMetC-23
94KinMetF-3827
Turley, Bob (Robert)
54OriEss-33
54Top-85
55ArmCoi-23
55Top-38
55TopDouH-63
56Top-40
56TopPin-31
57Top-264
58JayPubA-23
58Top-255
58Top-493
58YanJayP-12
59ArmCoi-19
59Baz-22
59HowPhoSP-2
59Top-60
59Top-237
59Top-570
59TopVen-60
60Lea-103
60NuHi-30
60Top-270
60YanJayP-12
61NuSco-430
61Pos-5
61Raw-12
61Top-40
61TopStal-200
61Yan61RL-21
61YanJayP-12
62Top-589
63Top-322
70FleWorS-55
78AtlCon-24
79DiaGre-200
79TCM50-136
81TCM60I-459
83YanASFY-49
87AstSer1-24
88PacLegI-52
91OriCro-464
91RinPos1Y3-9
92YanWIZ6-132
92YanWIZA-84
94TopArc1-85
94TopArc1G-85
Turley, Jason
96AubDouB-4
Turnbull, Anthony
93ElmPioC-23
93ElmPioF-3828
94BreCouMF-17
Turnbull, Keith
83EriCarT-8
Turner, Brian
90GreHorB-26
90GreHorP-2678
90GreHorS-23
90OneYanP-3374
91GreHorP-3069
92ForLauYC-20
92ForLauYTI-31
92Ft.LauYF-2623
93SanBerSC-20
93SanBerSF-780
94TamYanC-27
94TamYanF-2400
95NorNavTI-35
96StLucMTI-27
Turner, Chris
91BoiHawC-17
91BoiHawP-3884
92QuaCitRBC-6
92QuaCitRBF-814
93Bow-525

93VanCanF-2602
94AngLAT-20
94AngMot-13
94Bow-95
94ColC-277
94ColChoGS-277
94ColChoSS-277
94Don-567
94Fin-370
94FinRef-370
94FleMajLP-35
94FleUpd-22
94Lea-291
94Pac-92
94Pin-405
94PinArtP-405
94PinMusC-405
94Sco-500
94ScoGolR-500
94ScoRoo-RT85
94ScoRooGR-RT85
94Sel-205
94SpoRoo-65
94SpoRooAP-65
94SpoRooS-65
94StaClu-92
94StaCluFDI-92
94StaCluGR-92
94StaCluMOP-92
94Top-322
94TopGol-322
94TopSpa-322
94Ult-29
94UppDec-29
94UppDecED-29
95Don-361
95DonPreP-361
95Fle-237
95Lea-199
95Sco-55
95ScoGolR-55
95ScoPlaTS-55
95StaClu-82
95StaCluFDI-82
95StaCluMOP-82
95StaCluSTWS-82
95Ult-25
95UltGolM-25
96VanCanB-28

Turner, Earl
50PirTeal-22

Turner, Gregory
91SydWavF-6

Turner, Jerry (John Webber)
75HawIslC-8
75IntLeaASB-35
75PacCoaLAB-35
75OPC-619
75Top-619
76OPC-598
76Top-598
77PadSchC-60A
77PadSchC-60B
77Top-447
78PadFamF-34
78Top-364
79Top-564
80Top-133
81Don-244
81Fle-504
81Top-285
81TopSti-229
82Don-609
82Top-736
82TopTra-121T
83Fle-345
83Top-41

Turner, Jim
41HarHarW-24
43YanSta-27
52Top-373
62Top-263
63RedFreBC-29
73OPC-116
73Top-116A
73Top-116B
79DiaGre-204
83TopRep5-373

Turner, John
86PeoChiP-24

Turner, Jose
78DayBeaAT-25

Turner, Lloyd
78WatIndT-24
79WauTimT-10

Turner, Luis
76VenLeaS-104

Turner, Matt (William Matthew)
87SumBraP-2
88BurBraP-5
89DurBullS-24
89DurBulTI-24
90GreBraB-12
90GreBraP-1128
90GreBraS-20
91LinDriAAA-446
91RicBraBC-17
91RicBraLD-446
91RicBraP-2569
91RicBraTI-25
92TucTorF-487
92TucTorS-621
93EdmTraF-1136
93FleFinE-72
93MarPub-24
93PacSpa-472
93StaCluMarl-27
93TopTra-56T
94Don-593
94Fle-478
94Pac-251
94Sco-306
94ScoGolR-306
94StaClu-319
94StaCluFDI-319
94StaCluGR-319
94StaCluMOP-319
94StaCluT-78
94StaCluTFDI-78
94Top-587
94TopGol-587
94TopSpa-587
94Ult-200

Turner, Rick
82DanSunF-7
83RedPioT-24
93AngMot-28

Turner, Rocky
94PitMetC-22
94PitMetF-3537

Turner, Roy
04FanCraAL-46

Turner, Ryan
91BenBucC-16
91BenBucP-3709
92Bow-346
92UppDec-710
92VisOakC-17
92VisOakF-1028
93CenValRC-24
93CenValRF-2907
93Top-537
93TopGol-537
93TopInaM-537
93TopMic-537
94NewHavRF-1564

Turner, Shane
86FloStaLAP-47
86Ft.LauYP-23
87ColCliP-24
87ColCliP-9
87ColCliT-18
88MaiPhiC-13
88MaiPhiP-288
88PhiTas-27
89Fle-653
89FleGlo-653
89ReaPhiB-12
89ReaPhiP-655
89ReaPhiS-24
89ScoHot1R-67
90CMC-325
90ProAAAF-468
90RocRedWC-24
90RocRedWGC-22
90RocRedWP-711
91LinDriAAA-471
91RocRedWLD-471
91RocRedWP-1912
92CalCanF-3741
92CalCanS-71
92DonRoo-118
92FleUpd-58
93CalCanF-1176
93Fle-681
93StaClu-97
93StaCluFDI-97
93StaCluMOP-97
93Top-694
93TopGol-694
93TopInaM-694
93TopMic-694
94PhoFirF-1530
96BelGiaTI-33

Turner, Ted
91FouBal-24

Turner, Terry
05IndSouPSoCP-17
08RosComP-30
09ColChiE-291
09T206-360
10DomDisP-118
10SweCapPP-20
11E94-28
11MecDFT-43
11S74Sil-11
11SpoLifCW-353
11SpoLifM-51
11T205-173
12ColRedB-291
12ColTinT-291
12ColTinT-292A
12HasTriFT-8
12HasTriFT-72
12T207-185
14B18B-9A
14B18B-9B
14PieStaT-57
15SpoNewM-179
16ColE13-175
16SpoNewM-176

Turner, Tom
40WhiSoxL-21
77TCMTheWY-15
96Bro194F-28

Turner, Trent
88CapCodPPaLP-179

Turnes, Luis
80VenLeaS-102

Turnier, Aaron
92PulBraC-14
92PulBraF-3177
93IdaFalBF-4032
93IdaFalBSP-28
94MacBraC-23
94MacBraF-2205
95AusFut-67
95BreBtaTI-48

Turpin, Hal
43CenFlo-24
44CenFlo-25
45CenFlo-26

Turrentine, Richard
90TamYanD-27
91GreHorP-3070
92GreHorC-23
92GreHorF-790
96StLucMTI-33

Turri, Shawn
91NiaFalRC-22
91NiaFalRP-3632

Turtletaub, Greg
88LitFalMP-13

Turvey, Joe
90HamRedB-15
90SavCarP-2071
91HamRedC-20
91HamRedP-4042
92SavCarC-15
92SavCarF-665
93St.PetCC-24
93St.PetCF-2631

Tuss, Jeff
91Cla/Bes-364
91WesPalBEC-13
91WesPalBEP-1229
92WesPalBEC-7
92WesPalBEF-2089

Tutt, John
84ChaO'sT-24
85BeaGolGT-22
86LasVegSP-21

Tuttle, Bill
55Bow-35
56Top-203
57SwiFra-14
57Top-72
58A'sJayP-11
58Top-23A
58Top-23B
59Top-459
60A'sJayP-10
60A'sTeal-17
60Lea-32
60Top-367
61A'sTeal-21
61AthJayP-23
61Baz-36
61Pos-84A
61Pos-84B
61Top-536
61TopStal-167
61TwiCloD-28
62Jel-88
62Pos-88
62PosCan-88
62SalPlaC-87A
62SalPlaC-87B
62ShiPlaC-87
62Top-298
62TopStal-80
63Top-127
79TCM50-103

Tuttle, David
89AncBucTI-10
91TopTra-122T
91TopTraT-122T
92StaCluD-188
93SouAtlLAGF-56
93WesVirWC-23
93WesVirWF-2867
94WinSpiC-22
94WinSpiF-271
95ChaLooTI-23

Tuttle, John
96JohCitCTI-32

Twardoski, Michael
88CarLeaAS-38
88KinIndS-22
89CanIndB-12
89CanIndP-1299
89CanIndS-21
89EasLeaDDP-DD35
90Bes-155
90NewBriRSB-9
90NewBriRSP-1329
90NewBriRSS-18
90StaFS7-31
91LinDriAAA-357
91PawRedSDD-24
91PawRedSLD-357
92PawRedSF-932
92PawRedSS-369
92SkyAAAF-168
92TriA AAS-369
93NorTidF-2579
94PawRedSDD-26
94PawRedSF-954
97DunDonPPS-25

Twardy, Glenn
89BelMarL-14

Tweedlie, Brad
93BilMusF-3945
93BilMusSP-23
94WinSpiC-23
94WinSpiF-272

Twellman, Tom
74CedRapAT-18
75DubPacT-26
76DubPacT-36

Twiggs, Greg
93GenCubC-25
93GenCubF-3173
94DayCubC-25
94DayCubF-2354
96OrlCubB-26

Twins, Minnesota
61Top-542
61TopMagR-3
62GuyPotCP-13
62Top-584
63Top-162
64Top-318
64TopTatl-13
64TopVen-318
65OPC-24
65Top-24
66Top-526
66TopRubl-113
67Top-211
68OPC-137
68Top-137
68TopVen-137
69FleCloS-13
69FleCloS-47
69TopStaA-13
70FleWorS-62
70OPC-534
70Top-534
71FleWorS-63
71OPC-522
71Top-522
71TopTat-118
72OPC-156
72Top-156
73OPC-654
73OPCBTC-14
73Top-654
73TopBluTC-14
74OPC-74
74OPCTC-14
74Top-74
74TopStaA-14
74TopTeaC-14
78Top-451
82TwiPos-34
83FleSta-238
83FleSti-NNO
83TwiTeal-35
84MinTwiP-34
84TwiTeal-34
86TwiTeal-35
87SpoTeaL-17
88FleSluBC-C6
88FleWaxBC-C5
88PanSti-451
88PanSti-452
88PanSti-453
88PanSti-454
88PanSti-463
88RedFolSB-127
88TwiTeal-31
90PubSti-636
90RedFolSB-124
90TopMag-72
90VenSti-528
93TedWilPC-14
94ImpProP-9
94Sco-325
94ScoGolR-325
95PanSti-156
96PanSti-203

Twist, Jeff
94BenRocF-3599
97BenRocC-22

Twitchell, Lawrence
87OldJudN-518
88GandBCGCE-42
88WG1CarG-26

Twitchell, Wayne
71OPC-692
71Top-692
72OPC-14
72Top-14
73OPC-227
73Top-227
74Kel-26
74OPC-419
74Top-419
74TopSta-79
75OPC-326
75Top-326
76OPC-543
76Top-543
77ExpPos-31
77Top-444
78ExpPos-15
78OPC-189
78Top-269
79OPC-18
79Top-43
91MetWIZ-415
94BreMilB-368

Twitty, Doug
90BenBucL-21

Twitty, Jeff
80OmaRoyP-24
81Fle-49
82RicBraT-8

Twitty, Sean
91BelMarC-7
91BelMarP-3682
92PenPilC-15
92SanBerSF-973
93PriWilCC-24
93PriWilCF-671
94TamYanC-28
94TamYanF-2401

95GreBatTI-26
Twogood, Forest
34DiaMatCSB-183
Twomey, Mike
92NiaFalRC-30
93PalSprAC-29
94LakElsSC-29
Tyler, Brad
91KanCouCC-20
91KanCouCP-2667
91MidLeaAP-MWL35
92ClaFS7-109
92FreKeyC-6
92HagSunF-2565
93BowBayF-2198
94ExcFS7-16
94OriPro-99
94RocRedWF-1005
94RocRedWTI-22
95RocRedWTI-36
96RocRedWB-27
Tyler, Dave
81BriRedST-19
Tyler, Josh
95BelBreTI-1
96StoPorB-20
Tyler, Lefty (George)
12T207-186
14B18B-54A
14B18B-54B
14B18B-54C
14FatPlaT-49
15CraJacE-146
16BF2FP-58
16ColE13-176
16SpoNewM-177
17HolBreD-106
21E121So8-98
22AmeCarE-71
22W575-140
Tyler, Mike
76DubPacT-37
78ChaChaT-18
79ChaChaT-7
80PorBeaT-1
Tyler, Peter
63GadFunC-71
Tyler, Tarzan
72Dia-131
Tyner, Marcus
93IdaFalBF-4033
93IdaFalBSP-27
94IdaFalBF-3585
94IdaFalBSP-23
95MacBraTI-26
Tyner, Matt
90HagSunDGB-34
Tyng, James
87OldJudN-519
Tynon, Don
94ElmPioF-3476
94ElmPioC-22
Tyrell, Jim
93UtiBluSC-24
93UtiBluSF-3534
94UtiBluSC-27
94UtiBluSF-3820
95MicBatCTI-29
Tyrone, Jim
74OPC-598
74Top-598
76SSP-604
77SanJosMC-7
78Top-487
Tyrus, Jason
94SpoIndC-23
94SpoIndF-3338
Tyson, Jeremy
94LSUTig-14
Tyson, Mike
74OPC-655
74Top-655
74TopSta-120
75OPC-231
75Top-231
76CraDis-65
76OPC-86
76SSP-283
76Top-86
77BurCheD-18
77Car5-28
77CarTeal-27
77PepGloD-38
77Top-599
78CarTeal-24
78Top-111
79Car5-31
79OPC-162
79Top-324
80OPC-252
80Top-486
81CokTeaS-23
81Fle-315
81Top-294
81TopSti-155
81TopSupHT-30
82Don-435
82Fle-606
82FleSta-100
82Top-62
Tyson, Terry
76BatTroTI-27
77WatIndT-26
Tyson, Ty (Albert T.)
90DodTar-1088
Ubiera, Miguel
91GulCoaRSP-20
92GulCoaRSP-9
Ubinas, Alex
90BriTigP-3157
90BriTigS-24
91BriTigC-9
91BriTigP-3609
Ubri, Fermin
84JacMetT-24
Uchinokura, Tokashi
92SalSpuC-24
92SalSpuF-3765
Uchiyama, Kenichi
90SalSpuCLC-122
90SalSpuP-2713
Uecker, Bob
62Top-594
63BraJayP-12
63Top-126
64Top-543
65Top-519
66OPC-91
66Top-91A
66Top-91B
66TopVen-91
67CokCapPh-10
67Top-326
75BreBro-3
78BraTCC-14
93ActPacA-152
Ueda, Joe
88FreSunP-1238
Ueda, Sadahito
83SanJosBC-16
Ufret, Ricardo
89AncBucTI-15
89BlaYNPRWL-17
Ugueto, Hector
93JohCitCC-26
93JohCitCF-3692
94SavCarC-26
94SavCarF-518
95NewJerCTI-29
96NewJerCB-27
Ugueto, Jesus
91JohCitCC-10
91JohCitCP-3987
92JohCitCF-3128
93SavCarC-25
93SavCarF-696
94MadHatC-23
94MadHatF-144
95LinVen-192
Uhal, Bob
88LitFalMP-8
Uhey, Jackie
76CliPilT-30
82ElPasDT-18
85EveGialC-19
86EveGiaPC-34
Uhlaender, Ted
66Top-264
66TopVen-264
67DexPre-211
67Top-431
68DexPre-74
68OPC-28
68Top-28
68TopVen-28
69MilBra-279
69MLBOffS-72
69OPC-194
69Top-194
69TopFou-19
69TopSta-200
69TopTeaP-15
69TwiTealC-10
70Ind-12
70MLBOffS-204
70Top-673
71Ind-12
71MLBOffS-384
71OPC-347
71Top-347
72MilBra-349
72Top-614
78TCM60I-161
78TwiFri-47
90GreHorB-28
90GreHorP-2682
91Ft.LauYC-8
91Ft.LauYP-2445
92ColCliP-2
Uhle, George E.
20WalMaiW-56
21Nei-16
22E120-43
22W572-108
22W573-133
26SpoComoA-44
26SpoNewSM-10
27YorCarE-11
28Exh-44
28StaPlaCE-68
28W502-11
28W56PlaC-D5A
28Yue-11
29ExhFou-24
31Exh-23
33ButCre-26
33ExhFou-12
33Gou-100
34GouCanV-22
40PlaBal-239
61Fle-146
77Ind192T-19
79DiaGre-279
82OhiHaloF-43
83DiaClaS2-69
91ConTSN-224
Uhrhan, Kevin
91LynRedSC-10
91LynRedSP-1200
92NewBriRSF-435
92NewBriRSS-479
93NewBriRSF-1221
Ujdur, Gerry
80EvaTriT-10
81EvaTriT-8
81Top-626
82EvaTriT-10
83Don-600
83Fle-346
83Tig-28
83Top-174
Ulises, Pedro
94OriPro-100
Ullan, Dave
94SpoIndC-24
94SpoIndF-3326
Ullger, Scott
80OrlTwiT-21
82OrlTwi8SCT-10
82TolMudHT-22
83TwiTeal-4
84Don-438
84Nes792-551
84TolMudHT-12
84Top-551
84TopTif-551
85IntLeaAT-27
85TolMudHT-18
86TolMudHP-22
87RocRedWP-7
87RocRedWT-21
88VisOakCLC-170
88VisOakP-99
89CalLeaA-25
89VisOakCLC-118
89VisOakP-1433
90CalLeaACLC-25
90VisOakCLC-79
90VisOakP-2170
91LinDriAA-499
91OrlSunRLD-499
91OrlSunRP-1865
92PorBeaF-2681
92PorBeaS-424
93PorBeaF-2396
93TriAAAGF-48
94SalLakBF-831
86STaoftFT-22
Ulrich, Dutch
94ConTSN-1298
94ConTSNB-1298
Ulrich, George
89CalLeaA-55
Ulrich, Jeff
80PenPilBT-22
80PenPilCT-16
81OklCit8T-26
82OklCit8T-17
Ulvenes, Gregg
85RedWinA-6
86RedWinA-21
Umbach, Arnie
66Top-518
Umbarger, Jim
76OPC-7
76SSP-257
76Top-7
77Top-378
78SSP270-90
79Top-518
79TucTorT-24
81RocRedWW-8
93RanKee-362
Umbria, Jose
96MedHatBJTI-30
Umbricht, Jim
60Top-145
60TopVen-145
62Col.45B-20
62Col45'HC-19
63Top-99
64Top-389
89AstCol4S-9
Umdenstock, Bob
79AppFoxT-19
82ChaRoyT-11
Umont, Frank
55Bow-305
Umphlett, Tom
53Bri-24
53RedSoxTI-26
54Bow-88
55Bow-45
57SeaPop-38
61UniOil-S11
Underhill, Pat
91GulCoaRSP-15
Underwood, Bill
92OneYanC-20
93GreHorC-24
93GreHorF-886
Underwood, Bobby
88WatPirP-13
89AugPirP-500
90AugPirP-2463
91SalBucC-15
Underwood, Curtis
92SavCarC-10
92SavCarF-672
Underwood, Devin
95ButCopKtl-20
Underwood, Kent
93GreHorF-887
Underwood, Pat
80OPC-358
80Top-709
81Don-368
81EvaTriT-9
81Fle-469
81Top-373
82Top-133
83Don-29
83EvaTriT-10
83Fle-347
83TigAlKS-70
83Top-588
Underwood, Tom
75OPC-615
75Top-615
76OPC-407
76SSP-461
76Top-407
77Car5-29
77Top-217
78BluJayP-20
78Top-531
79BluJayBY-18
79OPC-26
79Top-64
80OPC-172
80Top-324
81Don-108
81Fle-97
81OPC-114
81Top-114
81TopTra-846
82Don-323
82Fle-109
82Top-757
83A'sGraG-31
83Don-391
83Fle-535
83FleSta-202
83FleSti-191
83Top-466
84Don-253
84Fle-460
84FleUpd-121
84Nes792-642
84OPC-293
84Top-642
84TopSti-335
84TopTif-642
84TopTra-123T
84TopTraT-123T
85Fle-194
85Top-289
85TopTif-289
86BluJayGT-10
89PacSenL-169
89T/MSenL-108
91OriCro-465
92YanWIZ8-194
Undorf, Bob
90NiaFalRP-26
91FayGenC-27
91FayGenP-1170
92LakTigC-1
92LakTigF-2280
92ProFS7-68
93LonTigF-2307
Unglaub, Robert
08AmeCarE-94
08RosComP-7
09AmeCarE-111
09ColChiE-292A
09ColChiE-292B
09ColChiE-292C
09RamT20-119
09SenBarP-10
09T206-361
10SenWasT-6
11SpoLifCW-354
11SpoLifM-134
12ColRedB-292A
12ColRedB-292B
12ColRedB-292C
12ColTinT-292B
12ColTinT-292C
Ungs, Mike
79WisRapTT-2
80OrlTwiT-15
81WisRapTT-10
Unitas, John
58HarSta-22
60Pos-9
66AurSpoMK-5
Unrat, Chris
94ChaRivC-21
94ChaRivF-2677
Unrein, Todd
91KanCouCC-11
91KanCouCP-2658
91KanCouCTI-23
Unroe, Tim
92HelBreF-1724
92HelBreSP-18
93ExcFS7-195
93StoPorC-24
93StoPorF-754
94ElPasDF-3156
95Bow-226
95BowGolF-226
95Exc-76
95ExcLeaL-17
95Sel-169
95SelArtP-169
95Sum-150
95SumNthD-150
95UppDec-264

95UppDecED-264
95UppDecEDG-264
95UppDecML-181
96ColCho-662
96ColChoGS-662
96ColChoSS-662
96Sco-222
96Spo-121
96SpoArtP-121
97PacPriGotD-GD58
95UppDecMLFS-181

Unruh, Paul
51BerRos-C11

Unser, Al
47SigOil-17
49W72HolS-23

Unser, Del
69MilBra-280
69SenTeal-15
69SenTeal8-18
69Top-338
69TopTeaP-23
70DayDaiNM-135
70MLBOffS-287
70OPC-336
70Top-336
71MLBOffS-551
71OPC-33
71SenTealW-24
71Top-33
72MilBra-350
72Top-687
73OPC-247
73Top-247
74OPC-69
74PhiJohP-25
74Top-69
74TopSta-80
75MetSSP-4
75OPC-138
75Top-138
76ExpRed-32
76MetMSAP-3
76OPC-268
76SSP-535
76Top-268
77BurCheD-155
77ExpPos-32
77OPC-27
77Top-471
78OPC-216
78Top-348
79OPC-330
79Top-628
80OPC-12
80PhiBurK-13
80Top-6
80Top-27
81Don-164A
81Don-164B
81Fle-26
81OPC-56
81Top-566
81TopSupHT-90
82Don-273
82Fle-261
82Top-713
83PhiPosGM-10
85PhiTas-7
85PhiTas-8
86PhiTas-25
87PhiTas-xx0
88PhiTas-29
91MetWIZ-416

Upchurch, David Wayne
94EugEmeC-23
94EugEmeF-3713

Updike, John
78ReaRem-20

Upham, John
67Top-608
81TCM60I-473

Upp, Jerry (George)
09AmeCarE-112

Upshaw, Cecil
67OPC-179
67Top-179
68CokCapB-1
68Top-286
68TopVen-286
69Top-568
70OPC-295
70Top-295
71MLBOffS-23
71OPC-223
71Top-223
72OPC-74
72Top-74
73OPC-359
73Top-359
74OPC-579
74Top-579
74TopTra-579T
75OPC-92
75Top-92
76SSP-138
86BraGreT-11
92YanWIZ7-156

Upshaw, Lee
88DurBulS-22
89BurBraP-1598
89BurBraS-21
90Bes-25
90GreBraB-1
91GreBraC-7
91GreBraLD-220
91GreBraP-3001
91LinDriAA-220
93GreBraF-349

Upshaw, Willie
76ForLauYS-21
78BluJayP-21
79OPC-175
79SyrChiT-4
79SyrChiTI-26
79Top-341
80SyrChiT-21
80VenLeaS-59
82Don-652
82Fle-624
82OPC-196
82Top-196
83AllGamPI-8
83Don-558
83Fle-442
83FleSta-203
83OPC-338
83Top-556
83TopSti-128
84AllGamPI-99
84BluJayFS-30
84Don-315
84Fle-168
84FunFooP-94
84Nes792-453
84OPC-317
84Top-453
84TopRubD-30
84TopSti-363
84TopTif-453
85AllGamPI-9
85BluJayFS-30
85BluJayPLP-4
85Don-10
85Don-71
85DonActA-52
85DonSupD-10
85Fle-118
85Fle-635
85FleLimE-41
85Lea-10
85OPC-75
85OPCPos-14
85SevCoi-S15
85Top-75
85TopMin-75
85TopRubD-31
85TopSti-358
85TopTif-75
86BluJayAF-23
86BluJayFS-31
86Don-195
86Fle-72
86GenMilB-3I
86Lea-128
86OPC-223
86Spo-98
86Top-745
86TopSti-188
86TopTif-745
87BluJayFS-32
87Don-367
87DonOpeD-30
87Fle-239
87FleGlo-239
87GenMilB-1I
87Lea-231
87OPC-245
87RedFolSB-107
87SpoTeaP-5
87SyrChi1A-2
87Top-245
87TopSti-186
87TopTif-245
88BluJay5-11
88Don-271
88Fle-124
88FleGlo-124
88FleUpd-25
88FleUpdG-25
88IndGat-20
88Lea-131
88OPC-241
88PanSti-217
88PanSti-218
88Sco-279
88ScoGlo-279
88ScoRoo-42T
88ScoRooG-42T
88Spo-214
88StaLinBJ-19
88Top-505
88TopSti-185
88TopTif-505
88TopTra-123T
88TopTraT-123T
89Don-492
89Fle-415
89FleGlo-415
89OPC-106
89PanSti-324
89Sco-188
89Top-106
89TopTif-106
89UppDec-157
92Nab-8
93BluJayDM-1
93RanKee-441
96BluJayOH-33
97BluJayS-29

Upshur, Takashi
80WauTimT-11

Upton, Jack
80QuaCitCT-16
80VenLeaS-153
82IowCubT-12

Upton, Thomas
52Top-71
83TopRep5-71

Uqueto, Jesus
92JohCitCC-9

Urban, Jack E.
58A'sJayP-12
58Top-367
59Top-18
59TopVen-18

Urban, Luke
92ConTSN-405

Urbanek, Jason
91MarPhiC-6
91MarPhiP-3465
92MarPhiC-11
92MarPhiF-3067

Urbani, Tom
89AncBucTI-17
90JohCitCS-27
91SprCarC-27
91SprCarP-742
92ArkTraS-48
92LouRedF-1888
92SkyAA F-21
93Bow-583
93FleFinE-132
93LouRedF-214
93StaCluCa-15
94CarPol-23
94StaClu-392
94StaCluFDI-392
94StaCluGR-392
94StaCluMOP-392
94StaCluT-321
94StaCluTFDI-321
94Top-83
94TopGol-83
94TopSpa-83
95FleUpd-163
95Top-376
96CarPol-26
96LeaSigEA-204

Urbanski, Bill
33DelR33-9
33Gou-212
34DiaMatCSB-184
34BatR31-59
34DiaStaR-37
34ExhFou-1
35DiaMatCS3T1-142
36ExhFou-1
36GouWidPPR-A103
36NatChiFPR-72
36WorWidGV-71
37ExhFou-1
92ConTSN-408

Urbina, Dan
93LinVenB-106
93LinVenB-249
95LinVen-30
95VerBeaDTI-27
96SanBerSB-28

Urbina, Ugueth
92AlbPolC-21
92AlbPolF-2306
92Bow-261
92ClaFS7-379
92UppDecML-297
93BurBeeC-24
93BurBeeF-159
93ExcFS7-63
93LinVenB-101
93MidLeaAGF-32
94ActPac-26
94Bow-88
94BowBes-B79
94BowBesR-B79
94Cla-44
94ClaGolF-91
94ExcFS7-229
94ExcLeaLF-19
94HarSenF-2092
94UppDecML-83
94UppDecML-264
94VenLinU-32
95Bow-146
95Bow-261
95BowBes-B64
95BowBesR-B64
95Exc-228
95LinVen-29
95SP-9
95SPCha-14
95SPChaDC-14
95SPSil-9
95UppDec-239
95UppDecED-239
95UppDecEDG-239
95UppDecML-204
95UppDecMLOP-OP17
95UppDecSE-137
95UppDecSEG-137
95Zen-141
96Bow-190
96BowBes-119
96BowBesAR-119
96BowBesR-119
96ColCho-28
96ColCho-217
96ColChoGS-28
96ColChoGS-217
96ColChoSS-28
96ColChoSS-217
96Fin-B329
96FinRef-B329
96LeaPre-139
96LeaPreP-139
96LeaSig-90
96LeaSigPPG-90
96LeaSigPPP-90
96Sco-234
96SelArtP-174
97Bow-96
97BowChr-119
97BowChrI-119
97BowChrIR-119
97BowChrR-119
97BowInt-96
97Cir-62
97CirRav-62
97ColCho-166
97DonEli-123
97DonEliGS-123
97DonRatR-14
97Fle-388
97FleTif-388
97Lea-22
97LeaFraM-22
97LeaFraMDC-22
97Pac-355
97PacLigB-355
97PacSil-355
97Pin-162
97PinArtP-162
97PinIns-91
97PinInsCE-91
97PinInsDE-91
97PinMusC-162
97Sco-86
97ScoPreS-86
97ScoShoS-86
97ScoShoSAP-86
97Top-414
97Ult-234
97UltGolME-234
97UltPlaME-234
97UppDec-112
95UppDecMLFS-204

Urbina, William
92HigSchPLS-3
93MadMusC-25
93MadMusF-1822
93SouOreAC-25
93SouOreAF-4063
94WesMicWC-22
94WesMicWF-2295

Urbon, Joe
89BatCliP-1933
90SpaPhiB-22
90SpaPhiP-2505
90SpaPhiS-22
91ClePhiC-25
91ClePhiP-1636

Urcioli, John
91MiaMirC-24
91MiaMirP-418

Urdaneta, Jose G.
93LinVenB-60

Uremovich, Mike
75CliPilT-16

Urena, Fausto
92GulCoaDF-3576

Uribe, Dilone
93YakBeaC-24
93YakBeaF-3886

Uribe, George
84ButCopKT-24

Uribe, Jorge
86WauTimP-26
87SalSpuP-2
88VerMarP-953
89SanBerSB-12
89SanBerSCLC-78
93LinVenB-253
94VenLinU-56
95LinVen-10

Uribe, Jose
85FleUpd-124
85GiaMot-13
85GiaPos-28
85TopTifT-125T
85TopTra-125T
86Don-236
86Fle-552
86GiaMot-13
86OPC-12
86Top-12
86TopSti-87
86TopTat-13
86TopTif-12
87Don-436
87DonOpeD-99
87Fle-286
87FleGlo-286
87GiaMot-13
87OPC-94
87Top-633
87TopTif-633
88Don-559
88DonBasB-303
88Fle-99
88FleGlo-99
88GiaMot-13
88Lea-218
88Nes-13
88OPC-302
88PanSti-425
88Sco-165
88ScoGlo-165
88StaLinG-19
88Top-302
88TopBig-95
88TopSti-91
88TopTif-302

89Bow-471
89BowTif-471
89Don-131
89DonBasB-106
89Fle-345
89FleGlo-345
89GiaMot-13
89OPC-8
89PanSti-217
89Sco-56
89Spo-61
89Top-753
89TopBig-258
89TopSti-82
89TopTif-753
89UppDec-181
90Don-335
90DonBesN-122
90Fle-74
90FleCan-74
90GiaMot-17
90GiaSmo-20
90Lea-225
90OPC-472
90PanSti-372
90PubSti-84
90Sco-455
90Spo-79
90Top-472
90TopBig-213
90TopTif-472
90UppDec-188
91Bow-627
91CadEllD-58
91Don-375
91Fle-275
91GiaMot-17
91GiaPacGaE-12
91GiaSFE-15
91Lea-433
91OPC-158
91PanFreS-70
91Sco-628
91StaClu-267
91Top-158
91TopDesS-158
91TopMic-158
91TopTif-158
91Ult-330
91UppDec-207
92Don-453
92Fle-649
92GiaMot-17
92GiaPacGaE-34
92OPC-538
92PanSti-215
92Sco-546
92StaClu-371
92Top-538
92TopGol-538
92TopGolW-538
92TopMic-538
92UppDec-270
93AstMot-12
93Fle-539
93PacSpa-483
93Top-201
93TopGol-201
93TopInaM-201
93TopMic-201
93UppDec-729
93UppDecGold-729
94Fle-502
94Pac-277
Uribe, Juan
88BelBreGS-8
90StoPorB-18
90StoPorCLC-170
90StoPorP-2179
Uribe, Milciades
88WytCubP-1975
89ChaWheB-3
89ChaWheP-1744
Uribe, Relito
89DunBluJS-20
Urman, Mike
88PulBraP-1764
89SumBraP-1109
Urrea, John
76ArkTraT-9
77Car5-30
77CarTeal-28
78CarTeal-26
78Top-587
79Top-429
81Don-190
81Top-152
81TopTra-847
82Don-313
82Fle-583
82Top-28
Urrieta, Ulises
76VenLeaS-100
Urshan, Ross
92LetMouSP-9
Urso, Joe
92BoiHawC-17
93PalSprAC-24
93PalSprAF-80
94LakElsSC-24
94LakElsSF-1674
95LakElsSTI-25
95MidAngOHP-35
95MidAngTI-28
96LakElsSB-22
Urso, Sal (Salvy)
91PenPilC-12
91PenPilP-378
92SanBerC-23
92SanBerSF-954
94RivPilCLC-9
95PorCitRTI-24
96TacRaiB-26
Usher, Bob
51Bow-286
52Top-157
57IndSoh-15
58Top-124
83TopRep5-157
Usiyan, Thompson
82MonNew-19
Ussery, Brian
96BoiHawB-29
Utecht, Tim
83BelBreF-20
Utting, Ben
94IdaFalBF-3595
94IdaFalBSP-26
95DanBraTI-27
96MacBraB-20
Uurat, Chris
96TulDriTI-27
Uzcundun, Paolino
28W513-88
Vaccaro, Sal
86JamExpP-27
87BurExpP-1072
87SanJosBP-4
Vachon, Mad Dog (Maurice)
72Dia-133
Vachon, Paul
72Dia-134
Vachon, Viviane
72Dia-135
Vagg, Richard
90IBAWorA-42
90IBAWorA-49
91MelBusF-11
95AusFut-83
Vail, Michael
75TidTidTI-23
76Hos-55
76HosTwi-55
76OPC-655
76SSP-534
76Top-655
77MetDaiPA-27
77Top-246
78Top-69
79Top-663
80OPC-180
80Top-343
81Don-554A
81Don-554B
81Fle-311
81Top-471
81TopTra-848
82Fle-84
82RedCok-22
82Top-194
83Don-597
83ExpPos-24
83Fle-605
83GiaMot-19
83Top-554
83TopTra-119T
84ExpPos-33
84Fle-290
84FleUpd-122
84Nes792-766
84OPC-143
84Top-766
84TopTif-766
84TopTra-124T
84TopTraT-124T
89TidTidC-6
90DodTar-812
91MetWIZ-417
Vaji, Mark
81QuaCitCT-24
Valandia, Jorge
93NiaFalRF-3399
Valazquez, Fred
71RicBraTI-17
Valdes, David
94YakBeaC-27
Valdes, Ismael
94LeaLimR-43
95ColCho-223
95ColChoGS-223
95ColChoSS-223
95DodMot-23
95DodPol-26
95Don-29
95DonPreP-29
95DonTopotO-273
95Emo-146
95Fin-316
95FinRef-316
95Fla-157
95Fle-550
95Lea-13
95Pac-226
95PacLatD-35
95Pin-139
95PinArtP-139
95PinMusC-139
95Sco-272
95ScoGolR-272
95ScoPlaTS-272
95SelCer-99
95SelCerMG-99
95StaClu-161
95StaCluFDI-161
95StaCluMOP-161
95StaCluSTWS-161
95StaCluVR-85
95Sum21C-TC8
95Top-66
95TopCyb-48
95Ult-400
95UltGolM-400
95UppDec-323
95UppDecED-323
95UppDecEDG-323
95UppDecSE-171
95UppDecSEG-171
96ColCho-588
96ColChoGS-588
96ColChoSS-588
96DodMot-11
96DodPol-29
96Don-318
96DonPreP-318
96EmoXL-216
96Fla-299
96Fle-448
96FleDod-17
96FleTif-448
96Lea-184
96LeaLim-87
96LeaLimG-87
96LeaPre-101
96LeaPreP-101
96LeaPrePB-184
96LeaPrePG-184
96LeaPrePS-184
96LeaSig-65
96LeaSigA-225
96LeaSigAG-226
96LeaSigAS-226
96LeaSigPPG-65
96LeaSigPPP-65
96Pac-108
96PacEstL-EL32
96PacPri-P39
96PacPriG-P39
96Pin-296
96PinFoil-296
96Sco-137
96ScoDugC-A86
96ScoDugCAP-A86
96Sel-34
96SelArtP-34
96SelCer-52
96SelCerAP-52
96SelCerCB-52
96SelCerCR-52
96SelCerIP-22
96SelCerMB-52
96SelCerMG-52
96SelCerMR-52
96SP-104
96StaClu-348
96StaCluEPB-348
96StaCluEPG-348
96StaCluEPS-348
96StaCluMOP-348
96StaCluVRMO-85
96Stu-103
96StuPrePB-103
96StuPrePG-103
96StuPrePS-103
96Top-324
96TopChr-128
96TopChrR-128
96TopGal-124
96TopGalPPI-124
96TopLas-128
96Ult-226
96UltGolM-226
96UppDec-96
96Zen-33
96ZenArtP-33
97Cir-212
97CirRav-212
97ColCho-142
97Don-79
97DonLim-104
97DonLimLE-104
97DonPre-129
97DonPreCttC-129
97DonPreP-79
97DonPrePGold-79
97DonTea-109
97DonTeaSPE-109
97Fin-264
97FinRef-264
97FlaSho-A158
97FlaSho-B158
97FlaSho-C158
97FlaShoLC-158
97FlaShoLC-B158
97FlaShoLC-C158
97FlaShoLCM-A158
97FlaShoLCM-B158
97FlaShoLCM-C158
97Fle-372
97FleTif-372
97Lea-145
97LeaFraM-145
97LeaFraMDC-145
97MetUni-106
97NewPin-95
97NewPinAP-95
97NewPinMC-95
97NewPinPP-95
97Pac-340
97PacLatotML-30
97PacLigB-340
97PacPri-116
97PacPriLB-116
97PacPriP-116
97PacSil-340
97PinCar-8
97Sco-16
97ScoDod-1
97ScoDodPl-1
97ScoDodPr-1
97ScoPreS-16
97ScoShoS-16
97ScoShoSAP-16
97StaClu-141
97StaCluMOP-141
97Top-166
97TopGal-96
97TopGalPPI-96
97Ult-224
97UltGolME-224
97UltPlaME-224
97UppDec-93
Valdes, Marc
92TopTra-121T
92TopTraG-121T
93StaCluM-20
94Bow-646
94BowBes-B35
94BowBesR-B35
94Cla-177
94ClaGolF-119
94ClaGolN1PLF-LP15
94ClaGolREF-RE15
94KanCouCC-1
94KanCouCF-161
94KanCouCTI-28
94Pin-431
94PinArtP-431
94PinMusC-431
94Sco-555
94ScoGolR-555
94Top-750
94TopGol-750
94TopSpa-750
95Bow-266
95BowBes-B78
95BowBesR-B78
95BowGolF-266
95ChaKniTI-27
95Exc-198
95KanCouCLTI-14
95Top-649
95UppDecML-86
96ChaKniB-27
96ColCho-553
96ColChoGS-553
96ColChoSS-553
96Fle-396
96FleTif-396
96Top-433
97Fle-618
97FleTif-618
95UppDecMLFS-86
Valdes, Pedro
95Bes-58
96BesAutSA-80
96Exc-143
96IowCubB-28
97Fle-288
97FleTif-288
95OrlCubF-24
97Pac-260
97PacLigB-260
97PacSil-260
97Ult-172
97UltGolME-172
97UltPlaME-172
Valdes, Ramon
88GreFalDTI-25
Valdes, Rene
49PorBeaP-4
57Top-337
61UniOil-SP11
90DodTar-813
Valdespino, Sandy
65OPC-201
65Top-201
66OPC-56
66Top-56
66TopVen-56
66TwiFaiG-15
67CokCapTw-12
67DexPre-212
68Top-304
68TopVen-304
69MilBra-281
70BreMcD-30
76ForLauYS-30
77WesHavYT-23
78TwiFri-48
81TCM60I-329
85RocRedWT-25
87AstShoSTw-18
94BreMilB-82
Valdez, Amilcar
88BakDodCLC-241
88BlaYNPRWL-177
Valdez, Angel
82MiaMarT-17
Valdez, Carlos
92EveGiaF-1691
93CliGiaC-23
93CliGiaF-2490
94SanJosGC-23
94SanJosGF-2817
96PhoFirB-25
Valdez, Doug
94ButCopKSP-24
Valdez, Efrain
88TulDriTI-5

89CanIndB-6
89CanIndP-1311
89CanIndS-22
90CMC-456
90ColSprSSC-4
90ColSprSSP-35
90ProAAAF-216
91Bow-60
91ColSprSSLD-96
91ColSprSSP-2183
91LinDriAAA-96
91OPC-692
91Sco-723
91StaClu-483
91Top-692A
91Top-692B
91TopDeb90-156
91TopDesS-692
91TopMic-692
91TopTif-692
92DenZepF-2640
92DenZepS-146
92StaClu-838
93LimRocDWB-70
Valdez, Frank (Francisco)
88KenTwiP-1393
89GasRanP-1020
89GasRanS-23
89SouAtlLAGS-40
89VisOakCLC-108
89VisOakP-1440
90CMC-722
90OrlSunRB-14
90OrlSunRP-1094
90OrlSunRS-21
91LinDriAA-479
91OrlSunRLD-479
91OrlSunRP-1864
Valdez, Ismael
91KisDodP-4186
94SanAntMF-2470
95StaCluSTDW-D161
Valdez, Jose
83PeoSunF-12
90KisDodD-27
Valdez, Julio
81PawRedST-17
82Don-560
82Top-381
83Fle-199
83Top-628
85DomLeaS-202
85IowCubT-7
86IowCubP-25
87IowCubTI-17
88PitCubP-1357
88WytCubP-1988
86STaoftFT-7
Valdez, Ken
92BriTigF-1430
93BriTigC-23
93BriTigF-3655
95BoiHawTI-29
Valdez, Mario
96HicCraB-25
96MidLeaAB-56
96SouBenSHS-26
97Fle-753
97FleTif-753
Valdez, Mica
90SanAntMGS-28
Valdez, Miguel
80ElmPioRST-44
93IdaFalBF-4049
93IdaFalBSP-9
94DanBraC-29
94DanBraF-3547
94MacBraC-24
94MacBraF-2221
Valdez, Pedro
91HunCubC-27
91HunCubP-3351
92GenCubC-1
92GenCubF-1575
92PeoChiC-21
93MidLeaAGF-44
93PeoChiC-1
93PeoChiF-1097
93PeoChiTI-30
94ClaGolF-53
94OrlCubF-1400
Valdez, Rafael
87ChaRaiP-15
88ChaRaiP-1201
89RivRedWB-18
89RivRedWCLC-4
89RivRedWP-1398
89WicChaR-16
89WicUpdR-10
90Bow-210
90BowTif-210
90CMC-523
90FleUpd-58
90LasVegSC-20
90LasVegSP-125
90ProAAAF-13
90ScoRoo-93T
90UppDec-775
91Bow-663
91LasVegSP-236
91Sco-360
91Sco100RS-31
91TopDeb90-157
91UppDec-253
92LasVegSF-2797
93LimRocDWB-67
Valdez, Ramon
89BlaYNPRWL-18
89PriPirS-22
Valdez, Sergio
85UtiBluST-7
87IndIndTI-21
88IndIndC-8
88IndIndP-501
89IndIndC-2
89IndIndP-1215
90Don-405A
90Don-405B
90IndTeal-41
90Lea-496
90OPC-199
90Top-199
90TopTif-199
91ColSprSSLD-97
91ColSprSSP-2184
91Don-344
91Fle-380
91LinDriAAA-97
91OPC-98
91Top-98
91TopDesS-98
91TopMic-98
91TopTif-98
92IndIndF-1859
92IndIndS-196
92StaClu-789
93Fle-465
93LimRocDWB-15
93OttLynF-2436
93StaClu-171
93StaCluFDI-171
93StaCluMOP-171
94PawRedSDD-27
94SarRedSC-28
94SarRedSF-1952
95Pac-47
95PhoFirTI-34
96ColCho-716
96ColChoGS-716
96ColChoSS-716
96Don-57
96DonPreP-57
96Fle-598
96FleTif-598
Valdez, Sylverio
80UtiBluJT-8
83AndBraT-18
Valdez, Trovin
94AlbPolF-2252
94BluOriC-21
94BluOriF-3577
Valdez, Victor
93AshTouC-21
93AshTouF-2276
Valdivielso, Jose
55DonWin-40
56Top-237
57Top-246
59SenTealW-17
60Top-527
61Top-557
61TwiCloD-29
61TwiJayP-11
61TwiPetM-25
62Top-339
Valeandia, Jorge
92BriTigC-22
Valencia, Gil
89MarPhiS-31
90BatCliP-3083
90SpaPhiB-23
90SpaPhiP-2506
90SpaPhiS-23
Valencia, Jose
88SumBraP-399
Valennia, Max
92BoiHawC-2
Valente, John
88CapCodPPaLP-2
Valenti, Jon
96WesMicWB-27
Valentin, Eddy
89AubAstP-2160
Valentin, Javier (Jose Javier)
94EliTwiC-24
94EliTwiF-3736
95ForWayWTI-15
96BesAutS-90
96Bow-311
96BowBes-151
96BowBesAR-151
96BowBesMI-8
96BowBesMIAR-8
96BowBesMIR-8
96BowBesR-151
97Bow-116
97BowBes-143
97BowBesAR-143
97BowBesR-143
97BowChr-134
97BowChrI-134
97BowChrIR-134
97BowChrR-134
97BowInt-116
97Don-389
97DonPreP-389
97DonPrePGold-389
97Top-4
Valentin, John
88BlaYNPRWL-178
88CapCodPB-11
88CapCodPPaLP-138
89WinHavRSS-25
90Bes-283
90NewBriRSB-21
90NewBriRSS-19
91LinDriAA-473
91NewBriRSLD-473
91NewBriRSP-361
91PawRedSDD-25
92DonRooP-BC19
92FleUpd-4
92PawRedSF-933
92PawRedSS-370
92SkyAAAF-169
93Bow-690
93DenHol-21
93Don-251
93Fle-183
93Lea-87
93OPC-220
93PacSpa-363
93Pin-224
93Pin-482
93RedSoxWHP-26
93Sco-243
93Sel-344
93StaClu-508
93StaCluFDI-508
93StaCluMOP-508
93Top-424
93TopGol-424
93TopInaM-424
93TopMic-424
93Toy-10
93UppDec-387
93UppDecGold-387
94ColC-278
94ColChoGS-278
94ColChoSS-278
94Don-517
94ExtBas-26
94Fin-128
94FinRef-128
94Fla-16
94Fle-44
94Lea-77
94Pac-67
94PanSti-33
94Pin-126
94PinArtP-126
94PinMusC-126
94Sco-417
94ScoGolR-417
94Sel-49
94StaClu-483
94StaCluFDI-483
94StaCluGR-483
94StaCluMOP-483
94StaCluMOP-ST16
94StaCluST-ST16
94Stu-165
94Top-568
94TopGol-568
94TopSpa-568
94TriPla-208
94Ult-318
94UppDec-373
94UppDecED-373
95ColCho-409
95ColChoGS-409
95ColChoSE-189
95ColChoSE-265
95ColChoSEGS-189
95ColChoSEGS-265
95ColChoSESS-189
95ColChoSESS-265
95ColChoSS-409
95Don-89
95DonPreP-89
95DonTopotO-28
95Emb-10
95EmbGolI-10
95Emo-16
95Fin-53
95FinRef-53
95Fla-14
95Fle-41
95Lea-12
95LeaLim-89
95Pac-48
95Pin-75
95PinArtP-75
95PinMusC-75
95Sco-8
95Sco-314
95ScoGolR-8
95ScoGolR-314
95ScoPlaTS-8
95ScoPlaTS-314
95Sel-98
95SelArtP-98
95SP-128
95SPCha-124
95SPChaDC-124
95Spo-88
95SpoArtP-88
95SPSil-128
95StaClu-62
95StaCluFDI-62
95StaCluMOP-62
95StaCluSTDW-RS1T
95StaCluSTDW-RS62
95StaCluSTWS-62
95StaCluVR-38
95Stu-164
95Sum-145
95SumNthD-145
95Top-36
95TopCyb-28
95UC3-10
95UC3ArtP-10
95Ult-16
95UltGolM-16
95UppDec-163
95UppDecC-3A
95UppDecED-163
95UppDecEDG-163
95Zen-54
96Baz-120
96Bow-96
96BowBes-88
96BowBesAR-88
96BowBesR-88
96Cir-13
96CirRav-13
96ColCho-471
96ColChoGS-471
96ColChoSS-471
96Don-83
96DonPreP-83
96EmoXL-19
96Fin-S91
96FinRef-S91
96Fla-28
96Fle-37
96FleRedS-16
96FleTif-37
96Lea-166
96LeaPre-109
96LeaPreP-109
96LeaPrePB-166
96LeaPrePG-166
96LeaPrePS-166
96MetUni-20
96MetUniP-20
96Pac-255
96PacEstL-EL10
96PacPri-P80
96PacPriG-P80
96PanSti-141
96Pin-84
96PinAfi-140
96PinAfiAP-140
96ProSta-109
96Sco-33
96ScoDugC-A32
96ScoDugCAP-A32
96Sel-126
96SelArtP-126
96SelCer-34
96SelCerAP-34
96SelCerCB-34
96SelCerCR-34
96SelCerMB-34
96SelCerMG-34
96SelCerMR-34
96Spo-71
96SpoArtP-71
96StaClu-196
96StaClu-376
96StaCluB&B-BB10
96StaCluMO-42
96StaCluMOP-196
96StaCluMOP-376
96StaCluMOP-BB10
96StaCluVRMO-38
96Stu-25
96StuPrePB-25
96StuPrePG-25
96StuPrePS-25
96Sum-140
96SumAbo&B-140
96SumArtP-140
96SumFoi-140
96Top-164
96TopChr-46
96TopChrR-46
96TopGal-12
96TopGalPPI-12
96TopLas-93
96TopRoaW-RW17
96Ult-21
96UltGolM-21
96UppDec-25
96Zen-86
96ZenArtP-86
96ZenMoz-9
97Bow-19
97BowBes-37
97BowBesAR-37
97BowBesR-37
97BowChr-15
97BowChrI-15
97BowChrIR-15
97BowChrR-15
97BowInt-19
97Cir-233
97CirRav-233
97ColCho-280
97Don-163
97DonPreP-163
97DonPrePGold-163
97DonTea-49
97DonTeaSPE-49
97DunDonPPS-26
97Fin-251
97FinRef-251
97Fle-31
97FleTif-31
97Lea-167
97LeaFraM-167
97LeaFraMDC-167
97MetUni-25
97NewPin-96
97NewPinAP-96
97NewPinMC-96
97NewPinPP-96
97Pac-47

97PacLigB-47
97PacSil-47
97Sco-101
97ScoPreS-101
97ScoRedS-3
97ScoRedSPl-3
97ScoRedSPr-3
97ScoShoS-101
97ScoShoSAP-101
97SpolII-141
97SpolIIEE-141
97StaClu-241
97StaCluMat-241
97StaCluMOP-241
97Top-134
97TopChr-51
97TopChrR-51
97TopGal-128
97TopGalPPI-128
97Ult-401
97UltGolME-401
97UltPlaME-401
97UppDec-309
Valentin, Jose Antonio
87SpoIndP-23
88ChaRaiP-1198
89BlaYNPRWL-155
89CalLeaA-7
89RivRedWB-19
89RivRedWCLC-8
89RivRedWP-1415
89WicUpdR-18
90WicWraRD-20
91Cla/Bes-33
91LinDriAA-620
91WicWraLD-620
91WicWraP-2606
91WicWraRD-16
92DenZepF-2652
92DenZepS-147
92SkyAAAF-72
93ClaFS7-265
93NewOrlZF-981
93Top-804
93TopGol-804
93TopInaM-804
93TopMic-804
94Bow-93
94BreMilB-83
94BrePol-27
94ColC-474
94ColChoGS-474
94ColChoSS-477
94Don-544
94Fle-194
94LeaLimR-33
94Pac-346
94Pin-249
94PinArtP-249
94PinMusC-249
94ScoRoo-RT101
94ScoRooGR-RT101
94SpoRoo-80
94SpoRooAP-80
94StaClu-456
94StaCluFDI-456
94StaCluGR-456
94StaCluMOP-456
94Top-251
94TopGol-251
94TopSpa-251
94UppDec-303
94UppDecED-303
95Bow-318
95ColCho-176
95ColChoGS-176
95ColChoSE-72
95ColChoSEGS-72
95ColChoSESS-72
95ColChoSS-176
95Don-68
95DonPreP-68
95DonTopotO-104
95Emb-7
95EmbGolI-7
95Fin-26
95FinRef-26
95Fle-192
95Lea-50
95Pac-241
95PacPri-77
95Pin-127
95PinArtP-127
95PinMusC-127
95Sco-190
95ScoGolR-190
95ScoPlaTS-190
95SP-167
95SPSil-167
95StaClu-402
95StaClu-451
95StaCluMOP-402
95StaCluMOP-451
95StaCluSTWS-402
95StaCluSTWS-451
95StaCluVR-242
95Top-527
95TopCyb-312
95Ult-69
95UltGolM-69
95UppDec-55
95UppDecED-55
95UppDecEDG-55
95UppDecSE-233
95UppDecSEG-233
96ColCho-598
96ColChoGS-598
96ColChoSS-598
96Don-443
96DonPreP-443
96Fla-108
96Fle-160
96FleTif-160
96FtMyeMB-5
96LeaSigA-226
96LeaSigAG-227
96LeaSigAS-227
96Pac-353
96PacPri-P111
96PacPriG-P111
96Sco-184
96SP-41
96SP-111
96StaClu-391
96StaCluMOP-391
96StaCluVRMO-242
96TeaOut-82
96Top-122
96Ult-86
96UltGolM-86
96UppDec-122
97Bow-280
97BowInt-280
97Cir-255
97CirRav-255
97ColCho-375
97Don-240
97DonPreP-240
97DonPrePGold-240
97Fin-42
97FinRef-42
97FlaSho-A70
97FlaSho-B70
97FlaSho-C70
97FlaShoLC-70
97FlaShoLC-B70
97FlaShoLC-C70
97FlaShoLCM-A70
97FlaShoLCM-B70
97FlaShoLCM-C70
97Fle-138
97FleTif-138
97Lea-60
97LeaFraM-60
97LeaFraMDC-60
97MetUni-70
97NewPin-85
97NewPinAP-85
97NewPinMC-85
97NewPinPP-85
97Pac-128
97PacLigB-128
97PacPri-42
97PacPriLB-42
97PacPriP-42
97PacSil-128
97Sco-445
97ScoHobR-445
97ScoResC-445
97ScoShoS-445
97ScoShoSAP-445
97SP-101
97SpolII-153
97SpolIIEE-153
97StaClu-113
97StaCluMOP-113
97TopChr-2
97TopChrR-2
97TopGal-135
97TopGalPPI-135
97Ult-83
97UltGolME-83
97UltPlaME-83
97UppDec-405
Valentine, Bill
76ArkTraT-10
80ArkTraT-23
Valentine, Bobby
71OPC-188
71Top-188
72OPC-11
72Top-11
73LinPor-38
73OPC-502
73Top-502
74OPC-101
74Top-101
74TopDecE-11
74TopSta-150
75OPC-215
75Top-215
76HawIslC-6
76OPC-366
76Top-366
77PadSchC-61
77Top-629
78MetDaiPA-24
78Top-712
79OPC-222
79Top-428
80Top-56
85MetTCM-5
85RanPer-2
85SpoIndGC-22
85TopTifT-126T
85TopTra-126T
86RanPer-2
86Top-261
86TopTif-261
87RanMot-1
87RanSmo-19
87Top-118
87Top-656
87TopTif-118
87TopTif-656
88RanMot-1
88RanSmo-8
88Top-201
88Top-594
88TopTif-201
88TopTif-594
89RanMot-1
89RanSmo-33
89Top-314
89TopTif-314
90DodTar-814
90OPC-729
90RanMot-1
90Top-729
90TopTif-729
91MetWIZ-418
91OPC-489
91RanMot-1
91Top-489
91TopDesS-489
91TopMic-489
91TopTif-489
92OPC-789
92RanMot-1
92RanTeal-25
92Top-789
92TopGol-789
92TopGolW-789
92TopMic-789
93RanKee-363
93RedKah-8
94NorTidF-2936
96NorTidB-1
Valentine, Corky (Harold)
55Top-44
55TopDouH-45
79TCM50-61
Valentine, Ellis
76ExpRed-33
76OPC-590
76SSP-342
76Top-590
77BurCheD-158
77ExpPos-33
77OPC-234
77RCColC-65
77Top-52
78Kel-19
78OPC-45
78RCColC-31
78Top-185
79ExpPos-29
79Hos-50
79OPC-277
79Top-535
80ExpPos-32
80Kel-21
80OPC-206
80Top-395
81AllGamPI-162
81Fle-148
81OPC-244
81OPCPos-7
81Top-445
81TopScr-80
81TopSti-186
81TopTra-849
82Don-605
82FBIDis-25
82Fle-541
82FleSta-83
82MetPhoA-23
82OPC-15
82Top-15
82TopSti-69
82TopStiV-69
83Fle-558
83FleSta-204
83FleSti-235
83Top-653
83TopTra-120T
84AngSmo-29
84Fle-529
84Nes792-236
84OPC-236
84Top-236
84TopTif-236
86ExpGreT-6
91MetWIZ-419
93ExpDonM-21
93RanKee-364
Valentine, Fred
64Top-483
66Top-351
66TopVen-351
67CokCapS-18
67DexPre-213
67OPC-64
67SenTeal-12
67Top-64
67TopVen-220
68AtlOilPBCC-45
68SenTeal-12
68Top-248
68TopVen-248
69MilBra-282
69SenTeal8-19
91OriCro-466
Valentinetti, Vito
57Top-74
58Top-463
59Top-44
59TopVen-44
Valentini, Vincent
80WicAerT-19
Valenzuela, Benny
77FriOneYW-76
Valenzuela, Derek
94ChaWheF-2707
Valenzuela, Fernando
81AllGamPI-180
81Dod-12
81DodPol-34
81Fle-140
81LonBeaPT-10
81PerAll-9
81Top-302
81TopTra-850
82DodPol-34
82DodUniOV-24
82Don-462
82Fle-27
82Fle-635
82Fle-636A
82Fle-636B
82FleSta-1
82FleSta-108
82FleSta-111
82Kel-9
82MonNew-20
82OPC-334
82OPC-345
82PerCreC-12
82PerCreCG-12
82Squ-20
82Top-6
82Top-166
82Top-345
82Top-510
82TopSti-11
82TopSti-50
82TopSti-119
82TopSti-257
83DodPol-34
83DodPos-18
83Don-1
83Don-284
83DonActA-53
83Fle-224
83FleSta-205
83FleSti-112
83Kel-7
83KelCerB-1
83OPC-40
83PerCreC-18
83PerCreCG-18
83SevCoi-8
83Top-40
83Top-681
83TopGloS-10
83TopSti-250
83TopStiB-1
84DodPol-34
84DodUniOP-9
84Don-52
84DonActAS-13
84Fle-115
84FleSti-81
84FunFooP-7
84MilBra-27
84Nes792-220
84OCoandSI-34
84OPC-220
84RalPur-10
84SevCoi-W9
84Top-220
84TopCer-10
84TopRubD-32
84TopSti-16
84TopSti-79
84TopSup-30
84TopTif-220
85AllGamPI-180
85DodCokP-31
85Don-52
85DonActA-37
85DonHig-6
85DonHig-28
85Fle-387
85FleLimE-42
85FleStaS-114
85GenMilS-12
85KASDis-18
85KitCloD-18
85Lea-184
85OPC-357
85SevCoi-W16
85ThoMcAD-45
85Top-440
85Top3-D-21
85TopRubD-32
85TopSti-71
85TopSup-52
85TopTif-440
86BasStaB-115
86BurKinA-3
86DodCokP-30
86DodPol-34
86DodUniOP-21
86Don-215
86DonAll-27
86DonHig-25
86Dra-36
86Fle-145
86Fle-641
86FleMin-31
86FleSlu-41
86FleStiC-123
86GenMilB-5J
86Lea-91
86MeaGolBB-15
86MeaGolM-12
86MeaGolSB-2
86MSAJifPD-14
86OPC-178

86OPCBoxB-P
86QuaGra-17
86SevCoi-C6
86SevCoi-E6
86SevCoi-S6
86SevCoi-W6
86Spo-12
86Spo-60
86Spo-72
86Spo-132
86Spo-143
86SpoDecG-66
86SpoRoo-47
86Top-207
86Top-401
86Top-630
86Top3-D-30
86TopGloS-3
86TopMinL-47
86TopSti-64
86TopSup-58
86TopTat-24
86TopTif-207
86TopTif-401
86TopTif-630
86TopWaxBC-P
86TruVal-6
87BurKinA-20
87ClaGam-91
87DodMot-4
87DodPol-17
87DodSmoA-36
87Don-94
87DonAll-54
87Dra-29
87Fle-457
87Fle-631
87FleAll-10
87FleAwaW-40
87FleBasA-43
87FleGamW-42
87FleGlo-457
87FleGlo-631
87FleMin-109
87FleSlu-43
87FleStiC-120
87GenMilB-6J
87HosSti-11
87K-M-33
87KayB-32
87KraFoo-32
87Lea-148
87MandMSL-19
87MSAJifPD-15
87OPC-273
87RalPur-11
87RedFolSB-57
87SevCoi-W16
87Spo-119
87Spo-120
87Spo-150
87SpoDeaP-2
87SpoRea-40
87SpoSupD-6
87SpoTeaP-14
87StaStiV-1
87StaStiV-2
87StaStiV-3
87StaStiV-4
87StaStiV-5
87StaStiV-6
87StaStiV-7
87StaStiV-8
87StaStiV-9
87StaStiV-10
87StaVal-1
87StaVal-2
87StaVal-3
87StaVal-4
87StaVal-5
87StaVal-6
87StaVal-7
87StaVal-8
87StaVal-9
87StaVal-10
87StaVal-11
87StaVal-12
87StaVal-13
87StuPan-6
87Top-410
87Top-604
87TopCoi-47
87TopGloA-11
87TopGloS-53
87TopMinL-16
87TopSti-75
87TopTif-410
87TopTif-604
88CheBoy-24
88DodMot-4
88DodPol-34
88DodSmo-24
88Don-53
88DonBasB-316
88Fle-528
88FleBasM-40
88FleExcS-43
88FleGlo-528
88FleMin-86
88FleStiC-94
88GreBasS-68
88K-M-31
88KinDis-19
88Lea-61
88MSAIceTD-20
88OPC-52
88PanSti-304
88Sco-600
88ScoGlo-600
88Spo-40
88StaLinAl-34
88StaLinD-20
88Top-489
88Top-780
88TopBig-18
88TopCoi-58
88TopMinL-54
88TopRevLL-14
88TopSti-70
88TopStiB-30
88TopTif-489
88TopTif-780
88TopUKM-80
88TopUKMT-80
89Bow-337
89BowTif-337
89DodMot-4
89DodPol-22
89DodSmoG-97
89DodStaSV-15
89Don-250
89Fle-76
89FleGlo-76
89K-M-32
89OPC-150
89PanSti-103
89RedFolSB-123
89Sco-437
89Spo-124
89Top-150
89TopBasT-61
89TopSti-60
89TopTif-150
89TopUKM-78
89UppDec-656
90DodMot-2
90DodPol-34
90DodTar-815
90Don-625
90DonBesN-90
90DonLeaS-39
90Fle-409
90Fle-622
90FleCan-409
90FleCan-622
90Lea-68
90MLBBasB-7
90OPC-340
90PanSti-269
90PubSti-21
90Sco-54
90SupActM-14
90Top-340
90TopSti-59
90TopTif-340
90UppDec-445
91BasBesRB-18
91ClaGam-73
91DodUno7P-3
91DodUno7P-4
91Don-127
91DonBonC-BC11
91Fle-222
91FleWaxBC-5
91OPC-80
91PanFreS-356
91PanSti-5
91PanSti-59
91Sco-449
91Sco-703
91SevCoi-SC15
91StaClu-90
91StaCluCM-30
91StaCluP-45
91Top-80A
91Top-80B
91TopDesS-80
91TopMic-80
91TopTif-80
91UppDec-175
92DodStaTA-24
93Fla-159
93FleFinE-166
93Lea-472
93LinVenB-312
93OPCPre-47
93PacJugC-17
93PacSpa-352
93StaClu-661
93StaCluFDI-661
93StaCluMOP-661
93Ult-503
93UppDec-550
93UppDecGold-550
94Don-408
94Fla-418
94Fle-22
94FleUpd-171
94Pac-46
94PacSilP-14
94PanSti-25
94Sco-190
94ScoGolR-190
94StaClu-69
94StaCluFDI-69
94StaCluGR-69
94StaCluMOP-69
94Top-175
94TopGol-175
94TopSpa-175
95ColCho-364
95ColCho-566T
95ColCho-TC5
95ColChoGS-364
95ColChoSE-168
95ColChoSEGS-168
95ColChoSESS-168
95ColChoSS-364
95DodROY-10
95Fle-406
95FleUpd-190
95Pac-339
95PadCHP-9
95PadMot-8
95UppDec-142
95UppDec-375
95UppDecED-142
95UppDecED-375
95UppDecEDG-142
95UppDecEDG-375
96Cir-189
96CirRav-189
96ColCho-299
96ColCho-334
96ColChoGS-299
96ColChoGS-334
96ColChoSS-299
96ColChoSS-334
96EmoXL-284
96Fla-382
96Fle-579
96FleTif-579
96Pac-190
96PacEstL-EL33
96PacPri-P64
96PacPriG-P64
96PadMot-8
96Ult-563
96UltGolM-563
96UppDec-114
97ColCho-207
97Don-203
97DonPreP-203
97DonPrePGold-203
97Fle-471
97FleTif-471
97MetUni-225
97Pac-433
97PacLatotML-35
97PacLigB-433
97PacPri-146
97PacPriGotD-GD211
97PacPriLB-146
97PacPriP-146
97PacPriSH-SH12B
97PacSil-433
97Pin-127
97PinArtP-127
97PinMusC-127
97ProMag-39
97ProMagML-39
97Sco-272
97ScoPreS-272
97ScoShoS-272
97ScoShoSAP-272
97Ult-288
97UltGolME-288
97UltPlaME-288
97UppDec-166
97UppDec-195

Valenzuela, Guillermo
83KinBluJTI-27

Valera, Julio
87ColMetP-26
88BlaYNPRWL-78
88ColMetGS-11
89BasAmeAPB-AA28
89BlaYNPRWL-88
89BlaYNPRWLU-71
89JacMetGS-29
89St.LucMS-23
89TexLeaAGS-26
90Bow-123
90BowTif-123
90CMC-364
90MetColP-52
90ProAAAF-277
90TidTidC-13
90TidTidP-546
90TopTVM-65
91Don-39
91Fle-164
91LinDriAAA-571
91MetColP-50
91MetWIZ-420
91OPC-504
91Sco-353
91TidTidLD-571
91TidTidP-2511
91Top-504
91TopDeb90-158
91TopDesS-504
91TopMic-504
91TopTif-504
91UppDec-534
92Bow-422
92Cla2-T4
92DonRoo-119
92Fle-517
92FleUpd-11
92Lea-490
92MetColP-30
92Pin-267
92ProFS7-276
92Sco100RS-17
92SkyAAAF-257
92StaClu-304
92StaClu-646
92TidTidF-897
92TidTidS-573
92TopTra-122T
92TopTraG-122T
92UppDec-747
92UppDecSR-SR23
93AngMot-11
93AngPol-14
93Don-5
93Fle-578
93Lea-430
93OPC-368
93PacSpa-374
93Pin-139
93Sco-427
93Sel-288
93StaClu-386
93StaCluAn-30
93StaCluFDI-386
93StaCluMOP-386
93Top-374
93TopGol-374
93TopInaM-374
93TopMic-374
93Ult-169
93UppDec-343
93UppDecGold-343
94Fle-72
94Pac-93
94Sco-223
94ScoGolR-223
96LeaSigEA-205
97PacPriGotD-GD52

Valera, Willy
95WatIndTI-29

Valera, Wilson
83WatIndF-10
85WatIndT-2
86LynMetP-23
87LynMetP-26
88SouBenWSGS-11

Valette, Ramon
91EliTwiP-4309
92EliTwiC-18
93ForWayWC-24
93ForWayWF-1977
94ForMyeMC-25
95HarCitRCTI-26

Valez, Rafael
86ChaRaiP-27

Valiente, Nestor
84ButCopKT-25

Valla, Mike
88WatPirP-26

Vallaran, Miguel
77LodDodT-22

Vallarelli, Mike
94BoiHawC-27
94BoiHawF-3359

Valle, Dave
80SanJosMJitB-20
81LynSaiT-14
82SalLakCGT-20
83ChaLooT-26
84SalLakCGC-176
85FleUpd-125
85MarMot-17
86CalCanP-24
87Don-610
87DonOpeD-120
87MarMot-9
87SpoTeaP-25
87TopTra-122T
87TopTraT-122T
88Don-393
88Fle-389
88FleGlo-389
88MarMot-9
88OPC-83
88PanSti-184
88Sco-126A
88Sco-126B
88ScoGlo-126A
88ScoGlo-126B
88StaLinMa-18
88Top-583
88TopBig-210
88TopSti-220
88TopTif-583
89Bow-208
89BowTif-208
89ChaLooLITI-30
89Don-614
89DonBasB-248
89Fle-561
89FleGlo-561
89MarMot-9
89RedFolSB-124
89Sco-27
89Top-459
89Top-498
89TopBig-56
89TopTif-459
89TopTif-498
89UppDec-320
90Bow-473
90BowTif-473
90Don-129
90DonBesA-55
90Fle-527
90FleCan-527
90Lea-166
90MarMot-5
90MarRedAP-1
90MLBBasB-120
90OPC-76
90PanSti-156
90PubSti-444
90RedFolSB-97
90Sco-109
90Top-76
90TopBig-266

90TopTif-76
90UppDec-451
91Bow-251
91Don-366
91Fle-463
91Lea-511
91MarCouH-6
91OPC-178
91PanFreS-227
91RedFolS-95
91Sco-262
91StaClu-32
91Stu-120
91Top-178
91TopDesS-178
91TopMic-178
91TopTif-178
91Ult-344
91UppDec-595
92Bow-134
92Don-462
92Fle-295
92Lea-170
92MarMot-5
92OPC-294
92PanSti-54
92Pin-232
92Sco-343
92StaClu-56
92Stu-240
92Top-294
92TopGol-294
92TopGolW-294
92TopMic-294
92TriPla-5
92Ult-130
92UppDec-182
93DiaMar-110
93Don-507
93Fla-275
93Fle-315
93Lea-425
93MarMot-7
93PacSpa-291
93PanSti-58
93Pin-179
93Sco-200
93StaClu-483
93StaCluFDI-483
93StaCluMari-20
93StaCluMOP-483
93Stu-68
93Top-370
93TopGol-370
93TopInaM-370
93TopMic-370
93TriPla-152
93Ult-273
93UppDec-100
93UppDecGold-100
94BreMilB-369
94ColC-627
94ColChoGS-627
94ColChoSS-627
94Don-385
94Fin-378
94FinRef-378
94Fla-17
94Fle-300
94Lea-430
94Pac-584
94PanSti-123
94Pin-514
94PinArtP-514
94PinMusC-514
94Sco-493
94ScoGolR-493
94Sel-241
94Top-736
94TopGol-736
94TopSpa-736
94Ult-319
94UppDec-333
94UppDecED-333
95RanCra-33
96Fle-265
96FleRan-16
96FleTif-265
96LeaSigEA-206
96RanMot-20
97PacPriGotD-GD100

Valle, Hector
65Top-561
66Top-314
66TopVen-314
89BlaYNPRWL-99

Valle, John A.
77EvaTriT-24
78IndIndTI-14
79IndIndTI-25
80RocRedWT-14
81RocRedWT-17
82RocRedWT-18
83RocRedWT-18
84RocRedWT-6

Valle, Lazaro
90IBAWorA-32

Valle, Tony
89IdaFalBP-2026
90BurBraB-8
90BurBraP-2350
90BurBraS-26

Vallero, Rich
95OdgRapTI-27

Vallette, Ramon
92EliTwiF-3689
94ForMyeMF-1177

Valley, Chick
77SalPirT-24
78SalPirT-17
79BufBisT-14
80ColAstT-6
81ElPasDT-16
82VanCanT-18

Valley, Jason
94BatCliC-24
94BatCliF-3446

Vallone, Gar
95BoiHawTI-30
96CedRapKTI-24

Vallone, Jim
78QuaCitAT-27

Vallot, Joey
91GulCoaRSP-24
92GulCoaRSP-20

Valo, Elmer
49Bow-66
49Lea-29
49PhiBul-56
50Bow-49
51TopRedB-28
52Bow-206
52Top-34
53Top-122
54Top-145
55A'sRodM-43
55A'sRodM-44
55Top-145
55TopDouH-85
56A'sRodM-11
56Top-3
57Top-54
58Top-323
60Lea-107
60Top-237
61Top-186
61TwiPetM-12
76A'sRodMC-28
79DiaGre-343
79TCM50-148
81TCM60I-316
83TopRep5-34
84TCMPla1-22
89PacLegI-187
90DodTar-816
91TopArc1-122
92YanWIZ6-133
94TopArc1-145
94TopArc1G-145

Valois, Frank
72Dia-136

Valrie, Kerry
90UtiBluSP-12
91Cla/Bes-243
91SouBenWSC-25
91SouBenWSP-2872
92MidLeaATI-46
92SouBenWSC-7
92SouBenWSF-192
93SarWhiSC-27
93SarWhiSF-1385
94BirBarC-24
94BirBarF-636
95NasSouTI-27
96NasSouB-26

Valverde, Joe
89SanDieSAS-27

Valverde, Miguel
88AugPirP-361
89SalBucS-23

Van Atta, Russ
33Gou-215
36GouWidPPR-A104
36R31PasP-50
79DiaGre-16
92ConTSN-611

Van Bever, Mark
78CliDodT-31

Van Blaricom, Mark
83ButCopKT-22
85Ft.MyeRT-10
86Ft.MyeRP-25
87MemChiB-6
87MemChiP-12
88MemChiB-3

Van Brabant, Ozzie
55JetPos-18

Van Brunt, Jim
87AncGlaP-37

Van Brunt, Lefty
85AncGlaPTI-28
86AncGlaPTI-35
87AncGlaP-30
89AncGlaP-26

Van Burkleo, Ty
82BelBreF-6
86PalSprAP-20
86PalSprAP-29
87MidAngP-7
92EdmTraF-3548
92EdmTraS-169
93Bow-497
93VanCanF-2606
94ColSprSSF-743
96LakElsSB-27

Van Cuyk, Chris
52Top-53
82Bow195E-255
83TopRep5-53
90DodTar-819
91RinPosBD3-9
95TopArcBD-7

Van Cuyk, John
53MotCoo-41

Van De Weg, Ryan
96RanCucQB-26

Van DeBrake, Kevin
91YakBeaC-13
91YakBeaP-4257

Van DeCasteele, Mike
78TidTidT-26
79TidTidT-19

Van Der Beck, Jim
75WatDodT-21

Van Deren, Steve
78QuaCitAT-28

Van Duzer, Donna L.
88FreSunP-1249
91ChaRanC-26

Van Dyke, Gordon Keith
49W725AngTI-28

Van Dyke, Rod
91BoiHawC-7
91BoiHawP-3879
92PalSprAC-17
92PalSprAF-841
93CedRapKF-1738

Van Dyke, William
87OldJudN-438
87OldJudN-520

Van Every, Jason
93MisStaB-45

Van Gilder, Elam
22E120-104

Van Gorder, Dave
79NaSouTI-24
80IndIndTI-8
81IndIndTI-6
82IndIndTI-12
83Don-188
83IndIndTI-27
83Top-322
84WicAerRD-10
85Don-384
86Don-550
86Fle-195
86Top-143
86TopTif-143
87RocRedWP-2
87RocRedWT-11
89IndIndC-24
91OriCro-467

Van Graflan, Roy
94ConTSN-1194
94ConTSNB-1194

Van Haltren, George
03BreE10-145
11SpoLifCW-355
87FouBasHN-10
87OldJudN-521
88AugBecN-28
88GandBCGCE-43
88WG1CarG-17
95NewN566-180

Van Heyningen, Pat
85NewOriT-20

Van Horn, Dave
83AndBraT-24

Van Houten, Jim
85SprCarT-4
87ColAstP-11

Van Iten, Robert
96MarPhiB-28

Van Kemper, John
85EveGialC-20

Van Landuyt, Jules
94HunCubF-3555
94HunCubC-27

Van Ornum, John
80GiaPol-42
84GiaPos-29

Van Pelt, Dennis
94BoiHawF-3371

Van Pelt, Mark
91AdeGiaF-14
94BoiHawC-28

Van Poppel, Todd
90ClaDraP-14
90MadMusB-1
90ProAaA-160
90SouOreAB-1
90SouOreAP-3422
90TopMag-38
91Bow-218
91Cla/Bes-386
91Cla1-T75
91Cla1-T77
91Cla1-NNO
91Cla2-T77
91ClaGam-151
91ClaGolB-BC6
91DonRoo-7
91HunStaC-24
91HunStaLD-296
91HunStaP-1795
91LeaGolR-BC9
91LinDriAA-296
91Sco-389
91SevCoi-T14
91SevCoi-NC13
91Stu-109
91UppDec-53
91UppDecFE-12F
92Bow-270
92Cla1-T91
92Don-9
92DonPre-12
92Fle-269
92FleRooS-2
92Lea-248
92OPC-142
92Pin-574
92PinRoo-12
92PinRool-12
92PinTea2-72
92ProFS7-129
92Sco-865
92ScoHotR-4
92ScoImpP-37
92ScoRoo-1
92SkyAAAF-244
92StaClu-129
92StaVanP-1
92StaVanP-2
92StaVanP-3
92StaVanP-4
92StaVanP-5
92StaVanP-6
92StaVanP-7
92StaVanP-8
92StaVanP-9
92StaVanP-10
92StaVanP-11
92TacTigF-2501
92TacTigS-545
92Top-142
92TopDeb91-175
92TopGol-142
92TopGolW-142
92TopMcD-44
92TopMic-142
92TriPla-142
92Ult-118
92UppDec-22
92UppDecML-75
93Bow-371
93Bow-681
93ClaYouG-YG25
93ExcFS7-219
93Lea-448
93SelRoo-79T
93SP-45
93StaClu-48
93StaCluAt-22
93StaCluFDI-48
93StaCluMOP-48
93TacTigF-3033
93Top-673
93TopGol-673
93TopInaM-673
93TopMic-673
93Toy-62
94A'sMot-9
94Bow-548
94ColC-279
94ColChoGS-279
94ColChoSS-279
94Don-557
94Fin-182
94FinPre-182P
94FinRef-182
94Fle-275
94FUnPac-59
94Lea-151
94OPC-56
94Pac-464
94PanSti-114
94Pin-357
94PinArtP-357
94PinMusC-357
94Sco-607
94ScoBoyoS-28
94ScoGolR-607
94Sel-86
94StaClu-562
94StaCluFDI-562
94StaCluGR-562
94StaCluMOP-562
94Top-559
94TopGol-559
94TopSpa-559
94Ult-414
94UppDec-195
94UppDecAJ-2
94UppDecAJG-2
94UppDecED-195
95A'sCHP-7
95AthMot-13
95ColCho-137
95ColChoGS-137
95ColChoSS-137
95Don-48
95DonPreP-48
95Fla-77
95Fle-256
95Lea-169
95Pin-247
95PinArtP-247
95PinMusC-247
95Sco-210
95ScoGolR-210
95ScoPlaTS-210
95StaClu-225
95StaCluFDI-225
95StaCluMOP-225
95StaCluSTWS-225
95Top-407
95TopCyb-207
95Ult-322
95UltGolM-322
95UppDec-284
95UppDecED-284
95UppDecEDG-284
95UppDecSE-106
95UppDecSEG-106
96A'sMot-25
96Cir-75
96CirRav-75
96ColCho-643
96ColChoGS-643

96ColChoSS-643
96Don-258
96DonPreP-258
96EmoXL-108
96Fla-154
96Fle-221
96FleTif-221
96LeaSigA-227
96LeaSigAG-228
96LeaSigAS-228
96Sco-432
96Ult-119
96UltGolM-119
96UppDec-413
Van Robays, Maurice
47RemBre-18
47SigOil-57
47SmiClo-7
48SigOil-23
48SmiClo-9
49BowPCL-32
49RemBre-29
77TCMTheWY-71
Van Rossum, Chris
96BelGiaTI-4
Van Ryn, Ben
91Cla/Bes-31
91SumFlyC-11
91SumFlyP-2334
92VerBeaDC-26
92VerBeaDF-2875
93SanAntMF-3005
94AlbDukF-844
94BowBes-B73
94BowBesR-B73
94ClaGolF-147
94ExcFS7-220
94ExcLeaLF-20
94Top-783
94TopGol-783
94TopSpa-783
94UppDecML-212
96SigRooOJ-34
96SigRooOJS-34
Van Rynback, Casper
90KinMetB-19
90KinMetS-23
91PitMetC-14
91PitMetP-3424
Van Ryssegem, Guido
96TulDriTI-28
Van Schaack, Tom
90WatIndS-27
Van Scoyoc, Aaron
89OneYanP-2115
90GreHorB-20
90GreHorP-2672
90GreHorS-24
91Ft.LauYP-2437
Van Scoyoc, Jim
91NiaFalRC-6
91NiaFalRP-3652
92BriTigC-28
93BriTigC-29
94FayGenC-28
94FayGenF-2165
Van Slyke, Andy
82ArkTraT-19
83LouRedR-18
84Car-31
84Car5x7-30
84Don-83
84Fle-339
84Nes792-206
84Top-206
84TopSti-150
84TopTif-206
85CarTeal-32
85Don-327
85Fle-242
85OPC-341
85Top-551
85TopMin-551
85TopSti-138
85TopTif-551
86CarIGAS-13
86CarKASD-19
86CarSchM-23
86CarTeal-41
86Don-412
86Fle-48
86KayB-32
86OPC-33
86Top-683
86TopSti-51
86TopTif-683
87Don-417
87DonOpeD-161
87Fle-311
87FleGlo-311
87FleUpd-121
87FleUpdG-121
87OPC-33
87SpoTeaP-12
87Top-33
87TopSti-51
87TopTif-33
87TopTra-124T
87TopTraT-124T
88Don-18
88Don-291
88DonBasB-157
88DonBonM-BC8
88DonSupD-18
88Fle-341
88FleGlo-341
88FleLeaL-43
88FleMin-105
88FleStiC-116
88FleTeaL-44
88Lea-18
88Lea-102
88OPC-142
88PanSti-380
88RedFolSB-92
88Sco-416
88ScoGlo-416
88Spo-109
88StaLinPi-20
88Top-142
88TopBig-184
88TopSti-126
88TopTif-142
88TopUKM-81
88TopUKMT-81
89Bow-424
89BowTif-424
89CadEllD-59
89ClaTraO-111
89Don-54
89DonAll-61
89DonBasB-45
89DonBonM-BC10
89Fle-222
89FleBasA-42
89FleBasM-40
89FleGlo-222
89FleHeroB-41
89FleLeaL-41
89FleWaxBC-C27
89KinDis-19
89MSAIceTD-17
89OPC-350
89PanSti-173
89PirVerFJ-18
89Sco-174
89ScoHot1S-92
89ScoSco-38
89Spo-166
89Top-350
89Top-392
89TopAme2C-30
89TopBasT-79
89TopBig-255
89TopCoi-27
89TopDouA-19
89TopGloS-4
89TopHilTM-30
89TopMinL-33
89TopSti-150
89TopStiB-54
89TopTif-350
89TopTif-392
89TopUKM-79
89TVSpoM-9
89UppDec-537
89UppDec-685
90Bow-171
90BowTif-171
90ClaYel-T30
90Don-244
90DonBesN-119
90DonLeaS-3
90Fle-481
90FleAwaW-40
90FleCan-481
90FleLeaL-40
90Hot50PS-47
90Lea-117
90MLBBasB-36
90OPC-775
90PanSti-324
90PirHomC-29
90PubSti-166
90RedFolSB-98
90Sco-440
90Sco100S-78
90Spo-101
90Top-775
90TopBig-217
90TopMinL-72
90TopSti-124
90TopTif-775
90UppDec-536
91Bow-529
91ClaGam-45
91Don-552
91Fle-53
91Lea-310
91OPC-425
91PanCanT1-106
91PanFreS-121
91PanSti-118
91RedFolS-96
91Sco-475
91Sco-698
91Sco100S-22
91StaClu-118
91StaCluP-46
91Stu-230
91Top-425
91TopDesS-425
91TopMic-425
91TopTif-425
91TopTriH-N9
91Ult-287
91UppDec-256
92Bow-35
92Cla1-T92
92Cla2-T64
92ClaGam-153
92Don-383
92DonMcD-17
92Fle-570
92Hig5-95
92HitTheBB-35
92Lea-43
92LeaGolP-9
92LeaPre-9
92Mr.TurS-25
92New-29
92OPC-545
92PanSti-257
92Pin-9
92PirNatI-23
92Sco-655
92ScoCokD-21
92ScoProaG-17
92SevCoi-7
92SpoIllFK1-145
92SpoStaCC-47
92StaClu-232
92StaCluD-189
92Stu-89
92StuHer-BC10
92Top-545
92TopGol-545
92TopGolW-545
92TopKid-23
92TopMic-545
92TriPla-6
92TriPla-148
92TriPlaP-3
92Ult-262
92UltAwaW-10
92UppDec-132
92UppDec-711
92UppDec-715
93Bow-218
93ClaGam-93
93ColAllG-12
93DenHol-19
93DiaMar-111
93Don-414
93DonDiaK-DK9
93DonEli-32
93DonEliS-14
93DonPre-9
93DurPowP2-8
93Fin-185
93FinRef-185
93Fla-117
93Fle-122
93FleAll-NL8
93FleAtl-24
93FleFruotL-62
93FlePro-B1
93FleTeaL-NL10
93FunPac-148
93FunPac-151
93Hos-1
93HumDumC-46
93JimDea-4
93Kra-30
93Lea-79
93LeaGolA-R7
93MetBak-39
93OPC-355
93OPCPre-88
93PacSpa-253
93PanSti-285
93Pin-19
93PinTeaP-9
93PirNatI-33
93Pos-27
93PosCan-11
93Sco-12
93Sco-524
93Sco-535
93ScoFra-23
93ScoGolDT-4
93Sel-35
93SelChaS-6
93SelStaL-5
93SelStaL-10
93SelStaL-16
93SelStaL-24
93SelStaL-42
93SP-188
93StaClu-294
93StaClu-394
93StaCluFDI-294
93StaCluFDI-394
93StaCluM-14
93StaCluMOP-294
93StaCluMOP-394
93Stu-132
93Top-275
93Top-405
93TOPBLAG-21
93TopGol-275
93TopGol-405
93TopInaM-275
93TopInaM-405
93TopMic-275
93TopMic-405
93TriPla-8
93TriPlaA-1
93TriPlaP-8
93Ult-103
93UltAwaW-8
93UppDec-124
93UppDec-480
93UppDecDG-19
93UppDecGold-124
93UppDecGold-480
93UppDecIC-WI18
93UppDecICJ-WI18
93UppDecOD-D25
93USPlaCA-11D
94Bow-50
94BowBes-R77
94BowBesR-R77
94ColC-280
94ColC-346
94ColChoGS-280
94ColChoGS-346
94ColChoSS-280
94ColChoSS-346
94ColChoT-15
94DenHol-26
94Don-375
94DonSpeE-375
94ExtBas-352
94Fin-408
94FinRef-408
94Fla-426
94Fle-622
94FleSun-24
94FUnPac-18
94KinDis-23
94Kra-30
94Lea-41
94LeaL-143
94OPC-86
94OscMayR-30
94Pac-509
94PanSti-240
94Pin-16
94PinArtP-16
94PinMusC-16
94PirBloP-2
94PirQui-24
94ProMag-109
94RedFolMI-3
94Sco-18
94ScoDreT-8
94ScoGolR-18
94ScoGolS-19
94Sel-129
94SP-144
94SPDieC-144
94SPHol-38
94SPHolDC-38
94Spo-76
94StaClu-687
94StaCluFDI-687
94StaCluGR-687
94StaCluMOP-687
94StaCluMOP-ST11
94StaCluST-ST11
94Stu-150
94Top-650
94TopGol-650
94TopSpa-650
94TopSupS-42
94TriPla-189
94TriPlaM-12
94Ult-560
94UppDec-83
94UppDecAJ-27
94UppDecAJG-27
94UppDecDC-C9
94UppDecED-83
95ColCho-390
95ColCho-564T
95ColChoGS-390
95ColChoSE-180
95ColChoSEGS-180
95ColChoSESS-180
95ColChoSS-390
95Don-389
95DonPreP-389
95Fin-216
95FinRef-216
95Fla-225
95Fle-490
95FleUpd-7
95Pac-353
95PacPri-114
95Pin-396
95PinArtP-396
95PinMusC-396
95RedFol-30
95Sco-352
95ScoGolR-352
95ScoPlaTS-352
95ScoYouTE-352T
95Sel-182
95SelArtP-182
95StaClu-153
95StaClu-541
95StaCluFDI-153
95StaCluMOP-153
95StaCluMOP-541
95StaCluSTWS-153
95StaCluSTWS-541
95Top-260
95TopCyb-141
95Ult-427
95UltGolM-427
95UppDec-149
95UppDec-368
95UppDecED-149
95UppDecED-368
95UppDecEDG-149
95UppDecEDG-368
96Don-11
96DonPreP-11
96Fle-510
96FleTif-510
96Pac-153
96Sco-171
96ScoDugC-A97
96ScoDugCAP-A97
96StaClu-52
96StaCluMOP-52
Van Stone, Paul
85EveGialC-21
86CliGiaP-25

Van Tiger, Tom
91WatIndC-29
91WatIndP-3384
92KinIndC-24
Van Vuren, Bob
86Ft.MyeRP-26
Van Winkle, Dave
89UtiBluSP-1
90SouBenWSB-4
90SouBenWSGS-19
91CalLeLA-5
91PalSprAP-2015
Van Wyck, Jim
74TacTwiC-21
76TacTwiDQ-20
77TacTwiDQ-1
Van Zandt, Jon
93ElmPioC-24
93ElmPioF-3823
Vanacore, Derek
85Ft.MyeRT-29
VanBuren, Chris
87BelMarTI-32
Vance, Dazzy (Clarence A.)
25Exh-15
28Exh-8
28PorandAR-A37
28PorandAR-B37
28StaPlaCE-69
28W512-10
28W56PlaC-S6
29ExhFou-3
29PorandAR-93
30SchR33-45
31Exh-3
31W517-36
33CraJacP-23
33ExhFou-2
33Gou-2
33GouCanV-2
34DiaMatCSB-185
34ButPreR-59
35GouPuzR-4C
35GouPuzR-7C
35GouPuzR-12C
50CalHOFW-72
51R42SmaS-109
60Fle-51
61Fle-81
61GolPre-26
63BazA-28
72FleFamF-4
72LauGreF-21
74Car193T-23
76GrePlaG-31
76RowExh-11
76ShaPiz-77
77GalGloG-104
77GalGloG-266
80DodGreT-9
80PerHaloFP-79
80SSPHOF-79
83DiaClaS2-68
89DodSmoG-29
89HOFStiB-73
90DodTar-817
92ConTSN-377
92YanWIZH-33
93ConTSN-929
94ConTSN-1055
94ConTSNB-1055
95ConTSN-1371
Vance, Sandy (Gene)
71OPC-34
71Top-34
75YanDyn1T-47
85SpoIndGC-23
90DodTar-818
Vancho, Bob (Robert)
89HelBreSP-18
90BelBreB-23
90BelBreS-22
90MidLeaASGS-22
91StoPorC-4
91StoPorP-3032
VandeBerg, Ed
81SpoIndT-15
82TopTra-122T
83Don-100
83Fle-488
83FleSta-206
83FleSti-180
83OPC-183
83Top-183
83TopSti-317
84Don-604
84Fle-623
84MarMot-8
84Nes792-63
84OPC-63
84Top-63
84TopTif-63
85Don-511
85Fle-504
85MarMot-5
85OPC-207
85Top-566
85TopMin-566
85TopSti-336
85TopTif-566
86DodCokP-31
86DodPol-31
86DodUniOP-22
86Don-637
86Fle-479
86FleUpd-121
86OPC-357
86Top-357
86TopTif-357
86TopTra-118T
86TopTraT-118T
87Don-376
87Fle-458
87FleGlo-458
87FleUpd-120
87FleUpdG-120
87IndGat-36
87OPC-34
87Top-717
87TopTif-717
87TopTra-123T
87TopTraT-123T
88AlaGolAA'TI-22
88Fle-619
88FleGlo-619
88OklCit8C-6
88OklCit8P-52
88Top-421
88TopTif-421
89Fle-534A
89Fle-534B
89FleGlo-534
89IowCubC-4
89IowCubP-1710
89Top-242
89TopTif-242
90CalCanC-8
90CMC-435
90DodTar-820
91CalCanLD-73
91CalCanP-517
91LinDriAAA-73
92CalCanF-3731
93RanKee-365
Vandemark, John
94BatCliC-25
94BatCliF-3447
95ClePhiF-217
Vandenberg, Hy
40PlaBal-209
44CubTeal-23
79DiaGre-106
Vanderbush, Matt
96ForWayWB-26
Vanderbush, Walt
83BeaGolGT-5
84LasVegSC-229
85LasVegSC-111
VanderGriend, Jon
95BoiHawTI-31
96CedRapKTI-25
96HilStaHWB-35
VanderMeer, John
38CinOraW-27
38CinOraW-28
39ExhSal-59
39OrcPhoAP-31
39OrcPhoAP-33
41DouPlaR-5
41HarHarW-25
41PlaBal-56
43MPR302-1-23
47Exh-227
47HomBon-47
48BluTin-46
48SweSpoT-10
49Bow-128
49EurSta-96
49Lea-53
50Bow-79
51Bow-223
60NuHi-5
61Fle-147
67TopVen-175
72LauGreF-7
74LauAllG-38
76LauDiaJ-12
76TayBow4-42
77GalGloG-73
77GalGloG-243
77Spo-624
77TCMTheWY-68
79DiaGre-263
80PacLeg-110
82OhiHaloF-21
84OCoandSI-128
84OCoandSI-215
87SpoRea-10
88PacLegI-30
89SweBasG-11
90BasWit-80
90HOFStiB-36
90SweBasG-99
91SweBasG-61
92ConTSN-367
92ConTSN-368
94ConTSN-1181
94ConTSNB-1181
94TedWil-24
94UppDecAH-2
94UppDecAH-38
94UppDecAH1-2
94UppDecAH1-38
97FleMilDM-7
Vandersall, Mark
92Min-22
VanderWal, John
87JamExpP-2551
88FloStaLAS-23
88WesPalBES-25
89JacExpB-25
89JacExpP-161
90Bes-90
90JacExpB-13
90JacExpP-1388
91IndIndLD-197
91IndIndP-476
91LinDriAAA-197
91TriA AAGP-AAA17
92Bow-232
92Cla2-T32
92Don-414
92ExpDonD-16A
92ExpPos-28
92FleUpd-99
92Lea-416
92OPC-343
92Pin-559
92ProFS7-255
92ScoRoo-105T
92StaClu-385
92Top-343
92TopDeb91-174
92TopGol-343
92TopGolW-343
92TopMic-343
92Ult-523
93Don-144
93Fle-80
93Lea-19
93OPC-376
93PacSpa-189
93PanSti-229
93Pin-322
93Sco-359
93Sel-323
93StaClu-442
93StaCluFDI-442
93StaCluMOP-442
93Top-69
93TopGol-69
93TopInaM-69
93TopMic-69
93Ult-419
93UppDec-619
93UppDecGold-619
93USPlaCR-5H
94Don-571
94Fle-553
94Pac-391
94Sco-180
94ScoGolR-180
94StaClu-161
94StaCluFDI-161
94StaCluGR-161
94StaCluMOP-161
94Top-563
94TopGol-563
94TopSpa-563
95Don-73
95DonPreP-73
95Fle-529
95Pac-146
95Sco-198
95ScoGolR-198
95ScoPlaTS-198
95StaClu-86
95StaCluFDI-86
95StaCluMOP-86
95StaCluSTWS-86
96ColCho-133
96ColCho-757
96ColChoGS-133
96ColChoGS-757
96ColChoSS-133
96ColChoSS-757
96Fle-376
96FleRoc-15
96FleTif-376
96RocPol-24
97ColCho-102
97Pac-290
97PacLigB-290
97PacSil-290
97StaClu-350
97StaCluMOP-350
VanderWeele, Doug
91EveGiaC-2
91EveGiaP-3912
92ClaFS7-368
92CliGiaC-17
93SanJosGC-24
93SanJosGF-8
94SanJosGC-24
94SanJosGF-2818
96PhoFirB-26
Vanderwel, Bill
86SalAngC-84
87PalSprP-13
88PalSprACLC-94
88PalSprAP-1457
89QuaCitAB-15
89QuaCitAGS-16
90SouBenWSB-23
Vanegmond, Tim
92ClaFS7-390
92LynRedSC-23
92LynRedSF-2908
92UppDecML-121
93ClaGolF-24
93NewBriRSF-1222
94Bow-63
94ExcFS7-22
94PawRedSDD-28
94PawRedSF-948
94UppDecML-137
95ColCho-412
95ColChoGS-412
95ColChoSE-21
95ColChoSEGS-21
95ColChoSESS-21
95ColChoSS-412
95FleUpd-15
95UppDec-399
95UppDecED-399
95UppDecEDG-399
97PacPrlGotD-GD59
Vangilder, Elam
27AmeCarE-47
92ConTSN-569
Vanhof, Dave
94BelMarC-1
94BelMarF-3236
94Bow-89
95UppDecML-156
95UppDecMLFS-156
Vanhof, John
92FroRowDP-85
93ClaGolF-146
95Exc-122
96WisTimRB-27
Vaninetti, Gene
94HagSunC-25
94HagSunF-2741
94MedHatBJF-3691
94MedHatBJSP-4
VanLandingham, Bill (William)
91EveGiaC-24
91EveGiaP-3913
92ClaFS7-251
92CliGiaF-3598
92ProFS7-356
92SanJosGC-4
93SanJosGC-25
93SanJosGF-9
94Bow-491
94ExcFS7-295
94Fla-447
94FlaWavotF-B10
94FleUpd-198
94LeaLimR-20
94ShrCapF-1608
94SpoRoo-70
94SpoRooAP-70
94TopTra-105T
94UppDec-521
94UppDecED-521
94UppDecML-138
95Bow-354
95ColCho-255
95ColChoGS-255
95ColChoSE-109
95ColChoSEGS-109
95ColChoSESS-109
95ColChoSS-255
95Don-12
95DonPreP-12
95DonTopotO-359
95Emb-82
95EmbGolI-82
95Fin-6
95FinRef-6
95Fla-212
95Fle-592
95FleRooS-19
95GiaMot-16
95Lea-51
95Pac-386
95PacPri-122
95PanSti-102
95Pin-351
95PinMusC-351
95Sco-181
95ScoGolR-181
95ScoPlaTS-181
95StaClu-158
95StaCluFDI-158
95StaCluMOP-158
95StaCluSTWS-158
95StaCluVR-83
95Stu-63
95Top-611
95TopCyb-379
95Ult-246
95UltGolM-246
95UltSecYS-14
95UltSecYSGM-14
95UppDec-84
95UppDecED-84
95UppDecEDG-84
95UppDecSE-201
95UppDecSEG-201
96ColCho-309
96ColChoGS-309
96ColChoSS-309
96Don-129
96DonPreP-129
96EmoXL-295
96Fla-393
96Fle-599
96FleTif-599
96GiaMot-13
96LeaSigEA-207
96MetUni-246
96MetUniP-246
96Pac-214
96PanSti-108
96Sco-164
96SP-167
96StaClu-158
96StaCluMOP-158
96StaCluVRMO-83
96Ult-299
96UltGolM-299
96UppDec-196
97Cir-71
97CirRav-71
97ColCho-216
97Fin-123

97FinEmb-123
97FinEmbR-123
97FinRef-123
97Fle-486
97FleTif-486
97Sco-418
97ScoHobR-418
97ScoResC-418
97ScoShoS-418
97ScoShoSAP-418
97SP-162
97StaClu-129
97StaCluMOP-129
97Top-131
97UppDec-171
Vann, Brandy
86SalAngC-80
87QuaCitAP-12
88QuaCitAGS-29
89PalSprACLC-53
89PalSprAP-471
90PalSprACLC-218
90PalSprAP-2577
91ElPasDLD-198
91LinDriAA-198
91StoPorP-3033
92ElPasDF-3923
92ElPasDS-223
93NorTidF-2570
Vannaman, Tim
88SouOreAP-1693
89MadMusS-22
90ModA'sCLC-159
90ModA'sP-2227
Vannell, Dan
90BenBucL-20
Vanni, Edo
47CenFlo-30
57SeaPop-39
Vantrease, Bob
83IdaFalAT-12
84IdaFalATI-26
Vanzytveld, Jeffrey
89VerBeaDS-26
90FloStaLAS-19
90VerBeaDS-26
91VerBeaDC-26
Vardijan, Dan
96KanCouCTI-27
96KanCouCUTI-12
Vargas, Angel
76VenLeaS-98
Vargas, Cesar
94VenLinU-220
Vargas, Eddie
78ChaPirT-24
80BufBisT-15
81BufBisT-23
82PorBeaT-17
Vargas, Eric
91ButCopKSP-15
Vargas, Gonzalo
89St.CatBJP-2083
Vargas, Guillaume
52LavPro-109
Vargas, Hector
87OneYanP-5
87PriWilYP-21
88BlaYNPRWL-21
88OneYanP-2049
89BlaYNPRWL-187
89PriWilCS-23
90Ft.LauYS-21
90StaFS7-42
91AlbYanLD-22
91AlbYanP-1018
91LinDriAA-22
92AlbYanF-2235
92AlbYanS-21
93OttLynF-2444
94BowBayF-2422
Vargas, Hedi
85HawIslC-236
88BlaYNPRWL-51
88ChaLooB-8
88NasSouTI-24
89BlaYNPRWL-188
89ChaLooLITI-31
89MidAngGS-29
Vargas, Jose
86OscAstP-27
86SalRedBP-26
87OscAstP-15
87PorChaRP-17
88ColAstB-8
88TulDriTI-7
89OscAstS-26
90ArkTraGS-29
91LinDriAA-645
91WilBilLD-645
91WilBilP-294
Vargas, Julio
89MarPhiS-32
89Sta-145
90PriPatD-25
91BatCliC-5
91BatCliP-3487
Vargas, Leo (Leonel)
82RicBraT-20
83RicBraT-21
84RicBraT-12
85DomLeaS-90
85GreBraTI-23
Vargas, Miguel
87ReaPhiP-5
Vargas, Ramon
83AndBraT-19
Vargas, Roberto
53BraSpiaS3-26
Vargo, Ed
81TCM60I-423
Varitek, Jason
92TopTra-123T
92TopTraG-123T
93StaCluM-197
94SigRooDP-14
94SigRooDPS-14
95ARuFalLS-19
95PorCitRTI-25
95SPML-153
96BesAutS-91
96PorCitRB-27
Varnell, Dan
90EveGiaB-2
90EveGiaP-3144
Varnell, Richard
89OneYanP-2117
Varner, Buck
88ChaLooLTI-29
Varney, Pete
76OPC-413
76SSP-154
76Top-413
Varni, Patrick
88CapCodPPaLP-182
90MiaMirIS-25
Varoz, Brett
85AncGlaPTI-29
Varoz, Eric
86BeaGolGP-24
Varsho, Gary
84MidCubT-23
86PitCubP-24
87IowCubTI-23
88CubDavB-24
88FleUpd-81
88FleUpdG-81
88IowCubC-22
88IowCubP-535
89Fle-441
89FleGlo-441
89Sco-604
89Top-613
89TopTif-613
89UppDec-321A
89UppDec-321B
90CMC-96
90IowCubC-21
90IowCubP-332
90ProAAAF-639
90PubSti-206
90TopTVCu-61
91Bow-510
91Don-671
91Fle-435
91FleUpd-114
91Lea-500
91ScoRoo-72T
91UltUpd-104
92Don-644
92Fle-571
92Lea-388
92OPC-122
92PirNatI-24
92Sco-481
92StaClu-568
92Stu-90
92Top-122
92TopGol-122
92TopGolW-122
92TopMic-122
92Ult-561
92UppDec-217
93Don-42
93PanSti-287
93RedKah-27
93Top-326
93TopGol-326
93TopInaM-326
93TopMic-326
94Pac-163
95Phi-32
95PhiMel-23
95Sco-204
95ScoGolR-204
95ScoPlaTS-204
Varva, Joe
92YakBeaC-24
Varverde, Miguel
86WatPirP-26
Vaske, Terry
94WilCubC-23
94WilCubF-3774
95MacBraTI-28
Vasquez, Aguedo
88BasCitRS-23
88FloStaLAS-50
89MemChiB-5
89MemChiP-1186
89MemChiS-22
90JacMetGS-19
91LinDriAA-646
91WilBilLD-646
91WilBilP-295
Vasquez, Angelo
85BurRanT-13
Vasquez, Archie
96BirBarB-20
Vasquez, Armando
95NegLeaLI-14
Vasquez, Chris
90BilMusP-3235
91ChaWheC-26
91ChaWheP-2901
92CedRapRC-19
92CedRapRF-1087
93WinSpiC-24
93WinSpiF-1583
94WinSpiC-24
94WinSpiF-285
Vasquez, Danny
95ChaRivTI-15
95HudValRTI-10
Vasquez, Dennis
80AppFoxT-11
81GleFalWST-7
Vasquez, Eddy
93MedHatBJF-3747
93MedHatBJSP-8
94St.CatBJC-26
94St.CatBJF-3655
Vasquez, Francisco
79ElmPioRST-18
Vasquez, George
73CedRapAT-12
75SacSolC-9
Vasquez, Jesse
80BurBeeT-12
85NewOriT-22
86HagSunP-26
Vasquez, Julian
89ColMetGS-25
90ColMetGS-15
90ColMetPPI-3
91Cla/Bes-359
91St.LucMC-16
91St.LucMP-710
92BinMetF-515
92BinMetS-68
92Bow-357
92ClaFS7-27
92MetColP-31
92ProFS7-283
92SkyAA F-31
92TidTidF-898
92UppDecML-72
93ExcFS7-80
93VanCanF-2599
Vasquez, Julio
91IdaFalBSP-12
Vasquez, Luis
85ElmPioT-23
86FloStaLAP-48
86WinHavRSP-26
87NewBriRSP-5
88EasLeaAP-24
88NewBriRSP-889
89NasSouC-10
89NasSouP-1285
89NasSouTI-25
91LinDriAAA-272
91NasSouLD-272
91NasSouP-2156
94VenLinU-93
95LinVen-249
Vasquez, Marcos
90DurBulTI-10
92DurBulC-19
92DurBulTI-20
92GreBraF-1154
93GreBraF-350
95ChaLooTI-24
Vasquez, Rafael
77SalPirT-25
80TacTigT-9
80Top-672
81BufBisT-11
Vasquez, Tony
89CedRapRB-27
Vatcher, James
87UtiBluSP-9
88SouAtlLAGS-26
88SpaPhiP-1045
88SpaPhiS-2
89ClePhiS-23
89Sta-14
90CMC-243
90ProAAAF-315
90ScrRedBC-17
90ScrRedBP-613
91Don-753
91Fle-708
91LasVegSLD-296
91LasVegSP-251
91LinDriAAA-296
91OPC-196
91PadMag-11
91PadSmo-37
91Sco-341
91Top-196
91TopDeb90-159
91TopDesS-196
91TopMic-196
91TopTif-196
91UppDec-604
92Don-563
92LasVegSF-2808
92LasVegSS-244
92SkyAAAF-119
92StaClu-78
93LasVegSF-959
94NorTidF-2935
Vatter, Scott
94ButCopKSP-7
Vaughan, Arky (J. Floyd)
33Gou-229
34BatR31-21
34Gou-22
34GouCanV-70
35ExhFou-7
36ExhFou-7
36GouWidPPR-A105
36NatChiFPR-73
36R31PasP-47
36R31Pre-L13
36SandSW-47
36WheBB3-11
36WheBB4-10
36WorWidGV-6
37ExhFou-7
37KelPepS-BB16
37WheBB14-16A
37WheBB14-16B
37WheBB6-5
37WheBB7-29L
37WheBB9-16
38ExhFou-7
38WheBB15-10
39ExhSal-60
39GouPreR303A-44
39GouPreR303B-22
39PlaBal-55
39WheBB12-9
39WorWidGTP-44
40PlaBal-107
41DouPlaR-33
41PlaBal-10
42DodTeal-22
43DodTeal-21
49SomandK-18
60Fle-11
61Fle-148
74LauAllG-41
74NewYorNTDiS-12
75ShaPiz-15
77GalGloG-77
80PacLeg-122
80PerHaloFP-192
80SSPHOF-193
82DiaCla-8
83ConMar-32
83TCMPla1942-29
87SpoCubG-3
88ConNatA-22
89DodSmoG-30
89HOFStiB-21
89PacLegI-200
90DodTar-821
90PerGreM-71
91ConTSN-38
93ActPacA-109
93ActPacA2-43G
93DiaStaES-151
94ConTSN-1102
94ConTSNB-1102
Vaughan, Charles
67OPC-179
67Top-179
Vaughan, Glenn
77FriOneYW-45
Vaughan, Porter (Cecil Porter)
77TCMTheWY-59
Vaughan, Rick
88St.CatBJP-2033
89MyrBeaBJP-1629
Vaughn, Billy
76LauIndC-10
76LauIndC-38
Vaughn, Derek
91SpoIndC-8
91SpoIndP-3964
92WatDiaC-16
92WatDiaF-2155
93PocPosF-4221
93PocPosSP-20
94LakElsSC-25
94LakElsSF-1679
95LakElsSTI-26
Vaughn, DeWayne
82LynMetT-7
84JacMetT-1
86TidTidP-28
87TidTidP-2
87TidTidT-8
88DonRoo-25
88RanMot-24
93RanKee-366
Vaughn, Farmer (Henry)
98CamPepP-81
Vaughn, Fred
47SigOil-18
Vaughn, Greg
87BelBreP-2
88BasAmeAAB-24
88ElPasDB-20
88TexLeaAGS-35
89BlaYNPRWL-129
89BlaYNPRWLU-50
89BlaYNPRWLU-58
89DenZepC-23
89DenZepP-36
89FleUpd-41
89TriA AAC-8
89TriAAP-AAA42
90Bow-396
90BowTif-396
90BreMilB-28
90BrePol-23
90ClaBlu-60
90Don-37
90DonBesA-107
90DonRoo-16
90El PasDAGTI-25
90Fle-339
90FleCan-339
90Hot50RS-44
90Lea-111
90LeaPre-9
90OPC-57

90Sco-585
90Sco100RS-30
90ScoRooDT-B8
90ScoYouSI-13
90Spo-135
90Top-57
90TopDeb89-128
90TopTif-57
90ToyRoo-27
90TriAAAC-8
90UppDec-25
91Bow-33
91BreMilB-29
91BrePol-26
91Cla3-T91
91ClaGam-46
91Don-478
91Fle-599
91OPC-347
91Sco-528
91Sco100RS-65
91StaClu-135
91Stu-79
91Top-347
91TopDesS-347
91TopMic-347
91TopRoo-30
91TopTif-347
91TopTriH-A8
91ToyRoo-29
91Ult-183
91UppDec-526
92Bow-496
92BrePol-27
92DenHol-17
92Don-224
92Fle-192
92Hig5-69
92Lea-276
92OPC-572
92PanSti-41
92Pin-92
92Sco-639
92StaClu-666
92Stu-198
92Top-572
92TopGol-572
92TopGolW-572
92TopKid-83
92TopMic-572
92TriPla-122
92Ult-86
92UppDec-97
92UppDec-232
92UppDecHRH-HR20
93Bow-295
93BrePol-26
93BreSen5-6
93Don-103
93Fla-231
93Fle-258
93FunPac-72
93Lea-56
93OPC-373
93PacSpa-166
93PanSti-44
93Pin-318
93PinHomRC-30
93Sco-160
93Sel-222
93SP-71
93StaClu-122
93StaCluFDI-122
93StaCluMOP-122
93Stu-197
93Top-153
93TopGol-153
93TopInaM-153
93TopMic-153
93TriPla-150
93Ult-225
93UppDec-563
93UppDecGold-563
93UppDecHRH-HR15
94Bow-449
94BowBes-R29
94BowBesR-R29
94BreMilB-84
94BreMilB-370
94BrePol-28
94ColC-585
94ColChoGS-585
94ColChoSS-585
94Don-339
94DonDiaK-DK20
94DonMVP-22
94DonSpeE-339
94ExtBas-109
94Fin-89
94FinRef-89
94Fla-309
94Fle-195
94FleAllS-24
94FleTeaL-8
94FUnPac-144
94Kra-13
94Lea-321
94LeaL-47
94OscMayR-15
94Pac-347
94PanSti-88
94Pin-37
94PinArtP-37
94PinMusC-37
94PinRunC-RC16
94ProMag-75
94Sco-49
94ScoGolR-49
94ScoGolS-47
94Sel-303
94SP-61
94SPDieC-61
94Spo-103
94StaClu-378
94StaCluFDI-378
94StaCluGR-378
94StaCluMOP-378
94Stu-48
94Top-225
94TopGol-225
94TopSpa-225
94TriPla-59
94Ult-380
94UppDec-288
94UppDec-445
94UppDecAJ-9
94UppDecAJG-9
94UppDecED-288
94UppDecED-445
95Baz-43
95Bow-410
95BowBes-R55
95BowBesR-R55
95ColCho-170
95ColChoGS-170
95ColChoSE-70
95ColChoSEGS-70
95ColChoSESS-70
95ColChoSS-170
95DenHol-27
95Don-130
95DonPreP-130
95DonTopotO-105
95Emb-23
95EmbGolI-23
95Fin-114
95FinRef-114
95Fla-55
95Fle-193
95FleTeaL-8
95Lea-261
95LeaLim-133
95Pac-242
95Pin-110
95PinArtP-110
95PinMusC-110
95Sco-379
95ScoGolR-379
95ScoPlaTS-379
95SelCer-87
95SelCerMG-87
95SP-165
95SPCha-164
95SPChaDC-164
95SPSil-165
95StaClu-210
95StaClu-423
95StaClu-517
95StaCluCC-CC24
95StaCluFDI-210
95StaCluMOP-210
95StaCluMOP-423
95StaCluMOP-517
95StaCluMOP-CC24
95StaCluSTWS-210
95StaCluSTWS-423
95StaCluSTWS-517
95StaCluVR-220
95Stu-96
95Sum-60
95SumNthD-60
95Top-452
95TopCyb-248
95TopPre-PP3
95UC3-94
95UC3ArtP-94
95Ult-300
95UltGolM-300
95UppDec-300
95UppDecED-300
95UppDecEDG-300
95UppDecSE-100
95UppDecSEG-100
96Baz-28
96Bow-90
96BowBes-27
96BowBesAR-27
96BowBesR-27
96Cir-190
96CirRav-190
96ColCho-413
96ColCho-590
96ColChoGS-413
96ColChoGS-590
96ColChoSS-413
96ColChoSS-590
96ColChoYMtP-41
96ColChoYMtP-41A
96ColChoYMtPGS-41
96ColChoYMtPGS-41A
96Don-206
96DonPreP-206
96EmoXL-78
96Fin-S179
96FinRef-S179
96Fla-109
96Fle-161
96FleTif-161
96Lea-19
96LeaLim-80
96LeaLimG-80
96LeaPre-44
96LeaPreP-44
96LeaPrePB-19
96LeaPrePG-19
96LeaPrePS-19
96LeaSig-82
96LeaSigPPG-82
96LeaSigPPP-82
96MetUni-74
96MetUniP-74
96PanSti-196
96Pin-129
96PinAfi-62
96PinAfiAP-62
96PinAfiFPP-62
96ProSta-27
96Sco-56
96ScoDugC-A49
96ScoDugCAP-A49
96Sel-114
96SelArtP-114
96SelCer-55
96SelCerAP-55
96SelCerCB-55
96SelCerCR-55
96SelCerMB-55
96SelCerMG-55
96SelCerMR-55
96SelTeaN-28
96SP-110
96StaClu-79
96StaCluMOP-79
96StaCluVRMO-220
96Stu-39
96StuPrePB-39
96StuPrePG-39
96StuPrePS-39
96Sum-36
96SumAbo&B-36
96SumArtP-36
96SumFoi-36
96Top-147
96TopChr-42
96TopChrR-42
96TopGal-24
96TopGalPPI-24
96TopLas-111
96Ult-87
96UltGolM-87
96UppDec-363
96Zen-81
96ZenArtP-81
96ZenMoz-14
97Bow-242
97BowBes-53
97BowBesAR-53
97BowBesR-53
97BowInt-242
97Cir-197
97CirRav-197
97ColCho-208
97Don-128
97DonEli-78
97DonEliGS-78
97DonLonL-5
97DonPre-39
97DonPreCttC-39
97DonPreP-128
97DonPrePGold-128
97Fin-221
97FinRef-221
97Fle-472
97FleTif-472
97Lea-314
97LeaFraM-314
97LeaFraMDC-314
97MetUni-226
97NewPin-43
97NewPinAP-43
97NewPinMC-43
97NewPinPP-43
97Pac-434
97PacLigB-434
97PacPriSL-SL12C
97PacSil-434
97PinCer-64
97PinCerMBlu-64
97PinCerMG-64
97PinCerMR-64
97PinCerR-64
97PinIns-65
97PinInsCE-65
97PinInsDE-65
97PinTotCPB-64
97PinTotCPG-64
97PinTotCPR-64
97PinX-P-68
97PinX-PMoS-68
97Sco-194
97ScoHeaotO-26
97ScoPreS-194
97ScoShoS-194
97ScoShoSAP-194
97Sel-66
97SelArtP-66
97SelRegG-66
97SP-158
97StaClu-214
97StaCluMat-214
97StaCluMOP-214
97Stu-99
97StuPrePG-99
97StuPrePS-99
97Top-397
97TopChr-138
97TopChrR-138
97TopGal-75
97TopGalPPI-75
97Ult-289
97UltGolME-289
97UltPlaME-289
97UppDec-169

Vaughn, Harry
87OldJudN-522

Vaughn, Heath
91GulCoaRSP-26
92GasRanF-2254
93ChaRaiC-21
93ChaRaiF-1911

Vaughn, Hippo (James)
10E98-27
10W555-60
11PloCanE-63
11T205-174
12HasTriFT-38A
12HasTriFT-68A
12T207-187
14PieStaT-58
15CraJacE-176
15SpoNewM-180
16BF2FP-71
16ColE13-177
16SpoNewM-178
17HolBreD-107
19W514-111
20NatCarE-103
21E121So8-99A
21E121So8-99B
22AmeCarE-72
22W575-141
23WilChoV-164
61Fle-82
69Baz-1
72FleFamF-14
72LauGreF-39
90HOFStiB-17
92ConTSN-348
92ConTSN1N-800
92CubOldS-26
93ConTSN-800

Vaughn, Mike
76CliPilT-31
77WatIndT-27

Vaughn, Mo (Maurice)
88CapCodPB-16
88CapCodPPaLP-93
90Bow-275
90BowTif-275
90PawRedSDD-28
90PawRedSP-471
90ProAAAF-443
90Sco-675
90TopMag-45
90TopTVRS-64
91Bow-112
91Cla1-T24
91ClaGam-152
91Don-430
91DonRoo-36
91FleUpd-7
91LeaGolR-BC7
91LinDriAAA-370
91MajLeaCP-10
91OPCPre-124
91PawRedSDD-26
91PawRedSLD-370
91PawRedSP-49
91Sco-750
91ScoRoo-6
91StaClu-543
91Stu-20
91TopTra-123T
91TopTraT-123T
91TriA AAGP-AAA32
91Ult-387
91UppDec-5
92Bow-397
92ClaGam-73
92Don-514
92Fle-49
92Fle-705
92Hig5-10
92Lea-103
92OPC-59
92OPCPre-50
92PawRedSF-934
92Pin-205
92PinTea2-54
92ProFS7-15
92RedSoxDD-27
92Sco-556
92Sco100RS-100
92ScoImpP-21
92SpoIllFK1-297
92SpoIllFK1-553
92StaClu-325
92Stu-139
92Top-59
92TopDeb91-176
92TopGol-59
92TopGolW-59
92TopMic-59
92TriPla-79
92Ult-23
92UppDec-445
93Bow-536
93ClaGam-94
93DiaMar-112
93Don-429
93Fin-165
93FinRef-165
93Fla-168
93Fle-184
93Lea-432
93OPC-393
93PacSpa-37
93PanSti-92
93Pin-189
93PinHomRC-40

93RedSoxWHP-27
93Sco-132
93Sel-214
93SP-206
93StaClu-334
93StaCluFDI-334
93StaCluMOP-334
93Stu-134
93Top-51
93TopGol-51
93TopInaM-51
93TopMic-51
93Toy-53
93Ult-156
93UppDec-396
93UppDecGold-396
94Bow-315
94BowBes-R80
94BowBesR-R80
94ColC-281
94ColChoGS-281
94ColChoSS-281
94DenHol-27
94Don-42
94DonDiaK-DK2
94DonMVP-16
94DonSpeE-42
94ExtBas-27
94ExtBasGB-28
94Fin-258
94FinRef-258
94Fla-18
94Fle-45
94FleTeaL-2
94FUnPac-42
94Kra-14
94Lea-285
94LeaL-12
94LeaMVPC-A14
94LeaMVPCG-A14
94OPC-259
94Pac-68
94PanSti-34
94Pin-17
94PinArtP-17
94PinMusC-17
94PinPowS-PS3
94PinRunC-RC12
94Pos-8
94ProMag-14
94RedFolMI-26
94Sco-57
94ScoGolR-57
94ScoGolS-51
94Sel-116
94SP-157
94SPDieC-157
94Spo-122
94StaClu-440
94StaCluFDI-440
94StaCluGR-440
94StaCluMOP-440
94Stu-166
94Top-690
94TopGol-690
94TopSpa-690
94TopSupS-43
94TriPla-209
94Ult-19
94UppDec-71
94UppDec-282
94UppDecAJ-12
94UppDecAJG-12
94UppDecED-71
94UppDecED-282
94UppDecMLS-MM19
94UppDecMLSED-MM19
94USDepoT-3
95Baz-17
95Bow-411
95BowBes-R42
95BowBes-X8
95BowBesJR-10
95BowBesR-R42
95BowBesR-X8
95ClaPhoC-8
95ColCho-421
95ColChoGS-421
95ColChoSE-194
95ColChoSEGS-194
95ColChoSESS-194
95ColChoSS-421
95Don-52
95DonPreP-52
95DonTopotO-29
95Emb-139
95EmbGolI-139
95Emo-17
95EmoN-11
95Fin-86
95FinPowK-PK8
95FinRef-86
95Fla-15
95FlaInfP-9
95Fle-42
95FleTeaL-2
95FleUpdH-19
95Kra-15
95Lea-269
95LeaLim-152
95LeaLimG-21
95LeaLimIBP-12
95LeaLimL-8
95Pac-49
95PacPri-16
95PanSti-37
95Pin-216
95PinArtP-216
95PinMusC-216
95RedFol-11
95Sco-12
95Sco-563
95ScoGolR-12
95ScoGolR-563
95ScoHaloG-HG17
95ScoPlaTS-12
95ScoPlaTS-563
95Sel-97
95SelArtP-97
95SelCer-10
95SelCerMG-10
95SelCerS-10
95SP-125
95SPCha-121
95SPCha-125
95SPChaDC-121
95SPChaDC-125
95Spo-98
95SpoArtP-98
95SPPlaP-PP20
95SPSil-125
95SPSpeF-3
95StaClu-350
95StaClu-511
95StaCluCC-CC20
95StaCluMOP-350
95StaCluMOP-511
95StaCluMOP-CC20
95StaCluSTDW-RS350
95StaCluSTWS-350
95StaCluSTWS-511
95StaCluVR-184
95Stu-39
95StuGolS-39
95Sum-94
95Sum-200
95SumBigB-BB20
95SumNthD-94
95SumNthD-200
95TomPiz-18
95Top-205
95TopCyb-117
95TopTra-9T
95TopTraPB-9
95UC3-6
95UC3-136
95UC3ArtP-6
95UC3ArtP-136
95UllHomRK-11
95Ult-17
95UltGolM-17
95UppDec-161
95UppDecED-161
95UppDecEDG-161
95UppDecSE-210
95UppDecSEG-210
95Zen-77
96Baz-85
96Bow-21
96BowBes-16
96BowBesAR-16
96BowBesP-BBP25
96BowBesPAR-BBP25
96BowBesPR-BBP25
96BowBesR-16
96Cir-14
96CirAcc-2
96CirBos-4
96CirRav-14
96ColCho-4
96ColCho-273
96ColCho-480
96ColCho-706
96ColChoCtG-CG6
96ColChoCtG-CG6B
96ColChoCtG-CG6C
96ColChoCtGE-CR6
96ColChoCtGG-CG6
96ColChoCtGG-CG6B
96ColChoCtGG-CG6C
96ColChoCtGGE-CR6
96ColChoGS-4
96ColChoGS-273
96ColChoGS-480
96ColChoGS-706
96ColChoSS-4
96ColChoSS-273
96ColChoSS-480
96ColChoSS-706
96ColChoYMtP-42
96ColChoYMtP-42A
96ColChoYMtPGS-42
96ColChoYMtPGS-42A
96DenHol-5
96DenHolGS-9
96DenHolGSAP-9
96Don-505
96DonDiaK-2
96DonEli-64
96DonHitL-6
96DonPowA-7
96DonPowADC-7
96DonPreP-505
96DonPurP-8
96DonRouT-5
96EmoLegoB-11
96EmoXL-20
96Fin-B288
96Fin-G64
96Fin-S151
96FinRef-B288
96FinRef-G64
96FinRef-S151
96Fla-29
96FlaDiaC-11
96Fle-38
96FleChe-9
96FleLumC-11
96FleRedS-17
96FleRoaW-9
96FleTeaL-2
96FleTif-38
96FleUpd-U244
96FleUpdTC-U244
96FleZon-11
96Kin-2
96Lea-130
96LeaAllGMC-7
96LeaAllGMCG-7
96LeaGolS-12
96LeaHatO-4
96LeaLim-47
96LeaLimG-47
96LeaLimL-6
96LeaLimLB-6
96LeaPicP-11
96LeaPre-49
96LeaPreP-49
96LeaPrePB-130
96LeaPrePG-130
96LeaPrePS-130
96LeaPreSG-22
96LeaPreSP-2
96LeaPreSte-22
96LeaSig-73
96LeaSigA-228
96LeaSigAG-229
96LeaSigAS-229
96LeaSigEA-208
96LeaSigEACM-30
96LeaSigPPG-73
96LeaSigPPP-73
96MetUni-21
96MetUniHM-9
96MetUniP-21
96MetUniT-9
96Pac-248
96Pac-260
96PacGolCD-DC23
96PacPri-P81
96PacPriFB-FB19
96PacPriG-P81
96PacPriRHS-RH20
96PanSti-122
96PanSti-137
96Pin-78
96Pin-141
96Pin-261
96PinAfi-58
96PinAfiAP-58
96PinAfiFPP-58
96PinAfiMN-4
96PinAfiR-3
96PinAfiR-4
96PinAfiR-6
96PinAfiR-8
96PinAfiR-9
96PinAfiR-11
96PinAfiSP-6
96PinArtP-28
96PinArtP-68
96PinArtP-161
96PinEssotG-12
96PinFan-9
96PinFirR-3
96PinFoil-261
96PinPow-2
96PinSam-PP2
96PinSky-6
96PinSlu-5
96PinSta-28
96PinSta-68
96PinSta-161
96PinTeaS-8
96ProMagA-8
96ProMagDM-6
96ProSta-106
96Sco-62
96Sco-370
96Sco-513
96ScoAll-5
96ScoBigB-13
96ScoDiaA-17
96ScoDugC-A54
96ScoDugC-B95
96ScoDugCAP-A54
96ScoDugCAP-B95
96ScoGolS-18
96ScoNumG-17
96ScoPowP-9
96ScoRef-3
96ScoTitT-3
96Sel-48
96Sel-158
96SelArtP-48
96SelArtP-158
96SelCer-67
96SelCer-141
96SelCerAP-67
96SelCerAP-141
96SelCerCB-67
96SelCerCB-141
96SelCerCR-67
96SelCerCR-141
96SelCerIP-2
96SelCerMB-67
96SelCerMB-141
96SelCerMG-67
96SelCerMG-141
96SelCerMR-67
96SelCerMR-141
96SelCerSF-8
96SelClaTF-5
96SelEnF-7
96SelTeaN-8
96SP-40
96Spo-31
96Spo-105
96SpoArtP-31
96SpoArtP-105
96SpoDouT-6
96SpoHitP-5
96SpoPowS-9
96SpoPro-3
96SPPreF-4
96SPSpeFX-41
96SPSpeFXDC-41
96SPx-10
96SPxGol-10
96StaClu-184
96StaClu-303
96StaCluEPB-303
96StaCluEPG-303
96StaCluEPS-303
96StaCluMeg-MH10
96StaCluMO-43
96StaCluMOP-184
96StaCluMOP-303
96StaCluMOP-MH10
96StaCluMOP-PP7
96StaCluMOP-PS9
96StaCluPP-PP7
96StaCluPS-PS9
96StaCluVRMO-184
96Stu-104
96StuHitP-10
96StuPrePB-104
96StuPrePG-104
96StuPrePS-104
96Sum-31
96SumAbo&B-31
96SumArtP-31
96SumBal-4
96SumBigB-4
96SumBigBM-4
96SumFoi-31
96SumHitI-2
96SumPos-1
96TeaOut-83
96TeaOut-C97
96Top-274
96TopBroLL-4
96TopChr-110
96TopChrR-110
96TopChrWC-WC14
96TopChrWCR-WC14
96TopGal-150
96TopGalPPI-150
96TopLas-94
96TopLasPC-7
96TopMysF-M19
96TopMysFR-M19
96TopPro-AL10
96TopRoaW-RW18
96TopWreC-WC14
96Ult-22
96Ult-591
96UltDiaP-11
96UltDiaPGM-11
96UltGolM-22
96UltGolM-591
96UltHomRKGM-11
96UltHomRKR-11
96UltRBIK-10
96UltRBIKGM-10
96UltRes-10
96UltResGM-10
96UppDec-18
96UppDecDD-DD10
96UppDecDDG-DD10
96UppDecDDS-DD10
96UppDecHC-HC13
96UppDecPD-PD18
96UppDecPHE-H9
96UppDecPRE-R9
96UppDecPRE-R19
96UppDecPreH-H9
96UppDecPreR-R9
96UppDecPreR-R19
96UppDecRunP-RP19
96Zen-30
96Zen-136
96ZenArtP-30
96ZenArtP-136
96ZenDiaC-2
96ZenDiaCP-2
96ZenMoz-9
96ZenZ-6
97Bow-277
97BowBes-7
97BowBesAR-7
97BowBesR-7
97BowChr-93
97BowChrI-93
97BowChrIR-93
97BowChrR-93
97BowInt-277
97Cir-42
97CirBos-19
97CirLimA-15
97CirRav-42
97CirSupB-19
97ColCho-50
97ColCho-327
97ColChoAC-37
97ColChoBS-16
97ColChoBSGS-16
97ColChoCtG-7A
97ColChoCtG-7B
97ColChoCtG-7C

97ColChoCtGIW-CG7
97ColChoNF-NF31
97ColChoPP-PP8
97ColChoPPG-PP8
97ColChoS-27
97ColChoTBS-11
97ColChoTBSWH-11
97ColChoTotT-T8
97Don-108
97Don-420
97Don-445
97DonDiaK-3
97DonDiaKC-3
97DonEli-12
97DonEli-10
97DonEliGS-12
97DonFraFea-10
97DonLim-47
97DonLim-76
97DonLim-95
97DonLimFotG-57
97DonLimLE-47
97DonLimLE-76
97DonLimLE-95
97DonLonL-3
97DonPowA-9
97DonPowADC-9
97DonPre-103
97DonPre-183
97DonPreCttC-103
97DonPreCttC-183
97DonPreP-108
97DonPreP-420
97DonPreP-445
97DonPrePGold-108
97DonPrePGold-420
97DonPrePGold-445
97DonPrePM-19
97DonPreS-19
97DonPreTB-25
97DonPreTBG-25
97DonPreTF-25
97DonPreTP-25
97DonPreTPG-25
97DonRocL-5
97DonTea-48
97DonTeaSPE-48
97DunDonPPS-27
97Fin-153
97Fin-202
97Fin-311
97FinEmb-153
97FinEmb-311
97FinEmbR-153
97FinEmbR-311
97FinRef-153
97FinRef-202
97FinRef-311
97FlaSho-A42
97FlaSho-B42
97FlaSho-C42
97FlaShoDC-18
97FlaShoLC-42
97FlaShoLC-B42
97FlaShoLC-C42
97FlaShoLCM-A42
97FlaShoLCM-B42
97FlaShoLCM-C42
97Fle-32
97Fle-719
97Fle-724
97FleBleB-9
97FleGouG-15
97FleGouGF-15
97FleLumC-18
97FleMilDM-42
97FleTeaL-2
97FleTif-32
97FleTif-719
97FleTif-724
97Lea-151
97LeaBanS-8
97LeaDrefS-15
97LeaFraM-151
97LeaFraMDC-151
97LeaGet-13
97LeaLeaotN-11
97MetUni-26
97MetUniBF-12
97NewPin-98
97NewPinAP-98
97NewPinIE-7
97NewPinMC-98
97NewPinPP-98
97NewPinPP-I7B
97Pac-48
97PacCar-6
97PacCarM-6
97PacCerCGT-8
97PacLigB-48
97PacPri-17
97PacPriLB-17
97PacPriP-17
97PacSil-48
97PacTriCD-3
97Pin-190
97PinArtP-190
97PinCer-2
97PinCerCMGT-8
97PinCerCT-8
97PinCerLI-3
97PinCerMBlu-2
97PinCerMG-2
97PinCerMR-2
97PinCerR-2
97PinHom-15
97PinHom-16
97PinIns-44
97PinInsC-7
97PinInsCE-44
97PinInsDD-8
97PinInsDE-44
97PinInsFS-11
97PinMin-5
97PinMinB-5
97PinMinCB-5
97PinMinCG-5
97PinMinCGR-5
97PinMinCN-5
97PinMinCS-5
97PinMinG-5
97PinMinS-5
97PinMusC-190
97PinPasttM-7
97PinSha-6
97PinTotCPB-2
97PinTotCPG-2
97PinTotCPR-2
97PinX-P-88
97PinX-PF&A-4
97PinX-PMoS-88
97PinX-PMW-16
97PinX-PMWG-16
97PinX-PMWS-16
97PinX-PSfF-17
97PinX-PSfFU-17
97ProMag-48
97ProMagML-48
97Sco-93
97Sco-510
97ScoBla-1
97ScoHigZ-3
97ScoHobR-510
97ScoPitP-12
97ScoPreS-93
97ScoRedS-2
97ScoRedSPI-2
97ScoRedSPr-2
97ScoResC-510
97ScoShoS-93
97ScoShoS-510
97ScoShoSAP-93
97ScoShoSAP-510
97ScoSteS-13
97ScoTitT-12
97Sel-2
97SelArtP-2
97SelRegG-2
97SelToootT-6
97SelToootTMB-6
97SkyE-X-11
97SkyE-XACA-7
97SkyE-XC-11
97SkyE-XEC-11
97SkyE-XHoN-18
97SP-35
97SPInsI-7
97SPMarM-MM15
97SpoIll-139
97SpoIllEE-139
97SpoIllGS-8
97SPSpeF-14
97SPSpxF-3
97SPSPxFA-3
97SPVinAu-31
97SPx-14
97SPxBoufG-6
97SPxBro-14
97SPxCorotG-9
97SPxGraF-14
97SPxSil-14
97SPxSte-14
97StaClu-42
97StaClu-377
97StaCluFR-F11
97StaCluMat-42
97StaCluMOP-42
97StaCluMOP-377
97StaCluMOP-FB11
97StaCluMOP-PG17
97StaCluPG-PG17
97Stu-36
97StuMasS-7
97StuMasS8-7
97StuPor8-18
97StuPrePG-36
97StuPrePS-36
97Top-450
97TopChr-159
97TopChrR-159
97TopChrSB-14
97TopChrSBR-14
97TopGal-109
97TopGalGoH-GH10
97TopGalPPI-109
97TopHobM-HM17
97TopIntF-ILM13
97TopIntFR-ILM13
97TopSeaB-SB14
97TopSta-27
97TopStaAM-27
97TopSweS-SS15
97TopTeaT-TT11
97Ult-21
97UltDouT-2
97UltGolME-21
97UltHRK-11
97UltPlaME-21
97UltPowP-B11
97UltRBIK-10
97UltThu-2
97UltTop3-16
97UltTop3GM-16
97UppDec-25
97UppDec-417
97UppDecAG-AG18
97UppDecHC-HC15
97UppDecLDC-LD8
97UppDecP-8
97UppDecPP-PP17
97UppDecPPJ-PP17
97UppDecRP-RP18
97UppDecU-8
97UppDecUMA-MA9
97Zen-41

Vaughn, Randy
88EugEmeB-10
89AppFoxP-850
90BasCitRS-23

Vaughn, Ron
89UtiBluSP-28

Vaughn, Tim
87MacPirP-9

Vaught, Craig
93St.CatBJC-24
93St.CatBJF-3984

Vaught, Jay
93Tex-6
94WatIndC-26
94WatIndF-3937
95KinIndTI-27
96CanIndB-27

Vavra, Joe
85AlbDukC-153
86AlbDukP-25
89GreFalDSP-9
90GreFalDSP-30
91YakBeaC-29
91YakBeaP-4264
92YakBeaF-3468
93VerBeaDC-28
94YakBeaC-30
94YakBeaF-3867
95YakBeaTI-34
96YakBeaTI-NNO

Vavrek, Michael
95AshTouUTI-7
96SalAvaB-25

Vavrock, Rob
82MadMusF-24

Vavruska, Paul
76CliPilT-32

Vazquetelles, Darren
93IdaFalBF-4041
93IdaFalBSP-12

Vazquez, Archie
92SpoIndF-1294
94HicCraC-23
94HicCraF-2178
94SouAtlLAF-SAL26
95Exc-32
95PriWilCTI-25
96Exc-38

Vazquez, Armando
91NegLeaRL-14
92NegLeaK-5
93TedWil-113
95NegLeaL2-5

Vazquez, Arthur
92SpoIndC-21

Vazquez, Ed
89KinMetS-24
90PitMetP-22

Vazquez, Javier
96DelShoB-29
97Bow-387
97BowChr-256
97BowChrI-256
97BowChrIR-256
97BowChrR-256
97BowInt-387

Vazquez, Jose
89OneYanP-2126
92JohCitCC-8
92JohCitCF-3133
93St.PetCC-25
93St.PetCF-2642

Vazquez, Manny
96HudValRB-8
96WesOahCHWB-11

Vazquez, Marcos
88BlaYNPRWLU-46
88SumBraP-403
89BlaYNPRWL-19
89SumBraP-1115
91DurBulUP-4
91MacBraC-11
91MacBraP-864
94ChaLooF-1359

Vazquez, Pedro
90AppFoxBS-29
90AppFoxP-2106
91BasCitRC-22
91BasCitRP-1408

Vazquez, Ramon
96EveAquB-25

Veach, Robert
15CraJacE-174
15SpoNewM-181
16BF2FP-31
16ColE13-178
16SpoNewM-179
17HolBreD-108
19W514-88
20NatCarE-104
21E121So1-108
21E121So8-100A
21E121So8-100B
21Exh-180
21Nei-33
22AmeCarE-73
22E120-59
22W572-109
22W573-134
22W575-142
23W501-5
23WilChoV-165
25Exh-71
81TigDetN-118
81TigSecNP-6
91ConTSN-159
92ConTSN-486

Veach, William
87OldJudN-523

Veal, Coot (Orville)
59Top-52
59TopVen-52
61Top-432
62Jel-68
62Pos-68
62PosCan-68
62SalPlaC-84
62ShiPlaC-84
63Top-573

Veale, Bob
62Top-593
63PirIDL-25
63Top-87
64Kah-28
64PirKDK-27
64Top-501
65Baz-13
65Kah-43
65OPC-12
65OPC-195
65Top-12
65Top-195
65TopTral-32
66Kah-31
66PirEasH-39
66Top-225
66Top-425
66TopRubI-95
66TopVen-225
67CokCapPi-4
67DexPre-214
67Kah-38
67PirTeal-22
67Top-238
67Top-335
67TopPirS-23
67TopVen-333
68Baz-3
68Kah-A12
68Kah-B35
68OPC-70
68PirKDK-39
68PirTeal-22
68Top-70
68TopActS-11A
68TopVen-70
69Kah-B21
69MilBra-283
69MLBOffS-189
69OPC-8
69Top-8
69Top-520
69TopSta-90
69TopTeaP-16
70MLBOffS-108
70OPC-236
70Top-236
71MLBOffS-215
71OPC-368
71PirActP-11
71Top-368
72MilBra-351
72Top-729
73LinPor-31
73OPC-518
73Top-518
78GreBraT-28
78TCM60I-114
92UppDecS-19

Vecchioni, Jerry
96DanBraB-26

Veeck, Bill
48IndTeal-30
49IndTeal-25
53IndPenCBP-27
76ChiGre-19
80PerHaloFP-211
82OhiHaloF-44
84OCoandSI-191

Veeck, Michael
90MiaMirIS-29

Veeck, William
31CubTeal-26
32CubTeal-25

Vega, Jesus
77BurBeeT-3
78OrlTwiT-21
79TolMudHT-20
80TolMudHT-11
81TolMudHT-16
82TwiPos-26
83Don-650
83Fle-624
83TolMudHT-17
83Top-308

Vegely, Bruce
88BenBucL-18
89QuaCitAB-19
89QuaCitAGS-12
90QuaCitAGS-7
91PalSprAP-2016

Veil, Bucky
11SpoLifCW-356

Veilleux, Brian
89ModA'sC-17

89ModA'sCLC-268
90HunStaB-12
Veintidos, Juan
74TacTwiC-12
75OPC-621
75TacTwiK-18
75Top-621
76TacTwiDQ-21
77TacTwiDQ-22
Veit, Steve
90AshTouC-17
90AubAstB-3
90AubAstP-3400
91AshTouP-578
Velandia, Jorge
92BriTigF-1423
93FayGenC-23
93FayGenF-139
93LinVenB-87
94LakTigC-24
94LakTigF-3047
94SprSulC-23
94VenLinU-226
95LinVen-49
95MemChiTI-5
96Bow-203
96MemChiB-28
Velarde, Randy
86AppFoxP-26
87AlbYanP-7
87IntLeaAT-13
88ColCliC-17
88ColCliP-22
88ColCliP-324
88Fle-646
88FleGlo-646
88TriAAC-20
89ColCliC-13
89ColCliP-17
89ColCliP-741
89ScoHot1R-18
89Top-584
89TopBig-239
89TopTif-584
89TriA AAC-19
89TriAAP-AAA19
89UppDec-189
90AlbDecGB-19
90Bow-434
90BowTif-434
90Don-630
90OPC-23
90Sco-524
90Top-23
90TopBig-68
90TopTif-23
90TopTVY-28
90TriAAAC-19
90YanScoNW-27
91OPC-379
91Sco-134
91StaClu-438
91Top-379
91TopDesS-379
91TopMic-379
91TopTif-379
92Bow-207
92Don-679
92Fle-246
92Lea-368
92OPC-212
92Sco-337
92StaClu-237
92Top-212
92TopGol-212
92TopGolW-212
92TopMic-212
92UppDec-399
92YanWIZ8-195
93Don-153
93Fle-287
93OPC-337
93PacSpa-214
93PanSti-148
93Pin-314
93Sco-219
93StaClu-32
93StaCluFDI-32
93StaCluMOP-32
93StaCluY-9
93Top-174
93TopGol-174
93TopInaM-174
93TopMic-174
93Ult-250
93UppDec-93
93UppDecGold-93
94ColC-498
94ColChoGS-498
94ColChoSS-498
94Don-439
94ExtBas-141
94Fin-41
94FinRef-41
94Fle-249
94Pac-440
94Pin-383
94PinArtP-383
94PinMusC-383
94Sco-216
94ScoGolR-216
94StaClu-156
94StaCluFDI-156
94StaCluGR-156
94StaCluMOP-156
94StaCluT-189
94StaCluTFDI-189
94Top-461
94TopGol-461
94TopSpa-461
95ColCho-513
95ColChoGS-513
95ColChoSS-513
95Don-491
95DonPreP-491
95DonTopotO-127
95Fle-83
95Pac-305
95Sco-384
95ScoGolR-384
95ScoPlaTS-384
95StaClu-247
95StaCluFDI-247
95StaCluMOP-247
95StaCluSTWS-247
95Top-566
95TopCyb-342
96AngMot-14
96ColCho-481
96ColChoGS-481
96ColChoSS-481
96Don-369
96DonPreP-369
96Fla-44
96Fle-60
96FleTif-60
96FleUpd-U22
96FleUpdTC-U22
96Pac-375
96Sco-55
96ScoDugC-A48
96ScoDugCAP-A48
96StaClu-44
96StaCluMOP-44
96Top-361
96Ult-328
96UltGolM-328
96UppDec-485U
97ColCho-257
97Fle-53
97FleTif-53
97Pac-15
97PacLigB-15
97PacSil-15
97Top-185
97Ult-32
97UltGolME-32
97UltPlaME-32
97UppDec-297
Velasquez, Al
82ReaPhiT-12
Velasquez, Carlos
75SacSolC-17
Velasquez, Frank
96ChaRivTI-9602
Velasquez, Gil (Guillermo)
88ChaRaiP-1203
88SouAtlLAGS-12
89RivRedWB-20
89RivRedWCLC-3
89RivRedWP-1394
90WicWraRD-21
91LinDriAA-621
91WicWraLD-621
91WicWraP-2607
91WicWraRD-17
92Bow-698
92LasVegSF-2805
92LasVegSS-245
92SkyAAAF-120
92TriA AAS-245
93Don-312
93FleFinE-146
93Lea-471
93PacBeiA-23
93PacSpa-604
93PadMot-17
93StaClu-744
93StaCluFDI-744
93StaCluMOP-744
93Top-724
93TopGol-724
93TopInaM-724
93TopMic-724
93Ult-479
94Don-300
94Fle-677
94Pac-536
94StaClu-278
94StaCluFDI-278
94StaCluGR-278
94StaCluMOP-278
94Top-556
94TopGol-556
94TopSpa-556
Velasquez, Ray
85VisOakT-16
86VisOakP-23
87CliGiaP-26
88SanJosGCLC-139
88SanJosGP-116
89SalSpuCLC-123
89SalSpuP-1807
90SalSpuCLC-125
Velasquez, Tony
72CedRapCT-27
Velazquel, Ildefonso
85MexCitTT-9
Velazquez, Carlos
94BreMilB-85
Velazquez, Edgar
96NewHavRB-25
96NewHavRUSTI-12
Velazquez, Edgard
94AshTouC-22
94AshTouF-1796
95SalAvaTI-11
96Bow-351
96BowBes-132
96BowBesAR-132
96BowBesR-132
96BowMinLP-15
97Bow-211
97BowBes-140
97BowBesAR-140
97BowBesR-140
97BowChr-193
97BowChrI-193
97BowChrIR-193
97BowChrR-193
97BowInt-211
97Top-491
Velazquez, Fred
80VenLeaS-242
83Pil69G-24
85DomLeaS-212
Velazquez, Jose
96GreBatB-30
Velazquez, Juan
83QuaCitCT-17
Velez, Jose
87GasRanP-25
88BlaYNPRWL-143
88GasRanP-1011
89PalSprACLC-46
89PalSprAP-484
Velez, Jose J.
91Cla/Bes-208
91SprCarC-28
91SprCarP-758
92SavCarF-678
93St.PetCC-26
93St.PetCF-2643
94St.PetCC-27
94St.PetCF-2601
95ArkTraTI-26
96ArkTraB-26
Velez, Noel
90Bes-54
90ChaWheB-18
90ChaWheP-2248
91CedRapRC-24
91CedRapRP-2734
91EriSaiC-12
91EriSaiP-4082
Velez, Otto
73SyrChiTI-28
74OPC-606
74SyrChiTI-27
74Top-606
74TopSta-219
75SyrChiTI-21
76SSP-455
77OPC-13
77Top-299
78BluJayP-22
78OPC-67
78Top-59
79BluJayBY-19
79OPC-241
79Top-462
80OPC-354
80Top-703
81Don-391
81Fle-410
81OPC-351
81OPCPos-23
81Top-351
81TopScr-44
81TopSti-138
82Don-304
82Fle-625
82FleSta-233
82OPC-155
82OPCPos-11
82Top-155
82TopSti-249
83ChaChaT-18
83IndPos-37
86BluJayGT-5
92Nab-26
92YanWIZ7-157
Vella, Greg
88MyrBeaBJP-1183
88SouAtlLAGS-19
89DunBluJS-21
Velleggia, Frank
84NewOriT-15
Veltman, Art
33ButCanV-49
34DiaMatCSB-186
Venable, Max
77CliDodT-28
78LodDodT-23
79GiaPol-49
80PhoGiaVNB-12
81Fle-443
81PhoGiaVNB-6
81Top-484
83Fle-275
83GiaMot-16
83Top-634
84Don-323
84Fle-385
84IndIndTI-15
84IndIndTI-28
84Nes792-58
84Top-58
84TopTif-58
85IndIndTI-9
86Don-650
86Fle-196
86RedTexG-9
86Top-428
86TopTif-428
87Fle-216
87FleGlo-216
87NasSouTI-22
87Top-226
87TopTif-226
89EdmTraC-23
89EdmTraP-556
90Lea-459
91Don-510
92Sco-477
94IdaFalBSP-27
95DanBraTI-28
95RicBraTI-29
96DurBulBlB-25
96DurBulBrB-21
Venafro, Mike
95HudValRTI-13
96ChaRivTI-9629
Venezia, Danny
93EliTwiC-21
93EliTwiF-3423
94ForWayWC-24
94ForWayWF-2019
Venezia, Mike
81RedPioT-8
Venezia, Rich
94WelPirC-28
94WelPirF-3506
Veneziale, Mike
93Top-726
93TopGol-726
93TopInaM-726
93TopMic-726
Venger, Tad
81ChaRoyT-24
Veniard, Jay
96DunBluJUTI-16
Venner, Gary
82BurRanF-9
83TriTriT-27
Ventress, Leroy
86BenPhiC-145
87UtiBluSP-2
88BatCliP-1666
89SouAtlLAGS-41
89SpaPhiP-1044
89SpaPhiS-23
90ClePhiS-23
91ClePhiC-26
91ClePhiP-1637
Ventura, Candido
77ChaPatT-24
Ventura, Jose
86BelBreP-24
89SouBenWSGS-16
90SarWhiSS-25
91BirBarLD-73
91BirBarP-1455
91Cla/Bes-271
91LinDriAA-73
92BirBarF-2584
92BirBarS-97
92SkyAA F-46
93LimRocDWB-129
93MemChiF-377
Ventura, Leonardo
94SouOreAC-29
94SouOreAF-3627
Ventura, Reynaldo
89BurIndS-25
Ventura, Robin
88StaVen-1
88StaVen-2
88StaVen-3
88StaVen-4
88StaVen-5
88StaVen-6
88StaVen-7
88StaVen-8
88StaVen-9
88StaVen-10
88StaVen-11
88TopTra-124T
88TopTraT-124T
89BasAmeAPB-AA21
89BirBarB-1
89BirBarP-106
89Bow-65
89BowTif-65
89ClaTraP-177
89FleUpd-23
89SouLeaAJ-2
89Sta-101
89Top-764
89TopBig-65
89TopTif-764
90BirBarDGB-1
90Bow-311
90BowTif-311
90ClaBlu-5
90Don-28
90DonBesA-60
90DonRoo-15
90Fle-550
90FleCan-550
90FleSoaS-4
90Hot50RS-45
90Lea-167
90LeaPre-8
90OPC-121
90Sco-595
90Sco100RS-96
90ScoRooDT-B6
90ScoYouS2-8
90Spo-222

90Top-121
90TopDeb89-129
90TopMag-76
90TopTif-121
90ToyRoo-28
90UppDec-21
90WhiSoxC-27
90WhiSoxC-28
91Baz-15
91Bow-358
91ClaGam-52
91Don-315
91Fle-139
91Lea-271
91OPC-461
91PanFreS-314
91PanSti-260
91RedFolS-97
91Sco-320
91Sco100RS-48
91StaClu-274
91Top-461
91TopDesS-461
91TopMic-461
91TopRoo-31
91TopTif-461
91TopTriH-A4
91ToyRoo-30
91Ult-86
91UppDec-263
91UppDec-677
91WhiSoxK-23
91WhiSoxK-NNO
92Bow-275
92Bow-655
92Cla2-T85
92ClaGam-49
92DenHol-8
92Don-145
92DonCraJ1-33
92DonPre-6
92Fle-101
92FleAll-19
92Fre-8
92Hig5-20
92Lea-17
92OPC-255
92OPCPre-132
92PanSti-127
92Pin-121
92Pin-286
92PinTea2-43
92PinTeaP-6
92Sco-122
92Sco100S-33
92ScoImpP-42
92ScoSam-3
92StaClu-70
92Stu-160
92Top-255
92TopDaiQTU-11
92TopGol-255
92TopGolW-255
92TopKid-102
92TopMic-255
92TriPla-17
92Ult-343
92UltAwaW-15
92UppDec-263
92UppDecF-6
92UppDecFG-6
92UppDecWB-T20
92WhiSoxK-23
93Bow-667
93CadDis-59
93ClaGam-95
93DenHol-27
93DiaMar-113
93Don-535
93DonDiaK-DK10
93Fin-93
93FinJum-93
93FinRef-93
93Fla-190
93Fle-211
93Fle-716
93FleFruotL-63
93FunPac-203
93FunPacA-AS5
93HumDumC-7
93Kra-14
93Lea-439
93LeaFas-14
93LeaGolA-R6
93OPC-387
93PacSpa-78
93PanSti-139
93Pin-28
93PinHomRC-24
93Sco-41
93Sel-30
93SP-261
93StaClu-295
93StaClu-387
93StaCluFDI-295
93StaCluFDI-387
93StaCluM-111
93StaCluMOP-295
93StaCluMOP-387
93StaCluWS-13
93Stu-78
93Top-770
93TOPBLAG-43
93TopGol-770
93TopInaM-770
93TopMic-770
93TopPos-1
93Toy-58
93TriPla-179
93Ult-537
93UltAwaW-14
93UppDec-51
93UppDec-263
93UppDec-838
93UppDecGold-51
93UppDecGold-263
93UppDecGold-838
93WhiSoxK-29
94Bow-295
94BowBes-R30
94BowBesR-R30
94ChuHomS-17
94ChuHomSG-17
94ColC-282
94ColChoGS-282
94ColChoSS-282
94Don-23
94DonSpeE-23
94ExtBas-54
94Fin-202
94FinJum-202
94FinRef-202
94Fla-281
94Fle-97
94FUnPac-163
94KinDis-21
94Lea-26
94LeaL-25
94OPC-33
94Pac-140
94PanSti-52
94Pin-29
94PinArtP-29
94PinMusC-29
94PinPowS-PS9
94ProMag-29
94Sco-347
94ScoGolR-347
94Sel-41
94SP-194
94SPDieC-194
94Spo-66
94StaClu-315
94StaCluFDI-315
94StaCluGR-315
94StaCluMOP-315
94StaCluT-126
94StaCluTFDI-126
94Stu-210
94Top-90
94TopBlaG-22
94TopGol-90
94TopSpa-90
94TriPla-270
94TriPlaM-9
94Ult-342
94UltAllS-5
94UltAwaW-4
94UppDec-263
94UppDecED-263
94WhiSoxK-28
95Baz-26
95Bow-329
95BowBes-R45
95BowBesR-R45
95ClaPhoC-14
95ColCho-505
95ColChoGS-505
95ColChoSE-237
95ColChoSEGS-237
95ColChoSESS-237
95ColChoSS-505
95D3-39
95Don-378
95DonDom-5
95DonPreP-378
95DonTopotO-55
95Emb-123
95EmbGolI-123
95Emo-30
95Fin-173
95FinRef-173
95Fla-28
95Fle-129
95Lea-215
95LeaCor-1
95LeaLim-192
95Pac-98
95PanSti-56
95Pin-257
95PinArtP-257
95PinMusC-257
95RedFol-14
95Sco-227
95ScoGolR-227
95ScoHaloG-HG32
95ScoPlaTS-227
95Sel-2
95SelArtP-2
95SelCer-52
95SelCerMG-52
95SP-138
95SPCha-138
95SPChaDC-138
95Spo-6
95SpoArtP-6
95SPSil-138
95SPSpeF-6
95StaClu-367
95StaCluMOP-367
95StaCluSTWS-367
95StaCluVR-193
95Stu-38
95StuGolS-38
95Sum-24
95SumNthD-24
95Top-479
95TopCyb-272
95UC3-53
95UC3ArtP-53
95Ult-277
95UltGolM-277
95UppDec-201
95UppDecED-201
95UppDecEDG-201
95UppDecSE-154
95UppDecSEG-154
95WhiSoxK-30
95Zen-90
96Baz-13
96Bow-50
96BowBes-55
96BowBesAR-55
96BowBesR-55
96Cir-30
96CirBos-7
96CirRav-30
96ColCho-361
96ColCho-505
96ColChoGS-361
96ColChoGS-505
96ColChoSS-361
96ColChoSS-505
96Don-535
96DonPreP-535
96EmoXL-43
96Fin-B67
96Fin-B280
96FinRef-B67
96FinRef-B280
96Fla-61
96Fle-79
96FleTif-79
96FleWhiS-18
96Lea-172
96LeaLim-52
96LeaLimG-52
96LeaPre-45
96LeaPreP-45
96LeaPrePB-172
96LeaPrePG-172
96LeaPrePS-172
96LeaPreSG-23
96LeaPreSte-23
96LeaSig-53
96LeaSigPPG-53
96LeaSigPPP-53
96MetUni-41
96MetUniP-41
96Pac-279
96PacPri-P92
96PacPriG-P92
96PanSti-172
96Pin-19
96PinAfi-100
96PinAfiAP-100
96PinAfiFPP-100
96PinArtP-59
96PinFirR-11
96PinSta-59
96ProSta-133
96Sco-326
96ScoDugC-B51
96ScoDugCAP-B51
96Sel-51
96SelArtP-51
96SelCer-46
96SelCerAP-46
96SelCerCB-46
96SelCerCR-46
96SelCerMB-46
96SelCerMG-46
96SelCerMR-46
96SelTeaN-27
96SP-57
96Spo-79
96SpoArtP-79
96StaClu-193
96StaClu-321
96StaCluEPB-321
96StaCluEPG-321
96StaCluEPS-321
96StaCluMOP-193
96StaCluMOP-321
96StaCluVRMO-193
96Stu-40
96StuPrePB-40
96StuPrePG-40
96StuPrePS-40
96Sum-79
96SumAbo&B-79
96SumArtP-79
96SumFoi-79
96TeaOut-84
96Top-310
96TopChr-124
96TopChrR-124
96TopGal-73
96TopGalPPI-73
96TopLas-32
96TopRoaW-RW19
96Ult-339
96UltGolM-339
96UppDec-44
96Zen-80
96ZenArtP-80
96ZenMoz-3
97Bow-7
97BowBes-77
97BowBesAR-77
97BowBesR-77
97BowChr-5
97BowChrI-5
97BowChrIR-5
97BowChrR-5
97BowInt-7
97Cir-330
97CirRav-330
97ColCho-70
97ColChoAC-12
97Don-22
97DonLim-23
97DonLimLE-23
97DonPreP-22
97DonPrePGold-22
97DonTea-61
97DonTeaSPE-61
97Fin-120
97Fin-248
97FinEmb-120
97FinEmbR-120
97FinRef-120
97FinRef-248
97FlaSho-A68
97FlaSho-B68
97FlaSho-C68
97FlaShoLC-68
97FlaShoLC-B68
97FlaShoLC-C68
97FlaShoLCM-A68
97FlaShoLCM-B68
97FlaShoLCM-C68
97Fle-73
97FleTif-73
97Lea-33
97LeaFraM-33
97LeaFraMDC-33
97MetUni-62
97Pac-65
97PacLigB-65
97PacPri-23
97PacPriLB-23
97PacPriP-23
97PacPriSL-SL2B
97PacSil-65
97ProMag-52
97ProMagML-52
97Sco-180
97ScoHeaotO-6
97ScoPreS-180
97ScoShoS-180
97ScoShoSAP-180
97ScoWhiS-8
97ScoWhiSPI-8
97ScoWhiSPr-8
97SkyE-X-16
97SkyE-XC-16
97SkyE-XEC-16
97SP-46
97SpoIll-150
97SpoIllEE-150
97StaClu-43
97StaCluC-CO6
97StaCluMat-43
97StaCluMOP-43
97Stu-14
97StuPrePG-14
97StuPrePS-14
97Top-425
97TopChr-150
97TopChrR-150
97TopGal-69
97TopGalPG-PG15
97TopGalPPI-69
97TopSta-56
97TopStaAM-56
97Ult-313
97UltGolME-313
97UltPlaME-313
97UppDec-330
97UppDecU-23

Venturini, Pete (Peter Paul)
86PenWhiSP-25
87BirBarB-22
88BirBarB-11

Venturino, Phil
86MidAngP-24
86PalSprAP-18
87MidAngP-29
88EdmTraC-8
88EdmTraP-566

Venuto, Nicholas
88SouOreAP-1695
89MedAthB-14

Veras, Camilo
84IdaFalATI-27
86MadMusP-21
86MadMusP-20
87MadMusP-20
87MadMusP-15
88HunStaTI-23

Veras, Dario
94RanCucQC-25
94RanCucQF-1640
95MemChiTI-21
96MemChiB-29
97Bow-173
97BowInt-173
97ColCho-23
97Fle-629
97FleTif-629
97UppDec-268
97UppDec-379

Veras, Juan
95ChaRivTI-21

Veras, Quilvio
91KinMetC-10
91KinMetP-3824
92ClaFS7-83

92ColMetC-25
92ColMetF-306
92ColMetPI-21
92ColMetPIISPI-7
92ProFS7-289
92UppDecML-187
93BinMetF-2344
93Bow-215
93ClaFS7-146
93ClaGolF-209
93ExcFS7-81
93ExcLeaLF-6
93LimRocDWB-110
93SouAtlLAIPI-4
93SouAtlLAPI-39
94Bow-428
94ExcFS7-239
94NorTidF-2930
94TedWilDGC-DG6
94TriAAF-AAA38
94Ult-538
94UppDecML-62
95Bow-171
95BowBes-R89
95BowBesR-R89
95ColCho-8
95ColChoGS-8
95ColChoSS-8
95DonTopotO-248
95Emo-133
95Fin-287
95FinRef-287
95Fla-356
95FleUpd-100
95Lea-233
95LeaLim-159
95SigRooOJ-33
95SigRooOJP-33
95SigRooOJPS-33
95SigRooOJS-33
95SP-21
95SPCha-13
95SPChaDC-13
95SPSil-21
95StaClu-555
95StaCluCB-CB10
95StaCluMOP-555
95StaCluMOP-CB10
95StaCluSTWS-555
95Sum-140
95SumNthD-140
95Top-540
95TopTra-145T
95UppDec-237
95UppDecED-237
95UppDecEDG-237
95UppDecPAW-H37
95UppDecPAWE-H37
95UppDecSE-248
95UppDecSEG-248
96Baz-122
96ColCho-5
96ColCho-148
96ColChoGS-5
96ColChoGS-148
96ColChoSS-5
96ColChoSS-148
96Don-446
96DonPreP-446
96EmoXL-191
96Fin-B148
96FinRef-B148
96Fla-269
96Fle-397
96FleRooS-15
96FleTif-397
96Lea-171
96LeaPrePB-171
96LeaPrePG-171
96LeaPrePS-171
96LeaSigA-229
96LeaSigAG-230
96LeaSigAS-230
96MetUni-170
96MetUniMFG-12
96MetUniP-170
96Pac-67
96PacEstL-EL34
96PacGolCD-DC8
96PacPri-P28
96PacPriG-P28
96PanSti-9
96PanSti-116
96PanSti-240
96Sco-78
96ScoDugC-A64
96ScoDugCAP-A64
96StaClu-189
96StaClu-344
96StaCluEPB-344
96StaCluEPG-344
96StaCluEPS-344
96StaCluMO-44
96StaCluMOP-189
96StaCluMOP-344
96Stu-120
96StuPrePB-120
96StuPrePG-120
96StuPrePS-120
96Top-141
96TopChr-40
96TopChrR-40
96TopGal-108
96TopGalPPI-108
96TopLas-95
96Ult-204
96UltGolM-204
96UppDec-74
97Cir-112
97CirRav-112
97Don-310
97DonPreP-310
97DonPrePGold-310
97Fle-562
97FleTif-562
97Lea-294
97LeaFraM-294
97LeaFraMDC-294
97Pac-309
97PacLigB-309
97PacSil-309
97Sco-393
97ScoHobR-393
97ScoResC-393
97ScoShoS-393
97ScoShoSAP-393
97Ult-437
97UltGolME-437
97UltPlaME-437
Veras, Wilton
96LowSpiB-27
Verban, Emil
47Exh-228
48Bow-28
49Bow-38
49EurSta-73
79DiaGre-314
83TCMPla1945-26
Verbanic, Joe
67Top-442
68OPC-29
68Top-29
68TopVen-29
69Top-541
70OPC-416
70Top-416
92YanWIZ6-134
92YanWIZ7-158
Verble, Gene
88ChaLooLTI-30
Verble, Gene Kermit
53Bri-27
Verdi, Frank
55JetPos-19
78TidTidT-27
79TidTidT-4
80TidTidT-24
81ColCliP-26
81ColCliT-17
82ColCliP-26
82ColCliT-25
83SanJosBC-1
84RocRedWT-9
85RocRedWT-24
Verdi, Mike
86SanJosBP-22
87SanJosBP-19
89ElmPioP-22
90ElmPioP-25
91WinHavRSC-5
91WinHavRSP-505
Verducci, John
85EveGiaC-17
86ShrCapP-26
87PhoFirP-18
Verdugo, Luis
89MiaMirIS-20
Verdugo, Mando
88SalLakCTTI-25
89MiaMirIS-20
90KinIndTI-21
Verduzco, Dave
92NiaFalRC-25
92NiaFalRF-3323
Verduzco, Steve
93AubAstC-24
93AubAstF-3454
94OscAstC-22
94OscAstF-1148
Veres, Dave (David Scott)
86MedA'sC-53
87ModA'sC-16
87ModA'sP-3
88CalLeaACLC-10
88HunStaTI-24
88ModA'sCLC-56
88ModA'sTI-32
89HunStaB-5
90CMC-579
90ProAAAF-137
90TacTigC-2
90TacTigP-90
91AlbDukLD-21
91AlbDukP-1141
91LinDriAAA-21
92TucTorF-488
93TucTorF-3059
94TucTorF-762
95AstMot-27
95Fla-149
95Fle-470
95Pac-195
95Top-525
95TopCyb-310
96Don-17
96DonPreP-17
96ExpBoo-6
96ExpDis-21
96Fle-421
96FleTif-421
96FleUpd-U153
96FleUpdTC-U153
96LeaSigEA-209
96Pac-88
96Ult-215
96UltGolM-215
97PacPriGotD-GD171
Veres, Randy
86BelBreP-25
87BelBreP-1
88StoPorCLC-179
88StoPorP-730
89ElPasDGS-17
89FleUpd-42
90Bow-390
90BowTif-390
90BreMilB-29
90TopDeb89-130
90TopTra-125T
90TopTraT-125T
91Cla1-T56
91Don-755
91Fle-600
91OPC-694
91RicBraP-2570
91Sco100RS-12
91Top-694
91TopDesS-694
91TopMic-694
91TopTif-694
92PhoFirS-397
94BreMilB-186
94IowCubF-1276
96Don-15
96DonPreP-15
96Fle-398
96FleTif-398
Vergez, Johnny
32R33So2-401
33ButCanV-50
33Gou-233
34DiaMatCSB-187
34BatR31-176
34DiaStaR-21A
34DiaStaR-21B
34TarThoBD-16
36WorWidGV-5
93ConTSN-811
Verheist, Edwin
76VenLeaS-124
80VenLeaS-205
Verhoeff, Will
77WesHavYT-24
Verhoeven, John
77Top-91
78Top-329
79TolMudHT-12
81Don-564
81Top-603
82Fle-547
82Top-281
Verkuilen, Mike
85OrlTwiT-13
Vermillion, Grant
95BoiHawTI-32
96CedRapKTI-26
Verna, Chris
89SanBerSCLC-92
90WilBilB-24
90WilBilS-27
Vernon, Mickey
46SpoExcW-12-12
47Exh-229A
47Exh-229B
47SenGunBP-11
49Bow-94
49IndTeal-26
49IndVisEl-14
50Bow-132
51Bow-65
51TopBluB-13
52Bow-87
52NatTeaL-39
52TipTop-44
52Top-106
53BowC-159
53Bri-25
53ExhCan-59
53IndPenCBP-28
53RedMan-AL21
54Bow-152
54RedMan-AL13
55ArmCoi-24
55BigLealS-18
55Bow-46
55DaiQueS-18
55DonWin-8
55RedMan-AL12
56Top-228
57Top-92
58Top-233
59ArmCoi-20
59RedSoxJP-10
59Top-115
59TopVen-115
60SenUniMC-19
60Top-467
61SenJayP-10
61Top-134
62Top-152
62TopVen-152
63Top-402
72Dia-48
76SSP-621
76TayBow4-23
77ExpPos-34
77GalGloG-45
77OPC-198
77TCMTheWY-67
79ColCliT-29
79TCM50-87
80PacLeg-78
83TCMPla1942-19
83TopRep5-106
84ColCliP-25
84ColCliT-21
84OCoandSI-68
85ColCliT-30
86SpoDecG-38
89SweBasG-54
91TopArc1-287
92BazQua5A-12
Verplancke, Joe
96AriBlaDB-33
96HonShaHWB-35
Verrall, Jared
96ButCopKB-29
Versalles, Zoilo
61Top-21
61TopStal-186
61TwiCloD-30
61TwiJayP-12
61TwiPetM-1
61TwiUniMC-13
62Jel-86
62Pos-86
62PosCan-86
62SalPlaC-51A
62SalPlaC-51B
62ShiPlaC-51
62Top-499
62TopStal-81
63Jel-3
63Pos-3
63Top-349
63TwiJayP-12
64Top-15
64TopVen-15
64TwiJayP-12
64WheSta-46
65MacSta-10
65OPC-157
65Top-157
65TopEmbl-33
66Top-400
66TwiFaiG-16
67CokCapTw-13
67DexPre-215
67Top-270
67TopVen-226
68Top-315
68TopVen-315
69MilBra-284
69MLBOffS-45
69OPC-38
69Top-38
69TopSta-100
69TopTeaP-13
70MLBOffS-288
70OPC-365
70Top-365
72MilBra-352
75OPC-203
75Top-203
78TwiFri-22
81TCM60I-442
82K-M-7
86TwiGreT-3
88PacLegl-107
90DodTar-822
92UppDecS-29
Verstandig, Mark
88SpolndP-1943
89ChaRaiP-990
90WatDiaB-25
90WatDiaP-2382
91HigDesMC-17
91HigDesMP-2400
Veryzer, Thomas
75OPC-623
75Top-623
76Hos-109
76OPC-432
76SSP-367
76Top-432
77OPC-188
77Top-145
78OPC-14
78Top-633
79Top-537
80OPC-145
80Top-276
81AllGamPI-25
81Don-199
81Fle-390
81Top-39
82Don-450
82Fle-381
82MetPhoA-24
82OPC-387
82Top-387
82TopTra-123T
83CubThoAV-29
83Fle-559
83Top-496
83TopTra-121T
84CubChiT-31
84Nes792-117
84Top-117
84TopTif-117
85Top-405
85TopTif-405
91MetWIZ-421
Veselic, Bob
80TolMudHT-19
81TolMudHT-9
82TolMudHT-6
83TucTorT-9
Vesling, Don
88FloStaLAS-51

88LakTigS-25
89BlaYNPRWL-29
89LonTigP-1374
90CMC-378
90ProAAAF-381
90TolMudHC-1
90TolMudHP-151
91LinDriAAA-598
91TolMudHLD-598
91TolMudHP-1933
92LonTigF-632
92LonTigS-421

Vespe, Will
88CapCodPPaLP-149
89WatIndS-22
90KinIndTI-15

Vessel, Andrew
94ChaRivC-22
94ChaRivF-2687
95Bow-186
96BesAutS-92
96BesAutSA-81
96Bow-148
96Exc-113
96WesOahCHWB-33

Vessey, Tom
81TucTorT-6
82TucTorT-4

Vetsch, Dave
85VisOakT-13
86OrlTwiP-22
87OrlTwiP-27

Vezendy, Gerry
65Top-509

Viano, Jacob
94AshTouC-23
94AshTouF-1781
94SouAtlLAF-SAL32
95Exc-191
95NewHavRTI-17
96BesAutSA-82
96Exc-159
96NewHavRB-26

Viarengo, Matt
91IdaFalBP-4328
91PulBraC-28
91PulBraP-4005

Viau, Leon
87OldJudN-525

Vice, Darryl
88CapCodPPaLP-152
89ModA'sC-26
90MadMusP-2280
90ModA'sC-30
91HunStaC-25
91HunStaLD-297
91HunStaP-1806
91HunStaTI-21
91LinDriAA-297
92HunStaF-3958
92HunStaS-322
93OrlCubF-2795

Vicente, Alberto
90MarPhiP-3419

Vick, Ernie
92ConTSN-402

Vick, Scott
89TenTecGE-28

Vickers, Mike
78AshTouT-26
79AshTouT-21
80TulDriT-25

Vickers, Randy
95EveAqaTI-29
96PitMetB-27
96WisTimRB-28

Vickers, Rube
12ImpTobC-37
90DodTar-1089

Vickery, Lou
62KahAtl-23
64TulOil-7

Vico, George
49Bow-122
49Lea-47
50Bow-150
53MotCoo-25
79DiaGre-394

Victery, Joe
96EveAquB-26

Vida, James
95SpoIndTI-28

Vidal, Gilbert
96PorRocB-30

Vidal, Jose
67Top-499
68Top-432
69PilPos-23
69Top-322

Vidmar, Donald
88BenBucL-26
89PalSprACLC-50
89PalSprAP-482
90PalSprACLC-225
90PalSprAP-2578
91MidAngOHP-30
91PalSprAP-2017
92EdmTraF-3540
92EdmTraS-170
92MidAngOHP-26
92ProFS7-36
92SkyAAAF-82

Vidro, Jose
93Bow-592
93BurBeeC-25
93BurBeeF-168
93ClaFS7-147
94WesPalBEC-25
94WesPalBEF-52
95HarSenTI-23
96HarSenB-27

Viebrock, Alan
76WatRoyT-32

Vieira, Scott
96RocCubTI-30

Viera, John
90PriWilCTI-26
91PriWilCC-23
91PriWilCP-1441
92AlbYanF-2240
92AlbYanS-22
92SkyAA F-11

Viera, Jose
90HunCubP-3295
90ProAaA-190
91PeoChiC-14
91PeoChiTI-21
92WinSpiC-4
93Bow-256
93ClaFS7-31
93ClaGolF-40

Vierra, Jeff
87HawRai-6

Vierra, Joey
87HawRai-21
88GreHorP-1574
89CedRapRB-8
89CedRapRP-915
89CedRapRS-21
89Sta-189
90CMC-128
90NasSouC-3
90NasSouP-234
90ProAAAF-546
91LinDriAAA-273
91MidLeaAP-MWL9
91NasSouLD-273
91NasSouP-2157
91PeoChiP-1352
92ClaFS7-319
92NasSouF-1833
92NasSouS-296
92SkyAAAF-137
92TriA AAS-296
92WinSpiF-1217
93AlbDukF-1461
93ExcFS7-14
93SanAntMF-3006
94BirBarC-25
94BirBarF-623
95NasSouTI-28

Viggiano, Matt
88BatCliP-1683

Vignaux, M.
87AllandGN-48
88GooN16-46

Vike, Jim
86AubAstP-27

Vila, Jesus
86VerBeaDP-26

Vilella, Lazaro
84ButCopKT-26

Vilet, Tom
91BatCliC-15
91BatCliP-3499
92BatCliC-26
92BatCliF-3280
93ClePhiC-24
93ClePhiF-2698

Villa, Jose
88St.CatBJP-2008
93LinVenB-94
94VenLinU-11
95LinVen-97

Villa, Mike
86FreGiaP-9
87TamTarP-30
88CliGiaP-719

Villa, Pancho
28W512-42

Villaescusa, Juan
81VerBeaDT-23

Villafana, Jose
95NewJerCTI-30

Villafuerte, Brandon
96HilStaHWB-30
96PitMetB-28

Villalobos, Carlos
96LanJetB-29

Villalobos, Gary
91LynRedSC-19
91LynRedSP-1209
92WinHavRSC-8
92WinHavRSF-1788

Villalobos, Oswaldo
94VenLinU-243

Villalona, Kadir
92MedHatBJF-3221
92MedHatBJSP-19

Villaman, Rafael
81NasSouTI-21
82NasSouTI-26

Villano, Mike
94EveGiaC-19
94EveGiaF-3656
96SanJosGB-21
97Bow-343
97BowInt-343
97Top-494

Villanueva, Gilbert
87ChaWheP-3
88StoPorCLC-188
88StoPorP-728
89RenSilSCLC-247

Villanueva, Hector
86WinSpiP-26
87PitCubP-3
88BlaYNPRWL-116
88EasLeaAP-28
88PitCubP-1355
89BlaYNPRWL-20
89IowCubC-13
89IowCubP-1696
90CMC-93
90CubMar-21
90FleUpd-10
90IowCubC-18
90IowCubP-322
90Lea-401
90ProAAAF-629
90ScoRoo-98T
90TopTra-126T
90TopTraT-126T
90TopTVCu-62
90UppDec-741
91CubMar-19
91CubVinL-30
91Don-296
91Fle-436
91Lea-75
91OPC-362
91Sco-71
91Sco100RS-51
91StaClu-213
91StaCluP-47
91Top-362
91TopDeb90-160
91TopDesS-362
91TopMic-362
91TopTif-362
91Ult-69
91UppDec-171
92CubMar-19
92Don-725
92Fle-394
92OPC-181
92PanSti-181
92Pin-419
92Sco-677
92StaClu-858
92StaCluNC-858
92Top-181
92TopGol-181
92TopGolW-181
92TopMic-181
92TriPla-28
92Ult-477
92UppDec-102
93CadDis-60
93CarPol-23
93Don-80
93LinVenB-297
93LinVenB-317
93PacSpa-637
93StaCluCa-28
93UppDec-621
93UppDecGold-621

Villanueva, Juan
86LynMetP-24
87LynMetP-2
88FloStaLAS-24
88St.LucMS-25
89JacMetGS-12
90WicWraRD-22

Villar, Maximo
96EriSeaB-24

Villareal, Juan
90PriPatD-26

Villarreal, Modesto
95SpoIndTI-29
96LanLugB-29
96SpoIndB-29

Villegas, Ismael
96RocCubTI-31

Villegas, Mike
84ElPasDT-8

Villegas, Ramon
85MexCitTT-6

Villodas, Luis
93UppDecS-17

Villone, Ron
92TopTra-124T
92TopTraG-124T
93Bow-223
93RivPilCLC-1
93StaCluM-18
94AriFalLS-21
94Cla-36
94ClaGolF-103
94ExcFS7-129
94JacSunF-1413
94UppDecML-52
95Bow-137
95BowBes-B41
95BowBesR-B41
95Fin-305
95FinRef-305
95Fla-303
95FleUpd-78
95StaClu-601
95StaCluMOP-601
95StaCluSTWS-601
95TacRaiTI-25
95UppDec-242
95UppDecED-242
95UppDecEDG-242
96Bow-172
96StaClu-317
96StaCluMOP-317
97Fle-619
97FleTif-619
97Pac-130
97PacLigB-130
97PacSil-130
97Top-459
97Ult-469
97UltGolME-469
97UltPlaME-469

Vilorio, Frank
79TolMudHT-19
83NasAngT-16

Viltz, Corey
87JamExpP-2552
88WesPalBES-26
89WesPalBES-23

Viltz, Eski
80CedRapRT-7
81WatRedT-17
82WatRedT-15
90CedRapRDGB-26

Vina, Fernando
91ColMetPI-15
91ColMetPPI-4
92ClaFS7-352
92St.LucMCB-18
92St.LucMF-1758
93ExcFS7-82
93MarMot-25
93PacSpa-627
93StaCluMari-9
93Ult-625
94ColC-449
94ColChoGS-449
94ColChoSS-449
94Fin-341
94FinRef-341
94MetColP-28
94ScoRoo-RT134
94ScoRooGR-RT134
94Sel-384
95Pac-290
95Sco-220
95ScoGolR-220
95ScoPlaTS-220
96ColCho-197
96ColChoGS-197
96ColChoSS-197
96Fle-162
96FleTif-162
96LeaSigA-230
96LeaSigAG-231
96LeaSigAS-231
96Pac-338
96PacPri-P112
96PacPriG-P112
96StaClu-299
96StaCluMOP-299
96Ult-370
96UltGolM-370
97Cir-49
97CirRav-49
97ColCho-148
97Don-201
97DonPreP-201
97DonPrePGold-201
97Fle-139
97FleTif-139
97Lea-305
97LeaFraM-305
97LeaFraMDC-305
97Pac-129
97PacLigB-129
97PacPri-43
97PacPriLB-43
97PacPriP-43
97PacSil-129
97Pin-64
97PinArtP-64
97PinMusC-64
97Sco-301
97ScoPreS-301
97ScoShoS-301
97ScoShoSAP-301
97StaClu-81
97StaCluMOP-81
97Top-213
97Ult-84
97UltGolME-84
97UltPlaME-84
97UppDec-98

Vinas, Julio
92SouBenWSC-6
92SouBenWSF-181
93SouBenWSC-22
93SouBenWSF-1434
94MidLeaAF-MDW29
94SouBenSHC-23
94SouBenSHF-598
96BirBarB-29
96NasSouB-27
92UtiBluSC-15

Vincent, Mike
86CedRapRT-12
87CedRapRP-19

Vindivich, Paul
94RocRoyF-579

Vindvich, John
93AubAstC-25
93AubAstF-3457
94AubAstC-23
94AubAstF-3774

Vines, Ellsworth
40WheM4-2B

Vineyard, Dave
65OPC-169
65Top-169
91OriCro-468

Vinson, Chuck
68Top-328
68TopVen-328

Vinson, Clay
89GeoColC-34
90GeoColC-31
Vinson, Mabel
40WheM4-13
Vinson, Rube (Ernest Augustus)
05IndSouPSoCP-18
Vinton, William
87OldJudN-526
Vinyard, Derek
93ForLauRSC-25
93ForLauRSFP-1611
Viola, Frank
82OrlTwi8SCT-24
82TolMudHT-7
83Don-382
83Fle-625
83Top-586
83TwiTeal-11
84Don-364
84Fle-575
84MinTwiP-29
84Nes792-28
84OPC-28
84Top-28
84TopSti-312
84TopTif-28
84TwiTeal-12
85AllGamPI-89
85Don-17
85Don-436
85DonSupD-17
85Fle-291
85FleStaS-84
85Lea-17
85OPC-266
85Top-266
85Top-710
85TopGloS-7
85TopMin-266
85TopSti-300
85TopTif-266
85TopTif-710
85Twi7-2
85TwiTeal-12
86Don-194
86Fle-408
86FleStiC-124
86KayB-33
86Lea-126
86OPC-269
86Spo-99
86Top-742
86TopMinL-25
86TopSti-284
86TopTat-18
86TopTif-742
86TwiTeal-11
87Don-196
87DonHig-24
87Fle-554
87FleGlo-554
87Lea-74
87OPC-310
87RedFolSB-127
87SpoTeaP-17
87Top-206
87Top-310
87TopSti-277
87TopTif-206
87TopTif-310
88CheBoy-15
88ClaRed-183
88Don-149
88DonBasB-214
88Dra-29
88Fle-25
88FleBasM-41
88FleGlo-25
88FleGlo-WS12
88FleMin-38
88FleRecS-42
88FleSluBC-C5
88FleStiC-47
88FleWorS-12
88Lea-94
88OPC-259
88PanSti-134
88Sco-475
88ScoGlo-475
88Spo-196
88StaLinTw-20
88Top-625
88TopBig-201
88TopMinL-25
88TopRitTM-33
88TopSti-25
88TopSti-282
88TopTif-625
88TopUKM-82
88TopUKMT-82
88TwiMasBD-2
88TwiSmoC-1
88TwiTeal-10
88Woo-19
88Woo-33
89Baz-21
89Bow-150
89BowTif-150
89CadElID-60
89ClaTraO-144
89Don-23
89Don-237
89DonAll-8
89DonBasB-74
89DonPop-8
89DonSupD-23
89Fle-127
89FleAll-12
89FleBasA-43
89FleBasM-41
89FleExcS-42
89FleGlo-127
89FleHeroB-42
89FleLeaL-42
89FleSup-41
89FleWaxBC-C28
89KayB-31
89KinDis-14
89MasBreD-1
89MetKah-U4
89MSAHolD-17
89Nis-17
89OPC-120
89PanSti-237
89PanSti-248
89PanSti-383
89PanSti-475
89RedFolSB-125
89Sco-290
89ScoHot1S-5
89ScoRoo-67T
89Spo-10
89SpollIFKI-35
89Top-120
89Top-406
89TopBasT-81
89TopBig-140
89TopCapC-4
89TopCoi-30
89TopDouA-10
89TopGaloC-11
89TopGloA-10
89TopGloS-18
89TopHeaUT-7
89TopHilTM-31
89TopMinL-64
89TopSti-153
89TopSti-292
89TopStiB-30
89TopTif-120
89TopTif-406
89TopUKM-80
89TVSpoM-103
89TVSpoM-134
89UppDec-397
89UppDec-658
89UppDec-691
89Woo-3
90Bow-122
90BowTif-122
90ClaBlu-91
90ClaYel-T37
90ClaYel-NNO0
90Don-353
90DonBesN-68
90Fle-219
90FleCan-219
90Lea-93
90MetColP-11
90MetFanC-29
90MetKah-29
90MSAIceTD-16
90OPC-470
90PubSti-297
90PubSti-339
90Sco-500
90Spo-122
90StaLonJS-7
90StaLonJS-18
90Top-470
90TopBig-162
90TopDou-67
90TopMag-108
90TopSti-95
90TopTif-470
90TopTVM-18
90UppDec-626
90USPlaCA-1D
90VenSti-469
91BasBesAotM-18
91Bow-477
91Cla3-T92
91ClaGam-1
91Don-529
91Fle-165
91Lea-180
91MetCol8-5
91MetColP-11
91MetKah-29
91MetTro-9
91MetWIZ-422
91OPC-60
91OPC-406
91PanCanT1-59
91PanCanT1-68
91PanCanT1-76
91PanFreS-87
91PanSti-84
91RedFolS-98
91Sco-460
91Sco-687
91Sco-882
91Sco100S-70
91Sev3DCN-15
91SevCoi-NE15
91StaClu-292
91StaCluCM-31
91Stu-210
91Top-60
91Top-406
91TopCraJI-4
91TopDesS-60
91TopDesS-406
91TopMic-60
91TopMic-406
91TopSta-34
91TopTif-60
91TopTif-406
91Ult-227
91UppDec-122
91USPlaCA-7C
92Bow-491
92Cla2-T80
92ClaGam-196
92Don-498
92DonUpd-U10
92Fle-518
92FleUpd-5
92Lea-221
92New-30
92OPC-510
92OPCPre-115
92PanSti-229
92Pin-407
92RedSoxDD-28
92Sco-220
92Sco100S-62
92ScoRoo-6T
92SpoStaCC-48
92StaClu-785
92StaCluD-190
92Stu-140
92Top-510
92TopGol-510
92TopGolW-510
92TopMic-510
92TopTra-125T
92TopTraG-125T
92TriPlaG-GS6
92Ult-319
92UppDec-277
92UppDec-733
93Bow-171
93Don-91
93Fin-33
93FinRef-33
93Fla-169
93Fle-185
93FunPac-166
93Lea-21
93OPC-228
93PacSpa-38
93Pin-76
93RedSoxWHP-28
93Sco-55
93Sel-94
93SP-207
93StaClu-147
93StaCluFDI-147
93StaCluMOP-147
93Stu-72
93Top-270
93TopGol-270
93TopInaM-270
93TopMic-270
93TriPla-178
93Ult-157
93UppDec-48
93UppDec-131
93UppDecGold-48
93UppDecGold-131
94Bow-35
94ColC-283
94ColChoGS-283
94ColChoSS-283
94Don-321
94ExtBas-28
94Fin-406
94FinRef-406
94Fle-46
94Lea-60
94OPC-88
94Pac-69
94Pin-348
94PinArtP-348
94PinMusC-348
94RedFolMI-26
94RedFolMI-27
94Sco-331
94ScoGolR-331
94Spo-137
94StaClu-569
94StaCluFDI-569
94StaCluGR-569
94StaCluMOP-569
94Top-140
94TopGol-140
94TopSpa-140
94TriPla-210
94Ult-320
94UppDec-127
94UppDecED-127
95ColCho-419
95ColChoGS-419
95ColChoSS-419
95Fle-43
95Pin-386
95PinArtP-386
95PinMusC-386
Viola, Lance
79NewCoPT-23
Violat, Juan
09T206-521
Viox, James
14B18B-82A
14B18B-82B
15SpoNewM-182
16SpoNewM-180
Virchis, Adam
96HicCraB-26
Virdon, Bill
55Bow-296
55CarHunW-28
56Top-170
57Top-110
58Hir-45
58Top-198
59Top-190
59Top-543
59TopVen-190
60KeyChal-48
60Lea-40
60PirTag-18
60Top-496
61PirJayP-12
61Pos-135
61Top-70
61Top-306
61TopStal-72
62Jel-175
62Kah-38
62Pos-175
62PosCan-175
62SalPlaC-168
62ShiPlaC-168
62Top-415
62TopStal-181
63Jel-142
63Kah-30
63PirIDL-26
63PirJayP-12
63Pos-142
63Top-55
64Kah-29
64PirKDK-28
64Top-268
64Top-495
64TopVen-268
65Kah-44
65OPC-69
65Top-69
72Top-661
73OPC-517
73Top-517A
73Top-517B
74SyrChiTI-28
75OPC-611
75SyrChiTI-22
75Top-611
75YanSSP-9
76OPC-147
76Top-147
77Top-327
78AstBurK-1
78Top-279
79AstTeal-1
79TCM50-100
79Top-381
80Top-82
81Don-384
81Fle-61
81Top-678
82Don-144
83ExpPos-25
83ExpStu-1
83OPC-6
83Top-516
84ExpPos-34
84ExpStu-2
84ExpStu-38
84Fle-658
84Nes792-111
84OPC-111
84Top-111
84TopTif-111
86AstGreT-12
88PacLegI-49
89SweBasG-119
91SweBasG-93
93PirNatI-34
94PirQui-25
94TopArc1-257
94TopArc1G-257
94UppDecAH-54
94UppDecAH1-54
Virgil, Ossie
77SpaPhiT-21
80CarMudF-3
81OklCit8T-19
82Top-231
83Don-606A
83Don-606B
83Fle-175
83PhiTas-28
83Top-383
84Don-326
84Fle-49
84Nes792-484
84PhiTas-26
84Top-484
84TopTif-484
85AllGamPI-135
85Don-82
85Fle-267
85Lea-250
85OPC-103
85PhiCIG-3
85PhiTas-10
85PhiTas-26
85ThoMcAD-46
85Top-143
85Top-611
85TopSti-110
85TopTif-143
85TopTif-611
86BasStaB-116
86BraPol-9
86Don-137

86DonAll-26
86Fle-456
86FleUpd-122
86OPC-95
86Top-95
86TopSti-115
86TopTif-95
86TopTra-119T
86TopTraT-119T
87BraSmo-12
87Don-67
87DonOpeD-45
87Fle-532
87FleGlo-532
87OPC-183
87Top-571
87TopTif-571
88Don-143
88DonAll-50
88DonBasB-85
88Fle-552
88FleGlo-552
88Lea-64
88MSAJifPD-17
88OPC-291
88PanSti-241
88RedFolSB-93
88Sco-129
88ScoGlo-129
88Spo-217
88StaLinBra-20
88Top-755
88TopBig-148
88TopSti-36
88TopStiB-24
88TopTif-755
89BlaYNPRWLU-33
89Don-145
89Fle-605
89FleGlo-605
89OPC-179
89RedFolSB-126
89Sco-111
89Spo-94
89Top-179
89TopSti-28
89TopTif-179
89UppDec-104
90BluJayFS-30
90CMC-348
90EliSenL-15
90ProAAAF-355
90SyrChiC-22
90SyrChiMB-26
90SyrChiP-575
91PacSenL-150
91PacSenL-159
93LinVenB-235
Virgil, Ossie Sr.
57Top-365
58Top-107
59Top-203
61Top-67
62Top-327
63RocRedWSP-8
65Top-571
67OPC-132
67Top-132
76ExpRed-34
76VenLeaS-1
77ExpPos-35
79ExpPos-30
80ExpPos-33
81TigDetN-135
84PadMot-27
84PadSmo-26
85Top-143
85TopTif-143
86MarMot-28
87MarMot-28
89PacSenL-22
91OriCro-469
91PacSenL-138
91PacSenL-159
96BelGiaTI-34
Virgilio, George
90PulBraB-19
90PulBraP-3089
91PulBraC-10
91PulBraP-4016
92MacBraC-5
92MacBraF-278
94HarSenF-2101
95BowBayTI-1
95HarSenTI-15
Viskas, Steve
79QuaCitCT-25
Visner, Joseph
87OldJudN-527
Vitale, Tony
86FreGiaP-28
Vitato, Richard
82ChaRoyT-14
83ChaRoyT-9
Vitiello, Joe
91Cla/Bes-404
91ClaDraP-5
91EugEmeC-15
91EugEmeP-3742
92BasCitRC-1
92BasCitRF-3855
92ClaDraP-94
92ClaFS7-24
92ProFS7-80
92UppDec-73
92UppDecML-309
93Bow-13
93Bow-367
93ClaFisN-1
93ClaGolF-83
93ClaGolLF-3
93ClaGolP-4
93ClaYouG-YG26
93ExcFS7-180
93MemChiF-384
93StaClu-570
93StaCluFDI-570
93StaCluMOP-570
93StaCluRoy-14
94Bow-415
94Cla-91
94ClaGolF-123
94OmaRoyF-1232
94SigRoo-50
94SigRooS-50
94Top-769
94TopGol-769
94TopSpa-769
94UppDecML-44
95ActPacF-37
95Bow-211
95Exc-68
95ExcLeaL-18
95FleUpd-50
95LinVen-274
95OmaRoyTI-28
95Pin-424
95PinArtP-424
95PinETA-3
95PinMusC-424
95Sel-198
95SelArtP-198
95SelCer-106
95SelCerMG-106
95StaClu-557
95StaCluMOP-557
95StaCluSTWS-557
95Sum-120
95SumNthD-120
95Top-637
95UC3-121
95UC3ArtP-121
95UppDec-247
95UppDecED-247
95UppDecEDG-247
95UppDecML-190
95Zen-126
96ColCho-177
96ColChoGS-177
96ColChoSS-177
96Don-304
96DonPreP-304
96Fla-96
96Fle-140
96FleTif-140
96Lea-159
96LeaPrePB-159
96LeaPrePG-159
96LeaPrePS-159
96LeaSigA-231
96LeaSigAG-232
96LeaSigAS-232
96Pin-175
96PinAfi-133
96PinAfiAP-133
96RoyPol-26
96Sco-243
96ScoDugC-A108
96ScoDugCAP-A108
96Sel-128
96SelArtP-128
96StaClu-24
96StaCluMOP-24
96Sum-29
96SumAbo&B-29
96SumArtP-29
96SumFoi-29
96Top-411
96Ult-76
96UltGolM-76
96UppDec-87
97Don-296
97DonPreP-296
97DonPrePGold-296
97Lea-267
97LeaFraM-267
97LeaFraMDC-267
97Pac-113
97PacLigB-113
97PacSil-113
97Pin-17
97PinArtP-17
97PinMusC-17
97RoyPol-22
97Sco-412
97ScoHobR-412
97ScoResC-412
97ScoShoS-412
97ScoShoSAP-412
95UppDecMLFS-190
Vitko, Joe
90ColMetGS-21
90ColMetPPI-3
90SouAtlLAS-45
91St.LucMC-15
91St.LucMP-711
92BinMetF-516
92BinMetS-69
92Bow-516
92ClaFS7-354
92SkyAA F-32
93Don-354
93UppDec-10
93UppDecGold-10
94BinMetF-705
Vito, Frank
91PacSenL-158
Vitt, Ossie (Oscar)
14FatPlaT-50
15SpoNewM-183
16ColE13-179
16SpoNewM-181
17HolBreD-109
21E121So1-109
21E121So8-101
22W575-143
23W501-9
40PlaBal-47
92ConTSN-495
Vivas, Domingo
91BilMusP-3753
91BilMusSP-7
Vivenzio, Augie
92PulBraC-18
92PulBraF-3183
Vizcaino, Jose
88BakDodCLC-240
88CalLeaACLC-47
89AlbDukC-23
89AlbDukP-82
90AlbDukC-20
90AlbDukP-355
90AlbDukT-29
90Bow-98
90BowTif-98
90ClaUpd-T49
90CMC-422
90DodTar-1090
90Fle-410
90FleCan-410
90ProAAAF-76
90Sco-613
90TopDeb89-131
90UppDec-44
91Bow-427
91CubMar-16
91CubVinL-31
91Don-724
91Fle-223
91Lea-323
91Sco-787
91Sco100RS-88
91UppDec-580
92CubMar-16
92Don-212
92Lea-270
92OPC-561
92Sco-169
92StaClu-359
92Top-561
92TopGol-561
92TopGolW-561
92TopMic-561
92Ult-182
93CubMar-28
93DiaMar-114
93Don-582
93Fla-23
93Fle-385
93Lea-499
93OPC-345
93PacBeiA-18
93PacJugC-36
93PacSpa-384
93StaClu-68
93StaCluCu-20
93StaCluFDI-68
93StaCluMOP-68
93Stu-218
93Top-237
93TopGol-237
93TopInaM-237
93TopMic-237
93Ult-322
93UppDec-211
93UppDecGold-211
94ColC-284
94ColC-532
94ColChoGS-284
94ColChoGS-532
94ColChoSS-284
94ColChoSS-532
94Don-291
94ExtBas-328
94Fin-312
94FinRef-312
94Fla-203
94Fle-400
94FleUpd-163
94Lea-68
94MetColP-29
94Pac-113
94PanSti-159
94Pin-141
94PinArtP-141
94PinMusC-141
94Sco-370
94ScoGolR-370
94ScoRoo-RT40
94ScoRooGR-RT40
94Sel-275
94SpoRoo-17
94SpoRooAP-17
94StaClu-89
94StaClu-662
94StaCluFDI-89
94StaCluFDI-662
94StaCluGR-89
94StaCluGR-662
94StaCluMOP-89
94StaCluMOP-662
94StaCluT-356
94StaCluTFDI-356
94Top-638
94TopGol-638
94TopSpa-638
94TopTra-120T
94TriPla-79
94Ult-167
94Ult-539
94UppDec-122
94UppDec-329
94UppDecED-122
94UppDecED-329
95ColCho-316
95ColChoGS-316
95ColChoSS-316
95Don-325
95DonPreP-325
95DonTopotO-298
95Fla-387
95Fle-385
95Lea-122
95Pac-291
95PacPri-94
95Sco-436
95ScoGolR-436
95ScoPlaTS-436
95StaClu-25
95StaCluFDI-25
95StaCluMOP-25
95StaCluSTWS-25
95StaCluVR-17
95Top-14
95TopCyb-12
95Ult-202
95UltGolM-202
95UppDec-363
95UppDecED-363
95UppDecEDG-363
96ColCho-626
96ColChoGS-626
96ColChoSS-626
96Don-431
96DonPreP-431
96EmoXL-239
96Fla-327
96Fle-490
96FleTif-490
96LeaSigA-232
96LeaSigAG-233
96LeaSigAS-233
96MetKah-33
96MetUni-206
96MetUniP-206
96Pac-138
96PacPri-P49
96PacPriG-P49
96PanSti-32
96ProSta-72
96Sco-214
96StaClu-360
96StaCluEPB-360
96StaCluEPG-360
96StaCluEPS-360
96StaCluMOP-360
96StaCluVRMO-17
96TeaOut-85
96Top-307
96Ult-248
96UltGolM-248
96UppDec-401
97Cir-201
97CirRav-201
97ColCho-452
97Fin-191
97FinRef-191
97Fle-91
97Fle-601
97FleTif-91
97FleTif-601
97Pac-81
97PacLigB-81
97PacSil-81
97Sco-449
97ScoHobR-449
97ScoResC-449
97ScoShoS-449
97ScoShoSAP-449
97StaClu-88
97StaCluMOP-88
97Top-297
97Ult-363
97UltGolME-363
97UltPlaME-363
Vizcaino, Julian
93BoiHawC-26
93BoiHawF-3925
94CedRapKF-1119
Vizcaino, Junior
87WatPirP-14
88CarLeaAS-18
88SalBucS-22
89HarSenP-293
89HarSenS-20
90HarSenP-1202
90HarSenS-19
Vizcaino, Romulo
94EliTwiC-25
94EliTwiF-3745
94ForWayWC-25
94ForWayWF-2024
95ForWayWTI-25
Vizquel, Omar
86WauTimP-27
87SalSpuP-19
88BasAmeAAB-4
88EasLeaAP-37
88VerMarP-946
89CalCanC-23

89CalCanP-537
89DonBasB-163
89DonRoo-53
89FleUpd-62
89MarMot-15
89ScoRoo-105T
89TopTra-122T
89TopTraT-122T
89UppDec-787
90Bow-474
90BowTif-474
90Don-483
90Fle-528
90FleCan-528
90Lea-88
90MarMot-12
90OPC-698
90PubSti-445
90Sco-264
90Sco100RS-37
90ScoYouSI-28
90Top-698
90TopBig-140
90TopDeb89-132
90TopGloS-59
90TopRoo-28
90TopTif-698
90UppDec-233
90VenSti-470
91Bow-245
91Don-231
91Fle-464
91Lea-91
91MarCouH-9
91OPC-298
91PanFreS-231
91Sco-299
91StaClu-195
91Top-298
91TopDesS-298
91TopMic-298
91TopTif-298
91Ult-345
91UppDec-593
92Bow-423
92Don-641
92Fle-296
92Lea-265
92MarMot-16
92OPC-101
92PanSti-58
92Pin-97
92Sco-162
92ScoProP-22
92StaClu-163
92Top-101
92TopGol-101
92TopGolW-101
92TopMic-101
92TriPla-137
92Ult-436
92UppDec-401
93Bow-599
93Don-25
93Fla-276
93Fle-316
93Lea-434
93LinVenB-23
93LinVenB-341
93MarMot-14
93OPC-379
93PacSpa-292
93PacSpaGE-20
93PanSti-61
93Pin-95
93Sco-102
93Sco-503
93Sel-164
93SP-135
93StaClu-67
93StaCluFDI-67
93StaCluMari-25
93StaCluMOP-67
93Top-68
93TopGol-68
93TopInaM-68
93TopMic-68
93TriPla-193
93Ult-274
93UppDec-301
93UppDecGold-301
94Bow-579
94ColC-285
94ColC-629
94ColChoGS-285
94ColChoGS-629
94ColChoSS-285
94ColChoSS-629
94Don-328
94ExtBas-70
94Fin-285
94FinRef-285
94Fla-290
94Fle-301
94FleUpd-38
94Lea-331
94OPC-267
94Pac-583
94PacAll-20
94PanSti-124
94Pin-64
94PinArtP-64
94PinMusC-64
94Sco-87
94ScoGolR-87
94ScoRoo-RT10
94ScoRooGR-RT10
94Sel-321
94SpoRoo-9
94SpoRooAP-9
94StaClu-93
94StaClu-572
94StaCluFDI-93
94StaCluFDI-572
94StaCluGR-93
94StaCluGR-572
94StaCluMOP-93
94StaCluMOP-572
94Top-593
94TopGol-593
94TopSpa-593
94TopTra-93T
94Ult-125
94Ult-352
94UltAwaW-5
94UppDec-486
94UppDecED-486
94VenLinU-42
94VenLinU-57
95ColCho-269
95ColChoGS-269
95ColChoSS-269
95Don-36
95DonPreP-36
95DonTopotO-69
95Fla-253
95Fle-150
95Lea-386
95LinVen-13
95LinVen-267
95Pac-131
95PacPri-42
95PanSti-69
95Pin-129
95PinArtP-129
95PinMusC-129
95Sco-429
95ScoGolR-429
95ScoPlaTS-429
95Spo-134
95SpoArtP-134
95StaClu-334
95StaCluMOP-334
95StaCluSTDW-I334
95StaCluSTMP-20
95StaCluSTWS-334
95StaCluVR-174
95Sum-64
95SumNthD-64
95Top-404
95TopCyb-205
95UC3-23
95UC3ArtP-23
95Ult-43
95UltAwaW-5
95UltAwaWGM-5
95UltGolM-43
95UppDec-338
95UppDecED-338
95UppDecEDG-338
95UppDecSE-26
95UppDecSEG-26
96ColCho-528
96ColChoGS-528
96ColChoSS-528
96Don-251
96DonPreP-251
96EmoXL-57
96Fla-77
96Fle-103
96FleInd-18
96FleTif-103
96LeaSigA-233
96LeaSigAG-234
96LeaSigAS-234
96MetUni-55
96MetUniP-55
96Pac-293
96PacEstL-EL35
96PacPri-P99
96PacPriG-P99
96Pin-113
96PinAfi-98
96PinAfiAP-98
96PinAfiFPP-98
96SchDis-5
96Sco-207
96Sel-42
96SelArtP-42
96StaClu-199
96StaClu-308
96StaCluEPB-308
96StaCluEPG-308
96StaCluEPS-308
96StaCluMOP-199
96StaCluMOP-308
96StaCluVRMO-174
96Sum-18
96SumAbo&B-18
96SumArtP-18
96SumFoi-18
96Top-84
96Ult-55
96UltGolM-55
96UppDec-56
97Cir-67
97CirRav-67
97ColCho-86
97Don-196
97DonPre-131
97DonPreCttC-131
97DonPreP-196
97DonPrePGold-196
97DonTea-81
97DonTeaSPE-81
97Fin-78
97FinRef-78
97Fle-92
97FleTif-92
97Lea-84
97LeaFraM-84
97LeaFraMDC-84
97MetUni-88
97Pac-82
97PacCar-9
97PacCarM-9
97PacGolCD-9
97PacLatotML-10
97PacLigB-82
97PacPri-28
97PacPriGA-GA6
97PacPriLB-28
97PacPriP-28
97PacSil-82
97Pin-154
97PinArtP-154
97PinCer-38
97PinCerMBlu-38
97PinCerMG-38
97PinCerMR-38
97PinCerR-38
97PinMusC-154
97PinTotCPB-38
97PinTotCPG-38
97PinTotCPR-38
97PinX-P-66
97PinX-PMoS-66
97Sco-153
97ScoInd-6
97ScoIndPl-6
97ScoIndPr-6
97ScoIndU-6
97ScoIndUTC-6
97ScoPreS-153
97ScoShoS-153
97ScoShoSAP-153
97StaClu-124
97StaCluMOP-124
97Stu-57
97StuPrePG-57
97StuPrePS-57
97Top-173
97TopGal-80
97TopGalPPI-80
97Ult-56
97UltGolME-56
97UltPlaME-56
97UppDec-54
97UppDec-146

Vizzini, Dan
90SouOreAB-21
90SouOreAP-3447
91SouOreAC-20
91SouOreAP-3846

Vlasis, Chris
91JohCitCC-13
91JohCitCP-3992
92SprCarC-13
92SprCarF-884
94SavCarC-27
94SavCarF-522

Vlcek, Jim
86SalRedBP-27
89SanDieSAS-28
92ChaRanC-17
93KanCouCC-22
93KanCouCF-916
93KanCouCTI-26

Vodvarka, Rob
83ButCopKT-12

Voeltz, Bill
87Ft.LauYP-16
87OneYanP-19
87PriWilYP-16
88Ft.LauYS-23

Vogel, George
84SavCarT-20

Vogel, Mike
92SouBenWSC-10
93SarWhiSF-1373
93SouBenWSF-1435

Vogelgesang, Joe
92GreFalDSP-28
93MedHatBJF-3738
93MedHatBJSP-10

Vogler, Peter
91BriBanF-13

Voigt, Jack
87NewOriP-7
88HagSunS-23
89FreKeyS-24
90Bes-103
90EasLeaAP-EL8
90HagSunB-15
90HagSunP-1430
90HagSunS-25
91HagSunLD-248
91HagSunP-2470
91LinDriAA-248
92RocRedWF-1953
92RocRedWS-472
92SkyAAAF-215
93Bow-678
93FleFinE-167
93LinVenB-246
93RocRedWF-255
93SelRoo-141T
93TopTra-27T
94Fle-23
94OriPro-101
94OriUSPC-5D
94OriUSPC-11C
94Pac-47
94Sco-580
94ScoGolR-580
94Sel-105
94StaClu-491
94StaCluFDI-491
94StaCluGR-491
94StaCluMOP-491
94StaCluT-292
94StaCluTFDI-292
94Top-117
94TopGol-117
94TopSpa-117
94Ult-10
94VenLinU-219
95ColCho-337
95ColChoGS-337
95ColChoSS-337
95Don-327
95DonPreP-327
95Fle-22
95RanCra-34
95Sco-249
95ScoGolR-249
95ScoPlaTS-249
95Ult-8
95UltGolM-8
96OklCit8B-23

Voigt, Paul
80WisRapTT-12
83AlbDukT-7
85NasSouTI-24

Voisard, Mark
92BenRocC-3
92BenRocF-1475
92ClaFS7-444
93CenValRC-25
93CenValRF-2894
93Top-476
93TopGol-476
93TopInaM-476
93TopMic-476
94CenValRC-24
94CenValRF-3204
95Exc-192
95NewHavRTI-NNO
95SalAvaTI-5

Voiselle, Bill
47Exh-230
47TipTop-134
49EurSta-27
79DiaGre-36
83TCMPla1944-37

Voit, David
89BelBreIS-23
89HelBreSP-12
90EriSaiS-30
91RenSilSCLC-26
91SydWavF-19

Voita, Sam
96WesOahCHWB-24

Volkert, Rusty
94MedHatBJF-3684
94MedHatBJSP-24
95StCatSTI-6
96HagSunB-22

Volkman, Keith
96BoiHawB-30

Vollmer, Clyde
50Bow-53
51Bow-91
52Bow-57
52Top-255
53BowC-152
53Bri-26
53Top-32
54Bow-136
55Bow-13
79DiaGre-267
83TopRep5-255
91TopArc1-32

Vollmer, Gus
90CliGiaB-11
90CliGiaP-2562

Vollmer, Robby
83WauTimF-16

Vollmer, Scott
94HicCraC-24
94HicCraF-2181
94SouAtlLAF-SAL27
96BirBarB-11

Voltaggio, Vic
88T/MUmp-32
89T/MUmp-30
90T/MUmp-29

Volunteers, Tennessee
95TenVolW-15

Von Der Ahe, Christian
87BucN28-105
87LonJacN-12
87OldJudN-528
90BasWit-77

Von Hoff, Bruce
68Top-529

Von Ohlen, Dave
79JacMetT-15
80TidTidT-1
81TidTidT-18
82TidTidT-23
83LouRedR-8
84Car-32
84Don-205
84Fle-340
84LouRedR-9
84Nes792-489
84Top-489
84TopTif-489
85Don-412

85Fle-243
85FleUpd-126
85Ind-33
85IndPol-38
85Top-177
85TopTif-177
85TopTifT-127T
85TopTra-127T
86Fle-597
86Top-632
86TopTif-632
87Fle-408
87FleGlo-408
87Top-287
87TopTif-287
Von Ohlen, David
77LynMetT-28
86MiaMarP-25
87TacTigP-7
88MiaMarS-24
VonDerleith, Scott
92BelBreC-2
Vondran, Steve
89BilMusP-2057
89FreStaBS-20
91CedRapRC-20
91CedRapRP-2723
91Cla/Bes-346
Vontz, Doug
87BurExpP-1095
Voorhees, Mark
77SpoIndC-NNO
Vopata, Nate
95HudValRTI-6
96ChaRivTI-9630
Vorbeck, Eric
91YakBeaC-2
91YakBeaP-4263
92BakDodCLC-26
93VerBeaDC-23
93VerBeaDF-2235
Vosberg, Ed
84BeaGolGT-6
85BeaGolGT-5
86LasVegSP-22
87LasVegSP-24
88BlaYNPRWL-62
88LasVegSC-7
88LasVegSP-222
89TucTorC-6
89TucTorJP-26
89TucTorP-192
90CMC-533
90PhoFirC-6
90PhoFirP-11
90ProAAAF-37
91EdmTraLD-172
91EdmTraP-1516
91LinDriAAA-172
91Sco-757
91Sco100RS-80
93IowCubF-2134
94TacTigF-3176
94TopTra-64T
94TriAAF-AAA20
95RanCra-35
96FleRan-17
96FleUpd-U91
96FleUpdTC-U91
96LeaSigEA-210
96RanMot-23
Vosik, Bill
90NebCor-27
91WatIndC-23
91WatIndP-3378
92SalLakTSP-2
Voskovitch, Milo
72CedRapCT-20
Vosmik, Joe
32OrbPinNP-35
32OrbPinUP-56
33DelR33-20
33DouDisP-40
33TatOrb-56
34BatR31-68
34ButPreR-60
34DiaStaR-8
34Gou-77
35GouPuzR-8I
35GouPuzR-9I
36ExhFou-11
36GouBWR-23
36GouWidPPR-B22
36GouWidPPR-B23
36GouWidPPR-B24
36GouWidPPR-C24
36NatChiFPR-74
36OveCanR-44
36SandSW-48
36WheBB4-11
36WorWidGV-76
37GouFliMR-2A
37GouFliMR-2B
37GouThuMR-2
38ExhFou-9
38GouHeaU-247
38GouHeaU-271
39GouPreR303A-45
39GouPreR303B-23
39PlaBal-107
39WorWidGTP-45
40DodTeal-22
40PlaBal-144
41DodTeal-9
41DouPlaR-143
90DodTar-823
91ConTSN-221
93ConTSN-767
Voss, Bill
66Top-529
68OPC-142
68Top-142
68TopVen-142
69Top-621
70OPC-326
70Top-326
71BreTeal-17
71MLBOffS-454
71OPC-671
71Top-671
72Top-776
94BreMilB-187
Voss, Strongman
88GooN16-47
Vossler, Dan
74OPC-602
74TacTwiC-13
74Top-602
Vota, Mike
96SouBenSHS-27
Vranjes, Sam
91SanBerSC-28
91SanBerSP-1991
Vuchinch, Steve
86A'sMot-26
90A'sMot-28
Vuckovich, Pete
77OPC-130
77Top-517
78CarTeal-25
78OPC-157
78Top-241
79Car5-32
79Hos-87
79Top-407
80OPC-31
80Top-57
81Don-189
81Fle-547A
81OPC-193
81Top-193
81TopTra-851
82BrePol-50
82Don-458
82Fle-156
82FleSta-141
82OPC-132
82Top-165
82Top-643
82Top-703
82TopSti-10
82TopSti-202
83BreGar-20
83BrePol-50
83Don-80
83Fle-49
83FleSta-207
83FleSti-14
83Kel-19
83OPC-375
83OPC-394
83Top-321
83Top-375
83Top-394
83TopSti-86
84BreGar-21
84BrePol-50
84Fle-217
84Nes792-505
84OPC-313
84Top-505
84TopTif-505
85BreGar-21
85BrePol-50
85Top-254
85TopTif-254
86Don-473
86Fle-504
86OPC-152
86Top-737
86TopTif-737
90SweBasG-83
92BreCarT-24
94BreMilB-280
Vujovic, Dragan
82MonNew-21
Vukovich, George
80VenLeaS-263
81Fle-21
81OklCit8T-20
81Top-598
82Fle-262
82Top-389
83Don-315
83Fle-176
83IndPos-38
83IndWhe-31
83Top-16
83TopTra-122T
84Don-468
84Fle-555
84Ind-31
84IndWhe-24
84Nes792-638
84Top-638
84TopTif-638
85Don-276
85Fle-458
85Ind-34
85IndPol-24
85Lea-120
85Top-212
85TopSti-249
85TopTif-212
86Don-346
86Fle-598
86OPC-337
86Top-483
86TopSti-214
86TopTif-483
87JapPlaB-34
91PacSenL-45
Vukovich, John
73OPC-451
73Top-451
74OPC-349
74Top-349
75OPC-602
75Top-602
76SSP-43
80PhiBurK-8
81Fle-22
82CubRedL-NNO
83CubThoAV-NNO
84CubChiT-32
84CubSev-NNO
85CubSev-NNO
86CubGat-NNO
87CubCan-36
87CubDavB-NNO
88PhiTas-38
89PhiTas-35
90PhiTas-34
91PhiMed-35
92PhiMed-31
93PhiMed-33
94BreMilB-371
94PhiMed-34
95Phi-33
96PhiTeal-33
Vuksan, Jeff
78AppFoxT-24
79AppFoxT-8
80AppFoxT-7
81DurBulT-12
Vukson, John
94YakBeaC-28
94YakBeaF-3852
95YakBeaTI-35
Vuz, John
87PocGiaTB-14
88CliGiaP-693
90SanJosGB-22
90SanJosGCLC-52
90SanJosGP-2001
90SanJosGS-24
Waag, Billy
81BufBisT-14
Wabeke, Doug
81ShrCapT-18
Wacha, Chuck
87GreHorP-7
89WinHavRSS-26
Wachs, Thomas
85LitFalMT-11
86ColMetP-26
87LynMetP-3
Wachter, Derek
92BelBreC-18
92BelBreF-421
93StoPorC-25
93StoPorF-759
94ExcFS7-89
95LinVen-194
Wacker, Wade
89EliTwiS-27
Waco, David
94SpaPhiF-1732
94SparPhiC-21
95ClePhiF-226
Wada, Hank (Hiromi)
83SanJosBC-2
86SanJosBP-23
Waddell, James
91PerHeaF-17
Waddell, Rube (George E.)
03BreE10-146
04FanCraAL-47
08AmeCarE-33
08RosComP-74
09ColChiE-294A
09ColChiE-294B
09ColChiE-294C
09PC7HHB-43
09T206-362
09T206-363
10StaCarE-27
10W555-62
11SpoLifCW-357
11SpoLifM-119
11TurRedT-39
12ColRedB-294A
12ColRedB-294B
12ColRedB-294C
12ColTinT-294A
12ColTinT-294B
12ColTinT-294C
36PC7AlbHoF-48
48ExhHoF-29
50CalHOFW-73
50H80FouMH-4
60Fle-61
61Fle-149
76ShaPiz-48
77BobParHoF-48
80LauFamF-11
80PerHaloFP-48
80SSPHOF-48
86ConSer1-35
88ConHar-6
88ConSer5-29
90PerGreM-52
93ConTSN-931
94OriofB-95
94UppDecTAE-13
96PitPosH-12
Waddell, Tom
84FleUpd-123
84Ind-32
84IndWhe-54
84TopTra-125T
84TopTraT-125T
85Don-582
85Fle-459
85Ind-35
85IndPol-54
85Top-453
85TopTif-453
86Don-94
86Fle-599
86IndOhH-54
86IndTeal-43
86OPC-86
86Top-86
86TopSti-209
86TopTif-86
87IndGat-54
87Top-657
87TopTif-657
Wade, Ben
50W720HolS-31
52Top-389
53Top-4
54Top-126
59DarFar-22
61UniOil-SD12
83TopRep5-389
90DodTar-824
91TopArc1-4
94TopArc1-126
94TopArc1G-126
95TopArcBD-29
95TopArcBD-38
95TopArcBD-74
Wade, Darrin
88DunBluJS-19
88St.CatBJP-2036
Wade, Gale
55Top-196
Wade, Jake
50WorWidGV-3
Wade, Scott
86NewBriRSP-25
87PawRedSP-71
87PawRedST-20
88PawRedSC-23
88PawRedSP-458
89PawRedSC-15
89PawRedSP-695
89PawRedSTI-27
90CMC-274
90PawRedSC-23
90PawRedSDD-29
90PawRedSP-476
90ProAAAF-448
90TopTVRS-65
91LinDriAAA-497
91ScrRedBLD-497
91ScrRedBP-2554
92IowCubF-4064
92SyrChiS-519
93IowCubF-2146
Wade, Terrell
92IdaFalGF-3514
92IdaFalGSP-9
93MacBraC-1
93MacBraF-1401
93SouAtlLAGF-43
94ActPac-32
94Bow-329
94BowBes-B23
94BowBesR-B23
94Cla-170
94Cla-AU2
94ClaCreotC-C12
94ClaGolF-118
94ColC-649
94ColChoGS-649
94ColChoSS-649
94ExcAllF-10
94ExcFS7-162
94GreBraF-415
94GreBraTI-26
94SP-17
94SPDieC-17
94Top-316
94TopGol-316
94TopSpa-316
94Ult-452
94UppDec-527
94UppDecAHNIL-13
94UppDecED-527
94UppDecML-7
94UppDecML-91
94UppDecML-255
94UppDecMLPotYF-PY5
95ActPacF-5
95Bow-111
95ColChoSE-5
95ColChoSEGS-5
95ColChoSESS-5
95Exc-159
95Fle-321
95RicBraRC-27
95RicBraTI-25
95Top-316
95UppDec-213
95UppDecED-213
95UppDecEDG-213
95UppDecML-5

95UppDecML-166
95UppDecMLMLA-9
95UppDecMLOP-OP1
95UppDecSE-18
95UppDecSEG-18
96BesAutSA-83
96Bow-367
96ColCho-461
96ColChoGS-461
96ColChoSS-461
96Don-533
96DonPreP-533
96Fin-B285
96FinRef-B285
96Fle-309
96FleBra-17
96FleTif-309
96Lea-144
96LeaPre-112
96LeaPreP-112
96LeaPrePB-144
96LeaPrePG-144
96LeaPrePS-144
96LeaSig-132
96LeaSigA-234
96LeaSigAG-235
96LeaSigAS-235
96LeaSigPPG-132
96LeaSigPPP-132
96Pin-169
96PinAfi-176
96PinAfiAP-176
96PinArtP-95
96PinSta-95
96Sco-501
96Sel-195
96SelArtP-195
96SelCer-133
96SelCerAP-133
96SelCerCB-133
96SelCerCR-133
96SelCerMB-133
96SelCerMG-133
96SelCerMR-133
96Spo-137
96SpoArtP-137
96Sum-185
96SumAbo&B-185
96SumArtP-185
96SumFoi-185
96Ult-446
96UltGolM-446
96Zen-129
96ZenArtP-129
97Cir-236
97CirRav-236
97ColCho-29
97Don-322
97DonEli-79
97DonEliGS-79
97DonLim-129
97DonLimLE-129
97DonPreP-322
97DonPrePGold-322
97DonTea-30
97DonTeaSPE-30
97Fle-270
97FleTif-270
97Lea-144
97LeaFraM-144
97LeaFraMDC-144
97NewPin-62
97NewPinAP-62
97NewPinMC-62
97NewPinPP-62
97PacPriGotD-GD115
97PinIns-69
97PinInsCE-69
97PinInsDE-69
97Sco-199
97ScoBra-11
97ScoBraPl-11
97ScoBraPr-11
97ScoPreS-199
97ScoShoS-199
97ScoShoSAP-199
97Top-3
97Ult-161
97UltGolME-161
97UltPlaME-161
97UppDec-14
95UppDecMLFS-5
95UppDecMLFS-166

Wade, Wallace
40WheM4-11

Wadley, Tony
82MiaMarT-7
83IdaFalAT-13

Waggoner, Aubrey
86AppFoxP-27
87PenWhiSP-8
89BirBarB-8
89BirBarP-114
90BirBarB-13
90BirBarP-1120
90CMC-817
91BirBarLD-72
91BirBarP-1468
91LinDriAA-72
92GreBraF-1167
92GreBraS-247
93CalCanF-1180
93ClaFS7-293
94GreBraTI-27

Waggoner, Jay
96LakTigB-28

Waggoner, Jimmy
89MedAthB-25
90MadMusB-9
90ModA'sC-31
90ModA'sCLC-166
90ModA'sP-2223
91Cla/Bes-89
91ModA'sC-26
91ModA'sP-3100
92CalLeaACL-20
92RenSilSCLC-55
93HunStaF-2091
94HunStaF-1340
95HunStaTI-27

Wagner, Adam
90Ft.LauYS-27
91PriWilCC-27
92PriWilCC-29

Wagner, Billy
93AubAstC-1
93AubAstF-3445
94Bow-642
94BowBes-B19
94BowBesR-B19
94Cla-140
94ClaGolF-18
94ClaGolN1PLF-LP16
94ClaGolREF-RE16
94ClaTriF-T34
94ColC-29
94ColChoGS-29
94ColChoSS-29
94ExcFS7-209
94MidLeaAF-MDW54
94Pin-264
94PinArtP-264
94PinMusC-264
94QuaCitRBC-1
94QuaCitRBF-532
94Sco-536
94ScoGolR-536
94SigRoo-49
94SigRooS-49
94SP-18
94SPDieC-18
94TedWil-134
94Top-209
94TopGol-209
94TopSpa-209
94UppDec-524
94UppDecAHNIL-14
94UppDecED-524
94UppDecML-86
95ActPacF-48
95Bow-1
95BowBes-B32
95BowBes-X14
95BowBesR-B32
95BowBesR-X14
95Exc-208
95ExcLeaL-19
95JacGenTI-8
95TusTorTI-28
95UppDecML-60
95UppDecMLOP-OP12
96Bow-336
96BowBes-148
96BowBesAR-148
96BowBesMI-10
96BowBesMIAR-10
96BowBesMIR-10
96BowBesP-BBP8
96BowBesPAR-BBP8
96BowBesPR-BBP8
96BowBesR-148
96BowMinLP-13
96ColCho-425
96ColChoGS-425
96ColChoSS-425
96Don-398
96DonPreP-398
96Fin-S313
96FinRef-S313
96Fle-422
96FleTif-422
96Lea-218
96LeaPre-121
96LeaPreP-121
96LeaPrePB-218
96LeaPrePG-218
96LeaPrePS-218
96LeaSig-80
96LeaSigPPG-80
96LeaSigPPP-80
96SP-12
96Top-212
96TopChr-74
96TopChrR-74
96TopGal-128
96TopGalPPI-128
96TusTorB-24
96UppDec-225
96UppDecBCP-BC11
96Zen-112
96ZenArtP-112
97Bow-54
97BowCerBIA-CA81
97BowCerGIA-CA81
97BowChr-42
97BowChrI-42
97BowChrIR-42
97BowChrR-42
97BowInt-54
97Cir-324
97CirRav-324
97ColCho-123
97Don-91
97DonEli-51
97DonEliGS-51
97DonLim-86
97DonLimLE-86
97DonPre-135
97DonPreCttC-135
97DonPreP-91
97DonPrePGold-91
97Fin-102
97FinEmb-102
97FinEmbR-102
97FinRef-102
97FlaSho-A13
97FlaSho-B13
97FlaSho-C13
97FlaShoLC-13
97FlaShoLC-B13
97FlaShoLC-C13
97FlaShoLCM-A13
97FlaShoLCM-B13
97FlaShoLCM-C13
97Fle-354
97FleTif-354
97Lea-5
97LeaFraM-5
97LeaFraMDC-5
97MetUni-141
97NewPin-34
97NewPinAP-34
97NewPinMC-34
97NewPinPP-34
97Pin-183
97PinArtP-183
97PinCer-102
97PinCerMBlu-102
97PinCerMG-102
97PinCerMR-102
97PinCerR-102
97PinIns-131
97PinInsCE-131
97PinInsDE-131
97PinMusC-183
97PinTotCPB-102
97PinTotCPG-102
97PinTotCPR-102
97PinX-P-98
97PinX-PMoS-98
97Sco-32
97ScoPreS-32
97ScoShoS-32
97ScoShoSAP-32
97SP-86
97SpoIll-52
97SpoIllEE-52
97StaClu-33
97StaCluMat-33
97StaCluMOP-33
97Stu-23
97StuPrePG-23
97StuPrePS-23
97Top-22
97TopAwel-AI19
97TopGal-178
97TopGalPPI-178
97TopStaFAS-FAS12
97Ult-212
97UltGolME-212
97UltPlaME-212
97UppDec-81
95UppDecMLFS-60
97UppDecTTS-TS7

Wagner, Bret
93BazTeaU-22
93TopTra-124T
94NewJerCC-27
94NewJerCF-3419
94SigRooDP-19
94SigRooDPS-19
94StaCluDP-86
94StaCluDPFDI-86
94TopTra-41T
95Bes-97
95Bow-128
95BowBes-B59
95BowBesR-B59
95Exc-276
95ScoDraP-DP2
95SPML-155
95StaClu-113
95StaCluFDI-113
95StaCluMOP-113
95StaCluSTWS-113
95Top-167
95UppDec-8
95UppDecED-8
95UppDecEDG-8
95UppDecSE-93
95UppDecSEG-93
96BesAutSA-84
96Bow-237
96Exc-232
96HunStaTI-25
96Top-430

Wagner, Bull (William G.)
14B18B-63
90DodTar-1091

Wagner, Butts (Albert)
90DodTar-1092

Wagner, Charlie
08AmeCarE-95
46RedSoxTI-22
78ReaRem-21
79DiaGre-238
80ElmPioRST-39
87ElmPio(C-33

Wagner, Dale
93JohCitCC-27
93JohCitCF-3679

Wagner, Dan
87PenWhiSP-29
88BirBarB-13
89BirBarB-5
89BirBarP-90
90MidAngGS-20

Wagner, Darrell
90BenBucL-16

Wagner, Gary
66OPC-151
66Top-151
66TopVen-151
67Top-529
68Top-448
69Top-276
69TopSta-158
70Top-627
71OPC-473
71Top-473
81TCM60I-437

Wagner, Gerald
86DurBulP-26
87SumBraP-28

Wagner, Harold
46RedSoxTI-23
47TipTop-13
77TCMTheWY-61
85TCMPla1-1

Wagner, Hector
88EugEmeB-6
89AppFoxP-849
90Bes-194
90MemChiB-18
90MemChiP-1008
90MemChiS-25
90ProAaA-34
91Bow-299
91LinDriAAA-347
91OmaRoyLD-347
91OmaRoyP-1036
91Sco-730
91TopDeb90-161
92StaClu-323

Wagner, Heinie (Charles)
08RosComP-8
09RamT20-120
09SpoNewSM-86
09T206-364
09T206-365
10DomDisP-119
10E-UOraBSC-22
10E12AmcCDC-36
10RedCroT-253
10SweCapPP-7
11BasBatEU-40
11SpoLifCW-358
11SpoLifM-18
11T205-175
12HasTriFT-10B
12HasTriFT-24
12RedSoxBASP-5
12RedSoxBDASP-3
12T207-188
12T207-189
14CraJacE-31
15CraJacE-31
15VicT21-28
42RedSoxTI-24

Wagner, Honus (John)
03BreE10-147
03WilCarE-29
06FanCraNL-49
08AmeCarE-96
08AmeLeaPC-15
08RosComP-156
09AmeCarE-113
09AmeCarE-114
09ColChiE-295
09MaxPubP-15
09PhiCarE-22
09SpoNewSM-11
09SpoNewSM-36
09T206-366
09WWSmiP-1
09WWSmiP-2
10CouT21-240
10DarChoE-32
10E-UOraBSC-23
10E101-44A
10E101-44B
10E102-25A
10E102-25B
10E12AmeCDC-37
10E12AmeCDC-38
10E98-28
10JuJuDE-40
10MelMinE-44A
10MelMinE-44B
10NadCarE-49A
10NadCarE-49B
10NadE1-56
10PeoT21-56A
10PeoT21-56B
10PeoT21-56C
10PeoT21-56D
10PirAmeCE-10
10PirHerP-11
10PirTipTD-4
10RedCroT-80
10RedCroT-163
10SepAnoP-5
10SepAnoP-24
10StaCarE-28
10W555-61
11BasBatEU-41
11DiaGumP-28
11E94-29
11PloCanE-64
11SpoLifCW-359

11SpoLifM-260
12ColRedB-295
12ColTinT-295
13NatGamW-41
13PolGroW-28
13TomBarW-37
14CraJacE-68
14TexTomE-44
14TexTomE-63
15AmeCarE-40A
15AmeCarE-40B
15CraJacE-68
15SpoNewM-184
16BF2FP-94
16ColE13-180
16FleBreD-97
16SpoNewM-182
16TanBraE-18
24MrsShePP-10
36NatChiFPR-75
36PC7AlbHoF-5
36R31PasP-47
36R31Pre-L13
40PlaBal-168
46SpoExcW-8-8
47TipTop-149
48ExhHoF-30
49Lea-70
50CalHOFW-74
51TopConMA-11
60ExhWriH-24
60Fle-62
61Fle-150
61GolPre-32
63BasMagM-83
63BazA-10
63HalofFB-20
67TopVen-143
68LauWorS-6
68SpoMemAG-14
69Baz-8
69Baz-12
69SCFOldT-5
70FleWorS-6
72FleFamF-21
72KelATG-9
73HalofFPP-18
76GalBasGHoF-29
76JerJonPC-6
76MotOldT-1
76OPC-344
76RowExh-15
76ShaPiz-5
76TayBow4-97
76TayBow4-NNO
76Top-344
77BobParHoF-49
77GalGloG-148
77ShaPiz-18
79Pew-7
80LauFamF-1
80MarExhH-30
80PacLeg-18
80PerHaloFP-5
80SSPHOF-5
81ConTSN-64
81SpoHaloF-1
82BHCRSpoL-10
83DiaClaS2-66
83DonHOFH-5
83Oco& SSBG-18
84GalHaloFRL-5
84OCoandSI-110
84OCoandSI-163
84OCoandSI-179
85UltBasC-2
86ConSer1-55
86PirGreT-3
86TCMSupS-38
87NesDreT-4
88FriBasCM-1
88GreBasS-54
89HOFStiB-14
89PacLegI-211
89SweBasG-4
90BasWit-84
90PerGreM-24
90SweBasG-50
91CadEllD-59
91ConTSN-8
91SweBasG-126
91USGamSBL-10C
91USGamSBL-10D
91USGamSBL-10H
91USGamSBL-10S
92RevLeg1-4
92RevLeg1-5
92RevLeg1-6
92Sco-880
92St.VinHHS-11
92WhiLegtL-4
92WhiPro-4
93ActPacA-86
93ActPacA2-20G
93CadDis-61
93ConMasB-4
93ConTSN-754
93CraJac-3
93Hoy-8
93LegFoi-12
93LegFoiP-2
93SpeHOF2-3
93UppDecAH-124
93UppDecAH-139
93UppDecAH-145
94ConTSN-1219
94ConTSNB-1219
94TedWil-81
94TedWilLC-LC17
94UppDecAH-55
94UppDecAH-163
94UppDecAH1-55
94UppDecAH1-163
94UppDecTAE-20
96ColCho-504
96ColChoGS-504
96ColChoSS-504
Wagner, Jeff
83AndBraT-33
84DurBulT-7
85DurBulT-31
Wagner, Joe
94BelBreC-25
94BelBreF-101
96StoPorB-18
Wagner, Ken
96WatIndTI-32
Wagner, Kyle
95BoiHawTI-33
Wagner, Leon
47Exh-231
59Top-257
60Top-383
61Top-547
61TopDicG-17
62AngJayP-11
62Jel-77
62Pos-77
62PosCan-77
62SalPlaC-57A
62SalPlaC-57B
62ShiPlaC-57
62Top-491
62TopBuc-90
62TopStal-71
63AngJayP-19
63ExhStaB-62
63Fle-21
63Jel-28
63Pos-28A
63Pos-28B
63SalMetC-55
63Top-4
63Top-335
64Kah-30
64Top-41
64Top-530
64TopCoi-6
64TopCoi-130
64TopGia-54
64TopVen-41
64WheSta-47
65Kah-45
65OldLonC-36
65Top-367
65TopEmbl-31
65TopTral-33
66Baz-8
66IndTeal-12
66OPC-65
66Top-65
66TopVen-65
67AshOil-11
67Baz-8
67CokCapA-33
67CokCapAAm-33
67CokCapI-12
67DexPre-216
67Kah-39
67OPC-109
67OPCPapI-24
67Top-109
67Top-360
67TopPos-24
67TopVen-207
68Kah-B36
68Top-495
69OPC-187
69Top-187
69TopFou-23
78TCM60I-125
86AngGreT-5
94CarLeaA-DJ17
Wagner, Mark
75CliPilT-18
77Top-490
79Top-598
80OPC-13
80Top-29
81Don-126
81Fle-478
81Top-358
81TopTra-852
82Don-163
82Fle-333
82Top-443
83Don-268
83Fle-582
83Top-144
84TacTigC-89
85Top-581
85TopTif-581
89PacSenL-170
91LinDriAAA-600
91PacSenL-112
91TolMudHLD-600
91TolMudHP-1948
92BriTigC-27
93FayGenC-25
93FayGenF-144
93RanKee-367
94LakTigC-27
96ChaLooB-3
Wagner, Matt
94SigRooDP-64
94SigRooDPS-64
95Bes-41
95Bow-70
95PorCitRTI-26
96Bow-370
96BowBes-116
96BowBesAR-116
96BowBesR-116
96TacRaiB-27
97Bow-83
97BowInt-83
97ColCho-384
97Fle-215
97Fle-528
97FleTif-215
97FleTif-528
97Ult-127
97UltGolME-127
97UltPlaME-127
Wagner, Paul
89WelPirP-26
90AugPirP-2464
91CarLeaAP-CAR38
91SalBucC-21
91SalBucP-951
92CarMudF-1181
92CarMudS-146
92DonRoo-120
92SkyAA F-68
93Bow-458
93Don-334
93FleFinE-121
93FleMajLP-B10
93Lea-466
93Pin-282
93PirNatl-35
93Sco-315
93SelRoo-148T
93StaClu-710
93StaCluFDI-710
93StaCluMOP-710
93TopTra-109T
93Ult-457
93UppDec-643
93UppDecGold-643
94ColC-433
94ColChoGS-433
94ColChoSS-433
94Don-611
94ExtBas-353
94Fin-309
94FinRef-309
94Fle-623
94Lea-220
94Pac-510
94PirQui-26
94Sco-578
94ScoGolR-578
94StaClu-505
94StaCluFDI-505
94StaCluGR-505
94StaCluMOP-505
94Top-157
94TopGol-157
94TopSpa-157
94Ult-261
94UppDec-383
94UppDecED-383
95ColCho-382
95ColChoGS-382
95ColChoSS-382
95Don-421
95DonPreP-421
95Fla-190
95Fle-491
95Lea-354
95PirFil-28
95Top-317
95Ult-428
95UltGolM-428
96ColCho-676
96ColChoGS-676
96ColChoSS-676
96Don-421
96DonPreP-421
96Fle-534
96FleTif-534
96LeaSigA-235
96LeaSigAG-236
96LeaSigAS-236
96Pac-171
96Ult-538
96UltGolM-538
96UppDec-438
97Cir-336
97CirRav-336
97UppDec-464
Wagner, Steve
77OrlTwiT-22
78OrlTwiT-22
Wahl, Kermit
79DiaGre-265
Wahl, Tim
88BelBreGS-17
89BelBreIS-24
Waid, Patrick
87AriWilP-17
88SalLakCTTI-1
89SalLakTTI-1
Wainhouse, Dave
89BowTif-358
89WesPalBES-24
90WesPalBES-25
91HarSenLD-272
91HarSenP-627
91LinDriAA-272
92ExpDonD-17B
92IndIndF-1860
92IndIndS-197
92ProFS7-260
92SkyAAAF-95
92TopDeb91-177
93ExcFS7-64
93FleFinE-276
93StaCluMari-3
93Ult-626
96CarMudB-11
Wainright, Helen
28W512-37
Waite, Jon
92HunCubC-21
92HunCubF-3149
Waite, Steve
92FayGenC-12
Waites, Steve
95ButCopKtl-27
Waitkus, Ed
47Exh-232A
47Exh-232B
47Exh-232C
47PM1StaP1-213
47TipTop-118
49Bow-142
49EurSta-151
49PhiBul-57
49PhiLumPB-12
50Bow-30
50Dra-12
50PhiPhil-4
51BerRos-C9
51Bow-28
51TopBluB-51
52Bow-92
52TipTop-45
52Top-158
54OriEss-34
55Bow-4
55OriEss-25
79TCM50-77
83PhiPosGPaM-7
83TopRep5-158
87Phi195T-4
91OriCro-470
Waits, M. Rick
74SpoIndC-32
75OklCit8TI-10
75SpoIndC-16
76OPC-433
76SSP-513
76Top-433
77BurCheD-61
77Hos-88
77PepGloD-16
77Top-306
78OPC-191
78Top-37
79Hos-35
79OPC-253
79Top-484
80OPC-94
80Top-168
81Don-201
81Fle-396
81OPC-258
81Top-697
82Don-33
82Fle-382
82Ind-35
82IndTeal-33
82IndWhe-10
82OPC-142
82Top-573
83Don-263
83Fle-422
83IndPos-39
83IndWhe-32
83Top-779
83TopTra-123T
84Nes792-218
84Top-218
84TopTif-218
85Don-368
85Fle-600
85Top-59
85TopTif-59
85VanCanC-219
86Fle-505
86Top-614
86TopTif-614
86VanCanP-27
89PacSenL-91
89T/MSenL-109
89TopSenL-60
91PacSenL-15
92MCIAmb-10
93RanKee-368
94BreMilB-86
Wakamatsu, Don
86TamTarP-24
87CedRapRP-16
88ChaLooB-12
89BirBarB-16
89BirBarP-107
90CMC-649
90ProAAAF-169
90VanCanC-22
90VanCanP-491
91LinDriAAA-648
91VanCanLD-648
91VanCanP-1598
92AlbDukF-724
92AlbDukS-22
92Sco-814
92TopDeb91-178
93AlbDukF-1465

Wakamatsu, Tsutomu
79TCMJapPB-20
Wakana, Josh
83TidTidT-25
Wakatabe, Kenichi
96MauStiHWB-26
Wakefield, Bill
64Top-576
65OPC-167
65Top-167
66Top-443
91MetWIZ-423
Wakefield, Dick
46SpoExcW-8-1B
47Exh-233
47TipTop-45
48KelPep*-BB5
49Bow-91
49Lea-50
50RemBre-25
77TCMTheWY-66
79DiaGre-391
79TCM50-90
83TCMPla1943-14
Wakefield, Tim
88WatPirP-27
89WelPirP-27
90SalBucS-23
91CarMudLD-119
91CarMudP-1087
91LinDriAA-119
92BufBisBS-24
92BufBisF-324
92BufBisS-45
92DonRoo-121
92FleUpd-117
92ProFS7-308
92ScoRoo-92T
92SkyAAAF-20
93Bow-570
93ClaGam-96
93Don-61
93Fin-37
93FinRef-37
93Fla-118
93Fle-123
93FleRooS-RSB9
93FunPac-152
93HumDumC-45
93LeaFas-2
93LeaGolR-R8
93OPC-227
93PacSpa-254
93PanSti-279
93Pin-401
93PinTea2-6
93PirNatI-36
93Sco-347
93Sel-307
93SelChaR-16
93StaClu-13
93StaCluFDI-13
93StaCluM-51
93StaCluMOP-13
93StaCluMP-12
93Stu-83
93Top-163
93TopGol-163
93TopInaM-163
93TopMic-163
93Toy-24
93TriPla-50
93Ult-104
93UppDec-66
93UppDec-480
93UppDecGold-66
93UppDecGold-480
93USPlaCR-13D
94BufBisF-1838
94Don-471
94Fle-624
94Lea-155
94Pac-511
94Pin-448
94PinArtP-448
94PinMusC-448
94Sco-418
94ScoGolR-418
94StaClu-152
94StaCluFDI-152
94StaCluGR-152
94StaCluMOP-152
94Top-669
94TopGol-669
94TopSpa-669
94Ult-262
95Fin-298
95FinRef-298
95PawRedSDD-27
95PawRedTI-NNO
95SPCha-126
95SPChaDC-126
95TopTra-95T
95UppDec-480T
96Baz-27
96Cir-15
96CirRav-15
96ColCho-474
96ColChoGS-474
96ColChoSS-474
96Don-487
96DonPreP-487
96DonSho-7
96Fin-B101
96FinRef-B101
96Fla-30
96Fle-39
96FleRedS-18
96FleTif-39
96Lea-111
96LeaPrePB-111
96LeaPrePG-111
96LeaPrePS-111
96MetUni-22
96MetUniP-22
96Pac-253
96PacPri-P82
96PacPriG-P82
96PanSti-140
96Sco-25
96ScoDugC-A24
96ScoDugCAP-A24
96StaClu-249
96StaCluMOP-249
96Top-138
96TopGal-43
96TopGalPPI-43
96Ult-23
96UltGolM-23
96UltSeaC-10
96UltSeaCGM-10
96UppDec-19
96UppDec-148
97Cir-286
97CirRav-286
97ColCho-284
97Don-219
97DonPreP-219
97DonPrePGold-219
97DonTea-52
97DonTeaSPE-52
97Fle-33
97FleTif-33
97ProMag-49
97ProMagML-49
97Sco-461
97ScoHobR-461
97ScoResC-461
97ScoShoS-461
97ScoShoSAP-461
97StaClu-264
97StaCluMOP-264
97Top-66
97Ult-441
97UltGolME-441
97UltPlaME-441
Walania, Alan
93ElmPioC-25
93ElmPioF-3824
94KanCouCC-25
94KanCouCF-162
94KanCouCTI-29
Walbeck, Greg
93PacSpa-385
Walbeck, Matt
87WytCubP-2
88ChaWheB-1
89PeoChiTI-15
90HunCubP-3285
90PeoChiUTI-U4
91CarLeaAP-CAR45
91WinSpiC-15
91WinSpiP-2832
92ChaKniF-2775
92ChaKniS-170
93Bow-384
93ExcFS7-15
93FleFinE-11
93Pin-607
93StaCluCu-28
93Top-812
93TopGol-812
93TopInaM-812
93TopMic-812
93Ult-323
93UppDec-509
93UppDecGold-509
94Bow-20
94ColC-670
94ColChoGS-670
94ColChoSS-670
94ExtBas-125
94Fin-436
94FinJum-436
94FinRef-436
94Fla-78
94FleUpd-66
94LeaGolR-14
94LeaLimR-39
94OPC-227
94Pin-487
94PinArtP-487
94PinMusC-487
94ScoRoo-RT154
94ScoRooGR-RT154
94SpoRoo-68
94SpoRooAP-68
94StaClu-561
94StaCluFDI-561
94StaCluGR-561
94StaCluMOP-561
94Stu-201
94Top-329
94TopGol-329
94TopSpa-329
94TopTra-69T
94Ult-396
94UppDec-130
94UppDecED-130
95ColCho-481
95ColChoGS-481
95ColChoSS-481
95Don-320
95DonPreP-320
95DonTopotO-116
95Fin-19
95FinRef-19
95Fle-216
95Lea-219
95Pac-258
95Pin-403
95PinArtP-403
95PinMusC-403
95Sco-265
95ScoGolR-265
95ScoPlaTS-265
95StaClu-76
95StaCluFDI-76
95StaCluMOP-76
95StaCluSTWS-76
95Top-471
95TopCyb-265
95Ult-79
95UltGolM-79
96ColCho-603
96ColChoGS-603
96ColChoSS-603
96Don-106
96DonPreP-106
96Fla-124
96Fle-179
96FleTif-179
96LeaSigA-236
96LeaSigAG-237
96LeaSigAS-237
96MetUni-83
96MetUniP-83
96Pac-363
96PanSti-205
96StaClu-75
96StaCluMOP-75
96Ult-97
96UltGolM-97
96UppDec-388
97Fle-159
97FleTif-159
97PacPriGotD-GD68
97Ult-517
97UltGolME-517
97UltPlaME-517
Walberg, Bill
82JacMetT-25
Walberg, Rube (George)
28W56PlaC-JOK
31W517-41
32OrbPinUP-57
33Gou-145
33Gou-183
33GouCanV-76
33RitCE-12S
33TatOrb-57
36NatChiFPR-76
81ConTSN-59
91ConTSN-91
94ConTSN-1151
94ConTSNB-1151
Walbring, Larry
76CliPilT-33
Walden, Alan
90BurIndP-3009
91ColIndC-17
91ColIndP-1484
92ColRedC-21
92ColRedF-2391
Walden, Ron
90ClaDraP-9
90ClaYel-T82
90GreFalDSP-1
91Bow-615
91OPC-596
91Sco-679
91Top-596
91TopDesS-596
91TopMic-596
91TopTif-596
93VerBeaDC-24
93VerBeaDF-2219
Walden, Travis
88ClePhiS-26
Waldenberger, Dave
89IdaFalBP-2019
92SanBerC-26
92SanBerSF-968
93RivPilCLC-21
Waldow, Joe
89GasRanP-998
Waldrep, Art
94BenRocF-3594
95AshTouTI-7
97BenRocC-23
Waldron, Joe
91ChaRaiC-11
91ChaRaiP-96
92WatDiaC-2
92WatDiaF-2142
93WatDiaF-1769
94WesPalBEC-26
94WesPalBEF-40
95JacGenTI-9
Waldrop, Tom
92IdaFalGF-3522
92IdaFalGSP-8
93MacBraC-26
93MacBraF-1416
94DurBulC-24
94DurBulF-342
94DurBulTI-26
95MacBraTI-29
Wales, Gary
91ParPatF-11
Walewander, James
86GleFalTP-23
87IntLeaAT-17
87TolMudHP-5
87TolMudHT-7
88Sco-571
88ScoGlo-571
88TigPep-32
88Top-106
88TopTif-106
89Don-415
89Fle-150
89FleGlo-150
89Sco-311
89TolMudHC-15
89TolMudHP-770
89Top-467
89TopTif-467
89UppDec-454
90CMC-212
90ColCliC-12
90ColCliP-21
90ColCliP-686
90ProAAAF-336
90TopTVY-65
91ColCliLD-122
91ColCliP-22
91ColCliP-607
91LinDriAAA-122
93VanCanF-2607
94EdmTraF-2883
Walgast, Ad
11TurRedT-53
Walk, Bob
81Don-393
81Fle-14
81Top-494
81TopTra-853
82BraBurKL-24
82BraPol-43
82Top-296
83Don-401
83Fle-149
83FleSti-93
83RicBraT-10
83Top-104
84HawIslC-141
85HawIslC-243
86Don-430
86TopTra-120T
86TopTraT-120T
87Don-203
87Fle-623
87FleGlo-623
87Top-628
87TopTif-628
88Don-514
88DonBasB-269
88Fle-342
88FleGlo-342
88Sco-162
88ScoGlo-162
88Top-349
88TopTif-349
89Bow-409
89BowTif-409
89Don-172
89DonAll-58
89DonBasB-145
89Fle-223
89FleGlo-223
89OPC-66
89OPC-151
89PirVerFJ-17
89Sco-224
89Spo-34
89Top-504
89TopSti-123
89TopTif-504
89UppDec-438
90Bow-163
90BowTif-163
90Don-370
90DonBesN-94
90Fle-482
90FleCan-482
90Lea-64
90OPC-754
90PirHomC-31
90PubSti-167
90Sco-21
90Top-754
90TopBig-23
90TopSti-125
90TopTif-754
90UppDec-596
90VenSti-471
91Bow-526
91Don-157
91Fle-54
91Lea-450
91OPC-29
91Sco-599
91StaClu-14
91StaCluP-50
91Top-29
91TopDesS-29
91TopMic-29
91TopTif-29
91UppDec-689
92Bow-666
92Don-88
92Fle-572
92Lea-353
92OPC-486
92Pin-410
92PirNatI-25
92Sco-54
92ScoProP-15
92StaClu-746

92StaCluNC-746
92Top-486
92TopGol-486
92TopGolW-486
92TopMic-486
92UppDec-619
93Don-546
93Fle-505
93Lea-134
93PacSpa-593
93PanSti-286
93Pin-380
93PirNatl-37
93Sco-144
93StaClu-421
93StaCluFDI-421
93StaCluM-77
93StaCluMOP-421
93Top-685
93TopGol-685
93TopInaM-685
93TopMic-685
93Ult-458
93UppDec-78
93UppDecGold-78
94Don-395
94Fle-625
94Pac-512
94Pin-457
94PinArtP-457
94PinMusC-457
94Sco-356
94ScoGolR-356
94Top-434
94TopGol-434
94TopSpa-434

Walkanoff, A.J.
95YakBeaTI-36
96VerBeaDB-28

Walkden, Mike
91GreFalDSP-23
91HigSchPLS-22
92BakDodCLC-27
92StaClu-852
92StaCluD-191
92StaCluECN-852
94BakDodC-24
95VerBeaDTI-29

Walker, Al
80BurBeeT-13

Walker, Andy
79QuaCitCT-20
83TopRep5-319

Walker, Bernie
87CedRapRP-25
88ChaLooB-23
89ChaLooB-20
89ChaLooGS-22
89SouLeaAJ-7
91ChaLooLD-173
91LinDriAA-173
91NasSouP-2171

Walker, Bert
85CloHSS-41

Walker, Bill
33Gou-94
33GouCanV-57
34DiaMatCSB-189
34BatR31-116
36NatChiFPR-77
74Car193T-24
93ConTSN-789

Walker, Billy
91MiaMirC-4

Walker, Cam (Cameron)
84ElPasDT-22
86ElPasDP-23
87ElPasDP-18
87WicPilRD-25

Walker, Chico
81PawRedST-22
83PawRedST-24
84PawRedST-16
85IowCubT-11
86IowCubP-26
87CubCan-37
87CubDavB-29
87Don-539
87OPC-58
87Top-695
87TopTif-695
88EdmTraP-561
89SyrChiC-23
89SyrChiMB-23
89SyrChiP-792
90ChaKniTI-7
91Cla3-T93
91CubMar-24
91CubVinL-32
91Lea-501
91UltUpd-74
92Don-439
92Fle-395
92FleUpd-107
92OPC-439
92Sco-578
92StaClu-564
92Top-439
92TopGol-439
92TopGolW-439
92TopMic-439
92Ult-183
92UppDec-617
93Don-410
93Fle-482
93Lea-149
93MetColP-49
93MetKah-34
93PacSpa-549
93Sco-399
93StaClu-114
93StaCluFDI-114
93StaCluMOP-114
93Ult-80
93UppDec-727
93UppDecGold-727
94Pac-419

Walker, Chris
88BatCliP-1677
89ClePhiS-24

Walker, Cliff (Clifton)
85BenPhiC-23
87SpaPhiP-16

Walker, Corey
96DanBraB-27

Walker, Curtis
21E121So1-110
21Exh-182
22E120-208
22W572-111
22W575-145
27AmeCarE-58
92ConTSN-417

Walker, Dane
92MadMusC-4
92MadMusF-1251
93ModA'sC-22
93ModA'sF-812
95HunStaTI-28
96WesMicWB-28

Walker, Darcy
86WinSpiP-27

Walker, Dave
94BluOriC-26
96HigDesMB-3

Walker, Dennis
89UtiBluSP-26
90SouBenWSB-12
90SouBenWSGS-20
91SouBenWSC-6
91SouBenWSP-2866
92SarWhiSCB-13
92SarWhiSF-216
93BirBarF-1201

Walker, Dixie (Ewart)
10SenWasT-7

Walker, Dixie (Fred)
34DiaStaR-12A
34DiaStaR-12B
34DiaStaR-12C
34Gou-39
34GouCanV-86
35GouPuzR-8E
35GouPuzR-9E
36R31PasP-38
39ExhSal-61A
39ExhSal-61B
40DodTeal-23
41DouPlaR-21
42DodTeal-23
43DodTeal-22
46SpoExcW-8-1A
47PM1StaP1-214
48BluTin-45
49EurSta-174
53Top-190
55CarHunW-29
61Fle-151
75YanDyn1T-48
76TayBow4-52
79DiaGre-82
80DodGreT-7
83TCMPla1945-30
88WilMulP-8
89DodSmoG-49
90DodTar-825
91RinPosBD4-11
91TopArc1-190
92BazQua5A-22
92ConTSN-506
95ConTSN-1387

Walker, Doak
51BerRos-B14
52Whe-28A
52Whe-28B

Walker, Duane
79NaSouTI-25
80IndIndTI-26
81IndIndTI-21
82IndIndTI-6
83Don-624
83Fle-606
83Top-243
84Don-325
84Fle-485
84FleSti-41
84Nes792-659
84RedEnq-10
84Top-659
84TopTif-659
85Don-608
85Fle-554
85Lea-52
85RedYea-18
85Top-441
85TopSti-52
85TopTif-441
86Don-500
86Fle-574
86Top-22
86TopTif-22
86TucTorP-23
87LouRedTI-28
88BriTigP-1878
88LouRedBC-17
88LouRedBP-425
88LouRedBTI-49
89MiaMirIS-24
93RanKee-369

Walker, Edsall
92NegLeaK-11
92NegLeaRLI-62
95NegLeaL2-8

Walker, Fleetwood (Moses F.)
63GadFunC-46
85UltBasC-7
86NegLeaF-28
87NegLeaPD-22
94OriofB-50
94TedWil-114
94UppDecTAE-8

Walker, Frank
22W575-144

Walker, Gee (Gerald)
33ButCanV-51
33DouDisP-41
34DiaMatCSB-188
34BatR31-118
34Gou-26
34GouCanV-81
35AlDemDCR3-21
35GouPreR-10
35GouPuzR-8F
35GouPuzR-9F
35TigFreP-20
36GouWidPPR-A106
36NatChiFPR-78
36WorWidGV-48
37OPCBatUV-110
38WheBB10-4
41DouPlaR-135
76TigOldTS-22
77TCMTheWY-82
78TigDeaCS-4
81ConTSN-99
81TigDetN-109
81TigSecNP-23
83TCMPla1944-31
91ConTSN-87
93DiaStaES-152
95ConTSN-1390

Walker, Glenn
81WauTimT-24
82LynSaiT-16
83SalLakCGT-20
84SalLakCGC-187
86MidAngP-25

Walker, Greg
80AppFoxT-20
81GleFalWST-16
83TopTra-124T
84Don-609
84Fle-73
84Nes792-518
84Top-518
84TopTif-518
84WhiSoxTV-30
85Don-366
85Fle-530
85OPC-244
85ThoMcAD-21
85Top-623
85TopSti-236
85TopTif-623
85WhiSoxC-29
86Don-135
86Fle-219
86MSAJayPCD-19
86OPC-123
86SevCoi-C16
86Spo-174
86Top-123
86TopSti-293
86TopTif-123
86WhiSoxC-29
87Don-25A
87Don-25B
87Don-59
87DonOpeD-233
87DonSupD-25
87Fle-508
87FleGlo-508
87FleLeaL-42
87FleMin-110
87Lea-25
87OPC-302
87SevCoi-C15
87SpoTeaP-26
87Top-397
87TopSti-291
87TopTif-397
87WhiSoxC-29
88Don-162
88DonBasB-193
88Fle-411
88FleGlo-411
88Lea-86
88OPC-286
88PanSti-56
88Sco-93A
88Sco-93B
88ScoGlo-93A
88ScoGlo-93B
88Spo-103
88StaLinWS-19
88Top-764
88TopBig-105
88TopSti-292
88TopTif-764
88TopUKM-83
88TopUKMT-83
88WhiSoxC-29
89Don-135
89PanSti-307
89Sco-37
89Spo-19
89Top-21
89Top-408
89TopBig-4
89TopTif-21
89TopTif-408
89UppDec-231
89WhiSoxC-27
89WhiSoxK-1
90CMC-318
90Fle-551
90FleCan-551
90OPC-33
90PanSti-45
90ProAAAF-469
90PubSti-402
90RocRedWC-18
90RocRedWP-712
90Sco-354
90Top-33
90TopTif-33
90UppDec-350
90VenSti-472
91OriCro-471

Walker, Harry
46SeaSLP-55
46SpoExcW-9-6
47Exh-234
48BluTin-39
49Bow-130
49EurSta-75
49Lea-137
50Bow-180
60Top-468
65Top-438
66PirEasH-3
66Top-318
66TopVen-318
67PirTeal-23
67Top-448
67TopPirS-24
69Top-633
70OPC-32
70Top-32
71OPC-312
71Top-312
72OPC-249
72Top-249
79TCM50-261
82GSGalAG-3
87AstShoSO-28
87AstShoSTw-24
89PacLegI-190
89SweBasG-34
90SweBasG-33
91SweBasG-94
94UppDecAH-43
94UppDecAH1-43
95ConTSN-1347

Walker, Hugh
89AppFoxP-856
89Bow-127
89BowTif-127
90BasCitRS-24
91Bow-313
91Cla/Bes-58
91LinDriAA-422
91LinDriP-422
91MemChiLD-422
91MemChiP-667
92BasCitRF-3859
92ClaFS7-184
92MemChiS-447
92SkyAA F-189
93ClaGolF-84
93WilBluRC-26
93WilBluRF-2012
94MemChiF-372

Walker, J. Luke
66Top-498
67OPC-123
67Top-123
68Top-559
69OPC-36
69Top-36
70OPC-322
70Top-322
71MilDud-68
71MLBOffS-216
71OPC-68
71OPC-534
71Pir-6
71PirActP-12
71PirArc-12
71Top-68
71Top-534
71TopSup-21
72MilBra-353
72OPC-471
72Top-471
73OPC-187
73Top-187
74OPC-612
74Top-612
74TopTra-612T
75OPC-474
75Top-474

Walker, James
87ChaLooB-5

Walker, Jamie
92AubAstC-17
92AubAstF-1354
93QuaCitRBC-23
93QuaCitRBF-101

94QuaCitRBC-22
94QuaCitRBF-533
95JacGenTI-10
96JacGenB-26
Walker, Jason
94WatIndC-27
94WatIndF-3938
Walker, Jerry
89BelMarL-35
Walker, Jerry Allen
58Top-113
59OklTodML-3
59OriJayP-10
59Top-144
59TopVen-144
60OriJayP-10
60Top-399
60Top-540
60TopTat-52
60TopTat-96
61AthJayP-24
61Top-85
62Top-357
62TopBuc-91
62TopStal-61
63AthJayP-12
63Top-413
64Top-77
64TopVen-77
84AstMot-27
85AstMot-27
91OriCro-472
Walker, Jim
88CalCanC-7
88CalCanP-791
94FreKeyF-2616
94OriPro-102
94FreKeyC-23
Walker, Joe
96PriWilCB-28
Walker, John
78LodDodT-24
79LodDodT-12
80TolMudHT-9
81TolMudHT-17
Walker, Johnny
90PulBraP-3112
91HigSchPLS-12
91IdaFalBSP-14
94UtiBluSF-3830
Walker, Keith
80KnoBluJT-23
82KnoBluJT-7
83SyrChiT-12
Walker, Kevin
96IdaFalB-27
Walker, Kurt
86BirBarTI-22
87VisOakP-8
88MidAngGS-2
94UppDec-274
Walker, Larry
85UtiBluST-16
86BurExpP-25
87JacExpP-429
87SouLeaAJ-8
89IndIndC-23
89IndIndP-1239
89TriA AAC-7
90Bow-117
90BowTif-117
90ClaUpd-T16
90Don-578
90DonBesN-91
90ExpPos-36
90Fle-363
90FleCan-363
90FleSoaS-3
90GreHorB-15
90GreHorP-2667
90GreHorS-25
90Lea-325
90OPC-757
90Sco-631
90ScoYouS2-9
90Top-757
90TopBig-296
90TopDeb89-133
90TopMag-95
90TopTif-757
90TriAAAC-7
90UppDec-466
90UppDec-702
90UppDecS-2
91Baz-19
91Bow-442
91Don-359
91ExpPos-22
91Fle-250
91Ft.LauYC-18
91Ft.LauYP-2431
91Lea-241
91MajLeaCP-80
91OPC-339
91PanFreS-145
91PanSti-65
91Sco-241
91Sco100RS-21
91StaClu-93
91StaCluP-48
91Top-339
91TopDesS-339
91TopMic-339
91TopRoo-32
91TopTif-339
91ToyRoo-31
91UltUpd-93
91UppDec-536
92Bow-648
92Cla2-T39
92Don-259
92ExpDonD-18
92ExpPos-29
92Fle-493
92ForLauYC-16
92ForLauYTI-32
92Ft.LauYF-2616
92Hig5-60
92Lea-201
92OPC-531
92PanSti-206
92Pin-194
92PinTea2-21
92Sco-199
92ScoImpP-29
92StaClu-256
92Stu-59
92Top-531
92TopGol-531
92TopGolW-531
92TopMic-531
92TriPla-89
92Ult-525
92UppDec-249
93Bow-100
93ClaGam-97
93DiaMar-115
93Don-540
93DonDiaK-DK6
93DonEli-30
93DonEliS-12
93DonLonBL-LL18
93DonMVP-9
93DonPre-6
93ExpColP7-7
93ExpDonM-7
93ExpPosN-22
93Fin-97
93FinJum-97
93FinRef-97
93Fla-87
93Fle-81
93Fle-715
93FleAll-NL6
93FleFruotL-64
93FunPac-98
93Hos-30
93HumDumC-42
93Lea-392
93MilBonSS-15
93NesQuiB-1
93OPC-384
93OPCPre-39
93PacSpa-190
93PanSti-231
93Pin-3
93Pin-299
93PinHomRC-14
93PinSlu-13
93PinTeaP-10
93PosCan-13
93Sco-5
93ScoFra-20
93Sel-27
93SP-107
93StaClu-299
93StaClu-320
93StaCluFDI-299
93StaCluFDI-320
93StaCluM-94
93StaCluMMP-11
93StaCluMOP-299
93StaCluMOP-320
93StaCluMP-24
93Stu-123
93Top-95
93Top-406
93TOPBLAG-22
93TopGol-95
93TopGol-406
93TopInaM-95
93TopInaM-406
93TopMic-95
93TopMic-406
93TopPreS-9
93Toy-23
93TriPla-42
93TriPlaA-6
93Ult-71
93UltAllS-8
93UltAwaW-9
93UppDec-144
93UppDec-481
93UppDecGold-144
93UppDecGold-481
93UppDecHRH-HR16
93UppDecTriCro-TC10
94Bow-500
94BowBes-R76
94BowBesR-R76
94ColC-286
94ColChoGS-286
94ColChoSS-286
94DenHol-28
94Don-371
94DonSpeE-371
94ExtBas-312
94Fin-216
94FinJum-216
94FinRef-216
94Fla-404
94Fle-554
94FUnPac-136
94Lea-397
94LeaCleC-1
94LeaL-127
94OPC-253
94OPCAllR-19
94OPCJumA-19
94Pac-392
94PanSti-213
94Pin-310
94PinArtP-310
94PinMusC-310
94PosCan-8
94PosCanG-8
94ProMag-85
94RedFolMI-27
94Sco-376
94ScoDreT-9
94ScoGolR-376
94ScoGolS-27
94Sel-18
94SelSki-SK9
94SP-86
94SPDieC-86
94Spo-77
94StaClu-280
94StaCluFDI-280
94StaCluGR-280
94StaCluMOP-280
94Stu-80
94Top-230
94TopGol-230
94TopSpa-230
94TopSupS-44
94TriPla-99
94Ult-526
94UltAwaW-17
94UppDec-370
94UppDecAJ-28
94UppDecAJG-28
94UppDecED-274
94UppDecED-370
95Baz-93
95Bow-290
95BowBes-R63
95BowBesR-R63
95ClaPhoC-25
95ColCho-238
95ColCho-579T
95ColCho-TC1
95ColChoGS-238
95ColChoSE-96
95ColChoSEGS-96
95ColChoSESS-96
95ColChoSS-238
95Don-492
95DonPreP-492
95DonTopotO-234
95Emo-126
95Fin-215
95Fin-274
95FinRef-215
95FinRef-274
95Fla-348
95Fle-361
95FleUpd-171
95Lea-305
95LeaLim-91
95LeaLimG-10
95LeaLimIBP-4
95LeaOpeD-8
95Pac-273
95PacGolP-30
95PacPri-89
95PanSti-75
95Pin-372
95PinArtP-372
95PinFan-28
95PinMusC-372
95RedFol-25
95RocPol-10
95Sco-346
95ScoGolR-346
95ScoHaloG-HG71
95ScoHaloGYTE-HG71T
95ScoPlaTS-346
95ScoYouTE-346T
95Sel-224
95SelArtP-224
95SelCer-89
95SelCerMG-89
95SelCerS-89
95SP-50
95SPCha-39
95SPCha-42
95SPChaDC-39
95SPChaDC-42
95Spo-139
95SpoArtP-139
95SPPlaP-PP7
95SPSil-50
95StaClu-148
95StaClu-618
95StaCluCT-10
95StaCluFDI-148
95StaCluMO-44
95StaCluMOP-148
95StaCluMOP-618
95StaCluMOP-SS15
95StaCluSS-SS15
95StaCluSTWS-148
95StaCluSTWS-618
95StaCluVR-77
95Stu-58
95Sum-45
95SumNthD-45
95Top-422
95TopCyb-221
95TopPre-PP1
95TopTra-20T
95UC3-90
95UC3-145
95UC3ArtP-90
95UC3ArtP-145
95Ult-409
95UltGolM-409
95UppDec-82
95UppDec-415
95UppDecED-82
95UppDecED-415
95UppDecEDG-82
95UppDecEDG-415
95UppDecPLL-R34
95UppDecPLL-R47
95UppDecPLLE-R34
95UppDecPLLE-R47
95UppDecSE-4
95UppDecSE-240
95UppDecSEG-4
95UppDecSEG-240
95Zen-67
95ZenZ-11
96Baz-26
96Bow-17
96BowBes-83
96BowBesAR-83
96BowBesMI-5
96BowBesMIAR-5
96BowBesMIR-5
96BowBesP-BBP21
96BowBesPAR-BBP21
96BowBesPR-BBP21
96BowBesR-83
96Cir-124
96CirRav-124
96ColCho-326
96ColCho-540
96ColCho-753
96ColChoCtG-CG16
96ColChoCtG-CG16B
96ColChoCtG-CG16C
96ColChoCtGG-CG16
96ColChoCtGG-CG16B
96ColChoCtGG-CG16C
96ColChoGS-326
96ColChoGS-540
96ColChoGS-753
96ColChoSS-326
96ColChoSS-540
96ColChoSS-753
96ColChoYMtP-43
96ColChoYMtP-43A
96ColChoYMtPGS-43
96ColChoYMtPGS-43A
96Don-342
96DonDiaK-11
96DonLonBL-7
96DonPreP-342
96EmoXL-178
96Fin-S13
96Fin-S302
96FinRef-S13
96FinRef-S302
96Fla-253
96Fle-377
96FleRoc-16
96FleTif-377
96Lea-63
96LeaLim-86
96LeaLimG-86
96LeaPre-80
96LeaPreP-80
96LeaPrePB-63
96LeaPrePG-63
96LeaPrePS-63
96LeaPreSG-37
96LeaPreSte-37
96LeaSig-77
96LeaSigPPG-77
96LeaSigPPP-77
96MetUni-159
96MetUniP-159
96Pac-65
96PacPri-P140
96PacPriFB-FB20
96PacPriG-P140
96PanSti-86
96Pin-150
96Pin-219
96PinAfi-68
96PinAfi-152
96PinAfiAP-68
96PinAfiAP-152
96PinAfiFPP-68
96PinArtP-77
96PinArtP-119
96PinFoil-219
96PinPow-19
96PinSta-77
96PinSta-119
96ProSta-114
96RocPol-25
96Sco-13
96Sco-374
96ScoAll-17
96ScoBigB-15
96ScoDiaA-13
96ScoDugC-A13
96ScoDugC-B99
96ScoDugCAP-A13
96ScoDugCAP-B99
96ScoGolS-27
96ScoNumG-20
96ScoPowP-8
96ScoRef-9
96ScoTitT-13
96Sel-98
96SelArtP-98

96SelCer-85
96SelCerAP-85
96SelCerCB-85
96SelCerCR-85
96SelCerMB-85
96SelCerMG-85
96SelCerMR-85
96SelTeaN-4
96SP-80
96Spo-72
96Spo-114
96SpoArtP-72
96SpoArtP-114
96SpoPowS-18
96SPx-23
96SPxGol-23
96StaClu-319
96StaCluEPB-319
96StaCluEPG-319
96StaCluEPS-319
96StaCluMO-45
96StaCluMOP-319
96StaCluMOP-PS11
96StaCluPS-PS11
96StaCluVRMO-77
96Stu-78
96StuPrePB-78
96StuPrePG-78
96StuPrePS-78
96Sum-61
96SumAbo&B-61
96SumArtP-61
96SumFoi-61
96TeaOut-86
96Top-5
96Top-363
96TopChr-5
96TopChr-147
96TopChrR-5
96TopChrR-147
96TopGal-179
96TopGalPPI-179
96TopLas-112
96TopLasPC-16
96TopPowB-5
96TopPro-NL10
96Ult-194
96UltGolM-194
96UltPowP-11
96UltPowPGM-11
96UppDec-60
96UppDec-421
96UppDecPD-PD19
96UppDecPRE-R38
96UppDecPreR-R38
96Zen-57
96ZenArtP-57
96ZenMoz-12
97Bow-275
97BowBes-67
97BowBesAR-67
97BowBesR-67
97BowChr-92
97BowChrI-92
97BowChrIR-92
97BowChrR-92
97BowInt-275
97BowIntB-BBI7
97BowIntBAR-BBI7
97BowIntBR-BBI7
97Cir-377
97CirRav-377
97ColCho-98
97ColChoBS-6
97ColChoBSGS-6
97Don-40
97Don-410
97DonArmaD-7
97DonLim-87
97DonLim-126
97DonLim-133
97DonLim-169
97DonLimFotG-28
97DonLimLE-87
97DonLimLE-126
97DonLimLE-133
97DonLimLE-169
97DonPre-10
97DonPreCttC-10
97DonPreP-48
97DonPreP-410
97DonPrePGold-48
97DonPrePGold-410
97DonTea-92
97DonTeaSMVP-16
97DonTeaSPE-92
97Fin-106
97Fin-335
97FinEmb-106
97FinEmb-335
97FinEmbR-106
97FinEmbR-335
97FinRef-106
97FinRef-335
97FlaSho-A76
97FlaSho-B76
97FlaSho-C76
97FlaShoLC-76
97FlaShoLC-B76
97FlaShoLC-C76
97FlaShoLCM-A76
97FlaShoLCM-B76
97FlaShoLCM-C76
97Fle-319
97FleTif-319
97Lea-238
97Lea-385
97LeaFraM-238
97LeaFraM-385
97LeaFraMDC-238
97LeaFraMDC-385
97LeaLeaotN-6
97MetUni-76
97NewPin-9
97NewPinAP-9
97NewPinMC-9
97NewPinPP-9
97Pac-291
97PacLigB-291
97PacSil-291
97PinCer-24
97PinCerMBlu-24
97PinCerMG-24
97PinCerMR-24
97PinCerR-24
97PinIns-114
97PinInsCE-114
97PinInsDE-114
97PinPasttM-24
97PinTotCPB-24
97PinTotCPG-24
97PinTotCPR-24
97PinX-P-1
97PinX-P-138
97PinX-PMoS-1
97PinX-PMoS-138
97PinX-PMP-4
97PinX-PSfF-31
97PinX-PSfFU-31
97Sco-176
97ScoPreS-176
97ScoRoc-8
97ScoRocPl-8
97ScoRocPr-8
97ScoShoS-176
97ScoShoSAP-176
97Sel-97
97SelArtP-97
97SelRegG-97
97SP-67
97SpoIll-111
97SpoIllEE-111
97SPx-25
97SPxBro-25
97SPxGraF-25
97SPxSil-25
97SPxSte-25
97StaClu-251
97StaCluMat-251
97StaCluMOP-251
97Stu-105
97StuPrePG-105
97StuPrePS-105
97Top-461
97TopChr-162
97TopChrR-162
97TopGal-72
97TopGalPPI-72
97TopScrSI-6
97TopSta-1
97TopSta1AS-AS13
97TopStaAM-1
97TopStaASGM-ASM9
97Ult-320
97UltGolME-320
97UltPlaME-320
97UppDec-182
97UppDec-353
97Zen-11
97Zen Z-Z-2

Walker, Lonnie
88LitFalMP-14
89ColMetB-27
89ColMetGS-26

Walker, M.J.
75TopPho-75

Walker, Matt
86CliGiaP-26
86EveGiaC-186
86EveGiaPC-35
87EveGiaC-1

Walker, Michael Charles
84IdaFalATI-28

Walker, Mickey
28W512-45

Walker, Mike (Michael Aaron)
86WatPirP-27
87HarSenP-23
87WatIndP-14
88HarSenP-850
88WilBilP-1310
89BlaYNPRWLU-39
89Bow-77
89BowTif-77
89ColSprSSP-239
90CalCanC-3
90CalCanP-652
90CMC-430
90CMC-453
90ColSprSSC-1
90ColSprSSP-36
90IndTeal-42
90ProAAAF-117
90ProAAAF-217
91Don-61
91Fle-381
91IndFanC-27
91OPC-593
91Top-593A
91Top-593B
91TopDesS-593
91TopMic-593
91TopTif-593
91UppDec-694
92CalCanF-3732
92DonRoo-122
92JacSunS-370
92TolMudHF-1044
92TolMudHS-594
93CalCanF-1167
93TopGol-825
94IowCubF-1277
94PhoFirF-1521
96TolMudHB-29

Walker, Pete
90PitMetP-16
91St.LucMC-14
91St.LucMP-712
92BinMetF-517
92BinMetS-70
93BinMetF-2335
94Bow-44
94ExcFS7-240
94Ult-540
95NorTidTI-29
96LasVegSB-29

Walker, R. Tom
73OPC-41
74OPC-193
75OPC-627
76OPC-186

Walker, Ray
88MarPhiS-32

Walker, Rich
88BatCliP-1681
89BatCliP-1935

Walker, Rod
89HigSchPLS-6
95HudValRTI-24

Walker, Rube (Albert)
49EurSta-74
52Top-319
53Top-134
54Top-153
55DodGolS-22
55Top-108
55TopDouH-15
55TopTesS-10
56Dod-28
56Top-333
57Top-147
58Hir-74
58Top-203
73OPC-257
73Top-257A
73Top-257B
74OPC-179
74Top-179
79TCM50-278
81TCM60I-407
82BraPol-54
83BraPol-54
84BraPol-54
89RinPosM1-36
90DodTar-826
91RinPosBD4-2
91TopArc1-134
94Met69CCPP-3
94Met69CS-2
94Met69T-32
94TopArc1-153
94TopArc1G-153
95TopArcBD-20
95TopArcBD-47
95TopArcBD-76
95TopArcBD-100
95TopArcBD-164

Walker, Shon
92ClaDraP-24
92ClaFS7-415
92FroRowDP-74
92UppDecML-83
93AugPirC-28
93AugPirF-1560
93ClaFS7-120
93ClaGolF-196
93StaCluM-155
93Top-658
93TopGol-658
93TopInaM-658
93TopMic-658
94AugGreC-25
94AugGreF-3023
94ClaGolF-188
96LynHilB-25

Walker, Steve
87SanBerSP-1
88BasCitRS-24
89MemChiB-23
89MemChiP-1196
89MemChiS-23
89Sta-46
91HunCubC-28
91HunCubP-3352
92HunCubC-18
92HunCubF-3167
93PeoChiC-23
93PeoChiF-1098
93PeoChiTI-31
94DayCubC-26
94DayCubF-2368
95RocCubTI-9
96DayCubB-24

Walker, The
90EveGiaB-7

Walker, Tilly (Clarence)
12T207-190
15CraJacE-173
15SpoNewM-185
16ColE13-181
16SpoNewM-183
21Exh-181
21Nei-6
22E120-89
22W572-110
23W501-100
23W515-7
23WilChoV-166
91ConTSN-137

Walker, Toby
88OklSoo-11

Walker, Todd
92LSUTigM-12
93BazTeaU-6
93LSUTigM-12
93TopTra-79T
94ClaUpdCotC-CC7
94LSUTig-2
94LSUTigMP-1
94SigRooDP-8
94SigRooDPS-8
95ActPacF-59
95ARuFalLS-20
95Bes-28
95Bes-103
95BesFra-F6
95Exc-89
95HarCitRCTI-27
95HarCitRCTI-28
95SigRooDDS-DD4
95SigRooDDSS-DD4
95SPML-10
95SPML-85
95SPMLDtS-DS10
95UppDecML-167
95UppDecML-170
95UppDecML-220
95UppDecMLOP-OP16
96BesAutSA-85
96Bow-159
96BowBes-135
96BowBesAR-135
96BowBesR-135
96BowMinLP-4
96Exc-83
96LeaSig-117
96LeaSigPPG-117
96LeaSigPPP-117
97Bow-293
97BowBes-107
97BowBesA-107
97BowBesAAR-107
97BowBesAR-107
97BowBesBC-BC19
97BowBesBCAR-BC19
97BowBesBCR-BC19
97BowBesP-13
97BowBesPAR-13
97BowBesPR-13
97BowBesR-107
97BowCerBIA-CA82
97BowCerGIA-CA82
97BowChr-201
97BowChrI-201
97BowChrIR-201
97BowChrR-201
97BowChrSHR-SHR6
97BowChrSHRR-SHR6
97BowInt-293
97BowIntB-BBI12
97BowIntBAR-BBI12
97BowIntBR-BBI12
97BowScoHR-6
97Cir-325
97CirEmeA-325
97CirEmeAR-AU6
97CirFasT-10
97CirRav-325
97ColCho-20
97ColChoNF-NF23
97Don-372
97DonEli-121
97DonEliGS-121
97DonEliTotC-4
97DonEliTotCDC-4
97DonFraFea-6
97DonLim-45
97DonLim-65
97DonLimFotG-36
97DonLimLE-45
97DonLimLE-65
97DonPre-146
97DonPre-199
97DonPreCttC-146
97DonPreCttC-199
97DonPreP-372
97DonPrePGold-372
97DonRatR-25
97DonRooDK-4
97DonRooDKC-4
97Fin-112
97Fin-341
97FinEmb-112
97FinEmb-341
97FinEmbR-112
97FinEmbR-341
97FinRef-112
97FinRef-341
97FlaSho-A12
97FlaSho-B12
97FlaSho-C12
97FlaShoLC-12
97FlaShoLC-B12
97FlaShoLC-C12
97FlaShoLCM-A12
97FlaShoLCM-B12
97FlaShoLCM-C12
97FlaShoWotF-12
97Fle-160

97FleNewH-14
97FleRooS-20
97FleTif-160
97Lea-170
97LeaFraM-170
97LeaFraMDC-170
97MetUni-215
97MetUniEAR-AU6
97MetUniMfG-10
97NewPin-165
97NewPin-199
97NewPinAP-165
97NewPinAP-199
97NewPinMC-165
97NewPinMC-199
97NewPinPP-165
97NewPinPP-199
97Pac-146
97PacLigB-146
97PacPri-48
97PacPriLB-48
97PacPriP-48
97PacSil-146
97Pin-171
97PinArtP-171
97PinCer-115
97PinCerMBlu-115
97PinCerMG-115
97PinCerMR-115
97PinCerR-115
97PinIns-144
97PinInsCE-144
97PinInsDE-144
97PinMusC-171
97PinTotCPB-115
97PinTotCPG-115
97PinTotCPR-115
97PinX-P-118
97PinX-PMoS-118
97Sco-324
97Sco-477
97ScoHeatO-36
97ScoHobR-477
97ScoResC-477
97ScoShoS-324
97ScoShoS-477
97ScoShoSAP-324
97ScoShoSAP-477
97Sel-103
97SelArtP-103
97SelRegG-103
97SelRooA-4
97SelRooR-12
97SelTooot T-16
97SelToootTMB-16
97SkyE-X-30
97SkyE-XC-30
97SkyE-XEAR-AU6
97SkyE-XEC-30
97SkyE-XSD2-13
97SP-5
97SpoIll-26
97SpoIllEE-26
97SPSpeF-43
97SPSpxF-10
97SPSPxFA-10
97SPx-32
97SPxBro-32
97SPxGraF-32
97SPxSil-32
97SPxSte-32
97StaClu-78
97StaClu-182
97StaCluM-M22
97StaCluMOP-78
97StaCluMOP-182
97StaCluMOP-M22
97Stu-154
97StuAut-3
97StuHarH-7
97StuPor8-12
97StuPrePG-154
97StuPrePS-154
97Top-377
97TopAwel-AI20
97TopChr-129
97TopChrR-129
97TopGal-180
97TopGalPPI-180
97Ult-548
97UltAutE-2
97UltGolME-548
97UltGolP-3
97UltPlaME-548
97UppDec-235
97UppDecBCP-BC5
95UppDecMLFS-167
95UppDecMLFS-170
95UppDecMLFS-220
97UppDecU-52
97UppDecUGN-GN17

Walker, Tom
72Dia-49
73Top-41
74Top-193
75Top-627
76Top-186
76TulOilGP-19
77ExpPos-36
77Top-652
78ColCliT-26
91HunCubC-29
91HunCubP-3345

Walker, Tony (Anthony)
81WatRedT-11
81WatRedT-21
82WatRedT-20
83DayBeaAT-27
86AstPol-20
86FleUpd-123
87Fle-71
87FleGlo-71
87Top-24
87TopTif-24

Walker, Wade
51BerRos-C14
93GenCubC-26
93GenCubF-3174
94PeoChiC-24
94PeoChiF-2267
96Bow-117
96OrlCubB-27

Walker, William C.
29ExhFou-7
31Exh-7

Walker, William H.
35DiaMatCS3T1-143

Walkup, James
39PlaBal-150
79DiaGre-184

Wall, Dave
81AppFoxT-27

Wall, Donne
89AubAstP-2182
90AshTouP-2749
91BurAstC-10
91BurAstP-2801
91MidLeaAP-MWL19
92OscAstC-19
92ProFS7-233
92UppDecML-138
93TucTorF-3060
94TucTorF-763
95TusTorTI-29
96Bow-318
96ColCho-568
96ColChoGS-568
96ColChoSS-568
96Don-456
96DonPreP-456
96Fle-423
96FleTif-423
96StaClu-179
96Top-341
96TusTorB-25
97Cir-131
97CirRav-131
97Fle-355
97FleTif-355
97Lea-80
97LeaFraM-80
97LeaFraMDC-80
97MetUni-142
97Pin-153
97PinArtP-153
97PinMusC-153
97StaClu-121
97StaCluMOP-121
97Top-223
97Ult-213
97UltGolME-213
97UltPlaME-213
97UppDec-82

Wall, Greg
89AncBucTI-19

Wall, Jason
90LSUTigP-11

Wall, Murray
53Top-217
58Top-410
59Top-42
59TopVen-42
83Bra53F-11
91TopArc1-217

Wall, Stan
74AlbDukTI-22
75AlbDukC-17
75IntLeaASB-36
75PacCoaLAB-36
76OPC-584
76Top-584
77Top-88
90DodTar-827

Wallace, Alex
85AncGlaPTI-30

Wallace, Arthur
88KimN18-45

Wallace, B.J.
90MisStaB-39
91MisStaB-47
92Bow-554
92ClaDraP-3
92ClaDraPFB-BC3
92ClaDraPP-BB3
92DEL-BB3
92FroRowDP-80
92FroRowDPPS-80
92MisStaB-44
92TopTra-126T
92TopTraG-126T
92UppDecML-2
93Bow-676
93ClaFS7-32
93ClaGolF-109
93OPCPreTDP-1
93Pin-456
93Sco-488
93Sel-310
93StaCluM-125
93StaCluM-142
93Top-33
93TopGol-33
93TopInaM-33
93TopMic-33
93WesPalBEC-1
93WesPalBEF-1341
94Bow-640
94Cla-42
94ClaGolF-191
94ExcFS7-230
94HarSenF-2093
94UppDecML-69

Wallace, Bobby (Roderick)
03BreE10-148
04FanCraAL-48
09AmeCarE-115
09ColChiE-297
09PC7HHB-44
09RamT20-121
09SpoNewSM-56
09T206-367
10DomDisP-120
10NadCarE-50
10SweCapPP-56A
10SweCapPP-56B
11MecDFT-48
11S74Sil-37
11SpoLifCW-360
11SpoLifM-120
11T205-176A
11T205-176B
11TurRedT-124
12ColRedB-297
12ColTinT-297
12HasTriFT-1A
12HasTriFT-1B
12T207-191
14B18B-35A
14B18B-35B
14PieStaT-59
50CalHOFW-75
76ShaPiz-69
80PerHaloFP-69
80SSPHOF-69
90BasWit-65
93ConTSN-916
94ConTSN-1017
94ConTSNB-1017
94OriofB-82
98CamPepP-82

Wallace, Brian
92BelMarC-27
92BelMarF-1454
93AppFoxC-23
93AppFoxF-2470
94AppFoxC-20
94AppFoxF-1064
95BurBeeTI-30

Wallace, Brooks
81TulDriT-24

Wallace, Curtis
76BatRouCT-21

Wallace, Dave
76OklCit8TI-21
81VerBeaDT-25
82VerBeaDT-28
84AlbDukC-245
86AlbDukP-26
95DodMot-28
95DodPol-30
96DodMot-28
96DodPol-8

Wallace, David
90AshTouC-24
91AshTouP-582
92BurAstC-1
92BurAstF-561

Wallace, Derek
92ClaBluBF-BC23
92ClaDraP-8
92ClaDraPFB-BC8
92ClaFS7-403
92PeoChiTI-29
92UppDecML-7
93Bow-4
93ClaPro-4
93ClaYouG-YG27
93DayCubC-22
93DayCubF-859
93Pin-460
93Sco-492
93Sel-357
93StaCluM-124
93Top-459
93TopGol-459
93TopInaM-459
93TopMic-459
93UppDec-429
93UppDecGold-429
94Bow-110
94Cla-134
94ClaGolF-133
94OrlCubF-1386
94UppDecML-201
95WicWraTI-23
96NorTidB-30
97Bow-147
97BowInt-147
97PacPriGotD-GD178
97UppDec-281

Wallace, Don
67Top-367

Wallace, Flint
96SouOreTI-13

Wallace, Greg
86MiaMarP-26

Wallace, Jeff
96LanLugB-30

Wallace, Jim
49RemBre-30
77TCMTheWY-90

Wallace, Joe
91OklStaC-28
92OklStaC-28
93JohCitCC-28
93JohCitCF-3683
94MadHatC-24
94MadHatF-136

Wallace, Kent
92OneYanC-22
93GreHorC-25
94TamYanC-29
94TamYanF-2384
95ColCliP-31
95ColCliTI-31
95NorNavTI-30
96ColCliB-29

Wallace, Mike
74OPC-608
74Top-608A
74Top-608B
75OPC-401
75SSP18-3
75Top-401
76SSP-290
77Top-539
92YanWIZ7-159
93RanKee-370

Wallace, Tim
83St.PetCT-15
84ArkTraT-5
86ArkTraP-25
86LouRedTI-28
86PeoChiP-25
87WinSpiP-15
88WinSpiS-21
89BoiHawP-1994
90PalSprACLC-216
90PalSprAP-2588
91LinDriAA-622
91WicWraLD-622
91WicWraP-2608
91WicWraRD-18

Wallach, Tim
81ExpPos-16
82Don-140
82ExpHygM-23
82ExpPos-40
82Fle-210
82OPC-191
82Top-191
83AllGamPI-126
83Don-392
83ExpStu-12
83Fle-299
83OPC-229
83Top-552
83TopSti-257
84AllGamPI-36
84Don-421
84ExpPos-35
84ExpStu-14
84Fle-291
84Nes792-232
84OPC-232
84Top-232
84TopSti-94
84TopTif-232
85AllGamPI-126
85Don-87
85Fle-412
85Lea-199
85OPC-3
85OPCPos-6
85Top-473
85TopSti-87
85TopTif-473
86BasStaB-117
86Don-219
86DonAll-25
86ExpPos-17
86ExpProPa-11
86ExpProPo-10
86Fle-263
86FleMin-56
86GenMilB-6I
86Lea-97
86OPC-217
86Spo-123
86Top-685
86Top-703
86TopSti-82
86TopTat-18
86TopTif-685
86TopTif-703
87Don-179
87DonOpeD-88
87ExpPos-32
87Fle-334
87FleGlo-334
87GenMilB-4H
87HosSti-5
87Lea-61
87OPC-55
87RedFolSB-117
87Spo-72
87Spo-115
87SpoTeaP-20
87StuPan-7
87Top-55
87TopSti-80
87TopTif-55
88AlaGolAA'TI-17
88Don-222
88DonAll-59
88DonBasB-258
88ExpPos-23
88Fle-198
88FleAwaW-44
88FleBasA-43

88FleBasM-42
88FleGlo-198
88FleMin-91
88FleStiC-98
88FleWaxBC-C15
88KayB-32
88Lea-193
88Lea-255
88MSAHosD-7
88MSAJifPD-18
88Nes-23
88OPC-94
88PanSti-327
88RedFolSB-94
88Sco-70
88ScoGlo-70
88Spo-151
88StaLinE-17
88Top-399
88Top-560
88TopBig-7
88TopCoi-59
88TopGloS-18
88TopMinL-58
88TopRevLL-6
88TopSti-85
88TopStiB-9
88TopTif-399
88TopTif-560
88TopUKM-84
88TopUKMT-84
89Bow-362
89BowTif-362
89Don-156
89DonBasB-34
89ExpPos-29
89Fle-395
89FleGlo-395
89K-M-25
89OPC-78
89PanSti-122
89RedFolSB-127
89Sco-220
89Spo-114
89Top-720
89TopBasT-117
89TopBig-215
89TopSti-70
89TopTif-720
89TVSpoM-16
89UppDec-102
90Bow-114
90BowTif-114
90Don-220
90DonBesN-55
90DonLeaS-28
90ExpPos-37
90Fle-364
90FleAwaW-41
90FleCan-364
90FleLeaL-41
90Lea-80
90OPC-370
90PanSti-286
90PubSti-189
90RedFolSB-99
90Sco-192
90Spo-182
90Top-370
90TopBig-70
90TopCoi-60
90TopDou-68
90TopMinL-64
90TopSti-74
90TopStiB-9
90TopTif-370
90UppDec-273
90USPlaCA-5D
90VenSti-473
91BasBesHRK-18
91Bow-437
91ClaGam-2
91DenHol-12
91Don-406
91Don-514
91Fle-251
91Lea-388
91LeaPre-6
91MSAHolD-3
91OPC-220
91OPCPre-125
91PanCanT1-102
91PanFreS-141
91PanSti-64
91PetSta-10
91PosCan-2
91RedFolS-99
91Sco-210
91Sco-865
91Sco100S-58
91StaClu-463
91StaPinB-51
91Stu-200
91SunSee-23
91Top-220
91TopCraJ2-21
91TopDesS-220
91TopMic-220
91TopTif-220
91Ult-210
91UppDec-96
91UppDec-235
92Bow-372
92Bow-557
92ClaGam-40
92Don-34
92ExpDonD-19
92ExpPos-30
92Fle-494
92HitTheBB-36
92Lea-298
92OPC-385
92PanSti-204
92PepDieM-22
92Pin-161
92PosCan-5
92Sco-595
92Sco100S-70
92StaClu-340
92Stu-60
92Top-385
92TopGol-385
92TopGolW-385
92TopKid-6
92TopMic-385
92TriPla-224
92Ult-226
92UppDec-228
93Bow-70
93DodMot-6
93DodPol-26
93Don-36
93ExpDonM-8
93Fin-118
93FinRef-118
93Fla-77
93Fle-82
93FleFinE-86
93HumDumC-33
93Lea-363
93OPC-225
93OPCPre-87
93PacSpa-191
93PanSti-215
93Pin-178
93Sco-211
93Sel-190
93SelRoo-27T
93StaClu-686
93StaCluD-11
93StaCluFDI-686
93StaCluMOP-686
93Stu-64
93Top-570
93TopGol-570
93TopInaM-570
93TopMic-570
93TopTra-127T
93TriPla-253
93Ult-408
93UppDec-547
93UppDecGold-547
94ColC-466
94ColChoGS-466
94ColChoSS-466
94DodMot-10
94DodPol-26
94Don-326
94ExtBas-297
94Fin-361
94FinRef-361
94Fla-184
94Fle-527
94Lea-21
94LeaL-122
94Pac-323
94Pin-484
94PinArtP-484
94PinMusC-484
94Sco-446
94ScoGolR-446
94Sel-139
94SP-81
94SPDieC-81
94StaClu-217
94StaCluFDI-217
94StaCluGR-217
94StaCluMOP-217
94Stu-73
94Top-143
94TopGol-143
94TopSpa-143
94TriPla-90
94Ult-220
94UppDec-408
94UppDecED-408
95Baz-51
95ColCho-219
95ColChoGS-219
95ColChoSE-94
95ColChoSEGS-94
95ColChoSESS-94
95ColChoSS-219
95D3-41
95DodMot-7
95DodPol-27
95Don-539
95DonPreP-539
95DonTopotO-274
95Emb-37
95EmbGolI-37
95Fin-62
95FinRef-62
95Fla-158
95Fle-551
95Lea-294
95LeaLim-140
95Pac-227
95PanSti-52
95Pin-384
95PinArtP-384
95PinMusC-384
95Sco-382
95ScoGolR-382
95ScoHaloG-HG104
95ScoPlaTS-382
95StaClu-259
95StaCluFDI-259
95StaCluMOP-259
95StaCluSTDW-D259
95StaCluSTWS-259
95StaCluVR-127
95Stu-165
95Top-38
95TopCyb-30
95Ult-401
95UltGolM-401
95UppDec-71
95UppDecED-71
95UppDecEDG-71
96AngMot-10
96ColCho-187
96ColCho-486
96ColChoGS-187
96ColChoGS-486
96ColChoSS-187
96ColChoSS-486
96Don-209
96DonPreP-209
96Fla-45
96Pin-58
96StaCluVRMO-127
96Ult-329
96UltGolM-329
97ColCho-136

Wallaesa, John
47TipTop-29
48WhiSoxTI-26

Wallen, Butch
87LitFalMP-2393

Wallenhaupt, Ron
85WatIndT-16

Wallenstein, John
74WicAerODF-127

Waller, Casey Lee
88CapCodPPaLP-113
90CMC-775
90ReaPhiB-19
90ReaPhiP-1229
90ReaPhiS-23
91LinDriAA-522
91ReaPhiLD-522
91ReaPhiP-1379
92ReaPhiS-546
92ScrRedBF-2457
92SkyAA F-239
93ScrRedBF-2553
93ScrRedBTI-26
95PorSeaDTI-27

Waller, K.C.
93ClaFS7-266

Waller, Kevin D.
80CedRapRT-25
82MadMusF-22

Waller, Reggie
80ColAstT-15
89AubAstP-2168

Waller, Rich
77BriRedST-20

Waller, Ty (Elliott)
78St.PetCT-25
79ArkTraT-9
82Fle-607
82IowCubT-13
82Top-51
84TucTorC-60
85TucTorC-64
86TucTorP-24
87TucTorP-6
88RivRedWCLC-233
88RivRedWP-1414
88SpoIndP-1923
89RivRedWCLC-30
90RivRedWCLC-27
94SpoIndC-25
94SpoIndF-3339
95PadMot-28

Walles, Todd
91BelMarC-8
91BelMarP-3676

Wallgren, Chris
90EliTwiS-23

Wallin, Craig
89SouBenWSGS-1

Wallin, Les (Leslie)
88WinHavRSS-25
89LynRedSS-20
90LynRedSTI-9
91WinHavRSC-21
91WinHavRSP-500
92WinHavRSC-21
92WinHavRSF-1789
93NewBriRSF-1231

Walling, Denny
77SanJosMC-17
77Top-473
79Top-553
80OPC-161
80Top-306
81Don-144
81Fle-66
81Top-439
82AstAstI-6
82Don-496
82Fle-236
82Top-147
83Don-419
83Fle-469
83Top-692
84AstMot-19
84Don-641
84Fle-244
84Nes792-36
84Top-36
84TopSti-73
84TopTif-36
85AstHouP-9
85AstMot-5
85Don-527
85Fle-365
85Top-382
85TopTif-382
86AstMilL-22
86AstPol-7
86AstTeaI-16
86Don-136
86Fle-314
86Top-504
86TopTif-504
87AstMot-13
87AstPol-12
87Don-554
87Fle-72
87FleGlo-72
87Lea-159
87OPC-222
87Top-222
87TopSti-33
87TopTif-222
88AstMot-13
88AstPol-23
88Don-384
88DonBasB-309
88Fle-458
88FleGlo-458
88Lea-224
88OPC-131
88PanSti-296
88Sco-145
88ScoGlo-145
88ScoSam-145
88StaLinAst-19
88Top-719
88TopSti-31
88TopTif-719
89CarSmo-23
89ChaLooLITI-32
89Don-279
89Fle-465
89FleGlo-465
89Sco-49
89Top-196
89TopTif-196
89UppDec-327
90CarSmo-26
90Don-677
90Fle-263
90FleCan-263
90OPC-462
90Top-462
90TopTif-462
90TopTVCa-30
91Fle-651
91RanMot-18
92Bow-530
93RanKee-371
96A'sMot-28

Walling, Kendall
86TriTriC-192
87QuaCitAP-25

Wallis, Joe
76OPC-598
76Top-598
77BurCheD-190
77Top-279
78SSP270-259
78Top-614
79Top-406
80Top-562

Walls, Doug
94AshTouC-24
94AshTouF-1782
94Bow-442
95SalAvaTI-7

Walls, Eric
94RocRoyC-27
94RocRoyF-580
95SprSulTI-30

Walls, R. Lee
53MotCoo-56
55Bow-82
57Kah-29
57Top-52
58Top-66
59Top-105
59TopVen-105
60Kah-42
60Lea-111
60Top-506
61Pos-119A
61Pos-119B
61Top-78
61TopStaI-60
62DodBelB-56
62Top-129A
62Top-129B
62TopStaI-160
62TopVen-129
63JeI-113
63Pos-113
63Top-11
64Top-411
90DodTar-828

Wallwork, Dave
86PenWhiSP-26
87PenWhiSP-18
88BirBarB-6
89BirBarB-25
89BirBarP-96
90BirBarB-27

Walraven, Randy
78DayBeaAT-26
Walsh, Christy
92MegRut-161
Walsh, Dave
84SyrChiT-21
86KnoBluJP-25
87KnoBluJP-1512
89AlbDukC-10
89AlbDukP-70
90AlbDukC-11
90AlbDukP-345
90AlbDukT-30
90CMC-413
90ProAAAF-66
90TriAllGP-AAA33
91AlbDukLD-22
91LinDriAAA-22
91OPC-367
91Sco-351
91Top-367
91TopDeb90-162
91TopDesS-367
91TopMic-367
91TopTif-367
Walsh, Dee
14B18B-28
Walsh, Dennis
91NiaFalRC-21
91NiaFalRP-3633
92FayGenC-23
92FayGenF-2169
93LakTigC-25
93LakTigF-1312
Walsh, Ed
07WhiSoxGWH-11
09AmeCarE-116
09ColChiE-299
09MaxPubP-16
09SpoNewSM-9
09T206-368
10ChiE-19
10DomDisP-121
10E98-29
10JuJuDE-39
10SepAnoP-25
10SweCapPP-14
11BasBatEU-42
11L1L-132
11MecDFT-39
11PloCanE-65
11S81LarS-107
11SpoLifCW-361
11SpoLifM-33
11T205-177
11TurRedT-125
12ColRedB-299
12ColTinT-299
12HasTriFT-22A
13NatGamW-42
13PolGroW-29
13TomBarW-38
14CraJacE-36
14PieStaT-60
14TexTomE-45
15CraJacE-36
15SpoNewM-187
16BF2FP-20
16SpoNewM-184
36PC7AlbHoF-49
48ExhHoF-31
49LeaPre-8
50CalHOFW-76
60Fle-49
61Fle-83
63BazA-7
69Baz-10
72FleFamF-23
76ShaPiz-49
77GalGloG-143
80LauFamF-34
80PerHaloFP-49
80SSPHOF-49
85WhiSoxC-34
85Woo-35
87HygAllG-45
88UtiBluSP-25
89HOFStiB-77
91ConTSN-273
92ConTSN-337
93ConTSN-703
93CraJac-23
94ConTSN-1013
94ConTSNB-1013
Walsh, Ed Jr.
60Fle-49
Walsh, James C.
11SpoLifM-242A
11SpoLifM-242B
12ImpTobC-20
14B18B-36A
14B18B-36B
14CraJacE-144
15CraJacE-144
17HolBreD-110
Walsh, Jay
83LynPirT-28
Walsh, Jim
16ColE13-182
50PirTeal-23
81QuaCitCT-11
82QuaCitCT-25
83MidCubT-4
Walsh, Joseph
87OldJudN-529
Walsh, Matt
94WesMicWC-23
94WesMicWF-2296
95ModA'sTI-29
96ModA'sB-11
Walsh, Rob
89MisStaB-36
Walter, Craig
85Ft.MyeRT-4
Walter, Gene
83MiaMarT-5
84BeaGolGT-9
85LasVegSC-112
86DonRoo-47
86Fle-644
86FleUpd-124
86TopTra-121T
86TopTraT-121T
87Don-511
87Fle-433
87FleGlo-433
87MetColP-49
87TidTidP-27
87TidTidT-21
87Top-248
87TopTif-248
88BlaYNPRWLU-12
88DonTeaBM-NEW
88Fle-153
88FleGlo-153
88MetColP-50
88MetKah-31
89BlaYNPRWLU-20
89Top-758
89TopTif-758
89UppDec-604
91MetWIZ-424
91PawRedSDD-27
92SyrChiF-1967
92SyrChiMB-25
92SyrChiS-520
93EdmTraF-1137
Walter, Jim
85RedWinA-24
Walter, Mike
94QuaCitRBC-23
94QuaCitRBF-534
96MidLeaAB-29
96QuaCitRB-29
Walterhouse, Dick
77SalPirT-26A
77SalPirT-26B
79BufBisT-19
Walters, Alfred
16ColE13-183
22E120-15
Walters, Brett
95MidLeaA-54
96RanCucQB-27
Walters, Bucky (William H.)
36GouWidPPR-A107
36WorWidGV-61
37ExhFou-6
38CinOraW-29
38ExhFou-6
39ExhSal-62
39OrcPhoAP-23
39PlaBal-22
40PlaBal-73
41DouPlaR-7
41DouPlaR-95
41HarHarW-26
41PlaBal-3
41WheM5-20
42GilRazL-1
47Exh-235
49EurSta-97
54BraJohC-31
55BraGolS-30
55BraJohC-31
79DiaGre-257
82OhiHaloF-34
83Bra53F-31
83TCMPla1943-29
89PacLegI-164
92ConTSN-537
93ConTSN-769
94ConTSN-1118
94ConTSNB-1118
Walters, Dan
86AshTouP-28
87OscAstP-8
88ColAstB-12
89WicWraR-11
90WicWraRD-23
91LasVegSLD-297
91LasVegSP-240
91LinDriAAA-297
92DonRooP-BC12
92DonUpd-U4
92FleUpd-126
92LasVegSS-246
92PadPolD-25
92ScoRoo-109T
92SkyAAAF-121
92TopTra-127T
92TopTraG-127T
93Don-48
93Fle-149
93Lea-156
93OPCPre-5
93PacSpa-605
93PadMot-19
93PanSti-257
93Pin-215
93Sco-332
93Sel-289
93StaClu-175
93StaCluFDI-175
93StaCluMOP-175
93Stu-81
93Top-273
93TopGol-273
93TopInaM-273
93TopMic-273
93TriPla-239
93Ult-125
93UppDec-172
93UppDecGold-172
93USPlaCR-4H
Walters, Darryel
85BelBreT-13
86StoPorP-25
87ElPasDP-21
88DenZepC-23
88DenZepP-1255
89DenZepC-16
89DenZepP-54
89ElPasDGS-29
90CMC-31
90DenZepC-6
90DenZepP-640
90ProAAAF-665
Walters, David
86ElmPioRSP-25
87GreHorP-26
88LynRedSS-24
89EasLeaDDP-DD24
89NewBriRSP-614
89NewBriRSS-20
90NewBriRSB-25
90NewBriRSP-1320
90NewBriRSS-20
91LinDriAAA-371
91PawRedSDD-28
91PawRedSLD-371
91PawRedSP-40
92PawRedSF-924
92PawRedSS-371
92SkyAAAF-170
97DunDonPPS-28
Walters, John
79WatIndT-28
Walters, Ken
60Top-511
61Pos-122A
61Pos-122B
61Top-394
62Top-328
63RedEnq-31
63RedFreBC-30
63Top-534
81TCM60I-317
Walters, Kent
88MisStaB-32
Walters, Leigh
91MelBusF-8
Walters, Mike
80ElPasDT-22
81SalLakCGT-13
82SpoIndT-9
82TolMudHT-8
83TolMudHT-10
84MinTwiP-30
84Nes792-673
84Top-673
84TopTif-673
84TwiTeal-22
85TolMudHT-11
85Top-187
85TopTif-187
Walters, Vic
78AppFoxT-25
79AppFoxT-24
Walther, Chris
96OgdRapTI-42
Walton, Bruce
86ModA'sC-20
86ModA'sP-26
87ModA'sC-17
87ModA'sP-14
88HunStaTI-25
89TacTigC-8
89TacTigP-1546
90CMC-583
90ProAAAF-138
90TacTigC-6
90TacTigP-91
91LinDriAAA-546
91ScoRoo-88T
91TacTigLD-546
91TacTigP-2306
92DonRoo-123
92FleUpd-52
92StaClu-563
92TacTigF-2502
92TopDeb91-179
92Ult-428
94ColSprSSF-735
96MedHatBJTI-31
Walton, Carlo
91KisDodP-4191
Walton, Danny
70BreMcD-31
70BreMil-24
70BreTeal-12
70OPC-134
70SunPin-18
70Top-134
71BreTeal-18
71Kel-22
71MLBOffS-455
71OPC-281
71Top-281
71TopCoi-88
73OPC-516
73Top-516
74TacTwiC-27
78Top-263
79SpoIndT-4
81Don-26A
83Pil69G-30
90DodTar-829
92YanWIZ7-160
93RanKee-372
94BreMilB-87
94BreMilB-372
Walton, Jerome
87PeoChiP-20
87PeoChiPW-5
88BasAmeAAB-5
88EasLeaAP-29
88PeoChiTI-30
88PitCubP-1374
89Bow-295
89BowTif-295
89ClaTraP-156
89CubMar-20
89DonBasB-172
89DonRoo-26
89FleUpd-80
89ScoRoo-85T
89ScoSco-2
89ScoYouS2-36
89StaWal-1
89StaWal-2
89StaWal-3
89StaWal-4
89StaWal-5
89StaWal-6
89StaWal-7
89StaWal-8
89StaWal-9
89StaWal-10
89StaWal-11
89StaWal/O-1
89StaWal/O-2
89StaWal/O-4
89StaWal/O-6
89StaWal/O-8
89StaWal/O-10
89TopAwaW-5
89TopTra-123T
89TopTraT-123T
89UppDec-765
90Baz-19
90Bow-35
90BowIns-10
90BowInsT-10
90BowTif-35
90BowTif-A10
90ClaBlu-34
90Col-15
90CubMar-22
90Don-285
90DonBesN-124
90DonPre-10
90Fle-44
90FleAwaW-42
90FleBasM-42
90FleCan-44
90FleLeaL-42
90FleSoaS-8
90FleWaxBC-C27
90Hot50RS-46
90K-M-7
90KinDis-15
90Lea-124
90MLBBasB-50
90MSAHolD-19
90OPC-464
90PanSti-230
90PubSti-207
90RedFolSB-100
90Sco-229
90Sco100RS-2
90Spo-67
90Top-464
90TopBig-267
90TopCoi-35
90TopDeb89-134
90TopDou-69
90TopGaloC-11
90TopGloS-39
90TopHeaU-24
90TopMag-6
90TopRoo-29
90TopSti-50
90TopSti-327
90TopStiB-21
90TopTif-464
90TopTVCu-34
90ToyRoo-29
90UppDec-345
90VenSti-474
90WonBreS-8
90Woo-6
91Bow-413
91Cla2-T29
91ClaGam-95
91CubMar-20
91CubVinL-33
91Don-72
91Fle-437
91Lea-39
91OPC-135
91PanFreS-48
91PanSti-44
91Sco-13
91StaClu-162
91Top-135
91TopDesS-135
91TopMic-135
91TopTif-135

91Ult-70
91UppDec-332
92Bow-27
92CubMar-20
92Don-528
92Fle-396
92OPC-543
92PanSti-187
92Pin-224
92Sco-457
92StaClu-421
92StaPro-11
92Top-543
92TopGol-543
92TopGolW-543
92TopMic-543
92Ult-184
92UppDec-463
92PacSpa-64
93Ult-526
93VanCanF-2611
94RedKah-32
95RedKah-33
95Sco-207
95ScoGolR-207
95ScoPlaTS-207
96Fle-356
96FleTif-356
96FleUpd-U107
96FleUpdTC-U107
96LeaSigA-237
96LeaSigAG-238
96LeaSigAS-238
97Ult-493
97UltGolME-493
97UltPlaME-493
Walton, Jim
73OPC-646
73Top-646
74Top-99
Walton, Reggie
75LafDriT-14
79SpoIndT-9
80SpoIndT-21
80VenLeaS-176
81Fle-609
81SpoIndT-14
82PorBeaT-22
82Top-711
Walton, Rob
88ChaKniTI-6
Walton, Tim
96MarPhiB-29
Wambsganss, Bill
16ColE13-184
16SpoNewM-185
17HolBreD-111
20NatCarE-105
21E121So1-111
21E121So8-102
21Nei-31
22AmeCarE-74
22E120-44
22W572-112
22W575-146
23MapCriV-29
23W501-22
25Exh-72
26Exh-112
27Exh-55
63GadFunC-59
68LauWorS-17
69SCFOldT-16
72LauGreF-49
76MotOldT-4
77GalGloG-262
77Ind192T-20
77Spo-4107
79DiaGre-277
81ConTSN-51
88ConSer4-29
90HOFStiB-24
91ConTSN-200
94ConTSN-1129
94ConTSNB-1129
95ConTSN-1358
Wampler, Samuel
94MarPhiC-28
94MarPhiF-3299
95MarPhiTI-29
Wandler, Mike
87PocGiaTB-20
Waner, Lloyd L.
28W502-59
28W513-73
28W56PlaC-D12
28Yue-59
29ExhFou-14
29PorandAR-94
30SchR33-2
30SchR33-16
30W554-17
31Exh-14
32USCar-13
33ButCre-27
33ExhFou-7
33GeoCMil-30
33Gou-164
33GouCanV-90
33RitCE-10H
33RitCE-12D
34DiaMatCSB-190
34BatR31-17
34BatR31-157
34ButPreR-61
34DiaStaR-16
34ExhFou-7
35DiaMatCS2-21
35DiaMatCS3T1-144
35GouPuzR-1E
35GouPuzR-3C
35GouPuzR-5C
35GouPuzR-14C
36GouWidPPR-A108
36NatChiFPR-96
36NatChiFPR-119
36R31PasP-39
36SandSW-49
38BasTabP-27
39PlaBal-89
40PlaBal-105
41DouPlaR-119
51R42SmaS-110
59OklTodML-2
60Fle-78
61Fle-84
67TopVen-167
72FleFamF-35
75SheGrePG-25
76GrePlaG-25
76RowExh-15
76ShaPiz-107
77GalGloG-86
79DiaGre-355
80PacLeg-24
80PerHaloFP-107
80SSPHOF-107
81ConTSN-62
83DonHOFH-22
84OCoandSI-147
85Woo-36
86ConSer1-58
89DodSmoG-32
89HOFStiB-42
89PacLegI-128
90DodTar-830
90PerGreM-15
91ConTSN-6
91ConTSN-265
92ConTSN-429
92ConTSN-562
92ConTSNCI-17
92MegRut-156
94ConTSN-1006
94ConTSN-1180
94ConTSNB-1006
95MegRut-9
Waner, Paul P.
26SpoComoA-45
28Exh-27
28PorandAR-A38
28PorandAR-B38
28W502-45
28W513-70
28W56PlaC-D3
28Yue-45
29ExhFou-14
29PorandAR-95
30SchR33-16
31Exh-14
31W517-34
32OrbPinUP-58
32R33So2-421
32USCar-2
33ButCanV-52
33ButCre-28
33CraJacP-24
33ExhFou-7
33GeoCMil-31
33Gou-25
33GouCanV-25
33NatLeaAC-1
33RitCE-5S
33RitCE-6D
33TatOrb-58
33TatOrbSDR-201
34DiaMatCSB-191
34ButPreR-62
34DiaStaR-83
34ExhFou-7
34Gou-11
34GouCanV-67
35DiaMatCS2-22
35DiaMatCS3T1-145
35ExhFou-7
35GouPuzR-1E
35GouPuzR-3C
35GouPuzR-5C
35GouPuzR-14C
36DiaMatCS3T2-23
36ExhFou-7
36GouBWR-24
36GouWidPPR-A109
36NatChiFPR-96
36PC7AlbHoF-62
36R31PasP-39
36SandSW-50
36WorWidGV-2
37ExhFou-7
37GouFliMR-10A
37GouFliMR-10B
37GouThuMR-10
37KelPepS-BB17
38ExhFou-7
38WheBB10-15
39PlaBal-112
40PlaBal-104
41DouPlaR-15
43DodTeal-23
50CalHOFW-77
51R42SmaS-111
59OklTodML-1
60Fle-76
61Fle-85
67TopVen-166
72FleFamF-24
75ShaPiz-2
75SheGrePG-9
76GrePlaG-9
76RowExh-15
76ShaPiz-62
77BobParHoF-50
77GalGloG-49
77GalGloG-209
80PacLeg-21
80PerHaloFP-62
80SSPHOF-62
81ConTSN-61
83ConMar-37
83DonHOFH-22
84OCoandSI-177
85FegMurCG-20
86ConSer1-8
86PirGreT-6
86SpoDecG-15
87HygAllG-46
88ConNatA-23
89HOFStiB-45
89PacLegI-127
90DodTar-831
90PerGreM-15
91ConTSN-5
91ConTSN-107
91ConTSN-315
92ConTSN-563
92YanWIZH-34
93ConTSN-672
94ConTSN-1099
94ConTSN-1180
94ConTSNB-1099
94ConTSNB-1180
95MegRut-9
Wanish, John
88BakDodCLC-261
89St.CatBJP-2086
90MyrBeaBJP-2778
91DunBluJC-11
91DunBluJP-207
Wanke, Chuck
90BenBucL-19
91EveGiaC-25
91EveGiaP-3914
92CliGiaC-16
92CliGiaF-3599
93SanJosGC-9
93SanJosGF-10
Wanz, Doug
81VanCanT-3
Wapnick, Steve
86AncGlaPTI-36
88MyrBeaBJP-1166
89DunBluJS-22
90Bow-346
90BowTif-346
90CMC-663
90ProAAAF-352
90SyrChiC-27
90SyrChiMB-27
90SyrChiP-572
91LinDriAAA-520
91SyrChiLD-520
91SyrChiMB-26
91SyrChiP-2481
91TopDeb90-163
92Don-743
92Sco-863
92StaClu-554
92VanCanF-2724
92VanCanS-627
93LinVenB-80
Warburton, John
89MisStaB-37
90MisStaB-40
91MisStaB-48
Ward, Aaron
20GasAmeMBD-18
20NatCarE-106
21E121So1-112
21E121So8-103
21Exh-183
21KoBreWSI-52
22E120-75
22W572-113
23W501-25
23W503-50
23W515-19
23WilChoV-167
25Exh-104
26SpoComoA-46
27AmeCarE-7
93ConTSN-747
Ward, Anthony
88St.CatBJP-2034
89MyrBeaBJP-1630
90DunBluJS-23
90FloStaLAS-47
90StaFS7-69
91KnoBluJLD-370
91KnoBluJP-1766
91LinDriAA-370
92SyrChiF-1968
92SyrChiMB-26
92SyrChiS-521
94SyrChiF-972
94SyrChiTI-28
Ward, Bryan
93ElmPioC-26
93ElmPioF-3825
94KanCouCC-26
94KanCouCF-163
94KanCouCTI-30
95PorSeaDTI-28
96PorSeaDB-28
Ward, Chris
73WicAerKSB-18
75OPC-587
75Top-587
Ward, Chuck
90DodTar-832
Ward, Colby
85AncGlaPTI-31
86SalAngC-89
87PalSprP-14
88MidAngGS-11
89EdmTraC-10
89EdmTraP-568
90CMC-454
90ColSprSSC-2
90ColSprSSP-37
90ProAAAF-218
91Don-330
91Fle-382
91OPC-31
91Top-31
91TopDeb90-164
91TopDesS-31
91TopMic-31
91TopTif-31
Ward, Colin
83BirBarT-19
84PhoGiaC-21
85PhoGiaC-198
86Fle-645
86ShrCapP-27
87PhoFirP-9
Ward, Dan
88PalSprACLC-95
88PalSprAP-1442
Ward, Daryle
94BriTigF-3514
95Bes-18
95FayGenTI-26
95SPML-57
96Exc-54
96LakTigB-29
96Top-425
97Bow-336
97BowChr-231
97BowChrI-231
97BowChrIR-231
97BowChrR-231
97BowInt-336
Ward, David
87SalLakTTT-12
Ward, Duane
83DurBulT-25
85GreBraTI-24
86BraPol-48
86FleUpd-125
87BluJayFS-33
87Don-45
87Lea-45
87OPC-153
87Top-153
87TopTif-153
88BluJayFS-30
88Don-567
88Fle-125
88FleGlo-125
88OPC-128
88Top-696
88TopTif-696
89BluJayFS-29
89Don-543
89DonBasB-216
89Fle-246
89FleGlo-246
89OPC-392
89Sco-359
89ScoYouS2-13
89Top-502
89TopTif-502
89UppDec-551
90BluJayFS-31
90Don-307
90Fle-95
90FleCan-95
90Lea-501
90OPC-28
90PubSti-528
90Sco-439
90Spo-107
90Top-28
90TopTif-28
90UppDec-653
90VenSti-475
91BluJayFS-28
91BluJayFS-30
91BluJayS-8
91Don-92
91Fle-187
91Lea-154
91OPC-181
91Sco-561
91StaClu-363
91Top-181
91TopDesS-181
91TopMic-181
91TopTif-181
91Ult-369
91UppDec-581
92Don-308
92Fle-344
92Lea-101
92OPC-365
92Pin-385
92Sco-48
92StaClu-781
92Top-365
92TopGol-365

92TopGolW-365
92TopMic-365
92Ult-154
92UppDec-450
93BluJayD-11
93BluJayD4-23
93BluJayFS-32
93Bow-307
93Don-379
93Fin-17
93FinRef-17
93Fla-296
93Fle-341
93Lea-135
93OPC-310
93OPCWorC-15
93PacSpa-330
93Pin-340
93Sco-436
93Sel-258
93SP-53
93StaClu-382
93StaCluFDI-382
93StaCluMOP-382
93Top-260
93TopGol-260
93TopInaM-260
93TopMic-260
93Ult-295
93UppDec-339
93UppDecGold-339
94BluJayUSPC-5D
94BluJayUSPC-13S
94Bow-225
94ColC-287
94ColChoGS-287
94ColChoSS-287
94Don-379
94DonSpeE-379
94ExtBas-197
94Fin-375
94FinRef-375
94Fle-346
94FleAllS-25
94FUnPac-97
94Lea-355
94OPC-160
94PanSti-10
94Pin-143
94PinArtP-143
94PinMusC-143
94Sco-481
94ScoGolR-481
94Sel-375
94Spo-58
94StaClu-377
94StaCluFDI-377
94StaCluGR-377
94StaCluMO-20
94StaCluMOP-377
94StaCluT-155
94StaCluTFDI-155
94Top-483
94TopGol-483
94TopSpa-483
94TriPla-39
94Ult-145
94UltFir-2
94UppDec-402
94UppDecED-402
95BluJayUSPC-2D
95BluJayUSPC-7S
95FleUpd-31
95Pin-250
95PinArtP-250
95PinMusC-250
95Sco-529
95ScoGolR-529
95ScoPlaTS-529
95Top-609
97BluJayS-38

Ward, Gary
77TacTwiDQ-15
79TolMudHT-1
80Top-669
80VenLeaS-15
81Don-594
81Top-328
82Don-571
82Fle-562
82FleSta-229
82Top-612
82TwiPos-27
83AllGamPI-70
83Don-429
83DonActA-18
83Fle-627
83FleSta-208
83FleSti-136
83Top-517
83TopSti-92
83TwiTeal-21
83TwiTeal-33
84AllGamPI-160
84Don-192
84Fle-576
84FleUpd-124
84FunFooP-95
84Nes792-67
84OPC-67
84RanJarP-32
84Top-67
84TopSti-303
84TopTif-67
84TopTra-126T
84TopTraT-126T
85AllGamPI-70
85Don-342
85Fle-572
85Lea-70
85OPC-84
85RanPer-32
85Top-414
85TopSti-353
85TopTif-414
86Don-20
86Don-98
86DonAll-51
86DonSupD-20
86Fle-575
86FleMin-113
86FleStiC-125
86Lea-20
86OPC-105
86RanPer-32
86Spo-197
86Top-105
86TopSti-239
86TopTat-21
86TopTif-105
87Don-427
87DonOpeD-242
87Fle-140
87FleGlo-140
87FleLimE-41
87FleRecS-40
87FleUpd-122
87FleUpdG-122
87Lea-177
87OPC-218
87Spo-91
87Top-762
87TopSti-235
87TopTif-762
87TopTra-125T
87TopTraT-125T
88Don-251
88DonReaBY-251
88Fle-224
88FleGlo-224
88OPC-235
88PanSti-160
88RedFolSB-95
88Sco-157
88ScoGlo-157
88Spo-125
88StaLinY-18
88Top-235
88TopBig-195
88TopSti-303
88TopTif-235
89Fle-273
89FleGlo-273
89FleUpd-33
89OPC-302
89Sco-435
89TigMar-32
89Top-302
89TopBig-206
89TopTif-302
89TopTra-124T
89TopTraT-124T
89UppDec-98
90Don-621
90Fle-618
90FleCan-618
90Lea-113
90OPC-679
90PanSti-68
90Sco-513
90TigCok-25
90Top-679
90TopTif-679
91Don-728
91Fle-356
91OklStaC-29
91OPC-556
91PanFreS-294
91Sco-637
91Top-556
91TopDesS-556
91TopMic-556
91TopTif-556
91UppDec-412
92OklStaC-29
92YanWIZ8-196
93RanKee-373
94RanAllP-13

Ward, Greg
87SavCarP-8
88RenSilSCLC-286

Ward, Jay (John F.)
61UniOil-H9
64Top-116
64Top-532
64TopVen-116
65Top-421
85CedRapRT-27
86VerRedP-23
88CarLeaAS-1
89WilBilS-24
92ExpPos-31
95PriWilCTI-29

Ward, Jon
96NewJerCB-28

Ward, Joseph
11MecDFT-49
12ImpTobC-6

Ward, Kevin
86PhiTas-xx
86ReaPhiP-25
87MaiGuiT-22
87ReaPhiP-12
88MaiPhiC-22
88MaiPhiP-278
89HunStaB-22
90CMC-602
90ProAAAF-156
90TacTigC-25
90TacTigP-109
91LasVegSLD-298
91LasVegSP-252
91LinDriAAA-298
91PadSmo-38
91TriA AAGP-AAA21
92Fle-623
92Lea-338
92PadCarJ-23
92PadMot-19
92PadPolD-26
92PadSmo-36
92Sco-862
92Sco100RS-42
92StaClu-253
92TopDeb91-180

Ward, Larry
95ChaLooTI-29
96ChaLooB-5

Ward, Max
87Ft.LauYP-12
88ColCliP-326

Ward, Montgomery (John Mont.)
76ShaPiz-101
77BobParHoF-51
80PerHaloFP-101
80SSPHOF-101
86OldJudN-13
87AllandGN-10
87BucN28-73A
87BucN28-73B
87BucN28-73C
87FouBasHN-11
87OldJudN-530
88GandBCGCE-44
88SpoTimM-26
88WG1CarG-45
89DodSmoG-33
89SFHaCN-18
90DodTar-833
90KalBatN-55
94OriofB-61
94UppDecTAE-10
95May-28A
95May-28B
95NewN566-586
95NewN566-587

Ward, Pete
47Exh-236
62AurRec-16
63Top-324
63WhiSoxJP-12
63WhiSoxTS-22
64ChatheY-48
64Top-85
64TopCoi-21
64TopGia-33
64TopSta-8
64TopStaU-73
64TopTatI-72
64TopVen-85
64WhiSoxTS-22
65Baz-8
65ChaTheY-47
65OldLonC-37
65OPC-215
65Top-215
65TopFmbl-64
65TopTral-71
65WhiSoxJP-11
66OPC-25
66Top-25
66TopRubl-96
66TopVen-25
66WhiSoxTI-12
67AshOil-12
67CokCapWS-4
67DexPre-217
67OPC-143
67Top-143
67Top-436
67TopVen-238
68AtlOilPBCC-46
68OPC-33
68Top-33
68TopActS-2A
68TopActS-15A
68TopVen-33
69KelPin-18
69MilBra-285
69MLBOffS-35
69MLBPin-29
69OPC-155
69Top-155
69TopDecl-44
69TopSta-159
69TopSup-11
69TopTeaP-11
69TraSta-20
69WhiSoxTI-12
70MLBOffS-251
70Top-659
71MLBOffS-501
71OPC-667
71Top-667
72MilBra-354
74SupBlaB-12
78TCM60I-120
80IowOakP-13
81PorBeaT-1
85WhiSoxC-32
91OriCro-473
92YanWIZ7-161

Ward, Preston
50Bow-231
53Top-173
54Bow-139
54Top-72
55Bow-27
55Top-95
55TopDouH-97
56Top-328
57Top-226
58Top-450
59Top-176
59TopVen-176
79TCM50-111
90DodTar-834
91TopArc1-173
94TopArc1-72
94TopArc1G-72

Ward, Ricky
90EveGiaB-20
90EveGiaP-3136
91CliGiaC-24
91CliGiaP-844
92SanJosGC-17
93SanJosGC-8
93SanJosGF-20
94NasXprF-396

Ward, Rube
90DodTar-1093

Ward, Todd
89GeoColC-35
90GeoColC-32

Ward, Turner
88ColCliC-19
88ColCliP-17
90CMC-472
90ColSprSSC-20
90ColSprSSP-52
90ProAAAF-233
91BluJayFS-31
91Bow-76
91Don-429
91Fle-383
91IndFanC-28
91Lea-449
91OPC-555
91Sco-732
91ScoRoo-4
91StaClu-593
91Stu-49
91Stu-138
91Top-555
91TopDeb90-165
91TopDesS-555
91TopMic-555
91TopTif-555
91Ult-118
91UppDec-762
92StaClu-621
92StaCluNC-621
92SyrChiF-1985
92SyrChiMB-27
93BluJayD-9
93BluJayD4-31
93BluJayFS-33
93Don-293
93Lea-427
93PacSpa-658
93Sco-473
94BreMilB-373
94BrePol-29
94ExtBas-110
94Fla-71
94Fle-347
94FleUpd-58
94ScoRoo-RT55
94ScoRooGR-RT55
94SpoRoo-21
94SpoRooAP-21
94StaClu-550
94StaCluFDI-550
94StaCluGR-550
94StaCluMOP-550
94Stu-49
94TopTra-104T
94Ult-381
95ColCho-177
95ColChoGS-177
95ColChoSS-177
95Don-74
95DonPreP-74
95Fle-194
95Pac-243
95Sco-263
95ScoGolR-263
95ScoPlaTS-263
95StaClu-495
95StaCluMOP-495
95StaCluSTWS-495
95Ult-70
95UltGolM-70
96LeaSigA-238
96LeaSigAG-239
96LeaSigAS-239
97PacPriGotD-GD60

Warden, Jon
68TigDetFPB-25
69Top-632
88TigDom-24

Wardle, Curt
83VisOakF-18
85FleUpd-127
85TwiTeal-26
86Fle-600
86IndTeal-44
86MaiGuiP-21
86Top-303

86TopTif-303
Wardle, Jack
28W512-34
Wardlow, Joe
88ButCopKSP-17
89GasRanS-24
89Sta-39
90Bes-208
90GasRanB-10
90GasRanP-2531
90GasRanS-24
91PriWilCC-20
91PriWilCP-1437
Wardlow, Mike
77CedRapGT-14
Wardwell, Shea
90ElmPioP-8
91Cla/Bes-295
91WinHavRSC-25
91WinHavRSP-504
Ware, Derek
87DunBluJP-950
Ware, Jeff
91ClaDraP-31
91TopTra-124T
91TopTraT-124T
92DunBluJC-2
92DunBluJF-2001
92OPC-414
92Pin-546
92StaCluD-192
92Top-414
92TopGol-414
92TopGolW-414
92TopMic-414
92UppDecML-323
93ClaGolF-88
95SyrChiTI-26
96BluJayOH-34
96Bow-232
96ColCho-663
96ColCho-752
96ColChoGS-26
96ColChoGS-663
96ColChoGS-752
96ColChoSS-26
96ColChoSS-663
96ColChoSS-752
96Pin-378
96PinAfi-195
96PinAfiAP-195
96PinFoil-378
Wareham, Ronnie
85CloHSS-42
Warembourg, Scott
94BenRocF-3595
97BenRocC-24
Wares, Buzzy (Clyde E.)
41CarW75-27
46SeaSLP-56
74Car193T-25
Warfel, Brian
87ElmPio(C-9
88ElmPio1C-8
88ElmPioC-26
88WinHavRSS-26
Warhop, John
09ColChiE-300
09T206-369
10CouT21-241
10CouT21-242
10DomDisP-122
10E-UOraBSC-24
10RedCroT-81
10RedCroT-164
10RedCroT-254
10SweCapPP-38
12ColRedB-300
12ColTinT-300
12T207-192
94ConTSN-1275
94ConTSNB-1275
Waring, Jim
91AubAstC-22
91AubAstP-4274
92BurAstC-6
92BurAstF-548
92MidLeaATI-47
93ClaGolF-156
93ExcFS7-50
94FloStaLAF-FSL36
94OscAstC-23
94OscAstF-1139
95JacGenTI-11
Warneke, Lon
32CubTeal-26
32OrbPinNP-4
32OrbPinUP-59
33CraJacP-25
33DelR33-16
33GeoCMil-32
33Gou-203
33NatLeaAC-8
33TatOrb-59
33TatOrbSDR-194
34DiaMatCSB-192
34BatR31-186
34ExhFou-3
35DiaMatCS2-23
35DiaMatCS3T1-146
35ExhFou-3
36ExhFou-3
36GouWidPPR-A110
36NatChiFPR-93
36R31PasP-33
36SandSW-51
36WheBB4-12
36WorWidGV-100
37ExhFou-8
38ExhFou-8
38WheBB11-8
39ExhSal-63
39GouPreR303A-46
39PlaBal-41
39WorWidGTP-46
40PlaBal-114
41CarW75-28
43CubTeal-23
55Bow-299
77GalGloG-222
81DiaStaCD-120
83ConMar-48
88ConNatA-24
91ConTSN-231
92ConTSN-371
92ConTSN-640
93ConTSN-687
94ConTSN-1106
94ConTSNB-1106
Warner, Bryan
94BurIndC-25
94BurIndF-3812
Warner, E.H.
87OldJudN-256
87OldJudN-531
Warner, Fred
80PenPilBT-5
80PenPilCT-8
Warner, Harry
77OPC-58
77Top-113
78BluJayP-23
80SyrChiT-19
80SyrChiTI-21
82BrePol-NNO
83VisOakF-13
92BreCarT-xx
Warner, Jack (John R.)
49W725AngTI-29
79DiaGre-302
90DodTar-835
92ConTSN-410
Warner, Jack D.
65Top-354
Warner, Jackie (John J.)
33Gou-178
65Top-517
66Top-553
Warner, Jim
47SigOil-72
47SunBre-23
Warner, John Joseph
03BreE10-149
08RosComP-86
11SpoLifCW-362
26Exh-96
Warner, Ken
93DanBraC-27
93DanBraF-3627
95DurBulTI-32
Warner, Michael
92IdaFalGF-3529
92IdaFalGSP-20
Warner, Mike
92FroRowDP-71
93DurBulC-22
93DurBulF-501
93DurBulTI-8
94CarLeaAF-CAR32
94DurBulC-25
94DurBulF-343
94DurBulTI-27
96GreBraB-29
96GreBraTI-7
Warner, Randy
92GulCoaMF-3495
93KinMetC-23
93KinMetF-3810
94CapCitBC-22
94CapCitBF-1765
95StLucMTI-32
96StLucMTI-16
Warner, Ron
91HamRedC-21
91HamRedP-4048
92SavCarC-6
92SavCarF-673
93St.PetCC-27
93St.PetCF-2637
94ArkTraF-3098
95ArkTraTI-27
96ArkTraB-27
Warner, W.M.
31CubTeal-27
Warrecker, Teddy
94BurIndC-26
94BurIndF-3794
96KenIndB-24
Warrecker, William
89BenBucL-11
90PalSprACLC-224
90PalSprAP-2579
Warren, Alan
88OneYanP-2066
Warren, Brian
90BriTigP-3167
91FayGenC-29
91FayGenP-1171
92ClaFS7-170
92ClaFS7-174
92LonTigF-633
92LonTigS-422
92ProFS7-67
92SkyAA F-177
93LonTigF-2308
94IndIndF-1813
95IndIndF-96
96IndIndB-26
Warren, Charlie
77WauMetT-22
Warren, Derrick
92BelMarC-3
92BelMarF-1460
Warren, DeShawn
92ClaDraP-31
93StaCluAn-25
93StaCluM-181
93Top-574
93TopGol-574
93TopInaM-574
93TopMic-574
94Bow-207
94BowBes-B12
94BowBesR-B12
94CedRapKC-1
94CedRapKF-1109
94Cla-159
94ClaTriF-T10
95Bow-87
95CedRapKTI-32
95MidLeaA-55
95UppDecML-92
96OgdRapTI-40
95UppDecMLFS-92
Warren, Earl
59FleWil-78
Warren, Glen
89EveGiaS-29
Warren, Joe
89BenBucL-12
91RenSilSCLC-10
Warren, Mark
84IdaFalATI-29
Warren, Marty
86AppFoxP-28
Warren, Mel
91KisDodP-4204
Warren, Mike
84A'sMot-20
84Don-631
84Fle-461
84Fle-639
84Nes792-5
84Nes792-338
84Top-5
84Top-338
84TopSti-288B
84TopTif-5
84TopTif-338
85A'sMot-19
85Don-278
85Fle-435
85Top-197
85TopTif-197
86OmaRoyP-28
89RenSilSCLC-248
92A'sUno7P-4
Warren, Randy
88UtiBluSP-12
89SouBenWSGS-17
Warren, Raymond
82BurRanF-7
82BurRanT-12
Warren, Ron
86ElmPioRSP-26
Warren, Tommy
77TCMTheWY-80
88KimN18-46
90DodTar-836
Warren, Travis
87ClePhiP-27
Warstler, Rabbit (Harold)
34DiaMatCSB-193
35DiaMatCS3T1-147
36GouWidPPR-A111
39PlaBal-120
40PlaBal-59
41Gou-21
91ConTSN-240
Warthen, Dan
72Dia-50
76ExpRed-35
76OPC-374
76SSP-347
76Top-374
77ExpPos-37
77OPC-99
77Top-391
79PorBeaT-17
80PorBeaT-26
81BufBisT-12
82AleDukT-20
87ChaLooB-2
88CalCanC-25
88CalCanP-789
89BlaYNPRWL-200
89CalCanC-25
89CalCanP-523
90CalCanC-24
90CalCanP-665
90CMC-451
90ProAAAF-130
92MarMot-27
94LasVegSF-885
96PadMot-28
Warwick, Carl
62Col.45B-21
62Jel-161
62Pos-161
62PosCan-161
62SalPlaC-160
62ShiPlaC-160
62Top-202
63Col45"P-16
63Col45'JP-12
63Jel-190
63Pos-190
63Top-333
64ChatheY-49
64Col.45JP-10
64Top-179
64TopVen-179
65CarJayP-11
65Top-357
66Top-247
66TopVen-247
90DodTar-837
91OriCro-474
Warwick, Clinton
86GenCubP-11
Wasdell, James
40DodTeal-24
41DodTeal-10
41DouPlaR-19
43PhiTeal-23
79DiaGre-56
90DodTar-838
93ConTSN-714
Wasdin, John
94Bow-660
94BowBes-B49
94BowBes-X101
94BowBesR-B49
94BowBesR-X101
94Cla-13
94ClaGolF-128
94ClaGolN1PLF-LP17
94ClaGolREF-RE17
94ModA'sC-23
94Pin-430
94PinArtP-430
94PinMusC-430
94Sco-571
94ScoGolR-571
94SigRoo-48
94SigRooS-48
94Top-749
94TopGol-749
94TopSpa-749
94UppDecML-209
95Bow-163
95BowBes-B14
95BowBesR-B14
95ColCho-30
95ColChoGS-30
95ColChoSS-30
95EdmTraTI-24
95Exc-113
95Top-207
95UppDecML-12
95UppDecML-168
95UppDecMLOP-OP20
96A'sMot-10
96Bow-174
96ColCho-15
96ColChoGS-15
96ColChoSS-15
96Don-354
96DonPreP-354
96Fle-222
96FleTif-222
96LeaPre-115
96LeaPreP-115
96LeaSig-74
96LeaSigPPG-74
96LeaSigPPP-74
96Pin-182
96PinAfi-193
96PinAfiAP-193
96Sco-497
96Sel-183
96SelArtP-183
96SelCer-118
96SelCerAP-118
96SelCerCB-118
96SelCerCR-118
96SelCerMB-118
96SelCerMG-118
96SelCerMR-118
96SP-16
96StaClu-284
96StaCluMOP-284
96Sum-175
96SumAbo&B-175
96SumArtP-175
96SumFoi-175
96Top-349
96TopChr-140
96TopChrR-140
96TopGal-134
96TopGalPPI-134
96UppDec-226
96UppDecBCP-BC7
96Zen-125
96ZenArtP-125
97ColCho-188
97DonRatR-9
97Fin-302
97FinEmb-302
97FinEmbR-302
97FinRef-302
97Fle-198
97Fle-574
97FleTif-198
97FleTif-574
97MetUni-132
97Pac-178
97PacLigB-178
97PacSil-178
97Sco-53

97Sco-344
97ScoHobR-344
97ScoPreS-53
97ScoResC-344
97ScoShoS-53
97ScoShoS-344
97ScoShoSAP-53
97ScoShoSAP-344
97Top-448
97Ult-116
97Ult-542
97UltGolME-116
97UltGolME-542
97UltPlaME-116
97UltPlaME-542
97UppDec-132
95UppDecMLFS-12
95UppDecMLFS-168
97UppDecTTS-TS19
Wasem, Jim
84EveGiaC-24
85FreGiaP-7
86ChaRaiP-28A
86ChaRaiP-28B
88ChaRaiP-1195
Washam, Jason
96HelBreTI-28
Washburn, Greg
70OPC-74
70Top-74
Washburn, Jarrod
95BoiHawTI-34
96Bow-297
96BowBesMI-10
96BowBesMIAR-10
96BowBesMIR-10
96Top-23
96TopPowB-23
97Bow-385
97BowBes-153
97BowBesAR-153
97BowBesR-153
97BowChr-254
97BowChrI-254
97BowChrIR-254
97BowChrR-254
97BowInt-385
97Top-207
Washburn, Ray
62Top-19
62TopVen-19
63Jel-168
63Pos-168
63Top-206
64Top-332
64TopVen-332
65CarTeal-27
65Top-467
66Top-399
67OPC-92
67Top-92
68Top-388
69Top-415
69TopTeaP-18
70DayDaiNM-86
70OPC-22
70Top-22
81TCM60I-404
Washington, Claudell
75GreHeroBP-3
75OPC-647
75Top-647
76Kel-2
76OPC-189
76OPC-198
76SSP-489
76Top-189
76Top-198
77BurCheD-115
77Hos-86
77OPC-178
77RCColC-66
77Top-405
77TopCloS-50
78RanBurK-19
78RCColC-46
78SSP270-88
78Top-67
79OPC-298
79Top-574
80Kel-34
80OPC-171
80Top-322
81BraPol-18
81Fle-329
81Top-151
81TopTra-854
82BraBurKL-25
82BraPol-15
82Don-58
82Fle-449
82FleSta-66
82OPC-32
82Top-126
82Top-758
82TopSti-22
83AllGamPI-161
83BraPol-15
83Don-249
83Fle-150
83FleSta-209
83FleSti-88
83OPC-235
83Top-235
83TopSti-216
84AllGamPI-71
84BraPol-15
84Don-310
84Fle-192
84Nes792-410
84OPC-42
84Top-410
84TopSti-32
84TopTif-410
85AllGamPI-160
85BraHos-22
85BraPol-15
85BraTBSAT-4
85Don-11
85Don-310
85DonSupD-11
85Fle-342
85Lea-11
85OPC-166
85Top-540
85TopSti-25
85TopTif-540
86BraPol-15
86Don-287
86Fle-531
86FleMin-107
86Lea-164
86OPC-303
86Top-675
86TopSti-39
86TopTat-17
86TopTif-675
86TopTra-122T
86TopTraT-122T
87A'sMot-15
87Fle-119
87FleGlo-119
87Top-15
87TopTif-15
88Don-340
88DonBasB-217
88DonReaBY-340
88Fle-225
88FleGlo-225
88OPC-335
88Sco-579
88ScoGlo-579
88StaLinY-19
88Top-335
88TopBig-178
88TopSti-301
88TopTif-335
89Bow-52
89BowTif-52
89Don-72
89DonBasB-227
89DonTra-46
89Fle-272
89FleGlo-272
89FleUpd-17
89OPC-185
89Sco-211
89ScoRoo-10T
89Spo-75
89Top-185
89TopDouM-17
89TopTif-185
89TopTra-125T
89TopTraT-125T
89TopUKM-81
89UppDec-310
89UppDec-794
90AngSmo-17
90Bow-297
90BowTif-297
90Don-52
90Fle-146
90FleCan-146
90OPC-705
90PanSti-30
90PubSti-380
90Sco-298
90ScoRoo-45T
90Top-705
90TopBig-12
90TopTif-705
90UppDec-395
90VenSti-476
90YanScoNW-8
91MetWIZ-425
92YanWIZ8-197
93RanKee-374
Washington, George (Sloan Vernon)
36NatChiFPR-104
Washington, Glenn
86QuaCitAP-31
87PalSprP-15
88PalSprACLC-111
88PalSprAP-1455
Washington, Herb
75OPC-407
75Top-407
Washington, Keith
80PenPilBT-9
80PenPilCT-18
81ReaPhiT-19
82ReaPhiT-19
83ReaPhiT-21
Washington, Kraig
89ChaWheB-4
89ChaWheP-1752
90PeoChiTI-7
Washington, Kyle
89KinMetS-25
90PitMetP-2
91CollndC-4
91CollndP-1503
91SouAtlLAGP-SAL19
92Canlndf-705
92CanlndS-122
92ClaFS7-41
92ProFS7-58
92SkyAA F-58
93BowBayF-2201
93ExcFS7-169
Washington, LaRue
76AshTouT-18
77TucTorC-7
78TucTorC-2
80Top-233
93RanKee-375
Washington, Lozando
76CedRapGT-30
Washington, Mal
75QuaCitAT-24
76CliPilT-34
Washington, Pete
91PomBlaBPB-23
Washington, Pres. (George)
63GadFunC-75
Washington, Randy
81BatTroT-24
82WatIndF-26
82WatIndT-25
83WatIndF-1
84BufBisT-20
85WatIndT-3
86IndTeal-45
86MaiGuiP-22
87BufBisP-12
88ColSprSSC-22
88ColSprSSP-1525
Washington, Ron
79TidTidT-9
80TolMudHT-6
81TolMudHT-18
82TopTra-124T
82TwiPos-28
83Don-431
83Fle-626
83OPC-27
83Top-458
83TwiTeal-24
84Don-391
84Fle-577
84MinTwiP-31
84Nes792-623
84OPC-268
84Top-623
84TopTif-623
84TwiTeal-25
85Don-391
85Fle-292
85Top-329
85TopTif-329
85TwiTeal-28
86Don-560
86Fle-409
86TolMudHP-23
86Top-513
86TopTif-513
86TwiTeal-26
87RocRedWP-19
87RocRedWT-16
87Top-169
87TopTif-169
88IndGat-15
88StaLinO-18
88TopTra-125T
88TopTraT-125T
89Don-468
89Fle-416
89FleGlo-416
89PacSenL-178
89T/MSenL-110
89TopSenL-44
89TucTorC-19
89TucTorJP-27
89TucTorP-190
89UppDec-519
90CMC-165
90DodTar-839
90EliSenL-31
90OklCit8C-15
90OklCit8P-442
90ProAAAF-688
91LinDriAAA-575
91OriCro-475
91PacSenL-47
91PacSenL-48
91TidTidLD-575
91TidTidP-2528
92TidTidF-914
92TidTidS-575
93CapCitBC-25
94CapCitBC-26
94CapCitBF-1767
95NorTidTI-3
96A'sMot-28
Washington, Tyrone
90ButCopKSP-25
91GasRanC-10
91GasRanP-2687
92Ft.MyeMCB-16
93ChaRanC-23
93ChaRanF-1942
Washington, U.L.
75OmaRoyTI-17
76OmaRoyTT-25
78Roy-23
78SSP270-236
78Top-707
79RoyTeal-11
79Top-157
80Top-508
81AllGamPI-27
81CokTeaS-80
81Don-460
81Fle-34
81OPC-26
81RoyPol-8
81Top-26
82Don-160
82Fle-424
82FleSta-203
82OPC-329
82Roy-21
82Top-329
83AllGamPI-26
83Don-490
83Fle-125
83FleSta-210
83FleSti-97
83OPC-67
83Roy-29
83RoyPol-7
83Top-687
84AllGamPI-117
84Don-543
84Fle-361
84Nes792-294
84OPC-294
84Top-294
84TopSti-282
84TopTif-294
85Don-521
85ExpPos-24
85Fle-215
85FleUpd-128
85OPCPos-4
85Top-431
85TopTif-431
85TopTifT-128T
85TopTra-128T
86Don-498
86Fle-264
86OPC-113
86Top-113
86TopTif-113
87VanCanP-1622
89PacSenL-205
89T/MSenL-111
89TopSenL-120
89WelPirP-30
90EliSenL-62
91PacSenL-102
92MemChiF-2437
92MemChiS-450
94MemChiF-375
95WicWraTI-30
96WicWraB-28
Washko, Patrick
76WilTomT-20
77WatIndT-28
Wasiak, Stan
74AlbDukTI-77
74AlbDukTI-23
77LodDodT-23
78LodDodT-25
79LodDodT-14
81VerBeaDT-27
83VerBeaDT-28
85VerBeaDT-26
86VerBeaDP-27
Wasilewski, Kevin
86AubAstP-25
87AshTouP-12
Wasilewski, Tom
86VenGulP-26
87ShrCapP-21
Wasinger, Mark
84BeaGolGT-17
85BeaGolGT-19
86LasVegSP-23
87LasVegSP-27
88Fle-100
88FleGlo-100
88GiaMot-23
88PhoFirC-17
88PhoFirP-54
88RedFolSB-96
88Sco-283
88ScoGlo-283
89ColCliC-22
89ColCliP-18
89ColCliP-738
90CMC-222
90ColCliC-22
90ColCliP-25
90ColCliP-687
90ProAAAF-337
91EdmTraLD-173
91EdmTraP-1525
91LinDriAAA-173
92EdmTraF-3549
92EdmTraS-171
92MidAngOHP-27
93MidAngF-336
97MidAngOHP-31
Waslewski, Gary
68CokCapRS-2
69Top-438
70Top-607
71MLBOffS-502
71OPC-277
71Top-277
72OPC-108
72Top-108
81RedSoxBG2S-125
92YanWIZ7-162
Wasley, Mel
40SolHug-18
47SunBre-24

Wassenaar, Robert
87SalAngP-5
88QuaCitAGS-25
89VisOakCLC-98
89VisOakP-1425
90OrlSunRB-18
90OrlSunRP-1084
90OrlSunRS-22
91LinDriAA-497
91OrlSunRLD-497
91OrlSunRP-1850
92PorBeaF-2668
92PorBeaS-422
Waszgis, B.J.
92KanCouCC-1
92KanCouCF-95
92KanCouCTI-29
92MidLeaATI-48
93AlbPolC-21
93AlbPolF-2029
93SouAtlLAGF-5
94CarLeaAF-CAR2
94FreKeyF-2618
94OriPro-103
95BowBayTI-41
95Exc-9
96RocRedWB-28
94FreKeyC-24
Watanabe, Curt
80BurBeeT-26
Watanabe, Hisanobu
87JapPlaB-33
Watanabe, Masahito
87MiaMarP-12
Waterbury, Steve
76TulOilGP-21
Waterfield, Bob
52Whe-29A
52Whe-29B
Waters, Darnell
76ForLauYS-13
Waters, Jack
60MapLeaSF-22
Wathan, Duke (John)
75OmaRoyTI-18
76OmaRoyTT-26
77Top-218
78Roy-24
78SSP270-233
78Top-343
79RoyTeal-12
79Top-99
80Top-547
81CokTeaS-81
81Don-221
81Fle-46
81OPC-157
81Top-157
82Don-86
82Fle-425
82OPC-383
82Roy-22
82Top-429
82TopSti-192
83AllGamPI-45
83Don-86
83Fle-126
83OPC-289
83Roy-30
83RoyPol-8
83Top-6
83Top-746
83TopSti-78
83TopSti-195
83TopSti-196
84AllGamPI-134
84Don-466
84Fle-362
84Nes792-602
84OPC-72
84Top-602
84TopSti-284
84TopTif-602
85Don-466
85Fle-216
85Top-308
85TopTif-308
86Don-496
86Fle-23
86RoyKitCD-12
86Top-128
86TopTif-128
87OmaRoyP-3
88RoySmo-1
88Top-534
88TopTif-534
89Top-374
89TopTif-374
90OPC-789
90Top-789
90TopTif-789
91OPC-291
91RoyPol-24
91Top-291
91TopDesS-291
91TopMic-291
91TopTif-291
93AngMot-28
Wathan, Dusty
95EveAqaTI-30
96LanJetB-30
Watkins, Bob C.
70OPC-227
70Top-227
71MLBOffS-93
Watkins, Bud
58UniOil-10
Watkins, Darren
87AppFoxP-12
87EugEmeP-2664
90BasCitRS-25
91DurBulUP-8
91LinDriAA-423
91MemChiLD-423
91MemChiP-668
Watkins, Dave
70OPC-168
70Top-168
Watkins, Don
49W725AngTI-30
95AngCHP-16
95PadCHP-16
Watkins, George
34Gou-53
35ExhFou-6
90DodTar-840
91ConTSN-222
Watkins, Jason
93SouBenWSC-23
93SouBenWSF-1430
94PriWilCC-21
94PriWilCF-1920
92UtiBluSC-17
Watkins, Jim
81BriRedST-22
Watkins, Keith
88ModA'sCLC-71
Watkins, Pat
93BilMusF-3961
93BilMusSP-12
94CarLeaAF-CAR52
94ExcFS7-182
94Top-743
94TopGol-743
94TopSpa-743
94WinSpiC-25
94WinSpiF-286
95Bes-64
95Bow-209
95BowBes-B23
95BowBes-X15
95BowBesR-B23
95BowBesR-X15
95ChaLooTI-25
95Exc-184
95SPML-39
95Top-647
95UppDecML-87
96Bow-151
96ChaLooB-29
95UppDecMLFS-87
Watkins, Scott
91OklStaC-30
92KenTwiF-605
92OklStaC-30
93ForWayWC-25
93ForWayWF-1970
94NasXprF-388
Watkins, Sean
95IdaFalBTI-33
96Bow-384
96RanCucQB-28
Watkins, Tim
87BelBreP-21
88DenZepC-6
88DenZepP-1265
89DenZepC-2
89DenZepP-41
89ElPasDGS-15
90CMC-28
90DenZepC-3
90DenZepP-627
90ProAAAF-652
91ChaKniLD-146
91ChaKniP-1690
91LinDriAA-146
Watkins, Troy
86Ft.MyeRP-27
Watkins, William H.
87OldJudN-532
Watlington, Julius
52Par-83
Watson, Allen
91Cla/Bes-427
91ClaDraP-17
91FroRowDP-44
91HamRedC-7
91HamRedP-4040
92Bow-634
92ClaFS7-282
92OPC-654
92Pin-304
92ProFS7-330
92Sco-799
92St.PetCC-1
92StaCluD-193
92Top-654
92TopGol-654
92TopGolW-654
92TopMic-654
92UppDecML-67
92UppDecML-153
93Bow-24
93Bow-358
93ClaFS7-148
93FlaWavotF-17
93LeaGolR-U1
93LouRedF-215
93SelRoo-90T
93SP-288
93StaCluCa-19
93TriAAAGF-24
93Ult-467
94Bow-480
94CarPol-24
94ColC-288
94ColChoGS-288
94ColChoSS-288
94Don-289
94Fin-331
94FinRef-331
94Fla-432
94Fle-648
94Lea-163
94OPC-15
94OPCDiaD-16
94Pac-606
94Pin-145
94PinArtP-145
94PinMusC-145
94PinNewG-NG8
94Sco-613
94ScoBoyoS-7
94ScoGolR-613
94Sel-376
94Spo-26
94StaClu-653
94StaCluFDI-653
94StaCluGR-653
94StaCluMOP-653
94StaCluT-322
94StaCluTFDI-322
94Top-196
94TopGol-196
94TopSpa-196
94TriPla-68
94Ult-570
94UppDec-235
94UppDecED-235
95ColCho-198
95ColChoGS-198
95ColChoSS-198
95Don-16
95DonPreP-16
95Fin-106
95FinRef-106
95Fla-196
95Fle-511
95Lea-124
95Pin-329
95PinArtP-329
95PinMusC-329
95Sco-480
95ScoGolR-480
95ScoPlaTS-480
95Sel-36
95SelArtP-36
95StaClu-165
95StaCluFDI-165
95StaCluMOP-165
95StaCluSTWS-165
95Stu-171
95Top-262
95TopCyb-142
95Ult-228
95UltGolM-228
95UppDec-307
95UppDecED-307
95UppDecEDG-307
96Don-150
96DonPreP-150
96EmoXL-296
96Fla-394
96Fle-558
96FleTif-558
96FleUpd-U210
96FleUpdTC-U210
96GiaMot-15
96LeaSigA-239
96LeaSigAG-240
96LeaSigAS-240
96Pac-217
96PanSti-80
96StaClu-64
96StaCluMOP-64
96Ult-572
96UltGolM-572
97Cir-297
97CirRav-297
97ColCho-253
97DonTea-12
97DonTeaSPE-12
97Fle-487
97FleTif-487
97Sco-78
97Sco-359
97ScoHobR-359
97ScoPreS-78
97ScoResC-359
97ScoShoS-78
97ScoShoS-359
97ScoShoSAP-78
97ScoShoSAP-359
97StaClu-363
97StaCluMOP-363
97Top-314
97Ult-299
97Ult-415
97UltGolME-299
97UltGolME-415
97UltPlaME-299
97UltPlaME-415
Watson, Andy
90ButCopKSP-27
91ButCopKSP-5
Watson, Bob
69Top-562
70OPC-407
70Top-407
71AstCok-10
71MLBOffS-94
71OPC-222
71Top-222
72OPC-355
72Top-355
72TopCloT-32
73LinPor-85
73OPC-110
73Top-110
74AstFouTIP-1
74Kel-11
74OPC-370
74Top-370
74TopDecE-69
74TopSta-39
75Hos-53
75Kel-6
75OPC-227
75Top-227
76CraDis-66
76Hos-5
76HosTwi-5
76Kel-27
76OPC-20
76SSP-60
76Top-20
77BurCheD-6
77Hos-39
77MSADis-60
77PepGloD-60
77Top-540
77TopCloS-51
78AstBurK-12
78Hos-28
78OPC-107
78TasDis-18
78Top-330
78WifBalD-77
79OPC-60
79Top-130
80OPC-250
80Top-480
81AllGamPI-9
81Don-225
81Dra-28
81Fle-93
81OPC-208
81Top-690
81TopSupHT-71
82BraBurKL-26
82BraPol-8
82Don-108
82Fle-54
82OPC-275
82Top-275
82TopTra-125T
83BraPol-8
83Don-551
83Fle-151
83FleSta-211
83FleSti-83
83Top-572
84BraPol-8
84Fle-193
84Nes792-739
84Top-739
84TopTif-739
85OPC-51
85Top-51
85TopTif-51
86A'sMot-27
86AstGreT-1
86AstMot-13
87AstShoSO-23
87AstShoSTw-26
87AstShoSTw-27
87AstShowSTh-29
88A'sMot-27
92YanWIZ8-198
94TedWil-37
Watson, D.J.
87AppFoxP-5
Watson, Dave
89PriPirS-23
91SalBucC-22
91SalBucP-952
92SalBucC-23
92SalBucF-64
Watson, Dejon
86Ft.MyeRP-28
88BasCitRS-25
89BasCitRS-26
Watson, Doc
96AugGreB-2
Watson, Frankie
88EugEmeB-28
Watson, John
22WilPatV-8
96BurBeeTI-18
Watson, John Reeves
22E120-135
22W573-135
Watson, Jonathan
95BelGiaTI-6
Watson, Kevin
94EveGiaC-4
94EveGiaF-3670
95BurBeeTI-31
96BurBeeTI-26
Watson, Mark
96HelBreTI-27
Watson, Marty
93ButCopKSP-13
94Bow-351
94ChaRivC-23
94ChaRivF-2688
Watson, Matt
89AlaGol-5
90St.CatBJP-3460
Watson, Milton

19W514-77
Watson, Phil
43ParSpo-71
77AshTouT-25
Watson, Preston
89BurBraP-1604
89BurBraS-22
90GreBraP-1129
90GreBraS-21
91GreBraC-8
91GreBraLD-221
91GreBraP-3002
91LinDriAA-221
92GreBraF-1155
92GreBraS-248
Watson, Ron
91BoiHawC-22
91BoiHawP-3880
92QuaCitRBC-13
92QuaCitRBF-810
93Bow-581
94MidAngF-2439
94MidAngOHP-31
94Top-713
94TopGol-713
94TopSpa-713
97MidAngOHP-32
Watson, Shaun
91KinMetC-18
91KinMetP-3814
92PitMetC-12
92PitMetF-3297
Watson, Steve
76CedRapGT-31
76SeaRaiC-19
83TamTarT-25
Watson, Todd
90Bes-94
90ChaWheB-19
90ChaWheP-2249
Watt, Eddie
66Top-442
67Top-271
68OPC-186
68Top-186
68TopVen-186
69Top-652
70OPC-497
70Ori-14
70Top-497
71OPC-122
71Ori-15
71Top-122
72MilBra-355
72OPC-128
72Top-128
73OPC-362
73OriJohP-39
73Top-362
74OPC-534
74Top-534
74TopTra-534T
75OPC-374
75Top-374
76HawIslC-3
76VenLeaS-176
81Ori6F-31
86TucTorP-25
87TucTorP-22
88TucTorC-25
88TucTorJP-23
88TucTorP-184
89TucTorC-24
89TucTorP-204
90BurBraB-12
90BurBraP-2367
90BurBraS-29
91OriCro-476
Watt, Gord
96AriBlaDB-4
Watters, Mike
86AlbDukP-27
87CalCanP-2310
88CalCanC-23
88CalCanP-798
86STaoftFT-15
Watts, Andy
86NegLeaF-17
Watts, Bob
87DunBluJP-925
88DunBluJS-20
89BelBreIS-25
Watts, Brandon
91KisDodP-4187
92GreFalDSP-24
93VerBeaDC-25
93VerBeaDF-2220
95VerBeaDTI-28
96SanAntMB-24
Watts, Brian
77SpaPhiT-16
Watts, Burgess
90GreFalDSP-11
91YakBeaC-14
91YakBeaP-4258
92YakBeaC-5
92YakBeaF-3450
93BakDodCLC-24
Watts, Craig
92GreFalDSP-13
93GreFalDSP-1
95AusFut-34
Watts, Josh
93MarPhiC-1
93MarPhiF-3492
94BatCliF-3462
95PiePhiF-201
Watts, Len
86ReaPhiP-26
87MaiGuiP-3
87MaiGuiT-20
87PhiTas-49
Watwood, Johnny
93ConTSN-963
Watychowics, Stanley
52LavPro-64
Waugh, James
53Top-178
91TopArc1-178
Wawruck, Jim
92FreKeyC-10
92FreKeyF-1821
92UppDecML-322
93BowBayF-2202
94OriPro-104
94RocRedWF-1012
94RocRedWTI-23
94UppDecML-72
95BowBayTI-9
95RocRedWTI-37
96RocRedWB-29
Way, Ron
89WelPirP-28
90AugPirP-2465
91SalBucC-23
91SalBucP-953
Wayne, Gary
86WesPalBEP-27
87JacExpP-450
88IndIndP-508
89DonRoo-27
89ScoRoo-91T
90Don-318
90Fle-387
90FleCan-387
90OPC-348
90PubSti-340
90Sco-527
90Sco100RS-15
90ScoYouS2-26
90Top-348
90TopDeb89-135
90TopTif-348
90UppDec-372
90VenSti-477
91Don-757
91Fle-626
91OPC-207
91Sco-283
91StaClu-491
91Top-207
91TopDesS-207
91TopMic-207
91TopTif-207
91TriA AAGP-AAA37
92Lea-424
92StaClu-261
92Ult-401
93Fle-645
93FleFinE-46
93PacSpa-179
93RocUSPC-3S
93RocUSPC-10D
93StaClu-10
93StaCluFDI-10
93StaCluMOP-10
93TopTra-16T
94DodMot-27
94DodPol-27
94Don-323
94Fle-456
94StaClu-648
94StaCluFDI-648
94StaCluGR-648
94StaCluMOP-648
Waznik, Allan J.
87IdaFalBP-13
88SumBraP-407
89BurBraP-1612
89BurBraS-23
Wearing, Melvin
89EriOriS-25
90Bes-293
90WauTimB-23
90WauTimP-2137
90WauTimS-24
91CarLeaAP-CAR9
91Cla/Bes-383
91FreKeyC-20
91FreKeyP-2374
92HagSunF-2566
92HagSunS-270
92SkyAA F-114
93ExcFS7-128
93RocRedWF-250
94OriPro-105
94RocRedWF-1006
Weatherford, Brant
86TamTarP-25
Weatherford, Joel
83BelBreF-29
Weatherly, Stormy (Roy)
39PlaBal-152
40PlaBal-49
41PlaBal-17
43YanSta-28
79DiaGre-283
93ConTSN-942
Weathers, David (John David)
88St.CatBJP-2023
89MyrBeaBJP-1476
90DunBluJS-24
91BluJayS-35
91KnoBluJLD-371
91KnoBluJP-1767
91LinDriAA-371
92Don-418
92ProFS7-167
92SkyAAAF-233
92SyrChiF-1969
92SyrChiMB-28
92SyrChiS-522
92TopDeb91-181
93BluJayD4-43
93Don-731
93EdmTraF-1138
93Fle-430
93StaCluMarl-26
93Top-739
93TopGol-739
93TopInaM-739
93TopMic-739
93TriAAAGF-11
94ExtBas-267
94Fin-355
94FinRef-355
94Fla-167
94Fle-479
94Pac-252
94SpoRoo-27
94SpoRooAP-27
94StaClu-673
94StaCluFDI-673
94StaCluGR-673
94StaCluMOP-673
94StaCluT-89
94StaCluTFDI-89
94Top-781
94TopGol-781
94TopSpa-781
94Ult-498
94UppDec-447
94UppDecED-447
95ColCho-307
95ColChoGS-307
95ColChoSS-307
95Don-306
95DonPreP-306
95Fla-142
95Fle-343
95Lea-58
95Pin-55
95PinArtP-55
95PinMusC-55
95Sco-141
95ScoGolR-141
95ScoPlaTS-141
95StaClu-75
95StaCluFDI-75
95StaCluMOP-75
95StaCluSTWS-75
95StaCluVR-47
95Top-73
95Ult-168
95UltGolM-168
95UppDec-118
95UppDecED-118
95UppDecEDG-118
96ColCho-157
96ColChoGS-157
96ColChoSS-157
96FleUpd-U134
96FleUpdTC-U134
96LeaSigA-240
96LeaSigAG-241
96LeaSigAS-241
96StaCluVRMO-47
97Fle-678
97FleTif-678
Weathers, Steven M.
75TucTorC-6
75TucTorTI-20
76TucTorCa-5
76TusTorCr-2
77SanJosMC-12
Weathersby, Leon
95SpoIndTI-30
Weaver, Art
11SpoLifCW-363
Weaver, Buck (George)
09MaxPubP-17
12T207-193
15SpoNewM-188
16BF2FP-21
16ColE13-185
16SpoNewM-186
16TanBraE-19
19W514-91
73FleWilD-11
75WhiSox1T-25
77SerSta-24
81ConTSN-40
87ConSer2-28
88PacEigMO-7
88PacEigMO-12
88PacEigMO-33
88PacEigMO-34
88PacEigMO-40
88PacEigMO-48
88PacEigMO-63
88PacEigMO-71
88PacEigMO-107
92Man191BSR-24
94ConTSN-1029
94ConTSNB-1029
Weaver, Colby
94IdaFalBF-3590
95DurBulTI-33
Weaver, D. Floyd
65Top-546
66Top-231
66TopVen-231
71OPC-227
71Top-227
73WicAerKSB-19
78TCM60I-176
94BreMilB-88
Weaver, Earl
69Top-516
70OPC-148
70Ori-15
70Top-148
71OPC-477
71Ori-16
71Top-477
72OPC-323
72OriPol-10
72Top-323
73OPC-136
73OriJohP-4
73Top-136A
73Top-136B
74OPC-306
74Top-306
75OPC-117
75Top-117
76OPC-73
76Top-73
77Spo-1816
77Top-546
78Top-211
79Top-689
80PerHaloFP-228
80Top-404
81Don-356
81Fle-178
81Top-661
82Don-27
83OriPos-28
83Top-426
85OriHea-18
85TopTifT-129T
85TopTra-129T
86Top-321
86TopTif-321
87Top-568
87TopTif-568
89PacLegI-179
89PacSenL-56
89PacSenL-219
89SweBasG-98
89T/MSenL-112
89T/MSenL-120
89TopSenL-76
90EliSenL-91
90PacLeg-108
91LinDri-12
91SweBasG-95
91UppDecS-3
92MCIAmb-1
93OriCroASU-8
93TedWil-85
93TedWil-147
93UppDecS-3
97TopStaHRR-14
97TopStaHRRA-14
Weaver, Eric
93BakDodCLC-25
94VerBeaDC-23
94VerBeaDF-73
95SanAntMTI-44
96SanAntMB-25
Weaver, James
83OrlTwiT-3
84TolMudHT-13
86MaiGuiP-23
87CalCanP-2311
88TucTorC-21
88TucTorJP-24
88TucTorP-172
89VanCanC-14
89VanCanP-583
90CalCanC-17
90CalCanP-663
90CMC-444
90ProAAAF-128
92VerBeaDF-2876
94RocRedWTI-24
Weaver, Jim (James B.)
68Top-328
68TopVen-328
69OPC-134
69Top-134
69TopFou-20
Weaver, Jim (James D.)
36NatChiFPR-96
36R31PasP-39
38CinOraW-30
92ConTSN-390
Weaver, Jim Francis
86IndTeal-46
Weaver, Monte
33Gou-111
35GouPuzR-1C
35GouPuzR-2C
35GouPuzR-16C
35GouPuzR-17C
79DiaGre-70
93ConTSN-853
Weaver, Roger
80EvaTriT-1
81EvaTriT-10
81Top-626
82RicBraT-9
Weaver, Scott
96FayGenB-29
Weaver, Terry
95BelGiaTI-31
96BurBeeTI-19

Weaver, Trent
89MedAthB-16
91ModA'sC-2
Weaver, William B.
87OldJudN-533
Webb, Ada
88KimN18-47
Webb, Ben
87WatPirP-1
88SalBucS-23
89HarSenP-311
89HarSenS-21
90HarSenP-1194
90HarSenS-20
91CarMudLD-120
91CarMudP-1088
91LinDriAA-120
92CarMudF-1182
92CarMudS-147
Webb, Chuck
88WauTimGS-19
Webb, Cleon Earl
34BatR31-98
85Woo-37
91ConTSN-261
94ConTSN-1226
Webb, Dennis
81QuaCitCT-9
Webb, Doug
94SigRooDP-35
94SigRooDPS-35
94StaCluDP-26
94StaCluDPFDI-26
95Top-406
96El PasDB-27
96Exc-74
Webb, Earl (William Earl)
31Exh-18
33ExhFou-9
79RedSoxEF-3
87ConSer2-25
94ConTSNB-1226
Webb, Hank
73OPC-610
73Top-610
75IntLeaAT-24
75MetSSP-2
75OPC-615
75Top-615
76OPC-442
76SSP-553
76Top-442
90DodTar-841
91MetWIZ-426
Webb, Kevin
92AshTouC-7
93AshTouC-22
93AshTouF-2287
95DurBulTI-34
Webb, Lefty (Cleon)
10PirTipTD-15
Webb, Lonnie
90GreFalDSP-7
92BakDodCLC-28
93VerBeaDC-26
Webb, Marvin
75WatDodT-22
Webb, Matthew
88AllandGN-50
Webb, Richmond
91StaCluCM-41
Webb, Sam
49EurSta-125
Webb, Skeeter (James)
39WhiSoxTI-21
40WhiSoxL-22
Webb, Spyder
87BelMarL-30
87BelMarTI-16
89BelMarL-33
91BelMarC-27
Webb, Tweed (Normal)
86NegLeaF-39
Webber, Chris
93StaCluMO-42
Webber, Les
42DodTeal-24
43DodTeal-24
77TCMTheWY-49
90DodTar-842
Weber, Ben
91St.CatBJC-19
91St.CatBJP-3396
92MyrBeaHC-6
92MyrBeaHF-2198
93DunBluJC-24
93DunBluJF-1797
93DunBluJFFN-27
93FloStaLAF-11
94ClaGolF-59
94DunBluJC-26
94DunBluJF-2558
95SyrChiTI-27
Weber, Bill (Charles)
87OldJudN-534
Weber, Brent
91IdaFalBP-4329
Weber, David
93HunCubC-26
93HunCubF-3236
94WilCubF-3765
Weber, Eric
93BriTigC-24
94BriTigC-26
94BriTigF-3503
96BurIndB-16
Weber, Lenny
94BurIndC-27
94BurIndF-3795
96KenIndB-25
Weber, Neil
93JamExpC-25
93JamExpF-3328
94WesPalBEC-27
94WesPalBEF-41
95AusFut-39
95Exc-229
95HarSenTI-10
96Bow-231
96HarSenB-28
Weber, Pete
87BufBisP-29
90CliGiaUTI-U8
91LinDriAA-323
91ShrCapLD-323
91ShrCapP-1837
92ShrCapF-3886
92ShrCapS-597
92SkyAA F-264
93ShrCapF-2774
Weber, Ron
89JohCitCS-22
90SprCarB-24
91St.PetCC-14
91St.PetCP-2277
92St.PetCC-9
92St.PetCF-2028
Weber, Steve
89BriTigS-30
90BriTigS-29
Weber, Todd
88AshTouP-1078
Weber, Wes (Weston)
86MedA'sC-65
87MadMusP-11
87MadMusP-21
88ModA'sTI-15
89HunStaB-13
89ModA'sC-18
90CMC-582
90ProAAAF-139
90TacTigC-5
90TacTigP-92
91HunStaP-1796
91HunStaTI-22
92TacTigF-2503
92TacTigS-546
94CalCanF-790
95TacRaiTI-26
96LasVegSB-30
Webster, Casey
86WatIndP-30
87KinIndP-13
88EasLeaAP-43
88WilBilP-1317
89CanIndB-5
89CanIndP-1318
89CanIndS-23
89EasLeaAP-19
90CanIndS-17
90CMC-473
90ColSprSSC-21
90ColSprSSP-47
90ProAAAF-228
Webster, Lenny
86KenTwiP-25
87KenTwiP-20
88KenTwiP-1392
88MidLeaAGS-31
89VisOakCLC-110
89VisOakP-1442
90Bes-45
90OrlSunRB-13
90OrlSunRP-1088
90OrlSunRS-23
90ProAaA-55
90Sco-638
90TopDeb89-136
90UppDec-728
91FleUpd-41
91LinDriAAA-422
91PorBeaLD-422
91PorBeaP-1569
92DonRoo-124
92Fle-220
92OPC-585
92Pin-276
92Sco-663
92ScoRoo-17
92StaClu-183
92Top-585
92TopGol-585
92TopGolW-585
92TopMic-585
92Ult-402
93Don-694
93Fle-646
93Sco-471
93StaClu-380
93StaCluFDI-380
93StaCluMOP-380
93Top-37
93TopGol-37
93TopInaM-37
93TopMic-37
93Ult-238
93UppDec-628
93UppDecGold-628
93USPlaCR-8D
94FleUpd-155
94StaClu-193
94StaCluFDI-193
94StaCluGR-193
94StaCluMOP-193
94Top-252
94TopGol-252
94TopSpa-252
95Don-541
95DonPreP-541
95Fle-362
95Phi-34
95PhiMel-24
95Sco-258
95ScoGolR-258
95ScoPlaTS-258
95Top-374
96ColCho-668
96ColChoGS-668
96ColChoSS-668
96Fle-511
96FleTif-511
Webster, Mike
89EugEmeB-2
90BasCitRS-26
Webster, Mitch
78CliDodT-32
79CliDodT-11
80SyrChiT-12
80SyrChiTI-22
82SyrChiT-23
82SyrChiTI-23
83SyrChiT-25
84BluJayFS-31
85BluJayFS-31
85DomLeaS-147
86Don-523
86ExpPos-18
86ExpProPa-5
86ExpProPo-5
86Fle-265
86GenMilB-6J
86Lea-253
86OPC-218
86Top-629
86TopTif-629
87Don-335
87DonOpeD-86
87ExpPos-33
87Fle-335
87FleAwaW-41
87FleGlo-335
87FleMin-111
87GenMilB-4I
87OPC-263
87Spo-177
87SpoTeaP-20
87StuPan-7
87Top-442
87TopSti-82
87TopTif-442
88CubDavB-28
88Don-257
88DonBasB-292
88ExpPos-24
88Fle-199
88FleGlo-199
88FleStiC-99
88Lea-198
88MSAHosD-1
88OPC-138
88PanSti-331
88RedFolSB-97
88Sco-345
88ScoGlo-345
88Spo-105
88StaLinE-18
88Top-138
88TopBig-150
88TopTif-138
89Bow-296
89BowTif-296
89CubMar-33
89Don-459
89DonBasB-261
89Fle-442
89FleGlo-442
89OPC-36
89PanSti-61
89Sco-71
89Spo-67
89Top-36
89TopTif-36
89TVSpoM-20
89UppDec-65
90Don-137
90Fle-45
90FleCan-45
90IndTeal-43
90Lea-312
90OPC-502
90PubSti-208
90Sco-85
90ScoRoo-4T
90Top-502
90TopBig-298
90TopTif-502
90TopTra-127T
90TopTraT-127T
90UppDec-153
90UppDec-730
90VenSti-478
91Bow-66
91Don-283
91Fle-384
91IndFanC-29
91OPC-762
91PanSti-175
91Sco-594
91ScoRoo-68T
91StaClu-448
91Top-762
91TopDesS-762
91TopMic-762
91TopTif-762
91Ult-119
91UppDec-120
92DodMot-26
92DodPol-20
92DodSmo-10692
92Don-714
92OPC-233
92Sco-643
92StaClu-403
92Top-233
92TopGol-233
92TopGolW-233
92TopMic-233
93DodMot-22
93DodPol-27
93Don-62
93Fle-455
93PacSpa-505
93StaClu-735
93StaCluD-18
93StaCluFDI-735
93StaCluMOP-735
94DodMot-12
94DodPol-28
94Don-457
94Fle-528
94Sco-130
94ScoGolR-130
94Top-382
94TopGol-382
94TopSpa-382
95DodMot-12
96YakBeaTI-NNO
Webster, Ramon
67Top-603
68OPC-164
68Top-164
68TopVen-164
69Top-618
72MilBra-356
75TucTorC-3
75TucTorTI-21
Webster, Ray G.
59Ind-20
59Top-531
60Top-452
Webster, Rich
82LynMetT-21
Webster, Rudy
86BelMarC-127
87WauTimP-25
88WauTimGS-17
Wechsberg, Von
90BurIndP-3010
91PocPioP-3783
91PocPioSP-7
92SpoIndC-18
92SpoIndF-1295
Weck, Steve
85IowCubT-31
Wedge, Eric
88CapCodPPaLP-51
89ElmPioP-32
90Bes-2
90Bes-319
90CMC-783
90EasLeaAP-EL41
90NewBriRSB-1
90NewBriRSP-1322
90NewBriRSS-21
90TopTVRS-66
91LinDriAAA-372
91PawRedSDD-29
91PawRedSLD-372
91PawRedSP-42
92PawRedSF-927
92PawRedSS-372
92ScoRoo-38
92SkyAAAF-171
92TopDeb91-182
93Don-44
93FleMajLP-A12
93Pin-239
93Sco-561
93ScoProaG-9
93Sel-401
93StaCluRoc-22
93Top-486
93TopGol-486
93TopInaM-486
93TopMic-486
93UppDec-653
93UppDecGold-653
94PawRedSDD-29
94Sco-643
94ScoGolR-643
94StaCluT-113
94StaCluTFDI-113
95PawRedSDD-28
95PawRedTI-35
96TolMudHB-30
97DunDonPPS-29
Wedvick, Jeff
86JamExpP-28
87BurExpP-1082
87JamExpP-2542
Weeber, Mike
75DubPacT-17
Weekley, Jason
96GreFalDB-30
96GreFalDTI-32
Weekly, Johnny
62Top-204
64Top-256
64TopVen-256
89AstCol4S-26

Weeks, Ben
91IdaFalBP-4330
91IdaFalBSP-8
92PulBraC-12
92PulBraF-3178
93ButCopKSP-11
Weeks, Thomas
87OneYanP-13
88Ft.LauYS-24
89PriWilCS-24
90PriWilCTI-27
Weems, Danny
86SumBraP-29
87ChaWheP-13
88CarLeaAS-39
88DurBulS-23
89GreBraB-13
89GreBraP-1157
89GreBraS-24
90GreBraB-16
90GreBraP-1130
90GreBraS-22
Weems, Jeff
94PitMetC-27
Weese, Dean
88HamRedP-1744
89SavCarP-348
90St.PetCS-25
91ArkTraP-1286
Weese, Gary
75SanAntBT-21
76WilTomT-21
Wegener, Mike
69ExpFudP-13
69Top-284
70ExpPos-5
70OPC-193
70Top-193
71ExpPS-27
71OPC-608
71Top-608
75TidTidTI-24
76PheGiaCr-35
76PhoGiaCa-10
76PhoGiaCC-23
76PhoGiaVNB-24
77PhoGiaCC-24
77PhoGiaCP-24
77PhoGiaVNB-24
Weger, Wes
92FroRowDP-77
92HelBreF-1725
92HelBreSP-10
93ElPasDF-2960
93ExcFS7-196
94ExcFS7-90
94ExtBas-111
94ExtBasMLH-10
94NewOrlZF-1478
94Ult-382
95ElPasDTI-23
96SigRooOJ-35
96SigRooOJS-35
Weglarz, John
92EugEmeC-27
92EugEmeF-3030
93RocRoyC-27
93RocRoyF-717
Wegman, Bill
82BelBreF-4
85VanCanC-216
86BrePol-46
86Don-490
86TopTra-123T
86TopTraT-123T
87BrePol-46
87BreTeal-15
87Don-109
87Fle-360
87FleGlo-360
87Top-179
87TopTif-179
88BrePol-46
88Don-151
88DonBasB-320
88Fle-177
88FleGlo-177
88OPC-84
88PanSti-119
88Sco-296
88ScoGlo-296
88StaLinBre-19
88Top-538
88TopBig-244
88TopSti-200
88TopTif-538
89Bow-135
89BowTif-135
89BreGar-9
89BrePol-46
89BreYea-46
89Don-293
89Fle-199
89FleGlo-199
89OPC-354
89Sco-335
89ScoYouS2-9
89Top-768
89TopTif-768
89UppDec-445
90BreMilB-30
90BrePol-46
90OPC-333
90PubSti-507
90Sco-188
90Top-333
90TopTif-333
90UppDec-629
90VenSti-479
91BreMilB-30
91BrePol-27
91FleUpd-35
91OPC-617
91Sco-483
91StaClu-398
91Top-617
91TopDesS-617
91TopMic-617
91TopTif-617
91UltUpd-33
91UppDec-292
92Bow-447
92BrePol-28
92Don-378
92Fle-193
92Lea-196
92OPC-22
92Pin-396
92Sco-374
92StaClu-758
92StaCluECN-758
92Stu-199
92Top-22
92TopGol-22
92TopGolW-22
92TopMic-22
92TriPla-185
92Ult-392
92UppDec-612
92UppDecTMH-53
93BrePol-27
93Don-17
93Fle-259
93Lea-144
93OPC-223
93PacSpa-517
93Pin-369
93Sco-190
93Sel-184
93StaClu-324
93StaCluFDI-324
93StaCluMOP-324
93Top-261
93TopComotH-9
93TopGol-261
93TopInaM-261
93TopMic-261
93TriPla-56
93Ult-226
93UppDec-416
93UppDecGold-416
94BreMilB-89
94BrePol-30
94ColC-289
94ColChoGS-289
94ColChoSS-289
94Don-633
94ExtBas-112
94Fin-145
94FinRef-145
94Fla-310
94Fle-196
94Sco-341
94ScoGolR-341
94Top-464
94TopGol-464
94TopSpa-464
94Ult-383
94UppDec-416
94UppDecED-416
95Don-333
95DonPreP-333
95DonTopotO-106
95Fla-56
95Fle-195
95StaClu-348
95StaCluMOP-348
95StaCluSTWS-348
95Top-159
96ProSta-30
Wegmann, Tom
90KinMetB-20
90KinMetS-24
91ColMetPI-27
91ColMetPI-31
91ColMetPPI-4
91St.LucMC-13
92BinMetF-518
92BinMetS-71
92SkyAA F-33
93NorTidF-2571
94RocRedWF-999
94RocRedWTI-25
95BowBayTI-31
95RocRedWTI-38
Wehmeier, Herm
47Exh-237
48Bow-46
49Bow-51
49EurSta-98
50Bow-27
51Bow-144
51FisBakL-28
51TopBluB-47
52Bow-150
52Top-80
53BowC-23
53Top-110
54Top-162
55Top-29
55TopDouH-131
56Top-78
56TopPin-22
57Top-81
58Top-248
59Top-421
79TCM50-126
83TopRep5-80
91TopArc1-110
94TopArc1-162
94TopArc1G-162
Wehner, John
88WatPirP-28
89SalBucS-24
90CMC-788
90EasLeaAP-EL26
90HarSenP-1203
90HarSenS-21
91CarMudLD-121
91CarMudP-1096
91FleUpd-115
91LinDriAA-121
92Bow-444
92BufBisF-330
92BufBisS-46
92Cla1-T93
92Don-731
92Fle-573
92OPC-282
92Pin-260
92ProFS7-306
92Sco-752
92Sco100RS-82
92SkyAAAF-21
92StaClu-831
92StaCluECN-831
92Top-282
92TopDeb91-183
92TopGol-282
92TopGolW-282
92TopMic-282
92UppDec-469
93Fle-506
93PirNatI-38
93StaClu-317
93StaCluFDI-317
93StaCluMOP-317
93Top-484
93TopGol-484
93TopInaM-484
93TopMic-484
93Ult-105
93UppDec-759
93UppDecGold-759
94BufBisF-1846
94Pac-513
96Fle-535
96FleTif-535
Wehrmeister, Dave
75HawIsIC-20
77PadSchC-62
77Top-472
78PadFamF-35
79HawIsIC-29
80ColCliP-30
80ColCliT-25
81ColCliP-28
81ColCliT-23
82ColCliP-28
82ColCliT-11
82Top-694
83ColCliT-6
84PhiTas-44
84PorBeaC-195
85BufBisT-26
86BufBisP-23
86Fle-220
92YanWIZ8-199
Weibel, Randy
83CliGiaF-27
Weibl, Clint
96JohCitCTI-33
Weidemaier, Mark
87SalAngP-32
89PriWilCS-27
Weidert, Chris
96WesPalBEB-16
Weidie, Stuart
86ElmPioRSP-27
87WinHavRSP-12
88LynRedSS-25
89LynRedSS-21
90NewBriRSB-13
90NewBriRSP-1332
90NewBriRSS-22
Weidman, George
87OldJudN-535
Weiermiller, Mike
82WisRapTF-4
Weigandt, Bryan
93MarPhiC-30
93MarPhiF-3486
94SpaPhiF-1733
94SparPhiC-22
Weigel, Ralph
48WhiSoxTI-27
49Lea-86
Weighaus, Thomas
82WicAerTI-20
Weik, Dick
53IndPenCBP-29
54Top-224
94TopArc1-224
94TopArc1G-224
Weiland, Ed
39WhiSoxTI-22
40WhiSoxL-23
Weiland, Robert
33ButCanV-55
34Gou-67
35GouPuzR-8C
35GouPuzR-9C
93ConTSN-895
Weilman, Carl
15SpoNewM-189
16ColE13-186
16FleBreD-98
16SpoNewM-187
17HolBreD-112
63GadFunC-28
Weimer, Jacob
06FanCraNL-50
08RosComP-123
09T206-370
11SpoLifCW-364
Weimerskirch, Mike
88CapCodPPaLP-96
91Cla/Bes-311
91MidLeaAP-MWL49
91RocExpC-26
91RocExpP-2061
92WesPalBEC-25
92WesPalBEF-2101
Weinbaum, Pete
91BelMarC-20
91BelMarP-3663
Weinberg, Barry
76ShrCapT-23
86A'sMot-26
90A'sMot-28
Weinberg, Mike
91FayGenC-26
91FayGenP-1185
Weinberg, Todd
94SouOreAC-30
94SouOreAF-3624
95WesMicWTI-35
96WesMicWB-29
Weinberger, Gary
86JacExpT-17
87JacExpP-438
Weinbrecht, Mark
80ElmPioRST-13
Weinert, Lefty
93ConTSN-958
Weinheimer, Wayne
88WytCubP-1977
89ChaWheB-1
89ChaWheP-1751
Weinke, Chris
91Cla/Bes-419
91St.CatBJC-6
91St.CatBJP-3405
92MyrBeaHC-1
92MyrBeaHF-2208
93ClaFS7-267
93DunBluJC-25
93DunBluJF-1806
93DunBluJFFN-28
93FloStaLAF-12
94ClaGolF-60
94ExcFS7-150
94KnoSmoF-1313
94UppDecML-179
95Bow-131
95Exc-146
95SyrChiTI-28
96KnoSmoB-25
Weinstein, Bobby
55GiaGolS-31
Weinstein, Jerry
93GenCubC-29
93GenCubF-3193
94WilCubC-26
94WilCubF-3781
87PanAmTUBI-NNO
Weintraub, Phil
36WorWidGV-135
37ExhFou-4
77TCMTheWY-51
83TCMPla1944-35
92ConTSN-610
Weir, Ike
87AllandGN-20
Weir, Jim
82CliGiaF-29
83CliGiaF-5
Weis, A.J.
25Exh-24
Weis, Al
63Top-537
63WhiSoxTS-23
64Top-168
64TopVen-168
65Top-516
66OPC-66
66Top-66
66TopVen-66
67CokCapWS-3
67Top-556
68Top-313
68TopVen-313
69MetNewYDN-20
69MilBra-286
69Top-269
70MetTra-21B
70MLBOffS-84
70OPC-498
70Top-498
71MLBOffS-168
71OPC-751
71Top-751
72MilBra-357
81TCM60I-425
81TCM60I-475
89RinPosM1-29
91MetWIZ-427
94Met69CCPP-32
94Met69CS-31
94Met69T-20

Weise, Phil
90CMC-709
Weisman, Skip
83AndBraT-3
89ColMetGS-4
Weismiller, Bob
77SalPirT-27B
Weiss, Alta
94UppDecTAE-16
Weiss, Bill
89CalLeaA-27
Weiss, Gary
80AlbDukT-13
81AlbDukT-19
81Fle-130
90DodTar-843
Weiss, George
76ShaPiz-126
80PerHaloFP-126
80SSPHOF-126
82MetGal62-32
88WilMulP-11
92YanWIZH-35
Weiss, Jeff
87DurBulP-3
Weiss, Marc
94BilMusF-3671
94BilMusSP-22
95BilRedTI-24
Weiss, Scott
91GenCubC-25
91GenCubP-4218
91PeoChiTI-32
92WinSpiF-1209
Weiss, Walt
86MadMusP-22
86MadMusP-26
87HunStaTI-23
88A'sMot-11
88DonRoo-18
88DonTeaBA-NEW
88Fle-652
88FleGlo-652
88FleMin-49
88FleUpd-56
88FleUpdG-56
88ModA'sTI-34
88ScoRoo-102T
88ScoRooG-102T
88TopBig-263
88TopTra-126T
88TopTraT-126T
89A'sMot-8
89A'sMot-28
89A'sMotR-3
89A'sMotR-4
89Baz-22
89Bow-196
89BowTif-196
89ClaLigB-68
89Don-446
89DonBasB-155
89DonGraS-3
89Fle-24
89FleBasM-42
89FleGlo-24
89FleGlo-WS10
89FleSup-42
89FleWorS-10
89K-M-4
89OPC-316
89PanSti-412
89PanSti-478
89Sco-165
89ScoHot1R-95
89ScoYouSI-20
89Spo-116
89TacTigP-1538
89Top-316
89Top-639
89TopBig-305
89TopCoi-31
89TopGaloC-12
89TopGloS-50
89TopRoo-21
89TopSti-168
89TopSti-326
89TopTif-316
89TopTif-639
89TopUKM-82
89ToyRoo-32
89TVSpoM-94
89TVSpoM-140
89UppDec-374
89UppDec-660
89Woo-5
90A'sMot-10
90Bow-461
90BowTif-461
90ClaBlu-46
90Don-67
90DonBesA-95
90Fle-22
90FleCan-22
90FleWorS-6
90Lea-239
90OPC-165
90PanSti-135
90PubSti-317
90Sco-110
90Spo-74
90Top-165
90TopTif-165
90UppDec-542
90VenSti-480
90Woo-26
91A'sMot-10
91A'sSFE-14
91Bow-228
91Don-214
91Fle-26
91Lea-50
91OPC-455
91PanFreS-195
91PanSti-147
91Sco-171
91StaClu-49
91StaCluP-49
91Top-455
91TopDesS-455
91TopMic-455
91TopTif-455
91Ult-255
91UppDec-192
92A'sUno7P-1
92AthMot-10
92Bow-651
92Don-71
92Fle-270
92Lea-380
92OPC-691
92PanSti-18
92Pin-56
92Sco-51
92ScoProP-13
92StaClu-248
92Top-691
92TopGol-691
92TopGolW-691
92TopMic-691
92UppDec-151
93Bow-290
93DiaMar-116
93Don-109
93Don-756
93Fla-55
93Fle-300
93FleFinE-73
93FunPac-122
93Lea-416
93MarPub-25
93MarUSPC-1C
93MarUSPC-2H
93MarUSPC-7C
93OPC-319
93OPCPre-101
93PacSpa-473
93Pin-231
93PinExpOD-6
93Sco-659
93Sel-192
93SP-143
93StaClu-370
93StaCluFDI-370
93StaCluMarl-5
93StaCluMOP-370
93Stu-69
93Top-580
93TopGol-580
93TopInaM-580
93TopMic-580
93TopPos-2
93TopPos-3
93TopTra-18T
93Ult-387
93UppDec-122
93UppDec-533
93UppDecGold-122
93UppDecGold-533
94Bow-582
94ColC-488
94ColChoGS-488
94ColChoSS-488
94Don-428
94ExtBas-255
94Fin-401
94FinRef-401
94Fla-377
94Fle-480
94FleUpd-131
94FUnPac-122
94FUnPac-222
94Lea-359
94OPC-244
94Pac-253
94PanSti-187
94Pin-486
94PinArtP-486
94PinMusC-486
94RocPol-25
94Sco-98
94ScoGolR-98
94ScoRoo-RT16
94ScoRooGR-RT16
94Sel-127
94SP-169
94SPDieC-169
94StaClu-581
94StaCluFDI-581
94StaCluGR-581
94StaCluMOP-581
94StaCluT-98
94StaCluTFDI-98
94Stu-181
94Top-256
94TopGol-256
94TopSpa-256
94TopTra-113T
94Ult-488
94UppDec-438
94UppDecED-438
95Baz-104
95ColCho-443
95ColChoGS-443
95ColChoSE-206
95ColChoSEGS-206
95ColChoSESS-206
95ColChoSS-443
95D3-59
95Don-14
95DonPreP-14
95DonTopotO-235
95Emb-112
95EmbGoll-112
95Fin-55
95FinRef-55
95Fla-134
95Fle-530
95Lea-55
95Pac-147
95Pin-20
95PinArtP-20
95PinMusC-20
95RocPol-11
95Sco-435
95ScoGolR-435
95ScoPlaTS-435
95StaClu-94
95StaCluFDI-94
95StaCluMOP-94
95StaCluSTWS-94
95Stu-161
95Top-110
95TopCyb-71
95Ult-377
95UltGolM-377
95UppDec-413
95UppDecED-413
95UppDecEDG-413
95UppDecSE-102
95UppDecSEG-102
96ColCho-541
96ColChoGS-541
96ColChoSS-541
96Don-203
96DonPreP-203
96EmoXL-179
96Fla-254
96Fle-378
96FleRoc-17
96FleTif-378
96LeaSigA-241
96LeaSigAG-242
96LeaSigAS-242
96MetUni-160
96MetUniP-160
96Pac-56
96PanSti-83
96Pin-107
96PinAfi-45
96PinAfiAP-45
96PinAfiFPP-45
96ProSta-115
96RocPol-26
96Sco-98
96Sel-136
96SelArtP-136
96SP-78
96StaClu-166
96StaCluMOP-166
96TeaOut-87
96Top-149
96Ult-476
96UltGolM-476
96UppDec-322
97ColCho-323
97DonTea-101
97DonTeaSPE-101
97Fin-180
97FinRef-180
97Fle-320
97FleTif-320
97MetUni-77
97Pac-292
97PacLigB-292
97PacSil-292
97Sco-38
97ScoPreS-38
97ScoRoc-3
97ScoRocPl-3
97ScoRocPr-3
97ScoShoS-38
97ScoShoSAP-38
97StaClu-287
97StaCluMOP-287
97Top-401
97Ult-190
97UltGolME-190
97UltPlaME-190
97UppDec-59
Weissman, Craig
81QuaCitCT-26
82QuaCitCT-13
86GleFalTP-24
87ArkTraP-17
89ArkTraGS-24
Weissmuller, John
28W512-38
Weitz, Bruce
91TopRut-3
Weitzel, Brad
90EriSaiS-31
Welaj, Johnny
50WorWidGV-8
77TCMTheWY-81
Welaj, Lou
50WorWidGV-40
Welborn, Frank
86JamExpP-29
Welborn, Sam
77SpaPhiT-23
80LynSaiT-21
81SpolndT-4
82SalLakCGT-21
83TucTorT-10
Welborn, Todd
85LitFalMT-12
86LitFalMP-29
87ColMetP-29
88JacMetGS-16
88MetColP-51
89JacMetGS-7
Welborn, Tony
87BurExpP-1070
88WesPalBES-27
Welch, Bob (Robert)
79Top-318
80DodPol-35
80Top-146
81DodPol-35
81Don-178
81Fle-120A
81Fle-120B
81LonBeaPT-13
81OPC-357
81Top-624
81TopSupHT-53
82DodPol-35
82DodPos-9
82DodUniOV-25
82Don-75
82Fle-28
82Top-82
83DodPol-35
83DodPos-19
83Don-410
83Fle-225
83OPC-288
83Top-454
84DodPol-35
84DodUniOP-10
84Don-153
84Fle-116
84Nes792-306
84Nes792-722
84OPC-227
84Top-306
84Top-722
84TopTif-306
84TopTif-722
85DodCokP-32
85Don-372
85Fle-388
85OPC-291
85Top-291
85TopTif-291
86DodCokP-32
86DodPol-35
86DodUniOP-23
86Don-459
86Fle-146
86Lea-223
86Spo-198
86Top-549
86TopMinL-48
86TopTif-549
87DodMot-9
87DodPol-18
87DodSmoA-37
87Don-475
87Fle-459
87FleGlo-459
87FleLeaL-43
87FleStiC-121
87OPC-328
87Top-328
87TopTif-328
88A'sMot-9
88Don-24
88Don-253
88DonBasB-134
88DonSupD-24
88DonTeaBA-NEW
88Fle-529
88FleGlo-529
88FleMin-50
88FleUpd-57
88FleUpdG-57
88Lea-24
88OPC-118
88PanSti-305
88RedFolSB-98
88Sco-510
88ScoGlo-510
88ScoRoo-15T
88ScoRooG-15T
88Spo-167
88StaLinAs-18
88Top-118
88TopMinL-55
88TopRevLL-15
88TopSti-73
88TopTif-118
88TopTra-127T
88TopTraT-127T
89A'sMot-9
89Bow-186
89BowTif-186
89ClaLigB-91
89DodSmoG-92
89Don-332
89DonBasB-267
89Fle-25
89FleGlo-25
89PanSti-416
89Sco-308
89ScoHot1S-89
89Spo-91
89SpollIFKI-261
89Top-605A

89Top-605B
89TopBasT-115
89TopSti-166
89TopTif-605
89UppDec-191
90A'sMot-16
90DodTar-844
90Don-332
90DonBesA-67
90Fle-23
90FleCan-23
90MLBBasB-76
90OPC-475
90PanSti-131
90PubSti-318
90Sco-159
90Spo-35
90Top-475
90TopBig-106
90TopMag-44
90TopSti-180
90TopTif-475
90UppDec-251
90UppDecS-2
90USPlaCA-1C
90VenSti-481
90WinDis-3
91A'sMot-9
91A'sSFE-15
91Baz-3
91Bow-215
91Cla1-T76
91ClaGam-199
91Col-5
91Don-20
91Don-54
91Don-645
91Don-727
91DonPre-5
91DonSupD-20
91Fle-27
91Lea-64
91MSAHolD-14
91OPC-50
91OPC-394
91PanCanT1-61
91PanFreS-174
91PanSti-151
91RedFolS-130
91Sco-311
91Sco-568
91Sco-877
91Sco100S-49
91SevCoi-NC14
91StaClu-79
91StaCluCM-32
91StaPinB-52
91Stu-110
91Top-50
91Top-394
91TopCraJ2-28
91TopDesS-50
91TopDesS-394
91TopGaloC-12
91TopGloA-10
91TopMic-50
91TopMic-394
91TopTif-50
91TopTif-394
91Ult-256
91UppDec-425
91Woo-4
92AthMot-9
92DodStaTA-19
92Don-190
92Fle-271
92Lea-390
92OPC-285
92Pin-409
92Sco-300
92StaClu-651
92Top-285
92TopGol-285
92TopGolW-285
92TopMic-285
92TriPla-124
92Ult-119
92UppDec-452
93AthMot-10
93Bow-77
93Don-579
93Fin-151
93FinRef-151
93Fla-264
93Fle-301
93Lea-94
93OPC-340
93PacSpa-227
93Pin-573
93Sco-208
93Sel-254
93StaClu-546
93StaCluAt-12
93StaCluFDI-546
93StaCluMOP-546
93Top-705
93TopGol-705
93TopInaM-705
93TopMic-705
93TriPla-192
93Ult-263
93UppDec-407
93UppDecGold-407
94A'sMot-10
94Bow-136
94ColC-574
94ColChoGS-574
94ColChoSS-574
94Don-282
94Fln-158
94FinRef-158
94Fle-276
94Lea-354
94OPC-213
94Pac-465
94PanSti-115
94Pin-329
94PinArtP-329
94PinMusC-329
94Sco-547
94ScoGolR-547
94Sel-126
94StaClu-297
94StaCluFDI-297
94StaCluGR-297
94StaCluMOP-297
94Top-521
94TopGol-521
94TopSpa-521
94Ult-114
94UppDec-429
94UppDecED-429
95Pac-322
95Sco-29
95ScoGolR-29
95ScoPlaTS-29
95Top-364
95Ult-323
95UltGolM-323
Welch, Bryce
89EveGiaS-32
Welch, Curt
76SSP188WS-8
87BucN28-106
87LonJacN-13
87OldJudN-537A
87OldJudN-537B
87OldJudN-538
87ScrDC-9
88GandBCGCE-45
88SpoTimM-27
89EdgR.WG-19
89SFHaCN-19
90HOFStiB-5
Welch, Dan
89MarPhiS-33
89Sta-146
90SpaPhiB-24
90SpaPhiP-2507
90SpaPhiS-24
Welch, David
92ColRedF-2392
93KinIndC-25
93KinIndF-2248
93KinIndTI-26
94KinIndC-20
94KinIndF-2642
Welch, Doug
89GenCubP-1864
90WinSpiTI-7
91ChaKniLD-147
91ChaKniP-1703
91LinDriAA-147
92ChaKniF-2785
92ChaKniS-171
Welch, Frank
22E120-90
25Exh-112
Welch, John V.
33Gou-93
33GouCanV-56
94ConTSN-1047
94ConTSNB-1047
Welch, Ken
90WatIndS-22
Welch, Mickey (Michael)
76ShaPiz-140
80PerHaloFP-140
80SSPHOF-140
81ConTSN-73
86OldJudN-14
87FouBasHN-12
87OldJudN-539
88AugBecN-29A
88AugBecN-29B
88AugBecN-29C
88GandBCGCE-46
94ConTSN-1250
94ConTSNB-1250
94OriofB-73
Welch, Mike
89SFHaCN-20
92ButCopKSP-20
93Bow-221
93ChaRaiC-22
93ChaRaiF-1926
93PitMetC-23
93PitMetF-3711
93SouAtlLAGF-9
94Bow-268
94CapCitBC-23
94CapCitBF-1752
94ExcFS7-241
94Top-713
94TopGol-713
94TopSpa-713
95StLucMTI-33
96BinBeeB-28
Welch, Rob
94SigRooDP-75
94SigRooDPS-75
95Top-429
96LowSpiB-28
Welch, Travis
94JohCitCC-28
94JohCitCF-3703
95Exc-277
95PeoChiTI-29
96BesAutSA-86
96MidLeaAB-24
96PeoChiB-29
Welchel, Don
80ChaO'sP-22
80ChaO'sW-23
81RocRedWT-18
81RocRedWW-9
82RocRedWT-8
84RocRedWT-14
85RocRedWT-23
86OklCit8P-24
88OmaRoyP-1511
91OriCro-477
Weldin, David
89HelBreSP-21
Weldon, Paul
91PocPioP-3792
91PocPioSP-21
Weleno, Doug
83MidCubT-8
Welish, Scott
89ChaRaiP-988
89SpoIndSP-16
Welke, Tim
88T/MUmp-55
89T/MUmp-53
90T/MUmp-51
Welles, Rob
94JamJamC-24
94JamJamF-3976
Wellman, Bob
52Par-95
52Top-41
79JacMetT-6
83TopRep5-41
Wellman, Brad
84Don-265
84Fle-386
84Nes792-109
84Top-109
84TopTif-109
85Fle-623
85GiaMot-26
85GiaPos-29
85Top-409
85TopTif-409
86Don-431
86Fle-553
86GiaMot-22
86OPC-41
86Top-41
86TopTif-41
87AlbDukP-23
88RoySmo-24
89Don-380
89Fle-289
89Sco-504
90DodTar-845
Wellman, Phillip
86DurBulP-27
87HarSenP-7
88PulBraP-1748
89PulBraP-1901
90BurBraP-2368
90BurBraS-30
91DurBulC-26
91DurBulP-1679
93LetMouF-4164
93LetMouSP-25
94LetMouF-3894
94LetMouSP-26
Wells, Beck
94ChaRivC-24
94ChaRivF-2678
Wells, Bob
90SpaPhiB-10
90SpaPhiP-2491
90SpaPhiS-25
91ClePhiP-1621
92ClePhiC-13
92ReaPhiF-576
94ReaPhiF-2063
95FleUpd-79
95MarMot-16
95MarPac-46
96MarMot-13
97ColCho-481
97Don-151
97DonPreP-151
97DonPrePGold-151
97DonTea-143
97DonTeaSPE-143
97Fle-216
97FleTif-216
97Pac-195
97PacLigB-195
97PacSil-195
97Sco-147
97ScoMar-5
97ScoMarPl-5
97ScoMarPr-5
97ScoPreS-147
97ScoShoS-147
97ScoShoSAP-147
97StaClu-304
97StaCluMOP-304
97Top-357
97Ult-128
97UltGolME-128
97UltPlaME-128
97UppDec-176
Wells, Boomer (Greg)
78DunBluJT-24
79SyrChiT-1
80SyrChiT-14
80SyrChiTI-23
81SyrChiT-16
81SyrChiTI-22
82OPC-203
82TolMudHT-17
82Top-203
87JapPlaB-30
Wells, David
83KinBluJTI-28
86VenGulP-27
87SyrChiT-9
88BluJayFS-31
88Don-640
88DonBasB-311
88DonRoo-26
88FleUpd-69
88FleUpdG-69
88TopTra-128T
88TopTraT-128T
89BluJayFS-30
89Don-307
89DonBasB-328
89Fle-247
89FleGlo-247
89OPC-259
89Top-567
89TopRoo-22
89TopTif-567
90BluJayFS-32
90Don-425
90Fle-96
90FleCan-96
90OPC-229
90Sco-491A
90Sco-491B
90ScoYouSI-31
90Top-229
90TopTif-229
90UppDec-30
91BluJayFS-29
91BluJayFS-32
91BluJayS-9
91Don-473
91Fle-188
91Lea-140
91OPC-619
91PanFreS-350
91PanSti-153
91Sco-474
91StaClu-133
91Top-619
91TopDesS-619
91TopMic-619
91TopTif-619
91Ult-370
91UppDec-583
92Bow-352
92Don-620
92Fle-345
92Lea-483
92OPC-54
92Pin-431
92Sco-49
92ScoProP-15
92StaClu-721
92StaCluNC-721
92Top-54
92TopGol-54
92TopGolW-54
92TopMic-54
92Ult-453
92UppDec-116
93BluJayD4-24
93Don-511
93Fla-210
93Fle-702
93FleFinE-214
93IdaFalBF-4034
93IdaFalBSP-26
93Lea-484
93OPC-321
93PacSpa-451
93Pin-114
93Sco-648
93SelRoo-113T
93SP-242
93StaClu-59
93StaCluFDI-59
93StaCluMOP-59
93TigGat-26
93Top-458
93TopGol-458
93TopInaM-458
93TopMic-458
93TopTra-50T
93Ult-296
93UppDec-699
93UppDecGold-699
94ColC-499
94ColChoGS-499
94ColChoSS-499
94Don-307
94Fin-108
94FinRef-108
94Fle-145
94Lea-39
94MacBraC-25
94MacBraF-2206
94Pac-231
94Pin-464
94PinArtP-464
94PinMusC-464
94Sco-369
94ScoGolR-369
94Sel-357
94StaClu-617

94StaCluFDI-617
94StaCluGR-617
94StaCluMOP-617
94Top-105
94TopGol-105
94TopSpa-105
94Ult-359
94UppDec-179
94UppDecED-179
95BluJayUSPC-8S
95Don-465
95DonPreP-465
95DonTopotO-223
95Fle-63
95Pac-162
95Pin-379
95PinArtP-379
95PinMusC-379
95Sco-526
95ScoGolR-526
95ScoPlaTS-526
95StaClu-182
95StaCluFDI-182
95StaCluMOP-182
95StaCluSTWS-182
95Top-434
95TopCyb-231
95Ult-52
95UltGolM-52
96ColCho-762
96Don-469
96DonPreP-469
96Fin-B252
96FinRef-B252
96Fla-14
96Fle-357
96FleOri-18
96FleTif-357
96FleUpd-U10
96FleUpdTC-U10
96Sco-471
96StaClu-20
96StaClu-240
96StaCluMOP-20
96StaCluMOP-240
96Top-311
96Ult-311
96UltGolM-311
96UppDec-483U
97Cir-334
97CirRav-334
97Don-335
97DonPreP-335
97DonPrePGold-335
97DonTea-134
97DonTeaSPE-134
97Fin-179
97FinRef-179
97Fle-15
97Fle-543
97FleTif-15
97FleTif-543
97Sco-256
97Sco-337
97ScoHobR-337
97ScoOri-15
97ScoOriPl-15
97ScoOriPr-15
97ScoPreS-256
97ScoResC-337
97ScoShoS-256
97ScoShoS-337
97ScoShoSAP-256
97ScoShoSAP-337
97StaClu-338
97StaCluMOP-338
97Top-228
97Ult-314
97UltGolME-314
97UltPlaME-314
97UppDec-251

Wells, Devil (Willie)
74LauOldTBS-13
83ConMar-58
86NegLeaF-71
87NegLeaPD-42
88ConNegA-11
89RinPosNL1-10
90NegLeaS-11

Wells, Ed
34Gou-73
92ConTSN-389

Wells, Forry
94BenRocF-3605
95SalAvaTI-24
96NewHavRB-27
97BenRocC-26

Wells, Frank
87OldJudN-541

Wells, Jacob
87OldJudN-540

Wells, Leo
47SunBre-25

Wells, Mark
94BenRocF-3611
95AshTouUTI-30
95SalAvaTI-21
97BenRocC-27

Wells, Matt
96BelGiaTI-1

Wells, Michael
94DavLipB-24
95DavLipB-24

Wells, Terry
86AshTouP-29
87OscAstP-1
88ColAstB-3
89ColMudP-144
89ColMudS-23
90AlbDukC-13
90AlbDukP-346
90AlbDukT-31
90CMC-415
90ProAAAF-67
91LinDriAAA-323
91OklCit8LD-323
91OklCit8P-180
91Sco-359
91TopDeb90-166
93ChaKniF-542

Wells, Tim
90ButCopKSP-28
91GasRanC-11
91GasRanP-2688

Wells, Vernon
97Bow-424
97BowChr-284
97BowChrI-284
97BowChrIR-284
97BowChrR-284
97BowInt-424
97TopSta-115
97TopStaAM-115

Welmaker, Roy
52MotCoo-37
53MotCoo-52
91PomBlaBPB-2

Welsh, Chris
79ColCliT-24
80ColCliP-34
80ColCliT-3
82Don-44
82Fle-584
82Top-376
83Don-94
83ExpPos-26
83Fle-374
83OPC-118
83Top-118
83TopTra-125T
84Don-498
84Fle-292
84IndIndTI-4
85RanPer-41
86Don-464
86Fle-576
86RedTexG-45
86Top-52
86TopTif-52
87Fle-217
87FleGlo-217
87Top-592
87TopTif-592
91BriBanF-5
91PacSenL-142
93RanKee-376

Welsh, Jimmy D.
29ExhFou-10
29PorandAR-96
92ConTSN-494

Welsh, William
75WesPalBES-16

Wendell, Turk (Steven)
88PulBraP-1755
89BurBraP-1616
89BurBraS-24
90Bes-122
90GreBraB-8
90GreBraP-1131
90GreBraS-23
91GreBraC-9
91GreBraLD-222
91GreBraP-3003
91LinDriAA-222
92Bow-693
92IowCubS-223
92LeaGolR-BC5
92OPC-676
92ProFS7-178
92SkyAAAF-109
92Top-676
92TopGol-676
92TopGolW-676
92TopMic-676
92UppDec-780
92UppDecML-85
93Bow-664
93FleFinE-12
93IowCubF-2135
93TopTra-49T
94Bow-550
94ColC-290
94ColChoGS-290
94ColChoSS-290
94Don-312
94Pac-114
94Pin-254
94PinArtP-254
94PinMusC-254
94Sco-616
94ScoGolR-616
94ScoRoo-RT89
94ScoRooGR-RT89
94Spo-170
94StaClu-499
94StaCluFDI-499
94StaCluGR-499
94StaCluMOP-499
94StaCluT-358
94StaCluTFDI-358
94Top-778
94TopGol-778
94TopSpa-778
95Pin-78
95PinArtP-78
95PinMusC-78
95Sco-285
95ScoGolR-285
95ScoPlaTS-285
95Top-149
96LeaSigA-242
96LeaSigAG-243
96LeaSigAS-243
96Sco-483
96StaClu-329
96StaCluMOP-329
97Cir-144
97CirRav-144
97Fle-289
97FleTif-289
97Pac-261
97PacLigB-261
97PacSil-261
97StaClu-256
97StaCluMOP-256
97Top-113
97Ult-381
97UltGolME-381
97UltPlaME-381

Wendelstedt, Harry
88T/MUmp-6
89T/MUmp-4
90T/MUmp-4

Wendlandt, Terry
84OmaRoyT-30
85OmaRoyT-5

Wendler, Doc
55DodGolS-30

Wendt, Glenn
78WatIndT-25

Wendt, Jason
92PulBraC-20
92PulBraF-3179

Wengert, Bill
88GreFalDTI-17
89BakDodCLC-188
90VerBeaDS-27
91AdeGiaF-8
91VerBeaDC-13
91VerBeaDP-774
92SanAntMF-3975
92VerBeaDC-24
93WicWraF-2978
94WicWraF-190

Wengert, Don
92FroRowDP-28
92SouOreAC-22
92SouOreAF-3417
93ClaGolF-181
93MadMusC-1
93MadMusF-1823
93MidLeaAGF-16
93StaCluM-114
94ModA'sC-24
94ModA'sF-3064
95Bow-29
95EdmTraTI-25
95UppDec-262
95UppDecED-262
95UppDecEDG-262
96A'sMot-23
96ColCho-247
96ColChoGS-247
96ColChoSS-247
96LeaSigEA-211
96Pac-387
96SigRooOJ-36
96SigRooOJS-36
96StaClu-371
96StaCluMOP-371
96Top-433
97Fle-551
97FleTif-551
97PacPriGotD-GD83
97UppDec-451

Wenrick, Bill
88BoiHawP-1623
88SalLakCTTI-26

Wenrick, John
88LitFalMP-23
89ColMetB-17
89ColMetGS-27
90WesPalBES-26

Wensloff, Charles
43YanSta-29
47TipTop-60

Wenson, Paul
87LakTigP-25
88GleFalTP-921
89TolMudHC-8
89TolMudHP-780

Wentz, Keith
86MedA'sC-75

Wentz, Lenny
91ChaWheC-20
91ChaWheP-2897
92ChaWheF-18
92ChaWVWC-22

Wentzel, Stan
78ReaRem-22

Wenz, Fred
69Top-628
71OPC-92
71Top-92

Wenzell, Marge
93TedWil-119

Wera, Julie
91ConTSN-100

Werber, Billy
34DiaMatCSB-194
34DiaStaR-61
34Gou-75
35DiaMatCS3T1-148
35ExhFou-9
35GouPuzR-8G
35GouPuzR-9G
36GouBWR-25
36GouWidPPR-A112
36GouWidPPR-B4
36NatChiFPR-79
36NatChiFPR-87
36OveCanR-45
37ExhFou-14
38CinOraW-31
38ExhFou-14
38GouHeaU-259
38GouHeaU-283
39OrcPhoAP-24
41DouPlaR-9
41HarHarW-27
79DiaGre-331
88ConSer5-30

Werd, Norm
75SanAntBT-22

Werhas, John
64Top-456
65Top-453
67Top-514
90DodTar-846

Werland, Hank (Henry)
90PulBraB-11
90PulBraP-3108
91Cla/Bes-42
91DurBulUP-2
91MacBraC-12
91MacBraP-865

Werle, William
47PM1StaP1-215
48SomandK-18
49EurSta-175
50Bow-87
50PirTeal-24
51Bow-64
51FisBakL-29
51TopRedB-33
52Bow-248
52Top-73
53RedSoxTI-27
53Top-170
54Top-144
61UniOil-H10
83TopRep5-73
91TopArc1-170
94TopArc1-144
94TopArc1G-144

Werley, George
91OriCro-478

Werley, Jamie
80NasSouTI-24
81NasSouTI-22
82ColCliP-15
82ColCliT-10

Werner, Dave
89EriOriS-29

Werner, Don
76IndIndTI-17
77IndIndTI-8
78Pep-25
78Top-702
79IndIndTI-22
80RedEnq-19
83Don-593
83OklCit8T-18
83Top-504
84IowCubT-16
85NasSouTI-25
86OklCit8P-25
87OklCit8P-5
88OklCit8C-21
88OklCit8P-37
89JamExpP-2150
91AugPirC-30
91AugPirP-822
92CarMudF-1195
92CarMudS-149
93RanKee-377
95CarMudF-175
96IdaFalB-28

Werner, Rick
93HelBreF-4095
93HelBreSP-24

Wernig, Pat
88MadMusP-25
88MidLeaAGS-52
89HunStaB-23
91LinDriAAA-547
91TacTigLD-547
91TacTigP-2307
92LasVegSS-247
93PalSprAC-25
93PalSprAF-71

Werrick, Joe
87OldJudN-542

Wert, Don
62Top-299
64Top-19
64TopVen-19
65OPC-271
65TigJayP-10
65Top-271
66Top-253
66TopVen-253
67CokCapTi-12
67DexPre-218
67TigDexP-9
67Top-511
67TopVen-253
68CokCapT-12
68OPC-178
68TigDetFPB-26

68Top-178
68TopVen-178
69MilBra-287
69TigTeal-12
69Top-443
69TopSta-180
69TopTeaP-1
70OPC-33
70Top-33
71MLBOffS-552
71OPC-307
71SenPolP-10
71Top-307
72MilBra-358
78TCM60I-163
78TigDeaCS-9
81TigDetN-65
88TigDom-25
Werth, Dennis
75ForLauYS-21
78TacYanC-9
79ColCliT-10
81Don-466
81Fle-102
81Top-424
82Fle-55
82Roy-23
82Top-154
82TopTra-126T
83LouRedR-22
84LouRedR-30
92YanWIZ7-163
92YanWIZ8-200
Werth, Jayson
97Bow-433
97BowChr-293
97BowChrI-293
97BowChrIR-293
97BowChrR-293
97BowInt-433
97TopSta-119
97TopStaAM-119
Wertz, Bill
90RenSilSCLC-280
90WatIndS-23
91Cla/Bes-138
91CollndC-18
91CollndP-1485
92CanIndF-692
92CanIndS-123
93Bow-529
93ChaKniF-543
93ClaGolF-8
93FleFinE-206
94ChaKniF-896
94Don-590
94Fle-123
94Pac-186
94StaClu-481
94StaCluFDI-481
94StaCluGR-481
94StaCluMOP-481
94Top-64
94TopGol-64
94TopSpa-64
94Ult-50
94VenLinU-37
95PawRedSDD-29
95PawRedTI-38
Wertz, Vic
47Exh-238A
47Exh-238B
49Bow-164
50Bow-9
51Bow-176
51TopBluB-40
52BerRos-66
52Bow-39
52RedMan-AL22
52StaCalL-72D
52StaCalS-86B
52Top-244
53BowC-2
53Top-142
54Bow-21
54OriEss-35
55Bow-40
55IndGolS-11
55RedMan-AL13
56Top-300
57IndSoh-16
57SwiFra-6
57Top-78
58Top-170
59Baz-23
59Top-500
60RedSoxJP-11
60Top-111
60TopVen-111
61Pos-49A
61Pos-49B
61Top-173
61Top-340
61TopStal-118
62SalPlaC-60
62ShiPlaC-60
62Top-481
63Top-348
78ReaRem-23
78TCM60I-227
79TCM50-45
81TigDetN-123
82OhiHaloF-54
83TopRep5-244
91OriCro-479
91TopArc1-142
92BazQua5A-1
Wesemann, Jason
96BatCliTI-25
Wesley, Tom
81CedRapRT-15
Wesolowski, Al
78NewWayCT-43
Wessel, Troy
89JamExpP-2139
90JamExpP-26
Wessels, John
88KimN18-48
Wessenaar, Rob
92SkyAAAF-194
Wessinger, Jim
79SavBraT-26
80RicBraT-21
Wesson, Barry
96AubDouB-18
West, Adam
96NewJerCB-29
West, Bobby
89PriPirS-24
West, Chris
89TenTecGE-30
93SpoIndC-22
93SpoIndF-3599
West, Dave
84LitFalMT-24
86LynMetP-25
87JacMetF-23
87MetColP-50
87TexLeaAF-29
88MetColP-52
88TidTidCa-28
88TidTidCM-2
88TidTidP-1592
88TriAAAP-41
88TriAAC-29
89ClaTraO-134
89Don-41
89Fle-51
89FleGlo-51
89MetCol8-16
89MetColP-57
89MetKah-29
89Sco-650
89ScoYouSI-32
89Spo-45
89TidTidC-7
89TidTidP-1973
89Top-787
89TopTif-787
89ToyRoo-33
89UppDec-7
90Bow-413
90BowTif-413
90ClaBlu-68
90Don-387
90Fle-388
90FleCan-388
90Hot50RS-47
90Lea-387
90OPC-357
90Sco-573
90Top-357
90TopBig-325
90TopRoo-30
90TopTif-357
90ToyRoo-30
90UppDec-15
90UppDec-562A
91Don-264
91Fle-627
91MetWIZ-428
91OPC-578
91Sco-158
91StaClu-34
91Top-578
91TopDesS-578
91TopMic-578
91TopTif-578
91UppDec-377
92Don-638
92OPC-442
92Pin-333
92PorBeaF-2669
92PorBeaS-423
92Sco-669
92StaClu-398
92Top-442
92TopGol-442
92TopGolW-442
92TopMic-442
92UppDec-548
93Don-501
93FleFinE-112
93Lea-460
93PacSpa-583
93PhiMed-34
93StaCluP-12
93Top-652
93TopGol-652
93TopInaM-652
93TopMic-652
93Ult-447
93UppDec-710
93UppDecGold-710
94Don-409
94Fla-419
94Fle-603
94Pac-489
94PhiMed-35
94PhiMel-24
94PhiUSPC-4S
94PhiUSPC-8D
94Sco-156
94ScoGolR-156
94StaClu-130
94StaCluFDI-130
94StaCluGR-130
94StaCluMOP-130
94StaCluT-220
94StaCluTFDI-220
94Top-266
94TopGol-266
94TopSpa-266
95Don-348
95DonPreP-348
95Fle-407
95Phi-35
95PhiMel-25
95StaClu-178
95StaCluFDI-178
95StaCluMOP-178
95StaCluSTWS-178
95StaCluVR-92
95Top-31
95TopCyb-24
95Ult-211
95UltGolM-211
96Fla-340
96StaCluVRMO-92
96Ult-528
96UltGolM-528
West, Dick
39OrcPhoAP-25
West, Jerry
66AurSpoMK-6
West, Jim
90SpoIndSP-15
91WatDiaC-13
91WatDiaP-1260
West, Joe
88T/MUmp-36
89T/MUmp-34
90T/MUmp-33
West, Lefty (Weldon)
96Bro194F-15
West, Matt
83DurBulT-26
85RicBraT-10
86RicBraP-25
87RicBraBC-22
87RicBraC-45
87RicBraT-8
88CalCanC-8
88CalCanP-788
89PulBraP-1902
90SumBraP-2451
91MacBraC-29
91MacBraP-884
92DurBulC-26
92DurBulF-1118
92DurBulTI-30
93DurBulC-29
93DurBulF-505
93DurBulTI-3
94DurBulC-27
94DurBulF-345
94DurBulTI-28
95DurBulTI-35
West, Milton
87OldJudN-543
West, Paul
92LetMouSP-14
West, Reggie
84EdmTraC-116
85EdmTraC-8
West, Samuel
31SenTeaPW-30
33Gou-166
34ButPreR-63
35GouPuzR-5D
35GouPuzR-6D
35GouPuzR-11F
35GouPuzR-13D
36ExhFou-15
36NatChiFPR-80
36OveCanR-47
37ExhFou-15
37KelPepS-BB18
37OPCBatUV-129
38ExhFou-15
39PlaBal-31
40PlaBal-22
60SenUniMC-20
77GalGloG-192
79DiaGre-51
91ConTSN-241
93ConTSN-679
94ConTSN-1090
94ConTSNB-1090
West, Tom
86DayBealP-29
86FloStaLAP-49
West, W. Max
36OveCanR-46
39PlaBal-149
40PlaBal-57
41DouPlaR-43
41PlaBal-2
52MotCoo-10
53MotCoo-19
74LauAllG-40
90DodTar-847
Westbrook, Destry
92AubAstC-21
92AubAstF-1355
94QuaCitRBC-24
94QuaCitRBF-535
Westbrook, Jake
96BesAutS1RP-FR8
97Bow-200
97BowChr-186
97BowChrI-186
97BowChrIR-186
97BowChrR-186
97BowInt-200
97Top-478
Westbrook, Mike
84LitFalMT-3
86LynMetP-26
88CarLeaAS-40
88KinIndS-23
89RenSilSCLC-251
Westbrooks, Elanis
88CliGiaP-716
89SanJosGB-13
89SanJosGCLC-225
89SanJosGP-435
89SanJosGS-25
90SanJosGB-14
90SanJosGCLC-32
90SanJosGP-2021
90SanJosGS-25
Westermann, Scott
88GreHorP-1565
Westfall, Fred
76WauMetT-24
77LynMetT-29
Westlake, James
09T206-522
Westlake, James Patrick
77FriOneYW-17
Westlake, Wally
46RemBre-8
46SpoExcW-4-11
47Exh-239
49Bow-45
49EurSta-176
50Bow-69
50PirTeal-25
51TopRedB-27
52BerRos-67
52NatTeaL-40
52StaCalL-81B
52StaCalS-93C
52Top-38
53Top-192
54DanDee-28
54Top-92
55IndGolS-18
55Top-102
55TopDouH-13
56Top-81
79DiaGre-368
83TopRep5-38
91OriCro-480
91TopArc1-192
94TopArc1-92
94TopArc1G-92
Westmoreland, Claude
79AlbDukT-21
80AlbDukT-11
Westmoreland, John
85CloHSS-43
Weston, Mickey
85LynMetT-6
86JacMetT-10
87JacMetF-11
88JacMetGS-22
89RocRedWC-6
89RocRedWP-1638
90CMC-304
90OPC-377
90RocRedWC-3
90RocRedWGC-10
90Sco-616
90Top-377
90TopDeb89-137
90TopTif-377
90UppDec-683A
90UppDec-683B
91LinDriAAA-521
91OriCro-481
91SyrChiLD-521
91SyrChiMB-27
91SyrChiP-2482
92ScrRedBF-2447
92ScrRedBS-496
95TolMudHTI-25
Weston, Tim
88OneYanP-2065
89AlbYanB-29
89AlbYanP-323
90AlbYanB-17
90AlbYanS-28
Westover, Richard
96VerExpB-29
Westray, Ken
94BatCliC-29
94BatCliF-3464
Westrum, Wes
47Exh-240
49EurSta-126
50JJKCopP-22
51Bow-161
51FisBakL-30
51R42SmaS-115
51TopRedB-37
52BerRos-68
52Bow-74
52CokTip-10
52RedMan-NL26
52TipTop-46
52Top-75
53RedMan-NL20
54Bow-25
54NewYorJA-36
54Top-180
55Bow-141
55GiaGolS-15
56Top-156

57Top-323
60Top-469
66Top-341
66TopVen-341
67MetTeal-12
67Top-593
75Gia-11
75Gia195T-29
75OPC-216
75Top-216
76SSP-113
79DiaGre-44
79TCM50-46
80GiaGreT-2
83TopRep5-75
84GiaMot-14
91TopArc1-323
92BazQua5A-10
94TopArc1-180
94TopArc1G-180

Wetherby, Jeff
86SumBraP-30
87GreBraB-21
88BlaYNPRWL-156
88RicBraC-16
88RicBraP-9
89BraDub-28
89RicBraC-16
89RicBraP-840
89RicBraTI-22
90CMC-474
90ColSprSSC-22
90ColSprSSP-53
90OPC-142
90ProAAAF-234
90Sco-540
90Sco100RS-44
90Top-142
90TopDeb89-138
90TopTif-142
90UppDec-611
91LinDriAAA-472
91RocRedWLD-472
91RocRedWP-1917
92CalCanF-3744
88RicBraBC-17

Wetmore, Michael
96HelBreTI-29

Wetteland, John
86BakDodP-28
87VerBeaDP-1
88BasAmeAAB-28
88BlaYNPRWL-189
88SanAntMB-21
88TexLeaAGS-7
89AlbDukC-11
89AlbDukP-63
89DodStaSV-16
89ScoRoo-90T
90Bow-82
90BowTif-82
90ClaBlu-110
90DodMot-19
90DodPol-57
90DodTar-1094
90Don-671
90Fle-411
90FleCan-411
90Hot50RS-48
90OPC-631
90Sco-388
90Sco100RS-25
90ScoYouSI-40
90Top-631
90TopDeb89-139
90TopRoo-31
90TopTif-631
90ToyRoo-31
90UppDec-377
91AlbDukLD-23
91AlbDukP-1142
91Don-614
91LinDriAAA-23
91Sco-267
91UppDec-668
92Bow-68
92Cla1-T94
92Don-627
92ExpDonD-20
92ExpPos-32
92FleUpd-100
92Lea-478
92OPCPre-108
92Pin-461
92Pin-593
92ScoRoo-78T
92StaClu-759
92StaCluNC-759
92Ult-526
92UppDec-788
93Bow-212
93Don-592
93Fin-129
93FinRef-129
93Fla-88
93Fle-83
93Lea-183
93MSABenSPD-11
93OPC-366
93PacSpa-538
93Pin-397
93Sco-165
93Sel-201
93SelStaL-72
93SP-108
93StaClu-344
93StaCluFDI-344
93StaCluMOP-344
93Stu-65
93Top-231
93TopGol-231
93TopInaM-231
93TopMic-231
93TriPla-206
93Ult-420
93UppDec-392
93UppDecGold-392
94Bow-172
94BowBes-R21
94BowBesR-R21
94ColC-410
94ColChoGS-410
94ColChoSS-410
94Don-293
94ExtBas-313
94Fin-133
94FinRef-133
94Fla-405
94Fle-555
94FUnPac-57
94Lea-414
94LeaL-128
94OPC-105
94Pac-393
94PanSti-214
94Pin-119
94PinArtP-119
94PinMusC-119
94Sco-390
94ScoGolR-390
94Sel-69
94SP-87
94SPDieC-87
94StaClu-446
94StaCluFDI-446
94StaCluGR-446
94StaCluMOP-446
94Stu-81
94Top-497
94TopGol-497
94TopSpa-497
94TriPla-100
94Ult-232
94UltFir-9
94UppDec-32
94UppDec-335
94UppDecED-32
94UppDecED-335
95Baz-121
95Bow-367
95ColCho-239
95ColCho-585T
95ColChoGS-239
95ColChoSE-102
95ColChoSE-252
95ColChoSEGS-102
95ColChoSEGS-252
95ColChoSESS-102
95ColChoSESS-252
95ColChoSS-239
95Don-516
95DonPreP-516
95DonTopotO-128
95Emb-137
95EmbGolI-137
95Emo-68
95Fin-81
95Fin-240
95FinFlaT-FT9
95FinRef-81
95FinRef-240
95Fla-289
95Fle-363
95FleUpd-28
95Lea-356
95Pac-274
95Pin-347
95PinArtP-347
95PinMusC-347
95Sco-85
95ScoGolR-85
95ScoPlaTS-85
95SP-179
95SPCha-174
95SPChaDC-174
95SPSil-179
95StaClu-472
95StaClu-615
95StaCluMOP-472
95StaCluMOP-615
95StaCluMOP-SS19
95StaCluSS-SS19
95StaCluSTWS-472
95StaCluSTWS-615
95StaCluVR-258
95Stu-94
95Top-22
95TopCyb-18
95TopTra-81T
95Ult-194
95UltGolM-194
95UppDec-78
95UppDec-439
95UppDecED-78
95UppDecED-439
95UppDecEDG-78
95UppDecEDG-439
95UppDecSE-146
95UppDecSEG-146
96Baz-101
96ColCho-633
96ColChoGS-633
96ColChoSS-633
96Don-161
96DonPreP-161
96EmoXL-98
96Fin-B17
96FinRef-B17
96Fla-139
96Fle-199
96FleTif-199
96Lea-140
96LeaPrePB-140
96LeaPrePG-140
96LeaPrePS-140
96MetUni-96
96MetUniP-96
96MLBPin-35
96Pac-381
96Pin-15
96Sco-99
96Sco-201
96ScoDugC-A71
96ScoDugCAP-A71
96SP-134
96StaClu-268
96StaCluMOP-268
96StaCluVRMO-258
96Top-95
96TopGal-50
96TopGalPPI-50
96Ult-108
96UltGolM-108
96UppDec-407
97Bow-69
97BowBes-63
97BowBesAR-63
97BowBesR-63
97BowChr-50
97BowChrI-50
97BowChrIR-50
97BowChrR-50
97BowInt-69
97Cir-340
97CirRav-340
97ColCho-63
97ColCho-224
97Don-139
97Don-286
97Don-437
97DonLim-92
97DonLimLE-92
97DonPre-26
97DonPreCttC-26
97DonPreP-139
97DonPreP-286
97DonPreP-437
97DonPrePGold-139
97DonPrePGold-286
97DonPrePGold-437
97Fin-222
97FinRef-222
97FlaSho-A89
97FlaSho-B89
97FlaSho-C89
97FlaShoLC-89
97FlaShoLC-B89
97FlaShoLC-C89
97FlaShoLCM-A89
97FlaShoLCM-B89
97FlaShoLCM-C89
97Fle-180
97Fle-609
97FleMilDM-40
97FleTif-180
97FleTif-609
97Lea-47
97Lea-214
97LeaFraM-47
97LeaFraM-214
97LeaFraMDC-47
97LeaFraMDC-214
97MetUni-124
97NewPin-27
97NewPinAP-27
97NewPinMC-27
97NewPinPP-27
97Pac-162
97PacLigB-162
97PacSil-162
97PinCar-16
97PinCer-7
97PinCerMBlu-7
97PinCerMG-7
97PinCerMR-7
97PinCerR-7
97PinIns-70
97PinInsCE-70
97PinInsDD-17
97PinInsDE-70
97PinTotCPB-7
97PinTotCPG-7
97PinTotCPR-7
97PinX-P-99
97PinX-PMoS-99
97Sco-134
97Sco-333
97Sco-524
97ScoAllF-19
97ScoHobR-333
97ScoHobR-524
97ScoPreS-134
97ScoResC-333
97ScoResC-524
97ScoShoS-134
97ScoShoS-333
97ScoShoS-524
97ScoShoSAP-134
97ScoShoSAP-333
97ScoShoSAP-524
97ScoYan-8
97ScoYanPI-8
97ScoYanPr-8
97Sel-19
97SelArtP-19
97SelRegG-19
97SP-176
97SpoIII-180
97SpoIIIEE-180
97StaClu-254
97StaCluI-I19
97StaCluMat-254
97StaCluMOP-254
97StaCluMOP-I19
97Top-90
97TopChr-36
97TopChrR-36
97TopGal-68
97TopGalPPI-68
97Ult-374
97UltGolME-374
97UltPlaME-374
97UppDec-267
97UppDec-548
97UppDecAWJ-15

Wetzel, Tom
84EveGiaC-29

Wever, Stefan
82NasSouTI-27
83ColCliT-10
92YanWIZ8-201

Wex, Gary
83AlbA'sT-8

Weyer, Lee
88T/MUmp-2
89T/MUmp-62

Weyhing, August
87OldJudN-544
89EdgR.WG-18
90DodTar-848
90KalBatN-56

Weyhing, John
87OldJudN-545

Weymouth, Marty
96EveAquB-27

Whalen, Mike
84NewOriT-12

Whalen, Shawn
90WatDiaB-17
90WatDiaP-2392
91Cla/Bes-337
91WatDiaC-24
91WatDiaP-1271
92WatDiaC-22

Whaley, Scott Lee
84MadMusP-5
85HunStaJ-23
85MadMusP-24
85MadMusT-3
86HumStaDS-32

Whaling, Albert
14B18B-55A
14B18B-55B
14B18B-55C
15CraJacE-163

Whalley, Jarrell
77SpaPhiT-5

Wharton, Greg
91MelBusF-1

Wharton, Joe
93OneYanC-24
93OneYanF-3504
94GreBatF-476
97GreBatC-26

Whatley, Fred
90CliGiaUTI-U9

Whatley, Gabe
93HunCubC-27
93HunCubF-3253
94WilCubC-24
94WilCubF-3775
95RocCubTI-18
96DayCubB-25

Wheat, Chris
90HelBreSP-6
91HelBreSP-20

Wheat, Danny
76SanAntBTI-26
83OklCit8T-24
85RanPer-NNO
86RanPer-NNO0
87RanMot-27
88RanMot-28
89RanMot-28
90RanMot-28

Wheat, Leroy
54Top-244
55JetPos-20
94TopArc1-244
94TopArc1G-244

Wheat, Mack (McKinley Davis)
90DodTar-849

Wheat, Zachary D.
09ColChiE-303
09SpoNewSM-80
09T206-371
10CouT21-243
10CouT21-244
10CouT21-323
10DomDisP-123
10RedCroT-82
10RedCroT-255
10SweCapPP-78A
10SweCapPP-78B
11MecDFT-3
11S74Sil-57
11T205-178
12ColRedB-303
12ColTinT-303

12HasTriFT-76
12T207-194
13NatGamW-43
13TomBarW-39
14B18B-64
14CraJacE-52
14PieStaT-61
14TexTomE-46
15CraJacE-52
15SpoNewM-186
15VicT21-29
16ColE13-187
16FleBreD-99
16SpoNewM-188
19W514-110
20GasAmeMBD-23
20NatCarE-107
21E121So1-113
21E121So8-104
21Exh-184
21Nei-117
21StaBis-78
22AmeCarE-75
22E120-150
22W572-114
22W573-136
22W575-147
22WilPatV-49
23W501-98
23W503-44
23W515-56
23WilChoV-168
25Exh-16
26Exh-16
27Exh-56
60Fle-12
61Fle-1
61Fle-86
69SCFOldT-3
75TCMAllG-34
76ShaPiz-84
77GalGloG-101
77GalGloG-151
80DodGreT-6
80PerHaloFP-84
80SSPHOF-84
89DodSmoG-34
90BasWit-82
90DodTar-850
91ConTSN-164
93CraJac-15

Wheatcroft, Bob (Robert)
89BluOriS-28
90WauTimB-10
90WauTimP-2123
90WauTimS-25

Wheaton, James
91FreStaBS-14

Wheeler, Bradley
88ElPasDB-18

Wheeler, Chris
84PhiTas-7
88PhiTas-39
90PhiTas-35

Wheeler, Dave
90BilMusP-3226

Wheeler, Duke
72CedRapCT-8

Wheeler, Earl
91OklStaC-31
92OklStaC-31
94ChaRanF-2497

Wheeler, Ed
75AppFoxT-28
90DodTar-851

Wheeler, Kenny (Kenneth)
90AshTouP-2750
91BurAstC-11
91BurAstP-2802
91MidLeaAP-MWL20
92OscAstC-4
92OscAstF-2531
93OscAstC-22
93OscAstF-628

Wheeler, Rocket (Ralph)
78DunBluJT-25
80KnoBluJT-24
85KinBluJT-25
86SyrChiP-26
87MyrBeaBJP-1453
90CMC-676
90ProAAAF-370
90SyrChiC-28
90SyrChiMB-28
90SyrChiP-590
91LinDriAAA-525
91SyrChiLD-525
91SyrChiMB-28
91SyrChiP-2498
92SyrChiF-1988
92SyrChiMB-29
93SyrChiF-1015
94DunBluJC-29
94DunBluJF-2574
96StCatSB-1

Wheeler, Rodney
86ClePhiP-24

Wheeler, Ryan
94BoiHawC-29
94BoiHawF-3366

Wheeler, Tim
82AleDukT-18
82BufBisT-9
83LynPirT-9
84HawIslC-140

Wheeler, Winston
90MarPhiP-3185

Wheelock, Gary
75SalLakCC-12
76SalLakCGC-2
77Top-493
78SanJosMMC-8
78Top-596
79SpoIndT-17
80SpoIndT-17
87BelMarL-12
87OklCit8P-2
89BelMarL-32
91BelMarC-27
91BelMarP-3684
92SanBerC-28

Wheelock, Warren
87OldJudN-546

Wherry, Cliff
83TucTorT-18
84OklCit8T-4

Whipple, Boomer
96AugGreB-28

Whipple, Jack
45CenFlo-27

Whipps, Joe
90JacMetGS-20

Whisenant, Matt
90PriPatD-27
91BatCliC-17
91BatCliP-3483
92SpaPhiC-20
92SpaPhiF-1264
92UppDecML-211
93Bow-38
93ClaFS7-149
93ClaGolF-136
93ExcFS7-88
93KanCouCC-23
93KanCouCF-917
93SouAtlLAIPI-6
93SouAtlLAPI-40
94Bow-206
94BreCouMC-22
94BreCouMF-14
95KanCouCLTI-15
95SPML-61
96ChaKniB-28
96Exc-168
93KanCouCTI-27

Whisenant, Pete
57Top-373
58RedEnq-41
58Top-466
59RedShiBS-23
59Top-14
59TopVen-14
60Top-424
61Top-201
61TopStal-187
61TwiPetM-11
83AlbA'sT-20

Whisenton, Larry
78RicBraT-17
79RicBraT-4
79Top-715
80RicBraT-4
81RicBraT-6
82BraBurKL-27
82BraPol-28
83Don-501
83Fle-152
83RicBraT-22
83Top-544
84RicBraT-5
85GreBraTI-25

Whisler, Randy
90GasRanB-27
90GasRanP-2537
90GasRanS-29
91GasRanP-2707
92TulDriF-2710
92TulDriS-625
93TulDriF-2750
94TulDriF-260
94TulDriTI-28
93TulDriTI-28

Whisman, Rhett
82WisRapTF-27

Whisonant, John
91BatCliC-23
91BatCliP-3484

Whisonant, Mike
89AncGlaP-27

Whistler, Clarence
88KimN18-49

Whistler, Randy
80AndBraT-19

Whitacre, Fred
75WesPalBES-4B

Whitaker, Darrell
85BurRanT-24
86SalRedBP-28
87GasRanP-26
88OklCit8C-11
88OklCit8P-43
88TulDriTI-6
89OklCit8C-10
89OklCit8P-1516

Whitaker, Jeff
91BurIndP-3311
92BurIndC-2
92BurIndF-1666

Whitaker, Jerry
96PriWilCB-29

Whitaker, Lou
78TigBurK-13
78Top-704
79Hos-117
79OPC-55
79Top-123
80OPC-187
80Top-358
81AllGamPI-16
81CokTeaS-58
81Don-365
81Fle-463
81OPC-234
81TigDetN-59
81Top-234
82Don-454
82Fle-284
82FleSta-156
82OPC-39
82Top-39
82TopSti-187
83AllGamPI-17
83Don-333
83Fle-348
83FleSta-212
83FleSti-249
83OPC-66
83Tig-29
83Top-509
83TopSti-65
84AllGamPI-107
84Don-227
84DonActAS-4
84Fle-92
84FleSti-13
84FleSti-30
84FunFooP-78
84MilBra-28
84Nes792-398
84Nes792-666
84Nes792-695
84NesDreT-2
84OCoandSI-84
84OPC-181
84OPC-211
84SevCoi-C16
84TigFarJ-15
84TigWavP-34
84Top-398
84Top-666
84Top-695
84TopGloS-30
84TopRubD-18
84TopSti-196
84TopSti-267
84TopStiB-1
84TopTif-398
84TopTif-666
84TopTif-695
85AllGamPI-17
85Don-5
85Don-293
85DonActA-42
85DonSupD-5
85Fle-24
85GenMilS-24
85Lea-5
85OPC-108
85SevCoi-D1
85SevCoi-S16
85TigCaiD-19
85TigWen-21
85Top-480
85TopGloA-14
85TopRubD-17
85TopSti-183
85TopSti-261
85TopTif-480
86BasStaB-118
86Don-49
86DonAll-11
86DonPop-11
86Fle-242
86FleLimE-44
86FleMin-51
86FleStiC-126
86GenMilB-1J
86Lea-33
86OPC-20
86SevCoi-S10
86Spo-48
86Spo-74
86SpoDecG-73
86SpoRoo-48
86TigCaiD-20
86Top-20
86TopGloA-3
86TopSti-156
86TopSti-272
86TopTat-23
86TopTif-20
86TruVal-25
87Don-107
87DonAll-3
87DonOpeD-218
87DonP-3
87Fle-168
87FleGlo-168
87FleMin-112
87FleRecS-41
87FleStiC-122
87HosSti-23
87Lea-78
87MSAJifPD-11
87OPC-106
87RedFolSB-88
87SevCoi-D12
87Spo-112
87Spo-137
87SpoTeaP-15
87TigCaiD-8
87TigCok-16
87Top-661
87TopGloA-14
87TopGloS-7
87TopSti-153
87TopSti-267
87TopTif-661
88Don-173
88DonBasB-315
88Fle-75
88FleGlo-75
88Lea-169
88OPC-179
88PanSti-92
88PanSti-122
88PanSti-443
88Sco-56
88ScoGlo-56
88Spo-30
88StaLinAl-35
88StaLinTi-20
88TigPep-1
88TigPol-14
88Top-770
88TopBig-99
88TopMinL-13
88TopSti-270
88TopStiB-38
88TopTif-770
89Bow-103
89BowTif-103
89ClaTraP-188
89Don-298
89DonBasB-35
89Fle-151
89FleGlo-151
89OPC-320
89PanSti-341
89Sco-230
89Spo-18
89TigMar-1
89TigPol-1
89Top-320
89TopBasT-162
89TopBig-22
89TopCoi-57
89TopSti-282
89TopStiB-6
89TopTif-320
89TopUKM-83
89UppDec-451
90Bow-356
90BowTif-356
90Don-16
90Don-298
90DonBesA-119
90DonSupD-16
90Fle-619
90FleCan-619
90Hot50PS-48
90KinDis-24
90Lea-34
90MLBBasB-89
90OPC-280
90PanSti-71
90PubSti-485
90RedFolSB-101
90Sco-75
90Sco100S-71
90Spo-103
90TigCok-26
90Top-280
90TopBig-130
90TopCoi-32
90TopDou-70
90TopSti-275
90TopStiB-39
90TopTif-280
90UppDec-41
90UppDec-327
90VenSti-482
91Bow-150
91CadEllD-60
91ClaGam-3
91Don-174
91Fle-357
91Lea-120
91OPC-145
91PanFreS-289
91PanSti-233
91Sco-297
91StaClu-101
91Stu-60
91TigCok-1
91TigPol-14
91Top-145
91TopDesS-145
91TopMic-145
91TopTif-145
91Ult-130
91UppDec-367
92Bow-630
92ClaGam-91
92Don-285
92Fle-149
92Hig5-50
92Lea-391
92OPC-570
92PanSti-106
92Pin-29
92Sco-255
92SpoIllFK1-204
92StaClu-550
92Stu-180
92Top-570
92TopGol-570
92TopGolW-570
92TopKid-77
92TopMic-570

92TriPla-117
92Ult-65
92UppDec-516
93Bow-11
93CadDis-62
93Don-686
93Fin-2
93FinRef-2
93Fla-211
93Fle-614
93FunPac-190
93Lea-148
93OPC-389
93PacSpa-116
93Pin-509
93Sco-596
93Sel-112
93SP-243
93StaClu-135
93StaCluFDI-135
93StaCluMOP-135
93Stu-76
93TigGat-27
93Top-160
93TopGol-160
93TopInaM-160
93TopMic-160
93TriPla-224
93Ult-555
93UppDec-273
93UppDecGold-273
94Bow-237
94ColC-291
94ColChoGS-291
94ColChoSS-291
94Don-360
94DonSpeE-360
94ExtBas-82
94Fin-364
94FinRef-364
94Fla-296
94Fle-146
94Fle-709
94Lea-80
94LeaL-35
94OPC-172
94Pac-232
94PanSti-70
94Pin-281
94PinArtP-281
94PinMusC-281
94ProMag-49
94Sco-79
94ScoGolR-79
94Sel-323
94StaClu-443
94StaCluFDI-443
94StaCluGR-443
94StaCluMOP-443
94Stu-195
94Top-410
94TopGol-410
94TopSpa-410
94TriPla-250
94TriPlaM-5
94Ult-60
94UppDec-414
94UppDecED-414
95ColCho-475
95ColChoGS-475
95ColChoSE-218
95ColChoSEGS-218
95ColChoSESS-218
95ColChoSS-475
95D3-30
95Don-45
95DonPreP-45
95DonTopotO-81
95Emb-97
95EmbGolI-97
95Emo-47
95Fin-220
95FinRef-220
95Fla-42
95Fle-64
95Lea-178
95LeaLim-142
95Pac-163
95PacPri-52
95PanSti-50
95Pin-117
95PinArtP-117
95PinMusC-117
95Sco-373
95ScoGolR-373
95ScoPlaTS-373
95SP-153
95SPCha-152
95SPChaDC-152
95SPSil-153
95StaClu-481
95StaCluMOP-481
95StaCluSTWS-481
95StaCluVR-262
95Stu-80
95Top-15
95TopCyb-13
95Ult-287
95UltGolM-287
95UppDec-188
95UppDecED-188
95UppDecEDG-188
95UppDecSE-230
95UppDecSEG-230
96ColCho-144
96ColChoGS-144
96ColChoSS-144
96Don-77
96DonPreP-77
96Fle-122
96FleGolM-10
96FleTif-122
96Pac-318
96Sco-487
96StaCluVRMO-262
96Ult-66
96UltGolM-66
96UppDec-107

Whitaker, Ryan
93SouOreAC-26
93SouOreAF-4064
94WesMicWC-24
94WesMicWF-2297
95ModA'sTI-30
96ModA'sB-19

Whitaker, Steve
91ClaDraP-29
91FroRowDP-40
92OPC-369
92SanJosGC-5
92StaCluD-194
92Top-369
92TopGol-369
92TopGolW-369
92TopMic-369
93ClaGolF-69
93SanJosGC-18
93SanJosGF-11
94ShrCapF-1607
95Exc-296
95UppDecML-189
96El PasDB-28
95UppDecMLFS-189

Whitaker, Steve (Stephen E.)
67Top-277
68Top-383
69MLBOffS-63
69OPC-71
69Top-71
69TopSta-189
69TopTeaP-7
70OPC-496
70Top-496
81TCM60I-445
83Pil69G-41
89PacSenL-67
92YanWIZ6-135

Whitaker, William
87OldJudN-548

Whitby, William
67Top-486

White Sox, Chicago
13FatT20-2
36NatChiFPR-88
36R31Pre-G21
38BasTabP-47
48WhiSoxTI-30
51TopTea-3
56Top-188
57Top-329
58Top-256
59Top-94
59TopVen-94
60Top-208
60TopTat-66
61Top-7
61TopMagR-9
62GuyPotCP-4
62Top-113
62TopVen-113
63GadFunC-64
63Top-288
64Top-496
64TopTatI-5
65OPC-234
65Top-234
66Top-426
66TopRubI-105
67Top-573
68LauWorS-3
68LauWorS-14
68Top-424
69FleCloS-6
69TopStaA-6
70FleWorS-3
70FleWorS-14
70FleWorS-16
70OPC-501
70Top-501
71FleWorS-4
71FleWorS-17
71Top-289
71TopTat-69
72OPC-381
72Top-381
73OPC-481
73OPCBTC-6
73Top-481
73TopBluTC-6
74OPC-416
74OPCTC-6
74Top-416
74TopStaA-6
74TopTeaC-6
75WhiSox1T-28
78Top-66
83FleSta-230
83FleSti-NNO
87SpoTeaL-26
87Top-356
87TopTif-356
88PacEigMO-4
88PanSti-458
88RedFolSB-117
90PubSti-639
90RedFolSB-110
90VenSti-520
91PanCanT1-136
91UppDec-617
94ImpProP-4
94Sco-320
94ScoGolR-320
95PanSti-146
96FleWhiS-19
96PanSti-171

White Sox, Yarmouth-Dennis
88CapCodPB-28

White, Al
49SolSunP-11
80PenPilBT-16
80PenPilCT-22

White, Andre
91BurIndP-3319
93ColRedC-25
93ColRedF-613
94KinIndC-21
94KinIndF-2659

White, Bill D.
59Top-359
60CarJayP-12
60Top-355
60TopTat-53
61CarJayP-13
61Pos-176A
61Pos-176B
61Top-232
61Top-451
61TopDicG-18
61TopStaI-96
62Baz-40
62CarJayP-12
62Jel-158
62Pos-158
62PosCan-158
62SalPlaC-115
62ShiPlaC-115
62Top-14
62TopBuc-92
62TopStaI-191
62TopVen-14
63BasMagM-84
63Baz-28
63CarJayP-20
63Fle-63
63Jel-158
63Pos-158A
63Pos-158B
63Top-1
63Top-290
63TopStiI-45
64CarTeal-8
64Top-11
64Top-240
64TopCoi-78
64TopCoi-141
64TopSta-10
64TopStaU-74
64TopVen-11
64TopVen-240
64WheSta-48
65CarJayP-12
65OPC-190
65Top-190
65TopEmbI-43
65TopTraI-72
66Baz-23
66PhiTeal-12
66Top-397
66TopRubI-97
67Baz-23
67CokCapPh-13
67DexPre-219
67PhiPol-13
67Top-290
68Baz-4
68OPC-190
68Top-190
68TopVen-190
69MilBra-288
69Top-588
69TopTeaP-8
72MilBra-359
78TCM60I-12
81TCM60I-414
82DanSunF-6
90PacLeg-56
90SweBasG-9
91LinDri-27
91SweBasG-96
92ActPacA-84
92CarMcD-25
93UppDecAH-125
94CarLeaA-DJ12
94UppDecAH-65
94UppDecAH1-65

White, Billy
89GenCubP-1884
90CarLeaA-50
90WinSpiTI-2
91ChaKniLD-148
91ChaKniP-1699
91Cla/Bes-363
91LinDriAA-148
91SydWavF-10
92ChaKniF-2781
92ChaKniS-172
92ClaFS7-64
92SkyAA F-78
94NewHavRF-1560
95NewHavRTI-11
96ColSprSSTI-31

White, Bob
79CliDodT-25

White, Brandon
93VerBeaDC-27
93VerBeaDF-2221

White, Chad
93AubAstC-26
93AubAstF-3458
94OscAstC-24
94OscAstF-1152
95QuaCitRBTI-29

White, Chaney
78LauLonABS-9
91PomBlaBPB-23

White, Charles
52Par-22
54BraJohC-24
55BraGolS-23
55BraJohC-24
55Top-103
55TopDouH-17
55TopTesS-11
89SprCarB-17

White, Charlie
90ArkTraGS-30
90AshTouP-2738
91ArkTraLD-47
91ArkTraP-1301
91LinDriAA-47
92BirBarF-2597
92BirBarS-98

White, Chris
91AubAstC-5
91AubAstP-4275
92AshTouC-14
93FloStaLAF-37
93OscAstC-23
93OscAstF-629
94JacGenF-218
95JacGenTI-12

White, Clinton
89WytCubS-28
90GenCubP-3042
90GenCubS-24

White, Craig
89GreFalDSP-29
90YakBeaTI-24

White, Darell
94SprSulC-24
94SprSulF-2036
95RanCucQT-22
96RanCucQB-29

White, Darren
91AdeGiaF-11
94TopTra-109T
95AusFut-65

White, Darrin
89HelBreSP-25
90BelBreB-14
90BelBreS-23
91BelBreC-12
91BelBreP-2106

White, Dave
79AppFoxT-5
80AppFoxT-21
86BirBarTI-4
86SouLeaAJ-19
87HawIslP-4

White, David
95AusFut-64
95AusFutSFP-SFFP3

White, Deacon (James)
76SSP188WS-18
87BucN28-35
87OldJudN-549
87ScrDC-18
88WG1CarG-27
94BatCliC-26
94BatCliF-3463

White, Derrick
91JamExpC-3
91JamExpP-3556
92ClaFS7-128
92HarSenF-469
92HarSenS-293
92ProFS7-271
92UppDecML-279
93ExcFS7-65
94OttLynF-2907
95TolMudHTI-26
96WesMicWB-30

White, Devon
82DanSunF-21
83PeoSunF-22
85MidAngT-8
86EdmTraP-27
87AngSmo-23
87ClaUpdY-140
87Don-38
87DonOpeD-5
87DonRoo-8
87Fle-646
87FleGlo-646
87FleUpd-123
87FleUpdG-123
87Lea-38
87SevCoi-W13
87SpoRooI-24
87SpoRooP-10
87SpoTeaP-11
87Top-139
87TopTif-139
88AngSmo-13
88ClaRed-178
88Don-8
88Don-283
88DonBasB-227

88DonSupD-8
88Fle-506
88FleExcS-44
88FleGlo-506
88FleMin-12
88Lea-8
88Lea-127
88OPC-192
88PanSti-43
88PanSti-49
88RedFolSB-99
88Sco-212
88ScoGlo-212
88ScoYouSI-12
88Spo-99
88StaLinAn-19
88Top-192
88TopBig-145
88TopCoi-31
88TopGloS-29
88TopRoo-5
88TopSti-183
88TopSti-313
88TopTif-192
88ToyRoo-33
89Bow-54
89BowTif-54
89Don-213
89DonBasB-27
89Fle-489
89FleGlo-489
89OPC-344
89PanSti-297
89Sco-323
89Spo-16
89Top-602
89TopAme2C-31
89TopBig-122
89TopSti-179
89TopTif-602
89TVSpoM-110
89UppDec-110
90AngSmo-18
90Bow-292
90BowTif-292
90ClaBlu-63
90Don-226
90Fle-147
90FleBasA-42
90FleCan-147
90FleLeaL-43
90Hot50PS-49
90Lea-76
90OPC-65
90PanSti-29
90PubSti-381
90RedFolSB-102
90Sco-312
90Sco100S-68
90Spo-210
90Top-65
90TopBig-299
90TopMinL-10
90TopSti-168
90TopTif-65
90UppDec-5
90UppDec-129
90VenSti-483
91BluJayFS-30
91BluJayFS-33
91BluJayS-23
91Bow-30
91Cla3-T94
91Don-150
91Fle-328
91FleUpd-69
91Lea-394
91OPC-704
91OPCPre-126
91PanFreS-185
91Sco-466
91ScoRoo-48T
91StaClu-444
91Stu-139
91Top-704
91TopDesS-704
91TopMic-704
91TopTif-704
91TopTra-125T
91TopTraT-125T
91UltUpd-64
91UppDec-517
91UppDec-783
92Bow-547
92Cla1-T95
92ClaGam-120
92Don-180
92DonMcD-G6
92Fle-346
92Hig5-120
92Lea-114
92MSABenSHD-4
92OPC-260
92PanSti-30
92Pin-17
92Sco-198
92ScoCokD-22
92ScoImpP-67
92ScoProP-2
92StaClu-41
92Stu-259
92SunSee-22
92Top-260
92TopGol-260
92TopGolW-260
92TopMic-260
92TriPla-240
92Ult-155
92UltAwaW-18
92UppDec-352
93BluJayCP1-11
93BluJayCP1-15
93BluJayD-20
93BluJayD4-13
93BluJayDM-16
93BluJayDM-21
93BluJayDM-31
93BluJayFS-34
93Bow-251
93Don-29
93Don-132
93Fla-297
93Fle-342
93HumDumC-24
93Lea-69
93OPC-341
93OPCWorC-16
93PacSpa-659
93PanSti-30
93Pin-138
93Sco-92
93Sel-72
93SP-54
93StaClu-485
93StaCluFDI-485
93StaCluMOP-485
93Stu-60
93Top-387
93TopGol-387
93TopInaM-387
93TopMic-387
93TriPla-89
93Ult-297
93UltAwaW-18
93UppDec-346
93UppDecGold-346
94BluJayP-9
94BluJayUSPC-5C
94BluJayUSPC-13H
94Bow-497
94ColC-292
94ColChoGS-292
94ColChoSS-292
94Don-285
94ExtBas-198
94Fin-125
94FinPre-125P
94FinRef-125
94Fla-351
94Fle-348
94FUnPac-79
94Lea-129
94LeaL-80
94OPC-159
94OPCWorC-2
94Pac-653
94PanSti-142
94Pin-85
94PinArtP-85
94PinMusC-85
94PinRunC-RC22
94Sco-97
94ScoCyc-TC10
94ScoGolR-97
94ScoGolS-53
94Sel-21
94SP-46
94SPDieC-46
94Spo-96
94StaClu-326
94StaCluFDI-326
94StaCluGR-326
94StaCluMOP-326
94StaCluT-174
94StaCluTFDI-174
94Stu-32
94Top-511
94TopGol-511
94TopSpa-511
94TriPla-40
94Ult-146
94UltAwaW-8
94UppDec-137
94UppDecED-137
95Baz-118
95BluJayUSPC-6S
95BluJayUSPC-13D
95Bow-397
95ColCho-143
95ColChoGS-143
95ColChoSS-143
95Don-382
95DonPreP-382
95DonTopotO-179
95Emb-68
95EmbGolI-68
95Emo-98
95Fin-180
95FinRef-180
95Fla-319
95FlaHotG-11
95Fle-107
95Lea-231
95LeaLim-112
95Pac-450
95Pin-186
95PinArtP-186
95PinMusC-186
95PosCan-4
95Sco-365
95ScoGolR-365
95ScoHaloG-HG109
95ScoPlaTS-365
95StaClu-335
95StaCluMOP-335
95StaCluMOP-SS9
95StaCluSS-SS9
95StaCluSTWS-335
95StaCluVR-175
95Stu-93
95Top-427
95TopCyb-225
95Ult-124
95UltAwaW-8
95UltAwaWGM-8
95UltGolM-124
95UppDec-42
95UppDecED-42
95UppDecEDG-42
96Baz-14
96Cir-132
96CirRav-132
96ColCho-351
96ColCho-557
96ColChoGS-351
96ColChoGS-557
96ColChoSS-351
96ColChoSS-557
96Don-464
96DonPreP-464
96EmoXL-192
96Fin-S256
96FinRef-S256
96Fla-270
96Fle-399
96FleTif-399
96FleUpd-U135
96FleUpdTC-U135
96MetUni-171
96MetUniP-171
96Pac-447
96Sco-28
96ScoDugC-A27
96ScoDugCAP-A27
96StaCluVRMO-175
96Top-209
96TopGal-35
96TopGalPPI-35
96TopLas-15
96Ult-482
96UltGolM-482
96UppDec-494U
97Cir-64
97CirRav-64
97ColCho-112
97Don-51
97DonPreP-51
97DonPrePGold-51
97Fin-83
97FinRef-83
97Fle-337
97FleTif-337
97Lea-272
97LeaFraM-272
97LeaFraMDC-272
97MetUni-180
97Pac-310
97PacLigB-310
97PacSil-310
97Pin-40
97PinArtP-40
97PinMusC-40
97Sco-385
97ScoHobR-385
97ScoResC-385
97ScoShoS-385
97ScoShoSAP-385
97StaClu-125
97StaCluMOP-125
97Top-359
97TopChr-122
97TopChrR-122
97TopGal-2
97TopGalPPI-2
97Ult-385
97UltGolME-385
97UltPlaME-385
97UppDec-151
97UppDec-191
97UppDec-358

White, Doc (Guy)
07WhiSoxGWH-12
08RosComP-20
09T206-372
09T206-373
10DomDisP-124
10JuJuDE-41
10RedCroT-83
10RedCroT-165
10SweCapPP-15
11S74Sil-10
11SpoLifM-34
11T205-179
12HasTriFT-22B
12T207-195
80LauFamF-15
95ConTSN-1353

White, Donald William
49PhiBul-58

White, Donnie
92KinMetF-1545
93CapCitBC-23
93CapCitBF-474
94St.LucMC-25
94St.LucMF-1210
95BinMetTI-23
95SigRooOJ-34
95SigRooOJS-34
95SigRooOJP-34
95SigRooOJPS-34
96BinBeeB-29

White, Elder
77FriOneYW-101

White, Eric
92BurIndC-29
92BurIndF-1667
93BurIndC-26
93BurIndF-3309
94ColRedC-22
94ColRedF-452
96KenIndB-26

White, Ernie
41CarW75-29
46SeaSLP-57
76Met63 S-18

White, Foley
09T206-523

White, Frank
74OPC-604
74Top-604
75OPC-569
75Top-569
76OPC-369
76SSP-174
76Top-369
77Top-117
78Roy-25
78SSP270-232
78Top-248
79OPC-227
79Top-439
80OPC-24
80Top-45
81AllGamPI-17
81CokTeaS-82
81Don-340
81Fle-44
81FleStiC-97
81Kel-34
81OPC-330
81RoyPol-9
81Top-330
81TopScr-47
81TopSti-83
82Don-286
82Fle-426
82Fle-629
82FleSta-209
82OPC-156
82OPC-183
82Roy-24
82Top-645
82Top-646
82TopSti-193
83AllGamPI-18
83Don-464
83Fle-127
83FleSta-213
83FleSti-94
83OPC-171
83Roy-31
83RoyPol-9
83Top-525
83TopSti-71
83TopSti-169
84AllGamPI-108
84Don-222
84Fle-363
84FunFooP-44
84Nes792-155
84OPC-155
84Top-155
84TopRubD-4
84TopSti-277
84TopTif-155
85AllGamPI-18
85Don-175
85Fle-217
85Lea-148
85Top-743
85TopRubD-4
85TopSti-274
85TopTif-743
86BasStaB-119
86Don-130
86Fle-24
86FleStiC-127
86GenMilB-2J
86Lea-54
86OPC-215
86RoyKitCD-13
86RoyNatP-20
86Spo-186
86Top-215
86TopSti-23
86TopSti-263
86TopTat-16
86TopTif-215
87Don-255
87DonAll-41
87DonOpeD-204
87Fle-383
87FleAwaW-42
87FleGlo-383
87FleMin-113
87FleStiC-123
87Lea-188
87OPC-101
87Spo-168
87SpoTeaP-13
87Top-256
87Top-692
87TopSti-260
87TopTif-692
88Don-225
88DonBasB-319
88Fle-273
88FleGlo-273
88FleStiC-35
88Nes-29

88OPC-326
88PanSti-105
88RedFolSB-100
88RoySmo-25
88Sco-79
88ScoGlo-79
88Spo-149
88StaLinRo-19
88Top-595
88TopBig-75
88TopSti-255
88TopStiB-39
88TopTif-595
89Bow-122
89BowTif-122
89Don-85
89DonBasB-175
89Fle-297
89FleGlo-297
89OPC-25
89PanSti-356
89RoyTasD-7
89Sco-390
89Top-25
89TopBasT-142
89TopBig-200
89TopSti-262
89TopTif-25
89UppDec-350
90Bow-371
90BowTif-371
90Don-262
90Fle-122
90FleCan-122
90Lea-204
90MLBBasB-108
90OPC-479
90PanSti-83
90PubSti-360
90Sco-372
90Top-479
90TopBig-105
90TopTif-479
90UppDec-382
90VenSti-484
91Fle-574
91OPC-352
91SimandSMLBL-45
91Top-352
91TopDesS-352
91TopMic-352
91TopTif-352
91UppDec-568
93RoySta2-14
94TedWil-39
94TedWil-142

White, Fred
88KenTwiP-1382
89VisOakCLC-102
89VisOakP-1446
90VisOakCLC-63
90VisOakP-2155
91Cla/Bes-278
91VisOakC-11
91VisOakP-1742
92OrlSunRS-523
93DayCubC-23
93DayCubF-860

White, G. Harris
04FanCraAL-49
09SpoNewSM-67

White, Gabe
90HigSchPLS-7
91Cla/Bes-61
91SumFlyC-12
91SumFlyP-2335
92Bow-279
92MidLeaATI-49
92ProFS7-268
92RocExpC-11
92RocExpF-2116
92UppDecML-202
93Bow-396
93ClaFS7-34
93ClaGolF-38
93ExcFS7-66
93HarSenF-270
94ActPac-34
94Bow-312
94Cla-86
94ColC-20
94ColChoGS-20
94ColChoSS-20
94ExcFS7-231
94Fla-406
94SigRoo-47
94SigRooHP-S12
94SigRooS-47
94Top-784
94TopGol-784
94TopSpa-784
94TopTra-31T
94Ult-527
94UppDec-30
94UppDecED-30
94UppDecML-55
94UppDecML-158
95Pin-419
95PinArtP-419
95PinMusC-419
95Sel-210
95SelArtP-210
95Spo-160
95SpoArtP-160
95Top-287
95Zen-114
96IndIndB-27
96Sco-480
96StaClu-173
96StaCluMOP-173

White, Gary
87ClePhiP-17
87UtiBluSP-12
88SpaPhiP-1044
91ParPatF-8
96HigDesMB-29

White, Harold
51Bow-320

White, Harry
79NewCoPT-13

White, Jarvis
93BluOriF-4140

White, Jason
92SouOreAC-11
92SouOreAF-3430
93MadMusC-26
93MadMusF-1832
94ModA'sC-25
94ModA'sF-3073
95ModA'sTI-31

White, Jerry
75IntLeaAT-1
75IntLeaAT-6
76ExpRed-36
76OPC-594
76SSP-340
76Top-594
77ExpPos-38
77OPC-81
77Top-557
79ExpPos-31
79Top-494
80ExpPos-34
80OPC-369
80Top-724
81Don-333
81Fle-161
81OPC-42
81OPCPos-11
81Top-42
82Don-621
82ExpHygM-24
82ExpPos-41
82Fle-211
82OPC-386
82OPCPos-24
82Top-386
83Don-602
83ExpPos-27
83ExpStu-19
83Fle-300
83OPC-214
83Top-214
86CarTeal-42
89PacSenL-185
89T/MSenL-113
89TopSenL-8
90EliSenL-32
91PacSenL-3
91UppDecS-23
94ForMyeMC-28
96FtMyeMB-2

White, Jimmy
90AshTouC-25
91AshTouP-583
92BurAstC-4
92BurAstF-562
93ClaFS7-294
93OscAstC-24
93OscAstF-641
94OscAstC-1
94OscAstF-1153

White, Jo-Jo (Joyner C.)
34DiaMatCSB-195
34DiaStaR-45
35GolMedFR-12
35TigFreP-21
35WheBB1-25
36GouWidPPR-A113
36R31PasP-30
36WorWidGV-74
46SunBre-20
47CenFlo-31
47SigOil-88
49BowPCL-14
60Top-460
76TigOldTS-23
79DiaGre-388
81TigDetN-27
81TigSecNP-30
92ConTSN-612

White, Joe
87AriWilP-18

White, John
82AmaGolST-13

White, John F.
09T206-473
12ImpTobC-4

White, Johnny
91JamExpC-1
91JamExpP-3560

White, K.G.
89BakDodCLC-199

White, Kelly
94JamJamF-3983

White, Kyle
92SpoIndC-4
92SpoIndF-1304
93SpoIndC-23
93SpoIndF-3592
94SprSulC-25
94SprSulF-2037

White, Larry
80WatIndT-4
81ChaLooT-21
82AlbDukT-10
83AlbDukT-8
83DodPol-47
84AlbDukC-158
85AlbDukC-168
90DodTar-852

White, Logan
84ButCopKT-27

White, Mac
94JamJamC-25

White, Marvin
89ButCopKSP-29
90GasRanB-26
90GasRanP-2538
90GasRanS-27
91ChaRanC-28
91ChaRanP-1331
92ChaRanC-27
92ChaRanF-2242
93ChaRanC-29
93ChaRanF-1957
94ChaRanF-2514

White, Maximo
93PriRedC-30
93PriRedF-4190

White, Mike
81LynSaiT-19
86BakDodP-29
87BakDodP-12
88FloStaLAS-25
88VerBeaDS-24
89SanAntMB-1
90SanAntMGS-29
91LinDriAA-546
91SanAntMLD-546
91SanAntMP-2990
92BinMetF-531
92BinMetS-72
92SkyAA F-34

White, Mike (Joyner M.)
64Top-492
65AstBigLBPP-11
65OPC-31
65Top-31
78TCM60I-155

White, Myron
77LodDodT-24
80AlbDukT-12
90DodTar-853

White, Oliver Kirby
09ColChiE-305
10PirTipTD-23
11S74Sil-115
11SpoLifCW-365
11T205-180
12ColRedB-305
12ColTinT-305

White, Phil
91AdeGiaF-13

White, Randy
83GreHorT-13
89IdaFalBP-2034

White, Reggie
91UppDecS-2

White, Rhett
89BirBarB-30

White, Rich
80UtiBluJT-2

White, Rick
91AugPirC-12
91AugPirP-806
92SalBucC-24
92SalBucF-65
93CarMudF-2055
93ClaFS7-35
94Bow-190
94ExtBas-354
94ExtBasRS-19
94Fin-383
94FinRef-383
94Fla-221
94FlaWavotF-A10
94FleUpd-177
94LeaLimR-13
94Pin-533
94PinArtP-533
94PinMusC-533
94PirQui-27
94SP-145
94SPDieC-145
94StaClu-589
94StaCluFDI-589
94StaCluGR-589
94StaCluMOP-589
94TopTra-121T
94Ult-561
95ColCho-383
95ColChoGS-383
95ColChoSS-383
95Don-35
95DonPreP-35
95Fle-492
95Lea-152
95Pac-354
95PirFil-29
95Sco-217
95ScoGolR-217
95ScoPlaTS-217
95StaClu-399
95StaCluMOP-399
95StaCluSTWS-399
95Ult-220
95UltGolM-220

White, Rondell
90ClaDraP-24
90ClaDraP-NNO
90ClaYel-T80
91Bow-450
91Cla/Bes-360
91Sco-390
91SumFlyC-25
91SumFlyP-2350
91UppDecFE-10F
92Bow-436
92ClaFS7-305
92ProFS7-266
92UppDec-51
92UppDec-61
92UppDecML-33
92UppDecML-65
92UppDecML-276
92UppDecMLTPHF-TP8
92WesPalBEC-1
92WesPalBEF-2102
93Bow-72
93ClaFisN-18
93ClaFS7-36
93ClaGolF-48
93ExcAllF-3
93ExcFS7-67
93FlaWavotF-18
93HarSenF-281
93SP-289
93Ult-421
93UppDec-510
93UppDecGold-510
94ActPac-25
94ActPac-64
94ActPac2G-10G
94Bow-360
94Bow-668
94BowBes-B33
94BowBes-X97
94BowBesR-B33
94BowBesR-X97
94Cla-70
94Cla-AU4
94ClaCreotC-C13
94ColC-293
94ColChoGS-293
94ColChoSS-293
94Don-320
94ExtBas-314
94ExtBasRS-20
94Fin-424
94FinJum-424
94FinRef-424
94Fle-556
94FUnPac-3
94FUnPac-205
94LeaGolR-2
94LeaLimR-54
94OPC-60
94OttLynF-2909
94Pac-394
94Pin-246
94PinArtP-246
94PinMusC-246
94PinNewG-NG19
94PinRooTP-6
94Sco-638
94ScoBoyoS-36
94ScoGolR-638
94ScoRoo-RT87
94ScoRooGR-RT87
94ScoRooSR-SU14
94Sel-201
94SelRooS-RS6
94SigRooDP-98
94SigRooDPS-98
94SP-88
94SPDieC-88
94Spo-174
94SpoRooRS-TR15
94SpoSha-SH6
94StaClu-435
94StaCluFDI-435
94StaCluGR-435
94StaCluMOP-435
94Top-784
94TopGol-784
94TopSpa-784
94TriPla-290
94Ult-233
94UppDec-237
94UppDecED-237
95Baz-128
95Bow-437
95BowBes-R52
95BowBesR-R52
95ColCho-235
95ColChoGS-235
95ColChoSE-103
95ColChoSEGS-103
95ColChoSESS-103
95ColChoSS-235
95Don-343
95DonPreP-343
95DonTopotO-288
95Emo-156
95Fin-5
95FinRef-5
95Fla-168
95Fle-364
95FleRooS-20
95Lea-48
95LeaLim-80
95LeaLim-128
95Pac-275
95Pin-339
95PinArtP-339
95PinMusC-339
95PinUps-US15
95Sco-147
95ScoGolR-147

95ScoHaloG-HG108
95ScoPlaTS-147
95Sel-11
95SelArtP-11
95SP-76
95SPCha-63
95SPCha-67
95SPChaDC-63
95SPChaDC-67
95Spo-129
95SpoArtP-129
95SPSil-76
95SPSpeF-44
95StaClu-349
95StaCluMOP-349
95StaCluSTWS-349
95StaCluVR-199
95Stu-75
95Top-196
95TopCyb-112
95Ult-410
95UltGolM-410
95UltSecYS-15
95UltSecYSGM-15
95UppDec-83
95UppDecED-83
95UppDecEDG-83
95UppDecSE-140
95UppDecSEG-140
95Zen-93
96Baz-3
96Bow-65
96Cir-153
96CirRav-153
96ColCho-215
96ColChoGS-215
96ColChoSS-215
96ColChoYMtP-44
96ColChoYMtP-44A
96ColChoYMtPGS-44
96ColChoYMtPGS-44A
96Don-408
96DonPreP-408
96EmoRarB-10
96EmoXL-227
96ExpDis-22
96ExpDis-23
96Fin-S52
96FinRef-S52
96Fla-314
96Fle-471
96FleTeaL-22
96FleTif-471
96FleTomL-10
96Lea-88
96LeaLim-12
96LeaLimG-12
96LeaPre-20
96LeaPreP-20
96LeaPrePB-88
96LeaPrePG-88
96LeaPrePS-88
96LeaPreSG-28
96LeaPreSte-28
96LeaSig-14
96LeaSigA-243
96LeaSigAG-244
96LeaSigAS-244
96LeaSigPPG-14
96LeaSigPPP-14
96MetUni-196
96MetUniP-196
96MetUniPP-10
96Pac-125
96PanSti-19
96Pin-234
96PinAfi-106
96PinAfiAP-106
96PinArtP-134
96PinFoil-234
96PinSta-134
96ProSta-50
96Sco-50
96ScoDugC-A43
96ScoDugCAP-A43
96Sel-25
96SelArtP-25
96SelCer-29
96SelCerAP-29
96SelCerCB-29
96SelCerCR-29
96SelCerIP-18
96SelCerMB-29
96SelCerMG-29
96SelCerMR-29
96SelTeaN-24
96SP-120
96Spo-64
96SpoArtP-64
96SPSpeFX-14
96SPSpeFXDC-14
96SPx-39
96SPxGol-39
96StaClu-12
96StaCluEPB-12
96StaCluEPG-12
96StaCluEPS-12
96StaCluMOP-12
96StaCluVRMO-199
96Stu-122
96StuPrePB-122
96StuPrePG-122
96StuPrePS-122
96Sum-15
96SumAbo&B-15
96SumArtP-15
96SumFoi-15
96Top-382
96TopChr-154
96TopChrR-154
96TopGal-116
96TopGalPPI-116
96TopLas-80
96Ult-238
96UltFreF-10
96UltFreFGM-10
96UltGolM-238
96UltRisS-10
96UltRisSGM-10
96UppDec-135
96Zen-4
96ZenArtP-4
96ZenMoz-17
97Bow-289
97BowBes-52
97BowBesAR-52
97BowBesR-52
97BowChr-99
97BowChrI-99
97BowChrIR-99
97BowChrR-99
97BowInt-289
97Cir-380
97CirRav-380
97ColCho-165
97ColChoTBS-31
97ColChoTBSWH-31
97Don-29
97DonEli-87
97DonEliGS-87
97DonLim-1
97DonLim-164
97DonLimFotG-12
97DonLimLE-1
97DonLimLE-164
97DonPre-58
97DonPreCttC-58
97DonPreP-29
97DonPrePGold-29
97Fin-296
97FinEmb-296
97FinEmbR-296
97FinRef-296
97FlaSho-A67
97FlaSho-B67
97FlaSho-C67
97FlaShoLC-67
97FlaShoLC-B67
97FlaShoLC-C67
97FlaShoLCM-A67
97FlaShoLCM-B67
97FlaShoLCM-C67
97Fle-389
97FleTif-389
97Lea-242
97LeaFraM-242
97LeaFraMDC-242
97LeaWarT-14
97MetUni-160
97NewPin-37
97NewPinAP-37
97NewPinMC-37
97NewPinPP-37
97Pac-356
97PacLigB-356
97PacSil-356
97Pin-56
97PinArtP-56
97PinCer-98
97PinCerMBlu-98
97PinCerMG-98
97PinCerMR-98
97PinCerR-98
97PinIns-104
97PinInsCE-104
97PinInsDE-104
97PinMusC-56
97PinTotCPB-98
97PinTotCPG-98
97PinTotCPR-98
97PinX-P-101
97PinX-PMoS-101
97PinX-PSfF-57
97PinX-PSfFU-57
97ProMag-26
97ProMagML-26
97Sco-413
97ScoHobR-413
97ScoResC-413
97ScoShoS-413
97ScoShoSAP-413
97Sel-89
97SelArtP-89
97SelRegG-89
97SP-115
97StaClu-224
97StaCluC-CO9
97StaCluMat-224
97StaCluMOP-224
97Stu-121
97StuHarH-18
97StuPrePG-121
97StuPrePS-121
97Top-331
97TopChr-112
97TopChrR-112
97TopGal-110
97TopGalPPI-110
97Ult-235
97UltGolME-235
97UltPlaME-235
97UppDec-425
97UppDecRSF-RS13

White, Roy Hilton
66TopVen-234
67CokCapYM-V18
67DexPre-220
68Top-546
69MilBra-289
69MLBOffS-81
69OPC-25
69Top-25
69TopSta-210
69TopSup-26
69TopTeaP-19
69TraSta-26
70DayDaiNM-90
70MLBOffS-252
70OPC-373
70Top-373
70TopPos-14
70YanCliDP-2
71Kel-43
71MilDud-32
71MLBOffS-503
71OPC-395
71Top-395
71TopCoi-34
71TopGreM-45
71TopSup-26
71TopTat-109
71YanArcO-12
71YanCliDP-16
72MilBra-360
72OPC-340
72Top-340
72TopCloT-33
73NewYorN-16
73OPC-25
73SyrChiTI-29
73Top-25
73Yan-6
74OPC-135
74SyrChiTI-29
74Top-135
74TopSta-220
75Kel-1
75OPC-375
75SyrChiTI-23
75Top-375
75YanSSP-6
76OPC-225
76SSP-435
76Top-225
77BurCheD-179
77OPC-182
77Top-485
77YanBurK-19
78OPC-48
78SSP270-8
78Top-16
78YanBurK-19
78YanSSPD-8
79OPC-75
79Top-159
79YanBurK-19
79YanPicA-34
80OPC-341
80Top-648
81TCM60I-453
83YanASFY-50
86YanTCM-29
90SweBasG-42
91SweBasG-97
92ActPacA-34
92YanWIZ6-136
92YanWIZ7-164
92YanWIZA-85

White, Sammy
47PM1StaP1-216
52Top-345
53BowC-41
53RedSoxFNSMS-4
53RedSoxTI-28
53Top-139
54Bow-34
54RedHeaF-31
54RedMan-AL14
54Wil-19
55Bow-47
56Top-168
57Top-163
58Hir-53
58RedSoxJP-11
58Top-414
59RedSoxJP-11
59Top-486
60Top-203
62Top-494
79DiaGre-248
79TCM50-95
83TopRep5-345
86RedSoxGT-1
91TopArc1-139

White, Sherman
51BerRos-B11

White, Sol
78LauLonABS-22

White, Steve
93CedRapKC-23
93CedRapKF-1739

White, Tom
77ReaPhiT-23

White, Trey
95PorCitRTI-27

White, Walter
94ElmPioF-3485
95KanCouCTI-21
96KanCouCTI-28
96MidLeaAB-35
94ElmPioC-23

White, William D.
87OldJudN-550

Whitecaps, Brewster
88CapCodPB-21

Whited, Ed
86AubAstP-26
87AshTouP-24
88GreBraB-1
88SouLeaAJ-16
89BraDub-29
89RicBraBC-27
89RicBraC-21
89RicBraP-837
89RicBraTI-23
90CMC-293
90OPC-111
90ProAAAF-413
90RicBraBC-16
90RicBraC-17
90RicBraP-268
90RicBraTI-29
90Sco-644
90Sco100RS-78
90Top-111
90TopDeb89-140
90TopTif-111
90UppDec-447

Whitehead, Chris
88ElmPioC-21
90LynRedSTI-10

Whitehead, James
89WinHavRSS-27

Whitehead, John
36GouWidPPR-A115
36GouWidPPR-C25
92ConTSN-568

Whitehead, Steve
76QuaCitAT-39
89JamExpP-2140
90RocExpLC-27
90RocExpP-2687
91RocExpC-28
91RocExpP-2048
92MidLeaATI-50
92RocExpC-17
92RocExpF-2117

Whitehead, Whitey (Burgess)
33ButCanV-53
34DiaStaR-51
36GouWidPPR-A114
36WorWidGV-59
39PlaBal-23
40PlaBal-92
41DouPlaR-27
41DouPlaR-89
74Car193T-26
79DiaGre-38

Whitehill, Earl
28Exh-47
29PorandAR-97
33ButCanV-54
33Gou-124
33TatOrbSDR-165
34ButPreR-64
35ExhFou-16
35GouPuzR-8H
35GouPuzR-9H
36ExhFou-16
36GouWidPPR-B25
36R31PasP-27
36WorWidGV-60
39CubTeal-24
81TigDetN-31
83ConMar-21
87ConSer2-60
88ConAmeA-24
91ConTSN-127

Whitehouse, Len
77AshTouT-26
78AshTouT-27
79TulDriT-3
83TopTra-126T
83TwiTeal-15
84Don-558
84Fle-578
84Nes792-648
84Top-648
84TopTif-648
85Don-513
85TolMudHT-12
85Top-406
85TopTif-406
85TwiTeal-17
93RanKee-378

Whitehurst, Todd
91BurIndP-3312
94PitMetC-23
94PitMetF-3531
95StLucMTI-34

Whitehurst, Wally
86MadMusP-23
86MadMusP-27
87HunStaTI-24
88TidTidCa-29
88TidTidCM-11
88TidTidP-1589
89Bow-373
89BowTif-373
89FleUpd-103
89MetColP-58
89TidTidC-6
89TidTidP-1958
89UppDec-737
90MetColP-53
90MetKah-47
90OPC-719
90Sco-599
90Top-719

90TopDeb89-141
90TopTif-719
90TopTVM-19
90UppDec-564
91Bow-470
91Don-511
91Fle-166
91Lea-333
91MetColP-51
91MetKah-47
91MetWIZ-429
91OPC-557
91Sco-529
91Sco100RS-91
91StaClu-458
91Top-557
91TopDesS-557
91TopMic-557
91TopTif-557
91ToyRoo-32
91UppDec-221
92Don-134
92Fle-519
92MetColP-20
92MetKah-47
92OPC-419
92Sco-299
92StaClu-476
92Top-419
92TopGol-419
92TopGolW-419
92TopMic-419
92UppDec-414
93Don-602
93FleFinE-147
93PadMot-24
93Top-271
93TopGol-271
93TopInaM-271
93TopMic-271
94ColC-381
94ColChoGS-381
94ColChoSS-381
94ExtBas-380
94Fla-237
94Fle-678
94Lea-216
94Pac-537
94PadMot-6
94Pin-109
94PinArtP-109
94PinMusC-109
94StaClu-652
94StaCluFDI-652
94StaCluGR-652
94StaCluMOP-652
94Top-486
94TopGol-486
94TopSpa-486
94Ult-284
94UppDec-129
94UppDecED-129
86HumStaDS-23

Whiteman, Charles
19W514-119

Whiteman, Greg
94JamJamC-26
94JamJamF-3965
94SigRooDP-67
94SigRooDPS-67
95FayGenTI-27
96Bow-162
96LakTigB-30

Whiteman, Tony
94BriTigC-27
94BriTigF-3504
95FayGenTI-28

Whiten, Mark
87MyrBeaBJP-1458
88DunBluJS-21
89KnoBluJB-26
89KnoBluJS-21
90CMC-350
90FleUpd-130
90Lea-396
90ProAAAF-367
90SyrChiC-24
90SyrChiMB-29
90SyrChiP-587
90TriAllGP-AAA2
91BluJayFS-31
91Bow-13
91ClaGam-65
91Don-607
91DonRoo-32
91Fle-189
91FleUpd-21
91Lea-234
91MajLeaCP-28
91OPC-588
91OPCPre-127
91Sco-358
91Sco100RS-24
91ScoAllF-6
91StaClu-452
91Stu-50
91Top-588
91TopDeb90-167
91TopDesS-588
91TopMic-588
91TopTif-588
91TopTra-126T
91TopTraT-126T
91Ult-371
91UltUpd-21
91UppDec-561
91UppDecFE-75F
92Bow-57
92ClaGam-84
92Don-325
92Fle-126
92IndFanC-29
92Lea-334
92LeaGolP-17
92LeaPre-17
92OPC-671
92OPCPre-178
92PanSti-49
92Pin-355
92Sco-587
92ScoImpP-15
92StaClu-51
92Stu-170
92Top-671
92TopGol-671
92TopGolW-671
92TopKid-74
92TopMic-671
92TriPla-95
92Ult-55
92UppDec-524
93Don-97
93Fla-130
93Fle-223
93FleFinE-133
93Lea-449
93OPC-378
93PacSpa-103
93PanSti-54
93Pin-420
93Sco-106
93Sel-146
93SelRoo-6T
93SP-81
93StaClu-352
93StaCluFDI-352
93StaCluMO-27
93StaCluMOP-352
93Stu-119
93Top-277
93TopGol-277
93TopInaM-277
93TopMic-277
93TopTra-20T
93TriPla-23
93Ult-193
93Ult-468
93UppDec-227
93UppDec-654
93UppDecGold-227
93UppDecGold-654
94Bow-40
94CarPol-25
94ColC-294
94ColChoGS-294
94ColChoSS-294
94Don-311
94ExtBas-365
94Fin-116
94FinRef-116
94Fla-229
94Fle-649
94FleGolM-1
94FUnPac-118
94Lea-29
94LeaL-148
94OPC-120
94Pac-607
94PanSti-250
94Pin-153
94PinArtP-153
94PinMusC-153
94PinPowS-PS20
94PinTri-TR11
94Pos-19
94ProMag-112
94Sco-315
94Sco-440
94ScoGolR-315
94ScoGolR-440
94Sel-164
94SP-67
94SPDieC-67
94Spo-142
94StaClu-37
94StaCluFDI-37
94StaCluGR-37
94StaCluMOP-37
94StaCluT-305
94StaCluTFDI-305
94Stu-56
94Top-54
94TopGol-54
94TopSpa-54
94TriPla-69
94Ult-273
94UppDec-150
94UppDecED-150
95Bow-306
95ColCho-58
95ColCho-195
95ColCho-576T
95ColChoGS-58
95ColChoGS-195
95ColChoSE-79
95ColChoSEGS-79
95ColChoSESS-79
95ColChoSS-58
95ColChoSS-195
95Don-79
95DonPreP-79
95Emb-88
95EmbGolI-88
95Fin-147
95Fin-265
95FinRef-147
95FinRef-265
95Fla-197
95Fla-232
95Fle-512
95FleUpd-16
95Lea-384
95Pac-418
95Pin-3
95PinArtP-3
95PinMusC-3
95Sco-376
95ScoGolR-376
95ScoHaloG-HG106
95ScoPlaTS-376
95StaClu-462
95StaClu-574
95StaCluMOP-462
95StaCluMOP-574
95StaCluMOP-SS10
95StaCluSS-SS10
95StaCluSTWS-462
95StaCluSTWS-574
95StaCluVR-251
95Stu-107
95Top-409
95TopCyb-209
95TopTra-102T
95UC3-83
95UC3ArtP-83
95Ult-229
95UltGolM-229
95UppDec-62
95UppDec-478T
95UppDecED-62
95UppDecEDG-62
95UppDecSE-214
95UppDecSEG-214
96ColCho-673
96ColChoGS-673
96ColChoSS-673
96Don-123
96DonPreP-123
96EmoXL-250
96Fla-341
96Fle-512
96FleTif-512
96Pac-162
96PhiTeal-34
96Pin-128
96Sco-387
96StaCluVRMO-251
96Ult-529
96UltGolM-529
96UppDec-426
97Don-352
97DonPreP-352
97DonPrePGold-352
97Fle-639
97FleTif-639
97Lea-301
97LeaFraM-301
97LeaFraMDC-301
97Pin-19
97PinArtP-19
97PinMusC-19
97Sco-216
97Sco-354
97ScoHobR-354
97ScoMar-11
97ScoMarPl-11
97ScoMarPr-11
97ScoPreS-216
97ScoResC-354
97ScoShoS-216
97ScoShoS-354
97ScoShoSAP-216
97ScoShoSAP-354
97Top-322
97Ult-352
97UltGolME-352
97UltPlaME-352
97UppDec-317

Whiteside, Matt
90ButCopKSP-29
91GasRanC-12
91GasRanP-2689
92ProFS7-157
92SkyAA F-277
92TulDriF-2697
92TulDriS-623
93Bow-283
93FleFinE-285
93Lea-508
93PacSpa-649
93Pin-590
93RanKee-435
93SelRoo-41T
93StaClu-474
93StaCluFDI-474
93StaCluMOP-474
93StaCluR-3
93Top-468
93TopGol-468
93TopInaM-468
93TopMic-468
93Ult-638
93UppDec-390
93UppDecGold-390
94Don-606
94Fle-323
94Pac-631
94Sco-304
94ScoGolR-304
94StaClu-502
94StaCluFDI-502
94StaCluGR-502
94StaCluMOP-502
94StaCluT-266
94StaCluTFDI-266
94Top-629
94TopGol-629
94TopSpa-629
94Ult-433
95Don-222
95DonPreP-222
95Fla-93
95Fle-298
95RanCra-36
95Top-254
95Ult-115
95UltGolM-115
96ColCho-736
96ColChoGS-736
96ColChoSS-736
96Fle-266
96FleRan-18
96FleTif-266
96LeaSigEA-212
96OklCit8B-24

Whiteside, Sean
92NiaFalRC-21
92NiaFalRF-3324
93FayGenC-24
93FayGenF-130
94LakTigC-25
94LakTigF-3037
95Bow-167
95FleUpd-24
95JacSunTI-27
95SigRoo-48
95SigRooSig-48
96JacSunB-29

Whitfield, Cat
80ChaO'sP-23
80ChaO'sW-24

Whitfield, Fred
62KahAtl-24
63Top-211
64Kah-31
64Top-367
64TopVen-367
65OPC-283
65Top-283
66Kah-32
66OPC-88
66Top-88
66TopVen-88
67CokCapI-13
67DexPre-221
67Kah-40A
67Kah-40B
67Top-275
67TopVen-249
68OPC-133
68Top-133
68TopVen-133
69MilBra-290
69Top-518

Whitfield, Ken
85KinBluJT-22
86KinEagP-25
89KinIndS-24
90RenSilSCLC-262
91CanIndLD-98
91CanIndP-994
91LinDriAA-98

Whitfield, Terry
75OPC-622
75SyrChiTI-24
75Top-622
76OPC-590
76SSP-443
76Top-590
76VenLeaS-34
78Hos-136
78Top-236
79GiaPol-45
79Hos-10
79OPC-309
79Top-589
80GiaPol-45
80OPC-361
80Top-713
81Don-435
81Fle-437
81Top-167
81TopScr-87
81TopSti-233
84DodPol-45
84FleUpd-125
85DodCokP-33
85Don-540
85Fle-389
85Top-31
85TopTif-31
86DodCokP-33
86DodPol-45
86Don-337
86Fle-147
86Top-318
86TopTif-318
90DodTar-854
92YanWIZ7-165

Whitford, Eric
92ClaFS7-238
92StoPorC-17
92StoPorF-44
93StoPorC-26

Whitford, Larry
86BelBreP-26

Whiting, Don
78HolMilT-23
79HolMilT-15
82ElPasDT-9

83BelBreF-14
Whiting, John
75BurBeeT-29
Whiting, Mike
86ElmPioRSP-28
Whitley, Kyle
96ButCopKB-30
Whitley, Matt
96AshTouB-30
Whitlock, Brian
96WatIndTI-33
Whitlock, Mike
88BelBreGS-22
89St.LucMS-24
96HagSunB-23
Whitman, Dick
49EurSta-51
51Bow-221
76TayBow4-74
84TCMPla1-28
90DodTar-855
Whitman, Jim
91EriSaiC-13
91EriSaiP-4083
Whitman, Ryan
92EriSaiC-9
92EriSaiF-1625
93Top-558
93TopGol-558
93TopInaM-558
93TopMic-558
94WicWraF-191
95RanCucQT-14
Whitmayer, Kurt
78OrlTwiT-23
Whitmer, Dan
79SalLakCGT-19B
80SalLakCGT-2
81SyrChiTI-23
82KnoBluJT-11
82SyrChiT-28
82SyrChiTI-24
83KnoBluJT-9
93TigGat-28
Whitmer, Joe
83ChaLooT-4
84ChaLooT-16
85CalCanC-99
Whitmore, Darrell
90BurIndP-3025
91WatIndP-3385
92ClaFS7-156
92KinIndC-22
92KinIndF-2490
93Bow-206
93ClaFS7-268
93EdmTraF-1150
93FlaWavotF-19
93FlaWavotF-20
93FleFinE-74
93MarPub-26
93SelRoo-77T
93SP-144
93StaClu-516
93StaCluFDI-516
93StaCluMarl-24
93StaCluMOP-516
93Top-697
93TopGol-697
93TopInaM-697
93TopMic-697
94Bow-123
94ColC-295
94ColChoGS-295
94ColChoSS-295
94Don-643
94EdmTraF-2888
94Fin-147
94FinRef-147
94Fle-481
94Pac-254
94Pin-399
94PinArtP-399
94PinMusC-399
94PinNewG-NG25
94Sco-556
94ScoBoyoS-57
94ScoGolR-556
94StaCluT-77
94StaCluTFDI-77
94Top-161
94TopGol-161
94TopSpa-161
94Ult-201
94UppDec-233
94UppDecED-233
95Don-22
95DonPreP-22
95Lea-95
95Pac-179
95Pin-267
95PinArtP-267
95PinMusC-267
95Top-225
95TopCyb-127
95UppDec-351
95UppDecED-351
95UppDecEDG-351
96ChaKniB-29
96Don-62
96DonPreP-62
Whitmyer, Steve
86WatIndP-25
Whitney, Arthur W.
31Exh-11
33TatOrb-60
87BucN28-92
87OldJudN-552
89SFHaCN-21
Whitney, G.
87OldJudN-553
Whitney, James
87BucN28-117
87OldJudN-551
88AugBecN-30
88WG1CarG-71
Whitney, Jeff
87ModA'sC-21
90RenSilSCLC-278
Whitney, Pinky (Arthur C.)
29ExhFou-12
29PorandAR-98
32OrbPinUP-60
33DouDisP-42
33RitCE-12C
34DiaMatCSB-196
36ExhFou-1
36NatChiFPR-81
37ExhFou-6
38ExhFou-6
38WheBB10-12
39PlaBal-98
79DiaGre-214
83PhiPosGPaM-10
91ConTSN-288
Whitson, Anthony
87WytCubP-1
89ChaWheB-14
Whitson, Ed
77ColCliT-22
78ColCliT-27
79Top-189
80GiaPol-32
80Top-561
81Don-74
81Fle-444
81OPC-336
81Top-336
81TopSti-240
82Don-251
82Fle-402
82Ind-36
82IndTeal-34
82IndWhe-20
82Top-656
82TopTra-127T
83Don-137
83Don-389
83Fle-423
83Top-429
83TopTra-127T
84Don-528
84Fle-316
84GiaMot-26
84Nes792-277
84PadMot-15
84PadSmo-27
84Top-277
84TopTif-277
85Don-446
85Fle-47
85FleUpd-129
85OPC-98
85Top-762
85TopMin-762
85TopSti-152
85TopTif-762
85TopTifT-130T
85TopTra-130T
86Don-225
86Fle-120
86OPC-15
86Top-15
86TopSti-301
86TopTif-15
86YanTCM-17
87Don-360
87Fle-434
87FleGlo-434
87PadBohHB-31
87Top-155
87TopTif-155
88Don-81
88DonBasB-322
88Fle-599
88FleGlo-599
88OPC-330
88PadCok-31
88PadSmo-30
88PanSti-401
88RedFolSB-101
88Sco-167
88ScoGlo-167
88StaLinPa-13
88Top-330
88TopBig-186
88TopSti-107
88TopTif-330
89Bow-449
89BowTif-449
89Don-229
89DonBasB-210
89Fle-321
89FleGlo-321
89OPC-21
89PadCok-20
89PadMag-22
89Sco-329
89Top-516
89TopBig-81
89TopTif-516
89UppDec-453
90Bow-204
90BowTif-204
90Don-26
90Don-205
90DonBesN-98
90DonSupD-26
90Fle-171
90FleCan-171
90Lea-246
90OPC-618
90PadCok-20
90PadMag-12
90PanSti-347
90PubSti-62
90Sco-373
90Sco100S-69
90Spo-212
90Top-618
90TopBig-152
90TopMinL-82
90TopSti-107
90TopTif-618
90UppDec-308
90VenSti-485
91Bow-651
91Don-186
91Fle-547
91Lea-337
91OPC-481
91PadMag-14
91PadSmo-39
91PanCanT1-67
91PanFreS-98
91PanSti-91
91Sco-789
91StaClu-246
91Stu-250
91Top-481
91TopDesS-481
91TopMic-481
91TopTif-481
91Ult-313
91UppDec-312
92Don-380
92Fle-624
92OPC-228
92PadCarJ-24
92Pin-104
92Sco-564
92StaClu-172
92Top-228
92TopGol-228
92TopGolW-228
92TopMic-228
92UppDec-103
92YanWIZ8-202
Whitson, Eric
95OdgRapTI-28
96HudValRB-13
Whitson, Tony
88WytCubP-1984
89ChaWheP-1763
Whitt, Ernie
78SyrChiT-20
78Top-708
79SyrChiT-3
79SyrChiTI-12
79Top-714
80VenLeaS-62
81Don-390
81Fle-411
81OPC-282
81OPCPos-20
81Top-407
82Don-381
82Fle-626
82OPC-19
82OPCPos-3
82Top-19
82TopSti-247
83Don-304
83Fle-443
83OPC-302
83Top-302
83TopSti-131
84BluJayFS-32
84Don-437
84Fle-169
84Nes792-506
84OPC-106
84Top-506
84TopSti-373
84TopTif-506
85AllGamPI-44
85BluJayFS-32
85BluJayPLP-5
85Don-268
85Fle-119
85Lea-181
85OPC-128
85Top-128
85TopMin-128
85TopTif-128
86BasStaB-120
86BluJayAF-24
86BluJayFS-32
86Don-559
86DonAll-48
86Fle-73
86GenMilB-3J
86Lea-217
86OPC-136
86Top-673
86TopTif-673
87BluJayFS-34
87Don-148
87DonHig-39
87DonOpeD-33
87Fle-240
87FleGlo-240
87GenMilB-1J
87HosSti-2
87Lea-69
87OPC-221
87StuPan-28
87SyrChi1A-5
87Top-698
87TopTif-698
88BluJayFS-32
88Don-394
88Fle-126
88FleGlo-126
88Lea-250
88MSAHosD-16
88OPC-79
88PanSti-216
88Sco-168
88ScoGlo-168
88StaLinBJ-20
88Top-79
88TopBig-239
88TopSti-187
88TopTif-79
89BluJayFS-31
89Bow-248
89BowTif-248
89Don-591
89DonBasB-255
89Fle-248
89FleGlo-248
89OPC-289
89Sco-98
89Top-289
89TopBig-224
89TopTif-289
89UppDec-118
90BluJayHS-4
90Bow-16
90BowTif-16
90BraDubP-30
90BraDubS-34
90Don-385
90Fle-97
90FleCan-97
90Lea-408
90OPC-742
90PubSti-529
90Sco-433
90ScoRoo-30T
90Top-742
90TopSti-189
90TopTif-742
90TopTra-128T
90TopTraT-128T
90UppDec-148
90VenSti-486
91Lea-391
91OPC-492
91OriCro-501
91Top-492
91TopDesS-492
91TopMic-492
91TopTif-492
92Nab-34
93BluJayDM-6
95StCatSTI-31
96BluJayOH-35
97BluJayS-39
Whitt, Mike
85EveGiaC-18
85EveGialC-22
86CliGiaP-27
Whittaker, Jerry
94SigRooDP-52
94SigRooDPS-52
94StaCluDP-24
94StaCluDPFDI-24
Whittaker, Stewart
89GeoColC-36
Whitted, Possum (George)
14B18B-90A
14B18B-90B
15CraJacE-151
15SpoNewM-190
16ColE13-188
16FleBreD-100
16SpoNewM-189
17HolBreD-115
19W514-92
20NatCarE-108A
20NatCarE-108B
21E121So1-114A
21E121So1-114B
21E121So8-105
21Exh-185
22W575-148
23W501-81
23WilChoV-169
90DodTar-856
Whittemore, Reggie
81BriRedST-5
83PawRedST-19
84PawRedST-15
85TolMudHT-19
Whitten, Casey
93WatIndC-1
93WatIndF-3562
94Bow-167
94Cla-64
94ClaGolF-187
94ExcFS7-51
94KinIndC-1
94KinIndF-2643
94Top-756
94TopGol-756
94TopSpa-756
95SPML-44
96BesAutS-93

96BesAutSA-87
96BowBes-133
96BowBesAR-133
96BowBesR-133
96CanIndB-28
Whitten, Mike
93HigDesMC-25
93HigDesMF-43
94PorSeaDF-677
94PorSeaDTI-29
95BreCouMF-247
Whitty, Todd
91CalLeLA-51
Whitworth, Clint
90OklSoo-17
93OneYanC-25
93OneYanF-3505
Whitworth, Dick
87NegLeaPD-13
Whitworth, Ken
91MiaMirC-12
91MiaMirP-408
Wick, David
82WatIndF-13
82WatIndT-10
Wickander, Kevin
87KinIndP-2
88BasAmeAAB-9
88EasLeaAP-44
88WilBilP-1315
89Bow-75
89BowTif-75
89ColSprSSC-5
89ColSprSSP-238
90Bow-327
90BowTif-327
90DonRoo-36
90IndTeal-44
90OPC-528
90Top-528
90TopDeb89-142
90TopTif-528
91ColSprSSLD-98
91ColSprSSP-2185
91Don-649
91Fle-385
91LinDriAAA-98
91OPC-246
91Sco-355
91Sco100RS-37
91StaClu-572
91Top-246
91TopDesS-246
91TopMic-246
91TopTif-246
92Bow-430
92ColSprSSS-98
92SkyAAAF-43
93Don-389
93Fle-602
93IndWUA-32
93RedKah-28
93Sco-358
93Top-358
93TopGol-358
93TopInaM-358
93TopMic-358
93Ult-547
94Fle-431
94Top-41
94TopGol-41
94TopSpa-41
95TolMudHTI-27
96FleUpd-U49
96FleUpdTC-U49
Wicker, Bob
06FanCraNL-51
11SpoLifCW-366
Wicker, Floyd
69ExpFudP-14
69Top-524
71MLBOffS-456
71OPC-97
71Top-97
94BreMilB-90
Wicker, Kemp
41DodTeal-11
75YanDyn1T-49
90DodTar-857
Wickersham, Dave
61Top-381
62Top-517
63Top-492
64TigLid-14
64Top-181
64TopCoi-105
64TopGia-35
64TopVen-181
65Baz-25
65OldLonC-38
65OPC-9
65TigJayP-11
65Top-9
65Top-375
65TopTral-34
66OPC-58
66Top-58
66TopVen-58
67CokCapTi-4
67DexPre-222
67OPC-112
67TigDexP-10
67Top-112
68PirKDK-40
68PirTeal-23
68Top-288
68TopVen-288
69RoySol-15
69RoyTeal-12
69Top-647
78TCM60I-195
Wickham, Alex
63GadFunC-73
Wickham, Mike
89StoPorB-26
89StoPorS-26
Wickman, Bob (Robert Joe)
90SouBenWSB-28
91Bow-353
91SarWhiSC-11
91SarWhiSP-1114
92ColCliF-354
92ColCliP-13
92DonRoo-125
92FleUpd-46
92UppDec-76
93Bow-455
93Don-417
93Fla-254
93Fle-288
93Lea-424
93Pin-226
93Sco-291
93Sel-343
93SP-269
93StaClu-53
93StaCluFDI-53
93StaCluMOP-53
93StaCluY-28
93Top-452
93TopGol-452
93TopInaM-452
93TopMic-452
93Toy-40
93TriPla-189
93Ult-251
93UppDec-372
93UppDecGold-372
93USPlaCR-9H
94ColC-296
94ColChoGS-296
94ColChoSS-296
94Don-231
94Fin-263
94FinRef-263
94Fla-325
94Fle-250
94Lea-206
94Pin-273
94PinArtP-273
94PinMusC-273
94Sco-147
94ScoGolR-147
94StaClu-494
94StaCluFDI-494
94StaCluGR-494
94StaCluMOP-494
94StaCluT-210
94StaCluTFDI-210
94Top-173
94TopGol-173
94TopSpa-173
94Ult-404
94UppDec-509
94UppDecED-509
95ColCho-509
95ColChoGS-509
95ColChoSS-509
95Don-282
95DonPreP-282
95DonTopotO-129
95Fle-84
95Pac-306
95StaClu-56
95StaCluFDI-56
95StaCluMOP-56
95StaCluSTWS-56
95StaCluVR-34
95Top-618
95TopCyb-386
95Ult-88
95UltGolM-88
96Fle-200
96FleTif-200
96LeaSigEA-213
96StaCluVRMO-34
97Cir-185
97CirRav-185
97Fle-140
97FleTif-140
97PacPriGotD-GD61
97Ult-450
97UltGolME-450
97UltPlaME-450
Wickware, Frank
78LauLonABS-19
Widger, Chris
92BelMarC-20
92BelMarF-1448
92ClaDraP-60
92FroRowDP-99
93RivPilCLC-22
93StaCluM-130
93Top-632
93TopGol-632
93TopInaM-632
93TopMic-632
94JacSunF-1415
95Bow-2
95Exc-123
95MarPac-47
95TacRaiTI-27
95UppDecML-98
96ColCho-732
96ColChoGS-732
96ColChoSS-732
96Pin-178
96Sco-503
96TacRaiB-28
97Bow-216
97BowInt-216
97ColCho-388
97Don-381
97DonLim-41
97DonLimLE-41
97DonPreP-381
97DonPrePGold-381
97FlaSho-A177
97FlaSho-B177
97FlaSho-C177
97FlaShoLC-177
97FlaShoLC-B177
97FlaShoLC-C177
97FlaShoLCM-A177
97FlaShoLCM-B177
97FlaShoLCM-C177
97Fle-646
97FleTif-646
97Ult-501
97UltGolME-501
97UltPlaME-501
95UppDecMLFS-98
Widmar, Al
51Bow-281
52Top-133
53MotCoo-14
74Top-99
83TopRep5-133
84BluJayFS-33
85BluJayFS-33
86BluJayFS-33
87BluJayFS-35
88BluJayFS-33
89BluJayFS-32
94St.CatBJC-30
95StCatSTI-27
Widmar, Tom
75SacSolC-15
76SpoIndC-4
Widner, Steven
77WatIndT-29
Widner, William
87OldJudN-536
Wieand, F. Ted
58RedEnq-42
59RedEnq-28
60Top-146
60TopVen-146
Wieczorek, Chet
40SolHug-19
Wieczorek, Ted
93AubAstC-27
93AubAstF-3459
Wiedenbauer, Tom
77CocAstT-25
80TucTorT-8
81TucTorT-26
83DayBeaAT-13
86OscAstP-28
87ColAstP-16
88ColAstB-25
89ColMudB-8
89ColMudP-130
89ColMudS-24
Wiegandt, Scott
89MarPhiS-34
90SpaPhiB-11
90SpaPhiP-2492
90SpaPhiS-26
91ClePhiC-11
91ClePhiP-1622
92ReaPhiF-577
92ReaPhiS-547
93ReaPhiF-296
94ReaPhiF-2064
95ScrRedBTI-28
96ScrRedBB-26
Wieghaus, Tom
80MemChiT-25
80VenLeaS-257
83ExpPos-28
83WicAerDS-23
84AstMot-18
Wielegman, Phil
86MiaMarP-27
Wieligman, Rich
87LakTigP-4
88GleFalTP-922
89TolMudHC-23
89TolMudHP-775
Wiener, Paul
79JacMetT-5
Wiens, Randy
78DunBluJT-26
Wiese, Phil
89EliTwiS-28
90VisOakCLC-64
90VisOakP-2156
91LinDriAA-498
91OrlSunRLD-498
91OrlSunRP-1851
Wieser, Dan
82OmaRoyT-18A
82OmaRoyT-18B
Wieser, Mike
93DanBraC-28
93DanBraF-3628
95DurBulTI-36
Wieser, Tom
84AriWilP-19
Wiesler, Bob
56Top-327
57Top-126
79TCM50-224
Wiesmiller, Bob
77SalPirT-27A
Wiesner, Doug
81AppFoxT-29
82AppFoxF-29
Wietelmann, Whitey (William)
52MotCoo-24
72PadTeal-27
73OPC-12
73PadDea-2
73Top-12A
73Top-12B
74PadDea-28
76SSP-598
77PadSchC-63
78PadFamF-36
79DiaGre-209
83TCMPla1944-38
Wieters, Rick
78GreBraT-29
79SavBraT-16
80GleFalWSBT-12
80GleFalWSCT-13
81GleFalWST-8
Wiggins, Alan
78QuaCitAT-29
79CliDodT-6
81HawIsIT-8
83Don-397
83Fle-375
83Top-251
84AllGamPI-18
84Don-568
84Fle-317
84FleSti-89
84Nes792-693
84OPC-27
84PadMot-10
84PadSmo-28
84Top-693
84TopRubD-6
84TopSti-153
84TopStiB-3
84TopTif-693
85AllGamPI-108
85Don-80
85Fle-48
85FleStaS-60
85Lea-68
85OPC-378
85OriHea-19
85Top-378
85TopRubD-7
85TopSti-150
85TopTif-378
86Don-607
86Fle-290
86Top-508
86TopTif-508
87DonOpeD-138
87FleUpd-124
87FleUpdG-124
87OriFreB-2
87TopTra-126T
87TopTraT-126T
88Sco-291
88ScoGlo-291
91OriCro-482
Wiggins, Dave
81PhoGiaVNB-14
Wiggins, Jimmy
91PriRedC-26
91PriRedP-3515
Wiggins, Kevin
86OrlTwiP-23
Wiggins, Tony
89TenTecGE-29
Wiggs, James
03BreE10-150
Wiggs, Johnny
89BelMarL-15
90SanBerSB-21
90SanBerSCLC-94
90SanBerSP-2634
91PenPilC-13
91PenPilP-379
Wight, Bill
48WhiSoxTI-28
50Bow-38
51Bow-164
52Bow-117
52Top-177
53BowC-100
53TigGle-28
55Bow-312
55IndGolS-22
56Top-286
57Top-340
58RedEnq-43
58Top-237
79DiaGre-143
79TCM50-131
83TopRep5-177
91OriCro-483
Wihtol, Sandy
77WatIndT-30
79TacTugT-16
80TacTigT-10
80Top-665
81ChaChaT-7
81Top-451
83ChaChaT-6
Wilber, Del
52Bow-225

52Top-383
53BowBW-24
53RedSoxTI-29
54Bow-178
74SpoIndC-45
77TacTwiDQ-26
83TopRep5-383
93RanKee-379
Wilbins, Mike
75CedRapGT-2
Wilborn, Ted
77ForLauYS-8
80NasSouTI-25
80OPC-329
80Top-674
81NasSouTI-23
83PhoGiaBHN-16
86HagSunP-27
87CedRapRP-20
92YanWIZ8-203
82PhoGiaVNB-3
Wilbur, Bob
80UtiBluJT-10
Wilburn, Fred
85MidAngT-4
Wilburn, Trey
89BilMusP-2041
90ChaWheB-11
90ChaWheP-2242
90GatCitPP-3355
90GatCitPSP-8
91BilMusP-3758
91BilMusSP-6
Wilcox, Chris
96Exc-96
Wilcox, Greg
90MedHatBJB-8
Wilcox, Luke
96Bow-223
96TamYanY-27
97Bow-301
97BowCerBIA-CA83
97BowCerGIA-CA83
97BowChr-209
97BowChrI-209
97BowChrIR-209
97BowChrR-209
97BowInt-301
Wilcox, Milt
70DayDaiNM-155
71OPC-164
71Top-164
72OPC-399
72Top-399
73OPC-134
73Top-134
74OPC-565
74Top-565
75OPC-14
75Top-14
76SSP-306
76VenLeaS-192
77EvaTriT-25
78OPC-136
78TigBurK-11
78Top-151
79Top-288
80OPC-204
80Top-392
81AllGamPI-90
81Don-247
81Fle-465
81Top-658
82Don-233
82Fle-285
82FleSta-157
82Top-784
82TopSti-186
82TopStiV-186
83Don-155
83Fle-349
83FleSta-214
83FleSti-248
83Tig-30
83Top-457
84AllGamPI-179
84Don-471
84Fle-93
84Nes792-588
84TigFarJ-16
84TigWavP-35
84Top-588
84TopTif-588
85Don-105
85Fle-25
85Lea-227
85OPC-99
85SevCoi-D6
85TigCaiD-20
85TigWen-22
85Top-99
85TopSti-10
85TopSti-17
85TopTif-99
86Fle-243
86MarMot-11
86Top-192
86TopTif-192
89PacSenL-13
89T/MSenL-114
89TopSenL-73
90EliSenL-16
91PacSenL-140
Wilcox, Steve
82CliGiaF-11
Wilczewski, Frank
79CliDodT-27
Wild, Jerry
64TulOil-8
Wildams, Jaime
85DomLeaS-106
Wilder, Bill
84MemChiT-11
Wilder, Dave
82IdaFalAT-29
83MadMusF-5
85ModA'sC-21
87PitCubP-18
Wilder, John
91PulBraC-27
91PulBraP-4006
92MacBraC-12
92MacBraF-269
93DurBulC-23
93DurBulF-487
93DurBulTI-18
93SouAtlLAPI-41
Wilder, Mike
83IdaFalAT-25
84MadMusP-4
Wilder, Paul
96BesAutS1RP-FR15
96NewJerCB-30
97Bow-170
97BowBes-132
97BowBesAR-132
97BowBesR-132
97BowCerBIA-CA84
97BowCerGIA-CA84
97BowChr-165
97BowChrI-165
97BowChrIR-165
97BowChrR-165
97BowInt-170
86HumStaDS-14
97Top-471
Wilder, Troy
76BatTroTI-28
78WatIndT-26
79WatIndT-5
Wilder, Willie
92PenPilC-18
92PenPilF-2947
93RivPilCLC-23
Wiles, Randy
75TulOil7-17
76ArkTraT-11
76TulOilGP-22
78ChaChaT-19
Wiley, Chad
92ButCopKSP-26
93ChaRaiC-23
93ChaRaiF-1912
94ChaRanF-2498
95TulDriTI-27
Wiley, Charles
91BelMarC-24
91BelMarP-3664
92PenPilC-2
92PenPilF-2933
93RivPilCLC-24
Wiley, Craig
87LasVegSP-21
88WicPilRD-12
89NiaFalRP-23
Wiley, Jim
90PriWilCTI-28
91Cla/Bes-167
91Ft.LauYC-15
91Ft.LauYP-2428
93PriWilCC-25
93PriWilCF-657
94AbaYanF-1443
Wiley, Joe
93NegLeaRL2-40
Wiley, Keith
88CapCodPPaLP-11
Wiley, Mark
74TacTwiC-14
75TacTwiK-1
76TacTwiDQ-22
79SyrChiT-5
79SyrChiTI-27
83RocRedWT-25
84RocRedWT-3
85RocRedWT-29
87OriFreB-31
88IndGat-35
89IndTeal-28
90IndTeal-45
91IndFanC-30
Wiley, Michael
91KanCouCC-12
91KanCouCP-2659
91KanCouCTI-22
Wiley, Skip
90AppFoxBS-30
90AppFoxP-2096
90ProAaA-108
91BasCitRC-12
91BasCitRP-1399
92MemChiF-2420
92MemChiS-448
92SkyAA F-190
Wilfong, Rob
76TacTwiDQ-23
77TacTwiDQ-16B
78TwiFriP-22
79Top-633
79TwiFriP-27
80Top-238
81Don-493
81Fle-569
81Top-453
82Don-130
82Fle-563
82FleSta-231
82Top-379
82TopSti-205
82TopTra-128T
82TwiPos-29
83Don-612
83Fle-101
83Top-158
84AngSmo-30
84Don-329
84Fle-530
84Nes792-79
84Top-79
84TopTif-79
85AngSmo-20
85Don-402
85Fle-315
85Top-524
85TopTif-524
86AngSmo-20
86OPC-393
86Top-658
86TopTif-658
87Don-258
87Fle-94
87FleGlo-94
87Top-251
87TopTif-251
Wilford, Eric
91HelBreSP-27
Wilhelm, Brent
96SouBenSHS-28
Wilhelm, Hoyt
50JJKCopP-23
52Top-392
53BowBW-28
53RedMan-NL21
53Top-151
54Bow-57
54NewYorJA-37
54Top-36
55Bow-1
55GiaGolS-6
55RedMan-NL12
56Top-307
57Top-203
58Top-324
59OriJayP-11
59Top-349
60Lea-69
60OriJayP-11
60Top-115
60Top-395
60TopVen-115
61Pos-80A
61Pos-80B
61Top-545
61TopStaI-107
62Jel-35
62Pos-35
62PosCan-35
62Top-423
62Top-545
62TopStaI-10
63SalMetC-39
63Top-108
63WhiSoxTS-24
64Top-13
64TopVen-13
64WhiSoxTS-23
65OPC-276
65Top-276
65WhiSoxJP-12
66Top-510
67CokCapWS-5
67Top-422
67TopVen-257
68Top-350
68TopVen-350
69AngJacitB-13
69MilBra-291
69Top-565
69TopDec-11A
69TopDecI-45
69TopSta-190
69TopTeaP-17
70DayDaiNM-12
70OPC-17
70Top-17
71MLBOffS-24
71OPC-248
71Top-248
71TopGreM-2
72MilBra-361
72Top-777
77GalGloG-23
77GalGloG-248
78HalHalR-19
78TacYanC-47
78TCM60I-100
79TCM50-270
79WesHavYT-27
80GiaGreT-4
80PacLeg-121
80PerHaloFP-193
80SSPHOF-196
82NasSouTI-28
83NasSouTI-25
83TopRep5-392
84FifNatCT-18
84NasSouTI-24
84OCoandSI-154
85WhiSoxC-43
86OriGreT-1
88PacLegI-76
89DodSmoG-35
89HOFStiB-81
89PacLegI-171
89SweBasG-45
89WhiSoxK-5
90DodTar-858
90PacLeg-57
90PerGreM-95
91OriCro-484
91TopArc1-151
91TopArc1-312
92BazQua5A-21
94TopArc1-36
94TopArc1G-36
Wilhelm, James W.
79HawIsIC-25
79HawIsIT-7
80Top-685
Wilhelm, Kaiser (Irvin)
09ColChiE-306
09T206-374
09T206-375
10CouT21-245
11SpoLifCW-367
11SpoLifM-164
11T205-181
12ColRedB-306
12ColTinT-306
14PieStaT-62
23WilChoV-170
90DodTar-859
Wilhelm, Spider (Charles Ernest)
55JetPos-21
Wilhelmi, Dave
80CliGiaT-1
81CliGiaT-4
84ShrCapFB-24
Wilhoit, Joe
16ColE13-189
Wilholte, Arnold
78AshTouT-28
79AshTouT-18
Wilie, Denney
12T207-196
Wilke, Matt
91MedHatBJP-4111
91MedHatBJSP-18
92MedHatBJF-3217
Wilkerson, Curt (Curtis)
82BurRanF-13
82BurRanT-13
82TulDriT-25
83OklCit8T-19
84Don-99
84FleUpd-126
84RanJarP-19
84TopTra-127T
84TopTraT-127T
85Don-99
85Fle-573
85OPC-342
85RanPer-19
85Top-594
85TopSti-349
85TopTif-594
86Don-256
86Fle-577
86OPC-279
86RanLit-7
86RanPer-19
86Top-434
86TopSti-244
86TopTif-434
87Don-223
87Fle-141
87FleGlo-141
87RanMot-14
87RanSmo-28
87Top-228
87TopTif-228
88Don-592
88Fle-481
88FleGlo-481
88RanMot-14
88RanSmo-21
88Sco-127
88ScoGlo-127
88StaLinRa-18
88Top-53
88TopBig-132
88TopTif-53
89Bow-292
89BowTif-292
89CubMar-19
89Don-402
89DonTra-34
89Fle-535
89FleGlo-535
89Sco-518
89Top-331
89TopTif-331
89TopTra-126T
89TopTraT-126T
89UppDec-465
90CubMar-23
90Don-608
90Fle-46
90FleCan-46
90OPC-667
90PubSti-209
90Sco-474
90Top-667
90TopTif-667
90TopTVCu-28
90UppDec-147
90VenSti-487
91Bow-511
91Fle-438

91Lea-317
91OPC-142
91Sco-603
91StaClu-512
91Top-142
91TopDesS-142
91TopMic-142
91TopTif-142
92Don-489
92Lea-387
92OPC-712
92Sco-382
92StaClu-46
92StaClu-849
92Top-712
92TopGol-712
92TopGolW-712
92TopMic-712
92Ult-377
92UppDec-490
93Fle-627
93PacSpa-142
93RanKee-380
93RoyPol-25
93StaClu-177
93StaCluFDI-177
93StaCluMOP-177
93StaCluRoy-23
94OmaRoyF-1233
94Pac-301
94StaCluMOP-ST21
94StaCluST-ST21
96LanLugB-2

Wilkerson, Marty
84OmaRoyT-12
85OmaRoyT-20
86OmaRoyP-29
86OmaRoyT-9

Wilkerson, Ron
82WesHavAT-18

Wilkerson, Steve
93BilMusF-3946
93BilMusSP-24
94ChaWheC-25
94ChaWheF-2704

Wilkerson, Wayne
77AshTouT-27

Wilkerson, Wayne Linwood
91PriRedC-21
91PriRedP-3530
92BenMusSP-5
92BilMusF-3372
93WesVirWC-24
93WesVirWF-2880

Wilkes, Greg
80HawIslT-13

Wilkie, Aldon
47RemBre-23
48SigOil-24
77TCMTheWY-47

Wilkie, James
91HelBreSP-13

Wilkins, Dean
88EasLeaAP-30
88PitCubP-1368
89IowCubC-10
89IowCubP-1690
90Bow-26
90BowTif-26
90CMC-84
90Fle-47
90FleCan-47
90IowCubC-9
90Sco-630
90TopDeb89-143
90TopTVCu-16
91TriA AAGP-AAA54
91TucTorP-2214

Wilkins, Dominique
93StaCluMO-43

Wilkins, Eric
80TacTigT-25
80Top-511
81ChaChaT-6
81Top-99

Wilkins, Marc
92WelPirC-25
92WelPirF-1323
93AugPirC-25
93AugPirF-1546
94SalBucC-23
94SalBucF-2324
95CarMudF-158
96CarMudB-12
97ColCho-428
97Fle-437
97FleTif-437
97Top-207
97Ult-267
97UltGolME-267
97UltPlaME-267

Wilkins, Mark
80QuaCitCT-10
81QuaCitCT-28

Wilkins, Michael
88FayGenP-1103
89LakTigS-24
90CMC-767
90EasLeaAP-EL46
90LonTigP-1269
91LinDriAA-547
91SanAntMLD-547
91SanAntMP-2976
92AlbDukF-722

Wilkins, Rick
87GenCubP-7
88PeoChiTI-31
89WinSpiS-17
90ChaKniTI-22
90TopTVCu-63
91Bow-419
91Cla3-T96
91DonRoo-38
91FleUpd-83
91IowCubLD-221
91IowCubP-1065
91LinDriAAA-221
91LinDriP-221
91ScoRoo-103T
91UltUpd-75
91UppDecFE-46F
92Bow-156
92Don-249
92Fle-397
92Lea-336
92OPC-348
92Sco-483
92Sco100RS-16
92StaClu-643
92StaCluNC-643
92Top-348
92TopDeb91-184
92TopGol-348
92TopGolW-348
92TopMic-348
92UppDec-373
93Bow-524
93CubMar-29
93Don-28
93Fle-28
93Lea-216
93PacSpa-65
93PanSti-202
93Pin-206
93Sco-185
93Sel-390
93SP-90
93StaClu-228
93StaCluCu-23
93StaCluFDI-228
93StaCluMOP-228
93Stu-63
93Top-721
93TopGol-721
93TopInaM-721
93TopMic-721
93TriPla-19
93Ult-25
93UppDec-598
93UppDecGold-598
94Bow-306
94ColC-297
94ColChoGS-297
94ColChoSS-297
94Don-444
94DonDiaK-DK5
94ExtBas-226
94Fin-86
94FinRef-86
94Fla-364
94Fle-401
94FUnPac-102
94FUnPac-234
94Lea-287
94LeaL-93
94Pac-115
94PacGolP-20
94PanSti-160
94Pin-84
94PinArtP-84
94PinMusC-84
94PinPowS-PS8
94PinRunC-RC44
94Sco-450
94ScoGolR-450
94Sel-16
94SP-74
94SPDieC-74
94Spo-27
94StaClu-2
94StaCluFDI-2
94StaCluGR-2
94StaCluMOP-2
94StaCluT-346
94StaCluTFDI-346
94Stu-65
94Top-244
94TopGol-244
94TopSpa-244
94TriPla-80
94TriPlaM-2
94Ult-168
94UppDec-154
94UppDecED-154
95Baz-65
95Bow-378
95ColCho-208
95ColChoGS-208
95ColChoSS-208
95Don-158
95DonPreP-158
95Emb-28
95EmbGolI-28
95Fin-38
95FinRef-38
95Fla-336
95Fle-426
95Lea-180
95LeaLim-63
95Pin-53
95PinArtP-53
95PinMusC-53
95Sco-348
95ScoGolR-348
95ScoPlaTS-348
95Spo-36
95SpoArtP-36
95StaClu-452
95StaCluMOP-452
95StaCluSTWS-452
95StaCluVR-243
95Stu-122
95Top-504
95TopCyb-294
95Ult-141
95UltGolM-141
95UppDec-313
95UppDecED-313
95UppDecEDG-313
96AstMot-11
96Don-445
96DonPreP-445
96Fle-424
96FleTif-424
96StaCluVRMO-243
96Ult-491
96UltGolM-491
96UppDec-496U
97Cir-57
97CirRav-57
97ColCho-458
97Fle-488
97FleTif-488
97Pac-449
97PacLigB-449
97PacSil-449
97Pin-125
97PinArtP-125
97PinMusC-125
97UppDec-498

Wilkins, Steve
76CedRapGT-32

Wilkins, Vern
74SpoIndC-43

Wilkinson, Bill
86CalCanP-25
87FleUpd-125
87FleUpdG-125
87MarMot-26
87TopTra-127T
87TopTraT-127T
88Don-568
88Fle-390
88FleGlo-390
88MarMot-26
88RedFolSB-102
88StaLinMa-19
88Top-376
88TopTif-376
89CalCanC-6
89LonTigP-1360
89Top-636
89TopTif-636
90OmaRoyP-67
90ProAAAF-602
92HunStaS-323
92TacTigF-2504

Wilkinson, Brian
87BelMarL-13
87BelMarTI-3
89WauTimGS-13
90RocExpLC-28
90RocExpP-2692
91WesPalBEC-14
91WesPalBEP-1230

Wilkinson, Don
81TCM60I-305

Wilkinson, Ray
23WilChoV-171
75WhiSox1T-26

Wilkinson, Ron
82MadMusF-16

Wilkinson, Spencer
88GasRanP-1019
89GasRanP-999
89GasRanS-25

Wilks, Ted
46SeaSLP-58
47TipTop-164
49Bow-137
49EurSta-199
51Bow-193
52Bow-138
52Top-109
53Top-101
79TCM50-218
83TCMPla1944-25
83TopRep5-109
91TopArc1-101

Will, Bob
59Top-388
60Top-147
60TopVen-147
61Top-512
61TopStaI-11
62SalPlaC-218
62ShiPlaC-218
62Top-47
62TopVen-47
63Top-58

Willard, Jerry
82ReaPhiT-11
83ChaChaT-8
84Don-520
84Ind-33
84IndWhe-16
85Don-346
85Fle-460
85Ind-36
85IndPol-16
85OPC-142
85Top-504
85TopMin-504
85TopTif-504
86Don-398
86Fle-601
86FleUpd-126
86OPC-273
86TacTigP-24
86Top-273
86TopTif-273
87Don-467
87Fle-409
87FleGlo-409
87TacTigP-19
87Top-137
87TopTif-137
89VanCanC-19
89VanCanP-587
90CMC-650
90ProAAAF-170
90TriAllGP-AAA37
90VanCanC-23
90VanCanP-492
91Don-634
91RicBraBC-36
91RicBraP-2573
91RicBraTI-20
92Bow-470
92BraLykP-29
92BraLykS-34
92Sco-188
92StaCluD-195
93RicBraBB-19
93RicBraF-188
93RicBraP-22
93RicBraRC-28
94CalCanF-794
95TacRaiTI-28

Willard, Jon
91SalLakTP-3212
91SalLakTSP-10

Willeford, Jerry
76DubPacT-38

Willes, David
87BriYouC-13

Willes, Mike
87BriYouC-3

Willett, Robert Edgar
07TigACDPP-27
09BusBroBPP-16
09ColChiE-307
09PhiCarE-23
09T206-376
09T206-377
09TigMorPenWBPP-14
09TigTaCP-19
10CouT21-67
10CouT21-246
10CouT21-247
10NadE1-57
10RedCroT-84
10RedCroT-256
11S74Sil-19
11SpoLifCW-368
11SpoLifM-72
11T205-182
12ColRedB-307
12ColTinT-307
12HasTriFT-55
14PieStaT-63

Willey, Carl (Carlton)
58Top-407
59Top-95
59TopVen-95
60BraLaktL-27
60BraSpiaS-25
60Top-107
60TopVen-107
61Top-105
61TopStaI-48
62BraJayP-12
62Jel-155
62Pos-155
62PosCan-155
62Top-174A
62Top-174B
62TopVen-174
63Top-528
64MetJayP-12
64Top-84
64TopCoi-75
64TopSta-44
64TopTatI-73
64TopVen-84
65Top-401
78BraTCC-15
91MetWIZ-430

Willhite, Nick
64Top-14
64TopVen-14
65Top-284
66OPC-171
66Top-171
66TopVen-171
67Top-249
78NewWayCT-44
90DodTar-860
91MetWIZ-431

Williams, Ace (Robert Fulton)
77TCMTheWY-63

Williams, Al (Alberto H.)
73CedRapAT-3
80TolMudHT-17
80VenLeaS-199
81Top-569
82Don-429
82Fle-564

82Top-69
82TwiPos-30
83AllGamPI-89
83Don-508
83Fle-628
83FleSta-215
83FleSti-137
83Top-731
83TwiTeal-20
84Don-316
84Fle-579
84MinTwiP-32
84Nes792-183
84Top-183
84TopTif-183
84TwiTeal-21
85ColCliP-23
85ColCliT-10
85Top-614
85TopTif-614

Williams, Barbara
59FleWil-64

Williams, Barry
90UtiBluSP-13

Williams, Bernie (Bernabe)
87Ft.LauYP-21
87OneYanP-4
88BlaYNPRWLU-13
88CarLeaAS-19
88PriWilYS-24
89BasAmeAPB-AA5
89BlaYNPRWL-189
89ColCliC-21
89ColCliP-23
89ColCliP-736
90AlbDecGB-33
90AlbYanB-1
90AlbYanP-1179
90AlbYanS-22
90Bes-26
90Bow-439
90BowTif-439
90ClaBlu-10
90CMC-789
90Don-689
90EasLeaAP-EL45
90OPC-701
90ProAaA-31
90Sco-619
90StaFS7-54
90Top-701
90TopTif-701
90TopTVY-66
91AlbYanCB-3
91Bow-173
91Cla2-T61
91Cla3-T97
91ColCliLD-123
91ColCliP-23
91ColCliP-612
91FleUpd-49
91LinDriAAA-123
91OPCPre-128
91RedFolS-112
91StuPre-7
91TriA AAGP-AAA8
91UltUpd-44
91UppDec-11
92Bow-407
92ClaGam-102
92ColCliF-365
92ColCliP-22
92ColCliS-123
92Don-344
92Fle-247
92OPC-374
92OPCPre-109
92Pin-229
92PinTea2-24
92ProFS7-106
92Sco-401
92Sco100RS-34
92SpoIllFK1-475
92StaClu-260
92Top-374
92TopDeb91-185
92TopGol-374
92TopGolW-374
92TopMic-374
92TriA AAS-123
92UppDec-556
92UppDecS-1
93Bow-623
93Don-577
93Fin-30
93FinRef-30
93Fla-255
93Fle-289
93Lea-130
93OPC-363
93PacSpa-215
93Pin-7
93PinTea2-15
93Sco-120
93Sel-393
93SP-270
93StaClu-364
93StaCluFDI-364
93StaCluMOP-364
93StaCluY-21
93Top-222
93TopGol-222
93TopInaM-222
93TopMic-222
93Toy-48
93Ult-252
93UppDec-332
93UppDec-470
93UppDecGold-332
93UppDecGold-470
94Bow-521
94ColC-298
94ColChoGS-298
94ColChoSS-298
94Don-259
94ExtBas-142
94Fin-279
94FinRef-279
94Fla-326
94Fle-251
94Lea-4
94OPC-35
94Pac-441
94PanSti-106
94Pin-139
94PinArtP-139
94PinMusC-139
94Sco-339
94ScoGolR-339
94Sel-140
94Spo-59
94StaClu-573
94StaCluFDI-573
94StaCluGR-573
94StaCluMOP-573
94StaCluMOP-ST24
94StaCluST-ST24
94StaCluT-198
94StaCluTFDI-198
94Top-2
94TopGol-2
94TopSpa-2
94TriPla-280
94Ult-103
94UppDec-86
94UppDecED-86
95ColCho-517
95ColChoGS-517
95ColChoSS-517
95Don-509
95DonPreP-509
95DonTopotO-130
95Fin-209
95FinRef-209
95Fla-290
95Fle-85
95Lea-105
95LeaLim-83
95Pac-307
95PacLatD-36
95Pin-248
95PinArtP-248
95PinMusC-248
95PinUps-US17
95Sco-124
95ScoGolR-124
95ScoPlaTS-124
95Sel-28
95SelArtP-28
95Spo-24
95SpoArtP-24
95StaClu-290
95StaCluMOP-290
95StaCluSTWS-290
95StaCluVR-150
95Stu-79
95Sum-22
95SumNthD-22
95Top-485
95TopCyb-277
95UC3-27
95UC3ArtP-27
95Ult-314
95UltGolM-314
95UppDec-209
95UppDecED-209
95UppDecEDG-209
96Baz-7
96Bow-109
96Cir-70
96CirRav-70
96ColCho-637
96ColChoGS-637
96ColChoSS-637
96Don-401
96DonPreP-401
96EmoXL-99
96Fin-S2
96FinRef-S2
96Fla-140
96Fle-201
96FleTif-201
96Lea-16
96LeaLim-35
96LeaLimG-35
96LeaPre-39
96LeaPreP-39
96LeaPrePB-16
96LeaPrePG-16
96LeaPrePS-16
96LeaSig-17
96LeaSigPPG-17
96LeaSigPPP-17
96MetUni-97
96MetUniP-97
96MLBPin-36
96Pac-369
96PacBaeS-3
96PacEstL-EL36
96PacPri-P123
96PacPriG-P123
96PanSti-156
96Pin-85
96PinAfi-71
96PinAfiAP-71
96PinAfiFPP-71
96PinArtP-47
96PinSta-47
96ProSta-140
96Sco-343
96ScoDugC-B68
96ScoDugCAP-B68
96ScoGolS-9
96Sel-78
96SelArtP-78
96SelCer-25
96SelCerAP-25
96SelCerCB-25
96SelCerCR-25
96SelCerMB-25
96SelCerMG-25
96SelCerMR-25
96SelTeaN-6
96Spo-76
96SpoArtP-76
96StaClu-210
96StaClu-289
96StaCluEPB-289
96StaCluEPG-289
96StaCluEPS-289
96StaCluMOP-210
96StaCluMOP-289
96StaCluVRMO-150
96Stu-44
96StuPrePB-44
96StuPrePG-44
96StuPrePS-44
96Sum-131
96SumAbo&B-131
96SumArtP-131
96SumFoi-131
96TeaOut-88
96Top-68
96TopChr-24
96TopChrR-24
96TopGal-31
96TopGalPPI-31
96TopLas-16
96Ult-109
96UltGolM-109
96UppDec-406
96Zen-20
96ZenArtP-20
96ZenMoz-22
97Bow-227
97BowBes-43
97BowBesAR-43
97BowBesR-43
97BowChr-56
97BowChrI-56
97BowChrIR-56
97BowChrR-56
97BowInt-227
97BowIntB-BBI4
97BowIntBAR-BBI4
97BowIntBR-BBI4
97Cir-51
97CirBos-20
97CirRav-51
97CirSupB-20
97ColCho-175
97ColCho-223
97ColChoAC-16
97ColChoTotT-T21
97Don-169
97Don-443
97DonLim-93
97DonLim-103
97DonLim-173
97DonLimFotG-42
97DonLimLE-93
97DonLimLE-103
97DonLimLE-173
97DonPre-111
97DonPreCttC-111
97DonPreP-169
97DonPreP-443
97DonPrePGold-169
97DonPrePGold-443
97DonPrePM-22
97Fin-45
97Fin-107
97Fin-331
97FinEmb-107
97FinEmb-331
97FinEmbR-107
97FinEmbR-331
97FinRef-45
97FinRef-107
97FinRef-331
97FlaSho-A51
97FlaSho-B51
97FlaSho-C51
97FlaShoDC-19
97FlaShoLC-51
97FlaShoLC-B51
97FlaShoLC-C51
97FlaShoLCM-A51
97FlaShoLCM-B51
97FlaShoLCM-C51
97Fle-181
97Fle-720
97FleMilDM-22
97FleTif-181
97FleTif-720
97Lea-111
97Lea-386
97LeaFraM-111
97LeaFraM-386
97LeaFraMDC-111
97LeaFraMDC-386
97LeaWarT-9
97MetUni-125
97Pac-163
97PacFirD-9
97PacGolCD-14
97PacLatotML-16
97PacLigB-163
97PacPri-55
97PacPriGA-GA11
97PacPriLB-55
97PacPriP-55
97PacPriSL-SL4B
97PacSil-163
97Pin-111
97PinArtP-111
97PinCar-20
97PinCer-10
97PinCerMBlu-10
97PinCerMG-10
97PinCerMR-10
97PinCerR-10
97PinInsDD-12
97PinMusC-111
97PinTotCPB-10
97PinTotCPG-10
97PinTotCPR-10
97PinX-P-46
97PinX-PMoS-46
97ProMag-67
97ProMagML-67
97Sco-5
97Sco-503
97ScoHeaotO-18
97ScoHobR-503
97ScoPreS-5
97ScoResC-503
97ScoShoS-5
97ScoShoS-503
97ScoShoSAP-5
97ScoShoSAP-503
97ScoStaaD-11
97ScoYan-1
97ScoYanPl-1
97ScoYanPr-1
97SkyE-X-36
97SkyE-XC-36
97SkyE-XEC-36
97SP-122
97SpoIll-127
97SpoIllEE-127
97SPSpeF-28
97StaClu-57
97StaCluI-I11
97StaCluMat-57
97StaCluMOP-57
97StaCluMOP-I11
97Stu-97
97StuHarH-19
97StuPrePG-97
97StuPrePS-97
97Top-150
97TopChr-57
97TopChrDD-DD2
97TopChrDDR-DD2
97TopChrR-57
97TopGal-103
97TopGalPPI-103
97TopIntF-ILM10
97TopIntFR-ILM10
97TopSta-90
97TopStaAM-90
97TopTeaT-TT3
97Ult-107
97UltGolME-107
97UltPlaME-107
97UltTop3-29
97UltTop3GM-29
97UppDec-124
97UppDec-248
97UppDec-250
97UppDecP-20
97UppDecU-26
97Zen-24

Williams, Bernie (Bernard)
70OPC-401
70Top-401
71MLBOffS-264
71OPC-728
71Top-728
72Top-761
73OPC-557
73Top-557
74PadDea-29
79TCMJapPB-10

Williams, Billy
88T/MUmp-3

Williams, Billy (William)
89CanIndB-8
89CanIndP-1317
94WatIndC-30

Williams, Billy Leo
47Exh-241
61Top-141
61TopStaI-12
62CubJayP-12
62PC7HFGSS-4
62SalPlaC-207
62ShiPlaC-207
62Top-288
62TopBuc-93
62TopStal-111
63CubJayP-12
63ExhStaB-63
63Jel-172
63Pos-172
63SalMetC-30
63Top-353
64Baz-17

64CubJayP-12
64Raw-8
64Top-175
64TopCoi-44
64TopGia-52
64TopSta-73
64TopStaU-75
64TopTatI-74
64TopVen-175
65Baz-17
65CubJayP-12
65OldLonC-20
65OPC-220
65Top-4
65Top-220
65TopEmbl-40
65TopTral-35
66Baz-48
66CubTeal-12
66Top-217
66Top-580
66TopRubl-98
66TopVen-217
67Baz-48
67CokCapC-13
67CubProPS-12
67DexPre-223
67ProPizC-14
67Top-315
67TopVen-337
68AtlOilPBCC-47
68Baz-14
68Kah-B37
68OPC-37
68Top-37
68TopActS-7C
68TopVen-37
69CubJewT-19
69CubPho-12
69CubTealC-10
69Kah-B22
69KelPin-19
69MilBra-292
69MLBOffS-126
69MLBPin-59
69OPC-4
69Top-4
69Top-450
69TopSta-20
69TopSup-39
69TopTeaP-4
69TraSta-38
70CubDunD-6
70Kel-37
70MLBOffS-24
70OPC-170
70SunPin-9
70Top-170
70TopSup-40
71BazNumT-26
71BazUnn-14
71Kel-61
71MilDud-69
71MLBOffS-48
71OPC-64
71OPC-66
71OPC-350
71Top-64
71Top-66
71Top-350
71TopCoi-75
71TopGreM-37
71TopTat-100
71TopTat-101
72CubChi-8
72CubTeal-12
72Kel-46A
72Kel-46B
72MilBra-362
72OPC-439
72OPC-440
72Top-439
72Top-440
72TopPos-21
73Kel2D-10
73LinPor-46
73OPC-61
73OPC-200
73Top-61
73Top-200
73TopCanL-53
73TopCom-23
73TopPin-23
74Kel-32
74OPC-110
74OPC-338
74Top-110
74Top-338
74TopSta-20
75OPC-545
75Top-545
76OPC-525
76SSP-496
76Top-525
80CubGreT-1
80MarExh-30
80PerHaloFP-199
80SSPHOF-197
81TCM60I-402
82CubRedL-NNO
83MLBPin-35
84A'sMot-27
84CubUno-1
84OCoandSI-62
85A'sMot-27
85CirK-18
86CubGat-NNO
86SpoDecG-51
86SpoDesJM-8
87CubCan-38
87CubDavB-NNO
87DonHig-20
87HygAllG-47
88PacLegI-90
88TopGloA-22
89HOFStiB-29
89PacLegI-184
89PerCelP-42
89SweBasG-120
89TopBasT-11
90IndTeal-46
90PacLeg-58
90PerGreM-69
90SweBasG-13
91Col-36
91IndFanC-30
91Kel3D-9
91LinDri-28
91MDAA-9
91SweBasG-98
91UppDecS-12
91UppDecS-15
91UppDecS-21
92ActPacA-18
92ActPacA2-18G
92CubMar-NNO
92CubOldS-27
92UppDecF-47
92UppDecFG-47
92UppDecHH-HI9
92UppDecS-28
92UppDecS-35
93ActPacAC-18
93CubMar-30
93CubOldSBW-1
93CubOldSBW-2
93CubOldSBW-3
93CubOldSBW-4
93TedWil-24
93UppDecS-21
95JimDeaAG-5
95TopLegot6M-12
96IllLot-5
97St.VinHHS-16
Williams, Bo
90SanBerSP-2648
Williams, Bob
12T207-197
86BurExpP-26
87NewOriP-15
88ChaKniTI-2
88HagSunS-25
Williams, Brent
91KisDodP-4192
Williams, Brian
91Cla/Bes-14
91OscAstC-12
91OscAstP-685
92Bow-125
92Cla1-T96
92ClaGam-112
92Don-416
92FleUpd-88
92Pin-540
92PinRoo-23
92ProFS7-228
92ScoRoo-108T
92SkyAAAF-278
92TopDeb91-186
92TopGol-787
92TopGolW-787
92TucTorF-489
92TucTorS-622
92Ult-498
92UppDec-23
93AstMot-20
93Bow-414
93Don-692
93Fle-56
93Lea-485
93OPC-369
93PacSpa-484
93Pin-339
93Sco-333
93Sel-287
93SelChaR-6
93StaClu-714
93StaCluAs-22
93StaCluFDI-714
93StaCluMOP-714
93Top-614
93TopGol-614
93TopInaM-614
93TopMic-614
93Toy-98
93Ult-48
93UppDec-286
93UppDecGold-286
93USPlaCR-5D
94AstMot-23
94BelMarC-29
94BelMarF-3237
94ColC-594
94ColChoGS-594
94ColChoSS-594
94Don-284
94Fin-44
94FinRef-44
94Fle-503
94Pac-278
94Pin-409
94PinArtP-409
94PinMusC-409
94Sco-150
94ScoGolR-150
94StaClu-205
94StaCluFDI-205
94StaCluGR-205
94StaCluMOP-205
94Top-249
94TopGol-249
94TopSpa-249
94Ult-211
95ColCho-347
95ColChoGS-347
95ColChoSS-347
95Fle-471
95FleUpd-191
95PadMot-12
96ColCho-358
96ColChoGS-358
96ColChoSS-358
96LeaSigA-244
96LeaSigAG-245
96LeaSigAS-245
Williams, Bruce
83BelBreF-9
Williams, Bryan
95StCatSTI-16
96DunBluJB-25
96DunBluJTI-29
Williams, Cary
90ClePhiS-24
91LinDrIAA-523
91ReaPhiLD-523
91ReaPhiP-1384
92ScrRedBF-2461
92ScrRedBS-497
93ScrRedBF-2557
93ScrRedBTI-27
94ScrRedBF-934
Williams, Charles Prosek
72OPC-388
72Top-388
75Gia-12
75OPC-449
75Top-449
76OPC-332
76SSP-98
76Top-332
77Top-73
78Top-561
79Top-142
91MetWIZ-432
Williams, Charlie
90KinMetB-24
90KinMetS-25
Williams, Charlie (Charles H.)
88T/MUmp-41
89T/MUmp-39
90T/MUmp-37
Williams, Clifford
91BenBucC-17
91BenBucP-3698
91RenSilSCLC-7
93AshTouC-23
93AshTouF-2280
Williams, Curtis
94JohCitCC-29
94JohCitCF-3618
Williams, Cy (Fred)
17HolBreD-116
20NatCarE-109
21Exh-186
21Nei-118
21OxfConE-19
22E120-209
22W573-138
22W575-150
22WilPatV-30
23W501-101
23WilChoV-172
27AmeCarE-42
27YorCarE-52
28StaPlaCE-70
28W502-52
28W56PlaC-D11A
28Yue-52
29ExhFou-12
31W517-18
76ISCHooHA-24
83PhiPosGPaM-1
91ConTSN-154
Williams, Dallas
80RocRedWT-2
81RocRedWT-23
81RocRedWW-2
82IndIndTI-26
83IndIndTI-7
84EvaTriT-12
86IndIndTI-26
87IndIndTI-22
91OriCro-485
Williams, Dan
81EdmTraRR-3
82GleFalWST-12
83BirBarT-3
88BurIndP-1799
89Sta-186
89WatIndS-23
90KinIndTI-22
91KinIndC-24
91KinIndP-342
93ColRedC-28
93ColRedF-616
94ColRedC-28
94ColRedF-462
Williams, Dana
86PawRedSP-27
87NewBriRSP-16
87PawRedSP-76
88PawRedSC-21
88PawRedSP-460
89PawRedSC-16
89PawRedSP-690
89PawRedSTI-28
90CMC-651
90Fle-648
90FleCan-648
90ProAAAF-182
90TopDeb89-144
90TopTVCu-64
90VanCanC-24
90VanCanP-504
Williams, Dave
85OrlTwiT-24
Williams, Dave (David Carlous)
52Bow-178
52Top-316
53BowC-1
53Top-120
54Bow-9
54NewYorJA-38
55Bow-138
55GiaGolS-17
75Gia195T-30
79TCM50-167
83TopRep5-316
91TopArc1-120
Williams, David
90PulBraB-12
90PulBraP-3091
91MacBraC-13
91MacBraP-866
92ColMetPI-33
92DurBulC-24
92DurBulF-1101
92DurBulTI-35
93GreBraF-351
Williams, Deb
40SolHug-20
Williams, Dee (Dewey Edgar)
77TCMTheWY-83
Williams, Dib (Edwin D.)
33Gou-82
33RitCE-8C
34GouCanV-36
35GouPuzR-1B
35GouPuzR-2B
35GouPuzR-16B
35GouPuzR-17B
93ConTSN-859
Williams, Dick H.
52Top-396
53Top-125
54NewYorJA-19
57Top-59
58Top-79A
58Top-79B
59Top-292
60A'sJayP-11
60A'sTeal-18
60Top-188
60TopVen-188
61Pos-86A
61Pos-86B
61Top-8
61TopStaI-168
62Jel-32
62Pos-32
62PosCan-32
62SalPlaC-48A
62SalPlaC-48B
62ShiPlaC-48
62Top-382
63Top-328
64Top-153
64TopVen-153
67OPC-161
67Top-161
67TopRedSS-26
68OPC-87
68Top-87
68TopVen-87
69RedSoxTI-11
69Top-349
71OPC-714
71Top-714
72OPC-137
72Top-137
73A'sPos-42
73OPC-179
73Top-179A
73Top-179B
75OPC-236
75Top-236
76OPC-304
76SSP-192
76Top-304
77ExpPos-39
77OPC-108
77Top-647
78OPC-27
78Top-522
79DiaGre-100
79ExpPos-32
79OPC-349
79TCM50-227
79Top-606
80ExpPos-35
80Top-479
81Don-453
81Fle-149
81RedSoxBG2S-66
81RedSoxBG2S-126
81Top-680
83Don-625

83Top-366
83TopRep5-396
84Fle-659
84Nes792-742
84PadMot-1
84PadSmo-29
84Top-742
84TopTif-742
85FleStaS-126
85PadMot-1
85Top-66
85TopTif-66
86DonAll-38
86MarMot-1
86RedSoxGT-12
86Top-681
86TopGloA-12
86TopTif-681
86TopTra-124T
86TopTraT-124T
87A'sMot-12
87MarMot-1
87Top-418
87TopTif-418
88MarMot-1
88Top-104
88TopTif-104
89PacSenL-166
89PacSenL-183
89T/MSenL-115
89T/MSenL-120
89TopSenL-22
90DodTar-861
90EliSenL-33
91OriCro-486
91RinPosBD2-6
91SweBasG-99
91TopArc1-125
92BazQua5A-6
92UppDecS-6
93UppDecS-3
93UppDecS-10
93UppDecS-13
95TopArcBD-33
95TopArcBD-46

Williams, Drew
91MisStaB-49
92MisStaB-45
93MisStaB-46
95BelBreTI-8
96StoPorB-7

Williams, Dwayne
87TamTarP-10

Williams, Earl
71OPC-52
71Top-52
72OPC-380
72Top-380
73OPC-504
73OriJohP-32
73Top-504
74OPC-375
74Top-375
74TopSta-130
75OPC-97
75Top-97
76Hos-108
76OPC-458
76SSP-13
76Top-458
77OPC-252
77Top-223
78Hos-16
78Top-604
89BluOriS-29
91OriCro-487
93UppDecS-2

Williams, Ed
86IndOhH-24
86IndTeal-47

Williams, Eddie L.
85CedRapRT-20
87BufBisP-13
87GenCubP-23
88ColSprSSC-17
88ColSprSSP-1547
88Don-46
88Fle-620
88FleGlo-620
88Lea-46
88PeoChiTI-32
88Top-758
88TopTif-758
89DonTra-29
89PeoChiTI-18
89ScoYouS2-39
89TopTra-127T
89TopTraT-127T
89UppDec-790
89WhiSoxC-28
90CedRapRDGB-10
90LasVegSP-131
90ProAAAF-19
90PubSti-403
90TriAllGP-AAA28
90UppDec-289
90VenSti-488
90WinSpiTI-25
91Cla/Bes-408
91ClaDraP-41
91Fle-548
91HigSchPLS-32
91JohCitCC-1
91JohCitCP-3980
91SanJosGC-12
91Sco-552
92Bow-331
92ClaFS7-366
92ProFS7-323
92RicBraF-3016
92RicBraRC-25
92RicBraS-447
92SavCarC-1
92SavCarF-666
92UppDecML-175
93ExcFS7-107
93NewOrlZF-982
93SprCarC-1
93SprCarF-1854
94FleUpd-191
94LasVegSF-877
94SavCarC-28
94SavCarF-511
95ColCho-345
95ColChoGS-345
95ColChoSE-167
95ColChoSEGS-167
95ColChoSESS-167
95ColChoSS-345
95Don-38
95DonPreP-38
95DonTopotO-346
95Fin-130
95FinRef-130
95Fla-423
95Fle-571
95Lea-42
95LeaLim-174
95PadCHP-14
95PadMot-18
95Pin-36
95PinArtP-36
95PinMusC-36
95Sco-113
95ScoGolR-113
95ScoPlaTS-113
95SP-111
95SPSil-111
95StaClu-370
95StaCluMOP-370
95StaCluSTWS-370
95StaCluVR-208
95Top-208
95TopCyb-118
95Ult-238
95UltGolM-238
95UppDec-133
95UppDecED-133
95UppDecEDG-133
95UppDecSE-265
95UppDecSEG-265
96Don-534
96DonPreP-534
96Fle-580
96FleTif-580
96FleUpd-U37
96FleUpdTC-U37
96Pac-182
96Sco-166
96StaCluVRMO-208
96Ult-289
96Ult-351
96UltGolM-289
96UltGolM-351

Williams, Edward
87PeoChiP-18

Williams, Eric
88GenCubP-1635
89ChaWheB-2
89ChaWheP-1756

Williams, Errick
95MarPhiTI-30

Williams, Flavio
88WatPirP-29
89AugPirP-505
89WelPirP-29
90SalBucS-24

Williams, Frank
84FleUpd-127
84GiaPos-30
84TopTra-128T
84TopTraT-128T
85Don-323
85Fle-624
85GiaMot-12
85GiaPos-30
85OPC-254
85Top-487
85TopMin-487
85TopSti-169
85TopTif-487
86Fle-554
86PhoFirP-24
86Top-341
86TopTif-341
87Fle-287
87FleGlo-287
87FleUpd-127
87FleUpdG-127
87RedKah-47
87Top-96
87TopTif-96
87TopTra-128T
87TopTraT-128T
88Don-512
88Fle-250
88FleGlo-250
88RedKah-47
88Sco-317
88ScoGlo-317
88StaLinRe-20
88Top-773
88TopTif-773
89Bow-100
89BowTif-100
89Don-478
89DonBasB-259
89Fle-174
89FleGlo-174
89FleUpd-34
89Sco-485
89TigMar-36
89Top-172
89TopTif-172
89TopTra-128T
89TopTraT-128T
89UppDec-449
90Don-327
90Fle-620
90FleCan-620
90OPC-599
90PubSti-486
90Sco-341
90Top-599
90TopTif-599
90UppDec-539
90VenSti-489

Williams, Fred
15SpoNewM-191
16ColE13-191
16SpoNewM-190
21E121So1-115
21E121So8-106
22AmeCarE-76
22W572-115
25Exh-48
28Exh-24
86StoPorP-26
87StoPorP-26
88ElPasDB-19
88TexLeaAGS-25
89JacExpB-18
89JacExpP-172
90WesPalBES-27

Williams, Gary
75WatRoyT-32
77JacSunT-22

Williams, George
63Top-324
64Top-388

Williams, George Erik
91SouOreAC-5
91SouOreAP-3851
92MadMusC-16
92MadMusF-1239
93HunStaF-2086
94ExcFS7-122
95EdmTraTI-26
96A'sMot-17
96ColCho-36
96ColChoGS-36
96ColChoSS-36
96Don-485
96DonPreP-485
96Fle-223
96FleTif-223
96LeaSigA-245
96LeaSigAG-246
96LeaSigAS-246
96Pin-385
96PinAfi-185
96PinAfiAP-185
96PinFoil-385
96Sco-258
96Sum-174
96SumAbo&B-174
96SumArtP-174
96SumFoi-174
96Ult-405
96UltGolM-405
96UppDec-162
97ColCho-409
97Don-171
97DonPreP-171
97DonPrePGold-171
97Sco-315
97ScoPreS-315
97ScoShoS-315

Williams, Gerald
87OneYanP-6
88PriWilYS-25
89PriWilCS-25
90Ft.LauYS-22
91AlbYanLD-23
91AlbYanP-1022
91Bow-161
91Cla/Bes-127
91Cla3-T99
91LinDriAA-23
91Ult-388
91UppDecFE-15F
92Bow-113
92ColCliF-366
92ColCliP-24
92ColCliS-122
92Don-697
92OPC-656
92ProFS7-115
92SkyAAAF-60
92Top-656
92TopGol-656
92TopGolW-656
92TopMic-656
92TriA AAS-122
93Bow-271
93ClaFS7-37
93ColCliF-1125
93ColCliP-20
93Don-49
93Fle-657
93Lea-130
93LeaGolR-R4
93OPC-386
93Pin-266
93PinRooTP-9
93Sco-298
93ScoBoyoS-11
93Sel-383
93StaClu-571
93StaCluFDI-571
93StaCluMOP-571
93StaCluY-26
93Top-654
93TopGol-654
93TopInaM-654
93TopMic-654
93Toy-36
93UppDec-360
93UppDecGold-360
94Don-390
94FleUpd-71
94LeaLimR-28
94Pac-442
94Pin-142
94PinArtP-142
94PinMusC-142
94Sco-590
94ScoGolR-590
94ScoRoo-RT81
94ScoRooGR-RT81
94Sel-402
94SpoRoo-87
94SpoRooAP-87
94StaCluT-190
94StaCluTFDI-190
94Top-383
94TopGol-383
94TopSpa-383
95Don-152
95DonPreP-152
95DonTopotO-131
95Fle-86
95Lea-226
95Sco-267
95ScoGolR-267
95ScoPlaTS-267
95Top-86
96Don-25
96DonPreP-25
96FleUpd-U69
96FleUpdTC-U69
97Fle-141
97FleTif-141
97Pac-131
97PacLigB-131
97PacSil-131
97Sco-457
97ScoHobR-457
97ScoResC-457
97ScoShoS-457
97ScoShoSAP-457
97StaClu-284
97StaCluMOP-284
97Top-287
97Ult-307
97UltGolME-307
97UltPlaME-307

Williams, Glenn
77AshTouT-28
94SigRooBS-P5
94SP-19
94SPDieC-19
94UppDecAHNIL-15
95AusFut-44
95EugEmeTI-28
95Exc-160
95UppDec-7
95UppDecED-7
95UppDecEDG-7
95UppDecML-34
95UppDecML-115
95UppDecSE-16
95UppDecSEG-16
96MacBraB-21
95UppDecMLFS-34
95UppDecMLFS-115

Williams, Greg
88St.CatBJP-2019
94ColRedC-23
94ColRedF-442
94StaClu-513
94Ult-441
95KinIndTI-28

Williams, Gus (August)
14B18B-37A
14B18B-37B

Williams, H.
86NasPirP-28

Williams, Harold
80AndBraT-25
81DurBulT-8
87SalBucP-15
88EasLeaAP-46
88HarSenP-861
89HarSenP-302
94HicCraC-25
94HicCraF-2186
94SouAtlLAF-SAL28
95Exc-33
95ExcLeaL-20
95PriWilCTI-12
95SPML-35
95Top-79
96BirBarB-9
96KanCouCTI-29

Williams, Harry
11PloCanE-66

Williams, Ike
51BerRos-C13

Williams, Jaime

84TucTorC-58
88OrlTwiB-10
Williams, James A.
87OldJudN-554
Williams, James Alfred
76LauIndC-3
76LauIndC-17
76LauIndC-29
76LauIndC-39
Williams, Jamie
82DayBeaAT-19
83DayBeaAT-16
86OscAstP-29
87VisOakP-1
90WicStaSGD-36
Williams, Jason
91MisStaB-50
93LSUTigM-14
94LSUTig-4
94LSUTigMP-16
Williams, Jay
88StoPorCLC-203
88StoPorP-744
89RocExpLC-29
90JacExpB-28
92HarSenF-NNO
94DurBulC-30
94DurBulTI-29
95DurBulTI-37
96GreBraB-4
96GreBraTI-TR
Williams, Jeff
81MiaOriT-19
84ChaO'sT-20
86RocRedWP-26
89ReaPhiP-675
89ReaPhiS-25
90WicStaSGD-37
91Cla/Bes-164
91FreKeyC-9
91FreKeyP-2364
92Bow-284
92ClaFS7-123
92HagSunF-2556
92HagSunS-271
92ProFS7-10
92SkyAA F-115
92UppDecML-318
93ClaGolF-60
93ColRedC-18
93ColRedF-598
93WatIndC-28
93WatIndF-3563
94CalCanF-791
94ColRedC-24
94ColRedF-443
Williams, Jeffrey Jay
89ReaPhiB-23
Williams, Jerrone
88WytCubP-2002
90PeoChiTI-18
91Cla/Bes-75
91WinSpiC-27
91WinSpiP-2844
92ChaKniS-173
92ProFS7-207
Williams, Jessie
87NegLeaPD-5
Williams, Jewell
96AppLeaAB-11
96BurIndB-29
Williams, Jim
70OPC-262
70Top-262
71OPC-262
71Top-262
75PhoGiaC-2
75PhoGiaCK-19
88CalLeaACLC-40
Williams, Jimmy
03BreE10-151
08RosComP-75
09PC7HHB-46
09T206-378
11SpoLifCW-369
76SeaRaiC-20
79SalLakCGT-22B
80ChaO'sP-24
80ChaO'sW-25
83OriPos-29
84OriTeal-29
87OriFreB-40
88AlaGolAA'TI-2
88VisOakCLC-163
89OrlTwiB-2
89OrlTwiP-1354
90CMC-562
90PorBeaC-10
90PorBeaP-179
90ProAAAF-249
91LinDriAAA-396
91PhoFirLD-396
91PhoFirP-68
93OrlCubF-2785
94VenLinU-209
95NorTidTI-30
96BufBisB-22
Williams, Jimy (James F.)
66Top-544
69TopTeaP-10
77SalLakCGC-1
78SprRedWK-13
84BluJayFS-34
85BluJayFS-34
86BluJayFS-34
87BluJayFS-36
87OPC-279
87Top-786
87TopTif-786
88BluJay5-12
88BluJayFS-34
88OPC-314
88Top-314
88TopTif-314
89BluJayFS-33
89OPC-381
89Top-594
89TopTif-594
90BraDubS-35
91BraSubS-38
92BraLykS-35
93BraLykS-36
94BraLykP-33
94BraLykS-32
Williams, Jody
87WatPirP-19
Williams, Joe
87UtiBluSP-21
90BoiHawP-3323
Williams, John
86BurExpP-27
Williams, Jon
86DavLipB-22
Williams, Juan
90PulBraB-25
90PulBraP-3111
91MacBraC-27
91MacBraP-880
92MacBraC-17
92MacBraF-283
93ClaFS7-269
93DurBulC-24
93DurBulF-502
93DurBulTI-17
94DurBulC-26
94DurBulF-344
94DurBulTI-30
94EliTwiC-26
94EliTwiF-3734
95BreBtaTI-37
95RicBraRC-28
96RicBraB-29
96RicBraRC-15
96RicBraUB-29
Williams, Keith
93EveGiaC-29
93EveGiaF-3785
94BowBes-B80
94BowBesR-B80
94ExcFirYPF-8
94ExcFS7-296
94SanJosGC-25
94SanJosGF-2831
95Bow-103
95Exc-297
95Top-658
96Exc-247
96PhoFirB-27
96Top-437
Williams, Ken
91MiaMirP-409
Williams, Kenneth Roy
21Exh-187
21Nei-52
22E120-105
22W572-116
22W573-137
22WilPatV-37
23W503-16
23W515-26
23WilChoV-173
25Exh-119
26Exh-119
26SpoComoA-47
27AmeCarE-48
27Exh-58
28StaPlaCE-71
92ConTSN-442
93ConTSN-940
Williams, Kenneth Royal
83AppFoxF-14
86BufBisP-24
87DonRoo-11
87FayGenP-25
87FleUpd-128
87FleUpdG-128
87HawIsIP-2
87SpoRoo2-41
88Don-334
88DonBasB-249
88Fle-412
88FleGlo-412
88FleMin-17
88FleSup-42
88GleFalTP-918
88OPC-92
88PanSti-65
88Sco-112
88ScoGlo-112
88ScoYouSI-6
88Spo-69
88StaLinWS-20
88Top-559
88TopSti-287
88TopTif-559
88WhiSoxC-30
89Don-337
89DonTra-17
89Sco-67
89TigMar-25
89TolMudHC-9
89TolMudHP-763
89Top-34
89TopTif-34
89TopTra-129T
89TopTraT-129T
89UppDec-506
89UppDec-714
90LonTigP-1270
90OPC-327
90PubSti-487
90TigCok-27
90Top-327
90TopTif-327
90UppDec-249
90VenSti-490
91BluJayFS-32
91Fle-190
91MiaMirC-13
91OPC-274
91Top-274
91TopDesS-274
91TopMic-274
91TopTif-274
91UppDec-89
92Sco-354
Williams, Kerman
85ElmPioT-24
86ElmPioRSP-29
Williams, Kevin
82OrlTwiT-1
83OrlTwiT-4
88ModA'sCLC-59
Williams, Landon
90PenPilS-24
Williams, Lanny
91ButCopKSP-11
92GasRanC-20
92GasRanF-2257
93ChaRanC-24
93ChaRanF-1945
Williams, Lefty (Claude)
16ColE13-76A
16ColE13-190A
16ColE13-190B
17HolBreD-117
19W514-35
75WhiSox1T-27
88PacEigMO-11
88PacEigMO-44
88PacEigMO-45
88PacEigMO-49
88PacEigMO-60
88PacEigMO-108
92Man191BSR-25
94ConTSN-1041
94ConTSNB-1041
Williams, Leroy
90KisDodD-28
93BakDodCLC-26
93YakBeaC-25
93YakBeaF-3892
Williams, Mark
92JohCitCF-3120
93GleFalRC-28
93GleFalRF-4006
93StaCluM-11
94NewJerCC-28
94NewJerCF-3421
Williams, Mark Westley
77SanJosMC-6
86BirBarTI-21
Williams, Marvin
86NegLeaF-87
Williams, Matt
92ClaDraP-73
92FroRowDP-53
92WatIndC-10
92WatIndF-3235
93ClaGolF-147
93KinIndC-26
93KinIndF-2249
93KinIndTI-27
94KinIndF-2644
96LynHilB-26
Williams, Matt (Matthew Derrick)
86EveGiaC-3
87DonRoo-45
87FleUpd-129
87FleUpdG-129
87GiaMot-22
87PhoFirP-2
87PocGiaTB-12
87SpoRool-25
87TopTra-129T
87TopTraT-129T
88ClaBlu-246
88Don-628
88Fle-101
88FleGlo-101
88PhoFirC-18
88PhoFirP-56
88Sco-118
88ScoGlo-118
88ScoYouSI-18
88StaLinG-20
88Top-372
88TopTif-372
89Don-594
89Fle-346
89FleGlo-346
89GiaMot-12
89PanSti-218
89PhoFirC-18
89PhoFirP-1485
89Sco-612
89Top-628
89TopTif-628
89TriA AAC-35
89TriAAP-AAA51
89UppDec-247
90Bow-238
90BowTif-238
90ClaBlu-73
90ClaUpd-T11
90Don-348
90DonBesN-61
90DonGraS-1
90Fle-75
90FleCan-75
90GiaMot-9
90GiaSmo-21
90Lea-94
90MotMatW-1
90MotMatW-2
90MotMatW-3
90MotMatW-4
90OPC-41
90PanSti-366
90Sco-503
90ScoMcD-6
90Spo-70
90StaMatW-1
90StaMatW-2
90StaMatW-3
90StaMatW-4
90StaMatW-5
90StaMatW-6
90StaMatW-7
90StaMatW-8
90StaMatW-9
90StaMatW-10
90StaMatW-11
90Top-41
90TopBig-96
90TopMag-35
90TopSti-88
90TopTif-41
90TriAAAC-35
90UppDec-577
90UppDecS-2
90USPlaCA-8H
90Woo-30
91Bow-378
91Bow-618
91CadEIID-61
91Cla1-T8
91Cla3-T95
91ClaGam-158
91Col-30
91Don-18
91Don-685
91DonEli-8
91DonGraS-8
91DonSupD-18
91Fle-276
91FleAll-3
91GiaActIS-3
91GiaMot-9
91GiaPacGaE-11
91GiaSFE-16
91KinDis-16
91Lea-93
91MajLeaCP-65
91OPC-190
91OPC-399
91PanCanT1-17
91PanFreS-69
91PanSti-76
91RedFolS-100
91Sco-189
91Sco-667
91Sco-689
91Sco100S-77
91SevCoi-NC15
91StaClu-295
91StaPinB-53
91Stu-259
91SunSee-24
91Top-190
91Top-399
91TopCraJ2-9
91TopDesS-190
91TopDesS-399
91TopMic-190
91TopMic-399
91TopSta-35
91TopTif-190
91TopTif-399
91TopTriH-N11
91Ult-331
91UppDec-79
91UppDec-157
91UppDecSS-SS13
92Bow-175
92Bow-579
92Cla2-T31
92ClaGam-45
92Don-135
92DonCraJ2-11
92Fle-650
92FleLumC-L6
92Fre-8
92GiaMot-9
92GiaPacGaE-35
92Hig5-130
92Hig5S-30
92Lea-373
92OPC-445
92OPCPre-144
92PanSti-214
92Pin-28
92PinTeaP-6
92Sco-230
92Sco100S-95
92ScoCokD-23
92ScoImpP-62
92ScoProP-7
92SpoIllFK1-64

92SpollIFK1-327
92StaClu-582
92Stu-120
92Top-445
92TopGol-445
92TopGolW-445
92TopKid-60
92TopMic-445
92TriPla-4
92Ult-296
92UltAwaW-13
92UppDec-154
92UppDecHRH-HR5
93Bow-56
93ColAllG-8
93DiaMar-117
93Don-182
93Fin-25
93FinRef-25
93Fla-148
93Fle-540
93FunPac-104
93GiaMot-3
93GiaPos-33
93Lea-158
93OPC-348
93PacSpa-278
93PanSti-239
93Pin-67
93PinHomRC-22
93Sco-46
93Sel-95
93SP-117
93SPPlaP-PP20
93StaClu-287
93StaCluFDI-287
93StaCluG-3
93StaCluMOP-287
93Stu-66
93Top-225
93TopGol-225
93TopInaM-225
93TopMic-225
93TriPla-171
93Ult-490
93UppDec-143
93UppDec-471
93UppDec-476
93UppDecGold-143
93UppDecGold-471
93UppDecGold-476
93UppDecHRH-HR21
94Bow-79
94BowBes-R8
94BowBes-X93
94BowBesR-R8
94BowBesR-X93
94ChuHomS-10
94ChuHomSG-10
94ColC-299
94ColChoGS-299
94ColChoSS-299
94Don-370
94DonDom-A4
94DonSpeE-370
94ExtBas-395
94ExtBasGB-29
94Fin-214
94FinJum-214
94FinRef-214
94Fla-448
94FlaHotG-10
94FlaInfP-10
94Fle-704
94FleLumC-10
94FlePro-3
94FUnPac-90
94FUnPac-188
94GiaAMC-24
94GiaMot-7
94GiaTeal-5
94GiaTeal-6
94GiaTeal-9
94GiaUSPC-1C
94GiaUSPC-7D
94Lea-334
94LeaCleC-10
94LeaL-160
94LeaLimGA-6
94LeaMVPC-N14
94LeaMVPCG-N14
94OPC-80
94Pac-559
94PacGolP-13
94PanSti-268
94Pin-298
94PinArtP-298
94PinMusC-298
94PinRunC-RC39
94PinTeaP-3
94PinTheN-16
94RedFolMI-9
94Sco-94
94ScoCyc-TC20
94ScoDreT-6
94ScoGolR-94
94ScoGolS-10
94Sel-269
94SP-95
94SPDieC-95
94Spo-139
94Spo-187
94SpoFanA-AS3
94SpoRooGGG-GG2
94StaClu-268
94StaClu-419
94StaClu-717
94StaCluFDI-268
94StaCluFDI-419
94StaCluFDI-717
94StaCluGR-268
94StaCluGR-419
94StaCluGR-717
94StaCluMO-8
94StaCluMOP-268
94StaCluMOP-419
94StaCluMOP-717
94StaCluMOP-ST14
94StaCluST-ST14
94StaCluT-22
94StaCluTFDI-22
94Stu-89
94Top-386
94Top-550
94TopBlaG-44
94TopGol-386
94TopGol-550
94TopPre-225
94TopSpa-386
94TopSpa-550
94TopSupS-45
94TopTraFI-3
94TriPla-110
94TriPlaBS-10
94Ult-296
94UltAllS-15
94UltAwaW-13
94UltHomRK-9
94UltRBIK-11
94UppDec-36
94UppDec-490
94UppDecAJ-6
94UppDecAJG-6
94UppDecED-36
94UppDecED-490
94UppDecMLS-MM20
94UppDecMLSED-MM20
94USPlaCA-8C
95Baz-64
95BazRedH-RH14
95Bow-278
95BowBes-R51
95BowBes-X13
95BowBesR-R51
95BowBesR-X13
95ClaPhoC-48
95ColCho-71
95ColChoCtG-CG20
95ColChoCtG-CG20B
95ColChoCtG-CG20C
95ColChoCtGE-20
95ColChoCtGG-CG20
95ColChoCtGG-CG20B
95ColChoCtGG-CG20C
95ColChoCtGGE-20
95ColChoGS-71
95ColChoSE-30
95ColChoSE-108
95ColChoSE-137
95ColChoSE-256
95ColChoSEGS-30
95ColChoSEGS-108
95ColChoSEGS-137
95ColChoSEGS-256
95ColChoSESS-30
95ColChoSESS-108
95ColChoSESS-137
95ColChoSESS-256
95ColChoSS-71
95DenHol-28
95Don-365
95DonAll-NL5
95DonBomS-1
95DonDiaK-DK12
95DonDom-5
95DonEli-53
95DonLonBL-4
95DonPreP-365
95DonTopotO-360
95Emb-134
95EmbGolI-134
95Emo-197
95EmoMas-10
95EmoN-12
95Fin-45
95FinPowK-PK15
95FinRef-45
95Fla-213
95FlaHotG-12
95FlaHotN-10
95FlaInfP-10
95Fle-593
95FleAllF-5
95FleAllS-4
95FleLeaL-7
95FleLumC-10
95FleTeaL-28
95FleUpdDT-10
95FleUpdH-20
95FleUpdSL-10
95GiaMot-7
95KinDis-9
95Kra-30
95Lea-28
95LeaCor-6
95LeaGolS-14
95LeaGreG-15
95LeaLim-144
95LeaLimG-17
95LeaLimL-11
95LeaSli-7A
95LeaSli-7B
95LeaStaS-9
95NatPac-2
95Pac-387
95PacGolP-20
95PacPri-123
95PanSti-54
95PanSti-116
95Pin-61
95Pin-294
95PinArtP-61
95PinArtP-294
95PinFan-17
95PinGatA-GA15
95PinMusC-61
95PinMusC-294
95PinPin-11
95PinPinR-11
95PinRedH-RH11
95PinTeaP-TP6
95PinWhiH-WH11
95Pos-9
95PosCan-14
95RedFol-33
95Sco-5
95Sco-552
95ScoDouGC-GC10
95ScoDreT-DG4
95ScoGolR-5
95ScoGolR-552
95ScoHaloG-HG2
95ScoPlaTS-5
95ScoPlaTS-552
95ScoRul-SR7
95ScoRulJ-SR7
95ScoSam-5
95Sel-112
95SelArtP-112
95SelBigS-BS11
95SelCer-67
95SelCerGT-7
95SelCerMG-67
95SP-113
95SPCha-95
95SPChaDC-95
95Spo-41
95SpoArtP-41
95SpoDet-DE2
95SpoDouT-4
95SpoHamT-HT11
95SpoPro-PM6
95SpoSam-DE2
95SPPlaP-PP8
95SPSil-113
95SPSpeF-48
95StaClu-191
95StaClu-315
95StaCluFDI-191
95StaCluMO-45
95StaCluMOP-191
95StaCluMOP-315
95StaCluMOP-PZ12
95StaCluMOP-RL11
95StaCluMOP-SS18
95StaCluPZ-PZ12
95StaCluRL-RL11
95StaCluSS-SS18
95StaCluSTWS-191
95StaCluSTWS-315
95StaCluVR-99
95Stu-24
95StuGolS-24
95StuPlaS-24
95Sum-13
95Sum-180
95Sum-200
95SumBigB-BB7
95SumNthD-13
95SumNthD-180
95SumNthD-200
95Top-10
95Top-386
95TopCyb-8
95TopFin-5
95TopLeaL-LL7
95TopLeaL-LL36
95TopTra-10T
95TopTra-158T
95TopTraPB-10
95UC3-70
95UC3-127
95UC3ArtP-70
95UC3ArtP-127
95UC3CycS-CS7
95UC3InM-IM6
95UllHomRK-12
95Ult-247
95UltAllS-20
95UltAllSGM-20
95UltAwaW-13
95UltAwaWGM-13
95UltGolM-247
95UltHomRK-6
95UltHomRKGM-6
95UltPowP-6
95UltPowPGM-6
95UltRBIK-7
95UltRBIKGM-7
95UppDec-85
95UppDec-106
95UppDecED-85
95UppDecED-106
95UppDecEDG-85
95UppDecEDG-106
95UppDecPAW-H9
95UppDecPAWE-H9
95UppDecPLL-R9
95UppDecPLL-R19
95UppDecPLLE-R9
95UppDecPLLE-R19
95UppDecSE-205
95UppDecSEG-205
95USPlaCMLA-1C
95Zen-74
95ZenAllS-8
95ZenZ-4
96Baz-25
96Bow-36
96BowBes-73
96BowBesAR-73
96BowBesR-73
96Cir-196
96CirAcc-30
96CirAcc-P30
96CirBos-50
96CirRav-196
96ColCho-720
96ColChoCtG-CG24
96ColChoCtG-CG24B
96ColChoCtG-CG24C
96ColChoCtGE-CR24
96ColChoCtGG-CG24
96ColChoCtGG-CG24B
96ColChoCtGG-CG24C
96ColChoCtGGE-CR24
96ColChoGS-720
96ColChoSS-720
96ColChoYMtP-45
96ColChoYMtP-45A
96ColChoYMtPGS-45
96ColChoYMtPGS-45A
96Don-365
96DonPreP-365
96DonSho-7
96EmoLegoB-12
96EmoN-10
96EmoXL-297
96EmoXLD-10
96Fin-B342
96Fin-G266
96Fin-S14
96FinBro-1
96FinRef-B342
96FinRef-G266
96FinRef-S14
96Fla-395
96FlaDiaC-12
96FlaHotG-10
96FlaPow-10
96Fle-600
96FleChe-10
96FleLumC-12
96FleRoaW-10
96FleTif-600
96FleUpd-U245
96FleUpdH-20
96FleUpdSL-10
96FleUpdSS-10
96FleUpdTC-U245
96FleZon-12
96GiaMot-4
96Kin-17
96Lea-52
96LeaLim-20
96LeaLimG-20
96LeaPre-18
96LeaPreP-18
96LeaPrePB-52
96LeaPrePG-52
96LeaPrePS-52
96LeaPreSG-26
96LeaPreSte-26
96LeaSig-36
96LeaSigEA-214
96LeaSigEACM-31
96LeaSigPPG-36
96LeaSigPPP-36
96MetUni-247
96MetUniHM-10
96MetUniML-12
96MetUniP-247
96MetUniT-10
96Pac-203
96PacPri-P68
96PacPriG-P68
96PanSti-105
96Pin-97
96Pin-160
96Pin-274
96PinAfi-66
96PinAfiAP-66
96PinAfiFPP-66
96PinAfiMN-9
96PinArtP-36
96PinArtP-87
96PinArtP-174
96PinEssotG-4
96PinFirR-8
96PinFoil-274
96PinPow-4
96PinSlu-8
96PinSta-36
96PinSta-87
96PinSta-174
96PinTeaP-3
96ProSta-51
96Sco-65
96Sco-360
96ScoAll-6
96ScoBigB-7
96ScoDiaA-26
96ScoDreT-4
96ScoDugC-A56
96ScoDugC-B85
96ScoDugCAP-A56
96ScoDugCAP-B85
96ScoGolS-8
96ScoNumG-14
96ScoPowP-5

96ScoTitT-5
96Sel-15
96SelArtP-15
96SelCer-87
96SelCerAP-87
96SelCerCB-87
96SelCerCR-87
96SelCerIP-23
96SelCerMB-87
96SelCerMG-87
96SelCerMR-87
96SelCerSF-17
96SelClaTF-13
96SelEnF-20
96SelTeaN-18
96SP-165
96Spo-56
96Spo-116
96SpoArtP-56
96SpoArtP-116
96SpoDouT-3
96SpoHitP-8
96SpoPowS-20
96SpoPro-14
96SPPreF-7
96SPSpeFX-37
96SPSpeFXDC-37
96SPx-52
96SPxGol-52
96StaClu-45
96StaCluEPB-45
96StaCluEPG-45
96StaCluEPS-45
96StaCluMOP-45
96StaCluVRMO-99
96Stu-71
96StuPrePB-71
96StuPrePG-71
96StuPrePS-71
96Sum-2
96Sum-161
96SumAbo&B-2
96SumAbo&B-161
96SumArtP-2
96SumArtP-161
96SumFoi-2
96SumFoi-161
96SumHitI-16
96SumPos-3
96TeaOut-89
96TeaOut-C98
96Top-12
96Top-360
96TopChr-12
96TopChr-145
96TopChrR-12
96TopChrR-145
96TopChrWC-WC15
96TopChrWCR-WC15
96TopGal-173
96TopGalPPI-173
96TopLas-96
96TopLasPC-8
96TopPowB-12
96TopPro-NL20
96TopRoaW-RW20
96TopWreC-WC15
96Ult-300
96Ult-592
96UltChe-A10
96UltCheGM-A10
96UltDiaP-12
96UltDiaPGM-12
96UltGolM-300
96UltGolM-592
96UltHitM-10
96UltHitMGM-10
96UltHomRKGM-12
96UltHomRKR-12
96UltPowP-12
96UltPowPGM-12
96UltPriL-14
96UltPriLGM-14
96UltRaw-10
96UltRawGM-10
96UltThu-20
96UltThuGM-20
96UppDec-455
96UppDecA-18
96UppDecDD-DD34
96UppDecDDG-DD34
96UppDecDDS-DD34
96UppDecG-GF8
96UppDecPD-PD20
96UppDecPHE-H39
96UppDecPRE-R39
96UppDecPRE-R49
96UppDecPreH-H39
96UppDecPreR-R39
96UppDecPreR-R49
96UppDecRunP-RP20
96Zen-77
96Zen-145
96ZenArtP-77
96ZenArtP-145
96ZenDiaC-13
96ZenDiaCP-13
96ZenMoz-4
96ZenZ-15
97Bow-66
97BowBes-6
97BowBesAR-6
97BowBesMI-MI9
97BowBesMIAR-MI9
97BowBesMIARI-MI9
97BowBesMII-MI9
97BowBesMIR-MI9
97BowBesMIRI-MI9
97BowBesR-6
97BowChr-47
97BowChrI-47
97BowChrIR-47
97BowChrR-47
97BowInt-66
97Cir-218
97CirIco-12
97CirRav-218
97ColCho-90
97ColChoCtG-13A
97ColChoCtG-13B
97ColChoCtG-13C
97ColChoCtGIW-CG13
97ColChoTBS-20
97ColChoTBSWH-20
97Don-19
97Don-271
97DonDom-15
97DonEli-137
97DonEliGS-137
97DonLim-14
97DonLim-99
97DonLim-193
97DonLimFotG-49
97DonLimLE-14
97DonLimLE-99
97DonLimLE-193
97DonPowA-23
97DonPowADC-23
97DonPre-7
97DonPreCttC-7
97DonPreP-19
97DonPreP-271
97DonPrePGold-19
97DonPrePGold-271
97DonPrePM-10
97DonRocL-9
97DonTea-84
97DonTeaSPE-84
97Fin-253
97Fin-308
97Fin-336
97FinEmb-308
97FinEmb-336
97FinEmbR-308
97FinEmbR-336
97FinRef-253
97FinRef-308
97FinRef-336
97FlaSho-A99
97FlaSho-B99
97FlaSho-C99
97FlaShoDC-20
97FlaShoLC-99
97FlaShoLC-B99
97FlaShoLC-C99
97FlaShoLCM-A99
97FlaShoLCM-B99
97FlaShoLCM-C99
97Fle-489
97Fle-655
97FleBleB-10
97FleDecoE-12
97FleDecoERT-12
97FleTif-489
97FleTif-655
97FleZon-20
97Lea-20
97Lea-212
97Lea-389
97LeaFraM-20
97LeaFraM-212
97LeaFraM-389
97LeaFraMDC-20
97LeaFraMDC-212
97LeaFraMDC-389
97LeaLeaotN-10
97MetUni-89
97MetUniMF-10
97MetUniML-12
97NewPin-4
97NewPinAP-4
97NewPinMC-4
97NewPinPP-4
97Pac-450
97PacLigB-450
97PacPri-150
97PacPriLB-150
97PacPriP-150
97PacSil-450
97Pin-197
97PinArtP-197
97PinCer-3
97PinCerMBlu-3
97PinCerMG-3
97PinCerMR-3
97PinCerR-3
97PinIns-111
97PinInsCE-111
97PinInsDE-111
97PinMusC-197
97PinTotCPB-3
97PinTotCPG-3
97PinTotCPR-3
97PinX-P-3
97PinX-PMoS-3
97PinX-PSfF-15
97PinX-PSfFU-15
97Sco-238
97Sco-361
97ScoHeaotO-14
97ScoHobR-361
97ScoIndU-1
97ScoIndUTC-1
97ScoPreS-238
97ScoResC-361
97ScoShoS-238
97ScoShoS-361
97ScoShoSAP-238
97ScoShoSAP-361
97ScoStaaD-20
97Sel-88
97SelArtP-88
97SelRegG-88
97SkyE-X-19
97SkyE-XC-19
97SkyE-XEC-19
97SP-61
97SpoIll-142
97SpoIllEE-142
97SPSpeF-37
97StaClu-203
97StaCluMat-203
97StaCluMOP-203
97Stu-101
97StuPrePG-101
97StuPrePS-101
97Top-385
97TopChr-132
97TopChrR-132
97TopGal-49
97TopGalPPI-49
97TopSta-60
97TopStaAM-60
97Ult-300
97Ult-364
97UltDiaP-12
97UltDouT-20
97UltFieC-18
97UltGolME-300
97UltGolME-364
97UltHRK-12
97UltPlaME-300
97UltPlaME-364
97UltPowP-A12
97UltTop3-28
97UltTop3GM-28
97UppDec-145
97UppDec-530
97UppDecAG-AG9
97UppDecPP-PP9
97UppDecPPJ-PP9
97UppDecU-19

Williams, Matt E.
82KnoBluJT-8
83SyrChiT-13
84SyrChiT-11
85SyrChiT-12
86OklCit8P-26
89SalSpuCLC-140
89SalSpuP-1825
93RanKee-381

Williams, Matthew
87IdaFalBP-19
88IdaFalBP-1842

Williams, Mel
83ReaPhiT-22

Williams, Michael
86DavLipB-23

Williams, Micheal
93StaCluMO-44

Williams, Mike
75WatRoyT-33
76WatRoyT-33
77LodDodT-25
79AlbDukT-3
80PhoGiaVNB-1
80VenLeaS-76
81PhoGiaVNB-8
87PocGiaTB-19
89PacSenL-16

Williams, Mike (Michael Darren)
90BatCliP-3067
91Cla/Bes-103
91ClePhiC-12
91ClePhiP-1623
92Bow-152
92DonRoo-126
92ReaPhiS-548
92ScrRedBF-2448
92SkyAA F-240
93Bow-568
93ClaFS7-38
93FleMajLP-B11
93ScrRedBF-2545
93ScrRedBTI-28
93StaClu-539
93StaCluFDI-539
93StaCluMOP-539
93Top-99
93TopGol-99
93TopInaM-99
93TopMic-99
93Ult-94
94PhiMed-36
94PhiMel-25
94PhiUSPC-10H
94StaCluT-230
94StaCluTFDI-230
94Top-447
94TopGol-447
94TopSpa-447
95Top-351
96Fle-513
96FleTif-513
96LeaSigEA-215
96PhiTeal-35
97PacPriGotD-GD187

Williams, Mitch
86DonRoo-19
86FleUpd-127
86RanPer-28
86SpoRoo-20
86TopTra-125T
86TopTraT-125T
87Don-347
87Fle-142
87FleGlo-142
87RanMot-17
87RanSmo-7
87SpoTeaP-1
87Top-291
87TopTif-291
87ToyRoo-32
88Don-161
88DonBasB-279
88Fle-482
88FleGlo-482
88FleRecS-43
88OPC-26
88RanMot-17
88RanSmo-19
88Sco-339
88ScoGlo-339
88ScoYouS2-31
88StaLinRa-19
88Top-26
88TopTif-26
89Bow-283
89BowTif-283
89CubMar-28
89Don-225
89DonBasB-60
89DonTra-38
89Fle-536
89FleGlo-536
89FleUpd-81
89OPC-377
89Sco-301
89ScoRoo-32T
89ScoYouSI-27
89Spo-151
89Top-411
89TopSti-247
89TopTif-411
89TopTra-130T
89TopTraT-130T
89UppDec-95
89UppDec-778
90Bow-25
90BowTif-25
90ClaBlu-23
90CubMar-24
90Don-275
90DonBesN-75
90Fle-48
90Fle-631
90FleAwaW-43
90FleBasA-43
90FleBasM-43
90FleCan-48
90FleCan-631
90Lea-156
90MLBBasB-48
90OPC-520
90PanSti-232
90PubSti-210
90RedFolSB-103
90Sco-262
90Sco-695
90Sco100S-93
90Spo-196
90Top-520
90TopBig-109
90TopDou-71
90TopGloS-47
90TopMinL-52
90TopSti-48
90TopStiB-33
90TopTif-520
90TopTVA-65
90TopTVCu-17
90UppDec-174
90VenSti-491
91Don-312
91Fle-439
91FleUpd-110
91Lea-420
91OPC-335
91RedFolS-101
91Sco-220
91ScoRoo-27T
91StaClu-261
91Top-335
91TopDesS-335
91TopMic-335
91TopTif-335
91TopTra-127T
91TopTraT-127T
91Ult-71
91UltUpd-101
91UppDec-173
91UppDec-769
92Bow-247
92Don-353
92Fle-547
92Hig5-80
92Lea-301
92OPC-633
92PhiMed-32
92Pin-406
92Sco-356
92Sco-892
92StaClu-499
92Stu-80
92Top-633
92TopGol-633
92TopGolW-633
92TopKid-20
92TopMic-633

92TriPla-220
92Ult-549
92UppDec-410
92UppDecTMH-54
93Bow-328
93CubRol-4
93Don-40
93Fin-49
93FinRef-49
93Fla-108
93Fle-498
93FunPac-147
93Lea-114
93OPC-226
93PacSpa-241
93PhiMed-35
93Pin-565
93RanKee-382
93Sco-367
93Sel-79
93SelSam-79
93SP-180
93StaClu-180
93StaCluFDI-180
93StaCluMOP-180
93StaCluP-29
93Stu-82
93Top-235
93TopGol-235
93TopInaM-235
93TopMic-235
93TriPla-125
93Ult-448
93UppDec-113
93UppDecGold-113
94AstMot-2
94Bow-446
94ColC-599
94ColChoGS-599
94ColChoSS-599
94Don-319
94Fin-242
94FinRef-242
94Fla-176
94Fle-604
94Lea-431
94OPC-99
94Pac-490
94PanSti-232
94Pin-218
94PinArtP-218
94PinMusC-218
94Sco-217
94ScoGolR-217
94StaClu-575
94StaCluFDI-575
94StaCluGR-575
94StaCluMOP-575
94Top-114
94TopGol-114
94TopSpa-114
94TriPla-30
94Ult-512
94UltFir-10
94UppDec-499
94UppDecED-499
95AngMot-16
95FleUpd-69
95Lea-310
95UppDecSE-130
95UppDecSEG-130

Williams, Norman
93BurIndC-27
93BurIndF-3315
94ButCopKSP-2

Williams, Otto
11MecDFT-50
11SpoLifCW-370

Williams, Paul
86ElmPioRSP-30
88WinHavRSS-27
90CarLeaA-11
90LynRedSTI-13
91LinDriAA-647
91WilBilLD-647
91WilBilP-303
92HagSunS-272

Williams, Quinn
86BenPhiC-131

Williams, Ray
88WauTimGS-13
90SanBerSB-22
90SanBerSCLC-112
92GulCoaRSP-25
94HudValRF-3396
94HudValRC-25

Williams, Ray R.
78St.PetCT-26
79ArkTraT-3
80ArkTraT-20

Williams, Reggie
83VerBeaDT-25
86AlbDukP-28
86DodPol-51
86DodUniOP-24
86DonRoo-5
86FleUpd-128
86SpoRoo-19
87DodMot-15
87DodPol-9
87Don-341
87Fle-460
87FleGlo-460
87FleHotS-42
87FleMin-114
87FleStiC-124
87SpoTeaP-14
87Top-232
87TopTif-232
88ColSprSSC-23
88ColSprSSP-1524
89BufBisC-23
89BufBisP-1685
89CliGiaP-893
90DodTar-862
90QuaCitAGS-26
91MidAngOHP-31
92EdmTraF-3552
92EdmTraS-172
93Don-253
93Top-543
93TopGol-543
93TopInaM-543
93TopMic-543
93VanCanF-2612
94AlbDukF-857
95FleUpd-178
95LinVen-3
96Sco-252

Williams, Rick
73CedRapAT-20
78ChaChaT-20
78MemChiBC-10
79MemChiT-13
79Top-437
80MemChiT-26
80Top-69
80TucTorT-4
81TolMudHT-10
82TolMudHT-9

Williams, Ricky
96PieBolWB-28
96PieBolWB-30

Williams, Rob
85UtiBluST-8
87WesPalBEP-657

Williams, Rodney
92LetMouSP-15

Williams, Roger
87PitCubP-21
88IowCubC-11
88IowCubP-545
89IowCubP-1691

Williams, Scott
85NewOriT-1
92KinMetF-1532

Williams, Scottie
92KinMetC-16

Williams, Shad
92MidLeaATI-53
92QuaCitRBC-7
92QuaCitRBF-811
93MidAngF-323
94MidAngF-2440
94MidAngOHP-32
96Bow-282
96VanCanB-29
97MidAngOHP-33
97PacPriGotD-GD8
97Ult-33
97UltGolME-33
97UltPlaME-33

Williams, Slim
88VisOakP-96

Williams, Smokey (Joseph)
74LauOldTBS-1
83ConMar-57
86NegLeaF-86
88ConNegA-12
88NegLeaD-8
90NegLeaS-27
93TedWil-114

Williams, Spin (Don)
60Top-414
77PadSchC-64
78PadFamF-37
84PriWilPT-20
85NasPirT-26
86NasPirP-27
87HarSenP-15
88HarSenP-839
89SalBucS-NNO
90EasLeaAP-EL28
90HarSenP-1209
90HarSenS-24
91CarMudP-1102
91LinDriAA-125
92BufBisBS-15
92BufBisF-340
93CarMudF-2072
94PirQui-28

Williams, Stan
59DodMor-6
59Top-53
59TopVen-53
60DodBelB-16
60DodJayP-15
60DodTeal-19
60DodUniO-20
60Lea-109
60Top-278
61DodBelB-40
61DodJayP-11
61DodUniO-22
61Pos-162
61Top-45
61Top-190
62DodBelB-40
62DodJayP-11
62Jel-115
62Pos-115
62PosCan-115
62Top-60
62Top-515
62TopVen-60
63Jel-122
63Pos-122
63Top-42
64ChatheY-25
64Top-505
65Top-404
68OPC-54
68Top-54
68TopVen-54
69OPC-118
69Top-118
69TopFou-22
69TopSta-170
70OPC-353
70Top-353
71MLBOffS-478
71OPC-638
71Top-638
72OPC-9
72Top-9
79ColCliT-6
84RedEnq-31
89DodSmoG-68
90DodTar-863
90RedKah-27
91RedKah-NNO
92YanWIZ6-137

Williams, Steve
75ShrCapT-23
86ClePhiP-25
87ReaPhiP-24
89EriOriS-26
90WauTimB-2
90WauTimP-2115
90WauTimS-26
91FreKeyC-10

Williams, Ted (Theodore Samuel)
39ExhSal-64A
39ExhSal-64B
39GouPreR303A-47
39PlaBal-92
39WorWidGTP-47
39WorWidGV-25
40PlaBal-27
41DouPlaR-57
41DouPlaR-81
41PlaBal-14
42RedSoxTI-25
43MPR302-1-24
46RedSoxTI-24
46SpoExcW-9-1B
47HomBon-48
47PM1StaP1-217
47PM1StaP1-218
47PM1StaP1-219
47PM1StaP1-220
47PM1StaP1-221
47PM1StaP1-222
47StaPinP2-41
48BluTin-44
48RedSoxTI-25
48SweSpoT-16
49Lea-76
49MPR302-2-101
50AmeNut&CCP-22
50Bow-98
51Bow-165
51R42SmaS-113
51Whe-6
52BerRos-69
52RedMan-AL23
52StaCalL-71B
52StaCalL-71C
52StaCalS-85A
52Whe-30A
52Whe-30B
53ExhCan-30
54Bow-66A
54Top-1
54Top-250
54Wil-20
55Top-2
55TopDouH-69
56Top-5
56TopHocF-A5
56TopHocF-B7
56TopPin-26
57Top-1
58HarSta-5
58RedSoxJP-12
58Top-1
58Top-321
58Top-485
59FleWil-1
59FleWil-2
59FleWil-3
59FleWil-4
59FleWil-5
59FleWil-6
59FleWil-7
59FleWil-8
59FleWil-9
59FleWil-10
59FleWil-11
59FleWil-12
59FleWil-13
59FleWil-14
59FleWil-15
59FleWil-16
59FleWil-17
59FleWil-18
59FleWil-19
59FleWil-20
59FleWil-21
59FleWil-22
59FleWil-23
59FleWil-24
59FleWil-25
59FleWil-26
59FleWil-27
59FleWil-28
59FleWil-29
59FleWil-30
59FleWil-31
59FleWil-32
59FleWil-33
59FleWil-34
59FleWil-35
59FleWil-36
59FleWil-37
59FleWil-38
59FleWil-39
59FleWil-40
59FleWil-41
59FleWil-42
59FleWil-43
59FleWil-44
59FleWil-45
59FleWil-46
59FleWil-47
59FleWil-48
59FleWil-49
59FleWil-50
59FleWil-51
59FleWil-52
59FleWil-53
59FleWil-54
59FleWil-55
59FleWil-56
59FleWil-57
59FleWil-58
59FleWil-59
59FleWil-60
59FleWil-61
59FleWil-62
59FleWil-63
59FleWil-64
59FleWil-65
59FleWil-66
59FleWil-67
59FleWil-68
59FleWil-69
59FleWil-70
59FleWil-71
59FleWil-72
59FleWil-73
59FleWil-74
59FleWil-75
59FleWil-76
59FleWil-77
59FleWil-78
59FleWil-79
59FleWil-80
59RedSoxJP-12
60Fle-72
60KeyChal-49
60NuHi-39
60NuHi-52
60RawGloT-35
60RedSoxJP-12
61Fle-152
61NuSco-439
61NuSco-452
63BasMagM-85
67TopVen-148
69SenTeal-16
69SenTeal8-20
69Top-539
69Top-650
70OPC-211
70Top-211
71OPC-380
71Top-380
72OPC-510
72Top-510
73HalofFPP-19
74LauAllG-46
74NewYorNTDiS-3
74NewYorNTDiS-12
75McCCob-16
75ShaPiz-10
75SpoHobBG-7
75SSP42-19
75SSP42-28
75TCMAllG-35
76GalBasGHoF-30
76LauDiaJ-27
76OPC-347
76RowExh-16
76ShaPiz-103
76TayBow4-21
76Top-347
77BobParHoF-52
77GalGloG-10
77GalGloG-230
77ShaPiz-23
77Spo-1303
78HalHalR-10
78SSP270-177
78TCM60I-260
79BasGre-75
79TCM50-10
80Lau300-6
80Lau300-20
80MarExhH-31
80PacLeg-61
80PerHaloFP-104
80SSPHOF-104
81RedSoxBG2S-65
81SanDieSC-8
81SanDieSC-9
81SpoHaloF-9
81TCM60I-444

82BasCarN-2
82DiaCla-21
82FleSta-237
82GSGalAG-9
83DonHOFH-9
83MLBPin-18
83TCMPla1942-6
83TigAlKS-68
83YanYealT-4
84DonCha-14
84OCoandSI-1
84OCoandSI-80
84OCoandSI-141
84SpoDesPW-20
85CirK-9
85DalNatCC-2
85DonHOFS-2
85Woo-38
86BigLeaC-8
86RedSoxGT-8
86SpoDecG-25
86SpoDesJM-1
86TCM-15
86TCMSupS-3
86TCMSupS-10
87HygAllG-48
87LeaSpeO*-H5
87NesDreT-18
87RedSox1T-6
87SpoRea-5
87WauTimP-12
88GreBasS-70
88PacLegI-50
88ScoBoxC-T1
89BowInsT-11
89BowRepI-11
89BowTif-R11
89HOFStiB-28
89Nis-20
89PacLegI-154
89PerCelP-43
89SweBasG-100
90BasWit-50
90Bes-138
90CMC-759
90Col-23
90HOFStiB-40
90PacLeg-59
90PerGreM-13
90PerMasW-41
90PerMasW-42
90PerMasW-43
90PerMasW-44
90PerMasW-45
90SweBasG-125
91MDAA-17
91SweBasG-100
91TopArc1-319
92BazQua5A-22
92MVP-9
92MVP2H-3
92TVSpoMF5HRC-14
92UppDec-HH2
92UppDecF-50
92UppDecFG-50
92UppDecHH-HI10
92UppDecHoB5-1
92UppDecS-32
92UppDecS-34
92UppDecWH-28
92UppDecWH-29
92UppDecWH-30
92UppDecWH-31
92UppDecWH-32
92UppDecWH-33
92UppDecWH-34
92UppDecWH-35
92UppDecWH-AU4
92UppDecWWB-28
92UppDecWWB-29
92UppDecWWB-30
92UppDecWWB-31
92UppDecWWB-32
92UppDecWWB-33
92UppDecWWB-34
92UppDecWWB-35
93RanKee-1
93TedWil-1
93TedWil-148
93TedWilLC-9
93TedWilLC-AU9
93TedWilP-1
93TedWilPC-23
93TedWilPC-26
93TolMudHF-1666
93UppDecAH-126
93UppDecAH-132
93UppDecAH-161
93UppDecAH-162
93UppDecAHP-1
93UppDecAHP-3
93UppDecAHP-4
94TedWil-1
94TedWil-143
94TedWil-P1
94TedWil-LP2
94TedWil5C-8
94UppDecAH-1
94UppDecAH-50
94UppDecAH-113
94UppDecAH-170
94UppDecAH1-1
94UppDecAH1-50
94UppDecAH1-113
94UppDecAH1-170
94UppDecAH1A-1
94UppDecAH1A-250
94UppDecS-8
94UppDecS-10
94UppDecTAE-51
94UppDecTAEGM-9
94UppDecTAELD-LD7
95EagBalL-5

Williams, Teddy
86BelMarC-123
87IdaFalBP-10
88CalLeaACLC-28
88SanBerSB-4
88SanBerSCLC-38
88SumBraP-419
89BurBraP-1622
89BurBraS-25
89EasLeaDDP-DD36
89WilBilP-636
89WilBilS-22
90WilBilP-1071

Williams, Terrell
90WilBilB-22
90WilBilS-23
91JacSunLD-348
91JacSunP-164
91LinDriAA-348
92KinMetC-15
92KinMetF-1542

Williams, Tim
84GreHorT-14
88CapCodPPaLP-143
89AlaGol-14

Williams, Todd
91GreFalDSP-25
92BakDodCLC-29
92SanAntMF-3976
93AlbDukF-1462
93Bow-182
93ClaFS7-39
93StaCluD-30
93TriAAAGF-16
94Bow-322
94Cla-157
94ClaGolF-11
94ExcFS7-221
94Top-713
94TopGol-713
94TopSpa-713
95DodMot-19
95DodPol-28
95Fla-371
95FleUpd-179
95TopTra-29T

Williams, Tom
88CapCodPPaLP-118

Williams, Troy
86BelMarC-118
87WauTimP-6

Williams, Vaughn
87GenCubP-24

Williams, Walt (Walter E.)
67Top-598
68OPC-172
68Top-172
68TopActS-6A
68TopVen-172
69Top-309
70MLBOffS-191
70OPC-395
70Top-395
70TopBoo-4
70WhiSoxTI-12
71OPC-555
71Top-555
71TopCoi-36
72MilBra-363
72OPC-15
72Top-15
73OPC-297
73Top-297
74OPC-418
74Top-418
75YanSSP-21
76OPC-123
76SSP-436
76Top-123
76VenLeaS-70
87SumBraP-4
88DurBulS-24
89PacSenL-123
89T/MSenL-116
89TopSenL-126
89TulDriGS-2
89TulDriTI-26
90EliSenL-120
90TulDriP-1173
90TulDriTI-27
91ChaRanC-29
92GasRanC-25
92GasRanF-2268
92YanWIZ7-166
93ChaRaiC-27
93ChaRaiF-1927
94ChaRivC-26
94ChaRivF-2689

Williams, Wayne
80CarMudF-1

Williams, Wes
79AshTouT-12

Williams, Willie D.
82DanSunF-18

Williams, Woody (Gregory Scott)
89DunBluJS-23
90Bes-210
90KnoBluJB-18
90KnoBluJP-1239
90KnoBluJS-20
91KnoBluJLD-372
91KnoBluJP-1768
91LinDriAA-372
92SyrChiF-1970
93FleFinE-297
93SyrChiF-999
93TopTra-118T
94BluJayUSPC-2H
94BluJayUSPC-8C
94ColC-300
94ColChoGS-300
94ColChoSS-300
94Fle-349
94Pac-654
94StaCluFDI-513
94StaCluGR-513
94StaCluMOP-513
94StaCluT-154
94StaCluTFDI-154
94Top-668
94TopGol-668
94TopSpa-668
94VenLinU-114
95Don-197
95DonPreP-197
95DonTopotO-180
95Fla-101
95Fle-108
95Top-299
96BluJayB-6
96BluJayOH-36
96Don-44
96DonPreP-44
96LeaSigEA-216
97BluJayS-12
97Fle-520
97FleTif-520
97PacPriGotD-GD107

Williams, Woody (Woodrow Wilson)
47SigOil-19
90DodTar-864

Williamson, Antone
94Cla#1DPMF-DD4
94ClaUpdCotC-CC4
94SigRooDP-5
94SigRooDPS-5
95ActPacF-55
95Bes-26
95ElPasDTI-24
95Exc-77
95Pin-169
95PinArtP-169
95PinMusC-169
95ScoDraP-DP6
95SigRooFD-FD5
95SigRooFDS-FD5
95SPML-81
95UppDecML-199
95UppDecML-218
95UppDecMLOP-OP15
96Bow-280
96BowBes-169
96BowBesAR-169
96BowBesR-169
96Exc-75
96SigRooOJTP-T6
97Don-395
97DonLim-84
97DonLimLE-84
97DonPreP-395
97DonPrePGold-395
97Lea-342
97LeaFraM-342
97LeaFraMDC-342
95UppDecMLFS-199
95UppDecMLFS-218

Williamson, Bret
87TamTarP-13

Williamson, Edward
87BucN28-26A
87BucN28-26B
87OldJudN-229
87OldJudN-555
87OldJudN-556
88WG1CarG-18
89EdgR.WG-14

Williamson, Greg
86WatIndP-31

Williamson, Jeremy
95SpoIndTI-31

Williamson, Joel
93WelPirF-3361
94AugGreC-26
94AugGreF-3013

Williamson, Kevin
87ModA'sC-18
87ModA'sP-16

Williamson, Mark
83BeaGolGT-8
85BeaGolGT-3
86LasVegSP-24
87DonRoo-3
87OriFreB-32
88Don-418
88Fle-574
88FleGlo-574
88SanDieSAAG-20
88StaLinO-19
88Top-571
88TopTif-571
89Fle-626
89FleGlo-626
89OriFreB-32
89SanDieSAG-20
89Sco-592
89Top-546
89TopBig-147
89TopTif-546
90Bow-248
90BowTif-248
90Don-406
90Fle-194
90FleCan-194
90Lea-461
90OPC-13
90PubSti-591
90Sco-332
90Top-13
90TopSti-236
90TopTif-13
90UppDec-173
90VenSti-492
91Bow-85
91Don-238
91Fle-495
91Lea-21
91OPC-296
91OriCro-488
91Sco-498
91StaClu-20
91StaCluMO-10
91Top-296
91TopDesS-296
91TopMic-296
91TopTif-296
91UppDec-510
92Don-511
92Fle-30
92OPC-628
92Sco-427
92Sco-487
92StaClu-177
92Top-628
92TopGol-628
92TopGolW-628
92TopMic-628
92UppDec-609
93FleFinE-168
93StaClu-613
93StaCluFDI-613
93StaCluMOP-613
93Ult-504
93UppDec-722
93UppDecGold-722
94Fle-24
94OriPro-106
94Sco-157
94ScoGolR-157

Williamson, Matt
94BatCliF-3457
94MarPhiC-29
95PiePhiF-196

Williamson, Mike
77AshTouT-29

Williamson, Ray
87WatIndP-22
88KinIndS-24

Williamson, Tyler
94EugEmeC-24
94EugEmeF-3717

Williard, Brian
93CedRapKC-24
93CedRapKF-1740
94CedRapKC-22
94CedRapKF-1110
95LakElsSTI-27

Willie, Prince
91PriWilCC-30

Willis, Alan
80WatIndT-7
82WatIndT-11

Willis, C.H.
87OldJudN-557

Willis, Carl
84EvaTriT-22
87Fle-218
87FleGlo-218
87NasSouTI-23
87Top-101
87TopTif-101
88VanCanC-4
88VanCanP-762
89EdmTraC-3
89EdmTraP-567
90CMC-460
90ColSprSSC-8
90ColSprSSP-38
90ProAAAF-219
91LinDriAAA-423
91PorBeaLD-423
91PorBeaP-1567
92Bow-466
92Don-665
92Lea-452
92OPC-393
92Pin-491
92Sco-482
92StaClu-779
92StaCluNC-779
92Ult-403
93Fle-275
93Lea-164
93OPC-388
93PacSpa-527
93Pin-372
93StaClu-182
93StaCluFDI-182
93StaCluMOP-182
93Top-747
93TopGol-747
93TopInaM-747
93TopMic-747
93Ult-239
94Don-581
94Fle-222

94Lea-198
94Pac-370
94Pin-378
94PinArtP-378
94PinMusC-378
94StaClu-484
94StaCluFDI-484
94StaCluGR-484
94StaCluMOP-484
94Top-621
94TopGol-621
94TopSpa-621
95Fle-217
95Sco-178
95ScoGolR-178
95ScoPlaTS-178
95Top-302

Willis, Dale
77FriOneYW-85

Willis, Jim
54Top-67
87AppFoxP-30
94TopArc1-67
94TopArc1G-67

Willis, Kent
87TamTarP-17
88RocExpLC-34
88VirGenS-22

Willis, Les
47IndTeal-26
47IndVanPP-25

Willis, Marty
89LakTigS-25
90LakTigS-25
91Cla/Bes-6
91LinDriAA-398
91LonTigLD-398
91LonTigP-1879
92LonTigF-634
92LonTigS-423

Willis, Mike
75IntLeaAT-18
75IntLeaAT-28
76SSP-382
76VenLeaS-177
77OPC-103
77Top-493
78BluJayP-24
78OPC-227
78Top-293
79OPC-366
79Top-688
80SyrChiT-7
80SyrChiTI-24
81Fle-426
81OPC-324
81Top-324
82OklCit8T-1
87MaiGuiT-25

Willis, Ron
67Top-592
68OPC-68
68Top-68
68TopVen-68
69Top-273

Willis, Scott
87CedRapRP-3

Willis, Steve
87AncGlaP-31

Willis, Symmion
96MedHatBJTI-32

Willis, Travis
89GenCubP-1867
90PeoChiTI-29
91CarLeaAP-CAR46
91WinSpiC-11
91WinSpiP-2830
92ChaKniF-2773
93OrlCubF-2786
94BufBisF-1839
94ExcFS7-171

Willis, Vic
03BreE10-152
06FanCraNL-52
08AmeCarE-97
09AmeCarE-117
09PC7HHB-45
09PhiCarE-24
09T206-379
09T206-380
09T206-381
10NadE1-58
11SpoLifM-279
11TurRedT-40
80PerHaloFP-224
86PirGreT-9

Willming, Gregory
93EriSaiC-25
93EriSaiF-3117
94ChaRivF-2675

Willoughby, Claude
29PorandAR-99
93ConTSN-792

Willoughby, Jim
73OPC-79
73Top-79
74OPC-553
74Top-553
75TulOil7-9
76OPC-102
76SSP-419
76Top-102
77Top-532
78Top-373
79Top-266
89PacSenL-37
89TopSenL-70
91PacSenL-88

Willoughby, Mark
86ColMetP-27A
86ColMetP-27B
89PitMetS-23
89Sta-165

Wills Moody, Helen
28W512-33

Wills, Adrian Charles
87GreBraB-8

Wills, Bump
76SacSolC-17
77SpoIIIAC-1
77Top-494
78Hos-21
78OPC-208
78RanBurK-12
78RCColC-100
78SSP270-95
78Top-23
79OPC-190
79Top-369A
79Top-369B
80OPC-373
80Top-473
81AllGamPI-18
81Don-25
81Fle-628
81OPC-173
81Top-173
81TopSti-134
81TopSupHT-96
82CubRedL-17
82Don-289
82Fle-334
82FleSta-175
82OPC-272
82Top-272
82TopSti-244
82TopTra-129T
83Don-351
83Fle-511
83FleSta-216
83FleSti-124
83Top-643
86RanGreT-6
88ButCopKSP-29
89ButCopKSP-24
91GasRanC-17
91GasRanP-2704
92ChaRanC-26
92ChaRanF-2240
93RanKee-383
95HudValRTI-28
96HudValRB-24

Wills, Frank
82OmaRoyT-10
84OmaRoyT-5
85CalCanC-85
85Don-374
86Fle-480
86MaiGuiP-24
86Top-419
86TopTif-419
87BufBisP-23
87IndGat-22
87Top-551
87TopTif-551
88SyrChiC-11
88SyrChiP-830
89BluJayFS-34
89SyrChiC-5
89SyrChiMB-24
89SyrChiP-794
90BluJayFS-33
90Fle-98
90FleCan-98
90TopTra-129T
90TopTraT-129T
91BluJayFS-33
91BluJayS-10
91Don-691
91Fle-191
91OPC-213
91Sco-521
91SyrChiMB-29
91Top-213
91TopDesS-213
91TopMic-213
91TopTif-213

Wills, Maury
47Exh-242
57HygMea-12
60DodBelB-20
60DodJayP-16
60DodTeal-20
60DodUnIO-21
60Top-389
61DodBelB-30
61DodJayP-12
61DodMor-6
61DodUniO-23
61Pos-164A
61Pos-164B
62DodBelB-30
62DodJayP-12
62Jel-104
62Pos-104
62PosCan-104
62SalPlaC-127A
62SalPlaC-127B
62ShiPlaC-127
63DodJayP-12
63ExhStaB-64
63Fle-43
63Jel-115
63Pos-115
63SalMetC-20
64DodHea-10
65DodJayP-12
65DodTeal-20
67CokCapPi-13
67DexPre-224
67PirTeal-24
67Top-570
67TopVen-321
68AtlOilPBCC-48
68Baz-1
68Baz-4
68OPC-175
68PirKDK-30
68PirTeal-24
68Top-175
68TopVen-175
69MilBra-293
69MLBOffS-162
69OPC-45
69OPCDec-23
69Top-45
69TopDec-24
69TopDecI-46
69TopSta-60
69TopSup-49
69TopTeaP-10
70DayDaiNM-3
70MLBOffS-60
70Top-595
71BazNumT-34
71DodTic-19
71MLBOffS-120
71OPC-385
71Top-385
71TopGreM-29
71TopTat-116
72MilBra-364
72OPC-437
72OPC-438
72Top-437
72Top-438
74GreHeroBP-6
75OPC-200
75Top-200
76SSP-592
77Spo-1411
77Top-435
78TCM60I-70
81Fle-595
81MarPol-14
81Top-672
82BasCarN-14
82K-M-2
83MLBPin-36
84DodUniOP-11
85Woo-39
87DodSmoA-38
87HygAllG-49
87Top-315
87TopTif-315
88DodSmo-7
89DodSmoG-69
90AGFA-12
90DodTar-865
90HOFStiB-66
92ActPacA-47
92DodStaTA-2
92MDAMVP-3
92UppDecS-29
93TedWil-17
93TedWilM-9
95MCIAmb-12
95SonGre-12
97FleMilDM-25

Wills, Shawn
92BatCliC-11
92BatCliF-3281
92ClaDraP-110
93SpaPhiF-1070
94SpaPhiF-1737
94SparPhiC-23

Wills, Ted
60Lea-56
61Top-548
62Top-444
65Top-488
78TCM60I-138

Willsher, Chris
81MiaOriT-22
84ChaO'sT-11

Willson, Rob
87EveGiaC-22

Wilmet, Paul
82LynMetT-10
85SprCarT-30
87ArkTraP-10
88EasLeaAP-18
88HarSenP-852
89OklCit8C-9
89OklCit8P-1509
90CMC-85
90IowCubC-10
90IowCubP-319
90ProAAAF-626
90SprCarDGB-16
90TopDeb89-145
93RanKee-384

Wilming, Greg
94ChaRivC-25

Wilmont, Walter
87OldJudN-558
88WG1CarG-72

Wilmore, Al
92NegLeaRLI-63
95NegLeaL2-18

Wilner, Dirk
90LSUTigA-9

Wilner, Eric
85AncGlaPTI-34

Wilridge, James
84IdaFalATI-30

Wilshere, Whitey
94ConTSN-1314
94ConTSNB-1314

Wilson, Alan
84LitFalMT-20
87ChaWheP-4

Wilson, Archie C.
52Bow-210
52Top-327
60MapLeaSF-23
83TopRep5-327

Wilson, Arthur Earl
10DomDisP-125A
10DomDisP-125B
10E12AmeCDC-39
10SweCapPP-122A
10SweCapPP-122B
11BasBatEU-44
11SpoLifM-222
12T207-198
14CraJacE-13
15CraJacE-13
15SpoNewM-192
16ColE13-192
16FleBreD-101
16SpoNewM-191
20NatCarE-110
27YorCarE-25
63Pos-83
65OPC-42
68OPC-10
68OPC-160
70OPC-95
71OPC-301
81TigDetN-51
88TigDom-26
91SweBasG-120
93UppDecAH-127
93UppDecS-6

Wilson, Artie (Arthur L.)
49RemBre-31
50RemBre-26
52MotCoo-40
75Gia195T-31
92NegLeaK-9
92NegLeaRLI-64
95NegLeaL2-9

Wilson, Barney
75CedRapGT-20
76CedRapGT-33

Wilson, Brad
89BriTigS-28
90BriTigP-3172
90BriTigS-25
91FayGenC-10
91FayGenP-1175
91LakTigP-270

Wilson, Brandon
91Cla/Bes-157
91MidLeaAP-MWL13
91SouBenWSC-7
91SouBenWSP-2867
92Bow-632
92ClaFS7-321
92ProFS7-47
92SarWhiSCB-4
92SarWhiSF-217
92UppDecML-251
92UppDecMLPotY-PY25
93BirBarF-1202
93Bow-7
93ClaFS7-90
93ClaGolF-80
93ExcAllF-10
93ExcFS7-157
93LeaGolR-R5
93StaCluWS-9
94Bow-267
94ExcFS7-41
94NasSouF-1260
94Top-158
94TopGol-158
94TopSpa-158
94UppDecML-8
96IndIndB-28

Wilson, Brian
92GulCoaRSP-11
94BilMusF-3680
94BilMusSP-9
95BilRedTI-13

Wilson, Bryan
91GulCoaRSP-28
91PeoChiC-15
91PeoChiTI-22
91WinSpiC-22
91WinSpiP-2839

Wilson, Bubba
76BatTroTI-29
77WatIndT-31

Wilson, Charles
36GouWidPPR-D38

Wilson, Chauff (W.H.)
76LauIndC-36

Wilson, Chaun
87NewOriP-17
88HagSunS-24

Wilson, Chief (John Owen)
08AmeCarE-98
08RosComP-157
09ColChiE-309
09T206-382
10CouT21-68
10CouT21-248
10DomDisP-126A

10DomDisP-126B
10E12AmeCDC-40
10NadE1-59
10PirAmeCE-11
10PirHerP-12
10PirTipTD-17
10RedCroT-85
10RedCroT-257
10SweCapPP-144
11BasBatEU-43
11S74Sil-116
11SpoLifM-261
11T205-184
11TurRedT-126
12ColRedB-309
12ColTinT-309
12HasTriFT-30C
12T207-199
14B18B-91A
14B18B-91B
14PieStaT-64
15CraJacE-148
15SpoNewM-193
16SpoNewM-192
85Woo-41
90HOFStiB-18

Wilson, Chris
94HelBreF-3627
94HelBreSP-16

Wilson, Craig
85SprCarT-12
87St.PetCP-2
88LouRedBP-439
88LouRedBTI-50
89ArkTraGS-25
89LouRedBTI-36
90CMC-115
90LouRedBC-15
90LouRedBLBC-42
90LouRedBP-413
90ProAAAF-527
90SprCarDGB-2
90TopDeb89-146
90TopTVCa-66
91CarPol-12
91Don-544
91Fle-652
91Lea-95
91OPC-566
91Sco100RS-97
91StaClu-566
91Top-566
91TopDesS-566
91TopMic-566
91TopTif-566
91TopTra-128T
91TopTraT-128T
91Ult-298
91UppDec-390
92CarPol-24
92Don-744
92JacSunF-3711
92JacSunS-371
92OPC-646
92Sco-557
92StaClu-361
92StaCluD-196
92Top-646
92TopDaiQTU-30
92TopGol-646
92TopGolW-646
92TopMic-646
92TopTraG-128T
93ClaFS7-150
93Fle-516
93MidLeaAGF-27
93RoyPol-26
93Sco-476
93SouBenWSC-24
93SouBenWSF-1441
93StaClu-88
93StaCluFDI-88
93StaCluM-105
93StaCluMOP-88
93Top-366
93TopGol-366
93TopInaM-366
93TopMic-366
94CarLeaAF-CAR12
94ClaGolF-162
94PriWilCC-22
94PriWilCF-1931
95Bow-145
95TolMudHTI-28
96BirBarB-28
96Bow-371
96HagSunB-24
96NasSouB-28
96Top-233

Wilson, Craig Gerald
87ElmPio(C-18
88LouRedBC-15
88LynRedSS-26
89LynRedSS-22
90NewBriRSB-8
90NewBriRSP-1323
90NewBriRSS-23
91LynRedSC-13
91LynRedSP-1203
92PenPilF-2937
92TopTra-128T

Wilson, Dan
88CapCodPPaLP-177
90Bes-232
90ClaDraP-7
91Bow-687
91ChaWheC-14
91ChaWheP-2891
91Cla/Bes-353
91OPC-767
91Sco-681
91StaClu-587
91Top-767
91TopDesS-767
91TopMic-767
91TopTif-767
91UppDecFE-6F
92Bow-471
92Don-399
92LeaGolR-BC18
92NasSouF-1834
92NasSouS-297
92ProFS7-217
92SkyAAAF-138
92TriPla-241
92UppDec-72
93Bow-202
93Don-6
93Fle-400
93OPCPre-35
93PacSpa-407
93Pin-255
93Sco-229
93ScoBoyoS-28
93Sel-345
93StaClu-662
93StaCluFDI-662
93StaCluMOP-662
93Top-813
93TopGol-813
93TopInaM-813
93TopMic-813
93Toy-65
93Ult-337
93UppDec-6
93UppDecGold-6
94Bow-173
94ColC-547
94ColChoGS-547
94ColChoSS-547
94Don-388
94ExtBas-174
94Fin-284
94FinRef-284
94Fla-342
94FleUpd-88
94Lea-329
94MarMot-24
94Pin-515
94PinArtP-515
94PinMusC-515
94Sco-355
94ScoGolR-355
94ScoRoo-RT22
94ScoRooGR-RT22
94Sel-343
94StaClu-656
94StaCluFDI-656
94StaCluGR-656
94StaCluMOP-656
94Top-154
94TopGol-154
94TopSpa-154
94TopTra-3T
94Ult-426
94UppDec-240
94UppDecED-240
95ColCho-291
95ColChoGS-291
95ColChoSS-291
95Don-24
95DonPreP-24
95DonTopotO-156
95Fla-304
95Fle-279
95Lea-228
95MarMot-12
95MarPac-48
95Pac-403
95Pin-407
95PinArtP-407
95PinMusC-407
95Sco-146
95ScoGolR-146
95ScoPlaTS-146
95Sel-187
95SelArtP-187
95StaClu-152
95StaCluFDI-152
95StaCluMOP-152
95StaCluSTDW-M152
95StaCluSTWS-152
95StaCluVR-79
95Top-263
95TopCyb-143
95Ult-106
95UltGolM-106
96Cir-83
96CirRav-83
96ColCho-319
96ColChoGS-319
96ColChoSS-319
96Don-79
96DonPreP-79
96EmoXL-119
96Fla-166
96Fle-245
96FleTif-245
96MarMot-15
96Pac-405
96Pin-332
96PinFoil-332
96Sco-177
96StaClu-30
96StaCluMOP-30
96StaCluVRMO-79
96Top-117
96Ult-131
96UltGolM-131
97Cir-135
97CirRav-135
97ColCho-228
97Don-327
97DonEli-136
97DonEliGS-136
97DonLim-163
97DonLimLE-163
97DonPre-12
97DonPreCttC-12
97DonPreP-327
97DonPrePGold-327
97DonTea-147
97DonTeaSPE-147
97Fin-220
97FinRef-220
97FlaSho-A152
97FlaSho-B152
97FlaSho-C152
97FlaShoLC-152
97FlaShoLC-B152
97FlaShoLC-C152
97FlaShoLCM-A152
97FlaShoLCM-B152
97FlaShoLCM-C152
97Fle-217
97FleTif-217
97Lea-46
97LeaFraM-46
97LeaFraMDC-46
97MetUni-151
97Pac-196
97PacLigB-196
97PacSil-196
97Pin-77
97PinArtP-77
97PinIns-109
97PinInsCE-109
97PinInsDE-109
97PinMusC-77
97Sco-185
97ScoMar-8
97ScoMarPl-8
97ScoMarPr-8
97ScoPreS-185
97ScoShoS-185
97ScoShoSAP-185
97SkyE-X-44
97SkyE-XC-44
97SkyE-XEC-44
97SP-169
97Spolll-53
97SpollIEE-53
97StaClu-123
97StaCluMOP-123
97Stu-144
97StuPrePG-144
97StuPrePS-144
97Top-63
97Ult-129
97UltGolME-129
97UltPlaME-129
97UppDec-503

Wilson, Danny
86DavLipB-24

Wilson, Dave
81CliGiaT-21
91AshTouP-569

Wilson, David
89NiaFalRP-24
90AshTouC-11
90AubAstB-4
90AubAstP-3404
91Cla/Bes-274

Wilson, Desi
92ButCopKSP-16
93Bow-337
93ChaRanC-25
93ChaRanF-1951
93ClaFS7-40
94Top-775
94TopGol-775
94TopSpa-775
94TulDriF-257
94TulDriTI-25
95UppDecML-99
96PhoFirB-28
97Fle-490
97FleTif-490
97PacPriGotD-GD220
97Ult-487
97UltGolME-487
97UltPlaME-487
97UppDec-482
95UppDecMLFS-99

Wilson, Don
67Ast-29
68Baz-13
68CokCapA-18
68OPC-77
68Top-77
68TopVen-75
68TopVen-77
69MLBOffS-143
69OPC-202
69Top-202
69TopFou-1
69TopSta-39
69TopTeaP-6
69TraSta-37
70AstTeal-11
70Kel-62
70MLBOffS-47
70OPC-515
70Top-515
71AstCok-11
71MLBOffS-95
71OPC-484
71Top-484
71TopCoi-41
72Kel-51
72MilBra-365
72OPC-20
72OPC-91
72Top-20
72Top-91
73LinPor-86
73OPC-217
73Top-217
74OPC-304
74Top-304
75OPC-455
75Top-455
81TCM60I-326
86AstMot-10
87AstShoSO-24
87AstShoSO-28
87AstShoSTw-28
87AstShowSTh-26
87AstShowSTh-28

Wilson, Doyle
87KinIndP-20
88WilBilP-1324

Wilson, Earl
60Top-249
61Top-69
63Jel-83
63Top-76
64Top-503
65Top-42
66Top-575
67CokCapTi-10
67DexPre-225
67TigDexP-11
67Top-235
67Top-237
67Top-305
67TopVen-234
68AtlOilPBCC-49
68CokCapT-10
68Kah-B38
68TigDetFPB-27
68Top-10A
68Top-10B
68Top-160
68TopActS-9A
68TopVen-10
68TopVen-160
69MilBra-294
69Top-525
69TopTeaP-1
70MLBOffS-216
70Top-95
71Top-301
72MilBra-366
78TCM60I-148
84WilMay-26

Wilson, Eddie
90DodTar-1095

Wilson, Enrique
93EliTwiC-22
94ColRedC-1
94ColRedF-453
95Bow-36
95Exc-44
95KinIndTI-29
95SPML-47
96BesAutS-94
96Bow-146
96BowBes-106
96BowBesAR-106
96BowBesR-106
96CanIndB-29
96ColCho-449
96ColChoGS-449
96ColChoSS-449
96Exc-47
96Top-427
96UppDec-261
97Bow-144
97BowCerBIA-CA85
97BowCerGIA-CA85
97BowInt-144
97Top-487

Wilson, Eric
86PenWhiSP-27

Wilson, Ewligul
93EliTwiF-3424

Wilson, Frank
52LavPro-3

Wilson, Gary
88BatCliP-1688
89SpaPhiP-1036
89SpaPhiS-24
90Bes-158
90CMC-737
90ReaPhiB-11
90ReaPhiP-1221
90ReaPhiS-24
91LinDriAAA-498
91ScrRedBLD-498
91ScrRedBP-2539

Wilson, Gary Morris
92WelPirC-26
92WelPirF-1324
93ClaGolF-197
93SalBucC-24
93SalBucF-433
94SalBucC-24
94SalBucF-2325
95Exc-259

95Fla-405
95FleUpd-152
95PirFil-30
95SigRoo-49
95SigRooSig-49
95StaClu-583
95StaCluMOP-583
95StaCluSTWS-583
Wilson, Gary Steven
76DubPacT-39
79ChaChaT-18
80TucTorT-5
Wilson, George H.
94TedWil-115
Wilson, George Washington
79TCM50-189
Wilson, Glenn
81BirBarT-10
83Don-580
83Fle-350
83Tig-31
83Top-332
83TopSti-318
84Don-618
84Fle-94
84FleUpd-128
84Nes792-563
84OPC-36
84PhiTas-40
84Top-563
84TopSti-270
84TopTif-563
84TopTra-129T
84TopTraT-129T
85Don-609
85Fle-268
85OPC-189
85PhiCIG-9
85PhiTas-12
85PhiTas-40
85Top-454
85TopTif-454
86BasStaB-121
86BurKinA-7
86Don-285
86DonAll-29
86Fle-457
86FleMin-95
86FleStiC-128
86Lea-160
86OPC-318
86PhiCIG-16
86PhiKel-6
86PhiTas-12
86Top-736
86TopMinL-56
86TopSti-118
86TopTat-9
86TopTif-736
87Don-62
87DonOpeD-158
87Fle-192
87FleGlo-192
87FleMin-115
87Lea-146
87OPC-97
87PhiTas-12
87Spo-166
87SpoTeaP-6
87Top-97
87Top-481
87TopSti-117
87TopTif-97
87TopTif-481
88Don-262
88DonBasB-306
88Fle-320
88FleGlo-320
88MarMot-12
88OPC-359
88PanSti-358
88PanSti-364
88RedFolSB-103
88Sco-405
88ScoGlo-405
88Spo-204
88StaLinMa-20
88StaLinPh-20
88Top-626
88TopBig-260
88TopSti-124
88TopTif-626
88TopTra-129T
88TopTraT-129T
89Bow-423
89BowTif-423
89Don-447
89DonBasB-241
89Fle-224
89FleGlo-224
89PirVerFJ-11
89Sco-106
89Spo-12
89Top-293
89TopBig-284
89TopTif-293
90AstLenH-26
90AstMot-22
90BirBarDGB-31
90Don-472
90Fle-240
90FleCan-240
90Lea-268
90OPC-112
90PubSti-168
90RedFolSB-104
90Sco-346
90Top-112
90TopBig-320
90TopTif-112
90UppDec-410
90VenSti-493
91Don-156
91Fle-519
91LinDriAAA-447
91OPC-476
91PanFreS-11
91RicBraLD-447
91RicBraP-2582
91RicBraTI-26
91Sco-298
91Top-476
91TopDesS-476
91TopMic-476
91TopTif-476
91UppDec-515
93BufBisF-532
Wilson, Hack (Lewis R.)
27YorCarE-25
28Exh-12
28PorandAR-A39
28PorandAR-B39
28StaPlaCE-72
28W502-25
28W513-74
28Yue-25
29ExhFou-5
29PorandAR-100
30ChiEveAP-10
30SchR33-14
30W554-18
31CubTeal-28
31Exh-5
31W517-42
33ButCre-29
33DouDisP-43
33Gou-211
33RitCE-9C
33RitCE-9S
34DiaMatCSB-198
34BatR31-73
46SpoExcW-9-4
60Fle-48
61Fle-87
69SCFOldT-29
72FleFamF-9
72LauGreF-27
77GalGloG-113
77Spo-7515
79Top-412
80CubGreT-10
80LauFamF-4
80PacLeg-97
80PerHaloFP-169
80SSPHOF-169
81ConTSN-86
82DiaCla-20
85Woo-40
86ConSer1-56
89DodSmoG-36
90BasWit-93
90DodTar-866
90HOFStiB-29
90PerGreM-80
91ConTSN-29
91ConTSN-267
92ConTSN-424
92ConTSN-585
92CubOldS-28
93ConTSN-736
94ConTSN-998
94ConTSNB-998
94UppDecAH-111
94UppDecAH-190
94UppDecAH1-111
94UppDecAH1-190
Wilson, Jack
40PlaBal-31
41PlaBal-29
86PhoFirP-25
Wilson, James George
28Exh-32
35DiaMatCS2-24
35DiaMatCS3T1-150
41HarHarW-28
81BriRedST-6
83BufBisT-14
83PawRedST-18
85IntLeaAT-25
85MaiGuiT-24
86IndTeal-48
86MaiGuiP-25
88EasLeaAP-38
89BlaYNPRWL-195
89CalCanC-22
89CalCanP-536
89TriA AAC-39
89TriAAP-AAA32
90TriAAAC-39
91LinDriAAA-397
91PhoFirLD-397
91PhoFirP-77
93LinVenB-315
Wilson, Jeff
83WisRapTF-4
86TamTarP-26
Wilson, Jim
88SanDieSAAG-21
88VerMarP-944
89SanDieSAG-19
Wilson, Jim A.
52Top-276
53BowC-37
53BraJohC-12
53BraSpiaS3-27
53Top-208
54Bow-16
54BraJohC-19
54BraMer-6
55Bow-253
55BraGolS-8
55BraJohC-19
55BraSpiaSD-18
56Top-171
57Top-330
58Top-163
58WhiSoxJP-11
79TCM50-130
82Bow195E-257
83Bra53F-19
83TopRep5-276
91OriCro-489
91TopArc1-208
92BazQua5A-18
Wilson, Jimmy
29ExhFou-15
30SchR33-30
31Exh-15
32R33So2-422
33ButCanV-56
33Gou-37
33GouCanV-37
33NatLeaAC-18
34DiaMatCSB-197
34BatR31-38
34ButPreR-65
34DiaStaR-22
34ExhFou-6
34WarBakSP-8
35ExhFou-6
35GouPuzR-6C
35GouPuzR-11E
35GouPuzR-13C
35GouPuzR-15C
36ExhFou-6
36NatChiFPR-114
36WheBB3-12
36WorWidGV-99
38CinOraW-32
39OrcPhoAP-26
40PlaBal-152
41CubTeal-25
43CubTeal-25
61Fle-88
69SCFOldT-50
77GalGloG-216
81ConTSN-87
91ConTSN-223
93ConTSN-683
93ConTSN-874
Wilson, John F.
39PlaBal-29
Wilson, Johnny
85LynMetT-24
86JacMetT-22
87JacMetF-17
Wilson, Jud
74LauOldTBS-12
90NegLeaS-34
91PomBlaBPB-23
94TedWil-116
Wilson, Kurt
89SalLakTTI-10
95OdgRapTI-29
Wilson, Mark
89HamRedS-26
92SanJosGC-30
Wilson, Matt
89GreFalDSP-32
90VerBeaDS-31
91CalLeLA-25
92BakDodCLC-32
95SanAntMTI-NNO
Wilson, Mike
77CliDodT-29
80AlbDukT-15
80QuaCitCT-26
87IdaFalBP-1
93BriTigC-25
94FayGenC-25
95FayGenTI-29
Wilson, Mookie
79TidTidT-7
80TidTidT-17
81Don-575
81Top-259
82Don-175
82Fle-542
82FleSta-86
82MetPhoA-25
82OPC-143
82RegGloT-10
82Top-143
83AllGamPI-162
83Don-56
83DonActA-32
83Dra-29
83Fle-560
83FleSta-217
83FleSti-233
83OPC-55
83Top-55
83Top-621
83TopGloS-2
83TopSti-266
84AllGamPI-72
84Don-190
84Dra-31
84Fle-603
84FleSti-91
84FunFooP-65
84JacMetF-13
84MetFanC-8
84Nes792-246
84Nes792-465
84OPC-270
84Top-246
84Top-465
84TopSti-108
84TopTif-246
84TopTif-465
85AllGamPI-161
85Don-482
85Fle-95
85Lea-122
85MetColP-28
85MetTCM-36
85OPC-11
85PolMet-M4
85Top-775
85TopMin-775
85TopSti-102
85TopTif-775
86Don-604
86Fle-97
86Lea-232
86MetColP-7
86MetTCM-29
86MetWorSC-21
86OPC-315
86RegGloT-1
86Top-126
86Top-315
86TopTat-6
86TopTif-126
86TopTif-315
87Don-487
87DonOpeD-129
87Fle-25
87FleGlo-25
87FleHotS-43
87Lea-176
87MetColP-9
87MetFanC-8
87OPC-84
87Top-625
87TopTif-625
88Don-652
88DonBasB-208
88DonTeaBM-652
88Fle-154
88FleGlo-154
88Lea-249
88MetColP-11
88MetKah-1
88PanSti-342
88PanSti-348
88Sco-474
88ScoGlo-474
88StaLinMe-20
88Top-255
88TopBig-182
88TopTif-255
89Bow-386
89BowTif-386
89Don-152
89Fle-52
89FleGlo-52
89MetColP-19
89MetKah-30
89OPC-144
89PanSti-141
89Sco-302
89ScoRoo-16T
89Top-545
89TopBig-231
89TopDouM-13
89TopTif-545
89UppDec-199
90BluJayFS-34
90Bow-516
90BowTif-516
90Don-442
90DonBesA-28
90Fle-99
90FleCan-99
90Lea-263
90OPC-182
90PanSti-174
90PubSti-147
90Sco-448
90Spo-128
90Top-182
90TopBig-179
90TopTif-182
90UppDec-481
90VenSti-494
91BluJayFS-34
91BluJayS-24
91Don-585
91Fle-192
91MetWIZ-433
91OPC-727
91PanFreS-341
91Sco-42
91StaClu-99
91Stu-140
91Top-727
91TopDesS-727
91TopMic-727
91TopTif-727
91Ult-372
91UppDec-512
92Fle-347
92OPC-436
92Sco-458
92Top-436
92TopGol-436
92TopGolW-436

92TopMic-436
92UppDec-391
94MetColP-30
94MetComR-2
96MetTeal-9
97FleMilDM-49
Wilson, Murray
72Dia-111
72Dia-112
Wilson, Nigel
88St.CatBJP-2017
89St.CatBJP-2081
90MyrBeaBJP-2791
91DunBluJC-24
91DunBluJP-222
91FloStaLAP-FSL10
92Bow-228
92ClaFS7-164
92KnoBluJF-3005
92KnoBluJS-397
92ProFS7-169
92SkyAA F-168
92UppDecML-286
93Bow-316
93Bow-351
93Don-737
93DonDiaK-DK27
93EdmTraF-1151
93ExcFS7-247
93FlaWavotF-19
93FlaWavotF-20
93Fle-431
93FleFinE-75
93LeaGolR-R16
93MarPub-27
93OPC-165
93StaClu-720
93StaCluFDI-720
93StaClul-A4
93StaCluMarl-1
93StaCluMOP-720
93StaCluMOP-MA4
93Top-426
93TopGol-426
93TopInaM-426
93TopMic-426
93TopMic-P426
93Ult-388
93UppDec-825
93UppDecGold-825
94ActPac-38
94Bow-590
94Cla-106
94ColC-301
94ColChoGS-301
94ColChoSS-301
94Don-537
94EdmTraF-2889
94FUnPac-30
94Lea-76
94Pac-255
94Pin-240
94PinArtP-240
94PinMusC-240
94PinNewG-NG22
94PinRooTP-8
94Sco-639
94ScoBoyoS-35
94ScoGolR-639
94Spo-158
94StaCluT-66
94StaCluTFDI-66
94Top-341
94TopGol-341
94TopSpa-341
94UppDec-103
94UppDecED-103
95IndIndF-109
95Top-506
96BufBisB-23
96Pin-186
Wilson, Parke
95NewN566-202
Wilson, Parker
80ElmPioRST-30
Wilson, Paul
93BazTeaU-10
93TopTra-107T
94Cla#1DPMF-DD1
94ClaUpdCotC-CC1
94MetShuST-5
94SigRooDP-2
94SigRooDPS-2
94SigRooFCD-5
94StaCluDP-82
94StaCluDPFDI-82
94TopTra-1T
94UppDecAHNIL-20
95ActPacF-52
95Bes-83
95Bes-109
95Bes-AU4
95BesFra-F12
95BinMetTI-40
95Bow-136
95BowBes-B5
95BowBesR-B5
95ColCho-20
95ColChoGS-20
95ColChoSE-9
95ColChoSEGS-9
95ColChoSESS-9
95ColChoSS-20
95Exc-240
95ScoDraP-DP3
95SelSurS-SS9
95SPML-5
95SPML-97
95SPMLA-24
95SPMLDtS-DS3
95StaClu-100
95StaCluFDI-100
95StaCluMOP-100
95StaCluSTWS-100
95Top-621
95UppDec-13
95UppDecED-13
95UppDecEDG-13
95UppDecML-169
95UppDecML-200
95UppDecML-215
95UppDecMLMLA-10
95UppDecSE-58
95UppDecSEG-58
96BesAutSA-88
96Bow-191
96BowBes-39
96BowBesAR-39
96BowBesP-BBP11
96BowBesPAR-BBP11
96BowBesPR-BBP11
96BowBesR-39
96Cir-162
96CirRav-162
96EmoXL-240
96Exc-192
96ExcAll-10
96ExcCli-10
96Fin-B245
96FinRef-B245
96Fla-328
96FlaWavotF-20
96FleUpd-U162
96FleUpdNH-20
96FleUpdTC-U162
96LeaLimRG-8
96LeaPre-127
96LeaPreP-127
96LeaPreSG-35
96LeaPreSte-35
96LeaSig-81
96LeaSigA-246
96LeaSigAG-247
96LeaSigAS-247
96LeaSigPPG-81
96LeaSigPPP-81
96MetKah-31
96Pin-369
96PinAfi-168
96PinAfiAP-168
96PinAfiSP-4
96PinFoil-369
96PinProS-1
96Sel-162
96SelArtP-162
96SelCer-111
96SelCerAP-111
96SelCerCB-111
96SelCerCR-111
96SelCerIP-21
96SelCerMB-111
96SelCerMG-111
96SelCerMR-111
96SP-5
96SPSpeFX-13
96SPSpeFXDC-13
96SPx-41
96SPxGol-41
96Stu-141
96StuPrePB-141
96StuPrePG-141
96StuPrePS-141
96Sum-152
96Sum-177
96SumAbo&B-152
96SumAbo&B-177
96SumArtP-152
96SumArtP-177
96SumBal-15
96SumFoi-152
96SumFoi-177
96Top-214
96TopChr-76
96TopChrR-76
96TopGal-127
96TopGalPPI-127
96TopLas-63
96TopLasBS-16
96Ult-516
96UltGolM-516
96UppDec-255
96UppDecHC-HC4
96UppDecPHE-H48
96UppDecPreH-H48
96Zen-117
96ZenArtP-117
96ZenMoz-24
97Cir-174
97CirRav-174
97ColCho-174
97ColChoTBS-33
97ColChoTBSWH-33
97Don-182
97DonEli-68
97DonEliGS-68
97DonPre-121
97DonPreCttC-121
97DonPreP-182
97DonPrePGold-182
97Fin-94
97FinRef-94
97Fle-405
97FleTif-405
97Lea-103
97LeaFraM-103
97LeaFraMDC-103
97LeaGet-12
97MetUni-199
97PacPriGotD-GD179
97Pin-120
97PinArtP-120
97PinCer-96
97PinCerMBlu-96
97PinCerMG-96
97PinCerMR-96
97PinCerR-96
97PinIns-29
97PinInsCE-29
97PinInsDE-29
97PinMusC-120
97PinTotCPB-96
97PinTotCPG-96
97PinTotCPR-96
97ProMag-29
97ProMagML-29
97Sco-9
97ScoPreS-9
97ScoShoS-9
97ScoShoSAP-9
97Sel-48
97SelArtP-48
97SelRegG-48
97StaClu-108
97StaCluC-CO2
97StaCluM-M20
97StaCluMOP-108
97StaCluMOP-M20
97Stu-133
97StuPrePG-133
97StuPrePS-133
97Top-89
97TopChr-35
97TopChrR-35
97TopGal-156
97TopGalPPI-156
97Ult-246
97UltGolME-246
97UltPlaME-246
97UppDec-117
95UppDecMLFS-169
95UppDecMLFS-200
95UppDecMLFS-215
97UppDecRSF-RS18
Wilson, Phil
82WatIndF-7
82WatIndT-13
83WatIndF-14
85VisOakT-1
86OrlTwiP-24
87PorBeaP-9
88PorBeaC-23
88PorBeaP-661
89JacExpP-171
Wilson, Pookie
92SalLakTSP-13
93KanCouCC-24
93KanCouCF-930
94BreCouMC-23
94BreCouMF-28
95PorSeaDTI-29
96PorSeaDB-29
93KanCouCTI-28
Wilson, Preston
92ClaDraP-117
92HigSchPLS-27
93Bow-594
93KinMetC-1
93KinMetF-3806
93StaCluM-27
93StaCluMMP-12
93Top-132
93TopGol-132
93TopInaM-132
93TopMic-132
94Bow-484
94CapCitBC-1
94CapCitBF-1760
94Cla-67
94ClaGolF-106
94ColC-650
94ColChoGS-650
94ColChoSS-650
94ExcFS7-242
94SP-20
94SPDieC-20
94UppDec-537
94UppDecAHNIL-16
94UppDecED-537
94UppDecML-219
95SPML-98
96BesAutS-95
96BesAutSA-89
96StLucMTI-22
97Bow-344
97BowChr-234
97BowChrl-234
97BowChrlR-234
97BowChrR-234
97BowInt-344
Wilson, Randy
84NewOriT-22
Wilson, Red (Robert)
53Top-250
54Top-58
56Top-92
57Top-19
58Top-213
59Top-24
59TopVen-24
60Top-379
61Pos-66
79TCM50-281
90DodTar-867
91TopArc1-250
94TopArc1-58
94TopArc1G-58
Wilson, Ric
82WauTimF-27
84ChaLooT-22
87WauTimP-27
Wilson, Rick
85EveGialC-23
94IowCubF-1293
Wilson, Roger
86MiaMarP-28
87WilBilP-21
Wilson, Ryan
92HigSchPLS-6
Wilson, Sam W.
23WilChoV-174
Wilson, Scott
89CalLeaA-51
89SanJosGB-17
89SanJosGCLC-234
89SanJosGP-454
89SanJosGS-28
90SanJosGB-27
90SanJosGCLC-55
90SanJosGS-30
91CalLeLA-49
91SanJosGC-30
Wilson, Steve
96YakBeaTI-33
Wilson, Steve Douglas
86TulDriTI-10
87PorChaRP-10
88TexLeaAGS-5
88TulDriTI-8
89Bow-280
89BowTif-280
89CubMar-44
89DonBasB-250
89DonRoo-10
89Fle-640
89FleGlo-640
89FleUpd-82
89TopTra-131T
89TopTraT-131T
89UppDec-799
90Bow-23
90BowTif-23
90CubMar-25
90Don-394
90Fle-49
90FleCan-49
90Lea-420
90OPC-741
90Sco-531
90ScoYouS2-28
90Top-741
90TopRoo-32
90TopTif-741
90TopTVCu-18
90TulDriDGB-9
90UppDec-341
91CubVinL-34
91Don-519
91Fle-440
91IowCubLD-222
91IowCubP-1062
91LinDriAAA-222
91OPC-69
91ParPatF-14
91Sco-306
91Top-69
91TopDesS-69
91TopMic-69
91TopTif-69
91UppDec-493
92DodMot-27
92DodPol-38
92DodSmo-5292
92Don-710
92Lea-161
92OPC-751
92Sco-812
92StaClu-626
92StaCluECN-626
92Top-751
92TopGol-751
92TopGolW-751
92TopMic-751
92Ult-510
93DodMot-23
93DodPol-28
93Don-34
93Fle-456
93Lea-145
93PacSpa-506
93RanKee-385
93StaCluD-27
93Top-133
93TopGol-133
93TopInaM-133
93TopMic-133
94Fle-529
94NewOrlZF-1470
94Pac-324
94Top-573
94TopGol-573
94TopSpa-573
95NasSouTI-29
96BriWhiSB-3
Wilson, Tack (Michael)
81AlbDukT-23A
82AlbDukT-23
83TolMudHT-18
84TolMudHT-22
85PhoGiaC-195
87EdmTraP-2070

89OklCit8C-22
89OklCit8P-1534
90HunStaB-23
91PacSenL-50
93DurBulC-28
93DurBulF-506
93DurBulTI-2
94RicBraF-2865

Wilson, Terry
89MyrBeaBJP-1475

Wilson, Tex
90DodTar-1096

Wilson, Tim
89HelBreSP-5
90HelBreSP-23

Wilson, Todd
86EveGiaC-181
86EveGiaPC-36
90BilMusP-3232
91CedRapRC-21
91CedRapRP-2730
94EveGiaF-3664
96SanJosGB-6

Wilson, Tom
86TamTarP-27
90PitMetP-17
91OneYanP-4158
92ClaFS7-308
92GreHorC-11
92GreHorF-783
93GreHorF-889
93SouAtlLAPI-42
94AbaYanF-1445
94ClaGolF-198
95NorNavTI-54
96BufBisB-24

Wilson, Trevor
85EveGialC-24
86CliGiaP-28
87CliGiaP-27
88BasAmeAAB-27
88BlaYNPRWL-126
88ShrCapP-1298
89Fle-347
89FleGlo-347
89PhoFirC-10
89PhoFirP-1481
89ScoHot1R-31
89Top-783
89TopTif-783
89UppDec-733
90CMC-535
90Don-414
90FleUpd-64
90Lea-489
90OPC-408
90PhoFirC-8
90PhoFirP-12
90ProAAAF-38
90Top-408
90TopTif-408
90UppDec-637
91Bow-630
91Don-263
91Fle-277
91GiaMot-22
91GiaPacGaE-9
91OPC-96
91Sco-657
91StaClu-212
91Stu-253
91Top-96
91TopDesS-96
91TopMic-96
91TopTif-96
91UltUpd-119
91UppDec-653
92Bow-119
92Don-575
92Fle-651
92GiaMot-22
92GiaPacGaE-36
92Lea-340
92OPC-204
92Pin-352
92Sco-608
92StaClu-86
92Top-204
92TopGol-204
92TopGolW-204
92TopMic-204
92TriPla-146
92Ult-297
92UppDec-337
93Don-578
93Fle-162
93GiaMot-23
93GiaPos-34
93Lea-477
93PacSpa-279
93Pin-210
93Sco-401
93StaClu-185
93StaCluFDI-185
93StaCluG-22
93StaCluMOP-185
93Top-364
93TopGol-364
93TopInaM-364
93TopMic-364
93TriPla-186
93Ult-491
93UppDec-197
93UppDecGold-197
94Don-572
94Fle-705
94GiaUSPC-3H
94GiaUSPC-10S
94Pac-560
94Pin-82
94PinArtP-82
94PinMusC-82
94Sco-140
94ScoGolR-140
94StaCluT-21
94StaCluTFDI-21
94Top-462
94TopGol-462
94TopSpa-462
95Fin-224
95FinRef-224
95FleUpd-197
95GiaMot-24
95StaClu-582
95StaCluMOP-582
95StaCluSTWS-582
95TopTra-117T

Wilson, Vance
94PitMetC-24
94PitMetF-3526
96StLucMTI-28

Wilson, Ward
76CliPilT-35
77LynMetT-30

Wilson, Wayne
84NewOriT-6
85NewOriT-11
86HagSunP-28
87HagSunP-16

Wilson, William D.
49SolSunP-12
54Top-222
55A'sRodM-45
55A'sRodM-46
55Top-86
55TopDouH-101
76A'sRodMC-29
94TopArc1-222
94TopArc1G-222

Wilson, William H.
67Top-402A
67Top-402B
69Top-576
70OPC-28
70Top-28
71MLBOffS-192
71OPC-192
71Top-192
72Top-587
73OPC-619
73Top-619

Wilson, Willie (batboy)
96DurBulBIB-11

Wilson, Willie J.
75WatRoyT-34
78Roy-26
78SSP270-241
79RoyTeal-13
79Top-409
80BurKinPHR-33
80OPC-87
80Top-157
80Top-204
81AllGamPI-70
81CokTeaS-83
81Don-223
81Fle-29
81Fle-653A
81Fle-653B
81FleStiC-106
81Kel-24
81OPC-360
81PerCreC-31
81RoyPol-10
81Top-208
81Top-360
81TopScr-20
81TopSti-16
81TopSti-81
81TopSti-247
82Don-448
82Fle-427
82FleSta-207
82Kel-62
82OPC-230
82Roy-25
82Top-230
82TopSti-189
83AllGamPI-71
83Don-15
83Don-112
83DonActA-13
83Dra-30
83Fle-128
83FleSta-218
83FleSti-104
83Kel-23
83OPC-16
83PerCreC-33
83PerCreCG-33
83Roy-32
83RoyPol-10
83Top-471
83Top-701
83Top-710
83TopFol-3
83TopFol-5
83TopGloS-23
83TopLeaS-1
83TopSti-15
83TopSti-73
83TopSti-161
84Don-175
84Fle-364
84FleSti-94
84FunFooP-82
84Nes792-525
84OPC-5
84Top-525
84TopSti-280
84TopStiB-5
84TopTif-525
85AllGamPI-71
85Don-297
85Fle-218
85KASDis-19
85KitCloD-19
85Lea-110
85OPC-6
85ThoMcAD-22
85Top-617
85TopSti-277
85TopTif-617
85Woo-42
86BasStaB-122
86Don-175
86Fle-25
86FleMin-5
86FleStiC-129
86Lea-106
86OPC-25
86RoyKitCD-15
86RoyNatP-6
86SevCoi-C14
86Spo-124
86Spo-128
86Spo-144
86Spo-180
86Spo-186
86Top-25
86TopMinL-22
86TopSti-258
86TopSup-59
86TopTat-21
86TopTif-25
86Woo-32
87Don-96
87DonOpeD-208
87Fle-384
87FleExcS-43
87FleGlo-384
87FleMin-116
87FleRecS-42
87FleStiC-125
87Lea-97
87OPC-367
87Spo-85
87SpoTeaP-13
87StuPan-20
87Top-783
87TopMinL-58
87TopSti-261
87TopTif-783
88Don-255
88DonBasB-263
88Fle-274
88FleGlo-274
88Lea-189
88OPC-222
88PanSti-113
88RoySmo-3
88Sco-102
88ScoGlo-102
88Spo-192
88StaLinRo-20
88Top-452
88TopBig-21
88TopMinL-17
88TopRevLL-25
88TopSti-263
88TopTif-452
89Bow-124
89BowTif-124
89Don-120
89Fle-298
89FleGlo-298
89OPC-168
89PanSti-361
89RoyTasD-5
89Sco-28
89Spo-186
89Top-168
89TopBatL-17
89TopBig-136
89TopMinL-56
89TopSti-268
89TopTif-168
89UppDec-244
90Don-440
90Fle-123
90FleCan-123
90KayB-31
90Lea-336
90MLBBasB-109
90OPC-323
90PacLeg-109
90PubSti-361
90Sco-104
90Top-323
90TopBig-45
90TopTif-323
90UppDec-349
90VenSti-495
91A'sMot-17
91Bow-230
91Fle-575
91Lea-299
91OPC-208
91OPCPre-129
91ScoRoo-15T
91StaClu-378
91Top-208
91TopDesS-208
91TopMic-208
91TopTif-208
91TopTra-129T
91TopTraT-129T
91UltUpd-48
91UppDec-609
92AthMot-17
92FleUpd-53
92OPC-536
92Sco-328
92StaClu-343
92Top-536
92TopGol-536
92TopGolW-536
92TopMic-536
92Ult-429
92UppDec-238
93Bow-468
93CubMar-31
93Fle-302
93FleFinE-13
93Lea-413
93OPC-370
93OPCPre-53
93PacSpa-228
93Pin-141
93RoySta2-15
93Sco-647
93Sel-395
93StaClu-622
93StaCluCu-5
93StaCluFDI-622
93StaCluMOP-622
93Stu-199
93Top-318
93TopGol-318
93TopInaM-318
93TopMic-318
93Ult-324
93UppDec-417
93UppDec-625
93UppDecGold-417
93UppDecGold-625
94DurBulTI-31
94Fle-402
94Pac-116
94Sco-134
94ScoGolR-134
94StaClu-311
94StaCluFDI-311
94StaCluGR-311
94StaCluMOP-311
94StaCluT-357
94StaCluTFDI-357
94Top-698
94TopGol-698
94TopSpa-698
94Ult-169
95DurBulTI-38

Wilson, Woodrow
94UppDecTAE-21

Wilstead, Judd
93HelBreF-4096
93HelBreSP-14
94BelBreC-26
94BelBreF-102
96El PasDB-29

Wilstead, Randy (Randon)
90JamExpP-6
91MidLeaAP-MWL50
91RocExpC-22
91RocExpP-2057
92WesPalBEC-22
92WesPalBEF-2097
93WesPalBEC-25
93WesPalBEF-1351
94HarSenF-2102

Wiltbank, Ben
78SalPirT-18
79PorBeaT-4
79Top-723
81BufBisT-5

Wiltse, Hal
93ConTSN-955

Wiltse, Hooks (George R.)
03BreE10-153
06GiaUllAFS-12
08RosComP-134
09AmeCarE-118
09ColChiE-310
09PhiCarE-25
09T206-383
09T206-384
09T206-385
10CouT21-249
10CouT21-250
10CouT21-251
10CouT21-252
10CouT21-253
10CouT21-254
10CouT21-324
10DomDisP-127
10E12AmeCDC-41
10PeoT21-57
10RedCroT-86
10RedCroT-87
10RedCroT-166
10RedCroT-167
10RedCroT-258
10RedCroT-259
10StaCarE-29
10SweCapPP-123
10W555-63
11MecDFT-34
11S74Sil-96
11SpoLifCW-371
11SpoLifM-223

11T205-183A
11T205-183B
11TurRedT-41
12ColRedB-310
12ColTinT-310
12HasTriFT-48J
12HasTriFT-74F
12T207-200
14B18B-73
14PieStaT-65
15AmeCarE-41
15VicT21-30
92ConTSN-332
Wiltse, Lew
06FanCraNL-53
Wiltshere, Vernon
35DiaMatCS3T1-149
36NatChiFPR-82
Wiltz, Stanley
92WelPirC-27
92WelPirF-1335
93WelPirC-27
93WelPirF-3370
Wimberly, Larry
94MarPhiC-30
94MarPhiF-3295
95PiePhiF-188
95SPML-129
95TopTra-88T
96BesAutS-96
96Exc-215
96MicBatCB-28
96SarRedSB-29
Wimmer, Chris
90WicStaSGD-38
91TopTra-130T
91TopTraT-130T
92StaCluD-197
92TopDaiQTU-28
92TopTra-129T
92TopTraG-129T
93SanJosGC-22
93SanJosGF-21
93StaCluM-42
94ClaGolF-152
94ExcFS7-297
94ShrCapF-1616
94UppDecML-21
95Bow-85
95PhoFirTI-8
95UppDecML-148
96LouRedB-27
95UppDecMLFS-148
Winawer, Larry
91HelBreSP-7
Winbush, Mike
86SalRedBP-29
Winchell, Derek
87SalAngP-34
88BenBucL-30
92CalLeaACL-50
Winchester, Marty
93SpoIndC-24
93SpoIndF-3593
94AppFoxC-21
94AppFoxF-1055
Winchester, Scott
95WatIndTI-30
Winders, Brian
94LSUTig-7
Windes, Cary
89FreStaBS-21
Windes, Rodney
88AubAstP-1955
89AshTouP-947
90OscAstS-26
91OscAstC-13
91OscAstP-686
92JacGenS-348
Windham, Mike
93GleFalRC-29
93GleFalRF-4003
94MadHatC-25
94MadHatF-132
96StPetCB-30
Windhorn, Gordon
62Top-254
90DodTar-868
Windmiller, Amy
91FreStaLBS-14
Windsor, Duchess of
83ASAJohM-10
Windsor, Duke of
83ASAJohM-10
Wine, Bobby (Robert)
69ExpPin-9
47StaPinP2-42
63Top-71
64PhiJayP-12
64PhiPhiB-26
64Top-347
64TopVen-347
65OPC-36
65PhiJayP-12
65Top-36
66Top-284
66TopVen-284
67CokCapPh-2
67Top-466
68Top-396
69Top-648
70ExpPin-14
70ExpPos-9
70MLBOffS-72
70OPC-332
70Top-332
71ExpLaPR-14
71ExpPS-28
71MLBOffS-144
71OPC-171
71Top-171
72Dia-51
72MilBra-367
72Top-657
73OPC-486
73Top-486A
73Top-486B
74OPC-119
74Top-119
78PhiSSP-32
78SSP270-32
78TCM60I-181
83PhiPosGPaM-4
85BraPol-7
86Top-51
86TopTif-51
89BraDub-30
96MetKah-34
96MetKah-32
Wine, Robbie
86TucTorP-26
87SpoTeaP-8
87TucTorP-3
88Don-508
88Fle-459
88FleGlo-459
88OklCit8C-22
88OklCit8P-42
88Sco-496
88ScoGlo-496
88Top-119
88TopTif-119
89RicBraBC-28
89RicBraC-11
89RicBraP-843
89RicBraTI-24
90CanIndB-17
90CanIndP-1295
91LinDriAAA-572
91TidTidLD-572
Winegarner, Ralph
34DiaMatCSB-199
35DiaMatCS3T1-151
36R31PasP-25
Winfield, Dave
74OPC-456
74PadDea-30
74PadMcDD-13
74Top-456
74TopSta-100
75Hos-37
75OPC-61
75Top-61
76Hos-83
76OPC-160
76SSP-133
76Top-160
77BurCheD-130
77Hos-44
77Kel-28
77OPC-156
77PadSchC-65A
77PadSchC-65B
77PadSchC-65C
77PadSchC-65D
77Spo-5702
77Spo-8803
77Top-390
77TopCloS-52
78Hos-63
78Kel-11
78OPC-78
78PadFamF-38
78Top-530
79Hos-125
79OPC-11
79PadDea-11
79Top-30
79TopCom-31
80BurKinPHR-22
80Kel-32
80OPC-122
80Top-203
80Top-230
80TopSup-18
81AllGamPI-71
81Don-364
81Dra-14
81Fle-484
81FleStiC-25
81Kel-21
81PerAll-18
81PerCreC-21
81Squ-19
81Top-370
81TopSti-111
81TopSupHT-72
81TopTra-855
82Don-18
82Don-31
82Don-575
82Dra-31
82FBIDis-26
82Fle-56
82Fle-646
82Fle-646B
82FleSta-110
82FleSta-113
82Kel-12
82OPC-76
82OPC-352
82PerCreC-14
82PerCreCG-14
82Squ-7
82Top-553
82Top-600
82TopSti-137
82TopSti-213
83AllGamPI-72
83Don-409
83DonActA-36
83Dra-31
83Fle-398
83Fle-633
83FleSta-219
83FleSti-39
83Kel-15
83OPC-258
83PerAll-7
83PerAllG-7
83PerCreC-34
83PerCreCG-34
83Top-770
83TopGloS-7
83TopSti-99
83YanRoyRD-12
84AllGamPI-161
84Don-51
84Dra-32
84Fle-143
84FleSti-5
84FunFooP-1
84MilBra-29
84Nes792-402
84Nes792-460
84NesDreT-6
84OCoandSI-63
84OPC-266
84OPC-378
84RalPur-7
84SevCoi-E7
84Top-402
84Top-460
84TopCer-7
84TopGloA-8
84TopGloS-16
84TopRubD-29
84TopSti-190
84TopSti-319
84TopSup-27
84TopTif-402
84TopTif-460
85AllGamPI-72
85Don-51
85Don-651A
85Don-651B
85DonActA-12
85DonHig-53
85Dra-32
85Fle-146
85Fle-629
85FleLimE-43
85FleStaS-5
85GenMilS-25
85KASDis-20
85KitCloD-20
85Lea-127
85Lea-140
85OPC-180
85PolMet-Y4
85SevCoi-C3
85SevCoi-E5
85SevCoi-G3
85SevCoi-S5
85SevCoi-W5
85SpoPro-4
85SpoPro-5
85ThoMcAD-23
85Top-180
85Top-705
85Top3-D-18
85TopGloA-17
85TopGloS-14
85TopRubD-30
85TopSti-186
85TopSti-308
85TopSup-60
85TopTif-180
85TopTif-705
86BasStaB-123
86BurKinA-2
86Don-248
86DonAll-15
86DonPop-15
86DorChe-19
86Dra-18
86Fle-121
86FleMin-26
86FleStiC-130
86FleStiWBC-S4
86Lea-125
86MeaGolBB-16
86MeaGolSB-7
86MSAJifPD-7
86OPC-70
86QuaGra-33
86SevCoi-E11
86Spo-49
86SpoDecG-74
86Top-70
86Top-717
86Top3-D-29
86TopGloA-8
86TopGloS-42
86TopMinL-29
86TopSti-160
86TopSti-298
86TopSup-60
86TopTat-1
86TopTif-70
86TopTif-717
86Woo-33
86YanTCM-36
87BoaandB-4
87ClaGam-11
87Don-20
87Don-105
87DonAll-2
87DonOpeD-243
87DonP-2
87DonSupD-20
87Dra-5
87Fle-120
87FleGlo-120
87FleLimE-42
87FleMin-117
87FleStiC-126
87GenMilB-2I
87KayB-33
87KraFoo-33
87Lea-20
87Lea-70
87MSAIceTD-9
87OPC-36
87OPCBoxB-H
87RalPur-4
87RedFolSB-28
87SevCoi-E15
87Spo-41
87Spo-153
87SpoTeaP-7
87StuPan-23
87Top-770
87TopCoi-26
87TopGloA-17
87TopSti-152
87TopSti-298
87TopTif-770
87TopWaxBC-H
88AlaGolAA'TI-16
88ClaRed-170
88Don-298
88DonAll-2
88DonBasB-244
88DonPop-2
88DonReaBY-278
88Dra-12
88Fle-226
88FleBasA-44
88FleBasM-43
88FleGlo-226
88FleMin-44
88FleSlu-43
88FleStiC-53
88KayB-33
88Lea-116
88MSAJifPD-19
88Nes-33
88OPC-89
88PanSti-161
88PanSti-231
88Sco-55
88ScoBoxC-8
88ScoGlo-55
88Spo-7
88SpoGam-7
88StaLinAl-36
88StaLinY-20
88StaWin-1
88StaWin-2
88StaWin-3
88StaWin-4
88StaWin-5
88StaWin-6
88StaWin-7
88StaWin-8
88StaWin-9
88StaWin-10
88StaWin-11
88StaWin-12
88StaStiW-1
88StaStiW-2
88StaStiW-3
88StaStiW-4
88StaStiW-5
88StaStiW-6
88StaStiW-7
88StaStiW-8
88StaStiW-9
88StaStiW-10
88Top-392
88Top-459
88Top-510
88TopBig-24
88TopGloA-8
88TopGloS-46
88TopSti-159
88TopSti-302
88TopStiB-54
88TopTif-392
88TopTif-459
88TopTif-510
88TopUKM-85
88TopUKMT-85
89Bow-179
89BowTif-179
89CadEllD-61
89ClaLigB-32
89Don-159
89DonAll-6
89DonBonM-BC11
89DonGraS-6
89DonPop-6
89Fle-274
89FleBasA-44
89FleBasM-43
89FleExcS-43
89FleGlo-274
89FleHeroB-43
89FleLeaL-43

89FleSup-43
89KayB-32
89KinDis-16
89MSAIceTD-13
89OPC-260
89OPCBoxB-P
89PanSti-240
89PanSti-409
89RedFolSB-128
89Sco-50
89ScoHot1S-3
89ScoSco-41
89Spo-24
89SpollIFKI-282
89Top-260
89Top-407
89TopAme2C-32
89TopBasT-42
89TopBig-314
89TopCoi-58
89TopDouM-15
89TopGloA-8
89TopGloS-21
89TopHilTM-32
89TopMinL-67
89TopSti-149
89TopSti-315
89TopStiB-20
89TopTif-260
89TopTif-407
89TopUKM-84
89TopWaxBC-P
89TVSpoM-81
89UppDec-349
89YanScoNW-7
90AllBasT-23
90Bow-432
90BowTif-432
90Don-551
90DonBesA-87
90Fle-458
90FleCan-458
90FleUpd-81
90KayB-32
90Lea-426
90MLBBasB-64
90OPC-380
90PubSti-298
90PubSti-550
90Sco-307
90ScoRoo-1T
90Spo-87
90Top-380
90TopAmeA-1
90TopBig-20
90TopHilHM-17
90TopMag-50
90TopTif-380
90TopTra-130T
90TopTraT-130T
90TopTVY-34
90UppDec-337
90UppDec-745
90VenSti-496
90VenSti-497
91AngSmo-3
91BluJayFS-34
91Bow-210
91Don-468
91Fle-329
91FouBal-27
91JimDea-22
91Lea-499
91OPC-630
91OPCPre-130
91PanFreS-184
91PanSti-132
91PetSta-5
91PosCan-28
91RedFolS-102
91Sco-83
91Sco100S-66
91StaClu-263
91StaCluMO-9
91StaPinB-54
91Stu-30
91Top-630
91TopDesS-630
91TopMic-630
91TopTif-630
91TopTriH-A3
91Ult-54
91UppDec-337
92Bow-315
92ClaGam-194
92Don-133
92DonUpd-U18
92Fle-72
92Fle-686
92FleUpd-67
92Hig5-15
92Lea-171
92LeaBlaG-171
92OPC-5
92OPC-792
92OPCPre-150
92PepDieM-30
92Pin-375
92PinRool-18
92Sco-32
92Sco100S-9
92ScoFacI-B10
92ScoProP-7
92ScoRoo-7T
92SpollIFK1-170
92StaClu-745
92StaCluMO-35
92Stu-260
92Top-5
92Top-792
92TopGol-5
92TopGol-792
92TopGolW-5
92TopGolW-792
92TopKid-96
92TopMic-5
92TopMic-792
92TopTra-130T
92TopTraG-130T
92Ult-454
92UppDec-28
92UppDec-222
92UppDec-734
92UppDecHRH-HR17
92YanWIZ8-204
92YanWIZA-86
93BluJayD4-14
93BluJayDWS-7
93Bow-565
93ClaGam-98
93DiaMar-118
93Don-643
93DonEli-35
93DonEliS-17
93DonSpiotG-SG1
93DurPowP1-24
93Fin-162
93FinRef-162
93Fla-243
93Fle-343
93FleFinE-241
93FleFinEDT-9
93FleGolM-A3
93FunPac-196
93HumDumC-12
93Lea-423
93Lea-DW
93MetBak-40
93OPC-371
93OPCPre-28
93OPCWorC-17
93OPCWorSH-4
93PacJugC-18
93PacSpa-528
93Pin-295
93Pin-438
93Pin-483
93Pin-486
93PinCoo-10
93PinCooD-10
93PinHomRC-32
93RaiFooW-1
93RaiFooW-2
93RaiFooW-3
93RaiFooW-4
93RaiFooW-5
93RaiFooW-6
93RaiFooW-7
93RaiFooW-8
93RaiFooW-9
93RaiFooW-10
93Sco-521
93Sco-620
93Sel-32
93SelRoo-9T
93SP-252
93StaClu-206
93StaClu-609
93StaCluFDI-206
93StaCluFDI-609
93StaCluM-1
93StaCluMO-28
93StaCluMOP-206
93StaCluMOP-609
93Stu-77
93Top-131
93TOPBLAG-44
93TopGol-131
93TopInaM-131
93TopMagJRC-2
93TopMic-131
93TopTra-83T
93TriPlaG-GS5
93Ult-589
93UppDec-40
93UppDec-786
93UppDecGold-40
93UppDecGold-786
93UppDecSH-HI19
93UppDecTAN-TN9
94Bow-300
94BowBes-R6
94BowBesR-R6
94ColC-302
94ColChoGS-302
94ColChoSS-302
94Don-336
94Don-550
94DonDiaK-DK29
94DonSpeE-336
94ExtBas-126
94ExtBasGB-30
94Fin-215
94FinJum-215
94FinRef-215
94Fla-79
94FlaOutP-10
94Fle-223
94FleGolM-3
94FUnPac-32
94FUnPac-202
94Kra-15
94Lea-137
94LeaL-52
94LeaStaS-8
94OPC-53
94Pac-371
94PanSti-97
94Pin-332
94PinArtP-332
94PinMusC-332
94PinTri-TR3
94ProMag-79
94Sco-407
94Sco-629
94ScoGolR-407
94ScoGolR-629
94Sel-84
94Sel-SS2
94SP-187
94SPDieC-187
94Spo-63
94StaClu-288
94StaCluDD-DD2
94StaCluFDI-288
94StaCluGR-288
94StaCluMOP-288
94StaCluMOP-DD2
94Stu-202
94Top-430
94TopGol-430
94TopSpa-430
94TriPla-260
94TriPlaM-15
94Ult-92
94UltCarA-5
94UppDec-81
94UppDecED-81
95BluJayUSPC-6D
95BluJayUSPC-13C
95Bow-434
95ColCho-54
95ColCho-280
95ColChoGS-54
95ColChoGS-280
95ColChoSE-115
95ColChoSEGS-115
95ColChoSESS-115
95ColChoSS-54
95ColChoSS-280
95Emo-40
95Fin-249
95FinRef-249
95Fla-254
95Fle-151
95FleUpd-43
95Lea-372
95Pac-259
95PacGolP-7
95PacPri-83
95Pin-367
95PinArtP-367
95PinMusC-367
95Sco-80
95ScoGolR-80
95ScoPlaTS-80
95Sel-226
95SelArtP-226
95SP-26
95SP-149
95SPCha-148
95SPChaDC-148
95SPSil-26
95SPSil-149
95StaClu-533
95StaCluMOP-533
95StaCluMOP-RL36
95StaCluRL-RL36
95StaCluSTWS-533
95Sum-75
95SumNthD-75
95Top-158
95TopCyb-38
95UC3-50
95UC3ArtP-50
95Ult-283
95UltGolM-283
95UppDec-95
95UppDecED-95
95UppDecEDG-95
95UppDecSE-160
95UppDecSEG-160
95Zen-23
96ColCho-123
96ColChoGS-123
96ColChoSS-123
96Don-275
96DonPreP-275
96Fle-104
96FleTif-104
96Pin-87
96PinArtP-49
96PinSta-49
96Sco-83
96ScoDugC-A66
96ScoDugCAP-A66
96Ult-56
96UltGolM-56
96UppDec-100
97BluJayS-43

Winfield, Steven W.
80MemChiT-27
82LouRedE-30
82SprCarF-11
83ArkTraT-8

Winford, Barry
88MisStaB-33
89ButCopKSP-7
89MisStaB-38
90Bes-187
90GasRanB-16
90GasRanP-2525
90GasRanS-25
91ChaRanC-15
91ChaRanP-1319
91Cla/Bes-25

Winford, Jim
74Car193T-27
90DodTar-869

Winford, Ron
88MisStaB-34
89MisStaB-39

Wing, Harry
79CedRapGT-25

Wing, Jim
84AriWilP-20
86AriWilP-19
87AriWilP-19
88AriWilP-15
90AriWilP-18
92AriWilP-20

Wing, Marc
84AriWilP-21

Wingard, Ernest
25Exh-120
26Exh-120
27Exh-60

Wingate, Ervan
92GulCoaDF-3577
93GreFalDSP-16
94BakDodC-25
95BakBlaTI-8
96SanBerSB-29

Winget, Jeremy
94OgdRapF-3744
94OgdRapSP-13

Wingfield, Fred
26Exh-72
27Exh-36

Wingo, Al
14FatPlaT-51
25Exh-95
92ConTSN-458
94ConTSN-1177
94ConTSNB-1177

Wingo, Ivey B.
12T207-201
13TomBarW-40
14CraJacE-130
15CraJacE-130
15SpoNewM-194
16BF2FP-74
16FleBreD-102
16SpoNewM-193
19W514-73
20NatCarE-111
20RedWorCP-24
21E121So1-116
21E121So8-107
21Exh-188
21Nei-83
22AmeCarE-77
22E120-180
22W572-117
22W575-151
23MapCriV-14
23W501-50
23W503-59
23WilChoV-175
25Exh-32
26Exh-32
27Exh-16
91ConTSN-235
93ConTSN-868
94ConTSN-1022
94ConTSN-1177
94ConTSNB-1022
94ConTSNB-1177

Wingo, John
52LaPat-17
52LavPro-83

Winham, Lave
90DodTar-870

Winiarski, Chip
91CollndC-19
91CollndP-1486
92KinIndC-14
92KinIndF-2477
93SouBenWSC-25
93SouBenWSF-1431

Winicki, Dennis
91KisDodP-4198
92GreFalDSP-20

Winkelsas, Joe
96DanBraB-28

Winkle, Ken
94EugEmeC-25
94EugEmeF-3714

Winkleman, George
87OldJudN-559

Winkler, Brad
84GreHorT-3
85AlbYanT-22

Winkles, Bobby
73OPC-421
73Top-421A
73Top-421B
74OPC-276
74Top-276
76SSP-624
77Gia-25
78Top-378
86ExpPos-19
86ExpProPa-14
87ExpPos-34

Winn, Jim
84HawIsIC-138
85DomLeaS-52
85HawIsIC-237
85Top-69

85TopTif-69
86Fle-624
86Top-489
86TopTif-489
87Don-312
87Fle-624
87FleGlo-624
87FleUpd-126
87FleUpdG-126
87Top-262
87TopTif-262
87TopTra-130T
87TopTraT-130T
87WhiSoxC-30
88Don-409
88Fle-413
88FleGlo-413
88OPC-388
88PorBeaC-9
88PorBeaP-642
88Sco-462
88ScoGlo-462
88Top-688
88TopSti-288
88TopTif-688
Winn, Randy
95ElmPioTI-30
95ElmPioUTI-30
96Bow-343
96KanCouCTI-30
96KanCouCUTI-13
96Top-235
97Bow-326
97BowChr-223
97BowChrI-223
97BowChrIR-223
97BowChrR-223
97BowInt-326
Winningham, Herm
82LynMetT-3
84TidTidT-5
85ExpPos-25
85FleUpd-130
85OPCPos-8
85TopTifT-131T
85TopTra-131T
86Don-279
86ExpProPa-22
86Fle-266
86Lea-153
86OPC-129
86Top-448
86TopSti-83
86TopTif-448
87ExpPos-35
87FleUpd-130
87FleUpdG-130
87OPC-141
87Top-141
87TopTif-141
88Don-581
88ExpPos-25
88Fle-200
88FleGlo-200
88Lea-242
88MSAHosD-4
88OPC-216
88PanSti-332
88Sco-142
88ScoGlo-142
88ScoRoo-43T
88ScoRooG-43T
88StaLinE-19
88Top-614
88TopSti-83
88TopTif-614
89Don-435
89Fle-175
89FleGlo-175
89RedKah-29
89Sco-496
89Top-366
89TopBig-94
89TopTif-366
89UppDec-636A
89UppDec-636B
90Don-478
90Fle-435
90FleCan-435
90OPC-94
90RedKah-26
90Sco-38
90Top-94
90TopTif-94
90UppDec-589
91Don-695
91Fle-82
91MetWIZ-434
91OPC-204
91RedKah-29
91RedPep-20
91Sco-656
91StaClu-546
91Top-204
91TopDesS-204
91TopMic-204
91TopTif-204
91UltUpd-78
92OPC-547
92Sco-574
92ScoRoo-43T
92StaClu-205
92StaClu-883
92StaCluNC-883
92Top-547
92TopGol-547
92TopGolW-547
92TopMic-547
92TopTra-131T
92TopTraG-131T
93Fle-566
93PawRedSDD-28
93PawRedSF-2423
93Top-377
93TopGol-377
93TopInaM-377
93TopMic-377
Winsett, Tom
90DodTar-871
Winslett, Dax
94BakDodC-26
94Top-755
94TopGol-755
94TopSpa-755
96OrlCubB-28
Winslow, Bryant
90WicStaSGD-39
91AubAstC-16
91AubAstP-4283
92AubAstC-10
92AubAstF-1364
92OscAstC-7
93QuaCitRBC-24
93QuaCitRBF-110
Winslow, Daniel
81ArkTraT-15
Winston, Darrin
88JamExpP-1918
89RocExpLC-30
90JacExpB-24
90JacExpP-1376
91IndIndLD-198
91IndIndP-463
91LinDriAAA-198
94HarSenF-2094
94OttLynF-2900
Winston, Hank
90DodTar-872
Winston, Todd
92AubAstC-14
92AubAstF-1357
93OscAstC-25
93OscAstF-642
94OscAstC-25
94OscAstF-1142
Winter, George
03BreE10-154
04RedSoxUP-14
08RosComP-9
11SpoLifCW-372
Winterburn, Robert
88BoiHawP-1631
Winterfeldt, Todd
79WauTimT-3
Winters, Dan
85FreGiaP-16
86LynMetP-27
87JacMetF-1
Winters, George
04FanCraAL-50
Winters, James A.
86PenWhiSP-28
87BirBarB-24
Winters, Lee
53MotCoo-1
Winters, Matt
83ColCliT-23
84ColCliP-24
84ColCliT-22
85ColCliP-24
85ColCliT-22
86BufBisP-25
87MemChiB-24
87MemChiP-7
87SouLeaAJ-9
88MemChiB-19
88SouLeaAJ-1
89OmaRoyC-21
89OmaRoyP-1728
90Fle-124
90FleCan-124
90Sco100RS-47
90TopDeb89-147
90UppDec-524
96KanCouCTI-31
Winzenread, Dickie
87NewOriP-22
Wipf, Mark
92KinMetC-14
92KinMetF-1546
93CapCitBC-24
93CapCitBF-475
94CapCitBC-24
94CapCitBF-1766
95StLucMTI-35
Wirsta, Mike
92MedHatBJSP-26
93MedHatBJSP-22
94MedHatBJSP-29
96MedHatBJTI-33
Wirtala, Allen
93AppFoxC-30
94AppFoxC-25
Wirth, Alan
79OgdA'sT-22
79Top-711
80OgdA'sT-17
81SpoIndT-25
Wirth, Greg
84NewOriT-10
Wisdom, Allen
87ClePhiP-24
Wise, Brett Wayne
81VerBeaDT-24
Wise, James
95DanBraTI-29
Wise, K. Casey
57Top-396
58Top-247
59Top-204
60Top-342
Wise, Rick
64PhiPhiB-27
64Top-561
65Top-322
67OPC-37
67Top-37
68Top-262
68TopVen-262
69MLBOffS-180
69OPC-188
69PhiTeal-12
69Top-188
69TopFou-5
69TopSta-80
69TopTeaP-8
70MLBOffS-96
70PhiTeal-12
70Top-605
70TopPos-8
71CarTeal-43
71MLBOffS-191
71OPC-598
71PhiArcO-13
71Top-598
71TopCoi-131
72Kel-23
72MilBra-368
72OPC-43
72OPC-44
72OPC-345
72Top-43
72Top-44
72Top-345
72Top-756
72TopPos-14
73OPC-364
73Top-364
74OPC-84
74OPC-339
74Top-84
74Top-339
74TopSta-139
75OPC-56
75Top-56
76Kel-35
76LinSup-112
76OPC-170
76RedSoxSM-15
76Top-170
77Top-455
78RCColC-99
78Top-572
79OPC-127
79Top-253
80OPC-370
80Top-725
81Don-3
81OPC-274
81Top-616
81TopSti-232
82Don-170
82Fle-585
82Top-330
83PhiPosGM-11
85MadMusP-25
85MadMusT-24
86MadMusP-27
86MadMusP-28
88AubAstP-1963
89AubAstP-2187
89PacSenL-31
89T/MSenL-117
89TopSenL-41
90EliSenL-106
91LinDriAA-475
91NewBriRSLD-475
91NewBriRSP-368
92NewBriRSF-450
93PawRedSDD-29
93PawRedSF-2426
94PawRedSDD-30
94PawRedSF-962
95PawRedSDD-30
95PawRedTI-40
Wise, Sam
87BucN28-13
87OldJudN-560
88WG1CarG-9
Wise, Will
95DanBraTI-30
96DanBraB-29
Wiseley, Mike
93NiaFalRF-3405
94LakTigC-26
94LakTigF-3051
Wiseman, Dennis
89JohCitCS-23
90Bes-142
90SprCarB-25
91ArkTraLD-48
91ArkTraP-1287
91LinDriAA-48
92ArkTraF-1131
92ArkTraS-35
93LouRedF-216
Wiseman, Greg
91ButCopKSP-23
92Ft.MyeMCB-23
92Ft.MyeMF-2759
Wiseman, Michael
88CapCodPPaLP-174
Wiseman, Tim
85OrlTwiT-21
Wishnevski, Mike
86ChaLooP-25
87CalCanP-2324
88CalCanC-20
88CalCanP-783
Wishnevski, Robert
88DunBluJS-22
89KnoBluJB-27
89KnoBluJP-1138
89KnoBluJS-22
89SouLeaAJ-21
90KnoBluJS-21
90SyrChiMB-30
91KnoBluJP-1769
92ClaFS7-335
92DenZepF-2641
92ElPasDS-213
93Bow-323
93NewOrlZF-974
94LouRedF-2982
Wisler, Brian
93BurIndC-28
93BurIndF-3298
94BurIndC-28
94BurIndF-3796
Wismer, Michael
89GreFalDSP-12
90VerBeaDS-28
Wisnaski, Len
52LavPro-44
Wissel, Dick
75IntLeaAT-30
75IntLeaAT-31
Wissler, Bill
92KenTwiC-18
92KenTwiF-606
93NasXprF-404
94SalLakBF-818
Wissman, Dave
77FriOneYW-83
Wistert, Francis
36GouWidPPR-D39
Witasick, Gerald
94ExcFS7-275
95Bow-212
97Bow-371
97BowInt-371
97Top-492
Witasick, Jay
93JohCitCC-29
93JohCitCF-3680
94BowBes-B87
94BowBesR-B87
94Cla-189
94MadHatC-26
94MadHatF-133
94MidLeaAF-MDW45
95Bes-96
95Exc-278
95SPML-154
95UppDecML-88
97UppDec-284
95UppDecMLFS-88
Witek, Mickey (Nicholas)
46SpoExcW-9-8
47TipTop-135
76TayBow4-70
Withem, Shannon
90BriTigP-3160
90BriTigS-26
91Cla/Bes-187
91FayGenC-13
91FayGenP-1172
91NiaFalRC-26
91NiaFalRP-3634
92FayGenF-2170
94TreThuF-2121
95JacSunTI-28
95SigRoo-50
95SigRooSig-50
96BinBeeB-30
Witherspoon, Richard
89ElmPioP-21
90WinHavRSS-25
Withrow, Corky
77FriOneYW-81
Withrow, Mike
82GleFalWST-24
83GleFalWST-21
Witkowski, Matt
89ChaRaiP-985
90Bes-68
90MidLeaASGS-52
90WatDiaB-18
90WatDiaP-2388
91HigDesMC-23
91HigDesMP-2406
92WicWraF-3665
92WicWraS-647
93LasVegSF-954
94LasVegSF-878
Witmer, Joe
86CalCanP-26
Witmeyer, Ronald
89ModA'sC-27
89ModA'sCLC-281
90CalLeaACLC-43
90ModA'sC-32
90ModA'sCLC-165
90ModA'sP-2224
91LinDriAAA-548
91TacTigLD-548
91TacTigP-2316
92SkyAAAF-245
92StaClu-435
92TacTigF-2513

92TacTigS-547
92TopDeb91-187
93TacTigF-3041
Witt, Bobby
85TulDriTI-18
86DonRoo-49
86FleSlu-42
86FleUpd-129
86RanPer-48
86SpoRoo-12
86TopTra-126T
86TopTraT-126T
87Don-99
87DonHig-25
87Fle-143
87FleExcS-44
87FleGlo-143
87Lea-112
87RanMot-25
87RanSmo-6
87Spo-39
87SpoTeaP-1
87Top-415
87TopTif-415
88Don-101
88Fle-483
88FleGlo-483
88PanSti-198
88RanMot-25
88RanSmo-7
88Sco-149
88ScoGlo-149
88StaLinRa-20
88Top-747
88TopTif-747
89Bow-222
89BowTif-222
89ClaLigB-77
89Don-461
89DonBasB-279
89Fle-537
89FleGlo-537
89OPC-38
89PanSti-448
89RanMot-14
89RanSmo-34
89Sco-463
89ScoYouSI-8
89Spo-82
89Top-548
89TopBig-191
89TopTif-548
89UppDec-557
90Don-292
90Fle-315
90FleCan-315
90Lea-337
90OPC-166
90PubSti-424
90RanMot-15
90Sco-457
90Top-166
90TopTif-166
90UppDec-636
90VenSti-498
91Bow-287
91Cla1-T87
91ClaGam-166
91Don-249
91Fle-304
91Lea-3
91OPC-27
91PanCanT1-78
91PanFreS-260
91PanSti-203
91RanMot-6
91Sco-410
91Sco-507
91SevCoi-T15
91StaClu-96
91Stu-130
91Top-27
91TopDesS-27
91TopMic-27
91TopTif-27
91Ult-357
91UppDec-627
92Bow-230
92Don-391
92Lea-305
92OPC-675
92Pin-451
92RanMot-6
92RanTeal-26
92Sco-381
92StaClu-677
92Top-675
92TopDaiQTU-5
92TopGol-675
92TopGolW-675
92TopMic-675
92TriPla-154
92UppDec-576
93AthMot-14
93Bow-301
93Don-51
93Fla-265
93Fle-303
93Lea-204
93Pin-365
93RanKee-386
93Sco-150
93Sel-363
93StaClu-150
93StaCluAt-16
93StaCluFDI-150
93StaCluMOP-150
93Top-398
93TopGol-398
93TopInaM-398
93TopMic-398
93TriPla-141
93Ult-264
93Ult-299
93UppDec-87
93UppDecGold-87
94A'sMot-14
94Bow-248
94ColC-471
94ColChoGS-471
94ColChoSS-471
94Don-308
94Fin-289
94FinRef-289
94Fla-334
94Fle-277
94Lea-102
94Pac-466
94Pin-276
94PinArtP-276
94PinMusC-276
94Sco-437
94ScoGolR-437
94Sel-128
94StaClu-91
94StaCluFDI-91
94StaCluGR-91
94StaCluMOP-91
94Top-255
94TopGol-255
94TopSpa-255
94TriPla-10
94Ult-115
94UppDec-120
94UppDecED-120
95ColCho-558T
95ColChoGS-123
95ColChoSS-123
95Don-391
95DonPreP-391
95DonTopotO-170
95Fin-71
95FinRef-71
95Fle-257
95FleUpd-101
95Pac-323
95Sco-152
95ScoGolR-152
95ScoPlaTS-152
95StaClu-368
95StaClu-594
95StaCluMOP-368
95StaCluMOP-594
95StaCluSTWS-368
95StaCluSTWS-594
95StaCluVR-194
95Top-461
95TopCyb-256
95TopTra-123T
96Don-449
96DonPreP-449
96Fla-180
96LeaSigA-247
96LeaSigAG-248
96LeaSigAS-248
96RanMot-13
96StaCluVRMO-194
96Ult-424
96UltGolM-424
97Cir-103
97CirRav-103
97ColCho-236
97Fle-233
97FleTif-233
97Pac-212
97PacLigB-212
97PacSil-212
97Sco-182
97ScoPreS-182
97ScoRan-10
97ScoRanPl-10
97ScoRanPr-10
97ScoShoS-182
97ScoShoSAP-182
97StaClu-262
97StaCluMOP-262
97Top-332
97UppDec-511
Witt, George
59Kah-38
59Top-110
59TopVen-110
60Top-298
61Top-286
62Top-287
Witt, Hal
78St.PetCT-27
Witt, Kevin
94MedHatBJF-3692
94MedHatBJSP-5
94SigRooDP-27
94SigRooDPS-27
94StaCluDP-88
94StaCluDPFDI-88
94TopTra-54T
95Exc-147
95HagSunF-79
95ScoDraP-DP17
95SelSurS-SS2
95SPML-163
95StaClu-101
95StaCluFDI-101
95StaCluMOP-101
95StaCluSTWS-101
95Top-341
96BesAutSA-90
96DunBluJB-26
96DunBluJTI-30
96DunBluJUTI-17
97Bow-339
97BowChr-232
97BowChrI-232
97BowChrIR-232
97BowChrR-232
97BowInt-339
Witt, Mike
81LonBeaPT-11
82Don-416
82Fle-473
82Top-744
83Don-416
83Fle-102
83Top-53
83Top-651
84AngSmo-31
84Fle-531
84Nes792-499
84Top-499
84TopTif-499
85AngSmo-1
85AngStrH-13
85Don-108
85Fle-316
85Fle-643
85FleStaS-111
85Lea-46
85OPC-309
85Top-309
85TopSti-195
85TopSti-227
85TopSup-45
85TopTif-309
86AngSmo-1
86Don-179
86DonHig-38
86Fle-171
86FleMin-36
86FleSlu-43
86Lea-112
86SevCoi-W12
86Spo-53
87AngSmo-3
87Don-58
87DonAll-51
87DonOpeD-2
87Fle-95
87Fle-641
87FleAwaW-43
87FleBasA-44
87FleGamW-43
87FleGlo-95
87FleGlo-641
87FleMin-118
87FleSlu-44
87FleStiC-127
87KraFoo-47
87Lea-111
87MandMSL-17
87OPC-92
87RedFolSB-4
87SevCoi-W15
87Spo-59
87SpoTeaP-11
87StuPan-16
87Top-556
87Top-760
87TopGloS-33
87TopMinL-48
87TopSti-179
87TopTif-556
87TopTif-760
88AngSmo-4
88Don-86
88DonAll-20
88DonBasB-307
88Fle-507
88Fle-626
88FleGlo-507
88FleGlo-626
88FleMin-13
88FleStiC-13
88FleSup-43
88GreBasS-15
88Lea-49
88OPC-270
88PanSti-38
88Sco-81
88ScoGlo-81
88Spo-32
88StaLinAn-20
88Top-270
88TopBig-4
88TopSti-174
88TopTif-270
88TopUKM-86
88TopUKMT-86
89AngSmo-19
89Bow-42
89BowTif-42
89Don-372
89Fle-490
89FleGlo-490
89OPC-190
89PanSti-286
89RedFolSB-129
89Sco-298
89Spo-197
89Top-190
89TopBasT-125
89TopCoi-59
89TopSti-176
89TopTif-190
89TopUKM-85
89TVSpoM-112
89UppDec-555
90AngSmo-16
90ClaYel-T49
90Don-580
90El PasDAGTI-33
90Fle-148
90FleCan-148
90OPC-650
90PubSti-382
90Sco-226
90ScoRoo-50T
90Top-650
90TopTif-650
90UppDec-548
90VenSti-499
90YanScoNW-14
91Don-282
91DonBonC-BC1
91Fle-680
91FleWaxBC-1
91Lea-74
91OPC-536
91Sco-430
91Sco-699
91StaClu-466
91StaCluCM-17
91Top-536
91TopDesS-536
91TopMic-536
91TopTif-536
91UppDec-429
92OPC-357
92StaClu-848
92Top-357
92TopGol-357
92TopGolW-357
92TopMic-357
93StaCluY-18
94Pac-443
Witt, Whitey (Lawton)
16ColE13-193
17HolBreD-114
20NatCarE-112
21OxfConE-20
23W515-37
23WilChoV-176
79DiaGre-13
90DodTar-873
Wittcke, Darren
91EveGiaC-26
91EveGiaP-3915
Witte, Dominic
96IdaFalB-29
Witte, Jerome
47TipTop-74
85TCMPla1-17
Witte, Trey
91BelMarC-18
91BelMarP-3665
92SanBerSF-955
93AppFoxC-24
93AppFoxF-2460
94RivPilCLC-23
96TacRaiB-29
Wittig, Paul
92GulCoaDF-3570
93GreFalDSP-24
94VerBeaDC-24
94VerBeaDF-76
95BakBlaTI-9
Witzel, Shane
93BilMusF-3947
93BilMusSP-14
Wizard, Wayne the
93ForWayWC-30
94ForWayWC-28
95ForWayWTI-30
96ForWayWB-31
Wizards, Fort Wayne
95ForWayWTI-32
Wobken, Bruce
88NebCor-18
Wockenfuss, John
76OPC-13
76Top-13
78TigBurK-3
78Top-723
79Top-231
80Top-338
81CokTeaS-56
81Don-245
81Fle-472
81Top-468
81TopSti-79
82Don-459
82Fle-286
82OPC-46
82Top-629
83Don-76
83Fle-351
83FleSta-220
83FleSti-254
83Tig-32
83Top-536
83TopSti-64
84Don-150
84Fle-95
84FleUpd-129
84Nes792-119
84PhiTas-27
84Top-119
84TopSti-274
84TopTif-119
84TopTra-130T
84TopTraT-130T
85Don-549

85Fle-269
85PhiTas-27
85Top-39
85TopTif-39
86FloStaLAP-50
86MiaMarP-29
88GleFalTP-917
89TolMudHC-25
89TolMudHP-771
92SalBucC-26
92SalBucF-79
Wodraska, Todd
92OklStaC-32
Wohler, Barry
85VerBeaDT-19
87SanAntDTI-8
88SanAntMB-2
Wohlers, Mark
89PulBraP-1908
89SumBraP-1099
90SumBraB-25
90SumBraP-2435
91Bow-582
91Cla/Bes-331
91ClaGolB-BC13
91GreBraC-10
91GreBraLD-223
91GreBraP-3004
91LinDriAA-223
91RicBraBC-30
91StaCluMO-30
91UppDecFE-77F
92Bow-396
92BraLykP-30
92BraLykS-36
92Cla1-T18
92Cla1-T97
92Don-1
92Don-616
92Fle-374
92Fle-700
92FleRooS-15
92OPC-703
92Pin-55
92PinRoo-21
92PinRool-4
92ProFS7-179
92RicBraBB-6
92RicBraF-3015
92RicBraRC-26
92RicBraS-448
92Sco-759
92Sco-787
92ScoImpP-38
92ScoRoo-5
92SkyAAAF-205
92StaClu-217
92Top-703
92TopDeb91-188
92TopGol-703
92TopGolW-703
92TopMic-703
92Ult-465
92UppDec-56
92UppDecSR-SR24
93BraLykP-30
93BraLykS-37
93ClaFS7-33
93Don-606
93Fle-16
93Lea-519
93OPC-7
93PacSpa-13
93Pin-379
93RicBraBB-20
93RicBraF-186
93RicBraRC-5
93RicBraRC-29
93Sco-193
93Sel-282
93StaClu-130
93StaCluB-25
93StaCluFDI-130
93StaCluMOP-130
93Top-8
93TopGol-8
93TopInaM-8
93TopMic-8
93Toy-55
93USPlaCR-3C
94BraLykP-34
94BraLykS-33
94BraUSPC-4C
94BraUSPC-12S
94Don-309
94Fla-133
94Fle-378
94Pin-444
94PinArtP-444
94PinMusC-444
94StaClu-522
94StaCluFDI-522
94StaCluGR-522
94StaCluMOP-522
94StaCluT-53
94StaCluTFDI-53
94Top-232
94TopGol-232
94TopSpa-232
94Ult-158
95Don-527
95DonPreP-527
95DonTopotO-194
95Fla-110
95Fle-322
95Lea-25
95Sco-507
95ScoGolR-507
95ScoPlaTS-507
95StaClu-128
95StaCluFDI-128
95StaCluMOP-128
95StaCluSTDW-B128
95StaCluSTMP-10
95StaCluSTWS-128
95Top-550
95Ult-356
95UltGolM-356
96Baz-70
96ColCho-47
96ColCho-380T
96ColChoGS-47
96ColChoSS-47
96Don-107
96DonPreP-107
96EmoXL-150
96Fin-S180
96FinRef-S180
96Fla-211
96Fle-310
96FleBra-18
96FleTif-310
96MetUni-137
96MetUniP-137
96MLBPin-37
96Pac-8
96Sco-202
96Sco-206
96StaClu-269
96StaCluMOP-269
96Top-49
96TopChr-18
96TopChrR-18
96TopGal-29
96TopGalPPI-29
96TopLas-64
96Ult-162
96UltGolM-162
96UppDec-3
96UppDecPHE-H49
96UppDecPreH-H49
97Cir-206
97CirRav-206
97ColCho-34
97Don-325
97DonLim-134
97DonLimLE-134
97DonPreP-325
97DonPrePGold-325
97DonTea-26
97DonTeaSPE-26
97Fin-234
97FinRef-234
97FlaSho-A143
97FlaSho-B143
97FlaSho-C143
97FlaShoLC-143
97FlaShoLC-B143
97FlaShoLC-C143
97FlaShoLCM-A143
97FlaShoLCM-B143
97FlaShoLCM-C143
97Fle-271
97FleTif-271
97Lea-130
97LeaFraM-130
97LeaFraMDC-130
97NewPin-36
97NewPinAP-36
97NewPinMC-36
97NewPinPP-36
97Pac-245
97PacLigB-245
97PacSil-245
97PinCar-11
97RicBraBC-6
97Sco-227
97ScoAllF-20
97ScoBra-13
97ScoBraPI-13
97ScoBraPr-13
97ScoPreS-227
97ScoShoS-227
97ScoShoSAP-227
97SkyE-X-60
97SkyE-XC-60
97SkyE-XEC-60
97StaClu-249
97StaCluC-CO3
97StaCluMat-249
97StaCluMOP-249
97Top-404
97TopAll-AS22
97TopChr-142
97TopChrAS-AS22
97TopChrR-142
97TopChrSAR-AS22
97TopGal-121
97TopGalPPI-121
97TopSta-82
97TopStaAM-82
97Ult-162
97UltGolME-162
97UltPlaME-162
97UppDec-17
Wohlford, Jim
73OPC-611
73Top-611
74OPC-407
74Top-407
75OPC-144
75Top-144
76OPC-286
76SSP-179
76Top-286
77Top-622
78Top-376
79Top-596
80GiaPol-9
80Top-448
81Don-316
81Fle-440
81Top-11
82Fle-403
82Top-116
83Don-524
83ExpPos-29
83ExpStu-21
83Fle-276
83Top-688
83TopTra-128T
84ExpPos-36
84ExpStu-24
84Fle-293
84Nes792-253
84OPC-253
84Top-253
84TopTif-253
85Don-585
85Fle-413
85Lea-82
85OPC-4
85Top-787
85TopTif-787
86Don-157
86ExpProPa-6
86OPC-344
86Top-344
86TopTif-344
87Fle-336
87FleGlo-336
87OPC-169
87Top-527
87TopTif-527
94BreMilB-188
Woide, Steve
88MyrBeaBJP-1172
90EriSaiS-27
Woinarowicz, Corey
94LetMouF-3883
94LetMouSP-22
Wojciechowski, Steve
91SouOreAC-29
91SouOreAP-3847
92ModA'sC-6
92ModA'sF-3900
92StaCluD-198
93ModA'sC-23
93ModA'sF-801
94HunStaF-1333
95Bow-204
95EdmTraTI-27
96A'sMot-13
96Fle-224
96FleTif-224
96StaClu-421
96StaCluMOP-421
96Ult-120
96UltGolM-120
97Fle-199
97FleTif-199
97PacPriGotD-GD84
97Top-432
97Ult-117
97UltGolME-117
97UltPlaME-117
Wojcik, Jim
81ShrCapT-5
Wojcik, John
63Top-253
Wojey, Pete
90DodTar-874
Wojna, Ed
83ReaPhiT-10
84LasVegSC-231
85LasVegSC-120
86Don-505
86Fle-338
86LasVegSP-25
86Top-211
86TopTif-211
87Don-589
87SpoTeaP-16
87Top-88
87TopTif-88
88VanCanC-5
88VanCanP-756
89ColSprSSC-4
89ColSprSSP-236
90CMC-588
90ProAAAF-140
90TacTigC-11
90TacTigP-93
Wojtkowski, Steve
93EugEmeC-27
93EugEmeF-3865
Wolak, Jerry
89UtiBluSP-27
90Bes-77
90MidLeaASGS-23
90SouBenWSB-13
90SouBenWSGS-21
91SarWhiSC-22
91SarWhiSP-1128
92SarWhiSCB-14
92SarWhiSF-223
93BirBarF-1206
94NasSouF-1264
95Bow-43
95NasSouTI-30
Wolcott, Bob
92ClaDraP-37
92ClaFS7-425
93BelMarC-29
93BelMarF-3210
93StaCluM-9
94RivPilCLC-14
95Bow-112
95MarPac-12
95MarPac-49
95PorCitRTI-28
95TacRaiTI-29
96Bow-179
96ColCho-23
96ColCho-381T
96Don-373
96DonPreP-373
96Fin-B251
96FinRef-B251
96Fle-246
96FleTif-246
96LeaSigA-248
96LeaSigAG-249
96LeaSigAS-249
96MarMot-23
96Pac-412
96Pin-184
96Sco-505
96Sel-168
96SelArtP-168
96Spo-127
96SpoArtP-127
96Sum-163
96SumAbo&B-163
96SumArtP-163
96SumFoi-163
96Top-353
96TopLasBS-8
96Ult-417
96UltGolM-417
96UppDec-248
97ColCho-229
97StaClu-368
97StaCluMOP-368
97Top-427
Wolf, Brian
92FroRowDP-86
Wolf, Michael
92BoiHawC-28
92BoiHawF-3645
Wolf, Mike
78KnoKnoST-25
80IowOakP-14
Wolf, Rick
77WauMetT-23
Wolf, Steve
89FreStaBS-22
90NiaFalRP-27
91LakTigC-13
91LakTigP-268
92LonTigF-635
93LonTigF-2309
Wolf, Waldo the
92WhiSoxK-0
Wolf, Wally (Walter)
63Top-208
70OPC-74
70Top-74
Wolf, William Van Winkle
87OldJudN-561
89EdgR.WG-17
Wolfe, Bill
11SpoLifCW-373
Wolfe, Donn
85FreGiaP-27
88St.CatBJP-2013
Wolfe, Joel
91SouOreAC-1
91SouOreAP-3865
92RenSilSCLC-56
92StaCluD-199
92UppDecML-193
93ModA'sC-24
93ModA'sF-813
94ClaGolF-129
94ExcFS7-123
94HunStaF-1341
94UppDecML-177
95HunStaTI-29
96ArkTraB-28
Wolfe, Larry
78TwiFriP-23
79Top-137
80Top-549
Wolfe, Scott
75LafDriT-4
Wolfenbarger, Scott
91OklStaC-32
Wolfer, Jim
89GreHorP-419
Wolff, Bryan
93SpoIndC-25
93SpoIndF-3594
94SprSulC-26
94SprSulF-2038
95Exc-290
95RanCucQT-29
96WilBluRB-20
Wolff, Jim
90HunCubP-3286
91HunCubC-26
91HunCubP-3338
92MidLeaATI-51
92PeoChiC-25
92PeoChiTI-30
92PeoChiTI-31
Wolff, Michael
93CedRapKC-25
93CedRapKF-1753
93MidLeaAGF-37

94MidAngF-2452
94MidAngOHP-33
95MidAngOHP-36
95MidAngTI-29
96FreKeyB-23
96VanCanB-30
Wolff, Roger
77TCMTheWY-75
79DiaGre-64
83TCMPla1943-22
83TCMPla1945-6
Wolff, Tom
93KinMetC-24
93KinMetF-3797
94KinMetC-24
94KinMetF-3825
95PitMetTI-24
Wolfgang, Meldon
15SpoNewM-195
16ColE13-146A
16SpoNewM-194
92Man191BSR-26
Wolkoys, Rob
86EugEmeC-26
87AppFoxP-21
Wollenburg, Doug
92IdaFalGF-3523
92IdaFalGSP-10
93DurBulC-25
93DurBulF-495
93DurBulTI-16
94GreBraF-423
94GreBraTI-28
95BreBtaTI-22
Wollenburg, Jay
86MacPirP-26
Wollenhaupt, Ron
80AppFoxT-30
82WatIndF-4
82WatIndT-28
Wollins, Paul
94IdaFalBF-3586
Wolten, Brad
87WatIndP-5
Wolter, Harry
10DomDisP-128
10JHDABE-16
10SweCapPP-39
11S74Sil-25
11SpoLifM-84
11T205-185
12HasTriFT-14A
12HasTriFT-15B
12HasTriFT-16A
12HasTriFT-61B
14TexTomE-47
95ConTSN-1370
Wolters, Mike
83ArkTraT-14
Wolverton, Harry
11SpoLifCW-374
12T207-202
Womack, Dooley
66Top-469
67CokCapYM-V4
67OPC-77
67Top-77
68Top-431
69Top-594
81TCM60I-339
92YanWIZ6-138
Womack, Tony
91WelPirC-2
91WelPirP-3584
92AugPirF-247
92ClaFS7-385
93CarLeaAGF-51
93ClaFS7-296
93SalBucC-25
93SalBucF-443
94BufBisF-1847
97Cir-124
97CirRav-124
97ColCho-434
97Don-394
97DonLim-39
97DonLimLE-39
97DonPreP-394
97DonPrePGold-394
97Fle-638
97FleTif-638
97Lea-345
97LeaFraM-345
97LeaFraMDC-345
97PacPriGotD-GD195
97Sco-469
97ScoHobR-469
97ScoResC-469
97ScoShoS-469
97ScoShoSAP-469
97TopSta-96
97TopStaAM-96
97Ult-492
97UltGolME-492
97UltPlaME-492
Womble, Brian
92DavLipB-25
93DavLipB-21
Wong, Dave
81ChaRoyT-3
82ForMyeRT-14
Wong, Kaha
89RenSilSCLC-257
90RenSilSCLC-273
Wong, Kevin
91PocPioP-3793
91PocPioSP-14
92SalSpuC-15
92SalSpuF-3766
93CliGiaC-24
93CliGiaF-2498
Wood, Andre
78DunBluJT-27
80KnoBluJT-22
82KnoBluJT-14
83KnoBluJT-13
Wood, Bicyclist
88GooN16-48
Wood, Bill
82TucTorT-22
Wood, Brian S.
86SpoIndC-155
88RivRedWCLC-215
88RivRedWP-1420
89SouAtlLAGS-8
89WicWraR-23
90WicWraRD-24
91LinDriAA-623
91WicWraLD-623
91WicWraP-2600
91WicWraRD-10
92HagSunF-2557
92SkyAA F-288
92WicWraS-648
94OriPro-107
Wood, Charles
88GooN16-49
88KimN18-50
Wood, Chris
75WesPalBES-18
Wood, Dave
76CliPilT-36
Wood, Fred
88AllandGN-25
Wood, Gary
76VenLeaS-154
Wood, George
87OldJudN-562
88AugBecN-31
88WG1CarG-54
Wood, Jake
61Top-514
62Jel-15
62Pos-15
62PosCan-15
62SalPlaC-83
62ShiPlaC-83
62TigJayP-12
62Top-72
62Top-427
62TopStaI-50
62TopVen-72
63TigJayP-12
63Top-453
64TigJayP-12
64Top-272
64TopVen-272
65Top-547
66Top-509
67CokCapTi-13
67Top-394
78TCM60I-186
Wood, Jason
89AncGlaP-28
91FreStaBS-15
91SouOreAC-12
91SouOreAP-3859
92Bow-262
92ClaFS7-191
92ModA'sC-1
92ModA'sF-3908
93HunStaF-2092
94HunStaF-1342
95EdmTraTI-28
96HunStaTI-26
Wood, Jeff
85ChaO'sT-17
86ChaOriW-30
87ChaO'sW-NNO
90RocRedWGC-36
Wood, Joe
03WilCarE-30
08AmeCarE-99
09ColChiE-311
09MaxPubP-18
09SpoNewSM-85
11SpoLifM-19
12ColRedB-311
12ColTinT-311
12HasTriFT-23
12HasTriFT-63
12RedSoxBASP-6
12SenVasS-5
12T207-203
13NatGamW-44
13PolGroW-30
13TomBarW-41
14CraJacE-22
14TexTomE-14
14TexTomE-64
15CraJacE-22
15SpoNewM-196
16BF2FP-7
16ColE13-194
16FleBreD-103
16SpoNewM-195
21E121So8-108
21Exh-189
22AmeCarE-78
22E120-45
22W572-118
22W575-152
23WilChoV-177
77Ind192T-21
81ConTSN-17
82DiaCla-3
87ConSer2-57
88ChaKniTI-10
90HOFStiB-16
91ConTSN-254
92ConTSN-336
93ConTSN-891
93UppDecAH-128
93UppDecAH-155
93UppDecAH-157
94UppDecTAE-24
95ConTSN-1354
95ConTSN-1408
93UppDecTR-10
Wood, John
90IdaFalBP-3249
Wood, Johnson
81BurBeeT-12
82BelBreF-5
84ElPasDT-2
Wood, Ken
50Bow-190
51Bow-209
52Top-139
53BowC-109
83TopRep5-139
Wood, Kerry
95Bes-130
96DayCubB-1
97Bow-196
97BowBes-154
97BowBesAR-154
97BowBesMI-MI3
97BowBesMIAR-MI3
97BowBesMIARI-MI3
97BowBesMII-MI3
97BowBesMIR-MI3
97BowBesMIRI-MI3
97BowBesR-154
97BowCerBIA-CA86
97BowCerGIA-CA86
97BowChr-183
97BowChrI-183
97BowChrIR-183
97BowChrR-183
97BowInt-196
97TopSta-110
97TopStaAM-110
Wood, Mathew
91MelBusF-13
Wood, Mike
84ButCopKT-5
93BatCliC-28
93BatCliF-3146
94SpaPhiF-1724
94SparPhiC-24
Wood, Pete
87BucN28-83A
87BucN28-83B
90KalBatN-57
Wood, Peter
87OldJudN-563
91PerHeaF-15
Wood, Robert Lynn
03BreE10-155
Wood, Stephen
88VerBeaDS-25
Wood, Ted
87PanAmTURB-15
88TopTra-130T
88TopTraT-130T
89ShrCapP-1842
89TopBig-308
90ShrCapP-1456
90ShrCapS-24
90TexLeaAGS-27
91LinDriAAA-398
91PhoFirLD-398
91PhoFirP-82
92Don-681
92Fle-678
92OPC-358
92PhoFirF-2836
92PhoFirS-398
92ProFS7-341
92Sco-768
92ScoRoo-11
92SkyAAAF-181
92StaClu-799
92Top-358
92TopDeb91-189
92TopGol-358
92TopGolW-358
92TopMic-358
92Ult-597
92UppDec-12
93Don-24
93PacSpa-539
93Pin-286
93StaClu-455
93StaCluFDI-455
93StaCluMOP-455
93Top-698
93TopGol-698
93TopInaM-698
93TopMic-698
94OttLynF-2910
87PanAmTUBI-11
Wood, Tony
96DurBulBIB-22
96DurBulBrB-23
Wood, Wilbur
64Top-267
64TopVen-267
65Top-478
67Top-391
68Top-585
69MilBra-295
69MLBOffS-36
69OPC-123
69Top-123
69TopFou-12
69TopSta-160
69TopTeaP-11
70MLBOffS-192
70OPC-342
70Top-342
71OPC-436
71Top-436
72Kel-4
72MilBra-369
72OPC-92
72OPC-94
72OPC-342
72Top-92
72Top-94
72Top-342
72Top-553
72Top-554
72TopPos-19
72WhiSox-12
72WhiSoxC-7
72WhiSoxDS-6
72WhiSoxTI1-12
73Kel2D-9
73LinPor-53
73OPC-66
73OPC-150
73Top-66
73Top-150
73TopCanL-54
74Kel-34A
74Kel-34B
74OPC-120
74OPC-205
74Top-120
74Top-205
74TopDecE-13
74TopSta-160
75Hos-68
75HosTwi-68
75OPC-110
75SSP42-1
75Top-110
76CraDis-67
76Hos-99
76OPC-368
76SSP-139
76Top-368
77Top-198
77WhiSoxJT-15
78SSP270-143
78Top-726
79OPC-108
79Top-216
81TCM60I-325
85WhiSoxC-50
89PacLegI-124
89SweBasG-127
91LinDri-35
91SweBasG-121
92ActPacA-53
92UppDecS-5
93UppDecS-24
Woodall, Brad
91IdaFalBP-4331
91IdaFalBSP-26
92DurBulC-23
92DurBulF-1102
92DurBulTI-11
92ProFS7-196
94RicBraF-2847
94SigRooTPD-T2
94SigRooTPS-T2
94TriAAF-AAA43
94VenLinU-175
95ActPacF-36
95Bow-222
95BowGolF-222
95RicBraRC-29
95RicBraTI-26
95Sel-199
95SelArtP-199
95SigRooOP-OP5
95SigRooOPS-OP5
95Top-91
96RicBraB-30
96RicBraUB-30
Woodall, Brent
93GenCubC-27
93GenCubF-3175
94PeoChiC-25
94PeoChiF-2268
Woodall, Kevin
91GulCoaRSP-10
92ButCopKSP-25
92GasRanC-13
93ChaRaiC-24
93ChaRaiF-1923
Woodall, Lawrence (Charles L.)
21Exh-190
21Nei-21
22E120-60
22W573-139
25Exh-96
27AmeCarE-53
28Exh-48
93ConTSN-784
Woodard, Darrell
81BirBarT-21
82BirBarT-3
Woodard, Mike
81WesHavAT-17
82WesHavAT-19

83TacTigT-13
85PhoGiaC-181
86Don-46
86Fle-645
86PhoFirP-26
87PhoFirP-10
87Top-286
87TopTif-286
88TriAAC-33
88VanCanC-14
88VanCanP-767
89ColCliC-12
89ColCliP-19
89ColCliP-742
89Fle-513
89FleGlo-513
Woodard, Steve
94SigRooDP-82
94SigRooDPS-82
95BelBreTI-2
96StoPorB-2
Woodbrey, Mark
75CedRapGT-25
76CedRapGT-34A
76CedRapGT-34B
Woodburn, Eugene
12T207-204
Wooden, Mark
86BelMarC-129
87WauTimP-16
88VerMarP-939
89WilBilP-628
89WilBilS-23
90WilBilB-23
90WilBilP-1059
90WilBilS-24
Woodeshick, Hal
59SenTealW-18
59Top-106
59TopVen-106
60Top-454
61Top-397
62Col.45B-22
62Col45'HC-20
62Top-526
63Top-517
64Col.45JP-11
64Top-370
64TopSta-78
64TopStaU-76
64TopVen-370
64WheSta-49
65CarTeal-28
65OPC-179
65Top-179
66Top-514
67AstTeal2-25
67Top-324
78TCM60I-123
86AstMot-2
87AstSer1-22
89AstCol4S-10
Woodfin, Chris
92SouBenWSC-17
92SouBenWSF-178
93SarWhiSF-1370
94CarLeaAF-CAR13
94PriWilCC-23
94PriWilCF-1921
95Exc-34
Woodfin, Olonzo
89BurIndS-26
Woodhouse, Kevin
84EveGiaC-9
Woodland, Bob
75WesPalBES-20
Woodling, Gene
47Exh-243A
47Exh-243B
47PM1StaP1-223
47StaPinP2-43
47StaPinP2-44
48SomandK-13
51BerRos-D1
51Bow-219
51R42SmaS-112
52BerRos-70
52Bow-177
52DixLid-24
52DixPre-24
52Top-99
53BowBW-31
53DixLid-24
53DixPre-24
53Dor-118
53RedMan-AL12
53Top-264
54Bow-209
54DixLid-17
54NewYorJA-59
54RedMan-AL15
54Top-101
55DonWin-41
55OriEss-26
55Top-190
56Top-163
56YelBasP-31
57IndSoh-17
57Top-172
58Top-398
59OriJayP-12
59Top-170
59TopVen-170
60OriJayP-12
60Top-190
60TopTat-54
60TopVen-190
61Baz-30
61Pos-70
61SenJayP-11
61SevElev-12
61Top-275
61TopStal-207
62Baz-45
62Jel-71
62Pos-71
62PosCan-71
62SalPlaC-96
62ShiPlaC-96
62Top-125
62TopBuc-94
62TopStal-101
62TopVen-125
63BasMagM-86
63Top-43
63Top-342
75JohMiz-20
79DiaGre-295
79TCM50-156
81Ori6F-32
82MetGal62-9
82OhiHaloF-65
83TopRep5-99
85TCMPla1-40
88PacLegI-5
89SweBasG-102
91MetWIZ-435
91OriCro-490
91SweBasG-101
91TopArc1-264
92ActPacA-23
92BazQua5A-4
94TopArc1-101
94TopArc1G-101
Woodmansee, Mark
83SalLakCGT-12
Woodridge, Dickie
93SpoIndC-26
93SpoIndF-3600
94SprSulC-27
94SprSulF-2047
95RanCucQT-10
95SPML-139
Woodring, Jason
94BurBeeC-25
94BurBeeF-1082
96DelShoB-30
Woodrow, James
95BelGiaTI-36
96BelGiaTI-19
Woodruff, Orville
09ColChiE-312A
09ColChiE-312B
11MecDFT-50
12ColRedB-312A
12ColRedB-312B
12ColTinT-312A
12ColTinT-312B
Woodruff, Pat
89BatCliP-1936
90ClePhiS-25
91LakTigC-28
91LakTigP-281
Woods, Al (Alvis)
76TacTwiDQ-24
77OPC-256
77Top-479
78BluJayP-25
78OPC-175
78SyrChiT-21
78Top-121
79BluJayBY-20
79OPC-85
79Top-178
80OPC-230
80Top-444
81Don-32
81Fle-422
81OPC-165
81OPCPos-17
81Top-703
81TopSti-141
82Don-180
82Fle-627
82OPC-49
82OPCPos-5
82Top-49
83Fle-444
83OPC-59
83Top-589
84SyrChiT-14
85TolMudHT-25
86BluJayGT-7
86TolMudHP-24
86TwiTeal-34
92Nab-4
86STaoftFT-21
Woods, Andy
86AncGlaPTI-42
Woods, Anthony
86WauTimP-28
87WauTimP-13
88SanBerSB-5
89SanBerSB-17
89SanBerSCLC-83
Woods, Brian
94SouBenSHC-24
94SouBenSHF-595
95PriWilCTI-26
96BirBarB-21
Woods, Byron
92IdaFalGF-3530
92IdaFalGSP-24
Woods, Clancy
79AppFoxT-7
Woods, Eric
88WinSpiS-22
89WinSpiS-18
Woods, Gary
76TucTorCa-4
76TusTorCr-3
77OPC-22
77Top-492
78OPC-13
78SyrChiT-22
78Top-599
79ChaChaT-5
80TucTorT-22
81Fle-75
81Top-172
82CubRedL-25
82Fle-237
82Top-483
82TopTra-130T
83CubThoAV-25
83Don-631
83Fle-512
83Top-356
84CubChiT-33
84CubSev-25
84Don-144
84Fle-507
84Nes792-231
84Top-231
84TopTif-231
85CubLioP-26
85CubSev-25
85Don-555
85Fle-71
85Lea-49
85Top-46
85TopTif-46
86Fle-385
86LasVegSP-26
86Top-611
86TopTif-611
Woods, George
49BowPCL-4
49W72HolS-24
50W720HolS-32
Woods, Jim
60Lea-104
61Top-59
Woods, Kelly
89PriPirS-25
89Sta-176
Woods, Kenny
92EveGiaC-7
92EveGiaF-1701
93CliGiaC-25
93CliGiaF-2503
94SanJosGC-26
94SanJosGF-2832
Woods, Lyle
87AncGlaP-41
89AncGlaP-29
Woods, Parnell
49RemBre-32
91PomBlaBPB-2
Woods, Preston
88CapCodPPaLP-54
Woods, Ron
69Top-544
70OPC-253
70Top-253
71MLBOffS-504
71OPC-514
71Top-514
72Dia-52
72OPC-82
72Top-82
73OPC-531
73Top-531
74OPC-377
74Top-377
92YanWIZ6-139
92YanWIZ7-167
Woods, Tony
83QuaCitCT-22
84MidCubT-24
86PitCubP-25
87MiaMarP-5
88TamTarS-24
88WauTimGS-22
Woods, Tyrone
89JamExpP-2134
90MidLeaASGS-24
90RocExpLC-29
90RocExpP-2709
91WesPalBEC-29
91WesPalBEP-1243
92MidLeaATI-52
92RocExpC-9
92RocExpF-2130
93HarSenF-282
94OttLynF-2911
95LinVen-12
95RocRedWTI-39
Woods, Walter
09ColChiE-313
12ColRedB-313
12ColTinT-313
Woodson, Dick
70OPC-479
70Top-479
71MLBOffS-479
71OPC-586
71Top-586
72Top-634
73OPC-98
73Top-98
74OPC-143
74Top-143
78TwiFri-49
92YanWIZ7-168
Woodson, George
69Top-244
Woodson, Kerry
89BelMarL-16
90Bes-308
90CalLeaACLC-19
90CMC-857
90ProAaA-136
90SanBerSB-25
90SanBerSCLC-90
90SanBerSP-2635
91Bow-264
92Bow-411
92CalCanF-3733
92DonRoo-127
92JacSunF-3707
92JacSunS-373
92SkyAA F-160
92TopTraG-132T
93Don-748
93FleMajLP-B2
93Sco-327
93Top-539
93TopGol-539
93TopInaM-539
93TopMic-539
93Ult-275
93UppDec-388
93UppDecGold-388
Woodson, Tracy
85VerBeaDT-2
87AlbDukP-24
87DodMot-22
88AlbDukC-17
88AlbDukP-256
88Don-499
88FleUpd-98
88FleUpdG-98
88TriAAAP-3
89AlbDukC-16
89AlbDukP-75
89DodPol-12
89Fle-77
89FleGlo-77
89Sco-586
89Top-306
89TopBig-92
89TopTif-306
89UppDec-108
90CMC-652
90DodTar-875
90ProAAAF-176
90VanCanC-25
90VanCanP-498
91LinDriAAA-448
91RicBraBC-23
91RicBraLD-448
91RicBraP-2579
91RicBraTI-15
92LouRedF-1896
92LouRedS-272
92SkyAAAF-130
93CarPol-24
93Don-652
93Fle-517
93PacSpa-638
93Sco-465
93StaCluCa-22
93Top-457
93TopGol-457
93TopInaM-457
93TopMic-457
93UppDec-728
93UppDecGold-728
94Fle-650
94RocRedWF-1007
95LouRedF-285
96ColCliB-30
Woodward, Chris
96HagSunB-25
Woodward, Jim
82JacMetT-17
Woodward, Rob
86DonRoo-53
86Fle-651
86PawRedSP-28
87ClaGam-69
87Don-652
87PawRedST-23
87Top-632
87TopTif-632
88PawRedSC-1
88PawRedSP-448
88Sco-403
88ScoGlo-403
89PawRedSC-10
89PawRedSP-699
89PawRedSTI-29
90CMC-303
90ProAAAF-460
90RocRedWC-2
90RocRedWGC-18
90RocRedWP-703
91LinDriAAA-473
91RocRedWLD-473
91RocRedWP-1904
Woodward, Vince
85CloHSS-44
Woodward, Woody (William)
64Top-378
65Top-487
66OPC-49
66Top-49
66TopVen-49

67CokCapB-8
67DexPre-226
67Kah-41
67Top-546
68CokCapB-8
68DexPre-75
68Top-476
69OPC-142
69Top-142
69TopFou-3
69TopTeaP-20
70DayDaiNM-83
70OPC-296
70Top-296
71MLBOffS-72
71OPC-496
71Top-496
72MilBra-370
Woodworth, John
80UtiBluJT-9
82KnoBluJT-23
83KnoBluJT-21
85SyrChiT-10
86SyrChiP-27
90DunBluJS-28
91DunBluJC-30
92DunBluJC-28
93DunBluJC-28
93DunBluJFFN-29
Wooldridge, Floyd
77FriOneYW-16
Woolf, Jason
96PeoChiB-30
Woolis, Danny
85IowCubT-35
Woolridge, Floyd
55CarHunW-30
Wooten, Daryl
89AubAstP-2189
Wooten, Earl
49Bow-189
Wooten, Greg
96MidLeaAB-8
96WisTimRB-29
Wooten, Junior
88ChaLooLTI-31
Wooten, Shawn
90HigSchPLS-14
93BriTigF-3649
94ExcFirYPF-9
94ExcFS7-63
94FayGenC-26
94FayGenF-2158
94Top-448
94TopGol-448
94TopSpa-448
Worden, Bill
82DanSunF-20
83RedPioT-25
84NasSouTI-25
86WatIndP-26
Workman, Michael
86WatIndP-32
87KinIndP-14
Workman, Widd
96IdaFalB-30
Works, Ralph
07TigACDPP-28
09TigTaCP-20
10JuJuDE-42
11SpoLifM-73
12T207-205
Worley, Bob
92BelMarC-17
92BelMarF-1445
93AppFoxC-25
93AppFoxF-2461
94RivPilCLC-24
95PorCitRTI-29
96PorCitRB-28
Worley, Roger
94SigRooDP-68
94SigRooDPS-68
Worrell, Steve
93MidLeaAGF-28
93SouBenWSC-26
93SouBenWSF-1432
94PriWilCC-24
94PriWilCF-1922
95PriWilCTI-27
96BirBarB-19
Worrell, Tim
91BriBanF-14
91MidLeaAP-MWL31
91WatDiaC-10
91WatDiaP-1257
92ClaFS7-314
92SkyAA F-289
92UppDecML-181
92WicWraS-631
93Bow-138
93ClaFS7-270
93ClaGolF-49
93ExcFS7-112
93FleFinE-148
93LasVegSF-945
93Ult-480
94ColC-434
94ColChoGS-434
94ColChoSS-434
94Don-318
94Fle-679
94StaClu-519
94StaCluFDI-519
94StaCluGR-519
94StaCluMOP-519
94Top-458
94TopGol-458
94TopSpa-458
95PadMot-17
96FleUpd-U201
96FleUpdTC-U201
96PadMot-24
97Cir-282
97CirRav-282
97ColCho-451
97Fle-473
97FleTif-473
97PacPriGotD-GD212
97Top-392
Worrell, Todd
83LouRedR-26
84ArkTraT-6
85LouRedR-28
86CarIGAS-14
86CarKASD-10
86CarSchM-24
86Don-43
86DonHig-29
86DonHig-54
86DonRoo-21
86Fle-49
86SevCoi-S15
86SpoRoo-35
86TopTra-127T
86TopTraT-127T
87CarSmo-2
87ClaGam-97
87Don-307
87Fle-312
87FleAll-8
87FleAwaW-44
87FleGlo-312
87FleHotS-44
87FleLeaL-44
87FleLimE-43
87FleMin-119
87FleRecS-43
87FleStiC-128
87Lea-218
87OPC-67
87Spo-33
87Spo-77
87SpoTeaP-12
87Top-7
87Top-465
87Top-605
87TopCoi-48
87TopGaloC-12
87TopGloS-10
87TopMinL-34
87TopRoo-22
87TopSti-11
87TopSti-12
87TopSti-55
87TopSti-310
87TopTif-7
87TopTif-465
87TopTif-605
87ToyRoo-33
87Woo-13
88Baz-22
88CarSmo-10
88CheBoy-8
88ClaRed-181
88Don-386
88DonBasB-268
88Fle-50
88FleGlo-50
88FleGlo-WS5
88FleLeaL-44
88FleMin-111
88FleRecS-44
88FleSlu-44
88FleStiC-122
88FleWaxBC-C16
88FleWorS-5
88K-M-32
88Lea-229
88OPC-135
88PanSti-386
88Sco-202
88ScoGlo-202
88Spo-61
88StaLinAl-37
88StaLinCa-20
88Top-715
88TopBig-149
88TopCoi-60
88TopMinL-73
88TopSti-54
88TopTif-715
88Woo-24
89Bow-429
89BowTif-429
89CadEllD-62
89CarSmo-24
89Don-82
89DonAll-60
89DonBasB-243
89Fle-466
89FleBasM-44
89FleGlo-466
89FleSup-44
89LouRedBTI-37
89OPC-291
89PanSti-179
89Sco-265
89ScoHot1S-94
89Spo-183
89Top-535
89TopBasT-154
89TopMinL-38
89TopSti-39
89TopTif-535
89UppDec-512
90BasWit-29
90Bow-185
90BowTif-185
90Don-319
90Fle-264
90FleCan-264
90MLBBasB-29
90OPC-95
90PanSti-340
90PubSti-231
90PubSti-274
90Sco-392
90Spo-165
90Top-95
90TopSti-43
90TopTif-95
90TopTVCa-22
90UppDec-467
90VenSti-500
90VenSti-501
91CarPol-38
91Fle-653
91LouRedTI-13
91Sco-807
92CarMcD-54
92CarPol-25
92FleUpd-121
92Lea-436
92Pin-479
92StaClu-703
92Stu-99
92Ult-574
93DodMot-21
93DodPol-29
93Don-72
93Fle-135
93FleFinE-87
93Lea-429
93OPC-374
93OPCPre-62
93Sco-635
93StaClu-728
93StaCluD-16
93StaCluFDI-728
93StaCluMOP-728
93Top-121
93TopGol-121
93TopInaM-121
93TopMic-121
93TriPla-253
93Ult-409
93UppDec-692
93UppDecGold-692
94ColC-567
94ColChoGS-567
94ColChoSS-567
94DodMot-13
94DodPol-29
94Don-397
94ExtBas-298
94Fla-185
94Fle-530
94Lea-362
94StaClu-612
94StaCluFDI-612
94StaCluGR-612
94StaCluMOP-612
94Top-611
94TopGol-611
94TopSpa-611
94Ult-221
95DodMot-18
95DodPol-29
95Don-474
95DonPreP-474
95DonTopotO-275
95Emo-147
95Fla-159
95Fle-552
95Lea-334
95Sco-213
95ScoGolR-213
95ScoPlaTS-213
95StaClu-53
95StaCluFDI-53
95StaCluMOP-53
95StaCluSTWS-53
95StaCluVR-33
95Top-204
95TopCyb-3
95Ult-185
95UltGolM-185
95UppDec-460T
96ColCho-585
96ColChoGS-585
96ColChoSS-585
96DodMot-25
96DodPol-30
96Don-144
96DonPreP-144
96EmoXL-217
96Fla-300
96Fle-449
96FleDod-18
96FleTif-449
96Pac-110
96Sco-157
96StaClu-88
96StaCluEPB-88
96StaCluEPG-88
96StaCluEPS-88
96StaCluEWB-EW10
96StaCluEWG-EW10
96StaCluEWS-EW10
96StaCluMOP-88
96StaCluVRMO-33
96Top-412
96Ult-227
96UltGolM-227
96UppDec-358
97Cir-96
97CirRav-96
97ColCho-63
97ColCho-369
97Fin-207
97FinRef-207
97Fle-373
97FleTif-373
97MetUni-107
97PacPriGotD-GD163
97Sco-392
97ScoHobR-392
97ScoResC-392
97ScoShoS-392
97ScoShoSAP-392
97SP-97
97StaClu-51
97StaCluMat-51
97StaCluMOP-51
97Top-226
97TopGal-13
97TopGalPPI-13
97Ult-387
97UltGolME-387
97UltPlaME-387
97UppDec-91
97UppDecAWJ-17
Wortham, Rich
80OPC-261
80Top-502
81Don-161
81Fle-347
81Top-107
82ReaPhiT-10
92TexLon-40
Worthington, Al
50JJKCopP-24
54NewYorJA-39
55GiaGolS-14
57Top-39
58GiaJayP-12
58GiaSFCB-25
58Hir-73
58Top-427
59Top-28
59TopVen-28
60Top-268
62AmeTraS-66
63RedEnq-33
63RedFreBC-31
63Top-556
64Top-144
64TopVen-144
65OPC-216
65Top-216
66OPC-181
66Top-181
66TopVen-181
66TwiFaiG-17
67CokCapTw-10
67Top-399
68Top-473
73OPC-49
73Top-49A
73Top-49B
78TwiFri-23
79TCM50-269
81TCM60I-405
86TwiGreT-11
Worthington, Bob
33ButCanV-57
Worthington, Craig
86HagSunP-29
87IntLeaAT-30
87RocRedWP-23
87RocRedWT-17
88DonRoo-23
88FleUpd-4
88FleUpdG-4
88RocRedWC-19
88RocRedWGCP-27
88RocRedWP-217
88RocRedWTI-26
88TriAAC-19
89Don-569
89DonBasB-282
89DonRoo-25
89Fle-627
89FleGlo-627
89OriFreB-11
89PanSti-252
89Sco-636
89ScoHot1R-6
89ScoYouS2-21
89Spo-134
89Top-181
89TopTif-181
89UppDec-725
90Baz-15
90Bow-253
90BowTif-253
90ClaBlu-31
90Don-141
90DonBesA-71
90Fle-195
90FleCan-195
90HagSunDGB-35
90Lea-170
90OPC-521
90PanSti-11
90PubSti-592
90Sco-234
90Sco100RS-21
90Spo-117

90Top-521
90TopBig-146
90TopGloS-49
90TopHeaU-22
90TopRoo-33
90TopSti-239
90TopSti-328
90TopTif-521
90ToyRoo-32
90UppDec-444
90VenSti-502
91Don-293
91Fle-496
91Lea-298
91OPC-73
91OriCro-491
91PanFreS-242
91PanSti-198
91Sco-503
91StaClu-467
91Top-73
91TopDesS-73
91TopMic-73
91TopTif-73
91Ult-26
91UppDec-141
92ColSprSSF-761
92ColSprSSS-79
92Fle-31
92OPC-397
92Sco-724
92StaClu-81
93IowCubF-2143
94IowCubF-1284
95IndIndF-105
96FleUpd-U92
96FleUpdTC-U92
96LeaSigEA-217
96RanMot-8
Worthy, Tommy
96MarPhiB-30
Wortman, Chuck (William)
16ColE13-195
Wortmann, Russ
82IdaFalAT-15
Wotus, Ron
82BufBisT-11
84HawIslC-128
86HawIslP-22
87OmaRoyP-20
89PhoFirC-19
89PhoFirP-1501
90CliGiaP-2567
91CalLeLA-47
91SanJosGC-23
91SanJosGP-27
92SanJosGC-26
93ShrCapF-2775
94ShrCapF-1622
96PhoFirB-2
Woyce, Don
86Ft.MyeRP-29
Woyt, Boris
50WorWidGV-29
Wozney, Kevin
93EriSaiC-26
93EriSaiF-3118
Wrangler, Wilbur T.
95WicWraTI-95
96WicWraB-30
Wray, David
94DavLipB-25
95DavLipB-25
Wray, James
88GreFalDTI-13
89BakDodCLC-189
89CalLeaA-16
90SanAntMGS-30
91LinDriAA-550
91SanAntMLD-550
91SanAntMP-2977
92VerBeaDC-15
92VerBeaDF-2877
Wren, Frank
80MemChiT-28
Wrenn, Luke
76ShrCapT-5
77ShrCapT-23
Wright, Ab
92ConTSN-407
Wright, Barry
77ModA'sC-2
Wright, Bill
87IdaFalBP-17
Wright, Bill (Burnis)
91NegLeaRL-10
92NegLeaK-12
93UppDecS-17
95NegLeaL2-2
95NegLeaLI-10
Wright, Brian
89IdaFalBP-2009
Wright, Clarence
90DodTar-876
Wright, Clyde
69Top-583
70OPC-543
70Top-543
71AngJacitB-10
71BazNumT-6
71BazUnn-24
71Kel-28A
71Kel-28B
71Kel-28C
71MLBOffS-359
71OPC-67
71OPC-240
71Top-67
71Top-240
71TopCoi-60
71TopGreM-18
71TopSup-39
71TopTat-117
72MilBra-371
72OPC-55
72Top-55
73OPC-373
73Top-373
74OPC-525
74Top-525
75OPC-408
75Top-408
76OPC-559
76SSP-258
76Top-559
86AngGreT-10
89AngSmo-6
93RanKee-387
94BreMilB-281
Wright, Dave
75ForLauYS-5
76ForLauYS-19
77ForLauYS-19
Wright, Don
87EugEmeP-2675
88AppFoxP-146
89AppFoxP-855
90BasCitRS-27
Wright, Ed (Henderson E.)
47TipTop-90
52Top-368
83TopRep5-368
Wright, Ernie
88MisStaB-35
89MisStaB-40
Wright, F. Glenn
25Exh-56
26Exh-56
26SpoComoA-48
26SpoNewSM-11
28Exh-28
28W502-47
28W512-5
28Yue-47
31Exh-4
33ButCre-30
33ExhFou-2
33Gou-143
33GouCanV-77
34ExhFou-2
35GouPuzR-4B
35GouPuzR-7B
35GouPuzR-12B
90DodTar-877
91ConTSN-208
Wright, George
36PC7AlbHoF-12
50CalHOFW-78
76ShaPiz-13
77BobParHoF-53
80PerHaloFP-12
80SSPHOF-12
84GalHaloFRL-13
89HOFStiB-15
94OriofB-25
Wright, George DeWitt
78AshTouT-29
79AshTouT-10
80TulDriT-10
81TulDriT-1
83Don-116
83Fle-583
83FleSti-160
83RanAffF-26
83Top-299
83TopSti-124
84AllGamPI-162
84Don-525
84Fle-435
84Nes792-688
84OPC-314
84RanJarP-26
84Top-688
84TopRubD-21
84TopSti-353
84TopTif-688
85Don-256
85Fle-574
85OklCit8T-16
85OPC-387
85Top-443
85TopRubD-21
85TopTif-443
86Don-220
86Fle-578
86Top-169
86TopTif-169
86TopTra-128T
86TopTraT-128T
89PhoFirC-24
89PhoFirP-1484
93RanKee-388
Wright, Goldie
83RedPioT-26
Wright, Harry (W. Henry)
50CalHOFW-79
75FlePio-2
76ShaPiz-70
77BobParHoF-54
80PerHaloFP-70
80SSPHOF-70
83PhiPosGPaM-11
87OldJudN-564
90KalBatN-58
94OriofB-21
94UppDecTAE-5
Wright, J.P.
89KenTwiP-1072
89KenTwiS-24
Wright, James L.
78PapGinD-18
79Top-722
80Top-524
81SyrChiTI-24
82Don-490
82SyrChiT-10
82Top-362
Wright, James R.
79OPC-180
79Top-349
80PenPilBT-13
80PenPilCT-7
81ReaPhiT-13
81Top-526
82Top-362
86PeoChiP-26
87PitCubP-5
87TolMudHT-12
88IowCubC-25
88IowCubP-542
89IowCubC-24
89IowCubP-1697
90CMC-249
90ProAAAF-316
90ScrRedBC-23
90ScrRedBP-614
91LinDriAAA-500
91ScrRedBP-2557
92ScrRedBF-2464
92ScrRedBS-500
93ScrRedBF-2560
93ScrRedBTI-29
94ScrRedBF-937
95ScrRedBTI-29
96ScrRedBB-2
Wright, Jamey
94AshTouC-25
94AshTouF-1783
94Bow-58
94Cla-178
94ClaGolF-28
94ClaGolN1PLF-LP18
94ClaGolREF-RE18
94Pin-268
94PinArtP-268
94PinMusC-268
94Sco-573
94ScoGolR-573
94SigRoo-46
94SigRooS-46
94Top-744
94TopGol-744
94TopSpa-744
95Bes-66
95Bow-181
95SalAvaTI-10
95SPML-52
95UppDecML-188
96BesAutSA-91
96Bow-137
96BowBes-157
96BowBesAR-157
96BowBesMI-9
96BowBesMIAR-9
96BowBesMIR-9
96BowBesR-157
96BowMinLP-5
96ColSprSSTI-32
96Exc-160
96NewHavRB-28
96NewHavRUSTI-21
97Bow-403
97BowBes-181
97BowBesAR-181
97BowBesR-181
97BowCerBIA-CA87
97BowCerGIA-CA87
97BowChr-266
97BowChrI-266
97BowChrIR-266
97BowChrR-266
97BowInt-403
97Cir-279
97CirRav-279
97ColCho-18
97Don-114
97DonPreP-114
97DonPrePGold-114
97DonTea-95
97DonTeaSPE-95
97Fin-28
97FinRef-28
97FlaSho-A49
97FlaSho-B49
97FlaSho-C49
97FlaShoLC-49
97FlaShoLC-B49
97FlaShoLC-C49
97FlaShoLCM-A49
97FlaShoLCM-B49
97FlaShoLCM-C49
97Fle-321
97FleTif-321
97Lea-86
97LeaFraM-86
97LeaFraMDC-86
97MetUni-78
97PacPriGotD-GD139
97Pin-170
97PinArtP-170
97PinMusC-170
97Sco-121
97ScoPreS-121
97ScoRoc-5
97ScoRocPl-5
97ScoRocPr-5
97ScoShoS-121
97ScoShoSAP-121
97SpoIll-27
97SpoIllEE-27
97StaClu-162
97StaCluMOP-162
97Stu-29
97StuPrePG-29
97StuPrePS-29
97Top-107
97TopGal-150
97TopGalPPI-150
97Ult-191
97UltGolME-191
97UltPlaME-191
97UppDec-228
95UppDecMLFS-188
Wright, Jaret
94ClaUpdCotC-CC9
94SigRooDP-10
94SigRooDPS-10
95ActPacF-58
95Exc-45
95SigRooDDS-DD5
95SigRooDDSS-DD5
95SPML-43
95SPMLA-25
95UppDecML-201
95UppDecML-221
96BesAutS-97
96CarLeaA1B-2
96CarLeaA2B-2
96Exc-48
96KenIndB-27
97Bow-398
97BowInt-398
97DonLim-151
97DonLimLE-151
97Fle-756
97FleTif-756
95UppDecMLFS-201
95UppDecMLFS-221
Wright, Jesse
77ModA'sC-6
Wright, Ken
70RoyTeal-38
71OPC-504
71Top-504
72Top-638
73OPC-578
73Top-578
76QuaCitAT-40
77QuaCitAT-29
92YanWIZ7-169
Wright, Larry
78CliDodT-33
79CliDodT-22
80AppFoxT-10
Wright, Margie
91FreStaLBS-12
Wright, Mark
80BatTroT-30
81WisRapTT-11
82WisRapTF-6
Wright, Mel
73OPC-517
73Top-517A
73Top-517B
83ExpPos-30
83ExpStu-25
Wright, Mike
79QuaCitCT-1
Wright, Mitch
79NewCoPT-21
Wright, Paul
82RedPioT-17
Wright, Ricky (Richard)
81AlbDukT-7
82AlbDukT-11
83DodPol-21
83Fle-226
85OklCit8T-9
86RanPer-24
86TopTra-129T
86TopTraT-129T
87TolMudHP-6
87Top-202
87Top-656
87TopTif-202
87TopTif-656
90DodTar-878
92TexLon-41
93RanKee-389
Wright, Ron
95Bes-56
95MacBraTI-30
95MacBraUTI-6
96Bow-337
96CarLeaA1B-12
96CarLeaA2B-12
96CarLeaA2B-25
96CarLeaAIB-B3
96DurBulBIB-27
96DurBulBrB-30
96Exc-135
96ExcSeaTL-10
96GreBraB-30
96GreBraTI-16
96Top-424
97Bow-165
97BowCerBIA-CA88
97BowCerGIA-CA88
97BowChr-161
97BowChrI-161

97BowChrIR-161
97BowChrR-161
97BowInt-165
97Top-489
Wright, Scott
95BilRedTI-12
Wright, Skipper
88SumBraP-404
89BurBraP-1626
89BurBraS-26
89Sta-112
90CarLeaA-27
90DurBulTI-11
Wright, Taft
39WhiSoxTI-23
40PlaBal-186
40WhiSoxL-24
41Gou-10
41PlaBal-32
47Exh-244
47TipTop-30
48WhiSoxTI-29
49Bow-96
49PhiBul-59
83TCMPla1942-17
Wright, Terry
94ButCopKSP-1
96DurBulBrB-10
96Exc-150
Wright, Thomas
51Bow-271
54Top-140
55Top-141
55TopDouH-75
94TopArc1-140
94TopArc1G-140
Wright, William S.
09T206-474
Wrightstone, Russell
21Exh-191
21Nei-61
22E120-210
22W573-140
26Exh-48
27AmeCarE-43
27Exh-24
91ConTSN-238
Wrigley, Charles
30SchR33-9
Wrigley, Phil
31CubTeal-29
76ChiGre-20
Wrigley, William
31CubTeal-30
32CubTeal-27
Wrigley, Zeke
90DodTar-1097
Wrona, Bill
86BeaGolGP-25
88WicPilRD-21
89LasVegSC-19
89LasVegSP-18
90CMC-91
90IowCubC-16
90IowCubP-328
90ProAAAF-635
90TopTVCu-65
Wrona, Dave
88CapCodPPaLP-39
90BelBreS-24
91BelBreC-23
91BelBreP-2113
91Cla/Bes-213
92CalLeaACL-6
92StoPorC-8
92StoPorF-45
Wrona, Rick
86WinSpiP-28
87PitCubP-17
88BlaYNPRWL-157
89DonRoo-38
90Don-512
90OPC-187
90Sco-557
90Sco100RS-73
90Top-187
90TopTif-187
90TopTVCu-21
90UppDec-582
91Sco-519
92NasSouF-1835
92NasSouS-298
93NasSouF-572
93StaClu-64
93StaCluFDI-64
93StaCluMOP-64
94BreMilB-374
96ScrRedBB-27
Wrona, Ron
76BurBeeT-33
77HolMilT-25
78SpoIndC-17
Wuerch, Jason
92GulCoaYF-3800
93GreHorC-26
93GreHorF-902
94SanBerSC-24
94SanBerSF-2773
95GreBatTI-27
Wulf, Eric
93KanCouCC-25
93KanCouCF-920
93KanCouCTI-29
Wulfemeyer, Mark
75QuaCitAT-19
Wulfert, Mark
96CliLumKTI-29
Wunsch, Kelly
94BelBreC-1
94BelBreF-103
94BrePol-5
94ClaGolF-20
94ClaGolN1PLF-LP19
94ClaGolREF-RE19
94Top-210
94TopGol-210
94TopSpa-210
95UppDecML-103
95UppDecML-173
96SigRooOJ-37
96SigRooOJS-37
95UppDecMLFS-103
95UppDecMLFS-173
Wurm, Garry
89BoiHawP-2005
90EriSaiS-28
Wuthrich, David
88PocGiaP-2074
Wyatt, Ben
96DanBraB-30
Wyatt, Chuck
91BilMusP-3754
91BilMusSP-10
Wyatt, Cortez
94WilCubC-25
94WilCubF-3766
Wyatt, Dave
83LynMetT-19
85LynMetT-10
86TidTidP-29
87TidTidP-14
87TidTidT-9
Wyatt, John T.
63Top-376
64Top-108
64TopVen-108
65OldLonC-39
65Top-590
66Top-521
67Top-261
67TopRedSS-24
68CokCapRS-4
68DexPre-76
68TigDetFPB-28
68Top-481
78TCM60I-159
81RedSoxBG2S-127
92YanWIZ6-140
Wyatt, Porter
78NewWayCT-45
Wyatt, Reggie
84MemChiT-6
Wyatt, Whit (John W.)
36GouWidPPR-A116
36OveCanR-48
39PlaBal-95
40DodTeal-25
40PlaBal-67
41DouPlaR-13
41Gou-18
41PlaBal-55
42DodTeal-25
43DodTeal-25
47PM1StaP1-224
60BraLaktL-28
60BraSpiaS-26
79DiaGre-281
83TCMPla1943-30
89DodSmoG-43
90DodTar-879
91RinPosBD3-3
Wyczawski, Paul
92MisStaB-49
Wyde, Rich
91EveGiaC-17
Wykle, David
89TenTecGE-31
Wylie, John
91BoiHawC-14
91BoiHawP-3881
92BoiHawC-12
92BoiHawF-3629
92PalSprAC-7
Wyman, Richie
95TenVolW-12
Wynegar, Butch
77BurCheD-53
77Hos-84
77Kel-56
77MSADis-61
77OPC-176
77PepGloD-3
77RCColC-67
77Top-175
78Hos-37
78OPC-104
78RCColC-10
78Top-555
78TwiFriP-24
79Hos-141
79OPC-214
79Top-405
79TwiFriP-28
80OPC-159
80Top-304
81AllGamPI-45
81Don-529
81Fle-558
81OPC-61
81Top-61
81TopSti-102
82Don-508
82Dra-32
82Fle-565
82OPC-222
82Top-222
82TopSti-208
82TopTra-131T
82TwiPos-31
83Don-325
83Fle-399
83OPC-379
83Top-617
83TopSti-101
84AllGamPI-135
84Don-458
84Fle-144
84Nes792-123
84OPC-123
84Top-123
84TopSti-321
84TopTif-123
85AllGamPI-45
85Don-417
85DonActA-45
85Fle-147
85Lea-165
85OPC-28
85Top-585
85TopSti-316
85TopTif-585
86Don-274
86Fle-122
86Lea-147
86OPC-235
86Top-235
86TopSti-299
86TopTif-235
86YanTCM-19
87AngSmo-10
87DonOpeD-6
87OPC-203
87Top-464
87TopTif-464
88AngSmo-23
88Sco-355
88ScoGlo-355
88Top-737
88TopTif-737
89Sco-140
92YanWIZ8-205
94AlbPolC-27
94AlbPolF-2254
Wyngarden, Brett
92AubAstC-15
92AubAstF-1358
94LakTigF-3041
Wynn, Early
49Bow-110
49IndTeal-27
50Bow-148
50IndNumN-22
50IndTeal-24
51Bow-78
51FisBakL-31
51TopRedB-8
52Bow-142
52IndNumN-6
52RedMan-AL24
52Top-277
53BowC-146
53IndPenCBP-30
53RedMan-AL14
53Top-61
54Bow-164
54DanDee-29
55Bow-38
55IndCarBL-11
55IndGolS-3
55RedMan-AL14
55RobGouS-14
55RobGouW-14
56Top-187
57IndSoh-18
57Top-40
58Top-100A
58Top-100B
58WhiSoxJP-12
59Top-260
60ArmCoi-20
60Baz-28
60NuHi-71
60RawGloT-36
60Top-1
60TopTat-55
60TopVen-1
60WhiSoxJP-12
60WhiSoxTS-22
61NuSco-471
61Pos-22A
61Pos-22B
61Top-50
61Top-337
61Top-455
61TopStal-131
61WhiSoxTS-20
62Jel-55
62Pos-55
62PosCan-55
62SalPlaC-97A
62SalPlaC-97B
62ShiPlaC-97
62Top-385
62TopBuc-95
62TopStal-30
62WhiSoxJP-12
62WhiSoxTS-22
63BasMagM-87
63Jel-43
63Pos-43
76LauDiaJ-23
76ShaPiz-133
77GalGloG-36
77SerSta-25
79BasGre-66
79TCM50-20
80Lau300-26
80PacLeg-73
80PerHaloFP-133
80SSPHOF-133
82OhiHaloF-22
83DonHOFH-42
83TopRep5-277
84OCoandSI-94
84OCoandSI-194
84OCoandSI-206
85TCMPla1-10
85WhiSoxC-30
86SpoDecG-36
88PacLegI-95
89SweBasG-60
90PerGreM-82
91TopArc1-61
92BazQua5A-5
93ActPacA-112
93ActPacA2-46G
Wynn, Jim
64Col.45JP-12
64Top-38
64TopCoi-2
64TopVen-38
65OPC-257
65Top-257
66Baz-35
66Top-520
66TopRubI-99
67Ast-30
67AstTeal1-12
67AstTeal2-24
67Baz-35
67Top-390
67TopGiaSU-24
67TopVen-316
68Baz-11
68CokCapA-17
68DexPre-77
68OPC-5
68Top-5
68Top-260
68TopActS-11C
68TopGamI-24
68TopPla-24
68TopPos-8
68TopVen-5
68TopVen-260
69MLBOffS-144
69MLBPin-60
69Top-360
69TopDec-11B
69TopDecI-47
69TopSta-40
69TopSup-43
69TopTeaP-6
69TraSta-41
70AstTeal-12
70DayDaiNM-26
70Kel-9
70MLBOffS-48
70OPC-60
70Top-60
70TopScr-23
70TopSup-35
70TraSta-4B
71AstCok-12
71BazNumT-43
71MLBOffS-96
71OPC-565
71Top-565
71TopCoi-69
71TopGreM-31
72MilBra-372
72Top-770
73OPC-185
73Top-185
74OPC-43
74Top-43
74TopSta-40
74TopTra-43T
75Hos-25
75HosTwi-25
75OPC-570
75Top-570
76CraDis-68
76Hos-129
76OPC-395
76SSP-89
76Top-395
77Top-165
77YanBurK-20
86AstGreT-5
86AstMot-7
87AstSer1-23
87AstSer1-28
87AstShoSO-25
87AstShoSTw-26
87AstShoSTw-27
87DodSmoA-39
88DodSmo-20
89DodSmoG-86
90DodTar-880
92DodStaTA-13
92UppDecS-8
92YanWIZ7-170
93ActPacA-156
93UppDecS-21
94BreMilB-375
94MCIAmb-4
Wynne, Billy
70Top-618
71MLBOffS-360

71OPC-718
71Top-718
91MetWIZ-436
Wynne, Jim
91JamExpC-18
91JamExpP-3546
92AlbPolC-13
92AlbPolF-2307
Wynne, Marvell
82TidTidT-16
83TidTidT-21
84Don-508
84Fle-269
84JacMetF-14
84Nes792-173
84Top-173
84TopSti-135
84TopTif-173
85AllGamPl-162
85Don-113
85Fle-481
85Lea-233
85OPC-86
85Pir-23
85Top-615
85TopMin-615
85TopSti-131
85TopTif-615
86Don-113
86Fle-625
86FleUpd-130
86OPC-293
86Top-525
86TopSti-128
86TopTif-525
87Don-411
87DonOpeD-144
87Fle-435
87FleGlo-435
87PadBohHB-16
87Top-37
87TopTif-37
88Don-237
88OPCBoxB-H
88PadSmo-31
88Sco-209
88ScoGlo-209
88StaLinPa-14
88Top-454
88TopTif-454
88TopWaxBC-H
89Don-347
89DonBasB-189
89Fle-322
89FleGlo-322
89PanSti-205
89Sco-203
89Top-353
89TopSti-107
89TopTif-353
89UppDec-154
90CubMar-26
90Don-255
90Lea-270
90OPC-256
90PubSti-63
90Sco-337
90Top-256
90TopTif-256
90TopTVCu-35
90UppDec-14
90VenSti-503
91Fle-441
91OPC-714
91Sco-531
91Top-714
91TopDesS-714
91TopMic-714
91TopTif-714
Wyrick, Chris
93BriTigC-26
93BriTigF-3656
Wyrostek, John
48Bow-44
49Bow-37
49EurSta-99
49Lea-19
50Bow-197
51Bow-107
51TopBluB-44
52Bow-42
52NatTeaL-41
52Top-13
53BowBW-35
53Top-79
55Bow-237
83TopRep5-13
85TCMPla1-35
91TopArc1-79
Wyse, Henry
43CubTeal-24
44CubTeal-24
47TipTop-119
51Bow-192
79DiaGre-108
83TCMPla1944-34
Wyszynski, Dennis
79WatA'sT-5
80WesHavWCT-2
X, Malcolm
93Pin-302
Xavier, Joe
86ModA'sC-21
87HunStaTI-25
88TacTigC-25
88TacTigP-613
89DenZepC-21
89DenZepP-53
90CMC-32
90DenZepC-7
90DenZepP-636
90ProAAAF-661
Yacopino, Ed
87MacPirP-20
88SalBucS-24
89HarSenP-291
89HarSenS-22
90HarSenP-1207
90HarSenS-22
91CarMudLD-122
91CarMudP-1099
91LinDriAA-122
92RocRedWF-1954
92RocRedWS-473
93RocRedWF-256
Yaeger, Chuck
86AlbYanT-20
Yaeger, Edward
52LavPro-41
Yagi, Richard
88FreSunCLC-14
88FreSunP-1239
Yagi, Yagi
72Dia-137
Yahmann, Jim
88JacExpB-26
Yahrling, Charles
52LavPro-48
Yamada, Tsutoma
92CalLeaACL-13
92SalSpuC-19
92SalSpuF-3757
Yamaguchi, Yuji
89SalSpuCLC-133
89SalSpuP-1813
Yamamoto, Kazunori
87JapPlaB-40
Yamamoto, Koji
79TCMJapPB-8
Yamamoto, Masahiro
88FloStaLAS-26
88SanJosGCLC-140
88SanJosGP-117
88VerBeaDS-26
Yamano, Mickey
86SanJosBP-24
87SanJosBP-11
Yamanouchi, Kenichi
90SalSpuCLC-140
90SalSpuP-2724
Yamashita, Daisuke
79TCMJapPB-7
Yamauchi, Kazuhiro
79TCMJapPB-90
Yamazaki, Hiroyuki
79TCMJapPB-16
Yamazaki, Kazu (Kazuharu)
92NiaFalRF-3325
Yamazaki, Kazuharu
92NiaFalRC-7
96HilStaHWB-16
Yampierre, Eddie
81WauTimT-12
Yan, Esteban
93DanBraC-29
93DanBraF-3619
94MacBraC-26
94MacBraF-2207
96BowBayB-27
Yan, Julian
87MyrBeaBJP-1435
88DunBluJS-23
88FloStaLAS-52
89DunBluJS-24
89Sta-118
90Bes-148
90KnoBluJB-13
90KnoBluJP-1253
90KnoBluJS-22
91KnoBluJLD-373
91KnoBluJP-1777
91LinDriAA-373
92KnoBluJF-3001
92KnoBluJS-398
92SkyAA F-169
93LimRocDWB-134
93SyrChiF-1008
94MedHatBJF-3699
94MedHatBJSP-27
94SyrChiF-980
94SyrChiTI-29
96VerExpB-4
Yan, Roberto
82DayBeaAT-9
Yanagida, Shikato
90CalLeaACLC-44
90SalSpuCLC-139
90SalSpuP-2723
Yancey, William
78LauLonABS-30
86NegLeaF-88
Yancy, Hugh
77IndIndTI-22
79TacTugT-10
Yandle, John
80HawIslT-12
81HolMilT-6
Yandrick, Jerry
77ChaPatT-25
Yanes, Eddie
86VisOakP-24
87OrlTwiP-19
88OrlTwiB-4
Yanez, Luis
96AubDouB-9
Yang, Chang
95BatCliTI-6
Yang, Charles
91DaiDolF-12
Yankees, Ft. Lauderdale
75ForLauYS-29
Yankees, Gulf Coast
92GulCoaYF-3708
Yankees, New York
13FatT20-5
36R31Pre-G25
38BasTabP-48
48ExhTea-4
48ExhTea-6
48ExhTea-8
48ExhTea-10
48ExhTea-14
48ExhTea-16
57Top-97
58Top-246
59Top-510
60NuHi-61
60Top-332
60TopTat-70
61Top-228
61TopMagR-2
61Yan61RL-1
62Top-251
63Top-247
64Top-433
64TopTatl-15
65Top-513
66OPC-92
66Top-92
66TopRubl-115
66TopVen-92
67OPC-131
67Top-131
68LauWorS-24
68LauWorS-33
68LauWorS-35
68LauWorS-39
68LauWorS-47
68LauWorS-48
68LauWorS-57
68LauWorS-59
69FleCloS-16
69FleCloS-48
69TopStaA-16
70FleWorS-19
70FleWorS-24
70FleWorS-33
70FleWorS-36
70FleWorS-38
70FleWorS-39
70FleWorS-40
70FleWorS-47
70FleWorS-48
70FleWorS-53
70FleWorS-57
70FleWorS-59
70OPC-399
70Top-399
71FleWorS-20
71FleWorS-25
71FleWorS-36
71FleWorS-37
71FleWorS-39
71FleWorS-40
71FleWorS-41
71FleWorS-45
71FleWorS-51
71FleWorS-54
71FleWorS-58
71FleWorS-60
71FleWorS-61
71FleWorS-62
71OPC-543
71Top-543
71TopTat-25
72OPC-237
72Top-237
73FleWilD-10
73OPC-556
73OPCBTC-17
73Top-556
73TopBluTC-17
74OPC-363
74OPCTC-17
74Top-363
74TopStaA-16
74TopStaA-17
74TopTeaC-17
75YanDyn1T-50
76OPC-17
77Spo-522
78SSP270-22
78Top-282
78YanSSPD-22
83FleSta-241
83FleSti-NNO
87SpoTeaL-7
88PanSti-464
88RedFolSB-125
89FleWaxBC-C18
89YanScoNW-33
90PubSti-646
90RedFolSB-121
90VenSti-531
93TedWilPC-10
94ImpProP-10
94Sco-326
94ScoGolR-326
95PanSti-144
96PanSti-155
Yano, Minoru
96MauStiHWB-1
Yanus, Bud
80MemChiT-29
83MemChiT-12
86WesPalBEP-28
87WesPalBEP-662
Yarbrough, Buddy
77DayBealT-27
Yard, Bruce
93YakBeaC-26
93YakBeaF-3893
95BakBlaTI-22
96SanAntMB-26
96VerBeaDB-29
Yaroshuk, Ernie
92OneYanC-3
93OneYanC-26
93OneYanF-3519
Yarrison, Rube
90DodTar-1099
Yaryan, Clarence
22E120-30
23WilChoV-178
Yastrzemski, Carl
47Exh-245
47PM1StaP1-225
47PM1StaP1-226
60Top-148
60TopVen-148
61Top-287
61TopStal-119
62Jel-61
62Pos-61
62PosCan-61
62RedSoxJP-11
62SalPlaC-27
62ShiPlaC-27
62Top-425
62TopBuc-96
62TopStal-20
63Baz-16
63Fle-8
63Jel-80
63Pos-80
63Top-115
63TopStil-46
64Baz-16
64ChatheY-50
64Top-8
64Top-182
64Top-210
64TopCoi-26
64TopCoi-134
64TopGia-48
64TopSta-23
64TopStaU-77
64TopTatl-75
64TopVen-8
64TopVen-182
64TopVen-210
64WheSta-50
65ChaTheY-48
65OldLonC-40
65Top-385
65TopEmbl-1
65TopTral-36
66Baz-22
66OPC-70
66Top-70
66Top-216
66TopRubl-100
66TopVen-70
66TopVen-216
67Baz-22
67CokCapA-17
67CokCapRS-2
67DexPre-227
67DexPre-228
67OPCPapl-5
67Top-355
67TopGiaSU-21
67TopPos-5
67TopRedSS-25
67TopRedSS-29
67TopTesF-23
67TopVen-193
68AtlOilPBCC-50
68Baz-2
68OPC-2
68OPC-4
68OPC-6
68OPC-152
68OPC-192
68Top-2
68Top-4
68Top-6
68Top-152
68Top-192A
68Top-192B
68Top-250
68Top-369
68TopActS-1B
68TopActS-6A
68TopActS-13B
68TopGaml-3
68TopPla-12
68TopPos-16
68TopVen-2
68TopVen-4
68TopVen-6
68TopVen-152
68TopVen-192
68TopVen-250
68TopVen-369
69KelPin-20
69MLBPin-30
69OPC-1
69OPC-130

69OPCDec-24
69RedSoxAO-12
69RedSoxTI-12
69Top-1
69Top-130
69Top-425
69TopDec-4
69TopDecI-48
69TopFou-25
69TopSta-140
69TopSup-5
69TopTeaP-3
69TraSta-19
70DayDaiNM-28
70MLBOffS-168
70OPC-10
70OPC-461
70RedSoxCPPC-16
70Top-10
70Top-461
70TopScr-24
70TopSup-29
70TraSta-13A
71AllBasA-24
71BazNumT-5
71BazUnn-23
71MLBOffS-336
71MLBOffS-576
71OPC-61
71OPC-65
71OPC-530
71RedSoxA-12
71RedSoxTI-12
71Top-61
71Top-65
71Top-530
71TopCoi-58
71TopGreM-40
71TopSup-49
71TopTat-13
71TopTat-14
72OPC-37
72OPC-38
72Top-37
72Top-38
72TopPos-2
73LinPor-32
73OPC-245
73Top-245
73TopCanL-55
73TopCom-24
73TopPin-24
74LauAllG-70
74OPC-280
74Top-280
74TopDecE-43
74TopPuz-12
74TopSta-140
75Hos-48
75Kel-51
75OPC-205
75OPC-280
75SSP42-23
75Top-205
75Top-280
76CraDis-69
76Hos-149
76Kel-24
76LauDiaJ-9
76LinSup-102
76OPC-230
76RedSox-9
76RedSoxSM-16
76SSP-409
76Top-230
77BurCheD-36
77Hos-4
77MSADis-62
77OPC-37
77PepGloD-23
77RCColC-68
77Spo-3003
77Spo-5408
77Top-434
77Top-480
77TopCloS-53
78OPC-137
78PapGinD-8
78Pep-39
78SSP270-187
78TasDis-16
78Top-40
78WifBalD-78
79Kel-45
79OPC-160
79Top-320
79TopCom-3
80Kel-27
80OPC-365
80PerHaloFP-204
80Top-1
80Top-720
80TopSup-22
81AllGamPI-72
81CokTeaS-11
81Don-94
81Don-214
81Dra-1
81Fle-221
81Fle-638
81FleStiC-13
81Kel-48
81OPC-110
81PerCreC-4
81RedSoxBG2S-65
81RedSoxBG2S-66
81RedSoxBG2S-128
81Top-110
81TopSti-45
81TopSupHT-12
82Don-74
82Fle-312
82Fle-633
82FleSta-162
82FleSta-237
82K-M-11
82Kel-43
82OPC-72
82OPC-358
82PerCreC-13
82PerCreCG-13
82RedSoxC-22
82Top-650
82Top-651
82TopSti-120
82TopSti-155
83AllGamPI-9
83Don-25
83Don-326
83DonActA-44
83Dra-32
83Fle-200
83Fle-629
83FleSta-221
83FleSti-60
83FraBroR-19
83Kel-9
83Oco& SSBG-19
83OPC-4
83OPC-126
83PerCreC-35
83PerCreCG-35
83Top-550
83Top-551
83TopFol-2
83TopGloS-1
83TopSti-6
83TopSti-31
84Don-B
84DonCha-10
84Fle-412
84Fle-640
84FleSti-97
84Nes792-6
84OCoandSI-10
84OCoandSI-124
84OCoandSI-170
84SpoDesPW-18
84Top-6
84TopGloA-11
84TopTif-6
85CirK-17
86RedSoxGT-9
86SpoDecG-47
86SpoDesJM-3
86TCMSupS-10
86TCMSupS-41
87K-M-11
87Top-314
87TopTif-314
89KahComC-2
89KahCoo-11
89PerCelP-44
89TopBasT-33
90AGFA-2
90BasWit-34
90Col-12
90Don-588
90HOFStiB-71
90PacLeg-61
90PerGreM-72
90PerMasW-46
90PerMasW-47
90PerMasW-48
90PerMasW-49
90PerMasW-50
90SweBasG-5
90TopGloA-22
91SweBasG-108
92ScoFacI-B15
92ScoFacI-B16
92ScoFacI-B17
92ScoFra-3
92ScoFra-4
92ScoFra-AU3
92ScoFra-AU4
92UppDecS-6
92Zip-4
93Pin-297
93SelTriC-2
93TedWil-7
93TedWilLC-8
93UppDecS-6
94CarLeaA-DJ1
94UppDecS-10
94Yoo-16
95JimDeaAG-6
95TopLegot6M-6

Yastrzemski, Mike
84DurBulT-3
85DurBulT-32
86BirBarTI-17
86SouLeaAJ-2
87HawIsIP-1
88VanCanC-19
88VanCanP-774
90BirBarDGB-32

Yasuda, Hideyuki
91CalLeLA-40
91SalSpuC-3
91SalSpuP-2248

Yates, Al
94BreMilB-91

Yates, Lance
90OklSoo-20

Yates, Peter
91DaiDolF-9

Yaughn, Kip
91CarLeaAP-CAR10
91FreKeyC-11
91FreKeyP-2365
92HagSunF-2558
92HagSunS-273
92SkyAA F-116
93Top-669
93TopGol-669
93TopInaM-669
93TopMic-669
94PorSeaDF-678
94PorSeaDTI-30

Yawkey, Mrs. (Tom)
79RedSoxEF-2
79RedSoxEF-11

Yawkey, Tom
59FleWil-42
80PerHaloFP-173
80SSPHOF-173
89HOFStiB-93

Ybarra, Jamie
95KanCouCTI-38

Yde, Emil
26SpoComoA-49
92ConTSN-546

Yeager Jr., Gary
95BatCliTI-33
96PieBolWB-29

Yeager, Eric
85AncGlaPTI-32
86AncGlaPTI-37
87AncGlaP-32

Yeager, Joe (Joseph F.)
03BreE10-156
09ColChiE-314
11SpoLifCW-375
12ColRedB-314
12ColTinT-314
12ImpTobC-84
90DodTar-881

Yeager, Steve
73OPC-59
73Top-59
74OPC-593
74Top-593
75OPC-376
75Top-376
76Hos-147
76LinSup-118
76OPC-515
76SSP-83
76Top-515
77BurCheD-151
77OPC-159
77Top-105
78Hos-51
78SSP270-73
78Top-285
79DodBlu-13
79OPC-31
79Top-75
80DodPol-7
80OPC-371
80Top-726
81AllGamPI-135
81DodPol-7
81Don-297
81Fle-129
81LonBeaPT-19
81OPC-318
81Top-318
81TopSupHT-54
82DodPol-7
82DodPos-10
82DodUniOV-26
82Don-201
82Fle-29
82OPC-219
82Top-477
82TopSti-259
83DodPol-7
83DodPos-20
83Don-201
83Fle-227
83OPC-261
83Top-555
84AllGamPI-45
84DodPol-7
84Don-581
84Fle-117
84Nes792-661
84OPC-252
84Top-661
84TopSti-86
84TopTif-661
85DodCokP-34
85Don-519
85Fle-390
85OPC-148
85Top-148
85TopMin-148
85TopTif-148
86Don-519
86FleUpd-131
86MarMot-5
86OPC-32
86Top-32
86TopTif-32
86TopTra-130T
86TopTraT-130T
87Fle-599
87FleGlo-599
87OPC-258
87Top-258
87TopTif-258
90DodTar-882
89MajLeaM-9
89MajLeaM-11

Yearout, Mike
86KnoBluJP-26
87KnoBluJP-1496

Yedo, Carlos
94OneYanC-25
95GreBatTI-24
96TamYanY-28

Yeglinski, John
75LafDriT-10
77ArkTraT-11A
77ArkTraT-11B

Yelding, Eric
85KinBluJT-23
86VenGulP-28
87KnoBluJP-1505
88SyrChiC-17
88SyrChiP-832
88TriAAAP-37
89AstLenH-12
89AstMot-21
89AstSmo-39
89DonRoo-34
89ScoHot1R-65
90AstLenH-27
90AstMot-24
90ClaYel-T58
90Don-123
90DonBesN-114
90FleLeaL-42
90FleUpd-18
90Hot50RS-49
90Lea-301
90OPC-309
90Sco-411
90Sco100RS-16
90ScoYouSI-15
90Top-309
90TopBig-317
90TopDeb89-148
90TopTif-309
90UppDec-427
91AstMot-7
91Bow-557
91ClaGam-71
91Don-277
91Fle-520
91Lea-100
91OPC-59
91PanCanT1-42
91PanFreS-12
91PanSti-13
91RedFolS-103
91Sco-329
91StaClu-16
91Top-59
91TopDesS-59
91TopMic-59
91TopTif-59
91Ult-141
91UppDec-197
92Don-148
92Sco-197
92StaClu-2
92TucTorF-502
92TucTorS-623
92UppDec-394
93CubMar-32
93PacSpa-129
94Fle-403
94IowCubF-1289
94StaCluT-337
94StaCluTFDI-337

Yellen, Larry
64Top-226
64TopVen-226
65Top-292

Yellowhorse, Moses
21Exh-192

Yelovic, John
43CenFlo-25

Yelton, Rob
91BriTigC-7
91BriTigP-3610
92FayGenC-15
92FayGenF-2173
93LakTigF-1315

Yennaco, Jay
96MicBatCB-29

Yerkes, Stephen
12T207-206
14TexTomE-49
14TexTomE-63
15SpoNewM-197
16ColE13-196
16SpoNewM-196

Yesenchak, Ed
76AppFoxT-27
77AppFoxT-29

Yeske, Kyle
92BluOriC-2
92BluOriF-2374
93AlbPolC-22
93AlbPolF-2041
94AlbPolC-26
94AlbPolF-2253

Yett, Rich
81WisRapTT-12
83OrlTwiT-15
84TolMudHT-5
85FleUpd-131
85TolMudHT-30
85TwiTeal-27
86IndOhH-42
86IndTeal-49

86MaiGuiP-26
87Fle-263
87FleGlo-263
87IndGat-42
87Top-134
87TopTif-134
88BlaYNPRWL-190
88Fle-621
88FleGlo-621
88IndGat-42
88Sco-484
88ScoGlo-484
88Top-531
88TopTif-531
89Bow-79
89BowTif-79
89Don-546
89Fle-417
89FleGlo-417
89IndTeal-27
89Sco-467
89Top-363
89TopBig-290
89TopTif-363
89UppDec-728
90Bow-412
90BowTif-412
90CMC-563
90Don-509
90Fle-504
90FleCan-504
90OPC-689
90PorBeaC-11
90PubSti-570
90Sco-274
90Top-689
90TopTif-689
90UppDec-595
90VenSti-504
Yi, Jiao
90IBAWorA-21
Yingling, Earl
16ColE13-197
90DodTar-1100
Ynclan, Rocky
87HawRai-24
Yobs, Dave
82GleFalWST-13
85BufBisT-16
86BufBisP-26
Yochim, Ray
49EurSta-200
Yockey, Mark
90EveGiaB-12
90EveGiaP-3128
91CliGiaC-10
91CliGiaP-835
92ShrCapF-3873
92ShrCapS-598
93ShrCapF-2761
94PorSeaDF-679
94PorSeaDTI-31
Yocum, David
95Bes-120
96Bow-269
96Exc-183
96SigRooOJPP-P8
96Top-236
96VerBeaDB-30
Yoder, Jeff
96Bow-299
96RocCubTI-32
97Bow-214
97BowInt-214
Yoder, Kris
76WilTomT-22
78RicBraT-18
79SavBraT-13
Yoder, P.J.
96PitMetB-29
95PitMetTI-20
Yogi, Great
76LauIndC-35
Yojo, Minoru
89VisOakCLC-115
89VisOakP-1424
Yokota, George
86SanJosBP-25
Yonamine, Wally
79TCMJapPB-89
York, Anthony
44CubTeal-25
47CenFlo-32
47SigOil-89
49BowPCL-22
York, Charles
92WatIndC-9
92WatIndF-3236
93ColRedC-26
93ColRedF-599
93SouAtlLAGF-16
94ClaGolF-46
94KinIndC-22
94KinIndF-2645
95BakBlaTI-21
York, Jim
72OPC-68
72Top-68
73OPC-546
73Top-546
75OPC-383
75Top-383
76OPC-224
76Top-224
87AstShoSTw-19
92YanWIZ7-171
York, Mike
86LakTigP-25
87MacPirP-7
88SalBucS-25
89HarSenP-310
89HarSenS-23
89Sta-21
90BufBisC-11
90BufBisP-374
90BufBisTI-27
90CMC-11
90ProAAAF-489
91BufBisLD-48
91BufBisP-543
91LinDriAAA-48
91OPC-508
91Sco-738
91Top-508
91TopDeb90-168
91TopDesS-508
91TopMic-508
91TopTif-508
91Ult-389
92LasVegSS-248
York, Ronald
91IdaFalBSP-1
York, Rudy
38ExhFou-12
38GouHeaU-260
38GouHeaU-284
39ExhSal-65
39GouPreR303A-48
39GouPreR303B-24
39WorWidGTP-48
40WheM4-6B
46RedSoxTI-25
47TipTop-14
48BluTin-27
60Top-456
72FleFamF-12
72LauGreF-3
74LauAllG-42
76GalBasGHoF-31
76TayBow4-62
81TigDetN-9
81TigSecNP-26
83TCMPla1942-13
85Woo-43
87RedSox1T-2
90HOFStiB-35
93ConTSN-773
Yorke, Christa
91FreStaLBS-11
Yorro, Jacinto
90St.CatBJP-3481
91St.CatBJP-3410
Yoshida, Takashi
89VisOakCLC-120
89VisOakP-1430
Yoshida, Yasuo
96HilStaHWB-3
Yoshimuru, Sadaaki
87JapPlaB-26
Yoshinaga, Yoshi
89SalSpuCLC-136
89SalSpuP-1810
Yoshitake, Shintaroh
96MauStiHWB-17
Yost, Eddie
49Bow-32
50Bow-162
51Bow-41
51R42SmaS-117
51TopBluB-1
52Bow-31
52NatTeaL-42
52RedMan-AL25
52TipTop-47
52Top-123
53BowC-116
53Bri-28
54Bow-72
54RedHeaF-32
55Bow-73
55DonWin-9
56Top-128
57SwiFra-11
57Top-177
58SenJayP-12
58Top-173
59Top-2
59TopVen-2
60TigJayP-12
60Top-245
61AngJayP-12
61Baz-6
61Pos-45
61Top-413
61TopStal-175
62AngJayP-12
62Jel-76
62Pos-76
62PosCan-76
62Top-176A
62Top-176B
62TopVen-176
73OPC-257
73Top-257A
73Top-257B
74OPC-179
74Top-179
79TCM50-88
81TCM60I-407
83TopRep5-123
85TCMPla1-11
89RinPosM1-31
90PacLeg-73
91SweBasG-122
94Met69CCPP-6
94Met69CS-5
94Met69T-33
94TedWil-90
94UppDecAH-206
94UppDecAH1-206
Yost, Ned (Edgar)
78SpoIndC-28
79Top-708
79VanCanT-13
80VanCanT-3
81Top-659
82BrePol-5
82Top-542
83BreGar-21
83BrePol-5
83Don-458
83Fle-50
83Top-297
84Don-271
84Fle-218
84FleUpd-130
84JacMetF-15
84Nes792-107
84RanJarP-7
84Top-107
84TopTif-107
84TopTra-131T
84TopTraT-131T
85Don-221
85Fle-575
85Top-777
85TopTif-777
87GreBraB-12
88SouAtlLAGS-3
88SumBraP-414
89SumBraP-1095
90SumBraB-30
90SumBraP-2450
91BraSubS-39
92BraLykS-37
92BreCarT-25
93BraLykS-38
93RanKee-390
94BraLykP-35
94BraLykS-34
94BreMilB-92
Yost, Steve
77LynMetT-31
Youmans, Floyd
84JacMetT-15
86Don-543
86ExpPos-20
86ExpProPa-24
86Fle-267
86Lea-210
86OPC-346
86Top-732
86TopTif-732
87ClaGam-98
87Don-257
87DonHig-22
87DonOpeD-89
87ExpPos-36
87Fle-337
87FleGlo-337
87FleMin-120
87FleRecS-44
87GenMilB-4J
87HosSti-6
87Lea-65
87Lea-206
87OPC-105
87Spo-103
87SpoTeaP-20
87StuPan-8
87Top-105
87TopMinL-19
87TopSti-79
87TopTif-105
88BlaYNPRWL-158
88Don-56
88DonBasB-314
88ExpPos-25
88Fle-201
88FleGlo-201
88Lea-66
88MSAHosD-9
88OPC-365
88PanSti-321
88Sco-327
88ScoGlo-327
88ScoYouS2-16
88Spo-108
88StaLinE-20
88Top-365
88TopSti-82
88TopTif-365
89Bow-396
89BowTif-396
89OPC-91
89PhiTas-36
89Top-91
89TopTif-91
89UppDec-459
89UppDec-730
90PubSti-252
90ReaPhiS-25
90VenSti-505
Young, Anthony
87LitFalMP-2394
88LitFalMP-24
89ColMetB-16
89ColMetGS-28
89SouAtlLAGS-22
90JacMetGS-26
90TexLeaAGS-31
91Bow-466
91Cla2-T56
91LeaGolR-BC23
91LinDriAAA-573
91LinDriP-573
91MetColP-52
91TidTidLD-573
91TidTidP-2512
91UppDecFE-65F
92Bow-268
92Cla2-T60
92ClaGam-144
92Don-409
92Fle-520
92Lea-356
92MetColP-32
92MetKah-19
92OPC-148
92Pin-558
92ProFS7-278
92Sco-756
92ScoImpP-39
92ScoRoo-14
92StaClu-85
92Stu-70
92Top-148
92TopDeb91-190
92TopGol-148
92TopGolW-148
92TopMic-148
92Ult-238
92UppDec-535
92UppDecSR-SR25
93Don-14
93Fle-96
93Lea-545
93MetColP-50
93MetKah-19
93OPC-380
93PacSpa-550
93Pin-350
93Sco-113
93Sel-284
93StaClu-582
93StaCluFDI-582
93StaCluMOP-582
93Top-734
93TopGol-734
93TopInaM-734
93TopMic-734
93Ult-81
93UppDec-71
93UppDecGold-71
93USPlaCR-3D
94ColC-303
94ColC-427
94ColChoGS-303
94ColChoGS-427
94ColChoSS-303
94ColChoSS-427
94Don-405
94Fin-167
94FinRef-167
94Fle-580
94FleUpd-112
94Lea-74
94MetShuST-8
94Sco-263
94ScoGolR-263
94ScoRoo-RT31
94ScoRooGR-RT31
94StaClu-28
94StaCluFDI-28
94StaCluGR-28
94StaCluMOP-28
94Top-359
94TopGol-359
94TopSpa-359
94TopTra-110T
94Ult-466
94UppDec-443
94UppDecED-443
95ColCho-201
95ColChoGS-201
95ColChoSS-201
95Don-358
95DonPreP-358
95Fle-427
96AstMot-21
Young, Babe (Norman)
40PlaBal-212
41DouPlaR-31
41DouPlaR-93
41Gou-23
41PlaBal-27
49Bow-240
76TayBow4-59
77TCMTheWY-89
84TCMPla1-44
93ConTSN-814
Young, Bob G.
52Bow-193
52Top-147
53Top-160
54Bow-149
54OriEss-36
54Top-8
55OriEss-27
83TopRep5-147
91OriCro-492
91TopArc1-160
94TopArc1-8
94TopArc1G-8
Young, Bobby
71RicBraTI-18
Young, Brian
90ElmPioP-24
91WinHavRSC-10
91WinHavRSP-490

2WinHavRSF-1778
3NewBriRSF-1223
4LynRedSC-25
4LynRedSF-1893
ng, Chris
3DavLipB-22
ng, Cliff
KnoBluJP-27
SouLeaAJ-24
KnoBluJP-1520
SyrChiC-8
SyrChiP-807
EdmTraC-4
EdmTraP-557
CMC-478
dmTraC-1
dmTraP-518
leUpd-82
roAAAF-94
ow-204
dmTraP-1517
e-330
pDeb90-169
dmTraS-173
e-73
yAAAF-83
aClu-562
aKniF-544
FinE-207
nVenB-90
, Curt
cTigT-8
cTigC-85
sMot-22
on-522
e-436
op-293
opTif-293
acTigP-25
op-84
opTif-84
'sSmoC-12
Don-344
DonOpeD-29
Fle-410
FleGamW-44
FleGlo-410
FleStiC-129
SpoTeaP-23
Top-519
TopSti-165
TopTif-519
A'sMot-17
Don-97
DonBasB-323
DonTeaBA-97
8Fle-296
8FleGlo-296
8FleStiC-58
88OPC-103
88PanSti-165
88RedFolSB-104
88Sco-125
88ScoGlo-125
88Spo-209
88StaLinAs-19
88Top-103
88TopTif-103
89A'sMot-14
89Bow-184
89BowTif-184
89Don-304
89Fle-26
89FleGlo-26
89Sco-29
89Top-641
89TopBig-254
89TopTif-641
89UppDec-392
90A'sMot-24
90Don-505
90Fle-24
90FleCan-24
90Lea-424
90OPC-328
90PubSti-319
90Sco-533
90Top-328
90TopTif-328
90UppDec-4
91A'sMot-24
91Bow-220
91Don-723
91Fle-28
91OPC-473
91Sco-236
91Top-473
91TopDesS-473
91TopMic-473
91TopTif-473
91Ult-257
92Don-469
92Fle-272
92OmaRoyS-348
92OPC-704
92Sco-722
92Top-704
92TopGol-704
92TopGolW-704
92TopMic-704
93Fle-658
Young, Cy (Denton T.)
03BreE10-157
04FanCraAL-51
04RedSoxUP-16
08RosComP-10
09AmeCarE-119
09AmeCarE-120
09BriE97-30A
09BriE97-30B
09ColChiE-315
09SpoNewSM-2
09T206-386
09T206-387
09T206-388
10DomDisP-129
10E101-45
10E98-30
10MelMinE-45
10NadCarE-51
10PeoT21-58
10RedCroT-88
10StaCarE-30
10SweCapPP-21A
10SweCapPP-21B
10W555-64
10W555-65
10W555-66
11DiaGumP-29
11E94-30
11S74Sil-12
11SpoLifCW-376
11SpoLifM-52
11T205-186
11TurRedT-42
12ColRedB-315
12ColTinT-315
12HasTriFT-50B
13NatGamW-45
13TomBarW-42
36PC7AlbHoF-13
48ExhHoF-32
50CalHOFW-80
60Fle-47
60NuHi-48
61Fle-153
61GolPre-33
61NuSco-448
63BazMagM-88
63BazA-6
63GadFunC-26
63HalofFB-28
67TopVen-150
69Baz-3
69Baz-6
71FleWorS-1
72FleFamF-11
72KelATG-12
72LauGreF-29
73HalofFPP-20
73OPC-477
73Top-477
75FlePio-19
75McCCob-14
76GalBasGHoF-32
76ShaPiz-8
77GalGloG-169
77GalGloG-270
77ShaPiz-3
77Spo-3217
77Spo-5103
79Pew-8
79Top-416
80Lau300-11
80LauFamF-30
80MarExhH-32
80PacLeg-91
80PerHaloFP-13
80SSPHOF-13
82BHCRSpoL-5
82OhiHaloF-14
83DonHOFH-27
84DonCha-31
84GalHaloFRL-8
85UltBasC-8
85Woo-44
86IndGreT-9
86RedSoxGT-3
87SpoRea-20
88ConSer4-30
89HOFStiB-59
89SweBasG-5
90BasWit-79
90HOFStiB-14
90PerGreM-10
90SweBasG-100
91HomCooC-5
91SweBasG-135
91USGamSBL-13A
91USGamSBL-13C
91USGamSBL-13D
91USGamSBL-13H
92St.VinHHS-12
92WhiLegtL-5
92WhiPro-5
93ActPacA-85
93ActPacA2-19G
93Hoy-9
93SpeHOF2-4
93UppDecAH-129
93UppDecAH-138
93UppDecAH-142
93UppDecAH-156
93UppDecAH-157
93UppDecAH-158
93UppDecAH-159
94TedWil-7
94TedWilLC-LC18
94UppDecAH-105
94UppDecAH-151
94UppDecAH-200
94UppDecAH1-105
94UppDecAH1-151
94UppDecAH1-200
95UppDecSHoB-2
93UppDecTR-3
98CamPepP-84
Young, Danny
92AshTouC-16
92ClaFS7-381
93AshTouC-24
93AshTouF-2277
95LynHilTI-29
Young, Del E.
39PlaBal-33
40PlaBal-101
48SomandK-27
49SomandK-21
Young, Delwyn
83CedRapRT-17
86VerRedP-24
87BurExpP-1081
87SanBerSP-11
88EasLeaAP-12
88GleFalTP-916
89TolMudHC-22
89TolMudHP-764
90CanIndB-14
90CanIndP-1306
90CanIndS-18
90CMC-734
96LanJetB-2
Young, Derrick
89ColMetB-3
89ColMetGS-29
90St.LucMS-26
91SanBerSC-25
91SanBerSP-2002
Young, Dick
90LitSunW-9
Young, Dmitri
91ClaDraP-4
91ClaDraPP-4
91JohCitCC-11
91JohCitCP-3993
91UppDecFE-7F
92ClaBluBF-BC8
92ClaDraP-89
92ClaFS7-272
92ClaRedB-BC8
92MidLeaATI-54
92ProFS7-322
92SprCarC-1
92SprCarF-879
92UppDec-58
92UppDecML-30
92UppDecML-62
92UppDecML-274
92UppDecMLPotY-PY7
92UppDecMLTPHF-TP9
93ClaFisN-13
93ClaFS7-AU8
93ClaGolF-96
93ClaYouG-YG28
93Don-638
93ExcFS7-108
93SP-290
93St.PetCC-1
93St.PetCF-2638
93UppDec-428
93UppDecGold-428
94ActPac-28
94ArkTraF-3099
94Bow-147
94BowBes-B75
94BowBes-X91
94BowBesR-B75
94BowBesR-X91
94Cla-161
94ClaCreotC-C24
94ClaGolA-SH2
94ClaGolF-173
94ExcFS7-276
94Ult-571
94UppDecML-30
94UppDecML-256
95ArkTraTI-28
95Sum21C-TC9
96BesAutS-98
96LouRedB-28
97Bow-414
97BowBes-180
97BowBesAR-180
97BowBesR-180
97BowCerBIA-CA89
97BowCerGIA-CA89
97BowChr-275
97BowChrI-275
97BowChrIR-275
97BowChrR-275
97BowChrSHR-SHR1
97BowChrSHRR-SHR1
97BowInt-414
97BowScoHR-1
97Cir-114
97CirRav-114
97ColCho-4
97Don-363
97DonFraFea-8
97DonLim-76
97DonLim-84
97DonLimFotG-59
97DonLimLE-76
97DonLimLE-84
97DonPre-142
97DonPreCttC-142
97DonPreP-363
97DonPrePGold-363
97DonRooDK-9
97DonRooDKC-9
97DonTea-164
97DonTeaSPE-164
97Fin-177
97FinRef-177
97FlaSho-A85
97FlaSho-B85
97FlaSho-C85
97FlaShoLC-85
97FlaShoLC-B85
97FlaShoLC-C85
97FlaShoLCM-A85
97FlaShoLCM-B85
97FlaShoLCM-C85
97Fle-455
97FleNewH-15
97FleTif-455
97Lea-176
97LeaFraM-176
97LeaFraMDC-176
97NewPin-177
97NewPinAP-177
97NewPinMC-177
97NewPinPP-177
97Pin-185
97PinArtP-185
97PinCer-121
97PinCerMBlu-121
97PinCerMG-121
97PinCerMR-121
97PinCerR-121
97PinIns-142
97PinInsCE-142
97PinInsDE-142
97PinMusC-185
97PinTotCPB-121
97PinTotCPG-121
97PinTotCPR-121
97PinX-P-124
97PinX-PMoS-124
97Sco-478
97ScoHeaotO-30
97ScoHobR-478
97ScoResC-478
97ScoShoS-478
97ScoShoSAP-320
97ScoShoSAP-478
97Sel-104
97SelArtP-104
97SelRegG-104
97SelRooR-11
97SelTooотT-6
97SelTooотTMB-6
97SpoIll-54
97SpoIllEE-54
97StaCluM-M39
97StaCluMOP-M39
97Stu-157
97StuPrePG-157
97StuPrePS-157
97Top-202
97Ult-470
97UltGolME-470
97UltPlaME-470
97UppDec-272
Young, Don
66OPC-139
66Top-139
69CubJewT-20
69Top-602
70OPC-117
70Top-117
89WatIndS-24
Young, Donald Wayne
66TopVen-139
Young, Eric O.
90FloStaLAS-20
90StaFS7-22
90VerBeaDS-29
91Cla/Bes-11
91LinDriAA-548
91SanAntMLD-548
91SanAntMP-2985
92AlbDukF-736
92AlbDukS-23
92DonRoo-128
92FleUpd-94
92SkyAAAF-11
93Bow-416
93Don-730
93Fin-48
93FinRef-48
93Fla-44
93Fle-69
93FleFinE-47
93Lea-415
93OPCPre-31
93PacSpa-440
93Pin-518
93PinExpOD-4
93RocUSPC-8D
93RocUSPC-11S
93Sco-586
93Sel-342
93SelRoo-130T
93SP-225
93StaClu-526
93StaCluFDI-526
93StaCluMOP-526
93StaCluRoc-27
93Top-145
93Top-551
93TopGol-145
93TopGol-551
93TopInaM-145
93TopInaM-551
93TopMic-145
93TopMic-551
93Ult-361
93UppDec-521
93UppDecGold-521

93USPlaCR-5C
94ColC-304
94ColChoGS-304
94ColChoSS-304
94Don-412
94Fin-186
94FinRef-186
94Fla-159
94Fle-457
94Lea-44
94Pac-209
94PanSti-178
94Pin-133
94PinArtP-133
94PinMusC-133
94RocPol-26
94Sco-472
94ScoGolR-472
94Sel-145
94StaClu-72
94StaCluFDI-72
94StaCluGR-72
94StaCluMOP-72
94StaCluMOP-ST4
94StaCluST-ST4
94StaCluT-104
94StaCluTFDI-104
94Top-712
94TopGol-712
94TopSpa-712
94Ult-190
94UppDec-252
94UppDecED-252
94USPlaCA-3H
95ColCho-446
95ColChoGS-446
95ColChoSS-446
95Don-544
95DonPreP-544
95DonTopotO-236
95Fla-135
95Fle-531
95Lea-188
95Pin-314
95PinArtP-314
95PinMusC-314
95RocPol-12
95Sco-71
95ScoGolR-71
95ScoPlaTS-71
95Top-517
95TopCyb-305
95Ult-159
95UltGolM-159
95UppDec-177
95UppDecED-177
95UppDecEDG-177
96Cir-125
96CirRav-125
96ColCho-128
96ColChoGS-128
96ColChoSS-128
96Don-214
96DonPreP-214
96EmoXL-180
96Fla-255
96Fle-379
96FleRoc-18
96FleTif-379
96Lea-177
96LeaPre-95
96LeaPreP-95
96LeaPrePB-177
96LeaPrePG-177
96LeaPrePS-177
96LeaSig-85
96LeaSigA-249
96LeaSigAG-250
96LeaSigAS-250
96LeaSigPPG-85
96LeaSigPPP-85
96RocPol-27
96Sco-122
96StaClu-412
96StaCluEPB-412
96StaCluEPG-412
96StaCluEPS-412
96StaCluMOP-412
96TeaOut-90
96Ult-477
96UltGolM-477
96UppDec-63
97Bow-49
97BowBes-23
97BowBesAR-23
97BowBesR-23
97BowInt-49
97Cir-98
97CirRav-98
97ColCho-59
97ColCho-99
97ColChoAC-38
97Don-200
97DonEli-76
97DonEliGS-76
97DonLim-57
97DonLim-87
97DonLimFotG-50
97DonLimLE-57
97DonLimLE-87
97DonPre-126
97DonPreCttC-126
97DonPreP-200
97DonPrePGold-200
97DonTea-97
97DonTeaSMVP-6
97DonTeaSPE-97
97Fin-146
97FinEmb-146
97FinEmbR-146
97FinRef-146
97FlaSho-A105
97FlaSho-B105
97FlaSho-C105
97FlaShoLC-105
97FlaShoLC-B105
97FlaShoLC-C105
97FlaShoLCM-A105
97FlaShoLCM-B105
97FlaShoLCM-C105
97Fle-322
97FleTif-322
97Lea-225
97Lea-390
97LeaFraM-225
97LeaFraM-390
97LeaFraMDC-225
97LeaFraMDC-390
97LeaGolS-31
97MetUni-79
97NewPin-113
97NewPinAP-113
97NewPinMC-113
97NewPinPP-113
97Pac-293
97PacLigB-293
97PacPri-99
97PacPriLB-99
97PacPriP-99
97PacSil-293
97PinCer-86
97PinCerMBlu-86
97PinCerMG-86
97PinCerMR-86
97PinCerR-86
97PinIns-58
97PinInsCE-58
97PinInsDE-58
97PinTeaP-2
97PinTeaP-10
97PinTotCPB-86
97PinTotCPG-86
97PinTotCPR-86
97PinX-P-40
97PinX-PMoS-40
97Sco-169
97ScoPreS-169
97ScoRoc-7
97ScoRocPl-7
97ScoRocPr-7
97ScoShoS-169
97ScoShoSAP-169
97ScoSteS-16
97Sel-18
97SelArtP-18
97SelRegG-18
97SP-68
97StaClu-37
97StaCluMat-37
97StaCluMOP-37
97Stu-109
97StuPrePG-109
97StuPrePS-109
97Top-71
97TopAll-AS6
97TopChr-26
97TopChrAS-AS6
97TopChrR-26
97TopChrSAR-AS6
97TopChrSB-24
97TopChrSBR-24
97TopGal-127
97TopGalPPI-127
97TopSeaB-SB24
97TopSta-55
97TopStaAM-55
97Ult-192
97UltGolME-192
97UltPlaME-192
97UppDec-55
97UppDec-218
97UppDecAWJ-8

Young, Erik
89WatIndS-25

Young, Ernest
75CedRapGT-32
75LafDriT-8
76CedRapGT-35
77SalPirT-28
79BufBisT-8
91MadMusC-18

Young, Ernie
87HagSunP-27
87NewOriP-25
88FreSunCLC-5
88FreSunP-1241

Young, Ernie (Ernest Wesley)
90SouOreAB-15
90SouOreAP-3438
91MadMusP-2145
92ModA'sC-10
93ModA'sC-25
93ModA'sF-814
94ClaGolF-98
94ExcFS7-124
94HunStaF-1346
94LeaLimR-75
94SpoRoo-50
94SpoRooAP-50
94UppDecML-203
94UppDecMLPotYF-PY3
95Bow-75
95EdmTraTI-29
95Pin-159
95PinArtP-159
95PinMusC-159
95Sco-576
95ScoAi-AM7
95ScoGolR-576
95ScoPlaTS-576
95Sel-195
95SelArtP-195
95Spo-154
95SpoArtP-154
95UppDec-33
95UppDecED-33
95UppDecEDG-33
96A'sMot-11
96ColCho-642
96ColCho-666
96ColChoGS-642
96ColChoGS-666
96ColChoSS-642
96ColChoSS-666
96Fin-S211
96FinRef-S211
96FleUpd-U77
96FleUpdTC-U77
96LeaSigA-250
96LeaSigAG-251
96LeaSigAS-251
96Pin-365
96PinFoil-365
96Sco-455
96Sum-71
96SumAbo&B-71
96SumArtP-71
96SumFoi-71
96Ult-406
96UltGolM-406
97Cir-342
97CirRav-342
97ColCho-189
97Don-205
97DonEli-69
97DonEliGS-69
97DonEliTotC-13
97DonEliTotCDC-13
97DonPreP-205
97DonPrePGold-205
97Fle-200
97FleTif-200
97Lea-67
97LeaFraM-67
97LeaFraMDC-67
97Pac-179
97PacLigB-179
97PacSil-179
97Pin-75
97PinArtP-75
97PinIns-33
97PinInsCE-33
97PinInsDE-33
97PinMusC-75
97Sco-432
97ScoHobR-432
97ScoResC-432
97ScoShoS-432
97ScoShoSAP-432
97SP-134
97Stu-45
97StuPrePG-45
97StuPrePS-45
97Top-329
97Ult-118
97UltGolME-118
97UltPlaME-118
97UppDec-128

Young, Floyd
36SandSW-52

Young, Ford
60DarFar-24

Young, Gary
87BriYouC-15

Young, Gerald
85OscAstTI-26
86ColAstP-25
87SpoRoo2-36
87TucTorP-11
88AstMot-3
88AstPol-24
88Don-431
88DonBasB-318
88Fle-460
88FleGlo-460
88HouSho-15
88Lea-210
88OPC-368
88Sco-442
88ScoGlo-442
88ScoYouS2-11
88StaLinAst-20
88Top-368
88TopTif-368
89AstLenH-20
89AstMot-3
89AstSmo-40
89Bow-333
89BowTif-333
89Don-207
89DonBasB-288
89Fle-370
89FleGlo-370
89OPC-95
89PanSti-93
89Sco-97
89ScoHot1S-72
89Spo-125
89Top-95
89TopCoi-28
89TopMinL-16
89TopSti-23
89TopTif-95
89TopUKM-86
89TVSpoM-56
89UppDec-135
90AstLenH-28
90AstMot-8
90Bow-72
90BowTif-72
90Don-325
90Fle-241
90FleCan-241
90Lea-214
90MLBBasB-40
90OPC-196
90PanSti-263
90PubSti-105
90PubSti-618
90Sco-43
90Top-196
90TopBig-49
90TopSti-22
90TopTif-196
90UppDec-196
90VenSti-506
90VenSti-507
91Don-689
91Fle-521
91LinDriAAA-623
91OPC-626
91Sco-844
91StaClu-494
91Top-626
91TopDesS-626
91TopMic-626
91TopTif-626
91TucTorLD-623
91TucTorP-2227
91Ult-142
92Don-477
92Fle-446
92OPC-241
92Pin-458
92Sco-346
92StaClu-355
92Top-241
92TopGol-241
92TopGolW-241
92TopMic-241
93RocUSPC-6S
93RocUSPC-9D
93StaCluRoc-14
93Ult-362
93UppDec-740
93UppDecGold-740
94LouRedF-2995

Young, Greg
91SouBenWSC-21
91SouBenWSP-2858
91UtiBluSC-9
91UtiBluSP-3241

Young, Irving
06FanCraNL-54
08RosComP-158
09T206-475
11SpoLifCW-377
11SpoLifM-35

Young, Jason
90CliGiaUTI-U10
90EveGiaB-21
90EveGiaP-3137
91CliGiaC-25
91CliGiaP-850

Young, Jim
91RocExpC-2
92RocExpC-30
93GenCubC-28
93GenCubF-3192

Young, Joe
94MedHatBJF-3685
94MedHatBJSP-25
95StCatSTI-2
96BesAutS-99
96Exc-120
96HagSunB-26
97Bow-102
97BowInt-102

Young, John
76ArkTraT-12
77ArkTraT-12A
77ArkTraT-12B
80IndIndTI-31
81IndIndTI-32
83SprCarF-15
84ArkTraT-22
87NasSouTI-24
88NasSouC-25
88NasSouP-495
88NasSouTI-25
88WatPirP-30
89NasSouC-9
89NasSouP-1276
90CMC-673
90NasSouC-26
90SprCarDGB-12
95IndIndF-114
96IndIndB-5

Young, Kenny
81BriRedST-14

Young, Kevin
90WelPirP-8
91Cla/Bes-239
91SalBucC-9
91SalBucP-963
92Bow-155
92BufBisBS-26
92BufBisF-331
92BufBisS-47

92DonRoo-129
92SkyAAAF-22
93Bow-682
93Don-452
93Fin-34
93FinRef-34
93FleFinE-122
93FleMajLP-A6
93FunPac-9
93LeaGolR-R1
93OPCPre-78
93PacSpa-594
93Pin-589
93PinRooTP-6
93PirHil-12
93PirNatl-39
93Sco-273
93ScoBoyoS-10
93ScoProaG-7
93SelRoo-51T
93SP-189
93StaClu-722
93StaCluFDI-722
93StaCluMOP-722
93Top-494
93TopGol-494
93TopInaM-494
93TopMic-494
93TopTra-52T
93Toy-9
93TriPla-72
93Ult-459
93UltAllR-10
93UppDec-536
93UppDecDG-36
93UppDecGold-536
94Bow-274
94ColC-438
94ColChoGS-438
94ColChoSS-438
94Don-578
94Fin-321
94FinRef-321
94Fla-222
94Fle-626
94Lea-23
94OPC-124
94Pac-514
94PanSti-241
94Pin-186
94PinArtP-186
94PinMusC-186
94PirQui-29
94Sco-492
94ScoGolR-492
94Sel-123
94StaClu-321
94StaCluFDI-321
94StaCluGR-321
94StaCluMOP-321
94Top-622
94TopGol-622
94TopSpa-622
94TriPla-190
94Ult-263
94UppDec-482
94UppDecED-482
95CedRapKTI-17
95Don-335
95DonPreP-335
95Pac-355
95Sel-53
95SelArtP-53
96Fle-536
96FleTif-536
96HilStaHWB-27
96LakElsSB-25
96OmaRoyB-30
97DonLim-29
97DonLimLE-29
97PacPriGotD-GD53
Young, Kip
79Top-706
80SpoIndT-11
80Top-251
81IndIndTI-8
82IndIndTI-3
Young, Larry
88T/MUmp-54
89T/MUmp-52
90T/MUmp-50
Young, Mark
88DunBluJS-24
89ButCopKSP-22
89DunBluJS-25
89MyrBeaBJP-1452
90DunBluJS-25
90PeoChiTI-30
91KnoBluJLD-359
91KnoBluJP-1778
91LinDriAA-359
Young, Matt
81CliGiaT-12
Young, Matt J.
81LynSaiT-12
82SalLakCGT-22
83TopTra-129T
84Don-16
84Don-16A
84Don-362
84Fle-624
84MarMot-9
84Nes792-235
84Nes792-336
84OPC-235
84SevCoi-W24
84Top-235
84Top-336
84TopRubD-9
84TopSti-386
84TopTif-235
84TopTif-336
85Don-267
85Fle-505
85MarMot-14
85OPC-136
85Top-485
85TopMin-485
85TopSti-340
85TopTif-485
86Don-267
86Fle-481
86MarMot-14
86OPC-274
86Top-676
86TopSti-220
86TopTif-676
87DodMot-12
87DodPol-19
87Don-193
87Fle-600
87FleGlo-600
87FleUpd-131
87FleUpdG-131
87OPC-19
87RedFolSB-123
87SpoTeaP-14
87Top-19
87TopSti-218
87TopTif-19
87TopTra-131T
87TopTraT-131T
88A'sMot-21
88Don-423
88DonTeaBA-NEW
88Fle-530
88FleGlo-530
88OPC-367
88PanSti-306
88Sco-357
88ScoGlo-357
88StaLinAs-20
88Top-736
88TopSti-72
88TopTif-736
90DodTar-883
90FleUpd-121
90Lea-509
90MarMot-16
90OPC-501
90Top-501
90TopTif-501
90TopTra-131T
90TopTraT-131T
90UppDec-787
91Bow-128
91Don-493
91Fle-465
91Lea-215
91OPC-108
91RedSoxP-20
91Sco-126
91ScoRoo-54T
91StaClu-426
91Top-108
91TopDesS-108
91TopMic-108
91TopTif-108
91UppDec-591
91UppDec-740
92Don-635
92OPC-403
92Pin-518
92RedSoxDD-29
92Sco-668
92StaClu-682
92StaCluNC-682
92Ult-320
92UppDec-505
93ChaKniF-545
93Don-459
93Fle-567
93FleFinE-208
93Lea-153
93MilBonSS-9
93PacSpa-39
93RedSoxWHP-20
93StaClu-428
93StaCluFDI-428
93StaCluMOP-428
Young, Michael Darren
81MiaOriT-23
82RocRedWT-19
83RocRedWT-22
84Don-621
84FleUpd-131
84RocRedWT-19
85Don-367
85Fle-195
85OriHea-20
85Top-173
85TopTif-173
86Don-123
86Fle-291
86FleMin-61
86Spo-199
86Top-548
86TopSti-234
86TopTat-11
86TopTif-548
87ChaRaiP-10
87Don-150
87Fle-483
87FleGlo-483
87OriFreB-43
87Top-309
87TopTif-309
88Don-396
88Fle-575
88FleGlo-575
88OPC-11
88PanSti-17
88PhiTas-26
88Sco-393
88ScoGlo-393
88ScoRoo-51T
88ScoRooG-51T
88StaLinO-20
88Top-11
88TopTif-11
89ColSprSSP-251
89Don-632
89RivRedWB-21
89RivRedWCLC-18
89RivRedWP-1399
89Sco-494
89Top-731
89TopTif-731
89UppDec-649
90GenCubS-25
90PubSti-571
90VenSti-508
91LinDriAAA-475
91OriCro-493
91RocRedWLD-475
91RocRedWP-1920
92RocRedWF-1957
94BreMilB-93
Young, Mike
86AriWilP-20
90WauTimS-28
91PerHeaF-2
Young, Mike (Michael Leslie)
90GenCubP-3046
90WauTimP-2143
91GenCubC-26
91GenCubP-4219
Young, Mike MG
89BluOriS-30
93WatIndC-29
93WatIndF-3579
94ColRedC-26
94ColRedF-460
Young, Pep (Lemuel)
16ColE13-198
16SpoNewM-197
19W514-107
20NatCarE-113
21E121So8-109
22AmeCarE-79
23W503-27
34BatR31-102
36NatChiFPR-83
39PlaBal-102
40PlaBal-106
92ConTSN-387
20W516-28
Young, Pete
88MisStaB-36
89JamExpP-2136
89MisStaB-41
90FloStaLAS-21
90WesPalBES-28
91Cla/Bes-189
91HarSenLD-273
91HarSenP-628
91LinDriAA-273
92DonRoo-130
92IndIndS-198
93Don-616
93FleMajLP-B17
93OttLynF-2437
93Sco-269
93Top-432
93TopGol-432
93TopInaM-432
93TopMic-432
94NewBriRSF-651
Young, Ralph S.
16BF2FP-32
17HolBreD-120
22W575-153
23WilChoV-179
Young, Randy
96AubDouB-20
Young, Ray
87DunBluJP-940
88ModA'sCLC-58
88ModA'sTI-16
89HunStaB-24
90CMC-578
90ProAAAF-141
90TacTigC-1
90TacTigP-94
90TriAllGP-AAA48
91Sco-761
93LasVegSF-946
Young, Rick
75QuaCitAT-1
Young, Scott
83St.PetCT-13
86ArkTraP-26
Young, Shane
84LitFalMT-10
86LynMetP-28
87JacMetF-7
87TexLeaAF-14
88MidAngGS-5
89MidAngGS-30
Young, Sly
83AlbA'sT-16
Young, Steve
92StaCluMO-42
93StaCluMO-53
Young, Thomas Jefferson
87NegLeaPD-28
Young, Tim
96VerExpB-30
Young, Ty
92GulCoaMF-3496
Youngbauer, Jeff
77OrlTwiT-23
79RocRedWT-1
91PacSenL-74
Youngblood, Joel
77Top-548
78MetDaiPA-25
78Top-428
79OPC-48
79Top-109
80OPC-194
80Top-372
81CokTeaS-95
81Don-277
81Fle-331
81OPC-58
81Top-58
81TopSti-195
82Don-613
82ExpPos-42
82Fle-543
82OPC-189
82RegGloT-10
82Top-655
82TopSti-65
82TopStiV-65
83Don-572
83Fle-301
83Fle-641
83GiaMot-17
83OPC-265
83Top-265
83TopSti-143
83TopSti-144
83TopTra-130T
84Don-480
84Fle-387
84GiaPos-31
84Nes792-727
84OPC-303
84Top-727
84TopSti-173
84TopTif-727
85Don-79
85Fle-625
85GiaMot-19
85GiaPos-31
85Lea-152
85OPC-97
85Top-567
85TopSti-168
85TopTif-567
86Don-567A
86Don-567B
86Fle-555
86GiaMot-26
86OPC-177
86Top-177
86TopTif-177
87Fle-288
87FleGlo-288
87GiaMot-20
87OPC-378
87Top-759
87TopTif-759
88GiaMot-20
88Sco-509
88ScoGlo-509
88Top-418
88TopTif-418
89Bow-315
89BowTif-315
89RedKah-12
89Sco-539
89ScoRoo-66T
89Top-304
89TopTif-304
89UppDec-458
90PubSti-42
90Sco-344
90VenSti-509
91FreKeyC-28
91MetWIZ-437
91PacSenL-131
92KanCouCC-26
92KanCouCF-108
92KanCouCTI-30
94RedKah-33
95RedKah-34
97FleMilDM-47
Youngblood, Todd
91BelMarC-25
91BelMarP-3666
92PenPilC-25
92PenPilF-2934
93RivPilCLC-25
Youngdahl, Raynor Lee
63RocRedWSP-9
Younger, Stan
81BirBarT-17
82BirBarT-1
83BirBarT-5
84EvaTriT-7
90BirBarDGB-33
Youngman, Pete
86GreHorP-25
87GreHorP-4
89NewBriRSP-601
89NewBriRSS-25

90PawRedSDD-30
93PawRedSDD-30
Youngs, Ross M.
20NatCarE-114
21E121So1-117
21Exh-193
21KoBreWSI-26
21Nei-106
22E120-195
22W573-141
22W575-154
23W501-68
23W515-29
23WilChoV-180
61Fle-154
75TCMAllG-36
76ShaPiz-134
77GalGloG-131
80PerHaloFP-134
80SSPHOF-134
87HygAllG-50
91ConTSN-26
Yount, Andy
95Bes-116
95SPML-113
96LowSpiB-29
Yount, Robin
75Hos-80
75HosTwi-80
75OPC-223
75Top-223
76BreA&P-15
76Hos-11
76HosTwi-11
76OPC-316
76SSP-238
76Top-316
77BurCheD-88
77Hos-34
77OPC-204
77PepGloD-1
77RCColC-69
77Top-635
77TopCloS-54
78Hos-138
78OPC-29
78RCColC-56
78Top-173
79Hos-55
79OPC-41
79Top-95
80OPC-139
80Top-265
81AllGamPI-26
81Don-323
81Fle-511
81FleStiC-38
81Kel-57
81OPC-4
81Top-515
81TopScr-10
81TopSti-95
81TopSti-244
82BrePol-19
82Don-510
82Fle-155
82FleSta-135
82Kel-28
82OPC-237
82PerAll-4
82PerAllG-4
82Top-435
82TopSti-203
83AllGamPI-27
83BreGar-22
83BrePol-19
83Don-258
83DonActA-56
83Dra-33
83Fle-51
83Fle-632
83FleSta-222
83FleSti-18
83Kel-14
83Oco& SSBG-20
83OPC-350
83OPC-389
83PerAll-9
83PerAllG-9
83PerCreC-36
83PerCreCG-36
83Top-321
83Top-350
83Top-389
83TopGloS-5
83TopSti-81
83TopSti-145
83TopSti-146
83TopSti-150
83TopSti-167
84AllGamPI-116
84BreGar-22
84BrePol-19
84Don-1
84Don-1A
84Don-48
84DonActAS-5
84DonCha-47
84Dra-33
84Fle-219
84FunFooP-29
84MilBra-30
84Nes792-10
84OCoandSI-17
84OCoandSI-221
84OPC-10
84RalPur-21
84SevCoi-C2
84SevCoi-E2
84SevCoi-W2
84Top-10
84TopCer-21
84TopGloA-5
84TopGloS-36
84TopRubD-32
84TopSti-295
84TopStiB-6
84TopSup-29
84TopTif-10
85AllGamPI-27
85BreGar-22
85BrePol-19
85Don-48
85DonActA-21
85Dra-33
85Fle-601
85FleLimE-44
85GenMilS-26
85Lea-44
85OPC-340
85SevCoi-G16
85Top-340
85TopMin-340
85TopRubD-32
85TopSti-284
85TopSup-37
85TopTif-340
86BasStaB-124
86BrePol-19
86Don-48
86DorChe-16
86Fle-506
86FleLeaL-44
86FleMin-103
86FleSlu-44
86FleStiC-131
86Lea-31
86MSAJayPCD-20
86MSAJifPD-5
86OPC-144
86SevCoi-C9
86Spo-42A
86Spo-42B
86Spo-54
86Spo-63
86Spo-71
86SpoDecG-73
86Top-780
86TopSti-197
86TopTat-9
86TopTif-780
86TruVal-11
87BoaandB-9
87BrePol-19
87BreTeal-16
87ClaGam-44
87Don-126
87DonOpeD-58
87Fle-361
87FleGlo-361
87FleLimE-44
87FleStiC-130
87FleWaxBC-C16
87GenMilB-2J
87HosSti-25
87KraFoo-23
87Lea-67
87OPC-76
87RedFolSB-126
87Spo-16
87SpoTeaP-19
87StuPan-21
87Top-773
87TopSti-196
87TopTif-773
88BrePol-19
88Don-295
88DonBasB-183
88Fle-178
88FleBasM-44
88FleGlo-178
88FleMin-33
88FleStiC-40
88FleSup-44
88GreBasS-44
88K-M-33
88Lea-106
88MSAJifPD-20
88OPC-165
88PanSti-129
88Sco-160
88ScoGlo-160
88Spo-34
88StaLinAl-38
88StaLinBre-20
88Top-165
88TopBig-66
88TopCoi-32
88TopMinL-21
88TopSti-201
88TopTif-165
88TopUKM-87
88TopUKMT-87
89Bow-144
89BowTif-144
89BreGar-2
89BrePol-19
89BreYea-19
89ClaLigB-83
89Don-5
89Don-55
89DonBasB-53
89DonSupD-5
89Fle-200
89FleExcS-44
89FleGlo-200
89FleHeroB-44
89FleLeaL-44
89KayB-33
89KinDis-13
89OPC-253
89PanSti-377
89RedFolSB-130
89Sco-151
89ScoHot1S-28
89Spo-199
89SpoIllFKI-127
89Top-615
89TopAme2C-33
89TopAwaW-6
89TopBasT-56
89TopBatL-21
89TopBig-249
89TopCapC-21
89TopCoi-60
89TopGloS-38
89TopHilTM-33
89TopMinL-59
89TopSti-205
89TopStiB-21
89TopTif-615
89TopUKM-87
89TVSpoM-74
89UppDec-285
90AllBasT-13
90Baz-2
90Bow-404
90BowIns-11
90BowInsT-11
90BowTif-404
90BowTif-A11
90BreMilB-31
90BrePol-19
90ClaBlu-147
90Col-9
90Don-146
90DonBesA-22
90DonLeaS-37
90Fle-340
90FleAwaW-44
90FleBasA-44
90FleBasM-44
90FleCan-340
90FleLeaL-44
90FleWaxBC-C28
90GooHumICBLS-26
90Hot50PS-50
90KayB-33
90KinDis-18
90Lea-71
90MLBBasB-82
90MSAHolD-7
90OPC-290
90OPC-389
90PanSti-92
90Pos-26
90PubSti-508
90Sco-320
90Sco100S-92
90ScoMcD-25
90Spo-18
90StaMit-1
90StaMit-3
90StaMit-5
90StaMit-7
90StaMit-9
90StaMit-11
90StaYou-1
90StaYou-2
90StaYou-3
90StaYou-4
90StaYou-5
90StaYou-6
90StaYou-7
90StaYou-8
90StaYou-9
90StaYou-10
90StaYou-11
90SunSee-6
90SupActM-6
90Top-290
90Top-389
90TopAmeA-5
90TopBatL-15
90TopBig-59
90TopCoi-1
90TopDou-72
90TopGaloC-12
90TopGloS-15
90TopMag-12
90TopMinL-22
90TopSti-198
90TopStiB-54
90TopTif-290
90TopTif-389
90TopTVA-23
90UppDec-91
90UppDec-567
90VenSti-510
90WonBreS-11
90Woo-1
90Woo-22
91BasBesHM-18
91Bow-55
91BreMilB-31
91BrePol-28
91CadEllD-62
91ClaGam-59
91Don-272
91Fle-601
91Lea-116
91MajLeaCP-43
91MooSna-17
91OPC-575
91OPCBoxB-P
91OPCPre-131
91PanCanT1-56
91PanFreS-208
91PanSti-166
91PosCan-21
91RedFolS-104
91Sco-525
91Sco-854
91Sco100S-38
91StaClu-509
91Stu-80
91Top-575
91TopCraJI-23
91TopDesS-575
91TopMic-575
91TopSta-36
91TopTif-575
91TopTriH-A8
91TopWaxBC-P
91Ult-184
91UppDec-344
91Woo-22
92Bow-700
92BreCarT-26
92BrePol-29
92BreSenY-1
92BreSenY-2
92BreSenY-3
92BreSenY-4
92BreUSO-4
92Cla1-T98
92Cla2-T30
92ClaGam-128
92Don-173
92DonCraJ1-8
92DonMcD-12
92Fle-194
92Fle-708
92FleUpdH-2
92Hig5-70
92JimDeaLL-4
92Lea-64
92Lea-397
92LeaBlaG-64
92LeaGolP-20
92LeaPre-20
92Mr.TurS-26
92OPC-90
92OPCPre-111
92PanSti-40
92Pin-38
92Pin-287
92Sco-525
92Sco100S-84
92ScoCokD-24
92ScoFacl-B11
92ScoProP-6
92SevCoi-17
92SpoStaCC-49
92StaClu-450
92StaClu-607
92StaCluECN-607
92StaCluMO-36
92Stu-200
92StuPre-6
92Top-90
92TopGol-90
92TopGolW-90
92TopKid-80
92TopMcD-17
92TopMic-90
92TriPla-81
92Ult-87
92UppDec-456
92UppDecF-44
92UppDecFG-44
93Bow-535
93BrePol-28
93BrePol-29
93BreSen-4
93ClaGam-99
93DenHol-6
93DiaMar-119
93DiaMarA-8
93Don-441
93DonDiaK-DK16
93DonEli-L3
93DonMasotG-15
93DonPre-17
93DonSpiotG-SG20
93DurPowP1-16
93Fin-192
93FinRef-192
93Fla-232
93Fle-260
93FleFinEDT-10
93FleFruotL-65
93FunPac-69
93FunPac-73
93Kra-15
93Lea-188
93LeaHeaftH-3
93OPC-365
93PacSpa-167
93PanSti-42
93Pin-118
93Pin-293
93PinCoo-3
93PinCooD-3
93Pos-30
93PosCan-6
93Sco-47
93Sco-518
93ScoFra-8
93Sel-22

93SelSam-22
93SelStaL-14
93SP-72
93StaClu-173
93StaCluFDI-173
93StaClul-A1
93StaCluMOP-173
93StaCluMOP-MA1
93Stu-118
93Top-1
93TopGol-1
93TopInaM-1
93TopMic-1
93TopMic-P1
93TopPre-1
93TriPla-188
93TriPlaA-16
93Ult-227
93UppDec-43
93UppDec-587
93UppDec-SP5
93UppDecDG-6
93UppDecGold-43
93UppDecGold-587
93UppDecSH-HI20
93UppDecTAN-TN15
94AmeYou-1
94BreMilB-94
94BreMilB-376
94BreSen-8
94ChuHomS-25
94ChuHomSG-25
94Don-15
94DonAnn8-2
94DonSpeE-15
94Fle-197
94FUnPac-202
94Pac-348
94PacSilP-1
94RedFolMI-28
94Sco-13
94ScoGolR-13
94Spo-24
94StaClu-1
94StaCluFDI-1
94StaCluGR-1
94StaCluMOP-1
94TomPiz-30
94Top-310
94TopGol-310
94TopSpa-310
94TriPla-60
94UppDecDC-C10
94UppDecS-3
95ColCho-47
95ColCho-54
95ColChoGS-47
95ColChoGS-54
95ColChoSS-47
95ColChoSS-54
95UppDec-446
95UppDecED-446
95UppDecEDG-446
95UppDecSHoB-7
Youppi, Mascot
93FunPacM-5
84ExpStu-1
85ExpPos-26
86ExpProPa-27
87ExpPos-37
90JamExpP-32
94MasMan-16
96ExpDis-24
Youse, Bob
73CedRapAT-23
74CedRapAT-2
Yselonia, John
93WelPirC-28
94AugGreC-27
94AugGreF-3019
Yuhas, John Ed
52Top-386
53CarHunW-26
53Top-70
54CarHunW-29
83TopRep5-386
91TopArc1-70
Yuhas, Marty
93WilBluRC-30
Yuhas, Vince
83OmaRoyT-10
84MemChiT-15
84OmaRoyT-16
Yurak, Jeff
75CedRapGT-8
76CedRapGT-36
77HolMilT-26
78HolMilT-24
79HolMilT-28
79VanCanT-18
94BreMilB-282
Yurcisin, Scott
90JamExpP-30
Yurtin, Jeff
86SpoIndC-176
88WicPilRD-11
89BlaYNPRWLU-24
89LasVegSC-20
89LasVegSP-20
90CMC-522
90LasVegSC-19
90LasVegSP-132
90LSUTigGM-10
90ProAAAF-20
Yvars, Sal
52Top-338
53Top-11
54Bow-78
54CarHunW-30
75Gia195T-32
83TopRep5-338
91TopArc1-11
Zabala, Ismael
94VenLinU-248
95LinVen-215
Zachary, Chink (Albert M.)
90DodTar-1101
Zachary, Chris
64Top-23
64TopVen-23
66Top-313
66TopVen-313
67Top-212
70OPC-471
70Top-471
71CarTeal-44
73OPC-256
73Top-256
87AstShoSTw-20
Zachary, J. Tom
21Nei-3
22E120-120
22W572-119
22W573-142
27YorCarE-26
28PorandAR-A40
28PorandAR-B40
29PorandAR-101
31Exh-1
33ButCanV-58
33Gou-91
34DiaMatCSB-200
34GouCanV-47
34TarThoBD-17
35GouPuzR-8A
35GouPuzR-8M
90DodTar-884
93ConTSN-693
Zacher, Elmer
10JuJuDE-43
Zacher, Todd
82CliGiaF-8
Zachmann, Rob
96EveAquB-1
Zachry, Pat
76OPC-599
76Top-599
77OPC-201
77PepGloD-57
77Top-86
78MetDaiPA-26
78OPC-172
78Top-171
79Kel-8
79OPC-327
79Top-621
80OPC-220
80Top-428
81CokTeaS-89
81Don-275
81Fle-334
81OPC-224
81Top-224
81TopSti-197
82Don-254
82Fle-544
82FleSta-88
82MetPhoA-26
82OPC-64
82Top-399
82TopSti-71
83DodPol-38
83Don-560
83Fle-561
83FleSta-223
83FleSti-237
83Top-522
83TopTra-131T
84DodPol-38
84Don-215
84Fle-118
84Nes792-747
84Top-747
84TopTif-747
85Fle-391
85PhiTas-9
85PhiTas-23
85Top-57
85TopTif-57
87VerBeaDP-8
88SanAntMB-27
88SanAntMB-28
89PacSenL-20
90DodTar-885
91MetWIZ-438
Zahn, Geoff
75OPC-294
75Top-294
76OPC-403
76Top-403
78Top-27
78TwiFriP-25
79Kel-27
79OPC-358
79Top-678
79TwiFriP-29
80Top-113
81Don-532A
81Don-532B
81Fle-564
81LonBeaPT-9
81Top-363
81TopTra-856
82Don-164
82Fle-474
82Top-229
83AllGamPI-90
83Don-66
83Fle-103
83FleSti-29
83OPC-131
83Top-547
83TopSti-42
84AllGamPI-180
84AngSmo-32
84Don-402
84Fle-532
84Nes792-276
84Nes792-468
84OPC-153
84Top-276
84Top-468
84TopTif-276
84TopTif-468
85AllGamPI-90
85AngSmo-15
85Don-301
85DonActA-33
85Fle-317
85Lea-53
85OPC-140
85SpoIndGC-24
85ThoMcAD-24
85Top-771
85TopSti-221
85TopTif-771
86Top-42
86TopTif-42
90DodTar-886
Zahn, Paul
74WicAerODF-102
Zahner, Kevin
92YakBeaC-9
92YakBeaF-3454
93YakBeaC-27
94VerBeaDC-25
94VerBeaDF-77
95BakBlaTI-10
Zajeski, Mike
88NebCor-27
90NebCor-28
Zaksek, John
88UtiBluSP-13
89SouBenWSGS-20
90Bes-165
90MidLeaASGS-25
90SouBenWSB-14
90SouBenWSGS-22
Zaleski, Richard
82DanSunF-15
83NasAngT-22
86MidAngP-26
87EdmTraP-2075
Zaletel, Brian
93EveGiaC-30
93EveGiaF-3781
94CliLumF-1992
94CliLumC-25
Zaltsman, Stan
86EriCarP-29
87SavCarP-22
88St.PetCS-25
Zambrana, Luis
81RedPioT-21
82RedPioT-18
83RedPioT-27
94VenLinU-206
Zambrano, Eddie (Eduardo)
85GreHorT-13
86GreHorP-26
87WinHavRSP-21
88NewBriRSP-895
89NewBriRSP-599
89NewBriRSS-21
89Sta-131
90KinIndTI-25
91CarMudLD-123
91CarMudP-1100
91LinDriAA-123
92BufBisBS-27
92BufBisF-337
92BufBisS-48
92TriA AAS-48
93IowCubF-2147
93LinVenB-260
93TriAAAGF-6
94Bow-337
94FleUpd-113
94Pac-117
94Pin-237
94PinArtP-237
94PinMusC-237
94Sco-385
94ScoGolR-385
94ScoRoo-RT93
94ScoRooGR-RT93
94Sel-400
94SpoRoo-129
94SpoRooAP-129
94Top-616
94TopGol-616
94TopSpa-616
94Ult-467
94VenLinU-197
94VenLinU-200
95ColCho-207
95ColChoGS-207
95ColChoSS-207
95Don-64
95DonPreP-64
95Fla-118
95Fle-428
95LinVen-116
95Pac-81
95Sco-202
95ScoGolR-202
95ScoPlaTS-202
95StaClu-297
95StaCluMOP-297
95StaCluSTWS-297
95Top-34
95TopCyb-26
Zambrano, Jose
91Cla/Bes-34
91LynRedSC-24
91LynRedSP-1214
92WinHavRSF-1793
93ForLauRSC-26
93ForLauRSFP-1612
93LinVenB-17
95LinVen-44
Zambrano, Roberto
85GreHorT-10
86WinHavRSP-27
87NewBriRSP-20
88NewBriRSP-911
90CanIndP-1307
90CanIndS-19
90CMC-777
91ColSprSSLD-94
91ColSprSSP-2199
91LinDriAAA-94
93LinVenB-239
94VenLinU-185
95LinVen-117
Zammarchi, Erik
91GreFalDSP-20
92YakBeaC-18
92YakBeaF-3467
Zamora, Oscar
75OPC-604
75Top-604
76OPC-227
76SSP-304
76Top-227
76VenLeaS-67
78Top-91
Zancanaro, Dave
90ProAaA-162
90SouOreAB-24
90SouOreAP-3423
91Cla/Bes-124
91Cla1-T77
91HunStaC-20
91HunStaLD-298
91HunStaP-1797
91HunStaTI-23
91LinDriAA-298
92Bow-99
92SkyAAAF-246
92TacTigF-2505
92TacTigS-548
92UppDec-54
96HunStaTI-27
96ModA'sB-13
Zane, Kelly
88SalLakCTTI-8
89RocExpLC-31
Zane, Lisa
91TopRut-4
Zanni, Dom
57SeaPop-40
59Top-145
59TopVen-145
60TacBan-21
61TacBan-21
62Top-214
63RedFreBC-32
63Top-354
66Top-233
66TopVen-233
Zanolla, Dan
93SpoIndC-27
93SpoIndF-3601
94OgdRapF-3745
94OgdRapSP-14
95KanCouCTI-29
Zapata, Gustavo
91KisDodP-4199
Zapata, Juan
96OgdRapTI-29
Zapata, Ramon
92AugPirC-11
92AugPirF-248
93AugPirC-26
93AugPirF-1556
94SalBucC-25
94SalBucF-2334
95LynHilTI-30
Zapelli, Mark
87AncGlaP-33
91MidAngOHP-32
92SkyAA F-202
Zapp, A.J.
96BesAutS1RP-FR13
97Bow-384
97BowChr-253
97BowChrI-253
97BowChrIR-253
97BowChrR-253
97BowInt-384
97Top-274
Zapp, Jim
86NegLeaF-46
92NegLeaRLI-65
Zappelli, Mark
89QuaCitAB-17
89QuaCitAGS-5
90MidAngGS-6

91LinDriAA-448
91MidAngLD-448
91MidAngP-435
92ClaFS7-340
92MidAngF-4029
92MidAngOHP-28
92MidAngS-473
93VanCanF-2600
94VenLinU-71
Zarate, Vincent
93PeoChiC-24
93PeoChiF-1099
93PeoChiTI-32
Zarilla, Al
46SeaSLP-59
47Exh-246
47TipTop-75
49Bow-156
49Lea-36
50Bow-45
51Bow-35
51R42SmaS-118
51TopRedB-49
52Bow-113
52StaCalL-73A
52StaCalS-87D
52TipTop-48
52Top-70
52WhiSoxH-10
53RedSoxTI-30
53Top-181
76TayBow4-102
79DiaGre-191
79HawIsIC-3
79HawIsIT-15
83TopRep5-70
91TopArc1-181
96Bro194F-11
Zarranz, Fernando
86GenCubP-27
86PeoChiP-27
87PeoChiP-29
88MidLeaAGS-29
88PeoChiTI-33
90ChaKniTI-12
90TopTVCu-66
Zaske, Jeff
82AleDukT-17
84HawIsIC-122
85HawIsIC-249
86HawIsIP-23
87OklCit8P-26
88TacTigC-6
Zastoupil, Rich
91BilMusP-3755
91BilMusSP-23
92ChaWheF-9
92ChaWVWC-6
Zauchin, Norm
55Top-176
56Top-89
57Top-372
58Top-422
59Top-311
79TCM50-252
Zaun, Greg
90WauTimB-15
90WauTimP-2128
90WauTimS-27
91Cla/Bes-209
91KanCouCC-14
91KanCouCP-2661
91KanCouCTI-24
91MidLeaAP-MWL36
92FreKeyC-7
92FreKeyF-1809
93BowBayF-2192
94Bow-271
94ExcFS7-17
94OriPro-108
94RocRedWF-1001
94RocRedWTI-26
94Ult-312
94UppDecML-24
95RocRedWTI-40
96ColCho-51
96ColChoGS-51
96ColChoSS-51
96Don-27
96DonPreP-27
96LeaSigA-251
96LeaSigAG-252
96LeaSigAS-252
96Sco-265
96ScoDugC-A110
96ScoDugCAP-A110
96Sel-170
96SelArtP-170
96Sum-167
96SumAbo&B-167
96SumArtP-167
96SumFoi-167
Zavala, Alfredo
74WicAerODF-121
Zavaras, Clint
86WauTimP-29
87SalSpuP-30
88VerMarP-960
89BlaYNPRWL-196
89CalCanC-11
90Don-662
90OPC-89
90Top-89
90TopDeb89-149
90TopTif-89
92CalCanS-73
92JacSunF-3708
94CalCanF-792
Zavershnik, Mike
96StCatSB-29
Zawaski, Vince
89St.LucMS-25
89Sta-25
Zayas, Carlos
85BenPhiC-24
87ClePhiP-6
88BlaYNPRWL-144
88SpaPhiP-1039
89BlaYNPRWL-21
89ClePhiS-25
Zayas, Felipe
77St.PetCT-3
78St.PetCT-28
80ArkTraT-19
81ArkTraT-1
Zayas, Pedro
89SpaPhiP-1051
89SpaPhiS-25
Zazueta, Mauricio
89PriWilCS-26
90CarLeaA-16
90PriWilCTI-29
Zdeb, Joe
76OmaRoyTT-27
76VenLeaS-10
78Roy-27
78Top-408
79Top-389
Zeber, George
73SyrChiTI-30
76VenLeaS-49
78SSP270-15
78TacYanC-20
78Top-591
78YanSSPD-15
92YanWIZ7-172
Zedalis, Craig
94DanBraC-26
94DanBraF-3533
Zehner, Kevin
93YakBeaF-3887
Zeider, Rollie
10ChiE-20
12T207-207
14CraJacE-60
14CraJacE-116
15CraJacE-116
15SpoNewM-198
16ColE13-199
16SpoNewM-198
19W514-32
Zeig, Robert
77WesHavYT-25
79WesHavYT-23
Zeigler, Bill
90RanMot-28
Zeihen, Bob
88OneYanP-2058
89Ft.LauYS-26
89Sta-81
90AlbYanB-24
90AlbYanP-1047
90AlbYanS-23
91EriSaiC-25
91EriSaiP-4087
92Ft.MyeMF-2761
Zeile, Todd E.
86EriCarP-30
87SprCarB-26
88ArkTraGS-7
88TexLeaAGS-2
89FleUpd-122
89LouRedBC-13
89LouRedBP-1267
89LouRedBTI-2
89LouRedBTI-3
89LouRedBTI-4
89LouRedBTI-5
89TriA AAC-1
89TriAAP-AAA14
89UppDec-754
89UppDecS-2
90Baz-12
90Bow-193
90BowTif-193
90CarSmo-27
90ClaBlu-90
90Don-29
90DonBesN-71
90DonPre-1
90DonRoo-31
90Fle-265
90FleCan-265
90FleSoaS-1
90Hot50RS-50
90Lea-221
90OPC-162
90PanSti-381
90Sco-600
90Sco100RS-6
90ScoRooDT-B3
90ScoYouS2-1
90Spo-177
90SprCarDGB-1
90Top-162
90TopBig-294
90TopDeb89-150
90TopTif-162
90TopTVCa-24
90ToyRoo-33
90TriAAAC-1
90UppDec-545
91Bow-404
91CarPol-27
91Cla2-T42
91ClaGam-173
91Don-71
91Fle-654
91Lea-327
91MajLeaCP-48
91OPC-616
91PanFreS-33
91PanSti-34
91Pos-25
91Sco-240
91Sco-869
91Sco100RS-81
91StaClu-255
91Stu-240
91Top-616
91TopDesS-616
91TopMic-616
91TopRoo-33
91TopTif-616
91TopTriH-N12
91ToyRoo-33
91Ult-299
91UppDec-164
92Bow-695
92CarPol-26
92ClaGam-25
92Don-132
92DonCraJ1-31
92Fle-596
92Hig5-100
92KinDis-4
92Lea-432
92OPC-275
92PanSti-174
92Pin-32
92Sco-52
92ScoImpP-34
92ScoProP-12
92StaClu-544
92Stu-100
92SunSee-3
92Top-275
92TopGol-275
92TopGolW-275
92TopKid-27
92TopMic-275
92TriPla-141
92Ult-273
92UppDec-40
92UppDec-533
92UppDecHRH-HR26
93Bow-628
93CarPol-25
93DiaMar-120
93Don-20
93Fin-21
93FinRef-21
93Fle-136
93Lea-8
93MilBonSS-10
93OPC-224
93PacSpa-305
93PanSti-195
93Pin-205
93Sco-119
93Sel-63
93StaClu-152
93StaCluCa-9
93StaCluFDI-152
93StaCluMOP-152
93Stu-62
93Top-428
93TopGol-428
93TopInaM-428
93TopMic-428
93TriPla-24
93Ult-115
93UppDec-569
93UppDecGold-569
94Bow-152
94CarPol-26
94ColC-305
94ColChoGS-305
94ColChoSS-305
94Don-460
94ExtBas-366
94Fin-410
94FinRef-410
94Fla-230
94Fle-651
94FUnPac-96
94Lea-61
94LeaL-149
94OPC-198
94Pac-608
94Pin-367
94PinArtP-367
94PinMusC-367
94ProMag-113
94Sco-358
94ScoGolR-358
94Sel-244
94SP-68
94SPDieC-68
94Spo-117
94StaClu-395
94StaCluFDI-395
94StaCluGR-395
94StaCluMOP-395
94StaCluMOP-ST12
94StaCluST-ST12
94StaCluT-306
94StaCluTFDI-306
94Stu-57
94Top-25
94TopGol-25
94TopSpa-25
94TriPla-70
94Ult-274
94UppDec-444
94UppDecED-444
95Baz-117
95Bow-389
95ColCho-188
95ColChoGS-188
95ColChoSE-74
95ColChoSEGS-74
95ColChoSESS-74
95ColChoSS-188
95D3-6
95Don-483
95DonPreP-483
95DonTopotO-207
95Emb-132
95EmbGolI-132
95Fin-80
95FinRef-80
95Fla-413
95Fle-513
95Lea-193
95LeaLim-153
95Pac-419
95PanSti-53
95Pin-118
95PinArtP-118
95PinMusC-118
95Sco-409
95ScoGolR-409
95ScoPlaTS-409
95SP-39
95SPCha-31
95SPChaDC-31
95Spo-23
95SpoArtP-23
95SPSil-39
95StaClu-274
95StaCluCC-CC19
95StaCluMOP-274
95StaCluMOP-CC19
95StaCluSTWS-274
95StaCluVR-139
95Stu-168
95Top-319
95TopCyb-173
95TopTra-121T
95Ult-434
95UltGolM-434
95UppDec-310
95UppDec-456T
95UppDecED-310
95UppDecEDG-310
95UppDecSE-91
95UppDecSEG-91
96ColCho-81
96ColCho-674
96ColChoGS-81
96ColChoGS-674
96ColChoSS-81
96ColChoSS-674
96Don-277
96DonPreP-277
96EmoXL-251
96Fin-B247
96FinRef-B247
96Fla-342
96Fle-333
96FleTif-333
96FleUpd-U173
96FleUpdTC-U173
96PhiTeal-36
96Pin-42
96Pin-360
96PinFoil-360
96Sco-402
96SP-142
96StaClu-420
96StaCluEPB-420
96StaCluEPG-420
96StaCluEPS-420
96StaCluMOP-420
95StaCluVRMC-139
96Stu-28
96StuPrePB-28
96StuPrePG-28
96StuPrePS-28
96TeaOut-91
96Top-35
96Ult-530
96UltGolM-530
96UppDec-36
96UppDec-431
97Cir-129
97CirRav-129
97ColCho-364
97Don-24
97Don-272
97DonPreP-24
97DonPreP-272
97DonPrePGold-24
97DonPrePGold-272
97DonTea-117
97DonTeaSPE-117
97Fin-236
97FinRef-236
97Fle-16
97Fle-605
97FleTif-16
97FleTif-605
97NewPin-16
97NewPinAP-16
97NewPinMC-16
97NewPinPP-16
97PinX-PSfF-59
97PinX-PSfFU-59
97Sco-257

97Sco-355
97ScoHobR-355
97ScoPreS-257
97ScoResC-355
97ScoShoS-257
97ScoShoS-355
97ScoShoSAP-257
97ScoShoSAP-355
97Top-473
97Ult-257
97Ult-379
97UltGolME-257
97UltGolME-379
97UltPlaME-257
97UltPlaME-379
97UppDec-540
Zell, Brian
80ElmPioRST-31
Zellers, Kevin
94YakBeaC-29
94YakBeaF-3861
95BakBlaTI-15
Zellner, Joey
86MacPirP-27
87VisOakP-20
88VisOakCLC-148
88VisOakP-98
Zello, Mark
91KanCouCC-30
91KanCouCTI-25
Zendejas, Tony
91StaCluMO-37
Zepp, Bill
70Top-702
71MLBOffS-480
71OPC-271
71Top-271
Zeratsky, Rod
86CedRapRT-13
87TamTarP-28
Zerb, Troy
87UtiBluSP-7
88BatCliP-1690
Zerbe, Chad
91KisDodP-4188
92GreFalDSP-4
93BakDodCLC-27
94VerBeaDC-26
94VerBeaDF-74
95SanBerSTI-27
Zernial, Gus
47Exh-247A
47Exh-247B
47PM1StaP1-227
47PM1StaP1-228
47SigOil-20
50Bow-4
51Bow-262
51FisBakL-32
51R42SmaS-119
51TopRedB-36A
51TopRedB-36B
52BerRos-71
52Bow-82
52RedMan-AL26
52StaCalL-76A
52StaCalS-89B
52Top-31
53BowC-13
53NorBreL-32
53RedMan-AL13
53Top-42
54DixLid-18
54RedHeaF-33
54Top-2
55A'sRodM-47
55RobGouS-2
55RobGouW-2
55Top-110
55TopDouH-123
56A'sRodM-12
56Top-45
56TopHocF-A13
56TopHocF-B15
56TopPin-15
56YelBasP-32
57Top-253
58Top-112
59Top-409
76A'sRodMC-30
79DiaGre-348
79TCM50-263
83TopRep5-31
91TopArc1-42
94TopArc1-2
94TopArc1G-2
Zettelmeyer, Mark
90Ft.LauYS-26
Zhigalov, Sergey
89EasLeaDDP-DD8
90IBAWorA-5
Zick, Bill
88QuaCitAGS-3
89QuaCitAB-4
89QuaCitAGS-4
92SalBucC-28
93SalBucC-28
Ziegler, Alma
94TedWil-98
Ziegler, Bill
84RanJarP-NNO
85RanPer-NNO
86RanPer-NNO0
87RanMot-27
89RanMot-28
Ziegler, Greg
87IdaFalBP-27
Ziegler, Shane
93BluOriC-24
93BluOriF-4126
94BluOriC-22
94BluOriF-3564
Ziem, Steve
84DurBulT-23
85GreBraTI-26
86GreBraTI-23
87RicBraBC-23
87RicBraC-19
87RicBraT-9
88GreBraB-15
89DurBullS-25
89DurBulTI-25
89RicBraBC-29
90RicBraBC-2
Zientara, Benny
49EurSta-100
85TCMPla1-39
Zimbauer, Jason
90HelBreSP-10
91BelBreC-10
91BelBreP-2104
Zimmer, Charles
03BreE10-158
11SpoLifCW-378
87OldJudN-565
Zimmer, Don
55Bow-65
55DodGolS-21
55Top-92
55TopDouH-97
56Top-99
57Top-284
58DodBelB-10
58Hir-41
58Top-77A
58Top-77B
59DodMor-12
59DodTeal-25
59Top-287
60DodBelB-17
60Top-47
60TopVen-47
61CubJayP-12
61Top-493
62Baz-43
62Jel-183
62MetJayP-12
62Pos-183
62PosCan-183
62SalPlaC-123A
62SalPlaC-123B
62ShiPlaC-123
62Top-478
62TopStal-161
63Top-439
64Top-134
64TopCoi-1
64TopSta-11
64TopVen-134
65OPC-233
65Top-233
72PadTeal-28
73OPC-12
73Top-12A
73Top-12B
74OPC-403
74Top-403
77Top-309
78SSP270-179
78Top-63
79DiaGre-98
79TCM50-228
79Top-214
80Top-689
81Fle-230
81TCM60I-482
81Top-673
82Don-195
84CubChiT-34
84CubSev-NNO
84OCoandSI-159
85CubLioP-27
85CubSev-NNO
87GiaMot-27
88CubDavB-4
88TopTra-131T
88TopTraT-131T
89CubMar-4
89SweBasG-23
89Top-134
89TopTif-134
90CubMar-27
90DodTar-887
90OPC-549
90Top-549
90TopTif-549
90TopTVA-66
90TopTVCu-1
91CubVinL-35
91MetWIZ-439
91OPC-729
91RinPosBD3-11
91Top-729
91TopDesS-729
91TopMic-729
91TopTif-729
92RedSoxDD-30
93RanKee-391
94RocPol-27
94TopArc1-258
94TopArc1G-258
95TopArcBD-83
95TopArcBD-99
95TopArcBD-125
95TopArcBD-148
Zimmer, Tom
72CedRapCT-3
89PacSenL-25
91PacSenL-136
Zimmerman, Brian
88LitFalMP-25
Zimmerman, Casey
89AncGlaP-30
Zimmerman, Cory
89AncGlaP-31
Zimmerman, Eric
83AleDukT-24
Zimmerman, Heinie (Henry)
09ColChiE-316
09ColChiE-317A
09ColChiE-317B
09MaxPubP-19
09SpoNewSM-95
09T206-389
10CouT21-255
10CouT21-325
10E101-46
10E102-26
10MelMinE-46
10NadCarE-52
10PeoT21-59A
10PeoT21-59B
11SpoLifCW-379
11SpoLifM-185
12ColRedB-316
12ColRedB-317A
12ColRedB-317B
12ColTinT-316
12ColTinT-317A
12ColTinT-317B
14CraJacE-21
14FatPlaT-52
14TexTomE-50
15AmeCarE-42
15CraJacE-21
15SpoNewM-199
16BF2FP-72
16ColE13-200
16SpoNewM-199
16TanBraE-20
92ConTSN-530
Zimmerman, Jennifer
89AncGlaP-32
Zimmerman, Jerry (Gerald)
59Top-146
59TopVen-146
60HenHouW-9
61TwiCloD-31
62Jel-130
62Pos-130
62PosCan-130
62Top-222
63Top-186
64Top-369
64TopVen-369
65Top-299
66OPC-73
66Top-73
66TopVen-73
67CokCapTw-9
67Top-501
68OPC-181
68Top-181
68TopVen-181
69MilBra-296
73OPC-377
73Top-377
74OPC-531
74Top-531
78TCM60I-117
78TwiFri-24
79TwiFriP-30
Zimmerman, Mike
88CapCodPPaLP-44
90WelPirP-31
91Bow-519
91SalBucP-954
92CarMudF-1183
92CarMudS-148
92SkyAA F-69
92UppDecML-230
93BufBisF-519
93ClaGolF-193
94CarMudF-1581
95ChaKniTI-28
95SigRooOJ-35
95SigRooOJP-35
95SigRooOJPS-35
95SigRooOJS-35
Zimmerman, Phil
92PulBraC-10
92PulBraF-3188
Zimmerman, Rick
89AncGlaP-33
Zimmerman, Roy
50RemBre-27
Zimmerman, Zeke
93BoiHawC-29
93BoiHawF-3932
Zinn, Frank
87OldJudN-566
Zinter, Alan (Alan Michael)
87AriWilP-20
88AriWilP-16
88CapCodPPaLP-29
89PitMetS-29
90Bow-135
90BowTif-135
90FloStaLAS-22
90Sco-671
90St.LucMS-27
90StaFS7-11
90TopTVM-66
91Cla/Bes-334
91LinDriAA-648
91MetColP-53
91WilBilLD-648
91WilBilP-297
92BinMetF-526
92BinMetS-73
92ClaFS7-28
92SkyAA F-35
93BinMetF-2338
94TolMudHF-1035
94UppDecML-17
95TolMudHTI-29
96PawRedSDD-29
Zinter, Eddie
88AlaGolTI-18
89SpoIndSP-2
90ChaRaiB-23
90ChaRaiP-2039
90ProAaA-74
91CalLeLA-10
91HigDesMC-13
91HigDesMP-2396
92HigDesMC-12
Zipay, Bud (Ed)
46SunBre-21
47SigOil-73
47SunBre-26
Zipeto, Ted
86ClePhiP-26
Zipfel, M. Bud
55DonWin-42
61SenJayP-12
63Top-69
Zisk, John
79WauTimT-11
80WauTimT-10
Zisk, Richie
72OPC-392
72Top-392
73OPC-611
73Top-611
74OPC-317
74Top-317
74TopSta-90
75Hos-139
75Kel-25
75OPC-77
75Top-77
76CraDis-70
76OPC-12
76SSP-574
76Top-12
77BurCheD-75
77Hos-127
77MSADis-63
77OPC-152
77PepGloD-27
77RCColC-70
77Top-483
77TopCloS-55
77WhiSoxJT-16
78PapGinD-30
78Pep-40
78RanBurK-20
78RCColC-39
78SSP270-98
78TasDis-14
78Top-110
78WifBalD-79
79Hos-140
79Kel-24
79OPC-130
79Top-260
80OPC-325
80Top-620
81Don-28
81Fle-620
81FleStiC-105
81MarPol-13
81OPC-214
81Top-517
81TopScr-16
81TopSti-127
81TopTra-857
82Don-11
82Don-127
82Dra-33
82Fle-519
82FleSta-223
82Kel-1
82OPC-66
82Top-769
82TopSti-229
83Don-559
83DonActA-54
83Fle-489
83FleSta-224
83FleSti-183
83MarNal-6
83OPC-368
83Top-368
83TopGloS-21
83TopSti-116
84Don-69
84DonActAS-30
84Fle-625
84Nes792-83
84OPC-83
84Top-83
84TopSti-342
84TopTif-83
90PeoChiTI-35
91CubMar-NNO
93RanKee-392

93UppDecAH-130
94RanAllP-6
96DayCubB-28
Zitek, Jeff
79AshTouT-9
Zitzmann, Billy (William)
28Exh-16
92ConTSN-570
Zizzo, Johnny
92BenRocC-26
92BenRocF-1489
Zlejo, Nigel
95KanCouCTI-31
Zmudosky, Tom
84AlbA'sT-20
84ModA'sC-28
Zoldak, Sam
46SeaSLP-60
48IndTeal-31
49Bow-78A
49Bow-78B
49IndTeal-28
50Bow-182
50IndNumN-23
50IndTeal-25
51Bow-114
51R42SmaS-120
52Top-231
53IndPenCBP-31
77TCMTheWY-73
83TopRep5-231
85TCMPla1-19
96Bro194F-34
Zolecki, Mike
94Bow-404
94CenValRC-25
94CenValRF-3205
94Cla-30
94ClaTriF-T25
95AshTouUTI-20
96NewHavRB-29
Zollars, Mike
91BurIndP-3313
92WatIndC-21
92WatIndF-3249
Zolzer, Rick
90SpaPhiB-29
Zona, Jeff
89IdaFalBP-2029
Zongor, Steve
93SouOreAC-27
93SouOreAF-4065
94WesMicWC-25
94WesMicWF-2298
95ModA'sTI-32
Zorrilla, Julio
96Exc-193
96StLucMTI-34
Zosky, Eddie
89FreStaBS-23
90Bes-23
90Bow-523
90BowTif-523
90CMC-812
90KnoBluJB-1
90KnoBluJP-1251
90KnoBluJS-23
90ProAaA-60
90Sco-665
90StaFS7-91
91BluJayFS-35
91BluJayS-30
91Bow-17
91Cla2-T25
91ClaGam-172
91LeaGolR-BC24
91LinDriAAA-523
91SyrChiK-5
91SyrChiLD-523
91SyrChiMB-30
91SyrChiP-2490
91TriA AAGP-AAA44
91Ult-390
91UppDec-734
91UppDecFE-14F
92Bow-381
92Cla1-T99
92ClaGam-123
92Don-8
92Fle-348
92OPC-72
92PinRool-11
92ProFS7-159
92ScoImpP-72
92SkyAAAF-234
92StaClu-873
92SyrChiF-1979
92SyrChiMB-30
92SyrChiS-523
92Top-72
92TopDeb91-191
92TopGol-72
92TopGolW-72
92TopMic-72
92TriPla-190
92Ult-156
92UppDec-544
93BluJayD4-32
93BluJayFS-35
93Don-57
93Fle-703
93Lea-190
93OPC-221
93PacSpa-660
93Pin-247
93Sco-297
93ScoBoyoS-15
93StaClu-460
93StaCluFDI-460
93StaCluMOP-460
93Top-689
93TopGol-689
93TopInaM-689
93TopMic-689
94BluJayUSPC-2D
94BluJayUSPC-9C
94SyrChiF-981
94SyrChiTI-30
95ChaKniTI-29
95FleUpd-102
96RocRedWB-30
Zottneck, Roger
86QuaCitAP-32
87PalSprP-16
Zuber, Jon
92BatCliC-23
92BatCliF-3275
92FroRowDP-97
93ClaGolF-137
93ClePhiC-25
93ClePhiF-2693
93ExcFS7-89
93FloStaLAF-29
94ClaGolF-40
94ReaPhiF-2073
94UppDecML-199
95ScrRedBTI-30
95UppDecML-203
96ScrRedBB-28
95UppDecMLFS-203
Zuber, William
43YanSta-30
47TipTop-15
77TCMTheWY-87
Zubiri, Jon
92BurIndC-11
92BurIndF-1658
93BurIndC-29
93BurIndF-3299
94ColRedC-25
94ColRedF-444
Zukertort, Chess
88GooN16-50
Zulzer, Rick
90SpaPhiS-29
Zumwalt, Rusty
95ButCopKtI-21
Zuniga, David
93PitMetC-24
93PitMetF-3721
94CapCitBC-25
94CapCitBF-1761
Zuniga, Tony
96BelGiaTI-3
Zupcic, Bob
87ElmPio(C-31
88CarLeaAS-20
88ElmPio1C-9
88LynRedSS-27
89NewBriRSP-600
89NewBriRSS-22
90Bes-108
90CMC-880
90NewBriRSB-6
90NewBriRSP-1333
90NewBriRSS-24
91LinDriAAA-373
91PawRedSDD-30
91PawRedSLD-373
91PawRedSP-53
92Don-720
92FleUpd-6
92OPC-377
92PawRedSS-373
92Pin-576
92Sco-850
92SkyAAAF-172
92StaClu-839
92Top-377
92TopDeb91-192
92TopGol-377
92TopGolW-377
92TopMic-377
93Don-531
93Fle-186
93FleRooS-RSB10
93Lea-65
93OPC-367
93Pin-404
93Sco-362
93Sel-292
93SelChaR-10
93StaClu-563
93StaCluFDI-563
93StaCluMOP-563
93Top-562
93TopGol-562
93TopInaM-562
93TopMic-562
93Toy-99
93Ult-158
93UppDec-277
93UppDecGold-277
93USPlaCR-12C
94Don-411
94Fle-47
94Pac-70
94PawRedSF-959
94Sco-221
94ScoGolR-221
94Top-661
94TopGol-661
94TopSpa-661
94WhiSoxK-29
95Top-229
96ScrRedBB-29
97DunDonPPS-30
Zupka, Bill
85ElmPioT-25
86GreHorP-27
87NewBriRSP-3
Zupo, Frank
58Top-229
91OriCro-494
Zurn, Rick
92BelBreC-24
92BelBreF-406
Zuvella, Paul
82RicBraT-17
83RicBraT-17
84RicBraT-23
85BraPol-18
85Fle-651
86Fle-532
86RicBraP-26
86Top-572
86TopTif-572
86TopTra-131T
86TopTraT-131T
87Top-102
87TopTif-102
88ColSprSSC-18
88ColSprSSP-1528
89ColSprSSC-17
89ColSprSSP-245
89Sco-598
89TriA AAC-34
89TriAAP-AAA33
89UppDec-236
90CMC-197
90OmaRoyC-22
90OmaRoyP-75
90ProAAAF-610
90RicBra2ATI-23
90TriAAAC-34
91LinDriAAA-348
91OmaRoyLD-348
91OmaRoyP-1044
92YanWIZ8-206
93CenValRC-26
93CenValRF-2908
94NewHavRF-1565
95NewHavRTI-14
Zuverink, George
52Top-199
55Bow-92
56Top-276
57Top-11
58Hir-66
58OriJayP-12
58Top-6
59Top-219
83TopRep5-199
91OriCro-495
Zweig, Ivan
91TopTra-131T
91TopTraT-131T
92StaCluD-200
Zwemke, Bryan
96BilMusTI-31
Zwilling, Dutch (Edward)
11SpoLifM-36
15SpoNewM-200
16SpoNewM-200
Zwisler, Josh
94HelBreF-3618
94HelBreSP-12
95AusFut-61
95BelBreTI-6
Zwolensky, Mitch
82WauTimF-19
83TulDriT-9
84OklCit8T-21
85OklCit8T-2
88PitCubP-1356
90CalLeaACLC-30
90StoPorB-28
90StoPorCLC-201
90StoPorP-2201
91StoPorC-25
91StoPorP-3048

Acknowledgments

Many
Thanks!

A great deal of diligence, hard work, and dedicated effort went into this First Edition. The high standards to which we hold ourselves, however, could not have been met without the expert input and generous amount of time contributed by many people. Our sincere thanks are extended to each and every one of you.

Each year we refine the process of developing the most accurate and up-to-date information for this book. I believe this year's Price Guide is our best yet. Thanks again to all the contributors nationwide (listed below) as well as our staff here in Dallas.

Those who have worked closely with us on this and many other books have again proven themselves invaluable: David Berman, Levi Bleam and Jim Fleck (707 Sportscards), Peter Brennan, Ray Bright, Card Collectors Co., Cartophilium (Andrew Pywowarczuk), Dwight Chapin, Barry Colla, Bill and Diane Dodge, Donruss/Leaf (Shawn Heilbron, Eric Tijerina), David Festberg, Fleer/SkyBox (Rich Bradley, Doug Drotman and Ted Taylor), Steve Freedman, Gervise Ford, Larry and Jeff Fritsch, Tony Galovich, Georgia Music and Sports (Dick DeCourcey), Dick Gilkeson, Steve Gold (AU Sports), Bill Goodwin (St. Louis Baseball Cards), Mike and Howard Gordon, George Grauer, John Greenwald, Greg's Cards, Wayne Grove, Bill Henderson, Jerry and Etta Hersh, Mike Hersh, Neil Hoppenworth, Jay and Mary Kasper (Jay's Emporium), David Kohler (SportsCards Plus), Paul Lewicki, Lew Lipset (Four Base Hits), Mike Livingston (University Trading Cards), Mark Macrae, Bill Madden, Bill Mastro, Michael McDonald (The Sports Page), Mid-Atlantic Sports Cards (Bill Bossert), Gary Mills, Brian Morris, Mike Mosier (Columbia City Collectibles Co.), B.A. Murry, Ralph Nozaki, Mike O'Brien, Oldies and Goodies (Nigel Spill), Pacific Trading Cards (Mike Cramer and Mike Monson), Pinnacle (Laurie Goldberg, Kurt Iverson), Jack Pollard, Jeff Prillaman, Pat Quinn, Jerald Reichstein (Fabulous Cardboard), Tom Reid, Gavin Riley, Clifton Rouse, John Rumierz, San Diego Sport Collectibles (Bill Goepner and Nacho Arredondo), Kevin Savage (Sports Gallery), Gary Sawatski, Mike Schechter, Scoreboard (Brian Cahill), Barry Sloate, John E. Spalding, Phil Spector, Frank Steele, Murvin Sterling, Lee Temanson, Topps (Marty Appel, Sy Berger and Melissa Rosen), Treat (Harold Anderson), Ed Twombly (New England Bullpen), Upper Deck (Steve Ryan, Marilyn Van Dyke), Wayne Varner, Bill Vizas, Bill Wesslund (Portland Sports Card Co.), Kit Young and Bob Ivanjack (Kit Young Cards), Rick Young, Ted Zanidakis, Robert Zanze (Z-Cards and Sports), Bill Zimpleman and Dean Zindler. Finally we give a special acknowledgment to the late Dennis W. Eckes, "Mr. Sport Americana." The success of the Beckett Price Guides has always been the result of a team effort.

It is very difficult to be "accurate" — one can only do one's best. But this job is especially difficult since we're shooting at a moving target: Prices are fluctuating all the time. Having several full-time pricing experts has definitely proven to be better than just one, and I thank all of them for working together to provide you, our readers, with the most accurate prices possible.

Many people have provided price input, illustrative material, checklist verifications, errata, and/or background information. We should like to individually thank AbD Cards (Dale Wesolewski), Action Card Sales, Jerry Adamic, Johnny and Sandy Adams, Alex's MVP Cards & Comics, Doug Allen (Round Tripper Sportscards), Will Allison, Dennis Anderson, Ed Anderson, Shane Anderson, Bruce W. Andrews, Ellis Anmuth, Tom Antonowicz, Alan Applegate, Ric Apter, Jason Arasate, Clyde Archer, Randy Archer, Matt Argento, Burl Armstrong, Neil Armstrong (World Series Cards), Todd Armstrong, Ara Arzoumanian, B and J Sportscards, Shawn Bailey, Ball Four Cards (Frank and Steve Pemper), Frank and Vivian Barning, Bob Bartosz, Nathan Basford, Carl Berg, Beulah Sports (Jeff Blatt), Brian Bigelow, George Birsic, B.J. Sportscollectables, David Boedicker (The Wild Pitch Inc.), Bob Boffa, Louis Bollman, Tim Bond (Tim's Cards & Comics), Andrew Bosarge, Brian W. Bottles, Kenneth Braatz, Bill Brandt, Jeff Breitenfield, John Brigandi, John Broggi, Chuck Brooks, Dan Bruner, Lesha Bundrick, Michael Bunker, John E. Burick, Ed Burkey Jr., Bubba Burnett, Virgil Burns, California Card Co., Capital Cards, Danny Cariseo, Carl Carlson (C.T.S.), Jim Carr, Patrick Carroll, Ira Cetron, Don Chaffee, Michael Chan, Sandy Chan, Ric Chandgie, Ray Cherry, Bigg Wayne Christian, Josh Chidester, Dick Cianciotto, Michael and Abe Citron, Dr. Jeffrey Clair, Derrick F. Clark, Bill Cochran, Don Coe, Michael Cohen, Tom Cohoon (Cardboard Dreams), Collection de Sport AZ (Ronald Villaneuve), Gary Collett, Andrew T. Collier, Charles A. Collins, Curt Cooter, Steven Cooter, Pedro Cortes, Rick Cosmen (RC Card Co.), Lou Costanzo (Champion Sports), Mike Coyne, Paul and Ryan Crabb, Tony Craig (T.C. Card Co.), Kevin Crane, Taylor Crane, Chad Cripe, Brian Cunningham, Allen Custer, Donald L. Cutler, Eugene C. Dalager, Dave Dame, Brett Daniel, Tony Daniele III, Scott Dantio, Roy Datema, John Davidson, Travis Deaton, Dee's Baseball Cards (Dee Robinson), Joe Delgrippo, Tim DelVecchio, Steve Dempski, John Derossett, Mark Diamond, Gilberto Diaz Jr., Ken Dinerman (California Cruizers), Frank DiRoberto, Cliff Dolgins, Discount Dorothy, Walter J. Dodds Sr., Bill Dodson, Richard Dolloff (Dolloff Coin Center), Ron Dorsey, Double Play Baseball Cards, Richard Duglin (Baseball Cards-N-More), The Dugout, Kyle Dunbar, B.M. Dungan, Ken

Edick (Home Plate of Utah), Randall Edwards, Rick Einhorn, Mark Ely, Todd Entenman, Doak Ewing, Bryan Failing, R.J. Faletti, Terry Falkner, Mike and Chris Fanning, John Fedak, Stephen A. Ferradino, Tom Ferrara, Dick Fields, Louis Fineberg, Jay Finglass, L.V. Fischer, Bob Flitter, Fremont Fong, Perry Fong, Craig Frank, Mark Franke, Walter Franklin, Tom Freeman, Bob Frye, Chris Gala, Richard Galasso, Ray Garner, David Garza, David Gaumer, Georgetown Card Exchange, Richard Gibson Jr., Glenn A. Giesey, David Giove, Dick Goddard, Alvin Goldblum, Brian Goldner, Jeff Goldstein, Ron Gomez, Rich Gove, Joseph Griffin, Mike Grimm, Neil Gubitz (What-A-Card), Hall's Nostalgia, Hershell Hanks, Gregg Hara, Zac Hargis, Floyd Haynes (H and H Baseball Cards), Ben Heckert, Kevin Heffner, Kevin Heimbigner, Dennis Heitland, Joel Hellman, Arthur W. Henkel, Kevin Hense, Hit and Run Cards (Jon, David, and Kirk Peterson), Gary Holcomb, Lyle Holcomb, Rich Hovorka, John Howard, Mark Hromalik, H.P. Hubert, Dennis Hughes, Harold Hull, Johnny Hustle Card Co., Tom Imboden, Chris Imbriaco, Vern Isenberg, Dale Jackson, Marshall Jackson, Mike Jardina, Hal Jarvis, Paul Jastrzembski, Jeff's Sports Cards, David Jenkins, Donn Jennings Cards, George Johnson, Robe Johnson, Stephen Jones, Al Julian, Chuck Juliana, Dave Jurgensmeier, John Just, Robert Just, Nick Kardoulias, Scott Kashner, Frank J. Katen, Jerry Katz (Bottom of the Ninth), Mark Kauffman, Allan Kaye, Rick Keplinger, Sam Kessler, Kevin's Kards, Larry B. Killian, Kingdom Collectibles, Inc., John Klassnik, Philip C. Klutts, Don Knutsen, Steven Koenigsberg, Bob & Bryan Kornfield, Blake Krier, Neil Krohn, Scott Ku, Thomas Kunnecke, Gary Lambert, Matthew Lancaster (MC's Card and Hobby), Jason Lassic, Allan Latawiec, Howard Lau, Gerald A. Lavelle, Dan Lavin, Richard S. Lawrence, William Lawrence, Brent Lee, W.H. Lee, Morley Leeking, Ronald Lenhardt, Brian Lentz, Tom Leon, Leo's Sports Collectibles, Irv Lerner, Larry and Sally Levine, Lisa Licitra, James Litopoulos, Larry Loeschen (A and J Sportscards), Neil Lopez, Allan Lowenberg, Kendall Loyd (Orlando Sportscards South), Robert Luce, David Macaray, Jim Macie, Joe Maddigan, David Madison, Rob Maerten, Frank Magaha, Pierre Marceau, Paul Marchant, Jim Marsh, Rich Markus, Bob Marquette, Brad L. Marten, Ronald L. Martin, Scott Martinez, Frank J. Masi, Duane Matthes, James S. Maxwell Jr., Dr. William McAvoy, Michael McCormick, Paul McCormick, McDag Productions Inc., Tony McLaughlin, Mendal Mearkle, Carlos Medina, Ken Melanson, William Mendel, Eric Meredith, Blake Meyer (Lone Star Sportscards), Tim Meyer, Joe Michalowicz, Lee Milazzo, Jimmy Milburn, Cary S. Miller, David (Otis) Miller, Eldon Miller, George Miller, Wayne Miller, Dick Millerd, Mitchell's Baseball Cards, Perry Miyashita, Douglas Mo, John Morales, William Munn, Mark Murphy, John Musacchio, Robert Nappe, National Sportscard Exchange, Roger Neufeldt, Bud Obermeyer, Francisco Ochoa, John O'Hara, Glenn Olson, Mike Orth, Ron Oser, Luther Owen, Earle Parrish, Clay Pasternack, Mickey Payne, Michael Perrotta, Doug and Zachary Perry, Tom Pfirrmann, Bob Pirro, George Pollitt, Don Prestia, Coy Priest, Loran Pulver, Bob Ragonese, Richard H. Ranck, Bryan Rappaport, Robert M. Ray, R.W. Ray, Phil Regli, Glenn Renick, Rob Resnick, John Revell, Carson Ritchey, Bill Rodman, Craig Roehrig, David H. Rogers, Michael H. Rosen, Martin Rotunno, Michael Runyan, Mark Rush, George Rusnak, Mark Russell, Terry Sack, Joe Sak, Jennifer Salems, Barry Sanders, Everett Sands, Jon Sands, Tony Scarpa, John Schad, Dave Schau (Baseball Cards), Bruce M. Schwartz, Keith A. Schwartz, Charlie Seaver, Tom Shanyfelt, Steven C. Sharek, Eddie Silard, Art Smith, Ben Smith, Michael Smith, Jerry Sorice, Don Spagnolo, Carl Specht, Sports Card Fan-Attic, The Sport Hobbyist, Dauer Stackpole, Norm Stapleton, Bill Steinberg, Bob Stern, Lisa Stellato, Jason Stern, Andy Stoltz, Bill Stone, Tim Strandberg (East Texas Sports Cards), Edward Strauss, Strike Three, Richard Strobino, Superior Sport Card, Dr. Richard Swales, Paul Taglione, George Tahinos, Ian Taylor, Lyle Telfer, The Thirdhand Shoppe, Scott A. Thomas, Paul Thornton, Carl N. Thrower, Jim Thurtell, John Tomko, Bud Tompkins (Minnesota Connection), Philip J. Tremont, Ralph Triplette, Mike Trotta, Umpire's Choice Inc., Eric Unglaub, Hoyt Vanderpool, Rob Veres, Nathan Voss, Steven Wagman, Jonathan Waldman, Terry Walker, T. Wall, Gary A. Walter, Mark Weber, Joe and John Weisenburger (The Wise Guys), Brian Wentz, Richard West, Mike Wheat, Richard Wiercinski, Don Williams (Robin's Nest of Dolls), Jeff Williams, John Williams, Kent Williams, Craig Williamson, Opry Winston, Brandon Witz, Rich Wojtasick, John Wolf Jr., Jay Wolt (Cavalcade of Sports), Carl Womack, Pete Wooten, Peter Yee, Wes Young, Dean Zindler, Mark Zubrensky and Tim Zwick.

Every year we make active solicitations for expert input. We are particularly appreciative of help (however extensive or cursory) provided for this volume. We receive many inquiries, comments and questions regarding material within this book. In fact, each and every one is read and digested. Time constraints, however, prevent us from personally replying. But keep sharing your knowledge. Your letters and input are part of the "big picture" of hobby information we can pass along to readers in our books and magazines. Even though we cannot respond to each letter, you are making significant contributions to the hobby through your interest and comments.

The effort to continually refine and improve this book also involves a growing number of people and types of expertise on our home team. Our company boasts a substantial Sports Data Publishing team, which strengthens our ability to provide comprehensive analysis of the marketplace. SDP capably handled numerous technical details and provided able assistance in the preparation of this edition.

Our baseball analysts played a major part in compiling this year's book, traveling thousands of miles during the past year to attend sports card shows and visit card shops around the United States and Canada. The Beckett baseball specialists are Theo Chen (Assistant Manager, Hobby Information), Mark Anderson, Steven Judd, Rich Klein and Grant Sandground (Senior Price Guide Editor). Their pricing analysis and careful proofreading were key contributions to the accuracy of this annual.

They were ably assisted by Jeany Finch and Beverly Mills, who helped enter new sets and pricing information, and ably handled administration of our contributor Price Guide surveys. Card librarian Gabriel Rangel handled the ever-growing quantity of cards we need organized for efforts such as this.

The effort was led by SDP Senior Manager Pepper Hastings and Manager of SDP Dan Hitt. They were ably assisted by the rest of the Price Guide analysts: Pat Blandford, Mike Jaspersen, Lon Levitan, Allan Muir, Rob Springs and William Sutherland.

The price gathering and analytical talents of this fine group of hobbyists have helped make our Beckett team stronger, while making this guide and its companion monthly Price Guide more widely recognized as the hobby's most reliable and relied upon sources of pricing information.

The IS (Information Services) department, ably headed by Airey Baringer, played a critical role in technology.

In the Production Department, Paul Kerutis, Marlon DePaula and Belinda Cross were responsible for the typesetting.

Don Pendergraft spent tireless hours on the phone attending to the wishes of our dealer advertisers. Once the ad specifications were delivered to our offices, Phaedra Strecher used her computer skills to turn raw copy into attractive display advertisements.

In the years since this guide debuted, Beckett Publications has grown beyond any rational expectation. A great many talented and hard working individuals have been instrumental in this growth and success. Our whole team is to be congratulated for what we together have accomplished. Our Beckett Publications team is led by President Jeff Amano, Vice Presidents Claire Backus and Joe Galindo, Directors Mark Harwell, Reed Poole and Dave Stock, and Senior Managers Jeff Anthony, Beth Harwell and Pepper Hastings. They are ably assisted by Pete Adauto, Dana Alecknavage, Kaye Ball, Airey Baringer, Rob Barry, Therese Bellar, Andrea Bergeron, Eric Best, Julie Binion, Louise Bird, Amy Brougher, Bob Brown, Joel Brown, Angie Calandro, Randall Calvert, Mary Campana, Cara Carmichael, Eric Cash, Susan Catka, Jud Chappell, Albert Chavez, Marty Click, C.R. Conant, Andy Costilla, Belinda Cross, Randy Cummings, Von Daniel, Aaron Derr, Gary Doughty, Lauren Drews, Ryan Duckworth, Amy Durrett, Kandace Elmore, Eric Evans, Craig Ferris, Gean Paul Figari, Carol Fowler, Loretta Gibbs, Mary Gonzalez-Davis, Rosanna Gonzalez-Oleachea, Jeff Greer, Mary Gregory, Robert Gregory, Jenifer Grellhesl, Julie Grove, Mike Gullatt, Tracy Hackler, Patti Harris, Steve Harris, Becky Hart, Mark Hartley, Joanna Hayden, Chris Hellem, Melissa Herzog, Tim Jaska, Julia Jernigan, Bob Johnson, Doug Kale, Justin Kanoya, Eddie Kelly, Keven King, Wendy Kizer, Gayle Klancnik, Rudy J. Klancnik, Tom Layberger, Jane Ann Layton, Sara Leeman, Benedito Leme, Lori Lindsey, Stanley Lira, Kirk Lockhart, Sara Maneval, Louis Marroquin, John Marshall, Mike McAllister, Teri McGahey, Matt McGuire, Omar Mediano, Sherry Monday, Mila Morante, Terrence Morawski, Daniel Moscoso Jr., Mike Moss, Randy Mosty, Allan Muir, Hugh Murphy, Shawn Murphy, Bridget Norris, Mike Obert, Stacy Olivieri, Lisa O'Neill, Clark Palomino, Mike Pagel, Clark Palomino, Wendy Pallugna, Laura Patterson, Missy Patton, Mike Payne, Susan Plonka, Tim Polzer, Bob Richardson, Tina Tackett, Lisa Runyon, Susan Sainz, David Schneider, Christine Seibert, Brett Setter, Len Shelton, Dave Sliepka, Judi Smalling, Sheri Smith, Jeff Stanton, Margaret Steele, Marcia Stoesz, Mark Stokes, Dawn Sturgeon, Margie Swoyer, Doree Tate, Jim Tereschuk, Roz Theesfeld, Jim Thompson, Doug Williams, Steve Wilson, Ed Wornson, Bryan Winstead, David Yandry, Mark Zeske and Jay Zwerner. The whole Beckett Publications team has my thanks for jobs well done.

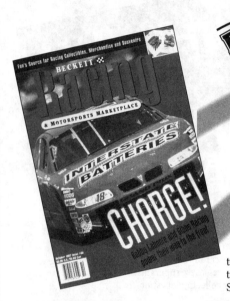